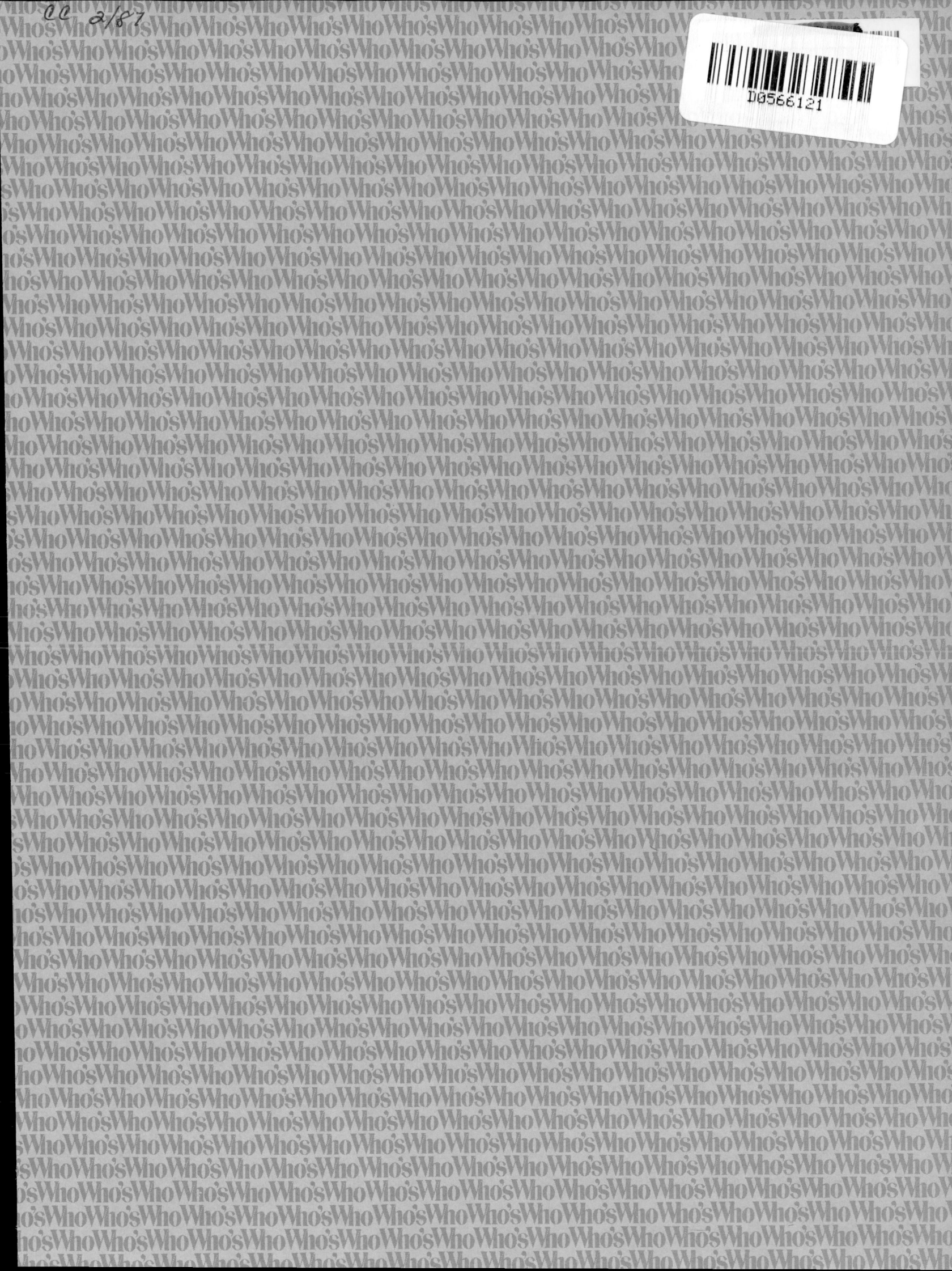

Who'sWho of American Women

Biographical Titles Currently Published by Marquis Who's Who

Who's Who in America
  Who's Who in America supplements:
    Who's Who in America Classroom Project Book
    Who's Who in America Index:
      Geographic Index, Professional Area Index
Who Was Who in America
  Historical Volume (1607–1896)
  Volume I (1897–1942)
  Volume II (1943–1950)
  Volume III (1951–1960)
  Volume IV (1961–1968)
  Volume V (1969–1973)
  Volume VI (1974–1976)
  Volume VII (1977–1981)
  Volume VIII (1982–1985)
  Index Volume (1607–1985)
Who's Who in the World
Who's Who in the East
Who's Who in the Midwest
Who's Who in the South and Southwest
Who's Who in the West
Who's Who in American Law
Who's Who of American Women
Who's Who in Finance and Industry
Who's Who in Frontiers of Science and Technology
Index to Who's Who Books
Directory of Medical Specialists

Who's Who
of American Women ®

15th edition
1987-1988

MARQUIS
Who's Who

Macmillan Directory Division
3002 Glenview Road
Wilmette, Illinois 60091 U.S.A.

Library of Congress Catalog Card Number 58–13264
International Standard Book Number 0–8379–0415–3
Product Code Number 030427

Distributed in Asia by
United Publishers Services Ltd.
Kenkyu–Sha Bldg.
9, Kanda Surugadai 2-Chome
Chiyoda-Ku, Tokyo, Japan

Manufactured in the United States of America

Table of Contents

Preface vi

Board of Advisors vii

Standards of Admission viii

Key to Information ix

Table of Abbreviations x

Alphabetical Practices xvi

Biographies 1

Preface

The fifteenth edition of *Who's Who of American Women* marks the twenty-eighth anniversary of publication of this reference book. As women have entered a variety of professions in greater numbers since 1958, when the first edition was published, there has been an increasing interest in and need for their biographical data.

In the first volume of *Who's Who of American Women,* volunteer workers in civic, religious, and club activities constituted almost 16 percent of the biographees. While the proportion of women in these areas has declined, increasing prominence has been achieved in many other fields. This directory includes women who are moving up in professional areas to which they are relatively new, as well as those at high levels in fields traditionally accessible to women. For example, the volume contains considerable representation of women in all areas of government: federal officials, high-level state positions, mayors, and judges. Outstanding women are found in many sectors of business, such as advertising, banking, insurance, and publishing. In addition, women entrepreneurs who head their own businesses constitute an important segment of the biographees. As always, women are prominent in the performing arts—dance, theater, opera—with increasing representation in music as, for example, players in symphony orchestras.

In preparing the contents of this edition—more than 25,300 sketches—the Marquis researchers have drawn on a variety of contemporary sources: newspapers, periodicals, professional associations, and other information. The result has been coverage of personal and professional biographical information about women in virtually every important field of endeavor.

In the great majority of cases, biographees have furnished their own data, thus assuring a high degree of accuracy. In some cases where individuals of high reference interest failed to supply information, Marquis staff members compiled the data through careful, independent research. Sketches compiled in this manner are denoted by an asterisk. As in previous editions, biographees were given the opportunity to review prepublication proofs of their sketches to make sure they were correct.

A new feature, avocations, has been introduced in the fifteenth edition. Biographees appearing for the first time in *Who's Who of American Women* were requested to indicate their avocations, thereby providing additional insights into their personal lives and interests.

Selection of a name for inclusion in *Who's Who of American Women* is based on one fundamental principle: reference value. Some women are eligible for listing because of position, while others have distinguished themselves by noteworthy achievements in their fields. Many listees qualify by virtue of both position and accomplishment.

In the editorial evaluation that resulted in the ultimate selection of the names in this directory, an individual's desire to be listed was not sufficient reason for inclusion; rather it was the person's achievement that ruled. Similarly, wealth or social position was not a criterion; only occupational stature or achievement influenced selection.

In assembling this comprehensive reference source on outstanding American women, Marquis Who's Who editors and researchers have exercised diligent care in the preparation of each biographical sketch. Despite all precautions, however, errors do occur. Users of this directory are invited to draw the attention of the publisher to any errors found so that corrections can be made in a subsequent edition.

The fifteenth edition of *Who's Who of American Women* continues the tradition of excellence established in 1899 with the publication of the first edition of *Who's Who in America*. The essence of that tradition is the continuing effort at Marquis Who's Who to produce reference works that are responsive to the needs of their users.

Board of Advisors

Marquis Who's Who gratefully acknowledges the following distinguished individuals who have made themselves available for review, evaluation, and general comment with regard to the publication of the fifteenth edition of *Who's Who of American Women.* The advisors have enhanced the reference value of this edition by the nomination of outstanding individuals for inclusion. However, the Board of Advisors, either collectively or individually, is in no way responsible for the final selection of names appearing in this volume, nor does the Board of Advisors bear responsibility for the accuracy or comprehensiveness of the biographical information or other material contained herein.

Mary S. Calderone, M.D.
Adjunct Professor
Health Education
New York University

Cardiss Robertson Collins
Congresswoman

Jean Dalrymple
Theatre Producer and Director

Mildred S. Dresselhaus
Professor
Electrical Engineering and Physics
Massachusetts Institute of Technology

Joseph J. Ellis
Dean of Faculty
Mount Holyoke College

John Guare
Playwright

Jill Krementz
Author and Photographer

Margaret M. Mills
Executive Director
American Academy and Institute of Arts and Letters

Jan Keene Muhlert
Director
Amon Carter Museum

Catherine R. Stimpson
Dean
The Graduate School-New Brunswick
Rutgers University

Standards of Admission

The major criterion for determining who will be included in *Who's Who of American Women* is the extent of a woman's reference value. Such reference interest is judged on either of two factors: (1) the position of responsibility held, or (2) the level of achievement attained by the individual.

Admission based on the factor of position includes the following examples:

High-level federal officials

Specified elected and appointed state officials

Mayors of major cities

Principal officers of selected businesses

Outstanding educators from major universities and colleges

Principal figures of cultural and artistic institutions

Heads of major women's organizations

Recipients of major awards and honors

Members of selected honorary organizations

Other women chosen because of incumbency or membership

Admission for individual achievement is based on objective qualitative criteria. To be selected, a woman must have attained conspicuous achievement. The biographee may scarcely be known in the local community but may be recognized in some field of endeavor for noteworthy accomplishment.

Key to Information

❶ **CHADWICK, ELIZABETH BATES,** ❷lawyer; ❸b. Mitchell, S.D., July 19, 1940; ❹d. Oscar William and Judith (Strait) Bates; ❺m. Richard T. Chadwick, Dec. 11, 1967; ❻children: Stephen Dwight, Mary Beth. ❼B.A., U. Okla., 1962, M.A., 1967; J.D., Rice U., 1970. ❽Bar: Tex. 1970, S.D. 1973, U.S. Dist. Ct. S.D. 1982, U.S. Supreme Ct. 1982. ❾Assoc. Newman, Calvin & Swain, Houston, 1967-73, ptnr., 1973-74; ptnr. Hoadley, Ellis, Chadwick & Gonzalez, Amarillo, Tex., 1974-78; sole practice, Rapid City, S.D., 1978-82; ptnr. Chadwick & Gibson, Rapid City, 1982—; lectr. Black Hills State Coll., Spearfish, S.D., 1984; mem. Gov.'s Task Force on Constl. Revision, Pierre, S.D., 1986—; bd. dirs. Custer Nat. Bank. ❿Contbr. articles to profl. jours. ⓫Trustee The Grove Sch., Rapid City, 1980—; active Pennington County United Way. ⓬Served with WAC, 1962-63. ⓭Named Outstanding Young Woman of Yr., Amarillo C. of C., 1975; Lincoln Found. grantee, 1980. ⓮Mem. ABA, S.D. Bar Assn., S.D. Assn. Def. Counsel, Pennington County Bar Assn., World Wildlife Fedn. ⓯Democrat. ⓰Lutheran. ⓱Clubs: Rushmore Hills Country, Noontime (Rapid City). ⓲Lodge: Order Easter Star. ⓳Avocations: golf, photography, quilting. ⓴Home: 5237 Woodbine Way Rapid City SD 57702 ㉑Office: Chadwick & Gibson 964 N Omaha St Rapid City SD 57701

KEY

❶ Name
❷ Occupation
❸ Vital Statistics
❹ Parents
❺ Marriage
❻ Children
❼ Education
❽ Professional certifications
❾ Career
❿ Writings and creative works
⓫ Civic and political activities
⓬ Military
⓭ Awards and fellowships
⓮ Professional and association memberships
⓯ Political affiliation
⓰ Religion
⓱ Clubs
⓲ Lodges
⓳ Avocations
⓴ Home address
㉑ Office address

Table of Abbreviations

The following abbreviations and symbols are frequently used in this book.

*An asterisk following a sketch indicates that it was researched by the Marquis Who's Who editorial staff and has not been verified by the biographee.

A.A. Associate in Arts
AAAL American Academy of Arts and Letters
AAAS American Association for the Advancement of Science
AAHPER Alliance for Health, Physical Education and Recreation
AAU Amateur Athletic Union
AAUP American Association of University Professors
AAUW American Association of University Women
A.B. Arts, Bachelor of
AB Alberta
ABA American Bar Association
ABC American Broadcasting Company
AC Air Corps
acad. academy, academic
acct. accountant
acctg. accounting
ACDA Arms Control and Disarmament Agency
ACLU American Civil Liberties Union
ACP American College of Physicians
ACS American College of Surgeons
ADA American Dental Association
a.d.c. aide-de-camp
adj. adjunct, adjutant
adj. gen. adjutant general
adm. admiral
adminstr. administrator
adminstrn. administration
adminstrv. administrative
ADP Automatic Data Processing
adv. advocate, advisory
advt. advertising
A.E. Agricultural Engineer (for degrees only)
A.E. and P. Ambassador Extraordinary and Plenipotentiary
AEC Atomic Energy Commission
aero. aeronautical, aeronautic
aerodyn. aerodynamic
AFB Air Force Base
AFL-CIO American Federation of Labor and Congress of Industrial Organizations
AFTRA American Federation of TV and Radio Artists
agr. agriculture
agrl. agricultural
agt. agent
AGVA American Guild of Variety Artists
agy. agency
A&I Agricultural and Industrial
AIA American Institute of Architects

AIAA American Institute of Aeronautics and Astronautics
AID Agency for International Development
AIEE American Institute of Electrical Engineers
AIM American Institute of Management
AIME American Institute of Mining, Metallurgy, and Petroleum Engineers
AK Alaska
AL Alabama
ALA American Library Association
Ala. Alabama
alt. alternate
Alta. Alberta
A&M Agricultural and Mechanical
A.M. Arts, Master of
Am. American, America
AMA American Medical Association
A.M.E. African Methodist Episcopal
Amtrak National Railroad Passenger Corporation
AMVETS American Veterans of World War II, Korea, Vietnam
anat. anatomical
ann. annual
ANTA American National Theatre and Academy
anthrop. anthropological
AP Associated Press
APO Army Post Office
apptd. appointed
Apr. April
apt. apartment
AR Arkansas
ARC American Red Cross
archeol. archeological
archtl. architectural
Ariz. Arizona
Ark. Arkansas
ArtsD. Arts, Doctor of
arty. artillery
AS American Samoa
ASCAP American Society of Composers, Authors and Publishers
ASCE American Society of Civil Engineers
ASHRAE American Society of Heating, Refrigeration, and Air Conditioning Engineers
ASME American Society of Mechanical Engineers
assn. association
assoc. associate
asst. assistant
ASTM American Society for Testing and Materials
astron. astronomical
astrophys. astrophysical
ATSC Air Technical Service Command
AT&T American Telephone & Telegraph Company

atty. attorney
Aug. August
AUS Army of the United States
aux. auxiliary
Ave. Avenue
AVMA American Veterinary Medical Association
AZ Arizona

B. Bachelor
b. born
B.A. Bachelor of Arts
B.Agr. Bachelor of Agriculture
Balt. Baltimore
Bapt. Baptist
B.Arch. Bachelor of Architecture
B.A.S. Bachelor of Agricultural Science
B.B.A. Bachelor of Business Administration
BBC British Broadcasting Corporation
BC, B.C. British Columbia
B.C.E. Bachelor of Civil Engineering
B.Chir. Bachelor of Surgery
B.C.L. Bachelor of Civil Law
B.C.S. Bachelor of Commercial Science
B.D. Bachelor of Divinity
bd. board
B.E. Bachelor of Education
B.E.E. Bachelor of Electrical Engineering
B.F.A. Bachelor of Fine Arts
bibl. biblical
bibliog. bibliographical
biog. biographical
biol. biological
B.J. Bachelor of Journalism
Bklyn. Brooklyn
B.L. Bachelor of Letters
bldg. building
B.L.S. Bachelor of Library Science
Blvd. Boulevard
bn. battalion
B.&O.R.R. Baltimore & Ohio Railroad
bot. botanical
B.P.E. Bachelor of Physical Education
br. branch
B.R.E. Bachelor of Religious Education
brig. gen. brigadier general
Brit. British, Brittanica
Bros. Brothers
B.S. Bachelor of Science
B.S.A. Bachelor of Agricultural Science
B.S.D. Bachelor of Didactic Science
B.S.T. Bachelor of Sacred Theology
B.Th. Bachelor of Theology
bull. bulletin
bur. bureau
bus. business
B.W.I. British West Indies

CA California

CAA Civil Aeronautics Administration
CAB Civil Aeronautics Board
Calif. California
C.Am. Central America
Can. Canada, Canadian
CAP Civil Air Patrol
capt. captain
CARE Cooperative American Relief Everywhere
Cath. Catholic
cav. cavalry
CBC Canadian Broadcasting Company
CBI China, Burma, India Theatre of Operations
CBS Columbia Broadcasting System
CCC Commodity Credit Corporation
CCNY City College of New York
CCU Cardiac Care Unit
CD Civil Defense
C.E. Corps of Engineers, Civil Engineer (in firm's name only or for degree)
cen. central (used for court system only)
CENTO Central Treaty Organization
CERN European Organization of Nuclear Research
cert. certificate, certification, certified
CETA Comprehensive Employment Training Act
CFL Canadian Football League
ch. church
Ch.D. Doctor of Chemistry
chem. chemical
Chem.E. Chemical Engineer
Chgo. Chicago
chirurg. chirurgical
chmn. chairman
chpt. chapter
CIA Central Intelligence Agency
CIC Counter Intelligence Corps
Cin. Cincinnati
cir. circuit
Cleve. Cleveland
climatol. climatological
clin. clinical
clk. clerk
C.L.U. Chartered Life Underwriter
C.M. Master in Surgery
CM Northern Mariana Islands
C.&N.W.Ry. Chicago & North Western Railway
CO Colorado
Co. Company
COF Catholic Order of Foresters
C. of C. Chamber of Commerce
col. colonel
coll. college
Colo. Colorado
com. committee
comd. commanded
comdg. commanding
comdr. commander
comdt. commandant

commd. commissioned
comml. commercial
commn. commission
commr. commissioner
condr. conductor
Conf. Conference
Congl. Congregational, Congressional
Conglist. Congregationalist
Conn. Connecticut
cons. consultant, consulting
consol. consolidated
constl. constitutional
constn. constitution
constrn. construction
contbd. contributed
contbg. contributing
contbn. contribution
contbr. contributor
Conv. Convention
coop. cooperative
CORDS Civil Operations and Revolutionary Development Support
CORE Congress of Racial Equality
corp. corporation, corporate
corr. correspondent, corresponding, correspondence
C.&O.Ry. Chesapeake & Ohio Railway
C.P.A. Certified Public Accountant
C.P.C.U. Chartered Property and Casualty Underwriter
C.P.H. Certificate of Public Health
cpl. corporal
C.P.R. Cardio-Pulmonary Resuscitation
C.P.Ry. Canadian Pacific Railway
C.S. Christian Science
C.S.B. Bachelor of Christian Science
C.S.C. Civil Service Commission
C.S.D. Doctor of Christian Science
CT Connecticut
ct. court
ctr. center
CWS Chemical Warfare Service
C.Z. Canal Zone

D. Doctor
d. daughter
D.Agr. Doctor of Agriculture
DAR Daughters of the American Revolution
dau. daughter
DAV Disabled American Veterans
DC, D.C. District of Columbia
D.C.L. Doctor of Civil Law
D.C.S. Doctor of Commercial Science
D.D. Doctor of Divinity
D.D.S. Doctor of Dental Surgery
DE Delaware
Dec. December
dec. deceased
def. defense
Del. Delaware
del. delegate, delegation

Dem. Democrat, Democratic
D.Eng. Doctor of Engineering
denom. denomination, denominational
dep. deputy
dept. department
dermatol. dermatological
desc. descendant
devel. development, developmental
D.F.A. Doctor of Fine Arts
D.F.C. Distinguished Flying Cross
D.H.L. Doctor of Hebrew Literature
dir. director
dist. district
distbg. distributing
distbn. distribution
distbr. distributor
disting. distinguished
div. division, divinity, divorce
D.Litt. Doctor of Literature
D.M.D. Doctor of Medical Dentistry
D.M.S. Doctor of Medical Science
D.O. Doctor of Osteopathy
D.P.H. Diploma in Public Health
D.R. Daughters of the Revolution
Dr. Drive, Doctor
D.R.E. Doctor of Religious Education
Dr.P.H. Doctor of Public Health, Doctor of Public Hygiene
D.S.C. Distinguished Service Cross
D.Sc. Doctor of Science
D.S.M. Distinguished Service Medal
D.S.T. Doctor of Sacred Theology
D.T.M. Doctor of Tropical Medicine
D.V.M. Doctor of Veterinary Medicine
D.V.S. Doctor of Veterinary Surgery

E. East
ea. eastern (used for court system only)
E. and P. Extraordinary and Plenipotentiary
Eccles. Ecclesiastical
ecol. ecological
econ. economic
ECOSOC Economic and Social Council (of the UN)
E.D. Doctor of Engineering
ed. educated
Ed.B. Bachelor of Education
Ed.D. Doctor of Education
edit. edition
Ed.M. Master of Education
edn. education
ednl. educational
EDP Electronic Data Processing
Ed.S. Specialist in Education
E.E. Electrical Engineer (degree only)
E.E. and M.P. Envoy Extraordinary and Minister Plenipotentiary
EEC European Economic Community
EEG Electroencephalogram
EEO Equal Employment Opportunity
EEOC Equal Employment Opportunity Commission

E.Ger. German Democratic Republic
EKG Electrocardiogram
elec. electrical
electrochem. electrochemical
electrophys. electrophysical
elem. elementary
E.M. Engineer of Mines
ency. encyclopedia
Eng. England
engr. engineer
engring. engineering
entomol. entomological
environ. environmental
EPA Environmental Protection Agency
epidemiol. epidemiological
Episc. Episcopalian
ERA Equal Rights Amendment
ERDA Energy Research and Development Administration
ESEA Elementary and Secondary Education Act
ESL English as Second Language
ESSA Environmental Science Services Administration
ethnol. ethnological
ETO European Theatre of Operations
Evang. Evangelical
exam. examination, examining
exec. executive
exhbn. exhibition
expdn. expedition
expn. exposition
expt. experiment
exptl. experimental

F.A. Field Artillery
FAA Federal Aviation Administration
FAO Food and Agriculture Organization (of the UN)
FBI Federal Bureau of Investigation
FCA Farm Credit Administration
FCC Federal Communications Commission
FCDA Federal Civil Defense Administration
FDA Food and Drug Administration
FDIA Federal Deposit Insurance Administration
FDIC Federal Deposit Insurance Corporation
F.E. Forest Engineer
FEA Federal Energy Administration
Feb. February
fed. federal
fedn. federation
FERC Federal Energy Regulatory Commission
fgn. foreign
FHA Federal Housing Administration
fin. financial, finance
FL Florida
Fla. Florida

FMC Federal Maritime Commission
FOA Foreign Operations Administration
found. foundation
FPC Federal Power Commission
FPO Fleet Post Office
frat. fraternity
FRS Federal Reserve System
FSA Federal Security Agency
Ft. Fort
FTC Federal Trade Commission

G-1 (or other number) Division of General Staff
GA, Ga. Georgia
GAO General Accounting Office
gastroent. gastroenterological
GATT General Agreement of Tariff and Trades
gen. general
geneal. genealogical
geod. geodetic
geog. geographic, geographical
geol. geological
geophys. geophysical
gerontol. gerontological
G.H.Q. General Headquarters
G.N. Ry. Great Northern Railway
gov. governor
govt. government
govtl. governmental
GPO Government Printing Office
grad. graduate, graduated
GSA General Services Administration
Gt. Great
GU Guam
gynecol. gynecological

hdqrs. headquarters
HEW Department of Health, Education and Welfare
H.H.D. Doctor of Humanities
HHFA Housing and Home Finance Agency
HHS Department of Health and Human Services
HI Hawaii
hist. historical, historic
H.M. Master of Humanics
homeo. homeopathic
hon. honorary, honorable
Ho. of Dels. House of Delegates
Ho. of Reps. House of Representatives
hort. horticultural
hosp. hospital
HUD Department of Housing and Urban Development
Hwy. Highway
hydrog. hydrographic

IA Iowa
IAEA International Atomic Energy Agency

IBM International Business Machines Corporation
IBRD International Bank for Reconstruction and Development
ICA International Cooperation Administration
ICC Interstate Commerce Commission
ICU Intensive Care Unit
ID Idaho
IEEE Institute of Electrical and Electronics Engineers
IFC International Finance Corporation
IGY International Geophysical Year
IL Illinois
Ill. Illinois
illus. illustrated
ILO International Labor Organization
IMF International Monetary Fund
IN Indiana
Inc. Incorporated
Ind. Indiana
ind. independent
Indpls. Indianapolis
indsl. industrial
inf. infantry
info. information
ins. insurance
insp. inspector
insp. gen. inspector general
inst. institute
instl. institutional
instn. institution
instr. instructor
instrn. instruction
intern. international
intro. introduction
IRE Institute of Radio Engineers
IRS Internal Revenue Service
ITT International Telephone & Telegraph Corporation

JAG Judge Advocate General
JAGC Judge Advocate General Corps
Jan. January
Jaycees Junior Chamber of Commerce
J.B. Jurum Baccalaureus
J.C.B. Juris Canoni Baccalaureus
J.C.D. Juris Canonici Doctor, Juris Civilis Doctor
J.C.L. Juris Canonici Licentiatus
J.D. Juris Doctor
jg. junior grade
jour. journal
jr. junior
J.S.D. Juris Scientiae Doctor
J.U.D. Juris Utriusque Doctor
jud. judicial

Kans. Kansas
K.C. Knights of Columbus
K.P. Knights of Pythias
KS Kansas

K.T. Knight Templar
KY, Ky. Kentucky

LA, La. Louisiana
lab. laboratory
lang. language
laryngol. laryngological
LB Labrador
lectr. lecturer
legis. legislation, legislative
L.H.D. Doctor of Humane Letters
L.I. Long Island
lic. licensed, license
L.I.R.R. Long Island Railroad
lit. literary, literature
Litt.B. Bachelor of Letters
Litt.D. Doctor of Letters
LL.B. Bachelor of Laws
LL.D. Doctor of Laws
LL.M. Master of Laws
Ln. Lane
L.&N.R.R. Louisville & Nashville Railroad
L.S. Library Science (in degree)
lt. lieutenant
Ltd. Limited
Luth. Lutheran
LWV League of Women Voters

M. Master
m. married
M.A. Master of Arts
MA Massachusetts
mag. magazine
M.Agr. Master of Agriculture
maj. major
Man. Manitoba
Mar. March
M.Arch. Master in Architecture
Mass. Massachusetts
math. mathematics, mathematical
MATS Military Air Transport Service
M.B. Bachelor of Medicine
MB Manitoba
M.B.A. Master of Business Administration
MBS Mutual Broadcasting System
M.C. Medical Corps
M.C.E. Master of Civil Engineering
mcht. merchant
mcpl. municipal
M.C.S. Master of Commercial Science
M.D. Doctor of Medicine
MD, Md. Maryland
M.Dip. Master in Diplomacy
mdse. merchandise
M.D.V. Doctor of Veterinary Medicine
ME Mechanical Engineer (degree only)
ME Maine
M.E.Ch. Methodist Episcopal Church
mech. mechanical
M.Ed. Master of Education
med. medical

M.E.E. Master of Electrical Engineering
mem. member
meml. memorial
merc. mercantile
met. metropolitan
metall. metallurgical
Met.E. Metallurgical Engineer
meteorol. meteorological
Meth. Methodist
Mex. Mexico
M.F. Master of Forestry
M.F.A. Master of Fine Arts
mfg. manufacturing
mfr. manufacturer
mgmt. management
mgr. manager
M.H.A. Master of Hospital Administration
M.I. Military Intelligence
MI Michigan
Mich. Michigan
micros. microscopic, microscopical
mid. middle (used for court system only)
mil. military
Milw. Milwaukee
mineral. mineralogical
Minn. Minnesota
Miss. Mississippi
MIT Massachusetts Institute of Technology
mktg. marketing
M.L. Master of Laws
MLA Modern Language Association
M.L.D. Magister Legnum Diplomatic
M.Litt. Master of Literature
M.L.S. Master of Library Science
M.M.E. Master of Mechanical Engineering
MN Minnesota
mng. managing
MO, Mo. Missouri
moblzn. mobilization
Mont. Montana
M.P. Member of Parliament
M.P.E. Master of Physical Education
M.P.H. Master of Public Health
M.P.L. Master of Patent Law
Mpls. Minneapolis
M.R.E. Master of Religious Education
M.S. Master of Science
MS, Ms. Mississippi
M.Sc. Master of Science
M.S.F. Master of Science of Forestry
M.S.T. Master of Sacred Theology
M.S.W. Master of Social Work
MT Montana
Mt. Mount
MTO Mediterranean Theatre of Operations
mus. museum, musical
Mus.B. Bachelor of Music

Mus.D. Doctor of Music
Mus.M. Master of Music
mut. mutual
mycol. mycological

N. North
NAACP National Association for the Advancement of Colored People
NACA National Advisory Committee for Aeronautics
NAD National Academy of Design
N.Am. North America
NAM National Association of Manufacturers
NAPA National Association of Performing Artists
NAREB National Association of Real Estate Boards
NARS National Archives and Record Service
NASA National Aeronautics and Space Administration
nat. national
NATO North Atlantic Treaty Organization
NATOUSA North African Theatre of Operations
nav. navigation
NB, N.B. New Brunswick
NBC National Broadcasting Company
NC, N.C. North Carolina
NCCJ National Conference of Christians and Jews
ND, N.D. North Dakota
NDEA National Defense Education Act
NE Nebraska
NE Northeast
NEA National Education Association
Nebr. Nebraska
NEH National Endowment for Humanities
neurol. neurological
Nev. Nevada
NF Newfoundland
NFL National Football League
Nfld. Newfoundland
NG National Guard
NH, N.H. New Hampshire
NHL National Hockey League
NIH National Institutes of Health
NIMH National Institute of Mental Health
NJ, N.J. New Jersey
NLRB National Labor Relations Board
NM New Mexico
N. Mex. New Mexico
No. Northern
NOAA National Oceanographic and Atmospheric Administration
NORAD North America Air Defense
Nov. November
NOW National Organization for Women
N.P.Ry. Northern Pacific Railway
nr. near
NRC National Research Council
NS, N.S. Nova Scotia

NSC National Security Council
NSF National Science Foundation
N.T. New Testament
NT Northwest Territories
numis. numismatic
NV Nevada
NW Northwest
N.W.T. Northwest Territories
NY, N.Y. New York
N.Y.C. New York City
NYU New York University
N.Z. New Zealand

OAS Organization of American States
ob-gyn obstetrics–gynecology
obs. observatory
obstet. obstetrical
Oct. October
O.D. Doctor of Optometry
OECD Organization of European
  Cooperation and Development
OEEC Organization of European
  Economic Cooperation
OEO Office of Economic Opportunity
ofcl. official
OH Ohio
OK Oklahoma
Okla. Oklahoma
ON Ontario
Ont. Ontario
ophthal. ophthalmological
ops. operations
OR Oregon
orch. orchestra
Oreg. Oregon
orgn. organization
ornithol. ornithological
OSHA Occupational Safety and Health
  Administration
OSRD Office of Scientific Research and
  Development
OSS Office of Strategic Services
osteo. osteopathic
otol. otological
otolaryn. otolaryngological

PA, Pa. Pennsylvania
P.A. Professional Association
paleontol. paleontological
path. pathological
P.C. Professional Corporation
PE Prince Edward Island
P.E.I. Prince Edward Island (text only)
PEN Poets, Playwrights, Editors, Essayists
and Novelists (international association)
penol. penological
P.E.O. women's organization (full name
  not disclosed)
pfc. private first class
PHA Public Housing Administration
pharm. pharmaceutical
Pharm.D. Doctor of Pharmacy
Pharm.M. Master of Pharmacy

Ph.B. Bachelor of Philosophy
Ph.D. Doctor of Philosophy
Phila. Philadelphia
philharm. philharmonic
philol. philological
philos. philosophical
photog. photographic
phys. physical
physiol. physiological
Pitts. Pittsburgh
Pkwy. Parkway
Pl. Place
P.&L.E.R.R. Pittsburgh & Lake Erie
  Railroad
P.O. Post Office
PO Box Post Office Box
polit. political
poly. polytechnic, polytechnical
PQ Province of Quebec
PR, P.R. Puerto Rico
prep. preparatory
pres. president
Presbyn. Presbyterian
presdl. presidential
prin. principal
proc. proceedings
prod. produced (play production)
prodn. production
prof. professor
profl. professional
prog. progressive
propr. proprietor
pros. atty. prosecuting attorney
pro tem pro tempore
PSRO Professional Services Review
  Organization
psychiat. psychiatric
psychol. psychological
PTA Parent–Teachers Association
ptnr. partner
PTO Pacific Theatre of Operations,
  Parent Teacher Organization
pub. publisher, publishing, published
pub. public
publ. publication
pvt. private

quar. quarterly
qm. quartermaster
Q.M.C. Quartermaster Corps
Que. Quebec

radiol. radiological
RAF Royal Air Force
RCA Radio Corporation of America
RCAF Royal Canadian Air Force
RD Rural Delivery
Rd. Road
REA Rural Electrification Administration
rec. recording
ref. reformed
regt. regiment

regtl. regimental
rehab. rehabilitation
Rep. Republican
rep. representative
Res. Reserve
ret. retired
rev. review, revised
RFC Reconstruction Finance
  Corporation
RFD Rural Free Delivery
rhinol. rhinological
RI, R.I. Rhode Island
R.N. Registered Nurse
roentgenol. roentgenological
ROTC Reserve Officers Training Corps
R.R. Railroad
Ry. Railway

S. South
s. son
SAC Strategic Air Command
SALT Strategic Arms Limitation Talks
S.Am. South America
san. sanitary
SAR Sons of the American Revolution
Sask. Saskatchewan
savs. savings
S.B. Bachelor of Science
SBA Small Business Administration
SC, S.C. South Carolina
SCAP Supreme Command Allies Pacific
Sc.B. Bachelor of Science
S.C.D. Doctor of Commercial Science
Sc.D. Doctor of Science
sch. school
sci. science, scientific
SCLC Southern Christian Leadership
  Conference
SCV Sons of Confederate Veterans
SD, S.D. South Dakota
SE Southeast
SEATO Southeast Asia Treaty
  Organization
SEC Securities and Exchange
  Commission
sec. secretary
sect. section
seismol. seismological
sem. seminary
Sept. September
s.g. senior grade
sgt. sergeant
SHAEF Supreme Headquarters Allied
  Expeditionary Forces
SHAPE Supreme Headquarters Allied
  Powers in Europe
S.I. Staten Island
S.J. Society of Jesus (Jesuit)
SJD Scientiae Juridicae Doctor
SK Saskatchewan
S.M. Master of Science
So. Southern

soc. society
sociol. sociological
S.P. Co. Southern Pacific Company
spl. special
splty. specialty
Sq. Square
S.R. Sons of the Revolution
sr. senior
SS Steamship
SSS Selective Service System
St. Saint, Street
sta. station
stats. statistics
statis. statistical
S.T.B. Bachelor of Sacred Theology
stblzn. stabilization
STD Doctor of Sacred Theology
subs. subsidiary
SUNY State University of New York
supr. supervisor
supt. superintendent
surg. surgical
SW Southwest

TAPPI Technical Association of the Pulp and Paper Industry
Tb Tuberculosis
tchr. teacher
tech. technical, technology
technol. technological
Tel.&Tel. Telephone & Telegraph
temp. temporary
Tenn. Tennessee
Ter. Territory
Terr. Terrace
Tex. Texas
Th.D. Doctor of Theology
theol. theological
Th.M. Master of Theology
TN Tennessee
tng. training
topog. topographical
trans. transaction, transferred
transl. translation, translated
transp. transportation
treas. treasurer
TT Trust Territory
TV television
TVA Tennessee Valley Authority
twp. township
TX Texas
typog. typographical

U. University
UAW United Auto Workers
UCLA University of California at Los Angeles
UDC United Daughters of the Confederacy
U.K. United Kingdom
UN United Nations

UNESCO United Nations Educational, Scientific and Cultural Organization
UNICEF United Nations International Children's Emergency Fund
univ. university
UNRRA United Nations Relief and Rehabilitation Administration
UPI United Press International
U.P.R.R. United Pacific Railroad
urol. urological
U.S. United States
U.S.A. United States of America
USAAF United States Army Air Force
USAF United States Air Force
USAFR United States Air Force Reserve
USAR United States Army Reserve
USCG United States Coast Guard
USCGR United States Coast Guard Reserve
USES United States Employment Service
USIA United States Information Agency
USMC United States Marine Corps
USMCR United States Marine Corps Reserve
USN United States Navy
USNG United States National Guard
USNR United States Naval Reserve
USO United Service Organizations
USPHS United States Public Health Service
USS United States Ship
USSR Union of the Soviet Socialist Republics
USV United States Volunteers
UT Utah

VA Veterans' Administration
VA, Va. Virginia
vet. veteran, veterinary
VFW Veterans of Foreign Wars
VI, V.I. Virgin Islands
vice pres. vice president
vis. visiting
VISTA Volunteers in Service to America
VITA Volunteers in Technical Service
vocat. vocational
vol. volunteer, volume
v.p. vice president
vs. versus
VT, Vt. Vermont

W. West
WA Washington (state)
WAC Women's Army Corps
Wash. Washington (state)
WAVES Women's Reserve, US Naval Reserve
WCTU Women's Christian Temperance Union
we. western (used for court system only)
W.Ger. Germany, Federal Republic of
WHO World Health Organization
WI Wisconsin

W.I. West Indies
Wis. Wisconsin
WSB Wage Stabilization Board
WV West Virginia
W.Va. West Virginia
WY Wyoming
Wyo. Wyoming

YK Yukon Territory (for address)
YMCA Young Men's Christian Association
YMHA Young Men's Hebrew Association
YM & YWHA Young Men's and Young Women's Hebrew Association
yr. year
YT, Y.T. Yukon Territory
YWCA Young Women's Christian Association

zool. zoological

Alphabetical Practices

Names are arranged alphabetically according to the surnames, and under identical surnames according to the first given name. If both surname and first given name are identical, names are arranged alphabetically according to the second given name. Where full names are identical, they are arranged in order of age—with the elder listed first.

Surnames beginning with De, Des, Du, however capitalized or spaced, are recorded with the prefix preceding the surname and arranged alphabetically, under the letter D.

Surnames beginning with Mac and Mc are arranged alphabetically under M.

Surnames beginning with Saint or St. appear after names that begin Sains, and are arranged according to the second part of the name, e.g. St. Clair before Saint Dennis.

Surnames beginning with Van, Von or von are arranged alphabetically under letter V.

Compound hyphenated surnames are arranged according to the first member of the compound. Compound unhyphenated surnames are treated as hyphenated names.

Parentheses used in connection with a name indicate which part of the full name is usually deleted in common usage. Hence Abbott, W(illiam) Lewis indicates that the usual form of the given name is W. Lewis. The name recorded as Abbott, (William) Lewis signifies that the entire name William is not commonly used. In both cases the parentheses are ignored in alphabetizing.

Who's Who of American Women

AADALEN, SHARON PRICE, educator, researcher; b. Manchester, N.H., June 26, 1940; d. Trevor Alaric Pryce and Beatrice (Dinsmore) Price; m. Richard Jerome Aadalen, July 27, 1963; children—Richard Andrew, Kirk Jeremy, Lora Elizabeth. B.A. magna cum laude, Radcliffe Coll., 1962, diploma in nursing, Radcliffe Coll.-Mass. Gen. Hosp., 1964; B.S. in Nursing, Western Res. U., 1967; M.S. in Pub. Health, U. Minn., 1979, Ph.D. in Edn., 1983. R.N., cert. pub. health nursing, Minn. Staff nurse pub. health Vis. Nurse Assn., Roxbury Dist. Boston, 1964-65; staff and charge nurse, Lakeside Hosp., Univ. Hosps., Cleve., 1965-66; staff and charge nurse neurol. rehab. Benjamin Rose Hosp., Univ. Hosps., Cleve., 1966; staff nurse coronary rehab., coronary ICU, Mt. Sinai Hosp., Mpls., 1974-76; instr. Sch. Nursing SUNY-Plattsburgh, 1967-69; instr. Sch. Pub. Health, U. Minn., Mpls., 1979-82, adj. faculty, 1982—, adj. asst. prof. Sch. Nursing, 1986—, prin. investigator Minn. Sudden Infant Death Center and Sch. Pub. Health U. Minn., 1978, prin. investigator dept. curriculum and instrn., adult edn., Coll. Edn., 1981-83; dir. nursing edn. and research United Hosp., St. Paul; cons. div. nursing and health scis. mgmt. Minot State Coll. (N.D.), 1982; workshop coordinator dept. family social sci. U. Minn., St. Paul, 1983, cons., 1983; instr. sch. nurse achievement program U. Colo., 1983; mem. maternal and child health external grants rev. com. Minn. Dept. Health, 1983; bd. dirs., exec. com. Midwest Alliance in Nursing, 1982-83; mem. task force Gov.'s White House Conf. on Family Stress and Work, 1981. Contbr. chpts. to books, articles to profl. jours.; speaker profl. confs. U.S., USSR. Bd. dirs. WYCA, Cleveland Heights, Ohio, 1969-73; speakers bur. Minn. affiliate Am. Heart Assn., 1975-77; mem. Citizens League, 1979—; mem. subcom. Citizens Adv. Task Force on Edn., Edina, Minn., 1975-77, com. Ind. Sch. Dist. 273 Edina Pub. Schs., 1983-84; active Edina Community Lutheran Ch., 1973—; mem. allocation and evaluation panels United Way Mpls., 1983-86; mem. Edina Health Adv. Bd., 1985—, chmn., 1986; mem. State Community Health Services Adv. Com., 1985-86; v.p. Council of Ministers, 1983, pres., 1984. Thompson scholar, 1960-61; Ruth Sherman fellow, 1962; scholar Mass. Gen. Hosp. Sch. Nursing, 1962-64; trainee div. nursing USPHS, HEW, Frances Payne Bolton Sch. Nursing, Western Res. U., 1966-67, Sch. Pub. Health, U. Minn., 1977-78; scholar reflective leadership seminar Hubert H. Humphrey Inst. Pub. Affairs, U. Minn., 1983-84. Mem. Am. Nurses Assn. (council nurse researchers, council continuing edn.), Minn. Nurses Assn. (coms.), Am. Pub. Health Assn., Minn. Pub. Health Assn. (Future Directions Task Force 1980-81), Am. Assn. Adult and Continuing Edn., Am. Assn. Nurse Execs., Minn. Assn. Nurse Execs., Twin Cities Assn. Nurse Execs., Midwest Nursing Research Soc., Minn. Mental Health Assn., World Futures Soc., U. Minn. Alumni Assn. (interim bd. dirs. Constituent Soc. Sch. Pub. Health), Sigma Theta Tau (bd. dirs. 1980-82, research award 1984), Phi Delta Kappa, Phi Kappa Phi. Home: 4924 Dale Dr Edina MN 55424 Office: Dept Nursing Edn and Research United Hosp 333 N Smith Ave St Paul MN 55102

AAKRE, S. MAUREEN, social services adminstr.; b. Granite Falls, Minn., Dec. 30, 1945; d. Bernard S. and Marjorie (Skjefte) Aakre; B.A. magna cum laude, No. Ariz. U., 1973, M.A., 1977; m. Glenn E. Williams, July 31, 1979. Sr. cons. Social Dynamics, Inc., under contract to HEW, San Francisco, 1974-75; pres. AAKRE Cons.'s; coordinator Fairbanks (Alaska) Native Assn. Adult Learning Center, 1976-77; instr. Tanana Valley Coll., Fairbanks, 1976-77; founder, exec. dir. Women in Crisis-Counseling and Assistance (WIC-CA), Fairbanks, 1977-78; dir. dept. human resources Esca-Tech. Corp.; cons. Tanana Chiefs Conf. Land Claims Coll., 1975; del. Alaska conf. Internat. Women's Year, 1977; bd. dirs. Tanana Valley Citizen's Council on Work and Edn., 1977—, Abused Women's Aid In Crisis, 1979—, pres., 1980—; chairperson com. tng. and tech. assistance Alaska Network Domestic Violence and Sexual Assault, 1980—; exec. dir. Alaska Women's Resource Center, 1980—. Named Alaska Outstanding Young Woman of Yr., Gen. Fedn. Womens Clubs, 1977. Mem. NOW (task force coordinator 1976-77), Am., Pacific sociol. assns., Soc. for Study Social Problems, Alaska Adult Edn. Assn. (treas.), Am. Tae Kwon Do Assn. (6th deg. Green Belt), Am. Chung Do Kwon Assn. Clubs: Sons of Norway, Fairbanks Noon Jaycees (dir. 1977—). Author: Guide to Nonprofit Organizations in Alaska; Resource Directory for Alaska Network, also supplementary tng. programs. Office: Alaska Women's Resources Center 111 W ith Ave Anchorage AK 99501

AANDRES, VIOLET SCHROCK, artist; b. Vancouver, Wash., July 14, 1943; d. Liscomb Edward and Helen Arlene (Swanson) Schrock; B.A. in Anthropology, Wash. State U., 1968. Counselor, Napoleon Hill Found., Boulder, Colo., 1971-73; social worker Del. Home and Hosp., Smyrna, 1968-69; Chautauqua artist Colo. Council Arts and Humanities, 1976; guest artist W. Colo. Ctr. for Arts, Grand Junction, 1977; dir. Draw "82, nat. juried show; art workshop coordinator Master Artists in Colo.; dir. Master Artists in Colo. One woman watercolor shows include Boulder Art Ctr., 1974, Club Santiago, Manzanillo, Mex., 1977, Blue Door Gallery, Taos Inn, Mex., 1977, W. Colo. Ctr. for Arts, 1977, Tamarron, Durango, Colo., 1977, Woman's Bank, Denver, 1981, Denver Nat. Bank, 1982, U. No. Colo., 1983, Nat. Ctr. for Atmospheric Research, 1984, F & B Gallery, Longmont, Colo., 1984, 85, 86, others; group shows include Boulder Pub. Library, 1976, U. Okla. Internat. Tng. Ctr., Colima, Mex., 1974, 75, 76, Albatross Gallery, Boulder, 1975-77, Red Rocks Campus-Community Coll. Denver, Arvada Ctr. for Arts, Colo., 1977, Wonderland Hill Corp., 1979, 80, Highland Bldg., Boulder, 1980; represented in permanent collections U. Okla. Internat. Tng. Ctr., Wonderland Hill, Boulder, State of Colo. Chautauqua Collection, Green peace Maui-Lahaina. Bd. dirs. Boulder Art Ctr., Mountain Artists' Guild. Recipient Gold Seal award Craig Spring Art Gala, 1975, 77, meritorious award Colo. State Fair, 1982, 85. Mem. Am. Watercolor Soc. (assoc.), Boulder Art Assn. (pres., Juror's award, annual show 1980, 81, 82. Home: Studio A PO Box 365 Nederland CO 80466

AARON, CHLOE WELLINGHAM, business executive; b. Santa Monica, Calif., Oct. 9, 1938; d. John Rufus and Grace (Lloyd) Wellingham; B.A., Occidental Coll., 1961; M.A., George Washington U., 1966; m. David Laurence Aaron, Aug. 11, 1962; 1 son, Timothy Wellingham. Free-lance journalist, contbg. articles on TV to various publs. including N.Y. mag., Art in Am. and Washington Post, 1965-70; dir. public media program Nat. Endowment for Arts, Washington, 1970-76; sr. v.p. programming Public Broadcasting Service, Washington, 1976-81; pres. Chloe Aaron Assos., Inc., N.Y.C., 1981—; producer Soldier's Tale (Emmy 1984), Pub. Broadcasting System, 1984. Mem. trustee com. on film Mus. Modern Art, N.Y.C.; mem. film and video com. Whitney Mus. Am. Art, N.Y.C.; bd. dirs. Pub. Devel. Corp. N.Y.C., Stowe Sch., Center Visual History. Recipient Alumni award Occidental Coll., 1983. Office: 609 Fifth Ave New York NY 10017

AARON, SHIRLEY MAE, tax consultant; b. Covington, La., Feb. 28, 1935; d. Morgan and Pearl (Jenkins) King; m. Michael A. Aaron, Nov. 27, 1976; m. Richard L. King, Feb. 16, 1952 (div. Feb. 1965); children—Deborah, Richard, Roberta, Keely. Adminstrv. asst. South Central Bell, Covington, La., 1954-62; acct. Brown & Root, Inc., Houston, 1962-75; timekeeper Alyeska Pipeline Co., Fairbanks, Alaska, 1975-77; adminstrv. asst. Boeing Co., Seattle, 1979—; pres. Aaron Enterprises, Seattle, 1977—. Bd. dirs. Burien 146 Homeowners Assn., Seattle, 1979—, pres., 1980-83. Mem. Nat. Assn. Female Execs. Avocation: singing.

ABAD, BERNADINE, state official, equal rights advocate; b. Phila., Jan. 13, 1949; d. Alexander Zachariah and Mamie Esther (Davis) Talmadge. B.S., Pa. State U.-Middletown, 1970; M.Ed., SUNY-Albany, 1971; postgrad. J.F. Kennedy Sch. Govt., Harvard U., 1982. Coll. admissions cons. SUNY-Oneonta, 1970-73; corrections counselor, supr. Pa. Dept. Justice Phila., 1973-76; dir. Alternatives for Exceptional Women, Phila., 1976-78; city planner CETA, City of Phila., 1978-80, mgr. employment and tng. program, 1980-81; dir. affirmative action and contract compliance Commonwealth of Pa., Harrisburg, 1981—; speaker, cons. in field. Mem. Internat. Personnel Mgmt. Assn., Nat. Inst. for Employment Equity (chmn. fin. com. 1983-84), Nat. Assn. Blacks in Criminal Justice, NAACP, Alpha Kappa Alpha (chmn. AKA connection 1984). Republican. Home: 2321 Market St Harrisburg PA 17103 Office: Executive Office Affirmative Action 510 Finance Bldg Harrisburg PA 17120

ABARBANEL, JUDITH EDNA, marketing executive; b. N.Y.C., Jan. 26, 1956; d. Albert Brandt and Dorothy Irene (Fennell) A.; m. Christopher George Lucas, June 17, 1984. B.A., UCLA, 1977; M.B.A., M.A., Ohio State U., 1980. Sales mgr. Columbus Magic, Ohio, 1979; account mgr. Mktg. Centre, St. Petersburg, Fla., 1980-82; asst. mktg. dir. MBI, Inc., Golden, Colo., 1983; dir. mktg. Colo. Outward Bound. Sch., Denver, 1983—; owner A Sporting Proposition, Boulder, Colo., 1984—. Mem. Denver Advt. Fedn., Ad 2. Avocations: mountain biking, race organizing. Office: Colo Outward Bound Sch 945 Pennsylvania St Denver CO 80203

ABARBANEL, KARIN, business communications specialist; b. N.Y.C., Feb. 23, 1950; d. Albert and Dorothy Irene (Fennell) A.; B.A. magna cum laude, Middlebury Coll., 1971; M.A., Columbia U., 1972, postgrad., 1972-73. Edn. coordinator Am. Film Theatre, N.Y.C., 1973-74; resume/career cons. Janice LaRouche Assos., N.Y.C., 1974—; assoc. editor Foundation News, N.Y.C., 1976-79; exec. editor The Exec. Female, N.Y.C., 1977—; dir. mktg. communications, editor Outlook mag. Booz, Allen & Hamilton, Inc., N.Y.C., 1979—; lectr., cons. in field. George W. Ellis fellow, 1971-72; Columbia U. fellow, 1972-73. Mem. Internat. Assn. Bus. Communicators, Advt. Women N.Y., Women's Inst. for Freedom of Press, Women in Founds./Corp. Philanthropy, Nat. Assn. Female Execs., Columbia U. Alumni Assn., Phi Beta Kappa. Co-author: Woman's Work Book, 1977, The Art of Winning Foundation Grants, 1975; also articles on career and fin. advancement, women in founds., youth employment, tech. and mgmt., community devel., grants planning and proposal writing. Office: Booz Allen & Hamilton Inc 101 Park Ave New York NY 10178

ABBADESSA, JOANN, lawyer; b. N.Y.C., Mar. 21, 1955; d. Joseph John and Jeanne (Pioppo) A. B.A., Adelphi U., 1976; J.D., Nova U., 1980. Bar: Fla. 1980, N.Y. 1982. Assoc. firm Levine & Green, Ft. Lauderdale, Fla., 1979-80, Dinkes, Mandel, Dinkes & Morelli, N.Y.C., 1981-84; sole practice, N.Y.C., 1984—; writer med. mag., MD/PC, 1983. Fellow N.Y. State Trial Lawyers Assn., N.Y. County Lawyers Assn., Met. Women's Bar Assn.; mem. ABA, Am. Trial Lawyers Assn., Lifespring. Office: 321 Broadway New York NY 10007

ABBEY, PATRICIA ANN, banker, cattle rancher; b. Coleman, Tex., Sept. 7, 1955; d. Charlie Ray and Betty Jeane (Traylor) Abbey. B.B.A., Tex. Tech. U., 1977. With Countrywide Ins., Coleman, Tex., 1973-74; student asst. Tex. Tech. U., Lubbock, 1975-77; asst. field supr. Employers Ins. Tex., Dallas, 1978-81; project mgr. Tex. Commerce Bank, Houston, 1982-84, sr. v.p., cashier Tex. Commerce Bank, Mid-land, 1984—; ptnr. Abbey Polled Herefords, Coleman, Tex., 1978—. Recipient Tuxwell award Tex. Tech. Rodeo Assn., 1977. Mem. Am. Bankers Assn., Nat. Assn. Female Execs., Tex. Polled Hereford Assn. (adv. dir. 1984—), Tex. Poll-Ettes (v.p. 1983-84, pres. 1984—, dir. 1982—, Miss Tex. Poll-Ette 1976-77), Phi Gamma Nu. Methodist. Club: Soroptimist. Home: PO Box 3294 Midland TX 79702 Office: Texas Commerce Bank PO Box 3905 Midland TX 79701

ABBOTT, FRANCES ELIZABETH DOWDLE, journalist, civic worker; b. Rome, Ga., Mar. 21, 1924; d. John Wesley and Lucille Elizabeth (Field) Dowdle; student Draughon's Bus. Coll., Columbia, S.C.; m. Jackson Miles Abbott, May 15, 1948; children—Medora Frances, David Field, Elizabeth Stockton, Robert Jackson. Feature writer, Mt. Vernon corr. Alexandria Gazette, Va., 1967-75; research assoc. Gadsby's Tavern Mus., Alexandria, 1977—. Chmn. ann. George Washington Birthnight Ball, Mt. Vernon, 1974-82; sec. 250th Washington Birthday Celebration Commn., 1979-82; chmn. publicity Waynewood Woman's Club, Waynewood Citizens Assn.; treas. Mt. Vernon Citizens Assn., 1967-82; dist. chmn. Mt. Vernon March of Dimes, 1960-62; sec. Waynewood Sch. P.T.A., 1962-64; tchr. 1st aid Girl Scouts U.S.A., 1964-65; den mother Cub Scouts, 1966; registrar DAR, 1968-77; chmn. publicity Mt. Vernon Women's Republican Club, 1955. Named Mrs. Waynewood by Community Vote, 1969. Mem. Audubon Naturalist Soc., Nat. Trust Historic Preservation. Episcopalian. Home: 8501 Doter Dr Alexandria VA 22308 Office: 134 Royal St N Alexandria VA 22314

ABBOTT, NANCY LEE, lawyer, nurse; b. Bklyn., Apr. 27, 1952; d. Michael and Louise Emma (Eklund) Abbott; m. Robert Andrew Feinschreiber, July 21, 1979 (div. 1984). B.A. in Econs., Rutgers U., Newark, 1978; M.B.A. in Acctg., NYU, 1981; J.D., U. Miami, 1982. Registered nurse, N.J., Fla; bar: Fla. Sec., treas. Interstate Tax Press Inc., Key Biscayne, Fla.; dir. Corp. Tax Press Inc., Key Biscayne, 1981-83; treas. Internat. Bus. Conf. Inc., Key Biscayne, 1982-83; tax cons. Feinschreiber & Assocs., N.Y.C., Key Biscayne, 1976-83; sole practice, Miami, Fla., 1983—; lectr. bus. orgns., others. Mng. editor Internat. Tax Jour., 1982-83; asst. editor, 1976-82; contbr. book; tax articles to profl. jours. Mem. ABA (tax sect.), Am. Assn. Critical Care Nurses, Fla. Bar Assn., Dade County Bar Assn., Omicron Delta Epsilon. Home: 187 Stirling Rd Warren NJ 07060

ABBOTT, ROSEMARY KENDALL, corporation executive; b. Chgo., May 13, 1951; d. Jesse Ray and Shirley Ruth (Pohl) Kendall; m. Gary Peter Abbott, Feb. 4, 1978. A.A., Kendall Jr. Coll., 1971; B.S. in Indsl. Psychology, U. Ill., 1973, M.A. in Indsl. Relations, 1974. Tng. and devel. rep. Union Carbide Corp., Texas City, Tex., 1974-76, employment assoc., 1976-77, non-exempt employee relations adminstr., 1977-79, labor relations adminstr., 1979-81, mgr. employment and salary adminstrn., 1981-86, mgr. employment, tng. and salary adminstrn., 1986—; bus. rep. Gulf Coast Pvt. Industry Council. Mem. Indsl. Relations Research Assn., Tex. Assn. of Bus. Club: Houstonian (Houston). Office: Union Carbide Corp Box 471 Texas City TX 77590

ABBOTT, SUSAN LEIGH, lawyer; b. Buffalo, Apr. 20, 1955; d. James Addison and Marguerite Louise (Hutchcraft) Abbott; m. Joseph A. Barbknecht, Nov., 1984. B.A., U. Okla., 1977, J.D., 1980. Bar: Okla. 1980, Tex. 1981. Assoc. Rex K. Travis, Oklahoma City, 1978-81, Shank, Irwin & Conant, Dallas, 1981—; vol. counselor Dallas County Young Lawyers, 1981—. Mem. Young Republicans, Dallas County, Dallas Symphony Innovators, Dallas Mus. Art. Mem. State Bar Tex., State Bar Okla., Dallas County Bar Assn., Phi Beta Kappa. Methodist. Office: Shank Irwin & Conant 1601 Elm St 4100 Thanksgiving Tower Dallas TX 75201

ABBOTT, VIRGINIA MILLER, speech-language pathologist, educator; b. Washington, Dec. 25, 1942; d. Edward Donald and Virginia Augusta (Grohs) Miller; B.A., George Washington U., 1964; M.Ed., Fitchburg State Coll., 1972; m. Henry L. Abbott, Jr., Aug. 30, 1966. Dir. speech and hearing clinic Burbank Hosp., Fitchburg, Mass., 1968-72; cons. tchr. Leominster (Mass.) Public Schs., 1972-76; chmn. evaluation team, spl. needs dept. Lunenburg (Mass.) Public Schs., 1977-81; dir. religious edn. Christ Ch., Fitchburg, Mass., 1980-82; speech-lang. pathologist Groton-Dunstable (Mass.) Public Schs., 1982—, elem. supr., 1984—. Mem. Am. Speech and Hearing Assn. (cert. clin. competence in speech pathology), Mass. Speech and Hearing Assn. (Disting. Service award 1986), Worcester Art Mus., NE Coalition for Ednl. Leadership, Sigma Alpha Eta, Zeta Tau Alpha. Republican. Home: 498 Valley Rd Mason NH 03048 Office: Pupil Personnal Services care Prescott Sch Groton MA 01450

ABDELLAH, FAYE GLENN, government official; b. N.Y.C., Mar. 13, 1919; d. H.B. and Margaret (Glenn) Abdellah. R.N., Ann May Sch. Nursing, N.J., 1942; B.S., Tchrs. Coll., Columbia U., 1945, M.A., 1947, Ed.D., 1955; LL.D. (hon.), Case Western Res. U., 1967, Rutgers U., 1973; Sc.D. (hon.), U. Akron, 1978, Cath. U. Am., 1981, Eastern Mich. U., 1982; D.P.H., Monmouth Coll., 1982. Commd. officer USPHS, 1949, advanced through grades to asst. surgeon gen. (Navy rear adm.), 1970; chief nursing edn. br., div. nursing, 1949-59; chief research grants br. Bur. Health Manpower Edn., NIH, HEW, 1959-69; dir. Office Research Tng. Nat. Center for Health Services Research and Devel., Health Services Mental Health Adminstrn., 1969; dep. surgeon gen., 1981—; chief nurse officer USPHS, Rockville, Md., 1970—; acting dep. dir. Nat. Center for Health Services Research and Devel., 1971, acting dep. dir. Bur. Health Services Research and Evaluation, Health Resources Adminstrn., 1973; dir. Office Long-Term Care, Office Asst. Sec. for Health, HEW, 1973—. Author: Effect of Nurse Staffing on Satisfactions with Nursing Care, 1959; Patient Centered Approaches to Nursing, 1960; Better Patient Care Through Nursing Research, 1965, 2d edit., 1979, 3d edit., 1986; Intensive Care, Concepts and Practices for Clinical Nurse Specialists, 1969; New Directions in Patient Centered Nursing, 1972. Contbr. articles to profl. jours. Charter fellow Am. Acad. Nursing (v.p.). Mem. Am. Psychol. Assn., AAAS, Assn. Mil. Surgeons U.S., Sigma Theta Tau, Phi Lambda Theta. Home: 3713 Chanel Rd Annandale VA 22003 Office: Room 18-67 5600 Fishers Ln Rockville MD 20852

ABEL, CLARE HOLLIE, lawyer; b. Lancaster, Pa., Feb. 14, 1955; d. Clarence Wallace and Laura Lee (Wilkinson) A.; m. Richard Stephen Bowman, Mar. 31, 1984. B.A. in Advertising with honors, Tex. Tech U., 1977; J.D., Ariz. State U., 1981. Bar: Ariz. 1981, U.S. Dist. Ct. 1981. Asst. regional mgr. Nationwide Advt., Inc., Phoenix, 1977-78; assoc. Richmond & Kelley, Phoenix, 1981-84, Burch & Cracchiolo, P.A., Phoenix, 1984—; dir., gen. counsel O.K. Community, Inc., Phoenix, 1983—; legis. aide, mem. rules com. Ariz. State House Reps., Phoenix, 1981. Vol., John Anderson for Pres. Campaign, Phoenix, 1980. Recipient Outstanding Customer Service Rep. 2nd Quarter award Nationwide Advt., Inc., 1978. Joe H. and Mary Lou Bryant scholar Tex. Tech Mass Communications, 1976; DuBois scholar, 1980. Mem. ABA, State Bar Ariz. (trial sect., various coms., arbitrator), Maricopa County Bar Assn., Assn. Trial Lawyers Am., Jr. League Phoenix, Ariz. State U. Coll. Law Alumni Assn. (bd. dirs. 1985-87), Phi Kappa Phi, Omicron Delta Kappa, Kappa Tau Alpha (v.p. 1976), Alpha Delta Sigma (charter), Alpha Delta Pi (pledge pres. 1975, Panhellenic del. 1976, 77-83, Phoenix Panhellenic Assn. (scholarship chmn. 1978-79, chmn. bird's nest 1979-83). Republican. Presbyterian. Office: Burch & Cracchiolo PA 702 E Osborn Rd Phoenix AZ 85014

ABEL, FLORENCE CATHERINE HARRIS, social worker; b. Phila., Dec. 28, 1941; d. Wilber Fiske and Melda Elizabeth (Beitzel) Harris; m. David Lynn Abel, Jan. 22, 1983. B.S., High Point (N.C.) Coll., 1963; M.S.W., U. Md., 1972. Social work asst. Calvert County (Md.) Dept. Social Services, Prince Frederick, 1964-69; social work asst. Prince George's County (Md.) Dept. Social Service, Hyattsville, 1969-71; social worker Md. Children's Aid and Family Service, Towson, Md., 1972-80, Crownsville (Md.) Hosp. Center, 1980—; field instr. U. Md. Sch. Social Work, 1985—; chairperson Social Work Peer Rev. Com., 1982-83; cons. Contact Balt., 1974-79; counselor Family Life Center, Columbia, Md., 1974-80; mem. citizens adv. council N.W. Mental Health Balt. County, 1977-78. sec. bd. dirs. Christian Counseling Assocs., Columbia, 1978—, family therapist, 1980—; mem. Faith at Work Team, Columbia, 1973-75, Calvert County Commn. on Aging, 1967-68, Evang. Women's Caucus, Washington, 1976—, N.W. Coalition Social Agys., Balt. County, 1978; cons. Nursing Home Ministry Evang. Presbyn. Ch., Annapolis, Md., 1978. Vice pres., treas. bd. dirs. Wheaton Animal Hosp., Inc., Kensington, Md. Lic. cert. social worker, Md. Mem. Nat. Assn. Social Workers, Register Clin. Social Workers, Assn. Certified Social Workers, Md. Conf. Social Concern, Christian Assocs. for Psychol. Studies. Democrat. Presbyterian. Home: 120 Hedgewood Dr Greenbelt MD 20770 Office: Sam Shoemaker Bldg Suite 203 11065 Little Patuxent Pkwy Columbia MD 21044

ABELAR, INA MAE, equipment technician; b. Jay Em, Wyo., July 18, 1926; d. Merritt Lyle and Leeta May (Worthen) Cameron; B.A., Calif. State Poly. U., 1978; m. Michael Sandoval Abelar, Nov. 17, 1951 (div. 1966); children—Debora Jean, Michelle Elaine, Randolph Lee. Lumber estimator Keith Brown Bldg. Supply, Salem, Oreg., 1946-48; with Whiting-Mead Bldg. Supply, Vernon, Calif., 1949-51, Trojan Lumber Co., Burbank, Calif., 1952-55; bookkeeper Jerry Kalior Bookkeeping Systems, North Hollywood, Calif., 1959-66; with Calif. State Poly. U., Pomona, 1967—, supervising equip. technician II dept. physics, 1979—, mem. campus staff council, 1970—, chmn., 1977-78. Recipient outstanding staff award Calif. State Poly U., 1983-84. Deaconess, Upland Christian Ch., 1978-81; mem. chancellery choir Bethany Bapt. Ch., 1984—. Mem. Mu Phi Epsilon. (chpt. pres. 1983—). Democrat. Home: 1833 Benedict Way Pomona CA 91767 Office: 3801 W Temple St Rm 8-238 Pomona CA 91768

ABEL HOROWITZ, MICHELLE SUSAN, advertising agency executive; b. Detroit, Mar. 31, 1950; d. Martin Louis and Phyllis (Berkowitz) A.; m. H. Jay Abel Horowitz, July 11, 1976; children—Jordan Michael, Stefanie Jennifer. Student Goucher Coll., 1967-70; B.A. in Econs., U. Mich., 1971; postgrad. in econs. U. Calif.-San Diego, 1973; M.A. in Econs., U. Detroit, 1974-76. Planning group supr. Hill Holliday Connors, Cosmopolus, Mass., 1976-78; econ. analyst Data Resources, Boston, 1978-79; v.p., media dir. Barkley & Evergreen, Southfield, Mich., 1979-80; v.p., dir. mktg. and media Yaffe/Berline, Southfield, Mich., 1980-82; sr. v.p., dir. client services, corp. treas. Berline Group, Birmingham, Mich., 1982—; instr. Oakland U., Rochester, Mich., 1982; trustee, chairperson mktg. com. Harbinger Dance Co., Farmington, Mich., 1983—. Named Advt. Woman of Yr., Women's Ad Club Detroit, 1982. Mem. Adcraft Club Detroit, Women in Communications. Democrat. Jewish. Office: Berline Group 6735 Telegraph Birmingham MI 48010

ABELING, PATRICIA ANN, retail contract furniture industry executive; b. Paterson, N.J., Mar. 15, 1947; d. Herbert Herman and Irene Elizabeth (Cleveland) Herron; m. m. (div. Oct. 1978); 1 child, Timothy Jon Blum; m. Michael Albert Abeling, June 1, 1979. Student Paier Sch. Art, 1965-67. Dining room mgr. Holiday Inn, Bridgeport, Conn., 1978-79; installation supr. Lubin Bus. Interiors, New Haven, 1979-83, project mgr., 1983-85, ops. mgr., 1985—, seminar leader. Author procedural manual: Installation Basics, 1986. Mem. Nat. Assn. Female Execs. Republican. Methodist. Lodge: Order of Rainbow (worthy advisor 1964-66, Grand Cross of Color 1964). Avocations: doll houses; English mysteries; bicycling. Office: Lubin Bus Interiors 620 Blvd New Haven CT 06516

ABELL, ALICE VIRGINIA SIMS (MRS. NORMAN ABELL), civic worker; b. Elizabethtown, Ky., June 29, 1902; d. Francis Leroy and Antoinette (Freeman) Sims; student N.Y. Sch. Design, Otis Art Inst., Cal. Sch. Fine Arts; student U. Ariz., 1921-22; m. Norman Abell, Mar. 19, 1927; children—Norman, Virginia Frances (Mrs. James Langdon Blake), Arlene Alice (Mrs. Francis Bruce Robertson). Pres., Abell Enterprises, Long Beach, Calif., 1954—. Gray Lady A.R.C., Long Beach, 1942-45; chmn. arts and crafts, 1945; mem. Pan Hellenic Bd., Long Beach, 1961; vol. Meml. Hosp. Aux., Long Beach, 1960—, occupational therapy chmn., 1960-62; organizer minimal universal lang. project, 1958; mem. Regional Arts Council; charter mem. research council Scripps U. Clinic. Recipient first prize Santa Ana (Calif.) Art Exhibit, 1941. Mem. D.A.R., Art Mus. Assn., Los Angeles World Affairs Council, Civic Light Opera Assn., Fine Arts Affiliates of Long Beach State U., Smithsonian Assocs., Town Hall of Calif., Gamma Phi Beta. Episcopalian. Clubs: Otis Art Associates (Los Angeles); Queen Mary. Home: 4022 Pacific Ave Long Beach CA 90807

ABELLE, PATSY CAPLES, lawyer; b. Waukegan, Ill., Aug. 20, 1935; d. Roy Lee Caples and Lee Self (Rosamond) Henderson. B.S. in Fin., DePaul U., 1964, J.D., 1967; LL.M., NYU, 1968. Bar: Ill. 1967, NY 1968, U.S. Dist. Ct. (no. dist.) Ill. 1967, U.S. Ct. Mil. Appeals 1968, U.S. Supreme Ct. 1968. Chief securities Fed. Res. Bank, N.Y.C., 1968-73; assoc. Willkie Farr & Gallagher, N.Y.C., 1973-78; sr. atty. Fed. Res. Bd, Washington, 1978-81; sr. assoc. Cravath, Swaine & Moore, N.Y.C., 1981—. Contbr. articles to law jours. Chmn. Fed. Women's Program Adv. Com., Washington, 1980. Mem. Blue Sky Lawyers Assn. (chmn. 1984-85). Office: Cravath Swaine & Moore 1 Chase Manhattan Plaza New York NY 10005

ABENDROTH, SUSAN MARIE, electric products company sales engineer; b. Berwyn, Ill., Aug. 7, 1960; d. Laurence Gerald and Ruth Eleanor (Karstens) A. B.S. in Indsl. Engring., U. Ill., 1982. Tech. mktg. trainee Gen. Electric Co., Placentia, Calif., 1982-83, quotations specialist, Plainville, Conn., 1983, sales engr., Salt Lake City, 1984-85, El Monte, Calif., 1985—. Mem. Christ Lutheran Ch. choir, Salt Lake City, 1984-85, asst. tchr. Sunday Sch., 1985. Mem. Nat. Assn. Female Execs. Republican. Avocations: needlework; playing the piano; singing. Home: 15123 S Brookhurst #232 Westminster CA 92683 Office: Gen Electric Co 9350 E Flair Dr El Monte CA 91731

ABERCROMBIE, VIRGINIA TOWNSEND, writer; b. Houston, Dec. 24, 1927; d. F. Lee and Yvonne (Burghard) Townsend; m. John B. Abercrombie, Apr. 1 1950; children—Virginia Lee Stonelake, John B. Jr., Gilchreas T. B.A., U. Tex., 1950. Poetry published in: Mississippi Arts and Letter, Poem, Roanoke Rev., Sam Houston Lit. Rev., Bluegrass Lit. Rev., Pudding, Midway Rev. 5, Rising Star, Madison Rev., and others; founder Brown Rabbit Presss, Houston, 1979—; co-author: Catering in Houston, 1977, Places to Take a Crowd in Houston, 1979, Catering to Houston 1981; co-editor: Christmas in Texas poem anthology, 1979. Social dir. women's aux. Houston Bar Assn., 1975-76, pres., 1976-77. Clubs: Houston Country, Jr League (puppet chmn.). Avocations: painting; sculpture. Home: 3 Smithdale Ct Houston TX 77024

ABERNATHY, MARGARET ANN STROUP, special education program coordinator, singer; b. South Pittsburg, Tenn., Nov. 29, 1950; d. Buford Lee and Kathryn (Amos) Stroup; m. Talmage L. Abernathy, Jr., Aug. 12, 1971. B.S., U. Tenn.-Chattanooga, 1973, Edn.M., 1978. Cert. spl. edn. tchr., Tenn. Asst. mgr. Suffolk Manor Apts., Lake Charles, La., 1973-74; client program coordinator Orange Grove Ctr., Chattanooga, 1974—; entertainer Sweet'n Savory Union Sq. Restaurant, Chattanooga, 1984—. Mem. speakers bur. United Way, Chattanooga, 1983-85; mem. task force Gov. Tenn., Nashville, 1983-84; female lead in musicals, 1966, 1974; soloist Brainerd United Methodist Ch., Chattanooga, 1974—. Recipient Jr. Miss Award South Pittsburg Jaycees, 1968; Grace Moore scholar, 1968, United Commercial Travelers Scholar, 1976. Mem. Chattanooga Assn. for Young Children. Avocations: lyricist; golf; water skiing; boating; knitting; crocheting. Home: 8342 Savannah Ln E Ooltewah TN 37363 Office: Orange Grove Ctr 615 Derby St Chattanooga TN 37404

ABERNATHY, MARI JESSICA WIRFS, nursing educator, consultant; b. San Diego, Oct. 4, 1947; d. Lewis Lenard and Bonnie Lee (Qualls) Wirfs; m. John M. Abernathy; children—John, Michael, Lindsey. A.S., DeKalb Coll., 1970; B.S.N., Ga. State U., 1972; M.N., Emory U., 1973; postgrad. U. New Orleans, 1983—. Staff nurse med. and intensive care units Grady Meml. Hosp., Atlanta, 1970-71, med. unit Ga. Bapt. Hosp., Atlanta, 1971-72; pvt. duty nurse Piedmont Hosp., Atlanta, 1972-73; instr. nursing Nell Hodgson Woodruff Sch. Nursing, Emory U., Atlanta, 1974, adj. instr., 1974-78; sr. staff nurse DeKalb County Alcohol and Drug Program, Central DeKalb Mental Health Ctr., DeKalb County, Ga., 1974-75; clin. nurse specialist, group therapy leader Salvation Army Resident Ctr. for Rehab., Atlanta, 1976-78; nursing supr. Ga. Regional Hosp., Atlanta, 1975; clin. nurse specialist/nursing supr. Fulton County Alcoholism Treatment Ctr., Atlanta, 1975; nurse specialist, clinic coordinator Atlanta Depression Clinic, 1977; community psychiatric-mental health cons. and educator to community instns., agys. and programs including hosps., schs. nursing, community health ctrs., high schs. and community orgns., Atlanta, 1973-78; adj. instr. nursing Sch. Pub. Health and Tropical Medicine, Tulane U., New Orleans, 1979-83; instr. nursing div. nursing Sch. Nursing La. State U. Med. Ctr., New Orleans, 1983—. Contbr. articles in field to profl. jours. Vol., Salvation Army, Atlanta, New Orleans, 1973-83, A.R.C., Atlanta, New Orleans, 1968-83. Ga. State Scholarship Commn. scholar, 1970-71, 71-72; HEW profl. nurse trainee, 1972-73, 73. Mem. Am. Nurses Assn. (council advanced practitioners in psychiatric-mental health nursing 1974—), Nat. League Nursing, Salvation Army Nurses' Fellowship, Nat. Nurses' Soc. on Alcoholism, Am. Nurses' Found. Century Club, La. State Nurses Assn., Sigma Theta Tau. Office: La State U Med Ctr Sch Nursing 420 S Prieur St New Orleans LA 70112

ABERNETHY, MARGARET MARY, computer education company executive; b. Old Greenwich, Conn., Mar. 16, 1949; d. Maury Francis and Margaret M. (Farrell) A. B.A., Marywood Coll., 1971; postgrad. William Patterson Coll., 1973, Glassboro State U., 1979; M.S., Troy State U., 1985. Cert. tchr., N.J., Del., Ala. Tchr., Corpus Christi Sch., Hasbrouck Heights, N.J., 1971-72, Dover High Sch., Del., 1972-74; substitute tchr. various schs., 1974-75; innovator curriculum for adult basic edn. Bergen Community Coll., Hackensack, N.J., 1975-78; coordinator computer based edn. Paterson Adult Learning Ctr., N.J., 1978-82; community edn. coordinator Legal Services Corp. Ala., Dothan, 1982-83; so. regional mgr. Compu*Tech Ednl. Services, Kenner, La., 1984—; counselor Woman's Discussion Group, Paterson, 1979-83; cons. in field. Editor, writer newsletters. Mem. Nat. Assn. Female Execs., Gamma Beta Phi. Democrat. Roman Catholic. Avocations: traveling; reading; theater; music; art. Home: 836-B Vouray Kenner LA 70065 Office: Compu*Tech Ednl Services Inc 1001 Veterans Blvd Kenner LA 70062

ABLES, JO ANGELA, state official, lawyer; b. Ada, Okla., Jan. 23, 1950; d. A.J. and George Ann (McKoy) A.; B.A., East Central U., Ada, 1972; J.D., Oklahoma City U., 1975. Bar: Okla. 1976, U.S. Dist. Ct. (no. dist.) Okla. 1976, U.S. Ct. Appeals (10th cir.) 1978, U.S. Dist. Ct. (we. dist.) Okla. 1982, U.S. Supreme Ct. 1984. Mem. staff Carl Albert, Speaker of Ho. of Reps., Washington, 1968-70; administrv. asst. to atty. gen. State of Okla., Oklahoma City, 1972-75, asst. atty. gen., 1976-78; asst. gen. counsel Okla. Ins. Commn., Oklahoma City, 1978-79, asst. ins. Commr., 1979-80, dep. ins. commr., 1980-84; mem. firm Kerr, Irvine & Rhodes, 1985—; arbitrator U.S. Dist. Ct. (we. dist.) Okla. Chmn. credentials com. Democratic Party, Oklahoma City, 1980; trustee East Central U. Found., Ada, 1982—. Recipient Outstanding Alumna award East Central U., 1983. Mem. Okla. Bar Assn. (sch. com. 1983—), East Central U. Alumni Assn. (pres. 1982), Chi Omega. Methodist. Office: 600 Fidelity Plaza Oklahoma City OK 73102

ABRAHAM, CHERYL GOODRICH, medical education company executive; b. Denver, Dec. 10, 1946; d. Herbert Linn and Frances Louola (Turner) Goodrich; m. Norman Dean Abraham, Aug. 7, 1982; children by previous marriage—Anthony, Matthew, Jeffrey, Kristin. B.A. in Mgmt./Journalism, St. Mary's Coll., 1978. Clk., Social Security Adminstrn., Kansas City, Kans., 1965-66; sec. Calif. Credit Union, Hayward, Calif., 1966-68; adminstrv. asst. San Ramon Schs., Danville, Calif., 1968-76; owner, mgr. Target Tng. Assocs., Danville, 1976—; exec. dir. Symposia Medicus, Walnut Creek, Calif., 1978—; columnist/freelance writer Herald News, Danville, 1976-82; cons., counselor, asst. organizer Venture Sch., Danville, 1978-79. Contbr. articles to profl. jours. Mem. Nat. League Am. Pen Women (state pres. 1979-80). Home: 802 Ackerman Dr Danville CA 94526 Office: Symposia Medicus 2815 Mitchell Dr Suite 108 Walnut Creek CA 94598

ABRAHAM, NANCY, business executive, lawyer; b. N.Y.C., Jan. 11, 1948; d. Alexander and Helene (Wilk) A.; m. Daniel Weiskopf, Mar. 13, 1969 (div. Aug. 1976); m. 2d, Larsh Mewhinney, Nov. 15, 1979; 1 dau., Antonia Abraham. B.A., Barnard Coll., 1970; J.D. (Harlan Fiske Stone Scholar), Columbia U., 1979. Bar: N.Y. 1980, U.S. Dist. Ct. (so. dist.) N.Y. 1980. Assoc., Sullivan & Cromwell, N.Y.C., 1979-82; sr. v.p. investments Shearson Lehman Bros. N.Y.C., 1983—; adviser to Senator D.P. Moynihan and exec. dir. Com. to Re-elect Senator Moynihan, N.Y.C. and Washington, 1976-79. Mem. Commn. on Presdl. Nominations, Washington, 1981-82; v.p. Abraham Found., N.Y.C.; bd. dirs. Internat. Rescue Com., Scenic Hudson, Inc., Burden Ctr. for Aging. Mem. ABA. Democrat. Club: Highlands Country (Garrison, N.Y.). Home: 983 Park Ave New York NY 10028 Office: Shearson Lehman Bros 660 Madison Ave New York NY 10021

ABRAHAMS, BETH, information services company executive; b. Springfield, Mass., June 14, 1954; d. Kenneth Gordon and Rosalie (Saffer) A.; cert. in data processing Computer Processing Inst., 1974. Customer software rep. Olivetti Corp., Hartford, Conn., 1974-77; regional customer service rep. Harris Corp., Burlington, Mass., 1977-79; product mgr. of devel. Shear Devel. Co., Boston, 1979-81; mgr. integration and test NEC Info. Systems Inc., Boxborough, Mass., 1981-85; account mgr. TAD Computer Services, Cambridge, Mass., 1985-86; personnel cons. Resources Objectives, Inc., Stoneham, Mass., 1986—. Home: 55D Staffordshire Ln Concord MA 01742 Office: 639 Massachusetts Ave Cambridge MA 02139

ABRAHAMS, MARJORIE, educational counselor; b. Orange, Tex., Feb. 3; d. Harvey and Naomi (Grice) Netherly; m. Joseph Rosario, June 22, 1969 (div. 1977); 1 son, Joseph; m. 2d Milford Abrahams, Apr. 22, 1978. B.S. in Biology, Prairie View A&M U., 1965; postgrad. Pepperdine U., 1969, U. So. Calif., 1969, UCLA, 1970, 71, Calif. State U., 1972, Chapman Coll., 1975; M.S. in Counseling, U. LaVerne, 1978. Tchr. sci. and phys. edn. Franklin Jr. High Sch., Port Arthur, Tex., 1965-66, Lincoln High Sch., Port Arthur, 1966-67; tchr., coach Markham Jr. High Sch., Los Angeles, 1967-68; tchr., coach Thomas Jefferson High Sch., Los Angeles, 1968—, counselor, 1981—; head coach girls interscholastic basketball and badminton Los Angeles Unified Sch. Dist., 1972-83. Mem. Thomas Jefferson High Sch. PTA, 1983-84. Named Outstanding Tchr., Thomas Jefferson High Sch., 1978. Mem. AAHPERD, United Tchrs. Los Angeles, Calif. Tchrs. Assn. Democrat. Baptist. Home: 776 E Meadbrook St Carson CA 90746 Office: Thomas Jefferson High Sch 1319 E 41st St Los Angeles CA 90011

ABRAHAMSON, INA JOAN SHAFER, librarian, media specialist, adult education administrator; b. Hartford, Conn., Dec. 19, 1930; d. Morris and Anne Rachel (Bishop) Shafer; m. Samuel Wilfred Abrahamson, Sept. 21, 1953; children—Jay M., Daniel J., Peter M., Steven R. B.A., U. Conn., 1952; postgrad. in library sci., So. Conn. State U., 1973; M.S., Central Conn. State U., 1977; postgrad. in sch. adminstrn., So. Conn. State U., 1982. Booklet author Conn. Gen. Life Ins. Co., Hartford, 1952-56; sch. librarian Middletown Dept. Edn. (Conn.), 1964-65; instr., librarian Vinal Regional Tech. Sch., Middletown, 1967—, media specialist, adult edn. supr., 1983—; dir. Reading Challenge Middletown, 1974-79; chmn. library media steering com. Conn. State Vocat. Tech. Schs., Hartford, 1969-72. Author: poetry Ascent to Myself (Wesleyan Writers Conf. scholarship 1979), 1979, New England's Child (Aspen Writers Conf. Invitation award 1983), 1983; manuscript Holocaust Commemoration, 1982, 83, 85. Pres., Sisterhood of Congregation Adath Israel, 1983-84, presidium, 1985-86. Recipient Panhellenic Scholarship award, 1952. Mem. ALA, Am. Assn. Sch. Librarians, Conn. Ednl. Media Assn., Adminstrn. and Supervision Assn., Am. Fedn. Tchrs., Phi Kappa Phi. Democrat. Jewish. Lodges: B'nai B'rith, Hadassah, Women's League Conservative Judaism. Home: 830 Long Hill Rd Middletown CT 06457 Office: Vinal Regional Vocat-Tech Sch 60 Daniels St Middletown CT 06457

ABRAHAMSON, SHIRLEY SCHLANGER, justice, lawyer; b. N.Y.C., 1933; d. Leo and Ceil (Sauerteig) Schlanger; A.B., N.Y.U., 1953; J.D., Ind. U., 1956; S.J.D., U. Wis., 1962; m. Seymour Abrahamson, 1953; 1 son, Daniel Nathan. Asst. dir. Legislative Drafting Research Fund, Columbia U. Law Sch., 1957-60; admitted to Wis. bar, 1962, since practiced in Madison; mem. firm Lafollette, Sinykin, Anderson & Abrahamson, 1962-76; justice Wis. Supreme Ct., 1976—; prof. U. Wis. Sch. Law, 1966—. Mem. Mayor's Adv. Com., Madison, 1968-70; mem. Gov.'s Study Com. on Jud. Orgn., 1970-73; mem. Wis. Bd. Bar Commrs., 1973-76; bd. visitors Ind. U. Law Sch., 1972—; adv. bd. Nat. Inst. Justice, Dept. Justice, 1980-82; commr. ins. Consumers Adv. Council. Bd. dirs. LWV, Madison, 1963-65, Union council Wis. Union, U. Wis., 1970-71; bd. dirs. Wis. Civil Liberties Union, 1968—, chmn. Capital Area chpt., 1969. Mem. Am. (mem. council sect. legal edn. and admissions 1976—), Wis. Dane County, 7th Circuit bar assns., Am. Law Inst. (council 1985—), Nat. Assn. Women Judges, Nat. Legal Aid and Defender Assn. (mem. appellate evaluation design adv. com. 1979-80), Wis. Jud. Council, Order of Coif, Phi Beta Kappa. Editor: Constitutions of the United States (National and State) 2 vols., 1962. Office: Wis Supreme Ct State Capitol Madison WI 53702

ABRALDES, GRACE ELIDA, aerospace components company executive; b. Buenos Aires, June 18, 1955; came to U.S., 1981; d. Antonio and Lucia Sabina (Pugliese) Boso; m. George Robert Abraldes, July 22, 1981; 1 child, Timothy Alan. Proficiency in English cert. Estudios Contemporáneos, Buenos Aires, 1977; law degree Universidad Belgrano, Buenos Aires, 1981; cert. in interior decorating, Los Angeles, 1984. Sec.-treas., bookkeeper Premach Corp., North Hollywood, Calif., 1982—. Mem. Smithsonian Instn., Human Soc. of U.S. Avocations: reading; travel. Home: 25435 Via Adorna Valencia Hills CA 91355 Office: Premach Corp 12030 Valerio St North Hollywood CA 91605

ABRAMS, ANNE, publicist; b. Bklyn., May 11, 1953; d. Sidney and B. Hilda (Langweber) A.; m. Mark Timothy Farmer, May 19, 1985. B.A., SUNY-Fredonia, 1974; M.A., U. Kans., 1976. Program coordinator Hashinger Arts Ctr., Lawrence, Kans., 1974-77; artistic/mng. dir. Crown Uptown Theatre, Wichita, Kans., 1977-79; dir. student activities Dickinson Coll., Carlisle, Pa., 1979-80; asst. gen. mgr. Am. Theatre Prodns., N.Y.C., 1980-81; account exec., publicist Fred Nathan Co., N.Y.C., 1981—; dir., founder Women's Resource Ctr., Carlisle, 1979-80; theatrical cons. and dir. Com. mem. Women in Bus. Against Cancer, Am. Cancer Soc., N.Y.C., 1983; bd. dirs. AIDS Resource Ctr., N.Y.C., 1986—. Democrat. Avocations: cooking; antiques; swimming; writing.

ABRAMS, DONNA ANNE, insurance agency executive; b. Phila., Dec. 3, 1952; d. John J. and Mary Ellen (Sharpless) Dean; m. Paul Abrams, July 24, 1983; 1 child by previous marriage, Jennifer Lynn. Student Camden County Coll., 1970-71. With Allstate Ins., Deptford, N.J., 1974-80, Hardenbergh Ins., Westmont, N.J., 1980-84; owner Turing-Abrams Ins., Cherry Hill, N.J., 1984—; agts. adv. council Hanover Ins. Co., Valley Forge, Pa., 1985—. Mem. Camden-Gloucester County Ind. Agts. Assn. (bd. dirs. 1985—), N.J. Ind. Ins. Agts. Assn. (instr. 1982—, bd. dirs.), N.J. Assn. Women Bus. Owners (publicity chmn. Camden County chpt. 1985—, now sec.), Profl. Ins. Agts. Assn. Avocations: snow skiing; crafts; field hockey. Home: 82 Farnwood Rd Mount Laurel NJ 08054 Office: Turing Abrams Ins Agy Inc 1940 Route 70 E Box 3922 Cherry Hill NJ 08034

ABRAMS, MARGARET SMITH, lawyer; b. Neptune, N.J., Sept. 8, 1954; d. Thomas Joseph and Jeanne Marie (Hanlon) Smith; m. Douglas Breen Abrams, May 15, 1976; 1 son, Noah Breen. B.A., Wake Forest U., 1976, postgrad., 1976-77; postgrad. Duke U., 1979-80; J.D., Wake Forest U., 1980. Bar: N.C., 1980. Research asst. N.C. Ct. Appeals, Raleigh, 1980-82; assoc. Blanchard, Tucker, Twiggs, Earls & Abrams, P.A., Raleigh, 1982—. Active Wake County Democratic Women, Raleigh, 1980—, N.C. Consumer's Council, 1981—, Wake County YWCA, Raleigh, 1983—. Hankins scholar Wake Forest U., 1972-76, tuition scholar, 1976-77, 77-79; Am. Jurisprudence award in contracts and criminal law, 1977; Corpus Juris Secundum award in contracts, 1977. Mem. Assn. Trial Lawyers Am., N.C. Acad. Trial Lawyers, N.C. Bar Assn., Wake County Bar Assn., N.C. Assn. Women Attys. Home: 5421 Huntingwood Dr Raleigh NC 27606 Office: PO Box 117 975 Walnut St Cary NC 27511

ABRAMS, ROSALIE S., state agency official; b. Balt.; d. Isaac and Dora (Rodbell) Silber; R.N., Sinai Hosp.; postgrad. Columbia U.; B.S., Johns Hopkins U., 1963, M.A. in Polit. Sci.; 1 child, Elizabeth Joan. Public health nurse, 1941-43; bus. mgr. Sequoia Med. Group, Calif., 1946-47; asst. bus. mgr. Silber's Bakery, Balt., 1947-53; mem. Md. Ho. of Dels., 1967-70; mem. Md. Senate, 1970-83, majority leader, 1978-82; chmn. Dem. Party of Md., 1978-83, chmn. fin. com., 1982-83; dir. Office on Aging, State of Md., 1983—; host Outlook TV show, 1983—; guest lectr., witness before congl. coms. Platform com. on nat. health care Dem. Nat. Com., 1979—; chmn. Md. Humane Practices Commn., 1978-83, mem., 1971-74; mem. New Coalition, 1979-83, State-Fed. Assembly Com. on Human Resources, 1977-83, Md. Comprehensive Health Planning Agency, 1972-75, Md. Commn. on Status of Women, 1968—, Am. Jewish Com.; bds. dirs. Sinai Hosp., Balt., 1973—, Balt. Jewish Council, Cross Country Improvement Assn., 1969—, Fifth Dist. Reform Democrats, 1967—; chmn. legis. com. Balt. Area Council on Alcoholism, 1973-75. Served with Nurse Corps USN, 1944-46. Recipient Louise Waterman Wise Community Service award, 1969, award Am. Acad. Comprehensive Health Planning, 1971, Balt. News Am. award, Women of Distinction in Medicine, 1971, traffic safety award, Safety First Club of Md., 1971, Ann London Scott Meml. award for legis. excellence, Md. Chpt. NOW, 1975, Md. Nurses Assn., 1975, service award Balt. Area Council on Alcoholism, 1975. Md. Order Women Legislators (pres., 1973-75), Nat. Conf. State Legislatures (human resources and urban affairs steering com. 1977-83), Nat. Legis. Conf. (human resources task force, intergovt. relations com. 1975-83). Jewish. Office: 301 W Preston St Suite 1004 Baltimore MD 21201

ABRAMS, RUTH I., state justice; b. Boston, Dec. 26, 1930; d. Samuel and Matilda B. A.; B.A., Radcliffe Coll., 1953; LL.B., Harvard U., 1956; hon. degrees Mt. Holyoke Coll., 1977, Suffolk U., 1977, New Eng. Sch. Law, 1978. Bar: Mass. 1957. Partner firm Abrams, Abrams & Abrams, Boston, 1957-60; asst. dist. atty. Middlesex County (Mass.), 1961-69; asst. atty. gen. Mass., chief appellate sect. criminal div., 1969-71; spl. counsel to Supreme Jud. Ct. Mass., 1971-72; asso. justice Superior Ct. Commonwealth of Mass., 1972-77; asso. justice Supreme Jud. Ct. Mass., Boston, 1977—. Mem. Gov.'s Commn. on Child Abuse, 1970-71, Mass. Law Revision Commn. Proposed Criminal Code for Mass., 1969-71. Recipient Radcliffe Coll. Achievement award, 1976, Radcliffe Grad. Soc. medal, 1977. Mem. Am. Bar Assn. (com. on Proposed fed. code 1977—), Mass. Bar Assn., Am. Law Inst., Am. Judicature Soc. (dir. 1978), Am. Judges Assn., Mass. Assn. Women Lawyers. Editor: Handbook for Law Enforcement Officers, 1969-71. Office: Supreme Judicial Ct 1300 New Courthouse Boston MA 02108*

ABRAMS, VICKI HALSEY, retail executive; b. Dallas, Aug. 2, 1952; d. William Gustavus, Jr., and Bobbie Gene (Stark) Halsey; m. Loryn T. Abrams, Aug. 25, 1974. B.A. in Criminal Justice, Calif. State U.-Fullerton, 1974. Sec., Ins. Records Pub. Co., Dallas, 1975-76; receptionist, sec. Joske's-Preston Forest, Dallas, 1976-77; personnel mgr. Joske's-Redbird Mall, Dallas, 1977-78, Joske's Dallas Downtown, 1978-81; corp. selling cost adminstr. Joske's of Dallas, 1981-83; ops. mgr. Joske's-Downtown Dallas, 1983—. Democrat. jewish. Home: 10230 White Elm Rd Dallas TX 75243 Office: Joskes of Dallas 1901 Main St Dallas TX 75201

ABRAMSON, ELAINE SANDRA, graphic designer, crafts artist; b. Cleve., Aug. 27, 1942; d. Norman Morris and Ruth Leah (Glassman) Splaver; m. Martin Stanley Abramson, May 27, 1977; children—Deborah Sue, Mitchell Lee. Hebrew tchr. cert. Hyam Greenberg Inst., Jerusalem, 1960-61; student Cleve. Inst. Art, 1954-64; B.S. in Edn., Kent State U., 1964. Illustrator Ednl. Research Council, Cleve., 1964-65 tchr. art Cleve. Bd. Edn., 1965-67; pres., owner Create-A-Craft, Ft. Worth, 1967—; founding artist, publicity designer Sassy Cat, Chagrin Falls, Ohio, 1967-71; adviser Women's Am. ORT Collection, Houston, 1983-84; designer Golden Gourmet dolls, Hobby Industries Am., Dallas, 1981, 85. Group shows of illustration, soft crafts, toys, enamelling include: Cleve. Mus. Art, 1964, Cleve. Inst. Art, 1964-71, Towson Courthouse Art Exhibit, Md., 1972-77; one-woman shows include: Kent State U., 1963-64, Central Nat. Bank Cleve., 1961-66; Md. Pub. Television Arts Exhibits, 1972-77. Designer, inventor, creator craft kits, toys, games., 1967—. Mem. Soc. Craft Designers (in Dallas Showcase of Designers 1985), Md. Art League (bd. dirs., workshop chmn.), Graphic Artist Guild, Cartoonists Guild, Am. Crafts Council, Nat. Enamelists Guild, Am. Mus. Natural History, Nat. Geographic Soc., Smithsonian Instn., Nat. Assn. Self-Employed, Am. Film Inst., Nat. Writers Club. Jewish. Avocations: sewing, painting, reading, travel. Office: Create-A-Craft PO Box 330008 Fort Worth TX 76163

ABRAMSON, ROCHELLE SUSAN, violinist; b. Detroit, Jan. 1, 1953; d. Seymour I. and Mayme (Tureck) A.; B.Mus., U. Mich., 1973; M.Mus., Juilliard Sch. Music, 1975, Profl. Studies degree, 1976. Founding mem. Trio N.Y., 1975-78, Muse-Arts Ensemble, Los Angeles, 1978—; 1st violin N.Y.C. Ballet Orch., 1976-78, Los Angeles Philharmonic Orch., 1978—; founding mem. Trio Candide, 1984—. Recipient awards Artists Internat. Young Musicians Auditions, 1977, Nat. Fedn. Music Clubs Biennial String Competition, 1973, Stillman-Kelly String Competition, 1968, Nat. Arts Club, 1976, Palm Beach Flagler-Matthews Competition, 1974, Charleston Symphony Competition, 1976, Kingsport Symphony Competition, 1975, Talman Prize, Soc. Am. Musicians, 1975, Young Artist award Music Study Club Detroit, 1978. Home: 1750 Camino Palmero Los Angeles CA 90046

ABRAMS-SMITH, PAULA SARA, psychologist; b. N.Y.C., Nov. 22, 1951; d. Arnold and Naomi Frances (Gettenberg) Abrams; cert. Institute Montesano, Switzerland, 1969; B.A., U. Wash., Seattle, 1972; M.S., Nat. Coll. Edn., 1974; Ph.D., Northwestern U., 1977; exec. tng. program Harvard Bus. Sch., Buffalo, 1980-81; m. James Theodore Smith, Nov. 23, 1979. Program coordinator spl. edn. programs Abraham Lincoln Center, Chgo., 1973-74; tchr., psychologist, program supr. Dysfunctioning Child Center, Michael Reese Hosp. and Med. Center, Chgo., 1974-78; research and child psychologist Fisher-Price Toys, East Aurora, N.Y., 1978-83, corp. cons., 1983—; asst. adj. prof. devel. psychology SUNY, Buffalo, 1980—. Mem. Amherst Players, 1978-79; dir. western N.Y. region U.S. Olympic Com.; bd. dirs. Children's Centre, Inc., 1984—; mem. exec. bd. Buffalo Dive Club; coach lightweight men's crew West Side Rowing Club. Mem. AAAS, N.Y. Acad. Scis., Am. Psychol. Assn., N.Y. Met. Assn. Applied Psychology, Nat. Assn. Underwater Instrs., Phi Delta Kappa. Asso. editor Sch. Psychology Internat. Jour., 1980—. Office: 4828 Bussendorfer Rd Hamburg NY 14075

ABRELL, BEVERLY JOANNE, publisher, graphic designer; b. St. Paul, Jan. 6, 1956; d. Stephen James and Audrey Victoria (Rice) Guter; m. Gregory Phillip Abrell; Mar. 18, 1978; children—Joshua G., Stephanie A., Heather E. Vice pres., co-pub. Wagons & Wheels Publs., Inc., Windsor, Vt., 1979—; pres., exec. dir. Green Mountain Graphics, Inc., Windsor, 1979—; pub., v.p. Abrell Publs., Inc., Windsor, 1982—; exec. dir., cons. Nat. Assn. Graphic Designers, N.Y.C., 1979-81. Pub. Down Home, 1984; Wagons and Wheels, 1982. Graphic design dir. Typography Designs, 1979. Sec. Brownville Pre-sch. Coop., 1984. Mem. Nat. Assn. Advt. Typographers, Nat. Assn. Newspaper Pubs. Roman Catholic. Avocations: snowsskiing; water skiing; gardening; horse back riding; home renovations. Office: Abrell Publs Inc 82 Main St Windsor VT 05089

ABRELL, JUDITH ARLENE, marketing executive; b. Indpls., July 4, 1937; d. E. Ellsworth and A. Ruth (Toms) Enlow; m. Joseph Kindred Abrell, Aug. 9, 1959; children—Lisa T., Bradford E. A.B., Ind. U., 1959. Tchr. English, Martinsville (Ind.) High Sch., 1959-60, So. Dade High Sch., Miami, Fla. 1963-64; program evaluator Dade County Mgrs. Office, 1973; pub. info. coordinator Dade County Mgrs. Office, South Fla. Employment Tng. Consortium, 1978-79; dir. account services Jack Kilpatrick Advt., Miami, 1982-83; mktg. dir. Richard Plumer Design, Miami, 1984—. Mem. Fla. Gov's. Commn. on Status of Women, 1975-83; mem. Dade County Council Arts and Scis., Miami, 1977-78; del Internat. Women's Yr. Tribune, Mexico City, 1975; mem. Lowe Mus. Adv. Com., U. Miami, 1975-76. Mem. Women in Communications. Democrat. Club: Beaux Arts (pres. 1975-76) (Miami). Office: Richard Plumer Design 155 NE 40th St Miami FL

ABREU, JUDITH ANN, broadcasting company executive; b. Franklin, Pa.; d. Paul Arthur Martin Mongomery and Dorothy Mozelle (Cast) Snyder; m. Ralph Francis Abreu, Nov. 16, 1974 (dec. 1980); children—Jennifer, Jessica. B.A., U. Tex., 1966, M.A., 1967; postgrad. NYU, 1978. Systems engr. IBM, Poughkeepsie, N.Y., 1968-70; sr. programmer Morgan Guaranty Co., N.Y.C., 1970-72; mgr. systems CBS, N.Y.C., 1972-76, dir. mgmt. info. systems edn., 1976-79, dir. systems assurance, 1979-83, dir. advanced office systems, 1983—; cons. Vol. Urban Cons. group, N.Y.C., 1979—. Instr. English, Internat. Club, N.Y.C., 1970-74; speaker Open Doors, N.Y.C. Pub. Schs., 1981—; leader Hudson County council Girl Scouts U.S.A., 1985. Recipient Outstanding Community award Am. Biographical Inst., 1975. Mem. Office Info. Systems Forum (pres. 1983-84), Office Products Exchange Forum, Assn. for Women in Computing, U. Tex. Alumni Assn., Phi Mu (pres. 1978-80). Club: 500 (N.Y.C.). Home: 1004 Palisade Ave Union City NJ 07087 Office: CBS Inc 51 W 52d St New York NY 10019

ABREU, SUE HUDSON, physician, army officer; b. Indpls., May 24, 1956; d. M.B. Hudson and Wilma Hudson (Jones) Black; m. Michael H. Abreu, Dec. 24, 1979. B.S. in Engring., Purdue U., 1978; M.D., Uniformed Services U., 1982. Commd. 2d lt. U.S. Army, 1978, recommd. capt., 1982; med. officer candidate, Bethesda, Md., 1978-82; intern Walter Reed Army Med. Ctr., Washington, 1982-83, resident in diagnostic radiology, 1983-85, fellow in nuclear medicine, 1985-87. Mem. Soc. Nuclear Medicine, Am. Coll. Nuclear Physicians, Soc. Women Engrs., Am. Med. Women's Assn., Am. Assn. Women Radiologists, Tau Beta Pi, Omicron Delta Kappa, Phi Kappa Phi. Avocations: calligraphy; sports. Home: 3520 Nimitz Rd Kensington MD 20895 Office: Nuclear Medicine Service Walter Reed Army Med Ctr Washington DC 20014

ABRIGO, MARIANNE MCKEON, real estate executive; b. Cleve., May 17, 1944; d. Frank Joseph and Marianne (Miller) McKeon; m. Rodney Rogelio Abrigo, Aug. 8, 1970; children—Timothy Michael, Ryan Mathew. B.S., Kent

State U., 1966. Speech therapist Tallmadge Pub. Schs. (Ohio), 1966-67, Lakewood Pub. Schs. (Ohio), 1967-68; lang. arts tchr. Waialua High Sch. (Hawaii), 1968-74, reading specialist, 1974-78; mgr. Mike McCormack Realtors, Haleiwa, Hawaii, 1978-83; pres., prin. broker Marianne Abrigo Properties, Haleiwa, 1983—. Mem. North Shore Neighborhood Bd.; com. mem. Trinity Luthern PTL; mem. Mayor's Small Bus. Adv. Council. Contbr. articles to profl. jours. Mem. Nat. Assn. Realtors, Honolulu Bd. Realtors, Hawaii Assn. Realtors, Hawaii Small Bus. Assn., North Shore Bus. and Profl. Orgn., Hawaii C. of C., Kent State U. Alumni Assn. Roman Catholic. Clubs: Honolulu, Waialua Bay. Home: 65-132 Hukilau Loop Waialua HI 96791 Office: Marianne Abrigo Properties PO Box 867 Haleiwa HI 96712

ABSHIER, SHIRLEY ANN, geologist; b. Vernon Center, N.Y., Oct. 19, 1936; d. Harry E. and Anna (Cuomo) Sauerhafer; B.Sc., U. Tex., El Paso, 1969; m. Jon F. Abshier, Nov. 5, 1964; children—Debrah, Gerald, Thomas, Patricia. Social services welfare caseworker N.Mex. Health and Social Service Dept., Grants, 1969-72; petroleum geologist Mobil Oil Corp., Denver, 1973-80, editor Mobil Denver E & P Newspaper, 1979-80, mem. speakers' bur., 1979-80; sr. geologist Sunmark Oil Co., Denver, 1980-81; dist. geologist Trans-Tex. Energy, Inc., 1981-82; geol. cons., 1982-86; v.p. A-W Systems, Ltd., 1986—, Corp. Mailings, Inc., 1986—. Chmn., N.Mex. Crippled Childrens Assn., 1970-72; charter mem. Grants Boys Ranch, 1970-72; mem. N.Mex. Gov.'s Com. on Mental Health, 1970-72; Jefferson County rep. to Republican County Conv., 1976—. Mem. Am. Assn. Petroleum Geologists, Rocky Mountain Assn. Geologists, Profl. Geologist, Clear Creek County Mining and Metals Assn. Republican. Episcopalian. Editor: RMAG Guidebook, 1979; editor Mobil Messenger, 1979. Home and Office: 19029 W 60th Pl Golden CO 80401

ABT, VICKI, sociologist, educator; b. N.Y.C., Dec. 9, 1942; d. Harold and Sylvia (Marcus) A.; student (tuition scholar) Mich. State U., 1960-61; B.A., Hofstra U., 1963; M.A., Pa. State U., 1966; Ph.D. (Univ. fellow), Temple U., 1972; 1 dau., Andrea Abt Jones. Teaching asst., research fellow Temple U., 1967-71; instr. Pa. State U. Ogontz Campus, 1966-71, assoc. prof. sociology, advisor women's studies, 1971—; research cons. Phila. Dept. Mental Health and Retardation. Chmn. Bucks County Community Devel. Citizens Com., 1975—. Mem. Am. Sociol. Assn., Am. Psychol. Assn., Popular Culture Assn., Assn. Anthrop. Study of Play, Soc. Psychol. Study Social Issues, NOW. Jewish. Club: B'rith Sholom. Author: (with others) The Business of Risk: Commercial Gambling in Mainstream America, 1985. Contbr. articles to profl. jours., chpts. to books. Home: 1617 Graham Rd Meadowbrook PA 19046 Office: Pennsylvania State University Ogontz Campus Sutherland Bldg Abington PA 19001

ACACIO, CORAZON, pediatrician; b. Manila, June 12, 1942; naturalized, 19 d. Deo and Lily Arabejo; ed. U. St. Thomas, Manila; m. I. P. Acacio, Mar. 27, 1971; children—Gerald, Joyce. Intern, N.Y.C., 1965; resident in medicine Univ. Hosp., Cleve., after 1966, then in pediatrics Michael Reese Hosp., Chgo.; practice medicine specializing in pediatrics; mem. staff Michael Reese Hosp.; physician Nutri-system Weight Loss Centers. Mem. Am. Women's Med. Assn., Kane County Women's Aux., Ill. State Med. Soc. and Aux.

ACHESON, ALICE BREWEN, publicist; b. Indiana, Pa., July 26, 1936; d. Stewart F. and Anna M.J. (Mohr) Brewen; A.B., Bucknell U., 1958; M.A., CUNY, 1963; m. Donald H. Acheson, Dec. 12, 1970 (dec.). Tchr. English and Spanish, Mt. Vernon (N.Y.) High Sch., 1958-69; exec. sec., then exec. asst. Media Medica, Inc., N.Y.C., 1969-71; with McGraw Hill Book Co., N.Y.C., 1971-78, asso. editor, 1971-76, publicity asso., 1977-78; asso. publicity dir. Simon & Schuster, N.Y.C., 1979-80, Crown Publishers Inc., N.Y.C., 1980-81; ind. publicist, prin. Alice B. Acheson, N.Y.C., 1981—; mem. faculty Wilamette Writers' Conf., 1981, Folio Pub. Week, 1983, 84, Face to Face Pub. Conf. and Expn., 1977, 79, 81, Howard U. Press Book Pub. Inst., 1984, NYU Pub. Inst., 1985. Recipient Partner-in-Edn. award N.Y.C. Bd. Edn., 1977, 78. Mem. Publishers Publicity Assn., Nat. Assn. Female Execs., Am. Soc. Profl. Cons. Address: 136 E 36th St New York NY 10016

ACHOR, SHIRLEY, educator; b. Dallas, June 3, 1928; d. Donald Glenn and Mary (Chambers) Coolidge; B.A. with honors, So. Meth. U., 1969, M.A., 1971, Ph.D., 1974; m. William Benson Parker, Oct. 7, 1950 (div. 1957); 1 dau., Tracy; m. 2d. Hubert Eugene Achor, Nov. 28, 1958. Instr., Richland Coll., Dallas, 1973-74; lectr. Tex. Women's U., Denton, Tex., 1974; asst. prof. anthropology East Tex. State U., Commerce, 1975-81, asso. prof., 1981—. Sec., bd. dirs. Involvement of Mexican Ams. in Gainful Endeavors, 1973. NSF traineeship, 1969-73; Ford Found. fellow, 1973-74. Fellow Am. Anthropol. Assn., Soc. Applied Anthropology, Inst. for Study of Earth and Man; mem. Council on Anthropology and Edn., Soc. Med. Anthropology, Southwestern Social Sci. Assn., Nat. Assn., Bilingual Educators, Phi Beta Kappa. Author: Mexican Americans in a Dallas Barrio, 1978. Office: Dept Sociology and Anthropology East Tex State Univ Commerce TX 75428

ACHTEN, ESTHER (MRS. ALFRED FRIEDMAN), physician; b. Dchurin, Russia, Nov. 27, 1919; d. Jacob and Lifsa (Lernerman) Achten; M.S., Escuela Preparatoria de Mexico, 1937; M.D. cum laude, Nat. U. Mex., 1943; m. Alfred Friedman, Dec. 3, 1944: children—Jack, Frank, Stanley, Melvin. Came to U.S., 1944, naturalized, 1950. Intern, Orange County Gen. Hosp., Orange, Calif., 1947-49, mem. Ross-Loos Med. Group, Los Angeles, 1951—, ptnr.; 1969—, historian, 1969—; practice medicine specializing in family pratice, Los Angeles, 1951—. Active Pioneer Women for Israel. Recipient plaque as clinician of yr. Cigna Health Plans, 1985. Fellow Am. Acad. Family Physicians; mem. AMA, Am. Israel, Calif., Los Angeles County med. assns. Home: 1222 S Genesee Ave Los Angeles CA 90019 Office: Ross-Loos Med Center 1711 W Temple St Los Angeles CA 90026

ACKEN, BRENDA THOMAS, business executive; b. Princeton, W.Va., Mar. 16, 1947; d. Murl Price and Pauline Farmer (Woolwine) Thomas; B.S. in Bus. Adminstrn., Concord Coll., Athens, W.Va., 1968. Sr. acct. Higgins & Gorman, attys. and C.P.A.s, Beckley, W.Va., 1968-74; sec.-treas., dir. South Atlantic Coal Co., Inc., Permac, Inc., REP Aviation, Inc., Bakertown Coal Co., Inc., REP Sales, Inc., Tri-States Sales Co., Bluefield, W.Va., 1974—; pres. Bluefield Health Systems, Inc. Treas., bd. dirs. Bluefield Community Hosp., 1979-81, vice chmn. bd. dirs., 1981-86; adv. bd. Bluefield Salvation Army, 1979-85; mem. mus. subcom. Pocahontas Coalfield Centennial Celebration, 1981-82; mem. adv. bd. Concord Coll., 1984-85; mem. Selective Service Bd., Selective Service Bd. Appeals. C.P.A., W.Va. Mem. Am. Inst. C.P.A.s (mem. at large council 1985-86, Upward mobility of women com. 1985-86), Nat. Assn. Accts., W.Va. Soc. C.P.A.s (pres. So. chpt. 1976-77, state dir. 1978-81, v.p. 1981-82 pres. 1983-84, Outstanding Chpt. Pres. award, 1977, Outstanding Com. Chmn. award 1979, Pub. Service award 1983). Republican. Mem. Ch. of God. Clubs: Fincastle Country, Quota Internat. (pres. Bluefield 1978-79, dist. gov. 1980-81, bd. dirs. East area 1983-85, treas. 1985-86). Home: 628 Parkway Bluefield WV 24701 Office: 127 North St Bluefield WV 24701

ACKER, LINDA JEAN, mental health therapist, administrative coordinator; b. Rock Springs, Wyo., Nov. 30, 1951; d. William James and Elaine Rose (Davis) Acker; m. John Dale Pallesen, Dec. 10, 1952. B.A. in Psychology, U. Wyo., 1974, M.A. in Psychology, 1976. Community coordinator Sweetwater County Drug/Alcohol Prevention Program, Rock Springs, 1976; mental health therapist S.W. Counseling Service, Rock Springs, 1976-81, co-dir., 1981-83, adminstrv. coordinator, 1983—. Pres. Sexual Assault Task Force, 1978-80; v.p. Youth Home, Rock Springs, 1980—. Democrat. Mem. Ch. of Jesus Christ of Latter-Day Saints. Home: 1326 Uinta St Rock Springs WY 82901 Office: Southwest Counseling Service 1124 College Rd Rock Springs WY 82901

ACKER, PHYLLIS ANN, executive, consultant; b. Mpls., Sept. 15, 1939; d. Glenn Kirt and Ruth Winnifred (Cropper) A. B.A., Augsburg Coll., 1961; postgrad. Columbia U. Sch. Social Work, 1962-63. Social worker Luth. Child Welfare Assn., N.Y.C., 1963-65, Ramsey County, St. Paul, 1965-69; vol. service coordinator, Ramsey County, Koochiching County, Dakota County, 1969-74; exec. dir. Info. and Vol. Ctr., Rochester, Minn., 1974-77; chief vol. service State Minn., St. Paul, 1977-83; sr. assoc. Energize Assocs., Phila./St. Paul, 1983—. Author/editor: Guidelines for Volunteer Transactions, 1980; contbr. articles to profl. jours. Del. Minn. Women's Consortium, 1982—, Interclub Council, 1982—, Gavel Club, St. Paul, 1982—, Joint Service Club Planning Com., St. Paul, 1980-82; active Luth. Women's Caucus, Twin Cities, 1983—; cons. Courage Ctr., Golden Valley, Minn., 1983—, Battered Women's Shelter, Rochester, 1976-77; bd. dirs. YWCA, Rochester, 1975-77; cons., trainer, bd. dirs. Nat. Ctr. Vol. Action, Washington, 1973-78; chmn. Community Service Coordinating Council, Rochester, 1975-76. Mem. Minn. Assn. Vol. Dirs. (pres. 1970-73), Assn. Vol. Adminstrn. (treas. 1979-80, pub. policy chair 1977-78). Democrat. Lutheran. Club: Zonta Internat. (pres. 1982-84). Office: Energize Assocs 203 Dejon Ct Woodbury MN 55125

ACKER, TERESA HOPTON, research analyst; b. Jackson, Miss., Nov. 25, 1957; d. Richard Gilbert and Carol Baggett (Fagan) H. m. James Alan Acker, Aug. 5, 1984. B.S., Miss. State U., 1979. Adminstrv. asst. Hampton Power Products, Jackson, Miss., 1979; with accounts payable dept. Lamar Communications, Jackson, 1979-80; sec.-treas. R.G. Hopton, Inc., Jackson, 1980-81, dir., 1979—; market research analyst Miss. Chem. Corp., Yazoo City, 1981-83, ops. research analyst, 1983-85; statis. research analyst U. S Ala., Mobile, 1985—. Mem. Am. Mktg. Assn., Alpha Chi Omega Alumni. Republican. Episcopalian.

ACKER, VIRGINIA MARGARET, nursing educator; b. Madison, Wis., Aug. 11, 1946; d. Paul Peter and Lucille (Klein) A. Diploma in Nursing, St. Mary's Med. Ctr., Madison, 1972; B.S. in Nursing, Incarnate Work Coll., San Antonio, 1976; M.S. in Health Professions, S.W. Tex. State U., 1980. R.N., Wis., Tex. Staff nurse St. Mary's Hosp., Milw., 1972-73, Kenosha Meml. Hosp., Wis., 1973-74, S.W. Tex. Meth. Hosp., San Antonio, 1974-75, Met. Gen. Hosp., San Antonio, 1975-76; instr. Bapt. Meml. Hosp. System Sch. Nursing, San Antonio, 1976-83; dir. nursing Meml. Hosp., Gonzales, Tex., 1983-84; dir., instr. Victoria Coll., Tex., 1984—; dir. Victoria Coll., Gonzales. Mem. Tex. Assn. Vocat. Nurse Educators, Nat. Assn. Female Execs., AAUW. Roman Catholic. Avocations: cross-stiching, reading, camping, fishing. Home: 102 1/2 Forest Ave Plymouth WI 53073 Office: Victoria Coll-Cuero Extention PO Box 807 Cuero TX 77954

ACKERMAN, DIANA FELICIA, philosophy educator; b. Bklyn., June 23, 1947; d. Arthur and Zelda (Sondack) A.; A.B. summa cum laude, Cornell U., 1968; Ph.D., U. Mich., 1976. Asst. prof. philosophy Brown U., Providence, 1974-79, assoc. prof., 1979—; vis. asst. prof. philosophy UCLA, 1976; sr. Fulbright lectr. Hebrew U., 1985. Mem. ACLU, Am. Philos. Assn., NAACP. Author articles in field. Office: Dept Philosophy Brown U Providence RI 02912

ACKERMAN, DIANE LEIGHTON, author; b. N.Y.C., Sept. 2, 1945; d. Lewis Charles and Florence Marie (Nicholls) Leighton; m. Martin S. Ackerman, June 29, 1971; 1 dau., Kelly Leighton. B.A., Barnard Coll., 1966. Publicity asst., Renault, Inc., N.Y.C., 1966-67, Curtis Publ. Co., 1967-68; beauty editor Status Mag., N.Y.C., 1968-79; publicity mgr. Clinique Labs., Inc., N.Y.C., 1969-71; pres. R.N.B. Leasing Corp., N.Y.C., 1971—, Sovereign Am. Arts Corp., N.Y.C., 1971—. Author: books including Money, Ego, Power: A Manual for Would-Be Wheeler Dealers, 1976; Living Rich: A Manual for Would-Be Big Spenders, 1978; Getting Rich: The Smart Woman's Guide to Successful Money Management, 1980; The Only Guide You'll Ever Need to Marry Money, 1982. Editor: Arthur B. Davies, Essays on His Art, 1973; The Drawings of Maurice Sterne, 1974. Mem. public relations com. Democrats Abroad, London, 1974-78; trustee Martin S. Ackerman Found., 1971—. Home and Office: 730 Park Ave New York NY 10021

ACKERMAN, FREDA STERN, investment research company executive; b. N.Y.C., Mar. 17, 1947; d. Alfred S. and Gertrude (Scher) Stern; B.A. in Polit. Sci., City U. N.Y., 1968. Analyst mcpl. bond research Dun & Bradstreet Inc., N.Y.C., 1968-71, sr. analyst mcpl. bond research, 1971-73; asst. v.p. mcpl. bond research Moody's Investors Service, Inc., N.Y.C., 1973-75, v.p., asso. dir., 1975-79, sr. v.p., dir. mcpl. bond dept., 1979-81, exec. v.p., dir. mcpl. bond dept., 1981—; faculty New Sch. Social Research. Mem. Mcpl. Forum of N.Y. (pres.), Council on Mcpl. Performance (bd. govs.), Soc. Mcpl. Analysts, Fin. Women's Assn., Women's Econ. Roundtable, Mcpl. Analysts Group of N.Y., Mcpl. Fin. Officers Assn. Democrat. Office: 99 Church St New York NY 10007

ACKERMAN, LOIS VOLK, retail executive; b. Sharon, Pa., Aug. 17, 1934; d. Louis and Sara Greenberger; B.B.A. magna cum laude, U. Pitts., 1955; m. Lawrence Volk, Dec. 25, 1955 (dec.); children—Valerie, David, Pamela; m. 2d, Sidney Ackerman, Sept. 3, 1978. Instr., demonstrator Burroughs Corp., Pitts., 1956; owner, mgr., pres. Star Pharmacy, Inc., North Fort Myers, Fla., 1971-81; pres. Star Gifts Inc., Fort Myers, Star Gifts Orlando Inc.; sec.-treas. Star Gifts Gainesville, Inc., Star Gifts Fla., until 1983. Mem. Gift and Decorative Accessories Assn., Jewelers Council, Fla. League Arts, Internat. Platform Assn., Beta Gamma Sigma. Democrat. Jewish (past v.p. Temple Judea). Club: InnerWheel. Home: 4510 SE 9th Pl Cape Coral FL 33904 Office: 16000 Chamberlain Pkwy Fort Myers FL 33913

ACKERMAN, LOUISE MAGAW, writer, civic worker; b. Topeka, July 9, 1904; d. William Glenn and Anna Mary (Shaler) Magaw; B.S., Kans. State U., 1926; M.A., U. Nebr., 1942; m. Grant Albert Ackerman, Dec. 27, 1926; children—Edward Shaler, Anita Louise. Free lance writer, 1930—. Mem. Lincoln Community Arts Council. Mem. Nat. Soc. Daus. Colonial Wars (nat. pres. 1977-80), Daus. Am. Colonists (regent Nebr. 1970-72), DAR (past v.p. gen.), Americans of Armorial Ancestry (sec. 1976-82), Nat. Huguenot Soc. (2d v.p. 1977-81), Nebr. Writers Guild (past sec.-treas.), Nat. League Am. Pen Women, Lincoln C. of C., Order Colonial Lords in Am., Nat. Gavel Soc., Soc. Descs. of Founders of Hartford, Conn., Phi Kappa Phi. Republican. Club: Nat. Writers, Order Eastern Star. Home: Eastmont Towers III Apt 428 6335 O St Lincoln NE 68510

ACKERMAN, MONA RIKLIS, foundation administrator; b. Tel-Aviv, Israel, May 22, 1946; d. Meshulam and Judith (Stern) Riklis; m. Irwin Ackerman, Dec. 18, 1966 (div. 1977); children—Ari, Gila. B.A., NYU, 1968; postgrad. Yeshiva U., 1982—. Story editor Frank Yablans Prodns., N.Y.C., 1975-77; editor Dell Publishing, N.Y.C., 1978-79; sr. editor Jove Books, N.Y.C., 1979-80; dir. Rapid Am. Corp., N.Y.C., 1976—; pres. Rapid Am. Found., N.Y.C., 1981—. Bd. govs. United Jewish Appeal of Greater N.Y., 1984-86; bd. dirs. United Jewish Appeal-Fedn. Jewish Philanthropies, 1986—; bd. dirs. Bd. Jewish Edn., N.Y.C., 1983-84, Am. Friends of Rechov Sumsum, 1984—; internat. bd. govs. Weizmann Inst. of Sci., 1985—; exec. com. Nat. Jewish Coalition, 1985—; mem. painting and sculpture com. Mus. Modern Art, 1985—. Republican. Office: Rapid American Found 595 Madison Ave New York NY 10022

ACKERMAN, SUSAN JANE, advt. agency exec.; b. Utica, N.Y., Oct. 10, 1941; d. Richard James and Annette Louise (Gardner) A.; B.A. cum laude, Harvard U., 1964, postgrad., 1963-64. Research project dir. Young and Rubicam Inc., N.Y.C., 1964-67; dir. of research Bresnick Co., Inc., Boston, 1967-69, Cambridge Mktg. Group Inc., N.Y.C., 1969-72; dir. mktg. Muir Cornelius Moore Inc., N.Y.C., 1973-75; assoc. dir. mktg. and research Grey Advt. Inc., N.Y.C., 1975-77, v.p. and sr. assoc. dir. mktg. and research, internat. research coordinator, 1978-83, dir. mktg. and research, Americas/Pacific, 1984—. Republican. Episcopalian. Office: Grey Advt Inc 777 3d Ave New York NY 10017

ACKLIN, NEVA CUNNINGHAM, machine shop owner; b. Cushing, Okla., Feb. 12, 1931; d. Ira W. and Eva Alene (Howerton) Sadler; m. George W. Cunningham, Apr. 28, 1960 (dec. July 1981); m. Jack L. Acklin, Feb. 14, 1983; children—Jennifer Figgins, Elizabeth Kinion, George W. II. Student Okla. State U., 1957-58, Central State U., 1959-60. Bookkeeper Cunningham Machine & Steel Co., Tulsa, 1968-81, pres., owner, 1981—. Mem. U.S. C. of C., Met. Tulsa C. of C. Republican. Mem. Christian Ch. Avocations: water skiing; snow skiing. Home: 6930 E 65th Pl Tulsa OK 74133 Office: Cunningham Machine & Steel Co 4832 S 83d E Ave Tulsa OK 74147

ACOR, GENEVA KEENE, veterinarian; b. Balt., Nov. 18, 1942; d. William Joseph and Geneva Irene (Ware) Keene; m. John Albert Acor, Nov. 18, 1966; children—J. Brannen, Erick Ryan. Student U. Md., 1960-62; D.V.M., U. Ga., 1966. Veterinarian, J. Brannen Murphy, Altamonte Springs, Fla., 1967-72; owner, mgr. Westside Animal Hosp., Vero Beach, Fla., 1972—. Chmn., Animal Control Bd. Indian River County, 1976-77; judge Regional Sci. Fair, Melbourne, Fla., 1982, 83, State Sci. Fair, 1984. AVMA scholar, 1964. Mem. Fla. Vet. Med. Assn. (Gold Star award 1982, pres. 1984-85), Treasure Coast Vet. Med. Assn. (pres. 1976), Central Fla. Vet. Med. Assn. (pres. 1970), Phi Zeta. Home: 3906 Indian River Dr Vero Beach FL 32963 Office: Westside Animal Hosp 1795 10th Ave Vero Beach FL 32960

ACOSTA, MARGARET ANN, educational administrator; b. Hanford, Calif., Jan. 23, 1946; d. Francisco Cordero and Tomasa (Reyes) A. B.A., UCLA, 1971; M.Ed., U. Houston, 1973. Tchr., Houston Ind. Sch. Dist., 1973-76, dir. ESEA Project, 1976-79; coordinator Tex. Family Inst., Houston, 1978-79; supr. U. Houston, 1979-81; planner/evaluator Houston Ind. Sch. Dist., 1981-83, gen. ops. mgr., 1984—; mem. task force on ednl. excellence, co-chmn., 1983-84; field rep. Inter-City Leadership Devel. Assn.; ednl. cons. Childhood Edn. Devel. Ctr., Inc. Past bd. dirs. Houston Council Human Relations, Houston Area Women's Ctr., Children's Edn. and Devel. Ctr., Inc., Ctr. Human Devel., Near Town Neighborhood Assn., Montrose Civic Club, Cameron County Cultural Arts Council. Bilingual Edn. doctoral fellow, 1979-81; Founds. of Edn. deptl. fellow, 1979-81. Mem. Tex. State Tchrs. Assn., Tex. Classroom Tchrs. Assn., NEA, AAUW, Nat. Assn. Bilingual Educators, Assn. Supervision and Curriculum Devel. Democrat. Roman Catholic. Home: 2410 Dunlavy Houston TX 77006 Office: 3703 Yoakum Suite 204 Houston TX 77006

ACREE, ANNE JOYCE, aerospace company official; b. Detroit, Oct. 31, 1945; d. Peter Joseph and Inez Marcella (Longville) Feliccia; student in bus. and adminstrn. Mt. San Antonio Coll., 1974-78; Assembler, Hoffman Electronics, El Monte, Calif., 1963-65; meat cutter, clk. P&J Meat Market, La Puente, Calif., 1965-70; with HTL Industries Inc. ATD (formerly Am. Standard), Monrovia, Calif., and Duarte, Calif., 1970—, supr. inventory control, 1978-79, supr. materials handling, 1980-81, prodn supr. contracts dept., 1981-84, product support supr., 1984-85; prodn. control specialist Simulaser Corp., 1986, prodn. control mgr., 1986—. Mem. Nat. Assn. Female Execs. Roman Catholic. Office: 15251 E Don Julian City of Industry CA

ACTON, ANN, planning/development consultant; b. Kankakee, Ill., June 7, 1942; d. Lawrence Donald and Yvonne Marie (Dionne) Boudreau; student Coll. St. Francis, Joliet, Ill., 1959-61; B.A. cum laude in Psychology, So. Ill. U., Carbondale, 1971, M.P.A., 1983; m. William Arden Acton, Aug. 26, 1961; children—Cory Francis, Michael Arden, Gregory Lee. Asst. dir. human resources Shawnee Community Coll., Ullin, Ill., 1973-74; health planner, adminstrv. asst. Miss.-Ohio Valley Regional Planning Commn., Mounds, Ill., 1974-75; health planner, planning coordinator, field dir., asso. dir. Comprehensive Health Planning in So. Ill., Carbondale, 1975-81; dir. planning and devel. Franklin Hosp., Benton, Ill., 1981-82; pres. Acton Assocs., West Frankfort, Ill., 1982—. Adv. com. Lions of Ill. Hearing Services, Ill. Com. Definitional Study of Devel. Disabilities; policy adv. com. Coal Miners Respiratory Disease Program; mem. Regional 208 Water Quality Com.; pres. Comprehensive Health Planning in So. Ill.; chairperson Greater Egypt Health Council. Mem. Am. Public Health Assn., Am. Assn. Hosp. Planning, Ill. Hosp. Assn., Am. Soc. Pub. Adminstrn., Nat. Assn. Female Execs., Phi Kappa Phi. Democrat. Roman Catholic. Club: Ladies Elks. Home: 108 N Horrell St West Frankfort IL 62896 Office: 108 N Horrell St West Frankfort IL 62896

ACZEL, SUSAN KENDE, mathematician; b. Budapest, Hungary, June 22, 1927; s. Lajos and Iren Kende; came to Can., 1965, naturalized, 1972; B.Sc., U. Budapest, 1948; M.Sc., U. Szeged, 1950; m. Janos D. Aczel, Dec. 14, 1946; children—Catherina Aczel Boivie Julie Aczel More. Teaching asst. U. Szeged, 1949-50; asst. prof. Tech. U. Miskolc, 1950-52; head cultural dept. City of Debrecen, 1953-55; research assoc. U. Waterloo, Ont., Can., 1965-71. Author bibliographies on math. books in Hungary and on works on functional equations, 1964-75. Home: 97 McCarron Crescent Waterloo ON N2L 5M9 Canada

ADAIR, JOAN, retail executive, school official; b. Spokane, Wash., Jan. 18, 1935; d. John Sherman and Laura Georgina (Barnes) Harris; student Santa Ana (Calif.) Coll., 1970-72; children—Laurie Gaye, Marcus Paul. Personnel asst. City of Tustin (Calif.), 1972-77; office mgr. Santa Ana Coll., 1977-78; agy. N.Y. Life Ins. Co., 1978-79; exec. sec. Tchrs. Mgmt. & Investment Co., Newport Beach, Calif., 1979-80, regional mgr., 1980-84; exec. sec. to dir. and bd. trustees Idyllwild (Calif.) Sch. Music and Arts, 1984—; co-owner The Pony Shop, 1983—. Mem. Nat. Assn. Securities Dealers, Am. Soc. Profl. and Exec. Women, Nat. Assn. Bus. and Indsl. Saleswomen, Internat. Assn. Fin. Planners, Nat. Assn. Female Execs. Home: 4802 SW Hinds #104 Seattle WA 98116 Office: 52500 Temecula Rd Idyllwild CA 92349 also 54200 N Circle Dr Idyllwild CA 92349

ADAM, CATHERINE, lawyer; b. Kiskunhalas, Hungary, Nov. 10, 1943; came to U.S., 1976; d. Matthew and Elizabeth (Battay) A., m. Joseph Szlapak, July 19, 1965 (div. 1972); 1 child, Matthew. J.D., Sci. U. Sch. Law, Budapest, 1966; LL.M., NYU, 1985. Bar: Hungary, N.Y. Legal cons. Patent and Trademark Bur., Budapest, 1967-75; tax adv. Feuerstein & Sinclair, N.Y.C., 1977-80; with Brooks & McNiely, Investments, N.Y.C., 1980—; cons. Manhattan Electronics, Inc., 1985—. Sci. U. Hungary scholar, 1963. Mem. N.Y. State Bar Assn., NYU Alumni Assn. (assoc.), Nat. Assn. Female Execs., Am. Mus. Natural History. Avocations: philately; hiking; music.

ADAM, RUTH COUFFER, infant wear company executive; b. Chgo., Nov. 6, 1897; d. William Elder and Roberta Wilson (Hanna) Couffer; m. James McIntosh Adam, Aug. 20, 1921; children—Virginia Ruth, Jean Elizabeth. Student Chgo. Normal Sch. of Phys. Edn. Sec., dir. phys. edn. YWCA, Evansville, Ind., 1919; dir. phys. edn. No. High Sch., Detroit, 1920, Carl Schurz High Sch., Chgo., 1921; playground dir. Chgo. Park System, Oak Park Park System, Ill.; designer Feltman Bros., N.Y.C., pres., cons., designer Personality Inc., Kansas City, Mo., 1981. Author: Personality Tails, 1981. Republican. Episcopalian. Home and Office: 1288 W 71st Terr Kansas City MO 64114

ADAMCZYK, PAULA MARCHEWKA, manufacturing company executive; b. Salem, Mass., Feb. 13, 1949; d. Stanley J. and Mariba M. (Markwuith) Marchewka; B.A. in English, Suffolk U., 1971, M.B.A., 1975. Tchr., Peabody (Mass.) High Sch., 1971-72; chief accountant Industrial Cab Co., Essex, Mass., 1972-74, asst. controller, 1974-75; corporate controller, treas. Madico, Inc., a Van Leer corp., Woburn, Mass., 1975-82; v.p. fin. VanLeer Plastics, 1982—; asst. treas. Keyes Fibre Co., 1982—; v.p. fin. adminstrn., treas., dir., minority owner Madico, Inc., 1984—. Bd. dirs. Woburn Council of Social Concern, 1976—. Mem. Nat. Assn. Accountants, Assn. M.B.A. Execs., Woburn C. of C., Audubon Soc., Jacques Cousteau Soc., NOW, Nat. Assn. Female Execs. Home: 5 Connolly Pl Beverly Farms MA 01915 Office: 64 Industrial Parkway Woburn MA 01810

ADAMOVICH, SHIRLEY GRAY, librarian; b. Pepperell, Mass., May 8, 1927; d. Willard Ellsworth and Carrie Elmer (Shattuck) Gray; m. Frank Walter Adamovich, Aug. 31, 1960; children—Carrie, Elizabeth. B.A., U. N.H., 1954; M.S., Simmons Coll., 1955. Cons., Vt. State Library, Montpelier, 1955-58; head cataloger Bentley Coll., Waltham, Mass., 1958-60; tchr. U. N.H. System, Durham, 1965-79; asst. state librarian N.H. State Library, Concord, 1979-81, state librarian, 1981—. Editor: A Reader in Library Technology, 1975. Served with USAF, 1949-53. Mem. ALA, N.H. Library Assn., New Eng. Library Assn., N.H. Library Trustees Assn., N.H. Ednl. Media Assn., Council State Library Agys. in Northeast. Office: NH State Library 20 Park St Concord NH 03301

ADAMS, ADDIE FULLER, principal; b. LaFayette, Ala., July 4, 1942; d. V. Wallace and Thelma (Wheeler) Fuller; m. Donald W. Adams, July 8, 1983. B.S., Jacksonville State U., 1963; M.Ed., Auburn U., 1970; postgrad. U. W. Fla., 1970, Auburn U., 1977, Fla. State U.-Tallahassee, 1985. Tchr. Carrollton High Sch., Ga., 1963-66, Benjamin Russell High Sch., Alexander City, Ala., 1966-68; counselor Mowat Jr. High Sch., Lynn Haven, Fla., 1968-72, prin., 1982-85; counselor Rutherford High Sch., Springfield, Fla., 1972-77, asst. prin., 1977-82, prin., 1985—. Named Outstanding Young Educator, Panama City Jaycees, Fla., 1970. Mem. Nat. Assn. Secondary Sch. Prins., Fla. Assn. Sch. Adminstrs., Sch. Adminstrs. Bay County (pres. 1984—). Democrat. Baptist. Office: Rutherford High Sch 1000 Sch Ave Panama City FL 32405

ADAMS, ALICE, sculptor; b. N.Y.C., 1930. B.F.A., Columbia U., 1953; postgrad. L'Ecole Nationale d'Art Decoratif, Aubusson, France, 1953-54. One-person exhbns.: Blemenfeld Gallery, N.Y.C., 1964; 55 Mercer St. Gallery, N.Y.C., 1971, 73, 74, 75; Hal Bromm Gallery, N.Y.C., 1979; Artemesia Gallery, Chgo., 1980; Pub. Art Fund, N.Y.C., 1980; The Globe, City Hall Park, 1980; Hal Bromm Gallery, N.Y.C., 1981; group exhbns. include: Spare, East Hall Gallery, Port Washington, N.Y., 1975; Working Drawings by Sculptors, Kans. State Coll., 1975; Herbert Lehman Coll. Gallery, N.Y.C., 1975, numerous others; recent commns. include: Bemis Park, Omaha, 1983; Dag Hammarskjold Plaza, N.Y.C., 1983; Crosby Gardens, Toledo, 1984; lectr. sculpture Manhattanville Coll., Purchase, N.Y., 1960-80; vis. assoc. prof. Calif. State Coll., Los Angeles, 1965; lectr. Sarah Lawrence Coll., N.Y., 1978, Princeton U., 1978, Pratt Inst., Bklyn., 1979-80, Sch. Visual Arts, N.Y.C., 1980-81, 82-83, U. Wis., 1979, Neuberger Mus., N.Y., 1980, Boston Mus. Sch., 1980, U. Chgo., 1980, Art Inst. Chgo., 1980, Parsons Sch., N.Y., 1981. Featured in numerous books, articles in profl. jours. and catalogs. Yale-Norfolk

Summer Art Sch. fellow, 1952; French Govt. fellow, Fulbright grantee, 1953-54; MacDowell Colony fellow, N.H., 1966; CAPS grantee, 1972, 76-77; NEA fellow, 1978-79; Princeton Humanities fellow, 1980; Guggenheim fellow, 1981-82; Am. Acad. and Inst. Arts and Letters grantee, 1984. Address: 117 W 26th St New York NY 10001

ADAMS, ALISON SARA MINET, lawyer; b. N.Y.C., Dec. 31, 1949; d. Ronald George and Selma Barbara (Silver) Minet; m. Jeffrey Norman Adams, June 17, 1971 (dec. 1979); 1 son, Thomas Gregory; m. Boris M. Young, Sept. 4, 1982; 1 dau., Natasha Zora Adams-Young. B.A., Tufts U., 1971; M.A., Simmons Coll., 1973; J.D., Loyola U.-Los Angeles, 1982. Bar: Calif. 1982, U.S. Dist. Ct. (cen. dist.) Calif. 1983. Staff atty. Isla Vista Legal Clinic, Goleta, Calif., 1982-83; pvt. practice law, Santa Barbara, Calif., 1983—. Mem. consol. grant programs Santa Barbara City Schs., 1983, dist. adv. council, 1984, sch. site com., 1984. Recipient commendation for Pro Bono Service, State Bar Calif., 1982. Mem. ABA, Calif. Attys. for Criminal Justice, Nat. Lawyers Guild. Democrat.

ADAMS, ALMA JEAN SHEALEY, Afro-American art educator, artist; b. High Point, N.C., May 27, 1946; d. Benjamen and Mattie (Stokes) Thomas Shealey; m. Billy Eugene Adams, Dec. 18, 1965 (div. July 1980); children—Billy Eugene II, Linda Jeanelle. B.S. in Art Edn., N.C. A&T State U., 1969, M.S., 1972; Ph.D., Ohio State U., 1981. Tchr., dept. chmn. Palmer Inst., Sedalia, N.C., 1969-70; prof., chmn. dept. visual arts/humane studies Bennett Coll., Greensboro, N.C., 1972-79, 81—; teaching assoc. dept. art edn. Ohio State U., Columbus, 1979-81; lectr., cons. Afro Am. art Bennett Coll., Greensboro, 1981—. Mem. sch. bd. Greensboro City Schs., 1984-86; coordiantor Jesse Jackson for Pres. Com., Guilford County, Greensboro, 1984. Recipient Martin Luther King Service award Greensboro br. NAACP, 1985; faculty curriculum devel. grantee Project Senegale, West Africa, United Negro Coll. Fund, Bennett Coll., 1985. Mem. Nat. Conf. Artists, AAUP Women, Nat. Art Edn. Assn., Kappa Pi, Alpha Kappa Alpha. Democrat. Baptist. Avocations: printmaker; singing; traveling; lecturing. Home: 508-B Savannah St Greensboro NC 27406 Office: Bennett Coll Box 11 900 E Washington St Greensboro NC 27420

ADAMS, ANNE MAYO, social worker; b. Cleve., Mar. 25, 1931; d. Edward L. and Kate S. (Hammond) Mayo; student Skidmore Coll., 1949-51; B.A. in Sociology, U. Wis., 1953; postgrad. Bridgewater State Tchrs. Coll., 1965-66; m. Charles B. Adams, Mar. 17, 1979; children by previous marriage—Michelle Morel Taylor, Jean Pierre Morel, Catherine Morel Zanartu, Andre Morel. Social worker with aged, blind, disabled and children, Akron and Medina, Ohio, 1969-72; social worker, West Palm Beach, Fla., 1972-73; social worker adult protective service State of Fla., West Palm Beach, 1972-80, social and rehabilitative counsellor II, 1980—; public speaker in field; participant seminars in law, psychology and counselling techniques. Founder gerontology program Meml. Presbyn. Ch., West Palm Beach, 1982; mem. session, choir, Christian edn. com. Lakewood Congl. Ch.; mem. Fla. Council on Aging, 1984—. Mem. Fla. Assn. for Health and Social Services, Alpha Chi Omega. Republican. Club: Cotillion of Palm Beaches (pres.). Home: 2287 Carambola Rd West Palm Beach FL 33406 Office: Health and Rehabilitation Services State of Fla Unit 23 3801 S Congress Ave Lake Worth FL 33460

ADAMS, AUDREY LEE, critical care physician, anesthesiologist, educator; b. Sioux Falls, S.D., Mar. 27, 1952; d. James Robert and Louise (Lewis) A.; m. Edward Lee Schumann, Dec. 9, 1983. B.S. in Medicine, U. S.D., 1975; M.D., Northwestern U., 1976. Diplomate Am. Bd. Anesthesiology. Intern Northwestern-McGraw Med. Ctr., Chgo., 1977, resident in anesthesiology, 1978-79, fellow, 1980; asst. prof. anesthesiology Pritzker Sch. Medicine, U. Chgo., 1981-82; asst. prof. anesthesiology U. Calif.-Irvine, 1982-85, assoc. prof., 1986—; dir. surg. intensive care, Long Beach VA Med. Ctr., Calif., 1982—. Named Outstanding Tchr., U. Chgo. Med. House Officers, 1982. Mem. Am. Soc. Anesthesiology, Soc. Critical Care Medicine, Internat. Anesthesia Research Soc., Am. Med. Women's Assn. Office: PO Box 6565 Orange CA 92613

ADAMS, BARBARA, English language educator, poet, writer; b. N.Y.C., Mar. 23, 1932; d. David S. Block and Helen (Taxter) Block Tyler; m. Elwood Adams, June 6, 1952; children—Steven, Amy, Anne, Samuel. B.S., SUNY-New Paltz, 1962, M.A., 1970; Ph.D., NYU, 1981. Adj. instr. Orange County Community Coll., Middletown, N.Y., 1970-77; grad. asst. NYU, N.Y.C., 1974-77; adj. lectr. SUNY-Albany, 1977-81; instr. Mt. St.Mary Coll., Newburgh, N.Y., 1980-81; asst. prof. SUNY-Cobleskill, 1981-83; adj. assoc. prof. Pace U., N.Y.C., 1983-84, asst. prof. English, 1984—, coordinator bus. communications, 1984—. Author: Double Solitaire, 1982. Contbr. poems, stories, articles to various mags. and jours. Recipient 1st prize for poetry NYU and Acad. Am. Poets, 1975; Penfield fellow NYU, 1977. Mem. MLA, Assn. Bus. Communication, Poets and Writers. Avocations: piano; bird-watching. Home: 57 Coach Ln Newburgh NY 12550 Office: Pace U Pace Plaza New York NY 10038

ADAMS, BETTY VIRGINIA, petroleum products company executive; b. Butler, Ga., Jan. 6, 1925; d. William Burton and Martha William (Duckworth) A.; B.A., U. N.C., 1946; B.A., Va. Intermont Coll., 1944. Chmn. Fuel Oil & Equipment Co., Inc., Roanoke, Va., 1949—. Methodist. Clubs: Roanoke Country; Yacht and Country (Stuart, Fla.). Office: PO Box 12626 Roanoke VA 24027

ADAMS, BEULAH GRACE JENKINS (MRS. ADDISON FRANK ADAMS), abstract co. exec.; b. Bastrop, Tex., Nov. 29, 1909; d. Hartford and Beulah Alice (Hemphill) Jenkins; B.A., Baylor U., 1930; postgrad. U. Tex., 1933, 39, U. Colo., 1934; m. Addison Frank Adams, Dec. 26, 1938; children—Forrest Jenkins, Alice Ann (Mrs. Charles Woodrow Miller). Tchr., Bastrop Pub. Schs., 1930-41; v.p., mgr. Bastrop County Abstract Co., Inc., 1942—. Mem. AAUW, Tex. Geneal. Soc., Am., Tex. land title assns., Am. Assn. Petroleum Landmen, Delta Kappa Gamma. Baptist. Home: 1707 Pecan St Bastrop TX 78602 Office: 901 Main St POB 550 Bastrop TX 78602

ADAMS, CAROLINE J. H., magazine advertising sales manager; b. Dallas, June 15, 1951; d. Bill G. and Anita N. (Murrah) Hickey. B.F.A., So. Methodist U., 1973. Office mgr., media planner Jim Leslie & Assocs., Dallas, 1973; continuity dir. Sta. KZEW-FM, Dallas, 1973-75; sec. Neiman-Marcus Co., Dallas, 1975-77; exec. sec. Harris Corp., Dallas, 1979-80; mgr. classified sales, circulation ADWEEK/Southwest Mag., Dallas, 1980—. Mem. Dallas Ad League, Am. Bus. Women's Assn. Republican. Methodist. Home: 5902 E University Blvd Dallas TX 75206 Office: ADWEEK 2909 Cole Ave Suite 115 Dallas TX 75204

ADAMS, CHRISTIE TEWKSBURY, marketing and public relations consultant; b. San Diego, Dec. 27, 1949; d. Henry Jackson and Lillian B. Adams, Jr.; student Am. Coll. Switzerland, Leysin, 1968-69; B.A. in Art History, Stanford U., 1972; postgrad. U. Hawaii, 1972-73. Advance publicist NBC Entertainment Corp., NBC TV/RCA, Burbank, Calif., 1974; advance rep. Ice Capades, Hollywood, Calif., 1974-76; asst. v.p. Pioneer Fed. Savs. and Loan, Honolulu, 1976-78; dir. public relations Kapiolani/Children's Med. Center, Honolulu, 1979-83; dir. pub. relations Hyatt Regency Waikiki, 1983; exec. dir. Hawaii Soc. AIA, 1984-86; founder Christie Adams & Assocs., mktg. and pub. relations, 1986—; site coordinator for Hawaii Health Fair '81. Judge, publicist Hawaii's Jr. Miss Scholarship Program, 1978; mem. Liberty House Consumer Bd., Honolulu, 1978; mem. working women panel Glamour mag., 1979; mem. cast Honolulu Press Club's Gridiron Shows, 1980, 81; TV hostess Friends of Hawaii Public TV's Festival Nights membership/fund-raising dr., 1981. Named to Mademoiselle mag. Coll. Bd., 1971; named 2d runner-up Miss Internat. Beauty Pageant, Honolulu, 1972; recipient awards including Galley award Hawaii Communicators Assn., 1979, 80, 1st place award for instl. newspapers and mags. Hawaii Med. Assn., 1980, cert. of appreciation YWCA, 1980, citation for 1st place in internal publs. div. splty. hosps. Acad. Hosp. Pub. Relations' ann. MacEachern Awards Competition, 1981; named 1 of 5 winners Hosp. Forum jour. Photography Contest, 1980. Mem. Am. Mktg. Assn., Hawaii Film Bd., Internat. Assn. Bus. Communicators (2d v.p., dir. and program co-chairperson Hawaii chpt. 1982), Nat. Assn. Female Execs. (charter), Pub. Relations Soc. Am., Arts Council Hawaii (charter), Daus. Hawaii, Friends of Iolani Palace, Hist. Hawaii Found. (charter), Honolulu Acad. Arts, Inventors Council Hawaii (charter; sec., dir. and publicist 1978-79, v.p., dir. 1979-80), Lovers of Arts (charter), Nat. Trust Hist. Preservation. Club: Stanford of Hawaii (sec. 1979-80, dir. 1979-81). Author various internal and external corp. publs., including ann. reports, brochures, other bus. lit., newsletters. Office: 6254 Kawaihae Pl Honolulu HI 96825

ADAMS, CYNTHIA D., health sciences educator; b. Detroit, Sept. 10, 1946; d. Walter Norbert Tokarz and Eugenia W. (Czastkiewicz) Tokarz; m. Charles Richard Adams, Feb. 18, 1978; children—Erik, Jessica, Kerensa. B.S., Wayne State U., 1968, Ed.D., 1973; M.A., Eastern Mich. U., 1970. Instr., Wayne State U., Detroit, 1970-71; chief technologist, ednl. coordinator Detroit Macomb Hosp. Assn., 1971-74; dir., asst. prof. health adminstrn. program Mercy Coll., Detroit, 1974-76; assoc. prof., chmn. dept. mediatech. Univ. of Health Scis., Chgo. Med. Sch., North Chicago, Ill., 1976-80, prof., dean, 1980—; dir. workshops Profl. Seminars Cons., N.Y.C., 1985—. Contbr. articles to profl. jours. Mem. adv. bd. Coll. Lake County, Grayslake, Ill., 1979-84; sci. fair judge Ill. Jr. Acad. Sci., 1980—; adv. bd. Lake County Urban League, Waukegan, Ill., 1980—; yearbook advisor Lake Bluff Jr. High Sch., Ill., 1983—; adv. bd. Lake County YWCA, Waukegan, 1984—. Recipient Cert. of Achievement for Outstanding Women in Edn., YWCA, Lake County, 1983, 84. Mem. Am. Assn. Allied Health Professionals, Am. Soc. Med. Technologists (cert. Omicron Sigma award 1980), Am. Soc. Clin. Pathologists (dir. workshops 1976—), Am. Soc. Allied Health Profls. (chmn. women's interest sect. 1984—), Am. Midwest Assn. Allied Health Deans, Ill. Med. Technology Assn. (chmn. sci. assembly 1979-80), Chgo. Soc. Med. Technologists (co-chmn. by-laws com. 1984-85, bd. dirs., 1984—). Home: 340 E Scranton Ave Lake Bluff IL 60044 Office: Univ Health Scis Chgo Med Sch 3333 Green Bay Rd North Chicago IL 60064

ADAMS, DARLENE MARIE, photographer, accountant; b. Lewisburg, Pa., Dec. 6, 1951; d. William and Betty Jane (Leicy) A. Grad. high sch., Ephrata, Pa. Clk., Armstrong Cork Co., Lancaster, Pa., 1969-71; asst. to controller CKM, Denver, Pa., 1971-73; acct. Ralph Stine and Co., Lancaster, 1973-78, Fleetmen, Kaneohe, Hawaii, 1980, Sir Speedy, Lancaster, 1981-82; owner, mgr. Adams Acctg. and Photography, Lancaster and Honolulu, 1977—. Author: Mixed Emotions, 1971. Recipient Outstanding Community Service award, 1969. Mem. Am. Bus. Women's Assn. (chpt. pres. 1981-82, Woman of Yr. 1982, nat. photographer 1983—), Nat. Assn. Female Execs. Avocations: writing poetry; music. Office Adams Acctg and Photography 38 W Orange St Lancaster PA 17603

ADAMS, EDA ANN FISCHER, nursing educator; b. Montclair, N.J., Jan. 27, 1943; d. Otto Gustav and Theresa (Yannotta) Fischer; m. Bruce Leonard Adams, June 12, 1970. Diploma, Mountainside Hosp. Sch. Nursing, Montclair, 1963; B.S.N., Fairleigh Dickinson U., 1969; M.A.T., Tchrs. Coll., Columbia U., 1977; Ed.M., 1979. Staff nurse Mountainside Hosp., Montclair, 1963-65, St. Barnabus Med. Ctr., Livingston, N.J., 1965-66; asst. head nurse Mountainside Hosp., 1967-71, head nurse, 1971-73, instr. Sch. Nursing, 1973-79; instr. Seton Hall U., South Orange, N.J., 1979-81; asst. prof. Bergen Community Coll., Paramus, N.J., 1983—. Vol., Hospice, Inc., Montclair, 1981—. Mem. Mountainside Hosp. Alumnae Assn., Sigma Theta Tau. Republican. Baptist. Home: 18 Holmehill Ln Roseland NJ 07068 Office: Bergen Community Coll Paramus Rd Paramus NJ 07652

ADAMS, EENA J. CARLISLE, dietitian, educator; b. Mt. Hope, Kans.; d. Alfred George and Nora Agnes (Kissick) Carlisle; student Ohio U., 1954-61; B.S. in Home Econs., Kans. State U., 1939; M.S. in Foods and Nutrition, 1970; m. Lawrence D. Adams, Dec. 11, 1940: children—Karen Jean Adams McCarthy, Maureen Janet Adams Mitchell. Tchr., Leonardville, Kans., 1939-40, Jan'es Pvt. Sch., Front Royal, Va., 1949-52, Forestdale Sch., McCracken County, Ky., 1952-53, Jackson (Ohio) County and City Schs., 1953-68, Head Start, Jackson, 1965-68; grad. teaching asst. Kans. State U., Manhattan, 1969-70; asst. prof. home econs. Wayne (Nebr.) State Coll., 1970-76; asst. prof. home econs. and dietetics Morehead (Ky.) State U., 1976-82, coordinator energy mgmt. asst. program, 1979-80; cons. dietitian, 1980—. Mem. Front Royal (Va.) Recreation Council. Delta Kappa Gamma Annie Webb Blanton scholar, 1968. Mem. Am. Dietetic Assn. (registered dietitian), Nutrition Today Soc., Soc. Nutrition Edn., Am. Home Econs. Assn., Inst. Food Tech., W.Va.-Ohio-Ky. Dietetic Assn., Ky. Dietetic Assn., Ohio Edn. Assn., Chi Omega, Delta Kappa Gamma (pres.), Alpha Lambda Delta. Home: Ka-Mel Farms Beaver OH 45613 also Crique Side Apt 4 Morehead KY 40351

ADAMS, FRANCES GRANT, office consultant; b. Springfield, Ill.; d. Daniel Harmon and Adah (Morris) Grant; A.B., U. Ill., 1960; student Ill. Wesleyan U., 1938-39, U. Miami, (Fla.), 1945, Am. Inst. Banking, 1959-60; m. Jack R. Adams, Oct. 24, 1945 (dec. 1975); children—Jack Richard, Jr., Alexander Beall, Frances Grant II. Sec., Ill. Senate, 1936; sec., bus. mgr. Wesleyan U. Ill., 1938-39; sec. to chief staff Flying Tng. Command, USAAF, 1951, personnel supr. U.S. Army Air Base, Ephrata and Moses Lake, Wash., 1941-42; job classification and adminstrv. survey analyst Canal Zone, 1942-44; sec. to comdr. USAF Res. Wing, Pitts., 1951-55; sec. to mayor City of Wheeling (W.Va.), 1955-59; sec. W.Va. Ho. of Dels., 1965-66, 77-80; legis. aide W.Va. Senate, 1981—; mem. D.A.R., 1947—, nat. vice chmn. service for vet. patients, 1968-71, editor W.Va. news, 1965-71, parliamentarian W.Va. soc., 1979, dir. No. dist. W.Va., 1980-83, state chmn. bylaws 1983—, state vice regent, 1986—; nat. chmn. public relations Nat. Soc. Women Descs. Ancient and Honorable Arty. Co., 1974-77; mem. Nat. League Am. Pen Women, 1949—, nat. 3d v.p., 1971-72, nat. rec. sec., 1966-68, nat. chmn. orgn., 1972-74, nat. chmn. commemorative endowment fund, 1976-80, nat chmn. fin. 1982-84, pres. Elkins br., 1986—. Mem. Magna Charta Dames, Colonial Order of the Crown, Order of Washington, Phi Beta Kappa. Democrat. Presbyterian. Home: Route 1 Box 63 Elkins WV 26241

ADAMS, HAZEL GREENLEE REDFEARN (MRS. PAYTON F. ADAMS II), teacher educator; b. Monroe, N.C., Nov. 12, 1905; d. Ephraim Eugene and Rebecca (Laney) Redfearn; student Radford Coll., 1924; A.B., U. Ky., 1940, M.A., 1953; postgrad. U. Nebr., 1955; m. Payton F. Adams II, July 11, 1928; children—Payton F. III, Juliette Greenlee (Mrs. J. B. Hawk). Elementary tchr. Larchmont Sch., Norfolk, Va., 1924-28, Winchester City Schs. (Ky.), 1943-53; supr. Clark County Schs. (Ky.), 1953-61; supr. student tchrs. Ky. Wesleyan Coll., 1945-48; instr. Wesleyan Coll., Macon, Ga., 1960; asst. and assoc. prof. edn. Dakota Wesleyan U., Mitchell, S.D., 1961-69; assoc. prof. early childhood edn. Pfeiffer Coll., Misenheimer, N.C., 1969—, supr. student tchrs., 1969-73. Chmn., Clark County Community Council, 1950-52, Clark County Recreation Bd., 1955-60; supr. Teen-Town Winchester, 1954-60; mem. adv. council Southeastern Christian Coll., Winchester, Ky., 1977—; aide Clark County Hosp. Aux. Mem. AAUW, AAUP, NEA, S.D. Edn. Assn., DAR (treas. chpt. 1975-80), Assn. Supervision Curriculum Devel., Assn. for Childhood Edn., Assn. Childhood Edn. Internat. (adviser Pfeiffer Coll. chpt. 1972-73), N.C. Assn. Supervisory Educators. Mitchell Bus. and Profl. Women Club, Albemarle Bus. and Profl. Women (pres. 1972-73), Ky. Hist. Soc., Nat. Trust Hist. Preservation, Phi Kappa Phi (pres. 1964-66), Delta Kappa Gamma (pres. 1964-66), Pi Gamma Mu. Methodist. Clubs: Irvine (Ky.) Garden, Daniel Boone Music, Christian Women's, Order Eastern Star. Home: 136 College St Winchester KY 40391 Office: Pfeiffer Coll Misenheimer NC 28109

ADAMS, IRENE FORSYTHE, oil and real estate investor; b. Kansas City, Mo., July 29, 1935; d. Max Leon and Dorothy (Frick) Drozda; m. James H. Forsythe, Aug. 3, 1958 (div. Feb. 1975); children—Nicole, Michael; m. Jerry Max Adams, Aug. 30, 1981. B.A. in English, Northwestern U., 1957, postgrad., 1958; postgrad. U. Cin., 1970, Columbia U., 1972. Sales rep. Gen. Foods Co., Anaheim, Calif., 1974-75; sr. account mgr. Dun & Bradstreet, Houston, 1975—; real estate cons., 1975—. Recipient Presdl. citation Dun & Bradstreet, 1983, regional citation, 1980, 82. Mem. Japanese Am. Soc., AAU, Jr. League (patron). Clubs: John Evans (Northwestern U.); Dads' (Tex. Tech U. 1982-84). Office: Dun & Bradstreet 2500 City West Blvd Houston TX 77042

ADAMS, JEAN LA VON, service company executive; b. Houston, Mar. 28, 1925; d. Ira Robbin and Frances Elizabeth (Ellison) Bryan; m. James Seymour Adams, Aug. 15, 1943; children—James S., Jr., Virginia Adams. Student pub. schs. Project dir. sr. citizens services Fort Bend County Commrs. Ct., Richmond, Tex., 1964-66; project dir. Fort Bend County Planning and Service Orgn., Inc., Rosenberg, 1966-72, aging services dir., 1972-73, exec. dir., 1973—. Group organizer Ft. Bend County Health Council, Richmond State Sch., 1983—. Clubs: Spring Branch County; Plantation County; Pecan Grove Country. Home: 2610 Precint Line Rd Richmond TX 77469 Office: Fort Bend County Planning and Service Orgn Inc 3720 Airport Rd PO Box 32 Rosenburg TX 77471

ADAMS, JEAN RUTH, entomologist; b. Edgewater Park, N.J., Aug. 17, 1928; d. Herbert Raymond and Gertrude Gladys (Budd) A.; B.S., Rutgers U., 1950, Ph.D. (Trubeck fellow), 1962. Lab. technician Rohm & Haas Co., Bristol, Pa., 1951-57; postdoctoral fellow U. Pa., Phila., 1961-62; research entomologist U.S. Dept. Agr., Agr. Research Center, Beltville, Md., 1962—; cons. insect pathology, electron microscopy, 1958—. Mem. nominating com. D.C. Bapt. Conv., 1977-79, dir. Acteens, Mission Youth Orgn., D.C. Bapt. Conv., 1972—, Sunday sch. tchr. 1st Bapt. Ch., Hyattsville, Md., 1962—, chmn. Christian edn. bd., 1973-74, mem. nominating com., 1974-77, mem. bd. missions, 1977-80, ch. treas., 1973-74, mem. choir, 1979—, diaconate, 1980—, vice chmn., 1981-82, chmn., 1982-84, trustee Bapt. Home, 1982—, sec., 1985—. Registered profl. entomologist. Mem. Electron Microscopy Soc. Am. (chmn. sci. exhibits ann. meeting 1982), Entomol. Soc. Am., Am. Soc. for Cell Biology, Soc. for Invertebrate Pathology (sec. 1982-84), Washington Soc. for Electron Microscopy (council 1976-83, sec.-treas. 1976-78, sec. 1980-82), Washington Entomol. Soc., Md. Entomol. Soc., Sigma Xi, Sigma Delta Epsilon. Contbr. articles to profl. jours. Home: 6004 41st Ave Hyattsville MD 20782 Office: US Dept Agr Agr Research Center-W Insect Pathology Lab Bldg 011A Room 214 Beltsville MD 20705

ADAMS, JEANNE MARIE, clinical social worker; b. Miami Beach, Fla., Apr. 4, 1951; d. John Hixson and Eula (Strickland) A. B.S., Fla. State U., 1973; cert. gerontology U. Utah, 1977; M.S.W., U. Kans., 1981. Lic. clin. social worker, Fla. Social worker United Way, Miami, Fla., 1974, Hallandale Social Services, Fla., 1975, Golden Triangle Mental Health Ctr., Great Falls, Mont., 1976-79; clin. social worker Fellowship House, Miami, 1981, Douglas Gardens Mental Health Ctr., Miami Beach, 1981—; field practicum instr. Barry U. Sch. Social Work, Miami, 1983—, Fla. Internat. U. Sch. Occupational Therapy, Miami, 1984—. Recipient award of excellence Nat. Council Community Mental Health Ctrs., 1978. Mem. Nat. Assn. Social Workers. Home: 10 NE 132 St North Miami FL 33161

ADAMS, JUDITH ROSE, home health care educator; b. New Haven, Mar. 14, 1943; d. Stephen Thomas and Bertha May (Vilforth) Oakley; m. Robert Neal Adams II, May 7, 1965; children—Robert, Lara. Diploma, Norwalk Hosp. Sch. Nursing (Conn.), 1964; B.S.Nursing, U. N.C., 1980. R.N., N.C. Supr., charge nurse various hosps., Conn., Ill., Fla., N.C., 1964-72; pvt. duty nurse, Durham, N.C., 1972-73; dir. inservice edn. McPherson Hosp., Durham, 1973-78; adminstrv. Med. Personnel Pool, Durham, 1980-82, regional dir. home care, Raleigh and Durham, 1982-83; dir. edn. N.C. Assn. for Home Care, Raleigh, 1983—, mem. assn. bd. dirs., exec. com., 1983—; mem. program com. N.C. Council Home Health Agys., 1981-82. Mem. profl. vol. com. Durham County Health Fairs, 1982, 83; mem. adv. bd. Durham County Community Alternative Program, 1982-83, Wake County Community Alternative Program, 1983. James M. Johnston scholar continuing edn. program, 1974, also U. N.C. Sch. Nursing, 1979. Mem. Am. Nurses Assn., N.C. Nurses Assn., N.C. Soc. for Prevention Blindness (nursing involvement com. 1977-78), N.C. Arthritis Assn., ARC, Am. Pub. Health Assn. Democrat. Home: 204 Lexington Rd Chapel Hill NC 27514 Office: NC Assn for Home Care 1037 Dresser Ct Raleigh NC 27609

ADAMS, LAURIE MARIE, art historian, psychoanalyst, educator; b. N.Y.C., Sept. 29, 1941; d. Daniel Edward and Helen Louise (Nelson) Schneider; B.A., Newcomb Coll., 1962; M.A. in Psychology, Columbia U., 1963, Ph.D. in Art History, 1967; m. John Brett Adams, July 24, 1970; children—Alexa, Caroline. Prof. art history John Jay Coll., City U. N.Y., 1966—; vis. asst. prof. U. Fla., Gainesville, 1967, Sarah Lawrence Coll., Bronxville, N.Y., 1967, Mt. Holyoke Coll., 1972; lectr. Columbia U., N.Y.C., 1968, instr. Sch. of Visual Arts, N.Y.C., 1976; pvt. psychoanalytic practice N.Y.C., 1978—. Recipient CUNY summer travel grantee, 1967, 68; Columbia summer travel grantee, 1966. Mem. Am. Psychol. Assn. (assoc.), Coll. Art Assn., N.Y. Center for Psychoanalytic Tng. (assoc.). Author children's books. Editor: Giotto in Perspective, 1974; Author: Art Cop, 1974; Art on Trial, 1976. Source: Notes in the History of Art. Contbr. articles to profl. jours. Office: 444 W 56th St New York NY 10019

ADAMS, MARGARET DIANE, taxi company exec.; b. St. Paul, Oct. 31, 1937; d. William Frank and Margaret Mary (O'Donnell) Rudolph; B.A., Met. State U., 1976; m. Ronald Earl Adams, Feb. 25, 1976; children—Margaret, Michelle and Mark (triplets); children by previous marriage—Roberta, Barbara, William, John, Dana. Bookkeeper, Universal CIT Credit Corp., 1956-59; clk. U. Minn., 1963-65; sec. Granville House, St. Paul, 1965-67, adminstrv. asst., 1967-72; adminstrv. asst. Assn. of Halfway House Alcoholism Programs of N.Am., Inc., St. Paul, 1972, project coordinator, 1973-74, project dir., 1974-78, acting dir., 1978-79, exec. dir., 1979-81; pres. Adams Enterprises, 1981-82; owner Adams Taxi, 1981—; cons. Nat. Center for Alcohol Edn.; lectr., adviser Lakewood Community Coll. Mem. Nat. Assn. Female Execs. (network dir. 1979-81), Nat. Assn. Alcoholism Counselors, Minn. Assn. Alcoholism Counselors, Minn. Assn. Alcoholism Counselors, Ind. Assn. Alcoholism and Drug Abuse Counselors (cert. alcoholism and drug counselor), Nat. Coalition for Adequate Alcoholism Programs, N. Am. Indian Women's Council on Chem. Dependency. Author: Women: On Women in Recovery, 1976; mem. editorial bd. Do It Now Found., 1978-79. Office: Adams Taxi & Dispatching Services 996 Bush Ave Saint Paul MN 55106

ADAMS, MARGARET PATRICIA, accountant; b. Washington, Pa., Feb. 5, 1931; d. Michael and Mary Ann (Kerin) A.; B.S., Point Park Coll., Pitts., 1974. From office clk. to acctg. supr. Indsl. Enterprises Washington, Inc., 1949-72; acctg. supr. Reliance Electric Co. div. Exxon Corp., Washington, Pa., 1972-75, plant controller, 1975—. Bd. dirs. Pa. Assn. Blind, Washington, 1982-84, fin. chmn., treas., 1984—; bd. dirs. Pvt. Industry Council (on-job tng.). Mem. Nat. Assn. Female Execs., Acctg. Assn. Washington County (dir.), World Affairs Council of Pitts., Bus. and Profl. Women's Club, Washington County History and Landmarks Found., Friends of Washington Library, Cath. Daus. Am. Club: Gaelic Arts (Pitts.). Home: 272 Crest Ave Washington PA 15301 Office: 320 Museum Rd Washington PA 15301

ADAMS, MARGIE MAE, nurse; b. Kilborn, La., July 20, 1936; d. Marion Edward and Beatrice (Jeffers) Smith; m. Hilton Ellis Baxter, Sept. 16, 1950; children—Brenda, J.R.; m. 2d, Howard Cornelius Adams, Sept. 23, 1955; children—Richard, Michael, Kathy, Sharon. Student Red River Vo-Tech, 1972; L.P.N., Assoc. in Nursing, So. Ark. U., 1982. Nurse, Ouachita County Hosp., Camden, Ark., 1972—. Home: Route 4 Box 123A Camden AR 71701

ADAMS, MARIE PAULINE, city official; b. Barrow, Alaska, Feb. 6, 1953; d. Baxter and Rebecca (Aiken) A. B.A. in Edn. and Human Devel., George Washington U., 1980. Ticket agt. Wien Air Alaska, Barrow, 1974-75; dep. borough clk. North Slope Borough, Barrow, 1975-76; summer camp dir. Arctic Slope Regional Corp., Barrow, 1978-79; legal intern VanNess Feldman & Sutcliffe, Washington, 1979-80; exec. dir. Alaska Eskimo Whaling Commn., Barrow, 1980-83; city mgr. City of Barrow, 1983—; spl. cons. Alaska Eskimo Whaling Commn., 1983—; U.S. del. Internat. Whaling Commn., Brighton, Eng., 1983. Vice pres. Barrow Basketball Assn., 1982-83, Barrow Athletic Assn., 1983—. Office: City of Barrow PO Box 629 Barrow AK 99723

ADAMS, MARILYN KNOX, pharmacist; b. Alpena, S.D., Jan. 23, 1932; s. Harry Stewart and Mary Etta (Richards) Knox; m. Arthur Roydon Fenn, Dec. 21, 1952 (dec. Dec. 1979); children—Loring Arthur, Douglas Roydon, Alan Lindsay. B.S., S.D. State Coll., 1953. Registered pharmacist, Nebr., S.D. Pharmacist, Steinwand Drug, Mobridge, S.D., 1953-58, Dady Drug, Mobridge, 1958-61, Williams Drug, Crawford, Nebr., 1962-64, Winter Drug, Lincoln, Nebr., 1964-69, Bryan Meml. Hosp., Lincoln, 1969-72, Glen's Pharmacy, Lincoln, 1972—. Den mother Cornhusker council Boy Scouts Am., Lincoln, 1967, 72-73; ambassador Friendship Force, Lincoln, 1980-83; vice moderator, bd. deacons Fairhill Presbyterian Ch., Lincoln, 1971, tchr. Sunday sch., 1967-71; bd. trustees First Plymouth Congregational Ch., Lincoln, 1981-83. Mem. Nebr. Pharmacists Assn., Sigma Lambda Sigma. Democrat. Club: PEO (corresponding sec. 1984-85). Avocations: knitting, world travel, bicycling, cooking. Home: 425 S 39th St Lincoln NE 68510 Office: 3145 O St Lincoln NE 68510

ADAMS, MARLYS, real estate broker; b. Ashland, Wis., July 16, 1931; d. Asa Earl and Vera Genevieve (Beck) Rhodes; m. Rodger Gustav Benson, Mar. 8, 1952 (div. Feb. 1967); children—Scott R., Jeffrey R., Valerie L.; m. Charles William Adams, Nov. 24, 1967. Student Eau Claire State Coll., 1950-51; grad. X-ray Technician, Fairview Hosp., Mpls., 1952. Grad. Realtors Inst.; cert. residential specialist. Real estate agt. Spring Co., Mpls., 1963-66, Bermel-Smaby Realty, Mpls., 1966-68; real estate agt. Charles W. Adams, Inc., Mpls., 1969-73, pres., broker, mgr., 1973—; bd. dirs. Realtors Credit Union, Mpls., 1971—, pres., 1978. Commr., City of Golden Valley, Minn., 1980-84; fund raiser Realtors Polit. Action Com., Mpls., 1983-84. Named Woman of Achievement, Twin West C. of C., Mpls., 1984; recipient Appreciation award Realtors Credit Union, 1978; Good Neighbor award Radio Sta. WCCO, Mpls., 1984. Mem. Nat. Assn. Realtors, Minn. Assn. Realtors (bd. dirs. 1983—, mem. exec. com. 1983—), Mpls. Bd. Realtors (bd. dirs., mem. exec. com. 1983—, pres. 1984, Realtor of Yr. 1984). Republican. Baptist. Avocations: reading, travel. Home: 1410 Mayland Ave N Golden Valley MN 55427 Office: Adams Assocs Realtors 7711 Country Club Dr Golden Valley MN 55427

ADAMS, MARY IRENE, banker; b. Orange, Tex., Oct. 23, 1954; d. Julius Huie and Frances Elizabeth (Dullahan) David; m. Robert Denton Adams, Oct. 18, 1980; children—Rebecca Elizabeth, Kathryn Barwick. B.A. in Fin., U. Houston, 1977. Interim processing officer 1st City Nat. Bank Houston, 1978-80, product devel. officer, 1980-81; asst. v.p. Tex Commerce Bank, Houston, 1981-82, v.p., 1982—. Mem. Bank Adminstrn. Inst. Forum (chmn. product devel. So. region 1985-86), Nat. Assn. Female Execs., Bus. and Profl. Women's Assn. Houston. Republican. Roman Catholic. Home: 3107 Lake Stream Dr Kingwood TX 77339 Office: Tex Commerce Bank PO Box 2558 711 Travis Houston TX 77252-8081

ADAMS, MARY PATRICIA, city official; b. Tarrington, Wyo., Nov. 3, 1954; d. Frank Austin and Mary Clare (Gabisch) Redle; m. John Patrick Adams, July 3, 1982; 1 child, Theresa Marie. B.S.W., U. Kans., 1977. Behavioral modification aide St. Joseph's Children's Home, Torrington, Wyo., 1971-76; psychotherapeutic counselor U. Kans. Med. Ctr., Kansas City, 1976-77; job service rep. Wyo. Employment Security Commn., Rock Springs, 1978-85; asst. to police commr. City of Rock Springs, 1980—; vol. tchr. Adult Right to Read, Rock Springs, 1980-85; vol. recruiter Campaign for Heart, 1979, Vial of Life, 1981; youth coordinator YWCA, Rock Springs, 1978; youth bd. sponsor Adult Cath. Youth Orgn., Rock Springs, 1981-82; vol. Council of Cath. Women. Republican. Avocations: back packing; reading; cooking; travel; gardening. Home: 1204 Adams Ave Rock Springs WY 82901

ADAMS, MARYELLEN, building services executive; b. Jersey City, Oct. 9, 1945; d. Edward C. and Mary (O'Loughlin) Koneski; children—Meredith Lynn, Leigh Anne, Lindsay Gayle. Student Fairleigh Dickinson U., 1962-64, Mo. State U., 1964-67, Wharton Sch., U. Pa., summer 1966, Duke U. Law Sch., 1972. Pres. Apple Comml. Bldg. Services, Inc., Albany, N.Y., 1980—. Mem. com. small bus. devel. N.Y. Assn. Learning Disabled, 1983-84; mem. Albany County Republican Com., 1981-84; fed. liaison Citizens for America, 1983—. Mem. State St. Bus. and Profl. Women (charter; 1st v.p. 1982-84), N.Y. State Bus. and Profl. Women (legis. dir. 1984-85), Guilderland C. of C. (dir. 1981—), Inst. Real Estate Mgmt., Nat. Assn. Women Bus. Owners. Avocations: tennis; swimming; skiing. Home: 708 Adams St Guilderland NY 12084 Office: 1900 Western Ave Albany NY 12203

ADAMS, PEGGY HOFFMAN, county agency administrator; b. Mpls., July 21, 1936; d. Donald Brooks and Margaret Jane (Gruber) Hoffman; B.S., Cedar Crest Coll., 1958; m. Harry C. Adams, Dec. 26, 1968; children—Frank, Harry, Edward, Irene. Tchr., Allentown (Pa.) Sch. Dist., 1958-69; sales rep./reporter Quakertown (Pa.) Free Press, 1974-76; advt. cons. Media Dynamics, Bedminster, Pa., 1973-76; dir. Bucks County Consumer Protection and chief sealer weights and measures, Doylestown, Pa., 1976—; dir. Blue Cross Greater Phila., 1977—. Sec.-treas. Bedminster Bicentennial Com., 1976-78, Bedminster Hist. Commn., 1978-82; active Opera Guild of Opera of Phila., 1970—; committeewoman Pa. Republican Com., 1974—; alt. del. Rep. Nat. Conv., 1972; co-chmn. fin. Bucks County Rep. Com., 1975—; chmn. pub. relations United Way of Bucks County. Mem. Upper Bucks C. of C. (dir. 1979—), Am. Standard Testing Materials, Soc. Consumer Affairs Profls. (treas. Delaware Valley chpt. 1981—), Pa. Assn. Weights and Measures (sec. 1983—), Nat. Conf. Weights and Measures (nat. chmn. W/M Week, liaison com. 1983—), N.E. Conf. Weights and Measures (chmn. consumer edn.), Nat. Assn. Consumer Agy. Adminstrs., Bucks County Fedn. Women's Clubs (legis. chmn.). Ch. of Christ. Club: Quakertown Women's (past pres.). Editor, co-pub. History of Bedminster, 1976; Richland, The Manor, The Township, Quakertown, 1978. Home: PO Box E Edge Hill Rd Bedminster PA 18910 Office: Court House Annex Broad and Union Sts Doylestown PA 18910

ADAMS, PHYLLIS HOLCOMB, county official; b. Elkin, N.C., Apr. 28, 1947; d. Arthur Lee and Bessie Novella (Swaim) Holcomb; m. Jasper Ray Adams, July 2, 1966; children—Kathy Danine, Melanie Jane. Student, Inst. of Fin. Edn., 1978, Inst. Govt., 1979, 80, 82, Winston-Salem Bus. Coll., 1965-66. Cert. tax supr. Dept. of Revenue. Purchasing clk. Western Electric, Winston-Salem, N.C., 1966-68; dental asst., bookkeeper, Dr. John Lee, Boonville, N.C., 1969-71; owner, mgr. day care service, Yadkinville, N.C., 1971-75; head teller, loan officer Mutual Fed. Savings & Loan Assn., Yadkinville, 1975-79; tax supr. Yadkin County, 1979—, equalization, review clk., 1979—. Sec. Yadkin Jaycettes, 1980; pres. Fall Creek Sch. Adv. Council, East Bend, N.C., 1982—; mem. Sch. Re-districting Com., Yadkinville, 1982. Mem. Internat. Assn. Assessing Officers, N.C. Assn. of Assessing Officers (bd. dirs.), Piedmont Regional Tax Suprs., N.C. Property Mappers Assn. Quaker. Club: Yadkin County Republican (pres. 1978-80). Avocations: cross stitch; painting; swimming; golfing; church youth work. Home: Route 5 Box 295 Yadkinville NC 27055 Office: PO Box 1217 Yadkinville NC 27055

ADAMS, ROSE MARY, real estate broker; b. Mexico, Mo., May 31, 1940; d. Olan Clifford and Mary Hayden (Pasley) Tratchel; m. Paul Delano Adams, Sept. 27, 1971. Student S.E. Mo. State Coll., 1958-60; B.S. in Edn., U. Mo., 1962. Lic. real estate broker; cert. lifetime tchr., Mo. Music dir. R-1 Sch. Dist., Auxvasse, Mo., 1962-63; dir. jr. high bands Jefferson City (Mo.) Pub. Schs., 1963-68; real estate sec. Welek Realty Co., Lake Ozark, Mo., 1969-74; closing officer C. Myers & Simpson, Lake Ozark, 1977—. Mem. Bagnell Dam Bd. Realtors, Mo. Assn. Realtors, Nat. Assn. Relators, VFW Aux., U. Mo. Alumni Assn. Democrat. Mem. Christian Ch. (Disciples of Christ). Home: Route 4 Box 139 Eldon MO 65026 Office: C Myers & Simpson Co Route 72 Box 12 Lake Ozark MO 65049

ADAMS, RUTH SALZMAN, foundation executive, editor, consultant, lecturer; b. Los Angeles, July 25, 1923; d. George Thomas and Josephine Amanda (Benson) Salzman; m. Mark F. Skinner, 1946 (div. 1951); children—Gail Beth Meagan; m. Robert McCormick Adams, Jr., July 24, 1953. B.A., U. Minn., 1946. Editorial sec. Econometrics of Cowles Commn., U. Chgo., 1953-55; mng. editor, editor, Bull. of Atomic Scientists, Chgo., 1955-68, editor, 1978-84; research assoc. Am. Acad. Arts and Scis., Cambridge, Mass., 1969-78; program dir. internat. security MacArthur Found., Chgo., 1985—. Editor: Contemporary China, 1965; (with William McNeill) Human Migrations: Policies and Implications, 1979; (with S. Cullen) The Final Epidemic: Scientists and Physicians on Nuclear War, 1981. Exec. dir. Ill. div. ACLU, 1971-74; governing bd. Internat. Centre of Insect Physiology and Ecology, Nairobi, Kenya, 1971-79; bd. dirs. Council for a Livable World, Washington, 1962—, Chgo. Women's Network, 1981—; participant Internat. Pugwash Confs. on Sci. and World Affairs, 1957—; adv. bd. on sci. and tech. for devel. Nat. Acad. Scis., 1973-78. Recipient Adlai Stevenson award for human understanding UN Assn., Chgo., 1978, award Forum on Physics and Society of Am. Phys. Soc., 1983, Pub. Service award Fedn. Am. Scientists. Fellow Am. Acad. Arts and Scis.; mem. Council on Fgn. Relations, AAAS. Home: 2810 31st St NW Washington DC 20008 Office: MacArthur Found 140 S Dearborn St Chicago IL 60603

ADAMS, SARAH FRANCES, real estate broker, educator; b. Pearsall, Tex., Aug. 3, 1930; d. Edwin Crawford and Nina (Ogden) Calhoun; m. William C. Hayes, Aug. 11, 1951 (div. 1969); children—Kempe Calhoun, Nina Clare, Ralph Aaron; m. 2d Edwin Eugene Adams, July 15, 1972; children—Charlotte Carol Cook, Jerry Lynn, Buff. B.A. in Speech and Drama, Trinity U., 1951; grad. Am. Coll. Real Estate, San Antonio, 1971. Cert. tchr., Tex.; lic. real estate broker, Tex. Tchr. English and drama Alice Ind. Sch. Dist. (Tex.), 1951-52; tchr. Falfurrias Ind. Sch. Dist. (Tex.), 1952-64, girls' counselor, 1965-68; tchr. English and drama Hale Center Ind. Sch. Dist. (Tex.), 1969-70, NW San Antonio Ind. Sch. Dist., 1970-72; real estate broker, San Antonio, 1970-72; real estate broker, Woods & Davenport Agy., Plainview, Tex., 1972—, realtor, 1985—; adv. bd. 1st Nat. Bank, Plainview, 1984—. Com. chmn. United Methodist Women, Plainview, 1965—. Mem. Tex. State Tchrs. Assn., NEA, Nat. Assn. Realtors, Tex. Assn. Realtors, Plainview Bd. Realtors (sec.-treas., pres. 1985-86; Doug Graham Meml. award 1983-84), Plainview C. of C.) founding chmn. women's div. 1967, pres. 1967-69). Clubs: PEO (pres. chpt. BL 1975-77), Women's.

ADAMS, SHARON MONTANO, lawyer, news reporter, educator; b. Camden, N.J., Sept. 1, 1954; d. Arthur D. and Ann B. (Durkin) Montano; m. Phillip Reese Adams, June 30, 1973. Student U. Pa., 1970-72; B.A., Chestnut Hill Coll., Phila., 1974; J.D., U. Houston, 1982. Bar: Tex. 1984. With promotions pub. relations dept. Phila. Phillies, 1971-74; asst. dir. Reproductive Services, Inc., Houston, 1974-75; news anchor ABC Radio, Houston, 1975-78; news reporter/anchor Sta. KHOU-TV, Houston, 1978-83; atty. Harris County Dist. Atty.'s Office, Houston, 1983-84, part-time news reporter Sta. KPRC-TV, Houston, 1983—; assoc. prof. journalism U. Nev., Reno, 1984—; instr. Nat. Coll. Dist. Attys., 1979-84. Bd. dirs. Tex. Abortion Rights League, 1983—; counselor Houston Rape Crisis Coalition, 1974—. Recipient award Houston Profl. Firefighters Assn., 1982, 83. Home: 1404 S Chilton Tyleron TX 75901 Office: Renolds Sch Journalism U Nev Reno NV 89557

ADAMS, TERRI, real estate company executive, broker; b. Manchester, Ga., Oct. 7, 1945; d. Terrell Buford and Hazel Ion (Millen) O'Neal; m. Lewis Leonard Adams, June 17, 1982; children—Dodd Mitchell Cooper, Brian Edward Cooper. B.B.A., Ga. State U., 1982. Revenue acctg. auditor Delta Airlines, Atlanta, 1968-72; pres. Community Living Concepts, Inc., Lawrenceville, Ga., 1972—; mgmt. cons. Metzger & Co., Doraville, Ga., 1975—, brokerage cons., 1979—. Charter mem. Republican Presdl. Task Force, 1983; permanent mem. Nat. Rep. Senatorial Com., 1983; mem. U.S. Senatorial Club, 1985, U.S. Def. Com., 1985, Nat. Rep. Congl. Com., 1983; mem. Johnson Rd. Civic Assn.; tchr. Mr. Paran Ch., Atlanta; counselor Key Rd. Prison Ministry, Recipient Cert. of Recognition and Dedication of Am. Flag in U.S. Capitol Bldg., 1984. Mem. Nat. Homebuilders Assn. (hon.), Gwinnett C. of C., Phi Chi Theta, Alpha Lambda Delta. Avocations: writing; psychology. Home: 995 Stone Mill Run Lawrenceville GA 30245 Office: Community Living Concepts Inc 3400 Club Dr Lawrenceville GA 30245

ADAMS, VALBORG T., secondary educator; b. Waterville, Iowa, Feb. 21, 1903; d. Theodore Ole and Oline Sophia (Hunstad) Pladsen; m. George Adams, Mar. 26, 1944; 1 child, Ronald Eric. B.A., U. No. Iowa U., 1933; M.A., U. Chgo., 1941. Cert. tchr., Iowa, Ind. Tchr. rural schs. Allamakee County, Iowa, 1921-26, consol. schs., Colesburg, Iowa, 1928-30, elem. schs., Waterloo, Iowa, 1930-34, Irving Sch., Hammond, Ind., 1934-44, secondary schs., Laporte, Ind., 1953-69; instr. Ind. U., South Bend, 1963-65; mem. editorial dept., social studies Scott, Foresman, Chgo., 1944-45. Pres. Ind. State Council Tchrs. Geography, 1965-66, LaPorte Community Concerts Assn., 1983-84; project chmn. Izaak Walton League Bicentennial SOS Project The Galien River, LaPorte County, 1975-76. Mem. AAUW (treas. 1959, sec. 1972-75), Ind. Fedn. Music Clubs (pres. dist. III 1981-83), Ind. State Tchrs. Assn. (chmn. geography dept. 1965-66), LaPorte County Ret. Tchrs. (pres. 1981-83), Kappa Delta Pi. Republican. Lutheran. Avocations: music; photography; nature study; travel Home: 912 Wright Ave LaPorte IN 46350

ADAMS, VERA GERTRUDE, market research data collection company executive; b. Denver, June 25, 1920; d. Hubert Charles and Margaret (Dawson) Farrow; m. Lawrence Elmer Adams, Dec. 30, 1937; children—George Gordon, Bettie Ann, Lawreen Edna. Student Metro State Coll., Denver, 1975-80. Interviewer Linda Calloway, Denver, 1948-62; supr. Knop Interviewing, Lakewood, Colo., 1962-71; owner Adams Research, Denver, 1971-72; mgr. Quality Controlled, Denver, 1972-75; pres. Info. Research, Denver, 1975—. Mem. Am. Mktg. Assn., Market Research Assn. Methodist. Club: Deer Creek Assn. (treas. 1984—) (Bailey, Colo.). Home: 3035 E Maplewood Ave Littleton CO 80121 Office Info Research Inc 1582 S Parker Rd Suite 303 Denver CO 80231

ADAMS, VICTORIA ELEANOR, administrative manager, realtor; b. San Francisco, Feb. 8, 1941; d. George Mulford and Sarah Louise (Dearborn) A.; m. Gene M. Richardson, 1965 (div. 1972); 1 son, Raymond; m. Franklin Carlisle Boosman, May 13, 1972; 1 son, Eric. A.A., Palomar Coll., 1976; B.B.A. summa cum laude, Nat. U., 1978. Sales adminstr. Evergreen Internat. Airlines, McMinnville, Oreg., 1983; corp. adminstr. N.N. Jaeschke, Inc., San Diego, 1984—; adminstrv. mgr. Tomlinson Agy., Inc., Spokane, Wash., 1980—; dir. Feline Enterprises, Spokane. Editor: Bravura, 1976; (text) Science Among Us, 1965. Designer Astrology game, 1974. Contbr. articles to profl. jours. Solicitor, Am. Heart Assn., 1985. Recipient Cert. Real Estate Sales Achievment, 1978, 1982, 85; Cert. Outstanding Contbn. to Real Estate Edn., 1980. Mem. Adminstrv. Mgmt. Soc. (publicity com. 1980), Nat. Assn. Realtors, Spokane Bd. Realtors (edn. officer 1979-80). Lodge: Eagles. Avocations: writing; educational research; fishing; camping. Home: N 11302 Lancelot Dr Spokane WA 99218 Office: Tomlinson Agy Inc N 9505 Division St Spokane WA 99218

ADAMSON, LUCILE FRANCES, consultant; b. Chetopa, Kans., Nov. 10, 1926; d. Truby Herbert and Anna Helen (Gail) A.; B.S., Kans. State U., 1948; M.S., State U. Iowa, 1950; Ph.D., U. Calif., Berkeley, 1956. Asst. prof. nutrition Hawaii Agrl. Expt. Sta., 1956-60; asst. prof. dept. pediatrics U. Mo., Med. Center, Columbia, 1960-64; research assoc., dir. Core Lab., Harvard U. clin. research unit Thorndike Meml. Lab., 1964-70; sr. research assoc. dept. biochemistry Monash U., Melbourne, Australia, 1970-72; staff scientist Environ. Def. Fund, Washington, 1972-74; prof., program adminstr. program macroenviron. and population studies Howard U., Washington, 1974-81; pres. Biolit, Inc., Corvallis, Oreg., 1981—; cons. environ. and occupational health, biomed. lit. revs., evaluations. Contbr. articles to profl. jours. Research on hormonal effects on amino acid transport and protein/mucopolysaccharide synthesis in vitro.

ADAMSON, MARY ANNE, geographer, environmental analyst; b. Berkeley, Calif., June 25, 1954; d. Arthur Frank and Frances Isobel (Key) Adamson; m. Richard John Harrington, Sept. 20, 1974. B.A., U. Calif.-Berkeley, 1975, M.A., 1976, postgrad., 1978—. Research asst. dept. geography U. Calif., Berkeley, 1974, reader, 1974-81, teaching asst., 1976, student rep. departmental rev. com. Acad. Senate, 1976-77; geographer, environ. and fgn. area analyst Lawrence Livermore Nat. Lab., Livermore, Calif., 1978-83, cons., 1983-86; systems engr. ESL, Sunnyvale, Calif., 1986—. Asst. editor Vulcan's Voice, 1982. Mem. Assn. Am. Geographers, Assn. Pacific Coast Geographers, Nat. Speleol. Soc. (geology, geography sects., sec., editor newsletter Diablo Grotto chpt. 1982-86), U. Calif. Alumnae Assn., Phi Beta Kappa. Contbr. articles to profl. jours. Home: 31 Blade Way Walnut Creek CA 94595

ADAMSON, SYLVIA JANE, public relations specialist; b. Atlanta, Mar. 25, 1952; d. Augustus Mays and Lela Inez (Jones) Adamson. B.A., W.Ga. Coll., 1974. Pub. relations asst. Atlanta Braves, 1976-78, promotions coordinator, 1978-79; sales mgr. Peber Prodns., Atlanta, 1979-80; pub. relations specialist to Ga. Sec. of State, Atlanta, 1980-83; owner Adamson & Co., Rex, Ga., 1983—; dir. Arts Clayton, Inc. Mem. Pub. Relations Soc. Am., Ga. Assn. Museums and Galleries (newsletter editor), Historic Oakland Cemetery (bd. dirs.), Phi Kappa Phi. Club: Atlanta Press (Atlanta). Office: Adamson & Co 6280 Hwy 42 Rex GA 30273

ADAMS-SELICO, SHIRLEY LUCILE, nurse; b. Marshall, Tex., Feb. 22, 1941; d. Gerald Hugo and Ella Mary (Hodges) Adams; B.S. in Psychology, Howard U., 1962; grad. with honors Los Angeles County Sch. Nursing, 1975; children—Sherilyn Marie Lum, E. Gerald Steven Lum, Michael J. Premmer. Staff nurse spl. care nurseries, newborn intensive care unit Los Angeles-U. So. Calif. Med. Center Women's Hosp., 1975-81, critical care nurse neonatalogy, 1976-81, clin. instr. nursing; staff nurse Queen of Valley Hosp., Covina, Calif., 1981-83. Social vice chmn. Young Democrats Am., Washington, 1962. Mem. Nat. Assn. Negro Women, Nat. Assn. Female Execs., Philathias Soc., ACLU, common Cause, Psi Chi. Roman Catholic. Home: 851 S Sunset Ave Apt 70 West Covina CA 91790

ADCOCK, BETTY-LEE, real estate brokerage executive; b. Waldo, Kans., Nov. 19, 1921; d. Ralph Preston and Hazel (Pangburn) Beatty; m. Charles Warren Adcock, Feb. 17, 1945; 1 dau., Roberta Lee. B.S. in Journalism, Kans. State Coll., 1946. Lic. real estate broker, Hawaii. Mem. pub. relations staff Boeing Airplane Co., Wichita, Kans., 1942-45; biographical staff AP, N.Y.C., 1945-46; real estate salesman and broker, Honolulu, 1972—; prin. broker, pres., owner Adcock, Ltd., real estate mktg., Honolulu, 1983—. Recipient Girl Scout Award of Merit, Kitzengen, Germany, 1960, spl. award Am. Cancer Soc., Middlebury, Vt., 1956. Mem. Nat. Assn. Realtors. Hawaii Assn. Realtors, Honolulu Bd. Realtors Realtors' Nat. Mktg. Inst., Nat. Trust for Historic Preservation, Honolulu Art Acad., Friends of Iolani Palace, Honolulu Symphony Assn., Bishop Mus., Hawaii Hist. Soc., Hawaii Humane Soc., Hist. Hawaii Found., Chi Omega. Republican. Episcopalian. Home: 2415 Aha Aina Pl Honolulu HI 96821 Office: Adcock Ltd 1188 Bishop St Suite 2805 Honolulu HI 96813

ADDAMS, MARTI, business executive; b. Kensett, Ark., Apr. 1, 1938; d. Raymond Martin and Barbara Lucile (Goodwin) Adams; m. A.R. Mittower, Feb. 1, 1958 (div. 68 and 73); children—Mitchell, Marcie, Mindy, Mark, Marvin. B.S. in Edn., Ind. U., 1972; M.B.A. in Mktg., Ball State U., 1977; postgrad. in humanities U. Dallas. Salesperson, Gibraltor Mausoleum Corp., Indpls., 1974-75; salesperson, mgr. Bill Frazier Mobile Homes, Muncie, Ind., 1975; salesperson Sears, Roebuck & Co., Muncie, 1975-76; lease records dept. Placid Oil Co., Dallas, 1981-84; owner Addams Cleaning Service, Dallas, 1984—. Reporter Dallas Downtown Democrats, 1984; social action clearing house Unitarian Ch., 1984; active Democratic Nat. Com., 1985—, People for Am. Way, 1985—. Recipient Acad. Excellence award Ind. U., 1965, 66. Mem. AAUW, Ind. U. Alumni Dallas, Nat. Assn. Female Execs., Tex. State Tchrs. Assn., NEA. Democrat. Unitarian. Avocations: chess; tennis; fencing; reading; music. Home: PO Box 501087 Dallas TX 75250

ADDELSON, KATHRYN PYNE, philosopher, educator; b. Providence, Apr. 22, 1932; d. Joseph Abraham and Catherine (Newton) Etchells; A.B., Ind. U., 1961; Ph.D., Staford U., 1968; m. Richard U. Addelson, Oct. 31, 1980; children—Catherine Casey, V. Shawn. Instr. philosophy Bryn Mawr Coll., 1965-66, CCNY, 1966-67; asst. prof. U. Chgo., 1967-72; prof. philosophy and history of sci. Smith Coll., 1972—; vis. prof. sociology Northwestern U., 1969, 80; vis. prof. philosophy U. Calif., Berkeley, 1971, Loyola U., Chgo., 1974-75. Fellow Nat. Endowment Humanities, 1978-79, Mellon Found., 1978-81. Mem. Soc. Women in Philosophy (exec. sec.), Am. Philos. Assn. Exec. editor Feminist Studies, 1976-80, now assoc. editor. Address: Dept Philosophy Smith Coll Northampton MA 01060

ADDIS, SARA ALLEN, franchise executive; b. El Paso, Tex., May 15, 1930; d. Waldo Rufus and Cordelia Dean (Kerr) Allen; m. Bobby Joe Addis, June 5, 1949; children—Craig Dell, Alan Blake, Neil Clark, Sara Kathleen. Sec. to adminstr. Southwestern Gen. Hosp., El Paso, 1948-49; sec. to dir. of personnel U. Tex., El Paso, 1964-65; pres., founder Sara Care Franchise Corp., El Paso, 1978—. Mem. Internat. Franchise Assn., Nat. Fedn. Ind. Businesses, Presidents Assn. Am. Mgmtm. Assn., El Paso Better Bus. Bur., El Paso C. of C., Assn. Pioneer Women. Named Entrepreneur of Yr., Bus. and Profl. Women El Paso, 1982. Republican. Club: Lower Valley Women's. Lodge: Order Eastern Star. Avocations: oil painting; music; travel. Home: 8417 Parkland St El Paso TX 79925 Office: Sara Care Franchise Corp 1200 Golden Key Circle Suite 368 El Paso TX 79925

ADDISON, ANNE SIMONE POMEX (MRS. JOHN ADDISON), television exec.; b. Antwerp, Belgium, Dec. 2, 1927; d. Eli and Mary Deborah (Rubinstein) Cleeman; B.A., Barnard Coll., 1947; M.A., Columbia U., 1952; m. Joseph B. Pomex, Mar. 6, 1947 (div. Apr. 1954); 1 son, Steven M.; m. 2d, John Addison, Sept. 1, 1966. Instr., Columbia U., 1947-48; circulation dir. Ford Found., N.Y.C., 1952-58; asso. dir. Broadcasting Found. Am., radio, N.Y.C., 1958-60; dir. NET (WNET-13) TV internat. dir., 1960—; pres. Communications Internat., 1980—; cons. cultural dept. Dept. State, Washington, 1961. Bd. dirs. Coll. Skills, Inc., N.Y.C. Recipient awards, medals for fostering understanding and cultural cooperation, Austria, Belgium, Holland, Israel, Italy, Brazil. Mem. Am. Women Radio and TV (1st v.p. 1972—), Advt. Club Am., Am. Women in Communications. Contbr. articles to profl. jours. Home: 1035 Fifth Ave New York NY 10028 Office: 767 Fifth Ave New York NY 10022

ADDISON, CONNIE LAWSON, cable television executive; b. Richlands, Va., Sept. 18, 1946; d. Douglas William and Margaret (Blanton) Lawson; children—Tracy Lynne, Cynthia Leigh. Grad. Richlands High Sch. Line supr. Eastern Isles Mfg. Corp., Richlands, 1965-78; dispatcher Teleprompter Corp., Richlands, 1979-82; office mgr. Group W Cable, Inc., Richlands, 1982-83, gen. mgr., 1983-85; gen. mgr. Richlands Cablevision, Inc., 1985—. Mem. Richlands C. of C. Democrat. Apostolic. Home: PO Box 665 Cedar Bluff VA 24609 Office: Richlands Cablevision Inc 306 Suffolk Ave Richlands VA 24641

ADDISON, MARY JANE, civic worker; b. Beaumont, Tex.; d. Henry Davis and Corinne (Carter) Pond; R.N., Jefferson Davis Sch. Nursing, 1945; student U. Houston; m. Eugene Morse Addison, Mar. 10, 1946; children—Eugene Morse, Paul Davis. Mem. choir First Bapt. Ch.; den mother Cub Scouts, 6 years, recipient Den Mothers award, 1961; pres. Huntsville (Tex.) PTA, 1955-56, v.p. dist. bd., 1956-57, state life mem. PTA, 1967; pres. Women's Missionary Union, First Bapt. Ch., 1965-68; chmn. heritage com. Mayor's Bicentennial Com., 1974-76; chmn. city beautification com. Tex. Sesquicentennial Celebration, 1982—; pres. Woman's Forum, Tex. Fedn. Womens Clubs, 1972-74, 80-81, named Woman of Year, 1974; charter and life mem. Hosp. Aux., pres., 1971-72; bd. dirs. Cultural Arts Center; active Sam Houston Meml. Mus., Walker County Hist. Commn., Tex. Hist. Found.; mem., dir., sponsor Community Choir. Decorated Grand Peiory of Am. Order St. John of Jerusalem, dame Knights Hospitaller. Mem. African Violet Soc. Am., Daus. Republic of Tex. (pres. Houston chpt. 1970-75, 79-81, registrar 1975—, state rec. sec. gen. 1973-75, state 1st v.p. gen. 1975-77, pres. gen. 1977-79), DAR (regent Mary Martin Elmore Scott chpt. 1972-74, 82-84), Daughters Am. Colonists (regent Capt. John Utie chpt., state corr. sec. 1977-79), UDC (dist. rec. sec. 1974-76, dist. gov. 1981-83), Colonial Dames Am., Dames of Ct. of Honor, Tex. Hist. Assn. (dir., cert. of commendation 1980, 81, mem. state heritage com.), Walker County Geneal. Soc., San Jacinto Mus. History Assn., Lone Star Drama Hist. Assn. (state adv. bd.), Victorian Soc. (charter mem. Tex. chpt.), Am., Tex. (pres. 38th Dist. 1977—) nurses assns., AMA, Spain and Tex. Soc., Tex., Tri-County (past pres.) med. auxs., Tex. Acad. Family Physicians (charter) Beautify Tex. Council. Clubs: Garden (past pres. chmn. city beautification com.); Univ. Women Sam Houston State U. (charter). Address: Huntsville TX 77340

ADDY, JO ALISON PHEARS, economist; b. Ger., May 2, 1951; d. William and Paula (Lee) Phears; B.A., Smith Coll., 1973; M.B.A., Adelphi U., 1975; postgrad. Stanford U., 1975-78; m. Tralance Obuama Addy, May 25, 1979; children—Mantse, Miishe, Dwetri. Economic analyst Morgan Guaranty, N.Y.C., 1973-75; econ. con. Nat. Planning Assn., Washington, 1976; economist Rand Corp., 1978; economist World Bank, Washington, 1979-80; asst. v.p., economist Crocker Bank, San Francisco, 1980-85; money market economist RepublicBank, Dallas, 1985—; lectr. in field. NSF fellow, 1976-79. Mem. Am. Econ. Assn., World Affairs Council, Dallas Women's Found. Home: 1904 Rockcliff Ct Arlington TX 76012 Office: RepublicBank Pacific and Ervay Sts Dallas TX 75201

ADELMAN, DOROTHY LEE MCCLINTOCK DELFS, artist, printmaker, educator; b. N.Y.C.; d. Erwin Lee and Phyllis (Slater) McClintock; student Art Students League, N.Y.C., Westchester Art Workshop, Hudson River Mus., Silvermine Guild for Artists, Sherman Bus. Sch., Mt. Vernon, N.Y.; m. Hamilton Delfs, Sept. 3, 1941; 1 son, David Hamilton; m. 2d, Emanuel L. Adelman, Sept. 16, 1961. Formerly sec. J. Walter Thompson, N.Y.C., with Saucy Susan Products, Inc., Briarcliff Manor, N.Y.; tchr. printmaking Westchester Art Workshop, White Plains, N.Y.; seminar lectr. in printmaking Elizabeth Seton Coll., Yonkers, N.Y.; one-man shows include: Katonah (N.Y.) Gallery, 1972, Mari Gallery, Mamaroneck, N.Y., 1974, Greenwich (Conn.) Art Barn, 1973, 75; group shows include: Hudson River Mus., Yonkers, N.Y., Graphic Soc. Internat., N.H., 1974, Nat. Arts Club; represented in permanent collections including: Hudson River Mus., Sears, Roebuck & Co., N.Y.C., Beneficial Life Ins. Co., N.Y.C., IBM Elmsford, N.Y., Microwave Communication Inc., Ryebrook, N.Y. mem. council Katonah (N.Y.) Gallery; bd. dirs. White Plains Outdoor Art Festival; cons. printmaking Girl Scouts U.S.A., Chappaqua, N.Y., 1973, 75; mem. arts, humanities and media com. Ogden P. Reid for Gov., 1972. Recipient Dirs. and Purchase award Westchester Art Workshop, White Plains, 1969; purchase award Hudson River Mus., Yonkers, 1971; 1st and 3d award Larchmont Printmaking, 1972; 1st and best in show, printmaking St. Lukes Hosp. Benefit Exhbn., N.Y.C., 1971. Mem. Art Students League (life), Mamaroneck Artists Guild, Yonkers Art Assn., Westchester Art Soc., Council for Arts in Westchester (visual arts affiliates exec. bd.), Abraxas Artists Group (treas.). Home and Studio: Heritage Hills of Westchester 36A East Hill Dr Somers NY 10589

ADELMAN, SANDIE SLOTKIN, educational administrator; b. Bkyn., Sept. 5, 1931; d. Sam and Ann (Kotick) Slotkin; m. Joseph Adelman, July 15, 1951 (dec.); children—Todd Fred, Beth Heidi. B.A., SUNY-Albany, 1952; M.A., Bklyn. Coll., 1954; M.S., L.I. U., Greenvale, N.Y., 1984. With N.Y.C. Bd.

Edn., 1952—, city-wide supr. curriculum and evaluation, 1972-75, coordinator tng. and testing, 1975-76, dir. job tng. program Rikers Island, 1976-83, coordinator adult basic edn./high sch. equivalency services, Queens, 1983—; cons. in field; guest lectr. Fordham U., L.I. U., 1972-74. Producer documentary: Manpower Training, the Next Decade, 1973. Sec. Nat. Council Jewish Women, Queens, 1959-66, v.p., 1960-62, pres., 1963-65; den mother, trainer Queens council Boy Scouts Am., 1963-67; treas. Queens Council Jewish Women, 1964; mem. exec. council Campfire Girls, Queens, 1965-70. Mem. Am. Vocat. Assn., Nat. Assn. female Execs. (network leader 1981—), N.Y. State Community/Continuing Edn., Women Adminstrs. in Vocat. Edn. (Who's Who award 1983), Am. Corrections Assn. (profl.), Internat. Corrections Assn. (profl.), Correctional Edn. Assn. Home: 89-51 208th St Queens Village NY 11427

ADERTON, JANE REYNOLDS, lawyer; b. Riverside, Calif., Dec. 22, 1913; d. Charles Low and Verna Mae (Marshall) Reynolds; B.S. in Merchandising, U. So. Calif., 1935; J.D., Southwestern U., 1965; m. Thomas Radcliffe Aderton, Oct. 16, 1964; children (by previous marriage)—Marshall Johnson, Jeannette Johnson Townsend. Jud. sec. to Dist. Ct. Appeal, Los Angeles, 1960-65; admitted to Calif. bar, 1968; practiced in Beverly Hills, Calif., 1968-79, Riverside, 1979—; assoc. firm Wyman, Bautzer, Rothman & Kuchel, 1970-79; del. Calif. Bar Conf., 1976, 77, 78. Mem. Founders' Club, Riverside Community Hosp., 1980—; mem. Women's Aux., Salvation Army, 1981—, pres., 1983-85; adv. bd., 1983—; v.p., pres.-elect Art Alliance of the Riverside Art Mus., 1984-85, pres., 1985-86; mem. Riverside Hospice, 1983—, Riverside Opera Guild, Friends of Mission Inn, 1986—. Mem. Am., Calif., Riverside, Beverly Hills (bd. govs. 1976-79, chmn. del. to Calif. Bar Conf. 1978) bar assns., Riverside Art Alliance, Soroptimist Internat., Phi Alpha Delta, Pi Beta Phi (pres. alumni club Riverside 1981-83). Clubs: Victoria Country (Riverside, Calif.); Newport Harbor Yacht (Newport Beach, Calif.). Home: 5190 Stonewood Dr Riverside CA 92506 Office: Riverside CA

ADKINS, BETTY A., state legislator; b. Mpls., June 4, 1934; d. John Edward and Barbara (Graff) Whalen; m. Wally Adkins, 1956; children—Patrick, Susan, Michael, Kathleen, Caroline, Nancy. Student North Hennepin Community Coll.; student U. Minn., 1952-53. Formerly dep. clk. Otsego Twp., vice chmn. Wright County Bd. Adjustment, Minn.; mem. Minn. Senate, St. Paul, 1982—. Formerly chmn. Wright County Democratic-Farmer-Labor Party. Office: State Capitol Saint Paul MN 55155*

ADKINS, DONNA MARIA, publicist; b. Gary, Ind., Dec. 28, 1945; d. Fred and Sadie (Lamar) Anderson; 1 dau., Tamara. Student, Ind. U.-Gary, 1962-63, Hammond Bus. Coll., 1964-65. Reader service mgr. Kiver Pubs., Inc., Chgo., 1969-70; collections mgr. Contemporary Books, Inc., Chgo., 1973-78, publicity dir., 1978—. Mem. Black Ind. Polit. Orgn., Chgo., 1983—. Mem. Chgo. Women in Pub. Democrat. Baptist. Home: 7819 S Kimbark Ave Chicago IL 60619 Office: Contemporary Books Inc 180 N Michigan Ave Chicago IL 60601

ADKINS, ELIZABETH ANNE, clin. social worker; b. Danville, Ill., Apr. 8, 1941; d. Albert William and Elizabeth Adele (Bahnke) A.; B.A., So. Ill. U., 1963; M.S.W., San Diego State U., 1969. Tchr., Clarence (N.Y.) Central Jr. High Sch., 1963-64; asst. adminstr. D'Youville Coll., 1964; caseworker Erie County Welfare Dept., Buffalo, N.Y., 1964-65; child welfare worker Los Angeles County Dept. Adoptions, 1965-72; public health social worker Los Angeles County Public Health Dept., 1972-74; corp. sec. Health Adv. Group, Inc., Los Angeles, 1978-80; social work supr. Los Angeles County-U. So. Calif. Med. Center, Los Angeles, 1974—. Mem. Los Angeles County Commn. on Life Support Policies, 1979-81; mem. adv. council bio-ethics NCCJ, 1977-78; mem. Santa Monica Symphony, 1970—. Lic. clin. social worker. Mem. Acad. Cert. Social Workers, Nat. Assn. Social Workers (chmn. public relations com.), Los Angeles County Bar Assn. Com. on Legal Aspects of Bioethics, Hastings Center of Soc. Ethics and the Life Scis., Mensa, DAR. Home: 2700 N Cahuenga Blvd E #2207 Los Angeles CA 90068 Office: 1200 N State St Room 6433 Los Angeles CA 90033

ADKINS, JUDITH KAYE, coal company executive; b. Pikeville, Ky., Oct. 8, 1947; d. James and Joyce Ann (Blair) Blackburn; m. Morgan Dean Adkins, Nov. 29, 1964 (div. Dec. 1979); children—Richard Dean, Christopher Morgan, Nicholaus Fayette. Student Pikeville Coll., 1966-70. Sec. Pike County Bd. edn., Pikeville, 1967-70; med. records adminstr. Mountain Comprehensive Care Ctr., Pikeville, 1971-76; owner, operator Beauty Corner, Regina, Ky., 1976-78; v.p. coal sales Ooten Coal corp., Pikeville, Ky., 1979-83; dir. coal sales Standard Elkhorn Coal Sales Corp., Prestonburg, Ky., 1983—; bd. dirs. Lexington Coal Exchange, 1986—; mem. N.C. Coal Exchange, Cin. Coal Exchange. Mem. Am. Soc. Mining Engrs., Coal Operators and Assocs. Republican. Baptist. Club: Green Meadows Country (Pikeville). Office: Standard Elkhorn Coal Sales Corp 328 N Lake Dr Prestonburg KY 41653

ADKINS, LINDA BERKLEY, word processor; b. Richmond, Va., May 30, 1943; d. Berkley Benjamin and Mary Virginia (Vassar) Adkins; B.S., James Madison U., 1965. Tchr. English and theater Fairfax (Va.) County Schs., 1966-74; supr., asst. mgr., mgr., word processing officer United Va. Bank Richmond, 1978—; cons. word processing. Mem. Office Automation Assn. of Richmond, Nat. Assn. Bank Women, Assn. Info. Systems Profls., NOW, Richmond Womensbooks/YWCA. Baptist. Office: United Va Bank 10 and Main Sts Richmond VA 23219

ADKINS, MARILYN BIGGS, lawyer; b. East Greenwich, R.I., July 3, 1945; d. John Elmer and Merle Bonita (Irish) Biggs; m. John C. Adkins, Oct. 12, 1965 (div. Feb. 1978); children—Christopher Troy, Shawneen Marie. B.A., U. Denver, 1967, J.D., 1982. Bar: Colo. 1982, U.S. Dist. Ct. Colo. 1982, U.S. Ct. Appeals (10th cir.) 1982. Owner, mgr. Texaco service stas., Denver, 1971-78, bookkeeping service, Denver, 1978-81; legal asst., paralegal Hubert M. Safran law firm, Denver, 1974-82; legis. dir. Colo. Trial Lawyers Assn., Denver, 1981—; ptnr. firm Safran & Adkins, Denver, 1982—. Instr. home fin. mgmt. Denver inner city parish Interdenomination Community Agy., 1970-75; mem. Dist. Atty.'s Automobile Repair Arbitration Panel, Denver, 1976; advisor petroleum mktg. practices act com. U.S. Senate, Washington, 1978; mem. civil rights com. Anti-Defamation League, Denver, 1983—; del. Democratic County Convs., Denver, 1975-78, 86. Mem. Colo. Trial Lawyers Assn. (dir. 1983—), Assn. Trial Lawyers Am., ABA, Colo. Bar Assn. (legal edn. and admissions com. 1983—), Denver Bar Assn., Trial Lawyers for Pub. Justice, U. Denver Alumni Assn. Jewish. (dir. temple 1986—). Home: 4512 E 17th Pkwy Denver CO 80220 Office: Safran & Adkins 1832 Clarkson St Denver CO 80218

ADLAKA, KAREN, consulting engineering company manager; b. Bannu, India, July 25, 1940; d. Nand R. and Maya W. Kathuria; m. Sat P. Adlaka, Nov. 28, 1962; children—Mala, Rajive, Nina. B.A. in Edn., Lucknow U., 1962; B.A. in Sociology, Ohio No. U., 1964; M.S. in Edn., Youngstown State U., 1970. Cert. tchr., Ohio. Tchr., Am. Embassy Sch., New Delhi, 1975-76; owner, operator D.Q., Youngstown, Ohio, 1978-83; mgr. adminstrn. Adlaka & Assocs., Youngstown, 1983—. Mem. Indian Assn. Greater Youngstown, 1985. Named Best Tchr. of Yr., Am. Embassy Sch., 1977. Hindu. Mem. Northeastern Soc. of Hindu Temple, New Neighbor of Youngstown Assn. Club: Internat. St. (sec. 1970). Avocations: tennis; reading; knitting. Home: 616 Squirrel Hill Dr Youngstown OH 44512 Office: Adlaka and Assocs 5600 Market St Suite 10 Youngstown OH 44512

ADLER, ELIZABETH THOMPSON (MRS. MILTON P. ADLER), civic worker; b. South Bend, Ind., Sept. 16, 1914; d. David Headley and Emma (Crawford) Thompson; B.S. in Phys. Edn. and Psychology, U. Wis., 1937; postgrad. Purdue U., 1934-35; m. Milton Pokorny Adler, Dec. 28, 1938; children—Ruth Louise (Mrs. Phillip Ruder), Coleman E. II. Instr. phys. edn. Sophie Newcomb Coll., New Orleans, 1937-38, McMain High Sch., New Orleans, 1938-39; supr. Dr. Alton Ochsner Cancer Clinic, Charity Hosp., New Orleans, 1946-49; mem. Touro Infirmary Bd. Aux., 1947-48; mem. citizenship awards com. Orleans Parish Sch. Bd., 1947-57, chmn., 1950-56; mem. vol. administrv. bd. Charity Hosp., 1947-50; life mem. Sara Mayo Hosp. Guild, 1953—, bd. dirs., 1961-62; exec. com. Nat. Conf. Christians and Jews, 1950, bd. dirs., 1951-61; mem. House of Detention Bd., City of New Orleans, 1951-54; mem. health edn. com. New Orleans YWCA, 1939-41, bd. dirs., 1939-52, v.p., 1948 pres., 1949-52, chmn. reconstrn. fund dr., 1947, del. regional conf., Atlanta, 1948, chmn. Y-Teens com., 1947-48, del. nat. conv., San Francisco, 1949, mem. resolutions com., 1949, del. regional conf., Houston, 1950, mem. nat. conv. com., discussion leader, 1950, del. nat. conv., Chgo., 1952, mem. centennial planning com., 1952-55, del. Y-Teen planning conf., Jackson, Miss., 1950, dean discussion leadership tng. conf. Gulf Park (Miss.) Coll., 1951-53, mem. nat. support com., 1948-53, rep. from La. to nat. bd. for centennial, 1952-55; chmn. New Orleans Com. Race Relations, 1952-53; mem. Tulane-Lyceum Assn. Bd., 1951-61, financial sec., 1954-59, treas., 1960-61; chmn. speakers bur. Mother's March on Polio, 1952; vice chmn. campaign United Fund, 1954; chmn. citizens com. services to children Dept. Pub. Welfare, 1954-61; mem. La. com. White House Conf. Children and Youth, 1959-60, La. del., 1960, exec. com., 1960; bd. dirs. Urban League, 1955-61; chmn. Eisenhower Birthday Dinner Celebration, 1956; chmn. women's div. pub. and pvt. schs. U.S. Treasury Bond Drive, 1957-58; hospitality chmn. Brandeis U. Area Conf., 1957; bd. dirs. inst. com. Community Vol. Service, 1952; hospitality chmn. Nat. and La. Conf. Social Work conv., New Orleans, 1953; v.p. bd. lay regents Xavier U., 1959, pres. 1960-61; bd. dirs. DePaul Hosp. Guild, 1961-69; mem. New Coll. Library Com., Sarasota, Fla.; mem. bd. Fed. Housing Authority, Ft. Myers, 1966-69, Girl Scouts U.S.A., 1965-67; pres. Blue Water Forest Assn., 1971-72; mem. Central Fla. Regional Library Bd., 1971-73; chmn. bd. trustees Context Industries Library Scholarship Fund, 1973-76. Free lance writer-photographer, 1973—. Recipient Merit certificate for distinguished service to City of New Orleans, from mayor of New Orleans. Mem. D.A.R., Needlework Guild Am., League Women Voters, Women's Auxiliary New Orleans C. of C. Presbyn. Author: Wakulla Springs, Its History, Legend, Birds and Wildlife, 1977; Wild Birds of Florida, 1981; Wild Bird Calendar, 1983 84; contbr. poetry to Caravan of Verse, An Anthology, 1949; contbr. stories and photos Fla. Wildlife mag.; contbr. photos Anatomy of a Waterfowl (Charles Frank, Jr.). Club: Sanibel-Captiva Shell Club (v.p. 1965-66). Home: Bay Plaza 1255 W Gulfstream Ave Sarasota FL 33577 Dec. Jan. 11, 1986.

ADLER, JANE EVE, internationally syndicated columnist and cartoonist-illustrator; b. Providence, Oct. 8, 1944; d. Frank Kozlov and Ruth Cohen; m. Edwin I. Adler, Feb. 19, 1961; children—Lindsay, Steven. B.A., U. R.I., 1971. Art dir. Trinity Sq. Theatre, 1971-72; T.V. talk show hostess, writer, artistic dir. original plays PBS 1971-72; weekly columnist/illustrator Boston Herald, Providence Journal, National Observer, 1972-77; News Am. Syndicate syndicated columnist/illustrator, 1977—; tchr., lectr., TV and radio guest in horticulture and writing. Author monthly nat. mag. columns; writer of books on children (with Hank Ketchum of Dennis the Menace), 1982—; columnist for Boston Herald on child healthcare, 1984—. Participant in numerous one woman and group art shows, 1965—. Organizer of free painting course for women at U. R.I.; active in numerous charity and cultural activities. Recipient awards for writing from various groups such as R.I. Fed. Garden Clubs. Mem. R.I. Horticulture Soc. (organizer), Garden Writers of Am., N.Y. Art Dirs. Club, Childhood and Adult Devel. Resources Inst. (founder, bd. dirs.) Jewish. Lodges: Masons, B'nai Brith. Office: 71 Faunce Dr Providence RI 02906

ADLER, JOYCE SPARER, literary critic, educator; b. N.Y.C., Dec. 2, 1915; d. Louis and Lillian (Solomon) Lifshutz; B.A. cum laude, Bklyn. Coll., City U. N.Y., 1935, M.A., 1951; m. Irving Adler, Sept. 16, 1968; children—Ellen, Laura. Tchr. English public high schs., N.Y.C., 1940-54, acting chmn. dept. English, 1950-52; editor Blood, Jour. Hematology, N.Y.C., 1954-55; tchr. English to fgn. dels. to UN, N.Y.C., 1956-63; tchr. English, Ramaz High Sch., N.Y.C., 1960-63; founding mem. U. Guyana, Georgetown, 1963-68, prof. lit., 1963-68, editor univ. newsletter, 1964-68; author books: Language and Man, 1970; War in Melville's Imagination, 1981; Attitudes Towards Race in Guyanese Literature, 1967; contbr. critical essays to anthologies, PMLA and lit. jours. U.S. and Commonwealth Countries; occasional mem. coll. faculties, 1981—; lectr. in field, China, Japan, India, Australia, Singapore, N.Z. invited main speaker Internat. Conf. on Commonwealth Lit., Liège, Belgium, 1974, Nat. Conf. African and Caribbean Lit., U. Mo., 1973, ann. Melville Soc. Meeting, 1978, Bennington Coll. Conf. on Am. Indian, 1977. Recipient Nat. Second prize English Jour., 1953. Mem. MLA, Internat. Assn. Commonwealth Lit. and Lang. Studies, Vt. Acad. Arts and Scis. (trustee 1981—, sec. 1981—), Melville Soc. (program chmn. 1985, conf. organizer Chgo. 1985, Nantucket, Mass. 1986). Free-lance writer song lyrics, short stories, plays, 1956-63; articles referee PMLA. Home and Office: North Bennington VT 05257

ADLER, LEONORE LOEB, psychologist; b. Karlsruhe, W. Ger., May 2, 1921; d. Leo and Elsie (Laemle) Loeb; m. Helmut E. Adler, May 22, 1943; children—Barry Peter, Beverly Sharmaine, Evelyn Renée. B.A. cum laude, Queens Coll., CUNY, 1968; Ph.D., Adelphi U., 1972. Research asst. Am. Mus. Natural History, N.Y.C., 1956—; adj. asst. prof. psychology Coll. S.I., CUNY, 1974-80; research assoc. Mystic Marinelife Aquarium (Conn.), 1976—; assoc. prof. dept. psychology, dir. Inst. for Cross-Cultural and Cross-Ethnic Studies, Molloy Coll., Rockville Centre, N.Y., 1980—; chmn. internat. and nat. confs. Author book chpts.; translator: This is the Dachshund, 1966, 2d rev. edit., 1975; co-editor: Comparative Psychology at Issue, 1973, Language, Sex and Gender: Does"la Difference" Make a Difference, 1979; editor; Issues in Cross-Cultural Research, 1977; Cross-Cultural Research at Issue, 1982; contbr. articles and chpts. to handbooks, profl. jours. and encys. Mem. to gov.'s com. on women N.Y. State Women's Com., 1977. Recipient Disting. Contbr. of Decade award, Internat. Orgn. Study Group Tensions, 1981. Fellow N.Y. Acad. Scis.; mem. Am. Psychol. Assn. (network of reps. of com. on women in psychology 1982—), Eastern Psychol. Assn. (bd. dirs. 1985—), N.Y. State Psychol. Assn. (pres. div. social psychology 1978-79, 80-82, 84-85; pres. div. acad. psychology 1982-83; mem. council reps. 1981-84; chmn. com. women's issues 1982-84, plaque for outstanding achievement from women's com. 1984, medallion from society div. 1984, Kurt Lewin award 1985), Internat. Assn. Cross-Cultural Psychology, Soc. Cross-Cultural Research, Internat. Orgn. Study Group Tensions (mng. editor Internat. Jour. Group Tensions, 1978-84, assoc. editor 1984-85), Animal Behavior Soc., Internat. Soc. Comparative Psychology, Assn. Women in Sci., Soc. Advancement Social Psychology, Internat. Council Psychologists (treas. 1983-85), Cheiron, the Internat. Soc. for History of Behavioral and Social Scis., Queens County Psychol. Assn. (pres.-elect 1985-86, pres. 1986-87), Psi Chi (faculty adviser Molloy Coll., 1980—), Alpha Sigma Lambda, Zeta Epsilon Gamma. Jewish. Home: 162-14 86th Ave Jamaica NY 11432 Office: Inst Cross-Cultural and Cross-Ethnic Studies Molloy Coll 1000 Hempstead Ave Rockville Centre NY 11570

ADONAYLO, RAQUEL, pianist, singer; b. Uruguay; came to U.S., 1975; d. Ruben and Felicia (Bornstein) A.; grad. W. Kolischer Conservatory of Music, Uruguay, 1944; student of E. Casal-Chapi and Lazare-Levy, France; vocal student of Ninon Vallin, 1951-56; m. Ziszko Peniazek, Apr. 26, 1952; children—Pablo, Eduard, Ana. Concert pianist, 1941—; soprano, appearances in opera and oratorio, also recitalist, performing throughout world, 1952—, including numerous contemporary world premieres; voice instr. Curtis Inst. Music, Phila., 1975—; pvt. piano tchr., Uruguay, 1947-62, Israel, 1963-75, Rosemont, Pa., 1976—; dir. Ninon Vallin Sch. Singing, 1953-58; faculty Rubin Acad., Jerusalem, 1963-64; vocal coach, 1956—; chamber music coach, dir. seminars, throughout world; rec. artist Columbia Records. Recipient Grand prize as soloist with orch. Record Circle of Critics, 1966. Address: 1118 Old Gulph Rd Rosemont PA 19010

ADORJAN, CAROL MADDEN, writer; b. Chgo., Aug. 17, 1934; d. Roland Aloysius and Marie (Toomey) Madden; m. William Walter Adorjan, Aug. 17, 1957; children—Elizabeth M., Katherine Therese and John Martin (twins), Matthew Christian. B.A. in English Lit., Mundelein Coll., 1956. Tchr. English, St. Scholastica High Sch., Chgo., 1956-57, substitute tchr., intermittently, 1957—; artist in residence Ill. Arts Council, 1982-83; leader various workshops for adults and children, 1980—. Author: Someone I Know, 1968; Jonathon Bloom's Room, 1972; The Cat Sitter Mystery, 1972; Pig Party, 1981; The Electric Man, 1981. Contbr. short stories, articles, features to various publs.; writer radio and stage plays. Home: 812 Rosewood Ave Winnetka IL 60093

ADREON, BEATRICE MARIE RICE, pharmacist; b. Huntington, W.Va., July 23, 1929; d. Lloyd Emerson and Beatrice (Odell) Rice; student Mary Washington Coll., 1947-49; B.S. in Pharmacy, Med. Coll. Va., 1952; M.A. in Spl. Studies and Women's Studies, George Washington U., 1976; m. Harry Barnes Adreon, Jr., Dec. 27, 1952. Summer vol. worker pharmacies De Paul Hosp., Norfolk, Va., 1949, U.S. Marine Hosp., Norfolk, 1950; pharmacist Washington Clinic, 1954-71; counselor George Washington U., 1976-77, cons. gerontology health scis. dept., 1977—; cons. medicine control traffic patterns nursing homes Cross & Adreon, Washington, 1962—; founder, pres. Pharmacy Counseling Services, Inc., 1978—. Instr. advanced first aid ARC, 1952—, civil def. instr., 1952—; vol. Spanish Edn. Devel. Center, Washington, 1972; mem. Arlington (Va.) Community Services Bd., chmn. com. substance abuse. Recipient Arnold and Marie Schwartz award in pharmacy, 1980. Mem. Acad. Pharmacy Practice, Am. Pharm. Assn., Va. Pharm. Assn., Potomac Pharmacists Assn., AAAS, Am. Inst. History of Pharmacy, Nat. Council Patient Info. and Edn. (task force pub. info.), Panhellenic Assn., Kappa Epsilon. Episcopalian (mem. bishop's com. neighborhood services 1967-69, chmn. services for aged div. 1967-69). Contbr. articles in field to profl. jours. Home: 4524 N 19th Rd Arlington VA 22207

ADRIAN, LINDA SUE, county health officer; b. Manchester, Iowa, Aug. 28, 1940; d. Lorenz Rhinehart and Lena Gladys (Henderson) Glass; m. Keith D. Reese, Apr. 7, 1961 (dec. Mar. 1975); children—Julie G., Boyd K.; m. Michael L. Adrian, Jan. 12, 1980; 1 child, Toni Lynne. Diploma Methodist Hosp. Sch. Nursing, Madison, Wis., 1960; pub. health cert. U. Wis.-Madison, 1968. Staff nurse Meth. Hosp., Madison, 1960-61; staff nurse Grant County Pub. Health Nursing Service, Lancaster, Wis., 1961-64, asst. dir., 1966-74, dir., 1981—; dir. nursing Quietdale Nursing Home, Platteville, Wis., 1965-66, Unified Counseling Services, Lancaster, 1974-81; bd. dirs. Grant County Diabetic Assn., 1983—, Health Planning Council, Madison, 1984—. Active S.W. Health Care Ctr. Aux., Platteville, 1961—, Lancaster Regional High Sch. Rodeo Assn., 1983-85, Wis. High Sch. Rodeo assn., Tomah, 1984-85. Mem. Wis. Pub. Health Assn., Wis. Council Pub. Health Adminstrs., Wis. Homecare Orgn. Lutheran. Avocations: rodeos; flower arranging; sewing; horses. Home: Rural Route 1 Box 190 Cassville WI 53806 Office: Grant County Nurses Office Courthouse Lancaster WI 53813

ADRIAN, PATRICIA LEE GRIMSHAW, association executive; b. Reliance, S.D., July 20, 1938; d. Walter George and Dorthy Veronica (Zastrow) Grimshaw; student Sinte Gleska U., 1973; m. Robert Earl Adrian, Oct. 12, 1957; children—James Robert, Thomas Edward, Kevin Patrick, David Duane. Sec., Cherry Todd Electric, 1956-57; tchr. White River (S.D.) Ind. Sch. Dist., 1970-71; dir. S.D. Beef Industry Council, 1970-73, pres., 1972-73, exec. v.p., 1973—; exec. sec., lobbyist S.D. Livestock Assn., part-time 1977—; pres. Mktg. Internat., Inc., 1981—; partner Prairie Press; dir. Nat. Livestock and Meat Bd. Gov.'s rep. to nutrition symposium Old West Regional Commn., 1979-80; mem. S.D. Indsl. Devel. Commn., 1979-82; mem. S.D. Agrl. Mktg. Commn., 1980-82; mem. adv. com. S.D. Vocat. Tech. Edn. Commn. for Agr.; bd. dirs. S.D. Livestock Expansion Found., 1981—. Recipient Disting. Service award S.D. Stockgrowers Assn., 1974, S.D. State U., 1976. Mem. Nat. Fedn. Press Women, Am. Soc. Assn. Execs., Nat. Cattlemen's Assn., S.D. Livestock Assn., Am. Agri-Women, U.S. Meat Export Fedn. (dir. 1980-82), S.D. Press Women's Assn., S.D. CowBelles (pres.). Republican. Roman Catholic. Home: Star Route Box 222 White River SD 57579 Office: 110 W Capitol St Pierre SD 57501

ADVINCULA, MARIETTA MAGSAYSAY, college dean, real estate broker; b. Manila, May 4, 1939; came to U.S., 1961, naturalized, 1978; d. Gregorio and Rosalia (Peralta) Magsaysay; m. Ronaldo C. Advincula, Dec. 4, 1965; children—Monica Rose, Ronna Marisse, Melanie Rhoda. B.S. in Home Econs., U. Philippines, 1959; M.S., U. Kans., 1965; cert. in hosp. adminstrn. U. Ill., 1980-81. Dietetic intern Philippine Gen. Hosp., Manila, 1960, U. Minn. Hosp., Mpls., 1962; reviewer/lectr. Bd. Exam. for Dietitians, Philippines, 1967-71; nutritionist YWCA, Philippines, 1971; tng. specialist applied nutrition program in Philippines, UNICEF, 1970-71; instr. food and nutrition Coll. Home Econs., U. Philippines, 1965-71; supr. menu selection West Suburban Hosp., Oak Park, Ill., 1971-72; clin. dietitian/teaching dietitian Weiss Meml. Hosp., Chgo., 1972-73, chief therapeutic dietitian, 1973-76; devel. specialist Malcolm X Coll., City Colls. of Chgo., 1976-78; reviewer/lectr. Northside Traineeship Council/U. Ill., 1974-81; clin. asst. prof. U. Ill. Sch. Associated Med. Scis., Med. Dietetics Curriculum, 1975-79; asst. dir. dept. dietetics U. Ill. Hosp., Chgo., 1976-79; asst. prof. dept. nutrition and med. dietetics U. Ill. Coll. Associated Health Professions, Chgo., 1979-81; asst. dean adult continuing edn. dept. Truman Coll., City Colls. Chgo., 1981—; cons. food service and nutrition education Intervention, 1979-80; cons., instr. inquiry edn. Augustana Hosp. Sch. Nursing, 1980; preceptor Am. Dietetic Assn. Traineeship, Weiss Hosp., 1973-76, Hosp. and Ednl. Food Service Suprs., 1973-76, Am. Dietetic Assn., U. Ill. Hosp., 1976-77; assoc. Nat. Inst. Edn. Inquiry, 1976-78; coordinator staff devel., continuing edn. seminars Weiss Hosp., 1973-76, U. Ill. Hosp., 1976-79; coordinator interviewing, counseling and med. recording skills workshop Am. Dietetic Assn., 1979-81; lectr. dept. nutrition and med. dietetics Coll. Associated Health Profs., U. Ill., 1979-80; cons. nutrition program Mayor's Office Sr. Citizen and the Handicapped, Chgo. City Wide Coll., 1981, Nutrition Edn. Tng. Program, Ctr. Urban Program, Bd. Edn., Chgo., 1981. Author videotape program: Sociocultural Aspect of Food Behavior Slide, 1981; chmn. revision com. Manual of Clinical Dietetics, 1981; author: Nutrition of Children, Mothers, and the Aged, 1973. Editor: The Home Economist, 1968-70. Contbr. articles to profl. jours. Mem. Arts and Humanities Task Force; organizer, liaison Filipino Community of OLM Parish, 1979-85; chmn. Ill. Minority Women's Caucus, 1986-87; bd. mem. Mother's Club, Our Lady of Mercy Sch., 1980-82; treas. Eugene Civic Neighborhood Assn., 1982-83, v.p., 1981-82; mem. sch. bd. Our Lady of Mercy Sch., 1982-85, pres., 1983-85; mem. Archdiocesan Pastoral Council, 1984-88; chmn. Task Force on Consolidation and Expansion, 1986; mem. adv. bd. Assn. Chinese from Indochina. U. Philippines scholar, 1955-59; named Most Outstanding New Citizen, Nutrition Care Adminstrn., Met. Chgo. Citizenship Council, 1979; recipient Certs. of Recognition, Filipino Spiritual Community Action, Philippines Week, 1983, Truman Coll. Student Govt., 1984-86. Mem. Am. Assn. Philippines Dietitians (chmn.), Am. Dietetic Assn., Ill. Adult and Continuing Educators, Ill. Dietetic Assn., Soc. Nutrition Edn., Women in Mgmt., Chgo. Nutrition Assn., Food and Instn. Systems Mgmt. Edn. Council, Filipino Am. Women's Network, Philippine Educators Assn., Chgo. Dietetic Assn., Ill. Consultation Ethnicity in Edn., Nutrition Today, Ill. Council Women's Programs, Am. Assn. Diabetes Educators, Nat. Assn. Female Execs., Cons. Dietitians in Health Care Facilities, Asian/Pacific Womens' Network, Northside Realty Bd., Minority Women's Caucus. Avocations: sewing; gardening; cooking; reading; swimming. Home: 5021 N Monticello Chicago IL 60625 Office: Truman Coll 1145 W Wilson St Chicago IL 60640

AERY, SHAILA ROSALIE, state official; b. Tulsa, Dec. 4, 1938; d. Silas C. and Billie M. (Brewer) A. B.S., U. Okla., 1964; M.S., Okla. State U., 1972, Ed.D., 1975. Tchr. history and govt. Oklahoma City Pub. Schs. System, 1964-68; mem. chancellor's staff Okla. State Regents, Oklahoma City, 1977; asst. prof. U. Mo., Columbia, 1978-81, spl. asst. to chancellor, 1978-80, asst. provost, 1980-81; dep. commr. State of Mo., Jefferson City, 1981, commr. higher edn., 1982—; exec. com. State Higher Edn. Exec. Office, Denver, 1983; commr. Edn. Commn. of the States, Denver, 1983. Contbr. articles to profl. jours. Democrat. Episcopalian. Office: Mo Coordinating Bd for Higher Edn 101 Adams St Jefferson City MO 65101

AFRIDI, PARVEEN NIAZ, psychiatrist; b. Farrukhabad, India, June 20, 1944; came to U.S., 1972; d. Niaz Mohammed and Zakia Sultana Khan-Afridi; M.D. (Merit scholar), S.M.S. Med. Coll., Japiur, India, 1968; m. Mohammed Kalimi, Apr. 26, 1970 (div. Nov. 1975); 1 son, Omar. Rotating intern S.M.S. Med. Coll. Hosp., Jaipur, 1968-69; attending med. officer dept. ob-gyn, Kota and Meerut, India, 1969-72; postdoctoral research Inst. Cancer Research, Columbia U., N.Y.C., 1972-73; resident in psychiatry N.Y. U.-Bellevue Med. Center, N.Y.C., 1974-77; attending psychiatrist Manhattan Psychiat. Center, N.Y.C., 1977-80; clin. instr. psychiatry Albert Einstein Med. Center, N.Y.C. and attending psychiatrist Jacobi Hosp., 1980-81; clin. instr. psychiatry Downstate Med. Center, N.Y.C. and sr. attending psychiatrist Kings County Hosp., N.Y.C., 1981-83, clin. asst. prof., sr. attending psychiatrist, 1984—. Named one of best psychiat. residents Manhattan Psychiat. Center, 1974-75; recipient Physicians Recognition award AMA, 1977, 83. Mem. Am. Psychiat. Assn., Menninger Found., N.Y. Acad. Scis., Am. Psychiatrists from India (life), N.Y. U.-Bellevue Psychiat. Soc. Home: 510 2d Ave Apt 13B New York NY 10016 Office: 451 Clarkson Ave Brooklyn NY 11203

AFTERGOOD, LILLA, biochemist, nutritionist; b. Krakow, Poland, Jan. 10, 1925; came to U.S., 1949, naturalized, 1956; d. Jacob and Zofia (Selzer) Anisfeld; B.S., Sorbonne U., 1948; M.S., U. So. Calif., 1951, Ph.D., 1956; m. Edgar Aftergood, Aug. 17, 1949; children—David, Steven, Annette. Sr. research asso. dept. biochemistry U. So. Calif., 1956-59; asso. research biochemist Sch. Public Health, UCLA, 1959-80. Mem. Am. Inst. Nutrition, Am. Heart Assn., Council on Arteriosclerosis, AAAS, Sigma Xi. Co-author: Nutrition for Today, 1973; Nutrition and Motherhood, 1982; mem. editorial bd. Nutrition and the MD; contbr. numerous articles to sci. jours.

AGAR-STEWART, BRENDA ANN, data processing executive; b. Cheltenham, Gloucestershire, Eng., Mar. 15, 1940; came to U.S., 1976, d. Edwin Walker/Leyden and Dorothy Marian (Hogg) Agar; m. Richard Bruce Stewart, July 6, 1976 (div. Sept. 1978). Higher Nat. Cert. in Computer Sci., Bournemouth Advanced Tech. Coll./Univ., Dorset, Eng., 1967. Data processing personnel cons. Data Search, Westminster, London, 1974-76; data processing recruiter Christopher & Long, St. Louis, 1977-79; gen. mgr. Exec. Resource, St. Louis, 1979-80; v.p. sales and mktg., pres. Exec. Connections, Inc., St. Louis, 1980-85; prin. Agar Assocs., St. Louis, 1985—. Bd. mgrs. Willowbrook Condominiums, St. Louis, 1983-85, sec., 1985. Mem. Assn. Systems Mgrs. (bd. dirs.), Data Processing Mgmt. Assn. Avocations: singing; music; dancing; tennis; writing. Home: 10439 Briarbend Dr Saint Louis MO 63146 Office: PO Box 41354 Saint Louis MO 63141

AGBAYANI, MARY ALLEN, travel company executive, educator; b. Philippines, Aug. 8, 1946; came to U.S. 1968; d. Constancio and Benita (Cagaanan) Arbotante; m. Randolph Del Prado, Sept. 6, 1973. B.S. in Edn., Philippine Normal Coll., 1965; M.Ed., Northeastern U., 1973. Travel cons. Winters World Travel, LaGrange, Ill., 1979-83; phys. edn. instr. Chgo. Bd. Edn., 1971-83; instr. Ill. Inst. Tech., Chgo., 1980-81, Triton Coll., River Grove, Ill., 1981—; pres. Berkeley Travel, Ill., 1983—; dir. Mary Allen Travel Sch., Berkeley, 1984—; cons. M.A. & Assocs., Berkeley, 1985—. Author: Passport to a New Horizon, 1985. Mem. Philippine Educators Assn. (sec. 1979), Am. Soc. Travel Agts., Am. Retail Travel Agts. Roman Catholic. Avocations: tennis; traveling. Office: Berkeley Travel Inc 555 Saint Charles Rd Berkeley IL 60163

AGEE, NELLE HULME, art history educator; b. Memphis, May 22, 1940; d. John Eulice and Nelle (Ray) Hulme; m. Bob R. Agee, June 7, 1958; children—Denise, Robyn. Student Memphis State U., 1971-72, postgrad., 1978; B.A., Union U., Jackson, Tenn., 1978; postgrad. Jackson State U., 1978, Seminole Okla. Coll., 1982, Okla. Baptist U., 1984. Cert. tchr. art, history, Ky., Tenn. Offices services supr. So. Bapt. Theol. Sem., Louisville, 1961-64; kindergarten tchr. Shively Heights Bapt. Ch., Louisville, 1965-70; editorial asst. Little Publs., agrl. mags., Memphis, 1973-75; tchr. art Humboldt High Sch., Tenn., 1978-82; vis. artist-in-schs. Tenn. Arts Commn., Nashville, 1978, 81, 82; adj. prof. art history Seminole Coll., Okla., 1985-86; frequent speaker art orgns., ch. groups; tchr. art workshops Humboldt City Sch. system; tchr. Cultural Arts Day Camp, Jackson, Tenn., 1982. Exhibited art in various shows. Active Salvation Army Aux., Shawnee; v.p. Union U. Woman's Club, 1976-77, pres., 1978. Recipient Disting. Classroom Tchr. award Tenn. Edn. Assn., 1982. Mem. Univ. Alliance, Okla Bapt. U., Shawnee Fine Arts Club, Alpha Delta Kappa. Republican. Baptist. Avocations: stained glass; pottery making; travel. Home: 616 University Pkwy Shawnee OK 74801

AGGER, CAROLYN E., lawyer; b. N.Y.C., May 27, 1909. A.B., Barnard Coll., 1931; M.A., U. Wis., 1932; LL.B. cum laude, Yale U., 1938. Bar: D.C. 1938, U.S. Tax Ct. 1943, U.S. Supreme Ct. 1950, U.S. Ct. Claims 1956, U.S. Ct. Appeals (6th cir.) 1958. Atty., NLRB, 1938-39; atty. tax div. U.S. Dept. Justice, Washington, 1939-43; now ptnr. Arnold & Porter, Washington. Mem. Order of Coif. Address: Arnold & Porter Thurman Arnold Bldg 1200 New Hampshire Ave NW Washington DC 20036*

AGIN, JOAN, educator; b. N.Y.C., Sept. 27, 1928; d. Jack and Lilly (Schwartz) Frucht; m. Arthur Agin, Oct. 1950 (div. Feb. 1985); children—Steven, Laurie-Debbie, Gary. B.S., NYU, 1949; M.A., Columbia U., 1951. Tchr. Bd. Edn., N.Y.C., 1962—; chpt. chmn. Pub. Sch. 40, N.Y.C., 1964-67; mem. women's rights com. Am. Fedn. Tchrs., Washington, 1973-80; dist. rep. United Fedn. Tchrs., N.Y.C., 1967—, mem. exec. bd., 1964—. Lobbyist United Fedn. Tchrs., Am. Fedn. Tchrs., N.Y. State United Tchrs., N.Y.C., Albany, and Washington, 1967—. Recipient Trachtenberg award United Fedn. Tchrs., 1965, Smalheizer award, 1967; Leadership award Council Suprs., N.Y.C., 1972; Cert. of Recognition, Community Sch. Bd., 1972; Disting. Service Citation, United Negro Coll. Fund, 1985. Avocations: dramatics; tennis. Office: United Fedn Tchrs 100-15 Queens Blvd Forest Hills NY 11375

AGNEW, JANICE JOANN, advertising agency executive; b. Pitts., Jan. 18, 1951; d. Michael A. and Josephine C. (Trangate) Coco; m. Bryant L. Agnew, May 29, 1971 (div. June 1979); 1 child, Darcy J. B.A. in English, Dickinson Coll., 1971. Health careers coordinator Pa. Health Council, Camp Hill, 1971-72; copy expeditor, corr. Lancaster newspaper, Pa., 1973-74; copywriter Kelly Advt., Lancaster, 1974-78; promotion supr. Armstrong World Industries, Lancaster, 1978-80; founder, chmn., pres., creative dir. Agnew & Corrigan Inc., Lancaster, 1980—; cons., vol. instr. Sch. Dist. Lancaster, 1985. Bd. dirs. DirPAC, Lancaster, 1984-85. Named Woman of Yr., Am. Bus. Women's Assn., Lancaster, 1979. Mem. Am. Advt. Fedn. (Addy award, 2d dist. 1982, 84), Central Pa. Advt. Fedn. (Addy award 1982, 83, 84), Lancaster Advt. Club (bd. dirs. 1983-84). Democrat. Roman Catholic. Avocations: writing; piano; reading; classical music; interior design. Office: Agnew & Corrigan 131 E Grant St Lancaster PA 17602

AGNEW, NETTIE LOU, nurse, administrator; b. Jasper, Mo., Jan. 23, 1948; d. Andrew Jackson and Mary Marie (Burton) Butler; m. Edwin John Agnew, Oct. 23, 1973; 1 dau., Rhian Mallorie. Diploma Burge Sch. Nursing, 1969; B.S. magna cum laude, Drury Coll., 1970; M.S., No. Ill. U., 1977. R.N., Mo. Staff nurse U.S. Air Force, Calif. and Ill., 1969-73; vis. nurse St. Clair County Vis. Nurse Assn., East St. Louis, Ill., 1973-75; staff nurse N. Kansas City Hosp., Mo., 1975; instr. Research Sch. Nursing, Kansas City, Mo., 1975-76; clin. nursing specialist N. Kansas City Hosp., 1978-79, v.p. nursing, 1979-85, v.p. clin. services, 1985—; mem. adv. bd. nursing dept. William Jewell Coll., Liberty, Mo., 1983, nursing dept. St. Mary's Coll., Leavenworth, Kans., 1982—. Mem. Am. Orgn. Nurse Execs., Mo. Assn. Nursing Service Adminstrs., Dirs. Nursing Greater Kansas City Hosp. Assn., Soroptimist Internat. (treas. Southwest Clay County 1984-86), Sigma Theta Tau. Home: 6801 N Mokane St Kansas City MO 64151 Office: North Kansas City Hosp 2800 Hospital Dr North Kansas City MO 64116

AGOSTINO-TRIOLI, MICHELE FRANCESCA, travel company executive, consultant; b. N.Y.C., Feb. 12, 1954; d. Vincent James and Diana Yolanda (Citti) Agostino; m. Luigi Trioli, Oct. 28, 1978 (div. July 1981). A.A. in Lang., U. Florence, Italy, 1975; B.A., Hofstra U., 1976; A.S. in Fin., N.Y. Inst., 1978. Adviser Nat. Model UN, N.Y.C., 1971-73; sr. acct. Joseph E. Seagram & Sons, N.Y.C., 1975-79; comptroller Halloran House, N.Y.C., 1979-81; dir. mgmt. services Tollman-Hundley Hotels, N.Y.C., 1981-84; v.p. fin. and adminstrn. Trafalgar Tours U.S.A., N.Y.C., 1984—; mng. cons. Divi Enterprises, Bethpage, N.Y., 1972—, Lava Hotel Mgmt., N.Y.C., 1984—. Active MacNeil-Mitchell Republican Club, N.Y.C., 1984—. Mem. Internat. Assn. Hospitality Accts., N.Y. Execs. Club, N.Y.C. Hospitality Accts. Roman Catholic. Avocations: reading; creative writing; song writing. Home: 1714 62d St Brooklyn NY 11204 Office: Trafalgar Tours USA Inc 21 E 26th St New York NY 10010

AGUIAR, JUDI KAY, training coordinator, consultant; b. Reading, Pa., Apr. 18, 1952; d. Clarence Elsworth and Roberta Mae (Melvin) Haussmann; m. Robert H. Aguiar, June 23, 1968; children—Shawn E., Kimberly Kay. Student schs. Orlando, Fla. State sales mgr. Penn Corp. Fin., Nashville and Orlando, 1973-85; tng. coordinator Source Video, Franklin, Tenn., 1985-86. Author: Women in the Business World, 1984; various tng. manuals, 1985-86. Coproducer seminars Penn Corp. Fin., 1974-83. Number one in sales in U.S. Penn Corp. Fin., 1983. Mem. Nat. Assn. Female Execs. Lutheran. Lodge: Order Eastern Star. Avocation: writing articles.

AGUIAR-VELEZ, DEBORAH, computer consultant, educator; b. N.Y.C., Dec. 18, 1955; d. Marcus and Margarita (Diaz) Aguiar; m. German Velez, Dec. 19, 1976; 1 child, Raquel Dagmar. B.S. in Chem. Engring. U. P.R., 1977; postgrad. Am. Women Econ. Devel., N.Y.C., 1984-86. Asst. instr. computer scis. U. P.R., Mayaguez, 1977-78; sr. analyst Exxon Corp., Florham Park, N.J., 1978-83; pres. Sistemas Corp., Kendall Park, N.J., 1983—; sr. programmer AT&T, Piscataway, N.J., 1983-84; sr. analyst Exxon Chems., Florham Park, 1984-85, Exxon Research and Engring., Florham Park, 1985—. Contbr. articles to profl. jours. Mem. Soc. Women Engrs., Am. Women Entrepreneur, Data Processing Mgmt. Assn. Republican. Mem. Ch. of Christ. Club: Toastmasters Internat. Avocation: reading. Office: Sistemas Corp PO Box 86 Kendall Park NJ 08824

AGUIRRE, BARBARA JEAN, librarian; b. Corinne, W.Va., Feb. 4, 1935; d. Paul F. and Mary Phyllis (Chambers) Kirk; B.S., Concord Coll., 1965; m. Thomas J. Aguirre, Dec. 22, 1953; 1 son, Thomas Kirk. Asst. librarian Bluefield Coll., 1965-67; asst. librarian Logan Campus, So. W.Va. Community Coll., 1971-73, librarian, 1973—. Mem. W.Va. Library Assn., W.Va. Edn. Media Assn., W.Va. Community Coll. Assn., LWV, Beta Sigma Phi. Methodist. Clubs: Woman's of Logan (pres. 1978), Order Eastern Star, Logan Bus. and Profl. Women's. Home: PO Box 334 Logan WV 25601 Office: Library So W Va Community Coll Logan WV 25601

AGUIRRE, ELEA ALICIA, city official; b. El Paso, Tex., May 25, 1948; d. Salvador Fernando and Elea (Hauchbaum) Aguirre; m. Jesus Antonio Uraga, Sept. 24, 1971 (div. 1975); 1 dau., Elea. B.B.A., U. Tex., 1969; postgrad. U. Americas, Puebla, Mexico, 1972. Adminstrv. asst. West Tex. Council Govts., El (treas. Edn. Found. 1981-83, urban planner El Paso Dept. Planning and Research, 1973-79; comml. loan officer Home Mortgage Co., El Paso, 1979-82; cons. real estate devel., financing, ops. analysis, El Paso, 1982-83; research and systems officer El Paso Central Appraisal Dist., 1983—; hon. prof. urban design Universidad Autonoma de Ciudad Juarez, Chihuahua, Mexico, 1977-79; actress Elenco Exptl., bi-lingual theater group, U. Tex.-El Paso, 1982—. Task force leader Goals for El Paso, 1976-79; asst. leader Rio Grande council Girl Scouts U.S., 1982-83; mem. El Paso City Planning Commn., 1983—. Recipient diploma for outstanding collaboration Universidad Autonoma de Ciudad Juarez, 1978, cert. for outstanding service to community City of El Paso, 1979. Mem. Tex. Assn. Assessing Officers, Am. Planning Assn. (treas. Edn. Found. 1981-83, honor award Tex. chpt. 1978). Office: El Paso Central Appraisal Dist 100 N Ochoa El Paso TX 79901

AGUIRRE, SHERRA L., building service contracting firm executive, real estate broker; b. Lufkin, Tex., Jan. 15, 1949; d. E.C. and Odell (Sweats) Johnson; m. Gene L. Locke, Sept. 4, 1969 (div. Apr. 1976); children—Tembekile, Attica; m. Ricardo Aguirre, Aug. 12, 1979. Student U. Tex.-Austin, 1966-68; B.A., U. Houston, 1970; M.Ed., Tex. So. U., 1973. Lic. real estate broker. Research assoc. Houston Ind. Sch. Dist., 1977-80; major account rep. Xerox, Houston, 1980-81; pres., chief exec. officer Aztec Maintenance Services, Inc., Houston, 1981—; mem. adv. council Enterprise Bank West, N.A., Houston, 1985—. Mem. Foster Parent Orgn., Houston, 1985—; supporter SHAPE Community Ctr., Houston, 1979—; mem. internat. affairs caucus Am. Friends Service Com., Phila., 1970-72. Mem. Bldg. Service Contractors Assn. Internat., Houston Bus. Council, Houston Bd. Realtors. Office: Aztec Maintenance Services Inc 5959 Westheimer Suite 101 Houston TX 77057

AHASAY, JULIE ANN, college public relations director, actress, b. Shell Lake, Wis., June 7, 1953; d. Marcus Leo and Helen Elizabeth (Erickson) A.; m. Steven M. Therrien, June 18, 1977 (div. 1983). B.S. magna cum laude, U. Wis.-Superior, 1975. Grad. asst. U. Wis., Superior, 1976; adminstrv. asst. Stewart-Taylor Co., Duluth, 1976-77; tchr. Head Start, Hayward, Wis., 1977-79; asst. promotion dir. Sta. KBJR-TV, Duluth, 1979-81; promotion dir. KDLH-TV, Duluth, 1981-82; dir. pub. relations Coll. St. Scholastica, Duluth, 1982—. Author, actress Colder by the Lake Comedy Theatre, 1983—; appeared in musicals and dramas Duluth Playhouse, 1981—(best supporting actress 1981, 83). Bd. dirs. Duluth Playhouse, 1984—; cons. Mayor's Higher Edn. Adv. Com., Duluth Area Vocational Tech. Inst., 1982—. Mem. Council for Advancement and Support of Edn., Lake Superior Advt. Club. Democrat. Office: Coll of St Scholastica 1200 Kenwood Ave Duluth MN 55811

AHEARN, SUSAN KAINS, environmental educator; b. Reading, Pa., Jan. 27, 1951; d. Archibald Sherwood and Eleanore (Larkby) Kains; m. Mark Joseph Ahearn, June 24, 1978; children—Andrew Agustin, Ian McMillan. B.S. in Edn., Bowling Green State U., 1972; M.S. in Natural Resources, Ohio State U., 1978; student The U. Minn., 1975; Ph.D. candidate, Columbia U., 1985—. Document analyst, environ. edn., sci. edn. ERIC/SMEAC Ctr. Ohio State U., Columbus, 1979-80; environ. edn. specialist Ohio Dept. Natural Resources, Columbus, 1981-82; nature preserves mgr. Ohio Dept. Natural Resources East Central Ohio Preserves, Columbus, 1982-84; dir. sch. programs Mus. L.I. Natural Scis., SUNY-Stony Brook, 1984; document analyst internat. urban edn. ERIC/CUE ctr. Tchrs. Coll., Columbia U., N.Y.C., 1985-86; tchr. spl. programs Ctr. of Sci. and Industry, Columbus, 1979-80; co-dir., tchr. Met. Sch. Columbus, 1980; teaching asst. wildlife Ohio State U. Dept. Wildlife, 1976, 77, 78; edni. cons. Glen Helen Smithsonian Exhibition at Yellow Springs, Ohio, 1981. Author: Nature Preserves and Other Wild Edibles, 1981; The Imagination Books of ODNR, anti-coloring books on ecology, 1981-82. Author guide to films on environment, peace and justice, 1982, 83. Dir. Nat. Film Festival for Peace and Justice, Washington, 1983, N.Am. Assn. Environ. Edn. Film Festival on Environment 1982, Silver Bay, N.Y.; group leader Hobson Conf, Episcopal Diocese So. Ohio, Dayton, 1983; adv., vol. Ctr. for Peace at St. Stephen's, Columbus, 1982-84, adv. wildlife dept. Muskingham Area Tech. Coll., Zanesville, Ohio, 1983-84. Scholar Nat. Audubon Soc., 1972, 78; grantee Ohio Biol. Survey, 1982. Mem. N.Am. Assn. for Environ. Edn., World Council for Curriculum and Instruction, Am. Nature Study Soc., The Nature Conservance Internat. Programs, League of Women Voters (natural resources com.), Latin Am. Parents Assn. L.I. Chpt., Internat. Families Through Adoption. Democrat. Episcopalian. Avocations: folk music, crosscountry skiing, backpacking, wildlife photography.

AHERN, ARLEEN FLEMING, librarian; b. Mt. Harris, Colo., Oct. 15, 1922; d. John R. and Josephine (Vidmar) Fleming; B.A., U. Utah, 1943; M.A., U. Denver, 1962; postgrad. U. Colo., 1967; m. George Irving Ahern, June 14, 1944; 1 son, George Irving. Library asst. Army Air Force Library, Salt Lake City, 1943-44; library asst. Colo. Women's Coll. Library (now U. Denver/CWC Campus), 1952-60, acquisitions librarian, 1960—, rep. Adult Edn. Council Denver, 1960—, reference librarian Penrose Library, WEC librarian, assoc. prof. librarianship. Committeewoman, Republican Com., Denver, 1958-59. Mem. ALA, Mountain Plains Library Assn., Colo. (1st v.p., pres. 1969-70, dir. 1971—), Library Assn., Altrusa Club of Denver (2d v.p. 1968-69, dir. 1971-74, 76, 78), Soc. Am. Archivists, Mountain Plains Adult Edn. Assn., AAUP. Home: 746 Monaco Pkwy Denver CO 80220 Office: U Denver Penrose Library University Park Denver CO 80208

AHERN, MARGARET ANN, nun, nurse, educator; b. Manchester, N.H., Nov. 23, 1931; d. Timothy Joseph and Helen Bridget (Kearns) Ahern; R.N., Sacred Heart Hosp. Sch. Nursing, 1952; B.S.N., Mt. St. Mary Coll., 1957; M.Nursing, Cath. U. Am., 1965. Entered Sisters of Mercy, Roman Catholic Ch., 1953; staff nurse Sacred Heart Hosp., Manchester, 1954-57, operating room supr., 1957-62, med.-surg. nursing instr., 1962-66, dir. Sch. Nursing, 1966-75; dir. Sch. Nursing, Cath. Med. Center, Manchester, N.H., 1975-79, dir. dept. edn. and mem. sr. mgmt., 1979—. Chmn. bd. dirs. Health Edn. Consortium, 1977—; bd. dirs. Vis. Nurse Assn., 1981—; adv. bd. Hesser Coll., 1980—, N.H. Voc-Tech. Coll., 1979—; mem. United Health Systems Agy., 1977-83; mem. adv. council on continuing edn. St. Anselm Coll., 1978—; mem. gen. chpt. Sisters of Mercy, 1968-70, 79-81, chmn. fin. bd., 1981-86, chmn. Bd. Conciliation and Arbitration, 1982—. Mem. Am. Nurses Assn., N.H. Nurses Assn., Nat. League for Nursing, New Eng. Cath. Hosp. Assn., New Eng. Edn. and Research Orgn., N.H. Heart Assn., Sigma Theta Tau. Democrat. Roman Catholic. Contbr. articles to profl. jours. Home: 647 Canal St Manchester NH 03104 Office: 100 McGregor St Manchester NH 03102

AHERN, MARY MARGARET, art director; b. N.Y.C., Aug. 12, 1940; d. Maurice Francis and Marie Hanora (Tonry) A. Cert., Cooper Union Art Sch., 1961, B.F.A. (hon.), 1976; B.Ed., NYU, 1968. Gal Friday, The Viking Press, N.Y.C., 1961-62; book designer Mus. Modern Art, N.Y.C., 1962-66; sr. book designer Random House, N.Y.C., 1968-71; juvenile art dir. Atheneum Publishers, N.Y.C., 1975—. Mem. The Typophiles, Am. Inst. Graphic Arts, Type Dirs. Club, Am. Printing History Assn. Home: Jackson Heights NY 11372 Office: Atheneum Publishers 115 Fifth Ave New York NY 10003

AHERN, VERONICA MARY, lawyer, poet; b. N.Y.C., Nov. 7, 1946; d. Frederick Michael and Rosemary (Schildknecht) Ahern. B.A., Rosemont Coll., 1968; J.D., Georgetown U., 1972. Bar: D.C. 1973. Atty., FCC, Washington, 1972-78; assoc. adminstr. Nat. Telecommunications and Info. Adminstrn., Washington, 1978-82; ptnr. firm Chadbourne, Parke, Whiteside & Wolff, Washington, 1982—. Office: Chadbourne & Parke 1101 Vermont Ave NW Washington DC 20005

AHGHARIAN, NARGESS HAKIMI, obstetrician, gynecologist; b. Tehran, Iran, July 11, 1947; came to U.S. 1974; d. Ahmad and Masoumeh (Shahriary) Ahgharian; m. Farhad Hakimi, Aug. 7, 1972; children—Tara, Tiana. M.D., Tehran U., 1972. Rotating intern New Rochelle Hosp. (N.Y.), 1974-75; resident, chief resident Roosevelt Hosp., N.Y.C., 1975-78; practice ob-gyn, N.Y.C., 1978—. Recipient Royal award for article about diabetes, Iran, 1972. Fellow Am. Coll. Ob-Gyn; mem. County Med. Soc., N.Y. State Med. Soc. Office: 125 E 63d St New York NY 10017

AHLSTROM, MARY LOU, lawyer; b. Pitts., Dec. 1, 1950; d. Albert Vincent and Violet Loretta (Myer) Donnelly; m. Michael Joseph Ahlstrom, Apr. 19, 1980. B.A., Miami U., 1972; J.D., Duquesne U., 1976. Bar: Pa. 1976, N.Y. 1979. Trademark atty. U.S. Patent and Trademark Office, Washington, 1976-78; assoc. Pennie & Edmonds, N.Y.C., 1978-81; trademark atty. Coca-Cola Co., Atlanta, 1981-82, internat. counsel (Europe), 1983—. Mem. ABA (corp. council com.), Pa. Bar, N.Y. Bar. Office: The Coca-Cola Co PO Drawer 1734 Atlanta GA 30301

AHR, DEIRDRE O'MEARA, lawyer; b. N.Y.C., June 2, 1946; d. Thomas Francis and Mary Veronica (Meehan) O'Meara; m. Paul Robert Ahr, June 8, 1968 (div.); children—Thomas Brady, Andrew Travers. B.A. cum laude, Trinity Coll., 1968; M.Ed., Va. Commonwealth U., 1976; J.D., U. Mo., 1982. Bar: Mo. 1982, U.S. Dist. Ct. (we. dist.) Mo. 1982. Tchr. Prince George's County Schs., Md., 1968-70, St. Michael's Sch., Richmond, Va., 1976-78; staff lawyer Mo. Supreme Ct., Jefferson City, 1981-83; gen. counsel State of Mo. Detention Facilities Commn., Jefferson City, 1983; gen. counsel State of Mo. Jud. Fin. Commn., Jefferson City, 1983-85; clk. of the ct. Mo. Ct. Appeals Eastern Dist., St. Louis, 1985—. Recipient Acad. Excellance award in environ. law U. Mo. Sch. Law, 1981. Mem. ABA, Mo. Bar Assn., Boone County Bar Assn., Cole County Bar Assn., Met. St. Louis Bar Assn., Am. Judicature Soc. Roman Catholic. Office: Mo Ct Appeals 111 N 7th St Saint Louis MO 63101

AHRENS, WENDY JOAN, data processing executive; b. Glen Cove, N.Y., Aug. 4, 1950; d. Thomas J. and Isabelle Taylor; student U. Md., Augsburg, W.Ger., 1969-71, SUNY, Farmingdale, 1972-74; m. Kent E. Ahrens, May 9, 1969; 1 son, Kenneth K. Sales rep. Met. Life Ins. Co., Huntington, N.Y., 1974-76, sales mgr., Flushing, N.Y., 1976-79; asst. dir. market devel. J. C. Penney Life Ins. Co., Dallas, 1979-81, dir. employment, 1981-82; mktg. cons. Informatics, Gen., Dallas, 1982-84, Incepts Inc., Dallas, 1984—; instr. ins. mktg. S. La. U., Lafayette, 1980. Chmn. recruiting Industry Task Force on Women and Minorities, Washington, 1980-83; mem. Plano Civic Com. Task Force, 1983—; chmn. United Way, L.I., N.Y., 1977; mem. telethon com. Easter Seals, N.Y.C., 1978. Recipient Pres.'s Conf. award Met. Life Ins. Co., 1974, 75; Nat. Quality award Nat. Assn. Underwriters, 1974, 75, Nat. Sales Achievement award, 1974, 75. Mem. Soc. Ins. Researchers, Nat. Assn. Life Underwriters, Gen. Agts. and Mgrs. Conf., Women's Life Underwriters Conf. Contbr. articles in field to profl. publs. Home: 4105 Early Morn Plano TX 75075 Office: 12770 Coit Rd Dallas TX 75234

AIELLO, BARBARA, educational puppeteering company executive, puppeteer; b. Pitts., Nov. 6, 1947; d. Antonio and Helen (Kaupiek) A.; m. Richard Laurie Dolph, June 8, 1985; 1 child, Rosanna. B.S. in Edn., Indiana U. of Pa., 1968; M.A. in Edn., George Washington U., 1971; postgrad. Harvard U., 1974-75. Spl. edn. tchr., pub. schs., Washington area, 1969-74; editor Teaching Exceptional Children, Council for Exceptional Children, Reston, Va., 1975-77; edn. cons. Learning mag., Palo Alto, Calif., 1977-78; pres., founder, script writer The Kids On The Block, Alexandria, Va., 1978—; mem. adv. bd. Inst. for Mental Health Initiatives, Washington, 1985—, Ctr. for Children of Div., Washington, 1986—; corr. N.Y. Times, 1974-85. Recipient One To One Media award N.Y. State Advocacy Bd. for Mentally Retarded, 1979; On Behalf of Youth award Camp Fire, Inc., 1980; Outstanding Pub. Service award Easter Seal Soc., 1984; Margaret Pope Hovey award People-To-People Com., 1984; Disting. Service award Pres.'s Com. on Employment Handicapped, 1985; Outstanding Achievement award Epilepsy Found. Am., 1982; award for The Invisible Children, Instructor mag., 1980. Mem. Council for Exceptional Children, Nat. Assn. Female Execs. Avocations: cross country skiing; running; reading biographies. Office: The Kids On The Block Inc 822 N Fairfax St Alexandria VA 22314

AIKEN, LINDA HARMAN, foundation executive; b. Roanoke, Va., July 29, 1943; d. William Jordan and Betty Philips (Warner) Harman; B.S. in Nursing, U. Fla., 1964; M.Nursing, 1966; Ph.D. in Sociology, U. Tex., 1973; children—June Elizabeth, Alan James. Nurse, U. Fla. Med. Center, Gainesville, 1964-65; instr. Coll. Nursing, U. Fla., Gainesville, 1966-67; instr. Sch. of Nursing, U. Mo., Columbia, 1967-70, clin. nurse specialist, 1967-70; program officer Robert Wood Johnson Found., Princeton, N.J., 1974-76; dir. research, 1976-79, v.p., 1979—; mem. Adv. Council on Social Security, 1982-84. NIH Nurse Scientist fellow, 1970-73; NIH fellow, 1965-66. Mem. Inst. Medicine, Nat. Acad. Scis., Am. Acad. Nursing (pres. 1979-80), Am. Sociol. Assn. (chmn. med. sociology sect. 1983-84), Council Nurse Researchers, Am. Nurses Assn. Author: Evaluation Studies Review Annual, 1985; Applications of Social Science to Clinical Medicine and Health Policy, 1986. Editor: Jour. Health and Social Behavior, 1979-81; assoc. editor Transaction Soc., 1985—; mem. editorial bd. Evaluation Quar., 1979-80, Medical Care, 1983—. Contbr. articles to profl. jours. Home: 242 Prospect Ave Princeton NJ 08540 Office: Robert Wood Johnson Found PO Box 2316 Princeton NJ 08540

AIKENS, MARTHA BRUNETTE, national park service administrator, consultant, educator; b. Jayess, Miss., Aug. 23, 1949; d. Walter and Elnora La Doris (Bridges) A. B.S. in Social Sci., Alcorn State U., 1971; postgrad. George Williams Coll., 1974, Fla. Internat. U., 1977, George Washington U., 1979, Pa. State U., 1979, U. So. Calif.-D.C. Ext., 1980. Social worker Pearl River County Devel. Corp., Picayune, Miss., 1971-72; environ. ednl. specialist Nat. Park Service, Homestead, Fla., 1973-76, environ. ednl. coordinator, 1976-78, communications specialist, 1976-78, park mgr., Bklyn., 1978-79, St. Augustine, Fla., 1979-83, Washington, 1983—; instr., cons. Coll. African Wildlife Mgmt., Tanzania, Africa, 1980, Mather Tng. Ctr., Harpers Ferry, W.Va., 1977—, Fed. Law Enforcement Tng. Ctr., Glynco, Ga., 1983—, Office of Internat. Affairs, Nat. Park Service, Washington, 1980—. Author tchrs. guides on Everglades Nat. Park, 1973-76, park brochure, 1977. Contbr. chpts. to books. Mem. Strategic Planning Task Force, Atlanta, 1981-83, Southeast Regional Equal Opportunity Commn., Atlanta, 1982-83, Dept. Interior's Partnership in Edn. Commn., Washington, 1983—, Fed. Interagy. Commn. on Edn., Washington, 1983—, Nat. Park Service Employee Relations Task Force, Washington, 1983—.

AIKMAN, ALICE ANNETT, marketing executive, consultant; b. Atlanta, Sept. 27, 1946; d. Howard Turner and Edith Alice (Johnson) Farmer; m. Ralph Coleman Aikman, June 14, 1965 (div. June 1975); 1 child, Candace Alicia; m. Danny Wayne Powell, May 4, 1985. Student West Ga. Coll., 1964-65, Northeastern U., 1968-71. Freelance photo-journalist, Boston, 1970-72, Boston and Atlanta, 1973-78; asst. to v.p. J. Walter Thompson, Atlanta, 1972-73; sr. editor Blue Cross & Blue Shield, Atlanta, 1978-80; pres. AAA Interior Maintenace, Inc., Roswell, Ga., 1980—. Staff photographer Carter for Pres. Campaign, New Eng. states, 1976. Republican. Avocations: photography, rafting, camping, refinishing antiques. Office: AAA Interior Maintenance Inc 9705 Coleman Rd Roswell GA 30075

AINSLEE, WINIFRED, public service agency writer; b. Zanesville, Ohio, Apr. 17, 1927; d. F. Bringle and Kathleen (Girton) Crowder McIntosh; student Randolph-Macon Women's Coll., 1942-43; B.A., Ohio State U., 1947; postgrad. N.Y. U., 1976—; m. James Preston Mar. 5, 1959 (div.); children—Heather Lee. Actress on Broadway and in road and stock prodns., 1947-63; featured roles include: Brigadoon, Paint Your Wagon, Seventh Heaven, Bus Stop, Cat on a Hot Tin Roof, Invitation to a March, Auntie Mame, others; with Port Authority of N.Y. and N.J., 1963—, staff info. officer public affairs dept., 1979-85, publs. editor, 1985—. Mem. Women in Communications, Port Authority Women's Equity, Mensa. Methodist. Home: 115 W 73d St Apt 3D New York NY 10023 Office: Port Authority of NY and NJ One World Trade Center 68W New York NY 10048

AIRTH, MISKIT, TV programming executive; b. Live Oak, Fla., May 29, 1939; d. George Edward and Dorothy A.; A.B., Randolph Macon Woman's Coll., 1961; M.A., Dallas Theater Center, Baylor U., 1963. Mem. repertory theater, tchr.-dir. Children's Theater, Dallas Theater Center, 1961-63; with Nat. Theater Co., touring children's theater, 1963-64, Phoenix Theater, Am. Place Theater, Shakespeare-in-the-Park, N.Y.C., 1964-69; producer Sta. WPIX-TV, N.Y.C., 1969-75; asso. producer Good Morning America, ABC-TV, N.Y.C., 1975-76; producer A Woman Is—With Bess Myerson, Sta. WCBS-TV, N.Y.C., 1976-77; exec. producer Sta. WABC-TV, N.Y.C., 1977-80; dir. program devel. for East Coast, Viacom Enterprises, N.Y.C., 1980-81; dir. programming and studio ops. Warner Amex Cable Communications, 1981-84, MBA Video Projects, 1984—; vis. scholar Boston U. Communications Inst.; lectr. Womanschool, N.Y.C., Randolph-Macon Woman's Coll., Lynchburg, Va., New Sch. for Social Research, N.Y.C., Inst. New Cinema Artist, N.Y.C. Mem. adv. com. So. Ohio Coll.; mem. planning com. Nat. Cancer Communications Conf., Houston; bd. dirs. Women's SPCA of Phila. Recipient 2 silver medals Internat. Film Festival N.Y., 1979, 80, EMMY awards: outstanding documentary, 1971, 72, 80, outstanding mag., 1980, outstanding entertainment, 1980, 2 awards of excellence, Communications Excellence for Black Audiences, 1979, 80, award Nat. Cable TV Assn., 1982. Mem. Nat. Acad. TV Arts and Scis. (gov. N.Y.C. chpt.), Am. Women in Radio and TV (dir. N.Y.C. chpt.), Women in Cable (founder, 1st pres. Cin. Tri State chpt.), Phi Beta Kappa. Prodns. include New York Closeup, weekly film documentary Sta. WPIX-TV, 1969-73 (8 N.Y. area Emmy awards, 2 personal awards), WABC Spl. Reports, documentary series, 1977-80, WABC YOU! show (Emmy for pilot show), WABC instant spl. Life Was Worth Living, N.Y.C.: You Can't Get There From Here (Emmy), The Town That Build N.Y., (Emmy), Elvis-Love Him Tender with Joel Siegel (Emmy), prodns. for QUBE Cable, Studio 30, on location, others.

AITCHISON, BEATRICE, transportation economist; b. Portland, Oreg., July 18, 1908; d. Clyde Bruce and Bertha (Williams) Aitchison; A.B., Goucher Coll., 1928, Sc.D. (hon.), 1979; A.M., Johns Hopkins, 1931; Ph.D. in Math., 1933; M.A. with honors in Econs., U. Oreg., 1937. Asso. prof. math. U. Richmond, 1933-34; lectr. statistics Am. U., 1934-44; instr. econs. U. Oreg., 1939-41; jr. statistician advancing to sr. statistician ICC, 1938-48, prin. transport economist, 1948-51; dir. transport econs. div. Office Transp., Dept. Commerce, 1951-53; dir. transp. research Post Office Dept., Washington, 1953-58, dir. transp. research and statistics, 1958-67, dir. transp. rates and econs., 1967-71; transp. cons., 1971—. Cons. Traffic Analysis and Forecasting Office Def. Transp., 1942-45; cons. mil. traffic. service U.S. Dept. Def., 1950-53. Recipient Alumnae Achievement citation Goucher Coll., 1954; First Ann. Fed. Woman's award, 1961, Career Service award Nat. Civil Service League, 1970. Fellow Am. Statis. Assn., A.A.A.S.; mem. Am. Econ. Assn., Am. Soc. Phi Beta Kappa, Sigma Xi, Pi Lambda Theta, Phi Delta Gamma. Episcopalian. Contbr. to numerous govt. publs. Home and office: 1929 S St NW Washington DC 20009

AITKEN, ROSEMARY THERESA, financial planner and consultant; b. Phila., June 26, 1946; d. John Francis and Mary Helen (Kinslow) A.; m. Frank Furch, June 24, 1983. A.A., Mundelein Coll., 1976. C.L.U. Mktg. Cons. Anchor Orgn., Chgo., 1974-76; assoc. dir. Big Bros.-Big Sisters of Chgo., 1975-76; fin. planner Phoenix Co., Chgo., 1976—; dir. ins. Lincoln Equities, Inc., Chgo., 1985—; pres. Capital Interests, Inc., Chgo., 1984—, Aitken Assocs., Chgo., 1980—; speaker, instr. Chgo. Women's Network, 1984—; cons., columnist Chgo. Tribune, 1980—, Chgo. Sun-Times, 1981—; lectr. Midwest Life Underwriters Assns., 1982—. Contbr. articles to profl. jours. Bd. dirs. Loop YWCA, 1974-81. Mem. Women Life Underwriters Conf. (bd. dirs., 1st v.p. 1984-85), Chgo. Life Underwriters Assn. (chmn. membership com. 1984-85), Million Dollar Roundtable (life and qualifying mem.), Internat. Assn. Fin. Planners. Republican. Roman Catholic. Club: East Bank. Avocations: marathon running; sailing; photography. Home: 2462 W Estes Chicago IL 60645 Office: Aitken Assocs 10 S Riverside Plaza Suite 1250 Chicago IL 60606

AJZENSTAT, JANET, educator; b. Toronto, Ont., Can., Apr. 19, 1936; d. George Leslie and Florence (Gibson) MacDonald; m. Samuel Ajzenstat, Sept. 10, 1959; children—Sandor, Oona. B.A., U. Toronto, 1959, Ph.D., 1979; M.A., McMaster U., 1972. Lectr. McMaster U., Hamilton, Ont., 1978-85, asst. prof., part-time, 1985—. Contbr. articles to profl. jours. Bd. dirs. Operation Lifeline Hamilton, 1979-80; coordinator Jewish Community (Hamilton) Refugee Com., 1979-80; pres. Hamilton Right to Life, 1984—. Recipient Jules and Gabrielle Léger award Social Scis. and Humanities Research Council, 1985. Mem. Can. Polit. Sci. Assn., Société Québécoise de Sci. Politique. Avocation: reading. Home: 172 Cline Ave North Hamilton ON L8S 3Z9 Canada Office: Dept Political Sci McMaster Univ Main St West Hamilton ON L8S 4M4 Canada

AKERS, JEANNE ANNE, communications executive; b. Olympia, Wash., Mar. 1, 1945; d. Stephen Elmer and Norma Jeanne (Bair) A.; student Radford Coll., 1963-64, U. Hawaii, 1965-66. Exec. asst. to Norman Vincent Peale, N.Y.C., 1971-75; assoc. dir. Guideposts Outreach Ministries, N.Y.C., 1975-77, dir. media services and planning Found. for Christian Living, Pawling, N.Y., 1978-83; owner features syndication entitled Positive Thinking (Norman Vincent Peale), 1980-83; exec. dir. Moynahan Med. Group, Inc., N.Y.C. Mem. Am. Women in Radio and TV. Mem. Dutch Reformed Ch. Home: 200 E 72d St Apt 25J New York NY 10021 Office: 1001 Fifth Ave New York NY 10028

AKINS, MARSHA HARRIET, designer and manufacturer of hats; b. N.Y.C., Nov. 13, 1945; d. Tovya Moldavsky and Shirley (Bendett) Lipson; 1 son, Cody Shaka Campbell. Student U. Ill., 1963-65, Bernard Baruch Coll., 1968-70, Fashion Inst. Tech., N.Y.C., 1971-74. Founder, pres., designer Makins Hats Ltd., N.Y.C., 1974—. Recipient Coty Fashion Critics award, 1977; Cutty Sark award, 1983. Office: Makins Hats Ltd 212 W 35th St New York NY 10001

AKLIN, EDNA ESTELL, psychiatric social worker; b. Georgetown, S.C., Nov. 15, 1948; d. Herbert and Almena (Rice) A. L.P.N., Eli Whitney Regional Vocational Tech., 1969; B.S.W., So. Conn. State Coll., 1977; M.S.W., Va. Commonwealth U., 1978. Staff nurse St. Raphael Hosp., New Haven, 1969-77; clin. dir. Morris Found., Waterbury, Conn., 1978-81; staff nurse Yale New Haven Hosp., 1982—, Med. Personnel Pool, New Haven, 1982—; community mental health specialist Hamden (Conn.) Mental Health Service, 1980—; clin. cons. Vietnam Vet. Ctr., New Haven, 1982—. Bd. dirs. Cornerstone, Inc., New Haven, 1982—; Big Sister, Big Bro./Big Sister South Central Conn., Hamden, 1981—; bd. dirs. Liberation House, Inc., New Haven, 1980-81. Mem. Nat. Assn. Black Social Workers (2d v.p. New Haven chpt. 1983). Democrat. Office: Hamden Mental Health Service 3000 Dixwell Ave Hamden CT 06511

AKOS, CATHERINE, voice educator; b. Budapest, Hungary, Apr. 8, 1925; came to U.S., 1954, naturalized, 1957; d. Ignatz and Berta (Zilzer) A.; m. Ernest White, Sept. 6, 1946; 1 child, George. Grad. opera and concert artist Lisst Ferencz Acad. Music, Budapest, 1944. Soloist with Budapest, Bucarest, Cluj Opera Romania, from 1945; mem. Radio Diffusion Francaise, Paris, 1947-52; soloist with Swiss Romande Orch., Switzerland, 1952; soloist in Israel, Germany, Can. Opera, Toronto, 1953-57; soloist with Boston Symphony, NBC, CBS, 1954-57; assoc. prof. voice So. Methodist U., Dallas, 1957—. Played leading role on Broadway in Menotti's opera The Saint of Bleeker Street, 1954; recs. RCA Records. Mem. Nat. Assn. Tchrs. of Singing, AAUP, Am. Guild Musical Artists, Dallas Goethe Soc. (bd. dirs.), Pi Kappa Lambda. Home: 3518 Gillon Ave Dallas TX 75205

AKSAMIT, BEVERLY JUNE, county official; b. Cleveland, Mo., Sept. 14, 1936; d. Richard Dwight and Edith Opal (VanEaton) Jacobs; m. Gerald Dale Aksamit, Apr. 13, 1957; children—Jeffrey Lynn, Jonnie Leland, Joel Leslie. Student Kansas City Bus. Coll., 1955. Sec. Bendix Corp., Kansas City, Mo., 1955-57; elected twp. collector Union Twp., Cass County, Mo., 1966-70; elected county treas. Cass County, 1976, 80, 84. Cass County Democratic Committeewoman, 1960-68; active Dem. Women's Club, 1976-85. Mem. Mo. Assn. of Counties (cert. of merit 1982), Bus. and Profl. Women U.S.A., (cert. of recognition 1985). Avocations: reading; swimming; writing; yard work. Home: 305 Lakeview Dr Cleveland MO 64734 Office: County Treas Cass County Seat County Courthouse Harrisonville MO 64701

ALANIS, PATTI MARLENE, auto repair company executive; b. Fresno, Calif., Oct. 18, 1951; d. Verner Walter and Marjorie Elaine (Terkelsen) Klinkby; m. Richard Raymond Alanis, Aug. 4, 1982. Diploma acctg. Heald Four C's, 1971. Bookkeeper Guy Gardner Volkswagen, Inc., Fresno, 1971-73; full charge bookkeeper Hugh A. McCargar, Jr., C.P.A., Fresno, 1973-76; office mgr., acctg. Corcoran Tire and Recapping Co., Corcoran, Calif., 1976-78; acct. J.G. Boswell Co. Inc., Corcoran, 1978-80; acct. Kings County Auditor/Controller, Hanford, Calif., 1980-81; office mgr., asst. mgr. Bookkeepers Bus. Services, Inc., Fresno, 1981; officer mgr., adminstr., co-owner Alanis Paint & Body, Fresno, 1981—. Avocations: photography; cross country skiing; trap/skeet shooting. Home: 1920 E Princeton Fresno CA 93703 Office: Alanis West Belmont Body Shop 1410 W Belmont Fresno CA 93728

ALAUPOVIC, ALEXANDRA VRBANIC, artist, educator; b. Slatina, Yugoslavia, Dec. 21, 1921; d. Joseph and Elizabeta (Papp) Vrbanic; student Bus. Sch., Zagreb, Yugoslavia, 1940-41, Acad. Visual Arts, Zagreb, Yugoslavia, 1944-48; postgrad. Acad. Visual Arts, Prague, Czechoslovakia, 1949, Art Sch., U. Ill., 1959-60; M.F.A., U. Okla., 1966; m. Peter Alaupovic, Mar. 22, 1947; children—Betsy, H. Clark Hyde. Came to U.S., 1958, naturalized, 1964. Sec., Arko Liquer & Yeast Factory and Distillery, Zagreb, 1941-44; instr. U. Okla., Norman, 1964-66; instr. three dimensional design sculpture Oklahoma City U., 1969-77, Okla. Sci. Found., Oklahoma City, 1969-75; one-woman shows at Okla. Art Center, Oklahoma City, U. Okla. Mus. Art, Norman, La Mandragore Internat. Galerie d'Art, Paris, 1984; exhibited art in group shows Springfield (Mo.) Art Mus., Okla. U. Mus., Norman, 7th Ann. Temple Emanuel Brotherhood Arts Festival, Dallas, Salon des Nation, Paris, 1983; represented in permanent collections Okla. U. Art Mus., Okla. State Art Collection, Mercy Health Center. Recipient Jacobson award U. Okla., 1964; hon. mention in sculpture Philbrook Art Center, Tulsa, 1967; 1st sculpture award Philbrook Art Center, Tulsa, 1970. Mem. Internat. Sculpture Center. Home: 11908 N Bryant St Oklahoma City OK 73111 Office: Route 1 Box 167A Oklahoma City OK 73111

ALBANESE, MICHELE OTTOLINO, optometrist; b. Oak Park, Ill., June 1, 1956; d. Michael Joseph and Ines Rosalie (Grolla) Ottolino; m. Lee Alan Albanese, June 7, 1980. B.S., Loyola U.-Chgo., 1978; O.D., Ill. Coll. of Optometry, 1982, now M.B.A. candidate. Optometric asst. to Dr. Edgar Fox, Des Plaines, Ill., 1981-82; eye clinic coordinator Infant Welfare Soc., Chgo., 1982-84; gen. practice optometry, Cicero, Ill., 1983-84; regional ops. mgr., Midwest dir. recruiting Dr. James Ellis & Assocs., Chgo., 1984—; cons. optometrist Eyeland Optical, Chgo., 1983-84; clin. instr. Ill. Coll. Optometry, Chgo., 1984. Mem. Nat. Assn. Female Execs., Am. Pub. Health Assn. Roman Catholic. Home: 2955 N Montclare St Chicago IL 60634 Office: Eyexam 2000 7153 Cermak Rd Berwyn IL 60450

ALBANTIDES, MARGARET ELOISE, button company executive, designer; b. N.Y.C., Oct. 14, 1942; d. Joseph E. and Hilda P. Bezares; m. Danny Albantides, Dec. 12, 1981; 1 child, Adam Edward Rodriguez. Student CUNY, 1960-65; postgrad. LaSalle Extension U., 1972-82, Comml. Art Sch., 1982-83, Ctr. Degree Studies in Bus. Adminstrn., 1984—. Graphic artist, 1981-85; info. asst. East Ramapo Central Sch. Dist., N.Y.; exec., graphic artist The Button Factory, 1981-84; bus. exec., designer cons. Buttons & Graphics, Inc., New City, N.Y., 1984—; lectr., cons. in field. Pub. relations vol. New City Am. Cancer Soc., 1981—; inspector New City Bd. Elections, 1982—; co-chmn. pub. relations com. New City C. of C. 1983-86, sec., 1984-85, trustee, 1985-86. Recipient numerous graphic art awards including 1st place award for graphics N.Y. State Chpt. Nat. Schs. Pub. Relations Assn., 1982, merit award, 1983; 1st place award for graphics Ednl. Press of Am., 1984. Mem. Am. Heart Assn., Nat. Alliance Homebased Bus. Women (steering com.), Am. Inst. Graphic Artists, Nat. Rifle Assn., Ramapough Revolver Club. Club: Spring Valley Racquet and Tennis (Nanuet, N.Y.). Avocations: swimming, dancing, crafts, art, reading. Office: Button & Graphics Inc 39 Carolina Dr New City NY 10956

ALBARELLA, JOAN KATHERINE, journalist, author; b. Buffalo, Sept. 22, 1944; d. John Anthony and Katherine (DiPasqua) A. B.S., SUNY-Buffalo, 1966, M.S.Ed., 1971. Tchr., Elma Central Sch., N.Y., 1966-71; actress, dir. Indigo Prodns., Buffalo, 1975-81; dir. performing arts Baker Hall, Lackawanna, N.Y., 1980-81; prodn. mgr. Real to Reel, Buffalo, 1983-84; journalist Western N.Y. Catholic, Buffalo, 1984—; owner, pub. Alpha Press, Gardenville, N.Y., 1973—. Author: Mirror Me, 1973; Poems for the Asking, 1975. Contbr. articles to poetry jours. Named Poet of Yr., Nat. Poetry Pubs. Assn., 1974, 75, 76. Mem. Poets and Writers, Catholic Press Assn., West Seneca Writers Club (founder, coordinator 1978-84). Roman Catholic. Avocations: fabric art; tutoring.

ALBERGA, ALTA WHEAT, artist; b. Ala.; d. James Richard and Leila Savannah (Sullivan) Wheat; B.A., M.A., Wichita State U., 1954; B.F.A., Washington U., St. Louis, 1961; M.F.A., U. Ill., 1964; m. Alvyn Clyde Alberga, Dec. 3, 1930. Mem. faculty Wichita (Kans.) State U., 1955-56, Webster Coll., St. Louis, 1962, Presbyn. Coll., Clinton, S.C., 1969-74; pvt. art tchr., Greenville, S.C., 1974—; substitute tchr. Greenville County Schs.; tchr. painting Tempo Gallery Sch., Greenville, 1974—, Greenville County Mus. Sch., 1975—; one-woman shows: Greenville County Mus., 1979, Greenville Artists Guild Gallery, 1979, 83, Wichita State U., 1954, St. Louis Artists Guild, 1956, N.C. State U., 1965; group shows include: Pickens County Mus., 1979, Inter/Art 81, Washington 1981, Greenville Artists Guild, 1982, Art/7, Washington, 1983; represented in pvt. collections; bd. dirs. Greenville Artists Guild, 1977-79, pres., 1985; bd. dirs. Guild Gallery, 1978, Guild Greenville Symphony, 1982-83. Recipient Richard K. Weil award St. Louis Mus., 1957; Purchase prize S.C. Arts Commn., 1972. Mem. Artists Equity (pres. St. Louis chpt. 1962), Internat. Platform Assn., Art Students League, Guild Greenville Artists (pres. 1984-85), S.C. Artists Guild, Southeastern Council Printmakers, Greenville Symphony Guild, Kappa Pi, Kappa Delta Pi. Democrat. Home: 11 Overton Dr Greenville SC 29609

ALBERGO, REBECCA MERYL, advertising agency executive; b. N.Y.C., Apr. 27, 1961; d. Norman Albin and Ann (Flaster) Hollander; m. Joseph Michael Albergo, Aug. 12, 1982. B.S. in Biology summa cum laude, Pace U., 1981, postgrad. in mktg., 1986. Account coordinator Rowland Co., N.Y.C., 1982-83, AC&R Advt., N.Y.C., 1983—. Mem. Nat. Assn. Female Execs. Republican. Jewish. Office: AC&R Advertising 16 E 32d St New York NY 10016

ALBERSHEIM, RENEE, information center manager; b. Boston, Mar. 13, 1961; d. Peter and Joyce Elizabeth (Johnson) A. B.A. in Psychology, U. Colo., 1983, M.B.A. in Info. Systems, 1985. Sec. Joint Inst. Lab. Astrophysics, U. Colo., Boulder, 1981-83, film series dir. Program Council U. Colo., 1982-83, dir. Trivia Bowl, 1983-84; mgr. Diners Club Info. Facility, Citicorp/Diners Club, Denver, 1985—. Vice chmn. U. Meml. Ctr. Bd., U. Colo., Boulder, 1983-85. Mem. Assn. M.B.A. Execs., Nat. Assn. Female Execs., Am. Film Inst., Nat. Trust for Hist. Preservation. Republican. Avocations: Mountain climbing; backpacking; stamp collecting; reading; drawing. Home: 9825 E Girard Ave 347 Denver CO 80231 Office: Citicorp/Diners Club 183 Inverness Dr W Englewood CO 80111

ALBERT, BEVERLY FOIT, architect; b. Buffalo, Apr. 28, 1938; d. Franklin and Ruth Marie (Fix) Foit; B.Arch., Cornell U., 1961; M.Arch., SUNY, Buffalo, 1975; Ph.D., Saybrooke Inst., 1978; m. James T. Albert, Dec. 28, 1963; children—James T., Jeffrey J., Richard A. Partner Foit, Baschnagel, Maharan & Albert, Buffalo, 1966-69; assoc. firm Castle, Hamilton, Houston & Lownie, Buffalo, 1970-71; prin. firm Foit-Albert and Assos., Buffalo, 1976—; assoc. prof. Sch. Architecture and Environ. Design, Buffalo, 1969—. Recipient Research award Progressive Architecture mag., 1975. Mem. Soc. Archtl. Historians, Constrn. Specifications Inst., Assn. Bus. and Profl. Women in Constrn., Assn. Minority Enterprises N.Y. Contbr. articles to profl. publs. Home: 10 Maple Dr Orchard Park NY 14127 Office: 700 Main St Buffalo NY 14202

ALBERT, CARRON MAGGI, personnel executive; b. West Trenton, N.J., May 4, 1952; d. Louis P. and Helen (Brailey) Maggi; m. Mark Douglas Albert, May 20, 1978; children—Heather C., Ryan C. B.A. in History, Wheaton Coll., 1974; Supervisory Mgmt. Cert., Rutgers U., 1984; Cert. of Completion, Mgmt. Devel. Inst., 1980; notary pub., N.J. Pub. service trainee N.J. Div. Youth and Family Services, Trenton, 1976-77, sr. personnel asst., 1977-79; labor relations officer N.J. Div. Youth and Family Services, Trenton, 1979-81; personnel asst. II, 1981-84; dir. personnel Thomas A. Edison State Coll., Trenton, 1984—. Mem. Mercer County Republican Capital Club, Lawrenceville, 1984, Ewing Twp. Republican Club, West Trenton, 1983—, Trenton Republican Club, 1983—, Delaware Rise Civic Assn., 1980—; trustee Mercer Regional Blood Council. Recipient Coordinator Award of Merit, Delaware Valley United Way, 1985. Fellow N.J. State Personnel Officers Council; mem. Wheaton Alumni Assn. Republican. Jewish. Avocations: tennis; bridge; swimming; gardening. Home: 20 Willis Dr West Trenton NJ 08628 Office: Thomas A Edison State Coll 101 W State St CN545 Trenton NJ 08625

ALBERT, CECELIA ANNE, editor; b. Balt., Sept. 22, 1954; d. Joseph Kenneth and Marion Cecelia (Fredrick) A.; m. Thomas Dale Reeg, Dec. 18, 1982. B.A. in Philosophy, U. Calif.-Santa Barbara, 1976. Editor Clio Books, ABC-Clio Info. Services Inc., Santa Barbara, 1979-85; assoc. editor ABC-Clio, 1985—, editor Clio Books, 1982-85; mng. editor ABC Polit. Sci., 1980-82; copy editor Coastlines, U. Calif.-Santa Barbara, 1982-85. Democrat. Home: 309 W Arrellaga 1 Santa Barbara CA 93101 Office: ABC-Clio 2040 Alameda Padre Serra Santa Barbara CA 93103

ALBERT, CHARLOTTE ELAINE, roofing company executive, metal company owner; b. Houston, July 1, 1947; d. Adolph Benedict and Myrtis Arlene (Sanders) Schneider; m. William Albert, June 3, 1966; children—William, Lance Matthew. Student South Tex. Jr. Coll., 1965-66, Am. Inst. Banking, 1982-84. Office supr. Gold Lance Corp., Houston, 1968-72; v.p., office mgr. Cliff Homes, Inc., Houston, 1972-80; pub. relations new accts., bus. devel. chmn. First-Taylor Nat. Bank, Taylor, Tex., 1981-84; v.p. A & B Roofing Co., Inc., Taylor, 1979—; co-owner, office mgr. A & B Sheet Metal, Taylor, 1984—; cons. mem. Taylor High Sch. Occupational Investigation Adv. Com., Tex., 1984-85. Active Hidden Valley Elem. Sch. P.T.A., 1979-80, North Houston Nat. Little League Assn., 1978-80, North Harris County Pee Wee Assn., 1978-80; mem., actress Taylor Community Theatre, 1985—; chmn. Taylor Area Cystic Fibrosis, 1985; publicity chmn. Thrall Community 4-H Future Farmers Am. Booster Club, 1985-86; fund raising chmn. Taylor Pop Warner Football. dir. Williamson County Youth Fair Bd., Georgetown, Tex., 1982—. Mem. Taylor Federated Bus. and Profl. Women's Club, 1983—, pres., 1984-85, 1st v.p., 1985-86, Taylor C. of C. Republican. Mem. United Ch. of Christ. Club: Backland Riding. Home: Route 1 Box 53 d Thrall TX 76578 Office: A & B Roofing Co Inc 313 Porter PO Box 105 Taylor TX 76574

ALBERT, DEBORAH GAIL FREIFELD, psychotherapist, educational administrator; b. Bklyn., Dec. 27, 1961; d. Stefan Allen and Sandra (Hirstreet) Freifeld; m. Daniel Albert, July 3, 1983. A.A., St. Pete Jr. Coll., 1979; B.A., U. South Fla., 1981, M.A., 1982, postgrad., 1982—. Cert. tchr., Fla.; Cert. in reality therapy; intermediate tng. in hypnosis. Research asst. indsl. psychology dept. U. S. Fla., Tampa, 1979-81, counselor, instr. counselor edn. dept., 1984—; tchr. Congregation Rodeph Sholom, Tampa, 1980-82; dir., coordinator Women's Peer Counseling Ctr., Tampa, 1980-81; counselor, tchr. Hillel Sch., Tampa, 1981-82; dir. edn. Congregation Schaarai Zedek, Tampa, 1982-85; therapist Discovery Inst., Tampa, 1985—; cons. Pinellas County Schs., Fla., 1985—; instr. continuing edn., Hillsborough Community Coll., Tampa, 1985—. Mem. edn. com. Anti-Defamation League, 1984—, Tampa Jewish Family Service, Tampa, 1983—; mem. young adult div. Jewish Fedn., Tampa, 1983—; bd. dirs. Fla. Ctr. for Reality Therapy, 1984—. Mem. Nat. Assn. Female Execs., Bus. and Profl. Women's Network (bd. dirs.), Fla. Assn. Counseling and Devel., NOW, Tampa Bay Area Assn. Marriage and Family Therapists. Democrat. Jewish. Avocations: aerobics; bicycling; reading; swimming; music. Office: Discovery Inst 1420 W Busch Blvd Tampa FL 33612

ALBERT, JANET CAVINS, personnel director; b. Wilmington, Ohio, June 1, 1948; d. Cloyce L. and Dorothy (Harris) Cavins; m. John Marvin Albert, Sept. 1, 1979. B.B.A., Ft. Lauderdale Coll., 1981; A.S., Broward Community Coll., 1979. Personnel asst. Holy Cross Hosp., Fort Lauderdale, Fla., 1969-72; dir. personnel Cypress Community Hosp., Pompano Beach, Fla., 1972-75; supr. employee relations Harris Corp., Fort Lauderdale, 1975-79; dir. personnel Cypress Community Hosp., 1979-81, North Beach Community Hosp., Fort Lauderdale, 1981—; mem. adv. bd. Healthcare Handbook, Earl R. Voorhies & Assocs., 1984-85. Photographer local Republican campaigns. Mem. Am. Soc. Personnel Adminstrs. (Merit award 1983, Superior Merit award 1984), Personnel Assn. Broward County (pres. 1982-84), S. Fla. Hosp. Personnel Dirs. Assn. (treas. 1981), Fla. Assn. Hosp. Personnel Dirs., Presbyterian. Avocations: photography; travel agent; marching band alumni. Office: North Beach Community Hosp 2835 N Ocean Blvd Fort Lauderdale FL 33308

ALBERT, JANYCE LOUISE, banker; b. Toledo, July 27, 1932; d. Howard C. and Glenola Mae (Masters) Blessing; student Ohio Wesleyan U., 1949-51; B.A., Mich. State U., 1953; M.S., Iowa State U., 1980; m. John R. Albert, Aug. 7, 1954; children—John R., James H. Asst. personnel mgr./tng. supr. Sears, Roebuck & Co., Toledo, 1953-56; tchr. adult edn. Tenafly (N.J.) Public Schs., 1966-70; personnel officer, tng. officer, tng. and edn. mgr. Iowa Dept. Transp., Ames, 1974-77; coll. recruiting coordinator Rockwell Internat., Cedar Rapids, Iowa, 1977-79, engrng. adminstrn. mgr., 1979-80; employee relations and job evaluation analyst Phillips Petroleum Co., Bartlesville Okla., 1980-81; v.p., dir. personnel Republic Bancorp., Tusla, 1981-83; v.p. human resources First Nat. Bank & Trust Co., Rockford, Ill., 1983—. Bd. dirs. United Way of Ames, 1976-77; publicity chmn. Tenafly 300th Anniversary Celebration, 1969; bd. deacons Presbyn. Ch., Ames, 1972-75; mem. adv. council Rockford YWCA; mem. bravo council Rockford Dance Co.; mem. mayor's task force Project Self-Sufficiency. Pres.'s scholar, 1951-53; Phi Kappa Phi Outstanding Student scholar, 1951-53. Mem. Am. Soc. for Personnel Adminstrn., Rockford Personnel Assn., Rockford C. of C., P.E.O., Employee Benefits Assn. No. Ill., Rockford Symphony Guild, Rockford Network (pres. 1985-86), Sigma Epsilon, Alpha Gamma Delta. Presbyterian. Home: 5587 Thunderidge Dr Rockford IL 61107 Office: 401 E State St Rockford IL 61110

ALBERTO, JUNE ELOISE, nursing educator; b. Clarkson, Ky., Oct. 17, 1941; d. Chester Owen and Carrie Edith (Logsdon) McClure; m. Leopoldo Caymo Alberto; children—Darwin Lee McClure Alberto, Leopoldo McClure Alberto. B.S. in Nursing, Spalding Coll., 1973; M.S. in Nursing, U. Ky., 1978; postgrad. in nursing Ind. U., 1984—. Registered nurse, Ky. Staff nurse St. Joseph Infirmary, Louisville, 1973; asst. instr. Spalding Coll., Louisville, 1976-77, instr., 1978-80; staff nurse Baptist Hosp. East, Louisville, summer 1979; asst. prof. nursing U. Louisville, 1980—. HEW nurse grantee, 1972-73. Mem. Ky. League for Nursing, Ky. Thoracic Soc., Nat. League for Nursing, Am. Nurses Assn., Ky. Nurses Assn., Oncology Nursing Soc., Sigma Theta Tau, Delta Epsilon Sigma. Republican. Roman Catholic. Office: Univ Louisville Sch Nursing Health Sciences Center Louisville KY 40292

ALBIN, MAJORIE ANN, banker; b. Tuscola, Ill., Aug. 8, 1930; d. George David and Mae L. (Perry) Martin; student Eastern Ill. U., 1948, 49, Wharton Sch., U. Ill., m. John S. Albin, Sept. 10, 1949; children—Perry S., Martin L., David A. Tax acct. Longview, Ill., 1963—; v.p., chief exec. officer Longview State Bank, 1978—, also dir.; dir. Newman Manor, Inc., Plant Pals, Inc., Longview Capitol Corp., Albi Pork Farm, Inc. Bd. dirs. Jarman Hosp., Tuscola, Continental Manor Nursing Home, Newman, Ill. Office: Longview State Bank Box 37 Longview IL 61852

ALBRECHT, GEORGENE LEE, science writer, graphic illustrator, editor; b. Pitts., Oct. 13, 1941; d. Harvey Howard and Effie Caroline (Ishman) Hetrick; m. Lawrence John Albrecht, Aug. 24, 1963; children—Brian James, Christopher Alan. Student in grahic art Inst. Pitts., 1959-61. Illustrator B K & T Advt., Pitts., 1961-63; free-lance artist, 1970-80; hort. columnist Gesneriad Saintpaulia News, Knoxville, Tenn., 1981—, contbg. editor, illustrator, 1981—, assoc. editor, Greenwood, Ind., 1985—; bd. dirs. Saintpaulia Internat. Knoxville, 1982-83, Cons., mem. Pitts. Civic Garden Ctr., 1984. Recipient Best in Show award Gesneriad Soc. Internat. Show, Indpls., 1983, Louisville, 1984, French Lick, Ind., 1985. Mem. Am. Orchid Soc., Am. Gloxinia and Gesneriad Soc., Orchid Soc. Western Pa. (dir. 1983-84). Democrat. Office: Gesneriad Saintpaulia News PO Box 102 Greenwood IN 46142

ALBRECHT, JANE KATHERINE, lawyer; b. St. Louis, Aug. 31, 1952; d. Edgar Samuel and Geraldine (Hendricks) A. B.S. magna cum laude, Regis Coll., 1974; J.D., Georgetown U., 1980. Bar: D.C. 1980, U.S. Ct. Appeals (fed. cir.) 1981, U.S. Ct. Internat. Trade 1981, U.S. Dist. Ct. D.C. 1982, Tax auditor IRS, St. Louis, 1975-77; law clk. Solicitor's Office, Gen. Legal Services, Dept. Interior, Washington, 1979; research asst. Georgetown U. Law Ctr., Washington, 1978-80; atty. Office Gen. Counsel, U.S. Internat. Trade Commn., Washington, 1980-84; assoc. Verner, Lippert, Bernhard & McPherson, Washington, 1984-85, Dewey, Ballantine, Bushby, Palmer and Wood, 1985—. Mem. Washington Fgn. Law Soc.

ALBRIGHT, DOROTHY JANE, sales and marketing executive; b. Charlotte, N.C., Sept. 16, 1945; d. George Franklin and Dorothy (Severs) A. Student Queens Coll., Charlotte, N.C., 1963-66. Mgr. sales and mktg. J.M. Garner Devel., Atlanta, 1978-82; account exec. sales and mktg. Bryant Lithographing, Atlanta, 1982-83; sr. account mgr. sales and mktg. COMPACK-Comprehensive Packaging, Atlanta, 1983-85; sales and mktg. mgr. Brock, Green & Assocs., Atlanta, 1985—. Bd. dirs. High Mus. Art, Atlanta, 1981-85. Mem. Am. Mktg. Assn. (bd. dirs. Atlanta chpt. 1983-84, sec. 1984-85, v.p. 1985-86). Republican. Episcopalian. Office: Brock Green and Assocs 2110 Powers Ferry Rd Suite 311 Atlanta GA 30339

ALBRIGHT, MADELEINE KORBEL, political scientist, educator; b. Prague, Czechoslovakia, May 15, 1937; d. Josef and Anna (Speeglova) Korbel; B.A. with honors, Wellesley Coll., 1959; M.A., Columbia U., 1968, cert. Russian Inst., 1968, Ph.D., 1976; children—Anne Korbel, Alice Patterson, Katharine Medill. Chief legis. asst. U.S. Senator Muskie, 1976-78; mem. staff NSC, 1978-81; fellow Woodrow Wilson Internat. Center for Scholars, Washington, 1980-81. Donner prof. internat. affairs and dir. women in fgn. service Sch. Fgn. Service, Georgetown U., 1982—; fgn. policy advisor Mondale for Pres. Campaign, 1984; to Geraldine A. Ferraro, 1984. Vice chair. Nat.

Democratic Inst. for Internat. Affairs, Washington, 1984—; trustee Wellesley Coll., 1983—; mem. U.S. Nat. Commn. for UNESCO; bd. dirs. Atlantic Council for U.S., 1984—, Ctr. for Nat. Policy; trustee Washington Urban League, 1981-84; bd. dirs. Beauvoir Sch., Washington, 1968-76, chmn., 1972-76; mem. exec. com. Chpt. of Washington Cathedral, 1972-76, mem., 1978—; mem. Black Student Fund Bd. Trustees, 1969-78, 81—; mem. exec. com. D.C. Citizens Better Public Edn., 1975-76; trustee Democratic Forum, 1976-78, Williams Coll., 1978-82; chmn. fgn. relations task force, polit. action com. Women's Nat. Dem. Club, 1975-76; Dem. campaign aide U.S. senators Mondale, 1972, Stevenson, 1974; Washington coordinator Maine for Muskie, 1975-76. Mem. Council Fgn. Relations, Am. Polit. Sci. Assn., Czeckoslovak Soc. Arts and Scis. Am., Women's Nat. Dem. Clubs, Am. Assn. Advancement Slavic Studies. Author: Poland, the Role of the Press in Political Change, 1983. Office: Sch Fgn Service Georgetown Univ Washington DC 20057

ALBRO, JOYCE MARIE, lawyer, judge; b. Louisville, June 10, 1951; d. Charles Wesley and Mary Rose (Anderson) Albro; m. H. Gene Taylor, Aug. 6, 1977. B.A., Eastern Ky. U., 1973; J.D., U. Ky., 1978. Bar: Ky. 1978. Sole practice, Frankfort, Ky., 1978-84; dist. judge Franklin County Cts., Frankfort, 1984—. Pres. Franklin County Pub. Defender Corp., Frankfort, 1980-81, 82-83. Mem. Franklin County Bar Assn. (sec./treas. 1981-82). Clubs: Frankfort Younger Women's (pub. affairs chmn. 1981), Democratic Women's (by-laws chmn. 1984). Home: 208 Hawthorne Dr Frankfort KY 40601 Office: PO Box 894 Frankfort KY 40602

ALCANTARA, ANITA LUISA, human resources consultant; b. Chgo., May 30, 1942; d. Francisco B. and Eleanor E. (Locke) A. A.A., Wright City Coll., 1962; B.Ed., Northeastern Ill. U., 1964. Field dir., ednl. services dir. Girl Scouts of Chgo., 1971-79, nat. tng. coordinator Girl Scouts U.S.A., N.Y.C., 1979-84; mgmt. devel. cons. The Equitable Corp., N.Y.C., 1984; adminstr. United Ch. of Rogers Park, Chgo., 1985—; cons. Contact Chgo., 1985—, Yule connection mgr., 1985-86. Author: You Make the Difference, Leaders' Guide; Council Guide, 1980. Bd. dirs. Rogers Park Children's Learning Ctr., 1985—. Recipient Chgo. Youth award Mayor's Commn. Youth Welfare, 1968; award Chgo. Pub. Library, 1970, Girl Scouts Chgo., 1975. Mem. Am. Mgmt. Assns., Nat. Assn. Female Execs., Ill. Tng. and Devel. Assn. Democrat. Methodist. Home: 1327 W Lunt Apt 2A Chicago IL 60626 Office: 1545 W Morse Ave Chicago IL 60626

ALCON, SONJA LEE DE BEY RYAN, medical social worker; b. Orange City, Iowa, Aug. 2, 1937; d. Albert Lee Gerard and Clarice Victoria (Brown) deBey; B.A., Western Md. Coll., 1959; M.S.W., U. Md., 1973; m. Richard J. Gebhardt, June 6, 1959; children—Russell, Cheryl, Kurt; m. George W. Ryan, Dec. 28, 1968; 1 dau., Alanna (dec.); m. David E. Alcon, July 20, 1985. Caseworker, Springfield State Hosp., Sykesville, Md., 1959-61; dir. social work dept. Hanover (Pa.) Gen. Hosp., 1966—; field instr. U. Md. Sch. Social Work; cons. Golden Age Nursing Home, Hanover, 1973-76, Carlisle (Pa.) Hosp., 1974-78, Hanover Vis. Nurse Assn., 1977-83; mem. profl. adv. com. Vis. Nurse Assn. of Hanover and Spring Grove, Inc., 1986-89; mem. social work adv. council Western Md. Coll., 1979, 80. Bd. dirs. Hospice of York, 1980-82, Hanover chpt. ARC, 1976-79, Adams-Hanover Mental Health, 1973-76; pres. Human Services Orgn., 1980, v.p., 1985-86; mem. adv. council Hanover Hospice Adv. Council, 1982-85; treas. Hanover Community Progress Com., 1976-80; mem. Adams-Hanover Sheltered Workshop Com., 1968-70; bd. dirs. Hanover Community Players, 1974-77, sec., 1982; organizer local chpt. Make Today Count and Preemie Parent Support Group, 1979; initiator Children's Cardiac Fund, 1979; mem. Hanover Oratorio Soc., 1964—; active YWCA, 1979-84; co-organizer Adams-Hanover chpt. Compassionate Friends, 1983; mem. vestry All Saints Episcopal Ch., 1973-74, 76-79, 83-86, vestry sec., 1975, diocesan del. Central Pa., 1978, 80-86, mem. altar guild, 1968—, treas. ch. women, 1979-83. Recipient York Daily Record Exceptional Citizen award, 1979, Spl. Recognition cert. Col. Richard McAllister chpt. DAR, 1980. Mem. Nat. Assn. Social Workers, Acad. Cert. Social Workers, Am. Hosp. Assn. Soc. Hosp. Social Work Dirs., Central Pa. Hosp. Social Workers (treas. 1981-85), Hosp. Assn. of Pa. Soc. for Hosp. Social Work Dirs., U. Md. Alumni Assn. (bd. dirs. 1983). Lodges: Order Eastern Star (worthy matron 1985-86), Order of Amaranth, White Shrine, Commandery Aux., Elks Aux. Home: 109 Frederick St Hanover PA 17331 Office: Hanover Gen Hosp 300 Highland Ave Hanover PA 17331

ALCOTT, SUSAN, writer, editor, public relations specialist; asst.; b. Los Angeles, June 7, 1940; d. William Kenneth and Hazel Stella (Pearson) Allin; student Los Angeles Harbor Coll., 1958-59, El Camino Coll., 1959-61, Calif. State U., 1961-64, Writers Guild Am. West, Inc., 1970-74, Arthur Alsberg's Advanced Screenwriting Workshop, 1980-81; div. Teaching asst., lab. technician Calif. State U., Los Angeles, 1963-64; with Musifon, Inc., Los Angeles, 1965-69; with Mickey Garrett & Assos., Public Relations, Los Angeles, 1967-68; freelance reader Screen Gems TV, Burbank, Calif., 1972; corp. sec.-treas., adminstrv. asst., dir. Don Perry Enterprises, Inc., Los Angeles, 1969-80; free-lance bus. and public relations writing service Susan Alcott's Scribe Services Ltd., Sherman Oaks, Calif., 1981—; pub. relations adminstr., editor, feature writer the Spl. Friends of Kenny Rogers Kenny Rogers Prodns. Inc., Los Angeles, 1981—; actress theatres So. Calif.; actress films, TV, comml s; poetry published Poetry Parade mag., Writers Guild Am. West Inc, newspapers; contbr. Ellery Queen Mystery Mag.;lyricist Nobody's Child. Recipient Writers Guild Found. award, 1972, cert., 1974. Mem. ASCAP, Screen Actors Guild, Am. Film Inst., Nat. Assn. Female Execs., Planetary Soc. Editor: Patterns, 1982.

ALDAVE, BARBARA BADER, educator, lawyer; b. Tacoma, Dec. 28, 1938; d. Fred A. and Patricia W. (Burns) Bader; B.S. (Nat. Merit scholar), Stanford U., 1960; J.D., U. Calif., Berkeley, 1966; m. Ralph Theodore Aldave, Apr. 2, 1966; children—Anna Marie, Anthony John. Bar: Oreg. 1966, Tex. 1982; assoc. law firm, Eugene, 1967-70; asst. prof. U. Oreg., 1970-73; vis. prof. U. Calif., Berkeley, 1973-74; vis. prof., asst. prof. to prof. U. Tex., Austin, 1974—, co-holder James R. Dougherty chair for faculty excellence, 1981-82, Piper prof., 1982, Joe A. Worsham Centennial prof., 1984—; disting. vis. prof. Northeastern U., 1985-86. Bd. dirs. Network, Austin Council on Fgn. Relations, NETWORK, Women's Advocacy Project. Recipient Teaching Excellence award U. Tex. Student Bar Assn., 1976, Teaching Excellence award Chicano Law Students Assn. of U. Tex., 1984, 1st ann. appreciation award Thurgood Marshall Legal Soc. of U. Tex., 1979, 81, 85. Mem. ABA (com. on corp. laws sect. corp., banking and bus. law), Stanford Alumni Assn., Am. Cath. Lay Network, Amnesty Internat. U.S.A., Bread for the World, Gray Panthers, United Campuses To Prevent Nuclear War, Lawyers Alliance for Nuclear Arms Control, Nat. IMPACT, Nat. Lawyers Guild, Pax Christi, U.S.A.-U.S.S.R. Citizens' Dialogue, Order of Coif, Phi Delta Phi, Iota Sigma Pi, Omicron Delta Kappa. Roman Catholic. Home: 803 Cedar Park Dr Austin TX 78746 Office: 727 E 26th St Austin TX 78705

ALDEGHI, JUDITH ANN, college public relations executive; b. Bklyn., Nov. 3, 1952; d. Dominick John and Vera Maxine (Firebaugh) Guido; m. Jonathan Robin Aldeghi, May 14, 1982. B.A., Glassboro State Coll., 1974, M.A., 1981. Editorial asst., reporter Cam-Glo Newspapers, Turnersville, N.J., 1972-80; elem. tchr. Maple Shade Pub. Schs., N.J., 1974-80; grad. asst. Ednl. Press Assn., Glassboro, N.J., 1980-81; asst. pub. relations mgr. Tropicana Hotel/Casino, Atlantic City, 1981-82; dir. pub. relations and publs. Spring Garden Coll., Phila., 1982—. Mem. Phila. Pub. Relations Assn., Council for Advancement and Support Edn., Coll. and Univ. Pub. Relations Assn. Pa., Pa. Hort. Soc. Avocations: skiing, traveling, gardening, needlework. Office: Spring Garden Coll 7500 Germantown Ave Philadelphia PA 19119

ALDEN, STACIA, board game manufacturing company executive; b. St. Louis, June 16, 1945; d. Henry J. and Mildred (Judkins) Ballas; m. Harvey A. Alden, Sept. 28, 1963 (div. Jan. 1979); children—Brian Gerald, Michael Todd. Student pub. schs. Grandview, Mo. Pres., owner S. Alden Inc., Kansas City, Mo., 1980—. Patentee Beverly Hills Game, The Plaza, The Golden Triangle, L.V. The Game, N.Y.C. The Big Apple. Sec., v.p. Boy Scouts Am., 1976-83; pres., v.p. PTA, 1976-83. Mem. Mchts. Assn. (v.p. 1979-82), Econ. Devel. Com. (exec. com. 1979-81). Home and Office: 2401 Martha Truman Rd Kansas City MO 64131

ALDERDICE, SUNNY PURL, newspaper editor; b. Dallas, Dec. 21, 1930; d. George Clark Purl and Bernice (Dillard) Purl Blanton; m. Barham Alderdice, Dec. 21, 1948; children—Barbara Emily Alderdice Anthony. Grad. Midlothian High Sch., 1948. Writer, editor Midlothian Mirror (Tex.), 1969—. Recipient various awards Texas Press, 1972—. Mem. park bd. Midlothian, Tex., 1975-79; mem. community edn. adv. bd., Midlothian, 1979-82; mem. sr. citizen adv. bd., Midlothian, 1979—; mem. home rule charter com., Midlothian, 1980; founder Midlothian Ch. Women, 1980—; life mem. Midlothian PTA, 1972. Sunny Alderdice Day proclaimed by City of Midlothian, 1973. Mem. Midlothian Cemetery Assn. Presbyterian. Club: Ladies of Leaf. Office: Midlothian Mirror 214 W Ave F PO Box 70 Midlothian TX 76065

ALDERMAN, DIXIE S., lawyer, stockbroker; b. Gainesville, Fla., Dec. 13, 1952; d. Earley DeWitt and Elizabeth Mae (Luckey) McFarland; m. James A. Alderman, II, Sept. 4, 1976. B.A., U. Fla.-Gainesville, 1974, J.D., 1976; diploma Instytutem Nauk Prawnych Polskiej Akademii Nauk, Warsaw, Poland, 1975. Bar: Fla. 1977. Corp. counsel Burger King Corp., Miami, 1978-80; sole practice St. Petersburg, Fla., 1980-82; assoc. Blackwell, Walker, Gray, Powers, Flick & Hoehl, Tampa, Fla., 1982—; dir. Premier Developers, Inc., Tampa, Premier Real Estate Services, Inc., Tampa. Mem. Fla. Bar Assn., Hillsborough County Bar Assn., Phi Beta Kappa, Phi Delta Phi (v.p. 1975-76).

ALDERMAN, MINNIS AMELIA, psychologist, business executive; b. Douglas, Ga., Oct. 14, 1928; d. Louis Cleveland and Minnis (Wooten) A.; A.B., Ga. Coll. at Milledgeville, 1949; M.A., Murray State U., 1960; fellow U. Utah, summers 1974, 75. Camp counselor Camp Sloan, Conn., summer 1949; music dir. Umatilla (Fla.) public sch., 1949-50, Campbell High Sch., Fairburn, Ga., 1950-54; music and drama dir., tchr. English and speech Wells (Nev.) High Sch., 1954-59; tchr. English and history Sinking Fork Sch., Hopkinsville, Ky., 1960; counselor White Pine High Sch., Ely, Nev., 1960-68; instr. psychology, guidance and counseling Murray (Ky.) State U., summers 1961, 62; instr. guidance and counseling U. Nev. Extension, 1963-68, mem. home econs. adv. bd., 1977—; psychologist Ely Mental Health Center, 1969-75, Nev. Job Service, 1975-79; owner Minisizer Exercising Salon, 1969-71, Minimimeo Mimeographing, 1969—, Knit Knook, 1969—, Gift Gamut, 1977—, Trip and Travel Agy., 1983-86, City Service Sta.; pres. Creative Crafters Gift Shoppe; sec.-treas. Great Basin Enterprises Corp., 1969-71; pvt. tchr. piano, violin, voice, 1981—; band dir. Sacred Heart Sch., 1982—; test supt. Coll. Entrance Exam. Bd. and Am. Coll. Testing, 1960-68. Pres. White Pine County Mental Health Assn., 1960-63, 78—; mem. Gov.'s Mental Health State Commn., 1963-65; bd. dirs. White Pine County Sch. Employees Fed. Credit Union, 1961-68, pres., 1963-68; 2d v.p. White Pine Community Concert Assn., 1965-67, drive chmn., 1981—, pres., 1967, 85—, treas., 1975-79; dir. Community Choir, 1962—; mem. Gov.'s Commn. on Status Women, 1968-72; sec.-treas. White Pine Rehab. Tng. Center for Retarded Persons, 1973-75; dir. Ret. Sr. Vol. Program, 1973-74; vice chmn. Great Basin Health Council, 1973-75; sec.-treas. Great Basin chpt. Nev. Employees Assn.; vice chmn. White Pine Council on Alcoholism and Drug Abuse, 1975-76, chmn., 1976-77; bd. dirs. White Pine chpt. ARC, 1976—, Nev. Hwy. Safety Leaders, 1977-81; grants author, originator Community Tng. Center for Retarded People, 1972, Ret. Sr. Vol. Program, 1974, Nutrition Program for Sr. Citizens, 1974, Sr. Citizens Center, 1974, Home Repairs for Sr. Citizens, 1974, Sr. Citizens Home Assistance Program, 1977, Creative Crafters Assos., 1976; mem. Nev. Gov.'s Commn. on Hwy. Safety, 1979-81; mem. White Pine Counties Adv. Bd. Sr. Citizens, 1982-86, chmn., 1983-86; reporter precinct ABC News, 1966; mem. adv. bd. U. Nev. Extension Service, 1977—; mem. adv. bd. for sr. citizens Lincoln and White Pine counties, 1982-86; mem. Commn. on Status and Role of Women, Calif.-Nev. ann. conf. United Meth. Ch., 1981. Mem. NEA (life), Nev. Edn. Assn., Counselors on Alcoholism, Addictions and Related Dependencies, AAUW (pres. 1964-65, state area rep. in edn. 1965-67; state implementation chmn. edn. 1967-69, state area adviser 1969-73, state handbook editor 1973-75), Bus. and Profl. Women's Club (1st v.p. 1965-66, pres. 1966-68, 85—, asst. dist. dir. 1967-68, state civic participation chmn. 1967-68, dist. dir. 1968-70, state 2d v.p. 1969-70, state rec. sec. 1968-69, state 1st v.p. 1970-71, state pres.-elect 1971-72, state pres. 1972-73), DAR, Internat. Platform Assn., Mensa (test adminstr. 1966—), Am. Personnel and Guidance Assn. (state memberships chmn. 1962-65), Am. Sch. Counselors Assn., Nat. Vocat. Counselors Assn., Nat. Fedn. Ind. Bus. (dist. chmn. 1971—), Nat. Assn. Women Deans and Counselors, Nat. Assn. Female Execs., NOW, Delta Kappa Gamma (2d v.p. 1964-66, state program chmn. 1965-69, 1st v.p. 1966-68, state 1st v.p. 1967-69, chpt. pres. 1968-72, state pres. 1969-71), Gen. Fedn. Women's Clubs (dist. pres. 1970-75, state chmn. CARE 1972-76), Beta Sigma Phi (chpt. sponsor 1970-72). Clubs: White Pine Knife and Fork (2d v.p. 1960-69, 1st v.p. 1969-70, pres. 1970-71, sec.-treas. 1978—), Ely Woman's (pres. 1969-70). Methodist (lay speaker 1967—, lay leader to regional conf. 1977—, choir dir. 1960-84). Author: Handbook for Counselors; Guidance Handbook for Teachers; Guidance Handbook for Administrators; Discipline Handbook; Handbook Workshop Career Development, also articles. Home: 945 Ave H PO Box 457 East Ely NV 89315 Office: Murry St PO Box 457 East Ely NV 89301 also 1113 Ave F PO Box 323 East Ely NV 89315

ALDERSON, MARGARET NORTHROP, arts administrator, educator, artist; b. Washington, Nov. 28, 1936; d. Vernon D. and Margaret (Lloyd) Northrop; m. Donald Marr Alderson, Jr., June 4, 1955; children—Donald Marr III, Barbara Lynn Hennesy, Brian, Graham. Student George Washington U., 1954-55; A.A., Monterey Peninsula Jr. Coll., 1962. Staff, tchr. Galerie Jaclande, Springfield, Va. 1972-73; artist/tchr. Studio 7, Torpedo Factory Art Ctr., Alexandria, 1974—, dir. ctr., 1979-85; tchr. Fairfax County Recreation, 1972-73, Art League Schs., Alexandria, 1978—; cons. in field; project supr. City of Alexandria for Torpedo Factory Art Ctr., 1978-83; ptnr. Soho Hubris Art Gallery (N.Y.), 1977-78; one woman shows at Way Up Gallery, Livermore, Calif., 1971, Lynchburg Coll. (Va.), 1978, Farm House Gallery, Rehobeth, Del., 1979, Art League Gallery, Alexandria, Va., 1980, 86; exhibited in group shows at Art League Gallery, Alexandria, 1972—; represented in permanent collections Phillip Morse Collection, United Va. Bank, CSX Corp., Office U.S. Atty. Gen., Office of Ins. Gen. EPA, Aerospace Corp. Festival chmn. City Festival Cultural Arts, Livermore, Calif., 1971; bd. dirs., juror Cultural Alliance, 1982—; bd. dirs. Torpedo Factory Art Ctr., 1978— mem. Partner's for Liveable Places, 1979—. Recipient 1st Place Awards in Watercolor, Art League, 1975, 76, 77, also numerous purchase awards. Mem. Va. Watercolor Soc. (pres. 1982, 1st place awards ann. exhibit 1980, 82), Potomac Valley Watercolorists (pres. 1978), Torpedo Factory Artists Assn. (pres. 1977-78), Springfield Art Guild (pres. 1977), Artists Equity, Am. Council on Arts, Am. Watercolor Soc., Am. Council of Univ. and Community Arts Ctrs., Nat. League Am. Pen Women, Am. Mgmt. Assn., Nat. Historic Trust. Republican. Home: 2204 Windsor Rd Alexandria VA 22307 Studio: Studio 7 Torpedo Factory Art Ctr 105 N Union St Alexandria VA 22314

ALDOUS, ELAINE MARIE, blood bank facility administrator; b. Isabell, S.D., Aug. 6, 1931; d. August G. Opp and Julia Elizabeth (Samuelson) Nightengale; m. Richard Robert O'Leary, July 23, 1946 (div. 1953); children—Sherry, Kathy, Vicky; m. 2d, James Henry Aldous, June 6, 1964 (dec.). Cert. in motel-hotel mgmt. Whitcomb Sch. Ltd., Clearwater, Fla., 1968; A.A., Fla. Jr. Coll. at Jacksonville, 1975; B.A. cum laude, U. North Fla., 1978. Self-employed in clerical mgmt., Aberdeen, S.D., 1947-50; gen. office mgr. Lavigne Ranches, Calexico, Calif., 1950-56; office mgr. Stan's Furniture Inc., El Centro, Calif., 1956-60; cashier mgr. Interstate Bakeries Corp., Glendale, Calif., 1960-64; acctg. tax/price cons. Standard Oil of Calif., Jacksonville, Fla., 1965-69, Louisville, 1969-73; personnel mgr. Jacksonville Blood Bank, 1976—. Mem. U. North Fla. Found. Inc., Jacksonville, 1978—; treas. Springfield Preservation and Restoration Soc., Jacksonville, 1982; activities dir. El Centro Recreation Dept., 1958-60. Mem. Am. Soc. Personnel Adminstrn. (cert.), N.E. Fla. Hosp. Personnel Assn., Jacksonville Personnel Women, Tiquana Jr. C. of C. of Mex. (hon.). Home: 159 Cottage Ave Jacksonville FL 32206 Office: Jacksonville Blood Bank PO Box 2758 Jacksonville FL 32203

ALDREDGE, THEONI VACHLIOTIS, costume designer; b. Athens, Greece, Aug. 22, 1932; d. Gen. Athanasios and Meropi (Gregoriades) Vachliotis; student Am. Sch., Athens, Goodman Theatre, Chgo., 1949-53; H.L.D. (hon.), De Paul U., 1985; m. Thomas E. Aldredge, Dec. 10, 1953. Mem. design staff Goodman Theatre, 1951-53; head designer N.Y. Shakespeare Festival, 1962—; designer numerous Broadway shows, Off Broadway shows, ballet, opera, television spls.; films include Great Gatsby, Network, Cheap Detective, Fury, Eyes of Laura Mars, The Champ, The Rose, Semi-Tough, You're a Big Boy Now; Broadway shows include Sweet Bird of Youth, Mary Mary, Who's Afraid of Virginia Wolf, A Delicate Balance, Championship Season, Sticks and Bones, Two Gentlemen of Verona, Three Penny Opera, A Chorus Line (Theatre World award 1976), Annie, Ballroom, Grand Tour, Dream Girls, 42nd Street, La Cage aux Folles, The Rink. Recipient Brit. Motion Picture Acad. award for The Great Gatsby, 1976; Obie award for Disting. Service to Off Broadway Theatre, Village Voice, 1976; Antoinette Perry award for Annie, 1977, for Barnum, 1981, for La Cage aux Folles, 1983; Maharam award for Peer Gynt; Drama Desk award for 42nd Street, 1981; numerous other Drama Desk and Critics awards. Mem. United Scenic Artists, Costume Designers Guild, Acad. Motion Picture Arts Scis. (Oscar award Great Gatsby 1975). Office: 890 Broadway New York NY 10006

ALDRICH, ANN, federal judge; b. 1927; children—James Mooney, Allen Mooney, Martin, William. Student Columbia U.; LL.B., NYU, 1950, LL.M., 1964, J.S.D., 1967. Mem. legal staff Internat. Bank for Reconstruction and Devel., 1951-52; pvt. practice, Washington, 1952-53, Darien, Conn., 1961-68; mem. legal staff FCC, 1953-60; prof. law Cleve. State U., 1968-80; judge U.S. Dist. Ct. (no. dist.) Ohio, 1980—; bd. visitors Case Western Res. U. Law Sch. Bd. dirs. Cleve. Play House, Cleve. Sun Players. Mem. Fed. Bar Assn., Cleve. Bar Assn., Nat. Assn. Women Judges. Office: 212 US Courthouse 201 Superior Ave Cleveland OH 44114

ALDRICH, LYNNE MERRILL, university administrator; b. Detroit, July 23, 1946; d. Claude E. and Irene (Suzanne) (Keil) Gardner; A.B. in Polit. Sci., W. Va. U., 1969; postgrad. Wayne State U. Asst., then acting area mgr. Fotomat Corp., Detroit, 1969-70; acad. service officer dept. biol. scis. Wayne State U., 1970-83; exec. asst. to sr. v.p. univ. relations Wayne State Univ., 1983—. Bd. dirs., sec. LaSalle Townhouse Coop. Assn., 1978-82. Recipient Humanitarian award Wayne State U., 1980, 81, bd. govs. Recognition Award Wayne State U., 1982. Mem. Nat. Assn. Female Execs. Mich. Council Advancement and Support Edn., AAUW (dir. Mich. div. bd., pres. 1986-88), Leadership Detroit VI. Club: Wayne State U. Faculty, Women's Econ. (Detroit). Office: Univ Relations Wayne State U Detroit MI 48202

ALDRICH, MICHELE L., historian, archivist; b Seattle, Oct. 6, 1942; d. Jean and Marion (Deasy) La Clergue; m. Mark Aldrich, Sept. 4, 1965. B.A., U. Calif.-Berkeley, 1964; Ph.D., U. Tex., 1974. Lectr., Smith Coll., Northampton, Mass., 1969-70; staff mem. Valley Women's Ctr., Northampton, 1970-73; asst. editor Henry Papers, Smithsonian Instn., Washington, 1974-75; field worker Women's History Survey, Mpls., 1976-77; archivist, project dir., mgr. computer services AAAS, Washington, 1977—; cons. Aaron Burr Papers, N.Y.C., 1975-76; research assoc. Calif. Acad. Scis., San Francisco, 1980—. Editor: (with N. Reingold, A. Molella) Joseph Henry Papers, 1975; (with A. Leviton, P. Rodda, E. Yochelson) Frontiers of Geology, 1982; author: (with P.Q. Hall) Programs in Science for Women, 1980; (with A. Leviton) John Anderson's Herpetology of Arabia, 1984; contbr. articles to profl. jours. U. Tex. fellow, Austin, 1965-66; NSF fellow, 1967-68. Fellow AAAS; mem. Soc. Am. Archivists, Geol. Soc. Am. (chair history div. 1979-80, sec.-treas. 1984-86), History Sci. Soc. (publicity officer 1978-83, co-chmn. women's com. 1984-86). Democrat. Home: 24 Elm St Hatfield MA 01038 Office: AAAS 1333 H St NW Washington DC 20005

ALDRICH, STEPHANIE RAE, chemist; b. Akron, Ohio, June 26, 1944; d. Steven Paul and Fannie Alberta (Beck) Hegedus; student Purdue U., South Bend (Ind.) Campus, evenings 1972-73; children—Todd Clifton, Robert LeRoy. Tchr. reality therapy, activities dir. Rehab. Center, Michigan City, Ind., 1972-74; metallurgy, sand control apprentice Josam Mfg. Co., Michigan City, 1978-79; with Manley Bros. div. Brit. Indsl. Sands, Ltd., Chesterton, Ind., 1979—, analytical chemist, mgr. quality control, research and devel. labs., 1980—. Mem. AAAS. Democrat. Lutheran. Contbr. poetry to various publs. Home: 1215 Earl Rd Michigan City IN 46360 Office: Manley Bros 128 S 15th St Chesterton IN 46304

ALDRIDGE, MARY HENNEN DELLINGER, chemistry educator; b. Sevier County, Ark., Jan. 11, 1919; d. Sadie Reeves Bonnie Dellinger; m. Alfred Owen Aldridge, May 18, 1941 (div. 1956); 1 child, Cecily Joan Aldridge Ward. B.S. in Chemistry, U. Ga., 1939; M.A. in Chemistry, Duke U., 1941; Ph.D. in Biochemistry, Georgetown U., 1954. Analytical chemist E.I. duPont de Nemours & Co., Buffalo, 1941-47; asst. prof. U. Md., College Park, 1947-55; assoc. prof. Am. U., Washington, 1955-62, prof. chemistry, 1962—, chmn. dept., 1979-83; pres. Washington Chromotography Discussion Group, 1974-75. Contbr. articles to profl. jours. Bd. dirs. Nat. Found. Cancer Research, Bethesda, Md., 1977—. Recipient Profl. Service award Alpha Chi Sigma, 1977; Charles L. Gordon Meml. award Chem. Soc. Washington, 1981; Honor Service award D.C. Inst. Am. Inst. Chemists, 1982. Mem. Am. Chem. Soc. (joint) bd.-council com. 1971-74), Washington Acad. Scis. (pres. 1978-79). Democrat. Methodist. Avocations: tennis; sailing. Home: 3209 D Sutton Pl NW Washington DC 20016 Office: Am Univ 4400 Massachusetts Ave NW Washington DC 20016

ALDRIDGE, RITA MARY, financial manager; b. N.Y.C., July 4, 1926; d. Howard and Helen Valentine (Maune) Dougherty; 1 dau., Jane Kathryn Aldridge Cooper. Student Fordham U. Exec. asst. Real Estate, N.Y.C., 1959-62; adminstrv. asst. Cornell U. Med. Coll., N.Y.C., 1964-72, adminstrv. mgr., 1972-77, fin. mgr., 1977—, mem. grievance panel, 1974—. Mem. Nat. Assn. Female Execs., Coll. Art Assn. Office: Cornell Univ Med Coll 1300 York Ave New York NY 10021

ALEMAN, MINDY R., advertising and public relations executive, freelance writer; b. N.Y.C., Nov. 23, 1950; d. Lionel Luskin and Jocelyn (Cohen) L.; m. Gary Aleman, Aug. 27, 1983. B.A., U. Akron, 1972, M.A., 1975. Instr. speech U. Akron, 1973-83; car salesperson Dave Towell Cadillac, Akron, 1977-79, mgr. fin. and ins., 1979; account exec., pub. relations dir. Loos, Edwards & Sexauer, Akron, 1980-82; mktg. services coordinator Century Products, Stow, Ohio, 1982-83; mgr. advt., pub. relations Century Products, Gerber Furniture Group, Stow, 1983—. Author: (play) Danny's Choice, 1972. Recipient various awards Am. Advt. Fedn., 1984, 86. Mem. Am. Mktg. Assn., Pub. Relations Soc. Am. (accredited mem.), Akron Advt. Club (various awards 1983-86), Am. Advt. Fed. (Addy awards 5th dist. 1984, 86), Akron Art Mus. Contemporaries. Office: Century Products Inc 1366 Commerce Dr Stow OH 44224

ALENIER, KARREN LALONDE, management analyst, poet; b. Cheverly, Md., May 7, 1947; d. Rona Lee (Bass) Keenan; 1 child, Ivan Ascher. B.A. with honors, U. Md., 1969. Computer programmer Fed. Power Commn., Washington, 1969-71; computer systems analyst Labor Dept., Washington, 1972-77; computer specialist Energy Dept., Washington, 1977-82; mgmt. analyst Justice Dept., Washington, 1982—; dir. Word Works, Inc., Washington, 1984—; bd. dirs. Poetry Com. Greater Washington, 1985—. Author: Wandering on the Outside, 1975, The Dancer's Muse, 1981, Whose Woods These Are, 1983. Recipient Dellbrook awards Shenandoah Coll., Va., 1978, 79; Billee Murray Denny award Lincoln Coll., Ill., 1981. Mem. Poetry Soc. Am. Jewish. Avocations: photography; gourmet cooking; foreign travel; cycling. Home: 4601 N Park Ave Apt 1212 Chevy Chase MD 20815 Office: The Word Works PO Box 42164 Washington DC 20015

ALES, EILEEN EHLERS, marketing executive, health care marketing consultant; b. Milw., June 8, 1943; d. Wilhelm Heinrich and Johanna (Hutsteiner) Ehlers; m. Larry Lowell Ales, June 12, 1965 (div. 1974). B.S., U. Iowa, 1965; M.A., U. No. Colo., 1977. RN. Field program supr. Denver Vis. Nurse Service, 1971-72, hosp. coordination program supr., 1972-77, dir. mktg., 1977-80; dir. home care programs Upjohn HealthCare Services, Kalamazoo, 1980-83, dir. program planning, 1983—; adj. faculty U. Mich., Ann Arbor, 1982-85; tech. adv. Nat. Network for Discharge Planning/Continuity of Care, Washington, 1982; home care liaison Am. Assn. for Continuity of Care, Washington, 1983-84; mktg. cons. ARC Kalamazoo County, 1985. Editor Baton (vol. I-V) monograph, 1983-85, Brook Lodge Symposium Discharge Planning to Home Care monograph, 1982. Contbr. articles to profl. jours. Bd. dirs. Kalamazoo Area Humane Soc., 1981-85, Area Council on Humanities, Kalamazoo, 1982-84; active mem. Profl. Execs. and Affiliates of Kalamazoo, 1981—, Kalamazoo Network, 1982-84. Mem. Nat. Assn. for Home Care (bd. dirs. 1982—, membership chmn. 1982-83, long term care com. chmn. 1984—), Am. Coll. Health Care Mktg. (bd. dirs. 1985—, co-chmn. ann. meeting, 1985), Am. Mktg. Assn. (adv. bd. mem. 1984). Republican. Presbyterian. Club: Civitan. Avocations: sailing; skiing; tennis. Home: 129 Pinecove Circle Kalamazoo MI 49002 Office: Upjohn HealthCare Services 2605 E Kilgore Rd Kalamazoo MI 49002

ALESCHUS, JUSTINE LAWRENCE, land broker; b. New Brunswick, N.J., Aug. 13, 1925; d. Walter and Mildred Lawrence; student Rutgers U.; m. John Aleschus, Jan. 23, 1949; children—Verdene Jan, Janine Kimberley, Joanna Lauren. Dept. sec. Am. Baptist Home Mission Soc., N.Y.C., 1947-49; claims examiner Republic Ins. Co., Dallas, 1950-52; broker Damon Homes, L.I., 1960-72; exclusive broker estate of Kenneth H. Leeds, L.I., 1980—; pres. Justine Aleschus Real Estate. Pres. Nassau-Suffolk Council of Hosp. Aux., 1981-82; hon. mem. aux. of St. John's Episcopal Hosp., Smithtown, N.Y., also pres. hosp. adv. bd.; pres. L.I. Coalition for Sensible Growth, Inc.; mem.

Smithtown Industry Adv. Bd.; bd. dirs. Suffolk council Boy Scouts Am.; mem. adv. bd. Suffolk County council Girl Scouts U.S.A. Mem. Advancement for Commerce and Industry, Hauppauge Industry Assn., Businessman's Assn., Eastern L.I. Execs. (v.p.), L.I. Bus. Profl. Women (dir., del.), wn Bus. and Profl. Women's Network, L.I. Assn., JEI Com. Republican. Lutheran. Office: 300 Hawkins Ave Lake Ronkonkoma NY 11779

ALEWINE, BETTY JOAN, abstracter; b. Galveston, Tex., Sept. 23, 1932; d. George Raymond and Ruth Elaine (Burney) Mulcahy; m. Tillman West Conovan, July 25, 1953 (div. Oct. 1970); m. Bennie Lee Alewine, May 23, 1984; children—Sharon Jeane Missildine, Jefferson Raymond Conovan, Kimberly Ruth Conovan. Grad. high sch., Teague, Tex. Typist, Fairfield Abstract Co., Tex., 1960-67; abstracter Am. Title Co., Houston, 1968-70; abstracter, owner Freestone County Title & Abstract Co., Inc., Fairfield, 1970—; organizer, dir. Citizens Nat. Bank, Teague, 1984—. Trustee Teague Ind. Sch. Dist., 1982—, 1st United Methodist Ch., Teague, 1982—. Mem. Tex. Land Title Assn., Gen. Fedn. Women's Clubs, Career Women's Club (pres. 1984—). Avocations: bridge; swimming; antiques. Home: PO Box 389 Mexia TX 76667 Office: Freestone County Title & Abstract Co Inc 117 S Mount St PO Drawer 908 Fairfield TX 75840

ALEXA, NANCY ANN, investment banker; b. Yonkers, N.Y., July 9, 1954; d. Harry and Mae (Poirier) Alexa; student Elizabeth Seton Jr. Coll., 1975; B.S. in Mgmt., Rutgers U., 1985. With Technicon Instruments Corp., Tarrytown, N.Y., 1974-80, asst. to gen. mgr., 1979-80; adminstrv. asst. to v.p. corp. communications Purolator, Inc., Piscataway, N.J., 1981; with NPO/Task Force Inc., N.Y.C., 1981-82; Holland Am. Line (USA) Inc., N.Y.C., 1982-83, Rothschild Inc., N.Y.C., 1983-84, Kelso & Co. (investment bankers), N.Y.C., 1984—. Home: 144 Lenox Ct Piscataway NJ 08854-3167 Office: Kelso & Co 350 Park Ave New York NY 10022

ALEXANDER, BARBARA LYNNE, film producer, literary agent; b. Los Angeles, Jan. 6, 1942; d. Henry and Esther (Weiss) Alexander; student U. Calif., Berkeley, 1960-61; B.A., UCLA, 1963. Tchr., Culver City (Calif.) Unified Sch. Dist., 1963-67; producer, dir., writer Comprenetics, Inc., Los Angeles, 1970-74; asso. producer Sutherland Prodns., Los Angeles, 1974-75; partner/producer Snow Prodns., Los Angeles, 1976-81; v.p. theatrical devel. Odyssey Communication, Inc., Culver City, 1977-81; v.p. prodn. Inst. for Career and Vocat. Tng., Culver City, 1979-81; ind. producer, Los Angeles, 1981-84; partner Pettit & Alexander Prodns., Los Angeles, 1984; lit. agt. The Wallerstein Co., Los Angeles, 1985. Recipient Info. Film Producers of Am. Bronze award, 1972, 76, 79; Am. Indian Film Festival Spl. Achievement award, 1978, 80, Bronze and Silver award Internat. Film and TV Festival of N.Y., 1978, 80; Columbus Film Festival Bronze award, 1979; U.S. Indsl. Film Festival Gold Camera award, 1979; Film Adv. Bd. award of excellence, 1976, others. Mem. Acad. TV Arts and Scis., Women in Film (bd. dirs. 1978-80), Los Angeles Cinimatheque (founding mem., bd. dirs. 1976-78). Address: 12310 Dorothy St Los Angeles CA 90049

ALEXANDER, BARBARA SHAPIRO, psychiatric social worker; b. St. Louis, May 6, 1943; d. Harold Albert and Dorothy Miriam (Leifer) Shapiro; B.Mus. Edn., Washington U., St. Louis, 1964; postgrad. U. Ill., 1964-66; M.S.W., Smith Coll., 1970; postgrad. Inst. Psychoanalysis, Chgo., 1971-73; grad. Child Therapy Program, 1980; cert. therapist Sex Dysfunction Clinic, Loyola U., Chgo., 1975; m. Richard E. Alexander. Research asst., NIMH grantee Smith Coll., 1968-70; probation officer Juvenile Ct. Cook County, Chgo., 1966-68, 70; therapist Madden Mental Health Center, Hines, Ill., 1970-72; supr., therapist, field instr. U. Chgo., U. Ill. Grad. Schs. Social Work, also Pritzker Children's Hosp., Chgo., 1972-80; therapist, cons., also pvt. practice, 1973—; instr. tng. and advanced tng. Effectiveness Tng. Assos., Chgo., 1974; instr. psychology Northeastern U., Chgo., 1975; intern Divorce Conciliation Service, Circuit Ct. Cook County, 1976-77; mem. postgrad. curriculum devel. com. Loyola U., 1981. Bd. dirs. North Am. Found., Grant Park Concerts Soc. Recipient Sterling Achievement award Mu Phi Epsilon, 1964. Cert. social worker, Ill. Mem. Acad. Cert. Social Workers, Nat. Assn. Social Workers, Ill. Soc. Clin. Social Work (pres., dir., chmn. services to mems. com., editor newsletter, dir. referral service), Am. Assn. Marriage and Family Therapists, Assn. Child Psychotherapists, Am. Assn. Sex Educators and Counselors, Nat. Rehab. Assn., Amateur Chamber Music Players Assn., Jewish Geneal. Soc., Smith Coll. Alumni Assn. (dir.). Democrat. Jewish. Contbr. to profl. publns. Home: 179 E Lake Shore Dr Chicago IL 60611 Office: 919 N Michigan Ave Suite 3012 Chicago IL 60611

ALEXANDER, BARBARA TOLL, securities analyst, investment banker; b. Little Rock, Dec. 18, 1948; d. Lawrence Jesser and Geraldine Best (Proctor) Toll; m. Lawrence Allen Alexander, Jan. 25, 1969 (div. 1980); m. Thomas Beveridge Stiles, II, Mar. 7, 1981; stepchildren—Thomas B. Stiles III, Jonathan E. Stiles. B.S., U. Ark., 1969, M.S., 1970. Asst. v.p. Wachovia Bank & Trust Co., Winston-Salem, N.C., 1972-76; security analyst Investors Diversified Services, Mpls., 1976-78; 1st v.p. Smith Barney Inc., N.Y.C., 1978-84; v.p. Salomon Bros., N.Y.C., 1984-86, dir., 1986—. Named No. 1 housing analyst in U.S., Instl. Investor, 1983. Mem. Inst. Chartered Fin. Analysts, Fin. Analysts Fedn., N.Y. Soc. Security Analysts, Constrn. and Bldg. Materials Analysts Group (pres. 1984-85). Presbyterian. Home: 18 Tuttle Ave Spring Lake NJ 07762 Office: Salomon Bros Inc One New York Plaza New York NY 10004

ALEXANDER, BEVERLY MOORE, mechanical engineer; b. Portsmouth, Va., Apr. 11, 1947; d. Julian Morgan and Ezefferlee (Griffin) Moore; m. Larry Ray Alexander, Mar. 4, 1978; m. Ronald Lee Rutherford, Dec. 21, 1969 (div. Dec. 1977). B.S., Aero. Engring., Va. Poly. Inst. and State U., 1969; postgrad. in bus. adminstrn. U. New Orleans. Registered profl. engr., La. Assoc. engr. McDonnell Douglas Corp., St. Louis, 1969-74; design engr. Bell Aerospace Textron, New Orleans, 1974-81; supr. systems integration, New Orleans, 1981-83, chief interface activities, 1983-84; chief engr. Bell Aerospace Textron, New Orleans, 1984-85, dir. engring. planning and control, 1985—. Mem. La. Engring. Soc., Nat. Assn. Female Execs., Mgmt. Club (pres.). Republican. Episcopalian. Clubs: HSC (treas. 1980-83); Pinewood Country. Avocations: golf; swimming; antique collecting. Home: 313 Margon Ct Slidell LA 70458 Office: Bell Aerospace Textron 6800 Plaza Dr New Orleans LA 70127

ALEXANDER, CAROL GREENE (MRS. KENNETH ALEXANDER), librarian; b. Washington, Oct. 13, 1933; d. Lawrence William and Inez Ages (Browne) Greene; student Ohio Wesleyan U., 1950-51; A.B., Brown U., 1954; M.S., Case Western Res. U., 1957; m. Kenneth Alexander, Oct. 14, 1968; 1 dau., Donna. Reference librarian sci. div. N.Y. Public Library, 1957-58; sci. reference librarian Library of Congress, Washington, 1959-66; adminstrv. librarian AEC, Germantown, Md., 1966-70, Nat. Agrl. Library, Beltsville, Md., 1970-72; librarian John Jay Coll. Criminal Justice, City U. N.Y., 1972-74; tech. info. officer ERDA, Washington, 1974-77; dir. U.S. nat. focal point UN environment program's internat. referral system, dep. chief Library Systems br. EPA, Washington, 1977-79; dir. Office of Library Systems and Services, EPA, Washington, 1979-83; chmn. exec. adv. com. Fed. Libraries Network, 1982-83; cons. environ. program UN, 1977—; cons. UNESCO Project on New and Renewable Energy Info. for E. Africa, 1983—; head sci. libraries dept. U. Calif.-Berkely. Mem. Am. Soc. Info. Sci., Alumni Assn. Brown U. (dir. 1973-74). Office: PO Box 7538 Landscape Sta Berkeley CA 94707

ALEXANDER, CAROL JEAN, personnel executive; b. Dayton, Ohio, June 11, 1935; d. Earl Edward and Catherine Louisa (Schroeder) Chenoweth; m. Robert Glenn Alexander, Sept. 19, 1953; children—John Robert, Susan Kay. A.Bus.Mgmt., Sinclair Community Coll., 1982. Adminstrv. asst. United Way Dayton (Ohio), 1977—, adminstrv. asst. personnel, 1977-78, personnel asst., 1978-79, personnel dir., 1979—. Author: Your Slip is Showing, 1969; Fascinating Foods, 1970. Adminstrv. chmn., dir. Greenmont Oak Park Community Ch., Kettering, Ohio, 1976. Mem. Am. Soc. Personnel Adminstrn. Democrat. Mem. United Ch. of Christ. Home: 2619 Talisman Dr Kettering OH 45420 Office: United Way Inc Dayton Area 184 Salem Ave Dayton OH 45420

ALEXANDER, CHERYL LEE, executive search and consulting firm executive; b. Mpls., Feb. 22, 1946; d. Wallace Einar and Dorothy Florence (Abrahamson) Arneson; m. Douglas Joel Hawkinson, Mar. 5, 1966; children—Tamara Lee, Alexander Lowell. Student, Gustavus Adolphus Coll., 1964-66, Nan Yang U., Singapore, 1971; B.A. summa cum laude, U. Minn., 1972. Personnel recruiter Nat. Recruiters, Mpls., 1972; pres. Alexander Recruiters, Mpls., 1973-79, Alexander Cos., (formerly Alexander Recruiters), Mpls., 1979—; former dir. Micro Application Systems, Inc., Proto Circuits, Inc.; lectr. numerous univs.; faculty, adv. David Campbell Assocs. Author: Up The Typewriter, 1977; Transition Management, 1980; subject of interviews by profl. jours, TV and radio. Advisor Hennepin County Pvt. Industry Council, Mpls., 1981-83; mem. St. Paul Set-Aside Adv. Com., 1981-82, Mpls. Tech. Enterprise Ctr., 1984—; participant White House Conf. on Small Bus., 1980; judge Internat. Sci. and Engring. Fair, 1980; bd. dirs. Children's Communication Exchange, 1981-82. Mem. Soc. Women Engrs. (founder, bd. dirs., sec.), Assn. Women in Computing (founder, bd. dirs., v.p. 1978-79), Nat. Assn. Women Bus. Owners (founder, bd. dirs. v.p., nat. sec. 1978-81). Republican. Avocations: tennis; public speaking; seminar leader; skiing; sailing. Office: Alexander Cos 3205 Casco Circle Wayzata MN 55391

ALEXANDER, DARLENE JANET, employment and training educator; b. Waco, Tex., June 28, 1937; d. Roy Lee and Pearl Ella (Cobb) Douglass; m. David Lavone, June 1, 1955 (div.); 1 child, David L. Alexander, III. B.S., Tex. So. U., 1971, postgrad., 1975. Adminstrv. asst. Tex. So. U., Houston, 1962-75, dir. exptl. learning program, 1975-78, asst. to dir. urban resources ctr., 1978-81; project assoc. Female Offender Project, Houston, 1981-82; mgr. employment Houston Urban League, 1982-86; mgr. summer youth employment and tng. program tng. Partnership Council, Houston, 1986—; dir. statewide tech. assistance adv. com. Tex. Dept. Community Affairs, Austin, 1983—. Editor: The Urban Collage, 1980. Bd. dirs. Coalition of 100 Black Women, Houston, 1984—. Recipient Outstanding Women of Yr. award Eta Phi Beta, 1985. Mem. Houston Personnel Assn., Alpha Kappa Alpha (Grammatues, 1980-82). Democrat. Baptist. Club: Jack and Jill of Am. (recording sec. 1969-71) (Houston). Avocations: reading; bridge; bicycling; movies. Home: 2619 Hopkins Houston TX 77006 Office: Tng Partnership Council 1919 Smith Suite 300 Houston TX 77002

ALEXANDER, DEANIE, bureau health administrator, city official; b. Cuthbert, Ga.; d. Dudley and Susie (King) Bridges; m. Alvin Neil Alexander, July 3, 1940. B.S., NYU, 1955, M.A., 1961. Tchr. N.Y. State Tng. Sch., Hudson, 1946-50; dir. recreation Dept. Social Services, N.Y.C., 1956-61; community organizer Neighborhood Conservation, N.Y.C., 1961-64; dir. Carnegie Project, N.Y.C., 1964-66; cons. N.Y.C. Dept. Health, 1966-75, dir. bur., 1975—. Mem. Nat. Conf. on Social Welfare, Internat. Council on Social Welfare, Nat. Recreation and Park Assn., Am. Camping Assn. Democrat. Roman Catholic. Club: Women's City (N.Y.C.).

ALEXANDER, ESTELLE R(AEFSKY), reference librarian, online searcher; b. Phila., Oct. 15, 1940; d. Morris and Sarah (Karp) Raefsky; m. Gerson J. Alexander, Sept. 4, 1960; children—Lee Ann, Lauren. B.A., Temple U., 1969; M.L.S., U. Md.-College Park, 1974. Reserve librarian Montgomery County Dept. Pub. Libraries, Gaithersburg, Md., 1971-73, reference librarian, Bethesda, Md., 1976, readers advisor, Rockville, Md., 1976-82, reference librarian, 1982-84, head reference librarian, Rockville Library, 1984—. Troop leader Brownies, Girl Scouts U.S.A., Commack, N.Y., 1968-69; mem. Nat. Women's Polit. Caucus, Washington. Mem. ALA, Md. Library Assn. (Community Info. Service Round Table, Balt. 1983-84), Montgomery County Pub. Library Staff Assn. (exec. bd. Rockville 1978-83), Women for Equality (chmn. 1984), AAUW, Beta Phi Mu. Democrat. Jewish. Home: 6102 Neilwood Dr Rockville MD 20852 Office: Rockville Library 99 Maryland Ave Rockville MD 20850

ALEXANDER, FRANCINE SUE, computer technical marketing executive; b. N.Y.C., Sept. 30, 1943; d. Henry Mathew and Renee (Hartblay) Librach; m. Howard George Youngstein, Aug. 25, 1965 (div. 1973); m. 2d, Robert Simon Alexander, Dec. 23, 1979. B.S. in Math., Syracuse U., 1964. Systems engr. IBM, N.Y.C., 1964-71, staff instr., 1972-75, mktg. support rep., 1975-80, adv. mktg. rep., 1980-81, adv. systems engr., 1982-85, sr. systems engring. specialist, 1985—. Chmn., Libertarian Abortion Action Group N.Y., 1972-74; mem. state com. Free Libertarian Party, N.Y., 1973-74; candidate for mayor Free Libertarian Party, N.Y.C., 1973; nat. treas. Libertarian Party, 1974-75, mem.-at-large exec. com., 1975-77; delivery mgr. Holiday Project, N.Y.C., 1980-81, nat. coordinator, 1981-82, pres., chief exec. officer, nat. chmn., 1982-83, ex-officio mem. nat. com., 1983-84, chmn. adv. bd. N.Y.C. com., 1985—. Mem. Assn. Computing Machinery, Am. Soc. Tng. and Devel. Office: IBM 33 Maiden Ln New York NY 10038

ALEXANDER, JACQUELINE PETERSON, librarian; b. N.Y.C., Aug. 28, 1928; d. Stephen Edgar and Anna (Boehm) Peterson; A.B., Hunter Coll., 1949; M.L.S., U. R.I., 1972; m. Lewis McElwain Alexander, Dec. 30, 1950; children—Louise, Lance. Asst. editor Law of the Sea Inst. Procs., 1966-71; reference librarian U. R.I., Kingston, 1971; research librarian Internat. Center Marine Resource Devel., 1973-79; regional librarian U.S. Naval Edn. and Tng. Support Center, Groton, Conn., 1979-81; asst. chief acquisitions sect. Dept. Transp., 1983-84; librarian Edwards & Angell, Providence, 1984—; tech. librarian, head books, periodicals div. Nav. Underwater Systems Center, Newport, R.I., 1971-72. Pres. South County Sr. Citizens Housing, 1974-82; bd. dirs., sec. South County Housing Improvement Found., 1966-83; bd. dirs. Washington County Vis. Nurse Assn., 1968-71; mem. South Kingstown Citizens Adv. Bd., 1965-71. Mem. Am. Assn. Law Librarians, Law Librarians of New Eng., Beta Phi Mu. Home: 28 Beech Hill Rd Peace Dale RI 02879 Office: Edwards & Angell One Hospital Trust Plaza Providence RI 02903

ALEXANDER, JANE, actress; b. Boston, Oct. 28, 1939; d. Thomas Bartlett and Ruth (Pearson) Quigley; student Sarah Lawrence Coll., 1957-59, U. Edinburgh, 1959-60; m. Robert Alexander, July 23, 1962 (div. 1969); 1 child, Jason; m. 2d, Edwin Sherin, Mar. 29, 1975. Appeared prodns. Charles Playhouse Boston, 1964-65, Arena Stage, Washington, 1965-68, 70—, Am. Shakespeare Festival including plays The Merry Wives of Windsor, Mourning Becomes Electra, Major Barbara, Stratford, Conn., summers 1971-72, Broadway prodns. Great White Hope, 1968-69, 6 Rms Riv Vu, 1972-73, Find Your Way Home, 1974, The Heiress, 1976, First Monday in October, 1978, Goodbye Fidel, 1980, Monday After the Miracle, 1982; appeared in The Time of Your Life, Plumstead Playhouse, Washington and Los Angeles; also appeared plays Present Laughter, 1975, Hamlet, 1975, The Master Builder, 1977, Losing Time, N.Y.C., 1979, Antony and Cleopatra, Atlanta, 1981, Hedda Gabler, Stamford, Conn., 1981; Old Times, 1983-84; appeared in films Great White Hope, 1969, A Gunfight, 1970, The New Centurions, 1972, All the President's Men, 1976, The Betsy, 1978, Kramer vs. Kramer, 1979, Brubaker, 1980, Night Crossing, 1982, Testament, 1983, City Heat, 1984, Sweet Country, 1985, Square Dance, 1986; appeared in TV films Welcome Home Johny Bristol, 1971, Miracle on 34th St., 1973, Death Be Not Proud, 1974, Eleanor and Franklin, 1976, Eleanor and Franklin: The White House Years, 1977, A Question of Love, 1978, Lovey, 1978, Playing For Time, 1980, Dear Liar, 1981, Calamity Jane's Diary, 1981, In the Custody of Strangers, 1982, When She Says No, 1984; appeared in TV spl. A Circle of Children, 1977, Calamity Jane, 1984, Malice in Wonderland, 1985, Blood and Orchids, 1986; author: (with Greta Jacobs) The Bluefish Cookbook; translator from Norwegian (with Sam Engelstad) The Masterbuilder. Recipient Antoinette Perry award, 1969; Theatre World award; Drama Desk award; TV Critics Circle award, 1977; Emmy award, 1981; Helen Caldicott leadership award, 1984; Western Heritage award, 1985.

ALEXANDER, JUDITH ANN, bank consultant; b. Fort Sill, Okla., Oct. 14, 1940; d. James Buchanan and Gerry Lee (Gibbs) Permenter; student U. Okla., 1958-59; B.A. in English, U. Tulsa, 1962; M.B.A., U. Okla., 1969; postgrad. U. St. Thomas, 1975-78; m. Robert Miles Turner, Oct. 28, 1962 (div. 1972); m. Clarence Withers Alexander, Dec. 19, 1975. Asst. cashier So. Nat. Bank of Houston, 1971-73, asst. controller, 1973-74, asst. v.p. and asst. controller, 1974, v.p., controller, 1974-77, sr. v.p., controller, 1977-79, cons., 1979—. Mem. Houston Mus. Fine Arts, Houston Bot. Soc., NOW, Nat. Wildlife Fedn., Nat. Audubon Soc., Am. Soc. Women Accountants, Beta Gamma Sigma, Gamma Phi Beta. Republican. Office: 2523 McKeever Rd Rosharon TX 77583

ALEXANDER, LINDA DIANE (GRAHAM), lawyer, educator; b. Winchester, Va., May 10, 1953; d. Kenneth A. and Edna Frances (Whitlow) Graham; m. Patrick B. Alexander, May 8, 1975. B.A. in Govt., George Mason U., 1975, B.A. in Philosophy, 1975; J.D., U. Okla., 1978. Bar: Okla. 1978, U.S. Dist. Ct. (we. dist.) Okla. 1979, U.S. Ct. Appeals (10th cir.) 1980, U.S. Ct. Appeals (8th cir.) 1984, U.S. Ct. Claims 1980. Legal intern Foliart, Mills & Niemeyer, Oklahoma City, 1976-79, assoc., 1979-81; sole practice law, Oklahoma City, 1981-84; ptnr. firm Niemeyer, Edmonds, Noland, Alexander & Hargraves, Oklahoma City, 1983—; prof. Sch. Law, Oklahoma City U., 1981-83. Mem. Okla. Bar Assn., Oklahoma County Bar Assn., Assn. Trial Lawyers Am. Democrat. Mem. Ch. of Christ. Office: 300 N Walker St Oklahoma City OK 73102

ALEXANDER, MARGARET CURRY, nurse practitioner; b. New Orleans, Dec. 28, 1950; d. Albert Mangum and Mildred Joanne (Hollinger) Alexander, Jr.; m. David Paul Swanson, Oct. 15, 1983; 1 child, Eric Alexander Swanson. A.S., DeKalb Community Coll., Clarkston, Ga., 1971; B.S., Ga. State U., 1973; Nurse Practitioner in Adult Health, Emory U., 1976. R.N., Ga., Fla. Nurse, Crawford W. Long Hosp., Atlanta, 1971-74; asst. dir. nursing and health programs ARC, Atlanta, 1974-77; nursing instr. DeKalb Tech. Sch., Clarkston, part-time 1977; nurse practitioner Grady Meml. Hosp., Atlanta, 1977-78; staff nurse critical care unit Palm Beach Gardens Hosp. (Fla.), 1978-79; nurse practitioner in doctors' offices, Palm Beach Gardens and Tequesta, Fla., 1979-80, Mid County Med. Center, West Palm Beach, Fla., 1980-82; occupational health nurse No. Telecom Electronics, West Palm Beach, 1982-83, mgr. health, safety and security, 1983-85, mgr. employment, 1985—. Vol., ARC, Atlanta, also West Palm Beach, 1971—; bd. dirs. Palm Beach County Safety Council, 1984-85. Mem. Am. Soc. Safety Engrs., Palm Beach Assn. Occupational Health Nurses (state newsletter editor 1984, chmn. relations and social affairs com. 1983-84), Fla. Nurses Assn. (dir. dist. 9, 1981-82, corr. sec. 1980-81, rec. sec. 1982-83), Nurse Practitioner Conf. Group, Am. Nurses Assn. Presbyterian. Home: 10105 Flag Dr Palm Beach Gardens FL 33410 Office: No Telecom Electronics 1601 Hill Ave West Palm Beach FL 33407

ALEXANDER, MARGO, nutrition and food service executive; b. Bklyn., May 10, 1952; d. Al and Ethel (Levinson) Isaacs; B.A., Bklyn. Coll., 1974; M.A., NYU 1977; postgrad. Pace U., 1980-81. Clin. dietitian Brookdale Med. Center, Bklyn., 1974-77; supervising dietitian Beth Israel med. Center, N.Y.C., 1977-78; assoc. dir. food service L.I. Coll. Hosp., Bklyn., 1978-82, dir., 1982—; cons., lectr. in field. Registered dietitian; accomplished health care food adminstr. Mem. Hosp. Food Adminstrs. Assn., (dir.; pres.-elect 1983-84 pres. 1984), Am. Hosp. Assn., Am. Dietetic Assn. (Young Dietitian of Yr. award 1983), Greater N.Y. Dietetic Assn. (past chmn. legis. and public policy com.). Office: LI Coll Hosp Food Service 340 Henry St Brooklyn NY 11201

ALEXANDER, MARY E., lawyer; b. Chgo., Nov. 16, 1947; d. Theron and Marie (Bailey) A.; m. Lyman Saunders Faulkner, Jr., Dec. 1, 1984; 1 child, Michelle. B.A., U. Iowa, 1969; M.P.H., U. Calif.-Berkeley, 1975; J.D., U. Santa Clara, 1982. Bar: Calif. 1982. Researcher, U. Cin., 1969-74; dept. dir., sr. environ. health scientist Stanford Research Inst., Menlo Park, Calif., 1975-80; cons. Alexander Assocs., Ambler, Pa., 1980-82; assoc. Caputo, Liccardo Rossi Sturges & McNeil, San Jose, Calif., 1982-84; assoc. Cartwright, Sucherman & Slobodin, San Francisco, 1984—. Com. mem. Cancer Soc., San Jose, 1983. Nat. Inst. Occupational Safety and Health scholar U. Calif.-Berkeley, 1975. Democrat. Home: 967 Clinton Rd Los Altos CA 94022 Office: Cartwright Sucherman & Slobodin 101 California 26th Floor San Francisco CA 94111

ALEXANDER, MARY LOUISE, health underwriter, financial planner; b. St. Cloud, Minn., Mar. 5, 1950; d. Thomas E. and Jean E. (Wichman) A.; B.F.A., Stephens Coll., 1972. Registered health underwriter. Riding dir. Hidden Valley Farms, Newton, N.J., 1974, El Dorado Ranch, Westtown, N.Y., 1974; riding instr. Frances Reker Sch. of Horsemanship, Rockford, Minn., 1975; instr. Area Learning Center, Dist. 742, St. Cloud, 1976, asst. dean of boys, 1976; sales rep. N.W. Nat. Life Ins. Co., St. Cloud, 1977-78; prin. Mary Alexander Ins. Agy., Cold Spring, Minn., 1978—; pres. M. Alexander & Assocs., Contempory Ins. Concepts, Maxi-Mktg. Inc., 1980—; owner, mgr. Bay Hill Farm. Mem. Nat. Assn. Health Underwriters, Minn. Assn. Health Underwriters, Nat. Fedn. Ind. Bus. Owners, Greater Twin Cities Chow Chow Club, Am. Quarter Horse Assn., Minn. Quarter Horse Assn., Minn. Horse Council. Lutheran. Home: Bay Hill Route 2 Cold Spring MN 56320 Office: 20 College Ave N Saint Joseph MN 56320

ALEXANDER, MARY LOUISE, educator; b. Ennis, Tex., Jan. 15, 1926; d. Emmett F. and Florence (Hill) Alexander; B.A., U. Tex., 1947, M.A., 1949, Ph.D., 1951. Instr., research asst. Genetics Found., U. Tex., 1944-51; postdoctoral fellow biology div. AEC, Oak Ridge, 1951-52; postdoctoral research fellow U. Tex., 1952-55; research asso. U. Tex.-M.D. Anderson Hosp. and Tumor Inst., Houston, 1956-58, asst. biologist, 1959-62; research scientist Genetics Found. U. Tex., Austin, 1962-67; research cons. Brookhaven Nat. Lab., Upton, N.Y., 1955; research participant Oak Ridge Inst. Nuclear Studies, 1951-77; asso. prof. biology S.W. Tex. State U., San Marcos, 1966-69, prof., 1970—. Nat. Cancer Inst. fellow Inst. Animal Genetics, Edinburgh, Scotland, 1960-61. Mem. Genetics Soc. Am., Radiation Research Soc., Am. Soc. Human Genetics, Sigma Xi, Gamma Phi Beta, Phi Sigma, Alpha Epsilon Delta. Home: Hunter's Glen Route 2 Box 119 San Marcos TX 78666

ALEXANDER, NANCY NICHOLS, veterinarian; b. Brookhaven, Miss., Oct. 24, 1955; d. Mack and Mary Alice (Cooke) Nichols; m. William Brent Alexander, Dec. 29, 1978. B.A., U. Tenn., 1977; D.V.M., 1980. Veterinarian Farragut Animal Clinic, Knoxville, 1980—, Cedar Bluff Animal Clinic, 1980—; vet. cons. Gifted Talented program, Knoxville, 1983—. Mem. AVMA, Tenn. Vet. Med. Assn., Knoxville Acad. Vet. Medicine, Alpha Epsilon Delta, Phi Beta Kappa, Chi Omega. Republican. Baptist. Home: 2115 Bishop's Bridge Rd Knoxville TN 37922 Office: Cedar Bluff Animal Clinic 9049 Middlebrook Pike Knoxville TN 37923

ALEXANDER, ROBERTA SUE, history educator; b. N.Y.C., Mar. 19, 1943; d. Bernard Milton and Dorothy (Linn) Cohn; m. Ronald Burett Fost, May 7, 1977. B.A., UCLA, 1964; M.A., U. Chgo., 1966, Ph.D., 1974. Instr. Roosevelt U., 1967-68; assoc. prof., dept. chmn. U. Dayton, Ohio, 1969—. Mem. editorial bd. Cin. Hist. Soc., 1973—. Author: North Carolina Faces the Freedmen: Race Relations During Presidential Reconstruction, 1985. Fellow NEH, 1975, 76-77, 82. Mem. Am. Hist. Assn., Organ. Am. Historians, So. Hist. Assn., Am. Soc. Legal History, Am. Contract Bridge Assn., (Life Master 1983), Mortar Board, Danforth Assocs., Phi Beta Kappa, Phi Alpha Theta. Jewish. Avocations: bridge, golf. Home: 72 Twin Lakes Dr Fairfield OH 45014 Office: Univ Dayton Dept History Dayton OH 45469

ALEXANDER, SHANA, journalist, author, commentator; b. N.Y.C., Oct. 6, 1925; d. Milton and Cecelia (Rubenstein) Ager; student Vassar Coll., 1942-45; m. Stephen Alexander, 1951 (div.); 1 child, Katherine. Feature writer PM newspaper, N.Y.C., 1944-47; with Harper's Bazaar, N.Y.C., 1946-47; entertainment editor Flair, N.Y.C., 1950; corr. Life mag., N.Y.C., 1951-59, columnist, 1961-64, writer monthly column The Feminine Eye, 1964-69; editor McCall's Mag., N.Y.C., 1969-71; commentator Sixty Minutes, CBS-TV, 1974-79; host What's Happening America, Sta. WOR-TV, 1980—. Founding mem. Nat. Women's Polit. Caucus; former dir. Am. Film Inst.; bd. dirs. N.Y. State Council on Arts. Author: The Feminine Eye, 1970; Shana Alexander's State-By-State Guide to Women's Legal Rights, 1975; Talking Woman, 1976; Anyone's Daughter, The Times and Trials of Patty Hearst, 1979; Very Much a Lady: The Untold Story of Jean Harris and Dr. Herman Tarnower, 1983; Nutcracker; Money, Madness, Murder: A Family Album, 1985. Office: 502 Park Ave New York NY 10022

ALEXANDER, SHARON GILES, advertising specialist executive; b. Orange, N.J., Sept. 12, 1951; d. William R. and Althea B. Giles; B.S., Morgan State U., 1973; M.Ed., Rutgers U., 1975. Pres., EPC Internat., Inc., East Orange, N.J., 1977—. Mem. N.J. Gov.'s Task Force on Minority Bus. Recipient Kizzy award, 1980, Chad Sch. award, 1981; Sharon A. Giles Day proclaimed by Mayor of West Orange, 1981. Mem. Advt. Splty. Inst., Am. Mktg. Assn., Splty. Advt. Assn. Internat., Splty. Advt. Assn. Greater N.Y., Coalition of 100 Black Women of N.J., Nat. Assn. Female Execs., NAACP, Urban League. Democrat. Baptist. Home: 1605 Plaza Dr Woodbridge NJ 07095 Office: 141 S Harrison St East Orange NJ 07018

ALEXANDER, SHARON KAY, medical technologist; b. Marion, Ill., Aug. 10, 1953; d. Clyde William and Jewell (Gibbons) Campbell; A.S. with honors, John A. Logan Jr. Coll., 1973; B.S. in Microbiology, So. Ill. U., 1975, postgrad., 1975-76; m. Mitchell H. Alexander, June 7, 1980; children—Christopher Mitchell, Sarah E. Registered med. technologist Am. Soc. Clin. Pathologists. Library asst. John A. Logan Jr. Coll., Carterville, Ill., 1973; med. asst., sec. Hugh D. McGowan, Carbondale, Ill., 1973-77; sec. Container Stapling Corp., 1977; co-asst. office mgr. Am. Investment, Carbondale, 1977; med. transcriptionist Marion Meml. Hosp., Herrin, Ill., 1978; med. technologist Herrin Hosp., 1978-83; med. technologist Paoli Meml. Hosp., 1984-85. Ill State scholar, 1971-72. Democrat. Home: 316 Glasgow St Pottstown PA 19464

ALEXANDER, STEPHANIE ANN, personnel administrator; b. Chicago Heights, Ill., Aug. 8, 1960; d. Arthur and Nadie Mae (Bowman) Alexander; B.A. in Psychology and Bus., Trinity Coll., Deerfield, Ill., 1983. Teenage pregnancy counselor Catholic Charities, Chgo., 1983; personnel mgmt. specialist Dept. Army, Ft. Sheridan, Ill., 1983—; counselor United Way Agy., San Francisco, 1980. Mem. choir Christ 1st Bapt. Ch., Harvey, Ill., 1968—. Fellow Assn. M.B.A. Execs., Nat. Assn. Female Execs. Democrat. Avocations: tennis; jogging; biking; bowling. Office: Dept Army CPO Bldg 35 Fort Sheridan IL 60037

ALEXANDER, STEPHANIE MARGOT, social worker; b. N.Y.C., Dec. 22, 1952; d. Charles Khalil and Margaret Frances (Kachur) A. B.A. in Phys. Edn., U. N.C., Chapel Hill, 1979, M.S.W., 1983. Wilderness instr. Group and Individual Growth, James Creek, Pa., 1980, Wilderness Sch., Goshen, Conn., 1981-82; co-dir. Southeastern Outdoor Women, Durham, N.C., 1980-83; adminstrv. intern Orange County Women's Ctr., Chapel Hill, 1982, N.C. Dept. Social Services, Durham, 1982-83; instr., cons. Project Venture, U. N.C.-Charlotte, 1984; instr. N.C. Outward Bound Sch., Morganton, 1983-85; case mgr. Blue Ridge Ctr., Asheville, N.C., 1985—. Avocations: rock climbing, cycling, canoeing, running. Address: 1 Coleman Ave Asheville NC 28804

ALEXANDER, SUSAN REED, economic analyst; b. Charleston, W.Va., Mar. 3, 1941; d. Andrew Stirling and Betsy Reed (Miller) A.; A.B. in Math., Sweet Briar Coll., 1963; M.B.A. in Fin., U. Houston, 1983. Adminstrv. asst. Earl and Wright, Cons. Engrs., San Francisco, 1965-72; programmer/analyst Bechtel, Inc., San Francisco, 1972-79, econ. analyst Bechtel Petroleum, Inc., Houston, 1979-81, study mgr., econ. analyst, 1981-83; bus. project mgr. ETSI Pipeline Project, San Francisco, 1984; study mgr., econ. analyst Bechtel, Inc., Houston, 1985—. Mem. Jr. League San Francisco, Am. Contract Bridge League (lifemaster 1974). Beta Gamma Sigma. Office: Bechtel Inc PO Box 2166 Houston TX 77252

ALEXANDER-KING, PEARL COQUEECE, nurse; b. Drumright, Okla., Dec. 21, 1936; d. Alonzo Cottrol and Marjorie Opal (Price) Alexander; degree Long Beach City Coll., 1961; R.N., Assoc. Sci., 1971; B.S.N., Calif. State U.-Long Beach, 1983; cert. psychiat./mental health nurse; m. Carl Dee King, Dec. 8, 1951; children—Carl Dee, Crystal, Michael (dec.), Marcus. Office nurse for gen. practitioner, Long Beach, Calif., 1961-66; nurse VA Hosp., Long Beach, 1966-69; nursing supr. outpatient alcoholism treatment and rehab. center Long Beach Gen. Hosp., 1971-78; dir. nursing Viewpark Community Hosp., Los Angeles, 1978-79; asst. nursing dir. Augustus F. Hawkins Psychiat. Facility, Los Angeles, 1981-84; mental health counselor Long Beach Mental Health Clinic, 1984—; dept. adminstr. chem. dependency services Kaiser Permanente Med. Ctr., Anaheim, Calif., 1984—; tchr. Long Beach City Coll., 1975. Mem. Calif. Women's Commn. on Alcoholism Rotary Club scholar, 1970-71; Cert. of Honor, Long Beach City Coll., 1971. Mem. Am. Nurses Assn., Calif. Nurses Assn., Sigma Theta Tau (Iota Eta chpt.). Democrat. Baptist. Office: 428 N Lakeview Ave Anaheim CA 92807

ALEXIOU, MARINA S., businesswoman; b. N.Y.C., Feb. 12, 1940; d. Stanley and Mary S. (Couloumbi) A.; bus. cert. in bus. mgmt. U. N.C., 1959; student in bus. mgmt. ICS Ctr. Degree Studies, Scranton, Pa., in Mgmt. Devel. Program, NAPC, 1985. Legal sec. Jordan, Wright, Henson & Nichols, attys., Greensboro, N.C., 1959-60; with North Am. Philips Co., 1961— (co. mergered with Consol. Electronics 1969 then became North Am. Philips Corp.), 1969—, adminstrv. asst. to chmn., chief exec. officer and dir., 1969-81; adminstrv. asst. to chmn. bd. U.S. Philips Trust, 1981-84, adminstrv. asst. to chmn. governing com. 1985-86. Mem. U.S. Senatorial Bus. Adv. Bd. and Steering Com., Washington; mem. adv. bd. Am. Security Council, Washington; mem. Republican Presdl. Task Force, Washington, Rep. Senatorial Inner Circle; asst. chmn. fund raising Am. Cancer Soc., 1978—; dep. chmn. exec. Republican Com. of Bronxville (N.Y.), 1980—. Mem. Nat. Assn. Exec. Sec., Nat. Assn. Female Execs., Am. Soc. Profl. and Exec. Women, Internat. Platform Assn., UN We Believe (exec. planning com.), Smithsonian Nat. Assocs., N.Y. Philharm. Soc. Greek Orthodox. Home: Northgate Alger Ct Bronxville NY 10708 Office: North American Philips Corp 100 E 42nd St New York NY 10017

ALEXIS, JODY RAE, real estate broker, lawyer; b. Langdon, N.D., Mar. 2, 1940; d. Raymond and Ada (Widwick) Armstrong; student Stephens Coll., 1959-61; B.A., U. Nebr., 1963; M.A., U. Colo., 1968; J.D., U. Denver, 1971; div.; 1 son, Clark Kendall. Asst. dir. USO, Colorado Springs, Colo., 1964-65; asst. to dir. adminstrn. Aircraft Mechanics, Inc., Colorado Springs, 1965-67, pub. relations dir. Red Ram of Am. Corp., Colorado Springs, 1967-70, The Woodman Corp., 1971; admitted to Colo. bar, 1971; exec. dir. Rocky Mountain Land Devel. Assn., Denver, 1970-74; pres. Alexis & Assocs., Denver, 1974—; broker assoc. Remax of Cherry Creek, Denver; individual practice law, Denver, 1974—; broker asssoc. Premier Assocs. Denver Ltd., 1979—; cons. Indian Mountain Corp., 1977—; br. mgr. Kentwood Co., 1982—; dir. Colo. Mgmt. Rocky Mountain Log Homes Inc., Designs Internationale. Bd. dirs. Colo. Convs. and Reservations. 1974—; chmn. Denver Art Mus.; active Denver Ctr. for Performing Arts, Jr. Symphony Guild, trustee Colo. Ballet. Republican. Roman Catholic. Home: 1313 Williams St Apt 1205 Denver CO 80218 Office: Remax of Cherry Creek 290 Fillmore #300 Denver CO 80206

ALFANO-VOSS, KATHY MARIE, flight crew coordinator; b. Los Angeles, May 29, 1956; d. Philip Blase and Katherine Alice (Thompson) Alfano; m. Gary Edward Voss, Jan. 6, 1979 (div. 1982); 1 child: Dallas Kristin Voss. A.B., Occidental Coll., Los Angeles, 1977; M.P.A., Calif. State U., 1984. Advisor, State Bd. Edn., Sacramento, 1972-73; flight crew acct. Continental Airlines, Los Angeles, 1978-80, flight crew controller, 1980-82, flight attendant, Houston, 1983; flight attendant coordinator Western Airlines, Los Angeles, 1984, flight crew coordinator, 1984—. Contbr. analysis and studies in transp. Recipient Leadership award Nat. Elk's Lodge, 1973; Achievement medallion Am. Legion, 1974; Achievement award in English, Bank of Am., 1974; Lyndon B. Johnson intern U.S. Congress, 1975. Mem. Am. Soc. Pub. Adminstrn., Acad. Polit. Scis., Evaluation Research Soc., Nat. Assn. Female Execs., Western Govtl. Research Assn., Delta Gamma (pres. Alumnae 1985-86). Republican. Roman Catholic. Club: Disneyland Alum (Anaheim, Calif.). Avocations: swimming; travel. Home: 7100 Cerritos Ave #42 Stanton CA 90680 Office: Western Airlines Inc 6060 Avion Los Angeles CA 90009

ALFONSO, MARIA C., marketing executive; b. Batabano, Havana, Cuba, Nov. 29, 1959; came to U.S., 1967; d. Rafael and Carmen (Menendez) Alfonso. A.A., Miami Dade Community Coll., 1978; B.A., Fla. Internat. U., 1981. Market research asst. Gang Nail Systems, Miami, 1979-81, market research mgr., 1981-84, market research mgr., adminstrv. asst. to v.p. mktg., 1984—. Roman Catholic. Home: 8284 Dundee Terr Miami Lakes FL 33016 Office: Gang Nail Systems 7525 NW 37th St Miami FL 33147

ALFORD, HELEN JOHNSON, lawyer; b. Murfreesboro, Tenn., July 3, 1951; d. Jack Ewing and Beulah Lee (Carter) Johnson; m. Woodrow Ellis Alford, June 27, 1975; 1 dau., Jacqueline Cecile. B.S. in Bus. Law, U. New Orleans, 1980; J.D., Tulane U., 1982. Bar: Ala. 1982, Miss. 1983. Office mgr. Brown Constrn. Co., Marrero, La., 1976-79; legal sec. Scariano & McCranie, Metairie, La., 1975-76, Billy F. Brown, Biloxi, Miss., 1973-75; assoc. Hand, Arendall, Bedsole, Greaves & Johnston, Mobile, Ala., 1982—. Mem. Ala. Bar, Miss. Bar, Ala. Def. Lawyers Assn. Republican. Presbyterian. Home: 1909 LaPine Dr Mobile AL 36618 Office: Hand Arendall Bedsole Greaves & Johnston 3000 First Nat Bank Bldg Mobile AL 36601

ALFORD, JOAN FRANZ, entrepreneur; b. St. Louis, Sept. 16, 1940; d. Henry Reisch and Florence Mary (Shaughnessy) F.; m. Charles Hebert Alford, Dec. 28, 1978; stepchildren—Terry, David, Paul. B.S., St. Louis U., 1962; postgrad. Consortium of State Univ., Calif., 1975-77. Head user services Lawrence Berkeley Lab., Calif., 1977-78, head software support and devel. Computer Ctr., 1978-82, dep. head, 1980-81; regional site analyst mgr. Cray Research, Inc., Pleasanton, Calif., 1982-83; owner, pres. Innovative Leadership, Oakland, Calif., 1983—. Contbr. articles to profl. jours. Chmn. income devel. com. Vol. Ctr. of Alameda, Oakland, 1985; campaign mem. Marge Gibson for County Supr., Oakland, 1984; mem. Oakland Piedmont Republican Orgn., 1985, Alameda County Apt. Owners Assn., 1982. Mem. Assn. Computing Machinery, Spl. Interest Group on Computer Personnel Research. (past chmn.), Nat. Speakers Assn. Republican. Clubs: Last Monday, Toastmasters, Claremont Pool and Tennis, Lakeview, San Francisco Opera Guild. Avocations: swimming; skiing; opera; horseback riding; gardening; reading. Home: 2605 Beaconsfield Pl Oakland CA 94611 Office: Innovative Leadership 1900 Embarcadero Dr Suite 200 Oakland CA 94606

ALFORD, MARY ANN, lawyer; b. Durham, N.C., June 18, 1954; d. Cecil Wylie and Charlotte Rose (Meadows) Alford; m. Thomas Wells White, Aug. 13, 1977 (div. 1981); m. Stephen Poltorzycki, Jan. 1, 1985. B.A., Wellesley Coll., 1976; J.D., Columbia U., 1979. Bar: D.C. 1980. Assoc. firm Sutherland, Asbill & Brennan, Washington, 1979-82; atty. Union Carbide Corp., Danbury, Conn., 1982—. Bd. editors The Trademark Reporter of the U.S. Trademark Assn., N.Y.C., 1983-86. Mem. ABA, Westchester Fairfield Corp. Counsel Assn. Democrat. Office: Law Dept Sect E-2 Union Carbide Corp 39 Old Ridgebury Rd Danbury CT 06817

ALFSEN, LOIS JEAN, home economist; b. Waupaca, Wis., Aug. 9, 1934; d. Allan William and Sara Margaret (Plowman) Schroeder; B.S., U. Wis., Stevens Point, 1956; m. George W. Alfsen, June 12, 1960; children—Geoffrey Wayne, Gregg Allan. Tchr. home econs. Hortonville (Wis.) High Sch., 1956-58, Preble High Sch., Green Bay, Wis., 1958-60, Waupaca High Sch., 1960-61; tchr. consumer edn. Gateway Tech. Inst., Kenosha and Racine, Wis., 1974-76; consumer info. coordinator consumer services Johnson Wax, Racine, 1975—; mem. home econs. vocat. edn. adv. com. Racine Unified Sch. Dist., 1981-84. Rep., Racine Women's Civic Council, 1967-68, 78-79; lay del. to state conf. Wis. United Meth. Conf., 1981-84. Mem. Internat. Fedn. Home Econs., Am. Home Econs. Assn., AAUW, Home Economists in Bus. (nat. public relations com. 1981-82), NOW, Nat. Consumer League, Wis. Home Economists in Homemaking (chmn. 1967-68), Wis. Rural Homemaking Instrs., Wis. Home Econs. Assn. (newsletter asst. editor, dist. meeting reservations chmn., exec. com., state council, state v.p.), Wis. Home Economists in Bus. (ways and means chmn., mem. exec. bd.), Wis. Women's Network, Wis. PTA, Racine Home Econs. Assn. (pres. 1967-68, 78-79), Phi Upsilon Omicron. Home: 1128 Shorecrest Dr Racine WI 53402 Office: 1525 Howe St Racine WI 53403

ALI, PERVEEN KHAN, systems analyst; b. Karachi, Pakistan, Jan. 1, 1957; came to U.S., 1972; d. Riaz Ahmed and Jamila (Begum) Khan; m. Ahmed Ali, Sept. 24, 1982; 1 child: Subhan Mustafa Ali. B.S., U. Southwestern La., 1977. Programmer analyst Ohio Nat. Life Ins., Cin., 1977-79; programmer analyst AT & T Communications, Cin., 1979-82, system analyst, Los Angeles, 1982—; v.p. Geo-Etka Inc., Fullerton, Calif., 1985—. Republican. Moslem. Avocations: reading. travelling; music. Home: 1944 Peaceful Hills Rd Diamond Bar-Walnut CA 91789 Office: AT & T Communications 611 6th St Los Angeles CA 90017

ALITO, MARTHA-ANN BOMGARDNER, librarian; b. Ft. Knox, Ky., July 31, 1953; d. Bobby Gene and Barbara Ann (Auwaerter) B.; m. Samuel Anthony Alito, Jr., Feb. 9, 1985; 1 child, Philip Samuel. Student Rutgers U. in France, 1973-74; B.A., U. Ky., 1975, M.S.L.S., 1977. Research asst. Info. for Bus., N.Y.C., 1977; reference librarian Neptune (N.J.) Public Library, 1977-79; librarian U.S. Atty. for Dist. N.J., Newark, 1979-82; head reference Main Library, Dept. Justice, Washington, 1982-83; library dir. Congl. Quar., Washington, 1983—. Mem. Am. Assn. Law Librarians, Law Librarians' Soc. of Washington, Law Library Assn. Greater N.Y. Office: Congl Quar Inc 1414 22d St NW 4th Floor Washington DC 20037

ALLAN, KATHLEEN ALYCE, radio station executive; b. Waukegan, Ill., June 20, 1952; d. George and Rosa (Urech) Adamek; m. Leigh Willard Allan, Dec. 1, 1979; 1 child, Leslie Alyssa. A.S., West Valley Coll., Campbell Calif., 1972. Legal sec. Hermann & Hall, Waukegan, Ill., 1976-81, Baxter/Travenol, Deerfield, Ill., 1975-76, Morgan, Beauzay & Hammer, San Jose, Calif., 1972-74; owner, operator Sta. WKED-AM, Frankfort, Ky., 1981—. Corr. sec. Welcome Wagon, Frankfort, 1982-83; pub. relations worker Bus. and Profl. Women Frankfort, 1983-84, Am. Cancer Soc., Frankfort. Democrat. Roman Catholic. Avocations: crafts; sewing; dollhouse construction. Home: 210 Papago Trail Frankfort KY 40601 Office: Sta WKED-AM 115 Myrtle Ave Frankfort KY 40601

ALLANACH, ELAINE JACQUELINE, nurse, army officer; b. San Jose, Calif., Mar. 26, 1954; d. William Burt and Edith Gwendolyn (Schindler) Moreland; m. Bruce Carlton Allanach, Oct. 8, 1976. B.S. in Nursing, U.Md., 1976. Registered nurse, Ga., Md. Commd. 2d lt. Nurse Corps, U.S. Army, 1972, advanced through grades to capt., 1978; staff nurse gen. medicine-oncology Walter Reed Army Med. Ctr., Washington, 1976-78, team leader gen. medicine-oncology, 1978-79, head nurse med. splty. ward, 1979-80; asst. head nurse gynecol. oncology unit Tripler Army Med. Ctr., Honolulu, 1980-81, head nurse med. splty. clinic, 1981-83, staff nurse orthopedics Eisenhower Army Med. Center, Ft. Gordon, Ga., 1983-84, patient edn. coordinator, 1984-85, head nurse recovery room, 1985—; mem. pub. edn. com. Am. Cancer Soc., Honolulu, 1982; guest lectr. Decorated Meritorious Service medal. Mem. Am. Diabetes Assn., Am. Assn. Diabetic Educators, Post Anesthesia Recovery Room Nurses Assn., Sigma Theta Tau. Avocations: Bible studies; jogging; movies. Home: 7 Woodbridge Way Evans GA 30809 Office: Patient Education Coordinator Dept Nursing Eisenhower Army Med Ctr Fort Gordon GA 30905

ALLANSMITH, MATHEA REUTER, ophthalmologist, educator; b. Santa Barbara, Calif., May 31, 1930; d. Harry Reuter; children—Lynn, Lauren, Kathryn, Carolyn, Andrew, Jennifer. B.A., U. Calif.-Berkeley, 1952, M.D., San Francisco, 1955. Diplomate Am. Bd. Pediatrics, Am. Bd. Ophthalmology. Intern, San Francisco Hosp., 1955-56; resident in ophthalmology Stanford U. Hosp., San Francisco, 1957, resident in pediatrics, 1958-59, staff mem., 1967-74; resident in pediatric U. Calif. Hosp., San Francisco, 1957-58, pediatric allergy fellow, 1959-60; resident in ophthalmology Stanford U. Sch. Medicine, 1969-72, postdoctoral fellow in immunology, 1960-63, research assoc. div. ophthalmology, 1963-67, research assoc. dept. med. microbiology, 1963-67, acting asst. prof. ophthalmology, 1967-68, asst. prof., 1968-74, head pediatric allergy injection clinic, 1960-67, head ophthalmic microbiology lab., 1967-74, head Stanford Eye Bank, 1970-74, chief cornea and external disease service div. ophthalmology, 1971-73; fellow in external disease Francis I. Proctor Found., San Francisco, 1959-60; asst. prof. ophthalmology Harvard U. Med. Sch., Boston, 1975-77, assoc. prof., 1977—; mem. assoc. staff Children's Hosp. Med. Ctr., Boston, 1975—; staff mem. Beth Israel Hosp. Boston, 1975—, head external disease service, 1981—; mem. staff Hosp. at Parker Hill, Boston, 1979—; Wilder Meml. lectr., Chgo., 1981. Author: The Eye and Immunology, 1982; mem. editorial bd. Am. Jour. Ophthalmology, 1973—, Survey of Ophthalmology, 1973-82, Ophthalmology, 1979-84. Recipient Woman of Yr. Creative Living award San Jose Mercury News, 1973; Physicians Recognition award AMA, 1979—. Mem. Assn. for Research in Vision and Ophthalmology, Am. Acad. Allergy, Am. Assn. Immunologists, Fedn. Am. Socs. for Exptl. Biology, Am. Acad. Ophthalmology, New Eng. Ophthalmol. Soc., Castroviejo Soc., Phi Beta Kappa, Sigma Xi. Office: 20 Staniford St Boston MA 02114

ALLARD, CHERYL ANNE, internal auditor; b. Norfolk, Va., May 24, 1961; d. Roy Joseph and Sandra Lee (Whiteside) Allard. B.S. in Acctg., U. N.C., Greensboro, 1985. Loan collector NCNB, Greensboro, 1984-85; internal auditor Burlington Ind., Greensboro, 1985—. Mem. Nat. Assn. Female Execs. Republican. Roman Catholic. Avocations: sailing; skiing; travelling. Office: Burlington Industries 3330 W Friendly Ave Greensboro NC 27406

ALLARD, JEAN, lawyer; b. Trenton, Mo., Dec. 16, 1924; d. Ben J. and Marion (Watson) McGuire; A.B., Culver-Stockton Coll., 1945, LL.D. (hon.), 1977; A.M., Washington U., St. Louis, 1947; J.D., U. Chgo., 1953; LL.D. (hon.), Elmhurst Coll., 1979; 1 son, John Preston. Dept. counselor, psychology dept. U. Chgo., 1948-51, research asso. Law Sch., 1953-58, asst. dean, 1956-58; admitted to Ill. bar, 1953, Ohio bar, 1959; asso. firm Fuller, Harrington, Seney & Henry, Toledo, 1958-59, Lord, Bissell & Brook, Chgo., 1959-62; sec., gen. counsel Maremont Corp., Chgo., 1962-72; v.p. for bus. and finance U. Chgo., 1972-75; partner firm Sonnenschein Carlin Nath & Rosenthal, Chgo., 1976—; dir. Commonwealth Edison Co., La Salle Nat. Bank., AM Internat., Inc., Maremont Corp. Trustee, Culver-Stockton Coll., 1976—; dir. Chgo. Sch. Fin. Authority, 1980—. Mem. ABA, Ill. Bar Assn., Chgo. Bar Assn., Am. Law Inst., Am. Judicature Soc., Am. Soc. Corp. Secs., Chgo. Assn. Commerce and Industry, Leadership Greater Chgo. Clubs: Economic, Chgo., Comml., Law. Home: 5844 Stony Island Ave Chicago IL 60637 Office: 223 S Wacker Dr Chicago IL 60606

ALLBRIGHT, MARTHA PHILLIPS, lawyer; b. Muscatine, Iowa, Sept. 12, 1952; d. Sherwood Roy and Ruth (Vetter) Phillips; m. Edwin T. Allbright, July 10, 1982. B.A., U. Denver, 1974, J.D., 1977. Bar: Colo. 1978. Atty., Saunders Snyder Ross & Dickson, Denver, 1978-83; spl. counsel Atler, Zall & Haligman, Denver, 1983-85; with Linton & Allbright, P.C., 1986—; real estate broker Centerline Properties, Denver, 1983—; v.p. mktg. Centerline Sports, Denver, 1982—; lobbyist water and environ. legislation, 1981—. Contbr. articles to profl. jours. Mem. Denver Bar Assn. (exec. council young lawyers sect.), Colo. Bar Assn. (exec. council young lawyers sect., vice chmn. environ. law sect.), ABA, Colo. Water Congress, Colo. Groundwater Assn. Gamma Phi Beta. Republican. Presbyterian. Club: P.E.O. Home: 5944 S Meadowbrook Dr Morrison CO 80465

ALLEGRA, MARISA IDA CALZOLARI, psychiatrist; b. Verbania, Torino, Italy; came to U.S., 1956, naturalized, 1962; d. Amilcare and Paola Bice (Alberizzi) Calzolari; M.D. summa cum laude, Bologna U., 1949; postgrad. Brown U., 1976; children—Ludwig Armand, David Paul, Christopher John. Pediatric and gen. practice medicine, Bologna, Italy, 1949-53; permanent staff physician Ospedale Maggiore, Bologna, 1953-56; resident in psychiatry Brown U., Providence, 1973-76; fellow in child psychiatry Bradley Hosp., Providence, 1976; practice medicine specializing in psychiatry, Providence, 1976—; cons. Family Service, 1976-80. Pres. R.I. Civic Choral and Orch., 1974-76, bd. dirs., hon. pres., life mem.; bd. dirs. R.I. Philharm. Orch.; active R.I. Sch. Design. Diplomate Am. Bd. Psychiatry and Neurology. Mem. AMA. Am. Psychiat. Assn., R.I. Med. Assn., Providence Med. Assn., N.Y. Acad. Scis., Butler Hosp. Staff Assn., Am. Med. Womens Assn., Providence Preservation Soc., Newport Preservation Soc. Clubs: Conamicut Yacht (Jamestown, R.I.); Faculty, Brown (Providence). Home: 220 Blackstone Blvd Providence RI 02906

ALLEMAN, AURELIA (LEA) RUSHTON, business executive; b. Fortville, Ind., Sept. 30, 1928; d. Frank M. and Mary M. (Davis) Rushton; m. Zachary T. Bunch, June 5, 1950; children—Zachary Taylor, Tanja Flame, Freeman Enmeier, Olivia Cutcher; m. 2d Ralph J. Alleman, May 7, 1973; children—Stephanie Miller, Bruce, Mark. Student Fortville, Ind. pub. schs. Owner, pres. Be Wise, Inc., Indpls., 1956-62, Miracles Happen, Inc., 1963-67, 20th Century Computer Matching, 1965-73; v.p. Dip-Er-Do Plane Co., Fort Lee, N.J., 1976-77; adminstr. Mgmt. Cleaning Controls, Inc., Chgo., 1981-84; dir. ASQ Clubs; chmn. Lee Parker Enterprises, Inc. Active LWV. Mem. Am. Bus. Women (ednl. com. mem., 1973-74). Author: How to Happily Kiss the Singles Scene Goodbye, 1979. Home: 5100 North Marine Dr Chicago IL 60640 Office: Berman Sales Co Inc 1728 S Michigan Ave Chicago IL 60616

ALLEN, ANNA JEAN, chiropractor; b. Henderson, Ky., Apr. 6, 1955; d. Harold D. and Aiko (Nakashima) Allen. A.S., U. Ky., 1973, B.S., 1976; Dr.Chiropractic, Palmer U., 1980; postgrad. Pan Am. U., 1981, San Antonio Coll., 1983. Health instr. Nautilus, Davenport, Iowa, 1978-80; dir. chiropractic, Harlington, Tex., 1980-81, Handley Chiropractic, San Antonio, 1982-83, NE Chiropractic Ctr., El Paso, Tex., 1983-84, Viscount Chiropractic, El Paso, 1984—. Mem. Am. Bus. Woman's Assn., Nat. Assn. Female Execs., Nat. Fedn. Ind. Bus., Am. Chiropractic Assn., Tex. Chiropractic Assn. (dist. dir. 1986). Avocations: scuba diving; weight lifting; running; bicycling; painting. Office: Viscount Chiropractic Health Ctr 8838 Viscount Suite 0 El Paso TX 79925

ALLEN, ANNE MONTEITH, realtor; b. Granite Falls, N.C., June 1, 1925; d. Nathan Young and Hattie Mae (Butler) Monteith; R.N., Watts Sch. Nursing, 1946; postgrad. U. N.C., 1961; m. Louis E. Allen, Apr. 2, 1949; children—Elizabeth Allen Fish, Louis Eugene, James Morris. Real estate salesman Brown Realty Co. Inc., Greensboro, N.C., 1960-71; owner Anne Allen & Assos., Greensboro, 1974-84; exec. v.p. Merrill Lynch Realty/Anne Allen Co., 1984—; dir. Community Bank of N.C. Gen. vol. chmn. Cerebral Palsy Campaign, 1973. Named Greensboro Realtor of Yr., 1975. Mem. Nat. Assn. Realtors (dir.), Greensboro Bd. Realtors (past pres., dir.), N.C. Assn. Realtors (pres. 1979-80), Better Bus. Bur., Sales and Mktg. Execs. (past chmn.), Greensboro C. of C. (dir.), Nat. Assn. Realtors, Nat. Mktg. Inst., Watts Alumnae Assn. Republican. Home: 15 Ramsgate Ct Greensboro NC 27403 Office: PO Box 10152 Greensboro NC 27404

ALLEN, ARCOLA JEANNE, anesthesia edn. cons., bus. exec.; b. Terre Haute, Ind., May 8, 1939; d. Monroe and Rosie E. (Bishop) Pickette; A.A., San Jose State Coll., 1960; B.S. in Nursing, U. Calif., Berkeley, 1963; B.A. in Psychology, Colombia Coll., 1977; postgrad. Wichita Clinic Sch. of Anesthesia, 1970-72, Wichita State U., 1980; M.Nursing Adminstrn., Columbia Pacific U., 1981, doctoral candidate, 1982; m. Robert Irving Allen, Feb. 19, 1959; children—Robert Irving, Michael, Brian, John, Mark, Jeffrey. Staff nurse surgery O'Connor Hosp., San Jose, Calif., 1962-64; mem. heart team St. Bernardines Hosp., Calif., 1964-65; mem. nursing staff surg. unit. St. Bernardette Hosp., Anchorage, 1965-67, St. Francis Hosp., Wichita, Kans., 1967-69; head nurse urology sect. Wichita Clinic, 1970-79, dir. Sch. of Anesthesia, 1974-79; inservice edn. staff St. Francis Hosp., Wichita, 1974-79; field underwriter Home Life Ins., of N.Y.C., Wichita, 1980-82; owner, chief exec. officer Dan'cer'cise of Wichita and Jenn-Arc Enterprises, 1982 ; anesthesia edn. cons., 1978—; co-developer courses and programs in anesthesia Wichita State U. Pres. Wichita chpt. Jack and Jills of Am., 1978—; sec., treas. Wind Rows Home Owners Assn., 1980—. Recipient Cert. of Achievement, Chgo. Musical Coll., 1958. Mem. Am. Assn. Nurse Anesthetists (cert.), Kans. Assn. Nurse Anesthetists Am. Nurses Assn., Progressive Women of Wichita (Cert. of Appreciation 1979), Nat. Assn. Female Execs., Nat. Assn. Life Underwriters. Republican. Roman Catholic. Home: 305 Wind Row Lake Dr Goddard KS 67052

ALLEN, BARBARA KIRKMAN, utility company executive; b. Asheville, N.C., July 23, 1931; d. Walter Alfred and Georgia Esmerald (Lewallen) Kirkman; m. Luke C. Allen, Jr., Sept. 9, 1949; 1 child, Michael Kirkman. With Carolina Power & Light Co., Raleigh, N.C., 1950—, mgr. adminstrv. services, 1979. Bd. dirs. N.C. Womens Forum, Wake County Council on Aging, N.C. Community Coll, Y.W.C.A. Wake County, Women's Adv. Council N.C.; bd. deacons New Hope Baptist Ch., Raleigh; mem. adv. bd. Wake County council Girl Scouts U.S.A.; mem. N.C. Symphony Soc., Wake County Hwy. Efficiency council N.C. Dept Transp.; bd. assocs. Meredith Coll., Child Adv. Council, Friends of the Coll. Mem. Nat. Assn. Female Execs., Exec. Women Internat. (pres.). Democrat. Clubs: Capital City, Women's of Raleigh. Office: 411 Fayettville St PO Box 1551 Raleigh NC 27602

ALLEN, BEATRICE, piano teacher; b. N.Y.C., June 30, 1917; d. Samuel and Rose (Krell) Hyman; student N.Y. U., 1933-36; diploma (scholar), Inst. Musical Arts, N.Y.C., 1939, postgrad. (scholar), 1939-40; diploma (fellow, letter commendation), Juilliard Grad. Sch., N.Y.C., 1943; B.A. magna cum laude, Cedar Crest Coll., 1980; m. Eugene Murray Allen, Jan. 23, 1937; children—Marlene Allen Galzin, Julian Lewis. Mem. faculty prep. div. Juilliard Sch. Music, 1957-69, Moravian Coll., 1967-68, Northampton County Area Community Coll., 1968-70, Manhattan Sch. Music, 1969—; founding faculty Community Music Sch., Allentown, Pa., 1982—; condr. Tchrs. Workshop, artist-in-residence Antioch Coll., Yellow Springs, Ohio, 1966; Bach lectr., recitals various univs.; concert appearances Town Hall, N.Y.C., Chautauqua, N.Y., others. Winner N.J. Artists contest, 1936. Mem. Music Tchrs. Nat. Assn. (program chmn. Lehigh Valley chpt. 1981-82), Pa. Music Tchrs. Assn. Address: 2100 Main St Bethlehem PA 18017

ALLEN, BERTHA LEE, social worker, family counselor; b. Bexley, Miss., Mar. 28, 1908; d. Charles H. and Winnie (McLeod) A.; student Maryville Coll., 1928-29; B.A., Miss. U. for Women, 1932; postgrad. U. Ala., 1936, La. State U., 1937, Miss. State U., 1939, U. Miss., 1940; M.S.W., Tulane U., 1949. Tchr. high sch. English and Latin, Rocky Creek and Lucedale, Miss., 1932-33, Agricola, Miss., 1933-36, Tchula, Miss., 1936-44; child welfare worker Miss. Dept. Public Welfare, Jackson, Columbus, Pascagoula, 1944-48; caseworker Columbia (Miss.) Tng. Sch., 1949-50; case work supr., chief social worker Osawatomie (Kans.) State Hosp., 1950-51; dir. casework Miss. Children's Home Soc., Jackson, 1952-54; casework supr. Child and Family Service, Mobile, Ala., 1954-58; supr. casework practice Family Counseling Center, Mobile, 1958-65; caseworker ARC Disaster Services, Hurricane Betsy, New Orleans, 1965, Family Service Soc., New Orleans, 1965-66, Jewish Family and Children's Service, New Orleans, 1966-71, Willow Wood, New Orleans Home for Jewish Aged, 1971-73; pvt. practice individual, marital and family counseling, New Orleans, Mobile, Lucedale, 1969—; cons. Wilmer Hall, Protestant Children's Home, YWCA, Mobile, 1954-65, Providence Nursing Home, New Orleans, 1972-77, Willow Wood, New Orleans Home for Jewish Aged, 1974-75. Bd. dirs. Mulherin Home for Spastic Children, Mobile, 1958-59; charter mem., sec. Miss. Mental Health Assn., 1953-54; mem. casework com. Mobile Council Social Agys., 1954-58, mem. inter-agy. planning com., 1958-62, mem. in-service tng. com., 1963-65; mem. program com. Southeastern Inst., Family Service Assn. Am., 1960; mem. planning com. Mobile County Mental Health Assn., 1964-65; sec. Assn. Maternity and Adoption Agys., New Orleans, 1969-70. Cert. first aid instr. ARC; life teaching cert., Miss.; social work cert., La., Ala. Mem. Nat. Assn. Social Workers, Acad.

Cert. Social Workers, La. Soc. Clin. Social Work, Internat. Platform Assn., Eta Sigma Phi, Oakliegh Garden Soc. Presbyterian. Home and Office: Route 9 Box 796 Lucedale MS 39452 also 1050B Palmetto St Mobile AL 36604

ALLEN, CATHERINE BRYANT, denominational executive, writer; b. Birmingham, Ala., Mar. 26, 1942; d. Leonard P. and Betty Lou (Durham) Bryant; m. Lee Norcross Allen, Aug. 24, 1963; children—Leland Norcross, III, Leslie Catherine. B.A., Samford U., 1964; M.B.A., Emory U., 1984. Editor Woman's Missionary Union So. Bapt. Conv., Birmingham, 1964-67, pub. relations dir., 1967-74, asst. to exec., 1974-83, dir. pub. and employee relations, assoc. exec. dir., 1983—; instr. journalism Samford U., Birmingham, 1970-71. Author: (with Alma Hunt) History of Woman's Missionary Union, 1976; The New Lottie Moon Story, 1980; Centennial History of Woman's Missionary Union, 1987; contbr. numerous guidebooks and articles to religious publs. Bd. dirs. Horizon 280 Assn., Birmingham, 1983-84. Named Alumna of Yr., Samford U., 1980. Mem. Women in Communication, Bapt. Pub. Relations Assn. (pres. 1971-72). Baptist. Office: PO Box C-10 Birmingham AL 35283

ALLEN, CHRISTINE ANN, educator; b. Alpena, Mich., May 16, 1955; d. Richard Lewis, Sr. and Rosemary M. (Detloff) A. A.A., Alpena Community Coll., 1976; B.S. in Edn. with honors, Central Mich. U., 1976-80, elem. endorsement cert., 1981. Jr. high sch. tchr. English, Spring Branch Ind. Sch. Dist., Houston, 1981—; counselor edn. Central Mich. U. Ednl. Skills Ctr., Mt. Pleasant, 1977-78; substitute tchr. Alpena Pub. Schs., 1979-80, Mt. Pleasant Schs., 1981; acad. tutor Cen. Mich. U. Counseling Ctr., 1980. Editor: The Pride, 1983. Coach, Oxbow Elem. Sch., Alpena, Mich., 1976; skills educator W. Intermediate Pub. Sch., Mt. Pleasant, Mich., 1978; mem. Landrum PTA, 1983—. Cynthia Cordell scholar Central Mich. U., 1978-79. Mem. Nat. Edn. Assn., Nat. Council Tchrs. English, Sigma Tau Delta (pres. 1979-80), Delta Psi Kappa (historian 1976-78), Phi Delta Kappa. Home: 2305 Hayes 9204 Houston TX 77077

ALLEN, CONSTANCE CHURCHYARD, state official; b. Tulsa, Aug. 12, 1924; d. Leonard S. and Elizabeth C. Allen; student U. Okla., 1942-43; B.A., U. Tulsa, 1948, postgrad. 1969-70; postgrad. U. Mich. extension, 1954-55, Lake Erie Coll., 1959. Adult program dir. YWCA, Tulsa, 1958-60; recreation supr. Tulsa Park and Recreation Dept., 1960-72; supr. Okla. Dept. Recreation, 1972-76, informational rep. services, 1976—, vol. coordinator; adj. clin. faculty Okla. Coll. Osteopathic Medicine, 1980—. Judge, Jr. Miss Pageant, 1975. Served with Army Service Clubs, Korea, 1956-58. Mem. Okla. Recreation and Parks Soc., U. Tulsa Alumni Assn., Chi Omega. Club: Diamond Head Country. Home: 111 Lakeview Dr Mannford OK 74044 Office: Route 4 Box 9 Sand Springs OK 74063

ALLEN, CYNTHIA GURNEE THORNDIKE, lawyer; b. N.Y.C., June 5, 1953; d. Hamilton Allen and Isabel (Phelps) Furland; m. Richard B. Seely, June 17, 1972 (div. Mar. 1981). B.A. with honors, U. Hawaii, 1975; J.D., Villanova U., 1980. Bar: Fla. 1981. Legal intern to judge, Phila., 1977-80; assoc. law clk. Lubin & Hamill, West Palm Beach, Fla., 1980-81;assoc. Sparber, Shevin, et al, Palm Beach, Fla., 1981-82; ptnr. Lesher & Allen, Palm Beach, 1982—; dir. Sr. Effectiveness Enterprises, West Palm Beach. Chmn. Palm Beach County Commn. on Status of Women, 1984-85; guild mem. Planned Parenthood; briefing leader Hunger Project, Inc., 1983-84; chmn. com. on ecology and environment Palm Beach County Democratic Exec. Com. Mem. Nat. Orgn. Women Bus. Owners, Palm Beach County Bar Assn., ABA, Fla. Assn. Women Lawyers, Exec. Women Palm Beaches (past pres., founder), West Palm Beach C. of C. Episcopalian. Clubs: Bath and Tennis (Palm Beach); Forum (West Palm Beach). Office: Lesher & Allen 189 Bradley Pl Palm Beach FL 33480

ALLEN, CYNTHIA LUDA, consulting company executive; b. Dallas, May 5, 1955; d. George Richard and Elizabeth Luda (Harris) A. B.A., U. Tex.-Dallas, Richardson, 1978; M.S., N. Tex. State U., 1980, M.A., 1983; Ph.D., U. Tex.-Dallas, Richardson, 1984. Market cons. Sun Oil Co., Dallas, 1980-83; pres. Aging Alternatives, Dallas, 1982—; mem. exec. com. Gas Requirements Com., Washington, 1980-83; adv. bd. Parents Anonymous, 1980—; founder and pres. Advocates for the Neurologically Disabled, 1983—. Author: Hospice: An Evolutionary Concept, 1983. Vol., SCAN, Dallas, 1982-83; vol. Old City Park, Dallas, 1980-84, Vista-Peace Corps, 1985—. Mem. Am. Gas Assn. (exec. com. 1980-83), Am. Gerontol. Soc., Tex. LP Gas Assn.

ALLEN, DELORES ANN, physical therapist, consultant; b. Walters, Okla., Feb. 10, 1934; d. Samuel Orestus and Golda Gertrue (Campbell) A. Student, U. Okla., 1955, Baylor Sch. Phys. Therapy, 1957; B.S., U. Tex., 1975. Staff phys. therapist D.C. Gen. Hosp., Washington, 1957-58; chief phys. therapist Dallas Soc. Crippled Children, 1959-61; chief phys. therapist Meth. Hosp., Houston, 1961-67; staff phys. therapist Dallas Soc. Crippled Children, 1967-68; cons., dir. rehab. services U. Tex. Health Sci. Ctr., dept. pediatrics, Dallas, 1968-78; cons. pediatrics Kaiser Found., 1978—; pvt. practice phys. therapy, Dallas, 1978—; allied health cons. phys. rehab. Children's Med. Ctr., Dallas, 1978—; cons. White House Conf. on Children, Washington, 1970; cons. Lamplighter Sch., Dallas, 1978—; profl. adv. counsel Dallas Soc. Crippled Children, 1982—. Bromberg-Myer scholar, Baylor Sch. Phys. Therapy, Dallas, 1956; Nat. Soc. Crippled Children and Adults scholar, 1960; recipient Amy Comstock Meml. award U. Okla., 1953. Mem. Am. Phys. Therapy Assn. Republican. Episcopalian. Club: Sierra (Dallas). Office: 5459 La Sierra Dallas TX 75231

ALLEN, DIANA UPTAIN, geriatric case manager; b. Guntersville, Ala., Mar. 3, 1948; s. Mann and Ruth (Bearden) Uptain; B.S. in Human Services, U. Tenn., Chattanooga, 1975; M.S.S.W., U. Tenn.-Knoxville, 1986; m. Charles Clay Allen, June 10, 1978; 1 son, Matthew Clay. Med. sec. Team Evaluation Center, Chattanooga, 1967-72; dir. social service Hamilton County (Tenn.) Nursing Home, Chattanooga, 1975-80, Meml. Hosp., Chattanooga, 1980-85; case mgr. Sr. Adult Assessment and Counseling Service, Chattanooga, 1986—; coordinator Lifeline Program. Expt. in Internat. Living Study Abroad Program scholar, 1974; Sarah Key Patten scholar, 1974. Mem. Soc. Hosp. Social Work Dirs., Am. Hosp. Assn., Nat. Assn. Social Workers, Pi Gamma Mu. Home: 1764 Pine Needles Trail Chattanooga TN 37421 Office: 204 High St Chattanooga TN 37403

ALLEN, DOROTHY EVELYN, state official; b. Glen Easton, W.Va., May 16, 1922; d. Anderson Andrew and Blanche M. (McCosh) Allen. A.B., West Liberty State Coll., 1944; M.S.W., Western Res. U., 1947. Sr. child welfare worker W.Va. Dept. Welfare, Charleston, 1947-49, dist. child welfare supr., Wheeling, 1949-59, chief child welfare, Charleston, 1959-64, div. dir., 1974-75, asst. commr. W.Va. Dept. Human Services, Charleston, 1975—; chmn. regional conf. Child Welfare League Am., Inc., 1976. Recipient award for dedicated services to children, W.Va. Welfare Conf., 1977; Service awards W.Va. Dept. Human Services, 1977, 84; Recognition award Pressley Ridge Sch., Pitts., 1985. Mem. Nat. Assn. Social Workers, Am. Pub. Welfare Assn., W.Va. Welfare Conf., Acad. Accredited Social Workers. Address: Div Social Service Dept Human Services 1900 Washington St E Charleston WV 25305

ALLEN, GENEVA LEONE, temporary service company executive, accountant; b. Richmond, Ind., Apr. 7, 1924; s. Melvin L. and Vida E. (Halstead) Smith; m. Dudley Brusher, Apr. 6, 1946 (div. Feb. 1953); m. Charles A. Allen, Mar. 5, 1954; children—Michael, Paula. Grad. high sch., Richmond, Ind. Licensed pub. acct. Clk. FBI, Washington, 1942-43; fin. officer ARC, Washington, 1943-44; pub. acct. William H. Thomas C.P.A., Richmond, 1954-63; pvt. practice acctg., Richmond, 1963-66; owner Franchise Manpower of Richmond, 1966—. Mem. Nat. Assn. Accts. (pres. 1975-76), Am. Bus. Women's Assn. (Woman of Yr. award 1973), Assn. Manpower Franchise Owners (bd. dirs. 1979-81), Richmond Area C. of C. (treas. 1980-82). Republican. Mem. Christian Ch. Club: Zonta (Richmond) (pres. 1984—). Avocations: boating; golfing. Home: 3820 Oakview Dr Richmond IN 47374 Office: Manpower of Richmond 301 NW 5th St Richmond IN 47374

ALLEN, GERTRUDE MARGARET, state day care consultant; b. Flint, Mich., Oct. 3, 1922; d. Leo and Florence Pearl (Mason) McPhillips; m. Joseph Anthony Allen, Feb. 18, 1946; children—Michael Joseph, Janice Lynn Marie Allen Tuke. B.S., Saginaw Valley State Coll., 1973; M.A., Central Mich. U., 1979. Sec. O'Keefe Law Firm, Saginaw, Mich., 1959-62, Vis. Nurse Assn., Saginaw, 1963-69; child day care cons. Mich. Dept. Social Services, Saginaw, 1974—; bd. dirs. Community Coordinated Child Care, Saginaw, 1980—; mem. Child Abuse and Neglect Council Saginaw, 1983—. Editorial bd. Chrysallis Jour., 1975. Bd. dirs. Chrysallis Ctr. for Human Devel., Saginaw Valley State Coll., University City, Mich., 1971—, v.p. 1971—). Served with USNR, 1943-45. Mem. Mich. League for Human Services, Mich. State Employees Assn. (chpt. pres. 1980—, arbitration com., legis. rep.), AAUW (Saginaw br.) pres. 1979-81, chmn. legis. com. 1982-84, fellowship named grant honoree 1981), Saginaw Valley State Coll. Alumni Assn. (v.p. 1982—), LWV. Office: Mich Dept Social Services 411 E Genesee Ave Saginaw MI 48605

ALLEN, GINA, writer; d. R.V. and Osa (Hanel) Hunkins; m. T.W. Allen (div.); 1 child, Ginita Wall. B.J., Northwestern U., 1940. Co-manager Allen Acres Dairy Farm, Las Cruces, N.Mex., 1946-64; corr. Guernsey Breeders Jour., N.Y.C., 1950-59; columnist Western Dairy Jour., Los Angeles, 1954-62; editor San Francisco Free Woman, 1968-73; freelance writer TV, radio, publs., 1946—; instr. English, Ahwaz Agrl. Coll., Iran, 1964-66; mem. editorial bd. The Humanist Mag., Amherst, N.Y., 1976—. Author: Gold!, 1964; Rustics for Keeps, 1948; Forbidden Man, 1961 (Anisfield-Wolf award 1962); Prairie Children, 1941; On the Oregon Trail, 1942; Gold Is—, 1964. Co-author (with Clement G. Martin) Intimacy, 1971; (with R.V. Hunkins) Tales of the Prairies, 1941, 42, 45 (3 books). Contbr. short stories and articles to leading mags., translations to fgn. publs., pieces on psychol. subjects to TV and radio. State v.p. PTA, N.Mex., 1954-62; leader 4-H Club, Las Cruces, 1958-62; chmn. N.Mex. Democratic Central Com., 1956-59. Recipient Friend of Children award Nat. Assn. Juvenile Judges, 1957. Mem. Am. Humanist Assn. (v.p. 1979-83, co-chmn. div. humanist counseling, 1981—, founding chmn. Feminist Caucus, 1977—, Merit award 1977, Pioneer award, 1983), Author's Guild, Sci. Writers No. Calif., NOW, Nat. Abortion Rights Action League, Internat. Soc. Gen. Semantics, Women's Polit. Caucus. Unitarian. Avocations: animals; travel; music; gardening; golf.

ALLEN, IRENE AMILHAT, teacher educator, consultant; b. Ypsilanti, Mich., July 2; d. Guilliaume Joseph and Ida Marie (Garceau) Amilhat; m. Roger Frank Allen, Nov. 29, 1958 (dec. 1965). B.S. in Edn., Johnson Tchrs. Coll., 1957; student U. Vt., summer 1959, U. Mich., 1973; M.A. in Edn., Ball State Tchrs. Coll., 1962; Ed.D. in Reading Ball State U., 1968. Elem. sch. tchr. Morristown Pub. Schs., Vt., 1957-59, Ft. Wayne Pub. Schs., Ind., 1959-66; doctoral fellow Ball State U., Muncie, Ind., 1966-68; asst. to full prof. Eastern Mich. U., Ypsilanti, 1968-77; vis. prof. Bulmershe Coll. Higher Edn., Earley, Reading, Eng., summer 1975; vis. exchange prof. U. Warwick, Coventry, Eng., 1980-81; prof., chief-of-party Swaziland Primary Curriculum Project, AID, Manzini, Swaziland, 1982-84; prof. Eastern Mich. U., 1984—; presentor papers at profl. association meetings, U.S., Africa and Europe. Co-author: Kollection of Kues from Kids, 1975; The Reading Skills Inventory, 1980; Effective Reading Instruction, 1984. Mem. editorial rev. bds. Fla. Reading Research Jour., 1981—, Jour. Edn. in Reading, 1984—. Bd. dirs. Cliffs on the Bay Condominium Assn., Ypsilanti, 1984—; mem. St. Ursula's choir, Ypsilanti, 1983—. Named Woman of Yr., Eastern Mich. U. Women's Commn., 1980, Outstanding Tchr. in Reading, Orgn. Tchr. Educators in Reading, 1979; recipient Josephine Nevins Keal Endowment award, 1980, 84, 85. Mem. Orgn. Tchr. Educators in Reading (pres.), Internat. Reading Assn., Assn. for Supervision and Curriculum Devel., Assn. Tchr. Educators, Mich. Reading Assn., Phi Delta Kappa (pres. 1979-80), Delta Kappa Gamma (pres. Beta). . Avocations: reading; traveling; mountain climbing, in U.S., Japan, Africa; bicycling; alpine skiing. Office: Eastern Mich U 234-P Boone Hall Ypsilanti MI 48197

ALLEN, ISABEL ELAINE, biostatistician, educator; b. N.Y.C., Oct. 18, 1948; d. John Thomas and Claire Isabel (Meldrum) Allen; B.A., Skidmore Coll., 1970; M.A., U. Evansville, 1975; Ph.D., Cornell U., 1979; m. Jeffrey Richard Seaman, Jan. 21, 1978; 1 son, Christopher Allen. Statis. cons. Historic New Harmony, Inc. (Ind.), 1975; research/teaching asst. dept. econs. and social stats. Cornell U., Ithaca, N.Y., 1976-78; asst. prof. stats. Wharton Sch., U. Pa., Phila., 1978-83, adj. assoc. prof., 1983-85, research assoc. in population studies, 1980—; sr. biostatistician, supr. clin. trials Wyeth Labs., Radnor, Pa., 1983—; research assoc. prof. Med. Coll. Pa., Phila., 1985—; cons. Dept. Revenue, Commonwealth of Pa., 1979-81, Def. Logistics Agy., U.S. Dept. Def., 1980-81. Bd. dirs. Parent-Infant Center, Phila., 1980-81, treas., 1980-81. Cornell fellow, 1977, research fellow in population, 1976; U. Pa. faculty summer fellow and grantee, 1979; Prudential fellow for inflation research, 1981-82. Mem. Am. Statis. Assn., Population Assn. Am., Biometric Soc., Classification Soc., Soc. for Computer Simulation, Internat. Assn. Statis. Computing, Phila. Fin. Assn. Contbr. articles to profl. jours. Home: Jug Hollow Rd Phoenixville PA Office: Biostatistics PO Box 8299 Wyeth Labs Philadelphia PA 19101

ALLEN, JANET RUTH, researcher; b. Houston, Mar. 10, 1957; d. John and Alena (Mayfield) Allen. B.S., Prairie View A&M, 1980; B.A., Houston U., 1983. Researcher Exxon, Houston, 1976—; paralegal Nat. Legal Forum, Houston, 1981—; cons. Youth Adv. Bd., Houston, 1981—; tutor Houston Ind. Sch. Dist., 1982-83. Tchr. Young Adult Christian Conf., Houston, 1983—. Prairie View A&M U. scholar, 1975. Mem. Tex. Paralegal Assn., NAACP. Democrat. Baptist. Clubs: Writers (Houston). Lodge: Order Eastern Star (chaplin 1981—). Home: 714 E 37th St Houston TX 77022 Office: Exxon Co 4400 Dacoma St Houston TX 77021

ALLEN, JEAN CURRY, lawyer; b. Atlanta, 1923. B.A., Vanderbilt U., 1944; J.D., Emory U., 1948. Bar: Ga. 1948. Now ptnr. Hansell & Post, Atlanta. Mem. ABA, Atlanta Bar Assn. Address: Hansell and Post 3300 First Atlanta Tower Atlanta GA 30383*

ALLEN, JESSIE LEE, nurse; b. Clarke County, Miss., Mar. 8, 1925; d. Roosevelt and Margie (Collins) Harper; G.E.D., Emily Griffith Opportunity Sch., Denver, 1963; A.A.S. in Mental Retardation Tech., Angelina Jr. Coll., 1972; L.P.N., Meridian Jr. Coll., 1976; m. Lawrence Allen, Oct. 26, 1974; 1 son, Renard Williams. Attendant, then head attendant and relief attendant supr. Ridge State Home and Tng. Sch., Denver, 1962-66; attendant, then attendant supr. I Tex. Research Inst. of Mental Scis., Houston, 1968-70; therapist asst. Lufkin (Tex.) State Sch., 1970-72; nurse Watkins Meml. Hosp., Quitman, Miss., 1976-77, staff nurse, 1981—; nurse Archusa Convalescent Center, 1977—. Mem. Am. Assn. Mental Deficiency, Nat. Fedn. L.P.N.'s. Baptist. Home: Route 3 Box 176 Vossburg MS 39366 Office: HC Watkins Meml Hosp Quitman MS 39355

ALLEN, JOAN RACHELLE, statistician; b. N.Y.C., June 24, 1947; d. Lester A. and Emma N. (Pinkofsky) Kraus; A.B., U. Mich., 1968; M.A., U. Calif.-Berkeley, 1969; children—Michael Zev, Lisa Arielle. Public health statistician Calif. Dept. Public Health, Berkeley, 1969-72; systems analyst Tex. Inst. Rehab. and Research, Houston, 1972-74; statistician Am. Optometric Assn., Washington, 1974-76; assoc. statistician George Washington U., Washington, 1977-78; cons. statistician Nat. Center for Health Stats., Hyattsville, Md., 1976-79, mem. faculty Applied Stats. Tng. Inst., 1977-81; research analyst Health Care Agy., Orange County, Santa Ana, Calif., 1979-85; adminstrv. analyst Orange County, 1985—. Pres., Sierra Broadmoor Community Assn., 1982. Mem. Am. Statis. Assn., So. Calif. Statis. Soc.

ALLEN, JOANN LONG, real estate investment company executive; artist; b. Laurens County, S.C., Nov. 25, 1932; d. Julius Vernon and Ruby Evelyn (Boland) Long; student Palmar Coll., 1964; B.A., Jacksonville U., 1970, M.A. in Math., 1974; m. Walter Gregory Allen, Jr., Oct. 12, 1952; 1 dau., Vivian JoAnn; 1 stepdau., Janet A. Henry. With Colonial Properties, Inc., Jacksonville, Fla., 1965—, dir., 1970—, sec., 1970-76, sec., treas., 1976-79, v.p., 1979—; group shows include: St. Augustine Art Assn., 1979—, Artists' Gallery, 1978—, Jacksonville U., 1980. Pres. Artists' Gallery, 1980; bd. dirs. Jr. Woman's Club Jacksonville, 1958-60, Garden Club Jacksonville, 1958, Duval County Hosp. Aux., 1960-61, Duval County Council Camp Fire Girls, 1973-75, Southside Women's Club, 1973-74, Empire Point Com. Council, 1976; mem. Mayor's Adv. Com. on Status of Women, 1978-79. Recipient various awards and hon. mentions for paintings and drawings. Mem. Jacksonville Symphony Guild, Jacksonville Art Mus., Arts Assembly, Jacksonville Watercolor Soc., Friends of Fine Arts, Friends Jacksonville U. Library, Jacksonville U. Alumni Assn., St. Augustine Art Assn., Art League Jacksonville. Republican. Episcopalian. Clubs: Ponte Vedra, River, Pilots (dir. 1974-75). Home: 3739 Duval Dr Jacksonville Beach FL 32250 Office: 3116 Atlantic Blvd Jacksonville FL 32207

ALLEN, KATHERINE YARNELL, state legislator; b. Pueblo, Colo., June 17, 1925; d. Paul and Gladys deFord (Meffley) Yarnell; m. William Allen, Jr., Sept. 20, 1947; children—Susan M. Southwick, Mary K., Barbara D. A.B. in Econs., U. Denver, 1947. State legislator Wash. House of Reps., Olympia, 1983—. Pres. Edmonds Sch. Dist. #15 Sch. Bd., Lynnwood, Wash., 1976, mem., 1973-77; mayor pro-tem, Edmonds, mem. Edmonds City Council, 1977-83. Recipient Thanks Badge, Totem Girl Scout Council, 1980, named Disting. Girl Scout, 1985; recipient Outstanding Service award Dist. PTA, 1978; Living Legend award Edmonds Sch. Dist. #15, 1985. Mem. LWV, AAUW, Elected Washington Women, Women's Polit. Caucus. Republican. Presbyterian. Home: 21712 85th Pl W Edmonds WA 98020 Office: House of Reps House Office Bldg Olympia WA 98504

ALLEN, LEATRICE DELORICE, psychologist; b. Chgo., July 15, 1948; d. Burt and Mildred Floy (Taylor) Hawkins; m. Allen Moore, Jr., July 30, 1965 (div. Oct. 1975); children—Chandra, Valarie, Allen; m. Armstead Allen, May 11, 1978. A.A. in Bus. Edn., Olive Harvey Coll., Chgo., 1975; B.A. in Psychology cum laude, Chgo. State U., 1977; M.Clin. Psychology, Roosevelt U., 1980. Clk., U.S. Post Office, Chgo., 1967-72; clin. therapist Bobby Wright Mental Health Ctr., Chgo., 1979-80; clin. therapist Community Mental Health Council, Chgo., 1980-83, assoc. dir., 1983—; cons. Edgewater Mental Health, Chgo., 1984—, Project Pride, Chgo., 1985—. Scholar Chgo. State U., 1976, Roosevelt U., 1978; fellow Menninger Found., 1985. Mem. Nat. Orgn. for Victim Assistance, Ill. Coalition Against Sexual Assault (del. 1985—). Avocations: aerobics; reading; theatre; dining. Home: 16603 S Paulina St Markham IL 60426 Office: Community Mental Health Council 1001 E 87th St Chicago IL 60426

ALLEN, LETTY CARMEN, research physicist; b. Quito, Ecuador, July 4, 1949; came to U.S., 1967, naturalized, 1978; d. Gustavo and Magdalena (Moreira) Carrera; m. Herbert Oswaldo Espinoza, Aug. 23, 1967 (div. 1977); children—Danny Javier, Dean Fernando; m. Robert Burnell Allen, Dec. 29, 1978; 1 child, Dianne Katherine. B.A. in Physics, U. Calif.-LaJolla, 1978; M.S. in Physics Rutgers U., 1980. Associate mem. tech. staff AT&T Bell Labs., Murray Hill, N.J., 1980-82, mem. tech. staff, 1982—. Contbr. articles to profl. jours. Recipient Second Prize in apparatus competition Am. Assn. Physics Tchrs., 1982. Mem. Am. Phys. Soc., Sci. Edn. Club. Office: AT&T Bell Labs 600 Mountain Ave Murray Hill NJ 07974

ALLEN, LISA JANE, television reporter, lawyer; b. Willimantic, Conn., Apr. 29, 1956; d. Myron and Nancy Lois (Sussman) A. B.A. summa cum laude, Tufts U., 1978; J.D., Emory U., 1982. Bar: Ga. 1982. News writer sta. WEEI-CBS Radio, Boston, 1977-78; anchor, reporter sta. WHYN-TV, Springfield, Mass., 1978-79; producer, reporter sta. WGBY-TV, Springfield, 1979; anchor, reporter sta. WGST, Atlanta, 1979-81; assignment editor, reporter sta. WSB-TV, Atlanta, 1981-82; TV corr. Cox Communications, Washington, 1983-85; med. reporter Sta. KTVI-TV, St. Louis, 1985—; mem. House/Senate Radio and TV News Galleries, Washington, 1983-85. Mem. ABA, Phi Beta Kappa.

ALLEN, LOUISE, writer, educator; b. Alliance, Ohio, Sept. 21, 1910; d. Earl Wayne and Ella Celesta (Goodall) A.; student Cleve. Coll. Western Res. U., 1963, Lakeland Community Coll., 1981-82; m. Benjamin Yukl, June 27, 1936; children—Katherine Anne Yukl Johnston, Kenneth Allen, Richard Lee, Margaret Louise Yukl Border. Co-founder, Sch. Writing, Cleve., 1961-62; founder, dir. Allen Writers' Agy., Wickliffe, Ohio, 1963—; editorial asso. criticism service Writer's Digest mag., 1967-69; instr. Lakeland Community Coll., Mentor, Ohio, 1973—, Cuyahoga Community Coll., 1975—. Mem. Mensa, Assn. Mundial de Mujures Periodistas y Escritoras, Women in Communications, Nat. League Am. Pen Women, DAR, Textile Arts Club of Cleve. Mus. Art. Republican. Congregationalist. Clubs: Shore Writers (founder), Euclid Three Arts; Women's City (Cleve.); Altrusa. Contbr. articles to mags. Address: 29308 Eddy Rd Wickliffe OH 44092

ALLEN, MARGERY J. MILNE, librarian; b. Montreal, Que., Can.; d. George Edwin Robinson and Wilhelmina Boyd (Pringle) Milne; m. William Gordon Allen, 1949 (div. 1964); children—Ian Drury, Peter Gershom. B.A., McGill U., 1942, B.L.S., 1946. Cataloger, NRC Library, Ottawa, Ont., Can., 1948-51; reviser Def. Sci. Info. Service, Def. Research Bd., Ottawa, 1951-54; classifier Engring. Socs. Library, N.Y.C., 1964-66; asst. librarian Clarkson Coll. Tech., Potsdam, N.Y., 1966-67; asst. univ. librarian for tech. services Sir. George Williams U. Library, Montreal, 1968-73; asst. dir. reference div. Met. Toronto Library, 1973—. Served to lt. Women's Royal Canadian Naval Service, 1943-45. Mem. Can. Library Assn., ALA, Ont. Library Assn., Canadian Assn. Coll. and Univ. Libraries, Corp. Profl. Librarians Que. Office: Met Toronto Library 789 Yonge St Toronto ON M4W 2G8 Canada

ALLEN, MARILYN MYERS POOL, theatre director; b. Fresno, Calif., Nov. 2, 1934; d. Laurence B. and Asa (Griggs) Myers; B.A., Stanford U., 1955, postgrad., 1955-56; postgrad. U. Tex., 1957-60, W. Tex. State U. summers 1962, 63; m. Joseph Harold Pool, Dec. 28, 1955; children—Pamela Elizabeth, Victoria Anne, Catherine Marcia; m. Neal R. Allen, Apr. 1982. Pvt. tchr. drama, speech, acting, directing, speech correction, Amarillo, Tex., 1960-82, Midland, Tex., 1982—; free-lance radio and TV actress; asst. mng. dir. Amarillo Little Theatre, 1964-66, mng. dir., 1966-68, play dir., 1980; mng. dir. Horsehoe Players, touring profl. theater, 1969-73; actress, multi-media prodn. Palo Duro Canyon, 1971; dir. touring children's theatre, 1978-79 guest actress in Medea, Amarillo Coll., 1981; guest reciter Midland-Odessa Symphony, 1984. Pres., Tex. Non-Profit Theatres, 1972-74, 75-77; 1st v.p. High Plains Center for Performing Arts, 1969-73; adv. mem. dept. fine arts Amarillo Coll., 1980-82. Adv. mem. Tex. Constnl. Revision Commn., 1973-75; mem. adv. council U. Tex. Coll. Fine Arts, 1969-72; community adv. com. for women Amarillo Coll., 1975-79; conv. program com. Am. Theatre Assn., 1978, program participant 1978-80, bd. dirs., 1980-83; bd. dirs. Amarillo Found. Health and Sci. Edn., 1976-82, program v.p., 1979-81; bd. dirs. Domestic Violence Council, 1979-82, March of Dimes, 1979-81, Tex. Panhandle Heritage Found., 1964-82, Friends of Fine Arts, W. Tex. State U., 1980-82, Amarillo City Library, 1980-82, Amarillo Symphony, 1981-82; publicity chmn. Midland Community Theatre, 1984—. Recipient cert. of appreciation Woman of Year, Amarillo Bus. and Profl. Women's Club, 1966; Best Actress award for Hedda Gabler role Amarillo Little Theatre 1965, Best Dir. award for Rashomon, 1967; named woman of Yr., Beta Sigma Pi, 1980; Travel fellow AAUW, 1973, 78. Mem. Am. Community Theatre Assn. (dir. 1969-72, 82-84, v.p. planning and devel. 1985—), S.W. Theatre Conf. (dir. 1973-76, 82—, exec. com. 1982-84), Tex. Theatre Council (dir. 1974-81, exec. com., pres. 1975-76), AAUW (br. pres. 1973-75, state chmn. cultural interests 1975-77, state bd. dirs. 1984—), DAR, (chpt. chaplain 1971-75, historian 1975-77), C. of C. (fine arts council), U.S. Judo Assn., Symphony Guild, Amarillo Art Assn., Midland Symphony Guild (arrangements chmn. 1983-84), Act IX, Amarillo Law Wives Club (pres. 1976-77), Hamhocks (v.p. 1985-86). Episcopalian.

ALLEN, MARY CATHERINE MITCHELL (MRS. WALTON ALBERT ALLEN), educator; b. Iva, S.C.; d. George Francis and Cinderella (Harris) Mitchell; A.A., Anderson Jr. Coll., 1946; B.S. in Edn., Central State Coll., Edmond, Okla., 1962; M.Ed., U. Ga., 1968; Ed.S., Atlanta U., 1974; m. Walton Albert Allen, Apr. 15, 1949; children—Susan Marie, Joel Walton, Barbara Ann. Tchr., prin. Anderson County (S.C.) Schs., 1946-52; tchr. West Clayton Sch., College Park, Ga., 1964-66, guidance counselor, 1966—. Active Girl Scouts U.S.A., 1946-68; bd. dirs. Cherokee Estates, Inc. Mem. NEA, Ga., Clayton County (public relations com. com. 1967-68, chmn. profl. devel. com. 1975-78) edn. assns., AAUW, Am. (state coordinator elem. counselors), Ga. personnel and guidance assns., Ga. Assn. Sch. Counselors, Alpha Delta Kappa (chpt. treas. 1970-72, dist. chaplain 1972—, chpt. pres. 1974-76), Kappa Delta Pi. Home: 2765 Jerome Rd College Park GA 30349 Office: 5580 Riverdale Rd College Park GA 30337

ALLEN, MARYON PITTMAN, former U.S. Senator, journalist, lectr., interior and clothing designer; b. Meridian, Miss., Nov. 30, 1925; d. John D. and Tellie (Chism) Pittman; m. Joshua Sanford Mullins, Jr., Oct. 17, 1946 (div. Jan. 1959); children—Joshua Sanford III, John Pittman, Maryon Foster; m. James Browning Allen, Aug. 7, 1964 (dec. June 1, 1978); 1 stepchild, James Browning. Student, U. Ala., 1944-47, Internat. Inst. Interior Design, 1970. Office mgr. for Dr. Alston Callahan, Birmingham, Ala., 1959-60; bus. mgr. psychiat. clinic U. Ala. Med. Center, Birmingham, 1960-61; life underwriter Protective Life Ins. Co., Birmingham, 1961-62; women's editor Sun Newspapers, Birmingham, 1962-64; v.p., partner Pittman family cos., J.D. Pittman Partnership Co., J.D. Pittman Tractor Co., Emerald Valley Corp., Mountain Lake Farms, Inc., Birmingham; mem. U.S. Senate (succeeding late husband James B. Allen), 1978; dir. public relations and advt. C.G. Sloan & Co. Auction House, Washington, 1981—; owner The Maryon Allen Co., "Cliff House," Birmingham, 1981—. Feature writer: Birmingham News, 1964; writer syndicated column Reflections of a News Hen, Washington, 1969-78; feature writer, columnist; Maryon Allen's Washington, Washington Post, 1979-81. Mem.

Ladies of U.S. Senate ARC Unit, Ala. Hist. Commn., Blair House Fine Arts Commn.; charter mem. Birmingham Commn. of 100 for Women; trustee Children's Fresh Air Farm, Ind. Presbyn. Ch., bd. dirs. Positive Maturity, Birmingham; mem. Fashion Group of Birmingham; Democratic Presdl. elector, Ala., 1968; bd. deacons Ind. Presby. Ch., Birmingham. Recipient 1st place award for best original column Ala. Press Assn., 1962, 63, also various press state and nat. awards for typography, fashion writing, food pages, several awards during Senate service. National Press Club. Clubs: Birmingham Country Washington, 1925 F Street, 91st Congress, Congressional. Presbyterian. Home: Cliff House 3215 Cliff Rd Birmingham AL 35205

ALLEN, MELISSA, marketing research analyst; b. Los Angeles, Oct. 27, 1959; d. Eugene and Elaine Joanne (Fox) A. B.A., U. Calif.-Santa Barbara, 1981. Project dir. J.D. Power & Assocs., Westlake Village, Calif., 1981-85; sr. mktg. research analyst Mattel Toys, Hawthorne, Calif., 1985—. Mem. Am. Mktg. Assn., Phi Beta Kappa. Avocations: reading; collecting antique dolls; jogging; swimming; bicycling. Office: Mattel Toys 5150 Rosecrans Blvd Hawthorne CA 90250

ALLEN, MYRNA LOIS, real estate broker; b. San Pedro, Calif., June 7, 1935; d. Frederick Alan and Jeraldine Ardina (Frohlich) Bucher; m. John Homan Allen, Apr. 18, 1958; children—Jillan, John, Laureen. Student Long Beach City Coll., 1955, Grau Bus. Coll., 1956. Salesman Wood-Geringer Realty Residential Homes, Placentia, Calif., 1969-71; assoc. broker U.S. Affiliated Brokers, Fullerton, Calif., 1971-73, Red Carpet Realty, Yorba Linda, Calif., 1973-76; land locator Westreal Investment and Devel. Co., Anaheim, Calif., 1976-79; assoc. broker Hillcrest Realty and Investment Co., Fullerton, 1979—. Sec. Young Republicans, 1963. Mem. Realty Investment Assn. Orange County (chmn. edn. com. 1983, v.p. edn., dir. 1984), Orange County Assn. Real Estate Investment Brokers (program chmn. 1983-84), Beta Sigma Phi. Home: 16722 Orange Dr Yorba Linda CA 92686 Office: Hillcrest Realty and Investment Co Inc 908 N Harbor Blvd Fullerton CA 92631

ALLEN, PAMELA KAY, nurse; b. Denton, Tex., June 4, 1949; d. Ruby Sauls Allen; L.V.N., Denton Sch. Vocat. Nursing, 1969; B.S. in Nursing, Tex. Woman's U., Denton, 1978. Hosp. and office nurse, 1973-76; dir. nurses Care Inn, Sanger, Tex., 1980; health care planning coordinator Nat. Living Ctrs., 1980; dir., tchr. vocat. nursing Irving (Tex.) Ind. Sch. Dist., 1979-80; nursing skills lab. asst. El Centro Coll., Dallas, 1979; staff nurse Tex. Woman's U., 1980-83; asst. head nurse emergency dept. Westgate Med. Ctr., Denton, Tex., 1982—; pub. health nurse Denton City-County Health Dept., 1981-82. Mem. Denton Police Res., 1981—. Mem. Am. Nurses Assn., Nat. League Nursing, Tex. Assn. Vocat. Nurse Educators, Tex. Women's U. Alumni Assn., Bus. and Profl. Women's Club. Methodist.

ALLEN, PAULINE VIRGINIA, accountant; b. Guntown, Miss., Feb. 7, 1909; d. Henry James and Madia Jane (Kennedy) A.; student Southwestern U., Memphis, 1927-29, 32-33, U. Miss., 1933-34; A.B., Duke U., 1935. Math. tchr. high sch., Pleasant Grove, Miss., 1936-37; clk. ins. agy., Tunica, Miss., 1940-48; bookkeeper, Tunica, 1952-56; accountant Tunica County Hosp., 1956—. Mem. Hosp. Fin. Mgrs. Assn. Democrat. Methodist. Club: Order Eastern Star. Home: Box 96 Tunica MS 38676

ALLEN, PHYLLIS H., hotel executive; b. Somerville, Mass., Nov. 8, 1939; d. Wilburt and Phyllis (Keough) Brown; m. Bruce B. Allen, June 12, 1958; children—Kim E., Bruce S., Jon M., William J. Student pub. schs., Medford, Mass. Window decorator Lerner Shop, Medford, Mass., 1956-57; mdse. staff Sears Roebuck Co., Cambridge, Mass., 1957-58; bookkeeper C. Carbone Co., Somerville, 1958-65; mgr. Tupperware, Westbrook, Conn., 1965-69; sale mgr., food and beverage dir., gen. mgr. Holiday Inn, Manchester, N.H., 1969-77, gen. mgr., Washington, 1977—. Group leader Girl Scouts U.S.A., 1967-68, Cub Scouts, 1969-70; mem. womens aux. Little League, 1971-73. Named Asst. Innkeeper of Yr., Holiday Inn, Memphis, 1977. Mem. N.H. Hospitality Assn. (dir. 1979-81). Roman Catholic. Office: Holiday Inn 1900 Connecticut Ave NW Washington DC 20009

ALLEN, RANDY LEE, management consulting executive; b. Ithaca, N.Y., June 24, 1946; d. Richard Hallstead and Mary Elizabeth (Howe) Hallstead Baker; m. Rodney Howard Allen, Jan. 24, 1969 (div. Nov. 1978); m. John James Meehan, Apr. 24, 1983; 1 child, Scott Hallstead; stepchildren Michael John, Kimberly Susan. B.A. in Physics, Cornell U., 1968; postgrad. Syracuse U., 1968, Seattle U., 1973-74. Cert. mgmt. cons., cert. systems profl. Programmer, IBM, Endicott, N.Y., 1968-69; product and industry mgr. Boeing Computer Service, Seattle, 1969-74; dir. mktg. Androcor subs. Boeing Computer, Calumet City, Ill., 1974-76; ptnr. Touche Ross & Co., Newark, 1976—; trustee N.J. Inst. Tech., Newark, 1984—. Author: OCR-A Cost/Benefit Guide; Pos Trends in the '80's; Bottom Line Issues in Retailing; also articles. Regional fund raiser Cornell U., 1983-84; chmn. long range plan United Methodist Ch. Bishop Janes, Basking Ridge, N.J., 1983. Recipient Acad. Women Achievers award YWCA, 1984. Mem. Inst. Mgmt. Cons. (nominating com.), Am. Mgmt. Assn., Am. Arbitration Assn., Exec. Women N.J. (pres. 1979-81, dir. 1981-85). Club: Cornell. Avocations: skiing, tennis, stamp collecting, symphony, art, swimming, boating, reading. Office: Touche Ross & Co Gateway One Newark NJ 07102

ALLEN, RAYE VIRGINIA, cultural historian; b. Temple, Tex., May 27, 1929; d. Irvin and Vivian (Arnold) McCreary; m. Henry Kiper Allen, June 9, 1951; children—Henry Kiper, Irvin McCreary, Rave Virginia. B.A., U. Tex.-Austin, 1951, M.A. in Am. Civilization, 1975, Ph.D. candidate. Mem. Am. Folklife Ctr. in Library of Congress, Washington, 1976-84, chmn., 1978-79; trustee, sec. Future Homemakers of Am. Found., 1983—; bd. dirs. Future Homemakers Akm., 1978-85; trustee U.S.-N.Z. Arts Found.; coordinator com. for Restoration of Ellis Island; mem. Centennial Commn. of U. Tex.-Austin and chmn. continuing edn. com., 1981-84, adv. council astronomy dept. McDonald Obs., 1984—; adv. council Inst. Texan Cultures; mem. Am. Revolution Bicentennial Commn. of Tex., 1971-75; co-founder, 1st pres. Cultural Activities Ctr. of Temple, Tex., 1957-59; bd. dirs. Tex. State Soc. of Washington, 1980-83, Tex. Cultural Alliance, Inst. Humanities, Salado, Tex., Tex. Folklife Resources (hon.). Recipient Outstanding Citizen of Temple award, 1973; Raye Virginia Allen State Pres. scholarship established in her honor Future Homemakers Am., 1986. Episcopalian. Home: 1537 33 St NW Washington DC 20007 also Green Oaks Farm #19 Hartrick Bluff Rd Temple TX 76502

ALLEN, REGINA ESTELLE, hotel sales executive; b. Rochester, N.Y., Sept. 21, 1941; d. Doyle and Violet (Skibski) A.; m. David Allen Westfall, Aug. 27, 1960 (div. June 1974); children—Betsy Suzanne, Todd Allan. B.A. in Mktg., Rochester Inst. Tech., 1963. Dir. mktg. Budget Rent-a-Car Systems Inc., Dallas, 1974-79; sales mgr. Loews Anatole Hotel, Dallas, 1979-82, nat. sales dir., Washington, 1982—. Mem. Nat. Assn. Female Execs., Hotel Sales Mktg. Assn. Internat. (Outstanding Mem. 1979), Sales Mktg. Execs. Internat. (Disting. Sales award Dallas chpt. 1980, chpt. award of merit 1982), Greater Washington Sales and Mktg. Execs. (bd. dirs. 1983—), Potomac Meeting Planners Internat. (chmn. hospitality 1983—). Republican. Home: 5222 Nebraska Ave NW B656 Washington DC 20015 Office: Loews Nat Sales Office 2000 L St NW Suite 200 Washington DC 20036

ALLEN, ROBERTA L., artist, fiction writer; b. N.Y.C., Oct. 6, 1945; d. Sol Allen and Jeanette (Waldner) Sanderson. A.A.S., Fashion Inst. Tech., 1964. Guest lectr. Corcoran Sch. Art, Washington, 1975, C.W. Post Coll., Glenvale, N.Y., 1979, Kutztown State Coll., Pa., 1979, Farleigh Dickenson U., Madison, N.J., 1980; panelist CAPS Graphic Artist Grants, N.Y.C., 1981-82. Author: The Traveling Woman, 1986; Partial Portrait, 1983. Author and artist: Pointless Acts, 1977; Everything in The World, 1981. One woman shows include John Weber Gallery, N.Y.C., 1974, 75, 77, 79. Recipient Monetary award CAPS, 1978-79, LINE grant, 1985; Residence award MacDowell Colony 1971, 72; Residence awards Ossabaw Island Project 1972, Yaddo 1983, Va. Ctr. Creative Arts 1985. Mem. Poets and Writers Inc. Avocation: photography. Home and Office: 5 W 16th St New York NY 10011

ALLEN, SHARON AMERINE, educational administrator; b. Alexandria, La., Apr. 22, 1942; B.A. in Speech Therapy, Northwestern State U., Natchitoches, La., 1965, M.A. in Speech Pathology, 1968; children—Lisa, Brooke. Speech therapist public schs., La., 1965-71; speech and hearing cons. Nicholls State U., Thibodaux, La., 1973-78; prin. TARC-Wonderland Houma, La., 1978—. Cert. tchr., La. Mem. Am. Speech, Lang. and Hearing Assn. (cert.), La. Speech and Hearing Assn., Am. Assn. Mental Deficiency, LAC Parents Anonymous. Home: 202 Lynwood Houma LA 70360 Office: 1 McCord Rd Houma LA 70360

ALLEN, SHEILA HILL, nursing executive; b. Imperial, Nebr., Sept. 28, 1935; d. Roger William and Lois Marion (Clayton) Hill; m. Everett Francis Allen Jr., Mar. 22, 1959 (div. 1975); children—Lee-Ann Hill, Todd Everett, Andrew James; m. Robert William Kositch, May 20, 1978 (div. 1985). R.N., St. Lukes Sch. Nursing, 1958; B.S., U. Denver, 1959. Asst. head nurse St. Lukes Hosp., Denver, 1959-62; dir. nursing Ridge Vista Mental Health, San Jose, Calif., 1973-75; primary care nurse O'Connor Hosp., 1981; dir. nursing services Westwood Mental Health Facility, Fremont, Calif., 1975—. Sec. Health Acctg. Services, Newark, Calif., 1984—; ptnr. Health Acctg. Services, Villa Maria Corp., Fremont, 1984—. Contbr. articles to profl jours. Home: 6513 Trinidad Ct San Jose CA 95120 Office: 4303 Stevenson Blvd Fremont CA 94538

ALLEN, SHEILA ROSALYND, television and motion picture writer, author; b. Elmira, N.Y., Mar. 8, 1942; d. Charles Judson and Doris Elizabeth (Beers) A. Ptnr. Allen & Ukra, Los Angeles, 1974-75; owner Allen Enterprises, Venice Beach, Calif., 1975-84; pres., chief exec. officer S.R.A., Inc., Venice Beach, 1984—; writer Columbia Studios Television, 1983-84, Aaron Spelling Prodns., 1984; mem. adv. bd. Whole Ocean Catalog, Dana Point, Calif., 1986, Insight for Learning, Ventura, Calif., 1978; dir. We the People, Santa Monica, S.R.A., Inc., Santa Monica, Author: Fire and Innocence, 1984, Victoria's Secret, 1986, The Mars Kill, 1987; author screenplay: Honeymoon, 1986; author episodic TV series, movies of the week, documentaries and films. Speechwriter, Democratic Party, Calif. Kick-Off Campaign, 1982; speaker Pub. TV, 1982. Recipient Teacher's award Insight for Learning, Ventura, 1978, Silver award Houston Film Festival, 1984. Mem. Writers Guild Am. (west arbitrator credits 1984-86), Authors Guild, Authors League, Romance Writers Am. (awards judge 1985-86), Mystery Writers Am., Nat. Writers Club. Democrat. Anglican Catholic. Club: Rose Ave. Beach (Venice, Calif.). Avocations: painting; cycling; vol. programs for disadvantaged would-be writers; classical music; culinary arts. Office: SRA Inc PO Box 5749 Santa Monica CA 90405-0749

ALLEN, SHIRLEY ANN, nurse, administrator; b. Joplin, Mo., Aug. 21, 1927; d. John Anthony and Ida Katherine (Willis) Feerick; m. William John Allen, Dec. 30, 1950 (dec. 1966); 1 child, John William. Diploma in Nursing, St. Mary's Hosp., 1948; postgrad. Margaret Hague Hosp., 1949. Staff nurse Margaret Hague Hosp., Jersey City, N.J., 1948-50, Christ Hosp., Jersey City, 1950-55; head nurse St. John's Hosp., Joplin, 1955-75; perinatal dir. Freeman Hosp., Joplin, 1975—. Mem. Nurses Assn. Am. Coll. Ob-Gyn, Am. Cancer Soc. (sec. dist. 8 1979-82). Roman Catholic. Avocation: bowling. Office: Freeman Hosp 1102 W 32d St Joplin MO 64801

ALLEN, SHIRLEY ANN, county constable; b. Palistine, Tex.; d. Al Colman and Ella Lorraine (Moore) Ray; m. Joseph Garcia, Mar. 3, 1950 (dec. Apr. 1977); children—Patricia Marie Garcia Huffman, Joe Ray, Kathleen Shirley Garcia Austin, Annimarie; m. John Henry Allen, May 4, 1978. Student in civil process procedures Ariz. State U., 1980; student constable tng. seminar Ariz. state U.-Tempe, 1980. Dep. sheriff Coconino County, Ariz., 1969-79, constable, 1979—. Mem. Frat. Order Police (chaplin). Democrat. Methodist. Avocation: pistol shooting. Home: 1804 E Maple Ave Flagstaff AZ 86001 Office: Constable's Office Flagstaff Precinct Courthouse Flagstaff AZ 86001

ALLEN, SUSAN BURDETTE, entrepreneur; b. Durham, N.C., Nov. 18, 1951; d. Malcolm Burdette and Louise (Lloyd) A.; B.S. in Interior Design, U. N.C., Greensboro, 1973. Mgr., designer Intra, Greensboro, 1973-75; designer Priba Interiors, W.Ger., 1976-78, Comml. Office Furniture, Washington, 1978-79; owner, mgr. Phasedesign, Greensboro, 1979-83; creator, v.p., co-owner Funnybusiness, Inc., Greensboro and Winston-Salem, N.C., 1979—; owner Funny U., Greensboro, 1982—; pres. Allen Resource Group (cons., speaker on morale and team building strategies), Greensboro, 1984—; pres., editor G/Golden Triad Mag., div. Piedmont Impressions, Inc., Greensboro, 1985—. Bd. dirs. Old Greensborough Preservation Soc., U. N.C.-Greensboro Sch. Home Econs. Found., 1983-87. Mem. Women's Profl. Forum, Nat. Speakers Assn. Home: PO Box 5492 Greensboro NC 27403 Office: PO Box 5492 Greensboro NC 27403

ALLEN, TONI DIANE, lawyer; b. King City, Calif., Dec. 28, 1952; d. Max Thayne and Amy G. (Medalen) Allen; m. Michael Stephen Matelli, June 30, 1979. A.A., Hartnell Coll., 1973; A.B. in Sociology, Stanford U., 1975; Secondary Edn. credential, San Francisco State U., 1977; J.D., U. Utah, 1981. Bar: Utah, 1981. Commd. capt., U.S. Army, 1981; atty., Ft. Ord, Calif., 1981—. Recipient William H. Leary award U. Utah, 1981. Mem. ABA, Utah State Bar. Democrat. Home: 215 Valencia Ave Aptos CA 95003 Office: Office of Staff Judge Advocate Fort Ord CA 93941

ALLENBAUGH, BEVERLY MARIE, county official; b. Kellogg, Idaho, July 16, 1935; d. Harry and L. Ethel (Simmons) Farmer; m. Andrew A. Clarke, Aug. 31, 1957 (dec.); children—Terry, Brian, Arthur, Brigid, Teresa; m. William J. Allenbaugh, Mar. 18, 1980; stepchildren—Diana, Robin, Bill Jr., J.J. B.A. in Edn., Central Wash. U., 1958, postgrad. 1960-70. Tchr. Reecer Creek Sch., Ellensburg, Wash., 1958-60, St. Andrew's Cath. Sch., Ellensburg, 1960-61; bookkeeper Fisher Mills Feed Store, Ellensburg, 1974-77; county auditor Kittitas County, Wash., 1977—, also co-chmn. voter outreach; chmn. Kittitas County Computer User Group, 1981—; sec. fin. com. Kittitas County, 1977—; mem. bus. adv. council, Ellensburg High Sch., 1981-84. Leader, Wash. 4-H Extension Service, 1979—; co-chmn. edn. com. Com. for Handicapped Accessibility for Voters in Wash. State, 1985-86. Mem. Wash. County Auditor's Assn. (sec. treas. 1983-84, co-chmn. edn. com. 1983-84, pres. 1984—, planning com. Crossroads '85), Internat. Assn. Clks., Recorders, Election Ofcls. and Treasurers, Nat. Assn. County Ofcls., Cowbells (sec.-treas.) Ellensburg Grange, Ellensburg Homemakers Club, Ellensburg Horse Club, Central Wash. U. Assn. Students in Religious Edn. (chmn. 1956, treas. 1956-57). Avocations: horse backpacking; fishing; sewing; children's activities, 4-H. Home: Route 4 Box 254 C Ellensburg WA 98926 Office: Kittitas County Auditor Room 105 Courthouse Ellensburg WA 98926

ALLEN-CLAIBORNE, JOYCE G., clinical and educational psychologist; b. Columbus, Ga., Feb. 23 1948; d. Homer W. Jr. and Berneda C. Allen; B.A. cum laude, Spelman Coll., 1970; M.A., U. Pitts., 1972, Ph.D. (NIMH pub. health fellow, 1972-74), 1975; m. Andrew J. Claiborne, Nov. 20, 1976; 1 child, Jomo Abd-Allah Kenyatta Claiborne. Teaching fellow U. Pitts., 1972, research assoc., 1975-77; clin. psychologist Hillcrest Children's Center, Washington, 1977-78; pvt. practice clin. psychology, Washington, 1980—; psychologist, Region D, D.C. Pub. Schs., Washington, 1979—; adj. prof. Union Grad. Sch., Clin., 1980-83. Adv. bd. St. Anselm's Abbey Day Camp, Washington. Mem. Am. Psychol. Assn., Delta Sigma Theta. Baptist. Home: 3729 Massachusetts Ave SE Washington DC 20019 Office: 45th and Lee Sts NE Washington DC 20019

ALLENTUCK, MARCIA EPSTEIN, English and art history educator; b. Manhattan, N.Y., June 8, 1928; m. 1949; 1 dau. B.A., NYU, 1948; Ph.D., Columbia U., N.Y.C., 1964. Lectr. English Columbia U., 1955-57, Hunter Coll., 1957; from lectr. to prof. English, CCNY, 1959—; prof. history of art Grad. Ctr. CUNY, 1974—. Author: The Works of Henry Needler, 1961; Henry Fuseli; The Artist as Critic and Man of Letters, 1964; Isaac Bashevis Singer, 1969; John Graham's System and Dialectics of Art, 1971; contbr. articles to profl. jours. Morrison fellow AAUW, 1958-59; Howard fellow Brown U., 1966-67, Huntington Library fellow, 1968, 77; fellow Nat. Translation Ctr. U. Tex., 1968-69, Chapelbrook Found., 1970-71, Dumbarton Oaks Harvard U., 1972-73; sr. fellow NEH, 1973-74; vis. fellow Wolfson Coll. Oxford U., 1974—; fellow Brit. Acad. Newberry Library, 1980; Murray research fellow Radcliffe Coll., Harvard U., 1982; fellow Inst. Advanced Studies in the Humanities, Edinburgh U. (Scotland), 1984; Am. Philos. Soc. grantee, 1966-67; recipient Sussman Meml. medal N.Y.U., 1946. Fellow Royal Soc. Arts London; mem. Brit. Soc. Archtl. Historians, MLA, Milton Soc. Am., Augustan Reprint Soc., Soc. Archtl. Historians, Coll. Art Assn., Phi Beta Kappa.

ALLERS, MARLENE ELAINE, law office business manager; b. Crosby, Minn., Dec. 29, 1931; d. Robert Prudent and Tressa Ida May (Hiller) Huard; m. Herbert Dodge Allers, Aug. 29, 1950 (dec. Aug. 1977); children—Melanie Lynn, Geoffrey Brian. B.S. in Math., U. Minn.-Mpls., 1966, B.A. in Acctg., 1968, M.B.A. in Personnel and Fin. Mgmt., 1972. Bus. mgr., Earl Clinic, St. Paul, 1959-68, Lindquist & Vennum, Mpls., 1968-79, Stacker, Ravich & Simon, Mpls., 1979-82, Wagner, Johnston & Falconer, Ltd., Mpls., 1983—; lectr. Inst. of Continuing Legal Edn., Mpls., 1977. Recipient Outstanding Achievement award in Bus. Young Women's Christian Assn., Mpls., 1978. Mem. Minn. Legal Adminstrs. Assn., Mensa. Avocations: bridge; reading. Home: 608 Queen Ave S Minneapolis MN 55405 Office: Wagner Johnston & Falconer Ltd 80 S 8th St Minneapolis MN 55402

ALLEVA, PATTI ANN, lawyer; b. N.Y.C., Apr. 10, 1955; d. Arthur Louis and Lee (Verrone) A. B.A., Hofstra U., 1976; J.D., 1979. Bar: N.Y. 1980, U.S. Dist. Ct. (so. dist.) N.Y. 1980, U.S. Dist. Ct. (ea. dist.) N.Y. 1980, U.S. Dist. Ct. (no. dist.) Calif. 1982. Law clk. U.S. Dist. Ct. N.J., 1980; assoc. Proskauer Rose Goetz & Mendelsohn, N.Y.C., 1981—. Articles editor Hofstra Law Rev., 1978-79. John Cranford Adams scholar, 1976; N.Y. State Regents scholar. Mem. Assn. Bar City N.Y. (sec. council jud. adminstrn. 1983—), Phi Beta Kappa, Phi Alpha Theta. Office: Proskauer Rose Goetz & Mendelsohn 300 Park Ave New York NY 10022

ALLEY, CAROL SCOTT, senator's aide, communications specialist; b. Pitts., Apr. 12, 1932; d. Frank Joseph and Ruth Scott (McCracken) Carlson; m. Rembert Caven Alley, Jr., Apr. 29, 1961 (div. Apr. 1984); children—Rembert Caven III, Daniel Carlson. B.A., Muskingum Coll., 1954. Prodn. editor Together Mag., Chgo., 1956-61; editor Mus. N.Mex., Santa Fe, 1964-68; news dir., host KRAT, KSWS Radio, Roswell, N.Mex., 1970-75; producer, host KBIM-TV, Roswell, 1975-79; pub. info. dir. Eastern N.Mex. U., Roswell, 1981-83; senator's aide Senator Jeff Bingaman, Albuquerque, 1983—; mem. Talent Bank, Profl. Presbyerian Communicators, N.Y.C., 1986—. Editor El Palacio, 1964-68. Sec. bd. regents Roswell Mus., 1984-86; bd. dirs. Roswell Symphony, 1979-82; mem. City Planning and Zoning Bd., Roswell, 1978-81; bd. dirs. Chaves County United Way, Roswell, 1972-86. Recipient Best Documentary award N.Mex. Broadcasters, 1972. Mem. Roswell Profl. Women's Network. Democrat. Club: Symphony Guild (Roswell). Avocations: archaeology; reading; walking. Home: 611 Lead Ave Apt 511 Albuquerque NM 87102 Office: Senator Jeff Bingaman Room 9017 Dennis Chavez Fed Bldg 500 Gold SW Albuquerque NM 87102

ALLEY, NANCY LAY, state official; b. Newton, Miss., Mar. 5, 1949; d. Robert Harold and Cherry (Pearson) Lay; B.S., U. So. Miss., 1971; postgrad. Miss. State U. Tchr., Sykes Elem. Sch., Jackson, Miss., 1972-73; mgr. Firestone Tire & Rubber Co., Jackson, 1975-76; supr. new bus. dept. Allstate Ins., Jackson, 1977-78; staff asst. U.S. Congressman G.V. Montgomery, Washington, 1979; state supr. indsl. tng. Miss. Dept. Edn., Jackson, 1980—. Mem. Nat. Employment and Tng. Assn., Miss. Employment and Tng. Assn. (v.p. 1981-82), Miss. Assn. Vocat. Educators, State Employees Assn. Miss., Nat. Assn. Female Execs., Delta Delta Delta. Roman Catholic. Office: Miss Dept Edu PO Box 771 Jackson MS 39205

ALLGOOD, BEVERLY MARIE, contract hardware and building speciality company executive; b. San Antonio, Jan. 16, 1940; d. Tony William and Alma Belle (Core) Risner; m. Kenneth M. Allgood, Nov. 1, 1963 (dec. Aug. 1982); children—Kenneth W., Kevin L. Student pub. schs., Broken Arrow, Okla. Acct. Robbins Incubator Co., Denver, 1959-60; individual practice tax acctg. and bookkeeping, Tulsa, also Jenks, Okla., 1961-75; editor Jenks Jour., 1965-67; office mgr. Garrison Heating Co., Broken Arrow, 1975-78; office mgr. Murray Womble Co., Tulsa, 1978—, M.W. Interstate, Inc. subs., 1981—, corp. asst. treas. Murray Womble Co., E.S.O.P. tax cons., Broken Arrow, 1975—; co-founder Take Off Pounds Sensibly, Jenks, 1965. Founder local scouting groups, Jenks, 1964-65. Mem. Am. Soc. Profl. and Exec. Women, Assoc. Gen. Contractors Am. Lodge: Royal Neighbors (oracle 1968-69). Home: 12500 S 185th E Ave Broken Arrow OK 74011 Office: Murray Womble Co of Tulsa Inc 624 E 4th St Tulsa OK 74120

ALLIES, VICTORIA ROSSINI, chemical engineer; b. Southington, Conn., May 27, 1950; d. Leon and Lillian (Wanagus) Rossini; student Middlebury Coll., 1968-70; B.A. with honors, U. Conn., 1972, M.S., 1979; M.B.A., U. Phoenix, 1980; m. James M. McCarron, June 18, 1980; stepchildren—James Roy, Dolores, Lynn. Adhesive chemist Loctite Corp., Newington, Conn., 1972-76, adhesives engr., 1976-78; market devel. mgr. Gen. Electric, Laminated Materials Dept., Coshocton, Ohio, 1978-79; chem. process engr. ITT-Courier Terminal Systems, Inc., Tempe, Ariz., 1979-80; sr. chem. process engr., environ. engring. supr. Digital Equip. Corp., Tempe, 1980-82; pres./cons. Tng. 'n' Tech. Inc., Tempe, 1982—; facility design, review, and implementation cons. Digitran Co. div. Becton Dickinson, Kodak, Hewlett-Packard, Xebec, L.M. Ericcson, Sweden, Peoples Republic China; instr. chemistry Maricopa Community Coll., Phoenix, 1981-82. Mem. Am. Chem. Soc., Ariz. Printed Circuit Bd. Assn., Soc. Women Engrs. Patentee on temporary bonding adhesives. Home: 11455 S Half Moon Dr Phoenix AZ 85044 Office: 2121 W Univ Dr #108 Tempe AZ 85281

ALLISON, DOROTHY GRAHAM, typesetting-graphics firm executive, consultant; b. Oil City, Pa., Oct. 31, 1953; d. Harold Leroy and Helen Dorothy (Luke) Graham; m. Robert Edwin Allison, Sept. 21, 1974. Student Montgomery Coll., Rockville Md., 1974-78, Germantown, Md., 1980-82; student U. Md., 1976. Exec. sec. Aircraft Owners and Pilots Assn., Bethesda, Md., 1972-74; dir. membership Services Internat. Franchise Assn., Washington, 1974-78; v.p. Systems Corp. Am., Bethesda, 1978-82; pres., chmn., chief exec. officer The Word Ctr., Inc., Frederick, Md., 1982—; cons., instr. in word processing. Mem. Frederick County Pvt. Industry Council, Md., 1983-85; mem. discretionary rev. panel, office community service HEW, Washington, 1983-84, vice chairperson, 1983. Mem. Downtown Frederick Assn. (pres. 1984-85), Frederick County C. of C. (bd. dirs. 1985-86), Frederick Women's Exchange. Republican. Roman Catholic. Avocations: tennis; racquetball; photography. Office: Word Ctr Inc 5 W 3d St Frederick MD 21701

ALLISON, ELIZABETH MATHEWS, corporate treasurer; b. Newport News, Va., June 11, 1952; d. Charles Wesley and Marietta Gaynelle (Short) Mathews; m. William Walker Allison, Feb. 14, 1976; children—Elizabeth Erin Allison, Ryan Michael Allison. A.A., No. Va. Community Coll., 1973; Cert., Control Data Corp., Arlington, Va., 1972; postgrad. U. Va., 1980—. Asst. editor Chronicle Guidance Corp., Falls Church, Va., 1973-77; staff asst. Vocat. Indsl. Clubs of Am. Inc., Falls Church, 1977-80, supt. fin./personnel, Leesburg, Va., 1980-84, corp. treas., 1984—. Bd. visitors Paxton Child Devel. Ctr., Leesburg, 1984—; mem. Nat. Capital Area council Girl Scouts Am. Mem. Nat. Assn. Female Execs., Am. Soc. Profl. and Exec. Women. Methodist. Avocations: swimming; water skiing; traveling. Home: 2709 New Ambler Ct Herndon VA 22071 Office: Vocat Indsl Clubs Am 9 Miles N on Route 15 PO Box 3000 Leesburg VA 22075

ALLISON, JANE LEA, financial consultant; b. Oskaloosa, Iowa, July 17, 1953; d. Melvin Eldred and Jeneane Lucille (Maughan) Dykstra; m. Kennie Dean Allison, Mar. 2, 1985; 1 stepson, Colter Dean. B.S. in Bus., N.E. Mo. State U., 1974; Cert., Coll. Fin. Planning, Denver, 1976. Regional sales mgr. Great Western Fin., Newport Beach, Calif., 1974-77, Continental Ins. Co., Newport Beach, 1977-78; account exec., br. mgr. Equitec, Newport Beach, 1978-81; sales rep. Security First, Century City, Calif., 1981-83; br. mgr. BretCourt Fin., Santa Ana, Calif., 1983-84; ins. sales specialist Johnson & Higgins, Des Moines, 1984—. Mem. Internat. Assn. Fin. Planning, Nat. Assn. Exec. Women, Nat. Assn. Security Dealers, Alpha Sigma Alpha. Democrat. Roman Catholic. Avocations: horseback riding; snow skiing; water skiing; bowling; racquetball. Home: Rural Route 1 Lynndana Acres Oskaloosa IA 52577 Office: Johnson & Higgins 400 Locust Des Moines IA 50398

ALLISON, JANE SHAWVER, medical school administrator, management consultant; b. San Angelo, Tex., Dec. 29, 1938; d. Floyd McKinzie and Bertha J. (Hicks) Shawver; m. Cecil Wayne Allison, June 22, 1957; children—Jana Lea, David Wayne, Don McKinzie. Student U. Denver, 1954, Northwestern U., 1955, Tex. Tech. U., 1956-57, Midwestern U., Wichita Falls, Tex., 1958. Continuity writer, Sta. KFDX-TV, Wichita Falls, Tex., 1957-58; sec. Wichita Falls Symphony, Tex., 1968-70; adminstrv. asst. Coll. of Bus. Tex. Tech U., Lubbock, 1971-74, coordinator programs dept. family medicine Health Sch. Ctr., 1974-77, adminstr. dept. family medicine, 1978—; cons. Family Practice Residency, Amarillo, Tex., 1984, Temple, Tex., 1984-85. Bd. dirs. Lubbock Symphony Orch., Inc., 1976—, mem. nominating com., 1986; bd. dirs. Helen A. Hodges Charitable Trust, Lubbock, 1983—. Mem. Med. Group Mgmt. Assn., Acad. Practice Assembly, Assn. Family Practice Adminstrs. (bd. dirs. 1985, charter pres. 1984, chmn. steering com. 1983). Mem. Disciples of Christ. Club: Soroptimist Internat. (pres. 1986-87). Office: Dept Family Medicine Tex Tech Univ Health Sci Ctr Lubbock TX 79430

ALLISON, JOANNE MARIE, arts executive; b. Lockport, N.Y., Mar. 27, 1930; d. Jay Cuthbert and Kathleen Mary (Gibson) Tomkinson; m. Eugene Macwood Allison, Aug. 27, 1949; children—Cynthia, Lynn, Steven, Lizabeth. A.A.S., St. Joseph Bus. Inst., Lockport, N.Y., 1949; B.A., SUNY-Buffalo, 1975; postgrad. Arts Mgmt. Inst., Cambridge, Mass., Harvard Bus. Sch., 1972; D.F.A. (hon.), Niagara U., 1982. Ptnr., Joel Enterprises, Lockport, 1964-67; dir. Kenan Art Ctr., Lockport, 1967-74; exec. dir. Artpark, Lewiston, N.Y., 1974—; cons. art orgns.; panelist N.Y. State Council on Arts, 1969-73, 81—; program auditor Nat. Endowment Arts, 1981—; mem. continuing edn. adv. bd. N.Y. State Dept. Edn., 1980-84. Mem. Western N.Y. Inst. (bd. dirs.). Office: Artpark Box 371 Niagara NY 14092

ALLISON, LOYETTE E., construction, engineering manager; b. Delano, Calif., July 7, 1946; d. Dempsey Willard and Billie Wanda (Fink) Bogard; m. Robert Lee, Nov. 30, 1963; children—Cindy Kay, Ann Rena. Student Pima Coll., 1979, U. Denver, 1983. Sales mgr. K-Mart, Tucson, 1975-78; clk.-typist Fairfield Green Valley, Ariz., 1978-81; purchasing agt. Tobin Homes, Tucson, 1981-83; constrn. mgr. Fairfield La Cholla Hills, Tucson, 1983-86; ops. mgr. Fairfield Pusch Ridge, 1986—. Notary public State of Ariz. Mem. Nat. Assn. Female Execs. Baptist. Avocations: stock car racing; aerobics. Home: 2151 W Felicia Pl Tucson AZ 85741 Office: Fairfield La Cholla Hills 8700 N La Cholla Blvd Tucson AZ 85741

ALLISON, MARY ANN, financial company executive, author; b. Orange, N.J., Sept. 27, 1949; d. David S. and Mary (McNaughton) Burnet; m. Eric William Allison, July 17, 1971. B.A., Shimer Coll., 1971; M.B.A., L.I. U., 1977. Various position Avis Rent-A-Car, Garden City, N.Y., 1971-80; v.p. Citicorp N.Y.C., 1980—. Co-author: Through the Valley of Death, 1983; Managing Up, Managing Down, 1984; contbr. articles to profl. publs. and nat. mags. Mem. Am. Soc. for Tng. and Devel., Am. Soc. Personnel Adminstrn., Authors Guild, Mystery Writers Am., Japan Soc. Episcopalian. Office: Direct Access Dakota Dr 3d Floor Lake Success NY 11042

ALLISON, TOMILEA, mayor City of Bloomington, Ind.; b. Madera, Calif., Mar. 28, 1934; d. John and Edna (Archer) Radosevich; m. James Allison, 1958; children—Devon, Leigh. B.A. in Sociology, Occidental Coll., 1955; postgrad. Fresno State Coll., 1956. City council mem. City of Bloomington, Ind., 1977-82, mayor, 1983—. Active Citizens for Good Govt., Bloomington, 1960-65, Community Progress Council, 1980-85. Mem. LWV, Bloomington C. of C. Democrat. Home: 1127 E First St Bloomington IN 47402 Office: City of Bloomington PO Box 100 220 E Third St Bloomington IN 47402

ALLISON-BRYAN, BARBARA ANNE, pediatrician; b. Pitts., June 28, 1954; d. Robert Kay and Lillian Ann (Pasqual) Allison; m. Hugh McLellan Bryan, III, June 14, 1980; 1 dau., Sarah Payne. B.A., Wellesley Coll., 1976; M.D., Pa. State U., 1980. Diplomate Nat. Bd. Med. Examiners, Am. Bd. Pediatrics. Commd. capt. M.C., U.S. Army, 1980, advanced through grades to maj., 1984; intern Letterman Army Med. San Francisco, Ctr., 1980-81, resident in pediatrics, 1980-83, staff pediatrician, 1983-85, chief adolescent medicine, 1983-84, chief outpatient pediatrics, 1984-85; gen. pediatrician Children's Clinic, Clarksville, Tenn., 1985—. Wellesley Coll. Trustee scholar, 1976; Wellesley scholar, 1976. Fellow Am. Acad. Pediatrics; mem. AMA, Sigma Xi. Episcopalian. Office: Children's Clinic 1760 Madison Ave Clarksville TN 37043

ALLMAN, MARGO HUTZ, sculptor, painter; b. N.Y.C., Feb. 23, 1933; d. Werner H. and Avis (Newcomb) Hutz; student Smith Coll., 1950-51, Moore Coll. Art, 1952-54, Hans Hofmann Sch. Art, 1953, U. Del., 1967-70; m. William B. Allman, Feb. 19, 1954; children—Avis Louise, David Drue. One-person shows include: Wallingford (Pa.) Art Center, 1964, Windham Coll., 1974, Bloomsburg State Coll., 1976, 77, Moore Coll. Art, 1979, Marian Locks Gallery, Phila., 1984; group shows include: Phila. Art Alliance, 1954, Del. Art Museum, Wilmington, 1958 (Ann. Show Drawing prize), 65, 67, Print Club, Phila., 1959, U. Del., 1977, Del. State Arts Council, Wilmington, 1981, C. Grimaldis Gallery, Balt., 1983, Art in Form Gallery, Karlsruhe, W.Ger.; represented in permanent collections, including: Del. Mus., Phila. Mus.; works include: Ferro Cement Sculpture, Tidewater Pub. Co., Centerville, Md., 1975, Crocheted Sculpture of Herculon, Hercules Inc., Wilmington, 1975. Bd. dirs. Robert Small Dance Co., N.Y.C., 1979-80. Recipient Mildred Boericke prize Print Club, Phila., 1958, Landscape prize Wilmington Trust Bank, 1969. Mem. Moore Coll. Art Alumnae Assn., Del. Center Contemporary Arts, Del. Art Mus. Unitarian. Home: 202 E State Rd West Grove PA 19390

ALLMAND, LINDA F., librarian, consultant; b. Port Arthur, Tex., Jan. 31, 1937; d. Clifton James and Jewel Etoile (Smith) A. B.A., North Tex. State U., 1960; M.A., U. Denver, 1962. Children's librarian Denver Pub. Library, 1960-63; coordinator children's service Anaheim Pub. Library (Calif.), 1963-64; instr. North Tex. State U., Denton, 1967-80; br. mgr. Dallas Pub. Library, 1965-71, chief br. service, 1971-81; dir. Ft. Worth Pub. Library, 1981—; instr. Dallas County Community Coll., Dallas, 1981; bldg. cons. Haltom City Pub. Library (Tex.), 1983—, Carrolton Pub. Library (Tex.), 1979-81, Hurst Pub. Library (Tex.), 1977-78, Dallas Pub. Library, 1974-80. Author: Fort Worth Public Library 1981-2000, Facilities and Long Range Planning Study, 1982. Bd. dirs. City of Dallas Credit Union, 1973-81; com. chair Goals for Dallas, 1967-69; mem. Forum Ft. Worth, 1963-84; bd. dirs. Sr. Citizens' Ctrs., Inc., Ft. Worth, 1982; mem. Leadership Ft. Worth, 1982-83. Pilot Club scholar Port Arthur, Tex., 1954, Library Binding Inst. scholar, 1958, Disting. Alumnus award North Tex. State U., 1983. Mem. NOW, AAUW, ALA (pub. library goals, guidelines and standards 1974-78, local arrangements Dallas, 1970-71, 79-80), Am. Mgmt. Assn., Freedom to Read Found., Tex. Library Assn. (pres. pub. library div. 1980-81, chair planning 1982-84, Librarian of Yr. 1985, pres. elect 1985-86, pres. 1986-87), Dallas County Librarians Assn. (v.p. 1967-68, pres. 1968-69). Club: Zonta (bd. dirs. 1981-85) (Ft. Worth). Office: Ft Worth Pub Library 300 N Taylor Fort Worth TX 76102-7309

ALLMARAS, ALICE ANN, school administrator; b. New Rockford, N.D., Aug. 21, 1927; d. Hugh Charles and Anna (Roffler) O'Connor; m. Jacob William Allmaras, June 27, 1950; 1 child, Jean. B.A., Valley City State Coll., 1964; M.A., Moorhead U., 1972. Tchr. St. Catherine's Sch., Valley City, N.D., 1964-68; instr. English and phys. edn. Valley City State Coll., 1968-73; supt. of schs. Eddy County, N.D., 1973—. Roman Catholic. Avocation: travel. Office: Eddy County Supt Schs Courthouse New Rockford ND 58356

ALLOWAY, ANNE MAUREEN SCHUBERT, industrial waste inspector; b. Martinez, Calif., Oct. 19, 1954; d. James Benjamin and Mariel Ann (Phillips) Schubert; m. William Glenn Alloway, Jr., Apr. 27, 1974 (div.); children—Joseph Benjamin, Odinn Glenn, Aaron Dean. A.S. in Life Sci., Allan Hancock Coll., 1982, A.A. in Liberal Arts, 1982. Indsl. waste insp. City of Santa Maria, Calif., 1982—. Choir mem. Saint Mary's Catholic Ch., 1985-86. Mem. Calif. Water Pollution Control Assn., Water Pollution Control Fedn. Republican. Roman Catholic. Club: Santa Maria Racquetball. Lodge: Keepers of the Flame. Avocations: painting; writing; sports; reading. Home: 953 E Jones #228 Santa Maria CA 93454 Office: City of Santa Maria 110 E Cook St Santa Maria CA 93454

ALLRED, RITA REED, artist; b. Davenport, Iowa, Apr. 12, 1935; d. Edward Platt and Delia Marie (Quinn) Reed; m. Glenn Charles Scott, June 9, 1956 (div. Nov. 1977); children—Sheryl Marie, Laura Ann; m. Robert Yates Allred, Dec. 9, 1977. Student Marycrest Coll., Davenport, 1953-56; B.S. in Art Edn., Drake U., 1958. Art tchr. Fayetteville City Schs., N.C., 1961-64, Charlotte-Mecklenburg Schs., N.C., 1967-71; cons., project dir. PCA Internat., Matthews, N.C., 1981; artist, art cons. Rita Reed Allred & Assocs., Charlotte, 1972—, dir. workshops, 1976—; dir. drawing program Thora McElroy Sr. Citizens Ctr., Charlotte, 1985—; civilian artist U.S. Coast Guard, 1981—. Painter in oils; recent commns. include paintings for U.S. Army, USCG, portraits for ABCO Industries, U.S. Naval Inst. Service Head Portrait Series. Bd. dirs. Internat. House, Charlotte, 1985—; mem. Sister Cities Com., Charlotte, 1984-85. Recipient George Gray award USCG, 1983. Mem. Women Bus. Owners. Democrat. Club: Cedarwood Country (Matthews, N.C.). Avocation: golf. Home and Studio: 7217 Quail Meadow Ln Charlotte NC 28210

ALLUSHUSKI, BARBARA ELIZABETH, auto club executive; b. Davenport, Iowa, Apr. 7, 1952; d. Leonard F. and Genievieve E. (Heinen) Swoyer; m. Gregory Anthony Allushuski, June 22, 1974. B.A., Ohio U., 1974. Indsl. engr. Fisher Body Gen. Motors, Lansing, Mich., 1974-75; labor relation rep. Oldsmobile Gen. Motors, Lansing, 1975-79; adminstr. exec. compensation Gen. Motors Hdqrs., Detroit, 1979-80, arbitration-labor staff mem., 1980-82; v.p. personnel Auto Club of Mich., Dearborn, 1982-85, v.p. corp. ops., 1985—; dir. Blue Cross/Blue Shield, Detroit, 1985—. Mem. Greater Detroit Area Health Council. Mem. Detroit Econ. Club, Internat. Assn. Personnel Women, Greater Lansing Indsl. Personnel Assn. (past v.p.), Mich. Assn. Occupational Health Nurses, Women's Econ. Club. Republican. Roman Catholic. Avocations: piano; racquetball; tennis; skiing; antiques. Home: 4887 Starak Ln Ann Arbor MI 48103 Office: Auto Club Mich Dearborn MI 48126

ALMAN, EMILY ARNOW, sociologist, lawyer; b. N.Y.C., Jan. 20, 1922; d. Joseph Michael and Cecilia (Greenstone) Arnow; B.A., Hunter Coll., 1948; Ph.D., New Sch. for Social Research, 1963; J.D., Rutgers U., Newark, 1977; m. David Alman, Aug. 1, 1940; children—Michelle Alman Harrison, Jennifer Alman Michaels. Probation officer, N.Y.C., 1945-48; assoc. prof. sociology Douglass Coll. Rutgers U., New Brunswick, 1960-85, prof. emeritus, 1985—; admitted to N.J. bar, 1978; individual practice law, Highland Park, N.J., 1978—. Candidate for mayor, City of East Brunswick, 1972; chmn. Concerned Citizens of East Brunswick, 1970-78; pres. bd. trustees Concerned Citizens Environ. Fund., East Brunswick, 1977-78. Mem. Am., N.J. Middlesex County bar assns., Am. Sociol. Assn., Assn. Fed. Bar State of N.J., Assn. Trial Lawyers Am., Trial Lawyers Assn. Middlesex County, Law and Soc. Assn., Am. Judicature Soc., Nat. Assn. Women Lawyers, N.J. Assn. Women Lawyers, ACLU, AAUP, Women Helping Women. Author: Ride The Long Night, 1963; screenplay, The Ninety-First Day, 1963. Home: 611 S Park Ave Highland Park NJ 08904

ALONGI, PATRICIA LOUISE, interior designer, architects assistant; b. Lakewood, Ohio, Mar. 16, 1935; d. James A. and Elizebeth Alice (Hughel) Madden; children—Deborah, Felicia, G. Patty. Student in interior design Colo. State U., 1954-55, 80-82; B.B.A., Phoenix Coll., 1971. Designer Furniture Galleries, Denver, 1959-62; interior designer Interiors Unlimited, Denver, 1962-69, Hayden Furniture Galleries, Tucson, 1983—; realtor Watts Realty, Phoenix, 1972-79; mem. design dept. bd. Pima Coll., Tucson, 1983-85. Avocations: Wilderness backpacking; horseback riding. Home: 765 W Limberlost Dr #39 Tucson AZ 85705

ALONZO, PATRICIA CAREY, travel agency executive; b. Birmingham, Ala., Aug. 15, 1939; d. Hugh Joseph and Elizabeth (Bedgood) Carey; m. Frank O. Alonzo, Sept. 6, 1958 (div. Oct. 1983); children—Frank O., Jr., Reynolds, David. Student U. Ala., 1958-60, U. So. Ala., 1967-68. Service rep. S. Central Bell Telephone Co., Mobile, Ala., 1962-65; ticket agt. Republic Airlines, Mobile, 1970; travel agt. World Travel Internat., Oxford, Miss., 1970-72, Carter Gerald, Hattiesburg, Miss., 1972-77; owner, gen. mgr. Alonzo Travel Agy., Hattiesburg, 1977-85. Mem. Forest County Indsl. Bd., 1985, Miss. Econ. Council, 1982-85. Recipient Professionalism in Travel award Japan Air Lines, 1980; Waldoff Acheiver award Waldoff's, Hattiesburg, 1985. Fellow Am. Soc. Travel Agts., Assn. Retail Travel Agts., Hattiesburg C. of C. (bd. dirs. 1980-83), Profl. Bus. Women's Club. Republican. Roman Catholic. Clubs: Century, Big Gold, Hardwood (Hattiesburg). Home: 108 Rockabye Ln Hattiesburg MS 39401 Office: Alonzo Travel Agy 1910 Hardy St Hattiesburg MS 39401

ALOU, SUSAN HARMAN, savings and loan executive; b. McKeesport, Pa., Oct. 11, 1934; d. Donald Eicher and Marjorie Ann (Weaver) Harman; m. David Parry Moss, Nov. 18, 1955 (div. May, 1966) children—Marjorie Moss Clark, Charles David Moss. Student La. State U., 1979-82; B.B.A. in Bus. Adminstrn., Oglethrope U., 1983. Acctg. clk. various banks, 1956-68; acctg. supr. Nashville City Bank, 1969-72; ops. officer Hamilton Bank, Nashville, 1973-74; controller, Hamilton Bank, Atlanta, 1974-76; v.p., acctg. mgr., risk mgr. Nat. Bank of Ga., Atlanta, 1976-83; asst. v.p., acctg. and corp. planning Fulton Fed. Savs. and Loan, Atlanta, 1983—. Pres., 3200 Clairmont No. Homeowners, Atlanta, 1980; mem. Fulton Polit. Action Com., Atlanta, 1983-84. Served with WAC, 1953-54. Mem. Nat. Assn. Bank Women, Nat. Assn. Accts. (v.p. adminstrn. 1980-81, v.p. communications 1979-80, dir. community programs 1984-85). Republican. Presbyterian. Clubs: Officers Wives (pres. 1963-64) (Glynco, Ga.); Women's (pres. 1964-65) (St. Simons Island, Ga.). Home: 304 Lenox Way NE Atlanta GA 30324 Office: Fulton Fed Savis and Loan Assn 1 Park Pl S Atlanta GA 30303

ALPER, JOANNE FOGEL, lawyer; b. N.Y.C., Sept. 16, 1950; d. Ben R. and Florence (Schneider) Fogel; m. Paul Edward Alper, Aug. 4, 1973; children—Michael Ian, Brooke Lauren. B.A., Syracuse U., 1972; J.D., George Washington U., 1975. Bar: Va. 1975, D.C. 1976. Law clk. Leonard, Cohen & Gettings, Arlington, Va., 1973-75, assoc., 1975-79; ptnr. Cohen, Gettings, Alper & Dunham, Arlington, 1979—. Mem. Arlington Bar Assn. (pres. 1982-83), Va. State Bar (pres. conf. local bar assns. 1984-85, chmn. family law sect. bd. govs. 1985-86), Va. Trial Lawyers Assn. (dist. gov. 1983—), George Washington U. Law Alumni Assn. (bd. dirs. 1977-81), No. Va. Young Lawyers Assn. (pres. 1979). Home: 5601 Little Falls Rd Arlington VA 22207 Office: Cohen Gettings Alper & Dunham 1400 N Uhle St Arlington VA 22201

ALPERIN, GOLDIE GREEN, cons. librarian, lawyer; b. Des Moines, Aug. 16, 1905; d. Morris and Bessie (Miliwer) Green; LL.B., Drake U., 1927; m. Moses Alperin, Dec. 25, 1930 (dec. 1950); children—Herschel Burton, Judith Miriam. Admitted to Iowa bar, 1927, U.S. Supreme Ct. bar, 1959; practice in Des Moines, 1927-30; law librarian Chgo. Bar. Assn., 1951-63; dir. Def. Information Office, Chgo., 1963-65; librarian book selections Northwestern U. Law Sch. Library, 1966-72; ret., 1972. Named one of 20 rep. U.S. women lawyers of various phases practice Women's Adjustment Bd., London, Eng., 1957; One of Outstanding Women of Am. Bicentennial, Austin (Tex.) Bicentennial Com., 1976; cert. religious sch. tchr. Bd. Jewish Edn., Chgo., 1951. Mem. Am. (sec. 1960-65), Chgo. (past exec. bd., editor 1958-59) assns. law libraries, Nat. Assn. Women Lawyers (regional) dir. 1960-64). Jewish religion. Asst. editor Women Lawyers Jour., 1961-67, exec. bd., 1961-67. Home: 3100 Lake Shore Dr Chicago IL 60657

ALPERN, BARBARA BELLMAN, advertising agency executive; b. El Paso, Tex., Aug. 26, 1947; d. Benjamin David and Evelyn Ruth (Barnett) Bellman; m. Peter Larsen Beatson, Aug. 26, 1965 (div. 1972); children—Aric, Wyatt; m. Harvey L. Alpern, Mar. 21, 1982; 1 child, David. B.S. in Bus. Adminstrn., Ariz. State U., 1973. With sales communications Nat. Chemsearch Corp., Irving, Tex., 1974-75; pub. relations dir. Jewish Community Ctr., Dallas, 1976-78; pres. Beatson Communications, Dallas, 1978-80; pub. relations dir. Century City Hosp., Los Angeles, 1980-82; pres., creative dir. York/Alpern Advt. affiliate Doyle Dane Bernbach, Inc., Los Angeles, 1982—; lectr. in field. Contbr. articles to profl. jours. Bd. dirs. Westside Jewish Community Ctr.; mem. parents bd. Windward Sch. Recipient George V. Christi Meml. award Phoenix Advt. Club. Mem. Internat. Assn. Bus. Communicators, So. Calif. Soc. Hosp. Pub. Relations (Newsletter and Advt. Golden Advocate awards), Los Angeles Advt. Women (award of Excellence), Century City C. of C., Western Los Angeles Regional C. of C., Los Angeles Art Dirs. Club. Republican. Jewish. Office: York/Alpern 5757 Wilshire Blvd 723 Los Angeles CA 90036

ALPERN, MILDRED, history educator, consultant; b. Boston, Sept. 10, 1931; d. Samuel and Mary (Poncewicz) Rosoff; m. Hale Nissen Alpern, Aug. 27, 1954; children—Merry, Spenser. B.A., Boston U., 1953; M.A. summa cum laude, Columbia U., 1966. Cert. techr. social studies. Tchr. history Spring Valley (N.Y.) Sr. High Sch., 1966—; adj. instr. Rockland Community Coll., Suffern, N.Y., 1973-76; instr. Manhattan Coll., Riverdale, N.Y., summer 1983, 84, 85; mem. advanced placement European history test devel. com., Coll. Bd. 1979-82, chmn. 1982-86, mem. Coll. Bd. history and social scis. adv. com., 1983—, chmn., 1985—; master tchr. summer inst. Sarah Lawrence Coll., Bronxville, N.Y., 1984; mem. faculty Coll. Bd. Project Equality Inst., 1986. Co-editor history column, Am. Hist. Assn. Perspectives, 1982—; co-author (teaching guide) Household and Kin, 1981; contbr. articles to profl. publs. Recipient award for contbns. in edn. Rockland Community Coll. and Rockland County Women's Network, 1984; Fulbright Commn. study grantee, Italy, 1980; NEH grantee Tufts U., 1983. Mem. Orgn. Am. Historians (chmn. teaching div. 1982-83), Am. Hist. Assn. (teaching div.), Nat. Council for Social Studies, Women in Hist. Profession (coordinating com.), Phi Beta Kappa, Pi Gamma Mu. Democrat. Home: 13 Cragmere Rd Suffern NY 10901 Office: Spring Valley Sr High Sch Route 59 Spring Valley NY 10977

ALPERT, ANN SHARON, editor; b. Indpls., Feb. 24, 1938; d. Oscar and Adele Alpert; B.S. in Edn., Ind. U., 1959. Tchr., Indpls. public schs., 1959-60; librarian George Fry & Assocs., Chgo., 1960-62, DeLeuw, Cather & Co., Chgo., 1962-65, Arthur Young & Co., C.P.A.s, Chgo., 1965-74; statis. asst. Sargent & Lundy, Chgo., 1974-81, computer liaison agt., 1981-83, tech. editor, 1983—. Office: 55 E Monroe St Chicago IL 60603

ALPERT, ETTARAE LIPSY, retail store official; b. Syracuse, N.Y., Sept. 15, 1932; d. Myron and Belle Rebecca (Rubenstein) Lipsy; m. Herbert Alpert, May 2, 1954; children—Mark, Susan, Carol, Robert. B.S., Syracuse U., 1953. Exec. trainee A & S, Bklyn., 1953-54; copywriter Chappell's, Syracuse, 1954-56; advt. dir. Flah's, Syracuse, 1958-61; advt. dir. Dey's Dept. Store, Syracuse, 1974—; bd. dirs. Jewish Observer Newspaper, Syracuse, 1982-84. Pres. Sisterhood Congregation Beth Sholom, Dewitt, N.Y., 1963-64, bd. dirs., 1964-80; bd. dirs. Women's League of Conservative Judaism-N.Y. State, 1965-72; editor newspaper Syracuse Jewish Fedn., 1961-65; bd. dirs. Jewish Family Service, Syracuse, 1983-84. Mem. Nat. Retail Merchants Assn., Beta Gamma Sigma, Gamma Alpha Chi. Club: Hadassah. Avocations: tennis; gardening; sewing. Home: 7212 Woodchuck Hill Rd Fayetteville NY 13066 Office: Dey's 401 S Salina St Syracuse NY 13201

ALPERT, LINDA M., nurse, medical consultant; b. Boston, Jan. 25, 1941; d. Sidney M. and Blanche (Kaplan) Omansky; B.S.N., U. Ariz., 1963; children—Sandra, Jeffrey. Staff nurse Handmaker Nursing Home, 1964; staff relief nurse Tucson Med. Center, 1967-68, nurse recruiter, 1968-70, head nurse cystic fibrosis center, 1970-76, head nurse, dir. chest clinic and allergy clinic, 1976-82; adminstr., dir. Pulmonary Care Center, Good Samaritan Med. Center, Phoenix, 1982-84, also project leader customer relations program; dir. med. services Goodman's Office Systems & Furnishings, Phoenix, 1985—; program coordinator Ariz. Chest Symposium, 1971-82; mem. adv. com. Sch. Respiratory Therapy, Pima Community Coll., 1979-82; bd. dirs. Continuity of Care Assn., 1982—; co-founder, bd. dirs. Parents Asthma Network, 1982—. Bd. dirs. Tucson chpt. Cystic Fibrosis Found., 1971-82. Mem. Ariz. Nurses in Mgmt., Am. Thoracic Soc., Ariz. Thoracic Soc., Sigma Theta Tau. Jewish. Clubs: Soroptomist, Jewish Bus. Profl. Women (bd. dirs.). Home: 1608 E Gardenia Ave Phoenix AZ 85020 Office: 1400 E Indian School Rd Phoenix AZ 85006

ALSBERG, EVERYL PARKER, consultant; b. Springhill, Okla., Oct. 14, 1921; d. Airy Lasker and Pearl Ellen (Collinsworth) Snelson; student U. So. Calif., 1943; B.S., U. Tulsa, 1953; postgrad. UCLA, 1953-58, Occidental Coll., 1958-62; M.A. in Adminstrn., Calif. State U., Los Angeles, 1962, postgrad., 1962-74; Ph.D., Walden U., 1979; m. Willis Parker, Jr., 1942 (dec.); children—Richard, Pennye Ellen; m. 2d, Harold Alsberg, 1969. Tchr., Fairfax, Va., 1953-55, Los Angeles City Schs., 1956-57; tchr. La Canada (Calif.) Unified Sch. Dist., 1957-62, prin. Paradise Canyon Elem. Sch., 1962-76, dir. instrn. K-8, 1976-78; cons. ednl. adminstrn., 1978-81; mgr. Peck & Peck, Annapolis, Md., 1981-84; ind. cons. Mary Kay Cosmetics, Inc. dir. PDQ Bus. Services, 1979-81, v.p., 1980. Dir. jr. high fellowship Presbyterian Ch., 1960-62; pres. Annapolis Bon Haven Community Assn., 1981—. bd. dirs. Colonial Players Annapolis, 1979-82, sec., 1981-84, chmn., 1984-85. Mem. Assn. Supervision and Curriculum Devel., Elementary Sch. Sci. Assn. (past sec., v.p., pres.), Profl. Educators Group, NEA, PTA (life), Mortar Bd., Kappa Delta Pi, Delta Kappa Gamma (pres. 1980-82, 2d v.p. 1982-84, membership chmn. 1984-86), Phi Mu (past chpt. adviser, pres. Glendale alumna club, nat. pub. relations dir., nat. membership dir., nat. pledge dir., dist. alumnae dir.), Democrat. Club: Annapolis Panhellenic (scholarship chmn., pres. 1986—). Home: 778 Bon Haven Dr Annapolis MD 21401

ALSTON, LELA, Ariz. state senator; b. Phoenix, June 26, 1942; d. Virgil Lee and Frances Mae Koonse Mulkey; B.S., U. Ariz., 1967; M.S., Ariz. State U., 1971; children—Brenda Susan, Charles William. Tchr. high sch., 1968—; mem. Ariz. State Senate, 1977—. Named Disting. Citizen, U. Ariz. Alumni Assn., 1978. Mem. NEA, Ariz. Edn. Assn., Am. Home Econs. Assn., Ariz. Home Econs. Assn., Am. Vocat. Assn. Methodist. Office: Capitol Bldg Senate Wing Phoenix AZ 85007

ALSTON, SUSAN SHIELDS, university administrator; b. Trenton, N.J., Mar. 10, 1951; d. Eugene Harold and Eunice Williams (Potter) Shields; m. David P. Alton, Apr. 10, 1980; children—David P., Lindsay S. B.S., Douglass Coll., 1973; M.B.A., Rider Coll., 1982. Adminstrv. asst. Woodrow Wilson Nat. Fellow Found., Princeton, N.J., 1975-76; fin. adminstr. dept. civil engring. Princeton U., 1977-81, mgr., dir. corporate relations Interactive Computer Graphics Lab., 1981-85, asst. dean Sch. Engring., 1985—. Mem. Am. Mgmt. Assn., Nat. Assn. Female Execs., AAUW. Presbyterian. Home: 8 Cavalier Dr Hamilton Square NJ 08619 Office: Dean's Office Sch Engring and Applied Sci Princeton U Princeton NJ 08544

ALTEKRUSE, JOAN MORRISSEY, physician; b. Cohoes, N.Y., Nov. 15, 1928; d. William T. Dee and Agnes Kay (Fitzgerald) Morrissey; A.B., Vassar Coll., 1949; M.D., Stanford U., 1960; M.P.H., Harvard U., 1965; Dr. P.H., U. Calif., Berkeley, 1973; m. Ernest Brenton Altekruse, Dec. 17, 1950; children—Michael, Philip, Clifford, Lisa, Janice, Charles, Sean, Sam, Patrick. Med. officer USPHS, San Francisco, Boston, 1960-64; asst. health officer Fla. Bd. Health, 1964-65; med. officer, cons. Calif. Dept. Pub. Health, 1966-69; with dept. community psychiatry U. Heidelberg (W. Ger.), 1970-72; area med. dir. Fla. Dept. Health and Rehab. Services, 1972-75; chmn. health adminstrn. U. S.C. Sch. Pub. Health, Columbia, 1975-77, prof., chmn. dept. preventive medicine and community health, 1979—; trustee Am. Bd. Preventive Medicine; mem. comprehensive test com. part II, Nat. Bd. Med. Examiners. Mem. bd. Vol. Health Agys., pres., 1985-86; bd. dirs. S.C. Heart Assn., S.C. March of Dimes, Democratic Leadership Conf. S.C.; mem. S.C.-Am. Council Edn. Council for Women in Higher Edn. Adminstrn. Served with USMC, 1949-51; with USPHS, 1960-64. Recipient Disting. Vol. award March of Dimes, certificate of merit Heart Assn.; World Health fellow, 1974; USPHS fellow, 1964, 67-69. Fellow Am. Pub. Health Assn., Assn. Tchrs. Preventive Medicine (pres. 1986-87); mem. Am. Coll. Preventive Medicine, Pub. Health Polit. Action Com. Democrat. Roman Catholic. Home: 3918 W Buchanan Dr Columbia SC 29206 Office: Dept Preventive Medicine and Community Health Sch Medicine USC Columbia SC 29208

ALTENHAUS, CORRINNE BATLIN (MRS. JULIAN ALTENHAUS), psychologist; b. N.Y.C., July 27, 1926; d. Louis and Rose (Cuttler) Batlin; B.S., Purdue U., 1946; M.Ed., Rutgers U., 1955, Ed.D., 1964; postdoctorate certificate in child psychiatry and child guidance (postdoctorate fellow), Postgrad. Center Mental Health, N.Y.C., 1971; m. Julian Altenhaus, Nov. 27, 1947; 1 dau., Amy Louise. Sch. psychologist Orange (N.J.) Bd. Edn., 1951-64, Millburn (N.J.) Bd. Edn., 1964-67; pvt. practice as psychologist, Millburn, 1967—. Coadj. staff Rutgers U., 1964-65, Newark State Coll., 1965-68, Seton Hall U., 1969-70; psychologist Stevens Inst. Tech. Psychol. Lab., 1965-68; faculty Postgrad. Center Mental Health, N.Y.C., 1972-75. Mem. profl. adv. bd. Children's Inst., 1973—. Trustee Child Guidance Clinic Oranges and Maplewood, N.J., 1961-69. Diplomate Am. Bd. Psychol. Examiners in Sch. Psychology. Fellow Am. Orth-Psychiat. Assn.; mem. Am., N.J. (mem.-at-large exec. bd. 1977-79), Essex County (pres. 1976—, trustee) psychol. assns., Kappa Delta Pi, Phi Delta Kappa. Home: 49 Claremont Dr Maplewood NJ 07040 Office: 120 Millburn Ave Millburn NJ 07041

ALTER, ELEANOR BREITEL, lawyer, legal educator; b. N.Y.C., Nov. 10, 1938; d. Charles David and Jeanne (Hollander) Breitel; children—Richard B. Zabel, David B. Zabel. B.A. with honors, U. Mich., 1960; postgrad. Harvard U. Law Sch., 1960-61; LL.B., Columbia U., 1964. Bar: N.Y., 1965. Atty. Ins. Dept., State of N.Y., 1964-66; assoc. firm Miller and Carlson, N.Y.C., 1966-68; assoc. firm Marshall, Bratter, Greene, Allison & Tucker, N.Y.C., 1968-74, ptnr., 1974-82; ptnr. firm Rosenman Colin Freund Lewis & Cohen, N.Y.C., 1982—; adj. prof. family law NYU Law Sch. 1983—. Editor: N.Y. Law Jour., 1986—. Contbr., lectr. to profl. books and jours. Trustee N.Y. State Clients Security Fund, 1983—, chmn., 1985—; bd. visitors U. Chgo. Law Sch. Mem. Am. Law Inst., ABA, New York County Lawyers, Assn. Bar City N.Y., Am. Acad. Matrimonial Lawyers. Home: 935 Park Ave New York NY 10028 Office: Rosenman Colin Freund Lewis & Cohen 575 Madison Ave New York NY 10022

ALTER, LUCILE L(EVINE), publisher, editor; b. N.Y.C., Dec. 13, 1931; d. Harold Joseph and Sylvia (Moskowitz) Levine; m. Robert H. Alter, Aug. 21, 1954; children—Deborah, Amy, Marjorie. B.F.A., Ithaca Coll., 1953. Sec., CBS-TV, N.Y.C., 1953-54; editor The Enterprise, Hastings/Dobbs Ferry, N.Y., 1979-84, editor, pub. Hastings/Dobbs Ferry, Ardsley and Irvington, N.Y., 1982-84. Editor in-depth reporting Cable TV Franchise in Hastings, 1979 (award N.Y. State Press Assn. 1980). Mem. community adv. bd. St. Cabrini Nursing Home, Dobbs Ferry, 1983—, Group Home for Retarded Adults, Hastings, 1981—; mem. adv. bd. Young Adult Inst., N.Y.C., 1983—; mem.

community adv. bd. Graham/Windham Home, Hastings, 1982-85; village trustee Hastings-on-Hudson, N.Y., 1986—. Recipient Editor award Sr. Citizen Edit., N.Y. Press Assn., 1984. Home: 18 Terrace Dr Hastings-on-Hudson NY 10706

ALTERSON, LEONA ZWEIG, artist, realtor; b. St. Louis, Mar. 1, 1920; d. Harry and Bertha (Laufer) Zweig; m. Maury Alterson, Nov. 21, 1940 (dec. 1978); 1 child, Adrienne Liberman. Student U. Fla., Gainesville, 1981-83, Fla. Internat. U., 1983-85. Lic. realtor, Fla. Sec., treas. Ford Realty, Inc., Miami, Fla., 1968-78. Exhbns. include Miami Community Coll., Gallery 1031. Mem. Miami Bd. Realtors, Nat. Honor Soc., Pastel Soc. Democrat. Reformed Judaism. Club: Funtastic (originator in Miami). Avocations: Drama; bowling; tennis; ping-pong; dancing.

ALTHAUS, BARBARA DONALSON, realtor; b. Fort Worth, Mar. 20, 1937; d. Thomas Kyle and Lucille (Martin) Donalson; student U. Tex., 1955-57; m. Dudley Nolin Althaus, Dec. 25, 1969. Legal exec. sec. firm McCully & Christensen, Houston, 1959-64; office mgr. H.A. Bornefeld, Jr., Houston, 1964-69; owner, mgr. Althaus Acres Realtors and Auctioneers, Inc., Fredericksburg, Tex., 1969—. Chmn. Damenfest, 1977; pres. Tex. Auctioneers Assn. Aux., 1977, pres., 1981-84. Mem. Nat. Auctioneers Assn. Aux., (bd. dirs. 1983-86), Tex. Assn. Realtors, Gillespie County Bd. Realtors, DAR (organizing regent 1974-76, state chmn. jr. Am. citizens 1976-79, registrar 1980-82, state parliamentarian 1985—), Daus. Am. Colonists (state chmn. colonial heritage 1981-83), vice regent 1983-86), Fredericksburg C. of C. (ambassador 1980-84), Daus. of Republic Tex., Alpha Phi. Democrat. Methodist. Home: Althaus Ranch Fredericksburg TX 78624 Office: PO Box 312 1906 N Llano St Fredericksburg TX 78624

ALTMAN, AMY JEAN, adhesive manufacturing company executive, importing company executive; b. N.Y.C., Oct. 18, 1956; d. Harold L. and Rosalind (Rainer) Altman; m. Lester Ira Mallet, May 29, 1982. B.A. cum laude in Communications, CUNY-Hunter Coll., 1979; M.B.A. in Mktg., CUNY-Baruch Coll., 1985. Asst. account exec. Miller Advt., Inc., N.Y.C., 1977-79; account exec. Creative Decisions, Inc., N.Y.C., 1979-81; mktg. mgr. Quick Quality Restaurants, Inc., Edison, N.J., 1981-82; v.p. Glue-Fast Equipment Co., Inc., Carlstadt, N.J., 1983—; pres. Amsley Design Products, Inc., Carlstadt, N.J., 1986—; mem. Internat. Trade Round Table Ctr. Internat. Studies Bergen Community Coll., Paramus, N.J., 1985. Div. staff officer for publs. U.S. Coast Guard Aux., Governors Island, N.Y., 1985-86; flotilla staff officer for pub. affairs, 1985-86. Recipient George Robinson award U.S. Coast Guard Aux., 1984. Mem. Am. Mktg. Assn. Jewish. Avocations: stained glass; interior design; boating. Office: Glue-Fast Equipment Co Inc 590 Commercial Ave Carlstadt NJ 07072

ALTMAN, DEENA MELANIE, wholesale plant nursery executive; b. Los Angeles, Mar. 4, 1952; d. Meyer Mike and Jeanne Betty (Ehrlich) Kashkin; m. Kenneth Louis Altman, July 29, 1973; children—Matthew, Logan, Mara Rose. B.A. in Human Devel., Pacific Oaks Coll., 1973. Grower, mgr. Retail Plant Nursery, Los Angeles, 1972-76; pub., founder Catalog of Unusual Succulents, Los Angeles, 1975—; owner Altman Splty. Plants, Malibu, Calif., 1977—, San Marcos, Calif., 1981—. Mem. Cactus and Succulent Soc. Am., Women in Horticulture Support Group, Calif. Assn. Nurserymen, Quail Gardens Found. Avocations: cooking, tennis. Home: 553 Buena Creek Rd San Marcos CA 92069 Office: Altman Splty Plants 553 Buena Creek Rd San Marcos CA 92069

ALTMAN, ELLEN, librarian, educator; b. Pitts., Jan. 1, 1936; d. William and Catherine (Wall) Conley. A.B., Duquesne U., 1957; M.L.S., Rutgers, 1965, Ph.D., 1971. Instr., asst. research prof. Rutgers U., 1965-67, 70-72; asst. prof. U. Ky., 1972-73, U. Toronto, 1974-76; assoc. prof. Ind. U., 1976-79; prof. Grad. Library Sch., U. Ariz., Tucson, 1979—; cons. various research orgns., state libraries. Active Exec. Women's Council So. Ariz., 1980—. Author: Performance Measures in Pub. Libraries, 1973, A Data Gathering and Instructional Manual for Performance Measures in Public Libraries, 1976, Local Public Library Administration, 1980. Fulbright-Hayes sr. lectr., 1978. Mem. ALA, AAUP, Am. Mgmt. Assn. Office: Univ Ariz Grad Library Sch Tucson AZ 85721

ALTMAN, MARION WELTMAN, lawyer; b. Wilkes-Barre, Pa., Nov. 20, 1929; d. Morris and Margaret (Israel) Weltman; m. Martin Altman, Nov. 18, 1951 (div. May 1973); children—Anita, Gary, Robert. B.S., Wilkes Coll., 1951; M.A., L.I. U., 1972, M.L.S., 1976; J.D., Hofstra U. Law Sch., 1981. Bar: N.Y. 1982, Fla. 1983. Tchr. Ohev Zedek, Wilkes-Barre, Pa., 1950-51, Roslyn (N.Y.) Adult Edn., 1961-70, Roslyn pub. schs., 1963-69; curator Bryant Library, Roslyn, 1970-78, archivist, librarian, 1974-78; lawyer, law clk. Raoul Lionel Felder, N.Y.C., 1980-82; pvt. practice law, Mineola, N.Y., 1983—; cons. preservation Nassau Libraries, Roslyn, 1976-78; lectr. to civic, profl. groups, 1975-78. Pres. North Shore Coop. Nursery Sch., Roslyn, 1957; pres., organizer Bryant Library Staff Assn., Roslyn, 1978; trustee Roslyn Landmark Soc., 1975-77; mem. Am. Contract Bridge League. Grantee Nat. Endowment for Humanities, 1974, N.Y. State Council Arts, 1973. Mem. ABA, N.Y. Bar Assn., Nassau Bar Assn., Fla. Bar Assn., Nassau-Suffolk Women's Bar Assn., Am. Trial Lawyers Assn., NOW. Home: 31 Squirrel Hill Roslyn NY 11576 Office: 170 Old Country Rd Mineola NY 11501

ALTOBELLO, MILDRED FRANCES, realtor-assoc.; b. West Palm Beach, Fla., Mar. 3, 1953; d. Francis Anthony and Ethel Hamner (Martin) A. B.A., U. Ala., 1975; M.B.A., Samford U., 1977. Ter. mgr. Burroughs Corp., Miami, Fla., 1978-80; mgmt. trainee Coral Gables Fed. Savs. and Loan (Fla.), 1981; realtor-assoc. Keyes Co., Coral Gables, 1981—. Active, West Dade Jaycee Women, Miami, 1981, Coral Gables C. of C., 1978, Civic Opera Palm Beaches, 1969; chmn. Liturgical Co. U Ala., Tuscaloosa, 1973. Mem. Soc. Profl. Journalists, Women in Communications, Inc. Democrat. Roman Catholic.

ALTOBELLO, SUZANNE M., sales executive, consultant; b. Meriden, Conn., Aug. 11, 1953; d. Henry D. and Josephine A. (La Montagne) Altobello. A.S., Endicott Coll., 1973; B.F.A., Hartford Art Sch., U. Hartford, 1976. Beauty adviser Lord & Taylor, Washington, 1977-79; tng. mgr. Erno Laszlo Inst., N.Y.C., 1979-81; regional tng. supr. Chanel, N.Y.C., 1981-83; regional mgr. sales devel. Frances Denney Inc., N.Y.C., 1983-85; cons. C.A.'s Compliment, Seattle, 1983—; regional sales mgr. UNIPERF div. Unilever, 1985, Deputé div. DEP Corp., 1985—. Campaign worker Kennedy for Pres., Boston, 1979; mem. Dallas Mus. Art, 1984—. Mem. Nat. Assn. Female Execs. Democrat. Roman Catholic. Club: Cosmesis of Tex. Home: 4048 Prescott Dallas TX 75219

ALTOMARA, RITA ECKE, librarian, author; b. Englewood, N.J., June 27, 1950; d. Russell and Rita (Walsh) Ecke; m. Gary John Altomara, Dec. 14, 1969; 1 child, Ginevra Marie. B.A., Barnard Coll., 1972; M.S., Columbia U., 1975. Jr. librarian Ft. Lee Pub. Library N.J., 1974-77, sr. librarian, 1977-80, prin. librarian, 1980-82, asst. dir., 1982-84, dir., 1984—; coordinator Women's Info. and Referral Service, Ft. Lee, 1975—. Author: Hollywood on the Palisades, 1983. Exec. bd. Ft. Lee Hist. Soc., 1982—; liaison Bergen County Office Hist. and Cultural Affairs, Hackensack, N.J., 1978—. Mem. ALA, N.J. Library Assn. Roman Catholic. Home: PO Box 13 Cresskill NJ 07626 Office: Ft Lee Pub Library 320 Main St Fort Lee NJ 07024

ALTON, ANN LESLIE, lawyer; b. Pipestone, Minn., Sept. 10, 1945; d. Howard Robert and Camilla Ann (DeMong) Alton, Jr.; B.A., Smith Coll., 1967; J.D., U. Minn., 1970; m. Gerald Russell Freeman; children—Matthew Alton (dec.), Brady Michael Alton. Admitted to Minn. bar, 1970; asst. county atty., Hennepin County, Mpls., 1970—, felony prosecutor, criminal div., 1970-75, acting chief citizens protection div., 1975-76, chief citizen protection, econ. crime div., 1976-79, chief econ. crime unit, 1979-85, sr. atty. civil div., 1985—; instr. Hamline U. Law Sch., St. Paul, 1973-76; adj. prof. law William Mitchell Coll. Law, St. Paul, 1977—; adj. prof. law U. Minn. Law Sch., Mpls., 1978-82; lectr. in field, 1970—; vice. chmn. bd. dirs. Minn. Program on Victims of Sexual Assault, 1974-76; bd. dirs. Physician's Health Plan, Health Maintenance Orgn., 1976-80, exec. com. 1977-80; mem. legal drug abuse subcom. Gov. Minn. Adv. Com. Drug Abuse, 1972-74; bd. visitors U. Minn. Law Sch., 1979-85; chmn. corp. policy task force Hennepin County Med. Soc. Child Abuse Project Coordinating Com., 1982-83. Mem. Am., Minn. (criminal law sect.), Hennepin County (ethics com. 1973-76, criminal law com. 1973—, co-vice chmn. 1979-81, unauthorized practice law com. 1977-78, individual rights and responsibilities com. 1977-78, labor and employment law com. 1986—) bar assns., Nat. Dist. Attys. Assn., Minn. County Attys. Assn., Minn. Trial Lawyers Assn., Am. Judicature Soc., Minn. Women Lawyers, U. Minn. Law Sch. Law Alumni Assn. (dir. 1979-85). Author articles, pamphlet, manual. Home: 2105 Xanthus Ln Plymouth MN 55447 Office: 2000 Hennepin County Govt Center Minneapolis MN 55487

ALTSCHUL, B J, public relations counselor; b. Norfolk, Va., Jan. 28, 1948; d. Lemuel and Sylva (Behr) A. Student, Goucher Coll., 1965-67; B.A., U. South Fla., 1970, postgrad., 1980-84. Reporter St. Petersburg Times, Fla., 1973-74; dir. pub. relations Valkyrie Press, Inc., St. Petersburg, 1974-77; founding editor Bay Life, Clearwater, Fla., 1977-81, Tampa Bay Monthly, Clearwater, 1977-81; mng. editor Fla. Tourist News, Tampa and Orlando, 1981; founder Capital Communications of Tampa, 1981, since owner, prin., name changed to bj Altschul & Assocs., 1985; mgr. editorial and info. services Va. Port Authority, Norfolk, 1985—. Author: Cracker Cookin' & Other Favorites, 1984. Editor: The Underground Gourmet, 1983. Bd. dirs. Pinellas County Big Bros.-Big Sisters, 1980-82, Fla. Folklore Soc., 1984-85, Tidewater Friends of Folk Music, Norfolk, 1985—; newsletter editor Ybor City Mus. Soc., Tampa, 1984. Grant rev. panelist Fla. Fine Arts Council, 1981. Mem. Nat. Assn. Creative Children and Adults (governing bd. 1981—), Fla. Motion Picture and Television Assn. (treas. 1976-78), Fla. Freelance Writers Assn., Hampton Rds. C. of C. (co-chmn. pub. relations Internat. Azalea Festival 1985), Hampton Rds. Fgn. Commerce Club, World Affairs Council, Am. Mensa Ltd., Pub. Relations Soc. Am. (treas. Mid-Atlantic Dist. 1985—, accreditation chmn. Hampton Rds. chpt. 1985—). Avocations: sailing; classical music; folk music. Home: 836 Jamestown Crescent Norfolk VA 23508 Office: Virginia Port Authority 600 World Trade Ctr Norfolk VA 23510

ALTSHULER, CYNDE HARA, advertising agency executive, artist; b. Atlantic City, N.J., Oct. 28, 1954; s. Kiva Adrain Altshuler and Dorothy Lois (Friedman) Stuart; m. James Lee Adler, May 22, 1977. B.A., Ithaca Coll., 1977. Mgr., Copper Bay Saloon, Atlantic City, summer 1977; consultation and edn. asst. Family Service Assn. Atlantic County, Atlantic City, 1977-78; tng. coordinator Bally's Park Place Casino Hotel, Atlantic City, 1978-80; gen. mgr. Marine Printing Co., Inc., Atlantic City, 1981-85; exhibited in various shows and galleries, including Central Sq. Gallery, Linwood, N.J., Fine Arts Gallery of Ardmore (Pa.), others. Bd. dirs., past trustee Atlantic County Women's Ctr., Absecon, N.J., 1978—; bd. dirs. Big Brothers/Big Sisters, 1977-78. Mem. Am. Soc. Tng. and Devel. Democrat. Jewish. Office: Costal Composition Inc 3305 Atlantic Ave Atlantic City NJ 08401

ALTUS, GRACE MERRIMAN THOMPSON, psychologist; b. Santa Barbara, Calif., Jan. 6, 1924; d. James Roderick and Mary Augusta (Merriman) Thompson; B.A., Santa Barbara Coll., 1944; M.A. (Allan D. Wilson Jr. Meml. scholar 1947-48), U. Calif.-Berkeley, 1947, Ph.D., 1949; m. William David Altus, Dec. 24, 1951; children—Martha Helen, Elizabeth Diane, Deborah Elaine. Tchr. Redlands (Calif.) Jr. High Sch., 1944-46; psychologist Santa Barbara (Calif.) County schs., 1949-53, dir. guidance, 1953-56; psychologist Goleta (Calif.) Union Sch. dist., 1966—. Fellow AAAS, Am. Psychol. Assn.; mem. Calif. Tchrs. Assn., NEA, Goleta Edn. Assn., U. Calif. at Santa Barbara Faculty Women (pres. 1958), Sierra Club. Club: Channel City Women's Forum (Santa Barbara). Contbr. articles to profl. jours. Home: 767 Las Palmas Dr Santa Barbara CA 93110 Office: 401 N Fairview Ave Goleta CA 93117

ALVARADO, DONNA M., government administrator; b. Washington, Nov. 8, 1948; d. Ricardo and Rita A. B.A., Ohio State U., 1969, M.A., 1970. Asst. dir. U.S. Senate Com. on Judiciary, Washington, 1980-81, counsel, 1981-83; dep. asst. sec. Dept. Def., Washington, 1983-85; dir. ACTION, Washington, 1985—. Mem. Pres.'s Task Force on Legal Equity for Women, 1985—; mem. Republican Nat. Hispanic Assembly, 1985—. Mem. Mexican-Am. Women's Nat. Assn. (exec. v.p. 1983), Am. Soc. Pub. Adminstrn. Office: ACTION 806 Connecticut Ave NW Washington DC 20525

ALVARADO, KAREN SEDDON, sales executive; b. Teaneck, N.J., Aug. 8, 1948; d. Herbert Norman and Dorothy Elizabeth (Seward) Seddon; m. Albert F. Alvarado, Feb. 25, 1978; children—Douglas, Brennan. B.S.B.I., Bucknell U., 1970; postgrad. U. Calif.-Irvine, 1978-79. Lab. technician Valley Hosp., Ridgewood, N.J., 1970-71, instr. Technicon Corp., Tarrytown, N.Y., 1970-71, tech. specialist, Denver, 1971-76, diagnostic sales mgr., Los Angeles, 1976-80, area sales mgr., 1980-81, regional sales mgr., 1981—. Mem. Nat. Assn. Female Execs., Women in Bus., Am. Mgmt. Assn., Am. Assn. Clin. Chemists, Clin. Lab. Mgmt. Assn., AAUW. Roman Catholic. Club: Orange County Cath. Alumni (pres. 1978). Office: Technicon Corp 14791 Franklin Ave Tustin CA 92680

ALVARADO, MARILYN DEL MAR, legal assistant; b. Los Angeles, Dec. 5, 1960; d. Eliud Eric Del Mar; m. Vicente Rolando Alvarado, Jr., Nov. 1, 1984. ABA paralegal cert. in litigation U. West Los Angeles Sch. Paralegal Studies, 1983; student Calif. State U.-Los Angeles, 1978-80; B.A. in Psychology, Calif. State U.-Northridge, 1982. Litigation paralegal Overton, Lyman & Prince, Los Angeles, 1982; litigation paralegal Loeb & Loeb, Los Angeles, 1983-85, Graham & James, Los Angeles, 1985—; cosmetic rep. Avon Products, Inc., Los Angeles, 1985-86. Vol. intern Los Angeles Mayor's Office, 1980-81. Recipient cert. appreciation Los Angeles Mayor's Office, 1981; Calif. Scholarship Bd. grantee Calif. State U.-Los Angeles, then Calif. State U.-Northridge, 1978-82. Mem. Los Angeles Paralegal Assn., Nat. Paralegal Assn., Nat. Assn. Female Execs. Republican. Baptist. Avocations: photography; music; horses; painting. Home: 4416 Maplewood Ave Los Angeles CA 90004 Office: Graham & James Citicorp Plaza 725 S Figueroa St 34th Floor Los Angeles CA 90017

ALVARADO VAZQUEZ, GLADYS, travel counselor; b. Havana, Cuba, Nov. 21, 1942; came to U.S., 1962; d. Silverio Miguel and Vitalia (Breso) Vazquez; m. Eduardo Alfredo Alvarado, May 4, 1963; children—Eduardo Miguel, Alfredo Joaquin. Grad. Chgo. Sch. Dental Nursing, 1963; A.S. Travel and Tourism, U. Houston, 1980. Cert. travel counselor Inst. Cert. Travel Agts. Nurse's aide Luth. Deaconess Hosp., Chgo., 1962-63; med. sec. S.M. Vazquez Clinic, Houston, 1966-79; gen. mgr. Action Travel, Inc., Bellaire, Tex., 1980-82; sr. internat. travel counselor All Travel, Inc., Houston, 1983-84, Sage Plaza One Travel, Houston, 1984—. Mem. Pacific Area Travel Assn., Inst. Cert. Travel Counselors, Am. Soc. Travel Agts., Houston Exec. Women in Travel, Caribbean Tourism Assn., Cuban Assn. Profls. and Students. Home: 5754 Birdwood St Houston TX 77096 Office: Sage Plaza One Travel 5151 San Felipe St Houston TX 77056

ALVARE, ANITA MARIE, public relations consultant; b. Phila., Dec. 31, 1952; d. Louis John and Rosemary Audrey (Cosgrove) A.; art student Rosemont Coll., 1970-71. With Certain Teed Corp., Valley Forge, Pa., 1972-81, asst. mgr. communications, 1976-78, pub. relations mgr., 1978-81; owner, pres. Alvare Assocs., Wayne, Pa., 1981—; ptnr., sec. Executive Sports, Wayne, Pa., 1985—. Republican. Roman Catholic. Club: Publicity. Home: 417 Strafford Ave Wayne PA 19087 Office: 409 E Lancaster Ave Wayne PA 19087

ALVAREZ, AUDREY SALOME, nurse; b. Jersey City, June 26, 1954; d. Casimir and Norma M. (Foerch) K.; m. Raul Alvarez, June 5, 1976; children—Deanna Norma, Michelle Salome, Carolyn Rose. B.S.N., Rutgers U., 1976, cert. Lamaza tchr. tng. program, 1982; cert. ICU nurse United Hosp., Newark, 1977. Pub. health nurse Community Nursing Service Essex and West Hudson, Harrison, N.J., 1976; staff nurse Palisades Gen. Hosp., North Bergen, N.J., 1976-79; med. dir. N. Hudson Regional Council of Mayors, Union City, N.J., 1980-82; ambulatory care nursing unit coordinator St. Michael's Med. Ctr., Newark, 1982-85; healthy mothers/healthy babies coordinator Health Corp. Archdiocese of Newark, 1985—. Mem. Nat. League Nursing, Sigma Theta Tau.. Office: 268 Dr Martin Luther King Jr Blvd Newark NJ 07102

ALVAREZ, MARIA LUISA RODON, lawyer; b. Havanna, Cuba, June 17, 1956; d. Lincoln and Maria L. (de Cardenas) Rodon; m. Julio E. Alvarez, June 28, 1974; 1 dau., Katrina L. B.A., Fla. Internat. U., 1978; J.D., U. Miami, 1981. Bar: Fla., 1982. Ptnr. Schreiber, Rodon-Alvarez, P.A., Coral Gables, Fla., 1982—. Fla. Internat. U. scholar, 1977. Mem. ABA, Fla. Bar Assn., Am. Judicature Soc. Office: Schreiber Rodon-Alvarez PA 430 S Dixie Hwy Suite 10 Coral Gables FL 33146

ALVAREZ-RIONDA, MERCEDES, advertising agency executive; b. Havana, Cuba, Sept. 24, 1942; came to U.S., 1960, naturalized, 1971; d. Jose Manuel and Teresita (Rionda) Alvarez; B.B.A., U. Miami (Fla.), 1963; postgrad. Manhattanville Coll., Purchase, N.Y., 1964. Sr. research exec. J. Walter Thompson Co., N.Y.C., 1966-78; v.p., research dir. Isidore, Lefkowitz, Elgort, N.Y.C., 1978-79, Bozell and Jacobs Inc., N.Y.C., 1979-85; v.p., assoc. research dir. BBDO, Inc., N.Y.C., 1985—. Mem. Am. Mktg. Assn., Advt. Research Found., Copy Research Council, N.Y. Advt. Club. Republican. Address: 420 E 55th St New York NY 10022

ALVARIÑO DE LEIRA, ANGELES (ANGELES ALVARIÑO), biologist, oceanographer; b. El Ferrol, Spain, Oct. 3, 1916; came to U.S., 1958, naturalized, 1966; d. Antonio Alvariño-Grimaldos and Carmen Gonzalez Díaz-Saavedra; B.S. and Letters summa cum laude, U. Santiago de Compostela, Spain, 1933; M. Natural Scis., U. Madrid, 1941, cert. Doctorate, 1951, Dr. Sci. (Ph.D.) summa cum laude, 1967; Biologist-Oceanographer, Spanish Inst. Oceanography, 1952; m. Eugenio Leira-Manso, Mar. 16, 1940; 1 dau., Angeles. Prof. biology Coll. El Ferrol, Spain, 1941-48; fishery research biologist dept. Sea Fisheries Spain, 1948-52; histologist Superior Council Sci. Research, 1948-52; biologist, oceanographer Spanish Inst. Oceanography, 1950-57; biologist Scripps Inst. Oceanography, U. Calif., La Jolla, 1958-69; fishery research biologist Nat. Marine Fisheries Service Southwest Fisheries Center, NOAA, U.S. Dept. Commerce, La Jolla, 1970—; assoc. prof. U. Nat. Autonomous Mexico; assoc. San Diego State U. assoc. researcher U. San Diego; vis. prof. U. Parana (Brazil), Nat. Poly. Inst. (Mexico). Brit. Council fellow, 1953-54; Fulbright fellow, 1956-57; NSF grantee, 1961-69; U.S. Office Navy grantee; 1958-69, Calif. Coop. Oceanic Fishery Investigation grantee, 1958-69; UNESCO grantee, 1979. Fellow Am. Inst. Fishery Research Biologists, San Diego Soc. Natural History; mem. Assn. Natural History Soc., Western Naturalists Soc., Calif. Acad. Scis., Biol. Soc. Washington, Hispano-Am. Assn. Researchers on Marine Scis., Marine Biol. Assn. U.K., Sigma Xi. Contbr. articles to profl. jours., chpts. to sci. books. Discovered 20 new species of animals, plankton indicator species of ocean dynamics and fisheries, zoogeography of chaetognatha, siphonophorae for the world oceans. Home: 7535 Cabrillo Ave La Jolla CA 92037 Office: PO Box 271 La Jolla CA 92038

ALVERS, LINDA KAY, nursing bus. exec.; b. Evansville, Ind., June 26, 1952; d. Henry N. and Marian H. (Clark) Alvers; B.S. in Nursing, U. Evansville, 1974, M. in Nursing Sci., 1979. Staff nurse Vanderbilt Med. Center, Nashville, 1974-75, St. Mary's Hosp., Evansville, 1975-77, dir. pediatric intravenous therapy, 1977-79; instr. U. Evansville Sch. Nursing, 1977-79; v.p. and dir. continuing med. edn. Nat Audio Video Transcripts, N.Y.C., 1978-81; founder, pres. Nat. Nursing Network, Inc., N.Y.C., 1981—; producer, dir. continuing edn. programs on audio and visual tape for health care profls.; adj. prof. U. Evansville, 1979-83; instr. ARC, 1978-83. Recipient Outstanding Instr. award U. Evansville Sch. Nursing, 1979, Nat. Alumni Achievement award U. Evansville, 1980. Mem. Am. Nurses Assn., N.Y. State Nurses Assn., Nat. Assn. Female Execs., Women Bus. Owners N.Y. Editorial bd. Infusion mag., 1978—. Office: 250 W 49th St Suite 400 New York NY 10109

ALVINO, SYLVIA MARIE, reading educator, educational company executive, consultant; b. Chicago Heights, Ill., Oct. 17, 1948; d. John Joseph and Diane (Urbinati) A. B.A. in English, Loyola U., Chgo., 1970, M.Ed. in Reading, 1977. Mgr. High Sch. Renaissance Program, Chgo. Bd. Edn., 1984—; reading specialist Project Upward Bound., Loyola U., Chgo., 1972—; v.p. fin., cons. Assocs. for Career Devel., Inc., Chgo., 1980—; founder The Phoenix Devel. Group, Inc., Chgo., 1983—. Recipient awards Rush Med. Ctr., 1982, Loyola U. Upward Bound Program, 1982, Calumet High Sch., 1978. Author: Liberal Arts Curriculum for Health and Medical Career Studies, 1979; (with others) Tutorial Supervisor's Manual, 1977; Cable TV Training Manual, 1981; editor Vineyard, 1971-73. Mem. Mid-Am. Equal Ednl. Opportunity Program Personnel, Assn. Supervision and Curriculum Devel., Internat. Reading Assn., Nat. Council Tchrs. English, Ind. Voters Ill., Ill. Guidance and Personnel Assn., Phi Delta Kappa, Phi Chi Theta. Roman Catholic. Home: 915 W Margate Terr Chicago IL 60640 Office: Loyola U Project Upward Bound 1041 W Loyola Ave Chicago IL 60626 also 3100 S Kedzie Ave Chicago IL 60623

ALVIS, MARGARET (PEGGY) OLIVIER, nurse; b. New Orleans, Nov. 6, 1942; d. Pliny Louis and Esther Phyllis (Bossier) Olivier; m. James Fred Alvis, Apr. 26, 1965 (div. Apr. 1980); children—Todd James, Trent David. B.S. in Nursing, U. Southwestern La., 1964. Staff nurse Charity Hosp., Lafayette, La., 1964-65; operating room nurse Our Lady of Lourdes Hosp., Lafayette, 1964-65, Charity Hosp., New Orleans, 1965-66, St. Elizabeth's Hosp., Dayton, Ohio, 1966-67; supr. operating room Baptist Meml. Hosp., Memphis, 1967-69, nursing instr., 1969-73; mem. utilization rev. Methodist Hosp., Memphis, 1976-77; instr. practical nursing Fayette County Bd. Edn., Somerville, Tenn., 1977-79; staff nurse, obstetrics supr. Fayette County Gen. Hosp., Somerville, 1979-82; dir. nursing St. James Parish Hosp., Lutcher, La., 1982—. Organizer, chmn. Christian Service Group, Memphis, 1974-75; instr. CPR Am. Heart Assn., Memphis, 1977-82; instr. first aid ARC, Baton Rouge, 1983—. Club: People for Youth (chmn. Lutcher). Avocations: oil painting, cake decorating. Home: PO Box 699 Gramercy LA 70052 Office: St James Parish Hosp 515 Louisiana Ave PO Box 430 Lutcher LA 70071

AL-YAMANI, FAIZA YOUSEF, oceanographer, researcher; b. Kuwait, Kuwait; Apr. 24, 1953; came to U.S., 1976; d. Yousef Abdul-Aziz Al-Yamani and Noora (Hassan) Al-Sharaf. B.S. in Biology, Am. U., Beirut, 1975; M.S. in Parasitology, U. Pacific, 1979; Ph.D. in Oceanography, U. Miami, 1985. Research asst. Kuwait Inst. Sci. Research, 1975-76, research assoc., 1979-80, researcher Kuwait Inst.-NOAA, Miami, Fla., 1980—. Contbr. articles to profl. jours. Muslim. Avocations: Sailing; fishing.

AMARA, LUCINE, opera and concert singer; b. Hartford, Conn., Mar. 1, 1927; d. George and Adrine (Kazanjian) Armaganian; student Music Acad. of West, 1947, U. So. Calif., 1949-50; m. Jan. 7, 1961 (div. June 1964). Appeared in Hollywood Bowl, 1948; soloist with San Francisco Symphony, 1949-50; with Met. Opera, N.Y.C., 1950—; recorded Pagliacci, 1951, 60; singer with Hartford, Pitts., Central City, New Orleans operas, 1952-54; appeared Glyndebourne Opera, 1954, 55, 57, 58, Edinburgh Festival, 1954; singer Aida, Terme Di Caracalla, Rome, 1954, also Stockholm Opera, N.Y. Philharm., St. Louis Civic Light Opera, 1955-56; has appeared in leading or title roles in several operas including Otello, Carmen, Don Giovanni, Il Trovatore, Tosca; appeared in title role of Turandot with Toledo and Dayton Opera Cos., 1979, with Stamford Opera Co., 1981; sang title role of Aida with Seattle Opera Co., 1980; sang role of Amelia in Un Ballo in Maschera, Met. Opera, N.Y.C., 1981; appeared with St. Petersburg (Fla.) Opera in title role of Tosca, 1981; appeared Vienna, Stuttgart Stattsopers; appeared with Lyric Opera of Toledo in Gala Concert, 1983, with Met. Opera's Centennial Gala, 1983; opera and concert tour, Russia, 1965; concert, Manila, 1968; tours, Paris, 1966, Mex., 1966, Far East, 1968, Hong Kong and China, 1983; rec. artist Columbia, RCA Victor, Met. Opera Record Club, Angel. Recipient 1st prize Atwater-Kent Radio auditions, 1948. Mem. Sigma Alpha Iota. Office: Metropolitan Opera New York NY 10023

AMARAL, MARY ELLEN, telecommunications company executive, lawyer; b. Kenosha, Wis., Aug. 5, 1946; d. Nestor Johnson and Mary Louise (Parker) Thompson; B.A. in Journalism, U. Mich., 1968; J.D., U. Denver, 1973; M.S. in Advanced Mgmt., Pace U., 1979; m. Charles Patrick Amaral; children—Maura Patricia, Brian Patrick. With Mountain States Tel. and Tel., Denver, 1970-76; admitted to Colo. bar, 1974; with AT&T, N.Y.C., 1976-79, dist. mgr. regulatory planning, 1980-83; regional atty. AT&T-Govt. Relations, 1983—. Conf. Bd. congressional asst. U. S. Senate Banking Com., Washington, 1980. Mem. ABA, Colo. Bar Assn., Denver Bar Assn., Colo. Women's Bar Assn., Nat. Bus. and Profl. Women's Assn. (Outstanding Profl. Woman, Dist. I, 1982), Denver Women's Partnership. Republican. Club: Zonta of Denver (2d v.p. 1986-87). Home: 1725 Fillmore Ct Louisville CO 80027 Office: 1331 17th St Suite 601 Denver CO 80202

AMATNIEK, SARA BERLIN, artist; b. N.Y.C., Feb. 6, 1922; d. Alexander and Martha (Aranow) Berlin; m. Ernest Amatniek, Apr. 1, 1949; children—Kathie, Joan Cindy. B.A., Bklyn. Coll., 1942; M.A., Columbia U., 1952. Art tchr. Music and Art High Sch., N.Y.C., 1951-54, Port Chester High Sch., Port Chester, N.Y. and N.Y.C., 1954-58; v.p. Bioelectric Instruments, Hastings-on-Hudson, N.Y., 1960-70; artist, printmaker, N.Y., 1970—. One woman shows include Davidson Gallery, Port Chester, 1984, Katonah Gallery, N.Y., 1982, Lumen Winter Gallery, New Rochelle, N.Y., 1980, Window Gallery, Nassau County Library System, N.Y., 1975; exhibited in group shows at Hudson River Mus., Yonkers, N.Y., Hecksher Mus., Huntington, N.Y., Pace Coll., Briarcliff, N.Y., Bergen County Mus., N.Y., Parish Art Mus., L.I., N.Y., Nat. Acad. Art., N.Y. Recipient Red Devil Purchase award Printmaking Council N.J., 1985, 1st Prize Graphics Minature Art Soc. N.J. 1976, 1st Prize Graphics Miniature Art Soc. Fla. 1982. Mem. Nat. Assn. Women Artists (v.p. 1983-85, treas. 1979-83,

House of Heyendryk Jr. award 1981). Home and Office: 4797 Boston Post Rd Pelham Manor NY 10803

AMATO, CAMILLE JEAN, accountant; b. N.Y.C., Aug. 6, 1942; d. William and Mary Carmela (Lombardi) Tuorto; m. Thomas Amato, June 1, 1963; children—Dawn, Thomas. Assoc. Sci., SUNY-Albany, 1981, B.S., 1983; B.S., Empire State Coll., 1983, M. Bus. and Policy, 1986. Lic. realtor, notary, N.Y. Controller, owner Island Marine Inc., Bellmore, N.Y., 1977—; account mgr. L.I. Luth. Assn., Brookville, N.Y., 1983-84, Borden Inc. Chem., Glen Cove, N.Y., 1984-85; real estate agt. N. of 25A R.E. Inc., Locust Valley, N.Y., 1986—; cons. various areas. Cons. sub-com. edn. and safety N.Y. State Senate, 1976-77. Mem. Nat. Assn. Female Execs., L.I. Bd. Realtors. Roman Catholic. Avocation: classical piano. Home: Woodstock Manor Muttontown Oyster Bay NY 11771

AMATO, CAROL JOY, technical publications consulting company executive, writer; b. Portland, Oreg., Apr. 9, 1944; d. Sam Lawrence and Lena Dorothy (Dindia) A.; m. Neville Stanley Motts, Aug. 26, 1967 (div. 1978); children—Tracy, Damon. B.A., U. Portland, 1966; M.A., Calif. State U., 1986. Freelance writer, Westminster, Calif., 1969—; human factor cons. Design Sci. Corp., Los Angeles, 1979—; dir. software documentation Trans-Ed Communications, Westminster, 1980-84, pres. Advanced Profl. Software, Inc., Westminster, 1984-86, Systems Research, Inc., Westminster, 1986—; dir. Oasis, Redondo Beach, Calif. Editor, Cultural Futuristics, 1975-80; author numerous articles and short stories, 1978—; participant in numerous radio and TV interviews. Mem. com. Am. Astronaut Meml. Found., Los Angeles, 1986—. Mem. Am. Anthrop. Assn., L-5 Soc., Human Factor Soc., Writers' Club of Whittier, Inc., Soc. for Applied Anthropology, Southwestern Anthrop. Assn., Oasis. Home: 10151 Heather Ct Westminster CA 92683 Office: Advanced Profl Software Inc 10151 Heather Ct Westminster CA 92683

AMATO, DOLORES ROSE, author, educational consultant; b. Newark, Nov. 7, 1941; d. Amelio and Carmela Amato; B.A., Caldwell Coll., 1963; M.A. in Reading, Keane State Coll., N.J., 1966; postgrad. Tex. So. U., 1976-78. Elem. sch. tchr., Parsippany, N.J., 1963-66; nat. reading cons. Harcourt Brace-Jovanovich, N.Y.C., 1966-72; dir. reading K-12, Houston Ind. Sch. Dist., 1972-79; nat. reading cons. and author, Houston, 1979—. Recipient Outstanding Educator award Nat. Soc. Creative Intelligence, 1975. Mem. Internat. Reading Assn., Am. Bus. Women's Assn., Assn. Supervision and Curriculum Devel. Author: Frost Reading and Math Program, 1979; Economy Spanish Reading Keys Basal Readers, 1978, 79; Enrich Comprehension Reading Series Books, 1981-82; contbg. author: Reading Basics Plus, 1976, 80. Address: 1 Wind Poppy Ct The Woodlands TX 77381

AMATO, ROSEMARY MARCELLA, shoe company executive; b. Cleve., May 17, 1952; d. Sam Anthony and Elizabeth Barbara (Cherney) A.; B.S.B.A., John Carroll U., 1974; postgrad. Ga. State U., 1976, Samford U., 1981. Asst. to controller Mr. Coffee, Cleve., 1973-75; staff acct. Luria Bros., Cleve., 1975-76; capital acctg. mgr. Reliance Electric Co., Cleve., 1976-77, cost acct., Gainesville, Ga., 1977-79, modernization controller, Cleve., 1979-80, regional controller, Birmingham, Ala., 1980-85; asst. corp. controller, bus. systems analyst Pic 'N Pay Stores, Inc., Charlotte, N.C., 1985—. Mem. AAUW, Nat. Assn. Female Execs., Nat. Assn. Accts. Republican. Roman Catholic. Office: Pic 'N Pay Stores Inc PO Box 34000 Charlotte NC 28261

AMBLE, BECKY LAVONNE, sales and marketing executive; b. Grand Forks, N.D., Apr. 18, 1955; d. John L. and Tillie J. (Holien) A.; m. Marshall J. Gravdahl, Dec. 20, 1975. B.S. in Bus. Adminstrn. summa cum laude, U. N.D., 1975; M.B.A. in Mktg., Central Mich. U., 1978. New products research analyst, St. Paul Co., Minn., 1979; assoc. mktg., product mgr. Medtronic, Inc., Mpls., 1979-82; ptnr., corp. treas. Juniper House, Inc., Prescott, Ariz., 1983—; instr. Lakewood Community Coll., White Bear Lake, Minn., 1982-85; pres. Infinite Expressions, Woodbury, Minn., 1982—; sales and mktg. mgr., Comml. Factors of Minn., Bloomington, 1985—. Com. mem. Jaycees, Midland, Mich., 1976-78; exec. com. fellowship chmn., youth advisor, Woodbury Health Care Project, King of Kings Ch., Minn., 1980-83. J.F.T. O'Connor Hon. scholar U. N.D., 1973-75. Mem. Minn. Women's Network (dir. 1985—), Minn. Women's Trade Fair (chmn. com. 1981-85), Minn. Entrepreneurs Club, Mpls. C. of C., Bloomington C. of C., Alpha Lambda Delta. Club: Racquet & Golf (Woodbury). Avocations: lectures; speaking; reading; racquetball; music; photography; travel; art; skiing. Home: 6601 Stratford Rd Woodbury MN 55125 Office: Comml Factors of Minn 9801 Dupont Ave S Suite 185 Bloomington MN 55431

AMBROSE, JEAN LOTRUGLIO, university administrator; b. Jamaica, N.Y., Oct. 9, 1932; d. Peter Joseph and Madeline Emma (Vohringer) LoTruglio; children—Carolyn, Christopher, Peter, Veronica. A.B., Rutgers U., New Brunswick, 1954; M.A., Columbia U., 1955; J.D., Rutgers U.-Newark, 1981. Bar: N.J. Tchr., N.Y. and Mass., 1955-58; lectr. in Spanish, Union Coll., Cranford, N.J., 1970-73; asst. to dean Rutgers U., New Brunswick, N.J., 1973-77; asst. dean Rutgers U., Newark, 1977-81, acting assoc. provost, 1981-82, assoc. dean, 1982—. Mem. adv. com. for affirmative action N.J. Dept. Higher Edn. and N.J. Commn. on Status of Women, 1975-76, Project on Equal Rights in Edn., 1975-76; cons. N.J. Dept. Edn. and Sch. Dists., N.J., 1973-76. Contbr. articles to publs. Trustee Family and Children's Services, Montclair and Glen Ridge, N.J., 1982-83; bd. dirs. Ctr. for Women Affected by Alcohol, Newark, 1980-81, Douglass Adv. Services for Women, New Brunswick, 1976—, Integrity House, Newark, 1976-77, N.J. Coll. and Univ. Coalition on Women's Edn., 1986—; mem. N.J. planning com. Am. Council on Edn. Nat. Identification Program, 1983—. Democrat. Home: 31 Trinity Pl Montclair NJ 07042 Office: Grad School-Newark Rutgers University Newark NJ 07102

AMBROZIK, LINDA ANTOINETTE, educator; b. Chgo., July 3, 1948; d. Alexander Anthony and Lillian Mary (Juszczyk) Ambrozik. B.A., George Peabody Coll., 1970; M.A., Fairleigh Dickinson U., 1975. Cert. English tchr. high sch., Ill. Tchr., English, D.U. Fletcher Sr. High Sch., Jacksonville Beach, Fla., 1970-72, Franfurt Am. Sr. High Sch. (W. Ger.), 1972-75, W.C. Reavis High Sch., Burbank, Ill., 1975-76, New Trier High Sch., Winnetka, Ill., 1977—. Recipient Superior Performance as Tchr. award, Dept. Def., 1975; named Master Tchr., New Trier High Sch. Bd. Edn., 1982. Mem. NEA, Ill. Assn. Tchrs. English (fall conf. planning com. 1978), Nat. Conf. Tchrs. English, Phi Delta Kappa (bd. dirs. 1984—, co-editor newsletter 1982—, cert. achievement 1983). Office: New Trier High Sch 385 Winnetka Ave Winnetka IL 60093

AMBURGEY, VALERIA, mathematics and information sciences educator; b. Lexington, Ky., Feb. 22, 1952; d. Eugene and Glenna Compton Amburgey; m. Thomas Alexander Wark, May 20, 1972 (div. 1981). B.Ed., Stephen F. Austin State U., 1972; M.Ed., U. Houston, 1979, Ed.D., 1984. Resident hall asst. Stephen F. Austin State U., 1971-72; tchr. Galveston (Tex.) Ind. Sch. Dist., 1973-76, Aldine Ind. Sch. Dist., Houston, 1976-81; teaching asst., lectr. U. Houston, 1979-82, 84-85; cons. Region IV, Edn. Service Ctr., Houston, 1982-85; pres. VEGA Ventures, Inc. Contbr. book rev., software revs. to Arithmetic Tchr., 1983. Sec., bd. dirs. Pine Village North Homeowner's Assn., Houston, 1983. Mem. Nat. Council Tchrs. Math., Research Council Diagnostic and Prescriptive Math., Tex. Computer Edn. Assn., S.W. Ednl. Research Assn., Kappa Delta Pi. Home: 1387 IH 45 Apt 517 Huntsville TX Office: Sam Houston State U Div Math and Info Services Huntsville TX 77341

AMENTA, CAROLINE, travel agency executive; b. Tarrytown, N.Y., Sept. 30, 1928; d. Carmelo John and Rosaria (Cavalieri) Malandrino; m. Sebastian Amenta, Dec. 27, 1952; children—Paul, John, Frank. Student Wood Bus. Sch., N.Y.C., 1946-47. Office sec. Westinghouse Internat., N.Y.C., 1947-49, Polychrome Co. Inc., Yonkers, N.Y., 1949-52, N.Y. State Regional Health Office, White Plains, 1952-55; travel cons. McGregor Travel, White Plains, 1967-70; pres. ATC Travel, Inc., Tarrytown, 1970—; sec. PJF Properties Ltd., Tarrytown, 1984—. Fellow Profl. Bus. Women (v.p. 1983-85). Roman Catholic. Avocations: swimming, reading, travel. Office: ATC Travel Inc 239 N Broadway Suite 3 North Tarrytown NY 10591

AMERINE, ANNE FOLLETTETTE, aerospace engineer; b. San Francisco, Sept. 27, 1950; d. William T. and Wilma (Carlson) F.; m. Jorge Armando Verdi D'Eguia, July 4, 1970 (div.); m. Donald Amerine, Dec. 18, 1983. A.A., Coll. Marin, 1977; B.A. in Math. with honors, Mills Coll., 1979. Sr. computer operator Bank of Am. Internat. Services, San Francisco, 1972-74; mathematician Pacific Missile Test Ctr., Pt. Mugu, Calif., 1979-80; engr. Grumman Aerospace Corp., Pt. Mugu, 1979-83; engr. Litton Guidance and Control Systems, 1984—. Chmn. Marina West Neighborhood Council, 1982-85; vice chmn., 1985—; v.p. Litton Guidance and Control Women's Enhancement Orgn., 1986—; mem. NOW; chmn. subcom. Ventura County Community Coll. Dist. Citizen's Adv. Com. on Status of Women, 1983-84. Aurelia Henry Reinhart scholar, 1978-79; recipient Project Sterling award Grumman Aerospace Corp., 1982. Mem. Nat. Assn. Female Execs., Litton Guidance and Control Women's Enhancement Orgn. (founding, v.p., chmn. info. and edn. com. 1985-86, editor newsletter 1986-87), Soc. Women Engrs. (chmn. career guidance com. and speaker Ventura County sect.), Assn. Old Crows, Mills Coll. Alumni, Alpha Gamma Sigma (life). Office: Litton Guidance & Control Systems 5500 Canoga Ave Mail Sta 80 Woodland Hills CA 91365

AMES, LOUISE BATES, child psychologist; b. Portland, Maine, Oct. 29, 1908; d. Samuel Lewis and Annie Earle (Leach) Bates; A.B., U. Maine, 1930, M.A., 1933, Sc.D., 1957; Ph.D., Yale 1936; D.Sc., Wheaton, 1967; m. Smith Whittier Ames, May 22, 1930 (div. 1937); 1 dau., Joan Ames (Mrs. Robert Clifford Chase). Research sec., personal asst. to Dr. Gesell, Yale Clinic Child Devel. Yale Med. Sch., 1933-36, instr., 1940-44, asst. prof., 1944-50; curator Yale Films of Child Devel. 1944-50; co-founder Gesell Inst. Child Devel., dir. research, sec.-treas., 1950—, assoc. dir., chief psychologist, 1968, co-dir., 1971-77, acting dir., 1978, pres., 1978—; author daily syndicated newspaper column Parents Ask; weekly TV broadcast on child behavior WBZ, Boston, 1952-55. Cert. psychologist. Conn. Mem. Conn. Psychol. Soc., Am. Psychol. Assn., Soc. Research Child Devel., Internat. Council Psychologists (bd. dirs. 1945-47), Soc. Projective Techniques (pres. 1970), Sigma Xi. Author: (with Arnold Gesell and others) First Five Years of Life, Infant and Child, Child from Five-to-Ten, Years Ten to Sixteen, Child Behavior, Child Rorschach Responses, Rorschach Responses in Old Age, Adolscent Rorschach Responses, Mosaic Patterns of American Children, Parents Ask, Guidance Nursery School, School Readiness, Is Your Child in the Wrong Grade?, Child Care and Development; Stop School Failure, Don't Push Your Preschooler: Your Two Year Old; Your Three Year Old: Your Four Year Old: Your Five Year Old: Your Six Year Old; The Gesell Institue: Child from One to Six. Editorial bd. Jour. Genetic Psychology, Jour. Learning Disabilities. Home: 283 Edwards St New Haven CT 06511 Office: Gesell Inst of Human Devel 310 Prospect St New Haven CT 06511

AMES, MARGERY ELLEN, lawyer; b. Yonkers, N.Y., May 2, 1949; d. George Joseph and Marion (Patterson) A. B.A., Skidmore Coll., 1971; J.D., Cath. U., 1974. Bar: N.Y. 1975. Cons. on pub. policy Fed. Protestant Welfare Agys., N.Y.C., 1975-83; exec. dir. Interagy. Council of Mental Retardation Agys., N.Y.C., 1983—; instr. N.Y. Med. Coll., Valhalla, N.Y., 1984—; dir. VASCA, N.Y.C., Graham-Windham, N.Y.C. Co-editor: Legal Affairs of Non-Profit Corporations, 1981. Pres. Cluster, Inc., Yonkers, 1981—; v.p. Leake & Watts Children's Home, Yonkers, 1981—; sec. Ames Family Fund, Inc., N.Y.C., 1982—. Mem. Exec. Women in Human Services, Council N.Y. Law Assocs., N.Y. Women's Bar Assn. Democrat. Roman Catholic. Avocations: scuba diving; sailing. Office: Interagy Council 275 7th Ave New York NY 10001

AMES, SANDRA PATIENCE, sales office executive; b. Quincy, Calif., May 23, 1947; d. Bruce Ray Richards and Margaret Elizabeth (Steiner) Richards Johnson; m. Martin P.M. Bettenhausen, Dec. 10, 1965 (div. 1972); m. Thomas William Ames, Nov. 28, 1975. Student Yuba City Jr. Coll., 1965-66. Sales corr. Nat. Can Corp., Seattle, 1974-76, Lehigh Valley, Pa., 1976-79, nat. account sales corr., Chgo., 1979-81, dist. sales office mgr., 1981-82, sales analyst I, Oakbrook, Ill., 1982-84, regional sales office mgr., 1984—. Mem. Nat. Assn. Female Execs. Republican. Office: Nat Can Corp 1211 W 22d St Suite 620 Oakbrook IL 60521

AMICE, CAROL RIZZARDI, copywriter; b. Chambersburg, Pa., Aug. 11, 1955; d. Carl J. and Angela A. (Zagrosky) Rizzardi; m. Thierry Thymen Amice, June 12, 1980. Student U. Ill.-Chgo., 1983, U. Md., Munich, 1979-80; B.S.J., Northwestern U., 1978. Staff reporter Dayton (Ohio) Jour.-Herald, 1977, Pottsville (Pa.) Republican, 1976; asst. personnel and logistics U. Md., 1979-80; copy editor Stars and Stripes, Griesheim, W.Ger., 1980; asst. advt. mgr., pub. relations specialist Chas. Levy Circulating Co., Chgo., 1981-83; copywriter Better Homes and Gardens mag., Des Moines, 1983—; copy editor Comparative Law Yearbook, 1978; contbr. article to Women's mag. Mem. Women in Communications (v.p. membership/communications chpt. 1984-85, pres. 1986—), Advt. Profls. Des Moines (Gridiron producer 1985, sce.-treas. 1986—), ACLU, Iowa Civil Liberties Union, greater Des Moines Volkssport Assn. (founder 1984, pres. 1985-86), Am. Volkssport Assn. (pub. relations and spl. events com. 1986), Amnesty Internat., Democrat. Home: 9009 Maplecrest Dr Norwalk IA 50211 Office: Better Homes and Gardens Advt 17th and Locust Sts Des Moines IA 50336

AMICK, CAROL CAMPBELL, state legislator; b. Cleve.; d. Charles L. and Janet (Campbell) A.; m. William S. Moonan. B.S., Iowa State U.; M.P.A., Harvard U. Mem. Mass. Ho. of Reps., 1975-77, Mass. Senate, 1977—; mem. Mass. Gov.'s Commn. on Status of Women, 1975-82; state senate chmn. Mass. Legis. Water Policy Commn., 1978—. Mem. Mass. Caucus Women Legislators, 1975—, chmn., 1976; active Friends of Bedford Pub. Library, Mass. Mem. LWV, Alpha Lambda Delta, Sigma Kappa. Democrat. Office: Mass Senate State Capitol Boston MA 02133*

AMIDEI, NANCY JEAN, social service agency executive, writer, media commentator; b. Lake Forest, Ill., Mar. 27, 1942; d. Natale and Dema (Capitani) A. B.S. in Humanities, Loyola U., Chgo., 1963; M.S.W., U. Mich., 1968. Vol., Peace Corps, Nigeria, 1964-65; mem. staff, then staff dir. U.S. Senate Com. on Nutrition and Human Needs, Washington, 1969-72; dep. asst. sec. HEW, Washington, 1977-79; dir. Food Research Action Ctr., Washington, 1980-84; weekly columnist; Washington corr. Commonweal Mag.; commentator All Things Considered program Nat. Pub. Radio; vis. prof. Sch. Social Work, U. Mich., Ann Arbor, 1985, Sch. Social Work, Catholic U., Washington, 1986—. Co-author: Protest, Politics and Prosperity: Black Americans and White Institutions, 1940-75, 1978; prin. author: Hunger in the Eighties: A Primer, 1984; also numerous articles. Commn. mem. Hunger Watch, N.Y. State, 1983; mem. adv. bd. U.S.A. for Africa, Project Vote; bd. dirs. OMB Watch. Recipient Disting. Alumni award U. Mich. Sch. Social Work, 1984, Spl. Achievement award Kenny and Marianne Rogers Hunger Awards, 1984; alumna in residence U. Mich. Alumnae Assn., 1985. Mem. Nat. Assn. Social Workers (publs. com.), Nat. Anti Hunger Coalition.

AMIEVA, MARTA Z(ENAIDA), data processing consultant; b. Havana, Cuba, Oct. 11, 1945; came to U.S., 1961, naturalized, 1969; d. Jose and Alsina (Felipe) Ferreira; m. Carlos Amieva, Nov. 25, 1961. B.S. in Commerce, Corazon de Maria, Havana, 1961; student N.Y. Inst. Tech., Commack, 1973—. Clk. Phoenix of London, N.Y.C., 1963-65; mgr. A.M.C., N.Y.C., 1965-70, Gambit Mgmt., N.Y.C., 1970-75; v.p. Republica Bank N.Y., N.Y.C., 1975-81; pres. AMK Systems, Inc., N.Y.C., 1981—; assoc. cons. R&P Inc., Boston; cons. Goldman, Sachs & Co., N.Y.C., 1985—. Active Thirteen, N.Y.C., Nat. Cancer Inst. and Ptnrs. in Courage; mem. Republican. Presdl. Task Force, Washington, 1986-87. Named woman of yr. YWCA, N.Y.C., 1980. Mem. Women in Communications, N.Y. Acad. Scis., Am. Film Inst., Women in Computing, Nat. Assn. Female Execs., Smithsonian Assocs., Nat. Mus. Women in Arts (charter), NOW (charter). Club: Centurion. Office: 53-36 37 Rd Woodside New York NY 11377

AMIN, JAMILLAH MAARIJ (JOYCE MARIE JOSEPH), food technologist, real estate agent; b. Lake Charles, La., Jan. 11, 1947; d. Anthony Armo and Edna (LeMelle) Joseph; m. Yusuf D. Amin Sr., Aug. 31, 1968 (div. Dec. 1981); children—Laval Vallare, Yusuf, Ishmael, Harun, Caliph m. Guy R. Grant, July 27, 1985. Student San Jose City Coll., 1965-67, San Jose State Coll., 1967-68, Calif. Poly. Inst., 1970-71; A.A., Yuba Coll., 1970; B.S., Calif. State U.-Fresno, 1973, Quality control technician Adolph Coors Co., Golden, Colo., 1979, food technologist, 1979-80; asst. mgr. food service Am. River Coll., Sacramento, 1982-83; food service mgr. U. Calif., Davis, 1983-84; pub. service dir. KMFO Broadcasting, Aptos, Calif., 1984-85; real estate agent Cornish and Carey Realtors, Hollister, Calif., 1985—. Recipient Outstanding Service award Sabin Sch., 1977; Outstanding Service award Gold Oak Sch., 1981. Mem. Inst. Food Technologists, San Benito County Bd. Realtors, Santa Cruz-Watsonville Bd. Realtors. Republican. Avocations: writing poetry; aerobic dance; gardening; hiking. Home: 1431 Sunnyslope Rd Hollister CA 95023 Office: Cornish and Carey Realtors 200 Tres Pinos Rd Hollister CA 95023

AMIRA, SHELLEY HELFER, hospital administrator; b. Bridgeport, Conn., Nov. 16, 1955; d. Edward F. and Muriel (Friedman) Helfer; m. Stephen Alan Amira, May 1, 1983. B.S., U. N.H., 1976; M.P.H., Yale, 1979. Adminstrv. resident Beth Israel Hosp., Boston, 1979, mgr. ambulatory services, 1980-83; course adminstr. Harvard Med. Sch., Boston, 1980-83; dir. ambulatory surg. services Brigham and Women's Hosp., Boston, 1983—. Mem. Am. Hosp. Assn., Women in Health Care Mgmt. (treas. 1981-84), Health Care Mgmt. Assn., Assn. Women's Networks (network leader 1983—). Democrat. Jewish. Home: 107 Upland Ave Newton Highlands MA 02161 Office: Brigham and Women's Hosp 75 Francis St Boston MA 02115

AMMAN, MARGARET CASEY, historian, educator; b. Newport, R.I., Feb. 18, 1932; d. John Raymond and Beatrice Zita (Harrington) Casey; B.A., Salve Regina Coll., 1956, postgrad., 1976. Tchr. U.S. history Thompson Jr. High Sch., Newport, 1956-58, 64—, chmn. social studies dept.; tchr. U.S. Navy, San Miguel, Zambales, Philippines, 1958-59, Yokosuka, Japan, 1959-60, Newport, R.I., 1960-61; tchr. Creole Petroleum Corp., Judibana, Estado Falcon, Venezuela, 1961-63, Esso Internat. Co., Gach Saran, Iran, 1963-64. Rep. U.S.-Japanese intercultural exchange program Yokohama, 1959-60. Mem. Nat., R.I. edn. assns., Newport Tchrs. Assn. Roman Catholic. Club: Goat Island Yacht (dir.). Home: 105 Goat Island Newport RI 02840 Office: Thompson Jr High Sch Broadway St Newport RI 02840

AMMANN, LILLIAN ANN NICHOLSON, horticulturist; b. Pearsall, Tex., June 20, 1946; d. Harvey Franklin and Annie Laura (Matthews) Nicholson; B.A. magna cum laude, Southwestern U., 1968; m. Jack Jordan Ammann, Jr., May 31, 1967; 1 son, William Erik. Inventory mgr. Kelly AFB, San Antonio, 1967-70; employment counselor Tex. Employment Commn., San Antonio, 1970-75; owner, operator Lillie's Lovely Little Gardens, San Antonio, 1975-77; owner, operator Lillie's Interior Landscapes (Inc. 1983), San Antonio, 1980-82, pres., 1983—; pres. Cas Mann Inc. doing bus. as Lillie's & Sherry's Plants & Pottery, San Antonio, 1977-80; sec. Jack Ammann, Inc., San Antonio, 1983—. Mem. Interior Plantscape Assn., Nat. Council for Interior Hort. Cert. (charter cert. interior horticulturist), San Antonio Interior Landscape Assn., Women in Bus., Nat. Assn. for Self-Employed, North San Antonio C. of C. Episcopalian. Author: Lillie's Lovely Little Gardening Book, 1976. Home: 603 Mauze San Antonio TX 78216 Office: 119 W Blanco Route 10 Box 82E San Antonio TX 78216

AMOS, JOAN MARIE, insurance agency executive; b. Leominster, Mass., Nov. 22, 1935; d. Louis Adelard and Cecelia Irene (Lamoreux) LaBelle; m. Charles Clinton Amos, Feb. 2, 1962; 1 child, Johnathan Ashley. Cert. in Acctg., LaSalle U., Chgo., 1968; charter property and casualty underwriting courses Boston U., 1968-69. Sec., treas. Henry Leblanc Inc., Fitchburg, Mass., 1969-74, Marsolais Ins. Agy., Ayer, Mass., 1970-74, Aanco Underwriters, Inc., St. Petersburg, Fla., 1973—, Countryside Insurors, Inc., Tarpon Springs, Fla., 1982—; owner, operator Jomar Charter & Properties, St. Petersburg, 1973—. Bd. dirs. Fla. Orch., St. Petersburg, 1981-83, bd. govs., 1984-87; fund raising chmn. Pinellas Assn. for Retarded Children, St. Petersburg, 1982. Am. Nat. Novice Ladies Figure Skating Champion, Roller Skating Rink Operators Assn. Am., 1953. Mem. Nat. Assn. Ins. Women, Ins. Women of St. Petersburg, Nat. Assn. Ins. Agts. Democrat. Roman Catholic. Clubs: Cross of Lorraine Soc., Infinity. Home: 300 Rafael Blvd NE Saint Petersburg FL 33704 Office: Aanco Underwriters Inc 1901 9th St N Saint Petersburg FL 33704

AMOWITZ, GEORGETTE WEISZ, choreographer, educator; b. Paris, Oct. 26, 1929 (parents Am. citizens); d. Bela and Margaret (Goldman) Weisz; B.A., U. Wis., 1951; postgrad. Juilliard Sch., 1951-53; tchrs. cert. Labanotation, Dance Notation Bur., Inc., 1956, advanced cert. Labanotation, 1960; m. J. David Amowitz, Jan. 30, 1954 (dec. 1979); children—Michael Bennett, Steven Paul, Susan Lynn; m. 2d Nathaniel T. Gorchoff, Sept. 4, 1983. Choreographer, Va. Grass Roots Opera Theatre, Lynchburg, 1955-58, Briar Patch Summer Theatre, Sweet Briar, Va., 1956, Lynchburg Little Theatre, 1955, 60, 67, 76, Lynchburg Coll. Opera Theatre, 1958, 63, Lynchburg Fine Arts Center, 1969, 74, Randolph-Macon Woman's Coll. Dance Concerts, Lynchburg, 1958-74; instr. dance Randolph-Macon Woman's Coll., 1956, 58, 59-62, 63, 64-65, 70-71, lectr. dance 76-77, 78-79, 82; lectr. dance Hollins Coll., 1977, U. Wis.-Milw., 1981-82; reconstructor dance works Lynchburg Fine Arts Center, 1958, 59, 62, 70, 71, 75, Hollins (Va.) Coll., 1976, 77, 80, Sweet Briar Coll., 1963, U. Wis.-Milw., 1981, Dance Theatre of Central Va., 1983-84; Talent Trust instr. Lynchburg City Schs., 1974-75, Fine Arts Center, 1974-75; v.p. Dance div. Fine Arts Center, 1973-74, asso. dir., 1974-75, dir. Dance Players, 1969; dir. Jr. Dansnotators of Lynchburg, 1958-66, Little Dance Theatre, 1959-63, Lynchburg Dance Theatre Workshop, 1966-76; chmn. dance dept. Nat. Fedn. Music Clubs, 1975-77; pvt. tchr. technique and Labanotation, Lynchburg, 1958-76. Fellow Internat. Council Kinetography Laban; mem. Dance Notation Bur. (dir. 1956-57, 61-64), U. Wis. Alumni Assn. (life). Choreography registered for copyright includes Shepherds Dance from Amahl and the Night Visitors, 1959; And After the Journey, 1981.

AMPARAN, MARIA ELENA, personnel executive; b. Los Angeles, Aug. 19, 1945; d. John S. and Concepcion (Mendez) A.; A.A., East Los Angeles Coll., 1967; B.A. in Journalism, Calif. State U., Los Angeles, 1969. Sec., coordinator press and publicity Sta. KNBC, 1969-70; prin. public relations rep. model cities program East N.E. neighborhood City of Los Angeles, 1970-72; public info. aide Housing Authority, Los Angeles, 1972; editor So. Calif. Rapid Transit Dist., 1972-73; coordinator dept. community services County of Los Angeles, 1973-76; employment specialist Kaiser Permanente Med. Care Program, Los Angeles, 1976-79; personnel supr. McDonald's Corp., Denver, 1979—. Vol., coordinator Youth Motivation Task Force, 1976-79; mem. employer adv. com. Career Planning Center, Inc., 1978-79; bd. dirs. Denver Pvt. Industry Council; mem. Denver Mayor's Task Force on Youth. Recipient commendation award Los Angeles County Bd. Supervisors. Mem. Personnel Mgmt. Assn. San Diego, Personnel Mgmt. Assn. of Aztlan (chairperson ad hoc placement com., pres. San Diego chpt. 1982-84, nat. publicity chmn. 1982-84), Profl. Women's Journalism Soc., Beta Phi Gamma. Democrat. Roman Catholic. Home: 2110 India St Los Angeles CA 90039 Office: PO Box 3247 1913 Frank Stiles Rd South El Monte CA 91733

AMSTER, LINDA EVELYN, newspaper executive, consultant, researcher; b. N.Y.C., May 21, 1938; d. Abraham and Belle Shirley (Levine) Meyerson; m. Robert Lewis Amster, Feb. 18, 1961 (dec. 1974). B.A., U. Mich., 1960; M.L.S., Columbia U., 1968. High sch. tchr. Stamford, Conn., 1961-63; researcher Detroit News, 1965-67; researcher N.Y. Times, N.Y.C., 1967-71, research supr., 1971-74, news research mgr., 1974—. Author: Who Said What, 1972; The Watergate Hearings, 1973; The White House Transcripts, 1974; The End of a Presidency, 1974; contbr. articles to N.Y. Times and other publs. Bd. dirs. Council for Career Planning, N.Y.C., 1982—. Mem. Spl. Libraries Assn. Home: 336 Central Park W New York NY 10025 Office: New York Times 229 W 43d St New York NY 10036

AMSTUTZ, LEORA EDWARDS (MRS. MELVIN E. AMSTUTZ), former church association executive; b. Marion, Ind., Sept. 12, 1909; d. Charles W. and Josephine (Bouvier) Edwards; student Sherwood Coll. Music and Dramatic Art, 1926-28; also pvt. study; m. Melvin E. Amstutz, Nov. 21, 1931 (dec. Jan. 1970); children—Carol Dawn Amstutz Kozma, Joy Diane Amstutz Caldwell. Exec. sec. Waukegan Area Council Chs., 1952-69; founder Waukegan Area Ch. Women United, 1952; producer, commentator own radio program Religion in the News, Sta. WKRS, 1958—, producer, narrator Songs of Faith, 1978—, also chmn. Radio Ministry; sec. organizing bd. mgmt. Lake County Mental Health Clinic, 1959-69; profl. dramatic reader, soloist, dir. plays, actress in amateur plays, platform and pulpit speaker, 1923—. Council mem. Girl Scouts U.S.A., 1937-45, pres., 1940-43, v.p., 1939, treas., 1943-45; bd. dirs. YWCA, 1945-52; sec. bd. dirs. North Lake County Mental Health Soc., 1953-70; bd. dirs. Lake County Welfare Council, Community Chest, USO; v.p. orgn. bd. 1st v.p. Civic Music Assn.; sec. orgn. bd. Lake County Council on Alcoholism, now mem. adv. bd.; organizer 1st Interfaith Women's Council, 1964—; co-founder, mem. exec. bd. Waukegan Area Interfaith Conf. Religion and Race, 1963—; treas. Lake County Welfare Council, 1961-67; organizing mem. bd. dirs. Lake County Music Center; mem. Am. Field Service Exchange Student Orgn.; charter bd. mem. OEO Vol. Adv. Council; bd. mem. Chgo. Home Missionary Soc.; mem. edn. com. Am. Cancer Soc.; mem. adv. council Lake County Health Dept.; mem. Lake County Urban League; bd. dirs., charter mem. Christian Ch. Supplies, Inc., 1972—; bd. dirs., pres. Victory Hosp. Aux., also mem. hosp. governing bd.; mem. Victory Hosp. Assn.; bd. dirs. Friends Library Waukegan, pres., 1981-84; bd. dirs. Lake County Blumberg Meml. Blood Bank, 1976-82, Happy Day Nursery Sch., 1979—; com. mem. Lake County Bd. Welfare Services, 1978—; bd. dirs. Waukegan Area Crimestoppers, 1982—; mem. Community Concert Assn., (founder), Waukegan Symphony

Assn. (founder), LWV (radio chmn.), Family Service Agy., Nat. Assn. Council Secs. (nat. exec. bd. 1965-68), Planned Parenthood Aux. of Lake County, WCTU, Woman's Soc. of Christian Service (past pres.); mem. home service com. ARC; adv. com. Practical Nurse Program, 1955-70; religious coordinator, celebration producer Waukegan Bicentennial Commn.; mem. council of laity Garrett Theol. Sem., Evanston, Ill., 1981—; pres. adminstrv. bd. 1st United Meth. Ch., 1978—; voting mem. No. Ill. Conf. United Meth. Ch.; chmn. Waukegan Bicentennial Yr. Celebration of Am. Methodism, 1784-1984. Named Community Woman of Achievement, 1956; recipient Brotherhood award NAACP, 1957; Brotherhood award B'nai B'rith, 1959; Ann. Lake County Mental Health award, 1969; Appreciation award Happy Day Sch., 1967; Community Service award Met. Council NAACP, 1968; House resolution Ill. Legislature, 1975; Valiant Woman award Waukegan Area and Nat. Ch. Women United, 1978; Spl. Achievement award Victory Hosp., 1978 Community Service award Lake County Urban League Guild, 1981, Leadership award Ill. Hosp. Assn., 1983. Mem. Internat. Platform Assn. Republican. Methodist (numerous offices and com. memberships in ch. orgns.). Clubs: Altrusa (dir.; Outstanding Woman in Lake County History award 1976), Woman's. Home: 2200 Hyde Park Ave Waukegan IL 60085

ANABLE, ANNE CURRIER STEINERT, journalist; b. Boston, Feb. 18; d. Robert Shuman and Lucy Pettingill (Currier) Steinert; grad. West Hill Jr. Coll., Boston, 1951; m. Anthony Anable, Jr., 1962 (div. 1965); m. 2d Robert C. Henriques, 1973 (div. 1980). Reporter women's pages N.Y. Jour. Am., N.Y.C., 1961-66, World Jour. Tribune, N.Y.C., 1966-67; fashion editor Cleve. Plain Dealer, 1967-73; fashion and beauty editor New Woman mag., Ft. Lauderdale, Fla., 1973-75, 78-79; contbg. editor Conn. sect. N.Y. Times, 1977-81; beauty editor L'Officiel/USA, 1979, New Woman mag., 1982; fashion editor Am. Salon, 1984—. Recipient Fashion Reporting award N.Y., 1970. Mem. Soc. Profl. Journalists, Fashion Group. Home: 7 Flower Hill Pl Port Washington NY 11050

ANAGNOST, MARIA ATHENA, surgeon; b. Chgo., Oct. 21, 1943; d. Themis John and Catherine (Cook) A.; B.A., Northwestern U., 1965; M.D., U. Ill., 1973. Resident in surgery U. Chgo. Hosps. and Clinics, 1973-74; gen. surgery resident Michael Reese Med. Center, Chgo., 1975-79, chief resident, 1979-80; practice medicine specializing in surgery; surg. staff Oak Park (Ill.) Hosp., Westlake Community Hosp., Melrose Park, Ill., Gottlieb Meml. Hosp., Melrose Park, St. Anne's Hosp., Chgo., St. Anne's Hosp. West (also sec.-treas.), Northlake, Ill., Good Samaritan Hosp., Downers Grove, Ill., Michael Reese Med. Center. Candidate for alderman, Chgo., 1964. Diplomate Am. Bd. Surgery, Nat. Bd. Med. Examiners. Recipient Physicians' Recognition award AMA. Fellow ACS, Internat. Coll. Surgeons; (vice-regent); mem. AMA, Ill. Med. Soc., Chgo. Med. Soc., Hellenic Med. Soc., U. Ill. Alumni Assn., Northwestern U. Alumni Assn. Contbr. articles to profl. jours. Office: 1545 Clinton Pl River Forest IL 60305 also 3825 Highland Ave Downers Grove IL 60515 also 11 S LaSalle St Chicago IL 60603

ANAGNOSTOS, FREDA KOURY, civic worker; b. Woonsocket, R.I., Apr. 11, 1918; d. Albert (Abdullah) Gibran and Jamela (Lataash) Koury; m. James Anagnostos, Sept. 7, 1952; 1 child, Peter Koury. Cert. R.I. Sch. Design, 1942. Advt. mgr. Woonsocket Call, 1949-54, Tilden Thurber, Providence, 1963-84; sec. citizens adv. bd. City of Woonsocket, 1963-64; state pres. leukemia drive St. Jude's Hosp., R.I., 1958-60; rec. sec. No. R.I. unit Am. Cancer Soc., 1977-80; pres. Trinity Club, 1972-74; chairwoman spl. gifts No. R.I. area Catholic Charity, 1977-78; pres. women's sodality St. Elias Ch., 1950-52; pres., founder Mt. St. Francis Sch. Mothers Guild, 1962-64; chmn. Woonsocket Heritage Festival, 1986—. Mem. Women's Advt. Club R.I. (past pres., Advt. Woman of Yr. 1963). Democrat. Mem. Eastern Rite Catholic Ch. Home: PO Box 8 44 Bernice Ave Woonsocket RI 02895

ANARGYROS, NEDRA FLORENCE HARRISON, cytotechnologist; b. N.Y.C., Dec. 3, 1915; d. Leverette Roland and Florence Martha (Pickard) Harrison; student Emerson Coll., 1936; cert. in cytology U. Calif., San Francisco, 1957; m. Spero Drosos Anargyros, Oct. 21, 1940 (div. 1969). Supr. cytology San Francisco Gen. Hosp., 1957—. Mem. Am. Soc. Clin. Pathologists (affiliate mem.), Am. Soc. for Cytotech. (affiliate mem., cert. cytologist), Women Flyers of Am., DAR (1st vice regent La Puerta de Ora chpt., San Francisco), Nat. Soc. Colonial Dames of Am. in Calif., Huguenot Soc. of Calif. Republican. Christian Scientist. Club: Presidents of Mercer U. (Macon, Ga.). Home: 2503 Clay St San Francisco CA 94115 Office: 22nd and Potrero Sts San Francisco CA 94110

ANAST, PAMELA SUE ROGERS, fashion designer; b. N.Y.C., June 26, 1946; s. Francis Henry and Sophia (Nadler) Rogers; children by previous marriage—Lisa Lipskin, Terri Lipskin, Scott Lipskin; m. Marcus Anthony Anast, Sept. 10, 1951; children—Jaime Alexander, Noah Andreas. Grad. high sch., Elmhurst, N.Y. Sales mgr. Supermarket Reps. Convs., Valley Stream, N.Y., 1975-78; sales mgr. Jerry Sorbara Furs, N.Y.C., 1979-80; designer Delaware Street, Inc., N.Y.C., 1980—; design coordinator Anastos Design, N.Y.C., 1982—; cons. World Fox Furs, N.Y.C., 1985. Bd. dirs., nat. liaison Nat. Council Jewish Women, Five Towns, N.Y., 1967-75, advisor teen group, 1968-75. Avocations: interior design, loft conversions. Home: 14 E 4th St New York NY 10012 Office: Delaware Street Inc 14 E 4th St New York NY 10012

ANASTOLE, DOROTHY JEAN, electronics company executive; b. Akron, Ohio, Mar. 26, 1932; d. Leonard L. and Helen (Sagedy) Dice; student De Anza Jr. Coll., Cupertino, Calif., spring 1969; children—Kally, Dennis, Christopher. Various secretarial positions in mfg., 1969-75; office mgr. Sci. Devices Co., Mountain View, Calif., 1975-76; exec. adminstrv. sec. corp. office Cezar Industries, Palo Alto, Calif., 1976-77; office and personnel mgr. AM Bruning Co., Mountain View, 1977-81; dir. employee relations Consol. Micrographics, Mountain View, 1981-83; personnel mgmt. cons., 1983-84; mgr. adminstrn./employee relations Mitsubishi Electronics Am., Inc., Sunnyvale, Calif., 1984—. Bd. dirs. Agnew State Hosp., San Jose, Calif., 1966-72, div. chmn. program mentally retarded, 1966-72, staff tutor, 1966-72. Recipient Service award Agnew State Hosp., 1972. Mem. Am. Soc. Profl. and Exec. Women, Adminstrv. Mgmt. Soc. Office: 1050 E Argues Sunnyvale CA 94086

ANCELL, BARBARA BIBEN, public relations executive; b. Seneca Falls, N.Y., Feb. 26, 1943; d. David Hugh and Hilda (Zeitlin) Rubinstein; student Eastman Sch. Dental Hygiene, 1961-63; m. Nathan S. Ancell, Nov. 3, 1984; children—Matthew Lee Biben, Douglas Ross Biben. Dir. Germanow Art Gallery, Rochester, N.Y., 1973-75; free-lance artist, Rochester, 1972-80; producer-host Pub. TV Arts Show, Rochester, 1977; pub. service mgr. Gannett Rochester Newspapers, 1978, dir. public service and promotion, 1979-84, mgr. community relations, 1984—; pres. Ancell Assocs.; mem. N.Y. State Pubs. Newspaper in Edn. Commn., 1979-82. Bd. dirs. United Way, 1980—; Rochester Bus. Opportunities, 1979-83, GEVA Theatre, 1979-85; v.p. Lend-A-Hand Charity; mem. Monroe Community Coll. Advisory Com., for Community Services, 1980—; dir. Ad Council, 1980-85; bd. dirs. Jr. League, 1976-78, Arts for Greater Rochester, 1980-86, Women's Career Ctr., 1978-80, Ctr. Ednl. Devel., 1985—; campaign mgr. Robert L. Dey for N.Y. State Senate, 1978; bd. dirs. Bus. Commn. Arts Greater Rochester, 1980—; commr. Brighton Cable Commn. Recipient Lantern award for pub. service. Mem. Internat. Newspaper Promotion Assn. (pres. Eastern region), Women in Communication (dir.). Home: 110 Runnymede Rd Rochester NY 14618

ANCKER, CAROLYN ROSE, real estate sales associate, community service volunteer; b. Phila., Nov. 4, 1919; d. Laurence Loeb and Theresa (Rothenberg) A. B.A., Randolph-Macon Woman's Coll., Lynchburg, Va., 1941. Receptionist, Travelers Aid Soc., Phila., 1946; exec. sec. Women's com. Red Cross Drive, Phila., 1947; sales assoc. John J. McGroarty, Elkins Park, Pa., 1952-56, Century 21 Langsdorf-Adler, Elkins Park, 1977—. Mem. East Montgomery County Bd. Realtors, Randolph Macon Woman's Coll. Alumnae Assn. (1st v.p. 1966-69), AAUW (pres. Phila. br. 1960-62, internat. fellow 1962). Republican. Jewish. Clubs: Philmont Country, Phila., Altrusa (pres. 1976-78), Women's University (pres. 1960-62) (Phila.).

ANCKER-JOHNSON, BETSY, physicist, automotive executive; b. St. Louis, Apr. 29, 1927; d. Clinton James and Fern (Lalan) Ancker; B.A. in Physics with high honors (Pendleton scholar), Wellesley Coll., 1949; Ph.D. magna cum laude, U. Tuebingen (Germany), 1953; D.Sc. (hon.), Poly. Inst. N.Y., 1979, Trinity Coll., 1981, U. So. Calif., 1984, Alverno Coll., 1984; LL.D. (hon.), Bates Coll., 1980; m. Harold Hunt Johnson, Mar. 15, 1958; children—Ruth P. Johnson, David H. Johnson, Paul A. Johnson, Martha H. Johnson. Instr., jr. research physist U. Calif., 1953-54; mem. staff Inter-Varsity Christian Fellowship, 1954-56; physicist, Sylvania Microwave Physics Lab., 1956-58; mem. tech. staff RCA Labs., 1958-61; research specialist Boeing Co., 1961-70, exec., 1970-73; asst. sec. commerce for sci. and tech., 1973-77; dir. phys. research Argonne Nat. Lab. (Ill.), 1977-79; v.p. Gen. Motors environ. activities staff Gen. Motors Tech. Center, Warren, Mich., 1979—; affiliate prof. elec. engring. U. Wash., 1964-73. Trustee Wellesley Coll., 1972-77. AAUW fellow, 1950-51; Horton Hollowell fellow, 1951-52; NSF grantee, 1967-72. Fellow Am. Phys. Soc. (councillor-at-large 1973-76), IEEE; mem. Nat. Acad. Engring.; Phi Beta Kappa, Sigma Xi. Author, patentee in field. Office: Environmental Activities Staff GM Technical Center Warren MI 48090

ANDER, LISA MARIE, lawyer; b. Sharon, Pa., Sept. 14, 1954; d. John Frank and Estelle Frances (Dankoff) Conticelli; m. Gregg D. Ander, July 14, 1983. B.A., U. Pitts., 1976; J.D., McGeorge Sch. Law, U. of Pacific, 1981. Bar: Calif. 1982, U.S. Dist. Ct. (ea. dist.) Calif. 1982. Legal intern Pub. Defender's Office, Sacramento, 1980-81; legal asst. Irvine Company, Newport Beach, Calif., 1982; assoc. Law Offices Daniel Lang, Elk Grove, Calif., 1982-83; atty. Ticor Title Ins. Co., Los Angeles, 1983—; of counsel firm Westhoff, Kazenzadeh, Jacobs, Nefas & MacMillan, 1983—. Mem. Calif. Bar Assn. (Voluntary Legal Services award 1983), ABA, Los Angeles County Bar Assn., Women Lawyers Los Angeles. Democrat. Roman Catholic. Office: Ticor Title Insurance Co 1717 Walnut Grove Ave Rosemead CA 91770

ANDERES, BERTA, chemistry and mathematics educator, researcher; b. Havana, Cuba, Mar. 25, 1949; came to U.S., 1962; d. Humberto and Bertha (Ribas) A. B.A. in Chemistry, Hunter Coll., N.Y.C., 1972; M.A. in Chemistry, CCNY, 1975; Ph.D. in Chemistry, CUNY, 1983. Lab. technician Montefiore Hosp., Bronx, N.Y., 1972-78- Mount Sinai Hosp., N.Y.C., 1978-79; research asst. Hunter Coll. CUNY, N.Y.C., 1979-83; asst. prof. Hostos Community Coll., Bronx, N.Y., 1983-84; instr. math. and sci. Dade County Pub. Schs., Fla., 1985—.

ANDERS, BARBARA LYNNE, lyric soprano; b. Jackson, Miss., Sept. 4, 1938; d. William Reid and Eunice Jeannette (Simmons) Gainey; m. Dan Raney Anders; children—Melissa Lynne, Laurie Nan Anders Campbell. Student Belhaven Coll., 1956-57. Appeared as Marsinah in Kismet at Am. Light Opera Co., Washington, 1967; with opera chorus Washington Opera, 1971-78, Wolf Trap Opera Co., Vienna, Va., 1975-79; appeared at Kennedy Ctr., Washington, 1981, Piccolo Spoleto Festival, Charleston, S.C., 1981; soloist with numerous coll. performances, nationwide; rep. People to People Goodwill Tour, Nat. Music Council, Scandinavia and USSR. Rec. soloist Golden Age Rec., 1978. Pres. Am. Opera Scholarship Soc., Washington, 1980-81, Friday Morning Music Club, Washington, 1983-84. Mem. Nat. Fedn. Music Clubs (nat opera chmn. 1983—, Marie Morrisey Keith Vocal award 1956), D.C. Fedn. Music Clubs (chairperson jr. festivals 1977-78, pres. 1978-80), Am. Guild Mus. Artists, Internat. League Women Composers, Am. Women Composers, Delta Omicron. Christian Scientist. Office: 3216 Prince William Dr Fairfax VA 22031

ANDERS, SUSAN BETH, accountant; b. Toledo, Nov. 1, 1956; d. Hal Frederick and Janet Agnes (Jacobs) Anders. B.B.A., So. Methodist U., 1978; M.S., North Tex. State U., 1986. C.P.A., Tex. Staff acct. Philip Vogel & Co., Dallas, 1978-80, Sharp, Bausch & Co., Dallas, 1980-83, Dohm & Wolff, Dallas, 1984—. Nat. Merit scholar, Roper Corp., 1974-78; recipient Sr. award in acctg., So. Methodist U., 1978. Mem. Am. Inst. C.P.A.s, Tex. Soc. C.P.A.s, Am. Women's Soc. C.P.A.s, Beta Alpha Psi, Beta Gamma Sigma. Republican. United Methodist. Clubs: Am. Mensa Ltd., Intertel. Home: 7340 Skillman #1114 Dallas TX 75231 Office: Dohm & Wolff 2121 San Jacinto Suite 1850 Dallas TX 75201

ANDERSEN, DORIS EVELYN, real estate broker; b. Christian County, Ky., Oct. 30, 1923; d. William Earl and Blanche Elma (Withers) Johnston; m. Roger Lewis Shirk, July 9, 1944 (div. 1946); 1 dau., Vicki Lee Shirk Sanderson; m. DeLaire Andersen, July 6, 1946; children—Craig Bryant, Karen Rae, Kent DeLaire, Chris Jay, Mardi Lynn. Diploma, South Bend Coll. Commerce, 1942; diploma in banking Notre Dame U., 1946; student Ind. U., 1942-44. Tng. dir. First Nat. Bank, Portland, Oreg., 1963-69, assoc. broker Stan Wiley, Inc., Portland, 1969-79; prin. Doris Andersen & Assocs., Portland, 1979—; speaker at seminars; mem. Gov.'s Task Force Council on Housing, Salem, Oreg., 1985, 86. Contbr. articles to profl. jours. Mem. task force Oreg. Dept. Energy, Salem, 1984, 85. Mem. Nat. Assn. Realtors (dir. 1983—), Oreg. Assn. Realtors (dir. 1979—, pres. 1986—), Portland Bd. Realtors (pres. 1982), Women's Council Realtors (local pres. 1977, state pres. 1978, gov. nat. orgn. 1979). Avocations: reading, travel. Home: 459 Chestnut St Ashland OR 97520 Office: 1730 SW Skyline St Portland OR 97221

ANDERSEN, ELLEN MARIE, social worker; b. Kingman, Ariz., Jan. 25, 1948; d. William Franklin and Beatrice Ellen (Vanderberg) Cummings Kohlhase; student U. Puget Sound, 1966-68; B.A., U. Oreg., 1970; M.S.W., U. Mich., 1972; m. Larry H. Andersen, Feb. 17, 1973; children—Hans Harold, Anna Marie. Family services specialist Muncipality of Anchorage, 1972-75; clinic coordinator River Bluffs Child Guidance Center, Council Bluffs, Iowa, 1975-78; social worker Bur. Indian Affairs, Dept. Interior, Anchorage, 1978, Indian Health Service, HEW, Anchorage, 1978—; mem. Alaska Tech. Dependent Children Task Force, personal appearances on radio, TV and newspaper presentations in S.W. Iowa, 1975-78. Mem. Anchorage Child Abuse Task Force, 1973-74, Anchorage Child Abuse Bd., 1974-75; charter mem. Alaska chpt. Nat. Com. to Prevent Child Abuse, 1978. March of Dimes grantee, 1971-72. Mem. Nat. Assn. Social Workers (co-editor Alaska chpt. newsletter, sec. 1979-80, chpt. sec. 1979-80), Register Clin. Social Workers, Acad. Certified Social Workers, Soc. Hosp. Social Work Dirs., Phi Beta Kappa. Home: 2955 Drake St Anchorage AK 99508 Office: Alaska Native Med Center Box 7-741 care Social Services Anchorage AK 99510

ANDERSEN, LETA MAE, business executive; b. Hamilton, Kans., Jan. 8, 1926; d. Oscar T. and Coie D. (McCloud) Smith; m. William George Sherrill, July 4, 1947 (dec. Dec. 1980); children—Cynthia, Jeffery, Theresa; m. Stanley Louis Andersen, Oct. 17, 1982; children—Linda, Helen, Stanley, Bryce, Luetta. Student Emporia State U., 1946. Fountain mgr., Crown Drug Stores, Emporia and Wichita, Kans., 1945-64; engr. Western Controls, Wichita, 1965-70; owner Norge Laundry, Emporia, 1983—, also apts. and tavern. Mem. Emporia C. of C., Nat. Automatic Laundry and Cleaning Council, Harley-Davidson Owners Group, Am. Legion. Republican. Methodist. Lodge: Order Eastern Star (worthy matron 1975-76). Avocations: motorcycles; crafts. Home: 514 S East St Emporia KS 66801

ANDERSEN, LOA RAE, video production and modeling agency executive, educator; b. Redding, Calif., Sept 16, 1939; d. Edward Afton and Veryl (Vanderford) Kirk; m. Roger Eugene Blaisdell, Aug. 4, 1962 (div. 1967); children—Verilee Lynn, Roger Jeff; m. Charles Abe Andersen, July 19, 1970; children—Brian Reid, Anjali. Student Shasta Jr. Coll., 1957, Chico State Coll., 1957-59, Calif. State Coll., 1963; B.S., Brigham Young U., 1961. Cert. elem. tchr., Calif., Utah. Fashion model Sweitzer-Edwards, Germany and Calif., 1941-63; tchr. various sch. dists., Calif., Utah, 1961-70; dir. Cassandras Modeling Agy., Castro Valley, Calif., 1963-67; dir. Fort Lewis Army Base Child Care Ctr., Wash., 1971-74; realtor Hale Koa Realty, Honolulu, 1977-82; fashion coordinator 40-Plus mag.; dir. Key Images, Tacoma, Wash., 1982—; founder, pres. Nat. Task Force Mil. Child Care, Washington DC, 1972-76; cons. Dept. Defense, Washington, 1972-76. Author: Military Child Care Handbook, 1972; Step 3-Modeling for Fun and Profit, 1985: (video) Step One-Beginning Fashion Modeling, 1985. Vol. speaker various youth groups, 1962—. Named Army Wife of Yr., Fort Lewis Army Base, 1974; Vol. Recognition award Civics Club Assn., 1966. Mem. Better Bus. Bur. Republican. Mormon. Clubs: Young Models (advisor) (Tacoma); Officers Wives (Fort Lewis) (pres. 1975-76). Avocations: sewing; sign language; assisting Asian refugees; directing children's choir. Office: Key Images Inc PO Box 64323 Tacoma WA 98464

ANDERSEN, MARIANNE SINGER, psychologist, educational administrator; b. Baden nr. Vienna, Austria, June 18, 1930; came to U.S., 1940, naturalized, 1946; d. Richard L. and Jolanthe (Garda) Singer; B.A., Hunter Coll., City U. N.Y., 1950, M.A., 1974; Ph.D., Fla. Inst. Tech., 1980; 1 son, Richard Esten. Book editor specializing in psychology and psychiatry various pub. firms including W.W. Norton Co., Sterling Pub. Co., E.P. Dutton Co., N.Y.C., 1950-71; research assoc. Inst. for Research in Hypnosis, N.Y.C., 1974—, fellow in clin. hypnosis, 1976, dir. seminars, 1978-82, dir. edn., 1982—; psychotherapist specializing in hypnotherapy Morton Prince Center for Hypnotherapy, 1976—, dir. weight control clinic, 1980—, dir. clin. services, 1981-82; dir. adminstrn. Internat. Grad. U., N.Y.C., 1974-77; adminstrv. coordinator Internat. Grad. Sch. Behavior Sci., Fla. Inst. Tech., 1978; co-dir. The Melbourne Group, 1983—; lectr. hypnosis and hypnotherapy to mental and phys. health profls., 1977—; pvt. practice psychotherapy, 1977—. Mem. Soc. for Clin. and Exptl. Hypnosis, Internat. Soc. for Clin. and Exptl. Hypnosis, Am. Psychol. Assn., Am. Soc. Bariatric Physicians (affiliate), N.Y. Acad. Scis. Author: (with Louis Savary) Passages: A Guide for Pilgrims of the Mind, 1972; research on treatment obesity with hypnotherapy. Home: 60 W 57th St New York NY 10019 Office: 200 Park Ave Suite 303 E New York NY 10166

ANDERSEN, MARY SCHWARTZ, marketing educator, consultant; b. Ft. Wayne, Ind., Jan. 26, 1953; d. Victor L. and Agnes Marie (Eicher) Schwartz; m. Roger Curtis Andersen, Jan. 10, 1976. Student Manchester Coll., 1971-73; B.S., Purdue U., 1975; M.S., Frostburg State Coll., Md., 1980. Divisional mgr. Eyerly's, Cumberland, Md., 1976-77; store mgr. Fashion Wearhouse, LaVale, Md., 1977; adminstrv. sec. Allegany Community Coll., Cumberland, 1977-79, instrn. coordinator, 1979-80; inst. Frostburg State Coll., Md., 1981—; cons. Inst. for Small Bus., Frostburg, 1979-80. Author: (with others) Readings in Marketing, 1983. Vol. coordinator March of Dimes, Cumberland, 1983-84. Mem. Am. Mktg. Assn., Md. Fedn. Bus. and Profl. Women's Club, Inc. (rec. sec. 1984-86), Cumberland Bus. and Profl. Women's Local Orgn. (Named Young Careerist 1979-80, v.p., pres. 1980-84). Democrat. Avocations: reading, crafts, sewing, writing, gardening. Home: 13708 Brant Rd Cresaptown MD 21502 Office: Frostburg State Coll 314 Framptom Hall Frostburg MD 21532

ANDERSON, AGNES M., counselor, banker; b. Beloit, Wis., May 2, 1900; d. Albert C. and Rose E. (Welter) Anderson; student Am. Inst. Banking, 1920-50, also various coll. and night sch. courses. With Beloit State Bank, 1918-28; with 1st Wis. Nat. Bank of Milw., 1928-65, secretarial asst., 1928-48, mgr. women's dept., 1949-65, asst. cashier, 1951-65; travel counsellor Bay Travel Mart, Inc., Milw., 1971—; asso. v.p. customer service Univ. Nat. Bank, Milw., 1971-73. Wis. women's chmn. U.S. Savs. Bonds Program, 1953-70. Sec. to bd. dirs. Bishop Haas Social Service Fund, 1958-69. Bd. dirs. Cerebral Palsy of Greater Milw., 1960-70; treas. bd. dirs., mem. exec. com. Eisenhower Meml. Cerebral Palsy Work Tng. Center, Milw., 1970-80. Recipient Eisenhower award U.S. Savs. Bonds Com., 1956, Cerebral Palsy award, 1963. Mem. Am. Inst. Banking (nat. women's com. 1949), Nat. Assn. Bank Women (chmn. Milw. group 1956, chmn. Wis. membership com. 1958), Lalumiere League (publicity chmn. Milw. 1970-72, chmn. auditing com. 1976-80). Roman Catholic (past pres. Altar Soc.). Clubs: Woman's of Wis., Milw. Tiffany (v.p., mem. bd. 1959-73); Quarter Century (1st Wis. Nat. Bank Milw.). Co-author: Stretching the Dollar, Budget Book, 1951, rev. edit., 1961. Home: 4001 N Prospect Ave Milwaukee WI 53211 Office: Bay Travel Mart Inc 517 E Silver Spring Dr Milwaukee WI 53217

ANDERSON, ALEXANDRA, writer, editor; b. Boston, May 14, 1947; d. Henry Morrill and Marion (Thompson) Fuller; divorced; children—Lafcadio Cortesi, Genevieve, Oscar. B.A., Sarah Lawrence Coll. 1961. Assoc. editor Village Voice, N.Y.C., 1973-77; feature editor Vogue Mag., N.Y.C., 1977-78; sr. editor Portfolio Mag., N.Y.C., 1979-83; editor in chief, Art & Antiques Mag., N.Y.C., 1983-84; exec. editor Am. Photographer, N.Y.C., 1985—. Co-author: The Essential Guide to Art and Life in Lower Manhattan, 1979. Exec. com., Assoc. Council Mus. of Modern Art, N.Y.C., 1968—; trustee Skowhegan Sch. of Painting and Sculpture, 1970—; mem. Art Table, N.Y.C., 1981—; chmn. bd. dirs., Franklin Furnace Archives, N.Y.C., 1983-84. Club: Old Chatham Hunt. Office: CBS Publications 1515 Broadway 17th Floor New York NY 10036

ANDERSON, ALLAMAY EUDORIS, health educator, dietitian; b. N.Y.C., July 18, 1933; d. John Samuel and Charlotte Jane (Harrigan) Richardson; B.A., Queens Coll., CUNY, 1975; profl. mgmt. cert. Adelphi U., 1978; M.S. in Edn., Fordham U., 1984; m. Edgar Leopold Anderson, Jr., Apr. 14, 1957; 1 son, David Lancelot. Mem. staff sch. food service, dietitian Bd. Edn., N.Y.C., 1968 , tchr. jr. high sch., 1985—; profl. devel. cons., N.Y.C., 1978—; ptnr. Masiba Bldg. Corp., Corona, N.Y., 1973-82. Devel. coordinator League for Better Community Life, Inc., 1977—, treas. exec. bd., 1970-76; officer N.Y.C. Community Devel. Agy., 1980-83; mem. adv. council home econs. dept. Queens Coll.; mem. Kwanzaa Adv. Com. (P.R.) Urban Coalition, 1983; vestry mem. youth ministries local Episcopalian Ch. Mem. N.Y. State Sch. Food Service Assn., Nat. Soc. Fund Raising Execs., Queens Coll. Home Econs. Alumni Assn. (v.p., chmn. bylaws com.), Assn. Supervision and Curriculum Devel. Home: 100-13 34th Ave Corona NY 11368 Office: 40 Irving Pl New York NY 10003

ANDERSON, ANN MARIE CASSAGNE, microbiologist; b. New Orleans, Apr. 19, 1944; d. Charles Emile and Julie Marie (Sierra) Cassagne; B.S. magna cum laude, Loyola U. of South, 1966; M.S., La. State U., 1968, Ph.D., 1971; m. Robert B. Anderson, June 25, 1966. Med. technologist Touro Infirmary, New Orleans; instr. clin. hematology Tulane U. Sch. Pub. Health, New Orelans, 1969-72, instr. dept. environ. health scis., 1969-72, asst. prof., 1972-76, assoc. prof., 1976-86, prof., 1986—, mem. grad. faculty and internat. health faculty, 1977—, adj. assoc. prof. Sch. Engring., 1974—. Pres. women's aux. New Orleans chpt. La. Engring. Soc.; bd. dirs. Children's Carnival. HEW grantee, 1974-82. Mem. Am. Pub. Health Assn. (sect. council environ. 1978-82), Am. Soc. Microbiology, Am. Soc. Med. Technologists, Soc. Environ. Geochemistry and Health, Soc. Exptl. Biology and Medicine, La. Engring. Soc. Aux. (pres.), P.E.O., Sigma Xi, Delta Omega. Democrat. Roman Catholic. Clubs: New Orleans Opera Guild, Orleans, Le Petit Theatre de Vieux Carre, Tulane Med. Internat. (pres.). Home: 5920 Memphis St New Orleans LA 70124 Office: 1430 Tulane Ave New Orleans LA 70112

ANDERSON, ANNELISE GRAEBNER, economist; b. Oklahoma City, 1938. B.A., Wellesley Coll., 1960; M.A., Columbia U., 1965, Ph.D., 1974. Assoc. editor McKinsey and Co., Inc., 1963-65; researcher Nixon Campaign Staff, 1968-69; project mgr. Dept. Justice, 1970-71; from asst. prof. bus. adminstrn. to assoc. prof. Calif. State U.-Hayward, from 1975; now sr. research fellow Hoover Instn., Stanford U., Calif.; mem. Nat. Sci. Bd., 1985—. Office: Hoover Instn Stanford U Stanford CA 94305

ANDERSON, ANTOINETTE J(OSEPHINE), city official; b. Kansas City, Kans., Nov. 28, 1943; d. Raymond and Margaret (McCabe) Burwell; B.S.Ed., Central Mo. State U., 1965; M.B.A., Rockhurst Coll., 1983; m. Joe Neill Watkins, June 12, 1965 (div.); children—Sherrie Lynn, Neil Jason. Exec. asst. to pres. Dimensional Mktg. Inc., Kansas City, Mo., 1975-76; dir. public relations Westgate State Bank, Kansas City, Kans., 1976; mgr. acctg. dept. Ozark Nat. Life Ins. Co., Kansas City, 1976-81; revenue acctg. mgr. United Telecom Computer Group, Overland Park, Kans., 1981-84; dir. adminstrv. services City of Gladstone (Mo.), 1984—; fin. cons. City of Houston Lake, 1969-84; aviation mktg. cons., 1975—. Platte County rep. Kansas City Met. Commn. on Status of Women, 1979-81. Mem. Nat. Assn. Exec. Females, Northland Women's Polit. Caucus, Gladstone C. of C., Sigma Kappa, Pi Omega Pi, Kappa Delta Pi, Alpha Phi Delta, Alpha Phi Sigma. Democrat. Clubs: Pilot Internat. (chmn. internal affairs 1978, 80, pres.-elect 1985, pres. 1986-87), Northland Women's Breakfast (March exec. bd. chmn. 1986-87). Home: 7231 N Bales St Gladstone MO 64119 Office: 7010 N Holmes St Gladstone MO 64118

ANDERSON, BARBARA A., sociologist, educator; b. Ames, Iowa, Aug. 10, 1948; d. A.I. and Carolyn Anna (Barnes) Snow; A.B. in Math., U. Chgo., 1970; Ph.D. in Sociology, Princeton U., 1974; M.A., Brown U., 1977; m. Michael P. Anderson, June 14, 1969. Research assoc. Office Population Research, Princeton U., 1974-76; research assoc. Econ. Growth Center, Yale U., 1974-75, asst. prof. sociology, 1975-76; assoc. prof. sociology Brown U., Providence, 1976-84; prof. sociology U. Mich., Ann Arbor, 1984—; vis. mem. Inst. Advanced Study, 1974. NIH grantee, 1976-77, 82—. Guggenheim fellow, 1982-83; NSF grantee, 1980-82; Ford-Rockefeller grantee, 1975-76. Mem. Am. Sociol. Assn., Am. Hist. Assn., Assn. Advancement Slavic Studies, Population Assn. Am. (dir. 1983-85), Social Sci. History Assn. Co-author: Human Fertility in Russia Since the Nineteenth Century, 1979; Internal Migration During the Modernization of Russia in the Late Nineteenth Century, 1980. Office: Population Studies Center 1225 S University Ave Ann Arbor MI 48104

ANDERSON, BARBARA ANN, educator; b. Atlanta, June 2, 1928; d. Roy and Mary Louise (McCormick) Boling: A.B. in Lang. Arts, Fla. State U., 1950; M.Ed. summa cum laude, Central State U., Edmond, Okla., 1972; m. Robert Lee Anderson, June 6, 1950; children—Michael Lee, Lynnda Louise, Robert

Scott. Tchr. lang. arts, schs. in Okla. and Kans., 1964—; tchr. Putnam City High Sch., Oklahoma City, 1966—, chmn. lang. arts dept., 1983—; tchr. grammar for tchrs. Okla. State U. extension, 1978; mem. Okla. Profl. Practices Commn., 1974-81, Okla. Profl. Standards Bd., 1984—. Co-chmn. edn. project Okla. Bicentennial, 1975-76; Democratic precinct sec., 1976-77, dist. co-chmn., 1984—, del. Okla. Dem. Conv., 1979-80, dist. co-chmn. Dem. Party; active local Lyric Theatre, YMCA. Hilda Maehling fellow, NEA, 1976; named Tchr. of Yr., Putnam City Sch. Dist., 1978, 82; Okla. Congress Parents and Tchr. hon. mention Educator of Year, 1985. Mem. NEA (del. 1974-84), Nat. Fedn. Press Women, Okla. Edn. Assn. (dir. 1979-81, chmn. blue ribbon task force on edn. 1983-84), Putnam City Assn. Classroom Tchrs. (pres. 1974-75, editor publs. 1973—, exec. bd. 1972—), Okla. Press Women (sec. 1976-79, scholarship chmn. 1978-79), Sigma Kappa. Episcopalian. Author curriculum materials, articles in field. Office: 5300 NW 50th St Oklahoma City OK 73122

ANDERSON, BARBARA RAE, art director, photographic stylist, freelance graphic designer; b. Trenton, N.J., July 9, 1955; d. Charles and Ruth (Davidow) Wiener. B.A., Simmons Coll., 1978. Prodn. supr. G.K. Hall Pubs., Boston, 1978-80, art dir., 1980—. Designer: American Women Artists, 1983, Bookbuilders of Boston (best cover award), 1984. Home: 166 Saint Botolph St Boston MA 02115

ANDERSON, CAROL ELAINE, human resource development consultant; b. Detroit, Nov. 20, 1947; d. Harold Leroy and Marianna (Williams) Anderson. B.S. in Sociology and Bus., Western Mich. U., 1970; postgrad. Eastern Mich. U., 1974-76; M.A. in Telecommunication Arts, U. Mich., 1983, postgrad., 1986. Tchr., Dorsey Sch. Bus., Lincoln Park, Mich., 1970-72, Southwest Oakland Vocat. Ctr., Walled Lake, Mich., 1972-74; psychologist Plymouth (Mich.) Community Schs., 1977-81; cons. Ford Motor Co./Westvaco, Dearborn, Mich., 1983—, Charleston, S.C., 1983—, High Scope Ednl. Found., Ypsilanti, Mich., 1982-84, Westvaco, Cleve., 1984—, Mich. Bell Telephone, Southfield, 1986—. Cinematographer, editor film Reunion, 1982. Mem. adv. council Infant Preschool Spl. Edn. Program, Plymouth, Mich., 1979-80. Recipient ednl. merit award U. Mich., 1981-82; recipient videotape editing internship Nat. Acad. TV Arts and Scis., 1982. Mem. Women in Communications, Inc., Am. Soc. Tng. and Devel., Acad. TV Arts and Scis., Am. Film Inst., Mich. Media Project, Pi Lambda Theta. Democrat. Home and Office: 806 Sycamore Pl Ann Arbor MI 48104

ANDERSON, CAROL MCMILLAN, lawyer; b. Fla., Aug. 7, 1938; m. Philip Sloan Anderson, Oct. 9, 1965; 1 dau., Courtney. B.S., Fla. Atlantic U., 1969; J.D., Cumberland Sch. of Law, Birmingham, Ala., 1971. Bar Fla. 1971. Asst. U.S. atty. So. Dist. Fla., Miami, 1971-74; ptnr. Anderson & Anderson, P.A., Ft. Lauderdale, Fla., 1974—. Elder 1st Presbyn. Ch.; mem. women's div. Boy's Club Am. Mem. ABA, Assn. of Trial Lawyers, Fed. Bar Assn., Fla. Bar Assn., Broward County Bar Assn., Acad. Fla. Trial Lawyers, Broward County Women's Trial Lawyers Assn., Gold Circle Nova U., Royal Dames of Cancer Research (trustee), Mus. of Art, Hospice Hundred (bd. dirs.), 1000 Plus of Am. Cancer Soc., Fort Lauderdale Symphony Soc., Freedom's Found. Am. Club: Coral Ridge Yacht. Home: 32 Isla Bahia Dr Fort Lauderdale FL 33316 Office: Anderson & Anderson PA 1313 S Andrews Ave Fort Lauderdale FL 33316

ANDERSON, CAROLINE ANNE, marketing and communications consultant; b. Belfast, No. Ireland, Jan. 21, 1947; came to U.S., 1953; d. James J. and Christina (O'Neill) Toman; m. James Hugh Anderson, June 17, 1968; children—Keeli, Christina. Ed. Queens U., Belfast, No. Ireland. Dir. mktg. and research Rreef Corp., San Francisco, 1973-75; owner Carole Anderson Mktg., cons., condrs. career seminars, Orinda, Calif., 1975—. Recipient Salesperson of Yr. award Basic Accessories, 1981. Mem. Nat. Assn. Female Execs., Stanford U. Alumni Assn. Republican. Roman Catholic.

ANDERSON, CHERYL, international government adviser; b. Camp Campbell, Ky.; d. Edward Gustav and Virginia Leona (Case) A.; B.A., U. Wash., 1969; m. Richard T. Ney, July 4, 1975; children—Alexander Case, Justin Anderson. Asst. press sec. Senator Warren G. Magnuson, Washington, 1969-71; parliamentarian officer Australian Senate, Canberra, Australia, 1971-72; adminstrv. asst. Richard Ney Assoc., Inc., Washington, 1972-73, account rep., 1973-74, v.p., 1974-77; v.p., sec., dir. Advocacy Internat., Ltd., Washington, 1977—; dir. Bellhouse Med., Inc., Washington, 1986—. Contbr. articles to profl. jours. Mem. Am. Assn. Med. Instrumentation, Regulatory Affairs Profls. Assn. Home: 5304 Wehawken Rd Bethesda MD 20816 Office: Advocacy Internat Ltd 1825 Eye St NW Suite 400 Washington DC 20006

ANDERSON, CHERYL MARIE, shoe company executive; b. Columbus, Ohio, Oct. 13, 1950; d. Charles Joseph and Norma Claire (Humphrey) Robinson. Student Ohio State U., 1968, Parsons Sch. of Design, 1980, Am. Mgmt. Assn. N.Y., 1981, 82, 83. Fashion coordinator Sears, Columbus, Ohio, 1965-69; dir. fashion merchandising Nationwide Coll., Columbus, 1969-71; designer buyer Lazarus, Columbus, 1971-77; dir. licensing Calvin Klein, Inc., N.Y.C., 1977-80; dir. fashion, advt. and sales promotion G.H. Bass Shoe Co., N.Y.C., 1980—; freelance fashion and mktg. cons. Recipient Art Dirs. Merit award Art Dirs. Club N.Y., 1981. Mem. Assn. Women's Econ. Devel., Fashion Group, Footwear and Accessories Council. Baptist. Office: G H Bass & Co 1414 Avenue of the Americas New York NY 10019

ANDERSON, CLAUDIA SMITH, lawyer; b. Peoria, Ill., Mar. 21, 1953; d. Lester Berry and June Edda (Kopal) Smith; m. Curtis A. Anderson, Aug. 26, 1972. B.S., Rockford Coll., 1976; J.D., Gonzaga U., 1979; student Stephens Coll., Columbia, Mo., 1971-72. Bar: Ill. 1979. Tchr. elem. schs. Rockford (Ill.) Sch. Dist., 1976; assoc. firm. Acton, Meyer, Smith, Miller & Anderson, Danville, Ill., 1979-84, ptnr., 1984—. Bd. dirs. Danville YWCA, 1984. Mem. Ill. Bar Assn., Vermilion County Bar Assn., ABA, Ill. Trial Lawyers Assn., Am. Trial Lawyers Assn., Danville C. of C. (dir.), AAUW, Phi Delta Alpha. Republican. Roman Catholic. Club: Executive of Danville. Home: 3638 Whittier Ln Danville IL 61832 Office: Acton Meyer Smith Miller & Anderson 11 E North St Danville IL 61832

ANDERSON, DARLENE MARIE, real estate broker, property management firm executive; b. Biddeford, Maine, Feb. 10, 1951; d. Rene Jean Provencher and Marceline May (Leighton) Provencher Prejean; m. Ronald Horace Anderson, Mar. 4, 1967; children—Saundra, David, Kathy, Michael, Suzanne, Stacy. Student Monterey Peninsula Coll., 1973-74. Lic. real estate broker, Alaska. Sec., voice coach Dancing Bear Theatre, Ft. Richardson, Alaska, 1977-78; resident mgr. Property Mgmt. Services, Inc., Anchorage, 1978-79; owner, broker Action Property Mgmt., Anchorage, 1979—. Choir dir., chmn. music com. Ch. Jesus Christ of Latter-day Saints, Farmington, Maine, 1972-73, 74-75; choir dir. Ch. of Jesus Christ of Latter Day Saints, Eagle River, Alaska, 1977-79; active as playwright, composer, performer with several local theatre groups, Anchorage area, 1977—. Republican. Mormon. Avocations: sewing, needlecrafts, sign language for deaf, gardening.

ANDERSON, DAUN ROBIN, hardware communications analyst; b. Winchester, Mass., Oct. 15, 1950; d. Ernest Lawrence and Muryle Caroline (Sandgren) A.; B.A. in Modern Langs., Coll. William and Mary, 1972; M.A. in French, Pa. State U., 1975. Teaching asst. Pa. State U., 1972-73; info. analyst to tech. research analyst GTE Labs., Waltham, Mass., 1977-80; software specialist Comml. Union Assurance Cos., Boston, 1980-81; systems engr. Nixdorf Computer Corp., Waltham, Mass., 1981-83; sr. hardware communications analyst Cullinet Software, Westwood, Mass., 1983—. Mem. Assn. Systems Mgmt. Home: 126 Windsor Rd Waban MA 02168 Office: 400 Blue Hill Dr Westwood MA 02090

ANDERSON, DEBORAH GAIL COOK, educator; b. San Antonio, Dec. 26, 1956; d. Clarence Edward and Dorothy Mae (Colvin) Cook; m. Dwight Edward Anderson, June 22, 1980 (div. Sept. 1981). B.S., Tex. Woman's U., 1979; postgrad. U. Houston, 1982—. Spl. edn. tchr. Ashford Elem., Sch., Houston Ind. Sch. Dist., 1979-80, resource tchr., 1981—, sec. hospitality com., 1982—; substitute tchr. Marshall Elem. Sch., Detroit, 1980-81; spl. edn. pvt. tutor, Houston, 1982—; tutor Denton Assn. Student Helpers (Tex.), 1977; vol. behavior technician North Tex. State U. Ctr. Behavioral Studies, Denton, 1976-77; vol. Spl. Olympics, Denton, 1978, Lowry Hall, Denton, 1978. Mem. Young Women's Aux., Mt. Calvery Bapt. Ch., Denton, 1977-79, pres., 1978-79, mem. usher bd., 1977-79, youth worker, 1978-79; youth worker, Sunday sch. tchr., mem. outreach com., Christian debutante com. Liberty Bapt. Ch.; mem. Houston Council Edn., 1981—. Mem. Council Exceptional Children, Assn. Childhood Edn. Internat., NEA, NAACP (named most prominent black woman Tex. Woman's U. chpt. 1979), Nat. Assn. Black Social Workers, Tex. State Tchrs. Assn., Houston Tchrs. Assn., Mortar Board, Sarah Circle, Alpha Chi, Delta Sigma Theta. Democrat. Baptist. Home: 2020 Bentworth St Apt 414 Houston TX 77077 Office: Ashford Elementary Sch 1815 Shannon Valley Houston TX 77077

ANDERSON, DEL MARIE, college administrator; b.Vicksburg, Miss., Nov. 6, 1937; d. James Neely and Emma (Grissom) Williams; m. E. Frederick Anderson, Mar. 31, 1967 (div. Dec. 1984). A.B. in child Devel., San Diego State U., 1965; M.S.W., San Diego State U., 1967. Asst. prof. social work San Diego State U., 1969-73; asst. dir. social work Wadsworth VA Hosp., Los Angeles, 1973-76; counselor Grossmont Coll., El Cajon, Calif., 1976-77, dean counseling, 1977-82; dean of students Los Angeles Harbor Coll., Wilmington, Calif., 1982—. Co-developer model programs, 1983, 84. Ford Found. grantee, 1983, 85. Mem. Assn. Community Coll. Adminstrs., Calif. Community Coll. Chief Student Services Officers, Calif. Community Coll. Counselor Assn. (Friend of Counseling award 1983), Calif. Assn. Community Colls. (bd. dirs. 1984—). Democrat. Baptist. Avocations: reading; sewing; music; sports. Office: Los Angeles Harbor Coll 1111 Figueroa Pl Wilmington CA 90744

ANDERSON, DORIS EHLINGER, lawyer, author, editor; b. Houston, Dec. 1; d. Joseph O. and Cornelia L. (Pagel) Ehlinger; B.A., Rice U., 1946; teaching cert. Sam Houston Tchrs. Coll., 1947; LL.B., U. Tex., 1951, J.D., 1955; M.S., U. Okla. m. Wiley Newton Anderson, Jr., Aug. 26, 1946; children—Wiley Newton III, Joseph Ehlinger. Tchr., Houston Ind. Sch. Dist., 1946-48; admitted to Tex. bar, 1950, since practiced in Houston; mem. firm Ehlinger and Anderson, 1950-52, 55—; assoc. firm Price, Guinn, Wheat and Veltmann, Houston, 1952-55. Founder, bd. dirs. Liberty Belles and Beaux, Houston, 1975—; mem. Gov.'s Com. on the Rights of Women, 1972; parliamentarian Harris County (Tex.) Flood Control Task Force, 1973—; past bd. dirs. Friends of Fondren Library; bd. dirs. Mus. Am. Architecture and Decorative Arts, Houston Bapt. U. Named staff Tex. Navy; recipient Woman of Yr. award YWCA, 1978, 80, 83. Mem. Tex. Bar Assn., Am. Arbitration Assn. (panel of arbitrators), UDC, Coll. Women's Assn., Freedoms Found., Soc. Rice U. Women (pres. 1977-79), Am. Mus. Soc., Univ. Women's Alliance, Rice U. Women, San Jacinto Descs. (past pres. gen., past parliamentarian), Daus. Republic of Tex., Sarah Lane Lit. Soc., Houston Edn. Excellence Program, Bayou Bend Docent Sustaining Orgn. Kappa Beta Pi. Author: (with Roy Cullen and Louis Welch) Houston: City of Destiny, 1980; also articles and papers. Home: 5556 Cranbrook Dr Houston TX 77056

ANDERSON, DORRINE ANN PETERSEN, librarian; b. Ishpeming, Mich., Feb. 24, 1923; d. Herbert Nathaniel and Dorothy (Eman) Petersen; B.S. with distinction, No. Mich. U., 1944; postgrad. Northwestern U., summer 1945, U. Wash., summer 1967, U. Mich. Extension, 1958-65; M.S. in L.S., Western Mich. U., 1970; m. Harold Edward Anderson, Aug. 23, 1947; children—David Charles (dec.), Brian Peter, Kent Harold, Bruce Herbert, Timothy Jon. Tchr. English jr. high sch., Eaton Rapids, Mich., 1944-45; tchr. English, speech Arlington Heights (Ill.) High Sch., 1945-48; tchr. English high sch., Nahma, Mich., 1948-49, 54-61, Gladstone, Mich., 1961-62; librarian Gladstone Sch. and Pub. Library, 1962-70; dir. library services Gladstone Area Pub. Schs., 1971—, Bicentennial coordinator, 1975-76. Acting dir. Mid-Peninsula Library Fedn., 1965-66; chmn. Region 21 Media Advisory Council, 1972—; chmn. adv. com. Regional Ednl. Materials Center 21, 1973—; mem. planning com. Upper Peninsula Reading Conf., 1974—; regional del. Mich. White House Conf. on Libraries and Info. Services, 1979. Pres., Delta County League Woman Voters, 1970-72; mem. human resources subcom. Upper Peninsula Com. for Area Progress, 1964—; trustee Library of Mich., 1984—, bd. dirs. Found., 1985—; chmn. Gladstone Centennial History Com.; mem. com. for library devel. Upper Peninsula, chmn. Delta County Library Bd., 1967-76; mem. region 17, Polit. Action Team, 1968-70. County del. Delta County Democratic Com., 1968. Named Tchr. of Year, Region 17 (Mich.), 1969. Mem. N.E.A., Mich. Edn. Assn. (pres. region 17 council 1967-68, chmn. Upper Peninsula dels. to rep. assembly 1966-68), ALA, Mich. Library Assn., Internat. Reading Assn., Mich. Assn. Media in Edn. (state Library Week chmn. 1973-74); recipient leadership award 1977), Mich. Assn. Sch. Library Suprs., Am. Assn. U. Women, Assn. Ednl. Communications and Tech., Kappa Delta Pi, Phi Epsilon, Beta Phi Mu, Delta Kappa Gamma (recipient citation for seminars in mgmt. for women 1977). Home: 1723 Montana Ave Gladstone MI 49837 Office: Gladstone Area Sch and Pub Library Gladstone MI 49837

ANDERSON, ELISABETH MADGE KEHRER, physician, state administrator; b. Aberdeen, S.D.; d. Robert Ewald and Oriole (Johnston) Kehrer; m. Page Morris Anderson, Jan. 6, 1951; children—Bruce Statham, Catherine Mercer, Mary Elisabeth. B.A., U. Louisville, 1946, M.D., 1949; M.P.H., U. Hawaii, 1971. Intern Queen's Hosp., Honolulu, 1949-50, resident, 1950-51; physician, dir. research Pacific Inst. Rehab. Medicine, Honolulu, 1960-69; asst. to pres. Hawaii Med. Assn., Honolulu, 1972-75; chief med. health services div. Hawaii Dept. Health, Honolulu, 1980—; mem. Hawaii Cancer Commn., 1984—; mem. adv. bd. Hawaii Cancer Research Ctr., 1986—; mem. staff Queen's Hosp. Contbr. articles to profl. jours. Sec. bd. trustees Hawaii Loa Coll., Kaneohe, 1962-76; mem. exec. com. Women's Assn., ABA Conv., 1966-67; mem. exec. bd. Community Scholarship Program, Honolulu, 1966-71; mem. Stanford Biol. Preserve Docent Council (Calif.), 1978—; chmn. bd. Hawaii Nature Ctr., Honolulu, 1983—; vice chmn., trustee Multiple Sclerosis Found. Hawaii; mem. exec. bd. Health and Community Service Council Hawaii. Mem. Yosemite Nat. History Assn., Am. Coll. Preventive Medicine, Am. Pub. Health Assn., Hawaii Med. Assn., Honolulu County Med. Soc., Sierra Club, Honolulu Acad. Arts, Outdoor Circle, Hawaii Bot. Soc. Clubs: Punahou Tennis, Trail and Mountain, Outrigger Canoe. Office: Hawaii Dept Health 1250 Punchbowl St Honolulu HI 96813

ANDERSON, ELIZABETH JANE, lawyer; b. Woodstock, Va., Apr. 9, 1955; d. Robert Homer, Jr. and Betty S. Anderson. A.B., Duke U., 1977; J.D., T.C. Williams Sch. Law, 1982. Bar: Va. 1983. Staff atty. S.W. Va. Legal Aid Soc., Marion, 1983-84; assoc. Greer and Greer, P.C., Rocky Mount, Va., 1984-85; asst. commonwealth's atty., Norfolk, Va., 1986—. Chmn., Students for Ford, Durham, N.C., 1976; del. N.C. Student Legislature, Durham, 1974-76; v.p. Coll. Republicans, Durham, 1975-76. Recipient Book award for evidence, Am. Jurisprudence, 1982. Mem. ABA, ACLU, Assn. Trial Lawyers Am., Va. Trial Lawyers Assn., Va. Bar Assn., Va. Women Attys. Assn., Delta Theta Phi. Democrat. Lutheran. Office: 800 E City Hall Ave Suite 600 Norfolk VA 23510

ANDERSON, ELIZABETH JANE, advertising agency executive, nurse; b. Alton, Ill., June 14, 1942; d. Joseph Clyde Anderson and Maxine (McBride) LeMay. Student U. Ill.-Champaign, 1960-63; R.N., St. John's Sch. Nursing, Springfield, Ill., 1974; postgrad. U. Colo.-Boulder, 1974-75. Media planner Leo Burnett Co., Chgo., 1964-71; nurse various hosps., Denver, St. Louis, 1974-76; media planner Gardner Advt., St. Louis, 1976-78; sr. planner Tatham-Laird & Kudner, Chgo., 1978-79; media supr. Bloom Advt., Dallas, 1979-80; assoc. media dir. Tracy-Locke/BBDO, Dallas, 1980-84, N.W. Ayer, Chgo., 1984—. Active Ill. Republican Com., 1956-71. Mem. Nat. League Nursing, Ill. Nurses Assn. Presbyterian. Club: Jr. Women's Ad (events dir. 1964-68) (Chgo.). Office: NW Ayer 111 E Wacker Dr Chicago IL 60610

ANDERSON, ERICA SUE, copper mine supervisor, landscape and irrigation contractor; b. Tucson, May 18, 1949; d. Kent Jerome and Mary Louise (Fox) A. Student U. Ariz., 1967-69; B.S. cum laude, Springfield Coll., 1971; M.B.A. summa cum laude, U. Phoenix, 1983. Laborer Duval Corp., Sahuarita, Ariz., 1974-77, supr., 1977-86, reclamationist, 1977-86; packaging supr. Cyprus Minerals, Cyprus Sierrita Mine, Sahuarita, 1986—; pres. Green Valley Plants and Landscapes, Sahuarita, 1986. Vol. Therapeutic Riding of Tucson, 1979-81; sec. Ams. Concerned about Tomorrow, Tucson, 1981-82. Mem. Nat. Orgn. Female Execs. Avocations: landscaping; skiing; horses; swimming; reading.

ANDERSON, FRANCES JANE, communications company executive; b. Freeport, Ill., Oct. 1, 1931; d. Lillian Rose A.; A.B., Millikin U., 1953; student Salvation Army Sch. for Officers Tng., 1953; M.S., Northwestern U., 1970. Ordained minister, Salvation Army, 1953; editor youth publs. Salvation Army, Chgo., 1956-75; asst. dir. public relations for central states, 1975-77; writer, editor bd. communications Bapt. Gen. Conf., Arlington Heights, Ill., 1977-81, editorial mgr., public affairs, 1981-82; writer/producer Domain Communications, 1982-84; owner Anderson Communications, 1984—; mem. faculty Olivet Coll., Kankakee, Ill., 1981—; prof. communications Salvation Army Sch., Chgo., 1981—. Mem. Salvation Army Com. for White House Conf. on Children and Youth, 1960, 70. Mem. Women in Communications (rec. sec. 1980, newsletter editor 1981, treas. 1982, pres. North Shore chpt. 1983-84), Conf. Editors Ch. Mags. for Children and Youth, Northwest Suburban Assn. Commerce and Industry, MacDowell Artists Assn. Contbr. articles to religious jours. Home and Office: 7 Oak Creek Dr #2708 Buffalo Grove IL 60089

ANDERSON, FRANCES SWEM, former nuclear medical technologist; b. Grand Rapids, Mich., Nov. 27, 1913; d. Frank Oscar and Carrie (Strang) Swem; student Muskegon Sch. Bus., 1959-60; certificate Muskegon Community Coll., 1964; m. Clarence A.F. Anderson, Apr. 9, 1934; children—Robert Curtis, Clarelyn Christine Anderson Schmelling, Stanley Herbert. X-ray file clk., film librarian Hackley Hosp., Muskegon, Mich., 1957-59; student refresher course in nuclear med. tech. Chgo. Soc. Nuclear Med. Techs., 1966; radioisotope technologist and sec. Hackley Hosp., 1959-65; nuclear med. technologist Butler Meml. Hosp., Muskegon Heights, Mich., 1966-70, Mercy Hosp., Muskegon, 1970-79; ret., 1979. Mem. Muskegon Civic A Capella choir, 1932-39; mem. Mother-Tch. Singers, PTA, Muskegon, 1941-48, treas., 1944-48; with Muskegon Civic Opera Assn., 1950-51; mem. choir Forest Park Covenant Ch. (formerly Evang. Covenant Ch.), Muskegon, 1953-79, 83—, choir sec., 1963-69, tchr. Sunday sch., 1954-75, supt. Sunday sch., 1975-78, treas. Sunday sch., 1980-86, ch. sec., 1982-85, chmn. master planning council, also coordinator centennial com.; mem. Republican Presdl. Task Force, 1981—; co-chmn. Jackson Hill Old-Timers Reunion, 1982, 83, 85, registration and publicity chmn., 1984. Cert. nuclear medicine technologist. Mem. Am. Registry Radiologic Technologists. Home: 5757 E Sternberg Rd Fruitport MI 49415

ANDERSON, GAIL MARIE, librarian; b. St. Cloud, Minn., Apr. 26, 1945; d. George Elroy Carpenter and Blanche Doris (Flam) Carpenter Neel; m. Gordon Alexander Anderson, Aug. 24, 1971. B.S., St. Cloud State U., 1969. Cert. librarian, Minn.; cert. elem. tchr., Minn. Librarian, Cloquet Pub. Sch., Minn., 1969-70; jr. high media ctr. dir. Roseville Pub. Sch., Minn., 1970-78; asst. program dir., group dir. Afton Alps Ski Sch., 1973-82; library asst. U. Minn. Sch. Dentistry, Mpls., 1979—. Sec., Minn. Christian Youth Council, Mpls., 1960-63; mem. Minn. Ednl. Media Orgn. Methodist. Club: Pheasants Forever. Avocations: outdoor sports; hunting; gardening; travel. Home: 947 Monterey Ct N Shoreview MN 55126 Office: Univ Minn Sch Dentistry Learning Resource Ctr Moos H S Tower 8-425 Minneapolis MN 55455

ANDERSON, GERALDINE LOUISE, clinical laboratory scientist; b. Mpls., July 7, 1941; d. George M. and Viola Julia-Mary (Abel) Havrilla; B.S., U. Minn., 1963; m. Henry Clifford Anderson, May 21, 1966; children—Bruce Henry, Julie Lynne. Med. technologist Swedish Hosp., Mpls., 1963-68; hematology supr. Glenwood Hills Hosp. lab., Golden Valley, Minn., 1968-70; asso. scientist dept. pediatrics U. Minn. Hosps., Mpls., 1970-74; instr. health occupations and med. lab. asst. Suburban Hennepin County Area Vocat. Tech. Center, Brooklyn Park, Minn., 1974-81, St. Paul Tech. Vocat. Inst., 1978—; research med. technologist Miller Hosp., St. Paul, 1975-78; research asso. Children's and United Hosps., St. Paul, 1979—; mem. health occupations adv. com. Hennepin Tech. Centers, 1975—, chairperson, 1978-79; mem. hematology slide edn. rev. bd. Am. Soc. Hematology, 1976—. Mem. Med. Lab. Tech. Polit. Action Com., 1978—; resource person lab. careers Robbinsdale Sch. Dist., Minn., 1970-79; mem. Luth. Chaplaincy Aux. of Mpls., 1978-80; del. Crest View Home Assn., 1981—; mem. sci. and math. subcom. Minn. High Tech. Council. Recipient service awards and honors Omicron Sigma. Mem. Minn. Soc. Med. Tech. (sec. 1969-71), Am. Soc. Med. Tech. (del. to ann. meetings 1972—, chmn. hematology sci. assembly 1977-79, nomination com. 1979-81, bd. dirs. 1985-88), Twin City Soc. Med. Technologists, Twin Cities Hosp. Assn. (speakers bur. 1968-70), Assn. Women in Sci., World Future Soc., AAAS, AAUW, Minn. Med. Tech. Alumni, Am. Soc. Hematology, Soc. Analytical Cytology, Nat. Assn. Female Execs., Sigma Delta Epsilon (corr. sec. Xi chpt. 1980-82, pres. 1982-84), Alpha Mu Tau Lutheran. Contbr. articles to profl. publs. Office: United Hosp Inc Harris Cancer Research Lab 333 Smith Ave N Saint Paul MN 55102

ANDERSON, HELEN ELAINE, retail co. exec.; b. Barnesville, Ohio, June 10, 1952; d. Charles Edward and Wilma Imelda (Kemp) Anderson; B.A., Marietta Coll., 1974. Nat. advt. copywriter Sears Roebuck & Co., Chgo., 1975-77, asst. nat. catalog mktg. mgr., 1977-79, asst. nat. buyer accent furniture and wall decor, 1979-81, nat. retail mdse. sales coordinator home fashion accessories, 1981-84, mgr. promotional planning, drapery dept., 1984—. Mem. Nat. Assn. Female Execs., Intaglio, Pi Delta Epsilon, Chi Delta Phi. Alpha Sigma Tau. Home: 235 Spring Hill Dr Roselle IL 60172 Office: Sears Roebuck & Co D/624 Sears Tower Chicago IL 60684

ANDERSON, HELEN SHARP, civic worker; b. Ennis, Tex., June 10, 1916; d. John H. and Eula (King) Sharp; A.B., U. Tex., 1937; m. Thomas Dunaway Anderson, Feb. 21, 1938; children—John Sharp, Helen Shaw, Lucille Streeter. Mem. Mt. Vernon Ladies Assn. of the Union, vice regent, 1967—, regent, 1982—; bd. dirs. Nat. Cathedral Assn., Washington, 1971-75, also mem. various spl. coms.; mem. Garden Club Am., 1945—, zone vice-chmn., 1959-62, nat. dir., 1975-77, nat. v.p., 1977-79, nat. chmn. long-range planning, 1979-80; bd. dirs. Japan Am. Soc. Houston, 1974-78; mem. fine arts adv. com. U. Tex., Austin, 1963—; chmn. Jr. Gallery, Mus. Fine Arts, Houston, 1953-54, docent, 1964-70; bd. dirs. Houston and Harris County council Girl Scouts U.S.A., 1966-67, Sheltering Arms, 1964-67; bd. dirs. Harris County Heritage Soc., 1963-65, v.p., 1965-66; mem. River Oaks Garden Club, Houston, 1945—, pres., 1958, 59; mem. coms. Christ Ch. Cathedral, Houston; mem. Houston Jr. League. Republican. Episcopalian. Clubs: Sulgrave (Washington); River Oaks Garden (Houston); Assembly; Bolero. Address: 3925 Del Monte Dr Houston TX 77019

ANDERSON, JACQUELINE CONNELL, social work administrator; b. N.Y.C., Jan. 25, 1948; d. Henry Morgan and Rosalee Stevens; m. Lawyer Cleveland Anderson, Oct. 29, 1966; 1 child, Rhakeem Malik. A.A.S., Manhattan Community Coll., 1978; B.S., summa cum laude, N.Y. Inst. Tech., 1980; M.S.W., Columbia U., 1982. Case worker Harlem Dowling Childrens Services, N.Y.C., 1980-81; psychiatric social worker, N.Y. State Psychiatric Inst., N.Y.C., 1981-82; psychiat. social worker Health and Hosps. Corp., Harlem Hosp., N.Y.C., 1982-83, project coordinator, social work supr., 1983—. Recipient Community Mental Health award N.Y. Inst. Tech., 1980. Mem. Nat. Assn. Social Workers, Nat. Black Child Devel. Assn., Nat. Assn. Female Execs. Democrat. Baptist. Office: Dept Psychiatry Harlem Hospital 506 Lenox Ave New York NY 10037

ANDERSON, JACQUELINE JONES, educator; b. Hartford, Conn., July 13, 1935; d. Ella B. (Jones) Anderson; B.A., N.H. Coll., 1979; cert. Hartford U., 1971, Hartford Coll. for Women, 1971, U. Conn., 1978; children—Wilfred, Gregory, Kevin, Kyle. With Community Renewal Team, CAP Agy., Hartford, 1966-69; freelance tng. cons., Hartford, 1974—; dir. Health Care Dept., Hartford Hosp., 1969—. Bd. dirs. Ambulatory Health Care Planning, Inc., 1970-71, PIT I Drugs, 1972-75, YMCA, 1973—, Toward an Allied Health Career Today, 1973-77, Get the Lead Out, 1974—, Child Guidance Center, 1974-78, AMISTAD Group Home for Girls, 1977—, Upper Albany Community Orgn., 1977—, Health Systems Agy., 1977—, Bergdorf Health Planning Com., 1977-79, Black Coalition on Health Issues, 1978—, Elderly Crisis Intervention, 1979—; mem. Conn. Stroke Program, 1972, Blue Hills Clinic task force on drugs, 1972-73, Mayor's Health Services Com., 1973-77, Community Health Adv. Com., City of Hartford, 1978—; resource person Planned Parenthood, 1972-77; Justice of the Peace, Hartford County, 1972-75; mem. Republican Town Com., 1973—; councilwoman Hartford Ct. of Common Council, 1975-77, many others. Recipient Cert. of Merit, CRT of Greater Hartford, 1972; Outstanding Woman of Yr. award Conn. Women's Soc., 1979; Cert. of Appreciation, Health Systems Agy. of N.C. Conn., 1980; Upper Albany Community Orgn. Service to Community award, 1981; others. Mem. Am. Public Health Assn., Conn. Hosp. Assn., New Eng. Public Health Assn., Soc. for Patient Reps., Alliance of Black Social Workers. Republican. Methodist. Contbr. articles to profl. jours. Home: 101 Tower Ave Hartford CT 06120 Office: 80 Seymour St Hartford CT 06115

ANDERSON, JACQUELINE PHILLIPS, telecommunications engineer; b. Dayton, Ohio, June 15, 1957; d. Stuart E. Phillips and Joan E. (Yeagler) Kerdolff; m. Michael L. Anderson, May 22, 1982. B.S. in Econs. and Stats., U. Mo., 1979. Communications cons. Southwestern Bell Telephone Co., Kansas City, Mo., 1978-80, Houston, 1980-82, Dallas, 1982-83; telecommunications analyst Frito-Lay Inc., Dallas, 1983-85; software engr. No. Telecom, Inc., Irving, Tex., 1985—. Mem. North Tex. Telecommunications Assn., Delta Sigma Pi (past officer), Chi Omega. Republican. Methodist. Home: 3309 Scarlet Oak St Dallas TX 75234

ANDERSON, JANE LOUISE BLAIR, librarian, horse breeder, poet; b. Wilkinsburg, Pa., Nov. 6, 1948; d. Francis Preston and Mary Louise (Maxwell) Blair; B.S. in Edn., Clarion State Coll., 1971; M.S.L.S., Duquesne U., 1974; m. Russell Karl Anderson, Jr., Apr. 20, 1973; children—Christina Lynn, Melissa Jane. Substitute tchr. Wilkinsburg Schs., 1971, tchr. Head Start, 1971; librarian Franklin Regional Schs. Intermediate High Sch., Murrysville, Pa., 1971—; breeder quarter horses, Fenelton, Pa., 1978—. Contbr. poems to various anthologies. Vol. mem. Rescue 5 Ambulance, Murrysville, 1974-76, Medic I ambulance, 1976-78; sec. Franklin Area REACT, 1976-78; first aid instr. ARC, Murrysville, 1975-80; instr. CPR, Am. Heart Assn., Westmoreland County, 1976-80; vol. worker with deaf, 1978-83; vol. United Cerebral Palsey, Butler, Pa., 1981—. Cert. public librarian, Pa. Mem. Westmoreland County Library Assn., Pa. Library Assn., Am. Quarter Horse Assn., Pa. Quarter Horse Assn. Methodist. Home: Fern Valley Farm PO Box 12 Fenelton PA 16034 Office: 3220 School Rd Murrysville PA 15668

ANDERSON, JANICE CAROLYN, nurse, cardiac sonographer; b. Savannah, Ga., Aug. 27, 1939; d. James Carswell and Lois Elizabeth (Robbins) Milligan; m. James Mixon Anderson, Sr., Sept. 5, 1959; children—James Mixon, Joseph, Jill. Diploma nursing U. Sch. Nursing, Augusta, Ga., 1966; B.S., Med. Coll. Ga., 1977. Staff nurse U. Hosp., Augusta, Ga., 1966; staff nurse coronary care unit St. Joseph Hosp., Augusta, 1967, head nurse coronary care unit, 1968, adminstrv. supr. coronary care unit, 1969-73, nurse instr. coronary care tng. program, 1970-73; nurse coordinator Augusta area cardiovascular facility Univ. Hosp., Augusta, 1972-73; inservice ednl. instr., coordinator continuing nursing edn. Hosp. and Clinics, Med. Coll. Ga., Augusta, 1973-75; cardiovascular nurse cons. Meml. Hosp. Washington County, Sandersville, Ga., 1974-75; cardiovascular nurse clinician Paul E. Cundey, Jr., M.D., cardiologist, Augusta, Ga., 1975-85; prin. JMA Communications; co-owner Alpine Video, Helen, Ga. Contbr. articles to profl. ultrasound jours. Chmn. nursing edn. com. Am. Heart Assn., Ga. affiliate, 1973-74; bd. dirs. Am. Heart Assn., Ga. affiliate, Richmond County unit, 1973-85, co-chmn. high blood pressure com. Recipient Bronze Service medallion, Ga. affiliate, Am. Heart Assn., 1971, Silver Service medallion, 1973, Gold Service medallion, 1975. Mem. Am. Heart Assn., Am. Soc. Echocardiography. Home: PO Box 388 Helen GA 30545 Office: PO Box 569 Helen GA 30545

ANDERSON, JANICE LARAE ALDEN, telecommunications executive; b. Frederic, Wis., Dec. 1, 1935; d. Clifford Oscar and Kathleen Harriet (Streed) Alden; m. Thomas Anderson Roden, Jr., Aug. 31, 1957 (div. July 20, 1971); children—Jacquelyn Lee, Thomas Alden; m. 2d, Robert William Anderson, July 29, 1973. Exec. sec. Pillsbury Co., Mpls., 1953-60; water safety instr., trainer ARC, Mpls., Rocky River, Ohio and Shoreview, Minn., 1962-70; supervising analyst-forecasting Continental Telephone Co., Mpls., 1971—. Vol. dir. ARC vision-hearing screening program, St. Paul, 1968-71; sec. dist. 55, chair precinct 4 Ind. Republicans, 1978-85. Named Toastmaster of Yr., Woodbury, Minn., 1981. Mem. United Ch. of Christ. Clubs: St. Paul-Mpls. Heathkit Computer Users Group (treas. 1982-83), Monterey Jacks Toastmasters (Bloomington, Minn.) (pres. 1984). Home: 1265 Kolff Ct Newport MN 55055 Office: Continental Telecom Inc 1300 Mendota Hts Rd PO Box 50770 Saint Paul MN 55150

ANDERSON, JANICE SCOTT, health care administrator; b. Magnolia, Miss., Apr. 22, 1949; d. Stafford and Mable (Holden) Scott; m. Willie James Anderson, (div. Jan. 1976); children—James Patrick, Christopher Scott. B.A., Millsaps Coll., 1970; M.A., U. Wis., 1972, M.A., 1974, Ph.D., 1981. Writer, City Milw., 1975-76; news analyst WISN-AM, Milw., 1974-76; staff cons. Office Mayor, Milw., 1976-84; pres., chief exec. officer Health Reach HMO, Milw., 1984—. Columnist, The Bus. Jour., 1985—, Milw. Community Jour., 1983—. Pres., founder Reach for the Stars, Milw., 1985; mem. Sojourner Truth House; pres.-elect Milw. Mental Health Assn.; bd. dirs. Leukemia Soc. Wis., United Cerebral Palsy, Goals for Greater Milw.-2000, Girl Scouts Am.-Milw. Mem. Am. Mgmt. Assn., Am. Med. Care and Rev. Assn., Wis. HMO Assn., Speech Communication Assn. Am., Milw. Press Club. Office: Health Reach HMO 2266 N Prospect Ave Suite 612 Milwaukee WI 53202

ANDERSON, JEAN, author, editor; b. Raleigh, N.C., Oct. 12, 1931; d. Donald Benton and Marian March (Johnson) Anderson; B.S., Cornell U., 1951; M.S. (Pulitzer Traveling scholar), Columbia, 1957. Women's editor N.C. Agrl. Extension Service, 1951-54, Raleigh Times, 1954-56; asst. editor Ladies' Home Jour., N.Y.C., 1957-59, editorial asso., 1959-62, mng. editor, 1963; sr. editor Venture Mag., 1964-71; sr. editor contbg. editor Family Circle mag., 1975—. Recipient So. Women's Achievement award Reed & Barton, 1963, George Hedman Meml. award, 1971; R.T. French Tastemaker award, 1975, 80. Mem. Am. Home Econs. Assn., Home Economists in Bus., Les Dames d'Escoffier (v.p. 1981-83), N.Y. Women's Culinary Alliance, Author's League, N.Y. Travel Writers, Gamma Phi Beta, Phi Kappa Phi, Omicron Nu. Author: (with Yeffe Kimball) The Art of American Indian Cooking, 1965; Food Is More Than Cooking, 1968; Henry the Navigator, Prince of Portugal, 1969; The Family Circle 16-Volume Illustrated Library of Cooking, 1972; The Haunting of America, 1973; The Family Circle Cookbook, 1974; (with Elaine Hanna) The Doubleday Cookbook, 1975; Recipes from America's Restored Villages, 1975; The Green Thumb Preserving Guide, 1976; The Grass Roots Cookbook, 1977; Jean Anderson's Processor Cooking, 1978; (with Ruth Buchan) Half a Can of Tomato Paste and other Culinary Dilemmas, 1980; Jean Anderson Cooks, 1982; Unforbidden Sweets, 1982; Jean Anderson's New Processor Cooking, 1983; Jean Anderson's New Green Thumb Preserving Guide. Home: care William Morrow & Co Inc 105 Madison Ave New York NY 10016

ANDERSON, JEAN VALERIE, business executive; b. Cheshire, Eng., Jan. 25, 1944; came to U.S., 1969, naturalized, 1979; d. Harry Ewart and Audrey Constance (Reece) A.; m. Martin Robert Pollner, Jan. 28, 1984. Student Lowther Coll., Eng., 1956-60, Foulkes Bus. Sch., 1960-62, Hunter Coll., N.Y.C., 1973-75, New Sch. Social Research, 1980-81, real estate div. NYU, 1983, N.Y. Sch. Interior Design, 1984—. Adminstr., Sir. Hugh Casson & Partners, Architects, London, 1963-65, Stucke, Harrison, Ritchie & Partners, Architects, Johannesburg, South Africa, 1966-67; asst. to area comptroller Hilton Internat. Co., Montreal, Que., Can., 1967-69; asst. to comptroller Intercontinental Hotels, N.Y.C. 1969-71; asst. to U.S. rep. to U.N., sr. partner Amen, Weisman & Butler, N.Y.C., 1973-76; asst. to pres. Nat. Econ. Research Assocs., N.Y.C., 1976-78; mgmt. exec. Imperial Chem. Industries, Limited, N.Y.C., 1978-83; founder, pres. Anderson Assocs., N.Y.C., 1983—. Coordinator, Expo '67, Montreal, 1969; vol. Mount Sinai Hosp., N.Y.C., 1976-77. Mem. Nat. Passenger Traffic Assn., Corp. Travel Assn. Republican. Clubs: Royal Liverpool (Eng.); Indian Hills Golf. Home: 245 Asharokon Ave Northport NY 11768 Office: 1391 Madison Ave New York NY 10029

ANDERSON, JILL ELIZABETH, accountant; b. Washington, June 30, 1957; d. Daniel G. and Bernice E. (Nordlund) A. B.S. in Commerce with honors, U. Va., 1979. C.P.A., Va., D.C. Staff acct. Price Waterhouse & Co., Washington, 1979-80; staff internal auditor Marriott Corp., Washington, 1980-82, internat. acctg. mgr., 1982-84, mgr. internat. fin. planning and control, 1984—. Mem. Am. Inst. C.P.A.s, Nat. Assn. Female Execs., U. Va. Alumni Assn., Beta Gamma Sigma, Beta Alpha Psi. Clubs: Sporting (Tysons Corner, Va.); Washington Ski. Avocations: racquetball; softball; skiing; aerobics; piano. Home: 2418 Lee Oaks Pl #202B Falls Church VA 22046 Office: Marriott Corp One Marriott Dr Washington DC 20058

ANDERSON, JOAN BROWNELL, economics educator; b. Colorado Springs, Colo., Oct. 15, 1938; d. John Wesley and Emily Margarite (Baer) Brownell; m. Fredric Clifford Anderson, July 1, 1961; children—Carolyn Anne, Fredric Brownell, Jo Ellen. B.A. in Econs., San Diego State U., 1960; M.A. in Econs., Standford U., 1961; Ph.D. in Econs., U. Calif.-San Diego, 1971. Teaching asst. Stanford Univ., Palo Alto, Calif., 1960-61; lectr. San Diego State U., 1961-64, 70-71, 72-81; teaching asst. U. Calif.-San Diego, 1965-67; asst. prof. econs. U. San Diego, 1981-83, assoc. prof., 1983—; sr. economist Calif. Border Area Resource Ctr., San Diego, 1979-81. Contbr. articles to profl. jours. Mem. steering com. San Diego Chpt. Nat. Emergency Response Network, 1985; mem. Presbyterian Synod Task Force on Central Am., San Diego, 1984—, Synod Task Force for Just Polit. Econ., Border Task Force Presbytery of San Diego; elder Point Loma Community Presbyn. Ch.; lectr. numerous community groups, 1982—. Recipient 1984 Women of Achievement award Pres.'s Council, 1985. Stanford U. fellow, 1960; Regional Employment Tng. Consortium grantee, 1979. Mem. Am. Econs. Assn., Western Econs. Assn., Assn. Borderland Scholars (sec. 1984—), Western Social Sci. Assn., Bus. Adminstrn. in Latin Am. Studies of Rocky Mountain Council on Latin Am. Studies, Altrusa Club of San Diego. Democrat. Avocations: skiing; swimming; guitar; camping. Home: 5422 Drover Dr San Diego CA 92115 Office: Sch of Bus Univ San Diego Alcala Park San Diego CA 92110

ANDERSON, JOAN SCHEUERMANN, clin. psychologist, educator; b. New Orleans, Mar. 17, 1933; d. Leonhard Naef and Margaret Scheuermann; B.A., Sophie Newcomb Coll., 1954; Ph.D., U. Houston, 1969; m. Frank Clayton Anderson, Jr., Apr. 30, 1954; children—Frank Clayton III, Mollie Elise. Pvt. practice clin. psychology, Houston, 1969—; clin. assoc. prof. Baylor Coll. Medicine, Houston; chmn. Tex. Bd. Examiners of Psychologists, 1982. Bd. dirs. Living Bank, 1965—, Children's World, 1970-75, Homes of St. Mark, 1977—. Mem. Am. Psychol. Assn., Tex. Psychol. Assn. (pres. 1977), Houston Psychol. Assn. (pres. 1979). Episcopalian. Office: 1535 West Loop S Suite 222 Houston TX 77027

ANDERSON, JOAN WELLIN FREED, freelance journalist; b. Shreveport, La., Aug. 18, 1945; d. Cyril and Rose (Friedman) F.; m. Steven G. Rapfogel, 1966 (div. 1984); children—Lisa L., Robert B.; m. J. Warren Anderson, July 21, 1984. B.A. in Gen. Studies, Tex. Christian U. Freelance reporter Sta. KERA-TV, Dallas, 1979-80, Fort Worth Star-Telegram, 1980-83, Fort Worth bur. Dallas Morning News, 1980-82; pub. relations coordinator Amon Carter Mus., Fort Worth, 1982; med. writer Tex. Coll. Osteo. Medicine, Fort Worth, 1982-85; freelance writer, 1985—. Bd. dirs. Am. Cancer Soc., 1982-84, active Cancer Hotline. Mem. Women in Communications, Inc. (past dir.), Internat. Assn. Bus. Communicators, Sigma Delta Chi. Contbr. articles to popular mags.

ANDERSON, JOLENE SLOVER, publisher; b. Tulare, Calif.; d. James P. Sr., and Helen B. (Walters) Slover; ed. Victor Valley Coll., Riverside City Coll.; m. Douglas R. Anderson, June 14, 1975; 1 dau. by previous marriage—Sabrina Jo. Model, Connor Sch. Modeling, Fresno, Calif., 1955-65; actress M. Kosloff Studios, Hollywood, Calif., 1965; nat. sales mgr. Armed Services Publs., 1966-68; pres., dir. Sullivan Publs., Inc., Riverside, Calif., 1970-82; pres., chief exec. officer Heritage House Publs., 1983—. Mem. Riverside Tourist and Conv., 1981, public relations com. YWCA, 1981; mem. City Councils Cultural Heritage Bd.; treas. DeAnza Verde Homeowners, 1978; active U.S. Ski Team, Rape Crisis Center. Mem. Riverside C. of C., Printers Industries Am. Club: Soroptimists (chmn. 1981). Home: Riverside CA Office: PO Box 7453 Riverside CA 92513

ANDERSON, JUDITH MARIE, insurance company executive; b. LaCrosse, Wis., June 6, 1955; d. Mark Ray and Monica Dorothy (Knotek) A. A.A., Western Wis. Tech. Inst., 1979; B.A. in Bus. Adminstrn., Lakeland Coll., 1986. Personnel asst. Northwestern Mut. Life Ins. Co., Milw., 1980-82, info. systems cons., 1982—. Mem. Nat. Assn. Female Execs. Roman Catholic. Office: Northwestern Mutual Life Ins Co 720 E Wisconsin Ave Milwaukee Wi 53202

ANDERSON, JUDITH MURRAYLYNN, label manufacturer, public relations consultant; b. Dallas, May 7, 1942; d. Murray Maxwell and Zelma (Reckley) Cole; m. Roy Morgan Anderson, Nov. 30, 1973; 1 child, Amy Leigh. B.S., U. Tex.-Austin, 1965. Quality assurance technician, mgr. consumer relations Riviana Foods Inc., Houston, 1965-80; account exec. Metzdorf Advt., Houston, 1980-81; owner, pres. Art Style Printing, Inc., 1981—, Dataware, 1981—, Anderson & Assocs. Pub. Relations, Houston, 1981—. Bd. dirs. Chocolate Bayou Theater Co., Houston, 1981—. Recipient Silver Spur award Tex. Pub. Relations Assn., 1983. Mem. Am. Home Econs. Assn., Home Economists in Bus. (regional advisor 1973-75). Republican. Lutheran. Office: Art Style Printing Inc 7570 Renwick St Houston TX 77081

ANDERSON, KARYN DAWN, banker; b. Salt Lake City, Oct. 30, 1945; d. Terence William and Fern Mildred (Jensen) A.; m. Robert Anderson, June 5, 1964 (div. 1978); children—Michael, Sherrie, Brett, Tammy, Brandon. Student, U. Utah, 1964-65. Office mgr. Pacific Leasing Co., Salt Lake City, 1978-80, Pacific Mortgage Co., Salt Lake City, 1978-80; v.p. CD Mortgage Inc., Salt Lake City, 1980-83; div. liaison City Consumer Service, Salt Lake City, 1983-85; br. mgr. First Union Mortgage Co., Salt Lake City, 1985—. Author: Crystal Chandeliers, 1978; (children's book) Freddie Frog, 1984. Contbr. articles to profl. jours., mag. Bd. dirs. Utah State Elem. Sch. Poison Prevention Com., 1975-76; pres. Utah State Pharm. Aux., Salt Lake City, 1975-76; pres. Boulton Elem. Sch. PTA, 1977-78. Recipient Pres.'s award Utah State Pharm Aux., 1976, Utah State PTA, 1978, award Loan Officer Assn. Mem. Credit Women Internat. Nat. Assn. Female Execs., Women's Council Realtors, Assn. Profl. Mortgage Women, Intermountain Exec. Assn., Women in Bus. Republican. Mormon. Avocations: reading; writing; music; boating; skiing. Office: First Union Mortgage Corp 7090 S Union Park Ave #260 Midvale UT 84047

ANDERSON, KATHERINE S., natural gas liquids supply manager; b. Oceanside, Calif., Mar. 9, 1958; d. Donald Wayne and Willadene (Savage) Springer; m. Randall Lloyd Anderson, Aug. 25, 1979; 1 child, Brianne D. Student Okla. Christian Coll., 1976-79. Service analyst Dunhill Temps, Tulsa, 1979-80; with Mapco Gas Products, Inc., Tulsa, 1980—, supply mgr., 1986—; mem. propane adv. com. NYMEX, N.Y.C., 1986—. Mem., contbr. Polit. Action Com. for Mapco, Inc., Tulsa, 1984—. Mem. Nat. Assn. Female Execs., Theta Theta Theta. Republican. Mem. Ch. of Christ. Clubs: Windycrest Sailing (editor 1981 sec. 1982, activities capt. 1983), Riverfield Country Day Sch. Parent Assn. Avocations: sailing; ceramics; needlework; modeling. Home: 6709 S Peach Ave Broken Arrow OK 74011 Office: Mapco Gas Products Inc 1800 S Baltimore Ave Tulsa OK 74119

ANDERSON, KRISTI SUSAN, marketing and advertising executive; b. Stockton, Calif., Jan. 6, 1952; d. Ivar Ernest and Jeanne Shirley (Hicks) A. B.A., San Francisco State U., 1974. Account exec. J. Walter Thompson, N.Y.C., 1978-80, Benton Bowles, N.Y.C., 1981; account supr. Needham Harper, N.Y.C., 1982-84, Griffin Bacal, N.Y.C., 1984-85, GLAD, N.Y.C., 1985—. Mem. Advt. Women N.Y., Women in Communications, Advt. Club N.Y. Republican. Home: 120 E 62d St New York NY 10021 Office: GLAD 41 Madison Ave New York NY 10010

ANDERSON, LANNO CRANE, multinational trading company executive; b. Mobile, Ala., June 21, 1947; d. Thomas Eugene and Beatrice (Donoghue) Crane; m. Russell Frederick Anderson, June 12, 1976; 1 child, Eugenia Crane. Student St. Mary's Dominican Coll., 1965-66, U. South Ala., 1966-67. Vice pres. Sterling, Standard & Plate, Honolulu, 1976-80; pres. The Silver Service, Coronado, Calif., 1980-84; U.S. rep. Bird & Co., Hong Kong, 1984—; cons. San Diego Mus. Art, 1980-84, Newport Hist. Soc., R.I., 1984. Mem. Internat. Soc. Appraisers, New Eng. Soc. Appraisers. Republican. Roman Catholic. Avocations: collecting antiques and silver. Home: 6203 Capella Ave Burke VA 22015

ANDERSON, LILLIE MAE, social worker; b. Columbia, S.C., Apr. 15, 1918; d. Julius and Lillie (Thompson) Hardy; B.A. magna cum laude, Benedict Coll., 1959; postgrad. Howard U., 1960-61; M.S.W., Atlanta U., 1969; postgrad., U. S.C., 1975, 78, So. Regional Inst., 1976, U. Ala., 1980; m. Calvin R. Goff, Aug. 1, 1981. Beautician, Columbia, S.C., 1938-45; file clk. Office Dependency Benefits, Newark, 1945-46; group leader Utility Electric Corp., East Newark, N.J., 1946-52; owner, propr. A & W Store, Columbia, 1952-56; group worker Bethlehem Community Center, Columbia, 1959-60; social worker S.C. Mental Health, Columbia, 1960-63, 66-68, Pilgrim State Hosp., West Brentwood, N.Y., 1963-66; supr. Columbia Housing Authority, 1969-71; social worker VA, Lyons, N.J., 1971, Dorn VA Hosp., Columbia, 1971—, coordinator visually impaired service, instr. cardiac rehab. program. Mental health grantee, 1960-61; VA grantee, 1968-69. Mem. Nat. Assn. Social Workers, State of S.C. Bd. Social Work Registration, Richland and Lexington Counties Social Work Assn., Social Work Club (pres. 1973), Zeta Phi Beta, Alpha Kappa Mu. Democrat. Roman Catholic. Home: Route 5 Box 166 Columbia SC 29203 Office: Dorn VA Hosp Garners Ferry Rd Columbia SC 29201

ANDERSON, LINDA CAROL, lawyer; b. Los Angeles, May 25, 1955; d. Adrian Campbell Anderson and Laura Ann (Kroencke) Harvey. Student U. Utah, 1977; B.A. in English cum laude, Brigham Young U., 1978; postgrad. U. Tex., 1980; J.D. cum laude, high honors with distinction, Brigham Young U., 1981. Bar: Tex. 1981. Adminstrv. aide Brigham Young U. Honors Program, Provo, Utah, 1976-78; legal intern Oppenheiner, Rosenberg, Kelleher & Wheatley, San Antonio, summer 1980; briefing atty. Tex. Ct. Appeals, San Antonio, 1981-82, ct. clerk, 1982-83; asst. criminal dist. atty. Bexar County Dist. Atty.'s Office, San Antonio, 1983-84; assoc. atty. litigation sect. Fulbright & Jaworski, 1984—; chmn. legal com., chmn. writing com. Dist. Atty.'s Task Force Child Abuse, San Antonio, 1984—; chmn. writing com. Dist. Atty.'s Task Force Domestic Violence, 1983; atty. provider Pro Bono Legal Services, San Antonio, 1983—. Contbr. chpt. to book, articles to profl. jours. Recipient Fine Arts scholarship La Canada Town and Country Assn., 1973-77; Calif. State scholar, 1973; Soroptimist scholar, 1973-77; Heppe Meml. Found. scholar, 1973-77; Univ. scholar Brigham Young U., 1978. Mem. Bexar County Women's Bar Assn., San Antonio Bar Assn., ABA (2d pl. regional client counselling competition 1980), Am. Judicature Soc., Tex. Bar Assn. (chmn. com. on child abuse and neglect 1985—), San Antonio Trial Lawyers Assn., NOW, Young Lawyers Assn. Democrat. Clubs: Italian, English Circle, Job's Daus. (musician 1969-71). Office: Fulbright & Jaworski 2100 Interfirst Plaza 300 Convent St San Antonio TX 78205

ANDERSON, LINDA SUE, healthcare computer info. systems consultant; b. Columbus, Ohio, Aug. 13, 1947; d. Charles Robert and Arlene Faye (Wilhelm) Anderson; B.A. in Sociology, Pa. State U., 1969. Accounts receivable specialist Hahnemann Med. Coll. and Hosp., Phila., 1971-73, asst. patient accounts mgr., 1973-75; installation dir., account mgr. spl. projects Shared Med. Systems, Malvern, Pa., 1975-80, internat. installations specialist, 1981, installation project support specialist, 1982-83, systems conversion cons., account exec., Pitts., 1984—. Office: SMS One North Shore Ctr Pittsburgh PA 15212

ANDERSON, LYNN COOVER, veterinarian, pharmaceutical company executive; b. Erie, Pa., Jan. 4, 1954; d. Kenneth Oliver and Martha Claire (Coover) Anderson; m. John F. Carpenter, June 12, 1982. D.V.M., Iowa State U., 1977. Clinician Lisle Emergency Vet. Service, Lisle, Ill., 1978-79, Boone Animal Hosp., Western Springs, Ill., 1977-79; postdoctoral fellow U. Mich. Med. Sch., Ann Arbor, 1979-81; asst. prof. lab. medicine U. Minn. Med. Sch., Mpls., 1981-83; supr. lab. animal medicine Riker Labs., Inc., St. Paul, 1983—; cons. VA Med. Ctr., Mpls., 1981-83; adj. asst prof. U. Minn. Coll. Vet. Medicine, St. Paul, 1984—; vice chmn. adv. council Animal Health Tech., U. Minn.-Waseca. Editor Iowa State U. Veterinarian mag., 1976-77; author profl. meeting presentations and profl. audio-visual program; contbr. articles to profl. jours. Mem. Jr. League of Mpls., 1982—. Mem. Am. Assn. Lab. Animal Sci. (regional exam. bd. 1981—, com. on lab. animal technicians 1984—), Minn. Assn. Lab. Animal Sci. (dir. 1982—), AVMA, Am. Soc. Lab. Animal Practitioners (bd. dirs. 1985—), 3M Circle Tech Excellence, Nat. Soc. Med. Research, Twin City Alumnae Panhellenic Assn., Mortar Bd., Phi Zeta, Kappa Alpha Theta (dir. Mpls. alumnae chpt. 1982-84). Republican. Congregationalist. Home: 708 Westwood Dr S Golden Valley MN 55416 Office: Riker Labs Inc 3M Ctr Bldg 270-3S-05 Saint Paul MN 55144

ANDERSON, MADELINE CAROL, nurse, educator; b. Queens, N.Y., Dec. 1, 1942; d. Joseph and Dorothy Helen (Burke) Palumbo; m. Donald Robert Anderson, June 29, 1963; children—Mark Payson, Keith Charles. R.N., Queens Hosp. Ctr. Sch. Nursing, 1963; B.S. with highest honors in Edn., U. Tenn., 1984, postgrad., 1984—. Cert. critical care R.N., Tenn., N.Y.; cert. tchr. in health occupations, Tenn. R.N., Middle Tenn. Med. Ctr., Murfreesboro, 1963-66, VA Med. Ctr., Lebanon, Tenn., 1966-67; critical care R.N. Baptist Hosp., Nashville, 1967-73, supr. critical care unit, med. intensive care unit, 1967-73; physician asst. Carl E. Mitchell, M.D., Nashville, 1973-78; L.P.N. instr. Metro Nashville Bd. Edn., Nashville, 1978-79, health occupations instr., 1979—; nursing inservice instr. Parkview Hosp., Nashville, 1979; part-time asst. Mitchell, Shmerling & McCracken, M.D.s, Nashville, 1982—; guest lectr. Critical Care Program, Nashville, 1967-75; mem. faculty adv. com. Stratford High Sch., Nashville, 1983-84, mem. steering com., 1984-85; sec., tchr. rep. Health Occupation Adv. Com., Nashville, 1979—; cons. J. Brady Co., 1984-85; mem. textbook adoption commn. Metro Bd. Edn., 1982-83; mem. task force Health Occupation Edn. Curriculum Framework, Nashville, 1985; mem. curriculum com. Martin Luther King, Jr. Health Sci. Magnet Sch., Nashville, 1985; adv. Health Occupation Students Am.-Stratford High Sch. Chpt., Nashville, 1980—. Mem. nursing edn. com. Middle Tenn. Heart Assn., Nashville, 1967-73; vol. instr. ARC, Nashville, 1979—. Recipient cert. of recognition Channel 5 Health Fair, 1983, 84, 85; cert. of appreciation ARC, 1981-84. Mem. Am. Assn. Critical Care Nurses, Am. Vocat. Assn. Tenn. Vocat. Assn., Tenn. Hosp. Assn., NEA, Tenn. Edn. Assn., Middle Tenn. Edn. Assn., Health Occupations Students Am. (cert. appreciation 1984), Gamma Beta Phi Soc. Republican. Lutheran. Avocations: reading; gardening; crafts; camping; traveling.

ANDERSON, MARGARET LAVINIA, history educator; b. Washington, Oct. 18, 1941; d. David and Margaret Lavinia (Anderson) A.; m. Charles Raff, Sept. 12, 1972; 1 dau., Sarah Elizabeth. B.A., Swarthmore Coll., 1963; Ph.D., Brown U., 1971. Asst. prof. history Swarthmore Coll. (Pa.), 1970-77, assoc. prof., 1977-84, prof., 1985—; mem. com. Ednl. Testing Service, Princeton, N.J., 1983—. Author: Windthorst: A Political Biography, 1981. Woodrow Wilson Found. fellow, 1963, 66-67; NDEA fellow Brown U., Providence, 1963-66, grantee, 1972; Humboldt Found. fellow, Bonn, W.Ger., 1974; Lang fellow Swarthmore Coll., 1981-82; Flack Faculty award for teaching, Swarthmore Coll., 1985. Mem. Am. Hist. Assn., Cath. Hist. Assn. Democrat. Episcopalian. Office: Dept History Swarthmore Coll Swarthmore PA 19081*

ANDERSON, MARGARET (MICKEY) CAUGHMAN, secretary, civic and church worker; b. Wagener, S.C., Mar. 14, 1936; d. Carl Davis and Iola (Gantt) Caughman; m. Hal Cecil Anderson, June 8, 1958; children—Elizabeth Caughman Anderson Gruber, Jonathan Hal. A.B. in Edn., U. S.C., 1958. Tchr. North Charleston High Sch., S.C., 1958-60; sec. to dean Coll. Charleston, S.C., 1960-61; ch. sec. Grace Lutheran Ch., Rock Hill, S.C., 1969—, numerous activities include sec. ch. council, 1976-79, lay asst., 1980-84, lector, 1980—, mem. altar guild, 1982—, mem. com. on ministries, 1983—; active S.C. synod Luth. Ch. in Am., including co-lay vice-chairperson camping and conf. ministries appeal, 1979-83, mem. mgmt. com., sec. personnel subcom. and chairperson Lutheridge satellite com., 1979-84, and S.C. del. to Luth. Ch. Am. Biennial Conv., 1980; active Luth. Ch. Women, including circle leader and sec., mem. S.C. exec. bd., 1977-78, conv. del., 1977, 80, co-chmn. family enrichment seminar, 1978, chmn. learning resources com., 1978, and mem. constn. com., 1977; v.p. Ebinport PTA, Rock Hill, 1972-74; treas. York County Multi-Disciplinary Com., Rock Hill, 1973-79; active York County Med. Assn. Aux., Rock Hill, including pres., 1974; chmn. ch. scout com. Boy Scouts Am., 1979-83; pres. Accolade Garden Club, Rock Hill, 1982, scrapbook chmn. 1984-86). Mem. S.C. Med. Assn. Aux. (corr. sec. 1979).

ANDERSON, MARIAN, contralto; b. Phila., Feb. 27, 1902; d. John Berkeley and Anna Anderson; ed. Phila. pub. schs.; mus. edn. pvt. study in Phila., N.Y. and abroad; hon. degrees 23 Am. ednl. instns., 1 Korean; m. Orpheus H. Fisher, July 24, 1943. As child sang in Union Bapt. Ch. choir, Phila.; a fund raised through a church concert enabled her to take singing lessons under an Italian instr.; won 1st prize in competition with 300 others at N.Y. Lewisohn Stadium, 1925; began singing career, 1924; debut in Un Ballo in Maschera, Met. Opera, 1955; has made many concert tours of the U.S. and Europe; one of the leading contraltos in world; appearances in all famous concert halls, stadia, now ret. U.S. del. to UN, 1955, also 13th Gen. Assembly. Recipient Bok Award, 1940, Congl. Medal of Honor, 1977; awarded Finnish decoration "probenignitate humana," 1940; decorations from Sweden, Philippines, Haiti, Liberia, France, numerous states and cities in U.S.; Yokus Lo medal (Japan). Mem. Alpha Kappa Alpha. Author: My Lord, What a Morning. Home: Danbury CT 06810 Office: care ICM Artists Ltd 40 W 57th St New York NY 10019

ANDERSON, MARILYS D., med. technologist; b. Balt., June 15, 1950; d. Harry Kenneth and Bonnie Bolt (O'Shields) Dicely; B.S. in Med. Tech., Coll. Charleston (S.C.), 1972; m. Allen Franklin, Mar. 25, 1972; children—Hillary Erin, Lyndsey Morgan. Med. technologist Med. U. S.C., Charleston, 1972-73, Ga. Baptist Hosp., Atlanta, 1973-75; med. technologist, then supr. St. Joseph Meml. Hosp., Murphysboro, Ill., 1975-81; med. technologist chemistry Richmond Meml. Hosp., Rockingham, N.C., 1981— instr., 1982-85; instr. hematology Med. U. S.C., 1972-73. Mem. Am. Soc. Clin. Pathologists (affiliate), So. Ill. Med. Tech. Ednl. Group (charter, past sec.). Democrat. Baptist. Home: 909 Carlyle Way E #139 Mobile AL 36609

ANDERSON, MARLENE SUE, management consultant; b. Sterling, Ill., Mar. 8, 1931; d. Enos L. and Evelyn (Sundberg) Rohrer; B.S., No. Ill. U., 1956, M.Ed., 1956, M.S. in Counseling, 1971; children—Cynthia Lynn, David Paul. Instr., William Rainey Harper Coll., Palatine, Ill., 1975, Triton Coll., River Grove, Ill., 1979-81; pres., owner Anderson & Assocs., Mgmt. Tng., Hinsdale, Ill., 1970—; speaker in field. Counselor, PCM Psychology Assocs. Mem. Ill. Tng. and Devel. Assn., Am. Soc. Tng. and Devel., Women in Mgmt. (chpt. treas. 1979), Chgo. Assn. Commerce and Industry, Oak Brook (Ill.) Assn. Commerce and Industry, Oak Brook Execs. Club, Execs. Club Chgo., Nat.

Assn. Female Execs. Author: Health Assertive Management, 1978; also articles, chpts. in book. Address: Hunt Trail Lake Barrington Shores Barrington IL 60010

ANDERSON, MARTHA ALENE, risk management director, hazardous waste expert; b. Monessen, Pa., June 15, 1945; d. Jesse Lee and Helen Frances (Daugherty) Cain; m. James O. Anderson, Sept. 9, 1966; 1 dau., Heather Linn. B.S. in Biology, Calif. State Coll., 1967. Research asst. W.Va. U., Morgantown, 1967-72; tchr. Hokkaido Internat. Sch., Sapporo, Japan, 1972-73; research asst. Pa. State U., 1974-76 research assoc. U. Ariz., Tucson, 1976-80; mgr. chem. waste Dept. Risk Mgmt., U. Ariz., Tucson, 1980-81, asst. dir., 1981-85, dir., 1985—; mem. Pima County Environment Com., Tucson, 1985—; advisor Tucson C. of C. Environ. Quality Com., 1984—. Co-sponsor: Waste Exchanges newsletter, 1985. Trainer Am. Cancer Soc., Tucson, 1985—; del Nat. Council on Future of Women in the Workplace, Washington, 1986—. Named Woman of Yr., Bus. and Profl. Women, Tucson, 1985; Woman on the Move, WYCA, Tucson, 1985. Mem. Am. Soc. Safety Engrs. (sec. 1985-86, v.p. 1986—), Am. Indsl. Hygiene Assn., Risk and Ins. Mgrs. Soc., Bus. and Profl. Women of U. Ariz. (pres.), Ariz. Fedn. Bus. and Profl. Women (career task force chmn. 1985—), So. Ariz. Water Resources Assn. (water quality com. 1984—). Avocations: reading translated Japanese literature; sewing. Office: Dept Risk Mgmt 1143 N Cherry Ave Tucson AZ 85719

ANDERSON, MARY JANE, newsletter publisher, public relations specialist; b. Richmond, Va., May 27, 1930; d. Francis W. and Margaret G. (Esbrook) A.; B.A. in Journalism, Wayne State U., 1951. Staff writer Skyline mag. and Mich. Motor Carrier, Detroit, 1952-54; reporter Fairchild Publs., Detroit, 1954-57, Home Furnishings Daily/Footwear News, Chgo., 1957-67; food service editor Vend Mag., Billboard Publs., N.Y.C., 1967-72; owner Anderson Publs. (pubs. The Anderson Report, Catering Merchandiser, Foods By Mail); prin. MJA Pub. Relations, Chgo., 1979—. Active local Republican campaigns; broadcaster Chgo. Radio Info. Services for blind and print handicapped; vol. Rec. for the Blind, N.Y.C. Named Food Editor of Yr., Nat. Assn. Coll. and Univ. Food Services. Mem. Women in Communications (past pres.), Internat. Food Editorial Council (past v.p.). Office: 203 N Wabash Suite 718 Chicago IL 60601

ANDERSON, MARY JORGENSEN, mathematician; b. Winchester, Tex., Oct. 31, 1937; d. Roy Lewis and Nellie Joyce (Hart) Jorgensen; B.S., La. State U., 1965, M.S., 1968, Ph.D., 1979; m. Edmund Hughes Anderson, Oct. 10, 1975; children—Carolyne Gail Calvert, Gary Steven Calvert, Christopher Lewis Calvert. Engring. technician La. Dept. Hwys., Baton Rouge, 1957-60; grad. asst. La. State U., 1965-68, 76-78; instr. in math. Miss. State U., 1970-76, asst. prof. math., 1978-81; mathematician Superior Oil Co., Midland, Tex., 1981-85; sr. computer analyst Mobil Oil Corp., Denver, 1985—. Mem. Am. Math. Soc., Assn. Women in Math., Miss. Acad. Scis., Pi Mu Epsilon, Phi Delta Kappa. Episcopalian. Contbr. articles to profl. jours.; reviewer Math. Revs., 1984—. Home: 2075 Wright St Lakewood CO 80228 Office: Mobil Oil Corp PO Box 5444 Denver CO 80217

ANDERSON, MARY LOU, educator; b. Mount Pleasant, Iowa, Aug. 29, 1949; d. Carl Marion and Hazel Lucile (Mitchell) A. B.S. in Edn., Northeast Mo. State U., 1971, M.S. in Elem. Guidance, 1974. Lic. elem. tchr., Mo. Elem. tchr. Waynesville pub. schs., Mo., 1971-73, Hannibal pub. schs., Mo., 1973-79, Bel Ridge Elem. Sch., St. Louis, 1979—; ERA cons. ERAmerica, Washington, 1980-81, NEA, Washington, 1980-82; LEAST discipline cons. Mo. NEA, 1981—, state conf. workshop leader, 1979-83; co-founder, chmn. Mo. NEA Women's Caucus, 1975-78. Pres. Mo. ERA Coalition, 1980-82; pres. Polit. Action Com. St. Louis Women's Polit. Caucus, 1984-85; campaign mgr. Mo. State Rep. race, 1986; campaign worker Mo. Democratic Orgn., 1982—. Mem. NEA, Mo. NEA (Lorna Bottger Polit. Action award 1982), St. Louis Suburban Tchrs. Assn. (bd. dirs.), Normandy Tchrs. Assn., NOW, ACLU, Phi Delta Kappa. Mem. United Ch. of Christ. Avocations: playing piano; aerobics; reading; plays and movies. Home: 4497 Pershing St Apt 107 Saint Louis MO 63108 Office: Bel Ridge Elem Sch 8930 Boston Ave Saint Louis MO 63121

ANDERSON, MERLINE POWELL, fund raiser; b. Indianola, Miss., Jan. 7, 1946; d. Aruator and Catherine (Bishop) Powers; m. James A. Anderson, May 28, 1966 (div. 1968); 1 dau., Tracy Sherra. Student Forest Park Community Coll., St. Louis, 1964-65; B.S. in Bus. Adminstrn., Lindenwood Coll., St. Charles, Mo., 1978, postgrad., 1978-79. Sec., adminstrv. asst. Mo. State Agys., St. Louis, 1965-70; legal asst. Atty. Forriss D. Elliott, St. Louis, 1970-77; dir. devel. Central Med. Ctr., St. Louis, 1977-83; freelance fund raising cons., St. Louis, 1983—; mem. Nat. Health Screening Council, St. Louis, 1985—; sec., ptnr. United Entertainment & Investment Corp. Treas. St. Louis Urban Affairs Council, 1978—; bd. dirs. Nat. Urban Affairs Council, St. Louis, 1978—; v.p. Rosary High Sch. PTA, St. Louis, 1983-85; treas. Campaign for Eddie Davis for Bd. Edn., St. Louis, 1983. Mem. Nat. Soc. Fund Raising Execs. (sec. 1980-82), Nat. Assn. Hosp. Devel., Nat. Assn. Female Execs. Democrat. Baptist.

ANDERSON, MICHAEL LARSEN, personnel administrator; b. Nashville, Feb. 19, 1941; d. Ralph Michael and Vee (Allen) Larsen; m. William J. Anderson, III, June 4, 1958 (div. 1984); children—Alicia Sayle, William Joseph, Ralph Michael Larsen, Mollie Blair. Student, Vanderbilt U., 1958-60, Xavier Coll., 1977-78. Asst. personnel dir. PEDCo. Inc., Cin., 1979-81, personnel dir., 1981-83. Bd. dirs. Nashville Mental Health Assn., 1968-71; founding bd. dirs. Children's Regional Med. Ctr., Nashville; child advocacy chmn. Jr. League, Huntington, W.Va., 1974-75, v.p., 1975-76; child advocacy co-chmn. Jr. League Cin., 1977-78. Appeared on cover of Time mag., July 1965, Town & Country, 1974. Episcopalian. Address: Nashville TN

ANDERSON, PAMELA P., human resources specialist; b. Greensboro, N.C., Apr. 9, 1950; d. William Aldeen and Eula (Clapp) Priddy. B.A. with distinction in Mgmt., U. Redlands (Calif.), 1983; postgrad. in bus. administrn., Loyola Marymount U., 1984—. Personnel asst. Mfrs. Bank, Los Angeles, 1975-77; employee relations asst. Ameron Corp hdqrs., Monterey Park, Calif., 1977-78, employee relations adminstr. Ameron Pipe div., Monterey Park, 1978-79; tng. and affirmative action programs adminstr. Beneficial Standard Corp., Los Angeles, 1979-82; human resources adminstr. Mattel, Inc., Hawthorne, Calif., 1982-84; mgr. affirmative action programs TRW-Space & Tech. Group, Redondo Beach, Calif., 1984—; mem. Aerospace Industry Equal Opportunity Com., Los Angeles, 1982—. Recipient Outstanding Support award Amigos de Service Employment Redevel. Hawthorne, Calif., 1982, 83. Mem. Career Planning Ctr. Los Angeles (exec. planning com. 11th ann. women's employment options conf. 1984), Am. Soc. Personnel Adminstrs., Am. Soc. Tng. and Devel., Nat. Assn. Female Execs. Office: TRW Space & Tech Group One Space Park Redondo Beach CA 90278

ANDERSON, PEGGY JEAN, university administrator; linguist; b. Fargo, N.D., Mar. 28, 1945; d. Walter Raymond and Elizabeth (Snider) A.; B.S. in Edn., Emporia State U., 1967; M.A. in Linguistics, U. Kans., 1979; m. Richard John Robinson, Apr. 18, 1981. Tchr. spl. edn., English, Kansas City (Kans.) Public Schs., 1967-68; tchr. Somerdale (N.J.) Public Schs., 1968-73; dir. fgn. staff, instr. YMCA Japan, Fukuoka, 1973-77; instr. Applied English Center, U. Kans., Lawrence, 1977-79; coordinator English as Second Lang. Programs, U. Iowa, 1979-81; curriculum coordinator Intensive English Lang. Center, Wichita State U., 1981-82, asso. dir. center, 1982—; reviewer Scott-Foresman Pub. Co.; cons. to community groups, public schs., internat. bus. Nat. Assn. Fgn. Student Affairs grantee, 1980—. Mem. TESOL, Mid-Am. TESOL (1st v.p., pres.), Nat. Assn. Fgn. Student Affairs, Linguistic Soc. Am., Mid-Am. MLA. Democrat. Episcopalian. Research in second lang. acquisition, teaching methodology, curriculum design. Home: 2410 Bromfield Circle Wichita KS 67226 Office: Intensive English Lang Center Wichita State U Wichita KS 67208

ANDERSON, RUTH LUCILLE, interior designer, fabric designer, educator; b. Cyprus Hills, N.Y., Dec. 19; d. Arthur Albert and Marie Rose (Weston) Buehler; grad. N.Y. Sch. Applied Design for Women (Pratt Inst.), 1939; grad. N.Y. Sch. Interior Design, 1944; B.A., Adelphi U., 1979, M.A., 1981; m. Gunnar Bohlin Anderson, June 22, 1946; children—Anna Kristine Kornblatt, Deborah Val. Fabric cons. F. Schumacher & Co., N.Y.C., 1954-60; sr. interior designer W&J Sloane, N.Y.C., 1960-83; adj. asst. prof. Nassau Community Coll., 1979-84, Adelphi U., 1980; mem. faculty Parson (New Sch.), 1980-82; lectr. in field. Mem. Am. Soc. Interior Designers (profl. mem.), Nat. Home Fashions League. Paintings and sculptures exhibited at W&J Sloane and Adelphi U. Home: 127 2d St Garden City NY 11530

ANDERSON, SAUNDRA LEE, recreation therapist; b. Salt Lake City, Feb. 9, 1951; d. Arthur Ray and Betty Jane (Griffith) Carlston; m. Michael Thomas Anderson, Jan. 5, 1980. B.S., U. Utah, 1975. Cert. therapeutic recreation specialist. Recreation therapist Utah State Tng. Sch., Salt Lake City, 1974-75, West Jordan Care Ctr., Salt Lake City, 1976-78, Wyo. State Tng. Sch., Lander, 1978—. Treas. Lander Dist. Recreation Bd., 1983-85. Mem. Ch. of Jesus Christ of Latter Day Saints. Avocations: traveling, camping, cross country skiing, gardening. Home: PO Box 119 Hudson WY 82515

ANDERSON, THELMA KAY, pharmaceutical company official; b. Sims, Ill., Nov. 2, 1938; d. Henry Audry and Leota Zelma (Wells) Linder; B.S., McKendree Coll., 1961; student Sch. Med. Tech., Meth. Hosp. of Central Ill., 1962; M.B.A., Rutgers U., 1975; m. Raymond Francis Anderson, Apr. 18, 1964. Lab. asst. McKendree Coll., 1959-61; med. technologist Methodist Hosp. Central Ill., 1962-63; hematology supr. and instr. USAF Hosp., Scott AFB, Ill., 1963-65; hematology supr. VA Hosp., East Orange, N.J., 1965-66; teaching supr. Perth Amboy (N.J.) Gen. Hosp., 1966-69, chief technologist, lab. mgr., 1969-72; adj. faculty Middlesex Coll., 1972-73; gen. supr., adminstrv. dir. lab. ops. Center for Lab. Medicine, Metuchen, N.J., 1972-73; med lab. supr., dir. tng. Schwarz-Mann div. Becton-Dickinson & Co., Orangeburg, N.Y., 1973-74; nat. ednl. coordinator, tech. cons. services specialist Roche Diagnostics, Nutley, N.J., 1974-76, product sales mgr., 1976-80, product mktg. mgr., 1980—; adj. faculty Middlesex County Coll., also med. tech. adviser council. Mem. Clin. Ligand Assay Soc., N.J. Soc. Med. Tech. (dir., past pres. 1972-73, chmn. membership com. 1979-80), Am. Soc. Med. Tech. (asso. ed. Jour. 1979-81), N.J. Blood Bank Assn., Am. Soc. Microbiologists, Alpha Mu Tau. Home: 732 Van Nest Dr Martinsville NJ 08836 Office: 340 Kingsland St Nutley NJ 07110

ANDERSON, WILMA GRACE, business development company owner; b. Oak Park, Ill., July 6, 1947; d. Ben and Grace (DeVries) VanBeveren; m. Donald Leonard Anderson, Oct. 7, 1967 (div. 1977). B.S. in Chemistry, Northwestern U., 1969, B.B.A., 1969, M.A. in Mgmt. Engring., 1973. Lab. tech. Wilson Labs., Chgo., 1965-67; office mgr. Grove Dental Assn., Downers Grove, Ill., 1967-74; practice mgr. E.G. Leary, M.D., Downers Grove, 1974-77; dir. bus. devel. Lifemark Corp., Houston, 1977-79, clinic mgr., Pediatric Med. Group, Houston, 1979-81; dir. healthcare div. Aaronson & Susman, Houston, 1981-84; prin. Anderson-VanBeveren Bus. Devel. Mgmt. Engring., Houston, 1984—. Bd. dirs. Houston Child Guidance Ctr., 1979-83. Republican. Presbyterian. Club: Profl. Women Breakfast (Houston) (gen. mgr. 1982-83, v.p. 1983-84). Avocations: tennis, skiing, scuba diving. Home and Office: 3318 Durhill St Houston TX 77025

ANDERSON, WILMA PRATHER, legal adminstr.; b. Elizabeth, W.Va., June 5, 1923; d. Hugh and Debba Lewis Prather; student W.Va. U., 1940-42, Wayne State U., 1945-46; cert. Nat. Surety Bond Sch.; m. Jack Anderson, Jan. 26, 1945. Clk., Ford Motor Co., Dearborn, Mich., 1942-45; office mgr., bookkeeper Mims & Stephens Ins., Midland, Tex., 1946-55; ins. underwriter Lee Durrell & Co., Midland, 1955-58; gen. ins. agt. Anderson Ins. Agy., Midland, 1958-71; adminstr. firm Turpin, Smith, Dyer & Saxe, Midland, 1971—. Bd. dirs. La Floreicita Day Nursery. Lic. ins. agt., Tex. Mem. Nat. Assn. Legal Adminstrs., Permian Basin Assn. Legal Adminstrs. (charter mem., v.p., pres. 1982), Am. Bar Assn. (asso.). Office: Turpin Smith Dyer and Saxe 1st Nat Bank 3d Floor Midland TX 79701

ANDERSON-JONES, MARY ERNESTINE (TEENIE) ADKINS, ornamental iron and steel manufacturing company executive; b. Adams, Tenn., July 29, 1925; d. Dudley W. and Mary Ethel (Albright) Adkins; m. Louis P. Anderson, Oct. 18, 1947 (dec. 1966); m. Jack L. Jones, Sept. 18, 1981. Grad. high sch. Adams, Tenn.; grad. Comptometer Sch., 1946, Watkins Inst., 1963, Jo Susan Modeling Sch., 1984. Mem. office staff B.F. Goodrich Co., Clarksville, Tenn., 1943-48; sec., bookkeeper S. Henrichsen & Co., Springfield, Tenn., 1948-67; mem. engring. dept., sec. Nashville Bridge Co., 1967-68; office mgr., mem. sales dept. Springfield Products, Tenn., 1968-76, owner, pres., 1979—; sales rep. Belknap, Inc., Louisville, 1976-79. Mem. Springfield C. of C. Presbyterian. Club: Springfield Country (sec., treas. 1978-79, bd. dirs. 1978-85). Avocations: golf, swimming, football and basketball games, bridge, cooking and collecting recipes. Home: PO Box 594 Springfield TN 37172 Office: PO Box 268 Springfield TN 37172

ANDERSON OLIVO, MARGARET ELLEN, physiologist, educator; b. Omaha, June 17, 1941; d. Clarence Lloyd and Anita Emma (Kruse) Anderson; B.A., Augustana Coll., Sioux Falls, S.D., 1963; Ph.D. (NSF predoctoral fellow), Stanford U., 1967; m. Richard F. Olivo, Sept. 4, 1971. NIH postdoctoral fellow Harvard U., 1968-70; research asso. Lab. of Neuro-biology U. P.R., 1970-71; vis. asst. prof. Clark U., 1972; asst. prof. Bennington (Vt.) Coll., spring 1973; asst. prof. Smith Coll., Northampton, Mass., 1973-79, asso. prof. dept. biol. scis., 1979-85, prof., 1985—. NIH research grantee, 1974-86. Mem. Soc. for Neuro-sci., Soc. Gen. Physiologists, Biophys. Soc., Soc. Am. Zoologists. Office: Dept Biol Sci Smith College Northampton MA 01063

ANDES, JOAN KEENEN, information processing company executive; b. Clarksburg, W.Va., Apr. 23, 1930; d. Ree Martin and Mary Ruth (Pyle) Groghan; m. William Anderson Keenen, Oct. 15, 1949 (div. 1969); children—Paula Annette Keenen Skelton, William Ree Keenen; 1 foster child, Donald Monroe Dreyer; m. Ralph Paul Andes, Sept. 29, 1976. Pvt. sec. State Capitol, Charleston, W.Va., 1948-49; statis. typist various acctg. offices, Beaumont, Tex., 1949-60; owner Machine Acctg. and Computing, Beaumont, 1960-70, Automated Enterprises Keypunch Sch., 1962-72; pres. Applied Data Processing, Beaumont, 1970-83; owner Applied Info. Processing, Beaumont, 1983—. Active Better Bus. Bur., Beaumont C. of C., Democratic Party, Westgate Youth Group, 1985-86. Mem. Data Processing Mgmt. Assn. (pres. 1972-73, 80, awards chmn. 1985-86), Nat. Assn. Female Execs., Nat. Fedn. Ind. Bus. Republican. Mem. Ch. of Christ. Avocations: counted cross stitch; collecting Coke memorabilia; coin collecting; skiing. Home: 1410 Marshall Pl Beaumont TX 77706 Office: Applied Info Processing 855 IH 10 South Suite 135 Beaumont TX 77701

ANDINO-MONTES, JULIA MARGARITA, laboratory executive; b. Santurce, P.R., Mar. 31, 1954; d. Cruz and Aurora (Montes) Andino-Rivera. B.A. cum laude, U. P.R., 1975; M.S.W., Columbia U., 1981. Social worker, supr. Social Service Dept., San Juan, P.R., 1981-82; quality circles facilitator Westinghouse Co., Toa Baja Complex P.R., 1982-84; sr. facilitator problem solving groups quality control dept. Wang Labs., Juncos, P.R., 1984, with orgnl. devel. dept., 1984—; cons. Resources Devel. Assocs., San Juan, 1983, Massos Morales & Assocs., 1983. Sec. to bd. dirs. San Mateo Condominium Adminstrn., San Juan. Mem. Nat. Assn. Social Workers, Internat. Assn. Quality Circles, Colegio de Trabajadores Sociales de P.R. (dir. 1981-82) (chmn. occupational social work com. 1984—). Democrat. Roman Catholic. Home: 1625 Condominio San Mateo Apt 5D Santurce PR 00912 Office: Wang Labs of PR Inc Call Box FF Juncos PR 00666

ANDRE, BABETTE YVONNE, flight instructor, media consultant, publisher, pilot; b. San Francisco, Jan. 26, 1942; d. Leo Fred and Dorothy (Fisher) Andre. B.A. in Polit. Sci., U. Calif.-Berkeley, 1963; postgrad. San Francisco State Coll., 1966, U. Colo., Denver, 1970. Cert. tchr., Calif., Hawaii, N.Y.; cert. flight and ground instr., FAA. Peace Corps vol., Bafoussam, Cameroun, Africa, 1963-65; French tchr. Punahou Acad., Honolulu, 1966-68; pub. info. officer Commn. Community Relations City and County of Denver, 1970-71, info. writer, 1973-78; traffic reporter Sta. KOA-AM, Denver, 1978, Sta. KHOW Sky Spy, 1982; mem. faculty dept. aerospace sci. Met. State Coll., Denver, 1975-80; pub. AiReporter, Wings West Mag.; gold seal flight instr.; pub. relations/advt. cons. Active various social agys. and programs, including Head Start. Contbr. articles to Colo. Bus., Rocky Mountain News. Author and photographer various informational city publs. Accident prevention counselor FAA, 1982—. Mem. Colo. Flight Instrs. Assn., Aircraft Owners and Pilots Assn., CAP, Colo. Pilots Assn., 99's, Alpha Eta Rho. Clubs: Aspen Air Flying, PC Flyers, Denver Press. Home: 89 Sherman St Denver CO 80203 Office: Wings West Mag Jeffco Air Bldg B8 Jefferson County Airport Broomfield CO 80020

ANDREAS, JOYCE KAY, musician, conductor; b. Cedar Rapids, Iowa, June 27, 1940; d. Louis Frederick and Leoma Bernice (Shellhammer) Pech; B.Mus.Ed. cum laude, Morningside Coll., 1962; M.A. magna cum laude, U. Iowa, 1968; m. Reuben Peter Andreas, June 21, 1963; children—David Glenn, Jonathan Peter, Marc Louis. Tchr. music, Pasadena (Calif.) City Schs., 1962-63; violinist, violist with orchs. including Pasadena, Oklahoma City, Wichita Falls, Tex., Cedar Rapids, Sioux City, Iowa, Ridgewood, N.J., San Gabriel, Calif., Irvine, Calif., Pacific Symphony, Calif., Long Beach, Calif.; tchr. music Eastern Christian Schs., North Haledon, N.J., 1970-77; music dir., condr. Saddleback Community Symphony Orch., Saddleback Community Coll., Mission Viejo, Calif., 1977—; Suzuki Festival coordinator N.J., 1971-77, Orange County, Calif., 1977-84. Sioux City Symphony scholar, Aspen Music Festival, 1960. Mem. Am. String Tchrs. Assn. (founder chpt. Saddleback Coll. 1980), Music Tchrs. Assn. Calif. (state chmn. strings/cert. merit program), Music Educators Nat. Conf., Suzuki Assn. Americas, Suzuki Music Assn. Calif., Nat. Sch. Orch. Assn. Mem. Christian Reformed Ch. Address: PO Box 2000-61 Mission Viejo CA 92692

ANDREN, LINNEA KATHY, interior plantscaping company executive; b. Point Pleasant, N.J., July 21, 1950; d. Carl Walter and Eva Helen (ReMillong) Andren. B.S. in Elem. Edn., Trenton State Coll., 1972. Owner, Plants by Design, Upper Black Eddy, Pa., 1975—. Mem. Interior Plantscape Assn., Am. Hort. Soc. Avocations: sailing; snow skiing; wind sailing; scuba diving. Home: PO Box 72 Firehouse Ln Upper Black Eddy PA 18972 Office: Plants by Design Singley Rd Upper Black Eddy PA 18972

ANDRESS, CHARLOTTE FRANCES, emerita social work executive; b. Birmingham, Ala., Apr. 22, 1910; d. Francis Samuel and Tommie (Daniel) Andress; B.S., Birmingham-So. Coll., 1932; A.M. in Social Service Adminstrn., U. Chgo., 1943. Asst. dir. Girl Scouts Am., Birmingham, 1932-35, exec. dir., Nashville, 1935-41; instr. Loyola U., Chgo., 1942-45; dir. U.S.O., Augusta, Ga., 1945-48; asst. dir. YWCA, Chgo., 1948-50, exec. dir., St. Louis, 1950-53; dir. group work, youth service Fedn. Protestant Welfare Agys., N.Y.C., 1953-59; exec. dir. Inwood House, N.Y.C., 1959-82, exec. dir. emerita, 1982—. Chmn. adv. bd. Jefferson Park Center, 1959-65; nat. camp com. Camp Fire Girls, 1959-68; bd. Social Work Vocat. Bur., 1961-66; dir. Trail Blazer Camps, 1957-83, chmn. personnel com., 1982-83; mem. Camp Sharparoon com. N.Y.C. Mission Soc., 1960-76, mem. personnel com., 1962-66; adv. bd. social welfare Meth. Ch., 1958-63; mem. United Meth. Bd. Missions, 1964-72; bd. Bethel Meth. Home, 1965-72, sec. bd., 1966-72; women's com. Japan Internat. Christian U. Found., 1969—, exec. com., 1983; adv. bd. Isabella Thoburn Coll., 1967-75; chmn. nat. com. Wesleyan Service Guild, 1970-72; trustee Christ United Meth. Ch., 1975-84; trustee Martha Mertz Found., 1979—, sec., 1981—, v.p., 1983—; bd. United Meth. City Soc., 1980—. Named Disting. Alumna Birmingham So. Coll., 1981. Cert. social worker, N.Y. Mem. Nat. Assn. Social Workers (sec. bd. N.Y.C. chpt. 1958-60, chmn. personnel standards and practices 1960-69, 73-74), Acad. Cert. Social Workers, Nat. Conf. on Social Welfare, Bethany Deaconess Soc. (dir. 1971—, sec. 1974-76, pres. 1976—), Internat. Conf. Social Welfare, N.Y. Deaconess Assn. (dir. 1969—, sec. 1971—), Soc. Women Geographers, 1982—, Gamma Phi Beta. Democrat. Club: Cosmopolitan. Home: 3030 Park Ave Bridgeport CT 06604

ANDREW, BARBARA JEAN, testing organization executive, educational psychologist; b. Hollywood, Calif., Aug. 9, 1943; d. Orin Henry and Clara Belle (Morris) A. A.B., UCLA, 1965, M.A., 1966; Ph.D., USC, 1970. Instr. humanities div. Ventura Coll., Calif., 1966-68; research assoc. U. So. Calif. Sch. Medicine, Los Angeles, 1968-70, asst. prof. med. edn., 1970-72; dir. dept. allied med. evaluation Nat. Bd. Med. Examiners, Phila., 1972-74, dir. dept. research and devel., 1974-80, v.p. instl. devel. and research, 1980—; cons. WHO, 1972, U.S. Dept. Labor, 1975-76, Am. Bd. Emergency Physicians, Lansing, Mich., 1978-80, Nat. Bd. Examiners in Optometry, Washington, 1983-84. Author book chpts. Contbr. articles to profl. jours. Bd. dirs. Nat. Fund for Med. Edn., New Haven, 1985—; corp. mem. U.S. Com. for UNICEF, N.Y., 1984—; mem. ednl. adv. com. Nat. Fund for Med. Edn., 1978-84; pres. Phila. area com. for UNICEF, 1982—. Recipient Recognition award Assn. Physician's Assts. Program, 1980. Fellow Coll. Physicians of Phila.; mem. Assn. Am. Med. Colls., Nat. Council on Measurement in Edn., Am. Mktg. Assn., N.Am. Soc. for Strategic Planning. Office: Nat Bd Med Examiners 3930 Chestnut St Philadelphia PA 19104

ANDREW, JANE HAYES, ballet manager; b. Phila., Jan. 1, 1947; d. David Powell and Vivian Muriel (Saeger) Hayes; A.B., Barnard Coll., 1968; cert. Harvard Arts Mgmt. Seminar, 1972; m. Brian David Andrew, June 14, 1977; 1 son, Kevin Hayes. Theatre mgr. Minor Latham Playhouse, Barnard Coll., N.Y.C., 1970-74; co. mgr. Houston Ballet, 1974-77; editor Cultural Directory, Greater Phila. Cultural Alliance, 1977; co. mgr. Ballet West, Salt Lake City, 1978-83; gen. mgr. Pacific NW Ballet, Seattle, 1983—. Dorothy D. Spivack grantee, 1973. Club: Zonta. Office: Pacific Northwest Ballet 4649 Sunnyside Ave N Seattle Wa 98103

ANDREWS, ANN M., physical therapist; b. Scranton, Pa., Oct. 12, 1948; d. Charles and Virginia (Mullen) Speicher; m. Martin F. Andrews, Aug. 4, 1978; children—Martin and David. B.S. in Chemistry, Marywood Coll., 1970; cert. of proficiency in phys. therapy U. Pa., 1971. Pvt. practice phys. therapy, Jacksonville, Fla., 1977-78; staff phys. therapist Allied Services Rehab. Ctr., Scranton, Pa., 1971-77; contractor Allied Services Home Health, Scranton, 1985—; dir. phys. therapy St. Joseph's Hosp., Carbondale, Pa., 1978—; cons. YMCA, Carbondale, 1982—; adv. bd. U. Scranton Phys. Theraphy Program, 1980-81. Mem. Am. Phys. Therapy Assn. Democrat. Roman Catholic. Avocations: golf; tennis; racquetball. Address: 1 Hendrick Ln Carbondale PA 18407

ANDREWS, CAROL CORDER, political scientist, educator; b. Wilmington, Del.; d. Kenneth Wilson and Aurelia Moreland (Speer) Corder; B.A. (Gen. Motors nat. scholar), Duke U., 1960; Certificat d'Etudes Politiques, Institut d'Etudes Politiques, U. Paris (France), 1961; M.A. (East Asian Inst. fellow), Columbia U., 1964, Ph.D., 1978; postgrad. Inter-Univ. Program for Chinese Lang. Tng., Taipei, Taiwan, 1966-67; div.; 1 son, Ethan Andrews. Research contract for study Taiwanese-Mainlander polit. relations Brookings Instn., Washington, 1967; research Kuomintang Party Archives, Taichung, Taiwan, 1967-68; asst. prof. polit. sci. Holy Names Coll., Oakland, Calif., 1970-79, assoc. prof., 1979-81, chairperson dept. history and polit. sci., 1979-80; editor, writer, researcher, 1982—. Bd. dirs. Alameda County chpt. UN Assn. U.S.A., World Without War Council, 1979—. Recipient Contemporary China Studies Com. award, 1967-70. Nat. Def. Fgn. Lang. fellow, 1962-64, 65-67. Mem. Am. Polit. Sci. Assn., Women's Caucus for Polit. Sci., Assn. for Asian Studies, AAUP, Internat. Platform Assn., Phi Beta Kappa. Democrat. Episcopalian. Club: Commonwealth of Calif. Contbr. articles to profl. jours. Home: 612 Vincente Ave Berkeley CA 94707

ANDREWS, CAROLYN, broadcasting company sales executive; b. Ticonderoga, N.Y., Aug. 30, 1948; d. Norman Bruce and Ruth (Adams) A.; student U. East Anglia, Norwich, Eng., 1968-69; A.B., Mt. Holyoke Coll., 1970; M.B.A., Simmons Coll., 1975; m. James Garrett Walley, May 17, 1980. Recruiting rep. Seven Coll. Conf., Northampton, Mass., 1970-71, co-dir. conf., 1971-72; asst. dir. admissions Emma Willard Sch., Troy, N.Y., 1972-74; spls. project analyst, Treasury, CBS, Inc., N.Y.C., 1975-77; account exec. trainee CBS TV Network, N.Y.C., 1977-78. account exec. nat. sales, 1978-80, account exec. eastern sales, 1980-84, v.p. spls. and miniseries sales, 1984—. Vol. career counselor CBS, Mt. Holyoke Coll. Mem. Internat. Radio and TV Soc., Mus. Modern Art. Club: Mt. Holyoke, N.Y. Office: 51 W 52d St New York NY 10019

ANDREWS, ELAINE MARIE, judge; b. San Francisco, Apr. 19, 1951; d. Charles F. and Cecilia R. (Cull) A.; m. Roger W. Du Brock, Apr. 25, 1981; 1 child, Francesca; stepchildren—Christopher, Andrew, Fiona. B.A. in Psychology and Criminology, U. Calif.-Berkeley, 1973; J.D., Golden Gate U., 1976. Bar: Calif., 1976, Alaska, 1977. Atty. Alaska Jud. Council, Anchorage, 1976-78, Pub. Defender's Office, Anchorage, 1978-80; assoc. firm Lane, Powell, Ruskin, Barker and Hicks, Anchorage, 1980-81; asst. presiding judge Dist. Ct. Alaska, Anchorage, 1981-85; mem. Alaska Commn. on Jud. Conduct, 1983—. Mayor's Mem. Task Force on Drunk Driving, Anchorage, 1983-84; mem. Chem. People Task Force, 1983-84. Mem. Calif. Bar Assn., Alaska Bar Assn. (com. on bar rolls and elections, 1978-84), Nat. Assn. Women Judges, Anchorage Assn. Women Lawyers (pres., 1979-88), Nat. Assn. Women Lawyers. Club: Soroptimists (Anchorage). Office: Dist Ct 941 W 4th St Anchorage AK 99501

ANDREWS, JEAN, author, artist, educator; b. Kingsville, Tex., Dec. 23, 1923; d. Herbert and Katharine (Smith) Andrews; B.S., U. Tex., 1944; postgrad. So. Meth. U., 1957-58, U. Corpus Christi, 1960-61; M.S., A. and I. U., 1966; postgrad. Tex. A. and M. U., 1970-71; Ph.D., N. Tex. State U., 1976; m. Robert F. Wasson, May 5, 1944 (div. May 1969); children—Robert F., Jean A. (dec.); m. 2d, C.B. Smith, Mar. 8, 1980. Exhibited in 25 one man shows Tex.

Tech. U., 1956, Witte Mus., San Antonio, 1965, Bright Shawl Gallery, San Antonio, 1966, Little Theater, Midland, Tex., 1963, Ame./Gallery, N.Y.C., 1964, McNamarra-O'Connor Mus., Victoria, Tex., 1963, 67, A. and I. U., Kingsville, Tex., 1966; finalist Corcoran Biennial, 1965; Dallas; tchr. art Richard King High Sch., Corpus Christi, Tex., 1967-80; Master judge Nat. Council State Garden Clubs; mem. departmental vis. com. botany U. Tex.-Austin; chmn. edn. com. Sci. Adv. Council, U. Tex.-Austin. Bd. dirs. Planned Parenthood, Austin; sponsor Austin Symphony Assn., Laguna Gloria Art Mus.; bd. dirs. Art Mus. of S. Tex., Corpus Christi, 1960-63; co-chmn. Friends of Women's Studies, U. Tex.-Austin; mem. Pres.'s Council N. Tex. State U.; mem. Chancellor's Council U. Tex.; mem. Padre Island Biol. Survey, U.S. Dept. Interior, 1970-76. Jean Andrews Day declared by Mayor Corpus Christi, 1971; endowed Jean Andrews Smith professorships in human nutrition and tropical and econ. botany U. Tex., Austin; Alice G.K. Kleberg grantee, 1969; Caesar Kleberg Wildlife Fedn. grantee; research prin. grant Dallas Fashion Group N. Tex. State U. Mem. Am. Malacol. Union, Tex. Tchrs. Assn., D.A.R., Colonial Dames VII Century, Coastal Bend Shell Club (hon. life), Nat. Pepper Conf., Tex. Pepper Conf., Houston Conchological Assn., Zeta Tau Alpha. Episcopalian. Author: Sea Shells of the Texas Coast, 1971; Shells and Shores of Texas, 1977; Texas Shells: A Field Guide, 1981; Peppers: The Domesticated Capsicums, 1984. Home: Austin TX

ANDREWS, JILLIAN MARIE, shoe manufacturing executive; b. Eugene, Oreg., Sept. 24, 1958; d. David Neil and Beverly Diane (Brown) A. Student Portland Community Coll., U. Oreg. Dept. mgr. Nordstrom, Seattle, also Portland, Oreg., 1977-79; asst. mgr. Red Robin Burger-Emporium, Portland, 1979; catering mgr. Pike's Vintage Shop, Lake Oswego, Oreg., 1980-82; v.p. ops. L.J. Simone Shoes, Bklyn., 1983—. Mem. Nat. Assn. Female Execs., Alpha Omega Pi. Democrat. Avocations: travel; reading; hiking; cross country skiing. Home: 205 W 10th St #6A New York NY 10014 Office: L J Simone Shoes 810 Humboldt St Brooklyn NY 11222

ANDREWS, JUDITH LYNNE, financial services co. exec.; b. Chgo., July 7, 1948; d. Fred Woodrow and LaVerne Mildred (Johnson) Andrews; B.A. in Econs., So. Ill. U., 1971; M.B.A. in Fin. Mgmt., Ill. Benedictine Coll., 1979. Acctg. mgr. McDonald's Corp., Chgo., 1973-78, Wickes Corp., Chgo., 1978-79; dir. fin. Carte Blanche Corp., Los Angeles, 1979-82; mgr. fin. Crowley Maritime Corp., Long Beach, Calif., 1982-84; mgr. planning Geneva Corp., Santa Ana, Calif., 1984—. Office: 2923 Pullman St Santa Ana CA 92705

ANDREWS, JULIA COVELL, data communications marketing product executive; b. Prince Georges County, Md., Oct. 26, 1957; d. Richard Erwing Snyder and Nancy Mae (Covell) Miller; m. Mickey Wilder Andrews, Sept. 1, 1984. B.S. in Mktg. and Computer Sci., Fla. Atlantic U., 1981. Communication Systems rep. AT&T Info. Systems, Fort Lauderdale, Fla., 1982-84; product specialist Racal-Milgo, Sunrise, Fla., 1984—. Episcopalian. Avocations: reading; camping; waterskiing; racquet ball. Office: Racal-Milgo 1601 N Harrison Pkwy Sunrise FL 33323

ANDREWS, JULIE, actress, singer; b. Walton-on-Thames, Eng., Oct. 1, 1935; d. Edward C. and Barbara Wells; studied with pvt. tutors; studied voice with Mme. Stiles-Allen; m. Tony Walton May 10, 1959 (div.); 1 dau., Emma; m. 2d, Blake Edwards, 1969. Debut as singer Hippodrome, London, 1947; appeared in pantomime Cinderella, London, 1953; appeared Broadway prodn. The Boy Friend, N.Y.C., 1954, My Fair Lady, 1956-60, Camelot, 1960-62; films include Mary Poppins (Acad. award for best actress, 1964), 1964. The Americanization of Emily, 1964, Torn Curtain, 1966. The Sound of Music, 1966, Hawaii, 1966. Thoroughly Modern Millie, 1967, Star!, 1968. Darling Lili, 1970. The Tamarind Seed, 1973, 10, 1979, Little Miss Marker, 1980. S.O.B., 1981, Victor/Victoria, 1982, The Man Who Loved Women, 1983; made TV debut in High Tor, 1956; star TV series the Julie Andrews Hour, 1972-73, also spls. Recipient N.Y. Drama Critics award My Fair Lady, 1955-56; Golden Globe award Hollywood Fgn. Press Assn., 1964, 65; named World Film Favorite (female), 1967. Author: (as Julie Edwards) Mandy, 1971; The Last of the Really Great Whangdoodles, 1974. Office: care Triad Artists Inc Monica Blvd 16th Floor Los Angeles CA 90067*

ANDREWS, MARY ELLEN, public relations exec.; b. Corning, N.Y., Nov. 10, 1931; d. Edwin Hardy and Edith Marie (Lowe) Ober; B.A., Mt. Holyoke Coll., 1953; postgrad. Syracuse U., 1974-75; m. James A. Reynolds, Jan. 28, 1962; m. 2d, Richard Hale Andrews, July 14, 1970; 1 dau., Amy Elizabeth; stepchildren—R. Hale, D. Gage, Philadelphia M. French/English translator Les Ateliers de Construction Electrique de Charleroi, N.Y.C., 1954-55, French Nat. R.R., N.Y.C., 1955-56; public relations asst. Steuben Glass, N.Y.C., 1956-64; French/English translator Corning (N.Y.) Internat. Corp., 1964-67; research asst. Corning Glass Wks. Found., 1967-70; French/English translator Corning Internat. Corp., 1972-75; office mgr. Beak Assos., Ithaca, N.Y., 1975-77; corporate relations staff, devel. office, Cornell U., Ithaca, 1977-79; staff asst. evening programs, Elmira Coll., N.Y., 1979-80, dir. public relations, 1980—, advisor student newspaper, The Octagon, 1980—. Bd. dirs. Elmira Symphony and Choral Soc., 1982—. Mem. Public Relations Soc. Am., Council for Advancement and Support of Edn. Democrat. Presbyterian. Editor-in-chief Campus Mag., 1980—. Home: RD 2 Old Corning Rd Watkins Glen NY 14891 Office: Elmira Coll Park Pl Elmira NY 14901

ANDREWS, OLA JEAN, office administrator; b. El Dorado, Ark., Dec. 9, 1929; d. Joseph Henry and Leceola (Tobin) A. Sec., Oakland Dept. Health Service, 1958-69, supr. Dept. Social Services, 1968-78; music. dir. Christliches Zentrum, Berlin, Germany, 1978-81; exec. sec. Harsh Investment Co., Oakland, 1981-82; Wang system adminstr. San Francisco Dept. Treasury, 1982—; pres. Believers, Inc., Oakland, 1971—, fund raiser, 1972-78; disc jockey Sta. KRE, Berkeley, Calif., 1973-78; instr. Prison Fellowship, Washington, 1983—; office mgr. Mass. Indemnity & Life Ins. Co., Atlanta, 1985—. Recipient awards KQED-TV, San Francisco, 1974, San Francisco Dept. Treasury, 1985. Grantee Sta. KDIA, Oakland, 1962-65. Mem. Exec. Females, Encore. Democrat. Avocations: travel, piano. Office: Believers Inc PO Box 19102 Oakland CA 94619

ANDREWS, SUSAN LYNN, insurance agent, marketing specialist; b. Los Angeles, Feb. 1, 1962; d. John Morton Andrews and Charmaine Mary (Wells) Andrews Gordon. Student U. Colo., Boulder, 1980-83. Dir. Gordon Gen. Ins., Los Angeles, 1978-84; mortgage specialist Am. Internat. Group, Los Angeles and N.Y.C., 1984—; U.S. agt. confidential program Bayly Martin and Fay, Los Angeles, 1986—. Vol. City of West Hollywood City Hall, Calif., 1986. Mem. Am. Mgmt. Assn., Hispanic Acad. of Media Arts and Scis., Calif. Assn. of Affiliated Agys., Am. Film Inst., Nat. Assn. Female Execs., Kappa Kappa Gamma. Buddhist. Avocations: tennis; nordic skiing; travel; art deco; theatre.

ANDREWS, THEODORA ANNE, librarian; b. Carroll County, Ind., Oct. 14, 1921; d. Harry Floyd and Margaret Grace (Walter) Ulrey; B.S. with distinction, Purdue U., 1953; M.S., U. Ill., 1955; m. Robert William Andrews, July 18, 1940 (div. 1946); 1 son, Martin Harry. Asst. reference librarian Purdue U., West Lafayette, Ind., 1955-56, pharmacy librarian, instr., 1956-60, pharmacy librarian, asst. prof., 1960-65, pharmacy librarian, assoc. prof. library sci., 1965-71, prof. library sci., pharmacy librarian, 1971-79, prof. library sci., pharmacy, nursing and health scis. librarian, 1979—. Mem. Purdue Women's Caucus, 1973—, v.p., 1975-76, pres., 1976-77; mem. Internat. Women's Yr. Regional Planning Com., 1977; del. Ind. Gov.'s Conf. Libraries and Info. Services, 1978. U. Ill. grad. fellow, 1954-55. Mem. Spl. Libraries Assn. (John H. Moriarty award Ind. chpt. 1972), ALA, Med. Library Assn., AAUP, Am. Assn. Colls. Pharmacy, Kappa Delta Pi, Delta Rho Kappa. Baptist. Author: A Bibliography of the Socioeconomic Aspects of Medicine, 1975; A Bibliography of Drug Abuse Including Alcohol and Tobacco, 1977; A Bibliography of Drug Abuse, Supplement 1977-1980, 1981; Bibliography on Herbs, Herbal Remedies and Natural Foods, 1982; Substance Abuse Materials for School Libraries, an Annotated Bibliography, 1985; Guide to the Literature of Pharmacy and the Pharmaceutical Sciences, 1986; sect. editor Advances in Alcohol and Substance Abuse, 1981—; contbr. articles to profl. jours. Office: Pharmacy Bldg Purdue U West Lafayette IN 47907

ANDRIKOPOULOS, BONNIE J., oil and gas lease broker, consultant; b. Loup City, Nebr., Feb. 22, 1935; d. Delmar C. and Gladys B. (Haddix) Edson; m. Anthony Andrikopoulos, Feb. 8, 1959 (div. Feb. 1965); children—Kari Kay, Toni Lynn; m. W. Ted Schuett, Sept 9, 1984. B.S. in Nursing, U. Wyo., 1958. Surg. nurse Meml. Hosp., Casper, Wyo., 1958-59; oil and gas lease broker A. G. Andrikopoulas Oil Co., Cheyenne, Wyo., 1960-65; ind. oil and gas lease broker, Denver, 1965—; prin. Bonnie Andrikopoulas, cons., Denver, 1984—. Co-editor conf. procs.: Abortion in the 70's, 1976. Vice chairperson Colo. Commn. on Women, Denver, 1974-77; mem. Colo. Supreme Ct. Nominating Com., Denver, 1976-77; treas. Colo. Women's Polit. Caucus, Denver, 1972-76; bd. dirs. Colo. Blue Cross-Blue Shield, Denver, 1976-85. Mem. Leadership Denver Alumni Assn., Colo. Assn. Profl. Saleswomen, Colo. Speakers Assn., NOW. Republican. Avocations: racquetball; skiing; ballroom dancing; art shows; reading. Home and Office: 635 Ash Denver CO 80220

ANDRUS, KAREN ROGENE, county assessor; b. Alliance, Nebr., Apr. 24, 1942; d. Kenneth Lyle and Marie Blanche (Coleman) Bachelor; m. Ronald John Andrus, June 9, 1962; children—Kimberly, John. Dental asst. Dental Office, Valentine, Nebr., 1961-62; deputy, clerk Cherry County, Valentine, 1964-68; clk., Brown County, Ainsworth, Nebr., 1973-79, county assessor, 1979—. Mem. Nebr. Assessor's Assn., Ne. Assessor's Assn. Office: Brown County Assessor 148 4th St Ainsworth NE 69210

ANDRUZZI, ELLEN ADAMSON, nurse, marital and family therapist; b. Colon, Panama, Dec. 15, 1917 (parents Am. citizens); d. Charles and Annie Isabel (Grinder) Adamson; m. Francis Victor Andruzzi, May 28, 1941; children—Barbara F., Francis C., Judith E., Antonette T., John J. B.S. in Pub. Health Nursing, Cath. U. Am., 1947, M.S. in Nursing, 1951. Cert. clin. specialist, psychiat. nurse. Pub. health nurse Washington Health Dept., 1942-44; instr. psychiat. nursing St. Elizabeth's Hosp., Washington, 1948-57; dir. nursing Glenn Dale Hosp., Md., 1961-67; chief mental health nurse dept. human resources D.C. Govt., 1967-73; cons. NIMH, HHS, Rockville, Md., 1973-81; marital and family therapist TA Assocs., Camp Springs, Md., 1973—; assoc. GWITA, Rockville, 1975-79; instr. Charles County Community Coll., LaPlata, Md., 1976-78, Prince George Community Coll., Largo, Md., 1973-81; assoc. Ctr. for Study of Human Systems, Chevy Chase, Md., 1976—. Author chpts. in books. Dist. co-capt. Prince Georgians for Glendening, Prince George County, Md., 1985-86; chmn. plan devel. com. So. Md. Health Systems Agy., Clinton, 1984—, sec. governing body, 1978-80; chmn. Mental Health Adv. Com. Prince George County, Cheverly, Md., 1983-85. Recipient Disting. Nurse award St. Elizabeths Hosp., 1985, Paula Hamburger Vol. award Mental Health Assn. Md., 1985, Recognition of Service award Md. Nurses Assn., 1983. Fellow Am. Acad. Nursing, Am. Orthopsychiat. Assn.; mem. Am. Nurses Assn., Am. Assn. for Marriage and Family Therapy (clin.), Nat. Mental Health Assn. (v.p. 1984—), Mental Health Assn. Prince George County (pres. 1974-76), Sigma Theta Tau (Kappa chpt., Excellence in Nursing award 1984). Democrat. Roman Catholic. Avocations: theatre, ballet, swimming, foreign travel. Office: TA Assocs 4904 Henderson Rd Temple Hills MD 20748

ANEMA, CHERYL LYNN, nurse; b. Chgo., Oct. 21, 1958; d. Kenneth John and Bertha (Schaap) Anema. R.N., Wesley-Passavant Sch. Nursing, 1979; B.S. in Nursing, DePaul U., 1983; postgrad. Loyola U., Chgo. R.N., Ill. Unit sec. Northwestern Meml. Hosp., Chgo., 1978-79, staff nurse, 1979-83; team supr. Ingall's Meml. Hosp., Harvey, Ill., 1984—. Mem. Am. Nurses Assn., Ill. Nurses Assn., Chgo. Nurses Assn., Critical Care Nurses Assn. Republican. Home: 16413 Betty Ln South Holland IL 60473 Office: Ingall's Meml Hosp 1 Ingalls Dr Harvey IL 60426

ANGEL, HATTIE LAVERNE, music company executive; b. Memphis, Mar. 12, 1952; d. Alvaughn and Hattie Ethel (Gordon) Dean; m. Juan Ricardo Angel, Feb. 14, 1975 (div. Apr. 1982); 1 son, Juan Ricardo. B.A., So. Ill. U., 1982. Sec., Music Factory, Inc., Memphis, 1973-76; tax examiner IRS, Memphis, 1975-76; claims clk. Social Security Adminstrn., Memphis, 1976-78; corp. dir., adminstr. Al Green Music, Inc., Memphis, 1978—; v.p., 1978—; pres., treas. Angel's Acctg. Service, Memphis, 1980-84; sec. Lee County Publ. Co., Memphis, 1983-84; cons. Concert Bookings, Inc., Birmingham, 1983—. Spl. dep. Shelby Spl. Deputies Assn., 1983; assoc. Nat. Urban League, 1983. Recipient Outstanding Achievement award Social Security Adminstrn., 1976, Outstanding Performance award IRS, 1975. Mem. NAACP. Home: 2311 Marble Ave Memphis TN 38108 Office: Al Green Music Inc PO Box 9485 Memphis TN 38118

ANGEL, PHYLLIS JEAN, financial executive; b. North Platte, Nebr., Aug. 10, 1947; d. Ralph Henry and Lucille (Bussell) Shinn; m. Lewis Worth Angel, Jan. 11, 1969 (div. 1975). A.A., North Eastern Jr. Coll., 1967; student cosmetology Mile Hi Beauty Sch., 1969. Office rep. Standard Quarter Horse Assn., Lakewood, Colo., 1967-69, info. operator Mountain Bell, Denver, 1967, sec. King Soopers Bakery, Denver, 1973, Prudential Ins. Co., Denver, 1973-76; owner/operator Phyl's Styling Salon, Sedalia, Colo., 1976-77; fin. specialist Martin Marietta, Denver, 1978—; cons. Self Images, Denver, 1973-79, Frisbie & Frisbie, Denver, 1973-80; owner A & B Enterprises, Denver, 1974-76; owner Shaklee Product Distbn., Denver, 1982—. Author: A Wolf Pup Was Born, 1983; Grandma, 1984; Wax Doll, 1984. Coach, Wagon Wheel Softball Team, Champion, Nebr., 1963-65; active Muscular Dystrophy Telethon, Littleton, Colo., 1974, Multiple Sclerosis Ride A Thon, Cheyenne, Wyo., 1975; sponsor Little League Baseball Team, Sedalia, 1976. Recipient Grand Cross of Colors, Rainbow Girls, 1965; Golden Poet award, 1985. Mem. Career Womens Assn., Internat. Platform Assn., Nat. Mus. Women in Arts Club: Square Dance. Methodist. Clubs: 4-H, Rodeo. Lodges: Order Eastern Star. Home: PO Box 620215 Littleton CO 80162

ANGELINO, DOLORES KEATING, budget analyst; b. Hackensack, N.J., May 9, 1951; d. George Joseph and Catherine Margaret (Brady) Keating; B.A. in Math., William Paterson Coll., Wayne, N.J., 1973; M.B.A., LaSalle Coll., Phila., 1984; m. Rudolph Peter Angelino, Apr. 24, 1976. Supply systems analyst U.S. Navy, Bayonne, N.J., 1973-76, fiscal acctg. asst., 1976-77, mgmt. analyst Navy Internat. Logistics Control Office, Phila., 1978-83, budget analyst, 1983—. Mem. Nat. Assn. Female Execs., Phila. Women's Network. Roman Catholic.

ANGELO, GAYLE-JEAN, research and development analyst; educator; b. Winchester, Mass., Nov. 27, 1951; d. John William and Josephine Marie (Tavano) A.; B.A. in Physics with honor, Northeastern U., 1975, M.Ed. in Curriculum and Instrn. Sci. and Math., 1978; M.S. in Applied Stats., Columbia U., 1984, postgrad., 1984—. Clin. chemist Boston Med. Lab., Inc., 1971-73; exptl. physicist Northeastern U., 1975-76; tchr. natural scis., head sci. dept. Girls Cath. High Sch., Malden, Mass., 1977-78; research and teaching asst. Columbia U., N.Y.C., 1978-80, research assoc., 1982-83; research scientist Air Force Rocket Propulsion Lab., Edwards AFB, Calif., 1980-82; instr. math. Golden Gate U., Cerro Coso Community Coll., 1981-82, Columbia U., N.Y.C., 1982-83; instr. chemistry North Shore Community Coll., 1985-86. Served with USAF, 1980-82; mem. Air N.G., 1982-85. Decorated Air Force Commendation; cert. secondary tchr., Mass.; cert. community coll. tchr., Calif. Mem. Am. Assn. Physics Tchrs., Am. Phys. Soc., Am. Soc. Quality Control, Am. Statis. Assn., Assn. for Women in Sci., Inst. Mgmt. Scis., Nat. Council Tchrs. Math., Nat. Sci. Tchrs. Assn., N.Y. Acad. Scis., Ops. Research Soc. Am., Sch. Sci. and Math. Assn., Soc. Coll. Sci. Tchrs., Mensa, Sigma Xi, Phi Delta Kappa, Sigma Pi Sigma. Sigma Delta Epsilon, Kappa Delta Pi. Home: 113 Butler Ave Wakefield MA 01880 Office: Research and Devel Dept Varian/Extrion Div Blackburn Indsl Park Gloucester MA 01930

ANGLE, SHARON ANN, interior director; b. Fairland, Okla., Sept. 8, 1946; d. Bernie and Thelma Louise (Wilmoth) Pennington; cert. Paralegal Inst. Ariz., 1979; student N.E. Okla. A&M Coll., Miami, 1980-82; 1 son, David Scott. Service rep. Gen. Telephone Co., Belvidere, Ill., 1968-69, bus. office supr., 1969; sec. to dir. adult edn. Rock Valley Community Coll., Rockford, Ill., 1970-73; legal sec. Hall, Stockwell & Wooley, Miami, OK, 1975; legal asst. law firm Garrette & Stockwell, Miami, 1976-83, Brown & Brown, 1983—; owner, operator Wallpapering, Unltd., The Classic Touch, 1984—; sec. Ray Son, Inc., Miami, 1980—, Maverick Enterprises, 1980—. Mem. adv. bd. N.E. Okla. A&M Coll., 1980—. Club: Hi-Noon Bus. and Profl. Women's (pres. 1979-80). Home: 1401 13th NE Miami OK 74354 Office: 122 N Main Miami OK

ANGOTTI, CATHERINE MARIE, consulting nutritionist; b. Arlington, Va., Nov. 9, 1946; d. Frank William and Catherine Jeannette (Kolakoski) Poos; B.S., James Madison U., 1968; R.D., Med. Coll. Va., 1969; postgrad. Va. Poly. Inst. and State U., 1975; m. John Joseph Angotti, Sept. 15, 1973; 1 dau., Heather Jeannette. Home economist Washington Gas Light Co., 1968; clin. dietitian Fairfax Hosp., Fairfax, Va., 1969-73; pvt. practice as nutrition cons., Va., 1972—; nutrition cons. Manassas (Va.) Manor Nursing Home, 1973-74, Bio-Tech., Inc., Falls Church, Va., 1977-78; nutrition surveyor JWK Internat., Annandale, Va., 1980-81; nutrition cons. NASA, Washington, 1977—; pres. Nutrition Cons., Inc., 1980—; nutrition lectr. state and nat. meetings. Del. for Va. Dietetic Assn. to Va. Council on State Legis., 1974-76; mem. Com. for Pub. of Regional Diet Manual, 1971-73. Food Service Execs. awards scholar, 1967; Mem. Am. Dietetic Assn. (named outstanding Young Dietitian of Yr. 1975, state rep. for nutrition services payment system 1984—), Va. Assn. Allied Health Profls. (del. 1974-79, bd. dirs. 1975-77), Cons. Nutritionists (Va. state coordinator 1976-79), D.C. Dietetic Assn., Va. Dietetic Assn. (exec. bd. 1974-76, 82—, legis. chmn. 1974-76), No. Dist. Dietetic Assn. (exec. bd. 1970—, treas. 1980-82, pres. 1983-84, chmn. nominating com. 1984-85), Fairfax County Nutrition Com., Cons. Nutritionists of the Chesapeake Bay Area (nominating com. 1983), Nat. Assn. Female Execs., Soc. for Nutrition Edn. Democrat. Roman Catholic. Contbr. articles to profl. jours. Home: 2727 Oak Valley Dr Vienna VA 22180 Office: 10721 Main St Fairfax VA 22030

ANGUIANO, LUPE, business executive; b. La Junta, Colo., Mar. 12, 1929; d. Jose and Rosario (Gonzalez) A.; student Ventura (Calif.) Jr. Coll., 1948, Victory Noll Jr. Coll., Huntington, Ind., 1949-52, Marymount Coll., Palos Verdes, Calif., 1958-59, Calif. State U., Los Angeles, 1965-67; M.A., Antioch-Putney-Yellow Springs, Ohio, 1978. S.W. regional dir. NAACP Legal Def. and Ednl. Fund, Los Angeles, 1965-69; civil rights specialist HEW, Washington, 1969-73; S.W. regional dir. Nat. Council Catholic Bishops, Region X, San Antonio, 1973-77; pres. Nat. Women's Employment and Edn., Inc., San Antonio, 1978-81; pres. Lupe Anguiano & Assocs., 1981—; cons. Tex. Dept. Human Resources, Dept. Labor, Women's Bur.; proposal reader U.S. Office Edn.-Women's Equity Act; mem. Tex. Adv. Council on Tech.-Vocat. Edn. Calif. del. White House Conf. on Status Mexican-Ams. in U.S., 1967; founding mem. policy council Nat. Women's Polit. Caucus, from 1971; Tex. and nat. del. Internat. Women's Year, 1976-77; chmn. Nat. Women's Polit. Caucus Welfare Reform Task Force, from 1977; co-chmn. Nat. Peace Acad. Campaign, 1977-81; founder, bd. dirs. Nat. Chicana Found., Inc., 1971-78; bd. dirs. Calif. Council Children and Youth, 1967, Rio Grande Fedn. Chicano Health Centers, S.W. Rural States, 1974-76, Women's Lobby, Washington, 1974-77, Rural Am. Women, Washington, from 1978, Small Bus. Council Greater San Antonio; mem. Pres.'s Council on Pvt. Sector Initiatives, 1983. Recipient Community award Coalition Mexican-Am. Orgns., 1967, Outstanding Service award Washington, 1968, Thanksgiving award Boys' Club, 1976, Outstanding Service award Tex. Women's Polit. Caucus, 1977, Liberty Bell award San Antonio Young Lawyers, 1981, Vista award for exceptional service to end poverty, 1980, Headliner award San Antonio Women in Communications, 1978, Woman of Year award Tex. Women's Polit. Caucus, 1978; named Outstanding Woman of Yr., Los Angeles County, 1972; Woman of the 80s Ms. mag., 1980; Wonder Woman Found. award, 1982; Advocate of Yr., San Antonio SBA, 1984. Mem. Assn. Female Execs., Pres.'s Assn., Am. Mgmt. Assn. Democrat. Roman Catholic. Author: (with others) U.S. Bilingual Education Act, 1967, Texas A.F.D.C. Employment and Education Act, 1977; manuals Women's Employment and Education Model Program. Office: Lupe Anguiano & Assocs PO Box 28251 San Antonio TX 78228

ANIKEEFF, PAMELA TATIANA, psychologist; b. Detroit, Sept. 27, 1948; d. Alexis Michael and Josephine W. (Obroslinski) A.; A.B., U. Calif., Berkeley, 1970; M.A., U. Akron (Ohio), 1972; Ph.D. (grad. teaching assoc. 1973-77), Ohio State U., 1977. Research psychologist, then program mgmt. analyst U.S. Dept. Transp., Washington, 1978-81, mem. evaluation team Nat. Task Force for Safety Belts and Child Restraint Devices, 1982, evaluator Office Occupant Protection, 1982-84, sr. behavioral scientist, profl. staff Sec.'s Safety Rev. Task Force, 1984—. Named hon. Mayor of Natchitoches, La. Mem. Am. Psychol. Assn., Assn. Women in Sci., Nat. Assn. Female Execs., Soc. Psychol. Study Social Issues, Internat. Soc. Polit. Psychology, Washington World Affairs Council, Guild Natural Sci. Illustrators, Assn. Advancement Psychology, Women's Equity Action League, Sierra Club. Office: US Dept Dept Transp Washington DC 20590

ANITON, JEANNE PATRICE, regional sales manager, market researcher; b. Chgo., Oct. 29, 1951; d. Oscar Lee and Priscilla Lillian (Bradwell) Motley; m. Michael Ray Aniton, Dec. 6, 1975; 1 child, Michael Wesley. B.S. in Bus. Adminstrn., Ohio State U., 1972. Pricing analyst Shell Oil Co., Chgo., 1972; systems analyst, sales rep. Nat. Cash Register Co., Columbus, Ohio, 1972-75; sales mgr. Gen. Electric, Columbus, 1975-83; sales engr. Codex div. Motorola, Columbus, 1983-84; regional sales mgr. NEC America, Atlanta, 1984—; pvt. practice computer cons., Columbus, 1976-78; career counselor BSA/NTA, Columbus, 1978-79. Com. chmn. Friends of Art for Cultural Enrichment, Columbus, 1981-82, com. mem. Jerry Hammond Election Orgn., Columbus, 1979. Recipient Mark Makers award Gen. Electric, 1977, 80. Mem. Am. Mgmt. Assn., Delta Sigma Theta. Republican. Methodist. Avocations: lepidoptery; calligraphy; ballet.

ANKER, CHARLOTTE MIRIAM, playwright, educator; b. Wilmington, Del., July 13, 1934; d. Neil Morris and Helen Sarah (Price) Lubin; m. Jerry David Anker, Apr. 12, 1959; children—Deborah, Daniel. A.B. in Sociology, Temple U., 1955; postgrad. Columbia U., 1955-56. Adminstrv. asst. Ams. for Democratic Action, Washington, 1956-57; asst. edn. dir. Internat. Union of Electric, Radio and Machine Workers AFL-CIO, Washington, 1957-60; asst. book editor World weekly newspaper, Washington, 1961-62; lectr. sociology George Washington U., Washington, 1965-71; coordinator speakers Dem. Nat. Presdl. Campaign, Washington, 1972. Author: Last Night I Saw Andromeda, 1975 (Phila. Writer's Conf. 1st prize for children's lit. 1974). Co-author: Onward Victoria (Broadway musical); (dramas Stroke Three, 1982, Sand Castles, 1983, Third Child, 1984 (Margo Jones Playwriting award 1984, Jane Chambers Playwriting award 1985). Precinct vice chmn. Democratic Party, Montgomery County, Md., 1963-64, 69-70; dir. tutoring and enrichment program Bells Mill Elem. Sch., Montgomery County, 1969-72. Social Sci. Research Council fellow, 1955. Mem. Dramatists Guild, Authors Guild, Soc. Children's Book Writers, Washington Ind. Writers. Avocations: photography; art; stamp collecting.

ANKROM, BARBARA BURKE, journalist; b. Upper Darby, Pa., May 30, 1943; d. Joseph Anthony and Teresa Gertrude (Smart) Burke; A.B., Wheeling Coll., 1965; children—Joseph Burke Nied, Laura Ann Nied, Michele Marie Nied; m. 2d, Robert W. Ankrom, Sr. Asst. editor Jones & Laughlin Steel Corp., Pitts., 1965-66; reporter/photographer Democrat Messenger, Waynesburg, Pa., 1976-77; corr. McGraw-Hill & World News Pubs., N.Y.C., 1976—; writer Pitts. Bus. Times, 1981-82; tech editor, writer JWK Internat. Corp., Pitts., 1982-84; writer-editor W.Va. U. Energy Research Ctr., 1985—; freelance writer, 1984—. Public relations dir. Boy Scouts Am., Greene County, Pa., 1977-84; editor, pub. Democrat Messenger, 1976. Mem. AAUW. Democrat. Roman Catholic. Asst. editor Men and Steel mag., 1965-66; editor Pa. chpts. Pan American's U.S.A. Guide Book, 1979, 80. Home: RD 1 Box 234A Clarksville PA 15322 Office: WVa U Energy research Ctr Morgantown WV 26505

ANNS, ARLENE EISERMAN, pub. co. exec.; b. Pearl River, N.Y.; d. Frederick Joel and Anna (Behnke) E.; student Bergen Jr. Coll., 1946-48; B.S., Utah State U., 1950; postgrad. Traphagen Sch. Design, 1957, N.Y. U., 1958, Hunter Coll., 1959-60. Research and promotion asst. Archtl. Record, N.Y.C., 1952-56; asst. research dir. Esquire Mag., N.Y.C., 1956-62; research mgr. Am. Machinist, publ. McGraw-Hill, Inc., N.Y.C., 1962-67, mktg. service mgr., 1967-69, 1969-71, sales mgr., 1976-77, dir. mktg., 1977-78; v.p. mktg. services Morgan-Gramplan, Inc., N.Y.C., 1971-72; mktg. dir. Family Health & Diversion mag., 1972-74; dist. sales mgr. Postgrad. Medicine, 1974-76; advt. sales mgr. Contemporary Ob/Gyn, 1976-78; dir. profl. devel., 1978-80; pub. Graduating Engr., McGraw, Inc., N.Y.C., 1980—. Mem. Am. Mktg. Assn., Pharm. Advt. Club, Advt. Women N.Y., Advt. Club N.Y., Sales Exec. Club, Employment Mgmt. Assn., Coll. Placement Council, Pi Sigma Alpha. Home: 101 Brianwood Ct Lakes Quinton VA 23141

ANOZIE, LYNDA SUZANNE, publishing company executive; b. Camp LeJeune, N.C., June 21, 1949; d. Dalton W. and Mary (Winston) Hielscher; m. Sunday Ogbonna Anozie, Aug. 3, 1974; children—Mary-Margaret, Emily, Nathaniel. B.A., U. Tex., 1970; M.Sc., SUNY-Buffalo, 1980. Cert. tchr., Tex., N.Y. Tchr. Randolph AFB, Tex., 1971-73; managing editor Conch Mag., Ltd., Buffalo, 1974—, v.p. Conch Typesetting and Graphics Co., 1976—; lectr. SUNY, Buffalo, 1977—. Mem. United Univ. Professions. Episcopalian. Co-author: Phenomonology of Modern African Studies, 1982. Home: 102 Normal Ave Buffalo NY 14213 Office: EOC 465 Washington St State Univ NY Buffalo NY 14205

ANSELL, KATHLEEN KIRK, speech communication educator, consultant; b. Mason City, Iowa, Dec. 1, 1936; d. Willis J. and Marie B. (Barnett) Kirk; m. Edgar M. Ansell, Dec. 28, 1957; children—Mark W., Annette K. Student

California U. (Pa.), 1954-56; B.S. in Library Sci. and English, Sam Houston U., 1958; M.Ed. in English and Speech Communication, Edinboro U., 1974; Ph.D. in Orgnl. Communications, U. Pitts., 1981. Monographs cataloger Fondren Library, Rice U., Houston, 1957-59; monographs cataloger Hamilton Library, Edinboro U. (Pa.), 1966-69, assoc. prof. speech communications, 1974—; cons. communications. Vice pres. United Ministries in Higher Edn., Pa. Commn., 1981—. Mem. Speech Communication Assn., Eastern Communication Assn. (panel chairperson 1984 conv.), Internat. Assn. Bus. Communicators (charter adviser), Women in Communication Inc., AAUP, Orgn. for Study Lang. and Gender, AAUW (v.p. Edinboro br. 1979-82, pres. br., chairperson corp. relations Pa. div. bd. 1982—, br. Outstanding Woman of Yr. 1980, 83). Republican. Methodist. Clubs: Heather Garden (chairperson tree-planting community project 1970-76), Campus Ministry Bd. (Edinboro). Lodge: Order Eastern Star. Home: 116 Brookview Dr Edinboro PA 16412 Office: Dept Speech Communications Edinboro U of Pa 122 Leader Clinic Edinboro PA 16444

ANSLEY, NINA MCCABE, fashion writer; b. Mineral Wells, Tex., July 26, 1918; d. Rex and Ruth (Hillsman) McCabe; ed. Mary Hardin Baylor Coll.; also seminars and univ. extension courses; m. James Ansley, Nov. 15, 1941; 1 dau., Janis. Fashion copywriter Neiman-Marcus Co., Dallas, 1950-55; account supr. women's accounts Don L. Baxter Advt. Agy., Dallas, 1955-66; dir. public relations Security World Pub. Co., Los Angeles, 1967-70; fashion dir. color and fashion trend forecasting Merle Norman Cosmetics, 1970—; lectr. in field. Mem. Dallas Advt. League, Fashion Group, Color Mktg. Group, Dallas Press Club, Nat. Writers Club. Republican. Episcopalian. Contbr. numerous articles to mags. Home: 13080 Dronfield Ave 55 Sylmar CA 91342 Office: 9130 Bellanca Ave Los Angeles CA 90045

ANSLEY, REBECCA ANN, personnel administrator; b. Holden, Mo., Feb. 25, 1942; d. John Nelson Bird and Mary Margaret (Clarkson) Welch; m. William Harper, Oct. 6, 1958 (div. 1961); children—John C., Charles R.; m. Bill Harold, Feb. 13, 1981. B.A., Avila U., 1977; M.B.A., Rockhurst Coll., 1982. Checker with accounts payable dept. Mossie's Grocery, Lee's Summit, Mo., 1958-64; on assembly line Wilcox Electronics, Kansas City, Mo., 1964-68; mgr. SWB Telephone Co., Overland Park, Kans., 1968—; personnel mgr. AT&T, St. Louis, 1968—. Bd. dirs. Women's Chamber Commn., Kansas City, 1982-83, LWV, St. Louis, 1985—. Mem. Human Relations Assn., Am. Arbitration Assn., Am. Soc. Personnel Mgrs. Methodist. Avocations: reading, swimming, tennis, walking. Home: 182 N Greentrails Chesterfield MO 63017 Office: AT&T 12755 Olive St Louis MO 63141

ANSON, SHARON HADDOCK, lawyer; b. Indpls., Jan. 21, 1945; d. Charles Richard and Janet Bernice (Conard) Haddock; m. Robert Sam Anson, Oct. 19, 1974 (div. Apr. 1979); m. Venable Herndon, May 31, 1985. B.A., Denison U., 1967; M.Internat. Affairs, Columbia U., 1969; J.D., NYU, 1978. Bar: N.Y. 1979. Atty., Zimet, Haines, Moss & Friedman, N.Y.C., 1978-80, Reavis & McGrath, N.Y.C., 1980-84, Kay Collyer & Boose, N.Y.C., 1984-86, Olnick Boxer Blumberg Lane & Troy, N.Y.C., 1986—. Office: Olnick Boxer et al 757 Third Ave New York NY 10017

ANSTETT, NANCY ANN, nurse; b. Detroit, May 8, 1947; d. Vincent Victor and Georgia Rita (DuLac) Calamia; m. Raymond Louis Anstett, Oct. 31, 1970; 1 child, Timothy Vincent. Diploma Henry Ford Hosp. Sch. Nursing, 1969; student Mich. State U., 1965-66. Nurse, Providence Hosp., Southfield, Mich., 1969—. State rep. Tuberous Sclerosis Mich., 1984—. Eucharistic minister St. Marys Roman Catholic Parish, Royal Oak, Mich., 1985, vol. librarian, grade sch., 1984-85. Mem. Henry Ford Hosp. Sch. Nursing Alumni. Avocations: genealogy; camping; stamp and coin collecting. Home: 415 W Hudson St Royal Oak MI 48067

ANTAL, MARGARET GREIF (PEGGY), interior design company executive; b. Orange, N.J., Nov. 30, 1940; d. Charles Elwyn and Evelyn Alice (Peavey) Greif; m. Thomas Loren Malmer, Nov. 21, 1960 (div. 1976); children—Karen Beth Malmer Martin, Susan, Conan Michael; m. Charles Edward Antal, Aug. 21, 1983. Student DePauw U., 1958-60, U. Ill., 1960-62; B.A., Coll. St. Francis, Joliet, Ill., 1981. Owner, operator Creative Decor, Kankakee, Ill., 1965-79; mem. sales staff designer Curriculum Co., Kankakee, 1977-78, Benjamin Bros., Chgo., 1978-80, Maple Hall, Inc., Chgo., 1980-84; owner, pres. Peggy Antal Hotel Interiors, Ypsilanti, Mich., 1984—; cons. Advance Mfg., Orlando, Fla., 1984-85; presenter seminars. Author tng. manual. Parent vol. Kankakee Sch. Dist., 1966-68; Republican election judge, Kankakee County, 1973-75. Mem. Women in Design, Nat. Assn. Future Women, Assn. Female Owned Businesses in Constrn. Avocations: Pottery, crafts, gardening, sailing. Home: PO Box 250 Ypsilanti MI 48197 Office: Peggy Antal Hotel Interiors 913 Pleasant Dr PO Box 250 Ypsilanti MI 48197

ANTHONY, AMY STANLEY, state official; b. Cuba, May 3, 1944 (parents Am. citizens); d. William and Margaret (Bell) Stanley; m. Samuel English Anthony. B.A., Smith Coll., 1966. Exec. dir. Housing Allowance Project, Springfield, Mass., 1973-79; prin. Amy Anthony Assocs., Boston, 1979-83; sec. Exec. Office Communities and Devel., Mass., 1983—; mem. Community Devel. Fin. Corp., 1983—, Mass. Housing Fin. Agency, 1983—, Community Econ. Devel. Assistance Corp., 1983—; co-chmn. Mass. Housing Partnership, 1985. Bd. dirs. Citizens Housing and Planning Assn., Boston, 1978-80; del. Democratic State Conv., Springfield, Mass., 1985. Office: Exec Office Communities & Devel 100 Cambridge St 14th Floor Boston MA 02202

ANTHONY, BETTY ARLENE, medical center executive; b. Jacksonville, Fla., July 14, 1926; d. Glessner Earl and Florence Claudine (Smyth) Pratt; m. Yancey Lamar Anthony, II, Sept. 13, 1983. Student Jones Bus. Coll., Jacksonville, 1944, New Orleans Bapt. Theol. Sem., 1952, U. Fla., 1953-54, Tampa U., 1956. Promotion sec. Fla. Bapt. Conv., Jacksonville, 1945-53; sec. First Bapt. Ch., Tampa, 1955-59; sec. to asst. adminstr. Bapt. Med. Ctr., Jacksonville, 1960-65, sec. to exec. dir., 1966-80, corp. sec., 1980—; asst. sec., treas. Bapt. Health, Inc., Jacksonville, 1983—; sec. Bapt. Health Services, Inc., Jacksonville, 1983—, Bapt. Health Properties, Inc., Jacksonville, 1983—; asst. sec. N.E. Fla. Breast Ctr., Inc., Jacksonville, 1984—; sec., treas. Healthcare Mgmt. Services, Inc., Jacksonville, 1985—; sec., First Coast Systems, Inc., Jacksonville, 1985—; asst. sec., treas. So. Bapt. Hosp. of Fla. Inc., Jacksonville, 1985—. Mem. Fla. Hosp. Exec. Secs. Assn. (dir. 1973-76, pres. 1975-76), Am. Soc. Corp. Secs., Nat. Assn. Female Execs. Office: Bapt Med Ctr Corp Offices Suite 303 1300 Gulf Life Dr Jacksonville FL 32207

ANTHONY, BONNIE RUBIN, physician; b. N.Y.C., Dec. 29, 1943; d. Milton J. and Gertrude R. (Pollack) Belasco; student Hunter Coll., CUNY, 1961-64; Ph.D., Columbia U., 1969; M.D., Georgetown U., 1975; m. Robert N. Anthony Jr., June 7, 1965; children—Patricia, Michelle, Scott, Michael, Peter. Intern, Georgetown Univ. Washington D.C., 1975-76; resident Georgetown U. Hosp., Washington, 1975-77; chief resident VA Hosp., Washington D.C., 1977-78; practice medicine specializing in psychiatry; mem. staffs Montgomery Gen. Hosp. Shady Grove Adventist Hosp. Psy.; faculty Balt.-D.C. Inst. Psychoanalysis. Dir. Women Ctr. for Growth, Rockville 1982. Mem. Am. Psychoanalytic Assn., Internat. Psychoanalytic Assn., AAAS, Am. Psychiatric Assn., Am. Woman's Med. Assn., Nat'l Academy Sci. Home: 6901 Whittier Blvd Bethesda MD 20817

ANTHONY, CLARISSA BERNING, singer, educator; b. Redmond, Oreg., Jan. 17, 1935; d. John Henry and Eleanor (Edwards) Berning; m. Jack Williams Anthony, Jr., June 26, 1960 (dec. 1982); children—Rebecca Ellen, Julia Kathleen. B.A., U. Oreg., 1957, M.Mus., 1959. Voice instr. William Paterson Coll., Wayne, N.J., 1979-84, Fairleigh Dickinson U., Rutherford, N.J., 1983—; pvt. practice voice and flute tchr., Upper Montclair, N.J., 1971—; owner garden ctr. Jack and the Preacher's, Holmdel, N.J., 1972-83; profl. singer, 1959—; soprano soloist Montclair State Coll., 1981-85, William Paterson Coll., 1981-82, Temple Emanu-EL, N.Y.C., 1962-79, Union Congl. Ch., Montclair, 1973—. Chmn. youth com. Union Congl. Ch., 1983-86, mem. parish life, 1985—, mem. music com., 1983-85. Winner voice and oratorio N.J. Young Artists, Nat. Fedn. Music Clubs, N.J., 1966. Mem. Nat. Assn. Tchrs. of Singing (treas. N.J. 1984-86), N.Y. Singing Tchrs. Assn. (chairperson young artists auditions), Internat. Bach Soc. (performing fellow 1969), AAUW, Phi Beta (nat. grad. grantee 1964). Democrat. Clubs: Montclair Music (Young Artists Audition chairperson 1982—), Rehearsal. Home: 8 Waterbury Rd Upper Montclair NJ 07043

ANTHONY, GERALDINE CECILIA, educator; b. Bklyn., Oct. 5, 1919; d. William and Agnes Josephine (Murphy) A.; B.A., Mt. St. Vincent U., 1951; M.A. in Philosophy, St. Johns U., N.Y.C., 1956, Ph.D. in English, 1963. Joined Congregation of Sisters of Charity of Halifax, Roman Cath. Ch., 1942; tchr. jr. and sr. high schs., Boston, N.Y., 1942-62; prof. English, Mt. St. Vincent U., Halifax, N.S., 1965—. Recipient cert. in 17th Century poetry Exeter Coll., Oxford U., Eng., 1964; fellow in journalism U. Minn., 1965. Mem. Assn. Can. Univs. Tchrs. English, Assn. Canadian Theatre History (pres.). Author: John Coulter, 1976; Gwen Pharis Ringwood, 1981; editor: (series) Profiles in Canadian Drama, 1977; Stage Voices, 1978. Home and Office: Mount St Vincent U Halifax NS B3M 2J6 Canada

ANTHONY, JOAN CATON, lawyer; writer; b. South Bend, Ind., July 28, 1939; d. Joseph Robert and Margaret Catherine (McMeel) Caton; m. Robert Armstrong Anthony, Jan. 3, 1980; 1 child, Peter. B.A., Marquette U., 1961; M.A., Northwestern U., 1963; J.D., Catholic U. Am., 1979. Bar: D.C. 1980, Va. 1982. Instr. English, Marquette U., Milw., 1963-65; instr. English, George Washington U., Washington, 1965-69, asst. prof., 1969-70; spl. asst. student affairs HEW, Washington, 1970-72; dir. Office Student and Youth Affairs, U.S. Office Edn., Washington, 1972-74, legis. specialist, 1974-78; chief mgmt. ops. br. Fed. Wildlife Permit Office, U.S. Fish and Wildlife Service, Washington, 1978-81; assoc. firm Cate and Goodbread, Washington, 1981-86; mem. U.S. del. to 2d meeting Conf. Parties to Conv. on Internat. Trade in Endangered Species of Wild Flora and Fauna, San Jose, Costa Rica, 1979. Contbr. lit. revs., essays and articles on univ.-community relations, western settlement and internat. negotiations to various publs. Bd. dirs. McLean Citizens Assn., 1982-83, Fairfax County Humane Soc., 1983, Greater McLean Republican Women's Club, 1984-85; pres. Franklin Forest Frolickers, 1985-86. Recipient spl. achievement award U.S. Fish and Wildlife Service, 1981. Mem. ABA, D.C. Bar Assn., Va. Bar Assn. Roman Catholic. Home: 2011 Lorraine Ave McLean VA 22101

ANTHONY, NANCY JEAN, city official; b. Redding, Calif., Mar. 2, 1938; d. Forrest Mark Anthony and Marjorie (Hall) Anthony-Jaros. A.A., Coll. of Marin, 1982; student U. Calif.-Santa Cruz, 1974-75, 81-83. City clk. City of Larkspur, Calif., 1974—, city clk. and adminstrv. asst., 1982—; cons. Community Renewal, Larkspur, 1983-84; trainer pvt. cons., Larkspur, 1975—; mem. adv. com. Coll. of Marin, 1980-82. Contbr. photographs to profl. jours. Mem. Internat. Inst. Mcpl. Clks. (conf. program com. 1984, cert.), City Clks. Assn. Calif. (recording sec. 1978-79, corr. sec. 1979-80, co-editor newsletter 1984-85), No. Calif. City Clks. Assn. (pres. 1983-84). Avocations: photography; traveling; needlepoint; swimming. Office: City of Larkspur PO Box 585 Larkspur CA 94939

ANTLEY, PATRICIA TAMSITT, county auditor; b. Aurora, Ill., Dec. 12, 1940; d. Joseph Cooper and Teresa Margaret (Rice) Tamsitt; m. Philip John Randolph Antley, Aug. 28, 1965; children—John Randolph, Mary Josephine, Margaret O'Hagan. A.B., Coll. Notre Dame of Md., 1961; M.M., U. S.C., 1964. Tchr. math. Balt. City Schs., 1961-63; systems engr. IBM Corp., Columbia, S.C., 1965; tchr. Nashville Pub. Schs., 1965-66, Richland Dist. 2, Columbia, S.C., 1966-72; instr. math. Midlands Tech. Coll., Columbia, 1972-73; cons. instr. State Dept. Edn., Columbia, S.C., 1972-75; sec. treas. Creative Day Care, Inc., Columbia, 1970-78; auditor Richland County, Columbia, 1979—. Mem. Richland County Bd. Assessment Control, Columbia, 1975-78, chmn., 1978; exec. dir. Assn. for Better Child Devel., Columbia, 1976-78; bd. dirs., exec. com. Three Rivers Health Systems, Columbia, 1978-80; bd. dirs. Community Care, Inc., Columbia, 1982-85, chmn., 1985—. Mem. S.C. Women in Govt. (treas. 1985), Internat. Assn. Assessing Officers, S.C. Assn. Auditors, Treas. and Tax Collectors (chmn. com. 1984—), S.C. Assn. Assessing Ofcls. (v.p. 1982, pres. 1983), S.C. Assn. Counties (bd. dirs. 1983—). Republican. Roman Catholic. Clubs: Richland County Republican Women's (v.p. 1978-80), Altrusa of Columbia (treas. 1980-81, v.p. 1982-84, pres. 1984-86), Columbia Touchdown (bd. dirs. 1985—), Columbia Exec. Women's Network. Avocations: reading, sewing, needlework. Home: 3701 Overcreek Rd Columbia SC 29206 Office: Richland County Auditors Office PO Box 192 Columbia SC 29202

ANTOINE, MAGGIE KELLEY, nurse; b. Tuskegee, Ala., Jan. 28, 1946; d. James Lee and Thelma C. (Chambliss) Kelley; m. John H. Wilkerson, June 19, 1972 (div.); m. Merriel J. Antoine, July 14, 1977 (dec.); children—Darryl Keith, Michael Kyle. B.S., Tuskegee Inst., 1968, M.Ed., 1980; cert. in Gerontology, Auburn U., 1983. Cert. adult health nurse practitioner, gerontl. nurse practitioner. Head nurse John Andrew Hosp., Tuskegee, 1968-71; staff nurse VA Med. Ctr., Tuskegee, 1971-75, nurse practitioner, 1975-84, head nurse, 1984—; asst. project dir. Geriatric Psychosocial Rehab. Unit, 1985; cert. instr. Heart Assn., Montgomery, Ala., 1980—. Research on effects of lecithin, physostiamine and hydergine on elderly dementia patients. Recipient Incentive award spl. advancement VA Med. Ctr., Tuskegee, 1973, 83; Mother of Yr. award Bethel Bapt. Ch., 1976; Cert. of Appreciation, Ala. Heart Assn., 1982, 83, 84, 85; named to Troy Nurses Honor Soc., 1985. Mem. Am. Nurses Assn., Tuskegee Nurses Club (fin. sec. 1975—), Tuskegee Inst. Nat. Nurses (treas. 1981-84), Chi Eta Phi (v.p. 1981-84), Delta Sigma Theta (v.p. 1981-82). Baptist. Lodge: Order Eastern Star (sec. 1978—). Home: 801 Chappie James Ave Tuskegee AL 36083 Office: VA Med Center Loop Rd Tuskegee AL 36083

ANTON, CHERYL LYNN, sales manager; b. Toledo, Nov. 3, 1953; d. Ralph Herbert and Coletta Marie (Nickerson) Snyder; student U. Toledo, 1971-73; 1 son, John Daniel. With Kroger Co., Toledo, 1972-80, dept. supr. merchandising; sales dir. Growth Unltd., Toledo, 1979-80; owner CJ's Bar, Toledo, 1980-82; sales rep. Armour Food Co., Orlando, Fla., 1983-85; dist. sales mgr. Jones Dairy Farm, 1985—. Mem. Nat. Assn. Female Execs. (network dir. 1979—), Nat. Assn. for Women. Democrat. Home: 6105 Luzon Dr Orlando FL 32809 Office: 6105 Luzon Dr Orlando FL 32809

ANTON, DEBORAH ANN, business services executive; b. Grand Rapids, Mich., Apr. 1, 1960; d. Anthony and Sandra Lee (Suarez) A. Student Central Mich. U., 1978-79, Grand Valley State Colls., 1979-80, Northwestern U., 1985—. Asst. promotion dir. Eastbrook Mall Promotions, Grand Rapids, Mich., 1979-80; exec. sec. BBDO Chgo., Inc., 1980-82; exec. legal sec. Velsicol Chem. Corp., Chgo., 1982-84; mgr. legal adminstrn. Velsicol Chem. Corp., Chgo., 1984-86, MIS liason, 1982—; pres. Assoc. Bus. Services, Inc., 1986—. Mem. Nat. Assn. Female Execs. (network dir. 1982—), Windy City Network (dir. 1983—), Am. Mgmt. Assn. Presbyterian. Avocations: triathalons; running races; sailboating; skiing.

ANTONACCI, LORI (LORETTA MARIE), marketing and promotion consultant; b. Riverton, Ill., Mar. 31, 1947; d. Antonio and Gena Marie A. B.A., Bradley U., 1969; postgrad. NYU, 1975-77, New Sch. Social Research, 1977. Broadcast copywriter Sta. WIRL-TV, Peoria, Ill., 1969; communications specialist Walgreen Co., Chgo., 1970-72; creative supr. Nat. Assn. Realtors, Chgo., 1973; creative dir., producer Steve Sohmer, Inc., N.Y.C., 1974-77; owner, exec. producer Antonacci Prodns., N.Y.C., 1977-79; promotion specialist Ziff-Davis Publs., 1979-80; promotion mgr. Psychology Today, 1980-81; mktg. and promotion cons. Antonacci & Assocs., N.Y.C., 1982—. Bd. dirs. Artists Talk on Art, Inc., Artists Community Fed. Credit Union; founder Artists Talk on Art Panel series, 1974. Recipient Golden Eagle award CINE, 1976; award U.S. Indsl. Film Festival, 1977; CEBA award, 1979; Bronze medal Internat. Film and TV Festival N.Y., 1979. Mem. Advt. Women N.Y. (profl. devel. com. 1983—, career council com. 1984—), Women Bus. Owners N.Y., Women in Communications, Media Research Dirs. Assn. Am. Women in Radio and TV. Address: 15 E 10th St New York NY 10003

ANTONE, KAREN ANN, real estate executive; b. Mpls., Jan. 21, 1947; d. Carl Harry and Mildred Marion (Johnson) Olson. Student U. Minn., 1966-68. Mortgage closer F&M Bank, Mpls., 1968-73; mortgage dept. coordinator Guarantee Title, Inc., Mpls., 1973-74; real estate closer Bermel Smaby Realtors, Mpls., 1974-75; real estate assoc. Edina Realty, Inc., Mpls., 1976—, sales adv. com., 1986—. Active Minn. Real Estate Polit. Action Com., 1982. Mem. Greater Mpls. Area Bd. Realtors, Minn. Assn. Realtors, Nat. Assn. Realtors, Nat. Assn. Female Execs. Avocations: arts; jogging; reading. Office: Edina Realty Inc 4015 W 65th St Edina MN 55435

ANTONE, LINDA A., educational film producer, director; b. Mpls., Aug. 31, 1947; d. Richard and Mary Antone. B.A. in Internat. Relations, U. Minn.-Mpls., 1969; postgrad. in broadcast communications, 1977-80. Advt. prodn. mgr. Hoffman Press, Mpls., 1972-73; advt. dir. Medallion Pub., Inc., Mpls., 1974-75; assoc. producer Wilson Learning Corp., Eden Prairie, Minn., 1976-79, producer, dir., 1979-82, dir. video dept., 1982-83; producer, dir. video programs for firms including AT&T, Ford Motor Co., Consol. Freightways. Producer, dir. tng. program ARC, 1982-83, v.p. prodn., 1983-85, mem. Mpls. chpt. pub. relations com., 1983; producer, dir. pub. service announcements Minn. Women's Network, Mpls., 1982-83. Mem. Internat. Television Assn. (judge Golden Reel awards 1982), Am. Film Inst., Women in Communications (program com. Mpls.), NOW, Minn. Entrepreneurs Club, Women's Internat. League for Peace and Freedom (newsletter editor Mpls. 1975-77). Home: 4700 Ewing Ave S Minneapolis MN 55410 Office: Wilson Learning Corp 6950 Washington Ave S Eden Prairie MN 55344

ANTONIO, MARLENE JOAN, commission administrator; b. Moose Jaw, Sask., Can., Apr. 24, 1936; d. John Ewan and Ruby Irene (Bagg) Lauder; m. Harry Antonio, Apr. 27, 1957; 1 dau., Jolaine Ann. B.E., U. Sask, 1956, B.S., 1957; M.E., U. Calgary (Alta., Can.), 1969. Geologist, Texaco Exploration Co., Calgary, 1957-58; tchr. Calgary Bd. Edn., 1966-70, 79-80; instr. Mt. Royal Coll., Calgary, 1970-74, U. Calgary, 1976-78; chmn. Alta. Human Rights Commn., Edmonton, 1981-85; mem. Minister's Consultative Com. on Tolerance and Understanding, Alta., 1983-84. Sec.-treas. Calgary Home and Sch. Assn., 1976-78. Recipient Good Servant award Can. Council Christians and Jews, 1984. Nat. Council Jewish Women scholar, Saskatoon, Sask., 1955-57. Mem. Alta. Tchrs. Assn., Can. Assn. Statuatory Human Rights Agys. (pres. 1984-85), Assn. Profl. Engrs., Geologists and Geophysicists of Alta. (hon.). Office: Alta Human Rights Commn 10808 99 Ave Edmonton AB T5K OG2 Canada

ANTOUN, ANNETTE AGNES, newspaper editor-publisher; b. Franklin, Pa., Mar. 7, 1927; d. Adrien Uriel and Charlotte Mary (McMullen) Adelman; student Allegheny Coll., Meadville, Pa.; m. Frederic George Antoun, July 19, 1947; children—Frederic G., Gregory S., Lawrence J., Mark J. (dec.), Laurence A., Scott J., Jonathan M., Lisa A. Founder, editor-pub. Paxton Herald, Harrisburg, Pa., 1960—; founder, owner Graphic Services, advt. and graphics, Harrisburg, 1972—; owner Communications System Design, 1978—; pres. Susquehanna Valley Assos., Inc., 1978—; co-editor French Creek Patriot, community newspaper, Cochranton, Pa., 1972. Bd. dirs. Tb and Health Soc., 1967—, exec. bd., 1967—, sec., 1972—; mem. communications com. Tri-County United Fund, 1973, mem. com. children's services, 1975—; bd. dirs. Pa. sect. Am. Lung Assn., 1973—, treas., 1976, sec., 1979-80, v.p., 1980-81; sec. bd. Central Pa. Lung Assn., 1969-73; bd. dirs. Harris Commn., 1975-79, Cath. Social Service Harrisburg, 1972-76; mem. extension planning com. YMCA, 1975—; bd. govs. Camp Curtin YMCA, 1980—; rep. dir. Pa. Lung Assn., 1973—, treas., 1975-76, sec. bd., 1977—; exec. bd. Lower Paxton Coalition Community Groups, 1973—; mem. communications bd. Catholic Diocese Harrisburg, 1971—; co-chmn. Dauphin County Ethics Com., 1979-80; chmn. bldg. com. Juvenile Detention Home, 1976—; chmn. fund raising com. Greater Harrisburg Arts Council, 1977—; co-chmn. Dauphin County Ethics Com., 1980-81; mem. Dauphin County bd. Com. Children and Youth, 1982—; vice chmn. Dauphin County Election Voting Machine Com., 1982—; mem. Tri-County Solid Waste Mgmt. Com., 1983—. Recipient Advocate award Paxton Area Jaycees, 1969, 73; citation Am. Legion Pa., 1971, CAP, 1972, medallion Am. Legion Pa., 1972; award Am. Cancer Soc., 1969-79; March of Dimes award, 1969-79; numerous others. Mem. Internat. Platform Assn., Associated Public Communication Officers. Club: Pleasant Hills Community. Home: 4910 Earl Dr Harrisburg PA 17112 Office: 101 Lincoln St Harrisburg PA 17112

ANTOUN, SISTER M. LAWREACE, college president; b. Meadville, Pa., Dec. 30, 1927; d. George K. and Freda (Habib) Antoun; B.S. Villa Maria Coll., 1954; M.S., Notre Dame U., 1959, postgrad. (doctoral candidate). Instr. chemistry Villa Maria Coll., Erie, Pa., 1955-61, asst. prof. chemistry, 1965-66, pres. 1966—; mem. Pa. Commn. on Financing of Higher Edn.; mem. exec. com. Commn. Ind. Colls. and Univs.; evaluator Middle States Assn./Commn. Higher Edn.; trustee Middle States Assn.; mem. Erie Conf. on Community Devel.; chmn. Pa. Postsecondary Planning Commn.; chmn. Council Higher Edn.; mem. adv. com. edn. Pa. Bd. Edn.; bd. dirs. Sisters of St. Joseph. Mem. Commonwealth Jud. Council; chairperson adv. council McManis Ednl. Trust Fund; past mem. Home Rule Charter Com.; adv. bd. human ecology Cornell U.; bd. incorporators St. Vincent Health Center; bd. dirs. Hamot Med. Ctr., Erie Conf. on Community Devel. Mem. Am. Assn. Ind. Colls. and Univs., Pa. Assn. Coll. and Univs., Pa. Assn. Ind. Colls. and Univs. Home: Erie PA 16505

ANTRIM, MINNIE FAYE, rest home administrator; b. Rochester, Tex., June 30, 1916; d. Charles C. Montandon and Myrtle Caldona (Brown) Montandon Taylor; m. Cecil C. Antrim, Jan. 1, 1938; children—Linda Faye Antrim Hathway, Cecil C. Student Central State Tchrs. Coll., Edmond, Okla., 1937. Asst. purchasing agt. Scenic Gen. Hosp., Modesto, Calif., 1955-68, Health Dept., Probation Dept., Stanislaus, Calif., 1955-68; owner, operator Sierra Villa Rest Home, Fresno, Calif., 1968-77, Mansion Home, Fresno, 1977—. Mem. Am. Coll. Health Care Adminstrs. Methodist. Club: Garden. Avocation: glee clubs. Home: 6070 E Townsend Fresno CA 93727

AONA, GRETCHEN MANN, art educator; b. Omaha, June 25, 1933; d. Albert Paul and Gladys Louise (Mann) Andersen; A.B., San Jose State U., 1951, M.A. in Art, 1966; m. Daniel Kaleikoa Aona, Jr., June 16, 1979. Tchr. elem. schs., Sunnyvale, Calif., 1951-54; instr. art, tchr. elem. sch., 1954-60; textbook illustrator math. and stats. dept. Stanford U., 1960-63; grad. admissions clk. San Jose State U., 1966-67; sci. illustrator Melabs, Mountain View, Calif., 1967; instr. art, crafts, and photography Kapiolani Community Coll., Honolulu, 1967—, chmn. humanities dept., 1978-79; one-woman shows in photography include: Fantasy Images, Queen Emma Gallery, Honolulu, 1977, Foyer Gallery, Leeward Community Coll., Honolulu, 1980; group exhbns. include: Photo '70, '71, '72, Sixty Yrs. World in Color, Hague, Netherlands, 1973, Honolulu, Art Hawaii One, Honolulu Acad. Art, 1974, 75, Gt. Hawaiian Open Art Exhbn., 1981, Artists of Hawaii, Honolulu Acad. Arts, 1981, Honolulu Printmakers 55th Ann. Exhbn., 1983, Windward Artists Easter Art Show, 1984, 85, Hawaii Watercolor Soc. Exhibit, 1985. Recipient Purchase award Honolulu Acad. Art, 1981. Mem. Am. Crafts Council, World Crafts Council, Hawaii Craftsmen, Arts Council Hawaii, Hawaii Watercolor Soc., Internat. Guild Craft Journalists, Authors and Photographers. Democrat. Roman Catholic. Author: Creative Exploration in Crafts, 1976. Home: 45-453 B Mokulele Dr Kaneohe HI 96744 Office: Kapiolani Community Coll 620 Pensacola St Honolulu HI 96814

APELT, LISA JANE, bookkeeper; b. Sacramento, Calif., May 30, 1945; d. Crawford A. and Ethel M. (King) Williamson; m. John C. Apelt, Dec. 27, 1969; children—Michael, Laura. B.A. in Sociology, Gonzaga U., 1966; postgrad., U. Guam, 1972-73, Riverside Community Coll., 1977-79. Social worker County of Sacramento, Calif., 1966-68, adminstrv. analyst, 1968-70; owner, operator AWT, Lake Oswego, Oreg., 1982-83; bookkeeper D. Van Rooy, C.P.A., Lake Oswego, 1984—. Mem. Riverside Jr. League, Portland Jr. League. Home: 3886 Tamarack Ln Lake Oswego OR 97034 Office: D Van Rooy CPA 4040 Douglas Way Lake Oswego OR 97034

APKER, CAROLINE ANNE, public relations executive; b. Green Bay, Wis., May 7, 1938; d. Herbert Siegfried and Ethel Alice (Boehm) Foth; m. James Raymond Poh, Dec. 28, 1957 (div. Mar. 1979); children—Jennifer Anne, James Andrew, Daniel Herbert; m. 2d, David Apker, Sept. 15, 1979. B.S. in Journalism, Boston U., 1958. Advt. mgr. Select Publs., Madison, Wis., 1958-61; dir. publs. United Community Services, Milw., 1963-65; assoc. Lee Baker Assocs., Milw., 1972-77; pres. Interpretive Communicators, Madison, 1977-82; dir. pub. relations Brady Co., Madison and Milw., 1982—. Editor: The Life of Man, 1973; contbr. articles to profl. jours. Bd. dirs. Milw. Council on Alcoholism, 1966. Mem. Mystery Writers Am. Episcopalian. Home: 5001 Tonyawatha Trail Madison WI 53716 Office: The Brady Co 6320 Monona Dr Madison WI 53716

APPE, MARGRET JUNE, public administrator; b. Endicott, N.Y., Feb. 22, 1927; d. Fisher Hiram and Irene Florence (Anderson) Wallace; m. Robert N. Appe, Dec. 10, 1949; children—David Mark, Michael Craig, Donald Brian, Stephen Charles, Ellen Elizabeth. B.A., Russell Sage Coll., 1969; M.P.A., SUNY-Albany, 1978. Personnel clk. IBM, Endicott, N.Y., 1947-49; founder, exec. dir. Voluntary Action Ctr., Albany, 1968-72; div. head program services N.Y. State Dept. Correctional Services, Albany, 1972-84; 1st dep. supt. Coxsackie Correctional Facility, Coxsackie, N.Y., 1984—. Author: (booklet) Guidelines for Volunteer Services, 1976. Mem. bd. Meml. Hosp. Aux., Albany; assoc. bd. Cerebral Ctr. for the Disabled, Albany, 1983—. Mem. Nat. Assn. Vol. in Criminal Justice, Am. Correctional Assn. (assembly), N.Y. corrections and Youth Services (exec. v.p. 1982—), Exec. Women in Govt., Am. Soc. Pub.

Adminstrn. (council/dir. Capital dist.). Democrat. Club: Zonta. Office: Coxsackie Correctional Facility Coxsackie NY 12051

APPEL, NINA S., law educator, university administrator; b. 1936. J.D., Columbia U., 1959. Bar: N.Y. 1959. Prof., dean Loyola U. Law Sch., Chgo.; mem. Ill. Jud. Conf., 1973—. Address: Office of Dean Loyola U Law Sch Chicago IL 60611

APPELBAUM, JUDITH PILPEL, editor, consultant, educator; b. N.Y.C., Sept. 26, 1939; d. Robert Cecil and Harriet Florence (Fleischl) Pilpel; B.A. with honors, Vassar Coll., 1960; m. Alan Appelbaum, Apr. 16, 1961; children—Lynn Stephanie, Alexander Eric. Editor, Harper's Mag., N.Y.C., 1960-74; mng. editor Harper's Weekly, 1974-76; sr. cons. Atlas World Press Rev., 1977; mng. editor Publishers Weekly, 1978-81; founder Sensible Solutions, Inc., 1979; contbg. editor Publishers Weekly, 1981-82; columnist N.Y. Times Book Rev., 1982-84; mng. dir. Sensible Solutions, Inc., 1984—; assoc. dir. Ctr. for Book Research, U. Scranton, 1985—; book rev. editor Book Research Quar., 1984—; mem. faculty Pub. Inst. of U. Denver, 1981—, CUNY edn. in pub. program, 1982—; editorial adv. Book Industry Study Group Newsletter, 1980-83; mem. stats. com. Book Industry Study Group, 1984—; adv. bd. Coordinating Council of Lit. Mags., 1980—. Mem. Authors Guild, Women's Media Group, PEN, Com. Small Mag./Press Editors and Publishers, Soc. for Scholarly Pub. Author: (with Nancy Evans) How to Get Happily Published, 1978, rev. edit., 1982; editor: (with Tony Jones and Gwyneth Cravens) The Big Picture: A Wraparound Book, 1976; The Question of Size in the Book Industry Today, 1978; Getting a Line on Backlist, 1979; Paperback Primacy, 1981; Small Publisher Power, 1982; editor-in-chief Book Research Quar., 1986—. Office: Sensible Solutions Inc 6 E 39th St New York NY 10016

APPELBAUM, MARILYN MARY, non-profit child care educational center executive, educator; b. Cleve., Dec. 21, 1941; d. Manny and Renee (Goldstein) Slomovits; m. Sanford J. Appelbaum, June 19, 1959 (div. 1986); children—Tobi Carole Appelbaum Chapman, Martin Howard. B.A. in Psychology summa cum laude, Cleve. State U., 1970; Montessori diploma Nat. Ctr. Montessori Edn., Washington, 1979; M.A. in Edn., Am. U., 1980; M.A. in Behavioral Sci., U. Houston, 1980, postgrad., 1982—. Dir., co-owner Oak Point Acad., Houston, 1973—; exec. dir., editor, writer Nat. Ctr. Montessori Edn., 1979-81, dir., 1979—; exec. dir. Nat. Ctr. for Child Care Profls., Houston, 1980—; mem. proprietary sch. adv. commn. Tex. commr. edn., 1983; specialist speaker Criminal Investigations Task Force, Los Angeles, 1984; mem. day care standards devel. com. Tex. Dept. Human Resources, 1984; lectr. in field. Author: A Discipline Course, 1980; Let's Cook It Right, 1982; Practical Life and Home Living Skills, 1982; Reading and Writing Manual, 1983; Ground Rules for the Classroom, A Step-By-Step Approach, 1983; Child Care Professional Training Course, 1984; also articles. Mem. Nat. Assn. Child Care Mgmt., Nat. Ctr. Montessori Edn. (bd. dirs.), Tex. Licensed Child Care Assn., Am. Montessori Soc., Assn. Children with Learning Disabilities, Phi Delta Kappa. Jewish. Avocations: boating; reading; travel; research; writing. Office: 1330 Winrock Suite 2703 Houston TX 77057

APPENBRINK, MAXINE JEAN, contract engineering service company executive, employee leasing company executive; b. Minster, Ohio, Dec. 8, 1956; d. Vernon J. and Madge H. (Wise) Westerheide; m. Ronald D. Appenbrink, Sept. 19, 1981. Student Bowling Green State U., Ohio, 1975-76. Tech. recruiter Search Enterprise Inc., Oak Brook, Ill., 1978-79, Chem. Personnel Search, West Chester, Ill., 1979-81; office mgr. Midwest Strom Engring. Corp., Naperville, Ill., 1981-83; owner, pres. Avalon Hi-Tech Services, Warrenville, Ill., 1983—. Republican. Roman Catholic. Avocations: swimming; reading. Office: Avalon Hi-Tech Services Inc 28W 530 Batavia Rd PO Box 628 Warrenville IL 60555

APPLE, RITA ELLEN, real estate broker; b. Grand Haven, Mich., Aug. 11, 1949; d. Roland Bertram and Margaret Elizabeth (Engel) Lloyd; m. Thomas Bernard Hanley, Apr. 11, 1970 (div. Sept. 1983); children—Kevin Michael Hanley, Shannon Marie Hanley; m. Richard Pierce Apple, Oct. 12, 1983. Student Muskegon Jr. Coll., 1967-68, West Shore Coll., Ludington, Mich., 1968-70; B.A. in Acctg., Grand Valley State Coll., 1971; student Real Estate Sch. Edn., Chgo., 1981. Design cons. Harris Internat., Chgo., 1976-77; staff acct. Angel, Kaplan, Gomberg, C.P.A.s, Chgo., 1977-81; broker cons. Brannigar, Inc., Geneva, Ill., 1981-83; broker of record Regency Realty, Itasca, Ill., 1983-85; mng. broker Century 21-SNS Realty, Chgo., 1985—. Troop leader Chgo. council Girl Scouts U.S.A., 1977-80; founder Golden Triangle Civic Orgn., Chgo., 1981-84, pres., 1982, editor newsletter, 1982-84; participant Chgo. Neighborhood Media Group, 1984; chairperson Women for Alderman Gerald McLaughlin, Chgo., 1984, 85; hostess, interviewer Mayor of Chgo. Presentation, 1984. Mem. North Side Real Estate Bd., NW Suburban Real Estate Bd., Nat. Assn. Female Execs., NW Suburban Women in Sales. Democrat. Roman Catholic. Club: Lakeshore (Chgo.). Avocations: golf; riding and training Arabian horses; old house renovation; painting and drawing; reading. Home: 6007 N Sheridan Rd Chicago IL 60660 also 3030 Lakeshore Ave Benton Harbor MI 49022 Office: Century 21 SNS Realty Inc 2714 W Touhy Ave Chicago IL 60645

APPLEBAUM, SHEILA GAY, nursing educator; b. Chgo., Mar. 15, 1945; d. Herbert Irwin and Marilyn (Victor) Rockoff; m. Richard J. Applebaum, Aug. 4, 1985. A.D.N., Long Beach City Coll., 1966; B.S.N., San Francisco State Coll., 1970; M.S.N., Calif. State U.-Los Angeles, 1976. R.N., pub. health nurse, nursing instr., Calif. Staff nurse Meml. Hosp., Long Beach, Calif., 1966-67, Mt. Zion Med. Ctr., San Francisco, 1967-69; instr. nursing Hollywood Presbyn. Med. Ctr., Los Angeles, 1970-74; nursing supr. Orthopedic Hosp., Los Angeles, 1974-76; instr. nursing Ariz. State U., Tempe, 1976-78; nurse supr. Hoag Meml. Hosp., Newport Beach, Calif., 1977-78; nurse educator U. Calif.-Irvine and Orange, Calif., 1978-80, Santa Ana Coll. (Calif.), 1980—; nurse cons. Home Health Care Agy., Irvine, 1983. Mem. Calif. Nurses Assn. (chmn. com. 1970-73), Am. Heart Assn., Nat. League for Nursing, Am. Cancer Soc., Phi Kappa Phi. Democrat. Jewish. Home: 15 Hollowglen Irvine CA 92714 Office: Santa Ana Community Coll 17th at Bristol Santa Ana CA 92706

APPLEGATE, EDNA (KAY), civic worker; b. Las Vegas, N.Mex., May 15, 1919; d. George Washington and Dora Maude (Bearce) Howell; m. George Edward Applegate, Nov. 30, 1945 (dec. 1980); 1 child, Nancy Kay. R.N., Hotel Dieu Sch. Nursing, 1942; B.S., Columbia U., 1956, M.S., 1963. Sch. nurse tchr. Garden City Pub. Sch., N.Y., 1960-73; pub. health nurse Nassau County Dept. Health, Garden City, 1953-60. Author: Breakfast Book, 1976; Little Book of Baby Foods, 1979. Bd. dirs. Maternal and Child Health Ctr., Santa Fe, N.Mex., 1978-80; mem. steering com. March of Dimes Birth Defects Found., Santa Fe, 1979-85, mem. exec. com., 1985—, vol. coordinator N.Mex. chpt., 1985-86; bd. dirs. LWV, Santa Fe, 1974-80, Vol. Involvement Service, Santa Fe, 1977-83, Santa Fe Opera Guild, 1981-82, Santa Fe Cancer Soc., 1983-84; founder Santa Fe chpt. Gilbert & Sullivan Soc., 1984; mem. adv. bd. women's unit Charter Sunrise Hosp., Albuquerque, 1985—; bd. dirs. N.Mex. Myasthenia Gravis Found., 1986—. Served as 2d lt. Army Nurse Corp, 1942-44. Fellow Am. Sch. Health Assn., Royal Soc. Health; mem. N.Y. Mental Health Assn. Democrat.

APPLEGATE, MICHELE ILENE, government executive; b. Buffalo, Mar. 3, 1947; d. Justin H. and Elaine (Fink) Wilkes; m. Kenneth C. Applegate, Sept. 6, 1982. B.A. in History, SUNY-Buffalo, 1968. Social studies tchr., Brockport Central High Sch., N.Y. and Charles Carroll Jr. High, New Carrollton, Md., 1968-71; mgmt. intern Health Services and Mental Health Adminstrn., Rockville, Md., 1971-72; program analyst NIMH, HEW (now U.S. Dept. Health and Human Services), Rockville, 1972-73, spl. asst. to assoc. adminstr. extramural programs, Alcohol, Drug Abuse and Mental Health Adminstrn., 1973-77, extramural programs officer, 1978-79, dep. assoc. adminstr. extramural programs, 1979-82, assoc. adminstr. extramural programs, 1982—. Contbr. articles to profl. publs. Recipient Quality Increase award Alcohol, Drug Abuse and Mental Health Adminstrn., 1980, Outstanding Performance Rating, 1982, 83, 84, 85. Mem. Am. Soc. Pub. Adminstrn. Club: Potomac Commons Garden. Avocations: golf, gardening, aerobic dance, skiing. Home: 9020 Falls Chapel Way Potomac MD 20854 Office: Alcohol Drug Abuse and Mental Health Adminstrn 5600 Fishers Ln Room 13-103 Rockville MD 20857

APPLETON, DOLOROS MAXINE, real estate executive; b. Utica, Nebr., Dec. 27, 1929; d. John Wesley and Anna Elizabeth (Moravec) Vrana; m. Richard J. Elliott, Nov. 24, 1950 (div. 1952); m. 2d, Thomas Ellis Appleton, May 21, 1955; 1 dau., Jane Emily. Student U. Nebr., 1947-48, U. Ill., 1954, Belleville Coll., 1977-78. Tchr. Portland Heights Sch. Dist., Superior, Nebr., 1948-50; asst. supt. schs. Champaign County, Urbana, Ill., 1951-57; organizer, tchr. Horstmann Sub-Primary Sch., Loring AFB, Maine, 1957-59; salesman Smiley Homes, Inc., O'Fallon, Ill., 1963-69, First Nat. Holding Corp., 1970-82, Fulford Realty, Inc., 1982—. Mem. Nat. Assn. Realtors, Ill. Assn. Realtors, Belleville Bd. Realtors (dir. 1975-79, 83—), Nat. Women's Council Realtors, Ill. Women's Council Realtors (chpt. pres. 1983-84). Republican. Methodist. Home: 200 Fontainebleau St O'Fallon IL 62269 Office: Fulford Realty Inc 312 S Lincoln Ave O'Fallon IL 62269

APPLETON, MYRA, magazine editor, writer; b. Phila., Dec. 21, 1934; d. Joseph and Sylvia (Pouls) Magid; m. John Johnston Appleton, July 29, 1962. B.A., Temple U., 1955. Researcher, TV Guide, Phila., 1956-61; assoc. editor Show Bus. Illustrated, Chgo., 1961-62; contbg. editor Show mag., N.Y.C., 1962-64; free lance writer, N.Y.C., 1964-68; sr. editor Cosmopolitan mag., N.Y.C., 1968—. Author various mag. articles, film scripts, TV commercials. Office: Cosmopolitan Mag 224 W 57th St New York NY 10019

APPLEWHITE, SUE SMITH, county official; b. Benson, N.C., Nov. 25, 1925; d. Robert F. and Myrtle Irene (Weeks) Smith; m. James A. Applewhite, Jr., Aug. 14, 1948; 1 child, Jennifer A. Applewhite Pelletier. A.B. in Sociology, U. N.C.-Greensboro, 1946; M.S.W., U. N.C., 1962. Caseworker, Johnston County Dept. Pub. Welfare, Smithfield, N.C., 1947-48; child welfare worker New Hanover County Dept. Pub. Welfare, Wilmington, N.C., 1948-50, Onslow County Dept. Pub. Welfare, Jacksonville, N.C., 1950-52, 56-58; social work supr. Onslow County Dept. Social Services, Jacksonville, 1958-74, asst. dir., 1974-79, dir., 1979—; adv. bd. bus. sch. Coastal Carolina Community Coll., Jacksonville, 1979—; sec. Onslow United Transit System, Jacksonville, 1982—. Mem. Onslow Bus. Assn., Jacksonville, 1985—; bd. dirs. Onslow Women's Ctr., Jacksonville, 1982—, Onslow County Energy Commn., Jacksonville, 1980—, N.C. Social Work Coalition, Raleigh, 1984—; past. pres., mem. Onslow County Human Services Council, Jacksonville, 1974—. Recipient Isabelle Kirkland Carter award N.C. Social Workers in Mental Health, 1975; Named Boss of Yr. El Rio Nueva Am. Bus. Women's Assn., 1980, Jacksonville chpt., 1981. Mem. Nat. Assn. Social Workers (bd. dirs. 1973-74, 82-84, del. 1975, 77, 79; Social Worker of Yr. 1985), N.C. Social Service Assn. (pres. 1971-72; Employee of Yr. 1973), N.C. Assn. County Dirs. of Social Services (bd. dirs. 1981—, v.p. 1985). Democrat. Baptist. Clubs: Country, Cotillion. Lodge: Lioness (Lioness of Yr. 1982). Office: Onslow County Dept of Social Services 604 College St Jacksonville NC 28540

APTER, ROSALIND HELEN, restaurant management executive; b. Hartford, Conn., Aug. 28, 1916; d. Aaron and Rebecca (Shimelman) Kenig; m. Marvin Apter, Aug. 4, 1942 (dec. Nov. 1975); children—Ronnie, Anne, Janet, Philip, Ruth, Alan. Assoc. degree Hartford Fed. Coll., 1936. Mng. ptnr. CRQ Co. and Oak Mgmt. (Bonanza Restaurants in Conn.), East Hartford, 1977—. Democrat. Jewish. Office: GRQ Co 531 Main St East Hartford CT 06108

APUNA, SANDI ROSENBERRY, insurance company executive; b. Ft. Wayne, Ind., Sept. 21, 1947; d. Raymond Ralph and Ruth Mildred Rosenberry; B.A., U. Wash., 1972; diploma in spl. early childhood Bellevue Community Coll., 1976; grad. Hawaii N.G. Mil. Acad., 1980; fellow Life Underwriters Tng. Council fellow, 1981; student Am. Coll. Life Underwriters, Hawaii, 1982—; m. Samuel K. Apuna, Jr., Sept. 26, 1980. Owner, dir. Small World Sch., 1976-78; instr. Infant Lab., Bellevue (Wash.) Community Coll., 1976-77 sales rep. Met. Life Ins. Co., 1979-80, sales mgr., Honolulu, 1980-82; mktg. assoc. John Hancock Life Ins. Co., Honolulu, 1982-84, mktg. mgr., 1984—. Served to USAR. Named Met. Rookie of Yr., Hawaiian Dist., 1979; recipient ins. sales awards; qualifying mem. Million Dollar Round Table, John Hancock Pres.'s Club, Nat. Quality award, Nat. Sales Achievement award. Registered ins. rep., Hawaii. Mem. Hawaii Assn. Life Underwriters (sec. 1984-85), Honolulu Assn. Life Underwriters (sec. 1981-82, pres. 1983-84), Hawaii State Assn. Life Underwriters (sec. 1984-85), Nat. Women Life Underwriters Conf. (co-regional dir.), Gen. Agts. and Mgrs. Assn. (Met. Agt. of Yr., Hawaiian dist. 1981), Res. Officers Assn., Civil Affairs Assn. Club: Downtown Bus. and Profl. Women's (pres. 1981-83, ways and means chmn., young careerist sect. 1982, state young careerist bd. 1982-83), chmn. 1983-84, state young careerist judge 1982). Home: 98-1764-D Kaahumanu St Pearl City HI 46782 Office: 1144 10th Ave Suite 300 Honolulu HI 96816

AQUILA, DEBORAH ANNE, film and television casting director; b. Bklyn., Feb. 10, 1958; d. Dominick Anthony and Anne Annette (Caull) A.; m. Henryk Tzvi Cymerman, Apr. 25, 1982. B.F.A., NYU, 1980; student directing and acting Stella Adler Conservatory. Producer Advt. to Women, N.Y.C., 1981-84; head comml. TV div. Zoli Actors, N.Y.C., 1984; assoc. casting dir. for Bonnie Timmermann in assn. with Universal TV (Miami Vice), 1984-85; casting assoc. film C.A.T.S., NBC, 1985-86; talent coordinator East Coast pilots CBS Entertainment, 1986—; free lance acting tchr. Mem. N.Y. Women in Film, Am. Film Inst. Roman Catholic. Avocations: photography; guitar; singing.

ARABIE, DOROTHY TRIPP, nurse; b. Nichols, N.Y., Feb. 12, 1935; d. Norman R. and Mamie Ethel (Wilhelm) Tripp; m. Norman L. Miller, Feb. 12, 1954 (div. Sept. 1968); children—Glenn R., Faith A. Miller Castille, Christopher L., John D.; m. Francis Blanchard (dec. Jan. 1978); m. Emmett J. Arabie, Aug. 15, 1981. L.P.N., T.H. Harris Vocat.-Tech. Sch., 1968; A.D. in Nursing, La. State U., 1976; student U. So. La., 1973-74; B.S. St. Joseph's Coll., Windham, Maine, 1985. Hosp. cert. critical care. Housekeeping aide Fayetteville (Ark.) Hosp., 1951, Mercy Hosp., Durango, Colo., 1953; lic. practical nurse Charity Hosp., Lafayette, La., 1968; lic. practical nurse Lourdes Hosp., Lafayette, 1968-76, nurse CCU, 1976-78, nurse, shift dir., 1978—. Mem. Nat. League Nursing, Quality Assurance Assn. (sec. 1978-82), Oncological Nursing Soc. (chmn. publicity chpt.), VFW Aux., Women's Bowling Congress. Democrat. Roman Catholic. Club: African Violet. Home: Route 1 Box 159 Youngsville LA 70592 Office: Our Lady of Lourdes Hosp 611 Saint Landry St Lafayette LA 70506

ARAKAWA, EVA EIKO, import/export company executive, interior designer; b. Hilo, Hawaii, Oct. 6, 1924; d. Futoshi Frank and Haru (Tachibana) A. Diploma Sch. of Art. Inst., 1948. Interior designer, drafting Ivo Meucci Assoc., Chgo., 1949-53; instr. Chgo. Art Inst., 1951-53; sec., clk. Mitsui & Co. (U.S.A.), Inc., N.Y.C., 1954-71, from asst. to asst. gen. mgr., San Francisco, 1971—. Supporting mem. San Francisco Opera Guild, 1983—, San Francisco Symphony, 1983—; participating mem. Mus. Soc., 1982—. Mem. Japanese Citizen's League. Republican. Congregationalist. Avocations: painting; traveling; symphony. Home: 2941 St Cloud Dr San Bruno CA 94066 Office: Mitsui & Co Inc 1 California St San Francisco CA 94111

ARANGO, ANA, lawyer; b. N.Y.C., Feb. 14, 1952; d. Anthony and Angela (Alcalde) A.; m. Robert A. Chaffin, Sept. 1, 1984; 1 child, Angela V. B.A. in Econs., SUNY-Stony Brook, 1979; J.D., Hofstra U., 1982. Bar: N.Y. 1982, Tex. 1985. Mgr. Health Club, Lucille Robert, N.Y., 1974-77; advanced ground instr., N.Y., 1977-79; assoc. Speiser & Krause, N.Y. and Tex., 1982-86; sole practice, Houston, 1986—. Sponsor LULAC, Tex., 1986. Mem. Assn. Trial Lawyers Am., Tex. Trial Lawyers Assn., Pilot Bar Assn., ABA, Phi Beta Kappa. Avocations: weight lifting; bicycling; running; aerobic dance; flying. Office: 3500 Travis Houston TX 77002

ARANT, PATRICIA M., educator; b. Mobile, Ala., Dec. 2, 1930; B.A., Ala. Coll., 1952; A.M., Radcliffe Coll., 1957; Ph.D., Harvard U., 1963. Researcher, U.S. Govt., Washington, 1952-56; asst. prof. Russian, Vanderbilt U., Nashville, Tenn., 1963-65; asst. prof., assoc. prof., prof. Slavic langs. and lits. Brown U., Providence, 1965—, also assoc. dean Grad. Sch., 1981—. Am. Council Learned Socs.-Social Scis. Research Council grantee, 1969, Internat. Research and Exchange grantee, 1973. Mem. Am. Assn. Tchrs. Slavic and East European Langs., Am. Folklore Soc. Author: Russian for Reading, 1981. Home: 5-D Squire Ln East Providence RI 02915 Office: Box E Brown U Providence RI 02912

ARBUCKLE, SALLY RAE, nurse; b. Saginaw, Mich., Mar. 3, 1944; d. Raynold and Lydia (Sturtz) Schmick; m. John E. Arbuckle, Aug. 21, 1965; children—Cari Lynn, Amber Joy. B.S. in Nursing, U. Mich.-Ann Arbor, 1966; M.S. in Nursing, Wayne State U., 1983. Staff nurse U. Mich.-Ann Arbor, 1966-68; asst. supr. Mott Children's Hosp., Ann Arbor, 1968-70; charge nurse Health Care One, Southfield, Mich., 1971-78; staff nurse Mt. Carmel Hosp., Detroit, 1978-80, asst. head nurse, 1981-82; perinatal nurse practitioner Providence Hosp., Southfield, Mich., 1983—. Arthur Hill Meml. Scholarship awardee, 1962. Mem. Perinatal Assn. Mich. (trustee), Nat. Assn. Neonatal Nurses, Nurses Assn. of Am. Coll. Ob-Gyn, U. Mich. Alumni Soc., Sigma Theta Tau. Lutheran. Office: Providence Hosp 16900 W 9-Mile Rd Southfield MI 48075

ARBUS, LOREEN JOY, broadcasting executive; b. White Plains, N.Y.; d. Leonard H. and Isabelle (Weinstein) Goldenson; student U. Pa., Harvard U., N.Y.U.; B.A., New Sch. Social Research, 1971; m. Norm Chandler Fox, Jan. 31, 1970. Profl. dancer Charles Weidman Co., N.Y.C., 1969-71; free-lance designer, N.Y.C., 1972—; editor Cosmopolitan Mag., N.Y.C., 1971-72; free lance prodn. asst., film editor, Los Angeles, 1972-73; film coordinator Imagivision, 1973-74; story analyst ABC Network, Los Angeles, 1974-75; program coordinator Late Night TV, Good Morning Am., ABC Network, Los Angeles, 1975, program exec. spls., Late Night TV, Good Morning Am., 1975-77, program exec., 1977-78, exec. producer Prime Dramatic, Variety and Children's Spls., 1978-79; contbg. editor Los Angeles Mag., 1978—; freelance TV and mag. writer; v.p. in charge West Coast programming Showtime Entertainment, Los Angeles, 1979-82; v.p. programming Cable Health Network, Los Angeles, 1982-83; v.p. Viacom Prodns., Los Angeles, 1983—; bd. dirs. U. So. Calif. Cinema Circulus. Exec. dir. Media Office of Gov.'s Com. for Employment Handicapped; co-founder Los Angeles Com. to Implement Passage of ERA. Mem. Acad. TV Arts and Scis. (Showtime rep. pay cable adv. com.), Women in Film Found. (trustee), Writers Guild Am., Women in Communications, Women in Bus., Women in Radio and TV, Women in Cable, Hollywood Women's Press Assn. Co-creator comedy pilots, episodic writer Angie, Lou Grant, Tony Randall Show, Marcus Welby, M.D., Gen. Hosp., others, 1975—.

ARCHBOLD, RONNA RAE, college administrator; b. Duluth, Minn., Sept. 22, 1947; d. Wilton Reuden and Georgia Adeline (Smith) A. B.A., Walla Walla Coll., 1969; M.Ed., Worcester State Coll., 1981; postgrad. Boston Coll., 1983—. Registrar Monterey Bay Acad., Watsonville, Calif., 1969-72; from asst. to assoc. dean women Walla Walla Coll., College Place, Wash., 1972-76; from asst. to assoc. dir. admissions Atlantic Union Coll., South Lancaster, Mass., 1976-80, chief exec. officer pub. relations and recruitment, 1980-84, chief exec. officer fund raising and pub. relations, 1984-85, asst. to pres., 1985—, asst. prof. speech communication dept. English. Bd. dirs. Clinton Area C. of C., Mass., 1983—, Thayer Conservatory Orch., South Lancaster, 1981-83; organist, dir. choirs First Ch., Sterling, Mass., 1983—, St. Patrick's Ch., Rutland, Mass., 1977-83. Mem. Speech Communications Assn., Pub. Relations Soc. Am., Am. Guild Organists, Choisters Guild. Office: Atlantic Union Coll Main St South Lancaster MA 01561

ARCHER, CYD LOUISE, advertising agency executive; b. Detroit, Dec. 22, 1954; d. Norman Edward and Violet Clara (Eberhardt) A. Student Northwestern Mich. U., 1973-75; B.B.A., Western Mich. U., 1977. Communications cons. to trial lawyers Archer Studios, Chgo., 1977—, designer, 1977—; prodn. mgr. Frank C. Nahser, 1977-79; media planner Leo Burnett, 1979—. Benefit chmn. Met. Bd. Youth Guidance, 1983, treas., 1984. Mem. Chgo. Council of Fgn. Relations, English Speaking Union. Club: Chgo. Yacht. Home: 1 East Scott St Chicago IL 60610 Office: Leo Burnett Prudential Plaza Chicago IL 60606

ARCHER, JOAN MARGARET, college administrator; b. Beverly, Mass., Dec. 19, 1948; d. Clement Charles and Helen Margaret (Cantwell) Archer; m. Robert Fairbanks Merriam, June 30, 1984. A.B., Regis Coll., 1970; M.Ed., Salem State Coll., 1975. Tchr. Annunciation Sch., Danvers, Mass., 1970-74; supervising tchr., adj. prof. Salem State Coll., Mass., 1974-82; campaign mgr. State Senate candidate, 2d Essex Dist., Mass., 1982; exec. dir. alumnae activities Regis Coll., Weston, Mass., 1983—, contbg. editor Regis Today alumnae mag., 1983—. Campaign mgr. mayoral election, Beverly, Mass., 1984; mem. sr. adv. com., mayoral campaign, Salem, 1985. Mem. Boston Alumni Dirs. (coordinator 1984—), Council for Advancement and Support Edn., Women in Devel. Democrat. Home: 35 Country Club Rd Peabody MA 01960 Office: Regis Coll 235 Wellesley St Weston MA 02193

ARCHER, ROBERTA RUTH, court interpreter; b. Rupert, Idaho, Oct. 8, 1930; d. James Willis and Sibyl Mae (Sadue) A.; children—Charlotte Dianne Kellum Gandy, Belita Earline Kellum, H. Armando Kellum, James Willis Kellum. B.A., Dallas Sem., 1950; postgrad. Puebla, Mexico City, 1974. Cert. U.S. ct. interpreter. Supervisory tchr. Am. Sch., Puebla, Mexico, 1969-74; instr. English Preparatory Bus. Sch., 1969-74; insp., coordinator, prof. Autonomous U. Puebla, 1969-74; lang. coordinator, founding mem., tchr. Hist. Instn. IPECYT, Puebla, 1969-74; pres. Archer Profl. Translating Service, El Paso, 1973—, sr. staff ofcl. U.S. Ct. Interpreter, El Paso, 1981—. Contbg. writer Puebla daily, 1969-74. Mem. Internat. Assn. Constructive Christian Profl. Women (founder), Nat. Assn. Female Execs. Avocations: reading; camping; swimming; hiking. Home: 203 Fountain St El Paso TX 79912Office: US Courts 511 E San Antonio Suite 142 El Paso TX 79912

ARDOIN, CLARA JEAN, auditor, tax specialist; b. Nacogdoches, Tex., May 17, 1950; d. Clezell and Aljean (Booker) Bailey; m. Patrick Ardoin, June 15, 1980; 1 dau., Cheherazade. B.B.A., Tex. So. U., 1973. Agt., IRS, Houston, 1972-78; auditor Dept. of Energy, Houston, 1978-83; auditor internal affairs U.S. Customs Service, Houston, 1983—. Recipient Army Commendation medal Tex. Army NG, Houston, 1980, U.S. Army Res., Houston, 1981, Gulf Coast Leadership award United Way, Houston, 1979. Serves as capt. U.S. Army Res., 1974—. Mem. Res. Officers Assn. (jr. v.p.), Assn. Govt. Accts., Nat. Assn. Female Execs. Democrat. Mem. Ch. of Christ.

ARENAL, JULIE, choreographer, director; b. N.Y.C., July 22, 1942; d. Luis and Rose (Beagle) Arenal; m. Barry Primus, Dec. 23, 1960. B.A., Bennington Coll., 1962. Choreographer for original Hair on Broadway, Isabel's A Jezebel, London, For Alicia Alonso's Ballet National de Cuba, San Francisco Ballet, for movies including King of the Gypsies, Four Friends; dir., choreographer New York Express (Break and Boogie Dance Co.), N.Y.C., 1984—; mem. commn. Spoleto Festival, Italy, 1984. Named Best Show Dir.-Choreographer Swedish Govt., 1969; Choreographer of Yr. Saturday Review of Books, 1968; Nat. Endowment Arts grantee, 1973. Home: 2526 Vasanta Way Los Angeles CA 90068 Office: 205 E 10st New York NY 10003

ARENDT, KATHERINE LOCKHART, economist; b. Washington, Sept. 23, 1952; d. Luther Bynum and Betty Jane (Brodnan) Lockhart; B.A., Duke U., 1974; M.A., Tufts U., 1975; postgrad. U. Va., 1976-78; m. Douglas M. Arendt, May 9, 1981. Economist developing nations U.S. Dept. Treasury, Washington, 1978-79, Export-Import Bank U.S., Washington, 1979—. U. Va. Gov.'s fellow, 1976-78. Office: 811 Vermont Ave NW Washington DC 20571

ARENSON, KAREN WATTEL, journalist; b. Long Beach, N.Y., Jan. 3, 1949; d. Harold Louis and Sara (Gordon) Wattel; S.B., MIT, 1970; M. in Public Policy, Harvard U., 1972; m. Gregory Keith Arenson, Sept. 4, 1970; 1 child, Morgan Elizabeth. Russell Sage Found. fellow, 1972; assoc. dir. Nat. Affiliation of Concerned Bus. Students, Chgo., 1972-73; corr., Bus. Week Mag., N.Y.C., 1973-78, editor, 1977-78; reporter N.Y. Times, 1978-84, asst. fin. editor, 1985—; vis. com. dept. econs., MIT, ednl. counselor. Recipient Women in Communications Matrix award, 1982; recipient journalism award Washington Monthly, 1981. Author: The New York Times Guide to Making the New Tax Law Work for You, 1981. Home: 125 W 76th St New York NY 10023 Office: 229 W 43d St New York NY 10036

ARENT-GRIFFITH, JUDITH MARY, manufacturing official, writer, media consultant; b. Wausau, Wis., Aug. 15, 1952; d. David and Ruth Mary (Goetzman) Arent; m. T. David Griffith, Dec. 27, 1975. B.A. in Broadcast Journalism, U. Wis., 1974, M.A. in Consumer Affairs and Pub. Relations, 1976. Lic. media specialist-pub. info., Wis. Tech. writer pub. relations Minuteman, Inc., Waterloo, Wis., 1976; press sec. to Bud Stewart for Congress, Muskogee, Okla., 1976; mgr. mktg. Met. Tulsa Transit Authority, 1977-80; mktg. coordinator John Zink Co., Tulsa, 1980—; adj. prof. U. Tulsa, 1981-82; freelance writer, media cons. Community Relations, Unltd., Tulsa, 1980, Phillips & Johnson Advt., 1982—; editor, cons. John Cegielski, 1983—. Mem. Women in Communications (pres. Tulsa chpt. 1982-83, Margaret Garner Winston award 1974), Meeting Planners Internat. Home: 7617 S Urbana St Tulsa OK 74136 Office: John Zink Co 4401 S Peoria St PO Box 702220 Tulsa OK 74170

ARESTY, ESTHER BRADFORD, author, scriptwriter; b. Syracuse, N.Y.; d. Jacob and Bertha (Levin) Bradford; m. Jules Aresty, June 24, 1936; children—Robert Joseph, Jane Aresty Silverman. Student DePaul U., 1929-31. Radio commentator Sta.-WJJD, Chgo., 1931-35; advt. mgr. Mandel Bros., Chgo., 1934-36; free-lance radio advt. writer, Chgo., 1936-41; radio scriptwriter Elsa Maxwell Show, Mut. Broadcasting Corp., N.Y.C., 1945-47; free-lance radio scriptwriter, N.Y.C., 1947—. Author: (young adult novels) The Grand Venture, 1963, (as Elaine Arthur) Romance in store, 1983; (cookbook) The

Delectable Past, 1964 (Cookbook Guild choice 1964); (etiquette history) The Best Behavior, 1970; (French gastronomy) The Exquisite Table, 1980. Contbr. articles on cookbooks, Careme, Fanny Farmer, Etiquette, Escoffier, Cordon Bleu to Ency. Americana. Bd. dirs. Trenton Community Found., 1960-72, pres., 1962-64; bd. dirs. Mercer County Guidance Ctr., Trenton, 1965-80, McCarter Theatre Assocs., Princeton, N.J., 1972-83. Mem. Authors Guild, PEN, Am. Inst. Wine and food (adv. bd.). Avocations: collecting rare cookbooks; piano; painting; chamber music. Office: 41 Armour Rd Princeton NJ 08540

ARGIROPOULOS, KATHLEEN O'NEILL, lawyer, construction company executive; b. Washington, July 31, 1948; d. Thomas Grover O'Neill and Elizabeth Jean (Nesbit) Berry; m. John George Argiropoulos, July 10, 1976. B.A., Mary Washington Coll., U. Va., 1970; J.D., George Washington U., 1973. Bar: D.C. 1974, U.S. Ct. Appeals D.C. 1978, U.S. Supreme Ct. 1979. Atty., Consumer Product Safety Commn., Washington, 1973-74; asst. v.p. law, sec. Air Transport Assn. Am., Washington, 1974-84; v.p., gen. counsel, sec. Airlines Reporting Corp., Washington, 1985—; co-owner, dir., pres. Georgetown Roofing, Inc., Arlington, 1979—. Mem. ABA, Met. D.C. Corp. Counsel Assn. (dir. 1984—, treas. 1986). Home: 3857 N Tazewell St Arlington VA 22207 Office: Airlines Reporting Corp 1709 New York Ave NW Washington DC 20006

ARGO, DOROTHY PECK, chemical company executive; b. Cunningham, Ky.; d. Clifton Bolen and Dean (Brooks) Peck; m. Haralson Butler Argo, Apr. 28, 1937; 1 dau., Anne Evans. Student Union U., 1922-23, Memphis Acad. Arts, 1936-37, 44-45. Dress designer, mfr., Memphis, 1935-37; inventor, pres. Argosheen Products Corp., Argo & Co., Inc., Memphis, Spartanburg, S.C., 1942—. Contbr. articles to profl. jours. Div. chmn. ARC, 1957; chpt. capt. United Fund, 1967; patron Music Found., Spartansburg Little Theatre, Ballet Build. Mem. Hotel Sales Mgmt. Assn., Am. Hotel-Motel Assn., Fla. Hotel-Motel Assn., S.C. Hotel-Motel Assn., Internat. San. Supply Assn. Episcopalian. Clubs: Piedmont, Country of Spartanburg. Home: 705 DuPre Dr Spartanburg SC 29302 Office: 182-19 9 Ezell St Spartanburg SC 29304

ARGUELLES, LOUISE WATTS, bank officer; b. Turrell, Ark., Aug. 12, 1924; d. Arthur C. and Mary Evelyn (Greenhaw) Watts; student Iowa State Tchr.'s Coll., 1944, U. Md., 1948-49; basic cert. Am. Inst. Banking 1977; m. Alfred Arguelles; children—Paul M., Robert A., Raymond A. Adminstrv. sec. Nat. Airlines, Miami, Fla., 1957-63; sec. 1st Nat. Bank of Maitland (Fla.), 1963-64; officer mgr. for neurosurgeons office, 1964-69; corp. sec. S.E. Nat. Bank of Orlando (Fla.), 1973—, sec. to bd. dirs., 1975—, now fin. planning and trust adminstrn.; regional office adminstr. Central Fla. region IV, S.E. Banking Corp., Orlando, 1973—. Bd. dirs. Sheltered Community Residences, Inc., 1975-77; mem. Seminole County Republican Exec. Com., 1979-80, Orange County Rep. Exec. Com., 1981. Served with WAVES, USNR, 1944-48. Mem. Nat. Assn. Bank Women. Baptist. Office: SE Bank 601 A1A Ponte Vedra Beach FL 32082

ARIAS, SAUNDRA MCGEE, physician; b. Sandpoint, Idaho, Nov. 17, 1951; d. Carl Fred and Hazel Louise (Burks) McGee; m. Jim Richard Arias, Oct. 7, 1978. B.A., Walla Walla Coll., 1975; M.D., Loma Linda U., 1978. Diplomate Nat. Bd. Med. Examiners. Intern Valley Med. Ctr. of Fresno (Calif.), 1978-79; med. dir. Fairfield Family Med. Ctr., Winnsboro, S.C., 1979-81; staff physician S.C. State Penitentiary, Columbia, 1981-82; gen. practice medicine, Ridgeway, S.C., 1981-82, Atwater, Calif., 1982—; med. dir. Bloss Hosp. Preventive Med. Ctr., Atwater, 1983; med. adv. bd. Merced Hospice, 1983-84; med. advisor Sweatshop, Merced, Calif., 1983. Dir. choir Seventh Day Adventist Ch., Merced, 1983. Mem. Merced County Found. for Med. Care, Merced-Mariposa Med. Soc., Calif. Med. Soc., AMA, Atwater C. of C. Home: 232 W 23rd St Merced CA 95340 Office: Ridgeway Med Assocs 1251 Grove Ave Suite 4 Atwater CA 95301

ARISON, MARILYN BARBARA (LIN), arts foundation executive; b. N.Y.C., May 10, 1937; d. Louis and Leona (Berger) Hersh; m. Bill Harvey, 1955 (div. 1964); 1 child, Michael; m. Ted Arison, Aug. 6, 1968; children—Micky, Sharon. A.A., Miami Dade Community Coll., 1974; B.A., Skidmore Coll., 1976. Exec. sec. L.I. Water Co., N.Y., 1955-57; legal sec. Myers, Heiman & Kaplan, Miami, Fla., 1958-64; sec. Judge Lawrence King, Miami, 1965; freelance pub. relations, Miami, 1965-66; columnist Miami Rev., 1965-69; vice chmn., trustee Nat. Found. for Advancement in Arts, Miami, 1981—. Contbr. travel articles to Miami Herald, Miami News. Mem. ARC Com., Miami, 1983—; mem. vis. com. U. Miami, 1984—; com. mem. Cultural Arts Found., Miami Beach, Fla., 1985—; trustee Am. Ballet Theatre, N.Y.C., 1984—, Gov.'s Mansion Found., Tallahassee, Fla., 1984—. Mem. Lowe Art Mus. Friends of Art. Republican. Jewish. Office: Nat Found Advancement Arts 100 N Biscayne Blvd Suite 1800 Miami FL 33132

ARISTONE, DOROTHY, educational administrator; b. Camden, N.J., Mar. 16, 1939; d. Robert Joseph and Naomi (May) Mentz; m. Edmund M. Aristone, Oct. 26, 1956; children—Pearl, Debra, Edmund, Joseph, Thomas, Atla. Student Rutgers U., 1964, Old Dominion U., 1965. Adminstr. Am. Tng. Service, Cherry Hill, N.J., 1963-66; dir. admissions Phila. Career Sch., 1966-70; asst. dir. admissions Franklin Sch. Sci., Phila., 1970-73; v.p. mktg. Lyons Tech. Inst., Newark, N.J., 1973-74; asst. dir. admissions Health Careers Acad., Cherry Hill, N.J., 1974-77; pres., adminstr. Jedar Corp., Maple Shade, N.J., 1977—. Mem. Nat. Assn. Trade and Tech. Schs., Pvt. Career Sch. Assn. N.J., Nat. Assn. Health Career Schs., N.J. Assn. Fin. Aid Adminstrn., N.J. Bus. Adminstrn. Assn., Nat. Assn. Female Execs., Presidents Assn., Am. Assn. Univ. Adminstrs., Nat. Bus. Edn. Assn., DAR, Paralegal Assn. South Jersey. Roman Catholic. Home: 554 Cutler Ave Maple Shade NJ 08052 Office: Dorothy Aristone's Sch Route 38 and 73 Maple Shade NJ 08052

ARKIN, LUCILLE MAESE, interior plantscaping co. exec.; b. Bklyn., Feb. 18, 1951; d. Albert Joseph, Sr., and Grace Elizabeth (Addeo) Maese; student St. John's U., 1976-78; m. Stephen Robert Arkin, May 17, 1980. Sec., Hudson Pulp & Paper, N.Y.C., 1973-76; benefits coordinator Scali, McCabe, Sloves, N.Y.C., 1976-78; v.p., controller New Growth Plantscape, Ltd., N.Y.C., 1978—; dir. public relations Found. for Interior Plantscape Edn. and Research. Mem. Hort. Soc. N.Y., Adminstrv. Mgmt. Soc., Nat. Assn. Female Execs. Home: 785 West End Apt 2E New York NY 10025 Office: 129 W 28th St New York NY 10001

ARKUS, HELENA B., pianist, piano teacher; b. N.Y.C.; d. Aaron and Esther (Munstock) Bankoff; student N.Y.U., 1925-27, Boston U., 1936; piano student Alberto Jonas, Arthur Friedheim, Edwin Hughes; composition student Percy Goetschius; m. James H. Arkus, Aug. 9, 1927 (dec. 1949); children—Albert, Deanne Arkus Klein, Edmund, Muriel Arkus Celkupa. Pvt. tchr. piano, 1925—; writer program notes N.Y. Orchestral Soc., Jamaica Symphony Orch., 1965—; lectr. Piano Tchrs. Congress, 1976; chmn. N.Y. State Nat. Music Week, 1976, 77, 78; N.Y. state chmn. Mason and Hamlin Competition, 1976-77, 78-80, Stillman Kelley Competition, 1977; internat. Bach Soc. rep. to Internat. Music Council, Prague and Bratislava, 1977; U.S. rep. European Piano Tchrs. Assn., 1978—. Recipient Presdl. citation, 1976. Mem. Nat. (dir. N.Y. div., pres. dist. X and II, chmn. Nat. Music Week 1973-77, N.Y. State Jr. Festival chmn. 1973-76, chmn. biennial young artists competition N.Y. State 1978, 80, 82, 84), N.Y. (v.p. 1976-80, 1st v.p. N.Y. State 1980, acting pres. 1981—, chmn. Young Artists competition) fedns. music clubs, Music Tchrs. Nat. Assn. (N.Y. State and nat. cert. diplomas), Am. Coll. Musicians (faculty and judge mem.), Piano Tchrs. Congress N.Y. (past program chmn., rec. sec., hon. v.p., judge), Leschetizky Assn. (judge, ofcl. rep.), Internat. Bach Soc. (ofcl. rep.), Asso. Music Tchrs. League (rec. sec. 1968), Bklyn. Music Tchrs. Guild (judge, certification diploma), N.Y. Orchestral Soc. (exec. dir., hon. plaque 1965), Piano Tchrs. Congress (hon. v.p., bronze plaque 1973). Contbr. to Musicianship through Improvisation, 1966. Home: 141-17 72d Crescent Kew Gardens Hills NY 11367

ARMAGOST, ELSA GAFVERT, computer industry communication consultant; b. Duluth, Minn., Jan. 26, 1917; d. Axel Justus and Martina Emelia (Magnuson) Gafvert; grad. with honors Duluth Jr. Coll., 1936; B.J., U. Minn., 1938; Ph.D. (hon.), Internat. U. Found., 1985; m. Byron William Armagost, Dec. 8, 1945; children—David Byron, Laura Martina. Freelance editor, Duluth, 1939-42; procedure editor and analyst U.S. Steel, Duluth, 1942-45; fashion advt. staff Dayton Co., Mpls., 1945-48; systems applications and documentation mgr. Control Data Corp., Mpls., 1969-74, promotion specialist, mktg. editor, 1974-76, corp. staff coordinator info. on edn., 1976-78, instr. communications, publ. specialist, 1978-79, bus. products cons., 1979-83, industry cons., 1983—. Bd. dirs. LWV; v.p. Sewickley Valley Hosp. Aux., Sewickley Valley Mental Health Council; dir. publicity Sacred Arts Expo, World Affairs Council radio program, Pitts., 1962-68. Mem. AAUW (1st v.p. Venezuela), Women in Communications (job mart dir.), U.S. Congl. Adv. Bd., Assn. Devel. Computer-Based Instr. Systems, Internat. Platform Assn., Friends of Mpls. Inst. of Arts, U.S. Senatorial Bus. Adv. Bd., U. Minn. Alumni Assn., Phi Beta Music Soc., Minn. Press Club, Walker art Ctr. Home and Office: 9500 Collegeview Rd Bloomington MN 55437

ARMANTROUT, RAE, poet; b. Vallejo, Calif., Apr. 13, 1947; d. John William and Hazel Maud (Hackett) A.; m. Charles Matos Korkegian, Aug. 21, 1971; 1 child, Aaron Mark. A.B., U. Calif.-Berkeley, 1970; M.A., San Francisco State U., 1975. Lectr. San Diego State U., 1979-82, U. Calif., San Diego, 1982—. Author: (poetry) Extremities, 1978; The Invention of Hunger, 1979; Precedence, 1985. Mem. Poets and Writers. Democrat. Home: 3074 Dwight St San Diego CA 92104

ARMBRECHT, CAROL ANN, nurse; b. Youngstown, Ohio, Mar. 4, 1950; d. Albert A. and Angeline M. (Ciarniello) Salata; B.S. in Nursing, Case Western Res. U., 1972; M.S., Tex. Woman's U., 1979; m. Karl James Armbrecht, May 26, 1972; children—Abby, Lyn. Staff nurse Univ. Hosps. Cleve., 1972-73, 74-75, St. Elizabeth Hosp. Med. Center, Youngstown, 1973-74, clin. coordinator, 1976-79; instr. nursing Youngstown State U., 1975-76, Pa. State U., Sharon and Monaca, Pa., 1980—; grad. asst. Kent (Ohio) State U., 1979-81, asst. prof. nursing, 1981—; psychology intern Towne Sq. Psychol. Services, Canfield, Ohio, 1981—. Recipient Cushing-Robb award Case Western Res. U., 1973; research grantee Case Western Res. U. Nursing Alumni Assn., 1979. Mem. Am. Nurses Assn., Nurses Assn. Am. Coll. Ob-Gyn, Ohio Nurses Assn., Tex. Woman's U. Alumni Assn., Phi Delta Kappa, Sigma Theta Tau. Roman Catholic. Author articles in field. Home: 58 Overhill Rd Youngstown OH 44512 Office: Sch Nursing Kent State U Summit St Kent OH 44242

ARMENDARIZ, GERALDINE, lawyer; b. El Paso, Tex., Mar. 9, 1952; d. Juan Sotelo and Mary (Ybarra) A. A.A., Coll. of Marin, 1972; B.A. in Econs. and Spanish, U. Calif.-Berkeley, 1974; J.D., John F. Kennedy U., 1980. Bar: Calif. 1981, U.S. Dist. Ct. (no. dist.) Calif. 1981. Legal asst. Heller, Ehrman, White & McAuliffe, San Francisco, 1974-76, San Francisco Lawyers' Com. for Urban Affairs, 1974-76; law clk. to City Atty., also to Pub. Defender for City and County San Francisco, summer 1978; law clk. criminal div. Superior Ct. Calif., San Francisco, 1979-80; sole practice, San Francisco, 1981—. Home: 2844 Lyon St Apt 303 San Francisco CA 94123 Office: World Trade Center Suite 226 San Francisco CA 94111

ARMENGOL, MARGARITA, bank official; b. Havana, Cuba, Aug. 22, 1944; came to U.S., 1971, naturalized, 1975; d. Alberto and Margarita (Sierra) A.; m. Roberto Lopez, Dec. 14, 1961 (div. 1967); children—Roberto, Lourdes; m. Jorge Flor, Aug. 11, 1984. A.A., Miami Dade Community Coll., 1978; student Fla. Internat. U., 1981-83, Am. Inst. Banking, 1982-83. Asst. bookkeeper, then underwriter, customer service clk. Caribe Ins., Miami, 1971-73; mortgage supr. Washington Fed. Savs. & Loan, Miami Beach, 1973-81; credit mgr. Continental Nat. Bank, Miami, 1981-84; consumer compliance officer, loan officer Republic Nat. Bank of Miami, 1984—. Bd. dirs. Twin Execs. Towers Assn., 1976-81, treas., 1978-79, v.p., 1979-80, pres., 1980-81. Mem. Nat. Assn. Female Execs. Republican. Roman Catholic. Home: 10993 SW 7 Terr Sweetwater FL 33174 Office: Republic Nat Bank 10 NW 42d Ave Miami FL 33186

ARMENTO, MARIANNE, state official; b. Hampton, Iowa, Mar. 21, 1948; d. Ervin John Ernest and Margaret Wilma Caroline (Bessman) Meyer; B.A., Kalamazoo Coll., 1970; m. Paul A. Armento, III, Aug. 16, 1975. Personnel asst. Central Nat. Bank, Chgo., 1970, personnel adminstr., 1971-74, human resources officer, 1974-75; personnel analyst Ill. Dept. Personnel, Springfield, 1975-76, lead personnel analyst, 1976-78, supr. reconsiderations and appeals, div. tech. services, 1978-84, mgr. class standards and reconsiderations, 1984—. Asso. mem. and choir mem. 1st Congregational Ch., Springfield, 1977—. Mem. Am. Mgmt. Assn., Nat. Assn. Female Execs. Mem. United Ch. Christ. Office: Ill Dept Central Mgmt Services 504 Stratton Bldg Springfield IL 62706

ARMIJO, JACQULYN DORIS, interior designer; b. Gilmer, Tex., July 2, 1938; d. Jack King and Iris Adele (Cook) Smith; children—John, Christy, Mike. Student North Tex. State Coll., U. N.Mex. Profl. model, 1961-75; sec. State Farm Ins., Albuquerque, 1965-71; life ins. agt. Mountain States, Albuquerque, 1980; owner Interiors by Jacqulyn, Albuquerque, 1961—; cons., lectr. in field. Mem. Alby Little Theatre, fund raiser for Old Town Hist. Com., Arthritis Fund; mem. Albuquerque Symphony Women. Mem. Am. Soc. Interior Design (chmn. historic restoration Albuquerque), Internat. Soc. Interior Design, Internat. Platform Assn. Republican. Roman Catholic. Clubs: Albuquerque Jr. Women's, Las Amapolas Garden. Home: 509 Chamiso Ln NW Albuquerque NM 87107 Office: Interiors by Jacqulyn 509 Chamiso NW Albuquerque NM 87107

ARMIJO, MARGARET SUZZANE MAESTAS, librarian ednl. adminstr.; b. Las Vegas, N.Mex., June 3, 1951; d. Frank M. and Agneda S. Maestas; cert. in library mgmt. U. Ariz., 1975; B.A. in L.S., N.Mex. Highlands U., 1976; M.L.S. equivalent, State N.Mex., 1976; m. John Paul Armijo, Nov. 27, 1982; 1 dau., Monica Michelle. Part-time library work Donnelly Library, N.Mex. Highlands U., Las Vegas, 1973-76; library intern, Nat. Agrl. Library, Tech. Info. Systems, Library of Congress, Washington, 1975; learning resource ctr. dir. Luna Vocat. Tech. Inst., Las Vegas, 1977—; mem. coms. N.Mex. Learning Resource Center Council, pres., 1982-83. Mem. N.Mex. Library Assn., Consortium N.Mex. Acad. Libraries, SW Library Assn., Seminar on Aquisitions of Latin Am. Library Materials, ALA. Republican. Roman Catholic. Home: 2311 West Dr Las Vegas NM 87701 Office: PO Box 300 Las Vegas NM 87701

ARMIJO, ROSANNE LYLES, company executive, consultant; b. Ysleta, Tex., Sept. 4, 1927; d. George Bartholomew and Fermina (Soliz) Lyles; m. Joe Armijo, Sept. 4, 1948 (div.); children—Mark, Eugene, Candice, Robert, Duane. Student Phoenix Coll., 1968. Advt. designer Ariz. Jour., Phoenix, 1958-62; layout artist Phoenix Am., 1963-66; composing supr. Pueblo Pubs., Peoria, Ariz., 1966-81; pub. info. officer Glendale Elem. Sch. (Ariz.), 1981-82; exec., owner Duo-Type Services, Glendale, 1982—; tchr. in-service workship Glendale Elem. Sch. Dist., 1983-84, also convs. Author: Old Aquaintance, 1984; editor Integration/Desegregation, 1982; contbr. articles to jours. in field. Officer, bd. cons. Glendale Booster Club, 1973-76; events coordinator Inter-Club Council Ariz, Phoenix, 1979-83; coordinator Integration/Desegregation Adv. Council, 1982; town coordinator Chem. Prople, Glendale, 1983; judge Ariz. Newspaper Assn., Phoenix, 1967-70. Recipient Woman of Yr. award Am. Bus. Women's Assn., 1978; Spl. Participant award Glendale Leadership Adv./Devel., 1984. Mem. Am. Bus. Women's Assn. (pres. 1977-78, 81-82, Outstanding Pres. award 1981), Ariz. Assn. Mex./Am. Educators (historian 1977-78, logo selection award 1977), Women in Communications, Inc., Glendale Sister City Program (bd. dirs. 1984-85), Inter Club Council Ariz. (treas. 1984-85). Democrat. Methodist (mem. ch. bd.). Home: 5917 W Colter St Glendale AZ 85301

ARMISTEAD, KATHERINE KELLY (MRS. THOMAS B. ARMISTEAD III), travel consultant, interior designer, civic worker; b. Pitts., Apr. 14, 1926; d. Joseph Anthony and Katherine Arnold (Manning) Kelly; grad. Finch Jr. Coll., 1946; m. Thomas Boyd Armistead, III, Nov. 29, 1952; children—Katherine Kelly (Mrs. W. Michael Roark), Thomas Boyd IV. Editor news Sta. WOR, N.Y.C., 1946-51; with Dumont TV, 1951-52; editor Social Service Rev., 1956-57; interior designer, Los Angeles, 1963—; travel cons. Gilner Internat. Travels, Beverly Hills, Calif., 1980—. Editorial bd. Previews Mag., 1984—. Pres. Jrs. Social Service, Los Angeles, 1962-64; nat. chpt. chmn. Associated Alumnae of Sacred Heart, 1960-66; pres. La Floristas, 1967-68, Los Angeles Orphanage Guild, 1969-70; coordinator Jr. Mannequin Assisteens, Assistance League So. Calif., 1971-72; mem. patroness com. Hollywood Bowl; pres. docent council Los Angeles County Mus. Art, 1976-77, pres. decorative arts council, 1977-80, chmn. Am. antiques conf., 1979-81, mem. costume council, mem. past pres.' council, 1981—, mem. capital gifts campaign com.; bd. dirs. Los Angeles Orphanage Guild, 1970—; trustee Robinson Gardens Found., Beverly Hills. Cert. travel cons. Recipient Eve award Assistance League So. Calif. Republican. Roman Catholic. Clubs: Beach (Santa Monica, Calif.), Birnam Wood Golf (Santa Barbara, Calif.), Bel Air Garden. Home: Los Angeles CA

ARMITIGE, CHERYL YVETTE, real estate agent; b. Houston, Apr. 18, 1955; d. Wilburn, Jr., and Bobbie Joyce (Lowe) Armitige; m. Travis R. Cooper, June 18, 1977 (div. May 1980); 1 son, Kevin Releigh Cooper. B.B.A., Tex. So. U., 1979. Teller, supr. Standard Savs. Assn., Houston, 1973-76; credit analyst HREA Service Agy., Houston, 1976-78; br. mgr. Continental Savs., Houston, 1978-81; ptnr. Sivart Realty Co., Houston, 1981—. Home: 4119 Beran St Houston TX 77045 Office: Sivart Realty Co 4900 Fannin St Suite 202 Houston TX 77045

ARMSTRONG, ANNA MARIA EDUARDA (MIEKE), landscape designer; b. Stavoren, Netherlands, June 14, 1937; came to U.S., 1961; d. Sybrand Marinus and Marca Eduarda (Van Heloma) Van Haersma Buma; m. John Kremer Armstrong, Apr. 27, 1963; children—Marca Carine van Heloma, Jeb Stuart. Horticulturist, Huis te Lande, The Hague (Netherlands), 1960. Landscape designer, Leeuwarden, Netherlands, 1961; bookkeeper, mcpl. bond dealer Chas. E. Weigold & Co., N.Y.C., 1963-65; landscape designer, Bronxville, N.Y., 1970—; lectr. and instr. in field. Bd. dirs., asst. treas. Jr. League of Bklyn., 1965-68; transfer chmn., com. mem. Jr. League of Bronxville, N.Y., 1970-77; bd. dirs. Brookwood Child Care, Bklyn., 1965-68, Musica Sacra, N.Y.C., 1977-80. Mem. Am. Horticulture Soc., Bronxville Working Gardeners (pres. 1981-84). Episcopalian. Clubs: Netherlands (N.Y.C.); Bronxville Field. Avocations: sailing; swimming; skating; cross-country skiing. Home and Office: Bronxville NY 10708

ARMSTRONG, ANNE LEGENDRE (MRS. TOBIN ARMSTRONG), corporate director, educator; b. New Orleans, Dec. 27, 1927; d. Armant and Olive (Martindale) Legendre; grad. Vassar Coll., 1949; m. Tobin Armstrong, Apr. 12, 1950; children—John Barclay, Katharine A., Sarita S., Tobin and James L. (twins). Trustee Kenedy County (Tex.) Sch. Bd., 1968-74; mem. Rep. Nat. Com. from Tex., 1968-73, co-chmn., 1971-73; del. Rep. Nat. Conv., 1964, 68, 72, 84; counsellor to Pres. U.S., 1973-74; U.S. ambassador to Gt. Britain and No. Ireland, 1976-77; dir. Gen. Motors Corp., Halliburton Co., Am. Express Co., Boise Cascade Corp.; chmn. adv. bd., vice-chmn. exec. bd. Center for Strategic and Internat. Studies, Georgetown U., 1977-81 professorial lectr. in diplomacy, 1977—. Bd. dirs. Atlantic Council, 1977-82; trustee So. Meth. U., 1977—; chmn. Pres.'s Fgn. Intelligence Adv. Bd., 1981—. Guggenheim Found., 1980-84; mem. vis. com. Kennedy Sch. Govt., Harvard U., 1978-82; mem. pres.'s council Tulane U., 1977-80; bd. regents Smithsonian Instn., 1978—; bd. overseers Hoover Instn., 1978—; mem. Congl. Awards Bd., 1980-82; co-chmn. Reagan-Bush Campaign, 1980. Recipient Rep. Woman of Yr. award, 1979, Texan of Yr. award, 1981. Mem. English-Speaking Union (chmn. 1978-80), Council Fgn. Relations, Phi Beta Kappa. Club: Econ. N.Y. Home: Armstrong Ranch Armstrong TX 78338

ARMSTRONG, CHALLEN HEANEY, relocation management company executive; b. White Plains, N.Y., July 5, 1944; d. Edwin Joseph and Barbara (Gibbs) Heaney; m. Daniel Edward Armstrong, Sept. 2, 1972; 1 dau., Lindsay. B.B.A., Mitchell Coll., 1965; B.A., Hollins Coll., 1967; M.B.A., Pace U., 1980. Program mgr. Chemical Bank, N.Y.C., 1967-73; dir. communications United Way of Westchester, White Plains, 1974-75; pres. Challen Armstrong, Pub. Relations, White Plains, 1975-76; pres. Challen Armstrong Mktg. Communications, White Plains, 1981-82; mgr. mktg. and communications Merrill Lynch Relocation Mgmt. Inc., White Plains, 1982—. Recipient Gold Quill award Internat. Assn. Bus. Communicators. Mem. Women in Communications (treas. 1981-83), Women in Mgmt., Am. Mktg. Assn. Democrat. Home: 19 Maplewood Way Pleasantville NY 10570 Office: Merrill Lynch Relocation Mgmt Inc 4 Corporate Park Dr White Plains NY 10604

ARMSTRONG, CLARA JULIA EVERSHED, retired college administrator; b. Murray, Utah, Aug. 25, 1911; d. Elmer B. and Lenora K. (Tripp) Evershed; student Henager Bus. Coll., 1936-37; m. Rollin S. Armstrong, Sept. 29, 1956; foster children—Maxwell Rollin, Ruth Elizabeth, Robert Neil, Philip Samuel. Office mgr., credit mgr. D.N. & E. Walter & Co., Salt Lake City, 1937-48; with Latter Day Saints Bus. Coll., Salt Lake City, 1948-76, sec., 1948-52, fgn. student adviser, 1952-55, vet. coordinator, 1952-55, rehab. counselor, 1952-55, registrar, 1955-62, sec.-treas., after 1962, then entrance counselor and employment dir., to 1976. Mem. Ch. of Jesus Christ of Latter-day Saints (pres. Ward Mut. Improvement Assn. 1941-45). Home: 475 E 900 S Apt 512 Box 27 Salt Lake City UT 84111

ARMSTRONG, DAWN, creative company executive; b. San Francisco, Jan. 28, 1943; d. James Harrison and Rose Marie (Kapak) Armstrong. B.B.A. in Mktg., U. Portland, 1964. Vice pres., creative dir. Mktg. & Fin. Mgmt. Enterprises, Inc., Encino, Calif., 1976-82; v.p., creative dir. Direct Mktg. Corp. of Am./Direct Mktg. Internat., Los Angeles, 1982-83; pres., creative dir. High Altitude Graphics, Jackson, Wyo., 1983—, DM Creative Group, Los Angeles and San Francisco, 1983—. Recipient Lulu award Los Angeles Advt. Women, 1966, 67; ECHO award, 1982, 83. Mem. Direct Mktg. Creative Guild (dir.). Club: San Francisco Press. Address: DM Creative Group 150 Powell St Suite 303 San Francisco CA 94102

ARMSTRONG, DENISE GRACE, association executive. Diploma, Briarcliffe Secretarial Sch., Hicksville, N.Y., 1974. Sec., Klar, Klar & Tifford, law office, East Meadow, N.Y., 1974-76; exec. sec. Nassau Acad. Medicine and Nassau County Med. Soc., Garden City, N.Y., 1976-80; adminstr. Suffolk County Dental Soc., Hauppauge, N.Y., 1980—. Mem. Am. Soc. of Assn. Execs., Assn. of Component Soc. Execs. of ADA, Nat. Assn. for Female Execs. Office: Suffolk County Dental Soc 850 Veterans Memorial Hwy Hauppauge NY 11788

ARMSTRONG, JANE BOTSFORD, sculptor; b. Buffalo; d. Samuel Booth and Edith (Pursel) Botsford; student Middlebury Coll., 1939-40, Pratt Inst., 1940-41, Art Students League, 1962-64; m. Robert Thexton Armstrong, July 3, 1960. One-man shows: Frank Rehn Gallery, N.Y.C. 1971, 73, 75, 77, Columbus (Ohio) Gallery Fine Arts, 1972, Columbia (S.C.) Mus. Art, 1975, New Britain (Conn.) Mus. Am. Art, 1972, Johnson Gallery, Middlebury (Vt.) Coll., 1973, Mary Duke Biddle Gallery for Blind, N.C. Mus. Art, 1974, J.B. Speed Art Mus., Louisville, 1975, Buffalo State U., 1975, Marjorie Parr Gallery, London, 1976, Ark. Art Center, Little Rock, 1977, Columbus (Ga.) Mus. Arts and Crafts, 1977, Cummer Art Gallery, Jacksonville, Fla., 1977, spl. children's exhbn. Dallas Fine Arts Mus., 1978, Wichita Art Mus., 1978, 82, Wadsworth Atheneum, Hartford, Conn., 1979, Southeastern Center for Contemporary Art, 1980, Chautaqua Nat. Exhbn. Am. Art, 1980, Rollins Coll., Winter Park, Fla., 1981, Sid Deutsch Gallery, N.Y.C., 1983, The Sculpture Ctr., N.Y.C., 1981, Foothills Art Gallery, Golden, Colo., 1984, Foster Harman Galleries of Am. Art, Sarasota, Fla., 1984, Burchfield Ctr., Buffalo, 1985, Glass Art Gallery, Toronto, Ont., Can., 1985, others; exhibited in USIA group exhbn., Europe, 1975-76, Critics Choice, The Sculpture Center, N.Y.C., 1972, 81; group shows: Phila. Mus., 1972, Nat. Collection Fine Arts, 1971-72, Artists of Am., Colo. State Mus., Denver, annually 1981-86 (speaker 1985); represented in numerous acad., indsl., pub. and pvt. collections; now represented by Sid Deutsch Gallery, N.Y.C. Recipient Pauline Law Prize Allied Artists Am., 1969, 70, Gold medal, 1977; Ralph Fabri medal, 1978, Porton award, 1981; Council Am. Artists' Socs. prize Nat. Sculpture Soc., 1973, Bronze medal, 1976, Tallix Foundry award, 1985, Percival Dietsch prize, 1986; Dr. Maurice B. Hexter prize, 1980; Charles N. Whinston Meml. prize Nat. Assn. Women Artists, 1973, C.D. Murphy Meml. prize, 1979, Elizabeth S. Blake prize, 1980; Chaim Gross Found. award, 1980. Fellow Nat. Sculpture Soc.; mem. Nat. Arts Club (gold medal for sculpture 1968, 69, 71, best in show 1973, Edith W. Macguire award 1975, plaque of honor 1977), Audubon Artists (medal of honor 1972), Knickerbocker Artists (Alice Standish Buell Meml. prize 1972, Elliot Liskin award 1979), Sculptors Guild, Allied Artists Am. Home: 2909 S Ocean Blvd Highland Beach FL 33431 (summer, studio) High Meadows Manchester Center VT 05255

ARMSTRONG, JANICE LYNETTE, nurse; b. Santa Anna, Tex., Dec. 31, 1954; d. Charles Noel and Chloti (Brannan) Armstrong. B.S.N., Tex. Woman's U., 1977; postgrad. in health care adminstrn., 1984—. Newspaper typist Santa Anna News, 1972-73; audio-visual technician Tex. Woman's U., Dallas, 1975-76; student nurse Parkland Hosp., Dallas, 1976-77; staff nurse III, Meth. Hosp., Dallas, 1977-83, staff nurse II, 1983-85, staff nurse III in mgmt. cardiology, 1985—. Basic Edn. Opportunity grantee, 1975, 76. Mem. Am. Heart Assn. Republican. Presbyterian. Home: 329 W Page Dallas TX 75208 Office: Methodist Hosp 301 W Colorado Dallas TX 75208

ARMSTRONG, PAMELA ANN, former retail store manager; b. Opelousas, La., Dec. 21, 1948; d. David Albert and Margaret Ouida (Culley) A.; B.A., U. Iowa, 1970; postgrad. DeCordova Mus. Sch., 1977-78; grad. with honors Nat. Ctr. Paralegal Tng., 1986. Promotion mgr. Witt-Armstrong Equipment Co., Hopkinton, Mass., 1970-78; dept. head data processing interphase dept.

Tropicana Products, Inc., Bradenton, 1979-80; mgr. Burdine's, Sarasota, Fla., 1980-85. Mem. Jr. League, U. Iowa Alumni Assn., Ringling Mus. Assn. Home: 706 Pearl Ave Sarasota FL 34243

ARMSTRONG, PAMELA GAYLE, psychologist; b. Tulsa, Sept. 17, 1945; d. Bernard Charles and Julia Helen (Spillman) A. A.B. in Psychology, George Washington U., 1967; M.Ed., Advanced Grad. Specialist in Counseling, U. Md., 1970, Ph.D. in Counseling, 1981. Cert. rehab. counselor. Dir. out-patient rehab., supervisory rehab. therapist Psychiat. Inst., Washington, 1970-76; regional child devel. coordinator Tenn. Office Child Devel., Jackson, 1978-79; intern psychologist Prince George's County Directorate of Mental Health, Cheverly, Md., 1981-82, psychologist and vocat. coordinator, 1982—; practice psychology and rehab. cons. Rehab. Services Adminstrn. grantee, 1968-70. Mem. Am. Psychol. Assn., Md. Psychol. Assn., Prince George's County Mental Health Assn., Alliance for the Mentally Ill of Md., Assn. Employee Assistance Program Practitioners, Md. Assn. Psychol. Services (ednl. research com.). Home: 6518 Carlinda Ave Columbia MD 21046 Office: Prince George's County Health Dept 6100 Jost St Fairmount Heights MD 20743

ARMSTRONG, REGINA BELZ, economist; b. Chgo., July 10, 1938; d. William Lawrence and Regina Theresa (Genge) Belz; m. William Frederick Armstrong, Jan. 7, 1967 (div. Sept. 1981); 1 dau., Naja Regina. B.A., Rosary Coll., 1960; M.A., U. Pitts., 1965; postgrad N.Y. U., 1980—. Research fellow Center Regional Studies, Pitts., 1962-63; cons. Manchester Nat. Bank (N.H.), 1963; economist Regional Plan Assn., N.Y.C., 1964-67, sr. economist, 1967-70, chief economist, 1970-80, v.p. econs., 1980-84; ptnr. Urbanomics, 1984—; econ. cons., 1984—; adj. prof. econs. NYU, 1984—; econ. advisor N.Y. Statis. Yearbook, Rockefeller Inst. Govt., 1984—; cons. N.Y. State Dep. Controller for N.Y.C., 1977—, Real Property Tax Study N.Y.C., 1980; econ. adv. N.Y.C. Office Mgmt. Budget, 1980—; charter adviser Wharton Econometric Model for N.Y. Region, 1975-78. Author: The Regional Accounts, 1980; The Office Industry, 1972; Growth and Settlement in US, 1975. Bd. dirs. West Side Montessori Sch., N.Y.C., 1977-79; mem. steering com. Econ. Observers LWV, N.Y.C., 1982-83, N.Y. State Econ. Forum, 1982-83. Exchange visitor Stockholm Town Planning Div., 1983; U. Pitts. fellow, 1960-63. Mem. Am. Planning Assn. (sec. N.Y. 1983, v.p. programs 1984), N.Y. Regional Economists Soc. (program chmn. 1983), Lambda Alpha. Democrat. Roman Catholic. Home: 607 West End Ave New York NY 10024 Office: Regional Plan Assn 1040 Ave of Americas New York NY 10018

ARMSTRONG, RUBYE MITCHELL, health association administrator; b. Catlettsburg, Ky., Feb. 14, 1916; d. Hatler Landon and Anna Elizabeth (Vinson) M.; m. William Griffith Armstrong, Jan. 19, 1941; children—Lawrence Mitchell, William Griffith, Jr. Student U. Ky., 1951-53. Exec. dir. Eastern Ky. chpt. Nat. Multiple Sclerosis Soc., Lexington, 1966-77; residential campaign chmn. Ky. Affiliate Am. Heart Assn., Lexington, 1984—, dir., supr. Democrat. Baptist. Avocations. Archeology, poetry; geneaology.

ARMSTRONG, SUSAN DEE, advertising executive; b. Wichita, Kans., Feb. 18, 1949; d. John William and W. Delores (Woodman) Trout; m. Bruce Wayne Armstrong, Mar. 31, 1970; 1 child, Matthew Christopher. B.A. in English and Journalism, Ft. Hays State U., 1971. News reporter Hays Daily News, Kans., 1970-72; account exec. Campaign Assocs., Wichita, 1972-76; account supr. Stephan Advt. Agy., Wichita, 1976-80; owner Armstrong Creative Services, Wichita, 1981—; cons. Kans. Small Bus. Devel. Ctr., Wichita. Mem. Haysville Bd. Edn., 1985; bd. dirs. Big Bros./Big Sisters, Wichita, 1985. Mem. Women in Communications (pres. 1979-80), Nat. Assn. Women in Bus. Owners, Advt. Club of Wichita. Democrat. Methodist. Avocations: reading; photography, snow skiing; swimming. Office: Armstrong Creative Services 715 W 13th Wichita KS 67203

ARMSTRONG, SYNETTA SILVERSTEIN ANDERSON, communications professional; b. St. Louis, June 7, 1953; d. Clarence and Florine (Jackson) Anderson; children—Ebony C., Charles R. B.S., Northwestern U., 1975. Producer, host Sta. KPLR-TV, St. Louis, 1975-77; promotion dir., account exec. Belleville (Ill.) News-Democrat, 1977-79; communications coordinator Brown Group, Inc., St. Louis, 1979-80, communications mgr., 1980-85; staff mgr. pub. relations Southwestern Bell Publs., St. Louis, 1985—; producer video program 60-minutes/month, Brown Group-United Way (Emmy nomination), 1982; copywriter Jan Matzlinger-Yes I Can (Flair nomination), 1983. Recipient 1st place award Editor's Communication Competition, 1982, 83. Mem. St. Louis Assn. Black Journalists, Internat. Assn. Bus. Communicators. Office: Southwestern Bell Publs Inc 1625 Des Peres St Saint Louis MO 63131

ARMSTRONG-DEVRIES, EDNA, state legislator. mem. Alaska Senate, Juneau, 1985—. Republican. Office: State Capitol Juneau AK 99811*

ARMSTRONG-POPPELBAUM, SYLVIA FINCH, social service agency executive; b. Jamestown, N.Y., Sept. 28, 1939; d. Charles Leslie and Josephine Van Vliet (Phillips) Finch; A.B. cum laude, Syracuse U., 1961; postgrad. U. Buffalo, 1962-64, Utica Coll., 1975; m. Thomas L. Poppelbaum, June 16, 1979; children by previous marriage—Ronald C. Armstrong, Andrew D.G. Armstrong. Tchr. secondary social studies, Williamsville, N.Y., 1961-64; dir. Oneida County Youth Bur., Utica, N.Y., 1976-77; asst. for contract mgmt. Oneida County CETA Program, Utica, 1977-79; exec. dir. Planned Parenthood of the Mohawk Valley, Utica, 1979—. Chmn. Oneida County Youth Bd.; exec. com. Central N.Y. Health Systems Agy. Mem. Nat. Execs. Dirs. Council Planned Parenthood, Assn. Human Service Exec. Dirs. (co-chmn.), Utica Met. Bus. and Profl. Women. Home: 30 Hamilton Pl Clinton NY 13323 Office: Planned Parenthood of the Mohawk Valley 1424 Genesee St Utica NY 13502

ARMSTRONG-WATLINGTON, MARY ELIZABETH, lawyer; b. Ponce, P.R., Aug. 25, 1939; d. Robert A. and Marie A. (Tollinche) Armstrong; m. Eric I. Watlington, Sept. 1, 1962; 1 child, Neil Eric. J.D., U. P.R., 1963. Bar: P.R. 1963. Chief appeals div. Legal Aid Soc., San Juan, P.R., 1963-70; sole practice, San Juan, 1971-77; asst. gen. counsel Aqueduct and Sewer Authority, San Juan, 1977—, under-sec. bd. dirs., 1982—, mem. bd. awards, 1981—. Mem. P.R. Bar Assn., D.C. Bar Assn., Instituto de Derecho Registral y Notarial, Nat. Assn. Woman Lawyers. Home: R-3 D St Ext Alto Apolo Guaynabo PR 00657

ARNBERG, CHARLEEN FONTELLE, college official; b. Emmett, Idaho, Sept. 25, 1929; d. George Leslie and Lola Irene (Jensen) Little; m. William Lawson Arnberg, Mar. 8, 1952; children—Linda Jane Arnberg Nielsen, William Leslie, Lori Ann. B.A. in Journalism, San Jose State U., 1951, Gen. Secondary credential, 1972. Instr. Gilroy Unifed Sch. Dist., Calif., 1964-72; pub. info. officer Gavilan Community Coll., Gilroy, 1972—, also campus communications supr., 1983—. Mem. community services group United Way, Santa Clara, Calif., 1981-83; mem. pub. relations bd. Cancer Soc., Gilroy, 1980-82; mem. Gilroy Inter-Agy. Council, 1981—. Mem. Gilroy Women in Chamber (of commerce), AAUW (mem. bd. 1980—). Republican. Avocations: bridge, needlepoint, knitting, traveling, fishing. Office: Gavilan Community Coll 5055 Santa Teresa Blvd Gilroy CA 95020

ARNDT, CYNTHIA, educator; b. N.Y.C., Sept. 27, 1947; d. Charles Joseph and Pura Maria (Rios) A.; B.A., Hunter Coll., M.A., 1975; profl. diploma in bilingual adminstrn. Fordham U., 1981. Adminstrv. asst. to asst. registrar Hunter Coll., N.Y.C., 1968-69; cataloguer asst. Finch Coll. Library, N.Y.C., 1974; tchr. N.Y.C. Bd. Edn., 1974-82, bilingual coordinator Jr. High Sch. 143 M, N.Y.C., 1982—. HEW scholar. Mem. Nat. Assn. for Bilingual Edn., Am. Art Soc., Center for Inter-Am. Relations, Nat. Travel Club, Pi Delta Kappa, Kappa Delta Pi. Democrat. Roman Catholic. Home: 50 W 97th St New York NY 10025 Office: 515 W 182d St New York NY 10033

ARNDT, DIANNE JOY, artist, photographer; b. Springfield, Mass., Dec. 20, 1939; d. Samuel Vincent and Carrie Lillian Annino; student Art Students League, 1965-71; B.F.A. with honors in Painting, Pratt Inst., 1974; student photojournalism, Columbia U., 1979-80; M.A., Hunter Coll., 1981; m. Joseph Vincent Bower, June 16, 1979; 1 dau. by previous marriage—Christabelle Nita Arndt. Photojournalist, photo cons. to mags. and bus., N.Y.C., 1978—; pub. relations assoc. McGraw-Hill Book Co., 1975-78; artist, filmmaker, 1962—; recent exhbns. include: A.I.R. Gallery, 1982, Franklin Furnace, 1982, Just Above Midtown, 1978, Aldrich Mus. Contemporary Art, Ridgefield, Conn., 1976, Am. Inst. Architects. Washington, 1985, Kenkeleba Gallery, N.Y., 1985, Boricua Coll., Brklyn., 1985, Newark Pub. Library, 1985, Metro Cinema, 1985, Collective for Living Cinema, 1985, Printmaking Council of N.J., 1985, Pub. Image, 1985, N.Y. RAW Space, 22 Wooster Gallery, 1985, Storefront for Art & Arch., 1986, City Without Walls, 1986, Wiesner Gallery, Brklyn., 1986, Pub. Image, N.Y.C., 1986, Tulane U., New Orleans, 1986, Pyramid Arts Ctr., Rochester, N.Y., 1986, Food Stamp Gallery, N.Y.C., 1986, Storefront for Art and Post Architecture, N.Y.C., 1986, Post Machina Group, Bologna, Italy, 1986. Recipient Exptl. Writing award Columbia U., 1967, 1st prize in show Springfield (Mass.) Mus. Fine Art, 1967. Mem. Am. Soc. Mag. Photographers, Artists Talk on Art (bd. dirs., exec. dir.), Profl. Women Photographers, Publicity Club N.Y., Found. for Community of Artists.

ARNDT, MARTHA JANE, veterinarian; b. Flint, Mich., Mar. 12, 1946; d. Donald Niergarth and Roberta Agnes (Grimes) Arndt; m. John Kenneth Adams, May 23, 1974 (div. Mar. 1981); children—Kara Elizabeth, Kimberly Ann Roberta. B.S., Mich. State U., 1967, D.V.M., 1969. Veterinarian, Jones Vet. Hosp., Southfield, Mich., 1969-73, German Village Vet. Hosp., Columbus, Ohio, 1973-74; pres., veterinarian Grove City (Ohio) Vet. Hosp., Inc., 1974—. Mem. AVMA, Columbus Acad. Vet. Medicine, Ohio Vet. Med. Assn., Am. Animal Hosp. Assn. (assoc.). Home: 4350 Grove City Rd Grove City OH 43123 Office: Grove City Vet Hosp Inc 4350 Grove City Rd Grove City OH 43123

ARNESON, NANCY CAROL, personnel manager, consultant; b. Mpls., July 29, 1942; d. Lawrence and Albina A. (Goski) Nyberg. B.A., U. Minn., 1971, postgrad., 1973-75. Adminstrv. asst. to v.p.'s U. Minn.-Mpls., 1962-69; office mgr. Coll. Agrl., U. Minn.-St. Paul, 1971-72; personnel rep. U. Minn., Mpls.-St. Paul, 1972-80; personnel dir. Farm Credit Services, St. Paul, 1980-85; employee relations mgr. Park-Nicollet Med. Ctr., St. Louis Park, Minn., 1985—; recruiter Data Processing Profls., Minn., 1985—; landscape design and gardening, Mpls., 1984—; lectr. various groups. Vol., Home for Aged, St. Paul, Target Grade Schs., Mpls., gardener City of Mpls., 1984—. Mem. Twin Cities Personnel Assn., Am. Soc. Personnel Adminstrn., Indsl. Relations Alumni Soc., Minn. Women's Network. Avocations: Plants and gardens; landscape design; scuba diving; motorcycling. Home: 2116 Cedar Lake Pkwy Minneapolis MN 55416 Office: Park-Nicollet Med Ctr 5000 W 39th St Saint Louis Park MN 55416

ARNETT, DIANNE MIX, child care center administrator; b. Dallas, May 4, 1957; d. John Allen and Joanne Louise (Billingsly) Mix; m. Richard Lynn Arnett, Apr. 21, 1979 (div. Mar. 1984); 1 child, John Alden. B.A., U. Tex.-Austin, 1978. Social worker Travis County Emergency Assistance, Austin, 1978-79; owner, dir. Children's Discovery Ctr., Austin, 1980—; pres. Parents Warmline, Austin, 1984-85. Mem. Nat. Assn. Edn. Young Children, Child Care Action Coalition, Austin Assn. Edn. Young Children. Democrat. Roman Catholic. Avocations: needlepoint; swimming; gardening.

ARNEY, IMOGENE UNITA, county official; b. Lindsay, Okla., Mar. 12, 1932; d. Dewey and Pauline Unita (Byrd) Webb; m. Bert Travis Arney, Aug. 10, 1948; children—Marlene Arney Rand, Michael, Paula Arney Baldwin. Recreational therapist III, Mexia State Sch. (Tex.), 1976-80; treas. Limestone County, Tex., 1980—. Pres. PTA, Thornton, Tex., Tri-County PTA, Groesbeck, Tex. Democrat. Presbyterian. Club: Groesbeck Study. Lodge: Order Eastern Star (worthy matron). Home: Route 1 Box 45 Thornton TX 76687 Office County Treas PO Box 515 Courthouse Groesbeck TX 76642

ARNOLD, ANITA GOLDEN, communications executive; b. Tecumseh, Okla., Dec. 22, 1939; d. Ross Golden and Juanita (Winrow) Golden Davis; m. William Arnold, Mar. 1, 1958 (div. Nov. 6, 1975); children—William Christopher, Denise, Cynthia Renee. B.A., Memphis State U., 1975; A.D., Okla. State U., 1970; postgrad. U. Okla., 1977. Systems analyst, indsl. engr. U.S. Postal Service, Memphis, 1974-76, program analysis officer, Washington, 1976-77; info. systems staff mem. Western Electric Co., Oklahoma City, 1977-78, buyer, 1978-79, dept. chief, Springfield, N.J., 1979-81; dist. mgr. AT&T Co., Parsippany, N.J., 1981—; cons. Grambling State U. (La.), 1980—, New Engl. Tel. Co., Boston, 1984; lectr. Nat. Urban League, N.Y.C., 1981—; co-founder Les Mannequins Charm Sch., Oklahoma City, 1971. Recipient Black Achiever in Industry award Western Electric/YMCA, N.Y.C., 1980, Women in Fed. Service award U.S. Postal Service, 1975, Outstanding Contbn. award Grambling State U., 1981. Mem. AT&T Profl. Employees (pres. 1983—), Com. AT&T Black Mgrs. (pres. 1982-83), Assn. Systems Mgmt. Home: PO Box 1138 Union NJ 07083

ARNOLD, ANNETTA ALINE, lawyer; b. Columbia, S.C., May 16, 1945; d. Samuel Herbert Zimmerman, Jr. and Annetta Eloise (Lollis) Zimmerman; m. William Marshall Arnold, Jr., Oct. 14, 1967; 1 dau., Annetta Eloise. B.F.A., Wesleyan Coll., 1967; J.D., Cumberland Sch. Law, Birmingham, 1979. Bar: Ala 1979, U.S. Supreme Ct. 1983, U.S. Dist. Ct. (no. dist.) Ala. 1984, U.S. Ct. Appeals (11th cir.) 1984. Asst. registrar U. South Ala., Mobile, 1968; comml. artist Sears Roebuck and Co., New Orleans, 1969-74; dep. dist. atty. 10th Jud. Dist. Ala., Birmingham, 1979-84; assoc. firm Harrison & Jackson, Birmingham, 1984-85; ptnr. Jackson & Arnold, 1985—. Wesleyan Coll. scholar, 1963-67; Trustees honor scholar Wesleyan Coll., 1963-67. Mem. ABA, Assn. Trial Lawyers Am., Ala. Bar Assn., Birmingham Bar Assn., Nat. Dist. Attys. Assn., Phi Alpha Delta. Episcopalian. Club: Young Men's Bus. (Birmingham). Office: Jackson & Arnold #1 Independence Plaza Suite 500 Birmingham AL 35209

ARNOLD, BARBARA COOK, school librarian; b. Willimantic, Conn., June 24, 1933; d. Wendell Burnham and Frances (Waymire) Cook; m. Edmund Randolph Arnold, June 4, 1955; children—Steven E., Quin L., Lianne C. Peterson, Craig A., Kristin N. B.S., U. Conn., 1955; postgrad. U. Iowa, 1974-75, East Mont. Coll., 1980. Cert. tchr., librarian. Asst. librarian U. Conn., Storrs, 1955-56; media technician Billings Sch. Dist. (Mont.), 1976-80; librarian Lockwood Sch. Dist., Billings, 1980—. Sec. LWV, Mt. Vernon, Iowa, 1974-75; bd. dirs. HACAP Tutor Program, Mt. Vernon, 1974; leader Blue Birds, Camp Fire and Cub Scouts, Potsdam, N.Y. and Mt. Vernon, 1963-73; dir. costume design for Community Theatre, Potsdam, 1964-65. Mem. ALA, Am. Assn. Sch. Librarians, Mont. Library Assn. (legis. com. 1983—), Pacific Northwest Library Assn. (registration com. 1984). Home: 3009 Morledge St Billings MT 59102 Office: Lockwood Schools 1932 Hwy 87 Route 2 Billings MT 59101

ARNOLD, BARBARA EILEEN, state legislator; b. N. Adams, Mass., Aug. 3, 1927; d. Lester Flemming and Sarah (Van Hagen) Smith; m. William E. Arnold, Dec. 5, 1946; children—Wynn, Jeffrey, Gayle, Christopher. B.A. in Psychology, U. Mass.; postgrad. Keene State Coll. Spl. Edn. Clinic tchr. Keene State Coll., N.H., 1964-67; spl. edn. tchr. Easter Seal Rehab. Ctr., Manchester, N.H., 1967-74; state legislator N.H., 1982—, now Republican floor leader Ho. of Reps.; chmn. Manchester Rep. Del.; clk. exec. bd. Hillsborough County Rep. Del. bd. dirs. ARC, 1975—, chmn. bd. dirs., 1977-80; Manchester campaign chmn. Warren Rudman for U.S. Senate, 1980, 86; mem. adv. bd. Greater Manchester Federated Women's Club; mem. vestry, registered lay leader, mem. diocesan commns., del. gen. conv. Episcopal Ch. Mem. Kappa Kappa Gamma. Address: 374 Pickering St Manchester NH 03104

ARNOLD, ERMA ARNETTA, automobile dealership executive; b. Danville, Va., Dec. 25, 1947; d. James Edward Arnold and Annie (Streat) Bailey. Student Va. Sem. and Coll., 1968-69; B.A. in Polit. Sci., Va. Union U., 1972; grad. Ford Motor Co. dealer devel. tng. program, 1985. Sales rep. Exxon Corp., Richmond, Va., 1973-75, Hunt-Wesson Foods, hdqrs. Fullerton, Calif., 1975-76; parts and service zone mgr. Ford Motor Co., Washington Dist., Falls Church, Va., 1976-85; dealer, trainee Dick Strauss Ford, Inc., Richmond, 1984-85; pres., chief exec. officer Waynesboro Sales and Service, Inc., Va., 1985—. Active Nat. Republican Party Com. Named Mgr. of Yr. Ford Motor Co., Richmond, 1977, 79. Mem. Nat. Automobile Dealers Assn., Va. Automobile Dealers Assn., Waynesboro Automobile Dealers Assn., Black Automobile Dealers Assn., Waynesboro C. of C., Waynesboro Bus. and Profl. Women's Club. Baptist. Avocations: restoring old cars and homes; tennis; sewing; cooking; crossword puzzles. Office: 2021 W Main St Waynesboro VA 22980

ARNOLD, FLORENCE MILLNER, artist; b. Prescott, Ariz., Sept. 16, 1900; d. George Thomas and Cora Grace (Paxton) Millner; diploma Mills Coll., 1923; B.S. in Edn., U. So. Calif., 1937; postgrad. Claremont Coll., 1938-40; m. Archibald Adrian Arnold, Aug. 14, 1925; 1 dau., Adrienne (Mrs. Jonathon Chakerian). Supr. music Placentia (Calif.) schs., 1924-41; tchr. music Fullerton (Calif.) High Sch., 1941-48, Buena Park (Calif.) schs., 1948-66; one-woman shows Long Beach Mus. Art, 1961, 69, 70, Calif. State U. at Fullerton, 1967; retrospective Fullerton Arts Commn., 1974; numerous group shows including Esther Robles Gallery, Los Angeles, 1965, Laguna Beach Mus. Art, 1966-68, Women U.S.A., 1973; represented in permanent collections at Long Beach Mus. Art, Laguna Beach Mus. Art, Fullerton Coll., Mills Coll. Art, U. Calif., Fullerton. Cons. program for gifted children Buena Park Schs., 1973-74. Mem. goals com. City Fullerton, 1970. Bd. dirs. Muckenthaler Cultural Center, 1964-78; pres. Art Alliance Calif. U. Calif., Fullerton, 1976-77; bd. trustees Fullerton Sci. Mus., 1971-74. Named Woman of Year Fullerton C. of C., 1973. Mem. Los Angeles County Mus. Art, Laguna Beach Mus. Art (dir. 1967-69), Orange County Art Assn. (pres. 1960-62, 1968-69), Smithsonian Inst. (Archives Am. Art), Delta Kappa Gamma. Address: 1136 Valencia Mesa Dr Fullerton CA 92633*

ARNOLD, GAIL WALLACE, construction consultant; b. Oneida, N.Y., June 3, 1946; d. Earl Jay and Edith Evelyn (Allen) Devendorf; student Onondaga Community Coll., 1977-79; m. Claude Arnold, July 29, 1963 (div. Nov. 1969); children—Joseph Todd, Thomas Edwin. Restaurant owner, Chittenango, N.Y., 1974-76; asst. constrn. super Taylor Woodrow Blitman, Lowell, Mass., 1979; asst. contract adminstr. Cambridge (Mass.) Housing Authority, 1980-81; constrn. supt. Boston Housing Authority, 1981-82; cons. Drug abuse counselor, Chittenango, 1976-79; mem. Millis Alcohol and Drug Abuse Assn.; mem., sec. council on aging Millis Town Bd.; bd. dirs. King Phillip Elderly Services, Norfolk County; chmn. Chittenango chpt. March of Dimes, 1974. Democrat. Roman Catholic. Clubs: Fin, Fur and Feather Hunt, Oak Tree Women's League (Millis, Mass.). Home: 171 Plain St Millis MA 02054

ARNOLD, HENRIETTA DOWS, corporate executive; b. Cedar Rapids, Iowa, Oct. 19, 1921; d. Sutherland C. and Frances Daisy (Mills) Dows; student The Masters Sch., Dobbs Ferry, N.Y., 1936-37; student Greenwood Sch., Ruxton, Md., 1938-39, student Coe Coll., 1939-41, also hon. doctorate, 1978; student Chgo. Art Inst., 1945-46; m. Duane Arnold, Apr. 27, 1946; children—Margaret, Helen, Duane, Elizabeth, Mary. Sec., Iowa Electric Light & Power, Cedar Rapids, 1942-43; with advt. dept. Sunkist Fruit Growers, Los Angeles, 1943-45; v.p., dir. Central Iowa Telephone Co., Cedar Rapids, 1960-66; v.p., corp. dir. Dows Real Estate Co., Cedar Rapids, 1969—; v.p., dir. Dows Maniti Dairy Farm, Inc., Cedar Rapids, 1969-77; v.p., dir. Dows Farms, Inc., Cedar Rapids, 1969—; dir. Sutherland Sq., Cedar Rapids, Iowa Electric Light and Power. Bd. dirs. YWCA, Cedar Rapids Art Assn., Public Health Nursing Assn.; trustee, mem. exec. com., bldg. com. Coe Coll.; trustee, mem. fin. and edn. coms. Menninger Found., Topeka. Mem. Jr. League, Cedar Rapids Hist. Assn. Republican. Presbyn (mem. religious edn. com., instr., trustee). Home: 321 Crescent St Cedar Rapids IA 52403 Office: 212 Dows Bldg PO Box 409 Cedar Rapids IA 52406

ARNOLD, JANE SUTTON, sales and marketing executive; b. Chgo., Feb. 8, 1944; d. John Carr and Florence Kathryn (Salter) Sutton; children—John Nolte, Kathryn Nolte, Alan Zachary. B.S. summa cum laude, U. Wis.-Milw., 1971, M.S., 1976. Dir. Title III ESEA, Project Happe, Milw., 1974-76; dir. programs for gifted and talented Southeastern Wis. Gifted Consortium, Milw., 1976-82; dir. sales and tng. Marine Corp., Milw., 1982-84; v.p. sales and mktg. Marine Trust Co., 1984—. Mem. State Supt.'s Adv. Com. on Gifted and Talented, 1974-77; cons. Wis. Banking Assn., 1983—; pres. Wis. Council for Gifted and Talented, 1974-77, Wis. Assn. for Educators Gifted and Talented, 1975-77. Bd. dirs. Waukesha County Tech. Inst., 1985—, Girl Scouts Greater Milw., 1985—, YWCA Greater Milw., 1985—; mem. planning and allocation com. United Way Greater Milw., 1985—, planned giving com. U. Wis.-Milw. Found., 1985—. Author: Identifying the Gifted and Talented, 1976; Organizing Parent Discussion Groups, 1978. Recipient Ednl. Pacesetter award U.S. Office Edn., 1976. Mem. Mortar Board, Phi Delta Kappa. Office: Marine Corp 111 E Wisconsin Ave Milwaukee WI 53202

ARNOLD, JANET NINA, hospital administrator; b. Poughkeepsie, N.Y., Apr. 23, 1933; d. Paul Dudley and Pauline Katherine (Board) Bartram; A.B., Vassar Coll., 1955; postgrad. Sch. Med. Tech., Albany Med. Center, 1955-56; M.S., Vassar Coll., 1963, M.H.S.M., Webster Coll., 1981; m. Robert William Arnold, Dec. 19, 1954; children—Paul Dudley, Janet Elizabeth. Research asst., med. technologist H. Aird Boswell, M.D., Troy, N.Y., 1956-59; teaching supr., adminstrv. cons. Vassar Bros. Hosp., Poughkeepsie, N.Y., 1959-69; adv. to med. lab., lectr. med. mycology Vassar Coll., Poughkeepsie, 1961-66; asst. lab. mgr. Boulder (Colo.) Meml. Hosp., 1975-80; cons. hosp. planning Mercy Med. Center, Denver, 1981-82; lab. dir. Valley View Hosp. and Med. Ctr., Thornton, Colo., 1982-85; cons. health care mgmt. MRI, 1985—; acad./adminstrv. cons. U. Guam, Vassar Coll., Boulder Community Hosp., others. Sec., bd. dirs. Sanitas Fed. Credit Union, 1977-78, pres., 1979-82. Vassar Coll. teaching fellow, 1961-63; NSF research fellow, 1960-62. Mem. Am. Acad. Microbiology, Soc. for Gen. Microbiology, Am. Soc. Med. Technologists, Colo. Public Health Assn., Med. Mycological Soc. of the Ams. Republican. Episcopalian. Asso. editor Am. Jour. Med. Tech., 1980—; contbr. articles to profl. jours. Home: 4195 Chippewa Dr Boulder CO 80303

ARNOLD, JOANNE EASLEY, educator, university official; b. Hutchinson, Kans., June 18, 1930; d. Orland Royce and Bernice Anna (Daugherty) Easley; B.A., U. Colo., 1952, M.A., 1965, Ph.D., 1971; m. Sanders Gibson Arnold, June 7, 1952 (div. 1983); 1 son, Sanders Gibson. Reporter, mem. editorial staff Boulder (Colo.) Daily Camera, 1955-56; tchr. journalism, speech and English, Boulder High Sch., 1956-71, dir. publs., 1958-69, chmn. dept. English, 1967-69, asst. dir. Nat. Center for Higher Edn. Mgmt. Systems, Western Interstate Commn. for Higher Edn., Boulder, 1971-74; asso. prof. journalism U. Colo., Boulder, 1974—, asso. dean Sch. Journalism, 1974-75, 82—, asso. vice chancellor for acad. affairs, 1975-80; adviser Elem. and Secondary Edn. Act, Title III, Colo., 1972-75; cons. Bur. Communications, U. Colo., 1970-71; cons. elementary and secondary edn., organizational communication, lectr.; mem. Western Interstate Commn. for Higher Edn., 1975-84. . Commr., vice chmn. Boulder Public Libraries, 1973-76; mem. com. on fiscal policy City of Boulder, 1972-73; mem. Boulder Valley Sch. Dist. Re-2 Bd. Edn., 1975-79; mem. nat. adv. council Girl Scouts Am., 1977-84; trustee Boulder Library Found., 1974-76, Boulder Meml. Hosp.; mem. Women's Rep. Club, Boulder, 1968-76. Newspaper Fund fellow Wall St. Jour., 1961; Nat. Woman of Achievement, Nat. Fedn. Press Women, 1979. Mem. Nat. Soc. for the Study of Communication, Speech Assn. Am., Kappa Tau Alpha, Theta Sigma Phi, Alpha Delta Kappa, Phi Kappa Delta, Pi Beta Phi. Club: U. Colo. Alumni (dir. 1954) (Boulder). Editor: Higher Edn. Mgmt., 1971-74. Contbr. articles to profl. jours. Home: 815 Park Ln Boulder CO 80302

ARNOLD, JUDITH ELLEN, hotel exec.; b. Sedalia, Mo., Nov. 30, 1949; d. Bert and Alice Florianne (Messier) Saunders; B.A., U. Mex., 1969; 1 son, Robert Lawrence. Dir. public relations Biloxi Hilton Resort Hotel and Conv. Center, 1975—, asst. mgr., 1978—; dir. advt. B & H Advt. Agy., Biloxi, 1976—; mgr. Biloxi Condominiums, 1980—; Named Hon. col., Gov. Cliff Finch, 1976-79. Mem. Biloxi C. of C., Nat. Fedn. Press Women. Episcopalian. Office: 3580 W Beach Blvd Biloxi MS 39531

ARNOLD, KATHY, state senator; b. Miami, Fla., Oct. 25, 1941; d. John Keith and Mary Fay (Webber) Shay; m. Richard John Speitls, Feb. 16, 1964; m. Harold Grant Arnold, Jan. 31, 1982; children—Mindy, Meghan, Richard. B.A., U. Colo., 1963. Tchr. Bean Creek High Sch., Lakewood, Colo., 1963-64, 65-66; asst. to prodn. control mgr. Fordwerke, Cologne, Fed. Republic Germany, 1966-67; mem. Colo. Ho. of Reps., Jefferson County, 1978-83, Colo. State Senate from Jefferson County, 1983—, mem. numerous coms. Asst. campaign mgr. Bill Armstrong U.S. Senate, Denver, 1977-78; campaign mgr. Dan Schaefer for Ho. of Reps., Denver, 1976. Mem. Nat. Conf. State Legislators (senate rep. 1985—), U. Colo. Alumni Assn. (v.p. bd. dirs. 1970, 72, 73), South Jefferson and Lake wood C. of C. Republican. Presbyterian. Home: 6436 W Frost Dr Littleton CO 80123 Office: Colo State Senate State Capitol Denver CO 80202

ARNOLD, LUCILLE EDNA COCKRIEL, med. group adminstr.; b. Indpls., Oct. 14, 1926; s. George W. and Cleo A. (DuChemin) C.; student Purdue U., 1944-46, Ind. U., 1946-48; m. William Arnold, June 22, 1947; 1 son, Tab. With Foster Bros., Weber, Toledo, 1957-59; gen. bookkeeper, fin. bookkeeper Ind. Bank, Ft. Wayne, Ind., 1965-68; tchr. Payne (Ohio) Elem. Sch., 1966-68; bus. mgr. Pediatrics Assos., Hollywood, Fla., 1970-77; adminstr. Internal Medicine Assos. of Hollywood (Fla.), 1977—; dir. Prudential Bank Fla.; med./bus. cons. Mem. Am. Coll. Med. Group Adminstrs., Med. Group Mgmt. Assn., Fla. Med. Group Mgmt. Assn. (pres, past treas.). Club: Order Eastern Star. Home: 732 48th Ave Plantation FL 33317 Office: Internal Medicine Assos of Hollywood 750 S Federal Hwy Hollywood FL 33020

ARNOLD, MARTHA ROSE, educator; b. Sewanee, Tenn., Sept. 20, 1942; d. Zeddie Lee and Sally Ophelia (Jones) Walker; m. Melvin Parmer Arnold, Dec. 28, 1963; 1 child, Melva Lee. B.S., Middle Tenn. State U., 1964. Cert. elem. tchr., tchr. library service, Tenn., Ga. Elem. Tchr. Cole Sch., Nashville, 1964-66; media specialist Marietta City Schs., Ga., 1966—, West Side computer contact person, 1983—, media com. rep. and incentive plan judge, 1984—; West Side honor rep. Ga. Schs. Excellence, Gov.'s Rev. Commn., Atlanta, 1985; judge Dist. Media Festival, Marietta, 1985. Reviewer children's books. Tchr. sponsor Red Cross Youth, Marietta, 1968-74, 77—; active Democratic campaign, Marietta, 1984. Named outstanding instructional employee Marietta City Schs., 1983; work scholar Middle Tenn. State U., 1960-64. Mem. Marietta Edn. Assn. (bldg. rep. 1982-83), Ga. Assn. Educators, NEA, West Side PTA (chmn. membership 1978-79), Ga. PTA (hon. life), Tau Omicron, Kappa Delta Pi. Methodist. Lodge: Woodmen of World. Avocations: reading; piano. Home: 3430 Elm Creek Dr Marietta GA 30064 Office: West Side Elem Sch 344 Polk St Marietta GA 30064

ARNOLD, MARY BERTUCIO, pediatric endocrinologist; b. Fitchburg, Mass., Sept. 29, 1924; d. George and Louise (Byrolly) Bertucio; A.B., Vassar Coll., 1945; M.D., U. Vt., 1950; M.A., Brown U., 1974; m. John Hampton Arnold, July 28, 1956 (dec. Apr. 1972); children—John, Mark, Matthew. Intern, resident Hartford (Conn.) Hosp., 1950-52; asst./sr. pediatric resident Babies' Hosp., Columbia-Presbyn. Med. Center, N.Y.C., 1952-54; pediatric endocrinology research fellow Mass. Gen. Hosp., Boston, 1954-57; asst. in pediatrics Harvard U. Sch. Medicine, Boston, 1955-57; instr. pediatrics/asst. prof. U. N.C. Sch. Medicine, Chapel Hill, 1959-65; lectr. med. sci./assoc. prof. pediatrics Brown U., Providence, 1966-74, assoc. prof., 1974—; chmn. dept. pediatrics, dir. pediatric endocrinology Roger Williams Gen. Hosp., Providence, 1971—. Chmn., Heart Health in the Young Com., Am. Heart Assn., R.I. Affiliate, Inc., 1979-82; mem. adv. com. New Eng. Regional Hypothyroidism Screening Program, 1976—; mem. subcom. pediatric planning rev. guidelines Hosp. Assn. R.I., 1976—; mem. program com. R.I. Clin. Diabetes Assn., 1975—. Recipient Carrbee award U. Vt. Sch. Medicine, 1950, Excellence in Teaching award Brown U., 1978. Mem. Endocrine Soc., Lawson Wilkins Pediatric Endocrine Soc., Am. Fedn. Clin. Research, AAAS, Am. Med. Women's Assn., Am. Acad. Pediatrics, AMA, New Eng. Pediatric Soc., R.I. Clin. Diabetes Assn. (pres. 1975-77), Sigma Xi. Episcopalian. Contbr. articles to profl. jours. Office: 825 Chalkstone Ave Providence RI 02908

ARNOLD, MIRIAM KEBA, educational program administrator; b. Pensacola, Fla., Sept. 5, 1927; d. James and Pauline (Spears) Campbell; m. Cecil D. Arnold, Sr., Apr. 14, 1951; children—Cynthia Susan Arnold Jolly, C. Duaine, Jr. B.S., Fla. State U., 1949, M.S. in Adminstrn. and Supervision, 1972. Bus. edn., cooperative edn. tchr. Pensacola High Sch., Fla., 1958-70, adminstrv. dean, 1970-74; coordinator vocat. edn. Escambia County Schs., Pensacola, 1974-83, dir. vocat. edn., 1983—. Bd. dirs., past pres. Fiesta Frolickers; bd. dirs. Maids of Luna, Krewe of Aphrodite; Mem. Am. Vocat. Assn. (invited to address U.S. Congress 1982), Fla. Vocat. Assn., Escambia Vocat. Assn. (Outstanding Vocat. Educator award 1981), Nat. Bus. Edn. Assn., Fla. Bus. Edn. Assn., Escambia Bus. Edn. Assn., Fla. Assn. Distributive Edn. Tchrs., Fla. Assn. Distributive Edn. Suprs., Health Occupations Tchrs. Fla., Fla. Assn. Sch. Adminstrs., Escambia Assn. Adminstrs. Edn. (pres.; outstanding Contbn. award 1985), Escambia County Tchrs. Credit Union (chmn. credit com. 1979-82), Fla. State U. Alumni Assn. (life mem.), Fla. Council Local Adminstrs., Nat. Council Local Adminstrs. Democrat. Presbyterian. Clubs: Pensacola Seminole Boosters, Nat. Seminole Boosters, Inc.

ARNOLD, RACHEL LOONEY, secretary; b. Paint Bank, Va., Feb. 26, 1916; d. George Crockett and Mabel Clara (Haynes) Looney; student Lynchburg (Va.) Coll., 1934-35; cert. in theory and organ Randolph-Macon Woman's Coll., Lynchburg, 1940; student Phillips Bus. Coll., Lynchburg, 1955; m. Clarence Bryan Arnold, Jr., Aug. 20, 1941 (div.), 1 dau., Merlyn Dawn Arnold Cloyd. Receptionist, bookkeeper Dr. G.C. Looney, Optometrist, Lynchburg, 1941-42; pianist Madison Heights (Va.) Christian Ch., 1930-40, organist, 1940-54; organist Meml. Christian Ch., Lynchburg, 1954-74; cashier dept. circulation Lynchburg News & Daily Advance, 1956; sec. to dean coll. and dean students Lynchburg Coll., 1956-61, sec. to dean student affairs, 1961—. Adviser Lynchburg Coll. chpt. Cardinal Key Nat. Honor Sorority, 1966-84. Mem. Profl. Secs. Internat. Home: 204 E Cadbury Dr Lynchburg VA 24501 Office: Lynchburg College Lynchburg VA 24501

ARNOLD, SHEILA, state legislator; b. N.Y.C., Jan. 15, 1929; d. Michael and Eileen (Lynch) Keddy; coll. courses; m. George Longan Arnold, Nov. 12, 1960; 1 son, Peter; 1 son by previous marriage, Michael C. Young; stepchildren—Drew, George Longan, Joe. Mem. Wyo. Ho. of Reps., 1978—, mem. appropriations com., select com. on water devel.; dir. First Interstate Bank of Laramie. Former mem., sec. Wyo. Land Use Adv. Com.; past pres. Democratic Women's Club, Laramie; past vice-chmn. Albany County Dem. Central Com.; past mem. Dem. State Com.; mem. spl. task force on long term health care Nat. Conf. State Legislatures, 1986—. Mem. Laramie Area C. of C. (Top Hand award 1977; pres. 1982), LWV. Clubs: Faculty Women's (past pres.), Zonta, Laramie Women's, Cowboy Joe. Office: Capitol Bldg Cheyenne WY 82001

ARNOLD, SHIRLEY MAE, educational administrator; b. Knoxville, Tenn., Mar. 3, 1951; d. Alvin and Carrie Louise (Spear) A. B.A. cum laude, Knoxville Coll., 1972; M.A., Atlanta U., 1974. Program analyst Dept. Health Edn. and Welfare, Atlanta, 1974; learning skills coordinator OIC, Inc., Atlanta, 1976; counseling coordinator Ga. State U., Atlanta, 1978-83, asst. project dir., 1983-85, project dir., 1985—; career counselor. Mem. parks neighborhood planning council Bur. Parks and Recreation, Atlanta, 1976; mem. adv. council So. Bell's Affirmative Action Council-Disabled, Atlanta, 1980; citizen advocate Ga. Advocacy Office for Disabled, Atlanta, 1980. Mem. Am. Assn. Counseling and Devel., Assn. Multi-Cultural Counseling Devel., Nat. Assn. Female Execs., Southeastern Assn. Spl. Program Personnel (exec. council 1985-86), Ga. Assn. Spl. Program Personnel, Delta Sigma Theta. Avocations: aerobics; jogging; drawing. Home: 6100 Castlegate Dr Riverdale GA 30296 Office: Ga State U University Plaza-CPUR Atlanta GA 30303

ARNOLD, SUSAN BIRD, safety education products company executive; b. Reading, Pa., Feb. 28, 1951; d. Frank Edward and Esther (Savidge) Bird; B.A., Mercer U., Macon, Ga., 1972; m. Robert Melvin Arnold, Jr., Mar. 18, 1972; children—Jennifer Michelle, Amelia Michelle, Elizabeth Michelle, Elizabeth Michelle. Audio-video technician Internat. Safety Acad., 1971; with Internat. Loss Control Inst., 1974—, mgr. edni. products div., 1978-82, v.p. adminstrv. services, v.p. press div., Loganville, Ga., 1982-85, exec. dir., gen. mgr., 1985—. Contbr. to Risk Control Rev. Mem. adv. com. Inst. Safety, Health and Rehab. for the Exceptional, 1978-84. Mem. AVMA Aux. Methodist. Home: PO Box 609 Loganville GA 30249 Office: Internat Loss Control Inst Hwy 78 Loganville GA 30249

ARNOLD, VERNA ALINE, educator, administrator; b. Haskell, Tex., Apr. 7, 1931; d. Bert W. and Juanita V. (Brooks) Marchbanks; m. Walter Eugene Arnold, Sept. 6, 1969; 1 dau., Teresa Anderson. A.A., Eastfield Coll., 1973; B.B.A., N.Tex. State U., 1975, M.B.A., 1976, Ph.D., 1978. Asst. adminstr. Doctors Hosp., Dallas, 1959-60; adminstrv. asst. Baylor U. Med. Ctr., Dallas, 1960-66; hosp. adminstr. Ennis Mcpl. Hosp. (Tex.), 1966-70; asst. prof. mgmt. N.Tex. State U., Denton, 1979—, exec. asst. to chancellor, 1982—; v.p. Arnold Assocs., Denton, 1979-82. Contbr. articles to profl. jours. Mem. Am. Pub. Health Assn., Am. Hosp. Assn., Am. Acad. Mgmt., Tex. Hosp. Assn., SW Acad. Mgmt., Bus. and Profl. Women's Club (v.p. 1968-70), Beta Gamma Sigma, Sigma Iota Epsilon, Phi Theta Kappa. Republican. Baptist. Office: N Tex State U PO Box 13737 Denton TX 76203

ARNOLIE, LOUISE WILLIAMS, government official; b. Gramercy, La., Nov. 1, 1941; d. Alexander and Olivia (Johnson) Williams; div. Nov. 1979; 1 child, Anthony Arthur. B.S., La. State U., 1986; postgrad. Dillard U., 1983, 86, So. U., 1986. Sec., FDA, New Orleans, 1964-72, consumer affairs specialist, 1972-79; women's mgmt. assoc. Dept. Health and Human Services, Rockville, Md., 1984-85; area dir. Women's Edni. Service Assn., New Orleans, 1982-84; regional program analyst FDA, New Orleans, 1979—. Bd. dirs. La. Equal Opportunity Assn., 1983—; mem. exec. bd. United Way Greater New Orleans, 1984—; program chmn. New Orleans Com. on Handicapped Issues, 1982—; project coordinator Minority Outreach Demonstration Project, Dallas, 1982-83; com. mem. Mayor's Task Force on Human Services Needs, 1983—, Mayor's Anti Truancy Task Force, 1984-85; bd. dirs. Afro Am. pavilion, I've Known Rivers, Inc. World's Fair 1984, also charter mem. Women's Pavilion; bd. dirs. urban League Greater New Orleans, 1975-81; pres. Urban League Guild, 1983-84, exec. bd., 1983—; bd. dirs. La. Consumers League, 1975-79; mem. choir, mem. bd. Christian edn. Tulane Meml. Bapt. Ch., 1975—; mem. fed. exec. bd. Equal Employment Opportunity Council, 1980-83. Mem. FDA Commr.'s Nat. Employee Adv. Council, 1984—. Named Woman of Yr., Fed. Women's Program, Fed. Exec. Bd., 1975-76; recipient Outstanding Vol. Service award Jefferson Parish Community Action Agy., 1976. Mem. Nat. Assn. Female Execs., Delta Sigma Theta. Democrat. Avocations: singing; reading; sports. Office: FDA 4298 Elysian Fields Ave New Orleans LA 70126

ARNOT, SUSAN EILEEN, publishing company manager; b. East Orange, N.J., Aug. 10, 1957; d. Robert B. and Mae (Cockcroft) A. B.A., Coll. William and Mary, 1979; student Cambridge U., 1977; cert. Ctr. for Pub., NYU, 1979. Promotion asst. Viking Press/Penguin Books, N.Y.C., 1979-82; promotion mgr. Rizzoli Internat. Publs., N.Y.C., 1982-83; advt. promotion mgr. USA Today, N.Y.C., 1983-85; sales promotion mgr. Whitney Communications Co., N.Y.C., 1985—; career adv. Coll. William and Mary, 1980—. Writer/editor quar. newsletter Maturity Market Update, 1985—. Vol. cook, fundraiser Cathedral Soup Kitchen, St. John the Divine Cathedral, 1983-85. Mem. Women in Communications Inc. (chpt. publicity com. 1985—), Nat. Assn. Female Execs., NOW, Coll. William and Mary Alumni Soc. (chpt. pres. 1986—, exec. bd. 1983-86), AAUW (chpt. corr. sec. 1983-86, chair com. on women's work 1984-86). Methodist. Avocations: travel; theatre; reading. Home: 230 W 107th St Apt 3J New York NY 10025 Office: 850 3d Ave New York NY 10022

ARNSTEIN, SHERRY PHYLLIS, health care executive; B.S., UCLA, 1951; M.S. in Communications, Am. U., 1963; postgrad. in systems dynamics MIT, summer 1976. Washington editor Current Mag., 1961-63; staff cons. Pres. Com. on Juvenile Delinquency, 1963-65; spl. asst. to asst. sec. HEW, 1965-67; chief citizen participation advisor Model Cities Adminstrn., HUD, 1967-68; pub. policy cons., Washington, 1968-75; sr. research fellow HHS, Washington, 1975-78; v.p. govt. relations Nat. Health Council, Inc., Washington, 1978-85; exec. dir. Am. Assn. Colls. Osteo. Medicine, 1985—. Bd. dirs. Youth Policy Inst. Author: (with Alexander Christakis) Perspectives on Technology Assessment, 1975; editor: Government Relations Handbook Series, 1979-85, Washington Report Series, 1985. mem. editorial bd. Tech. Assessment Update, 1975-78, The Bureaucrat, 1975-83, Pub. Adminstrn. Rev., 1978-83, Health Mgmt. Quar., 1985. Contbr. articles to profl. jours. Office: Am Assn Colls Osteo Medicine 6110 Executive Blvd Suite 405 Rockville MD 20852

ARONSON, CATHLEEN ANN, court reporter; b. Chgo., Apr. 30, 1951; d. Wesley and Catherine Angela (Nehls) A. Student Chgo. Coll. Commerce, 1973-76. Cert. shorthand reporter. Ct. reporter Metro Reporting Service, Chgo., 1976-77; court reporter Central Reporters Associated, 1977-79, owner, 1979—; guest lectr. Chgo. Coll. Commerce, 1984. Mem. Nat. Shorthand Reporters Assn., Ill. Shorthand Reporters Assn. Republican. Roman Catholic. Avocations: reading; collecting porcelains; needlepoint. Office: Central Reporters Associated 130 E Randolph Dr Suite 2207 Chicago IL 60601

ARONSON, HELENE SALLY DAVIES, psychological consultant; b. Phila., July 9, 1921; d. Michael Laurence and Gertrude Peggy (Bloom) Davies; m. Bernard Aronson, Apr. 18, 1953; children—Sandra Morris-Bandt, Robert, Gary, Sharyl. A.B. in Journalism, Pa. State U., 1942; M.S. in Psychiat. Social Work, Bryn Mawr Coll., 1959; Ph.D. in Psychology, Newport Internat. U., 1977. Psychotherapist Temple U. St. Christopher's Hosp. for Children, 1959-62; pvt. practice psychotherapy, Phila., 1962-71, San Diego, 1971—; psychiat. social worker VA, Phila., 1967-70; cons., seminar leader Intergovtl. Tng., San Diego, 1972-76; chairperson psychiat. dept. U. Humanistic Studies, San Diego, 1978-81; clin. dir. Sunrise Lodge Inst., Dulzura, Calif., 1972—; lectr. Laissez-faire Soc., Owens Mills, Md., 1970. Editor newsletter Child Abuse Council, San Diego, 1983. Group leader Girl Scouts Am., Phila., 1950-63. Recipient Fellowship and Stipend, NIMH, 1957-59. Mem. Internat. Transactional Analysis Assn., Am. Group Psychotherapy Assn., Am. Acad. Psychotherapy, Acad. Certified Social Workers, Psychology and Law Soc., Delaware Valley Group Psychotherapy Assn. (bd. mem. 1970-72). Avocations: golf; interior decorating; stained-glass making; music; theatre; travel. Office: Sunrise Lodge Inst Box 140 Dulzura CA 92017

AROVA, SONIA, ballet educator, administrator; b. Sofia, Bulgaria, June 20, 1928; came to U.S., 1954; d. Albert and Rene (Melamedoff) Errio; m. Thor Sutowski, Mar. 11, 1965. Grad. Fine Arts Sch., Paris, 1940, Eng., 1944. Ballerina Internat. Ballet, London, 1944-47, Rambert Ballet, London, 1947-50, Royal Ballet, London, 1961, Festival Ballet, London, 1951-54, Ballet de-Champs-Elysees, Paris, 1950-51, Am. Ballet Theater, N.Y.C., 1956-58; artistic dir. Nat. Ballet, Oslo, 1964-70, Hamburg Ballet, Fed. Republic Germany, 1970-71; co-dir. San Diego Ballet, 1971-75; dir. State of Ala. Ballet, Birmingham, 1981—, instr. Sch. Fine Arts, 1975—. Recipient World Championship of Dance award Ballet Jury, Paris, 1939; decorated knight of First Order, King Olav of Norway, 1971.

ARRATEIG, LYNN (BERNADETTE) MURPHEY, occupational therapist; b. Denver, Mar. 19, 1943; d. Maurice Francis and Katherine Bernadette (Sturgess) Murphey; B.S., Colo. State U., 1965; m. Pierre Bernard Arrateig, Apr. 8, 1972. With Calif. Crippled Children's Div., 1966-76, sr. therapist physically handicapped Orange County Health Dept., 1969-72, Riverside County Health Dept., 1972-76; clin. supr. occupational therapy Riverside County, 1972-76; clin. instr. Loma Linda U., 1974-76, instr. occupational therapy, 1976—, also supr. pediatric occupational therapy Loma Linda U. Med. Center. Mem. Am. Occupational Therapy Assn. (vice chmn. council on edn. 1971-72), Occupational Therapy Assn. Calif. (v.p. Orange County chpt. 1970-71 sec. Inland chpt. 1979-80), Center Study Sensory Integrative Dysfunction. Democrat. Roman Catholic. Home: 2334 Indian Ave Perris CA 92370 Office: Sch Allied Health Professions Dept Occupational Therapy Loma Linda U Loma Linda CA 92350

ARRECHE, CANDY ANN, lawyer, blood bank exec.; b. Santurce, P.R., July 7, 1954; d. Candido C. and Olga (Holdun) A.; B.A. cum laude in History and Fgn. Langs., Fla. Technol. U., 1974; J.D. magna cum laude, Inter-Am. U., 1976. Donor recruiter P.R. Community Blood Center, Inc., Santurce, 1974-76; law clk. firm Calderon Rosa Silva y Vargas, San Juan, P.R., 1975-76; admitted to P.R. bar, 1977; atty. Coop. Devel. Corp., San Juan, 1977; law clk. San Juan Jud. Center, 1978; individual practice law, Santurce, P.R. 1978—; exec. dir. P.R. Community Blood Center, Hosp. Sagrado Corazon, Santurce, 1981—; treas. Hosp. Sagrado Corazon. Den mother Cub Scouts Miami council Boy Scouts Am., 1970-72; active gubernatorial election Fla., 1971; translator for Spanish-speaking voting population, presdl. election, 1972. Recipient Key to City Coral Gables (Fla.), 1971; notary public, P.R. Mem. P.R. Bar Assn., Am. Bar Assn., Internat. Bar. Assn., Fla. Assn. Blood Banks, Am. Assn. Blood Banks, Better Bus. Bur. of P.R., C. of C. of P.R., Fla. Technol. U. Alumni. Roman Catholic. Club: Rosecrusian Order. Office: 1301 Jesus T. Piñero Ave Puerto Nuevo PR 00920

ARREDONDO, JOY GRACE, real estate broker; b. Roswell, N.Mex., Jan. 24, 1929; d. Jess Dewaco and Pauline (Lozano) Dominguez; student West Valley Jr. Coll., 1975-76; m. Chris Franco Arredondo, Apr. 3, 1949; children—Nancy Lynn, Christopher Anthony, Leslie Ann. Engring. asso. Raytheon Semi-Condr., 1963-74; office mgr., co-owner Jude Realty, Campbell, Calif., 1974—. Notary public, lic. real estate salesman and broker, Calif. Mem. San Jose Real Estate Bd., Nat. Assn. Realtors, Calif. Assn. Realtors, Alpha Gamma Sigma. Democrat. Roman Catholic. Home: 5186 Meridian Ave San Jose CA 95118 Office: 101 W Hamilton St Campbell CA 95008

ARRINGTON, LILLIAN ALLEN SHAW, nursing home adminstr.; b. Dayton, Ohio, Nov. 29, 1929; d. John and Odessa (Cook) Allen; student Sinclair Coll., 1951, 65, 66, 71, 73; Asso. degree Nursing, U. Dayton, 1952; student Ohio State U., 1975; children—Gary R. Shaw, Victor C. Shaw, Steven R. Arrington. Sec., Wright Patterson AFB, Dayton, 1951-54, Inland Mfg. div. GMC, Dayton, 1957-70; staff nurse VA Center, Dayton, 1973-74; dir. nursing Crawford Convalescent Center, Inc., Dayton, 1974-75, staff devel. and facility standards, 1975-76, gen. mgr., 1976-78, chief adminstr., 1978—, now owner, pres., treas.; inservice edn. dir. Stillwater Health Center, Dayton, 1975-76. Sec., Dayton Area Nursing Home Assn., 1977, 80; mem. Madison Twp. Community Assn., 1980—; Mem. Nat. Assn. Female Execs. (network dir. 1980—), Better Bus. Bur., Dayton C. of C., Nat. Fedn. Ind. Bus. Home: 3727 Hermosa Dr Dayton OH 45416 Office: 806 W Fifth St Dayton OH 45407

ARRINGTON, NELLIE WEBB, marketing executive, consultant; b. Balt., Oct. 16, 1952; d. Elbert C. and Margaret Virginia (Webb) Arrington; m. Robert Stacy Evans, Jan. 3, 1981; 1 child, Elyse Anne. A.B., Western Md. Coll., 1974; M.S., Johns Hopkins U., 1980. Reporter, editor Stromberg Publs., Ellicott City, Md., 1974-79; mktg. exec. Henry Adams, Inc., Balt., 1980-84, Edmunds & Hyde, Inc., Balt., 1984-85; realtor Long & Foster Realtors, Inc., Columbia, Md., 1986—; mktg./mgmt. cons., Ellicott City, 1977—. Author news feature series The Crime of Rape (2d place award Md.-Del.-D.C. Press Assn. 1975); contbr. articles to profl. jours. Pres., Lawyer's Hill-Rockburn Area Assn., Elk Ridge, Md., 1975-77. Mem. Soc. Mktg. Profl. Services (founding pres. Chesapeake chpt. 1981-83, jury chmn. 1981-82, nat. conv. speaker 1984, sr. roundtable 1984), Columbia Jaycees (internal v.p. 1980-81, Officer of Yr. award 1981). Democrat. Episcopalian. Club: Md. Press (pres. 1981, 1st v.p. 1979).

ARROTT, SUSAN CUMBIE, interior designer; b. Bronte, Tex., Aug. 27, 1953; d. Edward McCuistion and Helen Jane (Luby) Cumbie; m. Nick Edward Arrott, Mar. 24, 1973; 1 child, Nicholas Edward, II. Student, Angelo State U., 1971-73. With engring. div. Mitsubishi Aircraft, Internat., 1971-74; exec. sec. First Nat. Bank, Bronte, Tex., 1973-78; interior designer Bowman's Ctr., San Angelo, Tex., 1978, Home Interiors & Gifts, Dallas, 1979—; owner Cumbie's Arrott Gen. Mercantile, 1985—. Bd. dirs. Coke County Hist. Commn., 1983—, Child Welfare, Coke County, Tex., 1985—; sec. Tex. Sesquicentennial Com., Bronte, 1985—. Mem. Young Homemakers (area sec.-treas. 1980, area v.p. 1982), Bronte Young Homemakers (pres. 1981). Republican. Baptist. Avocations: snow skiing; water sports; antiques; stained glass. Home and Office: Route 2 Bronte TX 76933

ARROWSMITH, MARIAN CAMPBELL, educator; b. St. Louis, Nov. 12, 1943; d. William Rankin and Elizabeth (Mitchell) Arrowsmith; m. William Earl Schroyer, July 23, 1983; stepchildren—Carey Jo, Amy Lynn. B.S., La. State U., 1961; M.Ed., Southeastern La. U., 1978. Lic. tchr., La.; cert. practicum supr. Inst. for Reality Therapy. Tchr. 1st grade McDonough #26, Jefferson Parish Sch. Bd., Gretna, La., 1966; 2nd grade tchr. Woodlawn High Sch., Baton Rouge, 1966-67; kindergarten tchr. Univ. Terrace Elem. Sch., Baton Rouge, summer 1967; 1st grade tchr. Westminster Elem. Sch., Baton Rouge, 1967-72, Elm Grove Elem. Sch., Harvey, La., 1972-73; kindergarten tchr. Westminster Elem. Sch., Baton Rouge, summers 1968, 69, 70, 71, Elm Grove Elem. Sch., summer 1973; 1st grade tchr. St. Andrews Episcopal Sch., New Orleans, 1973-74; kindergarten tchr. St. Tammany Parish Sch. Bd., Folsom, La., 1974-77; early childhood specialist St. Tammany Parish Sch. Bd., Covington, La., 1977—; off-campus coordinating asst. St. Tammany Parish for Dept. Continuing Edn., Southeastern La. U., 1985—; condr. workshops in field; selected ofcl. librarian Sunbelt Region of Reality Therapists, 1983; regional dir. La. and Miss. Reality Therapists, Sunbelt Bd. of Reality Therapists, 1983. Author: Helping Your Child at Home, 1982-83; Handbook for Early Childhood Tutorial Program, 1983-84. Mem. AAUW, Friends of Audubon Zoo, Vols. of Am., La. Assn. on Children Under Six, So. Assn. on Children Under Six, La. Assn. Sch. Execs., Nat. Assn. Female Execs., Sunbelt Assn. Reality Therapists (regional bd. 1982—), Internat. Assn. Reality Therapists, Assn. Tchr. Educators, Delta Kappa Gamma (v.p. 1986), Alpha Delta Kappa (v.p.). Democrat. Presbyterian. Club: Basset Hound Club of Greater New Orleans (dir.). Avocations: horticulture; reading; fishing; showing dogs; racquetball. Home: 2327 Livingston St Mandeville LA 70448

ARROYO, MARTINA, soprano; b. N.Y.C.; pupil Marinka Gurevich Mo Martin Rich, Joseph Turnau, Rose Landver; student Kathryn Long Course Met. Opera; L.H.D. (hon.), Hunter Coll., CUNY. Vis. prof. La. State U., Baton Rouge. Debut Carnegie Hall, 1958; leading soprano Met. Opera, N.Y.C., in roles including Il Trovatore, Aida, Madama Butterfly, Un Ballo in Maschera, Cavalleria Rusticana, La Forza del Destino, Vespri Siciliani, Don Giovanni, La Gioconda, Macbeth, Andrea Chenier, Tosca; performed opening night Met. season, 1970-71, 71-72, 73-74; performed at La Scala, Milan, Munich Staatsoper, Berlin Deutsche Oper. Rome Opera, Vienna State Opera, Covent Garden, Teatro Colon, Buenos Aires, San Francisco, Chgo. and all major opera houses; soloist N.Y., Vienna, Berlin, Royal (London), Paris philharms., San Francisco, Pitts., Phila., Chgo., Cleve. symphonies, Concertgebouw, other major orchs.; frequent performer Saratoga, Ravinia, Tanglewood festivals and festivals Vienna, Berlin, Edinburgh, Helsinki; oratorios include Verdi and Dvorak Reguiems, Beethoven Missa Solemnis and Choral Fantasy, Judas Maccabaeus, others; recs. for Columbia, London, Angel, DGG, Philips records, RCA. Trustee Carnegie Hall, N.Y.C. Address: care Thea Dispeker 59 E 54th St New York NY 10022

ARSENAULT, LEONA MARIE, financial executive; b. Saratoga Springs, N.Y., May 6, 1954; d. Joseph Abel and Elva M. (Gallant) A. Student Seminole Community Coll., 1982—. Asst. to mng. editor Orlando Sentinel, Fla., 1973-78; asst. to gen. mgr. Cardinal Industries, Inc., Sanford, Fla., 1979-81, asst. v.p., 1981-84, v.p. corp. fin., 1984—. Republican. Roman Catholic. Office: Cardinal Industries PO Box U 3701 S Sanford Ave Sanford FL 32771

ARSHT, MARJORIE MEYER, oil company executive, educator; b. Yoakum, Tex., Nov. 1, 1914; d. Marcell A. and Myrtle (Levy) Meyer; m. Raymond I. Arsht, Sept. 1, 1938 (dec. 1979); children—Alan M., Leslye A., Margot A. Lane (dec.) B.A., Rice U., 1933; Diplome Superieur, Sorbonne, Paris, 1934; M.A., Columbia U., 1935. Tchr. Houston Pub. Schs., Houston, 1936-38; real estate broker, Houston, 1973-79; tchr. U. Houston, 1977-79; oil co. exec. The Arsht Co., Houston, 1979—; exec. asst. to Fed. Housing Commr. HUD, Washington, 1983-85. Regent Tex. So. U., Houston, 1979-84; former state committeewoman Republican party; Rep. candidate Tex. Legislature. Mem. Tex. Ind. Producers and Royalty Owners (com. mem.), Ind. Petroleum Producers Assn. Am., Daus. of Confederacy, Phi Beta Kappa. Jewish. Home: PO Box 818 Bellaire TX 77401 Office: The Arsht Co PO Box 818 Bellaire TX 77401

ARTAZ, JEANNINE FORD, radio-television personality, fashion designer; b. San Antonio, May 22, 1929; d. Grady Carlton and Volahelen (Latham) Ford; m. Ches T. Von Baronofjski-Childres, Sept. 9, 1946 (dec. May 1964); children—Ginger Dona Watts, Honey Dawn Johnson, Carlton Ford Childres-Artaz, Grady Baron Childres-Artaz; m. Souvenir James Artaz, Jan. 24, 1968; stepchildren—Soundra Lee Crabtree, Bob Gene, Cheri Ann Bleyeu, Danny Joe, Bonnie Lynn Harris, Marlene Denise Halstad. Illustration degree Paris Art Inst., 1946; B.A., Tex. Christian U., 1949; student radio engring. Colo. State U., 1972-74; B.A. in Comml. Art, Art Inst. Chgo., 1949; student Coco Chanel's Studios, Paris, 1947-48. Designer, Originals by Jeannine, San Antonio, also Denver and Glenwood Springs, Colo., 1942—; disc jockey, announcer Stas. WOAI and KTSA, San Antonio, 1944-50; air personality Stas. KOA/KBTV and KIMN, Denver, 1951-68; women's program dir., announcer Radio Sta. KGLN, Glenwood Springs, Colo., 1970-82; dir. Tails Ranch, Garfield County Humane Assn., Glenwood Springs, 1982—. also mem. bd. dirs. humane assn., 1982—; tchr. radio/TV, J.F. Modeling Agy., Denver, 1956-60. Author, editor: (children's plays) Play Time, 1976 (Illustrating award 1976). Designer Gidetts household appliance covers (Am. Design award 1980). Leader, 4-H Club, Glenwood Springs, 1972-83; active Valley View Hosp. Aux., 1966—; chmn. Am. Hosp. Aux., Denver, 1963-64; mem. Glenwood Springs Parks and Recreation Commn., 1973—; counselor Children Against Drugs, Glenwood Springs, 1982—; advisor Parent Adv. Bd., Glenwood Springs, 1970-83. Named Vol. of Yr., Garfield Sch. Dist., Glenwood Springs, 1973; Woman Broadcaster of Yr., Am. Broadcasting System, N.Y.C., 1956, 58; recipient award for multiple sclerosis work Borden Co., 1980; Ford Found. grantee, 1984. Mem. Colo. Women Broadcasters Assn. (Colo. Woman Broadcaster of Yr. 1956, 58), Airplane Pilots and Owners Assn., Am. Weather Observers Assn., Am. Designers Inc. (Coty award 1959), Am. Design Assn. (sec. Denver 1955-57), Am. Humane Assn. (founding mem., local dir. 1982—). Avocations: flying, needlework, gardening, reading, drawing. Home: 509 W 12th St Glenwood Springs CO 81601

ARTER, ANNE MARY, recruiting specialist; b. Flushing, N.Y., Aug. 13, 1942; d. William Charles and Marguerite Joan (Aquais) Rollauer; m. Michael Anthony Arter, Aug. 1, 1981; children—Lisa Anne Martin, Christine Anne Martin. Student C. W. Post Coll., 1960-62, Skinner Bus. Sch., Great Neck, N.Y., 1962-63. Personnel mgr. AVX Corp., Great Neck, N.Y., 1979-80; editor Dominus Pub. Co., Roslyn, N.Y., 1980-85; pres. Anne Arter Inc., Great Neck, 1986—. Mem. NOW. Democrat. Avocations: weight-lifting; jogging; photography. Home: 1 Tom's Point Ln Port Washington NY 11050 Office: Anne Arter Inc 505 Northern Blvd Great Neck NY 11021

ARTERS, LINDA BROMLEY, public relations consultant; b. Phila., Dec. 18, 1951; d. Edward Pollard and Rosalyn Irene (Bromley) A.; B.A., Thiel Coll., Greenville, Pa., 1973. Customer relations dir. Artmann Devel. Corp. Inc., Media, Pa., 1973-74; with Southeast Nat. Bank, Malvern, Pa., 1974-78, public relations coordinator, 1976-78; propr. Linda B. Arters Public Relations and Advt., Media, 1978-84, Tempe, Ariz., 1984, Arters & Assocs., Tempe, 1984—; past mem. pvt. industry council County Delaware (Pa.) CETA Program. Bd. dirs. South Chester County Advanced Life Support, Inc. Mem. Phila. Indoor Tennis Corp., 1977-82; past mem. bd. dirs. United Cerebral Palsy of Delaware County. Mem. Internat. Assn. Bus. Communicators, Nat. Fedn. Ind. Bus., Nat. Assn. Female Execs., Public Relations Soc. Am. (counselors acad.; counselors group Phoenix chpt.), Central Ariz. Mountain Rescue Assn. (bd. dirs., pub. relations chmn.), U.S. Tennis Writers Assn. Republican. Presbyterian. Office: 1205 E Northshore Dr PO Box 27848 Tempe AZ 85282

ARTHUR, JUDY LYNN, long range plans program analyst; b. Memphis, Nov. 23, 1944; d. James Willard and Rubye Owen (Robinson) A.; B.S. in Journalism, Memphis State U., 1966; postgrad. Pepperdine U., 1977—; m. Thomas C. Findley, Jan. 26, 1979. Writer-editor U.S. Army, Ft. Knox, Ky. and Stuttgart, W.Ger., 1966-69; writer-editor U.S. Navy, Memphis, 1969-77, EEO specialist, 1977-85; free-lance reporter Memphis Press Scimitar, 1969, 70, 72, UPI, 1970-73. Recipient Merit award U.S. Navy Dept. Chief of Info., 1970. Mem. Women in Communications, Federally Employed Women, Am. Mgmt. Assn., Nat. Press Club, Toastmasters Internat., Bus. and Profl. Women, Gamma Phi Beta. Home: 3696 Vanderschaaf Dr Memphis TN 38134 Office: Code N23 Naval Tech Tng Command Naval Air Sta Millington TN 38054

ARTHUR, LEE, actress; b. Indpls., Oct. 14, 1942; d. Conrad and Florence (Sewell) Hammond; children—Jeffrey K., Stephen C. B.A. in English and Psychology, Butler U., 1961; postgrad. Ind. U., 1962. Actress, Hal Prince, N.Y.C., 1970-72; TV sports anchor WCBS-TV, N.Y.C., 1972, KDKA-TV, Pitts., 1972-75; asst. sports dir. WTVJ-TV CBS-TV, Miami, Fla., 1976-80; writer, host Gulf Pub. Video, Houston, 1981-82; actress various TV and radio commercials, Houston, 1981-84; nat. publicity dir. Am. Women Supporting the Pres., 1982-83; now mem. Rep. Nat. Coalition. Vol., Republican Women, Houston, 1983-84; mem. bd. Houston Film Festival, 1983—, Life Tng., Houston, 1983. Recipient First Lady award Miami Shores Men's Club, 1978; Mass Communications award Fla. Internat. U., 1977; Bronze award Houston Film Festival, 1978. Mem. Women in Communications, Am. Women in TV and Radio. Republican. Episcopalian. Clubs: Tower (Ft. Lauderdale, Fla.); Houston City. Home: 49 Briar Hollow #803 Houston TX 77027

ARTHURS, ALBERTA BEAN, found. exec.; b. Framingham, Mass., Dec. 20, 1932; d. Maurice and Eleanor Irene (Levenson) Bean; B.A., Wellesley Coll., 1954; Ph.D., Bryn Mawr Coll., 1972; m. Edward Arthurs, Dec. 20, 1960; children—Lee Michael, Daniel Jacob, Madeleine Hope. Editor, Liberty Mut. Ins. Co. Mag., Boston, 1954-56; dir. admissions Eliot-Pearson Sch., Tufts U., Medford, Mass., 1957-59, instr. English, 1958-62; instr., lectr. Rutgers U., New Brunswick, N.J., 1964-72, asst. prof., 1972-73; dean Radcliffe Coll., Cambridge, Mass., 1973-75, Harvard U., Cambridge, 1975-77; pres. coll., prof. English, Chatham Coll., Pitts., 1977-82; dir. arts and humanities Rockefeller Found., N.Y.C., 1982—; dir. Culbro Corp., Salzburg Seminar in Am. Studies. Bd. dirs. Harbridge House, 1980-82, Presbyn.-Univ. Hosp. of Pitts., 1979-82, Pitts. Symphony Soc., 1980-82, Pitts. Ballet Theater, 1978-82, Pine Manor Coll., 1976-80; trustee Hotchkiss Sch., 1975-83, Ellis Sch., 1977-82, Dalton Sch., 1983—. Mem. Council on Fgn. Relations, Signet Soc. Clubs: Duquesne (Pitts.); Harvard (N.Y.C.). Office: Rockefeller Found 1133 Ave of Americas New York NY 10036

ARTUSHENIA, MARILYN JOANNE, internist; b. Glen Ridge, N.J., Feb. 16, 1950; d. Gregory Artushenia and Julia (Markewicz) A. A.B. Boston U., 1970; M.D., Hahnemann Med. Coll., Phila., 1974. Diplomate Am. Bd. Internal Medicine. Intern Mt. Sinai Hosp., N.Y.C., 1974-75, resident in medicine, 1975-77; fellow in nephrology Bronx VA Hosp., Mt. Sinai Hosp., Bronx, N.Y.C., 1977-79, research fellow in endocrinology, 1979-80; asst. attending physician in medicine and psychiatry Elmhurst Gen. Hosp. (N.Y.), 1980-85; research cons. endocrinology, Bronx VA Hosp., 1980-81, med. staff Hillcrest Gen. Hosp., Flushing, N.Y., 1982—; instr. basic cardiac life support Regional Emergency Med. Services Council N.Y.C., 1980—. Mem. ACP, AMA, Med. Soc. State N.Y., AAAS, N.Y. Acad. Scis. Republican. Home and Office: 732 Weigold Rd Torrington CT 06790

ARTY, MARY ANN, state legislator; b. Phila., Nov. 24, 1926; d. Henry J. and Pearl (VanDike) Scheid; R.N., Med. Coll. Pa., 1946; B.S., West Chester State U., 1965; m. Thomas B. Arty; children—James Scheid, Janis Arty Hamilton, John Thomas. Supr., staff nurse instr. nursing of children Med. Coll. Pa., 1951-54; nurse educator, 1960-65; dir. dept. health, Springfield Twp., Delaware County, Pa., 1965-76; dir. Office Intercommunity Health Coordinator, County of Delaware, Pa., 1976-79; mem. Pa. Ho. of Reps., 1979—; mem. adv. bd. Grad. Sch. Nursing Widener U., 1980—; bd. overseers Coll. Nursing, U. Pa., 1982—. Commr., Springfield Twp., 1977-83; vice chmn. Delaware County Republican Exec. Com., 1976—; del. Rep. Nat. Conv., Miami, 1972; mem. Govt. Study Commn., Delaware County Home Rule Charter, 1973. Recipient Benjamin Rush award Delaware County Med. Soc., 1975, Award of Merit, Am. Acad. Pediatrics, 1981, Award of Merit, Delaware-Chester County Dental Soc., 1979; Keystone award Alcoholism and Addiction Assn. Pa.; Victims' Rights award Delaware County Domestic Abuse and Rape Crisis Ctr. Mem. Am. Nurses Assn., Nat. Order Women Legislators, Bus. and Profl. Women, Pa. Nurses Assn., Springfield LWV. Lutheran. Office: 312 S Bishop Ave Springfield PA 19064

ARUNDEL, GERALDINE PATTON, retired educator; b. Fremont, Nebr., Aug. 25, 1914; d. Guy Gerald and Lillian Armstrong (Spencer) Patton; B.A., Calif. State U., Long Beach, 1956; M.S., U. So. Calif., 1966, Ed.D., 1973; m. Frank Henry Arundel, July 2, 1935; children—Frank Gerald, Paul Henry. Tchr. elementary sch., Torrance and Long Beach, Calif., 1956-58; tchr. orthopedically handicapped Norwalk-La Mirada (Calif.) Sch. Dist., from 1963; substitute tchr., Compton, Bellflower and Paramount, Calif., 1958-63; home tchr., Norwalk, 1961-63; chmn. woman's com. for affirmative action policy statement by Bd. Edn., Norwalk-La Mirada Unified Sch. Dist., 1975. Grantee Crippled Children's Soc., 1962. Mem. Am. Assn. Mental Deficiency, Council Exceptional Children, AAUW, Calif. Ret. Tchrs. Assn. (dir. scholarship found.), Pi Lambda Theta, Phi Delta Gamma, Delta Epsilon. Democrat. Roman Catholic. Author: (transparency series and text) Mainstreaming a Physically Handicapped Student; (cassette with Helen Brown) Problems of Mainstreaming a Physically Handicapped Student. Home: 1888 Blackhawk St Oceanside CA 92056

ARVAY, NANCY JOAN, oil company executive; b. Pitts., Aug. 27, 1952; d. William John and Cora Cornelia (Prince) A. B.A. in History, Duke U., 1974; postgrad. Columbia U., 1974-75. Polit. and internat. communications research U.S. Senate Fgn. Relations Com., Washington, 1975-77; broadcast media relations rep. Am. Petroleum Inst., Washington, 1977-79, Chevron U.S.A., San Francisco, 1979-82, coordinator electronic news media relations, 1982-85; sr. media relations rep. Chevron Corp., San Francisco, 1985—; pub. relations chmn. Internat. Oil Spill Conf., Washington, 1984-85; lectr. Tng. Ctr., Dept. Interior, Beckley, W.Va., 1983. Contbg. author: This is Public Relations, 1985; author, coordinator research studies in bus. and the media. Mem. Am. Women in Radio and TV, Nat. Assn. Broadcasters (assoc.), Radio/TV News Dirs. Assn. (assoc.), Overseas Edn. Group (founding mem. San Francisco chpt.), San Francisco Women in Bus. Home: 135 Gardenside Dr San Francisco CA 94131 Office: Chevron Corp 225 Bush St San Francisco CA 94104

ARVEDON, MAELYN NORMA SIGAL, former bank security official; b. Boston, Nov. 21, 1954; d. Samuel and Sandra (Levin) Sigal; A.B. magna cum laude, Boston Coll., 1976; M.B.A., Boston U., 1981; m. David K. Arvedon, June 3, 1979; 1 son, Andrew Lowell. Successively teller, asst. head teller, research analyst, head teller, customer service rep., audit asst. Mut. Bank for Savs. and predecessor, Boston, 1976-81, loss prevention specialist, 1981-84. Adv. Com. to Elect Frank Rich Gov. of Mass., 1981; adv. Jr. Achievement, 1982-83. Recipient ins. sales awards; cert. in life ins. Mass. Savs. Bank. Mem. Nat. Assn. Female Execs., Old Girls Network, Savs. Bank Women of Mass., Mass. Police Fraudulent Check Assn. Jewish.

ASA, ALICE EVELYN, real estate broker; b. Long Pine, Nebr., June 25, 1932; d. Shelley Theodore and Minnie Margueretta (West) Moore; m. Leland Forrest Asa, June 25, 1952; children—Sandra Jayne Asa Lundberg, Bert Forrest. B.A. in Edn., Northwestern Coll., Mpls., 1955, M.Ed., Macalester Coll., St. Paul, 1957; postgrad. U. Wyo.-Laramie, 1963-64. Cert. tchr., Nebr., Ill.; lic. real estate broker Calif., B.C. Tchr. rural sch., Bassett, Nebr., 1949-52; tchr. Bensenville Pub. Schs. (Ill.), 1956-57, Omaha Pub. Schs., 1957-60; instr. edn. Trinity Western Coll., Langley, B.C., Can., 1962-67, 69-72; saleswoman Block Bros. Realty, Langley, 1972-75; saleswomen, broker Sunset Co. Realtors, Santa Barbara, Calif., 1976—. Author: (geneology) The Moore and West Families, 1983. Charter mem. Westbrook Evangelical Free Ch., Omaha, 1957-63; guide Pioneer Girls Club Evangelical Free Ch., Kearney, Nebr., 1967-69. Recipient numerous awards. Mem. Santa Barbara County Bd. Realtors (chairperson 1978-79, recipient plaque for disting. service 1979, Howard Gates award 1981). Republican. Home: 1460 Las Positas Pl Santa Barbara CA 93105 Office: Sunset Co Realtors 3019 State St Santa Barbara CA 93105

ASAI, JANINE MARCIA, public relations and telecommunications consulting executive, journalist; b. Phila., Aug. 12, 1954; d. Paul and Idelle Elaine Hoffman; B.S. in Chemistry, Calif. State U., Long Beach, 1978, M.S., 1979, B.A. in Journalism, 1980; m. Shinji Asai, Aug. 20, 1975; 1 dau., Michelle Mari. With Sun Rose U.S.A. Inc., 1975-80, dir. internat. sales and mktg., Huntington Beach, Calif.; exec. dir. Pacific Hosp. of Long Beach Found., 1980-81; owner, prin. Janine Asai & Assocs., Huntington Beach, Calif., 1981—; lectr., specialist AT&T divestiture; condr. seminars; instr. Golden West Coll., 1984—; cons. in field. Vol. historian Fountain Valley Community Hosp., 1977-79. Served as nurse USAF, 1974-75, Res., 1975-78. Mem. Nat. Assn. Female Execs. (network dir.), Internat. Sales and Mktg. Execs. (dir.), Women in Communications, N.Am. Telecommunications Assn., Internat. Orgn. Women in Telecommunications, Calif. Assn. Sch. Bus. Ofcls., Calif. Assn. Pub. Purchasing Ofcls., Women Writers West, Nat. Sporting Goods Assn., Public Relations Soc. Am., Jewish Profls. Club, AAUW, NOW, New Alliance for Gay Equality. Club: B'nai B'rith.

ASAI-SATO, CAROL YUKI, lawyer; b. Osaka, Japan, Oct. 22, 1951; came to U.S., 1953; d. Michael M. and Sumiko (Kamei) Asai; 1 child, Ryan Makoto Sato. B.A. cum laude, U. Hawaii, 1972; J.D., Williamette Coll. Law, 1975. Bar: Hawaii 1975. Assoc. firm Ashford & Wriston, Honolulu, 1975-79; counsel Bank of New Eng., Boston, 1979-81; assoc. counsel Alexander & Baldwin, Honolulu, 1981-83, sr. counsel, 1984—; mem. Med. Claims Conciliation Panel, 1983—. Williamette Coll. Law Bd. Trustees scholar, 1972-73. Mem. ABA, Hawaii Bar Assn., Hawaii Women Lawyers, Phi Beta Kappa, Phi Kappa Phi. Democrat. Office: Alexander & Baldwin Inc 822 Bishop St Honolulu HI 96813

ASBILL, PAULINE PORTER (MRS. DAVID ST. PIERRE ASBILL), office manager; b. Royston, Ga., Sept. 19, 1906; d. James Alexander and Ophelia Kathryn (Fowler) Porter; R.N., Med. Coll. S.C. Sch. Nursing, 1926; m. David St. Pierre Asbill, Feb. 9, 1928; 1 son, David St. Pierre. Nurse charge pediatrics dept. Roper Hosp., Charleston, S.C., 1926-28; nurse obstet. dept. N.Y. Polyclinic Med. Sch. and Hosp., N.Y.C., 1928-29; mgr. physician's office, Columbia, S.C., 1934—. State civil def. nurse Richland County Civil Def. Council, S.C., 1953—. Mem. Woman's Aux. Assn. Surgeons So. Ry. and Seaboard Air Line R.R. Systems; woman's aux. Columbia Med. Soc. (chmn. decorations 1948-55, v.p. 1942); S.C. Med. Assn. (charge decorations 1952-55). Mem. Columbia Art Assn. (art com. 1935-36), Delphian Soc., Internat. Platform Assn. Episcopalian. Clubs: Columbia Woman's (publicity chmn. 1940; decorations com. 1939), Forest Lake Country, Altrusa (Columbia). Home: 1551 Sam Rittenberg Blvd Apt 234 Charleston SC 29407 Office: 1417 Barnwell St Columbia SC 29201

ASBJORNSON, HELEN E. (LONGSTRETH), real estate investment co. exec.; b. N.Y.C., Dec. 8, 1935; d. Clyde Marion and Elizabeth (Rudolph) Longstreth; B.A., State U. Iowa, 1957, J.D., 1959, postgrad., 1960; M.Ed., Mont. State Coll., 1961; postgrad. U. Minn., 1961-62; cert. apt. mgr.; m. Norman H. Asbjornson, March 1963; children—Elizabeth Erica, Scott Marion. Mem. bus. adminstrn. staff Northwestern Bell Telephone Co., Omaha, 1959-60; bus. adminstrn. mgr. Diversified Equities, Mpls., 1961; research asst. U. Nebr., 1962; instr. Elkhorn (Nebr.) public schs., 1963-64. Vol. worker Children's Hosp.; active Omaha Symphony Guild, Women's Assn. of Joslyn Art Mus., Omaha Civic Music Assn. Mem. Am. Council Christian Ch., Amvets Aux., C. of C., Am. Legion Aux., State U. Iowa Alumni Assn., AAUW (legis. chmn.), Soc. Liberal Arts, Nat. Vocat. Guidance Assn., Inc., Am. Personnel and Guidance Assn., Inc., Nat. Soc. Profl. Engrs. Aux., Omaha Montessori Soc., Neb. Hist. Soc., Airplane Owners' and Pilots' Assns., Am. Citizens' Forum, Mont. Guidance Assn., DAR (bd. dirs.), Mensa (highest group, Intertel), NOW, Minn. Fencing Assn., English Interest Soc. (dir.), Les Amis du Vin, Bacchus Wine Soc., Psi Chi, Kappa Beta Pi (pres. chpt. 1957-58, del. Province conv. 1958). Republican. Protestant. Address: 6442 Margaret's Ln Edina MN 55435

ASBURY, ROBENA ISABEL, nurse; b. Kansas City, Kans., Aug. 16, 1928; d. Joseph William and Lucy Helen (Nason) Berg; m. Faye Smith, June 11, 1950; children—Joseph Ernest, Denise Earlene, Mark Edwin. Diploma Bethany Hosp., 1949; certs. U. Kans. Coll. Nursing, 1981, 84, Brigham Young U., 1982. Nurse, Cushing Hosp., Leavenworth, Kans., 1949; rehab. nurse Vets. Hosp., Wadsworth, Kans., 1950-52; relief nurse Bethany Hosp., Kansas City, Kans., 1953-54; staff nurse recovery room St. Margaret's Hosp., Kansas City, 1954-61; internist office nurse J. Warren Manley, M.D., Kansas City, 1961-69; occupational health nurse Fairbanks Morse Pump div. Colt Industries, Kansas City, 1969—; dist. rep. Kans. State Nurses Assn., Topeka, 1966; nursing rep. Pres.'s Roundtable City Kansas City, Kans., 1961-62. Author: Orthopedic Nursing, 1950. Coordinator, editor History Bethany Hospital School of Nursing, 1964. Leader, organizer Blue Birds, 1960-62; project leader 4-H Club; counselor Boy Scouts Am. Mem. Greater Kansas City Occupational Health Nurses Assn., Am. Assn. Occupational Health Nurses, Inc., Bethany Alumnae Assn. (pres. 1966-67). Republican. Mem. Ch. of Jesus Christ of Latter-day Saints. Office: Fairbanks Morse Pump div Colt Industries Operating Corp 3601 Fairbanks Ave Kansas City KS 66110

ASCHER, AMALIE ADLER, author, journalist, syndicated columnist; b. Balt.; d. Charles and Alene (Steiger) Adler; B.A., Goucher Coll., 1949; m. Eduard Ascher, May 18, 1954; children—Kenneth Charles Weinberg, Cynthia Cecille. Garden columnist Balt. Sunday Sun, 1976—, feature writer, 1968—, contbr. Sunday Sun mag., 1968—; hostess, writer The Flower Show, Md. Center for Public Broadcasting, 1973—; lectr. numerous states and fgn. countries, 1965—. Recipient Quill and Trowel award Garden Writers Assn. Am., 1980; Cert. of Merit for hort. lit. Nat. Council State Garden Clubs, Inc., 1975, named Flower Arranger of Year, 1973; Garden Writers award Bedding Plants, Inc., 1984. Mem. Garden Writers Assn. Am. (dir. 1975-76), Indoor Gardening Nat. Council State Garden Clubs, Inc. (dir., chmn. 1977-79), Authors Guild, Authors League, Am. Hort. Soc. Republican. Jewish. Author: The Complete Flower Arranger, 1974. Contbr. numerous articles to various mags. and newspapers. Home and Office: 610 W 40th St Baltimore MD 21211

ASCHER-APPEL, LAURA, orthodontist; b. N.Y.C., Nov. 16, 1912; d. Jay and Fannie Ascher; B.S., N.Y. U., 1933, D.D.S., 1937; cert. orthodontia, Columbia U. Dental Coll., 1962; m. Sidney J. Appel, 1941; children—John Philip, Marjorie Appel Scherer; m. 2d, David Siegel. Intern in pedodontics Guggenheim Dental div., N.Y.C., 1938-39; extern Grassland Hosp., Valhalla, N.Y., 1956; pvt. practice orthodontics, Cedarhurst, 1962-82; tchr. residents Peninsula Hosp. Centre, Far Rockaway, N.Y. Fellow Royal Soc. Health; mem. ADA, Am. Assn. Orthodontists, N.Y. State Dental Assn., 10th Dist. Dental Soc., Northeastern Assn. Orthodontists, 10th Dist. Assn. Orthodontists (pres. 1978-80), Middle Atlantic Assn. Orthodontists, Assn. Women Dentists N.Y. (v.p. 1977-80), Nassau County Dental Assn., Columbia U. Dental Alumni Assn., N.Y. U. Alumni Assn. Home: 9283 Vista del Lago Boca Raton FL 33433

ASCHER-NASH, FRANZI, writer; b. Vienna, Austria, Nov. 28, 1910; came to U.S., 1938, naturalized, 1944; d. Luise Frankl and Leo Ascher; grad. cum laude, Humanistisches Maedchengymnasium, Vienna, 1928; student Vienna Acad. Music, 1929-31; m. Edgar R. Nash, Nov. 21, 1959. Freelance short story writer, Vienna, 1934-38; after arrival in U.S., lectr. women's clubs under auspices of N.Y. Herald Tribune; music reviewer Neue Volkszeitung weekly, N.Y.C.; monthly light essay Austro-Am. Tribune; writer radio playlets German-Am. Writers Assn.; host short German lang. radio programs Sta. WBNX; tchr. New Sch. Social Research, N.Y.C.: writer annotations for classical records; host radio program The Story of the Art Song, Sta. WFUV-FM; readings of poetry, essays, short stories Sta. WNYC, N.Y.C.; lectr. on the art song; contbr. essays and poems German-Am. Studies mag., Lyrik und Prosa mag., Lyrica Germanica mag., Schatzkammer; author: (novella) Das Zwoelftonwunder, 1952; (novella) Confession in the Twilight (1st prize The Villager mag.), 1948; (books) Bilderbuch aus der Fremde, 1948, Gedichte eines Lebens, 1976, Lauf, lauf, Lebenslauf (a memoir), 1982; others; (anthologies) Reisegepaeck Sprache (pub. in bilingual version In Her Mother's Tongue 1982), 1980, Album of International Poets, 1981; also poetry. Recipient citation Soc. German-Am. Studies, 1973. Mem. Assn. German Lang. Authors in Am., Soc. German-Am. Studies (participant symposia on aspects of Am. music, pub. in various compendia entitled Occasional Papers), Literarische Union (W. Ger.), Tagore Inst. of Creative Writing (India). Club: B'nai B'rith. Home: 118 N George St Millersville PA 17551

ASEL, JANET, travel service company executive; b. Jefferson City, Mo., July 30, 1936; d. Vincent Joseph and Hilda Marie (Fechtel) Plassmeyer; m. William Elmer Asel, Feb. 6, 1960; children—Ron William, Lea Ann. Sec. State Hwy. Commn., Jefferson City, Mo., 1956-66, Trans-Mo Airlines, Jefferson City, 1966-67; owner, pres. Asel Travel Service, Jefferson City, 1971—; owner, Young Fashions, Jefferson City, 1978—. Mem. Am. Soc. Travel Agts., Jefferson City C. of C. Roman Catholic. Club: Jefferson City Country. Avocations: tennis, bridge, bowling, reading, traveling. Home: 704 Hobbs Rd Jefferson City MO 65101 Office: Asel Travel Service 202 E High St Jefferson City MO 65101

ASFAHL, ETHEL FAYE LOWE, children's dress company executive, designer; b. McPherson, Kans., Mar. 27, 1904; d. Charles Willard and Ethel Mary (Jesse) Lowe; m. Charles Raymond Asfahl, Sept. 8, 1922 (dec. 1963); children—Eloise Faye Asfahl Crowley, Charles Raymond, Paul William. Student McPherson Coll., 1920, Northwestern State Coll., Okla., 1921. Dress designer C. R. Asfahl Co., Enid, Okla., 1940—, owner, operator, designer, 1963—; real estate dealer. Author: When Marriage was in Fashion: The Story of the C. R. Asfahl Co., 1985. Recipient Design Oscar Peter Pan Fabrics, 1942; grantee franchise first washable corduroy Cone Mills, 1943; citation for Design Corduroy Council, 1962. Mem. Exhibitors Assn. Dallas Apparel Mart, Am. Fashions of Dallas, Kappa Alpha Theta (past pres.), Sigma Alpha Epsilon (past pres.), Republican. Methodist. Club: Minerva. Lodge: Kiwanis Queens (pres. 1956) (Enid). Home: 1221 W York St Enid OK 73703 Office: C R Asfahl Co 211 W Oak St Enid OK 73701

ASH, KAREN ARTZ, lawyer; b. N.Y.C., Dec. 23, 1955; d. Bernard and Helen (Liff) Artz; m. David Charles Ash, June 11, 1977; 1 child. A.B. in Econs., Georgetown U., 1976; J.D. magna cum laude, N.Y. Law Sch., 1980. Bar: N.Y. 1981. Mem. firm Kaye, Scholer, Fierman, Hays & Handler, N.Y.C., 1980-83, Amster, Rothstein & Ebenstein, N.Y.C., 1983—; mem. drafting com. Com. To Revise Model Bus. Code, N.J., 1983; lectr. trademark law Pracitising Law Inst., NYU Law Sch. Law rev. editor N.Y. Law Sch. Law Rev., 1978-80; contbr. articles to profl. jours. Com. mem. NOW, 1980-83; fundraiser Assn. for Help of Retarded Children, 1977-83. Mem. ABA (chmn. trademark div. 1982-86), N.Y. State Bar Assn. Democrat. Jewish. Office: Amster Rothstein & Ebenstein 90 Park Ave New York NY 10016

ASH, MARY KAY, cosmetics company executive; b. Hotwells, Tex., May 12; d. Edward Alexander and Lula Vember (Hastings) Wagner; m. Melville Jerome Ash, Jan. 6, 1966 (dec.); children—Marylyn Theard, Ben Rogers, Richard Rogers. Student U. Houston, 1943-44. Unit mgr. Stanley Home Products, Easthampton, Mass., 1938-52; officer World Gift Co., Dallas, 1952-63; chmn. bd. Mary Kay Cosmetics, Inc., Dallas, 1963—; TV appearances, including 60 Minutes, Today, Donahue Show, 700 Club; speaker in field. Mem. Tex. Gov.'s Commn. on Status of Women, 1970; mem. Chancellor's Council, U. Tex., 1974-75; vol. Dallas County Community Action Com., 1975. Recipient Mktg. Citizenship award Memphis chpt. Am. Mktg. Assn., 1973; Hall of Fame award Direct Sales Assn., 1976; Leadership award Dale Carnegie, 1978; Horatio Alger award, 1978; Cosmetic Career Woman of Yr. award Cosmetic Career Women, Inc., 1978; Golden Plate award Am. Acad. Achievement, 1980; named Outstanding Corp. Sales Exec., Gallagher's Report, 1981, Disting. Bus. Leader, U. Tex.-Arlington Coll. Bus. Adminstrn., 1982, Entrepreneur of Yr., Edwin L. Cox Sch. Bus., So. Meth. U., 1983, One of 100 Most Important Women, Ladies Home Jour., 1983. Republican. Baptist. Office: 8787 Stemmons Dallas TX 75247

ASH, SHARON KAYE, real estate company executive; b. Altus, Ark., July 21, 1943; d. William Clyde and Odus Marie (Drew) Cline; m. J.W. Ash, June 1, 1966 (div. Oct. 1978); 1 child, Brian Edward. B.S., Southwestern Mo. State U., 1985. Lic. real estate broker, Mo. Personal lines asst. Squibb Ins., Springfield, Mo., 1967-69; bookkeeper Hood-Rich, Architects and Engrs., Springfield, 1969—; owner Ash Computer Service, Springfield, 1985—; owner, broker Ash Real Estate, Springfield, 1985—. Mem. Mo. Assn. Realtors, Nat. Assn. Realtors, Nat. Assn. Female Execs. Democrat. Episcopalian. Avocations: golf; boating; reading; collectin clowns; jogging. Home: 712 McCann Springfield MO 65804 Office: Ash Real Estate 309 H Jefferson Suite 342 Springfield MO 65806

ASH, VIRGINIA MARIA, piano teacher; b. Rigby, Idaho, Apr. 22, 1918; d. Hugh Hastings and LaVera Maria (Jensen) Judd; student Colo. Woman's Coll., Denver, 1936-37, Coll. So. Idaho, 1981-84; m. Henry Woodrow Ash, June 1, 1938; children—Anthony Woodrow, Fredric Judd, Rosalie Marie, David Charles. High sch. tchr., Moore, Idaho, 1946-47, Richfield, Idaho, 1947-49; newspaper reporter Buhl (Idaho) Herald, 1955-57, Citizen Record, Filer, Idaho, 1957-60; pvt. piano tchr., 1947-84. Candidate for Mayor of Buhl, 1979; bd. dirs. Twin Falls Community Concert Assn., 1962-72; precinct committeewoman Buhl Democratic Com.; mem. Buhl City Planning and Zoning Commn., 1985—; elder Presbyn. Ch.; mem. campaign Peace Acad. Recipient award Senator Len Jordan short story contest, 1960's. Mem. Twin Falls Music Club, Magic Valley Chorale, Idaho Writers League, Common Cause, LWV, ACLU, NAACP, Fellowship of Reconciliation. Lodge: Order Eastern Star (past matron). Author various articles, poetry. Address: 809 11th St Buhl ID 83316

ASHBAUGH, ANN MARIE, air force officer, nurse; b. Wilkes-Barre, May 11, 1945; d. Valentine and Stella Theresa (Byczek) Kompinski; m. George Eric Ashbaugh, Nov. 9, 1972; children—Anita Louise, Aimee Susan. R.N., Mercy Hosp., Wilkes Barre, Pa., 1967; B.S., Wilkes Coll., 1972; diploma Air Command and Staff Coll., 1984. Commd. 2d lt. U.S. Army, 1968; commd. 1st lt. U.S. Air Force, 1972, advanced through grades to maj., 1984; charge nurse USAF Hosp., Loring, Maine, 1979-84, asst. chief nurse, 1984-85; charge nurse USAF Hosp. Nellis AFB, Nev., 1985—. Mem. Am. Nurses Assn. (council 1984-86), Nev. Nurses Assn., Assn. Mil. Surgeons U.S., Nurses Assn. of Am. Coll. Ob-Gyn., Air Force Hist. Found., Polish Geneal. Soc., AAUW, Bus. and Profl. Women's Assn., Polish Inst. Arts and Scis. Am., Wilkes Coll. Alumni. Avocations: genealogy; opera; needlepoint; knitting and crochet design. Office: SGHMP USAF Hosp Nellis AFB NV 89191

ASHBURN, SHIRLEY SMITH, nursing educator, author; b. Anderson, Ind., May 11, 1945; d. Ollie J. and Audrey Jeanette (Chandler) S.; 1 child, Jodi Lynn. B.S.N., Ohio State U., 1967, M.S., 1970. Instr., Ohio State U., Columbus, 1970-76; asst. prof. Capital U., Bexley, Ohio, 1976-80; inservice instr. Children's Hosp.-Orange County, Orange, Calif., 1980-82; prof. Cypress (Calif.) Coll., 1982—; cons. central lines Kaiser Permanente, So. Calif., 1983—; growth and devel. cons. Columbus Tech. Inst., 1977-78. Author: The Process of Human Development, 1980, 2d edit., 1985 Leader, Brownie Scouts, Saddleback Valley, Calif., 1981-82; v.p. cheerleading Pop Warner Football, Saddleback Valley; advisor Red Cross Youth Council, Columbus, Ohio, 1976. Named Outstanding Tchr., Nursing Students at Ohio State U., Columbus, 1972-76. Mem. Am. Nurses Assn., Mortar Board, Sigma Theta Tau. Democrat. Baptist.

ASHBY, KATHLEEN MARIE, insurance company executive; b. Lockport, N.Y., July 20, 1946; d. Robert Morrow and Mary Catherine (Purdy) B.; m. Robert Marvin Ashby, May 20, 1965; children—Mary Catherine, Kenneth Robert. Asst. supr. People's Life Ins. Co., Washington, 1969-71, claims examiner, 1972-78, claims adminstr., 1978-83; claims and corrs. mgr. Acacia Mut. Life Ins., Washington, 1984—. Mem. Ins. Women Washington, So. Md. Ins. Women (pres. 1978-79), Nat. Assn. Ins. Women (cert. profl. ins. woman 1977), Md.-D.C. Claims Assn. Home: 311 Bucknell St Bryans Road MD 20616 Office: Acacia Group 51 Louisiana Ave NW Washington DC 20001

ASHBY, NORMA RAE BEATTY, broadcaster; b. Helena, Mont., Dec. 27, 1935; d. Raymond Wesley Beatty and Ella Mae (Lamb) Beatty Watson

Mehmke; m. Shirley Carter Ashby, Sept. 5, 1964; children—Ann, Tony. B.A., U. Mont.-Missoula, 1957. Reporter, Helena Ind. Record, 1953-56; picture dept. Life Mag., N.Y.C., 1957-58; picture researcher MD Med. Newsmag., N.Y.C., 1959-61; producer, hostess TV Show Today in Mont., Sta. KRTV, Great Falls, 1962-85; editor Noon News, Sta. KRTV, 1985—; producer Great Falls Centennial program, 1984. Author: What Is A Montanan?, 1971; Montana Woman, 1977; Montanans, 1982; scriptwriter: Last Chance Gulch, 1964, Gentle Giants, 1969, Our Latchstring is Out, 1979; Paris Gibson, 1983; Martha, Pioneer Woman, 1984. Co-chmn. Cascade County Bicentennial Com., Great Falls, 1974-76; founder, chmn. C.M. Russell Auction, Great Falls, 1979; bd. dirs. Mont. Physicians Service, Helena, 1980—; co-chmn. Great Falls Centennial Com., 1982-84; co-chair Mont. Jefferson awards; pres. Cascade County Mental Health Assn., 1980-82; bd. dirs. Mental Health Assn. Mont., also editor. Recipient TV Program of Yr. award Greater Mont. Found. and Mont. Broadcasters Assn., 1982; Communication and Leadership award Mont. Toastmasters Internat., 1983; Tribune Most Influential Woman in Great Falls, 1984; hon. mem. Blackfeet Tribe Blackfeet Reservation, Browning, Mont., 1981—. Mem. Women in Communications, Great Falls Advt. Fedn. (dir., Silver medal 1980), AWRT (founder, pres. Mt. Big Sky chpt. 1967, recipient cert. of commendation 1982). Office: KRTV PO Box 1331 Great Falls MT 59403

ASHBY, ROSEMARY GILLESPY, college president; b. Farnham, Surrey, Eng., May 16, 1940; came to U.S. 1967; d. Robert Dymock and Margaret Lois (Gillespy) Watson; m. John Hallam Ashby, June 17, 1967. B.A., U. Capetown, S. Africa, 1960; B.A., Cambridge U., 1963, M.A., 1967, M.Litt., 1972. Head resident Radcliffe Coll., Cambridge, Mass., 1968-70, asst. dir. career planning, 1969-70; dir. residence, instr. French Pine Manor Coll., Chestnut Hill, Mass., 1970-71, dean students, 1971-75, acting pres., 1975-76, pres., 1976—; pvt. tutor Sao Paulo, Brazil, 1963-65; teaching asst. U. Capetown, 1959-60; panelist N.E. Assn. Schs. and Colls., Boston, 1983, Nat. Assn. Ind. Schs., Boston, 1985. Author chpt. in book. Adv. bd. Keimei Fund for Internat. Edn., N.Y.C., 1978—. Nat. Endowment of Humanities fellow, 1984. Mem. Mass. Commn. on Post-secondary Edn., Assn. Am. Colls. (exec. com. 1977-78), Assn. Ind. Colls. and Univs. in Mass. (exec. com. 1977-80), Women's Coll. Coalition (exec. com. 1985—). Home: 41 Crafts Rd Chestnut Hill MA 02167 Office: Pine Manor Coll 400 Heath St Chestnut Hill MA 02167

ASHDOWN, MARIE MATRANGA (MRS. CECIL SPANTON ASHDOWN, JR.), writer, lecturer; b. Mobile, Ala.; student Maryville Coll. Sacred Heart, Springhill Coll.; m. Cecil Spanton Ashdown, Jr.; children—John Stephen Gartman, Vivian Marie Gartman, Cecil Spanton III, Charles Coster. Feature star daily program Sta. WALA, also WALA-TV, Mobile; photographer, model for Louise Sheridan; instr. continuing edn. Marymount-Manhattan Coll.; now exec. dir. Musicians Emergency Fund, Inc., N.Y.C.,; cons. No. U. Ill., Coll. Visual and Performing Arts. Mem. Am. Women in Radio and TV, Am. Businesswomen's Assn. Recipient cert. of merit for extraordinary service March of Dimes. Mem. Nat. Inst. Social Scis. Contbr. to Opera Mementos, Time-Life Collectibles Series. Home: 25 Sutton Pl S New York NY 10022

ASHENFELTER, NATALIE SUE, banker; b. Richmond, Ind., Apr. 26, 1951; d. William Jason and Alice Jean (Fleisch) A. B.S., U. Montevallo, Ala., 1973, M.S., 1976. Speech pathologist LaGrange pub. schs., Ga., 1973-75, Hearing and Speech Ctr., Columbia, S.C., 1976-79; forms mgr. S.C. Nat. Bank, Columbia, 1979—. Guardian ad litem Richland County Family Ct., 1985—; referee YMCA Youth Soccer League, 1978—. Mem. Bus. Forms Mgmt. Assn., Am. Inst. Banking, Nat. Assn. Female Execs., Am. Speech and Hearing Assn., S.C. Speech and Hearing Assn., Chi Omega, Animal Protection League. Republican. Presbyterian. Avocations: Photography; tennis; skiing; needlework; watercolors. Home: 610 Hemphill St Columbia SC 29205 Office: SC Nat Bank 101 Greystone Blvd Columbia SC 29226

ASHER, JANE FITZGERALD (MRS. JACK O'HAIR ASHER), lawyer; b. Little Rock, Dec. 3, 1929; d. Sam L. and Georgia Duffey (Hubbert) Fitzgerald; A.A., Los Angeles City Coll., 1951; student UCLA, 1951-52; J.D., Tulane U., 1957; m. Jack O'Hair Asher, Aug. 22, 1957; children—Duffey Ann, William Michael Fitzgerald, John Russell II (dec.). Admitted to La. bar, 1957, Alaska bar, 1959, U.S. Ct. of Appeals bar, 1960, Ill. bar, 1968; law clk. U.S. Dist. Ct. of Alaska, Juneau, 1957-58; atty. Vets. Affairs Commn., Juneau, 1958-59; asst. atty. gen. State of Alaska, Juneau, 1959-60, reviser of statutes, 1960-67; counsel judiciary coms. Alaska Senate, 1963-66, Alaska House, 1965-66. Chmn. Alaska Am. Cancer Soc. Crusade, 1959; sec. Juneau-Douglas Concert Assn., 1961-62, treas., 1962-66; dir. Gold Creek Summer Theatre, 1964-66; v.p., mgr. Edgar County Concert Assn., 1969-79; bd. dirs. Juneau-Douglas Little Theatre, 1961-62, 64-65, YMCA, Paris, Ill., 1969-71; bd. dirs. Edgar County Children's Home, 1968-84, treas., 1981-84; v.p. Hangar, Inc., teen-age center, 1972-81; mem. regional adv. com. Ill. Dept. Children and Family Services, 1980—; pres. bd. dirs. Paris Tiger Tots Nursery, 1969-73; del. Ill. Conf. on Children's Priorities for 80s, 1981. Mem. Alaska, Am., La., Ill. bar assns., Nat. Women Lawyers (state del. 1959-67), Nat. LWV, AAUW, Phi Delta Delta. Club: Quota (treas. Juneau chpt. 1961-62, dir. 1962-64). Home: Box 501 Chicago Rd Paris IL 61944 Office: 236 W Court St Paris IL 61944

ASHINOFF, SUSAN JANE, menswear manufacturing company executive; b. N.Y.C., Dec. 7, 1949; d. Lawrence Lloyd and Thelma B. (Rubens) A.; m. Robert Mintz, June 18, 1983; 1 child, Geoffrey Harrison. A.A., Dean Jr. Coll., 1969; B.A., Finch Coll., 1971; M.P.A., N.Y.U., 1977. Advt. coordinator menswear advt. New Yorker mag., N.Y.C., 1971-72; asso. Staub, Warrmbold & Assos., exec. search co., N.Y.C., 1972-80; exec. v.p. Muhammad Ali Sportswear, Ltd., N.Y.C., 1980-81; pres. Forum Sportswear, Ltd., N.Y.C., 1981—; advt. dir. Coronet Group, N.Y.C., 1983—. Trustee Dean Jr. Coll. Mem. Nat. Assn. Men's Sportswear Buyers, Sporting Goods Mfrs. Assn., Men's Apparel Guild Calif. Office: 301 East 79th Street New York NY 10021

ASHKINAZE, CAROLE LYNNE, columnist, editorial writer, educator; b. N.Y.C., Jan. 20, 1945; d. Harry M. and Rose (Goldstein) A. French lang. cert. U. Rouen/Caen (France), 1964-65; A.B. with honors, St. Lawrence U., Canton, N.Y., 1966; M.S. in Journalism, Columbia U., 1967. Reporter, Newsday, Garden City, N.Y., 1967-74, Denver Post, 1974-75; producer Sta. WXIA-TV, Atlanta, 1975-76; columnist Atlanta Constn., 1976—, mem. editorial bd., 1982—; host About Women, weekly TV talk show; instr. Emory U., Atlanta, 1976—; commentator radio sta. WGST/Ga. Network, Atlanta, 1982—. Editor: Saturday Night, Sunday Morning: Singles & The Church, 1978. Chmn. Holiday Project, Atlanta, 1984—; elected mem. Leadership Atlanta, 1983; bd. dirs. Nat. Kidney Found. of Ga., 1985—. Recipient George Polk Meml. award L.I. U., 1967; Pub. Service award N.Y. State Publishers Assn., 1967, 70; Pulitzer prize, 1970; Media award for Econ. Understanding, Amos Tuck Sch. Bus. Adminstrn. Dartmouth Coll., 1979, Best Editorial award Ga. Press Assn., 1985. Mem. Soc. Profl. Journalists (dir. 1976—, v.p. 1983-84, chmn. 1st Amendment Congress 1980, chmn. profl. devel. 1983, recipient 1st place award in Criticism 1976), Columbia U. Grad. Sch. Journalism Alumni Assn. (regional v.p. 1985—). Jewish. Club: Sporting (Atlanta). Office: Atlanta Constitution 72 Marietta St Atlanta GA 30303

ASHLEY, ELIZABETH, seminary librarian; b. Waycross, Ga., July 8, 1943; d. James Bryant and Henrietta (Hargreaves) Lewis; m. Rhett Ashley, Sept. 9, 1973 (div. July 1977); m. 2d, Stefan Mellin, June 21, 1978. A.A. Stephens Coll., 1963; B.A., U. Fla., 1965; M.S., Fla. State U., 1969; M.A., Ariz. State U., 1975. Cataloging librarian Columbia U., N.Y.C., 1967; circulation librarian Fla. State U., Tallahassee, 1968-69; acquisitions librarian Ariz. State U., Tempe, 1969-76, No. Ariz. U., Flagstaff, 1977-78; approval librarian Baker & Taylor Co., Somerville, N.J., 1979-80; dir. tech. services Golden Gate Sem., Mill Valley, Calif., 1981—. Author: A Midsummer Madness, 1979; Abraham Steele, 1981; The Skull, 1982. Founder, exec. dir. Friends of Trees Soc., 1983—. Mem. ALA, Calif. Library Assn., Am. Theol. Library Assn., Phi Theta Kappa, Phi Kappa Phi, Beta Phi Mu. Presbyterian. Office: Golden Gate Sem Strawberry Point Mill Valley CA 94941

ASHLEY, GAYLE LYNN WEST, corporation executive; b. Dahlgren, Va., Feb. 2, 1951; d. Robert Keith and Marzella Mae (Denman) West; m. William David Ashley, July 17, 1971. B.B.A. in Mgmt., U. Tex.-Arlington, 1980. Cert. compensation profl. Project coordinator Am. Hosp. Supply, Grand Prairie, Tex., 1971-78, customer service rep., 1978, personnel asst., 1978-80; sr. compensation analyst Dresser Industries, Dallas, 1980-82; compensation adminstr. Mostek Corp., Carrollton, Tex., 1982-83, sect. mgr. employee benefits, 1983—. Mem. Am. Compensation Assn., Beta Gamma Sigma, Alpha Chi.

ASHLEY, KAREN ELIZABETH, veterinarian; b. Waterloo, Iowa, Feb. 13, 1952; d. Roy Edgar and Audrey Elizabeth (Maass) A.; m. Jerry Holmes Johnson, Sept. 15, 1979; children—Jared, Jonathan, Kaithlyn; 1 stepdau., Julee Ann. B.S., U. Mo.-Columbia, 1973, D.V.M., 1979. Practice vet. medicine, Lexington, Ky., 1979—; dir. Jerry H. Johnson D.V.M., P.S.C., Lexington, 1983—. Mem. AVMA, Central Ky. Vet. Med. Assn., Central Ky. Small Animal Vet. Med. Assn. Methodist.

ASHLEY, LINDA DIANE, nurse; b. Peru, Ind., May 19, 1950; d. Charles Albert and Ruth LaVonne (Spangler) Moore; m. David E. Karst, June 19, 1971 (div. 1981); m. 2d Michael Allan Ashley, July 9, 1983; 1 dau., Heather Ayne. Grad. Ind. U. Sch. Nursing, 1972. Student nurse Marion (Ind.) Gen. Hosp., 1970, Ind. U. Hosp., Indpls., 1970-71; student nurse VA Hosp., Marion, Ind., 1971-72; pediatric staff nurse Marion Gen. Hosp., 1972-73; psychiat. staff, head nurse VA Hosp., Marion, 1973-75; coordinator impatient services Grant-Blackford Mental Health, Inc., Marion, 1975—. Vice pres. Grant County Democratic Women's Club, 1980; bd. dirs. Grant County Vis. Nurse Assn., 1979—. Mem. Am. Nurses Assn., Ind. Community Mental Health Nurses Assn. (pres. 1980—), Ind. State Nurses Assn., Ind. U. Alumni Assn. Democrat. Methodist. Home: PO Box 542 501 S Washington St Swayzee IN 46986 Office: Grant-Blackford Mental Health Inc 505 Wabash Ave Marion IN 46952

ASHLEY, LORYANA KIM, painter; b. N.Y.C., Oct. 10, 1949; d. John A. and Teresa (Kamienska) Rogers; student Royal Acad. Art, London, Mus. Modern Art, N.Y.C. One-woman exhbns. include Harkness House Gallery, N.Y.C., 1978, Royal Acad. Art, 1978, Studio 5, Milan, Italy, 1970, Ramon Hall, Bombay, India, 1983.

ASHLEY, MARY GAYLE, lawyer; b. Charlottesville, Va., Oct. 21, 1948; d. Bruce Dodson and Jane (Monroe) Reynolds; m. William Lloyd Ashley III, June 7, 1970 (div. 1980); children—William Lloyd, David Monroe; m. Peter Randolph Holden, June 15, 1985. B.A. cum laude, Roanoke Coll., 1970; J.D., U. Va. 1980. Bar: Va. 1980. Tchr., U.S. Army, Ft. Benning, Ga., 1975-77; mem. firm Boothe, Prichard & Dudley, Fairfax, Va., 1980-83, Allen & Ashley, Sterling, Va., 1983-84; instr. U. Va.-Falls Church, 1983-85; assoc. Frank, Bernstein, Conoway & Goldman, 1985—; corp. counsel The Crippen Cos., Great Falls, Va., 1986—; newspaper columnist Legally Yours, 1983. Bd. dirs. Fairfax Choral Soc., Inc., 1983-86, Com. for Dulles Airport, 1984-86. Mem. ABA (com. on marital deduction), Va. Bar Assn., Va. State Bar, Fairfax Bar Assn., Fairfax Women Soccer Assn. Democrat. Episcopalian. Home: PO Box 104 Lincoln VA 22078

ASHLEY, MERRILL, ballerina; b. St. Paul; attended Sch. Am. Ballet. With N.Y.C. Ballet, 1967—, prin. dancer, 1977—, leading roles in George Balanchine's Ballo della Regina and Ballade; has appeared in Flower Festival at Genzano, The Four Seasons, Jewels, Allegro Brillante, Vienna Waltzes, In the Night, In G Major, Goldberg Variations, Raymonda, Cortege Hongrois, Suite #3, Square Dance, Dances at a Gathering, Donizetti Variations; appeared in Pub. TV series Dance in America, Gala of Stars. Author: Dancing for Balanchine, 1984. Office: New York City Ballet Lincoln Center Plaza New York NY 10023

ASHLINE, KATHRYN PATRICIA DARLING, educator, real estate saleswoman; b. Albany, N.Y., Aug. 26, 1951; d. Asa James and Mary Louis (Harvey) Darling; m. John William Ashline, Aug. 23, 1974. A.A.S., Adirondach Community Coll., Glens Falls, N.Y., 1971; B.S., SUNY-Plattsburgh, 1973; M.S., SUNY-Stony Brook, 1977; postgrad. Adelphi U., Garden City, N.Y., 1983—. Cert. elem. tchr., N.Y. Long distant operator Tel. Co., Glens Falls, 1968-73; tchr. Rockville Diocese, Rockville Centre, N.Y., 1974—, Diagnostic Learning, Dix Hils, N.Y., 1974-76, Patchogue Regional Catholic Sch., Patch, N.Y., 1974—, Adult Edn. Patchogue Sch. Dist., 1978-83; real estate sales Realty World Rustic, Patchogue, 1984—; tutor Patchogue Med. Sch., 1978-81; proctor, examiner Suffolk Civil Service, Hauppauge, N.Y., 1980—; union rep. Diocesan Forum, Patchogue, 1982—. Mem. Suffolk County council Girl Scouts U.S., 1957—; mem. Audobon Soc., Suffolk County, N.Y., 1973—; bd. dirs. Meals-on-Wheels, Blue Point, N.Y., 1985—. Mem. N.Y. State Tchrs. Assn., Kappa Delta Pi. Democrat. Clubs: Am. Assn. Univ. Women (pres. 1984-86), Womens. Avocations: antiquing, needlecrafts, nature studies, restoring antiques, photography. Home: 215 N Prospect Ave Patchogue NY 11772 Office: Realty World Rustic 382 Medford Ave Patchogue NY 11772

ASHMORE, CARRIE MAE, educator; b. Springfield, Tenn., Mar. 5, 1923; d. James Dean and Vera Louvenia (Osborne) Barbee; student Tenn. State U., 1941-43; B.S., Wilberforce U., 1946; postgrad. Atlanta U., 1957-60, Chgo. State U., 1965, 70, 71, Roosevelt U., 1967, 68, 73; m. Edward Travis Ashmore, July 23, 1945; children—Travis Dean and Edward Lane (twins), Juanita Sherri, Angela Jean and Angelo Gene (twins), Andre Bernard. Tchr., Bransford High Sch., Springfield, Tenn., 1946-48; sec. Murrays Superior Products, Chgo., 1948-49; adminstrv. asst. Atlanta U., 1949-60; tchr. Atlanta Public Schs., 1960-62, Gary (Ind.) Public Schs., 1962-64, Wendell Phillips High Sch., Chgo., 1964-68; tchr. Hyde Park Career Acad., Chgo., 1969—; mem. tchr. corps project of Hyde Park Career Acad. and Roosevelt U. Recipient Am. Legion medal, 1941. Mem. Chgo. Assn. of Mentally Retarded, Lambda Eta Sigma, Zeta Sigma Pi. Methodist. Home: 422 W 98th St Chicago IL 60628 Office: 6220 S Stony Island Ave Chicago IL 60637

ASHTON, DORE, author, educator; b. Newark; d. Ralph N. and Sylvia (Ashton) Shapiro; B.A., U. Wis., 1949; M.A., Harvard, 1950; Ph.D. honoris causa, Moore Coll., 1975, Hamline U., 1982; m. Adja Yunkers, July 8, 1952 (dec. 1983); children—Alexandra Louise, Marina Svietlana; m. Matti Megged, Mar. 5, 1985. Asso. editor Art Digest, 1951-54; asso. critic N.Y. Times, 1955-60; lectr. Pratt Inst., 1962-63; head humanities dept. Sch. Visual Arts, 1965-68; prof. Cooper Union, 1968—; art critic, lectr., dir. exhbns. Bd. dirs. Found. for Edn. in Arts; adv. bd. John Simon Guggenheim Found.; adv. bd. Inst. Advanced Visual Studies, Nat. Gallery; mem. Freedom to Write Com. of P.E.N. Recipient Mather award for art criticism Coll. Art Assn., 1963; Guggenheim fellow, 1964; Graham fellow, 1963; Ford Found. fellow, 1960; Nat. Endowment for Humanities grantee, 1980. Mem. Internat. Assn. Art Critics, Coll. Art Assn., Soc. Fellows N.Y.U., Phi Beta Kappa. Author: Abstract Art Before Columbus, 1957; Poets and the Past, 1959; Philip Guston, 1960; The Unknown Shore, 1962; Rauschenberg's Dante, 1964; Modern American Sculpture, 1968; Richard Lindner, 1969; A Reading of Modern Art, 1970; Pol Bury, 1971; New York (cultural guide), 1972; Picasso on Art, 1972; The New York School: A Cultural Reckoning, 1973; A Joseph Cornell Album, 1974; Yes, But, A Critical Biography of Philip Guston, 1976; A Fable of Modern Art, 1980; American Art Since 1945, 1982; About Rothko, 1983; Modern Artists on Art, 1985; co-author: Rosa Bonheur, A Life and Legend, 1981; co-editor: Redon, Moreau, Bresdin, 1961; N.Y. contbg. editor Studio Internat., 1961-74, Opus Internat., 1968-74, XXième Siècle, 1955-70, Arts, 1974—. Contbr. to Vision and Value series (Gyorgy Kepes), 1966, The New Art Anthology (Gregory Battcock), 1966, On Art (Rudolf Baranik). Home: 217 E 11th St New York NY 10003

ASHTON, KATE PEGGY, speech educator; b. Washington, Sept. 11, 1948; d. Lester and Louise (Blanton) Leopold; M.A., Bob Jones U., 1970; M.A., San Diego State U., 1979. Instr., Christian Heritage Coll., San Diego, 1970-76; assoc. prof. speech San Diego City Coll., 1976-85, San Diego State U., 1984-86; editor Where Mag., San Diego, 1980-83; communications cons. U.S. Marine Corps, 1979-85, various corps. and assns. Mem. Western Speech Communications Assn., Communication Arts Group, Tree House Animal Protection Inst., Nat. Assn. Corp. Speakers, Internat. Platform Assn., Nat. Speakers Assn. Republican. Home: 4379 Vivaracho Ct San Diego CA 92124

ASHTON, SISTER MARY MADONNA, state official; b. St. Paul; d. Avon B. and Ruth (Fehring) A.; B.A., St. Catherine's Coll., St. Paul, 1944; M.S.W., St. Louis U., 1946; M.H.A., U. Minn., 1958. Mem. Congregation of Sisters St. Joseph of Carondelet; dir. med. social service dept. St. Joseph's Hosp., St. Paul, 1949-56; dir. out-patient dept. St. Mary's Hosp., Mpls., 1958-59, asst. adminstr., 1959-62, adminstr., 1962-68, exec. v.p., 1968-72, pres., 1972-82; commr. health State of Minn., Mpls., 1982—; dir. Nat. City Bank, Mpls.; preceptor, mem. faculty U. Minn. Program in Hosp. Adminstrn.; Bush summer fellow Harvard Sch. Bus., 1976. Trustee Minn. Blue Cross Assn. Recipient Sabra Hamilton award Program in Hosp. Adminstrn., U. Minn., 1958; Minn. Health Citizen of Yr. award, 1977. Fellow Am. Coll. Hosp. Adminstrs.; sec. Nat. Catholic Health Assn. Office: Minn Dept of Health 717 Delaware St SE Minneapolis MN 55440*

ASHWORTH, KATHRYN FORSYTH, lawyer; b. Seattle, Nov. 19, 1941; d. Albert John Chisholm and Mary Catherine (Fickes) Forsyth; m. Thomas Ashworth III, Aug. 31, 1963; children—Sara Elizabeth, James Chisholm, Michael Stephen. B.A., Mills Coll., 1963; J.D., U. San Diego, 1981. Bar: Calif. 1981. Ptnr. Shea & Ashworth, San Diego, 1982—. Pres., Children in Placement Project, San Diego, 1982—; campaign chmn., bd. mgrs. YMCA Human Devel. Center, San Diego, 1983—; vice chmn. San Diego County Delinquency Prevention Commn., 1980—. Mem. ABA, Calif. Bar Assn. (mem. juvenile justice com. 1982-83), San Diego County Bar Assn. (chmn. law week com. 1984), Lawyers' Club San Diego, Women in Bus. San Diego (founding mem., program chmn. 1981), San Diego Bar Assn. Aux. (dir. 1968-74, 83-84). Republican. Roman Catholic. Club: Jr. League San Diego (dir. 1974-78, 80-81, mem. area VI council 1978-79). Office: Shea & Ashworth 1855 1st Ave San Diego CA 92101

ASHWORTH, PATRICIA LOU, English language educator; b. Moundsville, W.Va., May 5, 1926; d. Earl McCoy and Mabel Virginia (Pickett) Robinson; B.A., W.Va. U., 1948, M.A., 1950; m. John C. Ashworth, Sept. 2, 1950; children—Robin Ann Ashworth Tice, Melinda Lou. Instr., Waynesburg Coll., 1948-49, W.Va. U., 1950-51; instr. to prof. English, Beckley (W. Va.) Coll., 1964—, dean of women, 1966-78, chmn. English, chmn. div. fine arts, 1978—; mem. W.Va. Writing Project, 1980; adj. W.Va. Coll. Grad. Studies, 1980-81; chmn. film series W.Va. Ethics, 1983-85. Charter mem. Friends of Raleigh County Library, Community Concert Assn.; adv. bd. Woman's Resource Center, 1978-81; treas. Altar Guild, United Methodist Temple, 1978-82. Cert. life tchr., W.Va. Mem. W.Va. Coll. English Tchrs. (charter), W.Va. Speech Assn., W.Va. Writers (charter), Nat. Council Tchrs. of English, Southeastern Council Linguistics, Delta Kappa Gamma, Alpha Xi Delta. Clubs: Beckley Woman's (sec. 1980-84), W.Va. U. Alumni (life), W.Va. Bar Aux. Home: 300 Glenn Ave Beckley WV 25801 Office: Beckley College S Kanawha St Beckley WV 25801

ASKEW, MARY FRANCES, educator; b. Eufaula, Ala., Oct. 31, 1921; d. Emmett Tyler and Frances Perry (Warr) Brown; B.S., Troy State U., 1962; M.S., Auburn U., 1964, postgrad., 1972-73; postgrad. Ga. State U., 1979; m. William Henry Askew, III, 1945; 1 son, William Henry Askew, IV. Tchr. Ft. Rucker (Ala.) Elem. Sch., 1963-69; tchr. Ft. Benning (Ga.) Schs., 1969-72, reading specialist, 1979—. Night Circle pres. Women of the Ch., First Presbyn. Ch., Phenix City, Ala.; den mother Cub Scouts, Eufala and Ft. Benning; active Girl Scouts, 4 yrs.; 1st v.p. Ft. Benning PTA, 1977-78; past pres. Barbour County Dist. PTA, Eufala PTA. Mem. Ala. Hist. Assn., Ga. Hist. Soc., NEA, Ga. Assn. Educators, Benning Edn. Assn. (pres. 1976-77, 83-84), Internat. Reading Assn. (pres. Muscogee County Reading Council 1978-79), Ga. Reading Assn., Ala. Reading Assn., East Ala. Geneal. Soc., Old Muscogee Geneal. Soc., Russell County Hist. Commn., Eufaula Heritage Assn., Phenix City Preservation Soc., Chattahoochee Valley Assn. Children with Learning Disabilities (dir.), Ga. Assn. Children with Learning Disabilities, Nat. Assn. Children with Learning Disabilities, Nat. Registrar Children of Confederacy (chpt. organizing pres.), L.S. Raiford Soc. (organizer, pres. 1973-79), Children Am. Revolution, Daus. Am. Colonists, DAR, Children of Confederacy (Ala. dir.), UDC (pres. Russell County 1971-81, Jefferson Davis Gold medal for dedicated service 1980), Eufaula Bus. and Profl. Women's Assn. (pres.), Friends Confederate Naval Mus., Kappa Delta Pi. Presbyterian. Editor profl. studies. Home: 212 N Randolph Ave Eufaula AL 36027 Office: 300 First Division Rd Fort Benning GA 31905

ASKINS, NANCY PAULSEN, savings and loan official; b. St. Paul, Nov. 2, 1948; d. Charles A. and Stasia (Sawicki) Paulsen; B.S.H.Ec., U. Cin., 1970. B.S.Ed., 1971, M.Ed., 1972; postgrad. SUNY-Buffalo, 1974-76, Temple U., 1976-78; student C.L.U. program, 1979-81, Inst. Fin. Edn., 1982—, mgmt. program. Am. Mgmt. Assn./Monmouth Coll., 1982-84; m. Arthur J. Askins, Apr. 28, 1979. Camp counselor Girl Scouts U.S.A., summers 1966, 67; asst. aquatic supr. Cin. Recreation Commn., 1969-72; student affairs adminstr., mem. faculty U. Cin., 1970-72, Tex. Luth. Coll., 1972-73, SUNY, Geneseo, 1974-76, Temple U., 1976-78; tchr., drug awareness coordinator Harlandale Schs., San Antonio, 1973-74; career life ins. agt., fin. planning cons. Phoenix Mut. Life Ins. Co., Phila., 1978-81; registered rep., securities agt. Phoenix Equity Planning Corp., Phila., 1980-81; owner Paulsen-Askins Fin. Services, Somers Point, N.J., 1980-81; mem. women's task force Phoenix Cos., 1980-81; tng. services coordinator Collective Fed. Savs. & Loan Assn., Egg Harbor City, N.J., 1981-82, tng. dir., 1982—, asst. v.p., 1982—; owner, cons. Nancy Paulsen Askins, M.Ed., cons. leadership and managerial skills, 1982—; facilitator Assertiveness Tng. Group, Interpersonal Communications Group; sales adv. Jr. Achievement; instr. Inst. Fin. Edn., 1982—; Agy. chmn. United Way Campaign, Phila., 1979, 80; active ann. Muscular Dystrophy Telethon, Phila.; active Girl Scouts U.S.A., 1956-74; bd. dirs. S. Jersey Regional Theatre, 1983—, chmn., 1983-84; mem. parish council, choir St. Joseph Roman Catholic Ch., Somers Point, N.J., 1979—, mem., coordinator parish enrichment com., 1984—. Recipient Blue Vase sales achievement award Phoenix Mut. Life Ins. Co., 1978, named Asso. of Month, 1979. Mem. Greater Camden Assn. Life Underwriters (chmn. Life Ins. Week for South Jersey 1978-79, dir. 1979-81, public relations chmn. 1979-81, chmn. state edn. 1981), Am. Soc. Tng. and Devel. (chpt. treas. 1983; charter), Greater Mainland C. of C. (v.p., treas., membership coordinator 1980—; Pres.'s award 1983), U. Cin. Alumni of Greater Phila. Area. (pres. 1980—), Alliance The Women's Network (dir. 1983-84). Democrat. Home: PO Box 800 Somers Point NJ 08244 Office: 200 Philadelphia Ave Egg Harbor City NJ 08215

ASLANI, CAROLE SUE, public policy educator, training company executive; b. Big Rapids, Mich., Oct. 22, 1943; d. Dwaine Charles and Eula Ferne (Crysler) Voss; m. Iraj Aslani, Mar. 20, 1981. B.S., Mich. State U., 1965; M.P.A., Western Mich. U., 1984. Tchr., Marysville Pub. Schs. (Mich.), 1965-67; social worker Berrien County Dept. Social Services, Benton Harbor, Mich., 1967-72, casework supr., 1972-76; pub. policy educator Mich. Dept. Social Services, Lansing, Mich., 1976—; owner Human Resource Devel. Tng. Co. Home Extension Service scholar, 1961. Mem. Mid-Mich. Landlords Assn., Am. Soc. Tng. and Devel., Am. Pub. Welfare Assn. Methodist. Home: 315 Richard Ave Lansing MI 48917

ASPER, BERNICE VICTORIA, editor; b. Luck, Wis., Apr. 1, 1920; d. Harry L. and Christine Marie (Hilseth) Johansen; m. Verdie Sanford Asper, Dec. 23, 1942 (dec. 1944); 1 dau., Victoria Sharon Asper Johnson. Student Mpls. Bus. Coll., 1939. Office worker, Fed. Agr. Agy., Balsam Lake, Wis., 1942; bookkeeper Enterprise-Herald, Luck, 1942-44; cashier Thorp Fin. Corp., Frederic, Wis., 1946-51; bookkeeper Rudell Motor Co., Frederic, 1951-57; billing clk. Frederic Telephone Co., 1958-63; editor Inter-County Leader, Frederic, 1963—. Author: 75 Years in Frederic, 1976; 100 Years at St. Peter's, 1980. Bd. dirs. Western Wis. Health Systems Agy., LaCrosse, 1976-82, Frederic Municipal Hosp., 1981—; sec. Frederic Citizens Adv. Com., 1968-83; supt. St. Peter's Luth. Sunday Sch., Luck, 1948-78; sec. Frederic Devel. Corp., 1982-84. Named Frederic Citizen of Yr., C. of C., 1980. Mem. Wis. Press Assn., Polk County Jury Commn. Democrat. Lutheran. Home: 302 N Wisconsin Ave Frederic WI 54837 Office: Inter County Leader 303 N Wisconsin Ave Frederic WI 54837

ASTARITA, SUSAN GALLAGHER, communications company executive; b. Wilmington, Del., Oct. 6, 1941; d. Hugh Francis and Alice Clara (Pepper) Gallagher; A.B. in Polit Sci., Randolph-Macon Woman's Coll., 1963; M.A. in Comparative Govt., Georgetown U., 1973; postgrad. U. So. Calif., 1973-75; m. Bruce Thomas Astarita, May 24, 1969; 1 dau., Alice Catherine. Adminstrv. asst. George Washington U., Washington, 1964, Ford Found., Nat. Assn. Edn. Broadcasters, Washington, 1965-66; asst. producer Youth Wants To Know, Theodore Granik Enterprises, Washington, 1966-68; community and public relations dir. Del. Tech. and Community Coll., Georgetown, 1968-72; writer-editor Inst. Indsl. Relations, UCLA, 1975-77; pres. Susan Astarita Communications, Rolling Hills Estates, Calif., 1977—; lectr. Harbor Coll. Bd. dirs. The Assocs. (Palos Verdes Community Arts Assn.), 1977-79, Palos Verdes Symphony, 1978-79; mem. peninsula com. Calif. State U., Dominguez Hills; mem. Palos Verdes Transit Adv. Com. Mem. Women in Communications (dir. Los Angeles chpt. 1980-83), Torrance C. of C., Palos Verdes Community Arts Assn. (bus. council). Democrat. Episcopalian. Office: 777 Silver Spur Rd Suite 233 Rolling Hills Estates CA 90274

ASTERITA, MARY FRANCES, physiologist; b. N.Y.C.; d. Martin A. and Mary L. (diPalma) A.; B.A., Marymount Coll., 1961; M.S., N.Y.U., 1969; Ph.D., Cornell U., 1973. Postdoctoral fellow Yale Univ. Sch. Medicine, New Haven, 1973-75; asst. prof. physiology Ind. U. Sch. Medicine, Gary, 1975—, dir. clin. biofeedback programs, 1980-83; dir. clin. biofeedback programs St. anthony's Hosp., 1985—; pres. Biofeedback and Stress Mgmt. Services, 1983—; mem. research rev. com. Am. Heart Assn., 1979-84. NIH fellow, 1974-75. Mem. Biofeedback Soc. Am., Biofeedback Soc. Ill. (bd. dirs. 1980-83, pres. 1982-83), Am. Assn. Biofeedback Clinicians, Am. Physiol. Soc., Am. Heart Assn., Nat. Speakers Assn., Internat. Platform Assn. Author: Physiology of Stress: with Special Reference to the Neuroendocrine System; Physical Exercise, Nutrition and Stress. Contbr. articles to profl. jours. Office: 3400 Broadway Gary IN 46408

ASTIN, PATTY DUKE (ANNA MARIE DUKE), actress; b. N.Y.C., Dec. 14, 1946; d. John P. and Frances (McMahon) Duke; grad. Quintano's School for Young Profls.; m. John Astin, 1973 (div.); m. Michael Pearce, 1986. TV appearances include Armstrong Circle Theatre, 1955, The Prince and the Pauper, 1957, Wuthering Heights, 1958, U.S. Steel Hour, Meet Me in St. Louis, 1959, Swiss Family Robinson, 1958, The Power and the Glory, 1961, numerous others; theatrical appearances include The Miracle Worker, 1959-61, Isle of Children, 1962; motion picture appearance in The Miracle Worker (Acad. award as best supporting actress 1963), 1962, Valley of the Dolls, 1967, Me, Natalie (Golden Globe award as best actress 1970), 1969, My Sweet Charlie, 1970, The Swarm, 1978, By Design, 1982 appeared in TV series Patty Duke Show, 1963-66 (Emmy award as best actress 1964), All's Fair, 1981-82, TV film Before and After, 1979, Having Babies, III, 1978, Women in White, 1979, Hanging by a Thread, 1979, The Women's Room, 1980, miniseries Captains and the Kings (Emmy award as best actress 1977), miniseries George Washington, 1984, TV Series Hail to the Chief, 1985. Mem. corp. council Muscular Dystrophy Assns. Am. Office: care Creative Artists Agy Inc 1888 Century Park E Suite 1400 Los Angeles CA 90069*

ASTOR, BRENDA KAREN, diagnostic, educational and lifestyle planning center executive, holistic stress counselor, consultant; b. Haverhill, Mass., Sept. 9, 1941; d. George Lee and Bertha (Dublin) A.; m. Victor A. Freedman, May 30, 1963 (div. Apr. 1974); children—Lori Shayne, Evan Jon (dec.). Diploma in nursing Beth Israel Hosp. Sch., Boston, 1962; postgrad. Sch. Psychology, Ind. U. and Purdue U., Indpls., 1975; cert. in gestalt methodology Gestalt Inst. Cleve., 1978; also workshops, seminars. R.N., Fla. Neurosurg. and clin. nurse Lahey Clinic, Boston, 1962-64; mental health nurse coordinator Gallaghue Mental Health Ctr. Community Hosp., Indpls., 1973-75; head nurse, coordinator pain ctr. Community Hosp., Indpls., 1975-78; dir. Ctr. for Healing Arts, N.W. Community Mental Health Ctr., Miami Lakes, Fla., 1979-82; program coordinator adolescent addiction program Dodge Hosp., Miami, Fla., 1983-84; program coordinator, holistic stress counselor, program dir. Alt. Lifestyle Ctr., Miami Beach, Fla., 1984—; cons., lectr., facilitator in holistic health, pain control, stress mgmt., assertiveness tng.; founder, dir. Healing Arts Assocs., Miami, 1981—; cons. World Living Ctr., Miami, 1983, Arvida, Miami, 1984, Larkin Inst., Miami, 1985, Victoria Hosp., Miami, 1986; mem. bd. advisers Interlink Systems, Miami, 1984—. Active New Age Network, Inc., Miami, 1983, nuclear disarmament Physicians for Social Responsibility, Miami, 1983—, Goddess Group, Miami, Friends of Emmanuel, Miami. Named to Who's Who in '82, Miami Mag., 1982; Community Mental Health Ctr. grantee, 1979-80, 80-81. Mem. Am. Holistic Nurses Assn. (charter), Holistic Health Learning Labs (founding mem., bd. dirs.), Gestalt Inst. Cleve., Nat. Assn. Female Execs. Avocations: nature; theosophy; dancing; reading; art. Home: 5830 Red Rd Apt 104 South Miami FL 33143 Office: Alt Lifestyle Ctr 6801 Collins Ave Miami Beach FL 33141

ASWAD, BETSY (BECKER), writer, educator; b. Binghamton, N.Y., Feb. 10, 1939; d. George Marrinan and Jane (Sprout) Becker; B.A. with high honors in English, Harpur Coll., Binghamton, 1961; M.A., SUNY, Binghamton, 1965, Ph.D. with distinction, 1973; m. Richard N. Aswad, Sept. 22, 1962; children—Richard, Kristin. Mem. film editing staff Sta. WNBF-TV, Binghamton, 1957; apprentice So. Tier Playhouse, summers 1957, 58; asst. editor Link Log, 1962-63; teaching asst., then instr. English, SUNY, Binghamton, 1963-74, mem. adj. faculty, 1974-84, fellow Coll. in the Woods, 1973. Sec., Friends of Binghamton Public Library, 1977-78; co-program chmn. Tappan Circle, First Presbyn. Ch., Binghamton, 1979-80; vol. Probe, Binghamton Gen. Hosp., 1978-79, Meals on Wheels, 1979-82, St. Mary's Soup Kitchen, 1983—. Author: Winds of the Old Days (Edgar Allan Poe spl. award Mystery Writers Am.), 1980, paperback edit., 1983; Family Passions, 1985. Home: 192 Deyo Hill Rd Binghamton NY 13905

ATALAY, ANDREA SWERLING, software consulting manager; b. Lorain, Ohio, May 20, 1956; d. Richard Henry and Renee (Newman) Swerling; m. Carlos Tomas Atalay, Oct. 9, 1983; stepchildren—Estela, Carlos. B.A., Notre Dame Coll., Cleve., 1981. Data processing cons., Cleve., 1973-80; fin. control mgr. Gould, Inc., Cleve., 1980-82; cons. mgr. Deltak, Inc., Pitts., 1982; br. mgr. Info. Builders, Inc., Chgo., 1983—. Mem. Am. Mgmt. Assn. Avocations: reading; theater; golf; needlework; animals. Office: Info Builders Inc 1020 31st St Suite 100 Downers Grove IL 60515

ATHERTON, FLORA CAMERON, civic worker, former foundation executive; b. Waco, Tex.; d. William Waldo and Helen Emelyn (Miller) Cameron; m. Holt Atherton; children—Ike Simpson Iampmann, III, Megan Cameron Kampmann. Dir., mem. exec. com. Certain-Teed Corp., 1971-78; exec. com. San Antonio World's Fair, 1968; mem. Pres.'s Mission to Latin Am., 1969; U.S. del. Inter-Am. Commn. Women, 1969-72; mem. citizens stamp adv. commn. U.S. Postal Service, 1969-71; cons. Bur. Inter-Am. Affairs, Dept. State, 1972-75; vice chmn. exec. com. Tex. Republican Party, 1968-69; del. Rep. Nat. Conv., 1960, 64, alt. del., 1968, sec. platform com., 1960; mem. Rep. Nat. Fin. Com., 1965—, pres., chmn. 1976-78; past pres. KAMKO Found.; trustee Trinity U., San Antonio, 1965—, chmn., 1976-78; trustee Sweet Briar Coll., 1969-78; mem. Pres.'s Commn. German-Am. Tricentennial, 1983-84; bd. dirs. San Antonio Art Inst., 1984—, mem. nat. council Met. Opera. Mem. San Antonio Jr. League, Colonial Dames Am. Home: 315 Westover Rd San Antonio TX 78209 Office: 4600 Broadway San Antonio TX 78209

ATHEY-STRODE, JANICE MARIE, manufacturing company executive; b. Flint, Mich., Sept. 17, 1951; d. Donald Edgar and Shirley Ann (Kiefer) Athey; m. George Michael Strode, Oct. 8, 1983. B.S., Miami U., Oxford, Ohio, 1974. Dir., Columbus (Ohio) Indsl. Commn., 1974-76; personnel asst. Allstate Ins. Co., Hudson, Ohio, 1976-77, pub. relations div. mgr., 1978-82; dir. consumer affairs Firestone Tire & Rubber Co., Cleve., 1982-83, dir. consumer affairs and mktg., 1983—; TV and radio appearances. Bd. dirs. Akron Better Bus. Bur., 1982—; mem. consumer adv. council Nat. Better Bus. Bur., 1983-84; mem. exec. bd. Summit County Toy Library; team capt. United Way, 1976-78; mem. hospitality com. Nat. Soap Box Derby, 1976-80; coordinator March of Dimes, 1976—; chmn. Spl. Olympics, 1979—; chmn. Walter Hogen Cancer Soc. Golf Tournament, 1980-81; chmn. pub. relations World Series of Golf. Named Career Woman of Yr., Bus. and Profl. Women Cleve., 1977. Mem. Women in Communications, Internat. Assn. Bus. Communicators, Soc. Consumer Affairs Profls. (pres. Ohio chpt. 1981-82), Sales and Mktg. Execs. Club: Women's City (Cleve.). Home: 1161 Akron St San Diego CA 92106 Office: PO Box 81120 Brook Park Cleveland OH 44181

ATKERSON, JOANNE RUTH, radio announcer, news director; b. Lewis Station, Mo., Jan. 18, 1933; d. John Logan and Carolyn Ruth (Schneider) Gill; m. Virgil Riley Atkerson, Jan. 16, 1955; 1 child, Teresa Susan Atkerson Muhs. Grad. high sch., McAlester, Okla. Lic. FCC Hostess cable show Sta. KBLE, McAlester, 1973-76; staff announcer Sta. KNED, McAlester, 1974—, news dir., 1983—. Active Tiak council Girl Scouts U.S.A., 1955—, McAlester PTA, 1955—; bd. dirs. McAlester Alcoholism Bd., 1982-83, Girls' Club Bd., McAlester, 1982-83; adv. Kiamichi Vo-Tech Sch. Bd., McAlester, 1976-83; vice chair McAlester Pub. Library Bd., 1984—. Recipient Meritorious Service citation Am. Legion Post 79, 1981; DJ of Yr. Runner-up, Kiamichi Country Tourism Group, 1979; Named DJ of Yr. Little Dixie Hayride, 1980. Republican. Baptist. Avocations: swimming, wood carving, painting, reading, embroidery, crocheting. Office: Sta KNED Radio Box 1068 McAlester OK 74501

ATKIN, EDITH, artist, poet; b. Washington, Nov. 12, 1921; d. Phillip and Sylvia Hirschel; student Md. Coll. Art and Design, 1973-79, Strayers Bus. Coll., Alice Kilbaum's Coll. Music; m. Irwin Symour; children—Sharon Welch, Joan Atkin Winewriter. Group exhbns. at Lynn Kottler Galleries, N.Y.C., Gudowsky Gallery, Silver Spring, Md., Akademia Raymond Duncan, Paris, Ligoa Duncan, N.Y.C., Salon Surindependants, Paris; represented in numerous pvt. collections. Recipient award for creative achievement Holly Daly Herman Palm Beach Galleries, 1984. Mem. Nat. Tobacco Distbrs. Assn. Jewish.

ATKINS, CHRISTINE JANE, systems analyst, data processing designer, consultant; b. Birmingham, Ala., May 3, 1952; d. Stanley William and Mildred Jane (Blair) Atkins; m. Michael Duane Pedersen, Mar. 30, 1979. B.A. in Journalism, U. Okla., Norman, 1973. Stringer reporter AP, Mobile, Ala., 1969; reporter Mobile Press-Register, 1971, 72; women's editor The Ponca City News, Okla., 1973-74; computer analyst Continental Oil Co., Ponca City, 1974-77; material systems and graphics analyst The M.W. Kellogg Co., Houston, 1977—. Nat. Merit Scholar, 1970, John Will Journalism Scholar, Sigma Delta Chi, Mobile, 1971, MacMahon Journalism Scholar, U. Okla., 1971, Grace Ray Scholar, 1972. Office: The MW Kellogg Co Three Greenway Pl Houston TX 77046

ATKINS, EUNICE LEMONS, county official; b. Mayodan, N.C., May 11, 1934; d. Franklin Dennis and Mary (Craddock) Lemons; m. Noel Dudley Atkins, Aug. 15, 1953; children—Alan Dudley, Lori Ann Atkins Overman. Grad. high sch., Mayodan, Billing clk. Sears Roebuck, Greensboro, N.C., 1952-53; owner, operator restaurant, Mayodan, 1953-61; sec. Rockingham County, Wentworth, N.C., 1965-67, asst. vets. service officer, 1967-74, vets. service officer, 1974—. Vice chmn. Democratic Precinct Com., Mayodan, 1964-70, chmn., 1970-78. pres. Rockingham County Dem. Women, 1972-74; bd. dirs. Rockingham Community Coll. Found., Wentworth, 1985. Moravian. Avocations: gardening, canning, freezing, cooking, reading. Home: 603 Roach St Mayodan NC 27027 Office: Rockingham County Vets Service Office Courthouse Sq Wentworth NC 27375

ATKINS, KAY ROBERTA, association executive; b. Flint, Mich., Aug. 21, 1939; d. Robert Henry and Jessie Mary (Cummings) Bueschen; children—Robert, Karla, James. Student Albion Coll., 1957-60; B.S., Eastern Mich. U., 1963; M.S., Ohio U., 1975. Tchr. Raleigh City Schs., N.C., 1967-69; instr. Ohio U., Athens, 1972-73; trainer Ohio Family Planning Tng. Ctr., Columbus, 1974-80; dir. edn. Planned Parenthood of S.E. Ohio, Athens, 1973-74, asst. dir., 1974-75, exec. dir., 1975—. Mem. Kootaga Area council Boy Scouts Am., 1980—; treas. United Campus Ministry, Athens, 1983—; pub. relations com. chmn. United Appeal of Athens County, 1985—. Mem. Nat. Assn. Female Execs., Am. Pub. Health Assn., Am. Home Econs. Assn., Ohio Citizens Council, Planned Parenthood Affiliates of Ohio (pres.), Planned Parenthood Great Lakes Region Exec. Dirs. Council, Planned Parenthood Nat. Exec. Dirs. Council, Ohio Family Planning Assn. Democrat. Presbyterian. Avocations: travel; reading; singing; swimming; walking. Office: Planned Parenthood of Southeast Ohio 396 Richland Ave Athens OH 45701

ATKINS, PATRICIA BOWEN, legal services executive, lawyer; b. Trenton, N.J., Apr. 2, 1944; d. William and Marie (Reeves) Bowen; m. Richard Leonard, June 15, 1963 (div. 1973), 1 dau., Victoria; m. Robert Martin Atkins, July 7, 1973; children—Leeanne, Robert. B.A., Trenton State Coll., 1966; M.A., Kean Coll., 1970; J.D., Rutgers U., 1979. Bar: N.J. 1979, Pa. 1984. Tchr., Bd. Edn., Trenton, N.J., 1966-68, guidance counselor, 1968-70; instr. Mercer County Community Coll., Trenton, 1970-72; spl. dept. atty. gen., asst. prosecutor Mercer County Prosecutor's Office, Trenton, 1979-80; chief hearings and adminstrv. procedure N.J. Dept. Agr., Trenton, 1980-82; mng. atty. Burlington office Camden Regional Legal Services, 1982-83, exec. dir., 1983—. Recipient award for achievement in field of law, Met. Civic League, Trenton, 1980. Mem. Nat. Bar Assn., N.J. Bar Assn., N.J. Assn. Black Women Lawyers, South Jersey Lawyers Assn., Camden County Bar Assn., Burlington County Bar Assn., Salem County Bar Assn., Cumberland County Bar Assn., Tri-County Women Lawyers Assn., Alpha Kappa Alpha. Roman Catholic. Club: Jack and Jill of Am. Home: 319 Mimosa Pl Cherry Hill NJ 08003 Office: Camden Regional Legal Services Inc 530 Cooper St Camden NJ 08102

ATKINSON, JOAN LYON, English educator; b. Memphis, Nov. 23, 1939; d. Robert Hershal and Otye Blanche (Kilpatrick) Lyon, B.A., Harding U., 1961, M.A., U. Tex., 1963; M.L.S., Pratt Inst., 1970; m. Jon Franklin Atkinson, June 19, 1964; children—Jon Christopher, Amy Frances. Instr. English, Abilene Christian U., Abilene, Tex., 1963-65; tchr. English, librarian Erasmus Hall High Sch., Bklyn., 1965-70; asst. prof. U. Ala., Tuscaloosa, 1973-80, assoc. prof., 1980—; cons. in field; lectr. in field. Mem. Ala. Library Assn. (2nd v.p. 1981-82), ALA (pres. young adult services div. 1985-86, councilor 1986—). Democrat. Mem. Ch. of Christ. Editor: Yarns, 1976-81, Ala. Librarian, CSLD Newsletter, 1981-86. Home: 4135 Windermere Dr Tuscaloosa AL 35405 Office: PO Box 6242 University AL 35486

ATKINSON, LINDA MAE, chiropractor; b. Detroit, May 20, 1953; d. Ray and Mary (Paich) Elwart; D.C., Palmer Coll. Chiropractic, Davenport, Iowa, 1975; m. Warren Bernard Atkinson, Dec. 28, 1978; children—Devin Patrick, Derek Benjamin; stepchildren—Jenny T.M., Warren D. Exec. coordinator Romulus (Mich.) Chiropractice Clinic, 1968-78; Exec. coordinator Arbor Vitae Chiropractic Centre, Chelsea, Mich., 1978-81, dir., chiropractor, v.p., sec.-treas., 1979-84; pvt. practice, Jackson, Mich., 1984—; speaker Parker Sch. Profl. Success. Mem. Internat. Chiropractice Assn., Women Doctors of Chiropractice, Mich. Chiropractic Council. Republican. Roman Catholic. Address: 2397 Shirley Dr Jackson MI 49202

ATKINSON, REGINA ELIZABETH, medical social worker; b. New Haven, May 13, 1952; d. Samuel and Virginia Louise Griffin; B.A., U. Conn., Storrs, 1974; M.S.W., Atlanta U., 1978. Social work intern Atlanta Residential Manpower Center, 1976-77, Grady Meml. Hosp., Atlanta, 1977-78; med. social worker, hosp. coordinator USPHS, Atlanta, Palm Beach County (Fla.) Health Dept., West Palm Beach, 1978-81; dir. social services Glades Gen. Hosp., Belle Glade, Fla., 1981—; instr. Palm Beach Jr. Coll.; participant various work shops, task forces. Vice pres. Community Action Council South Bay, 1978-79. Whitney Young fellow, 1977; USPHS scholar, 1977. Mem. Nat. Assn. Black Social Workers, Nat. Assn. Social Workers, Soc. for Hosp. Social Work Dirs., Fla. Public Health Assn., Fla. Assn. Health and Social Services, Glades Area Assn. for Retarded Citizens. Home: 525 1/2 SW 10th St Belle Glade FL 33430 Office: 1201 S Main St Belle Glade FL 33430

ATKINSON, SHIRLEY RUTH, consulting executive; b. Albuquerque, Aug. 30, 1949; d. Robert Lawrence and Neta Irene (Landis) Atkinson. B.A., U. N.Mex., 1971. Personnel mgmt. specialist Dept. Army, Washington, 1971-73, Office Personnel Mgmt., Atlanta, 1973-74; employee devel. specialist Dept. Army, Honolulu, 1974-75; personnel mgmt. specialist Def. Contract Adminstrn., Marietta, Ga., 1975-77; personnel mgmt. cons. U.S. Forest Service, Atlanta, 1977-83; owner, pres. Selective Singles-Video Dating Service and Mgmt. Services Assocs., San Antonio, Tex., 1983—. Mem. Am. Soc. Tng. and Devel., Orgn. Devel. Network, Nat. Assn. Female Execs., Women in Bus., Adminstrv. Soc. Office: Selective Singles and Mgmt Services Assocs 8531 N New Braunfels Suite 209 San Antonio TX 78217

ATLEE, DEBBIE GAYLE, sales specialist, nurse; b. Oklahoma City, Jan. 8, 1955; d. Harold Phillip and Ella Ruth (Birks) A. B.S. in Nursing, U. Okla., 1977. Registered nurse, Okla. Team leader ob-gyn Bapt. Med. Ctr. of Okla., Oklahoma City, 1977-80, asst. clin. supr. urology, 1980-81, nursing educator, diabetes educator, 1981-84; sales specialist Boehringer Mannheim Diagnostics, Inc., Indpls., 1984—; mem. regional piloting adv. group Nat. Diabetes Adv. Bd., Oklahoma City, 1984-85. Named Outstanding Bus. Woman, Bus. and Profl. Women, Capitol Hill chpt., 1981. Mem. Am. Diabetes Assn. (exec. bd. Met. chpt. 1985—, pres.-elect 1986), Am. Assn. Diabetes Educators, Western Okla. Diabetes Educators (pres. 1984, Outstanding Service and Dedication award 1984, chpt. service award 1985, chpt. edn. award 1984), U.S. Power Squadron (bd. dirs. Oklahoma City 1984), U. Okla. Alumni Assn. (life). Republican. Roman Catholic. Avocations: sailing; photography; gardening; music. Home: 649 Woodland Way Oklahoma City OK 73127 Office: Boehringer Mannheim Diagnostics Inc 9115 Hague Rd Indianapolis IN 46250

ATTAL, DEBORAH KUEHN, writer, editor; b. Crosby, N.D., Oct. 9, 1959; d. Lloyd Daniel and Eileen Dorothy (Wilhelm) Kuehn; m. Zied Mohammad Attal, Nov. 9, 1984. B.A. with honors, U. Minn., 1983, postgrad., 1984—. News reporter Suburban Sun News, Mpls., 1976-77; alderman's aide City of Mpls., 1977-80, research asst., 1980-81; free-lance writer, Mpls., 1977-83; mktg. writer Comserv Corp., Mpls., 1983—; free-lance writer, editor Wordmasters, Inc., Mpls., 1985—. Contbr. articles to mags. and newspapers. George Pillsbury scholar, 1977. Mem. Mpls. Inst. Arts, Soc. Tech. Communicators, The Loft-A Place for Lit. and the Arts, Phi Beta Kappa. Avocations: writing short stories; poetry; film-making. Home: 128 E 18th St 1 Minneapolis MN 55403 Office: Comserv Corp 3400 Comserv Dr Eagan MN 55122

ATTARD, ADELAIDE, gerontologist, county commissioner, educator; b. N.Y.C., June 2, 1930; d. Consiglio and Elizabeth (Bonnici) Spitery; children—Ronald, Gary. B.A., Empire State Coll., 1974; post masters cert. in gerontology Adelphi U., 1976; M. Profl. Studies, New Sch. for Social Research, 1978. Asst. dir. sr. citizens unit Nassau County Dept. Recreation, 1966-68, recreation supr., 1968-69; supr. community services Dept. Recreation and Community Activities, Oyster Bay, N.Y., 1970-71; adj. prof. Adelphi U., Garden City, N.Y., 1975-77, New Sch. for Social Research gerontological services adminstrn., N.Y.C., 1979—; commr. Nassau County Dept. Sr. Citizen Affairs, Mineola, N.Y., 1971—; dir. Am. Assn. for Internat. Aging, Washington; chairperson Fed. Council on Aging, Washington, 1982—; chairperson Committee on Family and Community Support Systems, mem. nat. adv. com. White House Conf. on Aging, Washington, 1981; del. to UN World Assembly on Aging, Vienna, 1982, White House Conf. on Aging, 1971, 81; mem. County Exec.'s Task Force on Status of Women, Mineola, 1977-80, mem. Gov.'s Task Force on Aging, Albany, N.Y., 1977-78. Contbr. articles to profl. jours. Bd. dirs. Welfare Research, Inc., N.Y.C., 1982—, Health and Welfare Council of Nassau County, N.Y., 1981—; mem. Nat. and Regional Tng. and Edn. Task Force Adminstrn. on Aging, Washington, 1971-73; mem. policy/adv. council for Columbia U. Ctr. for Geriatrics and Gerontology Long-Term Care Gerontology Ctr., N.Y.C., 1980—; adv., mem. curriculum com. dept. nursing SUNY, Farmingdale, 1982-83; mem. adv. com. on gerontol. services adminstrn. New Sch. for Social Research, 1976—; mem. Nassau County Criminal Justice Coordinating Council, 1982—; mem. Nassau County Republican Com., 1969—. Named Boss of Yr., Nat. Sec.'s Assn., Long Island chpt., 1971; Recipient Congl. award for Meritorious Service, 1981; Long Island Women Achievers' award 110 Ctr. for Bus. and Profl. Women, 1977, cert. of Leadership, L.I. Assn. Commerce and Industry, 1978; Pacemaker award St. Francis Hosp., 1975; Cert. of Excellence, New Sch. Social Research, 1978-79, Disting. Contbns. in Field of Pub. Mgmt. award L.I. chpt. Am. Soc. Pub. Adminstrn., 1984. Mem. Nat. Assn. Area Agys. on Aging (bd. dirs. 1976-78), N.Y. State Assn. Area Agys. on Aging (pres. 1976-77), Am. Assn. Retired Persons (assoc. mem.), N.Y. Conf. on Aging. Republican. Office: Nassau County Dept Sr Citizen Affairs 222 Willis Ave Mineola NY 11501

ATTARDO, PATRICIA MARY, clothing company executive; b. S.I., N.Y., May 14, 1955; d. Charles C. and Evelyn M. (Holley) Duff; m. Michael A. Attardo, Dec. 2, 1978. A.S., Coll. S.I., 1975, B.S., 1977. Lab. technician Block Drug Co., Jersey City, 1977-78; pres. Bridal Dream, Inc., Bklyn., 1980—, Finishing Touches by Patricia, bridal shoe designs and accessories, Bklyn., 1982—; sec.-treas. La Memoiré Bridal Boutique, Bklyn., 1985—. Democrat. Roman Catholic. Office: Bridal Dream Inc 7514 20th Ave Brooklyn NY 11214

ATTAWAY, ETHEL EVELYN, health spa executive; b. Albuquerque, June 5; d. Alfred Lee and Beryl Agatha (Curtis) Beal; m. Robert Howard Attaway, June 28, 1975; children—Amanda Lynn, Jesse Howard. B.S., Eastern N.Mex. U., 1971. Tech. dir. Pres., Health Club, Fort Worth, 1973-74; adminstrv. asst. European Health Spa, Mpls., 1974-80, asst. mgr., Albuquerque, 1980-82; mgr. Nautilus Fitness Ctr., Albuquerque, 1982-83; owner, mgr. The Fitness Ctr., Clovis, N.Mex., 1984—; cons., speaker Christian Womens Club, Clovis, 1984—; cons. KMCC TV, Clovis, 1985—. Exec. dir. United Way, Clovis, 1985—; chmn. United Way Spl. Events, Clovis, 1985—. Mem. Internat. Phys. Fitness Assn., Beta Sigma Phi. Avocations: water skiing; reading; gardening. Home: 1313 E 21st St Clovis NM 88101 Office: The Fitness Ctr Inc 1420 N Prince Clovis NM 88101

ATTEAN, PRISCILLA ANN, state legislator, state official; b. Old Town, Maine, July 3, 1941; d. Elmer Norman Attean and Eunice M. (Lewey) Attean Crowley; m. Francis Leo Kelly, Nov. 8, 1957 (div. 1967); children—Cheryl, Mary, Richard, Maureen, Colleen. Student U. Maine-Orono. Asst. mgr. Pompeii Restaurant, Bridgeport, Conn., 1970-81; cons. Penobscot Nation, Old Town, 1982-84, tribal, state relations officer, 1984—; mem. Maine Ho. of Reps., Augusta, 1984—, chmn. Joint Select Com. on Indian Affairs, 1984—. Mem. census com. Penobscot Nation, Old Town, 1982-84, adult vocat. tng. com., 1985—, mus. com., 1985—. Roman Catholic. Avocations: genealogical research, rafting, arts, crafts. Home: PO Box 139 Old Town ME 04468 Office: Community Center Old Town ME 04468

ATTEE, JOYCE VALERIE JUNGCLAS, artist; b. Cin., Apr. 4, 1926; d. LeRoy Francis and Clara Marie (Becker) Jungclas; B.A., Rollins Coll., 1948; postgrad. U. Cin., 1952, 54, Art Acad. Cin., 1962-64, Edgecliff Coll., 1967; m. William Robert Attee III, Oct. 25, 1952; children—Robin Wilson, Wendy Ann. One-man shows: Loring Andrews Rattermann Gallery, 1964, Town Club, 1966, 69, 72, 75, 78, 81, 82, 83, 84, Jr. League Office, 1975, Court Gallery, 1969, Bissingers', 1970, 76, Cin. Nature Center, 1974, 78, Cin. Country Day Sch., 1974; 2 woman show: Town Club Cin., 1984, Bissinger's, 1984; group shows include: Cin. Art Mus., 1962, Zoo Arts Festival, 1961, 62, 66, Town Club Cin., 1973-75, 77-79, 80-84, 85, Palm Beach (Fla.) Galleries, 1974, Showcase of Arts, 1976, Ursuline Center, 1976, Court Galleries, 1977, Indian Hill Artists, 1957-76, 82, 83, regional and local shows Nat. League Am. Pen Women, 77, 78, also nat. biennial art exhibit, 1970, Nat. Bicentennial Show, Washington, 1976, James H. Barker Gallery, Palm Beach, Fla., 1979, 80, 81, 82, Nantucket, 1982, Cin. Women's Club Show, 1979, Cin. Nature Ctr., 1983; represented in permanent collections: Bissingers, Cin. Recipient 1st prize in still life or flowers Cin. Womans Art Club, 1965, 69; Marjorie Ewell Meml. award, 1975. Mem. Nat. League Am. Pen Women (past pres. Cin. br., past state art chmn. 1st prize graphics 1975), Women's Art Club Cin. (past v.p.), Jr. League Cin., Jr. League Garden Circle (pres. 1974-75). Episcopalian. Clubs: Town, University, Camargo Racquet, Indian Hill. Author: Elbey Jay, 1964. Home: 8050 Indian Hill Rd Cincinnati OH 45243

ATTEL, ELIZABETH ANN, nurse, administrator; b. El Paso, Tex., July 19, 1947; d. Remus F. and Bernadine E. (McKay) Thomas; B.S.N., U. Colo., 1969; M.S.N., U. Tex.-El Paso, 1983; m. William Anthony Attel, Aug. 23, 1969; children—Timothy Louis, Theodore William. Asst. head nurse Med. Unit, Highland Hosp., Oakland, Calif., 1969-70; public health nurse Alameda, Calif., 1970-73; dir. childbirth edn. Parenthood Edn. Assn. El Paso, 1974-83; exec. dir. Reproductive Services, Inc., El Paso, Tex., 1978-80; dir. Family Planning Services, R.E. Thomason Gen. Hosp., El Paso, 1980-85; v.p. maternal child health Parkland Meml. Hosp., Dallas, 1986—; childbirth educator cons.; family planning mgmt. cons. James Bowman & Assocs., Nova Health Systems. Med. adv. bd. March of Dimes, El Paso; trustee Tex. Family Planning Assn.; Named Outstanding Woman of El Paso, Internat. Yr. of Women, 1974. Mem. Am. Nurses Assn., Tex. Nurses Assn., Am. Soc. for Psychoprophylaxis in Obstetrics, Tex. Family Planning Assn. (pres. 1983-85), Nat. Family Planning and Reproductive Health Assn., Sigma Theta Tau. Contbr. articles to profl. jours. Office: 5201 Harry Hines Blvd El Paso TX 75235

ATTWOOD, CYNTHIA LOU, lawyer; b. Chgo., Dec. 12, 1946; d. John Gordon and M. Louise (Crenshaw) A.; B.A., Oakland U., 1969; J.D., U. Minn., 1973. Admitted to D.C. bar, 1973; atty. employment sect. civil rights div. U.S. Dept. Justice, Washington, 1973-74, atty. appellate sect., civil rights div., 1974-79; counsel appellate litigation mine safety and health div. Office of Solicitor, U.S. Dept. Labor, Arlington, Va., 1979-80, dep. assoc. solicitor, 1980-81, assoc. solicitor, 1981—. Mem. Women's Equity Action League, Women's Legal Def. Fund, Audubon Soc., Women's Bar Assn., D.C. Bar. Office: Office of Solicitor US Dept Labor 4015 Wilson Blvd Arlington VA 22203

ATWATER, EVELYN LOUISE LOWE (MRS. VERNE S. ATWATER), record company executive; b. Akron, Ohio, Aug. 21, 1921; d. Alvin Sylvis and Mary (Marcum) Lowe; B.A., Heidelberg Coll., 1943; m. Verne Stafford Atwater, May 29, 1943; children—Lynda Mary Atwater Pyfrin, Louise Christine Atwater Reinhart. Tchr. Kittery (Maine) Sch., 1944, Seaside (Oreg.) High Sch., 1944-45; co-founder Sing'N Do Co., Inc., Midland Park, N.J., 1955, pres., 1964—; rec. artist pub. Children's songs. Pres. YWCA, Ridgewood, N.J., 1968-70, bd. dirs., 1957-70, bd. dirs., 1957-70; trustee Ridgewood Library, 1971-75; mem. Ridgewood Choral, 1966-82; contralto soloist Ridgewood Meth. Ch., 1951-68; mem. nat. bd. YWCA, 1977—, chmn. tribute to women and industry project YWCA, Ridgewood, 1974-77, nat. bd. dirs., 1980-83; bd. dirs. United Way of Bergen County, 1983—; adviser TWIN mgmt. Forum, chmn. Internat. Twin; Mem. NEA, ASCP, N.J. Library Trustee Assn. Presbyterian. Clubs: Ridgewood College (program chmn. 1964-66), Ridgewood Women's (chmn. music dept. 1963-65, 72—), Am. Woman's (Buenos Aires, Argentina) (program chmn. 1962-63); Arcola Country; Cosmopolitan (N.Y.C.). Home: 6 Maynard Ct Ridgewood NJ 07450 Office: Sing 'N Do Co Inc PO Box 149 Midland Park NJ 07432

ATWOOD, GENEVIEVE, geologist; b. LaJolla, Calif., May 4, 1946; d. Eugene and Margaret (Fisher) A. B.A., Bryn Mawr Coll., 1968; M.A., Wesleyan U., Middleton, Conn., 1973. Field geologist Lamont Doherty/Honduras, Minas de Oro, 1971-72; staff geologist Nat. Acad. Scis., Washington, 1972-74; mem. Utah Ho. of Reps., 1974-80; sr. geologist Ford Bacon and Davis Utah, Salt Lake City, 1975-81; state geologist, dir. Utah Geol. and Mineral Survey, Salt Lake City, 1981—; dir. Salt Lake City Water and Sewer Bd., 1978—, Central Utah Project, Orem, 1981-84, Network Mag., Salt Lake City, 1983—. Editor: 3 books; contbr. articles to profl. jours. Bd. dirs. U. Utah Hosp., Salt Lake City, 1978—. Recipient Legislator of Yr. award Utah Assn. Social Workers, 1977, Jim Bridger award Utah State U., 1978, John F. Kennedy fellow Harvard U., 1978. Mem. Geol. Assn. Am., Utah Geol. Assn. Republican. Episcopalian. Clubs: Town (Salt Lake City); Wadawanuck (Stonington, Conn.). Office: Utah Geol and Mineral Survey 606 Black Hawk Way Salt Lake City UT 84108

ATWOOD, MARGARET ELEANOR, author; b. Ottawa, Ont., Can., Nov. 18, 1939; d. Carl Edmund and Margaret Dorothy (Killam) Atwood; B.A., U. Toronto, 1961; A.M., Radcliffe Coll., 1962. Mem. faculty U. B.C., 1964-65, Sir George Williams U., 1967-68, U. Alta., 1969-70, York U., 1971-72; writer-in-residence U. Toronto, 1972-73, now Oxford U., Don Mills, Ont. Recipient E.J. Pratt medal, 1961; President's medal U. Western Ont., 1965; Gov. General's medal, 1966; Union Poetry prize Poetry mag., 1969; 1st place Centennial Commn. Poetry competition, 1967. Author: (poetry) Double Persephone, 1961, The Circle Game, 2d edit., 1967, The Animals in That Country, 1968, The Journals of Susanna Moodie, 1970, Procedures for Underground, 1970, Power Politics, 1971; You Are Happy, 1974; Selected Poems, 1976; Two-Headed Poems, 1978; True Stories, 1981; Interlunar, 1984; (fiction) The Edible Woman, 1969, Surfacing, 1972; Lady Oracle, 1976; Dancing Girls, 1977; Life Before Man, 1979; Bodily Harm, 1981; Murder in the Dark, 1983; Bluebeard's Egg, 1983 (non-fiction) Survival: A Thematic Guide to Canadian Literature, 1972; also short stories, TV scripts. Address: care Oxford U Press 70 Wynford Dr Don Mills ON M3C 1J9 Canada

ATWOOD, MARY SANFORD, author; b. Mt. Pleasant, Mich., Jan. 27, 1935; d. Burton Jay and Lillian Belle (Sampson) Sanford; B.S., U. Miami, 1957; m. John C. Atwood, III, Mar. 23, 1957. Author: A Taste of India, 1969. Mem. San Francisco/N. Peninsula Opera Action, Hillsborough-Burlingame Newcomers, Suicide Prevention and Crisis Center, DeYoung Art Mus., Internat. Hospitality Center, Peninsula Symphony, San Francisco Art Mus., Mills Hosp. Assocs., World Affairs Council of San Francisco. Mem. AAUW. Republican. Club: St. Francis Yacht. Address: 40 Knightwood Ln Hillsborough CA 94010

ATWOOD, SAUNDRA LEE, communications company executive; b. Miami, Apr. 5, 1946; d. Norman R. and Helen S. B.S. in Advt., U. Fla., 1968. Editor Western Temporary Services San Francisco, 1968-70; advt. copywriter Jordan Marsh Stores, Miami, 1972-74; advt. copy chief Gold Triangle Stores, Miami, 1974; asst. dir. pub. relations Miami Heart Inst., 1975-77; dir. pub. relations Parkway Gen. Hosp., Miami, 1977-81; dir. mktg. and communications Parkway Regional Med. Ctr., Miami, 1981-84; v.p. Communications Strategies, Inc., Miami, 1984—. Recipient MacEachern award Nat. Coll. Hosp. Pub. Relations, 1976, 81, award for community service Fla. Hosp. Assn. Pub. Relations Council, 1978, awards for vol. effort in communications, community service, internat. program, 1979, awards for employee publs. and pub. programs, 1980. Bd. govs., treas. North Dade YMCA. Mem. Fla. Hosp. Assn. (chmn. health edn. com.), Am. Soc. Hosp. Pub. Relations (regional council, editor newsletter), Internat. Assn. Bus. Communicators, S. Fla. Hosp. Pub. Relations Assn. (pres.), Fla. Hosp. Pub. Relations Council (bd. dirs.), Women in Communications, Am. Mktg. Assn. (pres. Miami chpt. 1984—), Acad. Health Care Mktg. (Nat. Adv. Council), N. Miami Beach C. of C., N. Miami C. of C., Greater Miami C. of C. Home: 11223 SW 88th St Miami FL 33176 Office: Communications Strategies Inc 234 Altara Ave Coral Gables FL 33146

ATWOOD, THERESA ANN, nursing educator; b. Richmond Ind., Feb. 13, 1944; d. Richard Albert and Marie Ange (Roy) Wickens; m. James Phillip Atwood, May 20, 1972; children—Jerold Lee, Jody Marie. B. Health Sci., Ball State U., 1972; M.Ed., Purdue U., 1982. R.N., Good Samaritan Hosp., Cin., 1965. Staff nurse St. John's Hosp., Anderson, Ind., 1965-68; nursing educator St. Elizabeth Med. Ctr., Lafayette, Ind., 1972—. Mem. Right to Life, ARC, Am. Heart Assn., Nat. League for Nursing, Ind. Square Dance Caller's Assn. Republican. Roman Catholic. Clubs: Shindig Square Dancing, Fun Squares Dancing. Home: 1801 Maple St Lafayette IN 47904 Office: St Elizabeth Sch Nursing Lafayette IN 47904

AUBREY, CHERYL ALMA, cattle farmer, animal keeper; b. Balt., Apr. 12, 1946; d. Clifford Franklin Hudson and Helen (Ida) Risch; m. Raymond Wesley Aubrey, Jan. 18, 1965; children—Alma Dawn, Wesley Franklin, Tana Dale. Student Andrews U., 1964-65. Asst. to overseer, overseer Twin Hills Cattle Farm, Fork, Md. and Rural Retreat, Ba., 1963-85, owner, overseer, Rural Retreat, 1985—. Vol. Republicans for Reagan, Fork, 1984, Leukemia and Mental Health Socs., 1981-86; mem. Am. Cancer Soc. Recipient John Philip Sousa award, Musicians Assn. Greater Balt., 1963-64. Mem. Nat. Assn. Female Execs., Nat. Trust Hist. Preservation, Am. Mus. Natural History, Nat. Wildlife Assn., People for Ethical Treatment of Animals, World Soc. for Protection of Animals. Seventh-day Adventist. Club: Golf Club of North Shore Animal League. Avocations: Training and riding horses; fishing; wildlife. Office: Twin Hills Cattle Farm Rural Retreat VA 24368

AUBREY, JOANNE ESTELLE, lawyer; b. Youngstown, Ohio, Oct. 18, 1938; d. Emmanuel David and Frances (Schwebel) Solomon; m. Howard L. Aubrey, July 20, 1958 (div. Dec. 1962); 1 dau., Karen Susan. B.A. cum laude, N.E. Mo. State U., Kirksville, 1961; J.D., Capital U., Columbus, Ohio, 1980. Bar: Ohio 1981. Tchr. reading Youngstown Bd. Edn., 1964-67, Rochester (N.Y.) City Schs., 1967-68, Ohio Youth Commn., Lancaster, Ohio, 1971-74; prin. Nelsonville (Ohio) Children's Ctr., Ohio Dept. Mental Health and Retardation, 1974-75; legal intern George Ambro, Esquire, Columbus, 1978-81; sole practice law, Columbus, 1981—; atty. Legal Aid Referral Project, Columbus, 1982—; instr. Ohio State U., 1976. Tchr., Rodef Sholem Temple, Youngstown, 1966-67; vol. speaker Choices for Victims Domestic Violence, 1981, ACLU, 1983—; campaigner for Democratic candidates, 1980; treas. polit. action com., treas. Columbus chpt. Nat. Abortion Rights Action League, 1982; co-founder singles group Temple Israel, Columbus, 1977; past pres. Fairfield Sch. for Boys chpt. Ohio Youth Commn. Fedn. Tchrs. Mem. Columbus Bar Assn., Women Lawyers Franklin County, Youngstown Fedn. Tchrs. (sec. 1966-67). Office: 575 S 3d St Columbus OH 43215

AUBUCHON, PENNY AMELIA, bank executive; b. St. Louis, Oct. 21, 1952; d. Roy Frederick Aubuchon and Virginia Mary (Clem) A. B.S. in Psychology and Sociology, S.W. Bapt. U., 1975. Payroll supr. Four Seasons Country Club, Lake of the Ozarks, Mo., 1977-78; accounts payable analyst Banquet Foods Corp., St. Louis, 1979-81; grain settlement controller truck shipment Far-Mar-Co, St. Louis, 1981; asst. instr. adult program St. Louis Assn. Retarded Citizens, St. Louis, 1981-84, instr. adult program, 1984-85; checking supr. United Postal Savs. Assn., St. Louis, 1985—. Vol. Bellfontaine State Sch. Hosp., 1968-70. Recipient Outstanding Achievement award S.W. Bapt. U. Athletic Dept., 1972-73, 73-74. Mem. Nat. Assn. Female Execs. (outstanding achievement award 1984-85). Baptist. Avocations: piano; art; tennis; racquetball; computer programming. Home: 436 Shepley Dr St Louis MO 63137

AUERBACH, ANITA L., clinical psychologist; b. Flushing, N.Y., Dec. 23, 1946; d. Ben and Gussie (Zuckerman) Weiss; B.A. cum laude, SUNY, Buffalo, 1968, M.A., 1970; Ph.D. (N.Y. State Regents fellow 1970-72), George Washington U., 1977; m. Steven Miles Auerbach, May 25, 1969. Chief research youth crime control project D.C. Dept. Corrections, 1970-74; intern clin. psychology No. Va. Tng. Center, Fairfax, 1974-75, staff psychologist, then chief psychol. services, 1975-79; pvt. practice clin. psychology, dir. Commonwealth Psychol. Assocs., McLean, Va., 1979—; lectr. Washington Tech. Inst., 1972-74, George Mason U., 1978—; cons. in field. Adv. bd. family edn. project Joseph P. Kennedy, Jr. Found., 1977-79; mem. regional appeals bd. No. Va. Public Sch. System, 1977-79. Recipient N.Y. State Scholar Incentive award, 1969; diplomate Am. Bd. Behavioral Medicine. Mem. Am. Psychol. Assn., Am. Soc. Clin. Hypnosis, Va. Acad. Clin. Psychologists, Va. Psychol. Assn., No. Va. Soc. Clin. Psychologists, Washington Soc. Study Clin. Hypnosis, Psi Chi, Alpha Lambda Delta. Author articles in field. Office: 1449 Dolly Madison Blvd McLean VA 22101

AUERBACH, GLENDA FERN, market researcher, consultant; b. Jersey City, May 27, 1955; d. Abraham Jacob and Shirley (Maloyfsky) A. B.S., Syracuse U., 1975; M.Ed., Northeastern U., 1977; M.B.A., Boston U., 1981. Book prodn. mgr. Town House Press, Spring Valley, N.Y., 1976; tchr. Marshfield (Mass.) Schs., 1977-79, Brookline Schs., 1977; lectr., teaching asst. Boston U., 1979-81; research project dir. Kenyon & Eckhardt, Boston, 1981—; research cons. Fielding Inst., Santa Barbara, Calif., 1983—. Mem. Am. Mktg. Assn., Women's Mgmt. Assn., Beta Gamma Sigma. Democrat. Jewish. Office: Kenyon & Eckhardt One Boston Pl Boston MA 02108

AUERBACH, NINA JOAN, English language educator; b. N.Y.C., May 24, 1943. B.A., U. Wis., 1964; M.A., Columbia U., 1967, Ph.D., 1970. Instr. English, Cleve. State U., 1968; asst. prof. Calif. State U., Los Angeles, 1970-72; asst. prof. U. Pa., Phila., 1972-77, assoc. prof. English, 1977-83, prof., 1983—. FORD Found. research fellow, 1975-76; fellow Radcliffe Inst., Cambridge, Mass., 1975-76; Guggenheim fellow, 1979-80. Mem. MLA, Coll. English Assn., Northeast Victorian Soc. Author: Communities of Women: An Idea in Fiction, 1978; Woman and the Demon: The Life of a Victorian Myth, 1982; contbr. articles to profl. jours. Address: U Pa Dept English Philadelphia PA 19104

AUFDENKAMP, JO ANN, librarian, lawyer; b. Springfield, Ill, Mar. 22, 1926; d. Erwin C. and Johanna (Ostermeier) A.; B.A., MacMurray Coll. for Women, 1945; B.L.S., U. Ill., 1946; postgrad. U. Chgo., 1964-66; J.D., John Marshall Law Sch., 1976. Asst. librarian Commerce Library U. Ill., 1946-48; librarian Fed. Res. Bank of Chgo., 1948-80; adminstr. info. services legal dept. Lincoln Nat. Life Ins. Co., Ft. Wayne, Ind., 1980-81; asst. trust officer Central Trust and Savs. Bank, Geneseo, Ill., 1981-83; practice law, 1983-84; cons. Ill. Valley Library System, 1984—; with Office Nat. Planning, Liberia, 1963. Mem. Ill. Bar Assn., ALA, Spl. Libraries Assn., Ill. Library Assn. Republican. Lutheran. Home: 313-D Lakeside Pekin IL 61554 Office: 845 Brenkman Dr Pekin IL 61554

AUFDERHAAR, SUSAN, commercial professional services consulting company executive; b. Celina, Ohio, Feb. 14, 1951; d. Norman Robert and Eleanor Belle (Shook) Aufderhaar; B.G.S., U. Nebr., Omaha, 1978; cert. MIT, 1980; M.B.A., Webster U., 1985; divorced; 1 dau., Laura Michelle. Programmer/systems analyst Dept. Def., U.S. Air Force, 1969-75; sr. programmer, analyst, mgr. quality assurance Majers Market Research, 1978-79; staff mgr. bus. systems Northwestern Bell Telephone Co., Omaha, 1979-82; mgr. area consultative staff AT&T Info. Systems, 1982-83; sr. dir. mktg. Datapoint Corp., 1983-85; sr. exec. data processing cons. Boeing Computer Services, Seattle, 1985—. Served with USAF, 1969-75; Vietnam. Decorated Air Force Commendation medal. Mem. Assn. Computing Machinery (past sec.), Data Processing Mgrs. Assn. (exec. bd., sec.), Nat. Assn. Female Execs., Am. Mgmt. Assn., Smithsonian Instn., Cousteau Soc., Women Data Processing, Nat. Honor Soc. Republican. Mem. United Ch. of Christ. Club: Eastern Star. Office: 919 SW Grady May MS 6K-01 Renton WA 98055

AUGELLO, NINA CATHERINE, legal services administrator; b. N.Y.C., July 5, 1954; d. Angelo and Rose (Cirlincione) Augello; m. Steven Scott Miller, Apr. 24, 1983. B.A., Hunter Coll., 1975; postgrad. Cornell U., 1975; M.A. in English, NYU, 1976. Instr. Hunter Coll., N.Y.C., 1976-79; paralegal asst. firm Proskauer, Rose, N.Y.C., 1979-80; account mgr. Career Blazers Law Services Div. (subs. Personnel Pool 1983), N.Y.C., 1980-81, area account mgr., 1981-82, mgr. law services, 1982-85; dir. corp. devel. Career Blazers, 1985—, now v.p. Contbr. articles to profl. jours. Recipient Blanche Colton Williams award, Hunter Coll., 1975, Irene Steinman award, 1975; Jewish Found. Edn. of Girls grad. scholar, 1975. Mem. Sales Exec. Club N.Y., Women in Sales (v.p., program chmn. N.Y. chpt. 1982-83), Nat. Assn. Female Execs., Herbert F. Johnson Art Mus., NYU Alumni Assn., Mus. Modern Art, Met. Mus. Art, Phi Beta Kappa. Home: Apt 14F 425 W 23d St New York NY 10011 Office: Career Blazers 500 Fifth Ave New York NY 10110

AUGUST, JOAN FRIEDA, cosmetic company human resources executive; b. Paterson, N.J., Jan. 15, 1948; d. John Anthony and Frieda Marie (Schrieb) August; m. Robert Eugene DeBrecht, July 15, 1978; 1 son, Andrew August. B.A., Rutgers U., 1978. Sec., St. Joseph Hosp., Paterson, N.J., 1964-68, Manhattan Shirt Co., 1969-71; recruiter McGraw-Hill, Hightstown, N.J., 1971-74; employment mgr. Bulova Watch Co., Jackson Hights, N.Y., 1974-76; dir. compensation and benefits Revlon, Inc., N.Y.C., 1978—. Instr. Am. Compensation Assn., Scottsdale, Ariz., 1982—. Mem. Am. Soc. Personnel Adminstrn., Am. Compensation Assn., N.Y. Compensation Assn. Office: Revlon Inc 767 Fifth Ave New York NY 10153

AUGUSTINE, JAQUELINE ROSE, publisher; Jersey City, Nov. 2, 1950; d. Edward Francis and Sheila Diana (Geater) A.; m. Richard Joseph Leach, May 29, 1976. B.S. in Mktg., Rutgers U., 1979. Statis. aide GAF Corp., N.Y.C., 1968-71; advt. service coordinator Petersen Pub. Co., Los Angeles, 1972-73; asst. advt. service mgr., 1974-77, advt. sales rep., 1977-80, classification mgr., 1980-82, assoc. pub., 1982—. Mem. Am. Mktg. Assn., Photog. Mfrs. and Distbrs. Assn. Home: 14 Lincoln Ave Wood Ridge NJ 07075 Office: Petersen Pub Co 437 Madison Ave New York NY 10022

AUGUSTINE, OLIVIA JOAN, supervisory programmer analyst; b. Long Beach, Calif., Dec. 17, 1941; d. John Harold and Althair (Clark) Graham; m. Benjamin Adams, June 3, 1958 (div. 1960); m. 2d Samuel Leroy Augustine, June 6, 1970; children—Prettyce, Condace. Student schs. Long Beach. Cert. data processing mgmt. With Long Beach Naval Shipyard (Calif.), 1962—, computer operator, 1970-73, computer programmer, 1973-75, computer specialist, 1975-80, supr. computer specialist, 1980-81, supr. programmer analyst, 1981—, EEO counselor, 1976 (spl. achievement award); career trainer, devel. counselor for youth, 1979. Youth dir. New Testament Baptist Ch., Wilmington, Calif., 1977, Carson Parks (Calif.), 1980. Mem. Fed. Employed Women, Black Data Processing Mgrs. Democrat. Clubs: Stars (pres. Carson 1981—), Toastmistress (sec. 1974). Home: 20212 Amantha Ave Carson CA 90746 Office: Long Beach Naval Shipyard Long Beach CA 90822

AULD, ISABEL GEORGE, university official; b. Winnipeg, Man., Can., Sept. 21, 1917; d. Charles George and Maggie (Davidson) Hutcheson; m. W. Murray Auld, Sept. 21, 1942; children—Nancy Birt, Hedley, Catherine. B.A., U. Sask., 1938, M.A., 1940, LL.D., 1979. Cytogenetic researcher Canadian Dept. Agr., 1941-42; mem. nat. exec. Consumers Assn. Can., 1963-67; mem. bd. Middlechurch Home Winnipeg, Family Bur. Winnipeg, 1968-76; bd. govs. U. Man., 1968-73, 77—, chancellor, 1977—. Bd. dirs. Klinic, Inc., Winnipeg, 1976-80, Social Planning Council Winnipeg, 1975—, Can. World Youth, Montreal, 1979—, Winnipeg Health Scis. Centre, 1980—, Mount Carmel Clinic, 1977-79. Recipient Centennial medal, 1967, Queen Elizabeth Silver Jubilee medal, 1977, Woman of Yr. award YWCA, 1978. Clubs: Women's Canadian, Univ. Women's. Office: U Man 204 Adminstrn Bldg Winnipeg MB R3T 2N2 Canada

AULD-RIDGEWAY, JULIE ANNETTE, business exec.; b. Oak Park, Ill., July 30, 1949; d. Roger Martin and Evelyn Harriet (Strand) A.; m. Don G. Ridgeway, June 30, 1985. Student Valley City State Coll., 1967-68, De Anza Community Coll., 1968-70; B.A., U. Calif., Santa Barbara, 1971, postgrad. in edn.; postgrad. in bus. adminstrn. Santa Clara U., 1974-76; M.P.A., U. So. Calif., 1979. Prodn. control supr. Intel Corp., 1973-76; tchr. kindergarten, San Jose, Calif., 1976; tchr. elem. grades, Santa Barbara, 1972-73, Goleta, Calif., 1972-73, Shandon, Calif., 1976-77; instr. Cerritos Community Coll., Norwalk, Calif., 1977-78; coordinator vol. tutoring program Operation SHARE Found., Norwalk, 1977-78, vol. program cons., 1977-78; mgmt. cons. Williams & Co., Palo Alto, Calif., 1979-80; prodn. mgr. Rucker & Kolls, Mountain View, Calif., 1980-81; mfg. systems supr. Racal-Vadic Inc., Sunnyvale, Calif., 1982, prodn. planning mgr., 1982-85; pres. IntroAction, Inc., 1985—. Mem. Calif. Tchrs. Assn., Native Am. Awareness, Am. Soc. Public Adminstrn., Mcpl. Mgmt. Assn., Am. Prodn. and Inventory Control Soc., Amnesty Internat., Kappa Delta Pi.

AULETTA, JOAN MIGLORISI, real estate broker; b. N.Y.C., July 23, 1940; d. Angelo George and Ann (Passa) Miglorisi; A.B.S., Bklyn. Community Coll., 1957; m. E.V. Auletta, Oct. 5, 1958; children—Ann, Vincent, George, Jeanne. Owner-mgr. Auletta Realty, also owner-mgr. E&J Pancake House, L.I., N.Y., 1974-76; office and fin. mgr. Larchwood Constrn. Co., Farmingville, N.Y., 1976-77; prodn. mgr. Lawlor Industries, Holtsville, N.Y., 1977-79; real estate and fin. adv. Family Home Improvement Corp., Queens Village, N.Y., 1979-81; co-owner Total Home Constrn. Co., N.Y.C., 1981-83; assoc. broker Better Homes and Gardens, Port Jefferson and Stony Brook, N.Y., 1981-82, Century 21, Port Jefferson, 1982-83; owner, broker Century 21 Echo Hills Realtors, Inc., Miller Place, N.Y., 1983—. Roman Catholic. Home: 80 Smithtown Polk Blvd Centereach NY 11720 also 71-07 N 70th Ave Fort Lauderdale FL 33319 Office: 450 Route 25A Miller Place NY 11764

AULT, KATHY ANN, lawyer, photographer; b. Crockett, Tex., June 20, 1957; d. Manuel Edward Mark and Theresa Mae (Spaeth) Kuta; m. Richard Allan Ault, July 3, 1982. B.A., U. Okla., 1978, J.D., 1981. Bar: Okla. 1981, U.S. Dist. Ct. (we. dist.) Okla. 1982. Assoc. firm Birdwell & Pain, Oklahoma City, 1981-82, Robert E. Walker, Inc., Oklahoma City, 1982-83; sole practice law, Oklahoma City, 1983—. Photographs published: Bath, England, 1979 (pub. award 1980), Domestic Animals, 1982 (award 1982), Pampas Grass, 1984 (award 1984), Rothenberg, Germany, 1985 (award 1985). Mem. Okla. Bar Assn., Okla. County Bar Assn., Okla. Criminal Def. Lawyers Assn., Phi Alpha Delta (alumni advisor John Marshall Harlan chpt. 1981-83, cert. of outstanding service award 1982). Democrat. Roman Catholic. Office: 217 N Harvey Suite 309 Oklahoma City OK 73102

AULT, LINDA CAE, educator, learning disabled specialist; b. Dallas, Aug. 10, 1954; d. Carlos Desmond and Carol Beth (Yarborough) Wier; m. Gary Cecil Ault, Apr. 24, 1976; 1 child, Grant Clayton. B.S., U. Tex.-Austin, 1975; M.S. with honors U. Tex.-Dallas, 1981. Resource tchr. Richardson Ind. Sch. Dist. (Tex.), 1977—. Active 500 Inc., Dallas, 1982—; vol. Young Republicans, Dallas, 1980, Variety Club Tex. Mem. U. Tex.-Austin Ex-Students Assn., Council for Learning Disabilities, Richardson Assn. Children with Learning Disabilities, Richardson Edn. Assn., Delta Zeta. Baptist. Clubs: Daus. of Nile, Masons.

AULTMAN, GRETCHEN LEE BORST, lawyer; b. Colorado Springs, Colo., Apr. 20, 1948; d. Frederick Livingston and Emma Lois (Young) Borst; m. Robert Sherril Aultman, Sept. 14, 1968; children—Christi Renee, Mark Andrew. B.S. with distinction, Colo. State U., 1970; J.D., U. Denver, 1982. Bar: Colo. 1982. Apt. complex mgr. Perl Mack Co., Denver, 1971-74; law clk. Sumners & Miller, Denver, 1981-82, assoc., 1982-86; assoc. Burns, Wall, Smith & Mueller, Denver, 1986—. Vol. counselor Arapahoe Mental Health Ctr., Littleton, 1977-78; troop leader Mile High council Girl Scouts U.S., 1977-82; bd. dirs. Littleton-Englewood Recycling, Inc., 1978-81; chmn. internat. relations com. Arapahoe County chpt. LWV, 1978-79, 2d v.p., 1979-80, unit leader, 1977-78; mem. Columbine Knolls Homeowners Assn., 1984—, bd. dirs., 1985—. Mem. ABA, Colo. Bar Assn., Denver Bar Assn., Colo. Women's Bar Assn., Am. Assn. Petroleum Landmen, Colo. Fedn. Bus. and Profl. Women, Psi Chi, Alpha Lambda Delta. Republican. Methodist. Club: Toastmasters (Littleton). Home: 6840 W Walker Ave Littleton CO 80123 Office: Burns Wall Smith & Mueller 303 E 16th Ave Denver CO 80203

AUMAN, CHAR, furniture store executive, interior designer; b. Roby, Tex., Aug. 3, 1943; d. Wesley W. and Pansy B. (Peterson) Smith. children—Noel Joe, Kenneth Scott; m. Gary Auman, Oct. 1, 1984. Grad. Jessie Lee's Hair Design Inst., Lubbock, Tex., 1961. Ind. art tchr. and design contractor, Tex., 1976-82; v.p., sec. Char's Furniture Showcase, Keller, Tex., 1982—. Mem. Keller C. of C., Beta Sigma Phi (local sec. and chmn. social work 1961-68). Republican. Mem. Churches of Christ. Lodges: Rotary, Toastmasters. Avocations: painting; interior design. Office: Char's Furniture Showcase 500 N Main Keller TX 76248

AUMAN, ELIZABETH HARVEY, librarian; b. West Chester, Pa., Jan. 28, 1943; d. Edward Wickersham Harvey and Mary Alice (Mains) Harvey Dickey; m. Robert Luther Auman, June 26, 1967. B.S., U. Md., 1967; M.A., Cath. U., 1971. Deck attendant music div. Library of Congress, Washington, 1970-71, sec. music div., 1971, reference librarian music div., 1971-77, asst. head reference sect. music div., 1977-79, head reference sect. music div., 1979-83, head acquisition and processing sect., coordinator pub. events, 1983—; asst. prof. Sch. Music, Cath. U., Washington, 1977-83. Recipient Superior Service award Library of Congress, 1983. Mem. Music Library Assn., Internat. Assn. Music Libraries, Am. Brahms Soc. (v.p. 1983—). Home: 4617 Powder Mill Rd Beltsville MD 20705 Office: Music Div Library of Congress Washington DC 20540

AURELIA, ROCHELLE ABOUDE, columnist, radio personality, paranormal researcher; b. Glens Falls, N.Y., Aug. 10, 1954; d. Samuel and Betty Emma (Rock) Abbott; m. Jerry Joseph Aurelia, Sept. 3, 1977; children—Timothy Abbott, Samantha Abbott. Grad. high sch., Glens Falls. Editor, mgr. TV Data Inc., Glens Falls, 1974-76; computer data entry Off Track Betting, Schenectady, 1976-77; columnist United Media Syndicate, N.Y.C., 1974—, UPI, N.Y.C., 1975—; lectr. schs. and orgns. throughout N.Y. State, 1980—; advt. cons. to businesses, N.Y. State, 1984—; investigator Aboude Enterprises, Glens Falls, N.Y., 1974—; cons. Psychic Research Library, Lake George, N.Y., 1985—. Contbr. Harness Horseman Internat., 1978-81, There Ought To Be a Law cartoons, 1980-85; writer short stories; contbr. newspapers and mags. Hostess numerous city homeshows, N.Y., 1985. Mem. Nat. Assn. Female Execs. Smithsonian Assocs. Democrat. Roman Catholic. Avocations: breeding Siamese cats; international traveling. Office: Aboude Enterprises PO Box 905 Glens Falls NY 12801

AURELIAN, LAURE, medical sciences educator; b. Bucharest, Romania, June 17, 1939; came to U.S., 1963, naturalized, 1971; d. George I. and Stella (Ben-Joseph) A.; M.S., Tel-Aviv U., 1962; Ph.D., Johns Hopkins U., 1966; m. I.I. Kessler, Nov. 24, 1970; 1 dau., Amalia D. Asst. prof. dept. lab. animal medicine and microbiology Johns Hopkins U. Sch. Medicine, Balt., 1969-74, asso. prof. dept. biophysics and biochemistry, 1975-82, asso. prof. dept. comparative medicine and biophysics, 1974-82, prof. div. biophysics, 1982—; prof. dept. pharmacology U. Md., 1982—, dir. vinology/immunology labs., 1984—; mem. NIH study sects. internat. teaching, 1973. ACS grantee, 1970-74; NIH grantee, 1969—; WHO grantee, 1980—; others; named Disting. Young Scientist, Md. Acad. Sci., 1970. Mem. David Boyes Soc. Gynecol. Oncology, Brit. Coll. Can. (hon.) Am. Soc. Microbiology, AAAS, Am. Assn. Immunologists, Soc. Exptl. Biology and Medicine, Md. Acad. Sci., N.Y. Acad. Sci., Am. Assn. Cancer Research, Reticuloendothelial Soc. Editor Jour. Soviet Oncology, 1980—, European Jour. Gynecol. Oncology, 1982—; contbr. articles to profl. jours. Home: 3404 Bancroft Rd Baltimore MD 21215

AUSTIN, AURELIA, author; b. Decatur, Ga.; d. Herbert O. and Virgil Mary (Wells) A.; ed. So. Bus. U., Mpls. Sch. Art, Atlanta Conservatory of Music; pvt. organ studies. Pvt. sec. to pres. Ashcraft-Wilkinson, Atlanta, 1952-71, Duval Corp., Houston, 1972-77; author: Bright Feathers (award as best book of poems by a Georgian), 1958; Georgia Boys with Stonewall Jackson (award Ga. Writers Assn.), 1968; (anthology) Wind Across the Plain, 1983, Christmas is Beauty, 1983; editor: Poetry Prisms, 1956; Leaves of Life, 1964; contbr. articles to mags.; columnist 13 Ga. newspapers. Mem. Nat. League Am. Pen Women (award 1970, pres. Atlanta br. 1980-82, state pres. Ga. 1982-84), Ga. Poetry Soc., Atlanta Writers Club (pres. 1967-68). Baptist. Home: 526 Hardendorf Ave Atlanta GA 30307

AUSTIN, CAROL ELIZABETH, educator, musician; b. Wheeling, W.Va., May 27, 1936; d. Woodward Thomas Wilson and Estelle Mae (Johnson) Wilson Emerling; m. Walter Thomas Austin, Feb. 12, 1960; 1 son, Charles Randall. Student W. Liberty State Coll., 1954-56; B.S. in Elem. Edn., W.Va. U., 1958, postgrad. 1976-80; M.A. in Edn., U. Pitts., 1970. Tchr. Ohio County Schs., Wheeling, W.Va., 1958-71; elem./jr. high prin. Bellaire City Schs., Ohio, 1971-74, Union Local Schs., Belmont, Ohio, 1974-80; grad. teaching asst. W.Va. U., Morgantown, 1980-81; supr. curriculum instrn. Guernsey County Schs., Cambridge, Ohio, 1981—; mem. cons. Guernsey County Coordinated Services, Cambridge, 1983-85. Trustees session Bethlehem Presbyn. Ch., Wheeling, 1975-78, 83-86, dir. music, 1965—; mem., chmn. Oglebay Inst. Opera Bd., Wheeling, 1968—; bd. dirs. YWCA, Wheeling, 1986—. Recipient Spl. Citizen Service award Wheeling Jaycees, 1966, Spl. People award Wheeling News Register, W.Va., 1980, First Place Vocal award State W.Va., 1966. Mem. Internat. Reading Assn., Phi Delta Kappa, Delta Kappa Gamma (v.p. 1984-86), W.Va. U. Alumni Assn. Republican. Clubs: Friendship Diners (pres. 1983-85), Christian Women's (music chmn. 1983-85), Soroptimist (corr. sec., ways and means chmn. 1984-85), Wheeling Country, Ye Olde Country (Wheeling). Avocations: music; travel; gardening; sports. Home: Glenwood Rd

Beechwood Wheeling WV 26003 Office: Guernsey County Schs County Adminstrn Bldg Cambridge OH 43725

AUSTIN, CONSTANCE MCCARROLL, battery company executive; b. Rapid City, S.D., July 15, 1940; d. Hugh Woodburn and Emily Constance (Myhren) McCarroll; m. William Frederick Austin III, July 24, 1965 (dec. May 1978); children—Joy Constance, William Frederick IV. B.A., U. Ariz., 1962. Real estate lic., Fla. Tchr. Great Neck Sch. System, N.Y., 1962-63; tchr., guidance counselor Orange County Sch. System, Orlando, Fla., 1963-68; sec.-treas. Austin Fertilizer & Chem. Co., Inc., Sanford and Lake Placid, Fla., 1967-78, pres., chief exec. officer, 1978-80; pres., chief exec. officer Ellman Battery Co., Inc., Orlando, 1980—, Jacksonville and Bell Glade, Fla., 1981—; pres., chief exec. officer C.J.R. Corp., 1979—, Orlando Laminated Plastics, 1981-82; owner, operator rental warehousing, Orlando, 1983—; ptnr. ind. TV stas., Chgo., Cin., 1984—; mem. adv. bd. Nelson Investment Timing Service; speaker Women's bus. Ownership Confs. Corp. chmn. Coeur de Coeur, Am. Heart Assn.; mem. devel. council Winter Park Hosp.; vice chmn. Lake Mary Bd. Adjustments, Fla.; mem. bd. deacons First Presbyn. Ch.; bd. dirs. Fla. Symphony Orch.; mem. found. bd. Fla. Hosp./Altamonte. Named one of Orlando's Outstanding Businesswomen, Orlando Sentinel, 1984. Mem. Battery Council Internat. (data-book com. 1983-85), Nat. Women's Coalition, Fla. Exec. Women (trustee), Greater Orlando C. of C. (small bus. council), Greater Seminole C. of C. (bd. dirs.), Seminole County Young Republicans, Heart of Fla., Bullsnort Forum, Council of '76, Council Arts and Scis. Home: PO Box 667 Lake Mary FL 32746 Office: Ellman Battery Co Inc 2710 N Orange Blossom Tr Orlando FL 32804

AUSTIN, DENISE LYNN, editor, journalist; b. Indpls., Jan. 9, 1956; d. Glenn W. and Margery (Nicholson) Austin. B.A., Franklin Coll., 1978. L.B. Johnson fellow intern to Congressman Dave Evans, Washington, 1978; communications assoc. Eli Lilly & Co., Indpls., 1978-80; assoc. editor Hoosier Farmer mag., Ind. Farm Bur., Indpls., 1980—. Adviser Jr. Achievement of Central Ind., 1983-84. Mem. Women in Communications (v.p. membership services). Democrat. Home: 317 E 50th St Indianapolis IN 46205 Office: Ind Farm Bur Inc PO Box 1290 Indianapolis IN 46206

AUSTIN, EILEEN KAY, educator; b. Chgo., Mar. 6, 1947; d. Richard James and Alice Antoinette (Holefelder) Austin; B.S.N., Spalding Coll., 1968; M.Ed., U. Fla., 1971, Ed.D., 1976. Nursing instr. Edison Community Coll., Ft. Myers, Fla., 1971-74; asso. coordinator Interinstl. Registered Nurse Program, Jacksonville, Fla., 1974-75; dir. nursing edn. U. No. Fla., Jacksonville 1975-80; adj. instr. div. continuing edn. U. Fla., Gainesville, 1980—; pres. Eileen K. Austin, Inc., Jacksonville, 1980—; adj. prof. Central Mich. U., Offcampus Grad. program, 1981—. Bd. dirs. Oak Psychiat. Center, Jacksonville, 1977-85; treas. N.E. Fla. Nurses Council for Continuing Edn., 1981-83. Mem. Fla. League for Nursing (chmn. public affairs and legis. com. 1981-83), Fla. Nurses Assn., Dist. Nurses Assn. (2d v.p. 1978-79, dir. 1979-80), Nurse Cons. (assoc., membership com.), Phi Kappa Phi, Phi Delta Kappa, Phi Lambda Theta, Kappa Delta Pi. Democrat. Roman Catholic. Author: Guidelines for the Development of Continuing Education Offerings for Nurses, 1981; A Report of the 1982 Nursing Survey on the Impact of Rules and Regulations and Continuing Education; mem. editorial rev. bd. Fla. Nursing and Health Care. Home: 2001 Groveland Rd Palm Harbor FL 33563 Office: PO Box 168 Crystal Beach FL 34256-0168

AUSTIN, GRACE BALIUNAS, periodontist, educator; b. Vilnius, Lithuania, May 22, 1940; d. Adolph and Anna Catherine (Savage) Baliunas; B.S., U. Chgo., 1963; D.D.S., Northwestern U., 1967; cert. periodontics N.J. Dental Sch., 1976; m. Nov. 28, 1970. Asst. prof. Northwestern U. Dental Sch., Chgo., 1967-69; sr. clin. scientist Warner Lambert Co., Morris Plains, N.J., 1969-71; clin. assoc. prof. periondontics N.J. Dental Sch., Newark, 1977-84; pvt. practice periodontics, Berkeley Heights, N.J., 1978—; mem. staff Overlook Hosp., Summit, N.J., 1979—. Ill. State scholar, 1959; grantee Coll. Medicine and Dentistry N.J. Found., 1976; diplomate Am. Bd. Periodontology. Mem. Am. Acad. Periodontology, ADA, N.J. Dental Assn., Central Dental Soc., Internat. Assn. Dental Research, Psi Omega. Contbr. articles to profl. jours.; mem. editorial bd. Jour. Dental Edn. Home: 15 Dominick Ct Short Hills NJ 07078 Office: 576 Springfield Ave Berkeley Heights NJ 07922

AUSTIN, HARRIETTE AUSTIN, employment data specialist; b. Memphis, Dec. 4, 1919; d. Willis Fowler and Harriette Margaret (Colton) A.; 1 son, Mark Austin Segura. A.B., Barnard Coll., 1943; M.F.A., Yale U., 1962. Drama dir. Mitchell Coll., New London, Conn., 1964-69; instr. speech and drama Baldwin Coll., Tifton, Ga., 1970-72; dir. Madison County Child Devel. Center, Appalachian Pilot Project, Comer, Ga, 1974-76; mem. faculty U. Ga., Athens, 1976-83; sr. employment data specialist JTPA-OW, 1983—; instr. creative writing, 1974—; cons. TESOL, Athens Council on Aging, 1983—. Roman Catholic. Home: PO Box 235 Danielsville GA 30633 Office: U Ga Athens GA 30602

AUSTIN, IRMA CAROLINE, magazine publishing company official; b. Dothan, Ala., Oct. 29, 1941; d. Frank A. and Irma (Rocker) Marshall; m. Joseph H. Austin, May 20, 1972 (dec. Mar. 1975). B.A., Trenton State Coll., 1963; M.A., Columbia U., 1968. Tchr., Dutch Neck, N.J., 1963-66, El Monte, Calif., 1966-67, West New York, N.J., 1968-79; bus. and personnel mgr. Hal Publs. Inc. (pub. Working Woman and Success! mags.), N.Y.C., 1979—. Bd. govs. Palisades Gen. Hosp., North Bergen, N.J. Mem. Adminstrv. Mgmt. Soc., Am. Soc. Personnel Adminstrn., Women in Communication, NOW, Nat. Women's Polit. Caucus. Home: Cliffside Park NJ 07010 Office: Working Woman Mag 342 Madison Ave New York NY 10173

AUSTIN, JOANN CLARK, lawyer; b. Balt., Oct. 15, 1939; d. Thomas Winder Young and Aurie Austin Clark; A.B., Earlham Coll., 1961; M.A.T., Johns Hopkins U., 1965; J.D. with honors, U. Md., 1978; 1 son, Lawan Tarn Petty. Research biologist Nat. Cancer Inst., Bethesda, Md., 1961-63; tchr. Brookline (Mass.) Public Schs., 1965-67; sr. computer programmer Computer Usage Co., Inc., Boston, Los Angeles, 1967-70; bookkeeper, bus. mgr. Koinonia Found., Balt., 1974-76; admitted to Maine bar, 1979; individual practice law, South China, Maine, 1979—; staff atty. Legal Services for the Elderly, Augusta, Maine, 1980-82. Bd. dirs. Sch. of Living, York, Pa., treas., 1975-79; trustee Balt. Monthly Meeting of Friends Homewood, 1976-79, clk. Vassalboro Quar. Meeting, 1981—; bd. dirs. Oak Grove-Coburn Sch., Vassalboro, 1982—; mem. permanent bd. New Eng. Yearly Meeting of Friends; mem. exec. com. Am. Friends Service Com., 1977-78; bd. dirs. Sam Ely Community Land Trust, 1981—; bd. dirs. Maine Women's Lobby, 1981-82; selectman Town of China, 1981—; chmn. China Republican Town Com., 1982—; mem. exec. com. Kennebec County Extension Service, 1985—. Mem. ABA, Maine Bar Assn., China Area C. of C. (v.p.), Vassalboro Grange, NOW, Natural Resources Council. Address: PO Box 115 Rt 32 N South China ME 04358

AUSTIN, KATHRYN ELIZABETH, corporation financial executive; b. Scarsdale, N.Y., Sept. 4, 1956; d. Robert Paul and Marie Theresa (Kane) A. Student Georgetown U., 1974-76; B.S. in Acctg., Fordham U., 1978. C.P.A., N.Y. Staff acct. Gimbel Bros., N.Y.C., 1978-79; jr. acct. R. H. Macy & Co. Inc., N.Y.C., 1979-80, sr. acct., 1980; audit sr. Price Waterhouse, N.Y.C., 1980-83; mgr. fin. reporting BASIX Corp., N.Y.C., 1983-85; fin. and budget analyst Carroll, Mc Entree & Mc Ginley, 1985—. Mem. Am. Soc. Women Accts., Am. Women Soc. C.P.A.s, Am. Inst. C.P.A.s, N.Y. State Soc. C.P.A.s, Nat. Assn. Female Execs. Republican. Roman Catholic. Office: Carroll Mc Entree & Mc Ginley 40 Wall St New York NY 10005

AUSTIN, LORA EVELYN, med. technologist; b. Grand Rapids, Mich., Sept. 6, 1926; d. Carlton and Florence Evelyn (Tyson) Austin; B.A., Olivet Coll., 1948; M.S., Calif. State U., Dominguez Hills, 1981. Intern in med. tech. Butterworth Hosp., Grand Rapids, Mich., 1948-49, staff med. technologist, 1949-52; staff So. Calif. Permanente Med. Group Lab., Los Angeles, 1952—, regional chief immuno-serologist, 1970—; mem. adj. faculty Calif. State U., Dominquez Hills, 1974—. Leader, Campfire Girls, Grand Rapids, Mich., 1949-52; asst. leader Girl Scouts U.S.A., Los Angeles, 1970-81. Recipient Disting. Alumni award Olivet Coll., 1978; lic. med. technologist, Calif., Nat. Cert. Agy. Mem. Am. Soc. Clin. Pathologists (assoc.), Calif. Assn. Med. Lab. Technologists, Am. Soc. Med. Technologists, Olivet Coll. Alumni Assn., Smithsonian Assos., Nat. Wildlife Fedn. Republican. Presbyterian. Home: 10707 Moorpark St Apt 106 Toluca Lake CA 91602

AUSTIN, MAXINE ANGELINE, nurse administrator; b. Nassau, Bahamas, Feb. 25, 1950; came to U.S., 1954; d. Charles Ignacious and Lillian Marie (Strachan) Bonamy; m. Alfonzo Austin, June 18, 1971 (div.); children—Kimberly, Tanya Cooper, Jason Cooper. A.A., A.S., Miami-Dade Community Coll., 1974; B.S. in Nursing, Fla. Internat. U., 1979; M.S. in Human Resources, Biscayne Coll., Miami, 1982. Nursing asst. Community Hosp. South Broward, Hollywood, Fla., 1971-74, staff nurse, 1974-78, asst. supr., 1978-82; nurse adminstr. Metro-Dade Human Resources Health Ctr., Miami, 1982—. State advisor U.S. Congl. Adv. Bd./Am. Security Council, Washington, 1984—; mem. Dade County Women Polit. Caucus, Miami, 1986. Mem. Nat. Assn. Female Execs., Miami-Dade C. of C. Republican. Baptist. Club: Miami-Dade Bus. and Profl. Women (chmn. sunshine com. 1985—, legis. chmn. dist. 12, 1986). Lodge: Order Eastern Star. Avocations: exercising; reading. Home: 20613 NW 22d Pl Carol City FL 33055 Office: 2500 NW 22d Ave Miami FL

AUSTIN, MILDRED KELLER, educator; b. Chgo., Mar. 15, 1925; d. Raymond Lee and Mildred Elaine (Whitney) Keller; student Northwestern U., 1943-44; B.A., Randolph-Macon Women's Coll., 1947; M.S., U. Ill., 1950, postgrad. 1950-55; diploma Burnham Hosp. Sch. Med. Tech., 1972; m. James O. Austin, July 12, 1952; children—James O., David T., Richard D. Lab./teaching asst. Goucher Coll., Townsend, Md., 1947-48; research asst. dept. physiology U. Ill., Urbana, 1949-51, research assoc., 1951-55, dept. vet. physiology and pharmacology, 1964-71; coordinator spl. procedures Burnham Hosp. Lab., Champaign, Ill., 1972-73, instr. lab. inservice, asst. ednl. coordinator, 1973-74, assoc. edn. coordinator, 1975-77, edn. coordinator, 1977-80, program dir., 1980—; lectr. in field; cons. in field; site surveyor, team leader Nat. Accrediting Agy. for Clin. Lab. Scis., 1980-81, cons., 1981. Treas., Kindergarten PTA, 1959-60; den mother Boy Scouts Am., 1962-64. Mem. Am. Soc. Clin. Pathologists (cert.), Am. Soc. Med. Technologists, Ill. Soc. Med. Technologists, Midwest Assn. Clin. Resource Sharing, Sigma Xi, Sigma Delta Epsilon. Republican. Methodist. Contbr. articles to profl. jours. Home: 917 W Charles St Champaign IL 61820 Office: 407 S 4th St Champaign IL 61820

AUSTIN, PATRICIA DAVIS, school system administrator; b. Lynn, Mass., Oct. 7, 1943; d. Lorne Campbell and Margaret Mary (Baker) Davis; B.A., Jackson Coll., Tufts U., 1965; Ed.M., Salem State Coll., 1971; postgrad. Suffolk U., 1975-76; C.A.G.S., Harvard U., 1977; m. Arthur Leonard Austin, Oct. 16, 1966. Editorial asst. Sat. Rev., McCall Corp., N.Y.C., 1965-66; researcher Loomis Sayles, Boston, 1966; tchr. Boston pub. schs., 1967-68; tchr., curriculum designer Hamilton (Mass.) pub. schs., 1968-74; edn. specialist Mass. Dept. Edn., 1974-76; teaching fellow Harvard U., 1976-77; Fed. projects dir. Chpt. I Malden (Mass.) pub. schs., 1977—; mem. Mass. State Adv. Council Chpt. I, 1983—; dir. Early Childhood Inst. of Tufts U.; dept. edn. mem. Tufts U. Alumni Council, Alumni rep. ednl. policies com. bd. trustees, 1974-76. Mem. Mass. Council Adminstrs. Compensatory Edn., Mass., North Shore (v.p. 1974-76) tchrs. assns., Common Cause, Action for Children's TV, Phi Delta Kappa. Office: Malden Public Schools Malden MA 02148

AUSTIN, TRACY ANN, professional tennis player; b. Rolling Hills, Calif., Dec. 12, 1962; d. George and Jeanne A. Student public schs. Amateur tennis player, 1970-78, profl., 1978—, mem. U.S. Fedn. Cup Team, 1978-80, U.S. Wightman Cup Team, 1978, 79, 81. Named AP Female Athlete of year, 1979, 82, Player of the Yr. Women's Tennis Assn., 1980, Women's Sports Found. Profl. Sportswoman of Year, 1980; recipient Ann. Victor award, 1980, 81. Life mem. U.S. Tennis Assn.; mem. Women's Tennis Assn. Champion Gunze Invitational, Japan, 1978, 82, Porsch Classic, Stuttgart, W. Ger., 1978, 79, 80, 81, Emeron Cup, Tokyo, 1979, Avon of Washington, 1979, Wells Fargo Tennis Open, San Diego, 1979, 80, 81, 82, Family Circle Cup, Hilton Head, S.C., 1979, 80, Italian Open, 1979, U.S. Open, 1979, 81, Avon Championships, 1980, Clairol Crown, La Costa, Calif., 1980, BMW Challenge, Eastbourne, Eng., 1980, 81, Can. Open, 1981; champion mixed doubles with brother, Wimbledon, Eng., 1980, Wimbledon Jr. champion, 1978. Office: care US Tennis Assn 1212 Ave of the Americas New York NY 10036

AUSTIN-LETT, GENELLE, English language educator; b. Chgo.; d. Howard Joseph and Evelyn Gene (Reynolds) Blomquist; B.A., U. Ill., Chgo., 1969; M.A., No. Ill. U., 1972. Teaching and research asst. No. Ill. U., 1970-71; TV prodn. asst. Nat. Coll. Edn. High Sch. Workshop, 1972; prof. mass media and critical consumer Principia Coll., summer 1975; reviewer in interpersonal communication, media and behavioral scis. Houghton Mifflin, Harper & Row, William C. Brown, and Wadsworth Pub., 1972-83, also assoc. prof. speech communication and media Ill. Central Coll., East Peoria, 1971-79, editorial cons. Concordia Pub. House, 1970-82, program dir. Clayton (Mo.) U., 1978-82; instr. St. Louis Community Coll., 1980—; systems analyst Spaulding Racquetball Inc., 1982-83; English tchr. Principia, 1983—; coordinator performing arts multimedia presentations, publicity and recruitment; lectr. media consumerism, psychopolitics and advt.; instr. communications, cons. crisis intervention Fed. Police Tng., 1974-75. Group leader Community Devel. Council, 1974; organizer 9th Ward Teenage Republicans, Chgo., 1963, coordinator, 1967-69; adviser to Ill. Central Coll. Young Reps., 1971-75; clk., dir. exec. bd., chmn. bd. 1st Ch. of Christ, Scientist, Peoria; nat. advisory bd. Am. Security Council; mem. Rep. Nat. Com. Recipient Honors Day recognition U. Ill., 1968, hon. mention Nat. Arts and Letters playwriting contest, 1972; lic. life ins. agt. Clubs: U.S. Senatorial, Bible Investigation, Racquet. Author: (with others) Instructor's Manual for Mass Communication and Human Interaction, 1977; (with Jan Sprague) Talk to Yourself, 1976; editor series on sex edn., 1980, book on child devel., 1983; contbr. articles to Christian Sci. periodicals.

AUSTRIAN, SONIA GRACE, social worker, consultant; b. N.Y.C., Jan. 27, 1933; d. Arthur William and Feiga (Bern) Grace; m. Geoffrey D. Austrian, June 22, 1954; children—Susan E., Sarah G. B.A., Wellesley Coll., 1954; M.S.W., Columbia U., 1967, cert. in advanced social welfare, 1984. Lic. social worker, N.Y., Mass. Researcher, Columbia U., N.Y.C., 1966-71, asst. prof. social work, 1978-83, faculty adviser, 1983—; social worker Payne Whitney Clinic, N.Y.C., 1969-73, social work supr., 1973-78; cons. COHME, N.Y.C., 1983—. Mem. adv. bd. N.Y.C. Dept. Mental Health, 1974-78; mem. Health Systems Adminstrn. Dist. Bd., N.Y.C., 1976-78; mem. Community Bd. Health Com., N.Y.C., 1976-78; chmn. health com. Yorkville Civic Council, N.Y.C., 1976-78. Mem. Nat. Assn. Social Workers, Acad Cert. Social Workers. Democrat. Clubs: Cosmopolitan, Columbia Faculty (N.Y.C.). Home: 25 East End Ave New York NY 10028

AUTENREITH, ALTA VIVIAN, retail craft store owner; b. Jefferson, Iowa, Mar. 11, 1915; d. Cyrus Emanuel and Alta Lulu (Hiddleson) Radebaugh; B.A., Simpson Coll., 1937; postgrad. Columbia U., 1939; m. Herbert Dean Autenreith, Feb. 7, 1939; 1 son, Rory Dean. Tchr. elem. sch., Jefferson, Iowa, 1948-77; partner, mgr., sec. The Crafters, Inc., Jefferson, 1977—; pres. Radebaugh Autenreith Farms. Mem. Hobby Industry Am., Mid-Am. Craft Hobby Assn., Jefferson C. of C. Retail Bur., Delta Kappa Gamma, Sigma Lambda Phi. Republican. Baptist. Clubs: Soroptomists, Bus. and Profl. Women's. Home: 302 E State St Jefferson IA 50129 Office: 217 E Lincolnway Jefferson IA 50129

AUTMAN, CAROL LYNNE, TV manager talent contracts; b. Wilmington, Del., Sept. 20, 1939; d. George Francis and Edythe (McClure) Autman; B.A. in Speech and Theatre and Psychology, Grinnell Coll., 1961; M.A. in Speech and Theatre, Ind. U., 1964; guardian of Molly Clogg. Actress, Alley Theatre, Houston, 1964-65; actress, mem. faculty Alley's Children's Theatre, Houston, 1964-65; artistic, bus. dir. The Children's Theatre Assn., Balt., 1965-68; co. mgr. Dames at Sea, N.Y.C., 1968-71; tour dir. Nat. Shakespeare Co., N.Y.C., 1971, now bd. dirs.; mgr. talent contracts WNET/13 Public TV, N.Y.C., 1971—; cons. public TV stas., 1972-82, also Corp. Pub. Broadcasting, Ind. TV Producers, Vol. Lawyers for Arts. Block improvement capt., N.Y.C., 1971—; career counselor Grinnell (Iowa) Coll., 1978—; youth counselor Troubled Children and Families N.Y., 1970-82. Named Outstanding Contbr. to Ind. U., 1963. Ford Found. grantee, 1964. Mem. Nat. Acad. TV Arts and Scis., Nat. Assn. Ednl. Broadcasters, Am. Film Inst., Nat. Assn. Female Execs., Alumni Assn. Ind. Democrat. Methodist. Club: Swiss Ski. Home: 34 W 83d St New York NY 10024 Office: WNET/13 356 W 58th St New York NY 10019

AUTREY, AVIS KATHLYN, insurance agent; b. Easterly, Tex., Mar. 17, 1937; d. Albert Kelsey and Willie Mae (Scott) Autrey; student Sam Houston State U., 1957-60, U. Houston, 1964. Office mgr. McMahan Ins. Agy., Houston, 1960-63; office mgr., realtor Homes Jones Devel. and Ins. Agy., Houston, 1963-65; acct., office mgr. Office Services, Inc., Houston, 1966-69; mgr. acctg. Sam Proler Industries, Inc., Houston, 1969-74; with Raymond Internat., Inc., Houston, 1974-79, supr. corp. systems and procedures, 1976, hdqrs. fin. coordinator, 1976-77, adminstrv. fin. mgr., Ras Al Khaimah, Saudi Arabia, 1977-79; owner, mgr. AKA-Interiors/Exteriors, Houston and Plantersville, Tex., 1979-80, Bellfort Nursery and Florist, Inc., Houston, 1980-83; ins. agt. Met. Ins. Cos., 1983—. Republican. Home and office: 700 Euclid Houston TX 77009

AUVENSHINE, ANNA LEE BANKS, educator; b. Waco, Tex., Nov. 27, 1938; d. D.C. and Lois Elmore Banks; B.A., Baylor U., 1959, M.A., 1968, Ed.D., 1978; postgrad. Colo. State U., 1970-71, U. No. Colo., 1972; m. William Robert Auvenshine, Dec. 21, 1963; children—Karen Lynn, William Lee. Tchr. math. and English, Lake Air Jr. High Sch., Waco Ind. Sch. Dist., 1959-63, Ranger (Tex.) Ind. Sch. Dist., Ranger High Sch., 1964, Canyon (Tex.) Ind. Sch. Dist., Canyon Jr. High Sch., 1964-66; instr. English, Baylor U., 1963; tchr. math. Canyon Ind. Sch. Dist., Canyon High Sch., 1968-70; tchr. math. and English, St. Vrain Sch. Dist., Erie (Colo.) High Sch., 1970-71; tchr. English and reading Thompson Sch. Dist., Loveland (Colo.) High Sch., 1971-72; instr., reading program dir. Ranger Jr. Coll., 1972-84, chmn. humanities div., 1978-82; tchr. math. Hillsboro High Sch., 1984-85, adminstr. Hillsboro Ind. Sch. Dist., 1985—. Trustee, Ranger (Tex.) Ind. Sch. Dist., 1979-84, v.p. bd. trustees, 1980-82, pres., 1982-84; community chmn., publicity chmn., troop leader Ranger Girl Scout Assn., 1974-77; sec. Eastland County Heart Assn., 1975-77; ch. sch. supt. First United Meth. Ch., Ranger, 1979-81, organist, 1974-77, mem. adminstrv. bd., 1979-84. Mem. Internat. Reading Assn., Assn. Supervision and Curriculum Devel., Western Coll. Reading Assn., Tex. Assn. Sch. Adminstrs., Tex. Assn. Gifted and Talented, Tex. Jr. Coll. Tchrs. Assn. (cert. of appreciation 1979, mem. profl. devel. com. 1974-79, vice chmn. 1976-77, mem. resolutions com. 1979-80), Ranger PTA (parliamentarian 1978-79), Ranger Jr. Coll. Faculty Orgn. (pres. 1980-81), Baylor Alumni Assn. (life), Delta Kappa Gamma (pres. Beta Upsilon chpt. 1978-80, pres. Gamma Delta chpt. 1986—, achievement award 1980). Methodist. Clubs: 1947 (pres. 1977-78) (Ranger); Baylor Bear (Waco). Home: 412 Corsicana St Hillsboro TX 76645 Office: Hillsboro Ind Sch Dist Box 459 Hillsboro TX 76645

AVELAR, CARMEN MARIA, journalist, editor; b. San Francisco, Oct. 11, 1923; d. Miguel and Victoria Simon; grad. Merritt Bus. Coll., Oakland, Calif., 1943; m. Alfred J. Avelar, Jan. 19, 1946 (dec.); children—Richard M., Diana Avelar Kewell. Advt. copywriter Jackson Furniture Co., Oakland, Calif., 1942-46; women's feature writer Sparks Newspapers, Hayward, Calif., 1963-79, columnist, food editor, 1979-85; dir. Spectrum Inc. Service Agy., Hayward, Calif. Mem. Women in communications. Past mem. bd. dirs. Children's Hosp. Med. Center Aux., Oakland, Calif.; bd. dirs. Eden Hosp. Found., Castro Valley, Calif.

AVELLANEDA, MARIA ELIZABETH, air force officer, educator; b. Bogota, Colombia, Mar. 26, 1955; came to U.S., 1962; d. Luis Arturo and Nohemy (Ortiz) A. B.S., U. P.R., San Juan, 1977, M.C.L. in French, 1977, M. Translation, 1981. Commd. 2d lt. U.S. Air Force, 1981, advanced through grades to capt., 1985; exec. support officer 620MS, McChord AFB, Tacoma, Wash., 1981-83, squadron sect. com. 62AMS, 1983-84; asst. prof. Spanish U.S. Mil. Acad., West Point, N.Y., 1984—. Sec. Colombians Assn. P.R., 1976-80; comdr. Angel Flight Soc., P.R., 1979-81. Mem. Air Force Assn., Jr. Officers Council, Phi Kappa Phi. Home: 785 Buckner Hill Rd 207 West Point NY 10996 Office: Dept Fgn Lang MADN-G West Point NY 10996

AVENICK, KAREN REINHARDT, librarian; b. Phila., Dec. 22, 1946; d. Otto M. and M. Sophie (Quinn) Reinhardt; m. Joseph F. Avenick, Nov. 28, 1970 (div. Jan. 1984). B.A., Chestnut Hill Coll., 1968; M.S. in L.S., Drexel U., 1969. Reference librarian LaSalle Coll., Phila., 1969-77; supr. reference services Camden County Library, Voorhees, N.J., 1977—; trustee Palinet, Phila., 1984—. Contbr. articles to mags. Mem. Pa. Library Assn., N. J. Library Assn., ALA. Home: 204C Warwick Rd Stratford NJ 08084 Office: Camden County Library Laurel Rd Echelon Urban Ctr Voorhees NJ 08043

AVERSA, DOLORES SEJDA, business school executive; b. Phila., Mar. 26, 1932; d. Martin Benjamin and Mary Elizabeth (Esposito) Sejda; B.A., Chestnut Hill Coll., 1953; m. Zefferino A. Aversa, May 3, 1958; children—Dolores Elizabeth, Jeffrey Martin, Linda Maria. Owner, Personal Rep. and Public Relations, Phila., 1965-68; ednl. cons. Franklin Sch. Sci. and Arts, Phila., 1968-72; pres., owner, dir. Martin Sch. of Bus., Inc., Phila., 1972—; mem. ednl. planning com. Ravenhill Acad., Phila., 1975-76. Active Phila. Mus. of Art, Phila. Drama Guild. Mem. Nat. Bus. Edn. Assn., Pa. Bus. Edn. Assn., Am. Bus. Law Assn., Pa. Sch. Counselors Assn., Am.-Italy Soc., Phila. Hist. Soc., World Affairs Council Phila., Hist. Soc. Pa. Roman Catholic. Home: 2111 Locust St Philadelphia PA 19103 Office: 2417 Welsh Rd Philadelphia PA 19114

AVERY, CHRISTINE ANN, pediatrician; b. Bklyn., Mar. 30, 1951; d. Basil Steven and Mary P. Goerner; B.S. summa cum laude, U. Houston, 1972; M.D., U. Tex. Health Sci. Ctr., 1976; m. Henry Jakob Wachtendorf, June 7, 1973; 1 son, Henry James. Resident in pediatrics U. Tex. Health Sci. Center, San Antonio, 1976-79, now clin. asst. prof. pediatrics and otorhinolaryngology; dir. Otitis Media Study Center, NIH, San Antonio, 1980—. Recipient Physician Recognition award, 1979, 82, 85. Mem. Am. Acad. Pediatrics, Tex. Pediatric Soc., San Antonio Pediatric Soc. Republican. Roman Catholic. Contbr. articles to profl. jours. Office: 519 W Houston San Antonio TX 78285

AVERY, CYNTHIA GAIL, health care consultant; b. Jacksonville, Fla., Sept. 11, 1948; d. Henry and Mary Ruth (Halverson) Avery. B.A., Boston U., 1970; M.S.W., U. Pitts., 1976. Lic. social worker, S.C. Community bd. trainer United Mental Health, Inc., Pitts., 1971-73; cons. specialist St. Joseph's Hosp., Pitts., 1973-77; dir. South Hills Health System, Pitts., 1977-80, 80-81; health care cons. Dept. Health and Environ. Control, Greenville and Anderson, S.C., 1981—; trainer Pa. State U., 1976-77; field instr. U. Pitts. Sch. Social Work, 1977-81; cons. Continuum of Care for Emotionally Disturbed Children, Anderson, 1986—. Editor-co-pub. Greenville's Gold, 1984; copywriter: Greenville Pleasure Guide, 1985; editor Communiqué, 1985. Mem. Gov.'s Task Force on Veneral Disease Prevention, Harrisburg, Pa., 1972, Gov.'s Council on Drug and Alcohol Abuse, 1977. Gov.'s Council on Drug and Alcohol Abuse grantee, 1979. Mem. Nat. Assn. Female Execs., Nat. Assn. Social Workers, Creative Bus. Exchange (dir.), S.C. Soc. Clin. Social Work, NOW, AAUW, LWV (v.p.), Boston U. Alumni Assn., Nat. Mus. of Women in Arts, Friends of the Library. Avocations: ink drawing; Chinese brush painting; tennis; travel.

AVERY, MARSHA CAROL, child care center executive, psychotherapist; b. Greenwich, N.Y., Mar. 5, 1943; d. Raymond Samuel Jones and Emma Elizabeth (Bounds) Jones Whittemore; m. Donald Joh Hoernig, Dec. 21, 1963 (div. 1972) children—Jon David, David Michael, Michael Patrick; m. Leroy Shirrell Avery, Dec. 31, 1973; children—Laura Suzane, Buddy Stephen Shirrell. B.A. in Psychology, Kent State U., 1965; M.A. in Clin. Psychology, West Chester U., 1984; postgrad. Temple U., 1984—. Sec. asst. to dean Adirondack Community Coll., Hudson Falls, N.Y., 1961-62; group leader Akron Detention Home, Ohio, 1964-65; kindergarten tchr. Twin Oaks Nursery Sch., Kent, Ohio, 1965-67; research statistician Benjamin rose Inst., Cleve., 1967-69; owner, exec. dir. Young World, Inc., Wilmington, Del., 1969—; pvt. practive psychotherapy, Wilmington, 1984—. Mem. Am. Psychol. Assn., Nat. Assn. Educators of Young Children, U.S. Tennis Assn., Psi Chi. Avocations: competitive tennis; piano; art; reading. Home: 24 Whitetail Dr Chadds Ford PA 19317 Office: Young World Nursery Sch and Child Care Ctr Inc 2711 Carpenter Rd Wilmington DE 19810

AVERY, MARY ELLEN, pediatrician, educator; b. Camden, N.J., May 6, 1927; d. William Clarence and Mary (Miller) A.; A.B., Wheaton Coll., Mass., 1948, Sc.D., 1974; M.D., Johns Hopkins U., 1952; Sc.D. (hon.), Trinity Coll., 1976, U. Mich., 1975, Med. Coll. Pa., 1976, Albany Med. Coll., 1977, Med. Coll. Wis., 1978, Radcliffe Coll., 1978; M.A. (hon.), Harvard U., 1974; L.H.D., Emmanuel Coll., 1979, Northeastern U., 1981, Russell Sage Coll., 1983. Intern, Johns Hopkins Hosp., 1953-54, resident, 1954-57; reseach fellow in pediatrics, Boston, 1957-59, Balt., 1959-69; assoc. prof. pediatrics Johns Hopkins U., 1964-69; prof., chmn. dept. pediatrics McGill U. Med. Sch., 1969-74; prof. pediatrics Harvard U., 1974—; physician-in-chief Montreal Children's Hosp., 1969-74. Children's Hosp. Med. Center, Boston, 1974-85; mem. council Med. Research Council Can.; mem. study sect. NIH, 1967—. Trustee Wheaton Coll., Johns Hopkins U. Recipient Mead Johnson award in pediatric research, 1968; Markle scholar in med. scis., 1961-66. Fellow Am. Acad. Pediatrics, Am. Acad. Arts and Scis., Royal Coll. Physicians and Surgeons Can.; mem. Am., Canadian pediatric socs., Am. Physiol. Soc., Soc. Pediatric Research (pres. 1972-73), Inst. of Medicine, Phi Beta Kappa. Author: The Lung and Its Disorders in the Newborn Infant, 4th edit., 1981; (with A. Schaffer) Diseases of the Newborn, 1971, 5th edit., 1984; also articles; editorial bd. Pediatrics,

1965-71, Am. Rev. Respiratory Diseases, 1969—, Am. Jour. Physiology, 1967-73, Jour. Pediatrics, 1974-84, Johns Hopkins Med. Jour., 1978-82, Clin. and Investigative Medicine, 1978—, Medicine, 1985—. Office: Children's Hosp Med Center 300 Longwood Ave Boston MA 02115

AVGERAKIS, MARIA ROSA, audio-visual, video and computer animation production company executive; b. Lima, Peru, Sept. 8, 1953; came to U.S., 1975, naturalized, 1984; d. Mario Enrique and Doris Violeta (Cordova) Pastorelli; m. George Harris Avgerakis, June 20, 1977; children—Stephanie Luisa, Alexander Thomas. Student langs. Rosa de Am., Lima, 1969, Alliance Francaise, Lima, 1968-73, L'Istituto Italiano di Cultura, Lima, 1972-74, Goethe Institut, Lima, 1975. Adminstrv. asst. to pres. Roger Wade Prodns., N.Y.C., 1976-78; adminstr., asst. to internat. dir. COMIND Bank, N.Y.C., 1978-83; pres. Avekta Prodns. Inc., N.Y.C., 1983—. Mem. Park Hill Residents Assn., Rent Stblzn. Assn., N.Y.-N.J. Minority Purchasing Council. Roman Catholic. Office: Avekta Prodns Inc 164 Madison Ave New York NY 10016

AVILA, SUZANNE DOLORES, television executive; b. Sacramento, Apr. 4, 1952; d. Joseph and Rosario (Castellanos) Romero Avila. Student Allan Hancock Coll., 1971-72, U. Calif.-Berkeley, 1977-79. Tchr., Robert Bruce Elem. Sch., Santa Maria, 1970-72; flight attendant TWA, Kansas City, Mo., 1973; social worker City Ct. San Francisco, 1974-78; asst. head Spanish dept. U. Calif.-Berkeley, 1978-79; NW sales mgr. SIN TV Network, San Francisco, 1979—; Hispanic media cons., 1980—. Bd. dirs. Little Jim Club/Children's Hosp., San Francisco, 1984—, publicity dir., 1983—. Mem. San Francisco Ad Club (dir. 1982—, 1st women pres. 1984— 1st v.p. 1985). Democrat. Roman Catholic. Office: SIN TV Network 601 Montgomery St 2015 San Francisco CA 94111

AVRAM, HENRIETTE DAVIDSON, librarian, government official; b. N.Y.C., Oct. 7, 1919; d. Joseph and Rhea (Olsho) Davidson; student Hunter Coll., N.Y.C., George Washington U.; Sc.D. (hon.), So. Ill. U., 1977; m. Herbert Mois Avram, Aug. 23, 1941; children—Lloyd, Marcie, Jay. Systems analyst, methods analyst, programmer Nat. Security Agy., 1953-59; systems analyst Am. Research Bur., 1959-61, Datatrol Corp., 1961-65; supervisory info. systems specialist Library of Congress, Washington, 1965-67, asst. coordinator info. systems, 1967-70, chief MARC Devel. Office, 1970-76, dir. Network Devel. Office, 1976-80, dir. processing systems, network and automation planning, 1980-83, asst. librarian for processing services, 1983—; lectr. dept. library sci. Cath. U. Am., 1973—. Chmn. subcom. 2 sectional com. Z39, Am. Nat. Standards Inst., 1966—; chmn. working group on content designators Internat. Fedn. Library Assns., 1972-77; chmn. subcom. 4 working group 1 on character sets Internat. Orgn. for Standardization, 1971—; mem. Com. for Coordination of Nat. Bibliog. Control, 1976-79; mem. steering com. MARC Internat. Network Adv. Com., 1975—; chmn. profl. bd. Internat. Fedn. Library Assns. and Instns., 1979-83, program mgmt. com., 1983—, chmn. info. tech. sect., 1978-83, chmn. mgmt. and tech. div., 1979-83, mem. exec. bd., 1983—; chmn. RECON Working Task Force, 1968-73. Recipient Superior Service award Library of Congress, 1968, Margaret Mann citation in cataloging and classification, 1971, Fed. Woman's award, 1974; award for achievement in library and info. tech. ALA-Library Info. Tech. Assn., 1980, Melvil Dewey award 1981; co-recipient ACRL Acad./Research Librarian of Year award, 1979. Mem. World Future Soc., Assn. Coll. and Research Libraries, ALA (dir., past pres. info. sci. and automation div.), Am. Soc. Info. Sci., Assn. Computing Machinery. Bd. editors Jour. Library Automation, 1970-72; contbr. articles to profl. jours. Home: 1776 Elton Rd Silver Spring MD 20903 Office: Library of Congress Washington DC 20540

AWL, CHARLOTTE JANE, nursing educator; b. St. Louis, Apr. 28, 1935; d. Herbert Vincent and Elizabeth Edwards (White) Pate; diploma, Presbyn. Hosp. Sch. Nursing, Phila., 1956; B.S. in Gen. Nursing, Ind. U., 1960, M.S. in Nursing Edn., 1961; postgrad. (Ada Belle Clark Welsh scholar), Ill. State U., 1978—; m. Richard Allen Awl, Sept. 2, 1962; children—Deborah Jane, David Allen, Stephen Scott. Pvt. duty nurse, team leader women's surg. ward Presbyn. Hosp., 1956-57, head nurse, pvt. duty nurse, 1957-58; staff nurse Bloomington (Ind.) Hosp., 1958-60; pvt. duty nurse, 1960-62; instr. nursing DePauw U., 1961-63; instr., coordinator devel. sr. courses Meth. Med. Ctr. Sch. Nursing, Peoria, Ill., 1963-64, staff nurse, 1964-66; cons. dept. nursing Bradley U., Peoria, 1966-67, asst. prof., 1967-72, asst. prof., asso. chmn. dept. nursing, 1972-74, asso. prof., asso. chmn. dept., 1974-78, asso. prof., asso. dir. div. nursing, 1978—. Cert. CPR instr. Ill. Heart Assn. Mem. AAUP, Am. Nurses Assn., Assn. Operating Room Nurses, Council Baccalaureate and Higher Degree Programs of Nat. League for Nursing, Am. Heart Assn., Ind. U. Alumni Assn., Pi Lambda Theta, Sigma Theta Tau, Phi Kappa Phi, Kappa Delta Pi. Presbyterian. Home: 305 Dundee Rd East Peoria IL 61611 Office: Div Nursing Bradley U Peoria IL 61625

AWTRY, NELL CATHERINE, former real estate exec.; b. Dallas, Sept. 29, 1900; d. Henry Hibbler and Laura Jane (Harris) Jacoby; B.A., So. Meth. U., 1935; postgrad. Columbia U., 1941-42; m. John Hix Awtry, Apr. 24, 1922; 1 dau., Nell Catherine Awtry Gilchrist (dec.). Real estate saleswoman Prince & Ripley, Scarsdale, N.Y., 1948, Midgeley Parks, Scarsdale, 1949, Cleveland E. Van Wert Inc., Scarsdale, 1954-60, Julia B. Fee, Inc., Scarsdale, 1960—. Mem. Scarsdale Realty Bd., Westchester Realty Bd., Zeta Tau Alpha. Republican. Baptist. Mem. Order Eastern Star (worthy matron 1961, 67), Am. Legion Aux., Am. Assn. Ret. Persons. Clubs: Scardale (N.Y.) Golf; Dallas Athletic; Laguna Hills Rep. Women's, Leisure World Rep. Author poems and lyrics. Home: PO Box 2833 3337-2A Punta Alta Rossmoor Leisure World Laguna Hills CA 92653

AWTRY-SMITH, MARILYN JOAN, psychic research consultant; b. Amityville, N.Y., Feb. 11, 1933; d. William Arthur and Bertha Eliza (Wheland) Jackson; student N.Y. Inst. Applied Arts and Scis., 1950-51; grad. Morris Pratt Inst., Wis., 1972; m. Jack Awtry, Apr. 27, 1952 (div. 1963); children—Jacalyn Susan, Nancy Jean Awtry Harmon; m. Henry Donald Smith, Apr. 2, 1984. Procurement asst. U.S. Air Force, Patrick AFB, Fla., 1963-66; contract negotiator/adminstr. NASA, 1966-72; contracting officer U.S. Coast Guard, Washington, 1972-83; ordained minister and medium Nat. Spiritualist Assn. of Chs., 1973—, trustee, 1983—; pres. SAM, Inc., Arlington, Va., 1979-82; co-founder Harmonial Philosophy Assn., lectr. in field; counsellor-medium in parapsychology, 1965—, monthly columnist The Spotlight, The Nat. Spiritualist. Recipient Outstanding Performance awards U.S. Govt., 1961, 63, 65, 76, 81, 82. Mem. South Cassadaga Spiritualist. Assn., Assn. for Research and Enlightenment, Nat. Contract Mgmt. Assn., Morris Pratt Inst., Ednl. Bur. Spiritualism. Democrat. Clubs: Nat. Spiritualist Tchrs. and Ministerial Assn., Lily Dale Assembly. Author: (pamphlet) You and a Way, 1977; The History of the National Spiritualist Assn. of Churches; A Spiritualist View of the Bible; co-author: Educational Course in Modern Spiritualism, 1981; Brighten Your Way - A Daily Devotional, Natural Law; Contemporary Definitions of Psychic Phenomena and Related Subjects; The Sunflower, An Introductory Approach to Natural Law. Home: 447 Lake St Cassadaga FL 32706

AXELROD, JANET SUZANN, software company executive; b. N.Y.C., Nov. 1, 1951; d. Joseph P. and Sara Elizabeth (Munich) A. B.A., Barnard Coll., 1973. Mem. staff Haymarket People's Fund, Boston, 1974-79; adminstrv. mgr. Lotus Devel. Corp., Cambridge, Mass., 1981-82, v.p. human resources, 1982—. Organizer Amandla: A Concert for Humanitarian Aid to South Africa, Cambridge, 1979. Jewish. Office: Lotus Devel Corp 55 Cambridge Pkwy Cambridge MA 02142

AXELROD, LEAH JOY, tour company executive; b. Milw., Sept. 7, 1929; d. Harry J. and Helen Janet (Ackerman) Mandelker; m. Leslie Robert Axelrod, Mar. 10, 1951; children—David Jay, Craig Lewis, Harry Besser, Garrick Paul, Bradley Neal, Nell Anne. B.S., U. Wis., 1951. Creative drama specialist Highland Park Parks & Recreation Dept., Ill., 1962-82; program specialist Pub. Library, Highland Park, 1972-82; ednl. cons. Bd. Jewish Edn., Chgo., 1973-80; children's edn. specialist Jewish Community Ctr., Chgo., 1975-82; tour cons. My Kind of Town Tours, Highland Park, 1975-79, pres., 1979—. Editor: Highland Park: All American City, 1976. Author: Highland Park By Foot or By Frame, 1980; Highland Park: American Suburb, 1982. Bd. dirs. Midwest Fedn. Temple Sisterhoods, 1975-79; pres. B'nai Torah Sisterhood, 1982-84; founding mem., v.p. Highland Park Hist. Soc.; founder, bd. dirs. Chgo. Jewish Hist. Soc.; mem. Highland Park Historic Preservation Commn. Mem. Am. Theatre Assn., Ill. Theatre Assn. (dir. creative dramatics 1977-79). Club: Hadassah (Highland Park). Home: 2100 Linden Ave Highland Park IL 60035 Office: My Kind of Town Tours Inc PO Box 924 Highland Park IL 60035

AYCOCK, JACQUELINE LEE, nursing administrator; b. Belleville, Ill., Nov. 25, 1939; d. Elmer William and Manila Cova (Muskopf) Koch; m. Ray H. Aycock, Dec. 30, 1960; children—Andrea Lyn, Andrew Wayne. Diploma in nursing St. Luke's Sch. Nursing, 1957-60; B.S.N., St. Louis U., 1981, postgrad., 1982—. R.N., Ill. Head nurse pediatrics Christian Welfare Hosp., East St. Louis, Ill., 1961-65, supr., 1966-69; supr. Meml. Hosp., Belleville, 1969-72, 78-81, head nurse emergency room, 1972-76, paramedic instr., 1977-78, head nurse ICU, 1983—; instr. nursing Barnes Hosp., St. Louis, 1981-83; dir. continuing edn. for R.N.s Belleville Area Coll., 1979-82. Emergency med. technician, paramedic Columbia Ambulance Service (Ill.), 1978-82. Fellow Am. Heart Assn.; mem. Nat. League of Nursing, Emergency Dept. Nurses Assn. Republican. Mem. United Ch. of Christ. Home: 1334 Glenwood Dr Columbia IL 62236 Office: Meml Hosp 4501 N Park Dr Belleville IL 62221

AYDELOTTE, MYRTLE E. KITCHELL, nursing consultant; b. Van Meter, Iowa, May 31, 1917; d. John and Lavara Josephine (Gutshall) Kitchell; B.S., U. Minn., 1939, M.A., 1947, Ph.D., 1955; m. William Osgood Aydelotte, June 22, 1956; children—Marie Elizabeth, Jeannette Farley. Head nurse Charles T. Miller Hosp., St. Paul, 1939-41; surg. teaching supr. St. Mary's Hosp. Sch. Nursing, 1941-42; instr. U. Minn., 1945-49; dir. dean-elect State U. Iowa, 1949, prof., dean, 1949-57, prof., acting chmn. psychiat. nursing dept., 1957-58; prof. Coll. Nursing, U. Iowa, 1949-62, 65-76, 84—; dir. dept. nursing U. Iowa Hosps. and Clinics, 1968-76; asso. chief nurse VA Hosp., Iowa City, 1963-64, chief of nursing research, 1964-65; exec. dir. Am. Nurses Assn., 1977-81; cons., 1982—. Served as capt. U.S. Army Nurse Corps, 1942-46; asst. chief nurse 26th Gen. Hosp., Eng., Africa, Italy, 1942-45; chief nurse 52d Sta. Hosp., Italy, 1945. Recipient Outstanding Achievement award U. Minn., 1959, Distinguished Service award U. Iowa. Mem. Am. Nurses Assn., Inst. Medicine, Psi Chi, Pi Lambda Theta, Sigma Theta Tau (nat. pres. 1955-57). Contbr. articles to profl. jours. Home: 201 N 1st Ave Iowa City IA 52240 also 149 Oswegatchie Rd Waterford CT 06385

AYERS, PATRICIA JEAN, real estate saleswoman, municipal official, crafts store executive; b. Massillon, Ohio, Feb. 9, 1948; d. Russell Richard and Della May (Murphy) Rehm; m. James Patrick Ayers, June 26, 1971; children—Jason Patrick, Jennifer Patricia. B.A. in Bus. Adminstrn., Kent State U., 1972. Time clk., sec. Westinghouse, Orrville, Ohio, 1966-70; ins. processor Westfield Ins., Westfield Center, Ohio, 1972-74; acctg. clk. Spray A Lawn, Orrville, 1981-84; sales assoc. Tredway Real Estate, Orrville, 1974—; clk. of council City of Orrville, 1978—; owner, operator Pat & Patti's Crafts, Orrville, 1979—. Pres. Parent Tchr. Orgn., Orrville, 1983-85. Democrat. Clubs: Mother Study, Silver and Gold Club (treas. 1983-84). Avocations: crafts; fishing; swimming and other sports. Home: 827 S Main St Orrville OH 44667 Office: City of Orrville 207 N Main St Orrville OH 44667

AYLOUSH, CYNTHIA MARIE, aircraft components manufacturing company personnel executive; b. Jackson, Mich., July 2, 1950; d. Leonard Edward and Violet Caroline (Kroeger) Ullrich; m. Abbott Selim Aylouish, June 21, 1980; children—Sasha Christine, Nadia Marie. A.A., Fullerton Coll., 1970; Diploma in Fashion Mdse., Brooks Coll., 1975; B.S., Pepperdine U., 1980. Receptionist, Hydraflow, Commerce, Calif., 1968-74, personnel mgr., Cerritos, Calif., 1979—, treas., 1979—, corp. sec., 1985—; with sales dept. Robinson's, Cerritos, Calif., 1974-75, dept. mgr., 1975-79. Mem. Am. Soc. Personnel Adminstrs., Personnel Indsl. Relations Assn., Merchants and Mfrs. Assn., Cerritos C. of C. (dir. 1983—). Republican. Roman Catholic. Clubs: Soroptimist (sec. 1979—), Century, Pepperdine Univ. Office: Hydraflow 13259 E 166th St Cerritos CA 90701

AYRAULT, EVELYN WEST, psychologist, writer; b. Buffalo, Mar. 3, 1922; d. John and Evelyn (West) A.; B.S., Fla. State Coll. for Women, 1945; M.A., U. Chgo., 1947. Chief psychologist, asst. prin. Crippled Children's Sch., Jamestown, N.D., 1947-48; psychologist, tchr. spl. edn. dept. Sharon (Pa.) Public Schs., 1948-50; chief psychologist, instr. Med. Coll. Va., Richmond, 1950-52; pvt. practice, psychology N.Y.C., 1952-68; clin. psychologist, Erie, Pa., 1968—; dir. psychol. services United Cerebral Palsy Assn., Miami, Fla., 1952-54, Erie County (Pa.) Crippled Children's Soc., 1968-78; cons. NW Tri-County Intermediate Unit, Edinboro, Pa., 1978—. Mem. Am., N.Y. State, Pa. psychol. assns., Council for Exceptional Children, Psi Chi. Author: Take One Step, 1963; You Can Raise Your Handicapped Child, 1964; Helping the Handicapped Teenager Mature, 1971; Growing Up Handicapped, 1978; Sex, Love, and the Physically Handicapped, 1981. Home: 10054 W Law Rd North East PA 16428

AYRAULT, MARGARET WEBSTER, emeritus educator; b. Tonawanda, N.Y., Sept. 8, 1911; d. Miles and (Maud) Eleanor (Webster) A.; A.B., Oberlin Coll., 1933; B.S. in L.S., Drexel Inst. Tech., 1934; M.S. in L.S., Columbia U., 1940. Gen. asst. Drexel Inst. Tech. Library, Phila., 1934; cataloger Pratt Free Library, Balt., 1934-38; asst. reference dept. library Columbia U., 1939-40; head cataloger Carnegie Endowment for Internat. Peace Library, Washington, 1941-43; chief processing sect. library U.S. Dept. Agr., Washington, 1943-50; chief bibliog. control sec. Tech. Library, Naval Ordnance Test Sta., Inyokern, Calif., 1950-51; asst. librarian Bur. Budget, Washington, 1952-54; head cataloging dept. library U. Mich., Ann Arbor, 1954-65; prof. Grad. Sch. Library Studies, U. Hawaii, Honolulu, 1965-75, prof. emeritus, 1976—. Mem. Friends of Library of Hawaii, bd. dirs., 1979-85; chmn. library com. Arcadia Retirement Residence. Mem. ALA (past counselor, exec. bd. resources and tech. services div. 1958-62, orgn. com. 1968-70, Margaret Mann citation 1975), Hawaii Library Assn. (hon.; pres. 1974-75), U. Hawaii Library Assn., AAUP, Phi Beta Kappa, Beta Phi Mu. Contbr. articles to profl. jours. Home: 1434 Punahou St Apt 729 Honolulu HI 96822 Office: Grad Sch Library Studies U Hawaii Honolulu HI 96822

AYRES, LINDA L., art historian, curator; b. Berlin, Md., May 25, 1947; d. John Pershing and Hilda Margaret (Smallwood) A.; m. David Emmert Brewster, Apr. 21, 1977. B.A., Washington Coll., 1969; M.A., Tufts U., 1973. Bicentennial coordinator Fogg Art Mus., Cambridge, Mass., 1974-75, asst. to dir., 1975-76; research asst. Nat. Portrait Gallery, Washington, 1977-78, asst. curator Am. art, 1978-84; acting curator Am. art Nat. Gallery, 1983; curator painting and sculpture Amon Carter Mus., Ft. Worth, 1984—. Author exhbn. catalogue: Harvard Divided, 1976; Thomas Moran's Watercolors of Yellowstone, 1984; co-author exhbn. catalogue: An American Perspective, 1981; Bellows: Boxing Pictures, 1982; American Paintings, Watercolors and Drawings from the Collection of Rita and Daniel Fraad, 1985; contbg. author: John Hay Whitney Collection, 1983. Recipient New Eng. Book award, 1976. Mem. Coll. Art Assn. Democrat. Episcopalian. Office: Amon Carter Mus Art Fort Worth TX 76113

AYSCUE, FREDA JEAN, investment/insurance company executive; b. Winston-Salem, N.C., June 13, 1950; d. Fred Jennings and Bessie Elizabeth Hauser; B.S. in Family Studies and Consumer Sci. (FS/CS scholar, Stokeley Van Camp Outstanding Achievement award 1974), San Diego State U., 1974; m. John H. Ayscue, Jr., Sept. 12, 1970. Sales coordinator Norris Industries, Los Angeles, 1974-75; ind. sales rep., So. Calif., 1975-78; regional mgr. Geno Designs, Atlanta, 1978-79; div. supt. Roosevelt Nat. Investment Co., New Orleans, 1979-83; exec. conf. dir. Fin. Services div. Am. Guaranty, Atlanta, 1983-85; supt. agys., exec. mktg. staff Fin. Services Network, Atlanta, 1985—; cons. F.J. Ayscue & Assocs., 1980—; speaker in field. Mem. cons. council New Orleans/Bayou Health Systems Agy., 1981-82. Mem. Bus. and Profl. Women, Am. Soc. Profl. and Exec. Women, Nat. Assn. Female Execs., Home Economists in Bus., Womens Equity Action League, Women's Polit. Caucus, NOW (chpt. public relations chmn. 1979-81, del. nat. conv. 1980-81). Office: 2191 Northlake Pkwy La Vista Office Park Bldg 11 Suite 101 Atlanta GA 30084

AYVALIOTIS, MICHELE ANN, programmer analyst, educator; b. Rhinebeck, N.Y., Feb. 25, 1954; d. Peter and Virginia (Rifenburgh) A. A.A., Dutchess Community Coll., Poughkeepsie, N.Y., 1974; B.S. cum laude, State U. Coll., Brockport, N.Y., 1976; cert. programmer analyst Houston Community Coll. Tennis pro Seasons Racquet Club, Rochester, N.Y., 1976-78; tchr. Wheatland-Chill Central Sch., Rochester, 1978-79; tchr. Houston Ind. Sch. Dist., 1979-80, programmer, 1980-82; sr. programmer Cabot Petroleum, Houston, 1982-84; programmer analyst Digicon, Houston, 1984—. Mem. Women in Data Processing. Republican. Greek Orthodox. Home: 89 Elm St Saugerties NY 12477 Office: 3701 Kirby Dr Suite 112 Houston TX 77098

AZARES, REBECCA, publishing executive; b. Angeles, Philippines, Sept. 3, 1950; came to U.S., 1955, naturalized, 1960; d. Francisco Lim and Celerina (DelaCruz) A. B.S. in Nursing, U. Md., 1973. Pvt. duty nurse, Silver Spring, Md., 1975-82; owner, pub. Dynamic Publs., Inc., Silver Spring, 1982—; pub. Mid-Atlantic Rev., 1983—, Western Rev., 1985—, Southwest Rev., 1985—, Northern Rev., 1985; N.Y.-New Eng. Rev., 1985; Canadian Rev., 1985. Served to capt. Nursing Corps., U.S. Army, 1973-76. Walter Reed Army Inst. of Nursing scholar, 1969-73. Republican. Mem. Ch. of Scientology. Avocation: horseback riding. Home: 901 Bonifant Rd Silver Spring MD 20904 Office: Dynamic Publs Inc 10510 Insley St Wheaton MD 20910

AZZATO, JUDITH ANNE, social worker; b. Floral Park, N.Y., Dec. 23, 1946; d. John August and Eleanor (Buckley) Rissmeyer; B.A., Queens Coll., Flushing, N.Y., 1967; M.S.W., Fordham U., 1971; m. Michael J. Azzato, Jr., Aug. 19, 1967 (div. Aug. 1974). Caseworker, community organizer Suffolk County Dept. Social Services, Bay Shore, N.Y., 1967-73; lectr. Cornell U. Coll. Human Ecology, Ithaca, N.Y., 1974; social worker Northport-East Northport (N.Y.) Community Council, 1974-75; project dir. YMCA Outreach Project, Bay Shore, 1976-77; therapist Luth. Community Services, 1978-79; social worker L.I. Devel. Center, Melville, N.Y., 1978—; field instr. Adelphi U. Sch. Social Work. Bd. dirs. Econ. Opportunity Council of Suffolk, Inc., Patchogue, N.Y., 1974-77; mem. 2d Congressional Dist. Com. on Youth, 1976; bd. dirs. Suffolk County Youth Bd., 1974-75; mem. Suffolk County Conf. Juvenile and Criminal Justice, Inc., 1976-80; founding mem. Day Care Council of Suffolk, 1971-74, N.Y. State Assn. Child Day Care Councils, Inc., 1972-74; fundraiser Women's Polit. Caucus, 1973; mem. Youth Services Coordinating Council of Suffolk, 1975-77. Qualified cert. social worker N.Y.; recipient award Suffolk County Community Service, 1977; N.Y. State-Suffolk County Dept. Social Services scholar, 1969-71. Mem. Nat. Assn. Social Workers (del. 1977, 79, 81, 84, treas. Suffolk div. 1978-81, sec. Suffolk div. 1986-88, sec. N.Y. State council 1973-75; Clin. Register Social Workers 1978, 82, 85), Queens Coll. Alumni Orgn., Alpha Sigma Alpha. Contbg. author: First Directory of Child Day Care Centers in Suffolk County, 1972; newsletter editor Suffolk Nat. Assn. Social Workers, 1971-75; founding social worker Victims Info. Bur. of Suffolk, Inc., 1976-77.

BAACKE, MARGARETA IRMGARD, German educator; b. Berlin, July 10, 1923; d. Willibald Ludwig and Irmgard Karla (Zinke) B. Ph.D., Philipps U., 1953. Translator NYU Med. Ctr., 1954; instr. German, U. Ill., 1955; asst. prof. German, French, English lit. Western State Coll., Gunnison, Colo., 1955-57; asst. prof. German, Purdue U., West Lafayette, Ind., 1957-65; assoc. prof. German, Knox Coll., Galesburg, Ill., 1965—; instr. Ind. Fgn. Lang. Inst. for High Sch. Tchrs., Bloomington, Ind., summer 1963, NDEA Inst., Scranton, Pa., summer 1968, German Grad. Sch., Millersville, Pa., summers 1969, 70; dir., leader classes to Western and Eastern Germany, 1974, 79. Mem. MLA, Am. Assn. Tchrs. of German. Lutheran. Home: Rural Route 1 Box 170 Knoxville IL 61448 Office: Knox Coll South St Galesburg IL 61401

BAADH, VALERIE, producer, choreographer, dancer; b. Burbank, Calif., Sept. 16, 1952; d. Uffe and Shirley (Goldberg) B.; m. Michael Earl Garrett, May 20, 1979; children—John David Garrett, Rose Kaiulani Garrett. B.F.A., Calif. Inst. Arts, 1973. Choreographer Dancers' Group, San Francisco, 1981-83; ind. choreographer, San Francisco, 1984—; dir. Kadeka Dances for Kids, San Francisco, 1982—, Dancers Group/Footwork, San Francisco, 1983. Choreographer: Half Past Eight, 1981, White Dance, 1982, Spy in the House of Love, 1983, Mother Goose Suite, 1984; producer: Robin Williams and Friends, 1985; Nat. Dance Inst. Event of the Year, 1986; Bay Area Theatre Week, 1986. Home: 120 Solano St Brisbane CA 94005

BAAR, LILLIAN MARY, business executive; b. Chgo.; d. James and Frances (Stanek) Shuss; student evening sch. J. Sterling Morton Jr. Coll., 1934-36; m. William D. Baar, July 25, 1942; 1 dau., Judith Baar Topinka. Sec. to pres. Thordarson Mgr. Co., Chgo., 1935-37; sec. to ofcls. of Sears, Roebuck & Co., Chgo., 1937-43; broker, owner Baar Realty Co., Berwyn, 1944-69; real estate cons. Baar Realty, Inc., 1969-75; owner Baar & Baar Realtors, Berwyn, 1976—; ins. broker Lillian Baar Ins. Agy. Active ARC, Am. Heart Fund; v.p. Berwyn Community Chest, 1968-70, chmn., 1971-72, dir., 1973—; mem. Berwyn-Cicero Gov.'s Council Employment Handicapped, 1965-73; co-chmn. Berwyn Heart Fund, 1968-72; bd. dirs. Dialogue, 1st v.p., 1971-72, pres. (1st woman), 1972-74, trustee, 1973—; v.p. Ill. Council of Real Estate of City of Hope, 1976-77, chmn., 1978-79, hon. chmn., 1980—. Recipient Meritorious Service award Dialogue, 1971; Town of Cicero resolution as outstanding bus. and civic leader, 1972; Citizen of Yr. award Rotary Internat., 1976; Service award Grant Works Children's Center, 1981. Mem. Cermak Rd. Bus. Assn. (pres. 1961-64, v.p. 1985-86, dir. 1946—), West Towns Bd. Realtors (pres. 1965-66), Nat. (mem. women's council), Ill. assns. real estate bds., Nat. Inst. Real Estate Brokers, Ill. C. of C., Riverside C. of C., Berwyn C. of C. (treas. 1980—) Berwyn Bus. and Profl. Women's Club (pres. 1973-74), Czechoslovak Nat. Council Am. Clubs: Mothers of Alpha Gamma Delta, Ladies Aux. The Bohemian of Ceska Beseda, West Suburban Exec. Breakfast (dir. 1975—, treas. 1982—); Execs. (Chgo.). Home: Riverside IL 60546 Office: 6335 W Cermak Rd Berwyn IL 60402

BAAS, JACQUELYNN, art historian, museum director; b. Grand Rapids, Mich., Feb. 14, 1948. Ph.D. in History of Art, U. Mich. Registrar, U. Mich. Mus. of Art, Ann Arbor, 1974-78, asst. dir., 1978-82; editor Bull. of Museums of Art and Archaeology, U. Mich., 1976-82; chief curator Hood Mus. of Art, Dartmouth Coll., Hanover, N.H., from 1982, now dir. Nat. Endowment Humanities fellow, 1972-73; Nat. Endowment for Arts fellow, 1974-75, exhbn. grantee, France, 1981. Mem. Coll. Art Assn. Am., Print Council Am., Am. Assn. Museums. Contbr. articles to profl. jours. Home: 12 Valley Rd Hanover NH 03755 Office: Hood Museum of Art Dartmouth Coll Hanover NH 03755

BABA, MARIETTA LYNN, university official, b. Flint, Mich., Nov. 9, 1949; d. David and Lillian (Joseph) B.; m. David Smokler, Feb. 14, 1977 (div. 1982); 1 child, Alexia Baba Smokler. B.A. with highest distinction, Wayne State U., 1971, M.A. in Anthropology, 1973, Ph.D. in Phys. Anthropology, 1975. Asst. prof. sci. and tech. Wayne State U., Detroit, Mich., 1975-80, assoc. prof., 1980—, assoc. prof. anthropology, 1983—, spl. asst. to pres., 1980-82, econ. devel. officer, 1982-83, asst. provost, 1983-85, assoc. provost, 1985—; founder, corp. officer Applied Research Teams Mich., Inc., Detroit, Intelligent Techs., Inc., Detroit; evolution researcher Wayne State U., 1975-82; lectr. nat. and internat. symposia, profl. conferences. Contbr. numerous papers and abstracts to profl. jours, tech. publs. Bd. dirs. City-Univ. Consortium, Detroit, 1980-83; v.p. Neighborhood Service Orgn., Detroit, 1980-85; mem. State Research Fund Feasibility Rev. Panel, 1982-86; active Leadership Detroit Class IV, 1982-83; dir. Mich. Tech. Council (SE div.), 1984-85. Job Partnership Tng. Act grantee, 1981-86; NSF grantee, 1982, 84-85. Fellow Soc. Applied Anthropology; mem. Am. Anthrop. Assn., Nat. Assn. Practice Anthropology (pres-elect), Phi Beta Kappa, Sigma Xi. Office: Wayne State U 1050 Mackenzie Hall Detroit MI 48202

BABB, SANORA, writer; b. Leavenworth, Kans., Apr. 21, 1907; d. Walter Lacy and Jennie Anna (Parks) B.; student Kans. U., 1924; A.A., Garden City Jr. Coll., 1925; m. James Wong Howe, Sept. 18, 1949 (dec. 1976). Editor, The Clipper, 1940-41, Calif. Quar., 1951-52 (both Los Angeles); instr. short story UCLA Extension, 1959; novel; The Lost Traveler, 1958, Brit. edit., 1958; memoir: An Owl On Every Post, 1970, Brit. edit., 1971; contbr. short stories to anthologies (including Best American Short Stories 1950, 60), texts, mags., poems to mags. Mem. Authors Guild Am. Democrat. Office: care McIntosh & Otis 475 Fifth Ave New York NY 10017

BABBAGE, JOAN DOROTHY, journalist; b. Montclair, N.J., Jan. 10, 1926; d. Laurence Washburn and Dorothy A. (Davenport) B.; B.A. in English, Mt. Holyoke Coll., 1948; postgrad. Art Students League, New Sch. for Social Research; m. Vernon H. Ellsworth, Mar. 6, 1971. Publicist, Paramount Internat. Films, N.Y.C., 1952-58; reporter Newark News, 1960-67, food editor, 1967-72; feature writer, reporter Star-Ledger, Newark, 1972—. Vice pres. jr. group Women's Nat. Republican Club, N.Y.C., 1955. Recipient award N.J. br. Humane Soc., 1978; Outstanding Journalistic Achievement award North Jersey PICA Club, 1980. Contbr. restaurant revs., bus. articles to N.J. Bus. Mag., articles to Official Dog mag.; appeared in various TV documentary and feature programs. Home: Washington Ave Montclair NJ 07042 Office: Star-Ledger Court St Newark NJ 07101

BABCOCK, BETTY THOMPSON, author; b. N.Y.C., Sept. 27, 1900; d. Lewis Steenrod and Geraldine Livingston (Morgan) Thompson; student Art

Students League, N.Y.C., 6 yrs.; m. Richard Franklin Babcock, Feb. 7, 1920; children—Betsy Babcock Moulton, Geraldine Babcock Boone, Anne Babcock Bristow, Alice Babcock Lloyd (dec.). Author, illustrator Polo Horse and Horseman, The Sportsman, N.Y.C., 1931-40, Horse and Hound, The Field, London, 1932-39; assoc. editor Country Life, N.Y.C., 1940-42; illustrator Grolier Club, N.Y.C., 1938; Eastern rep. Bob & Betsy's Antique Nook. Active Arts and Skills Corps, ARC, 1942-45; dep. sr. warden CD, Woodbury, N.Y.; bd. dirs. Brearly Sch., Home Sch., Child Study Assn.; sec.-treas., mem. exec. com. Nassau-Suffolk Sch. Bd. Assn.; trustee Woodbury Bd. Edn.; mem. Central Sch. Dist. 2 Bd. Edn., Oyster Bay Twp., N.Y.; mem. Nat. Com. To Support Pub. Schs., N.Y. State Com. To Support Pub. Schs.; mem. adv. com. Nassau County Community Coll. Recipient N.Y. Pub. Library award, 1949, N.Y. State Tchrs. award, 1949; Disting. Service award Nassau-Suffolk Sch. Bds. Assn., 1967, N.Y. State Sch. Bds. Assn., 1969. Mem. Nat. Forest Assn., Am. Mus. Natural History, Nat. Audubon Soc. Quaker. Clubs: Colony (past gov.), Meadow Brook Hounds (hon. hunt sec. 1939-42). Author: The Expandable Pig, 1949; Betty Babcock's Illustrated Hunting Diary, 1948; illustrator: Just Hunting (H.T. Peters), 1935; Early American Sport (Robert Henderson), 1937. Home: Hark Away PO Box 404 Woodbury NY 11797

BABCOCK, JILL ANN, police chief; b. Buchanan, Mich., Aug. 16, 1944; d. Walter James and Elayne Mary (Blaney) B. B.S. in Edn., Central Mich. U., 1967; M.A. in Spl. Edn., Eastern Mich. U., 1970. Tchr. phys. edn. Marysville High Sch., Mich., 1967-69, Punahou Sch., Honolulu, 1969-70; spl. edn. counselor Kailua High Sch., Hawaii, 1970, 73-74, 76; phys. edn. instr. Peace Corps, Gambia, W. Africa, 1973-74; police officer Lyons Police Dept., Colo., 1978-81, chief of police, 1981—. Mem. Met. Assn. Chiefs of Police, Colo. Assn. Chiefs of Police, Colo. Assn. Women Police. Home: PO Box 235 Lyons CO 80540 Office: Police Dept Hdqrs PO Box 49 Lyons CO 80540

BABCOCK, NELLIE JO, clinical social worker; b. Bozeman, Mont., Mar. 26, 1951; d. Harold Chester and Patricia Ann (Alexander) Babcock; student St. Andrews Presbyn. Coll., 1968-70; B.A. summa cum laude, U. Minn., 1972; M.S.W., U. Minn., 1974; m. Christopher J. Krenk, July 3, 1977; 1 child, Hanna Jo. Psychiat. social worker Lane County Mental Health, Eugene, Oreg., 1974-75, Benton County Mental Health, Corvallis, Oreg., 1975-77, Clackamas County Mental Health, Marylhurst, Oreg., 1978; pvt. psychotherapist and cons., 1978—; dir. Family Growth Alternatives, Marylhurst, 1980-84; co-founder, dir. Portland Family Inst., 1983—. NIMH trainee, 1972-74; registered clin. social worker, Oreg. Mem. Nat. Assn. Social Workers, Acad. Cert. Social Workers, Am. Assn. Marriage and Family Therapy. Democrat. Office: 425 SW 2d St Lake Oswego OR 97034

BABCOCK, PATRICIA ANN, nurse; b. Shelbyville, Ind., Oct. 31, 1934; d. Laurence H. and Reba D. (Conway) Underwood; B.S. in Nursing, Ball State U., Muncie, Ind., 1957, M.A., 1975, Ed.D. (fellow), 1980; m. Robert A. Babcock, Mar. 30, 1958; children—Brett Alan, Richard Scott, Laura Ann. Office nurse, Muncie, 1957-60; staff nurse Porter Meml. Hosp., Valparaiso, Ind., 1961; head nurse St. Joseph Hosp., Logansport, Ind., 1963-65; sch. nurse, Gary, Ind., 1967-76; asst. prof. nursing Purdue U. North Central Campus, Westville, Ind., 1976-82, assoc. prof., 1982—, acting chmn. nursing, 1983-84, chmn. nursing, 1984—; cons. in field. Mem. AAUW (br. pres.), Am. Nurses Assn., Nat. League Nursing, Ind. League Nursing, Ind. Assn. Health Educators, AAUP (chpt. pres.), Nat. Assn. Female Execs., Concern for Dying, Ind. State Nurses Assn. (dist. pres.), Hospice of Porter County, Compassionate Friends, Eta Sigma Gamma, Sigma Theta Tau, Phi Delta Theta, Sigma Kappa. Republican. Methodist. Home: 115 Washington Ave Chesterton IN 46304 Office: Purdue U North Central Campus Westville IN 46391

BABEY, EVELYN RUTH, college official; b. N.Y.C.; d. Adam and Hedwig (Voigt) Babey; B.A., Queens Coll., 1967; M.S. in Edn. (intern) SUNY, Albany, 1969; Ph.D., N.Y.U., 1981. Asst. registrar N.Y.C. Community Coll., Bklyn., 1968-72, asso. registrar, 1972-74; registrar Kean Coll. of N.J., Union, 1974-82, adj. instr. dept. math., 1981—; dir. records Bklyn. Coll., City U. N.Y., 1982-84; registrar U. Calif.-Davis, 1984—; lectr. in field; mem. steering com. N.J./N.Y. Conf. Registrars and Admissions Officers, 1981-84, treas., 1981-84. Recipient cert. of appreciation N.J./N.Y. Conf. Registrars and Admissions Officers. Mem. Am. Assn. Higher Edn., Am. Assn. Collegiate Registrars and Admissions Officers, N.J. Coll. and Univ., Registrars, Albany Student Personnel Alumni Assn. (treas. 1975-77, cert. of appreciation 1979), Am. Personnel and Guidance Assn., Am. Coll. Personnel Assn., AAUW, Nat. Assn. for Female Execs., Nat. Micrographics Assn., Pacific Assn. Collegiate Registrars and Officers of Admissions, Crocker Nat. Mus. (patron), Sacramento Opera Assn. (sustaining), Bravo. Presbyterian. Club: Elizabeth (N.J.) Town and Country. Contbr. articles to profl. jours. Office: U Calif-Davis Davis CA 95616

BABICH, BETH ELLEN, marketing consultant; b. Columbus, Ohio, Nov. 29, 1947; d. Robert and Marilyn (Barnett) B.; B.A. in Psychology, Ohio State U., 1969; M.Internat.Mgmt., Am. Grad. Sch. Internat. Mgmt., 1977. Counselor, cons. Ohio Bur. Employment Services, 1969-73; propr. retail art gallery, Toronto, Ont., Can., 1973-75; mktg. and advt. mgr. Ellio's Frozen Pizza div. Purex, Inc., 1977-78; mktg. mgr. The Drop Shop Ltd., cable TV installation parts, Roselle, N.J., 1978-80; product mgr. cheese and butter products mfg. div. Atlantic & Pacific Tea Co. Inc., Montvale, N.J., 1980-82, mktg. mgr. pies and pie shells Mrs. Smith's Frozen Foods Co., Pottstown, Pa., 1982-83; product mgr. Respond Communications Software Software Synergy, New Rochelle, N.Y., 1984-85; sr. v.p. Strategic Directions Inc., 1985—. Chmn. med. research com. Alzheimer's Disease Soc., 1980—; founding mem. singles div. United Jewish Appeal, Fort Lee, N.J., 1978—. Recipient Outstanding Creativity award Am. Dairy Assn., 1981. Mem. Nat. Assn. Female Execs., Am. Grad. Sch. Internat. Mgmt. Alumni Assn., Phi Alpha Theta. Office: 1450 Palisade St 2J Fort Lee NJ 07024

BABICH, JOANNE MARIE, clin. psychologist; b. Sewickley, Pa., Oct. 9, 1951; d. John and Cookie Joanne B.; B.S. summa cum laude, U. Pitts., 1973; M.A., Ariz. State U., 1976, Ph.D. summa cum laude, 1980; m. Frederick W. Meister, June 12, 1982. Predoctoral intern in community medicine and clin. psychology Baylor Coll. Medicine, Houston, 1977-78; psychotherapist Terros Crisis Center, 1979-80; research fellow Tex. Research Inst. Mental Sci., Houston, 1978; mem. faculty Phoenix Coll., 1979-83; cons. psychologist Family Villas, Inc. and clin. supr. New Ariz. Family, Inc., 1980-83; pvt. practice, 1982—. Vol. gubernatorial campaign; planning com. Coronado Park Conservation Dist. Neighborhood. Mem. Am. Psychol. Assn., Assn. Women in Psychology, Maricopa Soc. Psychologists, Phoenix Soc. Clin. Hypnosis, Phoenix Psychoanalytic Study Group, Am. Assn. Suicidology, Phi Beta Kappa. Democrat. Office: 240 W Osborn Rd Suite 217 Phoenix AZ 85006

BABINEAU, ANNE SERZAN, lawyer; b. Jersey City, Dec. 16, 1951; d. Joseph Edward and Mary (Golding) Serzan; m. Paul A. Babineau, Apr. 7, 1973; children—John Regis, Matthew Paul. B.A. cum laude, Coll. New Rochelle, 1973; J.D. cum laude, Seton Hall Sch. Law, 1977. Bar: N.J. 1977, N.Y. 1983, U.S. Ct. Appeals (3d cir.) 1984. Staff atty. Dept. Pub. Adv., Div. Rate Counsel State of N.J., Newark, 1977-78; assoc. Wilentz Goldman & Spitzer, P.C., Woodbridge, N.J., 1979-85, ptnr., 1985—; instr. Seton Hall Sch. Law, 1977-78. Mem. ABA, N.J. Bar, Assn. Fed. Bar State N.J., Middlesex County Bar Assn., Urban Land Inst. Roman Catholic. Avocations: antiques, museums, gardening. Office: Wilentz Goldman & Spitzer PC 900 Route 9 PO Box 10 Woodbridge NJ 07095

BABINGTON, JUDITH ANN, credit union exec.; b. Wendell, Idaho, May 24, 1941; d. Edward F. and Thelma (McLean) Mathison; cert. credit union exec. Credit Union Nat. Assn., 1979; grad. credit union personnel course U. Wis., 1981; m. Jack W. Babington, June 26, 1959; children—Jaylene, Cara. Optometric asst. Caldwell (Idaho) Vision Clinic, 1968-72; mgr. Canyon Med. Health Credit Union (Idaho), 1971—; sec. bd. dirs. Idaho Corp. Credit Union, 1977-80, pres., 1980—; mem. adv. bd. credit unions Idaho Dept. Fin. Mem. Caldwell Credit Women Internat. (treas. 1981—), Am. Bus. Women Assn. (sec. 1981—), Credit Union Exec. Soc. (sec.-treas. Idaho 1981—). Democrat. Roman Catholic. Office: PO Box 158 Caldwell ID 83605

BABITZ, BRENDA LIPTON, medical center administrator, educator; b. Rochester, N.Y., June 20, 1940; d. Theodore Harris Lipton and Freida H. (Kroll) Lipton Levine; m. Paul B. Babitz, July 2, 1962; children—Roberta, Theodore. B.S., SUNY-Brockport, 1961; postgrad. U. Rochester, 1962, 63; postgrad. in learning disabilities Nazareth Coll., 1970, 71. Cert. tchr., reading specialist, N.Y. Tchr. Rochester City Schs., 1961-66; instr. reading and English, Rochester Inst. Tech., 1970-76; exec. dir. Children's Alliance, Rochester, 1977-78; community liaison dept. pediatrics U. Rochester Med. Ctr., 1978-79, spl. projects adminstr., 1980-83, asst. in pediatrics, 1983—, asst. dir. devel., 1983—, dir. community affairs Strong Children's Med. Ctr., 1983-85, creator/developer Health Habits for Strong Children, Israeli-U. Rochester Scholar Exchange Program, 1981. Editor: Youth Services Guide for Monroe County, 1974-76; creator, editor column: Concerning Children, 1978. Mem. auction bd. Sta. WXXI, 1971-75; head membership drive div. Rochester Meml. Art Gallery, 1972-76; mem. group homes task force N.Y. State Div. Youth, 1975-76; mem. steering com. Child Health Adv. Group, 1976-77; mem. edn. com. Temple B'rith Kodesh, 1977-78; mem. adv. bd. Community Ptnrs. for Youth, 1978; mem. exec. bd. Health Edn. Promotion Practitioners Assn., 1981; mem. Rochester met. adv. bd. N.Y. State Div. Youth, 1983; bd. dirs. Jefferson Awards, 1983, 84; bd. dirs. Vols. in Partnership (now Community Ptnrs. for Youth), 1973-76, pres., 1976-77; bd. dirs. Nat. Council Jewish Women, 1973-82, v.p. adminstrn., 1974-76, nat. bd. justice for children com., 1978-81. Recipient 13th ann. award Group on Pub. Affairs, Am. Assn. Med. Colls., 1984, 85; Grantsmanship Newsletter award, 1985; named Rochester Woman of Yr., 1985. Mem. Women in Communications (Clarion awards 1983, 84), Pub. Relations Soc. Am., Health Edn. Promotion Practitioners Assn. (exec. com. 1978—), Am. Acad. Hosp. Pub. Relations (com. chmn. 1983—, MacEachern awards 1981, 83, MacEachern citation 1982). Home: 210 Bonnie Brae Ave Rochester NY 14618 Office: Strong Children's Med Ctr U Rochester Med Ctr 601 Elmwood Ave Rochester NY 14642

BABLES, MARILYN MARIE, laboratory technician; b. Kans., Nov. 21, 1954; d. Leon B.; A.A., Kansas City (Kans.) Community Coll., 1976; B.A. in Biology, Park Coll., 1978; postgrad. U. Mo.-Kansas City. Quality control lab. technician Bayvet Labs., Shawnee Mission, Kans., 1979; microbiology lab. technician Bd. Pub. Utilities, Kansas City, Kans., 1979—. Foster parent Kans. Dept. Social Rehab., 1983—. Mem. Kans. Valley Med. Soc., Am. Water Works Assn., Nat. Assn. Female Execs., Women in Bus. (pres. 1980—), Urban League, Friends of Park Coll. Library. Republican. Mem. Christian Ch. (Disciples of Christ). Office: 3601 N 12th Kansas City KS 66104

BABNIS, LINDA LOUISE, investment company executive; b. Sharon, Pa., Mar. 31, 1952; d. Peter R. and Regina Mary (Krent) Babnis. B.S., Slippery Rock State Coll., 1973; M.Edn., St. John's U., 1976. Pres., founder, owner Olympus Capital Corp., N.Y.C., 1983-86; sec., treas. Nemetz Capital Corp., N.Y.C., 1982-86. Me. Nat. Assn. Female Execs., Internat. Assn. Fin. Planners. Democrat. Roman Catholic. Avocations: sketching; watercolors; racquetball; reading. Home: 304 E 89th St Apt 2B New York NY 10128

BACA, POLLY, state legislator; b. La Salle, Colo., Feb. 13, 1941; d. Jose Manuel and Leda (Sierra) B.; divorced; children—Monica, Mike. B.A. in Polit. Sci., Colo. State U., 1962; postgrad. Am. U., 1966-67. Editorial asst. dept. research and edn. Internat. Brotherhood Pulp, Sulphite and Paper Mill Workers, AFL-CIO, Washington, 1962-65; editor Airline News mag., legis. aide Brotherhood Ry. and Airline Clks., AFL-CIO, Washington, 1966-67; pub. info. officer Interagy. Com. on Mexican-Ams., The White House, Washington, 1967-68; nat. dep. dir. Viva Kennedy div. Nat. Robert F. Kennedy for Pres. Campaign, Washington, 1968; dir. research services and info. Nat. Council of La Raza, Phoenix, 1968-70; dir. div. Spanish-speaking affairs, spl. asst. to chmn. Democratic Nat. Com., Washington, 1971-72; dir., pres. Bronze Publs., Inc., Denver, 1972-74; mem. Colo. Ho. of Reps., 1975-78; chmn. Dem. caucus, 1977-78, vice chmn. house rules com., 1975-76; mem. Colo. Senate, 1979—; dir. Fed. Home Loan Bank, Topeka, 1979—; mem. nat. adv. council Fed. Savs. and Loan Assns., 1980-81. Mem. exec. com., state sec. Colo. Young Dems., 1960-62; del. or alt. Nat. Dem. Conv., 1974, 76, 78, 80, co-chmn., 1980, 84; Dem. nat. committeewoman from Colo., from 1973; vice chmn. procedures and rules com. Dem. Nat. Com., 1978, mem. compliance rev. com., 1979-80, mem. exec. com., from 1977, vice chmn., from 1981; chmn. Colo. del. to Nat. Dem. Mid-Term Conf., 1978; Rocky Mountain states coordinator Carter/Mondale Presdl. Campaign, 1979; Dem. candidate for U.S. Congress from Colo. Dist., 1980; mem. Adams County Dem. Central Com., from 1973, Colo. Dem. Exec. Com., from 1973; participant Camp David Domestic Summit, 1979; Am. Council Young Polit. Leaders legis. del. to USSR, 1978, mem. policyholders' adv. council Div. State Compensation Ins. Fund, from 1975; trustee St. Mary's Acad., Labor's Community Agy., from 1973; bd. dirs. La Unidad Broadcasting Corp., from 1980, Nat. Inst. Socio-Econ. Research, from 1979; mem. nat. steering com. Hispanic/Black Dem. Coalition, from 1978, Hispanic Am. Dems., from 1978; mem. nat. adv. bd. Nat. Women's Polit. Caucus, from 1978; mem. Nat. Overseas Edn. Fund of LWV, from 1980; mem. sec.'s adv. com. on rights and responsibilities of women HEW, 1979-81; mem. Colo. Gov.'s Commn. on Pub. Telecommunications, from 1980; mem. Nat. Women's Employment and Edn. Inc.; mem. adv. bd. Nat. Inst. for Women of Color; participant German Marshall Fund and European Coop. Fund fgn. policy seminar, Brussels, 1981. Recipient Outstanding Service in State Govt. award Adams County Fiesta Day Com., 1979; cert. of appreciation Colo. Migrant Council, 1979, Salute to Women award Big Sisters Colo., Inc., 1979; named One of 10 Women of Future, Ladies Home Jour., 1979, One of 80 Women to Watch in '80's, MS mag., 1980, One of 20 New Dem. Faces for '80s, Newsweek mag., 1980. Office: Colo Senate State Capitol Denver CO 80203*

BACASTOW, LOIS JUNE, cosmetics company consultant; b. Altoona, Pa., June 10, 1931; d. Lesin Ralph and Rose Tracy (Miller) Oldham; m. Arthur J. Bacastow, Nov. 26, 1950; children—Raelynn, Robert Keith. Assoc. degree Zeth Bus. Coll., 1949; Beauty Culture Tchr.'s cert., Bryland Beauty Sch., Norristown, Pa., 1963; advanced styling studies Brit. Culture Design, London, 1977. Tchr. beauty culture Bryland Beauty Sch., 1963-79; mgr. beauty salon in nursing home, Plymouth, Pa., 1963-66; owner beauty salon, King of Prussia, Pa., 1964-79; technician, regional mgr. Syntex Beauty Care, Palo Alto, Calif., 1980-84; cons., educator Turner Hall Corp., Jericho, N.Y., 1984—; judge beauty and fashion contests, condr. beauty seminars, Pa., N.Y., Mass., Md. and Va. Named Tech. Advisor of Yr., Syntex Beauty Care, 1981-82; recipient Indsl. Youth Devel. awards Vocat. Clubs Am., Northampton, Pa., 1982, Catonsville, Md., 1983. Mem. Nat. Assn. for Female Execs. Republican. Lutheran. Avocations: reading, music, researching and collecting antique jewelry. Home: 467 Dorothy Dr King of Prussia PA 19406 Office: Turner Hall Corp 2 Jericho Plaza Jericho NY 11753

BACCUS, ANITA LOUISE, health clinic executive; b. Tulsa, Nov. 13, 1945; d. James Benjamin and Mary (Griffin) B.; 1 child, Michael McKay Baccus-Williams. B.S., Okla. State U., 1968; Ph.D., Meharry Med. Coll., 1977. Med. scientist Moton Comprehensive Health Ctr., Tulsa, 1969-71; cyto-technician Meharry Med. Coll., Nashville, 1971-77; postdoctoral fellow Atlanta U., 1977-79; research assoc. Emory U., Atlanta, 1979; asst. prof. dept. biology Clark Coll., Atlanta, 1979-80; exec. dir. Southside Community Clinic, Mpls., 1980—. Mem. Communith Clinic Consortium (pres. 1982), Black Women's Health Orgn., Alpha Kappa Alpha. Democrat. Episcopalian. Club: Jack & Jill Am. (Mpls.) (parlimentarian). Avocations: down hill skiing; needlecrafts; piano. Home: 7412 W 22d St #105 Saint Louis Park MN 55426 Office: Southside Community Clinic Inc 4243 4th Ave S Minneapolis MN 55409

BACCUS, R. EILEEN TURNER, business executive; b. Oxford, N.C., Aug. 8, 1944; d. Nathaniel Benjamin and Gloria Constance (Davis) Turner; B.A., Fisk U., 1964; M.B.A., U. Conn., 1975, Ph.D., 1978; 1 son, Christopher Lloyd. Programmer, systems analyst IBM, N.Y., Mo., 1964-66; substitute tchr., Lakenheath AFB, Eng., 1967-69; asst. dir. fin. aid U. Conn., Storrs, 1970-74, asst. to dean Sch. Edn., 1974-77, dir. personnel services div., 1977-81; adminstr. treasury ops. Aetna Life & Casualty Co., Hartford, Conn., 1981-82, ops. mgr. discretionary asset mgmt., 1982—; cons. Ford Found., 1976, Tchr. Corps, 1977, Meriden (Conn.) Schs., 1979—; dir. Conn. Savs. & Loan Assn. Mem. planning com. Conn. Legis. Black Caucus, 1980; mem. mgmt. team Ujima, Inc., Hartford, 1978-80; co-chmn. bd. Hartford Scholarship Found., 1971-75; treas. bd. Community Council Capitol Region, 1982—; mem. community adv. bd. Jr. League Hartford, Inc., 1982—. Mem. Am. Ednl. Research Assn., Internat. Platform Assn., Phi Delta Kappa, Pi Lambda Theta, Delta Sigma Theta. Democrat. Episcopalian. Home: 71 Briarwood Dr Windsor CT 06095 Office: 151 Farmington Ave Hartford CT 06156

BACH, LORETTA WALKER, travel and convention services company executive; b. Clopton, Ala., Sept. 6, 1936; d. William Aaron and Myrtice (Stephens) Walker; m. William Stratton Bach, Sept. 18, 1956; children—Sandra Bach Richards, Lora Leita, Laura Linda, William Baron. Student Massey Draughon Bus. Coll., Montgomery, Ala. Sec. Asa Allen Co., Montgomery, 1954-55, asst. mgr., 1955-56, mgr., 1956-58; adminstrv. asst. Martin J. Darity Co., Montgomery, 1975-76; owner, mgr. Exec. Meetings, Conventions and Travel, Montgomery, 1977—, Exec. Gift Shop, Montgomery, 1984—. Active local charity, church and civic orgns.; del. to 1980 Republican convention, Detroit; mem. Montgomery County Republican Exec. Com., 1984—. Mem. Sales and Mktg. Execs., Montgomery C. of C., U.S. C. of C., Am. Soc. Travel Agts., Montgomery Fedn. Garden Clubs. Methodist. Clubs: Arrowhead Country, Capitol City (Montgomery). Avocations: gardening, writing, cycling, water sports. Home: 1833 Croom Dr Montgomery AL 36106 Office: Exec Meetings Conventions and Travel Suite 145 120 Madison Ave Montgomery AL 36104

BACH, MURIEL DUNKLEMAN, author, actress; b. Chgo., May 14, 1918; d. Gabriel and Deborah (Warshauer) Dunkleman; m. Joseph Wolfson, June 16, 1940 (div. Apr. 1962); 1 child, Susan; m. Ira J. Bach, Apr. 14, 1963 (dec. Mar. 6, 1985); stepchildren—Caroline Bach Marandos, John Lawrence; m. Josef Diamond, May 18, 1986. Student Carleton Coll., 1935-37; B.S., Northwestern U., 1939. Researcher original manuscripts for One-Woman Theatre, also costume designer, writer, set designer; actress TV commls., indsl. films, radio commls.; photog. model; tchr. platform speaking techniques to corp. execs. Active sr. citizens groups, youth groups. Recipient Career Achievement award Chgo. Area Profl. Pan Hellenic Assn., 1971. Mem. Screen Actors Guild, AFTRA, Zeta Phi Eta. Clubs: Arts, Tavern (Chgo.). Author: (plays) Two Lives, 1958; ... because of Her!, 1963; Madame, Your Influence is Showing, 1969; MS ... Haven't We Met Before?, 1973; Lady, You're Rocking the Boat!, 1976; Freud Never Said It Was Easy, 1978; Of All the Nerve, 1982; vignettes for theatre. Address: 4205 E Highland Dr Seattle WA 98112

BACHER, JUDITH ST. GEORGE, executive search consultant; b. New Rochelle, N.Y., July 14, 1946; d. Thomas A. and Rose-Marie (Martocci) Baiocchi; B.S., Georgetown U., 1968; M.L.S., Columbia U., 1971; m. Albert Bacher, Jan. 2, 1972; 1 son, Alexander Michael. Researcher, Time Mag., N.Y.C. 1968-71; librarian Mus. of Modern Art. N.Y.C., 1971-72; cons. Informaco Inc., N.Y.C., 1972-74; cons. Booz-Allen & Hamilton, N.Y.C., 1974-79; assoc. Nordeman Grimm/MBA Resources Inc. N.Y.C., 1979—. Mem. White House Adv. Com. on Personnel, 1979—. Mem. The Research Roundtable (co-founder 1979), Phi Beta Kappa. Office: 717 5th Ave New York NY 10022

BACHER, RENÉE MARGARET, travel company executive; b. Stamford, Conn., Feb. 4, 1944; d. Romeo and Rose (Killian) Bacher; student public schs. Nat. dir. retail and bus. travel Thomas Cook Travel, N.Y.C., 1975-78; dir. cons. services AAA World Wide Travel, Falls Church, Va., 1978-79; v.p., gen. mgr. Gelco Travel Services, N.Y.C., 1980-82; v.p. corp. travel Liberty Travel, Paramus, N.J., 1982—; regional sales mgr. Regency Cruises, N.Y.C. Office: 260 Madison Ave New York NY

BACHER, ROSALIE WRIDE, educational administrator, counselor; b. Los Angeles, May 25, 1925; d. Homer M. and Reine (Rogers) Wride; A.B., Occidental Coll., 1947, M.A., 1949; m. Archie O. Bacher, Jr., Mar. 30, 1963. Tchr., English, Latin, history David Starr Jordan High Sch., Long Beach, Calif., 1949-55, counselor, 1965; counselor Poly. High Sch., 1966; vocat. counselor Office Occupational Preparation, 1967-68; v.p. Washington Jr. High Sch., 1968-70; counselor Lakewood Sr. High Sch., Calif., 1965-66, asst. prin., 1970; vice prin. Jefferson Jr. High Sch., Long Beach, 1970-81, Marshall Jr. High Sch., Long Beach, 1981—. Chmn. vocat. guidance steering com Long Beach Unified Sch., Dist., 1963-68; mem. youth adv. com. Long Beach chpt. ARC. Mem. AAUW, Long Beach Personnel and Guidance Assn. (dir. 1958-60), Long Beach C. of C., Long Beach Sch. Counselors Assn. (sec. high sch. segment 1963-64), Phi Beta Kappa, Delta Kappa Gamma (chpt. pres. 1964-66, area dir. Calif., 1969-71, mem. state exec. bd. profl. affairs com. 1971-72, chmn. state profl. affairs com. 1972-74, Calif. needs assessment com. 1974-76), Phi Delta Gamma (pres. chpt. 1977-78, nat. by laws chmn. 1980-82, dir. 1984—), Pi Lambda Theta (pres. chpt. 1974-76, v.p. So. Calif. council 1975-77), Phi Delta Kappa (sec. chpt. 1977-78). Home: 265 Rocky Point Rd Palos Verdes Estates CA 90274 also 17721 Misty Ln Huntington Beach CA 92649 Office: 5870 E Wardlow Rd Long Beach CA 90808

BACHMAN, ANITA ANNABLE, furniture manufacturing company data processing executive; b. Kankakee, Ill., Sept. 9, 1955; d. Donald Carr and Ann (Redwood) Annable; m. Phillip Gerard Bachman, Sept. 17, 1977. B.S., Calif. State U.-Los Angeles, 1980. Customer service rep. Metrocomp, Santa Monica, Calif., 1980-81; systems analyst Automatic Data Processing, LaPalma, Calif., 1981-83; data processing adminstr. Hyundai Furniture Industries, Santa Ana, Calif., 1983—. Mem. Am. Prodn. and Inventory Control Soc., Pasadena-Foothill Alumnae Delta Zeta (treas. 1980-83). Republican. Roman Catholic. Home: 147 W Dunton Ave Orange CA 92665 Office: Hyundai Furniture Industries 3001 S Susan St Santa Ana CA 92704

BACHMAN/GOODWIN, ADELIA ANN, college president, clergywoman, counselor; b. Hutchinson, Kans., Nov. 1, 1936; d. Harold Perry and Mildred Adelia (Barnes) Guizlo; m. Donald K. Goodwin, June 25, 1954 (div. 1975); children—Sandra A., Douglas; m. V. Charles Bachman, Feb. 14, 1980 (dec. Mar. 1985). Student Wichita State U., 1965-70; B.A., Berean Christian Coll., 1981, M.A. in Ministry, 1982, Ph.D. in Ch. Edn., 1984; Ph.D. in Philosophy, Crossroads Grad. Sch., Farmland, Ind., 1985. Ordained to ministry Evang. Christian Ch., 1982. Illustrator, graphic artist Wichita State U., Kans., 1974-79; pres., owner, graphics artist Studio Dee, Long Beach, Calif., 1980-86; pres. Berean Christian Coll., Long Beach, 1985—; pastor, counselor Berean Ch. of the Scriptures, Long Beach, 1984—; chaplain Berean Hosp. Chaplains Corp., Inc., Long Beach, 1986—. Mem. United Assn. Christian Counselors (counselor), Berean Hosp. Champlain Corps Internat, Long Beach C. of C., U.S. C. of C. Home: 6801 Millmark Ave Long Beach CA 90805 Office: Berean Christian Coll 2238 E Broadway Long Beach CA 90803

BACHUR, BARBARA FURLONG, county government official; b. Balt., Oct. 3, 1946; d. William Herdman and Mary Regina (Finley) Furlong; children—Thomas, Regina, David. A.A., Essex County Coll., Balt., 1985. Mem. Baltimore County Council, Md., 1978—, chmn., 1983. Mem. Towson Manor Village Assn., 1970-85; vice chmn. Regional Planning Council, 1983-85; co-chmn. Baltimore County Task Force Drunk Driving, 1981-82; bd. dirs. Human Resources Devel. Agy., 1979-83. Pres. bd. dirs. Balt. Region Community Devel. Corp., 1982-84. Mem. Nat. Assn. Counties (chmn. Community devel. steering com.), Md. Assn. Elected Women (co-founder, 1979; pres. 1982-83). Democrat. Home: 109 Linden Terr Towson MD 21204 Office: Old Courthouse Towson MD 21204

BACIC, DIANA COPPOLA, business executive; b. Brooklyn Heights, N.Y., Oct. 23, 1946; d. Francis George and Josephine (Manco) Coppola; A.S., N.Y.C. Community Coll., 1966; B.A., Queens Coll., 1970; m. Peter Raymond Hinkle, Nov. 12, 1982; 1 child, Jason Scott. Media dir. Wesson & Warhaftig Advt., N.Y.C., 1972-77; advt. sales rep. Charles C. Cunningham, Inc. Park Ridge, N.J., 1977-78; dir. media/research MED Communications, Hopelawn, N.J., 1978-82; v.p. Zip Pac Inc., Highlands, N.J., 1982—; media cons. Strategic Med. Communications, Cranford, N.J., 1984—; mem. programs and seminars com. Pharm. Advt. Council, 1978—. Vol., Sports for the Handicapped Program, Garden State Rehab. Hosp., 1979—. Mem. Pharm. Advt. Council, Healthcare Bus. Woman Assn. Club: Irish Setter of Long Island. Home: 141 Portland Rd Highlands NJ 07732

BACKENSTOSE, MARY ELIZABETH, psychotherapist; b. Hershey, Pa., Oct. 29, 1943; d. Daniel Lee and Elizabeth Dorothy (Hyland) Backenstose; A.A., Hershey Jr. Coll., 1963; B.S. in Nursing, Cornell U., 1966; M.S. in Psychiat. Nursing, U. Md., 1971; postgrad. Georgetown U., 1972-73, 79-80. Gen. staff nurse Cornell U.-N.Y. Hosp., N.Y.C., 1966-67; gen. staff nurse Harrisburg (Pa.) Hosp., 1967, clin. nurse specialist in psychiatry, 1971-78; nursing supr. Polyclinic Med. Center, Harrisburg, 1967-68; instr. psychiat. nursing Harrisburg Hosp. Sch. of Nursing, 1968-71; co-dir., therapist Inst. for Family Care, Inc., Hershey, Pa., 1974—; adj. faculty, instr. nursing courses Pa. State U., Hershey, 1973-76; clin. faculty mem., psychiat. nursing Bloomsburg (Pa.) State Coll., 1977-78; vis. asst. prof. nursing U. Va., Charlottesville, 1979—; mem. Faculty Millersville U., 1984—; cons. Mem. Am. Family Therapy Assn. (charter), Group for Advancement of Family Systems (sec.-treas.), Am. Nurses Assn., Cornell U.-N.Y. Hosp. Sch. of Nursing Alumnae Assn., U. Md. Sch. Nursing Alumnae Assn., Am. Assn. Sex Educators, Counselor and Therapists, AAUW, Sigma Theta Tau. Republican. Club: Quentin Riding. Home: Box 505 S Market St Schaefferstown PA 17088 Office: Inst for Family Care Inc 218 Governor Rd Hershey PA 17033

BACKIS, PAMELA CRAYTON, options exchange administrator; b. Newark, Ohio, Nov. 28, 1947; d. Robert Porter and Catherine (Ector) Good; m. Clarence Edward Crayton, Nov. 7, 1968 (div. Nov. 1976); 1 child, Kimberly Meredith; m. Robert Joseph Backis, Apr. 20, 1985; 1 child, Alexandra Danielle. B.A., Morris Brown U., 1973, postgrad. Loyola U., Chgo. Cert. police instr., Ga. Pub. safety planner Dept. Pub. Safety, Atlanta, 1975-80; cons. Ga. Peace Officers, Decatur, 1980-81; office mgr. St. Vincent de Paul, Atlanta, 1982; project coordinator Chgo. Bd. Options, Chgo., 1983—; cons. Melear Multimedia, Marietta, Ga., 1981. Author radio script: Slam the Door on Death, 1976 (award); author, editor tng. curriculum: Basic and Advanced Arson Investigation Manual, 1981 (award). Organizer, dir. Commn. for Black Catholic Concerns, Atlanta, 1982; mem. adv. bd. Parents Anonymous of Ga., Atlanta, 1981, bd. dirs., 1982; catechist St. Anthony, St. Ignatius, Atlanta and Chgo., 1982-85. Mem. Nat. Assn. Female Execs., Am. Bus. Women's Assn. (treas. 1977-79). Democrat. Roman Catholic. Avocations: music; acting. Home: 1225 W. Chase #E-2 Chicago IL 60626 Office: Chgo Bd Options Exchange 400 S LaSalle Chicago IL 60605

BACKLUND, CLAUDIA MAI, lawyer; b. Spokane, Wash., Aug. 13, 1954; d. Fred William and Mary Bell (Bennett) Backlund. B.S., U. Pacific, 1976; J.D., McGeorge Sch. Law, 1980. Bar: Calif. 1981, Wa. 1981. Law clk. to justice Wash. Ct. of Appeals, Seattle, 1981-82; assoc. Nourse & Green, Seattle, 1982-83; assoc. Burns & Ricketts, Seattle, 1983-85, Hatch & Leslie, Seattle, 1985—. Mem. ABA, Wash. Women Lawyers Assn., Women's Network, Wash. State Bar Assn., King County Bar Assn., Am. Judicature Soc. Republican. Office: Hatch & Leslie 2700 Columbia Ctr Seattle WA 98101

BACKMAN, ZOE-MARCIA, chiropractor; b. Bklyn., Dec. 25, 1950; d. Norman and Florine Muriel (Behrman) B.; 1 dau., Janyne Natanya Holtzman. B.A., Hofstra U., 1971, M.A. in Biology, 1972; postgrad. NYU, 1975-78; D. Chiropractic Medicine, N.Y. Chiropractic Coll., 1981. Instr. biochemistry N.Y. Inst. Tech., 1976-77; research scientist biochemistry Endo div., Dupont, Garden City, N.Y., 1972-75; pvt. practice chiropractic medicine, Merrick, N.Y., 1977-81, 81—; team physician/trainer Am. de Quito Semiprofl. Spanish soccer league, 1982, 83; lectr. in field. Rec. sec., bd. dirs. Nassau Assn. Children with Learning Disabilities, 1975-84; Recipient Green Angel award from Girl Scouts U.S.A., 1980. Mem. N.Y. State Chiropractic Assn., Am. Chiropractic Assn., Internat. Chiropractic Assn., Nat. Upper Cervical Assn., Assn. Nutrition and Preventative Medicine, Am. Assn. Nutrition and Dietary Cons., Assn. Commerce and Industry, Centre for Bus. and Profl. Women, Internat. Platform Assn., U.S. Homeopathy Assn. Contbr. articles to profl. jours., also New Voices in American Poetry. Home: 3069 Wynsum Ave Merrick NY 11566 Office: 3069 Wynsum Ave Merrick NY 11566

BACKOR, NANCY BURTON, medical records administrator; b. Winters, Tex., Nov. 5, 1931; d. James Clyde and Billie Mae (Burke) Burton; m. Benedict Paul Backor, Sept. 17, 1951; children—Kathryn Backor Stasny, Ben Paul, Mark Burton. Student, Sul Ross State U., 1948-49, U. Tex., 1960, 63. Reporter, The Brazosport Facts, Freeport, Tex., 1960-63; kindergarten tchr., Brazoria, Tex., 1962-65; receptionist Dow Chem. U.S.A., Freeport, 1965-66, clk., 1966-73, stenographer, 1973-77, med. records, supr., 1977—. Mem. City Planning and Zoning Com., Brazoria, 1962; mem. parish council St. Joseph's Ch., Brazoria, 1963; pres. PTA, Brazoria, 1963; dept. chmn. Dow Employee's Contbn. Dr., 1982; mem. Employee's Polit. Action Com., 1980—; charter mem. Republican Presdl. Task Force, Washington, 1984—; charter contbr. Statue of Liberty Ellis Island Found., N.Y., 1984. Mem. Tex. Dow Inst. Roman Catholic. Clubs: Riverside Country (Lake Jackson, Tex.); Brazoria Dance (treas. 1980-82). Avocations: plate collecting; carnival glass collection; traveling; dancing. Home: PO Box 165 (213 Ave B) Brazoria TX 77422 Office: Dow Chem USA Tex Ops Hwy 288 Freeport TX 77541

BACKUS, ROBERTA, advertising agency executive; b. Miami, Fla., Dec. 15, 1950; d. Louis Alfred and Ann Marie (Bowney) Ritchie; m. Lawrence O. Turner, Jr., Dec. 17, 1983; 1 dau., Rene Lynn. Student, U. Miami, 1968; grad. Bank Mktg. Sch., Denver, 1974. Advt. dir. Levitz Furniture, Miami, Fla. and Los Angeles, 1975-76; assoc. media dir. Mike Sloan, Inc., Miami, 1976-78; v.p. advt. service, Ryder & Schild, Miami, 1974-78; pres., chief exec. officer Backus Advt., Miami, 1978—, Backus/SCF, Miami, 1983—. Author: The Sad Merry Go Round, 1984. Mem. adv. bd. Republican Party, Washington, 1983; bd. govs. Expo 500, Miami, 1982—; vice chmn. United Way, Grove Isle Nursery. Mem. Am. Mktg. Assn., Advt. Fedn. Greater Miami, Nat. Acad. Arts and Scis., Nat. Assn. Advt. Agys., Nat. Assn. for Am. Indians, Bus. Soc. Miami, Greater Miami C. of C. (gov., trustee). Republican. Roman Catholic. Club: 200. Office: Backus/SCF Advt Miami FL

BACON, AMY JOAN, company executive, consultant; b. Chgo., Dec. 2, 1950; d. Delbert and Jean (Roxas) Reynolds; m. A. Raymond Bacon, Jan. 1970 (div.). B.A., No. Ill. U. Pub. relations asst. Delnor Hosp., St. Charles, Ill., 1971; pub. relations writer Walgreen Co., Chgo., 1972; communication specialist Gen. Electric Inc., Chgo., 1972-75; account exec. D.J. Edelman Agy., Chgo., 1975-77; account supr. Container Corp. Am., Chgo., 1977-79, regional mgr., 1979-83, assoc. mgr. corp. communication, 1983-84, mgr. corp. communication, 1985—. Author brochure: Container Corp. Am. (gold award), 1982. Mem. Women in Communications, Inc. (No. Ill. chpt. pres. 1971-72; Chgo. chpt. v.p. 1976-77). Office: Container Corp Am One First Nat Plaza Chicago IL 60603

BACON, BARBARA MCNUTT, social worker; b. London, Nov. 6, 1946; came to U.S., 1952; d. Peter Joseph and Margaret (Stronge) O'Reilly; m. Michael McNutt, Nov. 15, 1969 (div. 1977); m. John Lockhart Bacon, Apr. 29, 1978; 1 child, Patricia. B.A., Ursuline Coll. for Women, 1968; postgrad. Harvard U., 1968-69; M. Edn., U. Ill., 1971; M.S.W., U. Iowa, 1981. Psychometrist, Child Devel. Lab., Mass. Gen. Hosp. and Harvard Med. Sch., Boston, 1968-69; research assoc. Inst. Child Behavior and Devel., U. Ill., Champaign, 1969-78; clin. social worker Family and Children's Services, Davenport, Iowa, 1979-83; psychologist Gt. River Mental Health Ctr., Muscatine, Iowa, 1978-79; behavioral sci. coordinator family practice residency program Mercy-St Luke's Hosp., Davenport, Iowa, 1979-82; family therapist Family Counseling Service, Albuquerque, 1984-85; social worker vets. health study Lovelace Med. Found., Albuquerque, 1985—; pvt. practice Profl. Counseling Assocs., 1984—; cons. CIBA-Geigy Corp., Summit, N.J., 1975-77, Council for Children at Risk, Rock Island, Ill., 1981-83. Mem. Nat. Assn. Social Workers, Phi Beta Kappa. Republican. Episcopalian. Office: Profl Counseling Assocs 109 Elm St SE Albuquerque NM 87111-1

BACON, CAROL ANN, nurse; b. Evergreen Park, Ill., Apr.2, 1941; d. Raymond Benjamin and Loretta Carolyn (Diimig) Hanson; R.N., St. Mary's Sch. Nursing, 1962; B.S., St. Francis Coll., 1979, postgrad., 1980—; div. Clin. charge nurse U. Ill. Hosp. and Clinics, 1962-71; supr. Oak Park (Ill.) Hosp., 1972-75; adminstr. Addison Med. Center, 1976-81; nurse v.p., occupational health program Doctors Emergency Officenter, Mt. Prospect, Ill., 1981-85; owner C.A.B. Cons., occupational health and wellness programs, Hillside, Ill., 1985—. Mem. Addison Indsl. Assn., Suburban Chgo. Assn. Occupational Health Nurses (v.p. 1981-82, 85—), Emergency Dept. Nurses Assn., Nat. Occupational Nurses Assn., Ill. State C. of C. and Industry, Am. Soc. Safety Engrs., Ill. State Occupational Health Nurses Assn. (fin. dir. 1982-84). Roman Catholic. Office: 503 N Clayton St Hillside IL 60162

BACON, CHARLOTTE ALZERA MEADE, educator; b. Alberta, Va.; d. Ollie and Pinkie Ann (Manson) Meade; B.S. with honors, Hampton Inst., 1946; M.Ed., U. Pitts., 1952; m. Edward D. Bacon, Jr., Aug. 11, 1962; children—Judith, Edward, Susan. Tchr., Downingtown (Pa.) Indsl. Sch., 1946-50; tchr. Aliquippa (Pa.) Pub. Schs., 1950—. Mem. program com. YMCA, Aliquippa, 1955-65; active Sewickley (Pa.) YMCA; vice chmn. Mayor's Commn. on Human Rights, 1972-76; mem. Citizens' Adv. Com., City of Aliquippa, 1975-77; former mem. task force Beaver Castle council Girl Scouts Am., also bd. dirs., leader Troop 77; bd. dirs. Sewickley Community Center; mem. long-range planning com. Aliquippa Sch. Dist.; pres. Willing Workers Missionary Soc.; mem. adv. bd. Aliquippa Better Community Assn.; mem. fund raising com. Women's Crisis Center, 1981-84; vol. Adult Literacy Council of Beaver County, 1982-84; supr. Pa. State Fedn. Girls' Clubs, 1974-79. Recipient Woman of Yr. award Aliquippa Negro Bus. and Profl. Women's Club, 1970, Community Involvement award Delta Sigma Theta, 1972. Mem. AAUW (Aliquippa corr. sec. 1971-73, pres. 1977-79, women's history chairperson; Sojourner Truth award 1976), Pa. Fedn. Negro Women's Clubs (pres. 1969-73), Aliquippa Edn. Assn. (rec. sec. 1969-72), Negro Bus. and Profl. Women's Club (pres. 1960-62, 63-77), PTA (life), NAACP, N.W. Dist. Fedn. Women's Clubs (pres. 1974-77, chmn. edn. com. 1984—), Northeastern Fedn. Women's Clubs (exec. bd. 1973—), Nat. Assn. Colored Women's Clubs (exec. bd.), Nat. Assn. Negro Bus. and Profl. Women's Clubs (chmn. internat. relations N. Central dist. 1981—), Daniel B. Matthews Hist. Soc. of Sewickley, Three Rivers Reading Council, Keystone Reading Council, Leotta C. Hawthorne Reading Council, Black Women's Polit. Crusade, Hampton Inst. Alumni Assn., U. Pitts. Alumni Assn., World Affairs Council Pitts., Pa. Assn. Gifted Edn., Sewickley Valley Players, Delta Sigma Theta. Baptist. Club: Aliquippa (1st v.p.). Home: 311 Chadwick St Sewickley PA 15143 Office: New Sheffield Sch 21st St Aliquippa PA 15001

BACON, DENISE, pianist, composer, musical instititution administrator; b. Newton, Mass., Mar. 20, 1920; d. James Flynt and Maude (Milling) Bacon. Soloist diploma Longy Sch. Music, 1944; Mus.B., New Eng. Conservatory Music, 1952, Mus.M., 1954; cert. Kodaly method Liszt Acad., Budapest, Hungary, 1968; cert. Orff method Orff Inst., Salzburg, Austria, 1968. Ltd. concert artist career, 1940-60; head music dept. Dana Hall Schs., 1948-68; founder, dir. Dana Sch. Music, Wellesley, Mass., 1957-69, Kodaly Mus. Tng. Inst., Wellesley, 1969-77, Kodaly Ctr. of Am., West Newton, Mass., 1977—; lectr., cons., 1965—. Author: Let's Sing Together, 1971; 46 American Two-Part Folk Songs, 1973; 185 Unison Pentatonic Exercises, 1979; 50 Easy Two-Part Exercises, 1977; also assorted choral music; contbr. articles to profl. nat., fgn. music jours. Recipient Kodaly Centennial Diploma and Medal, 1983; Disting. Alumni award New Eng. Conservatory, 1984; Braitmayer fellow for European study, 1967-68. Mem. Music Educators Nat. Conf., Mass. Music Educators Assn., Orgn. Am. Kodaly Educators, Internat. Kodaly Soc., Chattanooga Edn. in Mus. Arts Assn. (former trustee). Office: Kodaly Ctr of Am 295 Adams St West Newton MA 02158

BACON, DENISE RAE, store management executive; b. Downey, Calif., Dec. 27, 1956; d. Boyd B. and Cleora (Anderson) Bacon. Student pub. schs. Bagger Safeway Stores, Corona, Calif., 1974-75, checker, food clk., Corona and Fontana, Calif., 1975-79, bookkeeper, Fontana and Ontario, Calif., 1979-82, store mgr. trainee, Ontario, Calif., 1983—, 3rd person, 1983—, asst. checker coach, Corona, Calif., 1976-79, customer service rep., Fontana, Calif., 1980-82, sea rep., Fontana, Ontario, Riverside, Calif., 1981; mem. electronic store level systems tag team, 1984—; United Food and Comml. Workers service rep., Pomona, Calif., 1983. Democrat. Home: 2265 Bradford Ave #515 Highland CA 92346 Office: Safeway Stores Inc Bellflower Blvd Downey CA 90241

BACUS, CAROLINE MARGARET, educator; b. San Francisco, Dec. 25, 1948; d. William G. and Doris E. (Wesley) Bacus. B.Ed., U. Alaska, 1972. Cert. tchr., Alaska. Tchr., North Star Borough, Fairbanks, Alaska, 1972-74, Bur. Indian Affairs, Val D'Or, Que., Can., 1975-77; prin.-tchr. Kenai Sch. Dist., Soldotna, Alaska, 1977-83, tchr., 1984—. Fellow Am. Soc. Curriculum and Devel., Alaska State Writing Consortium. Methodist. Address: Box 3342 Homer AK 99603

BADAL, SHARON LEE, film company executive; b. Newark, June 10, 1958; d. John Roy and JoAnn (Romano) B. B.F.A. in Film and TV, NYU, 1980. Lic. motion picture operator, N.Y.C. Asst. mgr. Loews Theatres, N.Y.C., 1978-81; nat. print control mgr. United Artists, N.Y.C., 1981-83; head film booker Warner Bros., N.Y.C., 1983-85; nat. sales adminstr. Orion Pictures, N.Y.C., 1985—. Artist, producer animated cartoon; Pigment of My Imagination, 1980. Mem. Motion Picture Bookers Club, Tisch Sch. of Arts Alumni Group. Lodge: Order Eastern Star. Avocations: scrabble; swimming; boating. Home: 151 Throckmorton Ln Old Bridge NJ 08857 Office: Orion Pictures 9 W 57th St 15th floor New York NY 10019

BADDOUR, ANNE BRIDGE (MRS. RAYMOND F. BADDOUR), aviatrix; b. Royal Oak, Mich.; d. William George and Esther Rose (Pfiester) Bridge; student Detroit Bus. Sch., 1948-50; m. Raymond F. Baddour, Sept. 25, 1954; children—Cynthia Anne, Frederick Raymond, Jean Bridge. Stewardess, Eastern Airlines, Boston, 1952-54; instr. aeros. Powers Sch., Boston, 1958; co pilot, flight attendant Raytheon Co., Bedford, Mass., 1958-63; flight dispatcher, ferry Pilot Comerford Flight Sch., Bedford, 1974-76; adminstrv. asst., ferry pilot, Jenney Beachcraft, Bedford, 1976; mgr., pilot Baltimore Airways, Inc., Bedford, 1976-77; pilot, flight facility M.I.T. Lincoln Lab. Flight Test Facility, Lexington, Mass., 1977—; aviation cons., corp. pilot Energy Resources, Inc., Cambridge, Mass., 1974-84. Bd. dirs. Cambridge Opera, 1977-79; mem. campaign council Mus. Transp., Boston; mem. council assos. French Library in Boston; commr. Commonwealth of Mass., Mass. Aero. Commn., 1979-83; chmn. regional adv. council FAA, 1984—. Winner trophy Phila. Transcontinental Air Race, 1954, New Eng. Air Race, 1957. World Class speed records Boston to Goose Bay, Labrador, 1985, Boston to Reykjavik, Iceland, 1985, Portland, Me. to Goose Bay, 1985, Portland to Reykjavik, 1985, Goose Bay to Reykjavik, 1985. Mem. Fedn. Aeronautique International, Nat. Aero. Assn., Ninety-Nines, Aero Club New England (v.p., dir.), Aircraft Owners Pilots Assn., Nat. Pilots Assn., U.S. Sea Plane Pilots Assn., Assn. Women Transcontinental Air Race, Republican. Episcopalian. Clubs: Bostonian Soc., English Speaking Union, Friends of Switzerland, French Center Library, Belmont Hill, Aero of New Eng. (dir. 1978—), St. Botolph. Home: 96 Fletcher Rd Belmont MA 02178 Office: Draper Flight Test Facility Lincoln Lab MIT PO Box 98 Concord MA 01742

BADENHOP, SHARON LYNN, psychologist, educator; b. Roswell, N.Mex., Feb. 21, 1946; d. Charles Theodore and Anna (Burke) B.; B.A. in Ednl. Psychology, SUNY-Oneonta, 1967, M.S., 1969, M.S. in Counselor Edn., 1971. Cert. mental health adminstr. Tchr., Gilbertsville (N.Y.) Central Sch., 1968-70; guidance counselor Delaware Acad., Delhi, N.Y., 1970-71; instr. SUNY-Oneonta, 1971-75; prof. SUNY-Delhi, 1974-75; psychol. case worker United Cerebral Palsy Assn., 1977-78; psychologist in psychogeratrics Rochester (N.Y.) Psychiat. Center, 1979, dir. edn. and tng. dept., 1979-81, psychologist, 1981—; instr. Rochester Inst. Tech., 1981—, U. Rochester, 1978—; psychologist Securecare, 1984—. Lic. guidance counselor, N.Y. State; cert. mental health adminstr.; cert. tchr. grades 1-6, N.Y. State. Mem. Am. Psychol. Assn., Am. Edn. Research Assn., N.Y. State Personnel and Guidance Assn., Clin. Sociology Assn., Assn. Mental Health Adminstrs. Home: 18 Hollingham Rise Fairport NY 14450 Office: Rochester Psychiat Center 1600 South Ave Rochester NY 14620

BADGER, JULIA MARGUERITE, hospital executive; b. Houston, Feb. 16, 1919; d. John and Julia Bennetta (Amonette) Oliver; m. Newton Augustus Bryson, July 6, 1940 (dec. Mar. 1970); 1 son, Barry Lee Bryson; m. 2d, William Herbert Badger, June 7, 1975. Student Sinclair Coll., 1936-38, U. Houston, 1971, Baylor Coll. Medicine, 1972. Sec.-treas. Houston Concrete Co., 1937-41; v.p. Bryson Lumber Co., Houston, 1948-70; dir. admissions Hermann Hosp., Houston, 1973-76, dir. patient services, 1976-77, coordinator flight ops., 1977-78, dir. flight ops., 1978—; pub. relations dir. Hermann Hosp. and Life Flight, 1976—; chmn. Aircraft Assistance in Disaster, City of Houston, 1982-83. Named Woman of Yr., YWCA, Houston, 1979; Hon., Harris County Sheriff's Dept., Houston, 1979; Marritot/Carlson award for contbns. to hosp. air emergency services, 1985. Mem. Am. Soc. Hosp. Based Emergency Air Med. Services (sec.-treas. 1980-82), Am. Helicopter Soc., Helicopter Operators Tex. Republican. Presbyterian. Clubs: Houston Lumberwomen (pres. 1953-54), Am. Osteopathy Aux. Doctor's (Houston). Office: Hermann Hosp 1203 Ross Sterling St Houston TX 77030

BADGER, MARY MARGUERITE, nurse; b. Dallas, Apr. 21, 1941; d. Hannah (Lewis) Williams; m. John Smith, Dec. 9, 1961 (div. 1965); children—Timothy Anthony Williams, Mark Vincent Williams; m. 2d, Napoleon Badger, Dec. 9, 1967. A.A.S., El Centro Coll., 1979. R.N., Tex. Staff nurse St. Paul Hosp., Dallas, 1971-73, VA Med. Ctr., Dallas, 1973—. Instr., Am. Heart Assn., Dallas, 1979—. Recipient Superior Performance award VA Med. Ctr., 1983; named Woman of Yr., New Mt. Moriah Bapt. Ch., 1982. Baptist.

BADRAN, LYNDA LEE, engineering company executive; b. Norfolk, Va., Feb. 19, 1947; d. Edward Nicholas and Mildred Belle (Signaigo) Badran; m. Henry John Huelsberg, Jr., Aug. 1, 1970 (div. 1979); children—Henry John, III, Erin Elizabeth. B.A. in Modern Fgn. Langs., Mary Washington Coll., U. Va., 1968. Owner, sec., treas. Heritage Furniture, Norfolk, Va., 1972-78; exec. asst. Systems Engring. Assocs., Virginia Beach, Va., 1978-81; v.p., dir. contracts Am. Systems Engring. Corp., Virginia Beach, 1981—.

BAECKLER, VIRGINIA VAN WYNEN, librarian, writer; b. Englewood, N.J., June 18, 1942; d. Kenneth Gregg and Esther Grace (Thompson) Van Wynen; m. William W. Baeckler, Apr. 9, 1971; children—Gregg William, Sarah Angela. B.A., Cornell U., 1964, M.A., 1967; postgrad. Moscow State U. (USSR), 1967-69; M.L.S., Rutgers U., 1972. Head, Slavic acquisitions Princeton U. Library, 1969-71; head Mercer County Library, Ewing, N.J., 1972-75; dir. Sources, Hopewell, N.J., 1975—. Author: Go, Pep and Pop!, 1976, PR for Pennies, 1978, Sparkle!, 1980; Storytime Science, 1986. Vol., tchr. YWCA of Princeton, N.J., 1979—. Mem. Nat. Sci. Tchrs. Assn., ALA. Democrat. Home: 26 Hart Ave Hopewell NJ 08525 Office: Sources 26 Hart Ave Hopewell NJ 08525

BAER, ELLEN DAVIDSON, nursing educator; b. N.Y.C., Sept. 21, 1939; d. James Alexander and Ann Victoria (Nicholson) Davidson; m. Henry Philip Baer, June 11, 1962; children—Susan James, Henry Philip. B.S., Columbia U., 1962; M.A., N.Y.U., 1973, Ph.D., 1982. Staff nurse N.Y. Hosp., N.Y.C., 1962-63, Cambridge City Hosp., Mt. Auburn Hosp., Cambridge, Mass., 1968-70; coordinator inservice edn. Cambridge City Hosp., 1970-71; instr. nursing of the adult Herbert H. Lehman Coll., Dept. Nursing, CUNY, 1973-76, instr. growth and devel., 1976, acting coordinator nursing of the adult, 1976-77, instr., 1977-78; lectr. nursing process and the individual U. Pa. Sch. Nursing, Grad. Div., 1980, course coordinator role devel. in nursing undergrad. div., clin. instr. adult health and illness master's program, 1981-82, small group leader conceptual systems in nursing, 1982, course coordinator advanced clin. practicum in nursing undergrad. div., 1982-83, asst. prof., chmn. adult health and illness sect., 1982—; manuscript reviewer Prentice Hall, Inc., 1982—; accreditation site visitor Nat. League for Nursing, N.Y.C., 1982—. Contbr. articles in field to profl. jours. Pres., Parent's Assn., Williston Northampton Sch., East Hampton, Mass., 1982-83, bd. trustees, 1982-83; mem. parents bd. Brearley Sch., N.Y.C., 1981-82; mem. women's bd. Democratic Nat. Com., 1982—. N.Y. State regents scholar, 1959-62, Columbia U. Sch. Nursing scholar, 1959-62; HEW grantee, 1971-73; recipient Margaret French Service award Williston Northampton Sch., 1983. Mem. Am. Nurses Assn., Nat. League Nursing, Soc. Nursing History, Hastings Ctr. Study Ethics, AAUP, N.Y. Acad. Scis., Sigma Theta Tau, Kappa Delta Pi. Democrat. Roman Catholic. Office: U Pa Sch Nursing 420 Service Dr S2 Philadelphia PA 19104

BAER, JEAN LOUISE (MRS. HERBERT FENSTERHEIM), editor, author; b. Chgo., May 17, 1926; d. Fred E. and Helen (Roth) Baer; B.A., Cornell U., 1945; m. Herbert Fensterheim, June 20, 1968. Writer press dept. MBC, N.Y.C., 1945-46; publicist Air Features, Inc., N.Y.C., 1946-49, Coll & Freedman Public Relations, N.Y.C., 1949-51; program info. editor Voice of Am., N.Y.C. and overseas, 1953; publicity dir. Seventeen mag., N.Y.C., 1953-68, spl. projects dir., sr. editor, 1968-74. Mem. Overseas Press Club Am. (sec. bd. govs.), Newswomen's Club N.Y. Club: Woman Pays (N.Y.C.). Author: Follow Me!, 1965; The Single Girl Goes to Town, 1968; The Second Wife, 1972; How To Be an Assertive (Not Aggressive) Woman, 1976; co-author: Don't Say Yes When You Want to Say No, 1975; Stop Running Scared!, 1977; The Self-Chosen, 1982. Home: 151 E 37th St New York NY 10016

BAERWALD, SUSAN GRAD, television broadcasting company executive; b. Long Branch, N.J., June 18, 1944; d. Bernard John and Marian (Newfield) Grad; m. Paul Baerwald, July 1, 1969; children—Joshua, Samuel. Degre des Arts and Lettres, Sorbonne, Paris, 1965; B.A., Sarah Lawrence Coll., 1966. Script analyst United Artists, Los Angeles, 1978-80; v.p. devel. Gordon/Eisner Prodns., Los Angeles, 1980-81; mgr. mini-series and novels for TV, NBC, Burbank, Calif., 1981-82, dir. mini-series and novels for TV, 1982, v.p. mini-series and novels for TV, 1982—. Bd. dirs. The Paper Bag Players, N.Y.C., 1974—; vol. Los Angeles Children's Mus., 1978—; mem. awards com. Scott Newman Found., 1982-84. Recipient Vol. Incentive award NBC, 1983. Mem. Am. Film Inst., Acad. TV Arts and Scis. Office: NBC 3000 W Alameda Ave Burbank CA 91523

BAEZ, JOAN CHANDOS, activist, singer; b. Staten Island, N.Y., Jan. 9, 1941; d. Albert V. and Joan Chandos (Bridge) B.; H.H.D. (hon.), Rutgers U., 1980, Antioch Coll., 1980; m. David Victor Harris, Mar. 1968 (div. 1973); 1 son, Gabriel Earl. Appearances include: Ballad Room, Club 47, 1958-60, Gate of Horn, Chgo., 1958, Newport (R.I.) Folk Festival, 1959, 60; extended tour to colls. and concert halls, 1961—, Carnegie Hall, 1962, U.S. tour, 1975; rec. artist for Vanguard Records, 1960-72, A&M, 1972-75, Portrait Records, 1975-79, Arida France, 1983; concert tours Europe, 1965-66, 70, 72, 73, 80, 83, 84, Japan, 1966, 82, U.S. and Europe, 1967-68; began refusing payment of war taxes, 1964; extensive TV appearances and speaking tours U.S. and Can. for anti-militarism, 1967-68; arrested for civil disobedience opposing draft, 1967; made trip to Hanoi, 1972. Founder, v.p. Inst. for Study of Nonviolence, Palo Alto, Calif. (now Resource Center for Nonviolence, Santa Cruz, Calif.), 1965; mem. nat. adv. council Amnesty Internat., 1974—; founder, pres. Humanitas Internat. Human Rights Com., 1979, attended Geneva Conf. on Cambodia as rep. of Humanitas, 1980. Author: Daybreak, 1968; (with David Harris) Coming Out, 1971; (songbook) And Then I Wrote. . . . ., 1979. Office: Diamonds & Rust Prodns Inc PO Box 1026 Menlo Park CA 94025

BAGARIA, GAIL FRANCES, lawyer; b. Detroit, Oct 6, 1942; d. Vincent Benjamin and Inez Elizabeth (Coffey) Farrell; m. William James Bagaria, Nov. 28, 1964; children—Bridget Ann, William James, Benjamin George. B.A., U. Detroit, 1964; J.D., Catholic U. Am., 1980. Bar: Md. 1980, U.S. Dist. Ct. Md. 1982. Cons. Miller & Webster, Clinton, Md., 1980-82; sole practice, Bowie, Md., 1982—. Mem. Prince George's Women Lawyers Caucus (sec. 1984), ABA, Md. State Bar Assn., Women's Bar Assn. Md. Democrat. Roman Catholic. Office: Gail Farrell Bagaria PO Box 759 Bowie MD 20715

BAGDAN, GLORIA, milk company executive; b. Bronx, N.Y., May 24, 1929; d. Max and Molly (Trufelman) Green; student CCNY, 1947-49, Inst. Interior Design, 1964, Wharton Sch., 1977; m. Kenneth Bagdan, Nov. 25, 1948 (dec. 1974); children—Meryl Bagdan Robins, Scott, Stacy. Founder, 1st pres. Bronx Mcpl. Hosp. Aux., 1955-60; interior designer, Scarsdale, N.Y., 1964-84; v.p., treas. Gold Medal Farms, Bronx, 1974-79. Active in fundraising Grasslands Hosp. Heart Assn.; cons. Mental Health Assn., 1967—. Mem. Internat. Platform Assn. (congl. adv. bd.). Clubs: Atrium (N.Y.C.; Internat. Beaux Arts. Home: 20 Sutton Place S New York NY 10022

BAGGETT, MARY E., personnel executive; b. Kettering, Eng., Aug. 24, 1926; came to U.S., 1946; d. Robert Burgess and Kate Alice (Joy) Hulatt; m. L. C. Baggett; 1 child, Kay Davis; m. L. C. Baggett, Oct. 17, 1963. Student pub. schs., Bedford, Eng. Sec., timekeeper Coats & Clarks, Albany, Ga., 1948-57; personnel dir. Phoebe Putney Hosp., Albany, 1957—; cons. personnel dir. Ga. Hosp. Assn., Atlanta, 1961-66. Mem. Am. Hosp. Assn., Ga. Hosp. Assn., Albany Dougherty County Personnel Soc. Republican. Episcopalian. Avocations: gardening; cooking. Home: Route 9 Box 353E Albany GA 31705 Office: Phoebe Putney Meml Hosp 417 3d Ave Albany GA 31703

BAGGIANO, FAYE STONE, state official; b. Charleston, S.C., Feb. 14, 1943; d. William E. and Mae (Thompson) Stone; m. Anthony L. Baggiano, June 9, 1961; children—Tory, Tana, Seb, Toni and Andra (twins). B.S., Auburn U., 1979, M.P.A., 1981; postgrad. U. Ala., 1984. Exec. dir. Council on Aging, Montgomery, Ala., 1979-81; commr. Ala. State Welfare Dept., Montgomery, 1981-83, Ala. Medicaid Agy., Montgomery, 1982—; mem. Gov.'s Cabinet, State of Ala., Montgomery, 1981—. Mem. community council United Way, Ala., 1984—; mem. pres.'s com. Ala. Gerontol. Assn., 1984—; water safety instr. for handicapped ARC; judge Am. Water Ski Assn. Pub. Service fellow Fed. Govt., 1979; named Vol. of Yr., ARC, Montgomery, 1977. Mem. Am. Soc. for Pub. Adminstrn., Nat. Council State Human Services Adminstrs., Ala. Council Social Work, Am. Pub. Health Assn., Auburn Alumni Assn. (v.p. 1982—), State Medicaid Dirs. Assn. (bd. dirs. 1982—), Pi Sigma Alpha. Home: 113 Payne Rd Pike Road AL 36064 Office: Ala Medicaid Agy 2500 Fairlane Dr Montgomery AL 36130

BAGGOTT, NANCY MARIE, real estate company executive; b. Highland Park, Mich., Nov. 3, 1949; d. Sydney and Julia Catherine (Schiftar) B.; B.S. in Bus. Adminstrn. with honors, Columbia Coll., 1978. Draftsman, Fed. Mogul Corp., Southfield, Mich., 1972-73; enlisted in U.S. Army, 1973, advanced through grades to staff sgt., 1977; intelligence analyst U.S. Army, Okinawa, 1973-74, guidance counselor/recruiter, San Francisco dist. recruiting command, 1974-77, profl. devel. and sales trainer, 1977-79, resigned, 1979; tng. and mktg. dir. TICKET Corp., San Jose, Calif., 1979-82; owner/prin. TICKET West, 1982-83; owner, ptnr. Bang & Baggott Realtors, San Pablo, Calif., 1983—; pub. speaker. Decorated Army Commendation medal; lic. real estate agt. Mem. Nat. Assn. Female Execs., Real Estate Edn. Assn., Mil. Intelligence

Assn. Office: PO Box 2351 Alameda CA 94501 also 2732 El Portal Dr San Pablo CA 94806

BAGGS, LEAH L. BATES, social leader; b. Franklinville, N.Y.; d. William Henry and Arlie Mae (Bozworth) Bates; A.B., Barnard Coll., 1922; student spl. courses various univs.; m. Linton Daniel Baggs, Jr., Oct. 1, 1926; children—Joan Bates (Mrs. Herbert A. McKenzie, Jr.), Linton Daniel III. Hon. bd. dirs. Macon Community Concert Assn., 1968—, pres., 1959-64; bd. dirs. Middle Ga. Camellia Soc.; v.p. Macon Grand Opera Assn., 1954—; vice regent Magna Charta Dames, 1968-70, regent Ga. div., 1970-72; hon. state regent Daus. Am. Colonists, 1962, nat. chmn. colonial heritage com., 1962-64, Bicentennial chmn. Ga. br., 1974-76; com. chmn. Ga. br. Sons and Daus. of Pilgrims Soc., 1954-55. Mem. AAUW, Ga. Soc. Mayflower Descs. (corr. sec. 1960-62), Pilgrim John Howland Soc., DAR, Middle Ga. Hist. Soc. (charter mem.). Am., Atlantic Coast Camellia Soc., Nat. Trust for Historic Preservation, Sigma Alpha Iota. Presbyterian. Clubs: Barnard College (Atlanta, v.p. 1967-72), Morning Music (pres. 1951-53), Atlanta Music, Capital City Atlanta, Idle Hour Country (Macon, Ga.). Home: 1137 N Jackson Springs Rd Macon GA 31211

BAGLEY, COLLEEN, marketing executive; b. Mountain Home, Ark., Feb. 18, 1954; d. Roy Louis and Dorothy (Fry) B. B.A. cum laude, U. South Fla., 1975. Lic. radio broadcaster, FCC 3d class. TV and radio producer Sta. WUSF-TV-FM, Tampa, Fla., 1974-76; TV announcer Sta. WFLA-TV, Tampa, 1974-76, news reporter, 1976-77, news producer, 1977-79; sr. producer Sta. KSTP-TV, Mpls., 1979-80; exec. producer Sta. WPVI-TV, Phila., 1980-82; dir. mktg. Grand Traverse Resort, Traverse City, Mich., 1982—; cons., dir. Enough Seminars, Phila., 1981-82. Contbg. author Strategic Hotel/Motel Marketing (Am. Hotel and Motel Assn. award), 1985. Mem. Traverse City Ad Club (awards for advt. excellence 1984, 85), Traverse City C. of C. (air service transp. com. 1984—), Grand Traverse Conv. and Visitors Bur. (mktg. com. 1984—). Republican. Avocations: pvt. pilot; aerobics; jogging; weight-lifting; yoga. Home: 3471 Blackwood St Traverse City MI 49684 Office: Grand Traverse Resort 6300 US 31 N Grand Traverse Village MI 49610

BAGLEY, CONSTANCE ELIZABETH, lawyer; b. Tucson, Dec. 18, 1952; d. Robert Porter and Joanne (Snow) Smith. A.B. in Polit. Sci. with honors and distinction, Stanford U., 1974; J.D. magna cum laude, Harvard U., 1977. Bar: Calif. 1978, N.Y. 1978. Teaching fellow Harvard U., 1975-77; assoc. Webster & Sheffield, N.Y.C., 1977-78, Heller, Ehrman, White & McAuliffe, San Francisco, 1978-79; assoc. McCutchen, Doyle, Brown & Enersen, San Francisco, 1979-84, ptnr., 1984—; lectr. Calif. Continuing Edn. of Bar, San Francisco, 1983, Los Angeles, 1986, Stanford Graduate Sch. Bus. Bd. Dirs. Exec. Program, Calif., 1985; guest speaker, 1985. Author: (with G. Moody) Proxy Contests, 1983, Supplement, 1986; Mergers, Acquisitions and Tender Offers, 1983; contbr. articles to profl. jours.; contbg. editor: Calif. Bus. Law Reporter, 1983—. Vol., Moffitt Hosp., U. Calif.-San Francisco, 1983-84; mem. vestry Trinity Episcopal Ch., San Francisco, 1984-85; mem. corp. practice series adv. com. Bur. Nat. Affairs, 1984—; mem. planning com. Calif. Continuing Edn. Bar Securities Inst., 1985—. Mem. ABA, San Francisco Bar Assn., State Bar Calif., State Bar N.Y., Phi Beta Kappa. Republican. Club: Golden Gateway Tennis and Swim (San Francisco). Office: McCutchen Doyle Brown & Enersen 3 Embarcadero Ctr San Francisco CA 94111

BAGLIORE, VIRGINIA, poet; b. Bklyn., Mar. 14, 1931; d. James and Josephine (Brunetti) Coglietta; m. James Bagliore, Nov. 8, 1953; children—Rosanne, Lisa. Student NYU, Bklyn. Coll.; student of Kimon Friar. Model, 1952-56; freelance promotional model, 1975-80; poet-tchr. creative poetry workshops, 1975—; condr. workshops Assn. Humanistic Psychology, 1978, 5th Am. Imagery Conf., 1981, Carroll St. Sch., 1981, Public Sch. No. 65, 1981, others; lectr. workshop New Sch., 1982, 85; sponsor, judge High Sch. Poetry Contect, 1977—. Co-editor Eve's Legacy Mag., 1980-82, 86; contbr. poems to various poetry mags.; poems represented in anthologies; exhibited 5 poems at Cork Gallery, Loncoln Center, 1981, 84; poems translated into Urdu; essays in The Study and Writing of Poetry; developed communication technique for improving lang. Recipient Cert. of Merit, Alan Foss Leukemia Found., 1975; Bill Burke award, 1976; Louise Bogan Meml. award, 1977; Louise Louis award, 1978. Mem. World Poets' Resource Ctr. (Creative Service award 1979), Nat. League Am. Pen Women (v.p. letters 1978-82, pres. 1982—, Disting. Service award 1986), N.Y. Poetry Forum, Avalon Soc., Eleanor Gaylee Found., Shelley Soc. N.Y. (hon.), Composers, Authors, and Artists Am., Nat. Assn. Poetry Therapy, Bklyn. Poetry Circle (pres. 1986). Office: PO Box 244 Ryder Street Station Brooklyn NY 11234

BAGWELL, SARA RUTH, religious organization official; b. Gray Court, S.C., Nov. 20, 1919; d. Luther and Janie Sue (Weathers) Bagwell. B.A., Furman U., 1947; postgrad. So. Baptist Theol. Sem., 1958. Sch. tchr., China Grove, N.C., 1947-48; dir. associational missions Baptist Ch., Murphy, N.C., 1948-51, Salisbury, N.C., 1951-56; dir. religious edn. Eglin AFB, Ft. Walton, Fla., 1958-64; assoc. dir. Woman's Missionary Union, Fla. Bapt. Conv., Jacksonville, 1964—. Office: Florida Baptist Convention 1230 Hendricks Ave Jacksonville FL 32207

BAHCALL, NETA ASSAF, astrophysicist; b. Israel, Dec. 16, 1942; d. Yehezkel Oscar and Gita (Zilberstein) Assaf; m. John Norris Bahcall, Mar. 21, 1966; children—Ron Assaf, Dan Ophir, Orli Gilat. B.S., Hebrew U., Jerusalem, 1963; M.S., Weizmann Inst. Sci., Israel, 1965; Ph.D., Tel Aviv U., 1970. Research fellow Calif. Inst. Tech., 1970-71; mem. staff Princeton U., N.J., 1971-75; research astronomer, 1975-79, sr. research astronomer, 1979-83, now chief gen. observer br., 1983—; now with Space Telescope Sci. Inst., Balt. Contbr. articles to profl. jours. Mem. Am. Astron. Soc. Office: Space Telescope Sci Inst 3700 San Martin Dr Baltimore MD 21218

BAHNER, SUE (FLORENCE SUZANNA), radio broadcasting executive; b. Phila.; d. William and Florence (Quinlivan) McElwee; m. David S. Bahner; children—Suzanna Elizabeth, Carol Aileen. Grad. Columbia Bus. Coll., 1950. Various exec. sec. positions, 1954-74; office mgr. Sta. WYRD, Syracuse, N.Y., 1974, gen. mgr., 1974-80; gen. mgr. Sta. WWWG, Rochester, N.Y., 1980—; v.p. Brandon Radio, Rochester, 1985—. Active Eastern Hills Bible Ch. Mem. Greater Rochester Assn. Evangelicals (v.p. 1982—), Nat. Religious Broadcasters (pres. eastern chpt. 1984—, bd. dirs. 1983—). Office: Sta WWWG 1850 S Winton Rd Rochester NY 14618

BAILEY, BARBARA BRAYTON, interior decorator, artist; b. Cambridge, Mass., Apr. 26, 1932; d. Anthony and Marjorie Doris (Tupper) Brayton; m. Ralph Edwin Bailey, June 1, 1957 (div. 1984); children—Stephen, William, Susan. Student Centenary Jr. Coll., 1949-50; A.A., The Garland Sch., 1952. Buyer Jordan Marsh Co., Boston, 1952-57; interior decorator Decors by Bailey & Read, Boston, 1970—. Congregationalist. Avocation: painting. Office: Decors by Bailey and Read 437 Boylston St Boston MA 02116

BAILEY, CAROLYN FAULKNER, computer programmer analyst; b. Troy, Ala., Nov. 6, 1942; d. Martin C. and Sylvania (Knotts) Faulkner; B.S. in Computer Sci. and Mgmt., U. Ala., 1980; M.S. in Personnel Mgmt., Troy State U., 1982; postgrad. Auburn U., 1982—. Staff asst. Air War Coll., Maxwell AFB, Ala., 1970-74, editorial asst., asso. programmer, 1974-75; computer technician Air Force Data Systems Design Center, Gunter AFB, Ala., 1975—; planner, organizer, dir. edn. seminars, workshops for women, 1979—; investment and fin. mgmt. cons., 1970—; data elements mgr., dir. Med. Systems, 1980—. Vol. counselor Montgomery Area Mental Health, 1979; v.p., bd. dirs. El Matadon Condo Assn., Fort Walton Beach, Fla., 1983-85. Mem. LWV, AAUW (dir.), Federally Employed Women (pres.), Cottage Hill Hist. Assn., U. Ala. Alumni Assn., Okaloosa Island Improvement Assn., Alpha Xi Delta, Beta Gamma Phi. Episcopalian. Contbr. articles to various publs. Home: 3503 Castle Ridge Rd Montgomery AL 36116 Office: Turner Bldg Gunter Air Force Station AL 36114

BAILEY, CHARLENE GAYE, bookstore administrator; b. Paintsville, Ky., Oct. 9, 1948; d. Russell and Marvel (Brown) Boyd; m. Danny Gale Bailey, Aug. 26, 1972. B.S., Morehead State U., 1972, M.A. in Edn., 1977, M.B.A., 1985. Tchr. math. Anderson County Bd. Edn., Lawrenceburg, Ky., 1972, Franklin County Bd. Edn., Frankfort, Ky., 1972-73; bookstore mgr. Ashland Community Coll., Ky., 1973—. Mem. Nat. Assn. Coll. Stores (regional steering com. 1978, 82), Ky. Assn. Coll. Stores (bd. dirs. 1985-90, pres. 1983). Republican. Baptist. Avocation: tennis. Office: Ashland Community Coll 1400 College Dr Ashland KY 41101

BAILEY, CYNTHIA LEE, banker; b. Memphis, Feb. 15, 1947; d. Hildria Leon and Jackie (Garrett) B. A.B., Syracuse U., 1969; M.S., Ind. U., 1971; Ph.D. candidate NYU, 1973—. Dir. fin. aid Marymount Manhattan Coll., N.Y.C., 1971-77; dir. new student fin. aid NYU, N.Y.C., 1977-79; dir. fin. aid Poly. Inst. N.Y., Bklyn., 1979-81; program mgr., 2d v.p. Chase Manhattan Bank, N.A., N.Y.C., 1981—; lectr. women and money. Contbr. articles to jours. in field. Mem. Nat. Assn. Bank Women (com. chairperson 1983-84), N.Y. State Fin. Aid Adminstrs. Assn. (N.Y.C. councilperson 1977-79, treas. 1974-76), Chi Omega. Democrat. Methodist. Home: 304 W 88th St Apt 3D New York NY 10024 Office: Chase Manhattan Bank NA 1 Chase Manhattan Plaza New York NY 10081

BAILEY, DAWN KAREN, systems programmer; b. N.Y.C., Apr. 6, 1961; d. Donald J. and Dorothy (Pinkney) B. B.B.A., Pace U., 1983; M.B.A., Adelphi U., 1985. Jr. fin. analyst Life Extension Inst., N.Y.C., 1984-85; programmer/data analyst Schieffelin & Co., N.Y.C., 1983-84; brokerage asst. 299 10th Ave. Brokerage, N.Y.C., 1982; mgmt. asst. Amajon Medallion Services, N.Y.C., 1981-82; asst. statistician Program Planners, Inc., N.Y.C., 1980-81; computer programmer Matthew Bender, Inc., N.Y.C., 1985-86; dist. support specialist Wang Labs., Inc., N.Y.C., 1986—. Mem. Nat. Assn. Female Execs., Assn. M.B.A. Execs., Phi Chi Theta. Roman Catholic. Office: Wang Labs Inc 39 Broadway New York NY 10006

BAILEY, DEBBIE DENISE, educator; b. Atlanta, Sept. 24, 1957; d. Carl Haynes and Sally (Parham) Haynes; m. Robert L. Bailey, Oct. 3, 1975; children—Tamara, Roctavius, Nathan. Student Ga. State U., 1985, St. Leo Coll., 1984-86, Atlanta Jr. Coll., 1975-77; A.A., Ga. State U., 1977. Tchr., Ben Hill Sch., East Point, Ga., 1978-80; Sheltering Arms, Atlanta, 1980-81; youth dir. U.S. Army, Bad Hersfeld, Germany, 1981-84, recreation asst. Fort Stewart, Ga., 1984—. Mem. Nat. Assn. Female Execs. Baptist. Avocations: dance; fitness; travel. Home: 7366B Camp Ctr Fort Stewart GA 31313 Office: Community Recreation Ctr 750 Lindquist Ave Fort Stewart GA 31313

BAILEY, DIANNE, psychologist; b. West Point, Ga., Sept. 6, 1949; d. Odie Lee and Frances Georgia (Hester) Bailey; B.S. magna cum laude, U. Ga., 1972. M.Ed., 1974, Ph.D., 1976; postgrad. Masters and Johnson Inst., 1980. Community psychologist, co-dir. marital sexual co-therapy service U.S. Govt., W. Ger., 1976-79; psychologist Ogeechee Psycho-Ednl. Center, Midville, Ga., 1979; part-time instr. U. Alaska, Cordova, 1980-81; co-dir. Mental Health and Alcohol Clinic, Cordova, 1980-81; co-founder, co-dir. Frost Found., sex therapy clinic, Augusta, Ga., 1981-85; sex and marital therapist Westbank Ctr. for Psychotherapy, Clinic for Marital and Sexual Therapy, 1985—. Mem. Am. Assn. Sex Educators, Counselors, and Therapists (cert. sex therapist), Am. Psychol. Assn., Sex Info. and Edn. Council of U.S., NOW, Phi Kappa Phi, Phi Delta Kappa, Kappa Delta Pi. Office: The Bon Air 2101 Walton Way Suite 200A Augusta GA 30904

BAILEY, ELAINE TERHORST, financial consultant; b. Buffalo, July 21, 1950; d. James Irving and Rita Mary (Bermel) Terhorst; m. Ernest Neilsen Bailey, Jan. 18, 1975; 1 child, Zachary. B.A. in English, U. Ga., 1972; M.B.A. in Fin., Ga. State U., 1978. Cost acct. Texaco, Inc., Atlanta, 1973-78; planning analyst Ga. Power Co., Atlanta, 1979-80, fin. analyst, 1981-83, cash planning mgr., 1983-84, fin. analysis mgr., 1984-85; prin. Rawson, Klepper, Fowler & Bailey, Atlanta, 1985—. Bd. dirs. Mental Health Assn. Metro Atlanta, 1980-84, v.p. Gwinnett County, 1983, treas.-elect, 1984. Mem. Ga. Exec. Women's Network, Fin. Mgmt. Assn., Am. Mgmt. Assn., Toastmasters Internat. Roman Catholic. Home: 4840 Dunwoody Station Dr Dunwoody GA 30338 Office: Rawson Klepper Fowler & Bailey 2900 Chamblee Tucker Rd #3 Atlanta GA 30341

BAILEY, ELIZABETH ELLERY, university dean; b. N.Y.C., Nov. 26, 1938; d. Irving W. and Henrietta (Dana) Raymond; B.A. in Econs. magna cum laude, Radcliffe Coll., 1960; M.S. in Computer Sci., Stevens Inst. Tech., Hoboken, N.J., 1966; Ph.D. in Econs., Princeton U., 1972; div.; children—James L., William E. From sr. tech. aid to mem. tech. staff, research head and supr. econ. analysis group Bell Telephone Labs., Holmdel, N.J., 1960-77, adj. asst., then adj. asso. prof. econs. N.Y. U., 1973-77; commr. CAB, Washington, 1977-83, vice-chmn., 1981-83; dean GSIA, Carnegie Mellon U., 1983—; bd. editors Am. Econ. Rev., 1977-79; dir. Standard Oil of Ohio, 1984—, Honeywell, 1985—, Dart & Kraft Inc., 1986—. Vice pres. trustees, founding mem. Harbor Sch. Children with Learning Disabilities, Red Bank, N.J., 1969-72; trustee Princeton U., 1978-82; head parent action group St. Maurice Sch., Potomac, Md., 1979-80; bd. dirs. Presbyn. Hosp., 1984—; corp. vis. com. Alfred P. Sloan Sch. Mgmt., MIT, 1983-85; adv. bd. Center Econ. Policy Research, Stanford U., 1983-85, Inst. Research on Poverty, U. Wis.-Madison, 1983-84; mem. research com. Am. Enterprise Inst. Center Study Govt. Regulation, 1980—; Champion-Tuck awards com. Dartmouth Coll., 1985-86; research program in telecommunications and info. policy Columbia U., 1984-86. Doctoral support grantee, 1970-72. Mem. Am. Econ. Assn. (exec. com. 1981-83; head com. status of women in econs. 1980-82, v.p. 1985-86), Gov. Rel. Commn. Am. Assn. Collegiate Schs. Bus., 1984-87. Author: Economic Theory of Regulatory Constraint, 1973; also articles. Editor: Selected Economics Papers of William J. Baumol, 1976, Deregulating the Airlines, 1985. Office: GSIA Carnegie Mellon U Schenley Park Pittsburgh PA 15213

BAILEY, ELIZABETH LILLIAN, photographic company executive; b. Winthrop, Mass., Sept. 28, 1951; d. George L. and Alice D. (Wall) Bailey. Student London Poly. U., 1971; B.A., Simmons Coll., 1973; M.B.A., Harvard U., 1976. Economicst, Council Econ. Advisors, Washington, 1973; legis. asst. U.S. House of Reps., Washington, 1973-74; fin. analyst Polaroid, Cambridge, Mass., 1976-79; pres. Bailey's Studio, Revere, Mass., 1979—. Bd. dirs. Friends Child Find Kid Pix Program, North Shore, Boston, 1985. Mem. Revere C. of C. (sec. 1978—), Profl. Photographers Assn., Bus. Womens Assn. North Shore. Advocations: Sailing; skiing. Office: Bailey's Studio 7 Foster St Revere MA 02151

BAILEY, ETHA MAE, dietitian; b. Lee County, S.C., Mar. 10, 1937; d. Alva Laverne and Clara Eltie (Stokes) McCaskill; m. William Oscar Bailey, Jr., May 24, 1973. B.S., Winthrop Coll., Rock Hill, S.C., 1957; M.S., U. Tenn., 1963. Registered dietitian, lic. cosmetologist. Pub. health nutritionist Dept. of Pub. Health, Nashville and Knoxville, Tenn., 1963-66; instr. St. Mary's Sch. of Nursing, Knoxville, 1966-67; food service cons. Fla. Dept. of Edn., Tallahassee, 1968-69; food service supr. Pinellas Sch. Bd., Clearwater, Fla., 1969-80; food service dir. Indian River Sch. Bd., Vero Beach, Fla., 1980—. Contbr. articles to profl. jours. Named Boss of Yr. Bus. & Profl. Women's Club, 1977; Children's Bur. fellow, U. Tenn., 1962. Mem. Am. Dietetic Assn., Am. Sch. Food Service Assn., Soc. Nutrition Edn., Fla. Sch. Food Service Assn. (chmn. nutrition com. 1972, personnel com., supervisory sec. 1980-81). Republican. Methodist. Avocations: cosmetologist, camping, sewing. Home: 1170 6th Ave 9A Vero Beach FL 32960 Office: Indian River Sch Bd 1990 25th St Vero Beach FL 32960

BAILEY, JANICE LARUE, educational counselor; b. Duncan, Okla., Dec. 26, 1939; d. O.H. and Ara D. (Hearn) Jennings; m. A. Lloyd Bailey, July 19, 1963; children—Scott, Elizabeth. A.B. in Biology and Chemistry, Bethany Nazarene Coll., 1962; med. technologist U. Kans., 1963; M.Ed. in Counseling, U. Mo., 1972; postgrad. in counseling adminstrn. U. Mo.-St. Louis. Research technologist VA Hosp., Oklahoma City, 1964-69; tchr. biology and chemistry Ritenour Sch. Dist., St. Ann, Mo., 1969-73, Hazelwood Sch. Dist., Florrisant, Mo., 1973-80; guidance counselor Frances Howell Sch. Dist., St. Charles, Mo., 1980—; speaker at seminars, workshops and retreats. Author papers in field. Co-chmn. Nazarene Laymen Activities in Mo., 1980—. Mem. Am. Soc. Clin. Pathology, NEA, Assn. Supervision Curriculum Devel., Am. Ednl. Research Assn., Profl. Counselors Assn., Phi Delta Kappa. Home: 23 Spencer Valley Dr St Peters MO 63376

BAILEY, JOSELYN ELIZABETH, physician; b. Pine Bluff, Ark.; d. Joseph Alexander and Angeline Elaine (Davis) B.; B.Mus., Manhattanville Coll., 1952; M.Music Edn., Manhattan Sch. Music, 1954; M.D., Howard U., 1971. Straight med. intern Huntington Meml. Hosp., Pasadena, Calif., 1971-72, resident, 1972-74; fell in nephrology Wadsworth VA Hosp., Los Angeles, 1975-77; practice medicine specializing in internal medicine and nephrology, Torrance, Calif.; mem. active staff Torrance Meml., South Bay, Little Company of Mary hosps.; cons. staff Del Amo Hosp.; attending staff Harbor Gen. Hosp.; courtesy staff San Pedro Peninsula Hosp.; active staff Bay Harbor Hosp., trustee, 1982—; dialysis unit rep. Renal Network Coordinating Council No. 4. Mem. Renal Physicians Assn., Am. Soc. Internal Medicine, Calif. Soc. Internal Medicine, So. Calif. Pvt. Practice Assn., Torrance Area C. of C. Roman Catholic.

BAILEY, JOYCE ELAINE, government official; b. Dallas, Tex., Mar. 18, 1953; d. Douglas Lee and Sarah Ann (Lee) Bailey. M.S. in Speech Communication, Texas Christian U. Grants mgmt. specialist USPHS, Dallas, 1978—, instr. grants adminstrn. and career devel., 1981—. Office: USPHS 1200 Main Tower Room 1860 Dallas TX 75202

BAILEY, KAREN ANN, sales executive; b. Hobart, Ind.; d. Cecil Alonzo and Florence Elizabeth (Cihonski) Bailey. B.S. in Bus. Adminstrn. and Econs., Regis Coll., 1982. Various acctg. and fin. positions, Chgo. and Denver, 1975-78; fin. analyst II, Adolph Coors Co., Golden, Colo., 1979-82, distbr. econs./expansion analyst, 1982-83, supr. young adult mktg., 1983-85, sr. distbr. econs. analyst, 1984-85, area sales mgr., 1986—. Office: Coors Co 727 Sapphire St Suite 102 Pacific Beach CA 92109

BAILEY, LONA M., real estate company executive; b. Soltau, W. Ger., Mar. 29, 1928; came to U.S., 1949; d. August and Carolina (Fleischer) Meyer; m. Edward H. Bailey, Feb. 4, 1949; 1 son, Mark Eric. Ed., W. Ger., 1934-44. Lic. real estate broker, N.J. Salesperson Earl W. Calloway, Inc., Wildwood Crest, N.J., 1968-76, Parson Realty, North Wildwood, N.J., 1976-77; broker-salesperson Bailey & Frankenfield, Wildwood, N.J., 1977-78; pres., owner Bailey & Bailey Realty, Inc., Wildwood, 1978—, Wildwood Crest, 1983—. Recipient Million Dollar Sales award, N.J. Assn. Realtors; Real Estate Showcase Cape May County sales awards, 1977-83. Mem. Nat. Assn. Realtors (cert. residential specialist), Greater Wildwood-Cape May County Bd. Realtors (treas. 1980, 81, 2d v.p. 1982, 1st v.p., pres.-elect 1983, pres. 1984—), N.J. Assn. Realtors (grad. Realtor's Inst. 1977). Republican. Lutheran. Home: 217 Fishing Creek Rd Cape May NJ 08204 Office: Bailey & Bailey Realty Inc 5918 New Jersey Ave Wildwood Crest NJ 08260

BAILEY, MARTHA LEE, educator; b. Melville, La., Nov. 6, 1936; d. Tom and Lillian Vaughn Rash; m. Irinton James Lee, Oct. 17, 1954 (dec. 1970); 1 son, Irinton James Lee; m. 2d, Samuel Bailey, Oct. 21, 1976. B.A., So. U., 1960. M.Ed., 1970; Ed.D., U. Houston, 1977. Coordinator, tchr. Head-Start Program, Opelousas, La., 1965-69; instr. So. U., 1971-74, field supr. child-care model program, 1973-74; univ. supr. U. Houston, 1975-77; assoc. prof. edn. Prairie View A&M U., 1977—, coordinator early childhood edn., 1979-84; reading tchr. Houston Community Coll., 1977; cons. Head Start Regional Tng. Office, Baton Rouge, 1972-74. Vol. Tex. Children's Hosp., Houston, 1983. Mem. Nat. Assn. Edn. Young Children, Assn. Childhood Edn. Internat., Houston Area Assn. Young Children, Tex. Assn. Coll. Tchrs., Phi Delta Kappa. Democrat. Methodist. Lodge: Order Eastern Star (matron 1960-65). Home: 5802 Green Falls Houston TX 77088 Office: Prairie View A&M U PO Box 2593 Prairie View TX 77446

BAILEY, MINNIE LEMON, allied health educator, nurse consultant; b. Montgomery, Tex., Feb. 8, 1938; d. Redie and Lola (Warren) Lemon; m. Bunard Bailey, June 28, 1958; children—Patricia Ann, Kimberly Elise, Bill. B.Nursing Edn., Prairie View A&M U., (Tex.), 1958; B.Nursing Adminstrn., U. Minn., 1961; M.S., Tex. So. U., Houston, 1963; M.S., U. Tex.-Houston, 1972; Ph.D., U. Houston, 1977. R.N., Tex. Sch. nurse Houston pub. schs., 1962-66; supr. St. Elizabeth Hosp., Houston, 1966-70; indsl. nurse Am. Can Co., Houston, 1970-71; instr. pub. health U. Tex.-Houston, 1972-75; assoc. dir. allied health scis. Tex. So. U., 1977-80; pvt. practice allied health consulting, Houston, 1980—. Mem. Am. Nat. Red Cross, Houston, 1958—; active Glenwood Forest Civic Orgn., Houston, 1984. Mem. Allied Health Assn. (pres. 1975-77), Alpha Kappa Alpha (chairperson 1982-84, recipient Cert. of Merit 1983), Chi Eta Phi. Episcopalian. Lodge: Eastern Star (conductress 1978-80). Home: 8438 Gallahad St Houston TX 77078

BAILEY, NANCY MARTIN, university official; b. Chgo., July 26, 1944; d. Ross J. and Marian (Shepherd) Martin; B.A., U. Wis., Madison, 1967; M.A., U. Ill., Champaign-Urbana, 1981, Ph.D., 1985; children—Ryan Martin Malmgren, Stuart Martin Bailey. Specialist botanist U. Wis., 1967-71; mem. faculty English dept. Univ. High Sch., Urbana, 1977-80; dir. Sch. Life Sci. Placement, U. Ill., 1980-85, asst. dean student affairs Coll. Vet. Medicine, 1985—, Chmn. adv. com. Urbana Park Dist., 1982-83. Mem. Philosophy of Edn. Soc., Am. Ednl. Research Assn., Am. Ednl. Studies Assn., Phi Kappa Phi, Phi Delta Kappa, Kappa Delta Pi, Alpha Chi Omega. Episcopalian. Office: 2271 Vet Med Basic Scis Bldg 2001 S Lincoln St Urbana IL 61801

BAILEY, ODESSA, radio station executive; b. Florence, Ala., Feb. 12, 1941; d. Annie Bertha Vaughn; m. Bob Carl Bailey, Jan. 20, 1962; children—Tori Charmette, Jurado Levias. B.S. in Bus. Adminstrn., Tenn. Valley State Tech. Coll., 1965. Mgr., Sta.-WZZA, Tuscumbia, Ala., 1977—; sec., treas. Muscle Shoals Broadcasting, Inc., Tuscumbia, 1981—. Mem. HUD Community Housing Resource Bd., 1980; bd. dirs. Mt. Moriah Jr. Usher Bd., Florence, 1973—; mem. bd. overseers W. C. handy Headstart, 1985—. Mem. NAACP. Democrat. Baptist. Home: 135 Fayette St Florence AL 35630 Office: Sta-WZZA Muscle Shoals Broadcasting 1570 Woodmont Dr Tuscumbia AL 35674

BAILEY, PAMELA GILES, public affairs consultant; b. Reading, Pa., May 24, 1948; d. John S., Jr., and Nancy (Clymer) Giles; A.B., Mt. Holyoke Coll., 1970; m. William W. Bailey, Dec. 13, 1980; children—Suzanne, Robert, Nancy, Kathryn. Mem. White House staff, Washington, 1971-75, research asst. to Vice Pres., 1970-71, research asst. to Pres., 1971-73, staff asst. to Pres., dir. research, 1973-74, staff asst. Domestic Council, 1974-75, asst. dir. Domestic Council, 1975; mgr. govt. consumer affairs Am. Hosp. Supply Corp., 1975-79, dir. govt. relations, 1980-81; asst. sec. for public affairs Dept. Health and Human Services, Washington, 1981-83; spl. asst. for pub. affairs Pres. of U.S., dep. dir. White House Office Pub. Affairs, 1983-84; spl. asst. to Pres., dir. White House Office Communications Planning, 1984—; prin. Michael K. Deaver and Assocs., 1985—. Republican. Home: 5206 Lawn Way Chevy Chase MD 20815 Office: 1025 Thomas Jefferson St NW Washington DC 20007

BAILEY, PATRICIA ANN, health, nutrition coordinator; b. Salem, Mass., Feb. 18, 1931; d. James Joseph and Alice Gertrude (Tremblay) Doggett; m. Bainbridge Edward Bailey, Oct. 11, 1952; children—Peter E., Cynthia A. Bailey-Ouellette. Grad. nurse St. John's Hosp., Lowell, Mass., 1951; grad. med. asst. Whittier Vo-Tech., Haverhill, Mass., 1977-78. Staff nurse Salem (Mass.) Hosp., 1951-52; staff, head, supr. J. B. Thomas Hosp., Peabody, Mass., 1952-71; health/nutrition coordinator Community Action, Inc., Family Day Care Program, Haverhill, Mass., 1979—; founder, dir. Fairy Godmother Program, Haverhill, 1983—; mem. N.E. Child Passenger Safety Council, Danvers, Mass., 1982—. Advocate low income families/children, Haverhill/Newburyport area, 1979—; advocate seat belts/safety restraints N.E. Child Passenger Safety Council, 1982—. Recipient Cert. of Appreciation, Council for Children, 1982; Monetary award Prince Foods Canning Div., 1983. Mem. St. John's Hosp. Nurses Alumni. Democrat. Roman Catholic. Office: Community Action Inc Family Day Care Program 25 Locust St Haverhill MA 01830

BAILEY, PATRICIA ANN, university official b. Augusta, Ga., Mar. 29, 1950; d. Thomas Edward and Georgia Angela (Mulherin) Bailey. B.S. in Edn., U. Ga., 1972, M.P.A., 1978. Research asst. Med. Coll. Ga., August, 1972, grad. research asst. U. Ga., Athens, 1977-78; field investigator Ga. Dept. Human Resources, Athens, 1973-76; rep. intergovtl. affairs Council State Govts., Atlanta, 1978-79; staff asst. spl. project U. Tex.-M.D. Anderson Hosp., Houston, 1980-82; adminstr. of bd. regents U. Houston System, 1982—; mem. adv. council Am. Soc. for Tng. and Devel., Houston, 1983—. Contbr. articles to profl. jours. Assoc. Mus. Fine Arts, 1980—; mem Houston Jr. League, 1980—. Grantee environ. law U.S. Dept. Interior, 1977. Mem. Am. Soc. Pub. Adminstrn., Ga. Soc. Pub. Adminstrn. (exec. council 1977-78), Zeta Phi Eta. Roman Catholic. Home: 2125 Augusta Dr Apt 51 Houston TX 77057 Office: Bd Regents U Houston System 4600 Gulf Freeway Room 500 Houston TX 77023

BAILEY, PATRICIA SUSAN, physician; b. N.Y.C., Dec. 18, 1943; d. Joel and Ethel (Miller) Salzburg; B.S. magna cum laude, Central Mich. U., 1970, M.A., 1972; M.D., Mich. State U., 1977; m. Cynthia Gellman, July 1, 1985. Clin. instr. Mich. State U. Coll. Human Medicine, 1976-77; resident Los Angeles County-Harbor Gen. Hosp., UCLA Med. Center, Torrance, 1977-78; partner, physician in emergency medicine Kaiser-Permanente Hosp., Harbor City, Calif., 1978—; instr. Am. Heart Assn.; clin. instr. U. So. Calif. Coll.

Medicine. Trustee, Delta Coll., 1972-74. Mem. Am. Coll. Emergency Medicine, Am. Physicians for Human Rights, Am. Physicians for Social Responsibility, So. Calif. Women for Understanding, NOW. Jewish. Author: (novel) The Summer of the Flea, 1980; contbr. to Echoes from the Heart (poetry anthology), 1982; contbr. articles to various publs. Home: 4016 Miraleste Dr Rancho Palos Verdes CA 90274 Office: 1050 W Pacific Coast Hwy Harbor City CA 90710

BAILEY, PORTIA ANDREA, author, producer; b. Chgo., Aug. 5, 1945; d. A. Leon and Portia H. (Thomas) B. Student Lawrence U., 1961-64, Lake Forest Coll., 1965-66, MacMasters U., 1967-75, Peters/Long creative writing seminars, 1971-74, language, communications, dance and music tng., 1951-70, 77-78. Dir., producer Carey Temple theatrical prodns., 1958; tech. dir., producer Thomas Meml. Theatre, Chgo., 1962-65; lit. translator from and into German, 1969-75; guest lectr. German seminar, Lawrence U., 1971; lighting designer, tech. dir. touring Prosenium Players, 1971-73; guest dir., theatre prodn. cons.; developer exptl. designers research project Linguistic Cultural Communication Devel. Corp., 1972-74, music copyist, 1978; cons., demonstrator Skinner Sch. Gifted Program, 1974-78; co-producer Gil Helmsley's God Is My Lighting Designer, U.S. Inst. Theatre Tech. Midwest sect., 1978; producer, propr. Andrea Bailey Enterprises, 1979-82; producer Black Ind. Cinema, U.S.A. Film Festival, 1981, most films from 31st Berlin Internat. Film Festival. Editor Midwest Report, 1978-82. Author: (book) Christophe, One Among Giants; (plays) The Greatest of These, 1970, 84, (an adapted transl.) Iphigenia In Tauris, Part I, 1983, Depth of the Shadow, 1963. Author monographs including The Black Lifestyle and Period of Training, 1974, Communicators Coming into Being, 1974, Our Concept of God and Man, 1984, From Dream to Dream, 1985. Author: (TV scripts) 9 program series America—Our Ideal, Our Reality, 1983, 22 program series America—Our Ideal, Our Reality, 1984. Author of literal transls. Recipient First prize Dist. Twenty Sci. Fair, 1961. Mem. Am. Soc. Theatre Research Internat., Am. Fedn. TV and Radio Artists, U.S. Inst. Theatre Tech. (vice chmn. Midwest sect. 1981-82). Roman Catholic. Avocations: embroidery; fine arts photography. Office: 3400 W 111th St Box 134 Chicago IL 60655

BAILEY, RUTH ELIZABETH, accountant; b. Boston, Apr. 22, 1955; d. Harwood and Esther Hill) B.; m. Lee Tibbert, Sept. 22, 1984. B.A., Conn. Coll., 1977; M.B.A., Boston U., 1983. Service rep., patient accts Maine Med. Ctr., Portland, 1977-78; controller Tamarack Mgmt., Pembroke, Mass., 1978-82; staff acct. Price Waterhouse, Boston, 1983-85, sr. acct., 1985; fin. analyst New Eng. Electric System, Westborough, Mass., 1985—. 1985—. Treas., Edgewood Village Condominium Trust, Marshfield, Mass., 1980-81; mem. fin. com. Appalachian Mountain Club, Boston, 1983—, treas. Boston chpt., 1985—. Mem. Am. Soc. Profl. and Exec. Women. Avocations: mountaineering; skiing; tennis; gardening. Home: 17 Rock Point Rd Southborough MA 01772 Office: New Eng Electric System 25 Research Dr Westborough MA 01582

BAILEY, RUTH HILL (MRS. A. PURNELL BAILEY), found. exec.; b. Roanoke, Va., Sept. 17, 1916; d. Henry Palmer and Carolyn Ruffin (Andrews) Hill; student Hollins coll., 1936-38; B.S. in Edn., Longwood Coll., Farmville, Va., 1939; postgrad. Ecumenical Inst., Jerusalem, 1979; m. Amos Purnell Bailey, Aug. 22, 1942; children—Eleanor Carol Bailey Harriman, Anne Ruth Bailey Page, Joyce Elizabeth Bailey Richardson, Jeanne Purnell Bailey Dodge. High sch. tchr. in Va., 1939-48; tour dir. to Europe and Middle East, 1963-73; syndicated columnist family newspaper, 1954-70; exec. sec. Nat. Methodist Found., Arlington, Va., 1979—; pres. Va. Conf. Bishop Cabinet Wives, United Meth. Ch., 1963-64; pres. Richmond (Va.) Ministers Wives, 1965-66; chmn. bd. missions Trinity United Meth. Ch., McLean, Va., 1975-79, adminstrv. bd., 1971-82; sec. bd. dirs. Nat. Temple Ministries, Inc., 1981—; life mem. United Meth. Women. Div. sec. United Givers Fund, 1964-65. Recipient Staff award Bd. Higher Edn. and Ministry, United Meth. Ch., 1976. Clubs: Country of Va., Jefferson Woman's. Home: 7815 Falstaff Rd McLean VA 22102 Office: 1835 N Nash St Arlington VA 22209

BAILEY, SANDRA ANITA, insurance company executive; b. Los Angeles, May 13, 1949; d. Ernest and Mattie Mae (Nash) Bailey. Student, UCLA, 1967-68, Calif. State U.-Los Angeles, 1977-78, Pepperdine U., 1984—. Actuarial clk. Transamerica Occidental Life Ins. Co., Los Angeles, 1968-72, supr., 1972-75, asst. mgr., 1975-79, dept. mgr., 1979-83, asst. sec., 1981-83, asst. v.p., 1983-84, 2d v.p., 1984—, instr., 1980—. Fellow Life Mgmt. Inst. of Life Office Mgmt. Assn.; mem. Los Angeles Jr. C. of C. Office: Transamerica Occidental Life Ins Co 1149 S Hill St Los Angeles CA 90015

BAILEY, SHIRLEY JEAN, consultant medical sales representative; b. Greenville, Ohio, Aug. 9, 1943; d. Lester Gerald and Thelma Madge (White) B.; m. Theodore Eugene Mong II, Oct. 9, 1966 (div. July 1970). B.S., Bowling Green State U., 1966; M.S., Ohio U., 1975. Lic. real estate, securities, Ohio. Tchr., coach Grove City High Sch., Ohio, 1966, Newark Pub. Sch. System, Ohio, 1967-70; with Reit One/Furman Tinon, Securities-Real Estate, Columbus, Newark, 1969-70; faculty, coach Muskingum Coll., New Concord, Ohio, 1970-75, choreographer dance, swimming shows, 1974-75; med. sales rep. G.D. Searle & Co., Skokie, Ill., 1976—, supr. various products, dist. level, 1978-85; dir. sch. handicapped swimming program, Zanesville, Ohio, 1973-74. Founder, editor dist. newspaper Ohio Valley Tally, 1983-84. Recipient various awards G.D. Searle & Co., 1977, 78, 80, 83. Mem. Ohio State Hosp. Pharmacists Assn., Female Execs. Orgn., Delta Zeta. Republican. Methodist. Avocations: aerobics; gardening, antique collecting. Home: 7573 Tina Ct Worthington OH 43085

BAILLIE, MARY HELEN, accounting company executive; b. Clio, S.C., Aug. 18, 1926; d. Paul Clydus and Laurie (Easterling) Orr; children—William Sinclair, Carol Anderson. Grad. Carolina Bus. Coll., 1946. Controller, George I. Clarke, Inc., Atlanta, 1953-57, DuBose Reed Constrn. Co./W. Carroll DuBose, Inc., Ft. Lauderdale, Fla., 1970-74; asst. controller H.B. Fuller Co., Ft. Lauderdale, 1975-76; owner M.H. Baillie & Assocs., Inc., Ft. Lauderdale, 1977—. Mem. Sign adv. bd. City of Ft. Lauderdale, 1983-86; bd. dirs., treas. Women in Distress of Broward County, Inc., 1984—; mem. Broward County Commn. on Status of Women, 1985—. Mem. Nat. Accts. Assn. (bd. dirs. 1977-84, dir. spl. activities 1979—), Fla. Accts. Assn. (bd. dirs., sec. 1977-79), Ft. Lauderdale C. of C. (bd. dirs. 1979—), Internat. Assn. Fin. Planners, Leadership Broward Alumni, Tower Forum, Downtown Council. Republican. Clubs: Women's Execs. (dir. 1978-80, treas. 1978-80), Le Club Internat., Ft. Lauderdale Country. Home: 3471 NE 17th Terr Fort Lauderdale FL 33334 Office: MH Baillie & Assocs Inc 746 NE 3d Ave Fort Lauderdale FL 33304

BAIMAN, GAIL, real estate broker; b. Bklyn., June 4, 1938; d. Joseph and Anita (Devon) Yalow; m. James F. Becker, Oct. 1970 (div. 1978); children—Steven, Susan, Barbara. Student Bklyn. Coll., 1955-57. Lic. real estate broker, N.Y., Pa., Fla. Personnel-pub. relations dir. I.M.C., Inc., N.Y.C., 1970-72; pres., broker Gayle Baiman Assocs., Inc., N.Y.C., 1972-74; v.p., broker Tuit Mktg. Corp., Mt. Pocono, Pa., 1974-83; pres., broker Ind. Timeshare Sales, Inc., St. Petersburg, Fla. and Mount Pocono, Pa., 1983—. Mem. Nat. Assn. Exec. Women. Avocations: reading; metaphysics; bowling. Office: Independent Timeshare Sales Inc 5680 66th St N Saint Petersburg FL 33709

BAIN, CYNTHIA DIANE, interior designer; b. Ennis, Tex., June 7, 1957; d. Harley Millican and Anna Laura (Fallen) Schoeps. Student Am. Leadership Study Group, Europe, 1975; B.S. in Edn., Tex. A&M U., 1980; student in interior design, North Tex. State U., 1982—. Staff interior designer Bayne Yancey & Assocs., Dallas, 1980-82; pres. Cynthia Bain Interiors, Dallas, 1982—; design cons. Hilton Inn Corp., Dallas, 1981. Mem. Am. Soc. Interior Design, Tex. A&M Former Students Assn., Country Music Assn., Dallas County Young Republicans, Tex. Fedn. Rep. Women, DAR, Am. Film Inst., Chi Omega. Home: 6436 Wrenwood Dr Dallas TX 75252 Office: Cynthia Bain Interiors 6436 Wrenwood Dr Dallas TX 75252

BAIN, FRANCINA, educational adminstrator; b. Phila., Feb. 25, 1943; d. John Marion and Wilhelmina (Darby) Spires; m. Zelvas Bain, Sr., Mar. 21, 1968 (div. Oct. 1976); children—Jacqueline Wilhelmina, Regina Hilliard. B.S., Fla. A&M U., 1965; M.Ed., Fla. Atlantic U., 1975; Edn. Specialist, Nova U., 1978. Tchr. phys. edn. pub. schs., Palm Beach County, Fla., 1965-81; tchr. alternative to suspension pub. schs., Riviera Beach, Fla., 1981-83, human relations counselor, 1983-84; asst. prin. pub. schs., Jupiter, Fla., 1984-86, Jupiter Middle Sch., 1984—; youth project mgr. West Palm County Bd. Instrn., West Palm Beach, Fla., 1985. Mem. Pan Hellenic Council Palm Beach County, West Palm Beach, 1983-85; chmn. advt. com. for Woman's Day, Hurst Chapel A.M.E. Ch., Riviera Beach, Fla., 1983. Mem. Assn. Supervision and Curriculum Devel., Palm Beach County Asst. Prins. Assn., Urban League Palm Beach County, Smithsonian Inst. Delta Sigma Theta (recording sec. 1983-85, v.p. 1985—). Democrat. African Methodist Episcopal. Avocations: reading; sewing; listening to music. Home: 1314 W 26th Ct Riviera Beach FL 33404

BAIN, REBA JOYCE, nursing administrator; b. Pampa, Tex., June 9, 1930; d. Pink Oliver and Reba Faye (Ferrell) B.; diploma nursing U. Okla., 1953; B.S. in Nursing, Northwestern State U., 1957; M.A., N.E. Mo. State U., 1968; Ed.D., N.Mex. State U., 1974. Assoc. dir. nursing Ariz. State Hosp., Phoenix, 1958-65; supr. (part-time) nursing Laughlin Hosp., Kirksville, Mo., 1965-67; adminstrv. asst. Hotel Dieu Hosp., El Paso, Tex., 1968-71; grad. asst. N.Mex. State U., 1971-72; dir. nursing R.E. Thomason Gen. Hosp., El Paso, 1972-73; assoc. prof. dept. nursing Ind. U. Sch. Nursing, 1973-78, chmn. dept. nursing adminstrn., 1974-78; pres. Bain Systems, Inc., Nineveh, Ind., 1978—, cons. health care adminstrn., 1978—; assoc. prof. nursing Ball State U., Muncie, Ind., 1981—, assoc. dir. grad. program; vis. prof. nursing U. Ala. Sch. Nursing, 1979; condr. nursing workshops, 1974—. Mem. Am. Nurses Assn., Ind. Citizens League for Nursing (dir. 1975-76), Nat. League for Nursing, Ind. State Nurses Assn. (mem. commn. nursing service 1981-83), Kappa Delta Pi, Sigma Theta Tau, Phi Delta Kappa. Democrat. Baptist. Author: (with Doris J. Froebe) Quality Assurance Programs and Controls in Nursing, 1976; contbr. articles on nursing adminstrn. to profl. publs. Home: DF52B Dr5 Nineveh IN 46164 Office: PO Box 187 Nineveh IN 46164

BAIN-SMITH, PRISCILLA, art historian, artist; b. Trenton, Mo., May 29, 1947; d. Frank Hubbird and Dorothy Court (Finlayson) Bain; children—Christian Andrew, Alexandria Christine. B.A. in Art History, Fla. Atlantic U., 1976; M.A. in Art History, U. Ky., 1978; postgrad. Cornell U., 1978—. Instr., artist, Coconut Grove, Fla., 1971-74; art historian Phillips U., Enid, Okla., 1983-85, instr. drawing, painting, 1983-85; free-lance artist, 1971—. Exhibited in numerous art shows, one-woman and group shows. Recipient numerous awards; Goldring travelling fellow, 1983. Mem. Coll. Art Assn., AAUW. Democrat. Unitarian. Avocations: photography; travel. Home and Office: 547 Bergen St 2B Brooklyn NY 11217

BAIR, DONNA MARLENE, medical laboratory administrator; b. Howard, Kans., Oct. 17, 1936; d. Ray Joe Stark and Mary Electa (Webster) Barnes; m. Donald Everett Bair, Dec. 21, 1958; children—Jerald David, Rayburn Webster. Student, Kans. State Tchrs. Coll., 1954-56; A.S. in Mgmt., Eastfield Coll., 1978; cert. med. technology, St. Francis Hosp., Wichita, Kans., 1957. Cert. med. technologist. Lab. supr. East Town Hosp., Dallas, 1970-78; adminstrv. dir. clin. lab. Mesquite Community Hosp. (Tex.), 1978—. Mem. adv. bd. El Centro Coll., Dallas, 1978—. Mem. Am. Med. Technologists (Exceptional Merit nat. award 1983, Disting. Achievement nat. award 1979, jour. awards 1978, 79, 80, 81, 82, 83, del. nat. conv., program moderator nat. conv. 1979, 83), Tex. State Soc. Am. Med. Technologists (host seminars 1980, 82, 84, unification task force on nat. and state level, editor jour. 1978—), Republican. Lodge: Altrusa Internat. Home: 10436 Elam Rd Dallas TX 75217

BAIR, MYRNA LYNN, state senator; b. Huntington, W.Va., Oct. 26, 1940; d. Charles Thomas and Velma Elvera (Schoenlein) North; B.S. in Chemistry, U. Cin., 1962; Ph.D., U. Wis., 1968; m. Thomas Irvin Bair, Mar. 12, 1966; children—Thomas Irvin, Catherine Lynn. Asst. prof. chemistry Beaver Coll., Glenside, Pa., 1966-70; instr. chemistry U. Del., 1974-76, asst. prof. edn., 1977-79; asst. dir. pub. info. Del. Energy Office, Wilmington, 1978-79; mem. Del. Senate, 1981—. Bd. dirs. Del. Lung Assn.; trustee Wesley Coll.; mem. Nat. Republican Com., Brandywine Region Rep. Women's Club. Recipient Freshman award Chem. Rubber Co., 1959; DuPont Co. Teaching award, 1963; NSF fellow, 1964-66. Mem. AAUW, Delawareans for Energy Conservation, Phi Beta Kappa, Iota Sigma Pi, Alpha Lambda Delta. Author sci. articles. Office: Legislative Hall Dover DE 19901*

BAIRAN, (LIBBY) ANNETTE, nursing educator, gerontologist, sociologist; b. Quitman County, Ga., Dec. 4, 1935; d. Adrian Norton and Nell Beatrice (Wood) Grubbs; m. William Castillo Bairan, May 26, 1957; children—Adrian, Cindy. Diploma in Nursing, Crawford Long Hosp., 1956; B.S. in Nursing, Med. Coll. Ga., 1971; M.Nursing, Emory U., 1972; cert. in gerontology Ga. State U., 1979, Ph.D. in Sociology, 1985. Office nurse for urologists, Atlanta, 1956-57, Marietta, Ga., 1963-65; mem. staff Venice (Fla.) Meml. Hosp., 1957-59, Kennestone Hosp., Marietta, Ga., 1959-63, 1966-69; pub. health nurse Cobb County Health Dept., Marietta, 1970-71; instr., asst. prof., now assoc. prof. nursing Kennesaw Coll., Marietta, 1972—; cons. Marietta-Cobb Community Service Ctr., 1982—; cons. Midwest br. Ga. Lung Assn., Marietta, 1978-81, Cobb County Rape Crisis Ctr., Marietta, 1977-78. Mem. Am. Nurses Assn. (nurse researcher award 1985), Ga. Nurses Assn. (exec. bd.), 13th Dist. Nurses Assn. (pres. 1974-78, Nurse of Yr. award 1978), So. Sociol. Assn., Am. Sociol. Assn., Ga. Sociol. Assn., Ga. Gerontol. Assn., Gerontol. Soc. Am., Assn. Gerontology in Higher Edn., AAUP, Am. Pub. Health Assn., AAUW. Episcopalian. Home: 2550 Kennesaw Dr Kennesaw GA 30144 Office: Kennesaw Coll PO Box 444 Marietta GA 30061

BAIRD, BILLIE RUTH, temporary employment services executive; b. Tex., Apr. 4, 1930; d. William Perry and Ruth Lee (Meriwether) Gullett; m. William T. Baird, Apr. 11, 1951 (div.); children—Deborah R., Lynne A., William T., Kristi A. Student, Fresno City Coll., San Francisco State U., Calif. State U. Jr. acct. Alexander & Alexander, C.P.A.s, Fresno, 1950-60; auditor acctg. Frank Chessman, C.P.A., Fresno, 1962-63; controller San Francisco Floral Co., Fresno, 1963-74; sales rep. Kelly Temporary Services, Fresno, 1975-77; mgr. Am. Temporary Services, Fresno, 1978-85; owner, pres. Profl. Temporaries, Inc., Fresno, 1985—; cons. in field. Mem. Nat. Bus. and Profl. Women's Assn., Nat. Assn. Profl. Saleswomen, Am. Soc. Personnel Adminstrn., Women's Network, Women's Trade Club of Fresno County (charter), Fresno C. of C., Beta Sigma Phi. Home: 1181 E Ashlan St #E Fresno CA 93704 Office: Profl Temporaries Inc 5141 N 6th Suite 104 Fresno CA 93704

BAIRD, EMILY NADINE BLACKWOOD, marriage and family therapist, educator; b. Collingwood, Tenn., Oct. 18, 1921; d. John Henry and Flora Alice (Goff) Blackwood; B.A. in Journalism, U. Ala., 1946; M.A. in Psychology, U. West Fla., 1972; Ed.D., Nova U., 1976. Marital cons. U. West Fla., Pensacola, 1971-73; clin. counselor Community Mental Health Center, Pensacola, 1973-77; dir. Consultation and Edn., Lakeview Center, Pensacola, Fla., 1977-82; first pres. Favor House, 1979; cons. Rape Crisis Center, Make Today Count, 1978-79; Fla. chmn. cons. and edn. Fla. Council Community Mental Health Ctrs. Chmn. service com. Am. Cancer Soc., 1978-81; chmn. woman's com. YWCA, 1978-80; mem. Gov.'s Commn. on Status of Women, 1982—; bd. dirs. Mental Health Assn., 1978-85, sec. Fla. div., 1986—; chmn. Reach to Recovery, Am. Cancer Soc., 1976-78, bd. dirs., 1976-80; elder Gulf Breeze Presbyn. Ch., 1980-82; pres. Mental Health Assn. Escambia County, 1983-85. Recipient Citizenship award N.W. Fla. Social Workers, 1980; Woman of Yr. award YWCA, 1983; named Woman of Yr., In-Town Bus. Women, 1985. Mem. Am. Psychol. Assn., Northwest Fla. Psychol. Assn. (pres. 1980-81), Network of Exec. Women (pres.).

BAIRD, KATHY KAUFMAN, public relations consultant; b. Middletown, Ohio, Mar. 7, 1954; d. John Michael and Betty (Reddington) Kaufman; m. Gary Edward Baird, Dec. 14, 1974; children—Linda Lee, James Joseph. B.A. in Journalism, Ohio State U., 1975. News producer Sta. WTVN-TV, Columbus, Ohio, 1975-77; asst. dir. pub. relations St. Anthony Hosp., Columbus, 1977-79; pub. info. specialist Ohio State U. Hosps., Columbus, 1979-81; pub. relations cons. Baird Communications, Columbus, 1981—. Contbr. numerous articles to mags. Mem. Women in Communications (chpt. v.p. membership 1980-81, scholarship chmn. 1981-82, job placement chmn. 1983-84, treas. 1984-86), Internat. Assn. Bus. Communicators (various awards for publs.), Ohio Soc. for Hosp. Pub. Relations (charter). Roman Catholic. Office: Baird Communications 1467 Kirkley Rd Columbus OH 43221

BAIRD, MARSHENA MCCOY, educator; b. Washington, Oct. 26, 1945; d. Rhody Arnold, Sr., and Edith McCoy; B.A., Boston U., 1967; M.Ed., U. Mass., Amherst, 1973, Ed.D., 1980; m. Francis Bernard Baird, Aug. 26, 1978; children—Duane Gist, Christopher Gist, Francis Bernard. Tchr. public schs., N.Y.C., 1967-70; head tchr., dir. New World Day Sch., U. Mass., 1973-78; assoc. prof. edn. Bennett Coll., Greensboro, N.C., 1978—; also dir. scholar program. Mem. Internat. Reading Assn., Assn. Supervision and Curriculum Devel., AAUP. Democrat. Roman Catholic. Office: Bennett College 900 E Washington St Greensboro NC 27406

BAIRD, PAMELA, manufacturer's representative agency executive; b. Denver, Dec. 4, 1951; d. Robert Charles and Ellen Roann (Fehr) B.; m. Leo Harold Kelsey, Jan. 14, 1978. B.S. in Housing and Design with high distinction, Colo. State U., 1974. Cert. kitchen designer. Decorator, Sherwin/Williams, Denver, 1975; design, sales Carriage Cabinets, Denver, 1976-78, Designed Cabinetry, Boulder, Colo., 1978-79; factory rep. KB Assocs., Foster City, Calif., 1980—. Contb. articles to mags. Recipient Merit award Cert. Kitchen Designers 1984. Mem. Successful Women Assocs., AAUW, Soc. Cert. Kitchen Designers, Am. Soc. Interior Designers (bd. mem. 1983-84), Nat. Kitchen and Bath Assn. (program, publicity 1981-83), Colo. State U. Alumni Assn. Presbyterian. Avocations: aerobics; jogging; sewing; gardening. Office: KB Assocs 1169 Chess Dr Suite 1 Foster City CA 94404

BAIRD, PATRICIA A., zoologist; b. Burbank, Calif., Oct. 22, 1945; d. Richard Harry and Nelle Wenzel (Bumer) Baird; B.A. in Biology, Denison U., 1967; M.S. in Zoology, Calif. State U. at Los Angeles, 1970; Ph.D. in Zoology, U. Mont., 1976; m. Parker Read Waite III, June 13, 1970 (div. 1977). Biologist, Forestry Scis. Lab., U.S. Forest Service, Missoula, 1973-76; biologist U.S. Fish and Wildlife Service, Anchorage, Alaska, 1976-81; adj. prof. biology U. Alaska, Anchorage, 1978—; chmn. bd. Alaska Environ. Research, Inc. Task force mem. Missoula City Planning Bd., 1973-76; vol. Planned Parenthood, 1974-75. Chapman Fund grantee Am. Mus. Natural History, 1975. Mem. Cooper Ornithol. Soc., Wilson Ornithol. Soc., Am. Ornithologists Union, Kappa Alpha Theta, Phi Sigma, Phi Soc., Eta Sigma Phi. Research on ecology of ring-billed and Calif. gulls, gecko learning, logging practices and spruce budworm populations, ecology pelagic birds with respect to oil devel. on the outer continental shelf, land use planning in Alaska, 1982-84; contbr. articles to profl. jours. Home: 3608 Lors Dr Anchorage AK 99502 Office: Alaska Environ Research Inc PO Box 4-1316 Anchorage AK 99509

BAIRD, PATRICIA ANN, social worker; b. Hot Springs, Mont., Jan. 18, 1932; B.Sociology with highest honors, Ariz. State U., 1968; M.S.W., U. Mich., 1971; children—Darleen, Jeffrey. Maternal and child health supr. social services Maricopa County Dept. Health Services, Div. Public Health, Phoenix, 1971—; field instr. Ariz. State U., 1972—. Exec. bd. Ariz. Council on Sch.-age Parents, 1977—; mem. exec. bd. adv. council Ariz. Perinatal Program, 1974—; steering com. Teenage Pregnancy Coalition, 1979—; adv. bd. Planned Parenthood, 1977-79, Phoenix S. Community Mental Health, 1979—. Mem. Acad. Cert. Social Workers, Nat. Assn. Social Workers, U. Mich. Alumni Assn., Am. Public Health Assn., Phi Kappa Phi. Democrat. Club: U. Mich. Alumni of Phoenix. Editor Ariz. Perinatal News, 1975-77. Office: 1825 E Roosevelt St Phoenix AZ 85006

BAIRD, ROBERTA LEIGH, social service agency executive; b. Charleston, W.Va., Nov. 10, 1947; d. Daniel Emerson and Isabell Mae (Westfall) Baird. B.A., Marshall U., 1969; M.S.W., W.Va. U., 1976. Child welfare worker W.Va. Dept. Welfare, Welch, 1969-74; social worker Elkhorn Mental Health Clinic, Welch, 1974-75; counselor Charleston Job Corps Ctr., 1976-79; mgr. counseling Brunswick (Ga.) Job Corps Ctr., 1979-80; mgr. counseling Knoxville Job Corps Ctr., 1980-82, mgr. employability assurance, 1982—. Methodist. Home: 4311 Buffat Mill Rd Knoxville TN 37914 Office: Knoxville Job Corps Center 901 College St Knoxville TN 37921

BAIRD, SUSAN J., social services administrator; b. Cohoes, N.Y., Aug. 22, 1946; d. Kenneth A. and Alva J. (McCarthy) B. B.A., SUNY-Albany, 1969; postgrad. Russell Sage Coll. Social worker Saratoga County, Ballston Spa, N.Y., 1969-76; dir. Office for Aging Saratoga County, Ballston Spa, 1976-79; commr. Rensselaer County Dept. for Aging, Troy, N.Y., 1979—. Contbr. articles to profl. jours. Mem. County Exec.'s Human Resources Com., Rensselaer County, 1979—. Mem. Nat. Assn. Counties (bd. dirs. aging affiliate 1980—; Achievement awards 1979, 80, 81, 82, 84), N.Y. State Assn. Area Agys. Aging (pres. 1985—), N.Y. State Home Care Assn. Home: Rockport Ct East Greenbush NY 12061 Office: Rensselaer County Dept Aging 1600 7th Ave Troy NY 12180

BAIRSTOW, FRANCES KANEVSKY, educator, labor relations consultant, arbitrator, mediator; b. Racine, Wis., Feb. 19, 1920; d. William and Minnie (DuBow) Kanevsky; student U. Wis., 1937-42; B.S., U. Louisville, 1949; student Oxford U. (Eng.), 1953-54; postgrad. McGill U., Montreal, Que., 1958-59; m. Irving P. Kaufman, Nov. 14, 1942 (div. 1949); m. David Steele Bairstow, Dec. 17, 1954; children—Dale Owen, David Anthony. Research economist U.S. Senate Labor-Mgmt. Subcom., Washington, 1950-51; labor edn. specialist U. P.R., San Juan, 1951-52; chief wage data unit WSB, Washington, 1952-53; labor research economist Canadian Pacific Ry. Co., Montreal, 1956-58; asst. dir. indsl. relations centre McGill U., 1960-66, asso. dir., 1966-71, dir., 1971—, lectr., indsl. relations dept. econs., 1960-72, asst. prof. faculty mgmt., 1972-74, assoc. prof. faculty mgmt., 1974-83, prof., 1983—; spl. master Fla. Pub. Employees Relations Commn., 1985-87; dep. commr. essential services Province of Que., 1976—; mediator So. Bell Telephone, 1985; cons. on collective bargaining to OECD, Paris, 1979; cons., Nat. Film Bd. of Can., 1965-69; arbitrator Que. Consultative Council Panel of Arbitrators, 1968—, Ministry Labour and Manpower, 1971—; mediator Canadian Public Service Staff Relations Bd., 1973—; contbg. columnist Montreal Star, 1971—. Chmn. Nat. Inquiry Commn. Wider-Based Collective Bargaining, 1978. Fulbright fellow, 1953-54. Mem. Canadian Indsl. Relations Research Inst. (exec. bd. 1965-68), Indsl. Relations Research Assn. Am. (mem. exec. bd. 1965-68, chmn. nominating com. 1977), Nat. Acad. Arbitrators (bd. govs. 1977-80, program chmn. 1982-83, v.p. 1986—), Soc. Profls. in Dispute Resolution (adv. council). Home and Office: 1430 Gulf Blvd #507 Clearwater FL 33515

BAISAS, ESPERANZA DE JOYA, pharmacist; b. Batangas, Philippines, Dec. 22, 1927; came to U.S., 1955, naturalized, 1973; d. Prisco Santos and Natividad (Morente) de Joya; m. Roger Calingo Baisas, May 20, 1950; children—Rebecca Baisas Diaz, Rachael, Roxanne Baisas Petch. B.S. in Pharmacy, U. Santo Tomas, Manila, Philippines, 1950. Instr. Abada Meml. Colls., Mindoro, Philippines, 1951-55; propr. Farmacia Morente, Pinamalayan, Mindoro, 1951-55; research asst. Baylor Med. Sch., Houston, 1955-57; asst. pharmacist Ohio State U., Columbus, 1957-60, 65-67; research asst. Cornell Med. Coll., N.Y.C., 1967-69, pharmacy intern, 1970-72; pharmacist VA Med. Ctr., Castle Point, N.Y., 1973—; cons. Craig House Hosp., Fishkill, N.Y., 1984—. Vol., Cath. Group, Castle Point, 1980, Cath. Mus. Group, Castle Point, 1980—; chmn. Asian Pacific Heritage, Castle Point, 1983, coordinator, 1985; mem. United Way 500 Plus Club, Poughkeepsie, N.Y., 1983—. Mem. Am. Soc. Hosp. Pharmacists, Philippine-Am. Pharm. Soc. N.Y. (pres. 1980—, recognition award 1985), Neurosurg. Soc. Office: VA Med Ctr Castle Point NY 12511

BAISDEN, ELEANOR MARGUERITE, airline compensation executive, consultant; b. Bklyn., Nov. 7, 1935; d. Vernon McKee and Ethel Mildred (Cockle) Baisden. B.A., Hofstra U., 1970. Clk., Trans World Airlines, N.Y.C., 1953-55, sec., 1955-64, compensation analyst, 1964-75, compensation mgr., 1975-85, dir. compensation and orgn. planning, 1985—. Mem. Airline Personnel Dirs. Conf. (personnel com. 1984-85), Airline Tariff Pub. Co. (personnel com. 1978—), Nat. Fgn. Trade Council (compensation com. 1980-84), Internat. Personnel Assn. (co. rep. 1980-84), Mensa, Alpha Sigma Lambda (Scholar of Yr. 1965-66). Republican. Methodist. Club: Cortlandt Yacht. Avocations: boating, swimming, piano, travel. Home: PO Box 33 Croton-on-Hudson NY 10520 Office: Trans World Airlines 605 3d Ave New York NY 10158

BAITSELL, WILMA WILLIAMSON, artist, educator; b. Palmyra, N.Y., July 5, 1918; d. Glen Hiram and Luetta (Newell) Williamson; B.S.E., SUNY, Oswego, 1957; M.S.E., Western State U., 1958; postgrad. Iowa State Tchrs. Coll., Syracuse U., Ind. State U., Cooper Union, McGill U. (Montreal); H.H.D., World U., 1982; m. Victor Harry Baitsell, Oct. 29, 1941; children—Corin Victor, Coby Allan, Corrine Luetta. Tchr. rural sch., 1939-41, Phoenix Central Sch., 1957-71, SUNY, Oswego, 1971-77; ret., 1977; cons. area schs., Ford Found., 1965-68; art cons. N.Y. State Dept. Edn., summers 1968-70. Chmn. Republican Twp. Com.; pres. Oswego County Women's Rep. Club; chmn. Sch. Bldg. and Orgn. Com., 1954. Ford Found. sci. and math. grantee, 1958-59; recipient 1st prize Mid-States Art Show, 1981, hon. mention for painting, Yamiguchi, Japan, 1981, 1st prize Am. Craftsman's Show, 1973. Mem. N.Y. State Ret. Tchrs. Assn. (life), Internat. Soc. Edn. Through Art, Oswega Art Guild (life), Nat. Ret. Tchrs. Assn., Oswego County and Scriba Hist. Soc. (life), SUNY Oswego Alumni Assn. (life), N.Y. State Grange. Methodist. Lodge: Order Eastern Star. Author: Crafts for Children, 1976; Art for Campers, 1972; Nature Crafts, 1975; editor Summer Art, 1957-71. Home and Office: Route 4 Box 330 Oswego NY 13126

BAKEMAN, CAROL ANN, architectural firm administrator, singer; b. San Francisco, Oct. 27, 1934; d. Lars Hartvig and Gwendolyne Beatrice (Zimmer) Bergh; student UCLA, 1954-62; m. Delbert Clifton Bakeman, May 16, 1959; children—Laurie Ann, Deborah Ann. Singer, Roger Wagner Chorale, 1954—, Los Angeles Master Chorale, 1964—; librarian Hughes Aircraft Co., Culver City, Calif., 1954-61; head econs. library Planning Research Corp., Los Angeles, 1961-63; corp. librarian Econ. Cons., Inc., Los Angeles, 1963-68; head econs. library Daniel, Mann, Johnson & Mendenhall, architects and engrs., Los Angeles, 1969-71, corp. librarian, 1971-77, mgr. info. services, 1978-84, mgr. office services, 1979-84, mgr. adminstrv. services, 1983—. Pres., Creative Library Systems, Los Angeles, 1974—; library cons. ArchiSystems, div. SUMMA Corp., Los Angeles, 1972—, Property Rehab. Corp., Bell Gardens, Calif., 1974-75, VTN Corp., Irvine, Calif., 1974, William Pereira & Assos., 1975. Mem. Assistance League, So. Calif., 1956—, mem. nat. auxiliaries com. 1968-72, 75-79, mem. nat. bylaws com. 1970-75, mem. asso. bd. dirs., 1966-76. Mem. Am. Guild Musical Artists, Am. Fedn. TV and Radio Artists, Screen Actors Guild, Spl. Libraries Assn. (mem. So. Calif. adv. council 1960-73), Adminstrv. Mgmt. Soc. (pres. Los Angeles chpt. 1986—), Los Angeles Master Chorale Assn. (dir. 1979-83). Office: 3250 Wilshire Blvd Los Angeles CA 90010

BAKER, ANITA DIANE, lawyer; b. Atlanta, Sept. 4, 1955; d. Byron Garnett and Anita (Swanson) B. B.A. summa cum laude, Oglethorpe U., Atlanta, 1977; J.D. with distinction, Emory U., 1980. Bar: Ga. 1980. Assoc., Hansell & Post, Atlanta, 1980—. Mem. Atlanta Hist. Soc. Recipient Sally Hull Weltner award Oglethorpe U., 1977. Mem. ABA, State Bar Ga., Atlanta Bar Assn., Order Coif, Phi Alpha Delta, Omicron Delta Kappa, Phi Alpha Theta, Alpha Chi (v.p. 1976-77). Office: Hansell & Post 56 Perimeter Ctr E Atlanta GA 30346

BAKER, BARBARA ANN, management consultant; b. Baton Rouge, Nov. 29, 1949; d. Ralph William and Charlotte Maude (Brenneman) B. A.B. with honors, U. Calif., 1971; M.B.A., Harvard U., 1984. Systems analyst Pacific Gas & Electric Co., San Francisco, 1972-78; project mgr. Rand Info. Systems Co., San Francisco, 1979-81; mgr. Price Waterhouse, San Francisco, 1981-82; assoc. Theodore Barry & Assocs., N.Y.C., 1983, McKinsey & Co., Los Angeles, 1984—. Mem. Nat. Assn. Female Execs., Harvard Bus. Sch. Assn. So. Calif. Presbyterian. Club: Harvard Business School 29+ (charter mem./founder, v.p. 1982-84). Office: McKinsey & Co 400 S Hope St Los Angeles CA 90071

BAKER, BARBARA JEAN, media specialist; b. Chattanooga, Tenn., July 20, 1931; d. James L. and Idaline (Turner) Bookout; m. Richard L. Bajker, May 25, 1952; children—Vance P., Matt R. Mus.B., Samford U., 1953; M.A. in Edn., U. Ala., 1976, postgrad. specialist degree, 1981. Media specialist Woodlawn High Sch., Birmingham, Ala., 1972-74, Kennedy Elem. Sch., 1974-76, Central High Sch., Lawrenceville, Ga., 1976-81, Brookwood High Sch., Snellville, Ga., 1981—. Mem. Ga. Assn. Educators, ALA, Ga. Library Media Dept., Phi Delta Kappa. Office: Brookwood High Sch 1255 Dogwood Rd Snellville GA 30278

BAKER, BETTY LOUISE, educator; b. Chgo., Oct. 17, 1937; d. Russell James and Lucille Juanita (Timmons) B.; B.Ed. (PTA scholar), Chgo. Tchrs. Coll., 1961, M.A., 1964; Ph.D. (Univ. fellow), Northwestern U., 1971. Tchr. math. Harper High Sch., Chgo., 1961-69; tchr. math. Hubbard High Sch., Chgo., 1970-85, chmn. dept., 1977-85; tchr. math. Bogan High Sch., Chgo., 1985—; mem. Com. for Writing Criterion-Referenced Tests in Math., 1979-80; co-chmn. high sch. sect. Dist. 15 Math. Fair, 1982; part-time instr. Moraine Valley Community Coll., 1983—. Pres. Hubbard High Sch. P.T.S.A., 1979-81, 3d v.p., 1981-82, 1st v.p., 1982-84; organist, Sunday Sch. tchr. Hope Luth. Ch., 1963—. Mem. Nat. Council Tchrs. of Math., Ill. Council Tchrs. of Math., Math. Assn. Am., Assn. Supervision and Curriculum Devel., Sch. Sci. and Math. Assn., Chgo. Tchrs. Union, Luth. Collegiate Assn., Am. Guild Organists, Kappa Delta Pi. Pi Lambda Theta, Phi Delta Kappa. Lutheran. Club: Walther League Hiking. Contbr. articles to math. jours. Home: 3214 W 85th St Chicago IL 60652 Office: Bogan High School 3939 W 79th St Chicago IL 60652

BAKER, BONNI PERROTT, human resource consultant; b. Westfield, Mass., Nov. 4, 1938; d. George Duffy Clark and Winnifred Pearl (Whitcher) Clark Wiltsie; m. Ronald Perrott, Dec. 1955 (div. June 1960); children—Lisa, Ronald; m. Eugene R. Baker, June 19, 1976; stepchildren—Sarah, Elizabeth. B.B.A., U. Mass., 1982; M.A. in Health Edn., Ohio State U., 1986. Cert. 1st aid and CPR instr. ARC, smoking cessation workshop facilitator Central Ohio Lung Assn. Note dept. supr. 1st Agrl. Bank, Pittsfield, Mass., 1975-76, personnel dir. Phila. Bd. Pensions, 1977-79; v.p. personnel Franklin Fed. Savs. & Loan Assn., Columbus, 1979-81; employment mgr. Buckeye Fed. Savs. & Loan Assn., Columbus, 1983-84; owner, pres. YWEM Enterprises, Inc., Worthington, Ohio, 1984—. Life mem. Friends Belchertown Sch. for Retarded Citizens, Mass., 1981—; friend U. Mass. Fine Arts Ctr.; mem. A Cappella Aux., Columbus Symphony; mem., patron Columbus Mus. Art. Recipient Significant Contbn. to Higher Edn. award Capital U., Columbus, 1980. Mem. Am. Soc. Personnel Adminstrs., Personnel Assn. Central Ohio, Am. Pub. Health Assn., AAHPERD, U.S. Entrepreneurs Network, Eta Sigma Gamma. Clubs: Sawmill Athletic, Faculty (Ohio State U., Columbus). Avocations: golf; walking; reading; cooking; travel. Home: 37 W Southington Ave Worthington OH 43085 Office: YWEM Enterprises Inc Worthington OH 43085

BAKER, BONNIE ANN, real estate broker; b. Rock Springs, Wyo., Apr. 5, 1946; d. Clarence Heber and Vivian Doan Sargent; m. Joel Cheney Baker, Feb. 7, 1969; children—Michelle Leigh, Joelle Doan. A.A., Western Wyo. Coll., 1971; B.F.A., U. Wyo., 1984. Lic. broker Wyo. Mem. public relations staff Janss Corp., Rock Spring, Wyo., 1980-81; salesman Sweetwater Realty, green River, 1982-85; broker, owner Twin Pines Realty, green River, 1985—. Trustee, Western Wyo. Coll., 1977-84; mem. Democratic Precinct Com., Green River, 1977—; trustee Castle Rock Hosp. Spl. Dist., 1981-84. Mem. Sweetwater County Bd. Realtors (chmn. com. 1983—), Green River C. of C., Rock Springs C. of C. Avocations: reading; painting; sculpture-lost wax. Home: 392 Hillcrest Way Green River WY 82935 Office: Twin Pines Realty 489 W Flaming Gorge Way Green River WY 82935

BAKER, CAROL RENAE, health care administrator, nurse; b. Cin., Jan. 30, 1953; d. Russell Wayne Hill and Kathy (Lovette) Hill Suter; m. James D. Baker, May 10, 1974; 1 child, Andrea Marie. B.S.N., Mt. St. Joseph Coll., 1975; M.S.N., U. Cin., 1979. Staff nurse St. George Hosp., Cin., 1974-76; R.N. Bethesda Hosp. and Deaconess Assn., Cin., 1976-79; ICU nurse Cin. Gen. Hosp., 1977-79; clin. nurse specialist Drake Meml. Hosp., Cin., 1977-79; dir. nursing Bethesda Scarlet Oaks, Cin., 1979, asst. exec. dir., 1979—; perceptor Miami U., U. Cin. Chmn. pub. info. and edn. com. Alzeheimer's Disease and Related Disorders Assn. Recipient Young Career Woman of Yr. award Bus. and Profl. Women's Club, 1981. Mem. Ch. of Christ. Office: Bethesda Hospital 619 Oak Street Cincinnati OH 45206 Home: 2588 Little Dry Run Road Cincinnati OH 45244

BAKER, CAROLINE FRANCES, librarian; b. Muskegon, Mich., May 4, 1922; d. Frank Anthony and Cora Caroline (Kramer) Schnitzler; m. Joseph Gerard Baker, Aug. 31, 1940 (dec. 1957); children—Thomas Raymond, Joseph Francis, Mary Therese; m. 2d, Francis A. Baker, May 16, 1975. A.B., Aquinas Coll., 1962; A.M. in L.S., U. Mich., 1965; postgrad. Central Mich. U., 1970-74. Instr. English Davenport Coll., Grand Rapids, Mich., 1962-64; asst. librarian Aquinas Coll., Grand Rapids, 1964-67; documents librarian, asst. prof. library sci. Central Mich. U., Mt. Pleasant, 1967-75; reference/periodicals librarian Hackley Pub. Library, Muskegon, 1975—. Mem. Mich. Edn. Assn., ALA, Muskegon City Tchrs. Edn. Assn., Mich. Library Assn., Library Dirs. Adv. Council, Altar Soc., St. Joseph's Women's Guild, Cath. War Vets. Aux., Dominican Tertiary, Phi Alpha Theta, Beta Phi Mu, Delta Kappa Gamma. Roman Catholic. Club: Faculty Women's (Mt. Pleasant). Asst. editor: Dag Hammarskjold Collection on Developing Nations, 1968, 70. Home: 4894 Clearwater Ct Muskegon MI 49441

BAKER, COSETTE MARLYN, religious writer, editor; b. Miami, Fla., Sept. 22, 1933; d. Juel Marlyn and Corene Frances (Emery) Baker; B.B.A., U. Miami, Fla., 1955; M.R.E., So. Bapt. Theol. Sem., 1959. Dir. childhood edn. First Bapt. Ch., Knoxville, Tenn., 1959-63; minister to children South Main Bapt. Ch., Houston, 1964-73; asst. to minister of edn. Central Bapt. Ch., Miami, Fla., 1973-74; cons. in Sunday Sch. Dept., Bapt. Sunday Sch. Bd., Nashville, 1974—, children's program editor, 1974—, cons., children's program editor, 1985—. Recipient YWCA award outstanding woman in religious work U. Miami, 1955. Mem. Tenn. Assn. for Edn. Young Children, Gamma Alpha Chi. Baptist. Author: God's Outdoors, 1967; writer children's teaching tapes for Broadman Press, 1979-81; writer, on-camera person Bapt. Telecommunication Network, 1984—; editor Children's Leadership, 1985—. Home: 100 Longwood Pl Nashville TN 37215 Office: 127 9th Ave N Nashville TN 37234

BAKER, DEBORAH WARRINGTON, univ. adminstr.; b. Hohenwald, Tenn., Oct. 17, 1949; d. Edward Young and Mattie Nelle (Staggs) W.; married; 1 dau., Sarah Elizabeth. B.A., Memphis State U., 1971, postgrad., 1977-78. Asst. editor Holiday Inn Mag. for Travelers, 1971-73, mng. editor, 1973-74; editorial asst. Memphis State U. News Bur., 1975-76; asst. dir. Memphis State U. Office Media Relations, 1976-78; dir. communications and public relations Mid-South Fair, Libertyland, Inc., Memphis, 1978-79; dir. media relations Memphis State U., 1979—. Mem. publicity com. Am. Cancer Soc.; active Heart Fund; bd. dirs. Lowenstein House, 1984—. Mem. Public Relations Soc. Am., Tenn. Coll. Public Relations Assn. (sec. 1982). Democrat. Club: Memphis State U Tiger. Office: Adminstrn Bldg Rm 322 Memphis State U Memphis TN 38152

BAKER, EDNA MAE, home economist; b. Guthrie, Okla., May 18, 1922; d. Robert Beecher and Lydia Mae (Guthrie) B.; B.S., Okla. State U., 1950; M.S., U. Wis., 1960. Tchr. elementary sch., Clark County Kans., 1943-48; county extension 4H agt., Okla. State U., El Reno, 1950-53; county extension home demonstration agt Okla. State U., Kingfisher, 1953-60; Northeast, Central and Northwest dist. supr. coop. extension Okla. State U., Stillwater, 1961-84; co-dir. in-service tng. programs for coop. extension, 1967-83, acting dist. dir, coop. extension service, 1973. Kellogg Found. fellow, 1960; Superior Service award Okla. State U. Coop. Extension Service, 1983. Mem. Am. Home Econs. Assn., Okla. Home Econs. Assn. (dist. chmn. 1977-78), Extension Home Economists Assn. (sec. 1957, pres.-elect 1959), Okla. State U. Home Econs. Alumni Assn. (life), Okla. State U. Alumni Assn. (life), Epsilon Sigma Phi (life), Delta Kappa Gamma (sec. 1979, 2d v.p. 1981). Mem. Ch. of Nazarene (youth dir., Sunday sch. tchr., choir mem., Sunday Sch. bd., ch. bd., dist. ch. bd.).

BAKER, ELEANOR JEANETTE, investment company executive; b. Seattle, Aug. 1920; d. Crafton C. and Edith Elvira (Tidholm) Carroll; student Eugene (Oreg.) Bus. Coll., 1951, Marin Jr. Coll., Kentfield, Calif., 1967-68, 70-71; m. Wilson E. Baker, Aug. 24, 1962; children—Carroll Klingbile, Wayne D. McIntosh, Laurie A. Stitt. Legal sec., Oreg., 1957-62; asst. corp. sec. Life Ins. Co., San Francisco, 1963-68; v.p./corp. sec. Birr, Wilson & Co., Inc., San Francisco, 1968—; cons. broker/dealer and investment adv. start-up; mem. com. for item writing N.Y. Stock Exchange. Mem. council Emmanuel Lutheran Ch., Napa, Calif. Cert. profl. sec. Mem. Nat. Assn. Securities Dealers (CRD user com.). Republican. Club: Order of Amaranth (past honored matron). Home: 1067 Round Hill Circle Napa CA 94558 Office: 155 Sansome St San Francisco CA 94104

BAKER, GARNETT YOST, telephone company executive; b. North Augusta, S.C., June 7, 1954; d. Kenneth William and Lillian Grace (Tuten) Yost; m. Robert Leonard Baker, Jan. 28, 1972; children—Johnathan Robert, Pamela Michelle. Student U. S.C., 1971-75. Dental asst., North Augusta, part-time 1969-71; asst. mgr. millinery Berrys on Main, Columbia, S.C., 1972-75; directory telephone sales rep. So. Bell Co., Columbia, 1975-77, asst. mgr. Yellow Pages, 1977—. Mem. Nat Assn. Female Execs. Republican. Presbyterian. Avocation: choir singing. Home: 1813 Woodvalley Ct Columbia SC 29210 Office: Bell So Advt & Publ 810 Dutch Sq Blvd Columbia SC 29210

BAKER, HELEN MANHEIM, lawyer, advocate; b. Cleve., May 6, 1922; d. Harry and Belle (Speiser) Manheim; m. Marvin Baker, Nov. 10, 1944 (div.); children—Jon, Scott, Lauren. B.S., Northwestern U., 1943; J.D., Cleve. State U., 1977. Bar: Ohio 1979. Coordinator youth rights ACLU of Ohio, Cleve., 1977-79, researcher rights of instl. law, 1979; staff counsel ACLU of Cleve. Found., 1979-80, dir. Children's Rights Advocacy Project, 1980-82; child/parent advocate, Elmhurst, Ill., 1982—; cons. ACLU. Contbr. chpt. to book, articles to profl. jours. Vol. polit. campaigns, civil rights, anti-war movements, nuclear freeze movement, others. Named Civil Libertarian of Yr., ACLU of Cleve.; recipient Civil Libertarian award ACLU of Ohio, 1981, others. Home and Office: 440 Addison Ave Elmhurst IL 60126

BAKER, HELEN VAUGHAN BURDIN, philosophy educator; b. New Orleans, May 20, 1937; d. John Joseph and Helen Rose (Broussard) Burdin; m. Larry T. Baker, Aug. 22, 1959 (div. 1980); children—Larry Eugene, Elizabeth Vaughan, David Scott; m. Amos E. Simpson, Oct. 10, 1980. B.A., Newcomb Coll., Tulane U., 1959; M.A., U. Southwestern La., Lafayette, 1970, Ph.D. in History, 1975; postgrad. U. Wales. Tchr., Caddo Parish Schs., Shreveport, La., 1959-60, Plaquemine Parish Sch., Belle Chasse, La., 1960-61; asst. prof. history and humanities U. Southwestern La., 1975—, coordinator interdisciplinary humanities program, 1985—, dir. Women in La. Collection, 1977—; chmn. social studies Episcopal Sch. of Acadiana, Cade, La., part-time 1982-84; cons. La. Com. Humanities, New Orleans, 1978—; grant reader NEH, 1980-82. Co-author The World of Europe (textbook), 1971; co-editor France and North America: The State of Democracy, 1981, Louisianan Gothic, 1984. Charter mem. Mayor's Commn. Needs of Women, Lafayette, 1978-82; bd. dirs. Fine Arts Found., Lafayette, 1978-83. Grantee, U.S. Dept. Edn., 1981-82, NEH, 1981-82, La. Com. Humanities, 1977-82. Mem. La. Hist. Assn., So. Hist. Assn. (editor European hist. newsletter 1979—, John Snell Prize 1971), Am. Hist. Assn., Attakapas Hist. Assn. (pres. 1971-73), Southwestern Social Sci. Assn. Democrat. Home: 200 Arlette Dr Lafayette LA 70503 Office: Dept Philosophy U Southwestern LA Lafayette LA 70504

BAKER, JANET, school administrator; b. Hamilton, Ohio, Aug. 11, 1947; d. Robert Herman and Betty Jane (Brown) Thiel; m. Dewey Wayne Baker, Aug. 24, 1968; children—Joshua Bryce, Justin Reid. B.S. in Secondary Edn., Miami U., Oxford, Ohio, 1969; M.A., Eastern Ky. U., 1971. Librarian, media specialist Hamilton City Schs., 1971-73, 74, dean students, 1974-77, prin. Jr. High Sch., 1977-86, prin. Lincoln Elem. Sch., 1986—. Mem Ohio Assn. Secondary Sch. Adminstrs., Hamilton City Orgn. Secondary Sch. Adminstrs., Delta Kappa Gamma. Home: 1323 Cereal Ave Hamilton OH 45013 Office: Lincoln Elem Sch Grey and North E Sts Hamilton OH 45013

BAKER, JEAN HARVEY, history educator; b. Balt., Feb. 9, 1933; d. Frederick Barton and Rose (Hopkins) Harvey; m. R. Robinson Baker, Sept. 12, 1953; children—Susan D., Robinson S., Robert W., Jean H. A.B., Goucher Coll., 1961; M.A., Johns Hopkins U., 1964, Ph.D., 1971. Asst. prof. history Notre Dame Coll., Balt., 1966-68; assoc. prof. history Goucher Coll., Balt., 1971-77, prof., 1977—, Elizabeth Todd prof., 1983—. Author: Politics of Continuity, 1973; Ambivalent Americans, 1976; Affairs of Party, 1982; editor Md. Hist. Mag. Officer Urban League, Balt., 1960; trustee Md. Inst., 1970-79. Grantee Am. Council Learned Socs., 1976-77, NEH, 1983-84. Mem. Orgn. Am. Historians, Am. Hist. Assn., Women's Internat. League for Peace Freedom, Berkshire Conf. Women Historians. Democrat. Home: 8717 McDonogh Rd McDonogh MD 21208 Office: Goucher Coll Towson MD 21204

BAKER, JOANNE EVELYN, government official; b. Crucible, Pa., Dec. 1, 1933; d. George Joseph and Anna Leona (Kagle) Cormack; m. Warren Clair Baker, July 7, 1956 (dec. May 1968); m. James Lewis Wilson, June 2, 1970; (div. Sept. 1984); former stepchildren—James Lloyd, John Thomas, Charles Edward, Debra Ruth, Jeff Lee Wilson. Cert. applied music Waynesburg Coll., 1951. Various clerical positions, 1951-66; supr. U.S. Navy, Washington, 1966-71; pres., treas. Little Round Top Farm, Inc., Gettysburg, Pa., 1971—; logistician U.S. Navy-U.S. Army, 1974-81; insp. Office of Insp. Gen., U.S. Army, Ft. Ritchie, Md., 1981-84; chief supply and services div. Fort Detrick, Frederick, Md., 1984—. Author: Reflections, 1974. Bd. dirs. Adams County Mental Health Assn., Gettysburg, 1982—. Recipient Sustained Superior Achievement award Dept. Navy, 1975. Mem. Internat. Graphoanalysis Soc. (Pa. chpt.), Adams County Amateur Radio Soc. (sec. 1981-83). Roman Catholic. Avocations: handwriting analysis; writing children's stories; ceramics; piano; studying self-improvement and psychology. Home: 5605 Shookstown Rd Frederick MD 21701

BAKER, JOANNE O'REILLY, special education educator; b. N.Y.C., June 18, 1951; d. Laselve Rubert and Laura Mae (Campbell) O'Reilly. B.A., Queens Coll., 1975; M.S. in Edn., 1976. Tchr. Better Community League Day Care Ctr., Corona, N.Y., 1975-81; spl. edn. tchr. Pub. Sch. 214Q, Flushing, N.Y., 1982—. Mem. Nat. Assn. Female Execs., Queensboro Council Reading. Democrat. Episcopalian. Avocations: music; computer games.

BAKER, JOSEPHINE L. REDENIUS, civic worker, retired army officer; b. Oceanville, N.J., Aug. 31, 1920; d. Jacob and Josephine (Palmer) Redenius; student Columbia U., 1948-49, L.I.U., 1957-58, George Washington U., 1947-48; M.A. in Journalism, Am. U., 1963; L.H.D. (hon.), Temple U., 1964; postgrad. St. Charles Sem., 1978-81, Eastern Bapt. Theol. Sem., 1981—; m. Milton G. Baker (dec. 1976). Enlisted as pvt. WAAC, 1943, advanced through grades to lt. col. U.S. Army, 1963; intelligence officer atomic installations throughout U.S. and Can., 1943-53; asst. in Office Chief of Staff, Army Forces Far East, Japan, 1954-56; public info. officer Office Chief of Info., Washington, 1958-61; chief Women's Army Corps Recruiting, U.S. Army, 1962-66; info. liaison officer U.S. Army, 1966-67, ret., 1967; dir. public relations and devel. Valley Forge Mil. Acad. and Jr. Coll., Wayne, Pa., 1967-70, dir. found., 1970-76; pres. Intercounty Trading Co., Inc., Surfside, Fla., 1976-80, Potential Gift Shop & Boutique, Ardmore, Pa., 1979-82; pres. bd. dirs. Surf Club Apts., Inc., 1977-79. Dir., Republican Women of Pa.; bd. dirs. Freedom Valley council Girl Scouts U.S.A., 1970—, Opera Guild Miami (Fla.); pres. found. bd. dirs. Chapel of St. Cornelius the Centurian, Wayne, Pa., 1976—; novice Third Order St. Francis, 1986—; mem. aux. Miami Heart Inst. Decorated Legion of Merit, U.S. Army Commendation medal with 1st oak leaf; recipient Pa. Meritorious Service medal; Disting. Alumnus, Am. U., 1969. Mem. Public Relations Soc. Am., Am. Personnel and Guidance Assn., Am. Coll. Personnel Assn., Nat. Vocat. Guidance Assn., Am. Sch. Counselors Assn., Am. Legion Aux., Ret. Officers Assn., Assn. U.S. Army (Anthony J. Drexel Biddle medal 1968), Army-Navy Union, Assn. Measurement and Evaluation in Guidance, Emergency Aid of Pa., Am. Legion, Mil. Order World Wars, La Boutique des Huit Chapeaux et Quarante Femmes, Women in World Communications, AAUW. Episcopalian. Clubs: Acorn, St. David's Golf, Surf, Miami Beach Women's. Address: 5645 N Bay Rd Miami Beach FL 33140

BAKER, JUDITH GRLICKY, lawyer; b. Cleve., Jan. 1, 1946; d. John and Helen (Nyiri) Grlicky; m. Houston R. Baker, Jr., Sept. 26, 1966; children—Eva Halle Baker, Elke Zoe. B.A., Ohio State U., 1967; J.D., Am. U., 1974. Bar: Md. 1975, D.C. 1976, U.S. Dist. Ct. Md. 1975, U.S. Ct. Appeals for D.C. 1976, U.S. Supreme Ct. 1980. Pres., prin. atty. Judith E. Baker, P.A., Gaithersburg, Md., 1975—; juvenile commr. Dist. Ct. Md., 1978—; lectr. LWV, YWCA, Jr. League, A Woman's Place, Women's Legal Def. Fund, Montgomery County Bd. Realtors. Mem. Gifted and Talented Assn. Montgomery County, 1979—. Mem. ABA, Montgomery County Bar Assn. (sec. taxation sect. 1983), Md. Bar Assn., Women's Bar Assn. Washington, Women's Bar Assn. Md., Gaithersburg C. of C., Phi Alpha Delta. Office: 702 Russell Ave Gaithersburg MD 20877

BAKER, JUSTINE CLARA, engineer; b. Phila., Oct. 1, 1939; d. Michael Angelo and Justine Catherine (DeFlavia) Boni; A.B., Immaculata (Pa.) Coll., 1963; M.A.T.M., Villanova (Pa.) U., 1970; M.S. in Edn., U. Pa., Phila., 1973, Ph.D., 1986; m. Harold Jerome Baker, July 23, 1966. Tchr. math. and sci. pvt. and parochial schs., 1963-66; tchr. math. public secondary schs., Pa., 1968-69; tchr. math. and sci. parochial, pvt. and public schs., Pa. and N.J., 1973-80; instr. math., stats., and computer sci. Goldey Beacom Coll., Wilmington, Del., 1980-84; instr. stats. and computer sci. Del. County Community Coll., Media, Pa., 1984-85; systems engr. RCA, Moorestown, N.J., 1985—. Cert. tchr. math. and physics secondary schs., Pa.; cert. tchr. math. and comprehensive sci., N.J. Mem. Nat. Council Tchrs. of Math., Math. Assn. Am., World Future Soc., Am. Ednl. Research Assn., Assn. Computing Machinery, Phi Delta Kappa (pres. U. Pa. chpt. 1977-78, cert. of recognition 1976, 81, 82, 83, 85, Pres.'s award 1978, Service Key 1982). Republican. Roman Catholic. Author: The Computer in the School, 1975; Computers in the Curriculum, 1976; Microcomputers in the Classroom, 1982; contbr. articles to profl. jours. Home: 1021 Drexel Ave Drexel Hill PA 19026

BAKER, LILLIAN, author, historian, artist, polit. activist, lecturer; b. Yonkers, N.Y., Dec. 12, 1921; student El Camino (Calif.) Coll., 1952, UCLA, 1968, 77, m. Roscoe A. Baker; children—Wanda Georgia, George Riley. Continuity writer Sta. WINS, N.Y.C., 1945-46; columnist, freelance writer, reviewer Gardena (Calif.) Valley News, 1964-76; freelance writer, editor, 1971—; lectr. in field. founder/editor Internat. Club for Collectors of Hatpins and Hatpin Holders, monthly and semi-ann. newsletter, 1977—, conv. and seminar coordinator 1979-80; founder Ams. for Hist. Accuracy, 1972, Com. for Equality for All Draftees, 1973; chair S. Bay primary campaign S.I. Hayakawa, for U.S. Senator from Calif., 1976; witness U.S. Senate Judiciary Com., 1983, U.S. Ho. Reps. Judiciary Com., 1986. Recipient award Freedoms Found., 1971, Ann. award Conf. Calif. Hist. Socs., 1983, monetary award Stanford U. Press Pubs. Com., 1985. Fellow Internat. Biographical Assn.; mem. Nat. League Am. Pen Women, Nat. Writers Club, Art Students League N.Y. (life), Nat. Historic Soc. (founding), Nat. Trust Historic Preservation (founding), other orgns. Author: Collector's Encyclopedia of Hatpins and Hatpin Holders, 1976; 100 Years of Collectible Jewelry 1850-1950, 1978, rev. edit., 1986; Jewelry: Art Nouveau and Art Deco, 1980; The Concentration Camp Conspiracy: A Second Pearl Harbor, 1981 (Scholarship Category award of Merit, Conf. of Calif. Hist. Socs. 1983); Hatpins and Hatpin Holders: An Illustrated Value Guide, 1983; Creative and Collectible Miniatures, 1984; Fifty Years of Fashion Jewelry: 1925-1975, 1986; also articles poetry; editor: Insider; contbg. author Vol. VII Time-Life Encyclopedia of Collectibles, 1979; numerous radio and TV appearances. Home and office: 15237 Chanera Ave Gardena CA 90249

BAKER, LINDA FRAZEE, technical communicator; b. N.Y.C., Dec. 16, 1946; d. Charles Edward and Dorothy (O'Neill) Frazee; m. Paul L. Baker, Apr. 9, 1968 (div. Aug. 1980). A.B. summa cum laude, Wagner Coll., N.Y.C., 1966; M.A., Cornell U., 1968; Ph.D., U. Calif.-Berkeley, 1974; postgrad. Johns Hopkins U., 1983. Asst. prof. U. Muenster (W.Ger.), 1975, lectr., 1976-78; administrv. assoc. Am. Insts. for Research, Washington, 1979-80; mng. editor gen. govt. div. Gen. Acctg. Office, Washington, 1980—. Author: (dramas) Persephone, 1979; The Third Wish, 1980; Oenone, 1983. NDEA fellow Cornell U., 1966-68; Genevieve McErney fellow U. Calif.-Berkeley, 1971; recipient Cert. of Merit, Gen. Acctg. Office, 1980, 81, 82, Outstanding Performance award, 1983. Mem. Soc. for Tech. Communication. Office: Gen Acctg Office 441 G St NW Washington DC 20007

BAKER, LORRAINE, educational administrator; b. Los Angeles, Aug. 20, 1935; d. Herbert McDowell and Izalia Lewena (Fee) Young; A.A., Los Angeles City Coll., 1955; B.A., Calif. State U., 1972; cert. sch. mgmt. (Rockefeller Found. fellow), Center for Ednl. Leadership, 1975-76; M.Ed., U. LaVerne, 1979; m. Rolland Alvin Baker, Mar. 16, 1955; children—Glenn, Eric. Tchr., La Canada (Calif.) Unified Sch. Dist., 1972-76, prin. Paradise Canyon Sch., 1976-79, bldg. adminstr. Foothill Intermediate Sch., 1979-80, coordinator curriculum K-12, 1980-84, dir. instructional services, 1984—. Mem. Assn. Supervision and Curriculum Devel., AAUW (chmn. profl. interest network), Assn. Calif. Sch. Adminstrs., Women in Mgmt., Women in Bus.

BAKER, MARGIE SPARKMAN, government administrator; b. Leon, Ky., Jan. 28, 1943; d. Frank and Lora Jane (Allen) Sparkman; student No. Va. Community Coll., 1975-77, George Washington U., 1977-79; B.A. in Sociology, Columbia Coll. Arts and Scis., 1979; m. Richard L. Baker, Nov. 21, 1962; 1 dau., Cheri Michelle, Various secretarial and adminstrv. positions U.S. Dept. Def. and U.S. Dept. Agr., Washington area, 1961-69; staff asst. to dep. for programs Am. Revolution Bicentennial Adminstrn., Washington, 1969-75; mgmt. analyst Office of Surface Mining and Reclamation Dept. Interior, Washington, 1978; adminstrv. asst. to legal counsel, Commn. on Accident at Three Mile Island, Washington, 1979; program analyst Mine Safety and Health Adminstrn., U.S. Dept. Labor, Arlington, Va., 1979—. Recipient Sustained Superior Performance award Commn. on Three Mile Island, Outstanding Achievement award Mine Safety and Health Adminstrn., 1981, Sustained Superior Performance award, 1983. Mem. Nat. Assn. Female Execs., Federally Employed Women, Am. Fedn. Govt. Employees (steward local 12), Columbian Women of George Washington U. Home: 6826 Stoneybrooke Ln Alexandria VA 22306 Office: Wilson Blvd Arlington VA 22203

BAKER, MARY JORDAN, educator; b. Chgo. A.B., Stanford U., 1961; M.A., U. Va., 1964; Ph.D. in Romance Langs., Harvard U., 1969. Instr. French, DePauw U., 1964-65; asst. prof. U. Tex.-Austin, 1968-75, assoc. prof. French, 1975—. Mem. MLA, Am. Assn. Tchrs. French, Renaissance Soc. Am., Modern Humanities Research Assn. Co-author: Panaché Littéraire, 1978; contbr. articles to profl. jours. Address: French Dept Univ Tex Austin TX 78712

BAKER, MELODY GENTRY, stockbroker; b. Summit, N.J., May 19, 1954; d. George H. and Muriel R. (Pugh) B. Grad. Kathryn Gibbs Sch., Montclair, N.J., 1980; student Green Mountain Coll., Poultney, Vt., 1972-73. Assoc., John J. Davis Assocs., Millburn, 1980-82; account exec. Dean Witter Reynolds,

Millburn, 1982—. Mem. Greater Newark C. of C. Republican. Episcopalian. Club: Chatham Squash (Chatham, N.J.). Avocations: squash; tennis; golf; lacrosse. Office: Dean Witter Reynolds Inc 235 Millburn Ave Millburn NJ 07041

BAKER, MIRIAM F., accountant; b. Paonia, Colo., Mar. 28, 1912; d. Arthur Balista and Mary Frances (Johnson) Ullrey; m. Eugene Baker, Mar. 2, 1930 (dec.); children—Hugh, Faye, Alice Joan. Dr. Life Scis., Inst. Life Sci., 1945, M. Life Scis., 1947; cert. Internat. Acctg. Soc., 1952. C.P.A., Colo. Comptroller, Gay Johnson, Inc., Montrose, Colo., 1945-55; acct. Van Serenter, Anchorage, 1955-57; pvt. practice acctg., 1957-64; auditor State of Alaska, Juneau, 1964-66; acctg. technician Alaska Dept. Hwys., Anchorage, 1966-74. Author: Olin and the Great One, 1969; Our Angel and Our Mysteries, 1971. Home: Pouch 6577 Box 555 Anchorage AK 99502

BAKER, PHYLLIS ANNE, company executive; b. Webb City, Mo., Apr. 17, 1930; d. Fred Aaron and Beatrice Blanche (Bogner) Spille; children—Deborah Kay Baker Lundien, Ronald Eugene Baker. Student Kansas City Coll. Commerce, 1949-53, Mo. So. State Coll., 1978-80. Sec.-bookkeeper, Wendel Locker Plant, Webb City, Mo., 1948-49; inventory clk. Yates Furniture Co., Kansas City, Mo., 1949-53; sec. Stars and Stripes, Darmstadt, Ger., 1956-57, Allison div. Gen. Motors, Frankfurt, Ger., 1957-61, 62-63; asst. corp. sec. Tri-State Motor Transit Co., Joplin, Mo., 1963—. Active Metro 2000 Indsl. Devel., Joplin, 1983-84. Mem. Profl. Secs. Internat. (treas. Mo. div. 1980-81, 83-84, sec. div. 1981-82, pres. chpt. 1977), Nat. Assn. Exec. Secs., Nat. Assn. Corp. Secs. Republican. Methodist. Home: 4460 E 25th St Joplin MO 64802 Office: Tri-State Motor Transit Co E 7th St Rd PO Box 113 Joplin MO 64802

BAKER, SHIRLEY CLAIRE, distributing company executive; b. Melrose, Mass., Oct. 21, 1934; d. John Charles and Ruth Marie (Hodgson) Martin; m. Joseph William Bucci, June 7, 1952 (div. 1962); 1 child, Joseph James; m. Richard William Baker, Aug. 18, 1968 (div. 1979); m. Frank Bernard Mesmer, July 4, 1983. A.S. with high honors, Foothill Jr. Coll., Palo Alto, Calif., 1972. Office export mgr. Atomium, Inc., Billerica, Mass., 1961-63; office mgr., bookkeeper Geo Space Gravity, Woburn, Mass., 1963-64; sales office mgr. Amicon Corp., Lexington, Mass., 1965-68; treas., mgr. Berghof/Am., Bend, Oreg. and Derry, N.H., 1974-79; pres. Berghof Am., Raymond, N.H., 1980—. Mem. Am. Chem. Soc. (assoc.), Derry C. of C. (bd. dirs.). Republican. Avocations: sailing, theater, painting, reading, cooking. Home: 116 Haverhill Rd Chester NH 03036 Office: Berghof Am Inc 27 Main St Raymond NH 03077

BAKER, SHIRLEY HODNETT, marketing professional; b. Halifax, Va., Aug. 11, 1951; d. Charlie Thompson and Earlene (Dance) Hodnett; m. Robert H. Baker. Student Central Va. Community Coll., 1974-76. Sec. Lynchburg (Va.) Coll., 1969-72; sec. Leggett Dept. Store, Lynchburg, 1972-75, sales mgr., 1975-76; co-owner Decorating Den, Lynchburg, 1976-81; adminstrv. asst. TV Bur. Advt., Atlanta, 1981-82, mktg./sales exec., Dallas, 1982-84; mktg. dir. N.Y. Market Radio Broadcasters Assn., N.Y.C., 1985—. Mem. Am. Women in Radio and TV, Nat. Assn. Female Execs. Baptist. Home: 57 Warren St New York NY 10007 Office: NY Market Radio Broadcasters Assn 575 Lexington Ave New York NY 10022

BAKER, SUSAN PARDEE, public health educator, epidemiologist; b. Atlanta, May 31, 1930; d. Charles Laban aand Susan (Lowell) Pardee; m. Timothy Danforth Baker, June 23, 1951; children—Timothy D., David C., Susan L. A.B., Cornell U., 1951; M.P.H., Johns Hopkins Sch. Hygiene and Pub. Health, 1968. Research assoc. Office Chief Med. Examiner, Balt., 1968-81; research assoc. Johns Hopkins Sch. Hygiene and Pub. Health, Balt., 1968-71, asst. prof., 1971-74, assoc. prof., 1974-83, prof. health policy and mgmt., 1983—, joint appointee environ. health scis., 1975—, joint appointee with Sch. Medicine in pediatrics, 1983—; vis. prof. U. Minn. Sch. Pub. Health, 1975—, vis. lectr. injury prevention Harvard Sch. Pub. Health, 1984—; adv. bd. Md. Safety Council, 1969-74, Emergency Med. Services Com., Md. Dept. Health, 1973-74; vice chmn. Nat. Hwy. Safety Adv. Com., U.S. Dept. Transp., 1975-77; chmn. U.S. Dept. Transp. Rev. Panel Nat. Accident Sampling System, Washington, 1976-81; adv. com. Nat. Safety Council, Workshop Occupant Restraint Com., 1982—; vice chmn. com. trauma research NRC, Washington, 1984—. Author: monograph Fatally Injured Drivers (Prince Bernhard medal 1974), 1970, The Injury Fact Book, 1984; also chpts. and articles. City chmn. United Appeal, Balt., 1961; active Cornell U. Council, Ithaca, N.Y., 1974-76, task force choking Am. Acad. Pediatrics, 1983. Recipient John T. Law Meml. lectr. award U. Calgary, Can., 1984. Mem. Am. Assn. Automotive Medicine (pres. 1974-75, dir. 1971-76), Am. Pub. Health Assn. (governing council 1975-77, jour. bd. 1983—), Am. Trauma Soc. (bd. dirs. 1972—, Disting. Achievement award 1981, Stone Lectureship award 1985), Phi Beta Kappa, Delta Omega. Office: Johns Hopkins Sch Hygiene and Pub Health Dept Health Policy and Mgmt 615 N Wolfe St Baltimore MD 21205

BAKER, THERESE LOUISE, sociology educator, administrator, editor; b. Mpls., June 20, 1939; d. Lloyd L. and Gussie G. (Miller) Elzas; m. Keith Michael Baker, Oct. 25, 1961; children—Julian Charles, Felix James. B.A., Cornell U., 1961; Ph.D., U. Chgo., 1973. Div. head behavioral and social scis. DePaul U., Chgo., 1977-81, assoc. prof. sociology, 1978—, chairperson, 1981—; dir. Chgo. Area Studies Ctr., 1984—; cons. Chgo. Sch. Bd. Adv. editor Contemporary Sociology, U. Minn., 1983—, sociol. Quarterly, U. Ill.-Chgo., 1981—. Contbr. articles to profl. jours. Cornell U. scholar, 1957-61; NIMH trainee U. Chgo., 1967-70; grantee NIMH, 1976, 79-81. Mem. Am. Sociol. Assn., Midwest Sociol. Soc. (bd. dirs. 1982-84), Ill. Sociol Assn., Internat. Sociol. Assn., Sociologists for Women in Soc., NOW. Avocations: collecting plates, jogging, aerobic dancing. Home: 5540 S Kimbark St Chicago IL 60637 Office: DePaul U 2323 N Seminary St Chicago IL 60614

BAKER, VALERIE L., lawyer; b. Mpls., June 25, 1949; d. Glen R. and Lorraine (Guselc) Baker. B.A. in English, U. Calif.-Santa Barbara, 1971, M.A., 1972; J.D., UCLA, 1975. Assoc., Overtich, Lyman & Prince, Los Angeles, 1975-77; asst. U.S. atty. U.S. Atty.'s Office, Los Angeles, 1977-80; ptnr. Lillick, McHose & Charles, Los Angeles, 1980—; del. 9th Cir. Jud. Conf., 1985—. Mem. Fed. Bar Assn., Bus. Trial Attys. Assn., Los Angeles County Bar Assn. (antitrust sect.), Santa Monica Bar Assn. Clubs: Santa Monica Tennis; Pacific Palisades Tennis. Office: Lillick McHose & Charles 707 Wilshire Blvd Los Angeles CA 90017

BAKER, VIOLET AUXILIADORA, English language educator; b. Granada, Nicaragua, July 9, 1941; came to U.S., 1952, naturalized, 1960; d. Joseph Albert Albites and Elda Maria (Matus) Beteta; m. Mario Napoleon Re, Jan. 21, 1956 (div. Oct. 1968); children—Mario N. Jr., James S., Maureen E., Violet D.; m. Elmer Chester Lobb, Aug. 9, 1969 (div. Sept. 1977); 1 child, Jason C.; m. Travis Lee Baker, May 12, 1979; 1 child, Kathryn Ann. A.A., Indian Valley Colls., Novato, Calif., 1975; B.A., Sonoma State U., 1977; M.A. in Ednl. Adminstrn., U. San Francisco, 1984. Accredited secondary tchr., ednl. adminstr., Calif. Customer service rep. Blue Shield Calif., San Francisco, 1977-80; supr. billing dept. Novato Community Hosp., 1980-81; high sch. tchr. English as Second Lang., Calif. Dept. Corrections, Jamestown, 1982—, mem. recruiting team, 1984—; balanced work force mem. Sierra Conservation Ctr., Jamestown, 1984—, safety com. coordinator edn. dept., 1984—; battered women/rape survivor counselor Mother Lode Women's Crisis Ctr., Sonora, 1981—; owner, mgr. T.L.'s Rusty Spur, Sonora, Calif., 1985. Mem. Correctional Edn. Assn., Calif. Assn. Tchrs. English to Speakers of Other Langs., Chicanos Correctional Workers Assn. (sec. Sierra chpt. 1985), U. San Francisco Edn. Alumni Assn. Republican. Roman Catholic. Avocations: poetry, dancing, camping. Office: Sierra Conservation Ctr PO Box 497 Jamestown CA 95327

BAKER, WINDA LOUISE (WENDY), social worker; b. Suwannee County, Fla., July 16, 1952; d. Austin Sidney Baker and Jessie Mae (Williams) Baker Jones; B.A. in Theology, Berkshire Christian Coll., 1974. Clk.-typist State of Fla., Tallahassee, 1974-76; cashier Tallahassee-Eastern Theatres, 1975-76; field rep. Commn. Human Relations, 1976-77; asst. to dir. retirement living, sec., receptionist Advent Christian Village, Dowling Park, Fla., 1977-79, admissions counselor, social worker, after 1979, multi-purpose worker, 1980; with circulation dept. Daily Sun Jour., Brooksville, Fla., 1982-83; geriatric care worker Advent Christian Village. Vol. ARC and Asso. Charities, 1977—; housemother Macon Rescue Mission, Ga.; founder Suwannee County Overeaters Anonymous, Live Oak, Fla., 1982. Mem. Suwannee County Mental Assn., Assn. Informed Travelers, Christian Fin. Planning, Inc., Cheeks Sch. Gymnastics Alumni. Republican. Advent Christian. Home: 322 Pine Ave Live Oak FL 32060

BAKER-LIEVANOS, NINA GILLSON, jewelry store executive; b. Boston, Dec. 19, 1950; d. Rev. John Robert and Patricia (Gillson) Baker; m. Jorge Alberto Lievanos, June 6, 1981; children—Jeremy John Baker, Wendy Mara Baker, Raoul Salvador Baker-Lievanos. Student Mills Coll., 1969-70; grad. course in diamond grading Gemology Inst. Am., 1983; student in diamondtology designation Diamond Council Am., 1986—. Artist, tchr., Claremont, Calif., 1973-78; escrow officer Bank of Am., Claremont, 1978-81; retail salesman William Pitt Jewelers, Puente Hills, Montclair, Calif., 1981-83, asst. mgr., Montclair, 1983, mgr., 1983—. Artist tapestry hanging Laguna Beach Mus. Art, 1974. Recipient Cert. Merit Art Bank Am., 1968, High Sales award William Pitt Jewelers, 1983, 84. Mem. Nat. Assn. Female Execs., C. of C., Compassion Internat. Democrat. Unitarian. Avocations: tapestry weaving, creative writing.

BAKKE, RUTH MARIE, university dean, nursing educator; b. Madison, S.D., June 29, 1940; d. Selmar O. and Eva B. (Barg) Bakke. B.S.N., Carroll Coll., 1962; M.S.N., U. Colo., 1966; Ph.D., U. Tex.-Austin, 1984. Staff nurse, asst. head nurse U. Colo. Med. Ctr., Denver, 1960-61; instr. St. Joseph's Hosp. Sch. Nursing, Denver, 1962-64; cons. Tri-County Health Dept., Englewood, Colo., 1966-69; assoc. dir. maternal child health, asst. prof. and chmn. U. Colo. Sch. Nursing, Denver, 1969-72; chief nurse and asst. to dep. project dir. Child and Youth project, Project: Driscoll Found. Children's Hosp., Robstown, Tex., 1972-74; dir. nursing program Corpus Christi State U., Tex., 1974-79, dean Coll. Sci. and Tech., 1979—; cons. in field; nursing program reviewer Coordination Bd., Tex. Coll. and Univ. System, Austin, 1984. Bd. dirs. ARC, Corpus Christi, 1981—; adv. bd. Bot. Gardens, Corpus Christi, 1984—; steering com. Corpus Christi Women's Council, 1984—; adv. bd. Sr. Citizens Bd., Corpus Christi, 1985—. Mem. Am. Nurses Assn., Corpus Christi C. of C., Am. Nurses Found. Century Club, Tex. Deans and Dirs. of Schs. of Nursing (sec., treas.), Am. Assn. Higher Edn., Council of Coll. of Arts and Scis., Tex. Assn. Coll. Tchrs., Phi Delta Kappa, Sigma Theta Tau, Beta Beta Beta, Kappa Delta Pi. Democrat. Methodist. Avocations: tennis; painting; walking; aerobics.

BALABAN, ANN, sales executive; b. Clinton, Ind., Mar. 27, 1949; d. Nicholas and Virginia (Reed) B. B.A., Ind. State U., 1971; postgrad. Ball State U., 1974. Dir. pub. relations St. Mary of the Woods Coll., Terre Haute, Ind., 1973-76; account rep. The Gillette Co., San Diego, 1976-78, account exec., Los Angeles, 1978-79; account mgr. The Pillsbury Co., Detroit, 1979-80, sales services mgr., Mpls., 1980-82, sales mgr., Dallas, 1982—; fund raising com. chmn. Ind. State U. Alumni, Terre Haute, 1973, St. Mary of the Woods Coll., 1975. Pre-sch. vision screening chmn. Ind. Soc. Prevention Blindness, Terre Haute, 1974; com. chmn., selection com. for jr. bd. Wabash Valley Festival Assn., Terre Haute, 1974, 75; bd. dirs. Terre Haute Marathon-Marathon, 1975. Mem. Nat. Assn. Female Execs., Am. Mgmt. Assn., Pub. Relations Soc. Am., Delta Gamma. Office: The Pillsbury Co 17101 Kuykendahl St Suite 110 Houston TX 77068

BALAS, GLENDA BROWN, public relations consultant; b. Portales, N.Mex., Feb. 13, 1949; d. Delbert Wesley and Verla (Allen) Brown; m. John Michael Balas, (div.); children—Heather Catherine; Jason Christopher. B.S., Eastern N.Mex. U., 1974. Dir. pub. info. sta. KENW-TV, Portales, 1974-76, dir. programming, 1976-79, producer, 1984-85; dir. pub. info. sta. KCTS-TV, Seattle, 1979-81; exec. asst. Jay Roehl & Assocs., Albuquerque, 1981-84; owner, pres. Press Works, Portales, 1984—. Producer TV program People's Forum, 1984 (hon. mention award 1984). Contbr. articles to profl. publs. Mem. exec. bd. Friends of Library, Portales, 1985, Democratic Women of N.Mex., 1985; chmn. pub. relations Roosevelt County Democratic Women, Portales, 1985; mem. Roosevelt County Hist. Soc., Portales, 1985. Women of the West grantee N.Mex. Humanities Council, 1984. Mem. Eastern N.Mex. Press Women, N.Mex. Press Women, Altrusa. Baptist. Club: Portales Woman's (chmn. spl. projects). Avocations: horse breeding; antique collecting. Home: Route 2 Box 222 Portales NM 88130 Office: Press Works 101 W 2d Portales NM 88130

BALAZS, MARJORIE KARLENE, chemist; b. St. Louis, Nov. 9, 1932; d. Karl John and Marie Antoinette (Hoffman) Balazs; A.B., Washington U., St. Louis, 1954; M.A. (NSF grantee) Stanford U., 1963; M.S., U. San Francisco, 1969. Chemist, chief chem. lab, U.S. Geol. Survey, Denver, 1955-58; tchr. chemistry Jefferson County Schs., Lakewood, Colo., 1958-62; chemist life scis. Stanford (Calif.) Research Inst., 1963-68, chemist analytical physics and phys. scis., 1971-75; chemist semiconductor tech. Applied Materials, Santa Clara, Calif., 1968-71; pres. Balazs Analyt. Lab., Mountain View, Calif., 1975—. Named One of Savvy's Women of Yr., 1984. Mem. Electrochem. Soc., Filtration Soc., Am. Electronic Assn., ASTM, Peninsula Profl. Women's Network (pres. 1981-82). Contbr. articles to profl. jours. Office: 2284 Old Middlefield Way Suite 10 Mountain View CA 94043

BALCOM, GLORIA DARLEEN, computer administrative and marketing consultant; b. Porterville, Calif., July 23, 1939; d. Orel A. and Eunice E. Stadtmiller; A.A., El Camino Coll., 1959; student computer sci. Harbor Coll., 1976-77; m. Orville R. Balcom, July 23, 1971; stepchildren—Cynthia Lou, Steven Raymond. Personnel trainee AiResearch div. Garrett Corp., Los Angeles, 1959-60, sales promotion adminstr., 1960-64; sales rep. Volt Temporary Services, El Segundo, Calif., 1965-69, mgr., Tarzana, Calif., 1969-71; co-owner, co-operator Brown Dog Engring., Lomita, Calif., 1972-77; pres., owner, cons. MicroSly Mktg., Lomita, 1977—. Mem. Ind. Computer Cons. Assn., Nat. Assn. Female Execs., Am. Soc. Profl. and Exec. Women. Club: Torrance Athletic. Home and office: 24521 Walnut St Lomita CA 90717

BALDA, JO, banker; b. Oak Harbor, Wash., Oct. 3, 1922; d. Jake and Jennie (Fakkema) Balda. Student pub. schs., Oak Harbor. With Olympic Bank (formerly Everett Trust & Savs.), Oak Harbor, 1942-85, asst. cashier, 1968-79, asst. v.p., ops. officer, 1979-83, asst. v.p., mgr. Midway br., 1983-85; mgr. Midway office First Interstate Bank of Wash. (formerly Olympic Bank), 1985—; workshop leader. Treas., Am. Cancer Soc., Oak Harbor, 1963, Am. Heart Assn., Island County, Wash., 1971—, Oak Harbor Area council Navy League, 1976—, March of Dimes, Island County, 1978-81; mem. exec. com. Puget Sound chpt. March of Dimes, 1984; bd. dirs. Island Thrift Shop, Oak Harbor, treas., 1976-81; treas. Oak Harbor Hist. Soc., 1979—, bd. dirs., 1978; pres. Women's Mission Guild, Christian Ref. Ch., Oak Harbor, 1981-82; bd. dirs. Community Concerts, 1982—, treas., 1984; treas. Island County Republican Central Com., 1983—; mem. personnel adv. bd. City of Oak Harbor, 1984—; Sunday Sch. tchr. Christian Reformed Ch., 1962-82; candidate mem. United Way, 1985. Mem. Am. Inst. Banking (instr., workshop leader), Nat. Assn. Bank Women (pres. chpt. 1978-79), North Whidbey C. of C. (trustee 1977-78; Citizen of Year award 1976, Disting. Citizen award 1984). Clubs: Bus. and Profl. Women's (v.p. 1980-81, pres. 1981-82, 85—, treas. 1984-85, Woman of Achievement 1977), North Whidbey Republican Women's (pres. 1976, treas. 1986), Toastmistress (treas. council 1977-78, treas. region 1979-80, v.p. club 1984-85), North Whidbey Women's Bowling Assn., Soroptomist (treas. 1981-83, dir. 1983-84). Home: PO Box 345 Oak Harbor WA 98277 Office: PO Box 769 Oak Harbor WA 98277

BALDASSANO, CORINNE LESLIE, radio executive; b. N.Y.C., May 16, 1950; d. Nicholas and Olga (Phillips) Baldassano. B.A. cum laude, Queens Coll., CUNY, 1970; M.A. in Theatre, Hunter Coll., CUNY, 1975; M.B.A. in Fin., NYU, 1986. Program dir., ops. mgr. Sta. KAUM-AM, Houston, 1977-79; dir. programming Sta. WSAI-FM, Cin., 1979-81; dir. programming ABC Contemporary and FM Radio Networks, N.Y.C., 1981-84; regional mgr. affiliate relations United Stations Radio Networks, N.Y.C., 1985—; panelist conf. Am. Women in Radio and TV, Cin., 1981; panelist conv. Nat. Assn. Broadcasters, San Francisco, 1983; guest lectr. Wharton Sch. Bus., Phila., 1983, St. John's U., N.Y.C., 1983-84. Alumni mem. Govs. Com. Scholastic Achievement, N.Y.C., 1984-85. Mem. NYU Bus. Forum, Internat. Radio and TV Soc., Women in Communications, Am. Women in Radio and TV. Democrat. Roman Catholic. Club: Liberty (N.Y.C.). Advocations: travel; theatre; dancing; running. Office: United Stations Radio Networks 1440 Broadway New York NY 10018

BALDI, PATRICIA ANN, public health administrator; b. Muskogee, Okla., Feb. 1, 1943; d. Boxly William and Anne Nell (Smith) Waak; children—Cinira Anne, Rachel Nell. Student Tulane U., 1961-62, U. Houston, 1964-65, George Mason U., 1976-77; diploma Mather Sch. Nursing, 1964. R.N., Va. notary public, N.Y. Peace Corps nurse, Maceio, Alagoas, 1966-68; staff nurse U. Wis. Children's Hosp., Madison, 1968-70; dir. counseling Planned Parenthood, Washington, 1973-75; spl. asst. Devel. Support Bur., USAID, Washington, 1977-78; assoc. dir. Office of Population, AID, Washington, 1978-82; asst. dir. Ctr. for Population and Family Health, Columbia U., N.Y.C., 1982-85; dir. population Nat. Audubon Soc., 1985—; mem. U.S. del. UN Population Commn., 1981-82; cons. Family Planning Internat., 1973, Global Com. of Parliamentarians on Population and Devel., 1984-85; project design team U.S. AID, Zimbabwe, 1985; NGO participant UN Mid-Decade Conf. of Women, Copenhagen, 1981; moderator global population anniversary Peace Corps Conf., 1981; lectr. in field. Mem. McGovern-Shriver Presdl. Campaign Staff, 1972; vice chmn. Arlington Democratic Com., 1974; chmn. Arlington Com. on Status of Women, 1975; dep. campaign mgr. Shriver for Pres. Com., 1976; del. Va. Dem. Conv., 1976, 82. Mem. Am. Pub. Health Assn. (population sect. council, com. on women's rights), Nat. Council for Internat. Health (pub. policy com.), Assn. for Women in Devel., Nat. Women's Polit. Caucus, Soc. Internat. Devel. Home: 16 N Highland St Arlington VA 22201 Office: National Audubon Soc Nat Capitol Office 645 Pennsylvania Ave SE Washington DC 20003

BALDONI, GAIL HUEY, legal secretary, legislative coordinator, medical record administrator; b. San Antonio, Tex., July 30, 1947; d. Herbert Ming and Bernice (Lee) Huey; m. Luis A. Baldoni, Sept. 15, 1973. B.S., Incarnate Word Coll., San Antonio, 1968. Registered med. record adminstr., Tex. Sr. med. record adminstr. Bexar County Hosp., San Antonio, 1969-71; chmn. dept. med. records Incarnate Word Coll., San Antonio, 1971-72; chief clin. records Sch. Aerospace Medicine, Brooks AFB, Tex., 1972-73; mgr. med. records dept. Mederi Home Health, Miami, 1975-78; safety documentation librarian Raymond Kaiser Engrs.; Miami, 1978-83; legal sec., legis. coordinator M. Frank Powell's Assocs., Austin, 1983—; speaker in field. Mem. Am. Med. Records Assn., Tex. Med. Records Assn., San Antonio Med. Records Assn. Democrat. Methodist. Home: 8800 IH 35 N Apt 1076 Austin TX 78753 Office: M Frank Powell's Assocs Southwest Tower Suite 1200 Austin TX 78701

BALDRIGE, LETITIA, public relations consultant; b. Miami Beach, Fla.; d. Howard Malcolm and Regina (Connell) Baldrige; B.A., Vassar Coll., postgrad. U. Geneva (Switzerland); D.H.L. (hon.), Creighton U., 1979, Mt. St. Mary's Coll., 1980; Robert Hollensteiner. Personal-social sec. to ambassador Am. Embassy, Paris, France, 1948-51, intelligence officer, 1951-53; asst. to ambassador Am. embassy, Rome, 1953-56; dir. public relations Tiffany & Co., 1956-61; social sec. to The White House, 1961-63; pres. Letitia Baldrige Enterprises, Chgo., 1964-69; dir. consumer affairs Burlington Industries, 1969-71; pres. Letitia Baldrige Enterprises, Inc., N.Y.C., 1972—; dir. The Outlet Co., Fed. Home Loan Bank N.Y., Libra Fund; mem. Com. of 200. Bd. dirs. Woodrow Wilson Found., Inst. Internat. Edn., Women's Forum Inc.; trustee Kenyon Coll., Gambier, Ohio. Mem. Fashion Group, Am. Soc. Interior Designers (pub. relations assoc.). Republican. Author: Roman Candle, 1956; Tiffany Table Settings, 1958; Of Diamonds and Diplomats, 1968; Home, 1972; Juggling, 1976; revised Amy Vanderbilt's Book of Etiquette, 1978; The Entertainers, 1981; Letitia Baldridge's Complete Guide to Executive Manners, 1985. Contbr. to popular mags., also lectr. Office: Letitia Baldrige Enterprises Inc 230 Park Ave Room 805 New York NY 10169

BALDWIN, BARBARA ANN, social work administrator; b. Hearne, Tex., Dec. 26, 1953; d. Clarence Jesse and Sallie (Cook) Dupree; m. John Albert Baldwin, Aug. 11, 1973; children—Yvette Renee, Dashaunda Michelle. B.S.W., Tex. So. U., 1976, postgrad., 1983—; M.S.W., U. Houston, 1980. Cert. social worker, Tex. Child care worker Florence Crittenton Service, Houston, 1974-76; social worker Tex. Dept. Human Resources, Houston, 1976-78; child placement specialist Harris County Children's Protective Services, Houston, 1978-81, child placement supr., 1981—. Author: I Speak Of ......, 1983; No One Has Seen My Tears, 1983. Mem. Adopt Black Children Com., Houston; bd. dirs. Mental Health/Mental Retardation Adv. Council, Houston, 1983—. Recipient Humanitarian Cert. Tex. So. U. Social Work Program, 1983; People to People II Campaign award Tex. Soc. U., 1983. Mem. Assn. Black Social Workers (pres. Houston chpt.), Assn. Blacks in Criminal Justice, NAACP. Democrat. Baptist. Office: Harris County Children's Protective Services 2525 Murworth Suite 209 Houston TX 77054

BALDWIN, BARBARA GEARLDINE, counselor, church lay worker; b. Louisville, Ky., Jan. 24, 1935; d. Paul Gordon and Alice Elizabeth (Hash) Thompson; m. Harold Bernard Baldwin, Dec. 27, 1952; children—Brian Gordon, Cheryl Lynn Baldwin Rodgers, Robin Thomas. Counselor, His House Ministry, Campbellsville, Ky., 1970—. Author: Boycott Hell, 1972. Den mother Old Ky. Home council Boy Scouts Am., 1964; Sunday Sch. tchr. Campbellsville Baptist Ch., 1964-66; pres. Taylor County PTA, 1968; campaign worker local circuit judge campaign, Campbellsville, 1968. Republican. Avocations: collecting and creating silk flower arrangements; collecting ceramic angels; writing. Home: 304 Summit Dr Campbellsville KY 42718

BALDWIN, CYNTHIA ACKRON, lawyer; b. McKeesport, Pa., Feb. 8, 1945; d. James Alexander and Iona (Meriweather) Ackron; m. Arthur Lawrence Baldwin, June 17, 1967; children—James Ackron, Crystal Anita. B.A., Pa. State U., 1966, M.A., 1974; J.D., Duquesne Sch. Law, 1980. Bar: Pa. 1980, U.S. Supreme Ct. 1984. Tchr. English, McKeesport Sch., 1966-71; instr. study skills and English, Pa. State U.-McKeesport, 1974-76, asst. dean student affairs, 1976-77; law clk. Pitts. law firms, 1978-79; Reginald Heber Smith fellow Neighborhood Legal Services, McKeesport, 1980-81; dep. atty. gen. Pitts. Regional Office Bur. Consumer Protection, Pa. Office Atty. Gen., 1981-83, atty.-in-charge, 1983—; adj. prof. Duquesne U. Sch. Law, 1984—. Founder, dir. McKeesport Counseling and Tutoring Service, 1971-83, bd. dirs., 1977—; mem. black task force adv. com. Pa. State U., 1976—, mem. alumni council, 1981—, mem. exec. com., 1982—; bd. dirs. Pitts. Urban League, 1973-79; bd. dirs. Neighborhood Legal Services Assn., 1984—. Mem. ABA, Pa. Bar Assn., Allegheny County Bar Assn., Homer S. Brown Law Assn. (exec. com. 1981—).

BALDWIN, FREDERIKA, machinery company executive, consultant; b. N.Y.C., July 2, 1938; d. Henry M. and Lee (Buff) Noe; m. James F. Baldwin, Jr., 1960 (div.); 1 child, James F. III. Exec. asst. to pres. Data Dimensions, Norwalk, Conn., 1975-79, TPT Machinery, Stamford, Conn., 1979—; ind. cons. to small restaurants Fairfield County, Conn., 1975—. Home: 512 Lake Ave Greenwich CT 06830 Office: TPT Machinery Corp Stamford CT 06903

BALDWIN, GERALDINE SARAH, librarian; b. Glen Cove, N.Y., Dec. 1, 1950; d. Jeremiah J. and Alice M. (Henry) Mahoney; m. Donald Elliot Baldwin, Mar. 4, 1984. B.A., SUNY-New Paltz, 1972; M.L.S., L.I.U., 1975. Asst. librarian, Mahopac, N.Y., 1972-73, dir., 1973-79; founding dir. Alice and Hamilton Fish Library, Garrison, N.Y., 1980—; advisor Mid-Hudson Library System, Poughkeepsie, N.Y., 1978—; cons. Active LWV, Putnam Community Hosp. Aux., Carmel, N.Y., Literacy Vols. Putnam County, N.Y. (founding dir. 1977-80). Grantee, Richard Lousnberry Found., 1983, Hudson River Found., 1985-86. Mem. ALA, N.Y. Library Assn., Putnam County (N.Y.) Library Assn. (holder numerous offices). Democrat. Home: Elvins Ln PO Box 208 Garrison NY 10524 Office: Alice and Hamilton Fish Library Routes 403 and 9 D Garrison NY 10524

BALDWIN, IRENE S., financial and business consultant; b. Dodge City, Kans., Sept. 8, 1939; d. Albert A. McMichael and Eleanor L. (Johnson) McMichael McGrath; m. Miles Edward Baldwin, June 30, 1961. B.S., Friends U., 1961. Dress designer, Wichita, 1959-61; social worker Sedgwick County, Kans., 1963-65; owner motel chain, Kans., 1965—; comml. and agrl. real estate investor, 1971—; sec.-treas. Baldwin, Inc., Kans., 1970—, fin. advisor, 1970—; pvt. practice fin. cons., Scottsbluff, Nebr., 1975—; founder, advisor Charitable Found., Kans., 1980—. Fundraiser various charitable orgns., 1982—; child sponsor World Vision, 1982—; pvt. placement of homeless animals, Kans. and Nebr., 1965—. Mem. Panhandle Humane Soc. Avocations: horseback riding; hiking; travel; sewing; drawing. Home: RR 2 Box 290 Scottsbluff NE 69361 Office: Baldwin Inc RR 1 Box 12M Colby KS 67701

BALDWIN, JANET LEE, lawyer; b. Dallas, Nov. 23, 1956; d. James Lee and Marie Louise (Giles) B. B.A., Sweet Briar Coll., 1979; student Sorbonne, 1977-78; J.D., So. Meth. U., 1982. Bar: Tex. 1982. French instr. Sweet Briar Coll. (Va.), 1978-79; estate planning research asst. So. Meth. U., Dallas, 1981; law clk. Bishop, Lamsens & Brown, Ft. Worth, 1981-82; law clk. Thompson, Coe, Cousins & Irons, Dallas, 1981-82; assoc. trust counsel Merc. Bank Dallas, 1982-84; atty. Touchstone, Bernays, Johnston, Beall & Smith, Dallas, 1984—; research cons. trust law Bruner, McColl, England, McColloch & Trice, Dallas, 1983-84. Asst. Steve Bartlett Congrl. Campaign, Dallas, 1982-83; asst. Dallas Area Rapid Transit Campaign, 1982; resident asst. United Way, Dallas, 1981-83. Recipient Outstanding Achievement in Bibl. Studies, Am. Bible Soc., 1978. Mem. ABA, Tex. Bar Assn., Dallas Bar Assn., Phi Beta Kappa, Delta

Theta Phi (v.p. 1981-82). Republican. Presbyterian. Clubs: Cotillion, Slipper, Backstagers (Dallas). Author: Les Baigneuses de Fragonard, 1978. Office: Touchstone Bernays Johnston Beall & Smith 1201 Elm St Dallas TX 75270

BALDWIN, JANICE MURPHY, lawyer; b. Bridgeport, Conn., July 16, 1926; d. William Henry and Josephine Gertrude (McKenna) Murphy; m. Robert Edward Baldwin, July 31, 1954; children—Jean Margaret, Robert William, Richard Edward, Nancy Josephine. A.B., U. Conn., 1948; M.A., Mt. Holyoke Coll., 1950; postgrad. U. Manchester, Eng., 1950-51; M.A., Fletcher Sch., Tufts U., 1952; J.D., U. Wis., 1971. Bar: Wis. 1971, U.S. Dist. Ct. (we. dist.) Wis. 1971. Staff atty. Legis. Council, State of Wis., Madison, 1971-74, 75-78, sr. staff atty., 1979—; atty. adviser HUD, Washington, 1974-75, 78-79; Mem. Dane County Bar Assn. (legis. com. 1980-81), Wis. Bar Assn. (pres. govt. lawyers div. 1985—, bd. govs.), Wis. Women's Network, AAUW, NOW, LWV, Legal Assn. for Women, Wis. Women's Polit. Caucus, U. Wis. Univ. League, Older Women's League. Home: 125 Nautilus Dr Madison WI 53705 Office: Legis Council Room 147N State Capitol Madison WI 53702

BALDWIN, JOAN (JODY) BOLLING, lobbyist, consultant; b. Norton, Va., Aug. 31, 1930; d. Henry C. and Nelle E. (Mann) Bolling; A.B., Hollins (Va.) Coll., 1953; M.A., U. Va., 1955; m. Donald Winston Baldwin, Nov. 16, 1957; children—Winston Monroe, Elizabeth Bolling, Alan Henry. Sec. to asst. register of copyrights Library of Congress, Washington, 1955-59; mem. profl. staff U.S. Senate Republican Policy Com., 1959-62; press and research asst. to Senator Len B. Jordan of Idaho, 1962-64; research asst. Rep. Nat. Com., 1964; polit. researcher James N. Juliana Assocs., Washington, 1965-69; legis. asst. to Senator James B. Pearson of Kans., 1969-71; spl. asst. to asst. sec. HEW, 1971-73; dep. staff dir. and editor Legis. Notice, Senate Rep. Policy Com., 1973-85, dep. editor 1984 Rep. platform; Washington lobbyist, v.p. United Internat. Cons. 1985—. del., Va. Rep. Conv., 1973, 80; pres. Alexandria (Va.) Rep. Women's Club, 1965-66; 2d v.p., 1st v.p. Alexandria Jr. Women's Club, 1963-64; treas. The Twig, 1968-69. Mem. Chi Omega. Anglican. Clubs: Capitol Hill; Senate Staff; Belle Haven Country (Alexandria). Office: United Internat Cons Suite 600 1800 Diagonal Rd Alexandria VA 22314

BALDWIN, JOANNE VIRGINIA, veterinarian; b. N.Y.C., Jan. 9, 1946; d. Morris H. and Pearl (Blum) Goldsmith; m. J.F. Baldwin, Nov. 20, 1967; 1 dau., Dvora. Student Ohio State U., 1963-64; B.S. Kans. State U., 1971, D.V.M., 1973. Assoc. veterinarian Aqueduct Animal Hosp., Schnectady, 1973-74, Cary Street Vet. Hosp., Richmond, Va., 1974—; cons. Docktors Pet Ctrs., Richmond, 1974—. Active Girl Scouts U.S.A., 1977-78, 4-H Clubs Am., 1984-85. Mem. AVMA, Kans. Vet. Med. Assn., N.Y. State Vet. Med. Assn., Assn. Avian Veterinarians, Central Va. Vet. Med. Assn. (pres. 1985-86), Alpha Lambda Delta, Phi Zeta, Phi Kappa Phi, Gamma Sigma Delta (merit award, 1971, 1973). Republican. Jewish. Office: Cary Street Veterinary Hospital 3210 W Cary St Richmond VA 23221

BALDWIN, MARY LEOLA, rural manpower and training company executive; b. Conway, S.C., Feb. 22, 1947; d. John Emily and Leoma Evelyn (Davis) Avant; B.S., S.C. State Coll., 1970; postgrad. George Washington U., 1972, Am. U., 1978-79; m. Jesse O. Baldwin, July 11, 1965 (dec.); children—Valeria Leoma, Emily Claroda. Tchr. secondary sci. Aiken County Pub. Schs. (S.C.), 1970-71; supply contract specialist Naval Security Sta., Washington, 1971-73; personnel cons. Assoc. Recruiters, Inc., Suitland, Md., 1973-75; personnel dir. NFU-Green Thumb, Arlington, Va., 1975-77, v.p. mgmt., budgets, program analysis, 1977-81, specialist methods mgmt., 1981-82, dir. EEO/AA, 1982—; cons. zero-based budgeting, grantsmanship; grants documentator Dept. Labor, 1977-81. Adv., Nat. Urban Coalition, 1979—; sgt.-at-arms White House Conf. on Aging, 1981; guidance adv. Montgomery County (Md.) PTA, 1981-82. Named Employee of Yr., NFU-Green Thumb, 1977; recipient Port of Jeffersonville award Jeffersonville, Ind., 1978. Mem. Am. Mgmt. Assn., Am. Soc. Personnel Dirs., S.C. State Coll. Alumni Assn., NEA. Democrat. Mormon. Club: Relief Soc. (dir.). Research on quality of work life of older people, 1979-80. Home: 3938 Tynewick Dr Silver Spring MD 20906 Office: 1401 Wilson Blvd Arlington VA 22209

BALDWIN, MARY LIVINGSTON, advertising and public relations executive; b. New Orleans, Mar. 25, 1954; d. John Hall and Eilyeen (Broyles) Livingston; m. Dan Michael Baldwin, Oct. 25, 1980. B.A. in Journalism, Northeast La. U., Monroe, 1976. Reporter, Alexandria (La.) Daily Town Talk, 1976; editor South Towne Courier, Shreveport, La., 1976-79; editor weekend mag. Shreveport Jour. 1979-81; editor mgr. Shreveport Mag., 1981-85. Task Force mem. Downtown Shreveport Unlimited, 1983—; bd. dirs. La. Assn. Blind, Shreveport, 1979; mem. Holiday In Dixie Diplomats, Shreveport, 1979; participant Leadership Shreveport, 1983-84. Recipient Most Appreciated of News Media award, Shreveport Lions Club, 1977. Mem. Shreveport Advt. Fedn. (bd. dirs. 1983—, 1st v.p. 1984-85, pres. 1985-86), Shreveport Soc. Profl. Journalists (past bd. dirs.). Republican. Presbyterian. Club: Northeast La. U. Alumni (Shreveport) (regional v.p. 1978). Home: 323 Merrick Shreveport LA 71104 Office: Baldwin Enterprises Inc 625 Texas Suite 202 Shreveport LA 71101

BALDWIN, PATRICIA ANN, lawyer; b. Detroit, May 3, 1955; d. Frank Thomas and Margaret Elyne (Velghe) Mathews; m. Jeffrey Kenton Baldwin, Aug. 23, 1975; children—Matthew, Katherine, Timothy. B.A. summa cum laude, Ball State U., 1976; J.D., Ind. U., 1979. Bar: Ind. 1979, U.S. Dist. Ct. (so. dist.) Ind. 1979. Ptnr., Baldwin & Baldwin, Danville, Ind., 1979—; dep. pros. atty. Hendricks County Ind., 1980—; sec.-treas., dir. T.F.W., Inc., Danville, 1983—. Bd. dirs. Cummins Mental Health Ctr., 1982-86; mem. Hendricks County Republican Women, 1976—; mem. parish council Mary Queen of Peace Catholic Ch., 1978-80, 81-83; bd. dirs. Cath. Social Services, Archdiocese of Indpls., 1985—, sec. bd., 1986; active Girl Scouts U.S.A., 1964—. Mem. Hendricks County Bar Assn., Ind. Bar Assn., ABA, Phi Delta Phi. Club: Danville Conservation. Office: Baldwin & Baldwin PO Box 63 Danville IN 46122

BALDWIN, SUSAN OLIN, lawyer; b. Battle Creek, Mich., Sept. 1, 1954; d. Thomas Franklin and Gloria Joan (Skidmore) Olin; m. James Patric Baldwin, Sept. 15, 1979. B.A., Miami U.-Ohio, 1976; J.D., U. Cin., 1979. Bar: Ohio 1979, Mich. 1984. Assoc. editor Am. Legal Pub. Co., Cin., 1979-80; corp. atty. Hosp. Care Corp., Cin., 1980-84; legal counsel Peak Health Plan, Cin., 1984; assoc. Cook, Pringle, Simonsen & Goetz, P.C., 1984—. Contbr. articles to profl. jours. Pres. Hunter's Green Homeowner's Assn., Independence, Ky., 1982-83; charter mem. Young Republicans, Ashland, Ohio, 1972. Mem. ABA, Ohio Bar Assn., Mich. Bar Assn., Alpha Lambda Delta, Phi Alpha Delta. Club: Am Businesswomen's Assn. (v.p. 1980-81, editor 1980).

BALDWIN, VELMA NEVILLE WILSON, cons.; b. Meade, Kans., Aug. 31, 1918; d. Charles Chester and Anna Velma (Neville) Wilson; A.B., U. Kans., 1940; m. Claude David Baldwin, Jan. 31, 1942 (dec. Nov. 1976). Placement working students U. Kans., 1940-41; personnel War Dept., Washington, 1942-45; research asst. Dr. A.C. Kinsey, Ind. U., 1946; with Carter Oil Co., Denver, 1948-50; personnel Bur. Budget, Washington, 1951-55; asst. to dir. personnel Treasury Dept., 1955-59; personnel officer, dir. adminstrn. Office Mgmt. and Budget, 1959-79; cons. in field. Mem. Am. Soc. Pub. Adminstrn. (past exec. bd.), Soc. Personnel Adminstrn. (exec. bd.). Home: 2234 49th St NW Washington DC 20007 Office: Office Mgmt and Budget Washington DC 20503

BALDWIN, WENDY HARMER, social demographer; b. Phila., Aug. 29, 1945; B.A. magna cum laude, Stetson U., DeLand, Fla., 1967; M.A., U. Ky., Lexington, 1970, Ph.D. (NDEA fellow, spl. grantee Population Council), 1973. Research asst. Colombian Assn. Med. Faculties, Bogatá, 1971; research asst. sociology U. Ky., 1971-72; health scientist adminstr. behavioral scis. br. Center Population Research, Nat. Inst. Child Health and Human Devel., NIH, 1972-79, chief demographic and behavioral scis. br., 1979—. Recipient Merit award NIH, 1978; USPHS Superior Service award, 1985. Mem. Population Assn. Am. (dir. 1978-80, 2d v.p. 1984), Am. Sociol. Assn. (sec. population sect. 1977-80, chmn. 1985), So. Sociol. Assn., Phi Beta Kappa. Author articles in field. Office: 7910 Woodmont Ave Room 7C25 Bethesda MD 20892

BALE, CHARALOTTE ANN, artist, educator; b. Nacogdoches, Tex., Apr. 25, 1941; d. Emory Leon and Elva Louise (Tucker) Seelbach; m. Leonard Hardin Bale, Apr. 17, 1965; children—Laura Allison, Joanna Leigh. B.S., Sam Houston U., 1963. Cert tchr., Tex. Chmn. art dept. Spring Br. Ind. Sch. Dist., Houston, 1964-69, tchr., 1980—; chmn. art dept. Houston Ind. Sch. Dist., 1972-80; art instr. Rice U., Houston, 1983; archtl. designer Manson Industries, Spring, Tex., 1970-72; Mid-America Corp., Houston, 1970-72; adminstrv. sec., M.D. Anderson Hosp., Houston, 1979. Paintings exhibited in one-woman shows: Atelier Gallery, Houston, 1962, Houston Pub. Library, 1971; group shows: U.S. Cultural Exchange Exhibit, Mex., 1960, So. Assn. Univs. touring exhibit, 1963-64, Houston Art Educators Ann., 1967, 74, 78. Mem. Nat. Assn. Profl. Women, NEA, Houston Art Educators Assn., Art League of Houston. Republican. Southern Baptist.

BALFOUR, LINDA FRIER, university official; b. Houston, Mar. 29, 1944; d. Robert Henry and Ina Loyce (Riley) Frier; B.B.A., Southwestern U., 1966; postgrad. N.C. State U., 1968, U. N.C., Chapel Hill, 1980; m. Robert F. Hill, Jr., June 7, 1978; 1 son, James Burton. Tchr., Franklin (Tex.) High Sch., 1966-67; sec. N.C. Bd. Higher Edn., Raleigh, 1967-68, statis. analyst, 1968-73; social research asst. gen. adminstrn. U. N.C. System, Chapel Hill, 1973-77, social research asso., 1977-78, dir. data collection and reporting, 1979—; cons. to instnl. researchers on coll. campuses; N.C. Higher Edn. Gen. Info. Survey coordinator Nat. Center Edn. Stats., Dept. Edn. Active Nat. Found. Ileitis and Colitis, Nat. Arbor Found. Mem. N.C. State Employees Assn., N.C. Assn. Instl. Research (exec. com. 1978—), So. Assn. Instl. Research. Author: Statistical Abstract of Higher Education in North Carolina, 1967—; Higher Educational Opportunities in North Carolina, 1967—. Office: U NC-Gen Adminstrn PO Box 2688 Chapel Hill NC 27514

BALGROSKY, JEAN ANN, healthcare information systems executive, consultant; b. Berwyn, Ill., Oct. 17, 1952; d. Steven A. and Evelyn Margaret (Cook) B.; m. Parker Hinshaw, June 22, 1985; children—Melissa, Jessica, Sarah, Seth. B.S. magna cum laude, UCLA, 1974, M.P.H., 1980, Ph.D., 1986. Registered med. records adminstr. Research/teaching asst. UCLA Sch. Pub. Health, 1974, 79, 80, 81; adminstrv. analyst Harrington Meml. Hosp., Bremerton, Wash., 1974-75; USPHS Dept. HHS health profls. trainee, 1978-83; office mgr. UCLA Child Care Ctr., 1978-79; info. services mgr. UCLA Hosp. and Clinics, 1979-80; research assoc. Lutheran Hosp. Soc. of So. Calif., Los Angeles, 1980-81; sr. cons. Peat Marwick Mitchell & Co., Los Angeles, 1982-83; dir. info. mgmt. Community Hosp. Indpls., Inc., 1983-86; v.p. info. resources Holy Cross Health System, South Bend, Ind., 1986—; cons. in field; bd. dirs. Health Info. Systems Sharing Group, 1983-85. Contbr. to profl. publs.; author info. systems evaluation methodologies. Mem. parent adv. com. UCLA Child Care Ctr., 1979-80. Ray Goodman scholar UCLA, 1978-83. Fellow Am. Pub. Health Assn.; mem. Am. Med. Records Assn., Calif. Med. Records Assn., Nat. Assn. Grad. Women, Nat. Assn. Female Execs., NOW. Democrat. Home: 16099 Baywood Ln Granger IN Office: Holy Cross Health System Corp Office 3606 E Jefferson Blvd South Bend IN 46615

BALICK, HELEN SHAFFER, bankruptcy judge; b. Bloomsburg, Pa.; d. Walter W. and Clarissa K. (Bennett) Shaffer; J.D., Dickinson Sch. Law, 1966; m. Bernard Balick, June 29, 1967; Admitted to Pa. bar, 1967, Del. bar, 1969; probate adminstr. Girard Trust Bank, Phila., 1966-68; pvt. practice law, Wilmington, Del., 1969-74; staff atty. Legal Aid Soc. Del., Wilmington, 1969-71; master Family Ct. Del., New Castle County, 1971-74; U.S. bankruptcy judge Dist. of Del., 1974—; U.S. magistrate, Wilmington, 1974-80; guest lectr. Dickinson Sch. Law, 1981-84; lectr. Dickinson Forum, 1982. Pres. bd. trustees Community Legal Aid Soc., Inc., 1972-74; trustee Dickinson Sch. Law; mem. Citizens Adv. Com. Wilmington, 1973-74, Wilmington Bd. Edn., 1974. Mem. ABA, Del. Bar Assn., Fed. Bar Assn., Nat. Conf. Bankruptcy Judges (gov.), Nat. Assn. Women Lawyers, Nat. Conf. Spl. Ct. Judges, Del. Alliance Profl. Women (Trailblazer award 1984), Nat. Lawyers Club, Nat. Assn. Women Judges, Wilmington Women in Bus. (bd.), Dickinson Sch. Law Gen. Alumni Assn. (exec. bd. 1977-80, v.p. 1981-84, pres. 1984—), Phi Alpha Delta. Office: US Courthouse 844 King St 6th Floor Wilmington DE 19801

BALICK, LILLIAN ROSEN, music educator, pianist, arts administrator; b. Phila.; d. Joseph and Ida (Rabinowitz) Rosen; m. Jacob Balick; children—Stephanie, Jennifer, Michael, Robert, David, Andrea. B.S. in Edn., Temple U., 1948; M. Music, West Chester State U., 1978. Social worker Pa. Dept. Pub. Welfare, Phila., 1948-49; tchr. music Bd. Edn., Phila., 1949-52, tchr. music, orch. condr. Cheltenham Twp., Elkins Park, Pa., 1955-56; instr. Coll. Music, Temple U., Phila., 1956-58; arts specialist Del. State Arts Council, Wilmington, 1981—; organizer, chmn. Jewish Community Ctr. Music Com., Wilmington, 1968-73, founder, dir. Contest for Young Musicians, 1972—; organizer, coordinator Grand Opera House Young Artists' Program, Wilmington, 1974; lectr. Del. Humanities Forum, Wilmington, 1978—; founder, pres., artistic dir. Community Showcase Performances, Inc., Wilmington, 1979—; mem. citizens grant rev. panel Del. State Arts Council, Wilmington, 1979-80; talent coordinator Rollins Cablevision, Wilmington, 1980-82; bd. dirs. Del. Chamber Orch., Wilmington, 1980-83, Wilmington Ballet Co., 1981—. Author: The Delaware Symphony, 1984; Reflections on Music, 1985. Recipient Harry Cohen leadership award, 1979, numerous others; Pa Bd. Edn. music scholar, 1944. Mem. Music Tchr. Nat. Conf., Music Tchrs. Nat. Assn., Del. State Music Tchrs. Assn., Astron, Kappa Delta Epsilon, Pi Mu, Pi Kappa Lambda. Democrat. Jewish. Home: 15 Clermont Rd Wilmington DE 19803

BALINKY, JEAN LAHN, psychologist; b. N.Y.C., Jan. 3, 1933; d. Jackson A. and Amelia (Meyers) L.; m. Alexander S. Balinky, Mar. 29, 1951. B.A., Douglass Coll., 1953; M.A., Boston U., 1955; Ed.D., Rutgers U., 1964. Tchr., East Brunswick Schs., N.J., 1953-54, 55-56; sch. psychologist Bridgewater-Raritan Schs., N.J., 1956-79; vis. prof. sch. psychology GSAPP-Rutgers U., Piscataway, N.J., 1978—; cons. King's Daus. Day Sch., Plainfield, N.J., 1979—, Paradise Sch. for Boys, Abbottstown, Pa., 1980—. Mem. Am. Psychol. Assn., N.J. Psychol. Assn. (pres. 1981), N.J. Assn. Sch. Psychologists (pres. 1970-71), N.J. Acad. Psychology (trustee), N.J. Psychol. Trust (trustee). Club: Explorers. Avocations: wildlife photography; philately. Home: Box 777 RR 1 Martinsville NJ 08836 Office: GSAPP Rutgers U PO Box 819 Piscataway NJ 08854

BALL, ANNE H., writer, editor, public relations consultant; b. Dayton, Ohio, June 7, 1939; d. James Leonard and Frieda Engelke Hitch; B.A., Ohio State U., 1961; m. Alan Odendahl, July 21, 1968 (div. May 8, 1985); children—Laura Jean, Cynthia Leonard; m. Robert L. Ball, June 30, 1985. Reporter, Dayton Jour. Herald, 1961-63, Balt. Sunpapers, 1964-66; pub. relations dir. Md. Inst. Coll. Art, 1966, Balt. Mental Health Assn., 1967-68; account exec. Compton Jones Advt., Washington, 1969-71; free lance writer, pub. relations cons., Washington, 1971—; dir. news bur. Cath. U. Am., Washington, 1976-78; co-owner Ad/Ventures, 1986—. Mem. Zeta Tau Alpha. Democrat. Unitarian. Home: 14828 Fireside Dr Silver Spring MD 20904

BALL, HELEN MARIE, communications consultant; b. San Antonio, Dec. 10, 1938; d. George Fred and Helen (Smith) Franz; student public schs.; m. Davis Frederick Ball, Jan. 13, 1972; children—Scott Wade, Elizabeth Ann. Sec., 1959-66; tech. editor computer field Randolph AFB, Tex., 1966-71, advt. copywriter recruiting, 1971-75, EEO officer, 1975-80, personnel mgmt. specialist, 1980-82, also fed. women's program mgr., affirmative action officer, civilian personnel evaluation officer, speech writer for comdr. Air Tng. Command; tng. cons., 1979—; owner Ball Diversified, San Antonio; mem., 1st vice chmn. Randolph-Brooks Credit Union; presenter seminars on personal/prof. growth; mem. task force on human relations tng. Dept. Def. Recipient various govt. performance awards; named Employee of Yr. in Mgmt., Randolph AFB, Outstanding Woman of Yr. in Sr. Mgmt. Author publs. in field. Home: 2330 Nashwood Dr San Antonio TX 78232 Office: ATC/PA Randolph AFB TX 78150

BALL, JACQUELINE AUSANKA, publishing company executive; b. New Britain, Conn., May 1, 1945; d. Joseph John and Helen (Meizlaiskis) Ausanka; m. John Bakewell Ball, Sept. 13, 1969; 1 dau., Ashley Evans. B.A., Coll. New Rochelle, 1967. Editorial researcher Look Mag., N.Y.C., 1967-69; tchr. Glenrock Sch., Carbondale, Colo., 1969-70; writer, editor Field Publs., Middletown, Conn., 1970-77, new products mgr., 1977-80, mng. editor weekly reader paperback clubs, 1980-82, exec. editor weekly reader children's hardcover clubs, 1982—, mem. Speakers' Bur., 1975—. Contbr. articles to to various Xerox ednl. productlines; editor children's mystery series Grosset & Dunlap, 1978. Mem., Chester (Conn.) Conservation Commn., 1979-82; sec. Chester Bd. Edn., 1983—. Mem. Soc. Children's Book Writers, Nat. Women's Book Assn., Am. Mktg. Assn., Direct Mktg. Assn. Democrat. Home: 64 Cedar Lake Rd Chester CT 06412 Office: Field Publs 245 Long Hill Rd Middletown CT 06457

BALL, JOYCE, librarian; b. N.J., Oct. 31, 1932; d. Frank Geza and Elizabeth Martha (Hopper) Csaposs; m. Robert S. Ball, Sept. 10, 1955; children—Stephanie, Valerie, Steven Robert; m. Stefan B. Moses, Mar. 30, 1980. A.B., Douglass Coll., Rutgers U., 1954; M.A., Ind. U., 1959; M.B.A., Golden Gate U., San Francisco, 1979. Fgn. documents librarian Stanford U., 1955-66; head documents librarian, then head reference div. U. Nev., Reno, 1966-75, head public services, 1975-80; univ. librarian Calif. State U., Sacramento, 1980—; mem. Nev. Gov's Adv. Council on Libraries, 1974-78; mem. panel judges Am. Book Awards, 1980. Editorial bd.: Coll. and Research Libraries, 1975-80; editorial adv. bd. Am. Library Assn. Yearbook, 1985—. Contbr. articles to profl. jours. Mem. Assn. Coll. and Research Libraries (dir. 1978-84, pres. 1983-84), ALA, Calif. Library Assn., Nev. Library Assn. Democrat. Home: 8545 Folsom Blvd 102 Sacramento CA 95826 Office: 2000 Jed Smith Dr Sacramento CA 95819

BALL, JULIE A., mortgage brokerage executive; b. Los Angeles, Dec. 18, 1957; d. Claude Ernest and Jean Alma (Vose) B.; m. Robert Alan Shimp, Mar. 19, 1983; 1 child, Robert Ryan. Clk. T&H, Inc., Canoga Park, Calif., 1976-79; teletypist Deluxe Check, Chatsworth, Calif., 1979-82; loan processor Valley Wide Funding, Granada Hills, Calif., 1982; pres. The Mortgage Connection, Northridge, Calif., 1983—. Mem. Nat. Notorial Assn., Northridge C. of C., Better Bus. Bur. Avocation: bowling. Home: 18758 Lull St Reseda CA 91335 Office: The Mortgage Connection 8949 Reseda Blvd Northridge CA 91324

BALL, KAY EVANS, mental health administrator; b. Columbus, Ohio, Nov. 30, 1952; d. T. Quentin and Helen (Brubaker) Evans; m. David Keith Ball, May 12, 1983; children—Jason Keith. B.S., Manchester Coll., 1975; M.S.W., Western Mich. U., 1979. Social worker Warsaw Community Schs., Ind., 1975-77; exec. dir. Oaklawn Found., Elkhart, Ind., 1979—; mgr. public info. Oaklawn Ctr., Elkhart, 1979-81, dir. community services div., 1981—. Mem. Project Assist, YWCA, Elkhart, 1984—; bd. dirs. Planned Parenthood North Central Ind., 1980—. mem. Nat. Assn. Social Workers, Nat. Ctr. Health Edn. Democrat. Club: Zonta (chmn. scholarship 1985—). Office: Oaklawn Psychiat Ctr 2600 Oakland Ave Elkhart IN 46517

BALL, LINDA ANN, educator; b. Des Moines, Aug. 10, 1942; d. Vern Ray and Orletha Ann Carmichael; student Iowa State U., 1960-62; B.S. in Edn., Drake U., 1964; M.S. in Edn., Ill. State U., 1981; m. Robert Ray Ball, Aug. 15, 1964; children—Lindsay, Ryan, Justin. Tchr., Marshalltown, Iowa, 1964-68; TV tchr. Sta. WAND-TV, Decatur, Ill., 1969-71; tchr. Des Moines Public Schs., 1973-79; adv. Ill. State U. Panhellenic, Normal, 1979-80; tchr. Metcalf Lab. Sch., Ill. State U., Normal, 1980—; presenter workshops and confs. Past mem. Jr. Women's Club, Assn. Advocacy and Edn. Disabled Citizens, Mid-Central Planning Commn. for Handicapped, Friends of the Arts; past pres. JayceeEttes, Campfire Girls Council; bd. dirs. United Cerebral Palsy. Cert. reading specialist, early childhood tchr. Mem. Ill. Reading Council, Early Childhood Edn. Assn., Ill. Edn. Assn., Ill. Assn. Supervision and Curriculum Devel., Delta Zeta (collegiate province dir.), Delta Kappa Gamma. Democrat. Home: 208 Robert Dr Normal IL 61761 Office: Metcalf Lab Sch Ill State U Normal IL 61761

BALL, LINDA JEAN, personnel executive; b. Rochester, N.Y., Nov. 7, 1948; d. Henry A. and Geraldine I. T. (Cole) Davis; m. Joseph H. Ball, Aug. 13, 1972; 1 son, Darren Ian. B.S. in Bus. Adminstrn., Calif. State U., Northridge, 1970; M.B.A., National U., 1982. Personnel adminstr. ARA Transp., Encino, Calif., 1970-78; benefits/compensation adminstr. Everest & Jennings, Los Angeles, 1978; sr. wage and salary analyst Cubic Corp., San Diego, 1978-82, mgr. wage and salary adminstrn., 1982-83, dir. compensation and benefits, 1983—. Mem. Compensation Practices Assn., Internat. Assn. Personnel Women (founder, past pres. San Diego), Personnel Mgmt. Assn., Career Women's Assn., Health Systems Agy. (dir.). Democrat. Home: 2921 Denver St San Diego CA 92117 Office: 9333 Balboa Ave San Diego CA 92123

BALL, MARGARET ANN, insurance company executive; b. Lorimor, Iowa, Feb. 23, 1938; d. Edmund Carl and Lola Mary (Edwards) Porter; student Drake U., 1963-70; m. Gary Ernest Ball, June 29, 1954; children—Monte, Marla, Mark. Rater, Farm Bur. Mut., Des Moines, 1957-60; rater Gt. Am. Ins. Co., Des Moines, 1963-66; underwriter The Atlantic Cos., Des Moines, 1966-71; asst. sec. Multiple Line Underwriters, Des Moines, 1971-80; asst. v.p. Employers Mut. Cos., Des Moines, from 1980, now v.p.; mem. faculty Drake U., 1973-78, Simpson Coll., 1974-75. C.P.C.U. Republican. Mem. Christian Ch. (Disciples of Christ). Mem. Order Eastern Star. Home: 579 Lake Panorama Panora IA 50216 Office: 717 Mulberry St Des Moines IA 50309

BALL, MARGENE GLENN, personnel specialist, government official; b. Flagstaff, Ariz., Apr. 11, 1936; d. Eugene Myrwill and Marjorie Susan (Longaker) Conrad; m. Emory W. Ball, Jr., Oct. 9, 1954; 1 dau., Robin Renee. A.A. in Bus., Coll. of Desert, 1978; B.A. in Mgmt., Redlands U., 1980; M.B.A., Nat. U., 1986. Payroll supr. Marine Corps Combat Ctr., Twenty Nine Palms, Calif., 1968-78, dep. EEO officer, 1978-81, labor relations tng. officer, 1981-83, tng. officer/dep. EEO officer, 1983—, co-owner, mgr. B & G Distbrs., 1983—. Recipient numerous awards for work performance Marine Corps Combat Ctr., 1968, 70, 74, 81. Mem. Federally Employed Women, NOW, Fed. Mgrs. Assn. (local pres. 1980-81). Democrat. Avocations: public speaking; travel; sewing. Home: HCO-1 Box 909 Twenty Nine Palms CA 92277 Office: Marine Corps Air Ground Combat Ctr Civilian Personnel Office Twenty Nine Palms CA 92278

BALL, OTEKA ANN LITTLE, educator, author; b. Madill, Okla., Feb. 2, 1939; d. Reuel Winfred and Oteka Delores (Wilson) Little; student Okla. U., 1957-59; B.S., So. Methodist U., 1962; postgrad. Rice U., 1962; M.S., Okla. State U., 1976; m. M. Gerald Ball, Sept. 5, 1959; children—Jeremy D., Oteka Lyn. Prin., broker Oteka Ball Real Estate Firm, Shawnee, Okla., 1970-76; instr. Seminole Jr. Coll., 1976-78; asst. prof. home econs. and edn., head home econs. Okla. Baptist U., 1978—; partner Land Oil Co., 1980—. Bd. dirs. Jack Little Found., Madill, 1970—; v.p. bd. dirs. Child's World, Shawnee, 1973-76; bd. dirs. YMCA, Shawnee, Okla., 1978—; mem. Hockaway Alumni Bd., Dallas, 1980-82; mem. Okla. Gov.'s Com. on Children and Youth, 1976-80. Mem. AAUP, Am. Home Econs. Assn., Assn. Couples for Marriage Enrichment, Nat. Council Adminstrs. Home Economists, PEO, Omicron Nu, Phi Kappa Phi. Democrat. Methodist. Home: 1320 N Broadway Shawnee OK 74801 Office: 500 W University Shawnee OK 74801

BALL, PATRICIA ANN, physician; b. Lockport, N.Y., Mar. 30, 1941; d. John Joseph and Katherine Elizabeth (Hoffmaster) B.; m. Robert E. Lee, May 18, 1973; children—Heather, Samantha. B.S., U. Mich., 1963; M.D., Wayne State U., 1969. Diplomate Am. Bd. Internal Medicine, Am. Bd. Hematology, Am. Bd. Med. Oncology. Intern, resident Detroit Gen. Hosp., 1969-71; resident Jackson Meml. Hosp., Miami, Fla., 1971-72; fellow Henry Ford Hosp., Detroit, 1972-74; staff physician VA Hosp., Allen Park, Mich., 1974-77; practice medicine specializing in hematology and oncology, Bloomfield Hills, Mich., 1977—; mem. faculty dept. medicine Wayne State U. Sch. Medicine, Detroit, 1974—. Mem. Founders Soc., Detroit Inst. Arts. Mem. ACP, AMA, Mich. State Med. Soc., Oakland County Med. Soc., Alpha Omega Alpha. Avocations: photography; skiing. Office: 2515 Woodward Suite 290 Bloomfield Hills MI 48013

BALLANCE, SHARON MARIE, nurse; b. Aurora, Ill., Feb. 2, 1942; d. Arthur E. and Virginia M. Kuhn; A.S. in Nursing, Long Beach (Calif.) City Coll., 1977; B.S. in Nursing, Calif. State U.-Long Beach, 1980, M.S. in Nursing, 1982; m. Roderic O. Ballance, Feb. 11, 1961; children—Kelly Michelle, Britton Lewis, Ryan Kortney. Mem. nursing staff St. Mary's Hosp., Long Beach, 1975-78, pulmonary rehab. clinician, 1978-81, home health clinician, 1981-83; dir. home health dept. Alamitos Belmont Hosp., Long Beach, 1983—, asst. adminstr., 1985—. Mem. Long Beach Lung Assn. (women's council, mem. med. adv., fund-raising, edn. coms., pres. 1984), Am. Nurses Assn., Nat. Rehab. Assn., Long Beach C. of C., Long Beach City Coll. Alumni Assn. (sec.), Calif. State U. at Long Beach Alumni Assn. (dir. 1981-82), Internat. Hostesses. Republican. Roman Catholic. Clubs: Alamitos Bay Garden; Long Beach Yacht; Internat. City. Home: 42 64th Pl Long Beach CA 90803 Office: Alamitos Belmont Hosp 3901 E 4th St Long Beach CA 90814

BALLANFANT, KATHLEEN GAMBER, newspaper executive, public relations company executive; b. Horton, Kans., July 11, 1945; d. Ralph Hayes and Audrey Lavon (Heryford) G.; m. Burt Ballanfant; children—Andrea, Benjamin. B.A., Trinity U., 1967; postgrad. NYU, 1976, Am. Mgmt. Inst., 1977, Belhaven Coll., 1985. Pub. info. dir. Tex. Dept. Community Affairs, Austin, 1972-74; pub. affairs mgr. Cameron Iron Works, Houston, 1975-77, Assoc. Builders and Contractors, Houston, 1982-84; pres. Ballanfant & Assoc.,

Houston, 1977-82, 84—; pres. Village Life Inc., 1985—; owner Village Life newspaper; mem. adv. council on Construction Edn., Tex. So. U., Houston, 1984—; mem. task force on ednl. excellence Houston Ind. Sch. Dist., 1983—; chmn. prevailing wage com. Houston C. of C., 1983-84. Author: Something Special-You, 1972; Prevailing Wage History in Houston, 1983. Editor newspaper Bellaire Texan, 1981-82, Austin Times, 1971. Vice pres. West Univ. Republic Women's Club, Houston, 1984—; fgn. vis. chmn. Internat. Inst. Edn., Houston, 1980—; mem. pub. affairs task force U.S. C. of C., 1984; docent Houston Zoo, 1982. Recipient Apollo IX Medal of Honor Gov. Preston Smith, 1970, Child Abuse Prevention award Gov. Dolph Briscoe, 1974. Republican. Presbyterian. Avocations: travel, racquetball, reading. Office: Ballanfant & Assoc 2514 Tangley Houston TX 77005

BALLANTINE, MORLEY COWLES, newspaper executive; b. Des Moines, May 21, 1925; d. John and Elizabeth (Bates) Cowles; student Smith Coll., 1943-44, Stanford U., 1944-45, U. Minn., 1948-49; B.A., Ft. Lewis Coll., Colo., 1975; Litt.D., Simpson Coll., Indianola, Iowa, 1980; m. Arthur Ballantine, July 26, 1947 (dec. Nov. 1975); children—Richard, Elizabeth, William, Helen. chmn. bd., editor Durango (Colo.) Herald, 1983—; dir. 1st Nat. Bank Durango. Mem. Colo. Anti-Discrimination Commn., 1959-61, Colo. Com. on Ednl. Endeavor, 1959-63; mem. Colo. bd. LWV, 1954-57, mem. Durango bd., 1953-59; mem. Jud. Dist. Selection Com., 1967-72; pres. S.W. Colo. Mental Health Center, 1964-65; mem. State Welfare Adv. Com., 1967-71, Colo. Population Adv. Council, 1972-75; mem. Colo. Commn. Status Women, 1972-75, Colo. Land Use Commn., 1975-81; trustee Choate/Rosemary Hall, 1973-81, Fountain Valley Sch., Colorado Springs, 1976—, Simpson Coll., Indianola, Iowa, 1981—, U. Denver, 1984; pres. Four Corners Opera Assn., 1983—; mem. Colo. Supreme Ct. Nominating Commn., 1983—. Recipient 1st place award for editorial writing Nat. Fedn. Press Women, 1955, (with husband) Outstanding Journalist award U. Colo., 1967, Outstanding Alumna award Rosemary Hall, Wallingford, Conn., 1969, (with husband) Disting. Service award Ft. Lewis Coll., 1970. Mem. Colo. Press Assn. (dir. 1979-80). Clubs: Federated Woman's (Durango); Mill Reef (Antigua, W.I.); Colo. Press. Episcopalian. Home: 175 W Park Ave Durango CO 81301 Office: care Herald Drawer A Durango CO 81302

BALLARD, ALICE WALKER, lawyer; b. Phila., May 15, 1948; d. Frederic Lyman and Ernesta (Drinker) B.; m. Joshua Jan Mittledorf, July 5, 1981; 1 child, Sarah May. B.A., in Physics, Harvard U., 1970, J.D., 1973. Bar: Maine 1973, Pa. 1975. Staff atty. Pine Tree Legal Assistance, Bangor, Maine, 1973-74, Pub. Interest Law Ctr. Phila., 1974-76; ptnr. Samuel & Ballard, Phila., 1976—; lectr. U. Pa., Law Sch., 1979-80; adj. prof. Villanova Law Sch., 1985—. Bd. dirs. Profls. for Nuclear Arms Control, Phila., 1984—, HERS Found., 1985—, Temple U. Hosp., 1985—; mem. adv. bd. Lawyers Alliance Nuclear Arms Control, 1983—; mem. com. 24th Ward Democratic Exec. Com., 1977-81; bd. dirs. Community Edn. Ctr., 1980-81. Mem. ABA, Am. Law Inst. Democrat. Office: Samuel & Ballard 1500 Walnut St Suite 920 Philadelphia PA 19102

BALLARD, ANN MERIWETHER, accountant; b. Montgomery, Ala., Aug. 2, 1958; d. Carl Edward and Hilda (Wallace) Meriwether; m. Willie Lee Ballard, Jr., July 1, 1978. B.S. in Acctg., U. Ala., 1979. C.P.A., Tex. Acct., Tenneco Oil Co., Houston, 1979-82, Enstar Petroleum, Houston, 1982—; owner Body Expressions exercise salon, Houston, 1983—. Mem. Am. Inst. C.P.A.s, Tex. Soc. C.P.A.s, Houston Soc. C.P.A.s, Nat. Assn. for Female Execs. Republican. Baptist. Home: 19510 Coppervine Ln Houston TX 77084 Office: Capital Bank Plaza 333 Clay St Suite 3800 Houston TX 77002

BALLARD, BETTY RUTH WESLEY, x-ray equipment co. exec.; b. Birmingham, Ala., Nov. 11, 1924; d. Henry Gaston and Ruth Lorine (Whitfield) Wesley; degree Glenn Tech. Inst., 1942-46; m. Douglas Hayden Ballard, Oct. 24, 1941; 1 son, Douglas Hayden. Mgr., Nbc Restaurant, 1960-68; corp. sec. X-Ray Service and Sales, Inc., 1960-68; pres. Ballard X-Ray Co., Birmingham, Ala., 1968—. Exec. com. Democratic Party; election law commr. State of Ala.; hon. dep. sheriff Shelby County, Ala.; mem. adminstrv. bd. 1st United Methodist Ch., Montevallo, Ala. Mem. Ala. Soc. Radiol. Technologists, Ala. Hosp. Assn., Inst. Hosp. Auxilians, Ala. Cattlemen's Assn., LWV, 20th Spl. Forces Group Aux. Methodist (adminstrv. bd., trustee ch.). Clubs: Downtown (Birmingham); The Club Inc. Home: Flying-X-Ranch Route 1 Box 29 Montevallo AL 35115 Office: 2701 4th Ave S Birmingham AL 35233

BALLARD, DOROTHY MAE, labor union representative, consultant; b. Kansas City, Mo., Dec. 8, 1916; d. Frank and Eva (Powell) Cann; widowed; 12 children. Ed. in Labor Edn., Norman Coll. Machinist, N. Am. Aviation, 1942-46; assemblyline worker Gen. Motors Co., Kansas City, Mo., 1953-55, instr, in electronics; labor rep. local 31 United Auto Workers, Kansas City; now cons.; lectr. in labor edn. and prison reform, 1974-85; organizer seminars, Operation PUSH convs., Kansas City, also workshops for women; leader petition drives for women's rights and labor reform. Mem. Black Awareness Program, Lansing, Mo.; co-founder, pres. Greater Kansas City Minority Women's Coalition for Human Rights; pres. Met. United Citizens for Prison Reform and Assistance; adv. bd. Mid-Am. Regional Council, Jackson County Jail Com., Council on Crimes and Delinquency, Creative Enterprises, New Directions Ctr., Mo. Probation and Parole Bd., Salvation Army Task Force, Job Partnership Tng. Programs; past bd. dirs. Ann Skinner Women's Fellowship, Am. Bapt. Ch.; affirmative action chmn. Greater Kansas City Women's Polit. Caucus; mem. platform com. Mo. Democratic Party, 1978-80. Recipient numerous community service awards including Women's award U.S. Sec. Labor, Woman of Yr. award United Auto Workers, Jefferson award. Mem. Nat. Assn. Colored Women, Negro Bus. and Profl. Women (Woman of Yr. Central chpt. 1979), Coalition Labor Union Women (chpt. pres. 1975-82, task force leader 1985-86, nat. exec. bd., chmn. women's history week 1985), Assn. Blacks in Criminal Justice, NAACP, Nat. Alliance Bus. (task force), Mo. Leadership Assn., Urban League of Greater Kansas City. Address: 13517 Lowell St Grandview MO 64030

BALLARD, MARY MELINDA, financial communications, public relations firm executive; b. Sikeston, Mo., Apr. 21, 1951; d. Claude M. and Mary (Birnbach) B. B.A., NYU, 1976, M.B.A., 1977; postgrad., Columbia U., 1979. Vice pres. corp. communications United Brands Co., N.Y.C., 1970-80; pres., chief exec. officer Ficom Internat., Inc., N.Y.C., 1980—; cons. Nat. Assn. Christians and Jews, Newark, 1985—; dir. Sea Bright Corp., N.J. Aura Enterprises, Chgo.; dir., chief exec. officer Ficom Internat., 1980—. Contbr. articles to profl. jours. Cons. State of Israel Free Trade area, Tel-Aviv, 1984—. Mem. Internat. Assn. Bus. Communicators (Golden Quill 1984), Pub. Relations Soc. Am., N.Y. C. of C., Israel-Am. C. of C., Urban Land Inst., Nat. Investor Relations Inst. Roman Catholic. Club: Publicity. Avocations: collecting oriental art; thoroughbred race horses. Home: 40 E 9th St 6F New York NY 10003 Office: Ficom Internat Inc 237 Park Ave New York NY 10017

BALLENTINE, KATIE HALL, registered dietitian, real estate company executive, color analysis and cosmetic consultant; b. Oriental, N.C., Oct. 20, 1934; d. Fred and Mima M. (Moseley) Hall; m. Louis Robert Ballentine, Nov. 12, 1961; children—Louis R., Shawn Tearle. B.S. in Instl. Mgmt. and Nutrition, Shaw U., 1956. Registered dietitian. Staff dietitian Bellevue Hosp. Ctr., N.Y.C., 1959-62; head therapeutic dept. Maimonides Hosp., Bklyn., 1962-64; asst. mng. dietitian Hosp. Food Mgmt. div. Automatic Retailers Am., Inc., Lutheran Med. Ctr., Bklyn., 1964-66; chief dietitian Community Hosp. Bklyn., 1966-69; chief therapeutic dietitian St. Clair's Hosp., N.Y.C., 1969-72; head dietitian French adn Poly. Hosp. and Med. Ctr., N.Y.C., 1972-77; dir. food service Haven Manor Health Related Facility, Far Rockaway, N.Y., 1977-78; dir. food services and nutrition Prospect Park Nursing Home, Bklyn., 1980—; v.p. Robert Tearle Realty, Hollis, N.Y. Sec. The Hollis Concern Concern Citizen, Inc., Hollis, N.Y., 1984; mem. Guy Brewer Democratic Club, St. Albans, N.Y., 1979—. Congregationalist. Avocations: tennis; oil painting; ceramics; sewing; collector bears.

BALLINGER, BETH ELLEN, optometrist; b. Jersey City, July 25, 1951; d. Morton William and Rita Ballinger; m. Steven L. Cohn, Aug. 24, 1978. B.S. cum laude, Fairleigh Dickinson U., 1969; B. Visual Sci., Pa. Coll. Optometry, 1977, O.D., 1979. Pvt. practice optometry, Newport Beach, Calif., 1981—; visual cons. pub. and pvt. schs., Orange County, Calif., So. Calif. Recipient Speaker's award for excellence in communication to community. Fellow Coll. Optometrists in Vision Devel. (chmn. assistance to undergrads. com.); mem. Am. Optometric Assn., Calif. Optometric Assn. (best bull. in Calif. award, agy. relations com.), Orange County Optometric Assn. (trustee), Better Vision Inst., Assn. Children with Learning Disabilities, Calif. Reading Assn., Optometric Editors Assn., So. Orange County Optometric Council, AAUP; Clubs: Soroptimists, Charter 100. Author tech. papers for optometric continuing edn.; editor: Perceptions. Office: 833 Dover Dr Suite 9 Newport Beach CA 92660

BALLMAN, PATRICIA KLING, lawyer; b. Cin., May 1, 1946; d. John Joseph and Margaret Elizabeth (Stacy) Kling; children—Andrew J., Cara E. B.S. with honors, St. Louis U., 1967; J.D., Marquette U., 1977. Computer programmer, systems analyst Gen. Electric Co., Cin., 1967-70; lectr. computer scis. Marquette U., Milw., 1971; law clk., Milw., 1975, 76; ptnr. Quarles & Brady, Milw., 1977—. Vol., St. Francis Meal Program, Milw., 1983—. Mem. Assn. Trial Lawyers Am., ABA, Wis. Acad. Trial Lawyers, Wis. Bar Assn., Milw. Bar Assn. (courts com., legis. com., ct. of appeal bench/bar com.), Milw. Young Lawyers Assn. (chmn. courts com.), NOW. Roman Catholic. Office: Quarles & Brady 411 E Wisconsin Ave Milwaukee WI 53202

BALLONOFF, MARILYN SILVERMAN, real estate broker, psychologist, b. N.Y.C., Nov. 17, 1940; d. Albert and Mina (Sobel) Silverman; m. Aaron Ballonoff, Aug. 21, 1960 (div. May 1972); 1 child, Selene. B.S., Cornell U., 1963; postgrad. U. Calif.-Berkeley, 1963-65; M.A. in Sci. Teaching, San Jose State Coll., 1970; M.A. in Counseling Psychology, U. Santa Clara, 1975. High sch. tchr. biology/math., Los Altos, Palo Alto, Calif., 1970-74; sci. textbook editor Addison Wesley Pub. Co., Menlo Park, Calif., 1975-76; instr. psychology Community Coll., Los Altos, Saratoga, San Jose, Calif., 1971-79; counselor O'Connor Hosp., San Jose, 1977-78; v.p., co-founder Biometrics, San Jose, 1978; real estate broker, owner, founder Home Estates Realty, Los Altos, 1979—; cons., writer/editor Alan Lakein & Co., San Francisco, 1976-78; seminar leader, workshop dir. Assn. Humanistic Psychology, Unitarian Ch., San Francisco Jewish Community Ctr., Trellis, Treasure, 1974-82. Author: How to Catch a Man and Keep Him, 1976. Realtor, Open Space Dist., acquisition of Incerpi Ranch, Skyline Blvd., Palo Alto, Calif., Los Altos, Calif., 1983. NSF fellow U. Calif., Berkeley, 1963-65; recipient Best Real Estate Advertisement award Los Altos Bd. Realtors, 1982. Mem. Assn. Humanistic Psychology (pres. San Francisco 1977-78, program dir. 1977-78), Nat. Assn. Sci. Tchrs., Nat. Assn. Realtors, Calif. Assn. Realtors, Phi Kappa Phi. Club: Sierra. Home: 2055 Kent Dr Los Altos CA 94022

BALLSUN, KATHRYN ANN, lawyer; b. May 8, 1946; d. Zan and Doris B.; m. Paul L. Stanton, June 1, 1981; 1 child, Brian Paul Ballsun-Stanton. A.B. cum laude in English, U. So. Calif., 1968, M.A. in Edn., 1970; J.D., Loyola U.-Los Angeles, 1976. Bar: Calif. 1976, U.S. Dist. Ct. (central dist.) 1977; cert. secondary tchr., Calif. Ptnr., Stanton and Ballsun, Los Angeles, instr. Calif. Continuing Edn. of Bar, 1981-83; vis. prof. clin. program UCLA Law Sch., 1981-82, 84, Loyola U. Sch. Law, 1982; adj. prof. paralegal program U. So. Calif. Law Sch., 1983; lectr. various orgns. and cons. Editor: How to Live—And Die— With California Probate; Loyola U. Law Rev., 1975-76. Sec. polit. action com. Women in Bus.; advisor Am. Cancer Soc. Program; co-chmn. class of 1976 Greater Loyola Law Sch. Devel. Program, 1983; bd. dirs. com. profl. women Los Angeles Philharmonic Orch.; bd. dirs. Planned Protective Services, Inc. Mem. Beverly Hills Bar Assn. (sec. probate, trust and estate planning com. 1979-80, vice-chmn. 1980-81, chmn. 1981-82, founder, chmn. legis. subcom. 1980-82, bd. govs. 1982-84, chmn. 1984-86, vice chmn. resolutions com. 1982-83, sr. vice chmn. 1983-84, chmn. 1984-85, del. Conf. Dels.-Calif. State Bar Conv. 1981-84, whip, 1982), Los Angeles County Bar Assn. (trust and probate sec. exec. com. 1980-83, resolutions sub.-com. 1982, taxation sect.), State Bar Calif. (estate planning, trust and probate sect. bus. law sect. taxation sect. estate planning techniques pre-death com., co-vice chmn. estate planning techniques post death com. 1982-84), ABA (real property, probate and trust law sect., taxation sect. pre-death planning com.), Estate Counselor's Forum (trustee 1984-85), Estate Planner's Workshop, Calif. Women Lawyers Assn., Los Angeles Women Lawyers Assn., ACLU, West Los Angeles C. of C., Kappa Alpha Theta (chmn. Theta connection program). Office: Stanton and Ballsun AVCO Ctr 6th Floor 10850 Wilshire Blvd Los Angeles CA 90024

BALOG, IBOLYA, controller; b. Subotica, Yugoslavia, July 11, 1953; came to U.S., 1969; d. Balint and Adela (Dohocki) B. B.A., Lehigh U., 1975; M.B.A., Temple U., 1980. Adminstrv. asst. Chain Bike Corp., Allentown, Pa., 1975-77; controller Bicycle Corp. Am., Allentown, 1982—. Bd. dirs. YWCA, Allentown, 1986—. Mem. AAUW (treas. 1984 85, Outstanding Woman 1985), Nat. Assn. Female Execs. Democrat. Avocations: movies; bike riding. Home: 1522 1/2 Chew St Allentown PA 18102 Office: Bicycle Corp Am 361 Gordon St Allentown PA 18102

BALSER, MARY JANE, association executive; b. Attleboro, Mass., Dec. 3, 1943; d. Alfred Douglas and Josephine (Bozzo) DeLutis; m. Jeremiah William Balser, Apr. 28, 1961; children—Jeremiah W., James Aaron. Student Mass. Gen. Hosp. Sch. Nursing, 1961-62, Fitchburg State Coll., 1967-69, Yale U., 1984—. Program dir. Kearney Ctr., Danbury, Conn., 1969-71; exec. dir. Danbury YMCA, 1971-79; pres. Norwalk YMCA, Conn., 1979—; dir. Fairfield County Savs. Bank. Sec. bd. trustees Norwalk YMCA, 1979—. Recipient Adminstrv. Excellence award Nat. YMCA, 1985; Nat. YMCA fellow; mem. Assn. Profl. Dirs. YMCA. Democrat. Roman Catholic. Home: 4 Benson Dr Danbury CT 06810 Office: Norwalk YMCA 370 West Ave Norwalk CT 06810

BALSHAW-BIDDLE, KATHERINE, freelance writer; b. Battle Creek, Mich., May 17, 1952; d. Robert Gordon and Ellen Lena (Roos) Balshaw; m. Kevin Thomas Biddle, Apr. 3, 1980; 1 child, Nicholas Roos Biddle. Student Kellogg Community Coll., 1970-72; B.S., Mich. State U., 1974, M.S., 1977; Ph.D., Rice U., 1981. Field engr. Alaskan Resource Scis. Corp., Fairbanks, 1975-76; research asst. Rice U., Houston, 1977-80; writer Houston Woman mag., 1986; freelance writer, 1984—; research geologist Exxon Prodn. Research Co., Houston, 1980-83, sr. research geologist, 1983-84; sedimentologist Leg 59 Deep Sea Drilling Project, Philippine Sea, 1978, U.S. Antarctic Program, Ross Sea, 1979, 80. Contbr. articles to profl. jours. Rice U. fellow, 1977-78; Petroleum Research Fund fellow, Houston, 1979. Assn.

BALSLEY, IROL WHITMORE (MRS. HOWARD L. BALSLEY), educator; b. Venus, Nebr., Aug. 22, 1912; d. Sylvanus Bertrand and Nanna (Carson) Whitmore; B.A., Nebr. State Tchrs. Coll., Wayne, 1933; M.S., U. Tenn., 1940; Ed.D., Ind. U., 1952; m. Howard Lloyd Balsley, Aug. 24, 1947. Tchr. high schs., Osmond and Walthill, Nebr., 1934-37, Van Sant Sch. Bus., Omaha, 1938; asst. prof. Ind. U., 1942-49; lectr. U. Utah, 1949-50, Russell Sage Coll., 1951-52; prof. office adminstrn. La. Tech. U., 1954-65, head dept., 1963-65; prof. bus. edn. and secretarial adminstrn. Tex. Tech U., Lubbock, 1965-72, prof. edn., chmn. bus. tchr. edn. program, 1972-75; prof. office adminstrn. and bus. edn. U. Ark., Little Rock, 1975-79, prof. emeritus, 1980—; adj. prof. office mgmt. Hardin-Simmons U., 1980-81; coordinator of USAF clk.-typist tng. program Pa. State, 1951, instr., head office tng. sect. TVA, 1941-42; editorial asst. South-Western Pub. Co., 1940-41. Mem. Nat. Bus. Edn. Assn. (past pres. Research Found.), Nat. Collegiate Assn. for Secs. (co-founder, past nat. pres., nat. exec. sec. 1976-81, nat. adv. com. 1981—), Adminstrv. Mgmt. Soc., Phi Delta Kappa, Pi Lambda Theta, Delta Pi Epsilon (past nat. sec.), Beta Gamma Sigma, Pi Omega Pi, Sigma Tau Delta, Alpha Psi Omega, Delta Kappa Gamma. Author: (with Wanous) Shorthand Transcription Studies, 1968; (with Robinson) Integrated Secretarial Studies, 1963; (with Wood and Whitmore) Homestyle Baking, 1973; Century 21 Shorthand, Theory and Practice, 1974; (with Hoskinson) Century 21 Shorthand, Intensive Dictation and Transcription, 1974; Self Paced Learning Activities, Vol. I, Century 21 Shorthand Collegiate Series, 1977; Dictation: The Corporate View, 1980. Address: 6501 15th Ave W Bradenton FL 33529

BALTER, FRANCES SUNSTEIN, civic worker; b. Pitts.; d. Elias and Gertrude (Kingsbacher) Sunstein; student Sarah Lawrence Coll., 1939-41, New Sch. Social Research, 1941-43, Bennington Coll., summers 1941, 42; cert. Harvard Inst. Arts Adminstrn., 1973; m. James Stone Balter May 15, 1948; children—Katherine (Mrs. Ross Anthony), Julia Frances, Constance (Mrs. Owen Cantor), Daniel Elias; m. 2d, Harry Philip Blum, Mar. 1, 1982. Adminstrv. asst., asso. producer Ednl. Television WQED-TV, Pitts., 1963-67; producer, mng. dir. Freedom Readers, 1964-67; a founder, incorporator, sec. bd. dirs. Pitts. Council for Arts, 1967-70; cultural cons. Mayor's Office, Dir. of Office of Cultural Affairs, Pitts., 1968; a founder Three Rivers Arts Festival 1960; co-dir. Ohio and Miss. River Valley Art Festival, 1961-62; mem. Pa. Council on Arts, 1972-78, mem. exec. com., 1975-78; co-founder Pioneer Crafts Council Mill Run Pa., 1972; exec. dir. POETRY ON THE BUSES, 1974—; mem. council for arts MIT. Recipient Woman of Year award in art Post Gazette, 1969. Mem. Asso. Councils on Arts, Nat. Soc. Arts and Letters. Home: 1021 Devonshire Rd Pittsburgh PA 15213

BALTHROP, CATHERINE, broadcast management firm financial executive; b. Nashville, Aug. 14, 1950; d. Dan H. and Myra L. (Wright) Boggs; m. Travis B. Balthrop, June 12, 1970; children—Cory Travis, Bonnie Catherine. B.S. with high honors, U. Tenn., 1977. C.P.A., Tenn. Staff acct. Rodgers Constrn. Internat., Nashville, 1972-78; controller Elnic, Nashville, 1978-80; pvt. practice acctg., Nashville, 1980-82; controller UPI Media, Nashville, 1982-84; treas. Media Mgmt. Corp., Chgo., 1985—, also dir.; dir. TV Ptnrs. Inc., Nashville. Mem. Tenn. Soc. C.P.A.s, Nat. Assn. Female Execs. Baptist. Avocations: water skiing; swimming. Office: Media Mgmt Corp 333 N Michigan Ave Suite 2315 Chicago IL 60601

BALTHROPE, JACQUELINE MOREHEAD, educational consultant; b. Phila.; d. Jack Walton and Minnie Jessie (Martin) Morehead; B.S. in Edn. with honors, Central State U., Wilberforce, Ohio, 1949; M.A. in Edn. with honors, Case-Western Res. U., 1959; m. Robert Granville Balthrope; children—Robert Granville, Yvonne Gertrude, Robin Bernice. Elem. master tchr. Cleve. Bd. Edn., 1950-65, leadership devel. tchr., 1965-69, asst. prin. elem. sch., 1969-77, prin. elem. sch., 1977-80; ednl. cons., Cleve., 1980—. Active, Ch. Women United, Project Friendship, Missionary Soc., Bible Sch., Sunday Sch., Christian Edn. Com., ch. choir; vol. religious and civic orgns. Recipient ednl. and civic awards, ch. awards. Mem. Cleve. Council Adminstrs. and Suprs., Elem. Sch. Prins., Internat. Reading Assn., AAUW, LWV, Phi Delta Kappa, Delta Kappa Gamma, Alpha Kappa Mu, Zeta Sigma Pi, Pi Lambda Theta, Alpha Kappa Alpha, Phi Delta Kappa, Eta Phi Beta, Gamma Phi Delta. Methodist. Clubs: Top Ladies of Distinction (local founder, 1st pres.), Jr. League, Sen Mer Rekh. Author: African Boy Comes to America, 1960, also sequel; contbr. articles to profl. jours., mags., newspapers. Address: 16220 Delrey Ave Cleveland OH 44128

BALTIMORE, HENRIETTA B., personnel administrator; b. Crest Hill, Va., Jan. 4, 1934; d. William Gordon and Dorothy (Baltimore) Howard; children—Patricia, James, Renee. B.A. in History, U. Mass.-Boston, 1973, postgrad., 1975-79. Cert. tchr., Mass., Washington; Tchr. pub. schs., Washington, 1967-70, Boston, 1970-71; acad. adviser, asst. dir. admissions, U. Mass.-Boston, 1972-78; asst. to pres. Roxbury Community Coll., Boston, 1978-82; dir. personnel Central Boston Elder Services, Inc., 1982—; ednl cons. Black Sister Orgn., Boston and Phila., 1970-72. Author handbooks. Mem. Boston Citywide Planning Commn., 1971-73. Mem. Educators Alliance. Avocations: sewing, reading, walking.

BALZAC, AUDREY FLOBELLE, psychologist; b. N.Y.C., May 5, 1928; d. Allen Isaac and Mildred Florence (Brown) Adrian; m. Ralph P. Balzac, Jr., May 3, 1961; children—Stephen Rafael, Elena Adrian, Rebecca Lisa. B.A. in Psychology with honors, Hunter Coll., 1951; M.S. with honors, Purdue U., 1962; B.D., Columbia U., 1963. Intern in psychology Howard Rusk Inst., NYU and Bellevue Hosp., N.Y.C., 1956-57; clin. psychologist Westchester Community Mental Health Bd., and Children's Ct., White Plains, N.Y., 1957-63; psychol. cons. div. Vocat. Rehab., N.Y.C., 1957—; pvt. practice, 1963—; research psychologist Psychiat. Inst., Columbia Presbyn. Med. Ctr., N.Y.C., 1955-57; cons. Pound Ridge Elem. Sch., 1975-76. Chairwoman Community Relations bd. Pound Ridge Jewish Community Ctr., 1975-79, treas., 1978-79; mem. Westchester Women's Adv. Bd., 1986. Fellow Rusk Inst., 1956-57; research grantee Columbia U., 1960—. Fellow AAUW; mem. Am. Psychol. Assn., Eastern Psychol. Assn., N.Y. Soc. Clin. Psychologists, Soc. Psychol. Study of Social Issues, Am. Sociol. Assn., Sigma Xi, Psi Chi (treas. 1951-52). Jewish. Home: Route 4 Box 267 Pound Ridge NY 10576

BAMBERGER, JO ANN SAMSON, lawyer, toxicologist; b. Johnson City, N.Y., Nov. 26, 1943; d. Joseph Frederick and Jayne Marion (Mitchell) Samson; m. Charles Park Shaw, Apr. 5, 1969 (div. Feb. 1982); children—Matthew Samson, John Park; m. Thomas Edward Bamberger, May 19, 1984. B.A., SUNY-Binghamton, 1965; M.S., N.C. State U., 1969; Ph.D., Kans. State U., 1978; J.D., Franklin Pierce Law Ctr., 1981. Bar: N.H. 1981. Teaching asst. N.C. State U., Raleigh, 1966-68; tchr. chemistry and biology First Colonial High Sch., Virginia Beach, Va., 1968-72; instr. Coll. Vet. Medicine, Kans. State U., Manhattan, 1972-78; legal researcher Energy Law Inst., Concord, N.H., 1979-80; legal intern U.S. Atty. of N.H., Concord, 1980-81; ptnr. Bamberger & Pfundstein, Concord, 1981—; owner, operator Jo Ann Samson Bamberger, Toxicology/Physiology Cons., Concord, 1981—. Bd. dirs. N.H. Task Force on Child Abuse and Neglect, 1982-85, sec., 1984-85, v.p., 1985-86; bd. dirs. Philbrook Ctr. for Children's Services, 1985-86; alt. del. N.H. Democratic Mid-Term Conv., 1983. NSF fellow, 1964; NDEA fellow, 1965-66. Mem. ABA, N.H. Bar Assn., N.H. Trial Lawyers Assn., Sigma Xi (assoc.), Phi Kappa Phi, Phi Alpha Delta. Democrat. Home: 17 Princeton St Concord NH 03301 Office: Bamberger & Pfundstein 13 Green St Concord NH 03301

BAMBRICK, GAIL, newspaper editor, journalist, columnist; b. Boston, Mar. 17, 1953; d. William Lewis and June (Wacker) B. B.A., Hampshire Coll., 1975; cert. Internat. Sch. Music, Vienna, 1976; M.A. in English, Tufts U., 1979, postgrad. in English, 1979—. Cert. tchr., real estate broker, Mass. Instr. English, Tufts U., Medford, Mass., 1978-83; reporter Suburban World, Inc., Neddham, Mass., 1979-81, mem. editorial prodn. staff, 1979-81, editor, columnist, 1981—; cons. sch. newspapers Dover-Sherborn High Sch., 1984; author weekly newspaper column: Albeit, 1981-84. Active Dover Found., 1977-84, Mass. Fair Share, Boston, 1980-84; active pub. relations dept. March of Dimes, Dover, 1981-84. Mem. New Eng. Press Assn. (Outstanding Service award 1983). Republican. Clubs: Hampshire Alumni, Tufts Alumni. Home: PO Box 30 64 Walpole St Dover MA 02030 Office: Suburban World Inc 992 Great Plain Ave Needham MA 02192

BAMFORD, CLAUDIA JO, personnel executive; b. Oklahoma City, Feb. 22, 1949; d. Claudie D. and Martha K. (Groves) Teddy; m. Frank Richard Bamford, Apr. 13, 1973; children—Craig Allen, Brian Dean. B.S. in Psychology, Okla. State U., 1971, M.S., 1974; personnel cert. Tulsa Jr. Coll., 1980. Vocat. rehab. counselor Okla. State Rehab. Services, Tulsa, 1974-79, supervising counselor, 1979-80; methods analyst, Blue Cross and Blue Shield of Okla., Tulsa, 1980-81, compensation EEO coordinator, 1981-84, dir. compensation EEO, 1985—. Mem. Tulsa Personnel Assn. (com. mem., 1983-84, pres. 1985-86), Tulsa Area Survey Group (chmn. 1983—), Nat. Rehab. Assn., Okla. Rehab. Assn., Am. Soc. Personnel Adminstrn. Democrat. Home: 7909 South 70 East Pl Tulsa OK 74133 Office: Blue Cross and Blue Shield of Okla 1215 South Boulder Tulsa OK 74119

BANAGHAN, VERA STENSON, insurance representative; b. Woonsocket, R.I., Nov. 17, 1924; d. Raymond John and Lillian Pauline (Johnson) Stenson; m. Edward Leo Banaghan, June 13, 1968; children by previous marriage—William George Gessner, Donald Moore Gessner, Lyn Gessner Roy. Cert., Bryant Coll., 1942, U. R.I., 1968. Office mgr. IBM, Providence, 1944-47; sec. Pelletier & Rourke, Providence, 1964-69; ins. rep. Raphael Paola, Inc., Cranston, R.I., 1969—. Pres., Coventry PTA, 1954-56. Mem. Ins. Women of Greater Providence (treas. 1971-73), Nat. Assn. Ins. Women (bd. dirs. 1984-85), corr. sec. 1985-86). Republican. Episcopalian. Clubs: Evening Guild, Altar Guild. Home: 42 Country Club Dr Warwick RI 02888 Office: Raphael Paola Inc 687 Park Ave Cranston RI 02910

BANANTO, DORTHA JANE, nurse anesthetist; b. Horatio, Ark., Feb. 4, 1927; d. Louis Sager and Ressie (Lyon) Everett; m. Norman Joseph Bananto, May 11, 1957; 1 dau., Kerry Ressie. R.N., Tri-State Hosp., Shreveport, La., 1948; grad. in anesthesia Charity Hosp., 1952. R.N., La. Nurse anesthetist St. Anne's Hosp., Raceland, La., 1953-69; chief nurse anesthetist West Jefferson Gen. Hosp., Marrero, La., 1971-84. Treas. Meml. United Meth. Ch., Mathews, La., 1984-85. Mem. La. Assn. Nurse Anesthetists, Am. Assn. Nurse Anesthetists (dist. sec. 1977), Democrat. Clubs: Lioness, Woman's, United Meth. Women (Raceland). Home: PO Box 152 Raceland LA 70394

BANATTE, HETTY DEANE, nutrition educator, researcher; b. Georgetown, Guyana, Oct. 15,; came to U.S., 1973, naturalized, 1985; d. Christopher W. and Doris Z. (Cummings) Deane; m. Jean-Marie Banatte, Sept. 3, 1977; 1 child, Marc. B.S. in Dietetics, U. Leeds (Eng.), 1966; M.S. in Human Nutrition, U. Mo., 1975; Ph.D. in Adult Edn., Fla. State U., 1980. Cons. Pan Am. Health Orgn., Washington, 1974; pub. health nutritionist State Dept. Health, Tallahassee, 1978-79; coordinator internat. program Fla. A&M U., Tallahassee, 1979-83, asst. prof., 1977-79; assoc. prof. Norfolk State U., Va., 1983—, dir. research, 1984—; cons. Bank of Montreal, Can., 1982—. Co-author: Infant

Feeding Guide for Mothers-Guyana, 1968; Relationships of Rural Development Strategies to Health and Nutrition Status, 1979. Exec. bd. Am. Cancer Soc., 1981; active Am. Heart Soc., 1986. Mem. Am. Dietetic Assn., Am. Home Econs. Assn., N.Y. Acad. Scis., Am. Pub. Health Assn., Sigma Xi. Methodist. Avocations: exercise; gardening. Office: Norfolk State U Dept Community Health Norfolk VA 23501

BANBURY, SHERA, journal editor, electronics company marketing executive, financial planning consultant; b. St. Louis, Jan. 28, 1943; d. Harold Wellington Banbury and Dorothy Mary (LeVan) Banbury Kuper; student Mills Coll., 1960-62; B.A., Hanover Coll., 1964; M.A.Ed. (Ford Found. Project I scholar), U. Rochester, 1965; lic. real estate sales, N.Y.; lic. social studies tchr., N.Y.; lic. life ins. sales, N.Y.; children—Sean Lachlan Connin, Lance Banbury Connin. Tchr. art, English, social studies, public and pvt. schs., Rochester, N.Y., 1964-74; substitute tchr., tutor, public schs., Naples and Churchville, N.Y., 1974-76; mktg. sec., receptionist Bristol Harbour Village, Canandaigua, N.Y., 1976-77; dir. advt. and promotions Sonnenberg Gardens, Canandaigua, 1977-79; mgr. advt. and sales promotion EDMAC Corp., RoSPATCH Electronic Systems Div., Fishers, N.Y., 1979-85; mgr. internat. market devel., 1980—; fin. planning cons. Gradinger & Assocs., Rochester, 1982; adv. Canandaigua C. of C., 1978-79; reporter, co-editor Villager newspaper, Bristol Harbour Village, 1974-76. Founder, pres. Churchville-Chili Tchr. Aides, 1971-74; mem. Politics of Food Task Force/Rochester Peace and Justice Edn. Center, 1983-85, mem. steering com., personnel com., 1985. Recipient Gold Key, Nat. Scholastic Art Exhibit (2), 1959. Mem. Tech. Mktg. Soc. Am., Women's Action for Nuclear Disarmament, World Trade Council, Kappa Alpha Theta. Club: Churchville-Chili Garden. Contbr. articles to co. publs. Home: 7 Robinia Lodge Station Rd Brighton BN1 GSF Sussex England Office: Eldon Publs Ltd 30 Fleet St London EC4Y 1AH England

BANCROFT, ANNE, actress; b. N.Y.C., Sept. 17, 1931; d. Michael and Mildred (DiNapoli) Italiano; grad. Christopher Columbus High Sch., N.Y.C.; m. Mel Brooks. Broadway debut in Two for the Seesaw, 1958; starred on Broadway as Annie Sullivan in The Miracle Worker, 1959-60, The Devils, Golda, 1977; films include: Don't Bother to Knock, 1952, Treasure of the Golden Condor, 1952, Tonight We Sing, 1953, The Kid from Left Field, 1953, A Life in the Balance, 1954, Demetrius and the Gladiators, 1954, Gorilla at Large, 1954, The Raid, 1954, The Girl in Black Stockings, 1955, The Last Frontier, 1955, New York Confidential, 1955, Naked Street, 1956, Walk the Proud Land, 1956, Nightfall, 1956, The Miracle Worker, 1962, The Pumpkin Eater, 1964, Seven Women, 1966, The Slender Thread, 1966, The Graduate, 1967, Young Winston, 1972, The Prisoner of 2d Avenue, 1975, The Hindenburg, 1975, Lipstick, 1976, Silent Movie, 1976, The Turning Point, 1977, The Elephant Man, 1980, To Be or Not to Be, 1983, Garbo Talks, 1984, Agnes of God, 1985; dir., writer, actress Fatso, 1979; TV appearances include The Goldbergs, Danger, Suspense, Philco-Goodyear Playhouse; guest on Perry Como Show, Bob Hope-Chrysler Show; TV spl. Annie-The Woman in the Life of a Man, Tom Jones Show, Jesus of Nazareth. Recipient Tony award for Two for the Seesaw; Oscar award best actress of yr. for movie recreation of role in Miracle Worker, 1962, also Tony award for stage version; Emmy award for tv spl., 1970. Address: care 1888 Century Park E Suite 1400 Los Angeles CA 90067

BANCROFT, ELIZABETH A(BERCROMBIE), analytical chemist; b. Washington, Mar. 2, 1947; d. John Chandler and Ruth Abercrombie (Robinson) B.; A.B., Harvard U./Radcliffe Coll., 1979; postgrad. in forensic scis. John Jay Coll. Criminal Justice, 1982. Asst. dir. research Bagley Fordyce Research Labs., N.Y.C., 1979-83, dir. research and publs., Washington, 1984—. Mem. Assn. Ofcl. Analytical Chemists, Am. Chem. Soc., AAAS, Am. Inst. Chemists, Forensic Sci. Soc., Am. Assn. Clin. Chemistry, Am. Acad. Forensic Scis. (affiliate), Internat. Reference Orgn. Forensic Medicine, English Speaking Union. Republican. Episcopalian. Clubs: Harvard, Chemists (N.Y.C.). Author: Radon Daughters, 1983. Home: 1821 23d St NW Washington DC 20008 Office: 1718 Connecticut Ave NW Suite 310 Washington DC 20009

BANCROFT, MARGARET ARMSTRONG, lawyer; b. Mpls., May 9, 1938; d. Wallace David and Mary Elizabeth (Garland) Armstrong; m. Alexander Clerihew Bancroft, Mar. 14, 1964; 1 child, Elizabeth. B.A. magna cum laude, Radcliffe Coll., 1960; J.D. cum laude, NYU, 1969. Bar: N.Y. 1971. Reporter Mpls. Star and Tribune, 1960-61, U.P.I., N.Y. and N.J., 1961-66; assoc. Donovan Leisure Newton & Irvine, Paris, France, 1969-71, N.Y.C., 1971-78, ptnr., 1978-84; ptnr. Finley, Kumble, Wagner, Heine, Underberg, Manley, Meyerson & Casey, N.Y.C., 1984—. Bd. dirs. Vis. Nurse Service N.Y., 1980—. Mem. ABA (mem. subcom. proxy contests), Assn. Bar City N.Y., N.Y. County Lawyers Assn., N.Y. State Bar Assn. (com. securities regulation, exec. com.). Democrat. Office: Finley Kumble Wagner et al 425 Park Ave New York NY 10022

BANDY, ALICE MARIE, publishing executive; b. Dayton, Ohio, Aug. 14, 1947; d. Philip C. and Phyllis B. (Walker) Dow; m. G. Thomas Bandy, Feb. 19, 1972. B.A., U. Colo., 1969, M.B.A., Pepperdine U., 1980. Sales asst. Cahners Pubs., Los Angeles, 1973-75, office mgr., 1975-76; prodn. asst. Archtl. Digest, Los Angeles, 1976-77; adminstrv. asst. The Knapp Press, Los Angeles, 1977-79, adminstrv. mgr., 1979-81, v.p., gen. mgr., 1981-82, pres., 1982-84; v.p. Knapp Communications, Los Angeles, 1982-84; ptnr. The Cons. Group, Los Angeles, 1984—. Mem. Direct Mktg. Assn., Assn. Am. Pubs. Office: The Consulting Group 76 Crest Dr Manhattan Beach CA 90266

BANDY, MARY LEA, museum official; b. Evanston, Ill., June 16, 1943; d. DeWitt Clinton and Ruth (Coale) Gibson; m. Gary L. Bandy, June 3, 1967. B.A., Stanford U., 1965. Asst. editor Harry Abrams Co., N.Y.C., 1966-73; assoc. editor Mus. Modern Art, N.Y.C., 1973-76, assoc. coordinator exhbns., 1976-78, adminstr. dept. film, 1978-80, dir. dept. film, 1980—; mem. film adv. com. Japan Soc., N.Y.C., 1983—. Editor: Rediscovering French Film, 1983. Office: Museum of Modern Art 11 W 53d St New York NY 10019

BANE, ROSEMARY SULLIVAN, musician, educator; b. Clever, Mo., Jan. 15, 1925; d. Earl Tom and Rosa Ethel (Maples) Sullivan; B.S., S.W. Mo. State U., 1949; M.Ed., U. Mo., 1959; postgrad., U. Cin., Miami U., Oxford, Ohio, 1963-64; m. James Edward Bane, Dec. 22, 1985; 1 son, Tom Donald Chaney; stepchildren—Nancy Bane Schultejans, James William, Ruthmary Bane Brassfield. Tchr. music Clever Consol. Schs. and dir. music First Bapt. Ch., Clever, 1949-53; tchr. Aurora (Mo.) Elem. Schs. and dir. music First Bapt. Ch., Aurora, 1953-57; bass violinist Springfield (Mo.) Symphony Orch., 1949-56; social dir. S.W. Mo. State U., summers 1955-56 and 1957-58; early childhood music specialist Indian Hills Exempted Village Schs., Cin., 1961-80, ret., 1980, on spl. assignment Fine Arts Project, 1980-84; writer curriculum materials for Cin. Symphony Orch. In-Sch. Music Program and dir. tng. docents, 1978-85; speaker at numerous confs., workshops, radio programs. Named Tchr. of Yr., Indian Hill Schs., 1979; recipient award of appreciation Cin. Public Schs., 1981. Mem. NEA, Music Educators Nat. Assn., Am. Orff Schulwerk Assn. (bd. govs. Greater Cin. chpt. 1973-77), Mo. State Tchrs. Assn. (pres. 1948-49), Nat. Assn. State Tchrs. Assns.' Pres. (pres. 1949-50), Indian Hill Ret. Tchrs. Assn. (pres. 1982-83), Delta Kappa Gamma, Pi Beta Phi (pres. 1943-44), Sigma Alpha Iota (pres. 1943-44). Clubs: Cin. Woman's (dir. 1982-85), Coll. Cin. (pres. 1979-80), PEO (local pres., dir. Greater Cin. chorus). Compositions include: Clever High Sch. Alma Mater for Band and Chorus, 1949; prepared, presented numerous original children's musicals. Author: Recorder Fun; contbr. articles to profl. jours. Home: 857 S Rogers Springfield MO 65804

BANIK, DEBORAH K. SWANSON, nurse, administrator; b. Ada, Okla., Apr. 19, 1951; d. Duane C. and June T. (Norris) Swanson; m. David Lee Banik, July 29, 1977; 1 child, Robbie David. B.S.N., S.D. State U., 1985; diploma in nursing Trinity Sch. Nursing, Minot, N.D., 1973; cert. advanced studies in patient care adminstrn. U. Minn., 1982, postgrad., 1985—. R.N., S.D. Evening supr. Mobridge Community Hosp., S.D., 1974-77, day supr., 1978-79, dir. nursing, 1979-85, asst. adminstr., 1985—; psychiat. nurse N.E. Mental Health, Mobridge, 1977-78. Bd. dirs. Community Fund Drive, Mobridge, 1984—; pianist, singer local Ch. of God, 1974—; mem. S.D. State Bd. Nursing, 1981—. Named Outstanding Young Woman of Yr., Mobridge Jaycees, 1985. Mem. Am. Nurses Assn. (chair nominations com. 1984-85), S.D. Nurses Assn. (Dist. Nurse of Yr. 1983), Soc. Nursing Service Adminstrs. (nominations com. 1981), Am. Cancer Soc., Sigma Theta Tau. Republican. Avocations: cooking; collectors plates. Home: HCR 10 Box 881 Mobridge SD 57601 Office: Mobridge Community Hosp Mobridge SD 57601

BANISTER, JUDITH, demographer, educator; b. Washington, Sept. 10, 1943; d. William Price and Helen Barbara (Myers) B.; m. Dec. 17, 1966; children—Adrian Banard, Dawn Banard. B.A. in History, Swarthmore Coll., 1965; Ph.D. in Demography, Stanford U., 1978. Postdoctoral research fellow East-West Population Inst., Honolulu, 1978-80; statistician/demographer U.S. Bur. of Census, Washington, 1980-82, chief China br. Ctr. for Internat. Research, 1982—; part-time assoc. prof. George Washington U., Washington, 1981—. Author: China's Changing Population, 1986; contbr. articles to profl. jours. Mem. Population Assn. Am., Internat. Union for Sci. Study of Population. Office: Ctr for Internat Research US Bureau Of Census Room 105 Scuderi Bldg Washington DC 20233

BANKOFF, MARY NORMAN, lawyer; b. Sac City, Iowa, Aug. 18, 1950; d. Rufus and Mildred (Dresselhuis) Norman; m. Peter Rosner Bankoff, Aug. 8, 1974; children—Amy Elizabeth, Michael Jacob. B.F.A. cum laude, U. Utah, Salt Lake City, 1973; J.D., magna cum laude, Ind. U.-Indpls., 1979. Bar: Ind. 1980, Ariz. 1981. Consumer protection asst. dir. Ind. Atty. Gen.'s Office, Indpls., 1976-78; community arts coordinator Ind. Arts Commn., Indpls., 1978-80; staff atty. Ct. of Appeals, Indpls., 1980-81; hearing officer State of Ariz., Phoenix, 1982—. Mem. Ariz. Bar Assn., ABA. Republican. Presbyterian. Home: 2451 E Acoma St Phoenix AZ 85032 Office: 207 E McDowell St Office of Appeals Phoenix AZ 85032

BANKS, BARBARA S(HADIOW), lawyer; b. Indpls., Mar. 27, 1950; d. Dwain L. and Elaine Audrey (Peterson) Shadiow; m. Robert Henry Banks, Aug. 30, 1970; children—Gage, Lindsay. Qime degre U. Grenoble-France, 1970; B.A., Ind. U., 1972, J.D. magna cum laude, 1977. Bar: Colo. 1977. Tchr. Indpls. Pub. Schs., 1972-75; ptnr. Gorsuch, Kirgis, Campbell, Walker and Grover, Denver, 1977—; legal counsel Landlord Tenant Mediation Services, Denver Commn. Community Devel., 1977-79; faculty Continuing Legal Edn., Denver, 1982—. Column editor Colo. Lawyer, 1982; editor Ind. Law Rev., 1975-77; author article in field. Bd. dirs. Denver Urban Ministries, 1983-85. Hoosier scholar, 1968. Mem. ABA, Colo. Bar Assn. (pres. real estate sect. 1985), Denver Bar Assn., Colo. Women's Bar Assn. Democrat. Methodist. Office: Gorsuch Kirgis Campbell Walker and Grover 1401 17th St Suite 1100 Denver CO 80202

BANKS, BETTIE SHEPPARD, psychologist; b. Birmingham, Ala., June 8, 1933; d. Francis Wilkerson and Bettie Pollard (Woodson) Sheppard; B.A., Ga. State U., 1966, M.A., 1968, Ph.D., 1970; m. Frazer Banks, Jr., Mar. 22, 1952; children—Bettie Banks Daley, Lee Frazer III. Clin. asso. Lab. for Psychol. Services, Ga. State U., 1968-70; intern Ga. Mental Health Inst., Atlanta, 1970-71, psychologist, 1971-72, chief psychologist, 1973; pvt. practice, Atlanta, 1972— adj. prof. clin. psychology Ga. State U.; mem. peer rev. panel Ga. Med. Care Found., 1980—. Diplomate in clin. psychology Am. Bd. Profl. Psychology. Fellow Ga. Psychol. Assn. (chmn. div. E 1980); mem. Am. Acad. Psychotherapists (exec. com. 1980-82, sec. 1982-86), Am. Psychol. Assn., Am. Group Psychotherapy Assn., Atlanta Group Psychotherapy Soc. (exec. com. 1982), Southeastern Psychol. Assn. Episcopalian. Club: Jr. League. Cons. editor Voices, 1978-84. Office: 595 Wimbledon Rd NE Atlanta GA 30324

BANKS, LISA JEAN, government official; b. Chelsea, Mass., Dec. 19, 1956; d. Bruce H. and Jean P. (Como) Banks. B.S. in Bus. Adminstrn., Northeastern U., 1979. Coop trainee IRS, Boston, 1975-79, revenue officer, Reno, 1979-81, spl. agt., Houston, 1981-84, Anchorage, 1984—, fed. womens program mgr., 1980-81. Recipient Superior Performance award IRS, 1981. Mem. Nat. Assn. Treasury Agts., Nat. Assn. Female Execs. Democrat. Roman Catholic Home: Anchorage AK Office: PO Box 1500 Anchorage AK 99510

BANKS, MARGARET AMELIA, librarian; b. Quebec City, Que., Can., July 3, 1928; d. Thomas Herbert and Bessey (Collins) B.; B.A., Bishop's U., Lennoxville, Que., 1949; M.A., U. Toronto, 1950, Ph.D., 1953. Archivist Ont. Archives, Toronto, 1953-61; law librarian U. Western Ont., London, 1961—, assoc. prof. faculty law, 1974-86, prof., 1986—. Mem. Am. Assn. Law Libraries, Can. Assn. Law Libraries, Am. Inst. Parliamentarians, Nat. Assn. Parliamentarians, Osgoode Soc. Anglican. Author: Edward Blake, Irish Nationalist, 1957; Using a Law Library, 1st edit., 1971, 4th edit., 1985; Law at Western, 1959-84, 1981. Office: Faculty Law Library U Western Ont London ON N6A 3K7 Canada

BANKS, SHARON ELIZABETH, nurse, educator; b. Pitts., Apr. 5, 1950; d. John C. and Myrtle (Banks) Claughton. B.S. in Nursing, U. Pitts., 1974, M. Nursing, 1980. Critical care nurse Presbyn.-Univ. Hosp., Pitts., 1974-79, relief supr. critical care div., critical care instr., 1979-80; critical care educator Doctors Med. Ctr., Modesto, Calif., 1980-82; critical care nurse Lavina Hosp., Altadena, Calif., 1982—; cons. Doctors Med. Ctr., tchr. CPR, Am. Heart Assn. bd. dirs. Am. Lung Assn. of Valley Lode, 1981-82. Served to lt. USNR, 1983—. Mem. Am. Assn. Critical Care Nurses, Four County Council Educators, Female Execs. (dir.), Am. Nurses Assn. Democrat. Address: Command Fleet Activities FPO Seattle WA 98769

BANKSTON, PHYLLIS MARIE, economist; b. Houston, Dec. 3, 1953; d. Gilbert and Gladys (Harris) B. B.A., Vanderbilt U., 1976; postgrad. U. Leeds (Eng., 1975-76; M.B.A., U. Chgo., 1980. Internat. banker First Nat. Bank Chgo., 1978-81; fin. systems cons. Conoco Inc., Houston, 1981-82, economist, 1982—. Advisor, Jr. Achievement, 1981-83. Exxon Corp. fellow, 1977. Mem. Black Women's Alliance, Nat. Black M.B.A. Assn. Democrat. Home: 4215 Botany Ln Houston TX 77047

BANNER, BETTY LUE, cosmetologist; b. Stephens, Ark., Jan. 21, 1938; d. Irvin and Chrriseen (McCollough) Adair; m. James Edward Banner, Apr. 28, 1984; m. Jessie Dickerson, Dec. 24, 1978 (div. Mar. 1981). Tchrs. cert. Velvatex Coll. Beauty Sch., 1961, operators licence, 1958; student Morris Brown Coll., 1963-65. Sales technician Johnson Products Co., cgho., 1966-68; co-owner Hair Clinic, Atlanta, 1968-70; instr. Velvatex Coll. Beauty, Little Rock, 1970-80; owner Adair House Beauty, Dayton, Ohio, 1981—; owner, mgr. Banners Hairweave, Dayton, 1985—; founder Artistic Hair Designers, Dayton, 1986—. Pres, Missionary Soc., Dayton, 1982—; dean Nat. Missionary Ch., 1984. Fellow Ministers Alliance (sec. 1985), Nat. Beauty Culturists, Nat. Fedn. Ind. Bus.; mem. Nat. Assn. Female Execs. Democrat. Avocations: fishing; swimming. Home: 3400 Cornell Dr Dayton OH 45406 Office: Banner's Hairweave Studio 2102 Miracle Ln Dayton OH 45406

BANNISTER, MARGARET ALICE TRIMBLE, public relations specialist; b. Oklahoma City, Dec. 15, 1924; d. Clyde Waldrop and Mary Melissa (Murray) Trimble; m. Lawrence R. Bannister, Jan. 18, 1947 (div. 1968); children—Karen Bannister Torretta, Barbara Jean Bannister Jewett, Sally Ann. B.A. in Journalism, U. Okla., 1945; postgrad. U. Mo., 1970-71, U. Wash., 1973. Reporter Alva Review-Courier, Okla., 1945-46, Clinton Daily News, Okla., 1946-47; pub. relations asst. U. Okla., Norman, 1947-51; editorial asst. Consol.-Vultee Aircraft Corp., Ft. Worth, 1951-53; coordinator community relations Berkeley Sch. Dist., Mo., 1968-72, dir. community relations, 1973-81; communications dir. YWCA of Met. St. Louis, 1984—. Mem. Women in Communication (v.p. membership St. Louis chpt. 1983-85), Nat. Sch. Pub. Relations Assn. (officer Greater St. Louis chpt. 1969-71, 73-74), Soroptimists Internat. (charter mem. North St. Louis County chpt.). Methodist. Home: 2040 Argo Dr Florissant MO 63031 Office: 1015 Locust St Suite 310 St Louis MO 63101

BANNON, JOANNE LOUISE, marketing executive; b. Phila., Oct. 12, 1954; d. Thomas James and Jeanne Judith (Jennings) B. B.S., Pa. State U., 1975. Tchr. math. Marple Newton Sr. High Sch., Newtown Square, Pa., 1975-76, Chalres Ellis Sch., Newtown Square, 1976-77, Marple Newtown Jr. High Sch., 1977-80; installation dir. Shared Med. Systems, N.Y.C., 1980-83, mktg. rep., 1983-86, mktg. mgr., 1986—. Named Rookie Sales Rep. of Yr., Shared Med. Systems, 1983, Salesperson of Yr., 1984. Mem. Healthcare Fin. Mgmt. Assn. Republican. Roman Catholic. Avocations: gardening, downhill skiing. Home: 1767 Mountain Ave Scotch Plains NJ 07076 Office: Shared Med Systems 6th Floor 1 Penn Plaza New York NY 10119

BANNON, MARGARET MARY, lawyer; b. Chgo., Oct. 4, 1944; d. Joseph W. and Margaret M. (Lahart) B. B.A., Mt. Mary Coll., 1967; J.D., Ind. U., Indpls., 1975. Bar: Ind., 1975. Tchr. Notre Dame High Sch., DeKalb, Ill., 1967-69; coordinator DeKalb County Migrant Day Care Ctr., 1968-69; tchr. Sheridan Elem. Sch., Chgo., 1969, Hamilton S.E. High Sch., Noblesville, Ind., 1969-73; lawyer, cons. Ind. Dept. Pub. Instrn., Indpls., 1973-84, dir. legal services Evansville-Vanderburgh Sch. Corp., 1984-86; assoc. Bose, McKinney, Evans, Indpls., 1986—; chmn. dept. task force on violence and vandalism Ind. Task Forces on Community Crime Prevention, 1975-77, Juvenile Justice, 1975-79. Contbr. article to profl. jour. Mem. ABA, Ind. Bar Assn., Indpls. Bar Assn., Ind. Council Adminstrs. Spl. Edn. Democrat. Roman Catholic. Home: 5667 Crittendon Indianapolis IN 46220 Office: 1100 First Federal Bldg Indianapolis IN 46204

BANSLEY, MARCIA DEW, banker, lawyer, environmental activist; b. Atlanta, Oct. 4, 1941; d. James Harris and Martha Wyly (Carmichael) Dew; m. John David Bansley, III, Nov. 27, 1965 (div. 1978.) Lang. student Monterrey Tech. (Mex.), 1961, Syracuse U., Florence, Italy, 1962; B.A. in English, Vanderbilt U., 1963; J.D., Emory U., 1981. Bar: Ga. 1982, D.C. 1982. Acctg. assoc. J.D. Bansley and Co., C.P.A.s, Atlanta, 1966-77; legal asst., office mgr. Bansley and Bansley, Atlanta, 1966-77; law clk. to regional counsel EPA, Atlanta, summer 1980; Congl. legis. asst. (intern) to U.S. Senator Sam Nunn and U.S. Representative Newt Gingrich, Washington, 1981; atty., legis. analyst Ga. Trial Lawyers Assn., Inc., Atlanta, 1982; bus. analyst Trust Co. Bank, Atlanta, 1982—. Chmn. bd. Legacy Found., Atlanta, 1976—; sec. Friends of Chattahoochee River, Atlanta, 1980—; sec. League Conservation Voters, Atlanta, 1983; environ. chmn. Ga. Canoeing Assn., 1982—; mem. Regional Water Resources Task Force, 1977-78; trustee Girls' Club; officer Peachtree Presbyn. Ch. Recipient Presdl. recognition for Leadership in Nat. Park Legislation, 1978; Ga. Water Conservationist of Yr. award Sears, Roebuck and Ga. Wildlife Fedn., 1984; lang. study grantee Carnegie Found., Mex., 1961. Mem. Tax Study Assocs., Soc. Fin. Analysts, Jr. League Atlanta, Phi Delta Phi, Chi Omega. Home: 275-23 Collier Rd NW Atlanta GA 30309 Office: Trust Co Bank PO Box 4655 Center 115 25 Park Pl Atlanta GA 30302

BANTEL, LINDA MAE, art museum director; b. King City, Calif., May 30, 1943; d. Clifford Burnett and Helen Vernelle (Mallicotte) Bantel; m. David Hollenberg, June 15, 1980; children—Matthew Bantel Hollenberg. M.A., NYU, 1971. Research cons. N.Y. Hist. Soc., N.Y.C., 1975-76; guest co-curator Art Mus. of South Tex., Corpus Christi, Tex., 1977-79; research assoc. Met. Mus. Art, N.Y.C., 1978-80; curator, now dir. of mus. Pa. Acad. Fine Arts, Phila., 1980—. Co-author: (with James Flexner) The Face of Liberty: Founders of the U.S., 1975; author: The Alice M. Kaplan Collection, 1980; William Rush, American Sculptor, 1982; (with Marcus Burke) Spain and New Spain: Mexican Colonial Arts in Their European Context, 1979. Mem. Coll. Art Assn., Am. Assn. Mus., Assn. Art Mus. Dirs. Home: 255 S 44th St Philadelphia PA 19104 Office: Pa Acad of Fine Arts Broad and Cherry Sts Philadelphia PA 19102

BANTIVOGLIO, BARBARA MARIE, investment banking company executive; b. Camden, N.J., Feb. 19, 1944; d. Frank Andrew and Eleanor Josephine (DiBartolomeo) B.; B.A. cum laude, Rutgers U., 1965, M.L.S., 1973; m. William Wade Middleton, Nov. 9, 1974. Tchr. French and math. No. Burlington County Regional Sch. Dist., Columbus, N.J., 1965-76; asst. mgr. institutional sales Robinson-Humphrey Co., Inc., Atlanta, 1976-84; asst. v.p. Johnson Lane Space Smith & Co., 1984—. Mem. Atlanta Assn. Women in Securities, (sec. 1980—), Nat. Assn. Female Execs., AAUW, Alliance Francaise d'Atlanta. Republican. Roman Catholic. Office: 3333 Peachtree Rd NE Atlanta GA 30326

BANTLE, LYNNE, lawyer; b. Phila., Oct. 27, 1952; d. David William and Helen Louise (Raschke) B.; m. Per-Henrik Mansson, Sept. 25, 1976. Student Wells Coll., 1970-71; B.A. with honors, Mills Coll., 1974; M.A., Johns Hopkins U. Sch. Advanced Internat. Studies, 1976; J.D., Boalt Hall Sch. Law, 1979. Bar: Calif. 1979; U.S. Dist. Ct. (no. dist.) Calif. 1979. Press attache Consulate Gen. France, San Francisco, 1973-74; assoc. Pettit & Martin, San Francisco, 1979—. Participating atty. Legal Services Project for San Francisco, 1979—. Mem. Calif. State Bar, San Francisco Bar, ABA, Calif. Women Lawyers. Democrat. Office: Pettit & Martin 101 California St 35th Floor San Francisco CA 94111

BANZER, CYNTHIA DEANE, state representative; b. Portland, Oreg., Jan. 24, 1947; d. Robert Lewis Banzer and Dorothy (Dennison) Davis; children—McKean Banzer-Lausberg, Eric Banzer-Lausberg. B.S. in Polit. Sci., Oreg. State U., 1969; M.Ed., Ohio U., 1973. Tchr. corps intern Ohio U. Tchr. Corps Program, Parkersburg, W.Va., 1969-70; research assoc. Pres.'s Commn. on Sch. Fin., 1971; legis. asst. Com. on Edn. and Labor, U.S. Ho. of Reps., 1972; adminstrv. asst. Senate Edn. Com., State of Oreg., 1973; citizen participation coordinator Oreg. Land Conservation and Devel. Commn., 1974; community services dir. City of Beaverton, Oreg., 1975-77; presiding officer Met. Service Dist., Portland, Oreg., 1978-85; mem. Oreg. Ho. of Reps., Salem, 1985—. Contbr. articles to profl. jours. Bd. dirs. United of Columbia-Willamette; pres. bd. dirs. Met. Family Services; mem. Assocs. of Good Samaritan Hosp.; bd. dirs. Jr. League of Portland; bd. dirs. Loaves and Fishes; past alt. del. Democratic State Central Com., exec. bd. dirs. Multnomah County Dem. Central Com., other past polit. activities; past mem., chmn. numerous civic groups, assns., cultural orgns. Democrat. Club: Multnomah Athletic (Portland). Office: State Capitol Bldg Salem OR 97310

BAPTIE, LAURI LOUISE, nurse anesthetist; b. Seattle, Oct. 17, 1955; d. Charles Jack and Martha Georgia (Papadakis) B. B.S. in Nursing, Loma Linda U., 1978; M.S., Long Beach State U., 1981. Cert. registered nurse anesthetist, Calif. Operating room scrub technician Loma Linda U. Med. Ctr., Calif., 1975-77, nurse, 1977-78; nurse UCLA Med. Ctr., 1978-81; nurse anesthetist Anesthesia Care Assocs., San Diego, 1982—; nurse anesthetist Kaiser Hosp., San Diego, 1981—. Mem. Am. Assn. Nurse Anesthetists, Calif. Assn. Nurse Anesthetists, Am. Assn. Critical Care Nurses, Sigma Theta Tau. Republican. Avocations: running, swimming, cycling, racquetball. Home: 3642 Mission Mesa Way San Diego CA 92120 Office: Kaiser Permanente Hosp 4647 Zion Ave San Diego CA 92120

BAPTIST, SYLVIA EVELYN, data service company executive, consultant; b. Chgo., Feb. 15, 1944; d. Clarence Walter and Evelyn Alphild (Fagerberg) Bonin; m. Jeremy Eduard Baptist, July 21, 1962; children—Sarah, Margaret, Catherine. Student Mich. State U., 1961-62; B.S., Roosevelt U., 1965. Instr. IBM, Chgo., 1965-66, systems engr., Topeka, Kans., 1966-67; tchr. computer sci. Lawrence High Sch., Kans., 1968; pres. Multiple Data Services, Leawood, Kans., 1983—; cons. in field. Alumni Disting. scholar Mich. State U., 1961-62, Internat. Ladies' Garment Workers Union scholar Roosevelt U., 1964-65. Lodge: Vasa (master of ceremonies 1986—). Avocations: Scandinavian dancing; cooking; writing. Office: Multiple Data Services 3501 W 92d St Leawood KS 66206

BARAN, HELEN MARIE, vineyard executive, real estate broker; b. Rochester, N.Y., Mar. 22, 1941; d. Glenn Edward and Alice Louise (Morton) Stidd; m. Stephen Baran, Jan. 1, 1966; children—Elaine, Stephan, Juliann, Beth. A.A., SUNY-Alfred, 1961; profl. courses on med. tech. and hosp. adminstrn., 1962-78; student SUNY-Fredonia, 1984. Chief med. records, adminstrv. asst. Westfield Hosp., N.Y., 1961-78; asst. in physicians' and dental offices, 1960-66; ptnr. Baran Vineyards, Westfield, 1966—; salesperson Chautauqua Realty, Chautauqua, N.Y. and Westfield, 1984—; bd. dirs. N.Y. State Grape Country Coop., W. N.Y. Health Systems Agy. Author: Pesticide Poison Manual for Emergency Rooms, 1969. Commr. N.Y. State Dept. Equalization and Assessment, 1979—; mem. N.Y. State Rural Hosp. Council, 1978—, Chautauqua County Planning Bd., 1975—; bd. dirs. N.Y. State Hosp. Rev. and Planning Council, 1982-85; chmn. Physician Recruitment Com., 1980-83. Named Citizen of Yr., Westfield C. of C., 1980. Mem. N.Y. State Wine Grape Growers, N.Y. State Farm Bur. Democrat. Club: Union Relief. Avocations: travel; music; needlepoint; bicycling; tennis. Home: 191 W Main St Westfield NY 14787 Office: Realty World 150 E Main St Westfield NY 14787

BARANOWSKI, CAROLYN AGNES, hospital administrator; b. Somerville, N.J., Apr. 10, 1947; d. Stephen Robert and Agnes (Malinowski) Baranowski. B.A., Newark State Coll., 1972; M.S., East Stroudsburg State Coll., 1976; student in respiratory therapy U. Chgo. Hosps. and Clinics, 1976. Registered respiratory therapist. Tchr., coach Bridgewater-Raritan High Sch. W., N.J., 1972-74; respiratory therapist Easton Hosp., Pa., 1975-76, asst. tech. dir. pulmonary medicine dept., 1976-80, tech. dir. pulmonary medicine dept., 1980—; adj. faculty Lehigh County Community Coll., 1976 to present; adv. mem. respiratory therapy program Lehigh County Community Coll., 1980—; cons. respiratory therapy home care, 1984. Mem. Am. Assn. Respiratory Therapy, AAHPER, Nat. Bd. Respiratory Care, Pa. Soc. Respiratory Therapy, Hosp. Assn. Pa. Roman Catholic. Office: Easton Hosp 21 and Lehigh St Easton PA 18042

BARANOWSKI, MARTHA FAHS, environmental cleaning and restoration company executive; b. Phila., July 29, 1938; d. Kenneth Garabrant and Marion (Radley) Fahs; m. Richard Baranowski, Aug. 13, 1976; children—Jill, LeeAnn, Martha Lois, Boyd Richard; stepchildren—Lisa Marie, Richard Michael. Student, U. Pa., 1956-59. Occupational therapist Mental Health Center 1, Wilkes-Barre, Pa., 1969-77; real estate salesperson Howell & Jones, Wilkes-Barre, 1978-80; program coordinator Assn. Retarded Citizens, Wilkes-Barre, 1980-84; pres. BES Environ. Specialists, Inc., Kingston, Pa., 1982—. Author, editor newsletter Assn. Retarded Citizens, Wilkes-Barre, 1982—, co-chmn. planning and devel., 1984-85, pres., bd. dirs., 1985, chmn. ann. awards dinner, 1985. Named Adv. of Yr., Assn. Retarded Citizens, 1985. Episcopalian. Avocations: reading; gardening. Home: 370 Reynolds St Kingston PA 18704 Office: BES Environ Specialists Inc 58 Pierce St Kingston PA 18704

BARANSKI, JOAN SULLIVAN, publishing company executive; b. Andover, Mass., Apr. 6, 1933; d. Joseph Charles and Ruth (McCormack) Sullivan; m. Kenneth E. Baranski, Apr. 20, 1970. B.S., U. Lowell (Mass.), 1955. Tchr., Andover Pub. Schs., 1955-61; cons. Holt, Rinehart and Winston, N.Y.C., 1961-62, editor, 1961-66; promotion editor Harcourt Brace Jovanovich, N.Y.C., 1965-70, promotion coordinator, 1970-74, mgr. div. verifiability and testing, 1974-75; editor in chief Tchr. mag., N.Y.C., 1975-81; editor-in-chief sch. div. Harper & Row Pubs., N.Y.C., 1981-84; v.p., editor-in-chief Globe Book Co., Simon and Schuster Ednl. Pub., N.Y.C., 1984—; pres. Ednl. Press Assn. Am., Glassboro, N.J., 1983—. Contbg. author: Winston Basic Reading Program, 1962, Little Owl Program, 1963. Mem. Assn. Am. Pubs. (critical issues com. 1983—). Office: Globe Book Co 50 W 23d St New York NY 10010

BARBER, JANET KATHERYNE, minister of music; b. Shreveport, La., Dec. 31, 1949; d. Olen Cleon and Helen Teeple (Wilson) B. B.S., Southwestern Assemblies of God Coll., Waxahachie, Tex., 1972. Minister of music First Assembly of God, New Orleans, 1972-76, Baton Rouge, 1976-79, Honolulu, 1979—; dist. music dir. Hawaii Assemblies of God, Honolulu, 1980—; speaker Church Growth Hawaii, Honolulu, 1981-83, cons., speaker Choral Clinics, Hawaii, mainland U.S., Singapore, 1980-82. Producer, dir. music prodn. The Witness, 1980-81, The Singing Christmas Tree, 1980—; producer TV prodns. He is the Music, Celebrate Life, 1980-81; contbr. articles in field to profl. publs. Coordinator Family Court Services, Baton Rouge, 1978-79. Mem. Assemblies of God Music Dirs. Fellowship, Fellowship Christian Musicians and Dirs. (co-founder) Republican. Office: First Assembly of God 930 Lunalilo St Honolulu HI 96822

BARBER, LAVERNE GOODMAN, accountant; b. Elysworth, Okla., Sept., 6, 1936; d. Bert Edward and Ira Leona (Mcafee) Goodman; children—Patricia Ann, Marsha Marie, Lea Frances. A.A., Tulsa Jr. Coll., 1976; grad. Tulsa U., 1985. Cert. graphoanalyst. With Shell Oil Co., Tulsa, 1973; EDP auditor Sartain & Fischbein Co., Tulsa, 1974; with KRAV-KFMJ Radio, Tulsa, 1974-75; acct. Am. Airlines, Inc., Tulsa, 1976—. Mem. Internat. Graphoanalysis Soc., Assn. Profl. Bus. Women Accts. Democrat. Club: Profl. and Bus. (sec.-treas. 1981-82). Avocations: travel; flying. Office: American Airlines Inc 3800 N Mingo Rd Tulsa OK 74151

BARBER, LEONA FOX, government employee, civic worker; b. Wilton, N.H., Sept. 30, 1927; d. Archer Douglas and Mabel Elizabeth (Fuller) Fox; m. Albertus Vaut Barber, Mar. 7, 1959; children—Amy Sue, Albertus Vaut III. B.A. in English Edn., U. N.H., 1948; cert. pub. affairs Army War Coll., 1950; cert. personnel adminstrn. U.S. Naval Postgrad. Sch., 1957; tchr. cert. U. Va., 1971; M.Ed. in Adminstrn. and Supervisory Mgmt., George Mason U., 1974. Cert. tchr., sch.adminstr./prin., Va. Commd. ensign U.S. Navy, 1949, advanced through grades to lt. comdr., 1958; resigned, 1960; tchr. St. Agnes Sch., Alexandria, Va., 1968-73, sch. adminstr., 1974-81; staff asst. Senator Harry Byrd, Washington, 1982; exec. sec. to sr. specialist Library of Congress, Washington, 1983—, also mem. info. resources com., women's program adv. com., 1983-85. Author curriculum materials; also many articles in ednl. publs. Pres., mem. pub. relations com., bd. dirs. Guest Hosue, Alexandria, 1976—; vestry mem., former chairperson day sch. All Saints Sharon Chapel Episcopal Ch., Franconia, Va. AAUW scholar, 1982. Mem. Library of Congress Prol. Assn., AAUW (bd. dirs.). Republican. Avocations: restoring antiques; painting; traveling. Home: 4504 Dartmoor Ln Alexandria VA 22310 Office: Library of Congress Congl Research Service 101 Independence Ave SE Washington DC 20540

BARBER, PATRICIA SMITH, county extension administrator; b. Tuscaloosa, Ala., Jan. 19, 1949; d. Joseph Fleet and Viva Leola (Swindle) Williamson; m. Daryl F. Barber, Aug. 24, 1981; children—Daffiny Leana, Dena Leigh. B.S., U. Ala., 1971; M.S., Purdue U., 1977. Adminstrv. sec. U. Ala., 1967-71; grad. research asst. Purdue U., 1971-73; data processor Gulf States Paper Corp., Tuscaloosa, Ala., 1973-74; home econs. agent Charlotte County, Punta Gorda, Fla., 1974-75, county extension dir., 1975-79; asst. for extension energy programs U. Fla., Gainesville, 1979; home econs./4-H agt. Baker County, Macclenny, Fla., 1979-80, county extension dir., 1980—. Appearances on numerous consumer oriented radio and TV shows. Contbr. weekly news column to newspaper. Mgr. Baker County Fair Assn., 1980-81, bd. dirs., 1982-84; chmn. concession stand Baker County Shine Festival, 1982, mem. planning com., 1983-84; chmn. Baker County Cystic Fibrosis Bike-A-Thon, 1980-82. Grantee in field. Mem. Baker County C. of C. (certificate of recognition 1981, 82), Am. Home Econs. Assn., Fla. Home Econs. Assn., Nat. Assn. Extension Home Econs. Agts., Fla. Assn. Extension Home Econs. Agts. (Pub. Affairs award 1982), Nat. Assn. Extension 4-H Agts., Fla. Council Family Relations, Women In Mgmt., Epsilon Sigma Phi, Gamma Sigma Delta. Democrat. Baptist. Avocations: reading, remodeling, refinishing furniture.

BARBER, RITA, burial clothing company executive; b. Waxahachie, Tex., Mar. 28, 1900; d. William James and Artelia (Cliftan) Williams; m. Clyde Clinton Barber, May 11, 1925 (dec. 1927); 1 child, Clyde Harwell. Student Natiam Bus. Coll., 1917-18. City collector, Stamford, Tex., 1919-20; bookkeeper Buie Hardware and Implement, Itasca, Tex., 1922, Kenny Funeral Home, Stamford, Tex., 1928; pres., founder Rita Barber, Inc., 1928—. Co-founder, trustee Barber Found.; charter mem. Abilene Altrusa Club; past vice-pres. Sunday Sch. class Univ. Church of Christ; active in Herald of Truth radio and TV program. Mem. Casket Mfrs. Assn., Nat. Found. Funeral Service (assoc.), Tex. Funeral Dirs. Assn. (award 1980), Tex. Assn. Taxpayers, Nat. Fedn. Ind. Bus., Abilene Better Bus. Bur., Abilene C. of C., C. of C. of U.S.A. Club: Abilene Organ (past. sec.). Office: Rita Barber Inc 518 Butternut Abilene TX 79602

BARBETTA, MARIA ANN, hospital records administrator, consultant; b. Bristol, Pa., Mar. 20, 1956; d. Eugene Charles and Anna (Strozzieri) B. A.A., Bucks County Community Coll., 1976; B.S., Coll. Allied Health Professions, Temple U., 1978. Dir. med. records Cumberland Regional Health Plan, Vineland, N.J., 1978; dir. med. record dept. St. Mary Hosp., Langhorne, Pa., 1978—; cons. med. records St. Joseph's Home for Aged, Holland, Pa., 1983—; speaker on med. record topics to various orgns., Langhorne, 1983—. Mem. Am. Med. Record Assn., Lehigh Valley Med. Record Assn., Southeastern Pa. Med. Record Assn., Hosp. Assn. Pa. Avocations: teaching Sunday school; cross-country skiing; volunteer work; reading. Home: 4707 Grandview Ave Bensalem PA 19020 Office: St Mary Hosp Langhorne-Newtown Rd Langhorne PA 19047

BARBOUR, CAROL GOODWIN, psychologist; b. Morganton, N.C., Sept. 15, 1946; d. Jesse Otho and Edith Adele (Goodwin) B.; m. Sidney Gilman. A.B., Duke U., 1967; Ph.D., U. Mich., 1981. Research analyst State of Ill., Chgo., 1968-69; psychologist Med. Student Mental Health Service U. Mich., Ann Arbor, 1977-80, postdoctoral fellow in clin. psychology, adolescent inpatient psychiatry, 1980-82, psychodiagnostic supr., 1973-77, supr. Psychol. Clinic, 1982-83; pvt. practice psychotherapy, Ann Arbor, 1980—; dir. psychiat. services Lakewood Clinic, Novi, Mich., 1982-85, clin. supr., staff psychologist, 1985—. Fulbright grantee, U.S. Ednl. Found. in India, 1967-68. Mem. Am. Psychol. Assn., Psychologists Interested in Study of Psychoanalysis, Mich. Soc. Psychoanalytic Psychology, Mich. Psychol. Assn., Assn. Advancement of Psychology, Phi Beta Kappa. Home: 3411 Geddes Rd Ann Arbor MI 48105 Office: 555 E William Suite 23L Ann Arbor MI 48104

BARBOUR, CYNTHIA DIANE, lawyer; b. Cleve., Feb. 26, 1954; d. Edward Daniel and Elizabeth (Leedy) Powers; m. William Edward Barbour, Sept. 19, 1975. Cert., U. Salzburg (Austria), 1972; student Fla. So. Coll., 1972-74, Cleve. State U., 1974-76; B.A., Mt. Vernon Nazarene Coll., 1977; J.D., Ohio No. U., 1982. Bar: Ohio 1983. Asst. to adult probation officer City of Mt. Vernon (Ohio), 1978-79; co-owner Irish Hills Golf Course, Mt. Vernon, 1976—; asst. city law dir., mcpl. atty., asst. city prosecutor City of Mt. Vernon, 1983—; sole practice, Mt. Vernon, 1983—. Mem. legal com. New Directions Shelter for Domestic Violence, Knox County, Ohio, 1983—. Mem. ABA, Bus. and Profl. Women (corr. sec.), Ct. Practice Inst. (diplomate), Internat. Platform Assn., Mt. Vernon Players (co-choreographer 1977—), Phi Alpha Delta. Republican. Roman Catholic. Office: City Law Director's Office 111 E Chestnut St Mount Vernon OH 43050 also: 5 N Gay St Suite 222 Mount Vernon OH 43050

BARBOUR, DELTA RAE, trade association executive; b. Independence, Va., Apr. 28, 1937; d. Floyd McKinley an Nannie Ellen (Osborne) Boyer; student Strayer Bus. Coll., 1974-76, Prince Georges County Community Coll., 1976-77. Acct., Structural Clay Products Inst., Washington, 1962-66; office mgr. Joseph T. Hunt, D.D.S., Henderson, N.C., 1966-69, McGaughy, Marshall & McMillan, Washington, 1969-74; comptroller Sugar Assn., Inc., Washington, 1974—, asst. corp. sec., 1974-85, v.p., 1984—, sec.-treas., 1986—; realtor Century 21 J.D. Williams Real Estate, Lanham, Md., 1979—. Mem. polit. action com. Prince Georges County Real Estate Bd., 1977-78. Mem. Nat. Assn. Female Execs., Nat. Assn. Realtors, Prince Georges County Bd. Realtors, Am. Soc. Assn. Execs., Greater Washington Soc. Assn. Execs., Washington Assn. Fin. Mgmt. Democrat. Presbyterian. Club: Nat. Dem. Home: 9411 Van Buren St Lanham MD 20706 Office: 1511 K St Washington DC 20005

BARBOZA-CLARK, FRANCES E., med. technologist; b. Jersey City, June 22, 1938; d. Lawrence and Clementina Frances (Lopes) Barboza; diploma med. tech. Coll. Medicine and Dentistry N.J.-Rutgers U., 1970; div.; children—Donald, Renee, Edward. Chem. lab. technician, 1956-57; histology technician Coll. Medicine and Dentistry N.J.-Rutgers U. Med. Sch., 1969-72, research asst., 1972-75, med. technologist, 1975-81, sr. med. technologist, 1981—, also tchr., trainer students, supr. historology lab. Mem. Am. Soc. Clin. Pathologists (registered affiliate), Am. Soc. Med. Tech., Nat. Soc. Histotech., N.J. Soc. Histotech. (charter), NOW (chpt. coordinator 1979-81, dir. 1983—, mem. polit. action com. 1983—). Office: U Medicine and Dentistry NJ-Rutgers U Med Sch PO Box 101 Piscataway NJ 08854

BARCELOW, NANCY ELIZABETH, dietitian; b. Providence, Dec. 16, 1953; d. Gordon Gilbert and Elizabeth Louise (Zuill) Beardwood; m. Jerry Albert Barcelow, Jan. 4, 1976; children—Dean Alan, Rebecca Elizabeth. B.S., Atlantic Union Coll., 1976; M.S., Framingham State Coll., 1978. Dietetic intern Beth Israel Hosp., Boston; clin. dietitian St. Elizabeth's Hosp., Brighton, Mass., 1979-80; renal and acute care nutrition specialist Lahey Clinic, Med. Ctr., Burlington, Mass., 1980-81; clin. dietitian Dartmouth Hitchock Med Ctr., Hanover, N.H., 1981-82; instr. Community Coll. Vt., Barre, 1984—. Mem. White River Valley Health Promotion Council, Randolph, Vt., 1985. Mem. Vt. Dietetic Assn. (pres. 1985-86), Am. Dietetic Assn., Seventh-day Adventist Dietetic Assn. Seventh-day Adventist. Avocations: gardening; house restoration; sewing and needlework. Home: S Windsor St Box 265 South Royalton VT 05068

BARDELLI, DONA ALICE, economist, international management consultant; b. Irvington, N.J., Feb. 27, 1953; d. Alfred and Dona Ellen (Self) B.; m. Harry M. Bainbridge, May 23, 1981. Certificat de Langue, Sorbonne, U. Paris, 1974; B.A., U. Ky., 1975; M.A. in Internat. Studies, Am. U., 1978; M.Sc. in Econ. and Social Planning in Developing Countries, London Sch. Econs., U. London, 1979. Research assoc. Woodrow Wilson Internat. Ctr. for Vis. Scholars, Washington, 1976-77, World Bank, Washington, 1977-79; legis. asst. to Congressman Marc Lincoln Marks, Washington, 1979-80; internat. trade analyst Internat. Trade Adminstrn., U.S. Dept. Commerce, Washington, 1980-82; internat. mgmt. cons. Coopers and Lybrand, 1982—, mgr. indsl. devel. and export promotion services; Washington coordinator Coopers & Lybrand Internat. Mgmt. Cons. Services, Washington, 1982—. Chpt. pres. Am. Friends of London Sch. Econs., 1981-83, nat. bd. dirs., 1982-85. Mem. AAUW, Nat. Fedn. Bus. and Profl. Women's Clubs, Bus. and Profl. Women's Clubs Am. (acad. scholar 1971), Nat. Assn. Female Execs., Am. Platform Assn. Democrat. Lutheran. Office: Coopers & Lybrand 1251 Ave of Americas New York NY 10020

BARDEN, CAROL ISAAK, oil company executive, designer, writer; b. Ellensburg, Wash., Feb. 4, 1947; d. Alvin Earnest and Helen Laverne (Munson) Isaak; m. Bryce M. Barden, Aug. 23, 1970 (div. 1983); m. E.G. Wallace, Jr., Feb. 2, 1986. Student U. Oreg., 1968; B.A. in Home Econs., Seattle Pacific U., 1969; postgrad Western Wash. State Coll., 1969-73; U. Vienna, 1971, U. Houston, 1980-81. Tchr. Mt. Vernon (Wash.) Sch. Dist., 1969-79; internat. group travel cons. IAA World Travel, Mt. Vernon, 1976-80; freelance travel writer, Mt. Vernon, 1977-80; exec. asst. to bd. dirs. Republic Mineral Corp., Houston, 1980—; producer Broadway play Whodunnit, 1982. Contbr. to Connossieur Mag., 1984—, articles to newspapers. Chmn. Opera-on-Stage Dinner, 1981-85; bd. dirs. Houston Grand Opera, 1983—, Soc. for Performing Arts, 1983—, San Antonio Music Festival, 1983—; co-chmn. Opera Ball, 1983; founder costume inst. Mus. Fine Arts, Houston. Mem. Wash. Gen. Hon. Orgn., Seattle U. Women. Republican. Club: Warwick (Houston). Office: Republic Mineral Corp PO Box 27406 Houston TX 77027

BARDIA, CAROL SAILORS, public relations executive; b. Los Angeles, Aug. 2, 1945; d. Ovid Burr and Roberta Josephine (Smith) Sailors; m. Alexander Vilicaña Bardia, Sept. 5, 1981. B.S., U. So. Calif., 1967, M.B.A., 1974. Securities trader Lehman Bros., Inc., Los Angeles, 1971-74; mktg. services mgr. Hughes Aircraft Co., Carlsbad, Calif., 1975-78; dealer services cons. Nissan Motor Corp., Carson, Calif., 1978; mktg. dir. Mgmt. Resource Assocs., San Diego, 1979; mgr. fine jewelry Bullocks, Inc., Carlsbad, Calif., 1980-81; mgr. communications mktg. TRW LSI Products, San Diego, 1981-83, pub. relations exec., 1983—. Republican. Congregationalist.

BARDOS, MARIA ELENA, banker, data processing consultant; b. Canonsburg, Pa., Nov. 6, 1949; d. George Phillip and Victoria (Loutsion) B. B.S. in Math., U. Pitts., 1971, M.B.A., 1976; postgrad. Duquesne U., 1980—. Programmer, analyst Mellon Bank, Pitts., 1971-73; systems cons. Westinghouse Nuclear, Pitts., 1973-75; systems planning analyst Equibank, Pitts., 1975-76; corp. EDP auditor Rockwell Internat., Pitts., 1976-77; pres. Bardos Cons., Pitts., 1977-79; asst. v.p., software devel. mgr. Dollar Bank, Pitts., 1979-82, v.p. electronic banking dept., 1984-85; pres. Dollar Bank Adv. Group, Inc., 1986—; instr. Robert Morris Coll., 1983-84. Bd. dirs. Holy Cross Greek Orthodox Ch., Pitts., 1984—, youth coordinator, 1983-84; youth commr. Greek Orthodox Diocese, 1983-84; vol. Bapt. Ctr., 1982-83; bd. dirs. United Way of Southwestern Pa., 1986-87, Pitts. Bus. Acad., 1986; tech. adviser United Way of Allegheny County. Recipient Thyrsa Amos award U. Pitts., 1970, Helen Garyiannis nat. grantee Greek Orthodox Archdiocese, N.Y.C., 1968. Mem. Data Processing Mgmt. Assn., Assn. Women in Computing, Greek Orthodox Young Adult League (v.p. 1982), Mortar Board. Republican. Home: 14 Pocono Dr Pittsburgh PA 15220 Office: Dollar Savs Bank Oliver Bldg 535 Smithfield St Pittsburgh PA 15222

BARDWELL, VICTORIA ELAINE, pharmacist; b. Charleston, W.Va., July 5, 1954; d. Victor Nasiff and Carolyn Elizabeth (Norris) B. B.S., U. Cin., 1977. Registered pharmacist. pharmcist, mgr. Super X Drugs Inc., St. Albans, W.Va., 1977-80, dist. pharmacy supr., 1980-81, regional nursing home supr. Super X Drugs, Inc., 1981-82; pharmacist, mgr. Neurman Drug Co., Inc., Charleston, W.Va., 1982-84, Revco Drugs, Inc., 1984—. Cons. Dunbar Health Care Ctr., 1978-81, W.Va. Dept. Health, 1984—. Mem. Nat. Democratic Com., 1986. Recipient Gold Link award pub. edn. Nat. Assn. Chain Drug Stores/Women's Day, 1980. Mem. Am. Pharm. Assn., W.Va. Pharm. Assn., Kanawha Valley Assn. Pharmacists. Vice pres. Soc. Orthodox Youth Orgns., Charleston, 1985-86. Avocations: reading; playing guitar; basketball; tennis. Office: Revco Drug Stores Inc 5433 Big Tyler Rd Charleston WV 25313

BAREIS, BEVERLIE ELAINE, nurse; b. Rockland, Maine, July 22, 1925; d. Earle Raymond and Margaret Verrel (Long) Conant; R.N., New Eng. Deaconess Hosp., Boston, 1946; B.S. in Health Sci., Calif. State U., Northridge, 1976; M.A., Calif. State U., Los Angeles, 1981; m. David W. Bareis, Feb. 8, 1947; children—Ellen Ruth Bareis DiGiampaulo, Karl Frederick, Paul Arthur, Kathilynn Bareis Marquette. Inservice supr. Motion Picture Country Hosp., Woodland Hills, Calif., 1960-66; nursing educator Los Angeles City Unified Schs., 1965—; staff devel. coordinator, then dir. community relations Brotman Meml. Hosp., Culver City, Calif., 1970-77; asst. dir. nursing and health programs ARC, 1978-80; asst. prof. Calif. State U., Los Angeles, part-time, 1981—; nursing educator paramed. br. Abram Friedman Occupational Center, Los Angeles 1980—. Recipient Gold medal Los Angeles County Heart Assn., 1966, Clara Barton medal ARC, 1972. Mem. Am. Public Health Assn., Nat. League Nursing, NEA, Los Angeles County Heart Assn., Am. Diabetic Assn., Sex. Edn. and Info. Council U.S., New Eng. Deaconess Hosp. Alumnae Assn., Phi Kappa Phi. Address: Santa Monica CA 90402

BAREISH, SYLVIA J., village official; b. N.Y.C., Dec. 25, 1915; d. Nathan and Rebecca Ruth (Rosenbloom) Janowitz; m. Philip Bareish, Feb. 22, 1940 (dec. 1968); children—Carolyn Bareish Mandelker, Clifford. B.A., Hunter Coll., 1937; M.S., NYU, 1938. Cert. math. tchr., N.Y. Asst. to mdse. mgr. Bernard Altman, N.Y.C., 1937-49, asst. buyer, 1939-40; tchr. pub. schs., Bronx and Queens, N.Y., 1953-82; trustee Village of Lake Success, Great Neck, N.Y., 1982—. Author Lake Success Resident's Handbook, 1983. Liaison officer Civic Assn., Lake Success, 1953—; vol. L.I. Jewish Psychol. Tutorial Program, 1980—, Indsl. Home For Blind; treas. Lake Success Ladies' Golf Assn., 1984—. Mem. Orgn. Rehab. and Tng. Democrat. Club: Women's Golf (treas. 1984—) (Lake Success). Lodge: B'nai B'rith Women (local pres. 1984—). Avocations: golf; bridge; theater; travel.

BARFIELD, SHIRLEY ROSALIS, banking officer; b. Apalachicola, Fla., Sept. 6, 1940; d. Charles Manuel and Loretta Frances (Nasto) Rosalis; m. Wendell W. Barfield, Mar. 2, 1962; children—Wendell N. Barfield, Charles Darrin Barfield. A.S., Polk Community Coll., Fla., 1981; Standard and Advanced Tng., Am. Inst. Banking, Washington, 1983. Dep. clk. CCC Franklin County, Apalachicola, 1959-61; mgmt. trainee Apalachicola St. Bank, Fla., 1961-66; pub. relations staff Peoples Bank, Lakeland, Fla., 1967; br. mgr. Fla. Nat. Bank, Port St. Joe, 1968; fin. officer Sch. Bd., Franklin County, Apalachicola, 1968-70; compliance officer Barnett Bank of Polk County, Lakeland, 1970—; instr. Polk Community Coll., Winter Haven, Fla., 1981—. Mem. Nat. Assn. Bank Women (com. 1981—), Nat. Assn. Exec. Women, Am. Inst. Banking. Democrat. Roman Catholic. Clubs: Beta (pres. 1956-59), 4-H (Carabelle, Fla., pres. 1953-59). Avocations: piano; reading; history; camping. Home: 1125 Lakewood Rd Lakeland FL 33805 Office: Barnett Bank Polk County 331 S Fla Ave Lakeland FL 33802

BARGAGLIOTTI, LILLIAN ANTOINETTE, nursing educator; b. Millington, Tenn., Dec. 29, 1949; d. Bernard Wood and Georgeanne (Lowe) McIllwain; m. Ronald M. Prentice, Apr. 24, 1970 (div. 1975); m. 2d Bill L. Bargagliotti, July 8, 1978; 1 son, William Benard. R.N., Tacoma Gen. Hosp., 1971; B.S. in Nursing, U. Tenn., 1976; M.S., U. Calif.-San Francisco, 1978, D.Nursing Sci., 1984. Staff nurse Tacoma Gen. Hosp. (Wash.), 1971, St. Joseph's Hosp., Tacoma, 1971-75, City of Memphis Hosp., 1975-76; instr. Northwest Miss. Jr. Coll., Senatobia, 1976-78; inservice coordinator Eden Hosp., Castro Valley, Calif., 1978-79; instr. Ohlone Coll., Fremont, Calif., 1979-84; assoc. prof. nursing San Francisco State U., 1984-85; assoc. dean, assoc. prof. nursing U. San Francisco, 1985—. Clin. evaluator SUNY Western Performance Assessment Ctr., Long Beach and Palo Alto, Calif., 1982-85. Contbr. articles to profl. jours. Served to capt. U.S. Army Res., 1976-78. Mem. Am. Nurses Assn., Calif. Nurses Assn., Calif. Soc. Nursing Service Adminstrs., Western Soc. Nurse Researchers, Sigma Theta Tau. Republican. Mem. Ch. of Christ. Home: 731 Buena Vista Moss Beach CA Office: Sch Nursing U San Francisco Ignatian Hts San Francisco CA

BARGER, CAROL MARGARET, lawyer; b. Oakland, Calif., Jan. 6, 1946; d. Conrad Alvin and Irma Ruth (Dennis) Barger; m. Roger F. Thomson, July 11, 1975. B.A., Lynchburg Coll., 1967; M.A., So. Meth. U., 1970, J.D., 1973. Bar: Tex. 1973, U.S. Dist. Ct. Tex. 1973, U.S. Ct. Appeals (5th cir.) 1973. Staff atty. Dallas Legal Services Found., Dallas, 1973-76, Tarrant County Legal Aid Found., Ft. Worth, 1977; mng. atty. East Tex. Legal Services, Longview, Tex., 1977-79; dir. Southwest Office, Consumers Union, Austin, Tex., 1979—; cons. Rand Corp., Santa Monica, Calif., 1980-83; program chmn. consumer law sect. Tex. State Bar Conv., Ft. Worth, 1983, program chmn. utility law sect., 1982; speaker to various orgns., 1982-84. Mem. Tex. Sunset Adv. Com., Austin, 1981-83; mem. subcom. fuel use act, Tex. Energy and Natural Resource Adv. Com., Austin, 1980. Mem. Student Bar Assn. (pres. 1972-73), State Bar Tex. (mem. consumer law sect. governing council 1981—). Democrat. Mem. Disciples of Christ Ch. Clubs: Sierra (Dallas); Dallas Democratic Forum. Home: 6210 Bryan Pkwy Dallas TX 74214 Office: Consumers Union of US Inc 202 W 13th St Austin TX 78701

BARHAM, MARY LEA, librarian; b. Brent, Okla., Aug. 17, 1933; d. James Jacob and Mary Angeline (Hollis) B. B.S. in Edn., Okla. State U., 1956; M.L.A., U. Okla., 1962. Govt. documents asst. Okla. State U., Stillwater, 1951-52, vet. medicine librarian, 1962-63, established vet. medicine library, 1962; readers services librarian Midwestern U., Wichita Falls, Tex., 1963-65, organizer, established govt. documents depository library, 1964, established curriculum edn. library, 1964; asst. librarian San Jacinto Coll., Pasadena, Tex., 1965-80; head librarian San Jacinto Coll.-South, Houston, 1980—. Author: Library Handbook, 1981; patentee follow-block booktruck. Mem. Southwestern Library Assn., Tex. Jr. Coll. Tchrs. Assn. Democrat. Baptist. Home: 701 Princeton St Deer Park TX 77536

BARHAM, PATTE (MRS. HARRIS BOYNE), publisher, author, columnist; b. Los Angeles; d. Dr. Frank Barham and Princess Jessica Meskhi Gleboff; student U. So. Calif., U. Ariz.; Litt.D., Trinity So. Bible Coll. War corr., Korea; syndicated columnist; acting sec. of state State of Calif., 1980-81. Life mem. AAU, former v.p. pub. relations; mem. internat. com. So. Calif. Philharmonic; dir. Los Angeles Council on Internat. Visitors; mem. hospitality com. U.S. Olympic Com. Decorated dame Sovereign Order of Alfred the Great, grand cross, patron of honor; compagne de la Couronne d'Epines, Ancien Abbaye-Principaute de San Luigi. Mem. Nat. League Am. Pen Women, English Speaking Union, DAR, St. Anne's Hosp. Guild, Social Service Aux., Delta Gamma. Clubs: Outrigger Canoe, Waikiki Yacht (Hawaii); Wilshire Country, Ebell, Bel Air Country (Los Angeles); Metropolitan (N.Y.C.); St. James (London); Tokyo Corrs.; Round the World; Author: Pin up Poems; Rasputin: The Man behind the Myth. Address: 100 Fremont Pl Los Angeles CA 90005

BARIL, NANCY ANN, gerontological nurse practitioner, nurse consultant; b. Paterson, N.J., May 10, 1952; d. Kenneth Gerald and Jeanette Elenore (Girodet) Keiser; m. Joel Mark Baril, Apr. 15, 1984; 1 child, Jason Kenneth. A.A., Gulf Coast Community Coll., 1976; B.S. in Nursing, Fla. State U., 1978; M. in Nursing, UCLA, 1983. Registered pub. health nurse, Calif.; ANA cert. gerontol. nurse practitioner. Charge nurse, nurse preceptor Cedar Sinai Med. Ctr., Los Angeles, 1979-83; registered nurse Nursing Services Incorp., Sherman Oaks, Calif., 1980-83; nurse practitioner Santa Monica Peer Counseling Ctr., Santa Monica, Calif., 1983; nurse cons., gerontol. nurse practioner Summit Health Ltd., Burbank, Calif., 1983-85; nurse cons. Geriatric Assocs., Granada Hills, Calif., 1983-85; nurse cons., gerontol. nurse practitioner Care Enterprises West, Burbank, 1985—. Mem. PTA, Granada Hills, 1985. Mem. Calif. Coalition of Nurse Practioners, Am. Nursing Assn., Calif. Nursing Assn., Gerontol. Soc., Sigma Theta Tau (rec. sec. 1983-85). Democrat. Episcopalian. Avocations: reading; crossword puzzles; gardening; jetskiing. Home: 16921 Bircher St Granada Hills CA 91344 Office: Care Enterprises West 303 Glenoaks Blvd Suite 180 Burbank CA 91502

BARISH, ELLEN GAIL, lawyer; b. N.Y.C., Nov. 11, 1946; d. Aaron and Doris (Warman) Schwartz; m. Joel Stuart Barish, Oct. 20, 1968; 1 son, Howard Saul. B.A., Am. U., 1968; M.A., Towson State U., 1973; J.D., U. Balt., 1982. Bar: Md. 1982, U.S. Dist. Ct. Md. 1983, U.S. Bankruptcy Ct. 1983. Tchr., N.Y.C. Pub. Schs., 1968-70; assoc. Allen, Thiebolt & Alexander, Balt., 1982-83, Weinberg & Green, Balt., 1983—. Fund raiser Assoc. Jewish Charities, Balt., 1982-83. Mem. Bar Assn. Balt. City, Md. Bar Assn., Assn. Trial Lawyers Am. Democrat. Jewish. Club: Woodholme Country (Pikesville, Md.). Office: Weinberg & Green 100 S Charles St Baltimore MD 21201

BARKAN, VICTORIA LYNN KOEGLE, cable television executive; b. Dayton, Ohio, Dec. 17, 1946; d. Wilbur Robert and Lillian (Lauer) Koegle; m. John Nestor Barkan Jr., July 19, 1971 (div.). B.S.E., Bowling Green State U., 1969. Layout artist Art Staff Studio, Toledo, 1969-71, Higbees, Cleve., 1972-73; freelance artist, 1974-75; account exec. Media 2000, Hudson, Ohio, 1976-77; nat. advt. mgr. Continental Cablevision, Findlay, Ohio, 1977-80; mktg. coordinator United Cable TV Corp., Denver, 1980; dir. mktg. Metrovision, Atlanta, 1980—. Recipient Bronze Echo, Direct Mail Mktg. Assn., 1979. Mem. Women in Cable (v.p., pres. Atlanta chpt. 1982-84, nat. dir. 1984—), Cable TV Adminstrn. Mgmt., Delta Phi Delta. Club: Atlanta Ski. Office: Metrovision 930 211 Perimeter Ctr Atlanta GA 30346

BARKER, BARBARA ANN, ophthalmologist; b. Paterson, N.J., Nov. 10, 1943; d. Earle Louis and Dorothy Louise (Williamson) Barker; m. Joel Ira Papernik, July 28, 1972. B.A., Connecticut Coll., 1965; B.A., Yale U., 1967; M.A., Rutgers Med. Sch., 1974; M.D., Mt. Sinai Sch. Medicine, 1976. Diplomate Am. Bd. Ophthalmology. Intern, Beth Israel Med. Center, 1977; resident Mt. Sinai Sch. Medicine/Beth Israel Med. Center, 1980, fellow in glaucoma, 1980-81, fellow cornea, refractive surgery, 1981-82, now mem. staff; research technician The Rockefeller U., N.Y.C., 1965-66; tchr. Riverdale Country Sch., N.Y.C., 1967-68; research asst. Sloan Kettering Inst., N.Y.C., 1969-72; clin. instr. Mt. Sinai Sch. Medicine, N.Y.C., 1982—; pvt. practice medicine specializing in ophthalmology, N.Y.C., 1983—; mem. staff N.Y. Eye and Ear Hosp., Cabrini Hosp. Recipient Resident Paper award Beth Israel Med. Center, 1980; Beth Israel Research grantee, 1983; NSF grantee, 1966. Mem. Internat. Soc. Refractive Keratoplasty, AMA, Am. Med. Women's Assn., Women's Med. Soc. N.Y.C., N.Y. County Med. Assn. (mem. com.), Phi Beta Kappa. Home: 11 E 86th St #18B New York NY 10028 Office: 11 E 86th St #1B New York NY 10028

BARKER, JOANN SPARKS, construction executive, consultant; b. Gad, W.Va., Aug. 30, 1949; d. Clayton and Edith (Roberts) Sparks; m. H. David Barker, Dec. 24, 1969 (div. Feb. 1984). Student W.Va. Inst. Tech., 1967-69, U. Charleston, 1974, 76. Project engr. Glasgow, Inc., Glenside, Pa., 1975-81; project mgr. London Bridge Co., Ky., 1981-83, safety dir., 1983-84; project mgr. Kokosing Constrn. Co., Phoenix, 1984, V.O. Contracting Co., Tempe, Ariz., 1985; constrn. mgr. Harquahala Valley Irrigation Dist., Buckeye, Ariz., 1985—. James Ireland scholar, 1967. Mem. Delta Zeta. Democrat. Avocations: golf; collecting antiques; psychological research. Home: 208 Narramore Ave Buckeye AZ 85326 Office: Harquahala Valley Irrigation Dist Star Route 2 Box 397 Buckeye AZ 85326

BARKER, LAURENN RUSSELL, public relations executive, sculptor, artist; b. Morristown, Tenn., Mar. 17, 1945; d. George Herbert and Claire Hortense (Perkins) Prater; m. Rodney Gibson Russell, Aug. 27, 1967 (div.); children—Chelse Fore, Josh Barrett, Micaiah Lael; m. Paul Edward Barker, Feb. 16, 1981. Grad. cum laude Mt. Vernon Sem., 1963; grad. Inst. Am. Univs., France, 1966; B.A., So. Meth. U., 1967; postgrad. Dallas Art Inst., 1967. Graphic designer Taylor Pub., Dallas, 1968-69; art dir. First Nat. Bank-First Family mag., Dallas, 1969-70; graphic artist Tyler Courier Times (Tex.), 1971-74; dir pub. relations Marsco Engring., Tyler, 1974-79; owner R&L Design Studio, Tyler, 1979-81; dir. pub. relations Espey, Huston & Assocs., Austin-Houston, 1981—; design cons. S.W. Hist. Wax Mus., Arlington, Tex., 1979, Tex. Hist. Preservation Park, Austin, 1983, Neuroscis. Inst., Los Angeles, 1983; cons. pub. relations Gallery Contemporary Southwestern Art, Dallas, 1983. Featured artist Tyler Courier Times, 1979, Sta. KLTV-TV, Longview, Tex., 1979, Tex. Hwys. State mag., 1979, Austin mag., 1981, Sta. KTVV-TV, Austin, 1982. Active Tex. Fine Arts Assn., 1982—, Austin Heritage Soc., 1983—, Tex. Hist. Found., 1983—; exec. bd. Central Tex. Chpt. March of Dimes Benefit, Austin, 1985—. Recipient State Rep. award Nat. Cherry Blossom Festival, Washington, 1966; U.S. Rep.-Bal de Petit Lits Blanc, Monte Carlo, Monaco, 1967; Design/Modeling award Neiman Marcus, Dallas, 1967. Mem. Women in Communications, Inc., Tex. Presswomen's Assn., Glamour Mag. Orgn. Profl. Women, Austin Contemporary Visual Arts Assn., Soc. for Mktg. Profl. Services, Tex. Pub. Relations Assn. Democrat. Presbyterian. Home: 1436 Circle Ridge Dr Austin TX 78746 Office: Espey Huston & Assocs Inc 916 Capitol Tex Hwy Austin TX 78746

BARKER, SANDRA L., educator; b. Chgo., July 17, 1941; d. Eugene George and A. Norene (Sanders) Fields; 1 child, Richard Allen. B.A., U. Oreg., 1963, Ph.D., 1983; M.A.T., Portland State U., 1968; student Lewis and Clark Coll., 1959-61. Instr. Oreg. State U., Corvallis, 1968-73; curriculum specialist Salem pub. schs., Oreg., 1973-78, curriculum supr., 1978-79; asst. prof., prin. Eastern Oreg. State Coll., La Grande, 1983-85; asst. prof. edn. Seattle U., 1985—; cons. Central Sch. Dist., Independence, Oreg., 1980; mem. accreditation team State Dept. Edn., Salem, Oreg., 1979-80. Contbr. articles to profl. jours. Mem. Met. League, Seattle, 1986—, Citizens for Edn. N.W., Seattle, 1985. Mem. Nat. Assn. for Curriculum and Devel., Am. Assn. for Higher Edn., N.W. Women in Ednl. Adminstrn., Assn. for Study of Higher Edn., Wash. Assn. Sch. Adminstrs., NOW. Avocations: hiking; cultural events; cooking. Home: 1800 Taylor Ave N #400 Seattle WA 98109 Office: Seattle U 12 & Columbia Seattle WA 98122

BARKER, SARAH EVANS, lawyer, U.S. district judge; b. Mishawaka, Ind., June 10, 1943; d. James McCall and Sarah (Yarbrough) Evans; m. Kenneth R. Barker, Nov. 25, 1972. B.S., Ind. U., 1965; J.D., Am. U., 1969; postgrad. Coll. William and Mary, 1966-67, George Washington U.; LL.D., Ind. Central U., 1984. Bar: Ind., U.S. Dist. Ct. (so. dist.) Ind., U.S. Ct. Appeals (7th cir.), U.S. Supreme Ct. Legal asst. to senator U.S. Senate, 1969-71; spl. counsel to minority govt. ops. com. permanent investigation subcom., 1971-72; dir. research scheduling and advance Senator Percy Re-election Campaign, 1972; asst. U.S. atty. So. Dist. Ind., 1972-75, 1st asst. U.S. atty., 1976-77, U.S. atty., 1981-84; assoc., then ptnr. Bose, McKinney & Evans, Indpls., 1977-81; judge U.S. Dist. Ct. for So. Dist. Ind., Indpls., 1984—. Bd. dirs. New Hope of Ind. Recipient Woman of Yr. award Women in Communications, 1984. Mem. Indpls. Bar Assn. (v.p. 1982-84, bd. mgrs.). Republican. Methodist. Address: 210 US Courthouse 46 E Ohio St Indianapolis IN 46204*

BARKLEY, LINDA DOROTHY, reliability engineer; b. San Diego, Dec. 12, 1951; d. James Falls and Helen Patricia (Yoo) B.; B.A., U. San Diego, 1974; M.S., Loyola Marymount U., 1980. Sr. project engr. Hughes Aircraft Co., El Segundo, Calif., 1978—; So. Calif. coordinator women and math. program, 1979—. Recipient Sci. award Bausch and Lomb, 1970. Mem. Soc. Women Engrs., Assn. Women in Math., Am. Math. Soc., Soc. Indsl. and Applied Math., Math./Sci. Interchange-Los Angeles, Women's Sports Found., Alumnae Assn. Acad. Our Lady of Peace, Alumni Assn. U. San Diego, Greater Los Angeles Zoo Assn., Pi Mu Epsilon. Roman Catholic. Office: Hughes Aircraft Co PO Box 92919 Bldg S32/MS C314 Los Angeles CA 90009

BARKLEY, MARILYN JANE, accountant; b. Yakima, Wash., July 9, 1934; d. Philip and Pauline Marie (Coulter) Barkley; m. Frederick Paul Fazi, Nov. 26, 1968 (div. July 1970). Cert. Lawton Sch., 1953. Office nurse W.A. Blampin, M.D., Los Angeles, 1953-55; jr. acct. Markson Bros., Los Angeles, 1955-57; office mgr. Deaf Smith Research Labs., Hereford, Tex., 1958-59; acct. Roy M. Guest, P.A., Dallas, 1960-68; comptroller, gen. mgr. Restaurant Chablis, Dallas, 1970-78; acct. Tannebaum, Bindler & Co., P.C., C.P.A.s, Dallas, 1978—. Mem. Internat. Platform Assn. Republican. Presbyterian. Lodge: Order of Rainbow. Office: Tannebaum Bindler & Co PC CPAs 2323 Bryan Suite 700 Dallas TX 75201

BARKMAN, ANNETTE SHAULIS, real estate management executive; b. Somerset, Pa., Oct. 18, 1948; d. Norman Albert and Janice Lorraine (Robbins) S.; m. Jon A. Barkman, Dec. 1, 1983. B.A., Dickinson Coll., 1969; M.A., Indiana U. of Pa., 1975. Psychol. services asso. II Bedford/Somerset Mental Health Clinic, Somerset, 1972-78, Somerset State Hosp., 1978-79; pvt. practice hypnosis cons., Somerset, 1976—; pres. Habitability, Inc., real estate mgmt., Somerset, 1978—; exec. mgr. Gt. N.E. Land & Cattle Co., Somerset, 1980-82; owner, mgr. Somerset Credit and Collection Bur., 1981—; realtor James F. Custer Real Estate, 1980—; cons. Somerset County Headstart Program, 1977, 78. Squadron comdr. CAP, Somerset, 1977-78, recipient Meritorious Service award, 1977. Mem. Somerset Welfare League, Chi Omega. Home: RD 8 Box 9 Somerset PA 15501 Office: 118 N Center Ave Somerset PA 15501

BARKSDALE, DIXIE LEE BARKER, association executive; b. Elsinore, Utah, May 25, 1930; d. Aaron Glen and Fawn Lenore (Braithwaite) Whitney; student Brigham Young U., Provo, Utah, 1956, Utah State U., 1957; m. Bruce W. Barksdale; children—Viviann Rose, Vicki Joan Barker, Whitney Dwain Barker. Pres., gen. mgr. Moab Broadcasting and TV Corp., 1969-77; dir. community devel. Grand County (Utah), Moab, 1976-81; exec. dir. Canyonlands Travel Region, 1976-81; econ. devel. cons. Mountainland Assn. Govts., 1981—. Bd. dirs. Utah Econ. and Indsl. Devel., 1969-83, Utah Assn. Travel Regions, 1976-81; mem. Moab City Council, 1976-80; chmn. Grand County Democratic Com., 1968-69, Moab Drug and Alcohol Adv. Bd., 1973; mem. multiple-use adv. bd. Bur. Land Mgmt., 1980-82; mem. Provo City Planning Commn., 1982—, Provo City Site Plan Rev. Bd., 1982-86. Named Woman of Yr., Epsilon Sigma Alpha, 1960, Friend of Utah, State of Utah, 1978. Mem. Moab C. of C. (pres. 1974-75), Provo C. of C. (indsl. devel. com. 1981—), Canyonlands Natural History Assn. (chmn. 1979-81), Utah Indsl. Devel. Execs. Assn. Democrat. Mormon. Club: Moab Women's Lit. (pres. 1959-60). Address: 110 West Pkwy Provo UT 84604

BARLIN, CAROLE ARLENE, educational administrator; b. Oakland, Calif., Nov. 7, 1935; d. Carl Christian and Leona Lillian (Vielhauer) Barlin; B.A., U. Calif., Berkeley, 1958; M.S., U. Redlands, 1971; 1 dau., Lizette Leona Swanson. Tchr., San Francisco Unified Sch. Dist., 1966-69, Los Angeles County Supt. Schs., 1971-74, asst. prin., 1974-76, prin., 1976, personnel coordinator, 1976—; lectr. —The Profl. Woman—. Mem. Assn. of Calif. Sch. Adminstrs. (officer 1976-82), Assn. of Los Angeles County Sch. Adminstrs. (pres. 1981-82), Women in Ednl. Leadership, Am. Speech and Hearing Assn., Who's Who Internat. (exec. v.p.). Office: 9300 E Imperial Hwy Downey CA 90242

BARLOW, CAROLYN MARIE, community management company executive, consultant; b. Media, Pa., May 14, 1939; d. Russell Franklin Mand Adelaide Marie (Manetti) Moyer; m. Robert Eachus Barlow, Sr., July 7, 1962 (div. Mar. 1971); children—Robert Eachus, Jr., Melissa M.; m. Robert Morgan Edmonds, Dec. 30, 1984. Cert. profl. community assn. mgr. Fashion and interior design coordinator, Phila., 1960-71; project mgr. JWH Constrn., Inc., Haverford, Pa., 1971-76; pres. C.M. Barlow & Assocs., Inc., Uwchland, Pa., 1976—; cons. Office Econ. Devel., Washington, 1983. Bd. dirs. real estate adv. bd. Immaculata Coll., 1984-85. Mem. Community Assn. Inst. (bd. dirs. 1976-85, pres. Mid-Atlantic chpt. 1983-84). Republican. Episcopalian. Avocations: watercolor painting; skiing. Home: Park Rd RD #2 Downingtown PA 19335 Office: C M Barlow & Assocs Inc Village of Eagle PO Box 7 Uwchland PA 19480

BARLOW, CAROLYN ROBERTS, retail executive; b. Sylvania, Ga., Oct. 14, 1940; d. Calvin and Caroline (Warnock) Roberts; children—Taushalin Mikuel, Tavin Mikeenan (twins). B.S., Savannah State Coll., 1966; M.Ed., U. Louisville, 1972. Tchr., Louisville Bd. Edn., 1967-72, tchr. coordinator; dir. community services Louisville Urban League, 1972-76; with Footprints, Etc., Savannah, Ga., 1986—; cons. Aceco Mitchell's Service Ctr., Savannah, 1983—. Adminstrv. asst. crusade for Voters, Savannah, 1960-63; dir. public relations Ky. Task Force on Alcoholism, Louisville, 1968-71. Savannah State Coll. scholar, 1960-63; U. Louisville fellow 1971-72. Mem. Delta Sigma Theta. Democrat. Christian. Avocations: Writing; sports; singing; swimming; cycling. Home: PO Box 23913 Savannah GA 31405

BARLOW, PATRICIA ANNE, bank officer; b. Cheyenne, Wyo., May 5, 1954; d. Thomas Alvin and Mary Louise (Canning) B. B.A. cum laude, U. P.R., 1976. Bilingual instr. Berlitz Sch. Langs., Hato Rey, P.R., 1976-77, dir., 1977-78; personnel officer Citibank N.A., San Juan, P.R., 1979-81, human resources dir. instl. bank, 1981-84; human resources officer internat. fin. instns., N.Y.C., 1984—. Mem. Nat. Assn. Bank Women, Am. Soc. Personnel Adminstrs., Nat. Assn. Female Execs., P.R. C. of C. (quality of life com. 1983—), P.R. Mfrs. Assn. (indsl. relations com., 1983—). Office: Citibank NA 111 Wall St New York NY 10047

BARLOW, PAULINE, educator; b. Pflugerville, Tex., Jan. 9, 1927; d. Wesley and Scottie Lee (Jones) B.; B.S., Samuel Huston Coll., 1950; M.Ed., Prairie View A&M U., 1964; cert. edn. of deaf Tex. Woman's U., 1973; postgrad. Miss. U., 1973. Clk., St. Joseph Grand Lodge, 1950-58; matron juvenile dept. Order Eastern Star, 1958-59; counselor Sunshine Day Camp for Underprivileged Children, 1959-60; tchr. Ebenezer Child Devel. Center, 1961-62; substitute tchr. Austin Ind. Sch. Dist., 1960-61; tchr. Tex. State Blind-Deaf and Orphan Sch., Austin, 1962-66, Tex. Sch. for Deaf, Austin, 1966—. Supr., Girl Scouts U.S.A., Girls' Club; mem. Travis County Dem. Women's Com. Mem. NEA, Tex. State Tchrs. Assn., Tex. Soc. Interpreters for the Deaf, Austin Interpreters for the Deaf, NAACP (life), U. Tex. Inst. Texan Cultures (sustaining assoc.), Delta Sigma Theta. Mem. African Methodist Episcopal Ch. Home: 4911 Russett Hill Dr Austin TX 78723

BARNABY MERZ, CAROLYN, radio station sales executive; b. Allentown, Pa., Feb. 3, 1954; d. Agatha Roberts; m. John F. Merz, Apr. 18, 1981. Student Moravian Coll., Bethlehem, Pa., 1973; student Radio Advt. Bur. Sales Mgmt., Wharton Sch., Phila., 1984. Continuity dir. Sta. WKAP, Allentown, 1975-77; media buyer Jackson Advt., Phillipsburg, N.J., 1977-78, media dir., v.p. Contestabile, Inc., Rochester, N.Y., 1978-81; account exec. Sta. WBBF/WMJQ, Rochester, 1981-83, gen. sales mgr., 1983-85; gen. sales mgr. Sta. WIL-Am, St. Louis, 1986—; dir. Rochester Advt. Council, 1983-85. Bd. dirs. Vet's Outreach Ctr., Rochester, 1985. Recipient Community Service Recognition award Rochester Ad Council, 1983-84. Mem. Am. Women in Radio and TV. Home: 1126 Des Peres Rd Saint Louis MO Office: Sta WIL-AM/FM 300 N Tucker Blvd Saint Louis MO 63101

BARNARD, FRANCES FLYNN, university official; b. Fort Worth, Tex., Sept. 16, 1938; d. Elgate Daniel and Effie Danella (Ross) Hitch; B.S.R., Tex. Wesleyan U., 1975; postgrad. Tex. Christian U., 1975-77; m. Doyle Graves Flynn, June 12, 1958 (dec.); children—Stehlin, Shari, Shareese, Shawn; m. 2d, William Gene Barnard, Aug. 13, 1979. Employment developer City of Fort Worth, 1978-80; exec. dir. Am. Med. Consumers, Fort Worth, 1977-80; field dir. Circle T council Girl Scouts U.S.A., Fort Worth, 1980-81; cons. women's affairs; devel. specialist, Cassata Learning Center, 1981-82; bd. dirs. Widowed Persons Services, 1978-80; mem. task force Area 5 Health Systems Agy.; mem. acctg. staff Office of Controller, Tex. Christian U., 1983—; univ. ofcl. Tex. Coll. Osteo. Medicine. Mem. AAUW, Pax Christi U.S.A., Gray Panthers, Clergy and Laity Concerned, Inst. Peace and Justice, Widowed Persons Services, Hospice Assn., Alpha Kappa Delta. Roman Catholic. Democrat. Home: 6513 Armando St Fort Worth TX 76133

BARNARD, KATHLEEN RAINWATER, business education educator; b. Wayne City, Ill., Dec. 28, 1927; d. Roy and Nina (Edmison) Rainwater; B.S., So. Ill. U., 1949, M.S., 1953; postgrad. Ind. U., 1953; Ph.D., U. Tex., 1959; m. Donald L. Barnard, Aug. 17, 1947 (div. Mar. 1973); children—Kimberly, Jill. Tchr. public high sch. Wayne City, 1946-51; faculty asst. and lectr. Vocat. Tech. Inst., So. Ill. U., Carbondale, 1951-53; lectr. bus. edn. Northwestern U., Chgo., 1953-55; chmn. dept. bus. edn. San Antonio Coll., 1955-60; chmn. dept. bus., tchr. edn. DePaul U., Chgo., 1960-62; chmn. dept. bus. adminstrn. Chgo. City Coll., 1962-67, prof., 1968—. Cons. edn. and tng. div. Continental Ill. Nat. Bank & Trust Co., Chgo., 1967, Victor Corp., 1965—, First Nat. Bank Chgo., 1974; ednl. cons. Oak Park Pub. Schs., 1969-70. Exec. sec. bd. dirs. Coll. and Univ. Credit Union, 1975-78. Mem. Nat. Bus. Edn. Assn., Chgo. Bus. Edn. Assn., Nat., North Central bus. edn. assns., Delta Kappa Gamma, Phi Lambda Theta, Pi Omega Pi, Alpha Delta Pi (sponsor), Sigma Phi (sponsor, pres. Alpha Theta chpt. 1958), Delta Pi Epsilon. Contbg. author: College Typewriting, 1960; Business Correspondence, 1962. Collaborator Ency. Brit., 1969-70. Home: 920 Courtland Ave Park Ridge IL 60068 Office: 64 E Lake St Chicago IL 60601

BARNDT, JANE NILES, educator; b. Elkland, Pa., June 13, 1926; d. Homer Fred and Mamie E. (Spencer) Niles; B.S. in Bus. Edn., Bloomsburg (Pa.) State Coll., 1948; m. E. Ralph Barndt, Aug. 1956; 1 son, Fred S. Tchr. bus. Quakertown Community Sch. Dist. (PA), 1961—, coordinator dept. 1977—, area coordinator, 1980—; operator employment service for bus. students, Quakertown; mem. Pa. Adv. Council Bus. Edn., 1980—. Tchr. nursery sch. United Ch. of Christ, Perkasie, Pa., 8 yrs. Mem. Nat. Fedn. Bus. and Profl. Women's Clubs (pres. Pa. fedn. 1978-80), NEA, Nat. Bus. Edn. Assn., Pa. Ednl. Assn., Eastern Bus. Edn. Assn., Quakertown Community Ednl. Assn., Bucks County Bus. Edn. Assn. (past pres.). Republican. Nat. adv. bd. Today's Sec. mag. Home: 317 Market St Perkasie PA 18944 Office: Senior High Sch 600 Park Ave Quakertown PA 18951

BARNES, BARBARA JEAN, manufacturing company executive; b. Milw., Jan. 25, 1945; d. Edward August and Gertrude Barbara (Hacker) Treder; m. Michael Alan Barnes, Aug. 19, 1967. B.S. in Edn., Ill. State U., 1968; postgrad. North Hennepin Community Coll., 1976-83. Tchr. pub. high schs., Central Ill., 1968-70; asst. corp. prodn. inventory control supr. Valspar Corp., Mpls., 1972-78; corp. prodn. inventory control mgr. J-Mark Inc., Mpls., 1979; prodn. control mgr. Gage Tool, Mpls., 1980; materials mgr. Delta Systems, Mpls., 1981; purchasing mgr. Resistance Tech. Inc., St. Paul, 1982-84; materials mgr. Despatch Industries, 1985—. Tutor, ESL, Hennepin County, Minn., 1980-82. Mem. Twin Cities Purchasing Mgrs. Assn., Am. Prodn. and Inventory Control. Soc. Club: Wayzata Yacht. Home: 2800 78th Ave N Brooklyn Park MN 55444 Office: Despatch Industries 619 SE 8th St Minneapolis MN 55414

BARNES, BETSY, television producer; b. Elizabethton, Tenn., May 3, 1954; d. James Madison and Elva Lee (Snyder) Barnes. B.S., East Tenn. State U. Radio producer Bonneville Internat. Corp., Dallas, 1978-81; TV producer Quanta Prodns., Dallas, 1982-83, Hickox-Daniel Prodns., Hollywood, Calif., 1983—. Mem. Women in Communications, Tex. Film and Tape Profls. Assn., Dallas Communication Council, Women in Film. Home: 6101 Merrymount St Fort Worth TX 76107 Office: 6455 Westrock Fort Worth TX 76133

BARNES, CANDACE RAY, retail company executive; b. Kodiak, Alaska, Oct. 23, 1952; d. Marion Carlyle Welch and Virginia (Caldwell) Steineker; m. William L. Barnes, Oct. 8, 1972 (div. July 1979); children—Chadwick W., Kelly C. Student U. Louisville. Sales staff Casual Corner, 1972, J. Riggings, Mentor, Ohio, 1972-76; nat. supr. Dan Howard Industries, Chgo., 1979—. Avocations: tennis, baseball; needlepoint.

BARNES, CONSTANCE INGALLS (MRS. RUSSELL C. BARNES), retired librarian; b. Atchison, Kans., July 30, 1903; d. Sheffield and Lucy (Van Hoesen) Ingalls; B.A., U. Kans., 1925; M.A., U. Mich., 1950, M.A. in L.S., 1955; postgrad. Ecole du Louvre, France, 1960, Vergilian Soc., Cumae, Italy, summer 1963; m. Russell C. Barnes, Oct. 1, 1927; children—Lucie-Jeanne (Mrs. Todd Seymour), John J.I. Librarian, Cranbrook Acad. Art, Bloomfield Hills, Mich., 1955-74, 80-81. Mem. LWV, AAUW, Internat. Arthurian Soc., Alliance Francaise, Founders Soc. Detroit Inst. Arts, Kappa Alpha Theta. Club: Village Woman's (Bloomfield Hills). Home: 788 Randall Ct Birmingham MI 48009

BARNES, CORINNE ANN, pediatric nurse, educator; b. Greenock Heights, Pa., July 3, 1928; d. George Julius and Elizabeth Sarah (Smythe) Meerhoff. R.N., Allegheny Gen. Hosp., Pitts., 1949; B.S.N., U. Pitts., 1960, M.N.Ed., 1963, Ph.D. in Nursing, 1974. Pediatric nurse adminstr. Allegheny Gen. Hosp., 1950-58; pediatric nurse specialist Children's Hosp. and U. Pitts., 1966-70; undergrad. tchr. U. Pitts., 1965—, chmn. pediatric dept., 1970-72, program dir. grad. programs in nursing care of children, 1978—, cons. Co-editor Maternal-Child Nursing Jour., 1978—; mem. editorial bd. Jour. Am. Assn. Child Health, 1981-82. Mem. adv. com. Bright Beginnings; pres. Pitts. Women's Tennis Orgn., 1957. Recipient Disting. Alumnus award U. Pitts. Sch. Nursing, 1982; recipient nursing grants; named Disting. Dau. of Pa., 1984. Fellow Am. Acad. Nursing; mem. Am. Nurses Assn., Pa. Nurses Assn., Allegheny Gen. Nurses Alumnae (pres. 1952), U. Pitts. Alumnae Assn., Am. Assn. Pub. Health, Assn. Child Care in Health, Soc. Research in Child Devel., Nat. League Nursing, Council Nurse Researchers, Sigma Theta Tau. Republican. Methodist. Clubs: Pitts. Tennis Assn., Fox Chapel Racquet, Univ. Faculty. Lodge: Zonta. Office: 3500 Victoria Hall Sch Nursing Pittsburgh PA 15261

BARNES, CYNTHIA ALEE, nurse administrator, educator; b. Chgo., July 8, 1952; d. John and Bobbie Jean Barnes. Diploma Wesley Meml. Hosp., Chgo., 1973; B.S. in Nursing, U. Ill., 1975, M.S., 1979, doctoral candidate, 1982—. Mem. nursing staff U. Ill. Hosps., Chgo., 1973-76, head nurse, 1977-78, asst. dir. nursing, 1980—, asst. prof., 1981—; clin. nurse specialist critical care U. Chgo. Hosps., 1978; dir. nursing edn. Neonatal and Pediatric Services, Inc., 1978—; mem. faculty Symposia Medicus, U. Ill. Coll. Nursing. Mem. editorial bd. Neonatal Network. Contbr. articles to profl. jours. Recipient Bronze award Am. Acad. Pediatrics. Mem. Am. Assn. Critical Care Nurses, Soc. Critical Care Medicine, Am. Nurses Assn., Assn. Care Children in Hosps., Sigma Theta Tau. Democrat. Lutheran. Home: 1411 E 49th St Chicago IL 60615 Office: 1740 W Taylor St Suite 1500 Chicago IL 60620

BARNES, DALPHNA RUTH, nurse; b. Lamesa, Tex., May 11, 1933; d. Raymond Vernon and Hazel Blanche (Lemons) Boatright; A.A. in Nursing, Texarkana Coll., 1966; B.A. in Psychology, U. Houston, 1974; m. Alvin Burwell Barnes, Jan. 18, 1958; children—David Lynn, Jeanne Michele Barnes Boxley. Office nurse, 1966; staff nurse Little York Hosp., Houston, 1967-68, Belhaven Psychiat. Hosp., Houston, 1968; intensive care nurse Hermann Hosp., Houston, 1968-69; office nurse, therapist, 1969; from staff nurse to infection control nurse Parkway Hosp., Houston, 1970-77, infection control, employee health coordinator Houston Northwest Med. Center, 1977-86, patient advocate, 1986—; adv. bd. Houston Hospice, 1980-82, bd. dirs., 1982-84; meml. chmn. North Harris unit Am. Cancer Soc., 1979, v.p., 1980-81, founder, facilitator Cancer Interaction Group, 1978—, cons. death and dying; dir. Montrose Clinic, 1986—. Served with USN, 1957-58. Recipient Sword of Hope award North Harris chpt. Am. Cancer Soc., 1980, 81, 82, 83. R.N. Mem. Assn. Practitioners Infection Control (pres. Houston chpt. 1980-81), Tex. Soc. Infection Control Practitioners (William L. Benson Meml. award 1980), Am. Soc. Profl. and Exec. Women, Tex. Soc. Patient Reps. Club: Toastmasters (pres. Frankly Speaking Chpt. 1986). Home: 20319 Belleau Wood Dr Humble TX 77338 Office: 710 FM 1960 West Houston TX 77090

BARNES, GLENDA ELLEN, banker; b. Clinton, Mo., Jan. 10, 1944; Leo Glenn and Marjorie Ellen (Harryman) Inglish; m. Gary Neal Barnes, Oct. 14, 1962 (div.). Ed. Calif. Coll. Arts and Crafts, Contra Costa Coll., Am. Inst. Banking. Br. officer Central Bank, Oakland, Calif., 1963-68; analyst/mgr. Computer Dynamics, Oakland, 1968-81; group product mgr. Bank of Am., San Francisco, 1981, v.p. teleprocessing product mgmt., 1981-82, v.p. standards and policy, 1982—; mem. Am. Nat. Standards Inst., Washington, 1983—; U.S. rep. test Key and Key mgmt. working groups Internat. Standards Orgn., Geneva, Switzerland, 1983—; dir. Bus. Info. Solutions, Inc.; lectr. in field. Mem. Orgn. Bus. and Profl. Women, Am. Bankers Assn. (Women's com. 1965-68). Club: Commonwealth. Office: Bank of Am PO Box 37000 San Francisco CA 94137

BARNES, HELEN CROSS, banker; b. Portsmouth, Va., Mar. 26, 1945; d. Robert Lee and Frances Phyllis (Motley) Cross; m. L. Gary Barnes, Aug. 10, 1968. B.A. in Math., Westhampton Coll. of U. Richmond, 1967; spl. courses Am. Inst. Banking, Md. Bankers Sch. of U. Md. Tchr., York County Schs. (Va.), 1967-71; internal cons. Equitable Bank N.A., Balt., 1971-78, project mgr., 1978-82, v.p., dir. bank services, 1982—. Mem. exec. com., v.p. programs, corp. sec. Jr. Achievement Met. Balt., 1982—; mem. exec. bd., employment steering com., info. processing tng. ctr. steering com. Urban League, Inc., 1985—. Mem. Assn. Internal Mgmt. Cons., Assn. Info. Systems Profls., Office Tech. Mgmt. Assn., Am. Soc. Performance Improvement. Democrat. Methodist. Club: Argyle County (Silver Spring, Md.). Office: Equitable Bank NA 100 S Charles St Baltimore MD 21201

BARNES, ISABEL JANET, microbiologists, educator, college dean; b. Union City, N.J., Sept. 22, 1936; d. Carl Robert and Isabel Sarah (Cappelletti) B.; B.S., Pa. State U., 1958; M.S., Cornell U., 1960; Ph.D., Hahnemann Med. Coll., 1969; m. John D. Bowman, June 15, 1978. Asst. prof. Hershey Med. Center, Pa. State U., 1968-73; asst. prof., assoc. prof. Sangamon State U., Springfield, Ill., 1973-76; assoc. prof. med. tech. U. Wis., Madison, 1976-85, interim dean Sch. Allied Health Professions, 1981-84; prof. med. tech. Ferris State Coll., Big Rapids, Mich., 1985—, dean Sch. Allied Health, 1985—. Mem. AAAS, AAUP, Am. Soc. for Microbiology, Am. Soc. Med. Technologists. Office: 200 VFS Ferris State College Big Rapids MI 49307

BARNES, LILLIAN SIGRID, escrow officer; b. Point Roberts, Wash., Aug. 9, 1930; d. Dui Marino and Elin (Myrdal) Edvalds Andreas; m. Claude Joseph Hinds, Dec. 8, 1979; m. Robert Eric Barnes, Nov. 14, 1953 (div. May 1973); children—Elisabeth Darby Britt, Eric Albert, Thomas Arni. Student Stanford U., 1949-51. Asst. chief stewardess Pacific Northwest Airlines, Anchorage, Alaska, 1951-53; legal sec. Richard Nelle Blaine, Wash., 1966-75; escrow officer, pres., Blaine Escrow Inc., 1975—, also dir. Contbg. author: The Old Fir Tree, 1984. Sec., Blaine Bicentennial Comm., 1973-76; mem. Northwest Park and Recreation Dist. Commn., 1980-85. Recipient Disting. Service award Blaine Jaycees, 1974; Woman of Yr., Westside Record Jour., 1985, Blaine C. of C., 1984. Mem. Am. Escrow Assn., Escrow Assn. Wash., North Puget Sound Escrow Assn., Blaine C. of C. (sec. 1972-76), PEO. Roman Catholic. Avocations: sailing; painting; antique collecting; gardening; writing. Office: Blaine Escrow Inc 374 H St Blaine WA 98230

BARNES, LINDA SLAWSON, banker; b. Wilson, N.C., Dec. 2, 1952; d. Charles Frank and Helen (Hendricks) Slawson; m. Thomas Harrison Barnes, May 26, 1973. Student U. N.C.-Greensboro, 1972, Atlantic Christian Coll., 1973. Teller, 1st Union Nat. Bank, Wilson, 1973-76; regional mktg. dir., 1976-78, br. mgr., 1978-81; tng. officer Branch Banking Trust Co., Wilson, 1981, sales tng. mgr., 1982, v.p., retail tng. and devel. mgr., 1983—. Gen. chmn. Wilson's 135th Anniversary Celebration, 1984. Loan exec. chmn., bd. mgrs. United Way Wilson County, 1982—; bd. dirs. past treas. Arts Council Wilson,

1981—; vice chmn. community services div. of devel. council Atlantic Christian Coll., 1983—; mem. exec. com. Heart of Wilson Assocs., 1983—. Recipient Disting. Vol. award United Way, 1978, 82, 83. Mem. Am. Inst. Banking (exec. com. 1975—), N.C. Bank Trainers' Edn. Forum, N.C. C. of C. Democrat. Presbyterian. Club: Wilson Country. Home: 1118 Windemere Dr Wilson NC 27893 Office: Branch Banking & Trust Co 223 W Nash St Wilson NC 27893

BARNES, LYDIA JANE, computer software marketing executive; b. Ft. Knox, Ky., Oct. 11, 1955; d. Fred William and Anne Marie (Bentley) B. B.A., U. Calif.-Berkeley, 1978. Research analyst Approach Assocs., Oakland, Calif., 1976-78; mng. editor Scriptor Editorial Services, Alameda, Calif., 1978-79; account exec. Aviso Pub. Relations and Mktg. Communications, Alameda, 1978-79; mktg. adminstr. Comarc Design Systems, San Francisco, 1979-80; dir. mktg. communications MicroPro Internat., San Rafael, Calif., 1980-83; v.p. mktg. ITM, Walnut Creek, Calif., 1983-84; product line mgr. Paladin Software, Santa Clara, Calif., 1984—. Mem. Women in Communications. Democrat. Office: Paladin 3255 Scott Blvd Suite 7E Santa Clara CA 95051

BARNES, MAGGIE LUE SHIFFLETT (MRS. LAWRENCE BARNES), nurse; b. nr. Spur, Tex., Mar. 29, 1931; d. Howard Eldridge and Sadie Adilene (Dunlap) Shifflett; student Cogdell Sch. Nursing, 1959-60; Western Tex. Coll., 1972-76, grad. Meth. Hosp. Sch. Nursing, Lubbock, Tex., 1975; B.S. in Nursing, W. Tex. State U., 1977; m. T.C. Fagan, Jan. 1950 (dec. Feb. 1952); 1 son, Lawayne L.; m. 2d, Lawrence Barnes, Sept. 2, 1960. Floor nurse D.M. Cogdell Meml. Hosp., Snyder, Tex., 1960-64, medication nurse, 1964-76, asst. evening supr., 1976-78, charge nurse, after 1973, evening nursing supr., until 1980; nursing supr. Scurry, Borden, Mitchell, Fisher, Howard Counties, West Central Home Health Agy., Snyder, 1980-83; emergency room evening supr. Root-Meml. Hosp., 1983, 84—; regional coordinator home health services Beverly Enterprises, 1983. Den mother Cub Scouts Am., Holliday, Tex., 1960-61; mem. PTA, Snyder, Tex., 1960-69; adv. Sr. Citizens Assn.; mem. Tri-Region Health Systems Agency, 1979—; mem. adv. bd. Scurry County Diabetes Assn., 1982—. Mem. Vocat. Nurses Assn. Tex. (mem. bd. 1963-65, div. pres. 1967-69), Emergency Dept. Nursing Assn. Apostolic Faith Ch. (sec., treas. 1956-58). Home: Route 1 Box 9B Hermleigh TX 79526

BARNES, MARY D., state government official; b. Pitts., Oct. 22, 1913; d. John C. and Helen T. (Thompson) Dilworth; m. Richard Langley Barnes (dec.); 4 children. A.B., Vassar Coll., 1936; LL.B., U. Pitts., 1939; postgrad. U. Pitts. Grad. Sch. Pub. and Internat. Adminstrn., 1959-60. Bar: Pa. With Bur. Census, U.S. Dept. Commerce; former mem. Spl. Adv. Commn. on Pub. Opinion, 1970; mem. Commn. on Research and Demonstration, White House Conf. on Aging, 1971; council mem. Nat. Inst. Child Health and Human Devel.; liaison Nat. Inst. for Aging; mem. Pa. CSC, 1963—, chmn., 1983—. Bd. advisors Fed. Reformatory for Women, Pa. Citizens Council Home for Aged Protestant Women; mem. women's bd. West Pa. Hosp. Mem. Allegheny County Bar Assn., Pub. Personnel Assn., Internat. Personnel Mgmt. Assn., Urban League. Address: Civil Service Commn PO Box 569 Harrisburg PA 17120

BARNES, MARY LEE, telephone company executive; b. Springfield, Mass., Jan. 5, 1950; d. Leroy Lee and Viola (Baker) Melton; m. Rufus Earl Barnes Mar. 30, 1968 (div. Mar. 1982); children—Earl Timothy, Angel Anita. Assoc. Acctg., Essex County Coll., 1974; student, 1977; student Rutgers U., 1975-76. Dietician St. Mary's Hosp., Orange, N.J., 1969-70; office mgr. James Clark D.D.S., East Orange, N.J., 1970-71; customer sales rep. N.J. Bell Co., Newark, 1971—. Counselor, Neighborhood Youth Corps, Newark, 1968. Recipient Outstanding Service award Neighborhood Youth Corp, 1968; Community Service Achievement award Pride in Heritage Com., 1985; Disting. Citizens award Italian Am. Nat. Hall of Fame, 1985. Mem. Nat. Assn. Female Execs., Young Telephone Pioneers Am. Avocations: classical and jazz music; equestrian activities; water sports; nature walks; tennis. Home: 210 Branch Brook Dr Belleville NJ 07109 Office: NJ Bell 1 Washington Park Fl 16 Newark NJ 07101

BARNES, NORA GANIM, psychologist, marketing educator, consultant; b. Pawtucket, R.I., Jan. 28, 1950; d. George Dimitri and Rose Martha (Waian) G.; m. Scott Michael Barnes, Apr. 13, 1980; 1 child, Nicholas James Barnes. B.A., R.I. Coll., 1972; M.A., U.R.I., 1973; M.A., U. Ct., 1979, Ph.D., 1979. Instr. U. Ct., Storrs, 1976-78; asst. prof. Boston Coll., Chestnut Hill, Mass., 1978-85; assoc. prof. mktg. Southeastern Mass. U., North Dartmouth, 1985—; cons. Nat. Pharmaceutical Council, Washington, 1978-83, Brit. Parliament, London, 1983—. Contbr. articles to profl. jours. Consumer advocate R.I. Consumer's Council, Providence, 1975—; cons. Pawtucket YMCA, 1984—. Mem. Am. Mktg. Assn., Assn. Consumer research, Am. Psychol. Assn. Avocation: photography. Office: Southeastern Mass U North Dartmouth MA 02747

BARNES, SYMIRIA PETERS, educator, soprano; b. Bolton, Miss., July 10; d. V.J. and Matilda J. (Buckley) Peters; B.Music Edn. in Voice, Jackson State U., 1959; M.A. in Adminstrn. and Supervision, Roosevelt U., 1982; student of Dora Lindgren and William Browning, Am. Conservatory Music, 1972-78, with Robert McFerrin, Roosevelt U., 1976-78; children—Stanford, Cedrick, Audwin. Choral dir. Tilden High Sch., Chgo., 1980—; tchr. voice and piano Mallette Music Sch., Chgo., 1980—; soprano opera and oratorio including performance in Aida premiere performance of Opera/South, Jackson, Miss., 1971: recitalist Young Artist Recital series, Chgo., 1973, Am. Conservatory of Music, 1975, Centennial Alumni Performers Series, Jackson State U., 1977; debut in concert Wigmore Hall, London, 1973; guest artist Nat. Talent Hunt Demonstration, Omega Psi Phi, Cleve., 1958; profl. mem. Chgo. Symphony Chorus. Winner ann. commencement solo audition Am. Conservatory Music, Chgo., 1972; recipient music scholarship award, Am. League Pen Women, 1972. Mem. Chgo. Tchrs. Union, Chgo. Musicians Assn., Nat. Assn. Negro Musicians (first place winner nat. voice contest U. Ill. 1957), Am. Guild Mus. Artists, Zeta Phi Beta. Baptist. Contbr. music sect. Handbook on Instructional Program of Chicago Public Schools, 3 vols., 1981. Office: 4747 S Union Chicago IL 60609

BARNETT, ANITA LINEGAR, interior designer; b. Elwood, Ind., Jan. 16, 1954; d. Robert Lawson and Mary Alice (Ebrite) Linegar; m. Robert Lawrence Barnett, May 31, 1980. B.S., Purdue U., 1976. Store designer Carson Pirie Scott, Chgo., 1976-77; interior designer Cooler Schubert Olds, Indpls., 1977—; v.p. CSO Architects, Indpls., 1980-85, exec. v.p., 1985—; prin. CSO Interiors, Indpls., 1984—. Mem. "500" Festival Com., Indpls., 1984; bd. alumni advisors Purdue U., West Lafayette, Ind., 1984—. Recipient Stores of the Yr. award, 1981. Mem. Interior Bus. Designers (bd. dirs., sec. 1984), Alpha Chi Omega (com. nat. hdqrs. 1984—). Presbyterian. Office: CSO Architects 9100 Keystone Crossing Indianapolis IN 46240

BARNETT, DONNA NANCY, telecommunications analyst; b. N.Y.C., May 26, 1954; d. Jack Louis Gross and Beatrice (Slotnik) Hewsenian. Student Rutgers U., 1972-74; B.A. in Biology, Ind. U., 1976; M.S.W., Washington U., St. Louis, 1978. Communications cons. Southwestern Bell, AT&T, St. Louis, 1980-82; systems cons. United Technologies Co., St. Louis, 1982; telecommunications analyst Associates Bancorp Inc., Dallas, 1983—. Mem. North Tex. Telecommunications Assn. Office: Associates Bancorp Inc 250 Carpenter Freeway Dallas TX 75222

BARNETT, ELIZABETH, foreign service officer; b. San Bernardino, Calif., May 26, 1954; d. John E., Sr., and Joan Olga (Connor) B.; B.A. summa cum laude, U. Mass., 1976; M.A. (fellow), Yale U., 1978. Fgn. service officer Dept. State, Washington, 1979—; civilian observer Multinat. Force and Observers, Sinai, 1984-85. Mem. Am. Fgn. Service Assn., Secs. Open Forum, Consular Officers Assn., Phi Beta Kappa. Clubs: Yale (N.Y.C.); Fgn. Service. Address: care Fgn Service Lounge US Dept State Washington DC 20520

BARNETT, FLORENCE LLOYD JONES, newspaper executive. Pres. Tulsa Tribune Co. Office: Tulsa Tribune Co PO Box 1770 Tulsa OK 74102*

BARNETT, HELAINE, lawyer; b. N.Y.C.; d. Harry and Helen (Chafets) Meresman; m. Victor Jules Barnett, June 28, 1959; children—Craig Edward, Roger Lawrence. Bars: N.Y. 1964, U.S. Dist. Ct. (so. dist.) N.Y. 1970, U.S. Dist. Ct. (ea. dist.) N.Y. 1970, U.S. Ct. Appeals (2d cir.) 1972, U.S. Supreme Ct. 1967. B.A., Barnard Coll., 1960; LL.B., NYU, 1964. Assoc. appellate counsel Criminal Appeals Bur., Legal Aid Soc., N.Y.C., 1966-71, Civil Appeals Bur., 1971-74, asst.-atty.-in-charge Civil Div., 1974—; adj. prof. Law Benjamin N. Cardozo Sch. of Law, 1980-82, 84-85. Mem. N.Y. Gov.'s Adv. Com. to Establish Criminal Justice Inst., 1983. Recipient Am. Jurisprudence prize NYU Law Sch., 1962. Mem. N.Y. State Bar Assn. (chmn. com. pub. interest law 1984—), Assn. Bar City N.Y. (mem. coms. 1976—), ABA (mem. com. profession, standing com. ethics and profl. responsibility 1985—), Am. Law Inst. Contbr. articles to profl. jours. Office: Legal Aid Soc Civil Div Park Pl New York NY 10007

BARNETT, JACALYN F., lawyer; b. Bklyn., Jan. 7, 1952; d. Melvin and Bette (Epstein) Fischer; m. Michael H. Barnett, June 29, 1975 (div. 1982). B.A., U. Wis., 1974; J.D., Bklyn. Law Sch., 1977. Assoc. Robinson, Silverman, Pearce, Aronsohn, Sand & Berman, N.Y.C., 1977-78; assoc. Hahn, Hessan, Margolis & Ryan, N.Y.C., 1978-79; ptnr. Shea & Gould, N.Y.C., 1979—; lectr. to orgns., women groups. Mem. legal task force NOW; mem. Task Force on Marriage, Divorce, Fedn. Jewish Philanthropies, N.Y.C. Office: Shea & Gould 330 Madison Ave New York NY 10017

BARNETT, MARILYN, advertising agency executive; b. Detroit, June 10, 1932; d. Henry and Kate (Boesky) Schiff; children—Rhona Barnett Gorosh, Ken. B.A., Profl. model, Detroit, 1955-56; hostess, creator, producer for radio, TV, Detroit, 1956-58; nat. TV spokesperson A&P, Chevrolet, Nat. Bank, 1960-70; exec. v.p. Northgate Advt., Southfield, Mich., 1974; co-founder, exec. v.p. MARS Advt., Southfield, 1974-80, pres., 1980—. Named Advt. Woman of Yr., 1986. Mem. Am. Women in Radio and TV, Adcraft, Econ. Club, AFTRA (local bd. dirs. 1959-67), Screen Actors Guild (bd. dirs.). Avocations: sailing; reading. Office: MARS Advt 24209 Northwestern Hwy Southfield MI 48075

BARNETT, OLA WILMA, psychology educator; b. Los Angeles, Jan. 26, 1940; d. William and Ruth Carol (Phillips) King; B.A., UCLA, 1962, M.A., 1965, Ph.D., 1971; m. Donald Joseph Barnett, Nov. 27, 1941; children—Darlene Ola Blake, Donna Shirley Johnson. Research asst. UCLA, 1961-67; asst. prof. psychology Calif. State Poly. U., San Luis Obispo, 1967-70; assoc. prof. psychology Pepperdine U., Malibu, Calif., 1970-79, prof. psychology, 1979—; sponsor Camp David Gonzales Tutorial Program, 1974-77. Recipient Vol. Service award Atascadero State Hosp., 1970; Action grantee, 1972-73. Mem. Am. Psychol. Assn., Nat. Council Crime and Delinquency, Am. Soc. Criminology, Acad. Criminal Justice Soc., Am. Criminal Justice and Research Soc., Am. Psychology-Law Soc., AAUP, Western Psychol. Assn. Mem. Ch. of Christ. Mem. Nat. Coalition to Ban Handguns. Research in domestic violence. Home: 24301 Sylvan Glen Rd Calabasas CA 91302 Office: Social Sci Div Pepperdine U Malibu CA 90265

BARNETT, SARA MARGARET, educator; b. Sikeston, Mo., Aug. 6, 1941; d. Grady Marvin and Mary Elizabeth (Love) Mills; B.S. in Med. Tech., U. Tex., Arlington, 1963; M.S. in Edn., U. Central Ark., 1968; Ph.D., E. Tex. State U., 1984; m. Herman Howard Barnett, Oct. 16, 1959; children—Gregory Lynn, Lori Elizabeth. Intern Baylor U. Med. Center, 1961-62; asst. supr. lab. Wadley Hosp., Texarkana, Tex., 1963-65, night lab. supr., 1976-77; public sch. tchr., Texarkana, 1965-69; med. technologist Collom and Carney Clinic, Texarkana, 1969-72; tchr. biology Liberty-Eylau High Sch., Texarkana, 1972-76; tchr. biology, health occupations coordinator Tex. Sr. High Sch., Texarkana, 1977—; speaker in field. Named Tchr. of Yr., Texarkana Ind. Sch. Dist., 1982-83; Martin-Lowrance scholar Delta Kappa Gamma, 1981. Mem. NEA, Am. Soc. Clin. Pathologists, AAUW (chmn. edn. found. Tex. 1972-74), Tex. Tchrs. Assn., Tex. Classroom Tchrs. Assn. (student council advisor N.E. Tex. dist. XIX, 1984-86), Tex. Soc. Med. Tech., Am. Vocat. Assn., Tex. Health Occupations Assn., Ark. Acad. Sci., Tex. PTA (life), Delta Kappa Gamma (pres. chpt. 1984-86), Phi Delta Kappa. Democrat. Methodist. Author: Medical Laboratory Assistant, 1981. Home: 100 Pioneer St Texarkana TX 75501 Office: 2112 Kennedy Ln Texarkana TX 75503

BARNETT, THERESA ANN, lawyer; b. Evanston, Ill., Feb. 24, 1952; d. William Andrew and Evelyn (Yates) B. B.A., St. Mary's Coll., Winona, Minn., 1974; J.D., Loyola U., Chgo., 1981. Bar: Ill. 1981, U.S. dist. ct. (no. dist.) Ill. 1982. Sole practice, Chgo., 1981-83; sr. atty. Northeastern Ill. Regional Commuter R.R. Corp., Chgo., 1983—. Mem. ABA, Ill. Bar Assn., Chgo. Bar Assn. Office: Northeastern Ill Regional Commuter RR Corp 547 W Jackson St Chicago IL 60606

BARNETT, VIVIAN ENDICOTT, museum curator; b. Putnam, Conn., July 8, 1944; d. George and Vivian (Wood) Endicott; m. Peter Herbert Barnett, July 1, 1967; children—Sarah, Alexander. A.B. magna cum laude, Vassar Coll., 1965; M.A., NYU, 1971; postgrad. CUNY, 1981. Research asst. Solomon R. Guggenheim Mus., N.Y.C., 1973-77, curatorial assoc., 1978-79, assoc. curator, 1980-81, research curator, 1981-82, curator, 1982—. Author: The Guggenheim Museum: Justin K. Thannhauser Collection, 1978; Handbook: The Guggenheim Museum Collection 1900-1980, 1980; Kandinsky Watercolors, 1981; Kandinsky at the Guggenheim, 1983; Kandinsky and Science: The Introduction of Biological Images in the Paris Period, Kandinsky in Paris: 1934-1944, 1985. Mem. Internat. Council Museums (modern art com.), Am. Assn. Museums (curator com.), Coll. Art Assn., Internat. Found. Art Research. Office: Solomon R Guggenheim Mus 1071 5th Ave New York NY 10128

BARNEY, NINA ESTHER, office equipment company executive; b. Chgo., Mar. 11, 1954; d. Joshua Moten and Valada (Lovett) B. Student pub. schs. Sr. account exec. Xerox Corp., Schaumburg, Ill., 1974-83; account exec. Fed. Express Corp., Chgo., 1983—. Founding mem. Young Execs. in Politics, Chgo., 1983. Mem. Apostolic Ch. of God. Home: 4800 S Chicago Beach Dr Chicago IL 60615

BARNHART, DOROTHY KOHRS, coalition official, game company executive; b. Des Moines, Apr. 27, 1933; d. Oliver John and Lila Mabel (Smith) Kohrs.; m. 1954 (div. 1977); children—Jacqueline, Dwaine, Jr., Kelly; stepchildren—Billie Jo, Jack, Cindy. Student pub. schs., New Virginia, Internat. Acctg. Soc., Chgo. Bookkeeper Iowa Credit Union League, 1954-69, Grand Printing Art-O-Type, 1970-72; office mgr. Am. Bus. Forms & Systems, Inc., 1972-76; forms dept. mgr. Action Forms/Action Printers Co., 1976-77; office mgr. Elliott Beechcraft Flying Service, 1977-81; telephone selling rep. Coca Cola Co., 1983-84; adminstrv. asst. Coalition for Family and Children's Service in Iowa, Des Moines, 1985—; developed Wellness Game, 1982-85; pres., owner Wellness Games, Ltd., 1985—; coordinator Youth Services Hotline.; vol. pres., coordinator vols., maintainer youth services hotline Chronic Pain Outreach of Central Iowa, Mercy Hosp., 1982-84; Midwest regional dir. Nat. Chronic Pain Outreach, 1985—. Mem. Iowa Women's Polit. Caucus; mem. choir Grace United Methodist Ch., disability action com. of Des Moines Area Urban Mission Council. Mem. Nat. Assn. Female Execs., Women's C. of C. of Des Moines. Democrat. Home: 2525 SW 80th Ave Lot 15 Des Moines IA 50321 Office: Coalition for Family and Children's Services in Iowa 311 E 5th St Des Moines IA 50309

BARNHART, JO ANNE B., government official; b. Memphis, Aug. 26, 1950; d. Nelson Alexander and Betty Jane (Fitzpatrick) Bryant; m. David Lee Ross, Feb. 14, 1976 (div. June 1983); m. David Ray Barnhart, May 24, 1986. Student U. Tenn., 1968-70; B.A., U. Del., 1975. Space and time buyer deMartin-Marona & Assocs., Wilmington, Del., 1970-73; adminstrv. asst. Mental Health Assn. Wilmington, 1973-75; dir. SERVE nutrition program Wilmington Sr. Ctr., 1975-77; legis. asst. to Senator William V Roth, Jr., Washington, 1977-81; dep. assoc. commr. Office Family Assistance, HHS, Washington, 1981-83, assoc. commr., 1983-86; majority staff dir. U.S. Senate Govt. Affairs Com., 1986—. Mem. Nat. Assn. Title VII Nutrition Project Dirs. (v.p. 1976). Republican. Methodist. Office: US Senate Govt Affairs Com Senate Dirksen Bldg Washington DC 20501

BARNS, CAROLE SUSAN, telephone company executive; b. Nome, Alaska, Nov. 21, 1944; d. Anton Raymond and Dorothy Virginia (Nelson) Johansen; B.A., U. Wash., 1967; m. Lee Miller, July 11, 1970; children—Jeffrey Miller, Anthony Nelson, Stephen Eric. Internal communications asst. Gen. Telephone Co. N.W., Everett, Wash., 1967-69, internal communications mgr., 1969-70, public affairs mgr., 1973-78, govtl. affairs mgr., 1978-85, employee communications dir., 1985—; newswoman AP, 1970-73; freelance editor Washington Community Coll. Dist. 17, 1970-71. Recipient writing and editing awards Nat. Fedn. Press Women, Wash. Press Women. Mem. Women in Communications. Home: 4310 141st St SE Snohomish WA 98290 Office: 1800 41st St Everett WA 98206

BARNS, DORETHA MAE CLAYTON, librarian, orgn. exec.; b. Fairmont, W.Va., Nov. 28, 1917; d. Sylvester Richard and Della Pearl (Morgan) Clayton; A.B., Fairmont State Coll., 1939; M.A., W.Va. U., 1940; B.S. in L.S., Western Res. U., 1947; m. William Derrick Barns, Sept. 3, 1947. Tchr., librarian Wetzel County (W.Va.) Schs., 1940-41, Preston County Schs., 1944-46; teaching fellow dept. English, W.Va. U., 1941-43, sec. to dean grad. sch., 1942-44, cataloguer library, 1947-48; dir., Internat. relations chmn. LWV W.Va., 1969—, 2d v.p., 1981-83. Bd. dirs. W.Va. affiliate Council of Internat. Programs, 1975—. Mem. Women's Internat. League for Peace and Freedom, Kappa Delta Pi, Nu Alpha Phi. Republican. Mem. Soc. Friends. Club: Order Eastern Star. Author: An Outline of the West Virginia Merit System, 1957; West Virginia's Interest in Foreign Trade, 1971; International Services Available to West Virginia Businesses, 1980. Home: 512 Beverly Ave Morgantown WV 26505

BAROCAS, SUSAN HONEY, advertising and public relations agency executive; b. Bronx, N.Y., May 25, 1952; d. David Ralph and Shirley (Fleischmann) B. B.S. in Pub. Communication magna cum laude, Boston U., 1974; postgrad. film NYU, 1985. Dir. pub. relations Jewish Community Ctr., Denver, 1974-76; owner, operator SHB Communications, Denver, 1976—; mng. editor Western Wear & Equipment Mag., Denver, 1977-78; dir. pub. relations Loretto Heights Coll., Denver, 1980-81. Asst editor, contbr. articles Am. Horologist & Jeweler, 1977, Beverage Analyst, 1977-78. Adviser, United Synagogue Youth Am., Denver, 1974-75; chairperson publicity Mt. Scopus chpt. Hadassah, Denver, 1977-78; del. Colo. Dem. Conv., 1980; co-chairperson pub. and community relations com., mem. exec. com., bd. dirs. Am.-Israel Friendship League, Rocky Mountain Region, Denver, 1983—. Marsteller scholar, 1973-74; named to Outstanding Young Women Am., U.S. Jaycees, 1981. Mem. Women in Communication, Inc. (profl.). Office: SHB Communications 1001 Niagara St Denver CO 80220

BARON, HELENA, ballet company administrator, educator, choreographer; b. Prague, Czechoslovakia; came to U.S., 1959; d. Vladimir S. and Ljubow (Bohensky) Slepyan; m. Simon Michael Baron, Aug. 15, 1949; 1 child, Alexander. Student Olga Preobtajenska, Victor and Tatjana Gsovski and Jens Keith. Dancer Deutsche Opera Ballet of Berlin, 1945-59; ballet dir. Ballet Sch., Paramus, N.J., 1961-76, Baron Ballet Co., Waldwick, N.J., 1971—; artistic dir. Petite Ballet Troupe, Paramus, 1971—, Baron Ballet Co., Paramus, 1978—. Choreographer (ballets) Roumanian Rhapsody, 1967, Naiades, 1982, Bolero (Nat. Choreography prize 1985), Vivace, 1984, Andulko, 1986. Mem. Northeast Regional Ballet Assn. (performing co. regional honor 1984), Nat. Assn. Regional Ballet. Avocations: art; literature. Office: Baron Ballet Co 74 Oak St Ridgewood NJ 07450

BARON, JEAN SZEKERES, lawyer; b. Harrisburg, Pa., June 18, 1943; d. Gaza John and Mary Ann (Gustin) Szekeres; 1 son, Jay. B.S. with high honors, U. Md., 1976; J.D. with honors, U. Balt., 1981. Bar: Md. 1981, U.S. Dist. Ct. Md., 1982. Law clk. Prince George's County Circuit Ct., Upper Marlboro, Md., 1980-81; assoc. firm Ellin & Baker, Balt., 1981-82, Gebhardt & Smith, Balt., 1982-83; asst. atty. gen. State of Md., Balt., 1983—. Mem. ABA, Md. Bar Assn., Prince George's County Bar Assn., U. Md. Young Alumni Assn. (dir. 1977-79), Mortar Bd., Phi Kappa Phi. Home: 7714 Lakecrest Dr Greenbelt MD 20770 Office: Office Atty Gen 301 W Preston St Room 1502 Baltimore MD 21201

BARON, LINDA, insurance company executive; b. Blackfoot, Idaho, Jan. 9, 1948; d. Lynn Poole and Mildred Ruth (Tiger) Scott; m. Stanley Lloyd Baron, July 17, 1971; children—Bridget Michele, Eric Jon. B.S. in Edn., U. Idaho, 1970; M.A.T., Lewis and Clark Coll., 1975; student Coll. of Idaho, 1966-67; postgrad. American Coll., 1986. Tchr., Beaverton Sch. Dist. 48, Oreg., 1970-74, 76-81; field underwriter Home Life of N.Y. Ins. Co., Portland, Oreg., 1982; field underwriter, trainer Monarch Life Ins. Co., Portland, 1982-84, field underwriter, Kensington, Md., 1984-86, asst. dir. variable life sales, Springfield, Mass., 1986—. Sunday sch. choir dir. Meth. Ch., Rockville, Md., 1985-86; active PTA; pres. Farmington West Homeowners Assn., Oreg., 1975; organist Aloha United Meth. Ch., Oreg., 1974-80. Named Agt. of Yr., Monarch Life Ins., Portland, 1983. Mem. Women Life Underwriters, Nat. Assn. Female Execs., Am. Bus. Women's Assn. (corr. sec.), D.C. Life Underwriters. Republican. Avocations: reading; sewing; skiing; tennis; music. Home: 9 Maplewood Dr Wilbraham MA 01095 Office: Monarch Life Ins Co 1250 State St Springfield MA 01133

BARON, LINDA ANN, cosmetic company executive; b. Flushing, N.Y., Nov. 9, 1943; d. Leonard Michael and Margaret Mary Cotone; grad. Gardner Sch. Bus., 1968; student George Washington U., 1970. Adminstrv. asst. U.S. Underseas Cable Corp., Washington, 1968-69; analyst programmer Friden div. Singer Co., Washington, 1969, programming mgr., 1970, systems sales exec., 1971; acct. exec. Clinique Labs., Inc., Washington and Balt., 1972, regional mktg. mgr. Md. and Va. markets, 1973-75, regional mktg. dir. Washington and Mid-Atlantic states, 1976-81, regional v.p., S.E., 1982—; instr. merchandising, 1976—. Vol., ARC, Walter Reed and Bethesda Naval Hosp., Washington, 1969-71. Mem. Nat. Assn. Female Execs., U.S. Dressage Fedn., Potomac Valley Dressage Assn., Am. Horse Show Assn., Bass Anglers Sportsmen Soc., Washington Fashion Group. Roman Catholic. Home: 9224 Beech Hill Dr Bethesda MD 20817

BARON, NAOMI SUSAN, linguistics, computers educator; b. N.Y.C., Sept. 27, 1946; d. Leonard and Ruth Joan (Josephson) B.; B.A., Brandeis U., 1968; Ph.D., Stanford U., 1972. Asst. prof. linguistics Brown U., 1972-79, assoc. prof., 1979-85, assoc. dean, 1981-83; vis. instr. R.I. Sch. Design, 1982-83; vis. Nat. Endowment Humanities chair Emory U., 1983-84; Brown vis. chair Southwestern U., 1985—. Bur. Edn. Handicapped grantee, 1975-84; Nat. Endowment for Humanities grantee, 1979-81. Mem. Linguistic Soc. Am., Semiotic Soc. Am., Am. Assn. Computing Machinery. Author: Language Acquisition and Historical Change, 1979; Speech, Writing and Sign, 1981; Computer Languages: A Guide for the Perplexed, 1986. Office: Southwestern U Georgetown TX 78626

BARONE, ROSE MARIE PACE (MRS. JOHN BARONE), writer, former educator; b. Buffalo, Apr. 26, 1920; d. Dominic and Jennie (Zagara) Pace; B.A., U. Buffalo, 1943; M.S., U. So. Cal., 1950; cert. advanced study Fairfield (Conn.) U., 1963; m. John Barone, Aug. 23, 1947. Tchr., Angola High Sch. (N.Y.), 1943-46, Puente High Sch. (Calif.), 1946-47, Jefferson High Sch., Lafayette, Ind., 1947-50; dir. Warren Inst., Bridgeport, Conn., 1951-53; instr. U. Bridgeport, 1953-54; tchr. bus. subjects Bassick High Sch., Bridgeport, 1954-74, Harding High Sch., Bridgeport, 1974-80; instr. Fairfield U., 1969 freelance writer, 1980—. Recipient Playwriting prize Conn. Federated Women's Clubs, 1955, 1st prize for poetry, 1985; Auerbach Found. scholarship, 1956; Citizen award Bridgeport Dental Assn., 1982; State/Town Hero award, 1986. Mem. NEA, AAUW (treas. 1957-58), Nat. League Am. Pen Women (Bridgeport historian 1966-84, state historian 1983—, treas. br. 1985—, State pres. 1986—, Nat. Historian award 1976), UN Assn. U.S.A. (pres. Bridgeport, 1964-66, 68-70, chmn. area UN Days, 1960—, pres. Conn. 1971—, state chmn. UNICEF to 1984, area UNICEF Ctr., 1984—, state historian 1984—), Conn. Bus. Tchrs., Bridgeport Edn. Assn. (sec. 1966-68), Fairfield Philatelic Soc. (sec. 1971-78, founder advisor Philatelic Jrs. 1972-80), Pi Omega Pi. Clubs: Fairfield University Women's (founder, pres. 1950, 74—, v.p. 1973-74) Southport Woman's (garden dept. sec. 1981-85, chmn. 1985—) (Fairfield). Home: 1283 Round Hill Rd Fairfield CT 06430

BARONIAN, MAUREEN MURPHY, securities dealer, state legislator; b. White Plains, N.Y., Aug. 5, 1934; d. Charles Thomas and Margaret M. Reed Murphy; A.S., Larson Coll., 1954; student U. Hartford, 1975-76; m. K. Albert Baronian, 1960; children—John Albert, Margaret Reed, James Andrew. Vice pres., sec., prin. Investors Services, Hartford, Conn., 1976—; mem. Conn. Ho. of Reps., 1981—, mem. judiciary, appropriations, program rev. and investigation coms. vice chmn. 10th Dist. Com., Republican Party, 1976—; mem. West Hartford Rep. Town Com., 1976—; mem. Charter Revision Commn., 1976-69, sec., 1976-77; chmn. West Hartford Fin. Adv. Bd., 1979; mem. Com. to Rev. and Revise West Hartford Rep. Com. Rules, 1979-80; West Hartford chmn. primary day activities George Bush for Pres., 1980; chmn. credentials com.

Rep. Spl. State Conv., 1984; corporator Inst. of Living, 1973—, aux. pres., 1973-75; chmn. Friends of Bushnell Meml., 1980-84; bd. dirs. Hartford Symphony Soc., 1981—, Am. Sch. for Deaf, 1982. Registered stock broker. Mem. Nat. Assn. Securities Dealers. Office: Conn Ho of Reps Hartford CT 06115

BARR, FRANCINE MARIE, communications co. ofcl.; b. Cleve., Jan. 21, 1947; d. Frank Andrew and Regina Mary (Kawalec) Wrobel; B.A. (Nat. Honor Soc. Scholar), Notre Dame Coll., 1969; postgrad. Royal Holloway Coll., London, 1969; M.A., Wayne State U., 1974; m. Robert F. Barr, May 30, 1970 (div. 1985); 1 dau., Lisa Francine. Asso. editor Moving Out mag. Wayne State U., Detroit, 1971-74; editorial asst. Wilding div. Bell & Howell, Southfield, Mich., 1976, writer, 1977, account exec., 1978, sr. account exec., 1979-81; account supr. Maritz Communications Co., Southfield, 1982—. Mem. Nat. Assn. Female Execs. (network dir. 1979-80), Adcraft, Mich. Metaphys. Soc. Libertarian. Unitarian. Office: 600 Renaissance Ctr Suite 1700 Detroit MI 48243

BARR, GINGER, cemeterian; b. Kansas City, Mo., Dec. 4, 1947; d. W.M. and Ann (Armstrong) Barr; m. Edwin P. Carpenter, Jan. 2, 1984. B.S., Baker U., Baldwin, Kans., 1969. Cemetery mgmt. Topeka Cemetery, Kans., 1969-76, Graceland/Fairlawn Cemeteries, Decatur, Ill., 1976—. Bd. dirs. Humane Soc., Topeka, 1983; mem. Jr. League, Topeka, 1985. Mem. Am. Cemetery Assn. (dir. 1980-82), Kans. Cemetery Assn. (pres. 1979-80), Ill. Cemetery Assn. Republican. Home and Office: Box 58 Auburn KS 66402

BARR, MARGARET REBECCA, nurse, educator; b. New Brunswick, N.J., June 22, 1956; d. Harry Joseph and Elizabeth Francis (Kelly) B. A.A., Colby Coll., N.H., 1976; B.S. in Home Econs., Fla. State U., 1978, B.S. in Nursing, 1981. R.N., Fla. VISTA vol. Las Vegas, Nev., 1978-79; charge nurse Tallahassee Community Hosp., 1982—; assoc. prof. Fla. State U., Tallahassee, 1984—, Fla. Community Coll., 1982—. Editor: Fla. Home Econs. Jour., 1977-78. Author short stories, poems. Recipient award N.J. Lit. Soc., 1974. Mem. Am. Nurses Assn. Republican. Roman Catholic. Avocations: dance; body sculpture. Home: 1524 Bowman Dr Tallahassee FL 32308 Office: Fla State U Sch Nursing Tallahassee FL 32303

BARRELL, BRIGITTE ISOLDE, temporary services executive; b. Dresden, Germany, Dec. 7; came to U.S., 1952, naturalized, 1960; m. Nathaniel A. Barrell, 1957; children—Michael A., Thomas F., Brigitte A. Gen. mgr. Manpower Temporary Services, Buffalo, 1953—; hon. German consul for Western N.Y. State, 1972—. Bd. dirs. Children's Hosp. of Buffalo, Canisius Coll., Medaille Coll., Pvt. Industry Council; co-founder Buffalo chpt. Exec. Women Internat., Buffalo-Dortmund Sister City Com., Buffalo-Kanazawa Sister City Com.; mem. adv. bd. Dept. Sr. Services Erie County, SUNY-Buffalo Community Adv. Council; vice chmn. C. of C. Conv. & Tourism; mem. presdl. Task Force, Frontier Club of Republican Women. Decorated Disting. Service Cross 1st class (Fed. Republic Germany); named U. Buffalo Bus. Woman of Yr., 1976; recipient Manpower Power award, 1976-80. Club: Garret. Home: 1230 Delaware Ave Buffalo NY 14209 Office: 135 Delaware Ave Buffalo NY 14202

BARRELLE, ANN MARIE, educator; b. New Orleans, Aug. 5, 1946; d. Eugene Joseph and Claire (Fallon) B. B.S. in Secondary Edn., La. State U., 1970; M.Ed. with honors, U. Nev., 1980. Tchr. English, reading, history and govt. Milledon Middle Sch., Violet, La., 1970, Arabi Park Middle Sch., La., 1970-71, Christ the King Internat. Sch., Okinawa, Japan, 1973-74, Kubasaki Adult High Sch., Okinawa, 1974-76; adj. instr. English, Clark County Community Coll., Las Vegas, 1977—; tchr. William E. Orr Jr. High Sch., Las Vegas, 1978-86, Western High Sch., Las Vegas, 1986—. Mem. NEA, Nev. State Edn. Assn., Clark County Classroom Tchrs. Assn., Nat. Assn. Female Execs., Nat. Council Tchrs. English, Nev. State Council Tchrs. English, So. Nev. Tchrs. English (recording sec. 1979-80, program v.p. 1980-81, membership v.p. 1981-83). Democrat. Avocations: golf; travel. Office: Western High Sch 4601 W. Bonanza Rd Las Vegas NV 89107

BARRES, BERNICE, nurse; b. Phila., Apr. 15, 1927; d. Morris S. and Eleanor (Steinberg) Browndorf; m. Samuel L. Barres, Aug. 31, 1946; children—Rachel Barres Bick, Joanne Barres Shaw, Robert Alan. A.S. with high honors, Mt. Ida Jr. Coll., 1978; B.S. in Nursing, Boston U. Sch. Nursing, 1981. Cert. med. asst., R.N. Adminstrv. asst. to registrar Brandeis U., Waltham, Mass., 1965-67; asst. to v.p. Newton Coll. (Mass.), 1971-72; exec. sec. Martin D. Braver Co., Chestnut Hill, Mass., 1972-74; staff nurse Beth Israel Hosp., Boston, 1981-83, Hebrew Rehab. Center for Aged, Boston, 1983—; mem. med. asst. adv. bd. Mt. Ida Jr. Coll., Newton. Vol. reader for blind coll. students; play therapist for multi-handicapped children at Peabody Sch. for Crippled Children; vol. librarian elem. sch. and Temple, Boston Lying-in Hosp., Brookline Hills Nursing Home; mem. nat. women's com. Brandeis U. Mem. Am. Nurses Assn., Mass. Nurses Assn., Hebrew Coll. Women's Assn., Hadassah, Phi Theta Kappa. Democrat. Jewish. Home: 132 Sargent St Newton MA 02158

BARRETO, EVANGELINA C., banker; b. Cuba, July 16, 1942; came to U.S., 1961; d. Evangelio and Consuelo (Hernandez) Jiminez; m. Francisco Barreto, July 24, 1961; children—Francisco III, Eva G. B.S., Havana U., Cuba, 1961; B.S., Barry U., Miami, Fla., 1984. Ops. officer Glendale Fed. Bank, Miami Lakes, Fla., 1979-80, br. mgr., Hialeah, Fla., 1980-81, asst. v.p., North Miami Beach, Fla., 1981-83, v.p., 1983—; lectr. Fla. U. Contbr. articles to newspapers and mags. Coordinator Glendale United Way, 1983-86; team capt. Dade County March of Dimes, 1983-86; dir. community adv. bd. Metro Police, North Dade, 1985-86; dir. St. Bernadette Ch., 1983-86. Named Future Bus. Leader of Am., Pompano Sch. Bd., 1980. Mem. North Dade C. of C. (v.p. 1985-86, recipient awards 1985, 86), Toastmasters (pres. 1982-84), Bankers Forum (chmn. 1983-86), South Fla. Soc. Br. Mgrs., Hialeah and North Miami Beach C. of C., Nat. Hispanic Assembly, PAC. Home: 8010 SW 20th St Davie FL 33328

BARRETT, BETTY, sculptor; b. N.Y.C., Nov. 5, 1912; d. Charles and Jeanette (Kaufman) Palash; student N.Y.U., New Sch. Social Research, Art Students League, N.Y. Sch. Interior Design; m. Herbert Barrett, May 29, 1937; children—Nancy Jane, Katherine Louise. One-man shows include Library Performing Arts, Lincoln Center, 1973, The White House, 1976; exhibited in group shows Audubon Artists, 1970, Caravan House Gallery, N.Y.C., 1971, N.Y. Guild Sculptors, 1972; represented in pvt. collections, U.S. and Eng. Recipient sculpture award New Sch. Social Research show, 1968. Mem. English Speaking Union.

BARRETT, COLLEEN CROTTY, airline executive; b. Bellows Falls, Vt., Sept. 14, 1944; d. Richard Crotty and Barbara (Hennessey) Blanchard; 1 son, Patrick Allen Barrett. A.A. with highest honors, Becker Jr. Coll., 1964. Legal sec. Oppenheimer Rosenberg Kelleher & Wheatley, San Antonio, 1968-72, adminstrv. asst., paralegal, 1972-78; sec. Southwest Airlines, Dallas, 1978—, exec. asst. to pres. and chmn., 1980—; dir. Groos Nat. Bank, San Antonio. Mem. Soc. Consumer Affairs Profls., Leadership Tex. Democrat. Roman Catholic. Office: Southwest Airlines Co PO Box 37611 Dallas TX 75235

BARRETT, ELIZABETH ANN MANHART, nurse researcher, educator, psychotherapist, consultant; b. Hume, Ill., July 11, 1934; d. Francis J. and Grace C. (Manhart) Fridy; B.S. summa cum laude in Nursing, U. Evansville, 1970, M.A., 1973, M.S. in Nursing, 1976; Ph.D. in Nursing, N.Y. U., 1983; grad. Gestalt Assocs. for Psychotherapy, 1982; children—Joseph B., Jeffrey F., Paula G., Pamela M. Shetler Carpino, Scott D. Inst. nursing u. Evansville (Ind.), 1970-73, asst. prof., 1973-76; staff nurse Welborn Baptist Hosp., Evansville, 1975-76; staff nurse Bellevue Psychiat. Hosp., N.Y.C., 1976-79; clin. tchr. CUNY, 1977-82; group practice Nurse Healers, 1979-82; pvt. practice psychotherapy, 1980—; nurse researcher Mt. Sinai Med. Center, N.Y.C., 1982—, asst. dir. nursing, 1983—; asst. prof. Adelphi U., 1979-80. Mem. com. Regional Health Planning Council, Evansville, 1974-77. Mem. Am. Nurses Assn. (cert. psychiat.-mental health), Nat. League Nursing, Soc. Advancement in Nursing, NOW, Phi Kappa Phi, Sigma Theta Tau, Alpha Tau Delta. Home: 415 E 85th St New York NY 10028 Office: 1 Gustave Levy Pl New York NY 10029

BARRETT, JULIE ANN, radio station executive; b. Wichita, Kans., Sept. 21, 1957; d. David Theodore and Anita Ruth (Smith) West; m. Paul Wayne Barrett, Jan. 12, 1980. B.A. in Radio/TV, U. Tex.-Arlington, 1979. Mgr., Tandy Corp., Dallas, 1980-83; announcer, news dir. Sta. KSKY, Dallas, 1983—; adv. Nat. Broadcast Mus., Dallas, 1980—. Club: Dallas Press. Avocations: computer programming; music; swimming; photography. Home: 2624 E Park Blvd Plano TX 75074

BARRETT, MARGARET ANN, needlework designer, consultant; b. Concordia, Kans., Nov. 9, 1939; d. Thayne Arthur and Hilma Margaret (Larson) Coulter; m. Phillip Leroy Barrett, Dec. 29, 1958; children—Michael John, Debra Ann. Student Ariz. State U., 1957-61; B.S., U. Kans., 1986. Pres., designer Peggi Barrett Originals, Stilwell, Kans., 1974-83; rep. Leiter's Designer Fabrics, Kansas City, Mo., 1983—; pres., assoc. cons. Color Profiles, Ltd., Stilwell, 1984—; translator: Bergere de France, Bar-le-Duc, France, 1985—; cons. Coe Coll., Cedar Rapids, Iowa, numerous fabric retailers and clothiers; translator knitting patterns. Mem. presdl. adv. council Coe Coll., 1980-83. Mem. Nat. Assn. Female Execs., Kans. Council Commerce and Industry, Coe Coll. Alumni Council, Chi Omega. Republican. Methodist. Avocations: cross-country skiing, backpacking. Home: 18550 Metcalf St Stilwell KS 66085

BARRETT, MARIANNE, television executive; b. Scranton, Pa., Oct. 5, 1951; d. Patrick Joseph and Margaret (Ferguson) B. B.S., Kutztown U., Pa., 1973. Prodn. asst. WVIA-TV, Pittston, Pa., 1975-77, film dir., 1977-79, dir. TV programming, 1979—. Bd. dirs. Women's Resource Ctr., Scranton, Pa., 1984-85; 2d v.p. YWCA, Scranton. Mem. Nat. Assn. TV Program Execs. Avocations: traveling; biking; hiking; athletic walking. Office: WVIA-TV Old Boston Rd Pittston PA 18640

BARRETT, MARY KATHLEEN, educator; b. Brighton, Mass., July 31, 1952; d. Patrick Joseph and Rosanna Carmel (Meunier) Leonard; m. Stephen Michael Barrett, Aug. 9, 1980; 1 child, Patrick Mark. A.A., Massasoit Community Coll., 1972; B.A., Bridgewater State Coll., 1974. Instructional aide Easton Jr. High Sch., North Easton, Mass., 1977-78, tchr. history, 1978—. Mem. Easton Tchrs. Assn., Mass. Tchrs. Assn. Roman Catholic. Clubs: Braintree Jr. Philergians (newsletter chmn. 1975-76, pres. 1977-78), Mass. Fedn. Women's Clubs (internat. affairs chmn. 1978-80), Holbrook Hist. Soc. (v.p. 1985—), Weymouth Hist. Soc. Avocations: antiques; deepsea fishing; bowling. Home: 240 Centre St Holbrook MA 02343 Office: Easton Jr High Sch Columbus Ave North Easton MA 02356

BARRETT, THELMA FAYE, state employment and training consultant; b. Kingston, Jamaica, Nov. 11, 1942; came to U.S., 1977; d. Hubert Solomon and Ambrozine (Smith) Stewart; m. Aston Cebert Barrett, Apr. 20, 1963 (div. Mar. 1980); children—Debra Ann, Ian Courtney, Nicola Patrice. Cert. social work Univ. of W.I., Kingston, 1970, B.S. in Applied Social Studies, 1973; M.S. in Community Devel., U. Mo., 1974; postgrad. Fla. Internat. U., 1980-81. Ops. mgr. Broward Employment and Tng. Adminstrn., Ft. Lauderdale, Fla., 1978-81; program mgr. Youth Employment Program of Greater Miami, Fla., 1981-82; project dir. Miami-Dade Community Coll., Miami, 1982; project mgr. Middle Ga. Consortium, Inc., Macon, 1983-85; job tng. cons. Ga. Dept. Human Resources, Atlanta, 1985—. Editor (manual); A Manual for Teachers of Community Education, 1974. Mem. Mayor's Oversight Community-Minority Bus. Assistance Program, Macon, Ga., 1984-85; chairperson bd. dirs. Community Day Care Ctr., Macon, 1983-85; coordinator missionary edn. Community Ch. of God, Macon, 1984-85. U. Mo. curators scholar, 1975. Mem. Community Devel. Soc. of Am., Benevolent League of Macon. Home: 2976 Springmeadow Dr Macon GA 31206 Office: Ga Dept Human Resources 878 Peachtree St NE Atlanta GA 31309

BARRETT-BOLLS, PATRICIA LOUISE, educator; b. Fargo, N.D., Aug. 17, 1936; d. John Edward and Irene Marie (Sullivan) Yunker; A.A., San Joaquin Delta, Stockton, Calif., 1971; B.S. magna cum laude, Mankato State U., 1973, M.S., 1977; adminstrv. credential U. Calif.-Irvine, 1982; m. F. Dale Bolls; children—James P. Hesch, Janell Smith, John Hesch, Joel Hesch, Jerome Hesch. Mgr., Duebers Fabric Shop, Waseca, Minn., 1971; tchr. Waseca County Day Activity Center, 1973-74; spl. edn. tchr. Waseca Public Schs., 1974-77; dept. chmn. home and family services div. U. Minn., Waseca, 1977-79, specialist vocat. edn. for handicapped Riverside County Supt. Schs. Office, Riverside, Calif., 1979-85, special edn. curriculum, staff devel. specialist, 1985-86; instr. L.H. program U. Calif.-Riverside Extension, 1982—. Precinct chmn. Democratic Farm Labor party, 1978, mem. adv. com. region 9 Council on Aging, 1979-80; mem. adv. com. Waseca County Group Home for Retarded, 1978-80; program coordinator Rural Family Life Center, Waseca, 1978-80; mem. Mayor's Com. Employment of Handicapped. Mem. Assn. Children with Learning Disabilities, Council Exceptional Children, Phi Kappa Phi, Phi Delta Kappa. Author: Prevocational Skills Checklist for Severely Handicapped, 1980; Career and Vocational Education for the Handicapped, 1981; contbr. articles in profl. jours. Office: Spl Schs and Services Riverside County Supt Schs PO Box 868 Riverside CA 92502

BARRIS, BEVERLY SYDELL, toy design company executive; b. Bronx, N.Y., Jan. 28, 1946; d. Harry and Iris (Weiner) B.; 1 child, Janine Barris-Gerstl. A.A., Parsons Sch. Design, 1967; student Sch. Visual Arts, 1967-69, Art Student League, N.Y.C., 1984. Assoc. art dir. Bride's Mag., N.Y.C., 1968-73; sr. product designer Nat. Silver Co., N.Y.C., 1974-75; proprieter Beverly Barris Co., N.Y.C., 1976-83; product devel. Commonwealth Toy & Novelty Co., N.Y.C., 1984; design dir. Durham Industries, N.Y.C., 1985—; design cons. Stewart Mosberg Design Assocs., N.Y.C., 1981-83; tchr. sculpture, painting Art Ctr. of No. N.J., New Milford, 1984-85. Recipient Art Students League award oil painting, 1963, hon. mention, 1967; Pen and Brush award Pen and Brush Soc., 1985. Active Fairlawn PTA, 1985—. Mem. Nat. Assn. Female Execs. Avocations: jogging, nautilus workouts.

BARRON, BARBARA MARILYN, fibre artist; b. N.Y.C., June 12, 1937; d. Samuel Leo and Anna Laura (Rosenbaum) Weinstein; m. Donald Jerome Barron, June 21, 1959; children—Nancy Ellen, Ruth Allison, Steven Joel. B.A., Hunter Coll., 1958; M.A., Columbia U., 1965; cert. Oxford U., Eng., 1972, Royal Sch. Needlework, Eng., 1972. Cert. elem. tchr., N.Y., cert. elem. sch. prin., N.Y. Tchr., N.Y.C. Bd. Edn., 1959-61, Deer Park Bd. Edn., N.Y., 1961-65, Suffolk Mus., Dowling Coll., Stony Brook, N.Y., 1971, Old Bethpage Village Restoration, Woodbury Country Club, N.Y., 1975; pres. Knicely Knotted by Barbara Barron, Huntington, N.Y., 1973-79, Interior Design Crafts, Inc., Huntington, 1979—; sem. leader East End Arts Council, Riverhead, N.Y., 1983. Interviews given to Barry Farber, N.Y.C. Radio, Joan May Channel 67, Hauppauge, N.Y. One woman shows include Pindar Gallery, Soho, N.Y., 1982, Goff Gallery, Orlando, Fla., 1984, Suzanne Brown Gallery, Scottsdale, Ariz., 1984; exhibited in group shows: Art Expo, N.Y., Dallas, Los Angeles, 1982-85, Heckscher Mus., Huntington, 1983; selected commns. A.T. &T., Australian Film Inst., Price Waterhouse; commd. artist Kehillath Shalom Synagogue, Cold Spring Harbor, N.Y., 1985; featured artist Posner Gallery, Milw. Mem. Am. Cancer Soc., Long Island, N.Y., 1985. Mem. Huntington Twp. Art League, Am. Crafts Council, L.I. Craftsmen's Guild, Women in Design, Huntington Twp. C. of C. Democrat. Jewish. Avocations: gourmet cooking; gardening. Home: 5 Larkin St Huntington Station NY 11746 Office: Interior Design Crafts Inc 1943 New York Ave Huntington Station NY 11746

BARRON, ERMA WILLIAMSON, statistician; b. Balt., June 10, 1940; d. Levi and Viola Williamson; B.S., Morgan State U., Balt., 1963; postgrad. Johns Hopkins U., George Washington U., U. Md.; children—Michael, Jocelyn. Tchr. high sch. math., 1963-64; with Social Security Adminstrn., 1964-70, 73—, statistician, 1973-78, chief earnings and employment stats. br., 1978—, chmn. task force minority women, 1979—; with HEW, 1970-73, coordinator fed. women's program, 1972-73. Chmn. adv. com. women low-income Prince George's County Commn. Women, 1974-76; 2d v.p. Prince George's County Women's Polit. Caucus, 1975-76; bd. dirs. Project SAGA, P.G. Family Crisis Ctr. Mem. Am. Statis. Assn., NAACP, Nat. Council Negro Women, Nat. Polit. Congress Black Women. Jack and Jill of Am., Alpha Kappa Alpha (pres. Prince George's county chpt. 1984—). Democrat. Mem. United Ch. Christ. Author papers in field. Home: 8510 Nightingale Dr Lanham MD 20706 Office: 6401 Security Blvd Baltimore MD 21235

BARRON, ILONA ELEANOR, educator; b. Mass, Mich., Sept. 19, 1929; d. John and Nelma (Erickson) Makinen; state cert. No. Mich. U., 1951; B.S. in Elementary Edn., Central Mich. U., Mt. Pleasant, 1961; M.A. in Edn., U. Mich., Ann Arbor, 1966; postgrad. Mich. State U., East Lansing; m. George F. Barron; 1 son, Frederick Mark. Title I dir. Saginaw (Mich.) Twp. Community Schs., 1967-68, reading cons., 1971—; elementary internal cons. Mich. State U., 1968-71; elementary reading cons. Saginaw Twp. Public Schs., 1972—. Mem. NEA, Mich., Saginaw Twp. Edn. Assns., Saginaw Area Reading Council. Specialist in reading, methods of teaching developmental reading skills and enrichment. Home: 4891 Hillcrest Dr Saginaw MI 48603 Office: Plainfield Elementary Sch 2775 Shattuck Rd Saginaw MI 48603

BARRON, JOSEPHINE, real estate broker; b. Santa Maria, Durango, Mex., Mar. 20, 1961; came to U.S., 1973, naturalized, 1971. Grad. high sch., Alhambra, Calif. Real estate loan processor Union Fed. Savs. & Loan, Los Angeles, 1979-80; real estate loan adminstr. Union Bank, Los Angeles, 1980-81; real estate agt. Real Estate Network, Baldwin Park, Calif., 1980-83; owner, broker Barron Realty, Baldwin Park, 1984—. Named Salesperson of Yr., Latinos Realty, Baldwin Park, 1982; Most Outstanding Realtor, Internat. Real Estate Network, Baldwin Park, 1981; Bus. Women of Yr., San Gabriel Valley, 1984. Mem. San Gabriel Valley Bd. Realtors (rep. 1981-82, bd. dirs. 1982-83, edn. chmn. 1982-85, Realtor Assoc. of Yr. 1983), San Gabriel Valley Bd. Realtors (mem. exec. bd. 1984-85, orientation-edn. chmn. 1982-84). Roman Catholic. Avocations: reading, swimming, tennis, hiking. Home: 868 Windermere Ct San Dimas CA 91773 Office: Barron Realty 13366 Ramona Blvd Baldwin Park CA 91773

BARRON, MARY L., nurse; b. Troy, Ala., July 7, 1951; d. Ledel and Mary L. (Farrior) Parker; m. Melvyn Shenweather, Apr. 22, 1969 (div. 1976); 1 dau., Dawn; m. 2d Richards B. Barron, Sr., Nov. 7, 1981; children—Richard B. II, Josephine D. A.A., Miami Dade Jr. Coll., 1974, A.S., 1974; B.A., U. Miami (Fla.), 1978, B.S., 1978, B.S.N., 1978. Nurse Jackson Meml. Hosp., North Miami, Fla., 1976-78; pvt. duty nurse, 1979-80; staff nurse Regency Hall Convalescent Ctr., Newton, Mass., 1981-83; surg. nurse Leonard Morse Hosp., Natick, Mass., 1983—. Bd. dirs. Commonwealth Mass. Dept. Mental Health, Newton, 1983. Mem. Am. League Nursing, Student Nurses Assn. Democrat. Jewish. Clubs: Weston Golf (Mass.); Madison Square Garden (Boston). Home: 5 Shelley Rd Wellesley Hills MA 02181

BARROS, ANNAMARIE, management consultant; b. San Jose, Calif., Mar. 14, 1932; d. Anthony Clarence and Clara Magdalene Pacheco Vierra; B.A., Coll. Holy Names, Oakland, Calif., 1953; M.A., Central Mich. U., 1978; m. Richard L. Barros, June 11, 1960. Intern med. tech. O'Connor Hosp., San Jose, 1953-54; adminstrv. technologist Children's Hosp., San Francisco, 1958-65, Good Samaritan Hosp., San Jose, 1965-74; adminstrv. asst. public relations and mktg. Lab. Services, 1974-76; mgmt. devel. coordinator O'Connor Hosp., 1976-78; mgmt. cons., educator, propr. Health Mgmt. Analysts, Los Gatos, Calif., 1976—; adj. prof. grad. program clin. scis. San Francisco State U., 1976—; sec.-treas. Nat. Cert. Agy. Med. Lab. Personnel, 1977-83, v.p., 1983-84; presenter workshops. Bd. dirs. Santa Clara County chpt. ARC, 1980-84; pres. Rinconada Hills Homeowners Assn., 1977-80. Named Med. Technologist of Yr. in Calif., 1969, 77. Mem. Am. Soc. Med. Tech. (pres. 1973-74, chmn. personnel relations com. 1981-84; named Adminstrv. Technologist of Yr. 1973, Mem. of Yr. 1978, recipient Profl. Achievement award 1979), Am. Mgmt. Assn., Calif. Soc. Med. Tech. Am. Med. Technologists, Clin. Lab. Mgmt. Assn. Republican. Roman Catholic. Author articles, column in field. Address: 129 Callecita St Los Gatos CA 95030

BARROW, GERALDINE, tax accountant; b. St. Clairsville, Ohio, July 12, 1938; d. John B. and Campsie I. (Henry) Washington; m. Albert L. Barrow, Feb. 16, 1958 (div. Mar. 1983). A.A.B., Cuyahoga Community Coll., 1982. Tax dept. clk. Stouffer Corp., Solon, Ohio, 1968-70, tax asst., 1971-72, asst. tax acct., 1972-73, tax acct., 1974-81, state and local tax mgr., 1982—. Mem. Nat. Assn. Female Execs., Tax Club of Cleve. Democrat. Methodist. Home: 4538 Warrensville Center Rd North Randall OH 44128 Office: Stouffer Corp 29800 Bainbridge Rd Solon OH 44139

BARRY, GLORIA ANN, university administrator, gerontology consultant; b. Pitts., Mar. 11, 1927; d. Edward F. and Marie M. (Flaherty) Round; m. James Francis Barry, Sept. 10, 1949 (dec. July 1981); children—Eileen, Nora, Patricia, Maryellen, James, Colleen, David, Katherine. R.N., St. Francis Hosp., Pitts., 1948; B.S. in Nursing Edn., California U. of Pa., 1976; M.Ed., U. Pitts., 1978, Ph.D., 1983. R.N., Pa.; cert. nursing home adminstr., Pa. Hosp. supr. St. Francis Hosp., Pitts., 1950-60; adminstr., dir. nursing services Holmes House, Pitts., 1969-75; clin. faculty U. Pitts., 1975-80, mem. grad. faculty in pub. health, 1980-82; curriculum specialist Temple U., Phila., 1982-83, dir. edn. Inst. Aging, 1983—, dir. edn. program Geriatric Edn. Ctr. of Pa., 1985—, mem. adv. bd. Adminstrn. on Aging Nat. Directory, 1985; cons. VA Hosp., Coatesville, Pa., 1984—; sec. Nat. Long Term Care Ctr. Products, Washington, 1983—; mem. adv. bd. Meth. Home/Hosp., Pitts., 1979-82, Pa. Ombudsman Assn., 1974-79. Author monographs; co-author: Patient Care Services, 1978. Chmn. Allegheny County council Girl Scouts U.S.A., 1957-63; program chmn. PTA, Glenshaw, Pa., 1958-62; mem. Republican Assn. Allegheny County, Pa., 1965-80. U. So. Calif. fellow, 1979; Dept. Aging Pa. grantee, 1985. Mem. Gerontol. Soc. Am., Assn. Gerontologists in Higher Edn., Am. Research Assn., St. Francis Hosp. Alumnae Assn., California U. Alumni Assn., U. Pitts. Alumni Assn. Roman Catholic. Avocations: literature; needlework; golf; travel. Home: S1206 Cooper River Plaza Pennsauken NJ 08109 Office: Inst Aging Temple U 1601 N Broad St Philadelphia PA 19122

BARRY, JANE MARY, employee benefits executive, consultant; b. Brockville, Ont., Can., Mar. 21, 1947; came to U.S., 1949; d. James Joseph and Gertrude Frances (Halpin) B.; m. Robert Morgan Epler, Apr. 29, 1978 (dec. 1983). B.A., St. Lawrence U., 1969. Adminstr., New Eng. Life Ins., Boston, 1969-71; cons. Haber & Stoller, Inc., San Francisco, 1971-74; cons., v.p. Robert M. Epler Co., Inc., San Diego, 1974-83; cons., pres. The Epler Co., San Diego, 1983—; bd. mem. Western Pension Conf. ann. meeting, San Diego, 1983. Editor Epler Reports, 1977-85. Mem. Assn. Pvt. Pension and Welfare Plans, Western Pension Conf. (bd. dirs. 1984-86), Women in Bus., Girls Club of East County Found. Avocations: reading; swimming; racquetball. Home: 2727 Morena St Suite 105 San Diego CA 92117 Office: 770 B St Suite 417 San Diego CA 92101

BARRY, JANET CECILIA, educator; b. Jersey City, May 12, 1944; d. John Aloysius and Mary Elizabeth (Hart) B.; B.A., Paterson State Coll., 1966; M.A., Georgian Ct. Coll., 1978. Tchr., Paterson (N.J.) Public Sch. No. 12, 1966-68; tchr. Walnut St. Elem. Sch., Toms River (N.J.) Regional Sch. System, 1968—. Mem. Nat. Council Tchrs. English, NEA, N.J. Edn. Assn., Ocean County Edn. Assn., Toms River Edn. Assn., Assn. for Supervision and Curriculum Devel., N.J. Assn. for Supervision and Curriculum Devel., Internat. Reading Assn., Ocean County Reading Council (1st v.p.), Georgian Ct. Coll. Grad. Sch. Alumni Assn. (sec.), Delta Kappa Gamma (program chmn.). Address: 219 Wells Mills Rd Waretown NJ 08758

BARRY, JOAN LEBLANC, gerontologist, social service adminstr.; b. Providence, Oct. 28, 1937; d. Albert Richard and Elizabeth Rose (Edwards) LeBlanc; student U. R.I., 1957-58, R.I. Coll., 1955-56; B.A., Calif. State U., Sacramento, 1974, M.S.W., 1976; m. Edward Barry, Sr., May 26, 1958; children—Alexis, Leslie, Ted, Mark. Dir., Stanford Settlement Sr. Center, Sacramento, 1974-78; exec. dir. Serve Our Srs. Inc., Orangevale, Calif., 1978—; chmn. bd. Eldercize, Inc., 1982—; lectr. Calif. State U.-Sacramento; cons. community agys., pvt. industry. Cert. community coll. tchr., Calif. Mem. Nat. Assn. Social Workers, Acad. Cert. Social Workers, Am. Gerontol. Soc., Nat. Assn. Nutrition and Aging Services Providers (contbg. editor Jour.), Am. Assn. on Aging, Nat. Assn. Nutrition and Aging Service Programs, Calif. Assn. Nutrition Dirs. for Elderly (bd. dirs.), Western Gerontol. Soc. Club: Soroptomist (pres. Orangevale/Folsom). Research on transp. for the elderly, exercise and aging. Home: 5110 Ruscal Way Fair Oaks CA 95628 Office: 6236 Main Ave Orangevale CA 95662

BARRY, JOYCE ALICE, dietitian; b. Chgo., Apr. 27, 1932; d. Walter Stephen and Ethel Myrtle (Paetow) Barry; student Iowa State Coll., 1950-52, Loyala U., 1952-58; B.S., Mundelein Coll., 1955; postgrad. Simmons Coll., 1963-64, U. Ga., 1979, Calif. Western U., 1980—. Prodn. supr. Marshall Field & Co., Chgo., 1955-59; dir. food services Women's Ednl. and Indsl. Union, Boston, 1959-62; dir. food services Wellesley Public Schs., Mass., 1962-70; cons. Stokes Food Services, Newton, Mass., 1960-70; regional dietitian Canteen Corp., Chgo., 1970-83; gen. mgr. bus. devel. Plantation-Sysco, Orlando, Fla., 1983—; vis. lectr.; restaurant cons. Mem. Nat. Consumer Panel; research adv. council Restaurant Bus. Mag.; career adv. council, Am. Dietetics Assn.; treas. Dietitians in Bus. Mem. Am. Home Econs. Assn., Internat. Fedn. Home Economists, Home Economists in Bus., Am. Dietetics Assn., Soc. Nutrition Edn., Nat. Assn. Female Execs., Roundtable Women in Food Service. Republican. Roman Catholic. Club: La Chaine des Rotisseurs, Civitan. Home:

175 Heron Bay Circle PO Box 515 Lake Mary FL 32746 Office: Plantation Sysco 2515 Shader Rd Orlando FL 32804

BARRY, LEI, medical equipment manufacturing executive; b. Fitchburg, Mass., May 27, 1941; d. Leo Isaacson and Irene Helen (Melanson) Isaacson Godbout; m. Delbert M. Berry (div.); children—David M., Susan L.; m. Frank H. Mahan III, June 25, 1976; stepchildren—Jodi L., Sarah C., Amy S., Frank H. IV. Grad. high sch., Waltham, Mass. Advt. salesperson, broadcaster various radio and TV stas., N.C. and Tex., 1961-67; New Eng. sales rep. Hollister, Inc., Chgo., 1967-71, Northeastern sales mgr., 1971-76; v.p., ptnr. Mahan Assocs., Blue Bell, Pa., 1976—; pres. Blue Bell Bio-Med., Inc., 1982—, also dir. Elder, United Ch. of Christ, 1978—. Mem. Wissahickon Valley C. of C., Wissahickon Valley Hist. Soc. (bd. dirs.), Wissahickon Valley Watershed Assn., Nat. Bus. and Profl. Women's Club, Health Associated Reps., Nat. Assn. Female Execs., NOW. Republican. Avocations: tennis, skiing, gourmet cooking. Office: Blue Bell Bio-Med Inc PO Box 49 Blue Bell PA 19422

BARRY, MARILYN WHITE, educator; b. Weymouth, Mass., Sept. 12, 1936; d. Harland Russell and Alice Louise (Dwyer) White; m. Dennis Edward Barry, July 11, 1959; children—Dennis Edward, Christopher Gerard. BS in Edn. Bridgewater State Coll., 1958; Ed.M. in Spl. Edn., Boston U., 1969, Ed.D. in Spl. Edn., 1974. Tchr. Weymouth pub. schs. (Mass.), 1958-60; spl. edn. instr. Boston U., 1972-74; asst. prof. in spl. edn. Bridgewater State Coll., (Mass.), 1974-79, assoc. prof., 1979-83, prof., 1983—, chmn. spl. edn. dept., 1979—, coordinator dept. grad. programs, 1979—, adminstr. bilingual spl. edn. training grant, 1983—. Co-author human service workers curriculum materials. Boston U. fellow, 1967-74; 3 Disting. Service awards, Bridgewater State Coll., 1980, 82, 85; Bilingual Spl. Edn. grantee, 1980, 83. Mem. Council Exceptional Children (Mass. chpt. founder, past pres.), Mass. Assn. Children With Learning Disabilities (past v.p.), Phi Delta Kappa, Pi Lambda Theta. Democrat. Roman Catholic. Home: 138 Bedford St Lakeville MA 02346 Office: Bridgewater State Coll Burrill Ave Bridgewater MA 02324

BARRY, MARY ALICE, financial executive; b. Quincy, Mass., Dec. 31, 1928; d. Lawrence Joseph and Alice Mary (Blaisdell) Barry. B.S., Emmanuel Coll., 1950; postgrad. N.Y.U. With FBI, Boston, 1950-56, Nat. Assn. Investment Cos., N.Y.C., 1958-59, Dreyfus Fund, N.Y.C., 1959-62; v.p. Eberstadt Fund Mgmt., Inc.; corp. sec. Chem. Fund Inc., Surveyor Fund, Inc., 1965—, Eberstadt Energy Resources Fund, 1962-84, Eberstadt Internat. Fund, Inc., 1962-84; asst. v.p. Alliance Capital Mgmt. Corp., N.Y.C., 1985—. Home: 520 E 81st St New York NY 10028 Office: Chemical Fund Inc 1345 Ave of Americas New York NY 10105

BARRY, MARYANNE TRUMP, federal judge; b. 1937; married. B.A., Mt. Holyoke Coll.; J.D., Hofstra U. Bar: N.J. 1974. Asst. U.S. Atty. N.J., Newark, 1974-75, dep. chief appeals div., 1976-77, chief, 1977-82, 1st asst. U.S. atty., 1981-83; judge U.S. Dist. Ct. N.J., Trenton, 1984—. Address: US Courthouse PO Box 419 Trenton NJ 07102*

BARRY, MICHELLE LYNETTE, television station executive; b. Lynwood, Calif., Feb., 13, 1956; d. Garfield and Marian Lee (Powers) B.; m. Frederick Charles Hoyt, June 19, 1983; 1 child, Justin James-Garfield Hoyt. B.A. in Pub. Relations magna cum laude, Weber State Coll., 1980. Promotion asst. Sta. KIRO-TV, Seattle, 1980-81, writer, producer, 1981-83, dir. advt. and promotion, 1983—. Writer, producer TV promotion: Bad Habits, 1982 (Internat. Film and TV Festival award 1982). Mem. parent policy council Neighborhood House, Seattle, 1985. Mem. Nat. Assn. TV Arts and Scis., Ad Club. Democrat. Avocations: racquetball; writing. Home: 7327 23d Ave NW Seattle WA 98117 Office: Sta-KIRO-TV 2807 3d Ave Seattle WA 98121

BARRY, MIRANDA ROBBINS, TV development executive, writer; b. N.Y.C., Jan. 18, 1951; d. Philip Semple and Patricia Allen (White) B. A.B., Stanford U., 1972; postgrad Columbia Law Sch., N.Y.C., 1978-79. Chmn. drama dept. Miss Porter's Sch., Farmington, Conn., 1973-75; prodn. research coordinator The Best of Families/CTW, N.Y.C., 1975-77; freelance story analyst CBS Inc., N.Y.C., 1976-81; asst. mgr. spl. programs devel. Sta. WNET 13, N.Y.C., 1977-78; exec. coordinator Nat. TV Theatre, N.Y.C., 1981-82; story editor Am. Playhouse, N.Y.C., 1982-83, dir. program devel., 1983—; instr. TV writing New Sch. Social Research, N.Y.C., 1982-83; instr. screen writing Womens Interart Center, N.Y.C., 1981-83; adj. assoc. prof. Columbia U. Sch. Film, 1986-87; co-dir., organizer TV Theater Workshop Sta. KTCA, Mpls., 1983; creator TV series Mom and Dad/Embassy-NBC, 1983; co-author Quincy script Blood Ties, 1980; author: (play) Friends and Relations, 1981, (TV adaptation) A World to Care For, (TV series) Med School, 1980; scriptwriting resource person Sundance Inst., 1984—; story editor Eugene O'Neill Nat. Playwright's Conf., 1984—. Rape victim counselor St. Luke's Hosp., N.Y.C., 1979-81; mem. alumnae bull. com. Miss Porter's Sch., 1979-84. McKnight grantee Playwright's Center, Mpls., 1983. Mem. Writers Guild Am.-East, Dramatists Guild, N.Y. Women in Film (sec., bd. dirs. 1984-85). Office: American Playhouse 1776 Broadway New York NY 10019

BARSKY, MARILYN LEE, clinical psychologist; b. Detroit, Sept. 11, 1928; d. Lester Arthur and Helen Amy (Stein) Cannon; B.A., Smith Coll., 1950; B.Ed., U. Toledo, 1952; M.A., U. Mich., 1954; Ed.D., Rutgers U., 1966; m. James Barsky, June 30, 1957; children—Robert, Rosalind. Tchr., Public Schs. Evanston (Ill.), 1955-58; sch. psychologist, Livingston, N.J., 1965, Bloomfield, N.J., 1966-68; prof. Jersey City State Coll., 1968-69; sch. psychologist, East Orange, N.J., 1969-70; staff psychologist Family Service and Child Guidance Center of Oranges (N.J.), 1970-75, research assoc., 1973-75; sr. research scientist Postgrad. Ctr. for Mental Health, N.Y.C., 1976-78; pvt. practice clin. psychology, 1972—; cons. Montclair Acad., 1976-77, Rossi and Sperling Assocs., 1978-80, N.J. Rehab. Cons., 1966—; adj. prof. Montclair State Coll., 1977—. Mem. Doe Vs. Klein Com., State of N.J.; trustee Temple Shomrei Emunah. Diplomate Am. Bd. Profl. Psychology; lic. psychologist, N.J., Fla., Calif.; cert. psychologist, N.Y.; lic. sch. psychologist, N.J. Mem. Am. Psychol. Assn., N.J. Psychol. Assn. (sec., com. profl. standards), N.J. Acad. Psychology, San Diego Acad. Psychologists, San Diego Mental Health Assn., Kappa Delta Pi; fellow Am. Orthopsychiat. Assn. Democrat. Contbr. articles to profl. jours. Home: 3861 Bandini St San Diego CA 92110 Office: 327 Laurel St San Diego CA 92107

BARSNESS, WYLLA DECKER, psychologist; b. Denver, Oct. 21, 1924; d. Rutherford Losey and Gladys (Jarnagin) Decker; B.A., William Jewell Coll., 1949; M.S. in Psychology, Mont. State U., 1959; Ph.D. in Child Psychology (NIMH fellow), U. Minn., 1969; m. John Alton Barsness, June 9, 1951; children—John Alton, James David, Karen Elizabeth, Sarah Losey. Office mgr. Larimer County Hosp., Ft. Collins, Colo., 1942-45; instr. William Jewell Coll., 1949-53, Mont. State U., 1957-59; research dir. Bozeman (Mont.) Public Schs., 1966-69; asst. prof. psychology Boise State U., 1968-69, assoc. prof., 1969-73, prof., 1973—; devel. cons. St. Lukes's Hosp., 1972-82. Bd. dirs. Info. and Referral Bd., United Fund, 1978—; regional dir., state del. Democratic Party; chpt. mem. St. Michael's Cathedral, 1972-75, dir. religions edn., 1972-75; dep. to gen. conv. Episcopal Ch., 1979, 82; chmn. social concerns com. Provincial Council, Episc. Diocese; mem. Idaho Bd. Health and Welfare, 1985—. Recipient Disting. Teaching award Boise State U. Alumni, 1980, 81; Danforth asso., 1973—. Mem. Soc. Research in Child Devel., Idaho Psychol. Assn. (pres. 1978-80), Rocky Mountain Psychol. Assn., HERS/West (chmn. Boise State U. chpt.). Democrat. Home: 1922 Mortimer Dr Boise ID 83712 Office: 1925 University Dr Boise ID 83725

BARST, ROBYN JOAN, pediatric cardiologist, educator, researcher; b. Los Angeles, July 19, 1950; d. Stanley S. and Ruth (Piltzer) Walters; m. Samuel M. Barst, Aug. 24, 1980; 1 dau., Nomi. B.A., U. Rochester, 1972; M.D., U. N.C., 1976. Diplomate Am. Bd. Pediatrics and Pediatric Cardiology. Resident in pediatrics Columbia U., N.Y.C., 1976-79, pediatric cardiology fellow 1979-81, pediatric pulmonary fellow, 1981-83, asst. prof. pediatrics, 1983-85; asst. prof. pediatrics and pharmacology N.Y. Med. Coll., Valhalla, 1985—. Contbr. articles to med. jours. Recipient Clinican Sci. award Am. Heart Assn., 1984-87; Parker B. Francis Found. pulmonary research fellow, 1983-84; Nat. Heart, Lung and Blood Inst. grantee, 1984, clin. investigator award, 1984—. Mem. Am. Heart Assn., Am. Thoracic Soc., N.Y. Acad. Scis., N.Y. Heart Assn., Alpha Omega Alpha. Democrat. Jewish. Home: 31 Murray Hill Rd Scarsdale NY 10583 Office: NY Med Coll Valhalla NY 10595

BART, MURIEL, library educator; b. N.Y.C., May 9, 1926; d. Harry and Sarah Deborah (Israelite) Singer; m. Leonard Eugene Bart, Feb. 15, 1953; children—Andrew Harrison, Jonathan James. B.A., U. Conn., 1947, M.A., 1948; M.L.S., Queen's U., SUNY, 1966. Cert. sch. adminstr., N.Y. Tchr. social studies N.Y.C. Bd. Edn., 1949-54, library tchr., 1964-67, librarian-in-charge, 1967—, mem. editorial adv. bd. High Points, 1970—, asst. to bd. examiners, 1980—; lectr. in field; workshop leader. Contbr. articles, book revs. to profl. jours. NDEA/ESEA grantee, 1972. Mem. ALA (chmn. vocat. tech. panel 1983-85), N.Y.C. Sch. Librarians Assn. (chmn. edn. com. 1974-76), N.Y. Library Club (sec. 1978-80, pres. 1985-86).

BART, VIRGINIA KATERI, public relations consultant; b. Frankfurt, Ger., May 21, 1952; (parents Am. citizens); d. Edward William and Anastasia Helen (Pezanowski) Bart. B.A. in Journalism, U. S.C., 1974; M.B.A., Ga. State U., 1980. Advt. specialist Sullivan Advt. Agy., 1974-77; writer, Policy Mgmt. Systems, Columbia, S.C., 1977-78; mktg. specialist Equifax, Atlanta, 1978-79; advt. mgr. Mgmt. Control Systems, Atlanta, 1979-80; dir. mktg. Insac Software, Atlanta, 1980-82; pres. Bart Ackley & Co., Roswell, Ga., 1982—. Mem. Am. Mktg. Assn. (sec. 1985-86, com. chmn. 1983-84, 84-85). Democrat. Roman Catholic. Club: Ad Club 2 (v.p. 1981-82). Lodge: Toastmasters. Avocations: photography; tennis; water and snow skiing; sewing; gardening.

BARTEL, ANN PELCOVITS, economist; b. N.Y.C., Sept. 15, 1949; d. Harry W. and Helen (Lassman) Pelcovits; B.A. summa cum laude, U. Pa., 1970; M.A., Columbia U., 1973, Ph.D., 1974; m. Charles H. Bartel, Aug. 30, 1970; children—Joseph, Sharon, Jessica. Asst. prof. econs. U. Pa., Phila., 1974-76; asst. prof. bus. Columbia U., N.Y.C., 1976-78, assoc. prof., 1978—; research assoc. Nat. Bur. Econ. Research, N.Y.C., 1974—; cons. statis. and econ. analysis Title VII, 1977—. Herbert Lehman grad. fellow, 1970-74; Dept. Justice grantee, 1973-74; Dept. Labor grantee, 1979-80; Alfred Sloan Found. grantee, 1980-81; Found. Fund for Research in Psychiatry grantee, 1980-81. Mem. Am. Econ. Assn. Contbr. articles to profl. jours. Home: 1674 Buckingham Rd Teaneck NJ 07666 Office: 710 Uris Hall Columbia U New York NY 10027

BARTELS, ANN-MARIE, federation executive; b. Alton, Ill., Dec. 15, 1954; d. Norman William Bartels and Betty L. (Pruessing) Julian. Student, So. Ill. U., 1972-76. Pub. relations dir. Showtime, Inc., St. Louis, 1976-78; pub. relations coordinator Ringling Bros. and Barnum & Bailey Circus, Washington, 1978, pub. relations dir., 1979-81; pub. relations cons., Belleville, Ill., 1981-82; mktg. mgr. Am. Fedn. Info. Processing Socs., Reston, Va., 1982-84, dep. dir. confs., 1984—. Recipient merit cert. Graphic Arts/Printing Industries Am., 1982, excellence certs. for exhibit promotions Conv. Promotion Assn. Trends, 1983. Mem. Am. Soc. Assn. Execs. Republican. Office: Am Fedn Info Processing Socs 1899 Preston White Dr Reston VA 22091

BARTELS WILKINSON, JAMI ELIZABETH, innkeeper, rancher, art consultant, artist; b. Armstrong, Iowa, July 16, 1941; d. Homer Wesley and Dorothy Irene (Bunday) Wilkinson; m. Donald Lee Bartels, June 30, 1974; 1 child by previous marriage, Dina Lyn. Student Drake U., 1959; A.A., Orange Coast Coll., 1971; student Napa Valley Coll., 1980-82. Office mgr., asst. to v.p. Zinsco Elec. Products, Los Angeles, 1963-65; office mgr. Raif Realty Inc., Montebello, Calif., 1965-67; gen. mgr. Chris-Craft West, Inc., Newport Beach, Calif., 1967-69; exec. dir. Orange Coast Coll. Vol. Bur., Costa Mesa, Calif., 1970-72; v.p. Newport Pacific, Inc., Newport Beach, 1972-74; owner Willow House Antiques, El Sobrante, Calif., 1976-80; owner Bartels Ranch & Country Inn, St. Helena, Calif., 1979—; ptnr. Bartels Realtors & Investments, St. Helena, Richmond, Calif., 1974—; dir. Napa Valley Repertory, Calistoga, Calif., 1985—. Chmn. Christian Bookstore Benefit, Grace Episcopal, St. Helena, Calif., 1981; chmn. membership Napa Valley Symphony Assn., St. Helena, 1985; chmn. Hearts for the Arts Benefit, St. Helena, 1986; co-founder, dir., pres. Napa County Arts Council, Yountville, Calif., 1980-84; state/local planner Calif. Arts Council/Napa County Arts Council, Napa, Calif., 1982-83; bd. dirs. Napa Valley Visitors Assn., Napa, 1985—. Named Saleswoman of Yr., Bayliner Boat Corp., Orcas Island, Wash., 1973-74. Mem. Am. Bed and Breakfast Assn., Wine Country Artists (v.p. 1984), Napa Valley Bed and Breakfast Innkeepers Assn. (v.p. 1984), Bed and Breakfast Innkeepers No. Calif. (dir. 1984-86), Calif. Lodging Industry Assn., Napa County C. of C., St. Helena C. of C. (dir. 1985-86), Epsilon Sigma Alpha. Republican. Lutheran. Club: Orange Coast Coll Law (Costa Mesa, Calif.) (pres. 1969-70). Avocations: artist; water skiing; interior design; antiques collecting. Office: 1200 Conn Valley Rd St Helena CA 94574

BARTHLOME, RANDIE LEE, law enforcement administrator, consultant; b. Laramie, Wyo., May 4, 1948; d. Ralph Randall and Wilma Lee (Hawk) Benintendi; m. Edward Earl Barthlome, May 5, 1973; children—Sherri Lanee, Lori Lynn, Thomas Arthur, Greg Edward. Student Community Coll. of Denver, 1971-72, Idaho State U. Law Enforcement Acad., 1972-73, Idaho Peace Officer Acad., 1973, Idaho State U., 1977, Duke U., 1985. Advanced law enforcement cert.; cert. law enforcement instr. Advt., pub. relations dir. Consumer Enterprises, Denver, 1969-72; tutor Idaho State U., Pocatello, 1972; officer Blackfoot Police Dept. (Idaho), 1972-73; sec. Idaho Peace Officer Acad., Pocatello, 1973-74; crime prevention officer Pocatello Police Dept., 1974-80, dir., 1980-85; pres. SYNTAX, 1985—; pvt. practice cons., 1983—. Author weekly newspaper column: Police Watch, 1974-85, also articles. Adv. bd. Salvation Army, Pocatello, 1982-85; com. chmn. Mayor's Com. for Handicapped, Pocatello, 1982—; pres. Pocatello Community Services Council, 1975-76; founder Women's Advocates for Battered Women, Pocatello, 1976—. Named Citizen of Yr., Idaho Pros. Attys. Assn., 1982, Idaho Outstanding Supr., Manpower Consortium, 1981, Disting. Young Woman, Pocatello Jay-C-Ettes, 1979; recipient Nat. Award of Merit, Nat. Crime Prevention Coalition, 1981. Mem. Idaho Crime Prevention Assn. (founding, pres. 1981-82), Idaho Peace Officers Assn., Am. Soc. Tng. and Devel., Internat. City Mgmt. Assn., Idaho Press Club, Am. Bus. Women's Assn., Idaho Assn. for Affirmative Action. Baptist. Home: 1170 E Phillips Dr Littleton CO 80122 Office: Syntax 13111 E Briarwood Ave Suite 250 Englewood CO 80112

BARTHOLD, CLEMENTINE B., judge; b. Odessa, Russia, Jan. 11, 1921; came to U.S., 1925; d. Joseph Anton and Magdalene (Richter) Schwan; m. Edward Brendel Barthold, July 5, 1941 (dec.); children—Judith Anne Barthold DeSimone, John Edward; m. 2d, Joel L. Stokes, Jr., Feb. 7, 1981. Student Aberdeen Bus. Coll., 1940; B.G.S., Ind. U. Southeast, 1978; J.D., Ind. U.-Indpls., 1980. Bar: Ind. 1980, U.S. Dist. Ct. (so. dist.) Ind., 1980. Sec. and asst. to mgr. Clark County C. of C. (Ind.), 1959-60; chief probation officer Clark Circuit Ct. and Superior Cts., Jeffersonville, 1960-72; research cons. Pub. Action Correctional Effort, Clark and Floyd Counties, 1972-75; instl. parole officer Ind. Women's Prison, Indpls., 1975-80; atty. State of Ind., 1980-83; judge Clark Superior Ct. No. 1, Jeffersonville, 1983—. Active in developing and implementing juvenile delinquency prevention and alternative programs, group counseling for juvenile delinquents and restitution programs. Treas. Ladies Elks Aux., Jeffersonville. Recipient Good Govt. award Jeffersonville Jaycees, 1966, also Good Citizenship award, 1967; Outstanding Community Service award Social Concerns League, Jeffersonville, 1966. Mem. ABA, Ind. Bar Assn., Clark County Bar Assn., Ind. Correctional Assn. (pres. 1971, Disting. Service award 1967, 85), Nat. Assn. Women Judges, Ind. Judges Assn., Ind. Juvenile and Family Ct. Judges, Jefferson County Women Lawyers Assn., Older Women's League, Ind. U. Alumni Assn., Howard Steamboat Mus., LWV, Bus. and Profl. Women's Club. Democrat. Roman Catholic. Home: 948 E 7th St Jeffersonville IN 47130 Office: Clark Superior Ct No 1 500 E Court Ave Jeffersonville IN 47130

BARTHOLET, ELIZABETH IVES, art gallery executive; b. N.Y.C.; d. Frederick M. and Edith (Wetherill) Ives; B.A., Bryn Mawr Coll., 1924; student U. Grenoble, summer 1922, Harvard U., summer 1926; m. Paul Bartholet, May 14, 1932; children—Paul Ives, Chauncey Ives, Elizabeth. Writer, art and music column Cambridge (Mass.) Tribune, 1925-28; contbr. articles to numerous mags., 1925-28; research reporter Fortune Mag., 1929-32; owner, dir. Bartholet Art Gallery, N.Y.C., 1957—. Mem. Appraisers Assn. Am. Club: Cosmopolitan. Rediscoverer of a number of Am. period artists, including Cubist painter Jan Matulka (1890-1972). Home and Gallery: 55 E 76th St New York NY 10021

BARTHOLOME, PAULA TERESA, marketing consultant; b. Terre Haute, Ind., July 31, 1951; d. Paul Ralph and Lois Virginia (Bilderback) B. B.S. in Bus. with honors, Ind. U., 1973. Mgmt. trainee Irwin Union Bank, Columbus, Ind., 1973-74, systems officer, 1974-76, mktg. officer, 1976-78; asst. v.p. mktg. Pioneer Bank, Chgo., 1979-80, v.p. mktg., 1980; dir. research and product devel. WN Lane Interfin., Northbrook, Ill., 1980-81, dir. mktg. services, 1981-82, v.p. mktg., 1982-86; mktg. cons., 1986—; dir., past pres., Chgo. Fin. Advertisers; past pres. PTB. Mem. Bank Mktg. Assn., Bus. Vols. for the Arts, Chgo. Home: 828 Michigan Apt B3 Evanston IL 60202

BARTHOLOMEW, FLORA BEATRICE, city official, county official; b. Withee, Wis., Jan. 1, 1919; d. Herman and May Frances (Barber) B. Grad. Wis. Bus. U., LaCrosse, 1938. Sec. Snapp Electric, Wausau, Wis., 1940-45, asst. mgr., 1945-73, gen. mgr., 1973-77; alderman City of Wausau, Wis., 1980—; supr. County of Marathon, Wis., 1980—, bd. dirs. Devel. Corp., 1984—. Vice chmn. Housing Authority, Wausau, 1977—; chmn. Judiciary and Regulatory Com., Wausau, 1982—; bd. dirs. No. Valley Workshop, Wausau, 1984—, Performing Arts Found., Wausau, 1985—. Named Woman in Govt., Wausau Area Jaycee Women, 1985, Wis. Jaycee Women, 1985; Woman of Achievement, Marathon County Bus. and Profl. Women's Club, 1985. Mem. Elec. Apparatus Service Assn., Wausau C. of C. (bd. dirs. Central Wausau Progress 1980—). Republican. Club: Zonta. Lodge: Order Eastern Star. Home: 320 S 7th Ave Wausau WI 54401 Office: City of Wausau and Marathon County City Hall 407 Grant St Wausau WI 54401

BARTHOLOMEW, SHIRLEY KATHLEEN, county official; b. Marysville, Wash., Jan. 26, 1924; d. Clarence E. and Mary (Hall) B. Grad. high sch., Marysville. News dir. Sta. KRKO, Everett, Wash., 1943-80; sec., dir. Everett Broadcasting, Inc., 1955-76, First Pacific Broadcasting, Everett, 1976-80; county councilwoman Snohomish County, Wash., 1981—. Editor, reporter wire service reports (AP Mng. Editor award 1959, 78). Recipient Outstanding Contbn. award Wash. State Press Women, 1968. Mem. Nat. Assn. Elected Women, Wash. State Assn. Counties, Bus. and Profl. Women. Republican. Home: 4830 67th St NE/2 Marysville WA 98270 Office: Snohomish County Council Everett WA 98201

BARTLETT, ALAYNE LUCILLE, nursing administrator, clinical specialist, air force officer; b. Waukegan, Ill., Jan. 19, 1947; d. Robert Wilson Bartlett and Lucille Adeline (Andersen) Bartlett Villiard. Diploma in Nursing, Grant Hosp. Chgo., 1968; B.S. in Nursing, Catholic U. Am., 1975; M.S. in Cardiovascular Nursing, St. Louis U., 1980. Commd. officer U.S. Air Force, 1968, advanced through ranks to lt. col., 1984; clin. nurse intensive care 12th U.S. Air Force Hosp., Cam Ranh Air Base, Vietnam, 1969-70; flight nurse, instr. 2d Aeromed Evacuation Group, Rhein-Main Air Base, Germany, 1970-73; chief health profl. recruiting 3509 U.S. Air Force Recruiting Squad, San Bernardino, Calif., 1975-78; clin. coordinator Malcolm Grow Med. Ctr., Andrews AFB, D.C., 1980-82; asst. chmn. dept. critical care nursing Wilford Hall Med. Ctr., Lackland AFB, Tex., 1982-85; asst. chmn. dept. nursing Regional Med. Ctr., Clark Air Base, Philippines, 1985—; cons. in field. Author: Nursing Service Bylaws, 1982; programs: Generic Screening, 1984, Generic Occurrences, 1984. Scout leader Girls Scouts Am., Rhein-Main Air Base, 1970-73, Washington, 1973-75; instr. HEW-Instructed Physicians in Egypt, Cairo, and Alexandria, 1980; lay reader Protestant Chapel, Clark Air Base, Recipient Air Force Commendation medal, Meritorious Service medal. Mem. Am. Nurses Assn. (treas.), Am. Assn. Critical Care Nurses, Nat. Assn. Female Execs., Soc. Critical Care Medicine, Nat. Critical Care Inst. Edn., Sigma Theta Tau. Republican. Club: Women Officers. Avocations: computers; painting; golf; counted cross-stitch; tole painting; biking; traveling. Office: Regional Med Ctr Clark Air Base/SGN APO San Francisco CA 96432

BARTLETT, DIANE SUE, mental health counselor; b. Laconia, N.H., Dec. 6, 1947; d. Fred Elmer and Dorothy Pearl (Wakefield) Davis; m. Josiah Henry Bartlett, Aug. 23, 1980; 1 child by previous marriage, Fred Louis Hacker; 1 step child, Juliet. A.A., Plymouth State Coll., 1982; B.Gen. Studies summa cum laude, U. N.H. Sch. for Lifelong Learning, 1984. Police communications specialist Div. Motor Vehicles, Concord, N.H., 1970-76, br. office mgr., 1976-83, coordinator motor vehicles registrations, 1983-84; tax collector City of Dover, N.H., 1984; intern Lakes Region Mental Health Div., Laconia, N.H., 1985; counselor Latchkey Pastoral Counseling, Laconia, 1984—. Mem. Town of Moultonboro Sch. Feasibility Study Commn., 1978; adminstrv. bd. mem., chmn. pastor-parish relations com. United Meth. Ch., Moultonboro, N.H., 1983—, participant N.H. Ann. Conf. on Status and Role of Women, Concord, 1985—. N.H. Charitable Found. grantee, 1985. Avocations: skiing; swimming; reading; writing. Home: PO Box 14 Moultonboro NH 03254

BARTLETT, JENNIFER LOSCH, artist; b. Long Beach, Calif., 1941; B.A., Mills Coll., 1963; B.F.A., Yale U., 1964, M.F.A., 1965. One-woman shows include: Mills Coll., Oakland, Calif., 1963, Reese Paley Gallery, N.Y.C., 1972, Paula Cooper Gallery, N.Y.C., 1974, 76, 77, 79, 81, 82, 83, 85, Saman Gallery, Genoa, Italy, 1974, John Doyle Gallery, Chgo., 1975, Contemporary Art Center, Cin., 1976, Dartmouth Coll., 1976, Wadsworth Atheneum, Hartford, Conn., 1977, San Francisco Mus. Modern Art, 1978, U. Calif., Irvine, 1978, Hansen-Fuller Gallery, San Francisco, 1978, Balt. Art Mus., 1978, Margo Leavin Gallery, Los Angeles, 1979, 81, 83, U. Akron, 1979, Carleton Coll., 1979, Heath Gallery, Atlanta, 1979, 83, Galerie Mukai, Tokyo, Akron Art Inst., 1980, Albright-Knox Art Gallery, Buffalo, 1980, Tate Gallery, London, 1982, Gloria Luria Gallery, Bay Harbor Islands, Fla., 1983, Rose Art Mus., Brandeis U., Waltham, Mass., 1984, Long Beach Mus. Art (Calif.), 1984, U. Calif. Art Mus., Berkeley, 1984; group exbhns. include: Mus. Modern Art, N.Y.C., 1971, Whitney Mus. Am. Art, N.Y.C., 1972, 77, 81, Walker Art Center, Mpls., 1972, Kunsthaus, Hamburg, Germany, 1972, Paula Cooper Gallery, N.Y.C., 1973, Corcoran Gallery Art, Washington, 1975, Art Inst. Chgo., 1976, Kunstmuseum, Dusseldorf, W. Ger., 1976, Kassel, W. Ger., 1977, Contemporary Arts Mus., Houston, 1980, numerous others; retrospective exhbn. Walker Art Ctr., also on tour, 1985-86; represented in permanent collections: Mus. Modern Art, N.Y.C., Met. Mus. Art, N.Y.C., Whitney Mus. Am. Art, N.Y.C., Phila. Mus. Art, Walker Art Center, Yale U. Art Gallery, New Haven, Art Mus. South Tex., Corpus Christi, R.I. Sch. Design, Providence, Art Gallery South Australia, Adelaide, Goucher Coll., Balt., Amerada Hess, Woodbridge, N.J., Dallas Mus. Fine Arts, Richard B. Russell Fed. Bldg. and U.S. Courthouse, Atlanta; instr. Sch. Visual Arts, N.Y.C.; author: (art books) In the Garden, 1982; Jennifer Bartlett, 1985; Rhapsody, 1985; (novel) History of the Universe, 1985. Creative Artists Public Services fellow, 1974; recipient Harris prize Art Inst. Chgo., 1976; Lucas vis. lectr. award Carleton Coll., 1979. Address: care Paula Cooper Gallery 155 Wooster St New York NY 10012

BARTLETT, LINDA GAIL, lawyer; b. N.Y.C., Apr. 6, 1943; d. Manny Max and Lottie (Sandler) Katz; m. Randall David Bartlett, Feb. 10, 1979; children—Gregory, Jeremy, Brian. A.B., Bklyn. Coll., 1964; J.D., U. Miami, 1977. Bar: N.Mex. 1977, U.S. Dist. Ct. N.Mex. 1977, N.Y. 1979, Appeals (2d cir.) 1979, U.S. Ct. Appeals (10th cir.) 1977, U.S. Dist. Ct. (so. dist.) N.Y. 1979, U.S. Dist. Ct. (ea. dist.) N.Y. 1979, U.S. Supreme Ct. 1980, U.S. Ct. U.S. Ct. Appeals (5th cir.) 1980. Assoc. firm Klecan & Roach, P.A., Albuquerque, 1977-78, Benjamin Wyle, Esq., N.Y.C., 1978-81; dep. gen. counsel Dirs. Guild Am., Inc., N.Y.C., 1981—. Contbg. author: Women in Management, 1983. Mem. ABA, Assn. Bar City N.Y., N.Y. County Lawyers Assn., N.Y. State Bar Assn. (co-chairperson com. on practice and procedure before nat. labor relations bd.). Office: Directors Guild of America Inc 110 W 57th St New York NY 10019

BARTLETT, RITA LOUISE, shopping center council executive; b. Clarksburg, W.Va., Sept. 11, 1948; d. Arnold Goff and Ellen Marie (Hustead) Bartlett. B.S., W.Va. U., 1970. Adminstrv. asst. Gen. Motors Corp., Washington, 1973-75; legis. asst. U.S. Ho. of Reps., Washington, 1975-78; research analyst Ruder & Finn, N.Y.C., 1978-80; dir. consumer affairs Am. Nat. Standards Assn., N.Y.C., 1980-82; program mgr. Internat. Council Shopping Ctrs., N.Y.C., 1982—. Mem. Meeting Planners Internat., Am. Soc. Assn. Execs. Democrat. Episcopalian. Office: Internat Council Shopping Ctrs 665 5th Ave New York NY 10022

BARTLETT, SANDRA GERRENE, manufacturing company executive; b. Bakersfield, Calif., July 29, 1946; d. George Henry and Lena Christine (Holwick) Grundy; m. Roger Gale Bartlett, July 29, 1972; children—Gina Lynn, George Brent. A.A., San Jose State U., 1979; B.S., Golden Gate U., 1981. Mgr. dentist's office, Bakersfield, 1965-72; ind. wedding cons., Salinas, Calif., 1972-77; ptnr. DeSerpa & Assocs., Salinas, 1977-79; owner, mgr. Bartlett Mgmt., Inc., Salinas, 1979-82; office mgr. Casa Serena Skilled Nursing, Salinas, 1982-84; controller Ramsay Welding & Machine, Inc., Salinas, 1984—. Writer office mgmt. procedures manuals. Treas., bd. dirs. Door to Hope recovery ctr. for alcoholic women, Salinas, 1980—; chmn. Steinbeck Festival Tours, Salinas, 1984—. Mem. Nat. Assn. Female Execs., Soroptimist Internat. (treas. Salinas 1981-82, pres. 1982-84, bd. dirs. 1984-86, Sierra Pacific regional sec. 1986—). Republican. Baptist. Avocations: quilting, sewing, crafts, reading, walking. Home: 1305 Primavera St Salinas CA 93901 Office: Ramsay Welding & Machine Inc 478 Brunken Ave Salinas CA 93901

BARTLETT, VIRGINIA JOYCE, government pension specialist; b. Clarksburg, W.Va., July 20, 1951; d. Thomas Jefferson and Hazel Rae (Smith) B. B.S., W.Va. Wesleyan Coll., 1973. Employee plans/exempt orgn. specialist IRS, Balt., 1973-77; pension investigator Pension and Welfare Benefits Adminstrn., Dept. Labor, Washington, 1977—. Recipient Meritorious Achievement award Dept. Labor, 1979. Mem. Nat. Assn. Female Execs. Republican. Methodist. Avocations: reading; aerobics. Home: 1110 Fidler Ln Apt 806 Silver Spring MD 20910 Office: Dept Labor Pension and Welfare Benefits Adminstrn 200 Constitution Ave NW Washington DC 20210

BARTLETT KRESL, JOYCE, real estate development company executive; b. Everett, Mass., Dec. 24, 1950; d. Robert Allan and Joyce Mary (Malcolm) Bartlett; m. Stephen Kresl, Sept. 15, 1984; 1 child, Timothy Bartlett Kresl. Student Montserrat Coll., Beverly, Mass., 1986—. Dir. mktg. communications, The Computer Store, Sudbury, Mass., 1979-82; dir. mktg. and corp. communications, dir. corp. advt., creative dir. Lotus Devel. Corp., Cambridge, Mass., 1982-86; dir., sr. v.p. Mktg. and Sales Assocs., Boston, 1985—. Recipient Desi awards. Mem. Ad Club Boston, Boston Computer Soc. Congregationalist. Avocations: sailing; skiing; art; music. Home: 78 Pitman Rd Marblehead MA 01945

BARTLEY, GEORGETTA KATYE, computer systems programmer, behaviorist, stress consultant therapist; b. Jacksonville, N.C., Nov. 14, 1946; d. Talmadge Oliver and Louise Georgetta (Benton) B. A.A. in Data Processing, San Diego City Coll., 1967; B.S. in Info. Systems Mgmt., San Diego State U., 1978; M.S. in Mgmt. Orgn. Devel., U.S. Internat. U., 1981, Ph.D. in Mgmt. Orgn. Devel., 1981. Computer technician Fed. Civil Service, San Diego, 1971-74, computer programmer, 1974-79, computer systems analyst, 1979-84, computer specialist, 1984, computer systems programmer, 1984—, EEO counselor, 1978—; stress cons. therapist Bartley & Bartley, Inc., San Diego, 1981—. Mem. Nat. Urban League, San Diego, 1979—. Mem. Nat. Assn. Female Execs., Sharing Inc. (vol. 1979—). Democrat. Episcopalian. Office: Fleet Combat Directions Systems Support Activity 271 Catalina Blvd San Diego CA 92147

BARTLEY, MARION ELVINA, librarian, media specialist; b. Pitts., Sept. 16, 1937; d. William Warren and Elvina (Henry) B. B.S., Clarion State Coll., 1959; M.Ed., U. Pitts., 1964, M.L.S., 1968, advanced cert. in Library Sci., 1981. Cataloger U. Pitts., 1959-61; sch. librarian, Spanish tchr. E. Forest Joint Sch., Marienville, Pa., 1961-62; sch. librarian Duquesne Sch. Dist. (Pa.), 1962-69, Allegheny Interned. Univ, Pitts., 1969-79; part time reference librarian Point Park Coll., Pitts., 1980-81; sch. librarian Escuela Internat. Sampedrana, San Pedro Sula, Honduras, 1981-83, Am. Sch. Tegucigalpa, Honduras, 1983—. Newsletter editor Friends of Pub. Library, Wilkinsburg, Pa., 1977-79. Mem. ALA, Wilkinsburg Bus. and Profl. Women's Club (pres. 1979). Republican. Episcopalian. Home: 9 Love Pl Pittsburgh PA 15218

BARTLING, PHYLLIS MCGINNESS, oil company executive; b. Chillicothe, Ohio, Jan. 3, 1927; d. Francis A. McGinness and Gladys A. (Henkelman) Bane; m. Theodore Charles Bartling, Aug. 2, 1946; children—Pamela, Theodore. Student, Ohio State U., 1944-47. Bookkeeper, Bartling & Assocs., Bartling Oil Co., Houston 1974-80; sec.-treas., dir. both cos., 1980—. Co-chmn. ticket sales Tulsa Opera, 1956-61; bd. dirs. Tex. Speech and Hearing Ctr., Houston, 1967-70. Republican. Episcopalian. Avocations: tennis; gardening; bicycling; cooking. Home: 11 Inwood Oaks Houston TX 77024 Office: 8550 Katy Freeway Suite 128 Houston TX 77024

BARTLOW, ROSALIE DIANNE, television producer; b. Oakland, Calif., Jan. 3, 1955; d. Robert and Lillie Velma (Turney) B. B.A. in Journalism, Radio and TV, Calif. State U.-Long Beach, 1977, M.A. in Speech Communication, 1980. Adminstrv. asst. news. Sta. KTNQ Radio, Los Angeles, 1976-78; editorial dir. youth newspaper Long Beach Recreation Dept. (Calif.), 1978-79; prodn. sec. CBS-TV, Los Angeles, 1979-80, prodn. asst., 1980-81, researcher, 1982-83, sr. researcher, 1983-84, assoc. producer, 1984—. Contbg. Emmy award winning show Two on the Town show, sta. KCBS-TV, 1979-82. Mem. Women in Communications (cert. of appreciation 1982-83, exec. v.p. Los Angeles chpt. 1985—, Central area rep., 1982-83), Soc. Profl. Journalists, Am. Film Inst. Democrat. Mem. Unity Ch. Office: CBS-TV 6121 Sunset Blvd Los Angeles CA 90028

BARTOK, MARGARET RIVA, psychologist; b. Pitts., Dec. 5, 1942; d. Victor E. and Helen M. (McShane) Riva; B.A., Carnegie-Mellon U., 1964; M.Ed., U. Pitts., 1968, M.Ed., 1968, Ph.D., 1975; postgrad. Duquesne U., 1976; m. Frederick F. Bartok, Apr. 12, 1969 (div. Jan. 1978); children—Rory Elizabeth, Keri Helene. Tchr., Los Angeles City Schs., 1964-65; research asst. U. Pitts., 1966-68; counselor Gateway Schs., Monroeville, Pa., 1968-73; instr. psychology Community Coll., Allegheny County, Pa., 1970-76, Pa. State U., 1971—, Duquesne U., 1976-77; assoc. prof. counselor edn. Calif. U. of Pa., 1983—; lectr. St. Vincent's Coll., 1983—, Westmoreland County Community Coll., 1983—; pvt. practice psychology, Greensburg, Pa., 1975—; psychologist Woodland Hills Sch. Dist., 1980-82, inter-mediate unit 1, 1981-82; cons. Hempfield Sch. Dist., Greensburg, 1977-81 Mem. Pa. Psychol. Assn., Nat. Assn. Sch. Psychologists, Am. Personnel and Guidance Assn. Democrat. Roman Catholic. Home: PO Box 877 Greensburg PA 15601 Office: Greensburg Profl Bldg 226 S Maple Ave Greensburg PA 15601

BARTOLOMEI, JOAN MARIE, educator; b. Chgo., Oct. 24, 1943; d. Gordon Richard and Florence Mary (Gundry) Kennerley; m. Roland Bartolomei, June 25, 1966; children—Gordon Richard, Elizabeth Marie. B.S. in Edn., Nor. Ill. U., 1965. Tchr. Dist. 105, LaGrange, Ill., 1965-70, substitute tchr., 1975-80, tchr., 1985—. Rep. library com., Countryside, Ill., 1978-79; cub scout leader, Countryside, 1978-79; Sunday Sch. tchr. Grace Episcopal Ch., Hinsdale, 1977-78. Mem. Internat. Edn. Assn., Nat. Edn. Assn. Club: Countryside Women's (sec. 1980—).

BARTON, ANN ELIZABETH, fin. exec.; b. Long Lake, Mich., Sept. 8, 1923; d. John and Inez Mabel (Morse) Seaton; student Mt. San Antonio Coll., 1969-71, Adrian Coll., 1943, Citrus Coll., 1967, Golden Gate U., 1976, Coll. Fin. Planning, 1980-82; m. H. Kenneth Barton, Apr. 3, 1948; children—Michael, John, Nancy. Tax cons., real estate broker, Claremont, Calif., 1967-72, Newport Beach, Calif., 1972-74; v.p., officer Putney, Barton, Assos., Inc., Walnut Creek, Calif., 1975—; dir., officer Century Fin. Enterprises, Inc., Century Adv. Corp., F.F.A. Inc. Cert. fin. planner. Mem. Internat. Assn. Fin. Planners, (registered investment advisor), Calif. Soc. Enrolled Agts., Nat. Assn. Enrolled Agts., Nat. Soc. Public Accts., Inst. Cert. Fin. Planners. Office: 1705 N California Blvd Walnut Creek CA 94596

BARTON, BRIGID S., museum director; b. Honolulu, June 1, 1943; d. William M. and Ellen Shanahan. B.A., Barnard Coll. Columbia U., 1965; M.A., U. Calif.-Berkeley, 1968, Ph.D. (NEA fellow), 1976. Instr. art Coll. Marin, Kentfield, Calif., 1969-71; asst. prof. art U. Santa Clara, 1976-82, assoc. prof., 1982—; former dir. DeSaisset Mus. Office: U Santa Clara Dept Art Santa Clara CA 95053

BARTON, DENISE ELLEN, water inspection station company manager; b. San Francisco, Aug. 28, 1960; d. William Blackwell and Irma Augusta (Gumprecht) B. B.S., U. Pacific, 1982. Market research analyst VLSI Research, San Jose, Calif., 1982-84; product mktg. engr. Optical Specialties, Inc., Fremont, Calif., 1984—. Mem. Am. Mktg. Assn. Club: Peninsula Figure Skating (bd. dirs. 1985—). (Belmont, Calif.). Avocations: ice skating; ice skating judge. Home: 250 Loyola Dr Millbrae CA 94030 Office: Optical Specialties Inc 4281 Technology Dr Fremont CA 94538

BARTON, JUDITH MARIE, lawyer, lobbyist; b. Grosse Pointe, Mich., Feb. 19, 1953; d. Joseph J. and Shirley (Fisher) Barton; m. A. Scott MacGuidwin, Sept. 19, 1980; children—Stephen Fisher, Richard Joseph. B.A., U. Mich. 1975; J.D., Thomas M. Cooley Sch., Lansing, Mich., 1979. Bar: Mich. 1981, U.S. Dist. Ct. 1982. Bus. and circulation mgr. Football News, Basketball Weekly publ., Grosse Pointe, 1975-77; legis. asst. Mich. Ho. of Reps., Lansing, 1977-80; legal specialist, 1980-81; staff dir. Mich. State Senate, 1981-83; sole practice, Lansing, 1983—. Bd. dirs. Common Cause Mich., 1983—, treas., 1983-84; bd. dirs. Landlords of Mid-Mich., 1985-86. Mem. Women's Law Assn., ABA, Mich. Bar Assn. Pub. Action Com. (Lansing), Capitol Area Women's Network (bd. dirs. 1983-84), Ingham County Bar Assn., Pi Beta Phi. Republican. Roman Catholic. Club: Civitan Internat. Office: Law Offices Judith Barton 121 E Allegan St Lansing MI 48933

BARTON, MAXINE BELLE, lawyer; b. Los Angeles, May 11, 1934; d. Norman Nathan and Celia (Rosenthal) Livingston; m. Richard H. Bauman, July 4, 1984; 1 child, Norma Lynn. J.D., Western State U., 1980. Bar: Calif. 1982; lic. realtor. Legal sec., para-legal, mgmt. asst. Indsl. Indemnity Co., San Diego, Sacramento, Los Angeles, 1971—; in-house counsel Indsl. Indemnity, San Diego, 1982—. Mem. ABA, Calif. Bar Assn., San Diego Bar Assn., Calif. Trial Lawyers Assn. San Diego Trial Lawyers Assn., Law Office Adminstrs. Democrat.

BARTON, NELDA ANN LAMBERT, political worker, newspaper executive, nursing home executive; b. Providence, Ky., May 12, 1929; m. Harold Bryan Barton, May 11, 1951 (dec. Nov. 1977); children—William Grant (dec.), Barbara Lynn, Harold Bryan, Stephen Lambert, Suzanne. Student Western Ky. U., 1947-49, Norton Meml. Infirmary Sch. Med. Tech., 1950, Cumberland Coll., 1978. Lic. nursing home adminstr. Owner, operator rental townhouse apts. and duplexes Corbin, Ky., 1970—; pres., chmn. bd. Barton & Assocs., Inc., Corbin, 1977—, Hazard Nursing Home, Inc., Ky., 1977—, Williamsburg Nursing Home, Inc., Ky., 1977—, Health Systems, Inc., Corbin, 1978—, Corbin Nursing Home, Inc., Corbin, 1980—, Key Distbg., Inc., Corbin, 1980—, Barbourville Nursing Home, Inc., Ky., 1981—, The Whitley Whiz, Inc., Williamsburg, 1983—, Harlan Nursing Home, Inc., 1986—; chmn. bd. Tri-County Nat. Bank, 1985—; dir. Corbin Deposit Bank, 1979-83; mem. long-term care adv. com. Ky. Peer Rev. Orgn., 1978-81. Mem. Fed. Council on Aging, 1982—; bd. dirs. Leadership Ky., 1984—; v.p. Southeastern Ky. Rehab. Com., 1981—; mem. devel. bd. Cumberland Coll., 1981—; mem. Fair Housing Task Force, Corbin, 1981—; charter mem. Ky. Mansion Preservation Found., Inc., 1978; mem. Corbin Community Devel. Com., 1970-83; mem. adv. com. City of Corbin, 1960-72; den mother Bluegrass council Boy Scouts Am., 1965-67; pres. Corbin Central Elem. Sch. PTA, 1963-65; vice chmn. 9th Dist. PTA, 1958-59; mem. Am. and Ky. Ednl., Med. and Polit. Action Com., 1968—; mem. stewardship, property, edn., youth fellowship coms. 1st Christian Ch., Corbin; mem. Ky. Commn. on Women, 1968-72; pres. Corbin Republican Women's Club, 1968; mem. exec. com. Ky. Fedn. Rep. Women, 1963—, 2d v.p., 1968-70; Rep. nat. committeewoman for Ky., 1968—; charter mem. bd. dirs. Nat. Rep. Inst. for Internat. Affairs, 1983—, sec.-treas., 1984-86; regent Nat. Fedn. Rep. Women, 1981-85; co-chmn. Ky. Reagan-Bush Campaign, 1980, 84; mem. exec. com. Rep. Nat. Com., 1976-80, 84—, vice chmn., 1984—; del. Rep. Nat. Conv., 1976, mem. rules com., 1972, 76, 80, 84—; mem. adv. com. 5th Dist. Lincoln Club, 1970—, Ky. Rep. Com., 1974—; Presdl. inaugural coordinator for Ky., 1981, 85; active numerous other polit. orgns. Recipient recognition award Joint Rep. Leadership of U.S. Congress; Dwight David Eisenhower award, 1970; Ky. Woman of Achievement award Ky. Bus. and Profl. Women, 1983; Nelda Barton Day Proclaimed by Corbin mayor, 1973; named Ky. col., 1968; Ky. Rep. Woman of Yr., Ky. Fedn. Rep. Woman 1969; acad. scholar Western Ky. U., 1947-49. Mem. Am. Coll. Nursing Home Adminstrs., Ky. Assn. Health Care Facilities (Better Life award 1981), Ky. Assn. Nursing Home Adminstrs. (polit. action com. 1979—), Ky. Med. Aux. (chmn. health edn. com. 1978-81), Ky. Council on Econ. Edn. (bd. dirs. 1986—), Am. Health Care Assn., Women's Aux. So. Med. Assn., Whitley County Med. Aux. (pres. 1959-60), Bus. and Profl. Women's Club (v.p. 1983-84), Ky. Mothers Assn. (parliamentarian 1970—, hon. Mother of Ky. award 1983), Ky. C. of C. (bd. dirs. 1983—), Christian Women's Fellowship. Avocations: fishing; oil painting. Home: 1311 7th Street Rd Corbin KY 40701 Office: Health Systems Inc PO Box 468 Corbin KY 40701

BARTON, PHYLLIS JOAN LOSEKE, home economist, educator; b. Gem, Kans., Apr. 18, 1936; d. Fred William and Yelva (Knudson) Loseke; B.S. in Home Econs., Kans. State U., 1957; M.Ed. in Vocat.-Tech. Edn., Va. Poly. Inst. and State U., 1974; m. Benny Eugene Barton, June 6, 1960. Tchr. home econs. schs. in Kans. and Va., 1957-69; tchr. home econs. Hayfield Secondary Sch., Alexandria, Va., 1970-75, child care services coop. edn. coordinator, 1975-84. Vice pres., sec. Williamsburg Manor North Citizens Assn., 1975, 76. Recipient Outstanding Leadership award Nat. Capital Area March of Dimes, 1979, 80-84; named hon. Ky. col., 1979. Mem. Nat. Assn. Future Homemakers Am. Assn. (bd. dirs. 1981-84), Nat. Assn. Vocat. Home Econs. Tchrs. (sec. 1977-79, pres. elect 1980-81, pres. 1981-82, Service award 1978, 81), Va. Vocat. Assn. (Outstanding Citation award 1976, 82), Am. Vocat. Assn., Am. Home Econs. Assn., Home Econs. Edn. Assn., NEA, Va. Edn. Assn., Fairfax Edn. Assn., Va. Home Econs. Tchrs. Assn., Va. Assn. Future Homemakers Am. (hon.), AAUW (treas. chpt.), Delta Kappa Gamma, Phi Delta Kappa. Baptist. Club: Alexandria Jr. Woman's (past pres., Outstanding Mem. award 1966, 68). Author: (cookbook) Hush Puppies and Other Stories, 1977; also consumer edn. teaching units; adv. bd. Favorite Recipes Press, 1982-85; editorial staff Mini Page Publ., syndicated column. Home and Office: 3265 Rustler Dr Lake Havasu City AZ 86403

BARTON, SUSAN MEYER, county recreation administrator, dog breeder; b. Los Angeles, Sept. 4, 1946; d. Edward John and Catherine Dorothy (McInerney) Meyer; m. Richard Emmett Barton, June 29, 1974. B.A., Loyola-Marymount U., Los Angeles, 1972; A.A., Mt. St. Mary's Coll., Los Angeles, 1966. Instr. St. Mary's Acad., Inglewood, Calif., 1972-73; recreation supr. County of Los Angeles, 1973-84, City of Redondo Beach, Calif., 1984—; breeder Old English mastiffs Barton Kennels, Hawthorne, Calif., 1980—; constituency rep. Learning Resources Network, Thurston, Kans., 1985—. Mem. Nat. Assn. Female Execs., Calif. Parks and Recreation Soc., Mastiff Club Am., Western Mastiff Fanciers, Chi Kappa Rho. Republican. Roman Catholic. Avocation: aerobic dancing. Office: City of Redondo Beach Recreation Dept 1102 Camino Real Redondo Beach CA 90277

BARTSCH, JANE ELLEN, radio executive; b. Huntington, N.Y., July 5, 1949; d. Edward Paul and Dorothy Lenore (Muller) Bartsch. Asso. Bus. Adminstrn., Grace Downs Coll. Media supr. Kelly Nason, Inc., N.Y.C., 1972-78; media dir. Ash/Le Donne, N.Y.C., 1979-81; account exec. CBS, Inc., N.Y.C., 1981-82; account exec. NBC, Inc., N.Y.C., 1982-83, nat. sales mgr., 1983-84, gen. sales mgr., 1984—. Avocations: fishing; running. Home: 139 E 27th St New York NY 10016 Office: NBC Inc 30 Rock Plaza New York NY 10112

BARTSCHT, WALTRAUD ERIKA, educator, costume designer; b. Munich, Germany, Oct. 16, 1924; d. Bruno and Edith Frida (Snell) Gutensohn; came to U.S., 1952, naturalized, 1959; diploma Deutsche Meisterschule Füer Mode, Munich, 1949; M.A., So. Meth. U., Dallas, 1966; Ph.D., U. Tex.-Dallas, 1986; m. Heri Bert Barscht, Mar. 31, 1950; 1 son, Martin Donald. Fashion designer, 1949-65, Dallas, 1954-65; instr. German, U. Dallas, Irving, Tex., 1966-69, asst. prof., 1969-80, asso. prof., 1980—, chmn. dept. fgn. langs., 1981—; designer theatrical costumes Knox Street Theater, Dallas, U. Dallas Drama Dept.; textile compositions exhibited Dallas galleries, Purdue U., and elsewhere, 1961—; textile chancel appts. Perkins Chapel So. Meth. U., St. Paul's Luth. Ch., Brenham, Tex. Mem. Tex. Fgn. Lang. Assn., South Central Modern Lang. Assn., Assn. Computer in the Humanities, Assn. Lit. and Linguistic Computing, Am. Assn. German Tchrs. (regional chmn. N. Central Tex. 1972-75), Dallas Goethe Center (founding mem.). Lutheran. Transl. and analysis Goethe's Das Maerchen, 1972. Translator poems and articles in Kerygma, 1961, Constantin Review, 1974; Dragonflies, 1980; Dimension, 1980; contbr. articles to Schatzkammer, Rice U. Studies, Procs. of VI Internat. German Tchrs. Congress, Nurenberg. Home: 1125 Canterbury Ct Dallas TX 75208 Office: University of Dallas Irving TX 75061

BARTUCCI, JANET EVELYN, marketing communications executive; b. Flushing, N.Y., Jan. 14, 1952; d. Louis Joseph and Evelyn Doris (Montleon) Bartucci; m. Reuben Samuel, Oct. 18, 1981. A.A.S. in Communications, Fashion Inst. Tech., N.Y.C., 1972. Asst. account exec. Saul Krieg, N.Y.C., 1972-74; publicity mgr. Grosset & Dunlap, N.Y.C., 1974-76; account exec. Burson Marsteller, N.Y.C., 1976-79; v.p. Myers CommuniCounsel, N.Y.C., 1979-85; pres. Bartucci-Samuel, Inc., N.Y.C., 1985—. Mem. Nat. Assn. Female Execs., Women in Communications, Am. Soc. Profl. and Exec. Women, Am. Mgmt. Assn. Home: 60 Gramercy Park N New York NY 10010 Office: Bartucci-Samuel Inc 1 World Trade Ctr Suite 7967 New York NY 10048

BARWICK, JOANN R., editor. Ed. Wagner Coll., Parsons Sch. Design, Columbia U. Former press assoc. Am. Soc. Interior Decorators, exec. v.p. Nat. Home Fashions League; former home furnishings editor Modern Bride mag., Am. Home mag.; former home bldg. and decorating editor Good Housekeeping mag., 1976-78; editor-in-chief House Beautiful, 1978—; creator, former editor Country Living mag. Office: House Beautiful Hearst Corp 1700 Broadway New York NY 10019

BARZ, PATRICIA, lawyer; b. Mattoon, Ill. B.A. in Lit. cum laude, Yale U., 1974; J.D., U. Va., 1978. Bar: Va. 1979, Conn. 1982, Ohio 1985. Mgmt. trainee, asst. br. mgr. 1st and Mchts. Corp., Richmond, Va., 1974-75; summer assoc. Hunton & Williams, Richmond, 1976, assoc., 1978-81, mem. activities com. and continuing legal edn. com.; summer assoc. Gray, Cary, Ames & Frye, San Diego, 1977; assoc. Davis, Graham & Stubbs, Denver, 1981-82; counsel Aetna Life Ins. Co., Hartford, Conn., 1982-84; assoc. Jones, Day, Reavis & Pogue, Cleve., 1984—. Figure skating instr., Richmond, 1975-78. Mem. ABA, Ohio Bar Assn., Bar Assn. of Greater Cleve., Conn. Bar Assn., Va. Bar Assn. Met. Richmond Women's Bar Assn. (sec.).

BASEL, FRANCES RITA, printing company executive; b. Calumet City, Ill., Mar. 8, 1933; d. Henry Adolph and Genevieve Veronica (Novak) Kaminski; m. Raymond John Basel, Feb. 19, 1955; children—Cynthia, Laura, Mark. Grad. Griffith Sch., Ind., 1950. Sec., Aeroquip/Barco, Barrington, Ill., 1955-62; freelance typist, Barrington, 1962-68; bookkeeper, office mgr. R.A.G. Enterprises, Fox Lake, Ill., 1968-78; ptnr., owner Classic Printery, Round Lake, 1978—. Republican. Roman Catholic. Office: Classic Printery 316 Main St Round Lake Park IL 60073

BASHA, MARY BETH, business executive; b. Auburn, N.Y., May 6, 1955; d. Roger and Dolores Anne (Malec) B. A.A.S. cum laude, Auburn Community Coll., 1975; B.A. in Sociology and Pub. Justice, Oswego State Coll., 1977. Concierge, Hotel Syracuse, N.Y., 1977; sales rep. Prudential Ins. Co., Syracuse, 1978-83; owner, operator The Cleaning Hands, Syracuse, 1983—, Basha/Baer & Assocs., Syracuse, 1986—; speaker Oswego Coll. Career Devel. Seminar, 1984. Recipient various awards Prudential Ins. Co., 1980, 81. Mem. Nat. Assn. Female Execs., Oswego Alumni Assn. Roman Catholic. Club: Holiday Health. Avocations: photography; basketball; softball; writing; cross country skiing. Home: 303 Hampshire Dr Dewitt NY 13214

BASILE, ABIGAIL JULIA ELLEN HERRON, employment counselor, state official; b. St. Louis, June 15, 1915; d. Charles Arthur and Abigail (Edwards) Herron; student Kansas City Jr. Coll., 1948-50, U. Kans., 1959; B.S. in Bus. Adminstrn., Rockhurst Coll., 1965; M.Ed., U. Mo., 1967; m. Joseph Basile, Aug. 15, 1939. Employment security dep. Mo. Div. Employment Security, Kansas City, 1945-59, youth coordinator, employment counselor, 1959-65, counselor, supr., 1965-81. Mem. Mo. Assn. Social Welfare. Mem. Am. Personnel and Guidance Assn., Nat. Vocat. Guidance Assn., Am. Vocat. Assn., Internat. Assn. Personnel in Employment Security (pres. Mo. 1966-67, internat. sec. 1968), Nat. Rehab. Assn., Nat. Employment Counselors Assn., Urban League, Am. Legion Aux., Personnel Research Forum, Profl. Counselors Assn. Democrat. Episcopalian. Home: 5316 Paseo Kansas City MO 64110

BASILICK, LINDA F., banker, consultant, educator; b. Putnam, Conn., July 4, 1947; d. Joseph M. and Irene (Varieur) Hewko; m. Donald J. Bouthillier, June, 1965; (div. 1970); children—Thomas, James; m. 2d, Roger J. Basilick, May 27, 1977. B.A. magna cum laude, Eastern Conn. State U., 1976; M.A. with honors, U. Mo., 1977. Researcher, Harry S. Truman Hosp., Columbia, Mo., 1977-78; asst. dir. Conn. Poll, Storrs, 1978-81; sr. research analyst Conn. Nat. Bank, Hartford, 1981-82, dir. mktg. research, 1983—; tchr., lectr. Eastern Conn. State U., 1979, Quinebaug Valley Community Coll., 1979, Mohegan Community Coll., 1980; pvt. cons. Mem. Am. Mktg. Assn., Nat. Assn. Exec. Women. Home: 189 S Main St Manchester CT 06040 Office: Conn Nat Bank 777 Main St Hartford CT 06115

BASINAIT, MARY BOKMAN, county official; b. Albion, N.Y., Mar. 16, 1924; d. Michael J. and Mary R. (Smith) Bokman; m. L. Charles Basinait, Aug. 28, 1944; children—L. Michael, Martin, Charles, Joseph, Larry. Student Chown Bus. Sch., 1941-43. Asst. treas. Niagara-Orleans Prodn. Credit Assn., Medina, N.Y., 1943-48; ct. stenographer Justice Cts. Orleans County, Albion, part-time 1950-73; office mgr. Bokman Bros. Dodge-Plymouth Agy., Medina, 1959-63; treas., budget dir. Orleans County, 1973—. Mem. Orleans County Republican Com., 1953-73, N.Y. State Rep. Com., 1956—, N.Y. State Exec. Com., 1974-83; leader 4-H club; mem. N.Y. State Finance Sch. Com. 1973—; mem. Electoral Coll., 1980. Mem. N.Y. Assn. Counties, N.Y. Mcpl. Fin. Officers Assn. (gov., v.p., pres.-elect), N.Y. State County Treasurers and Fin. Officers Assn. (pres. 1983), Albion Bus. and Profl. Women. Republican. Roman Catholic. Home: 3893 Riches Rd Albion NY 14411 Office: 34 E Park St Albion NY 14411

BASKETT, ANNE HELEN, travel agy. exec.; b. Kalamazoo, Jan. 22, 1941; d. Robert Elton and Helen Gertrude (Menten) Serfling; B.A., Emory U., 1962. Vol., Peace Corps, Philippines, 1962-64; sales rep., mgr. Smith Bell Travel, Manila, 1964-70; mgr., owner Daly Travel Services, San Francisco, 1970—. Bd. dirs. Friends of Brain Tumor Research. Mem. Am. Soc. Travel Agts., Pacific Area Travel Assn. Pub., editor The Daly News. Office: Daly Travel Service 391 Sutter St San Francisco CA 94108

BASKIN, BONITA LEE, laboratory executive, researcher; b. Chgo., Mar. 14, 1949; d. Seymour and Beverly Bernice (Geller) B.; m. Max Isak Corndorf, Dec. 21, 1975 (div. 1985); children—Eric, Adam. B.S., U. Miami, 1970, Ph.D., 1975; postdoctoral NIH, 1975-77. Research scientist U. Minn., Mpls., 1979-81; owner, dir. ViroMed Labs., Inc., Mpls., 1981—. Contbr. articles to profl. jours. NIH fellow, 1975; Eli Lilly Co. fellow, 1977. Mem. Am. Soc. Microbiology, Pan Am. Soc. Rapid Viral Diagnosis, Minn. Med. Tech. Soc. Avocations: skiing; reading; knitting. Home: 4350 Sussex Rd Minneapolis MN 55416 Office: ViroMed Labs Inc 5100 Gamble Dr 55 Minneapolis MN 55416

BASKIN, VLASTA JANA MARIE, language educator; b. Klatovy, Czechoslovakia, Jan. 20, 1929; came to U.S., 1948, naturalized, 1953; d. Josef Kolena and Marie (Hoskova) Kolenova; m. Wade Jacob Baskin, Jan. 1, 1949 (dec.); children—Wade Jacob Jr., Daniel Gregory, Michael Kenmar. Ed. Gymnasium for Women, Cheb, Czechoslovakia. Instr. Russian, Southeastern Okla. State U., Durant, 1960—, adviser to internat. students, 1960-74, instr. German and Russian, research analyst, 1983—. Translator: Hysteria, Reflex, and Instinct (Ernst Kretschmer), 1960, also children's story. Official interpreter Okla. Tourism and Recreation Dept. Bicentennial Com., 1976; contbr. ethnic history project Okla. Image, 1978; mem. steering com. City Council of Durant, 1981. Mem. Okla. Edn. Assn., Okla. Fgn. Tchrs. Assn., Alpha Mu Gamma. Democrat. Baptist. Home: 1723 W Locust St Durant OK 74701 Office: Southeastern Okla State U Durant OK 74701

BASLER, SARAH JANE, financial consultant; b. Dayton, Ohio, Feb. 23, 1946; d. Frederick William and Helen Jane (Harvey) Fansher; m. Donald Steven Basler, Dec. 23, 1967; children—Tamery Katharine, Matthew Thomas. B.S., Ohio U., 1969. Tchr. pub. schs., Durham, N.C., 1969-70, Franklin County Schs., Columbus, Ohio, 1973-76; pres. Basic Concepts, Inc., Columbus, 1981—; substitute tchr. Columbus pub. schs., 1983—; v.p. bd. dirs. Health Exec. Adv., Columbus, 1983—. Bd. dirs. Westerville PTO, 1978-80; tchr. Sunday Sch., Sharon Woods Bapt. Ch., 1980, 83, 85, 86. Republican. Club: Women's (bd. dirs. 1981-82) (Minerva Park). Office: Basic Concepts Inc Columbus OH 43229

BASS, BETTY ZOE PASSMORE (MRS. ERIC BASS), artist; b. Burlington, Wis., Mar. 26, 1926; d. Dempster Stewart and Bettina (Rakow) Passmore; student U. Ariz., 1943, U. Miami, 1944-47; B.A., UCLA, 1955; M.A., Stanford U., 1963; m. Eric Bass, Oct. 10, 1948. Designer, partner haute couture firm Eric Bass, Beverly Hills, Calif., 1949-53; fine art painting, Lakeside and Los Angeles, Calif., 1953—; exhibited UCLA Art Gallery, 1955, Art Center, LaJolla, Calif., 1957, So. Calif. Exposition, 1961; Oriental art research travel to Japan, Thailand, India, 1959-60. Chmn. opening night dinners San Diego Opera Guild, also chmn. LaJolla Assos.; mem. Asian arts com. Fine Arts Soc.; v.p. San Diego com. Los Angeles Philharmonic; v.p. Women's Assn. Salk Inst.; chmn. benefit ball San Diego Symphony, 1971; chmn. dinners Civic Light Opera. Bd. dirs. U. Calif. at San Diego Hosps. Aux.; bd. dirs. women's com. San Diego Symphony Assn. Named a San Diego Woman of Elegance, 1972; Makua life patroness, 1972; chmn. Social Service League benefit for Darlington House, 1976; chmn. benefit fashion show for U. San Diego, 1979; chmn. Women of Dedication Benefit, Door of Hope, 1985. Mem. Soc. Mayflower Descs., DAR, Social Service League, La Jolla Civic Orch. Assn., Old Globe Theater 400, Klee Wyk Soc. Mus. Man, La Jolla Mus. Contemporary Art, World Affairs Council, Country Friends, Starlight Women's Assn. (v.p.), U. San Diego Aux. (v.p.), Delta Gamma. Club: Stanford (San Diego). Home: PO Box 2064 La Jolla CA 92038

BASS, MARY FAULK, executive recruiter; b. Gladewater, Tex., Dec. 13, 1942; d. Woodrow Wilson and Nettie (Newman) Faulk; m. John Keith Holman, Feb. 28, 1964 (div. 1976); children—Kelly Elizabeth, Kecia Elaine. B.B.A. in Acctg., U. Tex.-Austin, 1979. Sr. acct. Exxon Co. USA, Houston, 1979-80; asst. controller Durango Oil and Gas Co., Houston, 1980-81; acctg. mgr. R.E. Smith Interests, Houston, 1981; mgr., recruiter Exec. Search Assocs., Houston, 1981-84; owner, pres. Pro-File, Inc., Tyler, Tex., 1984-86; exec. recruiter Clark & Assocs., Austin, Tex., 1986—. Republican. Presbyterian. Home: 1003 Blanco Austin TX 78703 Office: Clark & Assocs 704 W 9th St Austin TX 78701

BASS, ONA LYNN, health care administrator, consultant nuclear medicine; b. Niles, Mich., May 1, 1956; d. Joseph Theodore and Martha Bell (Bass) Upthegrove. A.S. in Sci., Ind. U., 1975, B.S., 1977; diploma Henry Ford Hosp. Nuclear Medicine, 1978; B.S., Siena Heights Coll., 1982; M.A. in Bus., Central Mich. U., 1984. Cert. in radiologic tech., nuclear medicine. Technologist nuclear medicine Radiology Assocs., Detroit, 1978-79; radiologic technologist St. John's Hosp., Detroit, 1981-84; head dept. med. imaging Kirwood Hosp., Detroit, 1979-84; dir. med. imaging St. Thomas Hosp., Nashville, 1984-85; dir. diagnostic imaging Humana Audubon Hosp., Louisville, 1985—; cons. nuclear medicine Brent Hosp., Detroit, 1980-84. Lectr. Career Day Winterhalter Middle Sch., Detroit, 1982, Murphy Middle Sch., Detroit, 1983-84; chmn. United Fund, Kirwood Hosp., 1980-83; participant Project Health-o-Rama, Detroit, 1983-84. Simplicity Pattern Co. scholar, 1973-76. Mem. Soc. Nuclear Medicine, Am. Soc. Clin. Pathologists, Am. Radiology Adminstrs., Am. Registry Radiologic Technologists, Am. Coll. Hosp. Adminstrs., Am. Hosp. Radiology Adminstrs., Young Adminstrs. Avocations: tennis; aerobics, movies, travel. Office: Humana Hosp Audubon One Audubon Plaza Dr PO Box 17555 Louisville KY 40217

BASS, RENEE FEIN, lawyer; b. Stuttgart, Ger., Sept. 25, 1946; d. Morris and Helen (Flek) Fein; m. Harvey B. Bass, Dec. 1, 1967; children—Stephanie, Michelle, Bradley. B.S., DePaul U., 1972, J.D., 1976. Bar: Ill. Mem. buyers program staff Marshall Field & Co., Skokie, Ill., 1965-67; ptnr. law firm Bass & Bass & Assocs., Chgo., 1977-80; sole practice law, Chgo., 1980—. Vol., Adlai E. Stevenson Campaign, 1969, Dan Walker Campaign, 1970; mem. Glencoe (Ill.) Village Caucus, 1983. Mem. Am. Immigration Lawyers Assn., Chgo. Bar Assn., Ill. Bar Assn., ABA. Democrat. Jewish. Home: 90 Harbor St Glencoe IL 60022 Office: 20 N Clark St Chicago IL 60022

BASS, RUTH, art educator; b. Boston, Oct. 11, 1938; d. Samuel and Beatrice (Wexler) Gilbert; B.A. magna cum laude, Radcliffe Coll., 1960; M.A., N.Y. U., 1962, Ph.D., 1978; m. Harvey Bass, Apr. 15, 1967; 1 child, Michael. Lectr., U. Bridgeport (Conn.), 1963-64; lectr. Queens Coll., N.Y.C., 1965-66; instr. N.Y. U., N.Y.C., 1980-81; faculty Bronx Community Coll., City U. N.Y., 1965-69, asst. prof., 1970-78, assoc. prof., 1978-81, prof. art, 1981—, project dir. NEH ednl. grant, 1984; art critic Art News, 1979—; curator Contemporary Images, Mendik Co., 1986; art writer Arts mag., Art World, Art in Am., McGraw-Hill Dictionary of Art, Dictionary of 20th Century Art, others. Bd. advisors Artists Choice Mus., 1980; moderator Panel on Realist Art sponsored Bklyn. Mus. and Louis Abrons Arts for Living Center, 1980—. Arts and Soc. fellow, 1981; SUNY Research Found. grantee, 1975-76; Bronx Community Coll. fellow, 1979-80; CUNY Women's Research and Devel. Fund grantee, 1986-87. Mem. Coll. Art Assn., Internat. Assn. Art Critics, Art Students League N.Y., AAUP, Women in the Arts, Artists Equity Assn. N.Y., Am. Soc. Aesthetics. Contbr. articles to profl. jours.

BASS, SHIRLEY ANN, lawyer; b. Brockton, Mass., Mar. 1, 1938; d. Ernest Francis and Clarissa May (Atwood) Marcotte; m. Jerry J. Bass, Dec. 26, 1959; children—Thomas, Robert, John. Cert. Katharine Gibbs Sch., 1958; student San Diego State U., 1963-64; B.A., Portland State U., 1975; J.D., Lewis and Clark Law Sch., 1979. Bar: Oreg. 1980. Assoc., Knappenberger, Tish, Poole, Cyr & Moe, Portland, 1980-84, Cyr & Moe, P.C., Portland, 1985—; lectr. Portland Community Coll. (Oreg.), 1983—. Bd. dirs. Oreg. Fair Plan, 1982—; vol. lawyer Sr. Law Project, 1985—; mem. planned giving com. Loaves and Fishes, Inc., 1985—. Recipient Estate Planning award Am. Jurisprudence, 1979. Mem. Oreg. Bar (editorial bd., legis. com. estate planning sect.), ABA, Multnomah Bar Assn., Washington County Bar Assn., Estate Planning Council Portland, Inst. for Managerial and Profl. Women, P.E.O., Phi Alpha Delta. Republican. Episcopalian. Club: Portland City. Office: Cyr & Moe PC 1010 First Farwest Bldg 400 SW 6th Ave Portland OR 97204

BASSETT, ALICE COOK, state legislator; b. St. Johnsbury, Vt., May 16, 1925; d. Clayton Earlman and Alberta (Campbell) Fisher; m. Clinton Dana Cook, May 21, 1944 (dec. June 1969); children—Dana, Allison, Polly, Timothy, Cynthia; m. Thomas Day Seymour Bassett, May 12, 1979. A.A., Colby Jr. Coll., 1944; B.S., U. Vt., 1971. Bus. mgr. Royall Tyler Theatre, Burlington, Vt., 1977-79; asst. to editor NE Bibliography, Boston, 1979-81; mem. Vt. Ho. of Reps., Montpelier, 1983—. Author (newspaper column) Memo from Montpelier, 1984—; editor (legis. newsletter) Legis. Alert, 1984-85. Vice pres. LWV, Burlington, 1981-84; bd. dirs. Am. Friends Service Com., Brattleboro, Vt., 1980-85, ACLU, Montpelier, 1983—. Democrat. Mem. United Ch. of Christ. Office: State Legislature Montpelier VT

BASSETT, BARBARA WIES, editor, publisher; b. New Haven, Dec. 5, 1939; d. John Philip and Marie Elizabeth (Stevens) Wies; m. Norman Wilbur Bassett. B.A., U. Conn.; postgrad. New Sch. for Social Research. Cons. pub. relations, N.Y.C., 1959-66; author, tchr., Greensboro, N.C., 1968-72; author, editor Bestways, Inc., La Canada, Calif., 1972-76, editor, pub., Carson City, Nev., 1977—; with product devel. dept. Fearn Soya, Melrose Park, Ill., 1974-76; free-lance writer Charlotte Charles/Modern Products, Inc.; reviewer Greensboro Daily News, 1968-72; contbg. author Potpourri Press, Greensboro, 1970—, Hearst Corp., N.Y.C., 1972—, Keats Co., Conn., 1974—. Author: Wok, 1971, Wok and Tempura, 1969, Japanese Home Cooking, 1970, Natural Cooking, 1971, Super Soy, 1976, Healthy Gourmet, 1981, Healthy Gourmet International, 1982; guest appearances on TV. Mem. Inst. Food Technologists. Office: Bestways PO Box 2028 Carson City NV 89702

BASSETT, KATHRYN LYNN, guidance counselor, educator, consultant; b. Houston, Mar. 16, 1950; d. Roger Dean and Lorine (McGlamery) Shoemaker; m. Perry Eugene Bassett, May 22, 1971; children—Aaron Kyle, Scott Taylor. B.A. in Edn., Baylor U., 1971, M.S. in Counseling, 1977. Cert. tchr., Tex.; lic. profl. counselor. Tchr., Arlington (Tex.) Ind. Sch. Dist., 1971-75, LaVega Ind. Sch. Dist., Bellmead, Tex., 1975-77; tchr. Cypress Fairbanks Ind. Sch. Dist., Houston, 1977-79, counselor elem. sch., 1979-82, counselor jr. high sch., 1982—; instr. English, Houston Community Coll., 1981—; cons. in parent and tchr. tng., Houston, 1980—; presenter programs in field. Tchr. Sunday Sch., So. Baptist Ch., Arlington, Tex., 1971-73, Ben Hur, Tex., 1975-76, Houston, 1977-79. Mem. Tex. Personnel and Guidance Assn. (presenter state conv. 1982), Am. Assn. Counseling and Devel. (organizer workshop nat. conv. 1984), Nat. Assn. Female Execs. Office: Watkins Jr High School 4800 Cairnvillage Houston TX 77084

BASSETT, LAVONIA POPE, music supervisor; b. Houston, Nov. 11, 1925; d. Fred and Rosetta (Edwards) Pope; m. Searcy Bassett, Aug. 15, 1951; 1 dau., Ava LaVerne. B.S., Hampton U., 1946; M.A., Columbia U., 1948; Adminstrs. Cert., Tex. So. U., 1949. Music instr. Fayetteville Tchrs. Coll., N.C., 1946-47; choral instr. Edward Waters Coll., Jacksonville, Fla., 1948-49; music tchr. Houston pub. schs., 1949-65, music supr., 1965—. Democrat. Lutheran. Home: 3431 Wentworth St Houston TX 77004 Office: Houston Pub Schs 3830 Richmond St Houston TX 77027

BASSI, TERESA ANN, human services executive; b. Johnston, Pa., Apr. 28, 1956; d. Leo Joseph and Shirley Anne (Williams) B. B.A., Seton Hill Coll., 1979; M.A., Indiana U. Pa., 1985. Resident adviser Seton Hill Coll., Greensburg, Pa., 1978-79, dorm coordinator, 1979-81; residential program worker Life Mgmt. Assocs., Greensburg, Pa., 1979-80, residential supr., 1980-82, dir. residential services, 1982-85, adminstrv. officer, 1985—; pvt. counseling, 1985—; facilitator drug and alcohol service, 1985—. Lector, Holy Trinity Ch., Ligonier, Pa., 1984—. Mem. Am. Assn. Mental Deficiency, Nat. Assn. Pvt. Residential Facilities Dirs., Health and Welfare Council, Westmoreland Assn. Vol. Adminstrs. Democrat. Roman Catholic. Avocations: Reading; birding; sports; woodworking. Home: 803 Weaver St Apt 12 Greensburg PA 15601 Office: Life Mgmt Assocs Ltd 593 Rugh St Greensburg PA 15601

BASSO, SARA JANE ANGELI, lawyer; b. Iron River, Mich., May 27, 1952; d. Libero and Nora Mae (Singler) Angeli; m. Ronald Matthew Basso, Apr. 14, 1973; children—Gabriel, Nora Mae. B.A. in Humanities, St. Mary's Coll., 1974; J.D., Thomas M. Colley Law Sch., 1978. Bar: Mich. 1978. Assoc. firm Dunn & Zulakis, P.C., Lansing, Mich., 1978-79; prin. firm Basso & Basso, Lansing, 1979—. Bd. dirs. YWCA, Lansing, 1983—; mem. Lansing Bd. Zoning Appeals, 1982-84; pres. Friends of Turner-Dodge House, Lansing, 1981-82; campaign mgr. Com. to Elect Ron Basso Dist. Judge, Lansing, 1980; sustaining mem. So. Poverty Law Center; adv. council Mich. Women's Hall of Fame. Fellow ACLU, Mich. Bar Assn., Mid-Mich. Women Lawyers Assn. (co-chmn. program com. 1980-81), Mich. Women Lawyers Assn. (co-chmn. amicus com. 1980); mem. AAUW, NOW. Roman Catholic. Home: 1381 Sebewaing Okemos MI 48864 Office: Basso & Basso 2356 Science Pkwy Suite 110 Okemos MI 48864

BASTARDI, MARILYN PATRICIA, printing executive; b. Newark, Mar. 17, 1945; d. Anthony Frank and Janet Louise (Richliano) Petrozzino; m. Anthony Vincent Bastardi, June 24, 1967; children—Noelle, Anthony III, Matthew, Christian. B.A. in English, Caldwell Coll., 1966. Cert. elem. tchr., N.J. Tchr. Wayne Bd. Edn., N.J., 1966-68, supplemental tchr. learning disabilities, 1975-77; pres. Presto Printing Ctr., Parsippany, N.J., 1980—. Pres. GATEway No. N.J., 1978-80; mem. gifted edn. com. Hanover Twp. Bd. Edn., N.J., 1980; Named Rookie of Yr., Sir Speedy Franchises, 1981. Mem. Middle Atlantic Sir Speedy Owners Assn., U.S. C. of C., AAUW (chmn. scholarship com. 1982), Caldwell Coll. Alumnae Assn. (exec. com. 1985), Delta Epsilon Sigma. Republican. Roman Catholic. Avocations: piano; ice skating; gourmet cooking. Home: RD2 4 Southview Dr Boonton Twp NJ 07005 Office: Sir Speedy Printing 1543 Route 46 Parsippany NJ 07054

BASTEDO, HELEN WILMERDING, civic worker; b. N.Y.C., Jan. 5, 1917; d. Lucius and Helen (Cutting) Wilmerding; ed. pvt. sch.; m. Philip Bastedo, Feb. 4, 1937; children—Russell, Bayard, Cecily, Christopher. Active Planned Parenthood of Manhattan, Bronx, 1937-66, chmn. 1952-55; active Planned Parenthood N.Y.C., 1966—; chmn. fund raising com. Planned Parenthood Fedn. Am., 1952-53, vice chmn., 1968-71; mem. Women's Aux. Union Settlement, 1939-58; mem. Women's bd. Women's Hosp., 1954-58; vice chmn. Women's com. Lincoln Center for Performing Arts, 1958-63, co-chmn. seat endowment com. 1960-63; mem. Assn. Vol. Sterilization, 1951-73. Episcopalian. Clubs: River, Cosmopolitan. Home: 925 Park Ave New York NY 10028

BATCHELDER, SHARON KAY, broker, realtor; b. Oklahoma City, Okla., Aug. 13, 1939; d. George Wayland and Clyda Grace (Hodges) Boles; m. Michael Earl Batchelder, June 4, 1960; 1 child, Mark Wayland. M.Ed., Tex. Christian U., 1978; B.A. in Journalism, So. Meth. U., 1960. Lic. real estate broker, Tex. Pub. relations asst. Dallas Theater Ctr., 1959; tchr. Antelope Valley High Sch., Lancaster, Calif., 1968-69, Ft. Worth Ind. Sch. Dist., 1969-73; tchr. journalism and English Castleberry High Sch., 1973-79, Joshua Middle Sch., Tex., 1980-81; realtor Henry S. Miller, Realtors, Ft. Worth, Tex., 1982—, broker, 1984—; counselor Tarrant County Jr. Coll., spring 1979; instr. Evelyn Wood Reading Dynamics, Austin, Tex., 1979-82; counselor, instr. Family & Individual Services, 1979-80. Mem. Alzheimer and Related Disorders Assn., 1983-84; bd. dirs. YWCA, Ft. Worth, 1982-85. Recipient Nat. Merit award Nat. Merit Scholarship Corp., 1957. Mem. Nat. Assn. Realtors, Tex. Assn. Realtors, Greater Ft. Worth Bd. Realtors. Home: 4309 Lanark St Fort Worth TX 76109 Office: Henry S Miller Realtors 6031 Camp Bowie Blvd Fort Worth TX 76116

BATCHELOR-WHITE, MARGARET, government energy official; b. Savannah, Ga. B.S., Savannah State Coll., 1953; M.Ed., Springfield Coll., 1969, C.A.G.S., 1972; Ed.D. U. Mass., 1974. Cons., trainer Springfield Ctr. for Alcoholism (Mass.), 1975-77; psychologist, guidance counselor, coordinator, tchr. Springfield Dept. Edn., 1968-77; instr., counselor Springfield Tech. Community Coll., 1969-74; program analyst, asst. for ops. HUD, 1977; equal opportunity specialist fed. contract compliance Employment Standards Adminstrn., Dept. Labor, Washington, 1978-79; program analyst for mgmt. systems br. Office of Mgmt. and Program Coordination, Econ. Regulatory Adminstrn., Dept. Energy, 1979—; instr. U. Mass., 1973-74. Bd. dirs. Episcopal Diocese Western Mass., 1972; mem. Tri-city Council Springfield Action Commn., 1973. Named Outstanding Woman of Yr., Links, 1974; Vol. of Yr., Girls' Club, Springfield, 1975; recipient cert. appreciation and service award, 1976; cert. appreciation HUD, 1978. Home: 307 Yoakum Pkwy Alexandria VA 22304

BATEMAN, DOTTYE JANE SPENCER, Realtor; b. Athens, Tex.; d. Charles Augustus and Lillie (Freeman) Spencer; student Fed. Inst., 1941-42, So. Meth. U., Dallas Coll., 1956-58; m. George Truitt Bateman, 1947 (div. Apr. 1963); children—Kelly Spencer, Bethena; m. 2d, Joseph E. Lindsley, 1968. Sec. to state senator, Tyler, Tex., 1941-42; sec. to pres. Merc. Nat. Bank, Dallas, State Fair of Tex., Dallas, 1942-48; realtor, broker, Garland, Tex., 1956—; co-ptnr. Play-Shade Co.; appraiser Assoc. Soc. Real Estate Appraiser; auctioneer, 1963—; developer Stonewall Cave, 1964—, Guthrie East Estates. Pres., Central Elementary Sch. PTA, 1955-56, Bussey Jr. High PTA, 1956-57; den mother Cub Scouts Am., 1957-59; chmn. Decent Lit. Com., 1956-58; chmn. PTA's council, 1958; dir. Dallas Heart Assn., 1960, local chmn., 1955-57, county chmn., 1957-60; spl. dir. Henderson County Red Cross, 1945; local chmn. March of Dimes, 1961-63; mem. Dallas Civic Opera Com., 1963-64; mem. homemaker panel Dallas Times Herald, 1955-74. Named Outstanding Tex. Jaycee-Ette Pres., 1953, hon. Garland Jay-Cee-Ette, 1956, hon. Sheriff, Dallas County, 1963; headliner Press Club Awards dinner, 1963-68. Mem. Garland, Dallas (chmn. reception com., past dir., mem. comml.-investment div., mem. make Am. better com. 1973-78, mem. beautify Tex. council 1977-78, by-laws com. 1977-78) bds. realtors, Auctioneers Assn., Internat. Real Estate Fedn., Soc. Prevention Cruelty to Animals, Dallas Women's (project chmn.). Garland (chmn. spl. services com. 1955-56) chambers commerce, Consejo Internacional De Buena Vecindad, Delphian Study Club, Eruditis Study Club, D.A.R. (Daniel McMahan chpt.). Christian Scientist. Clubs: Garland (past v.p., pres.), Tex. (past treas., ofcl. hostess) Jaycee-Ettes, Garland Fedn. Women's (past pres.), Garland Garden, Trinity Dist. Fedn. Women's (past pres.), Pub. Affairs Luncheon, Dallas Press (dir. 1973-74), chmn. house com. 1973-74, chmn. hdqrs. com. 1973-74). Home: 6313 Lyons Rd Garland TX 75043 Office: 5518 Dyer St Dallas TX 75206

BATEMAN, SYLVIA LILAINE, lawyer; b. Chgo., Mar. 5, 1956; d. Russell Clayton and Mamie H. (Johnson) Jones; m. Paul Ehrich Bateman, Aug. 19, 1978; 1 child, Paul Ehrich, Jr. B.S. with honors, U. Ill.-Chgo., 1976; J.D., U. Mich., 1980. Bar: D.C. 1980. Acct. Natural Gas Pipeline Co. Am., Chgo., 1976-77; assoc. firm Hudson, Leftwich & Davenport, Washington, 1980-82; atty. II, Potomac Electric Power Co., Washington, 1982-83, asst. counsel, 1983-84, assoc. counsel, 1984; atty. United Air Lines, Inc., Chgo., 1984—. Mem. ABA, D.C. Bar Assn., Wash. Bar Assn. (panelist law fair 1983), Nat. Bar Assn. Democrat. Episcopalian. Office: United Air Lines Inc PO Box 66100 Chicago IL 60666

BATER, JENNIFER N(OEL), management consultant; b. Mt. Clemons, Mich., Dec. 25, 1955; d. Gene F. and Mary-Louise (Arnold) B. B.A. in Econs. with distinction, Wells Coll., 1977; M.B.A., Columbia U., 1981. Assoc. Data Resources Inc., N.Y.C., 1977-79; sr. assoc. Booz-Allen & Hamilton, N.Y.C., 1981—. Samuel Bronfman fellow, 1979-81. Mem. Phi Beta Kappa, Beta Gamma Sigma. Office: Booz Allen & Hamilton Inc 101 Park Ave New York NY 10178

BATES, BARBARA J. NEUNER, municipal official; b. Mt. Vernon, N.Y., Apr. 8, 1927; d. John Joseph William and Elsie May (Flint) Neuner; B.A., Barnard Coll., 1947; m. Herman Martin Bates, Jr., Mar. 25, 1950; children—Roberta Jean Bates Jamin, Herman Martin III, Jon Neuner. Confidential clk. to supr. town Ossining (N.Y.), 1960-63; pres. BNB Assocs., Briarcliff Manor, N.Y., 1963-83, Upper Nyack Realty Co., Inc., Briarcliff Manor, 1966-71; receiver of taxes Town of Ossining (N.Y.), 1971—. Vice pres. Ossining (N.Y.) Young Republican Club, 1958; pres. Young Womens Rep. Club Westchester County (N.Y.), 1959-61; regional committeewoman N.Y. State Assn. Young Rep. Clubs, 1960-62; mem. Westchester County Rep. Com., 1963—; mem. Ossining Women's Rep. Club, 1960—, pres., 1984-85; mem. Westchester County Women's Rep. Club, 1957—. Mem. Jr. League Westchester-on-Hudson, DAR, N.Y. State Assn. Tax Receivers and Collectors, Receivers of Taxes Assn. of Westchester County, (legis. liaison, v.p., pres. 1984-85), Hackley Sch. Mothers Assn. (pres. 68), R.I. Hist. Soc., Ossining Hist. Soc., Ossining Bus. and Profl. Women's Club, Am. Soc. Notaries, Westchester County Hist. Soc., Briarcliff-Scarborough Hist. Soc. Congregationalist. Home: 78 Holbrook Ln Briarcliff Manor NY 10510 also RFD 2 Chepachet RI 02814

BATES, BARBARA JEANNE, living history producer and administrator, library consultant; b. Mpls., May 31; d. Gale Pillsbury and Rhetta Hilyer; m. George Walter Bates, Dec. 12, 1951 (div. 1962); 1 child, Brenda Leigh. Student Beaver Coll., 1947-48; B.A. in Edn., U. Pa., 1950; M.A., Drexel Inst., 1951; Tchrs. Cert., Temple U., 1953. Librarian, Free Library of Phila., 1950-54, U.S. Army Overseas Schs., Mannheim, Germany, 1956-61, Lansdown Aldan Sch. Dist., Pa., 1961-71, Kulani Honor Camp, Hilo, Hawaii, 1976; library coordinator Springfield Sch. Dist., Erdenheim, Pa., 1971-82; reference librarian in charge Community Coll. Phila., evenings and weekends 1977-80; pres., producer Betsy Ross Living History Presentations, Valley Forge, Pa., 1982—; kindergarten tchr. Children's Learning Service, King of Prussia, Pa., 1985-86; co-founder, vice pres., sec. Global Edn. Motivators, Erdenheim, 1980-84. Author, producer, coordinator, actress of video film: Happy Birthday George Washington, 1982 (Freedom Found. award 1982); The Rainbow Experience, 1984. Mem. disaster action team ARC, Phila., 1982—; disaster reservist Fed. Emergency Mgmt. Agy. Eastern Div., 1984—; vol. soup kitchen worker Mother Theresa Convent, Norristown, Pa., 1984; vol. asst. to Archivist Medal of Honor Grove Freedoms Found., Valley Forge, 1980—. Recipient George Washington Honor medal Freedoms Found., 1982; Legion of Merit, Chapel of Four Chaplains, 1982. Mem. Springfield Tchrs. Edn. Assn. (sec. 1980), NEA (del. conv. 1980, 81), Govs.' Conf. on Libraries and Info. Services (del. 1977), White House Conf. on Libraries and Info. Services, Pa. Library Assn., Nat. Council for Social Studies, World Affairs Council, Book and Author Lecture Series Phila. Inquirer, Japan Study Group II, Valley Forge Hist. Soc., Kappa Delta. Democrat. Episcopalian.

BATES, BARBARA SNEDEKER, editor, writer; b. Phila., Apr. 28, 1919; d. R. Cuyler and Dorothy Stow (Roberts) Snedeker; m. Frederick Heston Bates, Jr., Jan. 20, 1945; children—Susan Penelope, Stephen Cuyler. B.A., Wellesley Coll., 1940. Reporter, Times-Chronicle, Jenkintown, Pa., 1940-41; editor story papers United Presbyn. Ch., Phila., 1941-44; editor fiction Westminster Press, Phila., 1944-46; editor books for young people, 1967-85; freelance writer, Jenkintown, 1946-67; lectr. Beaver Coll., Glenside, Pa., 1985—; juvenile editor Walker & Co., N.Y.C., 1985—. Author children's books including: The Real Book of Pets, 1952, The Real Book of Camping, 1953; New Boy Next Door, 1965; Bible Festivals and Holy Days, 1967; contbr. stories, articles and poems to childrens mags., articles to Sch. Library Jour., Phaedrus. Named to Century Club Cheltenham High Sch., Wyncote, Pa., 1984; recipient Drexel award, 1986. Mem. Phila. Booksellers Assn. (pres. 1981), Children's Book Council (dir. 1979-81), Phila. Childrens Reading Round Table, Phila. Art Alliance, Pa. Acad. Fine Arts. Presbyterian (elder 1980—). Club: Peale. Home: 104 Runnymede Ave Jenkintown PA 19046

BATES, BETSEY, artist; b. Dobbs Ferry, N.Y., Nov. 29, 1924; d. Homer Morgan and Dorothy (Graef) Smith; B.F.A. magna cum laude, Beaver Coll., 1946; m. Guy C. Bates, Aug. 30, 1947 (div. 1965); children—Carleton Jane, Leslie Collins; m. Joseph M. Gerhart, June 13, 1978. Designer, painter, illustrator, printmaker for advt. agys., corps. and pubs.; works include: Christmas card Easter Seal Soc., 1974, mural for RCA TV Studio, Switzerland, 1977; represented in collections: Washington Hilton Hotel, Houston Marriott, Syracuse Marriott, Chgo. Marriott, Texaco, World Book, Lynell, Grad. Hosp. of Phila, Butler Inst. Am. Art, Danskin, Inc., Episcopal Acad., Hahnemann Hosp., Friends Central Sch., Continental Bank, Fed. Res. Bank, Free Library Phila., Germantown Hosp., Montgomery Hosp. (10), Smith Kline Pharm., McNeil Pharm. (2). Recipient cert. of merit Nat. Consumer Fin. Assn., 1963; cert. of excellence Phila. Art Dirs. Club, 1964; award Nat. Community Arts Program, Golden Disc, Beaver Coll., 1975; Best of Show award Norristown Borough (Pa.) Council of Arts, 1980. Mem. Artists Equity Assn., Phila. Art Alliance, Nat. Trust Hist. Preservation, Artists Guild Delaware Valley (Gold awards 1977-84). Home and Office: 1330 Valley Forge Rd RD 1 Norristown PA 19401

BATES, BETTY LAMBERSON, state official; b. Stevens County, Kans., Dec. 20, 1934; d. Bur Raymond and Ida Bernice (Florence) Cox; m. Albert Eugene Lamberson, Mar. 28, 1952 (div. 1972); children—Charles, Rebecca, Kristy, Terry, Janna; m. Robert Duane Bates, Sept. 3, 1982. Mgr., B & B Motel, Hugoton, Kans., 1972-75; bookkeeper Ford. Bros. Supply, Hugoton, Liberal, Kans., 1975-77; dept. clk., bookkeeper Dist. Ct., Stevens County, Kans., 1977-78, clk. of dist. ct., 1978—. Sponsor Teen-age Republicans, Hugoton, 1973-74. Mem. Kans. Assn. Dist. Ct. Clks. and Adminstrs. (sec. 1980-81, v.p. 1981-82, pres. 1982-83, chmn. steering com. 1984—), Nat. Assn. Ct. Adminstrs., Liberal Legal Secs. Club. Home: 811 S Jackson St Hugoton KS 67951 Office: Dist Ct 200 E 6th St Hugoton KS 67951

BATES, JANET FLEISHHACKER, civic worker; b. San Francisco, Sept. 13, 1908; d. Herbert and Ethel (Berger) Choynski; student pub., pvt. schs.; m. Mortimer Fleishhacker, May 1, 1929 (dec.); children—Delia F. Ehrlich, Mortimer, David. Treas. women's bd. San Francisco Mus. Art, 1957-59; v.p. Youth Guidance Center, 1950-51; vice chmn. DACOWITS, 1961; v.p. Salesian Boys Club, 1963-64; chmn. bd. Am.-Italy Soc., 1963-64, pres., 1972-76; nat. pres. Camp Fire Girls, 1969-72; exec. v.p. Internat. Hospitality Center, San Francisco, 1973-76; bd. dirs. mem. bd. Bay Area U.S.O., 1974-84, v.p., 1977—; v.p. Fort Point and Army Museum Assn., 1976-85; trustee U. San Francisco, 1976-85, chmn. bd., 1977-85; Beaudry Found., 1978-81; bd. dirs. Inst. for Philos. Research, 1976—, Internat. House, Berkeley, 1976-85, Berkeley Found. U. Calif., 1978-81, Am. Assembly, 1981—, Trauma Found., 1983—, Internat. Visitors Ctr., 1984-86; bd. overseers U. Calif.-San Francisco, 1980—. Decorated Order of North Star (Sweden); recipient Outstanding Civilian Service medal U.S. Army, 1961; decorated Stella della Solidarità, Republic of Italy, Orde Nationale du Merite (France). Home: 2298 Pacific Ave Suite 6 San Francisco CA 94115

BATES, LURA WHEELER, trade association executive; b. Inboden, Ark., Aug. 28, 1932; d. Carl Clifton and Hester Ray (Pace) Wheeler; B.S. in Bus. Adminstrn., U. Ark., 1954; m. Allen Carl Bates, Sept. 12, 1954; 1 dau., Carla Allene. Sec.-bookkeeper, then officer mgr. Assoc. Gen. Contractors Miss., Inc., Jackson, 1958-77, dir. adminstrv. services, 1977—, asst. exec. dir., 1980—; adminstr. Miss. Constrn. Found., 1977—; sec. AIA-Assoc. Gen. Contractors Liaisonship Coms., 1977—; sec. Carpenters Joint Apprenticeship Coms., Jackson and Vicksburg, 1977—. Sec., Marshall Elem. Sch. PTA, Jackson, 1962-64, v.p., 1965; sec.-treas. Inter-Club Council Jackson, 1963-64; tchr. adult Sunday sch. dept. Hillcrest Bapt. Ch., Jackson, 1975-82; mem. First Bapt. Ch., Crystal Springs, Miss.; mem. exec. com. Jackson Christian Bus. and Profl. Women's Council, 1976-80, sec., 1978-79, pres., 1979-80. Named Outstanding Woman in Constrn. Miss., 1962-63; Outstanding Mem. Nat. Assn. Women in Constrn., various times. Fellow Internat. Platform Assn.; mem. Nat. Assn. Women in Constrn. (chpt. pres. 1963-64, 76-77, nat. v.p. 1965-66, 77-78, nat. dir. Region 5, 1967-68, nat. sec. 1970-71, 71-72, pres. 1980-81, coordinator cert. constrn. assoc. program 1973-78, 83-84 guardian-controller Edn. Found. 1981-82, chmn. nat. bylaws com. 1982-83, 85-86, nat. parliamentarian 1983-86), Nat. Assn. Parliamentarians, Delta Delta Delta. Editor NAWIC Image, 1968-69, Procedures Manual, 1965-66, Public Relations Handbook, 1967-68, Profl. Edn. Guide, 1972-73; author digests in field. Home: 272 Lee Ave Crystal Springs MS 39059 Office: 2093 Lakeland Dr Jackson MS 39206

BATES, MARY MARTHA, nurse; b. Georgetown, Tenn., Aug. 23, 1932; d. Ray Cuthbert and Charlie Pearl (Snodgrass) Marler; B.A., Carson Newman Coll., 1954; diploma Bapt. Meml. Hosp. Sch. Nursing, Memphis, 1957; student Southwestern Bapt. Theol. Sem., 1980-82; m. Stanley R. Bates, Sept. 21, 1957; children—Elizabeth Ann. Staff nurse, Bapt. Hosp., Jacksonville, Fla, 1957-58, Mrytle Beach AFB Hosp., S.C., 1958-60; office nurse Dr. A.B. Russell, Ft. Walton Beach, Fla., 1964-65; nurse ARC, 1966; substitute tchr. Glasgow, Mont., 1966-68, Dover, Del., 1969-71; ednl. counselor Glasgow AFB, Mont., 1968; sch. health nurse Merced (Calif.) City Schs., 1968-69; asst. night supr. Del. Home and Hosp., Smyrna, 1971-72; staff nurse Eisenhower Hosp., Colorado Springs, Colo., 1975-78; asst. dir. nursing and staff devel. dir. Highland (Calif.) House Health Care, 1975-76; staff nurse Plymouth Village Convalescent Hosp., Redlands, Calif., 1976-78, Harris Hosp. Meth., Ft. Worth, 1978-79; preadmissions nursing coordinator, quality assurance coordinator Huguley Meml. Hosp., Ft. Worth, 1979-82; nurse Calif. Healthcare Cons., Sacramento, 1982-84; office nurse Crosslands Med. Complex Ft. Worth, 1985—. Dir., Del. Girls in Action, 1971-72; mem. exec. com. Md. Womens Missionary Union, 1972; adv. bd. Health and Rehab. Services, Ft. Worth. Mem. Nat. Assn. Quality Assurance Profls., Am. Assn. Ret. Persons. So. Bapt. Social Workers Assn. Republican. Presbyterian. Home: 6517 Arthur Dr Fort Worth TX 76134

BATES, RUBY LEE, corporate administrator; b. Marion, La., July 14, 1940; d. Roy and Wordie B. (Boyette) Shelbon; m. Julius Green, Aug. 18, 1963 (div. 1968); 1 child, Dana; m. Charles Bates, June 30, 1976 (dec.). A.A., Castlemont Coll., Oakland, 1957; S.S.A., Heald Coll., Oakland, 1958. Exec. sec. Golden State Ins., Oakland, 1958-66; adminstrv. office mgr. Simmons & Travis, Oakland, 1966-74; adminstrv. asst. Castle & Cooke, San Francisco, 1975-77, office coordinator, 1977-81, corp. bookkeeper, 1981-85. Editor: Handbook for Temporary Personnel, 1979. Vol., Gospel Voices, Oakland, 1971-85. Recipient Service award Bible Fellowship Ch., Oakland, 1976. Mem. Nat. Assn. Female Execs., Gamma Phi Delta. Democrat. Baptist. Avocations: Gospel singing; walking; reading. Home: 3822 39th Ave Oakland CA 94619

BATES-NISBET, (CLARA) ELISABETH, piano teacher, poet, lawyer; b. Houston, Dec. 4, 1902; d. William David and Kate Broocks (Arnall) Bates; B.A., U. Tex., 1938; M.A., U. Houston, 1941; LL.B., S. Tex. Sch. Law, 1937. Bar: Tex. 1937. Tchr. public schs., Houston, 1923-49, prin., 1950-73, prin. Longfellow Elem. Sch., 1950-52, Mamie Sue Bastian Elem. Sch., 1952-60, James Arlie Montgomery Elem. Sch., 1960-73; tchr. piano, Houston, 1928—. Life mem. chancellor's council U. Tex., Tex. Congress Parents and Tchrs. Established John Pelham Border Meml. Fund, San Jacinto Mus. of History Assn. Mem. State Bar Tex., Houston Bar Assn., Tex. Tchrs. Assn. (life), Ex-Students Assn. U. Tex. Austin (life), Tex. Geneal. Soc., Magna Charta Dames (organizing charter mem. E. Tex. Colony, 3d vice regent courier Round Table Tex. div. 1962-66), Tex. Hist. Assn. (patron, life), Colonial Dames XVII Century (registrar Col. John Alston chpt. 1966-68, mem. nat. com. on Am. history 1966-68), Alston-Willems-Boddie-Hillard Soc. N.C., Colonial Order Crown, San Augustine County Hist. Soc. (charter), San Jacinto Descs., Daus. Republic Tex. (organizing charter mem. Ezekial Cullen chpt. 1953, rec. sec. gen. 1963-65, compiler, editor anns. 1963-65, 2d v.p. gen., chmn. orgn. 1965-67), Soc. Descs. Charlemagne, DAR (Tejas chpt. regent 1966-68, mem. nat. coms.), Soc. Descs. Knights of Most Noble Order of Garter, Daus. Am. Colonists (organizer charter mem. LaSalle chpt.), UDC, Sovereign Colonial Soc. Ams. Royal Descent, Plantagenet Soc., Dames of Ct. of Honor, Daus. of Founders and Patriots of Am., Freedoms. Found. Valley Forge, Internat. Platform Assn., Smithsonian Instn., Bates Family of Old Va. Assn., Jamestowne Soc. (organizing gov. First Tex. Co. 1982), Delta Kappa Gamma (life, 1st v.p. Eta Delta chpt. 1966-68), Nat. Soc. Poets, state chm. Daughters Republic of Tex., 1976—, state chm. Kate Broocks Bates Award for Hist. Research. Co-founder Perpetual Endowment Fund Daus. Republic Tex., also perpeutally endowed Presdl. scholarship in law, history, govt. or music U. Tex. at Austin, and Kate Broocks Bates award for research in Tex. history sponsored by Tex. State Hist. Assn.; founder Kate Harding Bates Parker Award Fund for Jr. Historians Orgns. of Tex. Hist. Assn., Kate Harding Bates Parker Fund for Library of Daus. Republic Tex., Emma Broocks Arnall perpetually endowed Geology Scholarship Fund at U. Okla. at Norman, perpetual endowment U. Tex. at Austin Fine Arts Center, Kate Broocks Bates Recital Hall named in honor of mother and children. Address: 2305 Woodhead St Houston TX 77019

BATESON, MARY CATHERINE, anthropologist; b. N.Y.C., Dec. 8, 1939; d. Gregory and Margaret (Mead) B.; B.A., Radcliffe Coll., 1960; Ph.D., Harvard U., 1963; m. J. Barkev Kassarjian, June 4, 1960; 1 dau., Sevanne Margaret. Mem. faculty Harvard U., 1963-66, Ateneo de Manila, 1966-68, Northeastern U., Boston, 1969-71; ednl. cons., Tehran, 1972-74; mem. faculty Damavand Coll., Tehran, 1975-77, U. No. Iran, Babolsar, 1977-79; prof. anthropology Amherst Coll., 1980—, dean faculty, 1980-84; vis. scholar anthropology Harvard U., 1979-80; pres. Inst. Intercultural Studies, N.Y.C., 1979—. Grantee NSF, 1968-69, Wenner-Gren Found., 1972-73. Mem. Am. Anthrop. Assn., Soc. Iranian Studies, Lindisfarne Assn., World Soc. Ekistics. Author: Structural Continuity in Poetry: A Linguistic Study of Five Early Arabic Odes, 1970, Our Own Metaphor: A Personal Account of a Conference on Consciousness and Human Adaptation, 1972; With a Daughter's Eye: A Memoir of Margaret Mead and Gregory Batesen, 1984; co-editor: Approaches to Semiotics, 1964.

BATHONY, BARBARA ILSE, health care administrator, nurse; b. Landsberg, Germany, June 27, 1939, came to U.S., 1961, naturalized, 1964, d. Erich and Johanna (Heidke) Reuter; m. Tibor Bathony, Mar. 30, 1962. B.S. in Nursing, U. Alaska, 1979, M.S., 1983. Chemist, Fed. Health Dept., Berlin, 1959-61, Vitaminerals, Glendale, Calif., 1962-67; photog. lab. adminstr. Rapid Color, Inc., Glendale, 1967-72; photographer Boeing Co., Auburn, Wash., 1972-75; instr. Nakoiya and Anch Community Coll., 1977-83; dep. dir. North Slope Borough Health and Social Services, Barrow, Alaska, 1983—; chairperson adv. bd. Anchorage Sch. Nursing, 1981. Mem. Alaska Nurses Assn. (chairperson econ. and gen. welfare 1982—), Alaska Pub. Health Assn. (membership com. 1980—). Republican. Lutheran. Clubs: WBCCI (past treas.), Last Frontier, Newfoundland (past treas.). Home: Star Route 1687-R 4310 Sunstone Circle Anchorage AK 99507 Office: North Slope Borough Health and Social Services PO Box 69 Barrow AK 99723

BATISTE, PEARL THERESA, educator; b. Jeanerette, La., Dec. 9, 1930; d. Erris and Pearl (Armelin) Edgerly; B.A., Calif. State U., San Francisco, 1975; M.A. in Edn., U. San Francisco, 1978; M.S., Pepperdine U., 1979; m. Berwick Batiste, Sept. 12, 1950; children—Michael, Keith, Ronald, Elissa, Ingrid, Patrick. Dir. counseling tng. dept. Amrick Advt., Oakland, Calif., 1976-77; public relations dir. San Francisco Ednl. Found., Oakland, 1977-78; fashion model, instr., substitute tchr. Barbizon Modeling Sch., 1975-76; program and project coordinator Oakland Public Schs., 1976—. Mem. Black Exec. Women Assts., Profl. Woman Exec. Corp. Am., Black Profl. Bus. Women Assts., Nat. Alliance Black Edn. Democrat. Roman Catholic. Club: Fashionnete Social. Author: The Influence of African on American Fashion, 1980. Home: 2509 Tulare Ave El Cerrito CA 94530

BATTEN, ANNE, state legislator, real estate broker; b. Flushing, N.Y., July 24, 1932; d. Francis and Jeanne N. Kelly; student Goddard Coll., 1979-80; m. James C. Batten, Aug. 16, 1952; children—Robert, Barbara. Real estate broker, East Hardwick, Vt., 1964—; mem. Vt. Ho. of Reps., 1980-81, 82-86, vice chmn. judiciary com., 1985-86. Mem. Hardwick Planning Commn., 1972-73, Republican Town Com., 1970-86; treas. Hardwick Hist. Soc., 1981-82; mem. Northeastern Vt. Devel. Assn., 1981-86; mem. Vt. Gov.'s Commn. on Status of Women, 1980-84; bd. dirs. Hardwick Area Health Ctr., 1981—, Hardwick Aware Group. Mem. Hardwick C. of C., Vt. Women's Polit. Caucus, Northeast Kingdom Bd. Realtors. Address: RD 1 Box 2490 East Hardwick VT 05836

BATTIN, PATRICIA MEYER, librarian; b. Gettysburg, Pa., June 2, 1929; d. Emanuel Albert and Josephine (Lehman) Meyer; m. William Thomas Battin, June 16, 1951 (div.); children—Laura, Joanna, Thomas. B.A., Swarthmore Coll., 1951; M.S. in Library Sci., Syracuse U., 1967. Asst. librarian SUNY-Binghamton, 1967-69, asst. dir. for reader services, 1969-74; dir. library services group Columbia U., N.Y.C., 1974-78, v.p., univ. librarian, 1978—; interim pres. Research Libraries Group, Stanford, Calif., 1981-82; trustee EDUCOM, Princeton, N.J., 1983—, Council on Library Resources, Washington, 1984—. Contbr. articles to profl. jours. Mem. Assn. Research Libraries (dir. 1983—). Office: Columbia U Libraries 535 W 114th St New York NY 10027

BATTIN, (ROSABELL HARRIET) RAY, clinical neuropsychologist, audiologist; b. Rock Creek, Ohio; d. Harry Walter and Sophia (Boldt) Ray; A.B., U. Denver, 1948; M.S., U. Mich., 1950; Ph.D., U. Fla., 1959; postgrad. U. Miami (Fla.) Sch. of Medicine, 1957, U. Iowa, 1958; m. Tom C. Battin, Aug. 24, 1949. Instr. in speech pathology U. Denver, 1949-50; audiologist Ann Arbor (Mich.) Sch., 1950-51; audiologist Houston (Tex.) Speech and Hearing Center, 1954-56; dir. speech pathology-psychology Hedgecroft Hosp. and Rehab. Center, Houston, 1956-59; audiologist with Drs. Guilford, Wright and Draper, Houston, 1959-63; pvt. practice in psychology, audiology and psycholinguistics, Houston, 1959—; clin. instr. dept. otolaryngology U. Tex. Sch. Medicine, Galveston, 1964-80; dir. of audiology vestibulography and speech pathology lab. Houston Ear Nose and Throat Hosp. Clinic, 1963-73; adj. clin. instr. U. Houston, 1981—; lectr. The First Word program Sta. KUHT-TV, 1959; guest lectr. to various workshops and schs., 1959—. Bd. dirs. Juvenile Ct. Vols., 1980-83, Children's Resource and Info. Service, 1981—. Lic. psychologist, Tex. Recipient Gold award for Ednl. Exhibit, Am. Acad. Pediatrics, 1969. Fellow Am. Speech and Hearing Assn. (profl. services bd. 1967-70, com. on pvt. practice 1971-74), World Acad. Inc.; mem. Acad. Pvt. Practice in Speech Pathology and Audiology (pres. 1968-70), Am. Psychol. Assn., Tex. Speech and Hearing Assn. (v.p. 1968), Cleft Palate Assn., Tex., Houston psychol. assns., Harris County Biofeedback Soc. (pres. 1984), Acad. of Aphasia, Internat. Assn. of Logopedics and Phoniatrics, Am. Auditory Soc., Orthopsychiat. Assn., Am. Biofeedback Soc., Tex. Biofeedback Soc., Sigma Alpha Eta. Author: (with C. Olaf Haug) Speech and Language Delay, 1964; Vestibulography, 1974; Private Practice: Guidelines for Speech Pathology and Audiology, 1971; editor (with Donna R. Fox) Private Practice in Audiology and Speech and Language Pathology, 1978; contbr. author: Seminars in Speech, Language, Hearing (Northern); Auditory Disorders in School Children (Roeser and Downs); Current Therapy of Communications Disorder (Perkins); editor Jour. Acad. Pvt. Practice in Speech Pathology and Audiology, 1981-84; contbr. articles in field to profl. jours.; author (with Irvin A. Kraft) The Dysynchronous Child (film), 1971; The Battin Clinic Language Learning Screening Test for Preschool Children, 1985. Home: 3837 Meadow Lake Ln Houston TX 77027 Office: Battin Clinic 3931 Essex Ln Houston TX 77027

BATTLE, ANNA LEE, nurse, supervisor; b. Ocala, Fla., Aug. 13, 1951; d. Clarence and Goldie (Hall) Stukes; children—Ernest Stukes, Ranyatda Brown, Stevvon Stukes. A.S., Santa Fe Jr. Coll., 1972; lic. practical nurse, Mercer County Vocat. Sch., 1978. Master-at-arms Flamingo Club NCO Club, Fort Dix, N.J., 1976-79; practical nurse New Lisbon State Sch., N.J., 1978-80; practical nurse Trenton State Hosp., N.J., 1980-86; head cottage tng. supr. Trenton Psychiat. Hosp., 1986—, instr. of self-medication program, 1984—. Recipient award Dept. Human Services, Trenton Psychiat. Hosp., 1984, 85. Mem. Nat. Assn. Female Execs. Democrat. Baptist. Avocations: bicycling; travel; cooking; bowling; entertaining. Home: 33 Bond St Trenton NJ 08618 Office: Trenton Psychiat Hosp Cottage #3 PO Box 7500 Trenton NJ 08625

BATTLE, LOIS, writer, actress; b. Subiaco, Australia, Oct. 6, 1941; came to U.S., 1946, naturalized, 1962; d. John Henry and Doreen Mary (White) B.; student Fullerton Jr. Coll., 1956-58; B.A., UCLA, 1962. Author books: Season of Change, 1980; War Brides, 1982; Southern Women, 1984; actress. Mem. Writers Guild, Actors Equity Assn., Screen Actors Guild, AFTRA. Office: care St Martin's Press 175 5th Ave New York NY 10010

BATTLE, LUCY TROXELL (MRS. J.A. BATTLE), educator; b. Bridgeport, Ala., June 28, 1916; d. John Price and Emily Florence (Williams) Troxell; student U. Ala., Montevallo, 1934-35; B.S. Fla. So. Coll., 1951; postgrad. U. Fla., 1954, Fla. State U., 1963, Oxford (Eng.) U., 1979, 80, 81; M.A., U. South Fla., 1970; m. Jean Allen Battle, Aug. 25, 1940; 1 dau., Helen Carol. Asst. postmaster, Bridgeport, Ala., 1936-40; asst. dir. personnel office Sebring (Fla.) AFB, 1942-44; tchr. Cleveland Court Sch., Lakeland, Fla., also Forest Hill Sch., Carrollwood Sch., Tampa, Fla., 1949-64; dean of girls Greco Jr. High Sch., Tampa, 1964-68. Bd. dirs. Tampa Oral Sch. for Deaf. Recipient Outstanding Service award Fla. So. Coll. Woman's Club, 1942. Mem. NEA, Am. Childhood Edn. Internat., AAUW, Delta Kappa Gamma, Kappa Delta Pi, Phi Mu. Methodist. Club: Carrollwood Village Golf and Tennis. Author: (with J.A. Battle) The New Idea in Education, 1968. Home and office: 11011 Carrollwood Dr Tampa FL 33618

BATTLE, MARY VROMAN, English language educator; b. Marshall, Minn., Sept. 8, 1926; d. Alois and Idalie (Vercoutere) Vroman; B.A. in English and French, Coll. of St. Teresa, 1948; M.A. in Speech and Drama, Cath. U., 1954; Ed.D. in Founds. of Edn., Memphis State U., 1986; m. Allen Overton Battle, June 14, 1952; 1 son, Allen Overton III. Tchr. English, Albany (Minn.) Sr. High Sch., 1948-49; jr. high sch. tchr. English, Latin and sci., Washington, 1952-56; dean of studies Southwestern High Sch. Scholars Program, Memphis, 1967-71; asst. prof. English, Memphis State U., 1956—. Founder, participant Melrose tutoring project. Mem. NEA, Conf. on Coll. Composition and Communication, Nat. Council Tchrs. of English, Tenn. Edn. Assn., Shelby-Memphis Council Tchrs. of English (co-founder). Roman Catholic. Co-author: The Psychology of Patient Care: A Humanistic Approach; contbr. numerous articles to profl. jours. Home: 2220 Washington Ave Memphis TN 38104 Office: Dept English Memphis State U Memphis TN 38152

BATTLE, WILLA LEE GRANT, clergyman, educational administrator; b. Webb, Miss., Sept. 30, 1924; d. James Carlton and Aslean (Young) Grant; m. Walter Leroy Battle, July 4, 1941. Diploma, Northwestern Coll., Mpls., 1956; B.A. cum laude, U. Minn., 1975, M.A., 1979; Ph.D. summa cum laude, Trinity Sem., 1982. Ordained to ministry, 1939. Founder, pastor Grace Temple Del. Ctr., Mpls., 1958—; founder, pres., Willa Grant Battle Ctr., Mpls., 1980—; founder House of Refuge Mission, Haiti, W.I., 1957—; adminstr., dir. Kiddie Haven Pre-Sch., Mpls., 1982—. Mem. Interdenominational Ministerial Alliance (sec. 1986—), Mpls. Ministerial Assn., AAUW, AAUP, U. Minn. Alumni Assn. (life), NAACP, Nat. Council Negro Women, Christian Educators, Nat. Assn. Female Execs. Home: 220 E 42d St Minneapolis MN 55409 Office: Willa Grant Battle Ctr 1816 Fourth Ave South Minneapolis MN 55404

BATTLE-WELLS, DOLORES FRANCINE, government and security contractor; b. Cambridge, Mass., Aug. 10, 1938; d. Frank F. and Viola Gwendolyn (Waithe) Newton; m. Curtis Battle, June 4, 1958 (div. Dec. 1978); children—Dawn Francine, Robin Sareese Battle Deck, m. Richard Wells, Jan. 5, 1983. Student bus. mgmt. Cambridge Coll., 1985—. Coordinator data processing Youville Hosp., Cambridge, 1967-74; nutrition dir. Somerville Cambridge Home Care, Somerville, Mass., 1976-80, coordinator vols., 1974-76; owner, pres. Choice Inst. Supply Corp., Arlington, Mass., 1980—, Cis Corp. Security Inc., 1984—. Founding mem. Boston chpt. Nat. Caucas Black Aged. Mem. Nat. Assn. Female Execs., Nat. Bus. League, Black Corp. Presidents New Eng., Arlington C. of C., Somerville C. of C. Democrat. Baptist. Lodges: Order Eastern Star (past matron, conductress, sec., treas.), Heroine of Jericho, Lady K.T., Daus. of Sphinx.Avocations: Sewing; cooking; fishing. Home: Route 225 Groton Rd Shirley MA 01464 Office: Choice Inst Supply Corp 13A Medford St Arlington MA 02174

BATTY, JANE GRUPPE, hospital safety professional; b. Rochester, N.Y., Dec. 29, 1933; d. Karl William and Stella (Johnson) Gruppe; B.S. in Nursing, Simmons Coll., Boston, 1957; m. Norman Coulston Batty, Jr., Aug. 8, 1959; children—Michael Lawrence, Deborah Johnson. Head nurse Faxton Hosp., Utica, N.Y., 1958-60, instr. edn. and tng. dept., 1969-71, infection control nurse, 1971-75, environ. health and safety coordinator, 1975-80, dir. environ. health and safety, 1980—; public health nurse City of Utica, 1961-62; dir. environ. health and safety Children's Hosp. and Rehab. Center; tchr., cons. area nursing homes and hosps. Cert. health care safety profl., health care safety profl. exec. Mem. Assn. Practitioners in Infection Control, Am. Soc. Hosp. Risk Mgmt., Am. Soc. Safety Engrs. (pres. Mohawk Valley chpt. 1983-85). Republican. Presbyterian. Home: 10 Sherman Circle Utica NY 13501 Office: Faxton Hospital 1676 Sunset Ave Utica NY 13502

BAUCHMOYER, MADELEINE ANNE, nurse, educator; b. Los Angeles, Feb. 19, 1945; d. William Frederick and Dorothy Rose (Dalton) Muller; B.S. in Nursing, Catholic U. Am., 1966; M.Ed., U. Miami (Fla.), 1973; M.Nursing, La. State U., 1980; Ph.D. candidate La. State U.; m. A.J. Bauchmoyer, Jan. 14, 1978; children—Regina Louise, Karl Celby, Kenneth Garrett. Nurse clinician Miami VA Hosp., 1970; mem. faculty Miami-Dade Community Coll., 1970-73, U. Miami Med. Sch., 1973-75; dir. nursing, coordinator health care program U. Miami, 1973-75; mem. faculty Nicholls State U., Thibideaux, La., 1976-78, La. State U. Sch. Nursing, New Orleans, 1978-80; asst. prof. nursing U. Southwestern La. Coll. Nursing, Lafayette, 1980—, dir. ednl. mobility track 1982—; symposia participant. Reader mass St. Jules Roman Catholic Ch., Lafayette, 1982—; Navy judge Internat. Sci. and Engring. Fair, 1982—. Served as capt. Nurse Corps, USNR, 1964-69, comdg. officer med unit, 1983—. Navy scholar, 1964-66. Mem. Am. Council Nurse Researchers, Am. Nurses Assn., Nat. League Nursing, AAUP, Mental Health Assn. Lafayette, Res. Officer Assn. (past chpt. v.p.), Naval Res. Assn., Southwestern La. Arts Council, Spring Fiesta Hist. Assn., Sigma Theta Tau. Republican. Club: Univ. Women's. Office: Coll Nursing U Southwestern La PO Box 42490 Lafayette LA 70504

BAUDRY, RITA LUCRETIA, real estate executive; b. Biloxi, Miss., Oct. 8, 1925; d. Michael and Marguerite (Misko) Marinovich; m. Clay Frank Baudry, Nov. 14, 1942; children—Clay Frank, Steve M. (dec.), Paul J., Cathy Lynn, Richard D. Student pvt. sch., Biloxi. Apt. owner, mgr. Baudry Apts., Chateaux Elegance Apts., Harrell Sq. Apts., Magnolia Ridge Apts., Biloxi, 1953—, SMB Enterprise, Biloxi, 1979—. Roman Catholic. Home: 2306 Miller Ave Biloxi MS 39530 Office: 2250 W Beach Blvd Biloxi MS 39530

BAUER, CAROLINE FELLER, author; m. Peter A. Bauer; 1 dau., Hilary A. B.A., Sarah Lawrence Coll., 1957; M.L.S., Columbia U., 1958; Ph.D., U. Oreg., 1971. Children's and reference librarian N.Y. Pub. Library, N.Y.C., 1958-62; librarian Hewitt Sch., N.Y.C., 1960-61, Eron Prep. Sch., N.Y.C., 1962-63, Colo. Rocky Mountain Sch., Carbondale, 1963-65; art editor Pacific N.W. Library Assn. Quar., 1967-72; producer, instr. Oreg. Edn. Pub. Broadcasting System, 1973-74; assoc. prof. Sch. Librarianship U. Oreg., 1966-79; cons. Ednl. Cons. Assocs., Denver, 1979-81; vis. storyteller N.Y. Pub. Library, 1962-63; producer/performer Caroline's Corner Sta. KSNO, Aspen, Colo., 1964-66, Caroline: Folktales Around the World, NET affiliate, 1965-66, Caroline's Corner, Oreg. Ednl. Pub. Broadcasting System, 1972-80. Author: Children's Literature, 1973; Storytelling, 1974; Getting It Together With Books, 1974; Caroline's Corner, 1974; What's So Funny? Humor in Children's Literature (cassette), 1977; Handbook for Storytellers, 1977; This Way To Books, 1981; My Mom Travels Alot, 1981; Too Many Books! 1984; Celebrations, 1985; Take a Poetry Break (video cassette) Creative Storytelling (video cassette), 1979, others; contbr. articles to profl. jours. Recipient Ersted award for disting. teaching U. Oreg., 1968; Christopher award Jr. Literary Guild; award of excellence Chgo. Woman in Pub., 1978. Mem. ALA (notable books com. 1977-79, chmn. 1980; chmn. Laura Ingalls Wilder com. 1973-75, mem. Newbery-Caldecott com. 1972-78), Pi Lambda Theta, Beta Phi Mu.

BAUER, ELIZABETH HALE WORMAN, legal services agency executive; b. Mpls., Dec. 28, 1937; d. James R. and Virginia Hale (Murty) Worman; m. George Bittner Bauer, Sept. 12, 1959; children—Anna Stuart, Robert Bittner, Virginia Hale, Edward Russell. B.A., Mt. Holyoke Coll., 1959; M.A., Ohio State U., 1975. Cert. tchr., spl. edn. (mental retardation), gen. edn. Speech therapist Morris County Easter Seal Rehab. Ctr., Morristown, N.J., 1959-60; travel coordinator AFS Internat./Intercultural Programs, Inc., N.Y.C., 1960-63; speech therapist St. Barnabas Home, Gibsonia, Pa., 1967-71; tchr., cons. spl. edn. Pontiac (Mich.) Schs., 1975-78; dir. tng. Plymouth Ctr. for Human Devel., Northville, Mich., 1978-80; adminstr. devel. disabilities placement unit Mich. Dept. Mental Health, Northville, 1980-81; exec. dir. Mich. Protection and Advocacy Service for Devel. Disabled Citizens, Inc., Lansing, 1981—; mem. profl. adv. bd. Mich. Soc. Autistic Citizens, Inc., 1981—, Wayne State U. Developmental Disabilities Inst., 1984—; dir. Mich. Acad. Dentistry to Handicapped, 1982—, Kenny Mich. Rehab. Found., 1984—; mem. bio-ethics com. Children's Hosp. Mich., Detroit, 1983—; mem. Oakland County Assn. for Retarded Citizens, Inc., 1975—; bd. dirs. Assns. Retarded Citizens, Columbus, Ohio, 1972-75; bd. dirs., treas., pres. Epilepsy Ctr. Mich., Inc., Detroit, 1975-80; bd. dirs. AFS Internat./Intercultural Programs, Inc., 1971-83, trustee, 1986—. Author: (monograph) Parenting the Child with Epilepsy, 1977; (book) Adult Special Education Programs, 1978; also articles. Named Outstanding Tchr., Pontiac, Mich., 1978. Mem. Am. Assn. Mental Deficiency, Council for Exceptional Children, Assn. Persons with Severe Handicaps, Nat. Assn. Devel. Disabilities Councils, Nat. Assn. Protection and Advocacy Systems (dir. 1981-83, 85—, sec. 1985), Epilepsy Found. Am. Episcopalian. Club: Mt. Holyoke of Detroit. Home: 1355 Lake Park Dr Birmingham MI 48009 Office: 313 S Washington Sq Lansing MI 48933

BAUER, ELIZABETH KELLEY (MRS. FREDERICK WILLIAM BAUER), consulting energy economist; b. Berkeley, Calif., Aug. 7, 1920; d. Leslie Constant and Elizabeth Jeanette (Worley) Kelley; A.B., U. Calif. at Berkeley, 1941, M.A., 1943; Ph.D. (fellow), Columbia U., 1947; m. Frederick William Bauer, July 5, 1944; children—Elizabeth Katherine Bauer Berg, Frederick Nicholas. Instr. U.S. history and studies Barnard Coll., N.Y.C., 1944-45; lectr. history U. Calif. at Berkeley, 1949-50, 56-57; research asst. Giannini Found., 1946-49, asst. research agrl. economist, 1957-60; exec. sec. Internat. Conf. on Agrl. and Coop. Credit, U. Calif. at Berkeley, 1952-53, exec. sec. South Asia Project, 1955-56; registrar Holy Names Coll., Oakland, Calif., 1971-72; research asso. Brookings Instn. and Nat. Acad. Public Adminstrn., Washington, 1973; fgn. affairs officer Internat. Energy Affairs, Fed. Energy Adminstrn. Washington, 1974-77; fgn. affairs officer Office of Current Reporting, Internat. Affairs, Dept. Energy, Washington, 1977-81; dir. policy analysis and evaluation Nat. Coal Assn., Washington, 1981-83. Mem. Calif. Com. to Revise the Tchrs. Credential, 1961; trustee Grad. Theol. Union, Berkeley, 1972-74; bd. dirs. St. Paul's Towers and Episcopal Homes Found, Oakland, 1971-72. Recipient Superior Achievement award Dept. Energy, 1980; U. Calif. Alumni citation, 1983. Mem. AAUW (Calif. chmn. for higher edn. 1960-62), Internat. Assn. Energy Economists, Prytanean Honor Soc., AAAS, P.E.O., Mortar Bd., Phi Beta Kappa, Pi Lambda Theta, Sigma Kappa Alpha, Phi Alpha Theta, Pi Sigma Alpha. Democrat. Episcopalian. Author: Commentaries on the Constitution, 1790-1860, 1952; (with Murray R. Benedict) Farm Surpluses: U.S Burden or World Asset?, 1960; (with Florence Noyce Wertz) The Graduate Theological Union, 1970. Co-author, editor: The Role of Foreign Governments in the Energy Industries, 1977. Home: 708 Montclair Dr Santa Rosa CA 95405

BAUER, JO ANN, nursing administrator; b. Woodbury, N.J., Nov. 27, 1955; d. William Henry and Doris Mae (White) Jefferys; m. Mark David Bauer, May 24, 1980. B.S., Trenton State Coll., 1978. Staff nurse Scripps Meml. Hosp., San Diego, 1982-83, unit supr., 1983—. Served to lt. USN, 1978-82. Democrat. Lutheran. Home: 1748 Hill Top Ln Encinitas CA 92024

BAUER, JUDY MARIE, minister; b. South Bend, Ind., Aug. 24, 1947; d. Ernest Camiel and Marjorie Ann (Williams) Derho; m. Gary Dwane Bauer, Apr. 28, 1966; children—Christine Ann, Steven Dwane. Ordained to ministry, 1979. Sec. adminstrv. asst. Bethel Christian Ctr., Riverside, Calif., 1975-79; founder, pres. Kingdom Advancement Ministry, San Diego, 1979—: founder, co-pastor Bernardo Christian Ctr., San Diego, 1981—; evangelism dir. Bethel Christian Ctr., 1978-81, undershepherd minister, 1975-79, adult tchr., 1973-81; condr. leadership tng. clinics, lectr. in field. Author syllabus, booklet, tng. material packets. Mem. Internat. Conv. Faith Ministries, Inc. (area bd. dirs. 1983—).

BAUER, SHARON ANN, lawyer; b. Cleve., Mar. 26, 1947; d. John and Gertrude (Dempsey) Bukovac; m. Robert H. Bauer, June 10, 1972. B.A., U. Dayton, 1968; M.S., Wright State U., 1970; J.D., Loyola U., Chgo., 1980. Bar: Ill. 1980. Personnel specialist HEW, Chgo., 1974-77; supervisory mgmt. specialist Social Security Adminstrn., Chgo., 1977-79; supervisory atty. Fed. Labor Relations Authority, Chgo., 1979-86, regional atty., 1986—. Vol. Children's Meml. Hosp., Chgo., 1983—; legal vol. Pro Bono Advocates, Chgo., 1983—. Mem. Chgo. Bar Assn., ABA. Office: Fed Labor Relations Authority 175 W Jackson St Suite A1359 Chicago IL 60604

BAUER, SUSAN CAROL, educator; b. N.Y.C., June 28, 1949; d. Ernest Benjamin and Helene Michalene (Siergiej) Bauer; B.S. in Bus. Edn., Baruch Coll., 1974; M.A. in Secondary Edn.-Bus., Adelphi U., 1976; profl. diploma in sch. adminstrn. C.W. Post Center, L.I.U., 1978. Exec. sec. Union Carbide Corp., N.Y.C., 1967-72; tchr bus. Sewanhaka High Sch., Floral Park, N.Y., 1974-76; assoc. prof. secretarial sci. and word processing SUNY, Farmingdale, 1976—; condr. word processing seminars. Cert. profl. sec. Mem. Internat. Info. Word Processing Assn. (pres. L.I. chpt. 1981-83), Profl. Secs. Internat. (chairperson cert. profl. sec. and edn. com. L.I. chpt. 1980-82, pres. 1983-85), Nat. Assn. Female Execs., Nat. Bus. Edn. Assn. Republican. Roman Catholic. Office: Whitman Hall SUNY Farmingdale NY 11735

BAUGE, CYNTHIA WISE, distributing company executive; b. Ottumwa, Iowa, Sept. 7, 1943; d. Donald Carlyle and Opal Dorthea (Douglas) W.; m. Harry Grant Bauge, May 1, 1965; 1 dau., Melissa Anne. Student Iowa State U., 1962-64, Area XI Community Coll., Ankeny 1974-75. Legal sec. City of Ames, Iowa, 1965-69; acctg. mgr. Vivan Equipment Co., Ames, Iowa, 1969; asst. mgr. Bavarian Motor Lodge, Des Moines, 1969-71; bookkeeper TCP of Iowa, Des Moines, 1971-72, Moffitt Bldg Material co., Des Moines, 1972-73, CS Capital/Mid Am Growth Corp., West Des Moines, 1973-75; v.p. Grant Sales Inc., Plano, Tex., 1976—. Bd. dirs. Power/North Tex. Rehab. Ctr., Allen, Tex., 1985—, Cultural Arts Council of Plano, 1985—; v.p. Classics, 1985—. Mem. Nat. Assn. Female Execs., Women's Div. C. of C. Plano (treas. 1981-82), Beta Sigma Phi. Republican. Lutheran. Avocations: Home decorating; gaming. Office: Grant Sales Inc 1701 Capital Ave Plano TX 75074

BAUGHMAN, DEBORAH LYNNE, relocation manager; b. Austin, Tex., June 19, 1956; d. Claude Randall and Marinelle (Pribble) Baughman Scott. B.A., Vassar Coll., 1978. Relocation counselor Merrill Lynch, Stamford, Conn., 1978-79, relocation coordinator, Norwalk, Conn., 1979-80, group move adminstr., White Plains, N.Y., 1980-82, group move mgr., 1982—. Democrat. Presbyterian. Club: Vassar (2d v.p. 1978-83). Office: Merrill Lynch Relocation Mgmt 4 Corporate Park Dr White Plains NY 10604

BAUM, HELEN RYBA, public relations executive; b. Darien, Conn., Jan. 11, 1932; d. Michael A. and Helen (Wissman) Ryba; m. Arthur H. Baum, Oct. 10, 1977. Student in public relations and mktg. Northwestern U., 1963-64, U. Wis.-Madison, 1977. With Union Trust Co., Stamford, Conn., 1950—, asst.

v.p., 1969-77, v.p. community relations, public relations and legis. affairs, 1977—; justice of peace, State of Conn., 1974—; public relations coordinator for two legislators State of Conn., 1970-75; instr. Am. Inst. Banking, 1965-70; public relations chmn. for state rep. from Darien, Conn., 1974; public relations chmn. Stamford Hosp. Women's Aux., 1970-74. Mem. public relations com. Stamford United Way, 1962-74; mem. Darien Town Meeting, 1970-74; chmn. publicity 1968 campaign, Stamford Republican Party. Mem. Stamford Area Commerce and Industry Assn. (Sacian award 1976), Conn. Bankers Assn. (mem. legis. com.), Conn. Bus. and Industry Assn., Stamford-Norwalk Jr. League (dir. 1976-80). Republican. Club: Landmark. Office: Union Trust Co 300 Main St Stamford CT 06904

BAUM, INGEBORG RUTH, librarian; b. Berlin, Sept. 20; d. Ella Koch; Oberlyceum (scholar), Kassel, Germany, 1926-33; postgrad. Georgetown U., 1963-70; m. Albert Baum, Feb. 16, 1938 (div. 1960); children—Harro Siegward, Helma Sigrun (Mrs. George Meadows). Came to U.S., 1951, naturalized, 1957. Export corr. Bitter-Polar, Germany, 1933-35, Henschel Locs, Germany, 1936; exec. sec. Fieseler Airplane Mfrs., Germany, 1936-38; interpreter, sec. UNRRA, Germany, 1946-48; payroll supr., civilian dept. U.S. Army, Wetzlar PX, Germany, 1948-51; asst. librarian Supreme Council, Ancient and Accepted Scottish Rite, Washington, 1951-70, librarian and museums curator, 1970—; appraiser rare books and documents; v.p. Merical Elec. Contractors, Inc., Forestville, Md., 1974—. Mem. Am. Soc. Appraisers, Calligraphers Guild. Mem. Ch. Jesus Christ of Latter-day Saints. Free-lance contbr. to Pabelverlag, Rastatt, Germany, Harle, Ofcl. Publs., Inc., others. Home: 2480 16th St NW Apt 416 Washington DC 20009 Office: 1733 16th St NW Washington DC 20009

BAUM, MARY CAROLYN, occupational therapist; b. Chgo., Mar. 26, 1943; d. Gibson Henry and Nelle LaVern (Curry) Manville; m. Harry Gene Baum, July 10, 1965 (div. Sept. 1980); 1 dau., Kirstin Carol. B.S. U. Kans., 1965; M.A., Webster U., 1979. Dir. occupational therapy services Research Med. Center, Kansas City, 1967-73, dir. rehab. services, 1973-76; dir. occupational therapy clin. services Irene Walter Johnson Inst. Rehab., asst. research prof. occupational therapy and neurology Washington U. Med. Sch., St. Louis, 1976—; vis. prof. NYU. Author: Occupational Therapy, 1978, 83; Understanding the Prospective Payment System: A Business Perspective, 1985; contbr. articles to profl. jours. Pres. bd. dirs. Project Start, St. Louis, 1983; mem. nominating com. Kansas City Health Systems Agy (Mo.), 1975; mem. adv. bd. Older Adult Service and Info. System, St. Louis, 1980-84. Named Employee of Yr., Research Med. Center, 1973. Fellow Am. Occupational Therapy Assn. (pres. 1982-83, Eleanor Clark Slagle lectureship 1980, award of merit 1984), Kans. Occupational Therapy Assn. (Occupational Therapist of Yr. 1973), Mo. Occupational Therapy Assn. (Clinician of Yr. 1985). Office: Irene Walter Johnson Inst Rehab Washington U Med Sch 509 S Euclid St Saint Louis MO 63110

BAUM, SELMA, consumer affairs specialist; b. Bklyn., Jan. 15, 1924; d. Samuel and Tillie (Bayer) Goldman; ed. NYU, New Sch. for Social Research; m. Milton W. Baum, Jan. 19, 1947; children—Victor C., Cynthia Baum-Baicker. Communications mgr. Sobel & Goldman, Inc., N.Y.C., 1941-48; public relations cons., 1948-65; comparison shopper Gimbels, Valley Stream, N.Y., 1965-67, mgr. comparison shopping office N.Y. div., N.Y.C., 1967-75, dir. consumer affairs East div., 1975-84; dir. corp. customer relations Saks Fifth Ave., N.Y.C., 1984—; arbitrator Met. N.Y. Better Bus. Bur. lectr., writer in field. Mem. Am. Mgmt. Assn. (industry panelist), N.Y. & N.J. Retail Mchts. Council (v.p.), Women in Communication (award N.Y. chpt. 1984), Nat. Retail Mchts. Assn. (consumer affairs com.), Nat. Assn. Female Execs., Fashion Group, Am. Council on Consumer Interests, Soc. Consumer Affairs Profls. in Bus. (chpt. pres. 1981-82, nat. dir. 1983-86, award N.Y. chpt. 1983), Greater N.Y. WINS (regional affairs com.). Home: 843 Longview Ave North Woodmere NY 11581 Office: Saks Fifth Ave 450 W 15th St 5th Floor New York NY 10011

BAUMAN, SANDRA SPIEGEL, nurse; b. N.Y.C., June 30, 1949; d. Siegmund and Ruth (Josias) S.; student Boston U., 1967-70; B.S in Nursing, Adelphi U., 1971, postgrad., 1973-74; M.S. in Community Counseling, Barry Coll., 1981; postgrad. Fla. Atlantic U./Fla. Internat. U., 1982—, Gestalt Inst. Miami, 1982—; clin. specialist psychiat./mental health; m. H. Lee Bauman, Nov. 3, 1978 (div.); 1 child, Brandon Spiegel. Staff nurse educator obstetrics Albert Einstein Hosp., N.Y.C., 1971-72, head nurse newborn nurseries, 1973-74; asst. instr. maternity nursing St. Johns Riverside Hosp., 1972-73; head nurse obstetrics and nurseries, high risk nursery Mt. Sinai Hosp., Miami Beach, Fla., 1974-78; clin. nursing supr., div. pediatrics Jackson Meml. Hosp., Miami, 1978, coordinator div. clin. edn., 1978-81, quality assurance coordinator Maternal-Child Hosp. Center, 1979-81, perinatal coordinator, 1980-81, also core nursing mem. child protection team, 1979-81, asst. administr. ob-gyn, 1981-82; administr. Meadowbrook Med. Center, Inc., Dania, Fla., 1982—; pvt. practice Psychotherapy, 1983—; asst. administr. nursing Miami Gen. Hosp., 1985, assoc. administr. pvt. care services, 1985—; instr. Sch. Nursing, Fla. Internat. U., North Miami, 1982-84, coordinator child bearing and child rearing courses, 1982-84; mem. Fla. Bd. Nursing, 1979—, vice chmn., 1981-82, chmn., 1982-85; CPR instr., 1978. Mem. Am. Nurses Assn. (regional editor 1980—), Fla. Nurses Assn., Fla. Soc. Nurse Execs., Fla. Nursing Administrn. Assn., Fla. Hosp. Assn., Fla. Nursing Administrn. Soc., Sigma Theta Tau. Contbr. articles to RN mag., Fla. Nursing News, Fla. Nurses Assn. Newsletter. Office: Miami Gen Hosp 17300 NW 7th Ave Miami FL 33169

BAUMANN, EUGENIA TREMAINE, lawyer; b. Houston, Nov. 4, 1949; d. Richard Shirley and La Fay (Doughtie) Tremaine; m. Michael Hunt Baumann, Nov. 30, 1974. Student, U. N.Mex., 1967-69; B.A. in Polit. Sci., Okla. State U., Stillwater, 1972; J.D. U. Tulsa, 1976. Bar: Okla. 1976. Sole practice, Oklahoma City, 1976-80; juvenile ct. referee Dist. Ct. Oklahoma County, Oklahoma City, 1979-80; atty. Oklahoma County Pub. Defender, Oklahoma City, 1980—. Mem. ABA, Oklahoma County Bar Assn., Okla. Bar Assn. Republican. Unitarian. Club: Soroptimist (treas.). Office: Oklahoma County Pub Defender 320 Robert S Kerr 409 County Office Bldg Oklahoma City OK 73102

BAUMANN, MARGARET HELBLING, industrial marketing executive, consultant; b. Phila., Dec. 2, 1950; d. Frederick Joseph and Margaret (Straubmuller) Helbing; m. Peter Smith Baumann, Mar. 27. B.S. in Chemistry, Chestnut Hill Coll., Phila., 1972; M.A. in Philosophy, U. Notre Dame, 1975; M.B.A., Northwestern U., 1980. Regional sales rep. Union Carbide Corp., Chgo., 1975-79, area sales rep., 1979-81, bus. analyst, Danbury, Conn., 1981-82, market research mgr., 1982-83; market devel. specialist Uniroyal Corp., Middlebury, Conn., 1983—; sales mgmt. council Union Carbide Corp., 1979, dir. council, 1980. Company coordinator Inroads, Inc., Chgo., 1978-79; pres. Gaslight Village Condominium Assn., Chgo., 1980; treas., sec. Park North Condominium Assn., Fairfield, Conn., 1982. Mem. Soc. Plastic Engrs., Women in Mgmt. Republican. Roman Catholic. Avocations: running, music, hiking. Home: 216 Fairfield Beach Rd Fairfield CT 06430 Office: Uniroyal Corp Middlebury CT 06749

BAUMANN, MARY JANE TREMBLE, lawyer; b. Teaneck, N.J., Mar. 19, 1944; d. Roland Smith and Mary Jane (Roberts) Tremble; B.A. with honors, Ramapo Coll. of N.J., 1974; M.A. (fellow), Eagleton Inst., Rutgers U., 1978, J.D., 1978; m. Ulrich A. Baumann, Feb. 4, 1963; children—Kristin, U. Roberts, Jeffrey. Legis. asst. to N.J. Assemblyman, 1974-75; chmn. Bergen County (N.J.) Mental Health Bd., 1975-77; dir. consumer affairs Bergen County, 1980; realtor asso.; Franklin Lakes, N.J., 1980—; admitted to N.J. bar, 1981; dir. adminstrv. services N.H. Bettigole, Design Engrs., Paramus, N.J., 1981-82; pvt. practice law, Oradell, N.J., 1982—; asst. county counsel, Bergen County, N.J. Mem. Wyckoff Fed. Grants Com., 1974. Dir. Friends of Ramapo Coll., 1977-85, Hackensack YWCA, 1983—; Ramapo Coll. Alumni, 1980—; Wyckoff Community rep., 1979; Dem. candidate N.J. State Assembly, 1979; mem. Bergen County Energy adv. bd., 1980. Recipient Am. Legion award, 1957. Mem. N.J. Realtors Assn., NOW. Episcopalian. Club: Altrusa (pres. elect). Home: 550 Lee Ct Wyckoff NJ 07481 Office: 370 Kinderkamack Rd Oradell NJ 07649

BAUMEISTER, ELEANOR H., club woman; b. Lake Linden, Mich., Oct. 2, 1909; d. Thomas and Sarah (Madigan) Hoskins; B. Music Edn., U. Minn., 1930; m. Carl Frederick Baumeister, Apr. 19, 1930; 1 son, Richard. Co-founder, advt. mgr. The Corn Belt Livestock Feeder, trade mag., 1948-51. Publicity dir. Patron's Council, Riverside-Brookfield High Sch., 1951-53; pres. MacNeal Meml. Hosp. Women's Aux., 1956, mem. adv. bd., 1957; sec. High Sch. Dist., 208 Caucus, 1965-67. Dir., rec. sec. S.W. suburban chpt. Am. Cancer Soc., pres.

---

central suburban unit, 1969-71, treas., 1972-84; mem. citizens adv. com. Morton Coll. Sch. Nursing. Bd. dirs. Riverside Pub. Library, 1960-72, pres. bd., 1967-71, sec. bd., 1971-72. Mem. Gen. Fedn. Women's Clubs, P.E.O. (pres. Riverside chpt. 1955-56, Ill. corr. sec. 1956, rec. sec. 1957-58, fin. officer Ill. home 1958-63, dir.). Republican. Presbyterian. Clubs: Riverside Woman's (pres. 1954-56); Chicago Farmers. Home: 120 S Delaplaine Rd Riverside IL 60546

BAUMER, BEVERLY BELLE, journalist; b. Hays, Kans., Sept. 23, 1926; d. Charles Arthur and Mayme Mae (Lord) B.; B.S., U. Kans., 1948. Summer intern reporter Hutchinson (Kans.) News, 1946-47; continuity writer, dir. women's program Sta. KWBW, Hutchinson, 1948-49; dist. editor Salina (Kans.) Jour., 1950-57; commd. writer State of Kans. Centennial Yr., 1961; contbr. Popular Mechanics, Travel, bus. publs., 1958—; owner, mgr. apts. Hutchinson, 1967—; broadcaster Radio Reading Room, Sta. KHCC-FM, Hutchinson, 1982—; mng. editor The Hutchinson Record (Kans.), 1984—, columnist, 1982—; freelance genealogist, 1970—. Hon. fellow Anglo-Am. Acad. (Cambridge, Eng.); mem. Nat. Fedn. Press Women, Kans. Press Women, New Eng. Historic Geneal. Soc., Nat. Soc. Magna Carta Dames, Nat. Soc. Sons and Daus. Pilgrims (chaplain Kans. br.), Nat. Soc. Daus. Founders and Patriots Am., Nat. Soc. Daus. Am. Colonists (chpt. organizing regent 1979, state resolutions com.), DAR, Colonial Dames of 17th Century (chpt. chaplain), Plantagenet Soc., Internat. Platform Assn. Home and Office: 204 Curtis St Hutchinson KS 67501

BAUMER, JOAN LESLIE, marketing educator; b. Cleve., Oct. 1, 1952; d. Joseph Philip and Helen Saundra (Cohen) Malinas; m. David Lee Baumer, May 23, 1976; children—Erik, Paul. B.S. in Social Work, Ohio State U., 1974; M.B.A., U. Miami, 1979. Administrv. asst. Am. Psychiat. Assn., Washington, 1975-76; summer intern NOAA, Washington, 1978; vis. lectr. N.C. State U., Raleigh, 1981—; market research cons., 1983—. Cons. fund raising and publicity Raleigh Presch., 1983—; fund raising co-chmn. Wiley Elem. Sch., 1985-86. Mem. Am. Mktg. Assn., N.C. State U. Women's (sec. 1981-82), N.C. State U. Faculty. Home: 1307 College Pl Raleigh NC 27605 Office: Dept Econs and Bus NC State U Hillsborough Bldg Room 311-C Raleigh NC 27695

BAUMGARDNER, ASTRID REHL, lawyer; b. Montclair, N.J., Mar. 16, 1952; d. W. Richard and Alicia (Stein) Rehl; m. John E. Baumgardner, Jr., Sept. 7, 1974; children—Jeffrey, Julia. B.A. magna cum laude, Mt. Holyoke Coll., 1973; J.D., Rutgers U., 1976. Bar: N.Y. 1977, U.S. Supreme Ct. 1980. Assoc. firm Weil, Gotshal & Manges, N.Y.C., 1976-79, Debevoise & Plimpton, N.Y.C., 1979-80, Edwards & Angell, N.Y.C., 1980-83; ptnr. O'Melveny & Myers, N.Y.C., 1983-85; of counsel Gide, Loyrette & Nouel, N.Y.C., 1985—. Mem. ABA, Assn. Bar City N.Y., Phi Beta Kappa. Home: 140 Riverside Dr Apt 3K New York NY 10024 Office: Gide Loyrette & Nouel 900 Third Ave New York NY 10022

BAUMGARTEN, ALICE MARIE, abstract and title company executive; b. Menominee, Mich., Mar. 30, 1939; d. Alson Alfred and Edith (Bueltemann) Minor; m. William Leonard Tappen, Apr. 26, 1958 (div. 1971); children—William Thomas, Jeffrey Scott, Gary Francis, James Alson; m. Roger Frederick Baumgarten, May 6, 1978. With Marinett County Abstract Co., Wis., 1972-75; owner, 1979—; agt. Ticor Title Ins. Co., 1979—; speaker seminars and workshops U. Wis., 1980—. Bd. dirs. Tri-Counties Safety Council, 1985—. Named Woman of Yr., Marinette Bus. and Profl. Women's Club, 1985. Mem. Wis. Land Title Assn., Am. Land Title Assn., Marinette County Realtors Assn., Tri-County Bankers Assn., Soc. Mayflower Descs. (sec. 1984—), Thomas Minor Soc. Home: 1209 Currie St Marinette WI 54143 Office: Tri-County Abstract and Title Co 2109 Ella Ct Marinette WI 54143

BAUMGARTNER, EILEEN MARY, govt. ofcl.; b. St. Cloud, Minn.; d. Florian H. and Kathleen (Keefe) B.; B.A., Coll. St. Catherine, St. Paul, 1964; M.P.A., U. Minn., Mpls., 1970. Tchr., U.S. Peace Corps, Ethiopia, 1964-66; researcher N.Y. Med. Coll., N.Y.C., 1967-68, Minn. State Planning Agy., St. Paul, 1970-73; legis. analyst tax com. Minn. Ho. of Reps., St. Paul, 1973-78; legis. asst. to Congressman Sabo, U.S. Ho. of Reps., Washington, 1979—. Bd. dirs. Alumni Assn., Hubert H. Humphrey Inst. Public Affairs, U. Minn., 1982—. Mem. Am. Soc. Pub. Administrn. Democrat. Roman Catholic. Office: 436 Cannon Office Bldg Washington DC 20515

BAUMGARTNER, LEONA, public health administrator, physician, educator; b. Chgo., Aug. 18, 1902; d. William J. and Olga (Leisy) B.; m. Nathaniel M. Elias, 1942 (dec. 1964); m. 2d Alexander D. Langmuir, 1970. A.B., U. Kans., 1923, D.S., 1925; postgrad. Kaiser Wilhelm Inst., Munich, 1928-29; Ph.D. (univ. fellow 1930-31, Sterling fellow 1931-32), Yale U., 1932, M.D., 1934, LL.D., 1970; D.Sc., Women's Med. Coll., 1950, NYU, 1954, Russell Sage Coll., 1955, Smith Coll., 1956, Western Med. Coll. Women, 1960, U. Mass., 1963, U. Mich., 1967, McMurray Coll., 1967, N.Y. Med. Coll., 1968, Clark U., 1969; L.H.D., Keuka Coll., 1963; LL.D., Skidmore Coll., 1959, Oberlin Coll., 1965. Mem. faculty Colby Community High Sch. (Kans.), 1923-24, Kansas City Jr. Coll., 1925-26, U. Minn., 1926-28; intern, then asst. resident, asst. in pediatrics N.Y. Hosp. and Cornell Med. Coll., 1934-36; lectr. nursing edn. Columbia U., 1939-42; with N.Y.C. Dept. Health, 1937-62, commr. health, 1954-62; exec. dir. N.Y. Found., 1953-54; assoc. chief U.S. Children's Bur., Fed. Security Agy., 1949-50, cons., 1950-56; mem. faculty Med. Coll., Cornell U., 1939-66, pediatrics and pub. health faculty, 1957-66; vis. lectr. maternal and child health Harvard Med. Sch. Pub. Health, 1948-62; vis. prof. social medicine Harvard Med. Sch., Boston, 1966-76; asst. administr. Office Tech. Coop. and Research, AID, Dept. State, 1962-65; exec. dir. Med. Care and Edn. Found., Inc., Boston, 1968-72; adviser Indian minister health, 1955, French Ministry Health, 1945; mem. exchange mission to USSR, 1958, leader for Tokyo Met. Govt., 1961; mem. nat. adv. council Peace Corps., 1961-63; mem. Inst. Medicine, Nat. Acad. Sci., 1978—. Bd. dirs. N.Y. Fund for Children; trustee council U. Mass., 1973—; trustee New Sch. Social Research, 1966-74, adv. council, 1964—. Recipient awards including Albert Lasker award Am. Pub. Health Assn., 1954; Elizabeth Blackwell award Hobart and William Smith Colls., 1961; Samuel J. Crumbine award Kans. Pub. Health Assn., 1961; Albert Einstein award, 1964; Herman M. Biggs award, 1968; Wilbur Lucius Cross medal Grad. Sch. Assn., Yale U., 1970; Pub. Welfare Gold medal Nat. Acad. Scis., 1977; others. Diplomate Am. Bd. Pediatrics, Am. Bd. Preventive Medicine and Pub. Health. Mem. Harvey Soc., History Sci. Soc., Am. Assn. History Medicine, Oxford Bibliog. Soc., Am. Pub. Health Assn. (pres. 1958-59), Am. Acad. Pediatrics, Am. Pediatric Soc., Child Welfare League Am. (dir.), Nat. Social Welfare Assembly (v.p.), Nat. Conf. Social Work (exec. com.), Nat. Health Council (pres. 1956), Am. Acad. Arts and Scis., N.Y. Acad. Medicine, Mortar Bd., Phi Beta Kappa, Sigma Xi, Pi Beta Phi, Phi Sigma. Club: Cosmopolitan. Contbr. med. and sci. articles to profl. jours. Home: Abel's Hill Chilmark MA 02535

BAUMLEIN, MARIANNE, sales representative; b. Fostoria, Ohio, Jan. 24, 1955; d. Arthur Russel and Glenna Ruth (McClain) Wolfarth; m. David Paul Baumlein, Jan. 8, 1977 (div. Apr. 1986); children—Adam Paul, Andrew Ryan. Cosmetician Lane Drug Co., Toledo, 1973, pharmacy technician, 1973-74, store mgr., 1974-85; sales rep. Russ Berrie, Reynoldsburg, Ohio, 1986—; pres. Findlay Downtown Mchts. Assn., Ohio, 1974-75. Retail rep. Hancock County Alcoholism Council, 1985-86, to Community Devel. Research Found., 1985-86. Recipient Happy Apple award Lane Drug Co., 1974, Faberge award, 1980. Mem. Findlay Area C. of C. (chmn. retail sales booths Community Showcase 1986), Nat. Assn. Female Execs. Roman Catholic. Avocations: photography; cross-stitch; architectural design; interior design. Home: 902 Summit St Findlay OH 45840

BAUMLER, JEAN ANN, nurse; b. West Union, Iowa, Apr. 22, 1951; d. Melvin John and Rita Theresa (Lansing) Baumler; B.S., Viterbo Coll., LaCrosse, Wis., 1973; M.S., San Jose (Calif.) State U., 1980. Health supr. Camp Ehawee Scout Camp, LaCrosse, 1973; staff nurse, then asst. head nurse Letterman Army Med. Center, San Francisco, 1972-75; staff nurse Palo Alto (Calif.) VA Hosp., 1975-83; adult day health coordinator Kuakini Med. Ctr., Honolulu, 1983—. Treas. Fair Oaks 90 Homeowners Assn., 1980-83; bd. dirs. Honolulu chpt. Alzheimer's Disease and Related Disorders. Served with Nurse Corps, U.S. Army, 1972-75. Mem. Geront. Soc. Am., Internat. Assn. Gerontology, Hawaii Pacific Gerontol. Soc., Long Term Care Network. Contbr. articles to profl. jours. Home: 3355 Pinao St Honolulu HI 96822 Office: Kuakini Med Ctr 347 N Kuakini St Honolulu HI 96817

BAUNACH, PHYLLIS JO, surveys and censuses consultant; b. Amityville, N.Y., July 29, 1947; d. Edward Lincoln and Josephine Caroline (Dayton) B.;

B.A. (scholar), U. Rochester, 1969; Ph.D., U. Minn., 1974; J.D., George Washington U., 1986; m. July 17, 1976. Instr., U. Minn., 1974; vis. asst. prof., 1975; mem. Gov.'s Com. on Crime Prevention and Control, 1974-76; asso. professorial lectr. George Washington U., Washington, 1977; instr. Univ. Coll., U. Md., College Park, 1980-82, lectr., 1981; correctional research specialist Nat. Inst. Justice, Washington, 1976-82; cons. Calif. Youth Authority, Murton Found. Criminal Justice. Treas., Evang. Lutheran Mission, 1975; div. choir, Our Saviors Luth. Ch., 1986—, mem. worship and music com. Nat. Inst. Justice fellow, 1978-79; AAUW Young scholar, 1982-83; recipient Outstanding Performance award Dept. Justice, 1979, 81, 84, 85. Mem. Am. Soc. Criminology (chmn. div. women and crime 1982—) Am. Correctional Assn. Am. Psychology Assn., Assn. Programs on Female Offenders, Resource Network Female Offenders, Nat. Trust Historic Preservation, Smithsonian Assos., Phi Beta Kappa. Author: Mothers in Prison, 1985; contbr. articles to profl. jours. Office: 633 Indiana Ave NW Room 1013 Washington DC 20531

BAUROTH, NANCY ANN, marketing executive; b. Phila., Oct. 12, 1949; d. Harry William and Mary Octavia (Coffman) B.; m. Albert Allen Meyer, Aug. 19, 1972 (div. Apr. 1980). B.J., U. Mo., 1971. Asst. dir. pub. relations U. Mo. Med. Ctr., Columbia, 1971-72; copywriter advt. dept. Federated Dept. Stores, Columbus, Ohio, 1973; pub. relations specialist advt. dept. Blue Cross/Blue Shield, St. Louis, 1973; dir. advt. and pub. relations Doubleday & Co., N.Y.C., 1974-80; dir. product advt. Merrill Lynch & Co., N.Y.C., 1980-82, dir. mktg. communications, cash mgmt., 1982-84; v.p., dir. mktg. Direct Access electronic banking Citibank, 1984—; lectr. advt. writing CUNY, 1978, 79. Honoree, Boston Soc. Fin. Analysts, 1982; Creative Workshop Honoree, Advt. Age, 1983. Mem. Fin. Communications Soc. (honoree 1982), Pubs. Advt. Club (v.p. 1976-80). Republican. Presbyterian. Home: 400 E 54th St Apt 25H New York NY 10022

BAUTISTA-MYERS, LILIAN, writer, editor; b. San Diego; d. Jose Delos Angeles and Juanita (Perez) Bautista; B.A. in English, Calif. State U., Northridge, 1970; M.S. in Edn., SUNY, Albany, 1972; Ed.D. in Ednl. Adminstrn., Okla. State U., 1980; m. Donald Allen Myers, Oct. 28, 1966; 1 son, David Allen; children by previous marriage—Sherri Lynn, Johnny Martin. Adminstrv. officer, writer Capitol Hill Educator, Albany, 1972-73; asst. to dir., tech. editor/writer, coordinator grant and contract activities, contracts and grants mgmt. officer Okla. State U., 1973-79; co-owner/writer The Last Word, writing and graphic arts, Omaha, 1979-81; freelance writer, copywriter, editor, 1972—; coordinator grants mgmt. and devel. Met. Tech. Community Coll., Omaha, 1981-83; devel. officer Cath. Dept. Edn., Archdiocese of Omaha, 1984-85; exec. dir. Cooperating Hampton Rds. Orgns. for Minorities in Engring., Norfolk, Va., 1985—. Mem. Regional NOW, LWV (chpt. exec. bd. 1974-75). Democrat. Author, editor in field. Home: 1272 Belvoir Ln Virginia Beach VA 23464

BAUTSCH, VIRGINIA BELLE, city official; b. Dallas, Dec. 9, 1923; d. Harry Clay and Sarah Adelle (Slaughter) Coleman; student Dallas Art Museum, summers, 1940, 41, Met. Bus. Sch., 1945; m. Hilton Basil Bautsch, Dec. 21, 1947 (div. 1961); 1 son, Robert Hilton. Various clerical and stenography positions for bus. firms and schs. in Dallas, 1938-41; black and white etch and color copyist Manzer Studios, Dallas, 1941-42; sec., 1943-44; stenographer dept. water works City of Dallas, 1942-43, City Mgr.'s Office, 1945, sec. water works dept., 1946-52, sec. to city property mgr. pub. works dept., 1972, sec. dept. revenue and taxation, 1972-77; sec. police psychol. services, 1977-82, police computer trainee, 1982, sec. crime stats./spl. reports, 1982, sec. field and tech. support coordinators, 1983—; exec. sec. A. Harris & Co., Dallas, 1954-55, Tex. Power & Light Co., Dallas, 1955-58, Republic Nat. Bank of Dallas, 1961-66, 67-68; notary pub., 1978—. Mem. Am. Philatelic Soc., Baptist. Home: 5735 Gaston Ave Dallas TX 75214 Office: Field and Tech Support Coordinators Police and Courts Bldg 106 S Harwood Room 418 Dallas TX 75201

BAUTZ, LAURA PATRICIA, astronomer; b. Washington, Sept. 3, 1940; d. Charles Kothe and Laura (Stauverman) B.; B.A. in Physics, Vanderbilt U., 1961; Ph.D. in Astronomy, U. Wis., Madison, 1967. From instr. to assoc. prof. astronomy Northwestern U., Evanston, Ill., 1965-75; sr. staff astron. NSF, Washington, 1975-79, dep. dir. physics div., 1979-81, dir. astronomy div., 1982—, acting dir. sci. and engring. edn., 1983-84. Mem. Am. Astron. Soc., AAAS, Internat. Astron. Union, Phi Beta Kappa. Home: 1325 18th St NW Apt 506 Washington DC 20036 Office: 1800 G St NW Washington DC 20550

BAXT, BARBARA STEFANIE, travel industry executive, editor; b. Paterson, N.J., Apr. 10, 1947; d. Sydney Joseph and Rita Luceille (Seidman) B. B.S. cum laude, Syracuse U., 1968. Dir. travel industry sales Sonesta Hotels, N.Y.C., 1969-73; Princess Hotels, Hamilton, Bermuda, 1974-76; pres. Hotels Internat., Paterson, 1976—; cons. Allegro Photos, Miami, Fla., 1977-79, 83-84, HIP Photos, Bayonne, N.J., 1977-80. Editor Bride to Be mag., 1983—. Design patentee mug shirt. Office: Bride to Be Mag PO Box 384 Totowa NJ 07511

BAXTER, BETTY CARPENTER, educational administrator; b. Sherman, Tex., Oct. 10, 1937; d. Granville E. and Nan Elizabeth (Caston) Carpenter; m. Comer Cash Baxter, July 30, 1959; children—Stephen Barrington, Catherine Elaine. A.A., Christian Coll., 1957; B.A. in Music, So. Methodist U., 1959; M.A., Tchrs. Coll. Columbia U., 1972, M.Ed., 1979, Ed.D. Cert. tchr., N.Y. Copywriter WLOF Radio sta., Orlando, Fla., 1959, WDBO-CBS Radio Sta., Orlando, 1960-61; tchr. Riverside Ch. Day Sch., N.Y.C., 1967-71; asst. dir. admissions Eipsc. Sch., N.Y.C., 1972, head., 1973—. Photo illustrator: Infant Caregiving, 1971. Mem. Nat. Assn. Episcopal Schs. (bd. dirs., sec. 1984—), Ind. Schs. Admissions Assn. Greater N.Y. (vice chmn. 1976-82). Republican. Presbyterian. Office: Episcopal Sch 35 E 69th St New York NY 10021

BAXTER, CARLA LOUISE CHANEY, insurance underwriter; b. Indpls., Nov. 4, 1955; d. Carlton S. and Jennie B. (Yates) Chaney; m. Andrew Louis Baxter, Sept. 20, 1980. B.A. in Mktg., Ball State U., 1979. Lic. realtor, Ind. Zoning technician Dept. Met. Devel., Indpls., 1975; dir. mktg. Urban Tng. and Devel. Systems Inc., Indpls., 1979-80; casualty underwriter Wausau Ins. Cos., Indpls., 1980-84; sr. casualty underwriter CNA Ins. Cos., Indpls., 1984-85; nat. accounts underwriter Nationwide Ins. Cos., Columbus, Ohio, 1985—. Speaker various chs. and civic groups; dir. choir Trinity Ch., Indpls., 1983—. Statonian scholar, 1975-76; N.G. Gilbert scholar Ball State U., 1978. Mem. Indpls. Assn. Ins. Women, Indpls. Underwriters Assn., Urban League, Alpha Kappa Alpha (Career Day group leader 1984, scholar 1974-75, 75-76). Methodist. Avocations: skating; racquetball; singing; dancing. Office: Nationwide Ins Cos 35 Chestnut Ave Columbus OH

BAXTER, DEE LYNN, government agency official; b. Chouteau, Mont., Dec. 23, 1953; d. Donald Kenneth and Dorothy Marie (Eide) Peterson; m. Robert Charles Baxter, Nov. 24, 1976; children—Ryan Robert, Brandon Charles. A.A., Eastern Mont. Coll., 1974, B.S. with high honors, 1975. Gen. clk. U.S. Govt. Bur. of Land Mgmt., Billings, Mont., 1973-77; pub. contact specialist, 1977-78, land law examiner, 1978—, EEO counselor, 1980—. Mem. Laurel Parent Tchrs. Orgn., Mont., 1984—; candy sales team leader Little League Baseball, Laurel, 1984; com. mem. Fed. Women's Program, Billings, 1977; treas. Bur. Land Mgmt. Athletic Assn., Billings, 1976—. Am. Cancer Soc. student fellow 1971; Karyl Johnston Meml. scholar Eastern Mont. Coll., 1973-74. Mem. Foreign Lang. Honor Soc. Lutheran. Avocations: golf; volleyball, softball, skiing. Home: PO Box 932 Laurel MT 59044 Office: Bur of Land Mgmt 222 N 32d St Billings MT 59107

BAXTER, HEDWIG GERDA KALVAITIS, histologist; b. Kellenhusen, Germany, Mar. 6, 1945; came to U.S. 1950, naturalized, 1964; d. Otto and Ane Kalvaitis; A.A., Clinton Community Coll., 1981; 1 dau., Marta Ane. With CV/PH Med. Center, Plattsburgh, N.Y., 1964-70; with hematology sect., animal health div. Ayerst Labs., Chazy, N.Y., 1970-71, histologist, 1972—. Mem. Nat. Soc. Histotechnology, N.Y. Histotechnological Soc., Am. Soc. Clin. Pathologists. Home: PO Box 223 West Chazy NY 12992 Office: Ayerst Research Labs Animal Health Division Chazy NY 12921

BAXTER, JAMESON ADKINS, investment banking firm executive; b. Decatur, Ill., Sept. 6, 1943; d. Charles Edson and Virginia (Durning) Adkins; m. Reginald Robert Baxter, Jan. 24, 1976; 1 son, Sean Lee. B.A., Mt. Holyoke Coll., 1965. Analyst, First Boston Corp., N.Y.C., 1965-73; asst. v.p., 1973-75, v.p., N.Y.C., 1975-76, Chgo., 1976—. Trustee, Emma Willard Sch., Troy, N.Y., 1980—, Mt. Holyoke Coll., South Hadley, Mass., 1981—. Mem. Fin. Women's Assn. Office: First Boston Corp 135 S LaSalle St Chicago IL 60603

BAXTER, PAMELA KATHRYN, cosmetic company marketing executive; b. Pawhuska, Okla., Feb. 14, 1949; d. William Desmond and Gloria Mae (Young) Lohman; m. Barry Richard Baxter, Aug. 17, 1968 (div. July 1971); 1 son, Shannon Richard. Student U. S.D.; cert. LaSalle U. Spl. rep. Charles of the Ritz, N.Y.C., 1973-77; account exec. Princess Marcella Borghese, N.Y.C., 1977-80; regional mktg. dir. Aramis, Inc., N.Y.C., 1980—. Mem. World Affairs Council, Los Angeles, 1981. Mem. Nat. Orgn. Exec. Women, Calif. Cosmetic Assn. Republican. Club: Marina City (Los Angeles).

BAXTER, RUTH HOWELL, educational administrator, psychologist; b. Washington; d. Robert R. and Georgie (Murray) Lassiter; B.S., D.C. Tchrs. Coll., 1958; M.A., George Washington U., 1961, cert. in Edn., 1965; cert. (N. Am. Com. of Oslo scholar) Oslo U., 1970; grad. Adminstr.'s Acad. Class, D.C. Public Schs., 1982; m. Dudley H.G. Baxter; children—Robert, Astrid, Mova, Mava. Tchr., D.C. Public Schs., 1958—; founder, dir., propr. Jewels of Ann Pvt. Day Sch., Washington, 1970—; tchr. Newlands Infant, Southampton, Eng., 1965-67; instr. math. demonstration lessons dept. edn. Howard U.; dir. early childhood edn. workshop Brent Elem. Sch., Washington, 1974; tchr. adult edn. Bel Air Sch., Woodbridge, Va., 1977; mem. Ednl. Instn. Licensure Commn. Task Forces, 1978; mem. Mayor's Pre-White House Conf. on Libraries and Info. Services, 1978; exec. high sch. internship program D.C. Public Schs., 1978. Mem. planning com. Eastern region Jr. Red Cross, Washington; cons. coll. youth motivation task force program Nat. Alliance for Bus. Fulbright scholar, 1965; North Atlantic scholar, 1964; named Outstanding Tchr. of Yr., Future Tchrs. Am.; recipient Outstanding Contbn. award Nat. Assn. Negro Women, 1976, Commemorative Medal of Honor. Mem. Bus. and Profl. Women, English Speaking Union, Columbia Women (sec.), Jaycees, Zeta Phi Beta (life), Phi Delta Kappa. Presbyterian. Author: A Norwegian Birthday Party, 1979; contbr. children's stories to various publs. Home: 13349 Delaney Rd Dale City Woodbridge VA 22193 Office: 2011 Bunker Hill Rd NE Washington DC 20018

BAYLESS, KATHRYN REED, lawyer; b. Princeton, W.Va., Feb. 24, 1950; d. Oswald Clifford and Virginia Ruth (Hartsock) Reed; m. Laurence Emory Bayless, Sept. 1972 (div. 1974); 1 child, Michael Shannon. B.S. in Chemistry, Concord Coll., 1972; B.S. in Bus. Adminstrn., W.Va. U., 1976, J.D., 1979. Bar: W.Va. 1979, U.S. Dist. Ct. (so. dist.) W.Va. 1979, U.S. Ct. Appeals (4th cir.) 1980, U.S. Dist Ct. (no. dist.) W.Va. 1982. Tchr., Mercer County Bd. Edn., Princeton, 1972-75; assoc. Garrett, Whittier & Garrett, Webster Springs, W.Va., 1979-80; sr. law clk. to judge U.S. Dist. Ct., Bluefield, W.Va., 1980-82; ptnr. Wiley & Bayless, Princeton, 1982-83, Johnston, Holroyd & Gibson, Princeton, 1984-85; ptnr. Bayless & Wills, 1985—; adj. instr. Bluefield State Coll., 1980—. Bd. dirs. Windy Mountain Learning Ctr., Bluefield, 1980—. Recipient James F. Brown prize W.Va. U. Coll. Law, 1979. Mem. ABA, Mercer County Bar, W.Va. State Bar, Am. Trial Lawyers Assn., Fourth Circuit Jud. Conf., W.Va. Law Rev. Assn. Democrat. Club: Quota (treas. 1984-85, dir. 1982-84) (Princeton). Office: Bayless & Wills 1625 N Walker St Princeton WV 24740

BAYLEY, MOLLY GILBERT, government executive; b. Spokane, Wash., Nov. 19, 1944; d. Frederick Wolcott and Clare Emily (Whitehouse) Gilbert; m. James Burt Bayley, June 29, 1968. B.A. in French, Wellesley Coll., 1967. Sr. analyst market surveillance Nat. Assn. Securities Dealers, Washington, 1972-74, supr. market surveillance, 1974-76, asst. dir. market surveillance, 1976-78, dir. market surveillance, 1978-79, v.p. NASDAQ ops., 1979-84; exec. dir. Commodity Futures Trading Commn., Washington, 1984—. Nominating dir. Assn. of Jr. Leagues, Inc., N.Y.C., 1985—; bd. dirs. Recording for the Blind, Inc., Washington, 1983—; trustee Trustees Assembly, United Way, Washington, 1982—; pres., v.p. Jr. League of Washington, Inc., 1981-83. Home: 3106 33d Pl NW Washington DC 20008 Office: Commodity Futures Trading Commn 2033 K St NW Washington DC 20581

BAYLIS, KATHRYN RUTH, lawyer; b. Cin., Oct. 10, 1945; d. Henry David Fischer and Margaret Louise (Keagy) Fischer Lueders; m. Clarke Owen Baylis, Jr., Dec. 30, 1971. B.A. in Communications, U. Wash., Seattle, 1970, J.D., 1977. Bar: Wash. 1977, Mont. 1980. Assoc., Jonson & Jonson, Seattle, 1978; sole practice, Seattle, 1978-79, Roundup, Mont., 1980-85; pub. defender Big Horn County, Mont., 1985—. Vice pres. Musselshell County Democratic Women's Club, Roundup, 1983-84; sec. Musselshell County Dem. Central Com., Roundup, 1983-84; bd. dirs. Musselshell Valley Hist. Mus., Roundup, 1984-85. Mem. State Bar Mont., ABA, Mont. Trial Lawyers Assn., Assn. Trial Lawyers Am., Wash. State Bar Assn., Bus. and Profl. Women. Unitarian. Office: Big Horn County Courthouse Drawer H Hardin MT 59034

BAYLISS-ALLEN, MADELINE THERESE, marketing executive; b. N.Y.C., Oct. 11, 1954; d. Eugene R. and Madeline D. Bayliss; B.A. with honors in Human Communications, Colgate U., 1975; M.B.A., NYU, 1983; m. Jeffrey Thomas Allen, June 20, 1981. Unit dir. United Way N.Y.C., 1976-77, indsl. div. dir., 1977-79; mgr. area communications, United Way Tri-State, N.Y.C., 1979; sr. cons. Urban Bus. Assistance Corp., 1979-80; v.p. corp. mktg. Mfrs. Hanover Leasing Corp., N.Y.C., 1980-85; v.p. mktg. CIT Group/Equipment Financing, Livingston, N.J., 1986—. Mem. Am. Mktg. Assn., Jr. League No. Westchester, Phi Beta Kappa.

BAYLOR-REED, CAROLYN L., telephone company executive; b. Cedartown, Ga., Apr. 18, 1950; d. Lewis Cary and Dorothy Ruth (Johnson) Baylor; m. Luther Delano Reed, Feb. 27, 1986. B.B.A. in Acctg., U. Ga., 1972, M. in Acctg., 1974; cert. real estate Atlanta Area Tech. Coll., 1981. Fiscal coordinator Athens Model Cities (Ga.), 1972-74; internal auditor Nat. Services Industries, Atlanta, 1974-76; staff analyst So. Bell Telephone Co., Atlanta, 1976-78, instr., 1978-81, staff mgr., 1981—. Mem. panel United Way funds allocation, 1983—, loaned exec., 1985; sch. leader Empty Stocking Fund, Archer High Sch., 1982-83; v.p. state at large, bd. mgrs., U. Ga. Alumni Soc., Athens, 1982—; mem. So. Bell Women's Bowling League, 1979-81, Shady Ladies Softball Team, 1977-81; motivator Metro Employment Youth Motivation Day, 1978—; treas. Atlanta Urban Bus. and Profl. Women, 1979-81, pres., 1981-82. Named Young Careerist Atlanta Urban Club-Bus. and Profl. Women, 1979. Mem. Nat. Assn. Female Execs., AAUW, U. Ga.-Athens Black Alumni Assn. (pres. Atlanta 1982-83; treas. 1979-81, Outstanding Alumni Atlanta chpt. 1981), U. Ga.-Athens Alumni Assn. (young alumni council 1979-81), Delta Sigma Theta (treas. Decatur alumnae 1977-70; pres. Athens alumnae 1972-74; pres. chpt. 1971, treas. 1969-70). Home: 703 Indigo Ln NW Atlanta GA 30318 Office: 19D59 So Bell Ctr 675 W Peachtree St Atlanta GA 30375

BAYLY, PATRICIA ANNE, psychologist; b. Troy, N.Y., Dec. 4, 1952; d. Richard Yeilding and Martha (Coffey) Bayly; B.A. cum laude with honors in Psychology (Kellas scholar), Russell Sage Coll., 1974; M.S. in Ednl. Psychology and Statistics, SUNY, Albany, 1975, Ed.S. in Sch. Psychology, 1976, doctoral studies in ednl. psychology, 1978-81, in sch. psychology, 1986—. Psychologist, North Colonic Central Schs., Loudonville, N.Y., 1976-77, Enlarged City Sch. Dist. of Troy, 1977—; adj. instr. psychology Russell Sage Coll., Troy, 1978—. Bd. dirs. Drug Abuse and Prevention Council Troy, 1979-80, sec., 1980-83; bd. dirs., edn. chmn. Jr. League Troy, 1978-79, adv. planning chmn., 1980-81, tng. chmn., 1982-83; bd. dirs. Am. Cancer Soc., 1982-84. Mem. Am. Psychol. Assn., N.Y. State Psychol. Assn., Psychol. Assn. Northeastern N.Y. (sec. 1984—), Nat. Assn. Sch. Psychologists, N.Y. Assn. Sch. Psychologists, Sch. Psychology Educators Council of N.Y. State, Russell Sage Coll. Alumnae Assn. (exec. bd. 1974-78, sec. 1978-82, 1st v.p. 1982-86, mem. at large 1986—), Athenian Honor Soc., Psi Chi. Roman Catholic. Club: Russell Sage Troy Alumni (pres. 1976-83). Home: 19 Brentwood Ave Troy NY 12180 Office: 1976 Burdett Ave Troy NY 12180

BAYM, NINA, educator, university official; b. Princeton, N.J., June 14, 1936; d. Leo and Frances (Levinson) Zippin; B.A., Cornell U., Ithaca, N.Y., 1957; M.A., Harvard U., 1958, Ph.D., 1963; m. Gordon Baym, June 1, 1958; children—Nancy, Geoffrey; m. 2d, Jack Stillinger, May 21, 1971. Asst., U. Calif., Berkeley, 1962-63; instr. U. Ill., Urbana, 1963-67, asst. prof. English, 1967-69, assoc. prof., 1969-72, prof., 1972—, dir. Sch. Humanities, 1976—. Recipient Scholar award U. Ill., 1985; Guggenheim fellow, 1975-76; AAUW hon. fellow, 1975-76; Nat. Endowment Humanities fellow, 1982-83. Mem. Robert Frost Soc. (adv. bd.), Am. Studies Assn. (exec. council 1982-84), MLA (exec. com. 19th century Am. lit. div., chmn. 1984, mem. adv. council Am. lit. sect., chmn. 1984). Author: The Shape of Hawthorne's Career, 1976; Woman's Fiction: A Guide to Novels by and about Women in America, 1978; Novels, Readers and Reviewers; Responses to Fiction in Antebellum America, 1984; also essays. Editor: Norton Anthology of American Literature, 1985; mem. editorial bd. Am. Quar., Jour. Aesthetic Edn., Am. Lit., Tulsa Studies in Women's Lit., New Eng. Quar. Office: 608 S Wright St Urbana IL 61801

BAYMILLER, LYNDA DOERN, social services administrator; b. Milw., July 6, 1943; d. Ronald Oliver and Marian Elizabeth (Doern) B.; student U. Hawaii, 1962, Mich. State U., 1965; B.A., U. Wis., 1965, M.S.W., 1969. Peace Corps vol., Chile, 1965-67; social worker Luth. Social Services of Wis. and Upper Mich., Milw., 1969-77, contract social worker, 1978-79; dist. supr. Children's Service Soc. Wis., Kenosha, 1977-78; social services supr. Sauk County Dept. Social Services, Baraboo, Wis., 1979—. Bd. dirs. Zoo Pride, Zool. Soc. Milw. County, 1975-77, life mem.; bd. dirs. Sauk County Mental Health Assn., 1979-85; pres. bd. dirs. Growing Pl. Day Care Center, Kenosha, 1977-78. Mem. Nat. Assn. Social Workers, Acad. Cert. Social Workers, Wis. Social Services Assn., AAUW (br. sec. 1982-84), U. Wis. Alumni Assn. (life), Am. Legion Aux., DAR, Nat. Soc. Magna Charta Dames, Eddy Family Assn. (life mem.), Nat. Soc. Ancient and Hon. Arty. Co. of Mass., Daus. Colonial Wars, Morris Pratt Inst., Internat. Crane Found. (patron), Sauk County Hist. Soc., Am. Bus. Women's Assn. (charter mem.), Friends of Baraboo Zoo, Eagles Aux., Alpha Xi Delta, Clubs: Sweet Adelines (chpt. pres. 1971), Order Eastern Star. Author: (with Clara Amelia Hess) Now-Won, A Collection of Feeling (poetry and prose), 1973. Home: 332 4th Ave Baraboo WI 53913

BAYNE, PATRICIA HARRIS, museum official; b. Houston, July 17, 1948; d. James Gus and Luella Elizabeth (Ross) Harris; m. Harry G. Bayne, Apr. 6, 1985; 1 child, Brett Harris. B.F.A. in Art History, So. Meth. U., 1970. Exec. tng. asst. buying offices Neiman Marcus, Dallas, 1971-74; registrar asst. Dallas Mus. Fine Arts, 1974-75, adminstrv. asst., 1975-78, exec. asst., 1978-80, bus. mgr., 1980-81, supr. accounts, 1981-83, lead computer operator acctg. dept., 1983-84, systems analyst, 1984-86. Vol. Channel 13 Pub. Broadcasting System. Mem. Tex. Assn. Mus., Smithsonian Instn., Alpha Delta Pi. Democrat. Methodist. Home: 9511 Mossridge Dr Dallas TX 75238 Office: 1717 N Harwood St Dallas TX 75201

BAYSINGER-DEAVER, SHARON LEONA, insurance company executive; b. Fulton, Mo., Aug. 12, 1951; d. Samuel H. and Orba L. (Mccuine) Baysinger; m. Michael R. Deaver, June 1, 1978 (dec. Feb. 1979); 1 stepchild, Shawn Allen. B.S., U. Mo., 1973. Asst. mgr. Ann's Fashion Ctr., Columbia, Mo., 1973-75; corp. sec., mgr. Charles E. Rice Co., Columbia, 1975-77; dir. alumni assn. U. Mo.-Columbia, 1977-81; dir., assn. mktg. F.T. Jones & Co., Kansas City, Mo., 1981-82; southwest regional mgr. Puritan Life-Gen. Electric Credit, Providence, 1982-85; mgr. spl. markets, v.p. mass mktg. Bus. Men's Assurance Co., Kansas City, Mo., 1985—. Mem. Boone County Library Bd., Columbia, 1977-80. Mem. U. Mo. Alumni Assn. Lodge: Order of Eastern Star. Home: 6720 Rockhill Rd Kansas City MO 64131

BAZIGIAN, ANITA KIZIRIAN, manufacturing company executive, jewelry designer; b. Whitinsville, Mass.; d. Serop John and Mary (Pilibosian) Kizirian; m. Paul Bazigian, Aug. 25, 1957; children—Lesley Karen, Craig Michael. Student Worcester Art Mus., 1949-53, Sch. Nursing, Cambridge City Hosp., 1953-54; A.S., Becker Coll., 1956. Clerical positions Blackstone Valley News, Northbridge, Mass., 1953-56; med. asst. Bennett I. Fielding, M.D., Worcester, Mass., 1956-58, Agostine Del Signore, M.D., Worcester, 1958-60; freelance artist, Worcester, 1960-64; tchr. Armenian lang. Lang. Sch., Worcester, 1960-64; tchr. art, sci. Worcester Pub. Schs., 1964-70; tchr. Southwest Ednl. Ctr., Walled Lake, Mich., 1970-75; designer fine jewelry Birmingham Jewelers, Mich., 1975—; pres. ANI Designs div. Birmingham Mfg. Corp., Troy, Mich., 1984—; designer copyrighted jewelry. Exhibited various jewelry trade shows, N.Y.C., San Francisco, Los Angeles, Dallas. Counselor Girl Scouts U.S.A., Farmington Conn., 1952-53. Mem. Jewelers Bd. Trade, Pacific Jewelers Trade Show, Dallas Jewelers Trade Show, Jewelers of Am. Inc., Internat. Jewelry Show. Republican. Armenian Apostolic. Club: Mr. and Mrs. (Southfield, Mich.). Avocations: piano; boating; tennis; surfing; skiing. Office: ANI Designs Div Birmingham Mfg Corp 2300 W Big Beaver Rd Suite 6 Troy MI 48084

BEACH, J. ADRIENNE LAURIE, health care manager; b. N.Y.C., May 17, 1951; d. Johnny and Charlotte Frances (Cox) Beach. B.A. in Health Edn., Hunter Coll., 1973, M.S. in Guidance Counseling, 1979. Cert. sch. counselor, N.Y.C. Youth counselor Ch. of Intercession, N.Y.C., 1973-75; higher edn. intern Hunter Coll., N.Y.C., 1970-78; asst. systems analyst N.Y.C. Health & Hosp. Corp., N.Y.C., 1978-79, skilled nursing facilities coordinator, 1979—, fin. mgr., vol. Harlem Heights Fed. Credit Union, N.Y.C., 1979-82, also bd. dirs. Ruth R. Rachlin Meml. scholar, 1975; Samuel Dickstein Lodge Gold Medal award, 1970. Mem. Am. Personnel and Guidance Assn., Assn. for Non-White Concerns, Nat. Assn. Female Execs., Kappa Delta Pi. Democrat. Episcopalian. Home: 226 W 97th St New York NY 10025 Office: New York City Health & Hosp Corp 230 W 41st St New York NY 10036

BEACH, MARGARET GASTALDI (MRS. EDWARD WOODBRIDGE BEACH), found. exec., nurse; b. Placerville, Calif., Aug. 10, 1915; d. Giovanni Batista and Josephine (Bisagno) Gastaldi; student Sacramento City Coll., 1934; grad. Mercy Coll. Nursing, 1938; m. Edward Woodbridge Beach, Feb. 15, 1946 (dec. Aug. 1968); children—Laura G. (Mrs. Robert L. Phillips), Edward Woodbridge, Margaret J. In charge urol. dept. Mercy Hosp., Sacramento, 1938-42; tchr. urology to student nurses, 1943-45. Treas., Germana M. Wilson Meml. Scholarship Found., 1967—. Mem. Woman's Aux. AMA, Sacramento County Women Med. Soc., Am. Legion Aux., Italian Cultural Soc. Clubs: Carriage Trade, Women of the Moose, Hon. Guild St. Patrick's Day Mummurs. Home: 6255 14th Ave Sacramento CA 95820

BEACH, ROSE MARY RANDALL, librarian; b. Waterloo, Iowa, Dec. 11, 1921; d. Charles Warren Milton and Rose Ellen (MacDonald) Randall; m. Thomas C. Beach, Jr., May 5, 1945 (div. 1979); children—Charles Randall, Thomas Christopher, Murray MacDonald. B.A., U. Iowa, 1943; M.S., Drexel U., 1971. News and feature writer Assoc. Press Radio, N.Y.C., 1944-47; faculty Green Mountain Coll., Poultney, Vt., 1950-53, Goldey Beacom Coll., Wilmington, Del., 1956-69, library dir., 1970—. Mem. ALA, Del. Library Assn., Eastern Bus. Tchrs. Assn., Phi Beta Kappa, Phi Beta Mu. Episcopalian. Home: 5 Deville Ct Newark DE 19711 Office: Goldey Beacom Coll 4701 Limestone Rd Wilmington DE 19808

BEAHLER, ELECTRA CATSONIS, lawyer; b. Washington, Aug. 6, 1933; d. Achilles and Anastasia (Carzis) Catsonis; B.A. with honors, Pa. State U., 1955; J.D. with honors, George Washington U., 1969; m. John Leroy Beahler, Feb. 7, 1973. Bar: D.C. 1970, U.S. Sup. Ct. 1974. Asst. editor Aero Digest, Washington, 1955-56, Fairchild Engine & Airplane Co., Washington, 1956-57; exec. asst. internat. pub. relations dept. Kaiser Industries Corp., Washington, 1957-60; sec. to pres. George Washington U., Washington, 1960-62; legis. asst. to Congressman Donald D. Clancy, Washington, 1962-67; adminstrv. asst. to Congressman John M. Ashbrook, Washington, 1968-73; minority csl. edn. House Com. Edn. and Labor, U.S. Ho. of Reps., Washington, 1981-85; free lance writer. Recipient Schaeffer award Phi Delta Delta, 1962. Mem. ABA, Lawyer-Pilots Bar Assn., Internat. Orgn. Women Pilots, Ninety-Nines, Airplane Owners and Pilots Assn., D.C. Bar, Fed. Bar Assn., Women's Bar Assn. D.C., George Washington U. Law Assn., Washington Ind. Writers, Nat. Trust Hist. Preservation, Internat. Platform Assn., Columbia Hist. Soc.

BEALE, BETTY (MRS. GEORGE K. GRAEBER), columnist; b. Washington; d. William Lewis and Edna (Sims) B.; m. George Kenneth Graeber, Feb. 15, 1969. A.B., Smith Coll. Columnist, Washington Post, 1937-40; reporter and columnist Washington Evening Star, 1945-81; weekly columnist News Am. Syndicate (formerly Field Newspaper Syndicate), 1953—; lectr. in field. Recipient Freedom Found. award, 1969. Mem. Nat. Press Club. Address: 2926 Garfield St NW Washington DC 20008

BEALE, GEORGIA ROBISON, historian; b. Chgo., Mar. 14, 1905; d. Henry Barton and Dora Belle (Sledd) Robison; A.B., U. Chgo., 1926, A.M., 1928; Ph.D., Columbia U., 1938; student Sorbonne and Coll. de France, 1930-34; m. Howard Kennedy Beale, Jan. 2, 1942; children—Howard Kennedy, Henry Barton Robison, Thomas Wight. Reader in history U. Chgo., 1927-29; lectr. Barnard Coll., 1937-38; instr. Bklyn. Coll., 1937-39; asst. prof. Hollins (Va.) Coll., 1939-41, Wellesley Coll., 1941-42, Castleton (Vt.) State Coll., 1968-70; vis. asso. prof. U. Ky., Lexington, 1970-72 professorial lectr. George Washington U., 1983-84. Mem. Madison (Wis.) Civic Music Assn. and Madison Symphony Orch. League, 1958—; hon. trustee Culver-Stockton Coll., 1974—. Univ. fellow Columbia U., 1929-30. Mem. AAUW (European fellow 1930-31), Am., So. hist. assns., So. French Hist. Studies, Western Soc. French History (hon. mem. exec. council), Am., Brit. socs. 18th century studies, Phi Beta Kappa, Pi Lambda Theta, Phi Alpha Theta, Pi Kappa Delta. Clubs: Reid Hall (Paris); Brit. Univ. Women's (London). Author: Revelliere-lépeaux, Citizen Director, 1938, 72; Academies to Institut, 1973; Bosc and the Exequatur, 1978; contbg. author Hisytorical Dictionary of the French Revolution, 1985; also articles. Address: The Ridge Orford NH 03777 also 2816 Columbia Rd Madison WI 53705 also 110 D St SE Washington DC 20003

BEALE, HELEN RUBY, insurance company administrative assistant; b. Michigamme, Mich., Mar. 29, 1922; d. Edwin Martin and Katherine Mae (Rahilly) Stensrud; m. Roland Earl Beale, June 19, 1944 (dec.); children—John Robert, Ann Marie Beale Trachtenberg, James Edward. Student Mich. State U., St. Catherine's Coll. Cert. adminstrv. mgr. Owner Beale Funeral Home, Michigamme, 1943-60; asst. to pres. Ind. Mgmt. Cons., Madison, Wis., 1966-73; sec. Sch. Dist. Office, Oregon, Wis., 1974-76; administrv. asst. Modern Kitchen Supply, Madison, 1976-81; agy. administrv. asst. Bankers Life, Madison, 1981—. State advisor U.S. Congl. adv. bd. Am. Security Council Found., Washington, 1983. Mem. Adminstrv. Mgmt. Soc. (pres. 1981-82), Am. Mgmt. Assn., Nat. Tax Limitations Com., Madison Deanery (v.p. 1982-84, regents 1981-85). Roman Catholic.

BEALL, JOANNA MAY, painter; b. Chgo., Aug. 17, 1935; d. Lester Thomas and Dorothy Welles (Miller) B.; student Yale U. Sch. Fine Arts, 1953-57, Art Inst. Chgo., 1957; m. H.C. Westermann, Mar. 31, 1959. One-man shows include: Great Bldg. Crack-Up Gallery, N.Y.C., 1973, James Corcoran Gallery, Los Angeles, 1974, Gallery Rebecca Cooper, Washington, 1975; group shows: Allan Frumkin, Chgo., 1960, 61, Whitney Mus., N.Y.C., 1973, Art Inst. Chgo., 1976, Univ. Galleries, Los Angeles, 1979, Xavier Fourcade, N.Y.C., 1980, 85; vis. artist U. Colo., Boulder, 1979, 84. Mem. Artists Equity Assn., Visual Artists and Galleries Assn. Article The World of Joanna Beall (Melinda Wortz) appeared in Art Week mag., 1974. Home: Box 28 Brookfield Center CT 06805

BEAM, FRANCES DELORES, county official; b. Greensboro, N.C., May 12, 1942; d. Clarence Sterling and Lorena (Fuller) B. Student Va. State Coll., 1960-62; B.S. in Sociology A&T U., Greensboro, N.C., 1966; postgrad. Va. Commonwealth U., 1980-81, U. Va., 1982. Registered social worker. Youth counselor St. Matthew United Meth. Ch., Greensboro, 1963-66; counselor YWCA and A&T Upward Bound, Greensboro, 1966-69; social worker Henry County Social Services, Martinsville, Va., 1969-70, supr., 1970-71, supr. in control, 1970-71, dir., Collinsville, Va., 1971—; dir. Safetynet, Inc., Martinsville. Bd. dirs., mem. budget com. Martinsville/Henry County United Fund, 1979—; bd. dirs. Neighborhood Youth Ctr., Martinsville, 1981-83; mem. Council Human Relations, Martinsville, 1968-70; mem. crisis planning com. CONTACT, Martinsville, 1970-72; mem. Commn. on Family Life, 1968; mem. Bd. Suprs. Long Term Care Council, 1983—; Recipient Appreciation and Recognition award Dept. Welfare, Richmond, 1979. Mem. Am. Pub. Welfare Assn., Nat. Welfare Fraud Assn., Va. Council Social Welfare, Va. Govt. Employment Assn. (bd. dirs., chmn. nominating com. 1978-81), 5th Congl. Dist. Assn. Local Welfare Dirs. and Bd. Mems. (bd. dirs., publicity chmn. 1981—), NAACP, Voter League, Eta Phi Beta (pres. Alpha Rho chpt. 1982—, regional journalist 1983—, presdl. award 1984), Delta Sigma Theta. Democrat. Methodist. Clubs: Estreilla (Martinsville, Va.); United Meth. Women, Young Adults (Greensboro, N.C.). Avocations: cooking; reading; house plants; gardening; pinochle. Office: Henry County Dept Social Services Drawer 788 Kings Mountain Rd Collinsville VA 24078

BEAMAN, JANICE ELLEN, nurse; b. Auburn, N.Y., Sept. 23, 1961; d. Jack Edward and Frances Mary (Kenney) Hole; m. Glenn Peter Beaman, June 6, 1981; 1 child, Nathan James. A.S., Cayuga County Community Coll., 1981. R.N., N.Y. Med.-surg. staff nurse Community Gen. Hosp., Syracuse, N.Y., 1981-84, labor and delivery staff nurse, 1984—. Roman Catholic. Avocations: softball; racquetball; tennis; sewing. Home: 147 Walrath Rd Syracuse NY 13205 Office: Community Gen Hosp Broad Rd Syracuse NY 13215

BEAN, ELIZABETH HARRIMAN, county legislator, civic worker; b. Buffalo, Sept. 23, 1923; d. Lewis Gildersleeve and Grace (Bastine) Harriman; m. Charles Palmer Bean, Sept. 13, 1947; children—Katherine Bean Yancey, Bruce P., Margaret E., Sarah H., Gordon T. B.A. in History, Smith Coll., 1945; M.A. in Polit. Sci., SUNY-Albany, 1985; cert. in social welfare adminstrn. U. Ill., 1948. Claims adjustor Liberty Mutual Ins. Co., Washington, 1945; instr. U.S. Armed Forces Inst., Manila and Okinawa, 1946; social caseworker Family Service Agy., Urbana, Ill., 1948-50; legislator Schenectady County Bd. of Reps., N.Y., 1976—, chmn. ways and means com. 1980-85, majority leader, 1986—; commr. Capital Dist. Regional Planning Commn., 1976-80; treas. Schenectady County Indsl. Devel. Agy., 1983—. Chmn., N.Y. State Citizens Info. Service, 1968-72; bd. govs. Albany Med. Ctr. Hosp., N.Y., 1977—; bd. dirs. Sunnyview Hosp., Schenectady, 1979—, N.E. Parent and Child Soc., Schenectady, 1981—, Schenectady Symphony Orch., 1983—, Schenectady Mus., 1986—; chmn. budget com. N.Y. State Legis. Forum, Albany, 1983—. Recipient Pub. Service Recognition award YWCA, 1979; Susan B. Anthony award LWV, 1980. Mem. N.Y. State Suprs. and County Legislators Assn. (legis. chmn. 1982—), N.Y. State Assn. of Counties, Bus. and Profl. Women's Club of Schenectady, AAUW (issues chmn. 1985-86). Republican. Episcopalian. Clubs: Niskayuna Rep. (pres. 1984-86), Torch. Lodge: Zonta. Avocations: dancing, tennis, hiking. Home: 2221 Stone Ridge Rd Schenectady NY 12309 Office: Bd of Reps 620 State St Schenectady NY 12307

BEAN, JENNIFER JANICE, court reporting agency owner; b. Chgo., Nov. 4, 1955; d. Charles Hadley and Barbara (Haasis) B. Assoc., Mile High Reporting Coll., Denver, 1977. Cert. shorthand reporter; registered proficient reporter. Ct. reporter Howard Henry & Co., Albuquerque, 1977-80, Jennifer Bean & Assoc., Albuquerque, 1980-82, Bean & Harris, Albuquerque, 1982—; cons. N.Mex. Supreme Ct., Santa Fe, 1983—. Contbr. articles to profl. jours. Chmn. chpt. Nat. Com. on Suicide Prevention. Mem. N.Mex. Ct. Reporters Assn. (pres. 1982-85, lobbyist 1983-85), N.Mex. Supreme Ct. Bd. Governing Ct. Reporters (pres. 1984-87), Nat. Shorthand Reporters Assn. (com. mem.), Albuquerque C. of C. Democrat. Unitarian. Avocations: skiing; volleyball. Office: Bean & Harris Ct Reporting 900 Gold SW Albuquerque NM 87102

BEAN, JOAN LUCENT, crisis line executive; b. Paterson, N.J., Dec. 7, 1945; d. Santos Bellint and Violet Eleanor (Conrad) Lucent; m. Alexander Keith Nagy, Nov. 22, 1968 (div. Jan. 1974); m. Donald Bean, Aug. 28, 1977. A.A. in Liberal Arts St. John Baptist Acad., Mendham, N.J. 1963; student in psychology and liberal arts Upsala Coll., 1964-66; cert. in dental assisting Lyons Inst., Newark, 1969. Judge figure skating North Jersey Figure Skating Club, Westwood, 1965-66; coach figure skating Westwood Ice Arena, 1966-68, Palace Ice Arena, Richardson, Tex., 1972-73; dir. figure skating Ice Sports, Inc., Addison, Tex., 1973-75; exec. dir. Sussex County Help Line, Newton, N.J., 1981-85; mem. Contact Morris/Passaic, 1985—, sec. bd. dirs., 1985—; fin. auditor Sparta United Methodist Ch. (N.J.), 1982—. Author, editor: Sussex County Resource Directory, 1983. Assoc. Republican Nat. Com., Washington, 1978; com. mem. Sparta United Meth. Ch., 1982, com. chmn., 1984. Mem. Profl. Skaters Guild Am. (cert. figure skating coach), U.S. Figure Skating Assn. (judge 1964, Bronze medal for figures 1965, Bronze medal for ice dancing 1966), Ice Skating Inst. Am. Clubs: Riverview Skating (Wayne, N.J.); North Jersey Figure Skating. Home: PO Box 763 Sparta NJ 07871

BEAN, NANCY ANN MORGAN, food service broker; b. Williamstown, Ky., Feb. 9, 1936; d. Dora Bell Morgan and Helen (Dunlap) Strother Morgan; m. Philip Lee Crume, Oct. 26, 1960 (div. 1974); children—Ann Morgan Crume Redmon, Lynn Ellis Bean; m. James Ellis Bean, July 26, 1980. B.S., Eastern Ky. U., 1959; M.Pub.Affairs, Ky. State U., 1976. Nutritionist, Ky. Health Dept., Georgetown, 1966-68; dietary cons. Central Ky. Nursing Home, Lexington, 1968-71; dir. food service Ky. Bur. Corrections, Frankfort, 1971-76; sales rep., account exec. A.J. Seibert, Louisville, also Lexington, Ky., 1976-81; owner, pres. Profl. Food Service, Louisville, 1981—. Mem. Louisville Dietetic Assn., Ky. Dietetic Assn., Am. Dietetic Assn., Ky. Restaurant Assn., Nat. Food Brokers Assn., Am. Sch. Food Service Assn. Democrat. Methodist. Lodge: Order Eastern Star. Avocations: gardening, reading. Home: Route 2 Box 266 Cox's Creek KY 40013 Office: Profl Food Service 1006 Phillips Ln Louisville KY 40213

BEANE, LEONA, lawyer, educator; b. N.Y.C. B.B.A., CCNY, 1958, M.B.A., 1962; M.S., Columbia U., 1964; J.D., N.Y. Law Sch., 1968. Bar: N.Y. 1969. Practice law, N.Y.C., 1969—; prof. law Baruch Coll., CUNY, N.Y.C., 1978—. Author: The Essentials of Partnership Law, 1982; The Essentials of Corporation Law, 1984; Legal Materials in the Study of Commercial Transactions,

1984; joint author: Materials in the Law of Business Contracts, 1982; contbg. editor/author 2 chpts. The New York Corporate Handbook, 1983; contbr. numerous articles to profl. jours. Recipient Speaker's award, N.Y. State Bar Assn., 1983, 84, 85; spl. master Supreme Ct. N.Y., 1981. Mem. ABA, Nat. Assn. Women Lawyers (corr. sec.), Arbitrators Assn. Small Claims (dir., v.p., treas.), Assn. Bar City N.Y., Am. Judges Assn., N.Y. Women's Bar Assn., Met. Women's Bar Assn., N.Y. State Trial Lawyers Assn., New York County Lawyers Assn. (corp. law com.), N.Y. State Bar Assn. (corp. law com.), Inst. Jud. Adminstrn., Am. Judicature Soc., Am. Arbitration Assn. (arbitrator). Home: 136 E 56th St New York NY 10022 Office: Baruch Coll 17 Lexington Ave New York NY 10010

BEARD, ANN SOUTHARD, art framing company executive; b. Denver, Jan. 13, 1948; d. William Harvey and Cora Alice Cornelia (Caldwell) Southard; m. Terrill Leon Beard, Dec. 20, 1970 (div. Oct. 1980); 1 son, Jeffery Leon. B.A., Willamette U., 1970; postgrad U. Calif.-San Diego, 1981-82. Exec. asst. Kidder Peabody & Co., San Francisco, 1970-72; adminstrv. aide Arthur Anderson & Co., Portland, Oreg., 1972-73; owner, mgr. Beard's Frame Shoppes, Inc., Portland, 1973-80; dir. mktg. Multnomah County Fair, Portland, 1979; owner, chief exec. officer Ann Beard Spl. Events, San Diego, 1980-82; pres. Frame Affair, Inc., San Diego, 1982—, Jack Oil Co., Inc., Greeley, 1982—; v.p. 146 Co., Inc., Greeley; lectr., cons. SBA, San Diego, 1980—; dir. Fashion Valley Shopping Ctr., San Diego. Bd. dirs. San Diego Master Chorale, 1981—; mem. citizens adv. bd. Drug Abuse Task Force/Crime Prevention Task Force, San Diego, 1983—. White House fellow, 1976. Mem. Am. Mktg. Assn., Profl. Picture Framers Assn., San Diego C. of C., Save Our Heritage Orgn., Combined Arts and Edn. Council, La Jolla Mus. Contemporary Art, Charter 100 San Diego, Delta Gamma. Home: 13079 Caminito Del Rocio Del Mar CA 92014 Office: Frame Affair Inc 412 Fashion Valley San Diego CA 92108

BEARD, ARLINE FORTENBERRY, nursing home administrator; b. Tylertown, Miss., Aug. 19, 1944; d. Aaron A. and Willine (Pittman) Fortenberry; m. Elbert E. Beard, May 7, 1984; m. James Merril Dillon, Oct. 13, 1963 (div. Sept. 1981); children—Mark Andrew, Patrick Stewart, Michelle. Student U. So. Miss. 1985. Cert., Miss. Bd. Nursing Home Adminstrs. Auditor, So. Bell Tel. Co., Jackson, Miss., 1962-63; social dir. Tylertown Extended Care Ctr., Miss., 1981-84; activity dir., 1981-84; adminstr. Beverly Enterprises, Tylertown, 1984—. Ombudsman, Gov.'s Office Fed.-State Programs, Jackson, 1985—. County chmn. Miss. Heart Assn., 1984; com. mem. Miss. Job Service, Pike, 1984-86. Recipient Outstanding Leader award Walthall Coop. Extension, 1981, Gold Clover 4-H award Miss. State U., 1984. Mem. Am. Coll. Health Care Adminstrs., Nat. Assn. Activity Profls., Nat. Assn. Female Execs., Am. Bus. Women's Assn., Miss. Gerontol. Soc., Walthall C. of C. Baptist Club: Homemakers (pres. 1980). Avocations: oil painting; piano; needlework. Office: Tylertown Extended Care/Beverly Enterpreies 200 Medical Circle Tylertown MS 39667

BEARD, BARBARA LEE, lawyer; b. St. Paul, Dec. 20, 1947; d. Richard Morris and Edna (Schroeder) Beard. J.D., U. West Los Angeles, 1982. Assoc. firm Hews, Munoz & Howard, Santa Ana, Calif., 1982-83, firm Lund & Caplan, Long Beach, Calif., 1983—. Mem. ABA, Calif. Bar Assn., Orange County Bar Assn., Los Angeles County Bar Assn., Am. Trial Lawyers Assn., Calif. Trial Lawyers Assn. Office: Lund & Caplan 354 W Ocean Blvd Long Beach CA 90802

BEARD, DOROTHY REGINA, newspaper editor; b. N.Y.C., Jan. 12, 1924; d. Thomas Joseph and Jane Marie (Kearney) McCarthy; m. Bruce Montgomery Beard, Jr., Jan. 22, 1955; children—Jane, Anne, Ellen, Bruce. Fashion publicist Lord & Taylor, N.Y.C., 1942-56; free lance author, 1956-74; editor West Windsor-Plainsboro Chronicle, Princeton Junction, N.J., 1974—. Office: West Windsor-Plainsboro Chronicle PO Box 189 Princeton Junction NJ 08550

BEARD, ELIZABETH LETITIA, science educator; b. New Orleans, Apr. 2, 1932; d. Howard Horace and Irene (Handley) B. B.A. cum laude, Tex. Christian U., 1952, B.S. cum laude, 1953, M.S., 1955; Ph.D., Tulane U., 1961. Teaching fellow Smith Coll., Northampton, Mass., 1953, Vanderbilt U., Nashville, 1954; instr. to prof. Loyola U., New Orleans, 1955—; prof. biology Tulane U. Sch. Medicine, New Orleans, 1968—; vis. prof. Harvard Sch. Medicine, 1984-85. Contbr. articles to profl. jours. Project rev. com. New Orleans Health Planning Council, 1974-77, bd. dirs., 1975-80; pres. sch. bd. Holy Name Elem. Sch., New Orleans, 1976-79; soprano soloist Christ Ch. Cathedral, 1967-83, Holy Name of Jesus Ch., New Orleans, 1967—. Grantee NIH, 1962-64, 67-69, Edward Schleider Found., 1974-77, La. Heart Assn., 1966-67, Loyola U., 1970-71; La. Heart Assn. fellow, 1958-61. Mem. N.Y. Acad. Scis., Am. Physiol. Soc., Soc. Exptl. Biology and Medicine, Am. Heart Assn., AAAS, AAUP, La. Hist. Soc., Met. Mus. Art, La. Landmarks, Sigma Xi. Clubs: La. Landmarks, Friends of Cabildo. Avocations: soprano soloist; travel. Home: 6127 Garfield St New Orleans LA 70118 Office: Loyola U 6363 St Charles Ave New Orleans LA 70118

BEARD, JANET MARIE, health care administrator; b. Olean, N.Y., Feb. 18, 1930; d. Paul Claude and Virginia Maria (Mahaney) B. R.N., St. Catherine's Hosp., 1951; B.S. in Clin. Nursing, St. John's U., 1959, M.S. in Nursing Adminstrn., 1961; M.S. in Adminstrv. Medicine, Columbia U., 1968. Adminstrv. supr. Mary Immaculate Hosp., Jamaica, N.Y., 1957-66; asst. adminstr. Cath. Med. Ctr. Bklyn. and Queens, Jamaica, 1968-70; asst. dir. Yale-New Haven Med. Ctr., 1971-72; asst. dir. St. Barnabas Hosp., Bronx, N.Y., 1972-78, v.p., 1978-83; exec. dir. Bethel Homes, Ossining, N.Y., 1983—. Contbr. articles to profl. jours. Active Bronx Community Bd., 1977-83; mem. indsl. com. Ossining C. of C., 1983—; active Fedn. Protestant Welfare Agys., N.Y.C., 1978—; planning com. Div. on Aging, N.Y.C., 1978—; adv. com. Aging in Am., Bronx, 1978—; treas. Ft. Schuyler House, Bronx, 1977-83; exec. bd. Columbia U. Sch. Pub. Health, 1981—. Fellow Am. Coll. Hosp. Adminstrs.; mem. Am. Coll. Health Care Adminstrs., Columbia U. Alumni Assn. (sec. 1976-78, treas. 1978-80). Office: The Bethel Homes 19 Narragansett Ave Ossining NY 10562

BEARD, ROBERTA JEAN, dryer manufacturing company executive; b. Kokomo, Ind.; d. Paul L. and Sareta Corine (Thompson) B.; m. William Jennings Beard, Feb. 26, 1950; children—Steven W. (dec.), Neal A., Diana J., Pamela A. B.S. in Home Econs., Purdue U., 1950. Cert. tchr. home econs., Tchr. Carrol County Schs., Cutler, Ind., 1950-51; sec., treas., v.p. Beard Inds., Inc., Frankfort, Ind., 1965—, Coal Field Reclamation, Frankfort, 1981—. Mem. Frankfort C. of C. Club: Women's Symphony (Frankfort). Lodge: Zonta Internat. (membership chmn., pres. 1978-80). Avocations: singing, needlework, sewing, playing piano.

BEARD, VIRGINIA HARRISON, psychologist; b. St. Louis, Sept. 9, 1941; d. Monroe Colemon and Lula Lucille (Spicer) Harrison; B.A.Ed., Harris Tchrs. Coll., 1964; M.S., So. Ill. U., 1968; Ph.D., St. Louis U., 1976; m. Otis Charles Beard, Aug. 21, 1965; children—Bostic Charles, Bonji Lucille. Counselor, jr. high sch., University City, Mo., 1969-71; psychologist King Fanon Community Mental Health Center, Center for Human Concerns, St. Louis Juvenile Ct., 1973-75; community staff coordinator Med. Sch. St. Louis U., 1976-78, also instr.; exec. dir. Center for Family Mental Health, St. Louis, 1978-80; dir. psychol. services Met. Comprehensive Mental Health Center, 1980—; vis. prof. George Warren Brown Sch. Social Work, 1978-79, Fontbonne Coll., 1979, U. Mo.-St. Louis, 1985-86, Met. Coll.; cons. Job Corps, Head Start, Salvation Army. Chmn., Gov.'s Adv. Council on Aging, 1976-78; mem. planning com. Regional White House Conf. on Families; mem. Regional Adv. Council for Psychiat. Services, 1978-82; 1st v.p. Annie Malone Children's Home, 1975-85; mem. Div. Family Service Child Consultative Treatment Team; bd. dirs. Conf. on Edn. Ford Found. fellow, 1971-72; Inst. Applied Gerontology fellow, 1973-75; active Mid City unit Am. Cancer Soc. Mem. Am. Psychol. Assn., Mo. Psychol. Assn., Chums, Inc., Nat. Council Negro Women, Alpha Kappa Alpha. Baptist. Home: 890 Berick Saint Louis MO 63132 Office: 4731 Delmar Blvd Saint Louis MO 63108

BEARDEN, HELEN RUDD, nurse; b. East Arlington, Vt., June 15, 1922; d. Edward Leland and Hazel Rosamond (Bromley) Rudd; m. Harlie Bearden, Feb. 10, 1947 (div. 1948); 1 son, John Edward. R.N., Henry W. Bishop III Nursing Sch., 1943. Staff nurse H.W. Putnam Hosp., Bennington, Vt., 1943-44, pvt. duty nurse, 1948-50, head nurse, supr., 1950-63; instr. Putnam Practical Sch., Bennington, 1961; indsl. nurse Union Carbide Corp., Bennington, 1963—. Multi-media instr. ARC, Bennington, Vt. Served to 1st lt. USAF, 1944-47. Mem. Am. Nurses Assn., Am. Assn. Occupational Health Nurses, DAR, Bennington County Registered Nurses. Democrat. Methodist. Home: Crow Hill Arlington VT 05250 Office: Union Carbide Corp 401 Gage St Bennington VT 05201

BEARDSHEAR, EVELYN ANDERSON, former nursing administrator; b. N.Y.C., Mar. 13, 1918; d. Edwin Andrew and Sophie (Seaquist) Anderson; m. Albert Nathan Beardshear, Apr. 27, 1945; children—Grant Downer, Craig Anderson. B.S.N. in Edn., Ind. U., 1960; M.S., Butler U., 1966; Ph.D., Internat. Coll., Los Angeles, 1980. R.N., N.Y., Calif., Ind. Staff nurse, clin. instr. Bellevue Psychiat. Hosp., N.Y.C., 1939-43; head nurse, supr., asst. to dir. nurses Langley Porter Inst., San Francisco, 1943-45; instr., asst. dir. nursing service and nursing edn. Larue Carter Hosp., Indpls., 1960-73; asst. prof. Ind. U. Sch. Nursing, Indpls., 1973-75, assoc. prof., coordinator sr. yr., 1975-83; ret. 1983; lectr. and cons., condr. workshops in field. Editor, author nursing sect. Mnemonic Bull., 1967-73; contbr. articles to profl. jours. Mem. Washington Twp. Planning Com., Indpls., 1964-65; mem. nominating com. Washington Twp. Sch. Bd., 1966; speaker career days and future nurses clubs, 1966-70. Recipient Disting. Service award Ind. U. Sch. Nursing Alumni Assn., 1983. Mem. Am. Nurses Assn., Ind. Nurses Assn., Nat. League Nursing, Ind. League Nursing, AAUP (pres. Indpls. 1978-79), Pi Lambda Theta, Sigma Theta Tau. Republican. Clubs: Ind. U. Women's. Home: 8811 Cholla Rd Indianapolis IN 46240

BEARE, MURIEL ANITA NIKKI, public relations executive, author; b. Detroit, Mar. 7, 1928; d. Elbert Stanley and Dorothy Margaret (Welch) Brink; m. Richard Austin Beare, June 15, 1946; 1 child, Sandra Lee. A.A., Miami Dade Community Coll., 1974; B.A., Skidmore Coll., 1979. Writer, Key West Citizen (Fla.), 1959, Miami News (Fla.), 1967; field dir. Fla. Project HOPE, 1967-68, southeastern area dir., 1968-69; asst. v.p. pub. relations I/D Assocs., Inc., Miami, 1969-70; pres. Nikki Beare & Assocs., Miami, 1971—; v.p. South Fla. office Cherenson, Carroll & Holzer, Livingston, N.J., 1973; sr. v.p. D.J. Edelman, Inc., 1981-83; moderator, producer Women's Powerline, Sta. WIOD, Miami, 1972-77; co-owner South Miami Travel Service, South Miami, 1976-78; pres. Gov.'s Sq. Travel, Inc., Tallahassee, 1979-85, Travel Is Fun, Miami, 1985—. Author: Pirates, Pineapples and People: Tales and Legends of the Florida Keys, 1961; From Turtle Soup to Coconuts, 1964; Bottle Bonanza, A Handbook for Antique Bottle Collectors, 1965. Chmn. adv. bd. Met. Dade County Library, 1964; vice chmn. Met. Dade County Com. Status Women, 1971-76; active Met. Gen. Land Use Master Planning Com., 1973-74; Gov.'s Com. Employment Handicapped, 1970-72; chmn. Met. Dade Fair Housing and Employment Appeals Bd., 1975-78; chmn. Handicapped and Elderly subcom. Met. Dade Transit Devel. Com.; mem. Fla. Ins. Commn. Task Force, 1975, Dade County Democratic Exec. com., 1972-76, South Fla. Health Planning Council, 1972-74; founding mem. Nat. Women's Polit. Caucus, 1971—; v.p. Herstory, 1971—; candidate Fla. Senate, 1974, Fla. Ho. of Reps., 1976; past pres. adv. bd. Inst. for Women, Fla. Internat. U.; pres. Fla. Feminist Credit Union, 1975-78; bd. dirs. Community Health Inst. South Dade County, 1975-77; mem. Jobs for Miami, 1980-85; chmn. Fla. Gov.'s Small Bus. Adv. Council, 1981-83. Mem. Greater Miami C. of C., Coral Gables C. of C., LWV, NOW, Hist. Assn. So. Fla., Friends of Everglades, Women's C. of C. So. Fla., Greater Miami Tourism Coalition, 1983—. Recipient Silver Image award Pub. Relations Assn., 1967-68. Mem. Nat. Assn. Women Bus. Owners, Antique Bottle Collectors Assn. Fla. Democrat. Clubs: Tiger Bay, Manatee Bay. Office: Nikki Beare & Assocs Inc 14301 SW 87th Ave Miami FL 33176

BEARMAN, TONI CARBO, university dean; b. Middletown, Conn., Nov. 14, 1942; d. Anthony Joseph and Theresa (Bauer) Carbo; m. David A. Bearman, Nov. 14, 1970; 1 dau., Amanda Carole. A.B., Brown U., 1969; M.S., Drexel U., 1973, Ph.D. in Mgmt. of Info. Resources, 1977. Supr. Phys. Sci. Library, Brown U., Providence, 1967-71; subject specialist Engring. Library, U. Wash., Seattle, 1966-67; teaching and research asst. Drexel U., Phila., 1971-73; exec. dir. Nat. Fedn. Abstracting and Info. Services, Phila., 1974-79; cons. strategic planning Instn. Elec. Engrs., London, 1979-80; exec. dir. Nat. Commn. on Libraries and Info. Sci., Washington, 1980-86; dean Sch. Library and Info. Sci., U. Pitts., 1986—; Regents lectr. U. Calif., 1984. Mem. editorial bds. several maj. publs. in field; contbr. articles to profl. jours. Dir. secretariat U.S. Nat. Com. for UNESCO Gen. Info. Program, 1982-86; mem. adv. bd. Info. Inst. of Internat. Acad. Santa Barbara, 1982-86; trustee Engring. Info., Inc., 1981—. Recipient Disting. Alumni award Drexel U. Coll. Info. Studies. Fellow AAAS, Inst. for Info. Scientists; mem. Am. Soc. Info. Sci. (bd. dirs. 1978-81, chmn. Delaware Valley chpt. 1976-77, mem. and council liaison Internat. Relations and Networking Coms., 1979-81, rep. to Network Adv. Com., chmn. coms., Watson Davis award 1983), Am. Nat. Standards Inst. (chmn., vice chmn. coms.), U.S. Dept. Tech. Adv. Bd. (com. on sci. and tech. info. policy 1978-79). Home: 907 E Capitol St SE Washington DC 20003 Office: Nat Com on Libraries and Info Science GSA Bldg Suite 3122 7th and D Sts SW Washington DC 20024

BEARN, MARGARET SLOCUM, lawyer, educator; b. Fanwood, N.J., June 20, 1924; d. Clarence W. and Emma (Elliot) Slocum; B.A. with honors, Swarthmore Coll., 1945; LL.B., Yale U., 1948; m. Alexander G. Bearn, Dec. 20, 1952; children—Helen Bearn Pennoyer, Gordon. Bar: N.Y. 1950. Assoc., Grossman & Grossman, N.Y.C., 1948-50, Lewinson, Lewinson & Fieland, 1950-55; dir. admissions Lab. Inst. Mdse., N.Y.C., 1953-54; 55-56, dean, 1956-73; asst. prof. N.Y. Law Sch., 1973-76, asso. prof., 1976-85, asst. dean, 1974-76, asso. dean, 1976-85, acting dean, spring 1980, dir. joint program with U. Bologna (Italy), 1976-85; assoc. prof. law St. John's U. Sch. Law, Jamaica, N.Y., 1985—; mem. N.Y.C. Mayor's Com. Judiciary, 1980, 83. Mem. N.Y.C. Community Bd. 1, 1979-85; sec., bd. dirs. Chambers-Canal Civic Assn., 1977-85. Woodrow Wilson fellow, 1979, 80, 83. Mem. ABA (law schs. insp. team 1978—, com. on jud. edn. and internat. law 1982—), Assn. Am. Law Schs. (chmn. sect. on teaching law outside law sch. 1980-81), N.Y. County Lawyers Assn. (chmn. com. on legal edn. and admission to bar 1980-85), U.S. Supreme Ct. Hist. Soc. (com. student chpts.), Internat. Assn. Jurists (v.p. Am. com. 1981—, chmn. 1983 conf.), Am. Law Inst., Scribes (pres. 1983-84). Presbyterian. Office: St John's U Sch Law Grand Central and Utopia Pkwys Jamaica NY 11439

BEARSS, JOYCE CLARKE, retired telephone company manager; b. Jamestown, N.Y., July 7, 1930; d. Garnet Garfield and Margaret Alberta (Mooney) Clarke; m. William S. Bearss, May 28, 1955. Sec., N.Y. Telephone Co., Buffalo, 1955-65, asst. dial service supr., 1965-66, dial service supr., 1966-80, community affairs mgr., 1980-85. Mem. exec. bd. dirs., pres. Niagara Frontier Industry Edn. Council; pres. Bry-Lin Hosp.; v.p. Coordinated Care Mgmt. Corp.; mem. examiners N.Y. State Nursing Home Adminstrs.; del. White House Conf. on Aging; mem. Victim-Witness Task Force County Erie; bd. dirs. U.S. Ski Team, Buffalo Support Group; mem. Soc. Community Affairs Profl.; mem. adv. bd. Erie County Dept. Sr. Services; mem. Senator Javitz Bd.; mem. exec. bd. Erie County Republican Com.; mem. Buffalo Susquicentenial Media Com.; pres. bd. trustees Medaille Coll.; bd. mgrs. Mus. of Sci.; active various community drives. Recipient Service awards Am. Lung Assn., 1981, Erie County Dept. Sr. Services, 1980; named Outstanding Woman in Bus. and Industry, SUNY-Buffalo, 1984; Woman of Distinction in Field of Bus., Gov. Mario Cuomo, 1984. Mem. Telephone Pioneers Am., Women for Downtown, Buffalo Area C. of C., Hamburg C. of C. (bd. dirs.). Clubs: Wanakah Country; Capitol Hill; Zonta (pres., dir.), Twentieth Century (Buffalo). Home: S-4934 Clifton Pkwy Hamburg NY 14075 Office: 608 Ellicott Sq Buffalo NY 14203

BEASLEY, BRENDA JENNINGS, nurse, educator; b. Gadsden, Ala., Feb. 16, 1947; d. W. Jack and Arzelia Nell (Brown) Messer; m. E. Paul Beasley, Aug. 29, 1981; stepchildren—David Paul, Melanie Lea. R.N., U. Ala., 1968; Assoc. degree Emergency Med. Tech., Gadsden State Jr. Coll., 1981. R.N., lic. paramedic, Ala. Staff, emergency room nurse Univ. Hosp., Birmingham, Ala., 1968-69; neurosurg. intensive care nurse Carraway Hosp., Birmingham, 1969-72, emergency charge nurse, 1972-76; inservice edn. dir. Wedowee Hosp. (Ala.), 1976-79; emergency med. service instr. So. Union State Coll., Wadley, Ala., 1979-81, emergency med. service program dir. Emergency Med. Tech., 1981—; chmn. exec. com., chmn. tng. and edn. com. E. Ala. Emergency Med. Service, Anniston, 1983—; instr. affiliate faculty Advanced Cardiac Life Support Inst., Am. Heart Assn., Ala. and Ga., 1980—; instr. basic trauma life support Am. Coll. Emergency Physicians, 1983—. Active defensive driving course Nat. Safety Council-Ala. Dept. Pub. Safety, since 1978—. Named Woman of Yr., Randolph Press, 1981. Mem. Randolph County Health Council, Nat. Red Cross Nurses, Am. Heart Assn., Nat. Assn. Emergency Med. Technicians. Republican. Methodist. Home: Route 3 Box 80 Goodwater AL 35072 Office: Southern Union State Coll Roberts St Wadley AL 36276

BEASLEY, CARLA JO, advertising agency executive; b. Memphis, Dec. 1, 1955; d. Joseph Edward Beasley and Gloria Aileen (Watson) Beasley Powell; m. Thomas H. Rosteck, Feb. 3, 1976 (div. Mar. 1982). B.B.A. in Mktg., Memphis State U. Sec. Fed. Compress, Memphis, 1976-78, State Tech. Inst., Memphis, 1978-79; media buyer Ward Archer & Assocs. Advt., Memphis, 1979-82, account exec., 1982—. Mem. Nat. Agri-Mktg. Assn. (treas. Mid-South chpt. 1983-84). Baptist. Home: 3135 Carnes Memphis TN 38111 Office: Ward Archer & Assocs 2996 Directors Row Memphis TN 38130

BEASLEY, MARCIA LOU TURPIN, dietitian, former army officer; b. Indpls., Feb. 27, 1938; d. D. John and Mona Belle (Albright) Turpin; B.S., Purdue U., 1960; M.H.A., Baylor U., 1969; m. Allen Oswald Beasley, Sept. 6, 1975; stepchildren—Gwendolyn Beasley Clemens, Ossie Allen Beasley, Michelle Beasley Campbell. Commd. 2d lt. U.S. Army, 1960, advanced through grades to lt. col., 1979; dietetic intern Walter Reed Army Med. Center, Washington, 1960-61; chief prodn. and service br. Food Service Div., Irwin Army Hosp., Ft. Riley, Kans., 1961-63; asst. instr. Kans. State U., Manhattan, 1963-64; asst. chief Clin. Dietetics Br., Food Service Div., Walter Reed Army Med. Center, Washington, 1964-67; dietetic cons. 43d Med. Group, Rep. of Vietnam, 1969-70; dir. Food Service Div., 2d Gen. Hosp., Landstuhl, Germany, 1970-72; chief clin. dietetics br. Food Service Div., Walter Reed Army Med. Center, Washington, 1972-73, chief prodn. and service br., 1973-75; dir. Food Service Div., Martin Army Hosp., Ft. Benning, Ga., 1975-80; ret., 1980; adj. instr. Coordinated undergrad. program in dietetics Auburn (Ala.) U., 1977-80. Decorated Legion of Merit, Army Commendation medals with 2 oak leaf clusters, Bronze Star medal, Meritorious Service medal; lic. and registered dietitian. Mem. Citrus County Hist. Soc. (pres. 1984-86, v.p., mus. chmn. 1986—), Citrus County Fair Assn. (dir.), Brentwood Found. (bd. dirs.), DAR, Phi Mu. Episcopalian. Club: Floral Garden (judge student flower show 1984—), Citrus County Rose Soc. Lodge: Order Eastern Star. Home: 9626 E Tsala Apopka Dr Floral City FL 32636 Office: Room 105 Old Courthouse 110 N Apopka Dr Inverness FL 32650

BEASLEY, MAURINE HOFFMAN, journalism educator, historian; b. Sedalia, Mo., Jan. 28, 1936; d. Dimmitt Heard and Maurine (Hieronymous) Hoffman; m. William C. McLaughlin, May 20, 1966 (div. 1969); m. 2d, Henry R. Beasley, Dec. 24, 1970; 1 dau., Susan Sook. B.J., B.A. in History, U. Mo., 1958; M.S. in Journalism, Columbia U., 1963; Ph.D. in Am. Civilization, George Washington U., 1974; Cert. in Brit. History, U. Edinburgh, Scotland, 1964. Edn. editor Kansas City (Mo.) Star, 1959-62; staff writer Washington Post, 1963-73; asst. prof. journalism U. Md., College Park, 1975-80, assoc. prof., 1980—. Author: (with others) Women in Media, 1977; editor: (with others) Voice of Change: Southern Pulitzer Winners, 1978, One Third of a Nation (hon. mention Washington Monthly Book Award 1982), 1981; editor: White House Press Conferences of Eleanor Roosevelt, 1983; mem. adv. bd. Am. Journalism, 1983—; contbr. articles to acad. jours. Violinist, Montgomery Coll. Symphony Orch., 1975—. Gannett Teaching Fellowships Program fellow, 1977; Pulitzer traveling fellow Columbia U., 1963; Eleanor Roosevelt studies grantee Eleanor Roosevelt Inst., 1979-80; named one of nation's outstanding tchrs. of writing and editing Modern Media Inst. and Am. Soc. Newspaper Editors, 1981. Mem. Assn. Edn. in Journalism and Mass Communications (standing com. on profl. freedom and responsibility 1985), Am. News Women's Club (bd. govs. 1986-87), Women in Communications (bd. dirs. Washington chpt. 1985-86), Nat. Fedn. Press Women, Phi Beta Kappa. Democrat. Unitarian. Home: 4920 Flint Dr Bethesda MD 20816 Office: College of Journalism U of Maryland College Park MD 20742

BEASLEY, NORMA LEA, land titles and real estate executive, lawyer; b. Springdale, Ark., Sept. 6, 1931; d. Alpha F. and Minnie Lee (Parham) B. LL.B., U. Ark., 1953, B.S., 1960; postgrad. So. Meth. U., 1958-60. Bar: Ark. 1953, Tex. 1958, Fed. cts. 1953, 58. With legal dept. Mid-Continent Petroleum Corp., Tulsa, 1953; with claims dept. Res. Life Ins. Co., Dallas, 1955-56; head exec. legal dept. Tex. Title Co., 1956-61; sole practice, Dallas, 1958—; house counsel, v.p. Fidelity Title Co., Dallas, 1961-68; ptnr. B&W Investments, Dallas, 1962—; chief exec. officer, chmn. bd. Trinity Abstract & Title Co., Waxahachie, Tex., 1966—; owner, mgr. Hillcrest office Hexter-Fair Title Co., Dallas, 1968-79; chmn. bd., chief exec. officer Safeco Land Title of Dallas, 1979—, Safeco Land Title of Kaufman, Safeco Land Title of Rockwall, North Tex. Title of Hunt, Safeco Land Title of Collin, Safeco Land Title of Denton, Safeco Land Title of Tarrant County; vice chmn. bd. Tex. Am. Bank-Prestonwood; mem. adv. bd. Tex. Nat. Bank, Dallas; organizer new Charter Nat. Bank, Plano, Tex.; dir. Coming Attractions, Inc., Jami, M.D. Labs. and Verarex Med. Corp.; co-ptnr. B P W Investments. Mem. Dallas Council on World Affairs, 1966, Citizens Traffic Commn., Dallas, 1965; campaign helper Multiple Sclerosis Soc., Dallas, 1967; bd. dirs. Dallas Juvenile Diabetes Found.; lectr. to various colls. and organizations; charter mem. Charter "100" Club of Dallas. Recipient Disting. Alumni award U. Ark. Sch. Law, 1986, U. Ark. Alumni Assn., 1986; founder Marie Mivelaz Scholarship fund at So. Meth. U. Mem. Ark. Bar Assn., Tex. Bar Assn., Dallas County Jr. Bar Assn., Bus. and Profl. Women's Club, Kappa Beta Phi (Eta Sigma Phi chpt.). Republican. Baptist. Clubs: Altrusa (treas. 1964-65), Bent Tree Country (Dallas). Office: Safeco Land Title of Dallas 8080 N Central Expressway Suite 120 Dallas TX 75206

BEATON-SIMMONS, KAREN, fundraiser; b. Providence, Mar. 9, 1944; d. Allan and Arlene Beaton; B.A., U. R.I., 1965; M.Ed., U. Ga., 1974; m. 1965 (div.); children—Laura, Andrew. Speech pathologist, 1965-79; part-time faculty U. R.I., 1978-79; dir. ann. giving Bryant Coll., Smithfield, R.I., 1979-80, dir. devel., 1980-83; v.p. membership services Greater Providence C. of C., 1983-84; dir. pub. relations and devel. Jewish Home for the Aged, 1985—; pvt. practice speech pathology, Cranston, R.I., 1979-81. Mem. State Advs. for Gifted Edn., 1980—, pres., 1980-81; mem. nat. adv. council Small Bus. Adminstrn., 1983-85. Mem. Nat. Soc. Fundraising Execs., New Eng. Assn. Hosp. Devel., Leadership R.I., Alpha Chi Omega, Kappa Delta Pi. Baptist (choir, deaconess). Office: Bryant Coll Box 40 Smithfield RI 02917

BEATTIE, ANN, novelist; b. Washington, Sept. 8, 1947; d. James and Charlotte (Crosby) B.; m. David Gates, June 5, 1973; 1 child, Rufus. B.A., Am. U., 1969; M.A., U. Conn., 1970. Vis. asst. prof. U. Va., Charlottesville, 1976-77, vis. writer, 1980; Briggs Copeland lectr. English, Harvard U., Cambridge, Mass., 1977. Author: Chilly Scenes of Winter, 1976; Distortions, 1976; Secrets and Surprises, 1979; Falling in Place, 1980; Jacklighting, 1981; The Burning House, 1982; author numerous short stories; lectr. profl. confs.; contbr. articles profl. jours. and popular mags. Recipient Disting. Alumnae award Am. U., 1980, award in lit. Am. Acad. and Inst. Arts and Letters, 1980, grantee, 1980; Guggenheim fellow, 1977. Mem. PEN, Authors Guild.

BEATTIE, BETTY LORENE, realtor; b. La Harpe, Ill., Nov. 30, 1927; d. Cecil William and Helen Caroline (Wilke) Shugart; m. John Feree Hamman, May 26, 1945 (div. 1964); children—Michael, Mark; m. 2d, Jacques Boni, Dec. 23, 1968. Student pub. schs., Abingdon, Ill. Adminstr. Knox Manor, Galesburg, Ill., 1970-72; realtor assoc. Dick Rozynek, Galesburg, 1972-80; realtor, owner Hamrick-Beattie Realtors, Galesburg, 1980—. Republican. Presbyterian. Office: Hamrick-Beattie Realtors 1383 N Henderson St Galesburg IL 61401

BEATTIE, NORA MAUREEN, ins. co. exec.; b. Bklyn., July 10, 1925; d. Robert Gamble and Eileen Benedict (Geaney) B.; B.A. summa cum laude, St. John's U., 1947, M.S., 1949, D. Comml. Sci. (hon.), 1980. With N.Y. Life Ins. Co., N.Y.C., 1948—, v.p., actuary 1974—; actuary, dir. N.Y. Life Ins. and Annuity Corp.; treas., dir. N.Y. Guarantee Corp. Mem. Soc. Actuaries, Am. Acad. Actuaries, Bus. and Profl. Women's Club. Republican. Roman Catholic. Office: NY Life Ins Co 51 Madison Ave New York NY 10010

BEATTY, CAROL LEE, insurance company executive; b. Youngstown, Ohio, May 21, 1951; d. Richard McKinley Beatty and Donna Carol (Harris) Beatty Cracraft. B.A. in English, Youngstown State U., 1973, postgrad., 1973-74. C.P.C.U. Substitute tchr. Mahoning County Schs., Youngstown, 1973-74; bookkeeper Lake Park Tool & Die Co., Youngstown, 1974-76; comml. property underwriter St. Paul Fire & Marine, Cin., also Bloomington, Ill., 1976-79, ins. instr. employee relations, St. Paul, 1979-80, traveling rep. employee relations, 1980-82, employee relations adminstr., 1982-84, project mgr. flexible benefits, 1982-83, program mgr. comml. ins., 1984—. speaker various profl. groups; working mem. Minn. Coalition on Health Care Costs, Mpls., 1983—. Vol. cons. Daytons Bluff Neighborhood Housing Services, St. Paul, 1983—. Mem. Soc. C.P.C.U.s, Twin City Personnel Assn., Am. Soc. for Personnel Adminstrn. Methodist. Clubs: Der Skilaufers Ski (1st v.p. 1982-83),

Capitol Ski, Bridge, Book (St. Paul). Home: 780 W Hoyt Ave Saint Paul MN 55117 Office: St Paul Fire and Marine 385 Washington St Saint Paul MN 55102

BEATTY, CAROLYN ANN, educator; b. Pitts., Apr. 17, 1942; d. Charles Anderson and Manualla Grace (Snyder) Beatty. B.A. in English, History, U. Houston, 1964; M.Ed., Houston Bapt. U., 1981; Cert., U. London, U. Liverpool, 1968. Tchr. Johnston Middle Sch., Houston, 1964—; cons. Fed. Land Bank, Houston, 1982; mem. central textbook com. Houston Ind. Sch., 1978; mem. instructional council Johnston Middle Sch., Houston, 1978—, mem. faculty adv. com., 1976-78, 1980—. Author: (with others) Pre-International Baccalaureate Program Grade 7, 1982-83. Vol. Meth. Hosp. Service Corps, Mus. Fine Arts, Harris County Heritage Soc., Channel 8 (Pub. TV). Mem. Houston Area Council Tchrs. English (pres. 1976), Tex. Council Tchrs. English (state workshop chmn. 1976), Nat. Council Tchrs. English (bd. dirs. 1975-77), Congress Houston Tchrs., Nat. Assn. Secondary Dept. Chmn., Delta Kappa Gamma (pres. 1978-80), Kappa Delta Pi, Kappa Kappa Iota (historian 1983—), Beta Sigma Phi (pres. 1968-70). Club: College Women's (Houston). Office: Johnston Middle Sch 10410 Manhattan St Houston TX 77025

BEATTY-DESANA, JEANNE WARREN, cytogeneticist, consultant, educator; b. Tuscaloosa, Ala., Sept. 18, 1920; d. William Charles and Anna Belle (Rice) Warren; B.S., U. Ala., Tuscaloosa, 1946; M.S. (fellow), Emory U., 1952; cert. tutorial-human cytogenetics U. Chgo., 1972; m. Alvin V. Beatty, May 23, 1951 (dec.); m. 2d, James A. DeSana, May 28, 1970; children—Susan Warren Beatty, Jane Warren Beatty. Research assoc. biology dept. Emory U., Atlanta, 1952-70; dir. cytogenetics services Ga. Retardation Center, Atlanta, 1970—; adj. assoc. prof. biology Ga. State U., Atlanta, 1972—; cons. Fernbank Sci. Center, DeKalb County, Ga., 1975—; cons. cytogenetics Scottish Rite Hosp., Atlanta, 1979—; mem. Genetics Task Force, State of Ga., 1978, 79, Biosafety com. Ga. Inst. Tech., 1980—; mem. nat. com. Cytogenetics Proficiency testing HEW, Center for Disease Control, 1978-79. Recipient Profl. of Yr. award Assn. Retarded Citizens, Atlanta, 1979, service to Youth award Hi-Y and Tri-Hi-Y Clubs, Decatur-De Kalb YMCA, 1980, Outstanding research award (with A.V. Beatty), Assn. SE Biologists, 1960, 63, 64, Outstanding Achievement award Emory U. Women's Club, 1956, Sigma Xi Research award Emory U., 1955, Woman of Achievement award Cumming-Forsyth Bus and Profl. Women's Club, 1983; Atomic Energy grantee (with A.V. Beatty), 1952-70. Mem. Atlanta Genetics Soc. (dir. 1971-81, chmn. 1973-75, 1978-80), AAAS (mem. S.E. sect. adv. com. 1978-79), Assn. S.E. Biologists, Ga. Conservancy (dir. 1968-71), Am. Soc. Human Genetics (program com. Atlanta meeting 1973), Mammalian Cell Genetics Soc. Contbr. articles to profl. publs. Home: 122 Greenwood Dr Box 601 Cumming GA 30130 Office: Ga Retardation Center Cytogenetics Sect 4770 N Peachtree St Atlanta GA 30338

BEATY, REBECCA LYNNE, media executive; b. Raleigh, N.C., Apr. 3, 1953; d. James Robert and Mabel Grey (Parker) B. B.A. in Sociology, N.C. State U., 1975. Media buyer, media planner McKinney Silver & Rockett, Raleigh, N.C., 1976-84; media dir. Hodskins Simone & Searls, Raleigh, 1985-86; media dir. Rockett & Burkhead, Raleigh, 1986—. Actor, technician Raleigh Little Theatre, 1979—. Recipient Charles V. York Vol. Service award Raleigh Little Theatre, 1981-82. Mem. Nat. Assn. Female Execs., Raleigh Music Club. Democrat. Baptist. Avocations: music; theatre; golf. Home: 4319 Lake Ridge Dr Raleigh NC 27604 Office: Rockett & Burkhead 6501 Six Forks Rd Raleigh NC 27609

BEAUCHAMP, DANIELLE MARIE, research editor; b. Paris, May 30, 1950; d. William Ellsworth and Veronica Ellen (Klimek) Beauchamp; m. Michael Francis Barrett, Jr.; 1 child, Elizabeth Veronica Winifred. B.A., Vassar Coll., 1972; M.P.A., Harvard U., 1979. Editor, Library of Congress, Washington, 1972; legis. asst. to Jaime Benitez, Resident Commr. from P.R., U.S. Ho. of Reps., Washington, 1973; research analyst energy and power subcom. U.S. Ho. of Reps., Washington, 1975-81; energy cons. McKinsey & Co., Washington, 1981-83; mgmt. cons. Home Health Line pub. group, Port Republic, Md., 1983-85, research editor Nat. Geographic Mag., 1985—. Mem. job discrimination study Capitol Hill Women's Polit. Caucus, 1975. Matthew Vassar scholar, 1968, 69. Mem. AAAS, Am. Soc. Public Adminstrn., Washington Assn. Profl. Anthropologists, Women's Council on Energy and the Environment (bd. dirs. 1983—, pres. 1985-86), Kennedy Sch. Alumni Assn. (exec. council 1980-84), Mensa, Phi Beta Kappa. Clubs: Vassar (class rep. to alumnae council 1982-86), Harvard. Home: 241 G St SW Washington DC 20024 Office: 1145 17th St NW Washington DC 20036

BEAUDOIN, CAROL ANN, psychologist; b. Lowell, Mass., Mar. 30, 1949; d. Adrien P. and Rita J. (LeBlanc) B.; B.A. with honors, U. Fla., 1971; M.Ed. in Counseling, Boston U., 1973, Ed.D. in Counseling Psychology, 1979. Psychiat. aide U. Fla.-Shands Teaching Hosp., Gainesville, 1970-71; trainee VA Hosp., Gainesville, 1971-72; attendant Boston State Hosp., 1972, intern, 1973; intern Univ. Hosp., also Counseling Center, Northeastern U., Boston, 1973-74, Dorchester Mental Health Center, also Carney Hosp., 1974-75; staff psychologist Human Resource Inst., Boston, 1974-80, treatment team leader, 1975-80; pvt. practice psychology, Brookline, Mass., 1980—. Mem. Am. Psychol. Assn. Office: 1101 Beacon St Brookline MA 02146

BEAUFAIT, DORIS ELAINE O'DONNELL, reporter; b. Cleve., June 21, 1921; d. John Laurence and Stella Agnes O'Donnell; student Case Western Res. U., 1940-44, John Carroll U., 1944-47; m. Howard Beaufait, Sept. 1957. With Cleve. News, 1944-58, Cleve. Plain Dealer, 1958-59; with Cleve. Zool. Soc., 1959-62; staff Univ. Hosps., Cleve., 1961-63; reporter Cleve. Plain Dealer, 1963-70; with News-Herald, Willoughby, Ohio, 1970-71, Office of the Mayor, Cleve., 1972-73; investigative reporter/writer Tribune Rev., Greensburg, Pa., 1973—. Mem. Pa. Jud. Merit Selection Commn., Westmoreland County, 1980-81. Mem. Ligionier Valley Hist. Soc., Women in Communications, Pa. Newspaper Women's Assn., Theta Sigma Phi, Sigma Delta Chi. Roman Catholic. Club: Press. Contbr. articles to profl. jours. Home: 180 Old Forbes Rd Ligonier PA 15658

BEAUMONT, MONA MAGDELEINE, artist; b. Paris, Jan. 1, 1927; came to U.S., 1942, naturalized, 1945; d. Jacques Hippolyte and Elsie M. (Didisheim) Marx; B.A., U. Calif., Berkeley, 1945, M.A., 1946; postgrad. Harvard U., 1945-46, Fogg Mus., Cambridge, 1945-46, Hans Hoffman Studios, N.Y.C., 1946; m. William G. Beaumont, Dec. 20, 1946; children—Garrett, Kevin. One-woman shows at Galeria Proteo, Mexico City, 1960, Gumps Gallery, San Francisco, 1962, 64, 65, Palace of Legion of Honor, San Francisco, 1964, L'Armitiere Gallery, Rouen, France, 1966, Hoover Gallery, San Francisco, 1967, San Francisco Mus. Modern Art, 1968, Galeria Van der Voort, San Francisco, 1969, William Sawyer Gallery, San Francisco, 1972, Palo Alto (Calif.) Cultural Center, 1975, Galerie Alexandre Monnet, Brussels, 1974, Honolulu Acad. Arts, 1980; exhibited in group shows at San Francisco Mus. Modern Art, 1954, 57, 68, San Francisco Art Inst., 1958-74, DeYoung Meml. Mus., San Francisco, 1960-62, Grey Found. Tour of Asia, 1963, Bell Telephone Invitational, Chgo., 1968, Richmond Art Center, 1968, Los Angeles County Mus. Art, 1973, Galerie Zodiaque, Geneva, 1974, others; represented in permanent collections: Oakland (Calif.) Mus. Art, City and County of San Francisco, Hoover Found., San Francisco, Grey Found., Washington, Bulart Found., San Francisco; also numerous pvt. collections. Recipient Jack London Sq. Ann. Painting award, 1965; Purchase award Grey Found., 1963; Ann. award San Francisco Women Artists, 1966, 68; Purchase award San Francisco Art Festival, 1966; One-Man Show award San Francisco Art Festival, 1975. Mem. Soc. for Encouragement of Contemporary Art, Bay Area Graphic Arts Council, San Francisco Art Inst., San Francisco Mus. Modern Art, Delta Epsilon, Delta Chi Alpha. Address: 1087 Upper Happy Valley Rd Lafayette CA 94549

BEAUPRE, LINDA JOANNE LYLE, librarian; b. Oakland, Calif., Aug. 5, 1943; d. John Gunnar and Virginia Helen (Johnson) Lyle; A.B. in History, U. Calif., Berkeley, 1965; A.M.L.S., U. Mich., 1967; m. Mark E. Cain, Mar. 15, 1985. Supr. microform reading room, periodicals reading room, interlibrary loan unit at grad. library U. Mich., 1967-69; mem. library staff U. Calif., Berkeley, 1969-78, reference, coll. devel. librarian Moffitt Undergrad. Library, 1969-72, coordinator public services Moffitt Undergrad. Library, 1972-75, adminstrv. asst. to assoc. univ. librarian for public services, 1977-78, instr. bibliography I, 1971, 74-75; head librarian reference services dept. gen. libraries, then acting asst. dir. public services U. Tex., Austin, 1978-80, assoc. dir. public services, 1980-84, assoc. dir., 1984—. Council Library Resources acad. library mgmt. intern, 1975-76. UCLA sr. fellow, 1985. Mem. ALA, Tex. Library Assn., Tex. Assn. Coll. Tchrs., ACLU, Sierra Club. Author articles in field. Editorial bd. Jour. Acad. Librarianship, 1980-83. Office: Gen Libraries PCL 3 200 U Tex Austin TX 78713

BEAUSOLEIL, DORIS MAE, housing specialist, govt. agy. ofcl.; b. Chelmsford, Mass., Jan. 9, 1932; d. Joseph Honorius and Beatrice Pearl (Smith) B.; student State Tchrs. Coll., Lowell, Mass., 1949-51; B.A. in Sociology and Psychology, Goddard Coll., Plainfield, Vt., 1954; M.A. in Human Relations, N.Y. U., 1957. With div. human rights N.Y. State, N.Y.C., 1960-69, housing dir., 1966-68; housing cons. Nat. Com. Against Discrimination in Housing, N.Y.C., 1969-70; housing cons. Edwin Gould Found., N.Y.C., 1970-71; human resources cons. interfaith housing strategy com., housing cons. Fedn. Prot. Welfare Agencies, Inc., N.Y.C., 1971-72; self-employed housing cons., 1972-74; equal opportunity compliance specialist Region II HUD, N.Y.C., 1975—, Fed. women's program coordinator, 1975-79; br. chief Title VI Sect. 109 Compliance div. fair housing and equal opportunity Region II, HUD, N.Y.C., 1979-84; founding mem. N.Y. State HUD Com.; adv. panel Housing Mag., 1979; cons., examiner N.Y. State Civil Service Commn., 1970—. Mem. Nat. Assn. Human Rights Workers (Outstanding Service award 1974), Citizens Housing and Planning Council, Federally Employed Women, Nat. Assn. Housing and Devel. Ofcls. Republican. Unitarian. Clubs: Women's City N.Y., Rep. Bus. Women's (N.Y.C.) (pres. 1985). Home: 392 Central Park W New York NY 10025 Office: 26 Federal Plaza Room 3532 New York NY 10278

BEAVER, BONNIE VERYLE, veterinarian, educator; b. Mpls., Oct. 26, 1944; d. Crawford F. and Gladys I. Gustafson; B.S., U. Minn., 1966, D.V.M., 1968; M.S., Tex. A&M U., 1972; m. Larry J. Beaver, Nov. 25, 1972. Instr. vet. surgery and radiology U. Minn., 1968-69; instr. vet. anatomy Tex. A&M U., College Station, 1969-72, asst. prof., 1972-76, asso. prof., 1976-82, prof., 1982-86, prof. vet. small animal medicine and surgery, 1986—. Vice pres. Brazos Valley Regional Sci. and Engrng. Fair, 1974-83, dir., 1983-85; bd. dirs. Am. Cancer Soc., Brazos Valley unit, 1976-83, v.p., 1977-83. Named Citizen of Week, The Press, 1981, Outstanding Woman Veterinarian Assn. Women Veterinarians, 1982. Mem. AVMA, Tex. Vet. Med. Assn., Brazos Valley Vet. Med. Assn., Am. Animal Hosp. Assn., Animal Behavior Soc., Am. Soc. Vet. Ethology, Am. Assn. Vet. Clinicians, Am. Vet. Computer Soc., Assn. Am. Vet. Med. Colls., Phi Sigma, Sigma Epsilon Sigma, Phi Zeta, Phi Delta Gamma. Author or Co-author 5 books; contbr. numerous articles on vet. medicine to profl. jours.; editorial bd. Applied Animal Ethology, 1981-84, VM/SAC, 1982-85, Applied Animal Behavior Sci., 1983—. Home: RFD 3 Box 354 College Station TX 77840 Office: College of Vet Medicine Texas A&M College Station TX 77843

BEAVERS, JESSIE MAE (MRS. LEROY A. BEAVERS), journalist; b. Los Angeles; d. Albert and Arnette Marie (Hoyt) Brown; m. LeRoy A. Beavers, Jr., June 27, 1948; children—Deborah Elaine, LeRoy Albert, Kimberly Arnetta. Social columnist Calif. Eagle, Los Angeles, 1940-48; social editor family sect. Los Angeles Sentinel, 1949-83, exec. editor family sect., 1983—; cons. So. Calif. Gas Co., 1959-61, Calif. Turkey Adv. Bd., 1962-64. Mem. Los Angeles Human Relations Commn., 1972—, pres., 1973-77, mem. Los Angeles County Music and Performing Arts Commn., 1976; bd. dirs. Stovall Found., Los Angeles School Vols. and Doves. Recipient Arch Angel award Los Angeles Bus. Assn., 1967; Ida B. Wells award Nat. Assn. Media Women, 1968; Mary McLeod Bethune award Nat. Council Negro Women, 1973; Ambassador of Goodwill award Women for Good Govt., 1973; Vol. Activist award Germaine Monteil, 1972; Human Relations award Soodo Women's U., Seoul, Korea, 1977. Mem. Nat. Assn. Media Women (founder Los Angeles chpt., 1965, Founder's Cup award, 1975), Women in Communications, Calif. Human Relations Assn., Links, Alpha Kappa Alpha, Iota Phi Lambda. Baptist. Office: 1112 E 43d St Los Angeles CA 90011

BEAVERS, MARIELLA ANN, histotechnologist; b. Aschaffenburg, W.Ger., Dec. 9, 1953; came to U.S., 1955; d. Joseph George and Elizabeth Marie (Valter) Pencak; m. Nov. 12, 1979 (div. Dec. 1982); 1 child, Kimberly Dyan. Cert. histotechnologist Am. Soc. Clin. Pathologists. Histologist, Mullins' Pathology and Cytology Lab., Augusta, Ga., 1972-73, Univ. Hosp., Augusta, 1973; lab. ckl. Doctors Hosp. Augusta, 1973-74; histologist-asst. supr. Ga. Bapt. Med. Ctr., Atlanta, 1974-80; histologist Kaiser Found. Hosp., Clackamas, Oreg., 1980-81, Houston Northwest Med. Ctr., Tex., 1982—. Democrat. Methodist. Office: Houston Northwest Med Ctr 710 FM 1960 W Houston TX 77090

BEBELLE, CAROL FRANCES, city official; b. New Orleans, Sept. 4, 1949; d. George Donald and Evelyn (Smith) Bebelle Rattler. B.A., Loyola U., New Orleans, 1970; M.Ed., Tulane U., 1973. Planning asst. Orleans Sch. Bd., 1970-74; planner Mayor's Bur. Drugs, New Orleans, 1974-81; spl. adminstrv. services coordinator New Orleans Health Dept., 1981—; instr. Loyola U., 1976-79; cons. Orleans Sch. Bd., 1983. Chmn. youth com. New Orleans Mayors Adv. Council Youth and Drugs, 1983. Named Woman of Yr., Mayor's Bur. Drug Affairs, 1975. Mem. Nat. Inst. Drug Abuse, Black Womens Council (chmn. membership 1983-84), Black Woman's Group, Women's Edn. Service Assn., Nat. Alliance Coalitions, Kappa Delta Phi. Democrat. Home: 1029 Hillary St New Orleans LA 70118 Office: New Orleans Health Dept 1300 Perdido St Room 8E13 New Orleans LA 70112

BECCARI, NANCY JUDITH HALL (MRS. ARMANO A. BECCARI), educator; b. Marietta, Ohio; d. Robert Earl and Bernice (Underwood) Hall; B.A. cum laude, U. Miami, 1958, M.Ed., 1961, postgrad., 1970—; m. Turner M. Hiers, Oct. 29, 1942; m. Armano A. Beccari, Aug. 31, 1974. Tchr. pub. schs., Ga., Fla.; dir. Reading Center, Nova High Sch., Fort Lauderdale, Fla., 1963—, Lauderdale Reading Clinic, 1965—. Author: Little Pitchers With Big Ears. Mem. Internat. Reading Assn., Am. Ednl. Research Assn., AAUW, Nat. Soc. for Study Edn., Kappa Delta Pi, Alpha Delta Kappa, Kappa Kappa Iota, Epsilon Tau Lambda, Phi Lambda Pi. Clubs: Le Club Internationale, Rolls Royce Owners. Home: 4000 NW 9th Ct Coconut Creek FL 33162

BECHT, JANET REGINA, lawyer; b. Springfield, Ohio, May 27, 1950; d. John Anthony and Marjorie Catherine (Conrad) B. B.S., U. Dayton, 1972, M.S., 1973; J.D., Ohio No. U., 1980. Bar: Ohio, 1983. Social worker Clark County Childrens Services, Springfield, 1973-75, Bethany Home, Moline, Ill., 1975-76; office mgr. Catholic Social Services, Sidney, Ohio, 1976-78; atty. Rural Legal Aid, Springfield, 1981—; Title III coordinator, supervising atty. Rural Legal Aid, Troy, Ohio; instr. Saturday Morning Enrichment Program, Wright State U., Dayton, 1981-83. Grad. asst. U. Dayton, 1972. Mem. ABA, Ohio Bar Assn., Miami County Bar Assn., Assn. Trial Lawyers Am., Phi Alpha Delta (marshall 1979-80). Democrat. Roman Catholic. Home: 243 Floral Ave Springfield OH 45503 Office: Rural Legal Aid of West Central Ohio 12 W Main St Troy OH 45373

BECK, AUDREY, data management company executive; b. Mpls., July 23, 1954; d. John George and Shirley Hope (Dahley) Neis. Student, Hennepin County Vo-Tech. Coll. Software engr. CPT Corp., Mpls., 1978-85, Datamyte Corp., Minnetonka, Minn., 1985; sr. system support rep. Moore Data Mgmt. Services, Mpls., 1985—; computer contractor, Mpls., 1980—. Avocations: programming; electronics; horses; carpentry. Home: 4694 West Arm Rd Spring Park MN 55384 Office: Moore Data Mgmt Services 1660 South Hwy 100 Minneapolis MN 55416

BECK, DOROTHY FAHS, social researcher; b. N.Y.C.; d. Charles Harvey and Sophia (Lyon) Fahs; A.B., U. N.C., 1928; M.A., U. Chgo., 1932; Ph.D. (Gilder fellow), Columbia U., 1944, postdoctoral study, 1955-56; Am.-German Student Exchange fellow, Germany, 1928-29; m. Hubert Park Beck, Aug. 20, 1930; 1 child, Brenda E.F. Dir. econ. research ADA, 1929-32; social worker Emergency Relief Adminstrn. N.J., 1933-34; statistician N.Y. State Emergency Relief Adminstrn., 1934-35, U.S. Office Edn., 1935-36; asso. social economist U.S. Central Statis. Bd., 1936-38; research supr., author Am. Coll. Dentists, 1940-42; statistician Am. Heart Assn., 1947-53, Cornell U. Med. Coll., part-time 1951-53; asst. prof. biostats. Am. U. Beirut, part-time 1954; dir. research Family Service Am., N.Y.C., 1956-81, dir. study counselor attitudes and feelings, 1982—, evaluation research cons., 1982—. Fellow Am. Sociol. Assn.; mem. Acad. Cert. Social Workers, Am. Assn. Marriage and Family Therapy (affiliate), Nat. Council Family Relations, Groves Conf., Am. Statis. Assn., Nat. Assn. Social Workers, Soc. Study Social Problems, Am. Pub. Health Assn., Phi Beta Kappa. Liberal. Unitarian-Universalist. Author: Patterns in Use of Family Agency Service, 1962; Marriage and the Family Under Challenge, 1976; New Treatment Modalities, 1978; How Counselor Characteristics Affect Outcomes, 1986; co-author: Costs of Dental Care Under Specific Clinical Conditions, 1943; Myocardial Infarction, 1954; Clients' Progress within Five Interviews, 1970; How to Conduct a Client Follow-Up Study, 1974, 2d enlarged edit., 1980; Progress on Family Problems, 1973. Home: 523 W 121st St New York NY 10027 Office: Family Service Am 254 W 31st St New York NY 10001

BECK, JANE MARIA, display company owner; b. Chgo. Dec. 27, 1930; d. Joseph Herman and Josephine Maria (Vigil) Bertolone; children—Gema, Sally, Michael. Owner, Economy Home Improvement Co., 1949-57, Jane's Hideaway Club, 1950-57; McCormick Display, Cicero, Ill., 1966—. Mem. Am. Soc. Assn. Execs., Carpenters Union, Cicero C. of C., Cicero Mfg. Assn. Democrat. Roman Catholic. Home: 5104 S Lawler Ave Chicago IL 60650 Office: McCormick Display 1800 S 54th Ave Cicero IL 60650

BECK, JOAN WAGNER, journalist; b. Clinton, Iowa, Sept. 5, 1923; d. Roscoe Charles and Mildred (Noel) Wagner; B.J. cum laude, Northwestern U., 1945, M.S. in Journalism, 1947; m. Ernest William Beck, Sept. 9, 1945; children—Christopher, Melinda. Radio script writer O.W.I. Voice of Am., 1945-46; copy writer Marshall Field & Co., 1947-50; feature writer Chgo. Tribune, 1950—, writer syndicated column about young people, 1956-61, syndicated column about children, 1961-72, editor daily features sect., 1972-75, mem. editorial bd., 1975—, syndicated editorial page columnist, 1974—. Hon. chmn. Mother's March of Met. Chgo. chpt. Nat. Found. March of Dimes, 1970-75; trustee Ill. Children's Home and Aid Soc., from 1971; mem. Women's Bd. Northwestern U. Recipient AP award for best newspaper feature series award, Ill., 1964, best feature, 1966, best columns, 1983, 84; Alumni Merit award Northwestern U., 1965, 77, Alumnae award, 1977; Nat. award of Achievement, Alpha Chi Omega, 1966; 1st place award Penney-U. Mo., 1973; UPI Ill. award for editorial writing, 1984; 1st place award for commentary Ednl. Writers Assn., 1986; Concern for Children award Children's Meml. Hosp., 1986. Mem. Chgo. Press Club, Chgo. Network, Chgo. Headline Club, Theta Sigma Phi, Alpha Chi Omega. Methodist. Clubs: Northwestern; Lake Forest. Author: How to Raise a Brighter Child, 1967; (with Dr. Virginia Apgar) Is My Baby All Right?, 1973; Effective Parenting, 1976; Best Beginnings, 1983. Home: 905 Castlegate Ct Lake Forest IL 60045 Office: Chgo Tribune 435 N Michigan Ave Chicago IL 60611

BECK, JOYCE, safety and occupational health specialist, author; b. Las Cruces, N.Mex., Oct. 4, 1954; d. George Robert and Alice (Romero) Jiron; m. Bobby Lyn Beck, July 31, 1976 (dec. Nov. 1982). A.A., El Paso Community Coll., 1985; postgrad. N.Mex. State U., 1985-86. Sr. billing clk. R.E. Gen. Hosp., El Paso, Tex., 1972-73; sec. U.S. Army, White Sands, N.Mex., 1974-82, safety and occupational health specialist, 1982—. Author: Ever, Never, Sometimes, 1978; Songs of the Crystal Night, 1981; Great Treasury of World Poems, 1981; The American Muse, 1984. Counselor, Widowed Persons Service, El Paso, 1982—. Mem. Federally Employed Women, Feminist Writers Guild, NOW, Nat. Assn. Female Execs., Nat. Women's Studies Assn., Hispanic/Black Com. Democrat. Roman Catholic. Avocations: writing; handicrafts; painting; sports; motorcycle riding; music. Home: 10285 Cermac St El Paso TX 79924 Office: US Army White Sands Missile Range White Sands NM 88002

BECK, KAREN LYNN, design coordinator, art curator; b. N.Y.C., Dec. 3, 1941; d. Edward and Lillian Marker; student N.Y.C. Community Coll., 1959-61, N.Y.U., 1961-62, New Sch., 1963-64, Ramapo Coll., 1976-77; children—Marni Jill, Julia Dawn. Owner antique bus., Vt. and N.Y., 1965-68; interior designer and antique restorer, 1968-78; ptnr. Interiors Group, Tenafly, N.J., 1978-85; design coordinator, arts curator Robert Martin Co., Elmsford, N.Y., 1985—. Active community art projects, programs to foster arts and emerging artists. Mem. Nat. Assn. Female Execs., Whitney Mus., Smithsonian Instn. Jewish. Home: 40 Dawn Ln Suffern NY 10901 Office: 101 Exec Blvd Elmsford NY 10523

BECK, MARGIT, artist; b. Tokay, Hungary; d. Samuel and Johanna (Blau) Beck; student Art Inst. of Oradeamare (Rumania), Student League, N.Y.C., 1945-46; m. Sidney Schwartz; children—Joan, John. Came to U.S., naturalized, 1938. Theatrical scenic designer formerly mem. art faculty Hofstra U.; now asst. prof. art faculty NYU, Empire State Coll., N.Y. State U., until 1979; exhibited works in one-man shows Contemporary Arts, N.Y.C., 1955, 58, 59, San Joquin Mus., Stockton, Calif., 1956, Hofstra Coll., L.I., 1958, Lincoln High Sch., N.Y.C., 1959, Mus. Fine Arts, Greenville, S.C., 1959, Babcock Gallery, N.Y.C., 1962, 64, 66, 68, 71, 72, 73, Phila. Art Alliance, 1968, Mansfield (Pa.) State Coll., 1965, Queens Coll., N.Y.C., 1973, Port Washington (N.Y.) Library, 1978; Mus. Fin. Art, Wichita, Kans., 1980, U. Wyo., 1980; exhibited in group shows Whitney Mus. Ann., Corcoran Biennial, Chgo. Art Inst. Ann., Pa. Acad. Ann., Allentown (Pa.) Mus. Fine Arts, Lehigh U., Bethlehem, Pa., Bklyn. Mus. Internat. W.C. Biennial NAD Ann., Butler Inst. Ann., U. Nebr. Ann., Springfield (Mass.) Mus., Akron Art Inst., Am. Acad. Arts and Letters, N.Y.C., Am. Soc. Contemporary Artists, Riverside Mus., N.Y.C., Southeby Parke Bernet, N.Y.C., Art U.S.A., Ringling Mus., Davenport (Iowa) Municipal Gallery, São Paulo Mus., N.Y. World's Fair, Am. Fedn. Arts Internat.; travelling exhbns. include State Dept. sponsored exhbns., Am. embassies and mus. abroad; represented in permanent collections Peabody Mus., Cambridge, Mass., Speed Mus., Louisville, Morse Mus., Rawlins Coll., Hofstra Coll., Hunter Coll., Herbert Lehman Coll., N.Y.C., Miami U., Oxford, Ohio, Norfolk (Va.) Mus., Sheldon Meml. Mus., Lincoln, Nebr., Glichtenstein Mus., Safaad, Israel, Lyman Allen Mus., New London, Conn., Mansfield (Pa.) State Coll., Whitney Mus., Ulrich Mus. Fine Art, Wichita, Kans., A.C.A. Gallery, N.Y.C. others; also many pvt. collections and pub. bldgs. Recipient Gold medal oil Hofstra Coll., 1954; Purchase prize watercolor, 1955, Silver medal, 1956, Gold medal, 1957; Medal of Honor, Nat. Assn. Women Artists, 1956, watercolor award, 1957, 63, oil award, 1958, 64; Winsor and Newton oil award, 1959, others; MacDowell Found. Residence fellow, 1957, 59, 60, 75; Walker award oil Audubon Artists, 1965, Medal Honor, 1968, 71, James D.H. Meml. award 1982; Henry Ward Ranger Fund Purchase award NAD, 1965, 73, Andrew Carnegie award, 1973; Child Hassam award Am. Acad. Arts and Letters, 1968, 69, 72. Mem. Artists Equity Assn. (past mem. exec. bd.), Audubon Artists (v.p. 1968-71, Stephen Hirsch award 1975, James D.H. Meml. award 1982), NAD (full academician, Edwin Palmer award 1975), Coll. Art Assn. Am., Women in Arts. Address: 22 Florence St Great Neck NY 11023

BECK, MARILYN MOHR, columnist; b. Chgo., Dec. 17, 1928; d. Max Mohr and Rose (Lieberman) Mohr; A.A., U. So. Calif., 1948; m. Roger Beck, Jan. 8, 1949 (div. 1975); children—Mark Elliott, Andrea; m. 2d, Arthur Levine, Oct. 12, 1980. Free-lance writer nat. mags., newspapers, Hollywood, Calif., 1959-63; featured Hollywood columnist Valley Times, Citizen News, Hollywood, 1963-65; West Coast editor Sterling Mags., Hollywood, 1963-74; featured free-lance entertainment writer Los Angeles Times, 1965-67; Hollywood columnist Bell-McClure Syndicate, 1967-72, also chief West Coast bur.; Hollywood columnist NANA Syndicate, 1967-72; syndicated Hollywood columnist N.Y. Times Spl. Features, 1972-78, United Features Syndicate, 1978-79, Chgo. Tribune-N.Y. News Syndicate, 1979—; Hollywood corr. nat. PM Mag., 1983—; radio personality Marilyn Beck's Hollywood News Reports, KFT Radio, 1974-76, Marilyn Beck's Hollywood Out-Takes Spl., NBC, 1977, 78; Hollywood corr. KABC-TV, 1981. Recipient Citation of Merit, Los Angeles City Council, 1973; press award Publicists Guild Am. Author: Marilyn Beck's Hollywood, 1973. Address: PO Box 11079 Beverly Hills CA 90213

BECK, MARY VIRGINIA, lawyer, public official; b. Ford City, Pa., Feb. 29, 1908; B.A., U. Pitts., 1929, LL.B., 1932, J.D., 1968. Bar: Mich. 1944. Elected to Common Council City of Detroit, 1950-70; bd. suprs. County of Wayne, Mich., 1950-69; exec. dir. Ukrainian Info. Bur., Detroit. Chmn. Policeman & Retirement Fund Commn., Detroit, 1958-62; chmn. Wayne County Port Commn., 1962-68; mem. Gov.s Commn. on Status of Women, 1962, Gov.'s Commn. on Econ. Devel., 1962. Recipient Cert. of Merit Fashion Group of Detroit, 1955; Ruth Houston Whipple award Plymouth Bus. and Profl. Woman's Club, 1956; Sport Guild award Sprots Guild Detroit, 1956; award Detroit Dental Soc., 1957; citation Detroit Cancer Fighters, 1959; Ukrainian Community Service award Ukrainians of the Free World, 1960; Ukrainian of Yr. award Ukrainian Grad. Club of Detroit and Windsor, 1963; award Amvets of World War II, 1967; Woman of the Yr. award Soroptimist Club, 1968, others. Mem. Mich. State Bar, Detroit Bar Assn., Women Lawyers Assn. Mich., Nat. Assn. Women Lawyers, Detroit Bus. Womans Club, Nat. Fedn. Profl. and Bus. Women, Internat. Platform Assn. *

BECK, NANCY MANN MCCONNICO (MRS. EARL C. BECK, JR.), civic worker; b. Memphis, Aug. 31, 1931; d. John Davis and Pauline (Hilton) McConnico; m. Dean Carlton DuBois, Aug. 19, 1950 (div. Nov. 1963); children—Denise Hilton, Dean Carlton; m. Earl Crafton Beck, Jr.; 1 son, John

McConnico Harrington. Grad. So. Sem. and Jr. Coll., 1949. Asst. buyer, sportswear John Gerber Co., Memphis, 1949-50; fashion coordinator J. Hilton McConnico, Designer, Paris, 1963-65; buyer, mgr. Bridal Salon, Goldsmiths, Memphis, 1965-72, French Room, 1970-72. Press relations Hunter Lane for mayor, 1967; v.p. West Memphis Fine Arts Center, 1977-79; chmn. Crittenden County-Memphis, regional chmn. Mid-South Billy Graham Crusade, May 1978; chmn. Children's Art Day, Memphis, 1976-78, Memphis Symphony Ball, 1981; chmn. Crittenden County Jim Guy Tucker for U.S. Senate; bd. dirs. Crittenden Fine Arts Center, 1979-82, Memphis Orchestral Soc., 1981—, Memphis Arts Council; bd. dirs. Am. Symphony Orch. League, v.p., conf. chmn. vol. council, 1974-75; bd. dirs. Memphis Symphony League, 1977-78, pres., 1980-81; trustee So. Sem. Jr. Coll., Buena Vista, Va., 1982—. Recipient nat. ednl. award for Children's Arts Day, 1978. Mem. Episc. Churchwomen (pres. 1983-85), Josephine Circle (pres. 1963-64), Woman's Exchange. Episcopalian. Club: Town and Country Garden (pres. 1975-77). Home: Casa Lorraine Plantation Hughes AR 72348 also 6504 Cherryhill Pkwy Memphis TN 38119 Office: Route 1 Box 50 Hughes AR 72348

BECK, NANCY MOYLE, auditor; b. Phillipsburg, N.J., Aug. 17, 1957; d. William James and Gloria (Drake) Moyle; m. Steven Kindt Beck, Aug. 18, 1979; 1 child, David Edward. B.A. in Econs., Eastern Nazarene Coll., 1979. Lang. lab. instr. Eastern Nazarene Coll., 1977-79; tech. editor Bank of Boston, 1979-81, staff auditor, 1981-82, sr. staff auditor, 1982-83, trust audit specialist, 1983—, audit officer, 1984—, mem. TEFRA adv. com., 1983-84. Contbr. articles to profl. jours.; news editor Campus Camera, 1978-79. Acad. advisor Eastern Nazarene Coll., Quincy, 1978-79; mem. Multi-Dist. Inst. for Polit. and Legal Edn., 1975; intern Ma. Ho. of Reps., Quincy, 1978; mem. Community for Justice, Quincy, 1979. Recipient Chmn.'s Profl. Recognition award Bank of Boston, 1983, 84. Clubs: Choral Union, Debate Soc. (pres. 1977-78).

BECK, PATRICIA ANN, physicist, researcher; b. Atlantic City, N.J., Sept. 13, 1958; d. Edward James and Geraldine E. (Kozubski) B. B.S. in Applied Physics with highest honors and dept. distinction, R. Stockton State Coll., N.J., 1980; M.S., Stanford U., 1983, postgrad., 1985—. Research assoc. SSC Solar House, Pomona, N.J., 1976-80; research assoc. AT&T Bell Labs., Murray Hill, N.J., 1979, sr. tech. assoc. Holmdel, 1980-82, 83-85, mem. tech. staff, 1985—; research asst. Kitt Peak Nat. Obs., Tucson, 1980; researcher, teaching asst. Stanford U., Calif., 1981-83; cons. in field. Contbr. articles to profl. jours. Rutgers grad. fellow, 1980-81; Garden State Grad. fellow, 1980-81. Mem. Robotics Internat., Soc. Mfg. Engrs., Am. Phys. Soc., Am. Astron. Soc., IEEE. Avocations: travel; drawing; pottery; horseback riding; piano. Home: 308 N Annapolis Ave Atlantic City NJ 08401

BECK, ROSEMARIE, painter; b. N.Y.C., July 8, 1924; d. Samuel and Margit (Weisz) Beck; A.B., Oberlin Coll., 1944; student Inst. Fine Arts, N.Y.U., 1944-45, Columbia U., 1945, Atelier of Robert Motherwell, 1950; m. Robert Phelps, Sept. 14, 1945; 1 son, Roger. One-man shows include Peridot Gallery, N.Y.C., 1953, 55, 56, 59, 60, 63, 65, 66, 68-70, 72, Vassar Coll., 1957, 61, Wesleyan U., Middletown, Conn., 1960, SUNY-New Paltz, 1962, Zachary Waller Gallery, Los Angeles, 1971, Duke U., 1971, Kirkland Coll., 1972, Washburn Gallery, 1972, Poindexter Gallery, 1975, 80, Middlebury (Vt.) Coll., 1979, Ingber Gallery, 1980, 85, Witherspoon Gallery, 1980, Cornell U., 1980; group shows include: Chgo. Art Inst., 1962, Pa. Acad. Fine Arts, 1954, 66, Whitney Mus., 1955-57, 58, Tate Gallery, London, Eng., 1958, Butler Inst., Indpls., 1962, Kootz Gallery, N.Y.C., 1951, Felix Landau Gallery, Los Angeles, 1962, Nat. Inst. Arts and Letters, 1968, 75, 78, 79; represented in permanent collections: Pa. Acad. Fine Arts, Whitney Mus. Am. Art, N.Y.C., Art Inst. Chgo., others; tchr. Vassar Coll., 1957-55, 61-62, 63-64, Middlebury (Vt.) Coll., 1958, 60, 63, Queens Coll., 1968—. Grantee Ingram Merrill Found., 1966, 79 Rockefeller EditionRellagio grantee, 1983, NEA grantee, 1986. Address: 6 E 12th St New York NY 10003*

BECKER, BETTIE GERALDINE, artist; b. Peoria, Ill., Sept. 22, 1918; d. Harry Seymour and Magdalene Matilda (Hiller) Becker; B.F.A. cum laude, U. Ill., Urbana, 1940; postgrad. Art Inst. Chgo., 1942-45, Art Student's League, 1946, Ill. Inst. tech., 1948; m. Lionel William Wathall, Nov. 10, 1945; children—Heather Lynn (dec.), Jeffrey Lee. Dept. artist Liberty Mut. Ins. Co., Chgo., 1941-43; with Palenskie-Young Studio, 1943-46; free lance illustrator N.Y. Times, Chgo. Tribune, Saturday Rev. Lit., 1948-50; pvt. tutor, tchr. studio classes; co-owner Pangaea Gallery, Fish Creek, Wis. Exhibited one-man show Crossroads Gallery, Art Inst. Chgo., 1973; exhibited group shows including Critics' Choice show Art Rental Sales Gallery Art Inst. Chgo., 1972, Evanston-North Shore exhbns., 1964, 65, Chgo. Soc. Artists, 1967, 71, Union League, 1967, 72; represented in permanent collection Witte Meml. Mus., San Antonio; executed mural (with F. Wiater) Talbot Lab. U. Ill., Urbana, 1940. Active Campfire Girls, Chgo., 1968, 70; art chmn., mem. exec. bd. local PTA, 1959-60; active various art festivals, 1967—. Recipient Newcomb award U. Ill., 1940. Mem. Chgo. Soc. Artists (rec. sec. 1968-77), Soc. Illustrators, Northeastern Wis. Arts Council (2d v.p. 1982-83), Alumni Assn. Art Inst. Chgo., Internat. Platform Assn. Contbr. poetry to various publs. Home: 3992 Juddville Rd Fish Creek WI 54212

BECKER, CAROL ANN, import company executive; b. Bronx, N.Y., Nov. 20, 1954; d. Isidore A. and Adele S. B.; B.S., Syracuse U., 1976. Staff writer public relations Schenley Industries, Inc., N.Y.C., 1976-77, exec. trainee, 1977-78, asst. brand mgr. Schenley Distillers Co. div., 1978-80, product mgr., 1980-84; v.p., dir. mktg. Shaw-Ross Internat. Importers, Inc., 1984—; dir. Lerner Shops, Inc. Jewish. Home: 201 E 62d St New York NY 10021 Office: 126 E 56th St New York NY 10022

BECKER, ELEANOR MARION, county official; b. Oroville, Calif., Aug. 7, 1919; d. William Wilson and Nancy Elizabeth (McKillop) Nisbet; m. Rudolph William Becker, Jan. 20, 1946; 1 child, Rudolph William, Jr. Grad. high sch., Oroville. Office mgr. acctg. Savercool Plumbing, Oroville, 1938-41, Vaughn Bros. Buick, Oroville, 1951-59; office mgr. acctg. audit Western Auto Supply Co., Oroville, 1941-49; pvt. practice acctg. service, Oroville, 1959-65; asst. registrar of voters Butte County, Oroville, 1965-82, clk.-recorder, 1982—. Mem. Calif. County Clks. Assn., Calif. County Recorders Assn., Calif. Assn. Elected Ofcls., Oroville Bus. and Profl. Women's Club (Woman of Achievement award 1974-75), Chico State Assocs. Clubs: Oroville Bus. and Profl., Women's (pres. 1955-56), Soroptimist Internat. (pres. 1982-83). Avocations: gardening, sewing, traveling. Home: 33 Montrose Dr Oroville CA 95965 Office: Butte County Clk-Recorder 25 County Center Dr Oroville CA 95965

BECKER, JANET ARLENE, medical technologist; b. Wheeling, W.Va., Dec. 1, 1940; d. Ralph Charles and Clara Elizabeth (Bock) B.; B.S. in Med. Tech., West Liberty State Coll., 1963; cert. med. technologist Ohio Valley Med. Ctr., 1963; M.A. in Health Edn., W.Va. U., 1978. Edn. coordinator Ohio Valley Med. Center, Wheeling, W.Va., 1964-65, 1974, med. tech. edn. coordinator, 1965-68, hematology supr., 1968-82; with St. Margaret Meml. Hosp., Pitts., 1982—; ; instr. Wheeling Coll. Clin. Hematology, 1982; instr. Ohio Valley Med. Center, West Liberty State Coll., W.Va. No. Community Coll., Wheeling. Mem. Am. Soc. Clin. Pathologists (cert. med. technologist, specialist in hematology, clin. lab. scientist). Republican. Methodist. Home: RD 2 PO Box 319 W Alexander PA 15376 Office: 815 Freeport Rd Pittsburgh PA 15215

BECKER, MADELINE SUSAN MIRABITO, lawyer; b. N.Y.C., July 9, 1950; d. Nicholas and Violet (Sarli) Mirabito; m. Bruce S. Becker, Sept. 11, 1976. B.A. magna cum laude, Boston U., 1972; M.A., U. Chgo., 1974; J.D. cum laude, Boston Coll. Law, 1980. Bar: Mass. 1980. Assoc. firm Herrick & Smith, Boston, 1980-83; asst. atty. gen. Govt. Bur., Office Atty. Gen., Boston, 1983-86; assoc. firm Morrison, Mahoney & Miller, Boston, 1986—; instr. research and writing program Boston U. Sch. Law, 1984-85; judge moot ct. and client counseling competitions Boston Coll. Law Sch., Newton, Mass., 1981—. Editor-in-chief Am. Jour. Law and Medicine, Boston Coll. Law Sch., 1979-80. Boston U. scholar, 1968-72; Deidre Symington scholar Boston U., 1971. Mem. U. Chgo. Alumnae Assn. (admissions com. Boston 1983—), Women's Bar Assn. (sec. legis./policy com. 1983-84, co-chair appointments com. 1986-87), Boston Bar Assn. (health law com. 1982—), Mass. Bar Assn. Home: 90 Boulder Rd Newton MA 02159 Office: Morrison Mahoney & Miller 250 Summer St Boston MA 02210

BECKER, MARGARET WEBB, society administrator; b. Richmond, Va., July 20, 1956; d. E. Lovell and Margaret Webb (Thompson) B. B.A., Marymount Manhattan Coll., 1979; M.B.A., Pace Grad. Sch. Bus., N.Y.C., 1981; Cert., U. Nice, France, 1978. Mktg. specialist Amano Inc., N.Y.C., 1982-83; fin. dir. Interchange Ltd., London, Eng., 1983-85; govt. securities Smith Barney Harris Upham & Co., Inc., 1986—. Contbr. to reference book Access New York, 1981-82. Mem. numerous coms. N.Y. Jr. League, 1974—. Recipient Maj. Vol. Action award, Jr. League N.Y. Mem. Colonial Dames. Club: Colony. Home: 133 E 64th St New York NY 10021

BECKER, MARTHA JANE, radio executive; b. Bluefield, W.Va., Aug. 2, 1916; d. Ben H. and Martha Mabel Williams; m. William Pritchard Becker, Aug. 24, 1944; children—Jane Becker Delbridge, Beverly. A.B., W.Va. U., 1937. With Sta. WHIS, Bluefield, 1937-38; with Ziv Advt. Agy., Cin., 1939; tchr. Bramwell Schs. (W.Va.), 1940-44; with Sta. WVOW, Logan, W.Va., 1954—, comml. mgr., 1956—; instr. So. W.Va. Community Coll. Author: Mountain Roots Branching Out, 1976. Mem. Logan Bus. and Profl. Women's Club, W.Va. C. of C. (bd. dirs.), Logan C. of C. (dir., past pres.), W.Va. Assn. Broadcasters, DAR. Democrat. Presbyterian. Address: PO Box 1776 Logan WV 25601

BECKER, MARY ANNE, banker; b. Chgo., May 14, 1937; d. Eugene Bunte and Kathryn (Byrne) Reiner; B.A. in Mgmt., Mundelein Coll., Chgo., 1985; married; children—Kathryn, Richard, Teresa. With No. Trust Co., Chgo., 1963—, head securities custody div., 1976—, 2d v.p., 1981—. Mem. Nat. Assn. Bank Women, Corp. Fiduciaries Assn. Home: 4000 Cleveland St Skokie IL 60076 Office: 50 S La Salle St Chicago IL 60675

BECKER, MARY GAINER, music management and production company executive, apparel manufacturing representative; b. Denver, Aug. 5, 1943; d. James McInnes Henderson and Mary Medora (Jones) Henderson James; m. John Thomas Marshall, Jan. 26, 1963 (div. Sept. 1969); 1 child, Meredith Frances; m. 2d Lawrence Becker, Apr. 20, 1973. Student Tex. Tech U., 1961-62; Teaching cert. U. Tex., 1964, student Law Sch., 1964-65. Conv. coordinator Fed. Bar Assn., Washington, 1965-67; advance person Citizens for Humphrey, Washington, also Dallas, 1968; broker trainee Walston & Co., Dallas, 1969-70; adminstrv. asst. to chmn. bd. Revlon, Inc., N.Y.C., 1970-71; mfr.'s rep. Olad Corp., Dallas, 1972—, sec.-treas., 1974-79, v.p., 1979—, also dir.; cons. Otis Conner Prodns., Dallas, 1982—; pres., owner Meribec Cos., 1984—. Asst. chmn. bid-auction Cerebral Palsy Guild, Dallas, 1979, chmn. advt., 1980-81; cons. Teens in Trouble, Dallas, 1975-78; sustaining mem. Republican Nat. Com., 1982-84, vol. Rep. presdl. campaign, Dallas, 1980, mayoral campaign, 1983. Mem. Chi Omega. Episcopalian. Office: Olad Corp Apparel Mart 2300 Stemmons Freeway Dallas TX 75258 also 10939 Bluffside Dr 21 Studio City CA 91604

BECKER, MARY JULIA, educator, author; b. Akron, Ohio, Aug. 29, 1928; d. Nick and Mary (Krieger) Lengyel; m. Samuel Becker, Dec. 3, 1953 (dec. May 1954); 1 child, Samuella Rebecca. B.S., U. Akron, 1962, M.S., 1965; postgrad. U. London, Cambridge U., Oxford U., U. New Delhi, U. Moscow. Sec. B.F. Goodrich Co., Akron, 1948-50, Goodyear Tire & Rubber Co., Akron, 1954-56; draftswoman Ohio Bell Telephone Co., Akron, 1950-51; tchr. Akron Pub. Schs., 1958—; counselor West Jr. High Sch., Akron, 1964-67. Guest editor Ohio Reading Tchr., Columbus, 1983; contbr. articles to profl. jours. Vol. Ohio Ballet, 1983; pres. Hadassah, 1985-86. Recipient Martha Holden Jennings Master Tchr. award Kent State U., 1978, Tchr. of Week award Scholastic mag., 1981. Mem. Women in Communications, Akron Assn. Childhood Edn. (pres. 1960-61), Canton Writers Guild, Internat. Reading Assn., Akron Manuscript Club, Ohio Speakers Bur., AAUW, Kappa Delta Gamma. Clubs: Toastmasters, College, Press (Akron). Lodge: B'nai B'rith. Home: 1894 Evergreen Ave Akron OH 44301

BECKER, MARY LOUISE, polit. scientist; b. St. Louis; d. W. R. and Evelyn (Thompson) B.; B.S., Washington U., St. Louis, 1949, M.A. (Blewett fellow), 1951; Ph.D. (resident fellow 1952-56), Radcliffe Coll., 1957; postgrad. (Fulbright scholar) U. Karachi (Pakistan), 1953-54; m. 1966 (div.); children—James, John. Intelligence research analyst Dept. State, Washington, 1957-59; internat. relations officer AID, Washington, 1959-64, community relations officer, 1964-66, sci. research officer, 1966-71, UN relations officer, 1971—; adviser U.S. dels. 19th, 21st, 23d, 26th, 28th and 30th governing council sessions UN Devel. Program; adv. U.S. del. 3d prep. com. meeting World Conf. UN Decade for Women; lectr. internat. relations civic orgns., student groups, 1954—. Mem. adv. bd., chmn. student placement Washington Citizenship Seminar, Nat. YMCA-YWCA, Washington, 1961-71. Mem. Am. Polit. Sci. Assn., Soc. Internat. Devel., Assn. Asian Studies, Asia Soc., Am. Soc. Public Adminstrn., AAUW, Mo. Soc. Washington (sec. 1959-60), Mortar Bd., Chimes, Alpha Lambda Delta, Beta Gamma Sigma, Eta Mu Phi, Pi Sigma Alpha. Presbyterian. Clubs: Harvard, International, Harvard (Washington). Author: Muhammed Iqbal, 1965. Contbg. editor: Concise Ency. of Middle East, 1973. Contbr. articles to govt. publs. Office: AID Washington DC 20523

BECKER, REGINA (JEAN) K., credit and finance executive, consultant; b. Balt., Apr. 13, 1936; d. John E. and Eva (Urbanski) Kaczynski; m. Eugene C. Brukiewa, Aug. 28, 1954 (div. 1965); 1 child, Carol; m. William E. Becker, Oct. 11, 1974. Student, Johns Hopkins U. Vice pres., dir. Tidewater Indsl. Leasing Co., Inc., Balt., 1962-72; asst. to fund ops. mgr. T. Rowe Price Assocs., Balt., 1972-75; owner, operator Becker Cons., Balt., 1975—; dir credit Interchange, Balt., Balt. Credit Women, also pres. Pres., fin. sec. Knollwood-Donnybrook, Balt., 1975-85; bd. dirs. Criminal Justice Commn., Balt., 1968-71; bd. dirs., fund raising chmn. Metro Crime Stoppers, Balt., 1981—. Avocations: gardening, travel, bridge. Home and office: One Southerly Ct Towson MD 21204

BECKER, SAMUELLA REBECCA, communications executive; b. Akron, Ohio, Sept. 23, 1954; d. Samuel and Mary Julia (Lengyel) Becker; m. Frank L. Maltese, Dec. 22, 1984. B.S.J., Ohio U., 1975. Editorial asst. Talk Mag., N.Y.C., 1976; mng. editor Argosy Mag., N.Y.C., 1976-78; media cons./writer Union Carbide Corp., N.Y.C., 1978-80; mgr. internal qommunications SCM Corp., N.Y.C., 1980-84; dir. communications First Investors Corp., N.Y.C., 1984—. Vol., Meml.-Sloan Kettering Cancer Research Ctr. AMem. Women in Communications, Public Relations Soc. Am., Internat. Assn. Bus. Communicators, Soc. Profl. Journalists, Am. Mktg. Assn., Alpha Delta Pi. Democrat. Contbr. articles to profl. jours. Home: 420 E 72d St New York NY 10021 Office: 120 Wall St New York NY 10005

BECKER, SHIRLEY NORMAN, realty firm executive; b. Dallas, Feb. 1, 1929; d. Thomas Jefferson and Emily Sue (Holcomb) Norman; m. William Albert Branscum, Jan. 10, 1942; children—Byron, Suzan Branscum Bush; m. Herbert Peter Becker, Oct. 5, 1969. Salesman Bob Hardy, Realtors, 1958-65; sales mgr. Hand Blanchard, Richardson, Tex., 1965-68; pres. One Real Estate, Inc., doing bus. as Shirley Becker, Realtors (formerly Hand Blanchard), Richardson, 1968—; mem. devel. bd. Met. Bank, Richardson, 1984-85. Active Richardson Women's Club; dir. edn. Collin County, 1984. Mem. Nat. Assn. Realtors, Tex. Assn. Realtors, Dallas Bd. Realtors, Collin County Bd. Realtors (bd. dirs. 1983-85), Dallas C. of C., Richardson C. of C., Plano C. of C. Republican. Episcopalian. Avocations: art and antiques; travel. Home: 6509 Laurel Valley Dallas TX 75248 Office: Shirley Becker Realtors 2007 N Collins Suite 401 Richardson TX 75080

BECKET, FLORA GRACE, accountant, management systems consultant; b. Calhoun, Ga., Dec. 20, 1943; d. Claude Huckabee and Jimmie Mae (Merritt) Harbor; B.S., SUNY, 1984; m. Michael P. Becket, Jan. 26, 1974; children—Roni Wagner, Lori Falk, Christi Holland. Customer service mgr. Gen. Electric Credit Corp., Oklahoma City, 1964-65; office mgr. HLS Inc., Sunnyvale, Calif., 1970-72; personnel/office adminstr. Arthur Andersen & Co., San Jose, Calif., 1971-73; office mgr. Phifer & Schink, C.P.A.s, Mountain View, Calif., 1973-76; mgmt. cons., San Jose, 1976—; mgmt. cons., acting chief fin. officer Allstate Investment Corp., San Jose, 1978-82; mgmt. cons., v.p., chief fin. officer Becket & Co., Inc., 1982—. Bd. dirs. Girl Scout Endowment Fund Santa Clara County, Inc. Mem. Nat. Assn. Female Execs., Am. Soc. Profl. and Exec. Women, San Jose Hist. Soc., San Jose C. of C., Nat. Assn. Refunders and Shoppers (pres., editor newsmag.), Nat. Tax Consultors. Republican. Baptist.

BECKETT, GRACE, educator; b. Smithfield, Ohio, Oct. 7, 1912; d. Roy Martin and Mary (Hammond) Beckett; A.B., Oberlin Coll., 1934, A.M., 1935; Ph.D., Ohio State U., 1939. Music supr. pub. schs., Kelleys Island, Ohio, 1935-36; grad. asst. econs. Ohio State U., 1936-39; asst. prof. econs. and music Ind. Central Coll., 1939-41; with U. Ill., Champaign-Urbana, 1941—, asst. prof. econs., 1945-51, assoc. prof. econs., 1951-73, assoc. prof. emerita Coll. Commerce and Bus. Adminstrn., 1973—. Mem. Am. Econ. Assn., Music Educators Nat. Conf., Econ. History Assn., Music Tchrs. Nat. Assn., Am. Fin. Assn., AAAS, N.Y. Acad. Scis., Ill. Music Educators Assn., Ill. Music Tchrs. Assn., Nat. Sch. Orch. Assn., Oberlin Friends of Art, Am. Hist. Assn., Ohio Acad. History, Ohio Geneal. Soc., Mary Ball Washington Mus. and Library, Met. Mus. Art (nat. asso.), Krannert Art Mus. Assos. (U. Ill.), Interlochen (Mich.) Alumni Assn., (life), Winchester-Frederick County (Va.) Hist. Soc., Nat. Honor Soc., Ohio State U. Alumni Assn., Phi Beta Kappa, Pi Lambda Theta, Phi Chi Theta, Alpha Lambda Delta. Methodist. Clubs: University of Illinois Women's; Oberlin Coll. Half Century. Author: Reciprocal Trade Agreements Program, 1941, 2d edit., 1972. Contbr. articles to profl. publs. Address: PO Box 386 Urbana IL 61801

BECKETT, JANE ELIZABETH, legal assistant; b. Akron, Ohio, Nov. 26, 1935; d. Arzie Lothair and Elizabeth Mary (Roberts) Howell; m. Joseph Karr Beckett, Aug. 26, 1961; 1 child, Linda Christine. B.S., U. Akron, 1957; postgrad. U. So. Calif., 1977, UCLA, 1981. Exec. sec. Gen. Tire Co., Akron, 1957-59, legal sec., 1960-61; sec. Japanese polit. affairs U.S. Dept. State, Washington, 1959-60; legal sec. Henry Hardy, Esquire, San Francisco, 1961-68; legal sec. Tenneco West, Inc., Bakersfield, Calif., 1970-75, legal asst., 1976—. Mem. Pet Pride, Pacific Palisades, Calif., 1974—; mem. Presdl. Task Force Washington, 1984, Kern Children's Service Ctr., Bakersfield, Calif., 1984, Ag Boosters for FFA, Tehachapi, Calif., 1984. Mem. Nat. Assn. Legal Assts. (cert.), UCLA Atty. Asst. Alumni Assn., UCLA Alumni Assn. Republican. Presbyterian. Avocations: travel; collecting cat figurines; piano; cooking; bicycling. Home: 28711 Gleneagle Ct Star Route 1 Box 2975A Tehachapi CA 93561 Office: Tenneco West Inc 10000 Ming Ave Bakersfield CA 93311

BECKETT, SUSAN KAY, television executive; b. Webster City, Iowa, June 5, 1948; d. Ed Logan and Doris Darlene (Beckett) Oard; children—Gabrielle, Jessica. B.S., Iowa State U., 1969; J.D., U. Iowa, 1974; LL.M., NYU, 1977. Bar: Iowa 1974, N.Y. 1975, D.C. 1978. Assoc., Dewey, Ballantine, Bushby, Palmer & Wood, N.Y.C., 1974-76; trial atty. U.S. Dept. Justice, Washington, 1977-78; sr. atty. law dept. NBC, Inc., N.Y.C., 1978-80, sr. counsel, 1980-81, v.p. bus. affairs enterprises div., 1981—; v.p. NBC Internat. Ltd., Bermuda, 1982—; dir., asst. sec. Living Music, Inc., N.Y.C., 1979, Spectacular Music, Inc., N.Y.C., 1979—; dir., vice chmn. NBC Enterprises, Inc., N.Y.C., 1980—; v.p. NBC Ednl Enterprises Inc., Del., 1982—. Recipient Am. Jurisprudence award Lawyers Coop Pub. Co., 1973. Mem. N.Y. State Bar Assn., Iowa Bar Assn., D.C. Bar Assn., Order of Coif. Office: Nat Broadcasting Co Inc 30 Rockefeller Plaza Amax Bldg Room 2828 New York NY 10112

BECKEY, SYLVIA LOUISE, lawyer; b. Los Angeles, Feb. 8, 1946; d. Andrew Gabriel and Rita Jane (Mayer) B. B.A. with spl. honors, U. Tex.-Austin, 1968, postgrad., 1968-69; J.D., Duke U., 1971; M.A. candidate Johns Hopkins Sch. Advanced Internat. Studies, 1973-74; LL.M., NYU, 1981. Bar: D.C. 1972, N.Y. 1975, U.S. Dist. Ct. (so. and ea. dist.) N.Y. 1975, U.S. Supreme Ct. 1975, U.S. Ct. Appeals (2d cir.) 1980. Legis. atty. Am. law div. Congl. Research Service, Library of Congress, Washington, 1971-74; assoc. Cole & Deitz, N.Y.C., 1975-76, Milberg, Weiss, Bershad & Specthrie, N.Y.C., 1976-78; law. clk. to judge U.S. Dist. Ct. (so. dist.) N.Y., 1979-80; asst. chief div. comml. litigation Office of Corp. Counsel of City of N.Y., 1980—; spl. master Supreme Ct. State of N.Y.-N.Y. County, 1984—; guest speaker U. Witwatersrand Sch. Law, Johannesburg, S. Africa, 1973; guest researcher Ct. Library, Nairobi, Kenya, 1973; pro bono Internat. League Human Rights, N.Y.C., 1974-75, 8th ann. Conf. for World Peace through Law, Abidjan, Ivory Coast, W. Africa, 1973. Co-author Handbook for Drafting Jury Instructions, U.S. Dept. Justice Civil Rights Div., 1970; assoc. editor The Constitution of the United States of America-Analysis and Interpretation, 1972; author legis. reports on Equal Credit Opportunity Act; referee Am. Bus. Law Jour., 1980-81. Bd. dirs. Chalon Cooperative Bldg., Washington, 1972-73; chmn. fine arts com., mem. bd. dirs. St. Bartholomew's Community Club, St. Bartholomew's Episcopal Ch., N.Y.C., 1982-83. Grantee EEO, 1966, Hinds Webbs Fund, 1967. Mem. Women's Bar Assn. City of N.Y., NYU Law Alumni Assn., Duke U. Law Alumni Assn., Fed. Bar Council, Am. Fgn. Law Assn., Consular Law Soc., Dramatists Guild. Protestant Lawyers Guild, English Speaking Union, Met. Mus. Art, Chelsea Block Assn. and Hist. Soc. Democrat. Home: 235 W 22d St New York NY 10011 Office: Office of Corp Counsel City NY 100 Church St 3d Floor New York NY 10007

BECKMAN, JUDITH KALB, financial counselor and planner, lecturer, writer; b. Bklyn., June 27, 1940; d. Harry and Frances (Cohen) Kalb; m. Richard Martin Beckman, Dec. 16, 1961; children—Barry Andrew, David Mark. B.A., Hofstra U., 1962; M.A., Adelphi U., 1973, cert. fin. planning, 1984. Promotion coordination pub. relations Mandel Sch. for Med. Assts., Hempstead, N.Y., 1973-74; exec. dir. Nassau Easter Seals, Albertson, N.Y., 1974-76; dir. pub. info. Long Beach Meml. Hosp., N.Y., 1976-77; account rep. First Investors, Hicksville, N.Y., N.Y.C., 1977-78; sales asst., then account exec. Josephthal & Co. Inc., Great Neck, N.Y., 1978-81; v.p., cert. fin. planner Arthur Gould Inc., Great Neck, 1981—; adj. instr. Adelphi U., Garden City N.Y., 1981-83, Molloy Coll., Rockville Centre, N.Y., 1982-84; lectr. SUNY-Farmingdale, 1984, 85; creater, presenter seminars, workshops on fin., investing, 1981—. Fin. columnist The Women's Record, 1985—. Coordinator meat boycott, L.I., 1973; co-founder, chairperson L.I. del. Cong. for High Profile Men and Women, Colonie Hill, Hauppauque, N.Y., 1985. Mem. Women's Econ. Developers of L.I. (bd. dirs. 1985—), Internat. Assn. Fin. Planners (L.I. chpt.) (cert.), L.I. Ctr. Bus. and Profl. Women (pres. 1984—), C.W. Post Tax Inst., Am. Soc. Women Accts. Republican. Jewish. Avocations: theater; classical music; opera; reading. Home: 2084 Beverly Way Merrick NY 11566 Office: Arthur Gould Inc 98 Cutter Mill Rd Great Neck NY 11021

BECKMAN, PATRICIA ANN, systems analyst; b. Clearwater, Nebr., Feb. 28, 1931; d. Rudolph Frank and Margaret Mary (McCarthy) Funk; A.A., Black Hawk Coll., 1975; B.A., Western Ill. U., 1977; m. Duane George Beckman, June 28, 1952 (dec. 1965); children—Douglas Duane, Annette Marie, Jeffrey Thomas, Debra Lynn, Timothy Joseph. C.P.A., Tex.; cert. data processor. Programmer-analyst, auditing asst., acctg. and personnel asst. First Nat. Bank of Moline (Ill.), 1967-77; programmer-analyst Tex. Eastern Transmission Corp., Houston, 1978-80; systems analyst Cabot Corp., Houston, 1980-83; systems analyst Digicon, Inc., Houston, 1983—. Roman Catholic. Office: 3701 Kirby Dr Houston TX 77478

BECKMANN, MARY LEE, nephrologist; b. Pitts., Aug. 27, 1948; d. Robert Bader and Barbara Jean (Lee) Beckmann; m. Melville Alexander Thomas, Feb. 23, 1984; 1 son, Charles Alexander. A.B. in French, U. Rochester, 1970; M.S. in Physiology, U. Ill., 1974; George Washington U., 1978. Diplomate Am. Bd. Internal Medicine. Intern, Los Angeles County-Univ. So. Calif. Gen. Hosp., Los Angeles, 1978-79; resident in medicine Georgetown U. Hosp., Washington, 1979-81, clin. fellow nephrology, 1981-82; clin. research fellow in nephrology Beth Israel Hosp., N.Y.C., 1982-83; NIH fellow in medicine Columbia U. Sch. Medicine, N.Y.C., 1983—. Contbr. articles to profl. jours. Bd. dirs. Adams-Morgan Community Orgn., Washington, 1977-78; bd. dirs., v.p. 1869 Mintwood Coop., Inc., Washington, 1981. Washington Heart Assn. fellow, 1975, 76. Mem. AMA, Eastern Hypertension Soc., AAAS. Democrat. Home: 249 W 101st St Apt 6 New York NY 10025 Office: Columbia U School Medicine Black Research Bldg 809 650 W 168th St New York NY 10032

BECKNER, JULIE ANN ZIMMER, marketing services executive; b. Berwyn, Ill., Mar. 12, 1953; d. Marshall E. and Gertrude Carolyn (Staples) Sanders; m. Mark Edwin Beckner, Apr. 12, 1986; 1 dau., Stephanie N. B.S. Ed., Western Ill. U., 1975. Cert. tchr., Ill. Tchr. math. United Township High Sch., Moline, Ill., 1974-75; programmer Zenith Radio Corp., Chgo., 1975-76; programmer, analyst RCA, Indpls., 1976-78; sr. systems analyst Fin. Boehringer Mannheim Corp., Indpls., 1978-84, mgr. sales analysis, 1984, mgr. contracts, pricing and sales analysis, 1984-85, mgr. mktg. services, 1985—; cons. and lectr. in field. Author: poetry and drawings. Tchrs. scholar, 1971; recipient numerous athletic awards. Mem., Fishers United Meth. Ch., Ind., 1981—, Indpls. Humane Soc., 1983—, Greenpeace, 1985—. Mem. Nat. Contract Mgmt. Assn. Club: Japanese Karate Assn. (Macomb, Ill.) (sec. 1972-75). Avocations: tennis; skiing; golf; karate; biking. Home: 3324 Beech Pl Carmel IN 46032 Office: Boehringer Mannheim Corp 9115 Hague Rd Indianapolis IN 46250

BECKNER, MARY KATHRYN, accountant; b. Mendota, Ill., Dec. 5, 1904; d. Edward J. and Mary (Hoerner) Cannon; student pub. schs.; m. Lester W. Beckner, Dec. 5, 1931. Pvt. sec., 1922-41; treas. Wayside Press, Inc., 1941—, also dir.; sec.-treas., dir. Kenneth B. Butler & Asso., 1944—; treas. Butler Typo-Design Research Center, 1951—, Surrey Hill Arabians, Inc.; dir., treas. Packaging Digest Inc., 1964-70. Mem. Red Cross Canteen, Mendota Community Hosp. Aux.; bd. dirs. LaSalle County unit Am. Cancer Soc. Mem. Ill., Mendota chambers commerce, Nat. Council Catholic Women, Nat. Secs. Assn. (Sec. of Yr. Aishi chpt., treas. 1977—), Internat. Arabian Horse Assn. Roman

Catholic. Elk. Clubs: Woman's (treas. pub. affairs dept.); Antique Automobile of America (sec.-treas. Mendota). Home: 1312 Burlington St Mendota IL 61342 Office: 700 14th Ave Mendota IL 61342

BECKOS, VERONICA ANNE, nursing home administrator; b. Detroit, July 20, 1936; d. Stefan and Anne (Gensko) Velky; m. Milton V. Beckos, Nov. 20, 1965; children—Stefanie, Katherine, John. R.N., St. Joseph's Inf., Atlanta, 1959; B.A., Calif. State U.-Los Angeles, 1975, M.S., 1978. Owner, founder Mil-Veron Enterprises Inc., Ontario, Calif., 1978—; adminstr. Cherrylee Lodge San., El Monte, 1980-84; dir. nursing Sierra Madre Community Health Care Ctr., Calif., 1985—. Served as lt. U.S. Army, 1960-62. Mem. Am. Coll. Health Care Adminstrs. (sec. 1983). Club: Pomona Valley Writers (pub. relations com. 1985). Avocations: creative writing.

BECNEL, MARY HOTARD, lawyer; b. New Orleans, Oct. 25, 1949; d. Edmond Nicholas and Delora Mary (Morvant) Hotard; m. Daniel E. Becnel, Mar. 5, 1978; children—Bradley Douglas, Ainsley Michael. Student, U. New Orleans, 1970-77; J.D., Loyola U., New Orleans, 1980. Bar: La. 1980. Ofcl. ct. reporter 29th Jud. Dist. Ct., Edgard and Hahnville, La., 1969-78; ptnr. law firm Becnel, Landry & Becnel, LaPlace, La., 1980—. Alt. del. Dem. Nat. Conv., 1980; sub-chmn. LaPlace United Way Fund Drive, 1983. Mem. La. Bar Assn., La Trial Lawyers Assn., Am. Trial Lawyers Assn., 29th Jud. Dist. Bar Assn. (sec.-treas. 1982-83, 83-84), Am. Businesswomen's Assn. (program chmn. 1983-84). Roman Catholic. Home: 1203 W 5th St LaPlace LA 70068 Office: Becnel Landry & Becnel 429 W Airline Hwy Suite E LaPlace LA 70068

BEDDINGFIELD, BENITA DODD, insurance agent; b. Gadsden, Ala., Aug. 13, 1948; d. Charles Clarence and Eularene (Smith) Dodd; m. C.G. Phillips, Nov. 21, 1963 (div. 1966); 1 child, Laura Lynette; m. Larry Floyd Beddingfield, Sept. 20, 1974; 1 stepchild, Amy Claire. A.B.S., Gadsden State Community Coll., 1967; student Jacksonville State U., 1967. Office mgr. So. Electric Supply, Gadsden, 1973-77; ins. agt. and office mgr. GBS, Inc., Gadsden, 1978-85; agt. State Farm Ins., Gadsden, 1985—. Named to State Farm Ins. Millionaire Club, 1985. Mem. Am. Bus. Women's Assn. (Woman of Yr. Dixie Belle Chpt. 1985), Gadsden-Etowah C. of C., Gadsden Assn. Life Underwriters. Baptist. Clubs: Altrusa. Avocations: Reading; stock market. Home: 504 Palace Ave Rainbow City AL 35901 Office: 900 S 4th St Gadsden AL 35901

BEDELL, BARBARA LEE, newspaperwoman; b. Annapolis, Md., July 10, 1936; d. Royal Lee and Kathryn Rosalee (Alton) Sweeney; m. Raymond Lester Bedell, July 1, 1955 (div. 1979); children—Patricia Bedell Pulito, Barbara Ann Bedell Porrini, Raymond, Robert. B.A., U. Wyo., 1967. Dir. woman's programming, host daily talk show Sta. KLME, Laramie, Wyo., 1962-68, Sta. WKIP, Poughkeepsie, N.Y., 1968-70; asst. society editor, feature writer Poughkeepsie Jour., 1968-70; dir. communications and publs. Spackenkill Sch. Dist., Poughkeepsie, 1970-73; columnist, feature writer Times Herald-Record Newspaper, Middletown, N.Y., 1973—; lectr. on various topics to civic, polit., religious, social orgns., 1961—. Mem. 75th Anniversary Com., Cheyenne, Wyo., 1965; mem. Republican Precinct Com., 1961-68, Albany County Bd. Electors, 1966-68; mem. history and heritage collection Orange County Community Coll., Middletown, 1984; mem. 100th Anniversary Com., Middletown, 1983-88. Recipient 1st in N.Y. feature writing award Am. Cancer Soc., 1973; Disting. Service award NAACP, 1980; Service awards from numerous service clubs and lodges, chs., assns.; named Mrs. Wyoming, Mrs. Am. Pageant, 1967; N.Y. State All-Am. Family, 1972. Mem. Nat. Fedn. Press Women (8 awards for feature writing 1967-70, top Wyo. state award for radio script writing 1966). Republican. Home: Basel Rd Walker Valley NY 12588 Office: Times Herald-Record Newspaper 40 Mulberry St Middletown NY 10940

BEDFORD, DOROTHY LYNN, banker; b. Boonton, N.J., Feb. 10, 1956; d. Nathaniel Forrest and Roberta (Skinner) B.; m. Rush Taggart III, Mar. 29, 1985. A.B., Princeton U., 1978; M.B.A., Harvard U., 1982. Research asst. Temple, Barker & Sloane, Lexington, Mass., 1978-81; asst. treas. Chem. Bank, N.Y.C., 1982-85, Banker's Trust, N.Y.C., 1985—. Pres. Princeton U. Class 1978, N.J., 1983—; mem. exec. com. Alumni Council of Princeton U., 1984—. Republican. Mem. United Ch. of Christ. Clubs: N.Y. Yacht, Princeton of N.Y. (N.Y.C.). Avocation: competitive sailing. Home: 392 Washington Ave Pelham NY 10803 Office: Bankers Trust 280 Park Ave 22W New York NY 10015

BEDFORD, MADELEINE ALANN PECKHAM, civic worker; b. Ontario, Calif., Jan. 25, 1910; d. Allen Lewis and Madeleine (Elliott) Peckham; A.B., U. Calif., Berkeley, 1930, M.A., 1937; LL.D. (hon.), Tex. Christian U., 1973; m. Charles Francis Bedford, Dec. 30, 1930; children—Madeleine Alann, Frances Ellen, Charlotte Jean. Supr. tchr. tng. and counseling, in charge testing Univ. High Sch., U. Calif., Berkeley, 1931-38; tchr. English to fgn. born San Leandro (Calif.) Evening Schs., 1931-38; treas. Tarrant County Day Care Assn., 1953-54; pres. Ft. Worth and Tarrant County council Camp Fire Girls, 1961-63, mem. Nat. council, 1968-75, pres. Nat. council, 1965-68, NGO rep. to UN, 1968-69, nat. bd. dirs., 1960-68, bd. dirs. Houston council, 1971-72, mem. congress of Nat. Camp Fire Girls, 1975—; pres. Ft. Worth Lit. Council, 1963-65; v.p. Tarrant County United Fund and Community Council, 1963-66, mem. exec. com. bd. dirs., 1963—; pres. Ft. Worth chpt. Am. Field Service, 1964-66; chmn. budget sub-com. United Fund, 1959-68, chmn. met. div. Tarrant County, 1970; chmn. speakers tours, films div., United Way Tarrant County Campaign, 1973, chmn. planning and research div., 1973-75; v.p. United Way Met. Tarrant County, 1973-75, chmn. community services div., 1985-86; mem. exec. com. United Way Tex., 1979—; sec. Tex. United Community Services, 1968-70, v.p., 1970-73, pres., 1973-75; mem. Mid-Am. Regional Vol. Task group United Way Am., mem. nat. com. agy. support, 1975-80; Tex. state rep. for UNICEF, 1969—, mem. coordinating bd. for U.S. Com. of UN Childrens Fund, 1981—; chmn. Mayor's Council on Youth Opportunity, 1972-73; del. White House Conf. on Children and Youth, 1970; sec. social services adv. com. Tex. Dept. Human Resources, 1975-76, chmn., 1976-77; mem. nat. bd. Nat. Conf. Social Welfare, 1976-80; colleague nat. assembly Nat. Vol. Health and social welfare orgns., 1978-80; bd. dirs. Tarrant County chpt. ARC; bd. dirs. United Cerebral Palsy, pres. Tarrant County Br., 1976-78, mem. nat. corp., 1976—, v.p., Tex., 1977-83, pres., 1983-85; bd. dirs. Tarrant County Community Action Agy., Tarrant County Community Council, Tex. Social Welfare Assn.; trustee Assn. Grad. Edn. and Research, 1971—; trustee Tex. Christian U., also bd. visitors; trustee Tex. Coll. Osteo. Medicine Found., 1980—; mem. adv. council Sch. Social Work, U. Tex., Austin, 1980—; mem. adv. council for fin. assistance Tex. Dept. Human Resources, 1980—; pres. Womens Haven Tarrant County, 1979-81, bd. dirs., 1979-86; mem. exec. com. Community Trust Tarrant County, 1981—; bd. dirs. Family and Individual Services Tarrant County, 1981—, pres., 1985—; bd. dirs. Ft. Worth Girls Club, 1979—; mem. nat. bd. dirs. Girls Club Am., 1983-86; bd. dirs. Ft. Worth Acad., 1985—; Fed. Emergency Mgmt. Act, 1985—; pres. bd. dirs. Family Service, 1985—; mem. adv. council for adult basic edn. Ft. Worth Ind. Sch. Dist., 1976—; fellow Forum of Ft. Worth, 1981—; mem. Dallas/Ft. Worth Chaplaincy Bd., 1983—; bd. dirs. Tarrant Area Community of Chs., 1979—, pres., 1984—. Recipient Gulick award, 1961, Wo-he-lo award, 1968 Camp Fire Girls; award of Excellence for Outstanding Leadership and Service Tarrant County Community Council, 1964, Civic award First Lady Ft. Worth Altrusa, 1966, Hercules award for Outstanding Vol. Leadership in Social Welfare United Way, 1977, award for service to students 1983, Alumni Royal Purple award 1983 (both Tex. Christian U.), award for human service Sertoma, 1983. Mem. Council World Affairs (pres. 1985—), Internat. Good Neighbor Council, Ft. Worth Lecture Found., DAR, Mortar Board, Family Service Assn. (bd. dirs.), Phi Beta Kappa (pres. Ft. Worth 1958-59), Alpha Chi Omega, Pi Sigma Alpha. Episcopalian. Clubs: Ft. Worth Woman's (past pres. history sect., Tex. Christian U. Woman's). Home: 7 Westover Rd Fort Worth TX 76107

BEDFORD, RUTH ALICE HAEDIKE (MRS. EDWIN GARRARD BEDFORD), librarian; b. Chgo.; d. William Henry and Alice (Lohr) Haedike; student Beloit Coll., 1932-33; B.S., U. Ill., 1936, M.S., 1954, postgrad.; m. Edwin Garrard Bedford, June 6, 1942; children—David Edwin, Ellen Louise. Instr. U. Ill. Library, Urbana, 1954-64; asst. prof. library sci. U. Utah Libraries, Salt Lake City, 1964-68; asso. librarian Butler Library, State U. Coll., Buffalo, 1968-79, mem. personnel com. tech. services div., 1972-75, chmn., 1974-75, mem. faculty advisory council instructional resources, 1971-73. Mem. tech. services com. Western N.Y. Library Resources Council, 1968-73. Mem. State U. N.Y. Librarians' Assn., Am. Assn. U. Profs., ALA, Kenan Center (charter mem.), Delta Phi Alpha. Club: Order Eastern Star. Home: 905 Charlesgate Circle East Amherst NY 14051

BEDKE, KATHRYN LYNN, lawyer; b. Kearney, Nebr., Nov. 3, 1951; d. Richard August Tatem and Helen Kathryn (Weitzel) Bedke. B.A. in English and German, Kirkland Coll., 1974; postgrad. U. Vienna-Austria, 1972-73; M.T.S. in Religion, Harvard Div. Sch., 1976; J.D., Case Western Res. U., 1979. Bar: N.Y. 1981. Assoc., Demov, Morris, and Hammerling, N.Y.C., 1979-81, White & Case, N.Y.C., 1981—. Pres., Kirkland Coll. Alumnae Assn., 1982—; mem. Hamilton Coll. Alumni Assn., 1981-84. George F. Baker Trust fellow, 1971-72, 73-74; Rockefeller fellow, 1974-75; Soc. Benchers award, 1979. Mem. Case Western Res. Jour. Internat. Law, 1976-77, Case Western Res. Law Rev., 1977-79. Mem. ABA, N.Y. State Bar Assn., (com. on internat. law 1984—), Nebr. Soc. of N.Y. Inc. (sec., legal advisor 1984—). Democrat. Home: 250 W 24th St Apt 1CE New York NY 10011 Office: 1155 Ave of Americas New York NY 10036

BEDOCK, KAREN SUE, interior designer, educator; b. San Antonio, Apr. 2, 1958; d. Leo Eugene and Constance Ann (Machesky) B. A.A. in Middle Mgmt., San Antonio Coll., 1978. Office asst. U. Tex. San Antonio Health Sci. Ctr., 1978-81; interior designer J.C. Penney, San Antonio, 1981-82, Joskes, San Antonio, 1982-83, DLS Design Ctr., San Antonio, 1983-85, J.C. Penney, San Antonio, 1985—; tchr. community edn. Northside Sch. Dist., San Antonio, 1985—. Mem. Internat. Guild Accredited Interior Designers, Nat. Assn. Female Execs. Republican. Roman Catholic. Avocations: needlework; diving and snorkeling; hunting; walking. Home: 9306 Dover Ridge San Antonio TX 78250

BEDSOLE, ANN SMITH, state senator; b. Selma, Ala., Jan. 7, 1930; d. Malcolm White and Sybil (Huey) Smith; m. Massey Palmer Bedsole, 1958; children—Mary Martin Bedsole Riser, John Henry Martin, Margaret Loraine. Student U. Ala., 1948, U. Denver, 1955-56. Mem. Ala. Republican Exec. Com., 1966-74; del. seconded nomination Nixon for Pres., Rep. Nat. Conv., 1972; Rep. Presdl. Elector, 1972; mem. S.E. Regional Adv. Com. Nat. Park Service; mem. Ala. com. Internat. Women's Yr., 1977; mem. Ala. Senate. Vice pres. Mobile Child Care Found.; active Huntington Coll., Mobile Hist. Devel. Found., Spring Hill Coll., Hist. Mobile Tours, Inc., Jr. League of Mobile, Recipient M.O. Beale Scroll of Merit award Mobile Press Register, 1971, 72; First Lady of Mobile for 1972. Methodist. Office: Ala Senate State Capitol Montgomery AL 36130*

BEE, ANNA COWDEN, educator; b. Birmingham, Ala., Feb. 17, 1922; d. Porter Guthrie and Marion Irene (McCurry) Cowden; A.B., Samford U., 1944; student Chalif Sch. Dance, N.Y.C., 1950-54; m. Alon Wilton Bee, Oct. 21, 1942; children—Anna Margaret Bee Foote, Alon Wilton. Mem. faculty Byram High Sch., Jackson, 1945-52; mem. faculty Hinds Jr. Coll., Raymond, Miss., 1952—, dir. Hi-Steppers, girls' precision dance group; chaperone Miss Mississippi to Miss Am. Pageant; condr. charm clinics for teenagers; judge beauty pageants. Bd. dirs. Multiple Sclerosis Soc., Jackson, 1966-72; state chmn. Miss. Easter Seal Soc. campaign, 1966, 79; chmn. women's div. United Way, Jackson, 1973. Named Woman of Achievement, Jackson Bus. and Profl. Women's Club, 1967-78; disting. faculty of the yr. award Hinds Jr. Coll., 1981; Miss. Legislature commendation for contbn. to youth, 1981. Mem. Nat. Faculty Dance Educators Am., Dance Masters Am., Miss. Edn. Assn., Miss. Assn. Health and Phys. Edn., Beta Sigma Omicron. Democrat. Baptist. Producer halftime shows Gator Bowl, 1958, 64, 81, Sugar Bowl, 1960, Hall of Fame Bowl, 1977, 79. Home: 304 Alta Woods Blvd Jackson MS 39154 Office: Hinds Jr Coll Raymond MS 39154

BEE, MARY RICE, marketing consultant; b. Homer, N.Y., Aug. 11, 1933; d. John Moak and Isabella A. (Gilkerson) Rice; student Cortland (N.Y.) State Tchrs. Coll., 1951-54, Russell Sage Coll., 1968; children—Heather Jo Bee Chestnut, Edward R., Jr. Co-founder, v.p. Bee Bus. Forms, Schenectady, 1964-68; sales mgr. Gideon Putnam Hotel, Saratoga Springs, N.Y., 1968-71; founder, 1971, pres. Madison North Mktg. Communications Agy., 1971-82; exec. v.p. Wallace Armer Hardware, Schenectady; mktg. and mgmt. cons.; dir. Flah's; mem. adj. faculty Union Coll., Schenectady. Former bd. dirs. United Cerebral Palsy Schenectady County, Ind. Living of Capital Dist., United Way Schenectady County, Jr. Achievement Capital Dist.; past trustee Schenectady Mus.; bd. dirs. Schenectady Symphony Orch., Schenectady chpt. ARC, Hospice of Schenectady County, Salvation Army of Schenectady County, Freedom Forum of Schenectady, Family and Child Service, Schenectady; Albany League Arts adv. council to Bd. Regents N.Y. State, Pvt. Industry Council; adv. council Proctor's Theatre, Schenectady, exec. com. Capital Dist. Region Joint Tng. Partnership Act; chmn. Schenectady County Tourism and Visitors Council; trustee Hospice Found. Recipient Crystal Prism award 2d dist. Am. Advertisers Fedn., 1975; Hans M. Rozendaal Hospice award, 1983. Mem. Northeastern Fedn. Profl. Communicators (Silver medal 1975), Schenectady County C. of C. (pres. 1979). Democrat. Mem. Dutch Reformed Ch. Home: Synder Rd Alplaus NY 12008 Office: 6 Union St Schenectady NY 12305

BEE, SARAH ANN, rehabilitation administrator; b. N.Y.C., Oct. 4, 1947; d. Edward F. and Toby Palasz; B.S., Boston U., 1969, M.S., 1975; m. David W. Bee, Aug. 2, 1970. Intern, VA Hosp., Boston, 1974-75; counselor Mass. Rehab. Commn., Boston, 1975-77; rehab. specialist Internat. Rehab. Assos., Inc., Boston, 1977-78, service unit adminstr., 1978-82; with Comprehensive Rehab. Assocs., Newton, Mass., 1982—; attended Pres. Com. on Employment of the Handicapped, Washington, 1981. Cert. rehab. counselor, ins. rehab. counselor. Mem. Nat. Rehab. Assn., Nat. Rehab. Counseling Assn., Mass. Rehab. Assn. (past pres.), Nat. Assn. Rehab. Profls. in Pvt. Sector. Home: 199 S Main St Randolph MA 02368 Office: 181 Wells Ave Newton MA 02159

BEECHER, RUTH DOWNTON, assn. exec.; b. Manchester, N.H., Dec. 26, 1936; d. Ray Eugene and Dorothy (Muir) Downton; student Keene State Coll., 1954-57, N.H. Coll., 1979-81, Inst. for Orgnl. Mgmt., U. Del., 1981; m. Floyd Beecher, May 10, 1958; children—Deborah, Thomas, David, Robert. With Amoskeng Nat. Bank, Manchester, N.H., 1957-59; with Waumbec Mills, Inc., Manchester, 1972-79; dir. membership services, v.p. small bus. devel. Greater Manchester C. of C., 1979—; bus. cons. SBA, 1980—, active core exec., 1980—, mem. Small Bus. Adv. Bd. State of N.H. Trainer leaders Girl Scouts U.S.A., 1972-80; mem exec. bd. Service Corp. Ret. Execs. (SCORE), 1980—; bd. dirs. WON, Inc., Manchester, 1981—; active United Way, 1979-81; chmn. Heart Fund, 1979; key person Manchester Federated Arts, 1980-81. Recipient SBA Outstanding Service award, 1980, United Way Appreciation award, 1980, 81. Mem. Am., New Eng., N.H. C. of C. execs., Am. Bus. Women's Assn., Nat. Assn. Female Execs., Inst. Organizational Mgmt., Nat. Notary Assn. Club: N.H. Opera League, Concord Luncheon Group. Office: 57 Market St Manchester NH 03101

BEECHLER, IRIS JEAN, nurse, health educator; b. Winchester, Ind., July 27, 1940; d. Charles William and Lela Helen (Ozbun) Bussear; m. Billy Edman Beechler, Aug. 6, 1967; children—Billy Jr., Jeffrey, Cathy. Student Marion Coll., 1958-59, Taylor U., 1959-60; diploma in nursing, St. Vincent's Sch. Nursing, Indpls., 1965. R.N. Head nurse Community Hosp., Indpls., 1965-66; asst. supr. Riverview Hosp., Noblesville, Ind., 1966-67, head nurse, 1967-69; jr. high sch. resource tchr. Hamilton Heights Sch. Corp., Arcadia, Ind., 1981-82, elem. health educator, 1982—, mem. pupil service bd., 1983—. Youth dir. Victory Chapel Community Ch., Noblesville, 1966-81, mem. ch. bd., 1970—, ch. treas., 1975—, adult Sunday sch. tchr., 1975—; chmn. policy and procedure com. Emergency Med. Service Hamilton County, Noblesville, 1977. Recipient Very Spl. People award Noblesville Daily Ledger, 1980. Mem. Ind. Assn. Women Hwy. Safety Leaders (pub. info. chmn. 1975), Ind. Extension Homemakers Assn. (dist. rep. 1973-74, Jane award 1979), Hamilton County Extension Homemakers Assn. (health and safety chairman 1971-72, Jane award 1979), Roaring 20s Home Extension Homemakers Club, (pres. 1971-72). Home: RD 1 Box 352 A Cicero IN 46034

BEELER, SUSAN JANE, clinical nurse specialist; b. Manchester, N.H., Jan. 17, 1944; d. William Lawrence and Dorothy Olive (Smith) O'Connor; m. Thomas Taylor Beeler; children—Ethan Thomas, Emily Susan. B.S. in Nursing, Columbia U., 1968; M.S. in Gerontol. Nursing, Boston U., 1982. Pvt. duty nurse Columbia-Presbyn. Med. Ctr., N.Y.C., 1968-71; staff nurse ICU, Elliot Hosp., Manchester, 1971-72, head nurse ICU, 1972-75, instr. intensive care, 1975-78, cardiac rehab. coordinator, head nurse, 1978-79; gerontol. nurse practitioner Concord (N.H.) Regional Vis. Nurse Assn., 1982-83; geriatric nurse practitioner, clin. specialist Home Health Services No. Essex, Haverhill, Mass., 1983—. Mem. Am. Nurses Assn., N.H. Nurse Practitioners Assn., Am. Heart Assn., Am. Diabetes Assn., Am. Alzheimer's Disease and Related Disorders Assn., Arthritis Found. Home: King Rd Hampton Falls NH 03844 Office: Home Health Services Northern Essex 87 Winter St Haverhill MA 01830

BEER, ALICE STEWART (MRS. JACK ENGEMAN), musician, educator; b. Redwood Falls, Minn., Sept. 29, 1912; d. Robert and Isabel (Montgomery) Stewart; Mus.B., Northwestern U., 1934, Mus.M., 1952; postgrad. Johns Hopkins U., 1954, 60, Mexico City Coll., 1956 U. Md., 1957; m. Jack Engeman, Dec. 14, 1974; children by previous marriage—W. Robert, Jane K. Beer Mosher, Elizabeth S. Beer-Shilling. Tchr. public schs., Lawton, Mich., 1934-39, Battle Creek, Mich., 1949-51; tchr. Balt. Public Schs., 1951-53, supr. music, 1953-77; tchr. summer sessions various colls. and univs., 1957—; adj. faculty Peabody Inst., John's Hopkins U., Balt., 1981—. Mem. Nat. Fedn. Press Women, Music Educators Nat. Conf., Md. Music Educators Assn., Md. Fedn. Press Women, Trust Historic Preservation, Soc. Preservation Md. Antiquities, Md. Hist. Soc., Balt. Mus. Art, Balt. Symphony Assn., Phi Beta. Democrat. Presbyterian. Clubs: Towson Univ., Women's (Johns Hopkins U.). Author: Teaching Suggestions, Birchard Music Series II and III, 1962; Teaching Music: What, How and Why, 1973; Teaching Music to the Exceptional Child: A Handbook for Mainstreaming, 1980; Teaching Music, 1982; Patriotic Color Sound Filmstrips, 1967-69. contbr. articles to profl. jours. Home: 611 Debaugh Ave Towson MD 21204 Office: Music Edn Dept Peabody Inst Johns Hopkins U Baltimore MD 21202

BEER, BETTINA KNUST, educational administrator; b. N.Y.C., July 31, 1941; d. Kenneth Percy and Katherine Elizabeth (MacElveny) Knust; m. Joachim Rudolf Beer, Dec. 23, 1966 (div. 1972); 1 child, Walter. A.B., St. Lawrence U., 1963; M.A., Vanderbilt U., 1966, Ph.D., 1976. Teaching asst. Vanderbilt U., Nashville, 1966-68; instr. history Clemson U., S.C., 1968-73; asst. prof. Rollins Coll., Winter Pk., Fla., 1973-84, registrar, 1977-82, assoc. dean faculty, 1982-84; head Prew Prep. Sch., Sarasota, Fla., 1984—; participant Bryn Mawr Summer Inst., 1979. Active Fla. Assn. Collegiate Registrars and Admissions Officers, 1977-82, Am. Assn. Collegiate Registrars and Admissions Officers, 1978-82, edn. com. Winter Pk. C. of C., 1982-84; mem. Holocaust Resource and Edn. Ctr. Central Fla., 1983-85, chmn. budget com., 1983. Mem. Omicron Delta Kappa, Pi Sigma Alpha, Pi Beta Phi. Home: 1835 Baywood Dr Sarasota FL 34241 Office: Prew Prep Sch 7201 State Rd 72 Sarasota FL 34241

BEER, BETTY LOUISE, lawyer; b. Waco, Tex., July 17, 1943; d. William Lester and Ruth (Parks) B.; m. Sherwood James Franklin, June 16, 1979; 1 son, Jacob Harrison. B.A., Oberlin Coll., 1965; J.D., St. Louis U., 1974. Bar: Ill. 1974. Assoc. Kavanagh Scully Sudow White & Frederick, Peoria, Ill., 1974-78; owner Allen and Beer, Aledo, Ill., 1978—; asst. states atty. Mercer County, Aledo, 1979-84. Editor St. Louis U. Law Jour., 1974. Bd. dirs. Mo. Pub. Interest Research Group, 1973-74, Peoria Civic Opera, 1975-78, Prairie State Legal Services, Inc., 1975-77; bd. dirs., pres. Peoria City Beautiful, 1975-78; active Tri County Women Strength, Peoria, 1975-76; founding mem. Greasepaint Guild Theater, Aledo, 1980-83, Mercer County Coalition Against Domestic Violence, 1984-85. Mem. Ill. State Bar Assn. (estate planning council 1982, lawyer referral com 1975-82, pres. 1981), ABA, Mercer County Bar Assn. (pres. 1985—). Republican. Baptist. Lodge: PEO. Home: 207 SE 6th St Aledo IL 61231

BEER, JEANETTE MARY AYRES, French language and literature educator; b. Wellington, N.Z.; d. Alexander Samuel and Una Doreen (Castle) Scott; B.A., Victoria U., N.Z., 1954, M.A. 1st class, 1955; B.A. 1st class, Oxford U., Eng., 1958, M.A., 1962; Ph.D. (fellow), Columbia U., 1967; m. Colin Gordon Beer, 1959; children—Stephen James Colin, Jeremy Michael Alexander. Asst. lectr. French, Victoria U., Wellington, 1956; lectrice French and English, U. Montpellier (France), 1958-59; instr. French, Otago U., Dunedin, N.Z., 1963-64, Barnard Coll., Columbia U., N.Y.C., 1966-68; asst. prof. French, Fordham U., Bronx, N.Y., 1968-69, assoc. prof., 1969-76, prof., 1976-80, acting assoc. dean Thomas More Coll., 1972-73, dir. medieval studies, 1972-80; prof. French, Purdue U., West Lafayette, Ind., 1980—, head dept. fgn. langs. and lits., 1980-83; mem. nat. bd. cons. Nat. Endowment for Humanities, 1977—, asst. dir. div. fellowships and seminars, 1983-84. Nat. Endowment for Humanities grantee, 1975, fellow, 1979; Ind. Com. for Humanities Summer Fellow, 1985; Am. Philos. Soc. grantee, 1986. Mem. MLA, Medieval Acad., Internat. Arthurian Soc., Soc. Rencesvals, Medieval Assn. of Midwest (councillor), Am. Assn. Tchrs. French. Anglican. Author: Villehardouin—Epic Historian, 1968; A Medieval Caesar, 1976; Medieval Fables Marie de France, 1981; Narrative Conventions of Truth in the Middle Ages, 1981; Master Richard's Bestiary of Love and Response, 1985; gen. editor Teaching Language through Literature, 1971—; contbr. articles to profl. jours. Mem. adv. bd. Dictionary of the Middle Ages, 1981—. Office: Dept Fgn Langs and Lits Purdue U West Lafayette IN 47907

BEER, PAMELA JILL, vocational educator; b. Denver, Sept. 23, 1941; d. Wyeth Wittwer and Mary (DuReece) Porr; m. Calvin George Beer, Dec. 25, 1968. B.S., Pittsburg State U., Kans., 1963, M.B.A., 1979. Bookkeeper Hubbard Auto Supply, Pittsburg, 1950-63; tchr. bus. edn. Sabetha High Sch., Kans., 1963-65; tchr. bus. edn. Nevada High Sch., Mo., 1965-71; head bus. dept. Nevada Vocat. Area Sch., 1971—; mem. nat. adv. bd. Today's Sec., N.Y.C., 1982-83. Contbr. articles to profl. jours. Mem. editorial adv. bd. Roxbury Pub. Co., 1984—. Mem. Nat. Bus. Edn. Assn., Am. Vocat. Assn., Delta Kappa Gamma, Delta Pi Epsilon, Alpha Gamma Delta. Methodist. Avocations: bowling, swimming, bridge, tennis, golfing. Home: 1827 J F Kennedy Pittsburg KS 66762 Office: Nevada Area Vocat Tech Sch 900 W Ashland Nevada MO 64772

BEERBOWER, CYNTHIA GIBSON, lawyer; b. Dayton, Ohio, June 25, 1949; d. Charles Augustus and Sara (Rittenhouse) Gibson; m. John Edwin Beerbower, Aug. 28, 1971; 1 son, John Eliot. B.A., Mt. Holyoke Coll., 1971; J.D., Boston U., 1974; LL.B., Cambridge U., Eng., 1976. Bar: N.Y. 1975. Assoc., Cadwalader, Wickersham & Taft, N.Y.C., 1975-76; assoc. Simpson, Thacher & Bartlett, N.Y.C., 1977-81, ptnr., 1981—. Mem. Assn. Bar City N.Y., N.Y. State Bar Assn., ABA. Home: 160 E 72d St New York NY 10021 Office: Simpson Thacher & Bartlett One Battery Park Plaza New York NY 10004

BEERHALTER, BARBARA SUSAN, state official; b. Duluth, Minn., Dec. 13, 1943; d. Erwin Callies and Marcelle Elaine (Westlund) B.; m. Richard Alan Chapman, May 23, 1973; stepchildren—Connie, Candace, Timothy, Michael. Student, U. Minn.-Mpls., 1961-65. Broadcast journalist Sta. WCCO, Mpls., 1965-71; dir. info. Minn. AFL-CIO, St. Paul, 1971-74; asst. commr. Minn. Dept. Econ. Security, St. Paul, 1975-82, commr., 1983—; pub. utilities commr. State of Minn., St. Paul, 1986—; mem. Gov.'s Job Tng. Coordinating Council, St. Paul, 1983, Gov.'s Task Force on Emergency Food and Shelter, St. Paul, 1983, State Adv. Council on Vocat. Edn., Mpls., 1983; dir. Minn. Job Skills Partnership, St. Paul, 1983-85. Mem. U. Minn. Indsl. Relations Council, Mpls., 1983—. Recipient Meritorious Service award Am. Legion, 1983. Mem. Minn. Soc. Profl. Journalists (pres. 1970-71), Nat. Assn. Regulatory Utility Commrs., Minn. Nat. Assn. Women Bus. Owners (assoc.), Women Execs. in State Govt., U. Minn. Alumnae Soc. (bd. dirs. 1986—). Mem. United Ch. of Christ. Office: Minn Pub Utilities Commn 780 Am Center Bldg St Paul MN 55101

BEERMANN, COUNTESA ANA, investment and real estate company executive; b. Falls City, Nebr., May 19, 1945; d. August and Minnie Sophie (Ohlensehlen) Biermann; m. William August Beermann, Feb. 13, 1977 (dec. Dec. 1979); children—Kristine Kay, Angeline Ann; m. Otto Von Bismarchi, June 24, 1984. M.A., Kans. State U., 1966; postgrad. Moana Coll., 1971. Saleslady, Rudy's, Falls City, 1960-61, with Kappala Donna Enterprises Systems Inc., Honolulu, 1967—, pres., exec. owner, 1984—; mem. Charles Schwab & Co., Inc., 1985. Del., Republican Conv., Honolulu, 1983-84. Mem. Am. Mgmt. Assn. Lutheran. Clubs: Kamabemaha, Rose of Hawaii, Club House Hawaii, Sorority Club Hawaii. Avocations: golf, water skiing. Home: 7316 Maple St Omaha NE 68134 Office: Kappala Donna Enterprises Systems Inc S King St and Ala Monina Honolulu HI 96813

BEERS, CATHY LOU MILLER, direct mail marketing company executive; b. Pekin, Ill., Oct. 2, 1951; d. Richard Leroy and Betty Jean (Taylor) Miller; m. Daniel Joseph Beers, May 6, 1978; 1 child, Sean Franklyn. Student Ill. Central Coll., 1979. Mgr., Meadowbrook Dairy, Pekin, 1968-70; asst. to buyers Foster Gallagher, Peoria, Ill., 1971-73; account mgr. Ruppman Mktg. Co., Peoria, 1974-81; v.p. Customer Devel. Corp., Peoria, 1974-86; Editor: Collections newsletter, 1980-85. Vol., Midwest chpt. ARC, 1979, Dream Factory, 1984-85, Mem. Direct Mktg. Assn., Fla. Mag. Assn., Fulfillment Mgmt. Assn. (pres. Midwest chpt. 1984, editor chpt. newsletter 1984-85, chmn. Chgo.

1984-86); assoc. mem. Western Publs. Assn., Bus. Publs. Audit Bur., Audit Bur. Circulations. Democrat. Roman Catholic. Avocations: canoeing; fishing; volleyball. Home: 4312 Meadow Dr Pekin IL 61554

BEERS, DORIS CREIGHTON, realtor; b. Enfield, N.H., Aug. 6, 1908; d. Harris Edgar and Ada (French) Creighton; grad. public schs.; m. Robert Clayton Beers, Sept. 22, 1934 (dec. Sept. 1965); children—Diane Elaine (Mrs. Edward C. Schmults), Bradford B. Head sec. to chmn. Democratic State Com. N.H., 1929-30; sec. Gen. Motors Acceptance Corp., 1930-32, J.R. Poole, Boston, 1932-36; saleswoman Town & Country Homes, Boston, 1956-58; founder Cedar Realty, Wellesley Hills, Mass., 1958, owner, 1958-81. Sec., Wellesley (Mass.) ARC Fund Drive, 1955; pres. Melrose (Mass.) Jr. High Sch. PTA, 1953; chmn. bus. Wellesley United Fund Drive, 1974. Mem. Greater Boston Real Estate Bd., Nat. Assn. Realtors, West of Boston Realtors (sec. Council 1966), Nat. Assn. Women Realtors, Wellesley C. of C. Congregationalist. (past sec. guild Melrose Highlands). Clubs: Wellesley Republican, Wellesley Women's (rec. sec. 1982-84). Home: 27 Livermore Rd Wellesley Hills MA 02181 Office: 33 Washington St Wellesley MA 02181

BEERS, SANDRA DARIA, international banker; b. Niskayuna, N.Y., Aug. 4, 1952; d. Milford Charles and Alma Bernadette (Gaynor) Beers; A.B., Mt. Holyoke Coll., 1974. Global credit trainee Chase Manhattan Bank N.A., N.Y.C., 1974-75, fin. analyst Banco del Comercio, Bogotá, Colombia, 1975; asst. treas., relationship mgr. East European Lending, 1975-77, 2d v.p., dep. rep., Moscow, 1977-79, team mgr. credit devel. program, 1979-82, v.p., mgr. mktg. devel., London, 1982-83; v.p., rep. Chase Manhattan Bank, N.A., Moscow Office, 1983—. Home: Leninsky Prospect 83 Moscow USSR Office: Krasnopresnenskaya Emb 12 Suite 1709 Moscow USSR

BEESON, BETTY SPILLERS, educator; b. Muncie, Ind., Sept. 30, 1930; d. George W. and Gladys Elizabeth (Mills) Spillers; B.S., Ball State Tchrs. Coll., 1954; M.S., U. Omaha, 1963; Ed.D., U. Nebr., 1975; m. John D. Beeson, Feb. 1, 1952. Tchr., Salina (Kans.) Public Schs., 1954-59; instr. edn. U. Omaha, 1963-66; instr. edn. Ball State U., Muncie, Ind., 1969-70, prof., 1975—; founder Muncie Children's Mus.; workshop presenter. Pres. bd. dirs. United Day Care Center, Muncie; bd. dirs. Home Learning Center, Muncie. Mem. Muncie Assn. Edn. Young Children (past v.p.), Nat. Assn. Edn. Young Children, Ind. Assn. Edn. Young Children (regional rep.), Assn. Childhood Edn., Assn. Tchr. Educators, Kappa Delta Pi (past pres.), Phi Delta Kappa, Alpha Chi Omega, Kappa Kappa Kappa. Republican. Methodist. Club: USAF Officers Wives (dir.). Contbr. articles to profl. jours. Home: 3204 Twickingham Dr Muncie IN 47304 Office: Tchrs Coll Ball State U Muncie IN 47306

BEESON, MARY RUTH (PETE), personnel mgmt. cons.; b. Glen Rose, Tex., Nov. 15, 1913; d. Quentin Orestes and Maude Elma (Embree) Gaither; student Wright's Law Sch., 1931, U. Tex., 1934, San Antonio Coll., 1937, St. Mary's U., 1937-39, Am. U., 1952-53; m. Charles Edward Beeson, Nov. 15, 1940; children—Peter Gaither Embree, Caroline Jane. Exec. asst. to state dir. of ops., Works Progress Adminstrn., San Antonio, 1935-40; certifying officer, adminstrv. asst. Civilian Personnel Office, Army Air Force, San Antonio Aviation Cadet Center, 1941-46; personnel officer IRS, Washington, 1957-63, employment officer, Austin Service Center, 1963-74, chmn. Fed. Women's Program Planning Com., 1963-68, chmn. Equal Employment Opportunity Planning Com., Austin Service Center, 1963-73, mem. regional commr.'s adv. com. on Fed. Women's Program, IRS, Dallas, Tex., 1972-74; cons. in personnel mgmt., Austin, 1976—; cons. on curriculum, Camp Gary Job Corps, 1965. Chmn. Parent Edn. Com., Falls Church Schs., 1952-54; mem. exec. com. Community Coordinated Child Care Com., Austin, 1968-72; mem. adv. commn. to Tex. Legis. Council's study on the handicapped, Austin, 1970-73; mem. adv. com. on vocat. office edn. to Austin Ind. Sch. Dist., 1965-69; chmn. mayor's Com. on Devel. Child Care, Austin, 1970-75; chmn. Austin Mayor's Commn. on Status of Women, 1970-75, mem., 1975—; mem. citizens adv. bd. Travis County Juvenile Bd., 1981—. Recipient Outstanding Service to the Deaf award Tex. Edn. Agy., 1967, Fed. Woman's Award Bd. citation, Disting. IRS Worker for the Handicapped award IRS Commr., 1972, Pres.'s Com. on Employment Handicapped award, 1974. Mem. Internat. Personnel Mgmt. Assn., Austin Personnel Assn., Am. Mgmt. Assn. Unitarian. Inventor: Hycab, insulated coaster, car wastebasket. Home and Office: 2700 Valley Springs Rd Austin TX 78746

BEESON, MONTEL EILEEN, human services administrator, gerontologist; b. El Dorado, Ark., Dec. 22, 1939; d. Waymon Willett and Myrtle May (Roach) B. B.S. in Recreation, Calif. State U.-Hayward, 1963; M.A. in Edn. and Human Devel., Holy Names Coll., Oakland, Calif., 1979. Lic. nursing home adminstr.; cert. community coll. instr.; cert. gerontologist. Dist. exec. Ariz. Cactus-Pine council Girl Scouts U.S.A., Phoenix, 1963-66; dist. exec. San Francisco Bay council Girl Scouts U.S.A., Oakland, 1966-69, bus. mgr., 1969-71; exec. dir. Shabonee council Girl Scouts U.S.A., Moline, Ill., 1971-73, Tongass-Alaska council, Ketchikan, 1973-74, Muir Trail council, Modesto, Calif., 1974-78; asst. adminstr. Beulah Home, Inc., Oakland, 1980—; rehab. cons. Career Advancement Ctrs., San Leandro, Calif., 1979-80; preceptor Bd. Examiners Nursing Home Adminstrs., Sacramento, 1985. Mem. Am. Coll. Health Care Adminstrs., Am. Soc. on Aging, Calif. Specialists on Aging, Calif. Assn. Homes for Aging. Avocations: cross-country skiing; history; travel; reading; music. Home: 3393 Kiwanis St Oakland CA 94602

BEETZ, MARGARET O'CONNOR, health and beauty business executive, modeling school executive, model; b. Addis Ababa, Ethiopia, Dec. 12, 1955; came to U.S., 1967; d. Kevin Gordon and Mary (Symonds) O'Connor; m. Stephen Paul Beetz, Aug. 19, 1978. Student Aurora Coll., 1974-75; B.S. in Bus. and Fin., U. Ill., 1978. With Paul & Steve, Mendota, Ill., 1978-83; bookkeeper Brookhill Corp., Mendota, 1983—; asst. dir. Montee Modeling Sch., Wheaton, Ill., 1980-83; owner, dir. Elan Sch. Modeling, Peru, Ill., 1983—; pres., co-owner Total Image, Inc., Peru, 1984—; owner Feminique Fitness Ctr., Inc., Morris, Ill., 1985—, Feminine Fitness Ltd., Mendota, 1985—; registered model Suzanne Johnson Modeling Agy., Chgo., 1980—; asst. dir. Mrs. Am. Preliminaries, Ill., Iowa, Wis., N.D., S.D., Minn., 1981; asst. dir., scholarship chairperson Miss. Ill. Valley, Peru, 1985; cons. in field. Vice pres. Ill. Assn. Pvt. Colls. and Univs., 1975-76; v.p. Mendota Community Hosp. Aux., 1981, pres., 1982-84. Named to Outstanding Young Women Am., U.S. Jaycees, 1981; recipient Leadership award Ill. Hosp. Assn., 1984. Mem. Chgo. Fashion Exchange, Mendota C. of C. (dir. Nat. Sweet Corn Pageant 1979-81, cons. to pageant 1981-85). Avocations: coin collecting; boating; travel; reading. Office: Total Image Inc 1913 4th St Peru IL 61354

BEFAME, JEANNETTE, reporter, writer; b. Wahpeton, N.D., July 15, 1919; d. Frederick and Sykea (Ashton) Befame; A.B., Stanford, 1941; m. John Allen Sontheimer, Aug. 10, 1968 (dec.); m. 2d, W. Gordon Eustice, May 7, 1976. Reporter, San Francisco News, 1941, Sacramento Union, 1942; now newspaper feature writer-reporter San Jose (Calif.) Mercury-News; radio work, news reporter, interviews, San Francisco, 1947; TV guest appearances, 1956; during World War II wrote journalists for overseas. Del. Asian-Am. Journalists Conf. at East-West Center in Hawaii, 1965. Sec. Santa Clara County unit Am. Cancer Soc. Recipient (1st woman) Edward McQuade Meml. award for outstanding pub. service in journalism, 1955, Top Story award, met. dailies div. Calif. State Fair, 1956, Theta Sigma Phi Matrix award, 1964. Mem. Am. Assn. U. Women, Calif. Press Women (chartering pres. peninsula dist.), Stanford Alumni Assn. (sec. San Jose area 1962-63), Women in Communications (chpt. organizer, 1st pres. 1960, pres. Palo Alto chpt. 1975-76), Sigma Delta Chi (dir. No. Calif. chpt.). Club: San Francisco Press. Home: 1560 Plateau Ave Los Altos CA 94022 Office: San Jose Mercury-News San Jose CA 95125

BEFOURE, JEANNINE MARIE, writer, accounting consultant; b. N.Y.C., Aug. 6, 1923; d. Thomas James and Frances Marie (Thompson) Nicholson; m. Willard Rockne, Oct., 1940 (div. 1946); children—Rodger Lloyd, Lenore Irene; m. Jean Maure Befoure, Aug. 3, 1974. B.S. in Communications magna cum laude, Woodbury U., 1979, M.B.A., 1981. Audit clk. Sears Roebuck, Seattle, 1946-50; supr. materials U.S. Navy, Guam, 1951-52; self-employed acct., Nev., Calif., Ariz., 1953-68; pres. Yearound Bus. Services, Las Vegas, Nev., 1969-73; writer, cons. The JM People, El Monte, Calif., 1982—; instr. bus. and indsl. mgmt. Calif. Community Colls., 1979-82; mem. IRS/Tax Practioner Bd., Las Vegas, 1972-73; tutor Lauback Literacy Action, Los Angeles, 1981—. Author children's stories and poetry. Trainer Kellogg Found.-United Way, Los Angeles; founding sec. Homeowners of Golden Valley, Ariz., 1961. Mem. World Future Soc., Assn. M.B.A. Execs., Greater Los Angeles Press Club. Republican. Religious Scientist. Avocations: photography; poetry. Office: The JM People El Monte CA 91733

BEGELMAN, HEDDA JOAN, psychotherapist; b. Bronx, N.Y., June 5, 1939; d. Reuben and Edith (Fink) B.; B.S., Adelphi U., 1960; M.S.W., Columbia U., 1965. Social worker Sheltering Arms Children's Services, N.Y.C., 1965-67; psychiat. social worker, Girls Town, N.Y.C., 1967-69, Mid-Nassau Guidance Center, Hicksville, N.Y., 1969-76, Hempstead (N.Y.) Consultation Ctr., 1969-74, Mid-Nassau Family Counseling Ctr., Hicksville, 1976-76; pvt. practice psychotherapy, Farmingdale, N.Y., 1975—; speaker on sexuality various univs. Vol., Am. Cancer Soc. Cert. in psychotherapy Ind. Bronx Consultation Center; cert. in hypnosis, L.I. Soc. Clin. Hypnosis; lic. cert. social worker, N.Y. Mem. Nat. Assn. Social Workers, Acad. Cert. Social Workers. Home: 140 A Williamson St East Rockaway NY 11518 Office: 3 Dolphin Dr Farmingdale NY 11735

BEGGS, ELIZABETH ANN, medical group administrator; b. Decatur, Ill., June 13, 1960; d. David Whiteford and Joann (Lytle) Beggs. B.S., Ind. U., 1982. Staffing coordinator Spectrum Emergency Care, Dallas, 1983-84, regional recruiter, 1984-85; mktg. rep. Medicus Med. Group, Dallas, 1985-86, regional mgr., 1986—. Mem. Tex. Hosp. Assn., PEO, Women In Communications, Zeta Tau Alpha. Indiana scholar, 1976. Baptist. Office: Texas Medicus PA 8435 N Stemmons St Suite 144 Dallas TX 75247

BEHAL, SHAMILA, auditor; b. Nairobi, Kenya, June 29, 1956; came to U.S., 1984; d. Ved Parkash and Savitri (Bassi) Behal. B.S. with Honors, London Sch. of Econs., 1978; M.B.A., McGill U., 1984. Economist, Ministry of Fin., Nairobi, 1978-79; auditor Touche Ross & Co., London, 1979-82; audit sr., N.Y.C., 1984—. Treas. UN Youth Orgn., London, 1977. Mem. Nat. Assn. of Accts., Nat. Assn. Female Execs., Inst. of Chartered Accts. Students Soc. Club: U. London Bridge (sec. 1975-76). Avocations: horseback riding; tennis; international affairs; reading. Office: Touche Ross & Co 1633 Broadway New York NY 10019

BEHELER, ANN FERRY, computer consultant; b. Oklahoma City; d. Clarence E. and Ardath (Blair) Ferry; m. Carl M. Beheler, May 23, 1970; children—Joey, Sarah, Jeremy, Katie. B.S., Okla. State U., 1970; M.S., Fla. Inst. Tech., 1974; postgrad. U. Tex.-Richardson, 1975-77. Programmer, Mobil Oil Co., Dallas, 1970-71; adj. prof. Fla. Inst. Tech., Melbourne, 1972-75; research asst. U. Tex.-Dallas, 1975-77; project mgr. Rockwell Internat., Dallas, 1977-81; owner, pres. Computer Plus Inc., Dallas, 1981—. Mem. Fin. Mgrs. Soc. Republican. Office: Computers Plus Inc 12900 N Preston 1010 Dallas TX 75230

BEHLER, MARTHA ANN (MARTY), school administrator; b. Norman, Okla., June 27, 1950; d. Billy G. and Edna (Sargent) Monica Dadds; m. Robert F. Behler, Jan. 18, 1969; (dec. 1974); 1 son: Christopher Robert. B.A., San Jose State U., 1979; A.A. cum laude, De Anza Jr. Coll., 1976. Title IV-A liaison Ameridian edn. Milpitas Unified Sch. Dist., Calif., 1980—; founder and organizer Inner Bay Women's Soccer League, 1981, commr., 1981; tournament dir. 1st Annual Coors/Bobcats Internat. Women's Soccer Tournament, 1981; coach CYSA All Dist. U-16 Girl's Select, 1983; coach JV Girls Soccer, Milpitas High Sch., 1981-82, varsity coach, 1982—; coach Leland H.Sch., 1983; coach, coordinator Humber Vogelsinger/Puma Soccer Clinics, 1981-82; coach/mgr. San Jose Bobcats, 1980-82. Mem. Bay Area Title IV-A Edn. Assn., Calif. Indian Educators Assn., Nat. Indian Educators Assn., Calif. Sch. Employees Assn., Smithsonian Sccos. Democrat. Christian Ch. Home: 1136 Starbird Cir #2 San Jose CA 95117 Office: Milpitas Unified Sch Dist 1331 E Calaveras St Milpitas CA 95035

BEHLES, JENNIE DEDEN, lawyer; b. Longmont, Colo., May 8, 1946; d. L.O. and Katheryn (Ball) Deden; m. Robert J. Walley, Jan. 10, 1981. B.S.S., Northwestern U., 1967; student law Loyola U., Chgo., 1968-69; J.D. cum laude, U. N.Mex., 1970. Bar: N.Mex. 1970, U.S. Ct. Appeals (10th cir.) 1979, U.S. Tax Ct. 1982, U.S. Dist. Ct. N.Mex. 1970, U.S. Dist. Ct. (we. dist.) Tex. 1980. Assoc., Rosenberg & Blendon, Carlsbad, N.Mex., 1970-72; ptnr. Behles & Behles, Carlsbad, 1972-73; mng. atty. Smiley Profl. Assn., Albuquerque, 1973-79; co-owner Behles, Bloom & Behles, Albuquerque, 1979-83; ptnr. Martin & Behles, Albuquerque and Carlsbad, 1983-85; pres. Jennie Deden Behles, J.D., P.A., 1985—; mem. N.Mex. Supreme Ct. Specialization Bd., 1976-79; pres. Continuing Legal Edn. of N.Mex., Inc., 1974-75. State treas. Ill. Young Republicans, Chgo., 1968; state corr. treas. Bus. and Profl. Women Carlsbad, 1972. Recipient N.Mex. State award for outstanding leadership, 1975, award for outstanding service, 1976. Mem. ABA, Albuquerque Bar Assn., Nat. Conf. Bankruptcy Judges (assoc.). Club: Albuquerque Altrusa (treas. 1972). Lodge: Eastern Star. Office: 1104 Park St SW Albuquerque NM 87102

BEHLING, DOROTHY CLARA, fashion professional; b. Scotia, N.Y., May 25, 1930; d. Paul Carl and Evelyn Elizabeth (Blinsinger) Bazar. m. William Herman Behling, May 21, 1949; children—Gary Paul, Bruce William, Corrine Elizabeth. Student profl. modeling Roemary Bischoff Studios, Milw., 1965. Cert. modeling instr., Wis. Payroll mgr. Sears, Roebuck & Co., Schenectady, N.Y., 1947-49; sec., treas. Maple Grove Oil Co., West Allis, Wis., 1957-70; staff instr. Rosemary Bischoff Studios, 1966-81, profl. model, 1966-85; free-lance fashion profl., Mequon, Wis., 1985—; staff model Boston Stores, Milw., 1967-68, Gimbel Stores, 1968-69; cons. Max Factor, 1970; fashion model, cons. Alston Stores, Cedarburg, Wis., 1980-85. Treas., PTA, Hales Corners, Wis., 1957-58; leader Hales Corners council Boy Scouts Am., 1962-63; chmn. Hales Corners council Girl Scouts Am., 1967-68; mem., coordinator Milw. Soc. Models for United Assn. for Retarded Citizens, 1972-76. Mem. Bus. and Profl. Women' Assn., River Oaks Assn. (sec. 1976). Republican. Roman Catholic. Club: Christian Women Orgn. Avocations: tennis; gardening. Home: 12504 N Emily Ln 15 W Mequon WI 53092 also 154 Palm Dr Naples FL 33962

BEHNER, JANICE ROSE, real estate broker; b. Phoenix, May 20, 1938; d. Jefferson Robert and Oveita (Lawrence) Moore; m. Harvey Lee Acridge, June 8, 1956 (div. Dec. 1968); children—Sharma L., Lainee A., Scott Michael; m. 2d Richard Leo Behner, Oct. 27, 1973. Student Ariz. State U., 1961-62. Lic. real estate broker; cert. residential specialist. Salesman Goebel Realty, Phoenix, 1969-71, Apollo Enterprises, Glendale, Ariz., 1971-73; pres. Metro Realty, Inc., Phoenix, 1974-78; broker Century 21 Metro, Phoenix, 1973-78; co-founder 50 States Real Estate franchise, Phoenix, 1978, broker 1983—, sec., treas., 1978—, dir., 1978—; cons. curriculum com. Glendale (Ariz.) Community Coll., 1978—. Mem. Valley Cathedral, Phoenix, 1969—. Mem. Women's Council Realtors (pres. 1983-84). Republican. Home: 223 W Palmaire Ave Phoenix AZ 85021 Office: 50 States Real Estate 8686 N Central St Suite 106 Phoenix AZ 85021

BEHR, MARION RAY, artist, author, business executive; b. Rochester, N.Y., Sept. 12, 1939; d. Justin Max and Sophie Gusta (Koffler) Rosenfeld; B.Art Edn., Syracuse U., 1961, M.F.A., 1962; m. Omri Marc Behr, June 24, 1962; children—Dawn Marcy Yael, Darrin Justin Mason, Dana Marisa Jana. Freelance contbr. illustrations for stories, crafts, mag. covers and toy designs to nat. mags. including McCall's, Good Housekeeping, Lady's Circle, 1962-77; artist, works exhibited Contemporary Am. Artists, Scarsdale, N.Y., 1964, Am. Women Artists, Douglass Coll., 1977; one-woman show: Douglas Coll., 1983; creator survey Women Working Home—the Invisible Workforce, 1978; pres. Women Working Home, Inc., Edison, N.J., 1980—; condr. workshops; books include: (with others) Women Working Home: The Homebased Business Guide and Directory, 1981, 2d edit., 1983; illustrator: Jewish Holiday Book, 1977; extensive radio and TV appearances rep. Nat. Alliance Homebased Businesswomen. Mem. Kean for Gov. campaign, 1981; mem. White House Conf. on Free Enterprise Zones, 1982; trustee Women's Bus. Ownership Ednl. Conf., Inc., N.J., 1985; Presdl. del. White House Conf. on Small Bus., 1986. Recipient N.J. Women in Bus. Advocate of the Yr. award SBA, 1984; Woman of Yr. in Bus. and Industry award, 1985; Syracuse U. alumni grantee, 1957. Mem. Nat. Alliance Homebased Businesswomen (pres. 1980-82, legis. chair 1982-85; originator, founder), Women's Caucus for Art. Jewish. Co-Author: Women Working Home: The Homebased Business Guide and Directory, 2d edit., 1983. Home and office: 24 Fishel Rd Edison NJ 08820

BEHRENS, JOSEPHINE STORY, lawyer; b. Atlanta, Aug. 15, 1935; d. King J. and Mollie Aline (Connady) Story; m. Edward J. Behrens (dec. Jan. 1978); children—Kathy Sharon, Deborah Jean, Gregory R. J.D., U. San Fernando, Los Angeles, 1969. Bar: Calif. 1975. Legal sec. Loeb & Loeb, Los Angeles, 1964-69; tchr., City of Los Angeles, 1967-69; sole practice, Beverly Hills, Calif., 1975—. Mem. San Fernando Valley Bar Assn., Los Angeles County Bar Assn., San Fernando Valley Women Lawyers Assn. (bd. dirs., officer, charter mem. 1977—). Republican. Baptist. Home: 13630 Addison St Sherman Oaks CA 91423

BEHRENS, SUSANNE IRENE, insurance company executive; b. Houston, Jan. 8, 1947; d. Jerry Woodard and Katherine Sophie (Yantz) Black; m. Roy Robert Behrens, Jr., Nov. 22, 1967; children—Kimberly Sue, Troy Michael. B.S., U. Houston, 1975, M.B.A., 1984. Benefit analyst Blue Shield of Calif., San Diego, 1968-70; supr. med. claims inst. Phila. Life Ins. Co., Houston, 1970-77, mgr. group med. claims, 1977-79, dir. group med. claims, 1979-80, dir. group adminstrn. and billing, 1980-82; mgmt. cons., Houston, 1982-84; 2d v.p. Phila. Am. Life Ins. Co., 1984, 86, v.p., 1986—. Troop leader Girl Scouts U.S.A., Houston, 1965-68, 80—; cons. Project Bus., Jr. Achievement, Houston, 1980; vol. Tenneco Inc.'s Vols. in Assistance, Houston, 1980-82. Recipient Franklin award U. Houston, 1965. Roman Catholic. Home: 12622 Pebblebrook Houston TX 77024

BEIDLER, MARSHA WOLF, lawyer; b. Bridgeton, N.J., Feb. 29, 1948; d. Benjamin and Esther (Lourie) Wolf; m. John Nathan Beidler, Aug. 18, 1974. B.A., Dickinson Coll., Carlisle, Pa., 1969; J.D., Rutgers U., Camden, N.J., 1972; L.L.M. in Taxation, NYU, 1979. Bar: Pa. 1972, Fla. 1973, N.J. 1975. Atty. IRS, Phila., 1972-74, Trenton, N.J., 1974-76; mem. McCarthy & Hicks P.A., Princeton, N.J., 1976-81; ptnr. Pinto & Beidler, Princeton, 1981-83; prin. Smith, Lambert, Hicks & Miller, Princeton, 1983—; sec. Mercer County Estate Planning Council, Trenton, 1977—; lectr. estate planning; prof. Am. Inst. for Paralegal Studies. Bd. dirs. Birth Alternatives, Princeton, 1980, Mercer Council on Alcoholism, 1985—. Mem. ABA (tax sect.), N.J. Bar Assn. (tax sect.), Fla. Bar Assn., Mercer County Bar Assn., Princeton Bar Assn., Mercer County Women's Lawyers Caucus, Princeton C. of C. Lodge: Soroptimists (Princeton). Office: Smith Lambert Hicks & Miller PA One Palmer Sq Princeton NJ 08542

BEIL, KAREN MAGNUSON, editor, writer; b. Boston, Feb. 15, 1950; d. Victor Berger and Dorothy (Hall) Magnuson; student Upsala Coll., 1967-68; B.A. Cum laude, Syracuse U., 1971; m. James A. Beil, Feb. 24, 1973; 1 dau., Kimberly Erika. News reporter City News Bur. of Chgo., 1971-72; environ. research editor N.Y. State Dept. Environ. Conservation, Albany, 1973-75; asst. editor N.Y. State Environ., Albany, 1975-76, editor, 1976-78; assoc. dir. info. services The Conservationist Mag., N.Y. State Environ. and Environ. Notice Bull. of N.Y. State Dept. Environ. Conservation, Albany, 1978-81; freelance editor and writer, 1981—; cons. in field. Mem. Nat. Audubon Soc., Lit. Advocacy Pals Soc., Friends of the Library (Olean, N.Y.), Soc. Children's Book Writers. Contbr. articles to profl. jours.

BEILER/GROSHONG, NAOMI KAE, advertising consultant; b. Chestertown, Md., June 22, 1955; d. Christian Fisher and Katie B. (Stoltzfus) Beiler; m. Karl Francis Groshong, Aug. 9, 1980; 1 son, Gabriel Stephen. B.A., U. Md., 1977. Film dir., editor Buller Films, Henderson, Nebr., 1978-80; media dir. Warwick Sch. Dist., Lititz, Pa., 1980-81; producer PM Mag., Lancaster, Pa., 1981-83; account exec. Cable Ad Net, Hershey, Pa., 1983-84; free lance cons., Lancaster, Pa., 1983—; mem. task force Pa. Dutch Tourist Bd., Lancaster, 1984. Editor films: The History of the Great Plains series, 1978-80; producer, dir., editor films: Call to Care, 1979. Bd. dirs. Am. Cancer Soc., Lancaster, 1983. Mem. Internat. Assn. Bus. Communicators, Am. Women in Radio and TV. Mennonite. Home: 515 E Marion St Lancaster PA 17602

BEISEIGEL, SHIRLEY-ANN, rehab. psychologist; b. Allentown, Pa., May 27, 1927; d. John Calvin and Dorothy Irene (Bear) Shumberger; C.A.G.S. in Psychology and Counseling, Assumption Coll., 1982; A.B. in Biology, Bucknell U., 1949; M.S. in Rehab. Counseling, Va. Commonwealth U., 1969; m. Howard Alan Beiseigel, June 18, 1949; children—Robert Alan, Barry John, John Howard. Supervisory guidance counselor Woodrow Wilson Rehab. Center, Fishersville, Va., 1963-64; spl. edn. tchr. Lansing (Mich.) Public Schs., 1964; asst. home life dir. VFW Nat. Home, Eaton Rapids, Mich., 1964-66; exec. dir. Easter Seal Soc. of Ingham County, Lansing, Mich., 1966; profl. rehab. counselor Woodrow Wilson Rehab. Center, Fishersville, 1966-70, supr. counselors evaluation dept., 1970-71; counselor II, N.H. State Prison, Concord, 1971-72; vocat. evaluation coordinator Vocat. Devel. Center, Manchester, N.H., 1972-77; supr. psychodiagnostic and vocat. evaluation services Good Shepherd Home and Rehab. Hosp., Allentown, Pa., 1977-79, dir. psychodiagnostic and counseling services, 1979—. Mem. N.H. bd. dirs. Pres.'s Com. on Employment of Handicapped, 1975-76. Cert. psychol. services supr., Pa.; nat. cert. rehab. counselor. Mem. Am. Psychol. Assn., Pa. Psychol. Assn., Am. Personnel Guidance Assn., Nat. Rehab. Assn., Nat. Rehab. Counseling Assn. (charter), Pa. Rehab. Assn., N.H. Rehab. Assn. (dir. 1973-76), N.H. Rehab. Counseling Assn. (past pres. 1975-76), Va. Rehab. Counseling Assn. (dir. 1967-70), Va. Rehab. Assn. (membership chmn. 1968-69), Phi Mu. Republican. Presbyterian. Club: Order of Eastern Star (matron 1961-62). Home: 438 W Locust Ln Nazareth PA 18064 Office: Sixth and St John Sts Allentown PA 18103

BEISLER, SALLY JEAN, market manager; b. Pitts., Aug. 14, 1945; d. Rexford C. and Sue (Hopta) Arnold; B.S., U. Pitts., 1971, M.B.A., 1978; m. Joseph L. Beisler, Feb. 5, 1977; children—Susan Marie, Michael Anthony. With nuclear fuel mgmt. and sales staff Westinghouse Electric Co., Pitts., 1969-74; mgr. mfg. and internat. mktg. Borg Warner Chem. Co., Parkersburg, W.Va., 1974-78; mem. mktg. staff St. Joe Zinc Co., Pitts., 1978-79; market mgr. Mobay Chem. Co., Pitts., 1980—; dir. Med. Planning & Cons., Pitts., 1979—. Mem. Exec. Womens Council Pitts., Soc. Plastics Engrs., Flexible Packaging Assn. Home: 4320 Centre Ave Pittsburgh PA 15213 Office: Mobay Rd Pittsburgh PA 15205

BEITZEL, MARY ELIZABETH, retail company executive; b. Swarthmore, Pa., Dec. 29, 1955; d. George Bickley and Mary Louise (Elliott) Beitzel. B.A., U. Vt., 1977. Buyer, Downhill Edge, Burlington, Vt., 1977-78; sales rep. IBM Corp., Waldwick, N.J., 1978-80, systems engr. specialist, N.Y.C., 1980-82; pres. Insport Design, Inc., Chappaqua, N.Y., 1982—. Foster parent, Warwick, R.I., 1982—. Mem. Nat. Assn. Female Execs. Congregationalist. Office: Insport Designs Inc 29 King St Chappaqua NY 10514

BEKSA, REGINA, computerized accounting firm executive, translator, consultant; b. Newport Beach, Calif., Aug. 13, 1962; d. Chester Beksa and Blanche Ruth (Hart) Beksa Hart. Student Jagiellonian U., Cracow, Poland; A.A., Orange Coast Coll. Adminstr. RMP Mktg., Ensign Corp., MVA Design Group, Costa Mesa, 1983-85; owner, operator Beksa Enterprises, Santa Ana, Calif., 1985—; cons. The Graphic Agy., Costa Mesa, 1985—; translator from Polish lang. Mem. Polish Nat. Alliance (debutante), Nat. Assn. Female Execs., Calif. Scholarship Fedn. Democrat. Roman Catholic.

BELAFSKY, BETTY MATILDA, lawyer; b. Detroit, July 7, 1941; d. Charles and Blanche Forman; m. Mark Lewis Belafsky, Dec. 25, 1962; children—Caryn, Peter. B.S., U. Pa., 1962; J.D., Rutgers U., 1983. Bar: N.J. 1983. Assoc. firm Supnick et al, Haddonfield, N.J., 1988—. Fellow N.J. Bar Assn., Pa. Bar Assn.; mem. Fla. Bar Assn.

BELETZ, ELAINE ETHEL, nurse, educator; b. N.Y.C., Jan. 5, 1944; d. Harry and Rose (Friedman) B.; R.N., Mt. Sinai Hosp., N.Y.C., 1968; B.S. in Nursing, Fairleigh Dickinson U., 1970; M.A., N.Y.U., 1974; M.Ed., Columbia U., 1978, Ed.D., 1979. Staff nurse ICU Mt. Sinai Hosp., 1968-70, asst. head nurse, 1970; adminstrv. supervisory relief nurse, 1973-74, 77-78; clin. instr. Roosevelt Hosp. Sch. Nursing, N.Y.C., 1970-73; nurse gerontologist St. Luke's Hosp. Center, N.Y.C., 1974; asst. dir. nursing Bklyn. Hosp., N.Y.C., 1975-77; asst. prof. nursing Hunter Coll., CUNY, 1978-81; v.p. nursing Mt. Sinai Hosp., Med. Center, Chgo., 1982-83; assoc. prof. nursing Villanova (Pa.) U., 1983—; lectr.; cons. nursing adminstrn., labor relations in health care; mem. task force on block grants. Ill. Dept. Health. Fellow Am. Acad. Nursing; mem. Am. Nurses Assn. (dir. 1982—), N.Y. State Nurses Assn. (treas. 1977-78, pres.-elect 1978-79, pres. 1979-81), cert. of appreciation 1981), Pa. Nurses Assn., Indsl. Relations Research Assn., Am. Hosp. Assn., Am. Soc. Nursing Service Adminstrs., N.Y. Counties Registered Nurses Assn. (nominating com. 1973, dir. 1975-78, Amanda Silvers award 1981), Shershower Benevolent Assn. Jewish. Contbr. articles to profl. jours. Office: Grad Program Coll Nursing Villanova U Villanova PA 19085

BELFIGLIO, IRMA AVERY, gerontologist, social worker; b. Detroit, July 11, 1954; d. Turner Eugene and Beatrice (Agostini) Avery; m. Valentine John Belfiglio, Oct. 4, 1980. B.A., Tex. Woman's U., 1978; M.S., North Tex. State U., 1984. Cert. social worker, Tex. Adminstrv. asst. Dallas C. of C., 1978-79;

grand. intern Sr. Citizens of Greater Dallas/Hospitality House Sr. Ctr., 1981-82, assoc. dir. Ret. Sr. Vols., Dallas 1982-83; social service coordinator Dept. Human Services/Nutrition Program, Dallas, 1983, ctrs. adminstr., 1984—. Vol. nursing home Heritage Village, Richardson, Tex., 1983-85; mem. adv. council Ret. Sr. Vol. Program, sec., 1985, chmn. recognition com., 1983-85; bd. dirs. Centro de Amistad, 1985. Mem. La Voz del Anciano Mexico Americano (adv. bd. dirs.), Nat. Hispanic Council on Aging (v.p. Dallas 1985), Jr. League (community adv. bd. dirs. 1984—), Southwest Soc. of Aging (election com. 1985—), Tex. Soc. to Prevent Blindness (com. on pub. edn. 1984—). Republican. Roman Catholic. Club: Hispanic Club of Garland (sec. 1985—) (Tex.). Lodge: Altrusa. Avocations: bowling; travel; entertaining; volunteer activities.

BELFIORE-GRECO, MADDALENA, music instructor; b. Kearny, N.J., May 27; d. Frank and Agata (Spoto) Belfiore; m. Mauro Charles Greco, Sept. 25, 1960; children—Natale, Frank. Student Juilliard Sch. Music, N.Y.C., 1945-50, Mannes Sch. Music. Pres., founder ATA of N.J., 1959-61; music instr. Belfiore Accordion Studio, Kearny, N.J. Author: 1st Steps in Bellows Shake, 1958. Editor: Myron Floren Accordion Method, 1957. Recipient Golden Lady award, Amita, 1978; Woman of the Year, Jersey Jour., 1980, Am. Accordionists Assn. R.I., 1981. Mem. Am. Accordionists Assn. (dir., nat. pres. 1971-73, 75-76, 79-80), Confedn. Internat. des Accordeonistes/Austria (1st v.p. 1975—), Am. Accordionists Assn. N.J. (dir.), Accordion Tchrs. N.J. (pres. 1985—). Avocations: golf; cooking; needlepoint. Home: 58 W Bennett Ave Kearny NJ 07032

BEL GEDDES, BARBARA, actress; b. N.Y.C., Oct. 31, 1922; d. Norman and Helen Belle (Sneider) Bel G.; m. Carl Schreuer, Jan. 24, 1944 (div. 1951); 1 dau., Susan; m. Windsor Lewis, Apr. 15, 1951 (dec.); 1 dau., Betsy. Student, Buxton Sch., Putney, Andrebrook. First stage role in School for Scandel, Clinton (Conn.) Playhouse, 1939; made Broadway debut in Out of The Frying Pan, 1940; appeared in: Little Darling, 1942, Nine Girls, 1943, Mrs. January and Mr. X, 1944, Deep Are the Roots, 1945 (Clarence Derwent award), The Moon Is Blue, 1952, The Living Room, 1954, Cat on a Hot Tin Roof, 1955, The Sleeping Prince, 1956, Silent Night, Lonely Night, 1959, Mary, Mary, 1961, The Porcelain Year, 1965, Everything in the Garden, 1967, Finishing Touches, 1973, Ah, Wilderness, 1975; motion pictures include The Long Night, 1946, I Remember Mama, 1948, Blood on the Moon, 1948, Caught, 1949, Panic in the Streets, 1950, Fourteen Hours, 1951, The Five Pennies, 1959, Five Branded Women, 1960, By Love Possessed, 1961, The Todd Killings, 1970, Summertree, 1971; appears regularly as: Eleanor Southward Ewing on TV show Dallas, 1978-84, 85—. Recipient Theatre World award 1946; Emmy award for best actress in a dramatic series, 1980. Author, illustrator: children's books I Like to Be Me, 1963, So Do I, 1972; designer greeting cards for, George Caspari Co. Office: care Lorimar Television Pub Relations 3970 Overland Ave Culver City CA 90230

BELINA, MARIA, government contracts manager; b. Mexico, Jan. 23; came to U.S., 1969; d. Manuel and Rosa (Murua) Garcia; m. July 28, 1979; 1 child, Joseph John. B.A., Tchr.'s Coll., 1965; M.A., Manhattan Coll., 1974; postgrad. in Japanese lang. and history, Japan Sch. Langs., 1965-68. Cert. tchr., N.Y., N.J. Coll. prof. Aoyama U., Tokyo, 1967-69; prof. Techologico de Monterrey, Mexico City, 1980-81; mgr. adminstrn. Sodick, Inc., Saddle Brook, N.J., 1982-85; import mgr. Eiseman Ludmar, N.Y.C., 1985—; counselor, tchr. St. Catherine of Genoa, N.Y.C., 1970-80. Author: Spanish for Japanese, 1968; The Nobody Bird, 1980; translator: Psychology, 1981. Mem. Multiply Handicapped of N.J. Assn. Republican. Roman Catholic. Office: Eiseman Ludmar Co Inc 330 W 34th St New York NY 10001

BELING, HELEN, sculptor; b. N.Y.C., Jan. 1, 1914; d. Morris and Eva (Hurwitz) B.; m. Lawrence R. Kahn, Sept. 30, 1937; children—Kathe, Victoria. Student NAD, 1930-36. Tchr. Westchester County Art Workshop; exhbns. include: Met. Mus. Art, N.Y.C., Whitney Mus., Pa. Acad. Fine Arts, Everson Mus., San Francisco Mus., City Mus., St. Louis, Albright Knox Art Gallery, numerous others; one-woman exhbns. include: John Heller Gallery, 1952-54, Krasner Gallery, 1959, 61, 64, 67, 69, 71, Hudson River Mus., 1960, Sculpture Ctr., 1974, Bridge Gallery, 1979; represented in permanent collections: Butler Inst. Am. Art, Syracuse U. Mus., Hirshhorn Mus. and Sculpture Garden, Norfolk Mus. Art, St. Lawrence U., others; numerous commd. works. Mem. Sculptors Guild (pres. 1972-74), Nat. Assn. Women Artists (Medal of Honor), Audubon Artists (Medal of Honor), Fine Arts Fedn. (bd. dirs., v.p.). Home: 287 Weyman Ave New Rochelle NY 10805

BELINSKY, ILENE BETH, lawyer; b. Boston, Jan. 30, 1956; d. Harry Lewis and Ann Natalie (Rubin) B. B.A., Simmons Coll., 1977; J.D. cum laude, New Eng. Sch. Law, Boston, 1980. Bar: Mass. 1980, U.S. Dist. Ct. Mass. 1981, U.S. Ct. Appeals (1st cir.) 1981, U.S. Supreme Ct. 1984. Assoc. firm Reservitz & Steinberg, P.C., Brockton, Mass., 1980-85; ptnr., 1985—; bd. dirs. Southeastern Mass. Legal Assistance Corp., New Bedford, 1982-86. Bd. dirs. Brockton unit Am. Cancer Soc., 1983, 84. Mem. Mass. Bar Assn. (dir. young lawyers div. 1984-86), Mass. Women's Bar Assn., ABA, Plymouth County Bar Assn., Assn. Trial Lawyers Am., Mass. Acad. Trial Lawyers, Nat. Acad. Criminal Def. Lawyers. Democrat. Jewish. Office: Reservitz & Steinberg PC 528 Pleasant St Brockton MA 02401

BELIVEAU, MARTHA OATES, business education educator; b. Gastonia, N.C., Sept. 25, 1944; d. Grady and Helen (White) Oates; m. Paul Roland Beliveau, May 27, 1977. B.S., We. Carolina U., 1967; M.A., 1969; Ed.S., Ga. State U., 1981. Cert. tchr., Ga. Sec. to Congressman B. Whitener, Washington, 1965; instr. Haywood Tech. Inst., Clyde, N.C., 1967-68; instr. Gaston Coll., 1968-73; adminstrv. asst. Pilot Internat. Hdqrs., Macon, Ga., 1973; instr. Macon Jr. Coll., 1973-75; asst. prof., coordinator bus. edn. Clayton Jr. Coll., 1975-82, assoc. prof., 1982—; communications cons. Mem., Mid-Ga. Symphony Guild. Mem. AAUW, Assn. Info. Systems Profls., Am. Vocat. Assn., Ga. Vocat. Assn., Nat. Bus. Edn. Assn., So. Bus. Edn. Assn., Ga. Bus. Edn. Assn., Delta Pi Epsilon. Lutheran (mem. Southeastern Synod ch. ext. com., mem. ch. council, fin. chmn.). Contbg. author: Business Writing: Concepts and Applications, 1983. Home: 732 Valley Trail Macon GA 31204 Office: Clayton Jr Coll Bus Edn Morrow GA 30260

BELKIN, JANET E., lawyer; b. N.Y.C.; d. Irving and Pauline H. Ehrenreich; B.A., Vassar Coll., 1958; Ph.D., St. Johns U., 1975; J.D., Hofstra U.; LL.M., NYU, 1983; m. Myron Belkin, June 29, 1958; children—Lisa, Gary, Kira. Tchr. spl. edn., N.Y.C., 1958-60; adj. faculty St. Johns U., 1970-75, Nassau Community Coll., 1971-75; pvt. counselor, 1971-75; admitted to N.Y. bar, 1979; atty. govt. relations Equitable Life Ins. Co., N.Y.C., 1978—. Chmn. Hudson group Democratic Nat. Com. Task Force, 1981—; mem. legis. com. N.Y.C. Commn. Status Women; bd. dirs. Merrick (N.Y.) Sr. Citizens Center. Mem. ABA (vice chmn. adminstrv. law com.), Assn. Calif. Life Ins. Cos. (dir.), N.Y. State Bar Assn., Assn. Bar City N.Y., Women in Housing and Fin., Women in Govtl. Relations. Clubs: City (N.Y.C.), B'nai Brith. Home: 3014 Hewlett Ave Merrick NY 11566 Office: 787 Seventh Ave New York NY 10019

BELL, BETTY JEAN, educator; b. Dallas, Jan. 1, 1950; d. Alphonso Lee and Hattie Antonia (Nemec) Ground; m. Ronald Thomas Bell, Aug. 1, 1974. B.A., U. Tex.-Arlington, 1970; M.Ed., East Tex. State U., 1975. Cert. tchr., counselor, Tex. Tchr. sci., art and English, Fred F. Florence Jr. High Sch., Dallas, 1971-76; tchr. English and journalism W.W. Samuell High Sch., Dallas, 1976—. Recipient award of Excellence, Dallas Ind. Sch. Dist. Communications Div., 1980, 81. Mem. Greater Dallas Council Tchrs. English (liaison with nat. orgn. 1980-83), Tex. Assn. Counseling and Devel., Tex. Assn. Journalism Dirs., Shakespeare Guild (membership sec. Dallas 1980-81), Nat. Council Tchrs. of English, Tex. Joint Council Tchrs. of English, Alpha Delta Kappa (chpt. treas. Beta 1978-80), Phi Delta Kappa. Democrat. Methodist. Home: 8319 Foxwood Ln Dallas TX 75217 Office: W W Samuell High Sch 8928 Palisade Dr Dallas TX 75217

BELL, BETTY LORENE, nurse; b. Lebanon, Tenn., Nov. 18, 1946; d. Henry Jackson and Helen Emaline (Pack) Johnson; m. James Howard Bell, Mar. 11, 1972 (dec. 1973); children—Catherine Michelle, Christopher Michael. A.D. in Nursing, Middle Tenn. State U., 1978. Staff nurse VA Med. Ctr., Nashville, Tenn., 1978-81, 84-85, Alvin C. York VA Med. Ctr., Murfreesboro, Tenn., 1985—; nurse coordinator Cedar Creek Home Health Services, Murfreesboro, 1981-82, dir. nursing Tenn. In-Home Health Services, Lebanon, 1982-84. Served as 2d lt. USAR, 1985—. Mem. Nat. Assn. Female Execs., Am. Assn. Critical Care Nurses. Baptist. Avocations: boating; camping; horseback riding; tennis; volleyball. Home: PO Box 312 Smyrna TN 37167

BELL, BRITTON, business executive, management consultant; b. Louisville, June 18, 1948; d. Elbert Pinckley and Betsy Ann (Gordon) Watts; B.A. in Bus. Mgmt. and Profl. Communications, Alverno Coll., Milw., 1981; m. James H. Bell, Jr., Mar. 15, 1969 (div. Dec. 1972); 1 son, Scott Elbert. Acct., Am. Mut. Reins. Co., Chgo., 1967-69; office services Shell Oil Co., Detroit, 1969-71; personnel asst. RTE Corp., Waukesha, Wis., 1973-74; law office adminstr. John W. Cusack, S.C., Waukesha, 1974-77; regional rep. Reynolds and Reynolds Co., Milw., 1977-79; dist. rep. Bur. Nat. Affairs, Inc., Washington, 1978-80; founder, owner, pres. Profl. Mgmt. Services, Brookfield, Wis., 1979-84, Britton Bell Co., 1984—, Exec. Environments, Inc., 1983—, speaker, cons., seminar leader in field; instr. continuing legal edn. U. Wis. Law Sch. Author: A Practical Approach to Managing Your Law Practice, 1982; Financial Management—Key to a Successful Practice, 1983. Active local election com., NOW; proj. bus. cons. Jr. Achievement; mem. fund raising com. Florentine Opera, 1983—; vol. ARC Disaster Action Team, 1986—; hospice vol. St. Mary's Hosp., 1986—. Served with USN, 1966-67. Mem. Am. Mgmt. Assn., Internat. Platform Assn., Nat. Assn. Female Execs., Acad. Mgmt., Nat. Assn. Accts., Am. Entrepreneurs Assn., Alverno Coll. Alumnae Profls. Assn. Republican. Roman Catholic. Home: 1569 S Carriage Ln New Berlin WI 53151

BELL, CAROLYN SHAW, educator, economist; b. Framingham, Mass., June 21, 1920; d. Clarence Edward and Grace (Wellington) Shaw; A.B. magna cum laude, Mt. Holyoke Coll., 1941; Ph.D., London (Eng.) Sch. Econs., 1949; D.H.L. (hon.), Babson Coll., 1983; m. Nelson S. Bell, Aug. 26, 1953; 1 child by previous marriage, Tova Marie. Economist, OPA, 1941-45; research economist London Sch. Econs., 1946-47, Social Sci. Research Council, Harvard, 1950-53; mem. faculty Wellesley Coll., 1950—, prof. econs., 1962—, chmn. dept., 1962-65, 79-82, Katharine Coman prof. econs., 1970—. Pub. mem. Fed. Adv. Council on Unemployment Ins., 1974-77, chairwoman, 1975-77; bd. econ. advisers Pub. Interest Econ. Center, 1973-83; bd. overseers Amos Tuck Grad. Sch. Bus. Adminstrn., Dartmouth, 1973-79; mem. econ. policy council UN Assn., 1976-82; trustee Joint Council Econ. Edn., 1975-83, Tchrs. Ins. and Annuity Assn., 1977-85; mem. NRC Commn. on Behavioral Scis. and Edn., 1977-83. Mem. Am. Econs. Assn. (chmn. com. on status of women in econs. profession 1972-74, mem. exec. com. 1975-77), Am. Statis. Assn., AAUP (pres. Wellesley chpt. 1965-66), AAUW (Shirley Farr fellow 1961-62), ACLU, Assn. Evolutionary Econs. (dir. 1973-75), Eastern Econ. Assn., UN Assn. (dir. 1980-83), Boston Econ. Club, Phi Beta Kappa (pres. chpt. 1978-80). Author: (with W.W. Cochrane) Economics of Consumption, 1956; Consumer Choice in the U.S. Economy, 1967; The Economics of the Ghetto, 1970; (with others) Coping in a Troubled Society, 1974; also articles. Radio and television commentator, cons. Mem. bd. editors Challenge, Jour. Econ. Lit., Jour. Econ. Edn. Home: 167 Clay Brook Rd Dover MA 02030 Office: Wellesley Coll Wellesley MA 02181

BELL, DOROTHY HAGLER, real estate broker; b. Port Arthur, Tex., Dec. 22, 1935; d. John D. and Amy F. Hagler; m. James D. Bell, June 16, 1956 (div. Mar. 1974); children—Suzanne Clifford, John McLauchlin; m. Thomas R. Serlo, June 25, 1983. B.B.A., U. Tex.-Austin, 1956. Real estate broker Duffy & La Roe, Houston, 1973-83, Helena Underwood Realtors, Dallas, 1983—. Finalist Mademoiselle Mag. Coll Bd., 1953. Active Republican Party, Houston, New Orleans and Dallas; tres. Park Cities Rep. Women; vol. Dallas Mus. Art. Mem. Houston Livestock Show and Rodeo, Greater Dallas Bd. Realtors (pub. affairs com., Summit award), Women's Council Realtors (edn. com.), Internat. Platform Assn., Southwestern Watercolor Soc., Million Dollar Club, Alpha Phi. Presbyterian. Club: Houston Panhellenic (sec. 1972-74). Office: Helena Underwood Realtors 5550 Preston Rd Dallas TX 75205

BELL, GLENNA SUSAN, accountant; b. Hobbs, N.Mex., Oct. 21, 1951; d. Keith Howard and Thelma Lucille (Parker) Peverley; m. Randell W. Bell, Feb. 27, 1983. B.A., U. Tex., 1974. Sec., Forrest & Cotton, Inc., Austin, Tex., 1974-75; adult probation officer Harris County, Houston, 1975-76; office mgr. Landmark Realtors, Lubbock, Tex., 1976-79; supr., acctg. operator West Texas Consultants Inc., Odessa, Tex., 1979-83, mgr. acctg. dept., 1983—. Mem. Fiesta del Arte com. Art Inst. Permian Basin, Odessa, 1983-84, also mem. guild, bd. dirs., 1984—, publicity chmn., 1984—; mem. Odessa Crimestoppers Inc., 1983-84. Mem. Delta Zeta Sorority. Office: West Tex Consultants Inc 1101 N Whitaker Odessa TX 79763

BELL, JAYNELLE KHAMILLAH, pharm. mfg. co. mgr.; b. Oakland, Calif., Feb. 26, 1953; d. William Hayes and Genieve Cartwright (Hilton) Jenkins; B.A., U. Calif., Berkeley, 1976; M.B.A. (Basic Edn. Opportunity grantee, Consortium fellow), U. So. Calif., 1979; m. James M. Bell, June 28, 1980; children—Robert, Semaj. Bus. mgr. U. Calif.-Berkeley publ. Blue and Gold, 1975-76; mktg. analyst Oakland Tribune/Gannett Publs., 1976-77; sales rep. Procter & Gamble Co., San Francisco dist., 1979-81; dist. mgr. Drackett Products div. Bristol Myers Corp., Dublin, Calif., 1981-84; sr. account mgr. Block Drug Co., Jersey City, N.J., 1984—. Participant Big Sister Program, San Francisco, 1974—; voter registrar for Congressional campaign, 1971—. Mem. Nat. Assn. Female Execs., Women in Advt., Nat. Council Negro Women (publicity dir. asst. 1979), LWV. Republican. Methodist. Club: Profl. and Bus. Women's. Editor United Meth. Women newsletter, 1982. Home: 345 Goheen Circle Vallejo CA 94590 Office: 345 Goheen Circle Vallejo CA 94591

BELL, JEANNE VINER, public relations counselor; b. Los Angeles, Feb. 27, 1923; d. Herman and Mary (Kaufman) Spitzel; m. Melvin A. Viner, Feb. 1, 1942 (dec.); children—Michael, Karen Viner Fawcett; m. 2d, J. Raymond Bell, Dec. 15, 1974 (dec.). Student UCLA, Am. U., George Washington U. Prin. Jeanne Viner Spl. Services, Washington, 1958-61, Jeanne Viner Assocs., Washington, 1961-82; pub. relations counselor, 1982—; dir. Independence Fed. Bank, Washington, Independence Fed. Service Corp., Washington. Contbr. articles to profl. jours. Presdl. appointee to adv. council SBA, 1983, Pres.'s Com. on Employment of Handicapped, 1982; bd. dirs. nat. adv. bd. Fedn. Am. Immigration Reform, Washington, 1984—; bd. dirs., mem. exec. com. Arthritis Found. of Met. D.C., 1982—; mayoral appointee to D.C. Adv. Com. on Resources and Budget, 1981—, D.C. Pvt. Industries Council, 1983—. Recipient Outstanding Leadership and Achievement award State Bus. and Profl. Women's Clubs, Washington, 1981. Mem. Pub. Relations Soc. Am., Capital Press Women (pres. 1980-82, Woman of Achievement 1982), Am. News Women's Club (officer 1976-78), Fin. Mktg. Council of Washington. Clubs: Am. News Women's (bd. govs. 1969-70), Nat. Press (Washington). Address: 3506 Winfield Ln Washington DC 20007 also 9460 Hidden Valley Pl Beverly Hills CA 90210

BELL, JUDY FRANZ, parks executive; b. Indiana, Pa., May 1, 1940; d. Robert Casper Franz and Ellen Kathrine (Parks) Pierce; m. Walter Claude Overby, May 11, 1962 (div. 1977); children—Jeffrey Pierce, Lee Turner; m. James Dwight Bell, Dec. 3, 1983. B.A. in Edn., U. Pitts., 1961; M.A. in Documentary Film, UCLA, 1969. Tchr. Roswell (N. Mex.) High Sch., 1964-67, Carmichael (Calif.) High Sch., 1968; adminstrv. aide to chief exec. officer Harris County, Tex., 1976—; bd. dirs. Bayou Preservation Assn., Houston, 1976—, Parks People, Houston, 1980-84); adv. Harris County Flood Control Task Force, 1977-80. Named among 84 Most Interesting People in Houston, Houston City Mag., 1984. Mem. Nat. Parks Conservation Assn., Nat. Recreation, Parks Assn., Tex. Recreation, Parks Assn. Republican. Roman Catholic. Home: 1002 Whitestone Ln Houston TX 77073 Office: Harris County #911 1001 Preston St Houston TX 77002

BELL, LINDA CRAWFORD, magazine editor; b. Harrisburg, Pa., Jan. 13, 1948; d. Elwood F. and Reba J. (Stakley) Crawford; student Pa. State U., 1965-68; m. Daniel Locke Bell II, July 18, 1970 (div.); children—Daniel Locke III, Ian Spencer. With Soviet Life Mag., Washington, 1969—, sr. editor, 1976—. Bd. dirs., public relations adv. Emerson Gallery Art, McLean, Va., 1976—. Democrat. Episcopalian. Office: Soviet Life Mag 1706 18th St NW Washington DC 20009

BELL, MARY, real estate and investment cons.; b. Bklyn., June 5, 1907; d. Alonzo Chandler and Emily (Cox) B.; student Skidmore Coll., 1924-25; grad. Pratt Inst., 1928; student Hunter Coll., 1926, Berlitz Sch., 1927, U. Fla., 1947; children—Chandler Rogers Dann, Diana Dann Smelser. Photographer, Thomas Cook Co., 1927, Mary Bell Studio, Westfield, N.J., 1928-31, Aero. Art and Advt. Surveys, Ayer, N.Y., 1932; silver designer; advt. work for Timken Detroit Axle Co.; with Bell Electric Motor Co., Garwood, N.J., 1920, mgr. Bell Factory Terminal, Garwood, 1939-41, sec. treas., 1941-45, pres., 1945-52; sec. Bell Haven Inc., Miami, Fla., 1945-51, v.p., 1951-82, also dir.; v.p. Bell Bros. Co., Miami, 1945-82, also dir.; sec. Noren Estates Co., Pt. Reyes, 1975-80, also dir.; founding mem. Central Valley Savs. and Loan (Calif.). Mem. Republican Nat. Com., Rep. Senatorial Com., Rep. Congl. Com.; founding mem. Marin Cultural Center, 1980. Mem. Ariz. State Horsemen, Calif. State Horsemen, Calif. Equestrian Patrol, Pratt Alumni Assn., Museum Soc. of San Francisco, Smithsonian Assocs. Contbr. articles to New Yorker, N.Y. Herald Tribune, N.Y. Times, Country Life, Popular Aviation, Sportsman Pilot, others. Episcopalian.

BELL, MARY ANNE, graphics art company executive; b. Cape May, N.J., July 16, 1956; d. Glenn Laross and Margaret Marie (Hinke) Bell. Student Northeast Bergen Tech. Sch., 1971-74; currently enrolled Parsons Sch. Design, N.Y.C. Graphic artist Graphics Workshop, Paramus, N.J., 1974-78; art dir. Filip Assocs., Paramus, from 1979. Mem. Bergenfield Council for Arts, 1985. Roman Catholic. Home: 67 Gordon Ave Dumont NJ 07628 Office: Filip Assocs Inc 299 Forest Ave Paramus NJ 07652

BELL, MARY CATLETT (COCABELL), artist; b. Weleetka, Okla., Sept. 26, 1924; d. Stanley Boulware and Alma Bertha (Cagle) Catlett; B.A. in Lang., U. Okla., 1946; m. J. Stewart Bell, Sept. 15, 1951; 1 son, William Catlett. One woman shows at R.S. Barnwell Art Center, Shreveport, La., 1980, Exhibit in Gov.'s Gallery, State Capitol, 1981, Okla. Art Center, 1984; exhibited in group shows at 61st ann. exhbn. Allied Artists of Am., N.Y.C., 1974, Watercolor U.S.A., Springfield, Mo., 1975, 150th, 153d exhbns. Nat. Acad. Design, N.Y.C., 1975, 78, Okla. Bicentennial Art Exhbn., 1976, Living Women Living Art, Okla. Art Center, Kerr Conf. Center, others; represented in permanent collections at Okla. Heritage Assn., Oklahoma City, Arts Council Oklahoma City, Omniplex Arts and Scis. Mus., Oklahoma City; numerous commns. Mem. Okla. Art Center, Okla. Watercolor Assn., Okla. Mus. Art, Jr. League of Oklahoma City, Delta Delta Delta. Republican. Methodist. Address: 2 Colony Ln Oklahoma City OK 73116

BELL, MARY ELIZABETH, accountant; b. San Antonio, Dec. 20, 1937; d. Thomas Alfred and Mary Elizabeth (McMurrain) Beniteau; B.B.A., Baylor U., 1959; M.B.A., U. Tex., 1960; m. William Woodward Bell, May 31, 1969; children—Susan Elizabeth, Carol Ann. Teaching asst. U. Tex., Austin, 1959-60; prin. Deloitte, Haskins & Sells, C.P.A.s, Dallas, 1960-69; county auditor Brown County (Tex.), 1972-78; pvt. practice acctg., Brownwood, Tex., 1969—; acct. Brownwood Regional Hosp. Women's Aux., 1969—. Named Outstanding Com. Chmn., Dallas chpt. C.P.A.s, 1968-69; C.P.A., Tex. Mem. Brownwood C. of C. (dir. 1979-82, sec.-treas. 1981-82), Tex. Soc. C.P.A.s (dir. 1979-82, trustee Ednl. Found. 1981—, sec.-treas. Found. 1982-84, pres. 1984—), Am. Inst. C.P.A.s, Am. Soc. Women Accts., Am. Woman's Soc. C.P.A.s, AAUW, Pi Beta Phi, Baylor U. Alumni Assn. (dir. 1979-82). Baptist. Clubs: Brownwood Woman's (pres. 1980-81), Rotary Ann (v.p. 1982-83, pres. 1983-84), Baylor U. Hankamer Sch. Bus. Alumni Bd. Home: PO Box 1564 Brownwood TX 76804 Office: 109 N Fisk St Brownwood TX 76801

BELL, MARY KATHERINE, retired mathematician, educator; b. Pensacola, Fla., Apr. 14, 1909; d. Charles Henry and Mary Elizabeth (Sellers) Walker; B.S., Fla. State U., 1931; M.A. in Math. (Laws fellow), U. Cin., 1932; m. Clarence Russell Bell, Aug. 11, 1937; 1 dau., Charlotte Ann Bell Layman. Tchr., P.K. Young Sch., 1932-33, Pensacola High Sch., 1933-37, Wilbanks Elem. Sch., 1952-57, Austin Jr. High Sch., 1957-62; prof. math. Lamar U., Beaumont Tex., 1962-85, Regents prof., 1976-85, Piper prof., 1978, prof. emeritus, 1979-85, assoc. prof. math., 1979-85, acting head math. dept., 1982-83. Former pres., bd. dirs. YMCA; v.p. AAUW, 1942; leader United Appeals, 1978-81; mem. Rothwell Student Center Bd., 1979—; pres. United Meth. Women, 1952-54; chmn. council ministries 1st United Meth. Ch., Beaumont, Tex., 1981—, chmn. com. on edn., 1978-85, chmn. adminstrv. bd., 1985-87; bd. dirs. Tchrs. Credit Union of Beaumont, Tex., 1985-88; treas. Wesley Found., Lamar U., Beaumont, 1984-86. Recipient Sabine Area Math. Tchr. of Yr. award, 1983. Mem. Tex. Assn. Coll. Tchrs., Math. Assn. Am., Nat. Council Tchrs. of Math., Sabine Area Council Math. (pres.), Tex. Council Tchrs. Math., Alethea Lit. Soc., Hist. Soc. S.E. Tex., Beaumont Art Mus., AAUW, Delta Kappa Gamma, Phi Kappa Phi, Pi Mu Epsilon, Beta Pi Theta. Democrat. Author: Computational Skills, 1975; Manual of Computational Skills, 1975. Home: 1900 Central Dr Beaumont TX 77706 Office: Box 10047 Lamar University Beaumont TX 77710

BELL, MARY-KATHERINE, lawyer; b. Los Angeles, July 7, 1910; d. Weldon Branch and Vina (Cowan) Morris; m. Robert Collins Bell, Mar. 22, 1941; children—Robert Collins III, Marianne Bell Reifenheiser. B.A., Stanford U., 1934; J.D., George Washington U., 1943. Bar: D.C. 1943, N.Y. 1952, Conn. 1960. Atty., Cummings & Lockwood, Stamford, Conn., 1944-45, Shearman & Sterling, N.Y.C., 1948-77, Ivey, Barnum & O'Mara, Greenwich, Conn., 1978-83; asst. sec. to Assn. Bar City of N.Y., 1946-47; atty. to Conf. on Personal Fin. Law, N.Y.C., 1947-48; sole practice, New Canaan, Conn., 1983-84; mem. Tax Adv. Com. of Am. Law Inst. Co-editor: U.S. Bankruptcy Guide, 1948. Mem. Democratic Town Com. Mem. Conn. Bar Assn., Delta Gamma. Clubs: Cosmopolitan (N.Y.C.), Tokeneke (Darien). Home: 528 Main St New Canaan CT 06840 Office: 16 Forest St New Canaan Ct 06840 Died May 24, 1984.

BELL, MELINDA LEE, motion picture official; b. Wauseon, Ohio, Sept. 16, 1957; d. Herbert Taft and Edith May (Ludwig) Bell; Student Adrian Coll. (Mich.), 1975-77, Bowling Green State U. (Ohio), 1976; B.A. in English, U. Notre Dame, 1980; postgrad. UCLA, 1982. Corr., New Day Prodns., Los Angeles, 1980-81; asst. to v.p. communications Vidal Sassoon, Inc., Los Angeles, 1981-83, editor newsletter, 1982-83; internat. film distributor, coordinator MGM/UA, Culver City, Calif., 1983-84, script coordinator, 1984—; cons. Ford-Eye Prodns., Venice, Calif., 1981—. Author: Reunion, 1981; (radio play) Ellen and Bobby, 1984. Mem. Office and Profl. Employees Internat. Union. Democrat. Methodist. Club: Notre Dame Alumni. Office: MGM/UA Entertainment Co 10202 W Washington Bl Culver City CA 90230

BELL, MIKI ZAK, convention services and personnel consulting company executive; b. Tel-Aviv, Israel, Jan. 29, 1934; came to U.S., 1964; d. Moshe Tourgeman and Rachel Zak; div.; children—Scott, Julia. Stewardess, El-Al, Israeli Airlines, Israel, 1958-62; pres. J & M Internat. Trade Co., Atlanta, 1975-77; real estate agt. Clover Realty, Atlanta, 1977-81; pres. Miki Bell Enterprises, Atlanta, 1981-86, exec. dir., 1986—. Contbr. articles to profl. jours. Del., White House Conf. on Small Bus., 1985-86. Named Outstanding Women Bus. Owner, Ga. Small Bus. Council, 1985. Mem. Nat. Assn. Exposition Mgrs., Meeting Planners Internat., Bus. and Profl. Women, Atlanta Assn. Interpreters and Translators, Nat. Assn. Female Execs., Atlanta Women Entrepreneurs. Republican. Avocations: traveling; theatre; music; swimming; good conversation. Office: Miki Bell & Assocs 590 Piedmont Ave NE Atlanta GA 30308

BELL, MILDRED BAILEY, law educator; b. Sanford, Fla., June 28, 1928; d. William F. and Frances E. (Williford) Bailey; m. J. Thomas Bell, Jr., Sept. 18, 1948 (div.); children—Tom, Elizabeth, Ansley. A.B., U. Ga., 1950, J.D., 1969; LL.M. in Taxation, N.Y. U., 1977. Bar: Ga. 1969. Law clk. U.S. Dist. Ct. No. Dist. Ga., 1969-70; prof. law Mercer U., Macon, Ga., 1970—; mem. Ga. Com. Constl. Revision, 1978-79. Mem. ABA, Ga. Bar Assn., Phi Beta Kappa, Phi Kappa Phi. Republican. Episciopalian. Bd. editors Ga. State Bar Jour., 1974-76; contbr. articles profl. jours., chpts. in books. Home: 516 High Point North Rd Macon GA 31210 Office: Mercer U Law School Macon GA 31207

BELL, MILDRED MARIE, counselor, educational consultant; b. Orange Park, Fla., Nov. 27, 1921; d. Arthur and Lucille (Nelson) Bryant; m. Richard Allen Bell, Sept. 10, 1943; children—Richard Bernard (dec.), Corlette Lucille. Student Stillman Jr. Coll., 1939-41; B.S., Ala. A&M U., 1943; M.Ed., 1965. Tchr. pub. schs., Cleve., 1953-64, counselor pub. schs., 1964-81; planner, dir. Learning Ctr. for Young Children, Inc., East Cleveland, 1976—. Author: Daycare, 1980. Mem. Custody Rev. Bd. Cuyahoga County, Ohio, 1977-79; pres. Bus. and Profl. Women, 2d dist. Christian Meth. Episcopal Ch., 1970-80; rep. 5th dist. World Fedn. Meth. Women, 1980-85; sec. edn. Women's Mission Council, 5th dist. Christian Meth. Episcopal Ch., 1980-85. Recipient merit ednl. award Bd. Edn., Cleve., 1965; Disting. Service award Ala. A&M U., 1976; Outstanding Citizen award City Council, Cleve., 1980; Leadership award 21st Congl. Dist. Ohio, 1980. Mem. Phi Delta Kappa (pres. Alpha Xi chpt. 1963-65, pres. Gamma Rho chpt. 1974-76). Avocations: theatre; travel; fashions. Office: Social and Cultural Learning Ctr for Young Children Inc 12960 Euclid Ave East Cleveland OH 44112

BELL, NONI BETH, commercial waterproofing and construction company executive, poet; b. Phila., Oct. 3, 1958; d. Samuel Bookbinder and Diantha Bethia (Morgan) Morgan; m. William J. Bell, July 2, 1977; 1 child, Jaime Ann. Student Rutgers U., 1977, Burlington County Coll., Pemberton, N.J., 1978, 82, Rancocas Valley Community Coll., Mount Holly, N.J., 1985. Owner, Noni's Maids, Voorhees, N.J., 1973-76; sec., asst. Diantha Morgan Pub. Relations, N.J., 1975-76; office mgr. Medford Auto Supply, Inc., N.J., 1979-81; office mgr. Carranza Racing & Porsche Restoration, Tabernacle, N.J., 1981-83; v.p. fin., controller, corp. sec. Bell & Leclair Assocs., Inc., Tabernacle, 1983—, East Coast Waterproofing Techniques, Tabernacle, 1983—. Author: (poetry) Laid Back, 1981, Alleycats, 1982, 911, 1983, Solitaire, 1984. Mem. Nat. Assn. Female Execs. Republican. Avocations: reading; automobiles; horseback riding; traveling. Office: Bell & LeClair Assocs Inc/East Coast Waterproofing Techniques PO Box 411 Tabernacle NJ 08088

BELL, NORMA ARLEEN, consultant; b. Oakdale, Ill., Aug. 30, 1940; d. Albert Wilhelm and Mildred Beckley (Brown) Zacheis; m. Darrell Bell, Sept. 26, 1961 (div. 1985); children—Sharon, Steven. B.Mus. Edn., So. Ill. U., 1960; postgrad. Bradley U. English instr. Peoria pub. schs., 1969—; modeling and personal improvement instr., Peoria, 1968—; prin., image cons. co., Peoria, 1980—. Bd. dirs. Miss Heart of Ill. Scholarship Pageant, Peoria, 1969—, pres., 1977—; bd. dirs. Peoria Civic Ballet, 1981, Miss Ill. Scholarship Pageant, Aurora, 1976-79. Mem. Profl. Image Cons., Peoria Jaycee Women (membership dir. 1967-68, pres. 1968-69). Republican. Presbyterian. Avocation: community theater. Home: 9406 N Northview Rd Peoria IL 61615 Office: Peoria Pub Schs 3202 N Wisconsin Ave Peoria IL 61603

BELL, PATRICIA LAUDERDALE, government administrator; b. Louisville, July 20, 1930; d. Harry Edward and Mary Theresa (Hayden) Lauderdale; m. Hugh Clay Bell, Jr., Aug. 1, 1953 (dec. Dec. 1974); children—Gordon Edwin, Joanne Marie, Gloria Patricia-Leigh. B.S. in Gen. Edn., Spalding U., Louisville, 1951, postgrad., 1968-69; M.S. in Community Devel., U. Louisville, 1970; postgrad. Fla. State U., Western Ky. State U., 1970-75; Ph.D. in Adult Continuing Extension Edn., Mich. State U., 1979. Continuity writer, announcer, receptionist Sta. WLOU, Louisville, 1952-54; file clk., spl. searcher IRS, Louisville, 1956-65, employment devel. specialist Detroit dist., 1980-83, tng. specialist Data Ctr., 1983—; tchr. St. Bartholomew Sch., Buechel, Ky., 1965-67; tchr. social studies Central High Sch., Louisville Pub. Sch. System, 1967-69; tchr. econs. and sociology Ahrens Nigh Sch., Louisville, 1966-69; supr. social studies Louisville Pub. Sch. System, 1969-70, coordinator Hill Adult Learning Ctr., 1970-73; instr. social sci. Univ. Coll., instr. Office Interdisciplinary Programs, Speed Sci. Sch., asst. dir. profl. devel. U. Louisville, 1973-75, 77-78, dir. Life Planning Ctr., 1978-80; workshop presenter adult and career edn. Chmn. bd. Sacred Heart Model Sch., 1966; mem. Young Artists Promotions, 1969-72; mem. citizens adv. com. Louisville and Jefferson County Air Bd., 1970-72; mem. nominating com. Metro United Way; former mem. adult edn. com. St. Agnes Parish; past mem. bd. dirs. Planned Parenthood, Louisville; former chmn. bd. dirs. Louisville Area Planning Council; mem. women's council Bellarmine Coll.; mem. adv. bd. Creative Employment Project. Recipient Disting. Citizen award Mayor of Louisville, 1980; Black Achiever's award, 1980; Disting. Service award IRS Dist. Office, Detroit, 1981; Service to Edn. award Lewis Coll. Bus., Detroit, 1985. Mem. Am. Soc. for Engring. Edn., Am. Personnel and Guidance Assn., Nat. Assn. Student Personnel Adminstrs., Women in Higher Edn. Adminstrn. (nat. identification program), Ky. Personnel and Guidance Assn., AAUP, Blue Monday Network, Urban League. Democrat. Roman Catholic. Clubs: Friday Niters, Federally Employed Women (Detroit). Avocations: bridge; camping; interior design; promoting unknown artists. Home: 1925 Orleans Detroit MI 48207 Office: IRS Data Center Treasury Dept 1900 John C Lodge Dr Detroit MI 48207

BELL, PHYLLIS RUTH, editor; b. Smith Center, Kans., Aug. 5, 1929; d. Oscar Lawrence and Bonnie Lenora (Schroeder) Bloomer; student public schs. Lebanon, Kans.; m. Lennie Dale Bell, Apr. 3, 1948; children—Risë Dale, Vicky Sue, Gloria Jeanne. With The Lebanon Times, 1962—, mng. editor, 1968—, bus. mgr., 1968—. Election bd. clk. Smith County Democrats, 1958-60; leader 4-H Club, 1957-71, 81-82. sec. Lebanon PRIDE, 1972, pres., 1973-75. Recipient awards Kans. Press Assn., 1970, 71. Mem. Lebanon Hub C. of C. (sec.-treas. 1970—), Kans. Press Women (dir. 1975-76), North Central Kans. Geneal. Soc., DAR, Am. Legion Aux., VFW Aux. Mem. Christian Ch. (Disciples of Christ). Clubs: Music Study, Christian Womens Fellowship, Kans. Farmers Union, Publicity. Author: History of William Slater Family, 1972; researcher genealogy, 1970—. Home: Route 1 Lebanon KS 66952 Office: 413 Main St Lebanon KS 66952

BELL, REGINA JEAN, steel company ececutive; b. Lebanon, Mo.;d. Stephen S. and Ida M. (Reaves) B.; B.A., Draughens U., 1948; postgrad. Butler U., Ind.-Purdue U., Indpls. Prodn. mgr. Howe Mfg. Co., Inc., Indpls., 1958-64; v.p. budgetary control Howe Engring. Co., Inc., Indpls., 1964-67; mgr. material control Nat. Aluminum Div., Indpls., 1968—; owner Brown County Letter Shop, Nashville, Ind. Mem. Purchasing Mgmt. Assn., Ind. Real Estate Assn.

BELL, ROXANNE BEAIR, carwash mfg. co. exec.; b. Coffeyville, Kans., Sept. 9, 1942; d. Clarence A. and Gravette Beair; student Coffeyville Coll., 1960-61, Kans. State Coll., 1963, Toledo U., 1968, Aurora Coll., 1969; 1 dau., Shelly. Sec. to athletic dept. Kans. State Coll., 1962-65; adminstrv. asst. The Rooney Co., Tulsa, 1965-67; supr. Sch. Sales div. Indsl. Arts Equipment, Toledo, 1967-69; with Indsl. Sales, Cedar Rapids, Iowa, 1969-72; v.p. Southern Pride, Inc., Burlington, N.C., 1975-80, pres., 1980—. Sec., NAACP, Aurora, 1968; sec. Bd. Local Improvements, Aurora, 1969; adminstrv. asst. Commn. Public Property, Aurora, Ill., 1970-72; campaign mgr. U.S. Ho. of Reps., Ill., 1972. Mem. Nat. Carwash Council, Internat. Carwash Assn. Republican. Office: Southern Pride Inc 1312 Whitsett St Burlington NC 27215

BELL, SHARON ELAINE, nursing adminstr.; b. Dayton, Ohio, Apr. 25, 1942; d. Jack and Sara (Sabo) Matusoff; B.S. in Nursing, Ohio State U., 1964, M.A. in Edn., 1975; m. George Michael Bell, Jan. 5, 1969; 1 son, Chad Michael. Camp nurse Boston YMCA Camp, N.H., 1964, 65; staff nurse Ohio Tb Hosp., Columbus, 1964-66, Columbus Public Health Dept., 1966-68; instr. Sch. Practical Nursing Columbus Public Schs., 1968-77, tchr. coordinator, 1977-78, supr. sch., 1978-80, supr. health occupation programs, 1978—; chmn. Tri-Rivers Sch. of Practical Nursing Adv. Bd.; ex-ofcl. mem. Ohio Commn. on Nursing. Mem. Ohio State Nurses Assn., Columbus Adminstrs. Assn., Ohio Orgn. Practical Nurse Educators, Central Office Adminstrs. Assn., Nat. League Nursing, Ohio Assn. for Adult Educators, Am. Vocat. Assn. Jewish. Office: 100 Arcadia Ave Columbus OH 43202

BELL, SUSAN FORBIS, sales and marketing executive; b. Columbia, Mo., Nov. 19, 1954; d. Jessie Ray and Evelyn Sue (Roberts) Forbis; m. Philip Earl Bell, July 23, 1983. Front office mgr. Breckenridge Corp., Columbia, Mo., 1978-79; regional sales mgr. Laquinta Motor Inns, New Orleans, 1979-82; dir. sales and mktg. Chancellor Hotel, Champaign, Ill., 1982-85, Aircoa-Read House, Chattanooga, 1985, Aircoa-Wilmington Hilton, Claymont, Del., 1985—. Pres., chmn. bd. Champaign-Urbana Conv. and Visitors Bur., 1983-85; bd. dirs. Central Ill. Tourism Council, Champaign, 1984-85. Named Young Careerist Profl. Bus. Women, Champaign, 1984. Mem. Am. Mktg. Assn. Club: Exec. Champaign County (bd. mem. 1984-85). Home: 3054 Greenshire Ct E Claymont DE 19703 Office: Wilmington Hilton I-95 and Naamans Rd Claymont DE 19703

BELL, SUSAN JANE, lawyer; b. Shelbyville, Ill., July 28, 1955; d. Ross Franklin and Wanda June (Swinford) B. B.S. in Advt. with highest honors, U. Ill., 1977; J.D., UCLA, 1981. Bar: Calif. 1981, D.C. 1982. Legal intern FTC, Washington, 1979; law clk. intern D.C. Superior Ct., 1979; assoc. firm Wilkinson, Cragun & Barker, Washington, 1981-82; law clk. U.S. Dist. Ct. for D.C., 1982-83; assoc. firm Crowell & Moring, Washington, 1983—. Staff mem. UCLA Law Rev. Mem. ABA, Am. Trial Lawyers Assn., D.C. Bar Assn. (litigation div., Bar Assn. D.C. (chmn. young lawyer's sect., law student membership com., vice chmn. pro se litigation com., mem. host com. 1985 ABA conv.). Home: 3750 39th St NW Washington DC 20016 Office: Crowell & Moring 1100 Connecticut Ave NW Washington DC 20036

BELL, SUSAN JANE, state legislator; b. Houlton, Maine, Dec. 19, 1948; d. Leighton H. and Geraldine G. (Grant) B.; B.S., U. Maine, Orono, 1970, M.A., 1971. Tchr., Houlton (Maine) High Sch., 1970-73; tchr., coach Oxford Hills High Sch., South Paris, Maine, 1973-77; health edn. coordinator Oxford Hills Sch. Dist., South Paris, 1977-80; mem. Maine Ho. of Reps., 1980—, mem. joint standing com. on state govt., 1980-82, joint select com. on alcoholism, 1981-82, joint standing com. on appropriations and fin. affairs, 1982-84. Bd. dirs. Androscoggin Home Health, 1977-78, Oxford County unit Am. Cancer Soc., 1977-80; coordinator drug alcohol team Oxford Hills, 1979-80; mem. Oxford Hills Area Devel. Corp., 1982—. Republican. Episcopalian. Club: Nordic Ski.

BELL, VIRGINIA INMAN, lawyer; b. Albany, Ga., Dec. 20, 1943; d. Joel Guy and Sara (Phillips) Inman; m. P. Jackson Bell. B.A. with honors, Oglethorpe U., 1967; J.D., Mercer U., 1979. Bar: Ga. 1979, Va. 1982. Trial atty. Dept. Justice, Washington, 1979-83, counsel Atty. Gen.'s Task Force on Family Violence, 1983-84; spl. asst. Office of Justice Programs, Nat. Inst. Justice, Dept. Justice, Washington, 1984-85; atty.-adivsor Exec. Office for U.S. Attys., Dept. Justice, 1985—. Mem. ABA, Va. Bar Assn., Ga. Bar Assn. Club: Jr. League of Washington. Office: Exec Office for US Attys Dept Justice Washington DC 20530

BELLA, JEAN, retail proprietor; b. Bklyn., Nov. 11, 1940; d. Philip and Jean (Puleo) Alaimo; m. Peter Bolognese, Sept. 3, 1964 (div. 1980); children—Julie Lynn, Lisa Jean, Peter Philip; m. James Bartolo, Aug. 7, 1982. Diploma, Hollywood High Sch., Propr. Seaport Spas of San Diego, 1981. Mem. Nat. Assn. Female Execs., Nat. Spa & Pool Inst., Nat. Fedn. Ind. Bus. Democrat. Roman Catholic. Avocations: books; artwork; cooking. Office: Seaport Spas of San Diego 4877 Convoy St San Diego CA 92111

BELLAH, MELANIE, lawyer, writer; b. New Orleans, May 16, 1928; d. Earl Hyman and Josephine (Meyer) Hyman Taber; m. Robert Neelly Bellah, Aug. 17, 1949; children—Thomasin, Jennifer, Abigail, Hally. A.B., Stanford U., 1949; J.D., U.C.-Berkeley, 1972. Bar: Calif. 1974; cert. specialist in family law 1980, 85. Law clk. 3d Cir. Ct. Appeals, Trenton, N.J., 1972-73; sole practice, Berkeley, Calif., 1974—. Author: (poetry) Poems of the Pacific, 1949; (juvenile) Bow Wow! Meow! A First Book of Sounds, 1963; (play) The Blue Toadstool, 1950. Bd. dirs. Cambridge Nursery Sch. (Mass.), 1959-66; pres. Agassiz Sch. PTA, Cambridge, 1962-63; v.p. Panoramic Hill Assn., Berkeley, 1974-76. Mem. Assn. Cert. Family Law Specialists, ABA, Alameda County Bar Assn., Berkeley-Albany Bar Assn., Women Lawyers Alameda County, ASH, NOW, ACLU, Compassionate Friends, Phi Beta Kappa. Democrat. Clubs: U. Calif.-Berkeley Women's Faculty, YWCA.

BELLAMY, SHERRY FRANCHESCA, lawyer; b. N.Y.C., Oct. 13, 1952; d. Athelston Alhama and Mary Elizabeth (Reeves) B.; m. George Alexander Bumbray, Jr., June 10, 1977; children—George Alexander, Rashida Irene, Miles Bellamy. B.A., Swarthmore Coll., 1974; J.D., Yale U., 1977. Bar: Conn. 1978, N.Y. 1982, D.C. 1984. Staff atty. New Haven Legal Assistance Assn., 1977-81; assoc. Chadbourne, Parke, Whiteside & Wolff, N.Y.C. and Washington, 1981—. Mem. Swarthmore Coll. Alumni Council, 1980-83, South Central Conn. Shelter Adv. Bd., New Haven, 1980-81. Earl Warren Legal Tng. Program fellow, 1974-77. Mem. ABA, N.Y. State Bar Assn., N.Y. Women's Bar Assn., Nat. Bar Assn. Democrat. Home: 1319 Holly St NW Washington DC 20012 Office: Chadbourne Parke Whiteside & Wolff 1101 Vermont Ave NW Washington DC 20005

BELLER, CORRINE MARKEY, cable television executive; b. Hartford, Conn., Oct. 19, 1948; d. Charles Frederick and Emma Lydia (Milkie) M.; m. Edward Martin Beller, Apr. 23, 1983. B.A. Northeastern U., 1971; M.B.A., Harvard U., 1980. Cons Assn. for Internat. Research, Cambridge, Mass., 1972-76; sr. bus. analyst Am. Can Co., Greenwich, Conn., 1980-81; dir. mktg. Viacom Cable Co., Cleveland Heights, Ohio, 1981-83; v.p., gen. mgr. Telcom Internat., Lake Mary, Fla., 1984—; cons. to small businesses needing financing, 1980—. Bd. dirs. Central Fla. chpt. Am. Diabetes Assn., Orlando, 1985—. Club: Harvard of Central Fla. Avocations: sports, reading, music, theater. Home: 5575 Brookline Dr Orlando FL 32819 Office: Telcom Internat Inc 1275 Lake Heathrow Ln Lake Mary FL 32746

BELLES, ANITA LOUISE, graphics company executive; b. San Angelo, Tex., Aug. 30, 1948; d. Curtis Lee and Margaret Louise (Perry) B.; m. John Arvel Willey, July 13, 1969 (div. 1978); children—Suzan Heather, Kenneth Alan. B.A., U. Tex., 1972; M.S., Trinity U., San Antonio, 1984. Registered emergency med. technician, 1971-82. Emergency med. services regional tng. coordinator Bus. Emergency Med. Services, State of La., Lake Charles, 1978-79, dir., 1982; exec. dir. Southwest La. Emergency Med. Services Council, Lake Charles, 1979-83; pres. Computype, Inc., San Antonio, 1983—; project coordinator Tulane U. Sch. Medicine, New Orleans 1982-85; pres. Emergency Med. and Safety Assocs., San Antonio, 1984—; pub. jour. Pre-Hosp. Care, San Antonio, 1984—. Author: Handbook of Emergency Care, 1982; govt. document for motorcycle helmet law in La., 1984. Author, producer audiovisual prodn. A Cry for Help, 1981. Mem., instr. Am. Heart Assn., Lake Charles, 1978-82; adviser Women's Shelter, Lake Charles, 1979-81; expert witness La. State Legislature, Baton Rouge, 1981-83; civilian coordinator Mil. Assistance to Safety and Traffic, State of La., 1982. Recipient numerous grants U.S. Govt., 1979-83; regional winner Assn. Univ. Programs in Health Adminstrn., 1983; recipient Outstanding Service award La. Assn. Emergency Med. Technicians, 1983, Southwest La. Assn. Emergency Med. Technicians, 1983. Mem. Am. Assn. for Automotive Medicine, Nat. Assn. Emergency Med. Technicians, Tex. Assn. Emergency Med. Technicians, Am. Coll. Hosp. Adminstrs., Trinity Univ. Health Care Alumni Assn., Jr. League of San Antonio. Clubs: Thousand Oaks Racquet, Thousand Oaks Homeowners Assn. (sec.-treas. 1985—). Avocations: greenhouse gardening; writing; water skiing; tennis. Office: Computype Inc 434 W Nakoma San Antonio TX 78216

BELLES, MARLENE ANN, financial executive; b. Cleve., Aug. 28, 1943; d. Leo Vincent and Irene Virginia (Hrubo) Bielawski; m. Gerald Duane Holderbaum, Sept. 1, 1962 (div.); m. James Wesley Belles, Dec. 10, 1983. B.B.A., Cleve. State U., 1970. Chief acct. Sta. KYW/WKYC-TV, Cleve., 1963-69, bus. dir., 1977-80; acctg. mgr. Sta. WKBF, Cleve., 1969-70; systems mgr. NBC, N.Y.C., 1970-75; mgr. fin. Sta. KNBC-TV, Burbank, Calif., 1975-77; controller Sta. KTVU-TV, Oakland, Calif., 1980—; lectr. broadcasting careers. Adviser Jr. Achievement, Burbank, 1975-77; speaker Explorers div. Boy Scouts Am., Oakland, 1981—; arbitrator Better Bus. Bur., Oakland, 1982—; bd. dirs. Oakland YWCA, 1983—. Nat. Geog. scholar, 1960. Mem. Am. Women in Radio and TV (chpt. pres. 1982-83, div., v.p. membership 1984-86, pres.-elect 1986-87), Broadcast Fin. Mgmt. Assn. (bd. dirs. 1985—), Nat. Acad. TV Arts and Scis. Club: Harbor Bay Isle (Alameda). Office: KTVU-TV 2 Jack London Square Oakland CA 94607

BELLINGER, CHRISTINE BOWMAN, grounds maintenance company executive, nurseryman; b. Kansas City, Mo., Mar. 28, 1955; d. Daniel Benson and Phyllis Joann (Purdy) Bowman; m. Randal Charles Bellinger, Oct. 22, 1977. B.S. in Forestry, Purdue U., 1977. Pub. relations coordinator Sears Lawn & Leaf, Wheeling, Ill., 1977; co-owner, pres. Bellinger's Profl. Grounds Maintenance, Inc., Lafayette, Ind., 1977—. Mem. Ind. Assn. Nurserymen, Am. Assn. Nurserymen, Profl. Grounds Mgmt. Soc., Greater Lafayette C. of C. (Marquis de Lafayette award 1985). Republican. Avocations: skiing; camping; hiking; boating; ice skating; bicycling.

BELLINGER, MARTHA EMILY, lawyer, clergywoman; b. Watertown, N.Y., Mar. 1, 1950; d. Raphael Luther and Cora Alma (Van Brocklin) B. B.A., Syracuse U., 1972; postgrad. Princeton Sch. Theology, 1972-74; M.Theology, Boston U., 1975; J.D., Whittier Coll., 1982. Bar: Calif. 1983; ordained in ministry United Methodist Ch., 1974. Minister, United Meth. Ch., Dolgeville, N.Y., 1975-77; probation officer Madison County, Wampsville, N.Y., 1978; assoc. firm Federman, Gridley, Mogab & Gradwohl, Los Angeles, 1983; dep. dist. atty. Los Angeles County, 1984—; counsel Pomona-Claremont (Calif.) Sch. Dist., 1984. Contbr. articles to legal jours. Editor-in-chief Whittier Law Rev., 1981-82. Mem. ABA, Los Angeles County Bar Assn., Calif. Dist. Attys. Assn., Los Angeles County Dist. Attys. Assn. Democrat. Home: 6927 Layton St Alta Loma CA 91701 Office: 550 S Flower St Los Angeles CA 90014

BELLO-REUSS, ELSA NOEMI, physician, educator; b. Buenos Aires, Argentina, May 1, 1939; came to U.S., 1972; d. Jose F. and Julia M. (Hiriart) Bello; B.S., U. Chile, 1957, M.D., 1964; m. Luis Reuss, Apr. 15, 1965; children—Luis F., Alejandro E. Intern J.J. Aguirre Hosp., Chile, 1963-64; resident in internal medicine U. Chile, Santiago, 1964-66; practice medicine specializing in nephrology Santiago, 1967-72; Internat. NIH fellow U. N.C., Chapel Hill, 1972-74; vis. asst. prof. physiology U. N.C., Chapel Hill, 1974-75; Louis Welt fellow U. N.C.-Duke U. Med. Center, 1975-76; asst. prof. medicine, physiology and biophysics Washington U. Sch. Medicine, St. Louis, 1976-86, assoc. prof. physiology dept. cell biology and physiology, 1986—; mem. faculty Jewish Hosp. St. Louis, 1976-83, asst. prof. medicine. Mem. Internat., Am. socs. nephrology, Am. Fedn. Clin. Research, Am. Physiology Soc., Am. Heart Assn., Kidney Council, Soc. Gen. Physiologists, Math. Assn. Am. Contbr. articles on nephrology and epithelial electrophysiology to med. and physiology jours., chpt. to nephrology text. Office: Washington U Med Sch Box 8101 660 S Euclid Saint Louis MO 63110

BELLOVICS, DONNA MAE, nurse, educator; b. Rock Island, Ill., June 24, 1932; d. Harry John and Mabel Anna (Krueger) Ohms; R.N. (Annie Yates scholar), Los Angeles County Gen. Hosp., 1954; B.S. N., Marycrest Coll., 1965; M.A., U. Iowa, 1969; Ed.D., Walden U., 1975; m. Stephen M. Bellovics, June 24, 1955; children—Michael, Anne, George. Staff nurse, asst. head nurse Moline (Ill.) Public Hosp., 1956-58; pvt. duty nursing, 1960-64; instr. lic. practical nursing, Davenport, Iowa, 1964-65; instr. Moline Pub. Diploma Nursing, 1965-67; asst. prof. Marycrest Coll., 1969-70; assoc. prof. assoc. degree nursing program, chmn. dept. Black Hawk Coll., 1970-83; chmn. dept. Cameron U., Lawton, Okla., 1983—. Chmn. nursing scholarship com. Henry County March of Dimes, 1974-83. Mem. Am. Nurses Assn., Nat. League Nursing, Am. Heart Assn., Sigma Theta Tau. Republican. Presbyterian. Club: Spring Creek Grange. Home: 1802 NW 80th St DC 8016 4 Lawton OK 73505 Office: Cameron U 2800 W Gore Blvd Lawton OK 73505

BELLOWS, CAROLE KAMIN, lawyer; b. Chgo., May 24, 1935; d. Alfred and Sara (Liebenson) Kamin; B.A., U. Ill., 1957; J.D., Northwestern U., 1960; m. Jason E. Bellows, June 28, 1958 (dec. June 1980); children—Marcia, Douglas, Daniel. Admitted to Ill. bar, 1960; law clk. Chief Justice Ill. Ct. of Claims, Chgo., 1962-72; partner Bellows & Bellows, Chgo., 1970-79, Reuben & Proctor, Chgo., 1979—. Bd. dirs. Uptown Poverty Law Center, 1982—. Recipient Maurice Weigle award for outstanding service to organized bar, 1970, U. Ill. Mothers Assn. medallion of honor, 1975, Northwestern U. Alumnae award, 1978. Fellow Am. Bar Found. (sec. 1982-83); mem. Am. Bar Assn. (sec. 1967-73, chmn. sect. individual rights and responsibilities 1975—, mem. ho. of dels. 1975—, com. on bar activities and services 1978—), Ill. Bar Assn. (chmn. Bill of Rights com. 1965-67, bd. govs. 1969-79, mem. assembly 1972-79, chmn. budget com. 1976-77, chmn. legis. com. 1978-79, pres. 1977-78), Chgo. Bar Assn. (chmn. constl. revision com. 1973-74), Am. Law Inst., League Women Voters of Ill., Womens Bar Assn. Ill., Decalogue Soc., Nat. Conf. Bar Presidents (exec. council 1977—), Northwestern U. Sch. Law Alumni Assn. (pres. 1982-83). Club: Law (Chgo.). Editor: Your Bill of Rights, 1967, 69. Home: 725 LaPorte Ave Wilmette IL 60091 Office: 11 S LaSalle St Suite 2001 Chicago IL 60603

BELMONT, SANDRA ANN, ophthalmologist; b. Red Bank, N.J., Aug. 22, 1952; d. Mario Thomas and Emma (Sconduto) Caputo; m. Jeffrey Howard Belmont, Nov. 29, 1980; children—Justin Michael, Eric Reid. B.A. summa cum laude, St. John's U., 1974; M.D. SUNY Downstate Med. Ctr., Bklyn., 1979. Intern L.I. Coll. Hosp., Bklyn, 1979-80; resident in ophthalmology Nassau County (N.Y.) Med. Ctr., 1980-83; fellow corneal disease Manhattan Eye Ear and Throat Hosp., N.Y.C., 1985-86. Mem. Am. Acad. Ophthalmology, AMA, N.Y. County Med. Soc., N.Y. State Ophthal. Soc., Gastro-Viejo Corneal Soc., Internat. Soc. Refractive Keratoplasty, Kappa Gamma Phi. Roman Catholic. Office: 755 Park Ave New York NY 10021

BELOVITCH, JEANNE ANN, public relations writer, editor; b. Cin., June 7, 1945; d. Charles and Mildred Jane (Flinchpaugh) Belovitch; B.S., Boston U., 1967. Asst. v.p. sales promotion Putnam Fund Distbrs., Boston, 1971-74; prin. Jeanne Belovitch & Assocs., Boston, 1974-75; account exec., creator, producer, moderator arts program Sta. WWEL, Medford, Mass., 1975 78; writer public affairs United Way of Mass. Bay, Boston, 1978-82; creator, pub. Boston Firsts poster, 1980; mgr. G&R Publs., Inc., Boston, 1982-86; staff writer South End News, Boston, 1983-85; founder, editor newsletter Remarriage, Boston, 1984-86; cons. fund raising Cambridge (Mass.) YWCA, 1979; instr. Fenway Free U., Boston; adv. creative writer's workshop Walpole Prison, 1981-82. Mem. Boston U. Alumni Assn. (dir. Coll. Basic Studies). Jewish. Contbr. articles to newspapers and mags. Home: 24 Appleton St Boston MA 02116 Office: 648 Beacon St Boston MA

BELTON, LINDA WEBER, hospital administrator, nurse; b. Erie, Pa., Jan. 26, 1950; d. James E. and Mildred E. (Dougherty) Weber; R.N., Jameson Sch. Nursing, 1970; student Westminster Coll., 1967-68, Mercyhurst Coll., 1976-77; B.S. in Nursing Adminstrn., Columbia Pacific U., 1981, M.S. in Nursing Adminstrn., 1983; B.S. in Psychology, SUNY, 1982; m. Lawrence Winfield Belton, June 27, 1969; children—Marshall LeMaster, Adrienne Elizabeth. Nursing supr. Chatham (Pa.) Extended Care Facility, 1973-75; clin. coordinator rehab. services St. Vincent Health Center, Erie, Pa., 1975-77; dir. nursing Shady Acres Nursing Home, Madison, Ohio, 1977-79; nurse adminstr. Meml. Hosp. of Carbon County, Rawlins, Wyo., 1979-81, asst. hosp. adminstr., 1981-83; v.p. Mercy Med. Ctr., Oshkosh, Wis., 1983—; adj. prof. nursing U. Wis.-Oshkosh, 1984—; cons. Rawlins Health Occupations Center. Mem. Wyo. State Continuing Edn. com., 1981-83; bd. dirs. Am. Cancer Soc., 1980-83; mem. Child Protection Team, Rawlins, 1979-80, Family Life Ministry team, 1981-83. Recipient Am. Cancer Soc. Participation award, 1981. Mem. Nat. League for Nursing, Am. Nurses Assn. (advanced cert. in nursing adminstrn.), Wis. Nurses Assn., Wis. Orgn. Nurse Execs., Oshkosh Pregnancy Lifeline. Club: Bus. and Profl. Women's. Contbr. articles to profl jours.

BELTRAM, ANGELA MARIE, mental health executive, legislative assistant; b. Balt., July 3, 1939; d. John and Mary Ann (Venditti) Linardi; m. Peter Edwin Beltram, June 14, 1964; children—Christina, Gina, Valerie. B.A. in Bus. and Govt., Coll. of Notre Dame, Balt., 1984. Tchr. phys. edn. Seton High Sch., Balt., 1960-63, Inst. of Notre Dame, Balt., 1963-64; administr. Howard County Govt., Ellicott City, Md., 1979-80; legis. aide Md. Gen. Assembly, Annapolis, 1980, 84, 85, adminstr. women's caucus, 1983; exec. dir. Mental Health Assn., Ellicott City, 1984—; dir. Mental Health Assn., Assn. Community Services, Sexual Assault Ctr. Founder, pres. Ellicott City Democratic Club, 1976, 80; founder Citizens Allied for Responsible and Effective Zoning, Howard County, 1983. Mem. AAUW, Am. Bus. and Profl. Women's Assn., Women's Network. Roman Catholic. Clubs: Howard County Citizens Assn., St. John's Community Assn. Avocation: sports participant and spectator. Home: 3125 Paulskirk Dr Ellicott City MD 21043

BELTZNER, GAIL ANN, educator; b. Palmerton, Pa., July 20, 1950; d. Conon Nelson and Lorraine Ann (Carey) Beltzner; B.S. in Music Edn. summa cum laude, West Chester State U., 1972; postgrad. Kean State Coll., Temple U., Westminster Choir Coll., Lehigh U. Tchr. music Drexel Hill Jr. High Sch., 1972-73; music specialist Allentown Sch. Dist., Pa., 1973—; tchr. Corps Sch. and Community Developmental Lab., 1978-80, Corps Community Resource Festival, 1979-81, Corps Cultural Fair, 1980, 81. Bd. dirs. Allentown Area Ecumenical Food Bank. Mem. Lehigh County Hist. Soc., Nat. Sch. Orch. Assn., Allentown Symphony Assn., Allentown Symphony Women's Com., Allentown Art Museum Aux., Allentown Fedn. Tchrs. (sec., mem. exec. com.), AAUW, Music Educators Nat. Conf., Pa. Music Educators Assn., Am. Orff-Schulwerk Assn., Soc. Gen. Music, Am. Assn. Music Therapy, Internat. Soc. Music Edn., Assn. Supervision and Curriculum Devel., Lenni Lenape Hist. Soc., Kappa Delta Pi, Phi Delta Kappa, Alpha Lambda. Republican. Lutheran. Home: 959 Tilghman St Allentown PA 18102

BELYEA, MARLOU, twp. ofcl., mayor; b. Burbank, Calif., Sept. 11, 1926; d. Allan Francis and Louise (La Rue) Rau; B.A., Scripps Coll., 1947; m. Robert C. Belyea, June 15, 1947; children—Marlou, Wendy Lee, Carolyn Anne. Legis. aide to assemblywoman Ann Klein, Morristown, N.J., 1973; mem. Pequannock Twp. Planning Bd., 1975-77, Pequannock Twp. Council, Pompton Plains, N.J., 1977-81, mayor Pequannock Twp., 1979-80. Mem. N.J. Fedn. Elected Women Ofcls., N.J. Fedn. Republican Women, AAUW, LWV (N.J. dir. 1969-71). Home: 134 Mountain Ave Pompton Plains NJ 07444

BEMBRY, LINDA SUE, corporation executive; b. San Francisco, Aug. 22, 1953; d. Charles M. and Lorraine Deaderick; B.S. in Bus., San Diego State U., 1975; postgrad. UCLA, 1977-80. Purchasing agt. Calif. Milling Corp., Los Angeles, 1976-77; sales mgr. Universal Storage Systems, San Gabriel, Calif., 1977-80; ter. mgr. Alcon Labs., Dallas, 1981; sales mgmt. dir. Ladd-Fab Inc., El Monte, Calif., 1981—. Recipient cert. of Achievement award Action In Mgmt. Forum, 1980. Mem. Internat. Material Mgmt. Soc. Conf. (cert. of achievement award 1980), Nat. Assn. Female Execs., AAUW. Republican. Home: 416 E Duarte Rd Arcadia CA 91006 Office: 17891 Arenth Ave City of Industry CA 91748

BEMPORAD, SONYA, child care executive; b. Phila., Oct. 31, 1934; d. Sam and Pauline (Nemez) Kaufmann Kasakoff; m. Jack Bemporad, Oct. 10, 1954 (div. Oct. 1976); children—Henry, Raphael. B.A., U. Cin., 1956; M.A., Sarah Lawrence U., 1961. Mem. faculty dept. psychology Sarah Lawrence U., Bronxville, N.Y., 1964-72, dir. Early Learning Ctr., 1970-72; lectr. psychiatry U. Tex. Health Sci. Ctr., 1981-85; exec. dir. Rhoads Terrace Children's Ctr., Dallas, 1974-76; exec. program dir. Child Care Dallas, 1976—; cons. Yonkers Headstart, 1969-71, Dallas County Mental Health-Mental Retardation, 1980-82, Dallas County Child Welfare, 1976—. Pres., Child Care 76, Dallas, 1974-76; mem. at large Women's Council, Dallas, 1974-84; co-chmn. Women's Issues Congress, Dallas, 1983-84; chmn. Mayor's Child Care Task Force, Dallas, 1983-84. Fellow Am. Orthopsychiat. Assn.; mem. Nat. Assn. Edn. Young Children, Phi Beta Kappa. Office: Child Care Dallas 1499 Regal Row Suite 400 Dallas TX 75247

BENARD, MARY ELLEN, judge; b. Lake Forest, Ill., May 15, 1947; d. Ralph H. and Mary Elizabeth (Ewing) Rockwood; m. David J. Benard, Aug. 17, 1968 (div.); 1 child, Mary Elizabeth. B.S. in Math., U. Ill., 1969, J.D., 1972. Bar: Ill. 1972, D.C. 1975. Counsel NLRB, Washington, 1972-76, asst. chief counsel, 1976-80, adminstrv. law judge, 1980—. Mem. outreach com. St. John's Ch., Lafayette Sq., Washington, 1976—; bd. dirs. Coop. Urban Ministry Ctr. Inc., Washington, 1983-85. Recipient cert. of commendation NLRB, 1980. Mem. ABA (com. devel. law under Nat. Labor Relations Act 1979—), Nat. Assn. Women Judges, NLRB Profl. Assn. (pres. 1975-76), Forum of U.S. Adminstrv. Law Judges (pres. 1985—). Democrat. Episcopalian. Club: Zonta (bd. dirs. 1983—, chmn. fin. com. Washington chpt. 1983-85, chmn. pub. affairs com. 1985—). Home: 7201 46th St Chevy Chase MD 20815 Office: Div of Judges NLRB 1717 Pennsylvania Ave NW Washington DC 20570

BENATAR, PAT (PAT ANDREJEWSKI), rock singer; b. Bklyn., 1953; m. Neil Geraldo; 1 child, Haley. Albums include: In the Heat of the Night, 1979, Chrysalis, 1979, Crimes of Passion, 1980, Get Nervous, 1982, Live From Earth, 1983, Tropico, 1984, Seven the Hard Way, 1985. Recipient Grammy award for best female rock vocal performance, 1981, 82, 83, 84. Office: care Premier Talent Agy 3 E 54th St New York NY 10022*

BENBOW, CAMILLA PERSSON, psychology educator, researcher; b. Lund, Sweden, Dec. 3, 1956; came to U.S., 1965, naturalized, 1985; m. Robert Michael Benbow, Jan. 5, 1975; children—Wystan R., Bronwen G., Trefor A., Evan M., A. Lovisa. B.A. with honors, Johns Hopkins U., 1977, M.A. in Psychology, 1978, M.S. in Edn. of the Gifted, 1980, Ed.D. with distinction in Gifted Edn., 1981. Project assoc. Study of Mathematically Precocious Youth, Johns Hopkins U., Balt., 1977-79, asst. dir., 1979-81, assoc. dir., 1981-85, co-dir., 1985—; assoc. research scientist dept. psychology Johns Hopkins U., 1981-86, asst. prof. sociology, part-time 1983-86; assoc. prof. psychology Iowa State U., Ames, 1985—. Contbr. articles to profl. jours.; sr. editor: Academic Precocity: Aspects of Its Development, 1983; editor Intellectually Talented Youth Bull., 1979. Recipient John Curtis Gowan prize Nat. Assn. Gifted Children, 1980, 81; research award Am. Ednl. Research Assn., 1981; Spencer fellow, alt., 1984, 85; research paper award (2) Mensa, 1985; Early Scholar award Nat. Assn. Gifted Children, 1985. Mem. Phi Beta Kappa, Sigma Xi. Office: Iowa State U Dept Psychology Ames IA 50011

BENCINI, SARA HALTIWANGER, concert pianist; b. Winston Salem, N.C., Sept. 2, 1926; d. Robert Sydney and Janie Love (Couch) Haltiwanger; m. Robert Emery Bencini, June 26, 1954; children—Robert Emery, III, Constance Bencini Waller, John McGregor. Mus. B., Salem Coll., 1947; postgrad. grad. Juilliard Sch. Music, 1948-50; M.A., Smith Coll., 1951; postgrad. in piano U. N.C.-Greensboro. Head piano dept. Mary Burnham Sch. for Girls, Northampton, Mass., 1949-51; pianist, composer dance and drama dept. Smith Coll., 1951-52; head music dept. Walnut Hill Sch. for Girls, Natick, Mass., 1952-54; pvt. piano tchr., High Point, N.C., 1954-66; concert pianist appearing in Am. and Europe, 1948—; duo-piano performances with PBS-TV, Columbia, S.C., 1967, Winston Salem Symphony, N.C., 1964-68, Eastern Mus. Festival, Greensboro, N.C., 1969. Democrat. Presbyterian.

BENCK, JUNE JOHANSEN, librarian; b. Fresno, Calif., June 4, 1917; d. Martin John and Blanche Dolly (Goodrich) Johansen; m. Ernest A. Benck, Aug. 19, 1941; children—Bonnie Benck Newman, Ernest A. B.A. in Drama, Calif. State U.-Fresno, 1939. Sch. library credential, San Jose State Coll., 1966. Jr. high sch. librarian Fresno Unified Schs., Calif., 1962-72, secondary dist. librarian, 1972-80, coordinator dist. libraries, 1980—; puppeteer Fresno County Library, summers 1966-72. Contbr. articles to profl. jours. Bd. dirs. Storyland of Fresno; mem. Soc. for Prevention of Cruelty to Animals. Mem. ALA, Am. Assn. Sch. Librarians, Calif. Media Library Educators Assn., Fresno Area Library Council, Central Sierra Library Assn., AAUW, Alumni Assn. Calif. State U. Fresno, Phi Delta Kappa (editor newsletter), Delta Kappa Gamma, Kappa Alpha Theta. Club: Delta Zeta Mothers (past pres.). Home: 739 N Ferger Fresno CA 93728 Office: Fresno Unified Sch Dist Tulare and M Sts Fresno CA 93721

BENCZE, EVA IVANYOS, mechanical engineer; b. Budapest, Hungary, Mar. 6, 1932; came to U.S., 1956, naturalized, 1977; d. Jozsef and Katalin (Szabo) Ivanyos; m. Joseph Steven Bencze, Aug. 4, 1956; children—Christina, Ingrid, Caroline, Andrew. M.Mech.Engring., Tech. U. Budapest, 1955. Mech. designer Lockwood Greene, Inc., N.Y.C., 1956-69, Elster's, Inc., Hollywood, Calif., 1972-74; mech. engr. DMJM, Los Angeles, 1974-75; sr. mech. engr. DMJM/KE, Balt., 1975-82, DMJM/HTC, Houston, 1982-83; sr. mech. engr. DMJM/Metro Rail Transit Consultants, Los Angeles, 1983-85, supr. mech. engring., 1985—. Assoc. mem. ASHRAE. Avocations: reading, listening to music. Home: 5326 Townsend Ave Los Angeles CA 90041 Office: DMJM/Metro Rail Transit 548 S Spring St Los Angeles CA 90013

BENDER, BETTY WION, librarian; b. Mt. Ayr, Iowa, Feb. 26, 1925; d. John F. and Sadie Augusta (Guess) Wion; student Drake U., 1942-44; B.S., N. Tex. U., 1946; M.A., U. Denver, 1957; m. Robert F. Bender, Aug. 24, 1946. Asst. cataloger N. Tex. State Coll., Denton, 1946-49; cataloger So. Meth. U., Dallas, 1949-51; reference asst. Ind. State Library, Indpls., 1951-52; periodicals librarian So. Meth. U., Dallas, 1952-53, head of acquisitions, 1953-56; grad. asst. U. Denver, 1956-57; acting head librarian Ark. State Coll., 1958, librarian, 1958-59; cataloger St. Louis Public Library, 1966-67; librarian Eastern Wash. State Hist. Soc., Spokane, 1960-66, 67; reference librarian Spokane Public Library, 1968, circulation librarian, 1968-73, library dir., 1973—; mem. Wash. State Library Commn., 1979—. Bd. dirs. Inland Empire Goodwill Industries, 1975-77, NW Regional Found., 1975-77. Recipient Outstanding Achievement award in govt. YMCA, 1985. Mem. ALA, Library Adminstrn. and Mgmt. Assn. (v.p. 1985-86, chmn. various coms. 1980-85), AAUW (Betty W. Bender fellowship named in her honor 1972), Pacific NW Library Assn. (conv. chmn. 1977), Washington Library Assn. (pres. 1977-78). Lutheran. Club: Zonta. Office: Spokane Public Library W 906 Main Ave Spokane WA 99201

BENDER, CATHERINE ANNE, association executive; b. Detroit, Aug. 17, 1955; d. Henry Anthony and Sophie (Psioda) Lachowicz; m. Michael Allen Bender, May 16, 1980. B.A. in Elem. Edn., Mercy Coll., Detroit, 1977; M.A. in Vocat. Tech. Edn., Eastern Mich. U., 1985. Prodn. control analyst Ford Motor Co., Dearborn, Mich., 1978-80; student services dir., mktg. asst. Nat. Inst. Tech., Livonia, Mich., 1981, dir. adminstrn., 1982-84; adminstrn. mgr. Chrysler Learning Inst., Warren, Mich., 1984-85; exec. dir. Soc. Mfg. Engrs. Robotics Internat. and N.Am. Mfg. Research Inst., Dearborn, 1985—. Recipient Outstanding Service award Nat. Inst. Tech., 1982. Mem. Am. Soc. Asns. Execs., Nat. Assn. Female Execs. Roman Catholic. Avocations: reading; needlepoint; swimming; aerobics; cake decorating. Office: Robotics Internat Soc Mfg Engrs 1 SME Dr PO Box 930 Dearborn MI 48121

BENDER, DIANE LOUISE WOLF, lawyer; b. Evansville, Ind., Oct. 21, 1955; d. Thomas Joseph, Sr., and Margaret Gertrude (Horn) Wolf. B.B.A. with highest honors, U. Notre Dame, 1977, J.D. cum laude, 1980. Bar: Ind. 1980; C.P.A., Ill. Assoc. Kahn, Dees, Donovan & Kahn, Evansville, 1980—. Bd. dirs. Vis. Nurse Assn. Southwestern Ind., 1983—, United Way Southwestern Ind., 1983—, Health Skills, Inc., 1984—; chmn. study group steering com. Leadership Evansville, 1983-84. Recipient Ernst & Ernst award U. Notre Dame, 1976. Mem. ABA, Ind. Bar Assn., Evansville Bar Assn., Am. Inst. C.P.A.s, Ill. Soc. C.P.A.s, Beta Gamma Sigma, Beta Alpha Psi. Roman Catholic.

BENDER, MICHELLE, museum public relations official, writer, editor, educator; b. Dayton, Ohio, July 30; d. Donald Henry and Annalee (Block) Bender. B.A., Northwestern U., student Cambridge U. (Eng.); Ed.M., Columbia U., 1983. Sr. editor Harcourt Brace Jovanovich, N.Y.C., 1972; writer, communications coordinator Charles F. Kettering Found., Dayton, 1976; cons. editor Monsanto Corp., Dayton, 1979—; writer, editor, employee info. Copeland Corp., Sidney, Ohio, 1982; pub. affairs assoc. Am. Mus. Natural History, N.Y.C., 1983—. cons. Bus. Week, N.Y.C.; Exhibited photography one-woman shows: Ziegfield Gallery, Modern Age Gallery. Vol. editor Performing Arts Fund Dayton, 1982; active Big Bros./Big Sisters, 1980—. Abbott scholar Boston U. Mem. Women in Communications, Internat. Assn. Bus. Communicators (chpt. treas. 1982-83, communication merit awards 1980, 82, 83), Toastmasters Internat. (chpt. v.p. 1981-82), Am. Assn. Museums. Home: 515 East Dr Oakwood OH 45419 Office: Am Mus of Natural History Central Park W at 79th St New York NY 10024

BENDFELDT, JOMARIE, missile system administrator; b. Columbus, Ga., July 7, 1953; d. Harvey Gottfried and Adra Weatherford (Clark) B. B.A., Fla. State U., 1975. Supply systems analyst Navy Internat. Logistics Control Office, Phila., 1976-78; supply systems analyst Naval Supply Systems Command, Washington, 1978-82; asst. program mgr. logistics fgn. mil. sales of airborne weapons Naval Air Systems Command, Washington, 1983-85, asst. program mgr. logistics Sparrow Missile System, 1985—. Deaconess Glen Carlyn Rd. Baptist Ch., Falls Church, Va., 1983-85. Recipient Outstanding Performance awards Navy Internat. Log Control Office, 1978, Naval Supply Systems Command, 1979-82, Naval Air Systems Command, 1983-85; named Woman of Yr., Naval Supply Systems Command, 1979. Mem. Nat. Assn. Female Execs. Democrat. Baptist. Avocations: racquetball; reading; aerobics. Home: 5606 Eastbourne Dr Springfield VA 22151 Office: Naval Air Systems Command Air 41811D Washington DC 20361

BENDICK, JEANNE LOUIS, author, illustrator children's science books; b. N.Y.C., Feb. 25, 1919; d. Louis Xerxes and Amelia Maurice (Hess) Garfunkel; m. Robert Louis Bendick, Nov. 24, 1940; children—Robert Louis, Jr., Karen Bendick Watson Holton. B.A., Parsons/New Sch., 1939. Author children's sci. books including: Super People; Scare a Ghost, Tame a Monster; Putting the Sun to Work; (with Marcia Levin) Take a Number; Take Shapes; Lines and Letters; Mathematics Illustrated Dictionary; Pushups and Pinups; (with Leonard Simon) The Day the Numbers Disappeared; (with Glenn Blough) Nature Sci. Series; author Sci. Experiences series, The First Books of series (space travel; satellites; automobiles, also others); author, co-author edn. materials: textbooks Ginn Sci. Program, multimedia programs, Starting Points, Learning Experiences, You and Me and Our World; author filmstrips: The Seasons; story editor, writer NBC children's series The First Look for TV. Recipient several Best Sci. Books of Yr. awards. Mem. Nat. Sci. Tchrs. Assn., ALA, Authors League, Authors Guild, Writers Guild of Am. East. Jewish. Home: Guilford CT 06437

BENDICKSON, SHARON ANN, newspaper editor; b. Mason City, Iowa, Feb. 10, 1943; d. Wilbur G. and Loretta E. (Butzler) Dalluge; m. Robert A. Bendickson, Sept. 30, 1961; children—Julie, Robert A., Holly. A.A., Dodge City Community Coll., 1982. Community life and foods editor Dodge City (Kans.) Daily Globe, 1981—. Active in pub. relations and publicity Dodge City Regional Hosp. Aux., 1983—, Mental Health Assn. Ford County, 1983—, United Parents for Youth, Dodge City, 1983; vol. coordinator 4-H, 1983. Mem. Dodge City Press Women, Nat. Fedn. Press Women; United Way Campaign, 1983; bd. dirs. Boot Hill chpt. Am. Diabetes Assn. Republican. Lutheran. Home: 905 Arapahoe Dodge City KS 67801 Office: Dodge City Daily Globe 705 2d Ave Dodge City KS 67801

BENDIG, JUDITH JOAN, computer systems specialist, computer company executive; b. Erie, Pa., Oct. 28, 1955; d. Richard W. and Rhea Agnes (Hain) B. B.S. in Music Edn., Edinboro State Coll., 1977. Tech. cons. Inco, Inc., Washington, 1982; sr. systems analyst Devel. Sci. Services, Inc., Washington, 1982-85; dir. computer systems ADEENA Corp., Arlington, Va., 1985—; v.p. F&B Computer Assocs., Bethesda, Md., 1985—. Mem. Arlington Community Band, 1986—. Served to lt. USNR, 1978—, with USN, 1978-82. Mem. Assn. Computing Machinery, IEEE (assoc.), Naval Res. Assn., Nat. Assn. Female Execs. Republican. Roman Catholic. Club: Arlington Bike. Home: 1900 S Eads St Apt 902 Arlington VA 22202

BENDT, NORMA JUNE, procurement professional; b. Hawthorne, Nev., July 25, 1955; d. William Boyd and Sally Lou (Ramsey) Worsham; m. Steven Eric Bendt, July 28, 1973; 1 child, Steven Eric, II. Student, Coll. Charleston, S.C., 1983—. Sec., Med. U. S.C., Charleston, 1974-76, staff asst., 1976-82, ops. mgr., 1982-83; procurement officer Coll. of Charleston, 1983—. Mem. Sea Island Bus. and Profl. Women's Club (Young Career Women award 1983, treas. 1984—), Nat. Assn. Edn. Buyers, Nat. Inst. Govtl. Purchasing. S.C. Assn. Govtl. Purchasing Ofcls. (conf. com. 1985, program con. 1985—, profl. devel. com. 1986—, bd. dirs. 1986—), Purchasing Mgmt. Assn. of Carolinas (bd. dirs. local chpt. 1986), Nat. Assn. Female Execs. Republican. Lutheran. Avocations: scuba diving; skiing; racquetball; boating; aerobics. Office: Coll Charleston Purchasing Office 66 George St Charleston SC 29424

BENEDETTO, LOIS LEONARD, mathematics educator; b. N.Y.C., Dec. 12, 1944; d. John James and Lillian Marie (Gramer) Leonard; B.A., Marymount Manhattan Coll., 1966; M.A., Fordham U., 1967; postgrad. in bus. U. Chgo.; m. William Benedetto, Apr. 20, 1968; children—Michael, William. Instr. mathematics CCNY, 1967-68, Marymount Manhattan Coll., N.Y.C., 1968-71, 82—; bd. dirs. Northwestern Meml. Hosp., Chgo., 1977-82, pres. Service Bd., 1976-80; exec. leader Spl. Gifts Div., Crusade of Mercy, Chgo., 1976-78; mem. Women's Bd., Lincoln Park Zool. Soc., Chgo., 1976-81; jr. governing bd. Chgo. Symphony Orch, 1975-76; mem. bd. govs. Chgo. Heart Assn., 1978-82; mem. pub. policy and govt. relations com. N.Y. Heart Assn., 1982—; mem. N.Y. bd. Nat. Com. for Prevention of Child Abuse, 1983-84. Roman Catholic. Clubs: Woman's Athletic, Jr. League, Saddle and Cycle. Address: 1105 Park Ave New York NY 10128

BENEKE, MILLIE STONG, civic worker, author; b. Prairie City, Iowa; d. Rueben Ira and Lillian (Garber) Stong; student Washington U., 1942-43, Mankato State Coll., 1951, 67; m. Arnold W. Beneke, Aug. 10, 1939; children—Bruce Arnold, Paula Rae, Bradford Kent, Cynthia Jane, Lisa Patrice. Exec. sec. chmn. Vol. Services, ARC, St. Paul, 1940-41; v.p. Pi House, St. Paul, 1972-77; founder, bd. dirs., chmn. Project Interaction Boutique, Minn. Correctional Instn. for Women, Shakopee, 1971—, supervising vol., 1970—. Republican chairwoman McLeod County (Minn.), 1969-73; mem. Rep. Minn. Platform com., 1970; McLeod County del. Rep. Minn. Central Com., 1969—; mem. Rep. Feminist Caucus; alderman Glencoe City Council, 1974-80; v.p. Friends of Library, 1975—; bd. dirs. Buffalo Creek Players, 1976—, v.p., 1980—; bd. dirs. Mpls. Children's Theatre Co. Housing for elderly named in her honor. Mem. Glencoe Bus. and Profl. Women (Woman of Year 1975), Dramatists Guild. Lutheran. Author: (play) The Garage Sale, 1978; Politics Unusual, 1979; The Househusband and the Working Wife, 1982, also children's plays. Home: 330 Scout Hill Dr Box 215 Glenview Woods Glencoe MN 55336

BENEKE, NIKKI J(EANNETTE), physical therapist; consultant; b. Ft. Worth, July 29, 1951; d. Nicholas J. and Orma Anne (Rudd) Massey; m. Terry L. Beneke, June 16, 1979. B.S. in Biology, U. Tex.-Arlington, 1974; B.S. in Phys. Therapy, Southwestern Med. Sch., 1975, cert. Postgrad. Phys. Therapy, 1975. Lic. phys. therapist. Phys. therapist Presbyn. Hosp., Dallas, 1975-76; dir. phys. therapy Rutherford Hosp., Mesquite, Tex., 1976-77; supr. devel. therapy Angel's Inc., Dallas, 1977-78; cons. phys. therapist Convalescent Center, Dallas, 1980-82; cons. pediatric phys. therapist, Region X Ednl. Service Center, Richardson, Tex., 1978-82; pvt. practice as phys. therapist, Dallas, 1978—; cons. spl. edn. dept. Duncanville Ind. Sch. Dist. (Tex.), 1981—; cons. deaf blind program Waxahachie Ind. Sch. Dist. (Tex.), 1983—; contract phys. therapist Home Health Services, Dallas, 1983—. Exec. bd. North Central Tex. Chpt. Nat. Hemophilia Found., Dallas, 1977-79. Mem. Am. Phys. Therapy Assn., Tex. Phys. Therapy Assn., North Tex. Dist. Phys. Therapy Assn., Tex. Pediatric Spl. Interest Group (vice chmn. 1978-82), North Tex. Pediatric Spl. Interest Group (program com. 1982-83). Republican. Roman Catholic. Home: 9131 Dusti Dr Dallas TX 75243

BENENSON, CLAIRE BERGER, investment and financial planning educator; b. N.Y.C.; d. Nathan H. and Alice E. (Zeisler) B.; m. Lawrence A. Benenson, Sept. 29, 1940; children—Harold, Gary. B.A., Wellesley Coll., 1938; postgrad. N.Y. Inst. Fin., New Sch. Social Research, 1965-69. Security analyst Merrill Lynch, N.Y.C., 1940-43; research assoc. Conn. Coll., 1943-45; lectr. NYU Mgmt. Inst., N.Y.C., 1960-68; lectr. New Sch. for Social Research, N.Y.C., 1968—, dir. annual conf. Wall St. and Economy, 1967—, dir. annual conf. Futures and Options, 1979—, chmn. dept. investment and fin. planning, 1974-85, dir. fin. confs., 1969—; mem. adv. bd. The First Women's Bank, N.Y.C., 1984—; dir. Drexel Burnham Fund, DBL Cash Fund, DBL Tax Free Cash Fund, Drexel Series Trust, N.Y.C., 1970—; pres. Money Marketeers, NYU, N.Y.C., 1979-80. Contbg. editor Exec. Jeweler, 1981-83; creator, moderator NBC TV series, Wall St. for Everyone, 1967-68. Mem. bd. overseers Parsons Sch. of Design, N.Y.C., 1974—. Named Disting. Alumnae, Wellesley Coll., 1968; Alt. fellow in econs. Columbia U., 1938-39. Mem. Fin. Women's Assn. (dir resource adv. com.), Econ. Club N.Y., N.Y. Assn. Bus. Economists, Money Marketeers NYU, Women's Bond Club, Nat. Assn. Bus. Econs. Jewish. Office: New Sch for Social Research 66 W 12th St New York NY 10011

BENENSON, ESTHER SIEV (MRS. WILLIAM BENENSON), gerontologist, educator, nursing home administrator; b. Jerusalem, Aug. 16, 1925; d. Joshua and Anna (Sanders) Siev; A.A.S., Queens Coll., 1957; B.S., Hunter Coll., 1972, M.S., 1974; Ed.M., Columbia U. Tchrs. Coll., 1976, Ed.D. in Gerontology, 1981; m. William Benenson, Sept. 15, 1957; children—Michael J., Sharon G., Amy L., Blanche S. Exec. dir. Flushing (N.Y.) Manor Nursing Home, 1959—, Flushing Manor Care Center, 1974—; mem. N.Y. State Bd. Examiners for Licensing Nursing Home Adminstrs., 1970-74; mem. adv. council N.Y. State Health Planning Commn., 1974; adj. assoc. prof. dept. health care and public adminstrn. C.W. Post Center, L.I. U., 1972-77. Bd. dirs. Queensboro Council for Social Welfare, Health Systems Agy. N.Y.C. Fellow Am. Coll. Nursing Home Adminstrs., Am. Assn. Med. Adminstrs., Royal Soc. Health; mem. N.Y. State Nursing Home Assn., Am. Public Health Assn., Soc. Public Health Educators, Gerontol. Soc. Office: 35-15 Parsons Blvd Flushing NY 11354

BENHAM, CAROLINE MARGARET (SZVETECZ), social worker, lawyer; b. Oklahoma City, July 30, 1941; d. Webster Lance, Jr., and Catherine (Collier) B.; B.A., Colo. Coll., 1963; M.S.W. (NIMH fellow), U. Denver, 1965; J.D., U. Colo., 1975; m. Frank C. Szvetecz, Mar. 21, 1975; children—Jason, Tynan; stepchildren—Charles, Anne, Matthew. Social worker, prin. social worker Ft. Logan Mental Health Center, Denver, 1965-69; pvt. practice social work, 1969-71; admitted to Colo. bar, 1975; individual practice law, Colorado Springs, Colo., 1975-76; juvenile ct. referee 4th Jud. Dist., State of Colo., Colorado Springs, 1976-79, juvenile ct. commr., 1979—, dist. ct. referee, 1981—. Vice chmn., acting chmn. El Paso County Placement Alternatives Commn., 1979—; bd. dirs. Chins Up Youth Care Homes, chmn. task force/planning com.; Jr. League community adv. bd., 1978-80; Colorado Springs Citizens Goals conferee; mem. Pikes Peak Children's Advocates. Lic. social worker, Colo. Recipient Legal Services award Pikes Peak Children's Advocates, 1983. Mem. Am. Bar Assn., Colo. Bar Assn., El Paso County Bar Assn. (chmn. alternative dispute resolution com.), Colo. Women's Bar Assn., Women Lawyers of Fourth Jud. Dist., Am. Trial Lawyers Assn., Colo. Trial Lawyers Assn., Nat. Assn. Social Workers, Acad. Cert. Social Workers, Nat. Assn. Counsel for Children, Nat. Council Juvenile and Family Ct. Judges, Profl. Women's Assembly, Delta Gamma. Democrat. Participant, lectr. seminars in field; contbr. to juvenile sect. District Court Judges Benchbook, 1981. Home: 2115 Payton Circle Colorado Springs CO 80915 Office: Judicial Bldg 20 E Vermijo Ave Colorado Springs CO 80903

BENIEN, RUTH MARIE, lawyer; b. Norton, Kans., May 25, 1957; d. Alfred Arthur and Genevieve Irene (Kirk) Benien. B.S. Journalism, U. Kans., 1979, J.D., 1982. Bar: Kans. 1982, U.S. Dist. Ct. Kans. 1982, U.S. Ct. Appeals (10th cir.) 1985. Assoc. Schnider, Shamberg & May, Chartered, Shawnee Mission also Kansas City, Kans., 1982-83; Shamberg, Johnson, Bergman & Goldman, Chartered, Merriam, Kans., also Kansas City, Kans., 1984—. Mem. Kans. Democratic Century Club, Topeka, 1984—, Friends of Arts of Nelson Art Gallery, 1983—. Mem. Kans. Trial Lawyers Assn., Assn. Trial Lawyers Am., Kansas City Bar Assn., Kans. Bar Assn., ABA, Kans. Trial Lawyers Assn. (bd. govs. 1984—), Johnson County Bar Assn., Wyandotte County Bar Assn., U. Kans. Alumni Assn. (journalism law soc.), Assn. Women Lawyers Greater Kansas City (exec. com. 1983—, dir. 1983-84, v.p. 1984-85, pres. 1985-86), Nat. Assn. Female Execs., Phi Alpha Delta. Club: Woodside Racquet (Westwood, Kans.). Home: 8352 Overbrook Rd Shawnee Mission KS 66206 Office: Suite 355 4551 W 107th St Overland Park KS 66207

BENJAMIN, CAROL JOY, human resources executive, psychotherapist; d. Max and Molly (Spiegel) Levenson; m. Alan A. Benjamin, Sept. 3, 1961; children—Edward Levenson Benjamin, Barry Martin Benjamin. Student Bryn Mawr Coll., 1958-60; B.A., NYU, 1961; M.S.W., Adelphi U., 1975. Cert. social worker, N.Y. Tchr. Port Washington (N.Y.) Schs., 1961-65; activities therapist L.I. Jewish-Hillside Hosp., Queens, N.Y., 1970-72; psychiat. social worker Cath. Charities, Roslyn, N.Y., 1975-76; clin. dir. Copay, Inc., Great Neck, N.Y., 1976-81; dir. human resources UPA Technology Inc., Syosset, N.Y., 1981—; pvt. practice psychotherapist, Great Neck, 1981—. Mem. Acad. Cert. Social Workers, Nat. Assn. Social Workers, Am. Soc. Personnel Adminstrs. Home: 33 Nassau Dr Great Neck NY 11021

BENJAMIN, ELLEN JANICE, foundation director; b. White Plains, N.Y., Nov. 14, 1953; d. Theodore Simon and Barbara Joyce (Bloch) Benjamin; m. Frederick Newcomb Bates. Student U. Copenhagen, 1973; B.A., SUNY-Buffalo, 1974; M.S.W., U. Mich., 1976. Adminstrv. asst. Am. Friends Service Com., Chgo., 1976-77; coordinator Ill. Women's Agenda, Chgo., 1977-80; pub. relations specialist Planned Parenthood Assn., Chgo., 1980-82; grants coordinator Borg-Warner Found., Chgo., 1982; dir. corp. contbns., 1983—. Trustee Mt. Sinai Hosp., Chgo.; bd. dirs. Chgo. N.Y. State Regents scholar SUNY-Buffalo. Mem. Chgo. Women in Philanthropy, LWV (adv. bd. ednl. fund) Phi Beta Kappa, Alpha Lambda Delta. Home: 622 Briar Pl Chicago IL 60657 Office: Borg-Warner Corp 200 S Michigan Ave Chicago IL 60604

BENJAMIN, FLEUR KATHLEEN, nurse; b. Vinton, Iowa, Dec. 9, 1934; d. Glenn Ripley and Dorothy Marie (Evans) Healy; m. Roy Glen Ives, June 10, 1956 (div. 1971); children—Mark Alan, John Glenn, Jeanine Renee; m. 2d. David Hinton Benjamin, Oct. 1, 1977. Student Drake U., 1953-54; grad. Broadlawn Sch. of Nursing, Des Moines, 1956. R.N., Iowa; cert. urology nurse. Asst. nurse Broadlawns Hosp., Des Moines, 1956-57; staff nurse Jennie Edmunson Hosp., Council Bluffs, Iowa, 1957-60, Mennonite Hosp., LaJunta, Colo., 1967-70, Flagstaff Community Hosp. (Ariz.), 1972-73; asst. head nurse St. Lukes Hosp., Cedar Rapids, Iowa, 1970-72; asst. unit mgr. Flagstaff Med. Ctr., 1975—. Bd. dirs. Am. Cancer Soc. Mem. Am. Nurses Assn., Am. Urol. Assn., Am. Diabetic Assn., VFW Aux. Republican. Mem. Christian Ch. Home: 60 Columbine Mt View Ranchos Flagstaff AZ 86001

BENJAMIN, JEANNE CLARK, furniture and boat restoration company executive; b. Wakefield, Mass., Dec. 30, 1931; d. Richard Foster and Ruth Arvilla (Glynn) Clark; m. Robert Allan Simon, May 18, 1952 (div. Nov. 1965); children—Lisa (dec.), Karen, Karl; m. 2d, Donald Arthur Benjamin, Feb. 9, 1968. Student Tufts U., 1949-52; B.Ed. cum laude, U. Miami, 1964; J.D., Temple U., 1974; cert. Continuing Legal Edn. Profl. Seminar, Peoples Republic China, 1982. Bar: Pa. 1974, N.H. 1980, U.S. Supreme Ct. 1978; cert. tchr., Fla., Pa., N.H. Tchr., Dade County Schs. (Fla.), 1964-65, CETA program, Jamison, Pa., 1978, Kingswood Regional High Sch., Wolfeboro, N.H., 1979-83; freelance writer, 1967—; ptnr. Benjamin & Johnsen, Doylestown, Pa., 1974-78; treas. Wolfeboro Restoration Center, 1978—; counselor Hospice of So. Carroll County, Wolfeboro, 1981—, mem. exec. bd., 1982— instr., 1982—, also coordinator. Mem. Plumstead Twp. Planning Bd. (Pa.), 1976-78; ballot clk. Town of Wolfeboro, 1981, 84; bd dirs. Aid for Girls Bucks County (Pa.), 1975-78. Contbr. articles, stories and poems to various pubs. Mem. ABA, Bucks County Bar Assn. (chmn. minor judiciary com. 1976, speaker women and law 1974-78), N.H. Bar Assn., Seacoast Writers Assn., AAUW (fellowship chmn. 1971, legis. chmn. Doylestown 1972), Women Outdoors Medford (staff writer mag. 1981—), Appalachian Mountain Club. Home: Elm St Box 1794 Wolfeboro NH 03894 Office: Wolfeboro Restoration Center Lehner St Wolfeboro NH 03894

BENJAMIN, JOYCE HOLMES, lawyer; b. Winnipeg, Man., Can., Jan. 27, 1931; d. George Andrew and Margaret E. (Wachter) Holmes; m. Jonathan S. Benjamin, July 20, 1951 (div. 1978); children—George Andrew Holmes, Emelia Jane, Elisabeth Ryden. B.A., U. Oreg., 1971, J.D., 1974. Bar: Oreg. 1974. Assoc., Miller, Moulton, Andrews, Eugene, Oreg., 1974-76, Johnson, Harrang, Swanson & Long, Eugene, 1976-81; ptnr. Benjamin, Waggoner, Chapman & Farleigh, Portland, Oreg., 1982-84; assoc. Acad. for State and Local Govt., Washington, 1984, dep. chief counsel State and Local Legal Ctr., 1985—; chmn. Lane County Personnel Rev. Bd., Eugene, 1976-77. Chair, State

Oreg. Edn. Reorgn. Commn., Salem, 1967-69; pres. Intermediate Edn. Bd. sect. Oreg. Sch. Bd. Assn., 1965-66; mem., chmn. Lane County Internat. Edn. Dist. Bd., Eugene, 1964-76; chmn. Gov.'s Commn. on Fgn. Lang. and Internat. Relations Orgn., 1980-82; mem., chmn. Oreg. Bd. Edn., Salem, 1976-84. Named Oreg. Edn. Citizen of Yr., 1970; named Outstanding Oral Advocate, U. Oreg. Law Sch., Eugene, 1972. Mem. Nat. Assn. State Bds. Edn. (dir. 1979-83), Oreg. State Bar (chair govt. law sect. 1980, continuing legal edn. com. 1983—). Clubs: Multnomah Athletic (Portland); Town (Eugene). Office: Acad State and Local Govt 440 N Capital St Washington DC 20001

BENJAMIN, PAMELA SOUTHWORTH, interior designer; b. Hartford, Conn., Oct. 20, 1952; d. James Rollins and Jeanne Marthe (Bouvier) Southworth; B.S., U. Conn., 1975; m. Thomas Gerard Benjamin, July 29, 1972; 1 son, Tyler Ross. Interior designer Continental Ill. Nat. Bank, Chgo., 1979-81; dir. design OFP Total Design Cons., Stamford, Conn., 1981; space planner Midwest Stock Exchange, Chgo., 1981; office planner, interior designer Abbott Labs., North Chicago, Ill., 1982—; regional sec. Inst. Bus. Designers, 1979-81, v.p., 1981-83, chairperson nat. admissions com., 1985—. Mem. social com. Lake Hinsdale Tower Assn., 1978-81; mem. congressional campaign com., 1972, Midwest Communications Assn., 1981-82. Recipient cert. of recognition for Outstanding Contbn., Inst. Bus. Designers, 1981; First prize Design-A-Toy Contest, Mansfield (Conn.) Tng. Sch., 1975. Mem. Am. Soc. Interior Designers, Inst. Bus. Designers, Lake Hinsdale Tower Assn. Home: 6340C Americana 218 Clarendon Hills IL 60514 Office: 1400 Sheridan Rd Abbott Park North Chicago IL 60064

BENN, INGRID ILEANA, publishing company executive; b. Arroyo, P.R., May 1, 1953; came to U.S., 1955; d. Roberto and Virginia (Cancel) B.; A.B. magna cum laude, Wilmington (Ohio) Coll., 1975; M.B.A. cum laude, Ohio State U., Columbus, 1977. With Charles E. Merrill Pub. Co., Columbus, 1977—, product mgr., 1979-81, mktg. mgr. trade pub., 1982, now dir. internat. sch. div.; pub. cons. to mayor Columbus, Ohio. Named Power Maker of Month, Bell & Howell Co., 1985. Mem. Assn. M.B.A. Execs., Nat. Assn. Female Execs., ALA, AAUW, Green Key, Beta Gamma Sigma Roman Catholic. Home: 545 Woodingham Pl Columbus OH 43213 Office: 1300 Alum Creek Dr Columbus OH 43216

BENN, PHYLISS ASHMUN, lawyer; b. Washburn, Wis., Aug. 26, 1924; d. Van Sanford and Margaret Fiege Ashmun; B.A., U. Wis.-Madison, 1946; J.D., Valparaiso U., 1975; m. Donald W. Benn, Aug. 30, 1947; children—David W., Martha Ann, Ruth L., Robert Samuel. City editor Niles (Mich.) Daily Star, 1946-47; editorial asst. Towndan Pub. Co., LaPorte, Ind., 1964-71; admitted to Ind. bar, 1975; assoc. firm Smith and Smith, LaPorte, 1975-79; sole practice law, LaPorte, 1979—. Chmn. City of LaPorte Human Rights Commn., 1980-82; precinct committeewoman Democratic County Com., 1974-86; chmn. La Porte County Election Bd.; del. Dem. Nat. Conv., 1976; vol. Girl Scouts U.S.A., No. Ind. Council, 1948-70, v.p., 1964-67. Mem. LaPorte City Bar Assn. (sec. 1981-82), Family Service Assn. (dir. 1979-85), AAUW (LaPorte br. grantee 1973, pres. 1958-59, state dir. 1960-63), Am. Bar Assn., Ind. Bar Assn., County Bar Assn., Family Mediation Service, Phi Beta Kappa. Home and Office: 1001 Maple Ave LaPorte IN 46350

BENN, SARA KITCHEN, educator, lawyer; b. Holden, Mass., Jan. 25, 1949; d. Charles G. and Helen (Mansfield) Kitchen; m. Joel Dennis Benn, Feb. 14, 1976; children—Julia Ruth, Leon Matthew. B.A. cum laude, Trinity Coll., 1971; J.D., Villanova U., 1975. Bar: Pa., 1975. Asst. pub. defender Pub. Defender-Bucks County, Doylestown, Pa., 1975-77; instr. Beaver Coll., Glenside, Pa., 1979, Temple U., Phila., 1980, Gwynedd-Mercy Coll., Gwynedd Valley, Pa., 1977-85; instr. law Temple U., Ambler, Pa., 1984-85; asst. prof. chmn. dept. sociology Chestnut Hill Coll., Pa., 1985—; resource person Juvenile Justice Center, Phila., 1975-77. Editor: Youth Diversion Handbook of Bucks County, 1979. Mem. legal staff Com. Seventy, Phila., 1974; bd. dirs. Alpha Pregnancy Services, Phila., 1983—. Mary D Walsh scholar Trinity Coll., 1967-71; Thomas J. Watson fellow Watson Found., 1971-72. Mem. ABA. Roman Catholic. Home: 10 Oak Rd Philadelphia PA 19118

BENNER, ANN WRIGLEY, sales executive; b. Brevard, N.C., Oct. 30, 1943; d. George and Edith Charlotte (Patton) Wrigley; student Converse Coll., 1961-62; children—Arthur, Paige. Store mgr. Heskett's Carpets DBA Gen. Floors, Inc., Oakland, Calif., 1972-76; Pacific Flooring distbr. Burlington House Carpets, Emeryville, Calif., 1976-78; ter. sales mgr. J.P. Stevens & Co., Inc., Gulistan Div., San Francisco, 1978-82; sr. mktg. rep. West Point Pepperell carpet and rug div. Cabin Crafts Carpet, 1982—; also condr. various seminars. Patron, Performing Artists Group, San Francisco, 1981—. Recipient Outstanding Sales award Pres.'s Council, Burlington House Carpets, 1977; named to Laurel Soc. and Million Dollar Club, J.P. Stevens & Co. Mem. San Francisco Floor Covering Assn., Internat. Platform Assn. Club: USMC Wives' (pres. 1968). Home: 8061 Peppertree Rd Dublin CA 94568 Office: 875 Stevenson Mart II Space 403 San Francisco CA 94103

BENNER, KAREN JO, home furnishings company sales director; b. Hartford, Conn., Mar. 14, 1952; d. Russell C. and Joan E. (Schmidt) Appler; m. Robert B. Benner, June 24, 1972; children—Patricia, Pamela, Robert A. Sec., Lockwood Folding Box, Valley Forge, Pa., 1975-78; dist. mgr. Creative Expressions, Reading, Pa., 1979-85; sales dir. World Odyssey, Phila., 1985—. Designer needlecraft used as fund raiser by Am. Lung. Assn. Mem. Bus. and Profl. Women (chmn. pub. relations 1985-86). Republican. Roman Catholic. Avocations: needlecrafts; bowling. Home and Office: PO Box 162 Route 162 Unionville PA 19375

BENNETT, BARBARA STANTON, historical society executive; b. Wilmington, N.C., Feb. 6, 1944; d. Allen and Barbara Stanton (Packard) B. B.A. in Humanities, U. South Fla., 1964; M.L.S., U. Ill., 1970. Tchr. U.S. Peace Corps, Leyte, Philippines, 1964-66; with reference and documents dept. Savannah Pub. Library, Ga., 1971-77; indexer Ga. Hist. Soc., Savannah, 1978-81, asst. dir., 1981-83, acting dir., 1983—; hist. researcher for authors. Mem. Soc. Ga. Archivists, Coastal Ga. Library Assn., Mortar Bd., Beta Phi Mu. Home: 402 E Victory Dr Savannah GA 31405 Office: Ga Hist Soc 501 Whitaker St Savannah GA 31405

BENNETT, BETTY BESSE, librarian; b. Omaha, Feb. 18, 1921; d. Gordon Stanley and Besse Harriet (Amos) B.; B.A., Mcpl. U. Omaha, 1942; B.S. in L.S., U. Ill., 1943; M.A., U. Iowa, 1948; M.L.S., Tex. Woman's U., 1960. Asst. documents librarian U. Iowa Library, Iowa City, 1943-50; reference and documents librarian Kans. State Tchrs. Coll. Library, Pittsburg, 1950-57, reference librarian, archivist, 1957-67; reference and research librarian Stephen F. Austin State U. Library, Nacogdoches, Tex., 1967-72, govt. documents librarian, 1972—; resource cons. Gov.'s Conf. on Libraries, Austin, Tex., 1974. Clk. session Presbyterian Ch., 1967-80, ruling elder, 1975—; exec. dir. Telephone Reassurance Program for Elderly Shut-Ins, 1977-80; mem. ad hoc com. on superseded documents U.S. Govt. Printing Office, 1985-86. Mem. ALA (state document classifcation com. 1974-80, state documents task force) Tex. (chmn. govt. documents round table 1975-76), Southwestern library assns., Tex. Assn. Coll. Tchrs., Nacogdoches Friends of the Library, Alpha Xi Delta. Presbyterian. Office: Stephen F Austin State U Library Nacogdoches TX 75962

BENNETT, BOBBIE JEAN, state official; b. Gwinnett County, Ga., July 13, 1940; d. William Claude and Clara Maude (Nichols) Holcome; B.B.A. magna cum laude, Ga. State U., 1973; 1 dau., Terri Lynne. With Ga. State Merit System, Atlanta, 1960—, sr. acct., 1967, asst. div. dir., 1968-70, fiscal officer, 1970-74, div. dir., 1975-78, asst. dep. commr., 1978—. Mem. Ga. Fiscal Mgmt. Council, Ga. Council Personnel Adminstrn., Nat. Assn. Deferred Compensation Adminstrs. (sec.), Beta Gamma Sigma, Phi Kappa Phi, Beta Alpha Psi. Democrat. Home: 2072 Malabar Dr NE Atlanta GA 30345 Office: State Merit System 200 Piedmont Ave Atlanta GA 30334

BENNETT, CATHERINE JUNE, data processing manager; b. Augusta, Ga., June 19, 1950; d. Robert Stogner and Catherine Sue (Jordan) Robinson; m. Danny Marvin Bennett, Sept. 5, 1971; children—Timothy Jordan, Robert Daniel. B.S. in Stats., U. Ga., 1971, M.A. in Bus., 1973. Programmer William M. Shenkel & Assocs., Athens, Ga., 1971-73; systems analyst U. Ga., Athens, 1973-76; product cons. Info. Systems Am., Atlanta, 1976-78, project leader, 1978-80, mngr. product support, 1980-85, hotline mgr., sr. fin. specialist, 1986—. Avocations: bridge; swimming; travelling. Home: 3458 Larch Pike Dr Duluth GA 30136 Office: Info Systems Am 500 Northridge Rd Atlanta GA 30338

BENNETT, CELESTINE C. T., librarian; b. Winston-Salem, N.C., Nov. 9, 1932; d. Arthur Loveliest and Mamie (Guerrant) Tutt; B.A., Winston-Salem State U., 1952; M.L.S., Columbia U., 1971, D.L.S., 1983; m. Henry McNeal Bennett, Dec. 28, 1977; children—Richard Bennett, Kathryn Bennett. Librarian, Urban Center, Columbia U., N.Y.C., 1971-73, asst. librarian Whitney M. Young Jr. Meml. Library Social Work, 1973-77, librarian, 1978-83; mem. papers adv. com. Whitney M. Young Jr., 1975-78, chmn., 1979-83; mem. adv. com. Whitney M. Young Jr. Disting. Lecture Series, 1983; adminstrv. analyst Oakland Pub. Library, Calif., 1985. Fellow Brookdale Inst. on Aging and Adult Human Devel., Columbia U., 1983—. Mem. ALA, Calif. Library Assn., Council Social Work Edn., Internat. Council Social Welfare, Bay Area Urban League. Home: 3831 Balfour Ave Oakland CA 94610

BENNETT, DEBORAH LYNN, marketing director; b. Ft. Benning, Ga., Oct. 6, 1958; d. David Coral and Lottie Judith (Hickman) Goodwin; m. Gary Steven Bennett, June 27, 1976 (div. Aug. 1981); 1 child, Jamison Ryan. Student Sam Houston State U., 1978, U. Tex.-Austin, 1983—. Office mgr., Robert Dernick, D.D.S., Woodlands, Tex., 1981-82; pub. relations mgr. Robert J. Jordan, D.D.S., Austin, 1982-84; mktg. dir. Kennedy Reporting Service, Austin, 1984—. Mem. Am. Mktg. Assn., Nat. Assn. Female Execs., Austin Assn. Female Execs., Travis County Ct. Reporters Assn., Nat. Shorthand Reporters Assn. Republican. Seventh-day Adventist. Club: Toastmasters. Avocations: snow skiing; water skiing; music-voice and piano. Office: Kennedy Reporting Service Inc 7800 Shoal Creek Blvd Suite 346-W Austin TX 78757

BENNETT, DEBORAH R., employment agency executive; b. Los Angeles, Apr. 8, 1941; d. William H. and Harriet (Hatch) Roome; m. Raymond James Bennett, July 10, 1969; 1 dau., Shauna. B.S., U. Redlands, 1962. Exec. sec. Los Angeles Tchrs. Credit Union, 1965-81; sec.-bookkeeper Ronald Sinclair, CLU, Encino, Calif., 1981-83, Gruenfelder's, Canoga Park, Calif., 1984; self-employed, Granada Hills, Calif., 1983-84; owner, mgr. D.R. Bennett and Assocs., Encino, 1984—. Mem. Nat. Alliance of Homebased Women (v.p. 1983-85), Calif. Assn. Personnel Cons., Nat. Assn. Personnel Cons., Granada Hills C. of C. Republican. Christian Scientist. Avocations: reading, sewing. Home: 17306 Trosa St Granada Hills CA 91344 Office: DR Bennett & Assocs 15910 Ventura Blvd Suite 813 Encino CA 91344

BENNETT, EILEEN DOROTHY, radiologic technologist; b. Cleve., Sept. 28, 1914; d. Harvey James and Alice Bernice (Harding) Gleason; B.A., Ursuline Coll., 1936; R.T., Mt. Sinai Hosp., 1937; m. Robert Huge, Nov. 17, 1938 (dec. 1964); children—Robert, John; m. 2d, Frank M. Bennett, 1971. Technologist x-ray dept. Akron (Ohio) City Hosp., 1937-38; chief x-ray technologist St. Joseph's Hosp., Warren, Ohio, 1938-39, Bay View Hosp., Bay Village, Ohio, 1954-61; chief technologist Dr. Maurice D. Sachs, Fairview Park, Ohio, 1961-67, also office mgr.; x-ray technologist St. John's Hosp., Cleve., 1968-71. Bd. dirs. women's com. Sch. Fine Arts, 1977-79; trustee Sch. Fine Arts, 1981-84. Mem. AAUW (pres. 1976-78), Am. Registry Radiologic Technologists. Republican. Roman Catholic. Club: Willoughby Woman's (dir. 1976-79). Home: 35830 Boyd Ct Willoughby OH 44094

BENNETT, ELLEN EARP, telephone company official; b. Durham, N.C., Oct. 9, 1941; d. LeRoy A. and Dixie (Walton) Earp; m. Michael Wayne Bennett, July 22, 1960; 1 child, Michael Wayne. A.A.S. with honors, Durham Tech. Inst., 1983. Staff asst. Liggett Group, Durham, 1972-78; travel coordinator Gen. Telephone Co. S.E./Gen. Telephone Co. Ky., Durham, 1978—; chmn. car rentals GTE Travel Mgmt. Com., Stamford, Conn., 1984—. Mem. NC. Profl. Women in Travel (chair nominating com. 1984—), N.C. Passenger Traffic Assn., Nat. Passenger Traffic Assn. Methodist. Home: 5610 Birch Dr Durham NC 27712 Office: Gen Telephone Co PO Box 1412 Durham NC 27702

BENNETT, ELSIE MARGARET, music school administrator; b. Detroit, Mar. 30, 1919; d. Sy and Ida (Carp) Blum; m. Morton Bennett, June 20, 1937 (dec.); children—Ronald, Kenneth. Cert., Ganapal Conservatory Detroit, 1941; B.Mus. in Theory, Wayne State U., 1945; M.A. in Music Edn., Columbia U., 1946; postgrad. Columbia U., Manhattan Sch. Music. Music studio mgr., tchr. Bennett Music Sch., Bklyn., 1946—, dir. 1946—; music arranger, 1946—; tchr. Schiff Sch. Music, 1972-80, owner, 1972—; tchr. Robotti Accordion Acad. and Pkwy. Music Sch., 1945-46; owner Margolies Sch. Music, Acad. of Music Sch.; editor Accordion World Mag., 1945-56; works include: Easy Solos for Accordion, 1946; Bass Solo Primer, 1948; Hebrew and Jewish Songs and Dances for Accordion, 1959, Vol. 1, 1951, Vol. 2, 1953; Hanon for Accordion, 1953; Accordion Music in the Home, 1953; Folk Melodies for Accordion, 1954; Five Finger Melodies for Accordion, 1954; First Steps in Scaleland for Accordion, 1956; First Steps in Chordland for Accordion, Vol. 1, 1961, Vol. II, 1961. Mem. Bklyn. Community Council. Mem. Am. Accordionists Assn. (governing bd., pres. 1973-74, plaque, 1962, service to governing bd. award 1942-60, Silver Cup 1974-75), Bklyn. Music Tchrs. Guild (dir., past sec.),, Accordion Tchrs. Guild, L.I. Music Tchrs. Assn.

BENNETT, EUDORA SMITH, hospital administrator; b. W. Franklin, Pa., July 16, 1924; d. Merton Henry and Ruby-Estelle Grace (Allen) Smith; R.N., Robert Packer Hosp. Tng. Sch. Nurses, Sayre, Pa., 1945; m. Raymond Leslie Bennett, Dec. 21, 1946 (div. Jan. 1967); children—Ann Marie, Donald Hasbrouck, Stanley Douglas. Gen. duty nurse Robert Packer Hosp., 1945-46, supr. pediatrics, 1947-48; pvt. duty nurse Carbondale (Pa.) Gen. Hosp., 1948-49; supr. Monmouth Meml. Hosp., Long Branch, N.J., 1950-51; adminstr. Montrose (Pa.) Med. Center, 1951—, also dir.; dir. Med. Arts Nursing Center, Montrose; a founder Med. Arts Clinic, Montrose Gen. Hosp. Inc. (formerly Med. Arts Hosp.), Med. Arts Nursing Ctr., Inc.; mem. exec. com. Pa. Statewide Health Coordinating Council, 1976—. Bd. dirs., mem. exec. com. N.Y.-Pa. Health Planning Council, 1969—, chmn. Susquehanna County chpt., 1971-72; mem. bd. Northeastern Human Parts Assn., 1971—; mem. Susquehanna County Ambulance and Emergency Services Assn., 1971—. Named Spirit of Nursing, Robert Packer Hosp., 1945. Mem. Am. Hosp. Assn., Pa. Hosp. Assn. (dir. 1982—, planning and devel. com. 1978—, small and rural hosp. com., trustee 1981—) hosp. assns., Hosp. Council N.E. Pa. (chmn. 1982-83), Health Care Facilities Assn. Pa. Republican. Presbyterian. Club: Y-Gradale (Montrose). Home: 42 Maple St Montrose PA 18801 Office: 3 Grow St Montrose PA 18801

BENNETT, F(RANKIE) KATHARINE, rehabilitation consulting company executive; b. Flagstaff, Ariz., Feb. 15, 1945; d. Charles Birge and Allie Kathleen (Tanner) Wilson. A.A., Stephens Coll., 1965; B.A., U. Ariz., 1967, M.S., 1969. Cert. rehab. counselor. Counselor severely disabled State of Calif., Van Nuys, 1969-77; counselor cons. Innovative Services, Portland, Oreg., 1977-79; co-owner, pres. Germain-Bennett Rehab. Cons., Inc., Lake Oswego, Oreg., 1979—. Commr., sec. Mossy Brae Water Dist. Clackamas County (Oreg.), 1978-81. Mem. Nat. Rehab. Assn., Oreg. Assn. Rehab. Profls. in Pvt. Sector (bd. dirs. 1983—, editor newsletter 1983-84, chmn. legis. com. 1984—), Tng. and Profl. Placement Service (handicapped employment com. 1978-79). Democrat. Avocations: cross-country skiing; boating; bicycling. Office: 1 Germain-Bennett Rehab Cons Inc 525 SW 1st St Lake Oswego OR 97034

BENNETT, JULIA WALSH, nurse; b. St. Paul, Sept. 8, 1958; d. James Lawrence and Arlene Mary (Stephani) Walsh; m. Joel Cutler Bennett, Oct. 16, 1981; 1 child, James Cutler. B.A., Coll. St. Catherine, 1980. Staff nurse Hennepin County Med. Ctr., Mpls., 1980-85, head nurse emergency dept., 1985—. Roman Catholic. Office: Hennepin County Med Ctr Emergency Dept 701 Park Ave Minneapolis MN 55415

BENNETT, KATHERINE ANN, cosmetics co. exec.; b. Alexandria, La., Dec. 12, 1939; d. Charles D. and Esther V. (Whaley) Ward; student Cambridge U., 1960, Mercer U., 1976-77; m. Preston G. Bennett; children—Kerry D. Wolfe, Michael W. Wolfe. Sec. treas. Yellow-Cab Co., Inc., Alexandria, 1962-70; dist. sales mgr. Avon Products, Inc., Atlanta, 1970-75, mgmt. asso., 1975-77, div. sales mgr., 1977—. Loaned exec. United Way Campaign, Atlanta. Mem. Nat. Assn. Female Execs. Republican. Roman Catholic. Office: 2200 Cotillion Dr Atlanta GA 30338

BENNETT, KATHLEEN MCMANUS, forest products company executive; b. S.I., N.Y., May 11, 1948; d. Leo Giblin and Rosemary Katherine (Keenan) McManus; m. Michael Canville Bennett, May 6, 1972; 3 children. B.A., Manhattanville Coll., 1970. Adminstrv. asst. Office Congressional Affairs, U.S. Gen. Services Adminstrn., Washington, 1971-72; rep. Pub. Affairs Analysts, Inc., Washington, 1972-74; dir. legis. affairs Am. Paper Inst., Washington, 1974-77; fed. affairs rep. Crown Zellerbach Corp., Washington, 1977-81; presdl. appointee asst. adminstr. air noise radiation EPA, Washington, 1981-83; dir. regulatory affairs Champion Internat. Corp., Stamford, Conn., 1983-86; dir. environ. planning James River Corp., Richmond, Va., 1986—; mem. nat. task force Acid Precipitation, Washington, 1984—; mem. adv. com. to U.S. trade rep. on negotiations implementing Geneva Trade Agreement, 1978-80; head U.S. delegation 1982 Conv. Acidification Environ., Stockholm. Mem. Air Pollution Control Assn., Air Quality Subcom. Prevention Significant Deterioration, Am. Paper Inst. Republican. Roman Catholic. Office: James River Corp PO Box 2218 Richmond VA 23217

BENNETT, LAURA ELAINE JEWELL, nurse; b. Racine, Wis., Sept. 5, 1957; d. Ralph P. Jewell and Lois June Foster (Jewell); m. Bradley Kirk Bennett, Dec. 19, 1981; 1 child, Brittiny Jewell. B.S. in Nursing, U. Akron, 1980. R.N., Ohio Clin. lab. technologist Buckeye Med. Labs., Inc., Wadsworth, Ohio, 1975-80, Ravenna-Kent Med. Labs., Ravenna, Ohio, 1977-80; nurse Cleve. Clinic Found., 1980-85, asst. head nurse, 1983-86; preceptor Cleve. Clin. Found. Active free lunch program United Methodist Ch. Akron, Ohio, 1984, mem. community service com., 1985—. Mem. Am. Cancer Soc. Am. Soc. Ophthalmic Registered Nurses, Alpha Gamma Delta (chpt. ritual chmn.). Home: 105 Price Pl Akron OH 44308 Office: Cleve Clinic Found 9500 Euclid Ave Cleveland OH 44106

BENNETT, MARGARET ETHEL BOOKER, psychotherapist; b. Spartanburg, S.C., June 15, 1923; d. Paschal and Ovie (Grey) Booker. B.S., N.C. A&T State U., 1944; M.S.W., U. Mich., 1947; Ph.D., Wayne State U., 1980. Caseworker, field instr. Family Services Soc. Met. Detroit, 1947-52; caseworker, field instr., casework supr. Wayne County Cons. Center, 1952-60, Psychiat. Social Service, Wayne County Gen. Hosp., 1960-62; psychotherapist, field instr., asst. dir. Wayne County Mental Health Clinic, 1962-76; asst. dir. psychiat. social service Wayne County Psychiat. Hosp., 1976-77; dir. med. social service Wayne County Gen. Hosp., 1977-78; treatment cons. Project Paradigm; pvt. practice psychotherapy, Detroit, 1965—; psychotherapist, pres. Booker Bennett & Assocs., 1980—; founder Consultation Center of Ecorse, Mich., 1961; instr. Immanuel Luth. Coll., 1944-45; lectr. U. Mich., 1975-76. Bd. dirs. Crossroads, 1980—; exec. council Episcopal Diocese of Mich., 1974-77, 80—, exec. com. 1982—; governing bd. Cathedral Ch. of St. Paul, Detroit, 1971-74, 76-77, 79-82, v.p. governing bd., 1977; bd. dirs. Cathedral Terrace, 1981—, U. Mich. Women, 1982—, Wayne State U. Sch. Social Work Alumni Assn., 1981—. Cert. marriage counselor, cert. social worker, Mich.; cert. Acad. Cert. Social Workers. Fellow Am. Orthopsychiat. Assn.; mem. Mich. Assn. Marriage and Family Therapy, Am. Assn. Marriage and Family Therapy, Mich. Assn. Clin. Social Worker's Nat. Assn. Social Workers, Phi Delta Kappa, Alpha Kappa Alpha. Democrat. Episcopalian. Co-author: The Handbook of Psychodynamic Therapy; contbr. articles to profl. jours. Home and Office: 1971 Glynn Ct Detroit MI 48206

BENNETT, MARIANNE, health coverage company executive, lawyer; b. Bklyn., Oct. 9, 1948; d. Thomas Maurice and Mary Jo (Freese) D.; m. Charles N. Rapson, Sept. 25, 1971; children—Sean Maurice Bennett Rapson, Liam Terrence Bennett Rapson. B.A., Coll. of New Rochelle, 1970; J.D., Bklyn. Law Sch., 1975. Bar: N.Mex., 1976. Dir. Pre-Paid Legal Services, Albuquerque, 1975-76; research asst. prof. Inst. Pub. Law, Albuquerque, 1976-77; dir. Comserv. Ctr. for Legal Rep., Los Lunas, N.Mex., 1977-80, Legal Services-Albuquerque Bar, 1980-81; v.p., gen. counsel N.Mex. Blue Cross and Blue Shield, Albuquerque, 1981—. Contbr. chpt. to book, articles to publs. Pres. bd. dirs. S.W. Maternity Ctr., Albuquerque, 1977-80; bd. dirs. Assn. for Children with Learning Disabilities, 1982-83; mem. Bernalillo County Foster Parents, 1977-78, Am. Assn. on Mental Deficiency, N.Mex. Assn. for Retarded Citizens. Mem. ABA, N.Mex. Bar Assn., Albuquerque Bar Assn. Democrat. Roman Catholic. Office: New Mex Blue Cross and Blue Shield 12800 Indian School NE Albuquerque NM 87110

BENNETT, NANCY HENDERSON, pharmaceutical closures manufacturing official, translator, interpreter; b. Nice, France, May 9, 1947, came to U.S., 1952; d. Harvey Craig and Aimee Paulette (Chabbert) Henderson; m. Craig Haldeman Bennett, Dec. 23, 1970 (div. Dec. 1981); 1 child, Severine Rose. B.A., Goucher Coll., Towson, Md., 1968; M.A., Johns Hopkins U., 1971. Adminstrv. asst. Md. Nat. Bank, Balt., 1969-71; asst. to pres. House of Wines, Washington, 1971-72; asst. to pres. Medcraft, Inc., Skippack, Pa., 1972-74; self-employed translator, interpreter, Royersford, Pa., 1974—; asst. to chmn. Certain-Teed Corp., Valley Forge, Pa., 1978-80; export mgr. The West Co., Phoenixville, Pa., 1980—. Editor Internat. Highlights, 1969-71. Activities dir. outreach div. The Pilot Club, Valley Forge, 1982-83; dir. Royersford Bapt. Ch. Sch. Bd., 1977-78. Mem. Women's Internat. Trade Assn., Internat. Trade Assn. Am. Roman Catholic. Office: The West Co International Div W Bridge St Phoenixville PA 19460

BENNETT, NELL WAYNE, farming operations executive, oil, real estate, historical restorations consultant; b. Midland, Tex.; d. Wayne and Nell (Carpenter) Carlisle; m. Harry Anthony Bennett, Apr. 28, 1949; children—Elizabeth Becker, Harry Anthony. B.A., Tex. Tech U., 1958, M.A., 1959; postgrad. U. Tex., 1960, Oxford U., 1961. Airline hostess Braniff Airlines, Dallas, 1940-41; air traffic controller FAA, San Antonio, 1943-49; instr. English, Tex. Tech U., Lubbock, 1959, Tex. Southmost Coll., Brownsville, 1960-67; chief exec. officer Empresa, Inc., Brownsville, 1970—. Contbr. articles to profl. jours. Sec. Good Neighbor Settlement House, Brownsville, 1960-65; bd. dirs. Ch. of the Advent, Brownsville, 1975. Mem. Am. Cotton Growners Assn., Cotton, Inc., Littlefield Coop. Grain and Cotton, Am. for Legal Reform, Mensa. Democrat. Episcopalian. Clubs: Water, Inc., Greenpeace. Avocations: bridge; chess; reading; hypnosis; expansion of consciousness reincarnational research. Home: 85 Calle Cenizo Brownsville TX 78520 Office: Empresa Inc 321 E 14th St Littlefield TX 79339

BENNETT, PAMELA MCHARDY, production company executive, actress; b. Chgo., Mar. 4, 1947; d. George and Iris McH.; m. Robert K. Bennett, Mar. 19, 1983. B.A., Carroll Coll., 1969. TV and radio spokesperson Allied Van Lines, 1978-80; pres. Square One Prodns. Inc., N.Y.C., 1980—. Appeared in various stage and TV shows, radio and TV commls., 1969-80. Mem. Judith Harris Selig Found., N.Y.C., 1979—; sec. Widow to Widowed Internat., Inc., N.Y.C., 1986—. Recipient Wis. Broadcasters award, 1967, 68. Mem. Screen Actors Guild, Actors Equity Assn., AFTRA, Nat. Assn. Female Execs., Internat. Exhibitors Assn., Delta Nu Alpha. Republican. Avocations: singing; piano; guitar; jogging; reading. Office: Square One Prodns Inc PO Box 5122 New York NY 10150

BENNETT, PATRICIA ANN, natural resources company executive, lobbyist; b. Clarkston, Wash., Mar. 27, 1949; d. Richard Guy and JoAnn (Rogers) Bennett; m. Mahlon Stanley Priest, Oct. 31, 1983; 1 child, Zachary. B.A., Boise State U., 1974; postgrad. U. Idaho Coll. Law, 1975-76. Coordinating dir. Nat. Soc. Energy Awareness, Washington, 1978; legis. asst. Senator Ted Stevens, Washington, 1978-81, Senator Malcolm Wallop, Washington, 1981-82; dir. legis. affairs Burlington, No. Inc., Washington, 1982-85; sr. ptnr. Bennett, Rock & Wilson, Washington, 1985—. Contbr. articles to profl. jours. Mem. Women in Govt. Relations, Nat. Assn. Female Execs. Avocations: reading; gardening; photography. Home: 110 W Highland Dr #211 Seattle WA 98119 Office: Bennett Rock & Wilson 110 W Highland Dr #211 Seattle WA 98119

BENNETT, PHYLLIS A., real estate brokerage manager; b. Bonham, Tex., Apr. 14, 1947; d. Joseph Thurman and Anne Alene (Seals) Hamilton; student Draughon's Bus. Sch., 1965; children—Benjamin Dwain, Robert Joseph. Sec., Sheraton-Dallas Hotel, 1965; sec. client service dept. Praetorian Mutual Life Ins. Co., Dallas, 1965-67; mgr. advt. sales aids, editor Compans mag. Life Ins. Co. S.W., Dallas, 1967-69; sales agt. Arlington (Tex.) Real Estate, 1972-73; sec.-treas. Becco, Inc., Arlington, 1973-83; office mgr. Rich Billings Inv., Inc., Arlington, 1983-85; mgr. Synergy Land Investments, Inc., Arlington, 1985—. Mem. Am. Bus. Women's Assn. (Woman of Year 1979), Nat. Assn. Female Execs. Office: Synergy Land Investments Inc 600 Six Flags Dr #616 Arlington TX

BENNETT, PHYLLIS REDMON, human services agency executive; b. Smithville, Tenn., Aug. 1, 1944; d. Henry Clarence and Evelyn Louise (Ours) Redmon; m. Weyman Herbert Bennett, Dec. 31, 1984; stepchildren—Nancy Lee, Gary Parks, Christian Elliot; m. Milburn Smith Rodgers, Jr., June 15, 1962 (div. June 1972); 1 child, Milburn Smith III. Student Tenn. Tech. U., 1963-69. Editorialist Smithville Rev., Tenn., 1963-65; teller First Nat. Bank, Smithville, 1965-68; site mgr. LBJ & C Devel. Corp., Monterey, Tenn., 1969-73; CETA dir. Upper Cumberland Human Resource Agy., Algood, Tenn.,

1973-75, transp. dir., 1975-78, exec. dir., 1978—; council mem. Tenn. Dept. Human Services, Cookeville, 1983—. Pres. Cancer Soc., Smithville, 1968-73; hon. mem. State Senate State of Tenn., 1985. Agy. recipient Nat. Rural Transp. award U.S. Dept. Transp., Kansas City, Kans., 1985. Mem. Tenn. Assn. Human Resource Agys. (state pres. 1985—), Tenn. Assn. Spl. Transp. (dir. 1984—), Bus. and Profl. Women's Club (sec.-treas. 1966-72). Democrat. Baptist. Club: Jaycettes (Smithville) (v.p. 1970, Jaycette of Yr. 1972). Home: Route 6 Box 24 Cookeville TN 38501 Office: Upper Cumberland Human Resource Agy 150 W Church St Algood TN 38501

BENNETT, SARAH ISABEL NEFF (SALLY), author, composer; b. Fountain Springs, Pa.; d. Franklin Daniel and Jennie Catherine (Bright) Neff; student Banks Bus. Coll., 1940-41, Gwen Shock Modeling and Dramatic Sch., 1941-42, U. Pa., 1942; m. Paul H. Bennett, Nov. 1, 1947. Model, John Wanamaker's, Phila., 1942; legal sec. Dept. Justice, Phila., 1945-46; writer, performer, disc jockey Radio and TV Sta. WLWA, Atlanta, 1954-56; playwright, actress Karamu Little Theater and Lakewood Little Theater, Cleve., 1957-59; founder, pres., owner Solar Record Co., Cleve., 1959—; composer Broadcast Music Co., Cleve., 1958—; founder, pres. Composers Showcase, Inc., Cleve., 1965—, Music Pub. Co., Cleve., 1966, First Big Band Hall of Fame, Cleve., 1975—; contbr. to Palm Beach (Fla.) Life, Palm Beacher Daily. Mem. nat. council Met. Opera, N.Y.C., 1967—; mem. John F. Kennedy Center, 1967—; founder, pres. Animal Welfare Vols., Inc., Cleve., 1969—; founding bd. dirs. Great Lakes Shakespeare Festival, Cleve., Cleve. Indian Basebelles. Mem. Nat. League Am. Pen Women (pres. 1962-63, music chmn. Palm Beach chpt., pres. br. 1982-83), Am. Guild Authors and Composers, Am. Women in Radio and TV, Am. Guild Variety Artists, Broadcast Music, Palm Beach Quills, Palm Beach Opera, Preservation Found. Palm Beach, Palm Beach Hist. Soc., Palm Beach C. of C., English Speaking Union (Palm Beach chpt.), DAR. Clubs: Cleve. Yachting, Racquet Internat., Women's City (Cleve.). Author: Sugar and Spice, 1972; composer: Magic Moments.

BENNETT-ALEXANDER, DAWN DEJUANA, lawyer, educator; b. Washington, Jan. 2, 1951; d. William H. and Ann P. (Liles) Bennett; m. Willie M. Alexander, Sept. 1, 1976 (div.); children—Jenniffer Dawn, Ann Alexis. B.A. magna cum laude, Fed. City Coll. (now U. D.C.), 1972; J.D. cum laude, Howard U., 1975. Bar: D.C. 1979, U.S. Ct. Appeals (D.C. cir.) 1982, U.S. Dist. Ct. D.C. 1982, U.S. Ct. Appeals (5th, 9th, 10th, 11th cirs.) 1982. Law clk. U.S. Ct. Appeals, Washington, 1975-76; asst. to assoc. dir. and counsel, The White House, Washington, 1976-77; law clk. FTC, Washington, 1977-78; instr. Antioch Sch. Law, Washington, 1979-81; atty., adviser Fed. Labor Relations Authority, Washington, 1981-82; assoc. prof. bus. and employment law, U. North Fla., Jacksonville, 1982—; cons. Kent Pub. Co., Boston, 1983. Contbr. articles to profl. jours. Bd. dirs., chmn. personnel com. Girls Clubs of Jacksonville Inc., 1983—; sec. bd. dirs., chmn. Personnel Com. Consumer Credit Counseling Service North Fla. Inc., Jacksonville, 1983—; gen. counsel Nat. Council Negro Women, Jacksonville, 1983—. Recipient Am. Jurisprudence award, Lawyers Coop. Pub. Co., 1975; citation for spl. achievement Fed. Labor Relations Authority Group, 1981; seed research grantee, U. North Fla., 1983. Mem. ABA, Fed. Bar Assn., Nat. Bar Assn., Nat. Assn. Black Women Attys., Am. Bus. Law Assn., LWV, NOW, AAUW. Democrat. Baptist. Home: 12924 Tree Way Lane Jacksonville FL 32223 Office: University North Florida 4567 St Johns Bluff Rd Jacksonville FL 32216

BENNETTS, GENI ALDRICH, physician, medical educator; b. Richmond, Va., July 4, 1946; d. George Aldrich and Naomi Clara (Puckett) B. B.A., Columbia Union Coll., Takoma Park, Md., 1967; M.A., Andrews U., Berrien Springs, Mich., 1969; M.D., Loma Linda U., 1973. Diplomate Am. Bd. Pediatrics, Nat. Bd. Med. Examiners. Intern, U. Calif.-Irvine, 1973-74, resident, 1974-75, fellow in pediatric hematology/oncology, 1975-77, asst. clin. prof., 1977-80, assoc. clin. prof., 1980-83, asst. adj. prof., 1983; staff physician hematology/oncology Childrens Hosp. Orange County, Orange, Calif., 1977-80, dir. dept. hematology/oncology, 1980—; coordiantor Oncology Ctr. Calif. Childrens Services, Orange, 1979—; prin. investigator Childrens Cancer Study Group, Orange, 1981—. Contbr. articles to profl. jours. Bd. dirs. Am. Cancer Soc. Orange County Unit, Newport Beach, Calif., 1980-83; mem. adv. bd. YMCA-South Orange County, 1981-83; bd. dirs. Pediatric Cancer Research Found. of Orange County, 1982-83; bd. dirs. Leukemia Soc. Am., Garden Grove, Calif., 1983. Am. Cancer Soc. grantee, 1980. Fellow Am. Acad. Pediatrics; mem. Am. Soc. Pediatric Hematology/Oncology, Orange County Pediatric Soc., Los Angeles Pediatric Soc., Orange County Med. Assn., Calif. Med. Assn. Office: Childrens Hosp Orange County 1109 W La Veta St Orange CA 92668

BENNINGTON, BRENDA LEE, videographer; b. Gary, Ind., Nov. 15, 1954; d. Paul Wayland and Shirley Ann (Havard) B. Student Principia Coll., Elsah, Ill., 1972-74, Sch. of Art Inst. of Chgo., 1982; B.A. in English with honors, U. Hawaii, 1977. Tchr. English, Peace Corps, Mbuji-Mayi, Zaire, 1977-79, Asahi Cultural Ctr., Osaka, Japan, 1981-82, Osaka Inst. Fgn. Trade, Osaka, 1981-82, Kansai U. of Fgn. Studies, Osaka, 1980-82, Matsushita Electric, Osaka, 1982; pres., owner Video Enterprises, North Palm Beach, Fla., 1983—. Mem. Exec. Women of Palm Beaches, Fla. Motion Picture and TV Assn., No. Palm Beach County C. of C. (co-chmn. spl. events 1985-86). Republican. Christian Scientist. Avocations: swimming; aerobics; long distance running. Office: Video Enterprises Crystal Tree 1201 US Hwy 1 Suite 250 North Palm Beach FL 33408

BENNINGTON, MARCY MARIE, former school psychologist; b. South Bend, Ind., Feb. 1, 1949; d. John William, Jr. and Constance Dorothy (Weingartner) Truemper; A.B., Ind. U., Bloomington, 1971; M.Ed., U. Mo., St. Louis, 1976; Ph.D. (teaching asst./instr.), St. Louis U., 1981; m. Mark Ian Bennington, Sept. 7, 1968. Adminstrv. asst. Psychol. Service Center, St. Louis, 1974-75; personnel asst. Orchard Corp. Am., St. Louis, 1975-77; sch. psychology intern Pattonville Schs., Maryland Heights, Mo., 1978-79; diagnostician, eval. coordinator Wentzville Schs., Mo., 1979-80, dir. spl. edn., 1980-85. Speaker to community groups. Phi Beta Kappa scholar. Mem. Am. Psychol. Assn., Nat. Assn. Sch. Psychologists, Am. Assn. Counseling and Devel., Council Exceptional Children.

BENNY, ELIZABETH MARY, lawyer, journalist; b. Flushing, N.Y., Mar. 8, 1956; d. Dennis J. and Betty (Toolan) Harrington; children—Bridget and Katy (twins). B.A., SUNY-Stony Brook, 1977, postgrad., 1983—; J.D., Pepperdine U., 1980. Bar: Calif. 1981. Assoc., Kapretz & Kasdan, Irvine, Calif., 1981-82; journalist L.I. Nitelife (N.Y.), 1983—. Contbr. articles to mags. Mem. ABA, Calif. Bar Assn., Orange County Women Lawyers, Phi Delta Phi. Libertarian. Roman Catholic. Home: 1 Waco Ct East Northport NY 11731

BENSEL, CAROLYN KIRKBRIDE, psychologist; b. Orange, N.J., Sept. 21, 1941; d. William Everitt and Margaret Mary (McGlynn) B.; A.B. with honors in Psychology, Chestnut Hill Coll., 1963; M.S., U. Mass., 1964, Ph.D. (Univ. fellow), 1967. Teaching asst. U. Mass., Amherst, 1963-64, research asst., 1964-66; human factors psychologist Grumman Aerospace Corp., Bethpage, N.Y., 1967-71; chief human factors group U.S. Army Natick (Mass.) Research and Devel. Labs., 1971—. Lic. psychologist, Mass. Fellow Human Factors Soc.; mem. Am. Psychol. Assn., Human Factors Soc., Ergonomics Soc., Soc. Engring. Psychologists, Internat. Ergonomics Assn., AAAS, Sigma Xi. Editor: Proc. 23d Ann. Meeting of Human Factors Soc., 1979. Office: Individual Protection Lab US Army Natick Research and Devel Labs Kansas St Natick MA 01760

BENSKINA, MARGARITA O. (PRINCESS ORELIA), dancer, singer, musician; b. Colon, Panama, Mar. 16; naturalized U.S. citizen, 1956; d. Jose and Amelia Benskina; student parochial schs., Havana, Cuba, and Colon, Panama, Harren High Sch., N.Y.C.; diploma for instrs. in modeling, N.Y. Acad. Theatrical Arts, 1962; grad. N.Y. Sch. Floral Designing, 1971; postgrad. Queens Coll., 1982; 1 dau., Pearl A. Quintyne. Has appeared in theatres, night clubs in various cities U.S., including Connie's Inn Broadway Night Club, Broadway Cotton Club, Leon and Eddie's; in Dance with Your Gods, Calling All Stars, Broadway Parade, N.Y.C., after 1935; mem. Afro-Cuban dance team, Orelia and Pete, 1942; toured with Asadata Dafora Dance Opera, Kykunkor, 1947; now appearing with own ensemble; toured Can. with own dance co., Bacanal, 1950; starred in UN program Stars of the West Indies, also TV program Tropical Holiday, CBS; toured with Sam Manning Calypso Concert Co., 1954; personal mgr. for modern jazz group Rouse-Watkins-Les Modes Quintet, 1956, also dance and mus. groups; prod., dir. concerts, N.Y.C., 1959; produced, directed, starred in concert program Princess Orelia's Pot Puree, Town Hall, N.Y.C., 1964; appeared on Ghana radio, 1971-77; owner, mgr. retail religious mdse. store, N.Y.C.; ordained to ministry Internat. Spiritual Healers Fellowship, 1956. Vol., Bellevue Hosp., N.Y.C. Recipient J.F. Kennedy Library for Minorities Heritage award, Am. Honorarium award, 1966, community service plaque Kappa Sigma chpt. Sigma Gamma Rho, 1984. Mem. Broadcast Music, Inc., Synanon, Negro Women's Guild, Washington, Council Negro Am. Women (life), Media Women. Author: (poetry) No Longer Defeated and Other Poems, 1972; The Inflammable Desire to Rebel, 1973; I Have Loved You Already, 1974; I Thank You, Father, 1975; Library To Whom It May Concern, 1978. Contbr. to New Voices in American Poetry, 1972-73. Home: 192-22 100th Ave Hollis NY 11423

BENSON, BETTY JONES, educator; b. Barrow County, Ga., Jan. 11, 1928; d. George C. and Bertha (Mobley) Jones; B.S. in Edn., N. Ga. U., Dahlonega, 1958; M.Ed. in Curriculum and Supervision, U. Ga., Athens, 1968, edn. specialist in Curriculum and Supervision, 1970; m. George T. Benson; children—George Steven, Elizabeth Gayle, James Claud, Robert Benjamin. Tchr. Forsyth County (Ga.) Bd. Edn., Cumming, 1956-66, curriculum dir., 1966—; asst. supt. for instrn. Forsyth County Schs., 1981—. Active Alpine Center for Disturbed Children; chmn. Ga. Lake Lanier Island Authority; mem. N. Ga. Coll. Edn. Adv. Com., Ga. Textbook Com.; adv. Boy Scouts; Sunday sch. tchr. 1st Baptist Ch. Cumming. Mem. NEA, Ga. Assn. Educators (dir.), Nat., Ga. (pres.) assns. supervision and curriculum devel., Assn. Childhood Edn. Internat., Bus. and Profl. Women's Club, Internat. Platform Assn., Ga. Future Tchrs. Adv. Assn. (pres.), HeadStart Dirs. Assn., Forsyth County Hist. Soc. Home: Route 1 Box 12 Cumming GA 30130 Office: 101 School St Cumming GA 30130

BENSON, CARLEE JEAN, restaurant owner; b. San Antonio, Apr. 28, 1938; d. Carl Hotopp and Margaret (Jinkins) Gladwin; m. Dean Ernest Benson, Aug. 22, 1959; children—Dina Carlee, Alysa Marie, Amy Diane, Devin Dean. B.A., U. Wyo., 1960; M.A., Adams State Coll., 1978. Pub. relations dir. Wolf Creek Ski Area, Pagosa Springs, Colo., 1974-76; owner Spruce Ski Lodge, South Fork, Colo., 1973-80; facilitator Alternatives in Edn., Alamosa, Colo., 1978-80; spl. edn. facilitator N.E. Ind. Sch. Dist., San Antonio, 1980-83; English facilitator Ctr. Sch. for Emotionally Disturbed Youth, 1985—; pres. Corky's Just for You, Inc., San Antonio, 1983—; dir. HiWay Haus Restaurants, La Vernia, Tex.; mem. profl. adv. bd. Hospice San Antonio, 1983-85; bereavement counselor, 1983-85. Vol., Foster Parents Assn., Suicide Prevention Ctr., Youth Halfway House, San Antonio. Mem. Tex. Restaurant Assn., Tex. Florist Assn., NEA, Tex. Edn. Assn., Pi Beta Phi. Republican. Lutheran. Club: Charger Spirit (San Antonio). Avocations: floral design; poetry; gardening; travel. Home: 15819 Blue Creek Dr San Antonio TX 78232 Office: PO Box 621 La Vernia TX 78121

BENSON, LINDA DARLENE, lawyer; b. Tallassee, Ala., Sept. 27, 1953; d. Waymon Edwin and Dorothy Louise (Hogan) B. A.S., Alexander City Jr. Coll., 1973; B.S., Auburn U.-Montgomery, 1975, M.P.A., 1976; J.D., Jones Law Inst. 1979. Bar: Ala. 1980. Sole practice law, Tallassee, 1980—. Mem. ABA, Ala. Bar Assn., Assn. Trial Lawyers Am., Ala. Trial Lawyers Assn., Phi Theta Kappa (v.p. Alexander City Jr. Coll. 1972-73), Sigma Delta Kappa. Democrat. Mem. Church of Christ. Home: Rt 4 Box 254 Tallassee AL 36078 Office: PO Box 818 East Tallassee AL 36023

BENSON, MAXINE FRANCES, editor, historian; b. Boulder, Colo., Sept. 5, 1939; d. Mac Walden and Roberta Frances (Ladwig) B. B.A., U. Colo., 1961, M.A., 1962, Ph.D., 1968; M.A., U. Denver, 1973. Dep. state historian Colo. Hist. Soc., Denver, 1964-65, state historian, 1967-71, curator documentary resources, 1972-82, state historian, 1980-82; dir. publs. Kans. State Hist. Soc., Topeka, 1983—; lectr. U. Denver, 1969, 70, 71, 75, U. Kans., Lawrence, 1984, 85. Co-author: A Colorado History, 1972, 76, 82; A Colorado Reader, 1982; contbr. A Taste of the West, 1983. Henry W. Schoolcraft fellow Hist. Soc. Mich., 1967; Nat. Hist. Publs. Commn. Editing fellow, Washington, 1971. Mem. Phi Beta Kappa, Phi Alpha Theta, Beta Phi Mu. Office: Kans State Hist Soc 120 W 10th St Topeka KS 66612

BENTEL, MARIA-LUISE RAMONA AZZARONE, architect; b. N.Y.C., June 15, 1928; d. Louis and Maria-Teresa (Massaro) Azzarone; m. Frederick R. Bentel, Aug. 16, 1952; children—Paul Louis, Peter Andreas, Maria Elisabeth. B.Arch., MIT, 1951; Fulbright scholar, Scuola d'Architettura, Venice, Italy, 1952-53. Registered profl. architect, Conn., N.Y., N.J., Va., Vt.; registered profl. planner, N.J. Partner Bentel & Bentel (Architects), Locust Valley, N.Y., 1955—; pres. Tesstoria Realty Corp., N.Y.C., 1961—; v.p., sec.-treas. Correlated Designs, Inc., Locust Valley, 1961—, partner Cobblestone Enterprises, 1967; founding mem. Locust Valley Bus. Dist. Planning Commn., 1968—; regional vice-chairperson MIT Ednl. Council; adv. mem. MIT Council for the Arts; asso. prof. architecture N.Y. Inst. Tech.; adj. prof. Queensboro Community Coll., Bayside, N.Y., 1971—. Archtl. works include C.W. Post Coll. L.I. U (N.Y. State Assn. Architects award 1975, Gold Archi award L.I. Assn. Architects 1974), Hempstead Bank, Nassau Centre Office Bldg., (L.I. Assn. Architects award 1972, N.Y. State Assn. Architects award 1975), North Shore Unitarian Sch, Plandome, N.Y. (L.I. Assn. Architects Silver Archi award 1967), Plandome, N.Y. (N.Y. State Assn. Architects award 1970), Shelter Rock Library, Searingtown, N.Y. (L.I. Assn. Architects award 1970), St. Anthony's Ch, Nanuet, N.Y. (N.Y. State Assn. Architects award 1972), Kinloch Farm, Va, Steinberg Learning Center-Woodmere (N.Y.) Acad, (N.Y. Library Assn. award 1972, L.I. Assn. Architects award 1975), St. Francis de Sales Ch., Bennington, Vt., Neitlich residence, Oyster Bay Cove, N.Y. (L.I. Assn. Architects Silver Archi award 1971), Oyster Bay Cove, N.Y. (N.Y. Assn. Architects award 1971), Amityville (N.Y.) Pub. Library, (Silver Archi award L.I. Assn. Architects, N.Y. State Assn. Architects award 1973), Jericho (N.Y.) Pub. Library, (N.Y. State Assn. Architects award, Silver Archi award L.I. Assn. Architects 1974), John B. Gambling residence, Lattingtown, N.Y. (Silver Archi award L.I. Assn. Architects 1974), Glen Cove (N.Y.) Boys' Club at Lincoln House, (Silver Archi award L.I. Assn. Architects 1978), Aquatics Component Mitchel Park, Nassau County, N.Y., Salten Hall, N.Y. Inst. Tech (award N.Y. State Assn. Architects 1977), N.Y. Coll. Osteo. Med. at N.Y. Inst. Tech., Old Westbury, Commack Pub. Library, Commack (N.Y. State Assn. Architects award 1977), St. Mary Star of the Sea Ch., Far Rockaway (Queens C. of C. grand prize 1977), Oberlin Residence (N.Y. State Assn. Architects/L.I. Assn. Architects Archi award 1983); Contbr.: religious architecture chpt. to Time Saver Standards (De Chiara and Callender), 1973. Mem. comml. panel Am. Arbitration Assn.; chmn. adv. panel on govt. bldg. projects GSA, 1976; chmn. Inst. Internat. Edn.; nat. adv.-selection com. Fulbright-Hays awards, 1976-78, 80, 82; Chairperson Locust Valley Library Adv. Bd., 1973—; bd dirs. L.I. Library Resources Council, 1982—. Recipient 1st place award for Islip Downtown Urban Renewal Competition, 1976; named Woman Architect of Year Nassau-Suffolk County, 1976. Fellow AIA (corp. mem., chmn. design com., dir. L.I. chpt.); mem. N.Y. State Assn. Architects (chmn. design awards com.), Nat. Council Archtl. Registration Bds., MIT Alumnae Assn., MIT Alumni L.I. (dir., v.p.). Home: 23 Frost Creek Dr Lattingtown NY 11560 Office: 22 Buckram Rd Locust Valley NY 11560

BENTLEY, ANTOINETTE COZELL, lawyer; b. N.Y.C., Oct. 17, 1937; d. Joseph Richard and Rose (LaFata) Cozell; B.A. with distinction, U. Mich., 1960; LL.B., U. Va., 1961; children—Robert S., Anne W. Bar: N.Y. 1962, N.J. 1971. Assoc. Sage Gray, Todd & Sims, N.Y.C., 1961-65; counsel Farrell, Curtis, Carlin & Davidson, Morristown, N.J., 1970-73; asst. sec. Crum and Forster, Morristown, 1973, sec., 1973-75, v.p., sec., counsel, 1975—; trustee Crum and Forster Found., Morristown. Vice-pres. Mendham (N.J.) Bd. Edn., 1976-79; pres., trustee N.J. Conservation Found., 1981—; trustee Morris Mus., 1981—, St. Peter's Coll. Mem. Women's Econ. Roundtable, LWV, ABA, Am. Soc. Corp. Secs. (v.p. N.Y. region), Assn. Corp. Counsel N.J. (mem. exec. com.), N.J. State Bar Assn., Order of Coif, Chi Omega. Home: 9 Knollcrest Rd Bedminster NJ 07921 Office: 305 Madison Ave Morristown NJ 07960

BENTLEY, DIANE KAY, word processing consultant; b. Wichita, Kans., Nov. 30, 1943; d. Ralph Franklin and Betty Jane (Hemsworth) Garrett; m. Philip Robert Bentley, Apr. 5, 1963; children—Cheryl Elaine, Shawn Philip. Student Butler County Community Jr. Coll., 1967, Wichita State U., 1972, 76, Tulsa Jr. Coll., 1986. With bookkeeping dept. Kans. State Bank, Wichita, 1960-62; sec. Ranson & Co., Inc., Wichita, 1962-64, Vickers Refining Co., Wichita, 1964-66; owner The Letter Shop, Haysville, Kans., 1966-75; exec. asst. Ranson & Co., Inc., 1975-80; owner Bentley & Assocs., Tulsa, 1980—; owner, ptnr. Satellite Office Systems, Tulsa, 1983-84; tchr. typing, shorthand, word processing; adj. instr. Tulsa Jr. Coll.; lectr., cons. in field; mem. steering com. S.W. Computer Conf., Tulsa, 1982, 83, S.W. Bus. and Equipment Show of Tulsa, 1983-85. Mem. office systems adv. com. Tulsa Jr. Coll., 1983-86; mem. word processing sec. adv. com. Tulsa Area Vocat.-Tech. Sch., 1984-86; dist. del. Kans. Republican State Conv., 1976. Mem. Assn. Info. Systems Profls. (charter pres. 1982-84), Okla. Word Processing Assn., Adminstrv. Mgmt. Soc. (dir.). Mem. Christian Ch. Home and Office: 2518 S 96 E Place Tulsa OK 74129

BENTLEY, GAIL ELIZABETH, manufacturing company executive; b. San Francisco, Apr. 22, 1954; d. Donald Homer and Margaret Kathryn (Abbett) Outsen; B.B.A., Tex. Tech. U., 1975; m. David O. Bentley, Aug. 31, 1980; children—Christopher Allen, Jason Thomas, Aileen Elizabeth. Owner, operator The Hayrick, Lubbock, Tex., 1973—, Bookkeeping & Bus. Adv. Service, Lubbock, 1976—; co-owner C&H Generator Shop, Lubbock, 1983—; treas. bd. dirs., mgr. Johnson Mfg. Fed. Credit Union, 1978-82. Mem. Phi Gamma Nu. Republican. Home and Office: Route 10 Box 5A Lubbock TX 79404

BENTLEY, HELEN DELICH (MRS. WILLIAM ROY BENTLEY), Congresswoman; b. Ruth, Nev.; d. Michael and Mary (Kovich) Delich; m. William Roy Bentley, June 7, 1959. Student, U. Nev., 1941-42, George Washington U., 1943; B.J., U. Mo., 1944; LL.D., U. Md., 1970, U. Alaska, 1973, U. Mich., 1974; D.H.L., Bryant Coll., 1971, U. Portland, 1972, L.I. U., 1976, Goucher Coll., 1979. Reporter Ely (Nev.) Record, 1940-42; polit. campaign mgr. for late Senator James G. Scrugham, White Pine County, Nev., 1942; bur. mgr. UP, Fort Wayne, Ind., 1944-45; reporter Balt. Sun, 1945-53, maritime editor, 1953-69; chmn. FMC, Washington, 1969-75, Am. Bicentennial Fleet, Inc., 1973-76; pres. Internat. Resources & Devel. Corp., Washington, 1976-85, HDB Internat., Inc., 1977-85; pub. relations adviser Am. Assn. Port Authorities, 1958-62, 64-67; mem 99th Congress from 2d Md. dist. TV and film producer world trade and maritime shows, 1950-64; Editor: Ports of Americas, 1961. Bd. dirs., mem. council Ch. Home and Hosp.; bd. dirs. United Seamen's Service, Oceanic Ednl. Found.; mem. council Md. Hist. Soc., Villa Julie Coll., Stevenson, Md., Montessori Soc. Central Md., Slavic-Am. Nat. Assn.; Republican nominee for Ho. of Reps. from 2d Dist. Md., 1980, 82, 84. Recipient numerous honors including awards from AFL-CIO Maritime Port Council Greater N.Y., 1965, Ironworkers and Shipbuilders Council AFL-CIO, 1966, AOTOS award United Seamen's Service, 1971, AOTOS award N.Y. Freight Forwarders and Brokers Assn., 1972, AOTOS award Am. Legion, 1973, AOTOS award Navy League U.S., 1973, Jerry Land medal Soc. Naval Architects and Marine Engrs., 1974; George Washington Honor medal Valley Forge Freedoms Found., 1971, 76; named GOP Woman of Year, 1972, Ethnic Woman of Yr., Republican Nat. Heritage Council, 1985. Mem. Greater Balt. Com. (chmn. rail com.). Republican. Greek Orthodox. 1st non-Briton to address and be honored by U.K. Chamber Shipping, 1973. Only woman to trek Northwest Passage on S.S. Manhattan, 1969. Home: 408 Chapelwood Ln Lutherville MD 21093 Office: PO Box 10619 Towson MD 21285-0619

BENTLEY, PAULA ELOUISE, public relations executive; b. Tulsa, Mar. 24, 1943; d. J.D. Hollingshead and Georgia Louise (King) Dressler; m. Phillip C. Bentley, May 30, 1963 (div. July 1984); 1 dau., Katherine E. B.A. in Journalism, U. Okla., 1965. Dir. pub. relations Virginia Mason Med. Ctr., Seattle, 1966-69; coordinator pub. relations Gresham Schs. (Oreg.), 1973-78; dir. Metro Crisis Intervention, Portland, Oreg., 1984, Our New Beginnings, Portland, 1984; dir. pub. relations Goodwill Industries, Portland, 1981—. Mem. Gresham City Council, 1976-80, Gresham Planning Commn., 1975. Mem. Women in Communications. Club: City (Portland). Office: Goodwill Industries of Oreg 1831 SE 6th St Portland OR 97214

BENTLEY-MCCALL, SHARON RUTH, banker; b. El Paso, Tex., Sept. 17, 1947; d. Ralph Richard and Ruth Garnet (Logue) Wood; m. Ronald Keith Bentley, June 6, 1975 (div. Feb. 1984); children—Deana Lashel, William Warren; m. Harry Mason McCall, June 12, 1985. Student Am. Inst. Banking, 1975-80, Jones Real Estate Coll., 1978, El Paso Community Coll., 1976-78. Lic. real estate salesman, securities dealer. Cashier, Bank of Ysleta, El Paso, 1969-78; real estate salesman Pan Am. Realty, El Paso, 1979-80; with First City Bancorp. Tex., Inc., 1980—, asst. v.p. First City Nat., El Paso, 1980-83, v.p., cashier First City Bank-East, El Paso, 1983—. Mem. vocat. adv. com. El Paso Job Corps, 1985-86; vol. fundraiser El Paso Lighthouse for Blind, 1984-85; vol. Amigo Air Show, 1984-85; treas. Eastwood High Class of 1965, El Paso, 1984-86; speaker El Paso Opportunity Ctr. for Handicapped, 1986. Recipient Honor Roll award United Way El Paso County, 1977, Outstanding Achievement awards, 1984, 85; YWCA REACH honoree, El Paso, 1981, 83, 84. Mem. Nat. Assn. Bank Women (pres. El Paso 1985-86, local scholarship 1985), Am. Inst. Banking (bd. govs. 1984-86), El Paso Assn. Personnel Adminstrs., Nat. Assn. for Female Execs., Bank Adminstrn. Inst. (dir. 1984-86). Democrat. Methodist. Avocations: reading; swimming; three wheeling. Home: 3117 Eads Pl El Paso TX 79935 Office: First City Bank-East PO Box 27300 1330 Lee Trevino St El Paso TX 79926

BENTLEY-SCHECK, GRACE MARY, artist, printmaker, educator; b. Troy, N.Y., Apr. 20, 1937; d. Franklin Paul and Gladys Serena (Sickles) Bentley; m. George Frederick Scheck, July 22, 1967. B.F.A., N.Y. State Coll. Ceramics, Alfred U., 1959, M.F.A., 1960. Cert. tchr., N.Y. One-person shows: Cayuga Mus. History and Art, Auburn, N.Y., 1977, Manlius Pub. Library, Syracuse, 1979, Oswego Art Guild, 1981, Lenore Gray Gallery, Providence, 1983; group shows include: Pratt/Silvermine Internat. Print Exhbn., 1986 (juror's award, patron award), Dulin Nat. Works on Paper Competition, 1986, R.I./Australian Exchange, Newport Art Mus., 1986-87, Hunterdon Nat. Print Exhbn., 1979, 81, 82, 85, 86 (honorable mention, 1986), N.C. Print and Drawing Soc. Eastern U.S. Exhbn., The Boston Printmakers Mems. Show, 1985, New Prints/Northeast Women's Studio Workshop, Rosendale, N.Y., Summer Graphics, Gallery on the Green, Lexington, Mass., Backyards, Wenniger Graphics, Boston, 1986, Rockford Internat. Biennale, 1981 (purchase prize), 85, Bradley Nat. Print and Drawing Exhbn., 1981-85 (merit award, 1985), Contemporary Am. Printmakers, Phila., Silvermine Guild of Artists, Nat. Print Exhbn., 1983, 57th Internat. Print Club of Phila. Exhbn., 1982, N.D. Print and Drawing Annual 1980-82; represented in permanent collections; tchr. Mary Warren Sch., Troy, N.Y., 1962-63, Riverhead (N.Y.) Jr. High Sch., 1963-67, North Colonie Central Sch., Latham, N.Y., 1967-72, SUNY-Oswego, 1979-80. Recipient N.C. Nat. Bank purchase award 9th Annual Eastern U.S. Print and Drawing Exhbn., 1986, purchase prize Hunterdon Nat., 1982. Mem. Print Club Phila., Boston Printmakers, World Print Council, Los Angeles Printmaking Soc., Internat. Graphic Arts Found. Democrat. Club: Oswego Art Guild (treas. 1976-77, pres. 1977-78).

BENTON, CHERYL ANN, medical school administrator; b. Pitts., Jan. 10, 1944; d. James Olden and Clara Elnor (Jackson) Benton; m. Melanie Lynn Benton (div. 1981). B.B.A. in Fin., U. Houston, 1984. Legal sec. Larry D. Stewart, Los Angeles, 1970-72, Anthony H. Barash, Los Angeles, 1972-79; asst. to chmn. dept. neurology U. Tex. Med. Sch., Houston, 1979—. Mem. Physicians for Social Responsibility, Houston, 1983. Mem. Nat. Coalition of 100 Black Women, Med. Group Mgmt. Assn., Am. Mgmt. Assn. Democrat. Roman Catholic. Home: 7900 Cambridge Apt 26-1C Houston TX 77054 Office: Tex Med Sch 6431 Fannin St Room 7044 Houston TX 77225

BENTON, ELIZABETH LAQUETTA, real estate marketing company executive, consultant, educator; b. Ozark, Ala., Apr. 1, 1936; d. Horace and Dovie Lee (Gulledge) Pippin; m. Charles Wayne Benton, Dec. 17, 1954; children—Lisa Ann, Charles W. Jr. Diploma Napier Bus. Coll., 1955; student Minot State Coll., 1963-64, U. Md., 1965, 67; grad. Realtors Inst. Cert. residential broker residential specialist. Sec., Aeronca Aircraft Corp., Ft. Rucker, Ala., 1955, Strachan Shipping, Savannah, Ga., 1956, USAF, Savannah, 1956-58; supr. Internal Revenue, Denver, 1959-60; adminstrv. asst. Chrysler Corp., Izmir, Turkey, 1961-63; substitute tchr. Dept. Edn., Honolulu, 1968-71; agt. Naomi Grout Real Estate, Ewa Beach, Hawaii, 1971-77; v.p., ptnr. Benton & Large Realty, Honolulu, 1977; pres., owner Liz Benton, Inc., Aiea, Hawaii, 1977—; dir. Founders Title & Escrow Co., Honolulu, 1983—; resource person, study on agy. Nat. Assn. Real Estate Lic. Law Ofcls., Salt Lake City, 1984, 85; mem. adv. council Hawaii Real Estate Research and Edn. Ctr., 1985—. Contbr. articles to profl. jours. Mem. Small Bus. Council Am., Honolulu, 1977—; mem. Aloha United Way, Honolulu 1974—; bd. dirs. Big Bros., Big Sisters, Honolulu, 1982—; chmn. Easter Seals VIP Panel, Honolulu, 1981—; mem. Realtors Polit. Action Com., Honolulu, 1980—; dir. ACS. Recipient Vol. of Yr. award ARC, 1965, Outstanding Service award Dept. of Air Force, 1966, Top Producer award Naomi Grout Real Estate, 1972, 73, 74, 75, 76, Cert. of Excellence award Nat. Research Co., 1980, 81, 82, 83. Mem. Hawaii Assn. Realtors (chmn. convention com. 1974, chmn. edn. com. 1979, dir.-at-large 1979, 80, bd. dirs. 1979, chmn. fin. and audit com. 1980, 81, sec. 1981, judge parade of homes 1982, treas. 1982, v.p. 1983, pres. elect 1986, mem. strategic planning com. 1984), Honolulu Bd. Realtors (bd. dirs. 1978, chmn. election com. 1979, sec. 1979, chmn. multiple listing service, 1980, 81, pres.-elect 1982, chmn. realtor of yr. selection com. 1983, pres. 1983, chmn. nominating com. 1984, Realtor of Month award June 1981, Realtor of Yr. award 1981, chair strategic planning com. 1986, chair nominating com. 1986, liaison to real estate commn. 1986), Nat. Assn. Realtors (chmn. convention activities subcom. 1984, nat. bd. dirs. 1984-86, prof. standards and arbitration com. 1986), The Investment Group Realtors, Leeward Regional Group, Realtors Nat. Mktg. Inst. (cert., Hawaii chpt., v.p. 1981, pres. 1982, treas. cert. residential brokers chpt. 1985), C. of C. Home: 94-1101 Penakii Pl Waipahu HI 96797 Office: 98-211 Pali Momi St Suite 411 Aiea HI 96701

BENTON, EVELYN FLEMING, librarian; b. Ponchatoula, La., Aug. 10, 1921; d. Walter Raleigh and Mabel Magdalene (Varnado) Fleming; B.F.A. with high distinction and spl. mention in music, Okla. State U., 1943; student U. Tex. Grad. Sch. Library Sci., 1959-60; m. Douglas C. Benton, Aug. 25, 1942; children—Walter Bradford, Christopher Paul. Circulation asst. Tulsa Public Library, 1944, 1st asst. tech. dept., 1945; reference asst. Okla. State U., Stillwater, 1946-48, jr. reference librarian, 1948-50; piano tchr., Baytown, Tex., 1958-60; asst. librarian Lee Coll., Baytown, 1960-66; library dir. Deer Park (Tex.) Public Library, 1968-83; acting exec. dir. Tex. Library Assn., 1983; lectr. Weight Watchers Internat., 1985—; mem. automation com. Houston Area Library System Long Range Planning Com.; mem. Library Services and Constrn. Act adv. council Tex. State Library, 1981-84, vice chmn., 1984—. Pres., San Jacinto Music Tchrs. Assn., 1960, Baytown Unitarian Fellowship, 1965; chmn. Heritage '76 Com., Deer Park Bicentennial Commn.; mem. Public Library Adv. Council, Sam Houston State U. Sch. L.S. Mem. Am., Tex. (chmn. nominating com. 1971-72, chmn. reference roundtable 1972-73, sec. dist. V, 1969, treas. dist. VIII, 1971, dist vice chmn., chmn. elect 1980—), Southwestern (conf. program com., Tex. (dist. chmn.), Public (editorial com.) library assns., Tex. Mcpl. Library Dirs. Assn. (pres. 1981-82), Phi Kappa Phi, Sigma Alpha Iota (treas. Iota Alpha chpt. 1942-43). Unitarian. Co-author: An Introduction to the Houston Area Library System Computer Access Network, 1979; contbr. articles to profl. jours. Home: 5874 Doliver Houston TX 77057

BENTON, KATHRYN M. BRADLEY, escrow co. exec.; b. Carnegie, Pa.; d. Charles A. and Mary (Halpin) Bradley; student U. Calif. at Los Angeles, 1929-35; m. Robert E. Benton, Sept. 14, 1935 (dec. Sept. 1965); 1 dau., Barbara A. (Mrs. Bernard P. Drachlis). Co-founder, pres. Eagle Rock Escrow Co., Los Angeles, 1962—. Charter exec. sec. United Orgns., 1966-68, N.E. Taxpayers Assn., 1966—; bd. dirs., founder, sec. Robert E. Benton Meml. Found. Mem. Eagle Rock Bus. and Profl. Womens Club, Eagle Rock C. of C. Club: Womens Twentieth Century. Office: 5012 Eagle Rock Blvd Los Angeles CA 90041

BENTON, LOUISE WHITE, harpist, educator; b. Henderson, Ky., Aug. 4, 1920; d. George Washington and Mai Elizabeth (Korb) White; m. William A. Benton, June 27, 1942; children—Bruce White, Boyd Allen. A.A., Christian Coll., 1940; B.S., U. Ky., 1942; postgrad. Morehead State U., summer, 1967. Second harpist Evansville Philharmonic Orch. (Ind.), 1963, 64-65; 1st harpist Owensboro Symphony Orch. (Ky.), 1966-77; music librarian Henderson Community Coll., 1968-70; harp instr., Henderson, 1975—, Owensboro Music Camp, Maple Mount, Ky. mem. adj. faculty Brescia Coll., Owensboro, 1975—, U. Evansville, 1975—; accompanist choruses and choirs. Active, Friends of Music, U. Evansville; mem. Philharmonic Guild, Evansville. Mem. Am. Harp Soc. (Outstanding Harpist in So. Region 1977-78), Ky. Fedn. Music Clubs, Phi Beta, Kappa Delta, Pi Kappa Lambda. Methodist. Club: Henderson Music. Home: 4 Philips Ct Henderson KY 42420

BENTON, MARLENE A. KEELING, insurance company executive; b. Sammonsville, N.Y., Jan. 14, 1938; d. Jacob W. and Annabelle (Lippert) Sammons; m. Donald H. Benton, Sept. 8, 1979; children—Richard W. Keeling, Debra Keeling. Adminstrv. asst. Farm Credit Service, Fultonville, N.Y., 1955-70; mng. officer Fulton and Montgomery Counties Farmers Mut. Fire Ins. Assn., Johnstown, N.Y., 1970—; mem. exec. com., v.p., dir. N.Y. Coop. Ins. Assn. Mem. Fulton and Montgomery Mut. Ins. Assn. (sec.-treas., mem. exec. com., dir.), Nat. Assn. Female Execs., Fulton County C. of C., Fulton County Ins. Womens Assn. (pres.), Fulton County Farm Bur., Am. Mgmt. Assn., N.Y. Coop. Ins. Assn., Profl. Ins. Agts., Nat. Fedn. Ins. Bus. Home: Route 5 Amsterdam NY 12010 Address: Fulton Montgomery County Farmers Mut Fire Ins Assn RD 1 Johnstown NY 12095

BENTON, NELKANE OLGA, broadcasting co. exec.; b. N.Y.C., June 15, 1935; d. Ruben and Olga Marie (Catchings) B.; m. Thomas J. Hill, June 1, 1979; children—Donna, Marie. Press and record promoter Bing Crosby; now dir. community relations KABC/KIOS Am. Broadcasting, Inc., Los Angeles. Former mem. Gov. Reagan's Consumer Task Force; mem. black adv. panel So. Calif. Gas Co.; consumer adv. panel Pacific Bell; bd. dirs. Los Angeles Beautiful. Recipient cert. achievement ABC, Inc., 1977, 79, 80. Mem. Women in Communications, Public Interest Radio and TV Ednl. Soc. (v.p.), Consumer Credit Counselors (dir.). Democrat. Office: 3321 S La Cienega Blvd Los Angeles CA 90016

BENTON, RUTH NANN, insurance executive; b. Cheyenne, Wyo., May 1, 1952; d. Allan McElheran and Armella Nann (Kirk) Benton; m. Robert Nolan Wilkinson, Sept. 25, 1979; 1 child, Jens Kirk Wilkinson. Student U. Wyo., 1970-71, Regis Coll., Denver, 1981-84. Systems analyst data processing BCBS of Colo., Denver, 1973-77, mgr. reimbursement, 1977-79, ADS cons., 1979; mgr. ops. HMO Colo., Inc., Denver, 1980-81, dir. fin. and ops., 1981—. Mem. Data Processing Dgmt. Assn. Republican. Office: HMO Colo Inc 700 Broadway Denver CO 80203

BENTON, SONIA, communications executive; b. Bogotá, Colombia, July 13, 1961; came to U.S., 1964, naturalized, 1970; d. Roberto and Helga (Winkler) Restrepo; m. Jim Bob Benton, Dec. 17, 1983. Student Tex. A&M U. Account exec., advt. dir. Star Tel, Bryan, Tex., 1983-84; account exec. University Communications, College Station, Tex., 1984-85; pres. Info. Station, College Station, 1986; cons. in field. Author company handbook: Effective Advertising, 1984. Mem. Exec. Female. Office: Info Station 1701 Southwest Pkwy Suite 108 College Station TX 77840

BENTON, SUZANNE, sculptor, mask performance artist; b. N.Y.C., Jan. 21, 1936; d. Alex and Florence (Matkoff) Elkins; B.A. in Fine Arts, Queens Coll., 1956; children—Daniel, Janet. Creator, Mask Ritual Theatre, over 150 mask story theatre performances throughout U.S. and Japan, Korea, Bali, India, Israel, Greece, Yugoslavia, Denmark, Eng., Holland, Fed. Republic Germany, Switzerland, and Turkey; affiliate Image Theatre, N.Y.C.; one woman-shows of sculpture include Wadsworth Atheneum, Hartford, Conn., 1975, Internat. Christian Coll., Tokyo, 1976, Chemould Gallery, Bombay, 1977, Hellenic Am. Union, Athens, 1977, Internat. House, New Orleans, 1978, BITEF Internat. Theatre Festival, Belgrade, Yugoslavia, 1978, Condon Gallery, N.Y.C., 1981, Korean Cultural Service Galleries, N.Y.C., 1982; Kolner Wercladen Gallery, Cologne, W.Ger., Gallerie Fuchs, Dusseldorf, W.Ger., Amerika Haus, Cologne, Gallerie Schuleit, Basel, Switzerland, 1983, Zem Swaite Gsicht, Basel, 1983, Wilton Gallery (Conn.), 1983, Coll. Tunis, 1983, Union Am. Hebrew Congregations, N.Y.C., 1984, Amerika Haus, 1986, Stuttgart, Asia Soc., N.Y.C., 1986; group shows include USIS, Eastern Europe, 1971-75, Stamford (Conn.) Mus., 1976, Expo '74, Seattle, Nat. Sculpture Conf., Kans. U., 1974; convenor Conn. Feminists in the Arts, 1970-72; nat. coordinator NOW Women in the Arts, 1973-76. Grantee Conn. Commn. on Arts, 1973, 74, United Methodist World and Women's Div., 1976, United Presbyn. Program Agency, 1976, United Ch. Bd. Homeland Ministries, 1976, USIS, Tunis, 1983, USIS, Istanbul, 1986. Mem. Artists Equity N.Y.C., Nat. Korean Women's Sculpture Assn. (hon.), Nat. Assn. Women Artists (Amelia Peabody award 1979). Author: The Art of Welded Sculpture, 1975; also poetry. Address: 22 Donnelly Dr Ridgefield CT 06877

BENTON-BORGHI, BEATRICE HOPE, educational consultant; b. San Antonio, Nov. 7, 1946; d. Donald Francis and Beatrice Hope (Peche) Benton; A.B. in Chemistry, North Adams State Coll., 1968; M.Secondary Edn., Boston U., 1972; m. Peter T. Borghi, Aug. 12, 1980; children—Kathryn Benton Borghi, Sarah Benton Borghi. Tchr. chemistry Cathedral High Sch., Springfield, Mass., 1968-69; tchr. sci. and history Munich (W.Ger.) Am. High Sch., 1969-70; tchr. English, Tokyo, Japan, 1970-71; tchr. chemistry and sci. Marlborough (Mass.) High Sch., 1971-80; project dir., adminstr. ESEA, Marlborough Pub. Schs., 1976-77; project dir., proposal writer Title III, Title IX, U.S. Dept. Edn., 1975-76, 76-77; evaluation team New Eng. Assn. Schs. and Colls., 1974, 78; mem. regional dept. edn. com., 1977-78; ednl. cons., lectr., 1978—. Energy conservation rep. Marlborough's Overall Econ. Devel. Com., 1976; chmn. Marlborough's Energy Conservation Task Force, 1975; dir. Walk for Mankind, 1972; sec. Group Action for Marlborough Environment, 1975-76; bd. dirs. Girls Club, Marlborough, 1979; pres. Sisters, Inc., 1979-83. Mem. Women's Polit. Caucus, Nat. Women's Health Network. Home and office: 2449 Edington Rd Columbus OH 43221

BENVENISTE, MARILYN B., lecturer, public speaking consultant; b. Atlanta, July 27, 1940; d. Irving and Rose (Silver) Berkowitz; m. Morris Benveniste, Apr. 7, 1963; children—Mark, Marshall, Melissa. B.S. in Edn., U. Ala.-Tuscaloosa, 1962. Tchr., Atlanta pub. schs., 1962-63; co-dir. Assertiveness Tng. Inst., Atlanta, 1977-78; pub. speaking cons., Atlanta, 1978—; spl. asst. on coll. relations to pres. Kennesaw Coll., Marietta, Ga., 1983-84; chmn. Leadership Cobb, 1984-85. cons., lectr. in field. Author, trainer: Gaining Awareness Through Education, 1979; author: Put the Lid on Pot, 1978; author/producer slide show: Pot The Quiet Persuader, 1979, Kennesaw Coll., A Place for All Seasons, 1983. Sec. Atlanta Jewish Community Ctr., 1979-81, v.p., 1981-83; pres. Alpha Omega Dental Aux., 1972-73; v.p. Brandeis Women's Com., 1968-70; pres. Temple Sinai Women's Com., Atlanta, 1972-74; bd. dirs. chpt. Am. Cancer Soc., 1984-85. Recipient Young Leader award Jewish Welfare Bd., 1976, Leadership Ga., 1982, Leadership Atlanta, 1981. Mem. Internat. Platform Assn., Am. Soc. Tng. and Devel., Atlanta Women's Network, Leadership Ga. (trustee), AAUW. Clubs: B'nai B'rith Women, Women's Am. ORT, U. Ala. Alumni Assn. Home: 14 Heards Overlook Ct NW Atlanta GA 30328 Office: PO Box 420123 Atlanta GA 30342

BENVENUTO, ELAINE ELIZABETH, public relations executive; b. Bklyn., Nov. 10, 1943; d. Michael John and Mildred (Di Brienza) De Santis; m. John Anthony Benvenuto, Jr., June 12, 1965 (div.); 1 dau.: Kecia. B.A., Conn. Coll., 1965. Fashion editor Bride & Home Mag., N.Y.C., 1965-68; reporter, columist Fairchild Pubs., N.Y.C., Washington, 1968-71; consumer specialist Giant Food Inc., Washington, 1971-73; dir. consumer relations Cosmetic, Toiletry and Fragrance Assn., Washington, 1973-76; v.p. Carl Byoir & Assoc., N.Y.C., 1976-85; mgr. pub. relations Avon Products, Inc., N.Y.C., 1985—. Bd. dirs. Medic Alert Found., N.Y.C., 1983-85. Recipient Silver Anvil, Pub. Relations Soc. Am., 1972. Mem. Soc. Consumer Affairs, Profls. in Bus., Women in Communications. Democrat. Roman Catholic. Office: Avon Products Inc 9 W 57th St New York NY 10019

BENWAY, LIANE THERESE MEYER, architect, consultant; b. Besancon, France, Oct. 24, 1943; came to U.S., 1950, naturalized, 1952; d. Henry and Marcelle Adrienne (Baudin) Meyer; m. John Harry Benway, May 26, 1962 (div. 1982); children—John M., Michele J., Ryan P. Student in Nursing, St. Benedict's Hosp., Ogden, Utah, 1961-62; B.Interior Arch., U. Oreg., 1972; M.Arch. in Urban Planning, U. Colo.-Denver, 1977. Designer, job shopper Gen. Devices Inc., Westminster, Colo., 1972; project architect design and constrn. GSA, Denver, 1973-78, architect, project dir., Atlanta, 1978-80, architect, team leader, Office Insp. Gen., Atlanta, 1980—; cons. Allgeier Assocs., Washington, 1982-86. Artist, painter (1st place award 1968). Victim service provider Cobb County Dist. Atty. Victim-Witness Assistance Unit, Marietta, Ga., 1986; coordinator charitable projects Denver Fed. Exec. Bd., 1973-77. Recipient Commendable Service awards GSA and Denver Fed. Exec. Bd., 1975, 76; named Outstanding Employee, GSA, 1976. Mem. AIA, Phi Theta Kappa. Democrat. Roman Catholic. Club: Toastmistresses (v.p. Denver 1975-77). Avocations: classical guitar; writing; art; graphics. Office: GSA Office Insp Gen JA-4 75 Spring St Atlanta GA 30303

BERARDELLI, BARBARA KUNKEL, court clerk, consultant; b. Garfield, N.J., Mar. 17, 1945; d. Everett Edward and Florence Hilda (Davidsen) Kunkel; m. Jack E. Decker, Nov. 23, 1966 (div. Nov. 1981); children—Tasha Jade, Lara Ashley; m. Victor F. Berardelli, Jr., Nov. 25, 1983. B.A. in Psychology and Pre-Theology, Elmira Coll., N.Y., 1966; M.A. in Human Devel., Fairleigh Dickinson U., 1983. Income maintenance supr. Sussex County Welfare, Newton, N.J., 1975-79; dept. supr. Colonial Penn Ins. Co., Phila., 1979-81; adminstrv. mgr. Velo-Bind, Inc., Mt. Laurel, N.J., 1982-83; mgmt., human relations cons. pvt. practice, N.J. and Maine, 1983—; clk. Supreme Jud. and Superior Cts., York County, Maine, 1985—. Artist stained glass windows. Teaching fellow Fairleigh Dickinson U., 1983-84. Mem. Mensa. Libertarian. Zen Buddhist. Avocations: canoeing, photography, furniture restoration. Home: Robert's Ridge Rd HCR 72 Box 5540 East Waterboro ME 04030 Office: Supreme Jud and Superior Cts PO Box 160 Alfred ME 04002

BERCKEFELDT, JANET ANN, foundation financial officer, consultant; b. Oakland, Calif., June 8, 1945; d. Herbert Louis, Jr. and Margaret Manita (Baldwin) Wildenradt; m. David Law Throndson, Dec. 21, 1968 (div. June 1972), Denis Ray Berckefeldt, Dec. 29, 1984. B.A., U. Redlands, Calif., 1967; M. in Pub. Adminstrn., U. So. Calif., 1978. Supr. Div. Labor Law Enforcement, State of Calif., San Francisco, 1968; asst. to v.p. Computer Time-Sharing Corp., Palo Alto, Calif., 1968-69; bus. mgr. Family Service Agy. of San Mateo County, Burlingame, Calif., 1969-77; program adminstr. Alameda County Tng. and Employment Bd., Hayward, Calif., 1978; v.p. Shelton Fin. Services, Encino, Calif., 1979-81; chief fin. officer, assoc. exec. dir. Constl. Rights Found., Los Angeles, 1981—; cons. in field. Speakers bur. United Way of Am., San Francisco, 1970-77, Los Angeles, 1981-83; congl. intern U.S. Congress, Washington, 1966. Mem. Am. Soc. Pub. Adminstrn., Western Govtl. Research Assn., Nat. Assistance Mgmt. Assn. Democrat. Presbyterian. Avocations: scuba diving, cross country skiing. Office: Constl Rights Found 601 S Kingley Dr Los Angeles CA 90005

BEREAL-FULTON, ARLENE RUTH, construction and maintenance company executive; b. Phila., Nov. 6, 1946; d. Moses and Ruth Fulton. Student Entrepreneurial Devel. Tng. Ctr., Phila., 1970, Antioch U., 1978-80, Temple U., 1977-78. Cert. gen. contractor, City of Phila., State of Pa. Mentor supr. pub. relations Juvenile Justice, Phila., 1975-77; Southeast Pa. dir. Project J.O.E.Y., Commonwealth of Pa. Dept. Children & Youth, Phila., 1978-80; chief exec. officer, pres. Bereal Constrn. and Maintenance Co., Inc., Phila., 1980—; mem. Pa. Dept. Transp. Cert. Appeals Bd., 1986—. Author alternative to prison youth program, 1977. Bd. dirs. Pa. Democratic Inst., Phila., 1985; chmn. youth dept. Chs. of God in Christ, Eastern Jurisdiction of Pa., Phila., 1978—. Recipient Humanitarian award Chapel of Four Chaplains, 1978. Mem. Nat. Assn. Minority Contractors, Coalition Minority Contractors (bd. dirs.1983—), Nat. Assn. Negro Bus. and Profl. Women, Nat. Polit. Congress Black Women (bd. dirs., officer 1985), Nat. Assn. Women in Constrn. (legis. awareness chmn. 1983-84). Democrat. Mem. Pentecostal Ch. Avocations: reading; music; creative writing. Office: Bereal Constrn and Maintenance Co Inc 4950 Parkside Ave Fifth Floor Philadelphia PA 19131

BERES, MARY ELIZABETH, management educator, organizational consultant; b. Birmingham, Jan. 19, 1942; d. John Charles and Ethel (Belenyesi) B. B.S., Siena Heights Coll., Adrian, Mich., 1969; Ph.D, Northwestern U., 1976. Joined Dominican Sisters, 1960; tchr., St. Francis Xavier Sch., Medina, Ohio, 1962-64, St. Edward Sch., Detroit, 1964-67; tchr. Our Lady of Mt. Carmel Sch., Temperance, Mich., 1967-69, asst. prin., 1968-69; tchr. math. St. Ambrose High Sch., Detroit, 1969-70; vis. instr. Cornell U., 1973-74; assoc. prof. orgn. behavior Temple U., Phila., 1974-84; assoc. prof. mgmt. Mercer U. Atlanta, 1984—; cons. in field. Contbr. chpts. to books. Bd. trustees Adrian Dominican Ind. Sch. System (Mich.), 1971-79; bd. dirs. Ctr. for Ethics and Social Policy, Phila., 1980-84. Recipient Legion of Honor membership Chapel of the Four Chaplains, Phila., 1982; Disting. Teaching award Lindback Found., 1982. Mem. Acad. Mgmt., Am. Inst. Decision Scis., Indsl. Relations Research Assn., Assn. Social Econs., Acad. Internat. Bus., So. Ctr. Internat. Studies, Nat. Assn. Female Execs. Democrat. Roman Catholic. Office: Mercer U Atlanta Sch Bus and Econs 3001 Mercer University Dr Atlanta GA 30341

BERESIN, MARCELLA GRACE SUSKIND, arts management and marketing consultant; b. N.Y.C., July 5, 1916; d. Borah Alexander and Anna (Abramson) Suskind; m. Victor E. Beresin, Nov. 24, 1948; children—Eugene Victor, Alice Freddi. B.A., Hunter Coll., 1938. Group sales mgr. Temple U. Music Festival, Ambler, Pa., 1968-69, advt. mgr., 1969-71, indsl. and spl. sales mgr., 1969-73; dir. audience devel., dir. ticket subsidy fund and outreach program Annenberg Ctr., U. Pa., Phila., 1974-84; arts mktg. and mgmt. cons., 1984—; vis. lectr. M.B.A. programs in the arts Temple U., Phila., 1980, Cabrini Coll., 1982-83, Drexel U., Phila., 1983, U. Pa. Grad. Sch. Edn., 1982, 83; nat. cons. Found. for Extension and Devel. of Am. Profl. Theatre, N.Y.C., 1975, 76; lectr. in field; cons. numerous regional arts orgns., 1975—. Mem. Direct Mktg. Assn., Women in Communication Internat., Sales and Mktg. Execs. Inc., Family Maintenance Orgn., Phila. Pub. Relations Assn., Univ. Citigroup (founder, officer 1975—). Home: 225 S Bonsall St Philadelphia PA 19103

BERESKA, JOAN BURRIER, city administrative officer; b. Balt., Apr. 3, 1932; d. Webster Kenwood and Ethel Blye (Sunderland) Burrier; m. George J. Bereska, Sr., June 23, 1961; 1 child, George J., Jr. B.A., Western Md. Coll., 1954; LL.B., U. Balt., 1967, M.P.A., 1982. Tech. publs. editor Martin Marietta Corp., Balt., 1956-57; asst. dir. Citizens Planning and Housing Assn., Balt., 1957-64; adminstrv. asst. Pres. of City Council, Balt., 1967-71; adminstrv. officer Mayor of Balt., 1971—. Co-host radio program Know Your Govt., 1969-74. Contbr. column to newspaper The Jeffersonian, 1958-61. Bd. dirs. U. Balt. Bd. Govs., Balt., 1982—, Mayor's Coordinating Council on Criminal Justice, Balt., 1984—, William Donald Schaefer Civic Fund, Balt., 1979—; bd. dirs., chmn. long-range planning com. Municipal Employees Credit Union, 1975—. Recipient Spl. Baltimorean award Balt. City Fair, 1973; Balt. is Best award City of Balt., 1976; Trustee Alumni Recognition award Western Md. Coll., 1977; Gov.'s award State of Md., 1982; Best in Balt. Advt. Club award, Advt. Club of Balt., 1982; Outstanding Women in City Govt. award East Baltimore Citizens' com., 1982; Alumnus of Yr award U. Balt., 1984, others; named Woman of Yr. Coll. of Notre Dame, 1977. Mem. Am. Soc. Pub. Adminstrn. (Janet Hoffman award 1983), Phi Alpha Alpha. Democrat. Methodist. Home: 5802 Kenmore Rd Baltimore MD 21210 Office: Office of Mayor 250 City Hall Baltimore MD 21202

BERG, JEAN HORTON LUTZ, author; b. Clairton, Pa.; d. Harry Heber and Daisy (Horton) Lutz; B.S., U. Pa., in 1935, M.A., 1937; m. John Joseph Berg, July 2, 1938; children—Jean Horton, Julie Joanne, John Joel. Tchr. English and Latin, Bridgeville (Del.) High Sch., 1936-38; tchr. creative writing Radnor Twp. Adult Edn., also U. Pa. Coll. Gen. Studies; lectr. in field; author: Three Mice and A Cat, 1950, The Jolly Jumping Man, 1950, The Noisy Clock Shop, 1950, The Playful Little Dog, 1951, Baby Susan's Chicken, 1951, The Big Jump-up Book of Farm Animals, 1952, Christmas In Song and Story, 1953, The Traveling Twins, 1953, It's Fun to Peek, 1955, The Big Jump-up Book of Trains, Trucks and Planes, 1955, Tuggy the Tugboat, 1958, Pierre, The Young Watchmaker, 1961, The O'Learys and Friends 1961, Baby Raccoon, 1963, The Little Red Hen, 1963, The Wee Little Man, 1963, Big Bug, Little Bug, 1964, Bright Candle Light, 1966, There's Nothing to Do, So Let Me Be You, 1966, Miss Kirby's Room, 1966, Miss Tessie Tate, 1967, Nobody Scares a Porcupine, 1968, What Harry Found When He Lost Archie, 1970, Mr. Koonan's Bargain, 1971, numerous others, latest being I Cry When The Sun Goes Down, 1976, The Story of Jesus, 1977, The Story of Peter, 1979, The Story of Moses, 1982, also others. Mem. exec. bd. Friends' Central Sch. Home and School Assn., 1965-67; bd. dirs. Wayne Art Center, 1950-57; bd. vols. Health and Welfare Council Phila., 1970-71; exec. bd. Infant Day Care Center of Young Great Soc., Phila., 1971-74; bd. dirs. St. Davids Christian Writers Conf. Recipient Medallion of Phila. award, 1963, Follett award, 1961, Alumni Merit award U. Pa., 1969, Disting. Alumna award Friends' Central Sch., 1978. Mem. Nat. League Am. Pen Women (pres. Chester County br. 1967-68), Parents Council Suburban Phila. (pres. 1966-67, exec. bd.), Radnor Hist. Soc., Gen. Alumni Soc. U. Pa., LWV, ASCAP, Authors League, Phila. Childrens Reading Round Table, Authors Guild, Assn. Alumnae U. Pa. (officer, exec. bd.), Kappa Alpha Theta, Eta Sigma Phi, Pi Lambda Theta. Christian Scientist. Home: 207 Walnut Ave Wayne PA 19087

BERG, JEAN SCHOLL, lawyer; b. LaPorte, Ind., Nov. 21, 1950; d. John David and Winifred Viola (Jourdain) Scholl; m. Raymond Charles Berg, June 13, 1970; 1 son, Raymond Christopher. B.A. in Social Sci. Edn., Purdue U., 1973; M.A. in Liberal Studies, Valparaiso U., 1976; J.D., Notre Dame U., 1982; postgrad. in internat. law Exeter U., summer 1981. Bar: Ind. 1982, U.S. Dist. Ct. (no. dist.) Ind. 1982. Cert. secondary tchr., Ind., real estate broker, Ind. Tchr. Diocese of Gary, Michigan City, Ind., 1973-79; mng. broker United Realty, LaPorte, Ind., part-time 1974-78; compliance officer, asst. to pres. Lakeshore Bank, Michigan City, 1983-84; EEO counselor U.S. Postal Service, Gary, Ind., 1984—. Notes editor, Jour. of Legislation, 1981-82. Campaign worker re-election Congressman Hiler and Senator Lugar, LaPorte, 1982. Mem. ABA, Ind. Bar Assn., AAUW, Am. Quarter Horse Assn. Republican. Roman Catholic. Office: US Postal Service PO Michigan City IN 46360

BERG, SYLVIA LOUISE, educator; b. N.Y.C., Dec. 29, 1939; d. Joe and Fay (Streim) Maydeck; B.S., Oswego Coll., 1958; M.S., Hofstra U., 1959; postgrad. N.Y. U., 1960-65; children—Mitchell Ian, Nancy Patricia. Tchr., Public Sch. 198, N.Y.C. Bd. Edn., 1965—; adj. prof. edn. N.Y. U., 1965—; pvt. tutor, 1965—; cons. in field; job presentations; adv. skills in speed reading; condr. sci. seminars Fordham U., Sci. Council; cons. Elaine Goldhill Travel Cons. Bd. dirs. 301 E. 78th St. Corp., N.Y.C., sec., 1979-81; treas. Singles Coordinating Com., N.Y.C. Mem. SUNY Assn., Nat. Assn. Female Execs., Audubon Assn., United Fedn. Tchrs. Home: 301 E 78th St New York NY 10021 Office: Public Sch 158 1458 York Ave New York NY 10021 also 330 E 33d St Suite 8G New York NY 10016

BERGEMANN, MARJORIE ANN, nurse anesthetist; b. Staten Island, N.Y., Nov. 24, 1930; d. David Archer and Anna Hilda (Bloch) Stamler; R.N., Fordham Hosp., 1953; B.A. in Edn., Ottawa U., 1979; doctoral candidate Nova U., 1979—; cert. R.N. anesthetist Prince Georges County Gen. Hosp., 1974; m. Till Bergemann, Mar. 22, 1953; children—Jill Susan, Carol Sarah, Eve Louise. Head nurse Fordham Hosp., 1953-54, Montefiore Hosp., 1954-55; head nurse Prince Georges Gen. Hosp., 1955, staff nurse, 1969-72, staff anesthetist, clin. instr., 1974-80; staff anesthetist, clin. instr. Johns Hopkins Hosp., 1980; staff anesthetist Georgetown U./NIH, Washington, 1981—; instr. Prince George's Community Coll., 1982-83; pres. Anesthesia Seminar Consultants, Inc.; edn. cons.; nurse anesthetist adv. council Md. Bd. Examiners of Nurses, 1982. Mem. Am. Nurses Assn. (mem. council continuing edn.), Md. Nurses Assn., Am. Assn. Nurse Anesthetists (nominating com.), Md. Assn. Nurse Anesthetists (pres. 1982-83), Am. Soc. Regional Anesthesia. Office: Box 346 Greenbelt MD 20770

BERGER, BARBARA DIANE, personnel consulting company executive; b. Chgo., May 4, 1931; d. Alfred and Ruth (Shapiro) Lubin; m. Howard M. Berger, June 25, 1950; children—Teri Lawton, Patricia Wisley, Lisa Berger. A.A., Pasadena City Coll., 1950. Real estate salesperson E. Dunham, Arlington, Va., 1960-63; cons., mgr. Beverly Cross Agy., Torrance, Calif., 1974-76; pres., chief exec. officer Justin-Time Services, Inc., Torrance, 1979—, Keats-Manhattan Inc./Justin-Bentley Agy., Torrance, 1977—. Mem. Calif. Assn. Personnel Cons. (pres. Los Angeles chpt. 1984—, state dir. 1985—, Kerr-Codera award 1983-84, Maxine Taylor award 1984-85), Torrance C. of C., Cerritos C. of C. Avocation: boating. Home: 2108 Via Fernandez Palos Verdes Estates CA 90274 Office: Justin-Bentley Agy/Keats-Manhattan 23332 Hawthorne Blvd Suite 101 Torrance CA 90505

BERGER, BONNIE GROSS, educator; b. Champaign, Ill., May 20, 1941; d. Bernard G. and Mildred G. Berger; B.S., Wittenberg U., 1962; M.A., Columbia U., 1965; Ed.D., 1972; 1 son, Stephen Casher. Tchr., George Rogers Clark Jr. High Sch., Springfield, Ohio, 1962-64; supr. phys. edn. Agnes Russell Elem. Sch., N.Y.C., 1964-65; asst. prof. N.Y. State U., Geneseo, 1965-66; asst. prof. Dalhousie U., Halifax, N.S., Can., 1969-71; asst. prof. dept. phys. edn. Bklyn. Coll., 1971-77, assoc. prof., 1978-81, prof., 1982—, dir. sport psychology lab.; cons. in field of sport psychology. Mem. N.Am. Soc. Psychology of Sport and Phys. Activity (outstanding dissertation of yr. award 1971), Am. Psychol. Assn., AAHPERD, Internat. Soc. Sports Psychology, Can. Soc. Psychomotor Learning and Sport Psychology. Author: Free Weights for Women, 1984; contbr. chpts. to The Psychology of Running, 1981, Running as Therapy: An Integrated Approach, 1984; contbr. articles to profl. jours. Home: 20 Waterside Plaza New York NY 10010 Office: Department of Physical Education Brooklyn College Brooklyn NY 11210

BERGER, FRANCINE ELLIS, radio executive, educator; b. Albany, N.Y., July 27, 1949; d. David George and Harriet Sylvia (Bookstein) Ellis; m. Jerome Morris Berger, Oct. 9, 1977. B.S. in Broadcasting and Film, Boston U., 1971; Ed.M. in Adminstrn., Planning and Social Policy, Harvard U., 1981. Traffic mgr. WCAS-AM Kaiser Globe Broadcasting, Boston, 1971, WJIB-FM, 1971; continuity supr. WBZ-AM-Westinghouse, Boston, 1971-75; producer, traffic dir. WMEX-AM/WITS-AM, Boston, 1975-78; newswriter CBS Radio, WEEI-AM, Boston, 1980; gen. mgr. WERS/FM, Emerson Coll., Boston, 1980—, asst. prof. radio dept., 1981—, head radio dept., 1983—. Mem. Nat. Acad. TV Arts and Scis., Kappa Gamma Chi, Alpha Epsilon Rho. Avocations: Music; Cooking. Office: WERS-FM Emerson Coll 126 Beacon St Boston MA 02116

BERGER, HARRIET SCHWARTZ, advertising executive; b. Rome, Ga., Dec. 22, 1951; d. Lawrence Harris and Lillian (Smolen) Schwartz; m. James Menline Berger, Nov. 2, 1980. A.B.J. in Journalism, U. Ga.-Athens, 1972. Traffic mgr. Kinro Advt. div. Rollins, Inc., Atlanta, 1973-74; media asst. Cargill, Wilson & Acree, Atlanta, 1974; media buyer/planner Cole Henderson Drake, Inc., Atlanta, 1974-80; v.p., media dir. Bowes Hanlon Advt. Inc., Atlanta, 1980—. Bd. dirs. Atlanta Jewish Community Ctr. Mem. Atlanta Media Planners Assn., Atlanta Broadcast Advertisers Club. Office: Bowes Hanlon Advt Inc 3925 Peachtree Rd Atlanta GA 30319

BERGER, JANE MAULDIN, psychologist, educator; b. Atlanta, July 28, 1945; d. John Frank and Lilly Belle (Casey) Mauldin; B.A., U. Ga., 1966; M.S. (NDEA fellow), U. Ga., 1967; Ph.D. in Psychology, U. Miami, 1971; M.B.A., Nova U., 1984; m. Michael L. Berger, Jan. 8, 1966; children—Louis Jefferson Mauldin, James Ivan Mauldin, Sarah Elizabeth Mauldin. Instr. psychology Miami-Dade Community Coll., 1968-71, asst. prof., 1971-73, assoc. prof., 1976-79, prof., 1979—; pvt. practice psychology, Miami, 1971—; guest lectr. U. Miami; cons. Dade County Rape Treatment Center; guest speaker civic groups. Cert. psychologist, Fla. Mem. Am. Psychol. Assn., Fla. Psychol. Assn., Dade County Psychol. Assn., Mental Health Assn. Dade County, S. Fla. Forum Death Edn. and Counseling, Phi Beta Kappa, Phi Kappa Phi, Psi Chi. Office: 9300 S Dadeland Blvd Suite 713 Miami FL 33156

BERGER, JUDITH ELLEN, physician recruitment and health care consulting firm executive; b. Bklyn., Mar. 17, 1948; d. Eugene and Lillian (Rosensweig) Frankel; m. Stephen G. Schoen, Feb. 15, 1982; 1 child by previous marriage: Scott Berger. Student Franklin Pierce Coll., 1966-67, New Coll. Social Research, 1971, 73-74. Recruiter, Fanning Personnel, N.Y.C., 1967-71; sales mgr. Roth Young, N.Y.C., 1974-77; v.p., sr. sales cons. Corson Group, N.Y.C., 1977-79; pres. MD Resources, Inc., Miami, Fla., 1979—. Contbr. articles and papers to profl. lit. Vol. worker Miami unit Am. Cancer Soc., 1984—. Named to Inc Mag. 500, 1984, Outstanding Young Working Woman, Glamour Mag., 1985. Mem. Nat. Assn. Physician Recruiters (bd. dirs., sec. 1985—), Am. Mktg. Assn. (chpt. bd. dirs. 1984—), Am. Group Practice Assn. (assoc.), Med. Group Mgmt. Assn. (assoc.). Avocations: skiing; scuba diving; body building. Office: MD Resources Inc 7385 Galloway Rd Suite 200 Miami FL 33173

BERGER, JULIE ANN, social worker; b. Newark, Sept. 18, 1950; d. Murray M. and Estelle C. (Sperber) Monestersky; student U. Wis., 1968-70; B.A., Tufts U., 1972; M.S.W., Rutgers U., 1973. Med. social worker dialysis unit VA Hosp., East Orange, N.J., 1974-76, med. social worker hosp.-based home-care program and outpatient clinic, 1976-77; med. social worker dialysis unit Morristown (N.J.) Meml. Hosp., 1977-81; asst./trainee Donna Aughey Ely and Assocs., Morristown, N.J., 1984; freelance market research, health care and telecommunications cons., 1984—; field instr. casework sequence Rutgers U. Grad. Sch. Social Work, 1978; social work rep. to N.J. Renal Network Council, Inc., 1979-81, mem. subcom. on allied health profl. practice, 1978-81, mem. by-laws com., 1978-79, sec. to full council, 1980-81. Social work vol. The Richmond Fellowship, Morristown, 1984. Mem. Acad. Cert. Social Workers, Nat. Assn. Social Workers, Register Clin. Social Workers, Nat. Assn. Patients on Hemodialysis and Transplant, Council Nephrology Social Workers (1974-82), N.J. Dialysis and Transplant Assn. (sec. 1976-78, pres. 1978-80). Home: 7 Hamilton Rd Apt 4B Morristown NJ 07960 Office: 10 Madison Ave Morristown NJ 07960

BERGER, MAUREEN, seminar management executive; b. Leicester, Eng., Mar. 10, 1941; came to U.S., 1962; d. George Frederick and Katherine Irene (Ridgeway) Hill; m. David W. Lucier; children—Deborah, Steven, Donna; m. Richard William Berger, Aug. 10, 1985. Student bus. adminstrn. Leicester U., 1961. Test proctor U.S. Air Force, Phalsbourg, France, 1965-66; asst. adminstr. Oversea Div., Gen. Electric Co., Ramstein, Germany, 1966-67; prodn. mgr. Norman Harwell Assocs., Dallas and Saigon, 1968-72; sec. Coopers & Lybrand, Springfield, Mass., 1972-75; owner Latent Image Photography, Springfield, 1975-77; v.p. Tech. Seminars, Inc., Great Neck, N.Y., 1978—. Mem. Nat. Assn. Female Execs., NOW, Atomic Indsl. Forum Inc., Assn. Research and Enlightenment. Avocations: golf; racquetball; aerobics; collecting antique bottles and Maxfield Parrish prints. Home: 122 Forest Ave New Rochelle NY 10804 Office: Tech Seminars Inc 425 Northern Blvd Great Neck NY 11021

BERGER, RITA ROSE, educator; b. Bronx, N.Y., Jan. 1, 1925; d. Jack Maurice and Helene (Abrevaya); B.Ed., U. Miami, 1949; M.A., U. South Fla., 1973; m. Nathaniel Leah Berger, Sept. 29, 1949; 1 son, Carl Franklin. Tchr., North Miami (Fla.) Christian Ch., 1960-61, East Zephyrhills (Fla.) Elem. Sch., 1962-63; tchr. spl. edn. Polk County, Fla., 1965-67, tchr., 1967-73, reading tchr., 1973-81, tchr. learning disabled Rochelle Elem. Sch., Lakeland, 1981—, reading tchr. Plant City (Fla.) campus Hillsborough Community Coll., 1974-75; sec.-treas. Nate's Bike and Mower Sales and Service, Inc., Lakeland, Fla., 1973—; sales assoc. Pre-paid Legal Services; West area dir. Polk Edn., 1970-71; sec. Polk County Schs. Title I Dist. Parent Adv. Council, 1980-81. Altar worker First Assembly of God Ch. Recipient award for meritorious service United Negro Coll. Fund, 1977; cert. in elem. edn., reading, and secondary social studies, also adminstrn. and supervision, specific learning disabilities, and gifted edn., Fla. Mem. Internat. Reading Assn. (treas., del. Gen. Assembly), Fla. Reading Council (life), Assn. Children with Learning Disabilities, Polk Edn. Assn. (chmn. human relations com.), Fla. Teaching Profession, NEA, Assn. Supervision and Curriculum Devel., Fla. Assn. Supervision and Curriculum Devel., Nat. Assn. Female Execs., Internat. Platform Assn., Kappa Delta Pi. Republican. Pentecostal. Club: Century of South Fla. Home: 811 Arietta Dr Auburndale FL 33823 Office: 1728 E Edgewood Dr Lakeland FL 33803

BERGER, SHIRLEY JUNE, corporate executive; b. Washington, June 28, 1932; d. Milton Chapel and Lillian (Pavis) Kurland; student public schs., Washington; m. Kalvin Berger, May 19, 1957 (dec.); children—Andrew Charles, Marilyn. Exec. sec. Mayer & Co., Washington, 1950-56, H.L. Merin Co., N.Y.C., 1957-58; owner, operator Custom Color Lab., Palo Alto, Calif., 1959—, pres., chmn. bd., 1978—; pres. Chutzpah, Inc., 1976-79; seminar leader; pub. speaker. Bd. dirs. Tmpel Beth David, Cupertino, Calif., 1973, Louise Salinger Acad. Fashion, San Francisco. Recipient Pub. Service award USO, 1952. Mem. Nat. Fedn. Ind. Bus. (action com.), Assn. Profl. Color Labs. (adv. bd.), Assn. Bay Area Profl. Labs. (past pres.), Photo-Mktg. Assn. Contbr. articles to profl. jours. Office: 947 Industrial Ave Palo Alto CA 94303

BERGERS, RITA MOSKO, home therapy company executive, consultant; b. Bklyn., Apr. 23, 1955; d. John Joseph and Mary Rita (McLaughlin) Mosko; m. William John Bergers, Apr. 26, 1980. B.S. in Nursing cum laude, U. Bridgeport, 1977. Registered nurse. Mem. staff Mt. Sinai Hosp., N.Y.C., 1977-78; mem. critical care staff/charge Yale New Haven Hosp., 1978-81; clin. cons. Park Plaza Hosp., Houston, 1981-83; regional coordinator Home Med. Support Services, Houston, 1982—; cons. Diatek, San Diego, 1985. Mem. Oncology Nursing Soc., Am. Soc. Parenteral and Enteral Nutrition, Nat. Assn. Female Execs., Sigma Delta Phi. Avocations: reading; bicycling; yoga. Home: 2120 El Paso Dr Apt 2002 Houston TX 77054 Office: Home Med Support Services 8275 El Rio Suite 140 Houston TX 77054

BERGERUD, MARLY KAY, educator, dean; b. Minot, N.D., July 27, 1942; d. Winton Ernest and Florence Martha-Carrie (Hall) Balsukot; Student U. N.D., 1960-63; B.A., Calif. State U., Fresno, 1965; M.S., U. So. Calif., 1968; 1 child, Christen Erik. Tchr., Brea-Olinda High Sch., Brea, Calif., 1966-70; prof. bus. div., dir. info. systems center Cypress (Calif.) Coll., 1970-73; dean bus. div. Saddleback Coll. Mission Viejo, Calif., 1983—; owner AIMS (Am. Info. Mgmt. Specialists), Los Alamitos, Calif., mgmt. cons. in field. Mem. Assn. Info. Systems Profls. (pres. chpt. 1979-81), AAUP, Calif. Bus. Edn. Assn., NEA, Am. Vocat. Assn., Am. Assn. Jr. Coll. Adminstrs., Internat. Assn. Telecommunications, Office Systems Research Assn., Delta Pi Epsilon. Co-author: Word/Information Processing Concepts, 2d edit., 1984; Word Processing: Concepts and Careers, 3d edit., 1984. Home: 33812 Diana Dr Dana Point CA 92629 Office: Saddleback Coll 28000 Marguerite Pkwy Mission Viejo CA 92692

BERGESON, MARIAN, state legislator; m. Garth Bergeson; 4 children. Student UCLA; B.A. Brigham Young U.; postgrad. UCLA. Pres., regional dir. Calif. Sch. Bds. Assn.; officer, dir. Orange County Sch. Bds. Assn.; mem. Newport Beach City Sch. Dist. Bd. Edn., 1964-65; mem. Newport-Mesa Unified Sch. Dist. Bd. Edn., 1965-77; mem. Calif. Assembly, 1978-82, Calif. Senate, 1984—. Past mem. Orange County Juvenile Justice Commn., Riles-Younger Task Force for Prevention of Crime and Violence in the Schs., Com. for Revision State Edn. Code, Joint Com. on Revision Penal Code; mem. Calif. YMCA Model Legislature/Ct.; mem. bd. advisors Calif. Elected Women's Assn. Edn. and Research; bd. dirs. Sta. KBIG Adv. Bd.; mem. govt. relations com. Orange County Arts Alliance. Recipient Marian Bergeson Community Services award Orange County Sch. Bds. Assn., 1975; Anchor award Newport Harbor C. of C., women's div., 1967; Community Services award AAUW, 1976; Disting. Women's award Irvine Soroptimists, 1981; Disting. Service award Brigham Young U., 1980-81; Women of Achievement award Newport Harbor Zonta Club, 1981; Silver Medallion, YWCA, 1983; Pub. Service award Calif. Speech-Lang.-Hearing Assn., 1983; named Outstanding Pub. Ofcl., Orange County chpt. Am. Soc. Pub. Adminstrn., 1983. Office: 4500 Campus Dr Suite 344 Newport Beach CA 92660*

BERGHERR, DIANA E., investment banking executive; b. N.Y.C., Dec. 15, 1952; d. William Vincent and Theresa (Tucci) B.; m. Carl Petrie, Dec. 2, 1972 (div. 1985). A.A., Queensbrough Community Coll., 1980; B.A. cum laude Queen's Coll., 1980, M.S. in Edn., 1981. Vault custodian Home Fed., Little Neck, N.Y., 1972-75, adminstrv. asst., 1975-80; tchr. Great Neck Sch. Dist., N.Y., 1981-82; program mgr. E.F. Hutton, Garden City, N.Y., 1983-84, mgr. pvt. placement ops., asst. v.p., 1984—. Queen's Coll. scholar, 1980. Mem. Kappa Delta Pi, Sigma Lambda. Roman Catholic. Avocations: horseback riding; dance; skiing; weightlifting; exercise. Office: E F Hutton & Co Inc 1225 Franklin Ave Garden City NY 11530

BERGLIN, LINDA, state senator; b. Oakland, Calif., Oct. 19, 1944; d. Freeman and Norma (Lund) Waterman. B.F.A., Mpls. Coll. Art and Design. Mem. Minn. Ho. of Reps., St. Paul, 1972-80; mem. Minn. Senate, St. Paul, 1980—, chmn. Health and Human Services Com. Mem. Democratic-Farmer-Labor Party. Office: Minn Senate State Capitol Saint Paul MN 55155*

BERGMAN, BERNA ROSE, manufacturing company executive; b. Fabrica, Philippine Islands, Oct. 27, 1936; came to U.S., 1955; d. Samuel William Real and Rose (Vail) Johnston; m. Thomas William Gaine, Dec. 17, 1960 (div. 1973); children—Janice Michelle Brender, Debra Ann, Catherine Marie. A.A. in Bus., San Francisco Coll. for Women, 1957; student Diablo Valley Coll., 1977. Asst. mgr. Stecher-Traung Credit Union, San Francisco, 1969-70; with gen. office Monsanto Chem. Co., Martinez, Calif., 1970-74; sr. buyer Systron Donner-Inertial div., Concord, Calif., 1974-80, safety systems div., Concord, 1981—; sales rep. Hi-Rel Components, Los Angeles, 1980-81. Mem. Nat. Assn. Female Execs., No. Calif. Area Small and Disadvantaged Bus. Council (assoc.), Fed./Industry Small Bus. Council (sec. 1984-85), Purchasing Mgmt. Assn. (metro chpt.), Industry Council for Small Bus. Devel. Democrat. Roman Catholic. Office: Systron Donner Safety Systems Div 935 Detroit Ave Concord CA 94518

BERGMAN, BETTY LAING, hospital executive; b. Evanston, Ill., May 14, 1923; d. John Crawford and Marion (Buchanan) Laing; m. Richard Joseph Bergman, Oct. 6, 1951. B.A., Lake Forest Coll., 1947; cert. Case Western Res. U., 1977; cert. in teaching No. Ill. U., 1966. Personnel mgr. Wieboldt Stores, Inc., Chgo., 1947-62; tchr. Wooddale (Ill.) Schs., 1962-66; instr. Lorain County Community Coll., Elyria, Ohio, 1975-77; personnel dir. Elyria (Ohio) Home, 1979-81; employment mgr. Lorain (Ohio) Community Hosp., 1981-84, personnel mgr., 1984-85, dir. personnel, 1985—. Chmn. personnel com., sec. bd. trustees ARC, Elyria, 1982—; mem. adv. bd. Lorain City Schs., 1982—, Lorain County Joint Vocat. Sch., 1982—, Lorain County Community Coll., 1986—, Lorain Bus. Coll., 1986—; com. mem. Lorain County Hometown Careers Day, 1982—, chmn., 1984; mem. job service employer com. Ohio Bur. Employment Services, 1985—; div. capt. Heart Assn. Fund Drive, Elyria, 1976; mem., chmn. Lorain County Hist. Soc., 1975—. Named Woman of Achievement, Lorain YWCA, 1983; vol. recognition Elyria Home, 1979, 1st Congl. Ch., 1974. Mem. AAUW, Am. Soc. Personnel Adminstrs., Greater Cleve. Personnel Council. Republican. Presbyterian. Clubs: Elyria Woman's (pres. 1978-80); Culture (v.p. 1976-77), Roundtable (v.p. 1982-83). Home: 313 Georgia Ave Elyria OH 44035 Office: Lorain Community Hosp 3700 Kolbe Rd Lorain OH 44053

BERGMAN, EMILY ANNE, psychology librarian; b. Tulsa, July 24, 1953; d. Arthur Lawrence and Jean Lucy (Anson) Bergman; m. Mark Andrew Allen, June 20, 1982; 1 son, Philip Isaac. Student Wroxton Coll., Banbury, Eng., 1974; B.A., Goucher Coll., 1975; M.L.S., U. Tex., Austin, 1976. Asst. research librarian Tracy-Locke Advt., Dallas, 1977; research librarian, 1977-78; cataloger Dallas Pub. Library, 1978-80, head spl. collections, 1980-81; info. specialist, Dallas, 1978-81; asst. library dir. Calif. Sch. Profl. Psychology, Los Angeles, 1981—. Mem. ALA, Assn. Coll. and Research Libraries, Spl. Library Assn. Democrat. Jewish. Home: 1001 N Geneva St Glendale CA 91207 Office: Calif Sch Profl Psychology 2235 Beverly Blvd Los Angeles CA 90057

BERGMAN, ESTHER S., manufacturing company executive; b. Germany, Feb. 21, 1947; came to U.S., 1949; d. Leon and Paula (Jakubowicz) Srebnik; m. Howard A. Bergman, Aug. 26, 1967 (div. 1983). Pres. Design Youth Mfg., Inc., Phila., 1983—. Republican. Jewish. Avocations: knitting; aerobics; dancing. Home: 8036 Jenkintown Rd Cheltenham PA 19012 Office: Design Youth Mfg Inc 3412 J St Philadelphia PA 19134

BERGMAN, JANICE JOAN, nurse; b. Axtell, Kans., Jan. 6, 1938; d. Alban Matthias and Angela Philomena (Karnowski) Haug; R.N., Marymount Coll., 1959; m. Paul Harold Bergman, Nov. 28, 1959; children—Janel, Julene, Jennifer. Staff nurse Seneca (Kans.) Hosp., 1959; charge nurse St. Mary's Hosp., Kansas City, Mo., 1960-62; asst. dir. nursing services N. Kans. Meml. Hosp., North Kansas City, Mo., 1963-67; dir. health occupations program Kans. Dept Edn., 1976; co-owner, dir. nursing Cresview Manor, Seneca, 1968—; gerontol. nurse cons. Kans. State Dept. Vocat. Edn., 1977; Am. Nurses Assn. rep. Nat. Task Force on Credentialing in Nursing, 1980-83; gerontol. nurse cons. NE Kans. Area Agy. on Aging; ad hoc adv. 1981 White House Conf. on Aging, Nat. Observer. Mem. Am. Nurses Assn. (exec. Com. div. gerontol. nursing practice), ANA Council of Nursing Home Nurses, Kans. Coalition on Aging, Kans. Public Health Assn., Kans. State Nurses Assn., NE Kans. Regional Adv. Com. for Nurses, Bus. & Profl. Women's Club (pres. 1973-75), Nemaha County Mental Health Assn. (pres. 1976-78), Nemaha County Hist. Soc., Dist. 13 Nurses Assn. (pres. 1976-78), Nemaha Valley Community Hosp. Guild, Jaycee Jaynes (pres. 1971), C. of C. Mem. editorial adv. bd. Geriatric Nursing, 1982—; contbr. articles to profl. jours. Home: 1011 Nemaha St Seneca KS 66538 Office: 808 N 8th St Seneca KS 66538

BERGMAN, SHERRI GAY, marketing research company executive; b. Bklyn., Dec. 25, 1953; d. David Israel and Minnie Neuwirth. B.A., SUNY-Stony Brook, 1974; M.Mgmt., Northwestern U., 1980. Tchr., Kings Park Sch. Dist., N.Y., 1975-77; office mgr. Regal Packaging Co., Roslyn, N.Y., 1977-78; research assoc. Quaker Oats Co., Chgo., 1979-80; project mgr. Elrick & Lavidge, Chgo., 1980-85, v.p., 1985—. Treas. 2658 N. Orchard Condo Assn., Chgo., 1983—; vol. tutor Fourth Presbyn. Ch., Chgo., 1984—. Mem. Am. Mktg. Assn., Northwestern U. Profl. Women's Assn. (program dir.), Sierra Club. Democrat. Jewish. Avocations: bicycling; swimming; hiking. Office: Elrick & Lavidge Inc 10 S Riverside Plaza Chicago IL 60606

BERGMANN, BARBARA ROSE, economist, educator; b. Bronx, N.Y., July 20, 1927; d. Martin and Nellie (Wallenstein) Berman; m. Fred H. Bergmann, July 18, 1965; children—Sarah Nellie, David Martin. B.A., Cornell U., 1948; M.A., Radcliff Grad. Sch., Harvard U., 1958, Ph.D., 1959. Economist, U.S. Bur. Labor Stats., 1949-53; instr. Harvard U., 1958-61; sr. staff economist Council Econ. Advisers, 1961-62; mem. sr. staff Brookings Instn., 1963-65; sr. econ. adv. AID, 1966-67; mem. faculty U. Md., 1965—, prof. econs., 1971—; columnist econ. affairs N.Y. Times, 1981—; mem. Price Adv. Com.; cons. in field. Ford fellow, 1970. Mem. Am. Econ. Assn. (v.p. 1976), AAUP (pres. Md. chpt. 1978-79), Econometric Soc., Eastern Econ. Assn. (pres. 1974). Democrat. Author: Projection of a Metropolis, 1961; Structural Unemployment in the U.S., 1967, Impact of Highway Investment on Development, 1966. Home: 6700 Selkirk Dr Bethesda MD 20817 Office: Dept Econs U Md College Park MD 20742

BERGNER, JANE COHEN, lawyer; b. Schenectady, N.Y., Apr. 6, 1943; d. Louis and Selma (Breslaw) Cohen; m. Alfred P. Bergner, May 30, 1968; children—Lauren, Justin. A.B., Vassar Coll., 1964; LL.B., Columbia U., 1967. Bar: D.C. 1968, U.S. Dist. Ct. D.C. 1968, U.S. Ct. Appeals (D.C. cir.) 1968, U.S. Ct. Claims, 1969, U.S. Ct. Appeals (fed. cir.) 1969, U.S. Tax Ct. 1979. Trial atty. tax div. U.S. Dept. Justice, Washington, 1967-74; assoc. Arnold & Porter, Washington, 1974-76, Rogovin, Huge & Lenzner, Washington, 1976—. Legal counsel Jewish Social Service Agy., Washington; troop leader Girl Scouts U.S.A.; mem. Nat. Women's Com. Brandeis U. Finalist, Harlan Fisher Stone Honor Moot Ct. Competition, Columbia U. Law Sch. Mem. Vassar Coll. Class Alumnae (class of 1964 treas.), Bar Assn. D.C., Fed. Bar Assn., Women's Bar Assn. D.C., Women's Legal Def. Fund, Nat. Assn. Women Lawyers, Tax Litigation Luncheon Group, ABA (sect. taxation, chmn. subcom. continuing legal edn., com. ct. procedure), Columbia Law Sch. Alumni Assn., Service Guild Washington. Clubs: Vassar (Washington); Hadassah. Office: 1730 Rhode Island Ave NW Washington DC 20036

BERGQUIST, KATHLEEN MARIE, government official; b. Coos Bay, Oreg., Apr. 10, 1952; d. Elroy Atlee and Margaret Mary (Connor) B. B.A. in Social Scis., Oreg. Coll. of Edn., 1976. Personnel asst. U.S. Dept. Transp., Fed. Hwy. Adminstrn., Portland, Oreg., 1977-78, personnel mgmt. specialist, 1978-81, asst. regional dir. civil rights, 1981-83; exec. dir. Fed. Exec. Bd., Portland, 1983—. Vol., Clackamas County Mental Health, Portland, 1980-83. Mem. Inst. for Managerial/Profl. Women, Am. Soc. for Pub. Adminstrn. Office: Federal Executive Bd Federal Bldg 1220 SW 3d Ave Portland OR 07204

BERGQUIST, SANDRA LEE, medical corporation executive, registered nurse; b. Carlton, Minn., Oct. 13, 1944; d. Arthur Vincent and Avis Lorene Portz; m. David Edward Bergquist, June 11, 1966; children—Rion Eric, Taun Erin. B.S. in Nursing, Barry U., 1966; M.A. in Mgmt., Central Mich. U., 1975; student U. So. Calif., 1980-82. R.N., registered nurse practitioner; cert. physician asst. Commd. 2d lt. U.S. Air Force, 1968, advanced through grades to lt. col., 1985; staff and charge nurse U.S. Air Force, 1968-76, primary care nurse practitioner, McConnell AFB, Kans., 1976-79, officer in charge Wheeler Med. Facility, Wheeler AFB, Hawaii, 1979-83, supr. ambulatory care services, Elgin AFB, Fla., 1983-84; co-founder, pres. Care Cons. Corp., Niceville, Fla., 1985—. Bd. dirs. Okaloosa County Council on Aging, Fla.; chairperson Niceville/Valparaiso Task Force on Child Abuse Prevention, Fla., 1985—; chmn. home and family life com. Twin Cities Women's Club, Niceville, 1985—; chmn. advancement com. Gulf Coast council Boy Scouts Am., 1985—; instr. advanced and basic cardiac life support Hawaii Heart Assn. and Tripler Army Med. Ctr., 1981-83. Decorated Commendation medal with 1 oak leaf cluster, USAF Meritorious Service medal, Air Force Commendation medal. Mem. Am. Assn. Critical-Care Nurses, Am. Assn. Physician Assts., Assn. Mil. Surgeons U.S., Fla. Assn. Physician Assts., Soc. Air Force Physician Assts., Twin Cities Women's Club. Lutheran. Avocations: computer programming, reading, handicrafts. Office: Care Consulting Corp PO Box 385 Niceville FL 32578

BERGSTEIN, DOROTHY INA, clin. social worker; b. Jersey City, Apr. 10, 1940; d. Melvin Louis and Marjorie (Knaster) Kramer; A.A., Centenary Coll. for Women, 1960; B.A. magna cum laude, Upsala Coll., 1973; M.S.W., Rutgers U., 1975; m. Melvyn H. Bergstein, Aug. 28, 1960; children—Merri Lee, Jodi. Clin. social worker Newark Family Service, 1974-75; mem. staff, clin. social worker Essex County Guidance Center, East Orange, N.J., 1975-76; adminstr. Jewish Family Service, Ledgewood, N.J., 1976-77; clin. social worker emergency psychiat. service Morristown (N.J.) Meml. Hosp., 1977—; owner, dir. Counseling and Consultation Services, Morristown, N.J. bd. dirs. Jersey Battered Women's Services, 1976-77; lectr.; cons. family life sect. N.J. Bar, 1977-79, correction reform com., 1976-77. Lic. marriage counselor. Mem. Nat. Assn. Social Workers, N.J. Assn. Women Therapists, Acad. Cert. Social Workers (cert. family therapist), Psi Chi. Jewish. Office: 20 Community Pl Morristown NJ 07960

BERGSTROM, ERICA JUNE, market research analyst; b. Los Angeles, June 30, 1951; d. Evert and Annette Bergstrom; B.A. with honors in psychology, Stanford U., 1973; Ph.D., U. Pa., 1981; m. Sidney Edward Croul, Dec. 29, 1979. Instr., U. Pa., Phila., 1975, 76; research psychologist Carrier Found., Belle Mead, N.J., 1980-82; market research analyst Scott Paper Co., Phila., 1982—; head Stanford in France Program for Emotionally Disturbed Children, 1970-71. Head Swedish lang. program Seamen's Ch., 1980—; active Am.-Swedish Mus. Fulbright fellow, 1974. Mem. Am. Psychol. Assn., World Affairs Council of Phila., Phi Beta Kappa. Contbr. articles to profl. jours. Home: 4557 Boone St Philadelphia PA 19128 Office: Scott Paper Co Scott Plaza I Philadelphia PA 19113

BERINO, ANN MARIE DRAP, office equipment service firm executive; b. Yonkers, N.Y., Sept. 6, 1951; d. Albert Stephen and Ethel Francis (Townsend) Drap. Mgr. Keneric Bus. Machines, N.Y.C., 1973-84; mgr. All Brand Office Equipment, N.Y.C., 1984—; pres. All Brand Typewriter Service, N.Y.C., 1984—. Bd. mgrs. Monterrey Condominium, Yonkers, 1983—. Mem. N.Y. Office Machine Dealers Assn. (bd. dirs. 1984—, exec. sec. 1981-84, pres. 1985-86). Democrat. Roman Catholic. Home: 357 N Broadway Yonkers NY 10701 Office: All Brand Typewriter Service Corp 251 W 30th St New York NY 10001

BERKA, MARIANNE GUTHRIE, health, physical education and recreation educator; b. Queens, N.Y., Dec. 25, 1944; d. Frank Joseph and Mary (DePaul) Guthrie; B.S., Ithaca (N.Y.) Coll., 1966, M.S. (grad. asst.), 1968; doctoral candidate NYU; m. Jerry George Berka, June 1, 1968; children—Katie, Keri. High sch. tchr. Northport High Sch., 1966-67; full prof. health, phys. edn. and recreation Nassau Community Coll., Garden City, N.Y., 1968—. Mem. Assn. Women Phys. Educators N.Y. State (chpt. chmn. 1973-74, chpt. treas. 1980-84), AAHPER, N.Y. State Assn. Health, Phys. Edn. and Recreation (J.B. Nash scholarship com. 1983—), Am. Assn. Sex Educators, Counselors and Therapists (cert. sex educator). Roman Catholic. Home: 90 Bay Way Ave Brightwaters NY 11718 Office: P226 HPER Nassau Community Coll Garden City NY 11530

BERKBIGLER, MARSHA LEE, gold mining company executive; b. Flint, Mich., May 2, 1950; d. Herbert Ules and Rosy Vernell (Grimes) Cornelison; m. Gary Robert Koontz, June 22, 1968 (div. Nov. 1976); children—Deron Robert, Alicia Michelle; m. James Herbert Berkbigler, Dec. 16, 1977. A. in Bus., Reno Bus. Coll., 1979. Hosp. coordinating sec. LaHabra Community Hosp., Calif., 1973-76; sec., office mgr. Sierra Med. Assocs., Reno, 1976-78; claims rep. Equifax, Reno, 1978-79; legal asst. Freeport Export Co., Reno, 1979-85; pub. and govt. coordinator Freeport-McMoRan Gold Co., Reno, 1985—; cons. Neva. Wilderness Minerals Exploration Coalition, Denver, 1985. Mem. Nev. Republican Woman's Caucus, Reno, 1986; apptd. Reno Commn. Status of Women, 1985. Mem. Nev. Mining Assn., Nev. Landman's Assn., Assn. Exec. Females, Nev. Council Econ. Edn. (exec. com.), Concerned Nevadans for Practical Wilderness. Avocations: skiing; golf; travel. Home: 2090 Allen St Reno NV 89509

BERKE, ANITA DIAMANT, literary agent; b. N.Y.C., Jan. 15; d. Sidney J. and Lea (Lyons) Diamant; widowed; 1 child, Allyson. B.S., NYU. Mem. editorial bd. Forum Mag., N.Y.C., McCalls Mag.; reporter Macy Newspapers; literary agt., pres. Anita Diamant Literary Agy., N.Y.C.; adj. prof. L.I.U. Contbr. articles to profl. jours. Mem. Women in Communications Assn. (past pres. N.Y. chpt.), Nat. Assn. Newspaper Women, Soc. Author's Reps. Club: Overseas Press (pres. 1981—). Home: 16 Fanton Hill Rd Weston CT 06883 Office: Anita Diamant Literary Agy 310 Madison Ave New York NY 10017

BERKE, JUDIE, artist, writer, publisher; b. Mpls., Apr. 15, 1938; d. Maurice M. and Sue (Supak) Kleyman; student U. Minn., 1956-60, Mpls. Sch. Art, 1945-59. Free lance illustrator and designer, 1959—; pres. Berke-Wood, Inc., N.Y.C., 1971-84, Manhattan Rainbow & Lollipop Co., subs. of Berke-Wood, Inc., 1971-82, pres. Get Your Act Together, club act staging, N.Y.C., 1971-82; pres. Coordinator Publs., Inc.; pub./editor-in-chief The Continuing Care Coordinator mag., Continuing Care Health-watch; pres. Coordinator Publs., Inc.; owner Judie Berke Publs.; ptnr. Continuing Care Congress, yearly conv. for health care profls.; guest lectr. at various colls. and univs. in Calif. and N.Y., 1973—; writer, illustrator, dir. numerous ednl. filmstrips, 1972—, latest being Focus on Professions, 1974, Focus on the Performing Arts, 1974, Focus on the Creative Arts, 1974, Workstyles, 1976, Wonderworm, 1976, Supernut, 1977; author, illustrator film Fat Black Mack (San Francisco Ednl. Film Festival award, Mus. Modern Art permanent film collection), 1970; designer posters and brochures for various entertainment groups, 1963—; head prodn. Advanced Audio Visual Systems, 1979—; writer, producer Holidays, read along films for United Learning Corp., 1979; cons. to numerous film and ednl. cos.; composer numerous songs, latest being Time is Relative, 1976, Love Will Live On in My Mind, 1976, My Blue Walk, 1976, Let Me Sing a Love Song, 1982, Best Friends Baby Sister, 1982, Let's Go Around Once More, 1982; composer/author off-Broadway musical Street Corner Time, 1978; contbr. children's short stories to various publs., articles to mags. and jours. Trustee The Happy Spot Sch., N.Y.C., 1972-82. Mem. Broadcast Music Inc., Nat. Writers Club. Address: 11417 Vanowen St North Hollywood CA 91605

BERKELEY, BETTY LIFE, educator; b. St. Louis, May 25, 1924; d. James Alfred and Anna Laura (Voltmer) Life; m. Marvin Harold Berkeley, Feb. 7, 1947; children—Kathryn Elizabeth, Barbara Ellen, Brian Harrison, Janet Lynn. A.B., Harris Tchrs. Coll., 1947; M.A. in Ednl. Adminstrn., Washington U., St. Louis, 1951; Ph.D., North Tex. State U., 1980. Tchr. St. Louis pub. schs., 1946-48, Clayton pub. schs., Mo., 1948-49, Lamplighter Pvt. Sch., Dallas, 1964-67; program devel. specialist Richland Coll., Dallas, 1980-84, instr., 1981—; adj. prof. North Tex. State U., Denton, 1981—, cons. sch. community services, 1981—; pres. Retirement Planning Services, Dallas, 1984—. Contbr. articles to profl. jours. Mem. Dallas Commn. on Status of Women, 1975-79; bd. dirs. Dallas Municipal Library, 1979-83, 1979. Mem. AAUW (pres. 1973-75; Outstanding Women of Tex.). Methodist. Club: Women's Council of Dallas County (v.p. 1977-79). Avocations: travel; cooking; gardening; needlework. Home: 13958 Hughes Ln Dallas TX 75240 Office: Richland Coll 12800 Abrams Rd Dallas TX 75243

BERKHEIMER, GERALDINE FAY, educator, librarian; b. York, Pa., Feb. 18, 1934; d. Walter Lewis and Lena Emma (Tresselt) Berkheimer. B.S. in Edn., Millersville State Coll., 1956; M.A. in French, Middlebury Coll., 1959; M.S.L.S., Syracuse U., 1965. Tchr. French, Penncrest High Sch., Lima, Pa., 1956-58, Westminster High Sch. (Pa.), 1960-61; part-time sec. Sorbonne, Paris, 1961-62; English asst. Jean de la Fontaine Girls' High Sch., Paris, 1962-63; lit. analyst ERIC, Syracuse U. (N.Y.), 1964-65; asst. prof. French, Onondaga Community Coll., Syracuse, 1965-69, 70-71; librarian Reading Area Community Coll. (Pa.), 1971-72; substitute tchr. and librarian pub. schs., Orange County, Calif., 1972-79; library asst. U. Calif.-Irvine, 1979—. Mem. Calif. Library Assn., Alliance francaise, NOW, So. Calif. Women for Understanding, Laguna Outreach, Inst. for Religion and Wholeness, Nat. Mus. Women in Arts, Abundant Light Found. Home: 3101 S Fairview St Apt 84 Santa Ana CA 92704

BERKHEMER-CREDAIRE, BETSY, public relations executive; b. Washington, Jan. 31, 1947; d. Robert Walter and Claire (Myers) Berkhemer; m. Criston Credaire, Aug. 3, 1984. B.S. in History, UCLA, 1968. Reporter Ventura (Calif.) Star Free Press, 1965-68; editor Gardena (Calif.) Valley News, 1968-70; writer Sta. KTTV Metromedia News, Los Angeles, 1970-71; publicist Disney Studios, NBC, Burbank, Calif., 1971-73; pres., owner Berkhemer & Kline Inc., Pub. Relations, Los Angeles, 1973—; dir. Alcoholic Info Council, Los Angeles, 1982—. Mem. Nat. Women's Polit. Caucus, Rep. Women's Com., Los Angeles. Office: Berkhemer & Kline Inc 261 S Figueroa Suite 250 Los Angeles CA 90012

BERK-LEVINE, MARGO, personnel service company executive; b. Bklyn., Mar. 5, 1942; d. Louis A. and Rose (Galanty) Berkman; m. Alan Levine, Apr. 12, 1964; children—Seth., Aron D. B.A., Bklyn. Coll., 1962. Freelance actress, model N.Y.C., 1962-66; personnel cons. Albers Personnel, Washington, 1965; founder, co-owner Career Blazers Temporaries, N.Y.C., 1967; owner, operator, pres. Temporarily Yours Personnel Service, Inc., N.Y.C., 1968—; founder Margo Berk Personnel, Inc., 1979—. Contbr. articles to profl. newspapers. Featured on various TV news, and documentary programs. Mem. Am. Women's Econ. Devel. Corp., N.Y. Assn. Women's Bus. Owners, Am. Mgmt. Assn., N.Y. Assn. Temporary Service (pres. 1976-78), Nat. Assn. Temporary Service of Alexandria (Va.) (bd. dirs. 1980-81, sec. 1981-82, 2nd v.p., 1983-84, 1st v.p., 1984-85 pres. 1985-86), N.Y.C. C. of C. Democrat. Jewish. Club: Sales Exec. Office: Temporarily Yours Personnel Service Inc 505 Fifth Ave New York NY 10017

BERKLEY, NANCY MARGOLIS, lawyer, former art consultant, educator; b. St. Paul, Nov. 12, 1940; d. Charles and Dorothy (Wine) Margolis; m. Peter L. Berkley, Aug. 2, 1964; children—James, Alison, John. B.A., U. Minn., 1961; M.A.T., Harvard U., 1962; J.D., Rutgers U., 1985. Tchr., Malden, Mass., 1962-63, Newton, Mass., 1963-64, South Orange, N.J., 1964-67; art cons., N.Y. and N.J., 1973-83; law clk. U.S. Dist. Ct. N.J., 1983; law clk. Proskauer, Rose, Goetz & Mendelsohn, N.Y.C., summer 1984; assoc. Sullivan & Cromwell, N.Y.C., 1985—. Editor: Rutgers Law Rev., 1984-85. Trustee Livingston Symphony Orch., N.J., 1981—, Theresa Grotta Rehab. Ctr., West Orange, N.J., 1967—; active Livingston Recreation Adv. Council, 1981—; trustee Northwest Essex Suburban Arts Council, 1981-83. Mem. ABA, Phi Beta Kappa, Pi Lambda Theta. Home: 16 Fordham Rd Livingston NJ 07039

BERKMAN, CLAIRE FLEET, psychologist; b. New Orleans, Dec. 5, 1942; d. Joel and Margaret Grace (Fishler) Fleet; B.A., Boston U., 1964; M.Ed., Harvard U., 1966; Ed.D., Boston U., 1970; m. Arnold Stephen Berkman, Apr. 27, 1975; children—Janna Samantha, Micah Seth Siegel. Asst. prof. Counseling Center, Mich. State U., East Lansing, 1971-75, assoc. prof., 1975-78, assoc. prof. dept. psychiatry, 1975-82; pvt. clin. practice, 1975—; cons. Cath. Family Social Service, Lansing, 1979-83. Vice pres. Kehillat Israel Synagogue, 1975-76; bd. dirs. Jewish Welfare Fedn., Lansing, 1974-75, 84-86. NDEA fellow, 1968-70. Mem. Am. Psychol. Assn., Mich. Psychol. Assn., Am. Mental Health Assn. of Israel, Mich. Soc. Forensic Psychologists. Home: 4780 Arapaho Trail Okemos MI 48864

BERKSHIRE, LAURA SELIG, association administrator; b. Highland Park, Ill., June 21, 1951; d. Sidney and Ruth (Lewis) Selig; m. Michael R. Berkshire, May 19, 1973; children—Amy Louise, Jill Danielle. B.S. in Home Econs., Purdue U., 1973. Placement clk. Purdue U., West Lafayette, Ind., 1973-74; home economist Food Distbn. Systems, Cleve., 1974-75; office mgr. Ind.-Purdue Univs., Ft. Wayne, 1975-80; dir. pub. relations and fund devel. Limberlost council Girl Scouts U.S.A., 1980-85, exec. dir. Wapehani council, 1986—. Recipient 1st place pub. service award Ft. wayne Advt. Club, 1983. Mem. Women in Communications (pres. Ft. Wayne chpt. 1984-85), Pub. Relations Soc. Am., Internat. Assn. Bus. Communicators (award of excellence and merit Ft. Wayne chpt. 1984 award of excellence 1985), Sigma Delta Chi. Home: 2402 Windmire Way Anderson IN 46011 Office: Girl Scout Council PO Box 587 Daleville IN 47334

BERLAGE, GAI INGHAM, sociology educator; b. Washington, Feb. 9, 1943; d. Paul Bowen and Grace (Artz) Ingham; B.A., Smith Coll., 1965; M.A., So. Meth. U., 1968; Ph.D., NYU, 1979; m.; 2 children. Tchr., Nelson High Sch., Lovingston, Va., 1965-66, Ridgefield (Conn.) Pub. Sch., 1966-67, Piner Jr. High, Sherman, Tex., 1968-69; faculty Southeastern Coll., Durant, Okla., 1968, Norwalk (Conn.) Community Coll., 1971-77; instr. sociology Iona Coll., New Rochelle, N.Y., 1971-74, asst. prof. sociology, 1974-83, assoc. prof., 1983—, chmn. dept. sociology, 1981—, coordinator urban studies program, 1984—, coordinator gerontology program, 1985—; research cons. Health Studies Inst., New Rochelle, 1980-83; lectr. in field; fellow N.Am. Faculty Network, Northeastern U. Ctr. Study Sport in Society, 1984—; reviewer articles in field. Mem. Wilton Task Force Com. on Public Health Nursing Assn., 1981-82; commr. Wilton Commn. on Aging & Social Services, 1980—, chmn., 1982—; advisor Wilton Assn. Gifted Edn., 1981-82, pres., 1980-81; bd. dirs. Wilton Meal-on-Wheels, 1983—, chmn. Wilton Task Force Com. on Day Care, 1983-84; mem. Wilton Sports Council, 1985—; chmn. Wilton Task Force Com. for Outreach Program Iona Coll. grantee, 1981, summer 1981, 80-81; NSF grantee, 1980-81, 79-80, traineeship award, 1967-68; Iona Coll. dissertation fellow, 1975. Mem. Am. Sociol. Assn., Nat. Council on Crime and Delinquency, Nat. Inst. for Sport and Social Analysis, N.Am. Youth Sport Inst., N.Am. Soc. Sociology of Sport (nominating com.), Internat. Sociol. Assn. (internat. com. for sociology of sport), N.Y. Sociol. Assn., Internat. Soc. Sports Psychology. Co-author: Experience With Sociology: Social Issues in American Society. contbr. articles to profl. jours.

BERLEY, DIANE EMILY, lawyer; b. Lynwood, Calif., Sept. 12, 1952; d. Lionel and Virginia Ann (Germain) Isenberg; m. Kenneth Barnett Berley, Mar. 27, 1977; 1 child, Hannah. B.A. cum laude, U. Calif.-Irvine, 1974; J.D., Southwestern U., 1980. Bar: Calif. 1980. Realtor assoc. Choice Equities, Inc., Forest E. Olsen, Inc., Van Nuys, Calif., 1975-77; atty. Fadem, Berger & Norton, Santa Monica, Calif., 1980-82, Benjamin George Williams, Los Angeles, 1982-83, Walleck, Shane & Stanard, Woodland Hills, Calif., 1983-86, Whitman & Berley, Los Ange;es. 1986—; jud. extern Hon. Joan Dempsey Klein, Calif. Ct. Appeal, Los Angeles, 1980. Recipient Am. Jurisprudence Book award Southwestern U., Los Angeles, 1979. Democrat. Jewish. Office: Whitman & Berley 11111 W Olympic Blvd 3d Floor Los Angeles CA 90064

BERLINCOURT, MARJORIE ALKINS, government official; b. Toronto, Ont., Can., June 2, 1928; came to U.S., 1950, naturalized, 1956; d. Herbert John and Ellen Florence (Barker) Alkins; B.A., U. Toronto, 1950; M.A., Yale U., 1951, Ph.D., 1954; m. Ted Gibbs Berlincourt, Feb. 28, 1953; 1 dau., Leslie Ellen Berlincourt Yale. Editorial dir. Tech. Publs., Rocketdyne, 1956-59; lectr. classics U. So. Calif., 1959-61; assoc. prof. classical history Calif. Luth. Coll., 1961-67, Calif. State U., Northridge, 1967-71; prof. Met. State Coll., Denver, 1971-72; program dir. div. fellowships Nat. Endowment Humanities, for summer seminars and fellowships Washington, 1972-78, dep. dir. div. research programs, 1978-84, dir. div. state programs, 1984—; vis. lectr. Georgetown U., 1972. Recipient Calif. Faculty Research award, 1970; Sterling fellow Yale U., 1950-53. Mem. Am. Assn. Ancient Historians. Episcopalian. Author: De Surprise en Surprise, 1953; Entrez Petits Amis, 1954; Victory as a Coin Type, 1973; contbr. articles to profl. jours. Office: 1100 Pennsylvania Ave NW Washington DC 20506

BERLOWE, PHYLLIS HARRIETTE, public relations counselor; b. N.Y.C.; d. Louis and Rose (Jachez) B. Student Hunter Coll., N.Y.C., 1940-42. Account exec. Ted Sills & Co., N.Y.C., 1959-63, Harshe-Rotman & Druck, N.Y.C., 1963-65; exec. v.p. Edward Gottlieb & Assocs., N.Y.C., 1965-78; v.p. Hill & Knowlton Inc., N.Y.C., 1978-79; v.p., group supr. Doremus & Co., N.Y.C., 1980-83; v.p., group supr. Marketshare div. Doremus/BBDO, N.Y.C., 1983—. Mem. Pub. Relations Soc. Am. (accredited; chmn. Counselors Acad. 1981, Silver Anvil award 1977, president's citations, 1976, 78, 81, 81, 82, 83,), Publicity Club N.Y. (sec., v.p., Disting. Service award 1960, 61, 62), Am. Women in Radio and TV, Pharm. Advt. Council, N.Y. Acad. Scis., World Future Soc., Women Execs. in Pub. Relations (pres. 1982). Club: Marco Polo (N.Y.C.). Office: Marketshare 41 Madison Ave New York NY 10010

BERMAN, ANN M., career and employment counselor, psychometrician; b. Montreal, Que., Can., Apr. 25, 1951; d. Samuel and Regina (Kaps) B. Grad. CUNY, 1978; M.A., Columbia U., 1980. Cert. life skills educator. With Andorn, Begida & Danks, N.Y.C., 1978; counselor Sta. WEME, N.Y.C., 1977; psychometrician/counselor Project FIND, N.Y.C., 1980; asst. ednl. services IEEE, N.Y.C., 1981-82; ind. career and employment counselor, 1983—; also writer. Mem. Am. Psychol. Assn., Am. Personnel and Guidance Assn., N.Y. State Personnel and Guidance Assn., Nat. Hospice Assn., Nat. Writers Union. Home: 644 Amsterdam Ave New York NY 10025

BERMAN, CARYN SANDRA, psychotherapist and consultant; b. N.Y.C., Sept. 15, 1952; d. Paul and Rachel Berman. B.A. in Sociology, SUNY-Stony Brook, 1973; M.A. in Social Service Adminstrn., U. Chgo., 1980. Cert. social worker. Pub. health advisor, epidemiologist CDC, Dept. HEW, N.Y.C., Chgo., 1974-78; program developer Mental Health Assn., Evanston, Ill., 1978-79; policy intern Office Population Affairs, Dept. HEW, Washington, 1979; caseworker III, dept. psychiatry Evanston Hosp., 1979-84; adminstr. Travelers and Immigrants Aid, Chgo., 1984—; cons. and psychotherapist in pvt. practice, Chgo., 1982—; conf. planner Horizons Psychotherapy, Chgo., 1982-85. Contbr. articles to profl. jours. Pres. Foster Magnolia Condo Assn., Chgo., 1981—; bd. dirs. Women in Theatre, Chgo., 1978; performer N.Y. Feminist Theatre Troupe, N.Y.C., 1974-76. Mem. Nat. Assn. Social Workers, Assn. Labor and Mgmt. Alcohol Council, Sex Info. Edn. and Counseling U.S., Avocation: theatre arts. Home: 5201 N Magnolia Chicago IL 60640

BERMAN, EVA, food broker; b. Havana, Cuba, Oct. 17, 1942; came to U.S., 1960, naturalized, 1965; d. Sender and Taiba (Dworin) Golman; student U. Mich., 1964, N.Y.U., 1967; 1 dau., Raquel. Asst. to intensive English coordinator U. Mich., Ann Arbor, 1964; asst. to univ. plaza residents coordinator N.Y.U., 1966-68; food broker John G. Martin, San Francisco, 1969-74; pres. Sunshine Food Sales, Inc., Miami, Fla., 1974-81; pres., owner E & R Internat. Seafood, Inc., Miami Beach, Fla., 1981—. Treas., Steve Fraser City Council, Sausalito, Calif., 1971. Mem. Nat. Oceanographic Found., Nat. Fisheries Inst., Southeastern Fisheries Assn., Organized Fisherman of Fla., Nat. Assn. Female Execs., Miami Food Brokers Assn., Miami Food Trade Assn. Address: 7640 Bayside Ln Miami Beach FL 33141

BERMAN, LINDA FRAN, lawyer; b. Phila., Feb. 26, 1952; d. Martin and Ruth (Krum) B.; m. Paul M. Perlstein, May 25, 1986. A.B., Princeton U., 1973; postgrad. U. Pa., 1973-74, 80; J.D., Villanova U., 1978. Bar: Pa. 1978. Asst. dir. grants Villanova U. (Pa.), 1978; dir. grants Wistar Inst., Phila., 1979; asst. dir. Am. Law Inst., Phila., 1980; exec. editor Pa. Law Jour., 1980-82; mem. firm Schwartzman & Hepps, Phila., 1982-84; assoc. Berger & Montague, P.C., 1984-85; asst. city solicitor, City of Phila., 1985—. Bd. dirs. Bus. and Profl. Women's Coalition-Fedn. Jewish Agencies, 1982-84; mem. adv. com. Women's Alliance for Job Equity, 1983—; mem. budget allocation rev. com. United Way, 1982—; bd. dirs. Phila. Vol. Lawyers and the Arts, 1984—. Mem. Pa. Bar Assn., Phila. Bar Assn. (chmn. lawyers and arts com. 1982-84), Princeton U. Alumni Schs. Com. ABA (chmn. lawyers and arts com. 1984—), Sigma Delta Chi. Lodges: Hadassah. Democrat. Jewish. Club: Jr. League. Home: 2020 Walnut St Apt 19M Philadelphia PA 19103 Office: Phila City Solicitor's Officer Philadelphia PA 19102

BERMAN, LORETTA ELISABETH, advertising executive; b. Brookline, Mass., Nov. 3, 1949; d. Robert Frederick and Ines (Steigmann) F.; m. Stuart Berman, June 24, 1973 (div. 1980). B.F.A., U. Mass., Boston, 1973. Model, Fashions First WCNB-TV, Boston, 1960-61; copyright asst. Machat & Kronfeld, N.Y.C., 1969-70; model, Boston, 1970-73; legal asst. Hertzberg, Childs & Shiotani, Beverly Hills, Calif., 1974-76; dir. pub. relations Parsons, Friedmann & Central, Boston, 1978—; pres. Projects, Boston, 1982—. Democrat. Jewish. Mem. Nat. Assn. Female Execs., Advt. Club Greater Boston.

BERMAN, MARGO RENEE, advertising agency executive; b. Jersey City, July 8, 1947; d. Jack H. and Blanche (Bram) Breitbart; m. Jack Robert Berman, June 25, 1978. Mus. B., U. Miami (Fla.), 1971, M.Music, 1974, postgrad., 1977. Cert. tchr., Fla. Program host, producer Sta. WLRN-FM, 1977-78; copywriter, Ellman's, Atlanta, 1978-79; advt. supr. Mktg. Services, Hollywood, Fla., 1980-81; writer, account exec. WWJF, Fort Lauderdale, Fla., 1981, WKQS, Fort Lauderdale, 1981-82; producer, copywriter, dir. Hume, Smith, Mickelberry, Miami, Fla., 1982-83; sr. copywriter, dir., producer The Ad Team, North Miami Beach, Fla., 1983-84; prin. Madison Ave. Advt. Co., Inc., Miami Beach, 1984-85, Margo Berman Creative Services, North Miami Beach, 1985—; lectr. in field; judge Miami Herald Cannes Awards, 1984, Clarion Awards, 1986. Author TV and radio commls.: Miami Citizens Against Crime, 1982. Recipient Bronze award Internat. Film Festival of N.Y., 1982, Nat. Advt. Agy. Network, 1982; Bronze Telly award TV Commls. Festival, 1982; 1st place Angel award Fla. Advt. Fedn., 1982; John Caples award for Fla. Power & Light comml., 1983; Addy, awards for Hilton Resort print campaign, 1983, Fla. Power & Light print ad, 1983, Pantry Pride Supermarkets radio campaign, 1983, AmeriFirst devel. radio, Perry Cable radio, J.C. Hillary radio, Security First Fed. Savs. radio, print campaigns; Clarion award, 1985. Mem. Women in Communications (profl. advisor 1982-83, rec. sec. Miami 1984-85, historian 1985-86), Nat. Acad. TV Arts and Scis. (judge Chgo. 1983), Miami Advt. Fedn., Phi Kappa Phi, Sigma Alpha Iota. Home: 3351 NE 164 St North Miami Beach FL 33160 Office: Margo Berman Creative Services 1869 NE 163 St North Miami Beach FL 33162

BERMAN, MONA S. (MRS. CARROLL Z. BERMAN), theatrical dir., producer; b. Jersey City; d. Edward and Mary (Auster) Solomon; m. Carroll Z. Berman; children—Marcie S. Berman Ries, Laura Jane. B.A., Beaver Coll., postgrad. Columbia U., M.F.A., Boston U. Tchr. English, drama Jersey City High Schs.; actress Mass. Valley Players, Holyoke; owner, dir. The Theatre Sch. and Producing Co., Maplewood, N.J.; chmn. drama edn. YM-MWHA of Met. N.J. Cons., Clark Center for Performing Arts, N.Y.C., 1965-66; instr. South Orange, Maplewood Adult Sch., 1967; artistic dir. Children's Theatre Co. Inc., Maplewood, 1968-70; cons. The Whole Theater Co., 1974—; dir. pub. relations Co. 3 by 2. Playwright: Hello Joe, 1967; That Ring in the Center, 1968; The Big Show, 1970; Interim, 1974; Who Can Belong?, 1979; Sudden Changes, 1985. Producer, dir. A Night of Stars. Guest theatre reviewer El Paso Herald Post, 1980-82. Active Boston United Fund, 1955-59, chmn. Boston residential area, 1957; bd. dirs. Greater Boston Girl Scouts Am., 1956-58, Tufts Med. Faculty Wives, 1956-58. Mem. Am. Theater Assn., Playwrights Unit 42d St. Theater Ctr. N.Y.C., Dramatists Guild. Address: #176 454 Prospect Ave West Orange NJ 07052

BERMAN, NIKKI SCHUKAR, marketing company executive; b. El Paso, Feb. 16, 1955; d. Louis M. and Lynn (Kohane) Schukar; m. Howard J. Berman, Sept. 15, 1979 (div. Jan. 1982). Student Stephens Coll., Columbia, Mo., 1973-74. Sales rep. Chiquita Brands, St. Louis, 1976-78, Comp-U-Check, St. Louis, 1978-79; br. mgr. Savs. Plus Systems, St. Louis, 1979-81; div. mgr. Entertainment/Sports Unltd., St. Louis, 1982; dir. mktg. Comet Corp./Cashex, St. Louis, 1982-83, ABKO, Inc., St. Louis, 1983—. Chmn. membership ORT, St. Louis, 1979. Mem. Sales and Mktg. Execs., St. Louis Advt. Club, Assn. Female Execs.

BERMAN, PATRICIA KARATSIS, visual arts specialist; b. San Francisco, Oct. 2, 1953; d. George Emanuel and Hermoine Linda (Foster) Karatsis; m. William Issachar Berman, May 15, 1979; children—Ian, Melissa. B.S., Duke U., 1975; M.A., NYU, 1977. Dir. Vorpal Gallery, N.Y.C., 1976-83; visual arts coordinator East End Art and Humanities Council, Riverhead, N.Y., 1983—; cons. N.y. State Council on Arts, N.Y.C., Suffolk Assn. Jewish Schs., Huntington, N.Y., 1985. Contbr. articles to East End Arts News. Trustee Commack Jewish Ctr., N.Y., 1984—. Home: 22 Daisy Ln Commack NY 11725 Office: East End Art and Humanities Council 133 E Main St Riverhead NY 11901

BERMAN, SIEGRID VISCONTI, interior designer; b. Bremen, Germany, May 22, 1944; came to U.S., 1951, naturalized, 1956; d. Walter L. and Annegrete M. (Wolf) Knapp; self-educated. Designer, Shepard Martin Assocs., N.Y.C., 1968-76; facilities mgr. Unifert, USA, N.Y.C., 1976-78; owner Siegrid Visconti Berman Interiors, N.Y.C., 1978—; dir. interiors DAT Cons., N.Y.C., 1980-83; dir. design Ralph Mancini Assocs., N.Y.C., 1983-85; sr. designer Karco Davis, Inc., dir. Ten Park Ave Corp., 1979-81. Bd. dirs. Temple Spiritual Research and Learning, 1981-82; reader Lighthouse for Blind. Colo. State Coll. scholar, 1962. Mem. AFTRA, Screen Actors Guild. Composer songs, illustrator book. 10007 Office: 52 Duane St New York NY 10017

BERMAN-OLIVO, ROXANNE, health services company executive; b. Durham, N.C., June 22, 1945; d. Morris and Sylvia (Rosenblum) Berman; m. Frank Olivo, Dec. 4, 1965 (div. Apr. 1981); children—Alex, Aaron. B.A., SUNY-N.Y.C., 1983. Asst. dir. pub. relations Assn. Vol. Sterilization, N.Y.C., 1965-69; freelance pub. relations NARAL/ARM, N.Y.C., 1969-80; exec. dir. Nat. Abortion Rights Action League, N.Y.C., 1974-75, Abortion Rights Mobilization, 1977-78; v.p. Comprehensive Profl. Systems, N.Y.C., 1980—. Pres. Lenox Hill Democratic Club, N.Y.C., 1974-76; vice chmn. Community Bd. 6, N.Y.C., 1976-78, Beth Israel Methadone Com., N.Y.C., 1976-78; mem. Labor Council, Queens, N.Y., Nassau Civic Club, N.Y.C., 1982—, Nat. Maritime Port Council, N.Y.C., 1983—, Assn. Benefit Adminstrn., N.Y.C., March of Dimes, 1985—. Mem. Nat. Assn. Female Execs. Jewish. Club: Herat (N.Y.C.) (nat. bd. dirs. 1984-85). Lodge: B'nai B'rith. Home: 333 E 23d St New York NY 10010 Office: Comprehensive Profl Systems 144 E 24th St New York NY 10010

BERN, PAULA R., company executive, author; b. Pitts., July 27, 1934; m. Joseph Bern, Dec. 21, 1954; children—Bruce, Caryn, Marshall, Samuel, Rona. B.A., Pa. State U., 1956; M.A., U. Pitts., 1978, Ph.D., 1980. Editor-in-chief Jaffe Pub. Co., Los Angeles, 1958-63; on-air producer Sta. WQED-TV, Pitts., 1963-65; dir. univ. relations and devel. Robert Morris Coll., Pitts. and Coraopolis, 1965-69, Point Park Coll., Pitts., 1969-72; pres. Bern Assocs., Inc., 1972—; vis. prof. journalism Duquesne U., Pitts., 1967—; faculty mem. sr. exec. seminars Carnegie Mellon U. Grad. Sch. Pub. and Urban Affairs, 1985—. Author: Point Park College: A History, 1980; How to Work for a Woman Boss* When You'd Really Rather Not*, 1986. Trustee Pitts. Ballet Theatre, Inc., 1973—; bd. dirs. Council for Internat. Visitors, 1975—, Exec. Women's Council, 1980—; mem. adv. council Internat. Poetry Forum, 1979—; com. mem. Strategic Planning Com., Mt. Lebanon Twp., 1982—. Mem. Women in Communications, Pub. Relations Soc. Am., Delta Sigma Rho, Phi Beta Kappa. Republican. Club: Women's Press. Office: Bern Assocs Inc 3 Parkway Ctr Pittsburgh PA 15220

BERNABEI, LORA, university business official; b. White Plains, N.Y., May 3, 1948; d. Antonio and Colomba Domenica (Barbati) B. B.A., Fordham U., 1970; M.A., City U. N.Y., 1972; M.B.A., NYU, 1985. Speech pathologist N.Y. State Dept. Mental Hygiene, Wassaic, 1972-74, New Rochelle Hosp. Med. Ctr. (N.Y.), 1974-75; faculty instr. U. Wis.-Stevens Point, 1975-76; systems analyst Medicaid Program, State of Wis., Madison, 1976-77, Systems Group, Inc., Washington, 1977-80; adminstr. Marine Tech. Soc., Washington, 1980-81; fin. analyst Fashion Inst. Tech., SUNY, N.Y.C., 1981-86; adminstr. King Main Hurdman, C.P.A.s, N.Y.C., 1986—; actress dinner theater, regional theater, cable TV, 1977-80. Pres. Rockville Musical Theatre (Md.), 1978; founder Montgomery Theatre Alliance (Md.), 1979; bd. dirs. Silver Spring Stage (Md.), 1979; active Commn. for Women, Portage County, Wis., 1976, ACLU, Wis., 1975-80; del. State Democratic Conv., Wis., 1976. U.S. Office Edn. fellow, 1971. Mem. Am. Speech and Hearing Assn., Nat. Assn. Coll. and Univ. Bus. Officers, Eastern Assn. Coll. and Univ. Bus. Officers. Home: 307 E 44th St New York NY 10017 Office: Fashion Inst Tech SUNY 227 W 27th St New York NY 10001

BERNARD, LOLA, social worker, educator; b. Rockaway Beach, N.Y., Nov. 9, 1928; d. Clark and Antoinette (Berger) Bernard. B.A., Roosevelt U., 1949; M.A., U. Houston, 1952; M.S.W., Tulane U., 1954; Ph.D., Bryn Mawr Coll., 1967. Dir. social service Touro Infirmary, New Orleans, 1957-60; prof. Tulane U., New Orleans, 1965-69; dean sch. social work Fla. State U., Tallahassee, 1969-79; dir. doctoral program Va. Commonwealth U., Richmond, 1979-85; exec. dir. Council on Social Work Edn., Washington, 1985—; cons. Council Social Work Edn., 1972—, chmn. commn. on accreditation, 1972-75. Editorial bd. Women and Social Work, 1985—. Contbr. articles to profl. jours. Bd. dirs. New Orleans Home for Incurables, 1960-62, Long Term Health Care, Richmond, 1983-85, Condo World, Panama City, Fla., 1985. Named Alumna of Year, Tulane U., 1977; Outstanding Faculty, Sch. Social Work, Va. Commonwealth U., 1984. Fellow Psi Chi; mem. Nat. Council Social Welfare Nat. Assn. Social Work, Council on Social Work Edn. Democrat. Avocations: kite flying; beachcombing; writing; reading; travel. Office: Council on Social Work Edn 1744 R St Washington DC 20009

BERNARD, MARY ELIZABETH, state legislator; b. Dover, N.H.; d. Arthur P. and Margaret (Donnelly) O'Gorman; m. Albert O. Bernard, June 29, 1935. Grad. Carney Hosp. Sch. Nursing, Boston, 1929; student McIntosh Bus. Coll. R.N., Mass. Mem., N.H. Ho. of Reps., 1967-75, 81-86, 5-term mem. regulated revenues com.; historian State of N.H., 1973-74; county clk. County of Strafford (N.H.), 1973-74. Treas., Democratic City Com., Dover, 1965-82; clk. Strafford County Delegation, 1973-74, 81-84; mem. St. Mary Parish Council, Dover, 1977-80. Mem. Catholic Daus. Am.

BERNAS, ELIZABETH ARLENE SNYDER, nurse; b. Mt. Pleasant, Pa., Nov. 25, 1934; d. James H. Snyder and Ruth Catherine (Ferry) Snyder Sprung; m. Albert Earl Bernas, Oct. 1, 1955; children—Debra, Mark, Jeffrey, Brian. R.N., Latrobe Hosp. Sch. Nursing, 1955; postgrad. Lynchburg Coll., 1981. Gen. duty nurse Latrobe Hosp. (Pa.), 1955-57; pvt. duty nurse LaPlata Hosp. (Md.), 1959; vol. nurse ARC, Lynchburg, Va., 1965—; gen. duty nurse Lynchburg Coll., 1969—, coordinator health edn., 1979—, dir. student health services, 1982—. Contbr. articles to profl. jours. Vol., Republican party, Lynchburg, 1968; sec. Blue Ridge Farms Civic Assn., Lynchburg, 1966-67; den mother Boy Scouts Am., Lynchburg, 1966-68; advisor Omni Club, Lynchburg, 1982-84, Sexual Awareness Peer Group, Lynchburg, 1983-84, Alcohol Awareness Group, 1979—. Mem. Am. Nurses Assn., Va. Nurses Assn., Am. Coll. Health Assn., Mid-Atlantic Coll. Health Assn. Presbyterian. Clubs: Blumont Garden (historian 1960-63), Order of DeMolay (treas. 1976, 78), Mothers (v.p. 1975-76, pres. 1976). Home: 3025 Cardinal Pl Lynchburg VA 24503 Office: Lynchburg Coll Student Health Services Lynchburg VA 24501

BERNAY, BETTI (MRS. J. BERNARD GOLDFARB), artist; b. N.Y.C.; d. David Michael and Anna Gaynia (Bernay) Woolin; grad. costume design Pratt Inst., 1946; student Nat. Acad., N.Y.C., 1947-49, Art Students League, N.Y.C., 1950-51; m. J. Bernard Goldfarb, Apr. 19, 1947; children—Manette Deitsch, Karen Lynn. One-Woman shows at Galerie Raymond Duncan, Paris, Salas Municipales, San Sebastian, Spain, Circulo de Bellas Artes, Madrid, Bacardi Gallery, Miami, Fla., Columbia (S.C.) Mus., Columbus (Ga.) Mus., Galerie Andre Weil, Paris, France, Galerie Hermitage, Montecarlo, Monaco, Casino de San Remo (Italy), Galerie de Arte de la Caja de Ahorros de Ronda, Malaga, Spain, Centro Artistico, Granada, Spain, Circulo de la Amistad, Cordoba, Spain, Galerie Andre Weil, Paris, France, Studio Gallery H, N.Y.C., Walter Wallace Gallery, Palm Beach, Fla., Museo Bellas Artes, Malaga, Spain, Harbor House Gallery, Miami Beach, Fla., Crystal House Gallery, Miami Beach, Fla., Internat. Gallery, Jordan Marsh, Miami, Fontainebleau Gallery, Miami Beach, Fla., Carriage House Gallery, Miami Beach; exhibited in group shows at Painters and Sculptors Soc., Jersey City (N.J.) Mus., Salon de Invierno, Museo Malaga, Spain, Salon des Beaux Arts, Cannes, France, Nat. Acad. Gallery, N.Y.C., Salon des Artistes Independants, Paris, Salon des Artistes Francais, Paris, Salon Populiste, Paris, Salon de Otono, Madrid, Spain, Salamagundi Club, N.Y.C., Nat. Assn. Painters and Sculptors Spain, Madrid, Phipps Gallery, Palm Beach, Fla., Lever House, N.Y.C., Knickerbocker Artists, N.Y.C., Artists Equity, Hollywood (Fla.) Mus., Nat. Arts Gallery, N.Y.C., Springfield (Mass.) Mus., ACA Gallery, N.Y.C., Argent Gallery, N.Y.C., Nat. Acad. Gallery, N.Y.C., Gables Art Gallery, Miami, Gibralter Internat. Art Exhbn., Gault Gallery Cheltenham, Phila., Century Gallery,

Miami, Fla., Met. Mus. and Art Center, Miami, Lord & Taylor Gallery, N.Y.C., Pageant Gallery, Galerie 99 (both Miami), Rosenbaum Gallery, Palm Beach, Fla., Planet Ocean, Miami, Jockey Club Art Gallery, Miami; represented in permanent collections at Museo de Malaga, Circulo de la Amistad, Cordoba, Spain, I.O.S. Found., Geneva, Switzerland, Columbia (S.C.) Mus., others. Recipient Medal for artistic merit City of N.Y., Sch. Art Leagues, N.Y.C.; Prix de Paris, Raymond Duncan, 1958; others. Mem. Nat. Assn. Painters and Sculptors Spain, Nat. Assn. Women Artists, Societe des Artistes Francais, Societe des Artistes Ind., Fedn. Francais des Societes d'Art Graphique et Plastique, Artists Equity, Am. Artists Profl. League, Women's Caucus for Art, Profl. Artists Guild, Nat. Soc. Lit. and the Arts, Am. Fedn. Art, South Fla. Shell Club. Address: 10155 Collins Ave Bal Harbour FL 33154

BERNHARDT, LINDA BAILEY, marketing executive; b. Baldwin, Wis., Oct. 31, 1947; d. Don and Jeanne (Olson) Bailey; m. Carlos Martin, 1972 (div. 1974); m. 2d David Bernhardt, 1977 (div. 1984); 1 son, Alexander Justin. B.A., Gustavus Adolphus Coll., St. Peter, Minn., 1969; M.B.A., U. Miami-Coral Gables, 1972. Mgr. consumer research Burger King Corp., Miami, Fla., 1972-74, 76-77; research mgr. grocery div. Pillsbury Co., Mpls., 1975; dir. mktg. services Arvida Corp., Miami, 1977-80; pres., owner Bernhardt & Assocs., Atlanta, 1980-83; v.p. mktg. Uniflex Corp., Atlanta, 1983-84; v.p. mktg. services Arvida Disney Corp., 1985—. Contbg. author: Modern Marketing, 1978. Recipient scholarship Student Project for Amity among Nations U. Minn., 1968. Mem. Am. Mktg. Assn., Urban Land Instr. Republican. Home: 4455 NW 27th Ave Boca Raton FL 33434 Office: Arvida Disney Corp 5550 Glades Rd Boca Raton FL 33432

BERNHEIM, BARBARA WELT, editor, civic volunteer; b. Chgo., Oct. 12, 1938; d. Bernard David and Ida (Zolte) Welt; m. Charles Alexander Bernheim, June 6, 1964 (div. 1972). B.A., Smith Coll., 1960; M.A. in English, NYU, 1966, Ph.D. in English, 1977. Editorial asst. Look mag., N.Y.C., 1967; tchr. English composition NYU, 1971-72; editor-in-chief Ark House Ltd., N.Y.C., 1978-80; editor UN, Econ. and Social Council, Offices of Sec.-Gen., Office of Secretariat Services for Econ. and Social Matters, N.Y., 1980-83; freelance editor, N.Y.C., 1984—. Sec., Jr. League of N.Y., Inc., 1972-74, bd. dirs., 1972-74, admissions com., 1974-76, 85-86, area council liaison, 1974-75, sec. admissions com., 1975-76, mem., 1968—; vice chmn. WOR-TV for Elderly, 1970-71, chmn. fund raising event, 1970, 71, mem. ways and means com., 1971-72; researcher 75th Ann. Observer, 1974-75, sec. fund raising event, 1974-75; tchr. English to foreigners, 1976-79, mem. sustainers com., 1980—, mem. long-range planning com., 1986—; bd. dirs. hospitality com. for UN Dels., Inc., 1968-70, mem., 1964—; bd. dirs. Drama League of N.Y., Inc., 1978-79; mem. com. for hosps. Nat. Entertainment Service, 1966-69; chmn. Young Friends of N.Y.C. Ctr., 1967-69; mem. Aux. of N.Y. Infirmary (now N.Y.Infirmary-Beekman Downtown Hosp.), 1974—, sec., 1979—; class fundraiser for N.Y.C. Smith Coll. Alumnae Fund, 1976-85; assoc. Mt. Sinai Hosp. Assocs. Program (jr. bd.), 1983-85; mem. women's com. N.Y.C. div. Am. Cancer Soc., 1983—, membership co-chmn., 1986. Mem. MLA, Friends of Dove Cottage. Clubs: River, Cosmopolitan (N.Y.C.).

BERNHEIM, HEATHER STANCHFIELD PETERSON (MRS. CHARLES BERNHEIM), civic worker; b. Houston; d. Weed and Mylla (Stanchfield) Peterson; student U. Tex., 1938-42; m. Charles A. Bernheim, July 18, 1973. Docent chmn. Harris County Heritage Soc., 1969-70, v.p., after 1970; vol. worker Hermann Hosp., 1968-69; team capt. Mus. Fine Arts Ball, Houston, 1969; maintenance fund drive worker Mus. Fine Arts, 1970, trustee, chmn. costume council; docent Costume Inst., Met. Mus. Art, N.Y.C., 1978, co-chmn. Costume Inst., 1980-81, chmn., 1981-82, mus. guide, 1978—; auction chmn. Bluebonnet Ball, Harris County Heritage Soc., 1984; bd. dirs. Planned Parenthood N.Y.C. Mem. N.Y. Jr. League, Kappa Alpha Theta Alumni Assn. Club: Houston. Home: 33 E 70th St Apt S-E New York NY 10021 also 173 Sage Rd Houston TX 77056

BERNHEIM, SADYE KERN, lawyer; b. Monroe, La., Aug. 10, 1955; d. Sadrian Kern and Arvenia (May) B.; m. Gerald Wayne Merritt, Nov. 7, 1981; children—Sadrian Kern, Cale Alexander. B.A., Northeast La. U., Monroe, 1976, J.D., Loyola U., New Orleans, 1979. Bar: La. 1980. Atty., Law Offices Sadye Kern Bernheim, Monroe, 1980—; cooperating atty. N. La. Legal Assistance Corp., Monroe, 1983—, Gen. Motors-UAW, Detroit, 1983-85, Pro Bono Elderly Project. Mem. Northeast La. U. Student Correctional Assn. (v.p., organizer), ABA, La. State Trial Lawyers Assn., La. State Bar Assn., Fourth Jud. Dist. Bar Assn. (mem. com. on profl. responsibility 1985-86), Am. Trial Lawyers Assn., Alpha Phi Sigma, Phi Alpha Delta (pres., sec. O'Niell chpt.), Blue Key. Republican. Jewish. Home: 1420 Park Ave Monroe LA 71201 Office: 1200 N 18th St Monroe LA 71201

BERNKRANT, PAULA SPENCE, publisher's representative; b. Bourne, Mass., Oct. 30, 1956; d. Alfred P. and Pauline (Anderson) Spence; m. Keith D. Bernkrant, Sept. 6, 1981. A.A., Brevard Community Coll., 1977; B.S. in Bus. Adminstrn., U. Central Fla., 1979. Pub.'s rep. Bus. Publs., Inc., Orlando, Fla., 1979-81, Los Angeles, 1982—; account mgr. Midas Systems, Santa Ana, Calif., 1981-82. Mem. Am. Mktg. Assn. Republican. Home: PO Box 715 Leona Valley CA 93550

BERNS, ELLEN MARSHA SCHIMMEL, designer, artist; b. Bklyn., Oct. 3, 1948; d. Milton O. and Ruth Mildred (Mall) Schimmel; student U. Okla., Norman, 1966-68; B.A. in Art History and Art, U. Tex., Austin, 1970; cert. in interior design, El Centro Coll., Dallas, 1978; postgrad. Parsons Sch. Design, N.Y.C., 1978-79, NAD, 1980—, Am. Watercolor scholar, 1982. Fashion coordinator Neiman Marcus, 1971-73, exec. trainee 1973-74; display designer Apparel Mart and Trade Mart, 1972; owner, operator Ellen S. Berns Interiors, Dallas, 1974-78; artist, interior designer LCL Design Assos., Inc., N.Y.C., 1980-81, Swanke Hayden Connell Architects, N.Y.C., 1981—; commns. include: art for conf. area Judi S. Hall Interiors, San Francisco, 1981, Nursery wall mural Marble Collegiate Ch., 1980, editorial and conceptual illustrations Nat. Assn. Credit Mgmt., 1981, sidewalk pedestal clock 52 Madison Ave.; works exhibited Temple Emanuel, Dallas, 1978, Parsons Sch. Design, 1979, 82, Suzanne's Gallery, N.Y.C., 1980; freelance artist, designer rugs Sylvan-Garret Showroom, 1978, Peter Wolf & Assocs., 1975; lectr. Parsons Sch. Design. Mem. Am. Soc. Interior Designers, Art Students League, Women in Design (assoc.). Home: 1365 York Ave Apt 35H New York NY 10021 Office: 400 Park Ave New York NY 10028

BERNSTEIN, CARYL SALOMON, lawyer; b. N.Y.C., Dec. 22, 1933; d. Gustav and Rosalind (Aron) Salomon; m. William D. Terry, June 12, 1955 (div. 1967); children—Ellen Deborah, Mark David; m. Robert L. Cole, Jr., Oct. 25, 1970 (div. 1975); m. George K. Berstein, June 17, 1979. B.A. with honors, Cornell U., 1955; J.D., Georgetown U., 1967. Bar: D.C. 1968, U.S. Dist. Ct. D.C. 1968, U.S. Ct. Appeals (D.C. cir.) 1968, U.S. Supreme Ct. 1971; Atty. Covington & Burling, Washington, 1967-73; staff atty. Overseas Pvt. Investment Corp., Washington, 1973-74, asst. gen. counsel, 1974-77, v.p. for ins., 1977-81; sr. v.p., gen. counsel, sec. Fed. Nat. Mortgage Assn., Washington, 1981-82, exec. v.p., gen. counsel, sec., 1982—; dir. Nat. Housing Conf., 1983—. Contbr. articles to profl. jours.; bd. editors: Georgetown Law Jour., 1966; editorial adv. bd. Housing and Devel. Reporter, 1986—. Mem. Women's Legal Def. Fund, Washington, 1981—; bd. regents Georgetown U., 1986—. N.Y. Regents scholar, 1951-55; recipient Leadership award Catalyst, N.Y.C., 1984. Mem. ABA, Fed. Bar Assn., D.C. Bar Assn., Am. Soc. Internat. Law, Phi Beta Kappa, Phi Kappa Phi. Office: 3900 Wisconsin Ave NW Washington DC 20016

BERNSTEIN, JOSEPHINE HELENA, clin. psychologist; b. Chgo., July 5, 1929; d. Emanuel Bernard and Bessie Birdie (Kaplan) Fink; B.A., UCLA, 1952, M.A., 1956, Ph.D., 1961; m. Joseph C. Bernstein, Dec. 18, 1965 (dec.); 1 son, Allen Emanuel. Intern, UCLA Clinic, 1953; clin. psychology trainee VA, Los Angeles, 1953-56, 58-60; caseworker Jewish Com. for Personal Service, Los Angeles, 1957-58; clin. psychologist VA Outpatient Clinic, Los Angeles, 1960-61; clin. psychologist Rancho Los Amigos Hosp., Los Angeles, 1962-63, Brentwood VA Hosp., Los Angeles, 1963-65, Gateways Hosp., Los Angeles, 1965-69, chief psychologist, 1966-69; asst. chief psychologist Westwood Meth. Ch. Clinic, Los Angeles, 1964-66; clin. psychologist Los Angeles County Mental Health Clinic, Juvenile Hall, 1972—; tchr. Calif. Grad. Inst., 1971—, pres. bd. trustees, 1979-81. Mem. Los Angeles County Psychol. Assn., Calif. State Psychol. Assn., Am. Psychol. Assn., Internat. Transactional Assn., Psi Chi, Pi Gamma Mu. Home: 2345 Longden Dr San Marino CA 91108 Office: 1605 Eastlake Los Angeles CA 90033

BERNSTEIN, LEA HOPE, lawyer; b. Chgo., Apr. 4, 1937; d. Boris and Rose (Tenenbaum) Kummel; m. Herbert A. Blum (div.); children—Merle S., Barry K., Howard E.; m. 2d, Robert Bernstein, Feb. 11, 1971 (div. 1979). B.S., DePaul U., 1976; J.D., 1980. C.P.A., Ill.; bar: Ill. 1980. Paralegal, D'Ancona & Pflaum, Chgo., 1971-77; acct. Fields & Fields, Chgo., 1977; controller Taico Design Products, Chgo., 1977-78; acct. Bernstein & Bank, Lincolnwood, Ill., 1978-80; assoc. Levenfeld, Eisenberg, Chgo., 1980-82; sole practice, Chgo., 1983—. Contbr. articles to profl. jours. Bell & Howell achievement scholar, 1975. Mem. Chgo. Soc. Women C.P.A.s, Am. Inst. C.P.A.s, Ill. C.P.A. Soc., Chgo. Bar Assn., ABA. Home: 8512 N Harding Ave Skokie IL 60076 Office: Lea Hope Bernstein & Assocs 175 N Franklin St Suite 303 Chicago IL 60606

BERNSTEIN, RHONDA, lawyer; b. Flushing, N.Y., June 2, 1955; d. Kurt and Sylvia (Kleiner) Leighton; m. David Alan Bernstein, July 2, 1978. B.A. cum laude, Washington U. St. Louis, 1977; J.D., Hofstra U., 1980. Bar: N.Y. 1981, Fla. 1981. Assoc. Krolick & DeGraff, Albany, N.Y., 1980-81; sr. assoc. George E. Mueller, Jr., P.A., Tampa, Fla., 1981—. Mem. ABA, N.Y. State Bar Assn., Hillsborough County Bar Assn., Fla. Indsl. Devel. Council, Pi Sigma Alpha, Omicron Delta Kappa. Democrat. Jewish. Home: 1599 Willow Brook Dr Palm Harbor FL 33563 Office: 4830 W Kennedy Blvd Tampa FL 33609

BERNSTEIN, SHERYL ANNE, retail store executive; b. Orange, N.J., Dec. 25, 1959; d. Lawrence Edward and Judith Fay (Bauch) B. B.S. in Bus. Adminstrn., Boston U., 1981. Salesperson, Bloomingdale's, Boston, 1978-81, Short Hills, N.J., summer, 1978, asst. buyer, N.Y.C., 1981-82, dept. mgr., Tysons Corner, Va., 1982-83, assoc. buyer, N.Y.C., 1983, buyer, 1983—; buying intern J.C. Penney Co., Inc., N.Y.C., summer 1980. Recruiter, interviewer Sch. of Mgmt., Boston U., 1982—. Mem. Boston U. Alumni Assn. Jewish. Home: 150 E 30th St Apt 3G New York NY 10016 Office: Bloomingdale's 1000 3d Ave New York NY 10021

BERNSTEIN, SUSAN POWELL, development and fundraising executive; b. Chgo., May 17, 1938; d. Herman and Frances (Dobkin) Powell; m. Phillip Bernstein, Sept. 4, 1957; children—Kenneth, Robert, Michael. B.A. in Human Services, Northeastern Ill. U., Chgo., 1978. Real estate assoc. Martin-Marbry, Inc., Skokie, Ill., 1971—; exec. dir. B'nai B'rith Women, Land of Lakes Region, Skokie, 1978-83; dir. resource devel. Travelers and Immigrants Aid, Chgo., 1984—. Founder Nat. Forum for Women, Woodstock, Ill., pres., dir., 1980-83; bd. dirs., treas. Y-Me Breast Cancer Program, Chgo., 1984-86; mem. planning com. Jane Addams Conf. for Peace in Nuclear Age; pro-peace march vol. Named Citizen of Yr., Lerner Life newspapers, Chgo., 1980. Mem. Nat. Soc. Fundraising Execs. (Chgo. chpt.), Women in Devel. Professions, NOW. Democrat. Jewish. Home: 8414 Kedvale St Skokie IL 60076 Office: Travelers and Immigrants Aid 327 S LaSalle St Suite 1500 Chicago IL 60604

BERO, MARILYN PROCINO, civic worker, corporate professional; b. Auburn, N.Y., Sept. 12, 1937; d. Jack Anthony and Mary Louise (Cefaratti) Procino; B.A. in Elem. Edn., Marywood Coll., 1959; postgrad. Syracuse U., 1961; m. James Donald Bero, Feb. 10, 1962; children—Mark J., Michael A., Matthew R. Tchr. 3d grade Auburn Sch. System, 1959-61. Sec.-treas. Hampton Rd. Constrn. Corp., Seneca Falls, N.Y. Mem. Seneca Falls (N.Y.) Sch. Dist. Bd., 1976-85, v.p., 1978, pres., 1980-83, dir., 1978—; co-chmn. bldg. fund drive Nat. Women's Hall of Fame, Inc., Seneca Falls, 1978-79, pres., 1980-83; bd. dirs. Seneca County Child Care Ctr., 1975-84, pres., 1976-79; bd. dirs. Alpha Day Sch., Seneca Falls, 1972-75, Happiness House, Geneva, N.Y., 1968-72, CAUSE; adv. commn. Women's Rights Nat. Hist. Park. Named Rotary Citizen of Yr., 1983. Mem. AAUW, Women's League Seneca Falls (pres. 1978-79). Republican. Roman Catholic. Home: 2934 Route 89 Seneca Falls NY 13148 Office: Hampton Rd Construction Corp 2934 Route 89 Seneca Falls NY 13148

BERRET, BETH ANN, employment manager; b. Endicott, N.Y., Oct. 12, 1956; d. Edward Harvey and Esther Caroline (Webber) Bachman; m. James Joseph Berret, Aug. 27, 1983. B.S., Bloomsburg U., 1978; M.B.A., Phila. Coll. Textiles & Sci., 1984. Asst. to adminstr. Homeland, Harrisburg, Pa., 1978; asst. adminstr. Cameron Manor, Indiana, Pa., 1978-80, employment rep. The Fairmount Inst., Phila., 1980-82; employment mgr. The Reading Hosp. and Med. Ctr., Pa., 1982—. Mem. Hosp. Employment Mgrs. Phila., Internat. Assn. Personnel Women, Am. Soc. Personnel Adminstrn., Nat. Assn. Nurse Recruiters. Home: 1840 Shellbark Dr Sinking Spring PA 19608 Office: The Reading Hosp and Med Ctr Reading PA 19603

BERRIAN VIOLA, DIANE, architectural lighting design company owner; b. N.Y.C., May 1, 1956; d. Thomas P. and Doris J. (Seifried) Berrian; m. Denis Francis Viola, June 6, 1981. B.F.A. in Environ. Design, Parson Sch. Design, 1981. Project mgr. Jules G. Horton Lighting Design, Inc., N.Y.C., 1980-81; lighting specialist Kallen & Lemelson Cons. Engrs., N.Y.C., 1981-83; pres., owner Berrian Viola Associates Inc., N.Y.C., 1983—; guest lectr. Cooper Union Sch. Architecture. Mem. Internat. Assn. Lighting Designers (sr. assoc. 1983—), Illuminating Engring. Soc., Archtl. League N.Y., Nat. Trust for Hist. Preservation. Roman Catholic. Office: Berrian Viola Associates Inc 153 Conant Valley Rd Pound Ridge NY 10576

BERRIEN, EDITH HEAL, author, professor emeritus; b. Chgo., Aug. 23, 1903; d. Charles Frederick and Eva (Page) Heal; m. Gil Meywier, Oct. 30, 1930 (div. 1944); m. Stephen Berrien, Nov. 22, 1944 (dec. 1982). P.H.B., U. Chgo., 1925; M.A., Columbia U., 1956. Copywriter advt. dept. Marshall Field & Co., Chgo., 1926-28, Sears Roebuck & Co., Chgo., 1930-35, Tucson Daily Citizen, 1935-42; copy chief promotions Conde Nast Publs., N.Y.C., 1944-53, 58-70; prof. Fairleigh Dickinson U., Rutherford N.J., 1953-74. Author: Robin Hood, 1928; The Topaz Seal, 1928; Siegfried, How the World Began, 1930; How the World is Changing, 1931; (as Margaret Powers) World of Insects, 1931; (as Eileen Page) Hound of Culain, 1931; Mr. Pink and the House on the Rook, 1941; (with Louis E. Asher) Send No Money, 1942; Dogie Boy, 1943; This Very Sun, 1944; The Golden Bowl, 1947; Teen-Age Manual, 1948; First Book of America, 1952; Tim Trains his Terrier, 1952; The Shadow Boxers, 1956; (with William Carlos Williams) I Wanted to Write a Poem, 1958; The Young Executive's Wife, 1958; What Happened to Jenny, 1962; (as Edith Heal Berrien) Visual Thinking in Advertising, 1963; Careers, 1966; August Break, 1984; contbr. short stories and articles to jours. in field. Past bd. dirs. Women's Met. Golf Assn. Mem. Soc. Midland Authors.

BERRONES, LUCIA JOSETTE, lawyer; b. East Chicago, Ind., Mar. 3, 1953; d. Florentino and Josephine (Castel) Berrones. B.A. in Polit. Sci. and Spanish, Ind. U., 1975; J.D., Valparaiso U., 1978. Bar: Ind., 1979, Hawaii, 1980. Law clk., atty. Walter J. Alvarez, Inc., Merrillville, Ind., 1978-80; staff atty. Corp. Counsel, Honolulu, 1980-82; staff atty. Legal Aid Soc. Hawaii, Honolulu, 1982—, Legal Aid Soc. Hawaii, Honolulu, 1982—. Mem. ABA, Hawaiis Womens Lawyers Assn., Hawaii Bar Assn., Ind. Bar Assn. Roman Catholic. Office: Legal Aid Soc Hawaii 1108 Nuuanu Ave Honolulu HI 96817

BERRY, ANN ROPER, diplomat; b. Cleve., Nov. 9, 1934; d. Frank Carson and Doris (Decker) Roper; m. Maxwell K. Berry, Feb. 11, 1959; children—Walter F., Helen D. B.A., Ohio Wesleyan U., 1956; M.Ed., U. Md., 1964. Asst. budget and fiscal officer Am. embassy, Baghdad, Iraq, 1958-59; various teaching positions, Turkey, Zambia and U.S., 1961-75; internat. economist Dept. of State, Washington, 1975-77, asst. chief textiles div., 1977-80; econ. officer Am. embassy, Athens, Greece, 1980-82; dep. chief textile negotiator U.S. Trade Rep., Washington, 1982-84; mem. NATO Def. Coll., Rome, 1984; counselor for econ. affairs Am. embassy, Paris, 1985—. Recipient Superior Honor award Dept. of State, 1980. Mem. Phi Beta Kappa. Office: Am Embassy APO New York NY 09777

BERRY, JOYCE T., government administrator; B.A., Howard U., 1969, M.A., 1970; Ph.D., Fordham U., 1976; J.D. Georgetown U., 1983. Edn. program officer AID, U.S. Dept. State, 1970-71; manpower devel. specialist U.S. Dept. Labor, 1971-74; edn. and tng. officer Adminstrn. on Aging, U.S. Dept. Health and Human Services, N.Y.C., 1974-77, assoc. commr. edn. and tng., 1980-83, dep. assoc. commr. program devel., 1983-85, assoc. commr. Adminstrn. on Aging, 1985—; adj. prof. New Sch. Social Research, 1976; spl. asst. to asst. sec. for rural devel. U.S. Dept. Agr., 1978-80; guest lectr. Recipient Spl. Achievement award U.S. Dept. Agr., 1979, Outstanding Achievement award, 1979. Mem. Nat. Bar Assn., Assn. Gerontology in Higher Edn., Gerontol. Soc., Nat. Council on Aging, Southeast D.C. Community Orgn., Nat. Ctr. for Black Aged. Office: 3015 Park Dr SE Washington DC 20020

BERRY, JULIA FRANCES, produce company executive; b. Uvalde, Tex., June 30, 1943; d. Claude McGill and Frances Courtenay (Stockley) Allen; m. Henry J. Berry (dec. 1982); children—Ferral Milton, Julie Faith, Claude McGill. Student Sul Ross U., 1965-67. Sec. Alpine Natural Gas Co., Tex., 1965-67; receptionist Universal Book Bindery, San Antonio, 1969-70, Watkins Bridge Co., Uvalde, 1970-75; owner, pres. Henry J. Berry Co., Uvalde, 1982—. Mem. Redbook (Bus. Charter award 1983-84), Produce Reporter Co., Tex. Watermelon Assn., Tex. Fruit and Vegetable Assn. Republican. Episcopalian. Club: Uvalde Green Thumb Garden. Avocation: raising and racing Am. quarter horses. Home: 8 Buena Vista Dr Uvalde TX 78801 Office: Henry J Berry Co PO Box 1687 Uvalde TX 78801

BERRY, KATHRYN ELIZABETH, public relations executive; b. Long Beach, Calif., Oct. 29, 1942; d. Richard Phillip and Dorothy Kathryn (Horton) Berry; 1 child, Christopher Richard. A.A., Long Beach City Coll., 1963; student Calif. State U.-Long Beach, 1963-65. Sec. advt. Press Telegram, Long Beach, Calif., 1962-64, pub. relations coordinator, 1964-68, sec. to editor, 1969-70, pub. relations mgr., 1971—; account exec. Ind. Jour., San Rafael, Calif., 1968-69; sec. to pres. Calif. State U.-Long Beach, 1970-71. Contbr. articles to profl. jours. Mem. adv. council Long Beach Children's Mus., 1984—; pres. Women's Council, Long Beach, 1984-85, bd. dirs., 1982—; chmn. pub. info. United Way, Region III, Los Angeles, 1983—; advisor Jr. League Long Beach, 1985—. Recipient 1st place pub. relations award Internat. Newspaper Promotion Assn., 1984. Mem. Internat. Newspaper Promotion Assn., C. of C., Publicity Club of Los Angeles. Avocations: travel; theater; music; needlepoint; collecting antiques; reading. Home: 2109 Rutgers Ave Long Beach CA 90815 Office: Press Telegram 604 Pine Ave Long Beach CA 90844

BERRY, LESTA JEAN, lawyer, holding company executive; b. Iowa City, Iowa, June 7, 1940; d. Lester Jacob and Mary Viola (Droll) Gafeller; m. William Joseph Berry, Mar. 21, 1964. B.B.A., U. Iowa, 1964; J.D., DePaul U., 1978. C.P.A., Ill.; bar: Ill. 1978. Tax acct., sr. income tax acct. United Airlines, Inc., Chgo., 1964-73, mgr. income taxes, 1977-80, dir. taxes, 1980-85, v.p. taxes, 1986—; sr. tax acct. Sears Roebuck & Co., Chgo., 1973-77. Mem. ABA, Ill. Bar Assn., Chgo. Bar Assn., Tax Execs. Inst. Office: UAL Inc PO Box 66919 Chicago IL 60666

BERRY, LYLA LOUISE, nurse, consulting firm executive; b. Pottawattime County, Iowa, Dec. 4, 1934; d. Lyle Edward and Letha Leota (Walter) Armstrong; m. Robert William Berry III, July 1, 1965 (div. 1971); children—Thelma Lynn, Bartholowmew Benjamin. R.N. diploma Mercy Hosp., Council Bluffs, Iowa, 1955; B.A. in Mgmt. St. Mary's Coll., Moraga, Calif., 1978; M.A. in Mgmt., U. Phoenix, 1983. R.N., Calif., Ariz.; adult edn. credential, Calif. Edn. dir. Health Maintenance Assn., Phoenix, 1975-77; instr., presenter Maricopa Community Coll., Phoenix, 1977-80; dir. nursing Doctors Hosp., Santa Ana, Calif., 1980-82; dir. edn. Vocat. Nursing, Garden Grove, Calif., 1982-83; edn. coordinator Care Unit Hosp., Orange, Calif., 1983-84; pres. Health Edn. Tng. Cons., Inc., Brea, Calif., 1983—; film set cons. Trainex Corp., Garden Grove, 1984—; exec. dir. Genesis III, Mission Viejo, Calif., 1985. Author patient handbook, 1977. Bd. dirs. Brea Jr. Athletic Assn., 1980-82. Mem. Inservice Health Edn. Council Los Angeles, Nat. Assn. Female Execs., Brea C. of C. (youth edn. council 1985). Republican. Roman Catholic. Avocations: swimming; motorcycle riding; tennis. Home: 4721 Santa Fe Yorba Linda CA 92686 Office: Health Edn Tng Cons PO Box 9125 Brea CA 92621

BERRY, MARY ELIZABETH, nurse, educator; b. Union, S.C., Mar. 22, 1935; d. Oliver Wendel and Nellie (Toney) Willard; m. Jack Ivey Berry, Dec. 6, 1963; children—Jackie, Tracey. Diploma, Bapt. Hosp. Sch. Nursing, 1956; B.S. in Nursing, U. S.C., 1961; postgrad. Case Western Res. U., 1962, U. Ala., 1968. R.N., N.C., S.C. Staff nurse S.C. Bapt. Hosp., Columbia, 1956-69, head nurse, 1959-60, supr., 1962-63; instr. Charlotte (N.C.) Meml. Hosp., 1964-66; coordinator nursing programs Southeastern Community Coll., Whiteville, N.C., 1967, mem. faculty, 1968-76; pub. health nurse Robeson County Health Dept., Lumberton, N.C., 1977-78; pub. health nursing supr. Bladen County Health Dept., Elizabethtown, N.C., 1979—; condr. numerous workshops on death and dying, hypertension and stroke, arthritis at area health edn. ctrs. Eastern N.C.; bd. dirs. Fayetteville Area Health Edn. Ctr., 1981-86. Youth dir. Pleasant Plains Baptist Ch., Whiteville, 1980-86; leader Coastal Carolina council Girl Scouts U.S.A., 1973-76. Served to capt. S.C. Air N.G., 1958-62; to capt. USAF, 1962-63. Mem. N.C. Conf. Nursing Cons. and Suprs. (chmn. South Central region 1982-83), N.C. Nurse Mgrs. Assn., N.C. Pub. Health Assn. Democrat. Home: Route 4 Box 177D Whiteville NC 28472 Office: Bladen County Health Dept Box 188 Elizabethtown NC 28337

BERRY, PAULA MASON GRIFFITH, advertising agency executive; b. Scranton, Pa., Mar. 5, 1950; d. Powell Mason and Helen May (Nageli) G. Student Luzerne County Community Coll., Nanticoke, PA., 1976-77; B.A. in Sociology, East Stroudsburg (Pa.) U., 1972. Layout artist, copywriter The Globe div. John Wanamaker & Co., Scranton, 1973-76; art instr., coordinator South Ctr. Vocat.-Tech. Sch., Scranton, 1977-79; owner The Studio, Dunmore, Pa., 1977-79; art dir. Lombardi Enterprises, Inc., Pensacola, Fla., 1979-80; v.p., owner Armour & Griffith, Inc., Pensacola, 1980—; art instr. Keystone Jr. Coll., LaPlume, Pa., 1977; tech. designer, illustrator Von Bergen, Ltd., Pensacola, 1979. Pub. relations com. Girl Scouts U.S.A., 1975; mem. Scranton Hist. Preservation Bd., 1976. Mem. Am. Assn. Advt. Agys., West Fla. Advt. Council, Internat. Soc. Artists (charter), Pensacola Mus. Art. Republican. Office: Armour & Griffith Inc 315 S Palafox St Pensacola FL 32501

BERRY, ROSE BRIGID, social worker; b. McBride Canyon, N.M., Mar. 5, 1926; d. Patrick James and Bertha Cecilia (MacDonald) Berry; B.A., Mount St. Scholastica Coll., 1947; M.S.W., St. Louis U., 1950. Med. social worker Colo. State Hosp., Pueblo, 1948-49; asst. dir. social service VA Hosp., Phoenix, 1951-55; dir., clin. social work cons. social service dept. Phoenix Indian Med. Center, 1956-82; individual practice clin. social worker, 1982—. Mem. Internat. Med. Soc. Paraplegia (asso.), Nat. Assn. Social Workers, Clin. Social Workers Soc., St. Louis U. Alumni Assn. Republican. Roman Catholic. Home: 3894 N 30th St Phoenix AZ 85016

BERRY, ROSEMARY BROWN, city clerk; b. Phila., Jan. 6, 1954; d. J. Nadyne (Browne) Brown; m. Robert A. Berry, Sept. 8, 1979; 1 son, Robert Andrew S. B.A., St. Francis Coll., Loretto, Pa., 1975. Relocation technician Harrisburg (Pa.) Redevel. Authority, 1975-76; planning analyst Pa. Dept. Community Affairs, Harrisburg, 1976-78; exec. asst. Council for Children, Inc., Atlanta, 1979-80; city clk. City of Harrisburg, 1980—. Participant career exploration program Urban League Met. Harrisburg, 1982—; sec., dir. Family and Children's Service, Harrisburg, 1981—; dir. Tri-County Planned Parenthood, Harrisburg, 1982—, long range planning com., 1983—. Mem. Pa. Mcpl. Secs. Assn. Democrat. Roman Catholic. Home: 703 N 17th St Harrisburg PA 17103

BERRY, SANDRA, real estate executive; b. Dallas, June 23, 1936; d. Leon M. and Anna (Pristash) Van De Kreeke; m. Art J. Berry, June 15, 1954 (dec. Dec. 1963); children—William Chanel Beverly Ann; m. Charles J. Filiatrault, Nov. 21, 1981; stepchildren—Michael, David, Robert, Jeffrey, Diane, Monique. Student Comml. Coll., 1963; grad. Real Estate Inst., 1973. Cert. shopping ctr. mgr., real estate broker, Tex. Sec. to pres. Nat. Bank Odessa (Tex.), 1963-64; sec. to J.H. Conine, Oil Operator, Midland, Tex., 1954-69; officer adminstr. Coldwell Banker Co., Houston, 1969-72; real estate salesperson James Cain Realtors, Houston, 1972; leasing agt. Hale-Mills, Inc., Houston, 1973; property mgr. Schneider-Moore Properties, Houston, 1973-75; pres. Canam Mgmt., Inc. (formerly Berry Property Mgmt. Inc.), Houston, 1975—; v.p., sec. Canam Properties, Inc., Houston, 1981—, Canam Achievement Network, Inc., Houston, 1984—; mem. faculty Internat. Council Shopping Ctrs., N.Y.C., 1975—. Editorial bd. Southwest Real Estate News, Atlanta, 1976—; contbr. articles to profl. jours. Chmn., March of Dimes, Ft. Stockton, Tex., 1957; mistress of ceremonies Republican Rally, Ft. Stockton, 1956; mem. econ. devel. com. Houston C. of C., 1972. Mem. Internat. Council Shopping Ctrs., Houston Bd. Realtors, Beta Sigma Phi. Clubs: River Oaks Bus. Women's Exchange, Delphian. Lodges: Order of Eastern Star, Women of Rotary. Home: 14703 Barryknoll #8 Houston TX 77079 Office: Canam Mgmt Inc 4800 San Felipe Suite 400 Houston TX 77056

BERRY, SHARON ELAINE, interior designer; b. Kansas City, Mo., May 27, 1945; d. Ralph Epping Hohmann and Ruth Justine (Sturm) Hohmann Gibson; m. Max Allen Berry, Apr. 8, 1984. Grad. Pierce Sch. Interior Design, 1972. Designer Danie Dunn Interiors, Kansas City, Mo., 1972-76, 1980-83; co-owner, operator Clift-Willard Interiors, Leawood, Kans., 1976-80; head decorating dept. Carpets by Johnson and Johnson, Overland Park, Kans., 1983-84; owner, operator Nouveau Interiors, Shawnee Mission, Kans., 1984—; publicity dir. Design Excellence Awards, Kansas City, Mo., 1982—; designer Designers Showhouse, Kansas City, Mo., 1975—; participant Design '81 Congress, Helsinki, Finland, 1981. Mem. Jr. Women's Symphony Alliance, Kansas City, Mo., 1983—. Recipient Gold medal Home Builders Assn. of Kansas City, 1977, Silver medal, 1978, 79, 81. Mem. Am. Soc. Interior Designers (assoc.). Office: Nouveau Interiors 9321 W 74th St Shawnee Mission KS 66204

BERRY, VIRGINIA EVA, translation company executive, interpreter; b. Bagshot, Surrey, Eng., June 22, 1940; came to U.S., 1972, naturalized, 1985; d. Thomas J. and Lois P. (Morgan) B.; m. R. Gerard Palmer, III, Jan. 8, 1983; 1 stepson, R. Gerard, IV. B.A. in History, London U., 1959. Rep., Textile Co., Bern, Switzerland, 1963-67; part owner, mgr. Hotel Rapallo, Italy, 1967-72; co-ordinator, interpreter to corps. and govts., 1962-72; owner, pres. Intercontinental Bur. Translators and Interpreters, Inc., N.Y.C., San Franciso, 1973—. Contbr. articles to profl. publs. Mem. adv. bd. continuing edn. NYU, 1983—. Mem. Am. Translation Assn. (dir. 1980-83, pres. 1983-85), Internat. Fedn. Translators (pub. relations chair 1984—), N.Y. Circle Translators (founder, pres. 1981-83). Anglican. Club: Zonta (membership chair 1984). Avocations: classical Spanish dance, tennis, gardening, swimming. Home: 54 Miller Blvd Syosset NY 11791 Office: Intercontinental Bur Translators and Interpreters Inc 14 W 40th St New York NY 10018

BERRYMAN, KARAN ANN, librarian; b. Cuthbert, Ga., June 26, 1956; d. John Robert and Wilda (Fowler) B.; A.A. cum laude, Andrew Coll., 1975; B.S. with high honors, Auburn U., 1977; M.S.L.S., U. N.C., Chapel Hill, 1979. Dir. library Andrew Coll., Cuthbert, 1980-84; head reference services Louise Wise Lewis Library, Flagler Coll., St. Augustine, Fla., 1984—; book reviewer regional publs. Mem. ALA, Southeastern Library Assn., Original Muscogee County Geneal. Soc., Ga. Library Assn., Phi Kappa Phi, Phi Theta Kappa. Club: Pilot (Cuthbert). Home: 111 W Harris St Cuthbert GA 31740 Office: Flagler Coll Library Saint Augustine FL 32086

BERSHAD, KAREN FRANCES, commercial printing company executive; b. Amityville, N.Y., Mar. 29, 1948; d. Wallace Franklin Haskins and Beverly June (Robinson) Rosenthal; m. Barry Gilbert Bershad, Apr. 2, 1978; stepchildren—Ira, Michael, Elissa. Student pub. schs., Amityville. Pres. Plaza Printing Co., Inc. Mem. Sales & Mktg. Execs.-Atlanta, Women Bus. Owners, Nat. Assn. Printers and Lithographers, Ga. Hospitality and Travel Assn., Women's C. of C. (bd. dirs.), Atlanta C. of C. Republican. Methodist.

BERT, CAROL LOIS, teachers aide; b. Bakersfield, Calif., Oct. 15, 1938; d. Edwin Vernon and Shirley Helen (Craig) Phelps; m. John Davison Bert, Sept. 26, 1964; children—Mary Ellen, John Edwin, Craig Eric, Douglas Ethan. B.S. in Nursing, U. Colo., 1960. Med. surg. nurse U.S. Army, Washington, 1960-62, Ascom City, Korea, 1962-63, San Antonio, 1963, Albuquerque, 1964-65; tchrs. aide Jefferson County Schs., Arvada, Colo., 1979—. Mem. Nonpracticing and Part Time Nurses Assn. Club: Colo. Quilting Council. Avocations: reading; quilting; camping; fishing; tennis. Home: 5844 Oak St Arvada CO 80004 Office: Allendale Elem Sch 5900 Oak St Arvada CO 80004

BERT, ELEANOR LUCILLE, school system business administrator; b. Fall River, Mass., June 14, 1939; d. Edward Joseph and Eleanor Lucille (Simpkins) Bertolini. B.S., Marist Coll., 1976; M.B.A., M.H.A., U. Miami, 1977, postgrad. Rider Coll., 1984, SUNY-Albany, 1984. Intergovtl. coordinator Ulster Co., Kingston, N.Y., 1977-78; bus. mgr. Stuyvesant Inns, Kingston, 1978-79, Morrisville Sch. Dist., Pa., 1979-82; dir. bus. mgmt. service Bensalem Towns Sch. Dist., Pa., 1982-84; bus. adminstr. Catskill Central Schs., N.Y., 1984—; presenter workshops in field. Bd. dirs. Ulster County council Girl Scouts U.S.A., 1977-78, Ulster County YWCA, 1977-78, Ulster County CAP, Kingston, 1985—. Mem. Delaware Valley Assn. Sch. Bus. Ofcls. (pres. 1981-82), Assn. Sch. Bus. Ofcls., N.Y. Assn. Sch. Bus. Ofcls., Pa. Assn. Sch. Bus. Ofcls. Home: UPO Box 3234 Kingston NY 12401 Office: Catskill Central Sch Dist 347 W Main St Catskill NY 12414

BERTANY, DOROTHY KREMPA, county official; b. New Brunswick, N.J., Sept. 13, 1937; d. Michael and Wanda B. (Garnecki) Krempa; m. Robert P. Bertany, June 8, 1957; children—Robert P., Jr., Theresa Lee. Grad. high sch., Metuchen, N.J. Typist, receptionist Camp Kilmer, Piscataway, N.J., 1954; sec. to twp. clk. Piscataway Twp., 1955; clk. transcriber Calif. Spray Chem. Corp., South Plainfield, N.J., 1955-60; switchboard operator Hunterdon Med. Ctr., Flemington, N.J., 1967; sec. Hunterdon County Bd. of Chosen Freeholders, Flemington, N.J., 1968-77, dep. freeholder clk., 1977-78, freeholder clk., 1978—. Vol. in Probation, 1980-84; chmn. March of Dimes Teamwalk, Hunterdon County, 1982-83; govt. chmn. United Way Hunterdon County, 1983-84; pres. Hunterdon County Republican Women's Club, 1983—; mem. Hunterdon County Exec. Com., Franklin Twp., 1985—, N.J. State Exec. Com., Hunterdon County, 1985—; mem. Hunterdon County Community Services Council, 1985. Mem. N.J. Assn. Freeholder Bd. Clks. (pres. 1983—), Municipal Clks. Assn. Hunterdon County, Municipal Clks. Assn. N.J., Internat. Inst. Municipal Clks. Roman Catholic. Club: Soroptimist (dir. 1982-83, 85-87, pres. 1983-85). Home: RD 1 Box 327 Pittstown NJ 08867 Office: Hunterdon County Bd of Chosen Freeholder Main St Flemington NJ 98822

BERTHA, BARBARA ANN, insurance underwriter; b. Phila., Dec. 11, 1953; d. Walter George and Aletha (Talbert) B. B.S., Elizabethtown Coll., 1975. Comml. lines underwriter St. Paul Fire & Marine Ins. Co., Fort Washington, Pa., 1977—, edn. coordinator, 1984—. Mem. Jenkintown Planning Commn., Pa., 1982—; alumni-admissions liaison vol. Elizabethtown Coll., Pa., 1983—; area v.p. Abington/Jenkintown unit Am. Cancer Soc., Fort Washington, 1985—; mem. Jenkintown Republican Com., 1982—; vice chmn. Jenkintown Regular Rep. Orgn., 1984—. Recipient Merit award St. Paul Fire & Marine Ins. Co., 1980, 82. Mem. Nat. Assn. Ins. Women (cert., region I legis. chmn. 1985-86), Women's Ins. Co. Phila. (pres. 1984-85, Rookie of Yr. award 1981), Nat. Assn. Female Execs., Pa. Assn. Notaries, Sigma Lambda Sigma. Presbyterian. Avocations: numismatics; travel; long-distance swimming. Home: 100 West Ave 413 S Bldg Jenkintown PA 19046 Office: St Paul Fire & Marine Ins Co Phila Service Ctr PO Box 488 Fort Washington PA 19034

BERTRAM, PHYLLIS ANN, lawyer; b. Long Beach, Calif., July 30, 1954; d. William J. and Ruth A. Bertram; A.A., Long Beach City Coll., 1975, B.S. in Accounting, U. So. Calif., 1977; M.B.A., Calif. State U., Long Beach, 1978; J.D., Western State U., 1982. Bar: Calif. 1982, U.S. Ct. Appeals (9th cir.), U.S. Dist. Ct. Instr., lifeguard City of Long Beach, Calif., 1972-78; sports ofcl. swimming, softball, volleyball, and basketball, 1972—; asst. commr. Met. Conf. Community and Jr. Colls., Long Beach, 1978-84; instr. seamanship, fire sci. and bus. adminstrn. Long Beach City Coll., 1977—; mgmt. cons., 1978—; mgr. Pacific Bell, 1983—. Instr. CPR, water safety, small craft, first aid ARC, 1972—; mem. Republican Nat. Com. Recipient resolutions Calif. Senate and Assembly, Long Beach City Council; numerous service awards Am. Red Cross; Ednl. research grantee, City of Long Beach, 1972. Mem. U. So. Calif. Alumni Assn., U. So. Calif. Commerce Assocs., Assn. of MBA Execs., So. Calif. Volleyball Ofcls. Assn., So. Calif. Basketball Ofcls. Assn., Women's Basketball Ofcls. Assn., Women's Swim Ofcls. Assn. (pres.), So. Calif. Softball Umpires Assn., State Bar Calif., ABA, Fed. Bar Assn. Los Angeles, Los Angeles County Bar Assn., Calif. State U. at Long Beach Alumni Assn., Delta Theta Phi. Republican. Club: Seal Beach Yacht. Home: 120 Summerwood Pl Concord CA 94518 Office: 2600 Camino Ramon San Ramon CA 94583

BERTRAM, VALEREE MICHELL, hotel company executive; b. Oklahoma City, Mar. 7, 1962; d. Earl William and Laveta Kathryn (Noakes) O'Neal; m. William Brian Bertram, Apr. 7, 1984; 1 child, William Dennis. B.S. in Polit. Sci., Ariz. State U., 1983. Personnel mgr. Capins Dept. Store, Phoenix, 1979-81; chief night auditor Ramada Inns, Phoenix, 1982-83; acctg. mgr. Desert Hills Hotel, Phoenix, 1983-84; asst. store mgr. Lionel Playworld, Phoenix, 1984-85; acctg. mgr., front office mgr., Scottsdale Fashion Square Resort, Ariz., 1985—. Leader Arcadia br. Monte Vista council Girl Scouts U.S.A., 1979-82. Mem. Nat. Assn. Female Execs. Republican. Roman Catholic. Home: 3813 N 37th St Phoenix AZ 85018

BERUBE, GEORGETTE B., state legislature. State senator 16th dist., Maine, 1985—. Democrat. Office: State Capitol Augusta ME 04333*

BERUBE, PAULINE JEANNE ESTACIO, real estate broker, appraiser; b. Fall River, Mass., July 3, 1943; d. Joseph Michael and Mary (Farias) Estacio; m. Edward Berube, Sept. 14, 1963; 1 child, Christopher. Student Lee Inst., Brookline, Mass., 1968, U. Ft. Lauderdale, Fla., 1974. Owner Berube & Estacio Realty, Westport, Mass., 1968-74; pres. A.A. Pickett Agy., Litte Compton, R.I., 1975-78, Star Homes, Tiverton, R.I., 1978—; Manufactured Home Distbr., 1978—; fin. cons. in field, Hampton, N.H., 1984—; dir. Residential Planning of New Eng. Roman Catholic. Avocations: interior design; landscape design; reading. Home: 2371 Main Rd Tiverton RI 02878 Office: Star Homes PO Box 240 Tiverton RI 02878

BERUBEY, CAROLINE, electronic coil manufacturing company executive; b. East Longmeadow, Mass., June 10, 1923; d. Felice Anthony and Theresa (Belcamino) Costantini; m. Leroy Anthony Berubey, Dec. 16, 1943 (dec. Sept. 1981); 1 dau., Carole Anne Berubey Chapdelaine. Student pub. schs., Springfield, Mass. With Electronic Coils, Inc., Springfield, 1948—, v.p. adminstrn.; 1980—; notary pub. Mem. Springfield Bus. and Profl. Women (sec.). Home: 68 Hill Terrace Ludlow MA 01056 Office: Electronic Coils Inc 40 Frank B Murray St Springfield MA 01103

BERUMEN, SUSAN KAREN, artist; b. Los Angeles, Sept. 2, 1957; d. Frank Manuel and Clara (Silva) B. A.A., Fullerton Coll., 1979; B.F.A., U. Calif.-Irvine, 1982; M.A., NYU, 1984. one woman show 8 Washington Sq. Art Galleries, N.Y.C., 1984; exhibited in group shows: Santa Barbara Contemporary Arts Forum, Calif., 1983, Tech. U. N.S., 1985, Southwest Craft Ctr., San Antonio, 1985; represented in pvt. collection in N.Y., Calif., Mass., Southwest; corp. collection S&S Inc., N.Y. Mem. NOW, NYU Alumni Fedn. Home: 14 Jones St #2D New York NY 10014

BERZINS, ERNA MARIJA, physician; b. Latvia, Nov. 27, 1914; d. Arturs and Anna (Steckenbergs) Meilands; came to U.S., 1951, naturalized, 1956; M.D., Latvian State U., 1940; m. Verners Berzins, Aug. 24, 1935; children—Valdis, Andis. Mem. pediatric faculty Latvian State U., 1940-44; intern Good Samaritan Hosp., Dayton, Ohio, 1951-52; resident in pediatrics Children's Hosp. of Mich., Detroit, 1953-55; practice medicine specialising in pediatrics, Detroit, 1956-60; with ARC, Cleve., 1961-63; physician pediatric outpatient dept. Cleve. Met. Gen. Hosp., 1963-84; asst. prof. emeritus Case-Western Res. U., Cleve., trustee Women's Gen. Hosp., Cleve. Mem. Am., Ohio med. assns., Acad. Medicine, No. Ohio Pediatric Soc., Am. Women's Med. Assn., Am. Med. Polit. Action Com. Lutheran. Address: 5460 Friar Circle Cleveland OH 44126

BERZON, FAYE CLARK, nursing educator; b. New Britain, Conn., Sept. 26, 1926; d. Bernard Francis and Elizabeth Tillie (Gross) Clark; m. Harry Berzon, June 18, 1961. Diploma Beth Israel Hosp., 1947; B.S.N., Boston U., 1957, M.S.N., 1959; postgrad. U. Mass., 1981—. Staff, head nurse, instr. Beth Israel Hosp., Boston, 1948-58; instr. nursing Simmons Coll., Boston, 1958-62, Cath. Labore Sch. Nursing, Dorchester, Mass., 1962-67; asst. prof. nursing Boston U. Sch. Nursing, 1967-70; div. chmn. human services Massasoit Community Coll., Brockton, Mass., 1973-79, prof. nursing, 1970—; mem. acad. adv. com. to Mass. Bd. Higher Edn., 1975-76. Author: (with Govoni, Berzon, Fall) Drugs and Nursing Implications, 1965. Vol., Milton (Mass.) Meals on Wheels, 1978—. Mem. Am. Nurses Assn., Nat. League Nursing (scholar 1963-79, accreditation visitor 1976—), AAUW (v.p. Milton br. 1981-83), Nursing Archives, Mass. Heart Assn., Sigma Theta Tau, Delta Kappa Gamma. Democrat. Jewish. Home: 37 Brandon Rd Milton MA 02187

BESEN, JANE PHYLLIS TRIPTOW, civic worker; b. Chgo., Aug. 6, 1921; d. Richard Herman and Rose (Krips) Triptow; student Northwestern U., 1946-47, East Los Angeles Coll., 1967-68; B.A. in English, Calif. State U., Los Angeles, 1978, postgrad. in English; m. Irving Besen, Mar. 25, 1951 (div. 1978); children—Glenn, Allen. Exec. sec. Chgo. Ordnance Dist., War Dept., 1941-46, Aubrey, Moore & Wallace, Advt. Agy., Chgo., 1946; exec. sec. sales office McGraw-Hill Pub. Co., Chgo., 1947-51; exec. sec. Security Pacific Nat. Bank, Los Angeles, 1978—. Publicity chmn. Am Field Service, 1967-68; sec. Citizens Com for Good Govt., 1961; capt. United Crusade, Monterey Park, Calif., 1967—; publicity chmn. Monterey Park Art Assn., 1966-67, coor. sec., 1968, dir., 1965—, past pres., dir. newsletter, 1970—; chmn. Monterey Park Arts and Culture Com.; dir. in charge Brugemeyer Library Shows, 1973-74; dep. registrar voters Calif. State U., Los Angeles, 1971-74; 3d v.p. in charge publicity Community Concerts Monterey Park. Recipient Top award Alhambra Open Show, 1972. Mem. Nat. League Am. Pen Women (rec. sec., treas. 1961-65), LWV (sec. Alhambra chpt. 1971-73 pres. chpt. 1973-74, action chmn., publicity chmn. 1977-78, hospitality chmn. 1980—), Residents Assn. Monterey Park. Club: Northwestern U. Alumni So. Calif. (corr. sec. 1979-80). Home: 1540 Arriba Dr Monterey Park CA 91754

BESHAR, CHRISTINE, lawyer; b. Paetzig, Germany, Nov. 6, 1929; d. Hans and Ruth (vonKleist-Retzow) vonWedemeyer; student U. Hamburg, 1950-51, U. Tuebingen, 1951-52; B.A., Smith Coll., 1953; m. Robert P. Beshar, Dec. 20, 1953; children—Cornelia, Jacqueline, Frederica, Peter. Admitted to N.Y. Bar, 1960; asso. mem. firm Casey, Lane & Mittendorf, N.Y.C., 1960-63; asso. mem. firm Cravath, Swaine & Moore, N.Y.C., 1964-70, partner, 1971—. Bd. dirs. UN Assn., 1975—, Catalyst for Women Inc., 1977—, N.Y. State Bar and Am. Bar founds., 1977—; trustee Colgate U., 1978-84. Inst. Internat. Edn. fellow, 1952-53; recipient Disting. Alumnae medal Smith Coll., 1974. Fellow Am. Coll. Probate Counsel; mem. Assn. Bar City N.Y. (exec. com., 1973-75, v.p. 1985—), N.Y. State Bar Assn. (ho. of dels. 1971-80, v.p. 1978-80), Fgn. Policy Assn. (dir.). Presbyn. Clubs: Down Town Assn., Wall St., Cosmopolitan. Home: 120 East End Ave New York NY 10028 also Stone House Somers NY 10589 Office: 1 Chase Manhattan Plaza New York NY 10005

BESONEN, JOANNE FRANCES, automation company buyer; b. Somerville, Mass., July 21, 1946; d. Leo Joseph and Rose Marie (Costa) Fava; m. David Eino Besonen, Apr. 21, 1968; children—David M., Mark R., Amy E., Mara R., Matthew P. Student, Regis Coll. Sales team leader Avon Products Inc., Ayer, Mass., 1975-77; br. office clk. Army and Air Force Exchange Service, Ayer, 1976; asst. to sales/service mgr. John E. Cain Co., Ayer, 1976-77; purchasing agt. Scopus Corp., Lowell, Mass., 1978-81; contract buyer Network Personnel, Billerica, Mass., 1983-84; sr. buyer Netco Automation, Haverhill, Mass., 1984—. Mem. PTO, South Row Sch., Chelmsford, Mass., 1980—, PTO, Keith Catholic High Sch., Lowell, 1983—. Mem. Nat. Assn. Purchasing Mgmt., Nat. Assn. Female Execs., Purchasing Mgmt. Assn. Boston. Democrat. Roman Catholic. Club: Chelmsford Art Advocates. Avocations: cooking; knitting; crocheting; aerobics; biking. Address: 55 Billerica Rd Chelmsford MA 01824

BESS, CONSTANCE A., manufacturing company executive; b. Canton, Ohio, June 24, 1944; d. Virgil and Jane Shyrock; m. Kenneth B. Bess Jr., June 7, 1966; children—Constance Jane, Kenneth Bethea, Ty Hamilton. Ed., U. Cin. Owner, chmn. bd. Constance Bess, Inc., Charleston, S.C., 1981—; owner, v.p. Bess & Bess Ltd., 1978-81. Office: Constance Bess Inc PO Box 31964 Charleston SC 29417

BESSERT, HELEN S., communications specialist; b. Milw., Mar. 14, 1927; d. Frank Edward and Hilda Henrietta (Schmasow) Stetler; m. Frederic Thomas Bessert, Oct. 3, 1953; children—Lynn Ellen, Barbara Ann. B.A., Milw.-Downer Coll., 1949. Newsletter editor Wis. Electronics Service Assn., Milw., 1956-70; communications specialist Wis. Bakers Assn., 1977—, Graef, Anhalt, Schloemer & Assocs., 1977—. Recipient Retail Brokers Am. award for best state assn. newsletter, 1980. Mem. Women in Communications. Republican. Lutheran. Home: 2124 N 74th St Wauwatosa WI 53213 Office: Wis Bakers Assn 161 W Wisconsin Ave Milwaukee WI 53203

BEST, NANCY DOUGHERTY, educator; b. New Holland, Pa., May 18, 1931; d. Frank Harold and Kathryn (Ebersol) Dougherty; B.S., Drexel U., 1953; M.A., Millersville State Coll., 1972; M.S., Central Conn. State Coll., 1981; Ph.D., Pa. State U., 1978; children—Randolph, Kathryn Best Thomas, John, James. Tchr., Upper Darby, Pa., 1953-55; faculty Flathead County Community Coll., Kalispell, Mont., 1968-73; curriculum writer/tchr., Lancaster, Pa., 1973-76; intern Western Interstate Commn. Higher Edn., Boulder Valley, Colo., 1977-78; adj. instr. Pa. State U., State College, 1978; assoc. prof. edn. Central Conn. State Coll., 1978-81; asst. prof. Oral Roberts U., Tulsa, from 1981; now faculty Life Bible Coll., Los Angeles; cons. in field. Vol., Mental Health Hotline, 1980-81, City of Faith, 1982-83. Pa. State U. grantee, 1975-78; recipient Phonetics award Millersville Summer Lang. Inst., 1971; Borden award Drexel U., 1952. Mem. Single Ministries AAUW, Am. Ednl. Research Assn., Am. Personnel and Guidance Assn., Phi Kappa Phi, Phi Delta Kappa. Christian Ch. Club: Women's Aglow. Contbr. articles to profl. jours. Office: Life Bible Coll 1100 Glendale Blvd Los Angeles CA 90026

BESTIER, SABINE, urban planner; b. Berlin, W. Germany, Dec. 11, 1950; came to U.S., 1977; d. Hans Rudolf and Ellen (Hesse) B. Student in law Freie U. (Berlin) 1971-73; M.A. in Landscape Planning, Tech. U. (Berlin), 1975; postgrad. in urban planning, Calif. Poly. Inst., 1977—. Jr. planner Prof. Nagel, Berlin, 1973-75; research analyst TUB, Berlin, 1975-77; project planner PBR, Newport Beach, Calif., 1978-80; econ. dept. liaison City of La Habra (Calif.), 1980; assoc. CRA-Inglewood (Calif.), 1980-82; city planning assoc. Community Redevel. Agy., Los Angeles, 1982-84, asst. project mgr., 1984—; mem. Inglewood Devel. Corp., 1981—; dir. Los Angeles Family Housing, 1983—. Mem. Am. Planning Assn., Nat. Assn. Female Execs. Office: Community Redevel Agy 354 S Spring St Los Angeles CA 90013

BETHKE, SUE WHITTAKER, personnel official; b. Tazewell, Va., July 27, 1941; d. Garland Eugene and Mona Ellora (Trivette) Whittaker; m. Chester G. Bethke, Jr., Oct. 8, 1960; children—Robert, Susan, Sarah. Student Radford (Va.) Coll., 1958-60; student bus. adminstrn. East Tenn. State U., 1968-71. Exec. sec. Radford Coll., 1960-61; office mgr. The Exec. Desk, Reston, Va., 1975-76, Reston Internat. Constrn., 1976-78; personnel admistr. CENTEC Corp., Reston, 1978—. Mem. Am. Soc. Personnel Adminstrn. Baptist. Clubs: Reston Bus. and Profl. Women's (sec. 1976-77), Zonta. Home: 2101 Deep Run Ln Reston VA 22090 Office: CENTEC Corp 11260 Roger Bacon Dr Reston VA 22090

BETTAN, AMY MALAMY, consumer electronics distributor; b. N.Y.C., June 9, 1942; d. Henry Robert and Rhoda Ann (Resnick) Malamy; m. Philip Warren Bettan; children—Gary, Richard, Daniel. B.A., CUNY, 1964. Advt. exec. Community Newspapers, Glen Cove, N.Y., 1979-81; pres., owner Broadfield Distributing, Inc., Glen Cove, 1980—. Pres. Glen Cove chpt. Children's Hosp. at L.I. Jewish Hosp., New Hyde Park, N.Y., 1973-75. Republican. Jewish. Home: 27 Broadfield Pl Glen Cove NY 11542 Office: Broadfield Distributing Inc 67A Glen Cove Ave Glen Cove NY 11542

BETTAN, ANITA ESTHER, public relations specialist, writer; b. Cin., Nov. 30, 1928; d. Israel and Ida Judith (Goldstein) Bettan. B.A., U. Cin., 1950; M.A., Columbia U., 1951. Copywriter, Shillito's, Cin., 1953-55; continuity dir. Sta. WSAI, Cin., 1955-57; copywriter, jr. account exec. William F. Holland Agy., Cin., 1957-61; account coordinator Stockton-West-Burkhart, Inc., Cin., 1962-67; asst. to info. officer U. Cin. Coll-Conservatory of Music, 1967-71; info. services writer U. Cin., 1971—, mem. com. on aging, 1981-84. Contbr. articles to mags. Dep. foreman Hamilton County Grand Jury, Cin., 1979, foreman petit jury, 1980; pres. career div. Council Jewish Women, Cin., 1962-64; vol. Jewish Hosp., Cin., 1954-59; mem. Sr. Olympics Com., Cin., 1981-84. Mem. Women in Communications. Home: 2101 Grandin Rd Cincinnati OH 45208 Office: U Cin Mail Location No 65 Cincinnati OH 45221

BETTERIDGE, FRANCES CARPENTER, lawyer, mediator; b. Rutherford, N.J., Aug. 25, 1921; d. James Dunton and Emily (Atkinson) Carpenter; m. Albert Edwin Betteridge, Feb. 5, 1949 (div. 1975); children—Anne, Albert Edwin, James, Peter. A.B., Mt. Holyoke Coll., 1942; J.D., N.Y. Law Sch., 1978. Bar: Conn. 1979, Ariz. 1982. Technician in charge blood banks Roosevelt Hosp., N.Y.C. and Mountainside Hosp., Montclair, N.J., 1943-49; substitute tchr. Greenwich High Sch. (Conn.), 1978-79; intern and asst. to labor contracts office Town of Greenwich, 1979-80; sole practice immigration law, Tucson, 1982—; vol. referee Juvenile Ct., Pima County Superior Ct., Tucson, 1981-85; commr. Juvenile Ct., Pima County Superior Ct., Tucson, 1985—; hearing officer Small Claims Ct., Pima County Justice Cts., Tucson, 1982—; mediator Family Crisis Service, Tucson, 1982—, judge pro-tem, 1985—. Pres. High Sch. PTA, Greenwich, 1970, PTA Council, 1971; mem. Greenwich Bd. Edn., 1971-76, sec., 1973-76; com. chmn. LWV Tucson, 1981; bd. dirs., 1984-85; bd. dirs., sec. Let The Sun Shine Inc., Tucson, 1981—. Mem. ABA, Conn. Bar Assn., State Bar Ariz., Ariz. Women Lawyers Assn., Am. Immigration Lawyers Assn., Soc. Profls. in Dispute Resolution (assoc.). Republican. Congregationalist. Club: Point o' Woods (N.Y.). Home and Office: 3442 N Richland Circle Tucson AZ 85719

BETTIN, JANENE EDNA, real estate broker; b. Schaller, Iowa, Nov. 11, 1943; d. Robert A. and Edna (Harris) Bath; m. Thomas L. Bettin, June 20, 1964; 1 son, Christopher. Student U. No. Iowa, 1961; B.S., Tex. A&I U., 1965. Grad. Realtors Inst; cert. residential specialist. Tchr. high sch., Corpus Christi, Tex., 1965-70; tchr. Village Acad., Mt. Lebanon, Pa., 1973-76; broker, assoc. Re/Max Metro Properties, Inc., Denver, 1977-86; broker, br. mgr. Perry & Butler, Littleton, Colo., 1986—. Chmn. Blood Bank, South Suburban Bd. Realtors, 1980, chmn. Schs. Com., 1980; pres. South Suburban Bd. Realtors, 1985-86. Bd. dirs., officer Bristol Cove Homeowners Assn., Littleton, Colo., 1983; officer, treas. Arapahoe Youth League-Warriors, 1981. Mem. Realtors Nat. Mktg. Inst., Womens Council Realtors (pres. 1982-83), Colo. Assn. Realtors (instr. 1981—, dir. 1984), Cert. Residential Specialists (pres. Colo. chpt. 1984 instr. 1984—). Republican. Methodist. Club: Mt. Lebanon Newsomers (pres. 1973-74). Home: 7540 S Cove Circle Littleton CO 80122 Office: Perry & Butler 8089 S Lincoln St Suite 103 Littleton CO 80122

BETTINO, ANNEMARIE CHRISTINE, human services director; b. Niagara Falls, N.Y., Aug. 3, 1957; d. Dominick and Rosemary (Yenzi) B. B.S., SUNY-Oswego, 1979; M.S. candidate, Syracuse U., 1986—. Asst. dir. Retired Sr. Vol. Program, Niagara County, N.Y., 1981-82, dir., 1982—; adminstrv. supr. Young Vols. in Action, Niagara County, 1983-84. Author: (newsletter) Retiree Reflections, 1982—; contbr. to handbooks and pamphlets in field. Bd. dirs. Literacy Vols., Niagara Falls, 1985—. Recipient Good Neighbor award Sta. WHLD-Radio and Niagara Frontier Services, 1985. Mem. com. United Way Communications, Community Leadership and Devel. Niagara County (bd. dirs. 1986—), N.Y. State Assn. Retired Sr. Vol. Program Dirs. (v.p. 1985—), Agy. Coalition Taskforce (pres. 1984-86), County Human Services Assn.; del. to People's Republic of China, N.Y. State Health Care and Services for Aging, 1984. Democrat. Roman Catholic. Club: Zonta (Niagara Falls) (sec. 1986—). Avocations: education; fine arts; quilting; travel. Office: Retired Sr Vol Program 1302 Main St Niagara Falls NY 14305

BETTIS, ANNE KATHERINE, communications company executive; b. Newark, June 19, 1949; d. Theophilus Alonzo and Jean Katherine (Smallwood) B. B.A. summa cum laude in English, Jersey City State Coll., 1972; M.B.A. in Mktg., Columbia U., 1979. Cert. tchr., N.J. Tchr. Bd. Edn., East Orange, N.J., 1972-73; editor Avon Products, Inc., N.Y.C., 1973-77; account exec. AT&T Long Lines, Parsippany, N.J., 1979-82; nat. account mgr. AT&T Info. Systems, Paramus, N.J., 1983-85, staff mgr., Morristown, N.J., 1985—. Pres. 8th Irving Park Condominium Assn., Plainfield, N.J., 1984—. Recipient Achiever's Club award AT&T Info. Systems, 1982, 83, 84; Bravo Zulu award AT&T Info. Systems, 1984. Council for Opportunity in Grad. Mgmt. Edn. fellow, 1978-79. Mem. Nat. Black M.B.A. Assn., Am. Coaster Enthusiasts. Avocations: reading; theater; travel; music. Home: 614-5 W 8th St Plainfield NJ 07060 Office: AT&T Info Systems 1 Speedwell Ave East Tower Room 771E Morristown NJ 07960

BETTS, BARBARA LANG (MRS. BERT A. BETTS), lawyer, rancher; b. Anaheim, Calif., Apr. 28, 1926; d. W. Harold and Helen (Thompson) Lang; B.A. magna cum laude, Stanford, 1948; LL.B., Balboa U., 1951; m. Roby F. Hayes, July 22, 1948 (dec.); children—John Chauncey IV, Frederick Prescott, Roby Francis II; m. Bert A. Betts, July 11, 1962; 1 child, Bruce Harold, stepchildren—Bert Alan, Randy W., Sally Betts Joynt, Terry Betts Marsteller, Linda Betts Hansen, LeAnn Betts Hoffman. Admitted to Calif. bar, 1952, U.S. Supreme Ct. bar, 1978; pvt. practice law, Oceanside, Calif., 1952-68, San Diego, 1960—, Sacramento, 1962—; partner firm Roby F. Hayes & Barbara Lang Hayes, 1952-60; city atty., Carlsbad, Calif., 1959-63; v.p. Isle & Oceans Marinas, Inc., 1970-80, W. H. Lang Corp., 1964-69; sec. Internat. Prodn. Assos., 1968—, Margaret M. McCabe, M.D., Inc., 1977—. Chmn., Traveler's Aid, 1952-53; pres. Oceanside-Carlsbad Jr. Chambrettes, 1955-56; vice chmn. Carlsbad Planning Commn., 1959; mem. San Diego Planning Congress, 1959; v.p. Oceanside Diamond Jubilee Com., 1958; dir. No. San Diego County Chpt. for Retarded Children, 1957-58. Candidate Calif. State Legislature, 77th Dist., 1954; mem. Calif. Dem State Central Com., 1958-66; co-chmn. 28th Congl. Dist., Dem. State Central Com., 1960-62; alt. del. Dem. Nat. Conv., 1960. Mem. Am. Judicature Soc., Nat. Inst. Mcpl. Officers, Am., Calif., San Diego County bar assns., Oceanside C. of C. (sec. 1957, v.p. 1958, dir. 1953-54, 57-59), AAUW (legislative com. 1958-59; local pres. 1959-60; asst. state legislative chmn. 1958-59), No. San Diego County Assn. Chambers of Commerce (sec.-treas.), Bus. and Profl. Women's Club (So. dist. legislation chmn. 1958-59), D.A.R. (regent Oceanside chpt. 1960-61), San Diego C. of C., San Diego Hist. Soc., Fullerton Jr. Assistance League, U.S. Supreme Ct. Hist. Soc., Calif. Scholarship Fedn., Loyola Guild of Jesuit High Sch., Phi Beta Kappa. Clubs: Soroptimist Internat. (pres. Oceanside-Carlsbad 1958-59, sec. pub. affairs San Diego, Imperial Counties 1954; pres. of pres.'s council San Diego and Imperial counties and Mexico 1958-59), Barristers, Stanford (Sacramento), Stanford Mothers. Author: (with Bert A. Betts) A Citizen Answers. Office: Betts Ranch PO Box 306 Elverta CA 95626 also 3119-A Howard Ave San Diego CA 92104

BETTS, DAHNA MAY, bank officer; b. Oak Park, Ill.; d. Henry Christian and Mildred Henrietta (Vlach) Dubs; student Triton Coll., 1973-76; student, North Central Coll., 1979-81; student Am. Inst. Banking, 1982-83; children—Judith, Wally, Ralph, Dyhana; m. Donald E. Betts. Supr., Bresnahan Computer Service, Addison, Ill., 1967-70; operator, programmer, analyst various cos., 1970-76; programmer, analyst Loyola U. Med. Center, Maywood, Ill., 1976-77; sr. systems analyst, programmer Long Range Systems Planning div. Blue Cross Blue Shield Assn., Chgo., 1977-78; systems officer First Nat. Bank of Chgo., 1979—. Mem. Nat. Assn. Female Execs. Home: 44 Bunting Ln Naperville IL 60565 Office: One First Nat Plaza Chicago IL 60670

BETTS, ELAINE WISWALL, headmistress; b. Albany, N.Y., Aug. 4, 1925; d. Frank Lawrence and Clara Elizabeth (Chapman) Wiswall; m. Darby Wood Betts, June 2, 1951; children—Victoria, Catherine, Darby Jr. B.A., Smith Coll., 1947; M.A., Holy Names Coll., Oakland, Calif., 1975. Head of upper sch. Anna Head Sch., Oakland, 1971-78; head Royce Sch., Oakland, 1978-80; headmistress Albany Acad. for Girls, N.Y., 1980-84, Dana Hall Sch., Wellesley, Mass., 1984—. Mem. Headmistresses of East, Nat. Assn. Prins. Schs. for Girls, Nat. Assn. Secondary Sch. Prins., Nat. Assn. Coll. Admissions Counselors (profl. edn. com. 1978-81). Office: Dana Hall Sch 45 Dana Rd Wellesley MA 02181

BETTS, GLYNNE ROBINSON, writer, photographer; b. Fredericksburg, Va., Feb. 23, 1934; d. Frederick Hampden and Jessie (Maguire) Robinson; children—Elizabeth, William, Katherine. A.B., Wells Coll., 1956; postgrad. in history of art Columbia U., 1957; postgrad. in journalism NYU, 1975; photography student. The New Sch., 1967, 71, of Ansel Adams, Yosemite, Calif., 1968, Paul Caponigro, Bethel, Conn., 1969-71. Cert. media specialist, N.Y.C. Bd. Edn. With news and publicity dept. Riverdale Neighborhood House, 1974-76; staff photographer, The Reporter, publ. Ethical Culture Schs., N.Y.C., 1974-76; condr. photostudy project, N.Y.C. pub. sch., 1974-75; guest lectr. U. Maine, 1979; condr. photog. workshop for jr. high sch. students sponsored by N.Y. Pub. Library, 1973. Works appeared in publs. including N.Y. Times, Washington Post, N.Y. Daily News, Christian Sci. Monitor, Village Voice, San Francisco Chronicle, Los Angeles Times, Vineyard Gazette, Asia; featured in Women At Their Work, 1977; author: Writers in Residence, 1981; one-woman photog. shows Soho Photo Gallery, N.Y.C., 1974, Wells Coll., 1973, N.Y. Pub. Library, 1973; participant group exhibits: Riverdale Neighborhood House, N.Y.C., 1968, Guild Hall, Easthampton, N.Y., 1970, Soho Photo Gallery, 1973, Wells Coll., 1974-75, Carnegie House, N.Y.C., 1978, Cosmopolitan Club, N.Y.C., 1976, Community Gallery Met. Mus. Art, 1976. Mem. Am. Soc. Mag. Photographers. Club: Cosmopolitan. Home: 116 E 63rd St New York NY 10021

BETTS, VIRGINIA TROTTER, nursing educator, legal consultant; b. Sevierville, Tenn., Mar. 10, 1947; d. Mell Emert and Alice (Robbins) Trotter; m. Stephen Carter Betts, Sept. 3, 1946; children—Jennifer Susann, Jessica Alice. B.S. in Nursing, U. Tenn.-Memphis, 1969; M.S. in Nursing, Vanderbilt U., 1971; J.D., Nashville Night Law Sch., 1978. R.N.; bar: Tenn. Head nurse City of Memphis Hosp., 1969-70; specialist Middle Tenn. Mental Health Inst., Nashville, 1971-72; dir. Nashville Drug Treatment Ctr., 1972-73; instr. mental health Vanderbilt U., Nashville, 1973-76, asst. prof. mental health, 1976-78, assoc. prof. mental health, 1978—, acad. chair behavioral scis. applied to nursing, 1981—; quality assurance cons. Mental Health Inst., Nashville, 1976-79; exec. council Am. Nurses Assn. Council of Specialists in Psychiat.-Mental Health Nursing, Kansas City, Mo., 1981-84. Editorial bd. Nursing Economics, 1982—; contbr. articles to publs. Bd. dirs. Womankind Health Center, Nashville, 1982—, Nashville Opportunity House, 1983—. Recipient Shirley Titus award for Excellence in Teaching, Vanderbilt U., 1983; named Outstanding Alumna, Coll. Nursing U. Tenn.-Memphis, 1982. Mem. Am. Nurses Assn. (exec. council psychiat.-mental health nursing 1980-83), Am. Hosp. Assn. (governing council psychiat. sect. 1984—), ABA, Sigma Theta Tau. Office: Vanderbilt Univ School Nursing 409 Godchaux Hall Nashville TN 37240

BEU, MARJORIE JANET, music director; b. Elgin, Ill., Nov. 22, 1921; d. Herman Henry and Hattie Belle (Beverly) B.; B.M., Am. Conservatory Music, 1949; B.M.Ed., 1949, M.M.Ed., 1953; advanced cert. No. Ill. U., 1969; D.Ed., U. Sarasota, 1979. Music tchr. Sch. Dist. 21, Wheeling, Ill., 1961-64; music and fine arts coordinator, 1964-68, asst. supt. instrn., 1968-79; minister of music United Meth. Ch., Sun City Center, Fla., 1980—; dir. Sun City Ctr. Kings Point Community Chorus, 1984—; pres. Council Study and Devel. Ednl. Resources, 1971-79. Pres., Wheeling Community Concerts Assn.; dir. Community Chorus; pres. Sun City Center Concert Series. Mem. NEA, Am. Guild Organists and Choir Dirs., Music Educators Nat. Conf., Assn. Supervision and Curriculum Devel., Ill. Edn. Assn., Ill. Council Gifted, No. Ill. Assn. Ednl. Research, Evaluation and Devel. (pres.), Mu Phi Epsilon, Phi Delta Kappa (sec. N.W. Suburban Cook County chpt.), Delta Kappa Pi (pres. alumni chpt.). Home: 610 Fort Duquesna Dr Sun City Center FL 33570

BEUGEN, JOAN BETH, communications company executive; b. Chgo., Mar. 9, 1943; d. Leslie and Janet (Glick) Caplan; B.S. in Speech, Northwestern U., 1965; m. Sheldon Howard Beugen, July 16, 1967. Founder, prin., pres. The Creative Establishment, Inc., Chgo., N.Y.C., San Francisco and Tokyo, 1969—; speaker on entrepreneurship for women. Del., White House Conf. on Small Bus., 1979; vice-chmn. Ill. Del. to White House Conf., 1979; trustee Mt. Sinai Hosp. Med. Ctr.; bd. dirs. Chgo. Network Named Entrepreneur of Yr., Women in Bus. Mem. Nat. Assn. Women Bus. Owners (pres. Chgo. chpt. 1979), Ill. Women's Agenda, Chgo. Assn. Commerce and Industry, Chgo. Audio-Visual Producers Assn., Chgo. Film Council, Women in Film, Com. of 200 Midwest chmn.), Nat. Women's Forum (YWCA leadership award 1985), Overseas Edn. Fund Women in Bus. Com. Contbr. articles in field to profl. jours. Office: 1421 N Wells St Chicago IL 60610

BEUTELL, NORMA JEAN, dance educator, administrator; b. St. Louis, Feb. 18, 1934; d. Albert Jacob and Gladene Mildred (Waller) B.; m. William George Van Sickle; children—Denise, Mark. Student pub. schs., Normandy, Mo. Owner, artistic dir. Beutell Sch. of Dance, St. Ann and Manchester, Mo., 1951—; artistic dir. Gateway Ballet of St. Louis, St. Ann, 1974—. Choreographer (ballet) Fugue, 1975, Bras et Jambe, 1981, Amron, 1983. Mem. Mo. Bot. Gardens, Friends of St. Louis Art Mus., Tchr., choreographer Miss Dance of Am., 1979, Jr. Miss, 1983. Mem. Dance Masters Am. (1st place 1985), Cecchetti Council Am., Dance Educators Am., West St. Louis County C. of C. Methodist. Avocation: travel. Home: 13570 Amiot Saint Louis MO 63146 Office: Gateway Ballet of Saint Louis 10674 St Charles Rock Rd Saint Ann MO 63074

BEUTLER, LISA, park ranger; b. Oakland, Calif., Sept. 28, 1953; d. Charles Stanley and Beth (Peterson) B.; m. Michael Steven Decker, (div.); 1 child, Emily Decker; m. Ronald Edward Rowan, Dec. 31, 1983; 1 child, Matthew Beutler. Student Coll. San Mateo, Calif., 1976, West Valley Coll., Saratoga, Calif., 1976-77; B.S., U. San Francisco, 1986. Park ranger Calif. Dept. Parks and Recreation, 1974—; spl. cons. Office of Lt. Gov., Sacramento, 1982-83; spl. cons. law enforcement and environ. affairs Calif. State Lands Commn., Sacramento, 1983—; mem. Park Mgmt. Adv. Bd., West Valley Coll., 1980—; advisor U.S. Fish and Wildlife Service, Newark, Calif., 1982; legis. coordinator Calif. Union of Safety Employees, Sacramento, 1982-83, legis. dir., 1985-86. Contbr. articles to profl. jours. Recipient Letter of Commendation for Rescue Assistance, Nat. Park Services, 1976; Letter of Commendation for Outstanding Performance Calif. Dept. Parks. Año Nuevo State Res., 1977; Award of Outstanding Achievement, Calif. Union Safety Employees, 1985. Mem. State Park Peace Officers Assn. (bd. dirs. 1981-84, 86), Calif. State Park Rangers Assn., Calif. Peace Officers Assn., Peace Officers Research Assn. Calif., NOW, Audubon Soc., Greenpeace, Sierra Club. Democrat. Avocations: performing arts. Office: Calif State Lands Commn 1807 13th St Sacramento CA 95814

BEVELACQUA, DARCY HENDRICKSON, marketing executive, personnel consultant; b. Mt. Kisco, N.Y., Aug. 14, 1949; d. Veryl Philip and Elizabeth Ralph) Bevelacqua; m. George Stanhope Wiedemann, III, Feb. 28, 1978 (div.); m. Antoine Bertram Giaume, Mar. 26, 1983; children—A. Pearson, Ashton. B.A. in Psychology, Hood Coll., 1971; M.A. in Human Resources, New Sch. for Social Research, 1976. Circulation mgr. Time, Inc., N.Y.C., 1971-72; chmn. dept. learning disabilities W. Frederick Jr. High Sch., Frederick, Md., 1972-73; mktg. mgr. Chem. Bank, N.Y.C., 1974-77; systems cons. Revlon, Inc., N.Y.C., 1977-78; personnel mgr. Pfizer, Inc., N.Y.C., 1978-80; dir. bus. devel. Am. Express Corp., N.Y.C., 1980-85; mgr. fin. services mktg. Trintex, White Plains, N.Y., 1985—; personnel cons. Counseling Women, N.Y.C., 1980-83; pvt. practice career counselor, N.Y.C., 1978—. Recipient Isadore Lubin award New Sch. for Social Research, 1976, Percy Johnson award Chem. Bank, 1976. Mem. Direct Mktg. Idea Exchange, Direct Mktg. Assn. (pres. salary group 1981-82), Amateur Comedy Club. Republican. Episcopalian. Home: 118 Cross Hwy Westport CT 06880 Office: Trintex 123 Main St White Plains NY 10601

BEVERIDGE, LYNN RUTH, speech pathologist; b. Hartford, Conn., Jan. 9, 1953; d. Russell David and Ruth Julia (Seagren) Beveridge; B.S. in Edn., U. Hartford, 1974; postgrad. So. Conn. State U. Aide in learning disabilities class, substitute tchr. West Hartford (Conn.) public schs., 1975; speech, hearing, lang. pathologist New Britain (Conn.) pub. schs., 1978-82. Lic. speech pathologist, Conn.; cert. speech and hearing specialist, Conn.; cert. elem. sch. tchr., Conn. Mem. Conn. Fedn. Tchrs., Am. Speech and Hearing Assn. (cert. clin. competence), Conn. Speech and Hearing Assn. Republican. Lutheran. Lodge: Order of Rainbow (worthy advisor 1970, state rep. 1971, recipient Grand Cross of Color 1972). Home: 47 Broadview St Newington CT 06111

BEVILACQUA, LINDA MARIE, university administrator; b. Jamaica, N.Y., Mar. 7, 1941; d. Michael and Eleanor B.; B.S. magna cum laude, Barry Coll., Miami, Fla., 1962; M.Ed., Siena Heights Coll., Adrian, Mich., 1969; Ph.D. (Outstanding Grad. Student 1980; Julius E. Barbour scholar 1980), Mich. State U., 1980. Joined Sisters of St. Dominic, Roman Catholic Ch., 1962; 1st grade tchr., Mich., 1964-69; asst. dean students, then dean students Barry U., 1969-78, dir. alternative programs, 1981-82, assoc. v.p. acad. affairs, dean Sch. Adult Edn., 1982—; trustee Siena Heights Coll., 1978-80. Mem. Am. Assn. Higher Edn., Am. Assn. Univ. Adminstrs., Kappa Gamma Pi, Kappa Delta Pi, Phi Delta Kappa. Home: 11300 NE 2d Ave Miami FL 33161 Office: 11300 NE 2d Ave Miami FL 33161

BEVIS, CAESI AILEEN, communications executive; b. Cin., Jan. 31, 1956; d. Harold Edward and Dorothy Leona (Bevis) Morgan; 1 foster child, Juadi (Indonesia). A.A. in Advt., Mauna Olu Coll., U.S. Internat. U., Maui, Hawaii 1975; B.B.A. in Mktg. and Fin., U.S. Internat. U., San Diego, 1982, M.I.B.A. in Fin. and Mktg., 1984, Ph.D. in progress, 1984—. Residential resale agt. Coldwell Banker, San Diego, 1978-79, Century 21, San Diego, 1979; leasing agt. Apartment Selector, San Diego, 1979-80; estate planning agt. State Mutual Life, San Diego, 1980-81; account rep. Cordura Publs., San Diego, 1983-85; equal access cons. Allnet Communications, San Diego, 1985—; lectr. in field; teaching asst. U.S. Internat. U., 1977. Author unpub. work used in univ. Speed Reading for the International Student, 1982; editor unpub. work used in univ. Learning English through the Music of Ireland, England and the U.S.A., 1982. Pres. local chpt. Am. Field Service, 1971-74; local coordinator Foster Parents Plan Inc., 1985—; mem., speaker World Future Soc., 1985—. Recipient Betty Crocker Homemakers award, 1974, Quill and Scroll award, 1974; Top Producer of Month award Apartment Selector, 1979-80; Ace award for rookie prodn. State Mutual Life, 1981; Top Producer awards Cordura Publs., 1983, 84. Mem. Assn. M.B.A. Execs., Nat. Assn. Female Execs. Democrat. Avocations: research writing; backgammon; chess; pingpong; sketching. Home: 3918 La Jolla Village Dr La Jolla CA 92037

BEVIS, PATRICIA ANN, financial and marketing executive; b. Florence, Ala., May 9, 1955; d. G. Joe and Billie (Grisham) B.; ed. U. Ala., 1977, Smith Coll.; cert. Sorbonne, Paris, summer 1977. Cosmetics buyer R. H. Macy's, N.Y.C., 1981-82; bank officer mktg. dept. Citibank, N.Y.C., 1982-83; fin. and mktg. analyst, v.p. E.F. Hutton Co., Inc., N.Y.C., 1983—. Bd. dirs. Mary Anthony/Phoenix Dance Co.; mem. vol. councal N.Y. Philharm. Symphony. Recipient Outstanding Young Alumni award U. Ala., 1982. Mem. Panhellenic (sec. 1980), U. Ala. Alumni Assn. (v.p. student affairs, v.p. alumni), N.Y. Jr. League, Fin. Women's Assn., Partnership Analyst Soc. N.Y. (founder), Mu Phi Epsilon, Alpha Delta Pi (Outstanding Alumna). Presbyterian. Club: Smith (N.Y.C.).

BEYER, CHARLOTTE BISHOP, banker; b. N.Y.C., Oct. 16, 1947; d. Edward Morton and Chrlotte Reid (Handy) Beyer; B.A., Hunter Coll., 1969; m. Warren P. Weitman, Jr., July 28, 1967; children—Catherine Scott, Michael Benjamin; m. Scott Edward Thomas, Dec. 17, 1983. With Bankers Trust Co., N.Y.C., 1970-81, v.p. trust services and securities ops., 1979-81; dir. Can. mktg. Technimetrics, 1981-83; new bus./mktg. trust officer Fidleity Union Bank, Morristown, N.J., 1983—. Head Sunday Sch., Grace Ch., Bklyn. Heights, N.Y. Mem. N.Y. State Bankers Assn. (trust ops. com.), Morris County C. of C. Episcopalian. Office: Fidelity Union Bank 55 Madison Ave Morristown NJ 07960*

BEYER, JACQUELYN L., geography educator; b. Mitchell, S.D., July 11, 1924; d. Hayes Rutherford and Olive Grace (Garver) B.; B.A. in Journalism, U. Colo., Boulder, 1944, M.A. in Geography, 1954; Ph.D. in Geography, U. Chgo., 1957. Asst. prof. geography U. Mont., 1957-58, 59-60; vis. lectr. U. Tex., 1958-59; lectr. U. Cape Town (South Africa), 1960-64; asst. prof. Rutgers U., 1964-69; assoc. prof. U. Colo., Colorado Springs, 1970-73, prof., 1973—. Bd. dirs. Social Service Edn. Consortium. Served with WAC, U.S. Army, 1944-48, 52. Water Resources Research Inst. grantee, 1968-69. Mem. Assn. Am. Geographers, Nat. Council Geog. Edn., AAAS, African Studies Assn., Consortium on Peace Research, Edn. and Devel., Western African Studies Assn., Colo. Women Studies Assn., Soc. Woman Geographers. Contbr. chpts., articles to profl. publs. Office: Dept Geog and Environ Studies U Colo Box 7150 Colorado Springs CO 80933

BEYER, KAREN ANN, social worker; b. Cleve., Jan. 30, 1942; d. William Pryor and Evelyn Ann Haynes; B.A., Ohio State U., 1965; M.S.W., Loyola U., Chgo., 1969; cert. Family Inst., Northwestern U., 1979; 1 dau., Jennifer. With Cuyahoga County Div. Child Welfare, Cleve., 1965, Dallas County Child Welfare Unit, Dallas, 1966, Luth. Welfare Services Ill., Chgo., 1967-73; pvt. practice clin. social work, Barrington, Ill., 1975—; therapist Family Service Assn. Greater Elgin (Ill.), 1973-77, dir. profl. services, 1977-83; pvt. practice family mediation, 1981—; dir. health and human services Village of Hoffman Estates (Ill.), 1983—. Mem. Mediation Council Ill., Acad. Cert. Social Workers, Am. Assn. Marriage and Family Therapy. Unitarian. Home: 640 E Illinois Blvd Hoffman Estates IL 60194

BEYER, SUZANNE, advertising agency executive; b. N.Y.C.; d. Harry and Jennie Hillman; grad. Conservatory of Musical Art, 1943-47, Nassau Community Coll., 1963-65; m. Isadore Beyer, Oct. 19, 1947; children—Pamela Claire, Hillary Jay. Singer, tchr. piano, N.Y.C., 1947-66; asst. to v.p. media dir. Robert E. Wilson, Advt., N.Y.C., 1967-72; media planner, media buyer Frank J. Corbett div. BBDO Advt., N.Y.C., 1972-77; media planner, media buyer Lavey/Wolff/Swift div. BBDO Advt., N.Y.C., 1977-80, sr. media planner, 1980-83, media supr., 1983—; soprano Opera Assn. Nassau, 1976—, United Choral Soc., Woodmere, L.I., N.Y., 1970—, Armand Sodero Chorale, Baldwin, L.I., 1980—. Mem. Pharm. Advt. Council, L.I. Advt. Club, Healthcare Businesswomen's Assn. Home: 66 Fonda Rd Rockville Centre NY 11570 Office: 488 Madison Ave New York NY 10022

BEYER-MEARS, ANNETTE, physiologist; b. Madison, Wis., May 26, 1941; d. Karl and Annette (Weiss) Beyer; B.A., Vassar Coll., 1963; M.S., Fairleigh Dickinson U., 1973; Ph.D., Coll. Medicine and Dentistry N.J., 1977; m. William H. Mears, Jr.; 1 son, Karl. NIH fellow Cornell U. Med. Sch., 1963-65; instr. physiology Springside Coll., Phila., 1967-71; teaching asst. dept. physiology Coll. Medicine and Dentistry N.J., N.J. Med. Sch., 1974-77, NIH fellow dept. ophthalmology, 1978-80; asst. prof. dept. ophthalmology U. Medicine and Dentistry N.J., N.J. Med. Sch., Newark, 1979—, asst. prof. dept. physiology, 1980-85, assoc. prof., 1986—, assoc. prof. dept. ophthalmology, 1986—; cons. Alcon Labs. Chmn. admissions No. N.J., Vassar Coll., 1974-79; mem. minister search com. St. Bartholomew Episcopal Ch., Ridgewood, N.J., 1978, fund-raising chmn., 1978, 79; del. Epis. Diocesian Conv., 1977, 78. NIH Nat. Research Service award, 1978-80; NIH Research awardee, 1980—; grantee Juvenile Diabetes Found., 1985, Pfizer, 1983, Found. CMDNJ Research award, 1980. Mem. Am. Physiol. Soc., N.Y. Acad. Scis., Soc. for Neurosci., Am. Soc. Pharmacology and Exptl. and Therapeutics, Am. Diabetes Assn., Assn. for Research in Vision and Ophthalmology, Internat. Soc. for Eye Research, AAAS, Sigma Xi, Aircraft Owners and Pilots Assn., CAP. Contbr. articles in field of diabetic lens and kidney therapy to profl. jours. Office: U Medicine and Dentistry NJ-NJ Med Sch Dept Physiology 100 Bergen St Newark NJ 07103

BEYERS, BERNICE WEST (MRS. ROBERT A. BEYERS), sculptor; b. N.Y.C., Apr. 26, 1906; d. E. Lovette and Bess (Palmer) West; A.A. in Fine Arts and Drama, Bennett Coll., 1925; pupil Alexander Archipenko, Edmond Amateis, Lu Duble, William Zorach, Winold Reiss, 1926-28, 1929, 1921-25, 1930; m. Robert A. Beyers, Mar. 2, 1940 (dec. Feb. 1962); children—Robert West, Arthur L. Exhibited one-woman shows Contemporary Arts Gallery, N.Y.C., 1931, Feragil Galleries, N.Y.C., 1933, Mid-Town Gallery, N.Y.C., 1932, Mint Mus., Charlotte, N.C., 1941, other galleries in South and Southwestern U.S.; group exhbns. include So. Vt. Art Center, Manchester, 1929-71, Mt. Dora (Fla.) Art League, 1935-40, Tex. Ann. and Dallas County Ann., 1946-67, Dallas Mus. Fine Arts, 1946-67, numerous others; represented in permanent collections including monument at Silver Springs, Fla., displays at Mead Bot. Gardens, Winter Park, Fla., Venice-Nokomis, Fla., Wadsworth Athenaeum, Hartford, Conn., Swarthmore Coll., Mint Mus. Mem. women's com. Dallas Theater Center; mem. Dallas Art Mus. League. Bd. dirs. Dallas Symphony Orch. League, Dallas Opera Guild; trustee Dallas Ballet Soc. (Trustee) Dallas Symphony Assn., Dallas Opera, So. Vt. Artists, Inc. Awarded 1st prize sculpture So. States Art League, 1940, Conn. Acad. Fine Arts, 1943; recipient Medal of Honor Nat. Assn. Women Artists, 1932. Mem. Craft Guild Dallas, Print Soc. Dallas, Dallas Hist. Soc., Local History and Geneal. Soc., So. Vt. Artists (hon. trustee), D.A.R., Soc. Mayflower Descs., Nat. Soc. Magna Carta Dames, Colonial Order of Crown, Soc. Descs. Most Noble Order Knights of Garter, Plantegenet Soc., Sovereign Colonial Soc., Ams. Royal Descent, Nat. Soc. Women Descs. of Ancient and Hon. Arty. Co., Soc. Old Plymouth Colony Descendants, Nat. Soc. Colonial Dames Am., Nat. Soc. New Eng. Women, Order Descs. Colonial Govs., Nat. Soc. Daus. Am. Colonists, Nat. Soc. Daus. Founders and Patriots Am., Order of Washington, Soc. Daus. Colonial Wars. Episcopalian. Clubs: Garden, Woman's Brook Hollow Golf (Dallas); Pen and Brush (N.Y.C.); Ekwanok Country (Vt.).

BEYNON-FAIR, BARBARA ELIZABETH, petroleum geologist; b. Fort Bragg, N.C., Dec. 7, 1955; d. James L. and Elizabeth (Bruns) Beynon; m. David Len Fair, Jan. 28, 1984. B.A. in Geology, Tex. A & I U., 1976. Geologist Valero Transmission Co., Corpus Christi, Tex., 1977-80, Transcontinental Gas Pipe Line, Houston, 1980-81, Champlin Petroleum Co., Corpus Christi and Houston, 1981-84, geol. cons., Newman Ga., 1984—. Mem. Am. Assn. Petroleum Geologists, Am. Inst. Profl. Geologists, Soc. Profl. Well Log Analysts. Office: PO Box 2212 Newnan GA 30264

BEYRER, MARY KATHERINE, health education educator; b. South Bend, Ind., Mar. 3, 1922; d. Charles H. and L. Marie (Brickell) B.; B.A., Macalester Coll., 1944; M.S., MacMurray Coll., 1950; Ph.D., Ohio State U., 1959. Tchr. health and phys. edn. Buffalo (Minn.) High Sch., 1944-47, Harrisonburg (Va.) High Sch., 1948-51; teaching asst. MacMurray Coll., 1947-48; asst. prof. health and phys. edn. Madison Coll., Harrisonburg, 1951-56; teaching assoc. Ohio State U., Columbus, 1956-57, instr. health edn., 1957-59, asst. prof., 1959-61, assoc. prof., 1961-64, prof., 1964—, dir. Sch. Health, Phys. Edn., and Recreation, 1977-81. Recipient Alumni citation Macalester Coll. 1964. AAHPERD scholar, 1978-79. Mem. AAHPERD. (Honor Fellow award 1969, exec. com. 1981-84, nat. pres. 1982-83; health edn. award Midwest dist. 1984), Am. Acad. Phys. Edn., Am. Pub. Health Assn., Am. Sch. Health Assn., Assn. Supervision and Curriculum Devel., Ohio Assn. Health, Phys. Edn., Recreation and Dance (cert. of merit 1967), Assn. Advancement Health Edn. (Profl. Service to Health Edn. award 1976, Scholar award 1978), Eta Sigma Gamma, Phi Delta Kappa. Republican. Presbyterian. Author: (with D. Oberteuffer) School Health Education, 1966; (with M.K. Solleder) Directory of Selected References and Resources for Health Education, 1969, 2d edit., 1981; editor: Health Education Completed Research, 1974, 2d edit., 1979. Home: 4012 Lyon Dr Columbus OH 43220 Office: 1760 Neil Ave Columbus OH 43210

BEZOUSKA, CHRISTINE ANN, surgeon; b. Atlanta, Nov. 27, 1949; d. Thomas Jones and Agnes Eleanor (Back) Bezouska; m. Jan Ladd Ditzian, Jan. 26, 1985. B.A. summa cum laude SUNY-Buffalo, 1974, M.D., 1978. Diplomate Nat. Bd. Med. Examiners. Clin. instr. SUNY-Buffalo, Sch. Medicine, 1978-84; resident in surgery Buffalo. Gen. Hosp., 1978-82, chief resident in gen. surgery, 1982-83, fellow colorectal surgery, 1983-84. Mem. AMA, Am. Soc. Colon and Rectal Surgeons, Am. Med. Women's Assn., Nat. Audubon Soc. Home: 131 Brennan Rd Wexford PA 15090 Office: 4815 Liberty Ave Pittsburgh PA 15224

BHALLI, SHERRY ARLENE BARLOW, renal dietitian, medical educator; b. Wichita Falls, Tex., Oct. 22, 1942; d. Fred Terry and Juanita Jean (Ballard) B. B.S. in Nutrition, U. Tex., Austin, 1964; M.S. in Nutrition, Tex. Woman's U., Houston, 1983. Registered dietitian. Chief research dietitian M.D. Anderson Hosp., Houston, 1965-68; renal dietitian U. Tex. Med. Br., Galveston, 1968-71, Charity Hosp., New Orleans, 1971-73; cons. renal dietitian Madisonville Hosp., 1977-81, Jacinto Dialysis Unit, San Jacinto, Tex., 1981—; renal dietitian, instr. medicine Methodist Hosp., Houston, 1973—; founding chmn. Council on Renal Nutrition, 1972-76; nutrition rep. ESRD Coordinating Council, 1976—. Author: Renal Diet Guide for Patients on Dialysis, 1976; All About Dialysis, 1977; contbr. articles to profl. jours. Bd. dirs. Houston Kidney Found. Mem. Am. Dietetic Assn., Tex. Dietetic Assn., Nat. Kidney Found. Council on Renal Nutrition, Houston Kidney Found., Internat. Platform Assn. Home: 2125 Nantucket St Apt 1 Houston TX 77057 Office: Community Dialysis Unit Methodist Hosp Annex 1130 Earle St Houston TX 77030

BIANUCCI, KATHERINE PETTAS, real estate broker; b. Chgo., Sept. 15, 1937; d. John and Celia (Dragonas) Pettas; m. Donald Bianucci, Nov. 4, 1956; children—Denise Bianucci Spetter, Angela. Student pub. schs. Installment loan staff Cicero State Bank (Ill.), 1963-70; broker Pav/Hanson Realty, Berwyn, Ill., 1974-75; broker owner Village Ctr. Realty, Berwyn, 1975; with Century 21 K-Rich Realty, Berwyn, Ill., 1976—, now co-owner, dir.; dir. West Town Bd. Realtors, Cicero, 1980-82, dir., 1984-86. Mem. Women's Council Realtors. Greek Orthodox. Office: Century 21 K-Rich Realty Inc 6508 W Cermak Rd Berwyn IL 60402

BIAZAR, CYNTHIA LYNN, business executive; b. Denver, Feb. 11, 1960; Loujuan S. and Pauline Ann (Jones) Green; m. Esfandiar Biazar, Dec. 12, 1981 (dec. Aug. 1984); 1 child, Chad Arash. B.S. in Bus. Adminstrn., Chapman Coll., Orange, Calif., 1982. Student asst. Chapman Coll. Student Store, 1979, sec., 1979-80, asst. mgr., 1980-82; mgr. United Art Co. div. Follett Corp., Chapman Coll. Bookstore, Orange, 1982-84; controller Sandco Am./Fed. Am. Fin. Corp., Newport Beach, Calif., 1984—. Recipient Internat. Youth in Achievement award Internat. Biog. Ctr., 1981. Mem. Nat. Assn. Female Execs., Beta Chi (sec., treas. 1979-81; Orange). Home: 1645 Riverview Ave Orange CA 92665 Office: Sandco Am 3931 MacArthur Blvd Suite 207 Newport Beach CA

BIBEAU, DOROTHY STEVENS, construction company executive, consultant; b. Springfield, Mass., Jan. 18, 1933; d. Miles Earl Stevens and Alma Rose (Castonquay) LaRoche; m. Ovila L. Bibeau, July 1, 1950; children—Julie Bibeau Eckerson, Lynn Bibeau Henderson. A.S. with honors, SUNY, 1983. R.N., N.Y. Sec., Bibeau Constrn. Co., Spring Valley, N.Y., 1968-85, project coordinator Neighborhood Health Assn. Mt. Vernon, Inc., N.Y., 1985—; cons. Med Sell, Inc., N.Y.C., 1984-85. Roman Catholic. Home: Turtle Point Rd Tuxedo Park NY 10987

BIBERGALL, JO ANNE, biology educator; b. Chgo., Feb. 6, 1942; d. Charles Frederick and Blanche Marie (Vavak) Barry; m. Gerald Reginald Bibergall, Nov. 28, 1964. B.S., U. Ill., 1964, M.S., 1966; postgrad. N.E. Ill. U., 1968-72, Govs. State U., 1977-78, No. Ill. U., 1978-79, 84—. Cert. high sch. tchr., Ill. Histologist, Field Mus. Nat. History, Chgo., summer 1961; entomol. technician of jr. sci. Ill. State Natural History Survey, Urbana, 1963-65; jr. high sch. tchr. Sch. Dist. 57, Mt. Prospect, Ill., 1964-66; med. transcriptionist Holy Family Hosp., Des Plaines, Ill., 1968-69; high sch. tchr. Sch. Dist. 214, Mt. Prospect, 1966—. Contbr. articles to profl. jours. NSF grantee U. Calif.-San Diego, 1970, Berkeley, 1973; Am. Cancer Soc. scholar Mt. Sinai Hosp., Chgo., 1979. Mem. Nat. Assn. Biology Tchrs. (named Outstanding Biology Tchr. Ill. 1979), No. Ill. Assn. Biology Tchrs., Ill. Sci. Tchrs., Ill. Earth Sci. Tchrs., Kappa Delta Pi. Club: Glenbard All Breed Obedience. Avocations: dog obedience training and showing, crafts. Home: 346 N Brandon Dr Glendale Heights IL 60139 Office: Wheeling High Sch 900 S Elmhurst Wheeling IL 60090

BIBLE, FRANCES LILLIAN, mezzo soprano, educator; b. Sackets Harbor, N.Y., Jan. 26; d. Arthur and Lillian (Cooke) Bible. Student Juilliard Sch. Music, 1939-47. Appeared throughout U.S., Australia, Europe including: Vienna Staatsoper, Karlsruhe Staatsoper, Dublin Opera Co., N.Y.C. Opera, NBC-TV Opera San Francisco Opera, Glyndebourne Opera, San Antonio Opera Festival, New Orleans Opera, Houston Grand Opera, Miami Opera, Dallas Opera; appeared in concert with major symphonies; artist-in-residence Shepherd Sch. Music, Rice U., Houston, 1975—. Mem. Am. Guild Mus. Artists (past 3d v.p.), Sigma Alpha Iota (hon.), Beta Sigma Phi (hon.). Republican. Episcopalian. Home: 2225 Bolsover St Houston TX 77005

BICHLMEIER, JOYCE ANNETTE, insurance agent; b. Los Angeles, July 1, 1940; d. Finis Arthur and Albina Frances (Cvikel) Brown; m. Germanus Joseph Bichlmeier, Feb. 7, 1959 (div.); children—Cary John, Terry Edward, Sherrie Ann; m. 2d Bruce Craig Bottrell, Oct. 16, 1982. With May Co., Los Angeles, 1955-59; ins. agt. J. Bichlmeier Ins. Agy., Los Angeles, also Carson, Manhattan Beach and Hermosa Beach, Calif., 1961—, prin. agt./broker, Hermosa Beach. Charter mem. Republican Presdl. Task Force, Washington, 1982-83; charter pack leader Cub Scouts, Carson, Calif., 1968-71, troop leader Boy Scouts, Manhattan Beach, 1971-75; treas. v.p. Leapwood Ave. PTA, Carson, 1964-70. Named South Bay Woman of Yr., YWCA, Torrance, Calif., 1982, Ins. Woman of Yr., Ind. Ins. Agts. and Brokers, Inglewood, Calif., 1974—. Mem. Profl. Ins. Agts. (chpt. pres. 1979-80, state sec. 1981-82, state v.p. 1980-84, state pres. elect 1984—, Agt. of Yr. award 1983), Nat. Assn. Ins. Woman (pub. relations chmn. S. Bay chpt., pres. pub. 1984—, relations award 1983), Hermosa Beach C. of C. (pres. 1982-83, Dir. of Yr. award 1982). Republican. Roman Catholic. Club: Dolphins. Office: J Bichlmeier Ins Agy PO Box 929 200 Pier Ave #30 Hermosa Beach CA 90254

BICK, KATHERINE LIVINGSTONE, scientist, government official; b. Charlottetown, Can., May 3, 1932; came to U.S., 1954; d. Spurgeon Arthur and Flora Hazel (Murray) Livingstone; m. James Harry Bick, Aug. 20, 1955 (div.); children—James A., Charles L.; M. Ernst Freese, 1986. B.Sc. with honors, Acadia U. (Can.), 1951, M.Sc., 1952; Ph.D., Brown U., 1957. Research pathologist UCLA Med. Sch., 1959-61; asst. prof. Calif. State U.-Northridge, 1961-66; lab. instr. Georgetown U., Washington, 1970-72, asst. prof., 1972-76; dep. dir. neurol. disorder program Nat. Inst. Neurol. and Communicative Disorders and Stroke, NIH, Bethesda, Md., 1976-81, acting dep. dir., 1981-83, dep. dir., 1983—. Editor: Alzheimer's Disease: Senile Dementia and Related Disorders, 1978; Neurosecretion and Brain Peptides, Implications for Brain Functions and Neurological Disease, 1981; contbr. articles to profl. jours. Pres. Woman's Club, McLean, Va., 1968-69; bd. dirs. Fairfax County YWCA (Va.), 1969-70; pres. Emerson Unitarian Ch., 1964-66, Bethesda Place Homeowner's Assn., 1982. Recipient Can. NRC award Acadia U., 1951-52, fellow, 1951-52; Universal Match Found. fellow Brown U., 1956-57; NIH Dir.'s award, 1978; Fed. Exec. Inst. Leadership fellow, 1980; Spl. Achievement award NIH, 1981, 83; Superior Service award USPHS, 1986. Mem. Am. Neurol. Assn., Am. Acad. Neurology, AAAS, Am. Soc. Zoologists, Western Soc. Naturalists, Assn. for Research in Nervous and Mental Disease, Internat. Brain Research Orgn., World Fedn. Neurology Research Group on Dementias (exec. sec. Am. region 1984—). Office: NIH Nat Inst of Neurol and Communicative Disorders and Stroke 9000 Rockville Pike Bldg 31 Room 8A52 Bethesda MD 20892

BICKAR, BETTY ARLENE, business systems executive; b. Plattville, Colo., Nov. 14, 1931; d. Leslie William and Kathryn Mabel (Rutherford) Clawson; children—Patricia J., Andrew L. Bookkeeper, office mgr. Manes Logging Co., Clallam Bay, Wash., 1958-70; stenographer, prodn. acct. Crown Zellerbach Corp., Sekiu, Wash., 1970-73; bookkeeper, acct., office mgr., A. W. Logging Inc., Corner Bay, Alaska, 1973-79; owner, operator Spectra Northwest, specializing in photo identification and plastic lamination, Bellevue, Wash., 1979—. Mem. Faith, Hope and Love Christian and Healing Ctr., Issaquah, Wash. Lic. ins. agt., Wash. Mem. Nat. Fedn. Ind. Bus. Home: 12612 S E 30th St Bellevue WA 98005 Office: Spectra Northwest 1840 130th Ave NE Suite 6 Bellevue WA 98005

BICKERS, CONSTANCE RADCLIFFE, ins. co. exec.; b. Lorain, Ohio, Aug. 11, 1933; d. Howard Hugh and Harriet Alice (Lipple) Radcliffe; student LaSalle U., Lorain Community Coll.; m. Herbert Bennett Bickers, Nov. 24, 1955. Bookkeeper, McGeachie Plumbing and Heating Co., Lorain, 1950-51, Penn Rubber Co., Lorain, 1951-52, office mgr. Packard Motor Co., Lorain, 1952-54, Bay View Hosp., Bay Village, Ohio, 1954-57, acct., 1957-65, asst. adminstr., 1965-76; dir. provider affairs Blue Cross N.E. Ohio, Cleve., 1976-81, v.p. benefits adminstrn., 1982—. Mem. Hosp. Fin. Mgmt. Assn. (recipient Frederick T. Muncie award 1973, Dale L. Reed award 1969, 70, 71, 73, William G. Follmer award; nat. dir. 1973-74), Am. Coll. Osteo. Hosp. Adminstrs. (bd. examiners), Am. Soc. Women Accts., Am. Coll. Hosp. Adminstrs., Ohio Hosp. Assn., Health Care Adminstrs. N.E. Ohio, Fedn. Community Planning, Citizens League Greater Cleve., Am. Coll. Nursing Home Adminstrs., Am. Hosp. Assn., Nat. Council for Prescription Drug Program, Am. Med. Record Assn. Club: Women's City (Cleve.). Contbr. articles to profl. jours. Home: 315 Harris Rd Sheffield Lake OH 44054 Office: 2066 9th St E Cleveland OH 44115

BICKERSTAFF, LINDA, lawyer; b. Oklahoma City, June 4, 1954; d. Robert H. and Lois Ruth (Holder) Bickerstaff; m. Jeffrey Scott Bolgren, Sept. 18, 1979; 1 child, Daniel Reade. B.A. magna cum laude, Oklahoma City U., 1976, J.D., 1980. Bar: Okla. 1983, U.S. Dist. Ct. (we. dist.) Okla. 1984. Grad. teaching asst. U. Okla., Norman, 1976-77; coordinator judiciary com. Okla. State Senate, Oklahoma City, 1980-83; atty. for ops. Rev. and Evaluation div. Okla. Dept. Transp., Oklahoma City, 1983—. Recipient Oklahoma City U. Law scholarship, 1978, Okla. Bar Assn. scholarship, 1977, Oklahoma City U. scholarship, 1972-76, Banning Found. scholarship, 1972-73, Frank Horton scholarship, 1975-76; recipient Virginia Goff award as Outstanding English Major, 1976; winner Okla. U. Scholar-Leadership Enrichment Program, 1976. Mem. Okla. Bar Assn., ABA, Southwest Attys. Assn., Fed. Bar Assn. Democrat. Home: 7211 NW 44th St Bethany OK 73008 Office: Okla Dept Transp 200 NE 21st St Oklahoma City OK 73105

BICKNESE, EVELYN HOLLISTER, advertising agency executive; b. Gary, Ind., Nov. 14, 1934; d. Ross R. and Leona Colburn (Metzker) Hollister; B.S., Clayton U., St. Louis, 1980; m. Donald Dale Bicknese, June 29, 1952; children—Ross, Leona, Ralph, Kent, Eileen, Susan. Owner, mgr. Bick Outdoor Advt. Co., Gary, Ind., 1957-80, Valparaiso, Ind., 1963-73, LaPorte, Ind., 1963—, St. Louis, 1981—; advt. exec. D'Arcy, Masius, Benton & Bowles, Inc., St. Louis. Leader Singing Sands council Girl Scouts U.S.A., 1972-75, Potawattomi council Boy Scouts Am., 1963-72; pres. Principia Patrons of Northwestern Ind., 1977-79; treas., exec. bd. Principia Mothers Club, 1981-82; 4-H vol. worker; co-founder Kent Hollister Bicknese Found. to prevent crime, 1983. Mem. Eight Sheet Outdoor Advt. Assn. (dir. 1975—, pres. 1982—), Ind. Sign and Display Assn. (editor newsletter 1979, dir. 1978-80), Michiana Advt. Exec. Club, C. of C., Advt. Fedn. St. Louis. Republican. Christian Scientist. Author: Mostly Manners and Survival Manners for Teenagers. Office: 0353 E 900 N LaPorte IN 46350 also 2122 S Mason Rd Saint Louis MO 63131

BIDDIX, DIANE SMELTZER, nurse; b. Swannanoa, N.C., Nov. 25, 1950; d. Henry Carter and Reba (Bright) Smeltzer; m. Charles Melvin Biddix, July 21, 1972. A.Nursing, Asheville Buncombe Tech. Coll., N.C., 1972; B.S. in Nursing, Western Carolina U., 1982. R.N., N.C. Staff nurse St. Joseph Hosp., Asheville, N.C., 1972—, mem. policies and procedure com., 1984—. Educator oncology Am. Cancer Soc., 1984—; active Profl. Cancer Soc., Asheville, 1984—; vol. Republican Com., 1984. Mem. Oncology Soc., Sigma Theta Tau (fellow). Democrat. Episcopalian. Avocations: swimming; tennis; aerobics; reading. Home: 180 Domeno Dr Swannanoa NC 28778

BIDDLE, FLORA MILLER, art museum administrator. Chmn. Whitney Mus. Am. Art, N.Y.C. Office: Whitney Museum Am Art 945 Madison Ave New York NY 10021*

BIDDLE, MARY GERALDINE STATON, nurse; b. Camden, N.J., May 16, 1943; d. Maurice Glen and Mary Dolores (McNamara) Staton; diploma in nursing, Pa. Hosp., Phila., 1964; m. Theodore Long Biddle, June 6, 1970; children—Katherine Mary and Margaret Ann (twins), Theodore Richard. Staff nurse hosps. in Phila. and Denver, 1964-70; mem. adminstrv. staff nephrology U. Rochester (N.Y.) Med. Center, 1970-84, nephrology nurse cons.; faculty mem. Sch. Nursing, U. Rochester, 1975-84. Named Profl. Person of Yr., Genessee Valley Kidney Found., 1976. Cert. hemodialysis nurse Bd. Nephrology Examiners. Mem. Am. Nephrology Nurses Assn. (dir. 1976-81, nat. pres. 1985-86; outstanding contbn. award 1985), Nat. Kidney Found. (nat. program chmn., nursing 1982), Am. Heart Assn., End Stage Renal Disease Network Coordinating Council (exec. com. 1979-84). Author papers in field. Home: 10 Pepper Ln Loudonville NY 12211 Office: ANNA North Woodbury Rd/56 Pitman NJ 08071

BIDWELL, DOROTHY KAY, high technology company executive; b. San Francisco, July 10, 1947; d. Gerald R. and Viola E. (Herker) Danks; m. Dennis A. Riggs, Feb. 10, 1968 (div. June 1973); m. John R. Bidwell, Aug. 31, 1973; 1 child, Tina Lyn Riggs. A.A., San Diego Evening Coll., 1978; paralegal cert. Paralegal Inst., Phoenix, 1984. Adminstrv. asst. to v.p. theoretical physics Sci. Applications, Inc., La Jolla, Calif., 1972-75; co-founder, corp. sec., dir. Jaycor, San Diego, 1975—. Mem. citizens adv. council Am. Inst. for Cancer Research; mem. San Diego Master Chorale, 1971—, sect. leader, 1982; mem. San Diego Symphony, 1981—. Mem. Nat. Notary Assn., Nat. Assn. Female Execs., Nat. Assn. Legal Assts., Am. Soc. Corp. Secs., Internat. Platform Assn., World Inst. Achievement, Am. Mgmt. Assn. Republican. Presbyterian. Home: 727 Sapphire St Apt 407 San Diego CA 92109 Office: Jaycor 11011 Torreyana Rd San Diego CA 92121

BIEBER, (BERNICE) JEAN, association executive; b. Newport, Ky., Feb. 7, 1920; d. Edward Griggs and Irene Gertrude (Bird) Nieder; m. Ralph Gordon Bieber, Oct. 2, 1942; children—Karen Anne Downing, Gail Bieber, Susan Jill Rowe. B.A. in Journalism, Ohio State U., 1942. Freelance writer trade mags. Universal Trade Press Syndicate, 1947-50; writer, photographer mental hygiene Dept. of State, Ohio, parttime 1951-53; writer, editor Univ. Film Producers Jour., part-time 1955-58; communications dir. Easter Seals, Columbus, Ohio, 1959—. Editor: Something "Crummy" Cooking for Easter Seals, 1983; The News Parade newsletter. Named Staff Person of Yr., Easter Seals, Columbus, 1977, 84; nat. photo contest winner Nat. Easter Seal Soc., 1982. Mem. Women in Communications (past chpt. pres., commendation cert. for newsletter and photo 1979). Republican. Baptist. Home: 6676 Feder Rd Galloway OH 43119 Office: Easter Seal Rehab Center PO Box 7166 565 Children's Dr W Columbus OH 43205

BIEBER, KAREN RUTH, lawyer; b. San Francisco, Dec. 12, 1949; d. Leo Anthony and Evelyn (O'Brien) Gambone; m. Clifford Ralph Pohl, Sept. 6, 1969 (div. 1978); m. 2d Scott Alan Bieber; Mar. 13, 1983. B.S. with honors, Wright State U., Dayton, Ohio, 1970; cert. grad. Inst. Paralegal Studies, Phila., 1973; J.D., U. Chgo., 1979. Bar: N.Y. 1980, Ill. 1982, U.S. Dist. Ct. (ea. and so. dists.) N.Y. 1980, U.S. Dist. Ct. (no. dist.) Ill. 1982. Tchr. Dayton City Schs., 1970-72; lawyer's asst. Harter, Secrest & Emery, Rochester, N.Y., 1973-76; assoc. Davis Polk & Wardwell, N.Y.C., 1979-81; assoc. Levy and Erens, Chgo., 1981-83, ptnr., 1984; counsel Goldberg, Kohn, Bell, Black, Rosenbloom & Moritz, Ltd., Chgo., 1984-85, ptnr., 1985—. Founder Chgo. chpt. Israel Cancer Research Fund, 1983; bd. trustees Congregation Rodfei Zedek, Chgo., 1984. Decalogue Soc. of Chgo. scholar, 1978. Mem. ABA, Chgo. Bar Assn., Chgo. Council Lawyers. Democrat. Home: 3012 Wilmette Ave Wilmette IL 60091 Office: Goldberg Kohn Bell Black Rosenbloom & Moritz Ltd 55 E Monroe St Suite 3900 Chicago IL 60603

BIEGEL, EILEEN MAE, hospital executive; b. Eau Claire, Wis., Nov. 13, 1937; d. Ewald Frederic and Emma Antonia (Conrad) Weggen; student Dist. One Tech. Inst., 1974, also part time, corr. student U. Wis., Madison; grad. mgmt. seminars; student Upper Iowa U., 1984—; m. James O. Biegel, Oct. 6, 1956; children—Jeffrey Alan, John William. Exec. sec. to pres. Broadcaster Services, Inc., Eau Claire, Wis., 1969-74; exec. sec. to exec. v.p. Am. Nat. Bank, Eau Claire, 1975-77; exec. asst. to pres. Luther Hosp., Eau Claire, 1977—, asst. corporate sec., 1984—; mem. exec. staff, 1985—; asst. corp. sec. Luther Health Care Corp., 1984—; mem. secretarial adv. council Dist. One Tech. Sch. 1975—. State pres. Future Homemakers Am., 1955. Cert. profl. sec., 1980. Mem. Eau Claire Womens Network (founder, mem. steering com.), Profl. Secs. Internat. (chmn. goals and priorities com., pres. Eau Claire chpt. 1982-83), Chippewa Valley Hist. Mus. Lutheran. Home: 4707 Tower Dr Eau Claire WI 54701 Office: 310 Chestnut St Eau Claire WI 54701

BIEHN, MARIAN ELEANOR, commercial art studio executive, commercial real estate company executive; b. Stockton, Ill., Aug. 27, 1951; d. Eugene Simon and Mary Jane (Rowe) Borsdorf; m. Donald Roy Biehn, Feb. 7, 1976; children—Erich Simon, Anna Catherine, Maria Elizabeth. B.A., Coll. St. Catherine, 1973. Dir. World Pen Pals, Internat. Inst. Minn., St. Paul, 1974-75, dir. intercultural affairs Internat. Inst. Minn., 1975-77; constrn. contractor, office renovator Don Biehn Advt. Art, Mpls., 1977, ptnr., comml. art sales rep., 1978—; real estate owner, mgr. Biehn Bldgs., Mpls., 1977—. Mem. Art Dir. and Copywriters Club. Mem. Democratic Farmer Labor Party. Roman Catholic. Avocations: sailing; downhill skiing; gardening. Home: 83 Otis Ave Saint Paul MN 55104 Office: Don Biehn Advt Art Inc 1206 3d Ave S Minneapolis MN 55404

BIELEFELDT, CATHERINE C., sales executive; b. Bellwood, Ill.; d. William Anton and Linda (Buchert) B. B.Music in Piano Performance, Chgo. Conservatory Coll.; student El Conservatorio de Mex., Mexico City; postgrad. Northwestern U., CBS Sch. Mgmt., 1980. Dept. mgr. Fair Store, Oak Park, Ill., 1950-62; piano sales cons. Lyon & Healy Co., Oak Park and Oak Brook, Ill., 1963-77; dir. Steinway Hall, dir. nat. sales tng. Steinway & Sons, Long Island City, N.Y., 1978-82; v.p. sales Hendricks Music Co., Downers Grove, Ill., 1983—; sales seminar instr. Jordan-Kitt's Music, Wells Music, Washington and Denver, 1983-85. Author: The Wonders of the Piano, The Anatomy of the Instrument, 1984. Mem. Women in Communications, Inc., Evanston Music Club, Sigma Alpha Iota (past pres. alumnae chpt., recipient numerous awards). Republican. Lutheran. Home: 190 S Wood Dale Rd Wood Dale IL 60191 Office: Hendricks Music 421 Maple Ave Downers Grove IL 60515

BIELSKI, IRENE S., educator; b. Bronx, N.Y., Sept. 24, 1942; d. Milton and Anna (Schneider) S.; B.S., SUNY, Potsdam, 1964; M.S., Hunter Coll., N.Y.C., 1969; m. George W. Bielski, Nov. 13, 1982. Tchr., N.Y. Schs., 1964—; tchr. Limekiln Sch., Suffern, 1967—; del. N.Y. State Retirement System, 1979-80, 83—; trustee Leland R. Meyer Scholarship Fund, 1978—. Librarian, Pomona Jewish Center, 1981-83, v.p. adult edn., 1983—; social action chmn., 1981-83, rec. sec., 1985—. Mem. NEA (del 1980—), N.Y. Educators Assn. (del. 1978—), East Ramapo Tchrs. Assn. (v.p. 1977—), PTA (life). Jewish. Club: B'nai B'rith (v.p. membership educators unit 1981-82, program chmn. 1982-83, pres. 1983—). Home: 60 Somerset Dr Suffern NY 10901 Office: Limekiln Sch Limekiln Rd Suffern NY 10901

BIENENSTEIN, KATHLEEN LINDA, engineering company executive; b. Detroit, June 20, 1951; d. Charles August and Emily Linda (Tomolillo) B.; m. Alfred Reginal Trainer, III, Sept. 11, 1970 (div. 1972). B.A. Oakland U., Mich., 1973; A.A. in Bus., Kellogg Community Coll., Battle Creek, 1980. Owner retail store, Livonia, Mich., 1973-75; designer Criterion Design, Royal Oak, Mich., 1975-77; designer Eaton Corp., Galesburg, Mich., 1977-81; v.p. engrng. services Charles S. Davis & Assoc. Inc., Pontiac, Mich., 1981—, gen. mgr., 1984-85. Patentee camshaft bushing. Sponsor, Star Theatre, Flint, Mich., 1983-86. Mem. Soc. Body Engrs., NOW, Nat. Assn. Female Execs. Democrat. Office: Charles S Davis & Assoc Inc 140 S Saginaw #780 Pontiac MI 48058

BIERCE, CAROL ANNE HOOVER, computer software specialist, city official; b. Pensacola, Fla., Jan. 30, 1954; d. Ralph Alwin Hoover, Jr. and Hazel Floyce (Warren) Roberts; B.A. in Math. with highest distinction, U. North Fla., 1975, B.A.E. with highest distinction, 1976, M.B.A., 1979; m. Daniel Ambrose Bierce, Oct. 17, 1975; children—Adam Anthony, Joseph Alexander. Programmer, Sav-A-Stop, Inc., Orange Park, Fla., 1975-76; with City of Jacksonville (Fla.), 1976—, sr. application analyst, 1980-82, asst. computer systems officer, dep. tech. dir., 1982—; project leader water and electric computer services, tech. support; cons. for Jacksonville Software Devel. Corp. Mem. Assn. M.B.A. Execs., Nat. Assn. Female Execs., Riverside-Avondale Preservation Soc., Fla. Epilepsy Found., Jacksonville Zool. Soc., Jacksonville Mus. Arts and Scis., St. Mark's Women of Ch., Phi Theta Kappa, Pi Mu Epsilon. Democrat. Episcopalian. Home: 1624 Cherry St Jacksonville FL 32205 Office: City Hall 200 E Bay St Jacksonville FL 32202

BIERENKOVEN, KELLY M., manufacturing company marketing executive; b. Albuquerque, N.Mex., Apr. 5, 1959; d. William John and Jacqueline (Godfrey) Bierenkoven; B.A., U. No. Colo., 1981; M.A., 1982. Audiologist Adco Hearing, Denver, 1982-83; sales mgr. US Homes, Denver, 1983-84; audiologist Bass Hearing, Raleigh, 1984-85; dir. mktg. Bernafon, Inc., Mountainside, N.J., 1985—; lectr. in field. Mem. Am. Speech and Hearing Assn., Am. Mktg. Assn. Republican. Avocations: reading; exercise; tennis; dancing. Home: 800 Forest Ave 13C Westfield NJ 07090 Office: Bernafon Inc 1125 Globe Ave Mountainside NJ 07092

BIERNAT, LILLIAN M. NAHUMENUK, interior designer; b. Phila., Apr. 27, 1931; d. Peter and Anna (Wolonick) Nahumenuk; student pub. schs.; m. Joseph Anthony Biernat, July 22, 1951; children—Joseph A., Daria Ann, Karen Marie, Mark Allen, Brent Hilary. Receptionist, sec. Mayer, Magaziner & Brunswick, lawyers, Phila., 1950-53; owner Town House Interiors, Columbia, Conn., also Newton Square, Pa., 1956—, Lillian Biernat Interiors, Avon and Columbia, Conn. Mem. fund raising com. Girl Scouts U.S.A., 1968; exec. bd. Conn. Opera Guild, Hartford Ballet; pres. Friends of Hartford Ballet. Clubs: Womens, Avon Garden (publicity chmn.), Garden (Newtown Square); Villagers Womens (Columbia). Address: 30 Hurdle Fence Dr Avon CT 06001

BIESEL, DUANE MACDONALD, manufacturing company executive; b. Chgo., June 9, 1931; d. Lorne Evan and Marie Eileen (Lyness) MacDonald; m. Garnett Biesel, May 1, 1954 (div. June 1970). B.S., Monmouth Coll., 1952; postgrad. Northwestern U., 1956-57. Chemist, Underwriters Lab., Inc., Chgo., 1952-56; Toni Co. div. Gillette Co., Chgo., 1956-61; chemist Gillette Co., Chgo., 1964-74; product devel. mgr., Boston, 1974—. Patentee in hosiery field. Mem. Soc. Cosmetic Chemists. Avocations: reading; classical music; travel; golf. Office: Gillette Co Gillette Park South Boston MA 02106

BIESELE, SUSAN CLEGG, county official; b. Elko, Nev., Aug. 5, 1953; d. Daris Rae and Betty Ida (Beal) Clegg; m. Calvin Paul Goff, May 20, 1973 (div.); m. 2d William Henry Biesele, Apr. 12, 1979; 1 stepson, William Michael. Student Utah Tech. Coll., 1971-72, U. Utah, 1979—. Adminstrv. sec. Model Cities, Salt Lake City, 1972-73; clk. stenographer Salt Lake County Office Personnel Mgmt., Salt Lake City, 1973-74, personnel specialist, 1974-78, personnel analyst, 1978, supervising analyst, 1978-80, mgr. classification and selection, 1980—. Author personnel and tng. manuals. Active Utah Commn. on Employment and Careers for Women, 1981-82. Recipient Miss Annex award Utah Tech. Coll., 1971; outstanding performance awards Salt Lake County Govt., 1973, 74, 83, 84, 85, extra-meritorious performance awards, 1977, 81, 10 yrs. county service award, 1983. Mem. Internat. Personnel Mgmt. Assn. (Utah chpt. pres. 1981), Internat. Personnel Mgmt. Assn. (acting membership chair assessment council 1978—, acting membership chmn. 1978), Am. Compensation Assn., (cert. compensation profl.), Am. Soc. Pub. Adminstrs. Home: 3303 E Oakcliff Dr Salt Lake City UT 84124Office: Human Resources Div 135 E 2100 So Bldg 2 Salt Lake City UT 84115

BIEWER, MARGARET MINNIE, equipment company executive; b. Hawley, Minn., July 1, 1927; d. William Martin and Lena (Luthi) Schultz; m. John H. L. Biewer, Sept. 13, 1946; 1 child, Sharon Kay Biewer Wiener. Student Hibbing Jr. Coll., 1962-63, Hibbing Area Voc-Tec Inst., 1984. Credit mgr. Montgomery Ward & Co., Hibbing, Minn., 1953-62; office mgr. Duluth Avionics, Hibbing, 1962-65; office mgr. Vermillion Equipment & Supply Co., Inc., Hibbing, 1965-83, pres., 1983—; Colby Mfg. Co., Cohasset, Minn., 1983—. Mem. AIME. Lutheran. Lodge: Women of Moose (sr. regent Hibbing 1964-65, recorder 1975-76). Avocations: sewing; gardening; fishing; walking. Home: 2817 4th Ave W Hibbing MN 55746 Office: Vermillion Equipment & Supply Co Inc 1605 1st Ave PO Box 156 Hibbing MN 55746

BIGELOW, BEVERLY, security agency executive; b. Providence, R.I., Mar. 28, 1947; d. Antonio Joseph and Josephine (Soccio) Tartaglia Zaccaria; m. Anthony Michael Alviti, Jan. 4, 1969 (div. Feb. 1977); children—Anthony, Kevin, Jason; m. Elwin L. Bigelow, May 14, 1983. Student R.I. Jr. Coll. Bookkeeper, Alan I. Maylor Co., East Providence, R.I., 1979-82, Escom Devel. Corp., Fort Lauderdale, Fla., 1982-85; v.p. Bigelow Security Agy., Inc., Ft. Lauderdale, Fla., 1986—. bd. dirs. Ravenswood Mgmt. Assn., Fort Lauderdale, 1984-85, 86—, sec., 1984-85, 86—, bookkeeper, 1982—. Republican. Baptist. Club: Ravenswood Social (Fort Lauderdale) (sec. 1982—). Avocations: sewing; cooking; collecting dresser boxes; doll making. Office: Ravenswood Estates 5201 Ravenswood Rd Fort Lauderdale FL 33312

BIGELOW, MARTHA MITCHELL, historian; b. Talladega Springs, Ala., Sept. 19, 1921; (div.) children—Martha Frances, Carolyn. B.A., Ala. Coll., Montevallo, 1943; M.A. (tuition fellow, Julius Rosenwald scholar 1943-44, Cleo Hearson scholar, summer 1944, Ency. Brit. fellow 1944-45), U. Chgo., 1944, Ph.D., 1946. Asso. prof. history Miss. Coll., Clinton, 1946-48, Memphis State U., 1948-49, U. Miss., 1949-50; asso. curator manuscripts Mich. Hist. Collections, U. Mich., Ann Arbor, 1954-57; prof. history Miss. Coll., 1957-71, chmn. dept. history and polit. sci., 1964-71; dir. Mich. Bur. History, Mich. Dept. State, sec., also state historic preservation officer, 1971—; coordinator for Mich., Nat. Hist. Publns. and Records Commn., 1974; Amer. asso. state and History fellow, summers 1958, 59. Contbr. articles profl. publns. Mem. Am. Assn. State and Local History (pres. 1979-81), Orgn. Am. Historians, Nat. Assn. State Archives and Records Assn., So. Hist. Assn., Mich. Hist. Soc., Miss. Hist. Soc. Home: 223 Cowley St East Lansing MI 48823 Office: 208 N Capitol St Lansing MI 48918

BIGGER, ANNE, interior designer; b. Dallas, Sept. 5, 1949. B.S. in Interior Design, U. Tex., Austin, 1971. Interior designer Carl Barnett Interiors, Dallas, 1971-77, Anne Bigger Interior Design, Dallas, 1978—. Mem. Jr. League of Dallas, 1983—. Mem. Am. Soc. Interior Designers (dir. pubs. 1980-85, state bd. dirs. for Tex. 1984-85, state sec., 1986, Presdl. Citation for Meritorious service Tex. 1983, 84), Kappa Kappa Gamma.

BIGGERT, JUDITH BORG, lawyer; b. Chgo., Aug. 15, 1937; d. Alvin Andrew and Marjorie Virginia (Mailler) Borg; m. Rody Patterson Biggert, Sept. 21, 1963; children—Courtney Ray, Alison Mailler, Rody Patterson, Adrienne Taylor. B.A., Stanford U., 1959; J.D., Northwestern U., 1963. Bar: Ill. 1963, Law clk. to presiding justice U.S. Ct. Appeals (7th cir.), Chgo., 1963-64; sole practice, Hinsdale, Ill., 1964—. Mem. bd. editors Law Rev., Northwestern U. Sch. Law, 1961-63. Pres., bd. dirs. Hinsdale Twp. High Sch. Dist. 86 Bd. Edn., 1983-84, 78—; pres. Jr. League Chgo., 1976-78, treas., bd. bd. mgrs., 1966—; chmn. Hinsdale Antiques Show, 1980; pres. Oak Sch. PTA, Hinsdale, 1976-78; pres.-treas. Chgo. jr. bd. Travelers Aid Soc., 1965-70; Sunday sch. tchr. Grace Episcopal Ch., Hinsdale, 1978-80, 82—; treas., 2d v.p., bd. dirs. Vis. Nurses Assn. Chgo., 1978. Recipient Servian award Jr. aux. U. Chgo. Cancer Research Found. Mem. ABA, Ill. Bar Assn. Republican. Episcopalian. Home and office: 425 E 6th St Hinsdale IL 60521

BIGGS, MARGARET KEY, educator, author; b. Troy, Ala., Oct. 26, 1933; d. Samuel Elbert and Maggie Lee (Jackson) Kay; m. Wayne Saunders Biggs, Apr. 1, 1956. B.S. in English Edn., Troy State U., 1954; M.A. in Humanities, Calif. State U.-Dominquez Hills, 1979. Instr. Port St. Joe Jr./Sr. High Sch., Fla., 1954—; adj. prof. Gulf Coast Community Coll., Port St. Joe, 1984—. Author poetry: Swampfire, 1980; Sister to the Sun, 1981; Magnolias and Such, 1982; Petals from the Womanflower, 1983; Plumage of the Sun, 1986; editor Red Key Press; contbg. editor Earthwise, Tempest, Negative Capability; contbr. articles to profl. jours., poems to anthologies. Recipient Gulf County Star Tchr. award, 1965; Port St. Joe Jr.-Sr. High Sch. Tchr. of Yr. award, 1973; Fla. Speech award, 1980; Insight Press award for teaching creative writing exceptionally, 1981, 83; Rusel Leavit Meml. award, 1980; Poetry Monthly First Poem award, 1981; award for Advancing the Growth and Devel. of Edn. in State of Fla., 1982; Nat. Fedn. State Poetry Socs. award, 1983; Ind. Hist. award, 1983; Katharine F. Gordy award, 1983; others. Mem. Gulf County Classroom Tchrs. Assn. (pres. 1955-56, 65-66), Fla. Teaching Profession, NEA, Fla. Council Tchrs. English, Fla. Forensics, Fla. State Poets Assn. Inc., Nat. Fedn. State Poetry Socs., Nat. League Am. Pen Women (award 1983), Panhandle Writers Guild, DAR, Delta Kappa Gamma, Alpha Omega. Democrat. Methodist. Office: Port St Joe Jr-Sr High Sch 800 Niles Rd Port Saint Joe FL 32456

BIGGS, RITTIE JEAN, county official; b. Martin County, N.C., Jan. 16, 1942; d. Dennis Robert and Marie (Wynn) B. B.S., East Carolina U., 1964, M.S., 1974. Tchr., Edenton City Schs., N.C., 1964-67, Martin County Schs., Williamston, N.C., 1967-68; social worker Martin County Dept. Social Services, Williamston, 1968-72, dir., 1972—. Named Outstanding Dir. Social Services in N.C., N.C. Assn. County Commrs., 1979-80. Mem. N.C. Assn. County Dirs. Social Services (pres. 1979-80), N.C. Social Services Assn. Democrat. Baptist. Club: Williamston Bus. and Profl. Women (pres. 1977-78).

Avocations: reading, quilting, crocheting, gardening, church work. Office: Martin County Dept of Social Services PO Box 809 Williamston NC 27892

BIGGS, ROBERTA ELIZABETH, educational administrator; b. Chgo., Oct. 3, 1929; d. Thomas Jesse and Claytie Agnes (Day) Allen; m. Horace S. Biggs, May 29, 1949; 1 child, Helena Elizabeth. B.S., Ariz. State U., 1947. Tchr. Navajo children Bur. Indian Affairs, Navajo Reservations, Ariz. and N.Mex., 1947-49; owner, dir. LaFloresta Childrens Ctr., Albuquerque, 1969—; chmn. bd. Learning Tech. Ctr., Albuquerque, 1984—, originator, 1982—; cons. St. Francis Nursing Home, Albuquerque, 1982; coordinator child care workshops N.Mex. Polit. Women, 1974-77. Contbr. articles to profl. jours. Bd. dirs. All Faiths Receiving Home, Albuquerque, 1972-84, Assn. Commerce and Industry, Albuquerque, 1981-84; chmn. Com. on Women's Issues 1983—; com. mem. Small Bus. Com., N.Mex., 1985—. Mem. Nat. Assn. Child Care Mgmt. (dir.), N.Mex. Lic. Child Care Assn. (pres. 1974-77). Avocations: collecting and recording Navajo folklore; storytelling; collecting out-of-print children's books. Office: Learning Tech Center 5528 Eubank NE Albuquerque NM 87111

BIGGS, SELENA LOVE, educator; b. Tulia, Tex., May 29, 1956; d. Kenneth Lyle and Doris Ann (Nunn) Love; 1 child, Jonathan David. B.S. in Edn., U. Houston, 1978, M.Ed., 1985. Cert. tchr., Tex. Program coordinator Houston Ind. Sch. Dist., 1978—; cons magnet sch. com. Tijerina Elem. Sch., Houston, 1980. Co-founder Brownie Scout troop, Pleasantville Elem. Sch., 1979-80. Named Outstanding Young Educator, Felix Tijerina Elem. Sch., Houston, 1982. Mem. Tex. Tchrs. Assn., Congress Tchrs. Orgn., Parent Tchr. Orgn., Delta Zeta. Republican. Baptist. Home: 6623 Wanda Ln Houston TX 77074

BIGGY, MARY VIRGINIA, college dean; b. Boston, Oct. 15, 1924; d. John J. and Mary C. (Dwyer) B. B.S., Boston U., 1945, Ed.M., 1946, Ed.D., 1953. Tchr. bus. edn. Needham High Sch., Mass., 1944-45; reading cons. Plainville Pub. Schs., Conn., 1946-47; coordinator elem. edn. Concord Pub. Schs., Mass., 1953-62; dir. N.E. instructional TV project, dir. instructional TV Eastern Ednl. Network, Boston, 1962-67; asst. supr., supr. Concord Pub. Schs. and Concord Carlisle Regional Sch. Dist., 1967-69; prof. edn. U. Lowell, Mass., 1969—, dean Coll. Edn., 1979—; pres. Designs for Edn., 1969—; cons. Corp. Pub. Broadcasting. Author: Independence in Spelling, 1966; (with others) Spell Correctly, 1965-85. Mem. Acton Boxborough Regional High Sch. Dist. Sch. Com., Mass., 1963-66; chmn. Mass. Bd. Library Commrs., 1973-78. Mem. NEA, Am. Assn. Sch. Adminstrs., Am. Ednl. Research Assn., Assn. Supervision and Curriculum Devel., Pi Lambda Theta (nat. pres. 1961-65), others. Democrat. Roman Catholic. Home: 162 Park Ln Concord MA 01742 Office: Coll Edn Univ Lowell Lowell MA 01854

BIGLER, MARY GLENN, educator; b. Stevens Point, Wis., May 5, 1944; d. Ernest Dean and Maxine (Dermody) Glenn; B.A. in History, Aquinas Coll., 1965; M.A. in History, Eastern Mich. U., 1968, M.A. in Reading, 1971; Ph.D. in Curriculum and Instruction, U. Mich., 1974; m. William Wayne Bigler, Aug. 20, 1965; 1 dau., Beth Ann. Tchr., St. John's High Sch., Ypsilanti, Mich., 1965-69; reading cons., tchr. Ann Arbor (Mich.) Public Schs., 1969-75; field cons. Ednl. Cons. Assos., Englewood, Colo., 1975-77; asso. prof. tchr. edn. Eastern Mich. U., 1977—; keynote speaker at numerous confs.; honors convocation and grad. speaker, various high schs.; banquet speaker Reading '82 Conf., York U.; cons., workshop presenter in field. Mem. Assn. Supervision and Curriculum Devel., Internat. Reading Assn., Nat. Council Tchrs. English, Mich. Reading Assn. (pres. 1982-83), Internat. Platform Assn., Delta Kappa Gamma. Author: Reading and the Language Arts, 1974; contbr. articles to profl. jours. Home: 1332 King George Blvd Ann Arbor MI 48104 Office: 338 Pierce Hall Eastern Mich U Ypsilanti MI 48197

BILES, MARILYN MARTA, painter; b. Wilmington, Del., Oct. 3, 1935; d. Albert Humbert and Anne Marie (DeRogatis) Marta; m. George Ronald Bower, June 30, 1956 (div. May 1970); children—Michele Bower Alvarado, Nancy Bower Guthrie, Randall William. Student Moore Coll. Art, 1953-54, St. Mary's Coll., 1959-61, Mus. Fine Arts, Houston, 1972-74. Art tchr. Contemporary Arts Mus., Houston, 1969-73, 80-81; head art dept. pre-primary div. Duchesne Acad., Houston, 1970-72; project coordinator Nan Fisher, Inc., Houston, 1983-84; one-woman shows: 1st Nat. City Bank, Houston, 1980, Christ Ch. Cathedral, 1981-82, Toni Jones Gallery, 1981, U. Houston, 1982, Station Gallery, Greenville, Del., 1984, Boyar Norton & Blair, 1986; group shows include: U. Houston, 1977, 79, Nat. Cape Coral Exhbn., Fla., 1979, Toni Jones Gallery, 1979, Assistance League of Houston, 1979, 80, Golden Crescent Gallery, Houston, 1984; coordinator, designer art programs Spring Branch Schs., Houston, 1968-70. Bd. dirs. Spring Branch YWCA, Houston, 1973-74; docent Harris County Heritage Soc., Houston, 1970-72; mem. bd., v.p. Arcs Found., Inc., Houston, 1983; bd. dirs., gala chmn. Houston Grand Opera Guild, 1983-84, governing bd. assn., 1984-85, co-chmn. gala, 1985; founder, pres. Mus. Med. Sci. Assn., Houston, 1986-87. Mem. Artists Equity (dir. Houston chpt. 1980), Art League Houston, Tex. Fine Arts Assn. Republican. Episcopalian. Clubs: Racquet, World Trade (v.p. women's assn. 1974-75) (Houston), Westlake. Home: 148 Litchfield St Houston TX 77024

BILHARDT, DIANE MARIE, marketing manager; b. Phila., Aug. 14, 1952; d. William Durkin and Elaine Claire (Rosato) B. B.A., Douglass Coll., 1974; M.B.A., Rutgers U., 1980. Asst. mktg. dir. Franklin State Bank, Somerset, N.J., 1975-79; staff mgr. AT&T, Basking Ridge, N.J., 1980-82, staff mgr. AT&T Info Systems, Morristown, N.J., 1983, dist. mktg. mgr., 1984—. Mem. Am. Mktg. Assn. (award No. N.J. chpt. 1980), Beta Gamma Sigma. Republican. Roman Catholic. Office: AT&T Info Systems One Speedwell Ave Room 88W-863W Morristown NJ 07960

BILIMORIA, ELEANOR JOSEPHINE DANNER, retired educator, writer, cinematographer; b. Seattle, June 12, 1909; d. William Sheridan and Gazella Marie (Young) Danner; m. Sorabji Burjorji Bilimoria, Apr. 23, 1941; children—Katharine Shereen, Dina Anne. B.A., U. Wash., 1931, M.Ed., 1963, M.Librarianship, 1967; student Chouinard Sch. Art, 1932, Internat. Sch. Art, Europe, 1934, 36. Art tchr. Pub. Schs. Bainbridge, Wash., Seattle, 1931-38; writer, cinematographer, editor Harmon Found., N.Y.C., 1938-39; film producer Pub. Schs., Seattle, 1939-41; head films div. Fgn. Info. Service of U.S., Bombay, India, 1942-43; head ednl. films div. Ama Ltd., Bombay, 1943-44; tchr., librarian Pub. Schs., Bellevue, Wash., 1959-74; co-founder, adminstr. West Wind Sch., Bombay, 1947-50. Cinematographer: (16mm film) Teaching Creative Design, 1938. Author: (recruiting film) Diary of a WAC, 1942 (Govt. India purchase prize). Editor: (35mm film) Stop That Risin' Sun, 1943. Author, photographer articles in profl. publs. Co-founder, pres. Coalition Women and Religion, Seattle, 1973-75; chmn. membership and edn. Seattle Women's Commn., Seattle, 1976-79; co-chmn. Sex Equity Commn., Seattle Pub. Schs., 1978-79. Recipient Salute to Women in Religion Edn. award Seattle Smashers, 1979; scholar Internat. Sch. Art, 1936, Vassar Summer Inst., 1951. Mem. NEA, Wash. Edn. Assn., Ret. Pub. Employees Council, Pacific N.W. Writers, NOW, Women's Polit. Caucus, Friends of LWV, Gray Panthers. Democrat. Unitarian. Clubs: Venture, U. Wash. President's. Avocations: Computer-word processing; women's history; opera. Home: 6803 47th NE Seattle WA 98115

BILKEY, BEVERLY YVONNE, medical technologist, county social services official; b. Madison, Wis., Oct. 14, 1926; d. Rush Hillary and Amalie (Christen) Watson; m. Frederick Williams Bilkey, June 29, 1950 (dec. Dec. 1974); children—Barry W., Frederick D., Lorelei. B.S. in Med. Technology, U. Wis.-Madison, 1948. Lic. medical technologist. Chief technician Levin-Delavan Clinic, Delavan, Wis., 1948-49; asst. supr. Meml. Hosp., Wausau, Wis., 1949-50; supr. Gen. Hosp., Dodgeville, Wis., 1950-74; staff technologist Meml. Hosp. of Iowa County, Wis., 1974-76; supr. Dodgeville Clinic Lab., Wis., 1976-84. Mem. Health Planning Council, Dodgeville, 1978-84; chmn. Iowa County Social Services, Dodgeville, 1980-84, Iowa County Pub. Health Agy., Dodgeville, 1979-84; Iowa County bd. suprs. Fin. Personnel Community Action Agy.; gov.'s appointee Regional Planning Commn., 1980-82; chmn. bd. trustees Dodgeville United Ch. of Christ; candidate for State for Rep., 1980. Mem. Registry Am. Soc. Clin. Pathologists. Republican. Lodges: Rainbow Girls (mother adviser 1960), Order of Eastern Star (worthy matron 1964). Avocations: politics, crafts. Home: 4929 Whitcomb Dr Madison WI 53711

BILLAUER, BARBARA PFEFFER, lawyer; b. Aug. 9, 1951; d. Harry George and Evelyn (Newman) Pfeffer; B.S. with honors, Cornell U., 1972; J.D., Hofstra U., 1975; M.A., N.Y. U., 1982. Admitted to N.Y. bar, 1976, Fed. Dist. Ct. N.Y., 1977, U.S. Ct. Appeals for 2d circuit, 1978; assoc. firm Bower & Garnder, N.Y.C., 1974-78; sr. trial atty. Joseph W. Conklin, N.Y.C., 1978-80; assoc. dept. head firm. Curtis, Mallet-Prevost, Colt & Mosle, N.Y.C., 1980-82; partner firm Anderson, Russell, Kill & Olick, N.Y.C., 1982—; adj. assoc. prof. N.Y.U. Grad. Sch., 1982—; adminstrv. law judge N.Y.C. Dept. Transp.; mem. jud. screening com. Coordinated Bar Assn.; mem. Spl. Panel on Citywide Ct. Adminstrn.; cons. in field. Mem. Met. Women's Bar Assn. (v.p. 1981-82, pres. 1983-84, chmn. bd. 1985—), ABA, Health Law Forum, N.Y. State Bar Assn., Nat. Conf. Women's Bar Assns. (bd. dirs., chmn. Media liaison com. 1983-85), Nat. Assn. Bar Presidents, Mems. Network of Bar Leaders, Am. Soc. Law and Medicine, Nat. Assn. Bar Pres., Nat. Conf. Women's Bar Assn., Network Bar Leaders, Am. Soc. Microbiology, Am. Arbitration Assn., Brit. Occupational Hygiene Soc., N.Y. Acad. Scis. AAUW, AAAS, Weizmann League of Weizmann Inst. Sci. (exec. com.). Home: 630 First Ave New York NY 10016 Office: 666 Third Ave New York NY 10017

BILLER, PATRICIA LOUISE, nurse; b. Harrisonburg, Va., Oct. 4, 1958; d. Donald Welton and Nellie Rose (Woerner) Biller. B.S.N. cum laude, W.Va. Wesleyan Coll., 1980; M.S. in Nursing, U. Colo., 1983. Cert. family nurse practitioner. Staff nurse charge relief Denver VA Med. Ctr., 1980-83; family nurse practitioner Cedar Ridge Family Physicians, Strasburg, Va., 1983-85; family nurse practitioner emergency dept. Johns Hopkins Hosp., Balt., 1985—. Author Palliative Treatment Program-A Ray of Sunshine booklet, 1982 (outstanding work with hospice). Author vol. 1 and 2 newsletters Cedar Ridge Health Notes, 1984. Active mem. Am. Guild of Organists, Buckhannon, W.Va., 1980. Named W.Va. 4-H All Star, 1976; recipient Outstanding Sci. and Math Achievement award Baush-Lomb, 1976; Robert C. Byrd scholar, 1976. Mem. W.Va. Nurses Assn., Am. Nurses Assn., Phi Kappa Phi, Epsilon Delta chpt. Sigma Theta Tau, Beta Beta Beta. Democrat. United Methodist. Club: Lost River Extension (W.Va.) (v.p. 1984-85).

BILLINGS, BARBARA RUTH BEAMES, lawyer; b. Oceanside, Calif., Feb. 6, 1953; d. Jimmye Ruth (Moore) Beames; m. Bryan L. Billings, Sept. 5, 1981. B.A., U. Okla., Norman, 1975, J.D., 1978. Bar: Okla. 1978. Atty. Legal Aid Service, Lawton, Okla., 1979-80; head. legal dept. Human Services (child support), Oklahoma City, 1980-81; mem. Billings, Wolfe, & Billings, Woodward, Okla., 1982—. Bd. Dirs. Western Plains Youth Shelter, 1982—; vol. United Fund, 1981—; mem. Woodwerd Bd. Adjustment, 1983-84. Mem. ABA, Okla. Bar Assn., Woodward County Bar Assn., (sec.-treas. 1983, v.p. 1984), Okla. Trial Lawyers, Assn. Trial Lawyers Am., Bus. and Profl. Women (Oklahoma City, Woodward, monthly award outstanding young careerist 1982). Democrat. Mem. Christian Ch. (Disciples of Christ). Home: 2603 3d St Woodward OK 73801 Office: Billings Wolfe & Billings PO Box 912 Woodward OK 73802

BILLINGSLEY, ANN VOORHEES, lawyer; b. Los Angeles, June 14, 1953; d. Eugene Perry and Eugenia Ann (Bates) Voorhees; m. Henry Edmund Billingsley II, Oct. 11, 1980. B.S., UCLA, 1976; J.D., Case Western Res. U., 1979. Bar: N.Y. 1980, U.S. Dist. Ct. (so. and eastern dist.) N.Y. 1980. Enforcement atty. U.S. EPA, N.Y.C., 1980-83; freelance writer/editor, N.Y.C., 1983-85; sole practice real estate law, N.Y.C., 1984—. Contbr. articles to profl. jours. Fundraising cons. Inwood Heights Parks Alliance, N.Y.C., 1983-85. Mem. ABA, Council N.Y. Coops. Democrat. Home: 3601 Lytle Rd Shaker Heights OH 44122

BILLINGSLEY, EDNA FAYE RICHARDSON, special educator; b. St. Louis, Nov. 13, 1955; d. Robert J. and Annie P. (Johnson) Richardson; m. Vaughn Michelle Billingsley, Jan. 7, 1984. A.A., Patrick Henry Coll., Ala., 1975; B.S., U. South Ala., 1978, M.Ed., 1981. Tchr. educable mentally retarded Washington County Schs., Chatom, Ala., 1978-81; tchr. learning disability, emotional disability and educable mentally retarded Reed's Chapel Sch., McIntosh, Ala., 1981—. Election poll clk., 1977-81. Mem. NEA, Ala. Edn. Assn., Ala. Assn. Children with Learning Disabilities, Washington County Tchrs. Assn. (rep. 1982-83), Nat. Assn. Female Execs. Democrat. Baptist. Home: 1504 E Carlisle Mobile AL 36618

BILLINGSLEY, JESSICA LOUISE, broadcasting executive; b. Marion, Ala., Nov. 2, 1955; d. Jesse David and Willie Mae (Holman) B. B.S., U. Tenn., 1978, postgrad., 1978-80. Cert. secondary tchr., Ala. Tchr. Perry County Schs., Ala., 1978-80; substitute tchr. Marion City Schs., 1980-81; traffic mgr. Sta.-WAJO, Marion Communications, Inc., 1981-82, sales mgr., 1982-84, ops. mgr., 1984—, intern coordinator Marion Communications, Inc., 1982-85; pub. speaker, area chs., Marion, 1979—. Host talks show For and About Women, 1983 (award of cert. 1983). Recipient Media Support award Ala. Mental Health, 1983, Media Support award U.S. Air Force, 1983, Selective Service award U.S. selective Service, 1984; named Bus. Woman of Yr., Perry County Civic League, 1985. Democrat. Baptist. Club: Elites (pres. 1981-82) (Marion). Avocations: sewing; writing poetry. Home: 11 Pine Manor PO Box 379 Marion AL 36756 Office: Sta-WAJO PO Drawer 930 Marion AL 36756

BILLOUPS, ESTHER JEAN, health and nutritional aids company recruiter; b. Los Angeles, July 19, 1948; d. Alvin Ray and Eunice Gertrude (Washington) Pope; m. Larry Raney Billoups, Sr., Dec. 31, 1969; children—Larry Raney Jr., Charles Eugene. B.S. in Bus. Adminstrn., Calif. State U.-Dominguez Hills, 1982. Med. transcriber Los Angeles County, 1972-74; med. sec. Los Angeles County MLK Hosp., 1974-81; adminstrv. asst. U. So. Calif., 1981-82; office asst. 1st Nationwide Savs., 1982-84; recruiter Herbalife Internat., Los Angeles, 1984—; cons., bus. mgr. Greater Compton Football for Youth Orgn., Calif., 1983-86. Editor: A Childs Book, 1974; A Book of Poems, 1984. Mem. NAACP, Urban League. Democrat. Baptist. Office: Herbalife Internat 9800 S LaCienega Blvd Los Angeles CA 90009

BILLOW, SANDRA JEAN, corporate insurance executive; b. Columbus, Ohio, July 9, 1948; d. Lawrence R. and Carol L. (Edwards) B.; B.A. in Psychology with honors, Hollins (Va.) Coll., 1970; M.B.A., Cleve. State U., 1985; m. Leland E. Teschler, Oct. 20, 1979. Research asst. Hollins Coll., 1968, 69; ins. adminstr. Motel Mgmt. Corp., Arlington, Va., 1972-77; corp. ins. mgr. Stouffer Corp., Solon, Ohio, 1978-80; adminstr. property-liability ins. Sherwin-Williams Co., Cleve., 1980-84, sr. adminstr., 1984—. Recipient Pres. award for cost reduction Sherwin-Williams Co., 1981. Mem. Nat. Assn. Female Execs., Soc. Chartered Property and Casualty Underwriters, Risk and Ins. Mgmt. Soc. (officer). Unitarian. Author articles in field.

BILLS, SHERYL JEAN, newspaper editor; b. Rushville, Ind., Aug. 4, 1945; d. Robert Jackson and Mary Elizabeth (Kehl) B.; B.A., Ind. U., 1968. Mem. staff Cin. Enquirer, 1967-82, asst. mng. editor features, 1979-80, mng. editor, 1980-82; planning editor USA Today, Gannett Newspapers, 1982, sr. editor, 1985—; speaker in field. mng. editor Life, USA Today, 1982-85; Recipient Writing award Ohio Newspaper Women's Assn., 1971, 74; Ohio AP award for enterprise in journalism, 1974; award mag. covers Outdoor Writers Ohio-Ohio Press Photographers Assn., 1976; Penney-Mo. award newspaper Lifestyle sect., 1978, Outstanding Career Woman award Cin. YWCA, 1981. Mem. Women in Communications, AP Mng. Editors Assn., Am. Soc. Newspaper Editors, Sigma Delta Chi. Office: USA Today PO Box 500 Washington DC 20004

BILLUPS, KATHY MAYS, former securities representative; b. Huntington, W.Va., Oct. 28, 1959; d. William Floyd and Patsy Jean (Pierce) Mays; m. Paul Arthur Billups, May 5, 1984. A.A.S., Marshall U., 1980, B.B.A., 1982, now postgrad. Adminstrv. asst. Nationwide Ins. Co., Ceredo, W.Va., 1977-82; sales asst. E.F. Hutton & Co., Inc., Huntington, 1982-83, account exec., 1983-85. Notary public, W.Va. Mem. Nat. Assn. Female Execs., Jr. League of Huntington. Democrat. Baptist. Home: PO Box 1046 151 B St Ceredo WV 25507

BILOON, SANDRA GREEN, personnel and labor relations executive; b. N.Y.C., Oct. 12, 1930; d. Morris and Helen (Antler) Green; m. June 7, 1951. B.A. magna cum laude, Radcliffe Coll., 1951; M.A., Trinity Coll., Hartford, Conn., 1971. Editorial asst. Am. Polit. Sci. Rev., Duke U., Durham, N.C., 1951-53; tng. supr., editor G. Fox & Co., Hartford, 1953-56; employment interviewer I, Employment Security div. State Conn. Labor Dept., 1956-57, asst. personnel adminstr., 1957-58, personnel adminstr., 1958-75, dep. personnel commr., 1975-76, personnel commr., 1976-77, dir. personnel and labor relations, 1977—. Author: (with Clyde D. McKee) Pre-Professionals and the Theory and Practice of Public Administration, 1971. Mem. planning and study coms. U.S. Dept. Labor Manpower Adminstrn., U.S. Civil Service Commn. Mem. Nat. Assn. State Personnel Execs. (past pres.), Internat. Personnel Mgmt. Assn. (pres.-elect, past agy. mem.-at-large nat. exec. council; personnelist of yr. award Conn. chpt. 1980, past pres. award region 1982), Am. Soc. Pub. Adminstrn. (past bd. dirs.; Bosworth Meml. award 1975), Interstate Conf. Employment Security Adminstrs. (past chmn. personnel and tng. com.). Office: State of Conn Personnel Div 165 Capitol Ave Hartford CT 06106

BILSEL, ZELIHA, pediatrician; b. Kirklarel, Turkey, Apr. 24, 1924; d. Ismet and Emine (Tanriover) M.D., Med. Sch., 1947; m. Yilmaz C. Bilsel, Oct. 29, 1960; children—Deniz, Kurt. Dir. orphanage in Turkey, 1947-49; resident in pediatrics, Turkey, 1949-52; dir. orphanage, practice medicine specializing in pediatrics, Kirklarel, 1952-57; resident in pediatrics Homer Phillips Hosp., St. Louis, 1957-61, chief resident newborn premature nursery, 1959-61; fellow in cardiology, Augusta, Ga., 1961-63; practice medicine specializing in pediatrics, Kirklarel, 1963-66, Fairview Heights, Ill., 1970—; pediatrician outpatient clinic St. Louis Children's Hosp., 1966-70; pediatrics cons. for Pediatrics Clinic; cons. staff mem.; mem. staff Cardinal Glennon, St. Louis, Meml. Hosp., Belleville, Ill.; former attending physician to high risk newborns and premature for So. Ill. Christian Welfare Hosp., East St. Louis, Ill. Mem. AMA, St. Clair Med. Soc., So. Ill. Med. Soc.

BILYEU, ANNE MARIE, software specialist; b. Fairbanks, Alaska, May 8, 1955; d. Hiram Pierce and Patricia (Downing) B.; m. Jack E. Buckingham, Jr., May 24, 1975 (div. Jan. 1984); children—J. Pierce, Shannen L. B.A. in Bus., Point Loma Coll., 1981; M.S. in Systems Mgmt., U. So. Calif., 1986. Teller, River City Bank, Sacramento, 1976-77; loan clk. Bank of Am., Sacramento, 1977; customer rep. Home Fed. Savs. & Loan, San Diego, 1979; with Manpower, San Diego, 1981-82; adminstr. Singer-Link SSD, Silver Spring, Md., 1982—; software quality assurance Computer Scis. Corp., Falls Church, Va., 1985—. Phi Kappa Delta scholar, 1974. Mem. Mensa. Home: 161 D Ave #6 Coronado CA 92118 Office: CSC 7150 Carroll Rd San Diego CA 92123

BINCER, WANDA LAWENDEL, psychiatrist; b. Warsaw, Poland, Oct. 4, 1930; came to U.S., 1950, naturalized, 1961; d. Leonard and Evelyn (Glocer) Lawendel; M.D., Royal Coll. Surgeons, Ireland, 1956; m. Adam M. Bincer, Apr. 2, 1972; children—Yvonne, Brian, Michael. Rotating intern St. Mary's Hosp., Rochester, N.Y., 1957-58; resident in psychiatry City Hosp., Elmhurst, N.Y., 1958-59, 61-63; house officer Princess Margaret Hosp., Nassau, Bahamas, 1959-60; staff psychiatrist Pontiac (Mich.) State Hosp., 1965-66; cons. psychiatrist Bur. Social Services, Grand Forks, N.D., 1966-68, Community Mental Health Center, Grand Forks, 1966-68; staff psychiatrist VA Hosp., Atlanta, 1968-70, Center for Interpersonal Study, Smyrna, Ga. and Brawner Hosp., 1970-72; practice medicine specializing in psychiatry, Madison, Wis., 1972—; med. cons. Office of Social Security Disability, 1983—. Mem. City-County Com. on Sexual Assault, Madison, 1978-80; cons. Parental Stress Center, 1978—; chpt. co-leader Parents of Murdered Children. Served with Polish Underground, 1944. Decorated Bronze Cross of Merit. Mem. Am. Psychiat. Assn., Wis. Psychiat. Assn. (com. on women), Am. Acad. Psychotherapists. Cons. editor Voices, 1978-80; contbr. to Problem Solver (ed. Zastro et al), 1976, Voices, 1983.

BINDER, LUCY SIMPSON, utility executive; b. Phila., May 12, 1937; d. James G. and C. Lucy (Underwood) Simpson; B.S. in Bus. Adminstrn., Drexel U., Phila., 1959, m. Robert A. Binder, Aug. 12, 1967. With Phila. Electric Co., 1959—, asst. corp. sec., 1977-78, sec., 1978—. Mem. Am. Soc. Corp. Secs. Address: Phila Electric Co 2301 Market St Philadelphia PA 19101

BINDER, MILDRED KATHERINE, retired county public welfare agy. exec.; b. York, Pa., Jan. 5, 1918; d. Jemie Irving and Emma Jane (Billet) Binder; B.A. magna cum laude in Sociology, Hood Coll., 1940. Sec., mgr. Stock's Appliances, York, 1940-42; caseworker York County Bd. Assistance, Pa. Dept. Public Welfare, 1942-49, 1953-58, supr., 1949-53, 1958-59, exec. dir., 1959-83. Past mem. exec. com. York County Employment and Tng. Com.; past mem. dept. task forces Social Service Delivery to Client Info. System, also mem. ops. rev. bd.; past mem. bd. York County Council Alcoholism, 1959-62, Community Progress Council, 1965-67; co-chmn. Community Dialogue Com., 1968-69; mem. bd. Pre-Paid Health York, Inc., 1979; mem. human services planning coalition United Way, 1978-83, chmn. council agy. execs., 1967-71, 1976-78; mem. consumer adv. councils Gen. Telephone, Met. Edison; bd. dirs. Literacy Council of York County, 1985—; mem. York County Human Services Adv. Com., 1983—. Named Boss of Yr., Am. Bus. Women, 1973; named in commendations Pa. gov., Pa. Ho. of Reps. Mem. Am. Public Welfare Assn., Exec. Dirs. Assn. Pa. (exec. com. 1979-83, sec. 1980-83), AAUW (bd. dirs. York br. 1984—), York County Hist. Soc. United Way of Pa. Clubs: Coll. of York, Hood Coll. (York). Home: 1611 W Market St York PA 17404

BINDER, SARA, editor; b. N.Y.C., May 3, 1955, d. David and Muriel (Reinitz) B. B.A., Harvard U., 1977. Editorial asst. Random House, N.Y.C., 1977-78; assoc. editor Simon & Schuster, N.Y.C., 1979; assoc. editor Self mag. Conde Nast Publs., N.Y.C., 1980-81, sr. editor, 1981-83; East Coast story editor Universal Pictures, N.Y.C., 1983—. Author: (poetry) The Procedure (Mademoiselle Poetry prize), 1976; Modigliani Nude, 1919 (Roger Conant Hatch prize), 1976. Trustee Harvard Advocate. Mem. Women in Communications. Office: MCA-Universal Pictures 445 Park Ave New York NY 10022

BINDLEY, ELLA FRANCES, county official; b. Denver, May 21, 1926; d. Foster and Annie (Dupree) Smith; m. Ira B. Bindley, Aug. 20, 1946; children—Anna Kay, Jack Burton, Eldon Lee. Student U. Colo., 1944-45. Bookkeeper Olesen Motors, Eagle, Colo., 1965; clk.-assessor office Eagle County, 1966-67, dep. assessor, 1967-77, assessor, 1978—. Mem. Internat. Assessors Assn., Colo. Assessors Assn. (pres. 1984-85), Eagle Profl. Bus. Women. Republican. Methodist. Lodge: Order Eastern Star. Avocations: cake decorating; sewing; knitting; china painting; hiking; fishing; skiing. Home: Box 214 Eagle CO 81631 Office: Eagle County Assessor 550 Broadway Eagle CO 81631

BINDRIM, PATRICIA MASTERILLI, marketing communications director, consultant; b. Phila., Mar. 9, 1954; d. Frank Anthony and Kathryn Susan (Crawford) Masterilli; m. Mark William Bindrim, June 7, 1975; 1 child, Kira Lee. B.S., Pa. State U., 1975; M.Ed., U. Md., 1979. Cert. secondary sch. tchr., Md. High sch. English tchr. Prince George County (Md.) Schs., 1975; account adminstr. U. Md., College Park, 1977-79; communications specialist Internat. Bank, Washington, 1979-82; communications dir. Heritage div. Beverly Enterprises, Rockville, Md., 1982-83; dir. corp. communications TU Internat., Inc., Falls Church, Va., 1984-86; mktg. communications mgr. Entre Computer Ctrs., Inc., Vienna, Va., 1986—; promotions cons. 1983, Hannover Healthcare, 1984-85. Mem. Pub. Relations Soc. Am., Pa. State U. Alumni Assn., Kappa Kappa Gamma. Methodist. Home: 4611 Powder Mill Rd Beltsville MD 20705 Office: Entre Computer Ctrs Inc 1951 Kidwell Dr Vienna VA 22180

BINEGAR, GWENDOLYN ANN, social worker; b. Phoenix, Sept. 23, 1924; d. Glenn Marvin and Mary Lenore (Cartwright) Redington; B.S. in Sociology, Iowa State U., 1948; M.S.S., Bryn Mawr Coll., 1967; m. Lewis Albert Binegar, Nov. 2, 1951; children—Glen Albert, Birne Thomas, William Lewis, Alan Martin. Coordinator vols. Santa Barbara Mental Health Services, Lompoc, Calif., 1964; psychiat. social worker Child Study Inst., Bryn Mawr (Pa.) Coll., 1967-71; sr. social worker Ruth Sch. for Girls, Seattle, 1972; med. social worker Casa Colina Hosp., Pomona, Calif., 1973-74; supervising counselor San Gabriel Valley Regional Center, Pomona, 1974-79; asst. chief counselor San Diego Regional Center, 1979-80, chief counselor, 1980—; sec. Nat. Com. on Peace and Social Welfare, 1973-74; mem. Calif. Community Care Adv. Com., 1983—, vice-chmn., 1984—. Lic. clin. social worker, Calif. Mem. Acad. Cert. Social Workers, Am. Assn. Mental Deficiency (nat. prevention com. 1983—; chmn. region 1983—), Nat. Assn. Social Workers, Assn. Regional Ctr. Agys. (sec., chief counselors com. 1983—). Presbyterian. Home: 28809 Lilac Valley Center CA 92082 Office: 4355 Ruffin Rd San Diego CA 92123

BINER, MARGARET LAVIN, communications company executive; b. Worcester, Mass., May 1, 1952; d. Walter Douglas and Ellen M. (Gilligan) Lavin; m. Stanley Biner, Sept. 4, 1983; 1 child, W.J. B.A., Assumption Coll., 1974; M.B.A., Clark U., 1976, postgrad., 1976-77. Asst. mgr. New Eng. Telephone and Telegraph, Boston, 1978-80; sr. rate analyst Am. Electric Power, Columbus, Ohio, 1980-81; mkt. supr. GTE Satellite Co., Stamford, Conn., 1981-83; staff mgr. AT&T Communications, Basking Ridge, N.J., 1983—; v.p. programs Am. Mktg. Assn., N.J., 1985—. Solicitor AT&T Polit. Action Com., Basking Ridge, 1985; outreach com. Temple Emanu-El, Westfield, N.J., sec., 1985. Mem. Am. Statis. Assn., Nat. Assn. Bus. Economists, Am. Mktg. Assn. Jewish. Office: AT&T Communications 295 N Maple Ave Basking Ridge NJ 07920

BINGHAM, JINSIE SCOTT, broadcasting company executive; b. Greencastle, Ind., Dec. 28, 1935; d. Roscoe Gibson and Alpha Edith (Robinson) Scott; student DePauw U., 1952-53, Northwestern U., 1953, Coe Coll., 1953-54; m. Richard Innes Bingham, June 24, 1964; children by previous marriage—

Douglas Scott Wokoun, Richard Frank Wokoun. Receptionist, Ind. House of Reps., Indpls., 1959; saleslady Avon Products, Greencastle, Ind., 1961-64; sales mgr. WJNZ Radio, Greencastle, Ind., 1969-77, owner, pres., gen. mgr., 1977—; corp. sec., dir. Main St. Greencastle, Inc., 1983—. Exec. sec. Ind. Young Democrats, 1958-60; mem. Legis. Awareness Seminar, 1977—; co-chmn. Matrix, 1984, Greencastle Gaelic Festval, 1984; bd. dirs. Greencastle Community Child Care Ctr., 1983—; v.p. Greencastle Zoning Bd., 1985—; mem. Greencastle 2001 Com., 1985—; dir. Greencastle Vol. Fire Dept., 1986—. Mem. Am. Women in Radio and TV (pres. Hoosier chpt. 1979-82), Indpls. Network Women in Bus., Women in Communications, Am. Legion, Ind. Broadcasters Assn. (v.p. 1981-82), Greencastle Bus. and Profl. Women's Club (pres. 1976-77, 79-80), Ind. Dem. Editorial Assn., Ind. C. of C., Greencastle C. of C. (dir. 1980-83, pres. 1982), VFW (past pres. aux.), Daus. of 1812 (pres. chpt. 1979-80); DAR, Nat. Assn. Women Bus. Owners, Greencastle Civic League, Soc. Ind. Pioneers, Milestone Car Soc., Delta Theta Tau. Protestant. Clubs: Job's Daus. (life); Women of Moose; Women's Press of Ind., Order Eastern Star. Office: PO Box 494 Greencastle IN 46135

BINION, LINDA DIANE, systems technologies researcher; b. Birmingham, Ala., Apr. 21, 1948; d. James Marvin and Sara Meredith (Moore) Binion; m. Norman Willard Holman, June 20, 1981 (div. 1983). Student, U. Ala.-Tuscaloosa, 1966-67, U. Ala.-Birmingham. Data base adminstr. Carraway Methodist Med. Ctr., Birmingham, Ala., 1970-78; mgr. systems and program Brookwood Health Services Inc., Birmingham, 1979-80; sr. v.p. Innovative Systems Inc., Birmingham, 1980-83; pres. Amitec Inc., Birmingham, 1983-85; dir. research-info. systems technologies Ala. Metal Industries Corp., Birmingham, 1986—; cons. in field. Designer: (software system) Innovative Healthcare Support System, 1980. Guest speaker U. Ala. Sch. Community Allied Health Services, 1986, numerous others. Mem. C. of C. (Birmingham), Mensa, Assn. Systems Mgmt. (past pres.). Democrat. Am. Baptist. Office: Ala Metal Industries Corp 3245 Fayette Ave Birmingham AL 35208

BINNS, SUSAN PATRICIA, soft drink company sales manager; b. New Orleans, Sept. 15, 1958; d. John Olin and Elizabeth Lou (Cooper) B. B.A., Emory U., 1980; student Duke U., 1978. Accountant, Wavetek Inc., San Diego, 1980-81; fin. analyst Bank South Corp., Atlanta, 1981-82; sales rep. Coca Cola USA, Atlanta, 1982—; fin. advisor Delta Delta Delta, 1979-80, 83. Mem. Am. Inst. Banking, Bank Adminstrn. Inst., Nat. Orgn. Female Execs., Phi Beta Kappa. Democrat. Clubs: Duke Track, Atlanta Sporting. Home: 3206 M Post Woods Dr NW Atlanta GA 30339 Office: Coca Cola USA 8601 Dunwoody Pl Suite 200 Atlanta GA 30338

BINOWITZ, LIANE SUE, lawyer; b. St. Louis, Mo., July 21, 1958; d. Hubert Irwin and Beryl (Kitchen) Binowitz. B.A. in English, Grinnell Coll., 1980; J.D., St. Louis U., 1983. Bar: Mo. 1983, Ill. 1984. Assoc. firm Goldstein & Price, St. Louis, 1983—. Mem. ABA, Mo. Bar Assn. (spl. rep. grievance com.), Met. Bar Assn. St. Louis, Ill. Bar Assn., Vol. Lawyers Assn., Health Law Assn., Mo. Orgn. Det. Lawyers, Phi Delta Phi. Club: Propeller of U.S. Office: Goldstein & Price 818 Olive St Saint Louis MO 63101

BINSFELD, CONNIE BERUBE, state senator; b. Munising, Mich., Apr. 18, 1924; d. Omer J. and Elsie (Constance) Berube; B.S., Siena Heights Coll., 1945, D.H.L. (hon.), 1977; postgrad. Wayne State U., 1966-67; m. John E. Binsfeld, July 19, 1947; children—John T., Gregory, Susan, Paul, Michael. County commr., Leelanau County, Mich., 1970-74; mem. Mich. Ho. of Reps., 1974-82; mem. Mich. Senate, 1982—, asst. majority leader. Del., Republican Nat. Conv., 1980. Named Mich. Mother of Year, Mich. Mothers Com., 1977; Northwestern Mich. Coll. fellow. Mem. Nat. Council State Legislators, LWV, Siena Heights Coll. Alumnae Assn. Republican. Roman Catholic. Home: Rural Route 2 Maple City MI 49664 Office: Mich Senate State Capitol Lansing MI 48909

BIRCH, ELEANOR MANSFIELD, management educator; b. Lowell, Mass., Oct. 17, 1928; d. Lawrence Edward and Bridget Josephine (Reardon) Mansfield; B.A. magna cum laude, Brown U., 1949; Ph.D., U. Iowa, 1969; m. John Joseph Birch, Feb. 3, 1951; children—Joanna M., Laura E. With U.S. Bur. Labor Statistics, Boston and Washington, 1949-52, U.S. Dept. Agr., 1952-53; with Harvard Grad. Sch. Bus. Adminstrn., 1954; instr. agrl. econs. U. Calif., Berkeley, 1954-60, agrl. econs. U. Nebr., Lincoln, 1961-64; asso. prof. mgmt. scis. U. Iowa, Iowa City, 1968—, chmn. dept., 1975-78, assoc. dean, dir. M.B.A. program, 1984—; dir. Hon. Industries. NSF fellow, 1964-67; Ford Found. fellow, 1967-68; recipient Hancher Finkbine award U. Iowa, 1975. Mem. Am. Econs. Assn., Am. Statis. Assn., Econometric Soc., Am. Inst. Decision Scis., Iowa Womens Polit. Caucus. Author: (with others) Land and People in the Northern Plains Transition Area, 1966. Home: Box 190 Route 2 Iowa City IA 52240 Office: Grad Programs Office Coll Bus Adminstrn U Iowa Iowa City IA 52242

BIRCH, GLORIA MARIE, information systems consultant; b. Duluth, Nov. 21, 1946; d. William Toivo and Ethel MaryBelle (Tennyson) Korhonen; m. Laurence Lee Birch, Sept. 9, 1966 (div. Mar. 1975); 1 dau., Julie Marcia. B.A., Coll. St. Catherine, 1981. Audit rep. Sears Roebuck, Columbus, Ohio, 1966-71; services rep. Ariz. Bank, Tucson, 1973-76; systems analyst Sage Co., Mpls., 1978-79; analyst Donovan Companies, St. Paul, 1981; info. systems mgr. Detector Electronics, Mpls., 1981-84; cons. R.J. York & Assocs., St. Paul, 1983—. Mem. Data Processing Mgmt. Assn., Assn. for Women in Computing. Democrat. Lutheran. Office: RJ York & Assocs 245 S 6th St Suite 245 Saint Paul MN 55101

BIRCH, GRACE MORGAN, library administrator, educator; b. N.Y.C., June 3, 1925; d. Milton Melville and Adeline Ellsdale (Springer) Morgan; m. Kenneth Francis Birch, Oct. 26, 1947; children—Shari R., Timothy F. B.A., U. Bridgeport, 1963; M.L.S., Pratt Inst., 1968. With Bridgeport Pub. Library, Conn., 1949-66; asst. town librarian Fairfield Pub. Library, Conn., 1966-69; dir. Trumbull Library System, Conn., 1969—; lectr. Housatonic Community Coll., Bridgeport, 1970—. Judge, Barnum Festival Soc. Bridgeport, 1971-73. Mem. ALA, New Eng. Library Assn., Conn. Library Assn. (pres. 1972), Southwestern Conn. Library Council (pres. 1975-77), Fairfield Library Adminstrs. Group (pres. 1976-77), Nat. Assn. Female Execs. Democrat. Episcopalian. Avocations: sketching; dancing; traveling. Home: 175 Brooklawn Ave Bridgeport CT 06604 Office: The Trumbull Library 33 Quality St Trumbull CT 06611

BIRCH, TOBEYLYNN, librarian; b. Los Angeles, Nov. 26, 1949; d. George Walter and Phyllis Jacqueline (Barnes) B.; m. Michael Frederick Cowan, May 17, 1975; children—Stephanie Gayle, Natalie Claire. B.A. in Psychology, U. Calif.-Santa Cruz, 1972; M.A. in Librarianship, U. Denver, 1976. Acquisitions asst. UCLA, 1976-79; asst. librarian Calif. Sch. Profl. Psychology, Los Angeles, 1980-81, dir. library, 1981—. Mem. ALA (sec. Library Instrn. Round Table 1985—), Spl. Libraries Assn., Calif. Library Assn., Beta Phi Mu. Democrat. Home: 4510 W 231st St Torrance CA 90505 Office: Calif School of Professional Psychology 2235 Beverly Blvd Los Angeles CA 90057

BIRCHETT, JO ANN, government official; b. Emporia, Kans., Feb. 19, 1944; d. Clarence Othel and Wilma Jane (Young) Birchett; B.S., Tex. A&I U., Kingsville, 1967. Cooperative edn. student NASA-Johnson Space Center, Houston, 1963-67, computer programmer, data analyst, 1967—. Mem. Fed. Women's Program com., 1979-81. Mem. Nat. Mgmt. Assn., Am. Fedn. Govt. Employees (women's coordinator 1980-81, treas. 1981—). Democrat. Mem. Christian Ch. Home: Route 2 Box 2222 7510 Sunflower St Pearland TX 77584 Office: NASA Johnson Space Center Houston TX 77058

BIRD, MARIANNE CLARA, journalist; b. Saginaw, Mich., Aug. 4, 1954; d. Lewis Wadsworth and Marian Clara (Heindel) Bird; A.A., Delta Coll. U., 1974; B.A., Central Mich. U., 1976. Reporter Schmitt Pub., Saginaw, Mich., 1976—; graphics specialist Hare Printing, St. Charles, Mich., 1982—. Editor: Voluntary Action Ctr. News, Saginaw, 1984—; Saginaw Crescent, United Comml. Travelers of America, 1981—. Dir. pub. relations Mid-Mich. Heritage Com., Saginaw, 1982; publicity chmn. Can-Amera Games, Saginaw, 1978-79; publicist Saginaw Camp Fire Girls, Inc., 1977; speaker Adopt-a-Sch. program, Saginaw Twp. Sch. Dist., 1977. Recipient Spl. Sch. Bell award Mich. Edn. Assn., 1978, 79, 80, 81, 82, 83; Disting. Service award Swan Valley Edn. Assn., 1980; Friend of Edn. award Saginaw Twp. Edn. Assn., 1980; cert. of excellence in photography Mich. Press Assn., 1980; cert. of recognition, Saginaw Twp. Bd. Edn., 1983. Mem. Saginaw Valley Press Club, Soc. Profl. Journalists, Women in Communications, Phi Kappa Phi. Presbyn. Home: 2324 Richard Ave Saginaw MI 48603 Office: The Township Times 2089 Wieneke Rd Saginaw MI 48603

BIRD, ROSE ELIZABETH, state chief justice; b. Tucson, Nov. 2, 1936; B.A. magna cum laude, L.I. U., 1958; J.D., U. Calif. at Berkeley, 1965. Admitted to Calif. bar, 1966; clk. to chief justice Nev. Supreme Ct., 1965-66; dep. pub. defender, sr. trial dep., chief appellate div. Santa Clara (Calif.) County, 1966-74; tchr. Stanford U. Law Sch., 1972-74; sec. Calif. Agr. and Services Agy., also mem. governor's cabinet, 1975-77; chief justice Calif. Supreme Ct., 1977—. Chmn. Calif. Jud. Council, Commn. Jud. Appointments Calif.; pres. bd. dirs. Hastings Coll. Law, U. Calif., San Francisco; bd. councilors U. So. Calif. Law Center, 1975-77. Past bd. assos. San Fernando Valley Youth Found.; mem. Western regional selection panel President's Commn. White House Fellows, 1976-77. Ford Found. fellow, 1960. Democrat. Address: 350 McAllister St San Francisco CA 94102*

BIRDSALL, JANE ELAINE, financial executive; b. Buffalo, Aug. 26, 1947; d. Roy George and Geraldine J. (Steffan) Fink; m. Arthur Anthony Birdsall, Jan. 28, 1967; children—Robert James, Thomas Michael, William Mathew. B.B.A., Saginaw Valley State Coll., 1982. Cert. Fin. Planner, Mich. Acct. exec. Thomson McKinnon Securities, Inc., Midland, 1982—. Mem. Tri City Task Force for Econ. Devel. of Women, Midland, Bay City, Saginaw, Mich., 1984—; bd. dirs. Bay County YWCA. Mem. Am. Bus. Women's Assn. (pres. 1985-86, Woman of Yr. award 1986-87), Bus. & Profl. Women's Assn. (v.p. 1984-86, pres. 1986-87), Inst. Cert. Fin. Planners, Internat. Assn. Fin. Planning, AAUW. Office: Thomson McKinnon Securities Inc 121 1/2 E Main St Midland MI 48640

BIRDSALL, SANDRA JILL, lawyer, mayor; b. Chgo., Nov. 16, 1942; d. Harlan R. and Marion (Beach) Hendrickson; m. James R. Birdsall, Aug. 22, 1964; children—Jeffrey, Leslie, Mark. B.S., Western Ill. U., 1964; J.D., Kent Coll. Law, Chgo., 1982. Bar: Ill. 1982. Tchr., Lake Park High Sch., Roselle, Ill., 1967-70; staff writer Addison Leader News, Ill., 1974-77; mayor Village of Roselle, 1981—; assoc. Guerard & Drenk, Wheaton, Ill., 1982—; pres. DuPage Mayors and Mgrs. Conf., 1984-85; chair DuPage Community Devel. Commn., 1981-83; vice-chair DuPage Civic Ctr. Authority, Wheaton, 1985—. Republican precinct committeeman, Bloomingdale Twp., 1983—. Recipient Am. Jurisprudence award, 1980. Mem. Kent Law Rev., 1981-82. Mem. DuPage Bar Assn. Republican. Methodist. Home: 420 E Walnut St Roselle IL 60172 Office: 31 S Prospect St Roselle IL 60172

BIRDWELL, GAYLE KAYE, manufacturer's representative company executive; b. Brookfield, Mo., Oct. 24, 1952; d. Joseph Isaac and Dorothy Rosella (Butterfield) Kaye; m. Jack Ken Birdwell, June 25, 1977; 1 dau., Natalie Kaye. B.B.A., U. Mo.-Columbia, 1974. Sales rep. Procter & Gamble, Dallas, 1974-77, Wallace Bus. Forms, Dallas, 1977-81; gen. mgr. Birdwell & Assocs., Garland, Tex., 1981—. Mem. Dallas Microcomputer Users Group (v.p., membership dir.), Dallas Computer Council, U. Mo. Alumni Assn. Methodist. Office: Birdwell & Assocs 5102 Willowhaven Garland TX 75043

BIRK, BETSY HUNTER, advertising executive; b. Hartford, Conn., May 9, 1952; d. Jack Robert and Lillian (Burgess) Hunter. B.A. cum laude, Colgate U., 1974; postgrad. Boston U. Publicity/media relations Mobil Oil, N.Y.C., 1975-76; account exec. Tracy-Locke Advt., Dallas, 1976-78, Burton-Campbell, Inc., Atlanta, 1978-79; v.p., account supr. Wells, Rich, Greene, S.W., Dallas, 1979-82, Tracy-Locke/BBDO, Dallas, 1982—. Republican. Methodist. Home: 9530 Viewside Dr Dallas TX 75231 Office: Tracy-Locke/BBDO PO Box 50129 Dallas TX 75250

BIRKENES, AMY JO, advertising agency executive; b. Detroit, Jan. 31, 1950; d. Milton Norman Zimmerman and Molly Ann (Winokur) Zimmerman Foreman; m. Robert Elling Birkenes, May 12, 1979; children—Katherine Ann, Molly Beth. Student U. Denver, 1967-68, U. Ga., 1968-70, Columbia Coll., Chgo., 1970-71. Copywriter Zimmerman & Assocs., Chgo., 1972-73; asst. Columbia Records, Los Angeles, 1973; asst. to pres. Compilation Albums, Warner Records, Los Angeles, 1974; trainee agt. Internat. Creative Mgmt., Los Angeles, 1975; agt., artists' rep. Zimmerman & Assocs., Chgo., 1976-79; pres., chief exec. officer Birkenes & Foreman Advt., Boca Raton, Fla., 1980—; guest tchr. continuing edn. Fla. Atlantic U., Boca Raton, 1984. Vice pres. Boca Raton Symphony League South Fla. Philharm., 1984-85; active Boca Raton Art Mus., Caldwell Playhouse, Boca Raton. Mem. Ft. Lauderdale Advt. Fedn. (numerous Addy awards 1981—), Palm Beach Advt. Fedn. (numerous Addy awards 1981—), Boca Raton C. of C., Palm Beach C. of C., Fla. Atlantic Builder's Assn., Boca Raton Hist. Soc. Jewish. Clubs: Boca Raton Hotel and Club Boca Raton, Boca Groves Country, St. Andrews Country, Jr. League Boca Raton. Avocations: swimming, tennis, reading, traveling. Office: Birkenes & Foreman Advertising 1388 NW 2d Ave Boca Raton FL 33432

BIRKENSTEIN, LILLIAN RAY (MRS. GEORGE ULMAN BIRKENSTEIN), ornithologist; b. Phila., Oct. 9, 1900; d. Morris and Stella (Schloss) Rosenzweig; B.A. (coll. scholar), Wellesley Coll., 1922; student U. Pa., 1920-21, Northwestern U., 1936-37, Instituto Allende (Mexico), 1951-55, Academia Hispana-Americana (Mexico), 1960-68; m. George Ulman Birkenstein, Sept. 2, 1922; children—Dorothy (Mrs. Jose Vidargas), Jean (Mrs. Atlee Washington). Pres., Anker-Holth Mfg. Co., Port Huron, Mich., 1944-51; researcher local Spanish and tribal Indian names of Mexican birds, 1952—; vol. librarian, San Miguel Allende, 1954-64, tchr. ornithology Institute Allende, San Miguel Allende, 1973. Bd. dirs. Public Library San Miguel Allende, 1954-67, Hot Breakfasts for Sch. Children, San Miguel, 1957-61. Mem. San Miguel Allende Audubon Soc. (founder 1967, pres. 1967-71, dir. 1971—), Am. Soc. Mfg. Engrs. (hon. life), Am. Ornithologists Union, Cooper Ornithol. Soc., Linnaean Soc., Wilson Ornithol. Soc., Cornell Lab. Ornithology, Mexican Natural History Soc. (dir. 1972—), Mexican Ornitholog. Soc. (dir.), Internat. Com. for Bird Preservation (treas. Mexican sect. 1968—), Women's Aux. AIME (hon.). Clubs: San Miguel Allende Garden (1st v.p. 1971—); Golf Malanquin. Author: Native Names of Mexican Birds, 1981. Contbr. articles to various publs. Home: Tenerias 45 San Miguel Allende Guanajuato Mexico

BIRKHOFF, DEBORAH LORRAINE, police officer; b. Roanoke, Va., Feb. 12, 1959; d. Cornelius F. and Anna S.M. (Anderson) B. B.S. in Econs., Radford U., 1981; cert. paralegal George Washington U., 1982. Sec., Radford U., Va., 1980-81; congl. asst. Congressman Robinson, Washington, 1981-83; police officer U.S. Capitol Police, 1983—, research analyst, 1985-86. Active congl. campaigns. Mem. Fraternal Order of Police, Internat. Narcotic Enforcement Officers Assn., Sigma Sigma Sigma. Republican. Baptist. Office: US Capitol Police 331 1st St NE Washington DC 20510

BIRKHOLZ, GABRIELLA SONJA, communication consulting company executive; b. Chgo., Apr. 11, 1938; d. Ladislav E. and Sonja (Kosner) Becvar; student Northwestern U., U. Wis.; B.A. with honors, Alverno Coll., 1983. Editor, owner Fox Lake (Wis.) Representative, 1962-65, MacFarland (Wis.) Community Life and Monona (Wis.) Community Herald, 1965-69; reporter Waukesha (Wis.) Daily Freeman, 1969-71; community relations Waukesha County Tech. Inst., 1971-73; publs. editor J. I. Case Co., Racine, Wis., 1973-80; v.p. Image Mgmt., Milw., 1980-82; pres. Communication Concepts Unltd., Racine, 1983—; mem. adj. faculty U. Wis., Parkside. Guest lect. coll. Bd. dirs. Big Bros./Big Sisters of Racine County, Inc.; mem. community adv. council pub. radio sta. WGTD. Named Wis. Woman Entrepreneur of Yr., 1985. Mem. Internat. Assn. Bus. Communicators (accredited), Women in Communications, Sigma Delta Chi, Downtown Assn. Racine, Downtown Racine Devel. Corp., Racine Area Mfr. Commerce, Alverno Alumnae Assn. (gov. bd.). Contbr. articles to profl. jours. Club: Ad of Racine (bd. dirs.). Home: 901 Kingston Ave Racine WI 53402 Office: 312 Main St Racine WI 53403

BIRKITT, LINDA ANN AYLMER, physical therapist; b. Oakland, Calif., Feb. 8, 1946; d. William Stanley and Phyllis Jane (King) Aylmer; student U. Md. at Munich, W.Ger., 1967-68; B.S., Calif. State Poly. U., 1963-69; M.A. (HEW scholar), U. So. Calif., 1973; m. John C. Birkitt, Sept. 13, 1980; children—Andra, Robert, Lowell, Daniélle. Staff phys. therapist Valley Presbyn. Hosp., Van Nuys, Calif., 1973-75; chief therapist Ingleside Mental Health Center, Rosemead, Calif., 1975-79, mem. Speakers Bur., 1976-79; lectr. Santa Monica City Coll., 1976-79; asst. chief phys. therapist Alhambra (Calif.) Community Hosp., 1979-81; pvt. practice phys. therapy, San Juan Capistrano, Calif., 1981; rehab. supr. Vis. Nurses Orange County, 1983; clin. rehab. coordinator Meml. Health Techs., 1984-85; dir. ops. and phys. therapy Health tech. Rehab. Inc., 1985-86. Contbr. to profl. publs. Vol. fire fighter, El Cariso Village, Calif., 1979—; organizer village home owners El Cariso Village, Lake Elsinore, Calif., 1981. Mem. AAUW, Nat. Assn. Female Execs. Episcopalian. Research in motivation as a factor in performance of phys. skill, verticality perception distortion in hemiplegic patients. Home: 32536 Ortega Hwy El Cariso Village Lake Elisinore CA 92330

BIRMAN, CAROLINE (CARINA), lawyer; b. Graz, Austria, June 1; came to U.S., 1941, naturalized, 1946; d. Armin and Anna (Fischer) Birman. J.D., U. Vienna, 1924; Licencée en droit, U. Paris, 1929; LL.B., Bklyn. Law Sch., 1946, J.D., 1967. Bar: conseil juridique Paris 1929; N.Y. 1947, U.S. Supreme Ct. 1960. Exec. sec. Internat. Commn. for Distbn. Rolling Stock of former Austro-Hungarian Monarchy, Vienna, 1923-26; legal adviser Austrian legation and consulate, Paris, 1930-38; French legal counsellor, Paris, 1930-40; sole practice, specializing in French, Austrian and German law, also U.S. copyright law, N.Y.C., 1947—. Mem. editorial staff Revue Internationale des Societes, Paris, 1933-38. Decorated knight's cross Austrian Order of Merit. Mem. ABA, N.Y. Women's Bar Assn., New York County Lawyers Assn. Mem. Liberal Party. Home and office: 104-60 Queens Blvd Suite 9-B Forest Hills NY 11375

BIRNBAUM, JOAN WELKER, religious foundation executive; b. Oil City, Pa., Apr. 26, 1923; d. George Ernest and Josephine Wilson (Powell) Welker; m. Theodore Birnbaum, Jan. 8, 1949 (div. 1977); children—Lyuba, Margaret Jane (Meg), L. Crispin. B.A. in Econs., Wellesley Coll., 1945; postgrad. Northwestern U. Grad. Sch. Bus. Adminstrn., summer 1945, Nat. Planned Giving Inst., 1979, Philanthropy Tax Inst. Jr. acct. Price, Waterhouse and Co., N.Y.C., 1945-50; sec. to asst. treas. Rockefeller Found., N.Y.C., 1950; acct. Rye Youth Council, N.Y., 1976-84; exec. dir. Mamaroneck/Larchmont LIFE Ctr., N.Y., 1973; assoc. dir. vols. United Hosp., Port Chester, N.Y., 1974; bus. mgr. Burke Rehab. Ctr. Day Hosp., White Plains, N.Y., 1974-78; planned giving officer Save the Children Fedn., Inc., Westport, Conn., 1979-82; exec. dir. N.Y.-Conn. Found. of United Meth. Ch., White Plains, 1982—. Bd. dirs. Rye United Fund, sec., mem. nominating com.; elder, deacon pres. Women's Assn. Rye Presbyterian Ch.; chmn. maj. reunion fund campaign Wellesley Coll. Class, 1980-85, chmn. reunion, 1975, class historian, 1965—, admissions chmn. for Wellesley in Westchester Club; bd. dirs., pres. Planned Parenthood of Eastern Westchester; pres. Rye Family Service; telephone listener and source of referral Rye/Larchmont/Mamaroneck Hot Line; treas., exec. com. Rye Youth Council; sec., treas., v.p., pres. 15th Twig of United Hosp., also bd. dirs.; past pres. Rye High Sch. Mothers' Guild, chmn. 1st direct solicitation fund drive; bd. dirs. Woman's Club of Rye, pres. jr. sect.; membership chmn., bd. dirs. Midland Sch. of Rye (voted Parent of Yr.). Mem. Nat. Assn. United Meth. Founds. (treas. 1983—), Planned Giving Group of Greater N.Y. (v.p. 1983-84, pres. 1984-85), Internat. Assn. Fin. Planners, Devel. Assn. of So. Conn. (chmn. program com. 1983-84), Nat. Soc. Fund Raising Execs., Assn. Westchester Devel. Officers. Republican. Presbyterian. Club: Wellesley (so. Conn.). Avocations: silversmithing; handweaving; piano; guitar; Great Books.

BIRNEY, MEREDITH BAXTER, actress; b. Los Angeles, June 21, 1947; m. David Birney, 1974; children—Mollie and Peter (twins); children by previous marriage—Ted, Eva. Films include "Ben", 1972, "Bittersweet Love", 1976, "All the President's Men", 1976; TV movies: "Little Women", 1978, "The Family Man", 1979; star TV series: "Family", 1976-80, The Interns, 1970-71, "Bridget Loves Bernie", 1972-73, "Family Ties", 1982—; miniseries include "Beulah Land", 1980. Address: care Jack Fields & Assocs Inc 925 W Sunset Blvd Suite 1105 Los Angeles CA 90069*

BIROS, LORRAINE, mental health counselor; b. Cleve., June 8, 1946; d. John A. and Ann L. (Ferrara) Biros; B.S., Ohio State U., 1967; M.A., Goddard Coll., 1979. Nat. cert. counselor. Tech. editor Am. Psychol. Assn., Washington, 1968-72; prodn. coordinator, sr. staff editor John F. Holman & Co., Inc., Washington, 1974-79; mem. core faculty Goddard Coll., 1980-81, cons., 1981-82; feminist counselor in pvt. practice, Silver Spring, Md., 1979—; bd. dirs. Whitman-Walker Clinic, Inc., Washington, 1979-80; co-founder/coordinator Lesbian Resource and Counseling Center, Washington, 1978-80, mem. core staff, 1985—, cons., 1980—; charter mem. D.C. Area Feminist Alliance, 1976-78; mem. core staff Washington Area Women's Center, 1976-78. Mem. editorial bd. Women and Therapy: A Feminist Quar. Mem. Am. Assn. Counseling and Devel., Assn. for Humanistic Psychology, Assn. for Women in Psychology, Himalayan Internat. Inst. Yoga Sci. and Philosophy, Nat. Gay/Lesbian Task Force, Nat. Assn. Lesbian and Gay Alcoholism Profls., NOW, Women's Nat. Health Network, Women Strike for Peace, Women's Internat. League Peace and Freedom. Democrat. Home: 806 Malcolm Dr Silver Spring MD 20901

BISCHAK, CYNTHIA D., technical writer; b. Columbus, Ohio, Apr. 1, 1956; d. Donald Rex, Jr., and Nancy May (Dawson) Barnes; m. Frank William Bischak, Mar. 16, 1977. B.S. in Botany and Marine Sci., U. Wash., 1981, M.P.A., 1985. Water quality technician Ohio EPA, Columbus, 1978; exec. sec. Dan A. Carmichael, AIA, Columbus, 1978-79; supr. publs. Vitro Corp., Silverdale, Wash., 1982-85; sr. tech. writer water pollution control dept. Municipality Met. Seattle (Metro), 1985—; bd. dirs. Hood Canal Enciron. Council, Seabeck, Wash., 1985—; chmn. conservation com. Kitsap Audubon, Poulsbo, Wash., 1982-84. Author: Citizen's Guide to Municipal Incorporation in the State of Washington, 1985. Tech. advisor and publicity co-chmn. Silverdale Inc. Com., 1983-85. Mem. Am. Soc. Pub. Adminstrn. (student rep. Evergreen Chpt. Council 1984-85), Western Govtl. Research Assn. Club: Cityclub (Seattle). Avocations: Backpacking; canoeing; scuba diving; gardening; stained glass. Home: PO Box 187 Seabeck WA 98380-0187 Office: Metro 821 Second Ave MS-82 Seattle WA 98104

BISEDA, MARLENE A., computer company executive; b. Charleroi, Pa., Nov. 30, 1946; d. John Stephen and Margaret (Farkas) B.; m. Stephen Sher, Apr. 17, 1982; 1 child, Jonathan. B.S. in Edn., Duquesne U., 1968; M.A. in Edn., U. Calif.-Santa Barbara, 1973; M.B.A., U. Pitts., 1975. Math. tchr. Pitts. City Schs., 1968-74; analyst crude and fleet tactics Gulf Oil Corp., Pitts., 1975-77; systems engr. IBM, Los Angeles, 1977-82, industry specialist health, 1980-81, adv. market support rep., 1983, systems engring. mgr., 1984—. Recipient Duquesne U. scholarship, 1964-68; NSF grantee, 1971-73; U. Pitts. fellow, 1975. Mem. Nat. Assn. Female Execs. Democrat. Roman Catholic. Avocations: photography; needlework; reading; gourmet cooking. Home: 2108 E Oakdale St Pasadena CA 91107 Office: IBM 9045 Lincoln Blvd Los Angeles CA 90045

BISHOP, CONNIE B., hospital administrator; b. Atlanta, June 4, 1953; d. Robert Richard and Catherine Virginia (Mato) Bossons; m. Benamin Benson Bishop, May 13, 1976. B.S.N., Duke U., 1975; M.N., U. S.C., 1980; M.B.A., U. New Haven, 1987. Human relations dir. Nautilus Sports Medicine and Phys. Fitness Ctr., Jacksonville, N.C., 1982-83; asst. adminstr. Clin. Services, HSA Brynn Marr Hosp., Jacksonville, 1983-85; asst. adminstr. Elmcrest Psychiat. Inst., Portland, Conn., 1985—. Mem. Nat. Assn. Female Execs., Sigma Theta Tau. Methodist. Club: Exchange of Middletown (program com. co-chmn.). Office: Elmcrest Psychiatric Inst 25 Marlborough St Portland CT 06480

BISHOP, DORIS JACKSON, retired government official; b. Rahway, N.J., June 26, 1927; d. Alfred Charles and Ella Mae (Snyder) Jackson; student Parsons Sch. Design, 1945, U. Nev., 1949, Coll. Charleston, 1971-72; m. Frank Davis Bishop (dec.). Statis. officer, mgmt. analyst Naval Supply Center, Charleston, S.C., 1958-73; dep. command EEO officer, Fed. Women's Program coordinator Naval Supply Systems Command, Washington, 1973-75; coordinator, dep. dir. EEO/Fed. Women's Program, Mil. Dist. Washington, U.S. Army, 1975-79; internal EEO program mgr. FHWA, Denver, 1979-80; regional EEO officer Nat. Park Service, Denver, 1980-85. Bd. dirs. Amberwick Homeowners Assn., 1980-82, Greenhouse Condominium, Alexandria, Va., 1977-79, Tibetan Found., Inc., 1984—. Served with USAF, 1951-53. Named Career Woman of Yr., Bus. and Profl. Women, Charleston, 1967; recipient Outstanding Performance awards, U.S. Navy, U.S. Army. Columnist, Alex Port Packet, weekly, 1977-79. Home: 128 S Holman Way Golden CO 80401

BISHOP, FRANCES BLACKBURN, civic worker; b. West Palm Beach, Fla., Mar. 3, 1925; d. Julius Magath and Adele Eleanor (Berg) Blackburn; B.Mus.Ed., Fla. State U., 1945; postgrad. Columbia, 1959-62; M.A. in Musicology, U. Mo., 1958; M.A. Teaching English as 2d Lang., Hunter Coll., 1986; m. Ben Bishop, May 20, 1946 (div. 1952); 1 dau., Jewel. Music tchr., Joiner, Ark., 1946-47, Franklin Square, N.Y., 1957-69; asst. placement dir. of internat. counselor exchange program. Assn. for World Travel Exchange, N.Y.C., 1970-74; exec. sec. Army Relief Soc., N.Y.C., 1975-76; adminstrv. sec. Am. Music Center, 1977-78; editorial asst. Sci. Digest, 1978—; violinist Bloomingdale Chamber Orch.; tchr. English adult evening classes, N.Y.C., 1972-75; mem. Met. Greek Chorale. Vol. Internat. Center. Author reading textbook for English; collaborator on Japanese English dictionary of new words. Mem. Soc. Asian Music. Home: 36 W 84 St New York NY 10024

BISHOP, ISABEL (MRS. HAROLD G. WOLFF), artist; b. Cin., Mar. 3, 1902; d. John Remsen and Anna Bartram (Newbold) Bishop; ed. Wicker Art Sch., Detroit, 1917-18, N.Y. Sch. Applied Design for Women, 1918-20, Art Students League N.Y., 1920-22, 1927-30; A.F.D. (hon.), Moore Inst., Phila., Bates Coll., Maine, Syracuse U., 1982, Mt. Holyoke Coll., 1983, New Sch. Social Research, 1983; m. Harold George Wolff, Aug. 9, 1934. Instr. life painting and composition Art Students League, N.Y.C., 1936-37; instr. Snowhegan Sch. Painting and Sculpture, 1957, lectr., 1957, 60, 62, 64, 66; represented in Mus. Bibliotheque Nationale, Paris, Victoria and Albert Mus., London, Des Moines Art Center, Brit. Mus., Met. Mus., Whitney Mus., others, also art galleries, collections Paul Sachs, Johnson Collection, others; exhibited expns.; 12 one-man shows in N.Y.C., one-man show Berkshire Mus., Pittsfield, Mass., 1957; retrospective exhbns. Whitney Mus. Art, 1975, U. Ariz., 1974, Wichita (Kans.) State U., 1974. Recipient awards including W.A. Clark Prize, Bronze medal, Corcoran Gallery, Washington, 1945; Mrs. H. S. Noyes and Am. Artists Group prizes, 1947; Benjamin Franklin fellow Royal Soc. Art, 1965; first Altman prize NAD, 1967; Asso. mem. NAD, 1940; elected Nat. Academician, 1941. Fellow Royal Soc. Arts London; mem. Nat. Inst. Arts and Letters, Am. Acad. Arts and Letters, Am. Soc. Painters, Sculptors and Gravers, Soc. Am. Etchers, Nat. Arts Club, Phila. Water Color Club, Am. Group Cosmopolitan Club.

BISHOP, JOYCE ANN, college counselor, educator; b. West Mansfield, Ohio, June 16, 1935; d. Frederic J. and Marjorie Vere (Stephens) Armentrout; A.B., Albion Coll., 1956; M.A., Western Mich. U., 1969, postgrad., 1972-84; children—Belinda Lee, Thomas James. Tchr. phys. edn., health and cheerleading Walled Lake (Mich.) Jr. High Sch., 1956-58; instr. slimnastics adult edn. Milw. Pub. Schs., 1959-65; demonstrator, co. rep. Polaroid Corp., Cambridge, Mass., 1960-81; research asst. fetal electrocardiography Marquette U., Milw., 1962-64; tchr. phys. edn., health and cheerleading Brown Deer (Wis.) High Sch., 1963-65; instr. slimnastics adult edn., instr. volleyball Lakeview High Sch., Battle Creek, Mich., 1966—; dir. student activities, counselor, asst. prof. Kellogg Community Coll., Battle Creek, 1971—, transfer counselor; asst. prof. Olivet (Mich.) Coll., 1971—. Sec. adult bd. Teens, Inc., 1965-68; bd. dirs. Battle Creek Day Care Ctrs., sec., 1984, pres., 1984-85; team capt. United Way Awareness Week, 1984, pres., 1984-86; vice-chmn. United Arts Fund Dr., 1985, chmn., 1986. Cert. social worker. Recipient Master Teaching award Lakeview Schs., 1969; mem. Battle Creek Leadership Acad. Mem. Mich. Assn. Collegiate Registrars and Admissions Officers (pres. 1979-80), Am. Assn. Collegiate Registrars and Admissions Officers (mem. com. 1984-86), Am. Personnel and Guidance Assn., Am. Coll. Personnel Assn., Mich. Personnel and Guidance Assn., Mich. Coll. Personnel Assn., Mich. Assn. Women Deans, Adminstrs. and Counselors, Mich. Assn. Coll. Admissions Counselors, AAUW, Alpha Chi Omega, Beta Beta Beta. Clubs: Battle Creek Road Runners (v.p. 1983-85), Battle Creek Altrusa. Home: 721 Eastfield Dr Battle Creek MI 49015 Office: 450 North Ave Battle Creek MI 49016

BISHOP, MARGARET, retired basic literacy educator, writer; b. Urbana, Ill., July 4, 1920; d. Charles Maxwell and Prudence Emily (Pratt) McConn; m. Edwin Samuel Bishop, Aug. 22, 1942; children—Peter Boehler, Margaret. B.A., Barnard Coll., N.Y.C., 1943. Reporter, wire editor York Gazette and Daily, York, Pa., 1942-45; remedial reading tutor, Queens, N.Y., 1958-68; in-house writer Appleton-Century-Crofts, N.Y.C., 1964-70, McGraw-Hill, N.Y.C., 1971-74; reading specialist Fortune Soc., N.Y.C., 1976-85. Author: The ABC's and All Their Tricks, 1978, Ode on Reason and Faith, 1981, (workbooks) Phonics with Write and See, 1968, also articles. Exec. sec. NAACP, York, 1943-48; mem. LWV, York, 1946-50, Reading Reform Found., N.Y.C., 1958—; pres. N.Y. met. chpt., 1981-85. Mem. Mayor's Profl. Exchange, Adult Basic Edn. Providers. Democrat. Humanist. Avocations: hiking; camping; backpacking.

BISHOP, MARGARET ANN, coal company executive; b. Owensboro, Ky., Mar. 2 1949; d. Vernon Lee and Emma Frances (Smith) Frashure; m. Allen Ray Bishop, Nov. 11, 1972; m. Paul David Anderson, Apr. 4, 1969 (div. May 1971). Student Victor Bus. Coll., 1970, U. Ky., 1983. Fingerprint technician FBI, Washington, 1968-69; supr. Thomas Industries, Beaver Dam, Ky., 1971-74; lab. mgr. Island Creek Coal Co., Madisonville, Ky., 1974—. Named Ky. Col., 1978. Mem. Bus. and Profl. Womens Club (woman of yr. Madisonville 1978, pres. 1980-81), LWV, Am. Mgmt. Assn., ASTM. Democrat. Presbyterian. Lodge: Order Eastern Star (assoc. conductress 1983-84). Home: Rt 1 Box 156 Sacramento KY 42372 Office: Island Creek Coal Co Madison Sq Shopping Center Douglas Oates Bldg Madisonville KY 42431

BISHOP, MARTHA PHYLLIS, financial planner, advisor, educator; b. Toledo, June 10, 1930; d. Herbert Richard Lord and Rose Ethel (McNally) Young; m. John Frances O'Connor, July 21, 1951 (dec. Oct. 1957); children—Therese Marie, Gerard Kevin; m. Thomas McEffe Bishop, Feb. 21, 1970 (dec.). Cert. Davis Bus. Coll., 1957, Stautzenberger Bus. Coll., 1960; student U. Toledo, 1949-50, 168-70. Mgr. Slenderama, Toledo, 1957; city mgr. Avon Products, 1958; Yellow Page salesperson Ohio Bell Telephone, 1958-59; registered rep. Investors Diversified, Toledo, 1956-66; real estate salesperson Grogan Real Estate Co., 1962-68; adminstrv. asst. to pres. Peerless Molded Plastics, 1966-67; adminstrv. asst. to treas. Craftmaster, Inc., 1962-66; owner Bishop Constrn. Co., Mc Cullock Land Devel. Generator, 1970-74; owner Desert Dov & Tomar Trading Co., 1976-83; pres. Bishop & Assocs., Inc., Phoenix, 1983—. Leader seminars. Author workbook: Controlling Your Money, 1986. Lectr. in field. Mem. Republican Bus. Council, Phoenix, 1954. Mem. Internat. Assn. Fin. Planners, Nat. Assn. Women Execs., Ariz. Networking Council Women Emerging (columnist 1954—). Roman Catholic. Avocation: dancing.

BISHOP, MARY LUCILLE, theater restoration consultant; b. Sapulpa, Okla., Mar. 18, 1918; d. Charles George and Lizzie Pearl (Little) York; A.A., Kansas City Jr. Coll., 1934-36; m. Kenneth Lawrence Bishop, June 5, 1937; 1 child, Robin Bishop Allen. Office mgr. Am. Mut. Liability Ins. Co., Kansas City, Mo., 1939-42; sec. to pres. Devonian Oil Co., Midland, Tex., 1942-44; adminstrv. asst. to pres. Shawan & Assos., Columbus, Ohio, 1966-76; chmn. bldg. and restoration com. bd. trustees Historic Ohio Theatre, 1969-79; dir. bldg., restoration and grants Columbus Assn. for the Performing Arts, Columbus, 1979-85; theater restoration and preservation cons. Mem. exec. com., bd. dirs. Columbus Symphony Orch., 1974-80, trustee emeritus, 1985—; v.p. Columbus Assn. for the Performing Arts, 1971-74. Republican. Clubs: Columbus Metropolitan, Scioto Country. Home: 1380 La Rochelle Dr Columbus OH 43221 Office: 1380 La Rochelle Dr Columbus OH 43221

BISHOP, VIRGINIA WAKEMAN, librarian, humanities educator; b. Portland, Oreg., Dec. 28, 1927; d. Andrew Virgil and Letha Evangeline (Ward) Wakeman; m. Clarence Edmund Bishop, Aug. 23, 1953; children—Jean Marie Bishop Johnson, Marilyn Joyce. B.A., Bapt. Missionary Tng. Sch., Chgo., 1949; B.A., Linfield Coll., McMinnville, Oreg., 1952, M.Ed., 1953; M.Librarianship, U. Wash., 1968. Ch. worker Univ. Bapt. Ch., Seattle, 1954-56, 59-61; pre-sch. tchr. Parent coop Presch., Seattle, 1965-66; librarian Northwest Coll., Kirkland, Wash., 1968-69, U. Wash. Undergrad. Library, Seattle, 1970; librarian, instr. Seattle Central Community Coll., 1970—. Leader Totem council Girl Scouts U.S., 1962-65; pres. Wedgwood Sch. PTA, Seattle, 1964-65; chairperson 46th Dist. Democratic Orgn., Seattle, 1972-73; candidate Wash. State Legislature, Seattle, 1974, 80. Recipient Golden Acorn award Wedgwood Elem. Sch., 1966. Mem. Wash. Commn. for Humanities (Humanist scholar 1979-80), Wash. Library Assn. (legis. rep. 1972), Community Coll. Librarians and Media Specialists, Seattle Community Coll. Fedn. Tchrs., LWV. Unitarian. Avocations: swimming, hiking, reading. Home: 3032 NE 87th St Seattle WA 98115 Office: Seattle Central Community Coll 1701 Broadway Seattle WA 98122

BISHOP, WILLALMA BROWN, banker; b. Whiteside, Mo., Sept. 29, 1926; d. William Joseph and Alma Fay (Horton) Brown; student public schs.; m. Glen G. Bishop, June 26, 1964; 1 son, Kevin Lail. With Boatmens Bank of Troy (Mo.), 1945—, v.p., 1977—. Treas., Lincoln County Youth Fair, 1956—, Lincoln County Heart Assn., 1956—; mem. adv. com. sch. dist. bus. dept. Lincoln County, 1979—. Mem. Am. Inst. Banking, Troy C. of C. (treas. 1952—; Woman of Yr. award 1964), Troy Bus. and Profl. Women's Club (pres. 1956; Woman of Yr. award 1962). Democrat. Presbyterian. Clubs: Martha Dyer Federated (past pres.), Order Eastern Star. Home: 411 W College St Troy MO 63379 Office: 200 Main St Troy MO 63379

BISHOPRIC, ANNIE MILLNER, former mayor Sarasota; b. Miami, Fla., Apr. 12, 1927; d. Bruce James Millner and Lillian Elizabeth (Dobbs) Millner Massey; m. George Andrew Bishopric, Mar. 29, 1949 (div. Oct. 1983); children—Nanette Hahr, Suzanne P., George A., Jr. Student Mary Baldwin Coll., 1945-47; B.A., Duke U., 1949. Commr., City of Sarasota (Fla.), 1981-85, vice mayor, 1982-83, mayor, 1983-85. Mem. Sarasota Planning Bd., 1974-80; 1st v.p. Gulf Coast Planning and Zoning Assn., 1983-84; bd. dirs. Van Wezel Performing Arts Hall. Democrat. Episcopalian. Club: Field (bd. dirs.) (Sarasota). Home: 3745 Almeria Ave Apt 7-S Sarasota FL 33579

BISORDI, EILEEN MARY, educational administrator; b. Jamaica, N.Y., Nov. 29, 1945; d. William J. and Florence (Smith) Quinn; B.A., SUNY, Potsdam, 1968; M.A., Columbia U., 1969, M.Ed., 1976; m. Richard Bisordi, May 31, 1969; children—Anthony, Lisa, Lance. Tchr. spl. edn. Soundview Sch., Yorktown Heights, N.Y., 1968-71; dir. spl. edn. Margaret Chapman Sch., Hawthorne, N.Y., 1971-76, co-dir., 1976-78, exec. dir., 1979—; adj. instr. Westchester Community Coll., 1976—; cons. in field. Bd. dirs. N.Y. State Poets in the Schs., 1977—; mem. exec. com. N.Y. Spl. Olympics, 1977-79, bd. dirs., 1977-79, 83-85, 85-87, area 3 coordinator, 1971-78, regional coordinator N.E., 1978-79, chmn., 1981—; mem. Met. adv. bd. Senate Select Com. on the Disabled. Mem. N.Y. Assn. Pvt. Residential Facilities, Council for Exceptional Children, Council Adminstrn. Spl. Edn., Am. Assn. for Mental Deficiency, Kappa Delta Pi. Roman Catholic. Home: 48 Gurley Rd Stamford CT 06902 Office: 5 Bradhurst Ave Hawthorne NY 10532

BISSELL, BETTY DICKSON, stockbroker; b. Salina, Kans., Sept. 9, 1932; d. Henry Shields and Alta May Dickson; student U. Kans., 1949-52; cert. fin. planner, Coll. Fin. Planning, 1976; m. Buford Lyle Bissell, Jr., Nov. 1, 1952; 1 son, Bradford Dickson. With Dean Witter Reynolds Inc., Menlo Park, Calif., 1975—, asst. br. mgr., 1978-82, asso. v.p. investments, 1980-82, v.p. investments, 1982-86, sr. v.p. investments, 1986—. Pres. Jr. League San Jose (Calif.), 1963-64. Mem. Internat. Assn. Fin. Planners, Peninsula Stock and Bond Club, Pi Beta Phi. Republican. Episcopalian. Clubs: Commonwealth Calif., Summit League (Saratoga-Los Gatos), Jr. League (San Jose, Calif.); Menlopolitans (Menlo Park, Calif.). Office: 720 Santa Cruz Ave Menlo Park CA 94025

BISSELL, ELAINE, novelist, writer; b. Chgo., Oct. 18; d. Harold Whitney and Edwinna Stuart (Biederman) Faulkner; m. John Cooper McMahon, May 31, 1941 (div. 1959); children—Mary Jane McMahon Christofferson, Kathleen Conroy, Susan; m. Nicol Bissell, Dec. 18, 1965. Student Goodman Theatre Sch. Drama, NYU. Reporter Daily Times, Mamaroneck, N.Y., 1956-61; woman's editor Standard-Star, New Rochelle, N.Y., 1961-74; social editor Gannett-Westchester Newspapers, White Plains, N.Y., 1974-77, lifestyles editor, 1977-84, restaurant critic, 1984—; author, novelist St. Martin's Press, N.Y.C. Author: Women Who Wait, 1978; As Time Goes By, 1983; Family Fortunes, 1985. Bd. dirs. Iona Coll. Inst. for Arts, New Rochelle, 1961-75. Recipient Penney-Mo. Journalism award U. Mo., 1978. Mem. Authors League of Am., Authors Guild, Overseas Press Club. Home: 6 Essex Ln Suffern NY 10901

BISSELL, KATHRYN A., government employee; b. Ottumwa, Iowa, Nov. 26, 1926; d. George and Anna L. (O'Connor) B. B.A., Marycrest Coll., 1952; M.A., Am. U., 1960, Ph.D., 1962. Fellow Internat. Consortium for Social Sci. Research, U. Mich., Ann Arbor, 1972; dir. grad. research Howard U. Grad. Sch., Washington, 1972-77; dir. research Internat. Devel. Corp., Washington, 1977-81; pres. Internat. Research Resources, Inc., Bethesda, Md., 1980—; asst. to commr. Nuclear Regulatory Commn., Washington, 1981—. Sec. bd. dirs. Wider Opportunities for Women, Washington, 1978—; mem. adv. bd. The Women's Inst., Am. U., Washington, 1980—. Delmar Found. research grantee, 1976; John XXIII Found. research grantee; NSF research grantee. Mem. Soc. Internat. Devel., Am. Polit. Sci. Assn., Inner-Am. Studies Assn. Democrat. Roman Catholic. Clubs: Pax Community (chmn. steering com.) (McLean, Va.); Christian Feminist (Washington). Home: 4603 Cheltenham Dr Bethesda MD 20014 Office: Nuclear Regulatory Commn Office Commn 1717 H St NW Washington DC

BISSET, JACQUELINE, actress; b. Weybridge, Eng., Sept. 13, 1946. Ed., French Lycée, London. Made film debut in: The Knack, 1965; other motion pictures include Cul de Sac, 1966, Two for the Road, 1967, Casino Royale, 1967, The Sweet Ride, 1968, The Detective, 1968, Bullitt, 1968, The First Time, 1969, Airport, 1970, The Grasshopper, 1970, The Mephisto Waltz, 1971, Believe in Me, 1971, The Life and Times of Judge Roy Bean, 1972, Stand Up and Be Counted, 1972, The Thief Who Came to Dinner, 1973, Day for Night, 1973, Murder on the Orient Express, 1974, The Spiral Staircase, 1974, End of the Game, 1974, St. Ives, 1975, The Deep, 1976, Le Magnifique, 1977, Sunday Woman, 1977, The Greek Tycoon, 1978, Secrets, 1978, Who is Killing the Great Chefs of Europe?, 1978, Amo Non Amo, 1979, When Time Ran Out, 1980, Rich and Famous, 1981, Together, 1981, Inchon, 1982, Class, 1983, Under the Volcano, 1984, Anna Karenina, 1985, Choices, 1986, Forbidden, 1985. Address: care Internat Creative Mgmt 8899 Beverly Blvd Los Angeles CA 90048*

BISSINGER, ELEANOR LEBENTHAL (MRS. H. GERARD BISSINGER II), investment banker; b. N.Y.C., Mar. 5, 1927; d. Louis S. and Sayra (Fischer) Lebenthal; B.A., Smith Coll., 1948; m. H. Gerard Bissinger II, May 11, 1950; children—Ann Louise, H. Gerard III. Editorial asst. UNIFRUITCO mag., 1948-50; letters corr. Life Mag., 1950-52; with market research dept. Norman Craig & Kummel, 1957-58; asst. to producer-dir. plays, motion picture Laurette, There Must Be A Pony, To Kill a Mockingbird, N.Y.C., 1960-63; v.p. Lebenthal & Co., Inc., N.Y.C., 1963-68, adminstrv. v.p., 1970-78, exec. v.p., 1976—, also dir.; exec. asst. Ladenburg Thalmann & Co., 1968-70. Decade chmn. fund raising drive Smith Coll. 1965-66 master of ceremonies Smith Coll. reunions, 1949, 53, 58, 63, 73. Bd. dirs. American Place Theatre; bd. advisers Sun Day, N.Y., 1978; adviser Roundabout Theatre. Clubs: Downtown Athletic, Smith College of N.Y. Office: 25 Broadway New York NY 10004

BISSON, SALLY BROWN, bank officer; b. Omaha, Mar. 31, 1956; d. John Lloyd and Mary Elizabeth (Schwertley) Brown; m. Bruce William Bisson, Sept. 18, 1981. B.A. cum laude, U. Nebr., 1978, J.D., 1981. Bar: Nebr. 1981. Law clk. Douglas County, Omaha, 1980; credit analyst U.S. Nat. Bank, Omaha, 1981-83; loan officer Norwest Bank Omaha, 1983—. Bd. dirs., counsel Alpha Xi Delta Housing Corp., Omaha, 1982—. Mem. ABA, Nebr. State Bar Assn., Omaha Bar Assn., Omicron Delta Kappa (scholastic program 1977-78, leadership hon. chmn.), Alpha Xi Delta. Democrat. Roman Catholic.

BITA, LILI, author, actress; b. Zante, Greece, Dec. 23, 1935; came to U.S., 1959, naturalized, 1969; d. George and Eleni (Makri) Bitas; fine arts degree in music, Greek Conservatory of Music, 1954, in drama, Athens Sch. Drama, 1956; M.A. in Drama, U. Miami, 1978; m. Robert Zaller, Jan. 19, 1968; children—Philip, Kimon. Performer in Greek repertory Art Theatre, Civic Theatre and Royal Palace Garden Theatre, 1955-57; instr. Emporia (Kans.) Coll., 1960-62, U. Toledo, 1963-65, Bklyn. Conservatory of Music, 1967-68; guest lectr., condr. master classes, performer classic theatre various univs., U.S. and Europe, 1970—; actress radio, TV and stage; writer; books include: Steps on the Earth, 1955; Lightning in the Flesh, 1968; Furies, 1969; Zero Hour, 1971; Blood Sketches, 1973; Sacrifice, Exile, Night, 1976; Fleshfire: New and Selected Love Poems, 1980; translator: Anais Nin, A Spy in the House of Love, 1974, 2d edit., 1983; anthologies include: City Lights Anthology, 1974; Contemporary Greek Women Poets, 1979; guest dir. Fla. Internat. U., Aegean Inst. Women's Studies; cons. Dade County Poetry in the Schs. Program; charitable performances include ACLU, Ethical Culture Soc., Nat. Women's Week, Poetry Therapy Program, Odyssey House, Jackson Meml. Hosp. Italian Inst. Study fellow, 1956-57; Circle in the Sq. Theatre fellow, 1967-68; recipient group performance award Austin Theatre, 1978. Mem. Southeastern Theatre Conf., Alpha Psi Omega. Greek Orthodox. Club: Order of Knights of St. Dennis of Zante. Home and Office: 5901 SW 51st St Miami FL 33155

BITKER, MARJORIE MARKS (MRS. BRUNO VOLTAIRE BITKER), writer, editor; b. N.Y.C., Feb. 9, 1901; d. Cecil Alexander and Rachel (Fox) Marks; A.B. magna cum laude (Caroline Duror Meml. fellow), Barnard Coll., 1921; M.A., Columbia U., 1922; m. James C. Jacobson, 1922 (div. 1942); children—Emilie J. Jacobi, Margaret J. Strange, Elizabeth J. Reiss; m. John C. Mayer, Oct. 24, 1942 (dec. June 1945); m. 3d, Bruno Voltaire Bitker, Oct. 10, 1957 (dec. Apr. 1984). Free lance writer, 1922—; editor Farrar Straus, N.Y.C., 1946-47, G.P. Putnam's Sons, N.Y.C., 1947-53, David McKay Co., N.Y.C., 1953-55; now editorial cons., book reviewer, feature writer. Lectr., Hunter Coll., Coll. City N.Y., 1949-53; Women's Chair for Humanistic Studies, Marquette U., 1972-73. Mem. pres.'s council Alverno Coll., 1975-77; bd. visitors U. Wis., 1962-68; alumnae trustee Barnard Coll., 1964-68, Barnard-in-Milw.; bd. dirs. Friends Wis. Libraries. Recipient Barnard Alumnae Recognition award, 1978. Mem. AAUW, Women's Nat. Book Assn., Bookfellows Milw. (pres. 1971-73, dir.), Council Wis. Writers (dir. 1971-77), Phi Beta Kappa. Author: (novels) Gold of Evening, 1975, A Different Flame, 1976; contbr. articles, and book revs. to mags. and newspapers. Address: 2330 E Back Bay St Milwaukee WI 53202

BITNER, LORELEY N(OGUÉS), exporter, consultant; b. Montevideo, Uruguay; came to U.S., 1980, naturalized, 1984; d. Raul L. and Elena (Godoni) Nogues; m. Marlin C. Bitner, Jan. 14, 1981; 1 child, Brian Raoul. Ph.D. in Fin. and Bus. Adminstrn., C.P.A. cert. U. of the Republic, Montevideo, 1975. Tax officer Montevideo City Hall, 1958-75; sr. ptnr. Estudio Contadores Asociados, Montevideo, 1975-80; internat. mktg. person Atlantic Breeders Coop., Lancaster, Pa., 1980—; dir. B.N. Internat., Richland, Pa.; cons. Contadores Asociados, Montevideo, 1978—. Author: Analysis of investment on a rice producing industry, 1975; author bimonthly Letter from the U.S.A., 1984—. Mem. Internat. Assn. C.P.A.s, Coll. Accts. Uruguay, Real Estate Investors Assn. (bd. dirs.). Club: Penarol (Montevideo). Avocations: reading; music; theatre. Home: 1935 Split Rock Rd Lancaster PA 17601 Office: Atlantic Breeders Coop 1575 Apollo Dr Lancaster PA 17601

BITTEL, MURIEL HELENE, managing editor; b. N.Y.C., Mar. 22; d. Ernest Henry and Helen Minnie (Seibel) Albers; m. Robert Gifford Walcutt, June 15, 1946; children—Lynn Lowell Walcutt, Mark James Walcutt, Judith Anne Walcutt; m. Lester Robert Bittel, May 8, 1973. B.A., Douglass Coll. Feature writer Daily Home News, New Brunswick, N.J.; editor Fawcett Pubs., N.Y.C., 1940-46; pub. relations dir. Electrovox/Walco Inc., East Orange, N.J., 1946-62; mng. editor Acad. Hall Pubs., Bridgewater, Va., 1974—. Mng. editor: Ency. Profl. Mgmt., 1978; Handbook Profl. Mgrs., 1985. Home: 106 Breezewood Terrace Bridgewater VA 22812

BITTERMAN, JOAN ASELTINE, college administrator; b. Evanston, Ill., Mar. 25, 1954; d. James Merrill and Lorraine Elizabeth (Hinks) A.; B.A., Aurora Coll., 1976; M.S.Ed., No. Ill. U., 1982, now postgrad. Asst. to registrar Ill. Benedictine Coll., Lisle, Ill., 1976-77; asst. registrar George Williams Coll., Downers Grove, Ill., 1977-79; dir. acad. advisement Aurora (Ill.) U., 1979-85, registrar, 1985—. Mem. Nat. Acad. Advisement Assn., Ill. Assn. Coll. Registrars and Admissions Officers, Adult Edn. Assn. Home: 872 Hill Ave Glen Ellyn IL 60137 Office: 347 Gladstone Ave Aurora IL 60506

BITTLE, CATHERINE WILLIAMS, professional rehabilitation consultant, health education specialist; b. Lake Charles, La., May 28, 1955; d. Thomas Humphrey and Jane Catherine (Caldwell) Williams; one child, Jennifer Catherine Bittle. B.S., Old Dominion U., 1978, M.S. summa cum laude, 1983; profl. nursing diploma Norfolk Gen. Hosp., 1978. Intensive care unit nurse DePaul Hosp., Norfolk, Va., 1979-80; rehab. cons. Internat. Rehab. Assn., Virginia Beach, Va., 1980-82; ptnr., pres., cons. OccuSystems, Norfolk, 1982-85; prin., pres. Cathy Bittle & Assocs., Norfolk, 1985—; health edn. cons. Peninsula Health Dept., Newport News, Va., 1985—; educator Diabetes Inst., Virginia Beach, 1984—; speaker in field. Com. mem. Tidewater Health Fair Task Force, Norfolk, 1983. Mem. Am. Assn. Counseling and Devel., Am. Assn. Phys. Health, Edn., Recreation and Dance, Old Dominion U. Grad. Student Assn. (pres. 1982-83), Phi Kappa Phi. Republican. Roman Catholic. Avocations: sailing; biking; skiing; running; rollerskating. Home: 1460 Ashland Circle Norfolk VA 23509 Office: Cathy Bittle & Assocs PO Box 8551 Norfolk VA 23503

BITTNER, BARBARA NEWMAN, educational administrator; b. Pitts., May 4, 1931; d. Daniel Stephen and Hallie Harper (Wager) Newman; B.A., U. Pitts., 1953; M.Ed., Fla. Atlantic U., 1966; 1 son, Benjamin J. Lectr. dept. speech U. Pitts., 1953-55; sec. to v.p. Farmers Bank of Pompano, Pompano Beach, Fla., 1956-57; tchr. Hillsboro Country Day Sch., Pompano Beach, 1957-68; tchr., div. chmn. A.D. Henderson U. Sch., 1968-73, dir., 1973—. Mem. Am. Assn. Sch. Adminstrs., Assn. Supervision and Curriculum Devel., Nat. Assn. Lab. Schs. (dir. 1983-84, rec. sec. 1984-85, pres. elect 1986-87), Fla. Assn. for Gifted, Fla. Assn. Supervision and Curriculum Devel., Phi Delta Kappa. Clubs: Pilot (Ft. Lauderdale, Fla.); Torch (Boca Raton, Fla.). Home: 4420 W Tradewinds Ave Lauderdale by the Sea FL 33308 Office: 500 NW 20th St Boca Raton FL 33431

BITTNER, JANET SUE, state human service administrator; b. Madison, Wis., Oct. 8, 1945; d. Austin Stewart and Alice (Hermanson) Osterhaus; m. Robert Bruce Bittner, Aug. 26, 1967; 1 child, Matthew. B.S., U. Wis., 1967; postgrad. Fulbright program Ghandian Inst., Varanasi, India, 1974. Dir. planning Action, Inc., Athens, Ga., 1967-73; dir. planning EOA, Inc., Atlanta, 1973-76, dir. adminstrn., 1976-83; dir. office aging Ga. Dept. Human Resources, Atlanta, 1983-84, dep. commr., 1984— ; designer; mem. Alliance for Human Services Planning, Atlanta, 1977-83; chairperson plan devel. Ga. Health Coordinating Council, Atlanta, 1978-83; chairperson, v.p. Atlanta Region Human Services Council, 1979-83. Pres. bd. dirs. Atlanta Women's Network, 1980-85; mem. adv. bd. Met. YWCA, Atlanta, 1981-83; sec. bd. dirs. Outstanding Atlanta, 1982—; bd. dirs. Rich's Enterprising Women, Atlanta, 1982—. Named one of Ten Outstanding People of Atlanta, Outstanding Atlanta, 1982; named Image Maker, Atlanta Profl. Women, 1984. Mem. Ga. Planning Assn. (v.p. and bd. dirs. 1975-80, Outstanding Service award 1976, 77), Am. Planning Assn., Ga. Gerontology Assn., Ga. Pub. Health Assn., Leadership Atlanta, Ga. Women's Polit. Caucus. Office: Ga Dept Human Resources 47 Trinity Ave Room 522H Atlanta GA 30334

BIVENS, JOYCE FEIDLER, postmaster; b. Denver, May 13, 1943; d. Norman Paul Chambers and Marguerite Clyde (Osborne) Vasilka; m. George Edward Feidler, June 2, 1962 (div.); children—Darcus Ann, Julie Deenette; m. Roger Adrian Bivens, Feb. 4, 1984. B.A., Metropolitan State, 1973. Postmaster, U.S. Postal Service, Dumont, Colo., 1973-80, Kremmling, Colo., 1980-84, Placida, Fla., 1985—. Mem. steering com. Clear Creek Sanitation Dist., Dumont, Colo., 1973, bd. dirs., 1974-79, W. Grand County Mental Health, Kremmling, Colo., 1984; capt. Dumont Vol. Fire Dept. Woman's Hose Cart Team, 1974. Mem. Nat. Assn. Postmasters (2d v.p. 1979-80), Woman's Program U.S. Postal Service (bd. dirs. 1984—). Republican. Episcopalian. Avocations: back packing; snow skiing; sewing; leaded glass windows. Home: PO Box 1 Placida FL 33946-0001 Office: US Postal Service Placida FL 33946-9998

BIVINS, LYN MORHARDT, advertising agency executive; b. Baldwin, N.Y., Sept. 6, 1948; d. Charles Harold and Kathryn (Maguire) Morhardt; m. Terry Bivins, May 15, 1976. B.A., Northwestern U., 1970. Research asst. Needham, Harper & Steers, Chgo., 1971-73, research supr., 1973-75; assoc. research dir. Benton & Bowles, Chgo., 1975-79, v.p. research dir., 1979—. Mem. Am. Mktg. Assn. Club: Execs. Office: Benton & Bowles Inc 233 N Michigan Ave Chicago IL 60601

BIVINS, SUSAN STEINBACH, systems engineer; b. Chgo., June 5, 1941; d. Joseph Bernard and Eleanor Celeste (Mathes) S.; B.S., Northwestern U., 1963; postgrad. U. Colo., 1964, U. Ill., 1965, UCLA, 1971; m. James Herbert Bivins, June 7, 1980. With IBM, 1967—, support mgr. East, White Plains, N.Y., 1977-78, systems support mgr., western region, Los Angeles, 1978-81, br. market support mgr., 1981-84, mgr. IBM ops. and support Los Angeles Summer Olympics, 1984, project office mgr. complex systems mktg., 1984—; pres. Jastech. Vol. tchr. computer sci. Calif. Mentally Gifted Minor Programs; vol. Los Angeles Youth Motivation Task Force. Recipient Kranz award Northwestern U., 1963; various engrng. and mgmt. awards IBM, 1969—. Mem. Systems Engrng. Symposium, Pi Lambda Theta. Developed program to retrieve data via terminal and direct it to any appropriate hardcopy device, 1973. Office: 12501 E Imperial Highway Norwalk CA 90650

BIXBY, KATHERINE COSTLOW (MRS. E. REW BIXBY), civic worker; b. Lusk, Wyo., Feb. 8, 1920; d. Jesse Patrick and Anna (Thompson) Costlow; student Cottey Coll., 1937-38; B.A., Doane Coll., 1941; m. E. Rew Bixby, May 30, 1942; children—Patrick William, Jean (Mrs. Hennessy). Tchr. elem. schs., Lusk, Wyo., 1941-42; exec. dir. Vol. Center, Los Angeles, 1971-84; tchr. vol. mgmt. U. So. Calif., Marymount Coll., Valley Coll.; cons. Exec. Service Corps, 1984-86; trainer Ctr. Non-Profit Mgmt., 1984-86. Bd. dirs. Welfare Planning Council 1962-72, USO, 1965-71, Comprehensive Health Planning Los Angeles County, 1969-72, United Crusades Calif., 1968-72, Mayor's Com. on Aging, 1970-72, Los Angeles Mental Health Commn., 1967-72, Planned Protective Services, 1969-71, Camp Fire Girls, 1950-59. Bd. dirs. United Way, Inc.,

1963-71. Recipient Gold Key United Way, 1963, Armed Forces Vol. award, 1966, Luther Gulick award Camp Fire Girls, 1959, Gold Medallion award USO, 1970, Koshland Found. award, 1977. Mem. Nat. Conf. Social Welfare (dir. 1976-78), Assn. Vol. Adminstrs. (regional chmn. 1981-82). Home: 920 Crestview Ave Glendale CA 91202 Office: 621 S Virgil St Los Angeles CA 90005

BJORNTON, GRETCHEN LEE, sonogram laboratory executive; b. Phillips, Wis., Jan. 5, 1942; d. Jack Walter and Grace Alma (Branzell) Blume; m. Arvid John Bjornton, Dec. 22, 1962; children—Anthony John, Wendy Elizabeth. Student Coll. St. Scholastica, Duluth, Minn., 1959, Eau Claire State U., Wis., 1960-62. Receptionist, Alaska Clin., Anchorage, 1970-76; sonographer Alaska Hosp., 1976-78; owner, operator Real Time Images, Inc., Anchorage, 1978—. Contbr. chpt. to book. Registrar teen insight Insight Transformational Sems., Anchorage, 1985—. Mem. Am. Inst. Ultrasound Medicine, Soc. Diagnostic Med. Sonographers (sec. 1982-84), Soc. Law in Medicine, Am. Registry Diagnostic Med. Sonographers, Am. Soc. Echocardiography. Avocations: horses; reading; cooking; interior decorating. Home: 3130 Wenoy's Way Anchorage AK 99503 Office: Real Time Images Inc 2490 E 42d Ave Anchorage AK 99508

BLACK, ALICE BRENDA HENRY, school administrator; b. Phila., Aug. 7, 1940; d. Allen Ernest and Hazel Alice (Peck) Henry; m. John Andrew Black, June 24, 1961 (dec.); children—John Andrew, Joseph Allen. B.S., Morgan State Coll., 1960, M.S., 1970; Ed.D., Temple U., 1978. Sci. tchr. Balt. City Pub. Schs., 1966-74, sci. dept. head, 1974-76, sci. edn. specialist, 1976-77, secondary asst. prin., 1977-81, secondary sch. prin., 1981—; dir., cons. Nat. Ednl. Services, Balt., 1983—. Youth chmn. Balt.-Gbarnga Sister Cities Com., 1983-85, vice chmn., 1985—; block capt. Hillen Rd. Improvement Assn., Balt., 1976—; bd. dirs. Citizens Adv. Council, Balt., 1983—. NSF grantee, 1968-70; Inst. Devel. Ednl. Activities fellow, 1983. Mem. Nat. Assn. Secondary Sch. Prins., Pub. Sch. Adminstrs. and Suprs. Assn., NAACP, Phi Delta Kappa. Democrat. Methodist. Avocations: ceramics; camping; traveling. Home: 1600 Shadyside Rd Baltimore MD 21218 Office: Pimlico Middle Sch 3500 W Northern Pkwy Baltimore MD 21215

BLACK, BONNIE LEE, writer, editor; b. Jersey City, May 18, 1945; d. Kenneth W. and Emily R. (Stanzlaus) B.; m. James Jason, 1964 (div. 1966); 1 child, Whitney Lee. B.A. in Lit. and Writing, Columbia U., 1979. Editorial asst. Rhodesian Farmer, Salisbury, Rhodesia, 1969-72; editor Inside Midlantic mag. Midlantic Banks, Inc., Newark, 1972-75, Thirteen mag., Sta. WNET TV, N.Y.C., 1975-76; copywriter John Wiley & Sons, Inc., N.Y.C., part time 1977-79; freelance writer, editor, N.Y.C., 1979-82; writer, editor Coopers & Lybrand, N.Y.C., 1982—; cons. Child Find, Inc., 1981—. Author: Somewhere Child, 1981. Active Nat. Women's Polit. Caucus, 1982—. Mem. The Author's Guild, The Writers Community. Club: Friends Book (N.Y.C.). Home: 310 Riverside Dr New York NY 10025

BLACK, BONNI-LEIGH ANNE, radio station sales manager, advertising agency executive; b. Rockville Center, N.Y., Feb. 29, 1952; d. Roy William and Marilyn Anne (Barker) Rogers; m. Roger Malcolm Black, May 19, 1979; 1 child, Kimberly Stacey. B.A., SUNY-Plattsburgh, 1972, M.A., 1977. Account exec. WKDR Radio, Plattsburgh, 1973-74, gen. sales mgr., 1975—; owner Adplan Advt. Agy., Plattsburgh, 1976—; instr. Guibord's Sch. Dance, Plattsburgh, 1979—. Mem. Clinton County Hist. Soc., Plattsburgh, 1978—; bd. dirs. No. N.Y. chpt. Nat. Multiple Sclerosis Soc., Plattsburgh, 1980-84, sec. Champlain chpt., Burlington, Vt., 1983-84; bd. dirs. Council on the Arts for Clinton County, Plattsburgh, 1984—, treas., 1985—. Mem. Profl. Dance Tchrs. Am., Plattsburgh and Clinton County C. of C. Methodist. Clubs: Plattsburgh Bobsled and Luge (treas. 1976-79), Norco Mixed Bowling League (v.p. 1978-84). Avocations: reading; travel; history; teaching; sailing. Home: 90 Peru Ln Peru NY 12972 Office: WKDR Radio North Country Shopping Ctr Plattsburgh NY 12901

BLACK, BRENDA CLEM, entrepreneur; b. Paris, Ark., Feb. 12, 1947; d. Lewis Ray and Myrtle Eunice (Yancey) Clem; m. Russell Owen Black, June 4, 1966; children—John Stephen, Jeffrey Richard. Peace Corps vol., Uttar Pradesh, India, 1966; asst. acct. Donrey Media Group, Inc., Ft. Smith, Ark., 1966-67; various secretarial positions Manpower, Inc., Ft. Smith, 1967-68; exec. sec. Conn. Mut. Ins. Co., Gainesville, Ga., 1972; founder, owner, mgr. Blackland Farms, Inc., Prairie Grove, Ark., 1974—; owner Blackland Florist, 1980—, Westwood Gardens, Fayetteville, Ark.; speaker to garden clubs. Bd. govs. Washington Regional Med. Center, Fayetteville, 1979—, chmn. community relations com., 1980-81, chmn. fin. com., 1982—, vice chmn., 1982-84, 1st woman chmn. bd., 1984—. Mem. Prairie Grove C. of C. (dir. 1979-80), Alpha Chi Omega. Home and office: Route 2 Prairie Grove AR 72753

BLACK, CATHLEEN, publisher; b. Chgo., Apr. 26, 1944; d. James and Margaret (Hamilton) Black; B.A., Trinity Coll., Washington, 1966; m. Thomas Harvey, May 20, 1982. Advt. sales Holiday, 1966-68, Travel and Leisure, 1968-70; advt. sales N.Y. mag., N.Y.C., 1970-72, pub., 1977-83; assoc. pub. Ms. mag., N.Y.C., 1972-77; pres. USA Today, Arlington, Va., 1983-84, now pub.; exec. v.p. mktg. Gannett Co., Inc. Recipient Matrix award Women in Communication, 1982. Mem. Women in Communication, Women's Forum, Advt. Women N.Y. Office: USA Today 1000 Wilson Blvd Arlington VA 22209

BLACK, DORIS ANN, nurse; b. Bedford, Va., Apr. 15, 1941; d. William Louis and Cora Mae (Farley) Rakes; R.N., Grace Hosp., Richmond, Va., 1962; m. Henry Peter Black, II, May 15, 1976; children—Roger, Robin, Henry. Dir. nursing Eastview Lodge, Richmond, Va., 1974; cert. officer Va. Dept. Health, 1974-78; adminstr., preceptor for adminstr.-in-tng. Richmond City, 1980; spl. projects, nursing home adminstr. Eastern div. Beverly Enterprises, 1980-83; pres. D&H, Ltd., Richmond, Va., 1983—; cons. in field. Mem. Va. Health Care Assn., Assn. Practitioners in Infection Control. Republican. Episcopalian. Author manuals. Home: 8400 Chelmford Rd Richmond VA 23235 Office: D&H Ltd 200 Turner Rd Richmond VA 23235

BLACK, EILENE (DODEE) MOORE, fundraiser, direct mail marketing executive; b. Tucson, Ariz., May 6, 1947; s. Alvan N. and Frances (Wixson) M.; m. Steven Richard Black, Apr. 3, 1982. B.A., Hood Coll., 1969. Tchr. grammar sch. Escola Americana do Rio de Janeiro (Brazil), 1969-71; asst. to dir., women's activities C. of C. of U.S., Washington, 1971-72; dir. ednl. programs Charles Edison Meml. Youth Fund, Washington, 1972-74; pres. Omega List Co., Vienna, Va., 1974-75; founder, v.p. The Name Exchange, Washington, 1975-76; exec. v.p., gen. mgr. Atlantic List Co., Inc., Washington, 1976—; fundraising cons. Nat. Republican Congress Campaign Com., Washington, 1976—, Republican Nat. Com., Washington, 1977—, Heritage Found., 1977—, Presdl. Adv. Task Force Nat. Rep. Senatorial Commn., Washington, 1982—, Inaugural Com., 1980, Statue of Liberty/Ellis Island Found. Mem. Mailing List Users and Suppliers Assn., Direct Marketing Assn., Direct Mktg. Club Washington. Office: Atlantic List Co Inc 1101 30th St NW Suite 109 Washington DC 20007

BLACK, EMILIE ANNABELLE, physician; b. New Haven, Apr. 14, 1919; d. Lewis Albert and Margaret Ann (Knopf) Black; m. Samuel James Solt, July 19, 1946; 1 child, Margaret Ann. B.S., George Washington U., 1942, M.D., 1945. Intern, Garfield Meml. Hosp., Washington, 1945-46, resident, 1946-47; resident Children's Hosp., Washington, 1949; practice medicine specializing in pediatrics, Bethesda, Md., 1949-66; clinic dir. D.C. Dept. Pub. Health, Washington, 1966-68; med. officer NIH, Bethesda, Md., 1968-84; cons. grants adminstrn., Washington, 1984—; mem. staff Children's Hosp., 1950-68. Contbr. articles to profl. jours. Mem. nat. bd. dirs. Med. Coll. Pa., Phila., 1985. Recipient Harvey Stuart Allen Disting. award Am. Burn Assn., 1982; NIH Dirs. award, 1984. Mem. Am. Burn Assn., Am. Assn. Surgery Trauma, Internat. Soc. Burn Injuries, Am. Trauma Soc. Club: Kenwood Golf and Country. Advocation: needlepoint. Home: 5201 Watson St NW Washington DC 20016

BLACK, ESTELLE MARY, librarian; b. Rockford, Ill., Jan. 27, 1932; d. Thomas and Esther Naomi (Parker) Elmore; m. Charles Robert Black, June 14, 1952; children—DeVonne Marie, Charles Thomas, Jeffrey Clinton, Lisa Lyn. B.S., Rockford Coll., 1977; M.A., U. Wis., 1979. Asst. librarian Rockford Pub. Schs., 1960-65; asst. librarian Rock Valley Coll., Rockford, 1965-66; spl. librarian Ipsen Industries, Rockford, 1966-67; assoc. dir. Social, Ednl., Research & Devel., Inc., Rockford, 1971-72; br. mgr. Rockford Pub. Library, 1972-79, reference librarian, 1979-80, asst. dir., 1980—; mem. adv. bd. Ednl. Resource Ctr., Rock Valley Coll., 1980-82. Pres., Nat. Council Negro Women, Rockford, 1970, Woman of Yr. award, 1975; bd. dirs. Crime Stoppers, 1981—; bd. dirs. Gannett News Agy. Lend-A-Hand, 1979-82, City-County Planning Commn., 1977-79, Winnebago County Energy Adv. Council, 1980-81, YWCA, 1967-68; exec. bd. dirs. Rockford Council Arts and Scis., 1975-80, S.W. Bus. Assn., 1973-77; mem. land utilitzation com. Rockford Pub. Schs., 1983-84; bd. dirs. bldg. better bds. com. Rock Valley Coll., 1983-84; panelist WROK Viewpoint, Rockford, 1980-82; co-chmn. Beattie Is Com.-Music and Dance, 1980-82; mem. community adv. council Jr. League of Rockford, Inc., 1985—. Recipient Rockford Coll. Alumnae of Distinction award, 1981; Alta Hewlett award for professions Rockford YWCA, 1984; Ill. State Library scholar, 1978. Mem. ALA (chmn. planning process discussion group 1982-84), Ill. Library Assn. (councilor to ALA 1984—), Pub. Library Assn., Taus Service Club, Delta Kappa Gamma (hon.). Democrat. African Methodist Episcopalian. Office: Rockford Public Library 215 N Wyman St Rockford IL 61101

BLACK, GAYLA MITCHELL, advertising executive; b. Hackensack, N.J., May 28, 1942; d. Edward and Edna (Mitchell) Black; 1 son, Jason. Student Tarkio Coll., 1960-62, New Sch., 1963-64, Fairleigh Dickinson U., 1965. With ABC-TV, N.Y.C., 1964-65; adminstrv. asst. Ted Bates & Co., N.Y.C., 1965-66; account exec. Ries Cappiello Colwell, N.Y.C., 1966-71; sales rep. McGraw-Hill, San Francisco, N.Y.C., 1971-76; media dir. Paul Pease Advt., Palo Alto, Calif., 1976; media dir. Sobel Advt., Inc., San Rafael, Calif., 1976-83, v.p., 1983—. Scout leader San Francisco Bay council Girl Scouts U.S., 1971-76, Bergen County council, 1969-71. Mem. Bus. and Profl. Advt. Assn. Methodist. Home: 2587 Heatherstone Dr San Rafael CA 94903 Office: Sobel Knight Advt Inc 35 Mitchell Blvd San Rafael CA 94903

BLACK, JAN KNIPPERS, political scientist; b. Lawrenceburg, Tenn., Mar. 10, 1940; d. Ottis J. and Opal (Moody) Knippers; B.A. in Art and Spanish, U. Tenn., 1962; M.A. in Latin Am. Studies, Am. U., 1967, Ph.D. in Internat. Relations, 1975; m. John D. Black, 1967 (dec. 1974); m. Martin C. Needler, 1976; stepchildren—John D., II, Marc Black, Steve Needler, Dan Needler; 1 foster dau., Mary Marfise. Singer, pianist, 1954-58; comml. artist Sta. WSM-TV, Nashville, 1960; vol. Peace Corps, Chile, 1962-64, mem. staff, 1965; research polit. scientist div. fgn. area studies Am. U., 1968-75, chmn. Latin Am. research team, editor area handbooks for Latin Am., 1975-76; program coordinator State Dept. funded study Latin Am. petroleum policies U. N.Mex., 1976-77, sr. research assoc. div. inter-Am. affairs, 1976—, coordinator interdisciplinary courses Latin Am. Inst., research assoc. prof. Div. Public Adminstrn., 1979—; mem. faculty World Campus Afloat, 1966, Dag Hammarskjold Coll., 1974, George Mason U., 1975-76; cons. in field; TV appearances include MacNeil-Lehrer Report, 1976. Del., Nat. Young Democrats Conv., 1965, N.Mex. Dem. Conv., 1978, 80, 82, 84; v.p. N.Mem. Dem. Council, 1983-86; mem. fgn. policy adv. team Dem. Presdl. Campaign., 1972; mem. Mayoral Transition Team, City of Albuquerque, 1977; mgr. various polit. campaigns. Recipient Outstanding Dissertation award Am. U., 1967. Mem. Latin Am. Studies Assn. (chmn. subcom. ethical guidelines 1976-78), Inter-Am. Council Washington (v.p. 1975-76), Am. Polit. Sci. Assn., Internat. Studies Assn., Phi Kappa Phi. Contbg. author books on Latin Am. and Caribbean, including: The Restless Caribbean, 1979; co-author 17 books in Area Handbook series, 1969-75; author: United States Penetration of Brazil, 1977; The Dominican Republic; Politics and Development in an Unsovereign State, 1986; Sentinels of Empire; The United States and Latin American Militarism, 1986; editor books on Latin Am. and Caribbean, including: Area Handbook for Cuba, 1976; Area Handbook for Trinidad and Tubago, 1976; Latin America: Its Problems and Its Promise, 1984. contbr. numerous articles to profl. jours., popular publs. Home: 421 Solano Dr SE Albuquerque NM 87108 Office: Dept Polit Sci U NMex Albuquerque NM 87131

BLACK, JANE KINGSTON, independent oil operator; b. Dallas, Nov. 28, 1921; d. Carlton W. and Edith (Diehm) Kingston; m. John R. Black, Jr., Oct. 17, 1948; 1 child, Robert Carlton. Student North Tex. State U., 1939-41. Ind. oil operator, Dallas, 1976—. Mem. Tex. Ind. Producers and Royalty Owners, Ind. Producers of Am. Assn. Republican. Episcopalian. Office: 800 Mercantile Commerce Bldg 1712 Commerce St Dallas TX 75201

BLACK, JOANNE MARTENA REINHARD, air force officer, nurse; b. Fish Creek, Wis., Apr. 5, 1939; m. Joe A. Black. Diploma Chgo. Wesley Meml. Hosp. Sch. Nursing, 1960; B.S. in Nursing, Columbia U., 1972; M.S. in Med.-Surg. Nursing, U. Calif.-San Francisco, 1974; Ph.D. in Clin. Nursing Research, U. Tex., 1983. Staff nurse med./surg. ICU, Chgo. Wesley Meml. Hosp., 1960-62, 63-64; staff nurse cardiothoracic unit Univ. Hosps., Madison, Wis., 1962-63; courier nurse Santa Fe Ry., Chgo., 1964-66; head nurse trauma unit Cook County Hosp., Chgo., 1966-68; nurse research asst. Hektoen Inst., Chgo., 1968-69; nurse research asst. dept. surg. metabolism Mt. Sinai Hosp., N.Y.C., 1969-70, staff nurse surg. ICU, 1970-72, clin. nurse, hemodialysis, renal transplant and cardiothoracic units, 1972-73; commd. capt. Nurses Corps, U.S. Air Force, 1973, advanced through grades to maj., 1982; staff nurse dept. surg. nursing Wilford Hall USAF Med. Ctr., Lackland AFB, Tex., 1974-76, clin. instr. dept. nursing edn., 1976-78, clin. nurse investigator div. nursing, 1983—; surg. nurse clin. specialist USAF Regional Hosp., Lakenheath, Eng., 1978-80. Contbr. chpt., articles to profl. publs. Office: Wilford Hall USAF Med Ctr/SGHN Lackland AFB TX 78236

BLACK, JOYCE MACWATTY, civic worker; b. Englewood, N.J., Nov. 27, 1928; d. Frank Lamont and Gladys Jeannette (Harkness) MacWatty; B.S., Skidmore Coll., 1948; m. Hiram Day Black, Mar. 5, 1949; 1 dau., Suzanne. Expert cons. ACTION, fed. agy., 1975-76; v.p. Volunteer: Nat. Center for Citizens Involvement, Washington, 1974—, League of Cities, U.S. Conf. Mayors, 1970; cons. to study future of voluntarism Office Policy Research, Washington, 1976-77; pres. Day Care Council, 1972—; v.p. Cancer Care, Inc. of Nat. Cancer Found., 1965—, v.p. Big Bros./Big Sisters Am., 1970—; chmn. N.Y. State Adv. Com. on Day Care, 1973-76; mem. N.Y. State Dept. Social Services Adv. Council, 1973—; co-chmn. Nat. Congress on Volunteerism and Citizenship '76, 1975-76; sect. chmn. Nat. Conf. Social Welfare, 1976—; bd. dirs. N.Y. State Assn. Human Services, 1971-76, N.Y. State Banking Bd., 1973-77, N.Y. State Council Humanities, 1973—, N.Y. State Council Voluntary Child Care Agys., Inc., 1974—, N.Y. State Temp. Commn. on Child Welfare, 1974-81, Welfare Research, Inc., 1974—; mem. women's exec. com. United Hosp. Fund, N.Y.C., 1954—; treas., v.p. N.Y. Jr. League, 1962-66; v.p. Hudson Guild Neighborhood House, N.Y.C., 1963—; v.p., treas. Planned Parenthood of N.Y., 1956-74; co-chmn. N.Y.C. Mayor's Voluntary Action Council, 1966—; v.p. Plays for Living, N.Y.C., 1966—, Fedn. Protestant Welfare Agys., N.Y.C., 1973—; pres. Voluntary Action Corp., N.Y.C., 1966—; v.p. YWCA, N.Y.C., 1968-76, YM/YWCA Day Care Corp., N.Y.C., 1973—; chmn. Resources Rev. Bd. of N.Y.C., 1973—; adv. bd. Sch. Spl. Studies Columbia U., 1975—; bd. dirs. Counseling and Human Devel. Center, 1977—; trustee Cultural Instns. Retirement Fund, 1973—; mem. adv. com. Agy. Child Devel., 1977—; v.p. Nat. Conf. Social Welfare, 1978; cons. HEW, 1978, Greater N.Y. Fund; mem. N.Y. State Bd. Social Welfare, 1979; pres. Big Bros. N.Y., Inc., 1977; chmn. Internat. Yr. of Child, N.Y.C., 1979, Joint Action for Children, 1978; mem. Gov.'s adv. com. N.Y. State Conf. Children and Youth; vice-chmn. Hosp. Trustees N.Y. State; chmn. Trustees N.Y.C. Hosps; trustee N.Y. U. Med. Center, 1967; mem. other N.Y.C. bds. Recipient Outstanding Citizen award N.Y. Med. Soc., 1969, Mayoral award Mayor N.Y.C., 1969, 72, Outstanding Alumnae award Skidmore Coll., 1972, Lizette Sarnoff award Albert Einstein Med. Sch., 1975. Mem. Nat. Conf. Social Welfare, N.Y. State Assn. Human Services, Nat. Soc. Arts and Letters, Nat. Council Orgns. for Children, Youth, Jr. League, Child Welfare League Am. (pres.), Council on Accreditation on Services for Families and Children, Hosp. Assn. N.Y. State, Nat. Soc. Colonial Dames. Episcopalian. Clubs: Univ., Englewood Field; Siasconset Casino (Nantucket). Office: Day Care Council of NY Inc 22 W 38th St New York NY 10018

BLACK, JULIA ELAINE, nurse; b. Wadley, Ga., Nov. 14, 1952; d. James Berry and Willie Julia (Purvis) Tapley; m. Walter Roy Black, Oct. 25, 1974; children—Jennifer Kristen, Jessica Michele. Diploma, Ga. Bapt. Hosp. Sch. Nursing, Atlanta, 1974. R.N., Ga. Nurse, Dr. William's Office, Wadley, Ga., 1974-76; charge nurse 1st floor Emanuel County Hosp., Swainsboro, Ga., 1976-78; staff nurse VA Hosp., Dublin, Ga., 1978; house supr. Emanuel County Hosp., 1978-80, asst. dir. nursing, 1980—, dir. nursing, 1983-84, 85—. CPR instr. ARC, Swainsboro, 1978—; advanced cardiac life support instr. Am. Heart Assn., Statesboro, Ga., 1985. Named Dept. Head of Yr., Emanuel County Hosp., 1982, 84, 85; Boss of Yr., N.G., 1984. Methodist (sec. bd.). Office: Emanuel County Hosp Kite Rd PO Box 7 Swainsboro GA 30401

BLACK, KRISTINE MARY, physicist; b. St. Paul, July 11, 1953; d. Jaurd Oliver and Dorothy Helen (Amos) B.; B.Physics, U. Minn., 1975, M.S. in Cell Biology, 1978, M.S. Metallurgy and Materials Sci., 1981. Analytical physicist Cardiac Pacemakers, St. Paul, 1978, qualifications engr., to 1981; biomaterials engr. St. Jude Med., Inc., St. Paul, 1981-83; quality assurance Sperry Semicondr. Ops., St. Paul, 1983—. Mem. ASTM, Am. Soc. Metals, Nat. Assn. Female Execs., U. Minn. Inst. Tech. Alumni Soc. (dir. 1980-84). Contbr. articles to profl. jours. Office: Sperry Semicondr Ops PO Box 64724 MSH2H26 Saint Paul MN 55164

BLACK, MARILYN HAMMER, non-profit organization executive; b. Sioux City, Iowa, Apr. 25, 1923; d. Franklin Wilfred and Ruth Marie (Gray) Hammer; m. Albert Scott Black; children—Barbara Black Miller, William Scott Black, Patricia Black Thompson. B.A., U. Without Walls, 1975; M.S., U. Houston-Clear Lake, 1980. Dir. religious edn. St. Francis Episcopal Ch., Houston, 1968-72; program dir. NCCJ, Houston, 1972-80; exec. dir. Support Ctr., Houston, 1982—. Mem. Am. Soc. Tng. and Devel., Non Profit Mgmt. Assn., Nat. Soc. Fund Raiser Execs. (dir. 1982). Episcopalian (mem. mission council 1982). Home: 2219 Wroxton Rd Houston TX 77005 Office: Support Center of Houston 500 Jefferson Bldg Suite 1910 Houston TX 77002

BLACK, MARTHA SUSAN LOWE, lawyer; b. Maryville, Tenn., Sept. 18, 1945; d. Ernest Broyles and Esther Charlotte (Carlson) Lowe; B.A. with honors, Mount Holyoke Coll., 1967; postgrad. (NDEA fellow), Rice U., 1967-69; J.D. (Green scholar), U. Tenn., 1973; m. David T. Black, June 7, 1975; children—Charlotte Carlson, Elizabeth Cannon. Admitted to Tenn. bar, 1974; asst., then asso. prof. U. Tenn. Coll. Law, Knoxville, 1973-81; mem. firm Kizer & Black, P.C., Maryville, Tenn., 1981—; chmn. U. Tenn. Commn. Women, 1979-80. Chmn., Blount County Foster Care Review Bd., 1976-83; bd. dirs., chmn. Blount County Children's Home; mem. community adv. council Maryville Coll.; mem. Blount County Hist. Trust. Recipient Am. Jurisprudence and Corpus Juris Secundum awards, 1972; named Grad. of Yr., U. Tenn., 1973. Mem. Am. Bar Assn., Tenn. Bar Assn., Order Coif. Home: Hollybrook Rd Rockford TN 37853 Office: 329 Cates St Maryville TN 37801

BLACK, MAUREEN, realty company executive; b. Manchester, Eng., Feb. 4, 1937; came to U.S., 1957, naturalized, 1962; d. William Henry and Kathleen Mary (Cleaver) Jackson; grad. Felt and Tarrant Comptometer Sch., Eng., 1953; student Alamogordo br. N.Mex. State U., 1959-60, 62-63; m. Charles J. Dugan, Nov. 1979; 1 dau., Karen Elizabeth Black. Office mgr., personnel dir. J.C. Penney Co., Alamogordo, 1958-66; exec. sec. to project mgr. Re-entry System div. Gen. Electric Co., Holloman AFB, 1967-68; soc. editor, columnist Alamogordo Daily News, 1968-73; regional corr. El Paso (Tex.) Times, 1968-75; free lance writer and photographer; script writer Film Unit 505, Alamogordo, 1971; realtor asso. Shyne Realty, Alamogordo, 1975-77, West Source Realtors, 1977-80; owner, broker Hyde Park West Realty Co., 1980—. Pres., Alamogordo Music Theatre, 1971-72. Mem. planning com. tourism, recreation, convs. Gov. of N.Mex., 1965; mem. N.Mex. State Film Commn., 1973-74; life mem. Aux. of Zia Sch. for Handicapped Children, pres. Aux., 1975-76, 80-82, mem. sch. bd., 1982-83; pres. Zia Found., 1984-85. Recipient service award Nat. Found., March of Dimes, 1971; Americanism medal DAR, 1972; named Career Woman of Yr., Alamogordo chpt. Am. Bus. Women's Assn., 1971. Mem. Alamogordo C. of C. (chmn. convs. and motion picture com. 1965—), Nat. Assn. Realtors, Realtors Assn. N.Mex., Internat. Realtors Assn. Alamogordo Bd. Realtors (chmn. public relations com., v.p. 1981-82, pres. 1983-84), N.Mex. Opera Guild. Home: 1206 Desert Eve Dr Alamogordo NM 88310 Office: PO Box 2021 Alamogordo NM 88310

BLACK, MELVA KATHRYN, music company executive; b. Abilene, Tex., Aug. 19, 1939; d. Lee Edward and Lottie Opel (Earnest) Rhodes; m. E.J. Black, Jr., July 22, 1959; children—Sandie, Tammie, Dwayne, Keith. Student, Stenograph Inst. of Tex., 1959-60; B.A. in Bus. & Acctg., Tex. State Tech. Inst., 1974; postgrad. Lisco Jr. Coll., 1986—. Interviewer county and state, Anson, Tex., 1960-65; test trainer tech. Timex, Abilene, 1965-76; quality assurance inspector Crown Cork & Seal, Abilene, 1978—; exec. producer Electro Symphonic, Houston, 1984—. Mem. Am. Mgmt. Assn., Nat. Assn. Female Execs., Found. for Women Inc., Toastmasters and Speakers Am. Avocations: music; art; writing; swimming; tennis.

BLACK, PAGE MORTON, civic worker; b. Chgo.; d. Alexander and Rose Morton; student Chgo. Mus. Coll.; m. William Black, Mar. 27, 1962. Singer, pianist, Pierre Hotel, N.Y.C., Warwick Hotel, One Fifth Ave. Sherry Netherland Hotel; singer Chock Full o' Nuts Radio Show; singer comml. Chock Full o' Nuts; hon. chmn., dir. Chock Full o' Nuts Corp.; rec. artist Atlantic Records; co-founder Page and William Black Post Grad. Sch. Medicine, Mt. Sinai Med. Sch., 1965—; chmn., mem. exec. bd. Parkinsons Disease Found., Columbia U. Med. Center. Home: Premium Point New Rochelle NY 10801

BLACK, RITA ANN, business communicator; b. Newark, Sept. 2, 1950; d. Henry and Mary (Solomon) Black; m. David Joseph Franus, Dec. 30, 1973. B.A. in English, U. Rochester, 1972; M.S. in Journalism, Columbia U., 1975. Sr. editor Book Prodn. Industry, mag., New Canaan, Conn., 1972-74, 75-76; mgr. publs. AAUP, N.Y.C., 1976-78; sr. communication specialist Ciba-Geigy Corp., Ardsley, N.Y., 1978-80, mgr. internal communication, 1980-84; exec. speechwriter IBM Corp., Armonk, N.Y., 1984—. Mem. Women in Communication, Pub. Relations Soc. Am., Internat. Assn. Bus. Communicators (dir. 1982-84, Gold Quill 1983, 84, Dist. I award of excellence 1982), Phi Beta Kappa. Office: IBM Corp 44 S Broadway 16B-04 White Plains NY 10601

BLACK, ROSALIE JEAN, human resources manager; b. Dunsmuir, Calif., Dec. 29, 1938; d. Allen Bensen and Margaret Rose (Albonico) Henry Lea; m. James H. Black, June 12, 1956 (div. 1965); 1 dau., Kimberly Elaine. A.A., Foothills and Ohlone, 1964-74. Contracts adminstr. U.S. Air Force, Los Angeles and Shelby, Ohio, 1956-58; ops. planner/adminstr. Lockheed Missiles & Space Co., Inc., Sunnyvale, Calif., 1958-61; mgr. human resources Dialog Info. Services, Inc., Palo Alto, Calif., 1961—; instr. Dialog Supervisory program, 1982—; mem. Lockheed Univ. Relations Council, Burbank, Calif., 1982—. Contbr. articles to profl. jours. Recipient Cert., Human Resources Inst., 1982; Achievement award in English, Bank of Am., 1956. Mem. Am. Soc. Personnel Adminstrn., No. Calif. Human Resources Council, Am. Compensation Assn., Santa Clara Valley Personnel Assn., Calif. Scholarship Fedn., Siskiyou County Hist. Soc. Democrat. Lutheran. Home: 1400 Fallen Leaf Ln Los Altos CA 94022 Office: Dialog Info Services Inc 3460 Hillview Ave Palo Alto CA 95014

BLACK, SANDRA, public relations consultant; b. N.Y.C., Apr. 5, 1951; d. David Eastern and Norma (Springer) B.; B.A., Cornell U., 1975; student NYU Sch. Law, 1977-78. Adminstrv. asst. Ctr. for Mgmt. Tech., Inc., N.Y.C., 1975-77; paralegal Queens Legal Services Corp., Jamaica, N.Y., 1978-79; legal asst. Corbin, Silverman, Sanseverino & Taylor, N.Y.C., 1980-82; adminstrv. cons. N.Y. Cons. Group Ltd., N.Y.C., 1982-83; prin., cons. Imago Pub. Relations, N.Y.C., 1983—. Resource person Cornell Alumni Career Resource File, 1978—, class corr. alumni news mag.; mem. Cornell Council, 1982-83; v.p. pub. relations Network of Black Career Women, 1982—; publicity dir. South African Liberation Com., 1972-74. N.Y. State Regents scholar, 1969-74; Cornell U. grantee, 1969-74. Mem. Pub. Relations Soc. Am. (mem. coms.), Cornell Black Alumni Assn., Cornell Alumni Assn. N.Y.C. (council 1982-83), NAACP. Democrat. Episcopalian. Office: PO Box 195 New York NY 10027-0195

BLACK, SUSAN HARRELL, federal judge; b. Valdosta, Ga., Oct. 20, 1943; d. William H. and Ruth Elizabeth (Phillips) Harrell; B.A., Fla. State U., 1964; J.D., U. Fla., 1967; m. Louis Eckert Black, Dec. 28, 1966. Bar: Fla. 1967. Asst. state's atty. 4th Jud. Circuit Fla.; asst. gen. counsel City of Jacksonville (Fla.); judge County Ct. Duval County, Fla.; judge 4th Jud. Circuit Ct. Fla.; U.S. dist. judge Middle Dist. Fla., Jacksonville, 1979—; mem. faculty Fed. Jud. Ctr.; former mem. faculty Nat. Jud. Coll., Reno. Mem. adv. bd., former trustee Jacksonville Hosp. Ednl. Program; mem. Jacksonville Council Citizen Involvement; trustee U. Fla. Law Sch. Mem. ABA, Fla. Bar Assn., Jacksonville Bar Assn., State Conf. Circuit Judges (past chmn. edn. com., dean New Judges Coll.). Episcopalian. Office: 311 W Monroe St Jacksonville FL 32202

BLACKBURN, AUDREY PEYTON, lawyer; b. Camden, N.J., July 10, 1938; d. Robert Leon and Catherine (Collins) Peyton; m. Lemuel H. Blackburn, May 1, 1959; children—Hope Renee, Lisa Dawn. B.A., Douglass Coll., 1960; J.D., Rutgers U.-Camden, 1974. Bar: N.J. 1974, U.S. Dist. Ct. N.J. 1974. Tchr.

English, Moorestown Jr. High Sch., N.J., 1961-64, Ewing High Sch., N.J., 1964-67; ptnr. Blackburn and Blackburn, Trenton, 1974—; mem. N.J. Supreme Ct. Ethics Com., 1985—. Mem. Mayor's Overall Devel. Com., Trenton, 1978—; commr. Trenton Housing Authority, 1980—; trustee Mercer County Community Coll., Trenton, 1979-82, Mercer council Girl Scouts U.S.A., 1985—. Recipient Outstanding Service award Carver Ctr. YMCA, 1981; Outstanding Service award Las Chaperones Sorority, 1982; cert. recognition for excellence in law Mt. Zion Women's Club, 1985. Mem. ABA, N.J. Bar Assn., Mercer County Bar Assn., Nat. Assn. Women Lawyers, Nat. Assn. Female Execs., Jack and Jill Am., AAUW. Democrat. Methodist. Avocations: piano; violin; singing; writing; reading. Home: 11 Kensington Ave Trenton NJ 08618 Office: Blackburn and Blackburn 224 W State St Trenton NJ 08618

BLACKBURN, CATHERINE ELAINE, lawyer, pharmacist; b. Columbus, Ohio, Nov. 5, 1953; d. Robert Jerome and Patricia Ann (Buchman) B. B.S. in Pharmacy with high honors, U. Ky., 1978; J.D. with honors, Ohio State U., 1982. Bars: Ohio 1982, U.S. Dist. Ct. (so. dist.) Ohio 1983. Chief pharmacist Louisa Community Hosp., Ky., 1978; pharmacist Riverside Meth. Hosp., Columbus, Ohio, 1978-82; law clk. Michael F. Colley Co., L.P.A., Columbus, 1980-82, assoc., 1982—; workshop leader Ohio Drug Studies Inst., Columbus, 1982, 83, 14th Nat. Conf. on Women and the Law, Washington, D.C., 1983, 15th Nat. Conf., 1985; lectr./speaker Iowa Trial Lawyers Assn., Iowa City, 1984. Contbr. article to profl. jour. Staff writer, editor Ohio State U. Law Jour., 1980-82. Trustee Women's Outreach for Women, Columbus, 1982-85, Amethyst, Inc., 1985—. Mem. Assn. Trial Lawyers Am. (lectr./speaker 1982—), Ohio Acad. Trial Lawyers, Columbus Bar Assn., Ohio Bar Assn., Am. Soc. Pharmacy Law, Order of Coif, Phi Beta Kappa, Rho Chi Soc. Democrat. Home: 2648 Summit St Columbus OH 43202 Office: Michael F Colley Co LPA 536 S High St Columbus OH 43215

BLACKBURN, MARY KATHERINE (KATHIE), business executive; b. Honolulu, Apr. 19, 1949; d. Joseph Gibson and Mary Louise (Anton) B.; m. Ron Bailey, 1968 (div. 1969); m. 2d, John David Howard, June 26, 1971 (div. Mar. 1976). Student Marjorie Webster Jr. Coll., 1967-68, U. Mo.-Kansas City, 1969; lic. real estate Stapleton Sch. Real Estate, Honolulu, 1976; cert. of completion U. So. Calif., Honolulu, 1976; cert. in CPR. Dir. mail order div. Am. Rental & Sales, Kansas City, Mo., 1974-76; media rep. Hawaii Tourist News, Honolulu, 1976-77; sales exec., sales mgr. Inflight Mktg., Honolulu, 1977-79; owner Kakalina o Maui, Kahului, Hawaii, 1979-81; membership dir. Maui C. of C., Kahului, 1981-83; dir. advt. HBH Publication Services, Kaanapali, Hawaii, 1983-85; prodn., sales dir. Uniquely Maui Catalog, 1985—; owner, mgr. Maui Gift Baskets, 1985—; cons. various firms. Photographer: Latitude 20, 1977-81; publisher, editor: (conv. bull.) Nat. Assn. Life Underwriters, 1980. Bd. dirs., sec. Big Bros./Big Sisters of Maui, 1980—; mem. Maui Community Coll. Adv. Com. on Coop. Edn., 1982-83; media chmn. Kemper Open Golf Tournament; mem. Maui Visitors Bur., 1983-84; vol. Hospice Maui, 1983-84; various coms. Aloha Week, 1985-86. Recipient Cert. of Appreciation Kiwani's Club Maui, 1982; Gov.'s cert. media Chair King Kamehameha Commn., 1984. Mem. Maui C. of C., Hawaii Hotel Assn., Made in Maui Assn. Home: 281 Awapuhi Pl Wailuku HI 96793 Office: Maui Gift Baskets PO Box 1263 Wailuku Maui HI 96793

BLACKBURN-FIELDS, DENISE, financial marketing executive; b. Williamson, W.Va., Dec. 7, 1955; d. Tracy Rupert and Newana Yvonne (Stevens) Blackburn; m. Stephen J. Fields, Apr. 2, 1983. A.A., So. W.Va. Community Coll., 1976; B.A., Marshall U., 1979, M.A., 1982. Accounts adjustor Ashland Fin. Co., South Williamson, Ky., 1973-74; dir. payroll Mingo County Bd. Edn., Williamson, 1974-77; sec. spl. projects coordinator Marshall U., Huntington, W.Va., 1978-79; market researcher First Huntington Nat. Bank, 1980-81; mktg. dir. First Bank Ceredo (W.Va.), 1981-83; mktg. officer Flat Top Nat. Bank, Bluefield, W.Va., 1983—; instr. Marshall U., 1980-83. Contbr. articles to profl. jours. Vol. Am. Heart Assn., Bluefield, 1983, United Way, 1983. W.Va. Bd. Regents ednl. scholar, 1974-82. Fellow Communicator's Roundtable of Vas., Am. Mktg. Assn., Quota Club of Am., Charleston Advt. Club, mem. Am. Inst. Banking (pub. relations office 1982-83), Kappa Delta Pi, Pi Omega Pi. Club: Leading Ladies. Address: The Flat Top Nat Bank 211 Federal St PO Box 950 Bluefield WV 24701

BLACKER, HARRIET, public relations company executive; b. N.Y.C., July 23, 1940; d. Louis and Rebecca (Siegel) B.; m. Roland Algrant, Aug. 6, 1970 (div. 1981). B.A., U. Mich., 1962. Exec. asst. Nat. Book Com., N.Y.C., 1965-67; dir. publicity Hawthorn Books, N.Y.C., 1967-69, Coward-McCann & Geoghegan, N.Y.C., 1969-74; exec. dir. publicity Random House, N.Y.C., 1974-79; East Coast v.p. Pickwick-Maslansky-Koenigsberg, N.Y.C., 1980-81; v.p. pub. relations Putnam Pub. Group, N.Y.C., 1981-85; pres. Harriet Blacker Pub. Relations, N.Y.C., 1986—. Mem. Publs. Publicity Assn. (sec. 1973-75, treas. 1982-83, pres. 1983-85), Women's Media Group. Club: Manhattan Theatre (bd. dirs. 1984—). Home: 310 E 75th St New York NY 10021 Office: 230 Park Ave Suite 552 New York NY 10169

BLACKHAM, ANN ROSEMARY (MRS. JAMES W. BLACKHAM JR.), realtor; b. N.Y.C., June 16, 1927; d. Frederick Alfred and Letitia L. (Stolfe) DeCain; A.B., Ohio Dominican Coll., 1949; postgrad. Ohio State U., 1950; m. James W. Blackham, Jr., Aug. 18, 1951; children—Ann C., James W. III. Mgr. br. store Filene & Sons, Winchester, 1950-52; broker Porter Co. real estate, Winchester, Mass., 1961-66; sales mgr. James T. Trefrey, Inc., Winchester, 1966-68; pres., founder Ann Blackham & Co., Inc., Realtors, Winchester, 1969—; dir. Bay State Health Care, Winchester Hosp.; trustee, corporator Neworld Bank. Mem. bd. econ. advisors to Gov., 1969-74; participant White House Conf. on Internat. Cooperation, 1965; mem. Presdl. Task Force on Women's Rights and Responsibilities, 1969; mem. exec. council Mass. Civil Def., 1965-69; chmn. Gov.'s Commn. on Status of Women, 1971-75; regional dir. Interstate Assn. Commn. on Status of Women, 1971-73; mem. Gov.'s Task Force on Mass. Economy, 1972; mem. Mass. Emergency Fin. Bd., 1974-75; 2d v.p. Doric Dames, 1971-73; mem. White House Fellows Com.; mem. DACOWITS Com. Dept. Def., 1977; sec. Mass. Speech and Hearing Found., 1984—; pres. Mass. Fedn. Republican Women, 1964-69, sec. 1976-78; Fedn. Rep. Women, 1967-71, 3d v.p., 1972-75, 2d v.p., 1976-78; New Eng. regional dir., 1967-78; pres. Women's Rep. Club Winchester, 1960-62, 83-84; dep. chmn. Mass. Rep. State Com., 1965-66; sec. Mass. Rep. State Conv., 1970, del., 1960, 62, 64, 66; state vice chmn. Mass. Rep. Fin. Com., 1970; alt. del. at large Rep. Nat. Conv., 1968, 72, del., 1984; v.p. Winchester Scholarship Found., 1975-77, pres., 1977-79; v.p. Rep. Club Mass., 1980—; corporator Winchester Hosp. Recipient Pub. Service award Commonwealth Mass., 1969, Merit award Rep. Party, 1969, Pub. Affairs award Mass. Fedn. Women's Club, 1975; Mass. Order Paul Revere Patriots; named Civic Leader of Yr. Mass. Broadcasters, 1962; honor citation Mass. Ho. of Reps., 1978. Mem. Greater Boston Real Estate Bd. (dir. 1973-75), Mass. (dir. 1976—), Nat. (women's council) assns. realtors, Brokers Inst. Real Estate Council (pres. 1983-84), Winchester C. of C. (dir.), Enka Soc. Clubs: Capitol Hill (Washington); Winchester Boat, Wychmere Harbor, Winchester Country, Ponte Vedra, Winton. Home: 60 Swan Rd Winchester MA 01890 Office: 11 Thompson St Winchester MA 01890

BLACKMAN, ANNE DUFF, newspaper editor; b. San Francisco, Oct. 2, 1936; d. Price Hope and Pauline (Lehning) Duff; m. Edward Galbreath Blackman, III, Aug. 31, 1956; children—Paula Blackman Thrasher, Edward Galbreath IV, Cristan, Tallie. Student Lindenwood Coll., St. Charles, Mo., 1954-55, Vanderbilt U., 1955-57, U. Nebr., 1933. Advt. mgr. Goldstein/Chapmans, Omaha, 1967-75; mng. editor Gautier (Miss.) Ind., 1975-79, Citizen Newspapers, St. Louis, 1980—. Mem. adv. com. Pascagoula (Miss.) Schs., 1976-79; mem. festival com. Judevine Ctr. Autistic Children, St. Louis, 1983—; editor stories for St. Louis chpt. Am. Cancer Soc., 1981. Recipient Outstanding Woman award St. Louis-Marketplace Forum, 1983; named 1st Mardi Gras Queen, Gautier Jaycees, 1979; Best Story award Miss. Press Assn., 1979; 1st place Media award Nat. Mental Health Assn., 1981; 2d place award Suburban News Assn., 1980; 1st Media award St. Louis chpt. Am. Cancer Soc., 1982. Mem. Creve Coeur Area C. of C. (dir. 1981—, v.p. 1984—), Chesterfield C. of C. Home: 15344 Thistlebriar Ct Chesterfield MO 63017 Office: Citizen Newspapers 12520 Olive Blvd Creve Coeur MO 63141

BLACKMAN, BETTY LOU, hospital social services administrator; b. Sarasota, Fla., Oct. 2, 1930; d. Jim and Ola Vastiah (Coker) Fowler; m. Frank Ogilvie Blackman, Aug. 26, 1951 (dec. 1964); children—Katherine Lynn, Brenda Sue; m. John Quincy Woosley, Dec. 4, 1970 (div. 1978). Student Columbia Bible Coll., S.C., 1948-51, So. Bapt. Theol. Sem., 1964-65; B.A. in Sociology and Psychology, Ky. So. Coll./U. Louisville, 1968; M.S.S.W., Kent Sch. Social Work, U. Louisville, 1970. Lic. clin. social worker, lic. marriage and family therapist Fla. Dept. Profl. Regulations, 1982—. Bank teller, Tex., Ky., Ga., 1951-66; child care nursery dir. Fowler's Toddler's Inn, Sarasota, Fla., 1968; social worker Ky. Dept. Child Welfare, Louisville, 1969, Family Relations Ctr., Louisville, 1970-72; sr. social worker River Region Mental Health-Mental Retardation, Louisville, 1972-78; clin. social worker, psychotherapist W. Central Fla. Human Resources Ctr., Ocala, 1978; treatment team Sarasota Palms Psychiat. Hosp., Fla., 1978-79; dir. social services Venice Hosp., Fla., 1979-81, Morton F. Plant Hosp., Clearwater, Fla., 1981—; sec. to dir. Louisville and Jefferson County Children's Home, 1956-57; recreational dir. Perrine Bapt. Ch., Miami, Fla., 1965; condr. workshops, speaker chs., schs. Greater Louisville area; field instr. grad. sch. students U. Louisville. Chmn. Agys. United Appeal, 1974, 75; mem. Greater Louisville Area Mental Retardation Com.; act. ch. activities, tchr., counselor, condr. workshops; sec. Venice Area Community Council, 1980, pres., 1981; bd. dirs., dir. edn. Widow to Widow Program; adv. com. Ctr. for Counseling and Human Devel; mem. resource com. NRC, Clearwater; mem. adv. council Independent Home Health Agy. Named one of Sarasota County's 10 Most Eligible Bachelorettes, 1980-81. Mem. Nat. Assn. Social Workers (county coordinator 1982-83, chairperson-elect Tampa Bay Unit 1982-83, chairperson 1983-85, named Social Worker of Yr. Tampa Bay Unit 1984), Acad. Cert. Social Workers (cert.), Nat. Assn. Hosp. Social Work Dirs., Fla. Assn. Hosp. Social Work Dirs. (treas. 1982-84, pres. elect 1984-85, pres. 1985-86), Fla. Chpt. Assn. Social Workers. Baptist. Home: 1710 Belleair Forest Dr Unit D Belleair FL 33516 Office: Morton F Plant Hosp 323 Jeffords St Clearwater FL 33517

BLACKMAN, GHITA WAUCHETA, residential energy consultant; b. Chgo., Feb. 19, 1932; d. William Harveston Joseph and Zelda (Booth) Harris; m. David Edward Blackman, June 7, 1953 (div. Oct. 1976); children—Anasa, Anthony, Cynthia, Tracy. Student NYU, 1949-50, U. Dayton, 1952-53. Various secretarial positions U.S. Air Force, Dayton, Ohio, then Am. Humanist Assn., Yellow Springs, Ohio, 1950-64; sec. Antioch Coll., Yellow Springs, 1964-66, Fels Research Inst., Yellow Springs, 1966-70; cons. direct sales Fashion Two Twenty, Dayton, 1966-72; mem. sales staff Prophet & Friends Inc., New Britain, Conn., 1972-76; customer relations clk. Conn. Natural Gas Corp., Hartford, 1976-80, natural energy cons., 1980—. Second violin Springfield Symphony, Ohio, 1956-64; v.p. Conn. Capitol Area chpt. Older Women's League, Hartford, 1985—; sec. Spiritual Assembly of the Bahais of West Hartford, Conn., 1977-78; corr. sec. Spiritual Assembly of the Bahais of Hartford, 1982—. Avocation: music. Home: 31 Woodland St Hartford CT 06105 Office: Conn Natural Gas Corp 100 Columbus Blvd Hartford CT 06103

BLACKMAN, JESSICA LYNN, lawyer; b. Bklyn., June 1, 1954; d. Norman Sidney and Sylvia (Bader) B.; B.A., Syracuse U., 1975; J.D., Western New Eng. Coll., 1978; m. Bruce Gary Freedman, July 14, 1985. Admitted to Mass. bar, 1978; legis. asst. Senator John Tower, 1978-79, D.C. Mayor's Office, 1979-80, Congressman Alvin Baldus, Washington, 1980-81, Congressman Gus Savage, Washington, 1981-83; legis. dir. Congressman Edward F. Feighan, 1983-84; owner Resumes for Success, 1984—; teaching fellow Northfield/Mt. Hermon Sch., 1974. Reginald Heber Smith fellow, 1978. Mem. ABA, Mass. Bar Assn., Mass. Women's Bar Assn., D.C. Women's Bar Assn., Phi Alpha Delta, Delta Delta Delta. Democrat.

BLACKMAN, KATHERYN SUE, employment agency executive; b. Lubbock, Tex., Feb. 8, 1946; d. Floyd Harlen and Elsie Rose (Helms) Browning; m. Dorman Ray Blackman, Dec. 7, 1973; 1 child, Nickie Suc. Cert., Columbia Secretarial Sch., Odessa, Tex., 1964; student Midland Coll., 1975—. Sec., office mgr. Dalton H. Cobb, Ind. Oil Producer, Midland, Tex., 1973-75; dist. sec. Tex. Oil & Gas Co., Midland, 1975-77; mgr. Southwest Personnel, Midland, 1977-80; owner, pres. Career Path, Inc., Midland, 1980—; cons., tchr. time mgmt. for employment agys., 1980—. Mem. Leadership Midland, 1981-85, v.p., 1985. Mem. Tex. Assn. Personnel Consultants (sec., v.p., bd. dirs. 1980-85, pres. 1983-84; named Cert. Personnel Cons. of Yr. 1983-84), Nat. Assn. Personnel Consultants (dist. regent 1983-85; Regents award 1984), Cert. Personnel Consultants Soc. (charter), Permian Basin Assn. Personnel Consultants (pres. 1985, founder 1980), Am. Soc. for Tng. and Devel., Midland C. of C. (mem. M-Squad 1982—, guidelines chmn. M Squad 1986), Bus. and Profl. Women Midland (chpt. membership chmn. 1982; Woman of Yr. 1984), Beta Sigma Phi, Mu Psi, Xi Pi Kappa (v.p. 1979). Avocations: bowling, gardening, soccer, all spectator sports. Home: 3211 Stutz Dr Midland TX 79705 Office: Career Path Inc 4410 N Midkiff Suite D-210 Midland TX 79705

BLACKMAN KOENIG, LISA ANDREA, audiologist; b. Boston, Dec. 10, 1952; d. Benjamin Alexander and Rebecca W.; B.A. cum laude, Queens Coll., 1973, M.A., 1975. Dir., adminstr. dept audiology Albert Einstein Med. Center, Phila., 1975-79; audiologic cons. Moss Rehab. Hosp., Phila., 1975-79; pvt. practice audiology, speech/lang. therapy, hearing aid dispensing, Phila., 1978—; N.E. rep. Widex Hearing Aid Co., also Hal-Hen Hearing Aid Accessory Co., 1980-81; 1980-81; dir. audiological research Cooper Med. Center, Camden, N.J., 1982-83; course dir. Council of Accreditation for Occupational Hearing Conservation; lectr., cons. and program coordinator in field; pres. Better Hearing Inst. N.J., Pa. cert. hearing aid specialist. Mem. Am. Speech Lang. and Hearing Assn., Deafness Research Found., N.Y. Audiology Study Group, Am. Auditory Soc., Alexander Graham Bell Assn., Indsl. Audiology Soc., Am. Tinnitus Assn., Acoustical Soc. Am., Pa. Speech and Hearing Assn. Democrat. Jewish. Author: A Hearing Aid Handbook, 1979; contbr. article to profl. jour.

BLACKMAN-WEAVING, JOAN SARA, marketing executive; b. N.Y.C., May 25, 1948; d. Samuel William and Clara (Gershunoff) B.; B.A., Case Western Res. U., 1968. Research trainee Grudin Appel Research Corp., N.Y.C., 1968-69; research analyst BBDO Advt., N.Y.C., 1969-70; research analyst, mgr. mktg. research new products Nabisco Inc., N.Y.C., 1970-74, mgr. consumer research, Biscuit div., 1974-76, product mgr., East Hanover, N.J., 1976-82; asst. v.p., dir. mktg. Equitable Life Assurance Soc., N.Y.C., 1982—; lectr. in field; condr. seminars. Mem. Am. Mktg. Assn., Nat. Assn. Female Execs., Nat. Assn. Securities Dealers, Am. Soc. Profl. and Exec. Women. Home: 15 Bumble Bee Ln Norwalk CT 06851 Office: Equitable Life Assurance Soc 1285 Ave of Americas New York NY 10019

BLACKSTEN-PLANTZ, ANNA MARIE, public safety officer, investigator; b. Fargo, N.D., Dec. 23, 1948; d. Ove Harold and Florence Mildred (Holsinger) Anderson; student Lane Community Coll., 1972-74; criminology cert. of competancy Inst. Applied Sci., 1978; m. Ralph H. Plantz; children—David, Angela, Brooke. Crime prevention officer, lab. technician Eugene (Oreg.) Police Dept., 1974-79; fire prevention technician, investigator Seaside Fire Dept., Seaside, Oreg., 1980-83. Bus. and Profl. Women's Club scholar, 1976-77; cert. radiol. monitoring Nat. Emergency Tng. Center, 1982. Mem. Oreg. Fire Marshal's, Bus. and Profl. Women, Internat. Assn. Arson Investigators, Exec. Females, Inc., Oreg. Fire Edn. Assn., Oreg. Peace Officers Assn. Home: 100 NE Shannon Hillsboro OR 97121 Office: Oreg Health Scis U 3181 SW Sam Jackson Park Rd Portland OR 97201

BLACKSTOCK, DOROTHY EVELYN LYONS, artist; b. Tacoma, Aug. 4, 1914; d. Frank and Mildred Aubrey (Potts) Lyons; student Whitman Coll., 1931, Coll. Puget Sound, 1932, U. Wash., 1933; m. Carl Mims Blackstock, July 12, 1942; children—Carl Lyons, Gregory Lee. One-man shows State Hist. Mus., Olympia, Wash., Handforth Gallery, Tacoma; exhibited art in group shows at Seattle Art Mus., Woessner Gallery, Kittredge Gallery, U. Puget Sound, Frye Art Mus., Frederick and Nelson Little Gallery and Exhbn. Hall, Puget Sound Area Shows, NW Watercolor Show, Nat. League Am. Pen Women Biennials, Wash. State Hist. Mus.; represented in permanent collections Wash. State Hist. Mus. at Tacoma, Wash. State U. at Pullman; illustrator two covers Tacoma News Tribune Mag. Sect., five covers Seattle Times Mag. Sect. Art chmn. Music and Art Found., Seattle, 1962-64, trustee, 1958-64; mem. Seattle hospitality com. Allied Arts; chaperone Seattle Seafair Princess, 1979-85. Named Woman of Year in art, 1959. Mem. Nat. League Am. Pen Women (br. pres. 1966-68, v.p. Seattle br. 1979-80), Seattle Co-arts and Quad-A Art Club, Fedn. Women's Clubs, Women's Edn. Club (pres. 1960-61), Women Painters Wash. (pres. 1972-74), Artist's Equity, Seattle Art Mus., Seattle Opera Guild, Assistance League of Seattle. Clubs: Seattle Golf; Sand Point Golf and Country; Wash. Athletic, 200 plus 1. Home: 5520 Coniston Rd NE Seattle WA 98105

BLACKSTOCK, MARTHA PAGE, hospital official; b. Dunn-Loring, Va., Apr. 5, 1917; d. Robert Grove and Margaret Lee (Mull) Porter; m. Lavon Sewell Miller, Aug. 25, 1936 (div. 1946); children—Ronald L., Robert L., Edward C.; m. Edward Joseph Blackstock, Sept. 1, 1948; children—Bruce N., Marjorie Ann. Student Colo. State Coll., 1933, Western State Coll., 1936. Accredited med. record technician. Sec. U.S. Rubber Co., Los Angeles, 1937-41, Porter & Klingsmith Attys., Gunnison, Colo., 1944-45, Elko Sch. Dist., Nev., 1965-67; dep. county assessor Gunnison County, Colo., 1945-48; dir. med. records Elko Gen. Hosp., 1975-80, dir. med. staff services, 1980—. Founder, parliamentarian Elko Gen. Hosp. Aux., 1973—; bd. dirs. Elko County Rep. Party, 1964—, Am. Nat. CowBelles, 1971-73, Elko County Planning Commn., Nev. affiliate Am. Heart Assn., 1983—; pres. Nev. State CowBelles, 1970-71. Mem. Nat. Assn. Med. Staff Services, Nat. Assn. Quality Assurance Profls., Am. Med. Records Assn. Episcopalian. Lodge: Eastern Star (worthy matron 1973-74). Avocations: piano; painting; photography; flower gardening; travel. Home: PO Box 69 Elko NV 89801 Office: Elko Gen Hosp 1287 College Ave Elko NV 89801

BLACKSTOCK, VIRGINIA LEE LOWMAN (MRS. LEROY BLACKSTOCK), civic worker; b. Bixby, Okla., July 2, 1917; d. Joseph Arthur and Winifred (Lundy) Lowman; student Tulsa Coll. Bus., 1935-37; m. Leroy Blackstock, Dec. 29, 1939; children—Vincent Craig, Priscilla Gay (Mrs. Richard S. Kurz), Birch Lee, Lore Anne (Mrs. Dwight Mitchell), Trena Jan (Mrs. Frank Dale). Legal sec. law firm, Tulsa, 1937-41. Chmn. program Internat. Students in Tulsa, 1955-65; mem. Tulsa Council Camp Fire Girls, 1963-66; mem. youth com. Tulsa Philharmonic Soc., 1969-70; now mem. women's assn.; pres. Eliot Elementary P.T.A., 1961-62, Edison High Sch. P.T.A., 1971-72; mem. Tulsa Opera Guild. Co-chmn. Democratic precinct No. 132, 1960-67. Mem. Tulsa County Bar Aux. (pres. 1954-55, sec. 1962-63, chaplain 1966-67). Baptist. Clubs: Summit, Petroleum. Home: 7213 S Atlanta St Tulsa OK 74136

BLACKSTONE, SANDRA LEE, lawyer, educator, former govt. ofcl.; b. Washington; d. Fred J. and Madeline S. Blackstone; B.A., U. Vt., 1969; J.D., U. Denver, 1977; Ph.D., Colo. Sch. Mines, 1979. Systems analyst Martin Marietta Aerospace, Denver, 1969-74; cons. legal, econ. and regulatory matters W.R. Grace & Co., Colo. Energy Research Inst., Colo. Sch. Mines, Dawson, Nagel, Sherman & Howard, Denver, 1976-79; mgr. bus. devel. for synthetic fuels Rocky Mountain Energy subs. Union Pacific Corp., Denver, 1979-81; dep. dir. energy and mineral resources Bur. Land Mgmt., Dept. Interior, Washington, 1981-83; prof. Denver Coll. Law, 1983—; mem. Colo. Adv. Council on Energy and Energy-Related Mineral Research, 1980-82; mem. Bd. on Mineral and Energy Resources, Nat. Acad. Scis., 1983—. Republican precinct committeewoman, 1970-74; del. Denver County Rep. Conv., 1971, 74, Colo. State Rep. Conv., 1972. Colo. Energy Research Inst. fellow, 1974-76; Mobil Oil Co. natural resources fellow, 1975-76; Kennecott Corp. fellow, 1976-77. Mem. Am. Bar Assn., Colo. Bar Assn., Denver Bar Assn. Republican. Contbr. articles to profl. jours. Office: U Denver Coll Law 1900 Olive St Denver CO 80220

BLACKWAY, MADELINE ENDERS, librarian; b. Halifax, Pa., June 8, 1934; d. A. Marlin and Bertha Ellen (Straub) Enders; m. William Henry Blackway, Jr., Nov. 25, 1960; children—Julie Anne Blackway Kotkiewicz, William Enders. B.A., Pa. State U., 1956; M.S.L.S., Shippensburg U., 1980, M.Ed., 1982. Tchr. Susquehanna Twp. Sch. Dist., Harrisburg, Pa., 1956-61, Millersburg-Upper Paxton Sch. Dist. (Pa.), 1962-64; tchr. Halifax (Pa.) Area Sch. Dist., 1967-68, elem. librarian, 1968—. Active Harrisburg Community Theatre, 1970's; active Twin Valley Players, Halifax, 1970—, bd. dirs., 1983-84, 86—. Mem. ALA, Pa. Sch. Librarian Assn., Pa. Edn. Assn., Halifax Edn. Assn. (pres. 1970-72, 78-80), Delta Kappa Gamma, Phi Delta Gamma. Republican. Lodge: Order Eastern Star (Esther 1956-57). Home: Mountain View Dr PO Box 168 Halifax PA 17032 Office: Halifax Elem Sch RD 3 PO Box 7 Halifax PA 17032

BLACKWELL, ANTOINETTE LYNN, systems analyst; b. Anderson, Ind., Apr. 14, 1960; d. Donald Hugh and Janet Louise (Slaughter) B. Student in Computer Sci., Purdue U., 1978-79, Anderson Coll., 1980. Programmer/analyst Community Hosp., Anderson, Ind., 1979-81, Dynamic Control, Boston, 1981-82, project leader, Winter Park, Fla., 1982-84, mgr. implementations, Longwood, Fla., 1984-85, sr. tech. cons., Longwood, 1985—. Recipient Vocat. Edn. award, Anderson Rotary Club, 1978. Mem. Office Edn. Assn. (parliamentarian 1977-78, awards 1977, 78), Electronic Computing Health Oriented, Common IBM Users Group, Nat. Assn. Female Execs. Avocations: photography; writing; reading; volleyball; racquetball. Office: Dynamic Control 587 E Sanlando Springs Dr Longwood FL 32750

BLACKWELL, LUCY WHITE, retired state official; b. Jackson, Tenn., Apr. 22, 1912; d. William Francis and Ethel (White) Blackwell; A.B., Lambuth Coll., 1933; postgrad. West Tenn. Bus. Coll., 1934-35. Stenographer, Tenn. Emergency Relief Adminstrn., Jackson, 1935; accounting clk. FSA, Jackson, Brownsville, Tenn., 1936-39; stenographer Tenn. Dept. Pub. Welfare, Jackson, 1939-40; clk., interviewer, local office mgr. Tenn. Dept. Employment Security, Jackson, 1940-73. Comdr. Am. Cancer Soc., Madison County, Tenn., 1943-54, dist. comdr. W. Tenn., 1947-48, rec. sec. Tenn. div., 1954-56, bd. dirs., 1945—, organizer Madison County unit, 1954, pres., 1954-55; bd. dirs. Jackson Community Chest, 1955-57; pres. League Women Voters, 1951. Treas., chmn. bd. trustees Jackson Free Library, 1948-57. Recipient R.E. Womack Alumni Achievement award Lambuth Coll. Alumni Assn., 1956; named Jackson-Madison Woman of Year, 1955. Mem. Internat. Assn. Personnel Employment Security (pres. Jackson chpt. 1956), Lambuth Coll. Alumni Assn. (pres. 1962-63). Presbyterian. Clubs: Pilot Internat. (past pres. Jackson, dist. gov. Tenn., internat. dir. exec. com.). Altrusa Internat. (chmn.). Home: 45 Belle Haven Dr Jackson TN 38305

BLACKWELL, PENNY LEE, lawyer; b. Coco Solo, C.Z., Sept. 24, 1948; d. Frank Charles and Norma Madeline (Bryant) B.; m. John Kenneth Sanstead, Apr. 15, 1978; 1 dau., Rebecca Randolph. B.S., Portland State U., 1971; J.D., Am. U., 1974. Bar: Md., Pa. Atty., Wapora, Bethesda, Md., 1975-76, U.S. EPA, Phila., 1976-78; ptnr. Wolfson & Blackwell, York, Pa., 1980—. Bd. dirs. Displaced Homemakers, York, 1983—, Jr. League of York, 1984-85; mem. steering com. Martin Meml. Library, York, 1984, bd. dirs. York County Literacy Council, 1985—. Mem. ABA, Pa. Bar Assn., Md. Bar Assn., York County Bar Assn. (chmn. profl. responsibilities 1984), Nat. Assn. Women Lawyers. Democrat. Presbyterian. Club: Young Women's (bd. dirs. 1983-84) (York). Office: Wolfson & Blackwell 29 E Princess St York PA 17401

BLACKWOOD, DIANE JEAN, real estate company executive; b. Cleve., July 26, 1939; d. Peter H. and Irene (Knaus) Schaffer; m. James E. Blackwood, Dec. 17, 1960; children—Thomas James, David Scott. B.A., Hiram Coll., 1961. Sales agt. Donahue Realtors, Columbus, Ohio, 1971-76, HER Realtors, Columbus, 1976-77; br. mgr. Donahue Realtors, Columbus, 1977-80; v.p., broker Buy Ohio Realtors, Columbus, 1980—. Vol. Westerville Civic Symphony, 1984—. Mem. Ohio Assn. Realtors (trustee 1985), Columbus Bd. Realtors Nat. Realtors Assn. Republican. Avocations: reading, swimming. Home: 721 Autumn Branch Rd Westerville OH 43081

BLADE, MELINDA KIM, educator, researcher, archaeologist; b. San Diego, Jan. 12, 1952; d. George A. and Arline A. M. (MacLeod) B. B.A., U. San Diego, 1974, M.A. in Teaching, 1975, M.A., 1975, Ed.D., 1986. Cert. secondary tchr., Calif.; cert. community coll. instr., Calif.; registered profl. historian, Calif. Instr. Coronado Unified Sch. Dist., Calif., 1975-76; head coach women's basketball U. San Diego, 1976-78; instr. Acad. of Our Lady of Peace, San Diego, 1976—, chmn. social studies dept., 1983—, counselor, 1984—, co-dir. student activities, 1984—, coordinator advanced placement program, 1986—; mem. archaeol. excavation team U. San Diego, 1975—, hist. researcher, 1975—; lectr., 1981—. Author hist. reports and research papers. Editor U. San Diego pubs. Vol. Am. Diabetes Assn., San Diego, 1975—; coordinator McDonald's Diabetes Bike-a-thon, San Diego, 1977, 78. Mem. Nat. Council Social Studies, Calif. Council Social Studies, Soc. Bibl. Archeology, Assn. Supervision and Curriculum Devel., Assn. Scientists and Scholars Internat. for Shroud of Turin, Medieval Acad. Am., Medieval Assn. Pacific, Nat. Council on Religion and Pub. Edn., Am. Hist. Assn., Western Assn. Women Historians, San Diego Hist. Soc., Phi Alpha Theta (sec.-treas. 1975-77), Phi Delta Kappa. Office: Acad Our Lady of Peace 4860 Oregon St San Diego CA 92116

BLAESE, LOIS PATIENCE, manufacturing company executive; b. Atlantic City, Jan. 23, 1937; d. Louis Frank and Erma (Mott) Lamp'l; student public schs.; m. Donald Frank Blaese, Feb. 14, 1959; children—Monique, Donald Frank, Niccole. Div. mgr. Beeline Fashions, Bensenville, Ill., 1963-73;

sec.-treas. Accurate Screw Machine Products Co. div. Blaese Enterprises, Columbus, N.J., 1973—. Coordinator Miss Columbus contest, 1981—; mem. Mansfield Twp. Bd. Edn., 1976-85, v.p., 1979-81; Mansfield Twp. liaison N.J. Motion Picture and TV Commn., 1984—. Mem. N.J. Sch. Bds. Assn., Columbus Civic Assn., Columbus Hist. Soc., Columbus Ladies Fire Co. Aux. Republican. Home: Mill Ln Columbus NJ 08022 Office: 12 Atlantic Ave Columbus NJ 08022

BLAIN, JACQUELYN ALICE NASH GRIPPIN, cosmetologist; b. Springfield, Mass., Sept. 21, 1928; d. Roger Warren and Kathleen Alice (Proctor) Nash; student Springfield Conservatory Music, 1944-47, Hartford Conservatory Music, 1971-72, with concertmaster Bill Dalton, 1963-78; grad. Cosmetic Acad., 1978, Mansfield Beauty Acad., 1980. children—Diana Grippin, Lea Grippin, Lyn Grippin. With Watkins Bros., Inc., Hartford, Conn., 1964-79, asst. to owner, 1974-79; cosmetologist, Longmeadow, Mass., 1982—; mem. Zotos Creative Design Group, 1982. Recipient Merit award Redkin Labs., 1977. Mem. Hammond Organ Assn., Mass. State Cosmetology Assn. (dir., Pres. of Yr. award 1985), Internat. Platform Assn., Springfield Cosmetology Assn. (pres. 1984-85). Home: 80 Kenmore Dr Longmeadow MA 01106

BLAINE, ALISON MACDONALD, advertising agency executive; b. Hammond, Ind., May 17, 1952; d. George Allen and Sidney Constance Hurt (Sitwell) B. B.A. in Speech Edn., Radio and TV, Purdue U., 1974. Cert. tchr., Ind. Tchr., Donald E. Gavit High Sch. and Middle Sch., Hammond, 1975-77; staff liaison CETA Adv. Planning Council, Lake County, Ind., 1977; print bus. adminstr. Henderson Advt., Greenville, S.C., 1978-79; traffic mgr. Leslie Advt., Greenville, 1979-80; account exec., traffic dir. Bozell & Jacobs, Inc., Phoenix, 1980-82, account exec., Dallas, 1982-84; account exec. Long, Haymes & Carr, Winston-Salem, N.C., 1984—. Episcopalian. Home: 100 Flintwood Ct Apt B-10 Winston-Salem NC 27106 Office: Long Haymes & Carr 140 Charlois Blvd Winston-Salem NC 27113

BLAINE, DOROTHEA CONSTANCE RAGETTÉ, lawyer, b. N.Y.C., Sept. 23, 1930; d. Robert Raymond and Dorothea Ottilie Ragetté; B.A., Barnard Coll., 1952; M.A., Calif. State U., 1968; Ed.D., UCLA, 1978; J.D., Western State U., 1981; postgrad. in taxation Golden Gate U. Mem. tech. staff Planning Research Corp., Los Angeles, 1964-67; asso. scientist Holy Cross Hosp., Mission Hills, Calif., 1967-70; career devel. officer and affirmative action officer County of Orange, Santa Ana, Calif., 1970-74, sr. adminstrv. analyst, budget and program coordination, 1974-78; spl. projects asst. CAO/Spl. Programs Office, 1978-80, sr. adminstrv. analyst, 1980-83; admitted to Calif. bar, 1982; sole practice, 1982—. Bd. dirs. Deerfield Community Assn., 1975-78, Orange YMCA, 1975-77. Mem. Orange County Trial Lawyers Assn., Calif. Trial Lawyers, Calif. Women Lawyers, Nat. Women's Polit. Caucus, ABA, Calif. Bar Assn., Orange County Bar Assn., Orange County Women Lawyers Assn. ACLU, Delta Theta Phi, Phi Delta Kappa. Office: 270 Newport Center Dr Newport Beach CA 92660

BLAIR, BETTY STEPP, association executive; b. Odessa, Tex., July 2, 1947; d. William Fleming and Barbara Jane (Thompson) Stepp; m. Stephen Randolph Blair, Mar. 25, 1968 (div. 1978); children—Stacy Rae, Brian Randolph. B.B.A., Southwest Tex. State U., 1970. Sales rep. KYXY and XETV stas., San Diego, 1975-77; owner, mgr. Royal Suite, San Diego, 1977-79; internat. design cons. T. Goodrich & Assocs., Del Mar, Calif., 1979-80; acct. Sickels O'Brien Co., San Diego and La Jolla, Calif., 1980-81; property mgr. Total Office/Koll, San Diego, 1981-83; asst. devel. dir. Am. Cancer Soc., San Diego, 1983-86; assoc. D'Agostino, Underwood & Assocs., 1986—; cons. Poway Firewood Co., Calif., 1980-84, Starflight Prodns., San Diego, 1985—. Mem. Republican Central Com., San Diego, 1977; mem. steering com. Young Connoisseurs, San Diego Mus. of Art, 1982-84; mem. San Diego Rep. Businesswomen, 1984-86; bd. dirs. Rep. Bus. and Profl. Club, San Diego, 1986; vol. charitable orgns. and theaters. Recipient State award Am. Cancer Soc., 1985. Mem. Nat. Soc. Fund Raising Execs., Chi Omega. Avocation: sailing. Home: 6455 La Jolla Blvd #252 La Jolla CA 92037 Office: D'Agostino Underwood & Assocs 3646 4th Ave San Diego CA 92103

BLAIR, MARIE LENORE, educator; b. Maramec, Okla., Jan. 9, 1931; d. Virgil Clement and Ella Catherine (Leen) Strode; B.S., Okla. A. and M. Coll., 1956; M.S., Okla. State U., 1961, postgrad., 1965-68; m. Freeman Joe Blair, Aug. 26, 1950; children—Elizabeth Ann Blair Crump, Roger Joe. Reading specialist Pub. Schs. Stillwater (Okla.), 1966—. Past bd. dirs. Okla. Reading Council. Mem. Internat., Okla., Cimarron (past pres.) reading assns., NEA, Okla. Edn. Assn., Stillwater Edn. Assn., Kappa Kappa Iota. Democrat. Mem. Christian Ch. (Disciples of Christ). Clubs: DeMoley Mothers, Rainbow Mothers, Lahoma, White Shrine Jerusalem (past worthy high priestess). Order White Shrine Jerusalem (past supreme queen's attendant), Internat. Order of Rainbow for Girls (Okla. exec. com.), Order Eastern Star (past grand Martha, grand rep. of Nebr. in Okla.). Contbr. to Okla. Reader. Home: Route 1 Maramec OK 74045

BLAIR, MATTIE D., city official, consultant; b. Chgo., Nov. 26; d. James and Geraldine (Oliver) Cannon; div.; 1 child, Lisa Marie. B.S. in Bus. Adminstrn. in Acctg., Roosevelt U., 1979; M.B.A. in Fin., DePaul U., 1985. Pub. auditor Arthur Andersen & Co., Chgo., 1978-81; controller Johnson Products & Co., Chgo., 1981-82; mgr. fiscal policies United Way of Chgo., 1982-86; dir. devel. fin. City of Chgo., 1986—; cons. on fin. and mgmt. to small non-profit orgns. Developer network to assist black profls. in fin. and acctg. Mem. League of Black Women (v.p. 1983—). Democrat. Mem. United Ch. of Christ. Avocations: Tennis; jogging; sports. Office: Dir Devel Finance City of Chgo 30 N Clark St Chicago IL 60606

BLAIR, PRUDENCE LEWIS, business owner; b. Boston, Mar. 9, 1946; d. Wolfram L. and Elsie (Cole) Lewis; student U. Madrid (Spain), 1966; m. J. Kent Blair, Jr., Jan. 26, 1986. Corr., John P. Maguire Co., N.Y.C., 1968-71; asst. to pres. Cromwell Corp., N.Y.C., 1971-72, also corp. sec.; adminstrv. asst. to the exec. v.p. Rinfret Assocs., N.Y.C., 1973-76; asst to chmn. Friedlich, Fearon & Strohmeier, N.Y.C., 1976-77; v.p. mgmt., sec.-treas. Morgan Newman Assocs., Inc., Washington, 1977-84; v.p. mgmt. Balloon-Age, Short Hills, N.J., 1984—; pres. Products for the Filthy Rich, 1985—. Cert. CPR. Mem. Smithsonian Assocs., Nat. Assn. Female Execs. Republican. Episcopalian. Club: Jr. League of Summit, N.J. Office: PO Box 334 Short Hills NJ 07078

BLAIR, PRUDENCE WADDOCK, public relations executive, editor; b. St. Louis, Oct. 23, 1925; d. Joseph Patrick and Annie Laurie (Page) Waddock; B.J., U. Mo., Columbia, 1947; postgrad. Northwestern U., Chgo. campus, 1953-54; m. Giles Allen Blair, Jr., June 6, 1959; children—Annie-Laurie, Giles Allen, Rebecca Ralls. With news dept. KXOK Radio, St. Louis, 1947-48; agrl. editor Pet, Inc., St. Louis, 1949-52; asst. dir. public relations Am. Angus Assn., Chgo., 1953-56, St. Joseph, Mo., 1956-57; editor Bank-Trust News, Centerre Bank, Inc., St. Louis, 1957-62; substitute tchr./tchr. aide Webster Groves (Mo.) Sch. Dist., 1971-78; dir. public relations Edgewood Children's Center, Webster Groves, 1979-83; community relations and devel. dir. Care & Counseling, Inc., Creve Coeur, Mo., 1983—; notary public, 1978-82. Active Chgo. Young Democrats, 1953-56; asst. Brownie leader Girl Scouts U.S.A., 1965-66, 69-70, asst. scout leader St. Louis council, 1970-71, troop cookie chmn., 1974-78; active PTA, 1965-82; active United Fund campaigns, 1958-62, 78—, loaned exec. United Way, 1981, recipient Grand award to indsl. publs. editor, 1959, certs. of excellence, 1960, 61; mem. planning com. local history project Community Sch., Webster Groves, 1978. Mem. Nat. Assn. Mental Health Info. Officers (1st Place newsletters and spl. projects communications contest 1982), Nat. Soc. Fund Raising Execs., Community Service Public Relations Council Greater St. Louis (dir. 1980-83; pres. 1983), Webster Groves Hist. Soc. (dir. 1983-84), Alpha Chi Omega. Episcopalian. Contbr. articles to nat. press. Home: 44 Sylvester Ave Webster Groves MO 63119 Office: Care and Counseling Inc 12145 Ladue Rd Creve Coeur MO 63141

BLAIR, SUSAN LEE, editor; b. Detroit, June 3, 1944; d. George Eugene and Alice Spottswood (DuVal) Blair; m. Robert Roy Metz, May 18, 1984; 1 son by previous marriage, Allen David Hahn. B. Journalism, U. Mo., 1966. Copyreader, Time mag., N.Y.C., 1970-74, dep. copy chief, 1974-78, copy chief, 1979—. Bd. dirs., sec. Chamber Opera Theatre of N.Y.

BLAIR, THERESA LUCILLE, records manager, electrical contractor; b. Hernandez, N.Mex., June 27, 1943; d. Ben and Lucy (Roybal) Lovato; m. Roger Charles Blair, Feb. 23, 1963; children—Darrell, Yvette, Sean, DeVonne. B.S. in Bus. Adminstrn., U. Albuquerque, 1979; M.B.A., Highlands U., Las Vegas, 1982. Office sec. Sandia Nat. Labs., Albuquerque, 1964-79, mem. lab. staff, records mgr., 1980—, dir.'s rep. employee contbr. program, 1981—; elec. contractor, owner, operator T.L. Blair Electric Co. Mem. planning and allocations panel United Way Greater Albuquerque, 1984. Mem. Assn. Records Mgrs. and Adminstrs. Democrat. Roman Catholic. Home: 2126 Matthew Ave NW Albuquerque NM 87104 Office: Sandia National Laboratories PO Box 5800 Albuquerque NM 87185

BLAIR, TINA MARYA HOLOWAY, physician; b. Boston, May 14, 1948; d. Edward and Mary (Minko) Holoway. B.Sc. cum laude, Tufts U., 1970; M.D. with honors, Rush Med. Sch., Chgo., 1974. Diplomate Am. Bd. Emergency Medicine. Surg. intern Ind. U. Med. Ctr., Indpls., 1974, gen. surg. resident, 1975; Robert Wood Johnson Found. emergency medicine fellow U. Calif. Med. Ctr., San Francisco, 1976-78; dir. emergency service Jeannette Dist. Meml. Hosp., Pa., 1978-79, Morton Hosp., Taunton, Mass., 1979-83; chief emergency services Brockton Hosp., Mass., 1983—; asst. clin. prof. emergency medicine U. Mass. Med. Sch., Worcester, 1982—; chmn. bd. dirs. BARI Group, Inc., Dallas, 1985—; lectr. in field. Co-author: Disaster Planning for Physicians, 1982. Mem. editorial bd. Med Con Rev. Fellow Am. Coll. Emergency Physicians; mem. AMA, Mass. Med. Soc. (chmn. emergency med. service com. 1985—), Plymouth Dist. Med. Soc. (council del.), Am. Med. Women's Assn., Univ. Assn. Emergency Medicine, Emergency Medicine Mgmt. Assn., Am. Trauma Soc., So. Med. Assn., Women in Emergency Medicine. Office: Brockton Hosp 680 Centre St Brockton MA 02402

BLAIR, VIRGINIA ANN, public relations executive; b. Kansas City, Mo., Dec. 20, 1925; d. Paul Lowe and Lou Etta (Cooley) Smith; m. James Leon Grant, Sept. 3, 1943 (dec. July 1944); m. 2d, Warden Tannahill Blair, Jr., Nov. 7, 1947; children—Janet, Warden Tannahill, III. B.S. in Speech, Northwestern U., 1948. Free-lance writer, Chgo., 1959-69; writer, editor Smith, Bucklin & Assocs., Inc., Chgo., 1969-72, account mgr., 1972-79, account supr., 1979-80, dir. pub. relations, 1980-85; pres. GB Pub. Relations, 1985—; judge U.S. Indsl. Film Festival, 1974, 75; instr. Writer's Workshop, Evanston, Ill., 1978; dir. Northwestern U. Library Council, 1978—. Emmy nominee Nat. Acad. TV Arts & Scis., 1963; recipient Service award Northwestern U., 1978, Creative Excellence award U.S. Indsl. Film Festival, 1976, Gold Leaf merit cert. Family Circle mag. and Food Council Am., 1977. Mem. Pub. Relations Soc. Am. (counselors acad.), Women's Advt. Club Chgo. (pres.), Publicity Club Chgo., Nat. Acad. TV Arts & Scis., Zeta Phi Eta (Service award 1978), Alpha Gamma Delta. Author dramas (produced on CBS): Jeanne D'Arc: The Trial, 1961; Cordon of Fear, 1961; Reflection, 1961; If I Should Die, 1963; 3-act children's play: Children of Courage, 1967. Home and Office: 463 Highcrest Dr Wilmette IL 60091

BLAIR THOMAS, SHIRLEY JEAN, steamship company manager; b. Birmingham, Ala., July 5, 1946; d. Charles and Mary (McClung) Thomas; m. Charles June Blair, Nov. 22, 1972; children—Rosharon, Amond Hotep. B.A., Howard U., 1967. Long distance operator C&P Telephone Co., Washington, 1964-67; adminstrv. asst. Beacon Assocs., Washington, 1967-69; asst. to pres. Advanced Internat. Mktg., Washington, 1969-72; sales dir. Columbia Assoc., Washington, 1972-74; sales rep. Moore McCormack Lines, Washington, 1975-83; sr. internat. accounts mgr. U.S. Lines, Inc., Washington, 1983—. Pres. PTA, Washington, 1984-85; chairperson Capitol Artists Prodns., 1984-85. Mem. Nat. Assn. Female Execs., Women in Community Services, NAACP, Nat. Mus. of Women in Arts. Methodist. Clubs: Propeller (Washington); Traffic of Balt. Avocations: reading; swimming. Home: 2638 M L K Ave SE Washington DC 20020

BLAKE, CAROL T., county social service administrator; b. Buffalo, Sept. 17, 1950; d. Robert Wilson and Constance Jane (Milburn) Temple; m. Charles Grierson Signor Blake, Nov. 3, 1973; 1 child, Andrea Lynn. Student Hobart and William Smith Coll., 1968-70; B.A. in Liberal Arts, SUNY-Geneseo, 1972. Outreach worker Orleans Community Action, Albion, N.Y., 1973; dir. resident services Orchard Manor Nursing Home, Medina, N.Y., 1973-75; dir. Orleans County Office for the Aging, Albion, 1975—; cons. Genesee County Office for Aging, N.Y., 1983-84. Treas. Orleans Coop. Extension, Albion, 1977-80, Orleans Community Counseling Ctr., Albion, 1979; asst. campaign mgr., bd. dirs. Orleans United Way, Albion, 1983-85. Mem. N.Y. State Assn. of Area Agys. on Aging (chmn. rural affairs 1985 statewide conf.), Western N.Y. Network on Aging (presenter edn. conf. 1983). Democrat. Episcopalian. Avocations: classical music; dance; gardening; reading; vocal music. Home: 13579 Waterport-Carlton Rd Waterport NY 14571 Office: Orleans County Office For Aging 14016 Route 31 Albion NY 14411

BLAKE, CHRISTINA ELAINE, publishing company executive; b. Bklyn., Dec. 12, 1941; d. Edward Najib and Ann Rita (Boutross) Boutross; m. Kevin Edward Blake, Jan. 24, 1966; children—Kevin Barry, Elaine Christina, Ronald Lucius, Edward, Christopher. Student pvt. sch., Bklyn., 1955-59. Asst. to mktg. mgr. Singer Sewing Machine, N.Y.C., 1959-64; exec. sec. Palmer, Serles, Delaney, Shaw & Pomeroy, N.Y.C., 1964-66; subs. rights mgr., asst. to dir. Rutgers U. Press, New Brunswick, N.J., 1976—; lectr. in field. Mem.-in-charge Tuesday bingo St. Francis Parish, Metuchen, N.J., 1978—. Mem. Women in Scholarly Pub. Republican. Roman Catholic. Club: St. Francis Athletic Assn. (Metuchen) (basketball league coordinator 1980—). Home: 17 Susan Pl Edison NJ 08817 Office: Rutgers U Press 109 Church St New Brunswick NJ 08903

BLAKE, DOROTHY GRACE, educator; b. Linwood, N.Y., Dec. 15, 1927; d. John William and Kathryn Louise (Donnelly) Campbell; m. Gerald J. Blake, Feb. 16, 1957. B.A. in Sociology, U. Buffalo, 1949; M.S. in Edn., Canisius Coll., 1971; postgrad. U. Buffalo, 1971-78. Personnel dir. Sattler's Dept. Store, Buffalo, 1948-57; high sch. math tchr. Diocese of Buffalo, 1957-70, asst. prin., 1970-74, prin. St. Mary's High Sch., 1974—; mem. prins. steering com. Diocese of Buffalo, 1979-81, 84-85, mem. diocesan negotiation com., 1981, bishop's task force on enrollement, 1976; condr. workshops in field. Mem. Nat. Cath. Edn. Assn., Cath. Sch. Adminstrs. N.Y. State, Am. Assn. Sch. Adminstrs., Nat. Assn. Secondary Sch. Prins. Republican. Roman Catholic. Club: Niagara Sailing. Avocations: sailing; antique refinishing. Home: 207 Northwood Dr Kenmore NY 14223 Office: Saint Mary's Diocesan High Sch 142 Laverack Ave Lancaster NY 14086

BLAKE, ILENE MILLS, county official; b. Kegley, W.Va., Aug. 31, 1932; d. Ile Sheron and Okley Fay (Reid) Mills; student Concord Coll., 1950-51; B.B.A., George Washington U., 1967; m. Warren Porter Blake, May 24, 1951; children—Ile Wayne, Edward Dean. Adminstrv. asst. Arlington County, Arlington, Va., 1959-67; adminstrv. asst. Fairfax County, Fairfax, Va., 1967-71, budget analyst, 1971-72, budget officer, 1972-73, dir. Office Mgmt. and Budget, 1973—; treas. Blake-Mills Ltd. Founder, bd. dirs. Blake Pvt. Sch. Mem. Municipal Fin. Officers Assn. Home: 125 Evergreen St Sterling VA 22170

BLAKE, JOANNE, radio station executive; b. Concord, N.H., May 27, 1952; d. John Baxter and Mathilda (Probst) B. B.A. in Communications, Wash. State U., 1974. News dir. Sta.-KOTY, Kennewick, Wash., 1974-75, Sta.-KPUG, Bellingham, Wash., 1975-76; reporter, editor, anchor Sta.-KIRO, Seattle, 1976-81; news and pub. affairs dir. sta.-KSEA, Seattle, 1981-85. Mem. Radio and TV News Dirs. Assn., Sigma Delta Chi (Spot News award 1979, Feature award 1984). Avocation: flying.

BLAKE, MARY HUMPHREY, corporate official; b. Greensboro, N.C., Sept. 9, 1951; d. Harold Gilmer Humphrey and Julia Ann (Moyer) Humphrey Pace; m. Kenneth Marshall Blake, June 18, 1973 (div.). B.S., U. N.C., 1973. Exec. sec. Odell Assocs., Inc., Greensboro, N.C., 1973, Am. Bank & Trust Co., Charlotte, N.C., 1973-74, Community Bank of Carolina, Greensboro, 1974-75, W.H. Weaver Constrn., Greensboro, 1975-76, asst. cash mgr. Ashland Exploration, Houston, 1977-80; corp. cash mgr. APS, Inc., Houston, 1980—. Mem. LWV. Mem. Nat. Corp. Cash Mgmt. Assn., Houston Corp. Cash Mgmt. Assn., AAUW. Methodist. Office: APS Inc 3000 Pawnee Houston TX 77054

BLAKE, ROBERTA SHARON SAVAGE, nurse; b. Scott County, Ill., Jan. 14, 1941; d. Carl Alvin Wesley and Helen Margaret (Price) Savage; R.N., Passavant Meml. Area Hosp., Jacksonville, Ill., 1961; m. Daniel H. Blake, Dec. 27, 1960; children—Heather Anne, Amber Noelle. Staff nurse White Hall (Ill.) Hosp., 1961-75, utilization rev. coordinator, 1976-79, inservice dir., 1979-83, acting dir. nurses, 1979-80, dir. nurses, 1980—. Mem. North Greene Adv. Council, 1976-82; bd. dirs. Two Rivers council Girl Scouts U.S.A., 1978-83, troop leader, 1976-83; mem. nominating com. Two Rivers Council Girl Scouts U.S., 1985—; mem. Greene County Bd. Health, 1985—; Greene County bd. dirs. Am. Cancer Soc., 1985—. Mem. Ill. Soc. Nurse Adminstrs. Republican. Methodist. Club: Royal Neighbors Lodge. Home: 217 S Carrollton St White Hall IL 62092 Office: 407 N Main St White Hall IL 62092

BLAKELY, CARRELL RAE, metal products company executive; b. Hemingford, Nebr., July 27, 1936; d. Ray Willard and Marjorie Darlene (Carrell) Stull; A.A. in Bus. Adminstrn. and Acctg., Trinidad State Coll., 1974; m. Herbert S. Blakely, Aug. 31, 1972; children by previous marriage—Mickey F. Pugh, Rickey K. Pugh. Various secretarial and bookkeeping positions, 1953-65; legal sec. Wright & Kastler, Raton, N.Mex., 1965-68; pres. Elco Metal Products Corp., Clayton, N.Mex. and Burns Flat, Okla., 1970—. Mem. Nat. Assn. Archtl. Mfrs. Republican. Roman Catholic. Author: True Marriage Vows, 1974. Home: 1005 Jenkins Rd Clayton NM 88415 Office: Elco Metal Products Corp Box 100 Burns Flat OK 73624

BLAKENEY, ANNE BACON, occupational therapist; b. Morristown, Tenn., Mar. 16, 1947; d. David Ray and Ruth Anne (Speck) Bacon; B.S. with honors, U. Tenn., 1969; M.S. in Occupational Therapy (trainee HEW), Boston U., 1974; m. Michael Louis Blakeney, Apr. 13, 1974; children—Ruth Ellen, Kathleen. Unit dir. overseas recreation program ARC, Korea, 1969-70, recreation specialist U.S. Army Hosp., Ft. Polk, La., 1971; staff occupational therapist USPHS Hosp., Carville, La., 1975-78; mem. faculty U. N.C., Chapel Hill, 1978-84, asst. prof. occupational therapy, 1981-84; asst. prof. occupational therapy Eastern Ky. U., Richmond, 1984—; cons. in field. Vol., FISH Orgn., Morristown, Tenn., 1972, Ft. Saunders Community Project, Knoxville, Tenn., 1968-69. Served as officer USPHS, 1976-77. Mem. Am. Occupational Therapy Assn., World Fedn. Occupational Therapists, Soc. Behavioral Kinesiology, Center Neurodevel. Studies, Assn. Women Faculty, La. Occupational Therapy Assn. (pres. 1976-77), N.C. Occupational Therapy Assn. Democrat. Author articles in field. Office: Dept Occupational Therapy Wallace 109 Eastern Ky U Richmond KY 40475

BLAKENEY, TERESA ANN PEÑA, respiratory technician; b. Dover, Del., May 31, 1954; d. Efrain and Mary Lillian Peña; B.S., U. Del., 1976. Asst. to a veterinarian, Bridgeville, Del., 1972-73; clin. study in respiratory therapy Nanticoke Meml. Hosp., Seaford, Del., 1977; physician's asst., respiratory technician, Milford, Del., 1978-82; physician's asst., mgr., Seaford, Del., 1982-86, ins. claims coordinator, 1986—. Mem. Del. Assn. Respiratory Therapy, Am. Assn. Med. Assts., Kent-Sussex-Del. Am. Assn. Med. Assts. (pres., treas.), Del. Am. Assn. Med. Assts. Soc. (pres.), Alpha Zeta. Home: 104 Hickory Rd Seaford DE 19973 Office: Shipley St Seaford DE 19973

BLAKESLEE, DIANE PUSEY, financial executive; b. West Chester, Pa., Apr. 12, 1933; d. Norman Solomon and Leona (Ruth) Pusey; student Hood Coll., 1951-54, Calif. Poly. State U., 1966; m. Earle Bevington Blakeslee, June 11, 1954; children—Samuel, Barbara, David, Ruth. With Nat. Bank of Avondale (Pa.), 1952-53, Bank of Am., Chino, Calif., 1954-55; registered rep. TMI Equities, San Luis Obispo, Calif, 1971-73, registered prin., br. mgr., 1973-78; registered prin., br. mgr. Walt Becker and Assos., San Luis Obispo, 1978-80; registered prin., pres. Blakeslee & Blakeslee, San Luis Obispo, 1980—. Bd. dirs. San Luis Obispo Child Devel. Center, 1978—, Pvt. Industry Council, 1980—; chairperson planned giving com. Cuesta Coll.; bd. regents Coll. Fin. Planning, Denver, 1980—; counselor Family Services; active fund raiser for ch., symphony, PTA. Named Nat. Cert. Fin. Planner of Yr., 1985. Mem. Inst. Cert. Fin. Planners (dir), San Luis Obispo Life Underwriters, Internat. Assn. Fin. Planners, Nat. Assn. Life Underwriters. Republican. Quaker. Clubs: Symphony Guild, Women's Network, Quota. Home: 88 Country Club Dr San Luis Obispo CA 93401 Office: 1110 California Blvd San Luis Obispo CA 93401

BLAKEY, CAROLYN E., interior designer; b. Austin, Tex., Nov. 19, 1944; d. John Erwin and Estine (Dorward) B. B.S. in Interior Design, U. Tex., 1967. Interior designer Howard Goldman Interiros, Dallas, 1967-72; pres. Interiors, Inc., Dallas, 1972—. Mem. adv. bd. Skyline High Sch., Dallas, 1979-81; mem. vis. bd. Found. Interior Design and Edn. Research, 1986. Mem. Inst. Bus. Designers (chpt. pres. 1977-79, nat. trustee 1979-81, nat. v.p. 1981-83, nat. sec. 1983-85), Am. Soc. Interior Designers, Soc. Mktg. Profl. Services. Office: Interplan Inc 2121 San Jacinto Suite 830 Dallas TX 75201

BLAKLEY, DIANE MARY, hospital administrator; b. DuBois, Pa., May 18, 1952; d. Steve Charles and Lillian Jean (Zaffuto) Skraba; m. Benjamin Spencer Blakley, III, Aug. 10, 1974; children—Michael Joseph (dec.), Benjamin Spencer IV. B.A., Mansfield U., 1974. Mem. placement staff Duquesne U. Sch. Law, Pitts., 1977-78; mem. advt. staff DuBois Courier-Express, 1978-79; dir. pub. relations DuBois Hosp., Pa., 1981-85; dir. pub. relations and devel. DuBois Regional Med. Ctr., 1985—; pres. DuBois Hosp. Aux., 1984-85; adminstrv. liaison DuBois Regional Med. Ctr. Aux., 1985—; bd. dirs. DuBois Hosp., 1984-85; bd. dirs. Clearfield County unit Am. Cancer Soc., 1981-84, chmn. pub. relations Gateway unit, 1984; publicity chmn. DuBois Area Prepared Childbirth Assn., 1978-81. Mem. Am. Soc. for Hosp. Pub. Relations, Nat. Assn. Hosp. Devel., Hosp. Council Western Pa. (pub. affairs adv. com.), Hosp. Assn. of Pa. Pub. Relations and Mktg. Soc., AAUW. Democrat. Roman Catholic. Avocations: writing; gourmet cooking; physical fitness activities; photography; the arts. Home: 10 S Highland St DuBois PA 15801 Office: DuBois Regional Med Ctr PO Box 447 DuBois PA 15801

BLALOCK, JOYCE, lawyer, government official; b. Huntsville, Tex., Dec. 5, 1929; d. William Ben Blalock and Minnie Sue (Robbins) Blalock Cohen; m. Dimitri B. Cocovinis, June 18, 1949 (div.); children—Dean B., Derek D., Dwight W. B.A., Tex. U., 1949; LL.B., Denver U., 1963; LL.M., Columbia U., 1968. Bar: Mass. 1963, U.S. Dist. Ct. Mass. 1964, N.Mex. 1969, U.S. Dist. Ct. N.Mex. 1969, U.S. Ct. Appeals (10th cir.) 1970, U.S. Supreme Ct. 1972, Md. 1975, D.C. 1975. Assoc. Choate, Hall & Stewart, Boston, 1962-67; asst. atty. gen. State of N.Mex., Santa Fe, 1969-74; dir. Legal Div., Internat. Assn. Chiefs Police, Gaithersburg, Md., 1974-76; trial atty. FDA, Rockville, Md., 1977-78; br. mgr. law Dept. of Def., Washington, 1978-79; insp. gen. D.C. Govt., Washington, 1979-85; insp. gen. U.S. Govt. Printing Office, 1985—; bd. govs. Inst. Internal Auditors, Washington, 1982-86; chmn. nominating com. U.S. Joint Fin. Mgmt. Improvement Program, Washington, 1984, mem. nominating com., 1983; chmn. Internat. Conf. on Corruption and Econ. Crime against Govt.; mem. steering com. Pres.' Council on Integrity and Efficiency, 1982—; adv. com. Interagy. Auditor Tng. Program, USDA Grad. Sch., 1985—. Bd. dirs. NOW, Washington chpt., 1977, Wash. Area Feminist Theatre, 1977-80; bd. dirs., bus. mgr. Santa Fe Community Theatre, 1971-73; mem. Colo. Mountain Club, Denver, 1964—; treas. Exec. Women in Govt., Washington, 1983. Mem. Fed. Bar Assn., ABA (com. adminstrv. law sect. Chgo., 1982—), Philos. Soc., Zonta Internat. (bd. dirs.). Club: Columbia U. of Washington (bd. dirs.). Author: Civil Liability of Law Enforcement Officers; editor: Corruption and Economic Crime Against Government, 1984; contbr. numerous articles to profl. jours.

BLALOCK, TAMARA JONELLE, broadcasting executive; b. Garden City, Kans., May 3, 1959; d. Wesley Eugene and Georgia Harriet (McGillivray) B. Diploma Colby Community Coll., 1978. Broadcaster Sta. KXXX, Colby, Kans., 1978-79, Sta. KULY, Ulysses, Kans., 1979-80, program dir., 1983—; broadcaster Sta. KBUF, Garden City, 1980-81; mgr. Pizza Hut, Ulysses, 1981-82; officer mgr. Randall Corp., Houston, 1981-82. Publicity chmn. Grant County Community Theatre, 1985—; Daisy leader Tumbleweed council Girl Scouts U.S.A., 1985—. Recipient God and Community award Girl Scouts U.S.A., 1970; Future Home maker award Future Homemakers Am., 1977, Key award, 1976. Mem. Am. Legion Aux. Republican. Mem. Christian Ch. (Disciples of Christ). Club: Ulysses W.B.A. (treas. 1982—). Avocations: bowling; reading; singing; piano; collecting stamps and music boxes. Home: 418 N Court Ulysses KS 67880 Office: KULY Radio PO Box 1420 Ulysses KS 67880

BLANCHARD, DONNA LEE, investment banker; b. Lawrence, Mass., Oct. 28, 1947; d. Gerard J. and Lucille A. (Michaud) B.; m. Steven S. Lieberman, Mar. 8, 1975; stepchildren—Debra, Erik. Student, St. Petersburg Jr. Coll., 1965-69, Wagner Coll., 1982-83. With First Boston Corp., N.Y.C., 1971-78, Paine, Webber, Jackson & Curtis, N.Y.C., 1978; asst. v.p. Blyth, Eastman, Dillon (merged with Paine, Webber, Jackson & Curtis 1979), N.Y.C., 1978-79; v.p. Paine, Webber, Jackson & Curtis, N.Y.C., 1979-81; v.p., preferred stock trader Kidder Peabody & Co., N.Y.C., 1981—. Treas., Oaks at LaTourette Condominium II, S.I., N.Y., 1980, 81, pres., 1982, 83. Republican. Roman Catholic. Club: Corp. Bond Traders of N.Y. Office: Kidder Peabody & Co Inc 10 Hanover Sq New York NY 10005

BLANCHARD, HELEN MAE, government official; b. Pender, Nebr., May 17, 1926; d. Frank and Anna Florence (Rihanek) Pallas; m. John J. Blanchard, June 25, 1946; (dec. June 1974); children—Bruce Alan, Cheryl Ann Sonnenwald. Phys. sci. technologist Navy Electronics Lab., San Diego, 1960-75; supervisory sci. technologist Naval Ocean Systems Ctr., San Diego, 1975-83, communications specialist, 1983-84, head visitors info. and presentations br., 1984-85, head tech. info. dir., 1985—. Author numerous tech. reports on fleet tests. Named Woman of Yr., Navy Electronics Lab., 1971. Mem. Nat. Speakers Assn., San Diego Navy League, Profl. Speakers Assn., Save Our Heritage Assn., Toastmasters Internat. (dist. gov. 1976-77, internat. dir. 1978-80, 3d v.p. 1982-83, 2d v.p. 1983-84, sr. v.p. 1984-85, pres. 1985-86). Office: Naval Ocean Systems Center San Diego CA 92152

BLANCHARD, JANET MAY, plastic and reconstructive surgeon; b. W. Chester, Pa., July 3, 1943; d. John Edward and Dorothy (Skinner) Hoopes; m. Kenneth Edward Blanchard, June 21, 1969 (div.); m. Kermit Roosevelt Beckmann, Nov. 13, 1982. B.S., U. Del., 1965; M.S., Hahnemann U., 1973, M.D., 1976. Intern Cleve. Clinic, 1976-77; resident in gen. surgery, 1977-79, resident in plastic surgery, 1979-81, hand surgery spl. fellow, 1981-82; practice medicine specializing in plastic and reconstructive surgery, Mentor, Ohio, 1983—; mem. staff Met. Gen. Hosp., Cleve., 1982-83, Lake County Meml. Hosp., Painesville, 1983—, Lutheran Med. Ctr., Cleve., 1982—; cons. ARC, Cleve. Contbr. articles to profl. jours. Mem. AMA, Ohio State Med. Assn., Am. Med. Women's Assn., Cleve. Med. Women's Assn., Cleve. Acad. Medicine, Nat. Assn. Residents and Interns, Northeast Ohio Soc. Plastic and Reconstructive Surgeons (First Place award 1980), Lake County Med. Soc. Office: 7923 Munson Rd Suite 9 Mentor OH 44060

BLANCHARD, LINDA MARIE, real estate appraiser, financial official, consultant; b. Dallas, Feb. 25, 1953; d. Carl Webster and Mary Lee (Hamm) McKee; m. Michael David Blanchard, Aug. 25, 1979. B.A., N.Tex. State U., 1974; M.B.A., U. Tex.-Austin, 1983. Lic. real estate broker, Tex. Editor, media coordinator Tex. Pub. Utility Commn., Austin, 1976-79; dir. fin. and adminstrn. ROTEC Engring., Inc., Duncanville, Tex., 1982-83; real estate appraiser, fin. cons. Carl W. McKee and Assos., Dallas, 1983—; treas. Temperature Specialists, Inc., Dallas, 1982. Fin. sec. Trinity United Methodist Ch., Duncanville, 1984-86; campaign worker county polit. campaigns, 1982. Republican. Office: Carl W McKee and Assos 4403 N Central Suite 220 Dallas TX 75205

BLANCHARD WILDMAN, SUZANNE, composer, educator; b. Boston, Jan. 4, 1940; d. Wells and Helen Lane Blanchard; grad. San Francisco Conservatory Music, Vocal major, 1957; A.B., Classics, Stanford U., 1958; m. Ben. H. Williams, July 28, 1952 (div. 1958); children—Helen LeRoy, Benjamin Henry, Ludwig Altmann. Concert pianist, performing at Palace of Legion of Honor, San Francisco, 1961, Temple Emmanuel, San Francisco, 1961, Meml. Ch., Stanford U., 1962; tchr. elem. piano San Francisco Conservatory, 1963-64. Foster parent Operation Happy Child, Taiwan; active Met. Opera Raffle, UNICEF; mem. Town Com., Republican Party, Manchester, Mass. Mem. Am. Security Council, Manchester Hist. Soc., Stanford U. Alumni Assn. Republican. Christian Scientist. Clubs: Pebble Beach (Carmel, Calif.); Singing Beach Beach (Manchester); Revolutionary Ridge Book (Concord, Mass.). Composer: The Governor Proposes, 1962, additional scenes, 1985; Five Christmas Duets for Teacher and Beginner, Preludes 1-3, Fugue, 1962, Prelude 4, 1984. Home: 27 Pine St Manchester-by-the Sea MA 01944 Office: University Ln Manchester MA 01944

BLANCO, AMANDA, photographer; b. San Salvador, El Salvador, Oct. 23, 1933; d. Felix and Julia Isabel (Raimundo) Blanco; M.F.A., Calif. Inst. Arts, 1981; B. Profl. Arts, Inst. Photography, Santa Barbara, Calif., 1971; m. Mario Escobar (div. 1966); children—Maurice, César-E., Rosa Eugenia, and Rocio E. Blanco. Instr., Calif. State U., Northridge, 1977-79; asst. course organizer Calif. Inst. Arts, Valencia, 1980-81; faculty Idyllwild Sch. Music and Arts, 1980-82; exhibits: U. Calif., Northridge, Getty Mus., Los Angeles Mus. Sci. and Industry, other galleries and mus.; free lance photographer, Los Angeles, 1981—. Ahmanson Found. scholar, 1980; Lew and Eddie Wasserman scholar, 1979. Mem. Calif. Women Higher Edn. (exec. bd. 1975-78), AAUW, Profl. Photographers Am. Club: Rounce and Coffin. Author: The Many Faces of Jake Zeitlin, 1970; About Norman Corwin, 1980; Richard Hoffman at Seventy, 1982; Isomata: The Place and Its People, 1983. Home and Office: 46 Ozone Ave Venice CA 90291

BLANCQ, KRISTINE CAROL, marketing executive; b. Newport News, Va., Aug. 11, 1946; d. Kenneth Crawford and Helyn Elizabeth (Bull) Dempster; m. John Paul Blancq, Mar. 22, 1969 (dec. Jan. 1985); children—Eugenie Marie, Laura Elizabeth. B.A., U. Fla., 1968. Mem. prodn. dept. WSPA-TV-AM/FM, Spartanburg, S.C., 1970-71; payroll mgr., billing clk. Harvis Constrn. Co., Honolulu, 1972-74; promotion asst. KHON, Honolulu, 1975; creative services producer/writer WSPA, Spartanburg, S.C., 1976-77, WFBC, Greenville, S.C., 1977-78; advt. and promotion dir. KITV, Honolulu, 1979-85; mktg. mgr. Hawaiian Tel Employees Fed. Credit Union, 1985—. Mem. Broadcast Promotion Assn., Honolulu Ad Club, Zeta Phi Eta (Margaret Lee Meml. scholarship 1968), Kappa Alpha Theta (editor 1964—). Avocations: scuba diving; swimming; theatre; sailing.

BLAND, CARMEN LORETTA, information systems executive; b. Panama City, Fla., Dec. 2, 1949; d. Fred Frank and Ouida Madelyn (Downs) B. B.Liberal Arts, Ariz. State U., 1971; student U. Mexico, 1970, Glendale Community Coll., 1969; M.A. in Mgmt., U. Phoenix, 1986. Supr., Mountain Bell Co., Phoenix, 1971-76, assessment mgr., 1976-77, procurement mgr., 1977-83, info. mgr., 1984—. Active Big Sisters Ariz., 1976. Mem. Purchasing Mgmt. Assn. Ariz., Women in Mgmt. (v.p. 1983-84), Black Mgmt. Assn., Phi Theta Kappa. Democrat. Mem. Ch. Religious Sci. Home: Phoenix AZ 85051 Office: Mountain Bell 2601 E Magnolia St Rm 100 Phoenix AZ 85034

BLANDFORD, BRENDA, association executive; b. Loretto, Ky., Mar. 16, 1948; d. James Daniel and Nell (Lanham) Blandford; m. George L. Brooks, May 5, 1979. A.B., U. Ky., 1971. Customer startup Hydra Computer Corp., Raleigh, N.C., 1971-73; br. liaison officer 1st Citizens Bank, Raleigh, 1973-77; br. mgr. Hydra Computer Corp., Raleigh, 1977-79; user services rep. First VA Bank, Falls Church, Va., 1979-80; office system planning analyst Suburban Bank, Hyattsville, Md., 1980-82; dir. mgmt. info. processing Am. Soc. Hosp. Pharmacists, Bethesda, 1982—. Mem. Assn. Systems Mgmt., Women in Info. Processing, Info. and Image Processing Assn., Data Processing Mgmt. Assn. (awards chmn. 1973-75). Home: 17929 Archwood Way Olney MD 20832 Office: Am Soc Hosp Pharmacists 4630 Montgomery Ave Bethesda MD 20814

BLANE, BRENDA JO, social services organization executive; b. Louisville, Sept. 3, 1945; d. Rozelle F. and Johneva (Owsley) Poignard; m. Doye E. Blane, June 10, 1967; children—Doye Anton, Crystal Shaton. B.S., Ky. State U., 1967; M. Edn., Miami U., Oxford, Ohio, 1976. Cert. tchr., Ohio. Computer specialist Wright Patterson AFB (Ohio), 1967-70; tchr. Dayton pub. schs. (Ohio), 1971-79; spl. services coordinator Atlanta U., 1979-80; project dir. Urban League, Dayton, 1980-81, v.p. adminstrn., 1980-84, interim pres., 1984-85; community relations and youth adv. Dayton Pub. Schs., 1985—; cons. Bd. dirs. Minority Purchasing Council, Miami Valley Regional Planning Commn. (Ohio), Dayton Pvt. Industry Council, Leadership Dayton. Grantee Ednl. Policy Fellows Program, George Washington U., 1981; recipient Leadership Dayton 83 award, 1983. Mem. Phi Delta Kappa, Alpha Kappa Alpha. Democrat. Club: Zonta. Home: 3564 Cornell Dr Dayton OH 45406

BLANKE, GAIL ANN, communications executive; b. Cleve., Jan. 20, 1941; d. Warren J. and Isabelle (Voigt) B.; m. Franklin James Cusick, Feb. 22, 1969; children—Katharine Jennings, Abigail Jennings. A.B., Sweet Briar Coll., 1963. Mgr., Lifetime Sports Found., Washington, 1965-66, CBS, N.Y.C., 1966-69; v.p. Allen & Dorwood Advt., N.Y.C., 1969-72; v.p. communications Avon Products, Inc., N.Y.C., 1972—. Mem. Am. Women in Radio and TV (bd. dirs. 1971) , Internat. Assn. Bus. Communicators. Clubs: Metropolitan (N.Y.C.); Lawrence Beach (L.I., N.Y.); Rockaway Hunt (Cedarhurst, N.Y). Office: Avon Products Inc 9 W 57th St New York NY 10019

BLANKENHEIM, MARY VICTORIA, printing company executive; b. Milw., Mar. 15, 1950; d. John Nicholas and Margaret Catherine (Carpenter) Flessas; m. Charles John Blankenheim, Aug. 9, 1975. B.A., Alverno Coll., 1972. Account exec. Blankenheim Printing Co., Inc., Milw., 1979-81, v.p. sales, 1981-83, sec.-treas., 1983—. Mem. Women in Communications, Printing Industries Wis., Milw. Metro C. of C., Midwest Mfrs. Assn., U.S. Power Squadron. Democrat. Roman Catholic. Club: Milw. Litho. Home: 12221 W Rockne Ln Hales Corners WI 53130 Office: Blankenheim Printing Co Inc 2256 S 22d St Milwaukee WI 53215

BLANKENHEIMER, SUSAN LESLIE, government lawyer; b. Washington, Aug. 25, 1952; d. Bernard and Rosalind (Drescher) B.; m. Joseph J. Geraci, Jan. 9, 1982. Student Johannesburg, South Africa, 1968-70, London Poly. U., 1973; B.A. with honors, Syracuse U., 1974; J.D., Vanderbilt U., 1977. Bar: Pa. 1979, U.S. Ct. Appeals (D.C. cir.) 1980, U.S. Ct. Appeals (fed. cir.) 1982, D.C. 1984, N.Y. 1984, U.S. Supreme Ct. 1984. Law clk. Presdl. Clemency Bd., White House, Washington, summer 1975, FCC, Washington, summer 1976, Office Opinions and Rev., FCC, Washington, 1977-78; atty. Bur. Domestic Aviation, CAB, Washington, 1979-84, Office of Chief Counsel, Comptroller of Currency, Washington, 1985—. Assoc. editor Vanderbilt Jour. Transnat. Law, 1975-76, contbr. article to law jour. Recipient Spl. Achievement award CAB, 1980. Mem. Fed. Bar Assn., ABA, Pa. Bar Assn., N.Y. Bar Assn., D.C. Bar Assn., Eta Pi Upsilon, Pi Sigma Alpha, Alpha Chi Omega. Club: Internat. Aviation (Washington). Home: 5800 Nicholson Lane Apt #806 Rockville MD 20852 Office: Office of Chief Counsel Legis and Regulatory Analysis Div Comptroller of Currency 490 L'Enfant Plaza E SW Washington DC 20219

BLANKENSHIP, JENNY MARY, marketing company executive, fund raiser; b. Mpls., Nov. 15, 1955. A.A., Weatherford Coll., Tex., 1984; B.B.A., U. Tex.-Arlington, 1986. List aquisition coordinator Fingerhut, Minnetonka, Minn., 1978-80; pub. relations Family Service, Ft. Worth, 1983-85; dir. pub. relations Hope, Inc., Mineral Wells, Tex., 1985-86; pres. Gloss Mgmt., Weatherford, Tex., 1986—. Exhibited oil paintings. Contbr. articles to profl. jours. Neighborhood leader March of Dimes, Weatherford, Tex., 1984-86; bd. dirs. Social Service Bd., Weatherford, 1985-86. Mem. Nat. Assn. Female Execs., Bus. and Profl. Women, Phi Theta Kappa. Clubs: UMW (officer 1984-86), Civic (officer 1985-86) (Weatherford). Avocations: painting; singing.

BLANKINSHIP, KATHLEEN FLO, personal and professional development company executive, cleaning service executive, cosmetologist; b. Loma Linda, Calif., Nov. 5, 1947; d. Boyde Jefferson and Nell (Miller) Henderson; m. Floyd Jerome Smith, Oct. 25, 1969 (div. 1972); m. 2d Edwin Allen Blankinship, Oct. 15, 1977; 1 son, Robert Allen Smith. Cert. bookkeeping/acctg. Calif. Bus. Sch., San Bernardino, 1966; A.A., San Bernardino Valley Coll., 1975; student Riverside (Calif.) City Coll., 1985. Lic. Cosmetologist. Bookkeeper Laurentide Fin. Co., San Bernardino, 1969-70; loan officer Avco Thrift, San Bernardino, 1972-74; waitress Agro Land & Cattle, Colton, Calif., 1974-76; mem. advt. staff Holcombe Pub., San Bernardino, 1976-80; stylist, mgr. Mane St. Hair Design, Loma Linda, Calif., 1980-83; owner, profl. speaker, cons. U.&&I Enterprises, Grand Terrace, Calif., 1983—; organizational analyst Pomona Valley Praise Temple, Calif., 1985—; mentor Positive Force, Highland, Calif., 1985—. Author: Seasons of My Times, 1980; Winning Isn't For Everyone, 1986. Contbr. monthly make-over column to mag., 1980-83. Mem. Vols. in Child Abuse and Neglect, 1978; campaign worker McCartney for Judge, 1969-70. Mem. Nat. Assn. Female Execs., Women in Networking, Greater Riverside C. of C. (Chmn. Bus. in Action), Redlands C. of C. (ambassador), Riverside C. of C. Republican. Club: Toastmasters. Avocations: skiing, reading, personal development. Home: 12168 Mt Vernon St #51 Grand Terrace CA 92324 Office: U & I Enterprises PO Box 1737 Colton CA 92324

BLANKS, ARLENE LYNNETTE, lawyer; b. Washington, June 6, 1950; d. Isaac Renell and Elouise (Curry) Blanks; m. Donald W. Robinson, Aug. 1, 1980. B.A., Wayne State U., 1977, J.D., 1980. Bar: Mich. 1981; Ill. 1982; Tex. 1983. Assoc., Baxter & Hammond, Grand Rapids, Mich., 1980-81; law clerk to presiding justice U.S. Dist. Ct., Houston, 1982-83; staff trial atty CNA Ins. Co., Houston, 1983—. Active Democratic Party, Detroit, 1982. Recipient Bd. Gov.'s scholarship Wayne State U., 1979. Mem. State Bar Assn. Tex., State Bar Assn. Mich., Ill. State Bar Assn., ABA, Am. Judicature Soc. Congregationalist. Office: CNA Ins Cos Legal Dept 6565 W Loop S Suite 435 Bellaire TX 77401

BLANKSTEIN, MARY FREEMAN, violinist; b. Rutherfordton, N.C., Oct. 26; d. Spurgeon Lee and Dexter (Forney) Freeman; diploma (Sch. scholar) Juilliard Sch. Music, 1955, B.S., 1958; student (Fulbright fellow) Brussels Conservatoire, 1958-59; Mus.M., U. Maine, 1975; student Emmett Gore, Christine and Edouard Dethier, Arthur Grumiaux, Joseph Fuchs, Erica Morini, others; m. Joseph Blankstein, Mar. 6, 1958; children—Margot, Philip. Violin soloist Little Orch. Soc. in Town Hall, 1955; asst. concermaster Am. Symphony, N.Y.C., 1965-68, concertmaster, 1968-72; tchr. violin, prep. div. Juilliard Sch. Music, 1968-69; tchr. violin Manhattan Sch. Music, 1969—; pvt. tchr. violin and chamber music, 1970—; head instrumental dept. Chapin Sch., N.Y.C., 1973—; co-founder, mem. N.Y. Lyric Arts Trio, 1974-84; solo recitals, U.S. and Europe; co-founder Downeast Chamber Music Center, Castine, Maine, 1977, also mem. faculty; rec. artists Musical Heritage Soc. Rec., also recs. with Am. Symphony under Leopold Stokowski. Mem. Am. String Tchrs. Assn., Music Tchrs. Nat. Assn.

BLANTON, SALLY SAPPINGTON, service company executive; b. Longview, Tex., Aug. 12, 1939; d. John Monroe and Vyra Sue (Neely) Sappington; m. John R. Blanton, Sept. 9, 1959 (div. Mar. 1983); children—Bryan, Brent, Whitney. B.S., Tex. Christian U., 1961. Tchr. Richardson (Tex.) Ind. Schs., 1964-67; sales rep. Transart, Atlanta, 1977-78; program coordinator Human Potential Assn., Dallas, 1980-81; mem. bus. staff Dallas Bar Assn., 1981-82; v.p. Executmatch, Dallas, 1983; pres. Ultimate Matchmakers, Dallas, 1983—; lectr., 1983—; ptnr. Sex, Love and Money Dynamics, 1985; asst. to v.p. San Juan Pools, Dallas, 1976-77; model Sara Norton Agy., Dallas, 1978-80. Contbr. articles to mags. Past v.p. Cerebral Palsy Guild, Dallas, 1977—; active Golden Charity Guild, Parkland Burn Ctr., Dallas, March of Dimes, Dallas, Plaza Theatre Guild, Dallas, Dallas Mus. Fine Arts, Dallas Symphony Guild. Club: Turtlecreek Racquet. Home: 4404 Normandy Dallas TX 75205

BLANTON, SHIRLEY ANN, manufacturing official; b. Connersville, Ind., Nov. 6, 1949; d. Lawrence Michael and Catherine Ann (Pflum) Risch; B.S. in Prodn. Mgmt. (Hoosier scholar), Ball State U., Muncie, Ind., 1982; m. Randell Blanton, Apr. 20, 1968; children—James Randell, Angela Marie. Sec. purchasing Stant Mfg., Connersville, 1968-72; sec. customer service H.H. Robertson, Connersville, 1974-77, prodn. control coordinator, supr., 1977-81, mgr. prodn. control, 1981-84, mgr. material control, 1984—. Supr. Fayette County Girls Club; com. Fayette County blood drives, Fayette County Investment Club. Mem. Golden Key, Beta Gamma Sigma. Roman Catholic. Club: K.C. Aux. Home: Route 1 Box 108 Connersville IN 47331 Office: 800 W 18th St Connersville IN 47331

BLASS, ELIZABETH VICTORIA, writer, editor; b. Little Rock, Aug. 30, 1949; d. Noland, Jr. and Elizabeth (Weitzenhoffer) B. B.A., Fla. Presbyn. Coll., 1969. Columnist, editor Ark. Gazette, Little Rock, 1968-77; asst. account exec. Marsteller, Inc., N.Y.C., 1980-81; copywriter, account exec. Robert Landau Assocs., N.Y.C., 1981-83; sr. copywriter Hanley Partnership, N.Y.C., 1983-84; freelance writer, N.Y.C., 1984—. Bd. dirs. Little Rock Drug Abuse Coordinating Com., 1975, Community Photo-Film Workshop, Newburgh, N.Y., 1979-80. Mem. Nat. Assn. Female Execs., Sigma Delta Chi. Club: Jr. League Little Rock. Avocations: fishing; gardening; snowmobiling. Home: 78 Pomona Rd Suffern NY 10901

BLASSINGAME, SANDRA LOU, nurse, educator, university dean; b. Dallas, Nov. 8, 1937; d. James and Jessie (Leonard) Sears; B.S.N., Baylor U., 1960; M.S., Tex. Women's U., 1970; Ed.D., Nova U., 1980; m. Kenneth E. Blassingame, Sept. 27, 1963. Instr., Meth. Hosp. Sch. Nursing, Dallas, 1960-70; asst. prof. Dallas Bapt. U. Sch. Nursing, 1970-74, assoc. prof., 1974-81, prof., 1981—, dean Sch. Nursing, 1970—, assoc. dean acad. programs, 1981-82, dean acad. affairs, 1982—, acting v.p./dean of coll., 1984-85. Mem. Dist. 4 Tex. Nurses Assn. (dir. 1980-84), Tex. Nurses Assn. (dir., sec. 1982-84), Am. Nurses Assn., Nat. League for Nursing, Sigma Theta Tau. Democrat. Baptist. Club: Altrusa. Home: 6227 Highgate Ln Dallas TX 75214 Office: 7777 W Kiest St Dallas TX 75211

BLASZCZYNSKI, CAROL ANNE, industrial relations executive, business educator; b. Los Angeles, Apr. 6, 1957; d. Vincent Edward and Eva (Myson) Blaszczynski. B.S. in Bus. Edn., Calif. State U.-Los Angeles, 1978, M.A. in Bus. Edn., 1982. Sec. Union Oil Co. Calif., Los Angeles, 1979-82, indsl. relations asst., 1982—; instr. bus. edn. Calif. State U.-Los Angeles, 1982-83; cert. profl. sec. rev. instr. Mt. St. Mary's Coll., Los Angeles, 1983—. Mem. Am. Bus. Communication Assn., Am. Soc. Tng. and Devel., Am. Vocat. Assn., Calif. Bus. Edn. Assn., Internat. Soc. Bus. Edn., Nat. Bus. Edn. Assn., Profl. Secs. Internat., Western Bus. Edn. Assn., Theta Alpha Delta, Phi Beta Lambda, Delta Pi Epsilon. Office: Union Oil Co of Calif 461 S Boylston St Los Angeles CA 90017

BLATCHLEY, MARY ELIZABETH, nursing educator; b. Cleve., June 28, 1927; d. Frank H. and Emma (Blache) Bailey; m. Ernest R. Blatchley, June 3, 1950 (dec. July 1982); children—Carol, Barbara, Elizabeth, Ernest, Thomas. B.S., Adelphi Coll.; M.S., Purdue U.; D.N.S., Ind. U. Head nurse Jameson City Hosp., New Castle, Pa., 1950-51, Burnham City Hosp., Champaign, Ill., 1951-54; research asst. dept. psychology Purdue U., West Lafayette, Ind., 1966-68, asst. prof. Sch. Nursing, 1969-74, assoc. prof., 1974—, chmn. baccalaureate sect., 1979-85. Author: (with Holle) Introduction to Leadership and Management in Nursing, 1981; also articles. Mem. Am. Nurses Assn., Ind. Nurses Assn., Dist. 8 Nurses Assn. (dir. 1982—), AAUP, Ind. Pub. Health Assn., Sigma Theta Tau (chpt. Excellence in Edn. award 1983). Presbyterian. Office: Purdue U Sch of Nursing West Lafayette IN 47907

BLATT, GENEVIEVE, judge; b. East Brady, Pa., June 19, 1913; d. George F. and Clara M. (Laurent) B.; A.B., U. Pitts., 1933, M.A., 1934, J.D., 1937; LL.D. (hon.), St. Francis Coll., 1959, Villanova U., 1960, St. Joseph's Coll., 1964, Barry Coll., 1966, Seton Hill Coll., 1968, LaSalle Coll., 1970, Elizabethtown Coll., 1974, Dickinson Coll. Law, 1974, York Coll., 1975, St. Charles Sem., 1975, Cedarcrest Coll., 1976, Allentown Coll. of St. Francis de Sales, 1976. Mem. faculty U. Pitts., 1934-38; admitted to Pa. bar, 1938; sec., chief examiner Pitts. Civil Service Commn., 1938-42; asst. solicitor City of Pitts., 1941-45; dep. treas., exec. dir. Pa. State Dept. Treasury, 1945-49, sec. internal affairs, 1955-67, dir. departmental audits Auditor Gen., 1969; asst. dir. Pres.'s Office Econ. Opportunity, 1967-68; counsel Morgan, Lewis & Bockius, 1970-72; judge Commonwealth Ct. Pa., 1972-83, sr. judge, 1983—; mem. Pa. Bd. Pardons, 1955-67; sec. Pa. Indsl. Devel. Authority Bd. and Gen. State Authority Bd., 1956-67; Pa. del. to Interstate Oil Compact Commn., 1955-67, vice chmn., 1959-60; mem. weights and measures adv. com. Nat. Bur. Standards, 1960-67; mem. Pres.'s Commn. on Law Enforcement and Adminstrn. of Justice, 1965-67. Founder, exec. dir. Pa. Intercollegiate Conf. on Govt., 1934-72; founder, v.p. James A. Finnegan Fellowship Found., 1960—; bd. dirs. Center for Research in Apostolate, 1966-75, 80—; vice chmn. adv. council Nat. Conf. of Cath. Bishops, 1972-75; chmn. Harrisburg Cath. Diocesan Bicentennial Com., 1974-76; mem. exec. bd. Pa. Fedn. Democratic Women, 1940-72; del. Dem. Nat. Convs., 1936-68; Pa. Dem. Nat. Committeewoman, 1970-72; bd. mgrs. 41st Internat. Eucharistic Congress, 1975-76. Recipient Disting. Dau. Pa. award, 1956; Outstanding Citizenship award LWV, 1964; Pro Ecclesia et Pontifice medal, 1966; Phila. FAME award, Greater Phila. Women's Clubs, 1978; Bene Merenti medal Pope John Paul II, 1979. Mem. Am. Bar Found., ABA, Pa. Bar Assn., Dauphin County Bar Assn., Am. Judicature Soc., Nat. Assn. Women Judges, Nat. Assn. Women Lawyers, Nat. Bus. and Profl. Women's Clubs, Phi Beta Kappa, Delta Sigma Rho, Pi Tau Phi, Pi Sigma Alpha, Beta Sigma Phi, Delta Kappa Gamma. Clubs: Nat. Cath. War Veterans Aux., Nat. Cath. Women's Union, Eagles Aux., Soroptimists Internat., Altrusa. Office: 504 S Office Bldg Harrisburg PA 17120

BLATT, SUSANNE RENATE, lawyer; b. Vienna, Austria, Sept. 21, 1937; came to U.S., 1940, naturalized, 1945; d. Walter and Flora (Singer) Schwarz; m. S. Leslie Blatt, Mar. 22, 1959; children—J. Daniel, Jeremy, Elliott. B.A. in Psychology, Douglass Coll., 1959; M.A. in Edn., Ohio State U., 1970, J.D., 1980. Bar: Ohio 1980, U.S. Dist. Ct. (no. and so. dists.) Ohio 1981. Asst. psychometrist Stanford (Calif.) U., 1959; statis. analyst Fairchild Corp., Mountain View, Calif., 1959-61; tchr. Newark (Calif.) Elem. Schs., 1961-62, Palo Alto (Calif.) Elem. Schs., 1962; tchr., evaluator Columbus (Ohio) Schs. 1974-77; ptnr. Cloppert, Portman, Sauter, Latanick & Foley, Columbus, 1980—; lectr. student and tchr. groups, vol. orgns.; adj. instr. legal writing Ohio State Coll. Law, 1984, 85. Mem. exec. com. Community Assn. Upper Arlington (Ohio) Schs., 1970-76; pres. North Side Jewish Community Assn., Columbus, 1973-74; bd. dirs. Vol. Action Ctr., Columbus, 1975-77. State of N.J. 4-yr. acad. scholar. Mem. ABA, Ohio Bar Assn. (sch. law com.), Columbus Bar Assn. (family law com.), Phi Delta Kappa. Office: Cloppert Portman Sauter Latanick and Foley 225 E Broad St Columbus OH 43215

BLATTNER, MEERA MCCUAIG, educator; b. Chgo., Aug. 14, 1930; d. William D. McCuaig and Nina (Spertus) Klevs; B.A., U. Chgo., 1952; M.S., U. So. Calif., 1966; Ph.D., UCLA, 1973; m. Minao Kamegai, June 22, 1983; children—Douglas, Robert, William. Research fellow in computer sci. Harvard U., 1973-74; asst. prof. Rice U., 1974-80; assoc. prof. applied sci. U. Calif. at Davis, Livermore, 1980—; adj. prof. U. Tex., Houston, 1977—; vis. prof. U. Paris, 1980; program dir. theoretical computer sci. NSF, Washington, 1979-80; NSF grantee, 1977-81. Mem. Soc. Women Engrs., Assn. Computing Machinery (editor SIGACT News 1981-84), IEEE Computer Soc. Contbr. articles to profl. jours. Home: 908 Florence Rd Livermore CA 94550 Office: Dept Applied Sci U Calif Davis/Livermore Livermore CA 94550

BLATZ, KATHLEEN ANN, state legislator; B.A. summa cum laude, U. Notre Dame, 1976; M.S.W., U. Minn., 1978; J.D. cum laude, U. Minn., 1984. Psychiat. social worker, 1979-81; mem. Minn. Ho. of Reps., St. Paul, 1978—, chmn. crime and family law, fin. instns. and ins. coms.; mem. Legis. Commn. to Rev. Adminstrv. Rules, Council on Econ. Status of Women. Mem. LWV, Minn. Mental Health Assn., Phi Beta Kappa. Independent Republican. Office: State Office Bldg Saint Paul MN 55155

BLAU, FLORENCE HARRIETT, public relations and editorial cons.; b. Bklyn., July 19, 1928; d. Henry Morris and Elsie Rebecca (Weiss) Berman; B.A., N.Y. U., 1948; m. Edmund J. Blau, Apr. 7, 1946; (div. Dec. 1967); children—Barbara, Richard, Henry. Retail account exec. Berry & Price Advt., Washington, 1971; editorial asst. U.S. C. of C., Washington, 1971-73; public relations and community relations specialist, dir. vol. services Greater S.E. Community Hosp., Washington, 1973-78; public relations cons., copy editor Smithsonian Expn. Books, 1979-81; public relations and editorial cons., Washington, 1981—; communications prodn. editor Nat. Assn. Mfrs., 1984—. Active Explorer program Boy Scouts Am., 1974-78; 2d v.p., spl. events chmn. S.E. unit Am. Cancer Soc., 1974-80, trustee D.C. div., 1976—. Community Service award, 1981; public relations chmn. D.C. Congress PTAs, 1978-79; bd. dirs. Potomac River Jazz Club, 1983. Recipient cert. of appreciation Nat. Press Club, 1985. Mem. Nat. Press Club, Public Relations Soc. Am., Capital Press Club, Lit. Group No. Va. Club: Potomac River Jazz. Copy editor: The American Land, 1979; Every Four Years: The American Presidency, 1980; Fire of Life: The Smithsonian Book of the Sun, 1981. Address: 720 Beall Ave Rockville MD 20850

BLAUCH, BRENDA GAIL, systems analyst; b. Lancaster, Pa., Nov. 16, 1956; d. Thomas William and Ruth Ann (Shannon) B. A.S., Hillsborough Community Coll., 1980. Programmer I.X. Software, Inc., Tampa, Fla., 1981-83; systems analyst Fotomat Corp., St. Petersburg, Fla., 1983—. Mem. Ms. Found. for Women, Women's Sports Found. Democrat. Avocations: softball; racquetball; reading. Office: Fotomat Corp 205 9th St N St Petersburg FL 33701

BLAUFELD, LOIS MYRA, weight control firm executive; b. Pitts., July 9, 1934; d. Nathan Morris and Bessie (Rosenburg) Katz; m. Samuel S. Blaufeld, Sept. 23, 1956; 1 child, Henry Neal. B.F.A., Chatham Coll., 1956. Apprentice, Lando Advt., Pitts., 1952-56; advt. mgr. Lane Bryant, Pitts., 1956-59; adminstr. Assoc. Artists, Pitts., 1959-62; dir. Diet Workshop Western Pa., Pitts., 1972—; instr. informal courses Chatham Coll., Pitts., 1975—; presenter various womens' networking confs., Pitts., 1970's—, 4th Ann. Civil Rights Conf., United Steelworkers Am., 1985; bd. dirs. Job Adv. Service, Pitts., 1984—. Contbg. editor Pitts. Preview Mag., 1983—. Mem. Exec. Women's Council, Bus. and Profl. Women Pitts., AAUW, Chatham Coll. Alumnae Assn. (bd. dirs. 1985—), Zonta Internat. (bd. dirs. 1984—), Am. Soc. for Tng. and Devel., Nat. Council Jewish Women. Democrat. Jewish. Lodge: Hadassah. Avocations: reading, walking. Office: Diet Workshop care Kaufmann's 400 5th Ave Pittsburgh PA 15218

BLAUVELT, MELINDA, photographer, educator; b. Northampton, Mass., Sept. 15, 1949; d. Theodore Orlando and Melba Alice (Miller) B.; student Mt. Holyoke Coll., 1967-69; B.A., Yale U., 1971, M.F.A., 1973; m. Edwin E. Wells, Jr., July 3, 1982. One person shows: Harvard U., 1977, 78, Bayly Mus. U. Va., 1980, Wright Art Center Beloit (Wis.) Coll., 1981, Southeastern Center Contemporary Art, Winston-Salem, 1981, Mattingly-Baker Gallery, Dallas, 1982; group shows include: Yale Art Gallery, 1973, Addison Gallery of Am. Art, 1975, Harvard U., 1975, Va. Mus., Richmond, 1980, Nexus, Atlanta, 1980, Corcoran Gallery Art, Washington, 1981, 82, The Photography Gallery, La Jolla, Calif., 1982; Mus. Fine Arts, Houston, 1982; represented in permanent collections: Mus. Fine Arts, Houston, Dallas Mus. Fine Arts, Bayly Mus. U. Va., Corcoran Gallery of Art; lectr. art Smith Coll., 1974; teaching asst. Harvard U., 1974-75, lectr. visual and environ. studies, 1975-76, research fellow Carpenter Center for the Visual Arts, 1977-78; asst. prof. art U. Va., 1978—. Contbr. articles in field to profl. jours. Office: McIntire Department of Art Fayerweather Hall University of Virginia Charlottesville VA 22903

BLAYTON, DORIS, lawyer, educator; b. Atlanta; d. Jesse Bee and Willa May Blayton; A.B., Spelman Coll.; postgrad. U. Chgo., 1943-44; J.D., John Marshall Law Sch., 1949; M.B.A., Atlanta U., 1962, M.Ed., 1977. Mem. staff Jesse B. Blayton, C.P.A., Atlanta, 1943-77; admitted to Ill. bar, 1950, Ga. bar, 1951; mem. firm Daugherty & Combs, Atlanta, W.M. Mathews and D.A. Blayton, Atlanta; mem. faculty Ga. State Indsl. Coll., 1944-45, Ark. A.M.&N. Coll., 1966-67; supply tchr., Atlanta, 1974—. Mem. Nat. Bar Assn., State Bar Ga., Atlanta Bar Assn., Gate City Bar Assn., Black Women's Coalition of Atlanta, Nat. Council Negro Women, NEA, Ga. Edn. Assn., Atlanta Consumers Clubs, Delta Sigma Theta. Home and office: 1235 ML King Jr Dr SW Atlanta GA 30314

BLAZEK, MARY ANNE, editor; b. Fairmont, W. Va., Oct. 15, 1951; d. Edward Joseph and Ida Elizabeth (Vincent) Blazek; m. Richard Carlton Gayle, Aug. 13, 1982; 1 son, Matthew Carlton. B.A., Memphis State U., 1981, Coll. William and Mary, 1974; M.S., U. Tenn.-Knoxville, 1976. Asst. editor U. Tenn. Office Continuing Social Work Edn., Knoxville, 1977-80; editorial asst. and copy editor Memphis Pub. Co., 1981; mktg. mgr. Memphis State U. Continuing Edn. Dept., 1981-84; editorial cons. U. Tenn. Ctr. for Health Sci., 1984; condr. workshops in field; freelance editor, editorial cons. Editor, copywriter, creative co-dir. continuing edn. catalogs, 1982. Vol. basketball coach Knoxville Youth Basketball League, YMCA, 1980. Home: 912 Onslow Dr Greensboro NC 27408

BLECHER, HILARY, theatre director, educator; b. Johannesburg, Transvaal, South Africa, Nov. 14, 1941; came to U.S., 1981; d. Julius Ralph and Zelda Sonia (Wulfsohn) Shotland Goldberg; m. Basil Blecher, Aug. 30, 1964; children—Lisa, Sara, Gabriele. B.A., U. Witwatersrand, Johannesburg, 1961, B.A. with honors in Theatre, 1976, M.A. in Theatre, 1981. Resident dir. The Market Theatre, Johannesburg, 1978-81; tchr., theatre dir. U. Witwatersrand, 1977-85; theatre dir. South Africa, U.S.A., Scotland, Eng., Australia, Can.; lectr. Smith Coll., Mass., 1983, on narrative theatre U. So. Fla., 1984. Dir.: New York, 1982-83, Poppie Nongena (recipient Obie, Outer-Critics award), Trio, 1984, From a Small Room, 1985. Bd. dirs. Arts at St. Anns, Bklyn., 1983—. Nominated for Laurence Oliver award, 1985. Home: 3 Pierrepont Pl New York NY 11201

BLECK, PATRICIA MEA, architect; b. Chgo., Sept. 6, 1958; d. William Joseph and Patricia Joan (Finn) Mea; m. Robert Frank Bleck, June 11, 1983. B.S., U. Ill., 1981. Intern architect Hightower/Alexander, architects/planners, Bellaire, Tex., 1981—. Mem. AIA, Tex. Soc. Architects (assoc.), Landmarks Preservation Council Ill., Ill. State Hist. Soc., Alpha Phi Omega. Office: Hightower/Alexander 411 1st St Bellaire TX 77401

BLECK, PHYLLIS CLAIRE, physician and surgeon, musician; b. Oak Park, Ill., Mar. 10, 1936; d. William Fred and Mildred A. (Jones) B.; B.S., U. Ill., 1958; M.M., Northwestern U., 1968; D.M.A., U. So. Calif., 1970; postgrad. Autonoma U. of Guadalajara, Mex., 1973-76; M.D., Rush Med. Coll., 1979; M.S. in Surgery, U. Ill., 1983. Prin. trumpet Fla. Symphony Orch., 1960-66, Orch. Sinfonica Nat. de Peru, 1965; instr. Thornton Jr. Coll., 1966-68; lectr. U. So. Calif., 1969-73; asst. prof. Whittier Coll., 1973; asst. in gen. surgery Rush Presbyn. St. Luke's Med. Center, Chgo., 1979-82, instr. gen. surgery, 1982-84; resident in cardiothoracic surgery U. Medicine and Dentistry N.J., 1984—. Mem. Kappa Delta Pi, Pi Kappa Lambda, Sigma Alpha Iota. Editor: Mozart Divertimento for Winds; research on vascular ischemia.

BLEICH, ANNA LORETTA, nurse; b. Mineville, N.Y., Feb. 18, 1924; d. John Francis and Louise Marie (Fields) McKown; R.N., Champlain Valley Hosp., Plattsburg, N.Y., 1944; B.S. in Nursing, Northwestern State U., Shreveport, 1970; M.Ed., Northwestern State U., Natchitoches, La., 1971; M.S. in Nursing U. Tex., 1973; m. LaMoyne Charles Bleich, May 6, 1946; children—Edward Joseph, John Francis, Anne Marie, Rebecca. Pvt. duty nurse, Washington, 1944; instr. Washington Vis. Nurse Soc., 1946-47; mem. nursing staff Park Ave. Hosp., Rochester, N.Y., 1947-48; vol. ARC, 1955-65; regional dir. continuing edn. in nursing Northwestern State U., 1971-72; instr. med.-surg. nursing Northeastern La. U., Monroe, 1972-73, asst. prof., then assoc. prof., 1973-74; asso. prof. Northwestern State U., Shreveport, 1975-76; pvt. practice psychotherapy, Ruston, 1976—; dir. religious edn. St. Thomas Ch. Pres. Mental Health Assn. Lincoln Parish, 1978-79, chmn. edn. program, 1979—; bd. dirs. Ruston Emergency Pregnancy Service, Ruston Alcohol and Substance Abuse Clinic; past pres., disaster chmn. ARC, Lincoln Parish. Served to 1st lt. Army Nurse Corps. 1945-46. Mem. Am. Nurses Assn., Nat. League Nursing, Council Advanced Practitioners in Psychiat.-Mental Health Nursing. Am. Personnel and Guidance Assn., Am. Orthopsychiat. Assn., La. Nurses Assn., Nurses Coalition for Action in Politics, Ruston Dist. Nurses Assn., LWV, Ruston Bus. and Profl. Women, Phi Kappa Phi, Sigma Theta Tau. Republican. Roman Catholic. Home: 1004 D'Arbonne St Ruston LA 71270 Office: 810 Carey St Ruston LA 71270

BLEVINS, ANNE HELEN, microbiologist; b. Kankakee, Ill.; d. George and Mary Anne (Hoffman) B.; R.N., Wausau Meml. Hosp. Sch. Nursing, 1927; student Columbia U., 1929-36, Marquette U., 1941, N.Y. U., postgrad. Med. Sch., Columbia U., 1936. Research asso. Post Grad. Hosp., Columbia U., N.Y.C., 1940-47; chief bacteriologist Univ. Hosp., N.Y.U. Bellevue Med. Center, 1948-53; chief supervising bacteriologist Meml. Hosp., Meml. Sloan-Kettering Cancer Center, N.Y.C., 1953-68, asst. to dir., 1968-85; cons. hosp. epidemiology. Recipient Elizabeth O. King award in clin. microbiology Am. Soc. Microbiology, 1970. Fellow Am. Acad. Microbiology; mem. Am. Soc. Microbiology, Am. Pub. Health Assn. (life), N.Y. Acad. Scis. (life). Club: Soroptimist International of New York. Home: 501 W 123d St New York NY 10027 Office: Memorial Hosp 1275 York Ave New York NY 10021

BLEVINS, SANDRA LEE COWAN, educator; b. Morristown, Tenn., Apr. 15, 1941; d. Thomas Ewing and Anna Marie (Russ) Cowan; m. Raymond Dean Blevins, Aug. 11, 1962; children—Raymond Dean, Robert Lee, Lisa Dawn, Mary Vee. B.S., East Tenn. State U., 1962, Ed.D., 1979; M.Math., U. Tenn., 1970. Cert. tchr., supr., prin., Tenn. Tchr., Va. High Sch., Bristol, 1962-64, Overton High Sch., Memphis, 1965-66, East Tenn. State U. High Sch., Johnson City, 1974-75, Happy Valley High Sch., Elizabethton, Tenn., 1978-79; adminstrv. asst. dept. ob-gyn East Tenn. State U. Coll. Medicine, Johnson City, 1980-82; tchr. math. Daniel Boone High Sch., Gray, Tenn., 1982—. East Tenn. State U. scholar, 1959-62; NSF fellow, 1969-70, doctoral fellow, 1976-79. Mem. Nat. Council Tchrs. of Math., Athean Lit. Soc. (life), Women of Coll. Medicine, Johnson City Christian Women's Club, Nat. Assn. Female Execs., NEA, Tenn. Edn. Assn. Sunday Sch. tchr. Central Bapt. Ch., Johnson City, also vacation Bible sch. prin., circle pres.; pres. Univ. Sch. PTA, 1974-75. Club: Altrusa (v.p. 1985-86). Avocations: reading; sewing; singing; piano; travel. Home: 1401 Buffalo St Johnson City TN 37601

BLIESE, KATHLEEN ANDERSON, physician, nutrition consultant; b. Elk Horn, Iowa, Mar. 23, 1940; d. Arnold and Leona Christine (Gregersen) Anderson; m. Arthur Paul Bliese, Jr., Sept. 2, 1959. Student Lutheran Bible Inst., Mpls., 1958-59; B.A. in Gen. Sci., Dana Coll., Blair, Nebr., 1962; M.D., U. Nebr., 1967; postgrad. Nancy Bounds, Internat., Omaha, 1985; drama student of David Varnay, 1985. Diplomate Am. Bd. Family Practice. Practice medicine specializing in family practice, Omaha, 1968-69; med. dir. refugee camps, mem. med. team Lutheran World Relief, Nigeria, 1969-70; med. dir., founder Lamb Hosp., Bangladesh, 1970-80; practice medicine Northwest Clinic, Omaha, 1980—; med. dir., assoc. dir. World Wide Ministries, Omaha, 1981—; owner A and K Assocs. style and nutrition cons., 1981—; nutrition cons. Shaklee, Inc., Omaha, 1983—; speaker on religion and nutrition. Author, dir. program on rural health devel. in Bangladesh, 1976-80 (Best Internat. Program award 1983). Speaker radio program Kindle the Flame, 1981—. Adviser to women's ministry bd. Christ Luth. Ch., Omaha, 1981—; bd. dirs. children's tv program Jean's Story Time, 1983—. Named Nebr. Outstanding Young Woman of Yr., 1968; recipient Disting. Alumnus award Dana Coll., 1978, Woman of Achievement award Mrs. Nebr. Pageant, 1984, 1st runner-up Mrs. Nebr. Pageant, 1985. Fellow Am. Acad. Family Practice; mem. AMA (nat., state and county chpts.), Women's Am. Med. Assn., World Med. Assn. Republican. Lutheran. Avocations: writing music; acting; trombonist; sewing; knitting; swimming; skiing. Home: 6024 N 110th Plaza Omaha NE 68164 Office: Northwest Clinic 2734 N 61st St Omaha Ne 68104

BLISS, ANNA CAMPBELL, artist, architect; b. Morristown, N.J., July 10, 1925; d. Leo Manning and Agnes McManus Campbell; m. Robert Lewis Bliss, Apr. 2, 1949. B.A., Wellesley Coll., 1946; M.Arch., Harvard U., 1950; postgrad. MIT, U. Minn., U. Utah. Ptnr., Bliss and Campbell, Architects, Salt Lake City, 1956—; cons. and lectr. to profl. orgns. and workshops in color for architecture. One-person shows, group shows, gallery exhibits, collections in art throughout the world. Contbr. articles to profl. jours. Recipient numerous awards and grants in art and architecture; Graham Found. grantee to support color research and experimentation, 1980. Mem. adv. bd. Repertory Dance Theatre, 1965-70, Utah Mus. Fine Arts, 1972—; bd. dirs. Utah Arts Festival, 1979-81; design bd. Salt Lake City Art Design Bd., 1979-84; exec. bd. Walker Art Ctr. Arts Council. Mem. Am. Soc. Interior Designers (chmn. del. 1976-84, Presdl. citation 1981), Inter-Soc. Color Council (bd. dirs. 1983-86), Artists Equity, Color Mktg. Group, Contemporary Arts Group (pres. 1984-85, conf. chmn. 1985). Home: 27 University St Salt Lake City UT 84102

BLISS, JUDITH S., software development company executive; b. Plainfield, N.J., Jan. 16, 1947; d. John C. and Mary (Gibriano) Serido; 1 child, David Anthony. A.A., Union Coll., N.J., 1968; B.A., Syracuse U., 1970. Tech. cons. Carrier Corp., Syracuse, N.Y., 1969-72; mgr. distbn. Polaroid Corp., Needham, Mass., 1972-80; v.p. Distbn. Mgmt. Systems, Bedford, Mass., 1980-81; pres. Methods & Solutions, Stoneham, Mass., 1981—. Mem. Smaller Bus. Assn. New Eng. Home: 6 Leeland Terr Lexington MA 02173

BLISSIT, MARY LOU, pharmaceutical company researcher; b. Corinth, Miss., Mar. 26, 1945; d. James Turner and Sarah Elizabeth (Haynes) B. B.A., U. Miss., 1969; M.Combined Scis., Delta State U., 1972; postgrad. U. Miss., 1973-76. Med. rep. Ciba-Gigey, Summit, N.J., 1976-77; regional dir. BBL-Microbiol., Cockey's Ville, Md., 1977-78; sales rep. Boehringer Ingelheim Pharms., Kansas City, Kans., 1978-81, hosp. rep., Chgo., 1981-84, clin. research assoc., Los Angeles, 1984—; instr. Sch. Pharmacy, U. Miss., 1973-76. Named Outstanding Educator, Am. Soc. Microbiology, 1971; Sponsor of Yr., YWCA-Little Rock, 1973. Mem. Assocs. Clin. Pharmacology, Nat. Assn. Female Execs. Avocation: sailing. Office: Boehringer Ingelheim Pharms PO Box 11356 Marina Del Rey CA 90292

BLITZ, JEANETTE, furniture co. exec.; b. Poland, May 8, 1927; came to U.S., 1949, naturalized, 1954; d. Moses and Tsylia (Katz) Sobol; student public schs., Europe; m. John P. Pollak, Nov. 18, 1973; children by previous marriage—Regina, Mark, Helen. With Original Arts Mfg. Corp., Linden, N.J., 1956—; chmn. bd., pres. Andre Originals, Linden, 1969—; cons. on furniture design. Office: 2301 E Edgar Rd Linden NJ 07036

BLIZNAKOV, MILKA TCHERNEVA, architect; b. Varna, Bulgaria, Sept. 20, 1927; d. Ivan Dimitrov and Maria Kesarova (Khorozova) Tchernev; came to U.S., 1961, naturalized, 1966; architect-engr. diploma, State Tech. U., Sofia, 1951; Ph.D., Engring.-Structural Inst., Sofia, 1955-59; Ph.D. in Architecture, Columbia U., 1971; m. Emile G. Bliznakov, Oct. 23, 1954 (div. Apr. 1974). Sr. researcher Ministry Heavy Industry, Sofia, 1950-53; practice architecture, Sofia, 1954-59; asso. architect Noel Combrisson, architect, Paris, 1959-61; designer Perkins & Will Partnership, White Plains, N.Y., 1963-67; project architect Lathrop Douglass, architect, N.Y.C., 1967-71; asso. prof. architecture and planning Sch. Architecture, U. Tex., Austin, 1972-74; prof. architecture and planning Coll. Architecture, Va. Poly. Inst. and State U., Blacksburg, 1972—; prin. works include Speedwell Ave. Urban Renewal, Morristown, N.J., 1967-69, Wilmington (Del.) Urban Renewal, 1968-70, Springfield (Ill.) Central Area Devel., 1969-71, Arlington County (Va.) Redevel., 1975-77. William Kinne scholar, summer 1970; NEA grantee, 1973-74, Am. Beautiful Found., 1973; Fulbright Hays research fellow, 1984. Mem. Am. Assn. Tchrs. Slavic and E. European Langs., Soc. Archtl. Historians, Nat. Trust Historic Preservation, Am. Assn. Advancement of Slavic Studies, Assn. Collegiate Schs. Planning, Assn. Collegiate Schs. Architecture, Inst. Modern Russian Culture (chmn. architecture). Home: 219 Pine Dr Blacksburg VA 24060 Office: DEUS Coll Architecture Va Poly Inst and State Univ Blacksburg VA 24060

BLIZNIK, LUENDINA BARBARA, printing plant executive; b. Binghamton, N.Y., July 24, 1927; d. Pasquale and Laura (Marcello) DiFulvio; m. Bernard Alfred Bliznik, Apr. 24, 1948; children—Bernard James, Mark Anthony, Brian James. Sec., Union Press Co., Inc., Endicott, N.Y., 1959—. Democrat. Roman Catholic. Avocations: shelling; swimming; crocheting; walking. Office: Union Press Co Inc 305 Garfield Ave Endicott NY 13760

BLOCH, BARBARA JOYCE, author, editor; b. N.Y.C., May 26, 1925; d. Emil William and Dorothy (Lowengrund) Bloch; m. Joseph B. Sanders, Aug. 3, 1944 (div. 1961); children—Elizabeth Sanders-Hines, Ellen Janice Benjamin; m. 2d, Theodore S. Benjamin, Sept. 20, 1964. Student NYU, 1943-45, New Sch. Social Research, 1966. Office mgr. Writers War Bd., N.Y.C., 1943-45, Westchester Democratic Com., White Plains, N.Y., 1955-56; mgr. Westchester Symphony Orch., 1957-62; mng. editor Cooking Ency., Rutledge Books, N.Y.C., 1970-71; pres. Internat. Cookbook Services, White Plains, 1978—; columnist House Beautiful, 1984—; cons. in field; tchr. cooking classes White Plains, 1975-80; lectr. in field. Author: Anyone Can Quilt, 1975; Meat Board Meat Book, 1977; If It Doesn't Pan Out, 1981; Garnishing Made Easy, 1983; editor/author: All Beef Cookbook, 1973; In Glass Naturally, 1974; Fresh Ideas with Mushrooms, 1977; Holly Farms Complete Chicken Cookbook, 1984; Gulden's Cookbook, 1985; Am. adapter The Cuisine of Olympe, 1983, Baking Easy and Elegant, 1984, Best of Cold Foods, 1985, Cakes and Pastries, 1985, series of 12 Creative Cuisine books, 1985, The Art of Cooking, 1986; editor contbr. various books; contbr. articles to profl. jours. Nat. bd. dirs. Emcampment for Citizenship, N.Y.C., 1966-72; bd. dirs. YWCA Central Westchester, 1965-71, Westchester Ethical Humanist Soc., 1968-70; exec. com., pres. Internat. Student Exchange of White Plains, 1955-70. Jewish. Home: 21 Dupont Ave White Plains NY 10605 Office: Internat Cookbook Services 21 Dupont Ave White Plains NY 10605

BLOCH, JULIA CHANG, government official; b. Chefoo, China, Mar. 2, 1942; came to U.S., 1951, naturalized, 1962; d. Fu-yun and Eva Chang; B.A., U. Calif., Berkeley, 1964; M.A., Harvard U., 1967; m. Stuart Marshall Bloch, Dec. 21, 1968. With Peace Corps, Sabah, Malaysia, 1964-66, tng. officer, Washington, 1967-68, evaluation officer, 1968-70; staff mem. minority staff Senate Select Com. Nutrition & Human Needs, 1971-76, chief minority counsel, 1976-77; dep. dir. Office African Affairs, U.S. Internat. Communication Agy., 1977-80; Inst. of Politics fellow Harvard U., Cambridge, Mass., 1980-81; asst. adminstr. Bur. for Food for Peace and Voluntary Assistance, AID, 1981—. Mem. adv. bd. Nat. Women's Polit. Caucus, 1978-84. Recipient Hubert Humphrey award internat. service, 1979. Mem. Orgn. Chinese Am. Women (chmn. bd. dirs.). Republican. Office: Agy for Internat Devel Dept of State Room 3938 Washington DC 20523

BLOCH, KAREN MARIE, systems engineer; b. Wilmington, Del., Apr. 11, 1963; d. Leonard J. and Elizabeth C. (Dzielak) B. B.S. in Computer Sci., U. Del., 1985. Programmer, U. Del., Newark, 1981-83, PNC Nat. Bank, Wilmington, 1983-85; sr. programmer JMI Software, Inc., Spring House, Pa., 1985-86; systems engr. Computer Task Group, Phila., 1986—. Avocations: skiing; hiking; biking; reading; needlework. Home: 405 Becker Ave Wilmington DE 19804 Office: 8 Penn Center Suite 1350 Philadelphia PA 19103

BLOCH, SUSAN LOW, law educator; b. N.Y.C., Sept. 15, 1944; d. Ernest and Ruth (Frankel) Low; m. Richard I. Bloch, July 10, 1966; children—Rebecca, Michael. B.A. in Math., Smith Coll., 1966; M.A. in Math., U. Mich., 1968, Ph.C., M.A. in Computer Sci., 1972, J.D., 1975. Bar: D.C. 1975. Law clk. to chief judge U.S. Ct. Appeals, Washington, 1975-76; law clk. to assoc. justice Marshall, U.S. Supreme Ct., Washington, 1976-77; assoc. Wilmer, Cutler & Pickering, Washington, 1978-82; assoc. prof. Georgetown U. Law Ctr., Washington, 1983—; contbr. Mich. Law Rev., Wis. Law Rev., Supreme Ct. Preview, 1984, Voice of Am., 1983. Active, Common Cause, ACLU, Women's Legal Def. Fund. Mem. ABA, D.C. Bar, Women's Bar Assn., Soc. Am. Law Tchrs., Inst. Pub. Representation (dir.), Order of Coif, Phi Beta Kappa, Sigma Xi. Home: 4335 Cathedral Ave NW Washington DC 20016 Office: Georgetown U Law Ctr 600 New Jersey Ave NW Washington DC 20001

BLOCK, JANET LEVEN (MRS. JOSEPH E. ROSEN), public relations executive; b. Chgo.; d. Benjamin J. and Rosebud (Goldsmith) Leven; student Brenau Coll. for Women, Gainesville, Ga., Northwestern U.; m. Albert William Block, Sept. 27, 1947; m. Joseph E. Rosen, Dec. 5, 1985; children—Mitchell, Stephanie. Reporter, Chgo. Am. Newspaper, 1939-40; catalog advt. Alden's Chgo. Mail Order Co., N.Y.C., Chgo., 1940-42; stylist and public relations dir. Fashion Advt. Co., N.Y.C., 1942-44; asst. account exec., stylist Buchanan & Co., Advt. Agy., N.Y.C., 1944-46; advt. agy account exec. Abbott Kimball Co., Chgo., 1946-47; free-lance merchandising and public relations rep., Cin., 1960-64; v.p. public relations Lazarus (previously Shillito's), Cin., 1964—. Bd. dirs. Children's Heart Assn., 1975—; bd. dirs. Friends of City Parks, 1979-80, treas., 1982; adv. bd. Hoxworth Blood Ctr., 1982—; bd. dirs. ARC, 1984—, Salvation Army, Great Rivers council Girl Scouts U.S.A., 1980-83 Family Service, 1985—. Named YWCA Career Woman of Achievement, 1982. Mem. Fashion Group Cin. (past regional dir.), Downtown Council (promotion chmn. 1975-76, 80-81), Public Relations Soc. Am. (dir. 1974-75, sec. 1976, treas. 1977), TV Soc. Am., Bus. and Profl. Women's Club, Advt. Club. Cin. (dir. 1967—, v.p. 1972, Advt. Woman of Yr. 1972, mem. Speakers Bur. 1973—, pres. 1973-74, AAF Silver medal 1976), Women in Communications. Home: Shillito's Pub Relations Dept 7th and Race Sts Cincinnati OH 45202

BLOCK, MARCENE BURGESS, lawyer; b. Salina, Kans., May 15, 1954; d. Richard Benton and Marcene (Reynolds) Burgess; m. Frank Emmanuel Block, Jr., Nov. 15, 1975; 1 child, Frank Emmanuel III. Student, Smith Coll., 1972-74; B.A., U. Va.-Charlottesville, 1976, J.D., 1979. Bar: N.C. 1980, Fla. 1984. Assoc. law firm Everett, Creech & Hancock, Durham, N.C., 1981-82; sole practice law, Durham, N.C., 1982-83, Vero Beach, Fla., 1984—. Mem. ABA, N.C. State Bar Assn., Fla. State Bar Assn. Republican. Anglican. Address: PO Box 3342 Vero Beach FL 32964

BLOCK, RITA LEE, financial executive; b. Utica, N.Y., Mar. 27, 1942; d. Robert Heine and Anne (Polivan) Block; student U. Miami, 1959-62, Syracuse U., 1962-64. Vice pres. corp. bonds Muller & Co., N.Y.C., 1973-81; agt. Barry J. Levien, Real Estate Broker, N.Y.C., 1975—; corp. bond, fixed income salesperson Wertheim & Co., N.Y.C., 1981-83; fixed income sales person Dillon Read & Co., N.Y.C., 1983—. Home: 245 E 87 St Apt 3A New York NY 10028 Office: 535 Madison Ave New York NY 10022

BLOCK, RUTH, insurance company executive; b. N.Y.C., Nov. 7, 1930; d. Albert and Celia (Shapiro) Smolensky; B.A., Adelphi U., 1952; m. Norman Block, 1952. With Equitable Life Assurance Soc., 1952—, v.p., planning officer, 1973-77, sr. v.p. in charge individual life ins., 1977-80, exec. v.p. individual ins. businesses, 1980—, chief ins. officer, 1984—; chmn., chief exec. officer Equitable Variable Life Ins. Co., 1981-84, also dir.; dir. Equitable Real Estate Group, Equitable Investment Mgmt. Co., Monumental Nat. Life Ins. Co. of N.Y., Integrity Life Ins. Co., Tandem Fin. Group, Donalson, Lufkin & Jenrette, Avon Products, Inc., gov.-at-large Nat. Assn. Securities Dealers, 1982-84; trustee Life Underwriters Tng. Council, 1982—; Mobil vis. exec. U. Iowa, 1978. Bd. dirs. Stamford (Conn.) YWCA, 1977-80; nat. chmn. Equitable United Way, 1978. Recipient Disting. Alumni award Adelphi U., 1979; Catalyst award, 1983; WEAL award, 1983. Office: 1285 Ave of Americas New York NY 10019

BLOCK, WENDY, ins. co. ofcl.; b. Amityville, N.Y., Jan. 16, 1952; d. Herbert and Frances (Schaffel) B.; B.B.A., Adelphi U., Garden City, N.Y., 1975, M.B.A., 1977. Data mgmt. supr. Ins. Co. N.Am., Garden City, 1976-78, mgr. adminstrv. ops., White Plains, N.Y., 1978-80, field support mgr., Garden City, N.Y., 1980-81, Houston, 1982-84, Los Angeles, 1984—; sr. project mgr. Mass. Mut., Springfield, 1982. Mem. Am. Mgmt. Assn. M.B.A. Execs., Westchester Women's Ins. Assn., Nat. Assn. Female Execs., Adminstrv. Mgmt. Soc. CIGNA 3700 Wilshire Pl Los Angeles CA 90010

BLOEDE, ELLEN LOUISE MILLER, social worker; b. Honolulu, Dec. 21, 1922; d. Ralph W. and Phoebe Miller; B.A., U. Hawaii, 1947, M.S.W., 1975; m. Victor C. Bloede, May 9, 1947; children—Karl A., Pamela E. Social worker, Md. Dept. Social Services, 1948-54, 58-61; social worker Hawaii Dept. Social Services, 1956-58, 1969-72; sr. social worker Hawaii Dept. Social Services and Housing, Kapiolani Children's Med. Center, Honolulu, 1974-82; spl. cons. Native Hawaiian Study Commn., 1981—. Founder, 1st chmn. Leasehold Reform Assn., 1974—; co-chmn. celebration Bishop Mus., 1983. Named An Outstanding Woman of Hawaii in Celebration of Nat. Women's History Week, 1983. Mem. Nat. Assn. Social Workers, Aboriginal Lands Hawaii Assn., Bishop Mus. Assn., Docent Bishop Mus. Co-founder, 1st Unitarian Ch. Honolulu, 1957. Club: Woman's Campus U. Hawaii. Home: 635 Onaha St Honolulu HI 96816

BLOMBERG, SUSAN RUTH, training executive, consultant, author; b. Troy, N.Y., Apr. 23, 1941; d. Philip J. and Marion (Burke) Beckman; m. Harvey Blomberg; children—Michael, Jonathan. B.S. in Edn., SUNY-Plattsburg, 1963. Cert. tchr., N.Y.; cert. tng. instr. Author, educator Nat. Textbook Co., Skokie, Ill., Stamford Bd. Edn. (Conn.), 1970-78; sales and mktg. dir., v.p., ptnr. B/D Assocs., Stamford, 1978-81; dir. mktg., v.p., owner Self Paced Learning Ctr., Stamford, 1981—; tchr. Bayshore/Brook Ave. Sch., Bayshore, N.Y., 1963-65; dir. and creator Creative Playtime ednl. sch., Stamford, 1969-70; writing cons. Stillmeadow Sch., Stamford, 1972-74; cons., inservice instr. seminars and workshops, Stamford Bd. Edn., 1974-77. Author ednl. series: Let's Create: Think and Write, 1978; lectr., author program Basic Skills in English and Creative Writing for Teachers, 1977; author Creative Writing Activity Cards, 1975. Mem. Internat. Reading Assn., Southwestern Area Commerce and Industry Assn., Am. Soc. Tng. and Devel. (So. Conn. br.).

BLOMQUIST, SUSAN GAIL, graphic artist; b. Chgo., Dec. 25, 1953; d. Howard Joseph and Evelyn Gene (Reynolds) B. A.A., Am. Acad. Art, 1973. Apprentice prodn. artist Am. Graphics, Chgo., 1973-74; prodn. mgr. Graphic Services, Chgo., 1974-77; gen. mgr. Graphic Connections, Chgo., 1977-80; free lance prodn. artist Source/Inc., Chgo., 1980-82, Perception, Chgo., 1982-84; prodn. art dir. Robert Case & Assoc., Chgo., 1984-86; freelance prodn. artist, 1986—. Illustrator: Talk to Yourself, Why Not, 1973. Mem. Nat. Assn. Female Execs., Soc. Typographical Arts. Club: Porsche of Am. (sec. 1981-82) (Chgo.). Avocations: auto racing; skiing; community theater. Home: 401 Fullerton Pkwy Apt 603 E Chicago IL 60614

BLOND, PATRICIA ANN, offset press educator and consultant; b. Denver, June 10, 1950; d. Howard Bennett Scholtz and Margaret Evelyn (Elliott) Whiteley; m. Robert Dale Blond, Nov. 7, 1969 (div. 1974); 1 child, Belinda Ann; m. Charles Martin Conrad, Aug. 3, 1974 (div. 1979); 1 child, Denny Martin. Student schs. Denver. Press person Mountain Bell System, Denver, 1968-69; supr. printing dept. J.C. Penney Co., Denver, 1969-71, lead press person, Salt Lake City, 1972-74; bindery press person Tektronix, Portland, Oreg., 1974-78; market support rep. AMInternational Multigraphics, Seattle, 1978—. Originator GraphMart Contest, 1986. Mem. Nat. Assn. Female Execs. (network dir. 1986), Inplant Printing Mgrs. Assn. Republican. Office: AMInternational Multigraphics 21222 68th Ave S Kent WA 98032

BLONIARZ BEACH, MARIANNE AGNES, health association administrator; b. Springfield, Mass.; d. Aloysius Anthony and Irene Marie (Redgate) Bloniarz; m. Richard Arthur Beach, June 14, 1980; 1 child, Lauren Elizabeth. B.A., Hampshire Coll., 1975; M.Ed., Antioch U., 1978. Lic. clin. social worker. Client program coordinator Mass. Dept. Mental Health, Northampton, 1976-78; child advocate coordinator Mass. Office Children, Holyoke, 1978-80; case mgr. supr. Mass. Office Children, Springfield, 1980-82, Mass. Dept. Pub. Health, Northampton, 1982—. Recipient scholarship Hampshire Assn. Retarded Citizens, 1978. Roman Catholic. Home: 53 Corticelli St Florence MA 01060

BLOODWORTH, WILLIE ETHEL, realty company executive, accountant, appraiser; b. Marion, Ala., Sept. 18, 1936; d. Willie and Ezelle (Edwards) White; m. William C. Bloodworth, May 29, 1958; children—Titus Jerome, William Darryl. Student Cleveland Community Coll., 1974-77, LaSalle Extension U., Chgo., 1974-78, John Carroll U., 1980-81, Real Estate Appraising Inst., 1980-81. Cert. real estate broker, pub. acct., appraiser. Pres., B&B Bookkeeping Taxes, East Cleveland, Ohio, 1965—, W.E. Bloodworth Realty Co., East Cleveland, 1976—, Midwestern Indsl. Ctr. Inc., East Cleveland, 1980—, Ethel's Enterprise, East Cleveland, 1980—, W.E. Bloodworth Appraising Co., East Cleveland, 1981—. Pres., Voters Service Club, Cleve., 1977; v.p. Citizens Against Neighborhood Deterioration and Overcrowding, East Cleveland, 1980—; com. mem. East Cleveland Democratic Club, 1983—; bd. dirs. East Cleveland LWV; com. mem. Ann. Jud. Scholarship Fund Inc. Recipient achievement awards U.S. Congress, 1977, Cuyahoga Community Coll., Cleve., 1980, City of Cleve., 1983; cert. of achievement Cleve. Pub. Schs., 1984; cert. Ann. Jud. Scholarship Fund Inc., 1984. Mem. Real Estate Appraisers Inst. (award 1981), Am. Bus. Women's Assn., Cleve. Area Bd. Realtors, Cleve. Area Real Estate Brokers Assn. (sec. 1981), Nat. Assn.

Female Execs., East Cleveland C. of C. (a founder, dir. 1984—), Euclid-Lee Bus. Assn. (sec.-treas.). Baptist. Club: Supper (Cleve.). Home: 1106 Mt Vernon Blvd Cleveland OH 44112 Office: B&B Bookkeeping & Tax Service/W E Bloodwrorth Realty Co 14916 Euclid Ave East Cleveland OH 44112

BLOOM, BARBARA JANE, medical finance firm executive, consultant, nurse; b. Glen Ridge, N.J, Mar. 12, 1947; d. Martin I. and Sylvia S. (Levitt) B. Student Ohio State U., 1965-67, Bloomfield Coll., 1967-68; B.S. in Nursing, Cornell U., 1970; M.B.A., Baruch Coll., 1979. Sr. clin. nurse Mt. Sinai Hosp., N.Y.C., 1974-75; supr. nursing St. Barnabas Hosp., Bronx, N.Y., 1975-76, asst. dir. nursing, 1976-80; dir. nursing St. Francis Community Health Ctr., Jersey City, 1980-82; med. auditor Med. Payments Processing Co., Orange, N.J., 1982-84, med. adminstr., 1984—; cons. Document Research, Orange, 1985—, Health Care Info. Services, Nat. Med. Fin. Services, Orange, 1985—. Mem. Am. Physicians Fellowship (assoc.). Jewish. Home: Apt 307 200 Winston Dr Cliffside Park NJ 07010 Office: Med Payments Processing Co PO Box 153 Orange NJ 07050

BLOOM, CLAIRE, actress; b. London, Feb. 15, 1931; d. Edward Max and Elizabeth (Grew) Blume; student Badminton Sch., Bristol, Eng., Fern Hill Manor, New Milton, Eng.; pub. schs., Fla., N.Y.; m. Rod Steiger, Sept. 19, 1959 (div.); 1 child, Anna. Appeared as Ophelia, Stratford-Upon-Avon, 1948; plays include Lady's Not for Burning, also Ring Around the Moon, London, 1949-51; in Romeo and Juliet, others, for Old Vic, also as Juliet in Old Vic tour of U.S.; film roles in Limelight, The Man Between, Richard III, Alexander the Great, Brothers Karamazov, Buccaneer, Look Back in Anger, Three Steps to Freedom, 1960, The Brothers Grimm, The Chapman Report, 1962, The Haunting, 1963, 80,000 Suspects, 1963, Alta Infidelita, 1963, Il Maestro di Vigeuono, 1963, The Outrage, 1964, The Spy Who Came in from the Cold, 1965, A Doll's House, 1973, Islands in the Stream, 1976, Clash of the Titans, 1981; appeared Broadway in Rashomon, 1959, at Royal Court Theatre, London, in Altona, 1960, A Doll's House, Hedda Gabler, 1971, Vivat! Vivat Reginal, 1972; New York appearance The Innocents, 1976; London appearances A Doll's House, 1973, A Streetcar Named Desire, 1974, Rosmersholm, 1977, The Cherry Orchard, 1981; also various roles Brit. and U.S. TV including Henry VIII, Brideshead Revisited. Address: care Michael Linnit Prince of Wales Theatre Coventry St London W1 England

BLOOM, JUDI LYNN, television reporter and producer; b. N.Y.C., July 30, 1950; d. Willard Earnest and Ann Felice (Lyons) Bloom; m. Dennis Hauswirth, Mar. 45, 1984; 1 child, Heather Willie Bloom Hauswirth. B.S., Cornell U., 1971; student film courses, Hunter Coll., N.Y.C. Asso. producer, undercover investigative reporter Sta. WNEW-TV, N.Y.C., 1971-73; producer, reporter Sta. WPLG-TV, Miami, Fla., 1973-74; anchor, host, producer Sta. WPBT-TV, Miami, 1974-75; reporter, anchor Sta. WINZ-AM, Miami, 1975-76; reporter Sta. WPVI-TV, Phila., 1976-78; reporter, anchor Sta. KTTV-TV, Los Angeles, 1978-85; ind. reporter/producer, 1986—; anchor, producer Satellite News Channel, 1981-83; guest lectr. Fla. Internat. U., Dade Community Coll.; instr. Sta. KIIS broadcasting workshop; producer documentary film Grandpeople, 1975. Mem. Nat. Assn. Female Execs., AFTRA, Women in Radio and TV, Nat. Acad. TV Arts and Scis. Club: Los Angeles Press. Office: KTTV-TV 5746 Sunset Blvd Los Angeles CA 90028

BLOOM, KAREN KELLY (BITTNER), computer processing company executive; b. Norwalk, Conn., May 30, 1951; d. Henry Alfred and Alice (Weichel) Bittner; m. Jerry Howard Bloom, July 16, 1983. A.S., Norwalk Community Coll., 1977. Word processing supr. Travelers Ins. Co., Hartford, Conn., 1976-80; word processing dept. head Computer Processing Inst., Bridgeport, Conn., 1980—. Recipient Bus. Club award Norwalk Community Coll., 1976-77. Mem. Nat. Assn. Female Execs., Assn. Info. Systems Profls. Conn. Democrat. Roman Catholic. Avocations: swimming; aerobics; bicycling; tennis. Home: 135 Tunxis Hill Rd Fairfield CT 06430

BLOOMINGDALE, TERESA BURROWES, writer, lecturer; b. St. Joseph, Mo., July 26, 1930; d. Arthur Victor and Helen (Cooney) Burrowes; m. A. Lee Bloomingdale, jr., July 2, 1955; children—A. Lee, John, Michael, James, Mary, Dan, Peg, Ann, Tim, Patrick. Columnist, Omaha Metro, 1972-77, Our Sunday Visitor, 1973-83, Omaha Sun, 1976-78; contbg. editor McCall's mag., N.Y.C., 1982-84; lectr. Keedick Lecture Bur., N.Y.C., 1983—. Author: I Should Have Seen It Coming When the Rabbit Died, 1979, Up a Family Tree, 1981, Murphy Must Have Been a Mother, 1982; Life Is What Happens When You're Making Other Plans, 1984; Sense and Momsense, 1986. Recipient Disting. Alumna award Duchese Alumnae Assn., 1983. Mem. Assoc. Alumnae of Sacred Heart, Children of Mary Sodality, Authors Guild, Nebr. Writers Guild, Catholic League for Religious and Civil Rights. Republican. Roman Catholic. Clubs: St. Joseph Women's Press (Mo.); Omaha Press. Office: Julian Bach Literary Agy 747 3d Ave New York NY 10017

BLOS, JOAN W., author, critic; b. N.Y.C., Dec. 9, 1928; m. Peter Blos, Jr., 1953; 2 children (1 dec.). B.A., Vassar Coll., 1950; M.A., CCNY, 1956. Assoc. publs. div., mem. tchr. edn. faculty Bank St. Coll. Edn., N.Y.C., 1958-70; lectr. Sch. Edn., U. Mich., Ann Arbor, 1972-80; U.S. editor Children's Literature in Education, 1976-81. Author: "It's Spring!" She Said, 1968; (with Betty Miles) Just Think!, 1971; A Gathering of Days: A New England Girl's Journal, 1830-32, 1979 (Newbery medal ALA, and Am. Book award 1980), Martin's Hats, 1984; Brothers of the Heart: A Story of the Old Northwest, 1837-1938, 1985. Office: care Charles Scribner's Sons 115 Fifth Ave New York NY 10010

BLOUNT, DELORES OVERMAN, radio executive; b. Goldsboro, N.C., Dec. 1, 1948; d. Joseph Aaron and Beatrice (Basden) Overman; m. Girard Martin Blount, Jr., Mar. 23, 1974. B.A., U. N.C., 1971. Acct. exec. sta. WKZQ, Myrtle Beach, S.C., 1973-81; sales mgr. sta. WKZQ, Myrtle Beach, 1981—. Ambassador Myrtle Beach Conv. Bur., 1982-83. Named Career Woman of Year, Bus. and Profl. Women's Club, 1982. Mem. C. of C. (bd. dirs. 1983-86), Coastal Ad Fed. (bd. dirs. 1983; sec. 1984; v.p. 1985).

BLOZIS, JOLENE MCCOY, society executive; b. Washington, Sept. 17, 1941; d. Wilbur Milton and Bernys Dovie (Adee) McCoy; m. Raymond LeRoy Blozis, Dec. 28, 1974. B.A., Roberts Wesleyan Coll., Rochester, N.Y., 1963; legal advocacy cert., George Washington U., 1981; M.L.S., Cath. U. Am., 1975. Abstracter, Lawyers Title Ins. Corp., Washington, 1962; indexer Nat. Geog. Soc., Washington, 1963-75, index editor, mgr. indexing div., 1975—. Legal adv. Emmaus Services to Aging, Washington, 1979-84. Mem. ALA, Am. Soc. Indexers, Am. Soc. Info. Sci., D.C. Library Assn., Bibl. Archaeol. Soc., Am. Sch. Oriental Research, Nat. Press Club, Austrian Soc. Republican. Methodist. Home: 2555 Pennsylvania Ave NW Washington DC 20037 Office: Nat Geog Soc 1600 M St NW Washington DC 20036

BLUDNICKI, MARY A., librarian; b. Derby, Conn., Oct. 28, 1950; d. Benjamin S. and Sue R. (Bensko) B. B.A. in Sociology, Sacred Heart U., 1972; M.A. in Librarianship, U. Denver, 1976; M.S. in Ednl. Media, So. Conn. State U., 1980. Librarian treas.'s dept. Richardson-Merrell Inc., Wilton, Conn., 1974-75; investment dept. statis. clk. People's Bank, Bridgeport, Conn., 1977-80; audio-visual librarian Clinton Community Coll., Plattsburgh, N.Y., 1980—. Audio-visual reviewer Sch. Library Jour., 1981—; contbr. articles to profl. jours. Mem. ALA, Assn. Ednl. Communications and Tech., Ch. and Synagogue Library Assn. (pres. Conn. chpt. 1980-81). Home: 6 McMartin St Plattsburgh NY 12901 Office: Audio-Visual Dept Clinton Community Coll Route 9S Plattsburgh NY 12901

BLUE, CATHERINE ANNE, lawyer; b. Boston, Feb. 17, 1957; d. James Daniel and Angela Devina (Savini) Mahoney; m. Donald Sherwood Blue, Oct. 4, 1980; children—Mairead Catherine, Edward Pierce. B.A., Stonehill Coll., North Easton, Mass., 1977; J.D., Coll. William and Mary, 1980. Bar: Pa. 1980. Atty., Aluminum Co. Am., Pitts., 1980-83, Pa. Dept. Revenue, Harrisburg, 1983-85, State Workmen's Ins. Fund, Pitts., 1985—. Mem. ABA Pa. Bar Assn., Allegheny County Bar Assn. Republican. Home: 7414 Richland Pl Pittsburgh PA 15208 Office: State Workmen's Ins Fund 1516 State Office Bldg 300 Liberty Ave Pittsburgh PA 15222

BLUE, EDNA JENKINS GOSSAGE, civic worker; b. Emory Gap, Tenn., Aug. 7, 1909; d. Arthur A. and Lennie Belle (Bailey) Jenkins; m. Roy Lee Gossage, Jan. 17, 1927; children—Dorothy, Daniel Arthur; stepchildren—Roy Lee, Margaret; 1 foster child, Helen Kendall; m. William F. Blue, Sept. 20, 1978. Student Tenn. Poly. U., 1926, U. Tenn., 1940-48, Tenn. Tech. U., 1950-60, Mars Hill Coll., 1965, Roane State Community Coll., 1977. With Tenn. Dept. Human Services, Clinton and Crossville, 1949-77, sr. counselor, 1970-77. Pres. Anderson County Parents Council Cerebral Palsy, Tenn., 1949-51; founder Daniel Arthur Ctr. Cerebral Palsy, 1950, Daniel Arthur Rehab. Ctr., Oak Ridge, Tenn., 1951—; chmn. New Eyes for Needy program, Cumberland County, Tenn., 1960-77; pres., bd. dirs., co-founder Cumberland County Girls Club, 1976-77; mem. steering com., founder Hilltoppers, Inc., Cumberland, 1975, bd. dirs., 1975—, sec. bd., 1976-79; pres. Cumberland County Assn. Retarded Citizens, 1978-79; pres. Janet Clark Meml. Group Home, Ind., 1977—; bd. dirs. United Fund, Cumberland, 1978-80, Four C's Cultural Found., 1978; vol. Local Group Homes for Developmentally Disabled, 1976-78; chmn. Santa for All Yr. Fund for Needy Children in Foster Care, 1975-78; ch. treas. Homesteads United Methodist Ch., 1964-78, ch. historian, 1978—. Author: Cumberland Homestead, 1933-1955, 2d edit., 56, A Church Is Born, 1961, A People Dared, God Cared, 1984; also articles, poems; columnist Cumberland Homesteader, 1935-39. Named Anderson County's Mother of Yr., 1951, Cumberland County's Woman of Achievement, 1963, Bicentennial Woman of History, 1976; recipient Silver plaque Cumberland County chpt. ARC, 1985, Golden Poet award, 1985, others. Mem. Cumberland County Bus. and Profl. Women's Club (pres. 1960-61, 69-70, 76-77), Tenn. Fedn. Bus. and Profl. Women (bd. dirs. East II 1967), Costeau Soc. (founding). Clubs: Homesteads United Meth. Women (pres. 1960-78, 83-85). Address: 12 Grassy Cove Rd Route 3 PO Box 202 Crossville TN 38555

BLUE, MARGARET AURELL, rehabilitation counselor; b. Cushing, Okla., Sept. 20, 1939; d. Herbert M. and Olive M. (Starkey) Aurell; A.B. in Social Work, Ind. U., 1961; postgrad. Patna U., Bihar, India, 1961-62; M.A. in Guidance and Counseling, Ill. State U., 1972; Ph.D. candidate U. Ill.; m. H. Darrell Blue, Jan. 11, 1981; children by previous marriage—Robert W. Porter, Sharon M. Porter. Caseworker, Cook County Dept. Public Aid, Chgo., 1963; referral worker Chgo. Council on Alcoholism, 1972; rehab. counselor Ill. Div. Vocat. Rehab., Decatur and Champaign, 1973-79; teaching asst. ednl. psychology U. Ill., 1979-81; psychometrist Center Children's Services, Danville, Ill., 1981-83; rehab. counselor Internat. Rehab. Assocs., Inc., Spokane, Wash., 1983—; mem stroke task force Ill. Heart Assn., 1977-79. Mem. Nat. Rehab. Assn., Ill. Rehab. Assn. (past chpt. pres., dir.). Democrat. Home: E 5803 15th Ave Spokane WA 99212 Office: Internat Rehab Assocs N 112 University Ave Spokane WA 99206

BLUE, ROSE, author, educator; b. N.Y.C.; d. Irving and Frieda (Rosenberg) Bluestone; B.A., Bklyn. Coll.; postgrad. Bank St. Coll. Edn. Tchr., N.Y.C. Public Schs.; writing cons. Bklyn. Coll. Sch. Edn. Mem. Authors Guild Am., Authors League Am., MENSA, Profl. Women's Caucus, Broadcast Music, Inc. Author: A Quiet Place, 1969; Black, Black Beautiful Black, 1969; How Many Blocks is The World, 1970; Bed-Stuy Beat, 1970; I Am Here (Yo Estoy Aqui), 1971; A Month of Sundays, 1972; Grandma Didn't Wave Back, 1972; Nikki 108, 1973; We Are Chicano, 1973; The Preacher's Kid, 1975; Seven Years From Home, 1976; The YoYo Kid, 1976; The Thirteenth Year, 1977; Cold Rain on the Water, 1979; My Mother the Witch, 1981; Everybody's Evy, 1983; Heart to Heart, 1985; Drama of Love, 1964; Let's Face It, 1961; My Heartstrings Keep Me Tied To You, 1963; Give Me A Break, 1962; Homecoming Party, 1966; (teleplays) Grandma Didn't Wave Back, 1982, My Mother the Witch, 1984; Contbg. editor, contbr. Teacher mag., Day Care mag. Home and Office: 1320 51st St Brooklyn NY 11219

BLUESTEIN, JUDITH ANN, rabbi, educator diversified industry executive; b. Cin., Apr. 2, 1948; d. Paul Harold and Joan Ruth (Straus) Bluestein; B.A., U. Pa., 1969; postgrad. Am. Sch. Classical Studies, Athens, Greece, 1968, Vergilian Soc., 1970, 76, 77, 78, Hebrew Union Coll., Jewish Inst. Religion, Jerusalem, 1971, 1979-80, Am. Acad. in Rome, 1975; M.A. in Religion (Univ. fellow), Case Western Res. U., 1973, M.A. in Latin, 1973; M.Ed., Xavier U., 1984; M.A.H.L., Hebrew Union Coll.-Jewish Inst. Religion, Cin., 1985. Ordained rabbi, 1985. Sec., Paul H. Bluestein & Co., Cin., 1964—; v.p. Panel Machine Co., 1966—, Blujay Corp., 1966—, Ermet Products Corp., 1966—; partner Companhia Engenheiros Industrial Bluestein do Brasil, Cin., 1971—; tchr. Latin, Cin. Public Schs., 1973-79; Revson fellow Jewish Theol. Sem. Am., 1984-85, rabbi Temple Israel, Marion, Ohio, 1980-84, Temple Sholom, Galesburg, Ill., 1985-86. Mem. Archeol. Inst. Am., Classical Assn. Middle West and South (v.p. Ohio 1976-79), Central Conf. Am. Rabbis, Am. Classical League, Ohio Classical Conf. (council 1976-79), Vergilian Soc., Soc. Bibl. Lit., Cin. Assn. Tchrs. Classics (pres. 1976-78), Am. Philol. Assn. Address: 3420 Section Rd Cincinnati OH 45237

BLUESTEIN, VENUS WELLER, psychologist, educator; b. Milw., July 16, 1933; d. Richard T. and Hazel (Beard) Weller; B.S., U. Cin., 1956, M.Ed., 1959, Ed.D., 1966; m. Marvin Bluestein, Mar. 7, 1954. Psychologist in tng. Longview State Hosp., Cin., 1956-58; sch. psychologist Cin. Pub. Schs., 1958-65; asst. prof. psychology U. Cin., 1965-70, assoc. prof., 1970-79, prof., 1979—, dir. undergrad. studies, 1976—, dir. sch. psychology program, 1963-70, co-dir., 1970-75; cons. child psychologist. Sec., U.S. exec. com. research Children's Internat. Summer Villages, 1964-68; chmn. Ohio Interuniv. Council on Sch. Psychology, 1967-68. Recipient George Barbour award; Psi Chi award. Diplomate Am. Bd. Examiners in Profl. Psychology. Mem. Am. Psychol. Assn., Cin. Psychol. Assn. (sec. 1961-62), Ohio Psychol. Assn. (editor Ohio Psychologist 1961-68, citation 1972, Disting. Service award 1968), AAUP, Forum for Death Edn. and Counseling, Kappa Delta Pi, Sigma Delta Pi, Psi Chi. Contbr. articles to profl. publs. Co-editor Ohio Psychologist, 1972-79. Office: Dept Psychology McMicken Coll Univ Cincinnati Cincinnati OH 45221

BLUITT, KAREN, software engineer, manager; b. N.Y.C., Oct. 25, 1957; d. James Bertrand and Beatrice Bluitt; B.S., Fordham U., 1979; M.B.A., Calif. State Poly. U., 1982; m. Kenneth Mark Curry, Nov. 24, 1979. Software engr. Hughes Aircraft Co., Fullerton, Calif., 1979-81, microprocessor engr. Beckman Instruments Co., Fullerton, 1981-82, Singer Co., Glendale, Calif., 1982-83; sr. software engr. Sanders Assocs., Nashua, N.H., 1983-86; software project mgr. GTE Corp., Billerica, Mass., 1985-86; with MICOM-Interlon, Boxboro, Mass., 1986—. Served to 1st lt. USAR, 1979—. N.Y. State Gov.'s Scholarship, 1975-79; Beta Gamma Sigma scholar, 1978—. Served to lt. USAR, 1979—. Mem. Nat. Assn. Female Execs., Assn. M.B.A. Execs., Res. Officers Assn., AAUW, Civil Affairs Assn., LWV. Office: 155 Swanson Rd Boxboro MA

BLUM, BARBARA DAVIS, banker; b. Hutchinson, Kans., July 6, 1939; d. Roy C. and Jo (Crawford) Davis; student U. Kans., Lawrence, 1955-56; B.S., Fla. State U., 1958, M.S.W., 1959; children—Davis, Devin, Hunter, Ragan. Faculty, Pediatric Psychiatry Clinic, U. Kans. Med. Center, Lawrence, 1960-62; acting adminstr. Suffolk County Mental Health Clinic, Huntington, N.Y., 1963-64; founder, partner, adminstr. Mid-Suffolk Center for Psychotherapy, Hauppage, L.I., N.Y., 1964-66; v.p. Restaurant Assos. of Ga., Inc., Atlanta, 1966-74; v.p. Blum's Oxford Road, Inc., Atlanta, 1975-76; dep. adminstr. EPA, Washington, 1977-81; Now pres. Women's Nat. Bank; Washington. Dir. ops. Carter/Mondale Transition Teams, Washington, 1976-77; dep. dir. Carter/Mondale Presdl. campaign, Atlanta, 1976; chief lobbyist Save Am.'s Vital Environment, 1972-76; vice-chmn. Fulton County (Ga.) Planning Commn., 1973-76; pres. Friends of the River, Inc., 1972-75; sr. adviser to exec. dir. UN Environ. Programme; chmn. U.S. delegation U.S./Japan Environ. Agreement, 1977, 79; mem. Undersecs. Group, 1977-81; chmn. Environ. Policy Inst.; bd. dirs. Environ. Law Inst., Nat. Water Alliance. Decorated Comdr.'s Cross of Merit (W.Ger.); recipient Spl. Conservation award Nat. Wildlife Fedn., 1976; Orgn. of Year award Ga. Wildlife Fedn., 1974; Sol Feinstone Environ. award, 1976, 77; award Federally Employed Women, 1978, award Ams. for Indian Opportunity, 1978. Democrat. Home: 2231 Bancroft Pl NW Washington DC 20008 Office: 1627 K St NW Washington DC 20006

BLUM, ELEANOR GOODFRIEND, educator; b. Detroit, July 16, 1940; d. William Henry and Dorothy Elaine (Oslander) Goodfriend; B.S. in Edn., Wayne State U., 1962, M.Ed., 1983; children—Beth Goodfriend, Sara Caroline. Kindergarten tchr. Livonia, Mich., 1962-63, Montgomery County, Md., 1963-64; tchr. Detroit Public Schs., 1977—, also reading coordinator King High Sch.; mem. edn. com. New Detroit Inc., 1981—. Vol. Detroit office of Senator Robert Griffin, 1972-74, asst. to appointments sec. to Pres. Nixon, Washington, 1972-74; chmn. March of Dimes Drive, Farmington, Mich., 1975; pres. Potomac Village Homeowners Assn., 1975; mem. 19th dist. Republican Com., 1975—, precinct del. 20th precinct, West Bloomfield, Mich.; alt. del. to Nat. Rep. conv., 1976; mem. exec. com. Oakland County Rep. Com., 1977-78; mem. Bloomfield Women's Rep. Club, West Bloomfield Rep. Women's Club; chmn. health com. Doherty Elem. Sch., 1975—; mem. library com. Temple Beth El, Birmingham, Mich., 1976, mem. library and arts coms., 1977-78; mem. urban affairs com. Jewish Community Council, 1977-78, community relations com., 1978-80, chmn. met. concerns com., 1979; mem. adv. bd. Oakland County March of Dimes, 1977-78, mem. bd., 1979; bd. dirs. Oakland Citizens League, 1983; mem. Friends of West Bloomfield Library, 1975—, NAACP, 1979—; mem. com. on sheltered workshops, dept. mgmt. and budget State of Mich., 1978-80. Address: 5123 Chestershire Dr West Bloomfield MI 48033

BLUM, JOAN KURLEY, fund raising exec.; b. Palm Beach, Fla., July 27, 1926; d. Nehad Daniel and Eva (Milos) Kurley; B.A., U. Wash., 1948; m. Robert C. Blum, Apr. 15, 1967; children—Christopher Alexander, Martha Jane, Louisa Joan, Danna Carolyn, Paul Helmuth. Cert. fund raising exec. U.S. dir. Inst. Mediterranean Studies, Berkeley, Calif., 1962-65; devel. officer U. Calif. at Berkeley Alumni Assn., 1965-67; pres. Blum Assocs., Fund-Raising Cons., San Anselmo, Calif., 1967—; mem. faculty U. Calif. Extension, Inst. Fund Raising, SW Inst. Fund-Raising U. Tex., U. San Francisco, U.K. Vol. Movement Group, London, Australasian Inst. Fund Raising. Recipient Golden Addy award Am. Advt. Fedn.; Silver Mailbox award Direct Mail Mktg. Assn., Best Ann. Giving Time-Life award, others. Mem. Nat. Soc. Fund-Raising Execs. (dir.), Nat. Advt. of Hosp. Devel., Women Emerging. Club: Tamalpa Running. Contbr. numerous articles to profl. jours. Home: Kentfield CA 94904 Office: 292 Red Hill San Anselmo CA 94960

BLUM, JOANNE LEE, development executive, educator; b. Pitts., Aug. 30, 1932; d. L. Herbert and Dorothy Ruth (Cimberg) Finkelhor; m. Arthur Marvin Blum, June 14, 1959; children—Sherry Ruth, Laurie Jill, Katie Jo. Student U. Chgo., 1947-49, Chatham Coll., Pitts., 1949-51; B.A., Brandeis U., 1953; M.Ed., Harvard U., 1954; postgrad. U. Pitts., 1963-65. Cert. fundraising exec. Tchr., Mt. Diablo Unifed Sch. Dist., Walnut Creek, Calif., 1954-55; asst. dir. Fgn. Policy Assn. Pitts. (now World Affairs Council), 1955-57, assoc. dir., 1957-61, assoc. producer Focus on World Affairs, 1959-61; pres. Pitts. Internat. Travel, 1961-62; chmn. dept. edn. Point Park Coll., Pitts., 1962-69, dir. Lab. Schs. Program, 1964-69, dir. intermediate level Lab. Sch., 1972-73; co-founder, dean San Francisco Sch. Arts, San Anselmo, Calif., 1976-78; co-owner, dir. Camps Wahconah and Potomac and New Eng. Summer Programs in the Arts, Pittsfield, Mass., 1978-82; devel. and membership coordinator World Affairs Council of No. Calif., San Francisco, 1983-85; pvt. practice devel. cons., Calif., 1986—; co-founder Pitts. Area Preschool Assn., 1965; lectr. Headstart program Carnegie Mellon U., Pitts., 1965; cons. Goodwill Industries Devel. Office, Internat. Visitors Ctr., 1985, Feedback Prodns., others, all San Francisco. Founding dir. Pitts. Ballet Theatre, 1965; cons. arts program for handicapped children Renaissance Ctr. for Arts, Mt. Lebanon, Pa., 1967, cons. preschool program, 1967. Mem. Nat. Soc. Fund Raising Execs., Devel. Execs. Roundtable (treas. 1986—). Jewish. Office: 1090 Butterfield Rd Suite 100 San Anselmo CA 94960

BLUM, MELANIE RAE, lawyer; b. N.Y.C., Aug. 6, 1949; d. Theodore and Gertrude (Brawer) Sands; m. Michael Phillip Blum, June 27, 1970; 1 dau., Megan Alyse. B.A., Calif. State U.-Northridge, 1971; M.B.A., Calif. State U.-Long Beach, 1978; J.D., Loyola U., Los Angeles, 1981. Bar: Calif. 1981. Acct. Shain & Cohen, Los Angeles, 1969-71, INA, Los Angeles, 1971-72, Louis Kelso, San Francisco, 1972-75, O'Asian, Inglewood, Calif., 1975-78; assoc. firm Richard Dickson, Newport Beach, Calif., 1982-83; sole practice law, Tustin, Calif., 1983-84, Newport Beach, 1984—; sec., dir. Michael P. Blum, P.C., Anaheim, Calif., 1979—. Mem. ABA, Calif. State Bar, Orange County Bar Assn., Am. Trial Lawyers Assn., Phi Kappa Phi, Beta Gamma Sigma. Republican. Jewish. Office: 4041 MacArthur Blvd Suite 250 Newport Beach CA 92660

BLUMBERG, BARBARA MARILYN, history educator, writer; b. Bronx, N.Y., Oct. 27, 1936; d. Albert A. and Yvette (Beneck) Schneck; m. Paul Marvin Blumberg, Aug. 25, 1955 (div. 1973); 1 child, Ira Joseph; m. Alan L. Krumholz, Apr. 12, 1974; 1 child, Mark Reuben. A.B. in History, U. Calif.-Berkeley, 1968, M.A. in History, 1962; Ph.D. in History, Columbia U., 1974, Prof. history Adelphi U., Garden City, N.Y., 1967-68, Queens Coll., Flushing, N.Y., 1968-75, Pace U., N.Y.C., 1971—. Author: The New Deal and the Unemployed: The View from NYC, 1979; Celebrating the Immigrant: An Administrative History of the Statue of Liberty National Monument, 1952-82, 1985. Editor NYC: Readings in History, Literature, and Culture, 1982. Mem. Inst. Research in History (dir. 1983-84, mem. exec. com., sec. 1985-86), Women in the Hist. Profession (co-chmn. coordinating com. N.Y. 1983-84), Am. Hist. Assn., Orgn. Am. Historians, Phi Beta Kappa. Office: Pace Univ Pace Plaza New York NY*

BLUMBERG, BARBARA SALMANSON (MRS. ARNOLD G. BLUMBERG), civic worker; b. Bklyn., Oct. 2, 1927; d. Sam and Mollie (Greenberg) Salmanson; B.A., DePauw U., 1948; postgrad. New Sch. for Social Reserach, N.Y.C.; m. Arnold G. Blumberg, June 19, 1949; children—Florence Ellen Blumberg, Martin Jay, Emily Anne. With pub. relations dept. Nate Fein & Co., N.Y.C., 1948-51; freelance writer, 1960—. With UN Assn. Great Neck, N.Y., 1967—, chmn. China Study Workshop, 1966-67; leader Fertile Crescent Study Group; pres. Shalom chpt. Hadassah, 1955-57; exec. v.p. Lakeville P.T.A., Great Neck, 1963-65; exec. v.p. Great Neck South Jr. High Sch., 1965-66; co-chmn. Great Neck com. for UNICEF. Area co-chmn. Nassau County McGovern for Pres., 1972; v.p. Reform Democratic Assn. Great Neck; bd. dirs. New Dem. Coalition of Nassau; councilwoman North Hempstead Town Council, 1975-81; counsel energy com. N.Y. State Assembly, 1982-83; issues com. Nassau County Dem. Com.; bd. dirs. Citizen's Sch. Com., Great Neck; mem. council Great Neck Sr. Citizens Center; mem. adv. com. on pub. policy N.Y. State Assembly; dir. spl. needs housing Div. Housing and Community Renewal, N.Y. State bd. dirs. Am. Jewish Com., Am. Jewish Congress, Day Care Council of Nassau County. Recipient award Anti-Defamation League, 1975; Alumni certificate DePauw U., 1977; award 3 dist. U.S. Coast Guard Aux., 1979; Israel Bonds award, 1980—. Mem. N.Y. Alumni Club DePauw U. (trustee), North Shore Archael. Soc., Alpha Lambda Delta, Theta Sigma Phi. Club: L.I. Women's Network (gov. 1979). Home: 12 Birch Hill Rd Great Neck NY 11020 Office: 2 World Trade Ctr New York NY 10047

BLUMBERG, GRACE GANZ, educator, lawyer; b. N.Y.C., Feb. 16, 1940; d. Samuel and Beatrice (Finkelstein) Ganz; B.A. cum laude, U. Colo., 1960; J.D. summa cum laude, SUNY, 1971; LL.M., Harvard U., 1974; m. Donald R. Blumberg, Sept. 9, 1959. Admitted to N.Y. bar, 1971; confidential law clk. Appellate Div., N.Y. Supreme Ct., 4th Dept., Rochester, 1971-72; teaching fellow Harvard Law Sch., Cambridge, Mass., 1972-74; prof. law SUNY, Buffalo, 1974-81; prof. UCLA Law Sch., 1979—; cooperating atty. ACLU. Baldy Summer Research fellow in law and social policy, 1977, 78; SUNY research Found. summer faculty fellow, 1975. Mem. Am. Soc. Comparative Law, Am. Assn. Law Schs., ACLU. Editorial bd. Am. Jour. Comparative Law, 1977-81; contbr. articles in field to profl. jours. Address: Law Sch UCLA 405 Hilgard Ave Los Angeles CA 90024

BLUMBERG, JULIA BAUM, community leader, educator; b. Hazleton, Pa.; d. Benjamin and Ida Ruth (Lurie) Baum; Ph.B. summa cum laude, Muhlenberg Coll., Allentown, Pa., 1937; postgrad. NYU, Columbia U.; m. Dr. Leo Blumberg, Aug. 9, 1938. Mem. faculty Bethleham (Pa.) Sr. High Sch., dir. placement comml. grads., 1938-46. Life mem. B'nai B'rith Women, organized Bethlehem group, 1938, pres. Bethlehem, 1938-39, pres. Dist. 3, 1945-46, mem. nat. exec. bd., 1957-59, rep. nat. orgn., 1957-59, chmn. nat. vocat. guidance, 1957-59, chmn. dist. 3 Klutznick scholarship award, 1966-69, mem. bd. B'nai B'rith Women of Wilmington, pres. vocational service bd., 1962-64; life mem. Temple Beth Emeth Sisterhood, mem. bd., 1949-59, 70-86; treas. Dist 8, Nat. Fedn. Temple Sisterhoods, 1952-56; mem. nat. exec. bd. nat. fedn., 1953-57; gen. chmn. Dist. 8 conv., Wilmington, 1957; pres. community adv. bd. Hillel Counselorship, U. Del., 1979-82; mem. bd. Wilmington City Fedn. Women's Clubs and Allied Orgns., 1951—, 1st v.p., 1961-63, pres., 1963-65; mem. bd. mgrs. Florence Crittendon Home of Del., 1955-61; mem. Women's div. Brandeis U.; life mem. Aux. Kutz Home for Aged, also bd. dirs. aux., 1972-86, named Hon. Life Chmn. Bd., 1983; mem. Nat. Commn. Vocational Service, 1957-59, Mayor's Com. for Christmas, Mayor's Com. for UN; mem. bd. UNICEF, 1972-82; mem. steering com. CARE, Inc., 1971-82; mem. Del. Nature Edn. Center, Inc., Del. Council on Crime and Justice; chmn. bldg. and furniture com., dedication com. Hillel Found. at U. Del., 1963-64, hon. life chmn. community adv. bd. B'nai B'rith Hillel Counselorship, U. Del.; mem. women's div. Jewish Fedn. Del.; mem. bldg. fund com. St. Francis Hosp., 1973; v.p. bd. dirs. Kutz Home Aux. Mem. Nat. Council Jewish Women (life), Greater Wilmington Fedn. Women's Orgns. (dir. 1965-69, 69-73, 73-77, 77-86, pres. Past Officers Club 1965-67, historian 1973-75, dir. 1975—), Del. Mental Health Assn., Crippled Children and Adults Soc. Del., Hadassah (life), B'nai

B'rith Women (life), Phi Sigma Iota. Jewish (life mem., pres. Sisterhood 1952-53, mem. bd. 1971—, dir. temple 1952-55). Clubs: Widener U. Faculty Wives (hon. life), Wilmington New Century (internat. relations com. 1978-84, edn. com. 1978-86). Home: 1401 Pennsylvania Ave Apt 406 Wilmington DE 19806

BLUME, ELIZABETH RENEE, executive secretary, clinical research coordinator; b. Warren, Pa., Aug. 29, 1953; d. William Wesley and Betty Josephine (Anderson) B. Grad. Little Valley Central Sch. Motor vehicle acct. Cattaraugus County, Little Valley, N.Y., 1971-76; asst. office mgr. Dr. Widger and Dr. Gutierrez, Salamanca, N.Y., 1976-80; adminstrv. sec. The U. Tex. Med. Sch., Houston, 1980; exec. sec. Stanley J. Dudrick, M.D., Houston, 1980—; exec. sec. Am. Soc. Nutritional Support Service, 1983—. Co-author Annals of Surgery, 1983, Transactions of the So. Surg. Assn., The Yearbook of Surgery. Co-chmn. United Way Campaign dept. surgery The U. Tex. Med. Sch., Houston, 1980. Recipient Sorosis Literary Guild award for English N.Y. State Fed. Women's Clubs, 1971, Eastern Star award, 1971. Mem. Stanley J. Dudrick Found. and Soc., Am. Soc. for Nutritional Support Services (co-author Sci. poster session 1982, 84, 85), Am. Soc. for Parenteral and Enteral Nutrition (co-author sci. poster session 1982, 84), Eur. Soc. Parenteral and Enteral Nutrition (co-author sci. poster session 1985), Theta Rho (pres. 1969-70). Republican. Home: 5939 Sanford St Houston TX 77096 Office: Office of Stanley J Dudrick MD 6720 Bertner Suite B619 Houston TX 77030

BLUME, GINGER (ELAINE), psychologist; b. Lock Haven, Pa., Apr. 8, 1948; d. Martin Luther and Virginia Ruth (Rudy) B.; B.A., U. Fla., 1970, M.A., 1975, Ph.D., 1979. Predoctoral intern in psychology VA Hosp., West Haven, Conn., 1976-77; postdoctoral intern in psychology Elmcrest Psychiat. Inst., Portland, Conn., 1977-78; pvt. practice clin. psychology, Middletown, Conn., 1978—; corp. cons., 1983—; assoc. Harrison Assocs., Inc., Cons., Berkeley, Calif.; co-owner, program dir. PMT Assocs.; affiliated faculty New Eng. Type Inst. mem. adj. psychology faculty Middlesex Community Coll., Antioch Grad. Sch., Keene, N.H.; bd. dirs. Gilead House halfway facility, SAFE sexual assault clinic, Family Resource Center; cons. in field. Mem. Am. Psychol. Assn., Conn. Psychol. Assn., Orthopsychiatry Assn., Internat. Imagery Assn., Am. Soc. Tng. and Devel., Orgnl. Devel. Network, AAUW (chairperson edn. found. program), Phi Kappa Phi, Kappa Delta. Club: Soroptomists. Home: 748 Long Hill Rd Middletown CT 06457 Office: 11 S Main St Middletown CT 06457

BLUME, JUDY SUSSMAN, author; b. Elizabeth, N.J., Feb. 12, 1938; d. Rudolph and Esther (Rosenfeld) Sussman; B.S. in Edn., NYU, 1960; m. John M. Blume, Aug. 15, 1959 (div. Jan. 1976); children—Randy Lee, Lawrence Andrew. Author juvenile fiction books including: Are You There God? It's Me, Margaret (selected as outstanding children's book 1970); Then Again, Maybe I Won't, 1971; It's Not the End of the World, 1972; Tales of a 4th Grade Nothing, 1972; Deenie, 1973; Blubber, 1974; Otherwise Known as Sheila the Great, 1976; Forever, 1976; Tiger Eyes (outstanding book for young adults 1981); The Pain and The Great One, 1984; others; author 2 adult novels: Wifey, 1978; Smart Women, 1984; (nonfiction) The Judy Blume Diary: The Place to Put Your Own Feelings, 1981. Mem. Authors League and Guild, Soc. Children's Book Writers. Office: care Harold Ober Assos 40 E 49th St New York NY 10017

BLUME, KAROLYN VREELAND, lawyer; b. N.Y.C., Aug. 16, 1952; d. Donald Walker and Margaretta (Waller) Vreeland; m. Peter Frederick Blume, Oct. 4, 1980; 1 dau., Susanna Vreeland. B.A., Skidmore Coll., 1974; J.D., Villanova U., 1977. Bar: Pa. 1977. Sole practice law, Allentown, Pa., 1977-83; ptnr. Blume and Schwartz, Allentown, 1983—. Bd. dirs. United Way Lehigh County, Allentown, 1983—, pres. Women's Div., 1983—; dir. Girls' Club of Allentown, 1984—; mem. Allentown Zoning Hearing Bd., 1978-84; dir., sec. Old Allentown Preservation Assn., 1980-82. Mem. ABA, Pa. Bar Assn., Lehigh County Bar Assn. (dir. 1980—, service award 1982). Democrat. Presbyterian. Home: 420 N 8th St Allentown PA 18102 Office: Blume and Schwartz 36 N Fifth St Allentown PA 18101

BLUME, SHEILA BIERMAN, psychiatrist, former state official; b. Bklyn., June 21, 1934; d. Benjamin and Rose (Lazar) Bierman; student Cornell U., 1951-54; M.D. cum laude, Harvard U., 1958; m. Martin Blume, June 12, 1955; children—Frederick, Janet. Intern, Children's Hosp. Med. Center, Boston, 1958-59; Fulbright fellow to Tokyo U., 1959-60; resident in psychiatry Central Islip Psychiat. Center, 1962-65; dir. Charles K. Post Alcoholism Rehab. Center, Central Islip Psychiat. Center, 1964-79; dir. N.Y. State Div. Alcoholism and Alcohol Abuse, 1979-83; med. dir. Nat. Council on Alcoholism, 1983; med. dir. Alcoholism and Compulsive Gambling Programs, South Oaks Hosp., 1984—; clin. assoc. prof. psychiatry Albany Med. Center, 1979-82; clin. prof. psychiatry SUNY-Stony Brook, 1984—; apptd. to Nat. Commn. Alcoholism and Other Alcohol Related Problems, 1980; mem. Nat. Commn. Confidentiality of Health Records, 1976-80, Nat. Council on Compulsive Gambling, adv. bd., 1972—. Recipient Dr. Milton Helpern Disting. Physicians award for contbn. field of alcoholism, 1980, Harold Riegelman award for contbn. to field of alcohol policy, 1983. Mem. L.I. Council Alcoholism (dir. 1972-79), Am. Med. Soc. Alcoholism (dir., pres. 1979-80), Nat. Council Alcoholism, (dir.). Editor: (with S. Zimberg and J. Wallace) Practical Approaches to Alcoholism Psychotherapy, 1978; editor Bull. Suffolk County Med. Soc., 1969-76; contbr. articles profl. jours., chpts. in books. Home and office: 284 Greene Ave Sayville NY 11782 also South Oaks Hosp Amityville NY 11701

BLUMENTHAL-MCGANNON, SALLY ANN, nurse; b. Rochester, N.Y., Mar. 6, 1948; d. Lester and Marion (Natapow) Blumenthal; m. Michael Linden McGannon, June 3, 1984. Student Boston U., 1966-68; R.N., Los Angeles County-U. So. Calif. Sch. Nursing, 1971; B.A., New Coll. Calif., San Francisco, 1979; postgrad. U. San Francisco, 1984-86. Charge nurse Los Angeles County-U. So. Calif. Med. Ctr., Los Angeles, 1971-74; dir. pediatrics Foothill Free Clinic, Pasadena, Calif., 1974-75; nursing care coordinator Hospice Caring Project, Santa Cruz, Calif., 1982-84, liaison hospice and AIDS program, 1985—; faculty Cabrillo Coll., 1982-85, U. Calif.-San Francisco, 1980; instr., cons. U. Alaska, Ketchekan, 1984—. Bd. dirs. Friends of Laurel Gardens, Santa Cruz, 1982-85. Mem. Theosophical Soc. Am., Nurse Healers Profl. Assn. (bd. dirs. 1978-82), NOW, Physicians Social Responsibility. Democrat. Avocations: travel. Home: 823 Cathedral Dr Aptos CA 95003 Office: Hospice Caring Project 115 Maple St Santa Cruz CA 95060

BLUMROSEN, RUTH GERBER, lawyer, educator, arbitrator; b. N.Y.C., Mar. 7, 1927; d. Lipman Samuel and Dorothy (Finklebrand) Gerber; m. Alfred William Blumrosen, July 3, 1952; children—Steven Marshall, Alex B. B.A. in Econs., U. Mich., 1947, J.D., 1953. Bar: Mich. 1953, U.S. Supreme Ct. 1967, U.S. Ct. Appeals (3d cir.). Sole practice, Detroit, 1953-55; cons. civil rights litigation, 1958-65; acting chief advice and analyses, acting dir. compliance EEOC, Washington, 1965; asst. to the dean Howard U., Washington, 1965-67; consul to chmn. EEOC, 1979-80; expert EEO HHS, Washington, 1980-81; assoc. prof. Grad. Sch. Mgmt., Rutgers U., Newark, 1972—. Adviser, N.J. Commn. on Sex Discrimination in the Statutes, 1983—. Mem. ABA, Fed. Bar Assn., Indsl. Relations Research Assn. Author: Layoff or Worksharing: The Civil Rights Act of 1964 in the Recession of 1975; (with A. Blumrosen) The Duty to Plan for Fair Employment Revisited: Worksharing in Hard Times, 1975; Wage Discrimination, Job Segregation and Title VII of Civil Rights Act of 1964, 1979; Wage Discrimination and Job Segregation: The Survival of a Theory, 1980; An Analysis of Wage Discrimination in N.J. State Service, 1983; Worksharing, STC and Affirmative Action in Shorttime Compensation: A Formula for Work-sharing. Home: 54 Riverside Dr New York NY 10024 Office: Grad Sch Mgmt 180 University Ave Newark NJ 07021

BLUNT, MARY KATHERINE, corporation managing director; b. N.Y.C., Aug. 21, 1952; d. James Wallace and Elsie Mary (Moore) B. B.A. cum laude, Bowdoin Coll., 1974; M.B.A., Wharton Sch. Bus., U. Pa., 1977. Asst. buyer Bloomingdale's, N.Y.C., 1977-79; with customer service Polo Fashions, Inc., N.Y.C., 1980, prodn. dir. knits, 1980, prodn. dir. Far East, 1980-81, prodn. dir. U.S.A. Prodn., 1981-83, mng. dir. Mountain Rose Co. Ltd. (sister corp. of Polo Fashions, establishing and directing), Hong Kong, 1983—. Purchasing mgr. Holiday Project, N.Y.C. Area, 1981. Nat. Merit scholar, 1970-74. Mem. Nat. Honor Soc., Am. C. of C. of Hong Kong (co-chmn. textile com.), Am. Women's Assn. Club: Mensa (treas. N.Y.C. 1981), Royal Hong Kong Jockey. Office: Mountain Rose Co Ltd Mandarin Plaza Tower A 9th Floor Rooms 910-913 Tsim Shatsui East Kowloon Hong Kong

BLUST, JEANNE ELIZABETH, nurse; b. N.J., Jan. 10, 1943; d. Vincent Maurice and Ellen Kennedy (Adams) B.; A.A., Union Jr. Coll., 1963; R.N., Elizabeth Gen. Hosp. Sch. Nursing, 1964; B.A., Marymount Manhattan Coll., 1978; M.A. in Bus. Mgmt. and Human Relations, Webster U., St. Louis, 1983. Supr. nursing Elizabeth Gen. Hosp., 1970-71; asst. and head nurse Mt. Sinai Hosp., N.Y.C., 1967-70, clin. nursing coordinator intravenous and transfusion therapy, 1971-78, coordinator IV therapy cert. course Sch. Continuing Edn. in Nursing, 1978-80; clin. supr. cardiothoracic surgery Mt. Sinai Med. Center, N.Y.C., 1978-80; cons., lectr. IV and transfusion therapy, 1978—; ednl. coordinator blood services ARC, Louisville, 1981-83, asst. to mgr. program devel. and evaluation, 1981-85; adminstr. Medicare for Quality Care Nursing Service, Louisville, 1985—; instr. St. Johns Coll. Pharmacy, 1977-80. Allentown Paint Co. scholar, 1961-64. Mem. Nat. Intravenous Therapy Assn., IV Therapist Assn. Greater N.Y. (past pres.), Hosp. Alumni Assn., Am. Assn. Blood Banks, Am. Nurses Assn. Nurse rep. nat. coordinating com. on large volume parenterals U.S. Pharmacopia, 1977. Mem. editorial bd. Am. Jour. IV Therapy, 1975—. Home: 208 Hopkins Ln Jeffersonville IN 47130 Office: 3901 Atkinson Dr Louisville KY 40218

BLUSTEIN, RUTH, social work director; b. N.Y.C., d. Hyman and Eva (Kaplan) Worhaftig; m. Irving Blustein, Dec. 25, 1946; children—Abby Blustein Franchitti, Bonnie Jean. B.A., Bklyn. Coll., 1957; M.S.W., Columbia U., 1959; postgrad. tng. Advanced Ctr. Psychotherapy, 1973-74; D.S.W., Wurzweiler Sch. Social Work, Yeshiva U., 1984. Social worker Kingsbrook Hosp., N.Y., 1959-61; supr. social work Bklyn. Bur. Community Services, 1961-64, 67-69; psychiat. social worker Jewish Community Services, N.Y., 1964-66; asst. prof. Columbia Sch. Social Work, N.Y., 1969-72; adminstrv. supr. L.I. Jewish-Hillside Med. Ctr. and Schneider Children's Hosp., New Hyde Park, N.Y., 1972-83, assoc. dir., 1983—. Mem. Nat. Assn. Social Workers, Assn. Pediatric Oncology Social Workers (rec. sec. 1982). Jewish. Home: 184 Hillturn Ln Roslyn Heights NY 11577 Office: LI Jewish Hillside Med Ctr & Schneider Children's Hosp New Hyde Park NY 11042

BLUTTER, JOAN, interior designer; b. London, July 6, 1928; came to U.S., 1947, naturalized, 1952; d. Samuel and Bertha Wernick; m. Melvyn Blutter, Oct. 29, 1948; children—Janet, Steven. Partner, Joslyn Interiors, Chgo., 1958-68; owner Joan Blutter/Designs, Chgo., 1968-81; pres. Blutter Design Group, Chgo., 1981—; cons. Wool Bur. Inc., N.Y.C. Vice pres. womens bd. United Cerebral Palsy. Fellow Am. Soc. Interior Designers (Presdl. citation 1975, 80, named Designer of Yr. 1979); mem. Home Fashion League; Fashion Group (bd. dirs.), Decorators Club. Clubs: Ravislo Country (Homewood, Ill.); Mchts. and Mfrs. (bd. govs.) (Chgo.). Contbr. articles in field. Home: 2801 N Sheridan Rd Chicago IL 60657 Office: 13-124 Merchandise Mart Chicago IL 60654

BOARDMAN, CATHY N., non-profit organization administrator; b. Middletown, Conn., Jan. 29, 1949; d. John Alden and Barbara Searls (Tuttle) Nichols; m. Gerald Charles Weir, May 1, 1982; 1 child by previous marriage, Julian. B.A., Lawrence U., 1971; M.B.A., U. Wis.-Oshkosh, 1984. Exec. dir. Wis. Religious Coalition for Abortion Rights, Appleton, Wis., 1979—. Bd. dirs. Appleton LWV, 1972-78, pres., 1977; treas. Outagamie County Democratic Party, 1977. Unitarian-Universalist. Avocations: racquetball, weaving, knitting, cross country skiing. Home: 838 W Prospect Ave Appleton WI 54914

BOATRIGHT, ALESIA DEAN, human resources executive; b. Dayton, Ohio, Dec. 31, 1960; d. Carl Hughes and Peggy Justine (Wilkerson) B. B.A., Univ. So. Calif., 1982. Tng. dir. Bullock's Co., Costa Mesa, Calif., 1982-84; coll. relations coordinator Xerox Corp., El Segundo, Calif., 1984—. Pub. speaker Girl Scouts U.S.A., Orange County, Calif., 1984. Mem. Women in Communications, Inc. (bd. dirs. 1982-84), AAUW, NAACP, Nat. Assn. for Female Execs., Inc., Am. Guild Variety Artists, U. So. Calif. Alumni Assn. Democrat. Office: Xerox Corp 880 Apollo St El Segundo CA 90245

BOATWRIGHT, MARY HOWARD, mem. Republican Nat. Com.; b. Houston, Apr. 8, 1920; d. Arch Franklin and Dorothy (Bennett) Howard; A.B., Trinity Coll., Washington, 1941; m. Victor Taliaferro Boatwright, Aug. 29, 1945; children—Mary Dorsey, John Lord, William Howard, Mary Taliaferro. Mem. Bd. Wardens and Burgesses Stonington (Conn.) Borough, 1960-64; mem. Conn. Ho. of Reps. from 43d Dist., 1962-66; mem. Rep. Nat. Com. for Conn., 1972—. Roman Catholic. Address: 16 Denison Ave Stonington CT 06378

BOAZ, DONALEE, pastoral counselor, consultant; b. Grand Junction, Colo., Apr. 8, 1934; d. Leon T. and Marian (Fonder) Hutton; m. Richard Boas, Apr. 7, 1956 (div. 1983); children—Roxanne, Annika, Becca. Cert. pastoral ministry Seattle U., 1978; cert. clin. pastoral edn. Va. Mason Hosp., 1979; B.A., Antioch West, 1980. Cert. neuro-linguistic programmer. Owner Donalee's Studio of Dance, Kirkland, Wash., 1952-63; adminstrv. asst. Ch. of Redeemer, Kenmore, Wash., 1974-76; counselor Eastside Mental Health, Bothell, Wash., 1976-79; psychotherapist, Seattle, 1979—; owner, cons. Optimum Options, Seattle, 1979—; mem. adj. faculty Seattle U. Northwest Coll. Holistic Studies and Huston Sch. Theology, 1980—; cons. various non-profit orgns., Phoenix, Los Angeles, Seattle. Vice pres. Episcopal Ch. standing com. on stewardship, 1979-81; active in local politics., 1968-80. Assoc. mem. Clin. Pastoral Edn., Nat. Speakers Assn., Wash. Assn. Counseling and Devel. Episcopalian. Avocations: philosophy; carpentry; bridge; entertaining; travel. Office: Optimum Options Grosvenor House 500 Wall St Suite 322 Seattle WA 98121

BOAZ-KOPP, MELINDA HILLARIE, beverage company executive; b. N.Y.C., Mar. 29, 1957; d. Richard Stuart and Iris Ann (Cohan) Boaz; m. Martin Andrew Kopp, Jan. 4, 1986. B.A., Lehman Coll. CUNY, 1978; M.B.A., Fordham U., 1982. Mktg. research asst., analyst project dir., Colgate-Palmolive Co., N.Y.C., 1978-81, mktg. asst., asst. product mgr., 1981-83; assoc. product mgr. Jhirmack Hair Care Products, Internat. Playtex, Inc., Stamford, Conn., 1983-84; assoc. brand promotion mgr. PepsiCo., Inc., Purchase, N.Y., 1984-86, allied channel mktg. mgr., 1986—. Mem. Nat. Assn. Female Execs. (vol. cons. project bus. jr. achievement program). Jewish. Avocations: skiing; tennis; swimming; aerobics. Home: 104 Oakridge Dr South Salem NY 10590 Office: PepsiCo Inc 700 Anderson Hill Rd Purchase NY 10577

BOBBETT, LYNN MARIA, community housing authority executive; b. Corona, N.Y., Nov. 5, 1954; d. Angelo Jose Olivencia and Joan Barbara (Morris) Davis. B.A., SUNY-Fredonia, 1982. Cert. in drama therapy. Librarian tech. asst. N.Y. Pub. Library, N.Y.C., 1972-78; with Cornell's Coop. Extension program of Chautauqua County, Jamestown, N.Y., 1982; assoc. community services coordinator Albany Housing Authority, N.Y., 1983—. Roman Catholic. Avocations: reading; poetry. Home: care Davis 400 Central Ave 7N Albany NY 12206 Office: PO Box 6105 Albany NY 12206

BOCELL, CATHERINE LONG, architect, interior designer; b. Kansas City, Mo., Nov. 11, 1948; d. Marshall and Elizabeth (Clark) Long; m. James Russell Bocell, Jr., July 18, 1970 (div. Feb. 1983); children—James Russell III, Marshall Long, Benjamin Clark. A.S. in Interior Design, Garland Jr. Coll., Boston, 1968; B.F.A., U. Houston, 1971, M.Arch., 1986; A.A. in Interior Design, Art Inst. Houston, 1983. Pres., Catherine Bocell Interiors, Houston, 1969—; watercolorist. Docent, Jr. League Houston, 1971-76, chmn. advt. charity ball program, 1980; chmn. sports Channel 8 Houston Pub. TV Auction, 1980-82. Recipient 1st place award for watercolor, 1975. Assoc. mem. Am. Soc. Interior Designers. Republican. Presbyterian. Home and Office: 7465 Brompton St Houston TX 77025

BOCHENKO, CAROLE ANNE, manufacturing company safety executive; b. Phila., Nov. 27, 1945; d. Walter Francis and Margaret Jane (Hindman) Thompson; m. Robert Bochenko, Nov. 22, 1980 (div. May 1983). B.A., Temple U., Phila., 1978. Cert. occupational health and safety, Temple U., Villanova U. Asst. safety supr. Phila. Coke Co. Inc., Phila., 1969-71, safety supr., 1971-73, dir. personnel and safety, 1973-78; div. mgr. safety and security Kelsey Hayes Co., Phila., 1978—; pres., chmn. Data Research, Inc., Phila., 1983—; dir. Affiliated Med., Phila., 1983—; lectr. Drexel U., 1983-84; cons in field Contbr. articles to profl. jours. Chmn. first aid and safety programs ARC, Phila., 1974-76. Recipient safety achievement awards Phila. Safety Council. Mem. Am. Soc. Safety Engrs. (treas. Phila. chpt. 1978-79, 80), Nat. Safety Mgmt. Soc., AAUW, Nat. Assn. Female Execs., Am. Soc. Personnel Adminstrs., Nat. Fire Protection Assn., Ind. Relations Assn. Phila., Am. Mgmt. Assn. Republican. Home: 206 Berkeley Trace Bensalem PA 19020 Office: Kelsey Hayes Co 11000 Roosevelt Blvd Philadelphia PA 19116

BOCK, CAROLYN ANN, education materials company consultant, writer; b. New Bavaria, Ohio, Jan. 25, 1942; d. Wilfred Ignatius and Marcella Mary (Birkemeier) Gerschutz; m. Donald Charles Bock, Sept. 10, 1974; 1 son, Jonathon Edward. Student Notre Dame Coll., 1960-62, John Carroll U., 1962-66; bus. degree in progress Lorain County Community Coll., 1986—. With sales dept. Schaffer Diversified Corp., Cleve., 1964-69; columnist, writer West Life Newspaper, Westlake, Ohio, 1980-83, Westlaker Times, Lorain, Ohio, 1983-84; cert. coordinator Personal Dynamics Inst., Mpls., 1985; cons. Dynamic Living Assocs., Westlake, 1986—. Writer in field. Author: Authors, Artists and Auras (forthcoming 1986); untitled history Gerschutz family (forthcoming 1986/87). Trustee Community Action Team, Westlake, 1980-85, Westlake Arts Council, 1985—, co-founder, 1983-84, pres., 1984-85; chmn. Morning Seminar, Rocky River, Ohio, 1981-85; pres. Westlake PTA Council, 1980-82, Parkside Jr. High PTA, Westlake, 1983-84; com. chmn., den leader Cleve. council Cub Scouts, Westlake, 1977-80; active mem. Clague Playhouse, Westlake, 1985—, Westlake Hist. Soc., 1985—, Nuclear Freeze Campaign, Cleve., 1984—. Recipient Outstanding Service award Westlake Cub Scouts, 1980; named hon. life mem. Ohio PTA, 1982; Ohio Arts Council grantee, 1985; Notre Dame scholar, 1960. Mem. Nat. Assn. Female Execs., Am. Entrepreneurs Assn., Sigma Delta Chi. Republican. Unitarian Universalist. Club: Cleve. Press. Avocations: traveling; reading; spending time at cottage; cooking. Home: 23553 Belmont Dr Westlake OH 44145 Office: Dynamic Living Assocs 23553 Belmont Dr Westlake OH 44145

BOCKIAN, DONNA MARIE, computer systems manager; b. N.Y.C., June 4, 1946; d. Forrest Mager and Mary C. (Lovelace) Hastings; m. James Bernard Bockian, Sept. 16, 1984; children—Vivian Shifra, Adrian Adena. B.A. in Psychology, Vassar Coll., 1968; diploma in systems analysis NYU, 1978. Computer programmer RCA, N.Y.C., 1968-71; systems analyst United Artists Corp., N.Y.C., 1971-78; project leader Bradford Nat. Corp., N.Y.C., 1978-81; project mgr. Mfrs. Hanover Trust, N.Y.C., 1981-83; project mgr. Chem. Bank, N.Y.C., 1983—. Mem. Assn. Women in Computing (exec. com. 1982-83). Club: Vassar (N.Y.C.). Avocation: photography. Home: 26 Farmhouse Ln Morristown NJ 07960

BOCKMAN, LOUANN LAIRD, civic worker; b. Watseka, Ill., Nov. 6, 1954; d. Lloyd Rex and Marjorie Mae (Stanley) Laird; m. James Harold Bockman, Sept. 2, 1978; children—Cortney, Natalie, Lindsey, James, Megan. Nursing diploma Copley Sch. Nursing, Aurora, Ill., 1979. R.N., Ill. Nurses's asst. Iroquois Meml. Hosp., Watseka, 1974-75; nurse's asst. Copley Meml. Hosp., Aurora, 1976-79, nurse, 1979-81; troop organizer, leader Fox Valley council Girl Scouts U.S. 1981—, council del, 1981—, service unit dir., 1984—; v.p. Parents-Tchrs. League, Aurora, 1985—; active St. Paul's Lutheran Ch., Aurora, including helper Vacation Bible Sch, 1979—, chairwoman nursery, 1983-85; active Woman's Bible Study, Aurora, 1984—, Prayer Ministry, Aurora, 1985—. Recipient Spl. Service award St. Paul's Luth. Ch. Youth Bd., 1984, Fox Valley Girl Scout Assn. award, 1985; aux. scholar Iroquois Meml. Hosp., 1973. Mem. Copley Sch. Nursing Alumnae Assn. (fin. com. 1985). Avocations: child development; swimming; sewing.

BODDEN, JANE ELLEN, airline reservations manager; b. George Town, Grand Cayman, British West Indies, Dec. 7, 1948; came to U.S., 1969; d. Clarence Vernon and Dorothy (Gressman) Thompson; m. Ashby A. Bodden, Sept. 10, 1969. Student Miami Dade Community Coll., 1984-85, Embry Riddle Aero. U., 1985—. Receptionist Coral Caymanian Hotel, Seven Mile Beach, Grand Cayman, 1965-66; teller Royal Bank Can., Georgetown, 1966-69; teller Pan Am. Bank, N. Miami Beach, Fla., 1970-73; reservations Mackey Internat. Airlines, Ft. Lauderdale, Fla., 1973-78; reservations mgr. Cayman Airways Ltd., Coral Gables, Fla., 1978—; mem. South by Southeast, Miami, 1983—. Elder Faith Presbyterian Ch., Pembroke Pines, Fla., 1984, chmn. Women of Ch. Ruth Circle, 1982-84. Mem. Fla. Airlines Reservations Mgrs. Assn. (pres. 1983-84). Office: Cayman Airways Ltd 250 Catalonia Ave Suite 602 Coral Gables FL 33134

BODE, BARBARA, foundation executive; b. Evanston, Ill., Aug. 4, 1940; d. Carl and Margaret Emilie (Lutze) B. B.A. magna cum laude, U. Md., 1962, M.A., 1966; scholar Ludwig-Maximillians-Universitat, Munich, Fed. Republic Germany, 1960-61; postgrad. UCLA, 1966-67. Woodrow Wilson teaching fellow N.C. Central U., Durham, 1965-66; community developer Community Devel. Dept. Prince George's County, Md., 1967-68; field dir. Nat. Council on Hunger and Malnutrition in U.S., Washington, 1968-70; pres. Children's Found., Washington, 1970—; mem. Food Industry Adv. Commn., Fed. Energy Adminstrn., 1975-76; cons., mem. steering and adv. coms., commns. and orgns. in field. Author: School Lunch Bag, 1971; Barriers to School Breakfast, 1979. Contbr. numerous articles to profl. jours. Mem. Citizens Bd. of Inquiry into Brookside Miners' Strike, Harlan, Ky., 1974; mem. nat. adv. com. Food Day, 1975, 76, 77, Rural Am. Women, 1978—; bd. dirs., exec. com. Human Services Inst. for Children and Families, 1973-75; bd. dirs., v.p. Am. Freedom From Hunger Found., 1973-78, U.S. Com. on Refugees, 1976-78; bd. dirs., co-founder RAINBOW TV Works, 1976—, Nat. Council on Women, Work and Welfare, 1976-77, Nat. Com. for Responsive Philanthropy, 1975—; bd. dirs. Am. Parents Com., 1974-78, Rural Am., Inc., 1975-79, Coalition for Children and Youth, 1975-79, Women's Campaign Fund, 1982—, Child Care Action Campaign, 1984—, Human SERVE Fund, 1984—, Washington Child Devel. Council, 1984—; convenor Nat. Women's Polit. Caucus, 1971; nat. adv. bd. dirs. Women's Campaign Fund, 1975-77; active inpress bur. Poor People's Campaign, 1968; mem. planning com. Women's Leadership Conf. Dem. Nat. Com., 1972, mwm. Women's Nat. Dem. Club; vice chmn. com. on regional conf. planning and strategy, 1969-70; active voting and civil rights campaigns, 1961—. Named One of Ten Outstanding Young Women of Am., various women's orgns., 1977; Woodrow Wilson fellow, 1963-64, NDEA fellow, 1966-67; English Speaking Union scholar, summer 1964, Bundesrepublik scholar Goethe Institut, summer 1965. Episcopalian. Office: 815 Fifteenth St NW Suite 928 Washington DC 20005

BODINE, DELLA L., nursing administrator; b. Trenton, Oct. 16, 1951; d. Richard Stauffer and Jessie Mae (Beck) White; m. Wayne H. Bodine, July 2, 1972; 1 child, Jessica Leigh. Diploma Helene Fuld Sch. Nursing, Trenton, 1972; B.S.N., Trenton State Coll., 1980; M.S.N., U. Pa., 1983. Lic. nursing home adminstr. N.J. Dir. nursing Lakewood House, Burlington, N.J., 1972-73, Moorestown Nursing Home, N.J., 1973-78; staff nurse Burlington County Meml. Hosp., N.J., 1978-80, head nurse, 1980-81; dir. nursing Mt. Holly Ctr., N.J., 1981-82; assoc. dir. nursing Hamilton Hosp., Trenton, 1983-85. Mem. N.J. Assn. Hosp. Recruiters. Leader, Brownies. Owner, mgr. Frank's Folly Family Campground, Lyndell, Pa., 1984—. Home: PO Box 257 Lyndell PA 19354 Office: Hamilton Hosp PO Box H Trenton NJ

BODKIN, JEAN FLETCHER, psychiatric social worker; b. Jackson Heights, N.Y., Oct. 4, 1919; d. William M. and Lillian (Pastor) Fletcher; m. Richard E. Bodkin, Oct. 4, 1952 (dec. 1983); children—Karen, Alec, Andrew. B.A., U. Chgo., 1942; M.S.W., U. Conn.-West Hartford, 1959; postgrad. Met. Inst. for Psychoanalytic Studies, N.Y.C., 1963-66. Reporter, City Press, Chgo., 1942-43, Times Picayune, New Orleans, 1943-44; promotion and advt. staff Knopf Pub., N.Y.C., 1949-52; psychiatric social worker Fairfield Family Service, Conn., 1959-62, Bridgeport Child Guidance Clinic, Conn., 1963-65; psychotherapist Norwalk Hosp. Psychiat. Clinic, Conn., 1965—; psychiat. cons. Elderhouse, Norwalk, 1980-82; field work faculty U. Conn., W. Hartford, 1974-81, N.Y. U., 1982-83; sec. Assn. Psychiat. Clinics of Conn., 1981-82. Legislator Rep. Town Meeting, Westport, Conn., 1977-83, R.T.M. Fin. Com., Westport, 1981-83, Environ. Com., Library Com., Westport, 1979-81; bd. dirs. Dept. Social Services, Westport, 1975-76; commn. mem. Westport Housing Authority, 1984—. Fellow Am. Orthopsychiat. Assn.; mem. Acad. Cert. Social Workers, Nat. Assn. Social Workers, Conn. Soc. Clin. Social Workers. Democrat. Unitarian. Office: Norwalk Hosp Psychiatric Clinic Stevens St Norwalk CT 06850

BODMAN, HELENE DUNN, musicologist; b. N.Y.C., Nov. 22, 1936; d. Kempton and Susan Barret (Gill) Dunn; m. Richard S. Bodman, Jan. 28, 1961; children—Taylor, James Martyn. Ed. New Eng. Conservatory, 1957-60; B.Mus., San Francisco Conservatory of Music, 1968; M.A., Am. U., 1982. Dir. Opera and Symphony Previews, San Francisco, 1966-67; instr. piano, music theory, San Francisco, 1969-71, Wilmington, Del., 1973-76; research and photography Here Today: San Francisco's Archtl. Heritage, 1969; staff Congressman William S. Mailliard, Washington, 1973; exhbn. coordinator Del. State Arts Council, 1977-78; music librarian Am. U., Washington, 1981-84; pres. Music Info. Specialists, 1984—, dir. Discovering Music, 1984—; cons. young artist program Boys Clubs Am., 1985—. Author: Chinese Music

Inonography: A History of Chinese Musical Instruments Depicted in Chinese Art, 1986. . Editor: Am. Women Composers News/Forum, 1984—; program annotator Dumbarton Ave. Concert Series, 1984—. Bd. dirs. Spring Opera of San Francisco, 1967-71, Wilmington Music Sch., 1973-78, Nat. Symphony Orch., Washington, 1979-82, Washington Performing Arts; trustee San Francisco Conservatory of Music, 1967-71; steering com. Friends of Music at the Smithsonian Instn., 1980—; bd. overseers New Eng. Conservatory, 1985—. Mem. Am. Musicol. Soc. Address: 1336 30th St NW Washington DC 20007

BODY, JANET, advertising agency executive; b. Chgo., Sept. 21, 1937; d. Donald Arthur and Ora (Blanchard) Nightingale; m. David Wayne Body, Oct. 31, 1967. B.A., Middlebury Coll., 1959. Sec., Irwin Wasey Ruthrauff & Ryan, Chgo., 1963-65; copywriter D'Arcy Advt., Chgo., 1965-67; copy chief Needham Harper & Steers, Chgo., 1967-70; owner, creative dir. Body & Co., Advt., Portland, Maine, 1970—. Trustee, Portland Mus. Art, 1981—; trustee Jr. Achievement, Portland, 1983; bd. dirs. Women's Resource Ctr., Portland, 1983—, Kennebec council Girl Scouts U.S.A., 1978. Recipient 17 Hatch awards for creative excellence Boston Ad Club, 1977-83; Mem. Advt. Club Greater Portland (dir., Conwell award 1980, 61 Broderson awards for creative excellence 1978-83), Am Assn. Advt. Agys. (New Eng. council), Greater Portland C. of C. (dir. 1981—). Address: Body & Co 39 Exchange St Portland ME 04101

BOE, LORI MARIE, computer analyst; b. Logansport, Ind., Mar. 21, 1961; d. James Kenneth and Alma Jane (Turner) B. B.S., Ind. State U., 1983. Data resource analyst Riggs Nat. Bank, Washington, 1984-85; systems analyst Texaco, Inc., Houston, 1985-86; tech. specialist Fed. Res. Bank, Atlanta, 1986—. Mem. inaugural dinner and ball com. Ind. Soc. Washington, 1985; actuality vol. Reagan-Bush, Washington, 1984; mem. Houston Ballet Guild, 1985-86, Soc. League Against Molestation, Houston, 1984-86, Young Republicans, Houston, 1985-86. Mem. Assn. Women in Computing. Republican. Lutheran. Club: Toastmasters (Washington) (sgt.-at-arms 1985). Avocations: tennis; theater; reading; skiing; volunteer work. Home: 1165 La Vista Rd Apt 310 Atlanta GA 30324 Office: Fed Res Bank 104 Marietta St Atlanta GA 30303

BOECKMANN-ROSS, LAVERNE, publishing executive, foundation executive; b. Glendale, Calif., Oct. 14, 1949; d. Herbert F. and Jane Boeckmann; m. Steven A. Ross, Apr. 14, 1984. A.A., Glendale Jr. Coll., 1969; B.A., San Diego State U., 1971. Elem. tchr. Los Angeles Sch. Dist., 1974-78; account exec. Valley Mag., Granada Hills, Calif., 1978—; v.p. Tara Labs., Panorama City, Calif., 1982—; account exec. KABC Let's Talk Mag., Granada Hills, Calif., 1985—; co founder World Research Found., Sherman Oaks, Calif., 1983—. Coordinator Beauty Contest, Northridge, Calif., 1983. Mem. San Fernando Valley Exec. Assn. (bd. dirs. 1982-83), Nat. Female Execs. Assn., Women's Network Assn. Republican. Avocations: painting; dancing; skiing; travel; singing. Office: World Research Found 15300 Ventura Blvd #405 Sherman Oaks CA 91403

BOEHM, MARY MAGDALENE, interior designer, space planning consultant; b. Bluffton, Ohio, June 23, 1944; d. Marvin George and Martha Leoda (von Stein) B. B.S. in Interior Design, U. Cin., 1967. Designer, Taylor Designs, Cin., 1967-68, Space Design/Interior Architecture, Cin., 1968-74, Caudill, Rowlett, Scott, Houston, 1974-76; dept. head interior design, The Klein Partnership, Houston, 1977-80; propr. Boehm Design Assocs., Houston, 1980—; expert witness Tex. Health Facilities Comm.; tchr. interior design Jewish Community Ctr., Cin., 1968. Contbr. articles on interior design to profl. jours., newspapers. Recipient Hexter award, 1969, 76, Nat. award Inst. Bus. Designers, 1974, Burlington House award Burlington House Corp., 1974. Mem. Neartown Civic Assn., Preservation Alliance, Tex. Soc. Architects, Houston chpt. AIA; assoc. mem. AIA.

BOEHRINGER, MONICA EMMA, college admissions recruiter; b. Yonkers, N.Y., June 9, 1963; d. William and Ernesta (Castellg) B. Student Emerson Coll., 1981-82; Assoc. Occupational Studies, Tobe Coburn Sch., N.Y.C., 1985. Owner, contractor Blade Williams Fashion Coordination, Jackson, N.J., 1982-86; account exec. Wendi Winters Public Relations, N.Y.C., 1984-85; dept. mgr. Abraham & Straus, Eatontown, N.J., 1985-86; ter. mgr. Tobe Coburn Sch., N.Y.C., 1985—. Fashion show coordinator DECA, N.Y.C., 1983-84; promotional model DeLeigh Agy., Lakewood, N.J., 1983—, career cons. Msgr. Donovan High Sch., Toms River, N.J., 1985—. Fellow nat. Asn. Female Execs., Toba Coburn Alumni Assn., Fashion Group, Cousteau Soc., Nat. Geog. Soc., Nat. Wildlife Fedn. Republican. Roman Catholic. Avocations: horseback riding; theatre; Egyptology; creative writing; costume design. Office: Tobe Coburn Sch 686 Broadway New York NY 10012

BOELCSKEVY, HEIDI M(ARIA), airline pension fund executive; b. Zwittau, Czechoslovakia, Feb. 20, 1943; came to U.S., 1955; d. Roland Smolka and Elfriede (Heinisch) Smolka von Boelcskevy; m. V. B. Boelcskevy, Mar. 29, 1969. B.A., Hunter Coll., 1964; M.B.A., Bernard Baruch Coll., CCNY, 1968. With Pan Am. World Airways, Inc., N.Y.C., 1968—, mgr. pension plans, 1981-82, mgr. pension systems, 1982-83, mgr. pension, 1983—; dir. Finleasco, Inc., N.Y.C., 1975—, Qubix (N.A.) Inc., N.Y.C., 1979—. Mem. Am. Mgmt. Assn. Nat. Assn. Female Execs., Internat. Found. Employee Benefits, Museum Modern Art (charter). Club: Atrium (N.Y.C.). Office: Pan Am World Airways Inc 200 Park Ave New York NY 10166

BOELENS, DENISE MARIE, psychologist; b. Wichita, Kans., May 6, 1953; d. Clyde Donald and Wilma Ruth (Espenshade) B.; Ph.D., U. Wash., 1980. Chief alcohol dependence treatment unit VA Med. Center, Salt Lake City; mem. clin. faculty dept. psychiatry, dept. family medicine U. Utah Med. Center. Mem. Am. Psychol. Assn., Utah Psychol. Assn. Home: PO Box 8561 Salt Lake City UT 84108 Office: 500 Foothill Dr 116A Salt Lake City UT 84148

BOEMI, PAMELA LYNNE BOGAN, marketing executive; b. Evanston, Ill., Jan. 11, 1953; d. Ralph A.L. and Margaret (Wickman) Bogan; m. Andrew A. Boemi, Nov. 4, 1978. B.A. in Journalism and English, Butler U., 1975; cert. bus. adminstrn. Keller Grad. Sch. Mgmt., Chgo., 1977. Mgr. client and industry planning Peat Marwick, Chgo., 1977-82; dir. mktg. Kupferberg, Goldberg & Neimark, Chgo., 1982—. Contbr. articles to profl. jours. Bd. dirs. Chgo. chpt. Nat. Com. Prevention of Child Abuse, 1983—; bd. dirs., residential fundraising chmn. Northfield United Way, 1984—, v.p. pub. relations, 1985—; chmn. membership com. Chgo. Council Volunteerism, 1983—. Mem. Am. Mktg. Assn., Women in Communications, Soc. Profl. Journalists. Clubs: Lake Geneva Country (fin. com. 1982—) (Wis.); Woman's Athletic (Chgo.). Office: Kupferberg Goldberg & Neimark 111 E Wacker Dr Chicago IL 60601

BOEPPLE, ELIZABETH DELAPP, psychologist; b. Syracuse, July 12, 1950; d. Howard W. and Irene (Gratien) DeLapp; B.A. cum laude, SUNY, Buffalo, 1971, M.Ed., 1974, Ph.D., 1977; children—Karen Anne, Kathryn Marie. Instr., SUNY, Geneseo, 1974-75; research coordinator Research and Devel. Complex, State U. Coll., Buffalo, 1976; psychologist West Seneca Devel. Center, 1977-79; psychologist N.Y. State Div. for Youth, Masten Park Secure Center, Buffalo, 1979—; instr. Erie Community Coll., 1973-75, Bryant & Stratten Bus. Inst., 1976. Cert. psychologist, N.Y. Mem. Phi Beta Kappa. Roman Catholic. Home: 46 Washington Hwy Snyder NY 14226 Office: 485 Best St Buffalo NY 14208

BOER, ELLEN S(TRAUSS), lawyer; b. N.Y.C., Oct. 15, 1941; d. Michael E. and Cecilia (Rosen) Strauss; m. F. Peter Boer, Aug. 9, 1963; children—Alexandra, Andrew. B.A., Mt. Holyoke Coll., 1963; J.D., South Tex. Coll. Law, 1977. Bar: Tex., Conn., U.S. Dist. Ct. Of counsel Simmons & Zwernemann, Houston, 1977-78; asst. town atty. Town of Greenwich (Conn.), 1980-83; sole practice law specializing in spl. edn. law, Washington, 1983—. Planning commr. Midland, Mich., 1972-73. Mem. Law Rev., South Tex. Coll. Law, 1977. Mem. ABA, Tex. Bar Assn., Conn. Bar Assn., Greenwich Bar Assn., Order of Lytae. Home: 325 Taconic Rd Greenwich CT 06830

BOERST, RITA ANNE, insurance company executive; b. Licata, Italy, June 14, 1946; came to U.S. 1951 (father Am. citizen); d. Angelo and Maria (Callea) Cellura; 1 child, Erik. B.Ed., Mary Manse Women's Coll., 1968. Legal sec. Law firms in Miami, Fla., 1971-77; pres., owner Caribbean Title Ins., Inc., Miami, 1978—. Named one of Most Outstanding Bus. Women Dade County, Am. Bus. Women Assn., 1984. Mem. Nat. Assn. Women Bus. Owners (charter pres. 1978-79). Republican. Roman Catholic. Club: Soroptimist (charter sec. 1980-81). Avocations: motorcycle riding; reading; body building. Office: Caribbean Title Ins Inc 9245 SW 158 Ln Suite 201 Miami FL 33157

BOGAD, ALICE ROSE, beverage company executive; b. Waterbury, Conn., July 26, 1922; d. Edward A. and Catherine A. (Wood) Rose; student Hunter Coll., 1943, U. Okla., 1944, Am. U., 1945; m. Alfred J. Bogad, Sept. 30, 1971; children by previous marriage—Nancy, Karen, Eric. Propr., dir. Mid-Hudson Floor & Wall Co., Poughkeepsie, N.Y., 1948-51, Hudson Valley Welding and Supply, Poughkeepsie, 1951-55; propr. Colonial Knolls Devel. Co., 1955-65; asst. mgr. Dutchess County (N.Y.) Airport, 1965-68; propr. and mgr. Queen's Ransom Gallery, Poughkeepsie, 1967-71; sec., treas., dir. G.H. Ford Tea Co., Inc., Poughkeepsie, 1974—; guest lectr. on tea various schs. and community orgns., 1974—. Pres., Arlington High Sch. PTA, 1963-64; chmn. scholarship com. Arlington Sch. Dist., 1960-64; sec. to zoning bd. Town of Poughkeepsie, 1955-60, dep. zoning adminstr., 1971-73, chmn. Zoning Bd. Appeals, 1976-78; trustee Vassar Temple, 1979—, chmn. membership, 1978—; bd. dirs. Dutchess County (N.Y.) Arts Council, 1979—, chmn. public funding com., 1979-80; mem. citizens' adv. com. Dutchess Community Coll. Served with WAVES, 1942-45. Recipient Life Member award PTA, N.Y. State, 1964, Outstanding Citizen award Dutchess County Bd. Legislators, 1981. Mem. Tea Assn. U.S. (assoc. bd. dirs. 1977-78, chmn. 1979). Culinary Inst. Am. (cons. 1975—, mem. corp. 1980—, chmn. fellows com.) Bus. and Profl. Women's Assn. Republican. Club: Zonta (sec. 1978-79). Contbr. articles on tea industry to bus. and trade jours. Home: 7 Wilbur Ct PO Box 3506 Poughkeepsie NY 12603 Office: 110 Dutchess Turnpike PO Box 3407 Poughkeepsie NY 12603

BOGAN, MARY FLAIR, stock brokerage company executive; b. Providence, R.I., July 9, 1948; d. Ralph A.L. and Mary Frances (Dyer) B. B.A. cum laude, Vassar Coll., 1969. Lic. stock broker. Actress Trinity Square Repertory, Providence, 1965-66, Skylight Comic Opera, Milw., 1970, Gretna Playhouse, Pa., 1971, Playhouse in the Park, Cin., 1972, nat. tour No Sex Please, We're British, 1973, Playmaker's Repertory, Chapel Hill, N.C., 1975, Sara Lee comml. Benton & Bowles, 1976; account exec. E. F. Hutton & Co., Inc., Providence, 1977—; fin. reporter WPRI-TV 12-ABC Affiliate, Providence, 1982—; tchr. adult edn. Community Coll. R.I., Warwick, Lincoln, 1980—. Treas. Nickerson Community Ctr. Bd. dirs., R.I., 1983-84. Recipient Century Club award E. F. Hutton, 1980, 81, 82, 83, Blue Chip Sales award, 1983, 85. Mem. Internat. Platform Assn., R.I. Fedn. Republican Women. Roman Catholic. Clubs: Providence Art, Turks Head, Brown Faculty (Providence). Avocations: tennis; skiing. Office: E F Hutton & Co Inc 1 Turks Head Pl Suite 600 Providence RI 02903

BOGARD-REYNOLDS, CHRISTINE ELIZABETH, stock brokerage executive; b. Aberdeen, Md., Apr. 15, 1954; d. Charles Francis and Donna June (Mosbaugh) Bogard; m. Lawrence Edward Reynolds, Sept. 22, 1979; 1 child, Zachary Kagan. Student, U. Colo., 1972-73. Adminstrv. asst. Lange Co., Broomfield, Colo., 1972-73; field sales and service rep. Bowman Products Div., Denver, 1973-75; cashier Regency Inn, Denver, 1975-76; gen. mgr., sec.-treas., Edison Agy. Inc., Denver, 1976-81; gen. mgr. Edison Press, Inc., Englewood, Colo., 1978-80, 81; dir. advt. and pub. relations Blinder, Robinson & Co., Englewood, 1981—; ptnr. Reynolds Assocs., Denver, 1982—. Co-chmn. fundraising Blinder Robinson Emergency Ctr. Children's Hosp., Englewood, 1982—; benefit com. mem. Blinder Research Found. for Crohn's Disease; exec. com. Phil Donahue Benefit for Passages, 1986. Home: 2150 Garrison St Lakewood CO 80215 Office: Blinder Robinson & Co 6455 S Yosemite Englewood CO 80111

BOGART, GRACE ELIZABETH, information scientist; b. Bolton, Mass., June 10, 1923; d. Francis Gould and Grace Effie (Smith) Mentzer; B.S., U. Mass., 1945; M.S., Simmons Coll., 1975; m. Lindsay Boyd, Aug. 6, 1944 (dec.); children—David Gordon, Bethanne, Sandra Lindsay; m. 2d, Victor Brociner, Nov. 13, 1971 (dec.); m. 3d, Stanley C. Bogart, Aug. 7, 1977. Librarian, Lincoln Lab. Library, MIT, Lexington, 1959-77; dir. info. services Roberts Info. Service, Inc., Fairfax, Va., 1977-78; pres. Bogart-Brociner Assocs., Bolton, Mass., 1978—; rep. to adv. bd. Nat. Transls. Center, John Crerar Library, Chgo., 1975—. Mem. Spl. Libraries Assn. (chmn. spl. com. translation problems 1973-76), Am. Soc. Info. Sci. (local arrangements chmn. nat. conf. Boston 1975, publicity chmn. nat. conf. 1980, mem. nat. conf. com. 1983), Soc. Fed. Linguists, Compiler; A Guide to Scientific and Technical Journals in Translation, 1972; How to Obtain a Translation, 1976. Home and Office: 295 Main St Bolton MA 01740

BOGART, LEE C., interior designer; b. Bklyn., Nov. 10, 1931; d. Frank M. and Anna (Rovere) Corigliano; m. Adrian T. Bogart, Apr. 19, 1952; children—Laurie, Cynthia, Adrian, Clinton F. A.A., Centenary Coll., 1951; student N.Y. Sch. Interior Design, 1970. Owner, mgr. Bogart Cons. Inc., Locust Valley, N.Y., 1971-74; head designer archtl. firm Bogart, Geldbaugh, Goldstein, Peters, Locust Valley, 1974-76; pres. Bogart Consultants, Locust Valley, N.Y., 1976—, distbr. Thimble Hall Ltd. for Hallie Greer. Mem. Am. Soc. Interior Decorators, Decorators Club N.Y. Home: Laurel Ln Locust Valley NY 11560 Office: 250 Birch Hill Rd Locust Valley NY 11560

BOGARTY, JEAN ANN, veterinarian; b. Fountain Green, Md., Apr. 30, 1947; d. Walter and Irene C. (Burton) B.; m. Jonathan Mitchell Senior, June 22, 1974. B.S. in Edn., Towson State Coll., 1969; student Johns Hopkins U., 1969-70, U. Md., 1970-71; V.M.D. U. Pa., 1976. Veterinarian, Reisterstown Vet. Clinic, (Md.), 1976-77, Jarrettsville Vet. Clinic (Md.), 1977-80, Hickory Vet. Hosp., Inc., Forest Hill, Md., 1980—. Mem. AVMA, Phi Zeta. Democrat. Roman Catholic. Office: Hickory Veterinary Hospital Inc 534 East Jarrettsville Rd Forest Hill MD 21050

BOGAS, KATHLEEN LAURA, lawyer; b. Detroit, Mar. 4, 1951; d. Edward Joseph and Eleanor Laura (Hughes) Bogas; m. Frank Kavanaugh Rhodes, III, Jan. 2, 1982; children—Katherine Bogas, Frank Kavanaugh IV. A.B., U. Detroit, 1972, J.D., 1975. Bar: Mich. 1975. Assoc. law firm Sachs, Nunn, Kates, Kadushin, O'Hare, Helveston & Waldman, P.C., Detroit, 1975-80, ptnr., Southfield, Mich., 1981—. Mng. editor Jour. Urban Law, 1974-75. Mem. Mich. Trial Lawyers Assn. (chmn. jud. qualifications com. 1981—, chmn. ct. rules com. 1983-84), Assn. Trial Lawyers Am., State Bar of Mich., Women Lawyers of Mich., Detroit Bar Assn., Oakland County Bar Assn. Democrat. Home: 268 N Williamsburg Rd Birmingham MI 48010 Office: Sachs Nunn Kates et al 17117 W Nine Mile Rd Suite 1742 Southfield MI 48015

BOGGS, BARBARA JEAN, educator; b. Beaumont, Tex., Oct. 13, 1940; d. Dennis M. and Helen Grace (Ferrell) B. B.S., Tex. Woman's U., 1962; Cert. in Elem. Edn., U. Houston, 1970; Cert. in Learning Disabled, Lamar U., 1974; M.Ed., Stephen F. Austin U., 1980; Ed. Diagnosticians Cert., U. Houston, 1984. Statistician, Humble Oil & Refining Co., Houston, 1963-67; tchr. Sheldon Ind. Sch. Dist., Houston, 1967-84, ednl. diagnostician, 1984-85. Mem. Sheldon Edn. Assn. (pres. 1982-84) Tex. Tchrs. Assn. Republican. Roman Catholic. Home: 3230 Elmridge St Houston TX 77025 Office: Sheldon Ind Sch Dist 8450 CE King Pkwy Houston TX 77025

BOGGS, CORINNE CLAIBORNE (LINDY), congresswoman; b. Brunswick Plantation, La., Mar. 13, 1916; d. Roland and Corinne (Morrison) Claiborne; m. Thomas Hale Boggs, Jan. 22, 1938 (dec.); children—Barbara (Mrs. Paul E. Sigmund, Jr.), Thomas Hale, Corinne (Mrs. Steven V. Roberts). B.A., Sophie Newcomb Coll., Tulane U., 1935; L.L.D. (hon.); Litt.D., U. St. Thomas; D.Pub. Service (hon.), Trinity Coll., Washington, 1975; hon. degree St. Mary of Woods; LL.D., Loyola U. Tchr. history and English, St. James Parish, La., 1936-37; elected to 93d Congress to fill vacancy caused by death of husband, 1973; re-elected to 93d-99th Congresses from 2d La. Dist., mem. appropriations com. majority mem. from Ho. of Reps., Am. Revolution Bicentennial Adminstrn. Bd., chmn. Commn. Ho. of Reps. Bicentenary; mem. campaign com. Democratic Nat. Com., 1974; chairwoman Dem. Nat. Conv., 1976; mem. Com. on Bicentennial of U.S. Constn. Pres., Dem. Congl. Wives Forum, 1953, Womans Nat. Democratic Club, 1957-58, Congl. Club, 1970-72; co-chmn. Inaugural Balls for Presidents John F. Kennedy, 1961, Lyndon Johnson, 1965; mem. Nat. Hist. Publications and Records Com. Bd. dirs. La. Council for Music and Performing Arts; hon. bd. dirs. Met. New Orleans chpt. Nat. Found. March of Dimes; bd. advisers. CLOSE-UP and Presdl. Classroom; regent emeritus Smithsonian Instn.; mem. president's council Tulane U. Recipient Weiss Meml. award NCCJ, 1974; Nat. Oak award La. Assn. Ind. Colls. and Univs., Disting. Service medal Saint Mary's Dominican Coll., 1976, Humanitarian award AMVETS Nat. Aux., Torch of Liberty award B'nai B'rith, 1976, Gala IV award Birmingham So. U., 1976, Eleanor Roosevelt Humanitarian award, 1977, E. Roosevelt Centennial award, 1984, Disting. Alumna award Tulane U., 1986; 1st woman recipient VFW Congl. award, 1986. Mem. Nat. Soc. Colonial Dames, LWV, Internat. Fedn. Catholic Alumni. Office: Rayburn House Office Bldg Room 2353 Washington DC 20515

BOGGS, PAMELA POLETE, advertising, marketing and publishing executive; b. Ironton, Mo., Nov. 26, 1943; d. John William and Rosemary (Carmack) Polete; m. Jan Parr Boggs, Aug. 18, 1963 (div. Jan. 1974). B.S., Southwestern at Memphis, 1965; M.B.A., Fairleigh-Dickinson U., 1982. Product mgr., sales rep. Warner/Chilcott Labs. div. Warner/Lambert Co., Morris Plains, N.J., 1973-77; product mgr. Winthrop Labs. div. Sterling Drug, N.Y.C., 1977; account supr. Sudler & Hennessey, Inc. div. Young & Rubicam, N.Y.C., 1978; dir. mktg. Ayerst Labs., Inc. div. Am. Home Products, N.Y.C., 1979-82; v.p., gen. mgr. Occupational Health Services, Inc., N.Y.C., 1982; pres. Conv. Mktg. Group, Inc., Nutley, N.J., 1983—. Patentee in field. Mem. Pharm. Advt. Council, Am. Mktg. Assn., Advt. Women N.Y. Unitarian. Home: 39 Ernst Ave Bloomfield NJ 07003 Office: Convention Mktg Group Inc 633 Franklin Ave Suite 103 Nutley NJ 07110

BOGLE, MYRA CRUMPTON, entrepreneur; b. Dexter, Ga., Oct. 10, 1923; d. Julius Mathew and Clara Naomi (Faircloth) Crumpton; m. Louis Neuburn Bogle, Feb. 8, 1975; children by previous marriage—Sheryl H. Deuster, Margaret H. Allison, Susan H. Garrett. Ed. ABC Sectl., Macon, Ga., 1945, Sch. Cosmetology and Hair Design, Macon, 1944. Owner, Myra's Beauty Salons, Milledgeville, Ga. and Macon, and Atlanta, 1946-84; owner Myra's Enterprises, Loganville, Ga. and Atlanta, 1974—; cons. in field. Tchr. Sunday Sch., Columbia, S.C., 1963-66; leader Girl Scouts U.S.A., Columbia, 1963-65, Macon, 1956-60; instr. YWCA, Columbia, 1964-65. Republican. Clubs: Briarcliff Garden (pres. 1951-52), Macon Hairdressers Assn. (pres. 1959-60). Avocations: sewing; gardening; piano; mandolin. Home: 601 Oneta Dr Norcross GA 30093 Office: 374 E Paces Ferry Rd Atlanta GA 30305

BOGORYA-BUCZKOWSKI, YVONNE, university dean, management educator, consultant; b. Warsaw, Poland, July 27, 1942; citizen of Can.; married, 2 children. M.Phil., U. Warsaw, 1966; M.A., York U., Toronto, Can., 1971, Ph.D., 1979. Instr. dept. humanities Atkingson Coll. York U., 1971-72; lectr. bus. communication dept. and mgmt. devel. inst. Ryerson Poly. Inst., Toronto, 1972-77; editor, pub. relations officer New Canadian Publs., 1977-78; dir. acad. affairs, prof. Canadian Sch. Mgmt. and Northland Open U., 1978-81, dean acad. affairs, 1981—, sec.-treas. bd. govs. 1977—, also v.p.; pres. Bogorya Cons., 1979—; chmn. acad. standards com. Univ. Without Walls Internat. Council, 1980—; vis. internat. prof. Internat. Mgmt. Centre from Buckingham, U.K., 1983—, bd. dirs. N.Am. Acad. Advs., 1983—; editorial dir. Mgmt. Decision Jour., Innovative Higher Edn., 1984—; mem. editorial adv. bd. Mgmt. Research News, 1984—. Author (with G. Korey): University Without Walls, 1980. Contbr. articles to profl. jours. Fellow Royal Soc. for Encouragement of Arts, Manufactures and Commerce; mem. Assn. Women Execs., Acad. Mgmt., Am. Bus. Communication Assn., Am. Mgmt. Assn./Canadian Mgmt. Centre, Internat. Council on Distance Edn., Council for Advancement of Experiential Learning, Am. Assembly of Collegiate Schs. Bus., Acad. Internat. Bus., Can. Soc. for Comparative Study of Civilizations (pres. 1983—). Office: Canadian Sch Mgmt Suite 715 150 Bloor St W Toronto ON M5S 2X9 Canada

BOGOSIAN, KAREN MARY, application systems consultant, educator; b. Medford, Mass., Feb. 24, 1951; d. Zaven and Mary (Balian) B.; married, 1969 (div. 1976); 1 child, Derek R. B.S., Lesley Coll., 1980; M.B.A., Suffolk U., 1985. Head spl. needs tchr. Gaebler Children's Ctr., Waltham, Mass., 1981-82, NUVA Inc., Gloucester, Mass., 1982-83, dir. alt. sch., 1982-83; application systems cons. McCormack & Dodge, Natick, Mass., 1984—. Shop steward Dept. Mental Health, Waltham, 1981-82. Democrat. Avocations: classical piano; tennis; languages; horseback riding. Home: Rockport MA 01966

BOGSTAHL, DEBORAH MARCELLE, pharmaceutical company executive; b. Irvington, N.J., June 5, 1950; d. Marcel and Helena Christina (de Jaroszynsky) Bogstahl; m. Richard Neil Press, Mar. 20, 1976; 1 child, Alexandra Boman. B.A. in English Edn., Trenton State Coll., 1972. Cert. tchr., N.J. Project dir. U.S. Testing Co., Hoboken, N.J., 1973-75; project dir. J. Walter Thompson Co., N.Y.C., 1975-77; research account exec. Dancer Fitzgerald Sample, N.Y.C., 1977-80; group research mgr. Bristol-Myers Co., N.Y.C., 1980—. Contbr. poetry to anthology. Mem. Am. Mktg. Assn. Democrat. Roman Catholic. Avocations: sailing; reading; writing; horticulture. Office: Bristol Myers Co 345 Park Ave New York NY 10154

BOHANNON, SHARI ANN, business executive; b. Bakersfield, Calif., July 27, 1946; d. Vernon David and Jacqueline Sharon (Kramer) Hobbs; A.A., West Valley Jr. Coll., 1968; B.S., San Jose State U., 1972; children by previous marriage—Michelle, Richard, Garld. Asst. dir. core area devel. San Jose C. of C., 1969-71; asst. dir. health occupations Modesto Jr. Coll., 1971-75; mgr. Microwave Assocs. Communications Co., Sunnyvale, Calif., 1978-81; field engring. supr. Four Phase Systems, Inc., Cupertino, Calif., 1981-83; mgr. Rayne Plumbing & Sewer Service Inc., 1983-84; mgr. M/A COM MAC, Inc., 1984—. Mem. Nat. Assn. Female Execs. (network dir.). Home: 6571 American Ct San Jose CA 95120 Office: 1494 Hamilton Ave Suite 204 San Jose CA 95125

BOHNING, ELIZABETH EDROP, emerita educator; b. Bklyn., June 26, 1915; d. Percy Tom and Marion Lothrop (Stafford) Edrop; B.A., Wellesley Coll., 1936; M.A., Bryn Mawr Coll., 1938, Ph.D., 1943; postgrad. Middlebury Coll., summer 1936, U. Cologne, 1936-37, U. Munich, summer 1955; m. William H. Bohning, Aug. 18, 1943; children—Barbara Bohning Young, Margaret Bohning Anderson. Faculty, Bryn Mawr Coll., 1938-39, Middlebury Coll. Summer Sch. German, 1956, 58, Grinnell Coll., 1940-41, Stanford U., 1939-40; prof. U. Del., Newark, 1967-85, emerita, 1985—, chmn. dept. langs. and lit., 1971-78; mem. exec. com. Del. Humanities Council, 1980-83. Pres., Del. Council Internat. Visitors. Recipient Lindback award for excellence in teaching, 1962. Mem. Am. Assn. Tchrs. German, East Central Soc. 18th Century Studies, Am. Council Study of Austrian Lit., Middle State Assn. Colls. and Schs. (trustee 1974-80), Phi Beta Kappa, Delta Phi Alpha, Phi Kappa Phi, Alpha Chi Omega. Episcopalian. Clubs: Wellesley Alumnae, Bryn Mawr Alumnae. Author: The Concept "Sage" in Nibelungen Criticism, 1944; contbr. articles on lit. to profl. jours. Home: Box 574 Newark DE 19715

BOIES, MARY MCINNIS, broadcasting company executive, lawyer; b. Newton, N.J., June 30, 1950; d. Norman Kenneth and Sara (Bollinger) McInnis; m. David Boies, Aug. 21, 1982; children—Mary Regency, Alexander McInnis. Student U. Calif.-Berkeley, 1968-70; B.A. magna cum laude, U. Wash., 1972, J.D., 1975. Bar: Wash. 1975, D.C. 1978. Counsel U.S. Senate Commerce Com., Washington, 1975-77; asst. dir. domestic policy staff White House, Washington, 1977-79; gen. counsel CAB, Washington, 1979-81; v.p. CBS, Inc., N.Y.C., 1982—. Home: 2 Middle Patent Rd Armonk NY 10504 also 535 Park Ave New York NY 10021 Office: CBS Inc 51 W 52d St New York NY 10019

BOJARSKI, JEANNE FRANCES, technical writer; b. N.Y.C., Dec. 20, 1951; d. Frank J. and Theodosia H. (Trzcinski) B.; 1 child, Jessica James (dec.). B.A. in Philosophy, New Coll., Sarasota, Fla., 1974; postgrad. U. Chgo., 1979-81. Adminstrv. asst. Nat. Bus. Lists, Inc., N.Y.C., 1974-76; freelance writer, N.Y.C., 1976-77; asst. to pres. Tribal Arts Gallery, N.Y.C., 1977-78; instr. econs. Roosevelt U., Chgo., 1980-83; sr. cons. Cooley/Baker, Inc., Chgo., 1981-83; tech. writer, Kansas City, Mo., 1984-85. Editor: The Grackle (jazz criticism), 1976. Bd. dirs. Studio Infinity Ltd., N.Y.C., 1976-77; hon. parent Gillis Home for Children, Kansas City, 1985. Mem. Nat. Assn. Female Execs. Republican. Clubs: Nat. Rifle Assn., Mutual Musician's Found. (Kansas City). Avocations: hunting; photography; bicycling; jazz.

BOK, SISSELA, writer, educator; b. Stockholm, Dec. 2, 1934; came to U.S., 1955; d. Gunnar and Alva (Reimer) Myrdal; m. Derek Bok, May 7, 1955; children—Hilary, Victoria, Tomas. B.A., George Washington U., 1957, M.A., 1958; Ph.D., Harvard U., 1970; hon. degrees Mt. Holyoke Coll., 1985, George Washington U., 1986. Lectr., Simmons Coll., Boston, 1971-72; lectr. med. ethics MIT div. health scis. and tech. Harvard U., Cambridge, Mass., 1975-82, lectr. on core curriculum, 1982-86; dir. Population Council, N.Y.C., 1971-77; mem. ethics adv. bd. HEW, Washington, 1977-80; assoc. prof. Brandeis U., 1985—. Author: Lying: Moral Choice in Public and Private Life, 1978; Secrets: On the Ethics of Concealment and Revelation, 1982; editor: The Dilemmas of Euthanasia, 1975; Ethics Teachings in Higher Education, 1980; mem. editorial bd. Ethics, 1981-85, Criminal Justice Ethics, 1982—, Literature and Medicine,

1982—; contbr. articles to profl. jours. Bd. dirs. Hastings Ctr., Hasting-on-Hudson, N.Y., 1976-84. Mem. Am. Philos. Assn., Phi Beta Kappa.

BOKROSS, AGNES HELEN, educator documentalist; b. Budapest, Hungary, Jan. 9, 1922; came to Can., 1957, naturalized, 1962; d. Lajos Ferenc and Andrea (Tömöry) Szakonyi; B.A. with honors in English, Sir George Williams U., Montreal, Que., Can., 1970; Ph.D. in Comparative Lit. (Woodrow Wilson fellow 1970-71, Ford fellow 1970-71, Can. Council doctoral awards 1972-74), McGill U., Montreal, 1974; m. Béla E. Bokross, 1943 (div. 1945); 1 dau., Apollonia Elizabeth Bokross Schofield. Indexer and archivist Internat. Civil Aviation Orgn., Montreal, 1957-72; lectr. in English lit. Concordia U., Montreal, 1974-80; multilingual annotator Nat. Library Can., Ottawa, Ont., 1975-81; documentalist Public Service Commn. Can., Ottawa, 1981—; tchr., cons. in field. Recipient Gold medal Gov. Gen. Can., 1970; McGill U. travel research grantee, 1973. Mem. MLA, Can. Soc. Comparative Study Civilizations, Nat. Geog. Soc. Roman Catholic. Author Nat. Library of Can. Annotations Manual, 1979; contbr. essays to lit. jours.; papers to confs. Office: Public Service Commn L'Esplanade Laurier West Tower 930 300 Laurier W Ottawa ON K1A 0M7 Canada

BOLAN, BARBARA RICHTER, handbag and accessory company designer and executive; b. Providence, R.I., May 23, 1942; d. Leonard and Mollie (Stanzler) Richter; m. Henry A. Bolan, Feb. 20, 1966. B.A., U. R.I., 1963; Ed.M., Wheelock Coll., 1967. Elem. tchr. Wayland Pub. Schs., Mass., 1966-67, Brookline Pub. Schs., Mass., 1967-70; master elem. tchr., asst. dir. Horace Mann Sch., N.Y.C., 1970-73; designer, exec. Carber Enterprises, N.Y.C., 1974-76; prin. Barbara Bolan Inc., N.Y.C., 1976—; mem. Fashion Group, N.Y.C., 1983—; cons. Am. Women's Econ. Devel., N.Y.C. Active in Action Com. Homeless, N.Y.C., 1985—. Recipient Prix De Cachel award Prince Matchabelli Corp. 1980. Democrat. Avocations: travel; language study; ballet; gymnastics. Office: Barbara Bolan Inc 33 E 33d St New York NY 10016

BOLAND, JANET LANG, judge; b. Kitchener, Ont., Can., Dec. 6, 1924; d. George William and Miriam Janet (Geraghty) Lang; B.A., Waterloo Coll., 1946; law degree Osgoode Hall, 1950; L.L.D. (hon.), Sir Wilfred Laurier U., 1976; m. John Brown Boland, Oct. 1, 1949; children—Michael, Christopher, Nicholas. Called to Ont. bar, 1950; mem. firm White, Bristol, Beck & Phipps, Toronto, Ont., 1959-69; partner firm Lang Michener, Toronto, 1969-72; county ct. judge, Toronto, 1972-76; judge Supreme Ct. of Ont., Toronto, 1976—; named Queen's counsel, 1965; co-chmn. Penal Reform for Women Joint Com., 1956-58. Mem. Jr. League Toronto. Roman Catholic. Home: 164 Inglewood Dr Toronto ON Canada Office: Osgoode Hall Queen St Toronto ON Canada

BOLAND, SUSAN ECKELKAMP, television executive; b. Washington, Mo., Nov. 13, 1958; d. Louis Bernard and Martha (Wood) Eckelkamp; B.A., St. Mary's Coll., Notre Dame, Ind., 1981. Sales mgr. Ramada Inn, Six Flags, Eureka, Mo., 1981; asst. producer CBS, St. Louis, 1981-83; news dir. Harris Broadcasting Co., Union, Mo., 1983-85; television producer Multimedia, Inc., St. Louis, 1985—; ind. TV producer/cons., 1985—. Nat. committeewoman Young Republicans, Mo., 1985, co-chmn., 1984; state committeewoman 23d Senatorial Dist., Mo., 1985; mem. Young St. Louisians Charities Orgn. Mem. Press Club Met. St. Louis, Am. Women in Radio and TV. Roman Catholic. Home: PO Box 512 Washington MO 63090

BOLDEN, HELEN ELAINE, social welfare exec.; b. Kansas City, Kans., May 28, 1934; d. Labrum Arthur and Retha (Norman) Fells; student Ohio State U., 1963; m. James L. Bolden, Sr. (div.); children—Leroy, David, Michael, James, Nugene, Rachelle. With Post Office Dept., Lima, Ohio, 1963-64; dir. Garfield Opportunity Center, Lima, 1965-74; founder Tot Lot, Inc., Garfield Sch., 1972; founder, exec. dir. Friendly Sr. Citizens and Disabled Persons Center, Inc., Lima, 1974—, Garfield Breakfast Program. Active, Black Elected Democrats, Ohio, Mem. Nat. Assn. of Black Aged, Social Workers Council Allen County, Nat. Urban Coalition, Regional Planning Commn. Baptist. Club: Order Eastern Star (Ct. of Colanthe). Home: 312 N Pine St Lima OH 45801 Office: 213 S Pine St Lima OH 45801

BOLDEN, KRISTIN ELIZABETH, educator; b. Marietta, Ohio, May 17, 1939; d. Howard Alfred Spindler and Thelma Kathryn (Totman) Spindler Williamson; m. Norman William Holt II, June 2, 1959 (div. Feb. 1966) m. James William Bolden, Oct. 8, 1966; children—James William, Bruce Douglas, Cynthia Sue. B.S. in Edn., Ohio No. U., 1961. Cert. elem. and secondary tchr., Ohio. Tchr. Spanish, Ohio No. U., Ada, 1961; tchr. Ada Elem. Sch., 1961-62; tchr. Spanish and English, Warren High Sch., Vincent, Ohio, 1962—; mem. Ohio Valley Fgn. Lang. and Lit. Project, Athens, 1983—. Jennings scholar, 1973-74. Mem. Am. Assn. Tchrs. Spanish and Portuguese, NEA, Ohio Edn. Assn., Warren Local Edn. Assn., Delta Kappa Gamma (1st v.p. 1984—). Republican. Presbyterian. Lodge: Belpre Shrinettes. Avocations: boating; swimming; bridge; needlework; piano. Home: Route 2 Box 213 Little Hocking OH 45742 Office: Warren High Sch Route 1 Vincent OH 45784

BOLDEN, ROSAMOND, state official; b. Beggs, Okla., May 5, 1938; d. Benjamin James and Mary Crosby; m. James Alan Bolden, Jan. 27, 1963 (dec. Dec. 1973); 1 child, Stacie Lenore. B.S., U. Calif.-Berkeley, 1961, M.A., 1971. Employment counselor to office mgr. Calif. Dept. Employment, Sacramento, 1965-75; asst. civil rights officer Calif. Dept. Health, Sacramento, 1976-77; cheif Office Bldg. and Grounds, Calif. Dept. Gen. Services, Sacramento, 1977—; chmn. merit award bd. dept. personnel adminstrn., State of Calif. Sacramento, 1979-85; mem. women's adv. bd. Calif. Personnel Bd., Sacramento, 1980-84. Bd. dirs. Tierra Del Oro council Girl Scouts U.S.A., Sacramento, 1984; mem. citizen rev. bd., chmn. admission/allocation subcom. United Way, Sacramento, 1984; founding mem. Sacramento Black Women's Network, 1981. Recipient award of appreciation United Calif. State Employee Campaign, 1980; cert. of appreciation Nat. Assn. Retarded Citizens, 1981 United Way, 1984. Mem. Bldg. Owners and Mgrs. Assn. (founder Sacramento chpt., mem. govt. bldg. com., Grand Prize Ambassador's Club 1985), NAACP, Black Advocates in State Service, Alpha Kappa Alpha. Home: PO Box 22457 Sacramento CA 95831 Office: State of Calif 915 Capital Mall Room 106 Sacramento CA 95831

BOLDUC, JEANNE MARIE, steel fabrication company executive; b. Worcester, Mass., Jan. 23, 1947; d. Wilfred Thomas and Rita Eleanor (Mallette) B. Diploma Chamberlayne Jr. Coll., Boston, 1967. Sec. to v.p. Franklin County Trust Co., Greenfield, Mass., 1967-68; sec. to pres. Wilfred T. Bolduc Co., Orange, Mass., 1968-72, office mgr., 1972-84; treas. W.T. Bolduc & Son Co., Inc., Orange, 1984—, asst. clk., 1984—, also dir. Mem. Nat. Assn. Female Execs. Roman Catholic. Club: Rod and Gun (Orange). Avocations: travel; theater; tennis; interior decorating; reading. Office: WT Bolduc & Son Co Inc 20 Cherry St Orange MA 01364

BOLEN, LANORA LUKE, educator; b. Oklahoma City, Mar. 12, 1934; d. Elmer Werthon and Nellie Lois (Owensby) Luke; student Okla. Bapt. U., 1952-55, Baylor U., 1953, Okla. Central State U., 1957, S.W. Mo. State U., 1960-61, St. Louis Inst. Music, 1964, So. Ill. U., 1968-70; B.Mus. Edn., So. Ill. U., 1970; postgrad. N. Tex. State U., 1975, Tex. Christian U., 1977; children by previous marriage—Paul Anthony DeOgny, Frederick Ronald DeOgny, Terri Sue DeOgny. Pvt. piano tchr., 1956-68; elem. music tchr. Clayton (Mo.) Sch. Dist., 1969-74; profl. musician TV comml. artist, 1967-75; exec. dir. Youth Orch. of Greater Ft. Worth, 1979-80; dir. founder Kinderplatz of Fine Arts, Inc., Ft. Worth, 1979—. Fin. chmn. LWV, St. Louis, 1966; pres. Republican Women's Club, Lewisville, Tex., 1976; vice chmn. Rep. Party, Tarrant County, Tex., 1977; bd. dirs. Youth Orch. Greater Ft. Worth, 1976-81, pres., 1979-81; chmn. Oktoberfest Symphony League, Ft. Worth, 1978; bd. dirs. Ft. Worth Symphony, 1980—; mem. exec. com. Youth Orch. div. Am. Symphony Orch. League, 1980—. Mem. Am. Orff-Schulwerk Assn., Nat. Music Educators Conf., Nat. Assn. for Edn. Young Children, Youth Orch. Assn., Nat. Fedn. Rep. Women, Am. Symphony Orch. League, Delta Kappa Gamma, Sigma Alpha Iota. Presbyterian. Clubs: Women's. Contbr. articles to profl. jours. Office: 3320 W Cantey Fort Worth TX 76109

BOLENE, MARGARET ROSALIE STEELE, bacteriologist, civic worker; b. Kingfisher, Okla., July 11, 1923; d. Clarence R. and Harriet (White) Steele; student Oreg. State U., 1943-44; B.S., U. Okla., 1946; m. Robert V. Bolene, Feb. 6, 1948; children—Judith Kay, John Eric, Sally Sue, Janice Lynn, Daniel William. Technician bacteriology dept. Okla. Dept. Health, Oklahoma City, 1946-48; asst. bacteriologist Henry Ford Hosp., Detroit, 1948-49; bacteriol. cons., also asst. bus. mgr. Ponce Gynecology and Obstetrics, Inc., 1956—. Organizing dir. Bi-Racial Council, 1963; lay adviser Home Nursing Service, 1967-68; mem. exec. bd. PTA, 1956-71; active various community drives; sponsor Am. Field Service; patron Ponce Playhouse; bloodmobile vol. ARC; vol. Helpline. Republican precinct organizer, 1960. Mem. AAUW (treas. 1964-66), DAR (sec.-treas. 1961-67, 1st vice regent 1972-73, chpt. treas. 1974-84), Kay-Noble County Med. Aux. (treas. 1957-58, 66-67), Ponca City Art Assn., Pioneer Hist. Soc., Okla. Heritage Assn., Daus. Founders and Patriots (state pres. 1980-84), Nat. Huguenot Soc., Daus. Am. Colonists (chpt. pres. 1982-84), Magna Charta Dames (treas. Okla. chpt. 1984), Order Colonial Physicians and Chirurgiens (life), Ancient and Honorable Arty. Co. Women Descs. Okla. Ct. (treas. 1983-84, registrar 1986—), Dames of Ct. of Honor, Colonial Dames of 17th Century, U. Okla. Assn. (life), Lambda Tau, Phi Sigma, Alpha Lambda Delta. Presbyterian (elder 1983-86). Clubs: Ponca City Country, Ponca City Music, Red Rose Garden (pres. 1983-84), Twentieth Century. Home: 2116 Juanito Ave Ponca City OK 74604

BOLEY BOLAFFIO, RITA, artist; b. Trieste, Italy; d. Angelo and Olga Senigaglia; came to U.S., 1939, naturalized, 1944; studied with Joseph Hoffmann, Kunstgewerbe Schule, Vienna, Austria; diploma violin Music Conservatory, Vienna; student of F. Ondricek; ek; m. Orville F. Boley; children—Lucius R., Bruno A. Fashion and textile designer Wiener Werkstatte, Vienna and Milan, Italy; murals and displays throughout U.S., maj. exhns. collage and assemblage include Mus. of Art, Columbia, S.C., Am. House, N.Y.C., J.L. Hudson Gallery, Detroit, Pen and Brush Club, N.Y.C., Richard Kollmar's Gallery, N.Y.C., Guild Hall Mus., East Hampton, N.Y., James Pendleton Gallery, N.Y.C. Washington Art Assn. Conn. Mem. arts group ARC, 1942-44. Mem. Composer, Author and Artists Am. Home and Studio: 310 W 106th St New York NY 10025

BOLIN-BARINEAU, TENA, counseling psychology, educator; b. Corpus Christi, Tex., July 14, 1943; d. Wayne Horace Bolin and Elsie Nadine (Bishop) Spencer; children—John Ben Harris II, Krista Lynne. A.A., Del Mar Coll., 1970; B.S., U. Houston, 1972, M.Edn., 1974, Ed.D., 1981. Licensed profl. counselor; nat. cert. counselor; cert. in spl. edn.; cert. supt.; real estate broker. Office mgr. real estate broker Sage Investments, Corpus Christi, Tex., 1966-68; personnel cons. Snelling & Snelling, Corpus Christi, 1968-70; asst. U. Houston, 1971, 72, 73-74; asst. to exec. dir. Ctr. for Retarded, Inc., Houston, 1972-73; psychometrician James Rice, Ph.D.-Psychologist, Houston, 1974; learning facilitator Houston Ind. Sch. Dist., 1974-78; pvt. practice counseling psychology, Houston, 1981—; asst. U. Houston, 1971, 72, 74. Mem. adminstrv. bd. Chapelwood Meth. C., Houston, 1984—; bd. dirs. Meml. Assistance Ministries, Houston, 1984—; chmn. social concerns Chapelwood Meth., Houston, 1984—; chmn. program com. U. Houston Council for Exceptional Children, 1971-72, treas., 1971-72. Mem. Council for Exceptional Children, Am. Psychol. Assn., Am. Assn. Counseling and Devel., Am. Mental Health Counselors Assn., Am. Assn. Mental Deficiency, Am. Edn. Research Assn., Tex. Psychol. Assn., Tex. Assn. Counseling and Devel., Mental Health Assn. Houston and Harris County, West Houston C. of C., Phi Kappa Phi, Kappa Delta Pi. Office: 11931 Wickchester Ln Suite 200 Houston TX 77043

BOLING, JEWELL, retired government official; b. Randleman, N.C., Sept. 26, 1907; d. John Emmitt and Carrie (Ballard) Boling; student Women's Coll., U. N.C., 1926, Am. U., 1942, 51-52. Interviewer, N.C. Employment Service, Winston-Salem, Asheboro, 1937-41; occupational analyst U.S. Dept. Labor, Washington, 1943-57, placement officer, 1957-58, employment service adviser, 1959-61, occupational analyst, 1962, employment service specialist counseling and testing, 1963-69, manpower devel. specialist, from 1969. Recipient Meritorious Achievement award U.S. Dept. Labor, 1972. Mem. AAAS, N.Y. Acad. Scis., Am. Assn. Counseling and Devel., Nat. Career Devel. Assn., Am. Rehab. Counseling Assn. (archivist 1964-68), Assn. Measurement in Counseling and Devel., Assn. Humanistic Psychology, Planetary Soc., Smithsonians, Sierra Club, Nature Conservancy, Internat. Platform Assn., Audubon Naturalist Soc., Nat. Capital Astronomers (editor Star Dust 1949-58). Author: Counselor's Handbook, 1967; Counselor's Desk Aid, Eighteen Basic Vocational Directions, 1967; Handbook for New Careerists in Employment Security, 1971; contbr. articles to profl. publs. Address: Route 2 Box 176 Randleman NC 27317

BOLING, JUDY ATWOOD, civic worker; b. Madras, India, June 19, 1921 (parents Am. citizens); d. Carroll Eugene and Marion Frances (Ayrer) Atwood; A.A., San Antonio Jr. Coll., 1940; student Rogue Community Coll., Grants Pass, Oreg., 1978-79, So. Oreg. State Coll., Ashland, 1982—; m. Jack Leroy Boling, Apr. 8, 1941; children—Joseph Edward, Jean Ann, James Michael, John Charles. First aid instr. ARC, various locations, 1940-65, chmn. vols., Calif., 1961-62, Eng., 1964-65; den mother cub scouts Boy Scouts Am., Monterey, Calif., 1951-52; active Girl Scouts U.S.A., 1953—, council pres., Winema (Oreg.) Council, 1971-73, 79-82, del. to nat. council, 1966, 72, 81, cons. for nat. pubs., 1971, 79; Sunday sch. tchr. Base Chapel, Pyote, Tex., 1949-51, choir dir., 1951; Sunday sch. adminstr. Base Chapel, Morocco, 1954-55; Sunday sch. tchr. Hermon Free Meth. Ch., Los Angeles, 1956-57; active United Way campaign, 1967-84, Childrens Festival, 1974—; former liaison with local people in Japanese-Am., Franco-Am., Anglo-Am. orgns.; mem. Rogue Craftsmen Bd., Grants Pass, 1972—, sec., 1972-78, v.p., 1978-85; bd. dirs. Rogue Valley Opera Assn., 1978—, Community Concert, 1979—; historian Josephine County Republican Women, 1982—; public speaker. Recipient Thanks badge Girl Scouts U.S.A., 1957, 60, 73, Girl Scouts Japan, 1959, United Kingdom Girl Guides, 1982; others; cert. of appreciation USAF, 1959, City of Hagi, City of Fukuoka (Japan), Gov. of Fukuoka Prefecture; citation Internat. Book Project; Oreg. Vol. award Sen. Packwood, 1983; Community Woman of Year award Bus. and Profl. Women, 1984. Mem. Josephine County Hist. Soc., So. Oreg. Resources Alliance, Am. Host Found., Friends of Library, Women's Investment Group, Grants Pass Art Mus. Republican. Club: Knife and Fork. Contbr. articles to profl. jours. Address: 3016 Jumpoff Joe Creek Rd Grants Pass OR 97526

BOLING, MAUDE CLIFTON, television producer, communications consultant; b. Anahuac, Tex., Dec. 25, 1957; d. Blaine Arlington and Edith Naomi (Joseph) B. B.S. in Radio, TV and Film, U. Tex., 1980. Researcher, State House Study Group, Austin, Tex., 1979-81; film producer ABA Prodn. Co., Austin, 1981-82; TV producer Storer Cable Communications, Houston, 1982—; dir. communications St. Andrews United Methodist Ch., 1980-83; speech coach asst. Tex. So. U., 1981-82. Author: A Dream, 1983; contbr. photography to newspapers. Active polit. campaigns; youth dir. St. Andrews United Meth. Ch., 1982-84, named Outstanding Mem., 1982-83; Sunday sch. tchr. Windsor Village United Meth. Ch. Mem. Nat. Assn. Female Execs., Am. Women in Radio-TV-Film, Women in Communications, Women in Cable (exec. bd.). Club: Juneteenth (Houston). Home: 6236 Maybell St Houston TX 77091 Office: Storer Cable Communications 2505 Bisbee St Houston TX 77017

BOLINGER, SHIRLEY GOODWIN (MRS. JOHN RANDOLPH BOLINGER), former librarian; b. Seattle, July 11, 1907; d. Ervin Shirley and Eda (Hague) Goodwin; B.S. in Library Sci., U. Wash., 1931; m. John Randolph, Feb. 20, 1932; 1 son, Ervin Michael. Librarian elementary schs., Arlington, Va. until 1972. Mem. bd., v.p., Seattle YWCA, 1947-49; bd. mem. Travelers Aid Soc. of Tacoma, 1940-41, Travelers Aid Soc. of D.C., 1958-59; mem. bd. Washington Home for Incurables, 1952-59, Rock Spring Garden Club of Arlington, 1952-58. Mem. Jr. League of Washington, Nat. Symphony Orch. (women's com.), Antique Porcelain Soc. of Washington (founder), Smithsonian Assos., Nat. Trust for Historic Preservation, Friends of Kennedy Center, Am. Ceramic Circle, Kappa Kappa Gamma. Episcopalian. Clubs: Farmington Country (Charlottesville, Va.); Neighbors (Arlington). Home: 3224 N George Mason Dr Arlington VA 22207

BOLITHO, LOUISE GREER, university official; b. Wenatchee, Wash., Aug. 13, 1927; d. Lon Glenn and Edna Gertrude (Dunlap) Greer; B.A., Wash. State U., 1949; m. Douglas Stuart Bolitho, June 17, 1950 (div. Dec. 1975); children—Rebecca Louise, Brian Douglas. Adminstrv. aide dept. geology Stanford (Calif.) U., 1967-70, adminstrv. asst. med. microbiology dept., 1970-74, adminstrv. asst. W.W. Hansen Labs. Physics, 1974-77, adminstrv. services mgr. Center for Research in Internat. Studies, 1977-84, dir. fin. and adminstrv. services Law Sch., 1984-86; cons., 1985—. Bd. dirs. Mid Peninsula Support Network, Peninsula Vols. Mem. AAUW, Palo Alto C. of C. Home: 3128 David Ave Palo Alto CA 94303 Office: 3128 David Ave Palo Alto CA

BOLLAR, MARJORIE ODESSA, nurse; b. N.Y.C., July 25, 1923; d. Charles Whitmore and Glenfield Ernesta (Griffith) Heath; grad. Central Islip Sch. Nursing, 1948; B.S. Edn. and Health, Coll. Oneonta, 1973; M.A., SUNY, Stony Brook, 1977; m. Wilbur B. Bollar, July 11, 1944; children—Diane Seaman, Ronald. Head nurse Central Islip (N.Y.) State Hosp., 1949-70; acting nurse adminstr. Central Islip Psychiat. Center, 1970-77, nurse adminstr., 1977-81, dir. nursing services, 1981-83, coordinator for geriatrics, 1980-83, overtime coordinator, 1980—, mem. instl. rev. com. on research proposals, 1975—, mem. bd. visitors, 1985—, supr. research programs, tng. activities, tchr. affiliating nursing students and therapy aides div. research, chmn. unit med. records rev. com.; examiner N.Y. State Civil Service, 1982. Sec. bd. Christian edn. Faith Bapt. Ch., Coram, N.Y., 1985. Recipient 8th ann. Community Service award Eastern Suffolk Fed. Credit Union, 1980; cert. sch. nurse tchr., in-service edn. medication trainer and lectr., N.Y. Mem. Am. Public Health Assn., L.I. Minority Educators Assn., Internat. Platform Assn., Nat. Council Negro Women, N.Y. State Nurses Assn., Am. Film Industry Assn., Central Islip, Stony Brook alumnae, Centereach (N.Y.) C. of C., N.Y. Acad. Scis., NAACP, Delta Sigma Theta (chmn. social actions com. Nassau alumni chpt.). Research on follow up of geriatric subjects, discharged alcoholics and disturbed children, on geriatric hyperbaric oxygen therapy. Home: 218 N Washington Ave Centereach NY 11720 Office: Central Islip Psychiat Center Central Islip NY 11722

BOLLING, CHERYL M., educator; b. Galveston, Tex., Feb. 19, 1949; d. Percy and Vallie Mae (Kidd) Sullivan; m. William Bolling, June 15, 1974 (div.). B.A. in Music, Huston-Tillotson Coll., 1971; M.S. in Curriculum and Instrn., Pepperdine U., 1979. Tchr. Hitchcock Ind. Sch. Dist., Tex., 1971-74, Oakland Pub. Sch., Calif., 1974—. Mem. Oakland Edn. Assn. (bd. dirs. 1980—), State Council Edn., Calif. Tchrs. Assn., NEA, Alpha Kappa Alpha. Democrat. Methodist. Avocations: jogging; playing board games; basketball; football. Home: 12 Emery Bay Dr Emeryville CA 94608 Office: Carl Munck Sch 11900 Campus Dr Oakland CA 94619

BOLLINGER, DEBRA MARIE, lawyer, state government official; b. Huron, S.D., May 2, 1956; d. Gerald Edmund and Mary Jean (Dunn) B. B.S. in Bus. Adminstrn., U. S.D., 1978, M.B.A., 1981, J.D., 1981. Bar: S.D. 1981. Franchise adminstr. State of S.D., Pierre, 1981-83, dep. dir. div. securities Dept. Commerce, 1983-86, dir., 1986—. Dir. Oahe Fed. Credit Union, 1982-86; party worker S.D. Republican Party and Rep. Women, 1981—; actress, asst. dir. Pierre Players, 1981-83. Mem. ABA, S.D. Bar Assn., N.Am. Securities Adminstrs. Assn. Roman Catholic. Club: Cen-Kota (pres. 1985—) (Pierre). Home: 319 E Church St Pierre SD 57501 Office: Div of Securities 910 E Sioux Ave Pierre SD 57501

BOLLMANN, BARBARA ANN, educator, organizational change consultant; b. St. Paul, Dec. 29, 1943; d. Robert John and Mildred Ruth (Rose) Bollmann. B.A., U. Mo.-Columbia, 1965; M.A., U. Chgo., 1969; postgrad. Tex. Woman's U., Denton, 1983—, San Diego State U., 1984-85. Program dir. YWCA, Denver, 1965-67; social worker Crittendon Comprehensive Care, Chgo., 1969-71; dir. vol. service Pub. Welfare, Colo. and Ala., 1971-74; assoc. dir. Girl Scouts U.S.A., Dallas, 1977-84; mem. faculty Colo. State U., 1972, St. Mary's Coll., Kans., 1976, San Diego Mesa Coll., Nat. U., San Diego State U., 1984-85; cons. NOW, Dallas, 1979-84. Vol., Parkland Hosp., Dallas, 1981, Am. Heart Assn., Dallas, 1982. NIMH scholar, 1967. Mem. Nat. Assn. Social Workers, Am. Soc. Tng. and Devel., Women Bus. Owner's Assn., Nat. Womens Polit Caucas. Democrat. Address: 405 W Washington Suite 39 San Diego CA 92103

BOLOGNA, JOANNE DENISE, systems analyst; b. Albany, N.Y., Mar. 22, 1961; d. Matthew Joseph and Viola Theresa (Audi) B. B.A. in Computer Sci., LeMoyne Coll., 1983; postgrad. Rensselear Poly. Inst., 1983, Russel Sage Coll., 1984. Documentation specialist McAuto Systems Group, Inc., Menands, N.Y., 1983-84, sr. programmer/analyst, 1984-85; systems analyst Empire Blue Cross & Blue Shield, Albany, N.Y., 1985-86; lead systems analyst Computer Scis. Corp., Menands, 1986—. Mem. Nat. Assn. Female Execs. Democrat. Roman Catholic. Avocations: aerobics; golf; jogging; reading; softball; tennis. Home: 852 Warren St Albany NY 12208 Office: Computer Scis Corp 800 N Pearl St Menands NY 12204

BOLSTER, JACQUELINE NEBEN, communications exec.; b. Woodhaven, N.Y.; d. Ernest W. B. and Emily (Guck) Neben; student Pratt Inst., Columbia U.; m. John A. Bolster, May 8, 1954. Promotion mgr. Photoplay mag., 1949-53; merchandising mgr. McCall's, 1953-64; dir. promotion and merchandising Harper's Bazaar, N.Y.C., 1964-71; dir. advt. and promotion Elizabeth Arden Salons, N.Y.C., 1971-77, dir. communications, 1977—. Recipient Art Dir.'s award 1961, 66. Mem. Fashion Group, Inner Circle, Advt. Women N.Y. (life), Fashion Execs. Round Table. Home: 8531 88th St Woodhaven NY 11421 also Halsey Neck Ln Southampton NY Office: Elizabeth Arden Inc 55 E 52d St New York NY 10022

BOLZ, SARAH DAVIS, local government administrator; b. Saginaw, Mich., Mar. 14, 1945; s. Siegel Bloore and Kathleen (McCarvey) Davis; m. Charles R. Bolz, Sept. 7, 1968 (div. 1973). B.A., Albion Coll., 1967; M.A., Mich. State U., 1970. Curator, O. Henry Mus., Austin, Tex., 1973-78, Elisabet Ney Mus., Austin, 1978-83; spl. event coordinator Park and Recreation Dept., Austin, 1983-86, resource mgr., 1986—. Vice commodore city land events Austin Aqua Festival, 1985. Mem. Austin Soc. for Pub. Adminstrn., Smithsonian Instn. Office: City of Austin Parks and Recreation Dept PO Box 1088 Austin TX 78767

BOMAR, PORTIA HAMILTON, psychoanalyst, clinical psychologist; b. Cleve., July 19; d. Charles Brooks and Marion (Clements) Goulder; m. William P. Bomar, July 1, 1966. B.A., U. Mich., 1923; postgrad. Oxford U. (Eng.), 1923-25; M.A., Columbia U., 1932, Ph.D., 1940. Pvt. practice psychoanalysis and psychotherapy, N.Y.C., 1930-58; dir. teaching clinic Columbia Presbyn. Med. Ctr., N.Y.C., 1942-50; assoc. prof. psychology U. Richmond, Va., 1964-66; lectr. psychology U. Tex.-Austin, 1968-71; mem. faculty Southwestern Grad. Sch. Banking, So. Meth. U., Dallas, 1975-78. Author: When 'Mid This Glory I Was Young, 1980; contbr. articles to profl. jours. Vice-chmn. Human Relations Commn., Ft. Worth, 1968-71; bd. dirs. Tarrant County Hist. Soc. (Tex.), 1968—, Child Study Ctr., Ft. Worth, 1972-78, Tarrant County Mental Health Assn., 1974-76, Casa Manana, Ft. Worth, 1974-76; mem. corp. Eye Research Inst. of Retina Found., Boston. Fellow Am. Psychol. Assn.; mem. Psychical Research Found., Parapsychology Assn., Chi Omega, AAUW. Clubs: Rivercrest Country (Ft. Worth); University, Womans' (Sarasota, Fla.). Address: 888 Blvd of the Arts Sarasota FL 33577

BOMBA, MARGARET ANN, lawyer; b. Bklyn., July 1, 1947; d. Fred S. and Mary (Alban) Bomba; B.S., St. Francis Coll., 1975; postgrad. Columbia U., 1977; J.D., Bklyn. Law Sch., 1982; m. John N. Pizzuto, May 27, 1978. Sec., adminstrv. asst. Fieldcrest Mills, Inc., N.Y.C., 1966-71, product mgr. textiles for the home 1973-84; sole practice, N.Y.C., 1984—; sales and product mgmt. Wamsutta Mills Inc., N.Y.C., 1972-73; prof. law Parsons Sch. Design, 1985—. Mem. N.Y. County Lawyers Assn. (trade regulation com.), ABA, Assn. Bar City of N.Y., Assn. Trial Lawyers Am., N.Y. State Bar Assn. Office: 115 Broadway Suite 1115 New York NY 10006

BOMBARDIERI, MERLE ANN, psychotherapist; b. Atlanta, Mar. 16, 1949; d. Sol and Sadie (Drucker) Malkoff; m. Rocco Anthony Bombardieri, Jr., Aug. 22, 1971; children—Marcella, Vanessa. B.A. in Psychology, Mich. State U., 1971; M.S.W., San Diego State U., 1976. Lic. clin. social worker, Mass. Crisis intervention worker and trainer Listening Ear, East Lansing, Mich., 1969-71; tchr. English as 2d lang. Instituto Brasil Estados Unidos, Rio de Janeiro, 1971-73; supr. infant unit Married Student Day Care Ctr., Mich. State U., East Lansing, 1973-74; psychotherapist/family life educator Family Service Assocs., San Diego, 1975-77; psychotherapist Dade Wallace Mental Health Ctr., Nashville, 1977-78; psychotherpist/workshop leader Met. Beaverbrook Mental Health Ctr., Waltham, Mass., 1980-81; pvt. practice psychotherapy, Acton-Belmont, Mass., 1982—; clin. dir. Resolve, Inc., infertility orgn., Belmont, 1982-84; cons. HealthData Internat., Westport, Conn., 1983—, Open Door Soc., Newton, Mass., 1983—, First Day Film Corp., 1985—; psychology seminar leader; radio and TV appearances. Author: The Baby Decision, 1981; also articles in profl. and med. jours. N.Y. State Regents scholar, 1967; NIMH trainee, 1970. Mem. Nat. Assn. Social Workers, Acad. Cert. Social Workers, Boston Inst. Devel. Infants and Parents, Phi Beta Kappa, Phi Kappa Phi. Home: 124 School St Acton MA 01720 Office: 26 Trapelo Rd Belmont MA 02178

BOMBECK, ERMA LOUISE, author, columnist; b. Dayton, Ohio, Feb. 21, 1927; d. Cassius Edwin and Erma (Haines) Fiste; B.A., U. Dayton, 1949; m. William Lawrence Bombeck, Aug. 13, 1949; children—Betsy, Andrew, Matthew. Syndicated columnist Newsday Syndicate, 1965-70, Pubs.-Hall Syndicate, 1970, now News America Syndicate; contbg. editor Good

Housekeeping Mag., 1969-74. Mem. Theta Sigma Phi (Headliner award 1969). Author: At Wit's End, 1967; Just Wait Till You Have Children of Your Own, 1971; I Lost Everything in the Post-Natal Depression, 1974; The Grass is Always Greener Over the Septic Tank, 1976; If Life Is a Bowl of Cherries-What Am I Doing in the Pits, 1978; Aunt Erma's Cope Book, 1979; Motherhood: The Second Oldest Profession, 1983. Address: care Los Angeles Times Syndicate Times Mirror Sq Los Angeles CA 90053

BOMGAARS, MONA RUTH, physician, educator; b. Orange City, Iowa, Feb. 15, 1939; d. Arie John and Artha H. (Korver) B. B.A., Westmar Coll., 1959; M.D., U. Nebr.-Omaha, 1963; M.P.H., U. Calif.-Berkeley, 1972. Diplomate Am. Bd. Family Practice. Intern, Wayne County Gen. Hosp., Eloise, Mich., 1963-64; resident U. Nebr. Hosp., Omaha, 1964-66; fraternal worker United Presbyn. Ch., N.Y.C., 1967-76, staff physician Francis Newton Hosp., Ferozepore, Punjab, India, 1968-69, chief med. officer Bhagwant Meml. Hosp., Christian Med. Coll., Ludhiana, Punjab, India, 1969-71, dir. Lalitpur Community Health Services, Kathmandu, Nepal, 1972-75; exec. officer for devel. U. Hawaii Sch. Medicine, Honolulu, 1976-81; chief communicable disease div. Hawaii Dept. of Health, Honolulu, 1981-84, acting med. dep. dir., 1983-84. asst. prof. dept. family practice and community medicine U. Hawaii Sch. Medicine, 1976-79, assoc. prof., 1979-81, clin. prof., 1982-84; assoc. prof. dept. family medicine, coordinator U. Medicine and Dentistry N.J.-Rutgers, 1984—. Contbr. articles to med. jours., chpts. to books. Bd. govs. Hawaii Med. Library, Honolulu, 1983-84; trustee Westmar Coll., 1986. Recipient Disting. Alumna award Westmar Coll., 1975. Fellow Am. Acad. Family Physicians (sec. Hawaii chpt. 1983, pres.-elect 1984; trustee N.J. chpt. 1986); mem. Am. Pub. Health Assn., AMA, Soc. Tchrs. Family Medicine.

BOMMICINO, LINDA, computer company executive; b. N.Y.C., Sept. 6, 1948; d. Frank P. and Mary R. (Ficaro) Bommicino; children—Jody Lynn, Peter Joseph. Student Katharine Gibbs Sch., 1967. With IBM, 1967—, word processing systems adminstr., 1975-76, systems mktg. support rep., 1976-81, tech. support analyst, 1981-84, marketing support adminstrn., 1984—. Recipient various IBM awards, including Achievement in Mktg. Support Conf. award, 1977, 78, 79, 80, Hdqrs. award, 1985. Nat. Assn. Female Execs., Mem. Internat. Word Processing Assn. (v.p. membership, newsletter editor Music City chpt.). Roman Catholic. Club: YWCA Cable. Author tech. publs. Home: 5421 Colonial Ct Flower Mound TX 75028 Office: Carpenter Freeway Irving TX 75015-2750

BONATTI, GERTRUDE CLARE, hospital foundation executive; b. Hoboken, N.J., May 8, 1925; d. Nathan and Sylvia Florence (Erinfeld) Itzcowitz; m. Joseph P. Bonatti, Aug. 20, 1944 (dec. Jan. 1973); children—Sylvia Florence, Joy Patricia; m. Victor T. Zotta, July 3, 1979. Student continuing edn. courses in pub. relations, fundraising mgmt. Bd. dirs. Mercer County chpt. Am. Heart Assn., Trenton, 1959-69, Pa. region Deborah Hosp. Found., Phila., 1969-84, chpt. services Deborah Hosp. Found., Browns Mills, N.J., 1984—, also author found. publs. Author elem. sch. publ. on non-smoking. Dir. pub. affairs Bordentown Twp., N.J.; mem. Burlington Planning Bd., N.J. Recipient nat. life membership Deobrah Hosp. Found., 1958, testimonial, 1965; recipient awards, certs. for lecturing on pub. relations and fundraising Trenton State Coll., awards Am. Heart Assn. Mem. Nat. Soc. Fund Raising Execs., Nat. Assn. Female Execs. Democrat. Jewish. Avocations: swimming; dancing. Office: Deborah Hosp Found Trenton Rd Browns Mills NJ 08015

BONAVENTURA, ELANA MARIA, professional fund raiser, secretarial and bookkeeping services company executive; b. Los Angeles, May 17, 1946; d. James Basil and Mary Eve (Magina) B.; divorced; 1 son, James Micocci. A.A., Bakersfield Coll., 1967; secretarial grad. Am. Bus. Sch., Rome, 1967. Personal sec. Mazzie Farms, Bakersfield, Calif., 1967-73; adminstrv. asst. to pres. Dynasonics Corp., Bakersfield, 1973-79; office mgr., asst. Kinney & Assocs., Los Angeles, 1979-80; owner, operator Bonaventura & Assocs., Bakersfield, 1980—. Dir., sec. bd. Sand Canyon Water Dist., Bakersfield, 1978—; assoc. mem. Calif. Republican Party, Los Angeles, 1975—; bd. dirs. Juvenile Diabetes Found., Bakersfield, 1982-84. Recipient Achievement in Fundraising award Juvenile Diabetes Found., 1984. Mem. Rep. Women Federated. Roman Catholic. Club: Republican (Bakersfield). Avocations: politics; archeology; theatre; gourmet cooking; travel. Home: 2819 Christmas Tree Ln Bakersfield CA 93306 Office: Bonaventura & Assocs 2819 H St Suite C Bakersfield CA 93301

BONCHER, MARY, talent agent; b. Green Bay, Wis., Jan. 19, 1946; d. Anthony Peter and Bernice Mary (Lannoye) Williams; m. Joseph Phillip Boncher, Jan. 7, 1967; children—Yvette, Noelle. Diploma, Rosemary Bischoff Sch. Modeling, Milw., 1965. Dir. Mary Boncher Model Agy. & Sch. Ltd., Bloomington and St. Charles, Ill., 1970-80, Mary Boncher Model Agy. Ltd., St. Charles, 1980-84, Mary Boncher Model Mgmt. Ltd., Chgo., 1985—; fashion reporter TV and radio Men's Fashion Assn., N.Y.C., 1975-80, Eleanor Lambert's Am. Designer, N.Y. Fashion Press, N.Y.C., 1975-80; fashion corr. Green Bay Daily News, 1975-76. Lector Cath. mass, 1983—. Republican. Roman Catholic. Office: Mary Boncher Model Mgmt Ltd Presidential Towers Suite 802 575 W Madison St Chicago IL 60606

BOND, BEVERLY JEAN, communications specialist; b. Chgo., Aug. 29, 1952; d. E. Monte and Betty Jane (McCollister) B.; B.A., Tex. Tech U., 1974. Exec. mgmt. trainee Sears Roebuck & Co., Lubbock, Tex., 1973-75; chief assigner Southwestern Bell Telephone Co., Houston, 1976, chief deskman, 1976-77, repair foreman, 1977-78, installation foreman, 1978, chief deskman, 1978-79, PBX foreman, 1979-80; staff specialist bus. transition task force AT&T, Basking Ridge, N.J., 1981-82, staff mgr., 1982—. Fin. dir. Jr. Achievement, 1977-78. Mem. Nat. Assn. Female Execs. Republican. Roman Catholic. Home: 8D Dorado Dr Morristown NJ 07960 Office: 99 Jefferson Rd Room 2039 Parsippany NJ 07954

BOND, CATHERINE ANN, advertising agency executive; b. Oak Ridge, Sept. 23, 1945; d. William Joseph and Elsie Evelyn (Snapp) B. B.S. in Advt., U. Fla., 1968. Estimator, Tucker Wayne Advt., Atlanta, 1969-70; asst. buyer Henderson Advt., Atlanta, 1970-71; media buyer, dir. Noble Dury Advt., Nashville and Memphis, 1971-72; media supr. William B. Tanner Co., Memphis, 1972-74; assoc. media dir. Burton-Campbell Advt., Atlanta, 1975-76; v.p. media dir. Austin Kelley Advt., Atlanta, 1976—. Named Advt. Woman of Yr., Mag. Advt. Rep. of the South, Atlanta, 1982. Mem. Atlanta Media Planners Assn. (pres. 1984), Atlanta Broadcast Advt. Club. Democrat. Office: Austin Kelley Advt Inc 5901 Peachtree Dunwoody Rd Atlanta GA 30328

BOND, CHARLENE ELLIS, anthropologist; b. Terrell, Tex., Dec. 2, 1950; d. Charles Thomas and Edith LaNell (Stephens) Ellis; B.S., Eastfield Coll., 1980; B.S., So. Methodist U., 1985, postgrad., 1985—; m. Robert Lee Bond, Aug. 16, 1969; 1 dau., Charity Katherine. Shipwreck mapper Tex. Hist. Commn., Austin, 1983—; lectr. marine archaeology. Mem. Am. Anthrop. Assn. Republican. Roman Catholic. Office: Dept Anthropology So Methodist Dallas TX 75275

BOND, JOYCE RHODA, hospital administrator, nurse; b. Tuxedo Park, N.Y., Dec. 12, 1949; d. Lionel Jesse and Charlotte Elizabeth Bond. B.S. in Nursing, U. Ariz., 1972. Intensive care nurse Tucson Med. Ctr., 1973-74; nursing supr. Tuxedo Meml. Hosp., Tuxedo Park, 1974-78, dir. nursing, 1978-80, dir. ops., 1980-81, adminstr., 1981—. Active Orange County sub. area council Hudson Valley Health Systems Agy., Sterling Forest, Tuxedo, 1985. Recipient Ariz. State U. Nursing Hon. award, 1972; named to U. Ariz. State Nursing Hon. and Arek Soc., 1972. Mem. Nursing Service Adminstrs. Orange and Rockland Counties (pres. 1981-82), Normet Hosp. Assn., Orange County Hosp. Assn., Women in Mgmt., Orange-Rockland-Sullivan Heart Assn. (emergency cardiac care com. 1978-81). Republican. Lodge: Order of Eastern Star (matron 1984-86). Avocations: golf; skiing; swimming; fishing; hunting; piano; needlepoint. Home: Box 44 Arden NY 10910 Office: Tuxedo Meml Hosp Meyers Rd Tuxedo Park NY 10987

BOND, MARY DUNCOMBE, retired nurse; b. Wattsburg, Pa., May 3, 1906; d. Wilbur Eli and Sarah Elizabeth (Hayes) Duncombe; m. George Edward Simmons, Sept. 21, 1932 (dec. Feb. 1978); m. 2d, Frederick Almond Bond, Jan. 21, 1980 (dec. Nov. 1982). R.N., Ellis Hosp., Schenectady, N.Y., 1928; postgrad. Broward Jr. Coll., Ft. Lauderdale, Fla., 1970, 1981, 82. Pvt. duty nursing, Schenectady, N.Y., 1928-40; nurse Blood Mobile, ARC, Schenectady, 1943-45; sch. nurse City Child Care Ctrs., Schenectady, 1945-47; head nurse John Knox Village Retirement Ctr., Pompano Beach, Fla., 1974-80; instr. home nursing, first aid ARC, Schenectady, 1940-43; owner art studio preserving early Am. decoration, 1950-68; del. Internat. Health Study Tour, People's Republic China, 1984. Recipient E award ARC, 1945; Retired award John Knox Village of Fla., Inc., 1980. Mem. Am. Nurses Assn. Republican. Lutheran. Home: 630 SW 6th St Pompano Beach FL 33060

BONDS, DUANE ROBINA, obstetrician-gynecologist; b. Washington, Sept. 23, 1947; d. Robert and Helen B.; B.S. in Biology, Rensselaer Poly. Inst., 1971; M.D., Albany Med. Coll., 1971. Jr. asst. resident in ob-gyn Albany Med. Center Hosp., 1971-72; resident in ob-gyn Johns Hopkins U. Hosp., 1972-76; cons. gynecology E. Balt. Med. Plan, 1976-77; perinatal research fellow U. Colo. Med. Center, 1977-79; asst. prof. ob-gyn Div. Maternal-Fetal Medicine, U. Pa., Phila., 1979—; presenter papers profl. confs. Mem. adv. bd. Nat. Women's Law Center, Washington. Recipient Kenneth M. Archibald prize in obstetrics, 1971; Clin. Investigator award Nat. Inst. Child Health and Devel., NIH, 1984; diplomate Am. Bd. Ob-Gyn., Am. Bd. Maternal-Fetal Medicine. Fellow Am. Coll. Ob-Gyn; mem. Am. Med. Women's Assn., AAAS, N.Y. Acad. Scis. Contbr. articles to med. jours. Office: Jerrold Golding Div Maternal-Fetal Medicine Dept Ob-Gyn U Pa Hosp Box 619 3400 Spruce St Philadelphia PA 19104

BONDS, MARLENE KRIEWALD, lawyers; b. Robstown, Tex., June 15, 1935; d. Bruno Louis and Alvina Alma (Loep) Kriewald; m. Billy Ivas Bonds, Jan. 11, 1958; children—Douglas Blaine, Lawrence Ivas. B.S., Tex. Lutheran Coll., 1957; J.D., La. State U., 1979. Bar: La. 1979. Lab. technician U. Tex. Med. Sch., Galveston, 1957-58; high sch. sci. tchr. Robstown Ind. Sch. Dist., 1959-62; substitute tchr. Spring Branch Ind. Sch. Dist., Houston, 1968-70; sole practice law, Baton Rouge, 1979—. Chmn. Commn. for Mission in Tex.-La., Luth. Ch. in Am., 1980-84, mem. mgmt. com. Div. for Mission in N.Am., 1982—, chmn. sub-com. on ch. in mission, 1982—, mem. study commn. on war and peace, 1983—. Mem. ABA, La. Bar Assn., Baton Rouge Bar Assn. (various coms. 1979—), Baton Rouge Assn. Women Attys., Alumni Assn. Tex. Luth. Coll. (pres. 1986-87), Phi Delta Phi. Democrat. Club: Bal Masque (Baton Rouge). Office: Marlene K Bonds Atty at Law 1346 Main St Baton Rouge LA 70802

BONE, JANET WITMEYER (JAN), author; b. Shamokin, Pa., Dec. 19, 1930; d. Paul Eugene and Kathryn (Bender) Witmeyer; B.A., Cornell U., 1951; m. David P. Bone, Oct. 27, 1951; children—Jonathan, Christopher, Robert, Daniel. Newspaper and trade mag. writer, freelance writer, 1962—; sr. writer spl. advt. sects. Chgo. Tribune, 1986—; co-author: Understanding the Film, rev. edit., 1985; author: Opportunities in Film Production, 1983; Opportunities in Cable Television, 1983; Opportunities in Telecommunications, 1984; Opportunities in Computer-Aided Design and Computer-Aided Manufacturing (CAD/CAM), 1986; Opportunities in Robotics, 1987; tchr. creative writing adult edn. Sch. Dist. 211, Palatine, Ill., 1974—. Trustee William Rainey Harper Community Coll., Palatine, 1977-85, sec. bd. trustees, 1979-85. Recipient Chgo. Working Newsman's award, 1968, Sch. Bell award Ill. Edn. Assn., 1968, Am. Polit. Sci. Assn. award disting. reporting public affairs, 1970. Mem. Phi Theta Kappa, Alpha Omicron Pi. Address: 353 N Morris Dr Palatine IL 60067

BONEBRAKE, MARIAN MASON, real estate executive; b. Wendell, Idaho, July 5, 1930; d. Walter Scott and Elsine Mildred (Reinert) Mason; m. Howard Potter Bonebrake Jr., Dec. 26, 1952; children—Clinton M., Clayton M., Karin E. B.S., Washington U., St. Louis, 1951; B.A., U. South Fla., 1965. Tchr. Conroe Sch. Dist. (Tex.), 1978-80; sales agt. Sue Luce, Inc., 1980-84, Tri Star Properties, Conroe, 1984—. Deacon, First Presbyterian Ch., 1983—. Mem. Nat. Assn. Realtors, Tex. Assn. Realtors, Montgomery County Bd. Realtors (treas. 1983—, Realtor of Yr. 1984), Womens Council Realtors (pres. 1984—). Republican. Home: 101 S Delmont W Conroe TX 77301 Office: 1022 W Lewis Conroe TX 77301

BONELLO, KATHLEEN PATRICIA, computer company executive; b. N.Y.C., Jan. 29, 1938; d. Vincent and Mary (Jones Wilson) O'Reilly; children—Philip Joseph, Susan Patricia. Programmer, IBM, 1960-61; analyst Shell Oil Co., 1962-63; founder, pres. Info. Systems Inc., Teaneck, N.J., 1964—. Pres. Paramus Coop Nursery Sch., 1971-72, bd. dirs., 1972-75, pres. Teaneck Little League, 1977-78, team mgr., 1974-77; pres. Bryant Sch. PTA, Mem. Assn. Computing Machinery, N.J. Network Bus. and Profl. Women (dir. 1980-85). Home: 843 Belle Ave Teaneck NJ 07666 Office: 322 Cedar Ln Teaneck NJ 07666

BONHAM, JEANNE CECIL, writer, editor; b. Uhrichsville, Ohio, Jan. 19, 1928; d. Jesse W. and Zola P. (McConnell) Cecil; m. Roger D. Bonham, May 17, 1952; 1 sons, Christopher Dean. B.A., Ohio State U., 1945-48. Editorial asst. Am. Ceramic Soc. Columbus, Ohio, 1949-52, tech. indexer, 1967-77, tech. editor, 1986—; editor publs. Med. Bur., Columbus, 1952-56; reviewer Columbus Dispatch, 1952-77; exec. dir. for Ohio, Am. Acad. Pediatrics, Columbus, 1970-78, Ohio Council Home Health Agys., Columbus, 1974-84; columnist, book page editor Columbus Dispatch, 1977-84; co-editer, co-pub. Columba: The Midwest Review of Books; contbr. book rev. segment Sta. WCOL; cons., lectr. Recipient Disting. Service award Worthington Friends of the Library, 1982, Dorothy Royce award Ohio Council Home Health Agys., 1984. Mem. Nat. Book Critics Circle. Co-author: Some People Would Rather Read than Eat, 1981; contbr. numerous articles to popular and profl. jours. Home and Office: 101 E Wilson Bridge Rd Worthington OH 43085

BONHAM-YEAMAN, DORIA, business law educator; b. Los Angeles, June 10, 1932; d. Carl Herschel and Edna Mae (Jones) Bonham Emanuel; widowed; children—Carl Q., Doria Valerie-Constance. B.A., U. Tenn., 1953, J.D., 1957, M.A., 1958; Ed.S. in Computer Edn., Barry U., 1984. Instr. bus. law Palm Beach Jr. Coll., Lake Worth, Fla., 1960-69; instr. legal environment Fla. Atlantic U., Boca Raton, 1969-73; lectr. bus. law Fla. Internat. U., North Miami, 1973-83, assoc. prof. bus. law, 1983—. Editor: Anglo-Am. Law Conf., 1980; Developing Global Corporate Strategies, 1981; editorial bd. Attys. Computer Report, 1984-85, Jour. Legal Studies Edn., 1985—. Contbr. articles to profl. jours. Bd. dirs. Palm Beach County Assn. for Deaf Children, 1960-63; mem. Fla. Commn. on Status of Women, Tallahassee, 1969-70; mem. Broward County Democratic Exec. Com., 1982—; pres. Dem. Women's Club Broward County, 1981; mem. Marine Council of Greater Miami, 1978—, Service award, 1979. Recipient Faculty Devel. award Fla. Internat. U., Miami, 1980; grantee Notre Dame Law Sch., London, summer 1980. Mem. Am. Bus. Law Assn., No. Dade C. of C., Am. Acctg. Assn., AAUW (pres. Palm Beach County 1965-66), Alpha Chi Omega (alumnae chpt. pres. 1968-71), Tau Kappa Alpha. Episcopalian. Office: Fla Internat Univ North Miami FL 33181

BONHOMME, DENISE, law firm employee; b. Paris, Jan. 20, 1926; came to U.S., 1947, naturalized, 1951; d. René Louis and Jeanne Anna (Giroud) B.; children—Claire Helen Quebedeau-Schreiner, Norman Quebedeau. Baccalauréat, Acad. de Lille, 1943; student Sorbonne, U. Paris, 1943-45; M.A., U. Oreg., 1969. French-English translator and interpreter U.S. Forces in Europe, 1945-47; legal and adminstrv. sec., Austin, Tex., 1954-64; instr., asst. prof. French lang. and lit. Mount Angel Coll., Oreg., 1964-72; office worker, Monterey, Calif., 1973-74; part-time tchr. French lang. and lit. Acad. Arts and Humanities, Seaside, Calif., 1975-76, Monterey Inst. Fgn. Studies, 1976; program sec. Electric Power Research Inst., Palo Alto, Calif., 1977-80; word processor, sec. Nat. Semiconductor, Santa Clara, Calif., 1981-83; tchr. night class French lang. and lit. Mission Community Coll., Santa Clara, 1982; with law firm Pillsbury, Madison & Sutro, San Jose, Calif., 1983—. Author: Le Collier Symbolique d'Alfred de Vigny, 1968; The Esoteric Substance of Voltairian Thought, 1975. Vol. lectr. esoteric lit. Soledad State Prison, Calif., 1973-74.

BONHOTAL, KAREN LOUISE, human resources consultant; b. Pitts., May 13, 1955; d. Robert Macklin and Ann Elizabeth (Poglitsch) Geiger; m. Fred Bonhotal, Sept. 4, 1976. B.A. in Edn., Fla. Atlantic U., 1974, M.Ed., 1979. Coordinator children's services Broward County ARC, Ft. Lauderdale, Fla., 1981-82; program evaluation specialist Eckerd Drug, Clearwater, Fla., 1983-84; regional cons. Devel. Dimensions Internat., Tampa, Fla., 1984—. Mem. Am. Soc. Tng. Devel., Inc. Avocations: exotic birds; woodcraft. Office: Devel Dimensions Internat 4902 W Cypress Suite 102 Tampa FL 33607

BONI, MIKI, advt. agy. exec.; b. Bklyn., Nov. 10, 1938; B.A., U. Guanajuato, 1974; m. Lawrence Boni, Nov. 16, 1956; children—Andrew, Viki. Dir. advt. and pub. relations Kebo, Inc., Natick, Mass., 1965-74; tchr. painting and drawing U. Guanajuato (Mex.), 1974-76; exec. dir. Kreativ Assos., Watertown, Mass., 1976—; cons. pub. relations and advt. Recipient spl. painting award Lincoln Center, 1978. Mem. Women Art Profls. (founder, v.p.). Clubs: Art Dirs., Advt. (Boston). Editor: Woman's World Gazette, 1976—.

BONIFACE, WENDY JANINE, nurse, educator; b. Syracuse, N.Y., Dec. 20, 1946; d. Theodore and Elizabeth (Rolli) Fibison; B.S., Russell Sage Coll., 1969; cert. U. Va., 1971; M. in Health Sci., McMaster U., Ont., Can., 1978; m. James Henry Boniface, July 5, 1969. Staff nurse U. Va. Hosp., Charlottesville, 1969-70; instr. asso. degree program Jefferson Community Coll., Watertown, N.Y., 1970-71; program coordinator dept. pediatrics U. Va., Charlottesville, 1971; pediatric nurse practitioner Covenant House Health Services, Phila., 1972-74, Children's Hosp. of Phila., 1974-76; lectr. primary care program for nurses faculty of health scis. McMaster U., Hamilton, Ont., Can., 1976-77; data gathering technician Montreal (Que.) Research Associates, 1977; instr. pediatric nursing program Yale U. Sch. Nursing, New Haven, 1978-80, research affiliate dept. human genetics, 1981—; instr. grad. faculty Sch. Nursing, U. Conn., Storrs, 1980—; cons. WHO, 1980. Mem. profl. adv. com. Nat. Found., March of Dimes, 1980—. Cert. pediatric nurse practitioner. Mem. Am. Nurses Assn., Inst. of Soc., Ethics and the Life Scis., Nurse Practitioner Assn. of Ont., Am. Soc. Human Genetics, Sigma Theta Tau. Presbyterian. Contbg. author: Interpersonal Skills for Health Professionals, 1980; guest editor: Issues in Health Care of Women. contbr. articles to jours. in nursing. Home: 352 Greene St New Haven CT 06511 Office: Sch Nursing Univ Conn Storrs CT 06268

BONIUK, VIVIEN, ophthalmologist, lawyer; b. Glace Bay, N.S., Can., Nov. 25, 1940; d. Hyman and Rachel (Luchtiker) B. M.D., Dalhousie U., 1964; J.D., N.Y. Law Sch., 1979. Bar: N.Y. 1980; diplomate Am. Bd. Ophthalmology. Intern, Victoria Gen. Hosp., Halifax, N.S., Can., 1963-64; resident MacMillan Hosp., Washington U. Sch. Medicine, St. Louis, 1964-67; fellow Rosales Hosp., San Salvador, El Salvador, 1967; fellow in ophthalmic pathology, Coll. Medicine, Baylor U., Houston, 1967-68; teaching fellow in ophthalmology Sch. Medicine, Yale U., New Haven, 1968-69; staff ophthalmologist Toronto Gen. Hosp. (Ont., Can.), 1969-72; staff surgeon Hosp. for Sick Children, Toronto, 1969-72; cons. in ophthalmology Ont. Crippled Children's Ctr., Toronto, 1970-72; asst. attending ophthalmologist Flower & Fifth Ave. Hosp., N.Y.C., 1972-75, assoc. attending, 1976-78; asst. vis. ophthalmologist Met. Hosp., N.Y.C., 1972-75, assoc. attending, 1976-79; attending L.I. Jewish Hosp., New Hyde Park, N.Y., 1979—; dir. ophthalmology Queens Hosp. Ctr., Jamaica, N.Y., 1979—; clin. instr. dept. ophthalmology U. Toronto, 1969-72, teaching fellow in ophthalmology, 1969-70; asst. prof. ophthalmology N.Y. Med. Coll., N.Y.C., 1972-75, assoc. prof., 1976; assoc. prof. SUNY-Stony Brook, 1980. Contbr. articles to profl. publs. Entrance scholar Dalhousie U., 1957; Math. Congress scholar, 1957, 58; Univ. scholar, 1958; entrance scholar Dalhousie U. Med. Sch., 1959; Fogarty Internat. Found. fellow, USSR, 1977. Fellow Royal Coll. Surgeons Can.; mem. AMA, Assn. Research in Vision and Ophthalmology, Can. Ophthalmol. Soc., Am. Acad. Ophthalmology and Otolaryngology, Am. Med. Women's Assn., Am. Soc. Law and Medicine, ABA, N.Y. State Bar Assn., Alpha Omega Alpha. Office: LI Jewish/Queens Hosp Affiliation 82-68 164th St Jamaica NY 11432*

BONNER, MARIE TOSH, educator, lectr., poet; b. Pottstown, Pa., Apr. 24, 1924; d. Fred W. and Annette M. (Tosh) B.; B.S., Albright Coll., 1946; M.A., Columbia U., 1954; M.Ed., U. Del., 1971; postgrad. Phila. Coll. Pharmacy and Sci., summer 1965, Villanova U., summer 1966, Beaver Coll., summer 1967, U. Del., 1970-71. Tchr., Kutztown (Pa.) High Sch., 1946-53; tchr. biology Scott Sr. High Sch., Coatesville, Pa., 1953-59; traveling sci. tchr. Oak Ridge Inst. Nuclear Studies, 1959-60; tchr. chemistry, chmn. sci. dept. Alexis I. duPont High Sch., Greenville, Del., 1960-80, on leave, 1977-78; mem. Del. Sci. Curriculum Com., Dover; cons., lectr. in field. Delta Kappa Gamma scholar, 1970-71; NSF summer grantee, 1962-70; recipient award as Outstanding Sci. Tchr. in Del., Am. Chem. Soc., 1969; Am. Psychiat. Assn. commendation, 1969; award of excellence, Nat. Sci. Fair Internat., Am. Inst. Mining, Metall. and Petroleum Engrs., 1968; Cert. of Honor, Westinghouse Sci. Talent Search, 1975; poetry awards Shelly Soc. N.Y., Irma Rhodes Meml. award. Mem. NEA, Del. Tchrs. Sci., Nat. Sci. Tchrs. Assn., Nat. Sci. Suprs. Assn., N.Y. Poetry Forum, AAUW, Vt. Hist. Soc., Nat. Audubon Soc., League Vt. Writers, Poetry Soc. Am., Internat. Platform Assn., Delta Kappa Gamma. Author: (poetry) Vermont Reflections, 1980. Address: Box 207 Saint Albans Bay VT 05481

BONNER, MARY WINSTEAD, educator; b. Nash County, N.C., Apr. 20, 1924; d. Charlie Edward and Mason Ann (Whitted) Winstead; B.S. cum laude, St. Paul's Coll., Lawrenceville, Va., 1946, L.H.D. (hon.), 1979; M.S., Va. State Coll., 1952; Ed.D., Okla. State U., 1968; cert. in Spanish, Emporia State U., 1979, postgrad., 1982; m. Thomas Edison Bonner, Aug. 9, 1956. Tchr. pub. sch. Greensville County, Va., 1946-52; supr. student tchrs., demonstration tchr. Lab. Sch., So. U., Baton Rouge, La., 1952-57; tchr. pub. schs. St. Louis, 1957-64; asst. prof. edn. Emporia (Kans.) State U., 1964-75, asso. prof., 1975-80, prof., 1980—; vis. prof. U. So. Calif., Los Angeles, summer 1968, Norfolk (Va.) State Coll., summers 1970, 72. Named Outstanding Alumna St. Paul's Coll., 1975; recipient citation Nat. Assn. Equal Opportunity in Higher Edn., 1985; postdoctoral fellow in spl. edn. U. Kans., 1974. Mem. AAUW, Council for Exceptional Children, Internat. Reading Assn., Kans., Emporia reading councils, Nat. Assn. for Retarded Citizens, Nat. Council Negro Women, Caribbean Assn. on Mental Retardation, Panel Am. Women, Internat. Platform Assn. Sigma Gamma Rho (nat. edn. chmn. 1969-74, Hall of Fame), Sigma Delta Pi. Episcopalian. Club: Eastern Star. Author: Bonner Dominance Checklist; Educators' Diagnostic Guidebook and Reference Manual for Problems in Reading. Home: 1008 Watson St Emporia KS 66801 Office: Emporia State Coll Emporia KS 66801

BONNER, PATRICIA ANNE, science writer, government official; b. N.Y.C., Sept. 19, 1944; d. Cornelius John Bonner and Mary Catherine (Donovan) Moakler. B.A. in English, Carnegie Inst. Tech., 1966; M.S. in Tech. Writing and Communication, Rensselaer Poly. Inst., 1968; postgrad. in mktg. UCLA, 1970-71. Cert. tchr. English and history, Pa., Calif. Writer, program control mgr. AiResearch Corp., Anaheim, Calif., 1968-69; sr. mktg. writer Beckman Instruments, Fullerton, Calif., 1969; copy contact Barnes Chase Advt., San Diego, 1970-71; info. dir. Integrated Environ. Mgmt. Project, San Diego, also communications advisor Environ. Devel. Agy., San Diego County, 1971-73; writer Gen. Analysis Corp., San Diego, 1973-74; head info. services U.S. Dept. State, Internat. Joint Commn. U.S. and Can., Windsor, Ont., Can., 1974-84; speaker in field. Author, editor publs. Internat. Joint Commn.; contbr. writings to publs., papers to confs. Mem. steering com. Gt. Lakes Info. Referral Ctr. (Sea Grant/Gt. Lakes Basin Commn.), 1979-81. Chmn. Windsor br. Can. Inst. Internat. Affairs, 1984-85; trainer United Way Campaign, Windsor, 1982; mem. steering com. Hazardous Waste Siting Project LWV Mich., 1979-82; trustee, chmn. communications com., publicity chmn. spl. fundraising Mich. chpt. Nat. Multiple Sclerosis Soc., 1983-84. Recipient tech. publs. awards, Nat. Assn. Counties, 1975, Tech. Communications Soc., 1983; Carnegie-Mellon U. scholar, 1962-66; teaching fellow, Rensselaer Poly. Inst., 1966-68. Mem. Women in Communication, Internat. Assn. Environ. Coordinators (charter mem., governing council N.Am. chpt.), AAUW, Soc. for Tech. Communications, Air Pollution Control Assn. (publicity chmn. confs.), Carnegie Alumni Assn., Rensselaer Alumni Assn., Kappa Kappa Gamma. Office: EPA Chesapeake Bay Program 410 Severn Ave Annapolis MD 21403

BONNEVIER, SUSAN GRETHER, preschool administrator; b. Dayton, Apr. 8, 1940; d. Stanley Edward and Jane Louise (Scholl) Grether; m. Gerald Louis Bonnevier, Apr. 13, 1968; children—Perry Stewart, Jeffrey James. B.S. in Edn., Ohio U., 1962; postgrad. Nat. Coll. Edn. Tchr., Green County Sch. System, Xenia, Ohio, 1961-64, Sch. Dist. 102, LaGrange, Ill., 1964-69, Sch. Dist. 101, Western Springs, Ill., 1969-72; co-creator pre-sch. Western Spring Village Ch., 1975-82, dir., 1982—; mem. ad hoc sub group chmn. LaGrange Park Pub. Library, Ill., 1984—; docent Nettie McKinnon Art Gallery, LaGrange, 1985. Vol. Women's Aux. Community Meml. Gen. Hosp., 1965-71, Am. Cancer Soc., Easter Seal Soc. Mem. Chgo. Assn. Edn. Young Children, Nat. Assn. Edn. Young Children, Parent and Childbirth Edn. Soc. Avocations: skiing; gardening; aerobics; artist; tennis. Home: 742 N Kensington St LaGrange Park IL 60525 Office: Western Springs Village Ch PO Box 265 45th and Wolf Rd Western Springs IL 60558

BONTEMPO, MARILYN ROSE, advertising agency executive; b. Waterbury, Conn., Oct. 18, 1949; d. Albert Edward and Mary Gertrude (Manner) B.; children—Carla Simone Rozman, Michael Charles Rozman. A.B., Bard Coll., 1971. Music tchr. Bd. Cooperative Ednl. Services, Poughkeepsie, N.Y., 1971-73; assoc. editor Hudson Valley Mag., Pleasant Valley, N.Y., 1973-75, editor, 1975-77; pub. relations dir. No. Dutchess Hosp., Rhinebeck, N.Y., 1979-80; pres., art dir. Mid-Hudson Mktg., Poughkeepsie, 1977—. Recipient merit photography award N.Y. Art Dirs. Club, 1974, Heritage Savs. Photography award Heritage Savs. Bank, Albany, N.Y., 1976, Third Design award Assn. Coll., Univ. and Community Arts Adminstrs., Inc., 1980. Avocations: music; sailing; canoeing; bicycling; hiking. Office: Mid-Hudson Mktg 35 Market St Poughkeepsie NY 12601

BOODY-BIERI, PAMELA JEANNE, journalist; b. San Francisco, Oct. 30, 1949; d. David Eldon Boody and Shirley (Bright) Boody Dustrud; m. Roland Alfred Bieri, June 14, 1981. B.A., Calif. State U.-Northridge, 1974; postgrad. Calif. State U.-San Francisco, 1974-75. Staff writer Desert Sun, Palm Springs, Calif., 1979-84, fashion editor, 1980, food editor, 1983-84; Society editor Palm Springs Life Mag., 1984—. Democrat. Episcopalian. Home: 40-216 Sagewood Dr Palm Desert CA 92260 Office: Palm Springs Life Mag 303 N Indian Ave Palm Springs CA 92262

BOOK, ANITA-BAKER, business executive, designer; b. Essex, Ill.; d. John Benjamin and Dora (Greenwald) Baker; student Chgo. Bus. Coll.; B.A., Columbia Conservatory, 1923, Grace Hickox Studios, 1926; student Chgo. Acad. Fine Arts; grad. Herzl Jr. Coll., 1936; grad. U. Chgo., 1941, U. Nebr., 1941; Ph.D. (hon.), Colo. State Christian Coll., 1978; m. William Ship Book, Mar. 14, 1941. Tchr., owner dramatic art studio, Chgo., 1926-32; receptionist radio shows, 1927-32; sec. William Lemle Studios, 1930-34; mgr. N.Y. import office S.S. Sarna, 1933-34; creator, designer Bells of Sarna, 1935, specialist in Balinese art, lectr. throughout U.S. with exhbn. wood carvings and handicrafts from Dutch East Indies, 1934-41; sec. Consairways, Fairfield, Calif., 1945; owner, exec. dir. Binita Fruit & Gift Wares, Skokie, Ill., 1945—, exhbns. major gift and trade shows throughout U.S.; past treas. Natural Hygiene Press; original radio player Sta. WMAQ, Chgo., 1924; appeared with KYW Book Theatre, Old Vic Theatre Nat. Theatre, 1928, Chgo. Playwrights Theatre, Billy Bryant's Show Boat, Cort Theatre, Hollywood Players, Chgo. Century Progress, 1933-34; 1st mem.-player original Jack & Jill Players; with original prodn. When Chicago Was Young, Goodman Theatre and revival Studebaker Theatre, 1937. Mem. Skokie Beautification and Improvement Commn., Skokie Bicentennial Commn.; mem. nat. women's com. Brandeis U. Hon. fellow Harry S. Truman Library Inst. Mem. Am. Natural Hygiene Assn., Gift and Decorative Art Assn. (charter), Natural Food Assns., Organic Growers Ill., LWV (dir., historian Internat. Assn. Cancer Victims and Friends Skokie-Lincolnwood chpt., chmn. pub. relations, chmn. observation program publs.), Nat. Health Fedn., Skokie C. of C. (chmn. beautification com. 1968), U. Chgo. Alumni Assn. (life), Art Inst. Chgo. (life), Skokie Valley Symphony Orch., Skokie Valley Bus. and Profl. Women's Club, Nat. Fedn. Ind. Bus., AAUW, Poets and Patrons, Nat. Geog. Soc., Smithsonian Assos., North Shore Pub. Relations, Chgo. Hist. Soc., Actors Equity, Skokie Hist. Soc., Pioneer Women, Hadassah (life), Golden Key (chmn.), Field Mus. Club: Quarter Century (hon.). Editor: (with others) Early Skokie. Created and designed Bells of Serna, 1935. Home and office: 3811 Wright Terr Skokie IL 60076

BOOKER, BETTY MAE, writer; b. Allentown, Pa., Nov. 26, 1948; d. Harold George and Bessie (Bealer-Miller) Bartholomew; m. Samuel Efford Booker III, June 27, 1970; 1 child, Liesel Tamarah. B.A. in English, Millersville State Coll., 1970. Contbr. poetry to jours. and lit. mags. including Plainsong, America, The Christian Century, Poetry Now. Bd. dirs. Plowshare Peace Ctr., Roanoke, Va.; environ./peace task group Va Synod, Luth. Ch. Am., 1981-84, social ministry newsletter editor. Home: 3511 Valley View Ave NW Roanoke VA 24012

BOOKER, JANICE LEAH, journalist, educator; b. Phila., July 25, 1929; d. Max and Rebecca (Cohen) Lekoff; m. Alvin Eugene Booker, Dec. 16, 1951; children—Ellis Carl, Susan Barbara. B.S., Temple U., 1951. Dir. pub. info. Oak Lane Day Sch., Blue Bell, Pa., 1970-80; instr. Temple U. Phila., 1976-82, Beaver Coll., Glenside, Pa., 1980-83; broadcaster Sta. WIBF-FM Radio, Jenkintown, Pa., 1976—; instr. U. Pa., Phila., 1984—; cons. Levinson Found., Boston, 1975-79, Making Words Work, Phila., 1979-81. Author: (with Bea Kaiser) All Our Hearts are Trump, 1976. Trustee Oak Lane Day Sch., 1975-86; bd. dirs. Jewish Ys and Ctrs., Phila., 1983—. Mem. Women in Communications Inc, Soc. Profl. Journalists, Am. Women in Radio and TV, Phila. Writers Orgn. Jewish. Club: Pen and Pencil. Office: WIBF Radio The Benson East Jenkintown PA 19046

BOONE, DEBORAH ANN, recording artist; b. Hackensack, N.J., Sept. 22, 1956; d. Charles Eugene and Shirley Lee (Foley) B.; student parochial schs.; m. Gabriel Ferrer, Sept. 1, 1979; 1 son, Jordan Alexander. Recorded hit song You Light Up My Life, 1977; debut album You Light Up My Life, including selections End of the World and He's a Rebel, 1977; other albums include Midstream, 1978, Debby Boone, 1979, Love Has No Reason, 1980, With My Song, 1980, Savin' It Up, 1980, Surrender, 1983; appeared on numerous TV shows, 1977—, including Tonight Show, Merv Griffin, Dinah, Good Morning America (with Rona Barrett), American Bandstand, The Midnight Special, John Denver Special, A Tribute to Elizabeth Taylor, The Billboards Awards, The Today Show, Gift of the Magi, 1978, 4 Pat Boone Family Specials, 1978-79, Jack Jones Hosts the Palace, Bob Hope Special, 1980, Cambodian relief special, 1980; star Debby Boone Special, 1980, 82; star stage prodn. Seven Brides for Seven Brothers, 1981-82; star ABC-TV movie of week Sins of the Past, 1984. Recipient Am. Music award for song of year, 1977; Grammy award for best new artist, 1977, for best gospel performance by duo or group for Keep the Flame Burning, 1984; Nat. Assn. Theatre Owners award for best new personality, 1977, Gold and Platinum records for You Light Up My Life, 1977, Country Music award for best new country artist, 1977, Golden Plate award, 1978, Grammy award, 1980, Dove award, 1980; named Singing Star of Yr., AGVA, 1978. Author: (autobiography) (with Dennis Baker) Debby Boone—So Far, 1981. Office: 205 S Beverly Dr Suite 205 Beverly Hills CA 90212

BOONE, LESLIE SPEARMAN, educator; b. W. Palm Beach, Fla., July 18, 1930; d. Robert Ewell and Zonise (Wood) Spearman; B.A., U.S. Fla., Tampa, 1975, M.Ed., 1981; m. Floyd E. Boone, June 3, 1950; children—Zonise Jeanette Boone Swanson, Robert Edward, William Gordon. Head Start tchr. Manatee County (Fla.), 1967-75, head tchr. Bradenton (Fla.) Center, 1973-75; kindergarten tchr. Orange Ridge Elementary Sch., Bradenton, 1975—. Sunday sch. tchr. Trinity United Methodist Ch., Bradenton, 1958-78; instr. swimming, social worker ARC; active local PTA, Girl Scouts, Heart Fund. Mem. UDC, DAR, Nat. Soc. Colonial Dames XVII Century, Alpha Delta Kappa (pres. 1984-86). Democrat. Club: Sons of Norway. Home: 2611 26th Ave Dr W Bradenton FL 33505 Office: 400 30th Ave W Bradenton FL 33505

BOONSHAFT-LEWIS, HOPE JUDITH, public relations executive; b. Phila., May 3, 1949; d. Barry and Leriel Gail (Rienzi) B. B.A., Pa. State U., 1972; postgrad. Del. Law Sch., Kellogg Inst. Mgmt. Tng. Program writer Youth Edn., N.Y.C., 1972; legal aide to judge, Phila., 1973; dir. spl. projects Guiffre Med. Center, Phila., 1975; Arlen Specter senatorial campaign fin. dir., Phila., 1975; fin. dir. Jimmy Carter Presdl. Campaign, Atlanta, 1976; nat. fin. dir. Democratic Nat. Com., 1977-78; dir. devel. World Jewish Congress, N.Y.C., 1978; dir. devel. Yeshiva U., Los Angeles, 1979; dir. communications Nat. Easter Seal Soc., Chgo., 1979-83; pres. Boonshaft-Lewis, pub. relations Los Angeles, 1983—; spl. adv. community relations The White House, 1977-80; guest lectr. U. Ill., 1982, May Co.'s Calif. Women in Bus. Named 1 of 6 Non Stop Achievers, GermaineMonteil. Mem. Nat. Soc. Fundraisers, Women's Nat. Dem. Club, Alpha Chi Omega. Home: 1234 N Wetherly Dr Los Angeles CA 90069 Office: 10100 Santa Monica Blvd Suite 350 Los Angeles CA 90067

BOOTH, BARBARA R., civic worker; b. N.Y.C., May 2, 1928; d. Benjamin C. and Ceclia (Lowe) Ribman; A.A., Centenary Jr. Coll., Hackettstown, N.Y., 1948; B.A., Barnard Coll., 1950; m. Mitchell B. Booth, July 13, 1952; 1 son, Brian S. Pres. women's alliance, chmn., Christmas fair 1st Congl. Ch. of City of N.Y., 1959-63; mem. vol. com. Sheltering Arms Children's Service, N.Y.C.; vol., coordinator high sch. visits, program chmn. aux. N.Y. Hosp.; trustee Florence K. Griswold Meml. Fund. Com., All Souls Unitarian Ch., N.Y.C.; dir. women's div. Jefferson Dem. Club. N.Y.C.; committeewoman N.Y. County Dem. Com.; bd. govs., v.p. N.Y. Fruit and Flower Mission, Inc.; del. city conv., chmn. East Manhattan br. LWV; mem. spl. events com. N.Y. Assn. for Blind. Home: 75 East End Ave New York NY 10028

BOOTH, BEATRICE CROSBY, oceanographer; b. Mpls., Aug. 29, 1938; d. George Christian and Beatrice (Goodrich) Crosby; B.A., Radcliffe Coll., 1960; M.A.T., Harvard U., 1962; M.S., U. Wash., 1969; m. Theodore William Booth, Dec. 23, 1960; children—Marguerite Morse, Kristina Wells, George Crosby. Teaching asst. U. Wash., Seattle, 1974, instr., 1975-78, research oceanographer, 1975-80, sr. oceanographer, 1980-83, prin. oceanographer, 1983—; oceanographer NOAA, Seattle, 1978-79. NSF grantee, 1978-80, 80-82, 82-84. Mem. Am. Soc. Limnology and Oceanography, AAAS, Phycological Soc. Am. Democrat. Contbr. articles to profl. jours. Home: 5521 17th Ave NE Seattle WA 98105 Office: Sch Oceanography Univ of Wash Seattle WA 98195

BOOTH, BONNIE NELSON, management development trainer, administrator; b. Lynn, Mass., Aug. 28, 1942; d. Vincent Carl and Merchelle Romaine (Eastman) Nelson. Student Mary Washington Coll., 1960-61, Columbia U., 1965, Carnegie-Mellon U., 1962, 78, 79-80; Ed.M., Harvard U., 1979. Exec. sec. Kenyon and Eckhardt, Inc., advt. agy., N.Y.C., 1964-65; exec. sec., asst. to assoc. dir. Am. Press. Inst., Columbia U., 1965; prin. sec. to chief housing sect. UN Hdqrs., N.Y.C., 1965-68; adminstrv. asst. sec. UN Mission, Magadiscio, Somalia, 1968, Tripoli, Libya, 1968-69; research asst. Stockholm Sch. Econs., 1970; adminstrv. sec. to dep. dir. UN Conf. Trade and Devel./GATT, Geneva, 1970; adminstrv. asst. Harvard U., 1970-74, personnel officer dept. psychology and social relations, 1974-75; adminstrv. asst. Dravo Corp., Pitts., 1975-76; assoc. dir. admissions Chatham Coll., Pitts., 1976-77, acting dir. admissions, 1977-78; mgmt. devel. trainer and adminstr. Westinghouse Credit Corp., Pitts., 1981—. Democratic committeewoman 7th Ward, Pitts., 1980—. Recipient hon. diploma for outstanding performance at Internat. Seminar on Rural Housing and Community Facilities, Venezuelan Govt., 1967, Outstanding Quality Circle Facilitator award Westinghouse Electric Corp., 1985. Mem. Am. Soc. for Tng. and Devel., Internat. Assn. Quality Circles (pres. Pitts. chpt. 1985—), Am. Soc. Exec. Women. Episcopalian. Home: 5825 5th Ave Pittsburgh PA 15232 Office: Westinghouse Credit Corp One Oxford Centre 7th Floor Pittsburgh PA 15219

BOOTH, PAULA, educational guidance counselor; b. Montclair, N.J., June 29, 1938; d. Louis and Vincenza (DiConza) Catalano; m. Llewellyn Hardin Booth, Apr. 17, 1966 (div. Mar. 1980); 1 child, Llewellyn Paul. B.A., Trenton State Coll., 1960; M.A., Montclair State Coll., 1971. Cert. prin., supr., dir. student personnel, secondary English tchr., N.J. Health and phys. edn. tchr. West Orange High Sch., N.J., 1960-61, Meml. High Sch., Cedar Grove, N.J., 1961-64, James Caldwell High Sch., West Caldwell, N.J., 1964-66; health and phys. edn. tchr. Parsippany High Sch., N.J., 1967-72, guidance counselor, 1972-85, dir. guidance, 1985—; ind. coll. cons., Boonton, N.J., 1972—. Sec., Boonton Area Citizen's Coalition for Youth, 1975-78; chmn. Boonton Recreation Commn., 1981—, citizen sect. N.J. Recreation and Parks Assn., 1980—; citizen rep. Mid-Atlantic Regional Council, 1985—. Recipient minigrant in career edn. Parsippany Bd. Edn., 1978. Mem. N.J. Edn. Assn., Profl. Counselors Assn., NEA, County Guidance Dirs. Assn., Nat. Assn. Female Execs., Scotch Plains Round Table for Women. Avocations: tennis, softball, dance, writing. Home: 16 Cypress Terr Boonton NJ 07005 Office: Parsippany High Sch Vail Rd Parsippany NJ 07054

BOOTHE, SABRINA ANNE, development corporation manager, security consultant; b. Bklyn., Mar. 26, 1958; d. Robert Stanley and Matilda Sulla (Edwards) B. B.A. in Econs., Fordham U., 1983; postgrad. Pace U., 1984—. Bus. mgr. Fay & Allen's Foodhalls, N.Y.C., 1979-80; bus. mgr. Ctr. for Study of Presidency, N.Y.C., 1980-84, bus. mgr. Am. Friends of Chung-Ang U., 1982-84; bus. mgr. Flatbush Devel. Corp., Bklyn., 1985—; managerial cons. Maverick Ctr. for Self Devel., Bronx, N.Y., 1980—; exec. dir. Global Women of African Heritage, N.Y.C., 1981—; security cons. Ambassador Investigations, Bklyn., 1983-85; bus. mgr. Presdl. Studies Quar., 1982-84. Editorial intern: The Majority Report, 1975-76. Staff asst. The Ethnic Woman, 1980—. Security cons. Easter Seals Telethon, N.Y.C., 1980-82. Named one of Outstanding Young Women of Am., 1984. Mem. Nat. Assn. Female Execs., UN Assn. of USA. Republican. Home: 2620 Beverly Rd #11B Brooklyn NY 11226 Office: Flatbush Devel Corp 1033 Flatbush Ave Brooklyn NY 11226

BORBA-DARRAS, MARLEEN MARIE, optic sales executive; b. Phillips Ranch, Calif., Oct. 29, 1960; d. Joseph Antonio and Doleen Doris (Bourgeois) Borba; m. Frank Nicholas Darras, Aug. 14, 1983. Student U. Dijon, France, 1979; B.A., U. So. Calif., 1981. Adminstrv. intern The White House, Washington, 1981; profl. sales rep. labs. div. Pfizer, Inc., N.Y.C., 1981-82; optics sales specialist Coopervision, San Jose, Calif., 1982—; opthalmic mgmt. cons., Los Angeles, 1984-85; exec. resume service, Pomona, Calif., 1985-86. Fundraiser Young Republicans, Los Angeles, 1982; self-defense coordinator Project Sister, Pomona, 1984-86; advocate speaker United Way, Pomona, 1984-86; counselor Suicide Prevention Ctr., Los Angeles, 1981-83. Named Civic and Community Outstanding Citizen, United Way, Pomona, 1985. Mem. Nat. Assn. Female Execs. Republican. Roman Catholic. Clubs: Toastmasters (Brea, Calif.); St. Elizabeth's (Chino, Calif.). Avocations: aerobics; kung-fu; church socials; world travel. Home: 34 Stagecoach Dr Phillips Ranch CA 91766 Office: Coopervision Inc 289 Orchard Pkwy San Jose CA 95134

BORBOA, ANN CAROLYN, realty company executive; b. Dos Palos, Calif., May 23, 1938; d. Joseph Lawrence and Ruth Leona (Cornett) Clark; m. Cecil D. Borboa, Feb. 12, 1955 (div. July 1975); children—Mark A., Lynn A. Herrnberger, Michael D. Student West Hills Jr. Coll., 1973-75. Exec. office mgr. Price Giffen Ranch, Five Points, Calif., 1965-75; exec. adminstr. Agri-Till, Inc., Five Points, 1975-81; owner, operator Second Hand Rose, Lemoore, Calif., 1981-85; exec. adminstr. Ted Gamby Realty, Hanford, Calif., 1985—; owner, mgr. Rent A Maid, Second Hand Rose Antiques, Temporary Office Service. Mem. Soc. Antique Appraisers (sec. Calif. 1981-85), Bus. and Profl. Women's Club, Kings County Trade Club. Clubs: Calif. Fedn. Jr. Women's (Dos Palos) (founding charter pres. 1961-63), Calif. Fedn. Women's (state sec.). Avocations: golf; walking; bicycling; oil painting.

BORCHELT, SHERYL LYNN, health care executive, model, consultant; b. Carrollton, Ky., Oct. 17, 1949; d. Ruben Carl and Jessie D. (Bartlett) Johnson; m. James Caldwell Borchelt, Feb. 25, 1967; children—Kristi Ann, Jennifer Lynn. Cert. hosp. mgmt. Xavier U., 1982; student Coll. Mount St. Joseph. Cardiovascular technician Christ Hosp., Cin., 1976-78, mgr. cardiac cath lab., 1978-84; profl. model Familiar Faces, Cin., 1980—; mgr. Optimum Services, Inc., div. Bethesda Hosp., Cin., 1984—; mktg./devel. cons. corp. fitness programs, Cin., 1985—. Recipient Human Relations and Achievement award Dale Carnegie Inst., Cin., 1985. Mem. Nat. Assn. Female Execs., Assn. Fitness in Bus., Am. Mgmt. Assn. Republican. Club: TCH Drama (Cin.) (v.p. 1981-82). Avocations: dancing; acting; white water rafting; gardening. Office: Optimum Services Inc 2368 Victory Pkwy Suite 500 Cincinnati OH 45206

BORCHERDT, WENDY HAWLEY, civic worker; b. Oakland, Calif., Apr. 12, 1936; d. Stuart Meek and Lois (Weinmann) Hawley; B.A., Stanford, 1958; m. Edward Rahr Borcherdt, Jr., July 5, 1958; children—Kimberley Borcherdt Bolt, Edward Rahr III. Assoc. dir. Presdl. personnel The White House, Washington, 1981, spl. asst. to Pres. for public liaison, 1981-82; acting under sec. edn for intergovtl. affairs U.S. Dept. Edn., 1982-83; sr. advisor U.S. del. to UNESCO Gen. Conf., 1983; mem. U.S. Nat. Commn. on UNESCO, 1982-85; exec. vice chmn. Citizens for the Republic, 1986—; vice chmn. Dept. State monitoring panel on UNESCO. Div. chmn. Community Chest, Los Angeles, 1960-61; active various community drives; Blue Bird leader Camp Fire Girls, 1966-68; tchr. leadership and mgmt. Teren & Co., 1976-77; pres. Tng. for Effective Mgmt., 1977-81; bd. dirs. Jr. League of Los Angeles, rec. sec., 1965-81, treas., 1969-70, pres., 1972-73; area rep. Assn. Jr. Leagues, 1973-75; vice chmn. Citizens for Law Enforcement, 1975-78; mem. subcom. on indsl. and comml. firm retention City of Los Angeles Econ. Adv. Council, 1976; bd. dirs., pres. Symphonians, 1961-66, Jr. Philharmonic com., 1971-81, bd. overseers Hoover Instn. War, Revolution and Peace, 1974-81, 1984—; bd. govs. Town Hall, 1980-81; bd. dirs. Harvard Sch. Boys, 1975-78, Hancock Homes Owners Assn., 1975-77, Good Samaritan Hosp. Aux., 1975-81, Pacific Legal Found., 1979-81, 84—, Jamestown Found., 1985—; vice chmn. Ind. Colls. So. Calif., 1975-81; div. chmn. Nixon, 1960, 62; area chmn. Goldwater, 1964, Reagan, 1966; asst. co-chmn. Women for Nixon, Los Angeles, 1968; area chmn. Samuel Yorty, 1969; campaign worker Ronald Reagan for Pres., 1976-81, regional fin. dir., 1979-81; vice chmn. adv. bd. Alcoholism Info. Center, Los Angeles; mem. exec. com. Ed Davis for Gov., 1978; mem. Nat. Republican Women's Club, Rep. Nat. Fed. Forum, League Rep. Women, Charter 100, Washington, Women's Forum of Washington, Women's Econ. Round Table, N.Y.C., Renaissance Women, Washington. Episcopalian (tchr. Sunday sch.). Clubs: Los Angeles Country, Beach, Stanford Women's (dirs., pres. 1965-69) (Los Angeles); Larchmont Republican (dir., v.p. 1975-80). Home: 400 S Bentley Ave Los Angeles CA 90049

BORCHERS, ELIZABETH STUHT, lawyer; b. Omaha, Oct. 13, 1951; d. William Churchill and Lois Ann (Chenoweth) Stuht; m. Darwin Walter Borchers, Jan. 2, 1971 (div. July 1979); 1 son, William W.; m. 2d Michael Wayne Honaker, Aug. 20, 1982. Student, Augustana Luth. Coll., Sioux Falls, S.D., 1969-70; B.A., Midland Luth. Coll., Fremont, Nebr., 1973; J.D., Creighton U., 1976. Bar: Nebr. 1976, U.S. Dist. Ct. Nebr. 1976. Legal intern U.S. Atty., Omaha, 1972-73; ptnr. Gunderson, Abrahamson, Borchers & Grewe, Omaha, 1976-82; assoc. Byrne, Rothery, Borchers & Lewis, Omaha, 1983-84; corp. counsel Lozier Corp., Omaha, 1984—; speaker Nebr. Continuing Legal Edn. Author: Family Law Form Book, 1982. Mem. Mayor's Commn. Task Force on Abused Women, Omaha, 1977-78. Mem. Assn. Trial Lawyers Am., Nebr. Bar Assn., Omaha Bar Assn., Nat Assn. Women Bus. Owners. Clubs: Omaha Connections (v.p. 1984—), Omaha Peddlers Bicycle (treas. 1981-82). Home: 755 N 58th St Omaha NE 68132 Office: Lozier Corp 4401 N 21st St Omaha NE 68101

BORDEN, SANDRA MCCLISTER, day care center administrator, dancer; b. Trenton, Oct. 18, 1946; d. Harry Arthur and Ruth West McClister; m. Robert Stetson Borden, Mar. 23, 1968; children—Robert Freeman, Randolph McClister, David Buckley, Christian Delano. B.A., Eastern Nazarene Coll., Quincy, Mass., 1968; M.A., Nova U., 1986. Tchr. kindergarten Doves Nest Day Care Ctr., Rockland, Mass., 1979-84, owner, adminstr., 1979—; owner, adminstr. Dove's Nest Day Care Ctr., Weymouth, Mass., 1980-82, Abington, Mass., 1980-83; owner, editor Barter & Trade Jour., Rockland, 1980-83; owner Dove's Nest Family Day Care System, Rockland, 1984—; co-owner Carriage House Day Care Ctr., Brockton, Mass., 1986—. Dancer Foggs Dancers, Boston, 1980—; dir. Country Dance Soc., Boston, 1982—, v.p. 1986—, dancer, 1984-85; co-founder, dancer Rapscallion Rapper Sword Team, 1985—. Bd. dirs. LWV, Rockland, 1972-73. Mem. Nat. Assn. Young Children, Royal Scottish Dance Soc., Nat. Assn. Female Execs., Assn. for Childhood Edn. Internat. Baptist. Clubs: Women Aglow (sec., bd. dirs.) (Brockton); New Eng. Folk Festival Assn. (Boston). Home: 1040 Plymouth St Abington MA 02351 Office: The Dove's Nest Day Care Ctr 18 North Ave Rockland MA 02370

BORDER, LAURA LEA BAKER, French language educator; b. Steamboat Springs, Colo., Nov. 25, 1945; d. Claude A. and Mary (Chivington) Baker; B.A. cum laude, U. Colo., 1967, M.A., 1971; m. William Border, June 28, 1975; 1 dau., Alison Anne. Instr., U. Denver, spring, 1972, U. Colo., Boulder, 1977—; lectrice d'anglais, UniversitéU. Bordeaux (France), 1969-70. U. Colo. teaching associateship, 1967-69, 70-72. Mem. Colo. Assn. for Internat. Edn., Colo. Congress Fgn. Lang. Tchrs., Am. Assn. Tchrs. French. Author: Collage: Révision de Grammaire, 1981; Collage: Conversation Activitiés, Collage: Lectures Littéraires, Collage: Variétés Culturelles, 1981; (with others) Collage: Cahier d'exercices oraux et écrits. crits. Office: Dept French and Italian Univ of Colo Boulder CO 80309

BORDINI-LANCASTER, LINDA LEE, biologist; b. Monongahela, Pa., May 21, 1942; d. Walter and Lucille F. (Archbold) Warren; stepdau. Wilfred Caster; B.S., California U. of Pa., 1976, M.S. in Biology, 1984; m. Jack L. Myers, Jan. 8, 1960; children—Dana M., Jacqueline L., Kimberly A.; m. Primo Bordini, Apr. 28, 1978; m. William Lancaster, Aug. 5, 1983. Process analyst environ. health services dept. U.S. Steel Co., Clairton, Pa., 1978-84. Mem. Bot. Soc. Am., Pa. Acad. Sci., Sierra Club, Nat. Audubon Soc., Bot. Soc. Westmorland County, Grad. Student Assn., Beta Beta Beta, Chi Gamma Psi. Democrat. Methodist. Home: Box 211 Windridge PA 15038 Office: Box 411 Sutersville PA 15083

BORDNER, MARJORIE RICH, educator, civic worker; b. McDonough County, Ill., Dec. 1, 1914; d. Harry R. and Merle (Turner) Rich; B.Ed., Western Ill. U., 1936; Ed.M., U. Mo., Columbia, 1940; m. Lawrence Inman Bordner, Apr. 21, 1946; children—Larry Richard, Larrilyn Louise. Tchr. various elem. and secondary schs., Ill.; instr. Western Ill. U. and Spoon River Coll.; acct., receptionist Bordner Air Conditioning-Refrigeration Co. Sec., Ill. orgn. DAR, mem. state bd. dirs., 1977, div. dir., regent, 1971—; pres. New Eng. Women Ill. Prairie Colony, 1974-76; sec. found. bd., exec. com. Western Ill. U., 1972—; mem. Western Ill. U. Alumni Council, 1972—, sec., 1981—; pres. Fulton County Hist. and Geneal. Soc., 1974-75, 80—, Spoon River Scenic Drive Assn., 1971-74; mem. Fulton County Planning Commn., 1971—; chmn. Fulton County Bicentennial, 1973-76; sec. Community Resource Devel. Exec. Council of Fulton County, 1979—; life mem. Ill. Hist. Soc., Ill. Geneal. Soc. Recipient Disting. Alumni award Western Ill. U., 1971, Achievement award, 1980, Jefferson award, 1981, Martha Washington award, 1986; hon. parade marshal Canton Friendship Festival Parade, 1976. Mem. Nat. Soc. Daus. of Founders Patriots (life). Author: A Spoon River Portrait, 1983 (Ill. State award for excellence); contbr. articles to periodicals.

BORENSTEIN, EMILY RUTH, poet; b. Elizabeth, N.J., May 6, 1923; d. Louis and Jennie (Molowitz) Schwartz; student Julliard Sch., 1941-42; B.S. in Comparative Lit., Columbia U., 1964, M.S. in Social Work, 1984; M.A. in English, N.Y. U., 1972; m. Morris Borenstein, June 27, 1942; children—Rachel, Sandra, Marc. Author: Woman Chopping, 1978; Finding My Face, 1979; Cancer Queen, 1979; Night of the Broken Glass, 1981; contbr. numerous poems to poetry and lit. mags., anthologies, including Voices Within the Ark, The Modern Jewish Poets, 1980, Phoenix Rising, An Anthology of Contemporary Jewish Voices, 1981; Anthology of Mag. Verse, 1981; Blood to Remember: American Poets on the Holocaust, 1986; lectr. poetry workshops, poetry readings. Recipient Ann. Poetry award, Jewish Currents, 1978. Mem. Poets and Writers, Inc., Poetry Soc. Am., Columbia U. Alumni Assn., N.Y. U. Alumni Assn. Jewish. Club: Women's Univ. Home: 189 Highland Ave Middletown NY 10940

BORGESE, ELISABETH MANN, author; b. Munich, Germany, Apr. 24, 1918 d. Thomas and Katia (Pringsheim) Mann; came to U.S., 1938, naturalized, 1941; diploma Conservatory of Music, Zurich, 1937; m. Giuseppe Antonio Borgese, Nov. 23, 1939; children—Angelica, Dominica. Research assoc., editor Common Cause, U. Chgo., 1945-51; editor Perspective USA, Diogenes Intercultural Publs., 1952-57; exec. sec. bd. editors Ency. Brit., Chgo., 1964-66; sr. fellow, asso. Center for Study Democratic Instns., Santa Barbara, Calif., 1965—; Killam sr. fellow Dalhousie U., Halifax, N.S., Can., 1978-79, prof. dept. polit. sci., 1980—; author: To Whom It May Concern, 1962; Ascent of Woman, 1963; The Language Barrier, 1965; The Ocean Regime, 1968; The Drama of the Oceans, 1976; Seafarm: The Story of Aquaculture, 1980: The Mines of Neptune, 1985; The Future of the Oceans: A Report to the Club of Rome, 1985; contbr. short stories, essays to mags. Chmn. planning council Internat. Ocean Inst.; advisor Austrian del. 3d UN Conf. on Law of Sea, 1976-86. Decorated Cross of Honor (Austria). Mem. Acad. Polit. Sci. AAAS, Am. Soc. Internat. Law, World Acad. Arts and Scis. Home: Sambro Head Halifax NS Canada Office: Dept Polit Sci Dalhousie U Halifax NS B3H 4H6 Canada

BORIS, DORIS JO, cable television executive; b. Buffalo, Dec. 15, 1944; d. Joseph Ralph and Doris (Rafal) Glownia; m. Walter Michael Boris, Apr. 16, 1966; children—Nicole Elizabeth, Melisa Cathryn, Andrew Michael. B.S., Kent State U., 1966. Communications dir. Cuyahoga Falls Sch., Ohio, 1966-67; traffic coordinator Sta. WKYC-TV, Cleve., 1967-68; planner Lake County CETA, Painesville, Ohio, 1978-79, evaluator, 1979-80; systems mgr. Continental Cablevision Ohio, Mentor, 1980—. Pres. Mentor Swim Team, 1985—. Mem. Nat. Cable TV Assn. (congressional team leader 11th Dist. 1985—), Ohio Cable TV Assn., Lake County Profl. Communicators, Mentor C. of C. (mem. exec. bd.), Painesville C. of C. Democrat. Roman Catholic. Avocations: photography; swimming. Home: 7033 Hopkins Rd Mentor OH 44060 Office: Continental Cablevision Ohio 7511 Mentor Ave Mentor OH 44060

BORKAN, VIVIENNE ELIANE, retail stores manager; b. Basel, Switzerland, Apr. 16, 1956; came to U.S., 1960, naturalized, 1963; d. Günter and Rita Klara (Sonderegger) Schwarzbart; m. William Borkan, Aug. 31, 1980. Student U. Miami, 1973-74; B.A., Wellesley Coll., 1977. Reporter, Sta. WBZ, Boston, 1976-77; account exec. Joan Spector Pub. Relations, Inc., Miami, Fla., 1977-78; credit coordinator Burdine's Dept. Stores, Miami, 1978-80, store fin. coordinator, credit promotion mgr., 1980-83, mgr. credit card mktg., 1983—. Home: 3364 NE 167th St North Miami FL 33160 Office: 7100 NW 32d Ave Miami FL 33147

BORKENHAGEN, CONSTANCE KATSON, stockbroker, lawyer; b. Albuquerque, June 30, 1942; d. Robert Virgil and Penelope (Papafrangos) Katson; B.A., Duke, 1964; J.D., U. N.Mex., 1975; m. Robert H. Borkenhagen, Apr. 23, 1965 (div.); children—Holly Gabrielle, Lea Monique. Legis. asst. U.S. Ho. of Reps., 1965-71; lobbyist Albuquerque Consumer Fedn., N.Mex. Legislature, 1971-75; admitted to D.C. bar, N.Mex. bar; with Dist. Atty.'s Office, 1974, County Pub. Defender's Office, 1975; legal journalist Doing Business in Europe; internat. law practice, London, Eng., 1976-83; dir., gen.

counsel Equator Petroleum Co., 1981-83; fin. cons. Merrill Lynch, 1983—; lobbyist Criminal Sexual Conduct Act, 1974-75. Publicity dir. N.Mex. Arts and Crafts Fair, 1971-72; counsel Am. C. of C., London, Europe, Mediterranean. Bd. dirs. Democrats Abroad, Women's Playhouse Trust, Devel. Ctr. Mem. ABA (ho. of dels. 1974-75; Disting. Service award 1974, 75), Internat. Bar Assn. (bus. law sect.), Internat. Assn. Women Lawyers, City Women's Network, Brit. Assn. Women Execs. (bd. dirs.), Inst. Dirs.; Internat. Platform Assn., Delta Theta Phi (sec. 1974-75). Author profl. articles. Home: 29 Cambridge St London SW1 England Office: 153 New Bond St London W 11 England

BORKOWSKI, CARMEN ANA CINTRÓN, lawyer; b. Ponce, P.R., Aug. 2, 1953; d. Miguel and Zaida (Rodríguez) Cintrón; m. John Joseph Borkowski, May 29, 1982. B.B.A. with high honors, U. P.R., 1975, J.D. with honors, 1978. Bar: P.R. 1978, U.S. Dist. Ct. P.R. 1978, U.S. Ct. Appeals (1st cir.) 1979, U.S. Supreme Ct. 1983. Atty., advisor Jud. Com. on Civil Law, P.R. Ho. of Reps., 1978-79; atty. Fed. Litigation div. Justice Dept., P.R., 1979-80, FCC, Washington, 1980—. Translator, screener Washington Free Clinic, 1981-82. Recipient Criminal Law award U. P.R., 1978. Mem. Fed. Bar Assn., ABA, Hispanic Bar Assn. (v.p.), P.R. Bar Assn. Episcopalian. Office: Federal Communications Commission 1919 M St NW Washington DC 20554

BORKOWSKI, JULIA MARIE, auditor; b. Charleston, W.Va., June 24, 1959; d. Elmer Paul and Helena Kay (Cantley) Borkowski. B.A. in Bus. Adminstrn., New Eng. Coll., 1981; postgrad. N.H. Coll., 1984—. Student advisor New Eng. Coll., Henniker, N.H., 1978-81; customer service rep. N.H. Savs. Bank, Concord, N.H., 1981-82, asst. auditor, 1982-83; internal auditor Chubb & Son, Warren, N.J., 1983-85, EDP auditor, 1985—; bank rep. Am. Inst. Banking, Concord, 1982-83, chmn. mktg. com., 1983; coordinator Employee Benefit Program, Concord, 1984—. Mem. Nat. Assn. Female Execs., Concord, 1986. Mem. Nat. Assn. Female Execs., EDP Auditors Assn. Republican. Episcopalian. Avocations: painting; sailing. Office: Chubb & Son 1 Granite Pl Concord NH 03301

BORLAND, BARBARA DODGE (MRS. HAL BORLAND), author; b. Waterbury, Conn.; d. Harry G. and Grace (Cross) Dodge; student Oberlin U., 1922-23, Columbia U. Sch. Journalism, 1923; m. 2d, Hal Borland, Aug. 10, 1945 (dec. Feb. 1978); 1 dau., Diana (Mrs. James C. Thomson, Jr.). Editorial cons. various pubs., 1923-35; contbr. Writers Workshop, N.Y.C., 1934-38; writer, also collaborator with husband, fiction for Colliers, McCalls, Good Housekeeping, Cosmopolitan, Redbook, others, 1946-56; garden columnist Berkshire Eagle, Pittsfield, Mass., 1960. Recipient Distinguished Alumna award St. Margaret's Sch., 1972. Congregationalist. Mem. Authors League Am. Author: The Greater Hunger, 1962 (chosen Ambassador Book, English Speaking Union 1963); This is the Way My Garden Grows ... and This is the Way My Garden Cooks, 1986; contbr.: New England: The Four Seasons, 1980; editor: Twelve Moons of the Year (by Hal Borland), 1979. Address: Weatogue Rd Salisbury CT 06068

BORN, BROOKSLEY ELIZABETH, lawyer; b. San Francisco, Aug. 27, 1940; d. Ronald Henry and Mary Ellen (Bortner) B.; A.B., Stanford U., 1961, J.D., 1964; m. Alexander E. Bennett, Oct. 9, 1982; children by previous marriage—Nicholas Jacob Landau, Ariel Elizabeth Landau. Admitted to Calif. bar, 1965, D.C. bar, 1966; law clk. U.S. Ct. Appeals, Washington, 1964-65; legal researcher Harvard U. Law Sch., 1967-68; assoc. firm Arnold and Porter, Washington, 1965-67, 68-73, partner, 1974—; lectr. law Columbus U. Sch. Law, Cath. U. Am., 1972-74; adj. prof. Georgetown U. Law Center, Washington, 1972-73. Bd. visitors Stanford U. Law Sch., 1977-79, 84—; bd. dirs. Nat. Legal Aid and Defenders Assn., 1972-79; trustee Center for Law and Social Policy, Washington, 1977—; bd. dirs. Nat. Women's Law Ctr., Washington, 1981—. Named Woman Lawyer of Yr., Women's Bar Assn. D.C. 1981. Mem. ABA (chairperson sect. individual rights and responsibilities 1977-78, chmn. fed. judiciary com. 1980-83, ho. of dels. 1978—), D.C. Bar (sec. 1975-76, bd. govs. 1976-79), Am. Law Inst., Lawyers' Com. for Civil Rights Under Law (trustee 1978—), Am. Judicature Soc. (bd. dirs. 1984—), Order of Coif. Pres. Stanford Law Rev., 1963-64. Office: 1200 New Hampshire Ave NW Washington DC 20036

BORN, CAROLYNNE IONA, writer, public relations and political campaign consultant; b. San Francisco, Feb. 2, 1953; d. Philip and Vivian Louise (Kline) Born. Student Coll. San Mateo, 1971-73, D.A. in Journalism, San Jose State U., 1975. Free lance writer Collage Mag., San Jose, Calif., 1976-78; advt. copywriter Hugo Schneider Prodns., San Jose, 1976-77; pub. relations asst. San Jose Hosp., 1977-78; communications specialist Calif. State Employees' Assn., Sacramento, 1978-83; corp. staff writer Guy F. Atkinson Co., South San Francisco, Calif., 1984-86; campaign cons. Woodward & McDowell, Burlingame, Calif., 1986; cons. Citizens Against Nuclear War, Washington, 1983, various polit. groups, Sacramento, 1983-84. No. Calif. coordinator Nat. Women's Polit. Caucus, 1979, state sec., 1978, state vice chmn., 1980, local chmn., 1982-83, 86, mem. nat. steering com., 1983—, mem. state steering com., 1985; chmn. 6th Assembly Dist. Democratic Com., Sacramento, 1979-80; mem. state platform com. Calif. Dem. Com., 1983—, also alt. mem. state central com.; mem. San Mateo County Dem. Central Com.; bd. mem. 20th Assembly Dist. Dem. Com., Sacramento Women's Campaign Fund, 1984—; chmn. 10th Assembly Dist. Dem. Com., 1984. Mem. Soc. Profl. Journalists, Women in Communications, Internat. Assn. Bus. Communicators. Home: 1018 Chula Vista Ave Apt 3 Burlingame CA 94010

BORNHOLDT, LAURA ANNA, university administrator; b. Peoria, Ill., Feb. 11, 1919; d. John and Barbara (Kohl) Bornholdt; A.B., Smith Coll., 1940, M.A., 1942; Ph.D., Yale U., 1945. Asst. prof. history Smith Coll., Northampton, Mass., 1945-52; internat. relations assoc. AAUW, Washington, 1952-57; dean Sarah Lawrence Coll., Bronxville, N.Y., 1957-59; dean women, adj. prof. history U. Pa., Phila., 1959-61; dean coll., prof. history Wellesley Coll. (Mass.), 1961-64; v.p. Danforth Found., St. Louis, 1964-73; sr. program officer Lilly Endowment Inc., Indpls., 1973-76. v.p. for edn., 1976-84; spl. asst. to pres. U. Chgo., 1984—; mem. bd. Council on Library Resources, 1983—; mem. nat. adv. com. Black higher edn. and Black colls. and univs. Dept. Edn., 1977-82. Mem. Yale Council, 1977-82; trustee Coll. of Wooster (Ohio), 1966-76, trustee emerita, 1976—; trustee St. Louis U., 1971-75; bd. govs. St. Meinrad Coll., 1984—. Recipient Yale U. Wilbur Cross medal, 1976. Mem. Am. Assn. Higher Edn., Phi Beta Kappa. Editorial bd. Jour. Higher Edn., 1970-76; cons. editor Change mag., 1981—. Home: 5200 S East End Ave Apt 25A Chicago IL 60615 Office: Adminstrn Bldg 5801 S Ellis Ave Chicago IL 60637

BORNSTEIN, SARAH BARBARA, personnel specialist; b. Phila., Nov. 3, 1947; d. Nathan and Frances (Goldberg) Bornstein; m. Alexander Cockrell O'Reilly, Aug. 27, 1975 (div.); 1 child, Kevin Bernard. B.A., Chatham Coll., 1969; M.A., Rutgers U., 1970; M.S.I.R., Loyola U., Chgo., 1985. Adminstrv. asst. Temple Sholom, Chgo., 1972-76; exec. sec. Borg-Warner Corp., Chgo., 1976-79, communications assoc., 1979-81, grants coordinator Borg-Warner Found., Chgo., 1980-81; sr. communications specialist Dart & Kraft, Inc., Northbrook, Ill., 1981-85, personnel specialist, 1985—; dir. Health Evaluation & Referral Services, Chgo., 1980—; mem. Jr. League of Chgo., 1983—. Trustee, Chatham Coll., 1984—. Recipient YWCA Leadership award Metropolitan Chgo., 1980; Woodrow Wilson fellow, 1969. Mem. Internat. Assn. Bus. Communicators (Gold Quill 1982, Spectra, Silver Quill 1983) local chmn. 1982-83), Phi Beta Kappa. Democrat. Jewish. Office: Dart & Kraft Inc 2211 Sanders Rd Northbrook IL 60062

BOROCHOFF, IDA SLOAN, real estate executive, artist; b. July 29, 1922; d. Louis and Eva (Bistrick) Sloan; ed. U. Ga., 1939-40, Ga. State U., 1940, Chgo. Sch. Interior Decorating, 1966, Allegro Sch. Ballet, Chgo., Atlanta Ballet, 1948-54, Emory U., 1971-72; m. Charles Zachary Borochoff, Jan. 11, 1942; children—Lynn Borochoff Gould, Jean Sue Borochoff Shapiro, Toby Ann Borochoff Bernstein, Lance Mark. Investor and owner real estate, 1941—; v.p. Designs Unltd., Inc., Atlanta, 1964—; pres. Sloan Borochoff Gallery, Atlanta, 1970—; art lectr. Met. Ednl. Service; Ga. Inst. Tech.-Free U.; producer live talk health show on cable TV, Atlanta, 1983—; exhibited several one-woman shows, 1961-71, including Lovett Sch., 1972, 75, Ga. Inst. Tech., 1972, 75, Atlanta Mdse. Mart; art rev. columnist Northside Neighbor Newspapers. Bd. dirs. Atlanta Ballet, 1950-57; bd. dirs. Atlanta Music Club, also co-editor Newsletter; hostess Atlanta Arts Festival; capt. Heart Fund, 1968-76, area chmn. dr.; active various multi-media groups; artistic dir. Atlanta Playhouse Theatre; active Dogwood Festival; chmn., trustee Atlanta Playhouse Theatre; mem. U.S. Congl. adv. bd. Am. Security Council, 1983—. Recipient several art awards; Caber award, 1984; named hon. alumnus Atlanta Art Inst.,

1968, One of Ten Leading Ladies of Atlanta, J.C. Singles, 1976; City grantee, 1985. Mem. Atlanta Press Club, Atlanta Writers Club (membership com.), Atlanta Artists Club, Atlanta Women's C. of C. (chmn. fine arts 1977-78), LWV, High Mus. Art, Ga. Writers Assn., Arts High Mus. (patron). Mem. B'nai B'rith Women (pres. chpt. 1975, mem. SE regional bd.). Clubs: Jockey, Progressive. Home: 3450 Old Plantation Rd NW Atlanta GA 30327 Office: 733 Glendale Rd Scottdale GA 30079

BORREGO, LILA KAIN TAPIA, travel consultant; b. Buenos Aires, Argentina, July 23, 1930; came to U.S., 1962, naturalized, 1967. d. Martin and Rosalia (Schertzer) Kain; m. Alberto J. Borrego, Feb. 26, 1979. Degree in acct., Escuela Comercial Temperley, Buenos Aires, 1948; Degree in interpretation Spanish-Hungarian, Faculty Econ. Sci., Buenos Aires, 1951; Degree in Actriz-Director, Teatro LaRueda, Buenos Aires, 1950. Profl. actress Assoc. Argentina de Actores, Buenos Aires, 1958-62; locution TV camaras Secretaria se Communinacions Direccion Fral de Difusion, Buenos Aires, 1959-61; T.V. asistent of produccion Ministerior de Educadusticia, Buenos Aires, 1960-61; acct., sec. Dress Shops, Miami Beach, Fla., 1964-78; travel cons. Miami Beach Travel, Frank's Travel, Miami Beach, 1978—; computer trainer, 1978—; drama dir. Miami Beach Sr. High Sch., 1969—; judge Dade Community Coll., Dist. Thespian Sr. High Schs. Conf., Miami, Fla., 1972. Mem. Ind. Travel Agts., Thespian Soc. (hon.). Home: Drawer 110 9700 E Bay Harbor Bay Harbor FL 33114

BORST-MANNING, DIANE GAIL, medical center executive; b. Rochester, N.Y., Nov. 5, 1937; d. Howard Louis and Emily Kathleen (Crew) Borst; m. Steven Manning, Sept. 11, 1979. B.A. cum laude, Wagner Coll., 1959; M.B.A., N.Y.U., 1966. Planner N.Y.U. Med. Ctr., N.Y.C., 1962-76, assoc. dir. planning, 1976-78, dir. mgmt. services, 1978-80; dir. human resources Mt. Sinai Med. Ctr., N.Y.C., 1980-85, dir. planning, 1985—; inst. dept. health care mgmt. Mt. Sinai Sch. Medicine, CUNY, 1982—. Editor: Managing Non-Profit Organizations, 1979. Author: (cassette) Managers and Secretaries - How to Achieve Teamwork, 1980. Mem. Health Systems Agy. Bd., N.Y.C., 1976-79. Fullbright fellow, 1959. Mem. N.Y. Personnel Mgmt. Assn. (bd. dirs. 1974-76), Greater N.Y. Hosp. Assn., Am. Compensation Assn., Bur. Nat. Affairs (personnel policy forum 1983-84), Am. Assn. Hosp. Planners, Assn. Am. Med. Colls. Group on Instrl. Planning. Avocations: gardening; auto mechanics; carpentry. Office: Mount Sinai Med Ctr 19 E 98 St New York NY 10029

BORTON, MARILYN MILLER, recreation therapist; b. Paterson, N.J., Oct. 3, 1930; d. Calvin Henry and Lillian (Bennett) Miller; B.A. in Recreation, Syracuse (N.Y.) U., 1951; B.S. in Edn., Paterson State Tchrs. Coll., 1953; postgrad. Fairleigh Dickinson U.; m. Lee John Borton, June 9, 1951; children—Lee John, Nancy Lee, James Christopher, Susan Elizabeth. Dir., Village Sch. Retarded Children, Ridgewood, N.J., 1951-53; elementary sch. tchr., Wyckoff, N.J., 1953-56; tchr. Abbott Nursery Sch., Prospect Park, N.J., 1956-59; dir. Robin's Nest Nursery Sch., Bernardsville, N.J., 1964-66; dir. recreation Birchwood Convalescent Center, Edison, N.J., 1975—; sec.-treas. Borton Bus. Forms, Inc., 1968—. Bd. dirs. St. David's Kindergarten, Peters Twp., Pa., 1961-62, Passaic Twp. Youth Center, 1971-74, Watchung Hills Pop Warner Football, 1972-74; chmn. Helping Hand program Passaic Twp. Jaycees Wives, 1970-72; mem. Millington First Aid Squad, 1966—; charter mem., bd. dirs. Passaic Twp. First Aid Squad, 1974 , pres., 1976-77, 83, capt., 1984, 85, 86; instr. CPR and 1st aid ARC, 1974—; sec. Bicentennial Commn. Passaic Twp., 1974-76. Named Chmn. of Year, Passaic Twp. Jaycee Wives, 1970-71. Mem. Nat. Therapeutic Recreation Assn. Republican. Episcopalian. Home: 151 Division Ave PO Box 406 Millington NJ 07946 Office: 1350 Inman Ave Edison NJ 08820

BORYSEWICZ, MARY LOUISE, editor; b. Chgo.; d. Thomas J. and Mabel E. (Zeien) O'Farrell; B.A., Mundelein Coll., 1970; postgrad. in English lit. U. Ill, 1970-71; grad. exec. program U. Chgo., 1982; m. Daniel S. Borysewicz, June 11, 1955; children—Mary Adele, Stephen Francis, Paul Barnabas. Tchr. advanced level English for fgn.-speaking adults Evanston Twp. (Ill.) High Sch., 1969-71; editor tech. publs. AMA, Chgo., 1971-73; exec. mng. editor Am. Jour. Ophthalmology, Chgo., 1973—; asst. sec., treas. Ophthalmic Pub. Co., 1985—; guest lectr. U. Chgo. Med. Sch., 1979, Harvard U. Med. Sch., 1978, Northwestern U. Med. Sch., 1979, Am. Acad. Ophthalmology, 1976, 81. Mem. Am. Soc. Profl. and Exec. Women, Council Biology Editors (fin. com.), Internat. Fedn. Sci. Editors Assns., Soc. Scholarly Pub. (contbr. articles to sci. publs.), editor: Ophthalmology Principles and Concepts, 4th edit., 1970, 5th edit., 1982, 6th edit., 1986. Home: 4415 N California Ave Chicago IL 60625 Office: 435 N Michigan Ave Chicago IL 60611

BOS, CAROLE DIANNE, lawyer; b. Grand Rapids, Mich., May 31, 1949; d. James and Alberdean (Kooiker) Berkenpas; m. James Edwin Bos, Apr. 3, 1969; B.A. with high honors, Grand Valley State Coll., 1977; J.D. cum laude, T.M. Cooley Law Sch., Lansing, Mich., 1981. Bar Mich. 1981. Asst. mgr. Army & Air Force Base Exchange, Soesterberg, Netherlands, 1969-73; mgmt. asst. Selfridge Air Nat. Guard Base, Mt. Clemens, Mich., 1973-74; legal asst. John Boyles, Grand Rapids, 1974-77; law clk. Cholette, Perkins & Buchanan, Grand Rapids, 1977-82; trial atty. Hecht, Buchanan & Cheney, Grand Rapids, 1982-84; ptnr., trial atty. Buchanan & Bos, 1984—; mem. adv. bd. Grand Valley State Coll., 1981—. Co-author: Video Techniques in Trial and Pretrial, 1983; Video Technology: Its Use and Application in Law, 1984; How to Use Video in Litigation, 1986; contbg. author: Women Trial Lawyers: How they Succeed in Practice and in the Courtroom, 1986; staff T. M. Cooley Law Rev.; contbr. articles to profl. jours. Bd. dirs. Jellema Ho., Grand Rapids; trustee Grand Valley State Coll. Found. Breen scholar, 1977. Mem. Grand Rapids Bar Assn. (library com. 1983—), Mich. State Bar Assn. (communications com. 1983—), ABA, Fed. Bar Assn. (regional dir. 1984—), Am. Trial Lawyers Assn. Republican. Home: 795 Sea Watch Rd Holland MI Office: Buchanan & Bos 6th Floor Frey Bldg Grand Rapids MI 49503

BOSCHEN, DIANA ELIZABETH, sr. marketing analyst; b. Kingston, Jamaica, May 19, 1944; came to U.S., 1968 naturalized; d. George Augustus and Beryl Lillian Elaine (Thorburn) Purcell; m. John Christian Boschen, Dec. 27, 1967; 1 child, Rachel Elizabeth. Student, Mercy Coll., Bronx, N.Y., 1986—. Supr. customer services, adminstr. spl. fund raising U.S. Com. for UNICEF, N.Y.C., 1968-76; bus. mgr. Vis. Nurse Service N.Y., N.Y.C., 1976-79; acct. rep. Design House, Inc., Teaneck, N.J., 1980; classified advt. rep. N.Y. Daily News, N.Y.C., 1981-82, supr. classified advt., 1982-85, sr. mktg. analyst, 1986—. Editor: Innovators Club Newsletter, 1985-86. Mem. Morris Park Community Assn., Bronx, 1979—; on-call-newscaster In-Touch Radio Network, N.Y.C., 1984—. Named Black Achiever of Yr., Harlem YMCA, N.Y., 1985. Mem. Bronx Bd. of Realtors (Community award 1985), Nat. Assn. Female Execs., Internat. Tng. in Communication (chmn. pub. relations, council 1985-86, 1st place speech contest 1986), Alpha Alumna Assn. (pub. relations chmn. 1983). Avocations: reading; painting; creative writing; music; travelling. Office: New York Daily News 220 E 42nd St New York NY 10017

BOSEKER, BARBARA JEAN, teacher educator; b. Milw., Dec. 2, 1944; d. Edward Herbert and Alice Margaret (Maas) B.; student U. Nigeria, Nsukka, 1966; B.S. (hon.) in Secondary Edn. (Elks Nat. and State Youth scholar), U. Wis., Milw., 1968; M.A. in Anthropology (Ford Found. fellow 1968-69, NDEA fellow 1970-71), U. Wis., Madison, 1971, Ph.D. in Edn. (NDEA fellow), 1978; m. Dale Lester Sutcliffe, Aug. 8, 1975. Chemistry lab. technician Allen-Bradley Corp., Milw., 1963; coordinator Neighborhood Youth Corps, Madison, 1970; program devel. specialist Tchr. Corps, Madison, 1976-77; asst. prof. edn. Occidental Coll., 1978-80; assoc. prof. Moorhead State U., 1980—; cons. Inst. Latin Am. Studies, U. Tex., Austin, 1980. Evan writer Fargo-Moorhead (N.D.) Indian Center, 1980. Cert. English tchr. grades 7 through 12, Wis. Mem. NEA, Am. Assn. Colls. Tchr. Edn., Mortar Bd., Phi Kappa Phi, Pi Lambda Theta, Kappa Delta Pi, Sigma Tau Delta, Sigma Epsilon Sigma. Democrat. Christian Scientist. Contbr. articles to profl. jours. Home: 2709 S 15th St Apt 301 Fargo ND 58103 Office: Moorhead State U Moorhead MN 56560

BOSLAUGH, LESLIE, judge; b. Hastings, Nebr., Sept. 4, 1917; d. Paul E. and Ann (Herzog) B.; m. Elizabeth F. Meyer, Aug. 10, 1943; children—Marguerite Ann, Sarah Elizabeth, Paul Robert. B.B.A., U. Nebr., 1939, LL.B., 1941. Bar: Nebr. bar 1941. Mem. staff Nebr. Statute Revision Commn., 1941-43; pvt. practice law, Hastings, 1946-47, asst. atty. gen. Nebr., 1947-48; mem. firm Stiner & Boslaugh, Hastings, 1949-60; judge Nebr. Supreme Ct., Lincoln, 1961—. Served to lt. AUS, 1943-46. Mem. Nebr. Bar Assn., Am. Judicature Soc., Appellate Judges Conf., Order of Coif. Office: Supreme Ct Lincoln NE 68509

BOSSETT, ANN JOYCE, hospital administrator; b. LaFayette, La., Mar. 25, 1933; d. Norman Joseph and Mabel Ann (Catalon) Mouton; B.B.A., Tex. So. U., 1979; M.B.A. U. St. Thomas, 1983; m. Webster D. Bossett; children—Jennifer Louise, Mark Bernard, Greta Michelle. Med. technologist Baylor Coll. Medicine, Houston, 1963-65; Tex. program dir. Xerox Corp., Houston, 1969-74; asst. adminstr. Houston Internat. Hosp. for Hosp. Affiliates, Inc., Nashville, 1977-78, asso. adminstr., Houston, 1978-79; hosp. adminstr. Houston Internat. Hosp., 1979—; cons. Gardner Lab., 1974-77. Chmn., Mental Health-Mental Retardation Adult Adv. Bd., 1982; trustee, rep. Greater Houston Hosp. Council, Mental Health Needs Council; mem. by laws com. Tex. Rehab. Commn., 1981-82. Mem. Am. Mgmt. Assn., Houston C. of C., AAUP, Tex. Hosp. Assn., Nat. Assn. Pvt. Psychiat. Hosps. (state legis. rep.; chmn. manpower com.), Am. Soc. Med. Technology, Tex. Soc. Med. Technology, Washington Bus. Group on Health, Fedn. Am. Hosps., Nat. Assn. Female Execs. Roman Catholic. Home: 6903 Vinewood Circle Houston TX 77088 Office: 6441 Main St Houston TX 77030

BOSSON, BARBARA, actress; b. Bellvernon, Pa., Nov. 1. Attended Carnegie Inst. Tech., Pitts.; m. Steve Bochco; children—Melissa, Jesse John. Joined improvisational group, The Committee, San Francisco, 1967; appeared in films "Bullitt", 1968, "Capricorn One", 1978, "The Last Starfighter", 1984; appearing in TV series, "Hill Street Blues", 1981—. Recipient Emmy nominations for best supporting actress, "Hill Street Blues". Address: care Writers and Artists Agency 11726 San Vicente Blvd Suite 300 Los Angeles CA 90049*

BOSTER, JEANNETTE REAL, educator, rancher; b. Kerrville, Tex., July 10, 1925; d. Caspar and Meta Nannie (Riley) Real; m. Raymond Gowdy Boster, June 8, 1945 (div. Mar. 1965); children—Michael, Stephen, Barbara. B.A., Angelo State U., 1967; M.A., So. Methodist U., 1970. Registered med. technologist, 1945. Tchr. San Angelo Schs., Tex., 1965-71; team leader Glenn Jr. High Sch., San Angelo, 1971-78; homebound tchr. San Angelo Schs., 1980—. Treas. Tom Green Dem. Club, San Angelo, 1984-85. Experienced tchr. fellow So. Meth. U., 1969-70, tuition grantee Learning Disorders Council, San Angelo, 1971-72; named Tchr. of Yr., San Angelo Classroom Tchrs., 1973-74. Mem. Tex. State Tchrs. Assn. (dist. legis. chmn. 1982—). Democrat. Presbyterian. Avocation: travel. Home: 2480 Harvard Ct C San Angelo TX 76904 Office: San Angelo Ind Sch Dist 1800 University St San Angelo TX 76904

BOSTER, JOLYNN BARRY, lawyer, state legislator; b. Maricopa County, Ariz., Aug. 21, 1951; d. Jack and M. Jackie (Hamilton) Barry. B.S., Ohio State U., 1973, J.D., 1976. Bar: Ohio 1976, U.S. Supreme Ct. 1981. Atty. Emens, Hurd, Kegler & Ritter, Columbus, Ohio, 1976-78, Eachus & Boster, Gallipolis, Ohio, 1978-81. Cowles & Boster Co. L.P.A., Gallipolis, 1981—; state rep. Ohio Ho. Reps., Columbus, 1983—. Bd. mem. Big Brothers/Big Sisters of Gallia, Meigs, Jackson, and Mason Counties, Ohio, 1981—; mem. adv. bd. Rio Grande Coll., Emerson Evans Sch. of Bus., Rio Grande, Ohio, 1985, Ohio U. Sch. Nursing. Recipient Woman of Yr. award Gallipolis Bus. and Profl. Womens Club, 1983, Outstanding Young Women of Am. award, 1983, 84. Mem. ABA, Ohio Assn. of Trial Lawyers, Ohio State Bar Assn., Gallia County Bar Assn. Democrat. Avocations: skiing; jogging; tennis; sports. Office: Cowles & Boster Co LPA 26 Locust St Gallipolis OH 45631

BOSTIC, STEPHANIE EVON, public relations executive; b. Jamaica, N.Y., Mar. 22, 1953; d. Joseph Edward and Maud Gertrude (Wilson) B. B.S. in Pub. Communications, Boston U., 1975. Pub. relations asst. U.S. Tennis Assn., N.Y.C., 1975-77, asst. dir. pub. relations, 1977-80, pub. relations coordinator women's circuit, 1983-85; media relations mgr. ASME, 1985—; pres. Bostic & Small Cons., Inc., 1985—; editorial asst. U.S. Tennis Assn. Player Records, 1975, 76, stats. coordinator U.S. Tennis Assn. Tennis Yearbook, 1976, project editor U.S. Tennis Assn. Player Records, 1977, 78, 79, U.S. Open Tennis Championships Media Guides, 1976, 77, 78, 79; dir. pub. relations Women's Tennis Assn., 1980, D. Parke Gibson Assocs., Inc., N.Y.C., 1981-82; feature writer Queens Tribune, 1981; press-publicity coordinator Mercedes Tournament Champions, World Championship Tennis, 1984. Chmn. pub. relations com., gen. vol. com. 4th Ann. United Negro Coll. Fund/Arthur Ashe Tennis Benefit, 1978; pub. relations-publicity co-coordinator Forest Hills/Pro-Celebrity Tennis Tournament-Juvenile Diabetes Found., 1984; com. mem. Harlem Jr. Tennis Tournament, 1984. Mem. Nat. Assn. Media Women (dir. publicity Met. N.Y. chpt. 1979), Nat. Coalition 100 Black Women, Pub. Relations Soc. Am. (com. on minorities), Boston U. Sch. Pub. Relations Alumni Assn., (CEBA awards judge), Delta Sigma Theta. Home: 412 Old Country Rd Garden City NY 11530

BOSTON, LEONA, organization executive; b. Joliet, Ill., Aug. 4, 1914; d. Dorie Philip and Margaret (Mitchell) B.; student LaSalle Extension U., 1936-37, 1946, U. Chgo., 1944-45. Tchr., Nat. Stenotype Sch., Chgo., 1937; stenotypist Rotary Internat., Evanston, Ill., 1937-44, sec. to comptroller, 1944-50, head personnel dept., 1950-65, exec. asst. to gen. sec., 1965-77; mem. exec. com. North Shore Festival of Faith, Northfield, Ill., 1978. Bd. dirs. YWCA, Evanston, 1961-63. Mem. Bus. Profl. Women's Club Evanston (chmn. fin. com. 1977-78). Evangelical (fin. sec. Bible Ch., Winnetka 1965-68, treas. 1979-80). Club: Zonta (v.p., chmn. program com. 1969-70, pres. 1970-71, chmn. membership com. 1976-78, historian 1979-84, mem. past pres.' com. 1972-86, mem. fin. com. 1985-86) (Evanston). Home and Office: 350 W Schaumburg Rd Schaumburg IL 60194

BOSTON, LUCILLE MARCELLA, farming and supply company executive, ceramic company executive; b. Toluca, Ill., Dec. 21, 1908; d. John and Paulina (Racki) Blazina; m. Everett A. Boston, Jan. 23, 1929 (dec. Dec. 1983); children—Rosemary, Everett A. Frances J., Laurel A., Nancy L. B.E., U. Wis.-Whitewater, 1966, M.S., 1972. Tchr. pub. schs., Fort Atkinson, Wis., 1958-68, Milton, Wis., 1968-78; owner, mgr. Boston Farms & Supply, Milton, 1951—, Boston Ceramic, 1975—; tchr.-aide continuing edn. U. Wis., 1972-78; Active Rock County 4-H, Wis., 1941—, key leader, 1978—; craft leader St. Martha Soc., Milton; active Choral Club, Milton; treas. Commn. on Aging, Janesville, Wis., 1977—; vol. Fort Atkinson Hosp. Aux., 1981; mem. Wis. Network Policy Com., 1983—; vol. Ret. Sr. Citizens, 1970—; sec. literacy program, 1970—. Mem. State Tchrs.' Retirement, Rock County Ceramic Assn. Democrat. Roman Catholic. Home: Route 1 Box 177A Milton WI 53563 Office: Boston Farms & Supply 177A Bowers Lake Rd Milton WI 53563

BOSTON, MARY, consultant; b. Jackson, Miss., June 15, 1930; d. James Alfred and Geneva Elmore White; m. Joseph Nathaniel Boston, June 22, 1952; children—Cheryl D. Williams, Kelvin J., Waymonn K. B.S., Tuskegee U., 1950; M.A., U.No. Colo., 1973, Ed.D., 1975; elem. cert. U. Denver, 1961. Tchr. home econs. McGee's Creek High Sch., Tylertown, Miss., 1950-51; teenage program dir. YWCA, Jackson, Miss., 1951-52; co-owner, adminstr. Kiddie Kollege Pre-Sch., Denver, 1957-59; elem. tchr. Denver Public Schs., 1960-85; instr. U. No. Colo., 1972-74; cons., owner Dynamic Concepts, Westminster, Colo., 1985—. Bd. dirs. Girl Scout Day Camps, Denver, 1982-86; mem. adv. com. Adams County Sch. Dist. 50 career enrichment, 1985. Mem. Sen. Hart's Acad. Selection Com., 1976-79; chmn. Citywide Martin Luther King Jr. Commemoration, 1982-85; del. Adams County Democratic Conv., 1982, 84, Colo. Dem. Conv., 1982, 84; mem. Martin Luther King Jr. State Holiday Commn., 1986. Mem. NEA, Colo. Edn. Assn., Assn. Childhood Edn., Nat. Assn. Female Execs., Phi Delta Kappa, Colo. Tuskegee Alumni Assn., Sigma Gamma Rho. Mem. African Methodist Episcopal Ch. Club: Finesse Bridge. Avocations: bridge; travel. Home: 8061 Osceola St Westminster CO 80030

BOSWELL, KATHERINE ANN SMITH, nurse; b. Mineral Wells, Tex., Mar. 31, 1951; d. Samuel Thomas and Frances (Logsdon) Smith; B.S.N., Tex. Woman's U., 1975, postgrad., 1985; m. David Boswell, May 30, 1980; children—Wendy Lee, Joe Neil, Joshua David. Charge nurse Parkland Hosp., Dallas, 1975-76; dir. nursing Resort Lodge Nursing Home, Mineral Wells, Tex., 1977-80; charge nurse Palo Pinto Gen. Hosp., Mineral Wells, 1980; dir. LVN program Weatherford Coll., Mineral Wells, 1980—. Mem. policy council Head Start Program, 1980-83; bd. dirs. Tejas Home for Youth; leader Girl Scouts U.S.A., 1979—; Sunday sch. tchr. St. Luke's Episcopal Ch., 1980—. Episcopal Women's Orgn. Mem. Tex. Assn. Vocational Nurse Educators, Tex. Jr. Coll. Tchrs. Assn. Home: 610 SW 6th St Mineral Wells TX 76067 Office: Route 2 Mineral Wells TX 76067

BOSWELL, WINTHROP PALMER, writer; b. Bklyn., Dec. 17, 1922; d. Carleton Humphries and Winthrop (Bushnell) Palmer; B.A., Smith Coll., 1943; postgrad. U. S.C., 1956-58; M.A., San Francisco State Coll., 1969; m. James Orr Boswell, Oct. 26, 1946; children—James Lowell, Rosalind Palmer, John

Winthrop. Research asst. G-2 Spl. Br., U.S. Army, 1943-46; research asst. Hoover Instn., Stanford, Calif., 1976; docent Filoli, 1979-80; writer; books include: Irish Wizards in the Woods of Ethiopia, 1971; The Snake in the Grove, 1972; The Killing of the Snake King in Abyssinia, 1973; Hisperica Famina or The Garden of God, 1974; Bruce and the Question of Geomancy at Axum: The Evidence from the Norman Bayeux Tapestry, 1986. Mem. Soc. History of Discoveries, Medieval Assn. of Pacific, Societe Francaise pour les Etudes Ethiopiennes. Club: Peninsula Country (San Mateo, Calif.), Francisca (San Francisco).

BOSWORTH, PATRICIA, writer; b. Berkeley, Calif., Apr. 24, 1933; d. Bartley Crum and Gertrude Bosworth; m. Mel Arrighi, Feb. 15, 1966. B.A., Sarah Lawrence Coll., 1955. Articles editor Woman's Day mag., 1965-68; sr. editor McCall's Mag., 1969-70; mng. editor Harper's Bazaar, 1972-73; exec. editor Viva, 1974-76; author: Montgomery Clift: A Biography, 1978, Diane Arbus: A Biography, 1984, also periodical articles. Democrat. Roman Catholic. Office: care Knopf Inc 201 E 50th St New York NY 10022*

BOSWORTH, RUTH JULIE, business executive; b. Santa Monica, Calif., June 15, 1963; d. Benjamin Perez and Eugenia (Rangel) Garcia; m. Robert Andrew Bosworth, Dec. 19, 1982. Student El Camino Coll., 1981—. Ptnr., acct. Avant Garde Products, Redondo Beach, Calif., 1983—; owner, acct. Valve Tech, Lawndale, Calif., 1985—; v.p. chief fin. officer Genetic Research, Inc., Redondo Beach, 1983—. Address: Genetic Research Inc 2704C Nelson Ave Redondo Beach CA 90278

BOTHWELL, CHUNG THI NGUYEN, financial planner; b. Saigon, Vietnam, Nov. 19, 1949; came to U.S., 1969, naturalized, 1978; d. Tang Van and Nghi Thi (Tran) Nguyen; B.B.A., U. Miami (Fla.), 1974, M.B.A., 1980; m. Anthony Peirson Xavier Bothwell, Dec. 22, 1973; children—Anthony Peirson Xavier II, Thomas Theodore Nguyen. Budget analyst Fla. Power & Light Co., Miami, 1973-78; asst. to assoc. dean grad. program Sch. Nursing, U. Wis., Madison, 1978-79; mgr. budgets and costs Central Life Assurance Co., Madison, 1980-83; sr. budget analyst Lawrence Livermore Nat. Lab., Calif., 1983-84, prin. acct., 1984-85, asst. to ops. mgr., laser isotope separation program, 1985—. Project chmn. Madison chpt. ARC, 1978-79; human services commr. City of Madison, 1982-83; mem. City of Livermore Social Concerns Com., 1984-85, chairperson, 1985-86; mem. Alameda County Human Relations Commn., 1985. Internat. student scholar, 1973. Mem. Nat. Assn. Accts. (bd. dirs., newsletter editor 1984-85, assoc. dir. hospitality 1985-86, dir. community responsibility 1986—), Am. Acad. Mgmt., AAUW (corp. relations chairperson 1984-85, membership v.p. 1985-86). Republican. Roman Catholic. Home: 1823 Paseo Laguna Seco Livermore CA 94550 Office: LLNL Box 808/L-467 Livermore CA 94550

BOTINE, KAREN ELIZABETH, educator, state official; b. Pocahontas County, Iowa, Mar. 21, 1942; d. Lester Ferdinand and Eleanor Barbara (Wiese) B.; B.S. in Home Econs. Edn., Iowa State U., 1963, M.S., 1970. Home econs. instr. Clarion (Iowa) Pub. Schs., 1963-68; dorm housemother Iowa State U., Ames, 1968-69, 69-70; asst. supr. home econs. edn. N.D. Bd. Vocat. Edn., Bismarck, 1970-76, state supr. home econs. edn., 1976—; cons. FHA/HERO, 1980, workshop instr., 1971, 76; mem. steering com. project on parenting edn. Bush Found., 1979-81; part-time adult edn. instr. Bismarck home econs. program, 1978-80; presenter Nat. Vocat. Home Econs. Conf., 1981. Mem. exec. com. to reactivate N.D. Commn. on Status of Women, 1972, Bismarck-Mandan Am. Lutheran Ch. Coordinating Council, 1978-80; mem. reorgn. com. N.D. Safety Council, 1979-80, sec., 1979. Mem. NEA, N.D. Edn. Assn., Home Econs. Edn. Assn., Am. Vocat. Assn., N.D. Vocat. Assn., Nat. Assn. State Suprs. Vocat. Home Econs., Internat. Fedn. Home Econs., Am. Home Econs. Assn., N.D. Home Econs. Assn. (pres. 1985), Bismarck-Mandan Home Econs. Assn., N.D. Nutrition Council, Bismarck-Mandan Nutrition Council, Missouri Valley Adult Edn. Assn., N.D. Adult Edn. Assn., Omicron Nu, Phi Kappa Phi, Delta Kappa Gamma. Office: State Capitol 15th Floor Bismarck ND 58505

BOTTA, MADELYN MARIE, county official; b. Olympia, Wash., Dec. 26, 1946; d. B. J. and Rose (Palermo) B.; m. William H. Mays, Apr. 8, 1978. Student Central Wash. U. County clk. Kittitas County, Wash., 1977-85, dir. superior ct. adminstrv. services, 1985—. Sec. Kittitas County Dem., 1977. Mem. Ellensburg C. of C., Wash. State Assn. County Clks., Wash. Judicial Council. Club: Tacoma Golf and Country. Avocations: riding horses; golf; swimming; travel. Office: Kitsap County Courthouse 614 Div St Port Orchard WA 98366

BOTTARI, MARIANNA TERESA, public relations exec.; b. Phila., Nov. 17, 1941; d. Guido and Malvina Rose (Seccia) Bottari; student U. Pa., 1962-64; cert. Charles Morris Price Sch. Journalism and Advt., 1965-66; student Temple U., 1966; grad. The Fund Raising Sch., 1980. News relations asst. Smith Kline & French Labs., Phila., 1962-64; public relations asst. St. Luke's and Children's Med. Center, Phila., 1964-66; adminstrv. asst. Goodway Printing & Pub. Co., Phila., 1966-69; public relation asst. Thomas Jefferson U. Hosp., Phila., 1969-71; public relations dir. Albert Einstein Med. Center, Phila., 1971-74, John Muir Meml. Hosp., Walnut Creek, Calif., 1974-77, Peralta Hosp., Oakland, Calif., 1977-80; community info. dir. Sequoia Hosp. Dist., Redwood City, Calif., 1980-82; community relations and mktg. dir. Valley Meml. Hosp., Livermore, Calif., 1982-84; owner PR Woman & Co., pub. relations agy., 1984; career advisor Charles Morris Price Sch. of Journalism & Advt., 1966-73. Bd. dirs. Coop Center Council, 1977-78; v.p. Sun Country Homeowners Assn., 1977-79. Served with USNR, 1979-81. Recipient MacEachern Award citation Acad. Hosp. Public Relations, 1973, Cert. of Merit, 1976. Mem. Nat. Assn. Female Execs., Nat. Assn. Hosp. Devel., Hosp. Public Relations Assn. No. Calif., Internat. Assn. Bus. Communicators, Acad. Hosp. Public Relations. Office: 101 Kinross Dr 4 Walnut Creek CA 94598

BOTTERBUSCH, HOPE ROLAND, educational administrator; b. Lancaster, Pa., Aug. 11, 1950; d. Harry John and Mary Ellen (Cartzdafner) Roland; m. Ronald Paul Botterbusch, Jan. 7, 1972 (div. 1980). B.S. in Edn., Millersville U., Pa., 1973; M.S.L.S., Wayne State U., 1978. Cert. tchr., Fla. Media specialist Clearwater Central Cath. High Sch., Fla., 1974-77, Sch. Bd. Pinellas County, St. Petersburg, Fla., 1975-77, 79-80, 81-83, Westwood Community Schs., Dearborn Heights, Mich., 1978-79, Hillsborough County Schs., Tampa, Fla., 1980-81; audiovisual/TV supr. Sch. Bd. Pinellas County, 1983—; ptnr., cons. HB Media, St. Petersburg, 1981—; owner, cons. HRB Prodns., St. Petersburg, 1981—. Author computer software in field. Contbr. articles and revs. to profl. jours. Mem. Pinellas Assn. for Library Media Specialists, Fla. Assn. for Media in Edn., Nat. Assn. Female Execs., Pinellas Suprs. Assn., Phi Delta Kappa. Democrat. Club: Marly Group Mus. Fine Arts (St. Petersburg). Avocations: reading; boating; scuba diving; drawing. Office: Sch Bd Pinellas County Dept Media Services 1956 E Druid Rd Clearwater FL 33546

BOTTICELLI, MARIE JOHNSON, technical services manager; b. Noble County, Ind., July 29, 1940; d. Edward R. Johnson and Emogene (Emrick) Johnson Sowle; m. James T. Botticelli, Jan. 1971 (div. 1976); 1 child, Jessica Marie. B.S., Manchester Coll., 1962; M.S., U. Wis.-Milw., 1976. Programmer, tng. coordinator Blue Cross/Blue Shield, Milw., 1967-71; customer support Burroughs Corp., Milw., 1976-81, systems specialist, 1981-84, dist. mktg. support mgr., 1982-84; mgr. tech. services Milw. Pub. Schs., 1984—. Mem. Data Processing Mgmt. Assn., Am. Mgmt. Assn. Home: 6107 W Calumet Rd Milwaukee WI 53223 Office: Milwaukee Pub Schs Drawer 10K Milwaukee WI 53201-8210

BOTTOMS, BARBARA ANN, nurse; b. Ozark, Ala., Sept. 8, 1948; d. Homer Eugene and Etta (Simmons) B. Assoc. degree in nursing, Wallace St. Community Coll., Napierfield, Ala., 1974; B.S. in Nursing, Auburn U., Montgomery, Ala., 1981. Registered nurse. Staff nurse Flowers Hosp., Dothan, Ala., 1974-75, evening supr., 1975-76; staff nurse, charge Enterprise Hosp., Ala., 1976; evening charge nurse Baptist Med. Ctr., Montgomery, 1976-77, head nurse, 1977-78; staff nurse VA Med. Ctr., Montgomery, 1978—. Mem. Am. Nurses Assn. (cert. med.-surg. nurse), Auburn U. at Montgomery Nursing Honor Soc. (sec. 1984-85). Avocations: reading; crocheting; knitting; watching sports; collecting matchbooks and stamps. Home: 5716 Bratton Dr Temple Terrace FL 33617 Office: VA Med Ctr 215 Perry Hill Rd Montgomery AL 36193

BOTTOMS, MARGUERITE CLAUDETTE, security company executive; b. Rochester, N.Y., July 19, 1961; d. Kenneth Francis and Claudette (Perron) Bernier; m. James Eric Bottoms, Sept. 3, 1983; stepchildren—Eric, Kerry. Student U. Ark.-Little Rock, 1981—. Dept. mgr. Magic Mart, Benton, Ark., 1976-78; L.P.N., St. Vincent Infirmary, Little Rock, 1979-81, VA Hosp., North Little Rock, 1981-83; co-owner Inter Phase Systems, north Little Rock, 1980-83, v.p., 1983—; v.p. Detection Systems Inc., North Little Rock, 1983—. Mem. Nat. Assn. Female Execs. Roman Catholic. Avocations: reading; scuba diving. Office: Detection Systems Inc 5305 McClanahan St Suite E4 North Little Rock AR 72116

BOTTS, MERCEDES ALBERTINA BLOW, government official; b. Chester, Pa.; d. Beverly York and Laura Mae (Wright) Blow; m. Samuel Douglas Botts, Apr. 19, 1944 (dec. 1982); children—Ronald Anthony, Samuel York, John Myron, Sidney Vincent. B.G.S., Am. U., 1983. With Def. Logistics Agy., Cameron Sta., Alexandria, Va., 1955—, coordinator fed. women's program, 1973-74, indsl. property mgmt. specialist, 1974-80, indsl. specialist, 1980—. Liaison officer Internat. Women's Year Secretariat to Nat. Commn. Observance Internat. Women's Year, 1975; mem. judges panel to select 10 outstanding young women of Am., 1977; mem. Montgomery County Commn. on Status Women, also mem. econs. com., 1977—, v.p., 1979-80; chairperson internat. component Md. Internat. Women's Year Conf., 1977; ofcl. observer Nat. Women's Conf., Houston, 1977; bd. dirs. Neighbors Inc., Brightwood Site, Washington, 1960-71; mem. Pan Am. liaison com. Women's Orgns. Washington, 1970—; bd. dirs. U.S. com. UN Fund for Women, v.p., 1983—. Mem. UN Assn. (mem. exec. com.; dir. Capital Area div. 1971—; Human Rights award Capital Area div. 1975), Cosmopolitan Bus. and Profl. Women's Club (charter: named Bus. Women of Year 1972), D.C. League Republican Women, Potomac Women's Rep. Club, Rock Creek Rep. Women's Club. (Rep. Woman of Achievement award 1983). Home: 12004 Edgepark Ct Potomac MD 20854 Office: Defense Logistics Agy Cameron Station Alexandria VA 22314

BOUCOT, KATHARINE ROSENBAUM (MRS. SAMUEL B. STURGIS), physician; b. Phila., Sept. 6, 1903; d. Morris and Hannah (Rottenberg) Rosenbaum; student U. Pa., 1922-23, Pa. State U., 1934-36; M.D., Woman's Med. Coll. Pa., 1942; M.P.H., Johns Hopkins U., 1954; L.H.D. (hon.), Keuka Coll., 1960; D.Sc. (hon.), Beaver Coll., 1967; D.M.Sc. (hon.), Woman's Med. Coll., 1968, Hahnemann Med. Coll., 1978; Litt.D. (hon.), Thomas Jefferson U., 1978; D.Pedagogy (hon.), Temple U., 1986; m. Joseph R. Boucot, Mar. 23, 1944 (dec. May 5, 1962); children—Arthur J., Nancy (Mrs. Milton Curtis Cummings, Jr.); m. 2d, Samuel Booth Sturgis, Nov. 18, 1964 (dec. Aug. 1983). Intern, Woman's Coll. Hosp., Phila., 1942-43; resident Herman Kiefer Hosp., Detroit, 1944; chest specialist, Phila., 1945—; cons. Woman's Coll. Hosp., Nat. Cancer Inst., Phila. Gen., Vets, Landis State hosps. (all Phila.); prof., chmn. dept. preventive medicine, 1952-68, clin. prof. medicine Woman's Med. Coll. Pa., 1952-68, emeritus prof. preventive medicine, 1968—; asso. medicine U. Pa. Grad. Sch. Medicine, 1951-63. Vice pres. William B. Lake Found., 1959-77; bd. dirs., hon. life mem. Phila. div. Am. Cancer Soc.; pres. Phila.—Montgomery Lung Assn., 1963-65 (Lawrence F. Flick award 1983); hon. trustee Beaver Coll. Recipient Elizabeth Blackwell award, 1956; Disting. Dau. Pa. award, 1964; Golden Plate award Am. Acad. Achievement, 1965; award Albert Einstein Woman's Aux., 1967; Phila. Gimbel award, 1968; named Woman of Year, Pa. State U., 1967; Trudeau medal Nat. Tb and Respiratory Disease Assn., 1969; Alumnae Achievement award Women's Med. Coll. Alumnae Assn., 1970; Penn Club award, 1972; Hall of Fame honoree Am. Lung Assn., 1980. Fellow Am. Pub. Health Assn., Am. Coll. Preventive Medicine (pres. 1969-70, Disting. Service award 1973; Katharine Boucot Sturgis ann. lectr. 1979—), A.C.P., Phila. Coll. Physicians (v.p. 1970-72, pres. 1972-74); mem. Am., Pa. (ho. of dels. 1961-72), Phila. County (pres. 1968, Strittmatter award 1972) med. assns., Am. Thoracic Soc. (v.p. 1960-61, hon. mem., past pres. Eastern sect.), Pa. Trudeau Soc. (pres. 1958), Acad. Occupational Medicine, Pa. Public Health Assn. (exec. com. 1963), Am. Med. Women's Assn. (hon.), Laennec Soc. (past pres.), Am. Epidemiol. Soc., Woman's Med. Coll. Alumnae Assn. (past pres.), Alpha Omega Alpha. Episcopalian. Club: Cosmopolitan. Contbr. articles to profl. jours. Chief editor AMA Archives of Environmental Health, 1960-71; Festschrift for Katharine R. Boucot, 1971. Address: 600 E Cathedral Rd A417 Philadelphia PA 19128

BOUDREAU, LORRAINE JEANETTE, nursing researcher; b. W. Warwick, R.I., Aug. 24, 1943; d. Joseph Onesime and Beatrice Violet (Lecuivre) Boudreau; Diploma in Nursing, Roger Williams Gen. Hosp., 1964; B.S. in Nursing, U. Va., 1974; M.Nursing, UCLA, 1977. Nurse specialist in alcohol rehab. VA Med. Center, Sepulveda, Calif., 1974-78, coordinator community psychiatry program, 1978-80; asst. chief nurse VA Med. Center, Kerrville, Tex., 1980-84, nurse researcher, 1984—; asst. clin. prof. UCLA, 1978-79. Served with Nurse Corps, U.S. Army, 1965-71. Recipient Sustained Performance award, VA, 1979, 82; Comdr.'s Spl. Recognition, 6222d USAR Sch., 1980. Mem. Res. Officers Assn., Assn. Mil. Surgeons of U.S., Tex. Soc. Hosp. Nursing Adminstrs., Tex. Hosp. Assn., Nat. League for Nursing, others. Republican. Roman Catholic. Home: 140 Deer Hollow Dr Boerne TX 78006 Office: Memorial Blvd Kerrville TX 78028

BOUGHN, PENNY LINDNER, information systems corporation consultant; b. Balt., Mar. 24, 1944; d. Raymond Lewis and Grace Genieve (Smith) Lindner; m. James Roland Jones, June 29, 1963 (div. Sept. 1980); children—Kevin Brian, Raymond Thomas; m. 2d, Stephen Robert Boughn, Jan. 9, 1981; stepchildren—Julie C., Christopher R., Stacie A. A.A., Howard Community Coll. (disting. scholar), 1977; B.A. summa cum laude, Loyola Coll., 1979. Sec., Howard County Bd. Edn., Columbia, Md., 1974-77; communications rep. C&P Telephone Co., Balt., 1979-81, acct. exec., 1981-83, account exec./industry cons. AT&T Info. Systems, Rockville, Md., 1983—; freelance cons. var. clients, Columbia, 1981—. Chmn. Long Beach Village Bd., Columbia, 1972-73; fundraiser Dem. candidate Ho. of Reps., 1978-82; commr. Howard County Commn. for Women, 1984—; mem. Howard County Community Housing Resource Bd., 1984. Mem. Am. Mktg. Assn., Ind. Petroleum Assn., Women in Energy. Roman Catholic. Office: AT&T Information Systems 5515 Security Ln Rockville MD 20852

BOUGHTON, MAUREEN ELLA, mktg. exec.; b. Sydney, Australia, Feb. 11, 1944; came to U.S., 1965, naturalized, 1973; d. Patrick Yelverton and Joan Patricia (Heath) Williams; student Australian schs.; divorced; children—Edward, III, Tracy Yelverton. Account exec. Sta. KKOP-FM, Redondo Beach, Calif., 1976-77; pres. MAV Enterprises, Ventura, Calif., 1977-83, Boughton Enterprises Inc., Ventura, 1980—; mng. dir. Bilmar Welding Ltd., U.S. subs. Henrob S.A., Geneva, 1984—; fashion and beauty editor South Bay mag., Calif. Good Life mag., Big Valley mag., also Skin Care mag., 1977-80. Mem. Nat. Assn. Female Execs., Am. Soc. Profl. and Exec. Women. Republican. Christian Scientist. Office: 278 Walnut Dr Ventura CA 93003 also 20655 S Western Ave #112 Torrance CA 90501

BOULANGER, CAROL SEABROOK, lawyer; b. N.Y.C., Sept. 14, 1942; d. John M. and Anne S. (Schlaudecker) Seabrook; B.A., Swarthmore Coll., 1964; LL.B., U. Pa., 1969; m. Jacques P. Boulanger, June 1, 1974; children—Rodolphe, Adriana. Admitted to N.Y. bar, 1970, U.S. Tax Ct., 1970; assoc. firm Baker & McKenzie, N.Y.C., 1969-71; assoc. Wender, Murase & White, N.Y.C., 1971-75, partner, 1975-82; partner firm Boulanger, Finley & Hicks, N.Y.C., 1982-84, Drinker, Biddle & Reath, N.Y.C., 1984—. Founding mem. ARCS Found., Inc., N.Y. chpt., 1973-80, sec., 1973-75, v.p., 1975-80; bd. mgrs. Swarthmore Coll., 1977-81. Mem. Am. Bar Assn., Assn. Bar City N.Y. (com. on internat. law 1980-84, com. fgn. and comparative law 1984-85, chmn. 1985—). Office: 405 Park Ave New York NY 10022

BOULDING, ELISE MARIE, sociologist, former educator; b. Oslo, July 6, 1920; came to U.S., 1923, naturalized, 1929; d. Joseph and Birgit (Johnsen) Biorn-Hansen; B.A., Douglass Coll., 1940; M.S., Iowa State Coll., 1949; Ph.D., U. Mich., 1969; m. Kenneth Boulding, Aug. 31, 1941; children—John Russell, Mark David, Christine Ann, Philip Daniel, William Frederic. Research asso. Survey Research Inst., U. Mich., 1957-58, Mental Health Research Inst., 1959-60, research devel. sec. Center for Research on Conflict Resolution, 1960-63; prof. sociology, project dir. Inst. Behavioral Sci., U. Colo., Boulder, 1967-78; prof., chmn. dept. sociology Dartmouth Coll., Hanover, N.H., 1978-85, prof. emerita, 1985—, Montgomery vis. prof., 1978-79; mem. program adv. council Human and Social Devel. Program, UN U., 1977-80, v.p. UN U. council, 1980—; editor Internat. Peace Research newsletter, 1983—; mem. UNESCO Peace Prize Jury, 1982—. Internat. chairperson Women's Internat. League for Peace and Freedom, 1967-70; bd. dirs. Inst. for World Order. Recipient Disting. Achievement award Douglass Coll., 1973, Ted Lentz Peace prize, 1977; named Woman of Conscience, Nat. Council of Women, 1980; Danforth fellow, 1965-67; Faculty fellow U. Colo., 1974; recipient Jesse Bernard award Am. Sociol. Assn., 1981. Mem. AAAS, Am. Sociol. Assn., Internat. Sociol. Assn., Internat. Peace Research Assn., World Future Studies Fedn., World Future Soc., Colo. Women's Forum. Quaker. Author: Image of the Future (transl. from Dutch), 1961; From a Monastery Kitchen, 1976; (with Nuss, Carson and Greenstein) Handbook of International Data on Women, 1976; The Underside of History: A View of Women Through Time, 1976; Women in Twentieth Century World, 1977; (with Burgess and K. Boulding) Social System of Planet Earth, 1980; Children's Rights and the Wheel of Life, 1979; Bibliography for World Conflict and Peace, 1979; (with others) Women and the Social Costs of Economic Development: Two Colorado Case Studies. Home: 624 Pearl Boulder CO 80302

BOULTON, ELAINE CAROL, business owner, real estate broker; b. Portsmouth, N.H., Feb. 16, 1922; d. Charles A. and Lillian (Lovejoy) B. Grad., Nashua Bus. Coll., 1941; Student U. N.H., 1941-45, LaSalle Corr. Sch., 1946-49, Boston Sch. Engraving, 1945-47. Asst. comptroller Nashua Mfg. Co., N.H., 1944-47; comptroller/buyer Philip Morris Co., Nashua, 1947-54; real estate broker, Milford, N.H., 1958—; nat. conf. dir. Soc. Exchange Counselors, San Diego, 10 yrs.; cons., travel coordinator Sr. Action Group, Milford, 1978—; pres. Gift & Art Assocs., Milford, 1953—; lobbyist N.H. State Legislature, 1965—. Contbr. articles to mags. and newspapers. Inventor artificial flower candle rings. Bd. dirs. N.H. State Legis. Com., 1983—, St. Joseph's Community Services, Merrimack, N.H., 1983—, Milford Mill Apts. for Elderly and Handicapped, Portland, Maine, 1982—; chair Milford Town Budget Com., 1970-81, Milford Town Wage/Union Negotiation Com., 1978-81, Monadnock Regional Assn., Peterborough, N.H., 1975-80; trustee Wadleigh Meml. Library, Milford, 1978-81. Mem. Gift and Decorative Assn., Milford C. of C. (past v.p.). Republican. Lodge: Lionesses (Milford). Avocations: philately; numismatics; antiques. Home: Federal Hill Rd PO Box 403 Milford NH 03055

BOULTON, SHAUNA DEE, educator; b. Salt Lake City, May 29, 1949; d. Melvin and Afton Lillie (Davidson) Boulton. B.S., U. Utah, 1971, M.Ed., 1981; hon. Doctorate in Philosophy of Edn., World U., 1985. Cert. elem., severely handicapped, spl. resource tchr., Utah. Tchr. Habilitation Ctr. for Multiple Handicapped, Salt Lake City, 1971-73, Hartvigsen Sch. for Multiple Handicapped, Salt Lake City, 1973-79, William Penn Elem. Sch., Salt Lake City, 1979-83, East Mill Creek Elem. Sch., 1983—. Vol., Spl. Olympics. Mem. NEA, Utah Edn. Assn., Granite Edn. Assn., Nat. Mus. Women in Arts, Cousteau Soc., Greenpeace, Internat. Platform Assn. Home: 1516 Glen Arbor St Salt Lake City UT 84105 Office: East Mill Creek Elem Sch 2965 E 3435 S Salt Lake City UT 84109

BOULWARE, VALERIE HAWKINS, psychiatrist, educator; b. Rochester, N.Y., June 15, 1947; d. Oscar Edward and Kathryn (Green) Hawkins; m. Alfred Larry Boulware, Nov. 29, 1968; children—Leigh Ebony, Laura Joy. A.B., Bryn Mawr Coll., 1969; M.D., Case Western Reserve Univ. Sch. Medicine, 1976. Diplomate Nat. Bd. Med. Examiners. Intern, Univ. Hosps. of Cleve., 1976-77, resident, 1977-79, now mem. staff; court psychiatrist Cuyahoga County Juvenile Ct., Cleve., 1981-83; pres. Interventions, Inc., Cleve., 1981-83, Psychassess, Inc., Cleve., 1983—; practice medicine specializing in psychiatry, Cleveland Heights, Ohio, 1981—; asst. clin. prof. psychiatry Case Western Reserve Univ. Sch. Medicine, Cleve., 1981—. Trustee, Harambee Services to Black Families, 1982-83; bd. advisors New Cleve. Woman Jour., 1982—. Mem. Am. Psychiat. Assn., Ohio Psychiat. Assn., Cleve. Med. Assn., Middleton H. Lambright Soc. (sec. 1983-84), Women's Faculty Case Western Res. U. Sch. Medicine. Democrat. Episcopalian. Office: 5 Severance Circle #511 Cleveland Heights OH 44118

BOUNDS, BRENDA ANN, marketing official; b. Balt., Nov. 19, 1951; d. Walter Morris and Margaret Ann (Cooper) Ward; 1 son, Andrew Ward. Student Catonsville Community Coll., 1978. Adminstrv. asst. Hertz Corp., Balt., 1974-76; facilities adminstr. Ellicott City (Md.) Bd. Edn., 1976-78; supr. registration Dept. Recreation and Parks, Ellicott City, 1978; adminstr. Data Gen., Balt., 1978-80; mktg. mgr. Penta Systems, Balt., 1980—. Mem. Meeting Planners Am., Nat. Composition Assn., Printing Industries Am., Am. Mgmt. Assn., Soc. Assn. Execs. Republican. Home: 230-H Stonecroft Rd Baltimore MD 21229 Office: Penta Systems Internat Inc 1511 Guilford Ave Baltimore MD 21202

BOUNDS, NANCY, modeling and talent company executive; b. Rodney, Ark.; d. William Thomas and Mary Jane (Fields) Southard; m. Robert S. Bounds, 1960 (div. 1965); 1 child, Ronnie Jean; m. Mark Curtis Sconce, Nov. 28, 1972. Student Northwestern U., 1950. Exec. dir. Internat. Fashion/Modeling Assn., N.Y.C., 1978; founding pres. Internat. Talent and Model Schs. Assn., N.Y.C., 1979-80; pres. Nancy Bounds Internat., Omaha, 1959—. Contbr. articles to profl. jours. Producer TV Heart Fund Auction, 1965; chairperson Douglas/Sarpy County Heart Assn., Omaha, 1966, 73-74. Recipient Nat. Tchr.'s award MiLady Pub. Co., 1965. Mem. Internat. Models and Talent Assn. Unitarian. Avocations: reading; painting; travel; golf tournament bridge. Home and office: 4803 Davenport Omaha NE 68132

BOUNDS, SARAH ETHELINE, historian; b. Huntsville, Ala., Nov. 5, 1942; d. Leo Deltis and Alice Etheline (Boone) Bounds; A.B., Birmingham-So. Coll., 1963; M.A., U. Ala., Tuscaloosa, 1965, Ed.S. in History, 1971, Ph.D., 1977. Tchr. social studies Huntsville City Schs., 1963, 65-66, 71-74; residence hall adv., dir. univ. housing U. Ala., Tuscaloosa, 1963-65, 68-71; instr. history N.E. State Jr. Coll., Rainsville, Ala., 1966-68; instr. history U. Ala., Huntsville, 1975, 78-80, 85—, dir. Weeden House Mus., 1981-83; asst. prof. edn., supr. student tchrs. U. North Ala., Florence, 1978. Mem. AAUW, Assn. Tchrs. Educators, Nat. Council Tchrs. Social Studies, NEA, Ala. Hist. Assn., Ala. Assn. Historians, Ala. Assn. Tchrs. Educators, Huntsville Hist. Soc., Historic Huntsville Found., Alpha Delta Kappa, Kappa Delta Pi, Phi Alpha Theta. Methodist. Club: Huntsville Pilot. Home: 1100 Bob Wallace Ave SE Huntsville AL 35801

BOURGEOIS, MARTHA L., nurse; b. Calsbad, N. Mex., Feb. 1, 1939; d. Roy A. Simmons and Mary Ruth (Powell) Die; m. Warren R.E. Bourgeois, Jr., July 3, 1955; children—Warren III, Christopher M., Michelle M. A.S. with honors, Miss. Gulf Coast Jr. Coll.-Jeff Davis Campus, Gulfport, 1983. R.N., Miss., La., Calif. Adminstrv. asst. Tulane U. Sch. Medicine, New Orleans, 1965-79; personnel mgr. Halter Marine Inc., Pearlington, Miss., 1979-80; staff nurse Meml. Hosp., Gulfport, Miss., 1983, Gulf Coast Community Hosp., Biloxi, Miss., 1984, Humana Hosp., New Orleans, 1985—. Editorial asst. monograph La. Tumor Registry, 1979. Mem. ANA, Miss. Nurses Assn. Democrat. Roman Catholic. Home: 419 Waveland Ave Waveland MS 39576

BOURKE, MARY CATHERINE, government official; b. Curraney, Belcarra, Castlebar, Ireland, Apr. 23, 1944; came to U.S., 1955; d. Thomas and Anne (Moran) B. Student Am. U., 1985. Sec. to football coaches U. Notre Dame, South Bend, Ind., 1965-67; adminstrv. sec. Riggs Nat. Bank, Washington, 1967-71, Fed. Bar Assn., Washington, 1971-74; spl. asst. to Pres. The White House, Washington, 1974, asst. to spl. cons. to Pres., 1974-76, asst. to press sec., 1976-77; asst. to dir. of campaign div. Nat. Rep. Congl. Com., Washington, 1977-79, exec. asst. to exec. dir., 1979-81; asst. for congl. relations HUD, Washington, 1981-82, spl. asst. to asst. sec. housing, 1982-83, exec. asst. to under sec., 1983-85, cons. to sec. 1985; spl. asst. to sec. of energy, Washington, 1985—. Vol. Parris for Congress, 1972, 74; sec. Alexandria Young Republicans, 1973-74, polit. action chmn., 1974-75, 1st vice chmn., 1975-76; mem. Alexandria Rep. Com., 1974-76, 76-78; co-chmn. Canada for lt. gov., Alexandria, 1977, Warner for Senate, Alexandria, 1978; mem. Reagan Steering Com., 1980. Named Outstanding Rep., Young Rep. Fedn. Va., 1975, Outstanding Young Rep., Alexandria Young Reps., 1974; recipient Chairman's award for Outstanding Service Nat. Rep. Congl. Com., 1978. Roman Catholic. Avocations: bridge, skiing, sailing, cooking. Home: 34 E Rosemont St Alexandria VA 22301 Office: Dept Energy Washington DC 20585

BOURNE, MARY BONNIE MURRAY (MRS. SAUL HAMILTON BOURNE), music publishing co. exec.; b. Salix, Iowa, Sept. 13, 1903; d. Thomas William and Kathryn (McDermott) Murray; student Morningside Normal Coll., 1922-23; student Am. Banking Inst., N.Y.C.; m. Saul Hamilton Bourne, Apr. 12, 1928 (dec.); 1 dau., Mary Elizabeth. Appeared with George White Scandals, Ramblers, Cocoanuts, Ziegfield Follies, 1925-28; owner, mgr. Bourne Co., N.Y.C., 1960—. Mem. social work recruiting com. United Hosp. Fund. Trustee S.H. Bourne Found., Coll. New Rochelle; trustee N.Y. Infirmary, 1945—, chmn. social service youth bd., 1947—, bd. visitors Sch. Music, Catholic U. Am., Washington. Mem. A.S.C.A.P. (dir., pubs. adv. com.). Home: 14 E 75th St New York NY 10021 Office: 437 Fifth Ave New York NY 10016

BOUSLEY, GLORIA DIANE PARRISH, educator; b. Evansville, Ind., Dec. 3, 1932; d. Thomas Clifford Parrish and Cecelia Elizabeth (Graul) Parrish Armstrong; B.A. in Bus. Edn., Evansville Coll., 19S3; M.S. in Bus. Edn., Ind. U., 1958; Ph.D. in Occupational Edn., So. Ill. U., 1977; m. Donald R. Bousley, Aug. 2, 1958 (dec.). Guidance counselor, bus. tchr. Bridgeport (Ill.) Twp. High Sch., 1953-71; bus. tchr., chmn. bus. and human devel. div. Olney (Ill.) Central Coll., 1971—; adj. asst. prof. vocat. studies So. Ill. U., Carbondale, 1979—; mem. Ill. State Adv. Panel for Coop. Edn. at Post Secondary Level, 1979; mem. U. Ill./Ill. State Bd. of Edn. Staff Devel. adv. com., 1977-79; active in Ill. State Competency Based Edn. project, 1977—. Sec., 1st v.p. N.W. Ter. Art Guild, 1968-71; chmn. found. com. Bus. and Profl. Women's Orgn., 1978, 79, chmn. dist. young careerist program; 1st v.p. Olney Bus. and Profl. Women, 1983, 84; vol. counselor Ill. State Dept. Vocat. Rehab., 1972—, Southeastern Ill. Mental Health Center, 1976-77. Recipient Nat. Office Mgmt. award, 1953, State Ill. grantee, 1979. Mem. Ill. Bus. Edn. Assn. (1st v.p. 1980, pres. 1981), Ill. Vocat. Assn. (dir. 1980), Am. Vocat. Assn. (state membership chmn. 1979), Nat. Bus. Edn. Assn. (state membership chmn. 1979), Nat. Secs. Assn., Internat. Soc., Eastern Ill. Bus. Edn. Assn., So. Ill. Bus. Edn. Assn., Phi Kappa Phi, Delta Kappa Gamma, Delta Pi Epsilon, Iota Lambda Sigma, Phi Mu (life). Contbr. articles to profl. publs.; co-author chpt. Business Education into the Eighties, 1979. Home: 13 Brian Dr Olney IL 62450 Office: Olney Central Coll Route 3 Olney IL 62450

BOUSQUET, LORRAINE ISABEL, rehabilitation specialist, nurse; b. Ossining, N.Y., Dec. 31, 1948; d. Herbert Vincent and Ruth Isabel (Jackson) B. B.A. in Theology, Dominican Coll., Blauvelt, N.Y., 1971; M.A. in Sacred Scripture, St. Joseph's Coll., Yonkers, N.Y., 1974; A.S. in Nursing Sci., Daytona Community Coll., 1976; B.A. in Psychology, U. No. Fla., 1984; D. Sacred Theology (hon.), Belmont Abbey, N.C., 1977. R.N., Fla. Joined Dominican Sisters, 1966, laicized, 1981; psychol. counselor N.C. Prison System, 1966-67; crisis counselor St. Dominic's Home, Blauvelt, N.Y., 1970-71; open heart surg. nurse Columbia Presbyterian Hosp., N.Y.C., 1971-74; dir. outreach program East Coast Migrant Health Project, Putnam County, Fla., 1979-82; dir. adolescent drug rehab. St. John's River Hosp., Jacksonville, Fla., 1982-84; rehab. specialist Internat. Rehab. Assn., Jacksonville, 1985—; co-dir., cons. Coping with Death and Positive Healing, Human Resource Ctr., Daytona Beach, Fla., 1976-78; cons. Fla. Hospice Assn., Jacksonville, 1978-86; cons. Northeast Fla. Council on Drug Abuse, Jacksonville, 1982-84. Contbr. articles to profl. jours. Mem. Com. Concerned Catholic, Washington, 1985-86. Fellow Fordham U., 1971, U. No. Fla., 1982-83. Mem. Fla. Nurses Assn., Nat. Rehab. Assn., Nat. Assn. Pastoral Psychologists, NOW, Phi Beta Kappa. Democrat. Clubs: Arts Assembly, Lesbian Ethics Assn. (Jacksonville). Avocations: quilting; riding horses; reading; traveling; theatre. Home: 5822 Michigan Ave Jacksonville FL 32211 Office: INTRACORP/Internat Rehab Assocs 9485 Regency Square Blvd #420 Jacksonville FL 32211

BOUTELLE, JANE CRONIN, fitness consultant; b. Arlington, Mass., Nov. 3, 1926; d. William Francis and Sara (Gillis) Cronin; m. G. William Boutelle, 1953 (dec. 1973); children—Jeanne E., William R., James G. B.S., Boston U., 1948; M.A., Columbia U., 1953. Cert. tchr., Mass. Tchr. dance and health edn. Newton High Sch., Mass., 1948-51, Scarsdale High Sch., N.Y., 1951-55, Marymount Coll., Tarrytown, N.Y., 1955-58, Manhattanville Coll., Purchase, N.Y., 1958-59; pres., fitness cons. The Boutelle Method, Inc., Greenwich, Conn., 1973—. Author: Lifetime Fitness for Women, 1978. Contbr. articles to mags. Pres Westchester Dance Council, Westchester County, N.Y., 1956-57; mem. Nat. Alumni Bd. Boston U., 1981—. mem. woman's com. Lighthouse, Westchester County, N.Y., 1983. Recipient Bravo award Greenwich YWCA, 1978. Mem. AAUW (chmn. edn. 1963—), Soroptimists Internat., Assn. Women in Phys. Edn. (chmn. 1954-55), Greenwich Assn. Pub. Schs. (chmn. 1968-73). Home: Huckleberry Ln Greenwich CT 06831 Office: The Boutelle Method Inc Huckleberry Ln Greenwich CT 06831

BOUTIN, FRANCES HAILEY, educational administrator, consultant; b. Port Arthur, Tex., Jan. 29, 1940; d. Clarence Hanceford and Tressie Ethyle (Miles) Hailey; m. William Hubert Boutin, June 29, 1957 (div. May 1968); 1 dau., Kelli Gay. B.S., Lamar U., 1968, M.Ed., 1969; Ed.D., U. Houston, 1980. Cert. tchr. Instr. Sycamore Pvt. Sch., Nederland, Tex., 1965-69; tchr. Westwood Elem. Sch., Spring Branch Ind. Sch. Dist., Houston, 1969-76; coordinator primary edn. Spring Branch Ind. Sch. Dist. Adminstrn. Bldg., Houston, 1976—; cons. to pub. cos. Contbr. articles to profl. jours. Garland scholar, 1966; Lang. Arts fellow, 1969; Westwood Elem. PTA scholar, 1972, 74. Mem. Internat. Reading Assn. (chmn. meeting subcom. Tex. Council 1983), Nat. Council Teaching English, Tex. Joint Council Tchrs. English, Orgn. Tchr. Edn. in Reading, Nat. Reading Conf., Assn. Tex. Lang. Arts Suprs., Tex. Assn. Gifted and Talented, Sci, Tchrs. Assn. Tex., Alpha Lambda Delta, Phi Kappa Phi. Clubs: Houston Underwater (sec., dir. 1980), Seaspace '83 (chmn. registration 1983). Home: 18514 Trail Bend Ln Houston TX 77084

BOVA, DENISE ABIGAIL, computer programmer; b. Norfolk, Va., Jan. 9, 1953; d. Marcel and Nancy (Tibbetts) St. Lawrence; m. Richard J. Bova, Aug. 23, 1980. Computer operator Marine Midland Bank, Syracuse, N.Y., 1972-75; computer operator Syracuse Savs. Bank, 1976-80, programmer analyst, 1980—, sr. programmer analyst, 1981—. Democrat. Roman Catholic. Avocations: reading; writing; crewel work; photography. Home. 216 Jane Dr Syracuse NY 13219

BOVARD, FAITH JEAN, economist; b. N.Y.C. Dec. 13, 1938; d. Martin and Grace vom Lehn; student CCNY, 1956-60; B.A., Hofstra U., 1969; M.B.A., U. Houston, 1980, C.M.A., 1985; children—Victoria, Jacqueline, Tracy. Staff mgr. Rayburn Country, Houston, 1973; exec. sec. Gulf Oil Corp., Houston, 1974-76, fin. analyst, 1976-80, sr. fin. analyst, 1980-83, sr. econ. analyst, 1984-85; economist Chevron Corp., San Francisco, 1985—. Mem. jr. bd. Kent County Hosp., Dover, Del., 1973; bd. dirs. Dover Newcomers Club, 1973; econ. advisor Jr. Achievement, 1984. Mem. Inst. Mgmt. Acctg., Beta Gamma Sigma. Republican. Club: Forum (Houston). Office: 6001 Bollinger Canyon San Ramon CA

BOVAY, HELEN JEPPESEN, diversified investments executive; b. Houston, Mar. 29, 1915; d. Holger and Ruby (Stone) Jeppesen; m. Harry E. Bovay, Jan. 9, 1942 (div. Sept. 1976); children—Mark Benson, Susan Stone. Student Sophie Newcomb Coll., 1933-35, Houston Bus. Coll., 1938-39. Sec., Humble Oil Co., Houston, 1939-42; co-owner Bovista Farms, Brenham, Tex., 1954-80, also Moscow, Tenn., Mid-South Telephone Co., Rienzi, Miss., 1957—, Lamar Telephone Co. (Ala.), Bovay-Lawler Real Estate Interests, Houston, Austin, Tex., Baton Rouge, Spokane, Wash.; ltd. ptnr. Bovista Interests, Ltd., Houston; mem. consumer adv. bd. Joske's Dept. Store, Houston, 1961-64. Leader, Boy Scouts Am., Houston, 1950-60, Girl Scouts U.S.A., Houston, 1950-60; vol. terminal patient care St. Lukes Hosp., Houston, 1960; vol. Magnificat Houses Inc., Loaves and Fishes Soup Kitchen, Casa de Esperanza. Mem. Internat Arabian Horse Assn., Arabian Horse Registry Am., Women's Inst., Theresians Am. (pres. Theresian Fifth Dimension Houston chpt. 1983), Am. Horse Shows Assn., Tex. Soc. Profl. Engrs. (bd. dirs. aux. to San Jacinto chpt.), Embroiders Guild Am., Alpha Delta Pi. Republican. Episcopalian. Gulf Coast Arabian Horse Club (meritorious service award, dir.), Beta Sigma Phi (pres. 1939-40).

BOVE, ANNETTE DEMARIA, cosmetics company executive, consultant; b. Paterson, N.J., Nov. 15, 1943; d. Joseph Emanuel and Sarah Corrine (Pratt) D.; m. Terence John Bove, Apr. 19, 1965 (div. Feb. 1970); 1 child, Tracey Ann. Student, U. Miami, 1961-63. Adminstrv. and exec. asst. DeMaria Enterprises, Miami, Fla., 1969-80, S.E. Investment Corp., Miami, 1980—; owner, pres. So. Cosmetics, Inc., Miami, 1985—. Republican. Roman Catholic. Avocations: gourmet cooking; crocheting. Home: 8210 SW 83d St Miami FL 33143 Office: So Cosmetics Inc 8888 Howard Dr #385 Miami FL 33176

BOWATER, MARIAN LARSON, retired art gallery director; b. Emmons, Minn., Sept. 5, 1924; d. James Melvin and Hannah Elvira (Olson) Larson; student Gustavus Adolphus Coll., 1941-42; m. John J. Bowater, Jan. 22, 1945; children—Christine, Julianna, John James. Owner, dir. Bowater Gallery of Fine Art, Los Angeles, 1975-86; active mus. shows; lectr. art clubs. Mem. Art Dealers Assn. So. Calif. Home: 1168 Wales Pl Cardiff-by-the-Sea CA 92007

BOWDEN, ANN, bibliographer; b. East Orange, N.J., Feb. 7, 1924; d. William and Anna Elisabeth (Herrstrom) Haddon; m. Edwin Turner Bowden, June 12, 1948; children—Elisabeth Bowden Ward, Susan Turner, Edwin Eric; m. 2d, William Burton Todd, Nov. 23, 1969. B.A., Radcliffe Coll., 1948; M.S. in Library Services, Columbia U., 1951; Ph.D., U. Tex., 1975. Cataloger, reference asst. Yale U., 1948-53; manuscript cataloger, rare book librarian, librarian Humanities Research Ctr., librarian Acad. Ctr., U. Tex., Austin, 1958-63, lectr., sr. lectr. Grad. Sch. Library and Info. Sci., 1964-85; coordinator adult services Austin Pub. Library, 1963-67, asst. dir., 1967-71, dep. dir., 1971-77, assoc. dir., 1977-86; bd. dirs. Tex. Info. Exchange, Houston, 1977-78; bd. dirs. AMIGOS Bibliog. Council, Dallas, 1978-82, chmn. bd., 1980-81; chmn. AMIGOS '85 Plan, 1984-86; scholar in residence Rockefeller Found. Villa Serbelloni, Bellagio, Italy, 1986. Editor: T.E. Lawrence Fifty Letters: 1921-1935, 1962; Maps and Atlases, 1978; assoc. editor Papers of the Bibliographical Soc. Am., 1967-82; contbr. articles to profl. jours. Served as cpl. USMC Women's Res., 1944-46. Mem. ALA (council 1975-79), Assn. Coll. and Research Libraries (chmn. rare book and manuscript sect. 1975-76), Tex. Library Assn. (chmn. publs. com. 1965-71), Bibliog. Soc. Am., Phi Kappa Phi, Kappa Tau Alpha. Club: Grolier (N.Y.C.).

BOWDEN, JOYCE NOBLE, nurse, educator; b. Detroit, June 7, 1940; d. Harold and Louise (Miller) Noble; m. Charles Bowden, Apr. 11, 1963; children—Cheryl, Robert. B.S. in Nursing, Wayne State U., 1962; postgrad. UCLA, 1967, 68, 69; M.Ed., U.S. Internat. U., San Diego, 1975. Nurse educator Grossmont Sch. Dist., LaMesa, Calif., 1967—; local coordinator Nurses Assn. Am. Coll., San Diego, 1975-76. Served to lt. (j.g.) USN, 1961-63. Mem. Vocational Educators Assn., Calif. Tchrs. Assn., Nurses Assn. Am. Coll. Ob-Gyn (chmn. 1975-76), Grossmont Educators Assn. (econ./polit. action com., rep. council mem. 1967—). Republican. Home: 2900 Palo Verde Ln #31 Yuma AZ 85364 Office: Health Career Ctr 5345 Timken St La Mesa CA 92041

BOWEN, ANNE SHAFFER, hospital administrator; b. Odessa, Tex., May 24, 1952; d. Paul D. and Thelma M. S.; m. Peter N. Bowen. B.S. in Biology, Tex. Christian U., 1974; B.S. in Nursing, U. Pa., 1975; M.H.A., Ga. State U., 1981. Staff nurse Pa. Hosp., Phila., 1976-77, Hosp. Med. Coll. Pa., 1977-79, Shallowford Community Hosp., Chamblee, Ga., 1980-81; adminstrv. resident, asst. to adminstr. Goddard Meml. Hosp., Stoughton, Mass., 1981-82; v.p. ancillary services Meml. Hosp., York, Pa., 1982—. Mem. Am. Hosp. Assn., Am. Coll. Hosp. Adminstrs., Sigma Theta Tau. Home: PO Box 9 Glen Rock PA 17327 Office: 325 S Belmont St York PA

BOWEN, BARBARA LYNN, computer company executive; b. Toledo, May 19, 1945; d. John Thomas and Grace Elizabeth (Spaulding) B. A.B., Oberlin Coll., 1967; M.S., So. Conn. U., 1968; Ph.D., Cornell U., 1972. Asst. prof. Queens Coll., Flushing, N.Y., 1979-81; mgr. mktg. support-tng. Logo Computer Systems, Inc., N.Y.C., 1981-83; dir. Apple Edn. Found., Apple Computer, Inc., Cupertino, Calif., 1983-84; program dir. edn. affairs Apple Computer, Inc., Cupertino, 1984-86, mgr. external research and devel. in edn., 1986—; mem. Nat. Task Force on Ednl. Tech., 1984-86; bd. advisers N.E. Regional Exchange Teleconference Project, Bolton, N.H., 1984-85, Nat. Ctr. on Computer Equity, N.Y.C., 1985—. Author: Apple Logo Training Manual, 1983. Mem. editorial bd. Nat. Rural Spl. Edn. quar., 1986—. Bd. dirs. Ctr. for Econ. Conversion, Mountain View, Calif., 1985, 86, pres. bd. dirs., 1986; trustee Saybrook Inst., 1986—. Mem. Am. Assn. Artificial Intelligence, Am. Ednl. Research Assn., Assn. for Supervision and Curriculum Devel. Home: 521 Benvenue Ave Los Altos CA 94022 Office: Apple Computer Inc 20525 Mariani Ave Cupertino CA 95014

BOWEN, BETTY SMITH, clothing manufacturing company executive; b. Waco, Tex., Nov. 5, 1927; d. J. Floyd and Mary Dee (Tanner) Smith; m. William George Bowen, Apr. 11, 1957; children—Mary Owen, William George, Sara Dee. B.B.A., So. Meth. U., Dallas, 1948. Teller, Mercantile Bank, Dallas, 1948-52; gen. office Southwest Savs. Assn., Dallas, 1952-57; fashion cons. Doncaster, N.C., 1966-70, dist. mgr., 1970—. Chmn. fund drive Houston Symphony Soc., 1960-61. Republican. Methodist. Clubs: Jr. League Houston, River Oaks Garden. Home: 5883 Sugar Hill Houston TX 77057

BOWEN, CHRISTINE LYN, computerized health-care billing company executive; b. Troy, N.Y., July 23, 1952; d. Joseph William and Evelyn Ann (Webster) Sneden; m. Alan Leslie Deyo, May 20, 1974 (div. Dec. 1977); 1 child, Jason Alan Deyo; m. Robert Charles Bowen, Sept. 12, 1981. D.Applied Social Sci., SUNY-Binghamton, 1979. Office mgr. Maine Med. Group, N.Y., 1977-78; med. edn. coordinator Binghamton Gen. Hosp., 1978-82; systems operation mgr. Med. Office Systems of So. Tier, Inc., Binghamton, 1983-85, chief operating officer, systems ops. mgr., med. edn. coordinator, med. office mgr., 1985—; owner, operator tanning company. Editor Erudition Digest newsletter, 1982. Mentor B-R-I-D-G-E, Binghamton, 1981-84; active Port Dickinson Community Assn., Binghamton, 1984—; co-chairperson disaster service, bd. dirs. Broome County chpt. ARC, 1984—, bd. dirs., chairperson evangelism Ogden Hillcrest United Methodist Ch., Binghamton, 1985—. Served to 1st lt. U.S. Army, 1970-73. Mem. Women's Network, MOSST User Group (bd. dirs. 1983—). Democrat. Lodge: Altrusa (local treas. 1982-83). Avocations: cross-country skiing; antique hunting; camping; swimming; golfing. Home: One Perkins Ave Binghamton NY 13901 Office: Med Office Systems of So Tier Inc 4513 Old Vestal Rd PO Box 897 Binghamton NY 13902

BOWEN, DEBRA LYNN, lawyer; b. Rockford, Ill., Oct. 27, 1955; d. Robert Calvin and Marcia Ann (Crittenden) Bowen. B.A., Mich. State U., 1976; Rotary Internat. fellow Internat. Christian U., Tokyo, 1975; J.D., U. Va., 1979. Bar: Ill. 1979, Calif. 1983. Assoc., Winston & Strawn, Chgo., 1979-82, Washington, 1985—, Hughes Hubbard & Reed, Los Angeles, 1982-84; sole practice, Los Angeles, 1984—; gen. counsel, mem. exec. com. State Employee's Retirement System Ill., Springfield, 1980-82; pres. Bowen & Assocs., Marina del Rey, Calif., 1984—; adj. prof. Watterson Coll. Sch. Paralegal Studies, 1985. Exec. editor Va. Jour. Internat. Law, 1977-78; contbr. articles to profl. jours. Mem. mental health law com. Chgo. Council Lawyers, 1980-82. Wigmore scholar Northwestern U. Sch. Law, Chgo., 1976. Mem. ABA, Los Angeles County Bar Assn., Calif. State Bar Assn., Phi Kappa Phi. Unitarian. Office: 1800 Ave of the Stars Suite 1000 Los Angeles CA 90067 also 2550 M St Suite 500 Washington DC 20037

BOWEN, GWEN LORRAYNE, dance educator, choreographer; b. Denver, May 9; d. Walter Lee and Estermae (Brandfas) B. B.A., Denver U., 1951, postgrad., 1951-52. Tchr. dance Cushing Sch., Denver, 1945-48; tchr. Denver Pub. Schs., 1951-53; tchr. dance, owner Gwen Bowen Sch. of Dance Arts, Denver, 1953—; mem. theater faculty Metro State Coll., Denver, 1973; artistic dir. Premiere Dance Arts Co., Denver, 1959—, hon. life artistic dir., 1963—; lectr. in field. Author graded system for ballet, tap dance. Choreographer numerous ballets. Mem. South Central Improvement Assn. Colo. Council Arts and Humanities grantee. Mem. Colo. Dance Tchrs. (v.p. 1963-64), Dance Educators of Am. (life, area chmn. 1974-85), Dance Masters of Am. (life), Arts Alliance of Colo., Dance Alliance, Kappa Delta. Lodge: Soroptimists. Avocations: knitting; gardening. Office: Gwen Bowen Sch of Dance Arts 714 S Pearl Denver CO 80209

BOWEN, JUDY WILLIAMS, speech and language pathologist; b. Atlanta, Mar. 30, 1939; d. Leslie Spencer and Jewell Winifred (Ivey) Williams; B.A., Mercer U., 1961; M.Ed., Emory U., 1964; m. Henry Horace Bowen, Feb. 21, 1965; children—Susan Elizabeth, Sally Winifred. Speech pathologist DeKalb County Bd. Edn., Decatur, Ga., 1963-65, Atlanta Speech Sch., 1963-65, Central State Hosp., Milledgeville, Ga., summer 1966, Clarke County Bd. Edn., Athens, Ga., 1966-68, Wilkes County Bd. Edn., Washington, Ga., 1977—. cons. in field; mem. Title 1 adv. council Washington-Wilkes Middle Sch., 1979-80, program chmn. Parent-Tchr. Group Bd. dirs. Friends of Savannah River, 1976-78; v.p. prodns. Washington Little Theater Co., 1977, bd. dirs., 1977—; v.p. Fidelis Sunday Sch. class 1st Baptist Ch., Washington, 1979, pres., 1980-81; pres. Washington-Wilkes Primary Sch. Parent-Tchr. Group, 1977-78; patron Augusta Ballet Co.; mem. Madison-Morgan Cultural Ctr. Lic. speech/lang. pathologist, Ga. Mem. Am. Speech and Hearing Assn. (cert. clin. competence), Ga. Speech and Hearing Assn. (sec. 1967-68), DAR, Phi Mu. Home: 202 Water St Washington GA 30673 Office: Wilkes County Bd Edn PO Box 279 Washington GA 30673

BOWEN, JULIA ROGNER, real estate development company executive; b. L.I., N.Y., May 19, 1922; d. Henry J. and Olga (Jaggi) Rogner; m. John Thomas Bowen, Oct. 19, 1947 (dec. 1982); children—William Rogner, John Frederick, Jule Bowen Doran. B.Music, Manhattanville Coll., 1943; postgrad. Columbia U., 1943-44; Diploma with honors, Trinity Coll Music, London, 1938; student Juilliard Sch. Music, 1942. Profl. pianist Am. Theatre Wing, N.Y.C., 1944, Navy Jr. League, N.Y.C., 1944; music tchr., McLean, Va., 1953; corp. sec. John Bowen & Co., Falls Church, Va., 1948-82; sec.-treas. Wycliffe Ct. Corp., Falls Church, 1967-82, pres., 1982—. Mem. Am. Fedn. Musicians. Roman Catholic. Clubs: Bus. and Profl. Women's, Westwood Country. Office: Wycliffe Ct Assocs 200 Park Ave Falls Church VA 22046

BOWEN, LAURA M., traveling photographer; b. Santa Monica, Calif., Jan. 9, 1957; d. Earl and Dorothy Marie (Oxborrow) Bowen. Grad. pub. schs., Lonoke, Ark. Machine operator Remington Arms, Lonoke, 1975-81; traveling photographer Photo Corp. Am., Matthews, N.C., from 1982, now trainer, photographer, sr. traveler, Irvine. Mem. Nat. Assn. Female Execs. Mormon. Avocations: reading; traveling. Home: 1417 E 3d #1 Long Beach CA 90802-3619 Office: Photo Corp Am 17982 Sky Park Co Suite J Irvine CA 92714

BOWEN, MARCIA KAY, customs house broker; b. Bradford, Pa., July 20, 1957; d. George Wadell Jr. and Katherine (Jema) Allen; m. Glenn Edward Rollins, June 26, 1975 (div. 1979); m. Michael James Bower, Dec. 27, 1983. Student Houston Community Coll., 1978-81. Lic. customs house broker. Asst. mgr. W.R. Zanes & Co. of La., Inc., Houston, 1975-76; sec. Westchester Corp., Houston, 1973-75; import br. mgr. Schenkers Internat., Inc., Houston, 1976-85; br. mgr. F.W. Myers & Co., Inc., El Paso, 1985—. Mem. Houston Customs House Brokers Assn. (sec. 1977-79, mem. U.S. customs com. 1979-83), El Paso Customs House Brokers Assn., Houston Freight Forwarders Assn., El Paso Fgn. Trade Zone Assn. Roman Catholic. Office: FW Myers & Co Inc 9801 Carnegie St El Paso TX 79925

BOWEN, MARTHA KAREN, cosmetologist; b. Ulysses, Kans., Apr. 12, 1943; d. William and Beatrice Viola (Wolfe) Elliott; m. Earnest Lee Smith, May 29, 1960 (div. Apr. 1981); children—Tammera Lea Smith Christenson, Lynette Yvonne Smith Alcala. Cert. in cosmetology with high honors, Garden City Community Coll., Kans., 1970. Cert. cosmetologist, Kans. Hair stylist Nina's Beauty Shop, Ulysses, 1970, Chat & Curl, Ulysses, 1970-71; owner, operator Karen's Beauty Nook, Ulysses, 1971—. Republican. Avocations: softball; bowling; singing; skiing. Home and Office: 117 E Central Ulysses KS 67880

BOWEN, ROSEMARY STARKS, social work administrator; b. Savannah, Ga., Apr. 29, 1926; d. Joseph and Lillie Mae (Clayton) Starks; B.S., Ga. State Coll., 1948; postgrad, DePaul U., 1952, U. Chgo., 1970; M.S.W., Loyola U., Chgo., 1960; Ph.D., Walden U., Mpls.; m. Robert C. Bowen, Oct. 1969; children—James Shaw, Christopher Shaw, Laurence Shaw. Caseworker supr. Ada McKinley Community House, Chgo., 1953-57; community tenants relations worker Chgo. Housing Authority, 1957-58; caseworker United Charities Chgo., Family Service Bur., 1960-64; field work instr. U. Chgo., 1964-66; asst. dist. sec. United Charities Chgo., 1966-67; dir. Children's Services, John J. Madden Mental Health Center, Hines, Ill., 1968-70; social work cons., group therapist STEP, Inc., Chgo., 1967-69; exec. dir. South Central Community Services, Inc., Chgo., 1970—; mem. diagnosis mental illness Ill. Mental Health Task Force, 1977-79; radio panelist Mental Health at Work, 1977. Bd. dirs. United Way Chgo.; chmn. program com. PACT, 1980-82; mem. housing subcom. CDAC; bd. dirs. Columbanus Sch., 1969-70; bd. dirs. STEP, Inc. Named Woman of Yr. Iota Phi Lambda, 1983, Most Valuable Vol., St. Columbanus Sch. Center, 1978; NIMH fellow, 1948-60; recipient Disting. Achievements award Chatham Bus. Assn., 1979; Outstanding Exec. award South Central Community Health Service Orgn., 1976; Disting. Services award Chatham YMCA, 1975; Outstanding Citizens award Club Calendar Mag.; Outstanding Community Leadership award STEP, 1973; Image award Fred Hampton Scholarship Fund. Mem. Nat. Assn. Black Social Workers, Nat. Soc. Autistic Children, Nat. Council for Aged, Exec. Service Corps, Chatham Avalon Park Community Council, Day Care Crisis Council, Ill. Assn. Community Mental Health Agencies, Child Care Assn. Ill., Nat. Assn. Social Workers, Nat. Conf. Social Welfare, Am. Orthopsychiat. Assn., Adminstrs. Pvt. Care Assn., Nat. Assn. Social Workers, Nat. Black Child Devel. Inst., Alliance for Mental Health, Opn. PUSH, Nat. Urban League, Black Exec. Dirs. Coalition, Ill. Assn. Community Mental Health. Roman Catholic. Office: 8316 S Ellis Ave Chicago IL 60619

BOWENS, GLORIA FURR, educational administrator; b. Detroit, Apr. 15, 1927; d. Leon Lewis and Iva Rose (Talbot) Furr; B.S., Tufts Coll., 1947; Ed.M., State Coll. Boston, 1968; Ed.D., Harvard U., 1975; 1 dau., Stephanie T. Sci. tchr. Boston Pub. Schs., 1961-71, asst. to the dir. orientation for integration, 1971-73, acting dir. personnel mgmt., 1981-82, instr. med. tech., 1982—; asst. supt. schs. Roosevelt (L.I., N.Y.) Sch. Dist., 1974-77; asst. dir. urban schs. collaborative Northeastern U., Boston, 1977-79, dist. IX coordinator curriculum and competency resources, 1979-81; ptnr. antique shop, Pickering Wharf, Salem, Mass., 1982—. Mem. Nat. Council Adminstrv. Women Edn. (exec. bd. 1970-73), Am. Assn. Sch. Adminstrs., North Shore Antiques Assn., Phi Delta Kappa. Office: Boston Pub Schs 26 Court St Boston MA 02121

BOWER, CARITA BARBARA, marketing and promotions executive; b. Mpls., Oct. 18, 1944; d. Frederick Charles and Margaret Mary (Lambrecht) B. B.A., U. Minn., 1965. Purser Pan Am. Airways, San Francisco, 1965-72, dir. sales Dunfeys Royal Coach, San Mateo, Calif., 1972-78; owner, prin. Fast Co. Ltd. div. Reebok Sales Agents, Santa Cruz, Calif., 1978-82; dir. mktg. Mal Hetzer & Assocs. div. Reebok Sales Agents, Santa Cruz, 1982—. Democrat. Roman Catholic. Avocations: tennis; running; skiing; scuba diving. Home: 331 Vista Dr La Selva Beach CA 95076 Office: Mal Hetzer & Assocs 167 Tiburon Ct Aptos CA 95003

BOWER, CINDY LOU, property management and resort hotel company executive; b. Scottsbluff, Nebr., Apr. 6, 1957; d. Raymond Eugene and Kathleen Coila (Roberts) B. B.S. in Psychology, U. Wyo., 1980. Profl. basketball player Washington Metros, 1979; asst. to mng. dir. Western Services Corp., Silver Springs, Md., 1980-82; v.p., gen. mgr. Key Resort Mgmt., Crested Butte, Colo., 1982—. Mnr. Crested Butte Soccer Team, 1982—; capt. Crested Butte Softball, 1982—; mem. Crested Butte/Mount Crested Butte Adv. Bd., 1983—. Named to Women's Collegiate All-Am. Basketball Team, region VII Nat. Scouting Assn. and Women Pro Basketball League, 1979. Mem. Nat. Assn. Female Execs., Denver/Colo. Conv. Bur., Colo. Soc. Assn. Execs., Am. Hotel/Motel Assn., Colo./Wyo. Hotel/Motel Assn., Crested Butte/Mount Crested Butte C. of C., Gunnison County C. of C., Crested Butte Bus. and Profl. Women's Club (v.p.). Republican. Lutheran. Home: PO Box 1087 92 Aspen Ln Crested Butte CO 81224 Office: Key Resort Mgmt 21 Emmons Rd Mount Crested Butte CO 81225

BOWER, CLAIR ANNETTE, industrial engineer; b. Shreveport, La., June 11, 1957; d. William Judson and Dora Louise (Rouse) Thomas; m. Brett Parker Bower, Jan. 14, 1984. B.S. in Indsl. Engring., U. Houston, 1980. Planning analyst United Gas Pipe Line Co., Houston, 1980-82, engr., 1982-84, advanced planning analyst, 1984-85, agreement analyst, 1985—. Mem. Natural Gas Men of Houston, Nat. Assn. Female Execs. Republican. Avocations: cooking; gardening; bridge. Home: 1114 Channels Ct Crosby TX 77532 Office: United Gas Pipe Line Co PO Box 1478 Houston TX 77251

BOWER, DIANE YVONNE, lawyer, sheet metal company executive; b. Jackson, Mich., May 28, 1951; d. Wayne Arthur and Alice Jane (Borders) Bailey; m. Richard E. Bower, Sept. 8, 1968; children—Brenda, Richard Jr., Bryan, Timmi. A.A., Jackson Community Coll., 1976; B.A., Eastern Mich. U., 1978; J.D., U. Mich., 1980. Bar: Mich. 1981. Assoc. Bilakos & Hanlon, Ann Arbor, Mich., 1978-80; assoc., then shareholder Marcoux, Allen, Abbott & McQuillan, P.C., Jackson, Mich., 1981—; pres., treas., bd. dirs. G.W. Quick Sheetmetal Inc., Jackson, 1982—. Bd. dirs. Retired Sr. Vol. Program Adv. Council, Jackson, 1981-84, Jackson Speech and Hearing Clinic, 1983—, Legal Services S.E. Mich., 1984—, Goodwill Industries, 1985—. Mem. Jackson County Bar Assn. (treas. 1983-85), Mich. Bar Assn., ABA, Estate Planning Council S. Central Mich., Fellows of Mich. State Bar Found., Phi Kappa Phi. Republican. Baptist. Office: Marcoux Allen Abbott & McQuillan PC 145 S Jackson St Jackson MI 49201

BOWER, FAY LOUISE, nurse educator, univ. dean; b. San Francisco, Sept. 10, 1929; d. James Joseph and Emily Clare (Andrews) Saitta; B.S., San Jose State Coll., 1965; M.S. in Nursing, U. Calif., San Francisco, 1966, D.Nursing Sci., 1978; m. Robert Davis Bower, July 2, 1949; children—R. David, Carol Jean Tomei, Dennis James, Thomas John. Office nurse, Palo Alto, Calif., 1950-55; staff nurse Stanford (Calif.) Hosp., 1964-66; charge nurse newborn nursery, summers 1966-67, staff nurse premature research center, 1967-73; asst. prof. nursing San Jose (Calif.) State Coll., 1965-70, assoc. prof., 1970-75, prof., 1975-81, chairperson, 1978-81; dean U. San Francisco, 1981—; lectr. U. Calif., San Francisco, 1975. Mem. AAUP, Health Edn. Media Assn., Public Health Assn. Calif., Santa Clara Health Edn. Council, Commonwealth Club San Francisco, Calif. Nurses Assn., Calif. Tchrs. Assn., Sigma Theta Tau, Phi

Kappa Phi. Author: Theoretical Foundations of Nursing, 3 vols., 1972, The Process of Planning Nursing Care, 1972, 77, 82; Fundamentals of Nursing Practice, 1978. Contbr. articles to profl. jours. Home: 1820 Portola Rd Woodside CA 94062 Office: U San Francisco 2130 Fulton St San Francisco CA 94117

BOWER, JEAN RAMSAY, court administrator, lawyer; b. N.Y.C., Nov. 25, 1935; d. Claude Barnett and Myrtle Marie (Scott) Ramsay; m. Ward Swift Just, Jan. 31, 1957 (div. 1966); children—Jennifer Ramsay, Julia Barnett; m. 2d, Robert Turrell Bower, June 12, 1971. A.B., Vassar Coll., 1957; J.D. Georgetown U., 1970. Bar: D.C. 1970. Exec. dir. D.C. Dem. Central Com., Washington, 1969-71; sole practice, Washington, 1971-78; dir. Counsel for Child Abuse and Neglect Office, D.C. Superior Ct., Washington, 1978—; mem. Mayor's Com. on Child Abuse and Neglect, Washington, 1973—, vice chmn., 1975-79; mem. Family Div. Rules Com., Washington, 1977—. Vice pres. Vassar Club Washington, 1973-75; bd. dirs. Ionia D. Whipper Home, Washington, 1979-84, Big Sisters Met. Area, Washington, 1980-83. Named Washingtonian of Yr., Washingtonian Mag., 1978. Mem. Women's Nat. Democratic Club D.C., Women's Bar Assn. D.C. (Women Lawyer of Yr. 1985). Home: 2729 Dumbarton Ave NW Washington DC 20007 Office: DC Superior Ct Room 4235 500 Indiana Ave NW Washington DC 20007

BOWER, MARGE EMILY, educator; b. Chgo., June 8, 1941; d. Elmore Arthur and Elsie Ruth (Sauer) B.; B.A., U. Mich., 1963; M.A., Loyola U., Chgo., 1967; postgrad. Loyola U., DePaul U., Bradley U., Western Mich. U., U. Mich. Tchr. English, sch. newspaper advisor South Shore High Sch., Chgo., 1963-67; guidance counselor, tchr. Elmwood Park (Ill.) High Sch., 1967-84; dir. guidance Immaculate Conception High Sch., Elmhurst, Ill., 1985—. Chmn. com. out-of-state admissions and scholarships U. Mich. Nat. Alumnae Council, 1972-75, governing bd., 1972-75. Wall St. Jour. Newspaper Fund fellow, 1967. Mem. Nat. Assn. Women Deans, Adminstrs. and Counselors (exec. bd. 1979-81), Ill. Assn. for Counseling and Devel., Ill. Sch. Counselors Assn., U. Mich. Alumni Assn. (5th dist. sec.). Club: North Shore U. Mich. Alumni (scholarship chmn. 1976—). Editorial bd. Ill. Guidance and Personnel Assn. Quar., 1981-85, NAWDAC Jour., 1981-83. Home: 555 W Cornelia Ave Apt 707 Chicago IL 60657

BOWER, MARY MARGARET, library adminstr.; b. Detroit, Mar. 15, 1932; d. Raymond Gladstone and Mary Elizabeth (Carothers) B.; A.B., Wayne State U., 1956; M.A., U. Mich., 1965; m. Michael O. Braun, May 10, 1954; (div. 1963); children—Kolya Marie, Deor Elizabeth. Librarian, Detroit Public Library, 1965-67; asst. librarian Ferris State Coll., Big Rapids, Mich., 1968-72, head reference librarian, 1972-75, head info. services, 1976-78, head public services dept., 1978-79, acting dir., 1979, dir. library, 1980—; trustee Mich. Library Consortium. Mem. AAAS, Am. Soc. Info. Sci., ALA, Spl. Libraries Assn., Assn. Mich. State Coll. and Univ. Library Dirs. Author: Black History: A Bibliography, 1970; Black Literature, 1972, 73. Home: PO Box 1181 15848 157th Ave Big Rapids MI 49307 Office: Ferris State College Library Big Rapids MI 49307

BOWERS, LEOLA DELEAN, educator, nurse; b. Birmingham, Ala., May 5, 1919; d. Jasper Wiley and Lonie (Dunsford) B. Diploma Carraway Methodist Hosp. Sch. Nursing, Birmingham, 1946, Brook Army Med. Ctr. Sch. Anesthesia, Ft. Sam Houston, Tex., 1953; student U. Ga., 1954, U. Md., 1955; B.S.N., U. Ala.-Tuscaloosa, 1959; class B cert. in secondary edn. Jacksonville State U., 1960, M.S. in Edn., 1961; postgrad. Spring Hill Coll., 1962, U. Ala.-Mobile, 1963; cert. Nat. Respiratory Disease Course for Nurses, New Orleans, 1969; postgrad. Pepperdine U., 1971-74; cert. health occupation edn. U. Ala., Birmingham, 1975. R.N., Ala.; cert. secondary tchr., Ala. Hosp. supr. Citizens Hosp., Talladega, Ala., 1946-47, surg. nurse, 1949-50; gen. duty nurse Sylacauga Hosp. (Ala.), 1948; instr. med.-surg. nursing Sylacauga Sch. Nursing, 1963-71; tchr. health occupations Talladega City Vocat. Ctr., 1971—, coordinator Health Occupation Edn. Student Clin. Citizens Hosp. and Nursing Home, 1971—. Instr. ARC, Talladega, 1975—; CPR instr. Am. Heart Assn., Talladega, 1979-82, adv. projects, 1978-83; mem. telephone com. for election legislators, Talladega, 1982. Served as capt. Nurses Corps, U.S. Army, 1950-58; ETO. Recipient CD cert. State Ala., 1980, cert. service City of Talladega, 1983; named Tchr. of Yr., Talladega City Vocat. Ctr. and Health Occupation Edn., 1979, 83, 84, Outstanding Ala. Tchr., Ala. Vocat. Dept., 1983. Mem. Am. Nurses' Assn., Ala. Nurses' Assn., Talladega Nurses' Assn., Health Occupation Students Am. (adviser local club 1976—, adviser Dist. III Ala. 1981-85). Methodist. Lodge: Order Eastern Star. Home: Route 4 Box 239 Talladega AL 35160 Office: Talladega City Vocat Ctr 110 Picadilly Circle Talladega AL 35160

BOWERS, MARIANNE, clergywoman; b. Lafayette, Ind., Feb. 5, 1919; d. Gilbert Melville and Mary Frances (Montgomery) Wilson; m. Carl Eugene Bowers, June 19, 1964 (dec.); children by previous marriage—Frederic Kelly, Deborah Kelly Kivisels, Karen Kelly Wootton. B.S., Purdue U., 1940; grad. Unity Ministerial Sch., 1980. Ordained to ministry Unity Ch., 1980. Exec. sec. Tex. Lic. Vocat. Nurses Assn., Austin, Tex., 1964-66; employment counselor Tarrant Employment Agy., Austin, 1966-68; owner, mgr. Horizons Unlimited (book stores), Austin and San Antonio, 1968-72; with devel., mktg., pub. relations depts. First Nat. Bank, Harlingen, Tex., 1973-76; exec. officer Rio Grande Valley Apt. Assn., 1976-78; minister Unity Ch. of San Angelo (Tex.), 1980—. Mem. Assn. Unity Chs., Internat. New Thought Alliance, AAUW, Scriveners, Alpha Lambda Delta, Delta Rho Kappa, Chi Omega, Nat. Assn. Female Execs., Internat. Platform Assn. Address: PO Box 1221 San Angelo TX 76902

BOWERS, MARY BEACOM, editor; b. Hamilton, Ohio, May 22, 1932; d. Howard Clay and Henrietta R. (Klenke) Alspaugh; m. John Bliss Beacom, Dec. 10, 1955 (dec. 1969); 1 dau., Susanna; m. 2d, David Jean Bowers, July 6, 1972 (dec. 1976). B.A., U. N.C.-Greensboro, 1954; M.A., Kent State U., 1978, postgrad., 1970-73. Registrar Akron (Ohio) Art Inst., 1958-62; teaching fellow Kent State U. (Ohio), 1970-73, lectr. English, 1973-75; editor Bird Watcher's Digest, Marietta, Ohio, 1978—; v.p. Pardson Corp., 1986—. Editor: Stories about Birds and Bird Watchers, 1981. Mem. MLA, Am. Soc. Mag. Editors, ACLU, NOW, Cornell Lab. Ornithology. Democrat. Home: 6 Upland Rd Baltimore MD 21210 Office: Bird Watchers Digest Pardson Corp PO Box 110 Marietta OH 45740

BOWERS, MARY ELLEN KATHRYN, quality control executive, chemist; b. Cleve., Nov. 3, 1949; d. Arthur L. and Dorothy Virginia (DeLura) Jaklic; 1 child, Matthew Anthony. A.A. with honors Lakeland Community Coll., 1985. Lab technician W.S. Tyler, Inc., Cleve., 1969-71, C-E Tyler, Cleve., 1974-76; quality control mgr. Morton Salt, Painesville, Ohio, 1977—. Active Boy Scouts Am., 1986. Mem. Nat. Assn. Female Execs., AAAS. Republican. Roman Catholic. Avocations: traveling; photography; tutoring math. Home: 1651 Mentor Ave Bldg 6 Unit 604 Painseville OH 44077 Office: Morton Salt Div Morton Thiokol Inc PO Box 390 Painesville OH 44077-0390

BOWERS, PATRICIA ELEANOR FRITZ, economist; b. N.Y.C., Mar. 21, 1928; d. Edward and Eleanor (Ring) Fritz; student (scholar) Goucher Coll., 1946-48; B.A., Cornell U., 1950; M.A., N.Y.U., 1953, Ph.D., 1965. Statis. asst. Fed. Res. Bank N.Y., N.Y.C., 1950-53; lectr. Upsala Coll., East Orange, N.J., 1953-59; researcher Fortune Mag., N.Y.C., 1959-60; teaching fellow N.Y.U., N.Y.C., 1960-62, instr., 1962-64; mem. faculty Bklyn. Coll., CUNY, 1964—, prof. econs., 1974—. Mem. Am. Econ. Assn., Econometric Soc., N.Y. Acad. Scis., Met. Econ. Assn. (sec. 1963-68, pres. 1974-75), Am. Statis. Assn. (univs. chmn. ann. forecasting confs. 1970-71, 71-72). Club: Talbot Country (Easton, Md.). Author: Private Choice and Public Welfare, 1974. Office: Dept Econs Brooklyn Coll CUNY Brooklyn NY 11210

BOWERS, VELVA NETTIE, mental health therapist; b. Washington, Mar. 28, 1926; d. Lewis Henderson and Estelle Pleasant (Fitzhugh) Shumate; Student James Madison U., 1944-46, Am. U., 1952-53, Harvard U., 1953; B.A., Upper Iowa U., 1976; M. Counseling, U. Del., 1981; cert. clin. mental health counselor, cert alcoholism counselor; m. John T. Bowers, June 6, 1959; 1 dau., Suzon Bowers. Public relations asst. Am. Truck Assn., Washington, 1950-56; sec., treas. John T. Bowers Constrn. Co., Falls Church, Va., 1959-75; adminstr. officer Sussex County Mental Hygiene Clinic, State of Del., Georgetown, 1975-80; site supr., psychiat. social worker Kent-Sussex Community Mental Health Ctr., Georgetown, 1980—. Bd. dirs. Sussex County Mental Health Assn., 1980-84; pres. Sussex County, Interagy. Council, 1983-84. Recipient exchange scholarship, Harvard U., 1953. Mem. Am. Assn. Counseling and Devel., Mental Health Counselors Assn. Democrat. Episcopalian. Home: Route 2 Box 90 Millville DE 19970 Office: Kent-Sussex Community Mental Health Center Georgetown DE 19947

BOWERS, ZELLA ZANE, real estate broker; b. Liberal, Kans., May 24, 1929; d. Rex and Esther (Neff) Powelson; m. James Clarence Bowers, Aug. 12, 1949; (div. 1977); children—Dara Zane. B.A., Colo. Coll., 1951. Cert. real estate brokerage mgr. Sec. Bowers Ins. Agy., Colorado Springs, Colo., 1955-59, Central Colo. Claims Service, Colorado Springs, 1959-63; pres. Premium Budgeting Co., Colorado Springs, 1962-67; pres., owner Monument Valley Realty, Inc., Colorado Springs, 1981—. Trustee The Palmer Found., Colorado Springs, 1980—, pres., 1983-84; pres. Vis. Nurse Assn., Colorado Springs, 1966-67, 74; dir. Colo. League Nurses, Denver, 1968; advisor Found. of the Robin, Colorado Springs, 1985—; sec. Care & Share, Colorado Springs, 1984; chmn. McAllister House Mus., Colorado Springs, 1973-74; docent chmn. Colorado Springs Fine Arts Ctr., 1969-70; pres. Friends of the Library, 1971-72; pres. Women's Ednl. Soc. Colo. Coll., 1974-77; civil adminstrv. staff asst. Air Def. Filter Ctr., 1956-57, ground observer, 1956, others. Named State Regent for Life, Daus. of Am. Colonists, 1973. Mem. Nat. Assn. Realtors, Colo. Assn. Realtors, Colorado Springs Bd. Realtors (dir., v.p.), Children of the Am. Revolution (pres. 1956-57), Daus. of Am. Colonists (state regent 1970-73), Nat. Soc. Colonial Dames of Am., DAR, Gamma Phi Beta. Avocations: geneology; travel. Home: 11 W Caramillo St Colorado Springs CO 80907 Office: Monument Valley Realty Inc 219 E Yampa St Colorado Springs CO 80903

BOWES, FLORENCE (MRS. WILLIAM DAVID BOWES), writer; b. Salt Lake City, Nov. 19, 1925; d. John Albreckt Elias and Alma Wilhelmina (Jonasson) Norborg; student U. Utah, 1941-42, Columbia, 1945-46, N.Y. U., 1954-55; grad. N.Y. TV Workshop, 1950; m. Samuel Ellis Levine, July 15, 1944 (dec. July 1953); m. William David Bowes, Mar. 15, 1958 (dec. 1976); 1 child, Alan Richard. Actress, writer Hearst Radio Network, WINS, N.Y.C., 1944-45; personnel and adminstrv. exec. Mut. Broadcasting System, N.Y.C., 1946-49, free-lance editor, writer, 1948-49; freelance writer NBC and ABC, 1949-53; script editor, writer Robert A. Monroe Prodns., N.Y.C., Hollywood, Calif., 1953-56; script and comml. dir. KUTV-TV, Salt Lake City, 1956-58; spl. editor, writer pub. relations dept. U. Utah, Salt Lake City, 1966-68, editor, writer U. Utah Rev., 1968-75; author: Web of Solitude, 1979; The MacOrvan Curse, 1980; Interlude in Venice, 1981; Beauchamp, 1983. Mem. Beta Sigma Phi. Home: 338-K St Salt Lake City UT 84103

BOWES, LORRAINE EDWARDS, city official; b. McComb, Miss., Oct. 11, 1938; d. James Franklin Edwards and Florence Lorraine (Gatlin) Edwards Gladden, m. Harry James Bowes, Aug. 14, 1956; children—Lorraine Bowes Pickich, Harry McRedmond. Student Miss. State U., 1980-83. Dep. Tax collector Harrison County, Miss., 1969-70; dep. clk. and tax collector City of Pass Christian, Miss., 1970-77, city clk., tax assessor-collector, 1977—; sec. Civil Service Commn., Pass Christian, 1970—. Active Miss. Hist. Soc., Jackson, 1980. Mem. Pass Christian C. of C., 1985, Miss. Clks.-Assessors-Collectors Assn. (mem. legis. com. 1985—), Internat. Inst. Mcpl. Clks. (cert.). Democrat. Roman Catholic. Avocation: genealogy. Home: 965 E 2d St Pass Christian MS 39571 Office: City of Pass Christian PO Drawer 368 Pass Christian MS 39571

BOWIE, CAROL A., city official; b. Detroit, Aug. 17, 1946; d. Harold V. and Margaret (Black) B. B.A., Wayne State U., 1974; M.B.A., U. Mich., 1985. Employee benefits adminstr. Gen. Motors Corp., Detroit, 1968-74; gen. assignment reporter Detroit Free Press, 1974-75; news reporter, anchor NBC Radio, Chgo., 1975-77; pub. relations asst. Ford Motor Co., Dearborn, Mich., 1977-83; mgr. news relations Burroughs Corp., Detroit, 1983-85; exec. asst. to mayor City of Detroit, 1985—. Mem. Women in Communications, Nat. Black MBA Assn., Nat. Assn. Black Journalists, Nat. Assn. Female Execs., Detroit Press Club. Democrat. Home: 18515 Pinehurst Ave Detroit MI 48221 Office: Mayor's Office City of Detroit 1126 City-County Bldg Detroit MI 48226

BOWIE, PENNY JO, advertising and graphic arts company executive; b. Columbus, Ga., Apr. 5, 1958; d. Gerald and Jo Ellen (Churchwell) B. B.A. in Art, LaGrange Coll., 1980. Prodn. asst. Gulf Coast Publ., San Antonio, Tex., 1980-81, Hearst Printing Press, LaGrange, Ga., 1981—. Office: Omni Advertising 11 Airport Pkwy LaGrange GA 30240

BOWIE, THELMA ROSEMARY, laboratory analyst; b. Temple, Tex., Oct. 6, 1949; d. Joe Willie and Theopia E. (Gaines) Smith; m. Michael Lowery Bowie, Feb. 16, 1979 (div. Feb. 1981); 1 child, Tanya Michelle. B.S. in Edn., North Tex. State U., 1972; M. in Guidance and Counseling, 1974; postgrad. U. Houston, 1985—. Tchr., Denton Ind. Sch. Dist., Tex., 1972-74; counselor, social worker LaMarque Ind. Sch. Dist., Tex., 1974-75; counselor HEART-Exoffender Program, Houston, 1975-76; lab. analyst Amoco Oil Co., Texas City, 1976—. Sec. Civic Improvement League, Texas City, 1984—; co-chmn. Adolescent Health Promotion Council, LaMarque, Tex., 1984—; trustee LaMarque Ind. Sch. Dist., 1984—; mem. nominating com. South Tex. council Girl Scouts USA, Lake Jackson, Tex., 1985—. Mem. Options (founder), Nat. Assn. Sch. Bd. Mems., Nat. Alliance Black Sch. Educators, Tex. Assn. Sch. Bd. Mems., Alpha Kappa Alpha (named Outstanding Citizen of Yr. 1984-85). Lodge: Ct. of Colanthes. Avocations: jogging; aerobics; reading. Home: 7600 Palmer Hwy #312 Texas City TX 77591

BOWLBY, DIANA JEAN, computer consulting company executive; b. Cambridge, Mass., Sept. 15, 1953; d. Roy Irving and Peggy Joyce (Hall) Bowlby; m. John Patrick Mahoney, Feb. 13, 1983. B.S. in Psychology and Secondary Edn., U. Lowell, 1976. Cert. secondary edn. tchr., Mass. Acctg. clk. Cambridge Memories, Inc., Bedford, Mass., 1976-78; adminstrv. asst. ATEX, Inc., Bedford, 1978-80, logistics inventory control administr., 1980-84; computer/procedure cons. Darlabs, Inc., Harvard, Mass., 1984-85; procedure devel. mgr., office mgr. MOD-TAP System, Harvard, 1985 ind. cons., 1985—. Author procedure mans. Mem. Bedford Bicentennial Com., 1975-76. Mem. Am. Mgmt. Assn., Am. Electronics Assn. Republican. Baptist. Avocations: reading; singing; swimming; bicycling; travel. Home: 93 Baldwin Rd Billerica MA 01821 Office: MOD-TAP System 285 Ayer Rd PO Box 706 Harvard MA 01451

BOWLES, BARBARA LANDERS, food company executive; b. Nashville, Sept. 17, 1947; d. Corris Raemone Landers and Rebecca Aima (Bonham) Jennings; m. Earl Stanley Bowles, Nov. 27, 1971; 1 son, Terrence Earl. B.A., Fisk U., 1968; M.B.A., U. Chgo., 1971. Chartered fin. analyst, 1977. Banker to v.p. First Nat. Bank of Chgo., 1968-81; asst. v.p. Beatrice Cos., Chgo., 1981-84; v.p. investor relations Dart & Kraft, Inc., Chgo., 1984—. Recipient Salute to Am.'s Top 100 Black Bus. and Profl. Women award Delta Sigma Theta and Dollars & Sense Mag., 1985. Mem. Fin. Analysts Fedn., Nat. Assn. Investment Clubs, Nat. Investor Relations Inst., Chicago Fisk Alumni Assn. (pres. 1983-85). Mem. United Ch. of Christ. Club: University (Chgo.). Avocations: tennis, bridge. Office: Dart & Kraft Inc 2211 Sanders Rd Chicago IL 60062

BOWLES, FRANCES MARIE, personnel executive; b. Paducah, Ky., Feb. 5, 1938; d. Jesse Raymond and Anna Lou (Varnell) Walker; student Murray State U., 1955-57; m. James Everette Bowles, July 9, 1973; children—Robert Wayne, Michael Ray, Benjamin Earl. Collection correspondent, office supr. Sears Roebuck & Co., Paducah, 1957-65; credit mgr. Jeans Dept. Store, Paducah, 1965-67; mgr., estimator Slay Plumbing & Heating, Paducah, 1967-72; office mgr. Amick & Helm C.P.A., Madisonville, Ky., 1972-74; mgr. Arch Mgmt. Corp., Madisonville, 1974—, exec. asst. to pres. of affilated cos., 1974-83; co-owner, sec.-treas. Sebree Dock Inc., 1983—; co-owner, pres. HBH Mgmt. Services, Inc., 1983—, Nat. Testing Labs., 1984. Vol. United Way, Madisonville, Cancer Soc., Madisonville. Mem. Profl. Sec. Assn. (v.p. Madisonville chpt. 1974, pres. elect 1975, pres. 1976), Nat. Assn. Exec. Secs., Nat. Assn. Female Execs. Democrat. Baptist. Home: 1061 Parkwood St Madisonville KY 42431 Office: PO Box 326 2515 S Main St Madisonville KY 42431

BOWLES, MARTHA THOMAS, utility company executive; b. Greensboro, N.C., Dec. 29, 1952; d. Hargrove Jr. and Jessamine Woodward (Boyce) B.; m. Geoffrey McKewen Curme, Dec. 31, 1977; 1 child, Jonathan Woodward Bowles Curme. B.A., U. N.C., 1975; M.B.A., Harvard U., 1979. Asst. treas. Chem. Bank, N.Y.C., 1975-77; mgr. spl. projects Belk Stores Services, Charlotte, N.C., 1979; sr. fin. analyst Duke Power Co., Charlotte, 1980-84, sr. fin. analyst long term fin., 1984-85, sr. fin. analyst cash mgmt., 1985—, dir. cash ops., 1985—; commr. Mecklenburg Co. Indsl. Facilities Pollution Control Fin. Authority, Charlotte, 1983-85. Mem. Charlotte Community Concert Assn., 1981-84; bd. trustees Sacred Heart Coll., Belmont, N.C., 1983-84. Mem. Women Execs., Phi Beta Kappa. Democrat. Episcopalian. Office: Duke Power Co 422 S Church St Charlotte NC 28242

BOWLIN, JUDY SUE, personnel executive; b. Mt. Vernon, Ill., Sept. 5, 1947; d. Howard Leonard and Thelma June (Dubois) Breiseacher; 1 son, Wade Shannon. A.A., Mt. Vernon Community Coll., 1967; B.S., So. Ill. U., 1979. Personnel clk. Good Samaritan Hosp., Mt. Vernon, Ill., 1969-73; adjudicator State of Ill., Mt. Vernon, 1975-76, manpower rep., Centralia, 1976; tchr. Dodds Sch., Mt. Vernon, 1979-80; adminstrv. asst. personnel mgr. Nutherm Internat., Inc., Mt. Vernon, 1980-82; personnel dir. Mt. Vernon Hosp., Inc., 1982—. Asst. chmn. March of Dimes, 1974. Mem. Am. Soc. Personnel Adminstrn., Am. Soc. Hosp. Personnel Adminstrn., Beta Sigma Phi. Democrat. Baptist. Home: Rural Route 3 Mount Vernon IL 62864 Office: Mount Vernon Hosp Inc #8 Doctors Park Mount Vernon IL 62864

BOWMAN, ARLEEN DRIMMER, fashion designer; b. Bklyn., July 14, 1945; d. Nathan and Minnie (Goldhor) Drimmer; student N.Y.C. Community Coll., 1962-63. Prodn. coordinator M.P.O., music and film TV commls., N.Y.C., 1966-67; prodn. mgr. Richard Druz and Victor Lukens Assocs., music and film TV commls., N.Y.C., 1967-68; producer Flickers Inc., TV commls., N.Y.C., 1969-72; owner, buyer Family Boutique, Amsterdam, Netherlands, 1972-74; owner, designer, pub. relations dir. Bowman Trading Co., Inc., N.Y.C., 1974-84; owner, designer, pub. relations dir. Arleen Bowman Industries, Inc.; cons. China Trade; speaker in field. Recipient Clio award for TV comml. campaign, 1970; Effie award for TV comml., 1970. Guest editor Fashion mag., 1978. Patentee compact for cosmetics, 1975. Profiled on ABC World News Tonight, 1978. Office: 209 W 38th St New York NY 10018

BOWMAN, C. DALE, educational administrator; b. Madison County, N.C., July 16, 1936; d. Cora Lee Fender Wilds; m. Robert E. Bowman, July 27, 1963; 1 child, Brett E. B.S., Berea Coll., 1958; M.S. in Ed., Ind. U., 1960. Residence hall dir. Berea Coll., Ky., 1958-59; resident hall dir. Ball State U., Muncie, Ind., 1960-63, asst. dir. student programs 1963-67, asst. to v.p. student affairs, 1969-76, assoc. dean students, 1976—. Active YWCA. Mem. Nat. Assn. for Women Deans, Adminstrs. and Counselors, Ind. Assn. for Women Deans, Adminstrs. and Counselors (pres. 1974), Ind. Coll. Personnel Assn. (bd. dirs. 1978-80), AAUW. Democrat. Lutheran. Club: Altrusa, Riley Jones Inc.

BOWMAN, DEBORAH ANNE, book company sales representative; b. Lansing, Mich., Dec. 20, 1957; d. Norman James and Christine Ruth (Levring) B. B.S. in Bus. Adminstrn., U. Fla., 1980. Sales rep. D. Van Nostrand Co., Gainesville, Fla., 1980-81, Mc-Graw Hill Book Co., Dallas, 1984—; sales and mktg. rep. Benjamin-Cummings Publishers, Dallas, 1981-84. Active mem. St. Rita Young Singles, Dallas, 1981-84. Named to Outstanding Young Women in Am., 1983. Mem. Assn. for Computing Machinery (assoc.), Nat. Assn. for Female Execs., Phi Kappa Phi, Alpha Lambda Delta, Alpha Omicron Pi, Kappa Sigma Little Sisters. Roman Catholic. Home and Office: 8215 Meadow Rd #2098 Dallas TX 75231

BOWMAN, GEORGIANA HOOD, state public utilities commissioner; b. Middletown, Ohio, Jan. 19, 1937; d. George Simpson and Corinne Lula (Hunter) Hood; B.S. in Edn., Wilberforce U., 1965; M.A. in Adult Edn., Ohio State U., 1973, Ph.D. in Humanities Edn., 1976; m. Harris C. Bowman, Sept. 10, 1961. Tchr., Columbus (Ohio) Public Schs., 1965-72, ethnic studies planner, 1972-73, research planning and auditing specialist Title III project, 1973-74; coordinator black student programs and devel. Ohio State U., 1974-80; pres. G.H. Bowman Co., Mgmt. Consultants, Columbus, 1980-85; edn. cons. Div. Equal Ednl. Opportunity urban programs sect. Ohio Dept. Edn., 1983-84; chief EEO sect. Pub. Utilities Commn. Ohio, 1984—, dep. dir., 1986—; human relations cons. Columbus Public Schs. Sec., bd. dirs. YWCA; bd. dirs. Columbus Urban League; 2d v.p., sec., bd. dirs. North Central Mental Health Center; bd. dirs., exec. bd. South Side Settlement House; 2d v.p. Columbus chpt. NAACP.; charter mem. Columbus Assn. Performing Arts Colleagues. Recipient cert. of appreciation Ohio Ho. of Reps., 1980, public service awards Delta Sigma Theta, Sertoma Club, Alpha Kappa Alpha, Big Bros./Big Sisters Assn. Mem. Youth Service Guild, Nat. Council Negro Women (Columbus pres., Pub. Service award), Ohio State Univ. Hosps. Aux., Phi Delta Kappa (chpt. pres.), Pi Lambda Theta. Home: 2671 Cleveland Ave Columbus OH 43211 Office: 2671 Cleveland Ave Columbus OH 43211

BOWMAN, HAZEL LOIS, educator; b. Plant City, Fla., Feb. 18, 1917; d. Joseph Monroe and Annie (Thoman) B.; A.B., Fla. State Coll. for Women, 1937; M.A., U. Fla., 1948; postgrad. U. Md., 1961-65. Tchr., Lakeview High Sch., Winter Garden, Fla., 1939-40, Eagle Lake Sch., Fla., 1940-41; welfare visitor Fla. Welfare Bd., 1941-42; specialist U.S. Army Signal Corps, Arlington Hall, Va., 1942-43; recreation worker, asst. procurement officer ARC, CBI Theater, 1943-46; lab. technician Am. Cyanamid Corp., Brewster, Fla., 1946-47; instr., asst. prof. gen. extension div. U. Fla., Fla. State U., 1948-51; free-lance writer, editor, indexer, N.Y., Fla., 1951-55; staff writer Tampa (Fla.) Morning Tribune, 1956; staff writer, telegraph editor Winter Haven (Fla.) News-Chief, 1956-57; registrar/admissions officer U. Tampa, 1957-59; coll. counselor, Atlantic states, 1959-60; registrar/freshman adviser Towson State Tchrs. Coll., Balt., 1960-62; dir. student personnel, guidance, admissions Harford Jr. Coll., Bel Air, Md., 1962-64; instr. York (Pa.) Coll., 1965-66, asst. prof. English, journalism, 1966-69; tchr. S.W. Jr. High Sch., Lakeland, Fla., 1969-70; tchr. learning disabled Vanguard Sch., Lake Wales, Fla., 1970-82; docent, hist. calendar research editor Polk County Hist. and Geneal. Library, Bartow, Fla., 1984—. Mem. AAUW, Mortar Bd., NOW, Alpha Chi Alpha, Chi Delta Phi. Editor: Tampa Altrusan, 1958-60. Home: 511 NE 9th Ave Mulberry FL 33860

BOWMAN, JACQUELYNNE JEANETTE, lawyer; b. Chgo., Dec. 4, 1955; d. Arthur E. Joyce and Sallye Mae (Coppedge) Edwards; m. David John Rentsch, Sept. 15, 1984. A.B., U. Chgo., 1979; J.D., Antioch U., 1979. Bar: Tenn. 1981, Mass. 1984. Fellow, Nat. Urban League, N.Y.C., 1982-83; staff atty. W. Tenn. Legal Services, Inc., Jackson, 1979-84; dir. Edn. Adv. for Children with Handicaps, Jackson, 1982; cons. JONAH, Brownsville, Tenn., 1979-84; supervising atty. Greater Boston Legal Services, Inc., 1984—. Mem., advisor Citizens United for Polit. Action, Jackson, 1982; advisor Parents for Ednl. Accountability, Brownsville, 1983—; advocate EACH, 1979-85; mem. battered women's working group Gov.'s Anti-Crime Commn.; mem. Mass. Gov.'s Foster Care Commn., also chmn. subcom. on legal and policy issues. Mem. ABA, Nat. Conf. Black Lawyers, Mass. Black Lawyers Assn., Mass. Assn. Women Lawyers, Mass. Bar Assn., Boston Bar Assn., George Edmund Haynes Fellowship Soc., Female Advocacy Group. Roman Catholic. Office: Greater Boston Legal Services Inc 68 Essex St Boston MA 02111

BOWMAN, KAREN, jazzercise instr.; b. Fall River, Mass., July 21, 1949; d. Albert F. and Kathleen C. (Lavigne) Doucette; A.S., Johnson & Wales Coll., 1970; m. Michael Allen Bowman, July 18, 1974. Sec., Dept. Army, Pentagon, Washington, 1970-71, AID, Vientiane, Laos, 1972-74, Am. embassy, Vienna, Austria, 1974-75, Beckman Microbics, Carlsbad, Calif., 1976-79, Am. embassy, Ankara, Turkey, 1979-81; jazzercise instr. Am. ambassador's residence, Ankara, 1979-81, Mem. Nat. Assn. Scuba Diving Schs. Office: Bank of Am 73700 Gorgonio Dr Twentynine Palms CA 92277

BOWMAN, MARTHA ALEXANDER, librarian; b. Washington, June 8, 1945; d. Lyle Thomas and Helen (Goodwin) Alexander; m. David Henry Bowman, June 11, 1965 (div. 1982); 1 child, Elaine. B.A., U. Md., 1967; M.L.S., Catholic U. Am., 1969. Librarian U. Md., College Park, 1969-72, head acquisitions, 1973-75; asst. univ. librarian George Washington U., Washington, 1975-78, assoc. univ. librarian, 1978-82; univ. librarian U. Louisville, 1983—; cons. World Bank, Washington, 1982. Account exec. United Way Campaign, Louisville, 1985. Higher Edn. Act Title II fellow, 1968-69. Mem. ALA (chmn. poster sessions, 1983—), Southeastern Library Network (bd. dirs. 1985—), U. Louisville Athletic Assn. (chmn. personnel 1984—), D.C. Library Assn. (pres. 1981-82), Women Acad. Library Dirs. Exchange Network. Democrat. Episcopalian. Office: U Louisville Louisville KY 40292

BOWMAN, PATRICIA IMIG, microbiologist; b. Evanston, Ill., Aug. 10, 1951; d. Walter Joseph and Elizabeth Jean (Lutton) Imig; m. Van Martin Bowman, Dec. 16, 1972; B.S., Ga. State U., 1972, M.S., 1975; Ph.D., St. John's U., 1981. Research assoc. Ga. State U., Atlanta, 1975-77; microbiology supr. Personal Products Co., Milltown, N.J., 1981-82, mgr. microbiology, 1982-84; mgr. microbiology Avon Products, Inc., Suffern, N.Y., 1984—. Contbr. articles to profl. jours. Mem. Am. Soc. Microbiology, Soc. Indsl. Microbiology, Cosmetics, Toiletries and Fragrances Assn. (microbiology com 1982—, raw materials subcom. 1982—), Soc. Cosmetic Chemists, Mortar Bd. Soc., Phi Kappa Phi. Republican. Methodist. Office: Avon Products Inc Division St Suffern NY 10901

BOWMAN, ROSE, state official. Director, state of Idaho Health and Welfare Dept. Office: Idaho Health & Welfare Dept State Ho Boise ID 83720*

BOWMAN, SUSAN RENEE, collections company executive; b. Cin., May 19, 1963; d. James Nelson and Patricia Ann (Lehman) Richards; m. Larry D. Bowman, Aug. 23, 1982 (div. Nov. 1985). Assoc. degree, Miami U., Middletown, Ohio, 1983. Customer service supr. J.C. Penney Credit Corp., Cin., 1984-86; collection acct. coordinator Parson Bishop Nat. Collections, Cin., 1986—. Fund raiser Cin. chpt. Am. Cancer Soc., 1980-83. Mem. Nat. Assn. Female Execs. Democrat. Mem. Ch. of God. Avocations: reading; hiking; swimming. Home: 1261 Troy Ct Mason OH 45040 Office: Parson Bishop Nat Collections 7870 Camargo Rd Cincinnati OH 45243

BOWMAN-DALTON, BURDENE KATHRYN, educator, computer consultant; b. Magnolia, Ohio, July 13, 1937; d. Ernest Mowles and Mary Kathryn (Long) Bowman; B.M.E., Capital U., 1959; M.A. in Edn., Akron U., 1967, postgrad. 1976—; m. Louis W. Dalton, Mar. 13, 1979. Profl. vocalist, various clubs in the East, 1959-60; music tchr. East Liverpool (Ohio) City Schs., 1959-62; music tchr. Revere Local Schs., Akron, Ohio, 1962-75, elem. tchr., 1975-80, elem. team leader/computer cons., 1979-85, tchr. middle sch. math., gift-talented, computer literacy, 1981—; local and regional dir., Olympics of the Mind, also problem capt. for computer problem for world finals. Mem. Citizen Com., Akron, 1975-76; profl. rep. Bath Assn. to Help, 1978-80; audit com. BATH, 1977-79; volunteer chmn. Antique Car Show, Akron, 1972-81. Martha Holden Jennings Found. grantee, 1977-78; Title IV ESEA grantee, 1977-81. Mem. Assn. for Devel. of Computer-Based Instructional Systems, Assn. Supervision and Curriculum Devel., Ohio Assn. for Gifted Children, Phi Beta. Republican. Lutheran. Home: 353 Retreat Dr Akron OH 44313 Office: 3195 Spring Valley Rd Bath OH 44210

BOWSER, EMILIE LOUISE, nurse, educator; b. Newark, Ohio, July 16, 1941; d. James Elbert and Geraldine Mae (Utts) Drumm; m. Gary L. Bowser, June 6, 1964 (div. July 1980); children—Deborah, Diana, David. B.S. in Nursing, Ohio State U., 1964; M.S. in Nursing, Wayne State U., 1984. R.N., Ohio. Charge nurse West Paces Ferry Hosp., Atlanta, 1972-73; clin. instr. St. Vincent's Hosp., Toledo, Ohio, 1976; staff nurse Toledo Hosp., parttime 1976—; staff nurse Flower Hosp., Toledo, 1978-79; clin. instr. U. Toledo, 1979; asst. prof. nursing Owens Tech. Coll., Toledo, 1979—, cons. continuing edn., 1981—; advisor Nat. Student Nurses Assn., Toledo, 1981—. Cub scout com. chmn. Wolverine council Boy Scouts Am., 1983—. Mem. Ohio Nurses Assn. (publicity com. 1980-82), Bedford Band Boosters, Nat. League Nursing. Republican. Episcopalian. Club: Tamaron Country (Toledo). Home: 1765 Heather Temperance MI 48182 Office: Owens Tech Coll Oregon Rd Toledo OH 43699

BOWSER, SARAH WRIGHT, private investigator, security specialist; b. Phila., Oct. 5, 1954; d. Albert Edward and Sarah Bernice (Reid) Wright; m. Gervis Annious Brown, Feb. 14, 1977 (div. Aug. 1980); m. John William Bowser, Jan. 26, 1984. Cert. in law enforcement adminstrn. Tidewater Community Coll., 1979, Assoc. Polit. Sci., 1979; B.S. in Polit. Sci., Old Dominion U., 1981. Resident mgr. William Bush, Kitty Hawk, N.C., 1974; charter bus driver James William Bus Service, Norfolk, Va., 1974-75; spl. police officer Tower Mall Shopping Ctr., Portsmouth, Va., 1975; undercover agt. Norfolk Police Dept., 1975-76; investigator, security officer Portsmouth Detective and Security Patrol, 1975-76; security mgr. Rices Nachman Dept. Store, Norfolk, 1975-79; port police officer Va. Port Authority, Norfolk, 1979; law enforcement officer Va. Nat. Guard, Richmond, 1979-80; model Charm Modeling Sch., Norfolk 1979-81; usherette Spl. Services Unltd. HREC, Inc., Norfolk, 1980-81; security guard Transco Co. Ohio, Cin., 1980-81; campus police officer Norfolk State U., 1981-84; security officer Sears Roebuck & Co., Virginia Beach, Va., 1984—; chief investigator State Wide Investigations, Chesapeake, Va., 1984—; security mgr. Convenient Food Mart, Norfolk, 1985—; sales rep. D & J Service Co., Virginia Beach, Va., 1984—; lt., exec. body guard Waldron Corp. Va., Chesapeake, 1984—; cons. worthless checks Sears Roebuck & Co., Virginia Beach, 1985—; cons. non-traditional students State Va. Dept. Higher Edn., Richmond, 1981—. Mem. Portsmouth Composite Squadron CAP, U.S. Air Force Aux.; mem. Interfaith Com. Against Blasphemy, Big Sisters Tidewater. Served with Air N.G., 1979-80. Mem. Internat. Assn. Arson Investigators, Internat. Assn. Investigators and Spl. Police, Internat. Police Congress (spl. agt.), Nat. Assn. Blacks and Minorities in Criminal Justice, Nat. Assn. Bailbond Investigators, Nat. Rifle Assn. Am. Mem. Assembly of God Ch. Club: Glenwood Garden (Norfolk). Avocations: student pilot; bicycling; large game hunting; fishing. Home: 5572 Stonehaven Dr Virginia Beach VA 23464 Office: State Wide Investigations Ltd PO Box 1214 Chesapeake VA 23320

BOWYER, JOAN ELIZABETH, medical technologist; b. Ellensburg, Wash., July 11, 1944; d. Chester Joseph and Rita Geneva (Newell) Howarth; children—Suzanne, Elise. B.A., Ft. Wright Coll. of Holy Names, 1966; grad. Real Estate Sch. Oreg., 1982. Lic. med. technologist. Med. technologist Lab. of Clin. Medicine, Seattle, 1967-69, Sacred Heart Gen. Hosp., Eugene, Oreg., 1969-73, 74-76, McKenzie Willamette Hosp., Springfield, Oreg., 1976-77, Mid-Columbia Hosp., The Dalles, Oreg., 1977-82; realtor Red Carpet/Rich Hall Realty, Hillsboro, Oreg., 1982-85, Century 21 Columbia Realty, Portland, 1985—; med. technologist ARC, Portland, 1982—. Co-editor The Dalles Gen. Hosp. Newspaper, 1980-82. Pres. Wasco County Edn. Service Dist. Parents Group, The Dalles, 1978-82; founder, pres. Mid-Columbia Parents of Deaf, 1978-82; parental spokesperson Spl. Edn. Adv. Com., Salem, Oreg., 1980-82; activist parent for deaf/hearing impaired, 1977—. Mem. Med. Technologists of Am. Soc. Pathologists, Nat. Assn. Realtors. Democrat. Mem. Ch. of Jesus Christ of Latter Day Saints. Avocations: photography; dancing; hiking; travel. Home: 704 SE 38th St Portland OR 97214 Office: ARC 3131 N Vancouver PO Box 3200 Portland OR 97208

BOX, JANET YVONNE HAYNES, interior architectural designer; b. Lexington, Ky., Nov. 19, 1944; d. Leonard Stallard and Ina Claire (Vest) Haynes; m. Frederick Clyde Box, Aug. 28, 1965 (div. 1978); children—Lisa Courtenay, Derrick Everett. Student U. Tex., 1963-66; B.S. cum laude, U. Houston, 1978. Instr., Inwood Elem. Sch., Houston, 1971-75; project designer/assoc. Lammey Assoc., 1978-79; project designer/dir. 3D/Internat., 1979-82; project designer/team leader Pierce, Goodwin, Alexander Architects, 1982; project designer, project dir. Sikes Jennings Kelly Architects, 1983—. Mem. AIA (interior architecture steering com.), Inst. Bus. Designers (edn. com.), Women in Architecture, Am. Assn. Textile Chemists and Colorist. Democrat. Roman Catholic. Office: Archtl Interior Services PO Box 263 Houston TX 77001-0263

BOXER, BARBARA, congresswoman; b. Bklyn., Nov. 11, 1940; m. Stewart Boxer, 1962; children—Doug, Nicole. B.A. in Econs., Bklyn. Coll., 1962. Stockbroker, econ. research with securities firms on Wall St., 1962-65; journalist and assoc. editor Pacific Sun newspaper, 1972-74; congl. aide Fifth Congl. Dist. Calif, 1974-76; elected mem. Marin County Bd. Suprs., 1976-82, pres., 1980-81; dir. Bay Area Air Quality Mgmt. Dist., 1977-82, pres., 1979-81; mem. 98th-99th Congresses. Dir., Golden Gate Bridge, Hwy. and Transp., 1978-82; founding mem. Marin Edn. Corps, Marin Nat. Women's Polit. Caucus, Marin Community Video; mem. civic, cultural and ednl. orgns. Address: 315 Cannon Bldg Washington DC 20515*

BOXX, RITA MCCORD, banker; b. Greenwood, S.C., Aug. 10, 1930; d. John Thomas Logan and Dempsie (Dixon) McCord; student public schs.; m. John Douglas Boxx, Apr. 17, 1949; children—John Stephen, Eric Wesley, Merry Christine. Asst. mgr. Greenwood Ins. Agy., 1951-65, mgr., 1967-80; with Bankers Trust S.C., Greenwood, 1951—, asst. v.p. charge ins. dept. 1980—; tchr. ins. seminars. Mem. Nat. Assn. Ins. Women, Ind. Ins. Agts. Greenwood, Ind. Ins. Agts. S.C., Ind. Ins. Agts. Am., Greenwood Assn. Ins. Women, Greenwood C. of C. (dir. 1974-76, chmn. environ., energy and conservation com. 1974, chmn. edn. com. 1977). Baptist. Club: Greenwood Country. Home: 434 Dogwood Dr Greenwood SC 29646 Office: PO Box 1058 Greenwood SC 29648

BOYARSKY, ROSE EISMAN, psychologist; b. Jersey City, Mar. 16, 1924; d. Isadore and Clara (Klingenstein) Eisman; B.S. in Chemistry, U. Vt., 1944; M.A., Columbia U., 1946; Ph.D., Duke U., 1969; m. Saul Boyarsky, June 17, 1946; children—Myer William, Terry Linda, Hannah Gail. Psychologist, Durham (N.C.) County Mental Health Clinic, 1969-70; counselor U. Mo. Counseling Center, St. Louis, 1971-72; research asso. Masters and Johnson Inst., St. Louis, 1972-75; pvt. practice psychology, Boyhill Center, St. Louis, 1975—; research assoc. depts. surgery and urology Washington U. Med. Center, St. Louis, 1977—; mem. assoc. staff Jewish Hosp. of St. Louis, 1971—; dir. Archway Community for Drug Rehab., 1973—; mem. Eastern Mo. Regional Adv. Council for Psychiat. Services, 1975-81; apptd. mem. Mo. State Com. Psychologists, 1983—, chmn., 1986-87. Trustee Judea Reform Congregation of Durham-Chapel Hill, N.C., 1967-69, Portland Place Assn., 1980-83; mem. adv. bd. Victim Service Council, 1985—. Mem. Psychologists in Pvt. Practice, Mo. Psychol. Assn. (pres. 1977-78), Am. Psychol. Assn., AAAS, Am. Women in Psychology, Soc. of Columbia Chemists, Phi Beta Kappa, Iota Sigma Pi. Contbr. articles in field to profl. jours.; editorial bd. Profl. Psychology, 1979—, Psychology and Pvt. Practice, 1983—, Young Couples Internat., 1983—; editor SCOP Newsletter, 1984. Home: 45 Portland Pl Saint Louis MO 63108 Office: 4625 Lindell Blvd Saint Louis MO 63108

BOYCE, CARLA HOLLAND, veterinarian; b. Arlington, Va., Jan. 9, 1952; d. Charles William and Martha Lucille (Baldridge) Holland; m. William Lockhart Boyce, June 12, 1977; 1 son, Wiley Allen. Student, N.C. State U.-Raleigh, 1970-73; D.V.M., U. Ga.-Athens, 1977. Veterinarian specializing in dermatology Animal Med. Clinic of Cardiff, San Diego, 1977-78; veterinarian Colonial Animal Clinic, Springfield, Va., 1978-79, Health Clinic, Nairobi, Kenya, 1979-81; veterinarian, ptnr. Boyce-Holland Vet. Services, Stuart, Va., 1981—; cons. riding program Mt. Kenya Safari Club, Nanyuki, Kenya, 1981; cons. equine breeding Grant's Game Reserve, Nanyuki, 1981; lectr. exotic diseases U. Ga. Continuing Edn. Tours, Nairobi, 1979-81; lectr. Nairobi Nat. Mus., 1980-81; cons. Colcheccio Game Res., Rumurutl, Kenya, 1981. Senator agl. and life scis. N.C. State U., 1971; instr. Kabete Pony Club, Nairobi, 1979-81; cons. Patrick Springs Boy Scouts, Stuart, Va., 1983—; elder Stuart Presbyn. Ch., 1983—; instr. Patrick Springs 4-H Horse Club, 1981. Recipient Patty Lynn Burton award, U. Ga. Vet. Sch., 1976; Southeastern profl. scholar Cons. Inc., 1977. Mem. San Diego Vet. Med. Assn., Am. Vet. Med. Assn., D.C. Acad., Va. Vet. Med. Assn. and Sml. Animal Acad., Kenya Vet. Med. Assn., N.C. Vet. Med. Assn. and Sml. Animal Acad., Forsyth County Vet. Med. Assn., Women's Vet. Med. Assn. Democrat. Presbyterian. Clubs: Am. Women's, Kabete Riding, Pohick Valley Hunt. Home: Route 1 Box 354A Stuart VA 24171 Office: Boyce Holland Vet Services Route 1 Box 354A Stuart VA 24171

BOYCE, DOREEN ELIZABETH, educational foundation executive; b. Antofagasta, Chile, Apr. 20, 1934; d. George Edgar and Elsie Winifred Vaughan; B.A. with honors, Oxford (Eng.) U., 1956, M.A. with honors, 1960; Ph.D., U. Pitts., 1983; m. Alfred Warne Boyce, Aug. 11, 1956; children—Caroline Elizabeth, John Trevor Warne. Lectr. and tutor in econs. U. Witwatersrand, South Africa, 1960-62; provost and dean of faculty, prof. econs. Chatham Coll., Pitts., 1963-79; prof. econs., chmn. dept. econs. and mgmt. Hood Coll., Frederick, Md., 1979-82; exec. dir. Buhl Found., Pitts., 1982—; dir. Duquesne Light Co., Dollar Bank, FSB, Microbac Labs., Inc. Del. White House Conf. on Small Bus., 1980; mem. Gov.'s Conf. Small Bus., 1979-82; trustee Franklin and Marshall Coll., 1982—, Frick Edn. Commn., 1980—, Buhl Sci. Ctr., 1982—; mem. citizens sponsoring com. Allegheny Conf. Community Devel., 1982—; mem. Fed. Jud. Nominating Commn., 1977-79, Pa. Gov.'s Commn. on Financing of Higher Edn., 1983-85 bd. dirs. World Affairs Council, 1984—. Mem. Am. Econs. Assn., Exec. Women's Council, Am. Assn. Higher Edn. (mem. com. prof. devel. Council Founds.), Grantmakers of Western Pa. (pres.). Office: Four Gateway Center Room 1522 Pittsburgh PA 15222

BOYD, CATHERINE ROBERTSON, home economist; b. Shawnee, Okla., June 10, 1938; d. James Marvin and Cleo Rebecca (Snyder) Robertson; B.S., U. Ky., 1959, M.S., 1962; Ph.D., U. Ala., 1982; m. Leroy H. Boyd, Jan. 28, 1958; children—Susanne, Diane. Tchr. jr. and sr. high sch., Versailles, Ky., 1959-62; med. research asst. U. Ky. Med. Center, Lexington, 1962-63; prof. home econs. Miss. State U., 1969—, dir. for Miss., Make It Yourself with Wool Contest, 1972—. Mem. adv. council Oktibbeha County 4-H; vol. 4-H leader. Recipient Teaching award Miss. State U. Coll. Agr., 1981, 83. Mem. Am. Home Econs. Assn., Assn. Coll. Profs. Textiles and Clothing, Mid-South Ednl. Research Assn., Miss. Home Econs. Assn., Phi Upsilon Omicron, Omicron Nu, Kappa Delta Pi, Gamma Sigma Delta, Kappa Omicron Phi, Phi Delta Kappa. Baptist. Club: Miss. State U. Women's. Author 4-H bulletins. Home: 9 Oriole Dr Starkville MS 39759 Office: Drawer HE Miss State U Mississippi State MS 39762

BOYD, ELISE STEPHENS, rural health project administrator; b. Nashville, Sept. 21, 1930; d. Elbert Montgomery and Elise (Robin) Stephens; m. Herschel Livingston Boyd, Dec. 22, 1951; children—Patrick Stephens, David Stephens. Gen. acad. diploma Ward-Belmont Coll., Nashville, 1950, U. Chattanooga, 1951; B.S. in Human Services Mgmt., U. Tenn., 1976. Project dir. Jackson County Rural Health Project, Scottsboro, Ala., 1978—; sec. Marion County Speech and Hearing Bd. Dirs., South Pittsburg, Tenn., 1975-76, pres., 1976-78; bd. dirs. North Ala. Health Edn. and Resource Ctr., Huntsville, Ala., 1979-82; council mem. North Ala. Health Systems Agy., Madison, Ala., 1980-82; pres. Jackson County Home Health Adv. Bd., Scottsboro, 1980—; mem. interdisciplinary adv. council Sch. Nursing, U. Ala., Birmingham, 1983-84, Marshall-Jackson Mental Health Adv. Bd., Guntersville, Ala., 1980—. Vice pres. Care Assurance System for Aged and Homebound, Scottsboro, 1982-84; bd. stewards Citizens for Industry, Scottsboro, 1983-84. Mem. AAUW, Orgn. Active Women-Stevenson, Ala. Rural Health Assn. (sec. 1981-83, v.p. 1983-84), Nat. Assn. Community Health Ctrs. Nat. Rural Primary Care, Assn. Am. Rural Health Assn., Scottsboro/Jackson County C. of C. (bd. dirs. 1983-85), Stevenson County C. of C. (sec. 1982-84). Club: DAR (Scottsboro). Office: Jackson County Rural Health Project 506 Gregory St Scottsboro AL 35768

BOYD, JANET SCOTT, nursing school administrator, nursing education and nursing research consultant; b. Haverstraw, N.Y., July 21, 1921; d. Russel Thomas and Nora (Burke) S.; m. Robert David Boyd, Mar. 21, 1953; children—Robert Jr., Bruce Scott, Keith Ian. B.S.N., Case-Western Res., 1948; M.A., U. Chgo., 1952; Ph.D., U. Wis., 1976. Asst. prof. U. Wis., Madison, 1961-65, dept. head nursing, 1965-69; asst. exec. adminstr. Wis. Nurses Assn., Madison, 1972-75; dir. nursing sch. Eastern Mich. U., Ypsilanti, 1976—; bd. dirs. Midwest Alliance Nursing, Indpls., 1982-84; pres. Mich. Colls. Nursing, 1978-82; v.p. Mich. League Nursing, Detroit, 1978-84; chmn. legis. com. Mich. Nurses Assn., East Lansing, 1977-83. Office: Eastern Mich U Dept Nursing Baccalaureat Ypsilanti MI 48197

BOYD, JESSIE GEORGEAN, electrical contractor; b. Paintsville, Ky., Feb. 24, 1929; d. Scott Forrest and Stella Mae (McFadden) Moore; m. George Herman Boyd, Sept. 1, 1951; children—Anthony Joe, Terri Lynn, Timothy George (dec.). Student in Bus. Adminstrn., Mayo Bus. Coll., 1948-50; student Ashland Community Coll., 1975, 80. With sales dept. R.H. Hobbs dept. Store, Paintsville, 1946-48; bookkeeper Royal Crown Bottling Co., Paintsville, 1950-51; proof machine operator Second Nat. Bank, Paintsville, 1952-54; greenhouse co-owner, mgr. Boyd-Emmons Greenhouse, Ashland, Ky., 1973-76; sec.-treas. Boyd Assoc. Electric Contractors, Ashland, 1962-70, pres., 1970—. Leader Wilderness Road council Girl Scouts U.S.A., 1964-68; mem. council Ashland PTA, 1968-70; messenger So. Bapt. Conv., 1974-84; associational dir. Ky. Woman's Missionary Union, 1978-80, pres., 1976-78, internat. rep. to Africa New Enlargement Plan of Kenya, 1985-86, mem. exec. bd. 1982-85; coordinator for emergency relief ARC, Ashland, 1979—; publicity chmn. Student Ally United of Boyd County, Ashland, 1980—. Recipient Tchr. of Yr. award Rose Hill Bapt. Youth Dept., 1973. Mem. Nat. Electric Contractors Assn. (20 Yr. Good Standing award 1965). Republican. Avocations. guitar; boating; international travel; motorcycling. Home: 6123 State Route 5 Ashland KY 41101 Office: Boyd Associated Elec Contractors 7545 Midland Trail Ashland KY 41101

BOYD, KAREN JEAN, chemical engineer; b. Cedar Rapids, Iowa, Sept. 6, 1956; d. Frank Russell and Beverly Jean (Carlson) Bartos; B.S.Ch.E., U. Iowa, 1978; M.B.A., Govs. State U., 1982; m. Bruce A. Boyd, Sept. 4, 1982. Constrn. engr. Amoco Chem. Corp., Chocolate Bayou, Tex., 1979; regional project/process engr. Mobil Chem. Co., Kankakee, Ill., 1979-82; cons. K.B. Enterprises, 1982-83; sales adminstr. SCM-Glidden Coatings & Resins, San Francisco, 1983—; mem. Chem. Engring. Product Research Panel, 1980-81. Mem. Am. Inst. Chem. Engrs., Scholastic All-Am. Soc., U. Iowa Alumni Assn., Tau Beta Pi, Alpha Chi Sigma, Omicron Delta Kappa, Beta Sigma Phi. Author: Iowa and You, 1977. Home: 34634 Wells Ave Fremont CA 94536

BOYD, KATHLEEN ANN, airline executive; b. Denver, June 11, 1958; d. Darrel Wayne and Charlotte Maurine (Van Winkle) Boyd. Degrees in econs. and managerial studies Rice U., 1980. Purchasing analyst Tex. Internat. Airlines, Houston, 1980, purchasing agt., 1980-82, sr. purchasing agt., 1982; purchasing agt. Continental Airlines, Los Angeles, 1982-83, Houston, 1983-84, mgr. product planning, 1984—. Assoc. editor KRISIS II, III, IV, 1983-86. Publicist Houston chpt. Amnesty Internat., 1984-86. Arthur B. Cohn scholar Rice U., 1980. Mem. World Airline Entertainment Assn., Inflight Food Service Assn. Office: Continental Airlines 2929 Allen Pkwy Houston TX 77019

BOYD, LEONA JOHNSTON POTTER, former county welfare administrator; b. Creekside, Pa., Aug. 31, 1907; d. Joseph M. and Belle (McHenry) Johnston; grad. Ind. Normal Sch., 1927; student Las Vegas Normal U., summer 1933; courses Carnegie Inst. Tech. Sch. Social Work, summer 1945, U. Pitts. Grad. Sch. Social Work, 1956-57; m. Edgar D. Potter, July 16, 1932 (div.); m. 2d, Harold L. Boyd, Oct. 9, 1972. Tchr., Creekside Pub. Schs., 1927-30, Papago Indian Reservation, Sells, Ariz., 1931-33; caseworker, supr. Indiana County (Pa.) Bd. Assistance, 1934-54, exec. dir., 1954-68; ret., 1968; cons. assoc. Community Research Assocs., St. Paul; mem. bd. Lake Havasu Counseling Center Aux. Former mem. bd. dirs. Indiana County United Fund, Salvation Army, Indiana County Guidance Ctr., Armstrong-Indiana Mental Health Assn. Recipient award for community services Indiana County Bus. and Profl. Women's Club, 1965, Ind. Jaycees award for Disting. Service, 1966. Mem. Daus. Am. Colonists, Indiana County Tourist Promotion Bur. (hon. life), Am. Assn. Ret. Persons (chpt. historian Lake Havasu City), Sierra County (N.Mex.) Hist. Soc., Internat. Platform Assn., Sierra Vista Hosp. Aux. Lutheran. Club: Hot Springs Women's. Home: 507 N Foch St Truth or Consequences NM 87901

BOYD, LINDA CAPPS, writer; b. Mangum, Okla., Feb. 29, 1940; d. Travis B. and Virginia (Dorrill) Capps; m. William C. Boyd, June 15, 1963; children—William C. and Stanford Scott. B.S. in English and Edn., Tex. Tech. U., 1962; B.A. in Journalism, U. Houston, 1978. Cert. tchr., Tex. Tchr. pub. schs., Amarillo, Tex., 1962-63, Pasadena, Houston and Spring Branch, Tex. 1965-80; writer-trainee Houston Chronicle, 1981-82; freelance writer, contbr. numerous articles to popular mags., 1982—. Active Houston Symphony, Alley Guild Houston Theater, Rep. Women, Nat. Fedn. Rep. Women. Mem. Tex. State Tchrs. Assn., Women in Communications. Presbyterian. Home and Office: 3632 Ella Lee Ln Houston TX 77027

BOYD, MARY DEXTER, newspaper editor; b. Columbus, Ga., Feb. 5, 1913; d. Charles Amory and Lydia Cook (Folwell) Dexter; m. Francis William Boyd, Jr., Sept. 1, 1934 (dec. July 1972); children—Robert Alexander, Richard Dexter, Mary Frances Boyd Logback, Elizabeth Folwell Boyd James. Student Agnes Scott Coll., 1930-31; B.S., Kans. State U., 1934. Cert. tchr., Kans. Tchr., Kensington High Sch., Kans., 1934-35; asst. editor Jewell County Record, Mankato, Kans., 1940-72, editor, 1972—. Mem. Comml. Devel. Assn., Mankato, 1972—, Mankato Endowment Assn., 1972—, Housing Authority City of Mankato, 1975—, Jewell County Fair Bd., 1980—. Mem. Kans. Press Assn., Kans. Press Women, Omicron Nu, Kappa Alpha, Xo Chi Omega (v.p. 1932-33). Clubs: Modern Minerva (pres. 1939-40), Desire Tobey Sears, DAR, P.E.O.. Home: 405 S Center St Mankato KS 66956 Office: Jewell County Record 111 Main St Mankato KS 66956

BOYD, NANCY LOUISE, controller; b. Ottumwa, Iowa, Aug. 3, 1945; d. Paul Judson and Dorothy Agnes (Pritchard) B.; m. James Mueller, Mar. 1969 (div. 1969). B.S. in Secondary Edn., N.W. Mo. State U., 1967; postgrad. U. Iowa, 1973, Los Angeles Valley Coll., 1978. Cert. lifetime tchr., Mo. Tchr. English, pub. high sch., 1967-69; adminstrv. sec. Legal Aid and Defender Soc., Kansas City, Mo., 1970; employment cons. Hallmark Personnel, Denver, 1971-72; inventory control staff U. Iowa Press, Iowa City, 1972-73; accounts payable supr. Beren Corp., Denver, 1973-75; vocat. rehab. counselor Alcoholism Ctr. for Women, Los Angeles, 1976-77; office mgr./full charge bookkeeper J.J. & Co., Los Angeles, 1977-79; owner Boydco, Los Angeles, 1979-82; full charge bookkeeper, acct. Shirt Designs, Inc., Santa Monica, Calif., 1979; full charge bookkeeper acct. Marcal Sportswear, Los Angeles, 1979-80; controller, acct. Charles Towne Classics, Los Angeles, 1980-81; controller, acct. William Pearson Inc., Los Angeles, 1981-83; controller, chief acct. The Field Co., Los Angeles, 1983-84; acctg. mgr./controller Stevi Brooks, Inc., 1984-85. Co-chairwoman nat. task force NOW, 1975; bd. dirs. Van Ness Recovery House, Los Angeles, 1981-83, treas., 1982-83. Marcus Community High Sch. Tchrs.' scholar, 1963. Mem. Am. Mensa, Anti-Vivisection Soc., Animal Protection Inst., Cousteau Soc., Green Peace, Met. Museum Art, Smithsonian Instn., Calif. Arboretum Found., Pembroke Welsh Corgi Club So. Calif. (bd. dirs. 1985—), Welsh Corgi League, Kappa Delta Pi. Mem. Unity Ch. Author: Fractured Images, 1970; editor Tower yearbook, 1967, The Guardian, 1985—. Office: 1834 E 22d St Los Angeles CA 90058

BOYD, VIRGINIA ANN, savings and loan representative; b. Suffern, N.Y., Mar. 14, 1954; d. Thomas Alexander Boyd and Margaret (Herbell) Boyd Phillips. Student Roanoke Coll., 1972-74; B.A., Fla. State U., 1976. Account exec. Cobal Internat., N.Y.C., 1977-78; location research analyst A & P Tea Co., Montvale, N.J., 1978-81; locations analyst Chem. Bank, N.Y.C., 1981; market selection analyst Red Lobster Inns, Orlando, Fla., 1981-82; project coordinator Westway Service, Dallas, 1983; real estate devel. rep. Richardson Savs. & Loan (Tex.), 1984—. Tex. State Ednl. grantee U. Tex.-Dallas, 1984. Mem. Xi Theta Chi. Republican. Christian Scientist. Home: 12890 Noel Rd Apt 2088 Dallas TX 75230 Office: Richardson Saving & Loan 12700 Park Central Dr Dallas TX 75251

BOYER, ALICE ELIZABETH, temporary service company executive; b. Detroit, Mar. 24, 1946; d. John William and Lucille Constance (Jurkiewicz) Otrompke; m. David F. Boyer, Dec. 31, 1974 (div. Apr. 1985); 1 child, Stacey Lee. Legal sec., para legal Levenson, Disner, Ruby & Fruitman, Southfield, Mich., 1967-77; account exec. Matchmakers, Madison Heights, Mich., 1979; br. mgr. Remedy Temporary Service, Long Beach, Calif., 1979-81; pres., owner Temporary Specialists, Southfield, 1981—. Mem. Nat. Assn. Women Bus. Owners, Profl. Women in Sales, Adminstrv. Mgmt. Soc., Mich. Profl. Bus. Women's Network, Nat. Assn. Female Execs. Republican. Office: Temporary Specialists Inc 24901 Northwestern Hwy Suite 508 Southfield MI 48075

BOYER, ALTA ESSOM, preservationist, medical librarian; b. Lodi, N.Y., Oct. 18; d. Lewis Tunison and Emma Edith (Lott) Essom; B.A., William Smith Coll., 1936; student Syracuse U., 1960; M.L.S., SUNY, Geneseo, 1963; m. Charles H. Boyer, May 8, 1940; children—Charles C., Elizabeth A.; m. 2d, Charles A. Blohm, July 9, 1980. Chief library services Willard (N.Y.) Psychiat. Center, 1957-78; cons. S. Central Research Library Council, Ithaca, N.Y., 1974-78; pres. 20th Century Club, Ovid, N.Y., 1980-82; preservationist documents Pa. Hosp., Phila., 1980—; cons. med. library archives materials. Trustee Finger Lakes Library System, 1978—; bd. dirs. Seneca County Community Health Services Agy., 1981—, chmn. mental health com., 1985—; chmn. bd. trustees Regional Conf. Hist. Agys., 1984—. Mem. Lodi Hist. Soc. (pres. 1977-78), Med. Library Assn. N.Y. and Canada (mem. exec. bd. 1972-75), N.Y. Library Assn. (mem. exec. bd. 1969-71), N.Y. Fedn. Women's Clubs (pres. Seneca County 1982-84), William Smith Alumnae Assn. (mem. exec. council 1969-71), DeWitt Hist. Soc., Geneva Hist. Soc., N.Y. Preservation League, Historic Ithaca. Home: 8678 Watkins Glen Rd Lodi NY 14860 Office: 11514 Briar Forest Houston TX 77077

BOYER, EUNICE BEALL, sociology and anthropology educator, county official; b. Eureka, Ill., Mar. 28, 1918; d. J. Frank and Hazel (Van Skiver) Felter; m. Merle W. Boyer, Nov. 1, 1941; children—Judith, Frank, Charles. B.A., Eureka Coll., 1939; M.A., U. Chgo., 1941; M.A., U. Wis.-Milw., 1971, Ph.D., 1973. Asst. prof. to prof. sociology anthrpology Carthage Coll., Kenosha, Wis., 1958—; supr. County of Kenosha, Wis., 1980—, chmn. pub. welfare bd., 1982—. Contbr. articles to profl. jours. Mem. Kenosha Unified Sch. Bd., 1970-73; mem. Southeastern Wis. Planning Com. for Health Adminstrn., 1984-85. Mem. Am. Anthropol. Assn., Assn. Anthropology/Gerontology (program chmn. 1982-83), Midwest Sociol. Assn., Am. Sociol. Assn., AAUW. Democrat. Lutheran. Home: 6127 5th Ave Kenosha WI 53140 Office: Carthage Coll Alford Dr Kenosha WI 53141

BOYER, JANICE K., radiological services company executive; b. Rivesville, W.Va., Apr. 12, 1944; d. Elmer E. and Lena Virginia (LaValle) B.; m. Teddy

K. Tuttle, Aug. 1962 (div. 1963). Cert., Fairmont Gen. Hosp. Sch. Radiol. Technologist, 1966, Am. Soc. Radiol. Technologist, 1977, 78, student W.Va. U. Sch. Radiol. Technologist, 1966, U. Va., 1977. Cert. mgmt. radiographic environments, Eastman Kodak Co., 1978. Sr. staff technologist dept. radiology Arlington Hosp., Va., 1969-74; chief technologist, Alexandria Hosp., Va., 1974-77; cons. Health Physics Services, Potomac, Md., 1977-78; pres. B&C Radiographic Services, Inc., Woodbridge, Va., 1978—, Dominion X-Ray, Inc., Woodbridge, 1983—. Author, editor ednl. slide programs. Mem. Am. Registry Radiol. Tech., Am. Soc. Radiol. Tech., Soc. Photo-Optical Engr., U.S. C. of C., Prince William C. of C. Democrat. Methodist. Avocations: oil painting; racquetball; boating; walking. Office: Dominion X-Ray Inc 13536 Jeff Davis Hwy Woodbridge VA 22191

BOYER, LAURA MERCEDES, librarian; b. Madison, Ind., Aug. 3, 1934; d. Clyde C. and Dorcas H. (Willyard) Boyer. A.B., George Washington U., 1956; A.M., U. Denver, 1959; M.L.S., George Peabody U., 1961. Pub. sch. tchr., Kankakee, Ill., 1957-58; asst. circulation librarian U. Kans., Lawrence, 1961-63; asst. reference librarian U. of Pacific Library, Stockton, Calif., 1963-65, head reference dept., 1965-84, coordinator reference services, 1984—. Compiler of Play Anthologies Union List, 1976. Author article in profl. jour. Mem. Am. Soc. Info. Sci., ALA, Calif. Library Assn., AAUP, Nat. Assn. Female Execs., Nat. Assn. Vietnamese Am. Educators, Phi Beta Kappa, Kappa Delta Pi, Beta Phi Mu. Republican. Episcopalian. Home: 5650 Stratford Circle Apt 29 Stockton CA 95207 Office: U of Pacific Library Stockton CA 95211

BOYER, LILLIAN BUCKLEY, artist, educator; b. Paterson, N.J., Mar. 1, 1916; d. George and Adele (Roomy) Buckley; B.A. in Art Edn., U. Ky., 1975; m. Floyd E. Boyer, Jr., Sept. 7, 1935; children—Karen Boyer Lloyd. Field interviewer Survey Research Center, U. Mich., 1963-68; 20 regional one-woman shows; instr. art U. Ky., Lexington; Ky. reporter for Sunshine Artists mag., 1976-85. Crusade chmn. Am. Cancer Soc., Anaheim, Calif., 1958, Orange County, Calif., 1959; active PTA, 1950-62, hon. life mem. Recipient 56 awards for print-making, painting and sculpture. Mem. Lexington Arts Council, Ky. Citizens for the Arts, Lexington Art League (pres. 1976-80, 82-83, 84-86, dir., life mem.), Ky. Guild Artists and Craftsmen, U. Ky. Alumni Assn., Living Arts and Sci. Ctr., Friends of U.K. Art Mus., Nat. Mus. Women in Arts, JB. Speed Art Mus., Headley Whitney Mus. Methodist. Address: 969 Holly Springs Dr Lexington KY 40504

BOYKIN, FRANCES LEWIS, retired social worker; b. Boston; d. Joel Randolph and Frances Virginia (Kenney) Lewis; B.S., Simmons Coll., 1945, M.S., 1946; m. Herbert Charles Boykin, Jr., Dec. 23, 1951 (div. 1958). Caseworker, Family Service of Orange, Maplewood, N.J., 1946-47; child welfare worker Riverdale Children's Assn., N.Y.C., 1946-51; supr., casework coordinator Asso. Day Care Services of Greater Boston, 1952-53; caseworker, advancing to sr. caseworker Salvation Army-Family Service, N.Y.C., 1955-74; psychiat. research, 1957-62; field supr. for student unit Salvation Army Corps and Community Centers, N.Y.C., 1974-79; adj. asst. prof. N.Y. U. Sch. Social Work, 1977-79. Bd. dirs. Assn. Bronx Community Orgns., 1964-73, v.p., 1968-69, treas., 1970-73; bd. dirs. N.Y.C. region NCCJ, 1976—, mem. exec. com., 1977—; mem. Bronx advisory com. Urban League, 1966-69. Cert. social worker, N.Y. State. Mem. Nat. Assn. Social Workers, Register Clin. Social Workers, Acad. Cert. Social Workers, Internat. Conf. Social Work (unofcl. agy. del. 1964—). Home: 2235 Fifth Ave New York NY 10037 Office: 361 W 125th St New York NY 10027

BOYKIN, MARY JONES, nursing administrator; b. Columbia, S.C., Mar. 9, 1948; d. Jim Bob and Jessie Bell (Watts) Jones; m. Eddie Boykin, Jr., May 1, 1971; children—Ginger Renee, Darrell Timothy. A.Nursing, U. S.C., 1975; B.S.N., N.C. Central U., 1983. Nurses' asst. Richland Meml. Hosp., Columbia, S.C., 1966-67, lic. practical nurse, 1968-75; staff nurse Duke U. Med. Ctr., Durham, N.C., 1975-80, nursing supr., 1980-85, asst. dir. nursing, 1985—, career counselor intern, 1985. Selected Outstanding Woman of Achievement, YWCA, 1984. Mem. Nat. Soc. for Children and Adults with Autism, Am. Assn. Critical Care Nurses, Am. Mental Health Counselors Assn., Nat. Employment Counselors Assn., Nat. Vocat. Guidance Assn., Am. Assn. Counseling and Devel. Club: Durham Adoptable Family Support Group (v.p. 1983-85). Avocations: camping; reading; traveling; interior decorating. Home: 5802 Sandstone Dr Durham NC 27713

BOYKIN, NANCY GERTRUDE MERRITT, educational administrator, social worker; b. Washington; d. Matthew and Mary G. (White) Merritt; m. John Lovell (dec.); m. Ulysses Wilhelm Boykin, Apr. 17, 1965; 1 child, Taunya Lovell Banks. B.S., M.A., M.S.W., 1965, all Howard U.; Ph.D. in Ednl. Adminstrn., U. Mich., 1976. Cert. tchr., Mich.; cert. social worker. Employee relations counselor to chief of fin. Dept. Army, Washington; adminstrv. asst. to civilian aide to Sec. Def., Washington; policewoman, Washington; social worker Washington Dept. Pub. Welfare; adminstrv. asst. to dir. Active Community Teams, Inc., Detroit; dir. continuing edn. for girls' program Detroit Pub. Schs., 1966—; mem. adv. council Community Coll. of Air Force, 1984—; cons. U.S. Dept. Edn.; mem. Mich. Youth Adv. Commn., 1984—, Nat. Adv. Council on Extension and Continuing Edn., 1973-80. Author: A Multi-Disciplinary National Workshop on School Site Selection, Planning and Development, 1974; also articles. Mem. Mich. Bd. Examiners for Social Workers, 1978-84; chmn. orgn. com. Republican State Com., 1975-80; sec. 1st Rep. Dist., 1973-77. Recipient Leadership award Spirit of Detroit, 1979; Service award Wayne County Commn., 1979; award Pres.'s Nat. Adv. Commn., 1980. Mem. Profl. Women's Network, Nat. Assn. Supervision and Curriculum Devel., Detroit Orgn. Sch. Adminstrs., Nat. Assn. Black Sch. Adminstrs., Mich. Assn. Concerned with Sch.-Age Parents (founder; pres. 1971-73), Phi Delta Kappa. Home: 17224 Fairfield Ave Detroit MI 48221 Office: Detroit Pub Schs 2200 Ewald Circle Detroit MI 48238

BOYKIN, SHIRLEY JEAN, city official; b. Troy, Ala., Feb. 8, 1949; d. Robert D. and Lousie (Grider) Boykin; B.A. in Indsl. Psychology, U. Central Fla., Orlando, 1976; M.S. in Mgmt., Rollins Coll., Winter Park, Fla., 1981; children—Stephen, Keith. Personnel asst. United Parcel Service, Atlanta, 1970; with mktg. dept. Am. Can Co., Cin., 1974; personal banker II, Sun 1st Nat. Bank, Orlando, 1977-79; asst. v.p. mortgage lending, community reinvestment coordinator, loan officer AmeriFirst Fed. Savs. and Loan Assn., Orlando, 1979-81; mgr. Orlando Minority Bus. Devel. Ctr., U.S. Dept. Commerce, 1981-85; constrn. project coordinator Orlando Utilities Commn., 1985—; mem. fin. adv. com. Valencia Community Coll., 1982, mem. bus. and industry adv. bd., 1985—, mem. adj. faculty bus., 1985—. Pres. bd. dirs. Met. Orlando Urban League, 1981-83; bd. dirs. United Way Orange County, 1981—, mem. budget rev. team, 1977—; mem. Statewide Black Coalition, 1979-82; mem. community housing resource bd., fair housing div. HUD, 1980-81; regional sec. Nat. Urban League, 1981-83; mem. regional coordinating council Vocat. Edn., Adult Gen. Edn. and Community Instructional Services. Recipient Community Service award United Way Orange County, 1977-81, Citizen of Yr. award, 1981. Mem. Nat. Assn. Female Execs., Am. Bus. Women's Assn., NAACP, Orlando Area C. of C. Alpha Kappa Alpha. Home: 2101 Good Homes Rd Orlando FL 32818 also PO Box 580328 Orlando FL 32858-0328 Office: Orlando Utilities Commn Stanton Energy Ctr PO Box 3163 Orlando FL 32802

BOYKINS-MONTGOMERY, BRENDA KAY, broadcaster; b. Chgo., Nov. 30, 1956; d. Clarence James Boykins and Mary Kathryn (Rickman) Boykins Farlow; m. Sylvester Montgomery, Jr., Oct. 27, 1979; 1 child, Nathan. A.B., L.A.S., U. Ill., 1978. Traffic reporter Lee Communications, Chgo., 1981-85; broadcaster WGCI AM/FM, Chgo., 1982—. Bd. dirs. Taproots, Chgo., 1985-87. Named Up and Coming Bus. and Profl. Woman, Dollars and Sense Mag., Chgo., 1985. Mem. League Black Women, Nat. Assn. Female Execs., Black Pub. Relations Soc., U. Ill. Alumni Assn., Alpha Kappa Alpha. African Methodist Episcopal. Avocations: cooking; sports; trivia games. Home: 1444 S Homan Ave Chicago IL 60623 Office: WGCI AM/FM Radio 6 N Michigan Ave Chicago IL 60602

BOYLAN, VIRGINIA WALKER, lawyer; b. Washington, Dec. 29, 1941; d. Robert D. and Dorothy Elizabeth (Compton) Walker; B.A., Am. U., 1964; J.D., Cath. U. Am., 1979; m. James George Boylan, May 28, 1966; 1 dau., Kaithlin Janine. Admitted to Va. bar, 1979; resource specialist LWV of U.S., 1968-71; legis. asst. to Rep. John Melcher, 1971-76; staff atty. Select Com. on Indian Affairs, U.S. Senate, Washington, 1979—. Trustee, Nat. Reyes Syndrome Found., 1980—. Democrat. Office: 838 Hart Senate Office Bldg Washington DC 20510

BOYLE, BARBARA DORMAN (MRS. KEVIN BOYLE), lawyer; b. N.Y.C., Aug. 11, 1935; d. William and Edith Dorman (Kleiman) Dorman; B.A. with honors, U. Calif., Berkeley, 1957; J.D., UCLA, 1960; m. Kevin Boyle, Nov. 26, 1960; children—David Eric, Paul Coleman. Admitted to Calif. bar, 1961, N.Y. bar, 1964, U.S. Supreme Ct. bar, 1973; atty. Am. Internat. Pictures, Los Angeles, N.Y.C., 1960-65, corp. asst. sec., 1962-65; partner Calif., Cohen & Boyle, Hollywood, 1967-74; exec. v.p. New World Pictures, Inc., 1974-82; sr. v.p. prodn. Orion Pictures Corp., 1982-85; exec. v.p. prodn. RKO Pictures, 1986—; dir. Murakami-Wolf Prodns., Inc., Fafinta, Inc., Los Angeles. Mem. vol. com. Marquez Elem. Sch., Pacific Palisades, Calif., 1970-73, chmn. resource com., 1972-73; legal adv. Park Century Sch., Santa Monica, Calif., 1973-74; mem. entertainment adv. com. UCLA Law Sch., 1976—, co-chairperson, 1979-81. Mem. N.Y., Calif., Hollywood, Los Angeles bar assns., Women in Film (charter mem., pres. 1977-78), Acad. Motion Picture Arts and Scis. Contbr. articles to profl. jours. Home: 557 Spoleto Dr Pacific Palisades CA 90272 Office: 1900 Ave of Stars Los Angeles CA 90067

BOYLE, CAROLYN MOORE, public relations practitioner, marketing communications manager; b. Los Angeles, Jan. 29, 1937; d. Cory Orlando Moore and Violet (Brennan) Baldock; m. Robert J. Ruppelt, Oct. 8, 1954 (div. Aug. 1964); children—Cory Robert, Traci Lynn; m. 2d, Jerry Ray Boyle, June 1, 1970 (div. 1975). A.A., Orange Coast Coll., 1966; B.A., Calif. State U.-Fullerton, 1970; student U. Calif.-Irvine, 1970-71. Program coordinator Newport Beach Cablevision (Calif.), 1968-70; pub. relations dir. Fish Communications Co., Newport Beach, 1970-74; mktg. rep. Dow Pharm. div. Dow Chem. Co., Orange County, Calif., 1974-77, Las Vegas, Nev., 1980-81; product publicity mgr. Dow Agrl. Products div. Dow Chem. Co., Midland, Mich., 1977-80; mgr. mktg. communications Dowell Fluid Services Region div. Dow Chem. Co. Houston, 1981-84; mktg. communications adminstr. Swedlow, Inc., Garden Grove, Calif., 1984-85; mktg. communications cons., 1985—; guest lectr. Calif. State U., Long Beach, 1970; seminar coordinator U. Calif., Irvine, 1972; mem. Western White House Press Corps, 1972; pub. relations cons. BASF Wyandotte, Phila., 1981-82. Author: Agricultural Public Relations/Publicity, 1981. Editor Big Mean AG Machine (internal mag.), 1977. Contbr. numerous articles to trade publs. Contbg. editor Dowell Mktg. Newsletter, 1983. Creator/designer Novahistine DMX Trial Size nat. mktg. program, 1977. Com. mem. Dow Employees for Polit. Action, Midland, Mich., 1978-80; bd. dirs. Dowell Employees for Polit. Action Com., Houston, 1983-84. Named Salesman of Yr. Pharm. div. Dow Chem. Co., 1975; scholar World Campus Afloat (U. Seven Seas), 1966-67. Mem. Pub. Relations Soc. Am. (cert.), Soc. Petroleum Engrs., Internat. Assn. Bus. Communicators. Episcopalian. Recipient first rights to televise President Nixon in Western White House. Home: 16488 Cabrillo Dr Victorville CA 92392 Office: 4981 Pearce St Suite B Huntington Beach CA 92649

BOYLE, KATHLEEN FRANCES, cable television executive; b. Norfolk, Va., Oct. 28, 1951; d. Thomas Henry and Mary Louise (Poole) Boyle, Jr.; B.F.A., Va. Commonwealth U., 1974; M.B.A., Old Dominion U., 1980. Asst. product mgr. Dow-Corning Co., Norfolk, 1980-81; sr. cons. Norfolk Bus. Devel. Ctr., 1982-83; research mgr. Telecable, Norfolk, 1983—. Mem. Cable TV Adminstrn. and Mktg. Soc., Am. Mktg. Assn. (past dir. Norfolk). Home: 2201 Waters Pointe Pl Virginia Beach CA 23455 Office: Telecable 740 Duke St Norfolk VA 23501

BOYLE, KAY, writer; b. St. Paul, Feb. 19, 1902; d. Howard Peterson and Katherine (Evans) Boyle; student Ohio Mechanics Inst., 1917-19; Litt.D. (hon.), Columbia U., 1971, So. Ill. U., 1982; L.H.D. (hon.), Skidmore Coll., 1977, Bowling Green State U., 1986; m. Richard Brault, June 24, 1922 (div.); m. 2d, Laurence Vail, Apr. 2, 1931 (div.); children—Sharon Walsh, Apple-Joan, Kathe, Clover, Faith Carson, Ian Savin; m. 3d, Baron Joseph von Franckenstein, Feb. 20, 1943 (dec. 1963). Mem. faculty San Francisco State U. Recipient O. Henry Meml. prize, 1936, 1941; San Francisco Art Commn. award, 1978. Guggenheim fellow 1934, 61; Nat. Endowment for Arts sr. citizen grantee, 1980. Mem. Am. Acad. Arts and Letters. Author: (poems) A Glad Day 1958; (short stories), Wedding Day 1930; (novels) Plagued by the Nightingale, 1931; Year Before Last 1932; Gentlemen, I Address You Privately, 1933; My Next Bride, 1934; Death of a Man (novel), 1936; The White Horses of Vienna (short stores), 1937; Monday Night (novel), 1938; The Crazy Hunter (short novels), 1940; Primer for Combat (novel), 1942; Avalanche (novel), 1943, American Citizen (poems), 1944; A Frenchman Must Die (novel), 1945; Thirty Stories, 1946; 1939 (novel), 1947; His Human Majesty (novel), 1949; The Smoking Mountain (novel), 1951; The Seagull on the Step (novel), 1955; Three Short Novels, 1958; The Youngest Camel (children's book), 1959; Generation without Farewell, 1960; Collected Poems, 1962; Breaking the Silence (essay) 1962; Nothing Ever Breaks Except the Heart (short stories), 1966; Pinky, the Cat (children's book), 1967; Being Geniuses Together (memoir), 1968; Pinky in Persia (children's book), 1968; Testament For My Students (poems), 1970; This Is Not a Letter (poems), 1985; The Long Walk at San Francisco State (essays), 1970; Words That Must Somehow Be Said (essays), 1985; The Underground Woman (novel), 1975; Fifty Stories, 1980; translator; Devil in the Flesh (Raymond Radiguet), 1931; Don Juan (Joseph Delteil), 1932; Babylon (RenéCrevel), 1984; editor: The Autobiography of Emanuel Carnevali, 1967; Contbr. short stories to mags. Address: care Watkins/Loomis Agy 150 E 35th St New York NY 10016

BOYLE, MARY LOU, business executive; b. Youngstown, Ohio, May 24, 1935; d. Harold G. and Mary Helen (Shook) Morris; m. Bryan Joseph Boyle, May 4, 1957; children—Bryan Jr., J. Thomas, Jamie L. Student Youngstown Coll., 1954, Miami-U.-Oxford, Ohio, 1953-54, Rollins Coll., 1964, U. Central Fla., 1981, 84. Account exec. WLOF Radio, Orlando, Fla., 1978-80, WESH-TV, Winter Park, Fla., 1980-82; pres. Boyle Advt., Inc., Orlando, 1982—; pres., chief exec. officer We're Cooking Now, Inc., Winter Park 1984—. Creator, exec. producer tv series, We're Cooking Now, 1984, 85; pub. book: We're Cooking Now, Vol. 1, 1984. Mem. Orlando Area Ad Fedn. Republican. Episcopalian. Avocations: writing; walking. Office: We're Cooking Now Inc 1140 Solana Ave Winter Park FL 32789

BOYLE, PATRICIA JEAN, judge; student U. Mich., 1955-57; B.A., Wayne State U., 1963, J.D., 1963. Admitted to Mich. bar; practice law with Kenneth Davies, Detroit, 1963; law clk. to U.S. Dist. judge, 1963-64; asst. U.S. atty., Detroit, 1964-68; asst. pros. atty. Wayne County, dir. research, tng. and appeals, Detroit, 1969-74; judge Recorders Ct. Detroit, 1976-78; judge U.S. Dist. Ct. Eastern Dist. Mich., Detroit, 1978-83; justice Mich. Supreme Ct., 1983—. Active Women's Rape Crisis Task Force, Vols. of Am. Named Feminist of Year, Detroit chpt. NOW, 1978; recipient Outstanding Achievement award Pros. Attys. Assn. Mich., 1978; Spirit of Detroit award Detroit City Council, 1978. Mem. Women Lawyers Assn. Mich., Fed. Bar Assn., Mich. Bar Assn., Detroit Bar Assn., Wayne State U. Law Alumni Assn. (Disting. Alumni award 1979). Office: Mich Supreme Ct 1425 Lafayette Bldg Detroit MI 48226

BOYLE, RENEE KENT, cultural organization executive, translator; b. Cairo, Egypt, July 4, 1926; came to U.S., 1946; d. Maurice Colin and Victoria Smith; m. John E. Whiteford Boyle, Feb. 2, 1950; children—Vanessa Whiteford Boyle Wayne, Christopher, Andrea Boyle Heller, Mara Boyle DeMarco. Diploma St. Clare's Coll., Heliopolis, Egypt, 1944; postgrad. Rice U., 1947-48, Santa Monica Coll., 1950-51. Dep. dir. Am. Friends of Middle East, Tehran, Iran, 1959-62, Les Amis Americains du Maghreb, Tunis, Tunisia, 1962-64; v.p. Fgn. Services Research Inst., Washington, 1964—; v.p. Whiteford Internat. Enterprise, Villars sur Ollon, Switzerland, 1967-74. Editor: Beyond the Present Prospect, 1978; The Indra Web, 1982; Graffiti on the Wall of Time, 1982. Mem. Dem. Nat. Com., Washington, 1982—. Mem. Ams. for Dem. Action, People for Ethical Treatment of Animals, Sierra Club. Unitarian. Avocation: cordon bleu cooking. Home: 2718 Unicorn Ln NW Washington DC 20015 Office: Fgn Services Research Inst Box 6317 Washington DC 20015

BOZARTH, MARIA WEEKS, real estate broker; b. Roanoke, Va., Apr. 7, 1944; d. Randall Logan and Vera Virginia (Tyree) Jones; m. David Ronald Bozarth, Dec. 10, 1977 (div. 1983); children—Daniel James, Christopher David, Richard Kirby. B.A., Mitchell Coll., 1964; student Rutgers U., 1974-75. Sales assoc. Dee Realty, Northfield, N.J., 1972-77; broker, pres. Weeks MacMurray Inc., Pleasantville, N.J., 1977—; appraiser Nat. Community, Linwood, N.J., 1978-80; sales dir. Iles Farm, Linwood, N.J., 1985—; cons. Atlantic City and County Housing Study, Bd. Realtors, Absecon, N.J., 1982. Author: Mirrors, 1981. Chmn. fund raising March of Dimes, Atlantic City, N.J., 1982-84. Named Sales Assoc. of Yr., Dee Inc., Northfield, 1973, 74, 75, 76. Mem. Nat. Bd. Realtors, Nat. Fin. Assn. Comptrollers (exec. dir. 1985, dir. revenue planning and control 1985-86), Internat. Orgn. Real Estate Appraisers (sr.), Atlantic County Bd. Realtors (bicentennial com. 1976, outstanding sales award 1973). Republican. Methodist. Avocations: travel; writing; golf; teen counseling. Home: 1105 Furman Dr RD 1 Linwood NJ 08221 Office: Weeks MacMurray Inc RD 2 Box 49 Pleasantville NJ 08232

BOZEMAN, DOROTHY WOODARD, day care administrator, owner; b. Bamberg, S.C., Dec. 22, 1923; d. Willie Leon and Maude Agnes (Kinsey) Woodard; m. Larence Rigdon Bozeman, Apr. 2, 1942; 1 child, Larence Rigdon Jr. Student Tampa Bus. Coll., Fla., 1952-53. Acct., Lindsay, Squire & Everett, Greensboro, N.C., 1958-60; bookkeeper United Fund, Greensboro, 1961-62; unit buying control office, sportswear dept. Sears, Roebuck & Co., Greensboro and Concord, N.C., 1962-72; pres. Dorothy W. Bozeman Inc., doing bus. as Wonderworld Day Sch., Salisbury, N.C., 1973—. Republican. Baptist. Office: Wonderworld Day Sch 305 Link Ave Salisbury NC 28144

BOZONE, BILLIE RAE, librarian; b. Norphlet, Ark., Oct. 7, 1935; d. Guy Samuel and Vera (Jones) B. B.S. in Library Sci. Miss. State Coll. for Women, 1957; M.A., George Peabody Coll. for Tchrs., 1958. Asst. ref. librarian Miss. State U., State College, 1958-61, serials librarian, 1961-63; asst. ref. librarian U. Ill. at Urbana, 1963-65; asst. librarian New Eng. Mut. Life Ins. Co., Boston, 1965-67; sr. ref. librarian U. Mass., Amherst, 1967-68; head circulation dept. Smith Coll., Northampton, Mass., 1968-69, asst. librarian, 1969-71, coll. librarian, 1971—; Bd. dirs. Hampshire Inter-library Center, Amherst, 1971—; mem. exec. com. NELINET, 1977-79; chmn. Five Coll. Librarians Council, 1980-82. Mem. ALA, Assn. Coll. and Research Libraries, Alpha Beta Alpha, Alpha Psi Omega. Home: 20 S Whitney St Amherst MA 01002 Office: Smith Coll Library Northampton MA 01063

BRAAS-WARREN, PATRICIA LEE, insurance company manager; b. Chgo., Sept. 13, 1958; d. Ronald Norman and Doris Marie (Jones) B.; m. Michael A. Warren, Apr. 26, 1986. B.S. in Acctg., Eastern Ill. U., 1979. Internal auditor State Farm Ins. Cos., Bloomington, Ill., 1979-82, acct. II, Dallas, 1982-85, monthly payment plan supt., 1985—; office mgr. Mike Warren-State Farm Ins. Agy., Dallas, 1985—. Chmn., mem. com. United Way of Met. Dallas, 1983—; com. mem. Wadley Blood Ctr., Dallas, 1985. Mem. Nat. Assn. Female Execs. Methodist. Avocations: landscaping; photography; travel. Office: State Farm Ins Cos 17301 Preston Rd Dallas TX 75240

BRABANT, SARAH CALLAWAY, sociologist, educator; b. LaGrange, Ga., Nov. 18, 1932; d. Enoch and Jennie Louisa (Crowell) Callaway; student Newcomb Coll., 1950-52, Auburn U., 1952-53; B.S., Memphis State U., 1967, M.A., 1968; Ph.D., U. Ga., 1973; m. Wilmer Everett Mac Nair, Aug. 14, 1973; children by previous marriage—Jennie Crowell, Enoch Callaway, Anne Delebart. Instr. sociology Memphis State U., 1968-70; vis. asst. prof. anthropology La. State U., summers 1973, 74; asst. prof. sociology U. Southwestern La., Lafayette, 1973-77, assoc. prof., 1977-83, prof., 1983—. Pres. Lafayette Mayor's Commn. on Needs of Women, 1977-79; bd. dirs. United Christian Outreach; pres. Faith House, 1982-83. Recipient Am. Personnel and Guidance Assn. Research award, 1977; Martin Luther King Humanitarian Service award Lafayette Council on Human Relations, 1978; Disting. Prof. award U. Southwestern La. Found., 1980, vol. activist award Acadiana, 1985; Blue Key Alumni Faculty Excellence award, 1986. Mem. Mid-South Sociol. Assn. (v.p. 1976-77), So. Sociol. Soc., Southwestern Sociol. Assn., Am. Sociol. Assn., AAUP, AAUW. Democrat. Episcopalian (vestry 1984—). Club: Jr. League of Lafayette. Co-editor Sociological Spectrum. Contbr. articles to profl. jours. Home: 149 Memory Ln Lafayette LA 70506 Office: PO Box 40198 University Southwestern Louisiana Lafayette LA 70504

BRABEC, BARBARA ANN, writer, publisher; b. Buckley, Ill., Mar. 5, 1937; d. William Jonas and Marcella Eliza (Williams) Schaumburg; m. Harry Joseph Brabec, Aug. 26, 1961. Student pub. schs., Buckley. Adminstrv. asst. Investment Guide Advt., Inc., Chgo., 1962-65; pub. Artisan Crafts mag., Reeds Spring, Mo., 1971-76; pub., gen. mgr. Countryside Books, Barrington, Ill., 1979-81; owner Artisan Crafts, Springfield, Mo., 1981—, Barbara Brabec Prodns., Naperville, Ill., 1984—. Author: Creative Cash, 1979, 81; Home-Made Money, 1984; pub. newsletter Nat. Home Bus. Report (formerly Sharing Barbara's Mail), 1981. Mem. Am. Soc. Journalists and Authors, Soc. Craft Designers, Nat. Alliance Homebased Businesswomen, Nat. Writers' Club. Home and Office: PO Box 2137 Naperville IL 60566

BRACE, FLORENCE HILGERMANN, retired librarian, former copywriter; b. Milw., Aug. 4, 1914; d. George and Mary Jane (Higgins) Hilgermann; m. Sears Webster Brace, Nov. 30, 1940 (div. 1950). Student U. Minn., 1932-36, 1953, U. Houston, 1968-70, Gulf Park Jr. Coll., Gulfport, Miss. Copywriter, Dayton's Mpls., 1937-40; sr. fashion copywriter, promotion adviser Stix, Baer & Fuller, St. Louis, 1943-48; mgr. advt. and pub. relations Mindlin's Fashion Store, Kansas City, Mo., 1948-50; sr. fashion copywriter Dayton's Mpls., 1951-59; librarian Friendswood Devel. Co. subsidiary Exxon Co., Houston, 1981—. Past bd. dirs., fundraiser Women's Advt. Clubs, St. Louis, Mpls., and Kansas City, Mo., past vol. fundraiser for various charities, Cuernavaca, Mex.; past vol. ARC. Mem. Tex. Assn. Realtors, DAR, Nat. Assn. Female Execs. Delta Gamma. Republican. Episcopalian. Clubs: University; Yanke Women's Service (Edmonton, Alta., Can.); Mpls. Women's. Home: 361 N Post Oak Ln Apt 336 Houston TX 77024

BRACE, SHAE, financial planner; b. Flat River, Mo., June 25, 1930; d. Walter H. and Ruth (McClenahan) Adkins; B.S., Wayne State U., 1975; children—Michael Allen, Kevin James, Mark William. X-ray technician, Warren, Mich., 1959-60; asst. to purchasing agt. Rexair, Inc., 1960-62; with programming dept. WWJ-AM/FM/TV, Detroit, 1963-71; tech. writer/office mgr. Communico, Inc., Warren, Mich., 1971-75; asst. to mgmt. research cons. Wayne County Intermediate Sch. Dist., Wayne, Mich., 1975-77; sales asst. Mandey, Bennett, McDonald & Co., Detroit, 1977-79; account exec. First of Mich. Corp., Grosse Pointe, 1979-82; regional mgr. Mass. Fin. Services of Boston, 1982-85; mgr. Korn, Womack, Stern & Assocs., 1985—. Vol., James Brickley's campaign for Detroit council, 1965, Roman S. Gribbs campaign for Detroit mayor, 1970, Ronald Reagan's campaign for Pres., 1979-80. Recipient Service award Channel 56 Auction, 1980, 81. Mem. Women's Ad Club, Women's Econ. Club, Parapsychology Soc. Internat., Econ. Club Detroit. Republican. Roman Catholic. Clubs: Hillcrest Country, Vic Tanney InterNat., Peachtree Racquet. Feature writer Update Mag., 1974-76; producer, writer, hostess Mich. Money Monitors, Grosse Pointe Cable TV, 1981-82. Home: 453 Saint Clair St Grosse Pointe MI 48230 Office: 17854 Maumee Grosse Pointe MI 48230

BRACIALE, VIVIAN LAM, immunologist; b. N.Y.C., June 5, 1948; d. Wing Ching and Wai Ching (Li) Lam; A.B. (N.Y. State Regent scholar), Cornell U., 1969; Ph.D., U. Pa., 1973; m. Thomas J. Braciale Jr., Aug. 5, 1972; children—Kara, Michael Stephen, Laura. Postdoctoral fellow U. Pa., Phila., 1974-75, Washington U. Med. Sch., St. Louis, 1975-76, research instr. immunology, 1978-83, research asst. prof. pathology, 1983—; NIH Research Service awardee, vis. fellow Australian Nat. U., Canberra, 1976-78; mem. clin. scis. study sect. NIH, 1985—. Mem. Am. Assn. Immunologists, Am. Diabetes Assn. Lutheran. Contbr. articles in immunology to profl. jours. Office: Washington University Medical School Dept Pathology 660 S Euclid St Louis MO 63110

BRACK, RITA MACDONALD, state legislator, educator, counselor; b. Roxbury, Mass., May 15, 1918; d. Daniel Joseph and Mary Ellen (O'Brien) MacDonald; B.S. in Edn., Boston State Coll., 1939; M.Ed., Rivier Coll., Nashua, N.H., 1966; Ed.D., Nova U., 1978; m. John Joseph Brack, Oct. 4, 1942; children—Joan R. Brack Asbury, Lynda M., Susan T., John J., Judith A. (dec.), Lisa Brack Dougherty, Anne M., Martha, Maura. Assoc. prof. N.H. Coll. Acctg. and Commerce, Manchester, 1963-68; prof. edn., dir. counseling and placement Notre Dame Coll., Manchester, 1968—; mem. N.H. Ho. of Reps., 1976—; chmn. N.H. Coll. and Univ. Council Placement Dirs. Com., 1973-75; v.p. New Eng. Assn. Sch., Coll. and Univ. Staffing; vice chmn. New Eng. Bd. Higher Edn., 1980—; mem. profl. standards bd. N.H. Dept. Edn.; mem. 50th ann. com. Eastern Coll. Personnel Officers. N.H. coordinator Women in Community Service; organizer, adviser Manchester Hot Line; rep. to N.H. Gen. Ct.; mem. Stop and Shop Consumer Bd.; bd. Incorporators, trustee Cath. Med. Center, Manchester, Mental Health Center; pres. Sacred Heart Hosp. Assocs., 1972-75; vice-chmn. bd. trustees Community Correctional Center, Manchester; mem. Gov. N.H. Commn. Pub. Edn.; del. N.H. Dem. Com., 1972, gen. chmn. conv., 1974; mem. Manchester Sch. Bd., 1976—; mem. Manchester Charter Revision Commn., 1981. Recipient various certificates of recognition; Woman of Achievement award Manchester chpt. Bus. and Profl.

Women, 1979. Mem. Am. Personnel and Guidance Assn., AAUP, Women in Community Service. Address: 60 Hubbard St Manchester NH 03104 Office: 2321 Elm St Manchester NH 03104

BRACKEN, ELIZABETH ANN, newspaper executive; b. Yonkers, N.Y., Dec. 31, 1952; d. Edward Francis and Josephine Augusta (Pfaff) B.; m. Gregory Ralph Albanese, Aug. 3, 1975 (div.). B.A., Coll. New Rochelle, 1974. Educator, Yonkers Pub. Sch. System (N.Y.), 1975; promotion coordinator Gannett Westchester Rockland Newspapers, White Plains, N.Y., 1976-79; community relations dir., 1979-83, v.p. promotion, 1983—. Exec. bd. Coll. Careers Westchester, Westchester County, 1979—; bd. dirs. United Way Westchester, 1984—, Jr. Achievement Westchester, 1980—; v.p. Lend-a-Hand, Inc., White Plains, 1982—. Named Miss Westchester County, 1974, Miss Rockland County, 1973, Miss Bergen County, 1974, Miss N.J., 1974-75. Mem. Internat. Newspaper Promotions Assn., Women in Communications (chpt. pres. 1984-85), Pub. Relations Soc. Am. (chairperson 1980—), Advt. Club Westchester. Republican. Roman Catholic. Home: 353 Country Club Ln Pomona NY 10970 Office: Westchester Rockland Newspapers 1 Gannett Dr White Plains NY 10604

BRACKEN, KATHLEEN ANN, nurse; b. Chgo., Mar. 14, 1947; d. Thomas James and Catherine Anastasia (Cowal) B.; R.N., CCRN, Little Company of Mary Hosp., Evergreen Park, Ill., 1968; B.S.N., Lewis U., 1984. Mem. staff Little Company of Mary Hosp., Evergreen Park, 1968-69, 71—, supr. ICUs, 1976-79, dir. ICUs, 1979—; staff nurse coronary care unit Little Co. of Mary Hosp., Torrence, Calif., 1969-70; staff nurse Chgo. Lying-In Clinic, U. Chgo., 1970-71; instr.-trainer cardiopulmonary resuscitation; bd. dirs., mem. CPR tng. com., chmn. nursing cardiovascular com. South Cook Heart Assn., 1977-83, recipient Meritorious Service award, 1979, 81, 82, 83, 84, 85. Mem. Am. Nurses Assn., Council on Nursing Adminstrn., Chgo. Heart Assn., Assn. for Advancement Med. Instrumentation, Am. Assn. Critical Care Nurses (pres. Southside Chgo. Area chpt. 1983-84, rec. sec. 1984-85), Am. Heart Assn. (cardiovascular nursing council), Ill. Assn. Nursing Execs., Delta Epsilon Sigma, Sigma Theta Tau. Home: 10321 S Campbell Ave Chicago IL 60655 Office: 2800 W 95th St Evergreen Park IL 60642

BRACKEN, PEG, author; b. Filer, Idaho, Feb. 25, 1918; d. John Lewis and Ruth (McQuesten) Bracken; A.B., Antioch Coll., 1940; m. Parker Edwards. Mar. 17, 1966; 1 dau., Johanna Kathleen. Author: The I Hate to Cook Book, 1960; The I Hate to Housekeep Book, 1962; I Try to Behave Myself, 1963; Peg Bracken's Appendix to The I Hate to Cook Book, 1966; I Didn't Come Here to Argue, 1969; But I Wouldn't Have Missed It for the World, 1973; The I Hate to Cook Almanack-A Book of Days, 1976; A Window Over the Sink, 1981. Mem. AFTRA, Screen Actors Guild, Authors Guild, PEN. Address: 25 Kahana Pl Lahaina HI 96761

BRACKSHAW, SUSAN LEE, lawyer; b. Arlington, Mass., Dec. 5, 1949; d. Sarah Elizabeth (Montgomery) Bacon; m. Thomas Phillip Brackshaw, Aug. 11, 1973 (div.). B.A., U. Mass., 1972; postgrad. Smith Coll., 1972; J.D. (Mooer's trophy), Am. U., 1982. Bar: D.C. 1982, U.S. Dist. Ct. D.C. 1983, U.S. Ct. Appeals (D.C. cir.) 1983, U.S. Ct. Appeals (fed. cir.) 1983, U.S. Ct. Mil. Appeals 1983. Cert. tchr., N.J. Tchr. English, Scotch Plains-Fanwood (N.J.) Pub. Schs., 1972-78; adj. prof. Edward Williams Coll., Fairleigh Dickinson U., Hackensack, N.J., 1974-78; assoc. Webster & Fredrickson, Washington, 1982—. Editor Western Mass. English Council Jour., 1971-72. Mem. D.C. Bar Assn., ABA, Assn. Trial Lawyers Am., Bar Assn. D.C. Democrat. Office: Webster & Fredrickson 1522 K St NW Suite 1030 Washington DC 20005

BRADBERRY, PEGGY BROWN, automobile custom accessory business executive; b. Monroe, Ga., Apr. 23, 1933; d. John Harry and Sally May (Thomas) Brown; m. Bobby Gene Criswell, Sept. 12, 1954 (div. 1979); m. Donald Luther Bradberry, Dec. 11, 1980 (dec. 1982). Student U. Ga., 1980. With acctg. dept. Walton Mill, Inc., Monroe, 1950-80; real estate agent Betty Camp Realty, Monroe, 1979-80; owner, pres. AAA T-Tops, Inc., Tucker, Ga., 1980—. Democrat. Baptist. 4466 Rowland Ct Stone Mountain GA 30083 Office: AAA T-Tops Inc 3443 Lawrenceville St Tucker GA 30084

BRADBURY, KIMBER LE, veterinarian; b. El Paso, Tex., Dec. 16, 1957; d. Charles Lee and Bobby (Hurley) Johnson; m. Thomas James Bradbury, Dec. 31, 1977; 1 dau., Kristin Lee. Student La. State U., 1974-77; D.V.M., U. Tenn., 1981. Lic. veterinarian, Tenn. Endocrinology research cons. U. Tenn., Knoxville, 1979, post-doctoral research fellow microbiology, 1981; pvt. practice vet. medicine Rocky Hill Animal Clinic, Knoxville, 1981-82; veterinarian Knoxville Pet Emergency Clinic, Knoxville, 1982—; dir. pet therapy Knox County Humane Soc., Knoxville, 1983—; bd. dirs. Knox County Humane Soc., 1982—, treas., 1984—. Recipient Mil. Order of World Wars award City of Baton Rouge, 1976; Acad. and Leadership awards Air Force ROTC, La. State U., 1976; Mortar Board award U. Tenn., 1978. Mem. AVMA, Tenn. Vet. Med. Assn., Knoxville Vet. Acad., East Tenn. Vet. Med. Assn. Republican. Episcopalian. Clubs: Rugby (sec. 1975-76), Flying (v.p. 1976). Lodge: Rotary Aux. Office: Pet Emergency Clinic 1819 Ailor Ave Knoxville TN 37917

BRADEN, DANA DANIELLE, lawyer; b. Detroit, June 8, 1951; d. William Anthony and Marjorie Louise (Badertscher) B. B.A., Mich. State U., 1973; J.D., Detroit Coll. Law, 1977; postgrad. U. Miami Law Sch., 1979-81. Bar: Mich., Fla. Asst. bank mgr. Community Nat. Bank, Pontiac, Mich., 1973-76; asst. trust officer Genesee Bank, Flint, Mich., 1976-78; trust officer Sun Banks of Fla., Orlando, 1978-79; assoc. firm Storms, Krasny, Normile, Dettmer & Gillin, P.A., Melbourne, Fla., 1979, Raymond & Dillon, P.C., West Palm Beach, Fla., 1979-81; prin. Dana D. Braden, P.A., West Palm Beach, 1981-85. Author monthly tax newsletter Current Devels. in Taxation of Ins., 1982—, articles on estate planning and planned giving. Precinct del. Rochester (Mich.) Republican Com., 1972; 2d vice chmn. Oakland County (Mich.) Rep. Com., 1972; bd. dirs. Big Bros./Big Sisters of Brevard County (Fla.), 1978. Joseph S. Burak scholar Detroit Coll. Law, 1977. Mem. ABA, Mich. Bar Assn., Fla. Bar Assn., Planned Giving Council Palm Beach County (pres. 1982—), Martin County Estate Planning Council (co-founder), Nat. Assn. Planned Giving Council (founder). Congregationalist. Office: Penthouse Suite 600 2290 10th Ave N Lake Worth FL 33461-3208

BRADFORD, BARBARA TAYLOR (MRS. ROBERT BRADFORD), journalist, author; b. Leeds, Eng., May 10, 1933; d. Winston and Freda (Walker) Taylor; student pvt. schs., Eng.; m. Robert Bradford, Dec. 24, 1963. Came to U.S., 1964. Women's editor Yorkshire (Eng.) Evening Post, 1951-53, reporter, 1949-51; editor Woman's Own, 1953-54; columnist London Evening News, 1955-57; exec. editor London Am., 1959-62; editor Nat. Design Center Mag., 1965-69; syndicated columnist Newsday Specials, L.I., 1968-70; nationally syndicated columnist Chgo. Tribune/N.Y. News Syndicate, N.Y.C., 1970-75, Los Angeles Times Syndicate, 1975—. Recipient Dorothy Dawe award Am. Furniture Mart, 1970, 71. Mem. Authors Guild, Nat. Home Fashions League, Nat. Soc. Interior Designers (Distinguished Editorial award 1969, Nat. Press award 1971), Am. Soc. Interior Designers. Author: The Innocent Are Wise, 1963; Complete Encyclopedia of Homemaking Ideas, 1968; A Garland of Children's Verse, 1968; How to Be the Perfect Wife, 1969; Easy Steps to Successful Decorating, 1971; Decorating Ideas for Casual Living, 1977; How to Solve Your Decorating Problems, 1976; (novels) A Woman of Substance, 1980; Voice of the Heart, 1983; Hold the Dream, 1985; Matrix award, 1985. Office: 450 Park Ave New York NY 10022

BRADFORD, CHRISTINA, newspaper editor. Mng. editor Democrat and Chronicle, Rochester, N.Y. Office: Democrat and Chronicle Gannett Co Inc 55 Exchange St Rochester NY 14614*

BRADFORD, LOUISE MATHILDE, social worker; b. Alexandria, La., Aug. 3, 1925; d. Henry Aaron and Ruby (Pearson) Bradford; B.S., La. Poly. Inst., 1945; cert. in social work La. State U., 1949; M.S., Columbia U., 1953; postgrad. Tulane U., 1962, 64, La. State U., 1967; cert. U. Pa., 1966. With La. Dept. Public Welfare, Alexandria, 1945-78, welfare caseworker, 1950-53, children's caseworker, 1957-59, child welfare cons., 1959-73, social services cons., 1973-78, state cons. day care, 1963-66; dir. social services St. Mary's Tng. Sch., Alexandria, La., 1978—; del. Nat. Day Care Conf., Washington, 1964; mem. early childhood edn. com. So. States Work Conf., Daytona Beach, Fla., 1968; mem. La. adv. com. 1970 White House Conf. on Children, also del.; mem. So. region planning com. Child Welfare League Am., 1970-73; mem. profl. adv. com. Cenla chpt. Parents Without Partners, 1970; adj. asst. prof. sociology La. Coll., Pineville, 1969—, lectr. Kindergarten workshop, 1970-72; mem. La. 4-C Day Care Licensing Rev. Com., Central La. 4-C Steering Com.; social services cons. La. Spl. Edn. Ctr., Alexandria, 1980—; del. Internat. Conf. on Social Welfare, Nairobi, 1974, Jerusalem, 1978, Hong Kong, 1980, Brighton, 1982, Montreal, 1984. Pres., Les Soignees, Alexandria, 1947-48. Bd. dirs. Cenla Community Action Com., Alexandria, 1966-68. Mem. Acad. Cert. Social Workers, Nat. Assn. Social Workers, La. Bd. Cert. Social Work Examiners, So., La. assns. children under six, La. Conf. Social Welfare, Internat. Council on Social Welfare, Am. Pub. Welfare Assn. (S.W. region planning com. 1965), Am. Assn. on Mental Deficiency, DAR, Central La. Pre-Sch. Assn. (dir. 1967-70), Marquis Biog. Library Assn. (adv.). Methodist (kindergarten bd. 1967—, ofcl. bd. 1974-75, 77-81, 83-85). Clubs: Rapides Golf and Country, Pilot (Alexandria). Home: 5807 Joyce St Alexandria LA 71302 Office: PO Box 7768 Alexandria LA 71306

BRADLEY, BARBARA GAY, small business owner; b. Littlefield, Tex., May 29, 1939; d. C.R. and Ruby L. (Cox) Damron; m. Kendall W. Kendrick, Dec. 23, 1959 (div. 1963); 1 son, Kyd William; m. James H. Bradely, Feb. 26, 1969. Student Tex. Tech. U., 1957-59, West Tex. State Coll., 1961-63. Owner, mgr. Rees Boutique, Ruidoso, N.Mex., 1979—. Mem. Zeta Tau Alpha. Christian Scientist.

BRADLEY, BARBARA JOANNE, entrepreneur; b. Wauseon, Ohio, May 9, 1941; d. Vincent A. and Helen J. (Waterston) Klopfenstein; m. Eugene H. Rolf, Nov. 5, 1960 (div. June 1964); 1 child, Renee Jean Rolf; m. Paul Arnett, Dec. 5, 1969. A.A., La Salle Extension U., 1982; cert. secretarial sci. Miami-Jacobs Bus. Coll., Dayton, Ohio, 1963; student Ohio State U., U. Calif., others. Lic. real estate sales, Ohio. Exec. sec. Mazer Corp., Dayton, 1964-66; gen. sales office mgr. ACDC Electronics, Burbank, Calif., 1966-68; legal sec., Dayton, 1968-70; bookkeeper, Dayton, 1971; dir. fin. Durnbaugh Investments, Fairborn, Ohio, 1972-81; owner Barbara Bradley Bookkeeping, Englewood, Ohio, 1981—; property mgr. R.V.B. Assos., Englewood, 1982—. Author mdse. manual. Vol., Am. Heart Assn.; mem. Ohio State Jr. Fair Bd., 1958-59; v.p. Jr. Achievement, Dayton, 1958-59. Mem. VFW Aux. (charter), Dayton Area Bd. Realtors (women's council), Dayton Area Real Estate Exchangers (treas. 1983-4), Nat. Assn. Female Execs. Republican. Lutheran. Avocations: literature; art; sailing; travel. Office: PO Box 275 Englewood OH 45322

BRADLEY, BONNIE, mezzo soprano; b. Wilmington, Del.; d. Archie Merill, and Blanche Ruth B.; Certs. in Oratorio, Song, Opera, Britten-Pears Sch. Advanced Musical Studies, Snape-on-Maltings, Eng., 1978; cert. in Opera, Inst. Musical Studies, Graz, Austria, 1977, Mozarteum Sommerakadamie, Salzburg, Austria, 1974; B.Mus. in Voice, Westminster Choir Coll., 1972; M.Mus. in Opera Performance, Manhattan Sch. Music, N.Y.C., 1975; m. Nicholas Nicosia, June 28, 1975; 1 dau., Francesca Maria Aida. Operatic and concert artist performing with opera cos. and maj. symphony orchs., recitalist U.S., Eng., Germany, Austria, the Caribbean, 1975—; instr. master classes colls. and univs.; adjudicater maj. vocal competitions. Helene Rubenstein Found. grantee; winner Artists Internat. Competition, Liederkranz Found. competition, Oratorio solo competition; recipient Minna Kauffman Ruud Found. competition award. Mem. Am. Guild Musical Artists, Nat. Assn. Tchrs. of Singing, Coll. Music Soc., N.Y. Arts Group. Office: care Metropolitan Musical Artists 2836 Flagmaker Dr Falls Church VA 22042

BRADLEY, CAROL ANN, educator; b. Sellersville, Pa., Apr. 20, 1943; d. John Joseph and Stella Theresa (Dykie) Roney; m. Milton Sanderson Bradley, Sept. 24, 1966 (div. 1970). B.A., Kutztown U., Pa., 1965, M.Ed., 1966; postgrad. Immaculata Coll., Pa., 1984. Cert. tchr., Pa. Tchr. Pennridge High Sch., Perkasie, Pa., 1966—, chmn. dept. fgn. lang., 1972—, humanistic edn. cons., 1976-78; facilitator community communication workshops, Perkasie, 1978-79. Mem. Pennridge Edn. Assn., Pa. State Edn. Assn., NEA, Am. Assn. Tchrs. French, Am. Assn. Counseling and Devel., Delta Kappa Gamma. Democrat. Roman Catholic. Avocations: travel, reading.

BRADLEY, CYNTHIA NEWINGHAM, business school administrator; b. Pontiac, Mich., Sept. 7, 1955; d. Plezzy Lee and Agnes Lou (Hampton) Newingham; m. Alan D. Bradley. Cert. Pontiac Bus. Inst., 1975; A.A.S. in Mgmt. Devel., Oakland Community Coll., 1981, B.S. in Office Adminstrn., Detroit Coll. Bus., 1982; postgrad., Central Mich. U., 1983—. Receptionist, Pontiac Bus. Inst., Mich., 1974-75, bookkeeper, 1975-76; adminstrv. asst. to pres. PBI Schs. Inc., Pontiac, 1976-78, asst. treas., 1978-81, treas., 1981—. Mem. Am. Mgmt. Assn., Nat. Assn. Female Execs., Mich. Bus. Edn. Assn., Oakland County C. of C. Office: PBI Schools Inc 28 N Saginaw St Suite 514 Pontiac MI 48054

BRADLEY, FLORENE JORDAN, librarian; b. Magnolia, Ark., Aug. 18, 1917; d. Thomas Scott and Nellie (Nipper) Jordan; student So. State Coll., Ark., 1935-37; B.A., Henderson State Tchrs. Coll., 1939; B.S. in L.S., Peabody Coll., 1947; m. Steve Bradley, Nov. 23, 1966. Librarian, tchr. Burdette High Sch., 1939-42, Calhoun High Sch., 1942-43, Magnolia High Sch., 1943-51; regional librarian Columbia-Lafayette-Ouachita-Calhoun Regional Library, Magnolia, 1951—. Pres., United Way Columbia County, 1979; sec. City Planning Commn., Columbia County Fair Bd. Named Magnolia Woman of Year service and civic clubs, 1963; Citizen of Yr., 1968. Mem. Magnolia Bus. and Profl. Women's Club (Woman of Year 1979), AAUW, Magnolia LWV, Ark. (past pres.), Southwestern (past chmn. pub. library div.) library assns., ALA (mem. notable books council adult services div. 1962-64), C. of C. (dir.), Delta Kappa Gamma. Methodist. Club: Quota. Home: 405 W Calhoun St Magnolia AR 71753 Office: 220 E Main St Magnolia AR 71753

BRADLEY, GWENDOLYN, opera singer, soprano; b. N.Y.C.; degree N.C. Sch. Arts, Curtis Inst., Acad. Vocal Arts. Debut with Lake George Opera as Nanette in Falstaff, 1976; debut with Met. Opera as Le Rossignol in Ravel's L'Enfant et les Sortileges, 1981; Met. Opera performances include Tales of Hoffman, Le Rossignol, Siegfried, Entführung und Serail, Arabella, Die Frau ohne Schatten, 1981; internat. operatic debut Corfu Festival, Greece, summer 1981; other European engagements include Netherlands Opera, Paris Radio, Hamburg Staatsoper, Glyndebourne Festival; has appeared with Phila., Cleve., Central City Operas, Mich. Opera Theater; recitalist, concert performer; soloist Phila. Orch., Nat., Seattle, Denver, Honolulu, St. Louis Symphonies, Kansas City Philharm., Aspen Festival Chamber Orch.; recitals include Carnegie Recital Hall, Phillips Gallery, Dumbarton Oaks, Washington, community concerts. Nat. finalist Met. Opera Guild auditions; winner 26 competitions and awards. Office: care Columbia Artists Management Inc 165 W 57th St New York NY 10019

BRADLEY, JANET, greeting card company executive, mental health worker; b. River Rouge, Mich., June 19, 1947; d. Chester Brown and Mildred (Bradley) Sutton. Lic., Detroit Sch. Cosmetology, 1965; A.A. in Mental Health, Wayne County Community Coll., 1977. Data processor Blue Shield & Blue Cross, Detroit, 1968-73; worker Mich. Osteo. Med. Ctr. Adult Mental Health Unit, Detroit, 1977—; pres. Softly Spoken Greeting Card Co., Inc., Detroit. Author: Something About Man and Something Else Women, 1984 (Spirit of Detroit, Artistic Accomplishment awards 1984), other poems. Songwriter. Team leader Clean Up Detroit Day, 1975-77; mem. nominating com. Democratic County Conv., Lansing, 1977, worker mayoral campaign, Detroit, 1977, precinct del., 1978, vol. city clk. campaign, 1978. Mem. Nat. Assn. Female Execs. Democrat. Baptist. Office: Softly Spoken Greeting Card Co Inc PO Box 38725 Detroit MI 48238

BRADLEY, JANET LITZ, state official, civil rights advocate; b. Balt., May 9, 1935; d. Francis Joseph and Ella Doris (Manning) Litz; m. Richard Alan Bradley, Dec. 27, 1958; children—Anne Marie, M. Katheryn, Alana, Richard Alan. B.A. magna cum laude, Dunbarton Coll., 1957; postgrad. U. Paris, 1957, U. Dijon, Cours Etrangers, France, 1957-58, U. Alaska, 1975-77; M.A. in French, U. Wash., 1973. Lectr. French, U. Alaska, Juneau, 1970-73; exec. sec. Arts and Humanities Council, Juneau, 1973; asst. dir. Alaska Commn. for Human Rights, Juneau, 1974-82, exec. dir., Anchorage, 1982—. Coordinator, Southeastern Alaska McGovern for Pres. campaign, 1972; v.p. U. Alaska Policy Adv. Council, Juneau, 1980, pres., 1982. Fulbright scholar, 1957-58. Mem. Nat. Assn. Civil Rights Workers, NAACP, NOW, Bus. and Profl. Women's Club, Alaska Women's Lobby, Nat. Women's Polit. Caucus, Internat. Assn. Ofcl. Human Rights Agys. (sec. to bd.). Democrat. Roman Catholic. Lodge: Soroptimists. Office: Alaska State Commn for Human Rights 800 A St Suite 202 Anchorage AK 99501

BRADLEY, KAREN JEAN, marketing executive, writer, consultant; b. Milw., June 8, 1942; d. James Edward and Dellora Ethel (Linder) Lee; m. James Alton Bradley, Apr. 7, 1962 (div. Oct. 1984); children—Rhonda, Gregory. Reporter, Burlington (Wis.) Standard Press, 1970-75; owner, mgr. K.J. Bradley Advt. Agy., Burlington, 1975-78; dir. pub. relations St. Catherine's Hosp., Kenosha, Wis., 1978-84; mktg. dir. Hillhaven Corp., Menasha, Wis., 1984—; lectr. Editor, Community Health mag., 1978-83, C. of C.-City Jour. mag., 1978. Campaign fundraiser Congressman Les Aspin, Racine, Wis., 1983-84; mem. Child Passenger Safety Com., Kenosha, 1982-84; pres. Am. Cancer Soc. Kenosha, 1975; chmn. communications Kenosha United Way, 1982-83. Recipient Pub. Relations award Nat. Fedn. Press Women, 1980. Mem. Wis. Press Women (interview award 1979, feature article award 1978), Women in Communication (dir., writing grant 1983), Kenosha C. of C., Milw. Advt. Club, Kenosha Bd. Health (chmn. 1978-80). Lutheran.

BRADLEY, RAMONA KAISER, curator; b. Hamilton County, Ohio, Aug. 9, 1909; d. Oliver Barnard and Grace Lytle (Edwards) Kaiser; student Oakhurst Coll., Cin., 1926-28, Schuster-Martin Sch. Drama, 1931-33; m. Judson M. Bradley, Sept. 4, 1954. Sec. to patent atty., Cin., 1939-54; curator Sherman Indian Mus., Riverside, Calif., 1970—; cons. Title IV Project, Indian edn. Riverside Sch. Dist. Bd. dirs. Riverside Library, 1966-74, Riverside Cultural Heritage, 1974-80. Recipient Appreciation award Sherman Indian High Sch., 1977, honored for civic service City and County Riverside, 1980, honor award D.A.R., 1981. Mem. Nat. League Am. Pen Women, D.A.R., Daus. Am. Colonists, Printing House Craftsmen, Inland Empire Mus. Consortium. Republican. Methodist. Club: Citrus Belt (hon.). Author: Glimpses Into the Past, 1940, Weavers of Tales, 1965. Home: 9130 Andrew St Riverside CA 92503 Office: 9010 Magnolia Ave Riverside CA 92503

BRADLEY, ROSALEE, psychologist; b. Calhoun, Mo., Sept. 20, 1939; d. Wayne Beecher and Alice Maureen (Shrout) B.; B.S., U. Mo., Kansas City, 1961; M.A., Hollins Coll., 1962; Ph.D., Wash. State U., 1969. Clin. psychologist No. State Hosp., Sedro-Wooley, Wash., 1968-73; psychologist, adminstrv. asst. Calif. Correctional Center, Susanville, Calif., 1974-78; pvt. practice, Susanville, Calif., 1978—; adj. faculty U. San Francisco; owner, breeder, trainer Sunflower Appaloosa Ranch. Bd. dirs. Conbela Assn. Seattle, 1972-74. Womens liaison rep. Calif. Dept. Corrections, 1975-78. Mem. Am. Psychol. Assn. Democrat. Home: Box 88 Janesville CA 96114 Office: 803 1/2 Main St Suite 101 Susanville CA 96130

BRADLEY, WANDA LOUISE, librarian; b. Havre de Grace, Md., June 6, 1953; d. William Smith and Josephine Viola (Miller) B. B.A. (scholar), U. Md., 1975; M.S.L.S. (scholar), Atlanta U., 1976; postgrad. Cath. U.; M.P.A. (scholar), U. Balt., 1986. Librarian, Harford County Pub. Library, Bel Air, Md., 1976, Harford County Bd. Edn., Bel Air, 1977-81, Nat. Grad. U., Arlington, Va., 1982, Md. State Dept. Edn., Balt., 1982-83, U.S. Dept. Labor, Washington, 1984, Balt. Gas and Electric Co., 1984-85, Morgan State U., Balt., 1985, Coppin State Coll., Balt., 1985-86, Montgomery County Pub. Sch. System, Rockville, Md., 1985—; acad. advisor George Mason U., Fairfax, Va., 1981-82. Dept. Edn. fellow, 1983-84; U. Balt. Merit scholar, 1984. Mem. ALA, Md. Library Assn., Spl. Libraries Assn., Med. Library Assn., ASIS. Methodist. Office: Coppin State Coll North Ave Baltimore MD

BRADLEY-AUSTIN, BETTY E., social services adminstr.; b. Newark, June 23, 1947; d. Linzey and Evelyn (Harris) Moss; I.C.B.O., Rutgers U., Newark, 1977; cert. N.J. Coll. Medicine and Dentistry, 1973; m. John Austin, Jr., Sept. 17, 1962; children—Oumar, Sadiq, Allen, m. 2d, Norman V. Bradley, Oct. 8, 1983. Customer relations rep. Cooper-Jarrett, Springfield, N.J., 1973; radiology coordinator N.J. Coll. Medicine and Dentistry, Newark, 1974; family enabler, social service dept. United Hosps., Newark, 1980—; founder, exec. dir. Neo-Fight, Inc. Cons., Concerned Community Women of Jersey City, 1978-80. Trustee, Marie L. Villani Civic Assn. Notary Public, N.J. Mem. Nat. Council Negro Women, Concerned Community Women of Jersey City, Black Social Workers of N.J., Nat., Am. Bus. Women's Assn. Democrat. Baptist. Club: United Hosps. Employees Activity (v.p.). Home: 965 Thorn St Rahway NJ 07065 Office: United Hosps 15 S 9th St Newark NJ 07107

BRADSHAW, AUDRA ROSE, lawyer; b. San Angelo, Tex., Oct. 27, 1937; d. Wonnie Beatrice and Chlotilde Pearl (Parris) Rose; m. Leo Herman Bradshaw, Jr., Apr. 11, 1955 (div. Nov. 1975); children—Leo Herman III, Dana R., Karen R., Andrew T. B.A., Baylor U., 1975, J.D., 1978. Bar: Tex. 1979. Assoc., Locilar, Kasir & Everton, Temple, Tex., 1979-83, atty. advisor HUD, Washington, 1983—. Mem. Waco and Washington Jr. Leagues, 1958—. Mem. ABA, Assn. Trial Lawyers Am. Episcopalian. Home: 2601 Woodley Pl NW Washington DC 20008 Office: Dept of Housing and Urban Development 451 7th St SW Washington DC 20410

BRADSHAW, CYNTHIA HELENE, educator; b. S.I., N.Y., May 9, 1954; d. Frederick Thomas and Audrey Helene (Stetter) B. B.S. in Elem. Edn., Wagner Coll., 1975; M.S. in Edn., U. Miami, 1979. Cert. elem. tchr., adminstr., and supr. Tchr. Young Scholars Montessori Sch., S.I., 1975-76, Lutheran Schs., Mo. Synod, S.I., 1976, Hialeah and N. Miami, Fla., 1976-80, Dade County pub. schs., Miami, 1980—; reliability study subject Fla. Dept. Edn., Tallahassee, 1984—. Sch. chairperson United Way, Miami, 1983—. Recipient Cert. of Recognition Dade County Pub. Schs., 1984. Mem. United Tchrs. Dade, United Tchrs. Dade Polit. Orgn., U. Miami Sch. Edn. Allied Professions Alumni Assn. (mem. alumni telephone funding campaign 1984), Alpha Delta Kappa. Republican. Lutheran. Lodge: Order Eastern Star. Avocation: Music. Home: 10870 Olive Ave Pembroke Pines FL 33026 Office: Parkview Elem Sch 17631 NW 20th Ave Opa-Locka FL 33055

BRADSHAW, DONNA SUE, credit union executive; b. Boynton, Okla., Aug. 26, 1948; d. George William and Frelia Margaret (Yocham) Morgan; m. Charles R. Castleberry, Jan. 19, 1976 (div. 1982); children—Derrick, Diana, Dwayne; m. Kenneth Paul Bradshaw, Nov. 19, 1983. B.S., Northeastern State U., Tahlequah, Okla., 1969, M.S., 1972; M.B.A., Okla. U., 1981. Cert. credit union exec. Tchr. Liberty Morris Pub. Sch., Morris, Okla., 1969-72; gen. mgr. Honeycutt & Assocs., Denver, 1972-79; acct. Alexander Grant & Co., Oklahoma City, 1979-80; adminstrv. asst. to pres. Tinker Credit Union, Oklahoma City, 1980-82; v.p. MAPCO Employees Fed. Credit Union, Tulsa, 1982-83; pres. Williams Employees Credit Union, Tulsa, 1983—; cons. to various credit unions, Okla., 1983—. Operating fund dir. Philbrook Art Ctr., Tulsa, 1985; chmn. Magic Empire Scholarship Com., Tulsa, 1984. Mem. Credit Union Exec. Soc., Nat. Assn. Female Execs., Fin. Mktg. Assn., Okla. Credit Unions (pres. Magic Empire chpt. 1983—). Avocations: tennis, hiking. Office: Williams Employees Credit Union One Williams Ctr PO Drawer 3448 Tulsa OK 74101

BRADSHAW, LILLIAN MOORE, former librarian; b. Hagerstown, Md., Jan. 10, 1915; d. Harry M. and Mabel E. (Kretzer) Moore; B.A., Western Md. Coll., 1937; B.L.S., Drexel U., 1938, D.Litt. (hon.), 1978; m. William Theodore Bradshaw, May 19, 1946. Asst. adult circulation dept. Utica (N.Y.) Public Library, 1938-41, asst. head, 1941-43; adult librarian Enoch Pratt Free Library, Balt., 1943-44, asst. coordinator work with young adults, 1944-46; br. librarian Dallas Public Library 1946-47, readers adviser, 1947-52, head dept. circulation, 1952-55, coordinator work with adults, 1955-58, asst. dir., 1958-62, dir., 1962-84; asst. Dallas city mgr., 1984. Mem. adv. group libraries Library of Congress, 1976-77; del. White House Conf. on Library and Info. Services, Washington, 1979; mem. bd. publs. So. Meth. U., 1970-78; mem. Tex. Gov.'s Commn. on Status of Women, 1970-72; Tex. del. to ad hoc com. for planning and monitoring White House Conf. follow up activities Nat. Commn. on Libraries and Info. Service, 1980; mem. Nat. Reading Council, Washington, 1970-73; Goals for Dallas, conferee, asst. task force leader, 1966-69, vice chmn. Goals Achievement Com. for Continuing Edn., 1971, chmn., 1972; mem. Com. to Plan the Future Goals for Dallas, 1973-74; chmn. Citizen Info. and Participation com. Goals for Dallas, 1976-77, trustee, exec. com., sec., 1977 treas., 1979-83; mem. curriculum com. Leadership Dallas, 1978-79, adv. com., 1978-80; mem. Charter 100 of Dallas; mem. Tex. Com. for Humanities, 1980-84, treas., 1982. Bd. dirs. Hoblitzelle Found., 1971—, Dallas Ballet, 1985—, Arboretum Bot. Soc., 1986—; trustee Lamplighter Sch., 1974-81, Dallas Hist. Soc., 1984—, Friends of Dallas Pub. Library, 1984—; bd. dirs. Univ. Med. Ctr., 1984—. Named Tex. Librarian of Year, 1961, Public Adminstr. of Yr., 1981; recipient Disting. Alumnus award Drexel U. Library Sch., 1970, Titche's Arete award for epitome of excellence in chosen field, 1970; Disting. Service in a Profession award Dallas Hist. Soc., 1981; Lillian Moore Bradshaw chair in library and info. studies named in her honor Tex. Woman's U. Mem. ALA (v.p. adult services div. 1966-67, pres. adult services div. 1967-68, council 1968-69, pres. 1970-71, endowment trustee 1984—), Tex. Public Library Assn. (pres. 1964-65, chmn. public libraries div. 1955-56, chmn.

awards com. 1973-74, 79-80, Disting. Service award 1975), Tex. Humanities Alliance (pres.). Club: Zonta (pres. chpt. I, Dallas, 1976-77). Home: 6318 E Lovers Ln Dallas TX 75214

BRADSHAW, NANCI MARIE GILCHRIST, business executive; b. Schenectady, Aug. 21, 1940; d. Leo Arthur and Angela Bertha (Bonk) Bradshaw; m. William Clayton Hoehn, Oct. 12, 1963 (div. 1979); children—Sharon Ann, Theresa Lynn; m. Eugene Augustine Gilchrist, July 13, 1980. B.S., Skidmore Coll., 1977. Asst. to pres. Schenectady Indsl. Drafting, 1978-79; bus. exec. math dept. SUNY, Albany, 1979-86, Evangelist Newspaper, Albany, 1986—; cons., lectr. Trustee Help Ctr., Inc., Troy, N.Y., 1982—. Mem. Nat. Assn. Female Execs., Math. Assn. Am., Albany Catholic Press Assn. Republican. Roman Catholic. Lodge: Soroptimist Internat. Avocations: refinishing antiques; reading; music; fitness. Home: 157 Maple Ave Troy NY 12180 Office: Evangelist Newspaper 39 Philip St Albany NY 12207

BRADSHAW, ROXANNE ELIZABETH, educator; b. Pueblo, Colo., Oct. 31, 1943; d. Foster Costin and Martha M. (Moore) Moore; B.A., Western State Coll., 1965, M.A., 1969; m. David Lee Reinke, Dec. 15, 1974; stepchildren—Lisa Ann, Alison Lee. Advisor, Dean of Women's office Western State Coll., Gunnison, Colo., 1963-64; tchr., Pueblo, Colo., 1965-68; kindergarten tchr., Monument, Colo., 1968-69; women's counselor Rangely (Colo.) Coll., 1969-70; instr./coordinator tchr. aid program Pikes Peak Community Coll., Colorado Springs, 1970-74, instr. psychology, 1974—; developer grad. level tchr. aide course and workshop So. Colo. State Coll., 1970-73. Nat. bd. dirs. People for the American Way; bd. dirs. Tchrs. Services Corp., Joint Council Econ. Edn. Named Outstanding Woman in Edn., Beta chpt. Alpha Delta Kappa, 1981-82; W.G. Carr Profl. Study scholar, 1981. Mem. NEA (sec.-treas., exec. com., dir., program and budget com.; mem. Employee Retirement Bd.; mem. PAC steering com. and council; sec. Mems. Ins. Trust; spl. com. structure and services; rep. UN regional seminar Venezuela 1983; del. World Confedn. Orgns., Togo 1984), Pikes Peak Community Coll. Faculty Assn., Colo. Edn. Assn., NOW, Alpha Delta Kappa. Democrat. Presbyterian. Office: 1201 16th St NW Washington DC 20036

BRADY, ADELAIDE BURKS, public relations agency executive; b. N.Y.C., June 27, 1926; d. Earl Victor and Audrey (Calvert) Burks; B.S., Boston U., 1946; m. James Francis Brady, Jr., June 22, 1946 (div. 1953); 1 son, James Francis III. Exec. v.p. Media Enterprises, 1952-55; dir. group relations Save the Children Fedn., N.Y.C., 1955-59; dir. public affairs div. Girl Scouts U.S.A., N.Y.C., 1959-69; pres. Communication Internat., Inc., Washington, 1969-73; pres. Burks Brady Communications, N.Y.C., Wilton, Conn., 1972—, Adelaid's Angel Shopper Inc., Wilton, 1976—; exec. v.p. Arts in the Parks, Inc., Washington, 1971—. Mem. Women's Nat. Republican Club, 1968—; active Girl Scouts U.S.A.; bd. dirs. ARCS Found. Inc., Lenox Hill Hosp., N.Y.C.; chmn. bd. dirs., pres. Animal Lovers, Inc. Recipient Silver Reel award for film The Children of Now, Save the Children Fedn., 1968; Disting. award of appreciation Am. Legion Aux., decorated comdr. Order St. John of Jerusalem (Eng.), 1974. Mem. Public Relations Soc. Am., AAUW, NEA, Am. Women in Radio and TV, Nat. Ednl. Broadcasters Assn., Nat. Assn. Press Women (past N.Y. State pres.), Women Execs. in Public Relations, N.Y. Press Women (pres.), First Families Va., D.A.R., Daus. Am. Confederacy, Women in Communication, Internat. Platform Assn., Women's Polit. Caucus. Episcopalian. Club: Capitol Hill (Washington). Home: 267 Westport Rd Wilton CT 06897 Office: 785 Park Ave New York NY 10021

BRADY, BARBARA C., psychologist; b. Burbank, Calif., May 29, 1946; d. Roger Ralph and Lespith (Albright) Crist; 1 son, Scott Thomas Bauer. B.A. in Psychology, San Jose State U., 1969; M.S. in Home Econs., Calif. Poly. State U., 1974, M.A. in Counseling, 1976; Ph.D. in Ednl. Psychology, Brigham Young U., 1981. Instr. psychology Cuesta Coll., San Luis Obispo, Calif., 1974-76, counselor, 1976-80; counselor Brigham Young U., Provo, Utah, 1980-81, lectr., 1981; psychol. asst. Pacific Profl. Assocs., San Luis Obispo, 1981-83; pvt. practice psychology, San Luis Obispo, 1983—; host radio show A Session with Dr. Brady; lectr. in field, 1976—; cons. San Luis Obispo County Mental Health Services. Bd. dirs. Family Services, San Luis Obispo, 1984—; active Boy Scouts Am., San Luis Obispo, 1976-78. Exec. Assn., Assn. Media Psychologists, Mem. San Luis Obispo County Psychol. Assn. (pres. 1984-85), Calif. Psychol. Assn., Am. Psychol. Assn., Western Psychol. Assn., Women's Network San Luis Obispo (membership chmn. 1983), San Luis Obispo C. of C. (bd. dirs.), Toastmasters (pres. 1984), Phi Kappa Phi, Psi Chi, Phi Upsilon Omicron, Kappa Alpha Theta. Office: 1461 Higuera San Luis Obispo CA 93401

BRADY, BENNETT MANNING, mathematician, government official; b. Orangeburg, S.C., Apr. 11, 1943; d. William Ellis and Elizabeth (Mays) Manning; student Agnes Scott Coll., 1961-62; A.B., Vassar Coll., 1965; Fulbright fellow Cambridge U., 1965-66; M.A. (NSF fellow), U. Calif., Berkeley, 1968; postgrad. George Washington U., 1969-72; m. Roscoe Owen Brady, June 10, 1972; children—Roscoe Owen, Randolph Owen. Sr. mgmt. cons. Ernst & Ernst, Washington, 1968-70; research asso. Pres.'s Commn. Fed. Statistics, Washington, 1970-71; U.S. internat. statis. liaison OMB, Washington, 1971-78; spl. asst. to commr. labor statistics Bur. Labor Statistics, Washington, 1978-79, dir. Office Program Coordination and Evaluation, 1979—; cons. ops. research USAF, 1967-68; mem. faculty U. Calif., Berkeley, 1968; mem. U.S. delegation UN Statis. Commn., 1972. NASA fellow, 1964. Mem. Am. Math. Soc., Am. Statis. Assn., Inst. Mgmt. Sci., Ops. Research Soc. Am., Washington Ops. Research/Mgmt. Sci. Council, Washington Statis. Soc., Am. Soc. for Quality Control, Phi Beta Kappa, Omega Rho. Republican. Presbyterian. Clubs: Vassar, Met. Toastmistress (pres.) (Washington). Author: (with J.S. Duncan) Statistical Services in Ten Years' Time, 1978; (with E. Robins and K.S. Tippet) Going Places with Children in Washington, 9th ed., 1979; editor OSD Statis. Notes, 1980—; contbr. articles on statis. devels. and research to profl. jours. Home: 9501 Kingsley Ave Bethesda MD 20814 Office: 4340 East West Hwy Bethesda MD 20814

BRADY, BEVERLY J(EAN) P(ETERSON), trade association executive; b. Evanston, Ill., Jan. 13, 1946; d. Walter H. and E. Jean (Foster) Peterson; m. William D. Brady, Oct. 4, 1980. Student York Coll. Pa., 1963-65. C.P.C.U., C.I.C. Personal lines mgr. Almeida & Carlson, Sandwich, Mass., 1977-80; edn. coordinator PIA of New Eng., Hopkinton, Mass., 1980-84; mktg. rep. Preferred Mut. Ins. Co., New Berlin, N.Y., 1984-86; dir. field services Ind. Ins. Agts. Mass., Boston, 1986—. Author profl. manuals. Mem. Soc. C.P.C.U.s, Soc. Cert. Ins. Counselors. Republican. Congregationalist. Club: 1752 (dir. 1985, membership chmn. 1985). Avocations: skiing; needlework; reading; racquetball.

BRADY, DEBRA PATRICIA, nurse, educator; b. Pitts., Jan. 15, 1953; d. Frank and Winifred Patricia (Griffin) Rizzo; m. Martin John Brady, Sept. 11, 1976. B.S.N. cum laude, U. Pitts., 1974, M.N.ed., 1981. Staff nurse Presbyn. Hosp., Pitts., 1974-76, Westmorland Hosp., Greensburg, Pa., 1976-79; instr., cons. U. N.Mex., Albuquerque, 1981-84; staff nurse, cons. Presbyn. Hosp., Albuquerque, 1981-84; nursing edn. cons. N.Mex. Bd. Nursing, 1984—; instr. ARC, Albuquerque, 1981-84. Author: Psychosocial Assessment Across the Lifespan; contbr. articles to publs. Bd. dirs. Nurses Polit. Action Com., 1982-84, vice chmn., chmn. polit. edn. com. Mem. Am. Nurses Assn., Sigma Theta Tau. Democrat. Roman Catholic. Office: N Mex Bd Nursing Albuquerque NM 87108

BRADY, EDWINA KAY, banker; b. Artesia, N.Mex., Jan. 2, 1941; d. Edwin B. and Eleanor (Rogers) McCaw; m. Robert E. Brady, June 12, 1959 (div. Feb. 1972); children—Matt Blaine, Vicki Lynn. Student Eastern N.Mex. U. Cashier, credit investigator Interstate Securities, Inc., Artesia, 1971-72; sec. to sr. v.p. First Nat. Bank, Artesia, 1972-77, computer programmer/operator, 1977-78, computer programmer, 1978-80, mgr. data processing ops. dept., 1980-83, tng./purchasing officer, 1983—. Founding mem. Artesia Arts Council, also bd. dirs., pres., treas. Mem. Am. Inst. Banking (chpt. dir. 1976—, chpt. pres. 1984-85), Am. Bus. Women's Assn. (chpt. charter mem. and pres. 1982, chair edn. com. 1984-85). Republican. Mem. Dawn Bible Student Assn. Avocations: pastel painting; writing poetry. Office: First Nat Bank 303 W Main St Artesia NM 88210

BRADY, JEAN MARIE, microbiologist; b. Lockport, N.Y., Mar. 3, 1933; d. William Aloysius and Agnes Alice (Perkins) B.; B.S., Siena Heights Coll., Adrian, Mich., 1953; M.S., L.I. U., 1967; Ph.D., NYU, 1974. Med. technologist Lockport Meml. Hosp., 1953-64, Niagara Falls (N.Y.) Meml. Hosp., 1964-65; research assoc. St. Luke's, also St. Vincent's hosps., N.Y.C., 1965-75; assoc. prof. biology Alphonsus Coll., Woodcliffe Lake, N.J., 1970-74, Felician Coll., Lodi, N.J., 1974-83; sr. microbiologist Becton-Dickinson Co., East Rutherford, N.J., 1979-83; dir. sterilization and tech. services Nat. Contract Sterilizing Corp., West Paterson, N.J., 1983-84; sr. staff sci. writer Lederle Labs., Pearl River, N.Y., 1984—; mem. edn. com. Bergen County Adv. Council Aging, 1977. Fellow Royal Soc. Health; mem. AAUP, Am. Soc. Med. Tech., N.Y. Acad. Scis., N.J. Coll. and Univ. Coalition Women's Edn. Roman Catholic. Author articles in field. Home: 39 Chestnut St Hillsdale NJ 07642 Office: Middletown Rd Pearl River NY 10965

BRADY, JEAN P., county clerk; b. Yorkville, Ill., June 17, 1921; d. William and Elva Louisa (Worsley) Fitzsimmons; m. Allan O. Brady, Feb. 16, 1941; 1 child, Douglas Allan. Clk. County Treas.'s Office, 1944-53; dep. county treas. Kendall County, Yorkville, Ill., 1954-58, dep. county clk., 1958-60, county clk., recorder, 1960—. Mem. Kendall County Women's Rep. Club. Mem. Ill. Assn. County Clks and Recorders (treas. zone 4 1979-80). Congregationalist. Avocations: camping; needlework; traveling. Home: 906 Bristol Rd Yorkville IL 60560 Office: Kendall County 110 W Ridge St Yorkville IL 60560

BRADY, LINDA CAROL, architect; b. N.Y.C., May 18, 1949; d. John Joseph and Irene H. (Olawska) B.; B.Arch., Pratt Inst., 1971. Staff technician, draftsperson Gruzen & Partners, 1970-72; staff designer Warner, Burns, Toan, Lunde, 1973-75; archtl. cons. Citibank N.A., N.Y.C., 1976-77, staff architect, 1977—, asst. v.p., 1981—, also sr. project mgr. corp. facilities; corp. sec. Citidel, Inc., 1982—. Registered architect, N.Y. Mem. Am. Legion Aux., Pratt Alumni Assn., Nat. Classical Soc., Internat. Facilities Mgmt. Assn. (charter mem. N.Y. chpt.). Office: One Citicorp Center New York NY 10043

BRADY, MARYBETH GAREY, social worker; b. Wilkes-Barre, Pa., Aug. 10, 1946; d. Willard Lewis and Hilda (Staub) Garey; children—Erin Garey, Sean Michael. A.B. in Sociology, Coll. Misericordia, 1968; M.S.W., Marywood Coll. Sch. Social Work, 1982. Tchr. socially and emotionally disturbed children Devereux Found., Devon, Pa., 1968-69, Centennial Schs., Warminster, Pa., 1969-71; asst. dir. coll. admissions Solebury Sch., New Hope, Pa., 1972-74; outreach worker, community health coordinator, community services dir. Phillips Barber Family Health Ctr., Lambertville, N.J., 1975-80; summer adminstrv. asst. to dir. family practice residency program Hunterdon Med. Ctr., Flemington, N.J., 1980; summer inter Health Systems Agy. of Northeastern Pa., Avoca, 1982; dir. social services John Heinz Inst. Rehab. Medicine, Wilkes-Barre, 1982—; cons. Leader West Nursing Ctr., Kingston, Pa., 1982—, Home Care, Inc., Wilkes-Barre, 1983—. Bd. dirs. Luzerne County Children and Youth, Wilkes-Barre, Human Services Council, Wilkes-Barre, 1985, Act 101 Coll. Misericordia, 1984; participant Leadership Wilkes-Barre, 1984; alumni annual giving chmn. Coll. Misericordia, Dallas, 1986; com. mem. United Way of Wyoming Valley, 1985. Mem. Nat. Assn. Social Workers, Soc. Hosp. Social Work Dirs. Republican. Roman Catholic. Avocations: gourmet cooking; reading. Home: PO Box 105 Lehman PA 18627 Office: 150 Mundy St Box 2096 Wilkes-Barre PA 18703

BRADY, MAUREEN ELIZABETH, educator; b. Chgo., Mar. 15, 1945; d. William James and Gertrude (Hunter) B.; B.S. in Edn., Ill. State U., Normal, 1967, M.S. in Ednl. Media, 1971; postgrad. Nat. Coll. Edn. Librarian, Sch. Dist. 47, Crystal Lake, Ill., 1967-69, Sch. Dist. 155, Crystal Lake, 1969-70; learning center tchr. Rugen Elem. Sch., Glenview, Ill., 1971-73, Sunny Hill Elem. Sch. Dist. 220, Barrington, Ill., 1974—. Mem. aux. Good Shepherd Hosp., Barrington. Mem. ALA, Ill. Library Assn., Assn. Ednl. Communications and Tech., Ill. Assn. Ednl. Communications and Tech., NEA, Ill., Barrington (bd. dirs.) edn. assns., Chgo. Suburban Audiovisual Roundtable (dir., sec.), Ill. Assn. Media in Edn., No. Ill. Media Assn., AAUW (dir. Barrington area br.), Friends of Minocqua (Wis.) Library, Friends of Barrington Area Library, Elgin Scottish Soc. (pres.), Alpha Beta Alpha, Kappa Delta Pi (dir.), Phi Delta Kappa. Cert. in geography, library sci., ednl. media, Ill. Home: 25955 W Cuba Rd Barrington IL 60010 Office: 2500 Helm Rd Carpentersville IL 60110

BRADY, PATRICIA ELLIS, fin. exec.; b. Wake Forest, N.C., Aug. 12, 1935; d. Fred Day and Pauline Clarice (Hagwood) Rogers; student Strayer Secretarial Sch., 1965-66; children—Michael, Timothy, Darlene. Bookkeeper Union Trust Co., Washington, 1952-55; with B.F. Saul Co., Chevy Chase, Md., 1957—, corporate sec., asst. v.p., 1976—, trustee profit sharing plan, 1979—; dir. Franklin Property Co., B.F. Saul Co. of Md., B.F. Saul Co. of Va., Columbia Credit Co. Mem. Am. Soc. Corporate Secs., Nat. Assn. Exec. Secs., Nat. Assn. Female Execs., Women of the Ch. of God. Home: 552 Bruce Ave Odenton MD 21113 Office: 8401 Connecticut Ave Chevy Chase MD 20815

BRADY, PATSY FAE, nursing adminstr.; b. King, N.C., Aug. 31, 1940; d. Esker Ray and Mildred Olivia (Tuttle) Smith; student U. N.C., Greensboro, 1958-60; R.N., Watts Hosp. Sch. Nursing, 1963; B.S. in Nursing, U. N.C., Chapel Hill, 1970; M.S. in Nursing, Duke U., 1977; m. Michael Wayne Brady, Nov. 30, 1963. Head nurse, supr. operating room Duke U. Hosp., Durham, N.C., 1963-66; instr. Sch. Nursing, Watts Hosp. Sch. Nursing, Durham, 1966-69, asst. dir. nursing, 1973-77; coordinator policy, procedures and materials Duke U. Hosp., Durham, 1978—. Instr. home health nursing ARC, 1977-78. Mem. Watts Alumni Assn. (bd. dirs., co-chmn. membership com. 1979—). Democrat. Baptist. Home: 1709 Cole Mill Rd Durham NC 27712

BRADY, PEGGY JOE, oil company executive, consultant; b. Grimsley, Tenn., May 24, 1941; d. Paul Earl and Daisy Elease (Demonbreun) Stults; m. Robert Collins Whited, Oct. 9, 1959 (dec. July 1975); children—Paula Diane, Robert Wayne, Wesley Dale (dec.); m. James Dexter Brady, Mar. 10, 1984. A.B., U. Tenn., 1972-73. Insp. Colonial Mfr., Jamestown, Tenn., 1957-60; clk. Frisch's, Inc., Dayton, Ohio, 1960-64, Tenn. Dept. Pub. Health, Nashville, 1967-69; acct. Tenn. Dept. Safety, Nashville, 1969-73; service rep. IRS, Nashville, 1973-74; pvt. practice acctg., Crossville, Tenn., 1977-79; exec. asst. Vol. Energy, Inc., Crossville, 1979-82; owner Brady Enterprises; corp. officer H. Stone Well Service, Inc., Crossville, 1982—; cons. to oil and gas industries. Com mem. Young Democrats, Nashville, 1967-69; officer/del. PTA, Nashville, 1966-68; counselor Wautauga council Boy Scouts Am., 1968-69; bd. dirs. Community Action Services Cumberland County, 1985-86; advisor Am. Inst. for Cancer Research, 1984. Mem. Tenn. Oil and Gas Assn., Nat. Assn. Female Execs. Club: Order Eastern Star. Office: Harold Stone Well Service Inc Hwy 127 PO Box 2768 Crossville TN 38555 also Brady Enterprises Hwy 127 PO Box 2646 Crossville TN 38555

BRADY, ROBERTA KAY, nurse; b. St. Louis, May 12, 1939; d. Robert Talmage and Teresa Grace (Stani) Johnston; m. Morey Joseph Brady, Oct. 15, 1960; children—Edward Talmage, Brian Joseph, James Anthony. R.N., St. Luke's Hosp. Sch. Nursing, 1960; B.S. in Nursing, Washington U., St. Louis, 1965; postgrad. Ohio State U., 1980—. Cert. sch. nurse, Ohio; R.N., Mo., Ohio. Staff R.N. St. Luke's Hosp., St. Louis, 1960-61, Lemaze instr., 1965-67, clin. instr., 1965; pub. health nurse St. Louis County Health Dept., 1961-63; sch. nurse Westerville City Schs., Ohio, 1980—. Co-chmn. ednl. com. Westerville Citizens Against Chem. Dependency, 1984—. Mem. Central Ohio Assn. Sch. Nurses, Ohio Assn. Sch. Nurses, Doberman Pinscher Club Am., Doberman Pinscher Club Columbus (pres. 1980—), Central Ohio Kennel Club (sec. 1980—). Democrat. Roman Catholic. Avocation: handling breeding, exhibiting Doberman Pinscher dogs. Home: 574 Old Coach Rd Westerville OH 43081 Office: Westerville City Schs 950 Smothers Rd Westerville OH 43081

BRAGA, LINDA JEAN, lawyer; b. Nottinghamshire, Eng., Dec. 15, 1953; came to U.S., 1955; naturalized, 1961; d. Douglas Colin and Jean (Sampson) B. B.A. summa cum laude, SUNY-Buffalo, 1974, J.D., 1978. Bar: Tex. 1978. Title atty. S.W. Land Title Co., Dallas, 1977-78; assoc. firm Green, Gilmore & Rothpletz, Dallas, 1979-82, ptnr., 1983—. N.Y. State Regents scholar; SUNY-Buffalo undergrad. research asst., and grad. teaching asst. grantee. Mem. ABA, State Bar Tex., Dallas Bar Assn., Dallas Assn. Young Lawyers, Dallas Estate Planning Council, SUNY-Buffalo Alumni Assn., SUNY-Buffalo Law Alumni Assn., English-Speaking Union U.S., Phi Beta Kappa. Office: 1800 N Market Dallas TX 75202

BRAGG, ANNA LOU SPENCER, real estate broker; b. Denton, Tex., May 25, 1943; d. Thomas Morris and Betty Lou Rachel (Bradham) Spencer; m. Bobby J. Bragg, Sept. 5, 1964; children—Robert Morris, Jennifer Suzanne. A.A., San Jacinto Coll., 1962; B.S., U. Houston, 1964. Aerospace engr. NASA Johnson Space Center, Houston, 1964-66, reliability and quality assurance engr., 1966-69; instr. adult edn. Coll. Mainland, Texas City, Tex., 1974-76, Alvin Community Coll. (Tex.), 1975-76; agt. Jim Baker Realtors, Dickinson, Tex., 1976-80; pres. Bayou Realtors, Inc., Dickinson, Tex., 1980—. Mem. Tex. Assn. Realtors, Gulf Coast Bd. Realtors (dir. 1983—), Dickinson C. of C. (dir. 1983-85, pres. 1986—), Nat. Assn. Realtors, AAUW (v.p.), Mortar Bd., Tex. Garden Clubs (bd. dirs. 1979-84, treas. 1981-83, dist. vice dir. 1983-85; master flower show judge). Home: 2706 Mt Vernon Dr Dickinson TX 77539 Office: Bayou Realtors Inc 1613 Pine Dr Dickinson TX 77539

BRAGG, MELANIE DAWN, lawyer; b. Dallas, July 16, 1957; d. Charles V. and Shirley Lee (Harrison) Bragg. B.A. cum laude, U. Tex., 1978; J.D., U. Houston, 1982. Bar: Tex. 1982. Law clk. Pennzoil Co., Houston, 1981-82; briefing atty. Ct. Appeals for 14th Supreme Jud. Dist. Tex., Houston, 1982-83; sole practice, Houston, 1983—. Editor Houston Jour. Internat. Law, 1981-82. Media chairperson Texans for Child Support, Houston, 1983. Mem. ABA, State Bar Tex. (mem. selection, compensation and tenure of state judges com. 1983—), Houston Young Lawyers Assn. (chairperson law day com. 1983-85, mem. courthouse visitation com. 1983-84), Tex. Young Lawyers Assn. (mem. drug and alcohol abuse com. 1983-84, mem. pub. service handbook com. 1983-84, internat. law com. 1983-84), Assn. Trial Lawyers Am., Tex. Trial Lawyers Assn. Democrat. Methodist. Home: 497 N Post Oak Ln Houston TX 77024 Office: 710 N Post Oak Rd Suite 312 Houston TX 77024

BRAGMAN, RUTH SUSAN, educator; b. Bklyn., Dec. 9, 1947; d. Benjamin and Miriam (Brown) Bragman; B.S., U. Wis., 1969; M.Ed., U. Tex., 1973; Ph.D., U. Md., 1980. Tchr./vol. Sherut La'Am, Tel Aviv, Israel, summer 1969-71; recreational therapist Austin (Tex.) State Sch., 1972; acad. asst. in phys. edn. for handicapped U. Tex., Austin, 1971-73, intern in adaptive phys. edn., 1972-73; head motility tchr. Diagnostic Edn. Sch., Tidewater Rehab. Inst., Norfolk, Va., 1973-76; water safety instr. for handicapped, ARC, Norfolk, 1975-76; grad. asst. in recreation U. Md., College Park, 1976; adaptive phys. edn. tchr. Alternative Sch., Washington, 1977; grad. asst. spl. edn. U. Md., 1977-79, intern in arts for handicapped, 1979-80; project coordinator Nat. Com. Arts for Handicapped, Washington, summer 1980; asst. prof. dept. spl. edn. and rehab. Memphis State U., 1980-83; program asst. coordinator South Atlantic Regional Resource Ctr., 1983—; cons. in field; condr. workshops in field. Asst. in cardiac prevention and rehab. program Jewish Community Center, Norfolk, 1974-75; founder, leader handicapped Girls Scouts U.S.A., Norfolk, 1974-75; com. mem. exec. com. Spl. Olympics, Norfolk, 1974-76; com. mem. ad hoc com. on arts for handicapped children State of Tenn., 1981; mem. state monitoring team spl. edn. Dept. Edn., State of Tenn., 1981; steering com. spl. edn. alliance Memphis, 1982-83. Memphis State U. faculty research grantee, 1982; U. Md. fellow, 1979-80, grad. assistantship in spl. edn., 1977-78, 78-79, in recreation, 1976-77; U. Tex. grad. study grantee, 1971-72, 72-73. Mem. Am. Ednl. Research Assn., Am. Psychol. Assn., Council for Exceptional Children, Evaluation Network, Nat. Council on Measurement in Edn., Phi Kappa Phi, Phi Lambda Theta. Contbr. articles to profl. jours. Home: 7804 Lakeside Blvd Apt G404 Boca Raton FL 33434 Office: South Atlantic Regional Resource Ctr 1236 University Dr N Plantation FL 33322

BRAHAM, DELPHINE DORIS, government accountant; b. L'Anse, Mich., Mar. 16, 1946; d. Richard Andrew and Viola Mary (Niemi) Aho; m. John Emerson Braham, Sept. 23, 1967; children—Tammy, Debra, John Jr. B.S. Summa Cum Laude, Drury Coll., 1983; M. in Mgmt., Webster U., St. Louis, 1986. Bookkeeper, Community Mental Health Ctr., Marquette, Mich., 1966-68; credit clk. Remington Rand, Marietta, Ohio, 1971-72; acctg. technician St. Joseph's Hosp., Parkersburg, W.Va., 1972-74; material mgr. U.S. Dept. Army, Ft. Leonard Wood, Mo., 1982-86, accountant, 1986—. Leader Girls Scouts U.S.A., Williamstown, W.Va., 1972-74, Hanau, W.Ger., 1977-79. Mem. AAUW, Nat. Assn. Female Execs., Fed. Women's Program Com. (chmn. recruitment subcom.). Lutheran. Home: 76 Sheppard Fort Leonard Wood MO 65473

BRAINARD, JAYNE DAWSON (MRS. ERNEST SCOTT BRAINARD), civic worker; b. Amarillo, Tex., Nov. 1; d. Bill Cross and Evelyn (McLane) Dawson; A.B., Oklahoma City U., 1950; m. Ernest Scott Brainard, Nov. 26, 1950; children—Sydney Jane, Bill Dawson. Sec.-treas. E.S. Brainard Inc., 1980-84, v.p., 1984—; v.p. J. Thornton Cattle Co., 1981—. Guardian, Camp Fire Assn., 1960-65; vol. N.W. Tex. Hosp. Aux., 1960-63; state chmn. Am. Heritage, DAR, 1963-67, regent chpt., 1966-67, parliamentarian chpt., 1975-79, state historian, state chmn. marshalls, 1967-70, 73-76, mem. state organizing com., 1967-70, nat. vice chmn. marshalls, 1969-79, state rec. sec., 1970-73, editor cookbook, 1972, nat. vice chmn. motion picture com., 1971-73, mem. nat. bd. mgmt., nat. chmn. state regent's dinner, 1980-81, mem. Nat. Officers Club, 1979—, Nat. Chmn.'s Assn., 1981—, mem. Tex. speakers staff, 1972-76, 76-79, Tex. vice-regent, 1976-79, pres. nat. vice-regents club 1977-78, vice chmn. state fin. com., 1976-79, Tex. DAR Gen. Conf. chmn., 1975, 78, state chmn. state regents project, 1973-76, area rep. nat. speakers staff, 1977-80, 82-83, editor Tex. Roster, 1976, mem. state by law com., 1973-76, pres. chpt. regents Club, 1973-74, pres. vice-regents club, 1977-78, Tex. state regent, 1979-82, pres. Tex. DAR State Officers Club, 1980-81, state parliamentarian, 1982-85; organizing pres. Children Am. Revolution, 1963-65, state chmn. mag. sustaining fund; organizing regent Daus. Am. Colonies, 1972, chmn., 1974-76; bd. dirs. Tamassee DAR Sch., 1979-85; bd. dirs. Kate Duncan Smith Sch., mem. fin. com., 1979-82; pub. relations Amarillo Little Theater, 1965-69, pres., 1968-69, dir., 1966-69; bd. mem., program com. chmn. Amarillo Camp Fire Council, 1965-67, 75—, vice chmn. council, 1976—, pres., 1977-78; chmn. Camp Fire Leaders Assn., 1964-65, bd. dirs., 1974-79, pres. Amarillo council, 1977-78; br. pres. AAUW, 1963-65, pub. relations, 1965-67, world affairs rep., 1965-67; sec.-treas. group League Democratic Women, 1964; pres. Panhandle Geol. Soc. Aux., 1959, Starlighters Dance Club, 1963-64; pres. Speaking of Living Study Club, 1962-63, sec., 1973-74, parliamentarian, 1976-77, pres., 1977-78; pres. Republican Woman's Club, 1968, 73, v.p., 1972; parliamentarian Rep. Party Patter County; steering com. Nat. Library Week, 1966, 67, 68, Amarillo Chischom Trail Centennial, 1967; mem. Revitalize Amarillo Com., 1972, Amarillo Heart Bd., 1972-73, Historic Markers Task Force; vol. St. Anthony's Hosp. Mem. Internat. Platform Assn., U.D.C. (rep. to Amarillo Geneal. Adv. Bd. 1973-74, 75-76, 76-77, pres. Amarillo Geneal. Adv. Bd. 1982-84), Nat. Assn. Parliamentarians (profl. registered, pres. Hazel Crowley unit 1980-81, v.p. 1985-86), United Daus. 1812 (organizing regent, state chmn. lineage and hist. records 1984-86), Daus. Colonial Wars, Nat. Soc. So. Dames. Mem. Christian Ch. (bd. parliament 1965-66). Home: 2119 S Lipscomb St Amarillo TX 79109 Office: Box 1101 Amarillo TX 79105

BRAINARD, LEOLYN VERNITA, newspaper editor; b. Tacoma, Wash., Jan. 17, 1923; d. Jack Clement Agnew and Evelyn Leolyn (Byrne) Shelby; m. Hubert Ellis Brainard, June 14, 1944; children—Terry, Bernedene, Jennifer, Christopher. Student Skagit Valley Coll., 1973-74. Disbursing clk. USN, Melbourne, Fla., 1944-45, undercover agt. USN Intelligence, French Morocco, 1949-50; bookkeeper Jetmore Togs, Olathe, Kans., 1952-54, Sunshine Industries, Olathe, 1956-57; personnel clk. USN, Olathe, 1957-58; newspaper columnist Kingsville (Tex.) Record, 1958-60; reporter, photographer Whidbey Press (Crosswind), Oak Harbor, Wash., 1968-75, editor, 1975-85; pub. Spindrift Two, 1977—. Recipient Outstanding Feature Photography award USN Office Info., 1977, Best Navy Newspaper award, 1980, 81; Best Mil. Newspaper award U.S. Dept. Def., 1980. Mem. Federally Employed Women Inc (charter), Soroptimist Internat. (Oak Harbor charter). Home: 2285A N West Beach Rd Oak Harbor WA 98277 Office: Spindrift Two 3102 300 W Oak Harbor WA 98277

BRAISTED, MADELINE CHARLOTTE, army officer, personnel administrator; b. Jamaica, N.Y., Nov. 23, 1936; d. Melvin Vincent and Charlotte Marie (Klos) B. A.A.S., Nassau Community Coll., 1968; B.A., Hofstra U., 1973, M.A., 1975. Enlisted woman U.S. Marine Corps., Cherry Point, N.C., 1954-57; reservations agt. Airline Industry, N.Y.C., 1957-64; reservations controller Auto Lease Industry, N.Y.C., 1964-66; nuclear medicine technician Queens Gen. Hosp., Jamaica, N.Y., 1969-70; lab. mgr. CUNY, 1970-80; commd. capt. U.S. Marine Corps, 1980, advanced through enlisted grades to major, 1984; cons. Energy Etcetera, Flushing, N.Y., 1979-85; capt. U.S. Army Res., Fort Totten, N.Y., 1977-80; major AMEDD Profl. Support Agy., U.S. Army, Washington, 1980—. Author, pub. Energy Etcetera catalog, 1981-85; artist On Shore painting (hon. mention 1974). Merit badge counselor Boy Scouts Am., Queens County, N.Y., 1980-83; active mem. PTA, Jamaica, 1980-84. Decorated Army Commendation medal with one oak leaf, Army Achievement medal; named Community Leader and Noteworthy Am., Hist. Preservation of Am., 1976. Mem. Assn. Mil. Surgeons of U.S., Res. Officers Assn., Nat. Assn. Female Execs., Am. Pub. Health Assn., Soc. Nuclear Medicine. Roman Catholic. Avocations: painting; sculpture. Home: 216-12 38th Ave Bayside NY

11361 Office: US Army Med Dept Officer Procurement PO Box 4649 Bay Terrace NY 11360

BRAITINGER-GOEHRING, MARLIESE URSULA, business executive; b. Stuttgart, Ger., Jan. 27, 1938; d. Raymond and Anna (Weber) Braitinger; B.A.; Thiel Coll., 1960; M.A., Syracuse U., 1962; m. Walter G. Goehring II, June 16, 1962; children—Heidi U., Marliese O. Test adminstr. Thiel Coll., 1959-60; staff dean of women Syracuse U., 1960-62; prof. German and Spanish, Endicott Coll., Beverly, Mass., 1962-83, also acting acad. dean, asso. dean women, dir. advanced studies, supervisory dept. head dept. fgn. langs.; v.p. Investment Soc., Inc., 1983—. Bd. dirs Danvers YMCA, 1980-83; mem. Am. Security Council, 1979—, Republican Nat. Com., 1979—. Named Most Distinguished Advisor Phi Theta Kappa, 1982. Mem. Women for Constl. Govt. Congregationalist Home: 5 Puritan Rd Wenham MA 01984 Office: 8 Essex Center Dr Beverly MA 01960

BRAM, ISABELLE MARY RICKEY MCDONOUGH, clubwoman; b. Oskaloosa, Iowa, Apr. 4; d. Lindsey Vinton and Heddy (Lundee) Rickey; B.A. in Govt., George Washington U., 1947, postgrad., 1947-49; m. Dayle C. McDonough, Jan. 20, 1949; m. 2d, John G. Bram, Nov. 24, 1980. Dep. tax assessor and collector Aransas Pass Ind. Sch. Dist., 1939-41; sec. to city atty., Aransas Pass, Tex., 1939-41; info. specialist U.S. State Dept., Washington, 1942-48. Treas., Mo. Fedn. Women's Clubs, 1964-66, 2d v.p., 1966-68, 1st v.p., 1968-70, pres., 1970-72, exec. com., dir., 1972—; exec. com. Missourians for Clean Water. Bd. dirs. Gen. Fedn. Women's Clubs; bd. dirs. DeKalb County Public Library, pres., 1966; bd. dirs. Mo. Girls Town Found.; bd. advs. Legal Aid Western Mo. Mem. Mo. Fedn. Woman's Clubs (parliamentarian), Am. Soc. in Glasgow (Scotland), DeKalb County Hist. Soc., Internat. Platform Assn., AAUW, Nat. League Am. Pen Women, Epsilon Sigma Omicron, Zeta Tau Alpha, Phi Delta Delta, Phi Delta Gamma. Democrat. Episcopalian. Clubs: Tri Arts, Wimodausis, Gavel, Ledgers (pres.), Isabelle McDonough Girls Town, DeKalb County Women's Democratic (pres. 1964), Shakespeare, Mo. Democratic, Fifty Year. Editor Mo. Clubwoman Mag. Home: Sloan and Cherry Maysville MO 64469

BRAMBLETT, BARBARA DOYLE, city official; b. Coral Gables, Fla., Nov. 27, 1951; d. D. E. and Joy (Baker) Doyle; B.A., Auburn U., 1973. Asst. city mgr. City of Auburn, Ala., 1973-84; city mgr. City of Conyers, Ga., 1984—. Bd. dirs. Rockdale House, Conyers, 1984—; bd. dirs. United Way, Auburn, 1979-84, chmn., 1984; active Mayor's adv. com. on community devel., Auburn., 1976-82; mem. adv. council pub. adminstr. U. Ga., 1985—. NEH fellow, 1978. Mem. Internat. City Mgmt. Assn., Govt. Fin. Officers Assn., Ala. City Mgmt. Assn. (pres. 1980-81), Ga. City Mgmt. Assn. (bd. dirs. 1985), AAWU (v.p. 1984). Democrat. Methodist. Club: Pilot. Home: 1250 Shadowlawn Dr Conyers GA 30207 Office: City of Conyers PO Drawer 1259 Conyers GA 30207

BRAMLETT, MARY LYNNETTE HARRIS, banker; b. Corona, Calif., Sept. 18, 1953; d. Kenneth Frank and Kathy Lee (Hill) Harris; student U. Md., 1974-77, Southwestern Grad. Sch. Banking. Bookkeeper, First State Bank & Trust, Houston, 1972; successively teller, sec., relief supr., mgr., br. mgr. Peoples Nat. Bank of Md., Suitland, 1972-77; with Post Oak Bank, Houston, 1977-82, asst. v.p. ops. mgmt., 1980-82; asst. v.p. comml. loan ops. First City Nat. Bank Houston, 1982—. Bd. dirs. Big Sisters-Big Bros. of Houston, 1981; vol., Spl. Olympics, 1981; mediator Neighborhood Justice Center, 1981; speaker Speakers Bur., Houston Bar Assn., 1981. Mem. Nat. Assn. Bank Women, Am. Soc. Indsl. Security, NOW, Alpha Sigma Lambda. Mem. Christian Ch. Clubs: Bank Women's, Forum. Contbr. articles to profl. jours. Office: 1001 Main St Houston TX 77001

BRAMMER, DAWNA GAYLE, broadcasting sales executive; b. Canton, Ohio, June 1, 1950; d. Roy Edward and Doris Grace (Dennis) B. B.S., L'Institute Tours (France), 1971; B.A., Am. U., 1972; M.A., George Washington U., 1983. Media dir. Needham Harper Steers, Washington, 1974-76; account exec. Sta. WTTG-TV Metromedia, Washington, 1976-79, sales mgr., 1981-84; nat. account exec. Metromedia MTVS, N.Y.C., 1979-81; gen. sales mgr. sta. KRIV TV Metromedia, Houston, 1981—. Mem. Greater Washington Bd. Trade, 1981; expert adviser Jr. Achievement, Washington, 1983. Mem. Washington Advt. Club (chmn. TV 1983), Washington Media Research Council (pres. 1977-78), Am. Women in Radio and TV (mem. mktg. com. INTV). Republican. Presbyterian.

BRAMMER, DOROTHY PATTON, county government administrator; b. Chattanooga, Tenn., May 17; d. John Roy and Inez (McNeal) Patton; m. Shelby Richard Brammer, Apr. 10, 1937 (dec. 1952); children—Shelby Richard, David Morgan, John Patton. Diploma, Edmondson Bus. Coll., 1934. Sec. Tenn. Electric Power Co., Chattanooga, 1934-37, Dixie Mercerizing Co., Chattanooga, 1937-42; registrar Hamilton County, Chattanooga, 1954—. Sec.-treas. Chattanooga's Armed Forces Week Celebration, 1955—; bd. dirs. United Cerebral Palsy, 1960-66, Kidney Found. of Southeast Tenn., 1981-83, Girls Club of Chattanooga, 1967-72; mem. allocations com. United Fund, 1961-71, chmn. Hamilton County employees, 1962-80; mem. recruiting and tng. com. Am. Cancer Soc., 1962-63; hon. bd. dirs. Big Sisters Assn., 1962; mem. adv. bd. Salvation Army, 1963-84, sec. 1970-76, mem. Bell Ringers Club; sec. Chattanooga's Sesquicentannial Celebration Parade Com., 1965; mem. Models of Ministry Com., 1973; mem. Am. Diabetes Assn., 1980-84. Recipient Cert. of Appreciation, Sertoma, 1956, 57, 58, 71, 72, U.S. Marine Corps, 1972, U.S. Navy and Naval Reserve, 1972, VFW, 1972, Hamilton County, 1981, Citation of Appreciation Am. Legion, 1958, 72, 76, Citation for Meritorious Service, 1960, 63, 72; Cert. of Appreciation, VFW, 1972; Citation for Humanitarian Service, Cerebral Palsy Assn., 1966; Disting. Service award Radio Sta. WNOO, 1972; Plaque of Appreciation, U.S. Air Force Res., 1972, Disting. Citizen award City of Chattanooga, 1982, Hamilton County Bd. Commrs., 1981; Freedon award Sertoma Club, 1978; Community Relations award of Excellence, U.S. Army, 1980. Mem. Tenn. Registers Assn. (sec., Plaque of Appreciation 1969), Nat. Assn. County Recorders, Internat. Assn. Clks., Recorders and Treas., Nat. Assn. County Officers, County Ofcls. Assn. Tenn. (charter mem.), Tenn. Fedn. Democratic Women. Club: Tenn. Valley Patriots.

BRAMNICK, LEA SHAPIRO, business executive; b. Phila., Aug. 23, 1938; d. Irving Benjamin and Sylvia (Bloom) Shapiro; B.S. in Edn., Temple U., 1959, M.S. in Edn., 1962; 2 sons, Michael Richard, Gary David. Tchr. elem. schs., Phila. Bd. Edn., 1959-65; project mgr., designer ednl. materials Instructo, McGraw Hill, Paoli, Pa., 1971-74; dir. home products unit Research for Better Schs., Phila., 1974-76; pres. The Lobster Factory, Inc., designers ednl. materials, Merion Station, Pa., 1976—; creator Cooking for Kids program. Author: The Great Cook's Guide to Children's Cookery, 1976; The Kids Kitchen Encyclopedia, 1979; The Parents Solution Book, 1983, softcover, 1984. Address: 519 Putnam Rd Merion Station PA 19066

BRAMSON, RUTH NANCY, human resources executive; b. N.Y.C., May 17, 1940; d. Max H. Bohrer and Frances (Rosenfeld) Sadolsky; m. Paul Reich, Mar. 25, 1961 (div. 1977); children—Marjorie, Amy, Deborah; m. Robert S. Cohen, Apr. 16, 1977 (div. 1982); m. Sheldon H. Bramson, Nov. 24, 1984. B.A. cum laude, Barnard Coll., 1961; postgrad. Cornell U. Personnel coordinator Estee Lauder Internat., N.Y.C., 1973-75; asst. dir. personnel Brandeis U., Waltham, Mass., 1975-79; dir. corp. personnel Zayre Corp., Framingham, Mass., 1979-83; v.p. human resources Scandinavian Design, Natick, Mass., 1983—; instr. Framingham State Coll., 1983-84; adviser M.B.A. students Babson Coll., Wellesley, Mass., 1985. Mem. secondary sch. com. Cornell U., 1980-84. Recipient cert. of appreciation Waltham Job Placement Program, 1979, U.S. Dept. Labor, 1983. Mem. Am. Soc. Tng. and Devel., Am. Soc. Personnel Adminstrs., Womens Network, Assn. Affirmative Action Profls., New Eng. Soc. Personnel Mgmt., LWV (dir. Wellesley chpt. 1969-72). Democrat. Jewish. Avocation: tennis.

BRANAN, CAROLYN BENNER, accountant, lawyer; b. Wiesbaden, Fed. Republic Germany, Mar. 7, 1953; came to U.S., 1958; d. Huebert Harrison and Kathryn Wilfreda (Diggs) Benner; m. Robert Edwin Branan, Oct. 3, 1981. B.A. in Philosophy, U. S.C., 1973, J.D., 1976. Bar: S.C. 1977, U.S. Dist. Ct. S.C. 1977, U.S. Ct. Appeals (4th cir.) 1977; C.P.A., N.C., S.C. Sole practice law, Columbia, S.C., 1977-79; mgr. Deloitte Haskins & Sells, Charlotte, N.C., 1979—; cons. Gov.'s Bus. Council Task Force on Infrastructure Financing, 1983. Contbr. articles to profl. jours. Mem. exec. com., v.p., chmn. budget com., former treas. Charlotte Opera Assn., 1981—; exec. com., chmn. 1st and 2d ann. funding campaigns N.C. Opera, 1982—; exec. com. mayor's study com. Performing Arts Ctr., Charlotte, 1983—; mem. adv. council, chmn. performing arts Springfest, Charlotte, 1982—; fin. chmn. Opening of New Charlotte Transit Mall, 1984-85; bus. adv. council Queens Coll., Charlotte, 1984—; v.p. Opera Carolina. Mem. ABA (chmn. important devels. regulated pub. utilities tax sect. 1984—), N.C. Bar Assn., S.C. Bar Assn., Charlotte Estate Planning Council, Nat. Assn. Accts. (bd. dirs., dir. profl. devel., dir. community affairs 1979-84), N.C. Assn. C.P.A.s, Founders Soc. of Charlotte Opera Assn. (life). Episcopalian. Club: Charlotte City. Home: 530-A N Poplar St Charlotte NC 28202 Office: Deloitte Haskins & Sells 2100 So Nat Ctr Charlotte NC 28202

BRANCA, INEZ OLGA, construction company executive; b. N.Y.C., Feb. 7, 1915; d. Charles and Charlotte (Vernocchi) Monza; student Columbia U., 1938-39, CCNY, 1936-37; m. Barney Joseph Branca, Oct. 6, 1940; children—Joseph, Charles, Richard, Bernard. Sec., Jay Hormel & Co., N.Y.C., 1934-42; treas., corp. sec., office mgr. Bergen Engring. Co., East Rutherford N.J., 1943—. Roman Catholic. Mem. Glen Ridge (N.J.), Lodi (N.J.) (past pres.) women's clubs. Home: 2432 Harmon Cove Towers Secaucus NJ 07094 Office: Bergen Engring Co 375 Murray Hill Pkwy East Rutherford NJ 07073

BRANCH, CLAUDINE, real estate company executive; b. Duncan, Okla., Aug. 7, 1940; d. H. C. and Earle (Fulton) Byford; m. James Lee Branch, July 16, 1960; children—Robert Juarez, Rodney Kyle. Student pub. schs., Comanche, Okla. Bookkeeper, teller Okla. Nat. Bank, Duncan, 1961-69; trust dept. officer, teller, 1st Nat. Bank, Oklahoma City, 1969-72; sales assoc. Chuck Bagley Realtors, Oklahoma City, 1971-74; broker, owner Branch Realtors, Oklahoma City, 1974-77; broker, owner, pres. Realty World Branch & Assocs., Oklahoma City, 1977—. Duncan, 1978—; owner, pres. Realty World Branch & Assocs., Okemah, Okla., 1983—; broker, v.p. Realty World Unltd., Mustang, Okla., 1983—. Mem. Realty World Broker Council (Outstanding Broker 1979, sec.-treas. 1981-82), Bus. and Profl. Women's Club (pres. 1965), Credit Women Internat. (pres. 1966-67, Okla. bd. dirs. 1967), Oklahoma City Women's Council, Oklahoma City Bd. Realtors. Democrat. Baptist. Lodges: Eastern Star (Star Point 1968), White Shriners. Home: 704 Skylark Dr Oklahoma City OK 73127 Office: Realty World Branch & Assocs 4028 NW 23, Oklahoma City OK 73127

BRANCH, ETHEL V., accountant; b. Newark, Feb. 3, 1951; d. Harry and Jacqueline Virginia (Brown) Brown. Student Riverside City Coll., 1984, West Los Angeles Coll., 1985-86. Asst. to controller Sta. KYW-TV, Phila., 1973-75; acct. Majestic Am., Los Angeles, 1975-77; account exec. Thompson Recruitment Advt., Los Angeles, 1977-82; Western regional mgr. Springhouse Corp., Los Angeles, 1982-84; asst. mktg. mgr. Moldex Metric, Culver City, Calif., 1984-86; mgr. acctg. dept. office Quick Ink, City of Commerce, Calif., 1986—; owner, operator Trac Records, Culver City, 1985—. Mem. Democratic Circle, Los Angeles, 1984. Recipient 2nd place Nat. Essay Contest, 1968. Mem. Am. Soc. Women Accts., Nat. Assn. Female Execs. Club: Christian Women in Bus. (co-chmn.). Avocations: writing; caving. also 24015 Amberly Dr Moreno Valley CA 92388 Office: Trac Records Accounting for Profit PO Box 5462 Culver City CA 90231-5462

BRAND, DORIS, business executive; b. Phila., Mar. 9, 1945; d. Ida (Yevelson) Brand. B.S. in Acctg./Bus. Law, Temple U.; postgrad. in acctg., data processing and computer programming Camden County Coll., Blackwood, N.J. Controller Shulman Record Co., Inc., Phila., 1968—; v.p., controller Wall to Wall Sound and Video, Inc., Cinnaminson, N.J., 1968—. Treas., ORT, Cherry Hill, 1976-78, Landmark, N.J., 1980-81. Recipient certs. of appreciation Pennsauken High Sch., N.J., Cinnaminson High Sch., Delran High Sch., N.J. Mem. South Jersey C. of C. Avocations: art; sewing; tennis; golf; swimming. Home: 908 Society Hill Cherry Hill NJ 08003 Office: Wall to Wall Sound and Video Inc 200 S Route 130 Cinnaminson NJ 08077

BRANDES-BOWEN, ILA ANN, merchandising executive; b. Charlotte, Apr. 3, 1954; d. Roddy Arthur and Marguerite (Johnson) Brandes; m. Timothy Ray Bowen, July 1, 1984. B.A., U. N.C., 1977. Asst. supr. quality control Ball Corp., Asheville, N.C., 1977-79, indsl. engr., Muncie, Ind., 1979-80, methods and standards engr., 1980-82, materials handling engr., 1982-85, customer service engr., 1985-85, cons. Porsche Market Group, Rockaway, N.J., 1985-86; owner, pres. IAM, Asheville, N.C., 1985—; addressed 1984 Internat. Exposition Food Processors (speech pub.). Counselor, Young Life, Greensboro, N.C., 1972-77, Jr. Achievement, Muncie, 1979-81; bd. dirs. Muncie Symphony Membership Dr., 1981, Corp. Challenge, Muncie, 1981-83, United Way Fund Dr., Muncie, 1982-83. Mem. Nat. Assn. Female Execs. Republican. Presbyterian.

BRANDNER, MARGARET ANNE SHAW, polygraph examiner; b. Denver, Sept. 4, 1937; d. Bertram and Bessie (Syme) Shaw; B.A. in Elem. Edn., Loretto Heights Coll., 1959; grad. polygraph examiner Rocky Mountain Security Inst., 1978; A.A.S. in Polygraph Tech., Pike's Peak Community Coll., 1982; diplomate forensic hypnotist Inst. Forensic and Investigative Hypnosis, 1980; m. Kenneth LeRoy Brandner, Dec. 26, 1970. Lic. polygraphist, Nebr., Utah. Accountant, Denver Children's Home, 1970, Keny's Equipment, Inc., Green River, Wyo., 1971-78; polygraph examiner, sec., treas. Brandner Corp., Green River, 1978—. Mem. Am. Acad. Forensic Hypnotists, Am. Polygraph Assn., Colo. Assn. Polygraph Examiners, Nat. Acad. Women Polygraphists, Utah Polygraph Assn., World Congress Profl. Hypnotists, Wyo. Polygraph Assn. (charter), Am. Mensa. Roman Catholic. Home and Office: PO Box 1147 Green River WY 82935

BRANDON, MARY JANE HOWARD, lawyer, social worker; b. New Orleans, Sept. 19, 1944; d. Victor Charles and Mildred Eileen (Neal) Howard; B.A., Southwestern at Memphis, 1966; M.S.W., U. Tenn., 1968; J.D., Loyola U., New Orleans, 1982. Social worker Head Start program City of Memphis, 1965; dir. adoptions St. Peter Home for Children, Memphis, 1968-71; dir. social services Ednl. Research & Treatment Center, New Orleans, 1971-77; social worker in pvt. practice, 1975-77; chief social worker Hope Haven-Madonna Manor, New Orleans, 1977-80; practice law, New Orleans, 1982—. Trustee, fin. sec. First Unitarian Ch., New Orleans; pres. adv. bd. ACC Adult Group Home, 1982-83; mem. children's com. Mental Health Assn.; bd. dirs. Parents Anonymous, pres. bd., 1984—. NIMH fellow, 1966-68. Mem. Nat. Assn. Social Workers, Acad. Cert. Social Workers, La. Assn. Bd. Cert. Social Workers, Nat. Soc. Autistic Children, Am. Orthopsychiat. Assn., Am. Group Psychiat. Assn. Am. Soc. Internat. Law, ABA (commn. on legal problems of elderly), La. State Bar Assn., Interam. Bar Assn., Internat. Bar Assn., La. Hist. Assn., Preservation Resource Center, La. Landmarks Soc. Republican. Roman Catholic. Office: Suite 2300 Camal Pl One New Orleans LA 70130

BRANDON-PEREZ, SILVIA ANTONIA, lawyer; b. Havana, Cuba, Feb. 10, 1949; came to U.S., 1960; d. Richard Anthony Brandon and Marta Silvia (Perez) Brandon Hernandez; m. Fernando Lopez, Dec. 8, 1967 (div.); children—Ernesto, Ivan; m. 2d, Raymond Del Conte, June 10, 1978; children—Alessandro, Carlo Antonio. B.A. magna cum laude, U. P.R., 1970; J.D., Seton Hall Law Sch., 1976. Bar: N.J. 1976. Sole practice, North Bergen, N.J., 1976—; instr. Silva Mind Control, North Bergen, 1983—; dir. Centro de Control Mental de N.J., North Bergen. Author: Lluvia en negro, 1970. Counselor to Cuban refugees from Mariel in N.J., 1980-81; cons., trustee Sunrise Sch., North Bergen, 1983—. Named Lawyer of Year and to Hall of Fame, Hispanic Research Assn. N.Y., 1983. Mem. ABA, Assn. Trial Lawyers Am., Hudson County Bar Assn., Nat. Assn. Women Lawyers, Silva Internat. Grad. Assn. (coordinator N.J. 1983). Roman Catholic. Office: One Marine Plaza Suite 302 North Bergen NJ 07047

BRANDT, AVRENE LAURA, clin. psychologist; b. N.Y.C., July 3, 1942; d. Max Bernard and Pauline (Slatin) Brandt; B.A., Hunter Coll., 1964; M.S. (NIMH fellow), U. Mass., 1968, Ph.D., 1971; m. William Hall, June 24, 1973; children—Wiley, Gabbriel, Elissa. Staff psychologist Ashbourne Sch., Elkins Park, Pa., 1969-71; chief psychologist Pottstown (Pa.) Area Mental Health Clinic, 1971-74; clin. service dir. Devereux Found., Devon, Pa., 1975—; cert. instr. Assertive Relations with Children, Phila. Bd. dirs. Resources for Human Devel., v.p. Albert Einstein Acad. Mem. Phila. Clin. Neuropsychol. Group, Am. Psychol. Assn. Office: Devereux Found 19 S Waterloo Rd Devon PA 19333

BRANNAN, ETHEL FORD, social scientist; b. New Castle, Del., May 27, 1911; d. Thomas Drennen and Helen Virginia (Gooding) Ford; B.S., Johns Hopkins U., 1951, M.Ed. with honors, 1956; profl. diploma Columbia U., 1964, Ed.D. cum laude, 1965; widow. Mem. staff Balt. Pub. Schs., 1930-42, 46-62, 65-66, adminstr., 1958-62, 1965-66; prof. social psychology and sociology U. Buffalo, 1966-67; prof. social studies edn. Glassboro (N.J.) State Coll., 1967-82, prof. emeritus, 1981—, chmn. social studies edn. curriculum com., 1972-81, dir. Global Edn. Ctr., 1977-79, pres. World Edn. Council, 1979-86; curriculum cons., bd. dirs. N.J. Council Social Studies; mem. President's Commn. Global Edn., N.J. Consortium Global Edn. Served with WAVES, 1942-46. Recipient various service awards; research fellow U. Nairobi and Olduvai Gorge, Africa, 1975-76; named Outstanding Coll. Social Studies Educator of Yr., 1981. Fellow Acad. Polit. Sci.; mem. NEA (mem. ednl. leadership team to China 1979), Nat. Council Social Studies (pres. inter-nation exchange council 1981-83), Social Studies Suprs. Assn., AAUP, N.J. Edn. Assn., N.J. Council Social Studies, UN Assn., Phi Delta Gamma (pres. chpt. 1981-83), Pi Lambda Theta, Kappa Delta Pi, Phi Delta Kappa. Republican. Methodist. Clubs: Town and Country Women's, Johns Hopkins, Columbia U. Author: Cultural Unity and Curriculum, 1966; Improving Educational Programs for Disadvantaged Children, 1968; A Philosophy of Education for the 1970's, 1970; Creativity—What Is It, 1971; Individualized Reading and Social Studies, 1972; editor, contbr. to The Irregular Verb: To Teach, 1972; Looking at Two Faces of Education in China Today; author curriculum materials, articles in field. Home: 34 Holly Ct West Apts Pitman NJ 08071 Office: Robinson Hall Glassboro State Coll Glassboro NJ 08028

BRANNOCK, JUANITA LEWIS, nursing home administrator; b. Rockingham, N.C., June 29, 1924; d. Goley Burkemore and Mary Ann (Hancock) Lewis; R.N., James Walker Meml. Hosp., Wilmington, N.C., 1945; student Henry Ford Community Coll., Detroit, 1976-79; m. James Edward Brannock, Apr. 11, 1964. Pvt. duty and gen. hosp. duty nurse, 1945-46; nursing supr. Moses H. Cone Meml. Hosp., Greensboro, N.C., 1962-64; clin. nursing supr. Wayne County Gen. Hosp., Westland, Mich., 1966-79; dir. nursing Park Nursing Center, Taylor, Mich., 1979-81, adminstr., 1981—; pres. Continuing Health Edn. S.E. Mich., 1980-82; sec. Dirs. Nurses Wayne-Oakland Counties; bd. dirs. Family and Neighborhood Services of Southeastern Mich. Mem. Am. Nurses Assn., Am. Coll. Nursing Home Adminstrs., Am. Bus. Women's Assn. Home: 14860 McLain St Allen Park MI 48101 Office: 12575 S Telegraph Rd Taylor MI 48180

BRANNON, EMMA COLLINS, writer, essayist, poet, speaker; b. Elbert County, Ga.; d. Oscar L. and Hannah M. (Bell) Collins; grad. Sam Houston Normal Inst., 1913, Washington Sch. Art, 1922; B.S., Stephen F. Austin U., 1957, M.A., 1959; m. Jameston R. Brannon, Nov. 25, 1915 (dec. 1965); 1 foster son, James; 1 son, Jameston R. Tchr. public schs., Carthage, Tex., 1911-12, 15-16, 33-35, Gary, Tex., 1913-15, 16-24; bus. mgr. Brannon's Farms and Grocery Store, Carthage, 1929-40; postmaster U.S. Post Office, Carthage, 1940-55; religious, patriotic, inspirational, humorous and historic poems, ch. and prison ministry tracts writer, 1913—. Active Blue Bird council Girl Scouts U.S.A., 1957-59; sponsor Camp Fire Girls, 1959-68; Sunday Sch. tchr. 1st Bapt. Ch., Gary, 1913-34, Carthage, 1936-70, Rose Park Bapt. Ch., Shreveport, La., 1970-78; mem. U.S. Congl. Adv. Bd.; presdl. guest White House staff briefing, 1984. Recipient Silver Tray award Carthage Postal Service Rural/City Carrier-Clk. group, 1955, plaque U.S. Postal Service; Silver medal Congl. Bd. Mem. Acad. Am. Poets, Poetry Soc. Tex., Panola Hist. Soc., Panola C. of C., Tex. Geneal. Soc., La. Geneal. Soc., DAR, Internat. Platform Assn., Am. Security Council, Nat. Fedn. Republican Women, Nat. Alliance Sr. Citizens, Sam Houston Alumni Assn., Stephen F. Austin State U. Alumni Assn. Baptist. Clubs: Altrua (dir. 1950-52), Carthage Garden (pres. 1967-69). Author: These Passed Our Way, 1972; Wayside Blossoms (collection of poems), 1979. Home: Carthage TX 75633

BRANSCOMB, ANNE WELLS (MRS. LEWIS MCADORY BRANSCOMB), lawyer, consultant; b. Statesboro, Ga., Nov. 22, 1928; d. Guy Herbert and Ruby (Hammond) Wells; B.A., Ga. Coll., 1949, U. N.C., 1949; M.A., Harvard U., 1951; J.D. with honors, George Washington U., 1962; m. Lewis McAdory Branscomb, Oct. 13, 1951; children—Harvie Hammond, Katharine Capers. Bar: D.C. 1962, Colo. 1963, U.S. Supreme Ct. 1972, N.Y. 1973. Research assoc. Pierson, Ball and Dowd, Washington, 1962; law clk. to judge U.S. Dist. Ct., Denver, 1962-63; atty. Williams and Zook, Boulder, Colo., 1963-66; sole practice law, Boulder, 1966-69; mem. firm Arnold and Porter, Washington, 1969-72; communications counsel TelePrompTer Corp., N.Y.C., 1973; chmn. bd. Kalba Bowen Assocs., Inc., communications cons., Cambridge, Mass., 1977-80, v.p., 1974-77, sr. assoc., dir., 1980-82; mem. organizing com. Telecommunications Policy Research Conf., 1976; pres. Moneyscan, Inc., fin. planning computer services, 1980—; pres. The Raven Group, 1985—; vis. scholar Yale U. Law Sch., 1981-82; inaugural fellow Gannett Ctr. Media Studies, Columbia U., 1985; Pub. relations dir. Montgomery County (Md.) LWV, 1954-57; mass media chmn. AAUW, Chevy Chase, Md., 1959-62; del. Nat. Conf. on Crime, 1967; adv. bd. communications law program UCLA; co-chmn. Coordinating Com. for Low Income Housing for Boulder, 1966-68; bd. dirs. HELP for Boulder, Inc., 1968-69; commr. Public Housing Authority, Boulder, 1969-70; bd. dirs. Nat. Public Radio, 1975-78; trustee EDUCOM, Interuniv. Communications Council, Inc., 1976-78; Colo. chmn. Nat. Democratic Women's Conf., 1966; vice chmn. Colo. Dem. State Central Com., 1967-69, del. Dem. Nat. Conv., 1968, hearing officer credentials com., 1972; spl. asst. to nat. campaign dir. McGovern-Shriver campaign, 1972; policy planning Carter campaign, 1976, trustee Rensselaer Poly. Inst., 1980—; vis. com. Harvard U. Office Info. Tech., 1977-83; mem. Carnegie Corp. Task Force on Public Broadcasting, 1976-77; adv. panel on public understanding of sci. NSF, 1977-78; vis. com. Inst. Computer Scis. and Tech., Nat. Acad. Scis., 1977-80; mem. Aspen Inst. Task Force on Telecommunications Policy, 1977; mem. tech. adv. bd. Dept. Commerce, 1978-81, WARC adv. com. Dept. State, 1978-79; pres. Goose & Gander Soc. for Protection of First Wives, 1982—; trustee Fund for Peace, 1984—; adv. bd. EIC Intelligence, 1983—. Recipient Alumni Achievement award Ga. Coll., 1980. Mem. ABA (chmn. communications div. 1980-84, mem. council of sci. and tech. sect. 1981-85), Nat. Conf. Lawyers and Scientists, N.Y., D.C., Colo. bar assns., Fed. Communications Bar Assn., Am. Polit. Sci. Assn., Computer Law Assn. (dir.), Am. Arbitration Assn., Pacific Telecommunications Council (trustee), Internat. Inst. Communications, Order of Coif, Valkyries, Phi Beta Kappa. Contbr. articles to profl. jours.; editorial bd. Info. and Soc., 1980—; contbg. editor Jour. Communication, 1980—.

BRANT, ROXANNE HEATHER, religious ministries center executive; b. Toronto, Ont., Can., June 23, 1943; came to U.S., 1950, naturalized, 1960; d. Arthur Albert and Lilli Tekla (Umbach) B. Student U. Colo., 1961-62; B.A. Boston U., 1964; student Div. Sch., Harvard U., 1967-68, Boston Sch. Theology, 1967-68; M. Div., Gordon Div. Sch. (now Gordon-Conwell Div. Sch.), 1968; Th.D., Internat. Bible Inst. and Sem., 1985; D.D.(hon.), So. Calif. Theol. Sem., Stanton, 1985. Founder, pres. No. Fla. Christian Ctr., Inc., also known as Roxanne Brant Ministries, O'Brien, Fla., 1968—; mem. adv. bd. to Christian Bible schs., S.C., Hawaii; featured conf. speaker at various denominational confs.; featured speaker TV programs Trinity Broadcasting Network, Author 14 Christian teaching and inspirational books, the most recent being: From Decision To Discipleship, 1973; Knowing God's Will For Your Life, 1981; Praying In The Spirit, 1985; The God Who Gives Ideas, 1986; also 3 booklets. Republican. Avocations: golfing; tennis. Office: No Fla Christian Ctr Inc PO Box 1000 O'Brien FL 32071

BRANTLEY, HELEN THOMAS, clinical psychologist; b. Palmerton, Pa., Jan. 29, 1942; d. Francis Clyde and Elizabeth (Jennings) Thomas; B.A., Duke U., 1963, Ph.D., 1973; m. John Croft Brantley, June 15, 1963; children—Elizabeth Ann, John Thomas. Psychologist pub. schs., Boothwyn, Pa., 1967; pvt. practice psychol. cons., Chapel Hill, N.C., 1971-77, 81—; research assoc. Duke U., Durham, N.C., 1975-78; postdoctoral fellow in child psychology U. N.C. Sch. Medicine, Chapel Hill, 1977-78, research asst. prof., 1978-79, asst. prof. psychology, 1979-81. NIMH fellow, 1980-81. Mem. Am. Psychol. Assn., N.C. Psychol. Assn. Contbr. articles to profl. publs. Home: 635 Totten Pl Chapel Hill NC 27514 Office: 109 Conner Dr Suite 204 Chapel Hill NC 27514

BRASHERS, ROSE MARY, telephone co. ofcl.; b. Little Rock, Apr. 17, 1952; d. George Phillip and Mae (Bradley) Rollman; student (scholar) Claremore Jr. Coll., 1974-76, Tulsa U., 1982—; m. Charles Brashers, Aug. 23, 1969; children—Charles W., Michael E. Asst. city clk. City of Chelsea (Okla.), 1971-73; sales rep. Reynolds Aluminum Supply Co., 1976-79; communications cons. Southwestern Bell Telephone Co., Tulsa, 1979-80, customer service supr., 1980-81, account exec., 1981—; speaker career edn. Mem. Nat. Assn. Legal Adminstrs. (assn.), Green Country Soccer Assn., Phi Theta Kappa. Democrat. Roman Catholic. Club: Amethyst Rev. Home: 13309 E 40th Pl Tulsa OK 74134 Office: 510 S Elgin St Room G118 Tulsa OK 74120

BRASSEAUX, LORNA MARIE, lawyer; b. Crowley, La., Apr. 28, 1957; d. Ervin and Mary Irene (Meche) Brasseaux. B.A. in English, U. Southwest La., 1979; J.D., La. State U., 1982. Bar: La. 1983. Law clk. 1st Cir. Ct. Appeals, La. State Cts., Baton Rouge, 1983—. Mem. ABA, La. State Bar Assn., Assn. Trial Lawyers Am., Am. Judicature Soc, Phi Delta Phi, Phi Kappa Phi. Democrat. Roman Catholic.

BRASWELL, FRANCES POSTEL, human relations counselor; b. St. Louis, Aug. 18, 1917; d. Philip Henry and Bessie Holnback Postel; B.A., Wellesley Coll., 1939; postgrad. Bowie State Grad. Sch., Austria, 1976, Amsterdam, 1977; M.A., Webster Coll., 1979; m. David M. Braswell, Dec. 7, 1942; children—Joan, David III, Philip, Carol. With world hdqrs. IBM, 1939-41; program dir. USO, Ft. Dix, N.J., 1941-42; with YMCA, Wilmington, Del., 1942-43; intern Met. Ch. Fedn. St. Louis Area, 1964-76; TV producer Journey Through Darkness, 1965-67; human relations counselor, Belleville, Ill., 1980—; v.p. Braswell and Assos. Ltd., Belleville, 1964; pres. Braswell-Postel Farm Ltd., Belleville, 1978—. Pres. St. Clair County Health and Welfare Council; bd. dirs. McKendree Coll., Belleville High Sch.-Jr. Coll., 1959-62; mem. Sesquicentennial Commn.; mem. adv. council Sta. KETC-TV, St. Louis; trustee Belleville Area Coll., 1985—. Recipient citation of honor Ch. Women United in Ill., 1967; named Outstanding Citizen, St. Clair County Health and Welfare Council, 1970; Woman of Yr., St. Louis Wellesley Club, 1969; profl. counselor N.Am. Soc. Adlerian Psychology. Mem. LWV, Urban League St. Clair County-Madison County, St. Clair County Hist. Soc., P.E.O. (pres. local chpt. 1977-79), Delta Kappa Gamma (hon.). Independent Republican. Methodist. Club: Wellesley (St. Louis). Home and Office: 12 Woodland Ct Belleville IL 62221

BRASWELL, JACKIE BOYD, educator; b. Leon County, Fla., Feb. 15, 1938; d. Chalmer Parks and Kathryn Iris (Johnson) Boyd; m. Fletcher Braswell, Nov. 28, 1957; children—Felicia Lori Braswell Berger, Carmen Ethelee. B.S., Fla. State U., 1964, M. Ednl. Adminstrn., 1976, postgrad. 1978-85; edn. cert. Valdosta State Coll., 1968. Lic. tchr. and adminstr., Fla. Single mgr., security clearance U.S. Air Force, Moody AFB, Ga., 1958-61; tchr. bus. edn. Berrien High Sch., Nashville, Ga., 1966-69, Rickards High Sch., Tallahassee, 1970-75; bus.-vocat. tchr. Lincoln High Sch., Tallahassee, 1975—; co-owner, fin. mgr. Rundown Farms, Tallahassee, 1969—. Editor, In Touch, 1979-80. Recipient Merit award Future Farmers Am., 1974. Mem. Nat. Bus. Edn. Assn., Fla. Vocat. Assn., Fla. Bus. Edn. Assn., Leon Vocat. Assn., Leon Classroom Tchrs. Assn., Dance Arts Guild, Leon County Farm Bur., Quill and Scroll, Phi Kappa Phi. Democrat. Home: Route 13 Box 358 Tallahassee FL 32312 Office: Lincoln High Sch 3838 Trojan Trail Tallahassee FL 32301

BRATAAS, NANCY, state senator; b. Mpls., Jan. 19, 1928; d. John Draper and Flora (Warner) Osborn; m. Mark Gerard Brataas, 1948; children—Mark, Anne. Ed. U. Minn. First elected to Minn. legislature, 1975; now mem. Minn. Senate; cons. Brataas Systems. Minn. Republican state chairwoman, 1963-69; state chairwoman Minn. Rep. Fin. Com., 1969-71. Mem. League Women Voters, AAUW, Zonta Internat. Episcopalian. Office: Minn Senate State Capitol Saint Paul MN 55155*

BRATCHER, GRACE JONES CORNELIA, librarian, educator; b. Charlottesville, Va., June 22, 1939; d. Philip Alexander and Evangeline (Opie) Jones; m. Willie Marcus Bratcher, Aug. 27, 1960; children—Yvette Bratcher Carter, Debra Bratcher Monroe, Willie Jr. B.S., Va. State U., 1960; M.A. in Curriculum and Instrn., U. No. Colo., 1976; postgrad. U. Tex., 1966-68. Cert. librarian, tchr., curriculum supr., Tex. Tchr. ESL, pub. schs., Clint, Tex., 1966-67; tchr. pub. schs., El Paso, Tex., 1967-70, tchr., librarian, 1970-73; librarian pub. schs., Colorado Springs, Colo., 1973-76; tchr. pub. schs., Houston, 1976-77, learning resource coordinator, 1977—; reading activity coordinator Pub. Library, Houston, 1977-80. Mem. Tex. State Tchrs. Assn. (rep. 1977—), Aldine Tchrs. Assn., NEA, Tex. Library Assn., Delta Sigma Theta (sec. Tex.-Colo. alumnae chpt. 1972-82, Pub. Service honor 1973). Democrat. Club: Jack & Jill of Am. (Houston).

BRATCHER, TWILA LANGDON, conchologist, malacologist; b. Smoot, Wyo.; d. Willis G. and Pearl (Graham) Langdon; m. Ford F. Bratcher, Sept. 10, 1942. Research assoc. Los Angeles Mus. Natural History, 1965—; mem. Ameripages Sci. Expedition to Galapagos Islands, 1971; author stories for blind children about skin diving, sea shells, creatures of the sea pub. Braille Inst., 1964-72; work with schs. for blind. Mem. Conchological Club So. Calif. (pres. 1966; life hon. mem.), Am. Malacological Union (councilor at large 1971), Western Soc. Malacologists (pres. 1973), Hawaiian Malacological Soc., Santa Barbara Malacological Soc., San Diego Shell Club, Pacific Shell Club (life hon. mem.). Club: So. Calif. Woman's Press (pres. 1977-79). Author: Living Terebras of the World; contbr. articles to sci. jours. Home: 8121 Mulholland Terr Hollywood CA 90046

BRATLEY, CAROL ANN, real estate development consultant; b. Yonkers, N.Y., Jan. 2, 1944; d. Cyril Oliver and Eleanor (Newcomer) B.; m. William Palfrey Lamb, June 24, 1978. B.A. magna cum laude with high honors, Brown U., 1966; postgrad. Yale U., 1967; M.S. in Mgmt., MIT, 1981. Planning cons. to towns, cities, cultural and other instns., Boston, 1969-76; transp. planner Met. Area Planning Council, Boston, 1977-79; v.p. UST Investment Advisors, Boston, 1982-85; mgr. real estate adv. services Laventhol & Horwath, Boston, 1985—, alt. del. Charlestown Econ. Devel. Corp., Mass., 1985; developer Residential Real Estate, Charlestown, 1977—. Contbr. articles to profl. jours. Mem. Boston Art Commn., 1976—, chmn., 1985—; mem. Browne Fund Com., Boston, 1981—; trustee Charlestown Preservation Soc., 1982-85; bd. designators Henderson Found., Boston, 1985. Mem. Greater Boston Real Estate Bd., Phi Beta Kappa. Office: Laventhol & Horwath 2 Center Plaza Boston MA 02108

BRATTIN, NELL, building materials company executive, development company executive; b. Faucett, Mo., June 30, 1936; d. Everett L. and Artie M. (Ashford) Tracy. m. Ronald R. Brattin, Oct. 16, 1953; children—Rhonda, Olen, Richard, Vicki, Susan. Student U. Mo.-Kansas City, 1969-70; cert. broker Weaver Sch. Real Estate, 1973. C.P.A. Vice-pres. Brattin Drywall Inc., Lee's Summit, Mo., 1967-75; pres. Kenell Bldg. Materials Inc., Greenwood, Mo., 1976—, exec. pres. Greenwood Leasing and Developing Inc., 1977—. Office: Kenell Building Materials Box 108 RD 1 Greenwood MO 64034

BRATTON, CINDY DICK, human resources director; b. Jasper, Ind., Apr. 5, 1952; d. Roman Frank and Elizabeth (Brenner) Dick; m. John Francis Bratton, Sept. 9, 1972; children—Sarah Beth. A.A., B.S., U. Cin., 1979, M.Indsl. Relations, 1980. Fringe benefits coordinator Moses Cone Hosp., Greensboro, N.C., 1980-81, asst. personnel dir., 1981-83; human resources dir. Alamance County Hosp., Burlington, N.C., 1984—. Mem., leader Girl Scouts U.S.A., Cin., 1979-80, cons., Greensboro, 1981-82; coordinator St. Paul's Cath. Ch., Greensboro, 1982-83. U. Cin. state scholar, 1979. Mem. Personnel Assn. Alamance County (treas.), N.C. Hosp. Personnel Assn., Am. Soc. Hosp. Personnel Adminstrs., Nat. Assn. Female Execs. Republican. Roman Catholic. Avocations: jogging; snow skiing; camping; reading. Home: 1602 Foxhollow Rd Greensboro NC 27410

BRATTON, IDA FRANK, educator; b. Glasgow, Ky., Aug. 31, 1933; d. Edmund Bates and Robbie Davis (Hume) Button; m. Robert Franklin Bratton, June 20, 1954; 1 son, Timothy Andrew. B.A., Western Ky. U., 1959, M.A., 1962. Cert. secondary tchr., Ky., cert. leader, Ky. Tchr. math. and sci. Gottschalk Jr. High Sch., Louisville, 1959-65; tchr. math. Iroquois High Sch., Louisville, 1965-79, Waggener High Sch., Louisville, 1979—. Mem. NEA, Ky. Edn. Assn., Jefferson County Edn. Assn., AAUW. Democrat. Methodist. Avocations: travel; needle crafts. Home: 304 Paddington Ct Louisville KY 40222 Office: Waggener High Sch 330 S Hubbards Ln Louisville KY 40207

BRATTON, KATHLEEN WILSON, insurance company official, lawyer; b. Wilmington, Del., Oct. 29, 1949; d. William Wilson and Julie Clare (Hallahan) B.; m. Brian F. Wruble, Apr. 20, 1985. A.B., Radcliffe Coll., 1971; J.D., U. Chgo., 1974. Bar: N.Y. 1975, Md. 1979, U.S. Dist. Ct. (so. dist.) N.Y. 1975, U.S. Ct. Appeals (2d cir.) 1975, U.S. Supreme Ct. 1978. Assoc. firm Reid & Priest, N.Y.C., 1974-78, William Wilson Bratton, Elkton, Md., 1979-80; asst. counsel Equitable Life Assurance Soc. U.S., N.Y.C., 1980, assoc. counsel, 1980-81, asst. gen. counsel, 1981-84, v.p. counsel, 1984—; mem. 1933 and 1934 Act Subcom. Am. Council Life Ins., Washington, 1982—. Mem. ABA, N.Y. State Bar Assn., DAR (head Elk chpt., Elkton, Md.), Daus. Am. Colonists. Democrat. Episcopalian. Home: 411 West End Ave Apt 14B New York NY 10024 Office: Equitable Life Assurance Soc US 1285 Ave of Americas New York NY 10019

BRATTON, MARGARET KATHERINE (PEG), nurse, nursing director; b. Balt., Oct. 7, 1938; d. Roy Thomas and Katherine Sydney (Sharrer) Bankard; m. David Connolly Bratton, Feb. 14, 1963; children—David, Michael, Shawn, Katherine. R.N., St. Alphonsus Sch. Nursing, Boise, Idaho, 1959. USPHS nurse, Laredo, Tex., 1965; pediatric nurse St. Joseph's Hosp., Laredo, 1966; critical care nurse Phoenix Baptist Hosp., 1980; geriatric nurse, Kivel Geriatric Ctr., Phoenix, 1980—, dir. nurses, 1981—. Pres. Luke AFB Officers Wives Club, Phoenix, 1979. Served to capt., Nurse Corps, USAF, 1960-63. Roman Catholic. Home: 5336 N 40th Ln Phoenix AZ 85019 Office: Kivel Geriatric Center 3020 N 36th St Phoenix AZ 84018

BRATYANSKI, DORIS MADELINE (DORI BRYANT), advertising manager; b. Perth Amboy, N.J., Oct. 8, 1952; d. Adolph Joseph and Frances Mae (Griffin) B. B.A., Douglass Coll., 1974. Tchr. Perth Amboy Bd. Edn., 1974-75; dist. sales mgr. Hertz Corp., N.Y.C., 1975-80; adv. acct. exec. N.Y. Daily News, N.Y.C., 1980-81, Omni Mag., Penthouse, N.Y.C., 1981-82; travel advt. mgr. USA Today/Gannett, N.Y.C., 1982-85; advt. mgr. Hanover Pub., N.Y.C., 1985—. Morris Goldfarb scholar, 1970. Mem. Nat. Assn. Female Execs., Am. Soc. Travel Agts., Caribbean Tourism Assn., Travel and Tourism Research Assn., Travel Industry Assn. Can. Democrat. Roman Catholic. Avocations: languages; writing plays and musical scores.

BRAUCHT, ELIZABETH ANNE SANTOWASSO, educator, resort hotel owner; b. Elizabeth, N.J., Mar. 5, 1938; d. Leo Carmen and Anne Marie (Radice) Santowasso; m. Bruce Allen Braucht, Oct. 2, 1965 (div. July 1976). A.B. in English and Fine Arts, U. Pa., 1960; M.A. in Reading, Kean Coll., 1971. Cert. secondary tchr., N.J. Exec. asst. John F. Kraft, Inc., N.Y.C., 1960-61; tchr. Jamesburg and Freehold Bds. Edn., N.J., 1962-66; tchr. English and reading Millburn Bd. Edn., N.J., 1966—; gen. mgr., owner Sylvan Hotel, Avon-by-the-Sea, N.J., 1972—; owner, operator Always Travel Centre, Seabright, N.J., 1975-77, tour operator student trips to Greece, 1975. N.J. Dept. Edn. study grantee Princeton U., 1985. Mem. N.J. Hotel-Motel Assn., NEA, N.J. Ednl. Assn., Millburn Edn. Assn. (grievance co-chairperson 1985—). Avocations: antiques collector and dealer. Home: 125 Sylvania Ave Avon-by-the-Sea NJ 07717 Office: Millburn Bd of Edn Millburn Ave Millburn NJ 07042

BRAUER, JACQUELINE SUE, purchasing executive; b. Saginaw, Mich., July 20, 1948; d. Russell Lewis and Flora Ann (Andreotti) Murphy; m. Max T. Brauer, Nov. 29, 1975 (div. Sept. 1983). B.A., Mich. State U., 1971. Editorial asst. Mich. State U., East Lansing, 1973-74; account exec. Tom O'Brien & Assocs., Lansing, Mich., 1974-77; info. coordinator Mich. State U. Info. Services, East Lansing, 1977-81; account exec. Anthony M. Franco, Inc., Detroit, 1981-82; purchasing mgr. Beurmann-Marshall Corp., Lansing, 1982—. Mem. Women in Communications, Inc. (publicity chmn. 1979-81), Internat. Assn. Bus. Communicators. Home: 322 Kipling Blvd Lansing MI 48912 Office: Beurmann-Marshall Corp 5840 Enterprise Dr Lansing MI 48910

BRAUN, BARBARA DICKEY, nurse; b. Washington, Apr. 22, 1933; d. William Kinchley and Helen Bertha (Randall) Dickey; m. James Milton Bruan, Feb. 13, 1953; children—James Milton, Jr., Jon Mark. Lic. Practical Nurse, Savannah Vocat. Sch., 1967; A.S., Brunswick Jr. Coll., 1975. R.N., Ga. Indsl. nurse Interstate Paper Co., Riceboro, Ga., 1968-72; nurse Liberty Meml. Hosp., Hinesville, Ga., 1972—; dir. nursing Midway Nursing Inn, Ga., 1980-81, Savannah Health Care, Ga., 1982-83; vol. nurse for indigent patients Liberty Meml. Hosp. and Liberty Manor Nursing Inn, Midway, 1972—; owner, operator Jims Oyster Bar, Midway, 1983—. Republican. Baptist. Home: PO Box 57 Lake Gale Midway GA 31320

BRAUN, BARBARA ILENE, advertising executive; b. Charleston, W.Va., May 8, 1944; d. Arthur Goodman and Charlotte C. Braun; B.S., Northwestern U., 1966; M.B.A., Pepperdine U., 1982. Supr., Leo Burnett Advt., Chgo., 1966-67; account coordinator Lake Public Relations, London, Eng., 1967-68; account exec. Beneficial Standard Corp., Los Angeles, 1968-70; assoc. Argosy Group, Los Angeles, 1970-73; owner Braun & Assocs., Los Angeles, 1973—, Charleston Tent & Awning Co., 1984—; lectr., cons. in field. Mem. Nat. Assn. Women Bus. Owners, Nat. Assn. Female Execs., Internat. Platform Assn., Phi Beta. Democrat.

BRAUN, ELISABETH MARIA, publishing executive, consultant; b. Cologne, Germany, May 24, 1938; came to U.S., 1959; d. Winand Maria and Anna Maria (Zimmer) Esser; m. Peter C.M.S. Braun, July 1, 1967 (div. Dec. 1980). Student Heidelberg U., 1957-58, Cambridge U., 1958, Valladolid U., 1958, Paris U., 1959; M.A., U. Ky., 1961, Ph.D., 1963; postgrad. Columbia U., 1966, Colegio de Mexico, 1966. Chief Am. sect. U.S. Ednl. Commn., Bonn, West Germany, 1964-65; asst. cultural attache U.S. Embassy, Bonn, 1966; internat. polit./econ. corr., N.Y.C., 1967-79; dir. corp. strategic planning Am. Express Co., N.Y.C., 1979-80; dir. bus. devel. Am. Express Pub. Corp., N.Y.C., 1980—; internat. cons. pvt. and pub. instns., Germany, 1979—. Contbr. articles on politics and econs. to profl. jours. Dir., Battle Harbour Found., Greenwich, Conn., 1978—; treas. East Manhattan Counseling Service, N.Y.C., 1983. Fulbright fellow, 1959-61; recipient awards U. Ky., 1962-63, AAUW, 1966. Mem. N.Y. Women in Communications. Home: 16 Indian Mill Rd Greenwich/Cos Cob CT 06807 Office: Am Express Pub Corp 1120 Ave of the Americas New York NY 10036

BRAUN, EUNICE HOCKSPEIER, author, religious exec., lectr.; b. Alta Vista, Iowa; d. George Phillip and Lydia (Reinhart) Hockspeier; student Gates Coll., 1932-34, Coe Coll., 1937-39, Northwestern U., 1944-47; m. Leonard James Braun, May 29, 1937. Freelance writer for mags., newspapers, 1947-52; bus. mgr. Baha'i Publishing Trust, Wilmette, Ill., 1952-55, mng. dir., 1955-71; internat. news editor Baha'i News, 1952-70; tchr. Baha'i schs., Alaska, Can., Europe and U.S., 1958—; tchr. Baha'i Faith in U.S., Central Am., Europe, Africa, Asia, 1953—; cons. Baha'i Pub. Trust, New Delhi, India, 1972; mem. aux. bd. Continental Bd. Counselors, Baha'i Faith in the Ams., 1972—. Mem. Nat. League Am. Pen Women, Baha'i Faith, Iota Sigma Epsilon. Author: Know Your Baha'i Literature, 1959; The Dawn of World Peace, 1963; Baha'u'llah: His Call to the Nations, 1967; From Strength to Strength, Half Century of the Formative Age of the Baha'i Faith, 1978; A Crown of Beauty, 1982; The March of the Institutions, 1984; A Reader's Guide: Baha'i Literature in the Development of English, 1986; contbr. essays to Baha'i World, Internat. Record. Home: 1025 Forestview Ln Glenview IL 60025

BRAUN, ISLETA GAYLE, realty company executive, civic worker; b. Gayle, La., Mar. 20, 1916; d. Arthur Craig Gayle and Alma (Roberts) Gayle-Gumble; m. Woodward Garber, 1940 (div. 1947); 1 dau., Linda Gayle; m. William Louis Braun, Sept. 27, 1952; 1 dau., Alma Pinet. Student U. Okla., 1935, UCLA, 1936, Tulane U., 1937, 38, 41, Cin. Coll. Music, Cin. Conservatory of Music, 1942-46, Columbia U., 1953. Singer, actress CBS, Hollywood, 1939-40; columnist New Orleans Item, 1938-39, Times Star, Cin., 1947-48; woman's program dir. Sta. WCKY, Cin., 1947-48; actress Cin. Stage Inc., 1944-49; v.p. Braun & Co. Realtors, Long Beach, Miss., 1965—; pub. relations vol. Children's Internat. Summer Villages. Dir. short plays, concert readings. Collector, dir. Children's Internat. Art Fairs, 1968. Co-founder Children's Internat. Summer Villages, Miss. Gulf Coast region, 1962, Treasury of Trees ecological group; chmn. Drug Abuse Jazz Concert; chmn. Children's Internat. Art Shows, 1968—; active mem. Miss. LWV, Common Cause, Family Planning; pub. relations work for Coast Episcopal Schs., 1958—. Winner of So. Region Jessee Lasky's "Gateway to Hollywood" in Drama and Voice, 1940; recipient Humanities Golden award Miss. Library Assn., 1976; grantee Miss. Arts Com. Mem. Miss. Bd. Realtors, Miss. Inst. Arts and Letters, Miss. Coast Arts Assn., MacDowell Hon. Soc., Pi Beta Phi. Republican. Episcopalian. Clubs: Pass Christian Yacht, Martha Guild (past pres.). Home: 822 E Beach Blvd Long Beach MS 39560 Office: Braun & Co Realtors 822 E Beach Blvd Long Beach MS 39560

BRAUN, LENORE MARIE (MUSIELSKI), behavioral scientist, writer, psychologist, educator, consulant, researcher; b. Bridgeport, Conn., Mar. 12, 1955; d. Joseph Stanislaus and Dolores Marie (Palumbo) Musielski; B.S. in Psychology (Silverstone grantee), U. Bridgeport, 1979, M.S. in Psychology, 1979; m. John Richard Braun, Mar. 9, 1979; 1 stepson, John Richard. Interviewer for unemployment compensation claims, security div. State of Conn., New Haven, 1976; fin. cons., rep. Investors Diversified Services, Fairfield, Conn., 1976-77; asst. supr. dept. customer service Bank Americard, Fairfield, 1977; mental health therapist Hall-Brooke Psychiat. Hosp./Found., Westport, Conn., 1977-79; adj. faculty/guest lectr. in psychology U. Bridgeport, 1980—, Albertus Magnus Coll., 1980—, Western Conn. State U., 1982—, Norwalk Community Coll.; psychotherapist/cons. in behavioral medicine; free-lance writer in psychology, 1980—; vol. psychotherapist St. Andrew Sch. Mellon grantee. Mem. Am. Psychol. Assn. (assoc.), Eastern Psychol. Assn., (assoc.), Conn. Psychol. Assn. (assoc.), New Eng. Psychol. Assn., Soc. Behavioral Medicine, Am. Soc. Profl. Exec. Women, Am. Assn. Univ. Profs., AAAS, Nat. Cons. League, Am. Arbitration Assn., N.Y. Acad. Scis., World Fedn. Mental Health, Nat. Writers Union, Inst. Advancement Health, Assn. Humanistic Psychology, Am. Mgmt. Assn., Internat. Women's Writing Guild, Nat. Writers Club. Democrat. Roman Catholic. Research on creativity, health psychology. Home: Bridgeport CT 06606 Office: 2335 Black Rock Tpke Fairfield CT

BRAUN, MONIKA THERESIA, accountant; b. Merring, Fed. Republic of Germany, Oct. 29, 1961; came to U.S., 1968; d. Emmeran and Theresia (Plach) Braun Klein. B.S. in Acctg., Bob Jones U., 1985. Acct. Emkay, Inc., Chgo., 1985—; jr. acct. Continental Materials Corp., Chgo., 1984-85. Mem. Nat. Assn. Female Execs. Office: 20 N Wacker Dr Suite 1900 Chicago IL 60606

BRAUN, ROSLYN ROTKIN, psychologist; b. N.Y.C., Aug. 27, 1921; d. Meyer M. and Emma (Honigman) Rotkin; M.A., N.Y. U. Sch. Edn., 1947; m. Monroe Jacob Braun, Mar. 29, 1942; 1 son, Simon David. Intern, Mt. Sinai Hosp., N.Y.C., 1947; sch. psychologist N.Y.C. Bd. Edn., 1947-52; pvt. practice clin. psychology, Jamaica Estates, N.Y., 1952—; parent-edn. cons. various nursery schs., 1952—. Mem. Am. Orthopsychiat. Assn. (life), Am. Psychol. Assn., N.Y. Soc. Clin. Psychologists, Soc. Projective Techniques, Soc. Pediatric Psychology. Asst. editor Jamaica Estates Civic Assn. Bull., 1980—. Home and Office: 81-10 Haddon St Jamaica Estates NY 11432

BRAVERMAN, CAROL PETERS, lawyer; b. Wilmington, Del., June 15, 1948; d. Edwin Albert and Blanche Irene (Hillis) Peters; m. Raymond Howard Braverman, Jan. 25, 1970; children—Christopher Marc. B.A., U. Del., 1970; J.D., Del. Law Sch., 1979. Bar: Del. 1979, U.S. Dist. Ct. Del. 1980. Tchr., Capitol Sch. Dist., Dover, Del., 1970-71; adminstrv. asst. Kent County McGovern Presdl. Campaign, Dover, 1972; law clk. Twilley, Jones & Feliceangeli, Dover, 1977-79, assoc., 1979-81, ptnr., 1981—. Chmn. criminal justice adv. bd. Del. Tech. and Community Coll., Dover, 1983—; sec. to Democratic Nat. committeewoman R.T. Gates, 1972-73. Mem. ABA, Del. Bar Assn., Assn. Trial Lawyers Am. Methodist. Club: Soroptimist. Home: 42 Duchess Circle Dover DE 19901 Office: Twiley Jones Feliceangeli 410 S State St PO Box 1012 Dover DE 19901

BRAVO, LEONORE MCCRYSTLE, biologist, psychologist, conservationist; b. Vallejo, Calif., July 14, 1914; d. Arthur Bernard and Geraldine Marie (Winslow) McCrystle; B.A., San Francisco State U., 1934; M.A., U. Calif., Berkeley, 1947; m. Ignacio Bravo-Caro, Aug. 2, 1939; children—Nacho E., Michael A. Tchr. Indian schs. in Nev. and Calif., 1937-40; tchr., adminstr. schs. in Calif., 1940-47; head psychologist Sacramento County schs., 1948-51; tchr. San Francisco secondary schs., 1953-62; asst. prin. Indio (Calif.) High Sch., 1962-63; psychologist Oakland (Calif.) pub. schs., 1963-72, cons., 1972—; lectr. San Francisco Community Coll. Dist., 1975—; exec. sec. Tamalpais Conservation Club, 1974-77, bd. dirs., 1974—; pub. mem. Calif. Cling Peach Processors Adv. Bd., 1975-79; mgr. honeybee exhibit San Francisco Flower Show, 1979—. NSF fellow, 1957, 59-62; scholar intergroup relations Stanford U. NCCJ, 1959; fellow OAS, 1970. Mem. Am., Interam., Calif. psychol. assns., Calif. Tchrs. Assn., Calif. Acad. Scis., Calif. Sch. Psychologists Assn., Western Apicultural Soc. (charter), People for Preservation of the Natural and Wild in Bay Area Open Space (founder, pres. 1977), San Francisco Beekeepers Assn. (founder 1976, pres. 1978, exec. sec. 1977-79), Women's Internat. League Peace and Freedom, Common Cause, Amnesty Internat., Calif. Wilderness Coalition, Am. Beekeeping Fedn., Calif. State Beekeepers Assn., Internat. Platform Assn., San Francisco Democratic Women's Forum (dir. 1978-81, v.p. 1979), San Francisco Women for Peace, ACLU, Tamalpais Conservation Club (v.p. 1984, pres. 1986), Am. Friends Service Com., Friends of Earth, UN Assn., Wilderness Soc., U. Calif. Alumni Assn. (life), Consumers Coop. Berkeley. Author articles. Address: 47 Levant St San Francisco CA 94114

BRAWER, PATRICIA ELAINE, securities brokerage exec.; b. N.Y.C., July 3, 1945; d. Oscar I. and Iris (Pashman) Brawer; student U. Edinburgh (Scotland), 1965; B.A., Smith Coll., 1966; postgrad. N.Y. Inst. Fin., 1968. Prodn. asst. Merrill Lynch, N.Y.C., 1967-69; asst. to br. mgr. Shearson Hammill, N.Y.C., 1969-71; with Thomson McKinnon Securities, N.Y.C., 1971—, now asst. v.p., mktg. project mgr. Bd. dirs. Village Light Opera Group Ltd., N.Y.C.; trustee Pop Warner Little Scholars; program dir. Regional Emergency Med. Services Council of N.Y.C. Mem. English Speaking Union, Internat. Mensa Soc. Club: N.Y. Smith Coll. Address: 250 E 73d St New York NY 10021

BRAY, CAROLYN SCOTT, educational administrator; b. Childress, Tex., May 19, 1938; d. Alonzo Lee and Frankie Lucille (Wood) Scott; m. John Graham Bray, Jr., Aug. 24, 1957 (div. May 1980); children—Caron Lynn, Kimberly Anne, David William. B.S., Baylor U., 1960; M.Ed., Hardin-Simmons U., 1981; Ph.D., N. Tex. State U., 1985. Registered med. technologist. Research asst. Fairleigh-Dickinson Research Ctr., Hardin-Simmons U., Abilene, Tex., 1979; adj. prof. bus. communication Hardin-Simmons U., 1981-84; dir. career placement, 1979-82, assoc. dean students, 1982-85; assoc. dir. career planning and placement N. Tex. State U., Denton, 1985—; cons. univs. Interim youth dir. 1st Baptist Ch., Abilene, 1972-73; organizer, mem. Abilene Women's Network, 1982-85; mem. Abilene Art Mus., 1975-86, Abilene Philharm. Assn., 1969-79. Mem. Assn. Sch., Coll. and Univ. Staffing, S.W. Placement Assn., Tex. Assn. Sch., Coll. and Univ. Staffing, Nat. Assn. Women Deans, Adminstrs. and Counselors, Coll. Placement Council, Abilene Jr. League. Republican. Baptist. Club: Abilene Country. Avocations: skiing; water skiing; tennis; golf; reading. Office: N Tex State U Box 13378 Denton TX 76203

BRAY, ELIZABETH ALICE (BETTY), cosmetics consultant, writer; b. Dallas, June 15, 1953; d. Willis Joseph and Mildred Alice (Gulledge) B.; m. Joe H. Hodges, Jr., Jan. 11, 1975 (div. 1976). Student Tex. A&M U., 1971-75, B.S., 1979. Instr. Cisco Jr. Coll., Abilene, Tex., 1983-85; v.p. Ednl. Design Systems, Inc., Abilene, 1981-84; pres. E.A. Bray & Assocs., Inc., Abilene, 1983-85; cons. CiCi Cosmetics, Abilene, 1984—; cons. Dr. Willis J. Bray, Abilene, 1979-80, Radiology Assocs., Abilene, 1980-81, Jimmy Partin Realty, Abilene, 1985-86. Editor: The Deacon, 1971; author poetry. Bd. dirs. Brazos de Dios, College Station, Tex., 1980-81; mem. Abilene Cultural Affairs Council, 1977-79, March of Dimes, Abilene and College Station, 1981-85. Named to Great Chefs of Abilene, Abilene Cultural Affairs Council, 1985. Mem. Am. Bus. Woman's Assn. (sec. 1980-81, regional scrapbook 1979), Dramatist Guild. Episcopalian. Avocation: Cooking. Home and Office: 1725 N 2d St Abilene TX 79603

BRAY, EVELYN LEWIS, oil company executive, civic leader; b. Los Angeles, Jan. 5, 1905; d. George Edwin and Emma Anna (Schwarting) Lewis; m. Ulric Bannister Bray, June 9, 1928 (dec. 1977); children—Georgianna Eugenia Bray Erskine, Judith Evelyn Bray Longyear, Bannister Royston, Lourinda Susannah. B.Music in Voice, U. So. Calif., 1928. Chmn. bd. Bray Oil Co., Los Angeles, Calif., 1976—. Bd. dirs. Assocs. Calif. Inst. Tech., also life mem., mem. president's circle; trustee Northrop U.; founder Pasadena Opera Guild; founder, chmn. Pasadena Opera Trust; patron Assistance League; mem. women's com., chmn. house tour Pasadena Symphony; patron, bd. dirs. Euterpe Opera; chmn. Linda Vistans; bd. dirs. Pasadena Republican Club, Pasadena Rep. Club, Pro-Am.; active Lowman Club, Orthopedic Hosp.; mem. Los Angeles County 200 Com. Recipient Gold Crown/Patron of Arts award Pasadena Arts Council, 1986. Mem. Soc. Fellows Huntington Library (life), Art Collections and Bot. Gardens, Los Angeles County Mus. Sci. and Industry, Pacific Asia Mus., Hist. Soc. Calif., Hist. Soc. So. Calif. (life), Pasadena Hist. Soc. (life), Fine Arts Club Pasadena, Com. To Preserve Chinese Culture, World Affairs Council, Pasadena Civic League, Los Angeles County Zoo Assn., Descanso Gardens, Los Angeles County Arboretum, Los Amigos del Pueblo, Phi Beta (founder), Alpha Gamma Delta. Episcopalian. Clubs: Valley Hunt, Annandale Golf Lake Arrowhead Yacht, Coll. Women's (bd. dirs.). Home: 1660 La Vista Pl Pasadena CA 91103

BRAY, JACQUELINE HELEN LANGLOIS, graphic designer; b. Mpls., Apr. 20, 1932; d. Irving Charles and Margaret May (Stone) Langlois; student art Mpls. Coll. Art and Design, U. Minn., U. Copenhagen, Cornell U., George

Mason U., Fairfax, Va.; divorced; children—Leslee Marie, Judith Mae, David Edward, Laura Ann. Med. illustrator textbooks U. Minn., also univ. comml. artist, 1953-55; tech. illustrator Battelle Inst. N.W., Richland, Wash., 1966-68; artist Richland City Planning Dept., 1968-70; propr. studio, Aiken, S.C., also tchr. art Mead Hall, Aiken, 1970-75; sr. illustrator, designer Potomac Research Inc., 1977-78; graphic arts cons. Xerox Co., Leesburg, Va., 1978-79; art dir. CENTEC Corp., Reston, Va., 1979-83; pres., owner JHB Graphics and Design Co., Reston, Va., 1983—; one-woman exhbn., Richland, 1968 art cons. Internat. Assn. Satellite Users: Martha Gould scholar, 1952. Mem. Indsl. Graphics Internat., Exec. Women's Assn. Illustrator: The Magic Machine, 1978. Home and Office: 2124 Whisperwood Glen Ln Reston VA 22091

BRAY, MAUREEN ELIZABETH, clergy; b. Medford, Oreg., Nov. 23, 1946; d. Jouett Philip and Edith Pearl (Cape) Bray. B.A., Trinity Bible Inst., Jamestown, N.D., 1970; B.A., Northwest Coll., Kirkland, Wash., 1971. Ordained to ministry Assemblies of God, 1972; assoc. pastor Lake City Tabernacle, Seattle, 1970—, youth dir., 1972—, Christian edn. dir., 1972—, asst. dir., 1970—, trustee, 1970—. Mem. Alumni Assn. Northwest Coll., Alumni Assn. Trinity Bible Inst. Democrat. Home: 529 Taylor Pl NW Renton WA 98055 Office: Lake City Tabernacle 3001 NE 127th St Seattle WA 98125

BRAY, SUSAN HIGLEY, nephrologist, consultant; b. Oak Park, Ill., Aug. 24, 1941; d. Joseph Brewster and Margaret (Snyder) H.; m. Robert John Bray, Oct. 27, 1967; children—Brian, Gavin, Tara, Brendan. B.S., Ursinus Coll., 1963; M.D., Woman's Med. Coll. Pa., 1970. Diplomate Am. Bd. Internal Medicine. Intern, Woman's Med. Coll. Pa., 1970-71, resident 1971-72; fellow in nephrology Phila. VA Hosp., 1972-74; chief nephrology service Chestnut Hill Hosp., Phila., 1978—; clin. assoc. prof. medicine Med. Coll. Pa., Phila., 1980—; med. dir. Chestnut Hill Dialysis Ctr., Phila., 1980—. Contbr. articles to profl. jours. Fellow Am. Coll. Physicians, Phila. Coll. Physicians and Surgeons; mem. Network 24 End Stage Renal Disease (pres. 1984), Pa. Soc. Nephrology, Phila. County Med. Soc., Pa. Med. Soc. Republican. Roman Catholic. Club: Phila. Cricket. Avocations; skiing; jogging; theatre; gardening. Office: Chestnut Hill Dialysis Ctr 86 Bethlehem Pike Philadelphia PA 19118

BRAYTON, MARIAN TOLINE, broadcasting company executive; b. Toledo, Ohio, Apr. 18, 1939; d. Milford and Eda (Toline) Peterson B. B.S., U. Nebr., 1961. Assoc. fellow, reviewer The Kirkus Reviews, N.Y.C., 1963-71; v.p. Tony Bill Prodns., Los Angeles, 1974-78; v.p. CBS, Los Angeles, 1978—. Writer comedy material, screenplays. Recipient Disting. Alumni award U. Nebr., 1979. Mem. Nat. Acad. TV Arts and Sci. Democrat. Lutheran. Office: CBS Television City 7800 Beverly Blvd Los Angeles CA 90036

BRAYTON, PATRICIA RUTH, child care center administrator, minister; b. Rochelle, Ill., Nov. 4. 1937; d. Edward Walter and Helen Maxine (Johnston) Collins; m. George Henry Brayton, July 7, 1959; children—William George, Robert Henry. Grad. Mt. Vernon Bible Coll., 1960; student Bowling Green U., 1973. Ordained to ministry Internat. Ch. of Foursquare Gospel, 1960. Minister Internat. Ch. Foursquare Gospel, Ill., Ind., Wis., Ohio, 1960—; owner, adminstr. Avalon Ctr. Creative Child Care, Mt. Vernon, Ohio; adminstr., dir. Kiddie Kollege, Danville, Ill., 1969-71; tchr. Mt. Vernon Bible Coll., Ohio, 1982. Republican. Office: Avalon Ctr 14 Avalon Rd Mt Vernon OH 43050

BRAYTON, SANDRA KING, advertising company executive; b. Torrance, Calif., Mar. 6, 1944; d. Walter Raymond and Eleanor Christinas (Mehehoff) King; m. George Brayton; 1 child, Beau King. B.B.A., U. Miami, Fla., 1966. Sales rep. Chart Pak, N.Y.C., 1966-67; mem. acctg. staff Air Calif., Newport Beach, 1967-69; mktg. rep. U.S. Fin., San Diego and Santa Ana, Calif., 1969-70, dir. pub. relations and advt., 1970-72, regional sales mgr., 1972-73; acct. exec. Hubert Advt. Co., Tustin, Calif., 1973-74; pres. King Advt. and Pub. Relations Co., Newport Beach, 1974—; lectr. Career Counciling Advt. Vol., Orangewood Home of Dependent Children Arthritis Telethon. Recipient Mame awards Bldg. Industry Assn., 1979-84, Target award Profl. Builder Mag., 1985, Lulu award Women in Advt., 1984. Mem. Orange County Advt. Fedn., Sales and Mktg. Council, Bldg. Industry Assn., Home Builders Council. Republican. Avocations: aerobics, flying, scuba diving, ice skating, skiing. Office: King Advt and Pub Relations Co 610 Newport Ctr Dr #820 Newport Beach CA 92660

BRAZER, WYNONA MARIE, acct.; b. Seattle, Mar. 6, 1937; d. Perry Henry and Katherine Emma Moler; A.A. in Tech. Arts, Olympic Community Coll., 1971; m. Henry Brazer, Dec. 1, 1955; children—Ronald, Kenneth, Gregory, Jeffory, Samuel, Nancy. Clk., Gt. No. and No. Pacific R.R., Laurel and Billings, Mont., 1955-63; office mgr., bookkeeper Denny's Music Co., Portland, Oreg., 1971-72; bookkeeper Acme Signs Inc., Portland, 1973-74; acct. The Old Spaghetti Factory Internat., Portland, 1974-75; close down mgr., lead acct. Portland Met. Steering Com.-EOA Inc., Portland, 1975-78; asst. controller Harsh Investment Corp., Portland, 1979; acctg. mgr. United Cerebral Palsy Assn., Portland, 1980-83, San Francisco Housing Authority, 1983—. Mem. Am. Bus. Women Assn. Home: 240 Dolores St Apt 236 San Francisco CA 94103 Office: 440 Turk St San Francisco CA

BRAZIER, SHARLENE, association executive; Palo Alto, Calif., Nov. 18, 1959; d. Rollie Dean and Corinne (Rogers) B. Student El Centro Coll., 1976-78; B.A., So. Meth. U., 1982. Edn. dir. Dallas Urban League, 1982 ; com. mem. Dallas Ind. Sch. Dist., 1982—, com. mem. Orgn. Task Force, 1982—. Vol., Rape Crisis Prevention, Dallas, 1980; mem. adv. com. NCCJ, 1982—. Mem. Delta Sigma Theta. Democrat. Baptist.

BRAZIL, ELIZABETH ANNE, educator, consultant, social worker, psychotherapist; b. Visalia, Calif., Feb. 5, 1941; d. Byron William and Mary Wallace (Fisher) Jennings; m. Ernest William Brazil, July 4, 1970 (div. 1975); 1 adopted child, Robert Dale. B.A., Calif. State U.-San Jose, 1963; M.S.W., Calif. State U.-Fresno, 1979. Tchr. Earlimart Sch. Dist., Calif., 1963-64, 64-65, Dept. Def., Naha, Okinawa, 1965-67, Wiesbaden, Germany, 1967-69; Visalia Unified Sch. Dist., Calif., 1969-85; travel agt. Calif. Internat. Travel, Fresno, 1986—; mgr. Personal Investment Portfolio, Visalia, 1980—; owner Better Scents by Anne, Visalia, 1981—; cons. Dinuba Pub. Schs., Calif., 1984; prof. Pacific Coll., Fresno, 1982-84; Creator game: Hysteria, 1978; author play: Monday Morning Live, 1979; author cassette tape: Self Esteem through Music, 1982. Organizer Toastmastress Internat., 1970-74; facilitator Turning Point Drug Diversion Group, 1971-75; active YMCA, Beyond War. Mem. Nat. Assn. Female Execs., NEA, Nas. Assn. Social Workers, Music Educators Nat. Conf., Soc. Lic. Clin. Social Workers. Democrat. Avocations: computers; Basset hounds; travel; sewing; reading; writing; theatre. Home: 1708 S Linwood Ave Visalia CA 93277 Office: Calif Internat Travel Service 2611 N Fresno St Fresno CA 93793

BREAKSTONE, KAY LOUISE, public relations executive; b. Allentown, Pa., Sept. 9, 1936; d. Morris H. and Mabel (Gruber) Senderowitz; B.S., N.Y. U., 1967; m. Jules L. Breakstone, Dec. 3, 1960; children—Enid, Jessica. With N.Y. Conf. Bd., 1967-69, Bache, Halsey Stuart, N.Y.C., 1969-70; securities analyst Dean Witter, N.Y.C., 1970-71; v.p. Burson Marsteller, Inc., N.Y.C., 1971-79, dir. investor relations, 1979-81, sr. v.p., 1981—; dir. investor relations Kennecott Corp., Stamford, Conn., 1979-81; dir. First Woman's Bank. Mem. Nat. Investor Relations Inst. (pres. 1980-81). Home: 7 E 74th St New York NY 10021 Office: 866 3d Ave New York NY 10022

BREBNER, J(EAN) ANN, film producer; b. New Zealand, Aug. 15, 1923; came to U.S., 1953; d. John Hallam and Jean McBey (Robertson) Don; m. John Philip Brebner, May 21, 1953; children—Alexander McBey, John Howard. B.A., U. New Zeland; postgrad. Old Vic Theatre Sch. (London), 1951-52. Instr. drama Coll. of Marin, Dominican Coll., San Rafel, Calif., 1958-63; co-founder, producer Marin Shakespeare Festival, Marin County, Calif.; pres. Brebner Agys. Inc., San Francisco; film developer "Hard Laughter" Devel. Co.; lectr., seminar leader, cons. Cons. Delancey St. Found., San Francisco. Recipient No. Calif. Women in Film 1st Ann. award, tribute No. Calif. Film Industry, 1983. Mem. Mill Valley Film Festival Assn. (pres.), No. Calif. Women in Film (founder). Home: 130 Palm Ave San Rafael CA 94901

BRECHAN, LINDA LEE LAUESEN, management consultant; b. Chgo., Feb. 1, 1939; d. Elstun Wilbur and Ella Cecilia (Boadry) Lauesen; student public schs., Mich. and Alaska; m. Robert L. Brechan, Sept. 20, 1963; children—Perri Lynn, Sheri Alyse, Michael Robert; stepchildren—Beverly, Kenneth, Curtis, Hollis, Scott, Donna, Lory, Kelly. Adminstrv. asst. North Pole Refining (Alaska), 1976-77; sec.-treas. PMS, Inc., Fairbanks, Alaska, 1977-79; owner, accountant Linda's Bus. Services, Fairbanks, 1979-81; owner, decorator Decorating Den/Alaska, Fairbanks, 1979-81; mgmt. cons., 1977—; owner Goo Goo Baloo's, Fairbanks, 1985—. Mem. Nat. Assn. Female Execs., Nat. Assn. Women Bus. Owners, Nat. Fedn. Bus. and Profl. Women's Clubs, Inc., Golden Heart Bus. and Profl. Women's Club, Alaska Fedn. Bus. and Profl. Women's Clubs (state pres. 1985-86), Am. Soc. Trainers and Developers. Democrat. Home: 1506 10th Ave Fairbanks AK 99701 Office: PO Box 60753 Fairbanks AK 99706

BRECHBILL, SUSAN REYNOLDS, government official; b. Washington, Aug. 22, 1943; d. Irving and Isabell Doyle (Reynolds) Levine; B.A., Coll. William and Mary, 1965; J.D., Marshall-Wythe Sch. Law, 1968; m. Raymond A. Brechbill, June 29, 1973; children—Jennifer Rae, Heather Lea. Admitted to Va. bar, 1969, Fed. bar, 1970; atty. AEC, Berkeley, Calif., 1968-73, indsl. relations specialist AEC, Las Vegas, Nev., 1974-75; atty. ERDA, Oakland, Calif., 1976-77; atty. Dept. Energy, Oakland, 1977-78, dir. procurement div. San Francisco Ops. Office, 1978-85, asst. chief counsel, 1985—; mem. faculty U. Calif. Extension; speaker Nat. Contract Mgmt. Assn. Ann. Symposiums, 1980, 81, regional symposiums, 1983, 84. speaker on doing bus. with govt. Leader Girl Scout Troop 999. Named Outstanding Young Woman Nev., 1974. Fellow Nat. Contract Mgmt. Assn. (pres. Golden Gate chpt.; regional v.p. 1985-86); mem. Nat. Assn. Female Execs., mem. Va. State Bar Assn., Fed. Bar Assn. Republican. Contbr. articles to profl. jours. Home: 67 Scenic Dr Orinda CA 94563 Office: 1333 Broadway Oakland CA 94612

BREDHOFF, FLORENCE MEADOW, real estate broker; b. N.Y.C., Nov. 7, 1922; d. Samuel and Sadie (Margolis) Meadow; m. Saul J. Bredhoff, May 21, 1950 (dec. Mar. 1980); children—Susan B. Cohen, Stacey. B.A., Hunter Coll., 1943. Buyer, Allied Stores, N.Y.C., 1944-50; pres. Yankee Pedlar Ltd., retail store, N.Y.C., 1970-78; v.p. David Ferguson Ltd., import and mfg. co., N.Y.C., 1978-80; real estate salesperson N.Y.C., 1981—. Jewish. Home: 160 E 84th St New York NY 10028

BREECE, JENANNE NELSON, lawyer; b. Evanston, Ill., Dec. 30, 1941; d. Oscar William and Anne L. (Moll) Nelson; B.S. magna cum laude, U. So. Calif., 1967, J.D., 1976. Admitted to D.C. bar, 1977, Calif. bar, 1983. sec., corporate officer Sta. KUPD-AM-FM, Phoenix, 1959-61; media dir. West, Weir & Bartel, Los Angeles, 1962-65; asso. media dir. Eisaman, Johns & Laws, Los Angeles, 1966-68; media supr. Ogilvy & Mathers, N.Y.C., 1968-69; v.p. media and mktg. services Smith-Gent Advt. Co., N.Y.C., 1969-71; media supr. The Media Dept., N.Y.C., 1971-72; v.p. media Perkal Advt. Co., Los Angeles, 1972-74; research asst. U. So. Calif. Law Center, 1975-76; atty. adv. FCC, Washington, 1977-80; gen. atty. U.S. Dept. Energy, Las Vegas, 1980—; pro bono atty. Friends of Animals, N.Y.C. Mem. D.C. Bar, Fed. Bar Assn., Am. Bar Assn., Los Angeles Advt. Women, U. So. Calif. Alumni, Mensa, Cactus and Succulent Soc., North Shore Animal League, Friends of Animals, Defenders Wildlife, Smithsonian Assocs., Met. Mus., Phi Beta Kappa, Beta Gamma Sigma. Presbyterian. Office: US Dept Energy PO Box 14100 Las Vegas NV 89114

BREEDEN, CAROLYN SULLIVAN, curriculum coordinator, educator, designer, consultant; b. Great Bend, Kans., Apr. 6, 1943; d. T.R. and Lillian Oleta (Weaver) Sullivan; m. Ronald Gene Breeden, Dec. 23, 1961; children—Ronald Gene, Jon Charles. B.A. in Home Econs., Kans. State U., Ft. Hays 1966; M.A. in Textile Sci. and Design (Outstanding Designer award), Calif. State U.-Long Beach, 1976; Ed.D., U. So. Calif., 1985. Instr., dept. chmn. Anaheim Union High Sch. Dist., 1966-73; instr. pub. relations Southwestern Bell Telephone, Hays, Kans., 1965-66; instr., dept. chmn. family and consumer studies Santa Ana (Calif.) Community Coll., 1974-82, curriculum coordinator, instr., 1982-85; dir. instructional media services, coordinator coll. curriculum Rancho Santiago Coll., Santa Ana, 1985—. Recipient Rotary Club Outstanding Citizen award 1965; Women in Community Coll. Adminstrn. Leaders of 80s award 1981. Mem. Am. Assn. Research Postsecondary Edn., Am. Assn. Women Community and Jr. Colls., Am. Home Econs. Assn., Calif. Home Econs. Assn., Assn. Coll. Profs. Textiles and Clothing, Interior Design Edn. Council, Am. Soc. Interior Designers, Kappa Omicron Phi. Author: Designing Home Interiors: A Study Guide for Telecourses, 1979; A Matter of Taste, 1980; Light Cuisine, 1981. Home: 1914 Victoria Dr Santa Ana CA 92706 Office: 17th at Bristol Sts Santa Ana CA 92706

BREEDING, ANN WARREN, lawyer; b. Atlanta, Aug. 18, 1942; d. Julian Benjamin and Martha Elizabeth (Malone) Warren; m. Earle Griffith Breeding, Aug. 16, 1980; 1 dau., Martha Malone. B.A., Tulane U., 1964, M.A., 1965; J.D., George Washington U., 1980. Bar: D.C. 1980. Instr. English, U. Hawaii, 1965-67; tchr., librarian Piedmont Acad., Monticello, Ga., 1970-71; librarian Jasper County Library, Monticello, Ga., 1968-70; tchr. Willingham High Sch., Macon, Ga., 1971-72; tchr., librarian Mt. De Sales High Sch., Macon, 1972-73; aide Congressman John J. Flynt, Jr., Washington, 1973-79; sole practice, Washington, 1980—. Bd. dirs. Capitol Hill Restoration Soc., Washington, 1984. Mem. ABA, D.C. Bar Assn., Fed. Bar Assn., Assn. Trial Lawyers Am., Nat. Cathedral Assn., Phi Beta Kappa, Phi Delta Phi. Home: 529 14th St SE Washington DC 20003

BREEN, FAITH FEI-MEI LEE, economist, management consultant; b. Burbank, Calif., Feb. 3, 1951; d. John Quong and Eleanor S.G. (Choy) Lee; m. George Edward Breen, Jr., Nov. 30, 1974; children—Erika Lee, George Edward III. B.A., U. Md., 1972; M.A., U. Pitts., 1975. Asst. dir. Ctr. for Health Policy Research, Am. Enterprise Inst. Pub. Policy, Washington, 1975-77; economist U.S. Dept. Labor, Bur. Internat. Labor Affairs, Washington, 1978; Nat. Gov.'s Assn., Ctr. Pub. Policy Research, Washington, 1978-79; expert cons., economist Pres.'s Adv. Com. Women, Washington, 1979-81; polit. econ. cons. Nat. Assn. State and Territorial Solid Waste Mgmt. Ofcls., Washington, 1981-82; expert cons., economist to dep. under sec. mgmt. U.S. Dept. Edn., Washington, 1980-83; adj. faculty dept. econs. Central Mich. U., Washington, 1978—; asst. prof. sch. bus. and dept. econs. Prince Georges Community Coll., Largo, Md., 1985—; lectr. in field. Contbr. articles to profl. jours.; exec. producer TV program: Saccharin and the Public Interest, 1978. Active Rennaissance Women, 1984—; pres. Inner Wheel of College Park, 1986—, Orgn. Chinese Am. Women, 1985—; mem. fin. com. University Park Republican Women's Club; chair youth com. Nat. Rep. Com.'s Nat. Rep. Heritage Group Council, 1985—. Recipient Nat. Def. Lang. fellow, 1973-75; cert. of appreciation Sec. U.S. Dept. Edn., 1983; Fulbright-Hays Seminar Abroad, 1986. Mem. Am. Econ. Assn., Nat. Assn. Exec. Women, U.S. Small Bus. Adminstrn.'s Active Core Execs. Roman Catholic. Club: University Hills Swim. Avocations: tennis; swimming; bridge. Home: 7207 Windsor Ln College Heights Estates MD 20782 Office: Prince Georges Community Coll 301 Largo Rd Largo MD 20772

BREEN, JEAN MARIE, lawyer; b. Neosho, Mo., Oct. 5, 1954; d. John David and Joan (Kirkpatrick) Breen. B.A. summa cum laude, Creighton U., 1976, J.D., 1980. Bar: Nebr. 1981, Ill. 1984, Mo. 1985. Lectr. U. Nebr., Omaha, 1982, Creighton Law Sch., Omaha, 1982, Washington U. Law Sch., St. Louis, 1985—; law clk. to justice Nebr. Supreme Ct., Lincoln, 1981-82, to judge U.S. Dist. Ct. (no. dist.) Ill., Chgo., 1982-84; assoc. Thurman, Smith, Howald, Weber & Bowles, 1984—. Editorial staff Creighton Law Rev., 1978-80. Mem. ABA, Nebr. Bar Assn., Chgo. Bar Assn., Mo. Bar Assn. Roman Catholic. Office: One Thurman Ct Hillsboro MO 63050

BREEN, PATRICIA CARLA, transportation company executive; b. Wenatchee, Wash., June 23, 1930; d. Carlyon Durrand and Marion Carter (Cameron) Whitener; m. Orville Clyde Breen, Aug. 1, 1948 (div. Aug. 1975); children—Steven C., Jay N., Janet C. Breen Hovik, Scott T. (dec.); m. John Damien Malloy, Oct. 23, 1976. Student Wash. State U., 1947-51. Electronics trouble shooter and coordinator Boeing Airplane Co., Renton, Wash., 1957-59; asst. regional cargo mgr. Pacific North Airline, Seattle, 1959-70; owner, mgr. Valley Produce Inc., Kent, Wash., 1968-73; owner, pres. Associated Couriers Inc., Renton, 1979—. Mem. Seattle C. of C. (transp. com. 1974-75), Air Cargo Assn. (v.p. Seattle chpt. 1966, 69, 74, 75), World Trade Club (sec. Seattle chpt. 1976-77, pres. chpt. 1978-79). Republican. Presbyterian. Office: Associated Couriers Inc PO Box 98870 Seattle WA 98188

BREEN, PATRICIA HELEN, financial consultant; b. Detroit, Sept. 15, 1926; d. John William and Ethel Viola (Mardian) Hall. B.B.A., U. Mich., 1949; postgrad. U. Mich.-Detroit, 1953-54. Policy and procedure sec. Gen. Motors Central, Detroit, 1949-50; trust investment analyst Nat. Bank of Detroit, 1950-51; investment analyst Baxter & Co., Cleve., 1952; fin. cons. Merrill Lynch, Southfield, Mich., 1957—; founder, pres., chief exec. officer Good Food Co. Mem. Nat. Assn. Female Execs. (pres. 1985—), U. Mich. Alumni Assn. (bd. dirs. 1973-74). Republican. Roman Catholic. Club: Detroit Boat (Belle Isle, Mich.). Avocations: silversmithing; oil painting; writing; lecturing on radio and television; water and snow skiing; golf. Home: 17959 University Park Dr Livonia MI 48152 Office: Merrill Lynch Pierce Fenner & Smith Inc 26250 Northwestern Hwy Southfield MI 48076

BREGER, ETTA, health care consultant; b. N.Y.C., Nov. 21, 1921; d. Jack and Bella (Lowenstein) Weiner; 1 son, Paul. Student Miller Bus. Coll., 1940, NYU, 1942. Writer, Office of War Info., N.Y.C., Washington; writer with pub. relations dept. Edward L. Bernays, N.Y.C.; adminstr. Dental Practices, N.Y.C., 1960-70; cons. Healthco, N.Y.C., 1970-80, Bayside, N.Y., 1980—; lectr. Columbia U. Sch. Dentistry, Booth Meml. Hosp., N.Y.C., profl. socs. Contbr.: Valuation of Dental Practice-American Dental Association, 1985. Mem. Dental Group Mgmt. Assn., Practice Valuation Study Group, Nat. Assn. Exec. Women. Office: Etta Breger Cons Profl Practices 12-08 Robin Ln Bayside NY 11360

BREGMAN, PAULA JEAN, pharmaceutical company executive; b. Chgo., Feb. 1, 1947; d. Fredrick and Florence (Silavin) B.; m. Alfred Donald Morris, May 16, 1981. B.A., U. Wis., 1969; M.A., U. Chgo., 1977. Researcher, Menaker, Dangerfield & Wright, Chgo., 1974-78; research supr. Harshe-Rotman & Druck, Chgo., 1978-80; research analyst G. D. Searle & Co., Skokie, Ill., 1980-81, asst. product mgr., 1981-83, assoc. product mgr., 1983-85, product mgr., 1985-86; dir. Mktg. Land McNally Map Distbg. Co., 1986—. Mem. Austin Schock Neighborhood Assn., Chgo., 1982—. Mem. Am. Mktg. Assn. Office: Searle Consumer Products 5200 Old Orchard Rd Skokie IL 60077

BREHMER, MARCIA LYNNE, executive director legal aid society, lawyer; b. Circleville, Ohio, July 31, 1949; d. Robert Louis, Jr., and Marilyn Elizabeth (Lutz) B. B.A., Miami U., Oxford, Ohio, 1971; J.D., Boston U., 1976. Bar: Ohio. Law Library clk. Supreme Ct. Ohio, Columbus, 1974; law clk. Leist & Kitchen, Circleville, Ohio, 1975; staff atty. Legal Aid Soc. Columbus, 1976-78, supervising atty., 1978-82, exec. dir., 1982—; commn. mem. Franklin County Pub. Defender, Columbus, 1983—. Vol. Am. Cancer Soc., Columbus, 1983-84, United Way, 1984-85. Mem. ABA, Ohio Bar Assn., Columbus Bar Assn., Women Lawyers Franklin County. Episcopalian.

BREIDENBACH, CHERIE ELIZABETH, lawyer, accountant, real estate broker; b. Aberdeen, S.D., Aug. 20, 1952; d. Neil Allen and Portia Elizabeth (Bradner) Johnson; m. Steven Theodore Breidenbach, Aug. 9, 1975. B.S., U. S.D., 1975, J.D., 1979. Bar: Calif., S.D.; lic. real estate broker, Calif. Intern assoc. firm Frieberg, Frieberg and Peterson, Beresford, S.D., 1979; sole practice, La Jolla, Calif., 1982-84; atty., acct. firm Sussman and Siegel, C.P.A.s, 1984—. Mem. ABA, Calif. Bar Assn., S.D. Bar Assn., Phi Delta Phi, Alpha Phi. Republican. Methodist. Home: 4858 Tinasa Way San Diego CA 92124 Office: 3585 4th Ave San Diego CA 92103

BREINING, ELEANOR BROADBENT, medical secretary, accountant; b. N.Y.C., Sept. 25, 1913; d. Harry I. and Anna M. (Loeble) Broadbent; m. John McCabe Breining, Apr. 25, 1936; children—Lynne M. Breining Carpenter, Warren Douglas. Student Gaines Secretarial Coll., N.Y.C., Nassau Community Coll., Friends Sem., N.Y.C., Westchester Collegiate Ins., White Plains, N.Y., CCNY. Acct., A&P Tea Co., Bronx, 1942-43; prin. acct. Hicksville Pub. Schs., N.Y., 1960-75; med. sec., New Port Richey, Fla., 1979—. Dir. religious edn. Hicksville Methodist Ch. Sch., 1955-73; bd. dirs., leader Girl Scouts U.S.A., 1953-55; pres. Hicksville Ednl. Secs., 1964-69. Served with USMC, 1943-45. Mem. Civil Service Employees Assn. Democrat. Avocations: painting; ceramics. Home: 414 Lotus Dr Jasmine Lakes Port Richey FL 33568 Office: 1 Valencia Dr E New Port Richey FL 33552

BREITBART, BARBARA RENEE, research institute executive, psychologist, editor; b. N.Y.C., July 2, 1935; d. Bernard John and Sally Etta (Horwitz) Garson; m. Sheldon Lewis Breitbart, Mar. 16, 1954; children—Stacey Jana, Kevin Harrison. A.B., Syracuse U., 1973; M.A., Adelphi U., 1975, Ph.D., 1978. Lic. psychologist, N.Y. Pres. Research Inst. Psychophysiology, Inc., N.Y.C., 1982—; dir. Autogenic Biofeedback Ctr., Inc., Great Neck, N.Y., 1979—; editor Who's Who in the Biobehavioral Scis., N.Y.C., 1984—; columnist, lectr. on behavioral medicine and psychophysiology, 1978—; guest on radio talk shows; psychophysiological therapist, N.Y., 1978—. Mem. Am. Psychol. Assn., Biofeedback Soc. Am., Eastern Psychol. Assn., N.Y. Acad. Sci., Am. Acad. Arts and Scis. Avocations: chess, classical music, tennis. Office: Research Inst of Psychophysiology 2 Park Ave New York NY 10016

BREMER, KENDA POWELL, health care executive; b. Versailles, Mo., Sept. 27, 1942; d. Kenneth Lee and Mildred Marie (Rasa) Spalding; R.N., Mo. Baptist Sch. Nursing, St. Louis, 1963; grad. in health systems mgmt. U. Mo., 1984; neuro nurse specialist Methodist Hosp., Houston, 1970; student social gerontology Central Mo. State U.; m. William Darrell Bremer, Aug. 5, 1972; 1 son, John Sanford Powell III. Infirmary dir. U. Corpus Christi (Tex.), 1964; staff nurse Thomas Spann Clinic, Corpus Christi, 1964-65, Meth. Hosp., 1965-70; unit coordinator Tex. Inst. Rehab. and Research, 1970-71; dir. nursing Westwood Nursing Center, Clinton, Mo., 1972; exec. v.p. ops. new projects and planning Brooking Park Geriatrics Inc., Sedalia, Mo., 1972—. Mem. Am. Nurses Assn., Mo. Nurses Assn., Am. Coll. Nursing Home Adminstrs., Am. Health Care Assn., Mo. League Nursing Home Adminstrs. Republican. Lutheran. Club: Sedalia Altrusa (dir., treas. 1978-82). Home: Route 6 Box 148 A Sedalia MO 65301 Office: PO Box 1567 Sedalia MO 65301

BRENNAN, DEBORAH ANN, operations marketing assistant; b. Phila., July 31, 1947; d. Harry Clay and Margaret Ann (McConnel) Ward; B.A., Pa. State U., 1971; children—James Robert, Timothy Alexander. Dir. adminstrn. Pine Run Community, subs. Life Care Soc. Am., Doylestown, Pa., 1977-78, dir. mem. services, 1979-81, dir. mktg., 1980-81, spl. asst. to pres. Life Care Soc. Am., Doylestown, 1978-81; dir. resident and vol. services Evang. Manor, Phila., 1981-83; cons. for mktg. operational retirement and life care facilities Life Care Services of Des Moines, 1983—; corp. sec. Wardco Systems U.S.A. Mem. Nat. Assn. Female Execs., Social Service Workers Assn. (nursing homes sect.), Coalition of Advocates for Rights of Infirm Elderly. Mennonite. Home: 69 Providence Ave Doylestown PA 18901 Office: PO Box 1361 Doylestown PA 18901

BRENNAN, DEBRA ANN, radio executive; b. Birmingham, Ala., Aug. 16, 1957; d. Dan MacAuley and Clara Nell (Russell) Brennan. Photography cert., U. Ala., 1976; Acctg. cert., Jefferson State U., 1975. Acctg. asst. Dowdy & Assos., Brimingham, 1975-76; office mgr. Dr. Clarke Brown, Birmingham, 1976-78; account exec. WRKK-FM, Brimingham, 1978-81; promotion dir. WAPI-AM and FM, Birmingham, 1981—; entertainment dir. for spl. campaign for City Birmingham, 1982-85, Magic City Art Connection, Birmingham, 1983-85. Doo Dah Day Com., Birmingham, 1983-84; dir. Entertainment and Publicity, 1984. Coordinator publicity and entertainment March of Dimes, Walk America, Birmingham, 1984-85. Avocations: Hiking; dancing; photography; swimming. Office: WAPI Radio 2146 Highland Ave South Birmingham AL 35205

BRENNAN, EILEEN REGINA, actress; b. Los Angeles, Sept. 3, 1935; d. John Gerald and Jeanne (Menehan) B.; m. David John Lampson, Dec. 28, 1969 (div. 1975); children—Samuel John, Patrick Oliver. Student, Am. Acad. Dramatic Arts, 1955-56. Appeared off-Broadway: Little Mary Sunshine (Theatre World award 1960, Obie award 1960, Newspaper Guild award 1960); appeared on Broadway: Hello, Dolly, 1964-66; appeared in nat. co.: The Miracle Worker, 1961-62; appeared off-Broadway in A Coupla White Chicks Sitting Around Talking, 1980-81; films include: Divorce American Style, 1967, The Last Picture Show, 1971, The Sting, 1974, Murder By Death, 1976, The Cheap Detective, 1978, FM, 1978, Private Benjamin, 1980, also TV series, 1980-81 (Emmy award as best supporting actress 1981), The Funny Farm, 1983, Clue, 1985, appeared in TV miniseries The Blue Knight, 1973, Black Beauty, 1978; TV films include: Playmates, 1972, My Father's House, 1975, When She Was Bad, 1979, Incident at Crestridge, 1981. Mem. Actors Equity, Screen Actors Guild, AFTRA. Roman Catholic. Office: care Creative Artists Agy Inc 1888 Century Park E Suite 1400 Los Angeles CA 90067*

BRENNAN, MARY LYNN, lawyer; b. Wallace, Idaho, Apr. 16, 1946; d. William McKinley and Brunelle Frances (Mullen) Vipperman; m. Grant Warren Brennan, July 11, 1964 (dec.); children—Patrick, Michael. B.A., Pitzer Coll., 1978; J.D., U. Calif. Hastings Coll. Law, 1981. Bar: Calif. 1981, D.C. bar 1981, U.S. Dist. Ct. (so. dist.) Calif. Assoc. firm Jenkins & Perry, San Diego,

1981-83; asst. counsel Wells Fargo & Co., San Francisco, 1984-85; mem. Real Property Legis. Subcom., San Diego, 1983. Mem. ABA (real property, probate and trust sect.), San Francisco Bar Assn., State Bar Calif. (real property law sect.). Democrat. Roman Catholic.

BRENNAN, SHARON CATHERINE, lawyer, former teacher, medical technologist; b. Chgo., July 2, 1937; d. Frank Joseph and Florence Anna (Brichetto) Wolf; m. John Joseph Brennan, Aug. 14, 1968 (div.); children—Colleen Brennan White, Pamela, Shawn, B.A. in Social Studies, U. Ill., 1966, M.A. in Social Studies, 1971; J.D., No. Ill. U., 1983. Cert. tchr., Ill., Scotland, U.K.; bar: Ill. 1983, U.S. Dist. Ct. (no. dist.) Ill. 1983. Chem. researcher G.D. Searle Co., Skokie, Ill., 1955-57; med. technologist Swedish Covenant Hosp., Chgo., 1957-62, Mercy Hosp., Urbana, Ill., 1962-66; tchr. Centennial High Sch., Champaign, Ill., 1966-67, Coultrap Middle Sch., Geneva, Ill., 1968-69, 71-72, West Chicago Jr. High Sch., 1969-70, 78-80; secondary tchr., Glasgow, Scotland, 1967-68; staff atty. legal research dept. 2d Dist. Appellate Ct., Elgin, Ill., 1983—. Exec. editor, contbr. No. Ill. U. Law Rev., 1982. Tchr. religion St. John Neumann Ch., St. Charles, Ill., 1982—. James scholar U. Ill., 1962-66; Dean's scholar No. Ill. U. Sch. Law, 1980-83; recipient Corpus Juris Secundum award No. Ill. U. Law Sch. Faculty, 1983. Mem. ABA (com. appellate staff attys.), Ill. Bar Assn., Kane County Bar Assn., Tau Epsilon Rho, Phi Alpha Theta. Home: PO Box Y5 Elburn IL 60119 Office: 2d Dist Appellate Ct 55 North St Elgin IL 60120

BRENNEN, PATRICIA MICHAL, natural sciences educator, poet, consultant; b. Leisenring, Pa., Oct. 11, 1930; d. John Joseph and Marguerite Costello (Gettings) Kearney; m. George Kehoe Brennen, Dec. 29, 1976. B.A., Seton Hill Coll., 1952; postgrad. in medicine U. Pitts., 1954-55, in law Duquesne U., 1955-58, in arts and scis., 1964-65, in microbiology Ill. Inst. Tech., 1977—. Instr. sci Allegheny Gen. Hosp. Sch. Nursing, Pitts., 1952-54, 56-59, adminstrv. asst. to dir., 1959-60, chmn. sci. dept., 1959-60; instr. chemistry dept. Pa. State U., East McKeesport, 1961-64, 66-74; instr. biology dept. Olive Harvey Coll., Chgo., 1974-79, asst. prof. biology, 1979—; developer and tchr. correlated sci. Rochester Hosp. Sch. Nursing, 1969-72; cons. integrated scis. Westmoreland County Community Coll., Youngwood, Pa., 1972-73; developer computer program anatomy and physiology NSF, Chgo., 1981-83. Reviewer American Biology, 1982-83; author poems in: Anthology of the Verse of American Youth, 1949; America Sings, Annual Anthology of College Poetry, 1949, 50, 51; Voice of America, Anthology of Anthologies of College Poetry, 1953; A Goodly Heritage, Poems of Pennsylvania, 1968; The Family Treasury of Great Poems, 1981; Our 20th Century's Greatest Poems, 1982. Pres., co-founder Community Singers, Scottdale, Pa., 1966-69; vol. organizer Primary Gubernatorial Campaign, Greensburg, Pa., 1966; candidate del. to nat. conv. Democratic Party, 35th Senatorial Dist., Pa., 1972; active Call to Action, Chgo., 1981—. Ctr. for Disease Control grantee, 1971, 81; Argonne Nat. Lab. grantee, 1978; AAAS grantee, 1983-84; recipient Mastery Tchr. award Olive Harvey Coll., 1981. Mem. Am. Soc. Microbiology, Nat. Assn. Female Execs., Cornell U. Ornithology Labs., Assn. Women Sci., Pa. Elected Women's Assn., Mensa, Chgo. Colloquium Latin Am., N.Y. Acad. Scis., AAAS, Internat. Platform Assn., Indian Council Fire, Irish Am. Cultural Inst. Democrat. Roman Catholic. Home: 10432 S Prospect Ave Chicago IL 60643

BRENNER, ARLEEN PASVANIS, nurse; b. Youngstown, Ohio, Oct. 8, 1947; d. Peter Alexander and Kathleen (Kefalos) Pasvanis; diploma Sch. Nursing Ohio Valley Hosp., 1968; m. Gary Rogers Brenner, June 19, 1976; 1 dau., Ashley Kate. Staff nurse Presbyn. U. Hosp., Pitts., 1968-69; asst. head nurse Ohio State U. Hosp., Columbus, 1969-72; staff nurse Dameron Hosp., Stockton, Calif., 1972-73; asst. clin. nursing coordinator, staff nurse Stanford (Calif.) U. Hosp., 1974—. Mem. Assn. Operating Rm. Nurses, Am. Women's Vol. Soc., Friends of Nursing Stanford U. Med Center. Greek Orthodox. Home: 1523 Altura Way Belmont CA 94002

BRENT, JOLEENE ADALIE, artist, interior designer; b. Dallas, Nov. 27, 1920; d. Joseph Herman and Bertha B. (Raphiel) Margules; m. Allan Rudolph Brent; 1 child, Joanna Raphiel Brent Leake. B.A. in Art Edn., UCLA, 1941, postgrad., 1944-45; postgrad. La. State U., 1948-49. Teaching cert., La. Tchr., supr. Calif. pub. schs., 1941-43; instr. La. State U., Baton Rouge, 1950-52, 80-83; tchr. St. Joseph Acad., Baton Rouge, 1953-64; museum dir. La. Arts and Sci. Ctr., Baton Rouge, 1962-79; interior designer Karl Harvey Assocs., Baton Rouge, 1983—; mem. Artist-in-Residence State Program, 1979-82; adviser Reddy Cultural Ctr., Baton Rouge, 1980—. Executed murals Cath. Life Ctr., Cath. Prep. Sch., 1970, Our Lady of the Lake Med. Ctr. chapel 1980, Baton Rouge Gen. Med. Ctr., 1986; stained glass windows include: La. State U. Law Ctr., 1970, La. Arts and Sci. Ctr., 1969, Cath. Life Ctr., 1968, Baton Rouge Gen. Med. Ctr. chapel, 1984, various churches. Decorated Oden Del Merito Civil (Spain). Mem. Delta Kappa Gamma, Delta Epsilon. Clubs: Baton Rouge Country, City (Baton Rouge). Avocations: tennis; walking; bicycling. Home: 3930 Floyd Dr Baton Rouge LA 70808 Office: Karl Harvey Assocs 2223 Quail Run Dr Baton Rouge LA 70808

BRESALIER-KOODIN, JUDITH ABBY, college administrator; b. Bklyn., Apr. 29, 1947; d. Alexander and Ruth Dorothy (Daneloff) Shapiro; B.A., SUNY, Stony Brook, 1967, M.S., 1968; m. William Stephen Bresalier, Dec. 18, 1971 (div. 1983); 1 son, Alexander; m. Jeffrey Koodin, 1985. Asst. dean for residence SUNY, Delhi, 1968-69; counselor Suffolk County Community Coll., Selden, N.Y., 1969-78, dir. acad. advisement programs, 1978-80, dir. student activities, 1980-85, counselor, 1985—. Mem. N.E. Assn. Pre-law Advisors, Nat. Acad. Advising Assn., Nat. Assn. Women Deans, Adminstrs. and Counselors, NOW, Temple Beth-El Sisterhood (v.p.), Alpha Beta Gamma, Phi Theta Kappa. Jewish. Club: Women's Assn. of Suffolk Community Coll. Contbr. article to profl. publ. Home: 136 E Woodside Ave Patchogue NY 11772 Office: Speonk-Riverhead Rd Riverhead NY

BRESCIA, BARBARA M., antique shop executive, artist, art researcher; b. N.Y.C., Mar. 6, 1923; d. Andreas and Lyna (Russell) Randel; m. Victor J. Brescia, Apr. 8, 1953; children—Valerie, Vance. Student Pratt Inst., 1941-44; B.S., Columbia U., 1945, M.A., 1946. Cert. art cons., N.Y. Tchr. art Union Free Sch. Dist., Elmont, N.Y., 1950-64, Unified Free Sch. Dist. L, Smithtown, N.Y., 1965-80, ret., 1980; pres. The Little Red Sled antiques, St. James, N.Y., 1981—. Mem. Smithtown Twp. Arts Council. Life mem. N.Y. Acad. Scis. Republican. Methodist. Home: 190 Asharoken Ave Northport NY 11768 Office: The Little Red Sled Antiques 555 Route 25A Saint James NY 11780

BRESLAUER, ELLEN GIRDLER, financial executive; b. Santa Monica, Calif., Nov. 13, 1947; d. Lew and Lorena E. (Stripp) Girdler; m. Russell Lynn Breslauer, Aug. 27, 1967. B.A., U. Calif.-Berkeley, 1968, M.B.A., 1975. C.P.A., Calif. Statis. clk. Bank of Am., San Francisco, 1968-71, salary survey analyst, 1971; asst. to treas. BankAm. Realty Services, Inc., San Francisco, 1971-73, asst. treas., 1973-80, treas., 1980—; cons. Project Bus., San Francisco, 1983—. Mem. fund council U. Calif.-Berkeley, 1982-83. Winner regional speaking contest Am. Inst. Banking, 1977. Mem. Am. Inst. C.P.A.s, Calif. Soc. C.P.A.s, Calif. Bus. Alumni (v.p. 1977-79), Phi Beta Kappa. Office: BankAmerica Realty Services Inc 555 California St Suite 4275 San Francisco CA 94104

BRESLIN, CATHERINE O'CONNELL, rehabilitation specialist; b. Newark, Aug. 17, 1952; d. Philip Francis and Mary Catherine (Boyle) O'Connell; m. Michael John Breslin; children—Mary, Margaret. B.S. in Occupational Therapy, Kean Coll., 1981, M.A. in Behavioral Scis. and Psychology, 1984. Cert. in clin. hypnosis and neuro-linquistic programming. Pvt. practice occupational therapy cons., Dunellen, N.J., 1981—; chief psychiat. rehab. services Somerset Med. Ctr., Somerville, N.J., 1986—; cons., lectr. in field. Contbr. articles to profl. jours. Mem. Am. Occupational Therapy Assn. (bd. dirs.), World Fedn. Occupational Therapy, N.J. Occupational Therapy Assn. (legis. chmn. 1983—, Award of Merit 1983, 85), Nat. Assn. Female Execs., Psi Chi.

BRESLIN, MARY B., college president; b. Chgo., Sept. 27, 1936; d. William J.B. and Margaret D. (Hession) B. B.A., Mundelein Coll., 1958; M.A., Marquette U., 1961; J.D., Loyola U.-Chgo., 1977. Internal auditor Fed. Res. Bank, Chgo., 1958-59; asst. bus. mgr. Mundelein Coll., 1964-67, bus. mgr., treas., 1967-75, v.p. bus. affairs, treas., 1975-85, pres., 1985—; cons., evaluator North Central Accreditation Assn., Chgo., 1979—, Middle State Accreditation Assn., Phila., 1981—. Office: Mundelein Coll 6363 N Sheridan Rd Chicago IL 60660

BRESNAHAN, PAMELA ANNE, lawyer, educator; b. Washington, Nov. 21, 1954; d. Harry Anthony and Marilyn (Thompson) B. B.A., U. Md., 1976, postgrad., 1976-77; J.D., 1980. Bar: Md. 1980, D.C. 1982. Teaching asst. U. Md., College Park, 1976-77; law clk. Dept. of Interior, Washington, 1977-78; law clk. Seidenman & Dugan P.A., Balt., 1978-80; ptnr. Seidenman & Bresnahan, P.A., Balt., 1980-82; assoc. Finley, Kumble, Wagner, et al, Washington, 1982—; lectr. U. Md., College Park, 1981—; faculty Nat. Coll. Advocacy, 1984. Vol. campaign Mayor William Donald Schaefer, Balt., 1983, Senator Charles Mac Mathias, College Park, Md., 1975-76. Mem. ABA (trial evidence com. litigation sect. 1983-84), Assn. Trial Lawyers Am., Md. Bar Assn. (sec.-treas. young lawyers 1984-85, vice chmn. 1985-86, chmn. edn. com. 1983-84), chmn. young lawyers 1986-87, Women's Bar Assn. Md. (chmn. long range planning 1983-85, v.p. 1985-86, pres.-elect 1986-87), Unified Bar D.C., Internat. Platform Assn., Alpha Omicron Pi (counsel 1980-84). Democrat. Lutheran. Club: Soroptimist (Washington). Home: 3925 Beech Ave Apt 111 Baltimore MD 21211 Office: Finley Kumble Wagner et al 1120 Connecticut Ave NW Washington DC 20036

BRESSANT, MICHELE RENÉE, government official; b. Perth Amboy, N.J., Aug. 7, 1956; d. Ronald and Evelyn Pauline (Hall) Bressant; B.S. in Psychology, U. Pitts., 1978. Undergrad. teaching fellow U. Pitts., 1978; info. operator Greyhound Buslines, Pitts., 1978; med. clk. typist VA Hosp., Houston, 1979-81, patient services asst., 1981-82, psychology technician, 1982; revenue officer IRS, Houston, 1982—. Vol. Rape Crisis Ctr., Houston, 1980, Income Tax Assistance Program, Houston, 1984. Recipient Golden Panther award U. Pitts., 1978, Suggestion award VA Hosp., Houston, 1981; named Employee-of-the Month group 1400 IRS, Oct., Nov., Dec. 1985. Mem. Nat. Assn. Female Execs., Fed. Bus. Assn. Democrat. Baptist. Office: IRS 3223 Briarpark Stop 5114H-BP Houston TX 77042

BRETSCHNEIDER, ANN MARGERY, histotechnologist; b. Newton, Mass., May 11, 1934; d. Herman Frederick and Elizabeth Louise (Brady) B.; B.S., Northeastern U., Boston, 1957; M.S., Rutgers U., 1979. Histopathologic technician NIH, Bethesda, Md., 1957-58; chief histologic technician U. Ala. Med. Center, Birmingham, 1958-61; chief med. technologist in histology, instr. Muhlenberg Hosp., Plainfield, N.J., 1961-67; instr. anatomy Northeastern U., 1967-68; research-teaching specialist U. Medicine and Dentistry-Rutgers U. Med. Sch., 1968—; workshop leader, cons. in field. Mem. Am. Soc. Clin. Pathologists (affiliate), Nat. Soc. Histotech., Electron Microscopy Soc. Am., N.J. Soc. Histotech. Co-author: Thin Is In: Plastic Embedding of Tissue for Light Microscopy, 1981. Office: Dept Anatomy Rutgers U Med Sch Piscataway NJ 08854

BRETT, MARY LYNN HOCKING MARBURG, educator; b. Balt., Apr. 8, 1924; d. Francis Grainger and Mary Robbins (Hocking) Marburg; m. E. T. Mudge, Nov. 18, 1944; children—Edmund Tileston, Lynn Mudge Shultz; m. E. A. Poe III, Apr. 20, 1955; 1 child, Edgar Allan Poe IV; m. John M. Morgan, Apr. 18, 1968 (div. June 1979); 1 child, William Hocking; m. William Howard Brett, Nov. 15, 1984. B.S. in Elem. Edn.; M. in Modern Studies, Towson State U., 1973; Loyola Coll., 1984. Educator pvt. and pub. schs., Va., Md., 1960-78; recorder and computer programmer Loyola Coll., Balt., 1979-84; vol. docent The Living Desert, Palm Desert Calif. 1985—. Democrat. Episcopalian. Club: Marrakesh (Palm Desert). Avocations: photography; tennis; drawing; writing; acting. Home: 47156 El Menara Circle Palm Desert CA 92260

BRETT, MAUVICE WINSLOW, educational administrator, consultant; b. Xenia, Ohio, May 24, 1924; d. Perle Alonzo and Lurena Belle (Hamilton) W.; m. John Woodrow Brett, Sept. 20, 1943; children—Diane, John, Anthony, Loretta. B.S. in Psychology, Howard U., 1944, M.S. in Psychology, 1946; Ph.D. in English, Union Grad. Sch., Cin., 1978. Tchr. English, Hertford County Schs., Winton, N.C., 1959-76, ednl. supr., 1977-80, dir. personnel, 1981—; cons. N.C. Council English Tchrs., Charlotte, 1979; com. mem. quality assurance program N.C. State Dept. Pub. Instn., Raleigh, 1980-81. Sec. Hertford County Arts Council, 1977; mem. Hertford County 400th Anniversary Com., 1982-83; trustee Elizabeth City State U., 1983—. Mem. N.C. Assn. Sch. Adminstrs. (dist. rep.), Am. Assn. Sch. Administrs., N.C. Assn. Supervision and Curriculum Devel., Bus. and Profl. Women's Club, Delta Sigma Theta. Home: Route 2 Box 260A Ahoskie NC 27910 Office: Hertford County Schs PO Box 158 Winton NC 27986

BRETZ, (ALMA) LINDA, library administrator; b. Far Rockaway, N.Y., Sept. 22, 1934; d. Rocco Joseph and Linda Alma (Ley) Mazza; B.S. in L.S., SUNY, Geneseo, 1956; M.F.A. in Dramatic Arts, Columbia U., 1959; m. Robert Lawrence Bretz, June 10, 1961; children—Erika Katharine, John Michael, David Reinhard. Librarian, N.Y.C. Public Library, 1956-59; asst. prof. library edn. SUNY Coll., Geneseo, 1959-66; librarian Lincoln br. Rochester (N.Y.) Public Library, 1966-67, head br., 1967-72; inservice tng. cons. Monroe County (N.Y.) Library System, Rochester, 1972-73, children's services cons., 1973-75, asst. dir. system, 1976-78, dir. Rochester Public Library and Monroe County Library System, 1978—; del. N.Y. Gov.'s Conf. Libraries, 1978, White House Conf. on Library and Info. Scis., 1979; trustee Reynolds Library. Bd. dirs. Opera Theatre of Rochester, 1981-84, Rochester Health Network, 1982—, Genesee Health Service, 1986—; mem. N.Y. State Profl. Librarians Cert. Exam. Com., 1973-78, chmn. 1977; registrar Rochester Bach Festival, 1975—; mem. statewide adv. com. on equal opportunity for women N.Y. State Edn. Commn., 1985—. Mem. N.Y. Library Assn. (councilor-at-large 1976-80, pres. 1982), ALA Am. Soc. Public Administrn. (pres. Rochester-Monroe County chpt. 1979-80). Home: 32 Audubon St Rochester NY 14610 Office: 15 South Ave Rochester NY 14604

BRETZFELDER, DEBORAH MAY, museum exhibit designer; b. Hazleton, Pa., Sept. 21, 1932; d. Joseph and Rose (Smulyan) Hirsh; student Syracuse U., 1950-53; m. Robert Bretzfelder, Dec. 24, 1955; children—Karl, Marc. Textile colorist, designer Cohn-Hall-Marx, N.Y.C., 1954-55; fashion coordinator Hecht's Dept. Store, Washington, 1956; free-lance artist, Washington, 1956-58; exhibits technician Smithsonian Mus., Washington, 1958-59, exhibits prodn. supr., 1959-63, exhibits specialist Smithsonian Mus., Nat. Mus. Am. History, 1963-75, visual info. specialist, project mgmt. officer, 1975—; acting chief of design, 1983-84, chief design, 1984—; cons. various firms, orgns., mus. personnel. Mem. violin sect. George Washington U. Orch. Mem. Am. Assn. Mus., Internat. Com. Mus., Nat. Soc. Historic Preservation, Tau Sigma Delta. Jewish. Club: Potomac Appalachian Trail. Home: 2748 Woodley Pl NW Washington DC 20008 Office: Smithsonian Nat Mus Am History 14th and Constitution NW Room 4212 Washington DC 20560

BREUM, LINDA GARVER, nurse; b. Akron, Ohio, Sept. 22, 1955; d. Richard Franklin and Betty Jane (Baxter) Garver; m. Robert Paul Breum, May 28, 1977; 1 child, Erik Franklin. B.S.N., Vanderbilt U., 1977. R.N., Fla.; cert. nursing adminstrn. Am. Nurses Assn., 1985. Triage nurse Parkland Hosp., Dallas, 1978-80; staff nurse Lucerne Hosp., Orlando, Fla., 1980-81; head nurse Central Fla. Regional Hosp., Sanford, 1981-86, diabetic outpatient instr., 1982—; instr. diabetic update Seminole Community Coll., Sanford, 1984. Mem. Am. Diabetic Assn. Home: 1701 Missouri Ave Sanford FL 32771

BREVETTI, LAURA ANNA, lawyer; b. Bklyn., Aug. 16, 1951; d. Domenico and Josephine (Ferraro) B. A.B. cum laude, Barnard Coll., 1973; J.D., Georgetown U., 1976. Bar: N.Y. 1977, U.S. Ct. Appeals (2d cir.) 1978. Asst. dist. atty. Office Dist. Atty., Bklyn., 1976-80; asst. atty.-in-charge Organized Crime Strike Force, U.S. Dept. Justice, Bklyn., 1980—; lectr. U.S. Dept. Justice, FBI and Fed. Law Enforcement Acads., 1981-82. Recipient Fed. Younger Lawyers award Fed. Bar Assn., 1985. Mem. ABA. Roman Catholic. Office: US Dept Justice Organized Crime Strike Force 35 Tillary St Brooklyn NY 11201

BREWER, ALAANA FAYE, medical technologist; b. Dayton, Tenn., Nov. 6, 1952; d. Gene Vance and Nola Faye (Gibson) Vance; m. Melvin Wayne Brewer, May 8, 1982. Diploma in med. tech. St. Thomas Hosp., Nashville, 1974; B.S., Middle Tenn. State U., 1974. Head, Radioimmunolassay and Electrophorsis Clin. Labs., Nashville, 1974-75; asst. chief technologist Murfreesboro (Tenn.) Med. Clinic, 1976-78; asst. bacteriologist Ruthford Hosp., Murfreesboro, 1979-80; chief med. technologist Woman's Clinic, Murfreesboro, 1980—. Mem. Am. Soc. Clin. Pathologists (assoc.), Rutherford County Humane Soc., Murfreesboro Obedience Tng. Club. Baptist. Home: Route 4 Box 444 Murfreesboro TN 37130

BREWER, JANE LYNN, plant scientist, seed technologist; b. Mount Pleasant, Mich., June 1, 1944; d. Charles Francis and Ruby Eileen (Grandon) Whitcomb; student Central Mich. U., 1962-64; B.A. with high distinction, Colo. State U., 1980; m. Jesse Wayne Brewer, Dec. 26, 1964 (div. 1978); children—Laura Elizabeth, Matthew Whitcomb. Technician, Potato Virus Lab., Colo. State U., Fort Collins, 1972, lab. asst. Colo. Seed Lab., 1976-78, seed analyst, mem. botany dept., 1978—, supr. germination dept., 1982-84; seed lab. mgr. J.G. Boswell Co., Corcoran, Calif., 1984—. Mem. Soc. Comml. Seed Technologists, Phi Kappa Phi. Home: 1040 Josephine Ave Corcoran CA 93212 Office: JG Boswell Co PO Box 457 Corcoran CA 93212

BREWER, JANICE KAY, state representative, property and investment firm executive; b. Hollywood, Calif., Sept. 26, 1944; d. Perry Wilford and Edna Clarice (Bakken) Drinkwine; m. John Leon Brewer, Jan. 1, 1963; children—Ronald Richard, John Samuel, Michael Wilford. Med. asst. cert. valley Coll., Burbank, Calif., 1963, practical radiol. technician cert., 1963; D. Humanties, (hon.), Los Angeles Chiropratic Coll., 1970. Pres., Brewer Property & Investments, Glendale, Ariz., 1970—; mem. Ariz. Ho. of Reps., Phoenix, 1983—. Committeeman, Republican Party, Phoenix, 1970, 1983; legis. liaison Ponderosa Rep. Women, Phoenix, 1980; bd. dirs. Westside Mental Healty Agy., Phoenix, 1983—. Named Woman of Yr., Chiropractic Assn. Ariz., 1983. Mem. Nat. Fedn. Rep. Women, Am. Legis. Exchange Council, Lutheran. Home: 6835 W Union Hills Dr Peoria AZ 85345 Office: Ariz State Capitol 1700 W Washington Ave Phoenix AZ 85007

BREWER-VAN HARTESVELT, BEVERLY, television station representative executive; b. Mercedes, Tex., Mar. 21, 1955; d. Howard Archie and Marjorie M. (MacVean) Brewer; m. John van Hartesvelt, Jan. 21, 1984; child, Blaire Marie. B.F.A., Southwestern U., Georgetown, Tex., 1977. Admissions counselor Southwestern U., 1977-78; legal asst. Oler & Hoffman, Dallas, 1978; sales asst. RKO TV Reps., Dallas 1979-80; account exec. Sta. KTXA-TV, Dallas, 1981-84, TeleRep, Inc., 1985, MMT Mkgt., 1986—; instr. basic bus. of broadcasting So. Meth. U., 1981. Mem. Am. Women Radio & TV (pres. Dallas chpt. 1983-84), Alpha Delta Pi. Republican. Methodist. Office: MMT Mkgt 12790 Merit Dr Suite 515 Dallas TX 75251

BREWSTER, ELIZABETH WINIFRED, educator, poet, novelist; b. Chipman, N.B., Can., Aug. 26, 1922; d. Frederick John and Ethel May (Day) Brewster; B.A., U. New Brunswick, 1946; M.A., Radcliffe U., 1947; B.L.S., U. Toronto, 1953; Ph.D., Ind. U., 1962; D. Litt., U. N.B., 1982. Cataloger Carleton U., Ottawa, Ont., Can., 1953-57, Ind. U. Library, Bloomington, 1957-58, N.B. Legis. Library, 1965-68, U. Alta. (Can.) Library, Edmonton, 1968-70; mem. English dept. Victoria (B.C., Can.) U., 1960-61; reference librarian Mt. Allison U. Library, Sackville, N.B., 1961-65; vis. asst. prof. English, U. Alta., 1970-71; mem. faculty U. Sask., Saskatoon, 1972—, asst. prof. English, 1972-75, assoc. prof., 1975-80, prof., 1980—. Recipient E. J. Pratt award for poetry U. Toronto, 1953; President's medal for poetry U. Western Ont., 1980. Mem. League Can. Poets, Writers' Union Can., Assn. Can. Univ. Tchrs. English. Author: East Coast, 1951; Lilloot, 1954; Roads, 1957; Passage of Summer, 1969; Sunrise North, 1972; In Search of Eros, 1974; Sometimes I Think of Moving, 1977; The Way Home, 1982; The Sisters, 1974; It's Easy To Fall on the Ice, 1977; Digging In, 1982; Junction, 1982; A House Full of Women, 1983; Selected Poems, 2 vols., 1985. Office: Dept of English Univ of Saskatchewan Saskatoon SK S7N 0W0 Canada

BREWSTER, OLIVE NESBITT, librarian; b. San Antonio, July 19, 1924; d. Charles Henry and Olive Agatha (Nesbitt) B.; B.A., Our Lady of Lake Coll., 1945, B.S. in L.S., 1946. Asst. librarian aeromed. library U.S. Air Force Sch. Aviation Medicine, Randolph AFB, Tex., 1946-60, chief cataloger aeromed. library Sch. Aerospace Medicine, Brooks AFB, Tex., 1960-83, chief tech. processing, 1983—. Mem. ALA, Am. Soc. Indexers, Mensa. Anglican. Home: 1906 Schley Ave San Antonio TX 78210 Office: Aeromed Library USAF Sch Aerospace Medicine Brooks AFB TX 78235

BREWSTER-WALKER, SANDRA JOANN, publishing executive, genealogist, historian; b. Copiaque, N.Y., June 16, 1942; d. Willis Hodges and F. Wilda (Scurlock) Brewster; m. Stuart M. Walker (div. 1984); children—Jeffrey, Carlton, Cassandra. Cert. Island Drafting Sch., 1965; B.A., Dowling Coll., 1972; M.A., SUNY-New Paltz, 1978. Acting asst. dir. Urban Ctr., Vassar Coll., Poughkeepsie, N.Y., 1972-74; tchr. Middletown Jr. High Sch., N.Y., 1974-78; elec. mfg. engr. Perkin-Elmer Corp., Norwalk, Conn., 1978-84; pub., editor Ram's Horn Pub. Co., Stamford, Conn., 1983-84; software mgr. Pergamon Press, Inc., Elmsford, N.Y., 1985—. Pub.-editor Conneticut Update, 1984; contbr. Westchester Women, 1985. Editor: Augustus M. Hodges Project, 1978-86, Fairfield County Black Biograph. Index Project, 1980—. Mem. Town of Walkill Bicentennial Com., 1976, Bicentennial Com., Middletown Pub. Schs., 1976; mem. Circleville Pub. Sch. PTA, 1975-77, v.p., 1977-78; instr. genealogy Greater Orange YMCA, Middletown, N.Y., 1975, 77, mem. planning bd., 1976; corp. campaign advisor United Negro Coll. Fund, Lower Fairfield, Conn., 1980-81; mem. John Anderson for Pres. Com., 1980; exec. dir. Conn. Legis. Black Caucus, Hartford, 1981-82; aide to State Senator J.C. Daniels, 1981-82; founder, dir. Bridgeport Black History Project, 1982-83; adv. com. Conn. Democrats, 1984; inaugural com. Mayor Serrani, Stamford, 1984-85; coordinator Lower Fairfield County Mondale/Ferraro Campaign, 1984; state coordinator Conn. Com. to Elect Jesse Jackson Pres., 1984; mem. Conn. chpt. Coalition of 100 Black Women, 1980-84, Nat. Project Vote, 1984, adv. com. black women's exhibit L.I. and Bklyn. Hist. Soc.; vol. Alberta Jagoes for Mayor campaign, Milford, Conn., 1982, Christine M. Niedermeier for Congress Com., 1984. Named Woman of Month, Conn. Women's Mag., 1983, Working Woman of Month, Essence mag., 1983. Mem. Coalition of 100 Black Women (Lower Fairfield chpt.), Nat. Assn. Female Execs. Avocations: golf; tennis; painting. Home: 101 Turn of River Rd Stamford CT 06904 Office: Pergamon Press Inc Fairview Park Elmsford NY 10523

BREYMAIER, ANN MEREDITH (MEREDITH CHENEY), writer, poet, educator; b. Elyria, Ohio, June 17, 1925; d. Harvey Chapman and Ethel Josephine (Steffen) Cheney; m. Robert William Breymaier, May 24, 1952; 1 foster child, Christina Lipe Torres; 1 adopted child, Walter William II. B.A., Ohio State U., 1947; M.A., Eastern Mich. U., 1972, M.A. in lang. and lit., 1986. Provisional secondary teaching cert., Mich. Asst. to editor Clintonville Booster, Columbus, Ohio, 1947-48; copywriter, performer continuity Sta.-WLEC, Sandusky, Ohio, 1948-49; typist Sta.-WERE, Cleve., 1950; record librarian, music shows producer Sta.-WDOK, Cleve., 1950-51, traffic mgr., 1951-52, also performer, writer, producer children's show, 1951-52; writer pub. info. Sta.-WEMU, Eastern Mich. U., Ypsilanti, 1977-80, also on-air work, 1978-80; substitute tchr. Ypsilanti Pub. schs., 1981—; coordinator newsletter writer Ypsilanti Food Coop., 1981-85; Latin tutor. Contbr. poems to lit. jours., anthologies. Recipient 4th prize Seven Mag. Jesse Stuart Internat. poetry contest, 1975, 2d Place award Terre Haute Poetry Soc. Winter Contest, 1975, 2d prize Seven Mag. Jesse Stuart Internat. poetry contest, 1978, 4th prize Mich. Poetry Soc., 1974, 1st prize Mich. Poetry Soc., 1974, 2d prize Mich. Poetry Soc., 1975, spl. mention certs. World of Poetry contests, 1984, Golden Merit award World of Poetry Conv., 1985. Mem. Women in Communications, Inc., Ypsilanti Area Garden Club (pres. 1981), Alpha Epsilon Rho, Phi Mu. Presbyterian. Avocations: reading; radio; television; writing newsletters; gardening. Home and Office: 1376 Skyway Dr Ypsilanti MI 48197

BRIAN, SHARON LYNN, information systems technician; b. El Dorado, Ark., Nov. 23, 1946; d. Raymond Elbert and Beulah Lynn (Cook) Smith; m. Alfred Thomas Brian, Aug. 10, 1968; children—Christopher Aron, Kelly Lynn. B.S. in Math., So. Ark. U., 1968; postgrad. U. Houston, 1971-73, So. Meth. U., 1974-75. Math. tchr. El Dorado Pub. Schs., 1968-69; computer programmer, systems analyst, systems mgr. Tex. Instruments, Dallas, 1969-85, sr. mem. tech. staff, 1985—; cons. dental offices, Tex., 1985—. Publicity chmn. PTA, Allen, Tex., 1985-86; treas. United Methodist Women, Allen, 1976. Mem. Am. Mgmt. Assn., Guide Internat. (group mgr. 1984—). Club: Plano Maple (Tex.) (pres. 1985-86). Avocations: reading, needlework; water skiing. Home: Box 1137 Allen TX 75002 Office: Tex Instruments Inc PO Box 225621 Dallas TX 75265

BRICK, ANN VETA, lawyer; b. Cheyenne, Wyo., Mar. 17, 1947; d. Gerald John and Margaret (Pasternack) Veta; m. Steven A. Brick, Dec. 29, 1968; 1 dau., Kate Elizabeth. B.A., Newcomb Coll., Tulane U., 1969; J.D., U. Calif.-Berkeley, 1975. Bar: Calif. 1975, U.S. Dist. Ct. (no. dist.) Calif. 1975, U.S. Ct. Appeals (5th cir.) 1977, (7th cir.) 1981. Staff statistician Pacific Telephone Co., San Francisco, 1969-72; law clk. to Alfonso J. Zirpoli, U.S. Dist. Ct. No. Dist. Calif., San Francisco, 1975-76; assoc. firm Howard, Rice, Nemorovski, Canady, Robertson & Falk, San Francisco, 1977-81, ptnr., 1981-84, of counsel, 1984—; dir. Legal Aid Soc. San Francisco, 1982—; mem. San Francisco Lawyers Com. for Urban Affairs, 1983—; co-operating atty. ACLU, 1978—. Mem. ABA, State Bar Calif., San Francisco Bar Assn. (judiciary com.), Order of Coif, Phi Beta Kappa. Democrat. Jewish. Office: Howard Rice Nemerovski Canady Robertson & Falk 3 Embarcadero Ctr San Francisco CA 94111

BRICKER, VICTORIA REIFLER, anthropology educator; b. Hong Kong, China, June 15, 1940; came to U.S. 1947, naturalized 1953; d. Erwin and Henrietta (Brown) Reifler; A.B., Stanford U., 1962, A.M., Harvard U., 1963, Ph.D., 1968; m. Harvey Miller Bricker, Dec. 27, 1964. Vis. lectr. anthropology Tulane U., 1969-70, asst. prof., 1970-73, assoc. prof., 1973-78, prof. 1978—. Guggenheim fellow, 1982; Wenner-Gren Found. Anthropl. Research grantee, 1971, Social Sci. Research Council grantee, 1972. Fellow Am. Anthrop. Assn. (mem. exec. bd. 1980-83); mem. Am. Soc. Ethnohistory, Linguistic Soc. Am., Seminario de Cultura Maya, Société des Americanistes. Author: Ritual Humor in Highland Chiapas 1973, The Indian Christ, The Indian King: The Historical Substrate of Maya Myth and Ritual 1981, A Grammar of Mayan Hieroglyphs, 1986; book rev. editor Am. Anthropologist 1971-73; editor: Am. Ethnologist 1973-76; gen. editor: Supplement to Handbook of Middle American Indians 1977—. Office: Department Anthropology Tulane University New Orleans LA 70118

BRICKLE, JUDITH HERRMANN, manufacturing company official; b. Evansville, Ind., Nov. 19, 1940; d. Edwin Frederick and Anna Zerilda (Fridy) Herrmann; B.S., Northwestern U., 1962; 1 dau., Anne Elizabeth. Asst. to advt. mgr. Fortune Mag., Boston, 1962; editorial asst. Am. Pharm. Assn., Washington, 1962; asst. editor Nat. Def. Transp. Assn., Washington, 1962-63; freelance writer, Washington, 1963-70; women's editor No. Va. Sun, Arlington, 1970-71; copy editor Evansville (Ind.) Courier, 1971-72; sr. writer Keller Crescent Co., Evansville, 1972-77; supr. creative programs Gen. Electric Advt., Louisville, 1977-82; mgr. employee programs Gen. Electric major appliance bus. group, 1982—. Mem. NOW, Internat. Platform Assn., World Future Soc., Mensa. Home: 10604 Linn Station Rd Louisville KY 40223 Office: Appliance Park 3 #232 Louisville KY 40225

BRIDEWELL, SHERRY HAZELWOOD, lawyer; b. Williamsburg, Va., June 3, 1956; d. Howell Percell, Jr. and Mary (Courtney) Hazelwood; m. Travis Arthur Bridewell, May 14, 1977. B.A., Coll. William and Mary, 1978, J.D., 1981. Bar: Va. 1981, U.S. Ct. Appeals (4th cir.) 1983. Reporter, Daily Report, Inc., Newport News, Va., 1978-80; dep. clk. of ct. Williamsburg-James City County Circuit Ct. Clk's. Office, Williamsburg, 1979-80; atty. Office Gen. Counsel, State Corp. Commn., Richmond, Va., 1981—, mem. Task Force for Telecommunications, 1981-84; adj. instr. Sch. Bus., Coll. William and Mary. Author: Resolution for Nat. Assn. of Regulatory Utility Commns., 1983; co-author rules and legis. in field. Clk. Liberty Baptist Ch., Lanexa, Va., 1981-82. Abby Aldrich Rockefeller scholar, 1974. Mem. ABA, Va. Bar Assn., Richmond Bar Assn., Women's Richmond Bar Assn., Phi Beta Kappa. Home: Box 31 Barhamsville VA 23011 Office: Office of Gen Counsel Va State Corp Commn PO Box 1197 1120 Bank St Richmond VA 23219

BRIDGER, GALE WESSON, educator; b. Minden, La., Jan. 15, 1939; d. George Dudney and Corrie Ethel (Bennett) Wesson; B.A. cum laude, La. Tech. U., 1960, M.A., 1965; Ed.D., U. Miss., 1974; m. Robert Dixon Bridger, Dec. 26, 1956; 1 son, Robert Jeffrey. Tchr., English Caddo Parish (La.) Schs., 1960-70, curriculum coordinator, 1970-72; supr. lang. arts-social studies Holly Springs (Miss.) Schs., 1972-73; adminstrv. coordinator Caddo Parish Schs., 1973-75; asso. prof., dir. profl. lab. experience, coordinator grad. studies La. State U., Shreveport, 1975-81, asso. prof., dir. instl. research and planning, 1981—, asst. vice chancellor acad. affairs for univ. planning, 1984—. Mem. Caddo Parish Sch. Bd., 1977; mem. Leadership Devel. Shreveport, 1982—. Mem. Assn. Tchr. Educators, Assn. Instl. Research, So. Assn. Instl. Research, Midsouth Ednl. Research Assn., La. Assn. Instl. Research (sec.-treas.), S.E. Regional Assn. Tchr. Educators, La. Assn. Tchr. Educators, Kappa Delta Pi, Sigma Kappa. Methodist. Home: 244 Roma Dr Shreveport LA 71105 Office: 8515 Youree Dr Shreveport LA 71115

BRIDGES, ANNITA MARIE, lawyer; b. Columbia, S.C., Dec. 21, 1951; d. John R. and Anne M. (Wharton) B.; m. Robert H. Alexander, Jr. B.A., Howard U., 1973; J.D., Georgetown U., 1976. Bar: Okla. 1979, Colo. 1976, U.S. Dist. Ct. Colo. 1976, U.S. Dist. Ct. (we. dist.) Okla. 1980, U.S. Ct. Appeals (10th cir.) 1976. Legal intern SBA, Washington, 1974-75; asst. atty. gen. State of Colo., Denver, 1976-78; staff atty. Kerr-McGee Corp., Oklahoma City, 1978—; lectr. U. Okla., Norman, 1982. Mem. Colo. Gov.'s Clemency Adv. Bd., 1977-78; mem. Gov.'s Adv. Commn. on Status Women; vol. in Oklahoma City Pub. Schs.; bd. dirs., past pres. Planned Parenthood Assn., Oklahoma City; bd. dirs. YWCA, Oklahoma City N.E. Devel. Corp., Black Liberated Arts Council, Oklahoma City Jr. League. Recipient Outstanding Community Service award Community Council Central Okla., 1984; Bruce Miller Meml. award for community contbns. Oklahoma City Neighborhood Devel. and Conservation Ctr., 1985. Mem. ABA, Okla. Bar Assn. (sec. labor law sect. 1979-80), Jr. League of Oklahoma City. Office: Kerr-McGee Corp PO Box 25861 Oklahoma City OK 73125

BRIDGES, ELEUTHERIA (ELTRIA), artist, sculptor, interior designer; b. Adrianople, Turkey, Nov. 28, 1905; came to U.S., 1917, naturalized, 1943; d. Constantine Nicolaides and Aikaterine (Constantinou) Bezas; A.A., Cooper Union, 1926; student Art Students League, N.Y.C., 1925-26, Indsl. Sch. Art, N.Y.C., 1926-28, Grand Central Sch. Art, N.Y.C., 1928-29, William O. Forrest Summer Art Sch., Brooklin, Maine, 1932; m. Robert Wallace Bridges, June 22, 1933; children—Constance Louise (Mrs. Phillip Bodley), Rosalind Ellen. Stylist, Dennison Mfg. Co., N.Y.C., 1922; artist W.W. Brown, Engravers, N.Y.C., 1922-24; interior designer Darling Studios, N.Y.C., 1924-27; asst. to credit mgr. Mallinkrot Chems., N.Y.C., 1927; specialist for subscriber services dept. Moody's Investors Service, N.Y.C., 1928; asst. to sales devel. mgr. Fred F. French Investing Co., N.Y.C., 1928-29; free-lance artist, sculptor, interior designer, poet, author, 1947—; exhibited one-woman show, Blue Hill, Maine, 1968; mem. traveling art exhibit, Proctor & Gamble, 1932-34; exhibited group shows: Indsl. Sch.-Art, N.Y.C., 1927, Art League, Huntington, N.Y., 1963, 64, 65, Artists Group, East Meadow, N.Y., 1967, Solon Soc., Hempstead, N.Y., 1968, 69, 70. Mem. Solon Soc., Carman Ave. Artists Group, Huntington Twp. Art League, Sedgwick Hist. Soc., Daus. Penelope. Club: The Maine. Author: What Now, Iphigenia, 1971. Address: 2825 NE 21st Ave Fort Lauderdale FL 33306 also Fairhill Sedgwick ME 04676

BRIDGES, EMMA LOU, cytotechnologist; b. Indpls., Mar. 25, 1924; d. James Alverson and Helen Carolyn (Baldock) B.; student DePauw U., Ind. U., Cornell U. Med. Coll. Research asst., instr. Papanicolaou Research Lab., Cornell U. Med. Coll., 1956-60; chief cytotechnologist Papanicolaou Cancer Research Inst., Miami, Fla., 1961-66; chief cytotechnologist, instr., research asst., teaching coordinator Hahnemann Med. Coll. and Hosp., Phila., 1966-70; chief cytotechnologist, instr. Temple U. Med. Coll. and Hosp., Phila., 1970-73; owner, supr. Mary G. Papanicolaou Lab. Diagnostic Cytology, Plainfield, Ind., 1979—; past chmn. tech. adv. com. Dade County (Fla.) Community Cervical Cytology Program; cons. in field. Mem. Am. Soc. Clin. Pathologists, Inter-Soc. Cytology Council, Am. Soc. Cytology (1st sec. cytotechnologists adv. com. 1957-59), Am. Soc. Cytotech., N.Y. Acad. Scis., Delta Alpha Gamma. Author research papers in field. Address: 1407 Miami Ct N Plainfield IN 46168

BRIDGES, JANET MICHON, nurse; b. New Orleans, July 21, 1951; d. Winfred John Lawrence, Jr., and Bonnie Lou (Odom) Michon; R.N., Los Angeles County Med. Center, 1973; student Calif. State U., Los Angeles, 1976-79; m. Paul Donnelly Bridges, Nov. 23, 1974; children—Amanda Leigh, Melissa Michon. Charge nurse med. floor, relief charge nurse, charge nurse emergency room, mem. triage team Los Angeles County-U. So. Calif. Med. Center, 1970-76; staff nurse ICU, 3-11 house supr., 3-11 charge nurse emergency room, asst. to dir. nursing Doctors Hosp., Montclair, Calif., 1976-80; nurse mgr. emergency dept. Carson-Tahoe Hosp., Carson City, Nev., 1980-82; nurse adminstr. Christian Hosp. Med. Center, Perris, Calif., 1982-84; mgr. emergency services Queen of Valley Trauma Center, West Covina, Calif., 1984—. Mem. Emergency Dept. Nurses Assn. Co-inventor intravenous tubing device. Home: 5452 Ranch Gate Rd Rancho Cucamonga CA 91701 Office: Queen of the Valley Trauma Center 1115 S Sunset Ave West Covina CA 91790

BRIDGFORTH PATTERSON, SHERYL KAYE, chemical company executive; b. Gideon, Mo., Sept. 5, 1950; d. Hartwell Brown and Mildred Pauline (Summers) Bridgforth; m. Harlan F. Monson, Jan. 11, 1971 (div.); m. 2d, M. Lee Patterson, Jr., Jan. 3, 1981. B.S., Evangel Coll., 1971; M.A., Columbia U., 1973. Mgr. Elaine Powers Figure Salon, Union, N.J., 1971; dir. residence and student activities Marymount Manhattan Coll., N.Y.C., 1971-73; assoc. dir. student activities St. Thomas Aquinas Coll., Sparkill, N.Y., 1973-74; indsl. relations trainee Continental Can Co., 1974; recruiter Exxon Corp., N.Y.C., 1974, benefit plans adminstr., 1974-76, benefits and compensation adminstr., Florham Park, N.J., 1976-78, personnel adminstr., N.Y.C., 1978-79, benefits and policies supr., Houston, 1979-82; employee relations mgr. Exxon Houston Chem. Plant, 1982-83; compensation and benefits mgr. Exxon Chem. Ams., Houston, 1983—. Mem. Am. Soc. Personnel Adminstrs., Houston Bus. Forum. Presbyterian. Office: Exxon Chem Americas 13501 Katy Freeway Houston TX 77079

BRIEFEL, RONETTE RUSSELL, epidemiologist, consultant; b. Westfield, N.Y., Oct. 13, 1954; d. Ronald Glenmore and Marlene Norma (Green) Russell; m. Kenneth A. Briefel, May 7, 1983. B.S. in Nutrition, Pa. State U., 1975; M.P.H. in Health Adminstrn., U. Pitts., 1976, Ph.D. in epidemiology, 1982. Registered dietitian. Research asst. Child Guidance, Pitts., 1976; cardiovascular research nutritionist U. Pitt., 1976-78, sr. research nutritionist and clinic dir., 1978-82; epidemiologist Nat. Ctr. for Health Stats., Hyattsville, Md., 1983—; cons. cardiovascular risk reduction project Med. Coll. Va., Richmond, 1984—. Contbr. articles to profl. jours. Nutrition com. Am. Heart Assn., Washington, 1982—; chairperson Community Assn's Communications and Recreation coms., Laurel, Md., 1982-84. Maternal and child health tng. grantee U. Pitts., 1975-76. Mem. Am. Heart Assn. Council on Epidemiology, D.C. Dietetic Assn. (bd. dirs., mgmt. chairperson 1984-85), Am. Heart Assn. (nutrition com., co-chairperson symposium com., Dedicated Service award 1983, Continued Service award 1984), Am. Dietetic Assn. Avocations: tennis; cooking; refinishing furniture. Office: Nat Ctr for Health Stats 2-58 PGC 3700 E-W Hwy Hyattsville MD 20782

BRIGDEN, CAROL ANNE, real estate agent; b. Olympia, Wash., June 13, 1946; d. Lawrence Eugene and Georgia Belle (Keeton) B.; children—David John Pittman, Christin Dyan Pittman. Student North Lake Jr. Coll., Dallas, 1978-86. Licensed real estate agt., Tex. Legal sec. Geary, Stahl, Spencer, Dallas, 1975-77; paralegal John Roach & Co., Dallas, 1977-79; sr. property mgr. Mgmt. Systems, Dallas, 1979-81; leasing agt. Vantage Co., Dallas, 1981—; mem. adv. bd. Centerpoint Nat. Bank, Arlington, Tex., 1986. Named to Multi-Millionaires Club, Vantage Cos., 1985. Mem. Nat. Assn. Indsl. Office Parks, Comml. Indsl. Div. Greater Dallas Bd. Realtors, Greater Ft. Worth Area Indsl. Devel. Assn., Comml. Real Estate Women (2d v.p. 1986-87). Republican. Methodist. Clubs: So. Meth. U. Mustang, So. Meth. U. Mothers'. Home: 9848 Williamsburg St Dallas TX 75220 Office: Vantage Cos 600 Six Flags Dr Arlington TX 76011

BRIGGS, CINDY JEAN, data processing firm executive; b. Detroit, Feb. 6, 1955; d. Kenneth Eugene and Dolores (Makos) B. Student Capitol Inst. Tech., 1983-85. Office mgr. Internat. Packaging & Assembling, Detroit, 1973-80; EEO counselor IRS Data Ctr., Detroit, 1981-82, computer specialist, 1980-82; owner, cons. Brigstar Data Processing, Sterling Heights, Mich., 1982—. Medication worker Children's Leukemia Found., Southfield, Mich., 1979-82, publicity dir., 1978-81. Recipient Service award Children's Leukemia Found., 1982; Mich. State Fund scholar, 1973. Mem. Assn. Women in Computing (Detroit and nat. chpts.). Avocations: reading; softball; soccer; photography; travel. Office: Brigstar Data Processing 5060 Bedford Detroit MI 48224

BRIGGS, HEATHER, lawyer; b. Bronxville, N.Y., Sept. 30, 1953; d. Philip and Jean (Sloan) B.; m. Peter Stephen Erly, Sept. 8, 1983. A.B., Middlebury Coll., 1975; J.D., U. Akron, 1978; LL.M., Georgetown U., 1982. Bar: D.C. 1979, Ga. 1983. Atty., Fed. Labor Relations Authority, Washington, 1979-82; assoc. Jackson, Lewis, Schnitzler & Krupman, Atlanta, 1982, Mack, Caldwell & Steckel, Atlanta, 1983—. Editor Law Rev., Akron, 1977-78. Mem. ABA, Bar Assn. D.C., Ga. Bar Assn. Republican. Office: Mack Caldwell & Steckel 134 Peachtree St Suite 600 Atlanta GA 30303

BRIGGS, NANCY ERICKSON, educator, bus. cons.; b. Huron, S.D., July 28, 1944; d. Otto Palmer and Clara Marie (Schwartz) Erickson; B.A., Augustana Coll., 1966; M.A., U. So. Calif., 1968, Ph.D. (NDEA fellow), 1970; m. Rod Briggs, Dec. 27, 1966; children—Eric, Nicole. Prof. speech communication Calif. State U., Long Beach, 1970—, ednl. cons. to Newport Sch. Dist., Fountain Valley Sch. Dist., Los Angeles Free Public Theatre. Pres. Am. Luth. Ch. Women, Palos Verdes, 1981; mem. Chadwick Mothers Assn., Joy Bible Study. Named Outstanding Woman South Bay Area, 1981, Outstanding Prof., Sr. Citizen Club Calif. State U. Long Beach, 1981. Mem. Internat. Communication Assn., Speech Communication Assn. Am., Western States Speech Communication Assn., Am. Oratorical Assn. Author: Children's Literature through Storytelling and Drama, 1977; contbr. article to profl. jour.; speaker profl. convs. Office: 1250 Bellflower Blvd Long Beach CA 90840

BRIGGS, TRUDY HANKINSON, educational administrator; b. Poughkeepsie, N.Y., July 3, 1935; d. Arthur C. and Caroline G. (Mesler) Hankinson; B.S., Skidmore Coll., 1957; M.A. in Edn., SUNY, New Paltz, 1960, C.A.S. in Ednl. Adminstrn., 1974; m. Kenneth R. Briggs, June 2, 1957; children—Jeffrey, Kenneth R. III. Tchr., Poughkeepsie City Schs., 1958-72; prin. Vassar Road Sch., Wappingers Sch. Dist., Wappingers Falls, N.Y., 1973—. Chmn. State wide Adv. Com. on Equal Opportunity for Women in Edn.; bd. dirs. Dutchess County Hist. Soc., Community Children's Theatre, Community Exptl. Repertory Theatre;s Bardavon 1869 Opera House, Jr. League. Mem. Sch. Adminstrs. Assn., Wappingers Falls Adminstrs. Assn., N.Y. State Sch. Adminstrs. Assn. (treas. region IV), Dutchess County Adminstrs. Assn., AAUW (past pres.), Phi Delta Kappa. Home: 90 Beechwood Ave Poughkeepsie NY 12603 Office: Vassar Road Sch Vassar Rd Poughkeepsie NY 12603

BRIGGS-MILTEER, LINDA DENESE, manufacturing and construction executive; b. Andalusia, Ala., Aug. 26, 1954; d. Esther and Ivy Lee (Huffman) Briggs; m. James Leon Milteer, Aug. 4, 1979. B.A., Fisk U., 1976; M.R.E., Duke U., 1978. Customer service rep. Nat. Data Corp., Atlanta, 1979-81; accounts payable clk. Drs. Meml. Hosp., Atlanta, 1981; office mgr. Skeeter's Marine, Mansfield, Ohio, 1981-82; sales mgr. Quality Bldg. Supplies, Mansfield, 1983-84; pres.-owner Red-E-Bilt Products, Mansfield, 1983—. Bd. dirs. Mansfield Sickle Cell & Health Care, 1985—; mem. Central City Econ. Devel. Corp., Mansfield, 1984-85, NAACP, Black Women United. Mem. Assn. Bus. and Profl. Women in Constrn. Baptist. Clubs: Roadrunner, Reach II (Mansfield). Lodge: Order Eastern Star. Avocations: reading; motorcycling; travel. Home: 501 Louise Ave Mansfield OH 44903

BRIGHT, GWENDOLYN NECIA, lawyer; b. Phila., Sept. 13, 1951; d. John Douglas and Vida Mae (Harris) B. B.A., Del. State Coll., 1972; M.A., Atlanta U., 1973; J.D., Temple U., 1976. Bar: U.S. Dist. Ct. (ea. dist.) Pa. 1977, Pa. 1977, D.C. 1980, U.S. Ct. Appeals (3d cir.) 1982. Law clk. City Solicitor's Office, Phila., 1976-77; staff atty. Housing Assn. Delaware Valley, Phila., 1977-78; asst. defender Defender Assn. Phila., 1978—; cons. Keepers of Shrine, Phila., 1980—, Coalition of A.M.E. Fed. Credit Unions, Phila., 1980—; instr. Free Law Sch., Phila., 1978. Co-founder Jones Tabernacle A.M.E. Ch. Free Legal Clinic, Phila., 1977-79; bd. dirs. Southeastern Pa. Legal Services for Deaf, Phila., 1980—. Recipient Achievement awards Zion A.M.E. Ch., Phila., 1977, Bishop John D. Bright Scholarship Inc., Phila., 1981; Service awards Coalition of A.M.E. Fed. Credit Unions, Phila., 1982, Barrister Assn., Phila., 1978, 79, Keepers of Shrine, Phila., 1982. Mem. Barristers Assn. (sec. 1978-80, treas. 1980-82), ABA, D.C. Bar Assn., Pa. Bar Assn., Phila. Bar Assn., Delta Sigma Theta, Phi Alpha Theta. African Methodist Episcopal.

BRIGHT, JERLENE ANN, information systems programs administrator; b. Norman, Okla., July 4, 1942; d. Hoyt David and Pearl J. Little; Asso. in Bus., Okla. Sch. Banking and Bus., 1964; student U. Okla., 1974-76; m. James Bright, July 25, 1959; children—Bridget, Michelle, Erika. Project coordinator U. Okla. Computing Center, 1965-68, dir. info. systems programs U. Okla., Norman, 1968-84; data processing dir. Dwight's Energydata, Inc., 1984—; participant UN energy meetings and workshops to third world meetings. Contbr. numerous papers and articles to profl. jours. Mem. Soc. Petroleum Engrs. Home: 4317 Lyrewood Ln Norman OK 73072

BRIGHT, JUNE LOUISE, systems engineer, mechanical engineer; b. Dover, N.J., June 17, 1956; d. Richard Otten and Lois Ann (Preuss) B. B.S. in Civil Engring., Bucknell U., 1978; M.B.A., Fla. Inst. Tech., 1984. Civil engr. Interpace Corp., Parsippany, N.J., 1978-79; mech. engr. Dept. Def. munitions systems div., Dover, N.J., 1979-82, systems engr. Infantry and Armor, 1981-84, recruitment cons., 1979-84; asst. program mgr. systems engr. space and strategic div. Hughes Aircraft Co., 1984—. Recipient Outstanding Young Employee Fed. Exec. Bd., 1981. Mem. Am. Def. Preparadeness Assn., Assn. U.S. Army, Tech. Mktg. Soc. Am. Zonta. Republican. Lutheran. Home: 4151 Via Marnia #402 Marina Del Rey CA 90292 Office: Hughes Aircraft Co PO Box 902 ES4 F204 El Segundo CA 90245

BRIGHT, KATHY SUZANNE, public relations executive; b. Marianna, Fla., July 19, 1957; d. Charley Travis and Mary Etta (Davis) B. A.A., Chipola Jr. Coll., 1977; B.S., U. W. Fla., 1980. Energy cons. Fla. Pub. Utilities, Marianna, 1981-86; mgr. customer relations First Bank Marianna, 1986—. Sec. Am. Cancer Soc., Marianna, 1984-85; dir. Chipola Area Builder's Assn., Marianna, 1985-86. Named Outstanding Young Careerist, Bus. and Profl. Women, Marianna, 1984. Mem. Nat. Assn. Female Execs. Democrat. Baptist. Club: Pilot (Marianna) (2d v.p. 1984-85). Avocations: skiing; woodworking; reading. Home: 307B Deering St Marianna FL 32446

BRIGHT, LINDA JEAN, accountant, university official; b. Pittsfield, Ill., Nov. 9, 1945; d. Homer and Beverly D. (Turnbaugh) Ator; m. Talmadge C. Bright, Mar. 19, 1982; 1 dau., Kelle. B.S.B.A., U. Albuquerque, 1979; postgrad. N.Mex. Highlands U., 1979-80; M.B.A., U. Houston. C.P.A. Acctg. supr. Lovelace Bataan Med. Ctr., Albuquerque, 1971-77; v.p., controller Empire Clarklift Inc., Albuquerque, 1977-81; asst. controller U. Houston, 1981-83, asst. v.p., 1983-84, treas., 1984—. Mem. Nat. Assn. Corp. Treasurers, Nat. Assn. Coll. and Univ. Bus. Officers, Nat. Corp. Cash Mgrs. Assn., So. Assn. Coll. and Univ. Bus. Officers, Tex. Assn. Coll. and Univ. Bus. Officers. Republican. Quaker. Home: 1042 Wakefield St Houston TX 77018 Office: U Houston 4600 Gulf Freeway Suite 300 Houston TX 77023

BRIGHT, MARY KATHERINE, institute ofcl.; b. Waukegan, Ill., Oct. 30, 1925; d. William Lincoln and Edna Belle (Wardlow) Manny; B.A. in English with honors, Calif. State U., Northridge, 1965; M.A. in English, U. So. Calif., 1968, postgrad. in linguistics and higher edn.; m. William Herbert Bright, Dec. 22, 1978; children—Marianne, Kurtina, Kristina. Instr., sr. lectr. English, English as second lang. Calif. State U., Northridge, and U. So. Calif., 1965-68, asst. dean summer session, exec. dir. summer session evening coll., 1969-74; dir. continuing edn. Calif. State U., Long Beach, 1974-78; assoc. dir. urban extension and non-credit programs Ohio State U., 1978-80; dir. office mgmt. devel. U. Ill. Coll. Bus. Adminstrn., Chgo., 1980-84; dir. continuing edn. div. Am. Inst. for Fgn. Study, Greenwich, Conn., 1984—; conf. presenter; pres. Council Non-Traditional Studies, 1972-78; cons. W.Va. Bd. Regents, 1978. Mem. Nat. Univ. Continuing Edn. Assn., Sigma Alpha Alpha. Presbyterian. Office: 102 Greenwich Ave Greenwich CT 06830

BRIGHTON, ERNESTINE JOHNSTON, nursing administrator; b. Memphis, Nov. 27, 1925; d. Ernest Leonard and Annie Lillian (Lunn) Green; R.N., Bapt. Meml. Hosp., Memphis, 1946; B.S. in Nursing, U. Tulsa, 1970, M.S., 1975; m. Robert Samuel Johnston, Jan. 6, 1973 (div. 1981); children—Ira Emmett Brighton, Harry Lee Brighton, Val Lynn Brighton. Head nurse obstetrics St. John's Hosp., Tulsa, 1961-63; supr. pediatrics Mabee Children's Hosp., Hillcrest Med. Center, Tulsa, 1963-64, instr. Sch. Nursing, 1964-66, maternal-child health coordinator, 1966; dir. nursing services Hissom Meml. Center, Sand Springs, Okla., 1966-85, coordinator health services, 1985—; active state-wide orientation in mental retardation to schs. of nursing; mem. Drs. of Nursing Service and Nursing Edn. Group, Tulsa. Active Tulsa Area Health and Planning Council, 1970—. R.N., Okla., Tenn.; cert. in mgmt., U. Ala., Birmingham, 1973. Mem. Am. Nurses Assn., Okla. State Nurses Assn. (hosting com. for state conv. 1979, publicity chmn. 1979-80, dir. Tulsa dist. 1980—, pres. dist. 1981-82, nominating com. 1983-84), Dist. Nurses Assn. (pres. 1983-84), Am. Assn. Mental Deficiency, Parent Guardian Assn.-Hissom Meml. Center, Theatre Tulsa, U. Okla. Alumnae. Democrat. Club: Sweet Adelines (Tulsa). Home: 2832 S Pittsburg St Tulsa OK 74114 Office: Hissom Memorial Center Route 4 Box 14 Sand Springs OK 74063

BRILES, JUDITH, financial planning company executive; b. Pasadena, Calif., Feb. 20, 1946; d. James and Mary (McKnight) Tuthill; C.F.P., Coll. Fin. Planning, Denver, 1978; M.B.A., Pepperdine U., 1980; D.B.A., Nova U., 1986; postgrad. U. Calif.-Berkeley, U. Calif.-Santa Cruz, U. Hawaii; children—Shelley, Frank (dec.), Sheryl. Account exec. E.F. Hutton, Palo Alto, Calif., 1972-78; pres. Briles & Assocs., Palo Alto, 1980—; instr. DeAnza Coll., Canada Coll.; adj. prof. Coll. Fin. Planning, Denver; assoc. Ctr. Research on Women, Stanford U. Bd. dirs. Foothill-DeAnza Colls. Found., Los Altos Hills, Calif. Mem. Commonwealth Club, Inst. Cert. Fin. Planners, Nat. Assn. Female Execs. (bd. dirs.), Beta Sigma Phi. Republican. Author: The Woman's Guide to Financial Savvy, 1981; Money Phases: The Six Financial Phases of a Woman's Life, 1984; bd. dirs. Bus. Woman mag. Home: 558 Cambridge Ave Palo Alto CA 94306 Office: 101 University Ave Suite 230 Palo Alto CA 94301

BRILEY, WANDA MARIE, basketball coach; b. Charleston, S.C., June 7, 1952; d. Alvin Joseph and Sarah Lou (Byrd) B.; B.S., U. S.C., 1974; M.A., Appalachian State U., 1977. Asst. volleyball and basketball coach, teaching asst. Appalachian State U., Boone, N.C., 1975-77; mem. faculty, head basketball and volleyball coach High Point (N.C.) Coll., 1977-79; head basketball coach Wake Forest U., Winston Salem, N.C., 1979—; dir. Lady Deacon Basketball Sch., 1981—, Wanda Briley Basketball Camp, 1979—; nat. volleyball ofcl., 1982—. Mem. exec. com. Wade Trophy Com., 1977—; mem. N.C. Ethics and Eligibility Com., 1980-82; pres. N.C. Bd. Volleyball Ofcls. Named Carolinas Conf. Coach of Yr. in volleyball and basketball, 1978-79, Nat. Coach of Yr. Assn. Intercollegiate Athletics for Women, 1979; recipient Key to City, High Point City Council, 1978, Letter of Resolution for outstanding service High Point Council and Mayor, 1979; named to Basketball Hall of Fame, 1979; coached High Point Coll. to assn. Intercollegiate Athletics for Women Nat. Championship, 1978. Mem. Nat. Coaches Assn. Democrat. Roman Catholic. Home: 3606 Heathrow Dr Winston-Salem NC 27107 Office: Box 7265 Reynolda Sta Wake Forest U Winston-Salem NC 27109

BRILL, ELIZABETH BAKER, arts administrator, stage manager, producer; b. Mt. Vernon, N.Y., July 21, 1954; d. Laurence Spencer and Joy (Piza) Baker; m. Robert Michael Brill, Oct. 16, 1983; 1 child, Daniel Kenneth. B.A., Sarah Lawrence Coll., Bronxville, N.Y., 1976. Gen. mgr. Potter's Field Theatre Co., N.Y.C., 1979-81, The Acting Co., N.Y.C., 1981; adj. prof. New Sch. for Social Research, N.Y.C., 1981-84; researcher CBS News, N.Y.C., 1982-85; assoc. dir. Greene County Council on the Arts, Catskill, N.Y., 1985—; cons. Art Awareness, Lexington, N.Y.

BRILL, NORA KENDALL, public relations and marketing executive; b. Worcestershire, Eng., Jan. 28, 1931; d. Kenneth William and Sibyl Winnifred (Brown) Kendall; B.A., Queens U., Kingston, Ont., 1971; m. Lawrence Brill Mar. 8, 1957 (dec.); children—Dianne, Jonathan, Troy, Michael. Tchr., Arthur Murray Studios, Toronto and Havana, 1950-52; reservation agt. United Airlines, Chgo., 1953-54; society columnist Tampa Times, 1975-82; dir. pub. relations HFI Medinorm Div., Houston, 1983-85; mktg. dir. River's Edge Club, Tampa, 1985—. Del., Fla. Democratic Conv., 1981; mem. Arts Watch Task Force, 1981; pres. Las Damas De Arte, 1972; bd. dirs. Tampa Symphony Guild, Guilders of Tampa Bay Art Center, Easter Seal Guild. Named Outstanding Vol., Tampa Bay Art Center, 1975; recipient Diana award NOW, 1979. Mem. Athena Soc. (dir.), PEN, Tampa Bay Press Club, Women in Communications. Democrat. Home: 10604 Ilex St Tampa FL 33618 Office: 2780 Riverside Dr Tampa FL 33602

BRIMACOMBE, DOROTHY DARTMOUTH REDENBAUGH (MRS. ALFRED JOHN BRIMACOMBE), printing, stationery co. exec.; b. Quincy, Ill., Oct. 30, 1901; d. William Alfred and Mary Louise (Farr) Redenbaugh; tchrs. diploma Ellensburg (Wash.) Normal Sch., 1922; B.S. in Edn., Oreg. State U., 1926; m. Alfred John Brimacombe, Aug. 2, 1935. Tchr. pub. schs., Wapato, Wash., 1922-23, Seattle, 1923-25, 26-28; instr. journalism Ellensburg Normal Sch., 1928-31; receptionist Six Cos., Inc., Boulder City, Nev., 1931; co-owner, asso. editor Las Vegas Age, Nev., 1933-44; co-owner Brimmies Comml. Printing & Stationery, Las Vegas, 1944-85. Sec., Nev. Safety Council, 1968-80. Bd. dirs., exec. com. Nev. Safety Council, 1967-80; Nev. mem. Nat. Assn. Women Hwy. Safety Leaders, 1969-71; bd. dirs. So. Nev. Drug Abuse Council, 1972-82; founder Nike House, home for girls, 1972, pres. bd. dirs., 1972-74, 80-85; sec.-treas. DDB Found., 1975—; sec. Nev. Treatment Ctr., 1980—. Pres., Nev. Fedn. Republican Women, 1952-53. Mem. AAUW (pres. Las Vegas sect. 1940-42, Nev. div. 1946-47), Las Vegas Bus. and Profl. Womens (pres. 1940-42), Nev. (pres. 1943-44), Nat. (treas. 1956-60) fedns. bus. and profl. women, Nat. Fedn. Press Women (regional v.p. 1946), Alpha Gamma Delta. Clubs: Mesquite (pres. Las Vegas 1940), Las Vegas Altrusa. Office: PO Box 150 Las Vegas NV 89125

BRIMER, DEBORAH ROSE, promotion consultant, performer; b. Dallas, Oct. 5, 1949; d. C.D. and Rose Annette (Taylor) B. Grad. Dallas Fashion Merchandising Coll., 1969. Salesperson Bollman Enterprises, Dallas, 1969-70; mgr. Rick Robinson Enterprises, Inc., Dallas, 1970-72; owner Debbi Brimer & Assocs., Dallas and Mesquite, Tex., 1972-74; assoc. pub. Country Billboard Mag., Dallas, 1974-75; country music columnist Tex. newspapers; founder, co-owner Brimer-Lane Promotions, Mesquite, 1978—; performer Dixie Rose mus. duo, 1975—. Songwriter; interviewer. Vice-pres. Mesquite Performing Arts Council, 1984-85. Hon. mem. U.S.C.G., 1975. Mem. Tex. Music Assn. (chmn. bd. and pres. 1983-86, state dir. 1980-86), BMI, Nashville Songwriters Assn., Country Music Assn., Nat. Assn. Female Execs., Nat. Assn. Rec. Arts and Scis., E. Dallas C. of C., Mesquite C. of C., Garland C. of C., Balch Springs C. of C. Republican. Episcopalian. Avocations: boating; fishing; swimming; antiques; interior decorating. Home: 1312 Oriole St Mesquite TX 75149 Office: Brimer-Lane Promotions PO Box 1585 Mesquite TX 75149

BRINEGAR, MARY METTA, non-profit organization executive; b. Dallas, Oct. 11, 1947; d. Ralph Franklin and Rosemary (Thornton) B. B.A., So. Meth. U., 1969. Pub. relations, vol. coordinator Children's Med. Center, Dallas, 1971-74; underwriter Hill-Brinegar Ins. Co., Dallas, 1974-76; owner Memorable Occasions, Dallas, 1976-78; auction coordinator KERA/Channel 13, Dallas, 1978-79, auction dir., 1979-81, assoc. dir devel., 1981—; regional conf. chmn. PBS stas., 1983; devel. cons. Shakespeare Festival Dallas, 1983-84. Mem. devel. council Meth. Hosp., Dallas, 1980-82; mem. devel. com. Vis. Nurses Assn., Dallas, 1981-82; pres., The 500 Inc., Dallas; bd. dirs. Jr. League Dallas, 1973—, Vol. Center, Dallas, 1979—, Turtle Creek Manor, 1983—, Dallas Summer Musicals, 1978-79, Theatre Three, 1974-79, Theatre Three Women's Guild, 1977—, Clean Dallas Inc., 1983—, Park Cities Republican Womens Club, 1980-82, Interlude Study Course, 1974—, Dallas Symphony Orch. League, 1974-77, U.S.A. Film Festival, 1975—; pres. Innovators League Dallas, 1977; mem. exec. com. Dallas Services Visually Impaired Children, 1976-81; adminstrv. bd. Highland Park United Meth. Ch., 1983—; founder Friends of Dallas Services, 1978, Stagehands, Theatre Three, 1977-78. adv. to bd. Dallas Met. Ballet, 1975; Northpark ticket chmn. Dallas Civic Opera, 1978; chmn. Designer Showhouse, 1975; phone bank coordinator Dallas Area Rapid Transit Bond Election, 1983, Tim Collins for Congress, 1983, others. Recipient Extra Mile award Bus. and Profl. Women Dallas, 1981, Mem. Nat. Soc. Fund Raising Execs., Dallas C. of C. (Leadership) Dallas. Club: Slipper (Pres. 1976-77). Home: 4148 Hyer St Dallas TX 75205 Office: KERA 3000 Harry Hines St Dallas TX 75201

BRINEY, NANCY WELLS, publisher; b. Louisville; d. Edmond Daniel and Elsie Mae (Bald) Wells; student U. Louisville, 1932-33, William Rainey Harper Community Coll., 1965; B.A. with honors, N.Y.U., 1979; m. Paul Wallace Briney, Mar. 31, 1936; 1 son, Timothy Paul. With Jenny Lind Shop, Louisville, 1933-36; co-founder The Fireside Theatre Book Club, N.Y.C., 1948, editor Curtain Time, 1949-50; founder Barrington (Ill.) Town Hall Series, 1962—, Brownstone Press, Barrington, 1968—; lectr. William Rainey Harper Coll., Palatine, Ill., 1974—. Mem. Pub. Relations Soc. Am., Costume Soc. Am. Episcopalian. Clubs: Yale of N.Y., Jr. League of N.Y., Garden of Am., Louisville Country. Home: PO Box 375 Barrington IL 60010 Office: Brownstone Press PO Box 375 Barrington IL 60010

BRINKER, MARLENE ANN, health care executive; b. Greene, Iowa, Apr. 12, 1934; d. Bernard Charles and Marian Bertha (Crimmings) Dailey; R.N., St. Mary's Hosp., Rochester, Minn., 1955; B.A. in Geology, Rutgers U., 1975; m. Ray Brinker, Jan. 12, 1957; children—Sally Jean, Marc Henry, Sheri Louise, Sara Jane, Lisa Ann, Wendy Renee. Staff med.-surg. nurse VA Hosp., Iowa City, Iowa, 1955-57; nurse radiology dept. Mason Clinic, Seattle, 1957-58; staff nurse USPHS Hosp., Staten Island, N.Y., 1958; instr. nursing Holy Name Hosp., Teaneck, N.J., 1963-64, St. Luke's Hosp., St. Louis, 1967-69; supr. Kelly Services, Ann Arbor, Mich., 1979-80; service dir. Kelly Health Care, Ann Arbor, 1980-81, dist. mgr. for Mich. and Ind., 1981-83; pres. Brinker Cons., Inc., 1983—; mem. program and sub area coms. Comprehensive Health Planning, 1980-83. Mem. Pres.'s community relations bd. Rutgers U., 1975. Mem. N.Y. Acad. Scis. Democrat. Roman Catholic. Home and Office: 2775 Tessmer Rd Ann Arbor MI 48103

BRINKLEY, ELISE HOFFMAN, nurse, educator, biofeedback counselor; b. Barry, Tex., Mar. 10, 1922; d. James Edward and Laura Jack (Foster) Gay; R.N., Hermann Hosp., Houston, 1966; B.A. in Psychology, U. Houston, 1971; M.Ed., Prairie View U., Tex., 1973; postgrad. U. Tex., Austin, 1975-76; Ed.D. in Coll. Adminstrn., Nova U., Ft. Lauderdale, Fla., 1976; B.S. in Nursing, Tex. Womans U., Houston, 1982; postgrad. U. Tex., Galveston, 1978—; m. Billy Clarence Hoffman, June 20, 1941 (div. Nov. 1980); children—Rosilyn Gay, Billy May; m. Roger M. Brinkley, Nov. 26, 1981. Staff nurse labor, delivery and emergency room, supr. operating room Polly Ryon Meml. Hosp., Richmond, Tex., 1960-63, dir. Sch. Vocat. Nursing, 1966-71; campus nurse supr. Tex. Dept. Mental Health and Mental Retardation, Richmond State Sch., 1971-72; dir. asso. degree nursing program Alvin (Tex.) Community Coll., 1972-79, chmn. Bicentennial Show Case, 1976, also mem. pres.'s merit award com. for faculty, fin. and scholarship com., fin. affairs com.; instr. San Jacinto Coll., Pasadena, Tex., 1981-83, Midland Coll., 1983-85, Lee Coll.,Baytown, Tex., 1985—; biofeedback, counselor, 1984—; mem. Red Cross Nursing and Health Programs Adv. Com., 1974—; mem. Council Deans and Dirs. Nursing Schs. in Tex., 1975—; instr. cardio-pulmonary resuscitation Am. Heart Assn., 1976—; mem., conv. speaker Statewide Com. on Competencies, 1977—. Pres., Rosenberg PTA, 1953-55, Ft. Bend County PTA, 1956-57, Band Boosters, 1957-59; Rosenberg city chmn. Mothers March on Polio, 1954-58; mem. Gov.'s Com. on Drug Use and Drug Abuse, 1971-72; leader 4-H Club, 1952-54, Girl Scouts U.S.A., 1953-56; sponsor Alvin Nursing Students Assn., 1974-76; parliamentarian Democratic Party Ft. Bend County, 1970-71; bd. dirs. Salvation Army, 1958-60. Life mem. Nat. PTA, Tex. PTA; mem. AAUP, Tex. Jr. Coll., Alvin Community Coll. tchrs. assns., Am., Tex. nurses assns., Nat., Houston Area leagues for nursing, R.N.s of Ft. Bend County. Methodist. Club: Rosenberg Rebekah Lodge (past dist. dep. pres.). Author: Neurological Conditions of the Newborn, 1975; works listed in ERIC Clearinghouse for Jr. Colls., 1975, 76, 78. Home: 5114 Hwy 3 Dickinson TX 77539 Office: Lee Coll Baytown TX 77522 also: 1601 Main St Suite 302 Richmond TX 77469

BRINKLEY, PHYLLIS, speaker and program artist, stained glass artisan; b. Madison, Wis., May 28, 1926; d. Reynale R. and Florence (Jarvis) Crosby; B.A. in Speech and English, U. Wis., 1948, postgrad. in speech and oral interpretation of lit., 1949; m. William Malry, Jr., Aug. 5, 1949. Speaker, program artist, 1956—, current programs include First Ladies of our Land, Portrait of the Lincolns, Mary and Abraham, Stained Glass: Gift of Light; radio artist Focus on Books, Sta. WHA, 1967-72; tchr. speech, 1951-56; interpretative reader, 1950-58. Vol. hosp. aux.; public affairs chmn. Madison Civics Club; pres. Madison Women's Mcpl. Golf League, 1959; chmn. Little Sisters of Sisters of St. Benedict, 1968-69. Recipient award of excellence Wis. Fedn. Women's Clubs; named hon. cannoneer St. Louis Civil War Roundtable. Mem. Internat. Platform Assn., Nat. League Am. Pen Women, Phi Beta. Author: Abraham Lincoln and His Wife, Mary: Two Human Beings, 1975; The Lincolns: Targets for Controversy, 1986. Home: 6115 Imperial Dr Route 2 Waunakee WI 53597

BRINKMAN, LINDA W., manufacturing company executive, dietitian; b. Medford, Wis., Jan. 15, 1952; d. Clarence and Elizabeth (Scheuer) W.; m. David P. Brinkman, Apr. 25, 1981; children—Sarah, Matthew. B.S. in Edn., No. Ill. U., 1973, M.S., 1976. Registered dietitian, Ill. Extension adviser U. Ill., Champaign, 1973-74; home economist Jewel Foods, Melrose Park, Ill., 1976-78; technologist Quaker Oats Research Labs., Barrington, Ill., 1978-82; owner Am. Cat Emporium, Elburn, Ill., 1981—, LaDace, DeKalb, Ill., 1985—; tchr. Waubonsee Community Coll., Sugar Grove, Ill., 1984—. Author mag. column, 1983. Mem. Am. Pet Products Mfg. Assn., Pet Industry Distbrs. Assn., Pet Industry Joint Adv. Council, Elburn C. of C. Avocations: gourmet cooking, needle crafts, spinning. Home: Box 2446 Route 2 Maple Park IL 60151 Office: Am Cat Emporium PO Box 745 Elburn IL 60119

BRINKMAN, MARY JO, quality assurance coordinator; b. Wahoo, Nebr., Jan. 25, 1942; d. William J. and Mary Angela (O'Keefe) McDermott; m. Michael Anthony Brinkman, May 18, 1968; children—Bridget Dierdre, Sean William. B.S., Coll. St. Mary, 1963; M.A., Central Mich. U., 1980; student Morningside Coll., Penn Valley Community Coll., N.E. Nebr. Tech. Community Coll., Wayne State Coll. Registered med. technologist; lic. in real estate, Nebr. Staff med. technologist St. Joseph's Hosp., Omaha, Nebr., 1963-64; asst. supr. microbiology St. Luke's Hosp., Kansas City, Mo., 1964-65; dir. lab. Drs. Ferris, Layton, Mueller & Hoadley, Kansas City, 1965-67; AFB microbiology specialist VA Hosp., Kansas City, 1967-74; chief med. technologist J.G. Desai, M.D., Norfolk, Nebr., 1975-80, Norfolk Med. Group, 1974-80; no. subarea coordinator Greater Nebr. Health Systems Agy., 1980-81; quality assurance and utilization rev. coordinator Our Lady of Lourdes Hosp., Norfolk, 1981-84, quality assurance coordinator, 1981—. Author: (with William Long and Vickie Britten) Primary Care Recruitment Guide, 1981. Sec., Nebr.-Madison County unit Am. Cancer Soc., 1982-83; Young Democratic Nebr. State committee woman, 1964, mem. Nebr. central com., 1983—; page Nat. Dem. Conv., 1964, del., 1984; bd. dirs., treas., pres. Nebr. C.P.A.'s Wives, 1975-80. Recipient VA Hosp. Suggestion award, 1971. Mem. Am. Soc. Med. Tech., Greater Kansas City Soc. Med. Technologists (treas. 1972), Am. Pub. Health Assn., Nat. Assn. Realtors, Nebr. Realtors Assn., Norfolk Bd. Realtors, Nat. Assn. Quality Assurance Profls., Lambda of Lambda Tau, Sigma Iota Epsilon. Democrat. Roman Catholic. Clubs: Am. Contract Bridge League, Our Lady of Lourdes Hosp. Aux. Home: 1204 Greenlawn Dr Norfolk NE 68701

BRINSON, CARYL ANN, lawyer; b. Milw., Oct. 22, 1946; d. Edward McKinley and Mildred Ann (Wenzel) Dieringer; m. Robert Francis Brinson, Jr., Dec. 18, 1967. B.S., Fla. State U., 1967; M.A.T., U. Fla., 1971, J.D., 1981. Bar: Fla. 1981. Instr., U. Fla., Gainesville, 1971-73; owner, mgr. The Kitchen, Ltd., Gainesville, 1973-77; asst. city atty. City of Gainesville, 1981—. Author, lectr. historic preservation. Bd. dirs. Fla. Trust for Historic Preservation, 1982—, Historic Gainesville Inc., 1982—, Nat. Alliance Preservation Commns., 1984—. Recipient Legal Protection of Environment book award U. Fla. Coll. Law, 1980. Mem. Nat. Trust for Phi Kappa Phi. Office: City Gainesville Law Dept PO Box 490 Gainesville FL 32601

BRINSON, ELAINE KOGER, real estate and securties broker; b. Charleston, S.C., Nov. 21, 1936; d. James Edgar and Hazel Elizabeth (Martin) Koger; m. Thomas Woodrow Brinson, Apr. 6, 1958 (div. 1979); children—Thomas Benjamin, Alise Michele; m. David Morris Wiggs, Mar. 27, 1983. B.A., Furman U., 1957; M.A.T., The Citadel, Charleston, S.C., 1978. Cert. secondary sch. tchr., S.C.; lic. real estate, securities , and ins. broker. Tchr., instr. jr. and sr. high sch. and tech. coll., 1972-83; ind. contractor comml. and investment real estate, 1981-84; assoc. realtor/broker Charleston Comml., Inc., 1984-86, Spectrum Properties, Charleston, 1986—. Founder, pres. Meml. Soc. of Charleston, 1969—, Givens Found. (local investment group), 1983-84; active various community activities, programs committee chairmanships; bd. dirs., transp coordinator HELP, 1969-71; rep. Lutheran Service Ctr., 1967-69; Luther League advisor, nursery chmn., adult Sunday sch. tchr., pres. and v.p. Churchwomen, Faith Luth. Ch., 1962-70. Named Mrs. South Carolina, 1969. Mem. Nat. Assn. Realtors, Trident Bd. Realtors, Comml. and Investment Properties Council of Charleston, Cert. Comml. Investment, Realtors Nat. Mktg. Inst., Nat. Assn. Female Execs., Am. Congress Real Estate Investors, Am. Soc. Prevention Cruely to Animals, NEA (del. 1983), S.C. Edn. Assn. (rep. 1982-83), Charleston County Edn. Assn. (rep. 1982-83), Charleston Women's Network, Trident C. of C., Beta Sigma Phi (pres. Alpha Tau chpt. 1965-66, pres. city-wide 1966-67). Avocations: rare coin collecting; gardening; gourmet cooking; sailing; swimming. Home: 16 Edenwood Ct Charleston SC 29407 Office: Spectrum Properties 1190 Ashley River Rd Charleston SC 29407

BRINTLE, PEGGY VENABLE, loan service officer, corporation executive; b. Mt. Airy, N.C., Aug. 16, 1943; d. Wade Bowman, Sr., and Myrtle Maude (Simpson) Venable; m. Henry Allan Brintle, Nov. 24, 1960; children—Lisa B. Brintle Handy, Laura Leigh, L. Lyn. Student Surry Community Coll., 1982-84, Ednl. Inst., 1975-84. Title clk. Slate Motor Co., Mt. Airy, N.C., 1961-63; ins. clk. First Mchts. Bank, Newport News, Va., 1963-64; title clk. Merrimac Motors, Hampton, Va., 1964-73; substitute tchr. Surry County Sch. System, Dobson, N.C., 1974-75; loan service officer Workmen's Fed. Savs. Bank, Mt. Airy, 1975—; sec. Unlimited Bodys Inc., 1986—. Author poetry (awards), loan service procedure manual, 1986; editor newsletters, 1985—. Charter mem. North Surry Athletic Boosters, 1978—; mem. Nat. Com. to Preserve Social Security and Medicare. Mem. Am. Bus. Women's Assn., Nat. Assn. Female Execs. Republican. Quaker. Club: White Plains Woman's (pres. 1975-77). Avocations: music; writing; bicycling; volunteer work. Home: PO Box 136 White Plains NC 27031 Office: Workmens Federal Savings Bank PO Box 1508 N Main St Mt Airy NC 27030

BRIOSO, GERALDINE B., TV production company executive; b. N.Y.C., May 5, 1949; d. Domingo M. and Virginia S. (Gentile) B. B.F.A., Pratt Inst., Bklyn., 1971. Graphic artist Sta. WLIW-TV, Garden City, N.Y., 1971-72, CBS-TV Network, N.Y.C., 1972-73; graphic arts dir. Children's TV Workshop, Sesame St., N.Y.C., 1972-85; graphic design cons. Children's Computer Workshop, 1980-82; pres. The Dovetail Group Inc., N.Y.C., 1983—; free lance graphic artist, N.Y.C., 1971-83; designer, cons. computer software for children; pioneer in computer graphics and animation for TV. Recipient Creativity award Ad Directions Mag., 1975, 78; Emmy nominee, 1975, 76, 78, 80; Emmy award, 1983. Mem. Nat. Acad. TV Arts and Scis., Am. Fedn. TV and Radio Artists, ASCAP, Am. Film Inst., Spl. Interest Group Computer Graphics. Avocations: Raquet ball; ice skating; singing; playing flute. Office: The Dovetail Group Inc 127 W 92d St Duplex B New York NY 10025

BRISCH-KANABA, JANYCE, media company executive; b. Chgo., Mar. 4, 1950; d. John W. and Genevieve F. (Kowell) Brisch; m. Stephen Paul Kanaba, July 3, 1976. B.A. in Painting and Philosophy, Maryville Coll. Sacred Heart, 1973. Profl. equestrian, Chgo., 1966-76; artist, prodn. asst., Chgo., 1976-78; producer, dir., Scottsdale, Ariz., 1978-79; pres. Media People, Inc., Scottsdale, 1979—. Co-author: Single Camera Video Productions, 1981. Producer and dir. numerous video tapes, film and multi-media projects. Mem. Assn. for Multi-Image (bd. dirs. 1984-85, v.p. 1985-86). Office: Media People Inc 6736 E Avalon Scottsdale AZ 85251

BRISCO, MARGARET, physician educator; b. Trieste, Italy; b. Anna Loncarica; children—Ralph C. Stefanelli, Anna Maria Stefanelli. M.D., U. Padova (Italy), 1956. Intern, Martland Med. Center, Newark, 1956-57, resident in ob-gyn, 1957-60; practice medicine specializing in ob-gyn, Belleville, N.J., 1961—; dir. ob-gyn Clara Maas Hosp., Belleville, 1978—; asst. clin. prof. N.J. Coll. Medicine. Mem. AMA, Am. Med. Women's Assn., NOW. Author: Woman Doctor and Her Patients, 1975. Office: 5 Franklin Ave Belleville NJ 07109

BRISCOE, ANNE M., scientist, educator; b. N.Y.C., Dec. 1, 1918; M.A., Vassar Coll., 1945; Ph.D. (Sterling jr. fellow, USPHS fellow), Yale U., 1949; m. William A. Briscoe, Aug. 20, 1955. From research asso. to asst. prof. Cornell U. Med. Coll., 1950-56; faculty Columbia Coll. Physicians and Surgeons, N.Y.C., 1956—, now asst. prof. medicine; lectr. Harlem Hosp. Center Sch. Nursing, 1968-77; adj. asst. prof. Hunter Coll., 1951-64, 73-75. Mem. N.Y.C. Commn. on Status of Women, 1979—, vice chairperson, 1982—; non-govtl. orgn. del. to UN; mem. adv. council Inst. Nuclear Power Ops., 1979-84. Fellow Am. Inst. Chemists (sec. N.Y. chpt. 1981-83. Recipient Yale medal, 1986.), N.Y. Acad. Scis. (chairperson women in sci. com. 1978—, bd. govs. 1981); mem. AAAS (mem. council 1982-85), Am. Chem. Soc., Am. Soc. Clin. Nutrition, Am. Fedn. Clin. Research, Harvey Soc., Fedn. Orgns. for Profl. Women (treas. 1978-80), Assn. Women in Sci. Ednl. Founds. (pres. 1978-82), Assn. Women in Sci. (editor newsletter 1971-74, nat. pres. 1974-76), Assn. Yale Alumni (assembly rep. 1978—, bd. govs. 1982-85), Yale Grad. Sch. Alumni Assn. (pres. 1981-82). Contbr. articles to profl. jours.). Contbr. articles to profl. jours. Home: 2 Peter Cooper Rd New York NY 10010 Office: Dept Medicine Harlem Hosp Center New York NY 10037

BRISCOE, CATHERINE GRAY, investment firm executive; b. Roanoke, Va., May 15, 1920; d. Wilfred Wysor and Virginia Lucille Gray; m. Dan Edward Briscoe, Jr., Nov. 22, 1939; children—Dana Briscoe Robinette, Cary Gray, David Edward. Student, East Tenn. State U., 1971, Va. Intermont Coll., 1982, King Coll., 1984. Ptnr., Briscoe Investment Co., Bristol, Tenn., 1950—; cons. interior design, Bristol, 1950—. Bd. dirs. Bristol YWCA, 1965-71, treas., 1969-71. Republican. Presbyterian. Avocations: collecting antique furniture and paintings; swimming; travel. Home: 221 Mapletree Dr Bristol TN 37620 Office: Briscoe's Motor Inn 2412 W State St Bristol TN 37620

BRISCOE, MARY LOUISE, educator; b. Hutchinson, Kans., May 24, 1937; d. Arthur D. and Charlotte B. B.; B.A., Kans. State U., 1959; M.A., Bowling Green State U., 1961; Ph.D., U. Wis., 1968; 1 dau., Brenna. Asst. prof. U. Wis., Whitewater, 1967-72; coordinator women's studies program U. Pitts., 1972-77, assoc. prof., chmn. dept. English, 1977-85, prof., 1985—. Mem. MLA. Author: Up Against the Wall, Mother, 1971; American Autobiography: A Bibliography, 1945-1980, 1982; assoc. editor: First Person Female American, 1980. Office: Dept of English University of Pittsburgh Pittsburgh PA 15213

BRISKIN, JACQUELINE ELIZABETH, author; b. London; came to U.S., 1938, naturalized, 1944; d. Spencer and Marjorie Orgell; m. Bert Briskin, May 9, 1948; children—Ralph, Elizabeth, Richard. Author: (novels) California Generation, 1970; Afterlove, 1974; Rich Friends, 1976; Paloverde, 1978; The Onyx, 1982; Everything and More, 1983; Too Much Too Soon, 1985. Mem. Authors Guild, PEN.

BRISSETTE, MARTHA BLEVINS, lawyer; b. Salisbury, Md., Apr. 30, 1959; d. Reuben Wesley and Miriam Rebecca (Walters) Blevins; m. Henry Joseph Brissette, III, May 24, 1980. B.A. summa cum laude, U. Richmond, 1980, J.D., 1983. Bar: Va. 1983. Research asst. Va. Appellate Rules Com., Richmond, 1981; intern Va. Atty. Gen., Richmond, 1982; law clk. Supreme Ct. Va., Richmond, 1983-84; atty. U.S. Dept. Justice, Washington, 1984—; teaching asst. T.C. Williams Law Sch., U. Richmond, 1981-82, faculty research asst., 1983; legis. aide Va. Gen. Assembly, Richmond, 1983. Williams Merit and Patterson scholar, 1980-83. Mem. ABA, Va. State Bar, McNeill Law Honor Soc., Phi Beta Kappa, Phi Alpha Delta. Roman Catholic. Office: Appellate Sect Tax Div US Dept Justice Washington DC 20530

BRISTOL, LINDA JANE, medical technologist; b. Houston, June 5, 1947; d. Carl Robert and Hattie (McKinney) Carlson; B.S., Lewis and Clark Coll., 1969; m. Thomas L. Bristol, Dec. 27, 1968; children—Robert, John, Elizabeth. Intern, Good Samaritan Hosp., Portland, Oreg., 1968-69; researcher U. Oreg. Med. Sch., 1969-70; staff microbiologist Kaiser Hosp., Portland, Oreg., 1971; staff med. technologist ARC Lab., Portland, 1971-72. Mem. Am. Soc. Clin. Pathologists, Alpha Gamma. Republican. Mem. Ch. of Christ.

BRISTOL, VIRGINIA MAY, school administrator; b. Denver, May 18, 1934; d. Terry Glenn C. and Faye Virginia (Hoffman) Cartee; m. James Arthur Bristol, Feb. 14, 1958 (div. Nov. 1982); children—Marlon Ray, Timothy James, Terry Franklin, Merri Lynn. Student Belleview Coll., 1949-52, B.A. in Bible Seminary, 1956. Prin. Almadale Christian Sch., Jacksonville, Fla., 1967—. Republican. Methodist. Avocations: bicycling; walking; music. Home: 155 Clark Rd Jacksonville FL 32218 Office: Almadale Christian Sch 145 Clark Rd Jacksonville FL 32218

BRITT, ANN ROBERTSON, educational administrator; b. Rocky Mount, N.C., May 21, 1948; d. Leon Whitfield and Virginia (Lancaster) Robertson; m. Morris F. Britt, Apr. 24, 1976. Certificat d'etudes, U. Poitiers, La Rochelle, France, 1966; student Meredith Coll., Raleigh, N.C., 1966-68; B.A. in French, U. N.C., 1970; M.Ed. in French, U. N.C.-Greensboro, 1974; 5; Ph.D. in Adminstrn. Higher Edn., Duke U., 1981. Dean women, asst. dean students High Point (N.C.) Coll., 1974-75; grad. asst. for dir. grad. studies, Duke U., Durham, N.C., 1976-78; dir. devel. Meredith Coll., 1978-80; dir. devel. Charlotte (N.C.) Country Day Sch., 1980-82; exec. dir. Community Sch. Arts, Charlotte, 1982—. Mem. Leadership Charlotte, 1985-86. Recipient award Am. Council on Edn., Council for Advancement and Support of Edn., 1981. Mem. Kappa Delta Pi, Pi Delta Phi, Kappa Kappa Gamma. Democrat. Presbyterian. Clubs: Zonta, Women Execs. Home: 5805 Sharon Rd Charlotte NC 28210 Office: Community School of Arts 200 West Trade St Charlotte NC 28202

BRITT, GEORGETTA LEE CULTON, corporate executive; b. Junction City, Ky., Feb. 21, 1932; d. James Thomas and Anabel (Nevius) Culton; m. William Edward Britt, Dec. 25, 1955; children—James Edward, Susan Lee, Laura Anne. Degree in Acctg., Spencerian Comml. Coll., Louisville, 1952. Acct. George C. Baird & Co., C.P.A., Augusta, Ga., 1963-65, E.H. Bridger, C.P.A., Raleigh, N.C., 1970-72; acct., asst. sec. Saleeby, Inc., Raleigh, 1972-74; corp. sec.-treas. Saieed Constrn. Co., Inc., Raleigh, 1974-77; sec.-treas., office mgr. Associated Fire Protection, Inc., Raleigh, 1977—. Co-chairperson Precinct for Republican Party, Raleigh, 1970-73. Mem. Nat. Assn. Accts., Nat. Assn. Women in Constrn. (bd. dirs. Raleigh chpt. 1976-77, 84-85, treas. 1977-78). Presbyterian. Avocations; swimming, dance, bicycling, bridge. Home: 425 Millbrook Rd Raleigh NC 27609 Office: Associated Fire Protection Inc PO Box 28022 Raleigh NC 27611

BRITT, RUTH EVANGELINE BURGIN, civic worker; b. Fayette, Mo., Mar. 15, 1907; d. Samuel Herschel and Lora (Miller) Burgin; student Wesleyan Woman's Coll., 1926-27; A.B., Tallahassee Woman's Coll., 1928; m. James T. Britt, Sept. 18, 1930; children—Thomas Burgin, Robert McCammon. Bd. dirs. Spofford Home for Children, 1937-38, Della Lamb Neighborhood House, 1937-38, YMCA, 1938-39; mem. Woman's City Club, Kansas City, Mo., 1931-72, chmn. hosp. com., 1931-35; mem. Guild Friends Art at William Rockhill Nelson Gallery, 1961-71; mem. fireside com. Kansas City Art Inst., 1948-49; mem. women's div. Kansas City Philharmonic Assn., 1966—, Kansas City Mus. Assn., 1966—; bd. mgrs. George H. Nettleton Home for Aged Women, 1968-73. Chmn. Christian-social relations Women's Soc. Christian Service, 1946-48, pres., 1937-38, chmn. missions, 1961-63; chmn. St. Francis Aux. of St. Francis Home for Boys, Salina and Ellsworth, Kan., 1946-48, supplies com. Community Chest Dr., 1951; vol. visitor for aged Mattie Rhodes Settlement House, 1948; Hosp. Gray Lady, 1948-50. Pres., Young Women's Democratic Club, 1931-33. Mem. UDC, D.A.R. (regent 1942-43). Methodist (mem. adminstrv. bd.). Address: 409 W 58th Terr Kansas City MO 64113

BRITTAIN, LAURA READING, dancer, educator; b. Longmont, Colo., July 25, 1945; d. David R. and Jeanne (McKibbin) Reading; A.A. in Theatre, Bakersfield Jr. Coll., 1965; B.A. in Theatre Arts, UCLA, 1968, M.A. in Dance, 1971; m. Darryl A. Brittain, June 28, 1969 (div.). Dancer, Gus Solomon's Dance Co., N.Y.C., 1971-73; asso. prof. dance and dance edn., artist-in-residence N.Y.U., 1973—, dir. N.Y. U. Washington Sq. Repertory Dance Co.; performer Michelle Berne Dance Co., Marjorie Gamso & Dancers, Linda Diamond Dance Co.; choreographer; regional co-dir. Am. Coll. Dance Festival, N.Y.C., 1978; guest lectr. Jerusalem Rubin Acad. Music and Dance, 1982. mem. Am. Dance Guild, N.Y. State Dance Assn., Dance Theatre Workshop. Democrat. Office: NYU 35 W 4th St New York NY 10003

BRITTON, DOROTHEA SPRAGUE, hospital public relations administrator; b. Cleve., Oct. 30, 1922; d. Paul Epworth and Ruth Emily (Horrocks) Sprague; A.B., U. Mich., 1948, M.A., 1949; postgrad. Columbia U., 1975; m. Alan B. Britton, Sept. 27, 1952; children—Dana Sprague Chabina, Deborah Beckwith Tracy Tuttle. Personnel mgr. George Worthington Co., Cleve., 1951-52; pres. Tacydot Products, Scarsdale, N.Y., 1964-70; adminstr. program devel. Nellie J. Crocker Health Center, Ossining, N.Y., 1971-72; adminstrv. dir. vol. services Roosevelt Hosp., N.Y.C., 1973-77; dir. community and public relations Peoples Bank for Savs., New Rochelle, N.Y., 1977-80; dir. public relations St. John's Riverside Hosp., Yonkers, N.Y., 1980—; lectr. women and mgmt., handicrafts, community banking. Mem. Am. Assn. Vol. Services Coordinators (cert.), N.Y. Assn. Dirs. Vols., Am. Soc. Hosp. Public Relations, Am. Soc. Dirs. Vol. Services, Am. Hosp. Assn., Savs. Bank Women N.Y., Pi Beta Phi. Clubs: Scarsdale Golf, Scarsdale Woman's. Author: An Op-Art Easter Bazaar, 1959; Dot Britton's 1969 Bazaar Book; Dot Britton's 1970 Christmas Bazaar Book; The Complete Book of Bazaars, 1973; The New Volunteer, 1976; The Legends of Christmas, 1978; 30 Years of Christmas Nonsense, 1981; Christmas in the Hudson River Valley, 1984. Home: 4 Rock Hill Ln Scarsdale NY 10583

BRITZ, DIANE EDWARD, investment company executive, chemical trader; b. York, Pa., June 15, 1952; d. Everett Frank and Billie Jacqueline (Sherrill) B.; m. Marcello Lotti, Sept. 9, 1978; children—Ariane Elizabeth, Samantha Alexis. B.A., Duke U., 1974; M.B.A., Columbia U., 1982. Asst. mgr. Columbia Artists, N.Y.C., 1974-76; gen. mgr. Eastern Music Festival, Greensboro, N.C., 1977-78; v.p. Britz Cobin, N.Y.C., 1979-82; pres. Pan Oceanic Mgmt., N.Y.C., 1983, bd. dirs., 1983—. Active Bedford Republican Party (N.Y.). Mem. Fin. Women's Assn., Columbia Bus. Sch. Club N.Y. Quaker. Clubs: Highland Field and Stream (Eldred, N.Y.); Doubles, Wings (N.Y.C.). Office: Pan Oceanic Mgmt Ltd Suite 205 122 E 42d St New York NY 10168

BROADBENT, AMALIA SAYO CASTILLO, advertising executive, graphic arts designer; b. Manila, May 28, 1956; came to U.S., 1980; d. Conrado Camilo and Eugenia de Guzman (Sayo) Castillo; m. Barrie Noel Broadbent, Mar. 14, 1981; children—Charles Noel Castillo, Chandra Noel Castillo. B.F.A., U. Santo Tomas, 1978; postgrad. Acad. Art Coll., San Francisco, Alliance Francaise, Manila, Kailangan Finishing Sch., Manila, Manila Computer Ctr.; B.A., Maryknoll Coll., 1972. Designer market research Unicorp Export

Inc., Makati, Manila, 1975-77; asst. advt. mgr. Dale Trading Corp., Makati, 1977-78; artist, designer, pub. relations Resort Hotels Corp., Makati, 1978-81; prodn. artist CYB/Young & Rubicam, San Francisco, 1981-82; art dir. Ogilvy & Mather Direct, San Francisco, artist, designer, owner A.C. Broadbent Graphics, San Francisco, 1982—. Works include: Daing na Isda, 1975, (Christmas coloring) Pepsi-Cola, 1964 (Distinctive Merit cert.), (children's books) UNESCO, 1973 (cert.). Pres. Pax Romana, Coll. of Architecture and Fine Arts, U. Santo Tomas, 1976-78, chmn. cultural sect., 1975; v.p. Atelier Cultural Soc., U. Santo Tomas, 1975-76; mem. Makati Dance Troupe, 1973-74. Recipient Quezon award U. Santo Tomas Coll. Architecture and Fine Arts, 1978, Inst. of Religion cert. Merit, 1977, cert. Distinctive Merit Pepsi-Cola Bottling Co., 1964. Mem. Alliance Francaise de San Francisco, Nat. Assn. Female Execs. Roman Catholic. Office: A C Broadbent Graphics 805 Leavenworth Suite 506 San Francisco CA 94109

BROADLEY, MARGARET ERICSON, writer; b. Hawarden, Iowa, May 8, 1904; d. Eric John and Josefina Amalia (Bostrom) Ericson; m. Charles V. Broadley, July 27, 1931 (dec. Apr. 1961); children—Barbara Beinhocker, Deborah Gale. B.S., Iowa State U., 1927. Publicist, speaker Nat. Dairy Council, Chgo., Phila. and New Haven, 1927-29; writer Sta. WGN, Lord & Thomas Advt., Chgo., 1929-30; writer, publicist Chgo. Milk Council, 1930-31, Dairymen's League, N.Y.C., 1931-35; asst. publicity dir. White House Conf. Edn., Washington, 1954-55; publs. writer USIA, Washington, 1955-63; writer Manpower Adminstrn., Labor Dept., Washington, 1963-69; freelance author, Washington, 1969—; dir. EPM Publs., McLean, Va. Author: Square Pegs in Square Holes, 1943; (with Charles Broadley) Know Your Real Abilities, 1948; Be Yourself, 1972; Your Natural Gifts, 1977, 4d edit., 1974; contbr. articles to popular mags. Trustee Haman Engring. Lab.-Johnson O'Connor Research Found., 1946—; bd. dirs. Hurt Home for Blind, Washington, 1977—. Mem. English Speaking Union, Women in Communications, Delta Delta Delta. Republican. Episcopalian. Club: International (Washington).

BROADWAY, ANGELA SHARON, lawyer; b. Charleston, S.C., Sept. 22, 1957; d. Reid Archie and Althea (Sineath) Broadway. B.S., Med. U. S.C., 1980; J.D., U. S.C., 1983. Bar: S.C. 1983. Law clk. Law Office Donald Rothwell, Columbia, part-time, 1981-82; assoc. Law Office Wheeler M. Tillman, Charleston, S.C., 1983—. Mem. ABA, Assn. Trial Lawyers Am., S.C. Bar Assn., Charleston County Bar Assn., S.C. Trial Lawyer's Assn., Pilot Club, S.C. Hist. Soc., Phi Delta Phi. Home: 1082 Meader Ln PO Box 935 Mount Pleasant SC 29464 Office: Suite 202 Post-Courier Bldg 6296 Rivers Ave North Charleston SC 29418

BROADWAY, NANCY RUTH, landscape design and construction company executive; b. Memphis, Tenn., Dec. 20, 1946; d. Charlie Sidney and Patsy Ruth (Meadows) Adkins. B.S. in Biology and Sociology cum laude, Memphis State U., 1969; postgrad. Tulane U., 1969-70; M.S. in Horticulture, U. Calif.-Davis, 1976. Lic. landscape contractor, Calif. Claims adjuster Mass. Mut. Ins., San Francisco, 1972-73; community garden coordinator City of Davis, Calif., 1976; supr. seed propagation Bordier's Wholesale Nursery, Santa Ana, Calif., 1976-78; owner, contractor Calif. Landscape Co., Stockton, Calif., 1978—. NDEA fellow Tulane U., 1969-70. Mem. Am. Hort. Soc., Net. Assn. Gen. Contractors, Calif. Native Plant Soc., Stockton C. of C. Democrat. Office: California Landscape Co PO Box 4724 Stockton CA 95204

BROADWELL, MARIE ELLEN ELANDER, nursing educator; b. Afton, N.Y., June 13, 1944; d. Kenneth Lawrence and Bernice Marie (Howe) Elander. A.A.S. summa cum laude, Broome Community Coll., 1974; B.S.N., SUNY-Binghamton, 1976; M.S.N., Villanova U., 1984. Staff nurse Wilson Meml. Hosp., Johnson City, N.Y., 1974-76; nursing instr. Presentation Coll., Aberdeen, S.D., 1976-77; patient edn. coordinator Carlisle Hosp. (Pa.), 1977-80; nursing instr. St. Joseph Hosp., Lancaster, Pa., 1981-85; mem. nursing faculty SUNY-Binghamton, 1985—. Mem. Am. Heart Assn., Lancaster, 1983. Mem. Am. Nurses Assn., N.Y. Nurses Assn., Am. Diabetes Assn., Phi Theta Kappa, Sigma Theta Tau. Republican. Methodist. Office: SUNY-Binghamton Science III Room 269 Binghamton NY 13901

BROCHIN, LEONA NELKIN, real estate management executive; b. Boston, Apr. 28, 1932; d. Samuel and Mary (Birnbach) Nelkin; m. Murry David Brochin, Sept. 20, 1959; children—James Lewis, Nathaniel Edward, Esther Elizabeth. B.A., Mt. Holyoke Coll., 1953; M.A., Columbia U., 1955, M. Philosophy, 1978. Pres. Ruxton Mgmt. Corp., Millburn, N.J., 1979—. Nat. chmn. steering com. for establishment of chair of Jewish studies Mt. Holyoke Coll., South Hadley, Mass., 1983—; bd. dirs. women's div. Jewish Community Fedn. of MetroWest, East Orange, N.J., 1984-85; v.p. B/Nai Keshet, Montclair, N.J., 1984-85; bd. dirs. Jewish Vocat. Services, East Orange, co-chairperson scholarship com.; bd. dirs. Jespy House, South Orange, Mem. Internat. Council of Shopping Ctrs., Exec. Women of N.J., Bus. and Profl. Women (steering com). Democrat. Avocations: art collecting; reading; singing; walking; raising labrador retrievers. Office: Ruxton Mgmt Corp 225 Millburn Ave Millburn NJ 07041

BROCK, BARBARA HANAUER, accounting educator; b. Milw., Oct. 3, 1933; d. Erwin R. and Alice M. (Lehmann) Hanauer; m. F.W. Lander, June 9, 1955 (div. 1968); 1 child, Martha J. Lander Schwegler; m. Douglas H. Brock, Mar. 21, 1970. B.S., SUNY-Buffalo, 1971, M.B.A., 1973, Ph.D., 1979. Cert. internal auditor, mgmt. acct. Assoc. prof. acctg. Canisius Coll., Buffalo, 1974—. Author: The Development of Public Utility Accounting in New York State, 1981. Mem. mgmt. assistance com. United Way, Buffalo, 1982—. Mem. Nat. Assn. Parliamentarians, Am. Inst. Parliamentarians, Inst. Internal Auditors (gov. Western N.Y. chpt. 1983-85), Am. Soc. Women Accts. (nat. pres. 1985-86), Beta Gamma Sigma (pres. Canisius Coll. chpt.). Republican. Home: 135 Meadow Rd Buffalo NY 14216 Office: Canisius Coll 2001 Main St Buffalo NY 14208

BROCK, CYNTHIA JEAN, energy company executive; b. Tiffin, Ohio, Aug. 10, 1954; d. Donald Vincent B. and Ruth Ann (Westrup) Kapp; m. Richard James Kunkle, Aug. 3, 1975 (div. Feb. 1979). B.A. in Polit. Sci. magna cum laude, Cleve. State U., 1978; student law, John Marshall Sch. Law, Cleve., 1978-81; M.B.A., Baldwin-Wallace Coll., Berea, Ohio, 1985; postgrad. Northwestern U., 1984—. Collector, Firestone Tire & Rubber Co., Brookpark, Ohio, 1975-79; credit mgr. Ketchum Distbrs., Wickliffe, Ohio, 1979-81; corp. adminstrv. mgr. CBI Industries, Chgo., 1981—. Mem. NOW, Nat. Assn. Female Execs., Nat. Assn. Credit Mgrs. Democrat. Home: 1260 N Dearborn Apt 907 Chicago IL 60610 Office: CBI Liquid Carbonic Corp 135 S LaSalle St Chicago IL 60603

BROCK, KATHLEEN KENNELLY, advertising agency executive; b. Casper, Wyo., Aug. 19, 1939; d. Frank Thomas and Margaret (Bigelow) Kennelly; m. Jonathan Brock, Apr. 5, 1969. Student U. Colo.-Boulder, 1957-59. Vice pres. Prescott Co., Inc., Denver, 1966-78; pres. Brock & Assocs., Inc., Denver, 1978—. Pres. Denver Dumb Friends League, 1983, dir., 1984—; bd. dirs. Inst. for Entrepreneurship, Met. State Coll. Mem. Denver Advt. Fedn. (dir. 1984—). Republican. Club: Denver Country. Avocations: golf; tennis; fly fishing; gardening. Office: Brock & Assocs Inc 3773 Cherry Creek N Dr Suite 615 Denver CO 80209

BROCK, LILLIE RUTH, citizens advocate, safety consultant; b. Atmore, Ala., Aug. 8, 1956; d. James T. and Linda L. (Whetstone) B. B.A., Carson-Newman Coll., 1978. Cert. sr. safety. Ednl. therapist Valley Psychiat. Hosp., Chattanooga, 1978-81, Ridgeview Inst., Atlanta, 1981-84; owner, regional dir. Citizens Against Crime, Orlando, Fla., 1984—; asst. coach women's basketball Rollins Coll., Winter Park, Fla., 1984—, cons. Alcohol and Drug Task Force, 1984—. Mem. Nat. Assn. Profl. Saleswoman, Nat. Assn. Female Execs., Women's Basketball Coaches Assn. Democrat. Avocations: drawing; running; singing. Home: 711 Briercliff St Orlando FL 32806 Office: Citizens Against Crime 1177 Louisiana Ave Suite 210 Winter Park FL 32789

BROCK, RETHA GAIL, home health agency administrator; b. Pineville, Ky., Sept. 14, 1947; d. Charles Edward and Virginia Rebecca (Smith) Hall; m. Johnny Patterson, Nov. 2, 1968 (div. 1981); children—John Scott, Stephanie Amanda; m. Foster Mullins Brock, Jan. 29, 1982. R.N., East Tenn. Bapt. Sch. Nursing, 1968. Staff nurse Pineville Hosp., Ky., 1968-69; project nurse maternity, infant care Ky. State Health Dept., 1969-71; dir. Pineville Hosp. Home Health Agy., 1971—; mem. adv. com. Middlesboro Home Health Ctr., Ky., 1982-84; mem. com. Am. Cancer Soc., 1982—, Council on Aging, Middlesboro. Mem. Nat. Assn. for Home Care, Ky. Home Health Assn. Republican. Baptist. Avocations: running; snorkeling. Home: Route 2 Box 84G Harrogate TN 37752 Office: Pineville Hosp Home Health Agy Pineville Hosp Pineville KY 40977

BROCK, THERESA JEAN, educator; b. Ft. Worth, Aug. 30, 1929; d. Theodore Roosevelt and Naomi (Jones) Roberson; B.A., San Francisco State Coll., 1951; M.A., Mills Coll., Oakland, Calif., 1981; m. Buddy LeRoy Brock, Apr. 6, 1952; children—Angela Lynn, Richard LeRoy. Classroom tchr. Oakland Public Schs., 1969—, tchr. Crocker Highlands Elem. Sch., 1974—; master tchr. San Francisco State U. and Mills Coll., 1970—; presenter tchr. workshops; cons. Piaget Conf., Stanford U., 1977; tchr. cons. Bay Area Writing Project, U. Calif.-Berkeley; facilitator Project Learning Tree, 1981-82; writer social sci. curriculum Calif. Dept. Edn., 1981; mem. policy bd. Alameda/Contra Costa County Tchr. Edn. and Computer Center. Active Crocker Highlands Parent-Tchr.-Student Assn. Teaching activities filmed by Fuji Telecasting Co., Ltd., Tokyo, 1978; recipient Service award Calif. Congress Parents and Tchrs., 1978; Oakland Tchr. of Yr. award, 1981; Alameda County Tchr. of Yr. award, 1981. Mem. Assn. Childhood Edn. Internat., Calif. Council Social Studies, East Bay Council Social Studies, Nat. Council Tchrs. of English, Assn. Supervision and Curriculum Devel., Nat. Council Tchrs. of Math., Calif. Math. Council, Alameda-Contra Costa Counties Math. Educators, NEA, Calif. Tchrs. Assn., Oakland Edn. Assn., NAACP, Nat. Council Negro Women, LWV (adminstrv. v.p. Oakland 1967-69), Delta Sigma Theta, Phi Delta Upsilon. Methodist. Home: 38 Drake Ln Oakland CA 94611 Office: 525 Midcrest Rd Oakland CA 94610

BROCKWAY, LAURIE SUE, journalist; b. N.Y.C., Dec. 18, 1956; d. Lee L. and Shirley Ruth B. A.A., Laguardia Community Coll., 1978; student Hunter Coll., 1978-81. Features editor The Bklyn. Paper, 1978-81; editor-in-chief The Iniator, N.Y.C., 1982-83; pub., editor The Transformer, N.Y.C., 1983-84; co-producer, writer The Brockway Good News Report, N.Y.C., 1984-85; N.Y. bur. chief Women's News, N.Y.C., 1982-85; account supr., chief writer Brockway Assocs., Inc., N.Y.C., 1985; co-producer, writer, host, news anchor/writer, moderator This Is the New Age, The One Show, Whole Life Expo. Contbr. articles to mags., newspapers. Recipient LaGuardia Meml. award, 1978; Laguardia Student Council scholar, 1978; Expository Writing award, LaGuardia English Dept., 1978. Mem. Transformedia (founding), Nat. Assn. Female Execs.

BRODER, PATRICIA JANIS, art historian; b. N.Y.C., Nov. 22, 1935; d. Milton W. and Rheba (Mantell) Janis; student Smith Coll., 1953-54; B.A., Barnard Coll., 1957; postgrad. Rutgers U., 1962-64; m. Stanley H. Broder, Jan. 22, 1959; children—Clifford James, Peter Howard, Helen Anna. Stock brokerage trainee A.M. Kidder & Co., N.Y.C., 1958; registered rep. Thomson & McKinnon Co., N.Y.C., 1959-61; ind. registered investment adviser, 1962-64; research, writing on art history Bronzes of American West, 1964-74, book pub., 1974 (Herbert Adams Meml. medal Nat. Sculpture Soc. 1975, Gold medal Nat. Acad. Western Art 1975); lectr., author on art of Am. West, 1970—. Recipient Wrangler award for best article Western Heritage, 1976, best art book award, 1981; Border Regional Library Assn. award, 1981; Trustees Gold Medal Cowboy Hall of Fame; Trustees Gold medal Nat. Acad. Western Art, 1984. Mem. Western History Assn., AAUW. Author: Bronzes of the American West; The World of the Hopis; Hopi Painting Today; Dean Cornwell, Dean of Illustrators; Great Paintings of the Old American West; Taos: A Painter's Dream; American Indian Painting and Sculpture; The American West: The Modern Vision, 1984. Address: 488 Long Hill Dr Short Hills NJ 07078

BRODERICK, LAURA ANNE, communications executive; b. Phoenix, Feb. 25, 1953; d. George Donald and Barbara Ann (Huls) B. B.A., Ohio Wesleyan U., 1975. Communications dir. to Congressman Dick Schulze, U.S. Ho. of Reps., Washington, 1976-78; press sec. to Congressman Phil Crane, U.S. Ho. of Reps., 1978-81; dir. multimedia outreach dept., editor Source, Republican Nat. Com., Washington, 1981-82; dir. pub. affairs/mgmt. Office of Mgmt. and Budget, Exec. Office of Pres., The White House, Washington, 1982—. Mem. Task Force on Corp. Volunteerism, Jr. League, Washington, 1984. Republican. Roman Catholic. Home: 6513 Potomac Ave Alexandria VA 22307

BRODEUR, MARIANNE, valve and instrument company executive; b. Springfield, Mass., May 1, 1951; d. Victor Louis and Miriam Alice (Malcolm) Bissonnette; m. Frederic Alcide Brodeur, III, Sept. 1, 1973; children—Frederic A. IV, Jaime Lynn, JoniBeth, Ashley Marie. Student Western New Eng. Coll., Springfield, 1980—. Salesperson, with customer relations dept. Atlantic Valve Corp., Westfield, Mass., 1976-82, sales mgr., 1979-82; founder, pres. Internat. Valve & Instrument, Springfield, Mass., 1982—, IVI Rebuilders, Inc., Springfield, 1983—. Mem. Nat. Assn. Power Engrs., Instrument Soc. Am. Republican. Roman Catholic. Avocations: sailing; tennis; aerobics. Home: 75 Joanne Circle Feeding Hills MA 01030 Office: Internat Valve & Instrument Corp 1 Allen St Bldg 212 Springfield MA 01108

BRODMAN, BARBARA ANTOINETTE, designer; b. Rochester, N.Y., Dec. 8, 1949; d. Adam John and Antoinette Macie (Adams) Brodman; m. John Robert Fassanella, May 29, 1969 (div. 1976); 1 son, Adam. B.A. in Art and Humanities, Nazareth Coll., Rochester, 1971; postgrad. U. Rochester, 1979-81. Buyer, Macy's Dept. Store, N.Y.C., 1977-79, art dir. N.Y. State Dept. Agr., Albany, N.Y., 1978-80; cons. to small businesses upstate N.Y., 1979-81; asst. to v.p. Wilmorite Inc., Rochester, 1981-83; pres. Barbara A. Brodman Designs, Rochester, 1984—; tchr. Cloversville Central Sch. (N.Y.), 1971-75; pres. The Bakery, Albany, N.Y., 1975-76. Exhibited prints, sculpture, paintings throughout U.S., also in Paris. Mem. fin. com. Monroe County Dem. Party, Rochester, Lodge: Zonta Internat. Home and Office: 45 Vassar St Rochester NY 14607

BRODMAN, ESTELLE, librarian, educator; b. N.Y.C., June 1, 1914; d. Henry and Nettie (Sameth) B.; A.B., Cornell U., 1935; B.S., Columbia U., 1936, M.S., 1943, Ph.D., 1954; D.Sc. (hon.), U. Ill., 1974; postdoctoral UCLA, 1959, U. N.Mex., 1960. Asst. librarian Cornell U. Sch. Nursing Library, N.Y.C., 1936-37; asst. to acting med. librarian Columbia U. Libraries, N.Y.C., 1937-49; asst. librarian for reference services Nat. Library Medicine, Washington, 1949-61; librarian, asso. prof. med. history Washington U. Sch. Medicine, St. Louis, 1961-64, librarian, prof. med. history, 1964-81; instr. Columbia U., 1946-52, 84, Cath. U. Am., 1957; vis. prof. Keio U., Tokyo, 1962, U. Mo., 1971, 73; cons. Am. Hosp. Assn., NIH, AID, others. Documentation expert UN Tech. Assistance Program, New Delhi, 1967-68; expert tech. assistance program S.E. regional office WHO, New Delhi, 1970, Western Pacific regional office, 1983, UN Econ. Agy. for Asia and Far East, Bangkok, 1973, UN Fund for Population Affairs, 1976-77; chmn. biomed. study sect. NIH, 1976-80. Mem. Pres.'s Commn. Libraries, 1966-68. Fellow Med. Library Assn. (spl. award 1957, Noyes award 1971; pres. 1964-65, Frank Bradway Rogers info. advancement award 1985); mem. ALA, MLA, Spl. Libraries Assn. (dir. 1949-52, John Cotton Dana award 1981), Bibliog. Soc. Am., Am. Assn. History of Medicine (council 1967-68). Author: Development of Medical Bibliography, 1954; Bibliographical Lists for Medical Libraries, 1950; editor Bull. Med. Library Assn., 1947-57. Home: 19-09 Meadow Lakes Hightstown NJ 08520

BRODRICK, LOIS HUNTER, real estate broker, securities account executive; b. Altoona, Pa., Aug. 31, 1920; d. Frank Mathew and Faye (McKague) Hunter; m. Richard Boyd Brodrick, Apr. 20, 1946 (dec.); children—Victoria, Barrie Bea. B.A., Pa. State U.-State College, 1942; postgrad. U. Calif.-Berkeley, extensions, 1978. Lic. real estate broker. Prin., Brodrick Real Estate and Devel., Shingle Springs, Calif., 1980-82; Brodrick Real Estate Co., Shingle Springs, 1982-84; rep. Fin. Network Security Corp., Sacramento, 1983—. Prss. Calif. Rep. Assembly, Lamorinda unit, Orinda, Calif., 1978; v.p. Orinda Rep. Women, 1977; bd. dirs. Hacienda Del Orinda Homeowners, 1978-79. Mem. Internat. Fin. Planners, Nat. Assn. Security Dealers (registered rep.), Kappa Kappa Gamma (past pres. Bay Area). Club: Cameron Park Country (Calif.). Home: 3490 Fairway Dr Shingle Springs CA 95682

BRODT, MARJORIE LOIS BENTON, state educational official; b. Bethlehem, Pa., June 16, 1925; d. Walter M. and Emma Bell (Beckeler) Benton; m. Robert E. Brodt, Nov. 3, 1950; children—Carl Lester, Carolyn Jeannie. B.S. in Commerce, Drexel U., 1946; M.A. in Elem. Edn., U. Calif.-Sacramento, 1960; Ph.D., U. N.C.-Chapel Hill, 1978. Cons. in higher edn. Commn. for Tchr. Preparation and Licensing, Sacramento, 1971-81; dir. Title III project Charlotte-Mecklenberg Sch. Dist., N.C., 1966-68; ednl. planning specialist Pace Ctr., Sacramento, 1968-69; supr. correctional edn., research and evaluation supr. Calif. Youth Authority, Sacramento, 1981—; prof. U. Calif.-Davis, 1961-62, Calif. State U.-Sacramento, 1970-71; cons. various Calif. sch. dists. Mem. AAUW, Am. Assn. for Curriculum and Devel. (v.p. No. Calif. sect. 1961). Republican. Home: PO Box 1107 Roseville CA 95678 Office: Calif Youth Authority 4241 Williamsbourgh Dr Sacramento CA 95823

BRODY, ANITA B(LUMSTEIN), judge; b. N.Y.C., May 25, 1935; d. David Theodore and Rita (Sondheim) Blumstein; m. Jerome I. Brody, Oct. 25, 1959; children—Lisa, Marion, Timothy. A.B., Wellesley Coll., 1955; J.D., Columbia U., 1958. Bar: N.Y., Pa. Asst. atty. gen. State of N.Y., N.Y.C., 1958-60; sole practice, Ardmore, Pa., 1972-79; ptnr. Brody, Brown & Hepburn, Ardmore, 1979-81; judge Ct. Common Pleas Commonwealth of Pa., Norristown, 1981—; lectr. Law Sch. U. Pa., Phila., 1978-79. Mem. ABA, Pa. Bar Assn., Montgomery Bar Assn. (dir. 1979-81), Pa. State Trial Judges Assn. Republican. Jewish. Office: Court House Swede and Airy Sts Norristown PA 19404*

BRODY, NANCY LOUISE, lawyer; b. Chgo., Nov. 17, 1954; d. Mitchell and Grace Yaden (Williams) Block; m. Daniel Matthew Brody, Oct. 28, 1979. B.A., U. Mich., 1975; J.D., Loyola U., Chgo., 1979. Bar: Ill. 1979, Pa. 1980, Ariz. 1981. Sole practice, Indiana, Pa., 1980—. Named one of Outstanding Young Women Am., 1983. Fellow Pa. Bar Found (dir. 1984—); mem. Ill. State Bar Assn., ABA, Pa. Bar Assn. (bd. govs. 1984—, chairperson Young Lawyers Div. 1985-86, treas. Young Lawyers Div. 1983-84), Zonta (parliamentarian Indiana chpt. 1985-86), Pi Beta Phi. Republican. Office: 39 N 7th St Indiana PA 15701

BRODY, NAOMI, advertising agency official; b. Quebec, Que., Can., Aug. 5, 1934; came to U.S., 1954, naturalized, 1959; d. David and Eva (Zaltsman) Barenholtz; m. Melvin Brody, June 23, 1954; children—Deborah Brody, Sharon Zughaft, Michelle Skolnick. B.A. summa cum laude, Queens Coll., 1979. Reference asst. Jaffe's Books, Calgary, Alta., Can., 1952-54; asst. to office mgr. Behrman House, Inc., N.Y.C., 1954-57; project dir. Decisions Ctr., Inc., N.Y.C., 1979-81; sr. project dir. D'Arcy Masius Benton & Bowles, Inc., N.Y.C., 1981-82, account research supr., 1982—; guest lectr. Queens (N.Y.) Coll., 1979—. Pres. women's league Young Israel of Laurelton (N.Y.), 1973-74. Mem. Am. Mktg. Assn., Mensa, Phi Beta Kappa, Psi Chi. Democrat. Jewish. Contbr. articles to profl. jours. Office: D'Arcy Masius Benton & Bowles Inc 909 3d Ave New York NY 10022

BROER, EILEEN DENNERY, insurance holding company personnel executive; b. Phila., Sept. 7, 1946; d. Vincent Paul and Jane Dorothy (Knight) Dennery; m. Paul Alan Broer, Nov. 26, 1970 (div. 1980); m. Charles Kenneth ReCorr, Sept. 10, 1981; 1 child, Matthew Vincent. B.A., Coll. Mt. St. Vincent, 1969. Media dir., control mgr. Merrill Anderson Co., N.Y.C., 1970-72; adminstrv. asst. fin. McCall Pattern Co., N.Y.C., 1972-74, personnel specialist, 1974-77, mgr. employee relations, 1978; dir. personnel Notions Mktg. Inc., N.Y.C., 1978-79; 2d v.p. personnel Manhattan Life Ins. Co., N.Y.C., 1979, v.p. human resources, 1980-82; v.p. human resources McM Corp., Raleigh, N.C., 1982-85; pres. The Human Factor, 1985—; lectr. bus. writing NYU, 1975-78. Mem. Human Resource Planning Soc., Orgn. Devel. Network, Am. Soc. Personnel Adminstrs., Raleigh-Wake Personnel Assn., Am. Compensation Assn. Office: The Human Factor 102 Wimbledon Ct Cary NC 27511

BROHARD, ELLEN BRADY, business educator; b. Ashland, Va., Aug. 11, 1942; d. Patrick L. and Effie B. Brady; B.S. in Bus. Edn., Longwood Coll., 1963; M.S. in Vocat. Tech. Edn., Va. Poly. Inst./State U., 1975; m. Thomas L. Brohard, Feb. 10, 1967; children—Bill, Mark. Bus. edn. tchr. Fairfax County Schs., George Marshall High Sch., Falls Church, Va., 1963-68; bus. edn. tchr., coordinator Fairfax County Adult Edn., Falls Church, 1969-74; program head office systems technology, asst. prof. No. Va. Community Coll., Loudoun Campus, 1974—, coordinator coop. edn. and coordinated internship, 1981-84; reviewer Choice, ALA, 1982, Reston Pub. Co., Prentice Hall Pub. Co., 1984—. Asst. soccer coach; mem. PTA, 1978—; sec. Cub Scouts, 1978-79; mem. fund raising com. Soccer League, 1979, Pee Wee League, 1979. Mem. Nat. Bus. Edn. Assn., So. Bus. Edn. Assn., Va. Bus. Edn. Assn., Va. Community Coll. Assn., Internat. Platform Assn., Bus. and Profl. Women's Club, Longwood Coll. Alumni Assn. (co-chmn.). Methodist. Home: Route 2 Box 218F Leesburg VA 22075 Office: 1000 H F Byrd Hwy Sterling VA 22170

BROKAW, DOROTHY GENE, brokerage company executive; b. Pontiac, Mich., Mar. 4, 1934; d. William Edward and Ruth Elanore (Williams) Giroux; m. William Arthur Brokaw, Jr., May 30, 1952; children—Gary Arthur, Kenneth Edward, Katherine Ruth, Lori Anne. Clerk-sec. Raymond James & Assocs., St. Petersburg, Fla., 1969-71, payroll clerk, 1971-80, purchasing mgr., 1980—; v.p. West Coast Purchasing Mgrs. Assn., Tampa-St. Petersburg, 1983-84. Republican. Roman Catholic. Home: 6219 14th Ave S Saint Petersburg FL 33707 Office: Raymond James & Assocs 1400 66th St N Saint Petersburg FL 33710

BROKENBOUGH, WILLA MAE, caterer; b. Clio, S.C., Dec. 5, 1921; d. Joseph and Rebecca (Ales) Burch; student Va. State U., 1940-41; m. John Robert Brokenbough, Feb. 4, 1942; children—Jack, Russell Allen, Diane Elaine Brown. Caterer, Elk's Lodge, Vineland, N.J., 1939-40; cafeteria mgr. Gen. Floor Co., Los Angeles, 1960-63, Schick Safety Razar Co., Culver City, Calif., 1963-66; owner, pres. Willa Brokenbough Parties, Los Angeles, 1963—. Recipient award SBA, 1978, 79, 81; Hennessy trophy USAF. Mem. Nat. Restaurant Assn., Calif. Restaurant Assn., Internat. Food Service Execs. Assn. Lutheran. Clubs: Eastern Star, Heroines of Jericho. Office: 4853 Crenshaw Blvd Los Angeles CA 90043

BROMERT, JEAN MARIE, agribusiness company executive; b. Carroll, Iowa, Dec. 23, 1953; d. Leonard Francis and Eulalia Frances (Schaefer) Bromert. B.S., Iowa State U., 1976, M.S. in Horticulture, 1979. Field rep. for Green Giant, Pillsbury Co., Blue Earth, Minn., 1979-81; edn. coordinator Control Data Corp., Bloomington, Minn., 1981-83; v.p. edn. Farm Info. Mgmt. Services div. Pioneer Hi-Bred Internat., Inc., Des Moines, 1983—. Roman Catholic. Home: 6804 Forest Ct Des Moines IA 50311 Office: Farm Info Mgmt Services Div Pioneer Hi-Bred International Inc PO Box 247 Johnston IA 50131

BROMLEY, CATHERINE REED, rancher; b. Bradford, Ark., June 7, 1940; d. Claude Brewer and Lena Lucille (Rains) Reed; student Iowa Wesleyan Coll., 1958-60, Brigham Young U., 1963-65; m. Michael Fredrick Bromley, Apr. 1, 1965; children—Michael, Reed, Jess, Lori, Trisha, John, James. Partner, Bromley Farms, Inc., American Fork, Utah, 1965—, auditor, 1965—, v.p., 1968—. City coordinator March of Dimes Mother's March, 1979-80; mem. Miss American Fork Pageant com., 1977, 84-86; commr. American Fork High Sch. Parent-Tchrs.-Students Assn., 1984-86. Recipient Latter Day Saints Golden Gleaner award, 1970. Mem. Pacific Egg & Poultry Assn., Farm Bur., Utah Egg Council, United Egg Producers, West Coast Egg Producers, Outstanding Farmers of Am. Fraternity, Pi Beta Phi (Iowa chpt.). Republican. Mem. Ch. of Jesus Christ of Latter-Day Saints. Clubs: Young Homemakers, Rotary. Home and Office: PO Box 265 American Fork UT 84003

BROMLEY, MERYL LUELLA MARJORIE, pallet and crate company executive; b. Three Oaks, Mich., Oct. 12, 1924; d. Charles Arthur and Blanch Hulda Marie (Mangold) Myers; m. Fred Russell Bromley, Sept. 26, 1942; children—Gary Thomas, Judith Lorraine, Kathryn Louise, Joyce Lucille. Grad. high school Buchanan, Mich. Sec. Brandt Coin Handling Systems Rep., Dowagiac, Mich., 1962-68, Western Mich. U., Kalamazoo, 1968-69; office worker Richmond Lumber Co., Dowagiac, 1969-70; office mgr. Lux Wood Products, Inc., Dowagiac, 1970-80; pres. B R Pallets & Crates, Inc., Dowagiac, 1980—. Patentee in field. Methodist. Avocations: golf; camping; reading; traveling. Home: 28548 Fairlane Dr Dowagiac MI 49047 Office: B R Pallets & Crates Inc 29160 Middle Crossing Rd Dowagiac MI 49047

BRONNENKANT, ANNA COLLIS, lawyer; b. Syracuse, N.Y., Aug. 13, 1949; d. Nicholas and Helen P. (Panarites) Collis; m. Rex P. Bronnenkant, Sept. 20, 1975; children—Tyler N. and Adam P. (twins), Andrew Rex. B.A., Skidmore Coll., 1971; J.D., Syracuse U., 1975. Bar: Ariz., U.S. Dist. Ct. Ariz. Atty. Community Legal Services, Phoenix, 1975-78; assoc. counsel 1st Fed. Savs. and Loan Assn. Ariz., Phoenix, 1978-85; counsel S.W. Savs. and Loan Assn., Phoenix, 1985—. Admissions corr. Skidmore Coll., Phoenix, 1980—. Mem. ABA, Ariz. Bar Assn., Maricopa County Bar Assn. (corp. counsel sect.), Assn. Women Lawyers (pres. 1983), Exec. Bus. and Profl. Women (com. chmn. 1983-84, v.p. 1984-85), Phi Delta Phi (v.p. 1974-75, J. Mark McCarthy award 1975). Republican. Greek Orthodox. Office: SW Savs and Loan Assn Ariz 3101 N Central Ave 3d Floor Phoenix AZ 85012

BRONOCCO, TERRI LYNN, telecommunications and electronics company executive; b. San Antonio, Jan. 7, 1953; d. Lawrence and Jimmie Doris (Mears) B.; m. Martin L. Lowy, July 5, 1975 (div. Jan. 1979). Student in communications U. Tex.-Austin, 1970-73. Pub. relations mgr. Assocs. Corp., Dallas, 1976-79; editor-in-chief Nat. Tax Shelter Digest, Dallas, 1979; fin. editor Dallas/Ft. Worth Bus., Dallas, 1979-80; pub. affairs dir. Gen. Telephone Co., Lewisville, Tex., 1980-82; pub. info. mgr. GTE Corp., Stamford, Conn., 1982-83, media communications mgr., 1983-84, media relations and communications mgr., 1984-86; v.p. external affairs U.S. Sprint Communications Co., Dallas, 1986—. Fundraiser, pub. relations counsel Am. Shakespeare Theatre, Stratford, Conn., 1984-86; bd. dirs. Music Found. for the Handicapped, Bridgeport, Conn., 1984-86; precinct chmn. Dallas County Democratic Party, 1982; bd. dirs. Far Mill River Assn., Stratford, 1983-86. Recipient spl. recognition award Dallas C. of C., 1978; award for newspaper series Dept. Transp., 1980; Matrix award for pub. relations Women in Communications, 1985. Mem. Internat. Assn. Bus. Communicators (best photograph award 1977), Women in Communications (Matrix award 1984), Women in Mgmt., Am. Mgmt. Assn. Roman Catholic. Home: 5826 Preston Valley Dr Dallas TX 75240 Office: 4160 Alpha Rd Suite 502 Dallas TX 75234

BRONSON, CLAIRE SEKULSKI, finance educator; b. Memphis, Oct. 14, 1947; d. Julian Bernard and Opal Geneva (Scruggs) Sekulski; m. George D. Bronson, May 28, 1968; children—Christopher, Kevin, Meredith. B.A., Conn. Coll. for Women, 1969; M.A., U. Conn., 1971, Ph.D., 1982. Substitute tchr. Enfield pub. schs., Conn., 1979-82; part-time instr. econs. Manchester Community Coll., Conn., 1974-76, Asnuntuck Community Coll., Enfield, 1975-79; asst. prof. econs. Western New Eng. Coll., Springfield, Mass., 1983, vis. asst. prof. fin., 1983-84, asst. prof. fin., 1984—, mem. investment inst. adv. com., 1983-84; book editor for various pubs. Contbr. articles to profl. jours. Mem. Enfield Cultural Arts Commn., 1983—; mem. adv. com. Enfield Bd. Edn., 1981-83; pres. Nathan Hale PTO, Enfield, 1980-81. Mem. Am. Fin. Assn., Am. Econ. Assn., Eastern Fin. Assn. Republican. Roman Catholic. Club: Twin Mothers (Hartford, Conn.). Avocations: collecting antique jewelry, tennis, golf, reading. Home: PO Box 2032 Enfield CT 06082 Office: Western New Eng Coll Wilbraham Rd Springfield MA 01119

BRONSON, PATRICIA ANN, educator; b. Leesville, La., Mar. 15, 1931; d. Glenn Cecil and Allie Lee (Copeland) Packer; student Northwestern State U., 1948-51; B.A., George Peabody Coll., 1960, M.A., 1962; m. John Orville Bronson, Jr., June 11, 1966; children—Richard Wayne McCoy, Victoria Patricia Elizabeth, Glenn Charles Stephen. Tchr., Nashville Met. Schs., 1962-65, Calhoun Tech. Jr. Coll., Decatur, Ala., 1965-67; asst. prof. math. Chesapeake Coll., Wye Mills, Md., 1967—. Mem. Math. Assn. Am., Nat. Council Tchrs. Math., AAUP, Miss., S.C. hist. socs., La. Hist. Assn., Theta Sigma Upsilon, Delta Kappa Gamma. Democrat. Episcopalian. Club: Order Eastern Star. Author: Index of the Census of 1850, Orangeburg and Pickens Districts, S.C., 1974. Home: Hopkins Hall Box 81 Wye Mills MD 21679

BRONTE, D. LYDIA, foundation executive; b. Memphis, Dec. 27, 1938; d. Paul and Dorothy Vivian (Hamilton) B. B.A. with high honors, Hendrix Coll., Conway, Ark., 1960; postgrad. U. d'Aix-Marseille, Aix-en-Provence, France, 1960-61; Ph.D., U. N.C., 1969. Instr. then asst. prof. French, George Washington U., 1965-70, asst. prof. English, 1969-71; spl. asst. to dir. Folger Shakespeare Library, Washington, 1970-71; dir. research and publ. Nat. Humanities Series, Princeton, N.J., 1971-73; cons. in humanities Rockefeller Found., N.Y.C., 1973-74, asst. dir. humanities, 1974-77, assoc. dir., 1977-79, program officer central adminstrn., 1979-80; cons. to program policy com. MacArthur Found., Chgo., 1980-82; cons. Carnegie Corp. N.Y., 1982—, cons., staff dir. The Aging Soc. project, 1983—. Editor: (with Alan Pifer) Our Aging Society: Paradox and Promise, 1986. Contbr. in field. Recipient cert. of appreciation Am. Inst. Character Edn., 1980; Nat. Merit scholar, 1956-60; Fulbright fellow, 1960-61, Woodrow Wilson fellow, 1961-62, 62-63. Mem. MLA, Women and Founds./Corp. Philanthropy. Democrat. Clubs: Princeton, Coffee House, Women's City (N.Y.C.). Office: Carnegie Corp NY 437 Madison Ave New York NY 10022

BROOK, GESELL SAVANNAH, administrative analyst, manufacturing company executive; b. Seattle, Nov. 28, 1946; d. Lloyd Edward and Shirley Jean (Karl) Anderson; m. Bradford Whiting; children—Rob, Chris. B.S. in Speech Pathology and Audiology with honors, U. Oreg., 1970; M.S. in Interdisciplinary Studies with honors, Oreg. State U., 1979. Linn-Benton speech and lang. specialist Edn. Service Dist., Albany, Oreg., 1970-81; speech cons. Monroe, Oreg., 1981-83; exec. dir. Benton County Jr. Achievement, Corvallis, Oreg., 1981-83; v.p. Oregon Electro-MEC, Corvallis, 1970—, vice chmn. bd., 1970-83; program adminstrv. budget analyst State Oreg., Salem, 1983—. Author books including What Do You Think, Lunch, The Shack, Checkers, Make a Rug, Can You Make a Ship?, On Mount Shasta, numerous others. Mem. City Corvallis Budget Commn., 1979-81; Oreg. del. White House Conf. Families, 1980; chmn. Corvallis Sch. Dist., 1980—; bd. dirs. Corvallis Arts Center, 1981-82. Mem. Womens Networking Alliance (v.p. program 1983), Oreg. Speech and Hearing Assn. (assoc. editor), AAUW (pres. 1979-81), Corvallis C. of C. (edn. com.).

BROOK, JOAN MICHAEL, travel agent; b. Kansas City, Mo., Sept. 28, 1934; d. David Herbert and Pearl Bresler Diamond; m. Gerald G. Brook, Dec. 24, 1955 (dec. Jan. 1962); children—Donna Brook Clark, David Michael, Kathy Lynn. B.S., Northwestern U., 1956. Tchr. audiology, various schs., Mo., Ill., 1956-62; legal stenographer firms, Calif., 1963-75; owner, mgr. What A Wonderful World, Pebble Beach, Calif., 1983—. Mem. San Francisco Visitors and Conv. Bur., Monterey Peninsula C. of C., Pacific Grove C. of C., Monterey Peninsula Mus. Art, Calif. Repertory Theater Guild, New Forum. Democrat. Jewish. Home: PO Box 72 Pebble Beach CA 93953 Office: What A Wonderful World PO Box 72 Pebble Beach CA 93953

BROOK, LINDA RIOS, television executive; b. Houston, Apr. 22, 1949; d. Jack Laverne and Geraldine (Yale) Tye Abell; m. Michael J. Rios, May 14, 1971 (div. Sept. 1980); m. Larry Ocono Brook, Dec. 6, 1980; children—Christopher Michael, Kirsten Nicole. B.A., U. Houston, 1971. Dir. mktg. Santikos Theatres, San Antonio, 1977-78; program dir. KENS-TV, San Antonio, 1978-81, sta. mgr., 1981-83, v.p., gen. mgr., 1983-85, pres., gen. mgr., 1985—. Bd. dirs., v.p. BCA ARC, San Antonio, 1985, Bus. Com. on the Arts, San Antonio, 1985; co-chmn. Vision 2000, San Antonio, 1985; bd. dirs. Arthritis Found., San Antonio, 1984-85; trustee Target 90, Goals for San Antonio, 1985; bd. dirs. ARC. Recipient Communicator award Women in Communications, San Antonio, 1981, Tribute to Women in Internat. Bus., YWCA, 1983. Republican. Episcopalian. Avocations: swimming; aerobics. Office: KENS-TV PO Box TV5 San Antonio TX 78299

BROOKS, ANDREE NICOLE, journalist, journalism educator; b. London, Feb. 2, 1937; d. Leon Luis and Lillian (Abrahamson) Aelion; m. Ronald J. Brooks, Aug. 16, 1959; children—Allyson, James. Journalism cert. Northwest London Poly., 1958. Reporter Hampstead News, London, 1954-58; story editor Photoplay Mag., N.Y.C., 1958-60; N.Y. corr. Australian Broadcasting N.Y.C., 1961-68; elected rep., Elstree, Eng., 1973-74; columnist N.Y. Times, N.Y.C., 1978—; free lance journalist, 1978—; adj. prof. journalism Fairfield (Conn.) U., 1983—. Recipient numerous awards including 1st place for news writing Conn. Press Women, 1980, 83, 84; Outstanding Achievement award Nat. Fedn. Press Women, 1981; 1st place award Women in Communications, Fairfield County chpt., 1982, 1983; 2d place award in mag. writing Nat. Assn. Home Builders, 1983; Spl. Service award Conn. chpt. Am. Planning Assn., 1983; 1st place award for mag. writing Nat. Fedn. Press Women, 1983. Mem. Conn. Press Women (chmn. nominating com. 1983-84), Women in Communications (contest co-chmn. 1983-86). Office: care New York Times 229 W 43rd St New York NY 10036

BROOKS, AURORA PRISCELLA, marble importing company executive, interior design consultant; b. Ardmore, Okla., Dec. 25, 1945; d. Ralph Wadkins and Pauline (Ligon) Brooks; m. Buddy Lee Engstrom, Feb. 5, 1966 (div.); 1 dau., Brandi Lynn. A.A., Western State Coll. Office mgr. The Waldinger Corp., Houston, 1973-78; v.p. Brittany Blake Interiors, Houston, 1978-83, Marobles, Inc., Houston, 1983—; mgmt. cons. Pearson Falcone Interiors, Houston, 1983—, Maaco Auto Painting, Houston, 1979-83. Treas. Musicfeast, Houston, 1983; asst. curator Asst. League of Houston, 1983. Mem. Am. Subcontractors Assn., Associated Builders and Contractors, Exec. Women of Tex. Republican. Baptist. Office: Marobles Inc 1920 Fountainview Houston TX 77057

BROOKS, BARBARA JORDAN, human services administrator; b. Jacksonville, Fla., Dec. 17, 1933; d. Howard J. Jordan and Bernice Marguerite (Simmons) Crews; m. William Jason Brooks, July 24, 1953; children—Deborah Lynne, William Dale, Daneece Marguerite, David Lindsay, Darrell Steven. B.S., Jacksonville U., 1968; grad. cert. U. Fla., 1970; M.S., U. North Fla., 1983. Cert. tchr., adult/community coll. instr., aging specialist, Fla. Head tchr. Duval County Schs., Jacksonville, 1968-71; owner, dir. Brooks Pvt. Sch., Jacksonville, 1971-74; dir. Youth Service Bur., Jacksonville, 1974-77; chief community services City of Jacksonville, 1977-85, chief children's services, 1985—; appointee Gov.'s Task Force on Delinquency, Tallahassee, 1975-77; pres. County Council on Aging, Jacksonville, 1980—; bd. dirs. Human Services Coalition, Jacksonville, 1982—, Child Guidance Clinic, Jacksonville, 1984—; liaison Mayor's Commn. on Children and Youth, Jacksonville; coordinator Yr. of Disabled, 1980-81; chmn. Employee Assistance Program, 1985—. Recipient Vol. award Learn to Read, Inc., 1982; Woman in Power award Nat. Council Jewish Women, 1985. Mem. Govt. Fellows of U. North Fla., Fla. Council on Aging. Democrat. Baptist. Avocations: piano/organ; reading; aerobics. Home: 1651 Edgewood Ave S Jacksonville FL 32205 Office: City Hall Rm 603 220 East Bay St Jacksonville FL 32202

BROOKS, CLAUDIA MARIE, lawyer; b. Oakland, Calif., Aug. 2, 1952; d. Rex E. and Colleen M. (Walker) Brooks; m. James A. Smith. A.B., U. Calif.-Berkeley, 1974; J.D., U. Calif.-San Francisco, 1979; postgrad. Monterey Inst. Fgn. Studies (Calif.), 1974, Institut de Francais, Villefranche-sur-Mer, France, 1979, 84, Oxford U. (Eng.), 1973, Hague Acad. Internat. Law (Netherlands), 1980. Bar: Calif. 1979, U.S. Dist. Ct. (no. dist.) Calif. 1979, U.S. Ct. Appeals (9th cir.) 1979. Extern for justice Calif. Supreme Ct., San Francisco, 1978; assoc. Smith & Brooks, Attys. at Law, Redlands, Calif., 1979-82, ptnr., 1982—. Editor-in-chief Hastings Internat. and Comparative Law Rev., 1978-79; contbr. article to law rev. Pub. mem. Fgn. Service selection bds. U.S. Dept. State, Washington, 1983; bd. dirs. Redlands Community Music Assn., Redlands Symphony Assn. Mem. San Bernardino County Bar Assn. (mem. jud. selection com. 1982-83). Clubs: San Francisco Press, Zonta. Home: Redlands CA Office: Smith & Brooks Attys at Law 130 W Vine St PO Box 672 Redlands CA 92373

BROOKS, DEBORAH DEE, data base administrator; b. Kingman, Kans., Jan. 18, 1951; d. Delbert Dexter and Ella Mae (Linscheid) B.; m. John S. Waterman, June 11, 1983. B.A. in Computer Sci., Kans. State U., 1973; M.L., Emporia (Kans.) State U., 1974. Asst. librarian Northwestern U., 1974-77; programmer, analyst Mgmt. Systems Tech., Inc., Chgo., 1977-78; tech. dir., systems analyst CALS project Elgin (Ill.) Community Coll., 1978-80; product mgr. Advanced Systems Inc., Elk Grove Village, Ill., 1980-81; data base adminstr. Wilson Jones Co., Chgo., 1981—; dir. CALS Services Group Ltd.; cons. in field. Mem. Assn. Computing Machinery, ALA, Am. Soc. Info. Sci. (chmn. Chgo. chpt. 1979). Presbyterian. Office: Wilson Jones Co 6150 Touhy Ave Chicago IL 60648

BROOKS, DIANA D., auction house executive; b. Glen Cove, N.Y., 1950. Grad. Yale U. Exec. v.p. Sotheby's North America, N.Y.C. Address: Sotheby's North America 1334 York Ave New York NY 10021*

BROOKS, DOROTHY LEE, telephone company official; b. Beaumont, Tex., Dec. 8, 1946; d. Carter and Bessie (Smith) Williams; m. Elmo Brooks, July 18, 1981; children—Uzooma, Lexie, Rodney, Paula. B.S., U. Houston, 1970; postgrad. Western State Coll. Law, San Diego, 1975-77. Systems reviewer Prudential Ins. Co., Houston, 1970-72; dir. Eboness House, San Diego, 1975; instr. Learning Center, San Diego, 1975-76; adminstrv. asst. San Diego Tng. Consortium, 1976-77; mfg. engr. Tex. Instruments, Dallas, 1977-78; forecaster Southwestern Bell, Dallas, 1978—. Author: (with others) Thermophysical Properties Data Manual, 1970. Vol. tchr. Pinkston High Sch., Dallas, 1981—. Mem. Soc. Telephone Engrs. Democrat. Home: 1126 Alexandria St Garland TX 75040 Office: Southwestern Bell 311 S Akard St Room 1901 Dallas TX 75202

BROOKS, ELOISE SILVER, oil company executive, trophies and frames company co-owner; b. Marion, N.C., Nov. 9, 1940; d. Robert Lee and Nellie Gladys (Haynes) Silver; m. Floyd Thomas Brooks, Nov. 5, 1959; children—Brona Brooks Clontz, Kelly Dolores. Grad. high sch., Marion, N.C. Office mgr. Marion Oil Co., Inc., N.C., 1961-65, sec., treas., 1966-82, pres., 1982—; ptnr. Craft Land Trophies & Frames, 1981—; mem. staff, instr. Festival of Champions, Appalachian U., 1974; guest performer, instr. Festival of Champions, Gatlinburg, Tenn., 1976-78; co-dir. Carolina Mountain Cloggers, 1971-80; co-organizer Wagon Masters Western Square Dancers, 1965. Author: (with Floyd Brooks) Carolina Mountain Cloggin', 1978. Mem. McDowell Com. of 100, Inc., Marion, N.C., 1984-85; mem. Nat. Write Your Congressman, Inc., Dallas, 1984-85. Democrat. Presbyterian. Club: Wagon Masters Western Square Dance (co-pres. 1965-68). Avocations: tennis; bowling; dancing. Office: Marion Oil Co Inc PO Box 1250 Marion NC 28752

BROOKS, GWENDOLYN, poet, author; b. Topeka, June 7, 1917; d. David Anderson and Keziah Corinne (Wims) B.; grad. Wilson Jr. Coll., Chgo., 1936; 10 hon. doctorates; m. Henry L. Blakely, Sept. 17, 1939; children—Henry L., Nora. Poetry cons. to Library of Congress, 1985-86. Named One of 10 Women of Year, Mademoiselle mag., 1945; recipient award for creative writing Am. Acad. Arts and Letters, 1946; Pulitzer prize for poetry, 1950; Friends of Lit. award for poetry, 1964; Thormod Monsen award for lit., 1964; others; named Poet Laureate of Ill., 1968; Guggenheim fellow in creative poetry, 1946-47. Mem. Soc. Midland Authors. Author: Harper: A Street in Bronzeville, 1945; Annie Allen (poetry), 1949; Maud Martha (novel), 1953; Bronzeville Boys and Girls (book for children), 1956; (poetry) The Bean Eaters, 1960, Selected Poems, 1963, In the Mecca, Riot, 1969, Family Pictures, 1970, Aloneness, 1971, To Disembark, 1981; Report from Part One, 1972, Beckonings, 1975; Primer for Blacks, 1980; Young Poets Primer, 1980. Address: 7428 S Evans Chicago IL 60619

BROOKS, HARRIETT BURCH (MRS. FRANCIS EARL BROOKS), nursing administrator; b. Deland, Fla., May 24, 1924; d. William A. and Mary (Cadwallader) Burch; diploma Grady Meml. Hosp. Sch. Nursing, Atlanta, 1945; B.S. in Pub. Health Nursing, U. N.C., 1962; m. Francis Earl Brooks, Mar. 6, 1946; children—Mary Anne, Eleanor Susan. Inst. staff nurse Hernando County Hosp., Brooksville, Fla., 1945-47; staff pub. health nurse Citrus County Health Dept., Inverness, Fla., 1951-60; field supr. pub. health nursing Palm Beach County Health Dept., West Palm Beach, Fla., 1962-64; dir. nursing service Leon County Health Dept., Tallahassee, 1964-77; family planning program mgr. Dist. II, Fla. Dept. Health and Rehab. Services, Gainesville, 1977-80; dir. nurses Eastbrook Health Care Center, 1983—; asst. prof. Fla. State U., 1972-73. Sec. continuing edn. com. Fla. Bd. Health, 1966-69, chmn. conf. adminstrs., suprs. and educators, 1969—. Bd. dirs. Tallahassee-Leon County Community Action Program, 1967-72. Mem. Fla. Nursing Assn. (dist. 1st v.p. 1967-68), Fla. Pub. Health Assn. (sec. 1969, 1st v.p. 1972, dir. 1973-74, pres.-elect 1975, pres. 1976—), Leon County Assn. Community Services. Baptist. Home: 12225 S Pleasant Grove Rd Floral City FL 32636 Office: 10295 N Howell Ave Brooksville FL 33512

BROOKS, JANET, international tax consultant; b. Seattle, Feb. 11, 1956; d. Jonathan P. and Nancy (Barker) B. B.A., Whitman Coll., Walla Walla, Wash., 1978; J.D., U. Puget Sound, 1982. Tax assoc. Coopers & Lybrand, Palo Alto, Calif., 1982-83; tax assoc. Price Waterhouse, San Jose, Calif., 1984-85, internat. tax cons., Palo Alto, Calif., 1986—. Mem. San Francisco Symphony Vols. Mem. AAUW (chmn. fin. planning 1985-86), Bay Area Lawyers for the Arts. Home: 202 Thomas Dr Los Gatos CA 95030 Office: 300 Hamilton Ave Palo Alto CA 94301

BROOKS, MARY JEANETTE TIDWELL, lobbyist; b. Dallas, July 14, 1951; d. Earl Carl Edwin and Leta Virginia (McDonald) Tidwell; m. Eldon Lloyd Brooks, Mar. 18, 1972 (div.); children—Kari Rene, Chad Ryan. B.A. in History cum laude, U. Tex.-Arlington, 1973; M.Social Sci., U. Okla., 1978. Tchr., Hurst (Tex.) Pub. Schs., 1975, Lawton (Okla.) Pub. Schs., 1976; research analyst Okla. Legis. Council, Oklahoma City, 1979; legis. rep. state govt. affairs Texaco USA, Houston, 1980-83; sr. rep. state govt. affairs Panhandle Eastern Corp., Houston, 1983-84, mgr. state govt. affairs, 1984—. Author: (with others) Agencies, Boards and Commissions of Oklahoma, 1979. Mem. Ohio Gas Assn. (legis. com., regulator com.), Ill. C. of C. (energy com.), Ill. Mfrs. Assn. (energy com.), Ohio C. of C. (pub. affairs com.), C. of C. (pub. affairs com.), Ohio Mfrs. Assn., Pub. Affairs Roundtable, U. Tex.-Arlington Alumni Assn., U. Okla. Alumni Assn., Alpha Chi, Phi Alpha Theta, Sigma Delta Pi. Methodist. Club: Third House (Ill.). Home: 7307 Treewater Houston TX 77072 Office: Panhandle Eastern Pipe Line Co 3000 Bissonnet Houston TX 77005

BROOKS, STEPHANIE PLEMMONS, nursing administrator; b. Knoxville, Tenn., Jan. 16, 1956; d. James Kelsey and Eleanor (Williams) Plemmons; m. William Bogan Brooks III, June 30, 1979. B.S. in Nursing, U. Tenn., 1978, postgrad. Dental Coll., 1984; M.S. in Edn., Memphis State U., 1981. Instr. nursing St. Joseph Sch. Nursing, Memphis, 1979-80; staff nurse Meth. Hosp., Memphis, 1979; staff nurse UpJohn Health Care, Memphis, 1980-82; course co-ordinator, instr. nursing Shelby State Comml. Coll., Memphis, 1980-81; research nurse Clin. Research Ctr., Memphis, 1980-81; patient care co-ordinator U. Tenn. Hosp., Memphis, 1981—, staff devel., cardio pulmonary coms., 1983; instr. health ARC, 1981-83; instr. fitness Davis YMCA, 1983. Ruth Barrett Smith scholar Pi Beta Phi, 1976-77. Mem. Mortar Board, Omicron Delta Kappa, Kappa Delta Pi, Pi Beta Phi (pres. 1976-77). Home: 326 N Watkins Ave Memphis TN 38104 Office: U Tenn Hosp Bowld 941 Court Ave Memphis TN 38163

BROOKSHIER, PEGGY ANN, mechanical engineer; b. Idaho Falls, Idaho, Mar. 14, 1955; d. Yutaka and Miyoko (Konishi) Morishita; B.S., Calif. State U., 1977; m. Alan L. Brookshier, Nov. 18, 1978. Mech. engr., project mgr. U.S. Dept. Energy, Idaho Falls, 1977—. Mem. ASME. Office: 785 DOE Pl Idaho Falls ID 83402

BROPHY, CAROLE ANN, real estate developer, broker; b. Missoula, Mont., Oct. 25, 1948; d. John A. and Theckula Margaret (Tucker) Frankovich; m. Patrick Joseph Brophy, Dec. 22, 1971; children—Elizabeth Ann, Nathan John. Student U. Mont., 1966-70, U. Ariz., 1971-73. Comml. and residential salesperson Tony Lee Realty, Tucson, 1976-78; regional project mgr. Mahoney Mktg., Denver, 1978—; exec. com. mgr. Dayton Fin., Dayton of Dallas, 1980; v.p. Brokers West Mktg., Denver, 1981-82; project mgr. Richmond Homes, Ltd., Denver, 1981-82; pres., owner Carlton Carruthers, Inc., Denver, 1982—; v.p., owner Carruthers Design, Inc., Denver, 1982—; pres., owner Todays Am. Builder, Rocky Mountain region, 1983—; owner, dir. Greenbriar Devel., Inc., Denver, 1983—, Carlton Inc., Denver, 1985—; cons. West Star Devel., Denver, 1983—, Intrawest of Denver, 1983—; dir. Starmount, Inc., Denver. Mem. Nat. Assn. Realtors, Realtors Nat. Mktg. Inst., Colo. Assn. Realtors (edn. com. 1984), Homebuilders Assn. Met. Denver, Sales and Mktg. Council of Homebuilders Assn. (chmn. edn. com. 1983-84). Roman Catholic. Home: 7 Spyglass Dr Littleton CO 80123 Office: Carlton Carruthers Inc 2865 S Colorado Blvd Suite 205 Denver CO 80222 Office: Carlton Carruthers Inc 6970 S Holly Circle Suite 211 Englewood CO 80112

BROPHY, MOIRA LETITIA, lawyer; b. Paterson, N.J., Feb. 16, 1954; d. Richard and Margaret Mary (Garvey) Brophy. B.A., Montclair (N.J.) State Coll., 1976; J.D., Seton Hall Law Sch., Newark, 1981. Bar: N.J. 1981. Assoc. firm Porzio, Bromberg & Newman, P.C., Morristown, N.J., 1981—. Mem. Seton Hall Law Rev., 1980-81. Mem. ABA, Am. Trial Lawyer Assn., N.J. Bar Assn., Trial Attys. N.J., Morris County Bar Assn., Passaic County Bar Assn. Democrat. Roman Catholic. Home: 234 Trenton Ave Clifton NJ 07011 Office: Porzio, Bromberg & Newman PC 163 Madison Ave Morristown NJ 07960

BROSNAN, CAROL RAPHAEL SARAH, musician, arts foundation official; b. Paterson, N.J., July 19, 1931; d. Basil Roger Warnock and Mary Ellen Carroll (McDonald) Brosnan; student Montclair State Tchrs. Coll., 1948-49, George Washington U., Washington, 1956-61, U. Va., 1975, U. Oxford (Eng.), 1975, U. Calif., Berkeley, 1975; B.A., George Washington U., 1981; pupil Iris Brussels, Helen Yakobson. Adminstrv. clk. depts. Army and Def., Pentagon, Office Asst. Chief Staff Intelligence, Washington, 1955-58; clk. fgn. sci. info. program NSF, Washington, 1958-60, adminstrv. clk., 1960-65, adminstrv. fellowship clk. grad. fellowship program, 1965-72; reports specialist Nat. Endowment for Arts, Washington, 1972—; tchr. piano, Paterson, N.J., 1945-53; piano recitalist U.S., Heidelberg, W. Ger. Served with WAC, 1953-55. Recipient Young People's Concerts award, 1945. Hon. fellow Harry S. Truman Library Inst. Nat. and Internat. Affairs, 1975. Fellow Internat. Biog. Assn.; mem. Am. Assn. Advancement Slavic Studies, Am. Hist. Assn., Am. Philol. Assn., Acad. Polit. Sci. (contbg.), Am. Classical League, Friends of Bodleian Library, Luther Rice Soc. of George Washington U. (life), Phi Alpha Theta. Home: 4201 Massachusetts Ave NW Apt 3030C Washington DC 20016 Office: Nat Endowment for Arts Nat Found on Arts and Humanities Old Post Office Bldg 1100 Pennsylvania Ave NW Washington DC 20506

BROSSEAU, IRMA FINN, association executive; b. Boston, Sept. 4, 1930; d. Harry and Alfreda (Zimmerman) Miller; B.S., Simmons Coll., 1952; hon. doctorate, Hawthorne Coll., 1984; m. George Brosseau, Jan. 14, 1978; children by previous marriage—Hester, Jonathan, Sarah. Asst. to prodn. mgr. Houghton Mifflin Pub. Co., Boston, 1952-56; desk editor, women's editor Quincy (Mass.) Patriot Ledger, 1956-58; desk editor, reporter, feature writer, women's editor Anchorage Times, 1958-60, 66-71; desk editor Anchorage News, 1965-66; program dir. Nat. Fedn. Bus. and Profl. Women's Clubs, Washington, 1972-78, exec. dir., 1978—; dir. Nat. Council on Future of Women in the Workplace. Mem. rev. panel Women's Ednl. Equity Act grants HEW; mem. scholarship rev. panel Girl's Clubs of Am.; mem. bd. advisors Ten Outstanding Young Women of Am.; mem. nat. steering com. Nat. Women's Agenda; speaker, panelist on women's issues. Mem. Am. Soc. Assn. Execs., Washington Soc. Assn. Execs., AAUW, ACLU, Va. Citizens Consumer Council, Nat. Women's Polit. Caucus, Women's Ednl. Action League, Potomac Bus. and Profl. Women's Club, Bus. Execs. for Nat. Def. Democrat. Office: Nat Fedn Bus and Profl Women's Clubs 2012 Massachusetts Ave NW Washington DC 20036

BROTHERS, JOYCE DIANE BAUER (MRS. MILTON BROTHERS), psychologist; b. N.Y.C.; d. Morris K. and Estelle (Rapoport) Bauer; B.S., Cornell U., 1947; M.A., Columbia U., 1949, Ph.D., 1953; L.H.D. (hon.), Franklin Pierce Coll., 1969; m. Milton Brothers, July; 1 dau., Lisa Robin. Mem. faculty Hunter Coll., 1948-53, Columbia U., 1948-53; research fellow UNESCO, 1949-50; host TV program Dr. Joyce Brothers, Sta. WNBC, 1958-63, Consult Dr. Brothers syndicated by ABC, 1961-66, Tell Me, Dr. Brothers syndicated by Triangle Films, 1964-70; syndicated on TV by Gen. Foods Co., Kohner Bros., 1972-77; Living Easy with Dr. Joyce Brothers syndicated by Trevira, 1972-75; radio program ABC, 1963-68; program Call Dr. Brothers, WNBC Radio, 1966-69, WMCA, 1969-71, NBC Radio Emphasis, 1966-75, NBC Monitor, 1966-75, NBC Radio Network Newsline, 1975—; newspaper column N.Am. Newspaper Alliance, 1961-71; columnist Good Housekeeping mag., 1964, King Features Syndicate, 1972—; news analyst Metromedia TV, 1975-76; Cable News Network corr., 1980-82; spl. feature writer Hearst papers, UPI; cons. Magee Carpet Co., Sperry and Hutchins Co., ABC Films, Greyhound Corp., Hoechst Fibers, Inc., Armstrong-Cork Co., Reading Devel. Center. Recipient wisdom award of honor, 1965; named Woman of Achievement, Fedn. Jewish Women's Orgn., 1964; Justice Lodge citation for unselfish devotion and inspired leadership and service to community, 1963; named Profl. Woman of Yr. dist. 1 Bus. and Profl. Womens Clubs, 1968; Merit award Bar-Ilan U., Ramat, Israel, 1968, award Parkinson Disease Found., 1971, Deadline award for excellence in broadcasting radio news Sigma Delta Chi, 1971. Mem. Sigma Xi. Author: Ten Days to a Successful Memory, 1960; Woman, 1962; The Brothers System for Liberated Love and Marriage, 1972; Better Than Ever, 1976; How to Get Whatever You Want Out of Life, 1979; What Every Woman Should Know About Men. Office: NBC 30 Rockefeller Plaza New York NY 10020

BROTHERS, KATHRYN ANN, lawyer, banker; b. Endicott, N.Y., June 26, 1955; d. Robert Douglas and Evelyn Juanita (Coffey) Brothers. B.A. in Polit. Sci., U. Ky., 1977, J.D., 1981, M.A. in Diplomacy and Internat. Commerce, 1983. Bar: Ky. 1982. Sole practice law and legal research, Lexington, Ky., 1982-84; internat. credit analyst Commerce Union Bank, Nashville, 1984—. Active adoption group Amnesty Internat., Lexington, 1982-84, YWCA, Lexington, 1982—; campaign worker Harvey Sloane for Gov. Ky., 1979. Mem. ABA, Ky. Bar Assn., Phi Beta Kappa, Phi Delta Phi. Democrat. Episcopalian. Home: 210 Brooksboro Terr Nashville TN 37217-3341 Office: Internat Banking Dept Commerce Union Bank One Commerce Pl Nashville TN 37219

BROTHERS, M(URIEL) ELIZABETH, college official; b. Bklyn.; d. Sydney Inman and Marguerite Olley (Taylor-Lindsay) B.; A.B. with distinction in Spanish, Vassar Coll., 1950; postgrad. Latin Am. Inst., N.Y. Sch. Employing Printers, Philanthropy Tax Inst. Various editorial positions McCall Corp., 1951-62; devel. officer Mt. Holyoke Coll., South Hadley, Mass., 1961-67, 71-73; dir. publs. and dir. public info., 1967-71, dir. devel., 1973-80; assoc. v.p. devel Rollins Coll., Winter Park, Fla., 1980—; dir. Mass. Congl. Fund, 1979-80; lectr., cons. fin. planning for women. Moderator, First Congl. Ch., Winter Park, 1986—; v.p. Christopher D. Smithers Found.; bd. govs. Crosby Found. Recipient Outstanding Profl. Fund Raiser award, 1985. Mem. AAUW, Mt. Holyoke Alumni Assn. (hon.). Republican. Clubs: Cosmopolitan (N.Y.C.); University (Winter Park); Vassar of Central Fla.; Fla. Exec. Women (dir.) (Orlando); Mt. Holyoke of Del. (hon.). Author handbooks in field; contbr. articles to profl. publs. Office: Rollins College Winter Park FL 32789

BROTHERTON, JUNE MARIE, public affairs executive, state official, author; b. Charlotte, N.C., May 29, 1953; d. Ralph Shellton and Mary Cathryn (Barnett) B. B.S. in Agr., N.C. State U., 1974. Editor, Sunny States Publs., Inc., Atlanta, 1975-76; alumni editor N.C. State U. Alumni Assn., Raleigh, 1976-77; editor, women and youth coordinator N.C. Assn. Electric Coops., Raleigh, 1977-79; asst. dir. pub. service and info. dept. City of Charlotte, N.C., 1979-82; dir. pub. affairs N.C. Dept. Agr., Raleigh, 1982—. Editor: The Ga. Farmer, 1975-76; The EMC Employee (communicator award 1979), 1977-79; Around City Hall, 1979-82; Agrl. Rev., 1982—; alumni editor The Stater, 1976-77. Communications/media relations com. ARC, Charlotte, 1981-82; pub. relations vol. Girl Scouts U.S.A., Charlotte, 1980-81; career resource vol. Mecklenburg Women's Commn., Charlotte, 1981-82; chair publicity, bd. dirs. Wake County Women's Polit. Caucus, Raleigh, 1983-84; active Wake Democratic Women, Raleigh, 1983—. Mem. Women in Communications, Inc. (treas. N.C. Triangle chpt. agr. 1983-84, pres. 1984-85), Communications Officers State Depts. (pres. 1984-85), N.C. Assn. Govt. Info. Officers (sec. 1983-84), N.C. Assn. Farm Writers and Broadcasters (planning com. 1983-84), So. Assn. Info. Officers State Depts. Agr. Democrat. Presbyterian. Club: Pilot of Raleigh, Inc., (membership chmn. 1984-85). Office: NC Dept Agr 1 W Edenton St Raleigh NC 27611

BROTHERTON, NAOMI, artist; b. Galveston, Tex., Apr. 8, 1920; d. Vernon Smart and Hunter Smith Macon; B.A., Baylor U., 1941; m. Lem Brotherton, Nov. 20, 1941; children—Betty Brotherton Crudden, Robert James. Tchr. watercolor painting various workshops, 1962—; partner Artisan's Studio-Gallery, Dallas; 39 one woman shows since 1955, including: Oak Cliff Soc. Fine Arts, Dallas, 1961, Western N.Mex. U., Silver City, 1967, Baylor U., 1967, S. Ark. Art Center, El Dorado, 1969, Irving (Tex.) Art Center, 1972, Artisans Studio-Gallery, Dallas, 1981, Carlsbad (N.Mex.) Art Mus., 1984, St. Edward's U., 1985; group shows include: Panhandle Plains Hist. Mus., Canyon, Tex., 1968, Laguna Gloria Gallery of Tex. Fine Arts Assn., Austin, 1969, Barnwell Art Center, Shreveport, La., 1974, Galleria de Arte de Saltillo (Mex.), 1978, Artisans Studio-Gallery, Dallas, 1981, 82, Dallas Public Library, 1980; awards in competitive shows include: Tex. Watercolor Soc., 1954, 66, 81, Tex. Fine Arts Assn., Dallas, 1963, 65, 67, 69, 70, 73, 74, Tex. Fine Arts Assn. State-wide, Austin, 1965, 67, 70, 73, 74, Southwestern Watercolor Soc., Dallas, 1964, 66, 67, 68, 69, 71, 72, 79, 81, Artists and Craftsmen Assoc. of Dallas, 1983, 84, Coppini Acad. Fine Arts, 1982, 83; numerous others; represented in permanent collections: Baylor U., Ft. Worth Public Schs., S. Ark. Art Center, Brownsville (Tex.) Art Center, Pecos (Tex.) Art Center, Carlsbad Mus. and Art Ctr., others. Mem. Tex. Watercolor Assn., Southwestern Watercolor Soc. (pres. 1967-68), Tex. Fine Arts Assn., Artists and Craftsmen Assn. Dallas, Coppini Art Assn. San Antonio, Okla. Watercolor Assn., West Tex. Watercolor Soc., Beta Sigma Phi. Episcopalian. Co-author: Variations in Watercolor, 1981. Home: 4808 Oak Trail Dallas TX 75232

BROTMAN, PHYLLIS BLOCK, advt. and public relations exec.; b. Balt., Mar. 22, 1934; d. Sol George and Delma (Herman) Block; ed. Balt. Jr. Coll., U. Va., Mary Washington Coll.; m. Don N. Brotman, Aug. 16, 1953; children—Solomon G., Barbara Gay. Asso., Channel 13 TV, 1953-55; free-lance pub. relations, 1960-66; coordinator pub. relations Md. Council Ednl. TV, 1965-66; pres. Image Dynamics, Inc., Balt., 1966—. Lectr., cons.; lectr. pub. relations Johns Hopkins; spl. lectr. pub. schs., Baltimore County, Inst. Politics, Miss., Ark., N.C., La.; cons. legis. info. program Md. Gen. Assembly, 1970; former coordinator spl. events Balt. Jr. Coll.; former program coordinator Wine Inst. Internat. pres. B'nai B'rith Girls, 1952-53. Bd dirs. Nat. Council Jewish Women, 1969-71, former coordinator pub. affairs, chmn. coll. program, program intellectual enrichment; bd. dirs. Levindale Home and Infirmary Ladies Aux., 1963-64, Asso. Placement and Guidance Bur., 1964-65, Sinai Hosp. Aux., 1964-65, Chamber Symphony of San Francisco; former bd. dirs. Asso. Jewish Charities, Nat. Jewish Welfare Fund; vice chmn. Nat. UN Day Com.; rep. to UN; nat. commr. B'nai B'rith Youth Orgn.; mem. compensation com. Md. Gen. Assembly. Recipient certificate of achievement Md. Ho. of Dels., Md. Senate, Asso. Jewish Charities, 1965, award for outstanding community service Beta Omega Kappa, 1952; Woman of Yr. award Balt. Cancer Ctr.-U. Md., 1984. Mem. Pub. Relations Soc. Am. (asso. mem., sec. Md. chpt., certificate of achievement Md. chpt.), Am. Assn. Polit. Consultants (dir., nat. pres.), Am. Assn. Advt. Agys., Internat. Assn. Polit. Cons., McDonough-Field Assn. (pres.), Balt. Council Pub. Relations, Md.-Del.-D.C. Press Assn., Council State Govts., Advt. Assn. Balt., Chesapeake Bay Flyers, Advt. Club D.C., Beta Omega Kappa (past pres.). Democrat. Jewish (pres. parents assn. 1968-70, mem. religious sch. com., bd. congregation). Mem. B'nai B'rith Women (v.p. Balt.), Hadassah (past chmn., speaker rep.). Instrumental in legislation to create state-wide endl. television network. Home: 8105 McDonogh Rd Baltimore MD 21208 Office: Horizon House 1101 N Calvert St Baltimore MD 21202

BROUDE, JOSEPHINE RACHEL, univ. exec.; b. N.Y.C., May 25, 1927; d. Emanuel and Eva (Lieberson) Rosen; A.B., Antioch Coll., 1949; m. Henry W. Broude, June 29, 1947. With Shepley, Bulfinch, Richardson & Abbott, Boston, 1950-54; interior designer, adminstrv. asst. Douglas Orr, AIA, New Haven, 1954-65; exec. asst. to provost, cons. for interior planning Yale U., New Haven, 1965—. Bd. govs. Mory's Assn., 1974—. Guest editor Mademoiselle mag., 1948. Office: Provost's Office Yale U New Haven CT 06520

BROUGHTON, KATHY ANN, tax service executive; b. Scott AFB, Ill., July 27, 1959; d. Walter Merritt and Jeanette Marie (Boatwright) Wooters; m. Ronnie Ray Broughton, July 16, 1977 (div. Nov. 1982); children—Amy Michelle, Bethany Ann. Cert. tax practitioner. Machine operator Primo Pants, Inc., Versailles, Mo., 1983-84; owner, operator Tax Service, Versailles, 1984—; client asst. Mo. Ozarks Econ. Opportunity Corp., Richland, Mo., 1985. Vice pres. Head Start program, 1984-85, pres., 1985—. Democrat. Mem. United Pentecostal Ch. Avocations: sewing; notary public. Office: Kathy Broughton's Tax Service 503 W DeKalb Versailles MO 65084

BROUSE, ANN GUSTINA, librarian, storyteller; b. Hornell, N.Y., July 22, 1948; d. Edward Daniel and Wanda Mary (Wenderlich) Gustina; m. Gary Eugene Brouse, Apr. 22, 1978. B.S. in Edn., SUNY-Cortland, 1970; M.L.S., George Peabody Coll. for Tchrs., 1971. Cert. pub. librarian, sch. library media specialist, N.Y. Librarian, Steele Meml. Library, Elmira, N.Y., 1971—, br. head Elmira Heights Br. Library, 1977-80, Southside Br. Library, Elmira, 1980-83, head tech. services dept., parent library, 1983—; storyteller, various local and regional events, Ithaca and Elmira, 1979—; speaker various regional library workshops, 1982—. Scriptwriter, announcer Library News Spots, Cable-TV, 1976-77; book reviewer Sch. Library Jour., N.Y.C., 1979—. Mem. Chemung County LWV, Elmira, 1981—, historian, 1983-85, v.p., 1985-86, pres., 1986—. Mem. ALA, N.Y. Library Assn., Internat. Reading Assn., N.Y. State Reading Assn., Nat. Assn. for Preservation and Perpetuation of Story Telling, Beta Phi Mu. Democrat. Roman Catholic. Home: 3261 Easterbrook Dr Horseheads NY 14845 Office: Steele Meml Library 1 Library Plaza Elmira NY 14901

BROUSSARD, DONNA BYRD, marketing representative, consultant; b. Omaha, Jan. 19, 1944; d. Harry Helton and Beulah Mabel (Heydt) Byrd; 1 dau., Ann Marie. B.A., Stephen F. Austin U., 1966; M.A., Sam Houston U., 1980. Juvenile probation officer Probation Dept., Houston, 1966-77; dean instrn. Dallas Sch. Dist., 1977-78; dir. magnet sch. Houston Ind. Sch. Dist., 1978-79; adminstr. placement Juvenile Probation Dept., Houston, 1979-83; mktg. rep. Lifemark Corp., Houston, 1983—; cons., tchr. Nat. Council Juvenile Ct. Judges, Reno, 1979—; lectr. Sam Houston Criminal Justice Ctr., Huntsville, Tex., 1979—. Mem. exec. com. Harris County Democratic Com., Houston, 1979-83; mem. coordinating com. John Glenn for Pres. Campaign, Houston, 1983. Mem. Nat. Council Juvenile and Family Ct. Judges, Tex. Corrections Assn. (sec., chmn. cert. com.), Am. Judiciary Soc., Am. Corrections Assn., Nat. Assn. Exec. Women. Democrat. Baptist. Home: 11711 Pecan Gap Houston TX 77065 Office: Lifemark Recovery Centers 3800 Buffalo Speedway Houston TX 77028

BROWDER, JOHNIE MAE GOMILLION, retired educational administrator; b. McKenzie, Ala., Oct. 2, 1919; d. Thad Jackson and Irene (Lee) Gomillion; B.S., Troy State U., 1949; M.Ed., Auburn U., 1956; m. Ralph J. Browder, Dec. 15, 1939; children—Ralph Thaddeus, Tempie Leah Browder Mutschler. Tchr. public schs., 1943-46; tchr., guidance counselor McKenzie High Sch., 1946-65; supr. guidance and evaluation Butler County Public Schs., 1965-71; prin. W.O. Parmer Elem. Sch., Greenville, Ala., 1971-82, ret., 1982. Treas., adult Sunday sch. tchr. New Home Baptist Ch. Mem. Ala. Edn. Assn., NEA, Ala. Dept. Elem. Prins. Assn., Butler County Edn. Assn. (pres. 1973-74), Internat. Platform Assn., Delta Kappa Gamma, Kappa Delta Pi. Home: Route 1 McKenzie AL 36456

BROWER, ANN M., retired newspaper executive; b. Stowe, Pa., Nov. 26, 1924; d. Ralph J. and Mary A. (St. Cross) Capaldi; student Pottstown Sch. Bus., 1942-43; m. Francis T. Brower, Oct. 22, 1949; children—Patricia A., Karen L., Richard A. Bookkeeper, sec. Levin's Dept. Store, 1943-48; payroll clk., bookkeeper Pottstown (Pa.) Mercury, 1948-52, 66-73, office mgr., 1974-79, comptroller, 1979-83; teller 1st Fed. Savs. and Loan, 1952-53. Active fundraiser Cub Scouts Am., Boy Scouts Am., 1969-79. Mem. Nat. Assn. Female Execs., North Coventry Fire Co. Aux. Home: 103 W Cedarville Rd Pottstown PA 19464

BROWER, MARGARET MERCEDES, real estate exec., state ofcl.; b. Sault Ste. Marie, Mich.; d. Robert F. and Helen L. (Houlihan) Wagner; B.A., U. Chgo.; postgrad. Nat. Coll. Physiotherapy, 1931-33; diploma Edison Tech. U., 1948; postgrad. U. Wash., 1969, Portland State U., 1973; 1 son, Scott Gerald. Salesperson Ewing & Clark Realty, Seattle, 1950-51; sales mgr. Junction Realty, Seattle, 1951-53; salesperson McQuaid & Pickart Realty, Seattle, 1953-56; asso. broker, appraiser Admiral Realty, Seattle, 1956-81; real estate commr. dept. licensing State of Wash., Olympia, 1978—; lectr. in field. Real Estate Salesman of the Yr. award, City of Seattle, 1958; Woman of the Yr., Wash. State Women's Council, 1979; Award for outstanding service to handicapped children, Variety Clubs of Am., 1979; Citizen of the Yr., W. Seattle Bus. and Profl. Women's Club, 1980; Award of Merit, Seattle-King County Bd. Realtors, 1980. Mem. Wash. Assn. Realtors (dir.), Women's Council of Realtors, King County Bd. Realtors, (dir.), Seattle C. of C. (chmn. hist. soc. 1984—), W. Seattle C. of C. (dir.), Nat. Assn. Women's Councils, Nat. Assn. Real Estate Appraisers, Am. Inst. Real Estate Appraisers, W. Seattle Bus. and Profl. Women's, V.F.W., Delphian Soc., Omega Tau Rho. Democrat. Roman Catholic. Clubs: Variety, Swedish, Washington Athletic, Glen Acres Golf, 34th Dist. Dem., Children's Orthopedic Hosp. Guild, Alki Community. Contbr. articles to profl. jours.; author: How You Can Go From Broke to Broker in Real Estate, 1981. Home: 2510 Alki Ave SW Seattle WA 98116 Office: 3222 California Ave SW Seattle WA 98116

BROWN, ALICE ROBERTA, customer service manager; b. Pottsville, Pa., July 5, 1952; d. Emmett Franklin and Ruth Minnie (Nagle) Miller; m. Edward Martin Brown, Dec. 7, 1974; children—Jeremy Scott, Travis Edward. B.S. in Psychology, Millersville U., 1973; M.S. in Human Resource Mgmt., U. Utah, Stuttgart, W.Ger., 1978. Lab. technician, Bio-Med Labs, Friedensburg, Pa., 1969-71; mgr. Sico, Lancaster, Pa., 1971-73; quality control mgr. Berkley Products Co., Akron, Pa., 1974-75, order dept. clk., 1978-79, customer service mgr., 1979—; switchboard operator U.S. Army, Stuttgart, 1975-77. Mem. Nat. Assn. Female Execs. Republican. Avocations: camping; gardening; motorcycling; reading. Office: Berkely Products Co PO Box E Akron PA 17501

BROWN, ANN CARLSON, psychiatrist; b. Lorain, Ohio, June 19, 1930; d. Benjamin and Edna (Dellinger) Carlson; B.S., Otterbein Coll., Westerville, Ohio, 1948; M.D., Case-Western Res. U., 1956; children—Catherine, Elizabeth, Robert, Andrew. Intern, St. Luke's Hosp., Cleve., 1956-57, resident in pediatrics, 1957-58; resident in psychiatry Hall Inst., Columbia, S.C., 1976-80; practice medicine specializing in psychiatry, Charlotte, N.C., 1980—. Recipient Ohio Gov.'s award for community action, 1974, Service to Mankind award Sertoma, Zanesville, Ohio, 1976. Office: 1900 Randolph Rd Charlotte NC 28207

BROWN, ANNE BARBARA, financial executive; b. Bronxville, N.Y., Sept. 22, 1949; d. Paul Robert and Anne (Brady) B.; m. William Lawrence Farrell, Sept. 28, 1975; 1 child, Lacey Erin. B.A., Trinity Coll., Washington, 1971; M.B.A., U. Pa., 1973. Fixed income salesperson Goldman, Sachs & Co., N.Y.C., 1973-78, v.p., 1978-83, v.p., fin. futures specialist, Dallas, 1983—. Mem. women's com. Girl Scouts of N.Y., N.Y.C., 1982-83. Heubner fellow Wharton Grad. Sch., U. Pa., 1972. Mem. Trinity Coll. Alumni Assn. N.Y., Wharton Grad. Alumni Assn., Phi Beta Kappa. Roman Catholic. Club: Wharton (N.Y.C.) (officer 1975-79). Office: Goldman Sachs & Co 100 Crescent Ct Dallas TX 75201

BROWN, ARLENE ANN, data communications company executive; b. Cleve., Feb. 21, 1951; d. Lawrence Francis and Irene Marie (Kandzer) Tamasovich; m. William David Brown, June 25, 1977; children—Raymond Noel, Lawrence Joseph. B.S., Notre Dame Coll., Cleve., 1971. System analyst Ohio Bell Telephone Co., Cleve., 1971-76; mktg. specialist So. Bell Telephone Co., Atlanta, 1977-78; acct. exec. Teletype Corp., Skokie, Ill., 1978-79, sales mgr., 1979-80, regional sales mgr., 1980-82; v.p. sales David Brown Assoc., Atlanta, 1982; computer cons. Notre Dame Coll., 1972-73. Sec. Stonehaven Homeowners Assn., Ga., 1986. NSF grantee, 1970; recipient Digilog Sales award Digilog, Inc., 1984-85. Mem. Am. Mgmt. Assn., Ga. Telecommunications Assn., Nat. Assn. Female Execs. Roman Catholic. Avocations: golf; tennis; sailing; travel. Office: David Brown Assos Inc PO Box 1048 Stone Mountain GA 30086

BROWN, ARLENE PATRICIA THERESA, artist; b. Elizabeth, N.J., Jan. 3, 1953; d. William J. and Adelaide Elizabeth (Von Krasa) B.; student Union Coll., 1971; B.A., Kean Coll., 1980. Owner, pres. Reni Co., Roselle, N.J., 1979—; pvt. tchr. art, Roselle, 1979—; owner Twinks, trademarked dolls and toys. Mem. Am. Women's Econ. Devel. Assn., 1979-83. Recipient 3d Pl. award Custom Car and Van Show, Meadowlands, N.J., 1981, 2d Pl. award Custom Car and Van Show, Asbury Park, N.J. Mem. Graphic Artists Guild, Artists' Equity Assn., Summit Art Assn., Found. Christian Living, Positive Thinkers Club, N.J. Art Dirs. Club, Nat. Assn. Painters in Acrylic and Caseins, Westfield Art Assn., Princeton Art Assn., Alumni Assn. Kean Coll. Patentee in field. Address: PO Box 186 Roselle Park NJ 07204

BROWN, AYLA SALIHA, investment broker, real estate consultant; b. Izmir, Turkey, Jan. 10, 1939; d. Kadri and Bedia Celikoglu; children—James Kadri, Kurt Richard. Grad. Am. Acad. for Girls, 1957; cert. Allan Hancock Coll., 1978. Exec. sec. U.S. Air Force, Ankara, Turkey, 1957-59, Tripoli, Libya, 1959-60; real estate broker Bill Tayon Realty, Belleville, Ill., 1973-75; real estate broker, mgr., cons. Century 21 Armstrong, Lompoc, Calif., 1976-82; mgr. land devel. and subdivs. Century 21 Armstrong (8 offices), Central Coast, Calif., 1983—; pres. Ayla Brown, Inc. Real Estate Cons. Firm, Lompoc, 1979—. Named Top Overall salesman Century 21 Region I, 1980, recipient Achievement in Mgmt. award, 1979. Mem. Nat. Assn. Realtors (cert. comml. investment mem.), Realtors Nat. Mktg. Inst., Real Estate Securities & Syndications Inst., Calif. Assn. Realtors, Lompoc Valley Bd. Realtors (dir. and membership chmn., polit. actions chmn. 1976—, pres. 1985), Century 21 Investment Soc. (membership chmn. 1981-82), Century 21 Six Million Dollar Club, Real Estate Cert. Inst., Lompoc Valley Contractors Assn. (legis. chmn.). Office: 701 E North Ave Suite D Lompoc CA 93436

BROWN, BARBARA ANN, city official; b. Phila., Oct. 17, 1936; d. Clement George and Patricia (Brown) Saxon; m. Vernon Joel Brown, Jan. 10, 1958; children—Vernon Joel, Jr., Arthur George. Grad. high sch., Phila. Registered tax collector. Office mgr. Loop Cold Storage Co., San Antonio, 1966-73; city sec. City of Floresville, Tex., 1973—. Pub. info. com. Am. Cancer Soc., Floresville, 1984—. Mem. Tex. Assn. Assessing Officers, Assn. City Clks. and Secs. of Tex., Internat. Inst. Mcpl. Clks., Refrigeration Service Engrs. Soc Aux. (treas. 1983-84). Lodge: Eastern Star (Worthy Matron 1982-83, 84-85), Avocations: knitting; crocheting; fishing. Office: PO Box 845 1003 C St Floresville TX 78114

BROWN, BARBARA JEAN, gift shop owner; b. Houston, Mar. 9, 1941; d. Ralph Barrett and Martha Jeanette (Burress) Lee; m. Sam J. Brown, III, Aug. 15, 1964 (div. July 1978); children—Sheryl Jean, Samuel Jones IV. B.B.A., Baylor U., 1963. Co-owner, Butterflies Cards & Gifts, Houston, 1978—; co-owner Namesakes Personalized Gifts, Houston, 1984—; ptnr. A Better Idea, Houston, 1980—; dir. Spur Land Co., Houston. Third v.p., then 4th v.p. Houston Jr. Forum, 1973-76, treas., 1976-78. Mem. Nat. Assn. Female Execs. Gift Assn. Am., Nat. Assn. Women Bus. Owners. Republican. Baptist. Home: 11131 Riverview Houston TX 77042 Office: Butterflies Cards & Gifts 2423 Post Oak Blvd Houston TX 77056

BROWN, BARBARA MAXINE, lawyer; b. St. John, Kans., June 29, 1936; d. Charles Robert and Oneida M. (Dawson) Garvin; student Phillips U., Enid, Okla., 1954-56; B.S. in Acctg. cum laude, U. Cin., 1976; J.D., No. Ky. U., 1980; m. Benjamin S. Brown, Aug. 21, 1955 (div. Jan. 1970); children—Candace M., Cynthia A. Acct., Cinderella Cleaners, Forest Park, Ohio, 1970-71; office mgr. High Voltage Systems, Inc., Sharonville, Ohio, 1971-73, Kanter Corp., Forest Park, 1974-75; mgr. corp. acctg. Silco, Inc., Norwood, Ohio, 1976-78; pension account exec. Union Central Life Ins. Co., Forest Park, 1978-81; admitted to Ohio bar, 1980; individual practice law, Cin., 1980—; mem. part-time faculty U. Cin., Mt. St. Joseph Coll., Mt. St. Joe, Ohio. C.P.A., Ohio. Fellow Life Mgmt. Inst.; mem. Am. Bar Assn., Ohio Bar Assn., Cin. Bar Assn., Ohio Soc. C.P.A.s, Delta Mu Delta. Mem. Christian Ch. (Disciples of Christ). Home: 692 Fairborn Rd Cincinnati OH 45240 Office: 650 Northland Blvd Suite 2E Cincinnati OH 45240

BROWN, BARBARA STEIN, environmental scientist; b. Newark, Aug. 5, 1951; d. Louis and Louise (Mumper) Stein; 1 child, Kristin Leigh. Student Am. U., 1969-71; B.S. in Biology, U. Miami, 1976, postgrad.; m. Ralph David Brown, Sept. 9, 1978. Staff scientist Environ. Sci. and Engring., Inc., Miami, 1978—. Mem. Ecol. Soc. Am., Am. Inst. Biol. Scis., Assn. Women in Environ. Professions. Home: 10942 SW 117th St Miami FL 33176 Office: 2822 NW 79th Ave Miami FL 33122

BROWN, BEATRICE, symphony conductor; b. Leeds, Eng., May 17, 1917; came to U.S., 1921, naturalized, 1927; d. Abraham and Sarah (Levinson) B.; B.A., Hunter Coll., 1937; M.A., N.Y.U., 1939; Berkshire Music Center scholar, 1948-49, m. Morris Rothenberg, Jan. 29, 1961. Condr., Chamber Music Assocs., N.Y.C., 1950-53; music dir., condr. Scranton (Pa.) Philharm. Orch., 1963-72, Ridgefield (Conn.) Orch., 1969—, Western Conn. Symphony Orch., Danbury, 1981—, Housatonic Chamber Orch., 1982—; condr. N.Y., N.J., Conn. opera cos.; TV appearances; lectr.; violist symphony orchs., 1944—, Chamber Music Group, Musique Vivante, Am. Symphony Orch., N.Y. Pops Orch., 1979—; instr. music Hunter Coll., 1937-43; tchr. music N.Y.C. Pub. Schs., 1944-61; adj. asst. prof. Lehman Coll., 1972-74, tchr. music Bronx High Sch. Sci., N.Y.C., 1970-79. Recipient Fulbright grant in conducting, 1953-55, Martha Baird Rockefeller grant in conducting, 1957-59, Peace award UN, 1980, Wellington award, 1981; named to Hunter Coll. Hall of Fame, 1972; named One of 100 Disting. Women in Conn., 1976, One of 5 outstanding Women in Ridgefield, Conn., 1979. Mem. Am. Symphony Orch. League (bd. dirs.), Condrs. Guild, Phi Beta Kappa.

BROWN, BEATRICE SANDRA, musicologist, educator, performing arts director; b. Louisville, July 14, 1950. B.M.Ed., U. Louisville, 1972; M.A., Ph.D., Columbia Pacific U., 1986. Music and choral dir. Holy Temple Ch., 1978—; music dir. AC-BAW Ctr. for Arts, 1982-84; dir., music tchr. Holmes elem. Sch., Mt. Vernon, N.Y., 1983-84; performing arts cons. N.Y. State Council for Arts, 1984—; founder, dir. Mt. Vernon African-Am. Music Arts Festival; dir., music dir. Musical Arts of Creative Expression, 1977—; founder, dir. Mus. Arts Inst. Creative Expression for Children, 1986—; choral dir., tchr. music U. Louisville, 1969-75; cons. N.Y. State Council for Arts, 1984—. Recipient letter of award U. Louisville, 1970; Songwriter award Sta. WLOU Radio, Louisville, 1971; cert. U. Louisville, 1974, Appreciation award African-Am. Music Arts Festival Commn., 1984. Mem. Sigma Gamma Rho (hon.). Office: Dir Musical Arts Creative Expression 201 Ravine Ave Suite 7P PO Box 255 Yonkers NY 10701

BROWN, BELVA JEAN, real estate broker; b. Atlantic, Iowa, Aug. 9, 1940; d. Leslie N. and Cecelia M. (Brown) Esbeck; m. William A. Brown, Apr. 17, 1961; children—Bradley Allen, Jody Jean, DeAnn Michelle. Real estate lic. Randall Sch. of Real Estate, Omaha, 1972, brokers lic., 1974. Saleswoman Wurdeman Real Estate, Omaha, 1972-83; owner, operator B. J. Brown & Assocs., Inc., Omaha, 1983—. Mem. Omaha Bd. Realtors (exec. bd. 1985), Omaha Home Builders Assn. Lutheran. Club: Greater Omaha Yacht. Avocations: boating; vacations. Home: Omaha NE 68130 Office: B J Brown & Assocs Inc 13068 Arbor St Omaha NE 68144

BROWN, BEVERLY RENEE, computer hardware distributor company executive; b. Tucson, Aug. 27, 1956; d. Frank F. and L. Nadine (Moody) Hutcheson; m. William Harold Brown, June 7, 1975 (div. June 1981). B.S. in Acctg., U. Ariz., 1982, B.A. in Mgmt. Info. Systems, 1982, B.A. in Phys. Edn., 1982. Systems acct. U. Ariz., Tucson, 1978-82; cons., Phoenix, 1982-83; systems analyst Internat. Data Systems, Phoenix, 1983; field sales systems specialist Hall-Mark Electronics, Phoenix, 1983-85; br. mgr. Elctronic Mktg. Specialist, Phoenix, 1985—. Redevel. adviser Scottsdale Mayor's Spl. Task Force, 1984; fund raising advisor Phoenix Boys Clubs, 1983—; com. chmn. Great Gatsby Gala, 1985—. Fellow Mgmt. Info. Systems Assn. (treas. 1981-82); mem. Nat. Assn. Female Execs., Republican. Methodist. Club: Soroptimist (v.p. 1983—). Avocations: dancing; racketball; skiing; scuba diving; volleyball; reading. Office: Electronic Mktg Specialists 4350 E Camelback #195C Phoenix AZ 85018

BROWN, BILLIE AUGUSTINE, educator; b. Pangburn, Ark., Aug. 1, 1924; d. Prince Colombus and Icy May Wood; m. James A. Brown, Nov. 26, 1969; children by previous marriage—Terry Wood, Dawn Elizabeth, Benjamin McLove, Laura Delphine. B.S. in Edn., Harding Coll., Searcy, Ark., 1962, M.S., 1966; M.A. in Guidance and Counseling, U. Central Ark., 1974. Librarian, White County, Ark. 1947-52; U.S. postal clk., 1954; pub. sch. tchr., 1959—; art specialist Pulaski County (Ark.) Spl. Sch. Dist., 1978-79, instructional coordinator art, 1979—; co-founder, bd. advisers Ark. Young Artists Assn. Democratic committeewoman, 1978-82. Recipient 1st place award in pastel White County Art Show, 1957, 1st place in illus. poetry Ark. Festival Arts, 1973, Patron of Arts award Ark. Young Artists Assn., 1985, Spl. Achievement award Phi Delta Kappa, 1985. Mem. Nat. Art Edn. Assn., Ark. Art Educators, Mid-So. Watercolorists, Ark. for Arts, Pulaski Assn. Classroom Tchrs., Delta Kappa Gamma. Democrat. Baptist. Home: 5302 Dreher Ln Little Rock AR 72209 Office: 1500 Dixon Rd Little Rock AR 72216

BROWN, BONITA STARLIPER, nursing home administrator; b. Winchester, Va., May 26, 1942; d. Howard P. and Margaret E. Starliper; R.N., Winchester Meml. Hosp., 1963; student Lord Fairfax Community Coll., Middletown, Va., Mary Baldwin Coll.; m. Richard F. Brown, Mar. 10, 1962; children—Elizabeth, Christopher. Office nurse, 1963-66; mem. staff Shawnee Springs Nursing Home, Winchester, 1973—, orientation coordinator, shift supr., 1978-81, dir. nursing, asst. adminstr., 1978—; mem. nursing craft adv. com. health occupations Dowell J. Howard Vocat. Sch., Winchester, 1977-79; adj. faculty nursing program Shenandoah Coll., 1980-82; adv. craft com. James Rumsey nursing asst. program Martinsburg (W.Va.) Vocat. Sch., 1978-81; mem. edn. and tng. com. Va. Health Care Assn., 1980-81, membership chmn., 1984—; employee adv. com. Va. Employment Commn., 1980-82; mem. adv. com. Beverly Enterprises, 1984—; mem. health tech. curriculum adv. com. Lord Fairfax Community Coll., 1984—; preceptor bd. examiners for nursing home adminstrs. State of Va., 1984—. Mem. Nat. League Nursing, Am. Coll. Nursing Home Adminstrs., Winchester-Frederick County C. of C., Winchester Women's Civic League, Winchester Bus. and Profl. Women's Club (chmn. Nat.

Bus. Women's Week). Baptist. Address: Route 1 Box 181 Stephenson VA 22656

BROWN, BONNIE LOUISE, state legislator; b. San Francisco, Oct. 5, 1942; d. Wilbert Lauren and Thelma (Asbury) Wonderley; m. Gary Leigh Brown, June 13, 1965; children—Mollie Shannon, Joel Alexander. Student, Oreg. State U., 1962-65, U. Idaho, 1965-69; B.A. in English, Morris Harvey Coll., 1971. Tchr. theatre Morris Harvey Coll., Charleston, W.Va., 1973; legis. coordinator W. Va. Citizen Action Group, Charleston, 1975-76; project dir. Com. for Humanities and Public Policy, Charleston, 1976-77; cons. Appalachian Ednl. Lab., Charleston, 1980; state legislator 23d Dist. Charleston, W.Va., 1982—; lobbyist W.Va. NOW, 1976-82; ERA field organizer, 1978-82. Contbr. articles to profl. jours. Chmn., South Charleston Human Rights Commn., 1976; advisor W.Va. Women's Commn., 1977—. Recipient 1st ann. Susan B. Anthony award, 1980. Mem. Order Women Legislators. Democrat. Home: 2328 Woodland Ave South Charleston WV 25303

BROWN, CAROL ANNE, manufacturers' representative; b. Detroit, Feb. 26, 1947; d. Bruno Walter and Irene Sabina (Derengowski) Siedlarz; student Los Angeles City Coll., 1971, DeAnza Community Coll., 1973; m. Leonard Brown, Apr. 24, 1976; 1 son, David. Sec., Fairchild Semicondrs., Detroit, 1965-69, inside sales rep., Mountain View, Calif., 1969-74; sales rep. Calif. Circuit Engring., Sunnyvale, 1974-76; owner, operator Brown Sales Co., Mission Viejo, Calif., 1976-79; pres., gen. mgr. S.W. Contemporary Sales, Inc., Scottsdale, Ariz., 1979—. Mem. Bus. and Profl. Women Am., Network Female Execs. Republican. Roman Catholic. Home and Office: 12580 N 84th Pl Scottsdale AZ 85260

BROWN, CAROL JEAN, personnel executive; b. Chgo., Mar. 20, 1951; d. Emmett Hiram and Mary Louis (Smith) Brown. B.A., Loyola U., Chgo., 1977. Travel agt. Aloha Hawaii Travel Co., Chgo., 1972-74; claim rep. Travelers Ins. Co., Chgo., 1977-78; registrar Law Sch., Loyola U., Chgo., 1978-81, dir. law placement, 1981-82, non-faculty advisor Black Am. Law Student Assn., 1979-82; hiring coordinator Isham, Lincoln & Beale, Chgo., 1982—: facilitator student leadership workshop Loyola U., Chgo., 1980-81; guest speaker Creighton U. Law Sch., Omaha, 1982, Valparaiso U. Sch. Law (Ind.), 1984. Recipient Service award Loyola U. Sch. Law, 1980. Mem. Nat. Assn. Law Placement (rep., Midwest regional coordinator 1984-85), Nat. Assn. Female Execs. Office: Isham Lincoln & Beale Three First Nat Plaza Chicago IL 60602

BROWN, CAROL OSMAN, writer, photographer, public relations consultant; b. Schenectady, Sept. 28, 1941; d. Sidney A. and Natalie (Charipper) Osman; B.A. in Mass Communications, Ariz. State U., 1963; m. James Carrington Brown III, Nov. 3, 1961; children—James Carrington IV, Bryan Lee. Reporter, Prescott Evening Courier, Ariz. Republic, summer 1960; reporter, photographer Phoenix Gazette, 1961-65; public relations account exec. John S. Turner & Assocs., Phoenix, 1965-66, Patton Agy., Phoenix, 1966-68; free-lance writer, 1961—, free lance photographer, public relations cons., 1968—; mem. faculty Rio Salado Community Coll.; participant Reader's Digest Writers Workshop, 1986. Editor Advt. Dentist Newsletter. Public relations exec. Childbirth Edn. Assn., Phoenix; den mother Cub Scouts, Theodore Roosevelt council Boy Scouts Am., 1978, 80; publicity chmn. Friendship Force, Phoenix; legis. rep. Balsz Sch. Dist., Phoenix, 1980. Named Outstanding Woman Journalist, Ariz. State U., 1962; recipient numerous awards for writing, photography and pub. relations, including Lulu, Los Angeles Advt. Women, 1968 (2); Writing competition winner Reader's Digest, 1979; Ariz. Edn. Assn. writing award, 1980. Mem. Ariz. Press Women (pres. 1985, 1st Pl. Writing award 1974, 75, 76), Nat. Fedn. Press Women (1st Pl. Photography award 1968), Ariz. Authors's Assn., Soc. Children's Book Writers. Republican. Presbyterian. Club: Phoenix Press. Home and Office: 3734 E Campbell St Phoenix AZ 85018

BROWN, CHARLOTTE ANN, apparel and gifts representation company executive; b. Salem, Oreg., May 24, 1945; d. Albert Robert and Hazel Mayo B. B.A., Lewis & Clark U., 1967; M.A, Portland State U., 1971. Publicity coordinator various govt. orgns., 1970-75; mgr. U.S. Postal Service, 1975-83; owner, mgr. Bebetex, Inc., Sausalito, Calif., 1983—. Mem. Am. Fashion Assn., Pacific Northwestern Apparel Assn. Democrat. Avocations: travel to South America; travel writing. Home and office: 1001 Bridgeway Suite 183 Sausalito CA 94965

BROWN, CONNIE YATES, businesswoman; b. Carthage, Mo., Apr. 29, 1947; d. Charles Lee and Eunice Jane (Farmer) Yates; m. Larry Edward Brown, June 19, 1982; 1 step-dau., Tammy Lynn Brown. B.S., Pittsburg State U., 1969. With White Shield Oil and Gas/Petro-Lewis, Tulsa, 1969-74, dept. supt., 1971-74; with Southwestern Bell Telephone Co., 1975-79; owner, mgr. Abbyco, Inc., rental, sales carpet cleaning equipment, Tulsa, 1978—; lectr. in field. Named Rookie of Yr., Tulsa div. Southwestern Bell Yellow Pages, 1976; sales award winner Rug Doctor Licensee of Yr., 1981, 85. Mem. Home Economists in Bus. (treas. Okla. chpt.), Am. Home Econs. Assn., Met. Tulsa C. of C., Equipment Rental Dealers Assn. Eastern Okla., Tulsa Alumnae Panhellenic (dir. scholarships), Phi Upsilon Omicron, Alpha Gamma Delta (nat. dir. alumnae devel. 1984—). Lodge: Order of Rainbow for Girls. Home: 7806 S Evanston Ave Tulsa OK 74136 Office: 8600 S Lewis Ave Tulsa OK 74137

BROWN, DALE SUSAN, government administrator, writer; b. N.Y.C., May 27, 1954; d. Bertram S. and Beatrice Joy (Gilman) B. B.A., Antioch Coll., 1976. Research asst. Am. Occupational Therapy Assn., Rockville, Md., 1976-79; writer Pres.' Com. on Employment of Handicapped, Washington, 1979-82, program mgr., 1982—; writer Am. Rehab. Mag., Washington, 1982—; cons. in field; instr. Open U., Washington, 1978; gen. assembly speaker nat. conv. Gen. Fedn. Women's Clubs, 1981; mem. Rehab. Services Adminstrn. Task Force on Learning Disabilities, 1981—. Author: Steps to Independence for People with Learning Disabilities, 1980; writer film: They Could Have Saved Their Homes, 1982; editorial bd. Perceptions, 1981-83. Pres. Assn. Learning Disabled Adults, Washington, 1979-80; bd. dirs. Closer Look Nat. Info. Ctr., Washington, 1980—. Found. for Children with Learning Disabilities grantee, 1982. Mem. Nat. Network of Learning Disabled Adults (founder, pres. 1980-81), Nat. Assn. Govt. Communicators, Assn. for Children and Adults with Learning Disabilities (bd. dirs. 1986), ALA. Democrat. Jewish. Office: Pres' Com on Employment Handicapped 1111 20th St NW Room 600 Washington DC 20036

BROWN, DALTHEA DENISE, physical therapist; b. Tallahassee, Oct. 8, 1956; d. Willie, Jr., and Carrie M. (Roberts) B. Student Montclair State Coll., 1974-76; B.S. in Phys. Therapy, U. Pitts., 1978. Lic. phys. therapist. Phys. therapist Riverview, Red Bank, N.J., 1978-80, United Cerebral Palsy, Bricktown, N.J., 1980-81, Bayshore Community Hosp., Holmdell, N.J., 1981-83, Ocean Physiotherapy Ctr., Neptune City, N.J., 1983-85; contract phys. therapist Early Intervention Program, Tinton Falls, N.J., 1984—, United Cerebral Palsy, Long Branch, N.J., 1985—, pvt. practice and home care, Monmouth County, N.J., 1985—. Mem. Am. Phys. Therapy Assn. Avocations: sports; community theater. Home: 2017 W Bangs Ave Neptune NJ 07753 Office: United Cerebral Palsy 75 Bath Ave Long Branch NJ 07740

BROWN, DARMAE JUDD, librarian; b. Jefferson City, Mo., Sept. 14, 1952; d. William Robert and Dorothy Judd (Curtis) B. B.A., W.Va. Wesleyan Coll., 1974; M.A., U. Denver, 1975; postgrad. Odessa Coll., 1982-84, U. No. Iowa, 1984—. Organist numerous chs. in Md., W.Va., Colo., Tex., 1969-84, St. Barnabas Episcopal Chapel, Odessa, 1981-84; searching assoc. Bibliog. Center for Research, Denver, 1975-76; librarian N.E. Colo. Regional Library, Wray, 1976-81; head tech. services Ector County Library, Odessa, Tex., 1981-84, Waterloo Pub. Library, Iowa, 1984—. Mem. ALA, Iowa Library Assn., Library and Info. Tech. Assn., Iowa OCLC Users Group (pres. 1986-87), Beta Phi Mu, Sigma Alpha Iota. Home: 1143 Lantern Sq #12 Waterloo IA 50701-5746

BROWN, DEBORAH ANN, economist, small business consultant; b. Falfurrias, Tex., Oct. 28, 1957; d. Paul Douglas and R. Gale (O'Keefe) Brown. B.S. in Econs., Tex. Woman's U., 1979, M.B.A., 1986. Economist Bur. Labor Stats., Dallas, 1978—. Mem. fin. com. Lakewood United Methodist Ch., 1985—, co-treas., 1986. Mem. Bus. and Profl. Women-Dallas (chairperson individual devel. program 1982, young career woman program 1986-87; Young Career Woman award 1986), Federally Employed Women (agy. rep.), Nat. Assn. Female Execs., Dallas Hispanic C. of C., Internat. Assn. Personnel in Employment Security, Thorstein Veblein Soc. Office: Bur Labor Statistics Federal Bldg 525 Griffin Room 221 Dallas TX 75202

BROWN, DEBORAH ANNE, publications manager; b. Altoona, Pa., Feb. 12, 1953; d. Abraham Samuel and Lula Mary (Nassif) Brown. B.S., Towson State U., 1971-75. Membership coordinator Nat. Assn. Plumbing, Heating and Cooling Contractors, Washington, 1975-76; publs. supr. Exec. Enterprise Publs. Co., Inc. N.Y.C., 1976-78, publs. ops. mgr., 1978—. nat. officer, coordinator for N.Am. council Youth Movement: SOYO, 1972-82, pres. Eastern region, 1978-80; treas. Ridge Chorale Inc., Bklyn., 1981-84; del. Bay Ridge Community Council, Bklyn., 1982-84. Md. Senatorial scholar Towson State U., 1971-75. Republican. Eastern Orthodox.

BROWN, DEBORAH ELAINE, research services company executive; b. St. Joseph, Mo., Mar. 1, 1956; d. Warren Hugh and Donna Jean (Dunken) Wright; m. David John German, May 9, 1979; children—Kathleen Colette, Amanda Wright. B.B.A., U. Wash., 1978. Mgr., Peppermill Restaurant, Houston, 1978-80; dir. Ark Children's Ctr., Houston, 1981-82, Nat. Child Care, Inc., Houston, 1982-83; owner/pres. Brown Research Services, Houston, 1982—, Tex. Photo, 1984—, Double D Enterprises, 1984—. Leader, San Jacinto Girl Scouts U.S.A., 1982-83. Mem. Houston Area Assn. for Edn. of Young Children, Small Bus. Owners Assn. Democrat. Home: 13006 Harwin St Houston TX 77072 Office: PO Box 770653 Houston TX 77215

BROWN, DEBORAH SHARON, oil company official; b. Shamokia, Pa., Feb. 6, 1955; d. John M. and Gloria Ann (Leshinski) Miller. A.A. in Bus., Brandywine Coll., 1975; B.S. in Bus. Mgmt., U. Md., 1978; M.S. in Bus. Communication, Am. U., 1978. Adminstr., Pentagon, Arlington, Va., 1975-77; press officer FDA, Washington, 1977-79; sr. bus. analyst Shell Oil Co., Houston, 1979-83, supr., 1983—; dir., sec. Tex. Ozonator, Houston, 1982-84. Mem. Assn. Info. Processors, Nat. Assn. for Female Execs. Office: Shell Oil Co 200 N Dairy Ashford PO Box 2906 Houston TX 77252

BROWN, DENISE SCOTT (MRS. ROBERT VENTURI), architect, urban planner; b. Nkana Zambia, Oct. 3, 1931; came to U.S., 1958, naturalized, 1971; d. Simon and Phyllis (Hepker) Lakofski; m. Robert Scott Brown, July 21, 1955 (dec. 1959); m. Robert Charles Venturi, July 23, 1967; 1 child, James C. Student U. Witwatersrand, South Africa, 1948-51; A.A. Dipl., Archtl. Assn., London, 1955; M.City Planning, U. Pa., 1960, M.Arch., 1965; D.F.A. (hon.), Oberlin Coll., 1977, Phila. Coll. Art, 1985, Parsons Sch. Design, 1985; D.H.L. (hon.), N.J. Inst. Tech., 1984. Registered architect, U.K. Asst. prof. Sch. Fine Arts, U.Pa., Phila., 1960-65; assoc. prof., head urban design program UCLA, 1965-68; vis. prof. Yale U., New Haven, 1967-70, fellow Morse Coll., 1970; vis. prof. U. Pa., 1982, 83; with Venturi, Rauch & Scott Brown, Phila., 1967—; mem. adv. com. MIT, 1973-83, dept. architecture Temple U., Phila., 1980—; mem. policy panel, design arts program Nat. Endowment Arts, 1981-83. Co-author: Learning from Las Vegas (Recognition award Nat. Endowment Arts), 1972, rev., 1977; A View from the Campidoglio: Selected Essays, 1953-1984, 1985. Contbr. articles to profl. jours. Works include: plans for City Edges-Schuylkill River Corridor, Phila. (Recognition award Nat. Endowment Arts), 1974; The Strand, Galveston, Tex. (Recognition award Nat. Endowment Arts), 1975; Franklin Court, Independence Nat. Hist. Park, Phila. (Fed. Design Achievement award U.S. Govt.), 1976. Jim Thorpe, Pa. (citation Progressive Architecture mag., commendation Pa. Hist. and Mus. Commn.), 1979; Washington Ave., City of Miami Beach (spl. mention HUD Nat. Awards), 1979; Crosstown Community (1968) and Old City, Phila. (Honor award HUD Nat. Awards), 1979; Borough of Princeton, N.J., 1980, Republic Sq. Dist., Austin, 1984; Center City, Memphis, 1985. Bd. dirs. Central Phila. Devel. Corp., 1985—; mem. Pa. Capitol Preservation Com., 1983—; mem. curriculum and adult edn. com. Phila. Jewish Children's Folkshul, 1980—. Recipient numerous profl. awards. Mem. Royal Inst. Brit. Architects, Am. Planning Assn., Archtl. Assn. (London), Alliance of Women in Architecture, Soc. Archtl. Historians (bd. dirs. 1981-84). Democrat. Jewish. Office: Venturi Rauch & Scott Brown 4236 Main St Philadelphia PA 19127

BROWN, DIANA LYNN, advertising agency executive; b. Grosse Point, Mich., Sept. 13, 1944; d. Samuel L. and Billie (Moss) Brown; m. John W. Thompson, June 18, 1980 (div. 1982). Student Columbia U., 1970-71. Sec. Lin Broadcasting Corp., Nashville, 1964-66; appearance coordinator Miss Teenage America Pageant, Dallas, 1966-69; media buyer, dir. Noble-Dury Advt. Agy., Nashville, 1971-73; media dir. Buntin Advt., Nashville, 1973-79; pres. D. L. Brown Media Services, Inc., Nashville, 1979—; advt. media cons. Mondale Presdl. Campaign, 1984. Active Am. Cancer Soc., Nashville, 1976-79, Am. Heart Assn., 1976-79; hon. sgt.-at-arms Tenn. Ho. of Reps., 1973. Recipient Silver medal as Advt. Person of Year, 1982. Mem. Nashville Advt. Fedn. (pres. 1981-82), Am. Women in Radio and TV. Republican. Office: DL Brown Media Services Inc 460 10th Crícle Nashville TN 37203

BROWN, DINAH LEE, counselor, teacher; b. Houston, Feb. 27, 1933; d. John G. and Bonnie M. (Van Pool) B. A.A., Miami Dade Jr. Coll., 1968; B.Ed., U. Miami (Fla.), 1971, M. Ed., 1975. Cert. tchr., Tex., Fla. With Exxon, 1962-65; tchr., counselor Dade County Sch., Miami, 1971-75, Briarwood Sch., Houston, 1975-78; counselor M.D. Anderson Hosp., Houston, 1978-83; pvt. practice counseling, Houston, 1983—; cons. Fla. Hosp. Assn., La. Hosp. Assn., Sisters of Charity Hosp. Served with USAF, 1951-53. Mem. Am. Personnel and Guidance Assn., Council for Exceptional Children, Nat. Assn. Female Execs., Epsilon Tau Lambda. Republican. Episcopalian. Home: 7630 Fawn Terrace Dr Houston TX 77071 Office: 900 Lovett Blvd Houston TX 77006

BROWN, EDITH, community development agency administrator; b. Milw., Nov. 25, 1935; d. Anton J. and Elizabeth K. (Kribitsch) Volk; m. Edward S. Brown. B.S., U. Wis., 1958, M. Social Work, 1964; M.S. in Mgmt., Cardinal Stritch Coll., Milw., 1985. Hosp. admissions worker, 1958-60; welfare worker, 1960-62; with Kiwanis Children's Ctr. and Children's Hosp. Psychiat. Clinic, Milw., 1962-64; social worker Luth. Social Services, Milw., 1964-67; foster care supr. Milw. County Dept. Social Service, Child Protection and Parent Services, Comprehensive Emergency Services and Coordinated Community Edn. and Support Services, 1967-71, social services adminstr., 1971-79; assoc. dir. Community Devl. Agy., City of Milw., 1979—; tech. advisor for child abuse, neglect, woman abuse, domestic violence; grantwriter, tchr., cons. in field. Mem. Summerfest adv. council, Mayor's Beautification com., chmn. Summerfest Planting, 1972—; chmn. Milw. County Child Abuse and Neglect Task Force, 1976-78; chmn. adv. council Milw. Boy's Club, 1981-84; vice chmn. Internat. Yr. for Disabled Persons, 1982; liaison Nat. Yr. for Disabled Persons, City of Milw., 1982-83; mem. Mayor's Youth Initiatives Task Force, 1984-85; mem. U. Wis. M.P.A. adv. panel, 1984—. Recipient grad. scholarship Office of Vocat. Rehab., 1962-64; Successful Women in Mgmt. award U. Wis., 1977; award Community Tchrs. Corps, 1977; Changemaker award Wis. Fed. Jr. Women's Clubs, 1978; Outstanding Community Services award Milw. County, 1979, Outstanding Services award, 1979, Exemplary Service award, 1982; Women of Yr. award Mcpl. Women's Assn., 1981; Exceptional Vol. award Milw. Boys and Girls Club, 1985. Mem. Acad. Cert. Social Workers, Nat. Assn. Social Workers, Internat. Council on Social Welfare, Internat. Fedn. Social Welfare, Am. Soc. for Pub. Adminstrn. (pres. Milw. chpt.; outstanding service and dedication award 1984-85), Research Clearinghouse, Am. Bus. Women's Assn. (Women of Yr. award 1975), Internat. Graphoanalysis Soc. (pres. Wis. chpt.). Tech. contbr. to profl., community, resource documents, 1971—; author print and broadcast programs. Office: Community Devel Agency 200 E Wells St Milwaukee WI 53202

BROWN, ELIZABETH MYERS, publishing company executive; b. Bklyn., Dec. 31, 1915; d. Garry Cleveland and Caroline (Clark) Myers; B.S., Cornell U., 1937; M.A., Case Western Res. U., 1960; m. Kent Louis Brown, June 26, 1940; children—Karen Elizabeth (Mrs. Lyman Anders Johnson), Kent Louis, David Stuart, Garry Myers. Tchr., Walden, N.Y., 1937-38, Auburn, N.Y., 1938-39, Cleveland Heights, Ohio, 1939-40; asst. Erie County (N.Y.) home demonstration agt. govt. extension service Cornell U., Ithaca, N.Y., 1940-42; editorial asst. Highlights for Children, Columbus, Ohio, 1962-64, asst. editor, 1964-66, assoc. editor, 1966—, asst. sec., 1968—, dir., 1960—; dir. Zaner-Bloser Co., 1972—; dir. Skillcorp Pubs., Inc. Mem. Metro Writers Workshop, 1970—; trustee New Day Press, 1972-79 (both Cleve.). Bd. dirs. Fedn. Cornell Women's Clubs, 1955-57, pres. Cornell Women's Club Cleve., 1953-55; bd. dirs. Nutrition Assn. Greater Cleve., 1964-68; trustee YWCA, Westfield, N.J., 1985—. Mem. Women's Assn. for Continuing Edn. (treas. 1959-61, pres. 1961-63), Women's Aux. Acad. Med. of Cleve. (pres. 1969-70), Ohio Med. Assn. Aux. (chmn. mems.-at-large com. 1970-71, mem. state bd. 1970-71, 75-77, dist. dir. 1975-77), Women's Nat. Book Assn. (dir. Cleve. chpt. 1978-82), Am. Soc. Mag. Editors. Home: 148 S Portage St Westfield NJ 14787 Office: 803 Church St Honesdale PA 18431

BROWN, ELLEN RUTH, theoretical physicist; b. N.Y.C., June 15, 1947; d. Aaron Joseph and Grace (Presser) Brown; B.S., Mary Washington Coll., 1969; M.S., Pa. State U., 1971; Ph.D. (Govs. fellow), U.Va., 1981. Physicist, Naval Weapons Lab., Dahlgren, Va., 1969; instr. physics Lord Fairfax Community Coll., Middletown, Va., 1971-74; summer faculty fellow NASA, Langley, Va., 1974-75; engr. EG&G Washington Analytical Services Center, Dahlgren, Va., 1979—, head dept. analysis and evaluation, 1982—; v.p. Windy Knoll Enterprises, Inc., Magnolia, Tex., 1981—. First violinist Community Coll. Orch., Fredericksburg, Va., 1981—; mem. North Ferry Farms Civic Assn., 1979—. NSF Summer Sci. Faculty fellow, 1973; IEEE Summer Sci. Faculty fellow NASA, 1974-75. Mem. Am. Assn. Physics Tchrs., Am. Phys. Soc., Sigma Xi. Club: Barry Lee Bressler Science (pres.). Home: PO Box 1397 Fredericksburg VA 22402 Office: EG&G PO Box 552 Dahlgren VA 22448

BROWN, ELLEN STOUDEMIRE, coin machine company executive; b. Columbia, S.C., Jan. 20, 1941; d. George Woodrow and Ruby Mae (Marsh) Stoudemire; m. Paul Albert Rogers, Jr., June 24, 1961 (div. May 1973); m. Charlie Watson Brown, Jr., Jan. 27, 1979; 1 stepchild, Joseph E. Brown. Assoc. Secretarial Sci., Newberry Coll., 1961. Exec. and membership sec. Golf Course Supts. Am., Jacksonville Beach, Fla., 1963-65; exec. sec. Phillip Morris, Inc., Jacksonville, 1965-72, U. North Fla., Jacksonville, 1973-75, S.C. Amusement Co., Inc., Summerville, S.C., 1976-77; pres., sec. Sea Coast Music Co., Inc., Summerville, 1977—. Mem. S.C. Coin Operators Assn., Amusement and Music Operators Assn. Republican. Methodist. Avocations: cross stitch; crochet; antique china; cooking; bowling. Address: 1113 W Dorchester Rd Summerville SC 29483

BROWN, EVA DONALDA AMUNDSON, civic worker; b. Langdon, N.D., Apr. 23, 1911; d. Elmer Fritjof and Alma Julia (Nelson) Hultin; m. Leif Amundson, Mar. 1, 1929 (dec. 1974); children—Constance, Eleanor, Ardis, Priscilla. Bd. dirs. Opportunity Workshop, Missoula, Mont., 1950—, Rockmont Group Homes, Missoula, 1976—, Bethany L'Arche (group home for girls), 1976—; mem. Missoula Sr. Citizen's Ctr., 1980-82, pres., 1982-85; tchr. Norwegian cooking and baking, 1954-56, Norweigan Rosemaling, 1975-79; treas. Sacakawea Homemakers Club, 1979-81; mem. Am. Luth. Ch. Women St. Pauls' Lutheran Ch., 1951—; active Easter Seal Program, Heart Fund, March of Dimes, United Way, Campfire Girls; mem. adv. council Area Agy. on Aging, Missoula, 1984—. Recipient Outstanding Sr. award Missoula Jr. C. of C., 1984. Mem. Sons. of Norway. Club: Orchard Homes Country (mem. art judging com.). Lodges: Order of Eastern Star, Elks. Avocations: rosemaling; oil painting; poetry. Home: 324 Kensington Ave Missoula MT 59801

BROWN, GAYLE PATRICIA, software consultant; b. Pitts., Aug. 17, 1961; d. William Roger and Betty Lou (Jones) Brown. B.A., Thiel Coll., Pa., 1983. Documentation coordinator Adventure Internat., Longwood, Fla., 1983-84; head tech. writer Armor Systems Inc., Maitland, Fla., 1984-85; head tech. writer Am. Fin. Industries, Orlando, Fla., 1985; ind. cons. in software, Orlando, 1986—. Vol., Missing Children Ctr., Longwood, Fla., 1985—. Mem. Nat. Orgn. Female Execs., Sigma Kappa Alumnae Assn. Republican. Presbyterian. Avocations: stained glass art; reading; modern dance.

BROWN, GERALDINE REED, lawyer; b. Los Angeles, Feb. 18, 1947; d. William Penn and Alberta Vernice (Coleman) Reed; m. Ronald Wellington Brown, Aug. 20, 1972; children—Kimberly Diana, Michael David. B.A. summa cum laude, Fisk U., 1968; J.D., Harvard U., 1971, M.B.A., 1973. Bar: N.Y. 1974, U.S. Dist. Ct. (so. and ea. dists.) N.Y. 1974, U.S. Ct. Appeals (2d cir.) 1974, U.S. Supreme Ct. 1977. Assoc. White & Case, N.Y.C., 1973-78; atty. J.C. Penney Co., Inc., N.Y.C., 1978—. Bd. dirs. Council Concerned Black Execs., N.Y.C., 1977—, Studio Mus. in Harlem, N.Y.C., 1980-81. Mem. Women's Econ. Roundtable, Harvard Bus. Sch. Club, Harvard Law Sch. Assn., Coalition 100 Black Women, ABA (mem. several coms. of sect. corp., banking and bus. law, sect. internat. law and practice), Assn. Bar City N.Y. (corp. law com. 1978-81), N.Y. County Lawyers Assn. (corp. law com.), N.Y. State Bar Assn. (mem. exec. com. corp. counsel sect., chmn. com. on SEC, fin., corp. law and governance), N.Y. Women's Bar Assn., Harvard Bus. Sch. Black Alumni Assn., Harvard Law Sch. Black Alumni Assn., Phi Beta Kappa, Delta Sigma Theta. Club: Harvard (N.Y.C.). Home: 180 Union St Montclair NJ 07042 Office: JC Penney Co Inc 1301 Ave of Americas New York NY 10019

BROWN, GERTRUDE S., library director, interior designer; b. N.Y.C., July 21, 1935; d. Samuel E. and Frances I. (Levine) Scheff; m. Julius I. Brown, June 17, 1956; children—Cathy, Susan. Student Bennington Coll., 1952-53; B.A., NYU, 1956; cert. N.Y. Sch. Interior Design, 1964; M.L.S., L.I.U., 1969. Interior designer Trudy Brown Interiors, Roslyn Heights, N.Y., 1965—; head. pub. services Commack (N.Y.) Pub. Library, 1970-74; coordinator children's services Manhasset (N.Y.) Pub. Library, 1974-77; dir. Harborfields Pub. Library, Greenlawn, N.Y., 1977—; cons. interior design various libraries on L.I., 1970—; guest lectr. Palmer Grad. Library Sch., Greenvale, N.Y., 1975-76. Mem. Roslyn Country Club Civic Assn., Roslyn Heights, N.Y., 1973—; mem. Reconstructionist Synagogue of North Shore. Mem. ALA, N.Y. Library Assn., Suffolk County Library Assn., Children's Librarian's Assn. Suffolk County (pres. 1973-74), Pub. Library Dirs. Assn. (sec. (1984-85), North Shore Univ. Hosp. Aux. (life). Office: Harborfields Pub Library 31 Broadway Greenlawn NY 11740

BROWN, GLENDA ANN WALTERS, ballet director; b. Buna, Tex., July 22, 1937; d. Jesse Olaf and Kathryn Jeanette (Rogers) Walters; m. David Dann Brown, Dec. 13, 1958; children—Kathryn Jean, Vanessa Lea. Grad. high sch., Beaumont, Tex. Asst. tchr. Widman Sch., Beaumont, 1952-55; owner, tchr. Walters Sch. of Dance, Jasper, Tex., 1955-59; assoc. tchr. Emmamae Horn Sch., Houston, 1964-81; owner, tchr. Allegro Acad., Houston, 1981—; assoc. dir. Allegro Ballet, Houston, 1974-81, artistic dir., 1981—. Mem. dance panel Cultural Arts Council, Houston, 1979; sec. Riedel Estates Civic Club, Houston, 1975-78; Republican poll worker, Houston, 1970-81. Mem. Dance Masters Am. (exam. chmn. chpt. 3 1980—), Southwestern Regional Ballet Assn. (exec. v.p. 1981—), Nat. Assn. Regional Ballet (bd. dirs. 1983—), Methodist. Avocations: camping; singing; golf; travelling. Office: Allegro Acad of Dance 1801 Dairy Ashford Suite 130 Houston TX 77077

BROWN, GLENDA CAROL, insurance agent; b. Jackson, Miss., June 30, 1949; d. Troy Snow and Bonnie Glebn (Gill) B., Jr. A.A. in Radio and TV, Marjorie Webster Jr. Coll., 1969; B.A. in Radio and TV, U. Md., 1974; M.A. in Bus. Mgmt. and Supervision, Central Mich. U., 1975. Adminstrv. asst. Dept. Navy (NTDA), Washington, 1970-78; tech., writer, editor VSE Engring., Alexandria, Va., 1979; agt. Aetna Life Ins. Co., McLean, Va., 1979-84; ind. ins. agt. various ins. cos., Washington, 1985; gen. agt. Western Fidelity Ins. Co., Washington, 1985—; real estate agt. Mount Vernon Realty, Vienna, Va. Mem. Nat. Assn. Female Execs., D.C. Assn. Life Underwriters, Profl. Ins. Agts., Arlington C. of C., No. Va. Bd. Realtors. Avocations: reading; piano; tennis; ice skating; physical fitness. Home: 8522 Raglan Rd Vienna VA 22180 Office: 8522 Raglan Rd Vienna VA 22180

BROWN, GWEN ODELL, marketing representative; b. Ryan, Okla., July 31, 1941; d. Hubert Curtis and Eula Mae (Smith) Mays; m. Charles L. Brown, Dec. 23, 1961; children—Sammie, Melinda, Candice. Personnel asst. Mongomery Ward Co., Dallas, 1966-71; banking officer First City Bank, Lewisville, Tex., 1972-80; mktg. dir. Tex. Title Co., Lewisville, 1980-81; adminstrv. asst. to pres. CATV Systems, Lewisville, 1981-82; mktg. rep. Grandy's Country Cookin', Lewisville, 1982—. Contbr. poetry to publs. Chmn. Mothers' March, March Dimes, Lewisville, Carrollton, Tex., 1967-72; bd. dirs. United Way, 1980-82; bus. chmn. Heart Fund, 1972-73; bd. advisors Vocat. Edn. Program, Lewisville Sch. Dist., 1980-81; liaison adv. bd. Lewisville Meml. Hosp., 1978-80; bd. advisors Cancer Soc., 1972-74. Mem. Lewisville C. of C. (life, bd. dirs. sec.-treas. 1974-80), Am. Inst. Banking (bd. govs. Denton County 1974-75). Lodge: Soroptimist Internat. (sec.-treas. 1978-79). Mem. First Christian Ch. Home 1912 Ruidoso Run Lewisville TX 75067

BROWN, HELEN GURLEY, author, editor; b. Green Forest, Ark., Feb. 18, 1922; d. Ira M. and Cleo (Sisco) Gurley; student Tex. State Coll. for Women, 1939-41, Woodbury Coll., 1942; m. David Brown, Sept. 25, 1959. Exec. sec. Music Corp. Am., 1942-45, William Morris Agy., 1945-47; copywriter Foote, Cone & Belding, Los Angeles, 1948-58; advt. writer, account exec. Kenyon & Eckhardt, Hollywood, Calif., 1958-62; editor-in-chief Cosmopolitan mag., 1965—, editorial dir. Brit. edit., 1972—, also 13 other overseas edits.; supervising editor EYE mag., 1967-68. Recipient Francis Holmes Achievement award for outstanding work in advt., 1956-59, Disting. Achievement award U. So. Calif. Sch. Journalism, 1971, ann. awards Am. Newspaperwomen's Assn.,

1972, Am. Soc. Journalism Sch. Adminstrs., 1972, Disting. Achievement award in journalism, hon. alumnus Stanford U., 1977. Mem. Authors League Am., AFTRA, Am. Soc. Mag. Editors, Eta Upsilon Gamma. Author: Sex and the Single Girl, 1962; Sex and the Office, 1965; The Outrageous Opinions of Helen Gurley Brown, 1967; Helen Gurley Brown's Single Girl Cookbook, 1969; Sex and the New Single Girl, 1970; Having It All, 1982. Home: 1 W 81st St New York NY 10024 Office: Hearst Corp 224 W 57th St New York NY 10019

BROWN, J'AMY MARONEY, journalist; b. Los Angeles, Oct. 30, 1945; d. Roland Francis and Jeanne (Wilbur) Maroney; m. James Raphael Brown, Jr., Nov. 5, 1967 (dec. July 1982); children—James Roland Francis, Jeanne Raphael. B.A., U. So. Calif., 1967. Reporter Los Angeles Herald Examiner, 1966-67, Lewisville Leader, Dallas, 1980-81; editor First Person Mag., Dallas, 1981-82; journalism dir. Pacific Palisades Sch., Los Angeles, 1983-84; freelance reporter, 1984—. Auction chmn. Assn. Pub. Broadcasting, Houston, 1974, 75; vice chmn. Dallas Arts Council, 1976-80; vice chmn. Met. March of Dimes, Dallas, 1980-82; del. Dallas Council PTAs, 1976-80. Recipient UPI Editors award for investigative reporting, 1981. Mem. Women Meeting Women, Women in Communications, Am. Bus. Women's Assn. Republican. Roman Catholic. Home: 13101 Nimrod Pl Los Angeles CA 90049

BROWN, JANE PRESCOTT, county official; b. Chgo., Jan. 24, 1933; d. James Connor and Eunice (Lyons) Prescott; m. Jerome Howard Brown, Mar. 1, 1952; children—Christine, Stephen, Lynn. B.A., Governors State U., 1975, M.A., 1976; Ph.D., Kensington U., 1983. Tchr. Young Men's Jewish Council, Chgo., 1956-72; dir. day care South Shore Community Ctr., Chgo., 1972-75, exec. dir., 1975-78; dir. day care/child devel. Community and Econ. Devel. Assn. Cook County, Inc., Chgo., 1978-81, dir. social services, 1981-83, dir. resource devel. and interagy. relations, 1983-84; owner McDonald's franchise; pres. JPB Enterprises; cons. Nat. Coll. Edn., Chgo., 1978-79, Kirshner & Assocs., Chgo., 1978-79; instr. Prairie State Coll., Chicago Heights, Ill., 1980-82. Author: Resources and Activities for Parents, 1976; Parents as Volunteers, 1978. Bd. dirs. Chinese Am. Service League, 1979—, Suburban Cook County Area Agy. Aging, Chgo. Jobs for Youth, Nat. Black Child Devel. Inst., St. Bernard Hosp. Recipient award South Shore Community Ctr., 1975; McDonald's Gold Hat award. named Boss of Yr., Community and Econ. Devel. Assn. Cook County, 1980; Phi Delta Kappa vis. scholar, 1984. Mem. Ill. Head Start/Day Care Assn. (pres. 1979-81, award for service), Region V Headstart Assn. (pres. 1980-82, bd. dirs. 1984), Suburban Cook County Area Agy. on Aging, South Shore Ministerial Assn. (council, community service award 1978), South Side Dirs. Assn. (pres. 1974-76), Black McDonald Owners Assn., Alpha Kappa Alpha. Democrat. Roman Catholic. Clubs: South Suburban Links (v.p. 1979-82) (Chgo.), Jack and Jill Am. (v.p. 1968-73) (Chgo.). Home: 17906 Tarpon Ct Homewood IL 60430

BROWN, JANET C., lawyer; b. Balt., Mar. 16, 1927. B.A., Wellesley Coll., 1949; LL.B., Yale U., 1952. Bar: N.Y. 1953. Ptnr. Chadbourne, Park, Whiteside & Wolff, N.Y.C. Mem. N.Y. State Bar Assn., N.Y. County Lawyers Assn., ABA. Address: Chadbourne Parke Whiteside & Wolff 30 Rockefeller Plaza New York NY 10112

BROWN, JANET LEE, defense electronics company executive; b. Elmhurst, Ill., Nov. 3, 1951; d. John Richard and Doris Mae (Corlew) B. B.S.B.A. cum laude, U. Wis., 1982; M.B.A., U. Ill.-Chgo., 1985. Dir. Goodwill Industries, Racine, Wis., 1974-82; supr. U.S. Dist. Ct., Chgo., 1983; fellow, research asst. U. Ill.-Chgo., 1983-84; analyst Northrop Corp. DSD, Rolling Meadows, Ill., 1984—; cons., trainer numerous orgns. and profl. assns., 1977—. Contbr. poetry to Chime, 1983. Cons., advocate Soc.'s Assets, Inc., Racine, 1976-77; deacon Bellwood P Presbyterian Ch., Ill., 1986, tchr., 1982-83, youth fellowship leader, 1982-83. Mem. Chgo. Council Fgn. Relations, Am. Mktg. Assn., Product Devel. and Mgmt. Assn., Phi Kappa Phi, Alpha Mu Alpha. Democrat. Avocations: poetry; computers; singing; rafting; canoeing.

BROWN, JO GIESE, television reporter, author, producer; b. Seattle, Jan. 14, 1947; d. James Albert and Gladys (Kenney) Giese; m. Barry K. Brown, Dec. 19, 1975. B.A., U. Tex., 1968. News and feature writer The Houston Post, 1969; editor-in-chief The Designer, N.Y.C., 1969-71; assoc. producer Brillig Prodns., N.Y.C., 1971; assoc. producer Sta. WNET-TV, N.Y.C., 1975-79; producer/writer/on-camera news reporter News Center 4, WNBC; consumer reporter nationally syndicated TV show, 1980-81; curator Mus. Am. Folk Art and Fashion Inst. Tech., N.Y.C., 1981; host Sta. CBS Cable, 1981; consumer food editor nationally syndicated TV show, 1982, Cable Health Network, 1982. Mem. Soc. Profl. Journalists, Soc. Nutrition Edn., Writers Guild Am., AFTRA, Women in Film. Author: The Good Food Compendium, 1981; Naked, 1984. Office: 228 Main St Venice CA 90291

BROWN, J(OAN) DEVON, lawyer; b. Stockton, Calif., Nov. 12, 1953; d. Nat and Laurie (Edwards) B. B.A. in Psychology, U. Calif.-Santa Cruz, 1975; M.A. in Criminal Justice, Calif. State U.-Sacramento, 1977; cert. in legal investigation Calif. Western Sch. Law, San Diego, 1978, J.D., 1979; postgrad. in bus. Bar: Calif. 1979, U.S. Dist. Ct. (so. dist.) Calif. 1979, U.S. Dist. Ct. (no. dist.) Calif. 1984; U.S. Ct. Appeals 1984. lic. in real estate, Calif. Legal intern Legal Services Project, San Diego, 1978, San Diego County Bd. Suprs., 1978; law clk. Office of G. Randolph Wright, San Diego, 1979, assoc., 1979; environ.-legal research atty. ballistic missile div. TRW, Inc., San Bernardino, Calif., 1980-81, subcontracts specialist space systems div., Redondo Beach, Calif., 1981-82; atty. Todd Shipyards Corp., San Francisco, 1982-85; gen. counsel Phone-Master Communications Corp., Walnut Creek, 1985—; atty. adv. Shipbuilders Council Am., Washington, 1982-83. Mem. ABA, AAUW, San Francisco County Bar Assn., Contra Costa Bar Assn., Barristers Soc. San Francisco, Attys. for Animal Rights, Maritime Law Assn. U.S. Phi Alpha Delta. Club: Commonwealth of Calif. Home: 320 N Civic Dr 315 Walnut Creek CA 94596 Office: 2255 Ygnacio Valley Rd Suite N Walnut Creek CA 94598

BROWN, JOLENE ROBISON, publisher; b. Ioka, Utah, Jan. 3, 1938; d. Russell Henry and Thelma (Goodrich) Robison; m. Lee Ashton Brown, Oct. 7, 1967 (div. Feb. 1973); children—Michael Dennis, Douglas Jay; m. Bruce Merriman Brink, Jr., Sept. 1, 1982. Fine arts degree Weber State Coll., 1968; student U. Utah, 1970; studied with Carolyn Rich, Ogden, Utah, 1967-70. Dir. acctg. office Bur. Indian Affairs, Fort Duchesne, Utah, 1956-62; prodn. asst. Thiokol Chem. Co., Brigham City, Utah, 1962-65; prodn. mgr. U.S. Air Force, Ogden, 1965-67; v.p. mktg. Phone Books Inc., Salt Lake City and San Francisco, 1969-72; pub., dir. sales Phone Directory Co., Price, Utah, 1972-74; publisher, pres. Names 'n Numbers Inc., Sun Valley, Idaho, 1974-85; mktg. dir. Ballet Sch., Ketchum, Idaho, 1984-85. One-women shows: Ogden, Utah, 1969, Park City, Utah, 1972; group shows: Ogden, 1968. Asst. dir. art gallery Jr. League, Odgen, 1968, instr. art, 1967, decorations chmn. Charity Ball, 1969; bd. dirs. The Ballet Sch. Found. Inc., Ketchum, 1984-85. Mem. Assn. N.Am. Directory Publishers (Gold Book awards 1984, 85, named Publisher of Yr. 1984). Republican. Avocations: painting; skiing; river rafting; traveling. Home: 309 Sage Rd Sun Valley ID 83353 Office: Names 'n Numbers Inc 500 S Main St Sun Valley ID 83353

BROWN, JOY ALICE, social service administrator; b. Redmesa, Colo., Mar. 19, 1917; d. Ezra E. and Alice M. (Pinkerton) Walker; B.A., Highlands U., 1958; M.A., U. No. Colo., 1967, Ed.D., 1970; m. Clayton Henry Brown, Apr. 9, 1941; children—Kimleigh Clayton, Loraleigh Joy. Tchr., La Plata County, Colo., 1936-41; prin. Bayfield (Colo.) pub. schs., 1942-46; tchr. Aztec (N.Mex.) pub. schs., 1946-63; spl. edn. coordinator primary schs., Palmer, Alaska, 1963-67; lab. sch. supr. U. No. Colo., 1967-70; asso. prof. edn. N.Mex. State U., 1970-75; dir. Open Door Center, Las Cruces, N.Mex., 1975—; cons. Tex. Edn. Service Center, Roswell (N.Mex.) schs.; sec. Dona Ana Human Services Consortium, 1977. Recipient Community Service award Las Cruces Eastside Center, 1972. Outstanding Contribution award N.Mex. Council of Exceptional Children, 1977. Mem. NEA, Council for Exceptional Children, Nat. Assn. Retarded Citizens, Phi Delta Kappa. Contbr. articles on edn. to profl. jours. Home: 1232 Barker Rd Las Cruces NM 88001 Office: 2325 E Nevada Las Cruces NM 88001

BROWN, JUNE GIBBS, government official; b. Cleve., Oct. 5, 1933; d. Thomas D. and Lorna M. Gibbs; B.B.A. summa cum laude, Cleve. State U., 1971, M.B.A., 1972; postgrad. Cleve. Marshall Law Sch., 1973-74; J.D., U. Denver, 1978; A.M.P., Harvard Bus. Sch., 1983; children—Ellen, Linda, Victor, Carol. Real estate broker, office mgr. N.E. Realty, Cleve., 1963-68; staff acct. Frank T. Cicirelli, C.P.A., Cleve., 1970-71; grad. teaching fellow Cleve. State U., 1971-72; dir. internal audit Navy Fin. Center, Cleve., 1972-75; mgr. fin. systems design burs. in Dept. Interior, Denver, 1975-79, insp. gen., Washington, 1979-81; insp. gen. NASA, Washington, 1981-85; v.p. fin. and adminstrn. Systems Devel. Corp. subs. Burroughs Co., 1985—; bd. dirs. Fed. Law Enforcement Tng. Ctr., 1984-85, Interagy. Auditor Tng. Program, USDA Grad. Sch., 1983-85; chmn. interagy. com. of info. resource mgmt. GSA, 1984-85. Recipient award Am. Soc. Women Accts., 1969, 70, 71; Raulston award Cleve. State U., 1971, Pres.'s award, 1971; Outstanding Achievement award U.S. Navy, 1973; Career Service award Chgo. region Fed. Exec. Bd., 1974, Outstanding Contbn. to Fin. Mgmt. award, Denver Region, 1977; Fin. Mgmt. Improvement award Joint Fin. Mgmt. Improvement Program, 1980; Outstanding Service award Nat. Assn. Minority C.P.A. Firms, 1980; Meritorious Exec. designee NASA, 1983, 84, exceptional service medal, 1985; named Woman of Yr., Bur. Land Mgmt., Dept. Interior, 1975. Mem. Assn. Govt. Accts. (nat. exec. com. 1977-80, 81-85, nat. pres. 1985-86, vice chmn. nat. ethics com. 1978-80), Service award 1973, 76, Outstanding Achievement award, 1979). Am. Inst. C.P.A.s, Am. Accts. Assn., Assn. Fed. Investigators, Beta Alpha Psi. Office: Systems Devel Corp 7925 Jones Branch Dr McLean VA 22102

BROWN, JUNE WILCOXON, writer; b. W. Lafayette, Ohio, Aug. 14, 1914; d. Ralph Foster and Pearl Almeda (Marx) Wilcoxon; B.A., U. Md., 1935; m. Albert W. Brown, Nov. 3, 1938; 1 son, Peter Wilcoxon. Freelance writer, 1945-60, 81—; editor Select mag., Madison, Wis., 1959-65; radio script writer Beverly Stark Radio Show, 1963-68, John Doremus Show, 1971-72; sit-in hostess Mary Brooks Jackson radio show, St. Thomas, V.I., 1966-75, Louise Noble Radio Show, St. Thomas, 1975-81; author monthly column Caribbean Corner, 1977-78; author fiction and articles in nat. magazines. Mem. Nat. League Am. Pen Women (pres. Madison 1954), St. Thomas Community Music Assn. (v.p. 1970-71), Women in Communications (Writers cup Madison 1951), Kappa Kappa Gamma. Republican. Address: Box 7396 Saint Thomas VI 00801

BROWN, KAREN LEE, paper company executive, former state legislator; b. Rumford, Maine, Apr. 14, 1953; d. Leland Richard and Barbara May (Dougherty) B.; B.A. in Psychology, U. Mass., 1975. Mem. Maine Ho. of Reps., 1976-84; public relations cons. Boise Cascade Corp., 1981-84, mgr. govtl. affairs for Maine, 1984—; orgnl. cons. Citizens for Congresswoman Olympia Snowe; cons. George Bush for Pres., 1980; mem. Oxford County Republican Com., 1975-80; vice chmn. 2d Congressional Dist. Conv., 1978-80, chmn., 1986—; chmn. Sen. William Cohen's U.S. Mil. Acad. selection com. Home: Box 32 Elm St Bethel ME 94217 Office: Boise Cascade Corp Rumsford ME 04276

BROWN, KAREN LYNN, energy company executive; b. San Antonio, Jan. 9, 1957; d. James Roscoe and Margaret Mary (Dauwe) B. B.B.A. magna cum laude, St. Mary's U., San Antonio, 1979. Assoc. acct. Valero Energy Corp., San Antonio, 1979-80, acct., 1980-81, div. supply and distbn. coordinator, acct., 1981-82, div. supr. natural gas liquids supply and distbn., acct., 1982—. Mem. campaign com. City Council Elections, San Antonio, 1979. Recipient Free Enterprise Scholar award Travis Savs. and Loan Assn., 1979. Mem. Gas Liquids Distbn. Assn. (dir. 1982—), St. Mary's U. Alumni Assn., Delta Epsilon Sigma. Democrat. Roman Catholic. Club: Belgian Am. (San Antonio). Home: 3225 Timmons Ln #40 Houston TX 77027 also 2203 W Travis St San Antonio TX 78207 Office: Valero Mktg Co Suite 900 Two Allen Ctr 1200 Smith St Houston TX 77002

BROWN, KATHARINE EISENHART, artist; b. Princeton, N.J., Mar. 21, 1921; d. Luther P. and Katharine S. (Schmidt) Eisenhart; B.A., Vassar Coll., 1942; M.S. in Journalism, Columbia U., 1944; spl. studies in sculpture, Corcoran Gallery, Washington; pottery workshop, Boston Mus. Sch.; m. W. Danforth Compton, June 13, 1942 (dec.); children—John, Christina; m. 2d, Robert P. Brown, Apr. 3, 1959. Exhbns. include: Main Gallery Boston City Hall, 1978, Copley Art Assn., Boston, 1980, 86, Clark Gallery, Lincoln, Mass., Cambridge (Mass.) Art Assn., 1981, Currier Art Gallery, Manchester, N.H., 1981, Hyatt Art Gallery, Cambridge, 1983, Simmos Coll., Boston, 1986, various art assns.; one person shows include: Cambridge Art Assn., 1976, Hilles Library of Randolph Coll., 1975, 82, 85, Frameworks Gallery, Cambridge, 1977, Johnson (Vt.) State Coll., 1977, Vassar Coll., 1977, Harvard Law Sch. Library, 1978, Stonehill Coll., Easton, Mass., 1979, World Affairs Council, Boston, 1981, Wordsmith Gallery, Cambridge, 1983, Marion (Mass.) Art Ctr., 1983 many pvt. collections including Boston Globe, Bank Am., First Nat. Bank of Boston, Hearthstone Ins. Co. of Mass., Charleston Savings Bank, others in Mich., Ariz., N.Mex.; dir. Martin St. Collage Dance Group. Recipient 1st prize Cambridge Art Assn., 1976, Quincy Coop. Bank award South Shore Art Center, 1977; hon. mention Concord Art Assn., 1979, juror's choice award, 1980; juror's award Cambridge Art Assn., 1981; Best of Show, medal of honor Concord Art Assn., 1983; Crumbacher Award, Concord, 1984, others. Mem. Boston Visual Artists Union, Cambridge Art Assn., Copley Soc. Boston, Mass. Craftsman's Council, Concord Art Assn., Sharon Art Center, N.H. Art Assn., Phi Beta Kappa. Democrat. Episcopalian. Home: 16 Avon St Cambridge MA 02138

BROWN, KAY (MARY KATHRYN), former state official; b. Ft. Worth, Tex., Dec. 19, 1950; d. H.C., Jr. and Dorothy Ruth (Ware) B.; m. William P. Dougherty, Dec. 15, 1978 (div. 1984). B.A., Baylor U., 1973. Reporter, UPI, Atlanta, 1973-76; reporter, feature writer Anchorage Daily Times (Alaska), 1976-77; reporter, co-owner Alaska Advocate, Anchorage, 1977; aide, researcher Alaska State Legislature, Juneau, 1979-80; dep. dir. div. of oil and gas (formerly div. minerals and energy mgmt.) Alaska Dept. Natural Resources, Anchorage, 1980-82, dir., 1982-86. Chmn. ways and means com. Alaska Woman's Polit. Caucus, 1982-84, mem. steering com., 1982-86; bd. dirs. Blood Bank Alaska, 1984—; del. Alaska Democratic Conv., 1984; candidate Alaska Ho. of Reps., 1986.

BROWN, KAY WIELAND, charitable organization executive; b. Cleve., Oct. 7, 1937; d. Ralph Gazelle Wieland and Viola (Watson) Munger; m. Arthur Merrill Brown III, June 30, 1961 (div. Feb. 1978); children—Michael Merrill, Courtney Wieland, Carter Leigh. B.A., Conn. Coll., 1959. Cons. United Way Orange County, Calif., 1976-77; exec. dir. Voluntary Action Ctr., Newport Beach, Calif., 1977-80; annual fund dir. South Coast Repertory, Costa Mesa, Calif., 1980-83; exec. dir. New Directions for Women, Newport Beach, 1983—; dir. Clock Constrn. Co., Irvine, Calif., 1984—. Advisor Jr. League Newport Harbor, Newport Beach, 1978—; class agent Conn. Coll., New London, 1980—; active in U. Calif. Med. Research, Irvine, 1984—; former dir., officer United Way, Girls Club, Jr. League, Environ. Nature Ctr.; western area chmn. Assn. Jr. Leagues, 1975-77; parent fund chmn. Cate Sch., Santa Barbara, Calif., 1981-82. Recipient Community Service award Carnation County and Vol. Ctr. 1984, Community Service award Pks. Beaches and Recreation Commn. Newport Beach 1984, Community Service award City Newport Beach. Mem. Nat. Soc. Fund Raising Execs., Conn. Coll. Alumni Assn. (pres. 1976, class agent 1980-85), Jr. League Newport Harbor. Republican. Avocations: golf; bridge; music; reading. Home: 1731 Skylark Ln Newport Beach CA 92660 Office: New Directions for Women 120 Newport Center Dr 225 Newport Beach CA 92660

BROWN, LAURA VENTRESCA, arts commissioner; b. Washington, Oct. 2, 1915; d. Francesco and Florence Vendla Elizabeth (Olson) Ventresca; B.A., U. Ill., 1936, B.S. in L.S., 1941; postgrad. U. Md., 1961-62; m. George Berdine Brown, July 17, 1938; children—David Alan, Donald Kent, Douglas Scott. Librarian, Falls Church, Va., 1952-53; arts coordinator Anne Arundel County Dept. Recreation and Parks, Annapolis, Md., 1972-76; mem. Anne Arundel County Commn. Culture and Arts, 1976-81, chmn., 1980; mem. Commn. of Md. Hall for Creative Arts, Annapolis, 1978—; dir. Cultural-Edn. Centre, Inc., Annapolis. Membership chmn. Arlington County Women's Com. for Nat. Symphony, 1953-54; fine arts chmn. Marshall Sch. PTA, 1953-54; membership chmn. Anne Arundel County Concert Assn., 1959; chmn. symphony com. Anne Arundel Gen. Hosp. Aux., 1970-72; trustee Balt. Mus. Art, 1978-80; patron Ballet Theatre of Annapolis, Annapolis Symphony Orch., Annapolis Colonial Players, Md. Fedn. Arts, Annapolis Summer Garden Theatre, Annapolis Children's Theatre, Annapolis Opera Soc., Hist. Annapolis, Balt. Mus. Recipient Vol. Service award Severna Park Jaycees, 1981, Anne Arundel County Exec., 1981, Md. Hall for Creative Arts, 1982, Gov. Md., 1982. Mem. Order Sons of Italy in Am., Sumi-E Soc. Am., Inc. (chmn. D.C. chpt. 1980; dir. 1980—; assoc. editor Quar. 1982—), Annapolis Watercolor Club, Walters Art Gallery, Balt. Music Club, Ikebana Internat. (chpt. dir.; chmn. Annapolis workshop 1981-82, 85—), Pi Delta Phi. Home: 200 Riggs Ave Severna Park MD 21146

BROWN, LEA LEA, food ingredient and packaging executive; b. Knoxville, Tenn., Aug. 8, 1940; d. Roy Hogan, Jr. and Jane (Hensey) B. Student U. Tenn., 1958-60. Pres., Golf House, Inc., Fla. and Ga., 1964-74; teaching professional Barwick Golf Club, Delray, Fla., 1970-74; pres. L.L. Brown & Co., Inc., Decatur, Ga., 1975—; pres. Tenn. Women's Golf Assn., 1957-59, Bakers Allied Assn. of South, 1981-82; bd. dirs. Allied Trades of Baking Industry, 1982-84; dir. Kern's & Assoc. Bakeries, 1978—. Life mem. Life for God's Stray Animals. Mem. Am. Inst. Baking, Am. Soc. Bakery Engrs., Bakers Club Chgo., Inst. Food Tech., DeKalb C. of C. Episcopalian. Clubs: Boca Raton Hotel and Country (Fla.); Druid Hills Golf, East Lake Country (Atlanta); Big Canoe Golf (Ga.). Avocations: golf, animals. Home: 1756 S Hidden Hills Pkwy Stone Mountain GA 30088 Office: LL Brown & Co Inc 4285 Memorial Dr Suite K Decatur GA 30032

BROWN, LEANNA, state senator; b. Providence, 1935; d. Harold and Esther Young; B.A. with honors, Smith Coll., 1956; m. W. Stanley Brown; children—William, Stephen. Mem. profl. staff govt. dept. Ednl. Testing Service, Princeton, N.J., 1956-60; councilwoman, Chatham Borough, 1969-72; mem. taxation and fin. com. Nat. Assn. Counties, 1976-79; dir. Morris County Bd. Chosen Freeholders, 1976, dep. dir., 1975, chmn. fin. com., 1975; freeholder, 1972-81; pres. N.J. Assn. Counties, 1978; chmn. N.E. N.J. Transp. Coordinating Com., 1979-80; mem. N.J. Assembly, 1980-83, N.J. Senate, 1984—; mem. N.J. Job Tng. Coordinating Council, 1984-86, Casino Revenue Fund Study Commn., 1984-86; mem. Gov.'s Commn. on Internat. Trade, 1986—, N.J. Hist. Commn., 1986—; mem. adv. com. N.J. Public Broadcasting, 1979—; mem. corp. United Way of Morris County, 1978—; trustee Morris Mus. Arts and Sci., 1975—; trustee Arts Council of Morris Area, 1973—; del. White Ho. Conf. on Children, 1970; merit badge counselor Loantaka council Boy Scouts Am., 1975—; Morris County coordinator Millicent Fenwick for Senate, 1982; mem. N.J. Republican Fin. Com., 1979-81. Mem. N.J. Assn. Elected Women (pres. 1982, 83). Home: 7 Dellwood Ave Chatham NJ 07928 Office: 123 Columbia Turnpike Florham Park NJ 07932

BROWN, LEILA CARTER, lawyer; b. Atlanta, Nov. 3, 1950; d. William Hansel and Minnie Lorraine (Thornton) Carter; m. Early D. Monroe, Jan. 30, 1978 (div. July 1984); 1 child, Thema Monroe. Student Atlanta U., 1972-73; B.A., Mundelein Coll., 1972; J.D., Howard U., 1977. Bar: Pa. 1977. Atty. pub. utilities FCC, Washington, 1977—. Lead articles editor Howard Law Jour., 1977. Recipient Am. Jurisprudence award Lawyers Co-op Pub. Co., 1975, 76. Mem. Toastmasters Internat. (chpt. pres. 1984—), Ampersand Investment Club (pres. Washington 1983—), Phi Delta Phi, Delta Theta Phi. Roman Catholic. Home: 3738 Jason Ave Alexandria VA 22302 Office: FCC 1919 M St NW Room 305-BB Washington DC 20554

BROWN, LENORA VIRGINIA, physician; b. Anderson, S.C., Aug. 31, 1918; d. James Newton and Willie Clara (Stevenson) B.; m. Massoud T. Simnad, May 28, 1954; children—Jeffrey, Virginia. M.D., U. Va., 1943. Diplomate Am. Bd. Psychiatry and Neurology. Intern, U. Va., 1944, clin. fellow internal medicine, 1944-46, asst. in pathology, 1946-47; resident in neurology Neurol. Inst., Columbia-Presbyn. Med. Ctr., N.Y.C., 1947-50; fellow Nat. Found. Infantile Paralysis, 1950-53, Rockefeller Inst. and Rockefeller Found., Virus Research Labs., U. Pitts., 1953-56, Salk Inst., LaJolla, Calif., 1962-69; practice medicine specializing in neurology, San Diego, 1957—; cons. neurology San Diego County Mental Health Services, VA Outpatient Clinic, San Diego; asst. clin. prof. dept. neurosci. Sch. Medicine, U. Calif.-San Diego, 1971. Mem. AMA, Am. Acad. Neurology, Calif. Med. Assn., San Diego County Med. Soc., San Diego Neurol. Soc., Alpha Omega Alpha. Republican. Office: 345 Dickinson St San Diego CA 92103

BROWN, LINDA GAY, city market executive; b. Delta, Colo., Jan. 14, 1949; d. Lester Allen and Ruth LaVern (Thomas) Doyle; m. B. Terry Brown, Dec. 21, 1967; children—Shannon, Evan, Kimberly, Misty. Student pub. schs., Cedaredge, Colo. Lab. foreman Holly Sugar Co., Delta, 1974-77; mgr. gen. mdse. dept. City Market Corp., Delta, 1979—. Coordinator Delta County Crisis Teams; mem. Delta Sch. Bd., 1985—, vo-tech bd. State of Colo., 1985—. Republican. Mormon. Avocation: herb gardening. Home: 1374 D Dr Delta CO 81416 Office: City Market 625 Meeker Delta CO 81416

BROWN, LINDA JENKINS, government official; b. Balt., Nov. 8, 1946; d. Dennie Richard and Naomi (Harris) Jenkins; B.S. in Edn. Morgan State U., 1971; M.P.A. (Fed. Hwy. Adminstrn. scholar), cert. mgmt., U. Balt., 1981; m. Charles E. Brown, II, July 3, 1965; 1 son, Charles E. III. Elem. tchr. Balt. County Bd. Edn., 1971-73; EEO specialist Dept. Def., Ft. Holabird, Md., 1973-75; EEO specialist Fed. Hwy. Adminstrn., Balt., 1975-78, regional contracts compliance officer, 1978-80, dep. chief internal EEO div., fed. women's program mgr., 1980-84, chief internal equal employment opportunity div., coordinator historically black colls. and univs. program, 1984—. Recipient Superior Performance award Fed. Hwy. Admistrn., 1980, Spl. Achievement award, 1982, Outstanding Performance award, 1982, 83; Outstanding Woman award Federally Employed Women, Inc., 1984. Mem. Am. Soc. Public Adminstrn., Internat. Personnel Mgmt. Assn., Nat. Assn. Female Execs., Exec. Women's Network, Am. Bus. Women's Assn., Nat. Council Negro Women, Morgan State U. Alumni Assn., Zeta Phi Beta (Meritorious award, Cert. of Appreciation), Alpha Kappa Mu (Cert. of Merit). Home: 2401 Poplar Dr Baltimore MD 21207 Office: 400 7th St SW Washington DC 20590

BROWN, LINDA JOYCE, food and nutrition educator; b. Jacksonville, Fla., Jan. 8, 1954; d. Willie James and Katie Lee (Taylor) Lockett; m. Thomas Lee Brown, Dec. 18, 1982; children—Ashanti, William, Timothy. B.S. in Agr., U. Fla., 1975, M.Agr., 1981. Chemist/microbiologist Green Giant Co., Alachua, Fla., 1975-77; lab. technologist II, U. Fla., Gainesville, 1977-81, extension agt. I, Ft. Myers, 1981—; nutrition cons. Congregate Meals, Ft. Myers, 1984—, Serenity House, Ft. Myers, 1985—. Contbr. articles to profl. jours. Mem. exec. bd. Community Coordinating Council, Ft. Myers, 1985; co-founder Friends of Hearing Impaired Youth, Gainesville, 1976; tutor-coordinator Sampson, Gainesville, 1973. Named Alpha Zeta Outstanding Jr., 1974; State U. System Bd. Regents grantee, 1980; Leadership and Service award, Office Student Services, U. Fla., 1981. Mem. Soc. Nutrition Edn. (legis. network chmn.), Caloosa Dietetic Assn. (sec.), Am. Dietetic Assn., Fla. Dietetic Assn. (minority issues chmn.), Nat. Assn. Female Execs., Alpha Zeta, Black Student Union. Avocations: singing; violin. Office: Coop Extension Service 3406 Palm Beach Blvd Fort Myers FL 33905

BROWN, LINDA LEE, graphic designer; b. Raton, N.Mex., Oct. 29, 1955; d. John Tom and Anna Helen (Willett) Brown; A.S., Amarillo Coll., 1975; student West Tex. State U., 1975-77, B.A. in Bus. Adminstr., Century U., Beverly Hills, Calif., M.B.A. Teaching asst. Amarillo (Tex.) Coll., 1974-75; drafter natural gas div. Pioneer Corp., Amarillo, 1975-76, sr. drafter exploration div. Amarillo Oil Co. 1976-77; drafting supr., engrng. services supr., dir. speakers' bur. Thunder Basin Coal Co., Atlantic Richfield Co., Wright, Wyo., 1977-86; ptnr. Rose Enterprises, 1986—. Bd. dirs. Campbell County Drafting Adv. Council, 1984-85; mem. Nat. Assn. Female Exec., 1979—; sec. bd. dir. exec. com. Am. Inst. Design and Drafting, 1984-85, tech. publ. chairperson, 1984-85. Named Most Outstanding Woman, Beta Sigma Phi, 1980, 81; recipient Woman in the Industry recognition Internat. Reprographics Assn., 1980; grand prize winner Wyo. Art Show with painting titled Energy, 1976. Mem. Am. Inst. for Design and Drafting (dir. 1982—, asst. editor Design and Drafting News 1982—), Am. Legion Aux., mem. Ocean Research Edn. Soc., Gloucester, Mass. (grant proposal writer, 1984). Clubs: Wright Writers, 4-H. Author (poetry): God was Here, but He Left Early, 1976, Gift of Wings, 1980; Solo, 1986; columnist, Wytech Digest. Home: PO Box 114 Wright WY 82732

BROWN, MABEL ESTLE, retired educator; b. Muscatine County, Iowa, Oct. 6, 1907; d. Chester Millar and Myrne (Bell) Estle; m. Robert G. Brown, Dec. 30, 1931; children—Patricia Jane Brown Hoback, Linnaeus Estle. B.A., U. Iowa, 1929; M.S., Iowa State U., 1953. Cert. secondary tchr., guidance counselor, sch. librarian, Iowa. High sch. tchr., Conesville, Iowa, 1930-32, 42-48, Nichols, Iowa, 1949-50; grad. asst. journalism Iowa State U., Ames, 1950-53; tchr., librarian Lone Tree High Sch., (Iowa), 1953-60, guidance counselor, 1960-70; chmn. Carrie Stanley Scholarship Com., Lone Tree, 1962-70. Author: The Fork of the Rivers: History Is People, 1978. Chmn., Muscatine County Farm Bur. Women, Muscatine, Iowa, 1938-42; judge, clk. Twp. Election Com., Conesville, 1970—. Mem. NEA (life), Iowa Edn. Soc. (life), ALA, Iowa Acad. Sci., Theta Sigma Phi. Republican. Home: Rural Route Conesville IA 52739

BROWN, MABEL ETHEL, tax accountant; b. Norwich, N.D., Dec. 2, 1910; d. Edward and Augusta (Schwab) Simmons; student Fosters Tax Sch., San Leandro, Calif., 1952-53, Del Mar Coll., 1954, Bancroft Adult Sch., 1955-56, Alameda Adult Sch., 1955-62, U. Calif., 1961-62, Chabot Coll., 1963, Sunset Hi Adult Sch., 1967-68, Tech. Adult Sch., Oakland, Calif., 1965-73; m. George Victor Brown, Feb. 25, 1954; children—Arthur Ralph, Edward James (dec.), Jerry Lee Larsen. Prin., Mabel's Tax Service, Oakland, 1943-54; owner Gilroy Motel (Calif.), 1945-47; owner, operator Chatterbox, Avoca, Iowa, 1947-49; owner, mgr. Brown's Bus. Service, Flour Bluff, Tex., 1954-55, Hayward, Calif., 1954-84; owner Rocks Rough & Ready, jewelry shop, Browns Bus. Service. Mem. VFW Aux. Democrat. Lutheran. Address: 28105 Mission Blvd Hayward CA 94544

BROWN, MAREL, writer; b. Carroll County, Ga., Dec. 17, 1899; d. George Britt and Olive (Summers) Snow; student Atlanta public schs.; m. Alex B. Brown, Oct. 8, 1919 (dec. Dec. 1975). Sec., asst. to editor Christian Index, Atlanta, 1924-30; sec., asst. to Baptist pastor, 1930-37; freelance writer, 1938—; books include: Red Hills, 1941; Hearth-Fire, 1943; Fence Corners, 1952; The Shape of a Song (Writer of Yr. award Atlanta Writers Club 1968-69, Poet of Yr. for Ga. award Dixie Council 1968), 1968; Lily May and Dan, 1946; The Greshams of Greenway, 1950; The Cherry Children, 1956; Three Wise Women of the East, 1970; Presenting Georgia Poets, 1979; instr. writing workshops; chmn. Ga. Poetry Day, 1957-59; participant World Congress Poets, Fla., 1985. Ga. chmn. Books for Russia, World War II; public relations coms. Atlanta Bond Drive, High Mus. Art; bd. dirs. Warren Boys Club, 1984-85, also mem. edn. com., funder Poetry Reading and Writing Program, 1984—. Recipient Ann. Spl. award Dixie Council Authors and Journalists, 1980. Mem. Nat. League Am. Pen Women, Poetry Soc. Am., Poetry Soc. Ga., Ga. State Poetry Soc., Internat. Acad. Poets, World Congress Poets, Am. Acad. Poets. Ladies Burns Club Atlanta, Dixie Council Authors and Journalists, Rader Poetry Group Miami, Atlanta Hist. Soc., DeKalb County His. Soc. Baptist. Home: 1938 N Decatur Rd NE Atlanta GA 30307

BROWN, MARGARET MARY, psychologist; b. Albany, Calif., Dec. 6, 1943; d. Daniel Francis and Ethel Lucille (Cliff) B.; B.A., U. Calif., 1965; M.A., U. Kans., 1968; Ph.D., NYU, 1982; m. Wayne A. Gordon, Nov. 9, 1979. Evaluator, dir. project devel. Kans. Regional Med. Program, Kansas City, 1969-73; health planner Mid-Am. Comprehensive Health Planning Agy., Kansas City, Mo., 1973-74; project coordinator Rehab. Indicators project Inst. Rehab. Medicine, N.Y.C., 1974-82, assoc. research scientist, 1982—; cons. United Cerebral Palsy of N.Y., 1978-85. USPHS fellow, 1965-68. Mem. Nat. Rehab. Assn., Evaluation Research Soc., Am. Psychol. Assn., Phi Beta Kappa. Office: 400 E 34th St New York NY 10016

BROWN, MARGARET RUTH ANDERSON, state legislator; b. Scottsbluff, Nebr., Oct. 11, 1944; d. Everett Howard and Ruth (Nichols) Anderson; m. Kermit Campbell Brown, 1966. B.A., U. Wyo., 1966; postgrad. Pepperdine Coll., 1967-68. Mem. Legis. Exec. Commn. on Reorgn. of State Govt., 1974-78; mem. Wheatland (Wyo.) Town Council, 1974-75, Carbon County Council of Govts., 1976—, chmn., 1980-83; mem. adv. council for Div. of Community Programs, 1979-85, chmn., 1983-85, adv. council Dept. Health and Social Services, 1982-85; mem. bd. dirs. Nat. Assn. Regional Councils, 1982—; mem. Wyo. Ho. of Reps., 1983—. Mem. AAUW, Soroptimists. Republican.

BROWN, MARILYN BRANCH, social service executive; b. Richmond, Va., Apr. 11, 1944; d. Elbert LeRoy and Edna Harriett (Eley) Branch; m. Winfred Wayland Brown, Jr., June 19, 1982; 1 dau., Lesli Antoinette; 1 dau. by previous marriage, Kara Rachelle Lancaster. B.S., Va. State U., 1966; M.S., U. Nebr., 1968. Nat. Tchr. Corps intern U. Nebr. at Omaha and Omaha Pub. Schs., 1966-68; tchr. McKlenburg County Pub. Schs., Boydton, Va., 1968-71; community organizer model cities health planning Capital Area Comprehensive Health Planning Council, Richmond, Va., 1971-72; asst. dir. com. mental health mental retardation services bd. Va. Dept. Mental Health & Mental Retardation, Richmond, 1972-75, spl. edn. dir., 1975-76; civil rights coordinator Va. Dept. Social Services, Richmond, 1976—, chmn. EEO adv. com., 1984—; chmn. adv. com. on Black adoption Va. Dept. Social Services. Program coordinator Swansboro Bapt. Ch., Richmond, 1979—; mem. Swansboro Ensemble, 1974—. Recipient Youth Motivation Commendation, Nat. Alliance of Bus., 1983. Fellow Am. Orthopsychiat. Assn.; mem. Am. Assn. Affirmative Action, Black Adminstrs. in Child Welfare, Alliance for Black Social Welfare, Psi Chi, Alpha Kappa Alpha. Baptist. Home: 5500 Larrymore Rd Richmond VA 23225 Office: Va Dept Social Services 8007 Discovery Dr Richmond VA 23288

BROWN, MARJORIE SCHMIDT, civic worker; b. Bklyn., May 24, 1928; d. Raymond and Elsie (Engstrom) Schmidt; student Packer Collegiate Inst., 1943-45; m. Edward George Brown, Oct. 28, 1960. Dir., Central Hudson Gas & Electric Corp., Poughkeepsie, N.Y. Chmn., Salvation Army Women's Div. of Greater N.Y., N.Y.C., 1971—, mem. Salvation Army Foster Home and Adoption Service Advisory Council, 1972—, mem. N.Y. State exec. planning bd., 1975, Manhattan adv. bd., 1974—; vice chmn. Manhattan Salvation Army Bd., 1983—, exec. sec. N.Y. State adv. bd., 1979; mem. nat. bd. USO, 1976—, N.Y. state rep., 1977; bd. dirs. United Way of Dutchess County (N.Y.), 1979. Recipient Pub. Service award Salvation Army, 1975, Service award USO, 1980. Mem. DAR, Nat. Inst. Social Scis. (dir.), Women's Nat. Farm and Garden Assn., English Speaking Union. Clubs: Everglades (Palm Beach); Millbrook (N.Y.) Garden, Millbrook Golf and Tennis; Women's Nat. Republican, York (bd. govs. 1973—), City Gardens (dir. 1972—), Barnard, Sorosis (N.Y.C.). Address: PO Box AD Millbrook NY 12545

BROWN, MARY ELEANOR, physical therapist, educator; b. Williamsport, Pa., Jan. 1, 1906; d. Sumner Locher and Mary Kate (Eagles) Brown. Student U. Wis.-Madison, 1927-28; B.A., Barnard Coll., 1931; M.A., NYU, 1941, postgrad., 1942-45, Western Reserve U., 1960-61; postgrad. U. Miami, Miami-Dade Jr. Coll., 1971-72, Cuesta Community Coll., 1977-79. Supervising phys. therapist, research asst. Inst. for Crippled and Disabled, N.Y.C., 1941-46; instr. edn. N.Y.U., 1942-46; phys. therapist Childrens Rehab. Inst., Cockeysville, Md., 1946; organizing dir. phys. edn. State Rehab. Hosp., West Haverstraw, N.Y., 1946-47; phys. therapy cons. Nat. Soc. for Crippled Children and Adults, Chgo., 1947-49; physical therapy cons., dir. prof. services, dir. cerebral palsy sch. N.Y. State Dept. Health, Albany, N.Y. and Eastern N.Y. Orthopedic Hosp. Sch., Schenectady, N.Y., 1949-53; chief phys. therapist Bird S. Coler Hosp. for Chronic Diseases, N.Y.C., 1953-54; chief phys. therapist, instr. edn. St. Vincents Hosp. and N.Y.U., 1954-58; chief research asso. hand research Highland View Hosp., Cleve., 1958-64, cons. on kinesiology, hand research, 1964-65; supr. continuing edn. for phys. therapists, asst. prof. phys. therapy Case Western Res. U., Cleve., 1964-68; dir. phys. therapy Margaret Wagner House of Benjamin Rose Inst., Cleve., 1968-70; free lance writer, 1970—; 1st Mary Eleanor Brown lectr. clin. phys. therapy research Inst. Rehab. and Research, Tex. Med. Center, Houston, 1979; active Planetary Initiative for the World We Choose. Adv. bd. Community Services Dept. Cuesta Community Coll., San Luis Obispo, Calif., 1977—. Recipient Award of Merit, Case-Western Res. U., 1970; award for clin. research Inst. Rehab. and Research, Tex. Med. Center, Houston, 1979; Lucy Blair Service award Am. Phys. Therapy Assn., 1984. Mem. Inst. Gen. Semantics, Internat. Soc. Gen. Semantics, World Confedn. Phys. Therapy, Am. Phys. Therapy Assn., Planetary Citizens, Morro Bay Art Assn. Contbr. articles in field to profl. jours. Home: 659 Bernado Ave Morro Bay CA 93442

BROWN, MARY ELSIE, funeral home executive; b. Gloster, Miss., Nov. 13, 1925; d. Edward Newton and Iva Mae (Hammack) Robertson; m. Emile Ludwig Brown, July 17, 1948 (dec. 1963); children—John Emile, Deborah Kay Brown Hopf, Cynthia Lou Brown Garrett. Student Southwest Jr. Coll., 1944-46, U. So. Miss., 1946-47, 73-74. Lic. funeral dir., Miss. Bookkeeper, gen. office worker Brown Funeral Home, Gloster, 1949-62, ptnr., pres., dir., office mgr., 1976—; sec., bookkeeper Gloster High Sch., 1965-68, Pine Hills Acad., Gloster, 1972-76. Mem. Gloster C. of C. Methodist. Lodge: Eastern Star. Avocations: Reading; traveling; swimming. Home: PO Box 249 Gloster MS 39638 Office: Brown Funeral Home Inc PO Box 279 Gloster MS 39638

BROWN, MARY LEE, lawyer; b. Cin., Mar. 14, 1947; d. Vernon Elmer and Marion (Boyle) Roberts; m. Allan Leslie Brown, Feb. 15, 1969; children—Meredith, Austin. B.A., U. Cin., 1973; J.D., U. Houston, 1980. Bar: Tex. 1980. Briefing atty. U.S. Ct. Appeals (1st cir.), Houston, 1980-81; assoc. law firm Bonham, Carrington & Fox, Houston, 1981-82; sole practice law, Houston, 1982—; mem. Com. for Appellate Judiciary, Houston, 1981—. Leader, San Jacinto council Girl Scouts U.S.A., 1976-79; campaign worker John Hill for Gov., 1979, Rob Mossbacher for Senator, 1983-84. Mem. ABA, Houston Bar Assn., First Ct. Assocs. (sec. 1984-85), Mensa. Office: 1025 Blackhaw Houston TX 77079

BROWN, MONA WRIGHT, research and development company executive; b. Washington, Feb. 18, 1958; d. Robert Albert Sylvester and Margaretha (Frank) B. Student U. Nev., 1977—. Receptionist, br. mgr. sect. Wells Fargo Mortgage Co., Las Vegas, 1980-81; resident installation control clk. Central Telephone Co., Las Vegas, 1981-82; sec. customer service asst. mgr., 1982-84; tour guide Grayline Tours of Nev., Las Vegas, 1985-86; model various agy., Las Vegas, 1984—; adminstrv. coordinator Sci. Applications Internat. Corp., Las Vegas, 1984—. Bd. dirs. Nev. affiliate Am. Diabetes Assn., Las Vegas, 1985—, chmn. fund raising, 1985—, ann. meeting chmn., 1985, 86; vol. Las Vegas C. of C. membership com., 1982. Recipient Appreciation award Central Telephone Co. for United Way campaign, 1982. Mem. Am. Bus. Women's Assn. (pres. Gambleier's chpt. 1984-85, chmn. assoc. night banquet 1983-84), Am. Diabetes Assn. (nat. task force on gen. membership 1986-87, Most Outstanding Mem. award Nev. affiliate 1985-86). Clubs: Toastmasters (sec. 1984), I'll Drink to That (Las Vegas) (bull. editor 1983-84). Office: Sci Applications Internat Corp 3349 S Highland Dr Suite 403 Las Vegas NV 89109

BROWN, MURIEL WINDHAM, librarian; b. Dallas, Nov. 19, 1926; d. Charles Wyatt and Gladys Mae (Patman) Windham; m. George W. Brown, II, Jan. 28, 1951; children—Laurence Windham, David Mitchum, Leslie Ann. B.A., So. Meth. U., 1949, M.A., 1950; M.L.S., North Tex. State U., 1974, postgrad., 1974—. Library assoc. Dallas Pub. Library, 1964-66, librarian lit. and history, 1966-66 children's librarian, 1966-72, head children's dept., 1967-69, children's selection new brs., 1972-77, children's lit. specialist, 1977—; cons. in field. Author: Books for You, 1981; compiler bibliographies for Behind the Covers, 1985. Mem. presch. edn. com. Am. Heart Assn., Dallas, 1982-83. Jesse Jones fellow, 1949. Mem. ALA (children's Notable books re-evaluation com. 1983—, Newbery award com. 1984-85), Tex. Library Assn. (chmn. children's round table), So. Meth. U. Alumni Assn. (sec. 1972-73), Alpha Theta Phi, Beta Phi Mu, Alpha Lambda Sigma. Democrat. Unitarian. Home: 10415 Church Rd Dallas TX 75238 Office: Dallas Pub Library 1515 Young St Dallas TX 75201

BROWN, NANCY JONES, social worker; b. Pitts., Jan. 27, 1943; d. Oliver Woodford and Alma (Wesley) Jones; B.A., Mt. Holyoke Coll., 1965; M.S.W., Smith Coll., 1967; m. George Dixon Brown, May 20, 1972; children—George Oliver Robinson, Janice Marileine. Caseworker 1, Child and Family Service, Norfolk, Va., 1967-68; sch. social worker, spl. services project Middletown (R.I.) Sch. System, 1969; sr. psychiat. social worker Newport County Mental Health Clinic, Newport, R.I., 1969-72; sch. social worker Wayne (Mich.)-Westland Community Schs., 1972-73; staff social worker Child Evaluation and Treatment Center, Barnert Hosp., Paterson, N.J., 1973-74; sr. social worker Community Center for Mental Health, Dumont, N.J., 1974-75; unit supr. Catholic Children's Aid Soc. Met. Toronto (Ont., Can.), 1975-76; exec. dir. Halton (Ont.) Family Services, 1976—. Mem. Nat. Assn. Social Workers, Acad. Cert. Social Workers, Ont. Assn. Profl. Social Workers, Ont. Coll. Cert. Social Workers, Ont. Assn. Family Mediation. Republican. Methodist. Home: 129 All Saints Crescent Oakville ON L6J 5Y6 Canada Office: 168 Lakeshore Rd E Oakville ON L6J 5C1 Canada

BROWN, NATALIA TAYLOR, former contract specialist; b. St. Louis, Mar. 3, 1928; d. Gentry and Olivia (Webb) Taylor; diploma with honors, Hubbard Bus. Coll., St. Louis, 1949; B.S., St. Louis U., 1983; m. Edward Brown, Sept. 30, 1951. Civilian with U.S. Army, St. Louis, 1964-86, contract specialist Troop Support and Aviation Material Command, 1973-86; substitute tchr. St. Louis Pub. Schs., 1986—. Mem. Coalition 100 Black Women, John N. Doggett Scholarship Found. Recipient Sustained Superior Performance award U.S. Army, 1970. Mem. NAACP, Knights of St. Peter Claver, Ladies Aux., Urban League Met. St. Louis, Women's Assn. of St. Louis Symphony Soc., Gamma Phi Delta (Elizabeth Garner Meml. award 1966). Roman Catholic. Home: 5160 Campfire Trail Apt J Florissant MO 63033 Office: PO Box 14263 Saint Louis MO 63178

BROWN, ORIL IRENE, psychologist; b. Maumee, Ohio, Sept. 16, 1908; d. Edwin Joseph and L. Irene (Remelsbecker) B.; student U. Toledo, 1926-28; B.S., Northwestern U., 1930; M.S., George Washington U., 1951, Ph.D., 1965. Asst., Medill Sch. Journalism, Northwestern U., 1930-36; copyreader Chgo. Tribune, 1933-36, European edition N.Y. Herald Tribune, 1936-37; editor Federal Writers Project, 1938-40, Northwestern U., 1940-41, Fgn. Broadcast Intelligence Service, 1942-51; research asst. Human Resources Research Office, 1952-53; sch. psychologist Portsmouth (Va.) Schs., 1953-54; staff psychologist N.D. State Hosp., 1955-56; instr. psychology Med. Coll. Va., 1957-60; staff psychologist Danville (Pa.) State Hosp., 1960-64; staff psychologist to dir. psychology Mental Hygiene Clinic, Toledo, 1964-77; pvt. practice psychology, Toledo, 1977—. Lic. psychologist, Ohio. Mem. Am. Psychol. Assn., Southeastern Psychol. Assn., Midwestern Psychol. Assn., Ohio Psychology Assn., N.W. Ohio Psychol. Assn., Am. Soc. Clin. Hypnosis, AAUW, Ohio Hist. Soc., Maumee Valley Hist. Soc., Nat. Trust for Historic Preservation, Sigma Xi. Episcopalian. Author: Youth under Dictatorship, 1940; contbr. articles in field. Home: 2270 Townley Rd Toledo OH 43614 Office: 2500 W Central Ave Toledo OH 43624

BROWN, PATRICIA BUFORD, travel agt.; b. Jacksonville, Fla., May 3, 1938; d. Herman and Mildred Wainwright (Newsome) Buford; B.A., Nat. U., San Diego, 1976, M.B.A., 1978; divorced; children—Andrew James, Allison Paige. Mem. Faculty Foothill Community Coll., San Diego, 1978-79; dir. admissions and records, registrar Western State U. Coll. Law, San Diego, 1969-79; dist. mgr. Victor Temp. Services, San Jose, Calif., 1979-81; v.p. sales Freedom Travel Service, San Jose, 1981—. Mem. Peninsula Profl. Women's Network, Women in Bus. (chmn. 1981), San Jose C. of C. (dir.). Address: 10895 Northview Sq Cupertino CA 95014

BROWN, PATRICIA WHITE, medical technologist; b. Houston, Nov. 30, 1951; d. Albert Carr and Willie Mae (Sneed) White; m. Herbert Charles Pete, May 24, 1980 (div.); 1 dau., Sheatri Denise; m. 2d, Arthur Lee Brown, Sept. 25, 1982 (div.). B.S., Tex. Christian U., 1974. Med. technologist, edn. coordinator Riverside Gen. Hosp., Houston, 1974-76; chief lab. technologist Almeda Med. Lab., Houston, 1976-80; med. technologist Jefferson Davis Hosp., Harris County Hosp. Dist., Houston, 1980—. Founder Coalition of Pre-Sch. Dirs., 1982—; dir. Parents Calling Parents, Houston, 1980—; 2d and 3d v.p. Vols. in Pub. Sch. Adv. Bd., Houston, 1981, 83; mem. Tex. State Bd. for Vols. in Pub. Sch., Tex., 1982—, 1st v.p., 1985, pres., 1986; chairperson Bucks for Belts Coalition for Sch. Bus Seat Belts, 1985; mem. Mayor's Task Force on Edn., Houston, Mayor's Com. on Child Abuse Prevention; mem. adv. bd. Blueridge Health Dept., Attucks Community Coll.; pres. Reynolds Elem. Parent Tchr. Orgn., 1982, treas., 1984; sec. Pershing Middle Sch., PTO, 1985; pres. Kings Row Child Care Parent Tchrs. Orgn., 1978; bd. dirs. Women in Action, 1984-85; mediator Dispute Resolution Ctr., 1984—; chair Salute to Sch. Vols., 1984-86. Recipient Vols. in Pub. Sch. Spl. Service cert., 1984; recipient numerous certs. of appreciation. Mem. NAACP, Women in Action, Delta Sigma Theta. Recipient Cert. of Appreciation, Vols. Am., 1980, Vols. in Pub. Schs., Houston Ind. Sch. Dist., 1981, 82, 83; Outstanding Service award Reynolds Sch., 1982. Democrat. Baptist. Club: Top Ladies of Distinction. Home: 3134 Sunbeam St Houston TX 77051

BROWN, PAULA, communications company executive; b. Washington, Aug. 19, 1944; d. Stanley and Pauline Prusch; m. Tom Brown. B.A., U. Md.; postgrad. NYU. In various managerial positions AT&T, N.Y., 1967-81; sr. v.p. Donaldson, Lufkin & Jenrette, N.Y.C., 1981-82; chmn., chief exec. officer Shared Communications Services Inc., N.Y.C., 1982—, also dir. Bd. dirs. United Way, Westchester, N.Y., 1979-81. Recipient Tribute to Women and Industry award YWCA, 1980. Office: Shared Communications Services 3 Landmark Sq Suite 400 Stamford CT 06901

BROWN, PAULA KINNEY, heating and air conditioning contractor; b. Portsmith, Va., June 19, 1953; d. Curtis Wade and Joan (Glascoe) Kinney; m. Wayne Howard Brown, Feb. 12, 1983; 1 child, Rebecca Jo. A.S., Lake Sumter Community Coll., 1973, 77; student Lake County Area Vocat. Ctr., 1979, 80. Pres. Kinney's Air Conditioning and Heating, Leesburg, Fla., 1981—; mem. adv. com. for Lake Air Conditioning and Heating Vo-Tech. Sch., Eustis, Fla., 1981-82. Mem. Ch. of Christ. Home: Route 1 Box 719B Fruitland Park FL 32731 Office: Kinney's Air Conditioning and Heating 409 N 13th St Leesburg FL 32748

BROWN, PEGGY THUNE, sheep rancher, nurse; b. Buffalo, S.D., May 4, 1938; d. Walton Thomas and Kathleen M. (Moore) Thune; m. Glenn A. Brown, May 16, 1960; children—Debra Kay, Sharlet Rene, Timothy Glenn. R.N., Presentation Sch. Nursing, Miles City, Mont., 1958. Dir. nursing St. Luke's Hosp., Bowman, N.D., 1958-60; owner Brown's Rambouillet Ranch, Buffalo, 1960—; inservice coordinator John Burns Hosp., Belle Fourche, S.D., 1974-75. Contbr. articles to sheep and sheep dog jours. Mem. State 4-H Horse Adv. Bd., Brookings, S.D., 1979-82, State Extension Adv. Bd., 1983; pres. Harding County Extension Bd. (S.D.), 1982—; mem. Harding County Bd. Edn., 1981—, Harding County Republican Club, 1975—; pres. Am. Lutheran Ch. Women, Spearfish, S.D., 1966. Recipient S.D. Master Lamb Producer award S.D. Lamb Producer Com., 1978. Mem. S.D. Sheepgrowers Assn., Am. Rambouillet Assn. (various coms. 1960—), Am. Border Collie Assn. (dir. 1982—), Nat. Woolgrowers Assn., Harding County Surface and Mineral Interests Assn. (sec. 1985—). Home: H C R 1 Box 29 Buffalo SD 57720

BROWN, QUINCALEE, association executive; b. Wichita, Kans., Nov. 9, 1939; d. Quincy Lee and Lorene (York) B.; B.A., Wichita State U., 1961; M.A., U. Pitts., 1963; Ph.D., U. Kans., 1975; m. James Parson Simsarian, June 24, 1978. Asst. prof. speech communications, dir. debate Wichita State U., 1963-69, Ottawa U., 1970-73; adminstrv. asst. Montgomery County (Md.) Commn. for Women, 1973-74, exec. dir., 1975-80; mgr. fed. women's program Govt. Printing Office, Washington, 1974-75; exec. dir. AAUW, Washington, 1980—. Recipient award for contbn. to public service Women for Equality, Montgomery County Govt., 1975, Outstanding Contbn. to Sex Equity, 1979; Career Achievement award Profl. Fraternity Assn., 1981. Mem. Speech Communications Assn., AAUW, Am. Soc. Assn. Execs. (bd. dirs. 1986-88), Greater Washington Soc. Assn. Execs. (cert.), Zeta Phi Eta (Outstanding Service award 1975). Contbr. articles to profl. jours. Office: 2401 Virginia Ave NW Washington DC 20037

BROWN, REBECCA DORTCH, government official; b. Camden, Ala., Nov. 26, 1945; d. Clarence and Alice Dortch; m. J. Arthur Brown, Sept. 5, 1970; children—Kamilah Autumn, Kwanita Alicia. B.A., Johnson C. Smith U., 1968. Acct. HUD, Washington, 1968-72, Fed. Nat. Mortgage Assn., Washington, 1972-73; tax auditor D.C. Govt., Washington, 1973-74, budget analyst, 1974-76; asst. budget and fiscal officer Dept. Treasury, Washington, 1976-83, fin. mgmt. officer, 1983—. Ford Found. fellow, 1967-68. Mem. Am. Assn. Budget and Program, Alpha Kappa Alpha, Sigma Rho Sigma (v.p. 1965-68). Methodist. Avocation: reading. Home: 8417 Bella Vista Terrace Fort Washington MD 20744 Office: Dept of Treasury 1111 20th St NW Washington DC 20226

BROWN, RHETT DELFORD (HARRIETT), artist, educator; b. Atlanta, Nov. 12, 1924; d. Robert J. and Irene (Fox) Gurney; B.A., Duke U., 1944; m. William A. Cone, Oct. 1945 (div. Nov. 1960); children—Peggy, Carol; m. 2d Robert Delford-Brown, Mar. 21, 1963. Actress in stock and community theatres, N.H. and N.Y., 1950-59; founder, dir. Cricket Theatre, N.Y.C., 1959-63; producer Happenings and Events, London, Nice, France, Great Neck, N.Y., 1963-70; co-founder Gt. Bldg. Crack-Up Gallery, N.Y.C., 1969-71, gallery dir., 1971-76; instr. L.I. U., 1978-79, Am. Inst. Textile Art, Pine Manor Coll., Chestnut Hill, Mass., Spring 1978, 79, 80, 84; studio artist Embroiderers Guild Am., N.Y.C., 1973—; exhibited work in one-woman show: Gt. Bldg. Crack-Up, N.Y.C., 1974; exhibited in group shows: Erotics Gallery, N.Y.C., 1975-80, Union Carbide Invitational, 1978, U. Del., Wilmington, 1980, Brookfield (Conn.) Craft Center, 82, Abigail Adams Mus., N.Y.C., 1982, Culdane Ctr., Brookline, Mass., 1982; represented in permanent collections: Smithsonian, Inst. Contemporary Art, London. Co-chmn., Friends of Jackson Sq. Park, N.Y.C.; bd. dirs. The Ridiculous Theatrical Co., N.Y.C., 1977—, Brookfield Craft Ctr. Cert. tchr. mixed-media stitchery, Valentine Mus., Richmond, Va. Mem Embroiderers Guild Am., Older Women's League, Nat. Standards Council, Am. Inst. Textile Art (dir.), Coll. Art Assn., Woman's Art Caucus. Home and Office: 251 W 13th St New York NY 10011

BROWN, RITA MAE, author; b. Hanover, Pa., Nov. 28, 1944; B.A., N.Y.U., 1968; Ph.D., Inst. for Policy Studies, 1976. Works include: The Hand That Cradles the Rock, 1971; Rubyfruit Jungle, 1973; Songs to a Handsome Woman, 1973; A Plain Brown Rapper, 1976; Six of One, 1978; (novel) Southern Discomfort, 1982, screenplay, 1984; Sleepless Nights, 1982; (novel) Sudden Death, 1983; (TV show) I Love Liberty, prod. ABC, 1982; (teleplay) The Long Hot Summer, 1984; (teleplay) Two Loves, prod. ABC, 1985; (novel) High Hearts, 1986; lectr. Fed. City Coll., 1970-71; mem. faculty Goddard Coll., 1973—; Emmy judge TV Acad. Arts and Scis., 1984. Office: Speakeasy Productions 1900 Stillhouse Rd Charlottesville VA 22901

BROWN, ROSALYN, radio station news director; b. Hudson, S.D., Jan. 20, 1956; d. Charles Kendall and Hope (Jans) B.; m. David Brent Grimm, Sept. 6, 1981. B. Music, U. Colo., 1979. Adminstrv. asst. Am. Research Corp., Boulder, Colo., 1980-81; announcer, producer Biological Sci. Cirriculum, Boulder, 1980-81; news dir. Sta KGNU Radio, Boulder, 1980-81; news reporter Sta. KBOL/KBVL Radio, Boulder, 1981-83; news dir., 1983—; mem. Colo. Press Women, Inc., 1981—. Organist Univ. Luth. Chapel, Boulder, 1981—. Recipient Best Documentary and Feature Story award Nat. and Colo. Assn. Press Women, 1983, Best Documentary for Radio award Nat. and Colo. Assn. Press Women, 1984, Best Prepared Newscast award Colo. Broadcasters Assn., 1984. Mem. Boulder Press Club (sec. 1984-85, pres. 1985-86). Democrat. Avocations: reading; travel. Office: Sta KBCL 3085 Bluff St Boulder CO 80301

BROWN, RUTH CUNNINGHAM, club woman; b. Brooksville, Miss., Jan. 6, 1914; d. George William and Ruth (Hambrick) Cunningham; student Sophie Newcombe Coll., 1933-34, U. Tex., 1934-36; m. William Russell Brown, Apr. 19, 1941; children—Betsy (Mrs. Thomas M. Smith III), Virginia, Russell. Bd. dirs. Houston Community Council, 1962-63; bd. dirs., mem. women's aux. Houston Bar Assn., 1956; horticulture chmn. Garden Club of Houston, 1955-57; bd. visitors Sullins Coll., Bristol, Va., 1966-67, 69-75. Mem. D.A.R. (dir. John-McKnitt Alexander chpt. 1963), Kappa Kappa Gamma (v.p. Houston alumnae assn. 1961). Republican. Episcopalian. Clubs: Houston, Houston Country. Address: 5816 Bayou Glen Rd Houston TX 77057

BROWN, RUTH GEISLER, engineering supervisor; b. Beaver Falls, Pa., Mar. 17, 1924; d. Carl Charles and Emily (Pletz) Geisler; student math. Johns Hopkins U., 1960-70; m. Stuart Fife Brown, Apr. 13, 1944. Service rep. Bell Tel. Co. of Pa., Pitts., 1942-43; from draftsman to group engr. Martin Marietta Co., Middle River, Md., 1944-49, 1950-63; design draftsman Bendix Corp., Balt., 1949-50; engrng. staff asso. Missile Programs and Microelectronics, Johns Hopkins U. Applied Physics Lab., Laurel, Md., 1963-75, sr. staff, supr. hybrid ops., 1975-79, div. staff engr., 1979-81, engrng. supr., 1981—. Mem. Internat. Soc. Hybrid Microelectronics, Internat. Electronics Packaging Soc., Nat. Assn. Female Execs., Johns Hopkins Alumni Assn. Republican. Home: 7724 Hanover Pkwy Apt 301 Greenbelt MD 20770 Office: Applied Physics Lab/Johns Hopkins U Johns Hopkins Rd Laurel MD 20707

BROWN, SANDRA JANE, pharmaceutical research company executive; b. N.Y.C., July 7, 1945; d. Walter Joseph and Ina Buckley (McClurg) B. A.S., Dean Jr. Coll., 1965. Med. sec. Bergen Pines County Hosp., Paramus, N.J., 1965-66; adminstrv. asst. Info. Handling Services, Englewood Cliffs, N.J., 1966-70; clin. research assoc. Biometric Testing, Inc., Englewood Cliffs, 1970-79; corp. sec., dir. Pharma Control Corp., Englewood Cliffs, 1979—; sec./treas. TDI Pharm. Systems, Englewood Cliffs, 1980-83; v.p. Chateau Condo Assn., Cliffside Park, N.J., 1982—. Office: Pharma Control Corp 661 Palisade Ave Englewood Cliffs NJ 07632

BROWN, SANDRA K., resort owner, real estate investor; b. Geneva, Ill., Sept. 30, 1956; d. Thomas James and Eleanor Marie (Roessler) Kolar; m. Robert James Brown, Jan. 30, 1944; children—Chauncey James, Erik James. Asst. mgr. Eventide Motel, Fort Myers Beach, Fla., 1974-77; owner, mgr. Sand Castle Island Resort, Fort Myers Beach, 1977-79; cons. Gulf Coast Vacations, Fort Myers Beach, 1980-81; owner, mgr. Mariner's Lodge, Fort Myers Beach, 1981—, Chauncey's Resort, Westfield, Wis., 1977—. Mem. Christian Bus. and Profl. Women's Assn. (pres. 1983-85, treas. 1985—, speaker 1985—), Fort Myers Beach C. of C., Sanibel Island C. of C., Estero Island Resort Assn. (co-treas. 1977-79), Estero Island Hospitality Assn. Clubs: Caloosahatchee Marching and Chowder Soc. (Fort Myers Beach); J-24 Yacht Racing (Fort Myers). Republican. Baptist. Avocations: traveling; yacht racing; white water rafting; tennis; skiing; aerobic dancing. Home: 1475 San Carlos Blvd Fort Myers Beach FL 33931 Office: Mariner's Lodge 1475 San Carlos Blvd Fort Myers Beach FL 33931

BROWN, SARA LOU, accounting firm executive; b. Houston, Oct. 11, 1942; d. William Hale and Ruth Elizabeth (Hearon) Rutherford; m. Joseph Kurth Brown, Dec. 21, 1965 (div. Mar. 1979); 1 son, Derek Kurth. B.A., Rice U., 1964; M.B.A., U. Tex., 1966. C.P.A., Tex. Mem. staff Peat, Marwick, Mitchell & Co., Houston, 1966-69, mgr., 1969-73, ptnr., 1973—. Treas. Houston Grand Opera, 1973-74, Parks and Recreation Bd., City of West University Place, Tex., 1983, 84. Mem. Am. Inst. C.P.A.s, Tex. Soc. C.P.A.s. Office: Peat Marwick Mitchell & Co PO Box 4545 Houston TX 77210 Office: Peat Marwick Mitchell & Co 3000 Republic Bank Ctr Houston TX 77210*

BROWN, SARAH E. (MRS. RALPH JASON TEMPLE), lawyer; b. Topeka, Kans., Aug. 9, 1936; d. Paul Shannon and Alice (Rafter) B.; A.B., Vassar Coll., 1958; LL.B., Georgetown U., 1963; m. Ralph J. Temple, July 17, 1960; children—Katherine Esme, John Anthony. Admitted to D.C. bar, 1964; staff mem. U.S. Senator Estes Kefauver, Washington, 1958; legis. aide U.S. Senator Vance Hartke, Washington, 1959-60; staff asst. John F. Kennedy Presdl. Campaign, Washington, 1960; asst. to dir. compliance surveys and research Pres.'s Com. on EEO, Washington, 1961-65; cons. Migrant div. Office Econ. Opportunity, Washington, 1965-66; practiced in Washington, 1968-71; staff atty. Pub. Defender Service, Washington, 1971—; adj. prof. criminal law George Washington U. Grad Sch., Washington, 1974-76; faculty Nat. Inst. Trial Advocacy Georgetown U. Law Center, 1980-81; mem. D.C. Bar Com. on D.C. Cts.; treas., dir. N.W. Investment Co., Washington, 1964-66; vol. atty. ACLU, Washington, 1969-71; bd. dirs. Women's Legal Def. Fund, 1976-77; mem. criminal justice com. D.C. Commn. on Status of Women; bd. dirs. Washington Halfway House for Women; mem. Criminal Practice Inst. Com.; exec. com., bd. dirs. Law Students in Ct., 1979-82. Mem. Fed., Women's bar assns., Washington Council Lawyers (dir. 1979-82), Women's Legal Def. Fund. Home: 300 11th St NE Washington DC 20002 also Dillons Run Rd Capon Bridge WV Office: 451 Indiana Ave NW Washington DC 20001

BROWN, SARAH MALONE, educational administrator; b. Alexandria, La., Nov. 20, 1944; d. Robert Taylor and Thelma (Lewis) Malone; m. Middleton Vance Brown, Mar. 29, 1969 (div. 1981); children—Kimberly Pleshette, Meredith Nicole, Andrea Monique. B.S., Prairie View A&M U., 1967; M.Ed., Tex. So. U., 1971; postgrad. Lamar U., 1973-75. Elem. tchr. Galena Park (Tex.), Sch., 1967-74, ednl. diagnostician, 1974-80; ednl. diagnostician Houston Ind. Sch. Dist., 1980—. Mem. Houston chpt. Nat. Coalition of 100 Black Women. Mem. NEA, Tex. Tchrs. Assn., Tex. Assn. Ednl. Diagnosticians, Houston Tchr. Assn., NAACP, Delta Sigma Theta, Gamma Theta Upsilon. Democrat. Episcopalian. Home: 4403 Lemac Houston TX 77096

BROWN, SHARON, association publishing executive; b. Toronto, Ont., Can. B.A., York U., Toronto. Reporter, editor Bus. Week mag., N.Y.C., 1968-73; project mgr. Govt. of Can., Ottawa, 1974-75; freelance writer, editor, N.Y.C. and Los Angeles, 1976-77; mng. editor Los Angeles County Med. Assn., 1978-81, dir. publs., 1981—; program coordinator, speaker, moderator for annual conf. on publishing, Am. Assn. Med. Soc. Execs., Chgo., 1978-81. Co-author: To See Ourselves; Five Views on Canadian Women, 1975. Recipient Sandoz award for med. journalism, 1978-81. Mem. Am. Assn. Med. Soc. Execs. (publs. adv. com.), Internat. Assn. Bus. Communicators (Golden Quill award 1972, Award of Merit 1979), Women in Communications Inc., Western Publs. Assn. Office: Los Angeles County Medical Assn 1925 Wilshire Blvd Los Angeles CA 90057

BROWN, SHARON GAIL, data processing executive; b. Chgo., Dec. 25, 1941; d. Otto and Pauline (Lauer) Schumacher; B.G.S., Roosevelt U.; m. Robert B. Ringo, Aug. 2, 1984; 1 dau. by previous marriage, Susan Ann. Info. analyst Internat. Minerals & Chems., Northbrook, Ill., 1966-71, programmer analyst, 1971-74; programmer analyst Procon Internat. Inc. subs. UOP Inc., Des Plaines, Ill., 1974-76, systems analyst, 1976-77, project leader, 1977-78; mgr. adminstrv. services, 1978-82; spl. cons. to pres. IPS Internat., Ltd., 1982-83; spl. cons. to pres. CEI Supply Co. div. Sigma-Chapman, Inc., 1984—; data processing cons. Mem. Buffalo Grove (Ill.) Youth Commn., 1978-82; mem. adv. com. UOP Polit. Action Com., 1979-82; Mem. Rep. Senatorial Com. Inner Circle. Mem. Am. Mgmt. Assn., Chgo. Council on Fgn. Relations, Lake Forest-Lake Bluff Hist. Soc. Home: 1381 N Lake Rd Lake Forest IL 60045

BROWN, SHARON HENDRICKSON, broadcasting company executive; b. Malta, Mont., Mar. 27, 1944; d. Elmer Theodore and Dorothy Harriet (Flom) Hendrickson; m. Monty Charles Brown, Oct. 24, 1962; children—Michael Charles, Misty Dawn. Cert. med. lab. technologist, Profl. Bus. Inst., 1962; student Alaska Meth. U., Meth. Coll. Lic. 3d class broadcaster, FCC. On-air, traffic, copywriter various radio stas., Alaska, Tex., Mont., 1967-73; asst. news dir., prodn. mgr. Sta. KIXS-Radio, Killeen, Tex., 1973-74; prodn. mgr., continuity dir. Cape Fear Broadcasting, Fayetteville, N.C., 1978-81, account exec., 1981-85; gen. mgr. Ad Channel (television), Fayetteville, 1985—, market cons., 1986. Judge Miss Ft. Bragg Pageant, N.C., 1983; mem. parade com. Dogwood Festival, Fayetteville, 1983, mem. publicity com., 1984-85. Mem. Tex. Press Women (pres. Dist. 10 1973-74, 1st place award 1973), Fayetteville Area Advt. Fedn. (Gold ADDY award 1984, Silver ADDY award 1984), Nat. Assn. Female Execs., Assn. U.S. Army, Fayetteville Area Bd. Realtors, Fayetteville C. of C. Lutheran. Avocations: painting; writing; photography. Home: 7317 Avalon Dr Fayetteville NC 28303

BROWN, SHIRLEY ANTOINETT MCGEE, legal administrator; b. Savannah, Ga., Nov. 24, 1948; d. Henry and Wilhelmina (Cutter) McGee; m. Sage Brown; children—Lavanda, Sagdrina, Sage W. B.S., Savannah State Coll., 1971; M.S., Central Mich. U., 1983. Tchr. Richmond County Sch., Augusta, Ga., 1971-73; owner, mgr. Southeastern Service System, Ltd., Savannah, Ga., 1975-80; legal adminstr., 1978—. Bd. dirs. Girl Scouts U.S.A., Savannah, 1980—; v.p. bd. dirs. Greenbriar Children's Ctr.; chmn. Mt. Olive Holiness Ch. Women's Assn., 1984—; pres. bd. dirs. Mt. Olive Holiness Ch., 1984—. Recipient Scroll of Thanks, Savannah Girl Scout Council, 1979. Mem. Hostess City Bus. and Profl. Women's Club, Sigma Iota Epsilon, Alpha Kappa Alpha. Club: Jack and Jill Inc. (Savannah, Ga.); Zonta Internat. Avocations: swimming; tennis; reading. Office: Southeastern Legal Service System 427 Montgomery St Savannah GA 31401

BROWN, STELLA CHANEY, advt. agy. exec.; b. East St. Louis, Ill., Apr. 1, 1924; d. James Oscar and Lela Elizabeth (Hartill) Chaney; student Northwestern U., 1941-42, Jefferson Coll., 1942-45; m. A. Harvey Brown, Nov. 1, 1946 (div. Nov. 1960); children—Wendy Alexandra Brown Kennedy, Deborah Elisabeth Brown Garrity. Advt. mgr. Sonnenfelds, St. Louis, 1943; dir. men's wear advt. Stix, Baer & Fuller, St. Louis, 1944; account exec., copy writer Hillman Shane Breyer Agy., Los Angeles, 1945; copy dir. Harry Serwer Agy., N.Y.C., 1945-46; advt. mgr. Libson Shops, St. Louis, 1946-47; asst. advt. dir. Edison Bros. Stores, Inc., 1947-53; copy dir., account exec. Hirsch-Tamm & Ullman Agy., 1957-58; pres. Stella Chaney Brown Advt., Inc., Clayton, Mo., 1959—; dir. St. Louis Broadcasting Co., Inc.; fashion editor Prom Mag., 1946—. Mem. Am. Fedn. Astrologers. Editor: Wheelspin, 1953-58. Address: 9180 Ladue Rd Saint Louis MO 63124

BROWN, STEPHANIE B., insurance company executive; b. Bangor, Maine, Apr. 4, 1943; d. Stephen A. and Marvia P. Barry; B.A. in Math. magna cum laude, U. Maine, 1965. EDP tng. coordinator Eastman Kodak, Rochester, N.Y., 1965-67; data processing cons. Arthur D. Little, Cambridge, Mass., 1967-73; with New Eng. Life Ins. Co., Boston, 1974—, asst. v.p., 1978-79, 2d v.p. corp. planning and research, 1979-82, v.p. corp. planning and research, 1982-84, v.p. fin. planning, 1984—; pres. New Eng. Fin. Advisors, Inc. Mem. Commonwealth of Mass. Gov.'s Mgmt. Task Force, 1975; bd. dirs., mem. strategic planning com. Boston YMCA. Mem. Internat. Assn. for Fin. Planning (bd. dirs. Greater Boston chpt.), Inter-Fin. Assn. Office: 501 Boylston St Boston MA 02117

BROWN, SUZANNE WILEY, museum executive; b. Cheyenne, Wyo., Aug. 28, 1938; d. Robert James and Catharine Helen (Schroeder) Wiley; B.S. with honors, U. Wyo., 1960, M.S., 1964; postgrad. U. Cin. Med. Sch., 1965-66, U. Ill., 1969-72; m. Ralph E. Brown, July 19, 1968; 1 dau., Nina M. Research asst. Harvard Med. Sch., 1962-63; research asst. U. Cin. Med. Sch., 1964-65; sr. lab. asst. U. Chgo., 1966-67; research assoc. U. Colo. Med. Sch., 1968; teaching asst. U. Ill., 1971-73; exec. asst. Chgo. Acad. Scis., 1974-82, asst. dir., 1982-86, assoc. dir., 1986—. NDEA fellow, 1960-62. Mem. Mus. Educators of Greater Chgo., Am. Assn. Museums, Internat. Council Museums, Chgo. Zool. Soc. (governing mem.), Phi Beta Kappa, Sigma Xi, Phi Kappa Phi. Club: Executive's of Chgo. Office: 2001 N Clark St Chicago IL 60614

BROWN, TERRANCE SUZETTE, owner day care center; b. Corpus Christi, Tex., Feb. 17, 1955; d. Earl Edward and Nora Ann (Rossow) Moore; m. Philip Lee Brown, Nov. 14, 1973; children—Tiffany Ann, Patrick Edward. A.English, San Antonio Jr. Coll., 1972-73; B.B.A., U. Tex.-Austin, 1977-79. Cert. tchr., Tex.; child care lic., 1981. Instr./model Ben Shaw Modeling Studios, San Antonio, 1972-74; distbr. Ideal Incorp., San Antonio, 1976; accounts clk. Scobey Moving Storage, San Antonio, 1974-76; CRT operator The Woman's Shop, San Antonio, 1976-77; resident asst. U. Tex., Austin, 1978-79; distributive edn. tchr. Austin Ind. Sch. Dist., 1979-80; owner/operator Terri's Tender Care, Dallas, 1981—, ednl. coordinator, nutritional cons., phys. activities dir., 1981—; managerial cons. P.L. Brown Service Contracting, Dallas, 1983—. Sustaining sponsor Living Bibles Internat., 1981—; mem. Nat. Republican Senatorial Club, 1984; sustaining mem. Republican Nat. Com., 1983-84; charter mem. Rep. Presdl. Task Force, Washington, 1982—; vol. nat. election, Dallas, 1980, gubernatorial election, 1982. Mem. Tex. Tchrs. Assn., Distributive Edn. Clubs Am., NEA, Austin Voc. Assn., Tex. Voc. Tchrs. Assn., Tex. Assn. Distributive Edn. Tchrs., Pi Omega Pi. Roman Catholic. Clubs: Altar Soc. (v.p.), St. Elizabeth's Cir., Pre Sch. Moms. Address: 11308 Gatewood Pl Dallas TX 75218

BROWN, VALERIE ANNE, psychiatric social worker, educator; b. Elizabeth, N.J., Feb. 28, 1951; d. William John and Adelaide Elizabeth (Krasa) B.; B.A. summa cum laude (fellow), C.W. Post Coll., 1972; M.S.W. (Silberman scholar), Hunter Coll., 1975. Social work intern Greenwich House Counseling Center, N.Y.C., 1973-74, Metro Cons. Center, N.Y.C., 1974-75; sr. psychiat. social worker, co-adminstr. Saturday Clinic, Essex County Guidance Center, East Orange, N.J., 1975-80; pvt. practice psychiat. social work, psychotherapy, 1979—; sr. psychiat social worker John E. Runnells Hosp., Berkeley Heights, N.J., 1980—; co-founder Women's Growth Ctr., Cedar Grove, N.J., 1979; counselor Passaic Drug Clinic, 1978-80; field instr. Fairleigh Dickinson U., Madison, N.J., 1981-86; field supr. Union Coll., Cranford, N.J., 1986—; instr. Sch. Social Work, NYU, N.Y.C., 1980-83, asst. prof., 1983-85. Fund raiser Am. Heart Assn. Mem. N.J. Assn. Clin. Social Workers, Nat. Assn. Social Workers, N.J. Assn. Women Therapists, Am. Soc. Tng. and Devel., Psi Chi, Pi Gamma Mu, Sigma Tau Delta. Office: 250 N 19th St Kenilworth NJ 07033

BROWN, VALERIE MARY, nurse, cancer program administrator; b. Meriden, Conn., Jan. 6, 1950; d. Lawrence Lester and Marian Gertrude (Hartin) Tompkins; m. Edward Francis Brown, Oct. 27, 1979; children—Jonathan Edward, Matthew Michael. Diploma in Nursing, Mass. Gen. Hosp., 1971; B.A., Emmanuel Coll., Boston, 1977. R.N., Mass., Ind. Unit tchr. Mass. Gen. Hosp., Boston, 1973-76; staff nurse coronary care unit Cooley Dickinson Hosp., Northampton, Mass., 1977-79; patient care mgr. Methodist Hosp. Ind., Indpls., 1979-81, project coordinator, 1981-84, cancer data system coordinator, 1984-86, assoc. dir. cancer ctr., 1986—. Mem. Ind. Cancer Registrars Assn. (pres. 1986-87), Assn. Community Cancer Ctr. Spl. Adminstrs., Symposium for Computer Applications in Med. Care Spl. Interest Group for Nurses (regional coordinator for Ind. 1985-86). Avocations: flower gardening; interior decorating. Home: 11336 Fieldstone Ct Carmel IN 46032 Office: Methodist Hosp Ind 1604 N Capitol Ave Indianapolis IN 46202

BROWN, VICKI LEE, construction company executive; Ada, Okla., Nov. 6, 1947; d. Roland Eugene Descans and Ora Lee (Albin) Fisher; m. Robert Anthony Brown, Feb. 20, 1983. B.A., East Central U., 1967-71. Interior decorator Davis Paint, Oklahoma City, 1976-77, Curtline, Oklahoma City, 1977, Roach Paint, 1977-79, Gladys Shockley, Oklahoma City, 1979-81; owner, sec., treas. Assoc. Constrn. and Drywall, Inc., Oklahoma City, 1980—. Mem. Am. Business Women's Assn. (rec. sec. 1983, pres. 1984-85, Woman of Yr. 1984-85). Democrat. Home: 8400 NW 87 St Oklahoma City OK 73132

BROWN, VICKIE ADAMS, gift items manufacturer, designer; b. Lubbock, Tex., Jan. 1, 1951; d. Weldon Travis and Dorothy Faye (Gardner) Adams; m. John Michael Brown, July 28, 1978. B.F.A., Tex. Tech. U., 1974. Advt. mgr. J.C. Penney Co., Lubbock, 1979-81; advt. sales rep. Lubbock Avalanche Jour., 1981-83; owner, mgr. Vickie B's, Lubbock, 1979—. Author: Florals Gift Shop Wreaths, 1986. Mem. Woodmere Art Gallery. Baptist. Avocations: cooking; painting. Home: 719 Marietta Dr Ambler PA 19002

BROWN, WENDY ELAINE, systems programmer; b. Los Alamos, N.Mex., Apr. 28, 1956; d. Leon J. and Dorothy (Stern) B. B.A., Northwestern U., 1978. Software engr. Prime Computer Inc., Natick, Mass., 1978-80; systems programmer Dialcom, Silver Spring, Md., 1980-85; systems programmer, analyst APA, Falls Church, Va., 1985—. Mem. Prime User's Group, (sec. treas. 1986), Electronic Networking Assn. Democrat. Jewish. Avocations: sewing; theatre/stage crew. Home: 2248 Washington Ave #203 Silver Spring MD 20910 Office: APA 131 W Great Falls Falls Church VA 22046

BROWN-DUGGAN, GLORIA LORENE, health care administrator; b. Alpine, Utah, July 22, 1927; d. George Alfred and Alice Cleora (Adams) Brown; B.S. with honors, San Diego State U., 1957, postgrad., 1964-74; m. George F. Duggan Jr., Aug. 25, 1972; 1 son, Gregory P. Maynard. Sch. nurse, tchr. Sweetwater Union High Sch., National City, Calif., 1966-68; resident head nurse Mary C. Wheeler Sch., Providence, 1968-70; sub regional trainer Calif. State Drug program Calif. Dept. Edn., 1970-71; hearing conservation program San Francisco Schs., San Francisco Dept. Pub. Health, maternal and child welfare, 1974; clin. lab. instr. community health R.I. Coll., Providence, 1975-76; exec. dir. Pawtucket (R.I.) Neighborhood Health Centers Inc., 1976—; lectr. in field. Publicity dir. LaJolla aux. San Diego Symphony Orch., 1966-68, chmn. symphony summer music festivals, 1967—; past chmn. health adv. com. Dept. Human Services, State of R.I.; exec. com. R.I. Health Ctr. Mem. Nat. Assn. Community Health Centers (past treas. region 1, program planning com. 1978-82), R.I. Health Center Assn. (exec. com., publicity dir. 1978), Mass. League Neighborhood Health Centers, New Eng. Community Health Center Assn., AAUW (publicity dir. chpt. 1966), Am. Pub. Health Assn., New Eng. Pub. Health Assn., Blackstone Valley C. of C., Phi Kappa Phi. Mem. Ch. Jesus Christ Latter-day Saints. Home: 7 Gilbert St Warwick RI 02886 Office: 401 Mineral Spring Ave Pawtucket RI 02860

BROWNE, CINDY RAE, broadcasting executive; b. Mpls., Oct. 27, 1952; d. Richard A. and Patricia (Hudson) B. B.S., U. Minn., 1974, M.B.A., 1983. Broadcast mgr. KTCA, St. Paul, 1983, dir. broadcasting, 1984—; cons. Infovision, Mpls., 1984; mem. adv. bd. KBEM-FM, Mpls., 1984—. Mem. Citizen's League, Mpls., 1982-84. Mem. Nat. Assn. Television Program Execs. (mem. membership com. 1985—), Assn. M.B.A.s. Office: KTCA TV 1640 Como Ave Saint Paul MN 55108

BROWNE, JANE JORDAN, literary agent; b. Los Angeles, Apr. 14, 1931; d. Francis Emmett and Margaret Eleanor (Gray) B.; m. William O. Petersen, Nov. 25, 1978. B.A., Smith Coll., 1952; Diplome de la Langue Francaise, U. Neuchatel, Switzerland, 1953; M.A., UCLA, 1962. Mng. editor Hawthorn Books, N.Y.C., 1963-65; editor Thomas Y. Crowell, N.Y.C., 1965-67; freelance writer, Beverly Hills, Calif., 1967-68; gen. editorial and prodn. mgr. Macmillan Ednl. Services Inc., Beverly Hills, 1968-70; lit. agt. Multimedia Product Devel. Inc., Beverly Hills and Chgo., 1970—. Ghostwriter: When Towns Had Walls, 1970; writer, editor: Architectural Digest Book of Celebrity Homes, 1976. Contbr. articles to consumer mags., profl. jours. Bd. dirs. Ill. Ctr. for the Book, Chgo., 1985. Mem. Modern Poetry Assn. (v.p. 1983—), Midwest Writers Assn. (bd. dirs. 1983—), Ind. Lit. Agts. Assn. Republican. Roman Catholic. Clubs: Fortnightly, Friday (Chgo.). Avocations: gardening; cooking; travel. Office: Multimedia Product Devel Inc 410 S Michigan Ave Chicago IL 60605

BROWNER, FRANCINE, clothing manufacturer; b. N.Y.C., Sept. 10, 1945; d. Arnold and Chickie (Ulrich) Lehrer; divorced; children—Stacy Lyn, Jacqueline Beth. Student Syracuse U., 1963-64, Parsons Sch. Design, 1964-66, Queens Coll., 1973-76. Designer Organically Grown, Los Angeles, 1978-79; designer, merchandiser Bronson of Calif., Gardena, Calif., 1979; designer Robyn's Nest, Los Angeles, 1979-80, Calif. Class, Los Angeles, 1982-83; dir. merchandising and design Spare Parts, Los Angeles, 1983-84; owner, pres. Rue de Reves, Los Angeles, 1984—. Active Los Angeles Mus. Contemporary Art. Democrat. Jewish. Avocations: tennis, sailing, yoga, dancing, writing. Office: Rue de Rêves 1936 Mateo Los Angeles CA 90015

BROWNING, BARBARA WILLIAMS, restaurateur; b. Danville, Va., Sept. 23, 1934; d. Floyd Brantley and Martha Ada (Pettigrew) Williams; m. Roy Leon Browning, Dec. 10, 1955; children—Lari Delyn Browning Young, John Hamilton. Med. Tech. degree, Stratford Coll., Danville, 1954, Meml. Hosp., Danville, 1955. Registered Am. Soc. Clin. Pathologists. Med. technologist Meml. Hosp., Danville, 1955-56; poultry research lab virologist Va. Poly. Inst., Blacksburg, Va., 1956-58; biochemist UCLA, 1958-61, Riker Pharm. Northridge, Calif., 1961-62; chemist N.Am. Aviation Research Sci. Ctr., Northridge, 1962-63; chief exec. officer, sec., treas. B.M.R., Inc., McLean, Va., 1970—. Stratford Coll. scholar, 1952. Mem. Met. Restaurant Assn., Nat. Restaurant Assn. Republican. Methodist. Avocations: skiing (water and snow), sailing, swimming, tennis.

BROWNING, HARRIETTE REGINA, county tax commissioner; b. Athens, Ga., May 10, 1951; d. Robert Preston and Lola Jane (Gunter) Moon; m. Clarence Millard Browning, Sept. 11, 1969; children—David Alan, Terri Leanne. Grad. high sch., Watkinsville, Ga. Tax commr., Oconee County, Ga., 1981—. Mem. Oconee County Pilot Club, Oconee C. of C. Office: Oconee County Tax Commr PO Box 106 Watkinsville GA 30677

BROWNING, HAZEL GAY, nurses association executive; b. Greenville, N.C., May 29, 1950; d. Daniel Robert and Helen Nelson (Shelton) Gay; B.S.N., East Carolina U., 1972, M.S. in Rehab. Counseling, 1976, M.S.N., 1979; m. James Fred Browning, Oct. 29, 1972 (div.); 1 dau., Lauran Shelton. Staff nurse Pitt Meml. Hosp., Greenville, N.C., 1972-73; office nurse Dr. David Pearsall, Greenville, N.C., 1973; nursing instr. East Carolina U., Greenville, 1973-77, asst. prof. nursing, 1977-80; asst. prof. nursing Duke U., Durham, N.C., 1980-82; assoc. exec. dir. N.C. Nurses Assn., Raleigh, 1982—. Mem. Am. Nurses Assn., Nurses Assn. of Am. Coll. Obstetricians and Gynecologists, N.C. Nurses Assn., N.C. Nurses Assn. of Am. Coll. Obstetricians and Gynecologists (mem. adv. council), Rho Lambda, Sigma Theta Tau. Democrat. Presbyterian. Home: 4305 Sunbelt Dr Raleigh NC 27612 Office: NC Nurses Assn 103 Enterprise St Raleigh NC 27605

BROWNING, LISA RITONDO, lawyer; b. Anniston, Ala., July 16, 1957; d. John Thomas and Rose Marie (Elwell) Ritondo; m. James Patrick Browning, Jr., Aug. 8, 1981. B.S., U. Ala., 1979, M.A., 1982, J.D., 1982. Bar: La. 1982. Acting treas.; dir. compliance, asst. corp. sec. New Orleans Commodity Exchange, 1982-83; v.p. and gen. counsel Howard, Weil, Labouisse, Friedrichs, Inc., New Orleans, 1983—. Mem. New Orleans Mus. Art, Friends of Audubon Zoo. Mem. ABA, La. Bar Assn., Futures Industry Assn., Omicron Delta Epsilon, Dobro Slovo. Home: 1429 Fern St New Orleans LA 70118 Office: Howard Weil Labouisse Friedrichs Inc Energy Centre 1100 Poydras St Suite 900 New Orleans LA 70163

BROWNING, MARILYN CROUCH, psychiatrist; b. McAlester, Okla., Apr. 8, 1944; d. Orbin E. and Juanita E. Crouch. B.S., Bethany Nazarene Coll., 1967; M.D., U. Okla., 1973. Diplomate Am. Bd. Psychiatry and Neurology. Resident in psychiatry Napa State Hosp. (Calif.), 1973-77, staff psychiatrist, 1977-78; staff Sonoma County Mental Health, Santa Rosa, Calif., 1978-80; pvt. practive psychiatry, Santa Rosa, 1980—; psychiat. cons. Sonoma State Hosp., Eldridge, Calif., 1980—. Docent, Bouverie Audubon Preserve, Valley of Moon Natural History Assn. Mem. Am. Med. Women's Assn., Calif. Med. Assn., Sonoma County Med. Assn., Am. Psychiat. Assn. Democrat. Buddhist. Club: Sonoma County Forum (Santa Rosa, Calif.). Office: 515 Farmers Ln Santa Rosa CA 95405

BROWNING, REBA SMITH, bus contractor; b. Jacksonville, Fla., Dec. 5, 1926; d. Reuben F. and Emmie Ruth (Hopkins) Smith; m. Richard McGuire, July 26, 1945 (div. July 1949); children—Michael Vernon, Patricia Gail; m. Elwood Likens Browning, Aug. 17, 1957; 1 child, Bruce Morgan. Ed. pub. schs., Jacksonville. Bus owner, contractor Duval County Schs., Jacksonville, 1969-75; owner, pres. Reba S. Browning, Inc., Jacksonville, 1975—; driver tng. instr. Mem., sec. Fla. Vol. Chaplain Cert. Com., Jacksonville, 1984-85. Recipient Outstanding Christian of Yr. award Hogan Baptist Brotherhood, Jacksonville, 1971; Nat. Safety Slogan of Yr. award Gateway Transp., 1972. Mem. Nat. Fedn. Ind. Bus., U.S. C. of C., Duval County Sch. Bus Contractor's Assn. (pres. 1970-73, 81-83, bd. dirs.), Nat. Save-the-Children Club, Jacksonville Be-a-Friend Club. Republican. Baptist. Avocations: public speaking; poetry; furniture refinishing. Office: Reba S Browning Inc 8655 Phillips Hwy Jacksonville FL 32216

BROWNING-SLETTEN, MELISSA ANN, mechanical engineer; b. Steubenville, Ohio, Aug. 31, 1947; d. Milton M. and Mabel (Steele) Trudix; m. Darwin N. Sletten. B.S. in M.E., U. Colo., Boulder, 1977. Purchasing agt. Eastman Kodak, Windsor, Colo., 1971-73; mech. engr. Public Service Co. of Colo., Denver, 1978-85, supr. prodn. standards, 1985—. cons. Hvar Service, Inc. Mem. ASME, CSE. Episcopalian. Home: 11023 Tennyson Pl Westminster CO 80030 Office: 1800 W Sheri Ln Englewood CO 80110

BROWNLEE, PAULA PIMLOTT, college president, chemistry educator; b. London, June 23, 1934; U.S., 1959; d. John Richard and Alice A. (Ajamian) Pimlott; m. Thomas H. Brownlee, Feb. 10, 1961; children—Kenneth Gainsford, Elizabeth Ann, Clare Louise. B.A. with honors, Somerville Coll., Oxford (Eng.) U., 1957; D.Phil. in Organic Chemistry, Oxford (Eng.) U., 1959; Postdoctoral fellow, U. Rochester, N.Y., 1959-61. Research chemist Am. Cyanamid Co., Stamford, Conn., 1961-62; lectr. U. Bridgeport, Conn., 1968-70, asst. prof. Rutgers Coll., Rutgers U., 1970-73, assoc. dean Douglass Coll., Rutgers U., 1973-75, acting dean, assoc. prof. chemistry, 1975-76; dean faculty, prof. chemistry Union Coll., Schenectady, N.Y., 1976-81; pres., prof. chemistry Hollins (Va.) Coll., 1981—; dir. Colonial Am. Bank; bd. dirs. Roanoke Valley Sci. Mus., Va. Sci. Mus., Roanoke Symphony. Author articles, lab. manual. Mem. Royal Chem. Soc. London, Am. Chem. Soc., Am. Women in Sci., Am. Assn. Higher Edn. (past chmn.), Soc. Values in Higher Edn., AAAS. Episcopalian. Office: Office of Pres Hollins College Roanoke VA 24020*

BROWNSON, ANNA LOUISE HARSHMAN, editor, publisher; b. Indpls., May 4, 1926; d. Walter W. and Jennie Andrea (Jensen) Harshman; B.A., Butler U., 1949, postgrad., 1950-51; m. Charles B. Brownson, Nov. 23, 1966; children—Dwight, Bruce, David, Catharine, Scott. Asst. biochemistry lab. Ind. U. Med. Sch., Indpls., 1944-47; grad. asst. Butler U., Indpls., 1949-51; adminstrv. asst. to U.S. congressman from 11th Dist. Ind., Indpls., 1951-58; asso. editor, treas. Congl. Staff Directory, Ltd., 1959-79, pres., 1980—; pub., owner, editor (with husband) Advance Locator for Capitol Hill, 1963—, Election Index, 1966—, Congl. Staff Directory, Fed. Staff Directory, Jud. Staff Directory. Mem. Former Mems. Congress Aux. (sec., past pres.), Corcoran Art Gallery, Save the Redwoods Soc., Internat. Oceanographic Found., Atlantic Council, English Speaking Union, Oceanic Soc., Fairchild Gardens, Kappa Alpha Theta. Presbyterian. Home: 4748 Neptune Dr Alexandria VA 22309 also 1261 S Alhambra Circle Coral Gables FL 33146 Office: Box 62 Mount Vernon VA 22121

BROWNSTEIN, CLARA DOMB, life insurance company executive; b. Buenos Aires, Argentina, Mar. 6, 1951; came to U.S., 1964, naturalized, 1967; d. Ruben and Felisa (Schecter) Domb; m. Bennett J. Zucker, Nov. 26, 1972 (div. 1982); 1 son, Jonathan; m. Arnold Brownstein, Feb. 11, 1984. B.A., Queens Coll., 1972; Ph.M., Columbia U., 1975. Instr. Bronx Community Coll., CUNY, 1973-77, Fashion Inst. Tech., SUNY, 1973-74, Medgar Evers Coll., CUNY, 1975-76, Marymount Manhattan Coll., 1975-76; with MONY, N.Y.C., 1977-81, sales mgr., 1980-81; sales mgr. Met. Life, N.Y.C., 1981—. Mem. Nat. Assn. Life Underwriters, Women Life Underwriters Conf. (dir. N.Y. chpt.). Office: Metropolitan Life 1 Madison Ave Area 14S New York NY 10010

BROWNSTEIN, NANCY, commercial lighting company executive; b. Phila., June 4, 1947; d. Melvin and Frances (Turetsky) Ruttenburg; m. Allen Brownstein, Nov. 2, 1968; 1 dau., Marla Michelle. B.A. in Bus., Temple U., 1968. Sales adminstr. Shelby Mfg. Co., Southampton, Pa., 1973-75; sales v.p. Global Mfg. Co., Phila., 1975-78; sales dir. Jaco Industries, Huntingdon Valley, Pa., 1978-82; pres. Marlan Industries, Phila., 1982—; dir. Banner Indsl. Supply, Huntingdon Valley, Global Mfg. Co., Lighting Industries, Trenton, N.J. Vol. Phila. Big Bros.-Little Sisters, 1986. Mem. Nat. Assn. Female Execs. Republican. Jewish. Home: PO Box 432 Southampton PA 18966 Office: Marlan Industries 251 Robina Pl A Philadelphia PA 19116

BROWN-WHISTLER, SUSAN DIANE, employment and training counselor; b. Brainerd, Minn., Oct. 14, 1950; d. Lloyd Clifford and Lorraine Doris (Callahan) Brown; m. James V. Whistler, Dec. 15, 1973 (div. May 1985); children—Shawn Robert-Lloyd, Katura Lorna-Brown. Student Bemidji State U., 1973-76; B.A. in Psychology/Math., Mo. So. State Coll., 1984. Dist. supr.

circulation Pioneer Newspaper, Bemidji, Minn., 1975-80; ct. transcriptionist Dist. Ct. Reporter, Beltrami County, Bemidji, 1977-80; research lab. asst. Mo. So. State Co., Joplin, 1982-84; program coordinator Econ. Security Corp., Joplin, 1985, counselor employment and tng., 1984—. Sec.-treas. Nat. Women's Polit. Caucus, local chpt., Joplin, 1985-86; referral counselor Crisis Intervention, Joplin, 1983-86; counselor Coalition for Battered Women, Bemidji, 1977-80. Mem. Nat. Assn. Female Execs. (network dir. 1986), Interagy. Assn., Mo. Assn. Community Action. Democrat. Methodist. Avocations: reading; writing; water sports. Home: 2330 Murphy St Joplin MO 64801 Office: Econ Security Corp 305 Virginia St Joplin Mo 64801

BROXMEYER, PAULA RUBIN, crime prevention association executive; b. Bklyn., Apr. 17, 1951; d. Samuel and Rhoda (Jablowitz) Rubin; children—Michael, Evan. Student Hofstra U. Pres., founder L.I.A.I.S.O.N. (L.I. Assn. to Increase Security in our Neighborhoods, Inc.), New Hyde Park, N.Y., 1982—; co-founder L.I. Crime Victims Services Task Force, Garden City, N.Y., 1986. Co-author: Playing It Safe, 1985. Chmn. health and safety Roslyn Country Club Civic Assn., Roslyn Heights, N.Y., 1982—. Recipient Pres.'s Vol. Action award for Pub. Safety, Nat. Vol. and Action Coms., Washington, 1986. Mem. Nat. Orgn. for Victim's Assistance, Internat. Soc. Crime Prevention Practioners, Families Aware of Childhood Traumas. Jewish. Avocations: drawing; painting; photography; tennis. Office: LIAISON Inc Herricks Community Ctr Herricks Rd New Hyde Park NY 11040

BROYLES, REBECCA ANN, real estate investment counselor; b. Hannibal, Mo., Dec. 4, 1946; d. Everette Franklin and Bessie Marie (Legg) Stevens; m. Jay Randall Broyles, May 12, 1970; children—Saramarie, Elizabeth Ann. B.S. in Edn., U. Mo., 1967. Tchr. North Kansas City Sch., Mo., 1967-73; salesman Coldwell Banker, Kansas City, Mo., 1973-79; pres. Nat. Investment Counselors, Kansas City, 1979—; instr. Met. Real Estate Bd. of Kansas City, 1983—. Active North Kansas City Hosp. Aux., 1980—. Recipient Pathfinder award Acad. of Real Estate, 1983; named to Million Dollar Club Mo. Assn. Realtors, 1973-80. Mem. Met. Bd. Realtors (chmn. awards com. 1980-82, election com. 1981-83), Nat. Assn. Realtors (instr. 1979-83), Nebr. Assn. Realtors (instr. 1982-83), Cert. Comml. Investment (edn. chmn. 1980-82, bd. dirs. 1982-83), Soc. Exchange Counselors, Kappa Alpha Theta. Democrat. Avocations: reading; attending plays; handcrafts. Home: 7616 N Olive St Gladstone MO 64118 Office: Nat Investment Counselors Inc 4444 N Belleview Suite 110 Kansas City MO 64116

BRTICEVICH, DIANA JULIA, trucking company executive; b. Chgo., May 21, 1933; d. Frank and Julia (Naccarato) Cosentino; m. Michael George Brticevich, Sept. 5, 1953; 1 child, Mark. Grad. Kelly High Sch. Clk., Little Company of Mary Hosp., Evergreen Park, Ill., 1958-61; inventory control supr. All-Bright & Nell, Chgo., 1961-66; pres. Fast Motor Services, Inc., Brookfield, Ill., 1966—; pres. U.S. Internat. Inc., Brookfield, 1984—, also dir. Treas. Citizens Com. of Jerry Cosentino, Brookfield, 1974—. Democrat. Roman Catholic. Avocations: reading, ceramics. Office: Fast Motor Services Inc 9100 W Plainfield Rd Brookfield IL 60513

BRUBAKER, GWENDOLYN LEE, choral conductor, educator; b. Leadville, Colo., Feb. 28, 1944; d. Harold Harry and Frances Helen (Frey) B.; B.M., Hastings Coll., 1966; M.M.E., Drake U., 1968; Ph.D., Northwestern U., 1982. Tchr. vocal music kindergarten through 12th grades Central Dallas Sch., Minburn, Iowa, 1967-69; tchr. vocal music Lane Jr. High Sch., West Allis, Wis., 1969-78; vis. lectr. in music edn. Roosevelt U., 1979-80; vis. lectr. in jr. high sch. music Northwestern U., 1980; instr. choral music edn. U. Wis., LaCrosse, 1980-85; asst. prof. choral music edn. Wright State U., Dayton, Ohio, 1985—; dir. music Trinity Lutheran Ch., LaCrosse; musical dir. community theaters, Milw., LaCrosse. Mem. Am. Choral Dirs. Assn., Music Educators Nat. Conf., Ohio Music Educators Conf., Phi Delta Kappa, Pi Kappa Lambda. Choral compositions: Love Is Come Again, 1972; Sing Praise, 1972; The Lone Wild Bird, 1978; Orientale, 1982; The Proud Mysterious Cat, 1983. Home: 2681 Corlington Dr Kettering OH 45440 Office: Creative Arts Ctr Wright State U Dayton OH 45435

BRUBECK, ANNE ELIZABETH DENTON, artist; b. Beardstown, Ill., Mar. 5, 1918; d. Harry B. and Helen Jean (Gibbs) Denton; student Christian Coll., 1935-36; B.Design, Newcomb Coll., Tulane U., 1939; postgrad. Art Inst. Chgo., 1939-40; A.A. (hon.), Wabash Valley Coll., 1981; m. William E. Brubeck, Dec. 14, 1940; children—Jean Brubeck Stayman, William E. Instr. painting Wabash Valley Coll., Mt. Carmel, Ill., 1962-67; painter; one-man shows include N.Y.C., 1961, 63-67, Evansville, Ind., 1963-69; retrospective, Wabash Valley Coll., 1980; juried exhbns. include: Evansville Mus., 1963, 64, 65, Swopes Gallery, Terre Haute, Ind., 1964, 68, Nashville, 1967. Trustee, Mt. Carmel Pub. Library, 1954—, chmn., 1975-6; mem. cultural events com. Wabash Valley Coll., 1976—. Brubeck Art Center named in her and her husband's honor, 1976; named to Mt. Carmel High Sch. Centennial Hall of Fame, 1982. Mem. Ill. Library Assn., Nat. League Am. Penwomen, PEO. Methodist. Club: Reviewers Matinee. Home and office: 729 Cherry St Mount Carmel IL 62863

BRUBECK, SHARON ANN, nurse, educator; b. Milw., Oct. 24, 1956; d. Richard Frank and Ann (Fizel) Metzel; m. Harry James Brubeck, May 21, 1983; children—Thomas Richard, Rachel Ann. A.A.S. in Nursing, Elgin Community Coll., 1978; B.S. in Nursing, Ill. Benedictine Coll., 1983. R.N., Ill. Nurse Luth. Gen. Hosp., Park Ridge, Ill., 1978-83; nursing supr. Allied Med. Home Health, Arlington Heights, Ill., 1983, dir. nursing, 1983-84, clin. supr., 1985—; instr. home care nursing William Rainey Harper Coll., Palatine, Ill., 1985—; mem. fin. com. Ill. Council Home Health Services, 1984. Mem. Am. Nurses Assn. Lutheran. Avocations: antiques; camping. Office: Allied Medical Home Health 1430 N Arlington Heights Rd Arlington Heights IL 60004

BRUCE, ANNE, public relations company executive; b. Bronx, N.Y., Dec. 20, 1952; d. Eugene Thomas and Grace Therese (O'Donnell) Carra; m. David W. Thomley, May 18, 1978; 1 child, Autumn Kelly Bruce. Student San Diego Mesa Coll., 1971, Bakersfield Coll., 1975, Sacramento State U., 1978. Independent TV producer CBS Affiliate Sta. KXTV, Sacramento, Calif., 1979—; pres. Anne Bruce, Inc., Sacramento, 1979—; mem. advisory bd. Sumitomo Bank of Calif., Sacramento, 1983—. Instr. Jr. Achievement, Sacramento, 1984—; assoc. Sutter Hosp., Sacramento, 1984—; fundraiser, mem. Sacramento Symphony, 1983—. Editor: (nat. newsletter) Womans' Advocate, 1979-83 (recipient several awards). Producer, writer documentary on first women astronauts, 1980. Contbr. articles to profl. jours., mags. Recipient Best and Brightest award Sacramento Mag., 1985; Women Helping Women award Soroptimist Internat., 1981, 82. Mem. Sacramento Met. C. of C. (Disting. Bus. Woman of Yr. 1980), Citrus Heights C. of C. Democrat. Roman Catholic. Avocations: writing; travel; family time. Office: Anne Bruce Inc 1555 River Park Dr #101 Sacramento CA 95815

BRUCE, CATHERINE MARY, savings and loan company executive; b. Indpls., Nov. 15, 1943; d. George Thomas and Mary Jo (Carton) O'Connor; m. Curtis Brian Bruce, Dec. 28, 1963; children—Krista, Kylie, Brian. Real estate agt. Realty World, Escondido, Calif., 1976-78; in pub. relations Blackshear Ltd., Okinawa, Japan, 1978-79; dir. pub. relations Am. Income, Richmond, Va., 1980-81; nat. trainer Nat. Fitness Virginia Beach, Va., 1981-83; ctr. mgr. Carnation Health & Nutrition, San Diego, 1983-84; dist. coordinator 1st Nationwide Savs. and Loan Assn., San Diego, 1984—. Pres. Marine Wives, San Diego, 1968-69. Mem. Community Services Commn., San Marcos, Calif., 1983—; bd. dirs. North San Diego County Community TV Found., Calif., 1985. Mem. Nat. Assn. Female Execs. Avocations: oil painting; flower arranging.

BRUCE, ELIZABETH (BETSEY) ALICE, broadcast journalist; b. Gary, Ind., Dec. 27, 1948; d. Kenneth Ashel Barnette and Mary Elizabeth (Lasher) Myers; m. Robert S. Bruce, Dec. 11, 1971. B.J., U. Mo., 1970. Writer, editor Sta. KMOX-TV, St. Louis, 1970-71, staff reporter, 1971—, 5 P.M. News co-anchor, 1973, 74-76, host Newsmakers program, 1976—, polit. editor, 1978—, weekend news anchor woman, 1978—; pub. speaker; seminar instr. Jr. League, St. Louis, 1980, 82; journalism advisor St. Louis Med. Soc., 1983. Trustee Cystic Fibrosis Found., 1979—; pres. adv. council Girl Scouts U.S.A., St. Louis, 1979—; trustee, pres. Carrswold Subdiv., Clayton, Mo., 1979—. Recipient honor cert. for broadcast reporting Valley Forge Freedom Found., 1982, Media award Mental Health Patient Advocacy Group, 1982, Emmy award, St. Louis chpt. Nat. Acad. TV Arts and Scis., 1981, 84, cert. of leadership St. Louis YWCA, 1983, Spl. Leadership award for communications, 1984. Mem. Soc. Profl. Journalists (2d v.p. 1982-84), Women in Communications (Philpott-Collins award 1978), Investigative Reporters and Editors, AFTRA, Women's Polit. Caucus, U. Mo. Alumni Assn., Kappa Alpha Theta. Office: KMOX-TV 1 Memorial Dr Saint Louis MO 63102

BRUCE, MELODY ANN, obstetrician-gynecologist; b. New Orleans, Apr. 26, 1953; d. John Markey and Irma Drusilla (Weisdorffer) B.; m. David Allan Ray, July 18, 1982; 1 child, Isaac Michael Ray. B.S., La. State U., Baton Rouge, 1975; M.D., La. State U.-New Orleans, 1978. Diplomate Am. Bd. Obstetrics and Gynecology. Intern, Albany (N.Y.) Med. Ctr., 1978-79, resident, 1979-81, chief resident, 1981-82; teaching cons. Kasturba Med. Coll., Manipal, Karnataka, India, 1982; practice medicine specializing in ob-gyn, Troy, N.Y., 1982—; asst. clin. instr. dept. ob-gyn Albany Med. Ctr., 1982-83; co-developer Capital Dist. Birthing Ctr., Troy, N.Y., 1983-84. Chmn. fund raising Saratoga County Teen Clinic, Clifton Park, N.Y., 1983; mem. adv. bd. Saratoga County Teen Clinic, Clifton Park, 1984; chmn. adult edn. B'nai Sholom Synagogue, Albany, 1984-85. Named Outstanding Young Woman of Am., Albany, 1980; Outstanding Woman Resident Am. Med. Women's Assn., Albany Med. Ctr., 1981. Fellow Am. Coll. Obstetricians/Gynecologists (jr.); mem. AMA, N.Y. State Med. Soc., Rensselaer County Med. Soc. Democrat. Home: 637 Englemore Rd Clifton Park NY 12065 Office: Ob Gyn Birthing Ctr Assocs 2001 5th Ave Troy NY 12180

BRUCK, PHOEBE ANN MASON, landscape architect; b. Highland Park, Ill., Nov. 26, 1928; d. George Allen and Louise Townsend (Barnard) Mason; m. F. Frederick Bruck, June 30, 1956. Student Bard Coll., 1946-49; B.S., Ill. Inst. Tech., 1954; M.L.A., Harvard U., 1963. Trainee, Nat. Gallery of Art, Washington, 1947, Mus. Modern Art, N.Y.C., 1948; head design dept. Design Research Inc., Cambridge, Mass., 1955-60; cons. The Architects Collaborative & Sert, Jackson Assocs., Inc., 1960-63; v.p. F. Frederick Bruck, Architect & Assoc., Inc., Cambridge; vis. design critic dept. landscape architecture Harvard U. Grad. Sch. Design, 1971-79. Contbr. to New Landscapes for Living, 1980. Judge, New Eng. Flower Show, Mass. Hort. Soc., 1971-79, Thoreau Awards, Assn. Landscape Contractors, 1980; mem. Sci. Adv. Group for Edn., Cambridge Pub. Schs., 1981-82. Mem. Mass. Bd. Registration of Landscape Architects (vice chmn.), Am. Arbitration Assn., Am. Soc. Landscape Architects, Boston Soc. Landscape Architects (pres. 1973-75, examining bd. 1978-81), Mass. Soc. Mayflower Descendants, Harvard Sq. Def. Fund (bd. dirs. 1984-85, pres. 1985-86), Harvard U. Grad. Sch. Design Alumni Assn. (officer 1972-78). Episcopalian. Home: 148 Coolidge Hill Cambridge MA 02138 Office: 148 B Coolidge Hill Cambridge MA 02138

BRUCKER, CONNIE, police officer, consultant; b. Detroit, June 29, 1946; d. Joseph Schwenk and Errawanna Coates; 1 child, Debra June Huegel. Student San Jose State Coll., 1980, East Los Angeles Coll., 1978. Legal sec. Lapin & Chester, West Los Angeles, Calif., 1972-75; police officer Santa Monica Police Dept., Calif., 1977—; instr. Santa Monica Jr. Coll.; speaker, lectr. Lady Beware Programs, Los Angeles Area; cons. Safety Products, Calgary, Can., Calif. Council Hosps., Los Angeles, TV movies and spls. and interviews, Los Angeles. Author writings in field. Bd. dirs. ARC, Santa Monica, 1984—. Recipient Medal of Courage, City of Santa Monica, 1979, Mayor's Commendation, 1982. Mem. Internat. Police Assn., Women Peace Officers Assn., Los Angeles Peace Officers Assn., Santa Monica Police Officers Assn., Sexual Assault Investigators Assn. (treas. Calif. 1981—). Office: Santa Monica Police Dept 1685 Main St Santa Monica CA 90401

BRUCK-LIEB, LILLY, consumer advisor, broadcaster, columnist; b. Vienna, Austria, May 13, 1918; came to U.S., 1941, naturalized, 1944; d. Max and Sophie M. Hahn; Ph.D. in Econs., U. Vienna; postgrad. Sorbonne, Paris, Sch. of Econs., London, Sch. of Bus., Columbia U., 1941-42, Sch. of Social Work, N.Y. U., 1964-66; m. Sandor Bruck, Mar. 7, 1943; 1 child, Sandra Lee (Mrs. John David Evans III); m. David L. Lieb, Dec. 7, 1985. Dir. consumer edn. Dept. Consumer Affairs, City of N.Y., 1969-78; project dir. Am. Coalition of Citizens with Disabilities, 1977-78; consumer advisor, broadcaster In Touch Networks, N.Y.C., 1978—; consumer affairs commentator Nat. Public Radio, 1980-82. Chmn. Westchester County, Bonds for Israel, 1960-64. Recipient Eleanor Roosevelt award Bonds for Israel, 1963; Woman of Yr. award Anti Defamation League, 1972; Community Service award local council Girl Scouts U.S.A., 1974. Mem. Soc. of Consumer Affairs Profls., Am. Women in Radio and TV, Authors Guild, Am. Workers for Blind. Democrat. Jewish. Author: Access, The Guide to a Better Life for Disabled Americans, 1978; contbr. articles on disability and rehab. to books, ency., and mags. Home: 25 Murray Hill Scarsdale NY 10583 Office: In Touch Networks 322 W 48th St New York NY 10036

BRUCKS, MERRIE LYNN, business administration educator; b. N.Y.C., May 29, 1955; d. Norman and Marilyn (Gafka) B.; m. Richard T. Snodgrass, July 14, 1979. B.S., U. R.I., 1977; M.S., Carnegie-Mellon U., 1979, Ph.D., 1984. Instr., U. N.C.-Chapel Hill, 1982-83, asst. prof., 1984—. Contbr. articles to profl. jours. Recipient Robert Ferber award for best doctoral dissertation in field of consumer behavior, 1984. Mem. Assn. Consumer Research, Am. Mktg. Assn. Democrat. Home: 24 Gloucester Ct Durham NC 27713 Office: U NC Carroll Hall 012A Chapel Hill NC 27514

BRUDNAK, PEGGY HELENE, fast-food chain executive; b. Chgo., Jan. 8, 1923; d. Michael and Theresa (Hricisin) Kundrat; m. George Andrew Brudnak, June 16, 1946; children—Teresa M. Brudnak Luddy, George A. II, Catherine A. R.N., Englewood Hosp. Sch. Nursing, Chgo., 1944; B.A. with distinction, U. Redlands, Calif., 1977; cert. occupational health nurse, U. Calif.-Riverside, 1977-79. Occupational health nurse Kaiser Cement Co., Lucerne Valley, Calif., 1971-73, City of San Bernardino, Calif., 1974-79; instr. trainer CPR, San Bernardino County Am. Heart Assn., 1973-78; franchisee, dir. ops. Burger King Restaurant, Hesperia, Calif., 1979—; cons., Victorville Burger King Restaurant, 1974—. Choir mem. Holy Family Ch., Hesperia, 1970-72, Sunday sch. tchr., 1971-72. Served as 2d lt. Nurses' Corps, U.S. Army, 1944-45, PTO. Recipient Key to City, San Bernardino, 1977; Service award Am. Heart Assn., 1977. Mem. Inland Ctr. Assn. Occupational Health Nurses (treas. 1974-75), Burger King Franchisee Orgn. Republican. Roman Catholic. Club: Shoreline Yacht (Long Beach, Calif.). Avocations: boating; scuba diving; swimming; hiking; golf. Home: 17433 Aspen St Box 104 Hesperia CA 92345

BRUDNER, HELEN GROSS, history educator; b. N.Y.C.; d. Nathan and Mae (Grichtman) Gross; B.S., N.Y. U., 1959, M.A., 1960, Ph.D., 1973; m. Harvey Jerome Brudner, Dec. 18, 1963; children—Mae Ann, Terry Joseph, Jay Scott. Tchr., N.Y.C. Bd. Edn., 1959-60; instr. Pratt Inst., Bklyn., 1959-61; asst. prof. history N.Y. Inst. Tech., N.Y.C., 1961-63, dir. guidance, 1962-63; assoc. prof. Fairleigh Dickinson U., Rutherford, N.J., 1963-73, prof. history and polit. sci., 1974—, dir. Honors Coll., 1972—, chmn. social sci. dept., 1980—, dep. chmn. dept. internat. studies, history, polit. sci., 1985—, pres. univ. senate, 1975-76, asst. provost, 1983, asst. dean Coll. Arts and Scis., 1984-85; v.p. HJB Enterprises, Highland Park, N.J., 1970—, vice chmn. WLC Inc., Highland Park, 1976—; cons. auto ednl. systems, 1971—. Bd. dirs. NSF Women in Politics project, 1981, Nat. Endowment for The Humanities and Woodrow Wilson Found. project Women in Am. History, Princeton, N.J., 1980, Woodrow Wilson Found. Project on Global Interdependence, 1984, Fairleigh Dickinson U. Fed. Credit Union, 1983—. Recipient Woman of Yr. award Am. Businesswomen's Assn., 1980. Mem. Am. Judicature Soc., Am. Hist. Soc., Acad. Polit. Sci. Contbr. articles in field to profl. publs. Home: 812 Abbott St Highland Park NJ 08904 Office: Fairleigh Dickinson Univ Social Sci Dept Rutherford NJ 07070

BRUEHL, MARGARET ELLEN, human relations consultant; b. Phila., Nov. 22, 1935; d. George Martin and Virginia (Fowler) Gauger; m. William Justice Bruehl, Aug. 4, 1956; children—Amelia Susan, Alexandra Anne. B.S., West-Chester State Coll., 1956. Elem. tchr., pub. schs., Lindenhurst, N.Y., 1956-58, 59-60, Ridley Park, Pa., 1958-59; trainer Margaret Bruehl Assocs., N.J., N.Y., Pa., 1976—; ptnr. Pneuman/Bruehl/Assocs., Ohio, N.Y., 1981—; coordinator human-relations programs Princeton Theol. Sem.'s Ctr. for Continuing Edn., N.J., 1980—. Co-author: Managing Conflict, 1982. Mem. Assn. Creative Change (profl.), Lab. Trainers/Cons. Network (profl.), Alban Inst. Conflict Cons. (profl.), Organizational Devel. Network, SUNY-Stony Brook Univ. Assn. Democrat. Avocations: cooking; hiking; canoeing; creative movement and dance; gardening. Home and Office: 107 Main St PO Box 2826 Setauket NY 11733

BRUEHL, MARY MARTHA, lawyer; b. Shawnee, Okla., July 17, 1945; d. Forrest and Earline (Dunagun) Nelson; m. Dennis Anthony Bruehl, Aug. 17, 1970; children—Gabriel Anthony, Curtis Nelson. M.A., U. Okla., 1968, J.D., 1979. Bar: Okla., 1979. Learning disabilities tchr. Boulder Valley Schs., Colo., 1968-69; speech pathologist Central Valley Schs., Oahu, Hawaii, 1969-70, Norman Pub. Schs., Okla., 1970-72; adult spl. reading tchr. Central State Hosp., Norman, 1974-75; assoc. Walker, Walker, & Corbyn, Oklahoma City, 1979-80; ptnr. Emery McCandless Gaitis Bruehl, Oklahoma City, 1980-84; ptnr. Moran & Bruehl, Oklahoma City, 1984—. Chmn. Pack 221 Cub Scouts, 1982—; asst. coach basketball Norman Optomist, 1984. Will Rogers scholar, 1967-68. Mem. Okla. Bar Assn., Oklahoma County Bar Assn., ABA. Democrat. Office: Moran & Bruehl 6401 N Pennsylvania Suite 203 Oklahoma City OK 73116

BRUEMMER, LORRAINE VENSKUNAS, funeral director, real estate broker, nurse; b. Waterbury, Conn., Jan. 25; d. Anthony George and Mary Agnes (Kritchman) Venskunas; m. Jay Porter Bruemmer, Oct. 28, 1973; 1 child by previous marriage: Linda L. Rocco Sovak. R.N., St. Francis Hosp. Sch. Nursing, 1950; B.S., Columbia U., 1958; M.Ed., U. Hartford, 1961. Head nurse pediatrics Cook Hosp., Hartford, Conn., 1953-56; instr. pediatrics Bellevue Hosp., N.Y.C., 1958-59; instr. med. surg. nursing New Britain Gen. Hosp., 1959-62; hosp. supr. New Britain Gen. Hosp., 1962-63; owner Venskunas Funeral Home, New Britain, 1962—; owner Bruemmer Venskunas Real Estate, New Britain, 1974—; commr. New Britain Health Dept., 1965-74; nurse blood bank ARC, N.Y.C., 1957-59, New Britain, 1960-69. Vol. Republican Party, New Britain. Mem. New Britain Funeral Dis. Assn. (pres. 1975-78), Conn. Funeral Dirs., Nat. Funeral Dirs., New Britain Bd. Realtors, Hartford Bd. Realtors, Nat. Bd. Realtors, Multiple Listing Service Greater Hartford. Roman Catholic. Clubs: Ladies Guild (pres. 1969), Shuttle Meadow Country. Avocations: antiques; golf; tennis; swimming; bicycling; gardening. Home: 36 Roslyn Dr New Britain CT 06052 Office: Venskunas Funeral Home 665 Stanley St PO Box 1612 New Britain CT 06051

BRUEMMER, MARY ADELE, university official; b. Madison, Ill., Feb. 26, 1920; d. Ignatius George and Adele M. (Bergrath) B.; A.B. in Edn., St. Louis U., 1938-42, M.Ed., 1960. Dir. Cath. Youth Orgns., Springfield, Ill., 1943-48; dir. continuity dept. Sta. WCVS, 1948-51; dir. publicity Lincoln Library, 1951-53; dir. adult edn. dept. Springfield Coll. in Ill., 1953-55; dir. Marguerite Hall, St. Louis U., 1956-59, dir. women's housing, 1959-67, dean of women, 1967-73, asst. v.p. student devel., dean of women, 1973-75, dean student affairs, 1975-85, spl. asst. to v.p. for devel., 1985—. Mem. Nat., Mo. (sec.-treas. 1958-64, pres. 1971-78) assns. women deans, adminstrs. and counselors, AAUW, Pi Lambda Theta, Alpha Sigma Nu (nat. v.p. 1979-82). Club: Altrusa. Roman Catholic. Address: 1531 4th St Madison IL 62060

BRUETT, KAREN DIESL, marketing company executive; b. N.Y.C., May 15, 1945; d. Francis J. and Dorothy (Peterson) Diesl; m. William H. Bruett, Jr., Mar. 18, 1967; 1 child, Lindsey Diesl. B.A. in English, St. Lawrence U., 1966; M.A., Hunter Coll., 1971. Tchr. English, Freeport pub. schs., N.Y., 1966-70; exec. interviewer, researcher Louis Harris & Assocs., N.Y.C., 1970-72; adult edn. dir. West Side YMCA, 1972-76; v.p. new bus. devel. Gaylord Adams & Assocs., Inc., N.Y.C., 1976-81; account exec. John Blair Mktg., N.Y.C., 1981-83, v.p. sales, 1983-84, sr. v.p., gen. sales mgr., 1984—. Trustee, St. Lawrence U., 1978—, chmn. alumni fund, 1983-84, chmn. annual giving, 1984—; mem. bd. mgrs. West Side YMCA, 1978-83; del. Am.-Soviet Youth Forum, Baku, USSR, 1974. Home: RR 1 Box 1740 Hinesburg VT 05461 Office: John Blair Mktg 1290 Ave of Americas New York NY 10104

BRUFF, BEVERLY OLIVE, public relations consultant; b. San Antonio, Dec. 15, 1926; d. Albert Griffith and Hazel Olive (Smith) Bruff; B.A., H. Sophie Newcomb Coll., 1948; postgrad. Our Lady of Lake Coll., 1956, Okla. Center for Continuing Edn., 1960-70. Asst. dir. New Orleans Theatre Guild, 1948-50; dist. dir. San Antonio Area council Girl Scouts U.S.A., 1958-70, public relations dir., 1970-83; free-lance pub. relations, 1983—; mem. Council of Pres., v.p., 1981-82, 84—; mem. Council of Internat. Relations. Zoning commr. Hill Country Village, Tex., 1973-76, 83-85; council woman Hill Country Village, 1985—; bd. dirs. Camp Fire, Inc. Mem. Pub. Relations Soc. Am., Tex. Pub. Relations Assn. (Silver Spur award), Women in Communications (historian 1969-70, v.p. 1970-71, treas. 1971-73), Tex. Press Women (recipient state writing contest awards 1971, 72, 73, 74, mem. exec. bd. dirs. 1970-71, 73-74, dist. treas. 1972-73, dist. v.p. 1973), Nat. Fedn. Press Women, Internat. Assn. Bus. Communicators, Speech Arts of San Antonio (pres. 1964-66, 70-72, 84—, dir. 1964-72, chmn. bd. dirs. 1966-69), Am. Women in Radio and TV (dir. chpt. 1974, sec. 1975, pres. 1979-80), San Antonio Soc. Fund Raising Execs. Home: 508 Tomahawk Trail San Antonio TX 78232

BRUHN, GALE ADRIAN, university administrator, city official; b. Flint, Mich., Feb. 1, 1947; d. Adreon Beauton and Irene Julia (Shayman) Johnston; children—Elizabeth Irene, Kelly Daniel. A.S., Solano Community Coll., 1986; cert. in mgmt. and supervision U. Calif.-Davis, 1984. Sec. II gifts and endowments devel. U. Calif.-Davis, 1980-84, adminstrv. asst. II services for internat. students and scholars, 1984—; city clk. City of Winters, Calif., 1978—. Project leader Winters 4-H Club, 1975—; actor Winters Community Ctr. Theater, 1975—, bd. dirs., 1984—; firefighter, emergency med. technician Vacaville Fire Dist., Calif., 1980-82; mem. Circle of Singers, Winters, 1975—; mem. adv. com. Student Health Ctr., U. Calif.-Davis, 1984-85. Mem. Calif. State Firefighters Assn. (cert., firefighter 1980), Internat. Inst. Mcpl. Clks., No. Calif. City Clks. Assn. Democrat. Presbyterian. Avocations: acting; singing; painting; horsemastership; sheep raising. Home: 832 Jefferson St Winters CA 95694 Office: City of Winters 318 First St Winters CA 95694

BRUIN, LINDA LOU, lawyer; b. Grandville, Mich., June 7, 1938; d. John and Tena (Groeneveld) B. A.A, Grand Rapids Jr. Coll., 1958; A.B., Hope Coll., 1961; student U. Stockholm, 1963-64; A.M., U. Mich., 1967; J.D., Wayne State U., 1973. Bar: Mich. 1973. Tchr. Georgetown Pub. Schs., Jenison, Mich., 1959-63; Bullock Creek Area Schs., Midland, Mich., 1964-70; legal supr. Legis. Service Bur., Mich. Legislature, Lansing, 1973-79; legal counsel Mich. Assn. Sch. Bds., Lansing, 1979—, Mich. Supreme Ct. rep. to Mich. State Bar Assembly, 1985-87; mem. Supreme Ct. Citizens Commn. To Improve Mich. Cts., 1986. Fellowship Inst. Ednl. Leadership Washington, 1982. Mem. LWV, ABA, State Bar Assn. Mich. (com. chmn.), Women Lawyers Assn. Mich. (v.p., 1983-84, pres. 1984-85). Democrat. Columnist Mich. Sch. Bd. Jour., 1981—. Home: 1610 Pepper Tree Ln Lansing MI 48912 Office: Michigan Assn. School Boards 421 W Kalamazoo St Lansing MI 48933

BRULÉ, A. LORRAINE, commercial property manager; b. Yakima, Wash., Aug. 16, 1925; d. Arthur E. and Helen (Auvé) Brulé; student Seattle U., 1943-44, Dominican Coll. San Rafael, 1944-45; B.S. in Sociology, Seattle U., 1947; m. Nolan D. Roach, Oct. 24, 1959 (div. Jan. 1978); children—Dusty Dean, Susan Marie, and Dean Patrick Roach, Gaylen Leigh Brulé. Bookkeeper, Harper Meggee, Inc., Seattle, 1947-48; sec. bookkeeper Griffin Envelope Co., Seattle, 1948-50; with Yukon Investment Co., Inc., Seattle, 1950-59, 75-85, treas., 1977-85, mgr. comml. properties, 1975-85, asst. sec., 1975-85; cons. property mgmt., 1985—. Mem. Seattle U. Alumni Assn., Bldg. Owners and Mgrs. Assn. Seattle, Bldg. Owners and Mgrs. Assn. Internat., Seattle Downtown Assn., AAUW, Nat. Assn. Female Execs. Roman Catholic. Club: Wash. Athletic. Home and Office: Seven Highland Dr Unit 703 Seattle WA 98109-3215

BRUMFIELD, DEBORAH JAGERS, medical sociologist; b. McComb, Miss., Sept. 16, 1954; d. Hugh Fitzhugh and Mary Francelia (Moore) Jagers; B.S., U. So. Miss., 1975, M.A., 1981; 1 dau., Autumn Richelle. Med. sociologist, Southwest Miss. Regional Med. Center, McComb, 1976-82; med. dir. MCM, Inc., Jackson, Miss.; pres., chief exec. officer Autumn Essence Ltd., Kentwood, La.; faculty stats. and research methodology Miss. Coll., 1982-83; cons., med. recruiter. County demographic cons. senatorial campaign of Thad Cochran; active March of Dimes; vol. Crippled Children's Clinic. Mem. Am. Soc. Hosp. Pub. Relations Dirs., Nat. Assn. Nurse Recruiters, Women in Communication, Miss. Soc. Hosp. Pub. Relations, Dirs. Republican. Methodist. Club: Porsche of Am. Home: 1855 Lakeland I-202 Jackson MS 39216

BRUMFIELD, PEGGY DARLINE, oil company executive; b. Washington, May 27, 1948; d. Stanley Warren and Bessie C. (Grant) Tapscott; B.A. in French, Ind. State U., Terre Haute, 1970; m. James Irving Brumfield; children—Koren, James Irving, Jonathan, Colette. Human relations rep. Pa. Human Relations Commn., Pitts., 1972-74; with Gulf Oil Corp., Pitts., 1974—, mgr. programs and systems devel., 1977-78, mgr. EEO support systems, 1978-80, dir. personnel practices and affirmative action, 1980—; bd. dirs. Pitts. Regional Engring. Program; tchr., lectr., speaker in field. Mem. Am. Soc. Tng.

and Devel., Orgn. Resource Counselors. Baptist. Author articles in field. Office: Gulf Oil Corp PO Box 1166 Pittsburgh PA 15230

BRUMITT, LOIS EILEEN, university administrator, dietitian; b. Kankakee, Ill., Sept. 1, 1926; d. William August and Nora May (Joliff) B. B.S., U. Ill., 1949; cert. dietitian Barnes Hosp., 1950. Clin. dietitian Barnes Hosp., St. Louis, 1950-55; adminstrv. dietitian, 1955-62; asst. dir. food service Washington U., St. Louis, 1962-65; asst. food service mgr. So. Ill. U., Carbondale, 1965-78, dir. residence halls food service, 1978—, guest lectr., 1978—. Mem. Bus. and Profl. Women's Club (pres. 1975-77, chmn. state conv. 1976, dist. chmn. 1981; Woman of Yr. award 1984), So. Ill. Dietetic Assn. (pres. 1968), Ill. Dietetic Assn. (state registration chmn. 1970), Am. Dietetic Assn., Nat. Assn. Female Execs., Nat. Assn. Coll. and Univ. Food Services, Epsilon Sigma Alpha (pres. 1967-68, sec. 1975—). Republican. Methodist. Avocations: reading; knitting; music; recipe collecting and testing. Home: 2008 Woodriver Dr Apt 3 Carbondale IL 62901 Office: So Ill U Housing Food Service Central Food Service Office Grinnell Hall Carbondale IL 62901

BRUMLEY, JOAN REYNOLDS, inservice health education specialist; b. Toledo, Sept. 3, 1934; d. Harold Schaeffer Reynolds and Doris (Elnora) Reynolds Chisholm; m. Robert Paul Eckel, Aug. 8, 1955 (div. 1965); children—Jerry Eckel Kroll, Kenneth H., Jennifer Eckel Holman, Robert; m. Ronald Phillip Brumley, Apr. 28, 1979. R.N. diploma Toledo Hosp. Sch. Nursing, 1955; B.S., Toledo U., 1955. R.N., Ohio, Calif. Head nurse operating room Fresno County Hosp., Fresno, Calif., 1967-68, supr. cardiovascular diagnostic unit, 1968-84; inservice educator Honeywell Med. Electronics Div., Pleasantville, N.Y., 1984—; mem. faculty Am. Heart Assn., Fresno, 1972-85, Fresno City Coll., 1978-84, Kings River Community Coll., Reedley, Calif., 1978-82. Pres. Clovis Art Guild, Calif., 1982. Named Vol. of Yr. Fresno County, 1978; recipient Meritorious Service award Am. Heart Assn., 1978-80. Mem. Soc. Western Artists, Calif. Nurses Assn., Clovis City C. of C., Am. Heart Assn. Republican. Baptist. Avocation: art. Home: 475 Bliss Clovis CA 93612 Office: Honeywell Med 2600 Kittyhawk Rd Livermore CA 94550

BRUMMELL, DARLENE MARIA, architect, interior designer; b. Easton, Md., Sept. 6, 1957; d. Lawrence and Marva Louise (Camper) B.; m. Seth Elliott Couslar, Apr. 30, 1983. B.Arch., Howard U., 1982. Architect, D.C., Ga., Md., Va. Draftsperson, Howard U. A&E Services, Washington, 1980-81; interior decorator Transart, Inc., Atlanta, 1981-82; architect NASA-GSFC, Greenbelt, Md., 1982—; cons. for residence office Ms. Rawlings, Waldorf, Md., 1984-85; interior designer Ms. Pamela Wilson, Arlington, Va., 1985—. Mentor, Fed. Womens Program, Greenbelt, 1984—. Mem. Nat. Trust for Hist. Preservation, Am. Soc. Interior Designers, Alpha Kappa Alpha. Avocations: reading; sewing; racquetball Home: 11923 Centerhill St PO Box 2475 Wheaton MD 20902

BRUNDAGE, KAREN FRANCINE, communications company executive; b. Tacoma, Wash., July 6, 1957; d. William and Elaine Marie (Fleming) Brundage. B.A. in Psychology Fairleigh Dickinson U., 1981. Asst. mgr. New Jersey Bell, West Orange, 1980-82; customer educator AT&T Info. Systems, Woodbridge, N.J., 1983; staff supr. AT&T Communications, Bedminster, N.J., 1983—. Editor: Vol. Directory, 1978. Vol. program coordinator Rutherford Student Vol. Program, 1977-79. Francis Nelson scholar Ferry Avenue United Meth. Ch., 1975-79; recipient Dean's award Dean of Students, Fairleigh Dickinson U., 1978-80. Mem. Nat. Assn. Female Execs., AT&T Black Mgrs. Assn. Methodist.

BRUNDAGE, PATRICIA LOUNSBURY, art gallery director; b. Orange, N.J., Sept. 11, 1953; d. John Denton and Ann (Lounsbury) Brundage; m. William Bryant Copley, Nov. 12, 1983; 1 child, Bryant. Student Washington & Jefferson Coll., 1971-73; B.F.A., U. Ga., 1975. Asst. to dir. Castelli-Sonnabend Tapes and Films, Inc., N.Y.C., 1976-77, dir., 1977—; dir. Leo Castelli Gallery N.Y.C., 1984—. Episcopalian. Club: Jr. League (N.Y.C.). Home: 38 W 9th St New York NY 10011 Office: Leo Castelli Gallery 420 W Broadway New York NY 10012

BRUNE, BARBARA JEAN, pump company executive, realtor; b. Chgo., Dec. 31, 1943; d. Frank C. and Isabell (Minkel) Sapinski; m. Louis Joseph Sandbote, Dec. 27, 1965 (div. Mar. 1973); m. Paul Daniel Brune, June 14, 1978; 1 son, Jon-Paul Payton. B.A., Rosary Coll., 1965; M.A., Baylor U., 1974. Tchr. English, Aledo Community High Sch. (Ill.), 1965-66, Grant Community High Sch., Fox Lake, Ill., 1966-67; Forrest Sherman Schs., Naples, Italy, 1967-70; sec. dean women Baylor U., Waco, Tex., 1970-71; chmn. English dept. Jefferson Moore High Sch., Waco, 1974-78; v.p. Brune Pump Co., Valley Mills, Tex., 1978—; broker, owner All Am. Real Estate, Valley Mills, Tex., 1982—. Sec., Young Republicans, River Forest, 1964, pres., 1965. Mem. Waco Bd. Realtors, Baylor Alumni Assn. Roman Catholic. Home: Route 2 Rivercrest Estates Valley Mills TX 76689 Office: Brune Pump Co E Hwy 6 Valley Mills TX 76689

BRUNE, PATRICIA LYNNE, government court finance officer; b. Kansas City, Kans., Nov. 23, 1949; d. Lowell William and Anna Lucretia (Hollander) B. B.S. in Bus. Adminstrn., Rockhurst Coll., 1984. Computer ops. person Comml. Nat. Bank, Kansas City, Kans., 1969-72; asst. sec. Greater Kansas City Women's Bowling Assn., Mo., 1972-76; asst. mgr. King Louie Bowling, Kansas City, Mo., 1976-78; with U.S. Dist. Ct., (western dist.) Mo., Kansas City, 1978—, fin. officer, 1983—. Pres. 600 Bowling Club, Kansas City, Mo., 1975-85; sec.-treas. Kansas City Bowling Council, Mo., 1976-78; pres. Greater Kansas City Women's Bowling Assn., Mo.; bd. dirs. United Cerebral Palsy, Kansas City, Mo., 1985-86. Mem. Mo. Women Bowling Writers (bd. dirs. 1985—, 2nd Place Feature Story award 1975, 1st Place Feature Story award 1985). Home: 8494 Lane Dr Apt 1 Raytown MO 64138

BRUNER, DARLENE HILDAGARDE, retired industrial company official; b. Creston, Nebr., Oct. 8, 1928; d. Otto Frederick and Hildegard Eleanor (Dasenbrock) Feye; B.A. in Bus. Adminstrn., Midland Luth. Coll., 1949; m. James L. Paulin, Oct. 23, 1949 (div., 1963); children—James D., Jamie L., Kathryn D. Paulin Lackey; m. 2d Robert T. Bruner, Dec. 23, 1970. Acctg. clk. Kavich's Furniture, Fremont, Nebr., 1948-50; asst. acct. Gamble-Skogmo, Fremont, 1950-51; acctg. clk., plant acct. Hydro-Conduit Corp., Fremont, 1962-65; acctg. clk., plant acct., mgr. services CF Industries, Inc., Fremont, 1965-84, ret., 1984; tax preparer H&R Block; bookkeeper Travel Faire, Inc. Mem. Mensa. Democrat. Presbyterian. Home: 2139 William Fremont NE 68025

BRUNER, LINDA POLLARD, management information consulting company executive; b. Sarasota, Fla., July 1, 1948; d. Donald Dunsmore and Elizabeth (Murley) Polland; m. G. Evans Bruner IV, June 7, 1969; children—John Evans, Leah Robinson. B.A. in Edn. and History, Erskine Coll., 1969; M.A. in Math., Fairfield U., 1979. Tchr., St. Thomas Sch., Tucson, 1971-73; tchr. math. West Rocks Middle Sch., Norwalk, Conn., 1977-79; computer instr. Norwalk High Sch., 1979-81; cons. Bruner Consulting Assocs., Inc., Bridgeport, Conn., 1981-83, v.p., 1983—. Author: Teaching Children Basic, 1980. Contbr. articles to profl. jours. Mem. adv. bd. Notre Dame High Sch., Fairfield, 1985-86; bd. dirs. LWV, Bridgeport, 1978—. Mem. Ind. Computer Cons. Assn. (bd. dirs. 1983-85), Fairfield Network of Exec. Women (chmn. bd. dirs. 1986—, treas. 1984-85), Data Processing Mgmt. Assn. Republican. Episcopalian. Club: Brooklawn Country (Fairfield). Avocations: golf; bridge. Office: Bruner Consulting Assocs Inc 1069 Briarwood Ave Bridgeport CT 06604

BRUNER, MARJORIE W., educator; b. Marion, Ind.; d. Frank Kemper and Deffalyn (Hedrick) Williamson; m. Henry Pfeiffer Bruner, Aug. 22, 1936; children—Henry Williamson, Philip Lane, Stephen Claycomb, David Carroll, Robert Frank. A.B., U. Chgo., 1929, Ph.D., 1933. Asst. prof., dean of women Kanawha Jr. Coll., Charleston, W.Va., 1933-34; asst. prof. English, N.Mex. State Coll., State College, 1934-36; asst. prof. English, Carthage Coll., Kenosha, Wis., 1962-66, assoc. prof., 1966-69, prof., 1969-76, ret., 1976; vis. prof. Chapman Coll., Orange, Calif., 1968-69; lectr. City-Wide Colls. of Chgo., 1977-83; gen. lectr. various clubs, 1979—. Mem. bd. edn. Unified Sch. Dist. 1, Racine County, Wis., 1961-70, pres. bd., 1964-65; bd. dirs. Art Mus., Women's Club, YWCA, Children's Theater Council, Racine. Named Woman of Year, Racine Women's Civic Council, 1962. Mem. AAUW, AAUP, Nat. Council Tchrs. English, MLA., Wis. Sch. Bds. Assn., Nat. Assn. Sch. Bds. Congregationalist. Author articles in field. Home: 1335 Astor St Chicago IL 60610

BRUNGARD, DEBORAH ANN, communications company professional; b. Petoskey, Mich., Sept. 24, 1954; d. Peter Paul and Betty Jane (Crossley) B. B.S. with honors, Stevens Inst. Tech., 1977; M.E.E., 1984. Mem. tech. staff Smith Kline & French Labs., Phila., 1979-82; teaching asst. elec. engring. dept. Stevens Inst. Tech., Hoboken, N.J., 1982-84; mem. tech. staff internat. transmission systems engring. AT&T Bell Labs., Holmdel, N.J., 1984—. Recipient Exceptional Contbn. awards AT&T Bell Labs., 1984, 85; Stevens Inst. Tech. scholar, 1974-77. Mem. IEEE, Tau Beta Pi, Eta Kappa Nu. Avocations: skiing; sailing; racquetball; tennis. Home: 9 Lafayette St Rumson NJ 07760 Office: Room 1B413 AT&T-Bell Labs Crawfords Corner Holmdel NJ 07733

BRUNK, BRENDA MOORE, cable television and radio company executive; b. Winston-Salem, N.C., Nov. 18, 1942; d. Garland Edward and Eusebia Mae (Watkins) Moore; m. Rollis Gene Brunk, May 22, 1963; children—Jeffrey Wayne, Kelly Lynn. Programming cert. Automation Inst., Charlotte, N.C., 1962. Personnel clk. R. J. Reynolds Industries, Winston-Salem, 1962-63; with Summit Communications, Inc., Winston-Salem, 1971—, system mgr., 1975-81, gen. mgr., 1981-82, v.p., 1982—; officer Summit Cable Services of Thom-A-Lex, Inc., Lexington, N.C., 1982—. Mem. Internat. Mgmt. Council (chpt. program chmn. 1982—), Bus. and Profl. Women's Club (local treas. 1984-85), Women in Cable (charter; pres. N.C. chpt.) Soc. Cable TV Engrs., Cable TV Adminstrn. and Mktg., N.C. Cable TV Assn., Am. Bus. Women's Assn., Davidson County Art Guild. Democrat. Methodist. Lodge: Toastmasters. Avocations: photography; backpacking; fishing; reading; charcoal landscapes. Home: 204 Ridgecrest Dr Lexington NC 27292 Office: Summit Cable Services of Thom-A-Lex Ins PO Box 667 Lexington NC 27293

BRUNKEN, DOROTHY ELIZABETH BOSWELL, banker; b. Beverly, N.J., May 19, 1930; d. E. Raymond and Mary Ashton (Davies) Brown; m. Harry G. Brunken, Aug 11, 1956 (div. Sept. 1982); 1 child, Carole Delight Dolbow. B.A. in History, Boston U., 1966; postgrad. Mundelein Coll., 1980-81. Account exec. A.J. Rosenthal & Co., Chgo., 1978-84; dir. mktg. Bank of Ravenswood, Chgo., 1984—. Contbr. articles to profl. jours. vice pres. Jersey City PTA, 1960-61; com. chmn. LWV, 1962, 65-66; Mem. Am. Mktg. Assn., Women's Advt. Club Chgo., Chgo. Fin. Advertisers, Bank Mktg. Assn., Am. Assn. Zool. Parks and Aquariums, Lincoln Park Zoo Docents (pres. 1971-73). Republican. Episcopalian. Home: 3440 N Lake Shore Dr Chicago IL 60657 Office: Bank of Ravenswood 1825 W Lawrence Ave Chicago IL 60640

BRUNNER, LILLIAN SHOLTIS, nurse, author, consultant; b. Freeland, Pa., Mar. 29; d. Andrew J. and Anna (Tomasko) Sholtis; m. Mathias John Brunner, Sept. 8, 1951; children—Janet Lillian, Carol Ann, Douglas Mathias. Diploma in Nursing, U. Pa., 1940, B.S., 1945; M.S.N., Case-Western Res. U., 1947; Sc.D. (hon.), Cedar Crest Coll., Allentown, Pa., 1978; Litt.D. (hon.) U. Pa., 1985. Supr. operating rooms, inst. operating rooms and nursing Hosp. U. Pa., Phila., 1942-45; surg. supr. Yale-New Haven Hosp., 1947-51; asst. prof. surg. nursing Yale U. Sch. Nursing, New Haven, 1947-51; project dir. Bryn Mawr Hosp. Sch. Nursing, Pa., 1973-77; mem. bd. overseers U. Pa. Sch. Nursing, Phila., 1982—; cons. nursing Presbyn. U. Pa. Med. Ctr., Phila., 1970—. Author: (with Eliason and Ferguson) Surgical Nursing, 10th edit., 1955; (with Bragdon) Teaching Medical and Surgical Nursing, 1955, Art of Clinical Instruction, 1959; (with Cardew) Study Guide for Clinical Nursing, 2d edit., 1961; (with Ferguson) Eliason's Surgical Nursing, 1959; (with Ginsberg and Cantlin) Manual of Operating Room Technology, 1966; (with Suddarth) Lippincott Manual of Nursing Practice, 4th edit., 1986, Textbook of Medical and Surgical Nursing, 5th edit., 1984; also articles. Co-founder, dir. History of Nursing Mus., Pa. Hosp., Phila., 1974. Recipient 25 Yrs. Outstanding Author award J.B. Lippincott Co., 1975; Disting. Alumnus award Case Western Res. U., 1980. Fellow Am. Acad. Nursing; mem. Pa. League for Nursing (pres. 1976-78; Disting. Recognition award 1984), Nat. League for Nursing (Disting. Service award 1979), Nat. League Am. Pen Women (sec. 1984—), Am. Nurses Assn., Am. Med. Writers Assn., Assn. Operating Room Nurses, Am. Assn. Critical Care Nurses, Oncology Nursing Soc., Am. Assn. for History of Nursing, Soc. Nursing History. Avocations: traveling, piano playing, lace making, needlework, collector of tatting shuttles and old nursing textbooks. Home and Office: 1247 Berwyn-Paoli Rd Berwyn PA 19312

BRUNNER, NANCY H., human resource development manager, educator; b. Williamsport, Pa., Apr. 18, 1930; d. Carl H. Hall and Marian E. (Dilks) Hall; m. Richard B. Brunner, June 27, 1953; (div. 1966); 1 son, Curtis Evan. A.B. magna cum laude, Lycoming Coll., Williamsport, Pa., 1952; M.A. cum laude, NYU, 1973; postgrad. Columbia U. Sch. Bus., 1977-78. Dir. publs. Rider Coll., Trenton, N.J., 1966-69; pub. relations specialist Hoffman-LaRoche Inc., Nutley, N.J., 1969-71, career devel. assoc., 1971-75, mgr. orgn. devel., 1975-81; mgr. tng., devel. Lehn & Fink Products Co., Montvale, N.J., 1981—; adj. prof. Fairleigh Dickinson U. Sch. Bus., 1977—, pres. New Directions, Montclair, N.J. Writer, composer, dir. 2 musical theatre shows, Williamsport; author film For Life's Sake, 1973; editor: The New School Architecture, 1969; contbr. article to profl. jour. Bd. dirs. Jr. League, Williamsport, 1966; mem. allocations com. United Fund, Lycoming County, Pa., 1965, 66. Recipient Time-Life publs. award for Distinction in Coll. Publs., 1965, 66, 68; Tribute to Women in Industry, N.J. Industries, 1977. Mem. Human Resource Planning Soc., Acad. Mgmt., Am. Mgmt. Assn., Phi Kappa Phi.

BRUNNER, SULTRA ELAINE, lawyer, county official; b. Meridian, Miss., July 20, 1950; d. Moses and Hazel Juanita (Davis) B.; B.A. in Psychology, UCLA, 1973; M.A., Calif. State U., Los Angeles, 1976; J.D., Southwestern U., Los Angeles, 1982. Bar: Calif. 1983. Resource cons. Los Angeles County Dept. Mental Health, 1970-74; with Los Angeles County Dept. Health Services, 1974—, program mgr., 1975-77, legis. analyst, 1977-82, budget analyst, 1982-85, program adminstr., 1985—. Office: 2250 Alcazar Los Angeles CA 90033

BRUNSON, DOROTHY E., broadcasting company executive; b. Glensville, Ga., Mar. 13, 1938; d. Wadis and Naomi (Ross) Edwards; children—Edward, Daniel. B.S., Empire State Coll. Entered print communications industry, 1960-62; asst. gen. mgr. radio sta. WWRL, N.Y.C., 1964-68, corp. coordinator, liason dir. 1968-72; v.p. Howard Sanders Advt., Inc., N.Y.C., 1972-79; corp. v.p. Inner City Broadcasting Corp., 1973-79, corp. gen. mgr., 1979; pres. Sta. WEBB, Balt., Sta. WIGO, Atlanta, Sta. WBMS, Wilmington, N.C., 1979—; lectr., speaker bus., econ. devel., affirmative action, communications, women rights, religious and human issues throughout country; panelist bus. and communications White House, 1977. Recipient awards including citation NCCJ. Methodist. Office: Brunson Communications Inc 2018 Dennison St Baltimore MD 21216

BRUNSTING, MELODY ANN, weekly publication manager; b. Santa Ana, Calif., Sept. 19, 1955; d. Wallace Charles and Colleen Adelene (Baker) Huber; m. Calvin Henry Brunsting, Aug. 18, 1974. B.S., Poly. U., Pomona, Calif., 1980. Assoc. editor, Community Woman, Anaheim, Calif., 1977-80; editor TV Digest, Pomona, 1980-81; mng. editor Butterfield Bull., Temecula, Calif., 1981-83; publ. cons. Trainable Type, Wildomar, Calif., 1981—; ops. mgr. Bargain Bull., Temecula, Calif., 1983—. Author: Get Wired, 1986. Editor: Do-It-Yourself Humor, 1985. Founding mem. Southwest County Disaster Preparedness Com., Riverside County, Calif., 1983; chmn. organizing com. Rancho Calif. Balloon and Wine Festival, 1985-86. Mem. Nat. Assn. Female Execs., Nat. Fedn. Press Women, Calif. Presswoman. Avocations: scuba diving; gymnastics; water skiing. Home: 21705 Como St Wildomar CA 92395 Office: 28069 Diaz Rd Temecula CA 92390

BRUNTON, HELEN ESTHER, retired county official; b. nr. Valley Falls, Kans., Dec. 5, 1915; d. Roy Ernest and Hallie Elizabeth (Bonar) Steffey; m. Lex Allen Brunton, May 14, 1939 (dec. Jan. 1961); children—Max Allen, Dale Gene, Bryce Arlan. Grad high sch., Ozawkie, Kans. Tchr. Ozawkie Grade Sch., 1934-39; clk. State of Kans., Topeka, 1961-66; registrar of deeds Jefferson County, Oskaloosa, Kans., 1967-85, ret. 1985. Pres. Jefferson County Women's Republican Party, Oskaloosa, 1978. Mem. Assn. Registrars of Deeds. Methodist. Club: Colonial. Lodges: Eastern Star, Rebekah's. Avocations: painting, reading.

BRUSH, PENELOPE, secretarial services executive, real estate broker; b. San Antonio, Feb. 10, 1946; d. Paul F. and Doris (Robison) Rhodes; m. Barry Brush, Dec. 24, 1970; children—Jennifer, Joanna. B.A. in Mgmt., Trinity U. Exec. asst. CIM, Dallas, 1975-76; facilities mgr. Insyte Corp., Dallas, 1976-77; regional mktg. mgr. Applied Data Research, Dallas, 1977-79; prin. real estate broker, Dallas, 1979—; pres. Profl. Secretarial Services, Dallas, 1979—; seminar dir. and leader, 1980—. Producer, TV programs for LWV of Dallas, 1982-84. Pub. relations dir. Dallas Music Tchrs., 1982—. Named Cable Producer of Yr. City of Dallas, 1982; Edn. Vol. Dallas Ind. Schs., 1980. Mem. Tex. Real Estate Brokers, Nat. Legal Sec. Assn., Nat. Music Tchrs. Assn., Am. Coll. Musicians, LWV (chmn. TV prodns. 1981—, mem. League Internat.). Presbyterian. Office: Penelope Brush Properties PO Box 3007 Dallas TX 75230

BRUSTEIN, CAROLE NIVASCH, lawyer, former restaurant executive; b. N.Y.C., May 7, 1944; d. Henry and Esther (Miaskoff) Nivasch; m. Joel M. Brustein, Jan. 30, 1965; children—Hope, Marshall, Samuel. A.A., Fullerton Jr. Coll. (Calif.), 1976; B.A. in Religious Studies, Calif. State U.-Fullerton, 1979; J.D., Loyola U., Los Angeles, 1982. Bar: Calif. 1982, U.S. Dist. Ct. (central dist.) Calif. 1983. Ptnr. firm Brustein & Barnes, Orange, Calif., 1982-85. Mem. staff Internat. and Comparative Law Jour., 1981-82; editor: Bus. Law and Litigation Jour., 1982. Mem. ABA, Orange County Bar Assn., Orange County Barristers (mem. com. Bridging the Gap program 1983), Calif. Women Lawyers. Democrat.

BRUTON, DEIRDRA CARLEN, management consultant; b. Washington, Nov. 20, 1949; d. Charles S. and Virginia A. (Boehm) Hill; m. Peter W. Bruton, Aug. 7, 1971. B.S., Tulane U., 1971; postgrad. American U., 1974. Research asst. Ctr. for Naval Analysis, Arlington, Va., 1971-72; assoc. Ops Research Inc., Silver Spring, Md., 1972-74; sr. cons. Touche Ross, Washington, 1974-78; practice unit dir. Deloitte, Haskins and Sells, Phila., 1978—. Author: Dollars and Cents of Shopping Centers, 1975-78; The ABC's of Case Mix, 1979. Participant Presdl. Pvt. Sector Survey, Grace Commn., Washington, 1982. Republican. Home: 124 Eaton Dr Wayne PA 19087 Office: Deloitte Haskins and Sells 2500 Three Mellon Center Philadelphia PA 19102

BRUZZONE, NORMA ELAINE, accounting administrator, professional chorister; b. Albany, Calif., Jan. 6, 1937; d. Norman Gale and Mary Aida Schaefer; grad. high sch.; children—Michael Alan, Dana Elaine. Sec., Chevron Research Corp., Richmond, Calif., 1955-61; profl. chorister San Francisco Opera Co., 1967-79; performer San Francisco Symphony Orch., 1967-74; adminstrv. mgr. Warren, McVeigh & Griffin, San Francisco, 1973-79; adminstrv. mgr. profl. liability div. Marsh & McLennan, San Francisco, 1979-80; adminstrv. mgr., dept. head Antonini, P.C., San Francisco, 1980—. Active PTA. Mem. Microcomputer Users Group for C.P.A.s, Calif. Soc. C.P.A.s (coordinator computer fairs 1982-85), Am. Guild Musical Artists, AFTRA. Office: 1700 Montgomery St Suite 225 San Francisco CA 94111

BRYAN, BILLIE MARIE (MRS. JAMES A. MACKEY), biologist; b. Norfolk, Va., Dec. 30, 1932; d. William B. and Marie (Fortescue) Bryan; B.A. in Biology, U. Richmond, 1954; M.Ed., Am. U., 1966; m. James A. Mackey. Bacteriologist, Arlington County Health Dept., Arlington, Va., 1954-58; med. bacteriologist Walter Reed Army Inst. Research, Walter Reed Army Med. Center, Washington, 1959-62; tchr. Fairfax (Va.) High Sch., 1962-66; biologist NIH, Washington, 1966—. Mem. Am. Pub. Health Assn., Am. Soc. Info. Sci., Am. Med. Writers Assn., DAR. Contbr. articles to profl. jours. Home: 201 Quaint Acres Dr Silver Spring MD 20904 Office: NIH—NIADDK Westwood Bldg Room 3A-17A Bethesda MD 20205

BRYAN, DARLENE ALETA, pharmaceutical company sales representative, educator; b. N.Y.C., Aug. 28, 1954; d. Hugh Leslie and Geraldine Marie (Prillerman) B. B.A., Hampton Inst., 1976. Retail salesperson, asst. stock mgr. Hempstead China, N.Y.C., 1977-79; profl. cons. Petro Internat., N.Y.C., 1979-80; account exec. Reuben H. Donnelley, N.Y.C., 1980-86; profl. med. rep. Ciba-Geigy, Cherry Hill, N.J., 1986—; tchr. dance, choreographer Trenton Bd. Edn., 1976—; profl. dancer, theatrical and film prodns., 1976-81. Choreographer summer stock Hamilton High West, 1976, Hamilton Theatre II, Trenton, 1980, Lawrence High Sch., N.J., 1983, 84. Named one of Outstanding Young Women of Am., U.S. Jaycees, 1983. Mem. Nat. Assn. Female Execs., North Hudson Exec. Profl. Assn., Alpha Psi Omega. Avocations: dancing; tennis; jazzobics; travel.

BRYAN, MARIE ELIZABETH, library administrator; b. Oakland, Calif., Jan. 21, 1952; d. Joseph Wheatley and Martha Marie (Stirling) B.; m. William Allen Krause, Apr. 19, 1980. B.A. in French, Holy Names Coll., 1972; M.L.S., U. Calif.-Berkeley, 1973. Library student asst. Contra Costa County Library, El Cerrito, Calif., 1969-73, children's librarian, Antioch, Calif., 1973-75, Walnut Creek, Calif., 1975-77; children's project dir. North State Coop. Library System, Willows, Calif., 1977-79; library dir. Willows Pub. Library, 1979—; chmn. Gladys English Collection Com., Sacramento, 1983-84. Chmn. Math. Sci. Conf. Young Women, Willows, 1983, 84. Mem. Calif. Library Assn. (councilor 1980), ALA (membership task force 1983-84), Library Adminstrs. Assn. No. Calif., Bus. and Profl. Women, AAUW. Democrat. Roman Catholic. Club: Book Collectors (sec. 1984-85). Home: 2 Glacier Peak Ln Chico CA 95926 Office: Willows Pub Library 201 N Lassen St Willows CA 95988

BRYAN, MARY ANN, interior designer; b. Dallas, Nov. 16, 1929; d. William C. and Harriet E. (Carter) Green; m. Frank Wingfield Bryan, Aug. 31, 1957; children—Frank Wingfield, Elizabeth F. B.S. in Interior Design U. Tex., 1950. Head of stock Foleys Dept. Store, Houston, 1952-53, asst. buyer, 1953-54, buyer, 1955-60, exec. tng. dir., 1960-61; owner, pres., Mary Bryan Interiors, Inc., Houston, 1961-84. Active Bluebird Circle, Houston, 1967-84, del. Friendship Among Women, 1983; mem. adv. bd. Houston Art Inst. Mem. Am. Soc. Interior Designers (nat. bd., 1984—, pres. Gulf Coast chpt. 1975), Chi Omega. Republican. Methodist. Home: 10023 Locke Ln Houston TX 77042 Office: Mary Ann Bryan Interiors Inc 4041 Richmond St Houston TX 77027

BRYAN, NANCY LEE CRAVENS, operations manager, management consultant, financial planner; b. Los Angeles, May 2, 1936; d. Mark Clarence and Susan Louise (Fernsil) Cravens; children—April Lynn Bryan, Robert Lee Bryan. B.S. in Bus. Adminstrn., Pepperdine U., 1978, M.B.A., 1980, Ph.D. (hon.), 1986. Dir. procurement Aircraft Govs., Burbank, Calif., 1966-71; bus. mgr. Motown Record Corp., Hollywood, Calif., 1971-76; controller Pepperdine U., Malibu, Calif., 1976-79; mgr. contracts Gen. Electric, Sunnyvale, Calif., 1979-82; pres. Redwood Corp., Sunnyvale, 1982—; cons. Apple/Macintosh, Freemont, Calif., Intel Corp., Santa Clara, Calif., Micro Systems, Sunnyvale, Victor Corp., San Jose, Calif., 1983-84. Painter oils; editor various TV plays; author: Manufacturing Manual for Installation CIM, 1983. Vol. Suicide Prevention Ctr., Fish; ch. ambassador. Recipient service awards Los Angeles City Schs. Mem. Artists in Industry, Nat. Soc. Women Accts., Am. Prodn. and Inventory Control Soc., Nat. Assn. Female Execs., Pepperdine Alumni Assn. Clubs: Photography (pres.) (North Hollywood); Swim (Soquel, Calif.); Ski (Sunnyvale); Personal Computer. Avocations: swimming; photography; painting; stained glass; cloisonne; computers; volleyball; skiing; racquetball. Home: PO Box 61833 Sunnyvale CA 94088 Office: Redwood Corp PO Box 61833 Sunnyvale CA 94088

BRYAN, SANDRA HICKS, banker; b. Beverly, Mass., Apr. 12, 1951; d. William Sample and Annie May (Covington) Hicks; divorced; children—William Robert, Jason Franklin. Student U. S.C. Teller Standard Fed. Bank, Columbia, S.C., 1971-73; savs. clk. Bankers Trust Co., Columbia, 1974-75, customer service rep., 1976-78, br. mgr., 1979-82, mktg. adminstr., 1983—; speaker in field, workshops, convs. Advisor Jr. Achievement, Dreher High Sch., Columbia, 1984; mem. Legis. Action Com., Columbia, 1984. Named Dixie Council Credit Woman of Yr., 1985, Internat. Credit Woman of Yr., 1985. Mem. Columbia Credit Women Internat. (1st v.p. 1985; Credit Woman of Yr. 1984), Mid-Carolina Consumer Credit Assn. (pres. 1985), Columbia C. of C. Republican. Baptist. Avocations: tennis; horseback riding; swimming. Office: Bankers Trust of SC PO Box 1028 Columbia SC 29202

BRYAN, SHARON ANN, medical writer, editor; b. Kansas City, Mo., Dec. 18, 1941; d. George William and Dorothy Joan (Henn) Goll; B.J., U. Mo., 1963; diploma Stanford Radio and TV Inst., 1961; postgrad. N.Y.U. Sch. Arts and Sci., 1963-64; cert. personal fin. planning UCLA, 1986; postgrad. U. So. Calif. Law Ctr., 1986—; m. James Wesley Bryan, Dec. 26, 1962; children—Lisa Ann, Holly Renee. Proofreader, copy editor Cadwalader, Wickersham, and Taft, N.Y.C., 1963-64; manuscript editor, writer nonsci. sects. N.Y. State Jour. Medicine, Med. Soc. State of N.Y., N.Y.C., also mng. editor Staffoscope, 1965-66; manuscript editor Transactions, also editor Perceiver, Am. Acad. Ophthalmology and Otolaryngology, Rochester, Minn., 1969-72, hist. writer, 1972—; v.p., sec. James W. Bryan, M.D., Inc., med. corp.; writer publicity articles Ft. Lee (Va.) Community Theatre. Mem. vol. honor roll Soc. of Meml. Sloan-Kettering Cancer Center; active N.Y. Hosp. Women's League, 1965-67, Doctors' Wives Guild, Little Company of Mary Hosp., Torrance, Calif.; docent Los Angeles County Mus. Natural History. Mem. Am. Med. Writers Assn. (editor conv. bull. 1966), AAAS, Internat. Platform Assn., N.Y. Acad. Scis.,

Kappa Tau Alpha, Kappa Alpha Theta (chmn. membership com. N.Y. chpt. 1966). Club: Stanford. Author: Pioneering Specialists: History of the American Academy of Ophthalmology and Otolaryngology. Home: 533 Via del Monte Palos Verdes Estates CA 90274

BRYAN, VIRGINIA ANN, lawyer; b. Wolf Point, Mont., May 18, 1953; d. Harvey W. and Lily Eldora (Stensland) Bryan. B.A., Rocky Mountain Coll., 1975; J.D. with honors, U. Mont., 1979. Dir. deferred prosecution program Yellowstone County Attys. Office, Billings, Mont., 1975-76; assoc. firm Hibbs, Sweeney & Colberg, Billings, 1979-83; atty., owner Virginia A. Bryan, atty. at law, Billings, 1983—; lectr. family law Rocky Mountain Coll. Paralegal Inst., Billings, 1983. Founding mem. Billings Rape Task Force, 1975, Yellowstone Valley NOW, Billings, 1979. Mem. ABA, State Bar Mont., Yellowstone County Bar Assn., Am. Judicature Soc., Mont. Assn. Female Execs. Democrat. Home: 1600 Ave E Apt 3 Billings MT 59102 Office: 344 Hart-Albin Bldg PO Box 3093 Billings MT 59103

BRYANT, ANN ALEACE, recreation therapist; b. Roanoke, Va., Apr. 13, 1961; d. John Junior Bryant and Alice Margaret (Davis) Bryant Rice. B.S., Longwood Coll., 1983. Cert. therapeutic recreation specialist. Recreation therapist VA Med. Ctr., Tuskegee, Ala., 1983—; therapeutic recreation cons. VA Med. Ctr., Montgomery, Ala., 1984—. Recipient Superior Performance award VA Med. Ctr. Recreation Service, Tuskegee, 1983, Outstanding Performance award, 1984; Spl. Recognition cert. U.S. Congress, 1985. Mem. Nat. Therapeutic Recreation Soc., Nat. Recreation and Parks Assn., Delta Psi Kappa, Phi Kappa Phi. Avocations: reading; cooking; crossword puzzles; walking. Home: Box 47 VA Med Ctr Tuskegee AL 36083 Office: VA Med Ctr Recreation Service (11K) Tuskegee AL 36083

BRYANT, BARBARA EVERITT, market research company executive; b. Ann Arbor, Mich., Apr. 5, 1926; d. William Littell and Dorothy (Wallace) Everitt; m. John H. Bryant, Aug. 14, 1948; children—Linda Bryant Valentine, Randal E., Lois B. A.B., Cornell U., 1947; M.A., Mich. State U., 1967, Ph.D., 1970. Editor art Chem. Engring. magazine McGraw-Hill Pub. Co., N.Y.C., 1947-48; editorial research asst. Univ. Ill., Urbana, 1948-49; free-lance editor, writer, 1950-61; with continuing edn. adminstrn. dept. Oakland Univ., Rochester, Mich., 1961-66; grad. research asst. Mich. State Univ., East Lansing, 1966-70; from sr. analyst to v.p. Market Opinion Research, Detroit, 1970-77, sr. vp., 1977—. Author: High School Students Look at Their World, 1970, American Women Today & Tomorrow, 1977. Contbr. articles to profl. jours. Mem. U.S. Census Adv. Com., Washington, 1980—, Mich. Job Devel. Authority, Lansing, Mich., 1980-85; state editor LWV of Mich., 1959-61. Mem. Detroit Chpt. of Women in Communications, Inc. (pres. 1974-75, Nat. Headliner award 1980), Detroit Chpt. of Am. Mktg. Assn. (pres. 1976-77), Am. Mktg. Assn. (midwestern v.p. 1978-80, v.p. mktg. research 1982-84), Detroit Press Club. Republican. Presbyterian. Club: Renaissance. Avocation: swimming. Home: 1505 Sheridan Dr Ann Arbor MI 48104 Office: Market Opinion Research 243 Congress St Detroit MI 48226

BRYANT, BETTY JANE, shopping center executive; b. Camden, Ind., June 19, 1926; d. Claude Raymond and Louise (Eckert) Wickard; B.S., Purdue U., 1947; m. Harry R. Bryant, Aug. 21, 1949; children—Susan, Patricia. Retail mgmt. and advt. L. S. Ayres, Indpls., 1947-49, Burdine's, Miami, Fla., 1950-51, Joske's, San Antonio, 1968, Dillard's, San Antonio, 1968-70; with Sterling Advt. Agy., N.Y.C., 1949; mktg. dir. Mary Ann Fabrics and Designer's Fabrics By Mail, Evanston, Ill., 1971-75; instr. Ray-Vogue Sch., Chgo., 1976; mktg. dir. Woodfield Shopping Center, Schaumburg, Ill., 1977—. Mem. council Fashion Group of Chgo. Bd. dirs. N.W. Area council Girl Scouts Am., 1982—, Greater Woodfield Conv. and Visitors Bur., 1985-86. Mem. N.W. Suburban Assn. (dir.), Commerce and Industry (v.p. 1981-82), Chgo. Area Shopping Center Mktg. Dirs.'s Assn., Women in Mgmt., Mortar Board, Kappa Kappa Gamma. Home: 2008 Bayberry Ln Hoffman Estates IL 60195 Office: Woodfield Merchants Assn 5 Woodfield Mall Schaumburg IL 60195

BRYANT, BETTY LOU, nursing educator; b. Parke County, Ind., Sept. 3, 1929; d. Odus A. and Latitia I. (Swaim) Ratcliff; Lic. Practical Nurse, Ivy Tech. Coll., 1972; B.S. Nursing, Ind. State U., 1980, postgrad. 1982-83; m. Bobby L. Bryant, Dec. 7, 1947; children—Taunnie Nelson, Greg, Chris. Nurse's aide Ind. State Sanitorium, Rockville, Ind., 1968-70; Lic. Practical Nurse, Vermillion County Hosp., Clinton, Ind., 1972-79; asst. adminstr. Lee Alan Bryant Health Care Facility, Rockville, 1979-80, dir. nursing service, 1980-82; cons. gerontol. program Ind. State U. Sch. Nursing, Terre Haute, 1981-82, continuing edn. cons.-aging, 1981-82, asst. instr. anatomy, physiology, sci. dept. univ., 1979-80. Sec., Women's Soc. Christian Service, 1960-62; brownie leader Boy Scouts Am., 1961-62; leader Meth. Youth Fellowship, 1969-70, ch. camp counselor, 1968-70; precinct com. person Republican party, 1968-72, active Ind. state senator campaign, 1980-81; diabetes screener, 1979. Cert. nurse practitioner Am. Nurses Assn., 1986. Mem. Ind. Assn. Quality Assurance Profls., Central Ill. Soc. Health Edn. and Tng., Ind. State U. Alumni Assn., Ill. Nurses Assn., Ind. U. Alumni, AAUW, Am. Soc. Aging, Mid-Am. Congress on Aging. Home: Rural Route 1 Bloomingdale IN 47832 Office: Lakeview Med Ctr Sch Nursing 812 N Logan Ave Danville IL 61832

BRYANT, ELIZABETH LEEDS NOE, nurse; b. Abington, Pa., Apr. 29, 1940; d. William Leeds and Dorothy Donaldson (Roney) Noe; diploma Peter Bent Brigham Hosp. Sch. Nursing, 1961; B.S. in Nursing, Boston U., 1965; M.Ed., Francis Marion Coll., 1979; children—Kimberly Haws, Peter Leeds. Staff nurse Peter Bent Brigham Hosp., Boston, 1961-65, Tufts-New Eng. Med. Center, Boston, 1965-66; dir. inservice McLeod Meml. Hosp., Florence, S.C., 1969-73, dir. nursing service, 1974-76; regional nurse coordinator Pee Dee Area Health Edn. Center, Florence, 1976-79; head nurse alcohol dependence treatment program Seattle VA Med. Center, 1979—; clin. asst. prof. Sch. Nursing U. Wash., 1980—. Bd. dirs. S.C. affiliate Am. Heart Assn., 1975-79, mem. nursing edn. com., 1974-78; bd. dirs. Upper Florence County Heart Unit, 1976-79. Mem. Am., Wash., King County nurses assns., Nat. League Nursing, Sigma Theta Tau. Republican. Office: 8 West Seattle VA Med Center 4355 Beacon Ave S Seattle WA 98108

BRYANT, EVA LOU, sales executive; b. Orrick, Mo., Aug. 15, 1941; d. William Maurice and Lena Mae (Gooch) Hall; m. David Lynn Bryant, Aug. 20, 1960; children—Alan, Karen, James, Diane, Jason, Zane. A.A., Purdue U., Ft. Wayne, 1982; A.A., Ind. U., 1982, B.S., 1983. Owner Day Nursery, Colorado Springs, Colo., 1973-76; asst. mdse. coordinator House of Fabrics, Hastings, Nebr., 1978-79; with GTE Directories Corp., Ft. Wayne, 1980-81, service rep., 1981-83, telephone sales rep., 1983-85, dist. sales mgr., 1985—. Vestry chmn. St. Alban's Episcopal Ch., Ft. Wayne, 1986—; active PTA, Episcopal Ch. Women, Girl Scouts U.S.A., Boy Scouts Am., 4-H, Little League, Am. Arthritis Found., Am. Cancer Soc., Am. Heart Assn. Recipient Pres.'s award, GTE, 1984, Top Gen. Sales award, 1984, Top Sales Travel Incentive, 1985, 86. Mem. Am. Bus. Women's Assn., AAUW, Nat. Assn. Female Execs., Delta Zeta. Republican. Episcopalian. Club: Lake Forest Swimming and Tennis. Avocations: needlework; reading; sports.

BRYANT, GAY, magazine editor. Founder, editorial dir. New Dawn, N.Y.C., editor, exec. editor Working Woman, N.Y.C.; v.p., editor Family Circle mag., N.Y.C. Mem. Acad. Women Achievers, Women's Media Group, Women in Communications, Inc., Am. Soc. Mag. Editors, NOW. Address: Family Circle 488 Madison Ave New York NY 10022*

BRYANT, JANICE ELAINE, airline holding company executive; b. Emporia, Kans., Oct. 26, 1950; d. William Howard and Gretta May (Rees) Thomas; m. Harold Robert Bryant, May 2, 1981. B.A., B.S., Coll. of Emporia, 1972, postgrad. in bus. adminstrn., Emporia State U., 1973-79. Cost acct. Iowa Beef Processors, Emporia, 1972-76; mgr. gen. acctg. Sauder Industries, Inc., Emporia, 1976-80; dir. fin. reporting Tex. Air Corp., Houston, 1981—. Bd. dirs. United Way, Emporia, 1980. Mem. Nat. Corp. Cash Mgmt. Assn. Republican. Club: Atascocita (Tex.) Country. Office: Tex Air Corp 4040 Capital Bank Plaza 333 Clay St Houston TX 77002

BRYANT, JUDITH WILDER, librarian; b. Jersey City, Sept. 28, 1940; d. Robert Dennison and Eloise (Hulphers) Wilder; m. Carter Harrison Bryant, II; 1 son, Sean. B.A., U. Del.-Newark, 1962; M.L.S., U. Tex.-Austin, 1974; certs. Pratt Inst., 1977, 80; Braille cert. ARC, 1978. Library clk. U. Tex., Austin, 1973-75; circulation librarian Collier County Library, Naples, Fla., 1975; nat. cons. Inst. for Intellectual Devel. of Children and Young Adults, Tehran, Iran, 1975-76; outreach librarian Ridgewood Pub. Library (N.J.), 1977-78; children's librarian Jersey City Pub. Library, 1978—, co-chmn. Hudson-Essex Summer Committed. Researcher, article, 1973. Friends of Tex. Libraries spl. scholar, 1973. Mem. ALA, N.J. Library Assn., Am. Mus. Natural History, Nat. Wildlife Fedn. Democrat. Office: Jersey City Pub Library Miller Br 489 Bergen Ave Jersey City NJ 07304

BRYANT, KATHY ANN, writer, editor; b. El Paso, Tex., Feb. 16, 1942; d. Arthur James and Katherine Louise (Pollock) Lingle; m. Clifford Eugene Bryant, June 5, 1965; children—Christopher Eugene, Sean Clifford. B.A., U. Denver; postgrad. U. Calif.-Irvine. Tchr. English, Placentia (Calif.) Sch., 1963-69; art critic Newport Ensign, Newport Beach, Calif., 1977-80, Daily Pilot, Costa Mesa, Calif., 1980-81, The Register, Santa Ana, Calif., 1981-83; mng. editor McFadden Pub. Co., Costa Mesa, 1981-84; editor Newport Beach (714), Baker Communications, Irvine, 1984-86; writer Orange County Register, Exec. mag.; contbg. editor Orange County mag. Mem. Am. Prss Women, Women in Communications (co-chmn. writers' conf. 1982), Mystery Writers Am., Women's Polit. Caucus, Ind. Writers So. Calif. Democrat.

BRYANT, (LOIS) JEAN, editor; b. South Bend, Ind., Dec. 31, 1925; d. Ford Happa and Iva May (White) Bunch; m. Harland Hiram Bryant, Feb. 14, 1944; children—Daniel Eugene, Janet Alyce, Clayton Max, Elizabeth Ann, Adam Lee. Exec. secretarial diploma South Bend Coll. Commerce, 1943; Grad. religious edn. Pacific Coast Bapt. Bible Coll., 1970; student Bapt. Coll., Springfield, Mo., 1957-59; Dr. Sacred Laws and Letters, (hon.), Clarksville Sch. Theology, 1981. Editor, pub. LOIS Mag., Rialto, Calif., 1978-81; asst. editor Here's Life Pubs., San Bernardino, Calif., 1981-83, assoc. editor, 1983-84, mng. editor, 1984—. Dir. publicity Calvary Bapt. Ch., Redlands, Calif., 1985—. Mem. Nat. Assn. Female Execs. Republican. Avocations: art; music. Home: 700 E Washington St #138 Colton CA 92324 Office: Here's Life Publishes Inc 795 S Allen St San Bernardino CA 92402

BRYANT, MARJORIE ESTHER, flight instructor; b. Concord, N.H., June 17, 1926; d. Herbert and Gladys (French) Tittemore; m. Jack Douglas Bryant, Dec. 14, 1945; children—Virginia, Dale, Robert. Flight instr. Pennridge Airport, Perkasie, Pa., 1967—, chief flight instr., fixed base operator; accident prevention counselor FAA, 1973—; speaker in field. Named Flight Instr. of Yr. Eastern Pa., 1974; recipient Pa. Gov.'s trophy for outstanding service to aviation, 1981; apptd. flight examiner FAA. Mem. Aircraft Owners and Pilots Assn., Nat. Pilots Assn., Internat. Flying Farmers, Nat. Assn. Flight Instrs., 99's, Aviation Council Pa. (dir. 1974—). Republican. Clubs: Soroptimist, Order Eastern Star; Woman's (Perkasie). Won last leg of Powder Puff Derby Race, Parkersburg, W.Va. to Wilmington, Del., 1976. Home: 235 Ridgeway Ct Perkasie PA 18944

BRYANT, MARY SNELL, accounting and consulting company executive; b. Mexico, Mo., Feb. 27, 1949; d. William Ernest and Marie Louise (Austin) Snell; m. Timothy Clark Bryant, Jan. 17, 1981. B.A., Northwestern U., 1971; M.B.A., U. Ill., 1973. C.P.A., Ill., Tex. Dir. eval. and projects G. D. Searle & Co., Skokie, Ill., 1977-78, spl. asst. to exec. v.p. fin., 1979; dir. planning Searle Med. Products, Dallas, 1980, controller ventures, 1981; dir. planning Pearle Health Services, Inc., Dallas, 1981-83, v.p. internat., 1983-85; mgr. mgmt. cons. services Alexander Grant & Co., Tampa, Fla., 1985—. Mem. Planning Execs. Inst., Am. Inst. C.P.A.s, Tex. Soc. C.P.A.s, Ill. Soc. C.P.A.s. Clubs: The 500 Inc. (Dallas); Chandler's Yacht. Home: 307 Brightwaters Blvd NE Saint Petersburg FL 33704 Office: Alexander Grant & Co 501 E Kennedy Blvd Tampa FL 33602

BRYANT, RITA YVONNE, child care administrator, consultant; b. Memphis, Apr. 14, 1937; d. William Woodrow and Emma Ray (Reed) B.; m. Richard Lee Bryant, Jan. 10, 1959; children—Rhonda Lynn Bryant Golightly. Student Wayland Bapt. U., 1955-56, Amarillo Coll., 1963-64, 75-76, W. Tex. State U., 1977-79. Child care adminstr. Amarillo Community Ctr., 1963-68; adminstrv. asst. Amarillo Ind. Sch. Dist., 1968-74, headstart tchr., 1974-76; owner, mgr. Tots Villa Child Devel. Ctr., Amarillo, 1978—; child care cons., 1981—. Mem. Tex. State Adv. Bd. Day Care Licensing, 1981-84, Regional Adv. Bd. for Headstart, 1982-85, Study Commn. Handicapped Children Day Care, 1983-85. Mem. Tex. Assn. Edn. Young Children (sec. 1984-85), Tex. Lic. Child Care Assn. (sec. 1982-84, 1st v.p. 1985—), Nat. Assn. Edn. Young Children, Womens Forum, Amarillo Art Alliance. Publicity dir. Lone Star Ballet Guild, 1982-83. Baptist. Avocations: tennis; reading. Home: 1228 Crockett St Amarillo TX 79102 Office: Tots Villa Child Devel Ctr 1400 W 10th St Amarillo TX 79101

BRYANT, TERESENA WISE, city administrator; b. St. Petersburg, Fla., Jan. 19, 1940; d. Mose and Mattie Lee (Cooksey) Gardner; 1 child, Donna Kay Drayton. A.A., St. Petersburg Jr. Coll., 1958; B.A. in Edn., Math. and Social Studies, Fla. A&M U., 1963; postgrad. Howard U., 1976, Manhattan Coll., 1967; M.P.A., NYU, 1977. Manhattan borough planner Office of Mayor, N.Y.C. Youth Bur., 1971-74, exec. asst. to dep. commr. field ops., 1974-75, exec. asst. to dept. commr. mgmr. and adminstrn./field ops., 1975-76, asst. to exec. dir., 1976-77, adminstrv. mgr., 1977-81, asst. exec. dir. contract mgmt., 1981-84, dir. planning exec. office, 1984—, asst. exec. dir. contracts; pres., chairperson T. Wise Enterprise, Inc.; legis. asst. N.Y. State senator, 1979-83; mem. N.Y. State Temp. Commn., 1983—; dir. recreation Mohegan Community Ctr., 1965-66, dir., 1966-71. Coordinator Com. of Bronx Blacks, N.Y.; bd. dirs. N.Y. Urban League, Bronx; mem. Bronx Polit. Women's Caucus. Recipient Outstanding Civic Leadership award Bronx Unity Democratic Club, 1981, certs. S.A.V.E./Dept. Labor, 1981-83, Woman of Yr. award Morrisania Edn. Council, 1982, certs. N.Y.C. Central Labor Rehab. Council, 1983, other awards. Mem. Am. Soc. Pub. Adminstrs., Nat. Forum of Black Pub. Adminstrs., Council of Concerned Black Execs., Nat. Assn. Female Execs., AAUW, NAACP, Nat. Black Bus. and Profl. Women's Club, Women Bus. Owners of N.Y., NYU Alumni Assn., Fla. A&M U. Alumni, Alpha Kappa Alpha. Democrat. Mem. Christian Methodist Episcopalian. Ch. Avocations: writing poetry; swimming; arts; sketching; antiques. Home: 950 Evergreen Ave Apt 16M Bronx NY 10473 Office: Office of Mayor New York City Youth Bur 44 Court St Brooklyn NY 11201

BRYANT-REID, JOHANNE, investment company executive; b. Farmington, W.Va., Mar. 11, 1949; d. Leslie David and Jessie Lee (Scruggs) Bryant; m. Keith Alexander Reid, Nov. 20, 1976. B.A. in Psychology, W.Va. U., 1971. Placement counselor, mgr. Ran Assocs., Cleve., 1971-78; exec. recruiter Merrill Lynch, N.Y.C., 1978-80, corp. employment mgr., 1980—. Mem. adv. bd. Nat. Council Negro Women. Recipient Black Achiever award YMCA of Greater N.Y.C., 1981. Mem. Employment Mgrs. Assn., Am. Soc. Personnel Adminstrs. Democrat. Baptist. Home: 147 St Marks Ave Brooklyn NY 11238 Office: Merrill Lynch 165 Broadway New York NY 10080

BRYDON, PATRICIA CAROL, nurse, educator; b. McLeansboro, Ill., Aug. 21, 1947; d. William Albert and Melba Lee (Adams) Moorman; m. James Collins Brydon, May 10, 1973. Diploma in nursing Jewish Hosp. Sch. Nursing, St. Louis, 1968; A.A., Saddleback Community Coll., 1976; B.S.N., Calif. State U.-Fullerton, 1977; M.S.N., Calif. State U.-Los Angeles, 1980; student Western State U. Coll. Law, 1984—. Cert. critical care nurse, advanced cardiac, pediatric home health care nurse. Surg. nurse Northwestern Meml. Hosp., Chgo., 1968-69; nursing supr. Kingstown Manor, North Kingstown, R.I., 1969-70; pediatric intensive care nurse U. Calif. Med. Center, Orange, 1970-72; critical care Victory Meml. Hosp., Waukegan, Ill., 1972-74; critical care unit nursing supr. Tustin Community Hosp. (Calif.), 1974-79; nursing instr. Golden West Coll., Huntington Beach, Calif., 1980-83, 84—; nurse educator VA Med. Center, Long Beach, Calif., 1983-84; ednl. cons. ACCESS, Corona Del Mar, Calif., 1983-84; pediatric nursing tutor. Author slide-tape program, Swan-Ganz Catheters, 1978; co-author simulated learning on pediatric nursing, 1982. Fundraiser, bd. dirs., vol. Seaside Child Devel. Center, Long Beach, 1983; vol. ARC, Santa Ana, 1979, Orange County Health Planning Council, Tustin, 1977, Make-A-Wish Found., 1983—. Mem. Calif. Assn., Calif. Nurses Assn. Am. Assn. Critical Care Nurses, Nat. Critical Care Inst., Am. Fedn. Tchrs. Democrat. Contbr articles to profl. jours. Home: 307 21st St Huntington Beach CA 92648 Office: Golden West Coll 15744 Golden West St Huntington Beach CA 92640

BRYNWOOD, MARCIA RAE, newspaper publishing company executive; b. Milw., Oct. 29, 1937; d. Erwin Paul and Lorraine E. (Zuehlsdorf) Lehmann; m. Thomas L. Brynwood, Aug. 25, 1956 (div. Aug. 1970); children—Laura L. Brynwood Kitchen, Brandon L. Student U. Wis.-Milw., 1955-57, Union Coll., 1975-77; B.A., Edison Coll., 1978; postgrad. mgmt. Harvard U., 1984. IBM computer operator Gen. Electric Co., Milw., 1957-59; accounts records bookkeeper Columbia Wax/U.S. Borax Corp., Glendale, Calif., 1959-61; supr. compensation, benefits Kearfott div. Singer Co., San Marcos, Calif., 1961-71, mgr. benefits, services, Little Falls, N.J., 1971-78; corp. dir. compensation, benefits N.Y. Times Co., N.Y.C., 1978—. Seminar leader comparative mgmt. N.Y.C. Police Dept., 1983. Recipient Tribute to Women and Industry award YWCA, N.J., 1978; scholar U. Wis., 1955-57, Clare Dreyfus Found., 1956. Mem. Am. Compensation Assn., Epsilon Sigma Alpha (v.p., edn. dir. Loveland chpt. 1963-69). Club: Harvard Business. Avocations: sailing; swimming. Home: Apt 25-T 375 South End Ave New York NY 10280 Office: NY Times Co 12th Floor 229 W 43d St New York NY 10036

BRYSON, JO-ANN KNIGHT, health care administrator; b. Newport, R.I., Mar. 25, 1943; d. George K. and Josephine E. (DeRosier) Knight; m. Neil F. Bryson, 1967 (div. 1975); 1 son, Neil Kerry. B.S.Nursing, Boston Coll., 1965; M.S.Nursing, U. R.I., 1974; Ed.D., Internat. Grad. Sch., 1985. Lic. nurse, Ohio, 1977. Staff nurse, supr. U.S. Navy, Newport, 1965-68; instr. Youville Hosp., Cambridge, Mass., 1969-73, U. R.I., Kingston, 1973-75; asst. dir. Decatur Meml. Hosp. (Ill.), 1975-77; dir. sch. nursing Bethesda Hosp., Cin., 1977-85; asst. v.p. paramed. services Bethesda Hosps., Inc., Cin., 1986—; cons.; mem. ad hoc com. nursing edn. Ohio Bd. Nursing, 1980-83. Author: Cost-Effective Management in Schools of Nursing, 1982; contbr. articles to profl. jours. Mem. Ohio Council Diploma Nurse Educators (chmn. 1980), Assembly of Hosp. Schs. Nursing (mem. governing council 1980-83), Am. Hosp. Assn., Ohio League for Nursing (v.p. 1981-83, mem. steering com. Ohio River Valley council 1981-83), Nat. League for Nursing (mem. bd. 1983—, chmn. council diploma programs), Phi Kappa Phi. Roman Catholic. Clubs: Boston Coll. Alumni, Moeller High Sch. Mother's (Cin.). Home: 1878 Stockton Dr Loveland OH 45140 Office: School of Nursing Bethesda Hosp Inc 619 Oak St Cincinnati OH 45206

BRYSON, NATALIE ELIZABETH, antique dealer; b. Weymouth, Mass., Feb. 20, 1931; d. Harry Follett and Amy Louise (Hill) Duncan; student public schs.; children—Elizabeth Alice, Muriel Anne, William MacLean, Rebecca Jane, David Duncan, James Hill. Owner, Antiques and Epicure, Silverdale, Wash., 1972—; instr. gourmet cooking and antiques Olympic Coll., Bremerton, Wash., 1971—, lectr. on China, 1979—; pub. relations rep. AAA Travel Agy. of Wash.; tour guide trip to China, 1982, 83, 84; cons., mem. Mus. History and Industry, Seattle; rep. Wash. Art Commn. Pres. Olympic View Community, 1978; bd. dirs. March of Dimes. Recipient Golden Acorn award Wash. PTA, 1970, Outstanding Achievement award Lockheed Mgmt. Assn., 1979; flag officer Keechong Soc., Mus. Am. China Trade, Milton, Mass., 1979—. Mem. Oriental Ceramic Soc. (London and Hong Kong), Nat. Assn. Female Execs., Nat. Assn. Dealers Antiques, Victorian Soc. Am., Kipsap County Hist. Soc., Seattle Antique Study Group, Decorative Arts Council, Seattle Art Mus., U.S. C. of C., Central Kitsap C. of C. Home: 15251 Olympic View NW Silverdale WA 98383 Office: 330 6th Ave N Seattle WA 98109

BUBENIK, PATRICIA JEAN HADLE, educational administrator; b. Denver, Jan. 12, 1947; d. H. Paul and Allie Hadle; B.A., Colo. State U., 1969; M.A., U. Calif., Santa Cruz, 1970; Ed.D., U. San Francisco, 1981; m. David M. Bubenik, June 21, 1969. Tchr. Madrone Sch., Sunnyvale Sch. Dist. (Calif.), 1970-77; tchr. Demonstration Sch. for Gifted, San Jose State U., 1977; lang. arts specialist Sunnyvale Sch. Dist., 1977-78, vice prin., Madrone Sch., 1978-79, prin. summer sch., 1979, prin. Lakewood Sch., 1979-82, Columbia Community Sch., Sunnyvale, 1982-85; asst. supt. Mountain View Sch. Dist., Calif., 1985—; ednl. cons. for writing, oral lang., sch. climate, Calif., 1977—; established Kids Can Write Project, Kids View mag.; founder Jr. Scribe, dist. wide student mag. Producer Video Connections: A View of Brains-On Classrooms. Bd. dirs. Calif. Young People's Theatre, Umbrella House, Community Sch. Music and Arts.; mem. exec. bd. Stanford Area council Boy Scouts Am.; founder Deaver Mayor's Youth Council, 1964. Fellow, Bay Area Writing Project, U. Calif., Berkeley, 1978; Sparks Meml. fellow; Boettcher Found. scholar, 1965. Recipient Vol. award Calif. Parks and Recreation Assn., 1983; named Am Outstanding Elem. Tchr. of Am., 1973. Mem. Assn. Calif. Adminstrs., Assn. Curriculum and Supervision Devel., Santa Clara Reading Council (exec. bd.), Calif. Reading Assn., Nat. Council Tchrs. English, Calif. Assn. Gifted, Calif. Assn. Tchrs. English, Internat. Reading Assn., Am. Assn. Sch. Adminstrs., Phi Delta Kappa, Phi Beta Kappa, Phi Kappa Phi, Phi Sigma Iota. Club: Women Leaders in Edn. Author: A New Direction: Focusing on the Whole Person Through the Affective Domain, 1977; Effects of Principal-Delivered Written Positive Reinforcement on Teacher and Class Behavior, 1981. Office: 220 View St Mountain View CA 94041

BUCHANAN, BEVERLY ANN, nurse; b. Jackson, Miss., Apr. 10, 1952; d. W.R. and Emma O. (McElroy) Camel; m. Harold Ralph Buchanan, Mar. 13, 1976; children—Alecia A., Dalano K. Student St. Dominic Sch. Nursing, 1975; A.A., Hinds Jr. Coll., 1979; B.S.N., William Carey Coll., 1981; M.S. in Community Health Nursing, U. So. Miss., 1984. Registered nurse. Staff nurse, charge nurse Saint Dominic Hosp., Jackson, 1975-81; registered nurse, staff nurse, charge nurse VA Med. Ctr., Jackson, 1977—, enterostomal resource person, 1981—. Community rep. March Dimes, Jackson, 1976-78; mem. Nat. Council of Negro Women, Jackson, 1981-84; assoc. mem. Ostomy Assn. Jackson, 1981-83. Mem. Am. Assn. Critical Care Nurses, Internat. Assn. Enterostomal Therapy, Am. Nurses Assn., Miss. Nurses Assn., Nat. Alliance of Postal and Fedn. Employees. Democrat. Baptist. Avocations: reading; bicycling; swimming.

BUCHANAN, BRENDA J., computer company executive; b. San Diego; d. Fred and Annie M. (Winston) B. B.S. in Math., Physics and Chemistry, U. Denver; M.A. in Math., Washington U., 1973; postgrad. McGill U., 1973-75, U. Cologne, Fed. Republic Germany. Math. instr. Washington U., St. Louis, 1969-71; programmer/analyst United Aircraft of Can., Longueil, Que., 1971-73; ops. research analyst Consol. Bathurst Ltd., Montreal, Que., 1973-76; corp. new product planning mgr. Digital Equipment Corp., Maynard, Mass., 1976-80, new product program mgr., Springfield, Mass., 1980-84, tapes bus. mgr., 1984-86, corp. purchasing program office mgr., Northboro, Mass., 1986—. Leader, Can. Girl Guides, Montreal, 1972-74; mem. mayor's blue ribbon com. Dept. Pub. Works, Springfield, 1983. Fulbright fellow, Fed. Rep. Germany; recipient Experiment in Internat. Living award Fed. Republic Germany, 19. Mem. Can. Ops. Research Soc., Alpha Kappa Alpha (Basileus Ivy of Yr., Denver chpt.). Democrat. Baptist. Club: Links, Inc. (Springfield) (treas. 1984—). Home: 4E Strathmore Shire PO Box 49 Uxbridge MA 01568-0049 Office: Digital Equipment Corp 30 Forbes Rd Northboro MA 01532-2598

BUCHANAN, EDITH CLAMPITT, radio station executive; b. Franklin, N.C., July 23, 1933; d. Renfro Lofton and Maude Mae (Howard) Clampitt; m. Charles Roger Buchanan, Jan. 23, 1948; children—Charles Roger, Jr., Deborah Gaye Buchanan Young, Kelly Stephen. Grad. high sch., Canton, N.C. With Belk Dept. Store, North Augusta, S.C., 1965-70; with sales dept., traffic coordinator Sta. WRDW-TV, Augusta, Ga., 1970-75; traffic, ops. mgr. Sta. WGUS AM/FM, Augusta, Ga., 1975-82, gen. mgr., 1982—. Bd. dirs. Easter Seal Soc., Augusta, 1982—. Mem. Augusta C. of C., North Augusta C. of C., Augusta Advt. Club. Baptist. Home: 821 Dunbarton Dr North Augusta SC 29841 Office: Sta WGUS AM/FM Radio PO Box 1475 Augusta GA 30913-1475

BUCHANAN, FAY ANNETTE PENDLETON, educator; b. Tampa, Fla., Sept. 16, 1936; d. George Cline and Annabel (Roberts) Pendleton; m. Kenneth W. Buchanan, Feb. 7, 1959 (dec. Mar. 1976); children—Ross Eric, Sean Andrew. B.S. in Edn., Fla. State U., 1958; M.S., Fla. Atlantic U., 1966. Cert. tchr. Elem. sch. tchr., Fla., 1958—, Treadway Elem. Sch., Leesburg, 1976—. Mem. choir 1st Baptist Ch., Eustis, 1971—; mem. Eustis Band Boosters, 1979-84. Mem. Reading Council. Democrat. Avocations: reading; bowling; music; travel; genealogy. Home: 407 S Mary St Eustis FL 32726 Office: Route 4 Box 870 Leesburg FL 32788

BUCHANAN, GWENDOLYN ANN JONES, nurse; b. New Straitsville, Ohio, June 17, 1927; d. Thomas Britton and Gwendolyn (McGrady) Jones; R.N., U. Cin., 1948; B.S. in Nursing, U. Okla., 1967, M.S. (Outstanding Achievement scholar), 1978; m. Jim Charles Buchanan, Oct. 2, 1948; children—Linda Sue Buchanan Laakman, Cynthia Dianne Buchanan Patterson, Jim Charles, Thomas Britton. Staff nurse, then head nurse neurosurgery and neurology VA Hosp., Memphis, 1949-59; head nurse neurosurgery and neurology rehab. VA Med. Center, Oklahoma City, 1960-65, clin. nursing supr. ambulatory care, 1968-80, asst. chief nurse surg./ambulatory care, 1981—; nurse coordinator, cons. Midwest City (Okla.) Hosp., 1966-68; clin. asst. prof. U. Okla. Coll. Nursing. Mem. Am. Nurses Assn., Nat. League Nursing,

Emergency Dept. Nurses Assn. (chmn. edn. and program com.), Assn. Ambulatory Care Nursing Service Adminstrs., Okla. League Nursing (recognition award for community service 1980, 81), Okla. Nurses Assn. (dir. 1969-71), Okla. Home Health Care Assn. (standards com. 1979-81, chmn. nominations com. 1981), Okla. Nursing Service Adminstrs., U. Okla. Coll. Nursing Alumni Assn. (chmn. nominating com. 1982), Sigma Theta Tau (chpt. pres. 1982). Lutheran. Club: Order Eastern Star. Author articles in field, chpt. in book. Home: 5301 Listen Circle Spencer OK 73084 Office: 921 NE 13th St Oklahoma City OK 73104

BUCHANAN, MARY CATHERINE, editor; b. Darby, Pa., Sept. 2, 1945; d. Edward Robb and Loretta Theresa (Cashin) B.A., Widener U., 1976. Editor, USDA Forest Service, Broomall, Pa., 1963—, fed. women's program mgr., 1985-86. Mem. Alpha Sigma Lambda.

BUCHANAN, MARY ELLA, nurse, army officer; b. Hot Springs, Ark., July 19, 1950; d. Robert Glynn and Georgia Catherine (Dobson) B.; B.S. in Nursing, Vanderbilt U., 1972; M.S., U. Tenn., 1974. Staff nurse Met. Health Dept., Nashville, 1972-73; commd. lt. Nurse Corps, U.S. Army, 1973, advanced through grades to maj., 1983; ambulatory care nurse clinician Family Practice Clinic, Ft. Belvoir, Va., 1974-76, Robinson Barracks Army Health Clinic, Stuttgart, Germany, 1976-77, 5th Gen. Hosp., 1977-79, Acad. Health Scis., Ft. Sam Houston, Tex., 1979-80; ambulatory care nurse clinician Walter Reed Army Med. Center, Washington, 1980-81, nurse researcher Nursing Research Service, 1980-82, Nurse Ward 72, 1982-84; head nurse Ward 4A Irwin Army Community Hosp., Ft. Riley, Kans., 1984-86, coordinator infection control, quality assurance, 1986—. Mem. Am. Nurses Assn. (cert. family nurse clinician, div. community health), Am. Pub. Health Assn., Council Primary Health Care Nurse Practitioners, Nurse Practitioner Assn. D.C. (pres.), Sigma Theta Tau. Methodist. Clubs: Smithsonian Assos., Franklin Mint Collectors Soc., Internationale Volkssportverband c.V. Home: 1601 Leavenworth Manhattan KS 66502 Office: Irwin Army Community Hosp Dept Nursing Fort Riley KS 66442

BUCHANAN, VIRGINIA LOUISE, purchases and contracts agent; b. Winfield, Kans., Nov. 17, 1945; d. Harley Bruce and Barbara Louise (Briscoe) Parsons; m. Enrique Escobar, May 20, 1968 (div. Dec. 1972); m. 3d, John Edward Buchanan, Mar. 15, 1980; stepchildren—Teresa C., David M. B.A. cum laude, Southwestern Coll., 1967; M.S., Emporia State U., 1969. Prof., U. Industrial de Santander, Bucaramanga, Colombia, 1968-70; tchr. English, Bi-Nat. Ctr., Bogotá, Colombia, 1970-72; campaign sec. Putnam Community Hosp., Carmel, N.Y., 1972-73; legal sec. Arent, Fox, et al, Washington, 1973-75; contract mgr. Devel. Alternatives, Washington, 1975-81; contracts and purchases agt. Bechtel Petroleum, Houston, 1981—. Southwestern Coll. scholar, 1963-67; Emporia State U. fellow, 1967-69. Mem. Nat. Contract Mgmt. Assn. (chpt. sec. 1983—), Am. Rose Soc., Phi Beta Tau. Methodist. Home: 14203 Stokesmount Dr Houston TX 77077 Office: Bechtel Petroleum Inc 5400 Westheimer Ct Houston TX 77056

BUCHANNAN, MARY CATHERINE, accountant; b. Milledgeville, Ga., Nov. 25, 1955; d. Henry Lawson Sanders and Martha Eugenia (Manning) Green; m. Ronald Lee Hunt, Aug. 16, 1975 (div. Aug. 1981); m. 2d, Robert Allen Buchannan, June 18, 1982. B.B.A., Sam Houston State U., 1977. C.P.A., Tex. Teller Republic State Bank, Houston, 1974-75, Am. Bank, Huntsville, Tex., 1976-77; acct. Franklin, Sylvester & Co., Houston, 1977—. Norman Bundy Meml. scholar South Houston High Sch., 1973; Freshman Leadership scholar Sam Houston State U., 1974; Jessie Jones scholar, 1975-76. Mem. Am. Inst. C.P.A.s, Tex. Soc. C.P.A.s, Alpha Lambda Delta, Alpha Chi. Methodist. Home: 1533 Gardenia Houston TX 77018 Office: Franklin Sylvester & Co 5718 Westheimer Suite 550 Houston TX 77057

BUCHENAU, PATRICIA LYNETTE (PATI), accountant; b. Perryton, Tex., Feb. 3, 1955; d. Roy Weldon and Joette Aline (Winger) Riley; m. George Howard Buchenau, Jr., Aug. 22, 1974; children—Micah Dawn, Jori Tad. B.B.A., West Tex. State U., 1984. Legal sec. Schroeder, Guest & Hoffman, Dallas, 1973; adminstrv. sec. athletic dept. West Tex. State U., Canyon, 1974-75; tax preparer, bookkeeper H & R Block, Plainview, Tex., 1977-79; owner, mgr. Amarillo Bookkeeping Systems, Tex., 1982-85; staff asst. Arthur Young & Co., Amarillo, 1985—. Mem. Petroleum Accts. Soc., Nat. Accts. Assn., Alpha Kappa Psi. Republican. Avocations: gardening, snow skiing, jogging; bicycling. Home: 2201 Woodbury Amarillo TX 79124 Office: Arthur Young & Co 300 First National Plaza 1 Amarillo TX 79101

BUCHENHORNER, MARIANNE, psychotherapist, psychoanalyst; b. Budapest, Hungary, Sept. 15; d. Tibor and Agnes Aczel (Marks) de Nagy; B.A., Vassar Coll.; M.S.W., Columbia U., 1966; cert. in psychotherapy and psychoanalysis Postgrad. Center for Mental Health, 1975, cert. mental health cons., 1976, cert. in supervision, 1977; m. Walter Buchenhorner, Aug. 16, 1965. Research asst., librarian Psychoanalytic Inst., Columbia U., N.Y.C., 1960-61; asst. to dir. of social sci. and humanities textbooks McGraw Hill Co., N.Y.C., 1961-63; case aide Youth House, N.Y.C., 1963-64; social worker Community Service Service Soc. N.Y.C., 1966-69; supr. State U. Hosp., Bklyn., 1969-71; dir. Multiple Service Center, Big Bros. Inc., N.Y.C., 1971-72; dir. counseling services Postgrad. Center for Mental Health, N.Y.C., 1976-81, tchr., 1974—, supr., pvt. practice psychotherapy, N.Y.C. Mem. Nat. Assn. Social Workers, Soc. Clin. Social Work Psychotherapists, Postgrad. Psychoanalytic Soc. Office: 200 E 33rd St New York NY 10016

BUCHHOLZ, CAROLYN LEIGH, lawyer; b. Boulder, Colo., Dec. 10, 1955; d. Glen Elvis and Alice Joy (McIntosh); m. Roger Alan Buchholz, Oct. 4, 1980; B.A. cum laude, Middlebury Coll., 1978; J.D., U. Colo., 1981. Bar: Colo. 1981, U.S. Dist. Ct. Colo. 1981. Research asst. Rocky Mountain Mineral Law Found., Boulder, Colo., 1979-80; assoc. firm Sisk, Foley, Hultin, & Driver, Denver, 1981-83, Hultin, Driver & Spaanstra, Denver, 1983-85, Hultin & Spaanstra, Denver, 1985—; mem., atty. program to provide legal services to indigent, Denver, 1982—. Mem. procedural rules subcom. Colo. Air Quality Control Commn., 1983-84. Mem. ABA, Colo. Bar Assn., Denver Bar Assn. (legal fees arbitration com. 1983-84), Am. Bus. Women's Assn. Democrat. Methodist. Office: Hultin, Driver & Spaanstra 1610 Emerson St Denver CO 80218

BUCHMANN, MOLLY O'BANION, choreographer, ballet educator; b. Baton Rouge, Nov. 22, 1949; d. James Dennis and Annie Laurie (Joffrion) O'Banion; m. Fred J. Buchmann, Aug. 23, 1969; children—F. Jason, Dennis Andrew. B.S. in Secondary Edn., La. State U., 1971, M.S. in Dance, 1973. Artistic dir. Baton Rouge Ballet Theatre, 1976—; choreographer Baton Rouge Little Theatre, 1983—; instr. dance Baton Rouge Magnet High Sch., 1979-85; owner, mgr. The Dancers' Workshop, Baton Rouge, 1973—; vis. artist Arts and Humanities Council of Greater Baton Rouge, 1976; choreographer Aubin Lane Dinner Theatre, Baton Rouge, 1980-82. Editor La. Dance News, 1976-77. Choreographer numerous ballets. State of La. Div. Arts Choreographic grant, 1982; Baton Rouge Alumni Fedn. scholar, 1967. Mem. Southwest Regional Ballet Assn. (bd. dirs., sec. 1984—). Democrat. Roman Catholic. Office: Dancers' Workshop 3875 Government St Baton Rouge LA 70806

BUCHWALD, NAOMI REICE, U.S. magistrate; b. Kingston, N.Y., Feb. 14, 1944; d. Albert and Sylvie Reice; B.A. cum laude, Brandeis U., 1965; LL.B. cum laude, Columbia U., 1968; m. Don Buchwald, Jan. 19, 1974; children—David Evan, Jennifer Anne. Admitted to N.Y. bar, 1968; litigation assoc. firm Marshall Bratter Greene Allison & Tucker, N.Y.C., 1968-73; with U.S. Atty.'s Office, So. Dist. N.Y., N.Y.C., 1973-80, chief civil div., 1979-80, dep. chief civil div., 1976-79; U.S. magistrate So. Dist. N.Y., 1980—. Recipient spl. citation Commr. FDA, 1978. Mem. ABA, N.Y.C. Bar Assn., N.Y. State Bar Assn., Fed. Bar Council, Phi Beta Kappa, Omicron Delta Epsilon. Editor: Columbia Jour. Law and Social Problems, 1967-68. Office: US Courthouse Foley Sq New York NY 10007

BUCK, BARBARA JAMISON, chemical company executive; b. Pitts., Sept. 21, 1951; d. George Gale and Mary Jane (Butler) Jamison; B.S. in Chem. Engring., Carnegie-Mellon U., 1973; m. John Ashley Buck, May 19, 1973; Process design engr. Union Carbide Corp., Tarrytown, N.Y., 1973-75, sales engr., Tarrytown, 1975-77, asst. region sales mgr., 1977-79, asst. to v.p., bus. analyst, N.Y.C., 1979-81, product mgr. custom catalysts, Danbury, Conn., 1981-82, mgr. fin. analysis and planning, 1982-84, product mgr. engring. polymers, 1985—. Mem. Soc. Women Engrs. (chmn. nat. conv. 1980, mem. adv. com. nat. conv. 1980, 81, 82, exec. com. 1982-83, nat. conv. treas. 1986), Delta Delta Delta. Office: Union Carbide Corp Old Ridgebury Rd Danbury CT 06817

BUCK, BARBARA NELL, agricultural trade association executive; b. Whittier, Calif., June 12, 1957; d. Brenton Otis and Mary Lou (Ralston) B.S. in Animal Sci., U. Calif.-Davis, 1979. Staff writer, intern Dairyman mag., Corona, Calif., 1979-80; pub. relations dir. Mustang Engring. Co., Santa Fe Springs, Calif., 1980; pub. relations asst. Western Growers Assn., Irvine, Calif., 1980-83; dir. pub. relations, 1983—. Media relations aide Modern Pentathlon Jr. World Championships, Coto de Caza, Calif., 1983; chmn. service project St. Andrews Presbyn. Becomers, Newport Beach, Calif., 1983-84; pres., 1984; mem. Citrus Inst. com. Nat. Orange Show. Mem. Nat. Assn. Female Execs., Am. Agri-Women, Calif. Women for Agr., Calif. Aggie Alumni Assn. U. Calif.-Davis (life). Republican. Office: Western Growers Assn 17620 Fitch St Irvine CA 92714

BUCK, KATHLEEN ANN, lawyer; b. South Bend, Ind., Nov. 14, 1948; d. Betty Jo and Cecil and Betty Jo (Parfitt) B.; m. Raymond Donald Battocchi, Aug. 20, 1975; 1 son, Adam. B.A. cum laude, St. Mary's Coll., Notre Dame, Ind., 1970; J.D., Ind. U., 1973; student U. Iberoamericana, Mexico City, 1968. Bar: D.C., Fla. Trial atty. F.R.L.S., Delray Beach, Fla., 1973-75; atty. Swift & Co., Washington, 1975-77; atty., asst. dir. govt. relations Esmark, Inc., Washington, 1977-81; asst. gen. counsel U.S. Dept. Def., Washington, 1981—; mem. Def. Privacy Bd., 1981—. Bd. dirs. Va. Fedn. Republican Women, 1979-81; mem. Fairfax County Rep. Com., 1978-81; Republican precinct capt., Great Falls, Va., 1978-81; mem. Great Falls Citizens Assn. Mem. ABA, D.C. Bar, Fla. Bar, Women in Govt. Relations (Most Disting. Mem. 1979), Pi Sigma Alpha. Clubs: Capitol Hill (Washington); Equestrian Soc. Home: 10120 Forest Brook Ln Great Falls VA 22066 Office: Room 3E988 The Pentagon Washington DC 22031

BUCK, LINDA DEE, executive recruiting company executive; b. San Francisco, Nov. 8, 1946; d. Sol and Shirley D. (Setterberg) Press; student Coll. San Mateo (Calif.), 1969-70; divorced. Head hearing and appeals br. Dept. Navy Employee Relations Service, Philippines, 1974-75; dir. personnel Homestead Savs. & Loan Assn., Burlingame, Calif., 1976-77; mgr. fin. placement VIP Agy., Inc., Palo Alto, Calif., 1977-78; exec. v.p., dir. Sequent Personnel Services, Inc., Mountain View, Calif., 1978-83; Founder, pres. Buck & Co., San Mateo, 1983—. Publicity mgr. for No. Calif., Osteogenesis Imperfecta Found. Inc., 1970-72; cons. Am. Brittle Bone Soc., 1979—. Mem. Nat. Assn. Personnel Cons., Calif. Assn. Personnel Cons., Am. Soc. Tng. and Devel., Internat. Platform Assn. Jewish. Home: San Mateo CA Office: Mills Sq Tower 9th Floor 100 S Ellsworth Ave San Mateo CA 94401

BUCK, NATALIE SMITH, former state official; b. Carlsbad, N.Mex., Jan. 10, 1923; d. Milton R. and Rosa Adele (Binford) Smith; student William and Mary Coll., 1940-41; B.B.S., U. Colo., 1943; postgrad. U. Tex., 1945-46; m. C. B. Buck, Sept. 12, 1948; children—Warren Z., Barbara Anne. Chief clk. N.Mex. Senate, 1951-53; sec. of state State of N.Mex., Santa Fe, 1955-59; formerly supr. personnel N.Mex. Dept. Public Welfare; formerly chief personnel N.Mex. Health and Social Services Dept. Mem. Kappa Alpha Theta. Democrat. Home: 108 W Alicante Rd Santa Fe NM 87501 Office: PO Box 2183 Santa Fe NM 87504

BUCKETT, BONNIE-JEAN, physical education educator; b. Port Chester, N.Y., Apr. 23, 1948; d. Victor Robert and Dorothy Jean (Burger) Buckett; student Tampa U., 1967; B.S., Springfield Coll., 1970, M.S., 1976; D.Arts (Mamaroneck Women's Club Chairmanship scholar 1981, doctoral teaching fellow 1981-83) Middle Tenn. State U., 1983. Tchr. phys. edn., coach Byram Hills Sch. System, Armonk, N.Y., 1970-71; tchr. health, phys. edn., coach Rye (N.Y.) City Sch. System, 1971-75; women's athletic dir., coach Springfield Tech. Community Coll., 1975-76, coach women's basketball and softball, 1976-77; assoc. prof. phys. edn., women's athletic dir. Castleton State Coll., 1976-85, coach women's basketball, 1976-80, women's lacrosse, 1977-78, women's softball, 1979-81, 84-85, women's field hockey, 1983, dir. coll. Girls' Basketball Camp, 1977-81; assoc. prof. phys. edn. U. S.C.-Aiken, 1985—; dir. Springfield Coll. Clinic for Mentally Retarded, 1967-70; dir. recreation Town Newtown (Conn.), 1969-71; dir. Summer 8-13 Year-olds Community Regional Opportunities Program, Chicopee, Mass., 1976-77; cons. for adaptive phys. edn. programs Louise Devel. Center, Murfreesboro, Tenn., 1981-83; mem. Vt. Council Phys. Edn. Instrn. and Curriculum Revision, 1983-85; coordinator Spl. Olympics basketball and cross-country skiing, 1983-85; vol. Tenn. Sr. Citizen's Olympics, 1983; area rep. Ednl. Sport Inst., 1984-85. Vt. State Colls. grantee, 1981-83; mem. exec. council. Aiken County Assn. Spl. Citizens, 1986—; mem. steering com. Aiken County Spl. Olympics; mem. exec. bd. Diabetes Support Group for Children Ages 5-18, 1985—. Mem. AAHPER and Dance, S.C. Assn. Health, Physical Edn., Recreation Dance (state adv. student sect. 1986—), Am. Softball Assn., Am. Fedn. Tchrs. Home: 26 E Fawn Wood Dr Aiken SC 29801 Office: Dept Edn U SC Aiken SC 29801

BUCKLAND, BONNIE KAY, university administrator; b. Chgo., Apr. 13, 1949; d. Arthur William and Margaret Louise (Schranz) Vick; m. George Alexander Buckland, Sept. 11, 1971; 1 child, Erin Elizabeth. B.S., Fla. State U., 1971; M.S., U. Tenn., 1982. Cert. tchr., Tenn. English instr. Grainger County Schs., Rutledge, Tenn., 1972-76; counselor spl. programs Lincoln Meml. U., Harrogate, Tenn., 1976-77, asst. dir. spl. programs, 1977-80, dir. spl. programs, 1980-83, dean students, 1982—. Recipient Outstanding Young Women of Am. award, 1978, 80. Mem. AAUW (pres. 1982-84), Pi Lambda Theta. Lutheran. Avocations: reading; jogging. Home: PO Box 25 Cumberland Gap TN 37724 Office: Lincoln Meml U 308 Campus Ctr Harrogate TN 37752

BUCKLES, MARLA DIANNE, nursing educator; b. Dumas, Tex., Oct. 31, 1952; d. Richard Milton and Doris Helen (Ohlenbusch) B. B.S. in Microbiology, Tex. Tech. U., 1975; B.S.N., Tex. Christian U., 1977; M.S.N., U. Tex.-Arlington, 1983. Staff nurse St. Joseph Hosp., Ft. Worth, 1978-81; dir. clinic ops. Ft. Worth Rehab. Farm, 1979; nurse practitioner Sanborn Western Camps, Florisant, Colo., summer 1983; asst. prof. nursing Tex. Christian U., Ft. Worth, 1982—; pres./owner Tex. Cornerstone Corp., residential real estate devel. co.; dir. S.W. Glazing Supply, Inc., Dallas, 1978-80, 84—. Recipient Sword of Hope, Am. Cancer Soc., 1983. Mem. Am. Cancer Soc., Am. Assn. Primary Health Care Nurse Pracititioners, Am. Pub. Health Assn., Nat. League Nursing, Tex. League Nursing, Am. Nurses Assn., Tex. Nurses Assn., Alpha Chi Omega. Office: Texas Cornerstone Corp PO Box 309 Aledo TX 76008-0309

BUCKLES-DEANS, DELORA ELIZABETH, educational diagnostician, consultant; b. Houston, Apr. 19, 1940; d. Joseph Bernhardt and Helen Elizabeth (Phillips) Blazek; m. Richard George Buckles, June 26, 1962 (div. Oct. 1969); children—Gregory, Deborah; m. 2d, Harry Alexander Deans, Jan. 1, 1975; 1 dau., Catherine; stepchildren—Laurie, Daniel, Melissa, Andrew. B.A., U. Tex., 1962; postgrad. Cornell U., 1962; M.Ed., Boston U., 1966, cert. advanced grad. study, 1966; Ed.D., U. Houston, 1981. Instr., Boston U., 1964-66; coordinator Harris County Dept. Edn., Houston, 1969-72; dir. resource services Klein Ind. Sch. Dist., Spring, Tex., 1972-75; coordinator, ednl. diagnostician area 6 Houston Ind. Sch. Dist., 1975-78; inservice coordinator Coll. Edn. U. Houston, 1979-81; ednl. diagnostician Vocat. Evaluation Ctr. for Handicapped, Houston, 1981—; cons. Aldine Ind. Sch. Dist., Houston, 1981-82, Harlingen Ind. Sch. Dist. (Tex.), 1982-83. Contbr. articles in field to profl. jours.; patentee in field. Campaign worker Democratic Party Tex., Houston, 1979-84. Named Outstanding Student, U. Tex., Austin, 1962. Mem. Council Ednl. Diagnostics Services (sec. 1981-83), Tex. Council Exceptional Children (chmn. 1980-82), Tex. Ednl. Diagnostics Assn. (pres. 1981-82), Phi Delta Kappa, Zeta Tau Alpha. Democrat. Episcopalian. Home: 1931 Wroxton St Houston TX 77005 Office: Vocational Evaluation Ctr for Handicapped Houston Ind Sch Dist 3517 Austin St Houston TX 77004

BUCKLEY, ANNA PATRICIA, state legislator; b. Brockton, Mass., Mar. 21, 1924; d. Michael and Ann (Fitzmaurice) Hernan; m. Daniel J. Buckley, 1946; children—Kevin Michael, Daniel J., Paul, Patrice, Nancy J. Grad. Williams Sch. Bus., 1943. Adminstrv. asst. to lt. gov. Mass., 1963-65, to Mass. auditor, 1965-72; councilperson-at-large Brockton City Council, Mass., 1971-72; mem. Mass. Senate, Boston, 1973—. Active Plymouth County Democratic League, Mass., 1956—; mem. Mass. Dem. State Com., 1960—; mem. Dem. Nat. Com.; del. Dem. Nat. Conv., 1980. Served with WAC, 1943-45. Recipient Legislator of Yr. award Mass. Mcpl. Assn., 1982. Roman Catholic. Office: Mass Senate State Capitol Boston MA 02133*

BUCKLEY, PRISCILLA LANGFORD, magazine editor; b. N.Y.C., Oct. 17, 1921; d. William Frank and Aloise (Steiner) Buckley; B.A., Smith Coll., 1943. Copy girl, sports writer UP, N.Y.C., 1944, radio rewrite, 1944-47, corr., Paris, 1953-56; news editor-Sta. WACA, Camden, S.C., 1947-48; reports officer CIA, Washington, 1951-53; with Nat. Rev. mag., N.Y.C., 1956—, mng. editor, 1959-86, sr. editor, 1986—. Mem. U.S. Adv. Commn. on Pub. Diplomacy, 1984. Clubs: Overseas Press; Sharon (Conn.) Country (sec. 1973-77, pres. 1978-80). Columnist One Woman's Voice Syndicate, 1976-80. Home: Great Elm Sharon CT 06069 Office: National Review 150 E 35th St New York NY 10016

BUCKLEY, SHARON LYNNE, sales representative; b. Chgo., July 25, 1952; d. Marion Stewart and Lillian June (Madsen) B. B.A., Cornell Coll., 1974; M.S., Purdue U., 1976. Clin. biochemist Chgo. Pub. Health, 1977-80; sales rep. Hewlett-Packard, Naperville, Ill., 1980—. Contbr. articles to profl. publs. Mem. Am. Chem. Soc., Chgo. Chromatography Discussion Group. Republican. Congregationalist. Home: 2832 N Orchard St Chicago IL 60657 Office: Hewlett-Packard 1200 E Diehl St Naperville IL 60566

BUCKLEY, THELMA CLAIRE, guidance counselor, social worker; b. Primrose, Pa., Apr. 24, 1927; d. John Harvey and Anna Matilda (Hesselmeir) Weiderhold; student Phila. Bible Coll., 1950; B.A., Glassboro State Coll., 1975, M.A., 1979; m. Harold Donald Buckley, Apr. 8, 1950; children—Donna Buckley Movsovich, Darlene Buckley Gilligan, Deane. Clk., typist Bell Telephone Co., Phila., 1945-52; evening supr. food services dept. Mohawk Valley Community Coll., Utica, N.Y., 1966-67; asst. dir. catering Syracuse U., 1967-68; case assignment, service coordinator, field supr. Vis. Homemaker Service of Cumberland County, Vineland, N.J., 1971-76; spl. instr. N.J. Dept. Health, Trenton, 1977-78; sch. social worker Commercial Twp. Sch. Dist., Port Norris, N.J., 1975-79, Cumberland Regional Bd. Edn., Seabrook, N.J., 1979-81, sch. guidance counselor, 1981-85, sch. social worker, 1985—. Dep. v.p. region V, Fedn. Democratic Women, 1975-79; committeewoman Cumberland County Dem. Orgn., 1975-84; mem. adv. bd. Cumberland County Home Health Care, 1977—, Cumberland County Coll. Equal Opportunity Fund and Student Devel. Bd.; bd. dirs. Sr. Citizens Day Care Program. Mem. NEA, Am. Personnel and Guidance Assn., N.J. Sch. Guidance Assn., Cumberland County Personnel and Guidance Assn. (pres.). Baptist. Home: 2263 Edgewood Dr Vineland NJ 08360 Office: Cumberland Regional High School Seabrook NJ 08302

BUCKMAN, VALERIE NELSON, personnel executive; b. Chgo., Mar. 11, 1950; d. Karl Gustave and Clara Elizabeth (Jonesku) Nelson; m. Joseph Fabian Buckman, Oct. 25, 1975; 1 son, Thomas Kelly; m. James W. Curley, Nov. 24, 1971 (div. Aug. 1975); children—Kirsten M., Valerie P. B.A., U. Northeastern Ill., 1975. Dir. pub. relations Village of Glendale Heights (Ill.), 1980-81; assoc. editor Examiner newspapers, Winfield, Ill., 1982-83; communications dir. Banner Personnel Services, Chgo., 1984—. Recipient Appreciation citation Am. Legion, 1981. Mem. Nat. Assn. Female Execs. Charismatic Catholic. Home: 2N241 Diane Ave Glen Ellyn IL 60139 Office: Banner Personnel Service Inc 7 W Madison St Chicago IL 60602

BUCKMANN, CAROL IRENE, lawyer; b. N.Y.C., Aug. 20, 1950; d. Edwin Henry and Viola (Santoro) Buckmann; m. Mayer Siegel, Jan. 23, 1983. B.A., Barnard Coll., 1972; J.D., NYU, 1976. Bar: N.Y. 1976. Assoc. firm Fried, Frank, Harris, Shriver & Jacobson, N.Y.C., 1976-80, Weil Gotshal & Manges, N.Y.C., 1980-82, White & Case, N.Y.C., 1982—. Co-author: Executive's and Professional's Guide to Pension and Retirement Benefits, 1982; Pension Outlook; monthly columnist on pension law devels. Mem. ABA, N.Y. State Bar Assn. (employee benefits com. tax sect.). Office: White & Case 1155 Ave of Americas New York NY 10036

BUCKNER, BONNIE R(EYNOLDS), management consultant; b. Atlanta, Oct. 29, 1948; d. William Gerald and Betty Louise Reynolds; m. George Buckner, II, Jan. 22, 1971 (div. 1974). B.A., West Ga. Coll., 1970, M.S., 1971. Chmn. sci. dept. Mt. Zion High Sch., Ga. 1971-74; indsl. engr. Milliken & Co., Spartanburg, S.C., 1974-76, mgr. indsl. engring. Burlington Industries, Wilson, N.C., 1976-78; sr. indsl. engr. Arcata Corp., Kingsport, Tenn., 1978-81; corp. indsl. engring. mgr. Baxter Travenol, Deerfield, Ill., 1981-85; mgr. Ernst & Whinney, Chgo.,, 1985—. Advisor Jr. Achievement, Tenn., 1979, 80. Mem. Inst. Indsl. Engrs., Soc. Am. Value Engrs., Soc. Mfg. Engrs., Computer and Automated Systems Assn., Robotics Internat., Nat. Assn. Female Execs. Episcopalian. Home: 487 Rustic Dr Wheeling IL 60090 Office: Ernst & Whinney 150 S Wacker Dr Chicago IL 60606

BUCKNER, LINDA IVERSON, computer software sales executive, consultant office automation; b. Lincoln, Nebr., July 14, 1950; d. Joseph Thomas and Henrietta Mae (McClure) Fisher; m. David Lynn Iverson, Dec. 29, 1967 (div. May 1980); children—Rachelle, Meggan, Elyssa; m. John David Buckner, Apr. 17, 1981. B.S. in Bus., U. S.D., 1974. Lic. life, accident and health ins. agt.; lic. property and casualty agt. Mktg. rep. ESCO, Northfield, Ill., 1975-76; sales mgr. Safecom, Inc., Schaumburg, Ill., 1976-79; account exec. CNA, Ins., Chgo., 1979-81; mktg. mgr. Computer Scis. Corp., Chgo., 1980-82; ptnr., v.p. mktg. Buckner & Assocs., Wheaton, Ill., 1981—; mgr. nat. accounts devel. Marsh-McLennan Group, 1984—; cons. Ins. Agy. Automation, 1979-81, CARA Corp., Lombard, Ill., 1983-84. Democratic election judge, DuPage County, Ill., 1977—; mem. DuPage County Citizens Adv. Com., 1978-80; mem. Hoffman Hallmark Choir, 1978-80, fundraiser Acad. Performing Arts, Chgo., 1981—. Mem. Nat. Assn. Female Execs., Data Processing Mgmt. Assn., Am. Mgmt. Assn., Am. Soc. Assn. Execs., Chgo. Soc. Assn. Execs., Internat. Platform Assn., Ins. Distaff Execs., Assn., Nat. Assn. Ins. Women, Soc. Mgmt. Info. Systems (assoc.). Home: 505 W Union St Wheaton IL 60187

BUCOSSI, SANDRA JO, educator; b. Red Bank, N.J., Nov. 13, 1950; d. Anthony Francis and Ann Marie (DePierro) Trufolo; m. Brian Albert Bucossi, Mar. 27, 1977; 1 child, Brian Jr. Student Monmouth Coll., 1970, U. London, 1971; B.S., U. So. Fla., 1972; M.A., Kean Coll., 1979. Cert. supr. Tchr. Middletown Twp. Sch., Middletown, N.J., 1972-73, Keansburg Schs., N.J., 1973—; cons. Ednl. Dynamics, Keansburg, 1976-77; dir. Trufolo Learning Clinic, Little Silver, N.J., 1983—. Author: Journeys Through Occupational Experiences. Mem. Keansburg Tchr.'s Assn. (treas. 1981—), N.J. Ednl. Assn., Monmouth County Ednl. Assn., NEA. Home: PO Box 43 309 2d Ave Bradley Beach NJ 07720 Office: Trufolo Learning Clinic 530 Pospect Ave Little Silver NJ 07739

BUDNEY, LINDA MCDONALD, computer analyst; b. Stamford, Conn., Nov. 26, 1946; d. Harold Thomas and Dorothy (Nungesser) McDonald; B.A. in Econs., Cath. U., 1969; postgrad. in tech. of mgmt., Am. U., 1972-75; m. Thomas J. Budney, Mar. 4, 1978. Computer specialist HEW, Washington, 1969-73; area mgr. computer measurement and evaluation Data Mgmt. Center, HEW, 1973-77, chief systems programming br., 1977-79; EDP project coordinator Pension Benefit Guaranty Corp., Washington, 1979-84, asst. dir. project computers, 1984; group dir. IMTEC, U.S. Gen. Acct. Office, 1984—. Mem. Reston (Va.) Chorale, 1976-78, treas., 1977; mem. Rockville (Md.) Community Chorus, 1978-79. Mem. Assn. Computing Machinery, Computer Measurement Group, Ops. Research Soc. Am., Pi Gamma Mu. Home: 9908 Newhall Rd Potomac MD 20854 Office: 2020 K St NW Washington DC 20006

BUDOFF, PENNY WISE, physician, author; b. Albany, N.Y., July 7, 1939; d. Louis and Goldene Wise; m. Seymour L. Budoff, June 24, 1962; children—Jeff, Cynthia. Student U. Wis.; B.A., Syracuse U., 1959; M.D., SUNY-Upstate Med. Sch., 1963. Intern, St. Luke's Meml. Hosp., Utica, N.Y., 1963-64; practice medicine specializing in family practice, Woodbury, N.Y., 1964—; lectr., TV guest on women's medicine; mem. Nat. Com. on Women in Family Medicine; clin. research on menstrual pain and women's health problems. Contbr. articles to profl. jours. Named Woman of Yr., C.W. Post Coll., L.I., 1981; recipient Nat. Consumers League award, 1983, Max Cheplove award Erie chpt. N.Y. State Acad. Family Physicians, 1983. Fellow Nassau County Med. Soc., Am. Acad. Family Physicians (nat. com. on pub. relations); mem. AMA, Am. Med. Women's Assn. (co-chmn. nat. women's health com.), Nassau Acad. Family Physicians (past pres.). Author: No More Menstrual Cramps and Other Good News, 1980; No More Hot Flashes and Other Good News, 1983. Home and Office: 11 Fairbanks Blvd Woodbury NY 11797

BUDOVEC, SUZANNE, telephone company manager; b. Pomona, Calif., Oct. 28, 1944; d. Frank Louis and Caroline May (Rimmer) Taricco; m. John Edward Budovec, Mar. 9, 1963; children—Keith Brian, Kimberly Dawn. Cert. Mt. San Antonio Coll., Walnut, Calif., 1971; A.A. in Indsl. Supervision, Coll.

of the Desert, Palm Desert, Calif., 1977; B.A. in Pub. Service Mgmt., U. Redlands, Calif., 1978. Customer rep. Gen. Tel., Pomona, Calif., 1963-72, customer rep. supr., Indio, Calif., 1972-78, phone mart mgr., Palm Springs, Calif., 1978-80, service mgr., Monrovia, Calif., 1980-84, customer billing mgr., Mentone, Calif., 1984—. Recipient Community Service award Gen. Tel. Co. Eastern Area Mgmt. Club, 1976; Cert. of achievement Gen. Tel. Co. and YWCA, 1985. Mem. Ind. Tel. Pioneers Assn. (pres. 1984-85), Calif. Fedn. Women's Clubs (pres. 1978, Club Woman of Yr. 1977), Duarte C. of C. (pres. 1983). Clubs: Good Govt. (trustee 1984-85), Toastmasters (pres. Indio 1976, Yucca Valley 1980, Upland and Mentone 1984, Toastmaster of Yr. 1976). Avocations: water skiing; camping; reading; tennis. Office: Gen Tel Co PO Box 136 Mentone CA 92359

BUECHE, KRISTINE LOUISE, director of human resources; b. Ithaca, N.Y., June 16, 1947; d. Arthur Maynard and Margaret Louisa (Bassler) B. B.A., U. Dayton, 1970; M.S., Wright State U., 1974. Pres., Behavior Mgmt. Inc., Dayton, 1972-74; specialist employee relations Gen. Electric, Cin., 1977-78, mgr. compliance mgmt., Utica, N.Y., 1978-79; mgr. Lord Lindsay, Knoxville, Tenn., 1979-80; mgr. salaried employee relations Gen. Electric, Wilmington, N.C., 1980-83, mgr. orgn. and staffing, Milw., 1983-85; dir. human resources Quantum Med. Systems, Issaquah, Wash., 1985—. Mem. Human Resource Planning Soc., Am. Electronics Assn., Am. Mgmt. Assn. Republican. Roman Catholic. Club: Jr. League (Seattle). Avocations: swimming; sailing. Office: Quantum Med Systems 1065 12th Ave NW Issaquah WA 98027

BUECK, JANE MARGARET, clinical social worker; b. Providence, July 6, 1929; d. James Francis and Mary Gertrude (Foley) Harahan; B.A., St. Mary-of-the-Woods Coll., 1951; M.S.W., Catholic U. Am., 1953; m. Robert Kesler Bueck, Feb. 22, 1958; children—Sharon, Carol, Barbara. Social worker Youth Service Bur., Detroit, 1953-56; agy. supr. Catholic Family and Children's Services, Portsmouth, Va., 1970-72; psychiat. social worker Tidewater Psychiat. Inst., Virginia Beach, Va., 1972-75; supr. Family Counseling Center, Clearwater, Fla., 1975-77; dir. social services Horizon Hosp., Clearwater, 1977-79; pvt. practice clin. social work, Clearwater, 1979—. Served with USNR, 1956-58. Mem. Acad. Cert. Social Workers, Nat. Assn. Social Workers, Fla. Soc. Clin. Social Work. Roman Catholic. Office: 1100 Cleveland St Suite 900 Clearwater FL 33515

BUESNEL, GAIL JULIE, marriage, family and child therapist, freelance writer, seminar speaker; b. Perth, Australia, Nov. 26, 1949; came to U.S., 1976; d. Francis and Sylvia Evelyn (Page) McCarte; m. Paul Gerald Buesnel, Jan. 23, 1971. Diploma, Commonwealth Bible Coll., Brisbane, Australia, 1969-70; B.A., Northwest Coll., 1977; M.A., Chapman Coll., 1981. Intern, Gitin & Assocs., Santa Ana, Calif., 1981; intern to coordinator Christian inpatient psychiat. program Charter Baywood, Long Beach, Calif., 1984; dir. outpatient practice Christ Centered Counseling, Port Townsend, Wash., 1985—; cons. Life Ctr., Port Townsend, 1985—. Contbr. articles to profl. jours. Mem. Nat. Assn. Female Execs. Mem. Assemblies of God Ch. Clubs: Alateen (Perth) (sec. 1964-65), Women's Ministries (Port Townsend) (pres. 1985—).

BUFFMIRE, JUDY ANN, rehabilitation services administrator, psychologist; b. Salt Lake City, June 5, 1929; d. William Henry Broyles and Audrey Francis (Cook) Broyles Ballinger; m. LaMar Lee Buffmire, Nov. 28, 1948; children—Kathryn Ann, Shanna Lee. B.S. cum laude, U. Utah, 1966, M.S., 1967, Ph.D., 1969. Lic. psychologist. Asst. prof. dept. spl. edn. U. Utah, 1967-76; state program specialist Utah State Office Edn., Salt Lake City, 1976-77; dep. dir. Utah Social Services, Salt Lake City, 1978-80; dir. State Div. Family Services, Salt Lake City, 1981-82, dir. State Div. Registration, Salt Lake City, 1982-83, dir. State Div. Rehab., Salt Lake City, 1983—. Contbr. articles to profl. publs. Mem. Presdl. Adv. Council on Ednl. and Profl. Devel., 1974-77; chmn. Utah Adv. Com. on Handicapped, 1975-77, chmn. State Mental Health Adv. Com., Salt Lake City, 1977-78, Regional VIII Adoption Resource Ctr., Salt Lake City, 1980; mem. State Bd. Fin. Instns., Salt Lake City, 1981-83; vol. therapist Parents United, Inc., Salt Lake City, 1982-84. Utah State Bd. Edn. scholar 1967; NDEA scholar, 1968-69; recipient Disting. Grad. award Wasatch Acad., 1976; named Bureaucrat of Yr., Utah Issues, 1982; Pub. Service Adminstr. of Yr., Nat. Assn. Social Workers, 1983. Mem. Utah Psychol. Assn., Delta Kappa Gamma (pres. 1983-84). Democrat. Presbyterian. Avocations: cooking; camping; fishing; running rivers; traveling. Home: 765 E 4255 S Salt Lake City UT 84107 Office: Div Rehab Services 250 E 500 S Salt Lake City UT 84111

BUFFUM, NANCY KAY, interior designer; b. Portland, Oreg., Aug. 10, 1941; d. William Cheely and Wanda (Camblin) Whitman; student Shasta Coll., 1959-60, U. Calif.-Berkeley, 1960-63; m. Jack Erwin Buffum, Mar. 24, 1961 (div. 1981); children—Andrew Lewis, Airenne. Exec. sec. Pacific Mut. Life Ins. Co., San Francisco, 1961-63; gen. cashier N.Am. Brokers, San Francisco, 1963-64; mgr. So. area office Lindsey & Co., Sacramento, 1964-65; escrow office, sales rep. Kennicott Constrn. Co., Redding, Calif., 1967-69; office mgr., gen. ptnr. Buffum & Assocs., Redding, 1969-72; asst. designer Penthouse Interiors, Redding, 1973-75; owner, designer The Design Works, Redding, 1975—; lectr. on design and antiques to community groups. Pres., Shasta County Easter Seal Soc., 1971-73; pres. Redding Elem. Sch. PTA, 1973-77, trustee, adv. com., sch. bd., 1975-78; bd. dirs. Redding Mus. League; adviser KIXE Pub. TV Sta.; mem. Redding Planning Commn., 1981—; mem. adv. bd. Council; mem. Redding Jazz. Festival (steering com.), Redding Airport Transporation Com., United Way (campaign cabinet), Private Industry Council, Downtown Redding Bus. Assn. Recipient award for community service Rotary Internat., 1976, named Business Woman of Yr. Redding C. of C., 1982. Mem. Nat. Home Furnishing Assn., Am. Soc. Interior Designers (assoc.), Inst. Bldg. Designers, DAR (hon. pub. service award), Redding C. of C. (v.p. 1984-85; pres. elect 1986). Republican. Club: Soroptimist. Office: 1600 California St #100 Redding CA 96001

BUFORD, EVELYN CLAUDENE SHILLING, printing company executive; b. Fort Worth, Sept. 21, 1940; d. Claude and Winnie Evelyn (Mote) Hodges; student Hill Jr. Coll., 1975-76; m. William J. Buford, Mar. 1982; children by previous marriage—Vincent Shilling, Kathryn Lynn Shilling Vassar. With Imperial Printing Co., Inc., Fort Worth, 1964-70, 77—, gen. sales mgr. comml. div., 1982—, corp. sec., 1977—; with Tarrant County Hosp. Dist., Fort Worth, 1973-77, asst. to asst. adminstr., 1981-84. Mem. Am. Mgmt. Assn., Exec. Women Internat. (dir., publs. chmn., v.p. 1984, pres. 1985, chmn. adv. com. 1986), Nat. Assn. Female Execs., Presidents Club Tex. Republican. Methodist. Home: 100 Kenneth Ln Burleson TX 76028 Office: 1429 Hemphill Fort Worth TX 76104

BUGBEE-JACKSON, JOAN, sculptor; b. Oakland, Calif., Dec. 17, 1941; d. Henry Greenwood and Jeanie Ogden (Abbot) B.; B.A. in Art, San Jose (Calif.) State Coll., 1964, M.A., 1966; student Nat. Acad. Sch. Fine Arts, N.Y.C., 1968-72, Art Students League, N.Y.C., 1968-70; m. John Michael Jackson, June 21, 1973; 1 dau., Brook Bond. Apprentice to Joseph Kiselewski, 1970-73; Instr. art Foothill (Calif.) Jr. Coll., 1966-67; instr. design De Anza Jr. Coll., Cupertino, Calif., 1967-68; instr. pottery Greenwich House Pottery, N.Y.C., 1969-71, Craft Inst. Am., N.Y.C., 1970-72, Cordova (Alaska) Extension Center, U. Alaska, 1973-79, Prince William Sound Community Coll., 1979—; one-woman exhbns. in Maine, N.Y.C., Alaska and Calif.; group exhbns. include Allied Artists Am., 1970-72, Nat. Acad. Design, 1971, 74; pres. Cordova Arts and Pageants Ltd., 1975-76; commns. include Marie K. Smith Commemorative Medal, 1973, Bob Korn Pool Commemorative Plaque, 1975, Eyak Native Monument, 1978, Alaska Pioneer's Home Ceramic Mural, 1979, Alaska Wildlife Series Bronze Medal, 1980, sculpture murals and portraits Alaska State Capitol, 1981, Pierre De Ville Portrait commn., 1983, Robert B. Atwood, 1985, Armin F. Koernig Hatchery Plaque, 1985, Cordova Fishermen's Meml. Sculpture, 1985, Alaska's Five Govs., bronze relief, Anchorage, 1986, also other portraits. Scholarship student Nat. Acad. Sch. Fine Arts, 1969-72; recipient J.A. Suydam Bronze medal, 1969; Dr. Ralph Weiler prize, 1971; Helen Foster Barnet award, 1971; Daniel Chester French award, 1972; Frishmuth award, 1971; Allied Artists Am. award, 1972; C. Percival Dietsch prize, 1973; citation Alaska Legislature, 1981, 82. Fellow Nat. Sculpture Soc. Address: Box 374 Cordova AK 99574

BUGGAY, DOLORES NELL (DEE), city personnel official; b. Winterville, Ga., Sept. 15, 1938; d. Forrest Brinkley and Marion Lucille (Culbertson) Hardeman; m. Louie Edward Powell, Aug. 30, 1958 (div.); 1 dau., Sandra Dee; m. 2d, Al Daniel Buggay Jr., Jan. 1, 1970. B.S. in Elem. Edn., U. Ga., 1960. Cert. tchr., Ga. Tchr. Jefferson Elem. Sch. (Ga.), 1960-61; office mgr. W.T. Grant Co., Decatur, Ga., 1961-75; adminstrv. asst. City of Conyers (Ga.), 1975-83, personnel adminstr., 1983—. Vol. United Way, Conyers, 1981—; charter mem. Atlanta Ballet Soc., Atlanta. Mem. Am. Soc. Personnel Adminstrn. (v.p. 1983-84), Am. Bus. Women's Assn. (pres. 1981-82, Woman of Yr. 1983, del. Atlanta area council 1983-84). Democrat. Methodist. Lodge: Order Eastern Star. Home: 910 Dawn Ct Conyers GA 30208 Office: City of Conyers 1184 Scott St Conyers GA 30207

BUHL, CYNTHIA MAUREEN, foreign policy educator and advocate; b. Los Angeles, Apr. 14, 1952; m. Albert Buhl and Dorothy Jane (Loth) Henry. B.A., Lewis & Clark Coll., 1974. Dir., Resource and Counseling Ctr., Portland Youth Advs., Oreg., 1971-72; resource coordinator S.E. Youth Service Ctr., Portland Action Coms. Together, 1975-77; sec., asst. Human Rights Office, Nat. Council Chs. Christ, N.Y.C., 1977-78; human rights coordinator Coalition for a New Fgn. and Mil. Policy, Washington, 1978-85; cons. Fgn. Policy Edn. Fund, Washington, 1986—; nat. adv. bd. U.S. Student Assn. Peace Program, Washington, 1984—, West-Central Am. Network, Stanford, Calif., 1985—, Nat. Network in Solidarity with Guatemalan People, Washington, 1985—, Caribbean Basin Info. Project, 1983-85. Co-editor: Central America 1985: Basic Information and Legislative History on U.S.-Central American Relations, 1985. Contbr. articles to various jours., mags. Co-chmn. Human Rights Working Group, Washington, 1978-81, chmn., 1982-85; chmn. Central Am. Lobby Group, 1983-85; mem. Commn. on U.S.-Central Am. Relations, 1983—. Home: Apt 101 1831 Summit Pl NW Washington DC 20009

BUIE, ELISSA PAULINE, financial planning officer; b. Anderson, S.C., Sept. 16, 1960; d. Richard Emerson and Eileen Elizabeth (Stanley) Buie; m. Wayne Ludwig Grove, July 20, 1985. B.S. in Commerce, U. Va., 1982, also postgrad. Lic. securities dealer Va. Due diligence officer Heritage Fin. Group Inc., Falls Church, Va., 1982—; v.p., dir. Heritage Fin. Advisors. Author case study in textbook, 1986. Mem. Internat. Assn. Fin. Planners. Republican. Office: Heritage Fin Group Inc 5113 Leesburg Pike 511 Falls Church VA 22041

BUKAR, MARGARET WITTY, former clinical laboratory administrator; b. Evanston, Ill., June 21, 1950; d. LeRoy and Catherine Ann (Conrad) Witty; m. Gregory Bryce Bukar, June 5, 1971; children—Michael Bryce, Caroline Nicole. B.S., DePaul U., 1972, M.B.A., 1981. Staff med. technologist The Evanston Hosp., Ill., 1972-75, lab. supr., 1975-77, lab. mgr., 1977-84, dir. lab. adminstrn., 1984-85. Den leader Cub Scouts, Boy Scouts Am., Wilmette, 1985-86; active PTA of St. Francis Xavier Sch., 1985-86; mem. Wilmette Hist. Soc. Recipient Emily Withrow Stebbins award Evanston Hosp., 1985. Mem. Am. Mgmt. Assn., Nat. Assn. Female Execs., Clin. Lab. Mgt. Assn., Am. Soc. Clin. Pathologists. Avocation: knitting.

BULBIN, JANE BRANDT, lawyer; b. Washington, Sept. 27, 1952; d. Frederick B. and Annette R. (Shapiro) Brandt; m. Samuel Spigel Bulbin, Mar. 10, 1982; children—David Henry, Max Spigel, Jessica Rose. B.A. cum laude Smith Coll., 1974; J.D., U. Md.-Balt., 1977. Bar: Va. 1982. Assoc. Gerald S. Klein Law Firm, Balt., 1979-81; legal counsel U. Md., College Park, 1979-81; gen. counsel Va. Poly. Inst. and State U., Blacksburg, 1981—; spl. asst atty. gen. Commonwealth Va., 1982—. Bd. commrs. Econ. Devel. Commn. City Roanoke, Va., 1982—. Clubs: University (Blacksburg); Jefferson (Roanoke, Va.). Home: 3071 Poplar Ln SW Roanoke VA 24010 Office: Va Poly Inst and State U Office Gen Counsel 218 Burruss Hall Blacksburg VA 24061

BULETZA, CAROL ANN, educator; b. White Plains, N.Y., Dec. 10, 1942; d. Robert Henry and Ann Catherine (Wighton) Pansky; m. George Francis Buletza, Aug. 14, 1966 (div. Dec. 1985). B.A., Wintthop Coll., 1964; M.S., Clemson U., 1966. Tchr. sci. D.W. Daniel High Sch., Clemson, S.C., 1966-67, Vallejo Sr. High Sch., Calif., 1967-68, Amador High Sch., Pleasanton, Calif., 1968—; computer operator IBM, Morgan Hill, Calif., 1982. Sec., Inkstone Arts, Newark, Calif., 1979-85, mentor, tchr., 1985-86. Mem. NEA, Amador Valley Secondary Educators Assn., Nat. Sci. Tchrs. Assn., Am. Chem. Soc. Div. Chem. Edn., Calif. Tchrs. Assn. Avocations: traditional Chinese brush painting; Japanese language; Asian cuisine and culture. Home: 176 Sierra Dr #4 Walnut Creek CA 94596 Office: Amador Valley High Sch 1155 Santa Rita Rd Pleasanton CA 94566

BULL, NANCY ANN, publishing executive; b. Muskegon, Mich., Nov. 9; d. Kenneth Earnest and Pauline Fern (Morrison) B. Ed. Kalamazoo Coll. UCLA, Detroit Inst. Tech. Customer mgr. Styker Corp., Kalamazoo; mktg. mgr. Circon Corp., Santa Barbara, Calif.; prodn. mgr. Hall Surg. Systems, Santa Barbara; now pres. Vet. Practice Pub. Co., Santa Barbara; mem. feline adv. bur. Cornell U., Ithaca, N.Y. Mem. comml. revitalization task force East Beach Homeowners Assn. Mem. Am. Vet. Exhibitors Assn. (past pres.), Mission Canyon Homeowners Assn., Am. Animal Hosp. Assn. (assoc.), various other local, state and nat. profl. and civic orgns. Clubs: University, Coral Casino Beach (Santa Barbara). Home: PO Box 5101 Santa Barbara CA 93108 Office: PO Box 4457 7 Ashley Ave S Santa Barbara CA 93103

BULL, TARA MAVOURNEEN, sales executive; b. Balt., Sept. 15, 1957; d. Michael H.P. and Lorraine K.A. (Shea) Finn; m. Michael Owen Bull, Mar. 1, 1980. B.A. in German, Denison U., 1979, B.A. in Soviet Area Studies, 1979. Meeting planner Assoc. Builders and Contractors, Balt., 1979-81; sales mgr. Columbia Inn, Md., 1981-85; nat. sales mgr. Melbourne Hilton at Rialto Pl., Fla., 1985—. Choreographer: Creme de Keesing, 1979. Mem. Am. Bus. Assn., Hotel Sales Mktg. Assn., Central Fla. Soc. Assn. Execs., Nat. Assn. for Female Execs., Delta Phi Alpha. Republican. Episcopalian. Avocations: stereo; current music; piano. Home: 1616 Airport Blvd Melbourne FL 32901 Office: Melbourne Hilton at Rialto Pl 200 Rialto Pl Melbourne FL 32901

BULLARD, HELEN (MRS. JOSEPH MARSHALL KRECHNIAK), sculptor; b. Elgin, Ill., Aug. 15, 1902; d. Charles Wickliffe and Minnie (Cook) Bullard; student U. Chgo., 1921-29; m. Lloyd Ernst Rohrke, June 11, 1924 (div. Feb. 1931); children—Ann Louise (Mrs. Ross DeWitt Netherton), Barbara Jane (Mrs. Valtyr Emil Gudmundson); m. 2d, Joseph Marshall Krechniak, Jan. 30, 1932 (dec. Feb. 1964); 1 dau., Mariana (Mrs. Wilfred Martin). With research dept. L.V. Estes, Inc., Chgo., 1920-22; operator Square D Co., Detroit, 1922-24; simple research Commerce and Adminstrn. Library, U. Chgo., 1924-25; dir. Crossville (Tenn.) Play Center, 1949-50; creator hand-carved dolls, 1949—, wood sculpture, 1959—; exhibited with Nat. Inst. Am. Doll Artists Exhbns., Los Angeles, 1963, Cin., 1964, Washington, 1965, Chgo., 1966, Boston, 1967, New Orleans, 1969, Detroit, 1970, Los Angeles, 1971, Omaha, 1972, Louisville, 1973, Miami, Fla., 1974, Milw., 1975, Watts Bar Dam, Tenn., 1976, Chgo., 1977, N.Y.C., 1979, also craftsmen's fairs, 1954-65, The Club, Birmingham, Ala., 1963, Oak Ridge Art Center, 1965, Children's Mus., Nashville, 1967, McClung Mus., Knoxville, 1969; one man show Tenn. State Mus., 1972. Campaign chmn. Cumberland County unit Am. Cancer Soc., 1947-52. Mem. So. Highland Handicraft Guild (dir. 1957-59), Nat. Inst. Am. Doll Artists (founder, pres. 1963-67, 69-71, chmn. bd. 1977—), United Fedn. Doll Clubs (2d v.p. 1977-79), Am. Craftsmen's Council, Tenn. Folklore Soc., Mensa. Democrat. Unitarian. Author: (with husband) Cumberland County's First Hundred Years, 1956; The American Doll Artist, 1965, Vol. II, 1974; A Bullard Family, 1966; Dorothy Heizer, the Artist and Her Dolls, 1972; Crafts and Craftsmen of the Tennessee Mountains, 1976; 1976; (monograph) My People in Wood, 1984; Faith Wick: Dollmaker Extraordinaire, 1986; Cumberland County, 1956-86, Vol. II, 1986.

BULLARD, MELISSA MERIAM, history educator; b. Berkeley, Calif., Mar. 12, 1946; m. 1969. A.B., Duke U., 1967; M.A., Cornell U., 1969, Ph.D. in History, 1977. Asst. prof. history U. N.C., Chapel Hill, 1977-81, assoc. prof., 1981—. Mem. Renaissance Soc. Am., Soc. Italian Hist. Studies (award 1977), Am. Hist. Assn. Author: Filippo Strozzi and the Medici: Favor and Finance in Sixteenth-century Florence and Rome, 1980. Contbr. articles to profl. jours. Address: Dept History U NC Chapel Hill NC 27514

BULLARD, SHARON WELCH, librarian; b. San Diego, Nov. 4, 1943; d. Dale L. and Myrtle (Sampson) Welch; m. Donald H. Bullard, Aug. 1, 1969. B.S.Ed., U. Central Ark., 1965; M.A., U. Denver, 1967. Media specialist Adams County Sch. Dist. 12, Denver, 1967-69; tchr., librarian Humphrey pub. schs., Ark., 1965-66, librarian, 1969-70; catalog librarian Ark. State U., Jonesboro, 1970-75; head documents cataloging Wash. State U., Pullman, 1979-83; head serials cataloging U. Calif.-Santa Barbara, 1984—. Canvasser, Citizens for Goleta Valley, 1985—. Mem. ALA, Nat. Assn. Female Execs., So. Calif. Tech. Processer Group. Avocations: Aikido; windsurfing; walking; reading.

BULLEN, ADELAIDE KENDALL (MRS. KENNETH SUTHERLAND BULLEN), anthropologist; b. Worcester, Mass., Jan. 12, 1908; d. Oliver Sawyer and Grace (Marble) Kendall; A.B. cum laude, Radcliffe Coll., 1943; postgrad. Harvard U., 1943-48, 50; m. Ripley Pierce Bullen, July 25, 1929 (dec. Dec. 1976); children—Dana Ripley II, Pierce Kendall; m. 2d, Kenneth Sutherland Bullen, Mar. 22, 1980. Research anthropologist Health Center, Radcliffe Coll., 1943-44, Fatigue Lab., Harvard U. Grad. Sch. Bus. Adminstrn., 1944-46; civilian cons. in anthropology U.S. War Dept., 1946; anthropologist Peabody Mus., Harvard U., 1946-48, Fla. State Mus., 1949—. Fellow Am. Anthrop. Assn., AAAS, Royal Anthrop. Inst. London, Soc. Applied Anthropology; mem. Am. Assn. Phys. Anthropologists, Am. Psychosomatic Soc., N.Y. Acad. Scis., Authors League Am., Authors Guild, Soc. Research in Child Devel. Clubs: Gainesville Golf and Country. University Women's, Gainesville Woman's. Author: New Answers to the Fatigue Problem, 1956, paperback edit., 1980; also articles in field; contbg. editor Anthropology, Handbook of Latin American Studies, 1969-71. Home: 2720 SW 8th Dr Gainesville FL 32601 Office: Fla State Museum U Fla Gainesville FL 32611

BULLOCK, BARBARA LEE, nursing educator; b. Los Angeles, Aug. 2, 1941; d. Harry Benjamin and Lois Maxine (Farr) Radford; m. Talmadge Glen Bullock, Apr. 13, 1968; children—Sheila Anne, Brian Glen, Douglas Allen. B.S.N., U. Colo., 1963; M.S.N., U. Tex.-San Antonio, 1977. Staff nurse Framingham Union (Mass.), 1963-65; asst. supr., instr. Meth. Hosp., Houston, 1965-68; supr. relief Good Shepherd Hosp., Longview, Tex., 1975; instr. Kilgore Coll. (Tex.), 1975-76; asst. prof. Samford U., Birmingham, Ala., 1977-85, asst. prof. U. Ala.-Birmingham, 1985—. Singer, Birmingham Concert Chorale, 1976—; mem. PTA, Vestavia Hills, Ala., 1983, Birmingham Ballet, 1983—. Mem. Am. Nurses' Assn., Sigma Theta Tau, Alpha Omicron Pi. Republican. Methodist. Author: Cardiovascular Nursing, 1971; researcher Comparative Study of Registered Nurses, 1980; editor: Pathophysiology, 1984.

BULLOUGH, NANCY TYDINGS, graphics and printing supervisor; b. Washington, Sept. 30, 1950; d. Richard Emmet and Marie Adele (Roversi) Tydings; m. William Reed Bullough, Dec. 19, 1970; children—Amanda Marie, James William, Thomas Reed. B.A., U. Md., 1972. Tech. illustrator Vitro Labs., Silver Spring, Md., 1972-74; graphics technician City of Rockville Govt., Md., 1974-76, graphics and printing supr., 1976—; cons., designer, artist Pub. Gaming Research Corp., Rockville, 1975-85. Recipient Outstanding Performance award Indsl. Graphics Internat., Washington, 1978. Mem. Postal Customers Council, In-Plant Printing Mgmt. Assn., Nat. Assn. Female Execs., Alpha Phi Internat. Frat. Alumnae (pres. chpt. 1975-76). Avocations: reading; family.

BULLWINKEL, MARY ANN, radio news director; b. Santa Monica, Calif., June 21, 1957; d. Robert Edward and Margaret Flonora (Budnick) Dickerson; m. James Conrad Bullwinkel, Sept. 2, 1978. B.A. in Journalism, Humboldt State U., 1979. Disc jockey Sta. KFMI, Eureka, Calif., 1975-76; news reporter Sta. KXGO, Arcata, Calif., 1977-79; disc jockey, news reporter Sta. KEKA, Eureka, 1979-80, news dir., 1980—. Vol. Easter Seals, Eureka, 1979-83, March of Dimes, Eureka, 1982. Mem. Humboldt Press Club (sec. treas. 1982-85, pres. 1985—), Soc. Profl. Journalists. Democrat. Roman Catholic. Avocations: running, photography; dogs. Home: 2110 Haeger Ave Arcata CA 95521 Office: KEKA Radio 540 E St Eureka CA 95501

BULMAHN, LYNN, journalist, free-lance writer; b. Waco, Tex., Feb. 18, 1955; d. Franklin Harrold and Louise (Stolte) B. B.A., S.W. Tex. State U., 1977. Gen. assignment reporter Waco Tribune Herald, 1977—, city desk rewrite person, 1977-78, editor/reporter religion page, 1978-81, human services reporter, 1978-83, med. reporter, 1978—, Help-Line columnist, 1981—; free-lance writer, 1975—. Voter registration chmn. Waco area LWV, 1977-80; vol. Family Abuse Ctr., Waco, 1982—. Recipient Anson Jones citation of Merit, Tex. Med. Assn., 1978; Outstanding Contbn. award Nat. Found. March of Dimes, 1980; Pub. Health award for media excellence Tex. Pub. Health Assn., 1980, 85; First Place award Readers Digest Mag. Workshop Tex. Competition, 1981; award for feature writing North and East Tex. Press Assn., 1983; Media Appreciation award McLennan County Med. Assn., 1985. Mem. Central Tex. Journalists, Waco Jaycees (Outstanding New Mem. of Quarter 1985), Sigma Delta Chi. Democrat. Methodist. Office: Waco Tribune-Herald 900 Franklin Ave Waco TX 76702

BULOW, KATHERINE, government official; b. Kansas City, Mo., 1943; 1 child, Dick. Grad. Acad. Notre Dame. Various positions to spl. asst. Fed. Res. Bank Examiner; with Office of Congl. Affairs, White House, 1969-73; adminstr. Petrochem. Energy Group, 1973-75; dir. bldg. mgmt. div. Republican Nat. Com., 1977-80; spl. asst. to asst. sec. for adminstrn. Dept. Commerce, Washington, 1981-83, dept. asst. sec. for adminstrn., 1983-84, asst. sec., 1984—. Office: Dept Commerce Adminstrn 14th between E and Constitution Ave NW Washington DC 20230

BULTMAN, ANNE TULLER, optometric technician; b. Columbia, S.C., Dec. 26, 1945; d. William Henry and Anne Cordelle (Ehrlich) T.; m. James Linwood Gibbs, Jr. (dec. June 1972); 1 child, James Linwood III; m. Neill O'Donnell Bultman, June 16, 1973. Student U. S.C., 1965-67. Registered optometric technician. Asst., technician Contact Lens Clinic of S.C., Columbia, 1967—; cons. Liberty Optical, Newark, 1983—; speaker pvt. labs. and assn. meetings, nationwide. Contbr. articles to numerous optical jours. Mem. S.C. Optometric Asst. Assn. (v.p. 1969, pres. 1970), Am. Optometric Assn. (paraoptometric sect.; named Nat. Paraoptometric of Yr. 1983). Republican. Episcopalian. Club: Charleston Yacht (S.C.). Avocations: sailing, backpacking, cooking. Office: Contact Lens Clinic of SC 3519 Medical Dr Columbia SC 29205

BULVANOSKI, MARY MARGARET, educational administrator; b. Long Branch, N.J., Dec. 9, 1954; d. Edmund Henry and Margaret Mary (Harbison) Holahan; m. Stephen Andrew Bulvanoski, Jan. 28, 1984; 1 child, Patrick Stephen. B.A. in English, Rosemont Coll., 1976; M.A.Teaching in English, Monmouth Coll., 1981. Cert. tchr., N.J. Tchr., Our Lady Star of Sea Grammar Sch., Long Branch, N.J., 1976-77; English tchr. Red Bank Regional High Sch., N.J., summers 1979, 80, Red Bank Cath. High Sch., 1977-82; adj. instr. English, Ocean County Community Coll., Toms River, N.J., 1982-83; adj. instr. English, Georgian Ct. Coll., Lakewood, N.J., 1983—, dir. alumni affairs, 1982—, editor, writer Alumni Rev., 1982—. Mem. Am. Fedn. Cath. Alumnae, Rosemont Coll. Alumnae Assn. Roman Catholic. Avocations: swimming; jogging; needlework; traveling. Home: 932 Ocean Ave Sea Bright NJ 07760 Office: Georgian Court Coll Lakewood NJ 08701

BULWIK, HELEN CHANA, apparel and cosmetic manufacturing company executive; b. Swabach, W.Ger., Apr. 2, 1949; came to U.S., 1950; d. Cedalja and Rosalie (Schotka) B. B.S., U. Calif.-Berkeley, 1971, M.B.A., 1972. Buyer, Macy's of Calif., San Francisco, 1972-78; div. merchandise mgr. Bullock's Dept. Store, Palo Alto, Calif., 1978-80, gen. mgr., 1980-82; exec. v.p., gen. mgr. Sanca Internat. Inc., San Francisco, 1982—, also dir.; dir. Sanca Internat. Inc., San Francisco. Author: Affirmative Action for Women in Business: Myth and Reality, 1971. Bd. dirs. Stanford Shopping Ctr., Palo Alto, Calif., 1980. Mem. U. Calif. Bus. Alumni Assn., Am. Mktg. Assn. Democrat. Jewish. Office: Sanca Internat Inc 360 Post St Suite 701 San Francisco CA 94108

BUMGARNER, ELIZABETH ALICE, audio visual company executive, consultant; b. Aurora, Ill., Dec. 9, 1945; d. John William and Shirley Mae (Housholder) B. B.S., No. Ill. U., 1967. Cert. technologies specialist. Tchr. Lena/Winslow High Sch., Lena, Ill., 1967-69, Argo Community High Sch., Summit, Ill., 1969-70; curriculum writer Waubonsee Community Coll., Sugar Grove, Ill., 1970-71; test specialist Houghton Mifflin Co., Geneva, Ill., 1971-73; editor, writer Laidlaw Brothers, Inc., River Forest, Ill., 1973-74; pres., chmn. bd. GMA Audio/Visual, Inc., St. Charles, Ill., 1975—; speaker, cons. various local chambers and clubs, St. Charles, Batavia, Geneva, Ill., 1975—. Phone vol. Am. Cancer Soc. Radio-thon, Chgo., 1976-77; campaign worker Republican Party, Lena, 1968; time vol. United Way, Aurora. Mem. Internat. Communications Industries Assn. (cert. techs. specialist), Phi Alpha Theta. Republican. Methodist. Avocations: reading, cooking, entertaining, knitting. Office: GMA Audio/Visual Inc 30 N Park Lombard IL 60148

BUMP, ELAINE BONNEVAL, public record reporting services executive; b. New Orleans, June 4, 1932; d. Elmo James and Catherine Antoinette (Calamia) Bonneval; m. Wilbur Neil Bump, Nov. 24, 1951; children—William Earl, Jeffrey Neil, Steven Bonneval. Student U. Iowa, 1957. Pres. Iowa Search, Inc., Des Moines, 1966—, Computer Info. Services, Inc., Des Moines, 1981—,

Search Network, Ltd., Des Moines, 1984—. Crew leader U.S. Census Bur., Des Moines, 1960; del. Republican State Conv., Iowa, 1965. Mem. Pub. Record Research Assn. (nat. treas. 1980—), C. of C. Republican. Roman Catholic. Clubs: P.E.O. (pres. 1968), Atty.'s Wives (v.p. 1960). Lodge: Daus. of Nile (pres. 1977-78). Avocations: artist; pilot; antique doll collecting. Home: Rural Route 2 Winterset IA 50273 Office: #2 Corporate Pl 1501 42d St West Des Moines IA 50265

BUNCH, ARLINE HAMMOND (MRS. ALFRED B. BUNCH), educator; b. Lowry City, Mo., Jan. 30, 1907; d. Hardin R. and Minnie (Slavens) Hammond; B.S., Springfield State Tchrs. Coll., 1928; m. Alfred B. Bunch, June 28, 1933 (dec.); children—Bryan H., Robert Dale, Barbara Bunch Fields (dec.). Tchr., St. Clair County (Mo.) Rural Schs., 1926-28, Springfield Draughon's Bus. Coll., 1928-30; mgr. Sarachon Hooley Secretarial Sch., St. Louis, 1930-35; tchr. advanced secretarial dept. Miss Hickey's Sch. for Secs., St. Louis, 1935-40; owner, mgr. Crescent Hall Secretarial Sch., Peoria, Ill., 1940-47; owner, corp. sec., dir. Midstate Coll., Peoria, 1966-83, chmn. bd. dirs., 1983—; bd. advs. Internat. Speedwriting Co., N.Y.C.; mem. adv. bd. Ill. State Pvt. Bus. and Vocat. Schs., 1968—; accrediting commr. Assn. Ind. Colls. and Schs., 1968-70, recipient disting. service award for 50 yrs. service, 1979. Trustee Barbara Fields Meml. Scholarship Fund, 1968—. Recipient Charlotte Danstrom award, 1982. Mem. Jubilee Bus. and Profl. Women's Assn. (pres. 1968-69, 82-83, Outstanding Woman cert. 1984-85), Nat. Assn. Women Bus. Owners (charter mem. Peoria chpt., Women of Achievement award for entrepreneur, 1982, cert. appreciation for services to orgn., 1985). Home: Byerly Hills East Peoria IL 61611 Office: 244 SW Jefferson St Peoria IL 61602

BUNCH, ZOE VESTAL, corrugated paperboard manufacturing company executive; b. Whitewright, Tex., May 28, 1931; d. Rolla Calhoun and Lora Adelaide (Robinson) Vestal; student Baylor U., 1948-49, Houston Community Coll., 1974, Houston Bus. Coll., 1949, Lollie Lowe Career Coll., 1974, Harvard U., 1975; children—Morgan Rainey III, Zoann Marie. Sec., Nifty Tablet Mfg. Co., 1948; sec. to gen. mgr. Gen. Motors Acceptance Corp., Houston, 1950-52; change and reinstatement clk. Prudential Life Ins. Co., 1952-55; clk./tchr. aide William P. Hobby Elem. Sch., Houston, 1967-72; exec. sec. to pres. Krafcor Corp., Houston, 1973-74, mgr. Houston office, 1974, dist. sales rep., 1974-80, mgr. adminstrv. services, 1980-82, v.p., dir., 1982—; pres., dir. Kraftex Enterprises, Inc., 1984—. Mem. Nat. Secs. Assn. (dir.), Houston Personnel Assn., Purchasing Mgmt. Assn. Houston, Nat. Assn. Fleet Adminstrs., Am. Soc. Profl. and Exec. Women, Women's Network, DAR, UDC, Children of Am. Revolution, Dau. Republic of Tex. Republican. Baptist. Clubs: Chi Omega Mother's, Prayer Key Family, Internat. 700, Exec. Bus. Women's Forum. Home: 5857 Valley Forge Houston TX 77057 Office: 2900 Wesleyan Suite 680 Houston TX 77027

BUNCIS, ERICA JEAN, city official; b. Boston, Feb. 12, 1947; d. George Joseph and Evelyn Marie (Sweeney) Peterson; m. Andrew Buncis, Aug. 17, 1968; 1 child, Mara Kristin. B.A. in Edn., U. Wis.-Madison, 1968; M.A. in Pub. Adminstrn. Gov.'s State U., 1976. Tchr. River Valley High Sch., Spring Green, Wis., 1968-69; publs. dir. BOCA Internat., Homewood, Ill., 1969-73; adminstrv. intern, grants coordinator Village of Park Forest, Ill., 1976-80, asst. fin dir., 1980-81, fin. dir., 1981—, dep. mgr., treas., 1983—. Author acctg. trade publs. Editor trade publs. on acctg., mcpl. code enforcement. Ill. Gov. fellow, 1974. Mem. Internat. City Mgmt. Assn., Govt. Fin. Officers Assn., Ill. Govt. Fin. Officers Assn. Home: 145 Hay St Park Forest IL 60466 Office: Village of Park Forest 200 Forest Blvd Park Forest IL 60466

BUNDY, BARBARA KORPAN, college president; b. Chgo., May 13, 1943; husband dec.; 1 child. B.A., U. Ill., 1964; Ph.D. in Comparative Lit., Ind. U., 1970. Asst. prof. Slavic and comparative lit., U. Calif., Berkeley, 1966-69; lectr. Russian and German, U. Calif., Santa Cruz, 1969-71; with Dominican Coll. of San Rafael, Calif., 1971—, now prof., pres., 1980—. Contbr. articles to profl. jours. Address: Dominican College of San Rafael San Rafael CA 94901

BUNDY, ORA BRINKLEY, newspaper editor; b. Houston, Dec. 15, 1915; d. Ellis and Essie Sanchez (Robinson) Mitchell; B.A., U. Wis., 1934; m. Robert Fleming Bundy, Dec. 15, 1973; children by previous marriage—Leon Brinkley, Jr. (dec.), Shirley Ayn Barber. Soc. editor Phila. Tribune, 1945-58, women's and soc. editor, 1975-80, social columnist, 1980—; soc. editor N.Y. Amsterdam News, N.Y.C., 1958-61; fashion editor Sepia Mag., Ft. Worth, 1961-64, Elegant & Elegant Teen Mags., Los Angeles, 1965-67; public relations dir. YWCA, Phila., 1967-75; cons. Music Fair Enterprises, Inc., Bala Cynwyd, Pa., 1979-81. Bd. dirs. S.W. Belmont YWCA, 1982—, chmn. bd. dirs., 1983—; 3d v.p., trustee YWCA of Phila.; mem. Phila. Crime Commn. Mem. NAACP, Nat. Assn. Media Women, Women in Communications, Phila. Urban League, Continental Socs. (founder, pres. 1950-54), Lambda Kappa Mu. Democrat. Episcopalian. Clubs: Links (chpt. charter mem.), Thirty Clusters. Office: Philadelphia Tribune 520-26 S 16th St Philadelphia PA 19146

BUNKER, SHERRIE DARLENE, mortgage banker; b. Jacksonville, Fla., Dec. 17, 1950; d. Joseph Frank and Marguerite Faye (Ponce) Dietz. Student, Fla. Jr. Coll., U. North Fla. Credit investigator Credit Bur. Jacksonville (Fla.), 1968-70; loan processor Tucker Bros., Inc., Jacksonville, 1970-72, Collateral Investment, Jacksonville, 1972-73; personnel officer Barnett Mortgage Co., Jacksonville, 1973-82, v.p., 1982—. Bd. dirs. Mental Health Assn. Jacksonville, 1982—; vol. Drug Abuse Program, Jacksonville, 1978-80. Mem. Young Mortgage Bankers Assn. (pres. 1978-79), Mortgage Bankers Assn. Jacksonville (pres. 1983-84, regional gov. of state assn. 1983-84), Am. Soc. Personnel Adminstrs. (dir. 1979-81). Democrat. Roman Catholic. Office: Barnett Mortgage Co 17 W Adams St Jacksonville FL 32202

BUNN, DOROTHY IRONS, court reporter; b. Trinidad, Colo., Apr. 30, 1948; d. Russell and Pauline Anna (Langowski) Irons; m. Peter Lynn Bunn; children—Kristy Lynn, Wade Allen, Russell Ahearn. Student No. Va. Community Coll., 1970-71, U. Va., Fairfax, 1971-72. Registered profl. reporter; cert. shorthand reporter. Pres., chief exec. officer Ahearn Ltd., Springfield, Va., 1970-81, Bunn & Assocs., Glenrock, Wyo., 1981—. Cons., Bixby Hereford Co., Glenrock, 1981—. Del., White House Conf. on Small Bus., Washington, 1986. Mem. Nat. Shorthand Reporters Assn., Wyo. Shorthand Reporters Assn. (chmn. com. 1984—), Colo. Shorthand Reporters Assn., Nat. Assn. Female Execs., Nat. Fedn. Ind. Businesses, Am. Indian Soc. Avocations: art; music. Home: PO Box 1602 Bixby Hereford Co Glenrock WY 82637 Office: Bunn & Assocs 506 W Birch St Glenrock WY 82637

BUNN, RITA MAE, nurse, insurance company consultant; b. Woodlawn, Va., Apr. 20, 1949; d. Arnold Basil and Mary Edith (Rippey) Burcham; m. Dewey Michael Bunn, Dec. 23, 1970; 1 child, Courtney Michelle. R.N., Forsyth Meml. Hosp., Winston Salem, N.C., 1969. Staff nurse Forsyth Meml. Hosp., 1969-70; ICU nurse Cape Fear Valley Hosp., Fayetteville, N.C., 1971-72; emergency room nurse Wesley Long Hosp., Greensboro, N.C., 1972-74; operating room nurse Moses Cone Hosp., Greensboro, 1974-79; ins. med. cons. Travelers Ins. Co., Greensboro, 1979—, also nurse staff cons. to home office, Hartford, Conn., 1979—. Mem. chancel choir Lawndale Bapt. Ch. Republican. Avocations: crafts; needlework; aerobics.

BUNT, LYNNE JOY, insurance broker; b. Corning, N.Y., Sept. 25, 1948; d. William Henry and Cleo Ann (Williams) Prentice. A.A., Foothill Coll., 1969; ins. studies IIAAC, IEA, WAIB; C.P.C.U. Vice-pres., account exec. Jardine Emmett & Chandler, Inc., San Francisco, 1979—; tchr. ins. seminars. Mem. Western Assn. Ins. Brokers, Underwriters Forum, Ins. Forum (program chair). Congregationalist. Republican. Office: 50 Francisco St San Francisco CA 94133

BUNTIN, LINDA ANNE, administrator; b. N.Y.C., Aug. 8, 1953; d. Edward J. and Gladys R. (Bedigian) Bormann; B.S. in Agr. with honors and distinction (Outstanding Sr. Woman Coll. Agr.), U. Del., 1975; M.S., Wash. State U., 1977; Ph.D., Iowa State U., 1983. First woman extension entomologist in U.S., mem. faculty Iowa State U., 1977-82, dept. animal sci., 1983-84; entomologist Ga. Dept. Agr., 1985; dir. Farm and Community Life Ctr., Ft. Valley, Ga., 1985—. Mem. Entomol. Soc. Am., Am. Registry Profl. Entomologists., Entomol. Soc. Can., Sigma Xi, Alpha Zeta, Phi Delta Gamma. Office: Farm and Community Life Ctr Fort Valley GA 31030

BUNTING, JOELLE, psychiatrist, psychoanalyst; b. San Francisco, Feb. 6, 1939; d. John Richard and Adella Virginia (Bristol) Bunting; B.A. with distinction, Stanford U., 1960; M.D., U. Calif., 1964; cert. N.Y. Med. Coll., 1976; m. Leo B. Mazer, Mar. 27, 1977; 1 son, Ross Arthur. Intern, Maimonides Med. Center, Bklyn., 1964-65; resident N.Y. Med. Coll.-Met. Hosp. Center, N.Y.C., 1965-68; pvt. practice medicine specializing in psychiatry and psychoanalysis, Tenafly and Harrington Park, N.J., 1968—; clin. instr. Westchester div., N.Y. Med. Coll., Valhalla, 1979—; assoc. chief dept. psychiatry Englewood (N.J.) Hosp. Fellow Am. Psychiat. Assn. (br. past pres.), N.J. Psychiat. Soc. (pres.), Am. Med. Women's Assn., Soc. Med. Psychoanalysts Am. Acad. Psychoanalysis. Club: Altrusa. Home and office: 92 Higgins Pl Harrington Park NJ 07640

BUNYAN, ELLEN LACKEY SPOTZ, chemist, educator; b. Clarks Mills, Pa., Aug. 14, 1921; d. Scott Richard and Mary Ellen (Beal) Lackey; B.S., U. Pitts., 1942; Ph.D., U. Wis., 1950; m. Arthur Hughborn Bunyan, Dec. 26, 1977; children—Mark Stephen Spotz, Leslie Claire Spotz, Elizabeth Grace O'Rourke. Sr. technologist Eastman Kodak Co., Kingsport, Tenn., 1942-44, summer fellow, Rochester, N.Y., 1976. instr. chemistry U. Wis., Milw., 1946-47; research assoc. dept. chemistry U. Wis., Madison, 1950-52; instr. physics St. Agnes Acad., Houston, 1965; Welch fellow chemistry Rice U., Houston, 1968-69; lectr. Montgomery Coll., Rockville, Md., 1970-72; asst. prof. chem. tech. U. D.C., Washington, 1972-78, assoc. prof., 1978—; guest worker Nat. Bur. Standards, 1976. Nat. Urban League fellow, 1976. Mem. Am. Chem. Soc., NEA, Sigma Xi, Sigma Delta Epsilon. Methodist. Contbr. articles to profl. jours. Office: Coll Phys Sci and Engring Univ of District Columbia 4200 Connecticut Ave NW Washington DC 20008

BURACK, SYLVIA E. KAMERMAN, editor, publisher; b. Hartford, Conn., Dec. 16, 1916; d. Abraham and Augusta (Chermak) Kamerman; m. Abraham S. Burack, Nov. 28, 1940 (dec.); children—Janet, Susan, Ellen. B.A. magna cum laude, Smith Coll., 1938; D.Litt. (hon.), Boston U., 1985. Editor, pub. Plays, The Drama Mag. for Young People, also the Writer Mag., 1978—. Mem. Brookline Sch. Com., 1949-69, Mass. Bd. Higher Edn., 1973-75; trustee Mass. State Coll. System, 1971-75, chmn., 1974-75; trustee U. Mass., 1975-81, Max C. Rosenfeld Fund. Recipient Disting. Service award Brookline Rotary Club, 1973; Sylvia K. Burack Library named in her honor, Brookline High Sch. Mem. Nat. Book Critics Circle, LWV, Friends of Library at Boston U. (dir., pres., 1981-83), Phi Beta Kappa. Editor: Little Plays for Little Players, 1952; Blue Ribbon Plays for Girls, 1955; Blue Ribbon Plays for Graduation, 1957; A Treasury of Christmas Plays, 1958; Children's Plays from Favorite Stories, 1959; Fifty Plays for Junior Actors, 1966; Fifty Plays for Holidays, 1969; Dramtized Folk Tales of the World, 1971; On Stage for Christmas, 1978; Christmas Play Favorites for Young People, 1982; Holiday Plays Rond the Year, 1983; (adult) Writing the Short Short Story, 1942; Book Reviewing, 1978; The Writer's Handbook, 1985; Writing and Selling Fillers, Light Verse and Short Humor, 1982; Writing and Selling the Romance Novel, 1983; Writing Mystery and Crime Fiction, 1985. Home: 72 Penniman Rd Brookline MA 02146

BURAS, BRENDA ALLYNN, public affairs executive; b. New Orleans, May 1, 1954; d. Allen Anthony and Gloria Violet (Short) B. B.A. in Commerce, Loyola U.-New Orleans, 1976, M.B.A., 1984. Stenographer Texaco Inc., New Orleans, 1974-76, engr.'s asst., 1976-78, natural gas contracts analyst, 1978-80, pub. affairs asst., 1980-83, pub. affairs coordinator S.E. region, 1983—; owner Achievements Unltd., motivational counseling; cert. lectr. Silva Method Mind Devel. and Stress Control. Loaned exec. United Way Greater New Orleans, 1978-79, mem. speakers bur., 1979-83. Mem. Pub. Relations Soc. Am., Women in Communications, Inc., Press Club New Orleans. Republican. Clubs: U.S. Figure Skating Assn., Dixieland Figure Skating, Lee Circle YMCA. Office: Texaco Inc 400 Poydras St New Orleans LA 70113

BURBANK, VIRGINIA COLLINS, lawyer; b. Mays Lick, Ky., Feb. 22, 1934; d. William Herman and Mabel Esther (Davis) Roberson; m. William Fitch, Aug. 29, 1975; m. Winter Howe Collins, June 18, 1955 (div. 1973); 1 dau., Wynter Reneaux. J.D., U. Ky., 1954. Bar: Ky. 1954. Acting librarian U. Ky., Lexington, 1954-55; staff atty. Ky. Dept. Revenue, Frankfort, 1955-64; mem. firm Henchey Mulloy & Walz, Louisville, 1973-76; prin. Virginia Collins Burbank PSC, Louisville, 1976-82; ptnr. firm Burbank & Gulick, Louisville, 1982—; dir. Triple Spries Farms, Inc., Simpsonville, Ky.; pres. Louisville Surgery, Inc., 1983—. Chmn. Ky. Women's Agenda Coalition, 1981-83. Recipient Fleur de lis award City of Louisville, 1978. Fellow Am. Assn. Matrimonial Lawyers; mem. ABA, Louisville Bar Assn. (dir. 1978-79), Ky. Bar Assn., Ky. Trial Lawyers Assn., Am. Trial Lawyers Assn., Bus. and Profl. Women Louisville (gen. counsel 1982, 83), LWV (officer Louisville 1960, Outstanding Woman award 1980). Democrat. Presbyterian. Home: 3616 Glenview St Glenview KY 40025 Office: Burbank & Gulick 200 S 7th St 500 Legal Arts Bldg Louisville KY 40202

BURBIDGE, ELEANOR MARGARET PEACHEY, astronomer; b. Davenport, Eng.; came to U.S., 1955; d. Stanley John and Marjorie (Stott) Peachey; B.Sc. with honors, U. London, 1939, Ph.D., 1943; D.Sc. (hon.), Smith Coll., 1963, U. Sussex, 1970, U. Bristol, 1972, U. Leicester, 1972, City U., London, 1974, U. Mich., 1978, U. Mass., 1978, Williams Coll., 1979, SUNY-Stony Brook, 1985. m. Geoffrey Burbidge, Apr. 2, 1946; 1 dau., Sarah. Mem. staff U. London Obs., 1946-51; research fellow Yerkes Obs., Harvard Coll. Obs., 1951-53, vol. research assoc. Cavendish Lab., Cambridge, 1953-55; research fellow Calif. Inst. Tech., Pasadena, 1955-57; Shirley Farr fellow Yerkes Obs., 1957-59, assoc. prof., 1959-62; assoc. research physicist U. Calif.-San Diego, 1962-64, prof. astronomy, 1964—, dir Ctr. for Astrophysics and Space Scis., 1979—, Univ. prof., 1984; dir. Royal Greenwich Obs., Herstmonceux Castle, Hallsham, Sussex, Eng., 1972-73; mem. Internat. Adv. Bd. for the Sci. Mus. of Minn.; mem.-at-large NASA Adv. Council. Trustee La Jolla Inst., San Diego Hall of Sci. Recipient (with husband) Warner prize in Astronomy, 1959; hon. fellow Univ. Coll., London, Girton Coll., Lucy Cavendish Coll., Cambridge Fellow Royal Soc., Nat. Acad. Scis., Am. Acad. Arts and Scis., Royal Astron. Soc., Catherine Wolfe Bruce Medal, Astron. Soc. Pacific, 1982; Nat. Medal Sci., 1985. Mem. Am. Astron. Soc. (v.p. 1972-74, pres. 1976-78, Heineman prize com.) AAAS (fellow 1982, pres. 1982), Am. Philos. Soc., Nat. Acad. Scis., N.Y. Acad. Scis., Astron. Soc. of the Pacific, Royal Astron. Soc., Am. Acad. Arts & Scis. Author: (with G. Burbidge) Quasi-Stellar Objects, 1967. Editor Observatory mag., 1948-52; editorial bd. Astronomy and Astrophysics, 1969-80; cons. editor W.H. Freeman & Co. Address: Ctr Astrophysics and Space Scis U Calif/San Diego La Jolla CA 92093*

BURCH, JEAN CONNELL, nurse; b. Conort, Alta., Can.; came to U.S., 1950; d. David and Rosie (Schaffer) Connell; m. Floyd Allison Boothe, Nov. 18, 1949 (div. Jan. 1968); children—Bonnie, Brian, David, Kimberly; m. Dale Edison Burch, May 14, 1971. Licensed vocat. nurse Highland Gen. Hosp., Pampa, Tex., 1967; R.N., NW Tex. Hosp., Amarillo, 1972; B.S. in Profl. Arts, St. Joseph's Coll., North Wyndham, Maine, 1981. Staff nurse Shamrock Hosp., (Tex.), 1963-68, N. Plains Hosp., Borger, Tex., 1972-74; night shift supr. McLean Hosp. (Tex.), 1968-71; day supr. Worley Hosp., Pampa, 1974-76; plant nurse Amarillo Beef Processing (Tex.), 1977-78, Asarco, Inc., Amarillo, 1978—. Mem. Assn. Occupational Health Nurses (Panhandle chpt.). Republican. Methodist. Home: Route 3 Box 177-B-2 Amarillo TX 79107 Office: Asarco Inc PO Box 30200 Amarillo TX 79120

BURCHAM, ZELDA DEANE, nursing administrator; b. Wilmington, N.C., Jan. 11, 1935; d. John James and Eunice Mae (Corbett) Peterson; m. Billy Brian Burcham, June 15, 1957; children—Daphne Deane, Billy Brian, Mary Catherine. Diploma, James Walker Meml. Hosp. Sch. Nursing, Wilmington, N.C., 1956. Supr. operating room Hardin Meml. Hosp., Kountze, Tex., 1963-69; home health nurse Tex. Home Health, Kirbyville, 1969-70; pub. health nurse Hardin County Health Dept., Kountze, 1970-73; dir. nurses Hardin Meml. Hosp., 1973-76; dir. nursing services Silsbee Doctors Hosp., Tex., 1976—. Service chmn. Am. Cancer Soc., Kountze, 1970-76. Mem. James Walker Meml. Hosp. Sch. Nursing Alumnae Assn., Tex. Hosp. Soc. Nursing Service Adminstrs. Democrat. Presbyterian. Club: Silsbee Country. Avocations: golf; collecting Norman Rockwell plates. Home: PO Box 1404 Silsbee TX 77656 Office: Silsbee Doctors Hosp PO Box 1208 Silsbee TX 77656

BURCHAM MADISON, TERI, advertising agency executive; b. Passiac, N.J., Nov. 20, 1953; d. Benjamin Pawlowski and Charlotte (Brvlczyk) Rydzewski. Student pub. schs. Advt. clk. community newspapers, Glen Cove, N.Y., 1970-72; advt. coordinator Newsday, Garden City, N.Y., 1972-76; account exec. Bernard Hode Advt., N.Y.C., 1976-80; br. mgr. Jon Rob Advt., Los Angeles, N.Y.C., 1980-81 ptnr. Transworld Mktg., Los Angeles, 1981-82; pres. Transworld Advt. Mktg., Inc., Dallas, 1982—. First v.p., membership chmn. Am. Women Owned Businesses Dallas, 1982—. Mem. Dallas C. of C. Office: 12820 Hillcrest Rd Suite 209 Transworld Advt Mktg Inc Dallas TX 75230

BURCIAGA, MARY RUTH JEFFERSON, civic worker; b. Centreville, Miss., Oct. 24, 1945; d. Samuel James and Irene Singleton Jefferson; m. Jesse Burciaga, Dec. 16, 1973; children—Jessmye Malia, Challise Jorene. Student Jackson State U., 1962-64; B.S., Ark. AM&N Coll., 1966; postgrad. Jackson State U., 1978-79, N. Ala. Coll. Commerce, 1969-70. Tng. instr. U.S. Army, Redstone Arsenal, Ala., 1966-67, file clk., 1967-73; asst. ward mgr. Univ. Med. Ctr., Jackson, 1973-74; claims clk. VA Med. Ctr., Jackson, 1974-76; personnel clk. VA Med. and Regional Ctr., Jackson, 1976-79; personnel clk. VA Regional Office Out Patient Clinic, Honolulu, 1979-80; personnel processing clk. VA Med. Ctr., Jackson, 1980—, mem. EEO com., 1981—. Pres., Nat. Council Negro Women, 1977-79, organizer, 1979-80, pres., 1981-84, nat. bd. dirs., 1983—; bd. dirs. Rape Crisis Ctr., 1984—; co-organizer Women for Progress, 1978; chmn. organizing com. Jackson Hinds Operation PUSH, 1981; mem. Lt. Gov.'s Bd. for Day Care, Honolulu, 1980; mem. Gov.'s Task Force on Appointments, 1984. Recipient Mary McLeod Bethune award Nat. Council Negro Women, 1978, Outstanding Woman award, 1979, Spl. Act award VA Med Ctr., Jackson, 1981. Democrat. Baptist. Avocations: sewing; speaking; bridal consulting; traveling. Home: 4691 Nordell Dr Jackson MS 39206 Office: VA Med Ctr 1500 E Woodrow Wilson Dr Jackson MS 39206

BURDE, MARY LOIS (PENNY), labor/mgmt. specialist; b. Newark, May 25; d. Thomas J. and Mae V. (Pennie) Duggan; D.Ed., Rutgers U., 1985; m. Francis R. Burde, July 4; children—Gregory, Christopher, Tracey. Pres., Bergen Community Coll. Supportive Staff Assos., 1969-72; labor lobbyist, cons. N.J. Indsl. Union Council, AFL-CIO, 1978-79; bd. mem. Pvt. Industry Council, Hackensack, N.J., 1979—; v.p. Penclaire Service Corp., Paramus, N.J., 1973—; chmn. pay equity task force N.J. Coalition Labor Union Women, 1979-82; mem. Com. on Pay Equity, Conf. Alt. State and Local Policies, 1981—; mem. panel Women's Affirmative Action Com., N.J. Indsl. Union Council, AFL-CIO, 1979-81; adv. bd. mem. Women's Inst., Bergen Community Coll., 1978—. Mem. Bergen County Commn. Status of Women, 1976—. Mem. NOW, Coalition Labor Union Women, N.J. Coll. and Univ. Coalition for Women's Edn. Office: Seven Chimneys Westwood NJ 07675

BURDEN, JEAN (PRUSSING), poet, editor, author; b. Waukegan, Ill., Sept. 1, 1914; d. Harry Frederick and Miriam (Biddlecom) Prussing; B.A., U. Chgo., 1936; m. David Charles Burden, Aug. 31, 1940 (div. May 1949). Sec., John Hancock Mut. Life Ins. Co., Chgo., 1937-39, Young & Rubicam Advt. Agy., Chgo., 1939-41; editor, copywriter Domestic Industries, Inc., Chgo., 1941-45; office mgr. Obrion Russell & Co., Los Angeles, 1948-56; mem. public relations staff Meals for Millions Found., Los Angeles, 1956-65; editor Stanford Research Inst., South Pasadena, Calif., 1965-66; owner Jean Burden & Assocs., Altadena, Calif., 1966-72; contbg. editor Woman's Day Mag., 1973-82; poetry editor Yankee Mag., 1955—; supr. poetry workshop Pasadena City Coll., 1960-61, 66, U. Calif., Irvine, 1975; lectr. poetry numerous groups, univs. and colls., 1960—. Recipient awards including Silver Anvil award, Public Relations Soc. Am., 1969; MacDowell Colony fellow, 1973, 74, 76. Mem. Poetry Soc. Am., Acad. Am. Poets, Authors Guild. Democrat. Author: Naked as the Glass, 1963; Journey Toward Poetry, 1966; The Dog You Care For, 1968; The Cat You Care For, 1968; The Bird You Care For, 1970; The Fish You Care For, 1971; A Celebration of Cats, 1974; The Classic Cats, 1975; The Woman's Day Book of Hints for Cat Owners, 1980, 2d edit., 1984; Contbr. numerous articles to mags. and jours. Home and Office: 1129 Beverly Way Altadena CA 91001

BURDEN, MARJORIE ANN, county treasurer; b. Keswick, Iowa, Oct. 6, 1932; d. Tunis and Edith Jennie (Jordan) DeBont; divorced; children—Alan C., Linda L. Burden Moxley, Nancy K. Burden Yotler, Christine M. Telephone operator Continental Telephone Co., Mt. Pleasant, Iowa, 1963-65; receptionist, clk. Henry County Health Ctr., Mt. Pleasant, 1966-67; clk. Henry County Treas. Office, Mt. Pleasant, 1971-75, County treas., 1975—. Mem. Henry County Health Ctr. Aux. Mem. Iowa State Assn. County Treas., Iowa State Assn. County Officers, Nat. Assn. County Treas. and Fin. Officers, Fifth Dest. Treas. Assn. (sec. treas. 1984), Bus. and Profl. Women, Nat. Assn. Female Execs. Republican. Baptist. Club: Barettes (treas. 1981). Avocations: fishing; hiking; camping; reading. Home: Rural Route 2 Box 64 Mount Pleasant IA 52641 Office: Henry County Treas PO Box 146 Courthouse Mount Pleasant IA 52641

BURDETTE, JANE ELIZABETH, association executive; b. Huntington, W.Va., Aug. 17, 1955; d. C. Richard and Jewel Kathryn (Wagner) B. A.A.S., Parkersburg Community Coll., W.Va., 1976; B.S., Glenville State Coll., W.Va., 1978; M.A., W.Va. U., 1984. Fund raiser, recruiter Muscular Dystrophy Assn., Charleston, W.Va., 1973, 74, 75; sec., bookkeeper Nationwide Ins. Co., Parkersburg, 1975; v.p. Burdette Funeral Home, Parkersburg, 1976—; intake and referral specialist Wood Sheltered Workshop, Parkersburg, 1984-85; exec. dir. Young Women's Christian Assn., Parkersburg, 1985—. Bd. dirs. Sheltered Workshop, Parkersburg, 1982—, Western Dist. Guidance Ctr., Parkersburg, 1984—; bd. advisors Parkersburg Community Coll., 1980—; mem. Wood County Commn. on Crime, Delinquency and Corrections, Parkersburg; liaison Gov. Commn. on Disabled Persons, Charleston, W.Va. Named Miss Wheelchair W.Va., 1981; Outstanding Young Woman of Yr. for W.Va., 1981; recipient Kenneth Hieges award Muscular Dystrophy Assn., 1982. Mem. Nat. Assn. Female Execs., World Communication Assn., W.Va. Women in Higher Edn., W.Va. Funeral Dirs. Assn. Democrat. Roman Catholic. Avocation: designing. Home: 2500 Brooklyn Dr Parkersburg WV 26101 Office: Young Women's Christian Assn 2501 Dudley Ave Parkersburg WV 26101

BURDICK, CAROLYN JANE, physiologist; b. Westerly, R.I., Jan. 10, 1938; d. Thomas John and Amy (Eaton) B.; B.A., Smith Coll., 1959; Ph.D., Harvard U., 1965. NIH fellow Harvard U., Cambridge, Mass., 1962-64, dept. cell biology Rockefeller U., N.Y.C., 1964-66; lectr. physiology Hunter Coll., N.Y.C., 1966; asso. prof. biology Bklyn. Coll., 1966—; mem. corp. Marine Biol. Lab, Woods Hole, Mass., 1972—. Mem. Am. Soc. Zoologists, Phi Beta Kappa, Sigma Xi. Author: Laboratory Manual for General Physiology, 1978; contbr. numerous articles in field to profl. jours. Office: Dept Biology Brooklyn Coll Brooklyn NY 11210

BURDINE, LINDA SHARON, educator, author; b. Milw., July 23, 1950; d. Carl and Ruby (Dirk) Wiedmann; m. Stephen Michael Burdine, May 16, 1975; children—Scott, Kristine. B.S., Ball State U., 1973; M.S., Ind. U., 1979. Tchr. bus. edn. Washington High Sch., Indpls., 1974-76; tchr. bus. edn. Perry Meridian High Sch., Indpls., 1976—; chairperson textbook adoption State of Ind., 1976. Author: Typing Bulletin Board Projects, 1985; Awards, Rewards Coupons, 1985; Learning General Business, 1985; Learning Shorthand Learning Typing, 1985. Mem. Ind. State Tchrs. Assn., Indpls. Bus. Edn. Assn., Perry Edn. Assn. (mem. negotiation team 1977, bldg. rep. 1985—), Phi Delta Kappa. Avocations: reading; writing; swimming. Office: Perry Meridian High Sch 401 W Meridian Sch Rd Indianapolis IN 46217

BURECH, JOANNE GREENE, occupational therapist, educator; b. Paterson, N.J., Apr. 8, 1946; d. Walter Louis and Rosalie (Shapiro) Greene; m. Dennis L. Burech, June 13, 1976; 1 dau., Melissa Patrice. B.S. in Occupational Therapy, Ohio State U., 1969. Registered occupational therapist. Occupational therapist Ohio State U. Hosps., Columbus, 1969; occupational therapist Children's Hosp., Columbus, 1969-71, dir. occupational therapy and patient activity dept., 1971-76; dir. occupational therapy Wheeling Soc. Crippled Children (W.Va.), 1976-78; occupational therapist No. Panhandle Mental Health Center, Wheeling, 1976-78; dir. hand rehab. program Plastic Surgery, Inc., Wheeling, 1978—; mem. profl. adv. com. Wheeling Soc. Crippled Children; clin. instr. occupational therapy Ohio State U., SUNY-Buffalo; cons. in field. Recipient Community Service award Key Club Internat., 1971. Mem. Am. Occupational Therapy Assn., Ohio Occupational Therapy Assn., W.Va. Occupational Therapy Assn., Am. Soc. Hand Therapists, Assn. Care Children in Hosps. Designer splint to minimize deformity of shoulder joint in burned children, 1969. Club: Jr. League. Home: 4 Fieldcrest Dr Wheeling WV 26003 Office: 1300 Chapline St Wheeling WV 26003

BURFORD, ANNE MCGILL, lawyer; b. Casper, Wyo., Apr. 21, 1942; d. Joseph John and Dorothy Jean (O'Grady) McGill; student Nat. U. Mexico, summers 1955, 56, 58, Regis Coll., Denver, summer 1959; B.A., U. Colo., 1961, LL.B., 1964; m. David Gorsuch, June 4, 1964 (div. 1982); children—Neil, Stephanie, J.J.; m. 2d, Robert Fitzpatrick Burford, Feb. 20, 1983. Bar: Colo. 1964, D.C., 1985. Fulbright scholar, Jaipur, India, 1964-65; asst. trust adminstr. First Nat. Bank of Denver, 1966-67; instr. Metro State Coll.,

1966-67; asst. dist. atty. Jefferson County, 1968-71; dep. dist. atty., Denver, 1971-73; hearing officer Real Estate Commn., State Bds. Cosmetology, Optometric Examiners, Profl. Nursing and Vet. Medicine, 1974-75; corporate counsel Mountain Bell Telephone Co., Denver, 1975-81; mem. Colo. Ho. of Reps., 1977-81, chmn. state affairs com., 1979-80, chmn. legal services com., 1980; del. Nat. Conf. State Legislators; mem. Nat. Conf. Commrs. on Uniform State Law, 1979, 80; loaned exec. mgmt. and efficiency task force Colo. Dept. Regulatory Agys., 1976; adminstr. EPA, Washington, 1981-82; now lectr. Former mem. bd. dirs. YMCA. Mem. Am., Colo., Denver bar assns., Mortar Bd., Phi Alpha Delta, Delta Delta Delta. Republican. Roman Catholic. Home: 5505 Seminary Rd 105N Falls Church VA 22041 Office: 1050 Thomas Jefferson St NW 6th Floor Georgetown Washington DC 20007

BURFORD, MARLEEN CHITTUM, communications executive; b. Pitts., Nov. 2, 1946; d. William and Louise (Karako) Houck; m. Joseph F. Burford, Aug. 21, 1981; 1 child by previous marriage; Matthew David. B.S.J., W. Va. U., 1968. Group asst. Ketchum MacLeod & Grove, Pitts., 1968-70; exec. sec. Chittum Auto, Morgantown, W.Va., 1970-75; account exec. WAJR-WVAQ, Morgantown, 1975; with Liken, Pitts., 1976; account asst. Burson-Marsteller, Pitts., 1976-77; dir. communications Snowshoe Co., W.Va., 1977-85; dir. pub. relations and alumni relations St. Pius X High Sch., 1985—. Editor The Spotter mag., 1982-85. Mem. Vo-Tech. Adv. Bd., 1980—; mem. Rebuild W.Va. Com., 1984. Mem. Pub. Relations Soc. Am., Internat. Assn. Bus. Communications, W.Va. Press Assn. (sec.), Eastern Ski Writers Assn., Dog Writers Assn. Republican. Roman Catholic. Clubs: Am. Kennel, Dalmatian of Am. Avocations: skiing; bridge; showing dogs. Home: PO Box 930157 Norcross GA 30093 Office: 2674 Johnson Rd NE Atlanta GA 30345

BURFORD, MARY ANNE, medical technologist; b. Paris, Ark., Aug. 24, 1939; d. Anthony John and Julia Elizabeth (Hoffmann) Elsken; B.S. in Biology, Benedictine Coll., 1961; grad. in med. tech. St. Mary's Sch. Med. Tech., 1962; m. Joseph Paul Burford, May 11, 1968 (div. 1983); children—Sarah Elizabeth, Shawn Anthony, Joseph Paul, Daniel Aaron. Evening supr. St. Vincent's Infirmary, Little Rock, 1962-65; med. technologist Holt-Krock Clinic, Ft. Smith, Ark., 1966-68, Ball Meml. Hosp., Muncie, Ind., 1971-72, Pathologist Assoc., Muncie, 1972-73; chief technologist Ob-Gyn Inc., Muncie, 1975—; instr. microbiology St. Vincent's Infirmary, 1962-65, Sparks Med. Ctr., Ft. Smith, 1966-68. Chmn. liturgical life, St. Mary's Catholic Ch.; treas. Met. Football League, 1983-84; Foster parent Del. Dept. Pub. Welfare, 1975-81. Mem. Am. Soc. Clin. Pathologists (affiliate mem., registered med. technologist), Am. Assn. Clin. Chemists, Am. Soc. for Microbiology. Club: Altrusa (chmn. community services com. 1984-85, materials and records com. 1985-86, constn. and bylaws com. 1985-86, rec. sec. 1986-87, budget chmn. 1986-87). Home: 1509 W Buckingham Dr Muncie IN 47302 Office: 2501 W Jackson St Muncie IN 47302

BURG, RUTH (THELMA) COOPER, administrative judge; b. Phila., Mar. 29, 1926; d. Philip and Rose Anna (Applebaum) Cooper; m. Max Gunter Breslauer, Dec. 21, 1956 (dec. Aug. 1964); m. Maurice Benjamin Burg, Dec. 30, 1967; children—Elizabeth, Lawrence, Joan, Robert. B.S. in Chemistry, George Washington U., 1945, postgrad. Sch. Medicine, 1945-46, J.D. with distinction, 1950. Bar: D.C. 1950, Md. 1953. Report analyst Naval Research Lab., Washington, 1946-48; clk. Tax Ct. of U.S., Washington, 1950-53; sole practice law, Washington, 1953-65; asst. to chmn. Emergy Commn. Bd. Contract Appeals, Bethesda, Md., 1965-72; adminstrv. judge Armed Service Bd. of Contract Appeals, Alexandria, Va., 1972—; lectr. in field. Taxation editor: George Washington Law Rev. Contbr. articles to profl. jours. Vice chmn. Harriet B. Burg Found., Washington, 1983—. Recipient John Bell Larner medal, 1950. Fellow Am. Bar Found.; mem. ABA (chairperson pub. contract law sec. 1984-85), Nat. Assn. Women Judges, Exec. Women in Govt., Order of Coif, Phi Sigma Sigma (internat. pres. 1954-56). Lodge: B'nai B'rith Women (founding pres. Kroloff chpt. 1960; pres. elect Md. 1968). Avocations: wilderness camping; needlepoint, weaving. Home: 3106 Que St NW Washington DC 20007 Office: Armed Service Bd Contract Appeals 200 Stovall St Alexandria VA 22332

BURGDORFF, JEAN T., real estate executive; m. Douglas Burgdorff (dec. 1968); children—Charles, Peter. B.A. in Edn., Columbia U.; postgrad. New Eng. Conservatory Music. Mem. piano faculty Douglass Coll., Rutgers U.; sales rep. Burgdorff, Realtors, 1958-68, pres., 1968; dir. Country Living Assocs. Recipient Summit Community Service award, 1964; Mem. Intercommunity Relocation (nat. pres.), N.J. chpt. Cert. Resdl. Brokers (pres.), N.J. Assn. Realtors (state dir.). Office: Burgdorff Realtors 480 Morris Ave Summit NJ 07901

BURGESS, ANNIE PEARL, cytotechnologist; b. Brookhaven, Miss., Oct. 10, 1945; d. Jerome and Bernice (Calcote) Ratliff; student Malcolm X Jr. Coll., 1972-73, Roosevelt U., 1973-75, U. Chgo. Med. Sch., 1975; certificate Mt. Sinai Sch. Cytotechnology, 1975; A.A., Kennedy-King Jr. Coll., 1975; student U. Miss., 1981-85, Thomas Edison State Coll., 1984—; children—Terree Terrinda, Kimetta Arlinda, Leander Marcellus. Catalog writer Sears Roebuck & Co., Chgo., 1972; service rep. Ill. Bell Telephone Co., Chgo., 1973-74; cytotechnologist Mason-Barron Labs., Chgo., 1975-76, North Miss. Med. Center, Tupelo, 1976-85, King Faisal Specialist Hosp. and Research Ctr., Riyadh, Saudi Arabia, 1985—. Mem. Am. Soc. Clin. Pathologists, Internat. Acad. Cytology, Am. Soc. Cytology, Am. Soc. Cytotechnology, Miss. Soc. Cytopathology, Miss. Soc. Med. Technology, So. Assn. Cytotechnologists, Ill. Soc. Cytology. Home: Route 2 Box 35 Belden MS 38826 Office: King Faisal Specialist and Research Ctr Dept Pathology Box 3354 Riyadh 11211 Saudi Arabia

BURGESS, CAROLYN JANE, counselor, musician; b. Columbus, Ohio, Sept. 26, 1933; d. John Anderson and Mabel (McCullough) Twitty; m. Braxton V. Burgess, Dec. 17, 1966; 1 son, John. Student Ohio State U., 1951-52; B.A. cum laude, Wilberforce, U., 1972; postgrad. Wayne State U., 1971-72. Pvt. music tchr., various cities, Ohio, W.Va. and Mich., 1948-80; counselor Greater Flint Opportunities Industrialization Ctr. (Mich.), 1982—; organist, choir dir., accompanist various chs. and musical groups; minister music Allen Temple African Methodist Episcopal Ch., Detroit, 1968-73, Freeman Ave United Ch. Christ, Cin., 1973-75, Allen Chapel A.M.E. Ch., Kalamazoo, 1975-80. Active Women's Missionary Soc. A.M.E. Ch., 1960—, pres. Mich. conf. br., 1980—, organizer, ex-officio mem. bd. Mich. conf. br. Quality of Life Ctr., Detroit, 1980—; mem. new dimensions workshop com. Ch. Women United, Flint, 1982—; mem. dialysis unit fund raising com. Hurley Med. Ctr., Flint, 1984—; mem. exec. bd. Kalamazoo br. NAACP, 1978-80, del. nat. conv., 1980; former mem. laity leadership dept., Southwestern Ohio assn. United Ch. Christ, task force on instl. racism Ohio conf. United Ch. Christ; bd. dirs. Flint YWCA, 1981—. Mem. Nat. Council Negro Women, World Fedn. Meth. Women, Nat. Assn. Negro Musicians, Am. Guild Organists, Ch. Women United, Alpha Kappa Mu, Sigma Omega, Delta Sigma Theta. Democrat. Office: Greater Flint Opportunities Industrialization Ctr 708 Root St Flint MI 48503

BURGESS, EUNICE LESTER, counselor; b. Madison, Fla., Dec. 17, 1935; d. Thomas and Rebecca (Royal) Lester; m. Miller Burgess, Jr., Aug. 18, 1958; children—Brenda, Joyce, Wanda Renee, Kenneth Bernard. B.S. in Elem. Edn., Tuskegee Inst., 1958, M.Ed. in Psychology and Guidance, 1963; postgrad. U. N.C., 1967-68, U. South Fla., 1980-83. Coordinator student affairs Tuskegee Inst., Ala., 1960-64; vocat. counselor Job Corps Ctr. for Women, St. Petersburg, Fla., 1964-66; vocat. rehab. counselor State Dept. Edn., St. Petersburg, 1966-68; elem. counselor Pinellas County Sch. System, Clearwater, Fla., 1968-77; guidance coordinator St. Petersburg Vocat.-Tech. Inst., 1977-80, coordinator outreach recruitment, 1980—; cons. in career edn.; staff devel. tchr. in humanistic edn. Bd. dirs. NAACP, 1975—; v.p. Pinellas County Black Polit. Caucus, 1976-77; co-chmn. St. Petersburg Community Alliance, 1974-75; mem. Guidance Adv. Bd. Pinellas County, 1975-76; sec., treas. St. Petersburg Fair Housing Bd., 1976-78; mem. Pinellas Profl. Democratic Women's Club, 1976—; v.p. Pinellas County Biracial Adv. Com., 1980-82. Recipient service award Elem. div. of Fla. Sch. Counselor Assn., 1975, service and leadership award St. Petersburg C. of C., 1975, outstanding performance award City of St. Petersburg, 1973, community service awards Bethune Cookman Alumni Assn., 1976, St. Petersburg C. of C., 1977, disting. educator award Fla. Grand Lodge of Free and Accepted Masons, 1983; named Outstanding Educator of Yr., Pinellas County Sch. Bd., 1983, Nat. Parent, Tuskegee Inst., 1983; Fla. Sch. Counselor Human Rights award named in her honor, 1984. Mem. Am. Personnel and Guidance Assn., Fla. Personnel and Guidance Assn., Suncoast Personnel and Guidance Assn. (sec. 1981-82), Am. Sch. Counselor Assn. (human rights coordinator 1977-82), Fla. Sch. Counselor Assn. (v.p. post-secondary 1980-82), Suncoast Sch. Counselor Assn., NEA, Am. Vocat. Guidance Assn., Fla. Vocat. Assn., Assn. Non White Concerns, Sickle Cell Found. Pinellas County, Zeta Phi Beta (Woman of Yr. 1976, treas. 1980-82). Democrat. Baptist. Home: 3012 DeSoto Way S Saint Petersburg FL 33712 Office: 901 34th St S Saint Petersburg FL 33712

BURGESS, JANET HELEN, interior designer; b. Moline, Ill., Jan. 22, 1933; d. John Joseph and Helen Elizabeth (Johnson) B.; student Augustana Coll., Rock Island, Ill., 1950-51, U. Utah, 1951-52, Marycrest Coll., 1959-60; m. Richard Everett Guth, Aug. 25, 1951; children—John Joseph, Marshall Claude, Linnea Ann Guth Layman; m. 2d Milan Andrew Vodick, Feb. 16, 1980. Artist, self-employed, El Pao, Estado Bolívar, Venezuela, 1952-62; producer, designer Playcrafters Barn Theatre, Moline, 1963-65; designer, gen. mgr. Grilk Interiors, Davenport, Iowa, 1963—; dir. Fine Arts Gallery, Davenport, 1978-84; owner Amazon Vinegar & Pickling Works Drygoods, Davenport, 1982—; chmn. bd. Product Handling, Inc., Davenport, 1985—. Bd. dirs. Quad Cities Art Council, Rock Island Art Guild; adv. bd. Interior Design Dept., Scott Community Coll., also tchr. adult edn.; bd. dirs. Village of East Davenport (Iowa) Assn., 1963-84, pres., 1981; mem. Mayor's Com. for Historic Preservation, Davenport, 1976-77, 85—; bd. dirs. Neighborhood Housing Services, Davenport, 1981; bd. dirs., mem. retail com. Operation Clean Davenport. Recipient Gov.'s award for Leadership, Gov. Ray of Iowa, 1982. Mem. Davenport C. of C., ASID, Interior Designers, Gift & Decorative Accessories Assn. (Nat. merit award for promotion 1969), Nat. Trust for Historic Preservation, The Preservation Group, State of Iowa Hist. Soc., Rock Island Arsenal Hist. Soc., 16th Iowa Civil War Re-enactment Union. Republican. Design work featured in Gift & Decorative Accessories mag., 1969, 80, Decor mag., 1979; contbr. articles to profl. jours. Home: 2801 34th Ave Ct Rock Island IL 61201 Office: 2200 E 11th St Davenport IA 52803 also 2218 E 11th St Davenport IA 52803

BURGESS, KAREN ELAINE, clinical nurse specialist; b. Milw., Jan. 12, 1954; d. Carlton Philip and Elaine Ethel (Kamrath) B. B.S. in Nursing, U. Wis.-Milw., 1975; M.S. in Nursing, U. N.C., 1983. R.N., Wis., Calif., N.C., Fla. Med.-surg. staff nurse Columbia Hosp., Milw., 1976-79; community health nurse Vis. Nurse Assn., Orlando, Fla., 1979-80, pub. health nurse, Milw., 1980-81; neuro nurse clinician N.C. Meml. Hosp., Chapel Hill, 1981-84; neuro/ortho/rehab clin. specialist Hungtington Meml. Hosp., Pasadena, Calif., 1984—. Contbg. editor: Nurses Drug Handbook; author articles. Sunday sch. tchr., choir pianist Covenant Luth. Ch., Milw., 1970-72; flutist Music for Youth Symphony Orch., 1968-70. Recipient James M. Johnston award, 1981-82, 82-83. Mem. Internat. Graphoanalysis Soc., Phi Kappa Phi, Sigma Theta Tau. Avocations: writing; photography; piano; quilting. Office: Huntington Meml Hosp 100 Congress St Pasadena CA 91105

BURGESS, MEREDITH NANCY STRANG, advertising agency executive; b. Rockland, Maine, Apr. 27, 1956; d. Walter P. and Charlene M. (Perkins) Strang; B.S., U. Maine-Orono, 1978; m. James L. Burgess, June 24, 1978; children—Christopher James, Matthew Strang. Store activities rep. McDonald's Corp., Boston, 1978-79; account exec. Arnold & Co., Inc., Portland, Maine, 1979-80, field account supr., 1980-81, account supr. for McDonald's advt. in Maine, 1981-83, account service mgr., 1984, v.p., 1985—. Mem. Camden (Maine) Republican Town Com., 1974-80, Cumberland (Maine) Rep. Town Com., 1980—; del. Rep. Conv. Maine, 1974, 76, 78, 80; 1st alt. to Rep. Nat. Conv., 1976; com. woman from Knox County, Maine Rep. Com.; bd. dirs. Ronald McDonald House, U. Maine Alumni Council. Mem. Greater Portland Advt. Club (bd. dirs.), Soil Conservation Soc. Am., Natural Resource Council Maine, Alpha Phi. Home: 12 Country Charm Rd Cumberland ME 04021 Office: Custom House Sq 111 Commercial St Portland ME 04101

BURGESS, MYRTLE MARIE, lawyer; b. Brainerd, Minn., May 3, 1921; d. Charles Dana and Mary Elzaida (Thayer) Burgess. B.A., San Francisco State U., 1947; J.D., Hastings Coll. Law, 1950. Bar: Calif. 1951. Pvt. practice law, San Francisco, 1951-52, Reedley, Calif., 1952—; judge pro tem Fresno County Superior Ct., 1974-77; now owner/operator Hotel Burgess. Bd. dirs. Reedley Indsl. Site Devel. Found., 1970-81; dir., 2d v.p. Kings Canyon unit Calif. Republican Assembly, 1973-75; pres., bd. dirs. Sierra Community Concert Assn., Reedley council Girl Scouts U.S.A., 1955-56; bd. dirs., treas. Reedley Downtown Assn., 1983—; bd. dirs., sec. Kings View Found. Recipient Woman of Year award Reedley C. of C., 1971; award for remodeling and preservation of old bldg. Fresno Hist. Soc., 1975, others. Mem. ABA, Calif. Bar Assn., Fresno County Bar Assn., World Peace Through Law Internat., Am. Trial Lawyers. Republican. Presbyterian. Clubs: Bus. and Profl. Women's (pres.). Lodge: Order Eastern Star. Home: 1076 N Kady Ave Reedley CA 93654 Office: 1107 "G" St Reedley CA 93654

BURGESS, PATRICIA ANN, nurse, educator; b. Carson City, Nev., Oct. 20, 1938; d. Joseph Cecil and Victorine Virginia (Sciarini) Morrison; children—Heather, Michael. Diploma, Mary's Help Coll. Nursing, 1959; B.S.N. (Profl. Nurse trainee), U. Nev., 1974, M.S., 1981. Cert. rural nurse practitioner, child and adolescent nurse. Staff nurse Marin Gen. Hosp., San Rafael, Calif., 1959; staff nurse Washoe Med. Ctr., Reno, 1959, head nurse emergency room, 1960, staff nurse ICU, 1961-64, head nurse ICU, 1965-66, staff nurse pediatrics, 1978, 82—; lectr. U. Nev., 1974-81, asst. prof. pediatrics, 1982—; clinic mgr. Genetics Clinic. Contbr. articles in profl. jours. Mem. Nev. Task Force on Child Abuse and Neglect. Mem. Am. Nurses' Assn., Nev. Nurses' Assn., Nat. Soc. Profs., Orvis Sch. Nursing Hon. Roman Catholic. Home: 1479 Coronet Circle Reno NV 89509 Office: Orvis Sch Nursing U Nev Reno NV 89557

BURGHARD, KATHERINE ANN, lawyer; b. Houston, Oct. 9, 1955; d. Joseph Leroy and Sheila (Keating) B. B.A., U. Ill., 1976; J.D., U. Tex.-Austin, 1979. Bar: Tex. 1979, N.Y. 1982. Atty. Exxon Co., U.S.A., Houston, 1979-81; counsel Exxon Corp., N.Y.C., 1981-83; assoc. gen. counsel Weeks Petroleum Ltd., Westport, Conn., 1983-84, gen. counsel, N.Y.C., 1984—; U.S. counsel The Bell Group Ltd., Perth, Australia, 1984—. Mem. State Bar Tex., N.Y. State Bar, Assn. Bar City of N.Y., Phi Beta Kappa. Office: Weeks Petroleum Ltd 115 E 57th St New York NY 10022

BURGIO, JANE, state government official; b. Nutley, N.J.; m. John Burgio; children: John E., James. Student, Newark Sch. Fine and Indsl. Arts. Mem. N.J. State Assembly, Trenton, 1973-81; sec. of state State of N.J., Trenton, 1982—. Mem. Essex County Improvement Authority; mem. Trustees for Support of Free Pub. Schs.; trustee devel. com. St. Barnabas Hosp., Livingston, N.J.; trustee Planned Parenthood Essex County; alt. del. Republican Nat. Conv. Recipient Alumni Recognition award Univ. Coll., Rutgers U., Newark; rcipient hist. award N.J. League Hist. Socs.; recipient cert. N.J. Humane Soc., Newark. Mem. Nat. Assn. Secs. of State, Nat. Conf. State Legislature, Bus. and Profl. Women's Assn. of Millburn, N.J. Home: 586 Mountain Ave North Caldwell NJ 07006 Office: New Jersey Dept State State House CN 300 Trenton NJ 08625

BURGOYNE, SHIRLEY JEAN, lawyer; b. Saginaw, Mich., Oct. 25, 1932; d. Marshall Albert and Beatrice Viola (Clements) Cox; A.B., J.D., U. Mich., 1956; m. Bert Burgoyne, Apr. 22, 1955 (div.); children—Deborah Jeanne, David Edward, Douglas Jeffrey. Law clk. Oreg. Supreme Ct., Salem, 1956-57; admitted to Oreg. bar, 1957, Mich. bar, 1959; practiced in Roseburg, Oreg., 1957-58, Lansing, Mich., 1959-63, Ann Arbor, Mich., 1963—; mem. firm Burgoyne & Burgoyne, Roseburg, 1957-58, Thomas C. Walsh, Lansing, 1959-63, Burgoyne & Morris, Ann Arbor, 1968-69, Burgoyne & Pratt, Ann Arbor, 1977—; legal counsel Mich. Abortion Referendum Com., 1969-73. Mem. Mich. Women's Commn., 1971-72; bd. dirs. Mich. Council for Study of Abortion, 1971-73. Mem. Am. (family law sect., chair codification com.), Mich. (council family law sect.), Oreg. bar assns., Am. Trial Lawyers Assn., Am. Judicature Soc., AAUW, Kappa Beta Pi. Presbyn. Home and Office: 206 Miller St Ann Arbor MI 48104

BURICK-HOREJS, MARY F., banker; b. Youngstown, Ohio, Dec. 22, 1952; d. Joseph and Carol Marie (Vlasic) Burick; m. Edward Robert Horejs, Jr., Sept. 22, 1984. B.A. in Econs., Youngstown State U., 1975; M.A. in Econs., U. Okla., 1981. Bank Examiner State of Ohio, Div. of Bank Supervision, Columbus, 1975; liquidator, FDIC-Div. Liquidation, Washington, 1975-83; credit officer NCB, Cleve., 1983-84; asst. v.p. credit and loan adminstrn. Society Nat. Bank, Cleve., 1984—. Mem. Internat. Platform Assn., Nat. Assn. Bus. Women, Council Smaller Enterprises, Nat. Assn. Bank Women (pub. affairs chmn.). Clubs: Cleve. Women's City, Cleve. Bus. Econ. Avocations: sailing; skiing; golf; reading. Address: 26523 Normandy Bay Village OH 44140

BURK, MARGUERITE CATHERINE, educator; b. Ottawa, Kans., July 12, 1915; d. Ralph G. and Clara A. (Eberhart) Burk; A.B., U. Kans., 1937, M.A., 1938; Ph.D. (fellow), U. Minn., 1948; postgrad. Am. U., 1938-40, U. Wis., 1940, Cambridge (Eng.) U., 1955-56. Statis. clk., economist U.S. Dept. Agr., Washington, 1939-45; head consumption sec. Bur. Agr. Econs., Washington, 1945-60; agrl. economist Econ. Research Service, Washington, 1960-61; prof. agrl. econs. and home econs. U. Minn., 1961-69; leader food consumption research group Dept. Agr., Washington, 1969-75; prof. program internat. studies in human ecology Howard U., Washington, 1975-80; cons. FAO program, Rome, 1961, Philippine Food and Nutrition Research Inst., Manila, 1977, 79; cons. U.S. Dept. Agr., 1980—, AID, 1983; cons. in field. Recipient Superior Service award U.S. Dept. Agr., 1954; USOE grantee internat. studies in human ecology, 1975-77. Mem. Am. Econ. Assn., Am. Home Econs. Assn., Soc. Internat. Devel.; fellow Am. Council Consumer Interests (pres. 1961-62). Author handbooks. Contbr. articles to profl. jours. Editor: The Nat. Food Situation, 1945-60.

BURK, SYLVIA JOAN, petroleum landman, author, free lance writer; b. Dallas, Oct. 16, 1928; d. Guy Thomas and Sylvia (Herrin) Ricketts; m. R. B. Murray, Jr., Sept. 7, 1951 (div. Jan. 1961); children—Jeffery Randolph, Brian BeVaughn; m. Bryan Burk, Apr. 26, 1973. B.A., So. Meth. U., Dallas, 1950, M.L.A., 1974; postgrad. U. So. Calif., 1973-74. Landman, E. B. Germany & Sons, Dallas, 1970-73; asst. mgr. real estate Atlantic Richfield Co., Los Angeles, 1973-74; landman Goldking Prodn. Co., Houston, 1974-76; oil and gas cons./landman, co-owner Burk Properties, Burk Ednl. Properties, Houston, 1976—. Author: Petroleum Lands and Leasing, 1983, 2d edit., 1987; contbr. articles to jours. Mem. Am. Assn. Petroleum Landmen (dir. 1980-82, 2d v.p. 1982-83), Houston Assn. Petroleum Landmen (dir. 1978-79), Nat. Writer's Club. Republican. Presbyterian. Clubs: Dallas Woman's, Sugar Creek Country. Office: Burk Properties Tex Am Bank Bldg Suite 565 12603 Southwest Freeway Stafford TX 77477

BURKA, LESIA ROMANIW, pharmacist; b. N.Y.C., Dec. 9, 1953; d. Omelan and Daria (Szpilman) Romaniw; student Rutgers U., Newark, 1971-73; certs. in piano Ukrainian Music Inst. Am., in Ukrainian lang. Ukrainian Acad., 1972; B.S. in Pharmacy, Temple U., Phila., 1976; m. Eugene Burka, Aug. 11, 1973; children—Adrian, Tanya. Pharmacist, nursing homes cons. Miles Pharmacy, Erdenheim, Pa., 1976-77; mgmt. trainee, supr. processing depts. McNeil Labs., Inc. and McNeil Consumer Products Co., Ft. Washington, Pa., 1977-80; group supr. multi-shift packaging dept. McNeil Consumer Products Co., 1980-81, group supr. projects in processing ops., 1981-83, group supr. compression and encapsulation ops., 1983-85, project mgr., 1985—, steering com. quality circle program, 1981-84. Mem. Am., Pa., Montgomery County pharm. assns.; Del. Valley Women in Pharmacy, Acad. Pharm. Scis. Ukrainian Catholic. Home: 1375 Harris Rd Dresher PA 19025 Office: Camphill Rd Fort Washington PA 19034

BURKE, ARLENE LOUISE, family practice physician, army officer; b. Long Beach, Calif., Jan. 20, 1947; d. Lester Blair and Margaret Ethelyn (Rives) Larch; m. Lyle Ray Burke, July 18, 1965; children—Mark, David, Christiene, Sandra. Vocat. nurse lic. Biola Sch. Missionary Medicine, Los Angeles, 1965; B.A. in Biol. Scis. with honors, Loma Linda U., 1976; D.O., U. Health Scis. of Osteo. Medicine, Kansas City, Mo., 1981. Clk. Biola Book Room, Los Angeles, 1965; bank teller, bookkeeper, Garden Grove, Calif., 1966-67; PBX operator, bookkeeper Tamarisk Country Club, Palm Springs, Calif., 1970-71; nurse Eisenhower Med. Ctr., Palm Desert, Calif., 1972, Desert Hosp., Palm Springs, Calif., 1974-76; commd. 2d lt., M.C., U.S. Army, 1978, advanced through grades to capt., 1981; intern Silas B. Hayes Army Community Hosp., Ft. Ord, Calif., 1981-82, resident, 1982-83; family practitioner U.S. Army, Ft. Irwin, Calif., 1983—, preventive medicine med. officer, med. dept. activities, 1983. Youth dir. Univ. Baptist Ch., Palm Desert, 1969, Seventh Day Adventist Ch., Palm Desert, 1983; foster parent Riverside county Health Dept., Palm Desert, 1970-77. United Spanish War Vets. Aux. nursing grantee, 1965; Loma Linda U. worthy student grantee, 1973-75; Mayr Found. scholar, 1974-75. Mem. Am. Osteo. Assn., Assn. Mil. Osteo. Physicians, Am. Med. Woman's Assn., Osteo. Physicians and Surgeons Calif., Alpha Phi Omega, Delta Omega. Republican. Adventist. Office: USA AHS Stud Det Fort Sam Houston TX 78234

BURKE, BARBARA JEAN, fundraising executive; b. Hartford, Ala., Oct. 24, 1948; d. Clarence Lee and Syble (Simmons) Peters; m. Michael Wayne Foster, 1966 (div. 1976); children—Michaele, Jonathan; m. Robert Edmund Burke, June 11, 1977; children—Mark, Kathleen, Colleen, Sean, Alan. A.A., Enterprise State Jr. Coll., 1970; B.A., U. South Fla., 1974; M.A., Trinity U., San Antonio, 1975; postgrad. Universidad Nacional Autonoma de Mexico, 1982. Instr., San Antonio Coll., 1975; planner Econ. Opportunities Devel. Corp., San Antonio, 1976, Alamo Area Council Govts., San Antonio, 1977-82; devel. officer Oblate Missions, San Antonio, 1982—; cons. Bob Burke & Assocs., San Antonio, 1982—. Author: Paratransit Provider Handbook, 1978. Contbg. author: Human Responses to Aging, 1976; Transportation for Elderly Handicapped Programs and Problems, 1978. Contbr. articles to profl. publs. Mem. Nat. Soc. Fund Raising Execs. (sec. San Antonio chpt.), Council Advancement and Support Edn. Democrat. Roman Catholic. Office: Oblate Missions PO Box 96 San Antonio TX 78291

BURKE, DEBORAH STANTON, lawyer; b. Galveston, Tex., Sept. 12, 1953; d. Rufus Hezekiah and Janice Dhaye (Splane) Stanton; m. William Tunnell Burke III, Mar. 13, 1981; 1 son, William Tunnell IV. B.B.A., U. Tex., 1975, J.D., 1982. Bar: Tex. 1983. Exec. trainee Foleys, Houston, 1975-76, asst. buyer, 1976-77, group sales mgr., 1977-78; buyer Joskes of Tex., San Antonio, 1978-80; ombudsman U. Tex., Austin, 1981-82; sole practice, Beaumont, Tex., 1983—. Bd. dirs. YWCA, Beaumont, 1984—. Mem. ABA, Tex. Bar Assn., NAACP, Friar Soc., Alpha Kappa Alpha, Phi Alpha Delta (treas. 1981-82). Home: 2100 Victoria St Beaumont TX 77701 Office: 1765 Washington Blvd Beaumont TX 77705

BURKE, DENISE WILLIAMSON, broadcasting executive; b. Bridgeport, Conn., Mar. 24, 1947; d. Philip Edmund and Ingrid (Williamson) Burke. A.S., Vt. Coll., 1967. Exec. sec. ABC, N.Y.C., 1967-73, 76-78; exec. sec. Pepsico, Purchase, N.Y., 1973-74, Am. Can Co., Greenwich, Conn., 1974-76; mgr. awards ABC, Inc., N.Y.C., 1978-81, dir. awards and spl. projects, 1981—. Mem. Nat. Acad. TV Arts and Scis., Am. Women in Radio and TV, Acad. TV Arts and Scis., Internat. Radio and TV Soc., Women in Communication. Home: 50 Barker St #637 Mt Kisco NY 10549 Office: ABC 1330 Ave of Americas New York NY 10019

BURKE, JANET LYNN, communications company executive, advertising, editor; b. Detroit, Mar. 2, 1950; s. William J. and Alice M. (Wozarik) Charkey; B.A., Wayne State U., 1974, postgrad. 1983—. Advt. layout Observer and Eccentric Newspapers, Livonia, Mich., 1973-76; dir. community relations Cranbrook Inst. Sci., Bloomfield Hills, Mich., 1976-78; dir. pub. relations Cranbrook Ednl. Community, Bloomfield Hills, 1978-84; pres., chief exec. officer JB Communications, Birmingham, Mich., 1984—. Editor: The Cranbrook Quar., 1978-84, (Grand Gold medal 1984, exceptional achievement award 1981-84); The Cranbrook Jour., 1984—. (Grand Gold medal 1985). Mem. Council for Advancement and Support of Edn., Women in Communications, Inc. (membership chmn. 1983—, Great Lakes award 1984), Women's Econ. Club of Detroit. Office: JB Communications 30600 Telegraph Suite 3394 Birmingham MI 48010

BURKE, KAREN KAESS, real estate broker; b. Boston, Feb. 12, 1948; d. Kenneth Richard and Marguerite Alice (Welch) Kaess; B.A., Briarcliff, 1969; m. Edwin M. Burke, Jr., June 6, 1970; children—Edwin M., James Van Vleck. Asst. editorial credit editor Glamour Mag., N.Y.C., 1969-70; tchr. Canterbury Sch., Charlottesville, Va., 1970-71; asst. dir. mktg. Vogue Mag., N.Y.C., 1971-72, asst. fashion editor, 1972-73; asst. mdse. editor House and Garden Mag., N.Y.C., 1972; tchr., vol. fund raiser Matheny Sch. Cerebral Palsy, 1976—; mktg. and brokerage Previews Inc., Greenwich, Conn., 1978-82, Estates Internat. Corp., Greenwich and New Canaan, Conn., 1978—; broker Realtech Realtors, New Canaan, 1982—; pres. Balloons Unltd., New Canaan; ptnr. E.B. Wallace Inc. Chmn. jr. com. Channel 13, 1984-85. Mem. Nat. Assn. Realtors, New Canaan Bd. Realtors. Jr. League. Democrat. Home: 33 Father Peter's Ln New Canaan CT 06840 Office: 39 Pine St New Canaan CT 06840

BURKE, LINDA BEERBOWER, lawyer; b. Huntington, W.Va., June 19, 1948; d. William Bert and Betty Jane (Weddle) Beerbower; m. Timothy Francis Burke, Jr., Aug. 26, 1972; children—Ryan Timothy, Hannah Elizabeth. B.A.,

Coll. William and Mary, 1970; J.D., U. Pitts., 1973; postgrad. acctg. U. Pitts., 1976. Bar: Pa. 1973, U.S. Claims Ct. 1982. Tax atty. ALCOA, Pitts., 1973-77, gen. tax atty., 1977-80, mgr. legal and planning taxes, 1980—. Industry coordinator Allegheny Conf. Partnerships in Edn., Pitts. pub. schs., 1981—; mem. United Way adv. com. for Vol. Action Ctr., Pitts.; trustee St. Edmund's Acad. Recipient salute Triangle Corner, Pitts., 1983. Mem. Tax Execs. Inst. (pres., bd. dirs.), Pitts. Internat. Taxation Soc., Pitts. Tax Club, ABA, Pa. Bar Assn., Allegheny County Bar Assn. Clubs: Pitts. Athletic Assn., Longue Vue, Rivers. Office: Aluminum Co Am 1501 Alcoa Bldg Pittsburgh PA 15219

BURKE, LUCILLE PENNUCCI, systems analyst, programmer; b. Morristown, N.J., Jan. 31, 1938; d. Bernard and Pauline Lucy (Corea) Pennucci. Student parochial schs., Morristown and Madison, N.J. Sr. console operator Beneficial Mgmt. Co., Morristown, 1955-66; asst. keypunch supr. Cessna, Inc., Morristown, 1966-68; control supr., keypunch supr. Keuffel & Esser, Morristown, 1968-71; encoding (data entry) mgr. Newsweek mag., Livingston, N.J., 1971-73; mgr. data entry, Litton Publs., Oradell, N.J., 1973-75; sr. systems analyst, trainer Gen. Computer Systems, N.Y.C., 1975-76; regional tng. coordinator, sr. system engr., customer rep. No. Telecom Systems Corp., Houston, 1976-79; contract programmer Houston Ind. Sch. Dist., 1979; contract programmer Bechtel Corp., Houston, 1979, data entry supr., 1979-81, sr. system analyst, 1981—. Vol., The Sheltering Arms, Houston, 1978—. Democrat. Roman Catholic. Home: 2660 MariLee #A59 Houston TX 77057 Office: Bechtel Inc 5400 Westheimer Houston TX 77056

BURKE, MARY JOAN THOMPSON, psychiatric social worker; b. Louisville, Apr. 1, 1933; d. Thomas Earl and Imelda C. (Mattingly) Thompson; B.S., Nazareth Coll., 1955; M.S.W., U. Pitts., 1969; m. Joseph Charles Burke, Sept. 1, 1956; children—Anne Maura, Colleen Elizabeth. Psychiat. social worker Homestead Community Mental Health Center, Pitts., 1969-70, Mental Hygiene Instr., Montreal, Que., Can., 1971-73, Champlain Valley Physicians Hosp., Plattsburgh, N.Y., 1973-79; also pvt. practice psychol. counseling. Bd. dirs. Assn. Retarded Children, Center Emotionally Disturbed, 1974-76, Clinton County Community Services, 1974—; mem. profl. adv. com. Clinton County Health Dept.; co-chmn. Conf. on Psychiatry and Medicine, 1974-82; mem. Lake Champlain Com. Bd. Mem. Nat. Assn. Social Workers, Am. Assn. Marriage and Family Counselors, Am. Acad. Certified Social Workers, LWV, Internat. Coll. Psychosomatic Medicine, N.Y. State Assn. Community Service Bds. (1st v.p.). Roman Catholic. Home: 134 Court St Plattsburgh NY 12901 Office: 60A Oak St Plattsburgh NY 12901

BURKE, MARY LOUISE, instrumentation laboratory executive; b. Holyoke, Mass., May 15, 1936; d. Edmund Anthony and Mary Louise (McCabe) B.; B.A., Elms Coll., 1957; cert in med. tech. Mercy Hosp. Sch. Med. Tech., Springfield, Mass., 1957. Hematologist, Mercy Hosp., Springfield, 1957-66, teaching supr., 1961-66; tech. rep. Hycel Inc., NE and Eastern Can., 1966-69, new product mgr. Houston, 1969, edn. mgr., 1969-71, dir. profl. consultation, 1971-73; product coordinator Instrumentation Lab., Inc., Lexington, Mass., 1973-74, mgr. tech. services, biomed. div., 1974—.Clay-Adams research grantee, Am. Soc. Med. Tech., 1963; recipient Disting. Alumnae Medal Elms Coll., 1982. Mem. Am. Soc. Med. Tech., Am. Assn. Clin. Chemistry, Mass. Assn. Med. Tech. (pres. 1966-67), Elms Coll. Alumnae Assn. (pres. 1963-67, Disting. Alumnae medal 1982). Roman Catholic. Home: 378 Park Ave Arlington Heights MA 02174 Office: 113 Hartwell Ave Lexington MA 02173

BURKE, MARYELLEN, manufacturing engineer; b. Orange, N.J., Feb. 28, 1958; d. Raymond Michael and Gloria Anne (Grube) Burke, Sr. B.S. in Chemistry and Classics, Tufts U., 1980; spl. student archeol. scis. U. Bradford, W. Yorkshire, Eng., 1979. Research organic chemistry Celanese Research Co., Summit, N.J., summers 1978, 79; researcher chem. engring. Celanese Plastics Co., Summit, summer 1980; mem. tech. staff, laser systems support engr. Hughes Aircraft Co., El Segundo, Calif., 1980—; v.p. intergroup woman's forum, 1983-84; cons. computer mfg. Euclid Computer Co., Torrance, Calif., 1983; pres. Ryell Enterprises, mktg. firm, Manhatten Beach, Calif., 1983—. Vol., Children's Mus., Los Angeles, 1981, Rec. for Blind, Los Angeles, 1982. Recipient Outstanding Leadership and Achievement Cert. Los Angeles YWCA, 1983. Mem. Am. Chem. Soc., Soc. Women Engrs (co-chmn. 1983-84), Nat. Assn. Female Execs. (network dir. 1982—), Tufts U. Alumni Admissions Council. Home: 14630 Saticoy St Apt 230 Van Nuys CA 91405

BURKE, PATRICIA ANNE, corrosion engineer, consultant, researcher; b. Norwich, Conn., Aug. 13, 1955; d. Edward Martin and Shirley Mae (Siedel) B.; m. Robert Mark Shammas, Nov. 12, 1977 (div. 1980). B.S. in Civil Engring., U. R.I., 1977; M.Sc. in Corrosion Sci. and Engring., U. Manchester Inst. Sci. and Tech., Eng., 1985. Constrn. engr. Chevron USA, Denver, 1977-79, chem./corrosion engr., Midland, Tex., 1980-81; sr. corrosion engr. Mitchell Energy Corp., Woodlands, Tex., 1981-84; staff engr. Cortest Labs., Cypress, Tex., 1986—. Editor: Advances in CO2 Corrosion II, 1985. Contbr. articles on CO2 corrosion, acid corrosion to profl. jours., 1984—. Mem. Nat. Assn. Corrosion Engrs. (com. mem., sec. and chmn.), Istn. Corrosion Sci. and Tech., Soc. Petroleum Engrs. (jr.), ASTM, Soc. Biomaterials, Soc. Am. Bus. Women. Republican. Roman Catholic.

BURKE, RANDEE LYNN, exercise physiologist, educator, consultant; b. Chgo., July 12, 1952; d. Anderson Walter and Gladys Emma (Shaver) Burke. B.S., U. Wis., 1976; M.S., Ft. Hays State U., 1977. Head athletic trainer U. Redlands (Calif.), 1977-79; cardiac rehab. staff U. Wis., Madison, 1979-82; therapist Richard Bachrach, D.O., N.Y.C., 1982-83; exercise physiologist Park E. Chiropractic, N.Y.C., 1983; fitness instr. Biofitness Inst., N.Y.C., 1983-84; health cons., therapist, N.Y.C., 1982-85; health cons. to Liza Minnelli, N.Y.C., 1982-85. Served with U.S. Army, 1985—. Recipient Outstanding Female Athlete award Wis. Interscholastic Athletic Assn., 1970; All-Am. Track award U.S. Track and Field Assn., 1975, 76. Mem. Am. Coll. Sports Medicine, Nat. Athletic Trainers Assn., N.Y. State Athletic Trainers Assn., Republican. Presbyterian. Clubs: Nat. W, U. Wis. Alumni. Home: 4800 Burt Mar Dr Apt 1 Columbus GA 31907

BURKES, SARAH BEATRICE, educator, insurance agent; b. Clarksdale, Miss., Feb. 28, 1948; d. Henry and Eldora (Abshaw) Burkes; student Jackson State U., 1966-68; B.S., Tex. Coll., 1970; M.A., East Tex. State U. With Progressive Community Center, Chgo., 1970-72; tchr. Chgo. Bd. Edn., 1972—; with Blue Cross-Blue Shield, Chgo., 1972-75; communications counselor Malcolm X Coll., Chgo., 1975-77; instr. reading and English, Accounter Community Center, Chgo., 1977-80; agt. Equitable Life Ins., Chgo., 1980—; rep. World Book-Childcraft Encyclopedia, 1981—. Mem. Internat. Reading Assn., Nat. Council Tchrs. English, MLA, Chgo. Reading Assn., Nat. Life Underwriters Assn., United Ednl. Employees Assn., Alpha Kappa Alpha. Home: 1109 S Troy St Chicago IL 60612 Mailing Address: PO Box 12051 Chicago IL 60612

BURKET, GAIL BROOK, author; b. Stronghurst, Ill., Nov. 1, 1905; d. John Cecil and Maud (Simonson) Brook; A.B., U. Ill., 1926; M.A. in English Lit., Northwestern U., 1929; m. Walter Cleveland Burket, June 22, 1929; children—Elaine (Mrs. William L. Harwood), Anne, Margaret (Mrs. James Boyce). Pres. woman's aux. Internat. Coll. Surgeons, 1950-54, now bd. dirs. mus.; nat. vice chmn. Am. Heritage of DAR, 1971-74; pres. Northwestern U. Guild, 1976-78; sec. bd. Northwestern U. Settlement, 1979-81, pres. Evanston Women's Bd., 1984-86. Recipient Robert Ferguson Meml. award Friends of Lit., 1973. Mem. Nat. League Am. Pen Women (Ill. state pres. 1952-54, nat. v.p. 1958-60), Soc. Midland Authors, Poetry Soc. Am., Women in Communications Inc., AAUW (pres. N. Shore br. 1961-63), Daus. Am. Colonists (state v.p. 1973-76), Colonial Dames Am. (chpt. regent 1974-80), Ill. Opera Guild (bd. dirs. 1982-84, 1st v.p. 1985—), Phi Beta Kappa, Delta Zeta. Author: Courage Beloved, 1949; Manners Please, 1949; Blueprint for Peace, 1951; Let's Be Popular, 1951; You Can Write a Poem, 1954; Far Meadows, 1955; This is My Country, 1960; From the Prairies, 1968. Contbr. articles, poems to lit. publs. Address: 1020 Lake Shore Dr Evanston IL 60202

BURKET, HARRIET, editor, consultant; b. Findlay, Ohio, June 14; d. John Franklin and Betty (Hoege) B.; m. Maurice Conrad Reinecke, Sept. 24, 1935 (div. Apr. 1952); 1 child, Rosalind Reinecke Eggum; m. Francis Brewster Taussig, Oct. 8, 1960 (dec. 1970). B.A., Vassar Coll., 1931. Assoc. editor Arts and Decoration, N.Y.C., 1932-35, Creative Design, N.Y.C., 1935-37; assoc. editor House and Garden, N.Y.C., 1937-44, home furnishings editor, 1952-55, exec. editor, 1955-58, editor-in-chief, 1958-70; interior design editor Woman's Home Companion, N.Y.C., 1944-52; ptnr. Editor's Inc., N.Y.C., 1970—. Editor: House and Garden's Complete Guide to Interior Decoration, 7th edit., 1970; House and Garden's Complete Guide to Creative Entertaining, 1971. Recipient Dallas Market award Dallas Market Assn., 1962. Mem. Nat. Home Fashions League (founder Trail Blazer awards 1948), Internat. Fashion Group (v.p. 1958-59), Internat. Platform Assn., Am. Soc. Interior Designers, Decorative Arts Trust. Republican. Episcopalian. Clubs: Vassar; Harvard; Decorators; Cosmopolitan (N.Y.C.) (bd. govs. 1976-79); Field (Sarasota, Fla.). Home: 14 Sutton Pl S New York NY 10022 Office: Editors Inc 14 Sutton Pl S New York NY 10022

BURKETT, MYRL HODGSON, advertising agency executive; b. Kansas City, Kans., Dec. 4, 1944; d. John Thomas, Jr. and Myrl O'Neill (Hodgson) B.; m. Dickinson Hale McGuire, Nov. 10, 1965 (div. Aug. 1974); children—Samuel D., John T.; m. 2d, John William Borecky, Mar. 25, 1977. A.A., Stratford Coll., 1964. Prodn. control mgr. L. Honold Mfg. Co., Folcroft, Pa., 1974-76; media dir. Arnold Advt. Corp., Reading, Pa., 1977—. Pub. relations dir., bd. dirs. YWCA, Reading; fin. developer Wallingford Fine Arts Ctr. (Pa.), 1970-73; active St. James Episcopal Ch. Women, Aston, Pa., 1969-75. Mem. Sales and Mktg. Execs. Reading, Am. Women in Radio and TV. Club: Monday. Home: RD 1 Box 1359 A Fleetwood PA 19522 Office: Arnold Advt Corp 3608 St Lawrence Ave Reading PA 19606

BURKHARDT, DOLORES ANN, librarian, educator; b. Meriden, Conn., July 28, 1932; d. Frederick Christian and Emily (Detels) Burkhardt; B.A., U. Conn., 1955, 6th year diploma, 1972; M.S., So. Conn. State Coll., 1960; postgrad. Central Wash. State Coll., 1962, Columbia, 1964—. Asst. librarian So. Conn. State Coll. Library, summers 1960, 62; sch. library tchr. Farmington High Sch., Unionville, Conn., 1955-66, North Haven High Sch., 1967-68; media specialist East Farms Demonstration Sch., Farmington, Conn., 1967-70; library coordinator Regional Dist. 13, 1970-72; library media coordinator Regional Dist. 10, Burlington-Harwinton, Conn., 1972-78. Instr. So. Conn. State Coll., New Haven, 1967-68, Boston U. Media Inst., 1970-71. Spl. cons. Conn. Dept. Edn., 1965-68; chmn. Conn. Sch. Library Standards Com., 1968-70. Mem. AAUW (sec. 1956-58, edn. chmn.), NEA, Conn. Edn. Assn., New Eng. (past pres.), Conn. (2d v.p. 1965-68) sch. library assns., Am. Assn. Sch. Librarians, New Eng. Media Assn., New Eng. Sch. Devel. Council, Am. Soc. Curriculum Devel., Nat. Council Tchrs. English, Phi Delta Kappa. Lutheran. Home: 812 Savage St Southington CT 06489 Office: 812 Savage St Southington CT 06489

BURKHARDT, JUDITH CAROL, youth advisor; b. Highland Park, Mich., Aug. 1, 1940; d. Edward Anthony and Angela Margarita (Gebell) B.; 1 dau., Barbara. B.A., Marygrove Coll., 1963; postgrad. Mich. Technol. U., 1968, U. Detroit, 1974; M.Ed., Wayne State U., 1974. Tchr., Holy Redeemer Sch., Detroit, 1964-67, St. Bede Sch., Southfield, Mich., 1967-69, St. Hugo Sch., Bloomfield Hills, Mich., 1969-73; children's supr. Oakland County Childrens Village, Pontiac, Mich., 1974; youth advisor Pontiac (Mich.) Police Dept., 1974—. Pres. Bloomfield Youth Guidance, Bloomfield Hills, 1971-73; sec. Cath. Social Services, Royal Oak, Mich., 1969-73; mem. community adv. bd. Woodland Hills Ctr., Troy, Mich.; founding mem. Bloomfield-Birmingham Ctr. for Human Devel., Bloomfield Hills, 1971; mem. Women's Polit. Caucus, Washington, 1983—. Mem. AAUW, Am. Assn. Female Execs., Am. Assn. for Counseling and Devel., Nat. Employment Counselors Assn. Democrat. Roman Catholic. Office: Pontiac Police Dept 110 E Pike St Detroit MI 48058

BURKHART-COBB, EVELYN LAVERNE, geologist, consultant; b. Lenoir City, Tenn., June 6, 1945; d. Walter Leo and Edith Almira (Snodderly) Burkhart; m. Cornelius Quincy Cobb, Oct. 26, 1962; children—Andrea, Aaron Schadwicke. B.S., U. Tenn., 1965, M.S., 1974. Teaching asst. U. Tenn., Knoxville, 1965-66, 73-74; geologist Texaco Bellaire Research Labs., Houston, 1974-76; geologist/project mgr. Office Nuclear Waste Isolation, Oak Ridge (Tenn.) Nat. Lab., 1976-78; mgr. geology Gruy Petroleum Tech., Inc., Houston, 1978-84; pres. L.B. Cobb & Assocs., Houston, 1984—. 1st v.p. LWV, Greenville, Tenn., 1969-70. NSF student fellow, Knoxville, Oak Ridge, 1959, 60, 61; named Grand Champion, So. Appalachian Sci. Fair, 1962. Mem. Am. Assn. Petroleum Geologists, Am. Inst. Profl. Geologists (cert.) Soc. Econ. Paleontologists and Mineralogists, Houston Geol. Soc. (asst. editor bull. 1983-84). Office: 27 E Shady Ln Houston TX 77063

BURKHOLDER, GRACE ELEANOR, educator, archeologist; b. Sumas, Wash., Sept. 21, 1920; d. George Lewis and Leah (Denke) Welch; m. Warren Stanford Burkholder, June 4, 1938 (div. Apr. 1957); children—Warren Stanford, Carol Joyce Van Dyke. B.Ed. cum laude, U. Miami, Fla., 1956; M.Ed., U. Okla., 1980. Tchr., Laurel Sch., Oceanside, Calif., 1956-58; elem. tchr. U.S. Navy, Kwajalein, M.I., 1958-59, Transport Co. Tex., Kwajalein, 1959-60, Arabian Am. Oil Co., Dhahran, Saudi Arabia, 1960-80. Author: An Arabian Collection: Artifacts from the Eastern Province, 1984; research, publs. on Ubaid sites and pottery in Saudi Arabia. Mem. Archeol. Inst. Am., Smithsonian Instn., Audubon Soc. Republican.

BURKS, JUDITH ANN, radio station executive; b. Gary, Ind., Oct. 19, 1946; d. Glen V. and Mary K. (Hatch) Reyome; m. Robert M. Burks, Sr., June 29, 1974; 1 child, Marybeth. Student Ind. U.-Gary, 1983—. FM operator, traffic reporter Sta. WIFE, Indpls., 1967-68; reciptionist, sec., traffic dir. Sta. WLTH, Gary, 1965-67, traffic, continuity, 1968-77, dir. broadcasting ops., 1977-81, v.p., gen. mgr., 1981—. Bd. dirs., past pres. Lake Area United Way, Griffith, 1984; bd. dirs. Gary Community Devel., 1984—, Northwest Ind. Forum, Merrillville, Ind., 1984—, United Way Ind., 1985-86; mem. cons. com. Gary Career Ctr., 1985; Named Outstanding Young Women Tradewinds, Easter Seals, 1979, 80. Mem. Gary C. of C. (bd. dirs.). Office: Sta WLTH Radio 3669 Broadway St Gary IN 46409

BURLEIGH, RITA JEAN, librarian, educator; b. Santa Monica, Calif., Mar. 19, 1943; d. Charles P. and Jeanne (DeWitt) Loftus; m. Thomas W. Scott, 1965 (div. 1975); children—Graham Robert, Shelly Amber; m. Edward William Burleigh, Oct. 23, 1980; children—Edward William, Rebecca Dawn. B.A., U. Redlands, 1965, M.A., 1967; M.L.S. Immaculate Heart Coll., 1969. Librarian, Pomona Pub. Library (Calif.), 1967-69, U. La Verne, Calif., 1970-72, Rio Hondo Coll., Whittier, Calif., 1973-79; learning resources dir., Citrus Coll., Glendora, Calif., 1979—. Pres. San Gabriel Community Colls. Library Cooperative, 1982—. Corr. sec. Pomona Valley Art Assn., 1979; mem. draft bd. U.S. Selective Service, 1981—; sr. warden Saint Paul's Episc. Ch., 1984. Recipient Woman of Distinction award Riverside (Calif.) City Coll., 1962; Leader of the '80's award Fund Improvement Post-Secondary Edn., 1983; fellow Claremont Grad. Sch., 1984, 85, 86. Mem. Calif. Community Coll. Librarians (sec.-treas. 1985), Citrus Coll. Faculty Assn. (sec. 1981-82), NEA, Calif. Tchrs. Assn. Democrat. Home: 474 E Chaparral Dr Claremont CA 91711 Office: Hayden Meml Library 1000 W Foothill Blvd Glendora CA 91740

BURLESON, CYNTHIA PERRYMAN, gallery owner; b. Atlanta, Dec. 18, 1946; d. William Marcus and Varnelle (Braddy) Perryman; m. James Weldon Burleson, Apr. 22, 1978. B.A., Agnes Scott Coll., 1968. Tchr., Atlanta, 1969-72; designer Vista Gallery, Decatur, Ga., 1972-77, owner, mgr., 1977—. Mem. Ga. Antiquarian Bookseller's Assn. Republican. Episcopalian. Avocations: watercolor painting; studying and collecting antique prints. Office: Vista Gallery 2840 La Vista Rd Decatur GA 30033

BURLESON, KAREN BRYANT TRIPP, lawyer; b. Rocky Mount, N.C., Sept. 2, 1955; d. Bryant and Katherine (Watkins) Tripp; m. Robert Mark Burleson, June 25, 1977. B.A., U. N.C., 1976; J.D., U. Ala., 1981. Bar: Tex. 1981, U.S. Dist. Ct. (so. dist.) Tex. 1982, U.S. Patent and Trademark Office 1981, U.S. Ct. Appeals (fed. cir.) 1983. Atty., Exxon Prodn. Research Co., Houston, 1981—; honor ct. justice U. Ala. Sch. Law, University, 1978-79. Contbr. articles to legal jours.; exec. editor Jour. Legal Profession, 1980-81, bd. editors, 1979-80. Treas. Student Bar Assn., U. Ala. Sch. Law, 1979-80. Recipient Am. Jurisprudence award, 1980; Dean's award U. Ala. Sch. Law, 1981. Mem. ABA, Houston Bar Assn. (internat. transfer of tech. com. 1983-84), Am. Intellectual Property Lawyers Assn., Houston Intellectual Property Lawyers Assn. (outstanding inventor com. 1982-84, student edn. com. 1985), Tex. Bar Assn., Bench and Bar, Phi Alpha Delta (clk. John Tyler Morgan chpt. 1979-80). Republican. Methodist. Office: Exxon Prodn Research Co PO Box 2189 Houston TX 77252

BURLEW, CANDACE LOUISE, lawyer, accountant; b. Greenville, S.C., July 5, 1946; d. Conover Herbert and Evelyn Louise (Galbraith) Burlew; m. Lewis M. Jones (div.); children—Amy, Robyn, Jeffrey. B.S. summa cum laude Lander Coll., 1979; J.D., U. S.C., 1982. Bar: S.C. 1982. acctg. lab. asst. Lander Coll., Greenwood, S.C., 1978-79; legal research asst. Lumpkin & Sherrill, Columbia, S.C., 1980-82; acct. Summersett & Babinec, Columbia, 1982; contracts atty. S.C. Dept. Social Services, Columbia, 1982-84; atty. adminstr. legal services S.C. Health and Human Services Fin. Com., 1984—. Vol., S.C. Republican party, Columbia, 1980-83. Recipient Scholastic awards Lander Coll., 1978, 79. Mem. ABA (coms.), S.C. Bar Assn., S.C. Bus. & Profl. Women, S.C. Trial Lawyers Assn., Blue Key, Alpha Chi, Alpha Kappa Psi, Phi Delta Phi. Episcopalian. Office: Adminstrv Legal Services SC Health and Human Services PO Box 8206 Columbia SC 29202

BURLEY, DELORES VIOLA, pediatric nurse; b. Balt., Oct. 23, 1939; d. Lemmie Mason and Thelma Irene (Baker) Wiltz; m. Bernard Burley, Oct. 23, 1966; children—Denise Antoinette, Lisa Michelle, Dwight. Student Franklin Sq. Hosp. Sch. Nursing, U. Md., 1965; R.N., Johns Hopkins U., 1974; postgrad. Coll. of Notre Dame, Balt., 1985. Cert. pediatric nurse practitioner. Staff nurse Franklin Sq. Hosp., Balt., 1965-66, asst. supr., 1965-66; staff nurse Balt. City Health Dept., 1966-74, pediatric nurse practitioner, 1974—; cons. Balt. City Schs., Balt. City Health Dept., 1975—. Bd. dirs. Foster Care Rev. Bd., Balt., 1982—; fin. sec. Urban Services Agy.; pastor's aide Waters A.M.E. Ch., Balt. 1984—. Named Community Health Nurse of Yr., Balt. City Health Dept., 1977. Mem. Am. Nurses Assn., Nat. Assn. for Pediatric Nurse Assocs. and Practitioners, Black Nurses Assn. of Balt. Democrat. Avocations: reading; bowling.

BURLINGAME, VIRGINIA SIMS, family therapist; b. Chgo., Mar. 30, 1930; d. Paul J. and Pauline Sims; B.A., Blackburn Coll., 1952; M.S. In Social Service, Boston U., 1955; Ph.D. in Psychology, Northwestern U., 1982; m. Leroy J. Burlingame, July 1954 (div. 1982); children—Elizabeth, John. Tchr., Carlinville (Ill.) Jr. High Sch., 1951-52; child welfare worker Rockford (Ill.) Dept. Child Welfare, 1953-54; caseworker Children's Aid of Boston, 1955-56; sch. social worker Rockford Public Schs., 1956-58; psychiat. caseworker Bacon Clinic, Racine, 1960-62; caseworker Children's Service Soc., Racine and Kenosha, 1966-72; dir. Big Sisters of Racine, 1973-75; clin. therapist Family Service Racine, 1976-78; dir. People Power Potential, 1978—; pvt. practice marital and family therapy, Racine, 1982—; cons. Southeastern Wis. Med. and Social Services; counselor Holy Communion Lutheran Ch., 1980-84. Wis. co-chmn. John Anderson for Pres., 1981; pres. bd. Taylor Children's Home; mem. nat. steering com. Nat. Unity Party, Wis. state chairperson Nat. Unity Com.; bd. dirs. Family Service Racine, Racine Symphony, Racine Urban League, Girl Scouts, U.S.A., Racine, Unitarian Ch. Racine, also PTAs and nursery sch. bds. Mem. Acad. Clin. Social Work, Am. Assn. Marital and Family Therapy, Am. Psychol. Assn., NOW, Phi Delta Kappa. Unitarian. Address: 4637 Bluffside Dr Racine WI 53402

BURLISON, BEVERLY NADINE, financial consultant; b. Los Angeles, Dec. 23, 1937; d. Austin Thomas and Dorothy (Gaby) Hodges; m. Herbert Ichinose, 1982. B.A. in Econs., UCLA, 1959; M.B.A. in Fin., Rutgers U., 1972. Mgr. research info. systems Stanford U., 1972-76; asso. dir. Inst. Med. Sci., Heart Research Inst., San Francisco, 1976-82; pres., mng. editor Acad. Research Info. Systems, Inc., 1976-82; exec. dir. Frank Gerbode Med. Research Found., 1979-82, ALS and Neuromuscular Research Found., 1980-82; fin. officer program rev. com. NIH, 1978-81; pres. Beverly Burlison Assocs., Inc., 1982—; pres., chief exec. officer Ichinose Food Systems, Inc., 1986—; Ichinose Securities, Inc., 1984—. Mem. Fedn. Am. Scientists. Republican. Roman Catholic. Home: 3 Richmond Pl New Orleans LA 70115 also 1515 Poydras Suite 2220 New Orleans LA 70116

BURNER, FAYE ALICE, lawyer, musician; b. Jacksonville, Fla., Aug. 30, 1955; d. George Clark and Alice Frances (Leighton) B. B.A., Wesleyan Coll., Macon, Ga., 1977; J.D., U. Fla., 1979. Bar: Fla., 1980; U.S. Ct. Mil. Appeals, 1983. Sole practice law, Jacksonville, 1984—. Soloist St. John's Cathedral, Jacksonville, 1979—; singer Pro Nobis, Jacksonville, 1982-84, Riverside Chamber Singers, Jacksonville, 1981—, Jacksonville Madrigal Singers, 1982—. Served from lt. (j.g.) to lt. USN, 1980-84. Nat. Merit scholar, 1973-77. Mem. ABA, Jacksonville Bar Assn., Assn. Trial Lawyers Am., Law Assn. for Women (pres. Gainesville 1978-79). Democrat. Episcopalian. Home: 718 Oaks Manor Jacksonville FL 32211 Office: 720 N Ocean St Jacksonville FL 32202

BURNETT, ANNICE JOHNSON, excavating company executive; b. Knoxville, Tenn., Jan. 8, 1924; d. Meno and May Elizabeth (Patty) Johnson; m. John Cecil Burnett, Sept. 5, 1950 (dec. May 1973); children—Capitola, Ronda V., Karla J. Student pub. schs., Knoxville. Pres., Jay Burnett Co., Inc. Democrat. Baptist. Avocations: U. Tenn. football fan; traveling; bowling; camping; gardening. Home: 6411 Burnett Creek Rd Knoxville TN 37920 Office: Jay Burnett Co Inc 611 John Sevier Hwy Knoxville TN 37920

BURNETT, BILLIE ANN, equal employment specialist; b. Wilmington, N.C., July 11, 1942; d. William Elijah and Anna (Gardner) B. B.A., Knoxville Coll., 1964, M.S.W., Howard U., 1968. Med. social worker D.C. Gen. Hosp., 1968-70; student program specialist Nat. Urban Coalition, Washington, 1970-73; equal opportunity officer U.S. Corps of Engrs., Wilmington 1973-77, SBA, Atlanta, 1977-79; equal employment specialist, EEOC, Atlanta, 1979—. Active LWV, Atlanta, 1981-83. Mem. Federally Employed Women, Blacks in Govt., Nat. Assn. Female Execs.; Alpha Kappa Alpha. Democrat. Roman Catholic. Home: PO Box 41704 Atlanta GA 30331 Office: Equal Employment Opportunity Comm 75 Piedmont Ave NE Atlanta GA 30335

BURNETT, BRENDA BULLOCK, government agency official; b. Red Mountain, Calif., Apr. 12, 1941; d. Miles Wallace and Harriet Jane (Wittmeyer) Bullock; student U. Redlands, 1959-60, 61-62; B.A., U. Md., 1967; m. Daniel George Burnett, Oct. 3, 1970. With U.S. Navy, various locations, 1969—, asso. head budget div. Naval Weapons Center Office Fin. and Mgmt., China Lake, Calif., 1975-77, head reports and analysis br., 1977-78, head fin. mgmt. Br. A, 1978-81, mem. staff Hdqrs. Dept. Def. Schs. Ger., 1982-84, head plans and programs br., 1984—. Mem. Ridgecrest City Council, 1980-81; instr. Stop Smoking Clinic, Am. Cancer Soc.; founding mem. Maturango Mus., Ridgecrest. Mem. Am. Soc. Public Adminstrn., Am. Soc. Mil. Comptrollers, Naval Aviation Exec. Inst., NAACP. Democrat. Baptist. Home: 735 Sonja St Ridgecrest CA 93555 Office: Code 0825 Naval Weapons Center China Lake CA 93555

BURNETT, DONNA SUE, lawyer; b. Houston, Apr. 6, 1948; d. Travis E. and Yvonne (Thompson) B.; m. Gary B. Conine, Sept. 2, 1983. B.B.A. with highest honors, U. Tex., Austin, 1975; J.D. magna cum laude, U. Houston, 1980. Bar: Tex. 1980. Ptnr. firm Liddell, Sapp & Zivley, Houston, 1980—. Editor-in-chief Houston Law Rev., 1979-80. Mem. ABA, Houston Bar Assn., Nat. Assn. Bond Lawyers, Houston Law Rev. Alumni Assn., Order of Barons, Beta Gamma Sigma. Republican. Mem. Disciples of Christ Ch. Club: Jr. League (Houston). Home: 3422 Gannett Houston TX 77025 Office: Liddell Sapp & Zivley 3500 Texas Commerce Tower Houston TX 77002

BURNETT, JUDITH JANE, property management executive; b. Muncie, Ind., Aug. 21, 1947; d. Albert Ward and Jane M. (Collins) Burnett; student public schs. Saleswoman, Collins Mobile Home Sales, Muncie, 1970-73; sales mgr. HiWay, Inc., Anderson, Ind., 1973-75; service dir., then ops. mgr. Indiana Homemakers, Inc., Indpls., 1975-80, exec. v.p., 1980-83, also dir.; corp. sec. Mgmt. Alternatives, Inc., Indpls., 1984—; exec. v.p., dir. Three—I Homemakers, Inc., Illini Homemakers, Inc., 1980-83; dir. Home Care Med. Products Co., 1980-82; mem. council Central Ind. Health Systems Agy., 1980-83; mem. Homemaker, Handyman, Home Health Aide Task Force, 1980-83, sec., 1980-81. Mem. Nat. Assn. Female Exec., Network Women in Bus., Indpls. Met. Bd. Realtors, Nat. Fedn. Rep. Women. Republican. Baptist. Home: 9459 Timber View Dr Indianapolis IN 46250 Office: 777 E 86th St Indianapolis IN 46240

BURNETT, SUSAN WALK, personnel service company executive; b. Galveston, Tex., Aug. 21, 1946; d. Joe Decker and Ruth Corinne (Lowe) Walk; m. Rusty Burnett, Dec. 27, 1973; stepchildren—Barbara, Sara. B.A. in Journalism, U. Ark.-Fayetteville, 1968. Asst. pub. relations mgr. sta. KATV, Little Rock, 1968-69; speech writer Assoc. Milk Producers, Inc., Little Rock, 1969-70; mgr. Allied Personnel, Houston, 1970-74; owner Burnett Cos. Consol., Inc., Houston, 1974—. Speaker Job Search Seminars, Houston, 1984; worker Easter Seals Telethon. Recipient Appreciation awards Lyndon Johnson Space Ctr., NASA, 1983, State of Tex., 1984. Mem. Tex. Assn. Personnel Cons. (v.p. 1985), Houston Assn. Personnel Cons. (pres. 1986), Nat. Assn. Personnel Cons., Houston C. of C., Chi Omega Alumnae. Republican. Methodist. Avocations: Reading; golf; flying; sailing. Office: Burnett Cos Consol Inc 3300 S Gessner Suite 250 Houston TX 77063

BURNEY, VICTORIA KALGAARD, management consulting and training company executive; b. Los Angeles, Apr. 12, 1943; d. Oscar Albert and Dorothy Elizabeth (Peterson) Kalgaard; children—Kim Elizabeth, J. Hewett. B.A. with honors, U. Mont., 1965; M.A., U. No. Colo., 1980; postgrad. Webster U., St. Louis, 1983-84. Exec. dir. Hill County Community Action, Havre, Mont., 1966-67; community orgn. specialist ACCESS, Escondido, Calif., 1967-68; program devel. and community orgn. specialist Community Action Programs, Inc., Pensacola, Fla., 1968-69; cons. Escambia County Sch. Bd., Fla., 1969-71; pres. Kal Kreations, Kailua, Hawaii, 1974-77; instr., dir. office human resources devel. Palomar Coll., San Marcos, Calif., 1978-81; chief exec. officer IDET Corp., San Marcos, 1981—; cons. County of Riverside, Calif., 1983. Mem. San Diego County Com. on Handicapped, San Diego, 1979; cons. tribal resource devel., Escondido, Calif., 1979; mem. exec. com. Social Services Coordinating Council, San Diego, 1982-83; mem. pvt. sector com. and planning and rev. com. Calif. Employment and Tng. Adv. Council, Sacramento, 1982-83; bd. mgrs. Santa Margarita Family YMCA, Vista, Calif., 1984-85; bd. dirs. North County Community Action Program, Escondido, 1978, Casa de Amparo, San Luis Rey, Calif., 1980-83; mem. San Diego County Pub. Welfare Adv. Bd., 1979-83, chairperson, 1981; assoc. mem. Calif. Republican Central Com., Sacramento, 1984-85; ofcl. San Diego County Rep. Central Com., 1985. Mem. Nat. Assn. County Employment and Tng. Adminstrs. (chairperson econ. resources com. 1983-84), Calif. Assn. Local Econ. Devel., San Diego Econ. Devel. Corp., Oceanside Econ. devel. Council (bd. dirs. 1982-85), Oceanside C. of C., San Marcos C. of C. (bd. dirs. 1982-85), Carlsbad C. of C. (indsl. council 1982-85), Escondido C. of C. (comml. and indsl. devel. council 1982-85), Vista C. of C. (vice chairperson econ. devel. com. 1983-84), Vista Econ. Devel. Assn., Nat. Mgmt. Assn. (charter mem. North County chpt.), Nat. Job Tng. Partnership, Job Tng. Assn. San Diego, Am. Mgmt. Assns., San Diego County Golden Eagle Club, Oceanside Rep. Women's Club Federated. Office: IDET Corp 1125 Linda Vista Dr Suite 101 San Marcos CA 92069

BURNHAM, HELEN ANDERSON, librarian; b. Seattle; d. Andrew and Fredrika (Johnson) Anderson; m. Wesley Burnham, Oct. 23, 1948; children—Barbara, Laurie, Ray. B.S. in L.S., U. Wash., 1932, postgrad., 1932-33. Children's librarian Seattle Pub. Library, 1933-41, Bklyn. Pub. Library, 1941-49; dir. Croton Free Library, Croton-on-Hudson, N.Y., 1968-84, trustee, 1985—, co-chmn. fund raising campaign. Testified before nuclear Regulatory Commn., Concerned Parents about Indian Point, 1983; adv. bd. United Fund, 1981, 83; mem. Adult Edn. Adv. Bd., 1981—. Recipient Recognition for personal achievements and contbns. to community Croton Cortlandt Women's Ctr., 1980; Cert. of Merit, Town of Cortlandt and Village of Croton, 1985. Mem. Pub. Library Dirs. Assn. (exec. bd.), ALA, Westchester Library Assn., N.Y. State Library Assn., Common Cause. Home: 38 Devon Ave Croton-on-Hudson NY 10520 Office: Croton Free Library 171 Cleveland Dr Croton-on-Hudson NY 10520

BURNHAM, LEAH LUCILLE, medical technologist; b. Fergus Falls, Minn., July 31, 1947; d. Dresden Gordon and Helen Lucille (Keller) Taylor; B.S., Millikin U., 1969; M.S., U. Vt., 1972; m. Frederick R. Burnham, II, Dec. 8, 1973; children—Russell Adam, Laurel Helene. Blood bank technologist Luth. Hosp., Cleve., 1969-70; gen. technologist Lake Forest (Ill.) Hosp., 1970; teaching fellow U. Vt., Burlington, 1970-72; edn. coordinator Tucson Med. Center Sch. Med. Tech., 1972-74; sr. technologist in clin. toxicology Univ. Med. Ctr. U. Ariz. Health Scis. Ctr., Tucson, 1974—; conductor workshops in field. Mem. Am. Soc. Clin. Pathologists. Contbr. articles to profl. jours. Office: Clin Pathology Univ Med Center Tucson AZ 85724

BURNHAM, MARSHA LYNN, corporation tax manager, tax consultant; b. Milw., June 30, 1952; d. Jack Laverne and Mildred Arlene (Burquam) B. A.A., Valencia Community Coll., 1972; B.S. in Bus. Adminstrn., U. Central Fla., 1977; M.A., U. South Fla., 1985. C.P.A., Fla. Sr. tax acct. Price Waterhouse, Tampa, Fla., 1978-81; tax mgr. Paradyne Corp., Largo, Fla., 1981-85; tax mgr. Harcourt Brace Jovanovich, Inc., Orlando, Fla., 1985—; pvt. practice tax cons. Tampa, 1981—. Campaign mgr. United Way, Largo, 1983. Mem. Am. Inst. C.P.A.s, Fla. Inst. C.P.A.s. Republican. Presbyterian. Avocations: artist; traveling; racquetball; reading. Office: Harcourt Brace Jovanovich Inc Orlando FL32887

BURNS, ANNE MARIE, educator; b. Providence, Apr. 13, 1921; d. James B. and Annie (Hagan) B.; Ph.B., Providence Coll., 1964; M.A., U. Conn., 1965. Tchr., Providence Sch. Dept., 1961—, also nursing asst. R.I. Hosp., Providence, 1972—. Sec. del. to Democratic Nat. Conv., 1980; appeared in BBC TV film on Dem. Nat. Conv., 1980. Mem. Providence Tchrs. Union, R.I. Hist. Soc. Roman Catholic. Club: Cath. Women's. Home: 1 Sheila Ln Smithfield RI 02917 Office: 195 Nelson St Providence RI 02908

BURNS, BARBARA JO, outfitter, lodge manager, ranch manager, horse trainer; b. Memphis, July 10, 1944; d. DuMont Glyn and Lois Evelyn (Murray) Caskey; m. Virgil B. Burns, Dec. 31, 1967; children—Braiden J., Shannon Rae. Student Colo. State U., 1970-74. Sec. Martin Marietta, Denver, 1962-64; sec., bus. mgr. Bus. Communications, Aspen, Colo., 1964-67; sec., bookstore mgr. Colo. Mountain Coll., Glenwood Springs, Colo., 1967-71; mgr. cultural programs Colo. State U., Ft. Collins, 1971-75; outfitter, lodge and ranch mgr., horse trainer Bob Marshall Wilderness Ranch, Seeley Lake, Mont., 1975—. Home and Office: Bob Marshall Wilderness Ranch Seeley Lake MT 59868

BURNS, BRENDA ELIZABETH, news librarian; b. Chattanooga, Nov. 9, 1953; d. Everett Keith and Martha Luella (Graham) McMahon; m. Patrick Gregory Burns, Jan. 28, 1977. B.A., U. Ga., 1975; postgrad. U. Tex.-Permian Basin, Odessa, 1981. Adminstrv. asst. U.S. Dept. Agr., Atlanta, 1975-77; freelance ct. reporter, Atlanta, 1977-80; news librarian Gazette Telegraph, Colorado Springs, Colo., 1982—. Mem. Spl. Libraries Assn. (newspaper div.), German Shepherd Dog Club Am., Working Dog Assn., Phi Beta Kappa. Republican. Presbyterian. Avocations: photography, dog training. Office; Gazette Telegraph 30 S Prospect St Colorado Springs CO 80903

BURNS, CINDY LEE, nurse; b. Hobbs, N.Mex., Apr. 3, 1960; d. Donald Ray and Dixie Lee (Kimmel) Burns. B.S.N., Baylor U., 1982. R.N., Tex. Clin. nurse II thoracic ICU, Baylor Med. Ctr., Dallas, 1982—. Trainer, Evangelism Explosion, Dallas, 1983-84; instr. CPR, Dallas, 1982-84. Mem. Baylor U. Sch. Nursing Honor Soc. (v.p. 1982-83), Alpha Tau Delta, Sigma Theta Tau. Baptist. Address: 8849 Fair Oaks Crossing Apt 2072 Dallas TX 75243

BURNS, ELIZABETH MURPHY, media executive; b. Superior, Wis., Dec. 4, 1945; d. Morgan and Elizabeth (Beck) Murphy; m. Richard Ramsey Burns, June 24, 1984. Student U. Ariz., 1963-67. Promotion and programming sec. Sta. KGUN-TV, Tucson, 1967-68; programming and traffic sec. Sta. KFMB-TV, San Diego, 1968-69; owner, operator Sta. KKAR, Pomona, Calif., 1970-73; co-owner, pres. Morgan Murphy Stas., Madison, Wis., 1976—; dir. Nat. Guardian Life Ins. Co., various media stas. and corps. Mem. adv. bd. Wis. Chamber Orch., Madison, 1983—; bd. dirs. Duluth/Superior Symphony, Minn., 1985, TV Bur. of Advt.; bd. dirs. N.E. Midwest Inst., 1984—, now chmn. bd. dirs. Mem. Nat. Assn. Broadcasters, Wis. Broadcasters Assn. Republican. Roman Catholic. Clubs: Madison, Nakoma Country, Northland Country (Duluth). Avocations: golf, tennis, travel. Home: 180 Paine Farm Rd Duluth MN 55804 Office: Sta WISC-TV 7025 Raymond RD Madison WI 53711

BURNS, ELLEN BREE, judge; b. New Haven, Dec. 13, 1923; d. Vincent Thomas and Mildred Bridget (Bannon) B.; B.A., Albertus Magnus Coll., 1944, LL.D. (hon.), 1974; LL.B., Yale U., 1947; LL.D. (hon.), U. New Haven, 1981; m. Joseph Patrick Burns, Oct. 8, 1955 (dec.); children—Mary Ellen, Joseph Bree, Kevin James. Bar: Conn. 1947. Dir legis. legal services State of Conn., 1949-73; judge Conn. Circuit Ct., 1973-74; judge Conn. Ct. of Common Pleas, 1974-76; judge Conn. Superior Ct., 1976-78, U.S. Dist. Ct. for Dist. of Conn., New Haven, 1978—. Trustee Fairfield U., 1978—, Albertus Magnus Coll., 1985—. Recipient John Carroll of Carrolton award John Barry Council KC, 1973; Judiciary award Conn. Trial Lawyers Assn., 1978; Cross Pro Ecclesia et Pontifice, 1981. Mem. ABA, New Haven County Bar Assn., Am. Bar Found. Roman Catholic. Office: 141 Church St New Haven CT 06510

BURNS, FRANCES CAREY, home economist; b. Woodhaven, N.Y., Dec. 7, 1939; d. Robert F. and Florence (Bohne) Carey; B.S., Immaculata Coll., 1961; postgrad. Villanova U., 1964, U. Pa., 1962, Columbia U., 1976, Parsons New Sch., 1979; m. Gerald E. Burns, Apr. 4, 1978; 1 son, Thomas Gerald. Home service dir. mags. Macfadden Barteil Co., N.Y.C., 1971-74; cons. to food dir. Weight Watchers Internat., Inc., Manhasset, L.I., 1974-75; advt. home economist Best Foods Co., Englewood, N.J., 1975-76; restaurants mgr. Lord & Taylor Co., N.Y.C., 1976-77; freelance cons., N.Y.C., 1977-82. Treas., Assn. to Improve Abbington Sq. Park, 1979-81; research librarian Council Fin. Aid to Edn., 1983. Mem. Am. Home Econs. Assn., Home Economists in Bus., Immaculata Alumnae. Roman Catholic. Home: 310 W 11th St New York NY 10014

BURNS, GLADYS KING, political scientist, author; b. Gadsden, Ala., Feb. 7, 1927; d. Leslie Cooper and Gladys (Angle) King; B.A., Huntingdon Coll., Montgomery, Ala., 1963; M.A., Auburn (Ala.) U., 1965; Ph.D., U. Ala., 1977; m. J.A. Burns, 1946 (div. 1963); 1 child, Elizabeth King. Mem. faculty N.E. State Jr. Coll., Rainesville, Ala., 1965-66; prof. polit. sci. Jefferson State Coll., Birmingham, Ala., 1966—, dir. Women's Center, 1980, dir. sex. discriminaton Ala. Gen. Assistance Center, U. Ala., 1975-77. Mem. Ala. Hist. Assn., Internat. Platform Assn., DAR, Phi Alpha Theta, Kappa Delta Pi. Home: 1163 Montclair Rd Birmingham AL 35213 Office: Jefferson State Jr Coll 2601 Carson Rd Birmingham AL 35215

BURNS, GLORIA KELLEY, construction company executive; b. San Antonio, Sept. 19, 1944; d. E. Lloyd and Yvonne (McGarry) Kelley; m. Jerry W. Burns, July 19, 1965; children—Brian Kelley, Julie Marie. B.B.A., Abilene Christian U., 1966. Exec. sec. Gen. Motors Inst., Flint, Mich., 1966-68, Fidelity Advt., Inc., Abilene, Tex., 1968-69; office sec. Duncan Constrn., Florence, Ala., 1969-84, corp. sec., exec. v.p., dir., 1975—. Vice chmn. Bd. Zoning Adjustments, Florence, 1980—. Mem. Nat. Secs. Assn. Republican. Mem. Ch. of Christ. Home: 1708 Shennandoah Rd Florence AL 35630 Office: PO Box 100 5336 E Hough Rd Florence AL 35631

BURNS, JAN MARIE, hosiery company executive; b. Windsor, Ont., Can., Aug. 24, 1953; d. Alex James and Mary Carmen (Cipparone) Boegner; m. Dennis Ray Burns, May 24, 1980. Student Olivet Coll., 1971-72; B.S., Western Mich. U., 1975; student John Robert Powers Sch., Chgo., 1980. Tchr., Union City Schs., Mich., 1975-78; estimator Coleman Fireproof Co., Chgo., 1978-79; regional mgr. Marshalltown Inst., Hastings, Nebr., 1979-80; store mgr. Fantles, Marshalltown, Iowa, 1980-81; sales trainer Kayser-Roth Branded Products, Greensboro, N.C., 1981—. Active Big Bros./Big Sisters, Hastings, 1986—. Named Sales Rep. of Yr., Kayser-Roth Branded Products, 1984-85. Mem. Bur. Wholesale Sales Reps., Nat. Assn. Female Execs., Christian Women's Assn. Democrat. Roman Catholic. Avocations: travelling; snow skiing; reading. Home: 1927 W 12th St Hastings NE 68901 Office: Kayser-Roth Branded Products PO Box 77077 Greensboro NC 24717

BURNS, MARETTA JO, accountant; b. San Antonio, Nov. 7, 1941; d. Joseph Wallis and Mary (Shepard) Burns; B.B.A., Baylor U., 1962. Supervisory cost acctg. asst. Pueblo (Colo.) Army Depot, 1962-65; employment security advisor U.S. Dept. Labor, Denver, 1965-68, Seattle, 1968-70, cost acctg. task force, 1969-70, budget and acctg. officer, Denver, 1970-83, systems acct., 1983—, regional automated system redesign task force, 1979-80. Mem. Nat. Assn. Female Execs., Phi Gamma Nu, Beta Alpha Psi, Beta Gamma Sigma. Baptist. Home: 3784 S Quince St Denver CO 80237

BURNS, MARSHA MERTZ, personnel manager; b. San Antonio, Aug. 17, 1951; d. Eugene Marshall and Shirley Jean (Gower) Mertz; m. Timothy Robert Burns, Aug. 14, 1976. B.S. in Edn., Jacksonville U., 1972; postgrad. U. North Fla., 1975. Probation officer State of Fla., Jacksonville, 1973-76; psychiatric therapist Northside Community Mental Health Ctr., Tampa, Fla., 1976; job developer Orange County Govt., Orlando, 1977-78, auditor, 1978-80, EEO/AA officer, 1980-81; personnel mgr. Advt. Checking Bur., Inc., Orlando, 1981—. Mem. Am. Soc. Personnel Adminstrn., Central Fla. Personnel Assn., Mid-Fla. Homebuilders Assn. Aux. Republican. Roman Catholic. Home: 439 River Isle Ct Longwood FL 32779 Office: Advt Checking Bur Inc 1010 Executive Center Dr Suite 251 Orlando FL 32803

BURNS, MARY L., laboratory administrator; b. Bridgeport, Conn., Jan. 21, 1955; d. Laurence Bertram and Edna Mary (Firmenich) Ford; m. William Luke Burns, III; Sept. 2, 1978; children—William Luke IV, Matthew Laurence. Student Coll. of Racine, Holy Family Coll.; B.A. in Chemistry, Lewis U., 1976. Lab. technician Econs. Lab., Joliet, Ill., 1976-79; lab. supr. Lake River Packaging, Berwyn, Ill., 1979-81, Lake River Terminals, Berwyn, 1981—. Mem. ASTM, Ill. Mfg. Assn., Am. Chem. Soc., Ind. Liquid Terminals Assn. Office: Lake River Corp Terminals Div 5005 S Harlem Ave Berwyn IL 60402

BURNS, NORMA DECAMP, architect; b. N.Y.C., Dec. 14, 1940; d. Cyrus and Stella (Werner) DeCamp; m. Robert Paschal Burns, Dec. 4, 1973; 1 child, Linda Paige. B.S., Fla. State U., 1962; M.Arch., N.C. State U., 1976. Registered architect, N.C. Tchr., high schs., Fla., Md., 1962-73; pres., owner Burnstudio Architects, P.A., Raleigh, N.C., 1977—, WorkSpace, Inc., 1981—. Past chmn. City of Raleigh Appearance Commn.; mem. Land Use Com. Triangle J Council Govts.; mem. Downtown Adv. Com. Raleigh; bd. advisers Historic Preservation Found. N.C., Raleigh, 1985—; mem. Bus. Adv. Council Peace Coll., Raleigh, 1985—; councillor-at-large Raleigh City Council, mem. comprehensive planning com.; law and fin. com. Recipient numerous awards including Owens Corning Energy award, 1984; Adaptive Reuse award Durham Preservation Soc., 1983, 84; cited in Ten Best Designs, Time Mag., 1984. Mem. AIA (nat. interiors com. 1981-84, nat. design com. 1985, chmn. N.C. historic resources com.), Nat. Trust for Historic Preservation.

BURNS, PATRICIA RAND, fragrance developer; b. N.Y.C., Jan. 30, 1953; d. Gerhard A. and Lisa (Peterson) Rand; m. Barrett Burns, Sept. 26, 1981. A.A., Pine Manor Coll., 1973; A.B., NYU, 1975. Fragrance evaluator, Roure Bertrand DuPont Co., Teaneck, N.J., 1975-76; mgr. product testing Estee Lauder Co., N.Y.C., 1976-77, product mgr. make up, 1977-78, product mgr. fragrance, 1978-79, dir. corp. fragrance devel., 1979-83. Mem. Cosmetic Exec. Women Jr. League Houston. Republican. Presbyterian. Clubs: Nantucket (Mass.) Yacht; Am. Yacht (Rye, N.Y.). Home: 9128 N 55th St Paradise Valley AZ 85253

BURNS, SANDRA KAYE, lawyer, educator; b. Bryan, Tex., Aug. 9, 1949; d. Clyde W. and Bert (Rychlik) B.; 1 child, Scott. B.S., U. Houston, 1970; M.A., U. Tex., 1972, Ph.D., 1975; J.D., St. Mary's U., 1978. Bar: Tex. 1978; cert. tchr., adminstr., supr., Tex. Tchr., Austin pub. schs., Tex., 1970-71; field coordinator depts. child devel./family life and home econs. tchr. edn. Coll. Nutrition, Textiles and Human Devel., Tex. Woman's U., Denton, 1974-75; lectr. Our Lady of the Lake Coll., San Antonio, 1975; instructional devel. asst., office ednl. resources, div. instructional devel. U. Tex. Health Sci. Ctr., San Antonio, 1976-77; legis. aide to Tex. State Senator Wm. T. Moore, Austin, 1978; clk.-counsel Tex. State Senate Com. on State Affairs, 1979; internat. legal cons. Colonbotti & Assocs., Aberdeen, Scotland, 1980; lectr. Tex. A&M U., 1981; contracted to Republic Energy, Inc., Bryan, Tex., 1981-82; sole practice, 1981-82; house counsel First Internat. Oil & Gas, Inc., Dallas, 1983; contracted to Humble Exploration Co., Inc., Dallas, 1984, ARCO, Dallas, 1985—. Contbr. articles to law jours. Mem. ABA, Am. Petroleum Inst., Delta Theta Phi, State Bar Tex., Kappa Delta Pi, Phi Delta Kappa, Phi Kappa Phi, Pi Lambda Theta. Methodist. Lodge: Daus. of the Republic of Texas. Avocations: water sports; collecting crystals. Office: 12126 Forestwood Circle Dallas TX 75244

BURNS, VICTORIA LEE, data processing consultant; b. Tulsa, July 18, 1954; d. Robert Otis and Virginia Lovina (White) Martin; m. William Michael Burns, Dec. 18, 1982. Student U. Tulsa, 1971-75. Assoc. systems analyst Sperry Co., Tulsa, 1975-77, sr. systems analyst, 1979-83; computer analyst City of Tulsa, 1978-79; systems specialist AES, Houston, 1983-84; owner Nat. Postal Ctr., Houston, 1984—. Sec. Bus. and Profl. Women, Tulsa, 1978-79; pres. West Airport Homeowners Assn., Houston, 1983-86. Mem. Data Processing Mgmt. Assn., Am. Prodn. and Inventory Control Soc., Kappa Delta. Republican. Roman Catholic. Home: 12003 Ripple Glen Houston TX 77071

BURNS-BLAGMON, DJUANA PHAE, public health analyst; b. Little Rock, Oct. 4, 1944; d. James Venice and Cleopatra (Diamond) Burns; student Little Rock U., 1964; B.S. in Zoology, Howard U., 1966; postgrad. U.S. Dept. Agr. Grad. Sch., 1970-71, also Am. Soc. Clin. Pathologists, Hawaii, 1SH, Paris and Montreal, Que., Can.; m. Lowell E. Blagmon, Aug. 29, 1981; 1 child, Vache Nieri. Histotechnologist, Georgetown U. Med. Sch., Washington, 1966-68; research technologist Washington Hosp. Center Research Found., 1968-69; cardiopulmonary research technologist Hosp. for Sick Children, Washington, 1969; med. technologist, supr. hematology Bur. of Lab., D.C. Dept. Pub. Health, 1969-77; Medicaid program specialist in lab. sci., pub. health analyst D.C. Commn. Pub. Health, Washington, 1978—; leader surveillance/utilization rev. team for nat. certification of D.C. Medicaid Mgmt. Info. System, 1982; cons./adviser to various orgns. and agys. Dancer, D.C. Recreation Dept. Showmobile, 1967; mem. community modeling group for charitable orgns., 1971-73. Recipient longevity sevice award D.C. Govt., 1980, sustained excellence in job performance award, 1983, outstanding job performance award, 1984; cert. in hematology U.S. Communicable Disease Center. Mem. Am. Soc. Clin. Pathologist (asso. mem., cert. in histology), Am. Pub. Health Assn., Am. Inst. Biol. Scis., AAUW, D.C. Neighborhood Health Center Technologists (rec./corr. sec. 1970-74). Methodist. Club: Bridge. Contbr. article to profl. jours. Home: 9801 Justina Ct Lanham MD 20706 Office: 1331 H St NW Suite 601 Washington DC 20005

BURNSIDE, MARY ARDIS, psychologist; b. Milw., May 14, 1950; d. Glenn Grover and Edna Mae Chrystine (Mueller) B.; B.A., Rice U., 1972; M.A., U. Houston, 1976, Ph.D., 1980; m. Bruce Edward Anderson, July 17, 1973; children—Aaron Hunter Anderson-Burnside, Andrew Chase Anderson-Burnside. Clin. asst. prof. dept. psychiatry Baylor Coll. Medicine, Houston, 1980—; adj. faculty psychology dept. U. Houston, 1984—, Rice U., 1986—. Lic. psychologist, Tex. Mem. Am. Psychol. Assn., Tex. Psychol. Assn., Houston Psychol. Assn., Phi Kappa Phi. Office: 4710 Bellaire Blvd Suite 160 Bellaire TX 77401

BURPULIS, EUGENIA G., telecommunications manager; b. Salem, N.J., Nov. 21, 1942; d. George S. and Thelma G. (Pirovolos) B. Student Kent State U., 1961-62, Tri-C Coll., Cleve., 1976. Operator, Ohio Bell Telephone Co., Cleve., 1961-62, supr., 1965-71, asst. mgr., 1972-75, course developer, 1975-78, mgr., 1978—. Loan exec. City of Cleve., 1984; adminstrv. sec. bd. trustees St. Demetrios Ch., 1986. Mem. Nat. Soc. Performance and Instrn., Am. Bus. Women's Assn. Republican. Greek Orthodox. Clubs: Women's Guild, Philoptochos. Avocations: writing; tennis; crafts. Home: 35270 Drake Rd North Ridgeville OH 44039 Office: Ohio Bell Telephone Co 45 Erieview Pl Suite 704 Cleveland OH 44114

BURR, CYNTHIA M., insurance company executive; A.A., Hartford Coll. for Women, 1953; B.A., Conn. Coll., 1955. With Conn. Gen. Life Ins. Co., Hartford, 1955—, supr. fin. reporting cont. dept., 1972, asst. sec., 1973-74, asst. sec., 1974-75, asst. dir. corp. devel. mgmt. services, 1974-76, dir. mgmt. services, 1976-77, 2d v.p. mgmt. services dept., 1977-78, 2d v.p. corp. personnel ops., 1978-80, v.p. personnel ops., 1980-83, sr. v.p. group pension, 1983—. Address: Conn Gen Life Ins Co PO Box 2975 Hartford CT 06104*

BURR, DEANNE MARIE, software design engineer; b. Brookings, S.D., Oct. 30, 1959; d. Arthur Dean and Derla Jean (Yada) B. B.S., Iowa State U., 1982. Cert. computer engr. Software design engr. Tex. Instruments, Dallas, 1982—. Programmer Blood Drive Program, Ames, Iowa, 1981; pres. O'Bryan House, Ames, Iowa, 1981. Mem. IEEE, Soc. Women Engrs. (pres. Ames 1981), Iowa State Alumni Assn. of Dallas (pres. 1982—). Home: 718 Prairie Creek Dr Princeton TX 75077 Office: Tex Instruments Hwy 380 McKinney TX

BURRAS, OUIDA MAE, ultrasonic cleaning specialist; b. Wewoka, Okla., July 2, 1934; d. James Shafter and Winona (Phillips) Read; m. Marland Lee Mitchell, Apr. 28, 1952 (div. Sept. 1975); children—Pamela Marie, Michael Lee, Carol Anne; m. 2d Samuel Thomas Burras, Sept. 3, 1983. Student Fluid Power Cylinder Sch., 1974. Inside saleswoman Tex-A-Droulic, Houston, 173-76; outside saleswoman Fluid Connectors, Houston, 1976-78, Thrust Hudraulics, Houston, 1978-79; saleswoman Air-Hydraulic, Houston, 1979-81, TEI Fluid Power, Houston, 1981-82; v.p. Fil-Clean Corp., Houston, 1982—, also dir. Mem. Fluid Power Soc. Republican. Baptist. Office: Fil-Clean Corp 6005 Milwee St Suite 921-J Houston TX 77092

BURROUGHS, BONNIE LEIGH, commercial artist, advertising executive; b. Appleton, Wis., July 4, 1950; d. Robert J. and Charlotte (Clausen) B.; children—John B. Zacherl, Paul B. Zacherl. Student Marian Coll., Fond du Lac, Wis. Media dir., artist understudy James Spallas & Assocs., Fond du Lac, 1969-75; artist, art dept. Mercy Marine, Fond du Lac, 1970-73; pres. Burroughs & Assocs., Fond du Lac, 1980—. Mem. County Bd. Suprs., Fond du Lac, 1979-81; bd. dirs., pres. Fond du Lac County Legal Aux.; bd. dirs. Fond du Lac County Hist. Soc., 1980—. Mem. Fond du Lac C. of C., Fond du Lac Home Builders. Avocations: tennis, reading, swimming, golf. Home: 86 Martin Pl Fond du Lac WI 54935 Office: Burroughs & Assocs 76 S Macy St Fond du Lac WI 54935

BURROUGHS, MARGARET TAYLOR GOSS, artist, former museum director; b. St. Rose, La., Nov. 1, 1917; d. Alexander and Octavia (Pierre) Taylor; m. Bernard Goss, 1937; 1 dau., Gayle; m. Charles Burroughs, 1949; 1 adopted son, Paul. B.A. in Edn, Art Inst. Chgo., 1946, M.A., 1948; L.H.D. (hon.), Lewis U., 1972; D.H.L. (hon.), Chgo. State U., 1983. Tchr. art Chgo. Public Schs., 1944-68; prof. humanities Kennedy King Coll., Chgo., 1969-79; exec. dir. DuSable Mus. African Am. History, Chgo., 1961-84, dir. emeritus, 1984—; group shows include: Los Angeles County Mus., 1976, Corcoran Gallery, 1980; mem. Chgo. Council Fine Arts, 1976-80, Nat. Commn. Negro History and Culture, 1981—; founder Nat. Conf. Artists, 1959. Fellow Nat. Endowment Humanities, 1968. Office: Dusable Museum 740 E 56th Pl Chicago IL 60657*

BURROUGHS, PAULINE HUFF, social worker; b. Carlton, Ga., Mar. 20, 1926; d. Arthur W. and Mattie E. (Huff) Huff; Ph.B., Northwestern U., 1952; M.S.W., Loyola U. Chgo., 1955; M.Ed., DePaul U., 1958; postgrad. U. Chgo. and Smith Coll., 1970-71; m. Stanley A. Burroughs, Mar. 9, 1972. Tchr., Bd. Edn., Chgo., 1956-60, 64; clin. social worker VA Hosp., Buffalo, 1960-62; clin. social worker psychiatry VA Hosp., Tomah, Wis., 1963-65; med. clin. social worker VA Hosp., Hines, Ill., 1965-66; clin. social worker psychiatry VA Hosp., Northport, N.Y., 1966-74; field experience supr. SUNY, VA Hosp., Northport, 1968-74; social worker VA Hosp., Battle Creek, Mich., 1974-76; cons., counseling therapist in pvt. practice, Chgo., 1977—; lectr. in field. Recipient award for superior performance in social work VA Hosp., Northport, 1970, others; cert. social worker, Ill., N.Y. Mem. Nat. Assn. Social Workers (registered clin. social worker), Acad. Social Workers, Council on Social Work Edn., Am. Soc. Profl. and Exec. Women, Nat. Assn. Female Execs., AAUW. Office: PO Box 49365 Chicago IL 60649

BURROUGHS, VIRGINIA LAKE, community arts coordinator, writer, photographer; b. Dayton, Ohio, Dec. 9, 1946; d. Otis F. and Josephine A. (Murlin) Lake; m. Herbert Kennon Burroughs, Aug. 20, 1973 (dec. 1980); children—Herbert, Veronica. B.F.A., U. Dayton, 1972; M.Humanities, Wright State U., 1985. Art cons. Dayton Bd. Edn., 1968-69, tchr., 1970-77; arts instr. Living Arts Ctr., Dayton, 1973-76; freelance writer, photographer Dayton newspapers, 1979-82; coordinator Hale Ch.'s Neighborhood Fine Arts Program, Dayton, 1980—; grad. teaching asst. Wright State U., 1982-84; dir. Dayton Children's Theater, 1983-84; speaker and workshop leader for various civic, ch., ednl. groups, 1978—; producer, hostess cable TV series on arts. Author, illustrator: (pre-sch. books) The Herbie Series, 1978; contbr. articles to mags., ch. publs., art criticism to Dayton Jour. Herald, Dialogue: an Art Jour., Art and Artists, New Art Examiner. Represented in permanent photog. collection Dayton Art Inst. Visual art rep. Miami Valley Arts Council, Dayton, 1981—; chmn. arts Dayton 1st Black Cultural Arts Festival, 1982; arts coordinator Goodwill Industries Art Affairs, Dayton, 1981, Jewish Community Ctr. Arts Knosh, Dayton, 1982. Recipient Humanitarian Service award United Cerebral Palsy Greater Dayton, 1980; Meritorious Service award Hale United Ch. of Christ, 1980. Mem. Dayton City Beautiful Council, Women in Communications, United Ch. of Christ Arts Fellowship. Democrat. Office: Hale United Ch of Christ's Neighborhood Fine Arts Program 200 Delaware Ave Dayton OH 45405

BURROUGHS-MARSH, LAROYCE CARRIE, legal fund administrator; b. Phila., Dec. 31, 1958; d. Leroy Theodore and Juanita (Williams) B.; m. Donald Keith Marsh, July 26, 1986. B.B.A., Rutgers U., 1982. Computer mgmt. system operator, Westat Research, Lawnside, N.J., 1976-79, supr. 1979-82; fund editor Laborers Edn. and Tng. Fund, Phila., 1982-84; fund adminstr. Laborers Prepaid Legal Fund, Phila., 1984—. Mem. from Lawnside Borough, N.J. Motion Picture Assn., Newark, 1984—. Mem. Internat. Found. Employee Benefits, Pa. Found., Delaware Valley Adminstrs. Assn. Democrat. Baptist. Avocations: photography; racquetball; traveling. Office: Laborers Prepaid Legal Fund 661 N Broad St Philadelphia PA 19123

BURROW, DONNA GALE, business systems analyst; b. Chgo., Sept. 21, 1952; d. Robert William and Lois Muriel (Eich) B.; m. Richard Burrow. B.S., Western Ill. U., 1974; M.B.A., Ball State U., 1981. Cert. systems profl. Phys. (program) dir. YMCA, Anderson, Ind., 1976-79; mgr. internal systems Mktg. Decisions, Inc., Woodland Hills, Calif. and Mpls., 1981-83; sr. systems analyst RCA Direct Mktg., Indpls., 1983—. Mem. Am. Mktg. Assn., Assn. Systems Mgmt. (cert. systems profl.), Mktg. Research Assn. Office: RCA Direct Mktg 6500 E 30th St Indianapolis IN 46219

BURROWES, HELENA, pharmacist; b. Clarkton, N.C., June 1, 1948; d. Ardrey H. and Zella (Jacobs) White; m. Astley S.E. Burrowes, Aug. 23, 1969; children—Tamara R., Lawrence J. B.S. in Biology, A&T State U., Greensboro, N.C., 1970; B.S. in Pharmacy, U. N.C.-Chapel Hill, 1975. Staff pharmacist Children's Hosp Nat. Med. Ctr., Washington, 1975-78; staff pharmacist Hadley Meml. Hosp., Washington, 1978-82, asst. dir. pharmacy services, 1982-85, dir. pharmacy services, 1985—; instr. hypertension class, 1982-83; sec. League Intravenous Therapy of Edn., Springfield, Va., 1982-83. Mem. Am. Soc. Hosp. Pharmacists. Home: 5407 19th Ave Hyattsville MD 20782 Office: Hadley Meml Hosp 4601 Martin Luther King Jr Ave SW Washington DC 20032

BURSON, ANNE TRIBBY, educator, consultant; b. St. Petersburg, Fla., Nov. 18, 1947; d. David Eugene and Ruth Louise (Mennen) Tribby; m. Ralph Taber Burson, Jan. 3, 1981. A.A., St. Petersburg Jr. Coll., 1967; B.A., U. S. Fla., 1969, M.A., 1974. Cert. tchr., Fla. Tchr., Clearwater Central Cath. High Sch., Fla., 1969-74; media specialist Dunedin Comprehensive High Sch., Fla., 1974—; cons. in field. Co-chmn. Dunedin High Sch. So. Assn. Evaluation, 1984—. Mem. Fla. Assn. Media in Edn., Pinellas Assn. Librarians and Media Specialists (sec. 1976-77), Pinellas County Tchrs. Assn. (faculty rep. 1976-80), Delta Kappa Gamma. Republican. Lutheran. Home: 2439 Indian Trails E Palm Harbor FL 33563 Office: Dunedin High Sch 1651 Pinehurst Rd Dunedin FL 33528

BURSTEIN, KAREN SUE, state civil service official; b. Bklyn., July 20, 1942; d. Herbert and Beatrice (Sobel) B. B.A., Bryn Mawr Coll., 1964; postgrad. Fisk U., 1964-65, New Sch. for Social Research, 1965; J.D., Fordham U., 1970. Bar: N.Y. 1971, U.S. Dist. Ct. (ea. and so. dist.) N.Y. 1971. Mem. faculty Fisk U., Nashville, 1965; film editor Colorvision Inc., N.Y.C., 1966; staff atty. Nassau County Law Service, N.Y., 1970-72; mem. N.Y. State Senate, Nassau County, 1972-78; spl. prof. law Hofstra U., N.Y., 1976-78; commr. Pub. Service Commn., Albany, 1978-80; exec. dir. Consumer Protection Bd., Albany, 1981-83; pres. Civil Service Commn., Albany, 1983—; chair Temp. Commn. on Workers' Compensation, Albany, 1984-86; co-chair Gov.'s Commn. on Domestic Violence, Albany, 1978—; pres. Ctr. for Women in Govt., Albany, 1979-83; co-leader govt. ofcls., labor leaders and academics to study pub. sector productivity in Japan, 1984. Contbr. articles and chpts. to profl. jours. and books. Del. Dem. Nat. Conv., N.Y.C., 1976, Am. Council Young Polit. Leaders Delegation to Soviet Union, 1979, Nat. Women' Conf., Houston, 1977; bd. Nat. Governing Council of Am. Jewish Congress; bd. dirs. Ctr. for Women in Govt., Empire State Day Care Service Inc., NCCJ. Recipient Lifetime Achievement award L.I. Nassau chpt. NOW, 1986, Outstanding Service award South Shore div. Am. Jewish Congress, Personal Devel. award Bus. & Profl. Women's Club of N.Y., Humanitarian award L.I. Rehab. Assn., Myrtle Wreath Achievement award Nassau Region Hadassah, Women of Action award B'nai B'rith Women, Benjamin Potokin award N.Y. State Employees Brotherhood Com. Mem. Coalition to Free Soviet Jews (exec. bd. dirs.), Nassau County Bar Assn., NAACP, Nat. Council Jewish Women, Wilderness Soc. Lodge: Hadassah. Office: New York State Civil Service Commn W Averell Harriman State Campus Albany NY 12239

BURSTEIN, ROSE ANNE KORNBLUM, librarian; b. N.Y.C., May 3, 1922; d. M.J.C. and Myrille (Soloman) Kornblum; m. Lucien Burstein, Nov. 15, 1943; children—Barton M., Emily M., Daniel. A.B. with honors, Olivet Coll., 1943; M.A., Yale U., 1949; M.S. with honors, Sch. Library Sci., Columbia U., 1965. Econ. analyst U.S. Dept. State, Washington, 1944-45; reference librarian New Haven Pub. Library, 1947-48; research librarian advt. agys., N.Y.C., 1949-52; library staff Sarah Lawrence Coll., Bronxville, N.Y., 1956—, library dir., 1974—; mem. N.Y. State Librarians' Task Force on Statewide Serials Database, 1979. Editor: Westchester Union List of Serials, 3d edit., 1979. Bd. vistors Pratt Grad. Sch. Library and Info. Sci., Bklyn., 1981—; trustee METRO: N.Y. Met. Reference and Research Library Agy., 1982—. Mem. ALA, N.Y. Library Assn., Westchester Library Assn. Office: Esther Raushenbush Library Sarah Lawrence Coll Glen Washington Rd Bronxville NY 10708

BURSTYN, ELLEN, actress; b. Detroit, Dec. 7, 1932; d. John Austin and Coriene Marie (Hamel) Gillooly; student pub. schs., Detroit; 1 son, Jefferson Jack. Appeared in: (films) Tropic of Cancer, 1970; Alex in Wonderland, 1970; The Last Picture Show (Acad. Award nomination for Best Supporting Actress; awards N.Y. Film Critics, Nat. Soc. Film Critics), 1971; The King of Marvin Gardens, 1972; The Exorcist (Acad. award nomination Best Actress), 1973; Harry and Tonto, 1974; Alice Doesn't Live Here Anymore (Acad. award Best Actress), 1974; Providence, 1977; A Dream of Passion, 1978; Same Time Next Year, 1978; Resurrection, 1980; Silence of the North, 1980; (Broadway play) Same Time Next Year, 1974-75 (Tony award Best Actress 1974-75); mem. corp. bd. Actors Studio, 1975—, co-artistic dir., 1982—; mem. corp. bd. Actor's Equity, pres., 1982. Office: care Todd Smith Creative Artists Agency 1888 Century Park E Los Angeles CA 90067

BURT, JOHANNA, real estate executive; b. Jamaica, W.I., May 10, 1926; came to U.S., 1958; d. Josephus and Cottilda (Ayre) Blake; m. Walter Lloyd Burt, Mar. 3, 1950 (div. 1962); 1 child, Walter Evon. Sr. Cambridge cert. Kingston Tutorial Coll. Dir. nurses Williamsbridge Manor Nursing Home, N.Y.C., 1972-74; pres. J.B. Inventions, Orlando, Fla., 1981—, J.B. Properties, Orlando, 1985—. Patentee spacer game. Pres., Williamsbridge Mchts. Assn., 1975-78; campaign worker Democratic congl. elections, New Rochelle, N.Y., 1982, 83. Served with Brit. Women's Royal Aux. Corps, 1948-50. Mem. Am. Nurses Assn., Gen. Nursing Council for Eng. and Wales, Jamaica Gen. Trained Nurses Assn., Nat. Assn. Female Execs., Nat. Assn. Negro Bus. and Profl. Women's Clubs (corr. sec. New Rochelle club). Democrat. Episcopalian. Avocations: reading, gardening, volunteer work. Home: 2125 Palm Vista Dr Orlando FL 32712

BURT, LAURA ELLEN, accountant, credit union executive; b. Galveston, Tex., May 8, 1954; d. Howard and Helen (Wilson) B. B.S., Trinity U., 1976. C.P.A., Tex. Staff acct. A. Burke Haymes & Co., Houston, 1976-77; acct. Simmonds & Co., San Antonio, 1977-81, ptnr., acct. Burt & Co., 1981—; pres. treas. San Antonio Womens Credit Union, 1981—. Contbr. articles to profl. jours. Treas. Pecan Valley Arts Ctr., San Antonio, 1978-83; pres. River City Divers, San Antonio, 1982-83; treas. San Antonio Women's Soccer Assn., 1983-85; bd. dirs. San Antonio council Girl Scouts U.S.A., 1984—; asst. to chmn. Women's Polit. Caucus of Bexar County, San Antonio, 1984-85. Mem. Am. Inst. C.P.A.s, Tex. Soc. C.P.A.s, Women in Bus. Republican. Episcopalian. Avocations: scuba diving; soccer; horseback riding; sewing. Office: Burt & Co Inc 15600 San Pedro #202 San Antonio TX 78232

BURT-EDWARDS, BARBARA, English language educator, lawyer; b. Paterson, N.J., Jan. 13, 1945; d. Edward Lee and Jane (Kennedy) Knopf; m. Richard Allen Burt, June 1, 1968 (div. 1978); children—Jennifer Ashley, Richard Allen; m. 2d, William Green Edwards, Nov. 26, 1980. Student Syracuse U., 1962-63; B.A., Kenne Coll., 1966; M.A., U. Miami, 1968, J.D., 1982. Tchr., Newark Bd. Edn., 1966-67, Dade County Bd. Edn., Miami, Fla., 1968-72; asst. project dir. Ministerial Alliance, Miami, 1976-77; assoc. prof. English, Miami-Dade Community Coll., 1977—, assoc. dean, 1985-86. Mem. Nat. Testing Network in Writing, Coll. English Assn., Fla. Assn. Community Colls., ABA, Assn. Trial Lawyers Am., Am. Judicure Soc., LWV. Home: 8465 SW 147th St Miami FL 33158 Office: Miami-Dade Community Coll 11011 SW 104th St Miami FL 33158

BURTNER, SUSAN BURNS, govt. ofcl.; b. Chgo., Nov. 30, 1942; d. William Grady and Margaret (MC Donald) Burns; B.A., Purdue U., 1964; M.S.L.S., U. Ill., 1967; M.A., George Washington U., 1979; m. Carrol E. Burtner, June 7, 1980. Catalog librarian HEW, Washington, 1967; librarian U.S. Air Force, Japan, 1968-70, Dept. Commerce, Washington, 1970-73; chief readers services Gen. Acctg. Office Library, Washington, 1973-75, library dir., 1975-80, dir. Office Info. Systems and Services, 1980-81, dep. dir. gen. services and controller div., 1981—. Mem. Spl. Library Assn., ALA. Roman Catholic. Home: 4013 N Tazewell St Arlington VA 22207 Office: General Services & Controller General Accounting Office Washington DC 20548

BURTON, ANN MCKAY, recreational center merchandise executive; b. Gainesville, Fla., July 12, 1949; d. Eli Osborne and Genevive (Agnew) McKay; m. Jeffrey Wade Burton, June 30, 1951; 1 child, Christopher Matthew. Student in marine biology U. South Fla., 1967-71. With Walt Disney World, 1971—, head retail design and bldg. project EPCOT Ctr., Burbank, Calif., 1979-82, mdse. mgr. EPCOT Ctr., Lake Buena Vista, Fla., 1982, mgr. mdse. Walt Disney World Resort Hotels, 1983-84, mgr. Magic Kingdom, Resorts, and EPCOT Ctr. for Human Resources and Devel., 1984-85, mdse. and retail sales mgr. Magic Kingdom, 1985—. Active United Way, 1976. Presbyterian.

BURTON, ANNA MARJORIE, nurse; b. Pontiac, Mich., May 1, 1931; d. Harold Vale and Sophia (Eaton) Kelly; m. Alexander Frank Burton; children—Julie A. Burton Stone, William A., Rory R., Kenneth G. Student Mich. State U., 1949-51; A.A., Fla. Keys Community Coll., 1976, A.S. in Nursing, 1983; R.N., Fla., Calif., N.Y. Orthodontic technician Birmingham, Mich., 1960-67; claims rep. Social Security Adminstrn., Lexington, Ky., 1967-71, Key West, Fla., 1972-79; pvt. duty nurse. Recipient Appreciation award Vets. Council, 1974; hon. Conch and Key, City of Key West, 1974. Mem. U.S. Coast Guard Aux (comdr. 1976), U.S. Power Squadron, Key West Power Squadron (sec. 1984-85), Am. Nurses Assn., Fla. Nurses Assn., Dist. 25 Nurses Assn., Bus. and Profl. Women, Handicapped Boaters Assn., Boat Owners Assn. of U.S., U.S. Yacht Racing Union, Key West Art and Hist. Soc., Am. Cancer Soc., Am. Diabetes Assn., Juvenile Diabetes Assn., Am. Heart Assn. Club: Marathon Yacht. Home: 1420 Von Phister St Key West FL 33040

BURTON, BRONDA PARKER, nurse; b. Durham, N.C., Mar. 22, 1955; d. Charlie Raymond and Mildred Frances (Brown) Parker; m. William Harold Burton, Feb. 15, 1976; children—Cory Michael, Amy Hope, Toby Parker. Diploma, Watts Sch. Nursing, Durham, 1976. Lic. R.N., N.C., Va. Occupational therapy aide Durham Rehab. Ctr., 1971-73; assoc. nurse, area programmer Murdoch Ctr., Butner, N.C., 1976; staff nurse Meth. Retirement Home, Durham, 1978-79; activity dir. Melody Manor Rest Home, Boydton, Va., 1980-82; nursing supr. Burnette's Retirement Village, Louisburg, N.C., 1982-84; head nurse, R.N. supr. Hillhaven Convalesence Ctr., Raleigh, N.C., 1985; patient coordinator, 1986—. Ch. pianist, asst. organist Centerville Bapt. Ch. (N.C.), 1982—, youth choir dir., 1982-84, program dir. Bapt. Young Women, 1982-84, dir. Women's Missionary Union, 1983-84; assoc. mem. N.C. chpt. Arthritis Found., 1983—. Mem. Am. Nurses Assn. (cert. gerontol. nurse), N.C. Nurses Assn., Century Club Am. Nurses Found., N.C. Long Term Facilities Assn., N.C. Bapt. Nursing Fellowship. Office: Hillhaven Convalescent Ctr 616 Wade Ave Raleigh NC

BURTON, CHARLOTTE LYETH, development and fundraising executive, consultant; b. Bethesda, Md., Dec. 20, 1943; d. John Mortimer Richardson Lyeth and Patricia (Dobson) Lyeth Webb; m. Michael Augustus Dively, June 17, 1978 (div. 1981); m. Bruce Robert Burton, Oct. 30, 1985. B.A., Principia Coll., 1965; cert. N.Y. Sch. Interior Design, 1966. Asst. to treas. fin. com. to re-elect Pres., Washington, 1972-73; congl. laison Adv. Council on Hist. Preservation, Washington, 1973-74, exec. asst. Capital Fund Campaign, N.Y. Bot. Gardens, 1976-78; regional chmn. Americans for an Effective Presidency, N.Y.C., 1980; pres. Mich. Assn. Community Arts Agys., Lansing, Mich., 1981-82; dir. area devel. U. Mich., Ann Arbor, 1983-85; dir. devel. N.Y. Bot. Garden, 1985—; cons. Capital Campaign Albion Coll., Mich., 1978-82; cons. Pathfinder Sch., Traverse City, Mich., 1978-79; dir. Longyear Realty Corp., Marquette, Mich., 1975—; dir., treas. Resource Exploration, Inc., Marquette, 1980—. Past pres. Human Relations Commn., Albion; former dir. Impressions V Mus., Lansing, Neighborhood Playhouse Repertory Theatre, N.Y.C., Richard Morse Mime Theatre, N.Y.C., Women's Nat. Republican Club, N.Y.C.; various positions numerous Jr. Leagues; mem. Marquette Hist. Soc., Albion Hist. Soc., Nat. Trust Hist. Preservation, Washington; bd. dirs., v.p. Hist. Soc. Mich., 1984-86; bd. dirs. Artrain, Inc., Detroit, 1984-86. Mem. Christian Sci. Ch. Avocations: sailing, skiing. Home: 21 Indian Spring Rd Rowayton CT 06853 Office: Dir Devel NY Botanical Garden New York NY 10458

BURTON, JACQUELINE COGER, geochemist, researcher; b. Little Rock, May 11, 1944; d. John Howard and Lura Virginia (Crippen) Miller; m. Stephen Dale Burton, Dec. 23, 1971 (div. Dec. 1983). B.S. in Geology cum laude, N.E. La. U., 1970, M.S. in Geology, 1974; Ph.D. in Geology, U. Tenn., 1978. Environ. geologist Dept. Transp., Salem, Oreg., 1972-74; grad. teaching asst. U. Tenn., Knoxville, 1974-78; sr. research geologist Exxon Prodn. Research Co., Houston, 1978-80; sr. research specialist Exxon Minerals Co., Houston, 1980-82, sr. research assoc., supr. geochem. research, 1983-86; ptnr. J and J Geochemistry Internat., Houston, 1986—. Contbr. articles and abstracts to profl. jours. Research grantee Sigma Xi, 1971, 77, Geol. Soc. Am., 1977; NASA research fellow, summers 1975-77. Mem. Geol. Soc. Am., Internat. Assn. Geochemistry and Cosmochemistry, Mineral. Assn. Can., Phi Kappa Phi, Sigma Gamma Epsilon. Episcopalian. Office: J and J Geochemistry Internat 12893 Westheimer Suite 43277001

BURTON, JACQUELINE JOYCE, college administrator; b. Tupelo, Ark., Dec. 11, 1939; d. Henry Lester and Amanda Elizabeth (Rice) Burton. B.S. in Edn., Ouachita Bapt. U., 1961; M. Religiou Edn., Southwestern Theol. Sem., Fort Worth, 1965; postgrad. U. Miss., Oxford, 1966, 68. Student librarian Ouachita Bapt. U., Arkadelphia, Ark., 1957-61; tchr. Newport Pub. Schs., Ark., 1961-63; girls' camp dir. Ark. Women's Missionary Union, Little Rock, 1965; counselor for women Southern Bapt. Coll., Walnut Ridge, Ark., 1965-80, dir. Bapt. Student Union, 1975—, dean of women, 1980—. Recipient Danfort Leadership award Danforth Found., 1957. Mem. Ark. Bapt. Student Dirs. Assn. (sec. 1979-80), Assn. Student Devel. in So. Bapt. Colls. and Univs. Democrat. Club: Southern Baptist College Women's (pres. 1984-85) (Walnut Ridge). Avocations: Music, piano, tennis. Home: Box 48 Southern Bapt Coll Walnut Ridge AR 72476 Office: Southern Bapt Coll Box 48 Walnut Ridge AR 72476

BURTON, PEGGY, advertising executive; b. N.Y.C.; B.S.B.A., NYU. Freelance TV producer, N.Y.C., 1964-67; TV producer Young & Rubicam, N.Y.C., 1967-69; sr. acct. exec. Daniel & Charles, N.Y.C., 1969-74; ptnr., v.p. Bruderer Hartnett Advt. Agy., N.Y.C., 1974-76; dir. Communications Am. Express Co., N.Y.C., 1976-83; v.p. advt. Dreyfus Corp., N.Y.C., 1983—. Mem. Internat. Advt. Assn., Advt. Women of N.Y. Office: Dreyfus Corp 767 Fifth Ave New York NY 10153

BURTON, SALA GALANT, congresswoman; b. Bialystok, Poland; Apr. 1, 1925; m. Phillip Burton; 1 child, Joy Temes. Ed. U. San Francisco Mem. 98th-99th Congresses from 5th Calif. Dist., mem. rules com., select com. on hunger. Assoc. dir. Calif. Pub. Affairs Inst., San Francisco, 1948-50; v.p. Calif. Democratic Council, 1951-54; former mem. Calif. Dem. Steering Com.; former mem. San Francisco County Dem. Com.; pres. San Francisco Dem. Women's Forum, 1957-59, Dem. Wives of House and Senate, 1972-74; former legis. chmn. Women's Nat. Dem. Club; del. Dem. Nat. Conv., 1956, 76, 80, 84; mem. Congl. Wives Task Force; mem. adv. com. Council on Soviet Jewry; mem. women's adv. com. Nat. Security Com. Recipient Woman of Yr. award Dem. Women's Forum, 1983. Club: Washington Internat. Club IV. Office: care Postmaster US Ho of Reps Washington DC 20515*

BURTON, THERESA LYNN, petroleum engineer; b. Baton Rouge, La., May 25, 1959; d. John Amos and Dorothy Jean (Abney) B. B.S. in Petroleum Engring., La. State U., 1981. Area engr. Conoco, Midland, Tex., 1981—, speaker, 1985—. Vol., ARC, Midland, 1982—; chmn. supervisory com. Conoco West Tex. Fed. Credit Union, Midland, 1984—. Mem. Nat. Assn. Female Execs., Soc. Petroleum Engrs. (treas. 1985—), Theta Rho. Republican. Baptist. Avocations: travel; reading; sailing; quilting. Home: 4626 Erie Midland TX 79703 Office: Conoco PO Box 1959 Midland TX 79702

BURTON, TRULY, government affairs director; b. Miami, Fla., Mar. 5, 1951; d. Harry John and Athena Minerva (Andreadis) Dourdis; m. Richard Jay Burton, June 11, 1972. B.A., U. Miami, 1973. Legis. asst. House Com. on Pub. Works and Transp., U.S. Congress, Washington, 1976-78; lobbyist Fed. Nat. Mortgage Assn., Washington, 1978-80; creative services mgr. Prose Mgmt. Co., Miami, 1980; pub. relations coordinator Arvida So., Miami, 1980-81; govt. affairs dir. Builders Assn. South Fla., Miami, 1981—; mem. Agr. Rev. Com. for Land Use Reform, Miami, 1985; chmn. Constrn. Industry Advisory Com., Miami, 1986. Contbr. articles to profl. jours. Mem., LWV, Miami, 1982—. Mem. Greater Miami Jewish Fedn. (events chair 1984-85). Jewish. Avocations: snow skiing; boating; entertaining; water sports; collecting art. Office: Builders Assn of South Fla 15225 NW 77th Ave Miami FL 33014

BURTON-GOODE, JULENE ELEANOR, clinical pharmacist, administrator; b. Kingston, Jamaica, Apr. 12, 1944, came to U.S., 1968, naturalized, 1974; d. Alman Sylvester and Mavis Maud (Miller) Burton; m. Alvin Bancroft Goode, Dec. 27, 1975; 1 dau., Pamella Nadjmi. B.S. in Pharmacy, Arnold and Marie Schwartz Coll. L.I. Univ., 1971; D.Pharmacy, Columbia U., 1973. Lic. clin. pharmacist. Resident Montefiore Hosp. and Med. Ctr., Bronx, N.Y., 1971-73; clin. research pharmacist Meml. Sloan Kettering Cancer Ctr., N.Y.C., 1973-80; asst. dir. pharmacy Bronx-Lebanon Hosp., N.Y., 1980—; adj. clin. assoc. prof. L.I. U. Grad. Sch., 1978-79; preceptor St. John's U., L.I., 1975-78. Active mem. Greenburgh Democratic Soc., Orchard Hill Civic Assn. Teacher's assistantship Columbia U., 1972-73. Mem. Nat. Assn. Female Execs., Westchester County Pharm. Soc., N.Y. State Soc. Hosp. Pharmacists, Am. Pharm. Assn., Am. Soc. Hosp. Pharmacists. Baptist. Avocations: traveling, reading, walking, music. Home: 846 Hartsdale Rd White Plains NY 10607

BURTT, ELIZABETH ALLENE, public health nurse; b. Exeter, N.H., July 31, 1926; d. William Abbot and Elizabeth Pride (Cole) Burtt; diploma in Nursing, Hillsborough County Gen. Hosp., 1947; B.S., Johns Hopkins U., 1961, M.P.H., 1977; M.S. in Public Health Nursing, Boston U., 1965. Staff nurse Mass. Gen. Hosp., Boston, 1948-49; head nurse, supr. emergency dept. Johns Hopkins Hosp., Balt., 1950-55; resident sch. nurse Oldfields Sch., Glencoe, Md., 1955-60; sr. public health nurse Balt. City Health Dept., 1961-63; instr. public health nursing U. R.I., Kingston, 1965-68; asst. prof. public health nursing U. N.H., Durham, 1968-72; public health nurse epidemiologist N.H. Div. Public Health Services, Concord, 1972-73, ednl. cons., 1973-75, chief Bur. Public Health Nursing, 1975-84, coordinator Tb Program and Refugee Health Program, 1984—; N.H. State Tb control officer, 1981—; summer camp nurse Vt., 1955-59, N.Y., 1965, Mass., 1966, R.I., 1968; public health nurse cons. Exeter Vis. Nurse Assn., 1967; adv. N.H. Student Nurse Assn., 1979-81. Chmn. Epping (N.H.) Health Com., 1969-70, N.H. Immunization Task Force, 1977-79. Mem. Am. Nurses Assn., N.H. Nurses Assn. (dir. 1979-81, chmn. legis. com. 1978-80). Am. Public Health Assn., Nat. League Nursing, N.H. League Nursing (dir. 1977-78, pres. 1981-83), Sigma Theta Tau. Contbr. to Nursing Clinics of North America, 1972. Home: Route 1 Exeter NH 03833 Office: Hazen Dr Concord NH 03301

BUSBEY, GAIL BOYD, city official; b. Cullman, Ala., Apr. 26, 1949; d. Ernest Jefferson and Irene (Sparks) Boyd; m. John Arthur Busbey, Jan. 11, 1973 (div. Apr. 1979). A.S. in Acctg. summa cum laude, Calhoun Community Coll., 1979; B.S. in Bus. Adminstrn. cum laude, Athens State Coll., 1982; M.S. in Adminstrn., U. Ala., 1986. Clk./stenographer City of Decatur, Ala., 1967-73, receptionist, 1973-74, account clk., 1974-77, asst. city clk. treas., 1977-80, clk.-treas., 1980—. Co.-chmn. Am. Cancer Soc., Morgan County, Ala., 1984-85; dir. Mental Health Assn., Morgan County, 1985. Mem. Internat. Inst. Mcpl. Clks. (cert. 1982), Ala. Assn. Mcpl. Clks. and Adminstrs. Baptist. Club: Altrusa (sec. 1983-84, pres. 1984—). Avocations: reading; needle work; antique and folk art shopping. Office: City Decatur PO Box 488 Decatur AL 35602

BUSBY, MAUREEN JENNINGS, investment adviser; b. Milw., June 9, 1947; d. David V. and Mary B. (Johnston) Jennings; m. Walter W. Busby, Dec. 27, 1969 (div. Aug. 1984); 1 child, Kate Fagan. B.A., Barat Coll., 1969. Chartered fin. analyst, 1974. Sr. trust investment officer Southeast Banking, Sarasota, Fla., 1970-76; asst. stock dir. Wis. Investment Bd., Madison, 1976-79; sr. v.p. Heritage Trust, Milw., 1979-82; exec. v.p. Heritage Invetment Advisors, Inc., Milw., 1982-83, pres., 1983-85; pres. Newton Funds, Milw., 1982-85, also dir.; v.p. Lipper Analytical Services, 1985—; pres. Lipper Adv. Services, 1985—. Bd. dirs. Mt. Mary Coll., Milw., 1983—; mem. adv. council Sch. Bus., Marquette U., Milw., 1984—; trustee Waukesha YWCA Found., Wis., 1982—. Mem. Milw. Investment Analysts Soc. (pres. 1982-83, dir. 1982—), No Load Mut. Fund Assn. (bd. dirs. 1984-85, exec. com.), Profl. Dimensions (hon., Sacajewea award 1983). Republican. Roman Catholic. Club: Milwaukee Athletic. Avocation: running. Home: 7857 N Lake Dr Fox Point WI 53217 Office: Lipper Adv Services McGeoch Bldg 3226 Michigan Ave Milwaukee WI 53202

BUSCH, NANCY ELIZABETH, marketing/communications consulting firm executive; b. Manitowac, Wis. Sept. 7, 1944; d. Edgar Wilhelm and Dorothy Janette (Blust) Putz; m. Charles Nels Busch, Aug. 21, 1965; 1 son, Alexander. B.A. in Journalism, U. Mich., 1966. Sales rep. Grosse Pointe News (Mich.), 1966-68; pres. Nels Advt. Co., Birmingham, Mich., 1968-75, Busch & Morris, Birmingham, 1975-80, Busch & Assocs., Birmingham, 1980—; cons. U. Mich. Devel. Bd., Ann Arbor, 1973-80. Mem. Econs. Club of Detroit, Adcraft Club of Detroit, Am. Mktg. Assn., Southeastern Mich. Hosp. Assn. (awards for concept and creative devel. in reports, brochures and other collateral materials 1975-80), Am. Hosp. Assn., Mich. Hosp. Assn. (awards for reports, brochures and other materials 1975-80), U. of Mich. Alumni Assn. Office: Busch & Assocs PO Box 1024 Birmingham MI 48012

BUSH, ANNA MARKLEY, lawyer; b. Evanston, Ill., July 28, 1949; d. Charles Woodrow and Marie Andrea (Olsen) Markley; m. Robert Eugene Bush, Mar. 4, 1972; 1 son, Scott Markley. B.A., Valparaiso U., 1971, J.D., 1977. Bar: Ill. 1977. Assoc. firm Irwin & Assocs., Barrington, Ill., 1977-78, White Nack & Louderman, Wilmette, Ill., 1978; owner Bush & Assocs., Barrington, 1979-80; sr. ptnr. firm Bush & Heise, Barrington, 1980—; instr. Harper Coll., Palatine, Ill., 1981—; cons. in field. Contbr. articles to profl. jours. Mem. ABA, Chgo. Bar Assn., N.W. Suburban Bar Assn., Ill. Bar Assn., Women's Bar of Ill., Bus. and Profl. Women Barrington (dir. 1979—). Democrat. Methodist. Home: 249 W Russell St Barrington IL 60010 Office: Bush & Heise 101 Lions Dr Suite 104 Barrington IL 60010

BUSH, BARBARA PIERCE, wife of vice president U.S.; b. Rye, N.Y. June 8, 1925; d. Marvin and Pauline (Robinson) Pierce; ed. Smith Coll.; L.H.D., Mt. Vernon Coll., Washington, 1981; LL.D., Cardinal Stritch Coll., Milw., 1981; H.H.D. (hon.) Hood Coll., Frederick, Md., 1983; m. George Herbert Walker Bush, Jan. 6, 1945; children—George Walker, John Ellis, Neil Mallon, Marvin Pierce, Dorothy Walker. Bd. dirs. Reading is Fundamental, Soc. for Meml. Sloan-Kettering Cancer Center, Children's Oncology Services of Met. Washington, Parent's Choice, The Washington Home, Bus. Council Effective Literacy; trustee Morehouse Sch. Medicine; nat. bd. govs. Nat. Adoption Exchange; trustee The U.S. Cap. Hist. Soc.; sponsor Laubach Literacy, Inc.; mem. adv. council Kingsbury Ctr.; hon. nat. chmn. Nat. Organ Donor Awareness Weeks, 1983, 84; mem. Leukemia Soc. Am. (nat. hon. chmn.), Ladies of the Senate (pres.), Internat. Club II, Republican Women's Fed. Forum (Wash. D.C.), Women's Nat. Rep. Club (N.Y.C.), Magic Circle Rep. Women's Club (Houston), Tex. Fedn. Rep. Women (life member). Recipient Nat. Outstanding Mother of Year, 1984. Espiscopalian. Address: The Vice President's House Washington DC 20501

BUSH, DELORES FAITH, nurse; b. Waterloo, Iowa, Aug. 22, 1946; d. Ted and Louise Grace (Aswegan) Jungling; m. Vincent Neil Bush, June 9, 1967; children—Anthony Neil, Angela Lou. R.N., St. Luke's Sch. Nursing, 1967. Registered nurse, Calif., Minn., Iowa. Staff nurse operating room U. Iowa Hosps., Iowa City, 1967-72; indsl. nurse E.F. Johnson Co., Waseca, Minn., 1975-76; staff nurse Community Hosp., St. Peter, Minn., 1979—. Council sec.

Our Savior's Luth. Ch., Cleveland, Minn., 1980-81, ch. treas., 1982—; leader Bible study Friendship Bible Coffees, Cleveland, 1982—. Mem. Assn. Operating Room Nurses. Republican. Avocation: hardanger needlecraft. Home: Route 1 Box 330 Madison Lake MN 56063 Office: Community Hosp 618 W Broadway Saint Peter MN 56082

BUSH, FREDDIE ANN, educator; b. Greensboro, N.C., June 30, 1942; d. Fred and Elizabeth (Hinton) B.; B.S., N.C. A&T State U., 1969; M.S., Hunter Coll., 1975. Editorial asst. McGraw-Hill Book Co., N.Y.C., 1969-76; instr. Spanish American Inst., N.Y.C., 1976—, also student counselor. Cert. tchr., N.Y.C., N.Y. State, N.J. Mem. Nat. Alumni Assn. N.C. A&T State U. (2d v.p. 1979-81, sec. NE Region 1972-79, pres. N.Y.C. chpt. 1978-80, young alumna award 1973, Chancellor's Council award 1974), Hunter Coll. Alumni Assn. N.Y.C. Club: Century Club of N.C. A&T State U. Alumni Assn. Author: The Woman's Personal Wardrobe Plan Book, 1981. Home: 419 W 34th St New York NY 10001 Office: 215 W 43rd St New York NY 10036

BUSH, GERALDINE TERESA, electronics company executive; b. Phila., Apr. 14, 1946; d. Charles William and Marie Frances (Barnes) B.; B.A., Temple U., 1968. Chemist, Union Camp Corp. Research and Devel., Princeton, N.J., 1968-71; asst. scientist N.L. Industries Corp., Hightstown, N.J., 1971-73; sales engr. UPA Tech., Syosset, N.Y., 1973-74, dist. mgr., 1974-75, field sales mgr., 1975-77, dir. sales and mktg., 1977-85; pres. Voss Electronic, Inc., Santa Ana, Calif., 1985—; lectr. in field. Recipient Salesman of Yr. award, 1973, 74, 75; Recognition award Dept. Commerce, 1978. Mem. ASTM, Am. Electroplaters Soc., Am. Soc. Quality Control, Am. Mgmt. Assn. Club: Internat. Bus. Roundtable (Adelphi U.). Contbr. articles to profl. jours. Office: 1812 E Carnegie St Santa Ana CA 92704

BUSH, MARGERY PECK, clinical social worker; b. Bristol, Conn., Mar. 22, 1934; d. Seymour Roe and Margery (Earl) Peck; B.A. in Psychology, Wells Coll., Aurora, N.Y., 1956; M.S.W., U. Conn., 1975; m. Edward Wallace Bush, Jr., Feb. 28, 1958; children—Kimberly, Barbara, David. Intern, Family Service Soc., Hartford, Conn., 1973-74, Inst. Living, Adult Outpatient Clinic, Hartford, 1974-75; cons., sch. social worker East Hartford Bd. Edn., 1976; family counselor Family Service, Inc., New Britain, Conn., 1976-79, Glastonbury Youth and Family Resource Center, 1980-82; pvt. practice individual, marital, and family counseling, West Hartford, 1979—; instr. program Living in Fuller Effectiveness (LIFE), 1979—. Corporator, Oak Hill Sch. Blind, 1968—; trustee Larrabee Fund Assn., 1970-73, chmn. Hartford com., 1970-72; bd. dirs. Hartford Interval House, 1977-78. Mem. Nat. Assn. Social Workers, Acad. Cert. Social Workers, Conn. Soc. Clin. Social Workers, Audubon Soc. Congregationalist. Clubs: Hartford Ski, Hartford Tennis. Address: 28 Church St Noank CT 06340

BUSH, MARJORIE EVELYNN GENUNG TOWER-TOOKER, educator, media specialist, librarian; b. Atkinson, Nebr., Mar. 12, 1925; d. Albert Ralph and Vera Marie (Rickover) Tower-Tooker; student U. Nebr., 1951, Wayne State Coll., 1942-47; B.A., Colo. State Coll., 1966, U. No. Colo., 1970; postgrad. Doane Coll., 1967-68, U. Utah, 1973-74, Ph.D. (hon.), 1973; m. Louis T. Genung, Feb. 2, 1944 (dec. Jan. 1982); 1 son, Louis Thompson; m. Laurence Scott Bush, Sept. 22, 1984; 1 stepson, Roger A. Bush. Elem. tchr. Atkinson Public Schs., 1958-69; dir. libraries and audiovisual communications Clay County Dist. I-C, Fairfield, Nebr., 1972-81; media specialist Albion (Nebr.) City Schs., 1981—; mem. Neb. Gov.'s White House Conf. on Libraries. Chmn. edn. adminstrv. bd. Park Hill United Meth. Ch.; sec. Denver Symphony Guild. Mem. NEA (life), Nebr., Colo. edn. assns., Assn. Childhood Edn. Internat., ALA, Nebr., Mountain Plains library assns., Nat. Council Tchrs. English, AAUW, Nebr. Ednl. Media Assn., Assn. Supervision and Curriculum Devel., Assn. Ednl. Communications and Tech., Internat. Visual Literacy Assn., Nat. Council Exceptional Children, Alumni Assn. U. No. Colo. (life charter), Women Educators Nebr., Am. Legion Aux., Nebr. Lay Citizens Edn. Assn. (exec.), Am. Nat. Cowbelles, Nebr. Cowbelles, DAR (regent 1971, dist. treas. 1968-71), Internat. Platform Assn., LWV, Women's Soc. Christian Service, Ak-Sar-Ben. Mem. Order Eastern Star. Club: Opti Mrs. Home: 9655 E Center Ave Denver CO 80231

BUSH, MELINDA JOHNSON, publisher; b. Champaign, Ill., June 14, 1940; d. Maurice R. and Margaret B. Johnson; B.S., U. Colo., 1962; postgrad. London Sch. Econs. and Polit. Sci.; postgrad. Advanced Mgmt. Program, Harvard U., 1984. With J. Walter Thompson, advt., N.Y.C., 1962-64, Paul Bradley Assns., public relations, N.Y.C., 1964-66; with Ziff-Davis Publishing Co., N.Y.C., 1966—, asst. to pres., 1974-76, pub. Hotel & Travel Index, 1976—, v.p. bus. div., 1983-85; v.p. Murdoch Mags. div., pub. Hotel & Travel Index, News Group Publs., Inc., N.Y.C., 1985—; advisor Cornell U. Hotel Sch., Lausanne Hotel Sch.; advisor tourism programs U. Mass., New Sch. for Social Research, Culinary Inst. Am. (also mem. corp. bd.); frequent speaker and panelist at industry assns. and convs. Nat. photography coordinator Model Cities Task Force, 1970-72; founder, chmn. Photography Youth Found., 1973-76. Named Woman of Year in Travel, Travel Industry Assn. Am., 1980. Fellow Inst. Cert. Travel Agts. (bd dirs.); mem. Hotel Sales Mgmt. Assn. Internat. (dir.), Am. Hotel and Motel Assn., Advt. Women N.Y. Club: Wings (N.Y.C.). Author articles in field. Office: Murdoch Mags Div News Group Publs Inc One Park Ave New York NY 10016

BUSH, VIRGINIA ANN, physician; b. Chickasha, Okla., Nov. 3, 1943; d. Clarence William and Frances Louise (Talla) B. B.S., Central State U., Edmond, Okla., 1966; M.D., U. Okla., 1970. Emergency physician St. Anthony Hosp., Oklahoma City, 1972-74, No. N. Mex. Emergency Med. Services, P.C., Taos, Los Alamos and Santa Fe, 1974—, also pres.; mem. active staff St. Vincent Hosp., Santa Fe, 1985; active staff Holy Cross Hosp., Taos, 1985; dir. emergency service Holy Cross Hosp., Taos, 1985; dir. Los Alamos Hosp. Emergency Dept., 1977-82. Mem. Am. College Emergency Physicians. Home and Office: Box 1285 Taos NM 87571

BUSH, VIRGINIA CARNITA, educator; b. Pima, Ariz., Dec. 17, 1933; d. John Gabriel and Elizabeth Harriet (Britkrite) Becht; m. Abraham L. Pennington, June 12, 1954 (div. Dec. 1968); children—Kay Pennington, Steven Pennington; m. John Augustus Bush, Aug. 2, 1969 (div. Apr. 1976). B.S., N.Mex. Western Coll., 1954; M.A., Western N.Mex. U., 1964. Cert. elem., secondary and community coll. tchr., Calif. High sch. Spanish and elem. tchr. Cliff Consol. Schs., N.Mex., 1956-57, 58-62; inst. Western N.Mex. U., Silver City, 1962-64; tchr. Spanish, Lincoln Jr. High Sch., Taft, Calif., 1964-72, tchr. fgn. langs., 1979—; tchr. Spanish, Singapore Am. Sch., Singapore, 1973-75; tchr. English, Roosevelt Sch., Taft, 1975-79. NEH stipendee U. Wyo. seminar on French metaphys. novel, 1984. Mem. Taft Elem. Tchrs. Assn. (pres. 1976-77), Calif. Tchrs. Assn., NEA, Bus. and Profl. Women (v.p. chpt. 1985-86). Republican. Mem. Ch. of Religious Science. Avocations: graphology; photography; gourmet cooking; travel.

BUSHER, ROBERTA MARIE, ambulance service executive; b. Atwater, Calif., Dec. 5, 1956; d. James Patrick and Gloria Patricia (Fisch) Collins; m. George Christopher Busher, July 17, 1983; 1 child, Jonathan James. A.A., Merced Jr. Coll., 1977. Registered dental asst. Dental ins. auditor Calif. dental Service, San Francisco, 1979-82, cons., 1982-83; ins. claims examiner Bankers Life and Casualty, Terra Linda, Calif., 1982-83; owner, operator Arcata Ambulance, Calif., 1983—. Mem. Calif. Ambulance Assn., Nat. Fedn. Ind. Bus. Republican. Roman Catholic. Avocations: photography; skiing; camping; reading; boating. Home: 1112 School Rd McKinleyville CA 95521 Office: Arcata-Mad River Ambulance 220 F St Arcata CA 95521

BUSHNELL, CATHARINE, property representative, photographer; b. Pullman, Wash., July 2, 1950; d. David and Catharine Howe (Goodfellow) B.; B.S. in Speech, Northwestern U., 1972; m. H. Michael Sisson, Oct. 31, 1975. Prodn. dept. Mike White Advt., Chgo., 1972; stage actress, Chgo., 1972-73; partner, dir. photography Mome, Raths and Outgrabe, Chgo., 1973-75; prodn. stills photographer Raggedy Ann and Andy, animated film, 1975-77; motion picture stills photographer for various feature films, N.Y.C., 1977—; exec. v.p., creative dir. Sisson Assos., N.Y.C., 1981—; pres. Illusion Gallery, Creative Service Co., N.Y.C., 1981—; mem. faculty Parsons Sch. Design, New Sch. for Social Research, 1984-85; judge ann. student photog. portfolio rev. High Sch. Art and Design, N.Y.C., 1979-83. Lic. property rep. Mem. Internat. Photographers Motion Picture Industry, Internat. Soc. Photography (charter), Actors Equity Assn., Northwestern U. Alumnae Assn., Delta Zeta. Author: Raggedy Ann and Andy in the Tunnel of Lost Toys, 1980; Raggedy Ann and Andy and the Pirates of Outgo Inlet, 1981; Linda's Magic Window, 1981; Frannie's Magic Kazoo, 1983. Office: 300 E 40th St New York NY 10016

BUSSE, NORMA VIRGINIA, lawyer, former army officer; b. San Francisco, Jan. 19, 1927; d. Erich Paul and Alwine (Westphal) B. B.A., U. Calif.-Berkeley, 1949; B.S. in Nursing, Incarnate Word Coll., San Antonio, 1976; M.A., Calif. State U.-San Francisco, 1962; J.D., St. Mary's U., San Antonio, 1979; grad. Army Command and Gen. Staff Coll., 1965, Army War Coll., 1971. Bar: Tex. 1980; R.N., Tex. Commd. 2d lt., U.S. Army, 1951, advanced through grades to lt. col., 1968; personnel staff officer, 1950-73; ret., 1973; nurse Villa Rosa Hosp., San Antonio, 1977; sole practice, San Antonio, 1980—. Advisor legacy and nursing councils Incarnate Word Coll., 1981—. Decorated Legion of Merit, Bronze Star medal. Mem. ABA, Tex. Bar Assn., Tex. Nurses Assn., U.S. Army War Coll. Alumni, Am. Legion (judge adv. 1982-83). Democrat. Home: 137 Wagon Trail Rd San Antonio TX 78231

BUSSEY, (FRANCES) LYNN, photography studio marketing executive, genealogist; b. Dallas, Apr. 10, 1949; d. Charles Dan Bussey and Lyda Lynn (Wood) Bussey Marchman; m. Charles Francis Guittard, June 11, 1971 (div. Feb. 1983); children—James Francis Guittard, Robert Bussey Guittard. B.A., Baylor U., 1970; postgrad. in math. So. Meth. U., 1971-72, U. Tex. Austin, 1969-70, U. Tex. Arlington, 1968-69. Tchr. math. high sch. Dallas Ind. Sch. Dist., 1970-72; mktg. ptnr. Dickens & Co. Photog., Dallas, 1985—; devel. adminstr. St. John's Episc. Sch., Dallas, 1984-85; genealogy book publ. specialist, Dallas, 1976—. Instr. astronomy The Sci. Place, Dallas, 1980-82. Author: Bussey Family Genealogy 1635-1978, Bussey Family Genealogy 1061-1635, 1986; Alpha Omega History 1927-79, 1979. Editor: Foundations of Dallas County, 1983. Mem. Nat. Geneal. Soc., Dallas Geneal. Soc., Bus. and Profl. Women, Jr. League Dallas, Dallas C. of C., Dallas Jr. Symphony League, Nat. Soc. Fundraising Execs., Pi Beta Phi. Baptist. Avocations: travel; photography; reading history and biography; violinist; astronomy. Home: 3849 Greenbrier Dr Dallas TX 75225 Office: Dickens & Co 6713 Snider Plaza Dallas TX 75205

BUST, DEBORAH ELIZABETH, surplus buyer, fashion accessories manufacturing executive; b. Bonne Terre, Mo., Sept. 20, 1950; d. William Hardage and Marilyn Elizabeth (Moore) B.; m. Gary Karl Bridges, Sept. 2, 1973 (div. 1983); 1 child, Stella Mariah Verker Bust. Student Drury Coll., Springfield, Mo., 1968-70; B. Journalism, U. Mo., 1972. Advt. sales Graham Hayes & Lange, Miami, Fla., 1972-73; nat. advt. dir. Jeans West, St. Louis, 1973-75; freelance stained glass artist, Mpls., 1976-77, Phila., 1980-83; pub. affairs dir. Planned Parenthood of S.E. Pa., Phila., 1978-80; owner, head product devel. H-Corps Products, Phila., 1983—; nat. lobbyist, state lobbyist Planned Parenthood of Pa., Washington and Harrisburg, Pa., 1978-80. Editor newsletter Planned Parenthood Pa., 1978-80, designer, artist, 1978-80, Organizer Teen Health Conf., Phila., 1979-80. Democrat. Presbyterian. Club: 3 HO. Avocation: yoga. Office: H-Corps Products PO Box 2387 Philadelphia PA 19103

BUSTAMANTE, DOLORES MORALES, social work administrator; b. El Paso, Tex., May 23, 1950; d. Hector M. Morales and Gloria (Lightbourn) Carreon; m. Daniel Ray Bustamante, Sept. 21, 1979; children—Rosalinda Danielle, Adrian Ramon. B.A., U. Tex.-El Paso, 1973; M.S.W., U. Houston, 1978. Research asst. Southwestern Schs. Study, El Paso, 1971-73; caseworker Mental Health Retardation, El Paso, 1974-76; intern pub. affairs Gulf Oil Corp., Houston, 1977-78; research cons. Tex. Commn. on Alcoholism, Houston, 1978-79; dir. youth services SER-Jobs for Progress, Houston, 1979-81, conf. coordinator, 1982; asst. dir. INROADS/Houston, Inc., 1983—; tech. translator CRS Group Engrs., Houston, 1981-82; audience developer Soc. Performing Arts, Houston, 1982. Mem. Minority Women's Assn., Trabajadores Sociales de Aztlan, Cultural Arts Council Houston. Roman Catholic. Home: 2719 Morrison St Houston TX 77009 Office: INROADS Houston Inc 711 Louisiana Suite 1270 Houston TX 77002

BUSTER, LISA B., sports agent; b. Phila., June 26, 1959; d. Leonard David and Arlene Linda (Segal) Buster. Student Georgetown U., 1977-79; B.A. in Spanish, U. N.C., 1981. Asst. to sports dept. WDVM-TV, Washington, 1978-79; sports reporter WCHL Radio, Chapel Hill, N.C., 1980; sports reporter, anchor WDCG-WDNC Radio, Durham, N.C., 1980-81; anchor, reporter KTVG-TV, Helena, Mont., 1982-83; dir. celebrity promotions, Starpower, Feasterville, Pa., 1984; pres., owner Promotion in Notion Internat., Ltd., Jenkintown, Pa., 1984—; asst. to dir. Nike-N.J. 10 Miler, Cherry Hill, 1985-86. Mem. Athletics Congress. Club: Delaware Valley Paleontological Soc. Avocations: horseback riding; travel; music. Address: Promotion in Motion Internat Ltd PO Box 181 Jenkintown PA 19046

BUSTIN, BEVERLY MINER, state legislator; b. Morrisville, Vt., Feb. 14, 1936; d. Donald Haze and Della Mae (Kenfield) Miner; div. children—Catherine Margaret, David Wayne. B.S., Thomas Coll. Mem. Maine Senate, Augusta, 1979—; chmn. joint select com. on alcoholism services, 1982-84; chmn. instl. services com., 1983-84. Vice chmn. Kennebec County Regional Health Agy., Maine, 1984—; vice chmn. Kennebec County Dem. Com., 1979—. Office: Maine Senate State Capitol Augusta ME 04333*

BUSTO, FELICE E., lawyer; b. Paterson, N.J., Jan. 12, 1953; d. Felix Henry and Ruth Elizabeth (Brown) Busto. B.A., Bucknell U., 1975; J.D., Cath. U., 1980. Bar: D.C. 1980. Legis. asst. U.S. rep. Henry Helstoski, Washington, 1975-77; assoc. Steptoe & Johnson, Washington, 1980—. Active Americans Democratic Action, Washington, 1976—, ACLU, Washington, 1976—. Recipient Best Brief award Cath. U., 1979. Mem. D.C. Bar Assn., Women's Bar Assn., Washington Council Lawyers. Democrat. Presbyterian. Home: 7300 Holly Ave Takoma Park MD 20912 Office: Steptoe & Johnson 1330 Connecticut Ave NW Washington DC 20036

BUSWELL, SUSAN ROWE, state legislator; b. Denver, Sept. 13, 1935; d. Kenneth Wyer and Leone (Krumling) Rowe; children—Janice, Scott. B.A., Carleton Coll., 1957; postgrad. U. Copenhagen, 1958. Analyst, Dept. Def., Washington, 1959-62; officer mgr. Green Street Coalition, Annapolis, Md., 1980-81; exec. dir. Md. Assn. Elem. Sch. Adminstrs., College Park, 1981-83; del. Md. Gen. Assembly, Annapolis, 1983—; exec. dir. Md. Assn. Nonpub. Spl. Edn. Facilities, 1985—. Mem. Howard County Bd. Edn. (Md.), 1973-83, Howard County Recreation and Parks Bd., 1975-79; bd. dirs. Howard County Commn. on Arts, 1975-80. Recipient Mortar Board award Carleton Coll., Northfield, Minn., 1957. Mem. LWV, Delta Kappa Gamma. Democrat. Mem. United Ch. of Christ. Club: Soroptimists. Office: Lowe Office Bldg Annapolis MD 21401

BUTEAU, MICHELLE DIANE, energy company executive; b. Oakland, Calif., Mar. 6, 1952; d. Bernard Lamonthe and June (Dowler) B.; m. Barry Crawford Anderson, Nov. 1974 (div. 1982); 1 child, Damon Buteau-Anderson. B.A. in Liberal Arts, Cath. U. Am., 1974, postgrad. Dir. U.S. Summer Sch. Inst., U.S. Dept. State/USIA, Posnan, Poland, 1975-76; bookkeeper Internat. Energy Assocs. Ltd., Washington, 1980-83, research asst., 1983-84, research assoc., 1984-85, staff cons., 1985—, asst. project mgr., 1984—. Actress and dir. dinner theatres, 1974—. Intern Senator E. Dirksen, Washington, 1968; pres. Catholic Youth Orgn., Bethesda, Md., 1968-70. Mem. Am. Mgmt. Assn., Nat. Assn. Female Execs. Roman Catholic. Avocations: acting; bodybuilding; dancing; singing; writing poetry. Home: Bethesda MD Office: Internat Energy Assocs Ltd 2600 Virginia Ave NW Washington DC 20037

BUTERA, JOANN TERESA, publishing company sales manager; b. Bronx, N.Y., Mar. 28, 1950; d. Anthony Ferdinand and Vivian Teresa (Moscato) B. B.A., St. John's U., 1972; M.A., Hofstra U., 1974; cert. Smith Coll. Mgmt. Program, 1983. Asst. buyer Henri Bendel, N.Y.C., 1971-75; mem. faculty dept. clin. communicology N.Y. Med. Coll., Valhalla, N.Y., 1975-79; mktg. asst. Springer-Verlag, Inc., N.Y.C., 1979-80; library sales coordinator, 1981-83; library sales mgr. John Wiley & Sons, N.Y.C., 1983—. Mem. ALA, Spl. Library Assn., Profl. Pub. Mktg. Group, Am. Assn. Pubs. Democrat. Roman Catholic. Office: John Wiley & Sons Inc 605 3d Ave New York NY 10158

BUTERA, M. LEE, publisher, publication executive, consultant; b. Darby, Pa., Mar. 3, 1943; d. Leo Yermack and Yolande Marie (Bosacco) Freed; m. James J. Butera, Aug. 2, 1969; children—Jennifer, Madelyn, Allison. B.A., Pa. State U., 1965; postgrad. George Washington U., 1974. Market research analyst, Procter & Gamble, Cin., 1965-66; claims supr. John Hancock, Phila., 1966-69; program dir. Arthritis Found., Washington, 1975-78; pub. relations cons. M. Lee Butera & Assocs., Washington, 1978-79; founder, pub. Fgn. Bank Focus, Washington, 1979—; pres. Focus Publs., Washington, 1979—; sponsor Fgn. Banking in Am. Conf., Washington, 1982—. Pub., editor: Foreign Banking in America, 1982, 83, 84, 85, 86. Mem. Nat. Assn. Women Bus. Owners. Avocations: jogging; furniture refinishing; dog breeding. Home: 4006 Virgilia St Chevy Chase MD 20815 Office: Fgn Bank Focus 4520 East-West Hwy #600 Bethesda MD 20814

BUTERBAUGH, CORINNE DEBOLT, marketing consultant; b. Stockton, Calif., Jan. 10, 1956; d. Merrill E. and Frances J. (Schooler) DeBolt; m. William R. Buterbaugh, May 27, 1978; 1 child. B.S. in Mktg., U. Va., 1978. Mktg. analyst Woodward & Lothrop, Washington, 1978-79; dir. mktg. Nat. Sch. Pub. Relations Assn., Arlington, Va., 1979-83; mktg. mgr. Assn. Trial Lawyers Am., Washington, 1983; account exec. MacDantz Direct, affiliate Needham, Harper Worldwide, McLean, Va., 1983-85; prin. Buterbaugh Ptnrs., 1985—. Mem. Am. Mktg. Assn., Assn. Mktg. Roundtable (v.p. 1983). Republican. Episcopalian. Home: 1624 Great Falls St McLean VA 22101 Office: Buterbaugh Ptnrs 1624 Great Falls St McLean VA 22101

BUTLER, BARBARA LOUISE, home economist; b. Rye, N.Y., Jan. 12, 1929; d. George and Mariella (Burgevin) Harvey; m. Charles Bradford Butler, Feb. 9, 1963; 1 child, Amy. B.S., Conn. Coll., 1950. Asst. restaurant mgr. Herpolshiemer Co., Grand Rapids, Mich., 1950-52; assoc. food editor Crowell-Collier Pub. Co., N.Y.C., 1952-56; home economist Gen. Foods Corp., White Plains, N.Y., 1957-66, supr. radio, TV, mag. publicity, 1966-68; cons. foods, Cos Cob, Conn., 1968-77; mgr. test kitchen services Gen. Foods Corp., White Plains, N.Y., 1977—. Mem. Am. Home Econs. Assn., Home Economists in Bus., Women in Mgmt., Internat. Microwave Power Inst. (com. mem. IMPI Handbook 1982—), Internat. Assn. Cooking Profls., N.Y. State Home Econs. Assn. Republican. Episcopalian. Club: Conn. Coll. (v.p. 1975-77). Home: Riverside CT 06878 Office: Gen Foods Corp 250 North St White Plains NY 10625

BUTLER, CAROL DENTON, government official; b. York, Nebr., Apr. 8, 1931; d. Robert Ralph and Fern V. (Mann) Denton; B.A. summa cum laude, York Coll., 1952; m. Charles Farrell Butler, Jan. 17, 1959; children—Robert Charles, Julie Ann. Reporter, staff asst. York (Nebr.) Daily News Times, 1952-54; claims rep. Social Security Adminstrn., Lincoln, Nebr., 1955-57, disability examiner, cons., policy specialist, staff assoc., Balt., 1957-69, sect. chief disability operations, 1970, chief med. policy, 1971-74, chief rehab. div., 1974-76, dep. asst. bur. dir. fed./state programs, 1976-78, dep. asst., bur. dir. systems and methods, 1978-79, dir. office pub. concerns, 1979-85; ret., 1985; disability examiner Div. Vocat. Rehab., State of Md., 1985—. Counselor, Howard County Sexual Assault Center, 1976-79, bd. dirs., 1979-85, pres. bd., 1981-83; mem. Md. Gov.'s Adv. Bd. on Rape and Sexual Offenses, 1982-84; bd. dirs. Baltimore County Sexual Assault and Domestic Violence Ctr., 1986. Recipient Commrs. citations Social Security Adminstrn., 1968, 78; citation Assoc. Commr. for Disability, 1985, 86. Mem. ACLU, Preservation Md., Women's Alliance Md., NOW, Nat. Assn. Disability Examiners, Am. Assn. Ret. Persons. Alpha Chi.

BUTLER, CAROL KING, radio advertising sales executive; b. Charlotte, N.C., May 29, 1952; d. Charles Snowden Watts and Marion (Thomas) King; m. James Rodney Butler, Aug. 12, 1972 (div. 1975). Student U. N.C.-Greensboro, 1970-72. Sales rep. Sta.-WKIX, Raleigh, N.C., 1978-82, N.C. Box, Inc., Raleigh, 1982-84; radio sales account exec. WRAL-FM, Raleigh, 1984—. Mem. Nat. Assn. Female Execs. Republican. Episcopalian. Avocations: water skiing; skiing; tennis; boating; bicycling. Home: 5501 Oldtowne Rd Raleigh NC 27612 Office: WRAL-FM 711 Hillsborough St Raleigh NC 27605

BUTLER, CAROLE ANN, advertising agency executive; b. Stoneham, Mass., July 7, 1945; d. Solomon Leopold Bogert and Ida Carmina (Iannillo) Stutzman; m. Lawrence Herb Zimmerman, Dec. 6, 1965 (div. 1970); children—Bryan Joseph, Erik Michael; m. James Charles Butler, Apr. 29, 1983. B.S. in Mktg., Pa. State U., 1972; L.P.N., Allentown Sch. Practical Nursing, 1965. Operating room technician Sacred Heart Hosp., Allentown, Pa., 1965-68; v.p. sales Graphic Spection, Allentown, 1973-75; mktg. dir. Sac-Car Advt., Allentown, 1975-79; creative dir. Varkond Advt., Allentown, 1979-81; pres. Guest Advt. Agy., Wilkes-Barre, Pa., 1982—; mktg. cons. Retailers N.E. Pa., Wilkes-Barre, 1982—. Mem. N.E. Advt. Ad Club (dir. 1982-85). Democrat. Roman Catholic. Avocations: skiing; writing; reading. Home: 610 A Thomas Ave Kingston PA 18702 Office: 77 E Market St Wilkes-Barre PA 18704

BUTLER, JOAN BOGLE, actress; b. Kingsthorpe, Northamptonshire, Eng., Aug. 5, 1906; d. Harold and Edith (Bogle) Hickson; m. Eric Norman Butler, Oct. 29, 1933; children—Nicholas Andrew Mark, Caroline Margaret Julia. Student Oldfield Sch., Swanage, Dorset, Eng.; diploma Royal Acad. Dramatic Art. Appeared in plays A Day in the Death of Joe Egg, Forget Me Not Lane, The Card, Bedroom Farce, The Freeway, Blithe Spirit, On the Razzle; films include The Guinea Pig, Seven Days to Noon, Yanks, The Wicked Lady, Clockwise; television appearances include Great Expectations, Nanny, Good Girls, Poor Little Rich Girls, Time for Murder. Recipient —Tony— award League of N.Y. Theatres, 1979. Mem. Ch. of Eng. Home: Rose Lane Wivenhoe Essex England Office: c/o Plunket Green Ltd 110 Jermyn St London SW1 England

BUTLER, JOSEPHINE DENATALE, dance educator; b. N.Y.C., Mar. 12, 1911; d. Domenico Tommaso and Maria Adelina deNatale; student Traphagen Sch. Fashion, N.Y.C., 1928-32, N.Y. U., 1939-40; m. Albert Shreve Butler, July 19, 1937. Fashion stylist Amos Parrish Fashion Cons., N.Y.C., 1932-36; tchr., historian Albert Butler Sch. Dancing, N.Y.C., 1936-84, also dir. Recipient Dance Masters of Am. awards, 1968, 72. Mem. Inst. Social Dance Studies (pres.), Internat. Dance Council, Dance Masters Am. Author: (with Albert Butler) Encyclopedia of Social Dance, 1971, 75, 80; contbr. articles in field to profl. jours. Home: 60 W 57th St New York NY 10019

BUTLER, MARY FRANCES, nurse; b. Elrode, Ala., Sept. 10, 1931; d. Leon and Beatrice (Nixon) Mosely; m. Harry M. Butler; children from previous marriage—Keith Wheeler, Pat Wheeler Clark. A.D. in Nursing, Kansas City Jr. Coll., 1974. R.N. Lic. practical nurse St. John's Hosp., Leavenworth, Kans., 1956-64, surg. technician, 1962-63; lic. practical nurse Cushing Meml. Hosp., 1963-65; lic. practical nurse VA Med. Ctr., Leavenworth, Kans., 1965-75, charge nurse, 1975—. Recipient Quality Increase award Leavenworth VA Hosp., 1971, 79, Advanced Proformance award, 1981. Ch. sch. tchr., 1976—. Baptist. Home: 104 Fern Cliff Lansing KS 66043

BUTLER, MATILDA LOU, psychologist, educator; b. Oklahoma City, Feb. 5, 1942; d. Edward Ainsworth and Flossie Jewel (Calderhead) Butler; m. William John Paisley, Oct. 16, 1970; children—Kenneth Earl, Edward Ainsworth, William John. Student U. Okla., 1960-62; B.S. magna cum laude, Boston U., 1964; M.A., Stanford U., 1966; Ph.D., Northwestern U., 1970. Research assoc. psychology dept. Stanford U., 1970, lectr., research assoc. Inst. for Communication Research, 1971-77; research assoc. U. Calif.-Berkeley Grad. Sch. Pub. Policy, 1971; v.p. Applied Communication research, 1974-77; v.p. Far West Lab. for Ednl. Research and Devel., San Francisco, 1977-82, dir., 1982—, dir. women and minorities mgmt./leadership program, 1977-78, leader women's concerns component, 1977-81, health edn. component, 1977-81, dir. Women's Ednl. Equity Communications Network, 1977-80, chmn. tech. and communications dept., 1980-82, dir. research and devel. div., 1982; pres. Edupro, 1982-86, Knowledge Access, Inc., 1986; cons. Coll. Bds., Lockheed-Technicon Info. Systems, Palo Alto Unified Sch. Dist., Nat. Cancer Inst., Nat. Center Health Services Research. NIMH trainee. Mem. Am. Psychol. Assn., Am. Assn. Pub. Opinion Research (program chmn. Pacific chpt. 1972, council mem. 1975), Assn. for Edn. in Journalism (co-chmn. com. status women 1975), Internat. Communication Assn. (co-chmn. com. status women in communications 1975-76), Am. Ednl. Research Assn., ALA, Am. Soc. for Info. Sci. (cabinet rep.), Am. Assn. Higher Edn. Author: (with W. Paisley) Women and the Mass Media: Sourcebook for Research and Action, 1980, Knowledge Systems in Education, 1983. Home: 717 Charleston Ct Palo Alto CA 94303 Office: 2685 Marine Way Suite 1305 Mountain View CA 94043

BUTLER, REBECCA BATTS, ednl. cons., author; b. Norfolk, Va.; d. William and Gussie Batts; diploma Va. State Coll., 1933; B.S., Glassboro (N.J.) State Coll., 1942; M.Ed., Temple U., 1950, Ed.D., 1965; m. Robert Butler (dec.). Tchr. one room sch., Charlotte County, Va., 1930-32, Caroline County, Va., 1933-35; tchr. Norfolk (Va.) Public Schs., 1935-36; tchr. and guidance counselor, Camden, N.J., 1937-65, supr. guidance, 1966-68; dir. State N.J. Adult Learning Center, Camden, 1968-69; dir. adult continuing community edn. program, Camden, 1969-74; adj. prof. Glassboro State Coll., 1971-82; ednl. cons., 1974—; condr. workshops. Trustee, Thomas Edison Coll., N.J., 1973-76; pres. Vis. Nurses and Health Assn. Camden County, 1974-82; bd. dirs. Camden County chpt. ARC, 1970-82, Planned Parenthood, 1970—; nat.

trustee Andrus Found., 1980—; civilian mem. adv. com. on women to Sec. Def., 1972-74; del. 1981 White House Conf. on Aging. Recipient numerous awards, including: Vol. Service award United Way, 1978; Achievement award N.J. Elks, 1977; Woman of Year, Zeta Phi Beta, 1977; Humanitarian award N.J. conf. United A.M.E. Chs., 1977. Mem. Am. Assn. Ret. Persons (chairperson nat. com., nat. dir. 1980—), AAUW, Nat. Assn. Adult Continuing Public Edn., Nat. Assn. Negro Bus. and Profl. Women's Clubs (Woman of Year 1982), Nat. Hook-up of Black Women (dir.), Phi Delta Kappa (nat. editor-in-chief 1973-77, nat. and regional chairperson second careers com. 1979—). Mem. African Methodist Episcopal Ch. Club: Cherry Hill Maturity. Author: Problems of Beginning Teachers: A Handbook of Suggestions. Address: 15 Eddy Ln Cherry Hill NJ 08002

BUTTERMAN, ELIZABETH B(IERMANN), apparel company executive; b. N.Y.C., Feb. 27, 1944; d. Carl O. and Lucille (Lacey) Biermann; m. John A. McTaggart, Dec. 19, 1965 (div. 1970); 1 dau., Elan Lacey; m. Donald J. Butterman, Apr. 7, 1976. B.A., Mt. Holyoke Coll., 1965. Asst. buyer J.C. Penney Co., N.Y.C., 1966-70; buyer Woolco, Secaucus, N.J., 1970-74, K-Mart, North Bergen, N.J., 1974-76; personnel dir. Korvettes, N.Y.C., 1976-79, AMC/Federated Dept. Stores, N.Y.C., 1979-82; v.p. merchandising Empire Shield Co. Inc., Bklyn., 1983-85; sales and mktg. exec. Elkay Industries, N.Y.C., 1986—. Mem. Am. Women's Econ. Devel. Orgn. Republican. Episcopalian. Office: Elkay Industries 1333 Broadway New York NY 10118

BUTTERWORTH, NONA ANGEL, artist; b. Spartanburg, S.C., Jan. 28, 1929; d. James Oscar and Joyce (Beatty) Angel; student Randolph Macon's Womans Coll., 1947-49, Ringling Sch. Art, 1949-50, Art Students League, N.Y.C., 1950-51; m. James Ebert Butterworth, Jr., Dec. 18, 1954; children—James Ebert III, Alison Angel, Joy Evans. Jr. curator art Pack Meml. Library, Asheville, N.C.. 1951-52; artist. advt. dept. Ivey's Dept. Store, Asheville, 1952-53; comml. artist Ayer & Gillette advt. agy., Charlotte, N.C. 1953-55; one woman show Charlotte Country Club, 1972, Charlotte Country Day Sch., 1977, Copeland House Art Gallery, 1982; 2-woman show Charlotte Meml. Hosp., 1985, Ivey's Dept. Store, 1985; exhibited in group shows First Union Bank, Charlotte, 1973, 74, 75, 76, 77, 85, Wachovia Bank, 1975, WSOC-TV, 1975-78; Lincolnton (N.C.) City Hall, 1974, 75, N.C. Nat. Bank, 1971, 72, 76-77, 84, 85, Charlotte Festival in the Park, 1972-86, Spl. Bicentennial Invitational Exhibit Queens Coll., 1976, N.C. Watercolor Show, High Point, 1976, Greenville, 1977, Fayetteville, 1986, Davidson Coll., 1979, Shelby Nat. Juried Show, 1983-84, 85, N.C. Nat. Bank, 1984, N.C. Watercolor Soc., 1985; represented in permanent collections, Phila., Charlotte, Asheville, Gastonia; tchr. art, children Mint Museum, Charlotte, 1973-76, Charlotte Country Day Sch., 1975-76, 77; watercolor tchr. Central Piedmont Community Coll., 1981—; pvt. tchr. art; free-lance writer Charlotte Mag., 1981-84. Pres. Friends of Mint Museum, 1972-73; v.p. Artists Guild, 1973-74, 2d v.p. Women's Aux. Mint Mus., 1975-76, chmn. overseas tours, 1975—; chmn. Christ Episcopal Ch. Fair, 1968; bd. dirs. Women's Assn. Charlotte Symphny, also co-chmn. Symphony Designerhouse, 1975; mem. artists' adv. bd. Mint Mus., 1977—; bd. dirs. Arts and Sci. Council, 1978-81, Guild Charlotte Artists, 1984-85, Charlotte Writers Club, 1984-85; mem. co. Charlotte Little Theater, 1981, 84, 85, Piedmont Community Coll. Summer Theater, 1983. Recipient Merit award Pa. State Hort. Soc., 1966; Purchase award Mint Mus., 1977; 1st prize WSOC-TV Invitational, 1978; honorable mention Guild Charlotte Artists, 1983, 3d prize, 1983. Mem. Guild Charlotte Artists (dir. 1983-84, pres. 1976-77), Affiliates Arts and Sci. Council (sec. exec. com. 1977—), N.C. Watercolor Soc. (sec., dir. 1978-79), Jr. League, Charlotte Writer's Club (pres. 1982-84, 1st prize children's story contest 1981). Republican. Epsicopalian. Club: Charlotte Country. Home: 1438 Queens Rd W Charlotte NC 28207

BUTTNER, ANN DANIELLE MECKLENBORG, nurse; b. Phila., July 29, 1952; d. Robert Henry and Helen Gail (Gallagher) Mecklenborg; m. Edward George Buttner, Jan. 7, 1978; 1 dau., Rachel Caroline. Assoc. Nursing, Gwynedd-Mercy Coll., 1972; B.S., 1974; M.A., U. No. Colo., 1980. Staff nurse Chestnut Hill Hosp., Phila., 1972-74; profl. pub. health nurse N. Pa. Vis. Nurse Assn., Ambler, 1974-75; nursing instr. community health U. Wyo., Laramie, 1978-81; staff pub. health nurse Health Cons. Services, Alamogordo, N.Mex., 1982, coordinator nursing program N.Mex. State U., Alamogordo, 1983-84, now sch. nurse Sembach Elem. Sch., Dept. Def. Dependents Schs., Germany; patient edn. cons./instr. Am. Lung Assn., Albuquerque, 1983; adv. bd. mem., cons. Alamogordo Home Care, 1983; pub. edn. chmn. Am. Cancer Soc., Dist. V Otero County Unit, Alamogordo, 1982-83, CPR instr. ARC, Phila., 1972-76, health careers cons. C. of C., Inc., Alamogordo, 1983. Served to 1st lt., Nurses Corps, USAF, 1976-78. Recipient awards Am. Cancer Soc., 1981—. Mem. Am. Nurses Assn., N.Mex. Nurses Assn. (nursing edn. planning com. 1983). Democrat. Roman Catholic. Club: Sembach AFB Wives (Germany). Home: PO Box 2052 APO New York NY 09130

BUTTNER, ELEANOR HOLLINGSWORTH, educator; b. Balt., Apr. 30, 1953; d. Walter Douglas and Sarah Alexander (Russell) B.; B.A., Hollins (Va.) Coll., 1975; M.B.A., U. Pa., 1977 Ph.D., U. N.C., 1986. Treas., dir. Camp Atahi, Inc., Conway, N.H., 1977-80; asst. prof. mgmt. U. N.C.-Greensboro, 1985—. Recipient Elizabeth Kennedy Chance award Hollins Coll., 1975. Mem. NOW (treas. Greater Lawrence chpt. 1980-81), AAUW (corp. rep. 1980-82), ACLU. Presbyterian. Clubs: Appalachin Mountain, Appalachin Trail Conf. Contbr. articles to profl. pubs. Home: 26 Fidelity Ct Carrboro NC 27510 Office: Dept Mgmt U NC Greensboro NC 27412

BUTTS, ALICE GOULD, property investment and management firm executive, writer; b. Elyria, Ohio, Aug. 18, 1942; d. Howard George and Helen (Baumann) Gould; m. Charles Lewis Butts, Aug. 10, 1963; children—John, Paul, Joanna, Helen. Student Baldwin-Wallace Coll., 1960-63; B.A., Millsaps Coll., 1964. Telephone investigator Liberty Mut. Ins. Co., N.Y.C., 1962; med. sec. Doctors Higley, Ray & McCline, Memphis, 1963-64; owner, mgr. FCH Property Mgmt., Cleve., 1980—; free-lance writer, 1985—. Mem. Ohio City Redevel. Assn., Cleve., 1973—, Detroit-Shoreway Devel. Corp., Cleve., 1973—; bd. advisers Neighborhood Housing Services, Cleve., 1984—. Mem. Democratic County Exec. Com., Cleve., 1974—; office mgr. Charles Butts' state senate campaigns, 1974, 78, 82; bd. dirs. West Side Community House, Cleve., 1967-70, Urban Community Sch., Cleve., 1978-84. Mem. Cuyahoga Woman's Polit. Caucus, LWV (bd. dirs. 1967-70). Mem. United Ch. of Christ. Avocations: sailing; piano; canoeing; gardening. Home: 4514 Franklin Blvd Cleveland OH 44102 Office: 4514 Franklin Blvd Cleveland OH 44102

BUTTS, DONNA KAY, insurance agent, insurance agency executive; b. Evansville, Ind., Dec. 30, 1946; d. Clarence Ellis and Erma Joyce (Morris) Hazlett; m. Robert Lee Butts, July 18, 1964; 1 child, Kimberly Kay. Student pub. schs., Mt. Vernon, Ind. Lic. in property and casualty ins., life and health ins., Ind. Agt., prin. Donna Butts Ins. Agy., Mt. Vernon, 1977—. Vice pres. Posey County United Way, Ind., 1984-85; sec. Greater Mt. Vernon Assn., 1984-86; organist Mt. Pleasant G.B. Ch., Mount Vernon, 1976—. Mem. Mt. Vernon Bus. and Profl. Women's Assn. (treas. 1983-86), Mount Vernon C. of C., Profl. Ins. Agts. Assn. State of Ind., Evansville Ind. Ins. Women's Assn. (officer 1967-75). Democrat. Avocations: painting; music; needlecraft; camping; bowling. Office: Donna Butts Ins Agy 122 W 3d St PO Box 603 Mount Vernon IN 47620

BUTTS, VIRGINIA, public relations executive; b. Chgo.; B.A., U. Chgo. TV producer, writer, performer Chgo.; writer Dave Garroway's NBC Radio Show, N.Y.C.; midwest pub. relations dir. Time-Life Publs., 1956-63; public relations dir. Field Enterprises, Chgo. Sun-Times and Daily News, 1963-74, v.p. pub. relations Field Enterprises, Inc., Chgo., 1974-84; v.p. pub. relations Field Corp., 1984—. Contbr. to Lesley's Public Relations Handbook, 1978, 83. Mem. Pub. Relations Soc. Am. (dir.), Chgo. Network, Fashion Group, Chgo. Acad. TV Arts and Scis. Address: The Field Corp 333 W Wacker Dr Chicago IL 60606

BUTVYDAS, KRISTINA RITONE, catering company executive; b. Newark, Apr. 1, 1953; d. Vincas and Viltis (Garunkstis) B. Student fine arts Boston Mus. Sch., 1971-75; B.A. in Fine Arts summa cum laude, Tufts U., 1975; M.S. in Historic Preservation, Columbia U., 1977; numerous postgrad. courses in bus. and arts. Historic preservation specialist Dept. of Interior, Washington, 1977, policy analyst, communications mgr. Heritage Conservation and Recreation Service, 1977-80; exec. dir. Victorian Soc. in Am., Phila., 1980-81; dir. art and advt. Boehm Porcelain, Trenton, N.J., 1982—; dir. Phila. Christmas Coalition, 1982; v.p. Raymond Haldeman Catering, Phila., 1983—. Mem. Pub. Relations Soc. Am., Internat. Assn. Bus. Communicators, Phila. Pub. Relations Assn., Meeting Planners Internat., Phila. Women's Network, Phi Beta Kappa. Home: 1905 Mt Vernon Philadelphia PA 19130 Office: Raymond Haldeman Catering 110-112 S Front St Philadelphia PA 19106

BUXTON, CHANDRA DAWN, travel agency executive; b. Balt., Aug. 24, 1948; d. Arthur Brent and Ruth Alverta (Whitcomb) Hall; m. James C. Pochron, Feb. 14, 1974 (div. 1980); 1 child, Douglas Stanley; m. Roger Basil Buxton, Jan. 24, 1981; children—Dustin Brown, Dallas Ramee. Cert. travel counselor. Travel agt. Aladdin Travel, Glen Burnie, Md., 1966-67; internat. travel agt. Travel Guide, Balt., 1967-70; mgr. Tobys Travels, Reisterstown, Md., 1970-72; owner, mgr. Welcome-Aboard Travel, Frederick, Md., 1972-80; mgr. Pardee Travel, Frederick, 1980-82; owner, mgr. Buxtons World of Travel, Damascus, Md., 1982—. Mem. Mid Montgomery Bus. and Profl. Women, Am. Soc. Travel Agts., Assn. Retail Travel Agts., Inst. Cert. Travel Agts. Democrat. Methodist. Avocations: swimming; redecorating. Office: Buxton's World of Travel 9830 Main St Damascus MD 20872

BUXTON, MARY PERRIN, development professional; b. Highland Park, Ill., Apr. 22, 1953; d. William Perrin and Anne (Taylor) B. A.A., Colby-Sawyer Coll., 1973; B.A. in Edn., U. Mich., 1975, A.M. in L.S., 1976; J.D., Wayne State U., 1980. Bar: Mich., Pa. U.S. Dist. Ct. (ea. dist.) Mich. Young adult librarian Monroe County Library System, Monroe, Mich., 1976-77; trust officer Pitts. Nat. Bank, 1980-82; instr. Pa. State U., 1981; instr. legal research Univ. Detroit Sch. Law, 1982, asst. dean 1982-84; dir. devel. and alumni affairs Villanova Law Sch., Pa., 1984-86; dir. devel. Miss Porter's Sch., 1986—; cons. Pa. Bar Found., 1984-85. Sec. to corp., fin. adviser Alpha Xi Delta Fraternity, Inc., Ann Arbor, 1983; judge Miss American Co-Ed Pageant, 1984, Outstanding Young Americans, 1983, 84, Miss Teen All-Am. Pageant, 1985. Mem. ABA, Mich. Bar Assn., Pa. Bar Assn., Main Line Bus. and Profl. Women (co-chmn. legis. com. 1984-85), Phi Theta Kappa. Democrat.

BUYER, SUSAN PATTERSON, health care agency program executive; b. Paterson, N.J., Nov. 8, 1949; d. Edward Michael and Marilyn Patterson (Stier) B.; student Wellesley Coll., 1967-69; B.A. in Polit. Sci., George Washington U., 1971, M.A. in Health Care Adminstrn., 1975; m. Eugene A. Slater, Feb. 9, 1980; children—Laura Patterson, Thomas Michael. Mgmt. intern. NIH, Bethesda, Md., 1971-72; sr. program analyst planning office, Nat. Library Medicine, Bethesda, Md., 1972-85, chief planning br., 1985—. Recipient Sustained High Quality Work Performance award Nat. Library Medicine, 1980. Mem. Am. Pub. Health Assn., NOW, Nat. Assn. Female Execs., Am. Soc. Pub. Adminstrn., Nat. Abortion Rights Action League. Office: 8600 Rockville Pike Bethesda MD 20209

BUYSE, MARYLOU, pediatrician, clinical geneticist; b. N.Y.C., June 27, 1946; d. George J. and Barbara M. (Sauer) B.; A.B., Hunter Coll., 1966; M.D., Med. Coll. Pa., 1970; m. Carl N. Edwards, Jan. 22, 1982. Intern, U. Mich., 1970-71; resident in pediatrics Los Angeles County-U. So. Calif. Med. Center, 1971-73, fellow, 1973-75; instr. Boston U., 1975; asst. prof. pediatrics U. So. Calif., 1973-75, Tufts U., 1976-84; coordinator Myelodysplasia Clinic, Tufts-New Eng. Med. Center, Boston, 1976-79, dir. Cystic Fibrosis Clinic and staff pediatrician Center for Genetic Counseling and Birth Defects Evaluation, 1975-82, med. dir. Center for Birth Defects Info. Service, 1978-82, dir. center, 1982—; pres. Medx, Ltd., 1985—; pres. Ctr. for Birth Defects Info. Scis., Inc., 1985—; dir. clin. genetics Children's Hosp., Boston, 1985—; mem. med. adv. bd. Mass. Cystic Fibrosis Found., 1977-79; cons. in field. Recipient Physicians Recognition award AMA, 1975. Diplomate Am. Bd. Med. Genetics. Fellow Am. Acad. Pediatrics, Mass. Med. Soc.; mem. Am. Assn. Mental Deficiency, Am. Med. Woman's Assn. (pres. Mass. br. 39 1986—), Am. Mgmt. Assn., Am. Soc. Human Genetics, AAAS, N.Y. Acad. Scis., Soc. Med. Decision Making, Am. Cleft Palate Assn., Am. Med. Writers Assn., Soc. Craniofacial Genetics (pres. 1986—), Am. Soc. Med. Systems and Info., Boston Computer Soc., Teratology Soc., Common Cause. Asso. editor Birth Defects Compendium, 2d edit., 1979; asso. editor Syndrome Identification Jour., 1977-82, editor, 1982; editor Jour. Clin. Dysmophology, 1982-86, Clinical Genetics, 1986—. Office: 300 Longwood Ave Boston MA

BUZZELL, LUCILLE EDITH, gerontologist, consultant, researcher; b. Waltham, Mass., Apr. 19, 1940; d. Thomas Vernon Wooley and Thelma Hope (Clark) Wooley Cunningham; divorced; children—Robert C. (dec.), Bruce Scott. B.A. cum laude, in Communication, U. So. Maine, 1980; M.A. in Liberal Studies, U. Maine, 1983. Manpower aide Maine Employment Security Commn., Augusta, 1970-77; dir. social services Augusta Convalescent Ctr., 1977-78, Pleasant Hill Healthcare Facility, Fairfield, Maine, 1978-81; gen. mgr. pub. relations Hill House Congregate Living, Fairfield, 1981; case mgr. Central Maine Area Agy. on Aging, Waterville, 1981-85; adult program dir. Found. for Sr. Living, Scottsdale, Ariz., 1986—; bus. cons. Soule's Respite Ctr., Sidney, Maine, 1981-85, Tebolt & Boldic, Inc., Waterville, 1985; chairperson Evaluation of Aging Com., Waterville, 1985; personal care instr. Kennebec Valley Vocat. Inst., Fairfield, 1985; workshop instr. on aging Project RISE, Waterville, 1985; mem. Nat. Task Force on Aging, 1985—. Bd. dirs. Citizens Adv. Council, Maine Dept. Social Welfare, Augusta, 1972, profl. adv. com. Kennebec Regional Health Agy., 1973, Waterville Hospice, Inc., 1984-85, Widowed Persons Service, Waterville, 1985. Recipient plaque of appreciation Waterville Area of Social Services, 1985. Mem. Nat. Assn. Female Execs., Gerontol. Soc. Am., Am. Soc. on Aging, Nat. Remotivation Therapy Orgn. (v.p. chpt. 1980). Democrat. Lodge: Zonta. Avocations: writing songs; writing poetry; swimming; classical music. Home: 3320 E University Dr Apt 2119 Mesa AZ 85203

BUZZELLI, CHARLOTTE GRACE, educator; b. Akron, Ohio, Mar. 21, 1947; d. Edmund Albert and Sarah Agnes (Russo) Buzzelli. B.S., U. Akron, 1969, M.S. in Edn., 1976. Tchr. St. Anthony Sch., Akron, 1969-76; program coordinator, tchr. Akron Montessori Sch. Continuing Edn. Program, Eastwood Ctr., Akron, 1976-77; dir. edn. Fallsview Psychiat. Hosp., Cuyahoga Falls, Ohio, 1977—; cons. in field pioneered first spl. edn. program in Ohio for adult state psychiat. hosp.; developed 1st community-based adult basic edn. program in state instn. in Ohio. Named Ohio Tchr. of Yr., 1979. Mem. Council Exceptional Children (chpt. pres., A key award), Assn. Supervision and Curriculum Devel., Assn. Children with Learning Disabilities, Internat. Reading Assn., U. Akron Alumni Assn., Pi Lambda Theta (pres.), Phi Delta Kappa, Delta Kappa Gamma, Gamma Beta (pres.). Clubs: Univ., Akron Women's City. Home: 662 Dayton St Akron OH 44310 Office: Fallsview Psychiat Hosp 330 Broadway East St Cuyahoga Falls OH 44221

BYARS, FRANCES CAROL, medical technologist; b. Calhoun City, Miss., Dec. 10, 1932; d. John G. and Elvie I. (Barton) Putman; B.S. in Bacteriology, Miss. State Coll. for Women, 1954; cert. Hendrick Meml. Hosp., 1958; divorced; children—John Randolph, Donna Dianne. Chief med. technologist Houston Hosp., 1954-56, Hendrick Meml. Hosp., Abilene, Tex., 1956-59; head bacteriology dept., tchr. med. tech. Coahoma County Hosp., Clarksdale Miss., chief med. tech., 1959-61; med. technologist Jackson (Tenn.) County Hosp., 1961-63, Children's Hosp., Birmingham, Ala., 1963-64, part-time, 1964-68; chief med. tech. Shades Mountain Clinic, 1968-75; head lab. Vestavia Pediatric P.A., Birmingham, Ala., 1975—. Mem. Am. Soc. Clin. Pathologists, Am. Soc. Med. Tech. Baptist. Address: 1915 Buttercup Dr Birmingham AL 35216

BYARS, ILA PEARL, organization executive, civic worker; b. Travis, Tex., June 25, 1908; d. William Lafayette and Sibyl Allen (Massey) B.; student public schs. With Mid-west States Telephone Co., Blanco, 1924-53; with Bigden Ins. and Real Estate, Tex., 1953-55; pvt. kindergarten tchr., Blanco, 1955-56; waitress various restaurants, 1956-62, 63-65; with Wall Furniture, also Wall Funeral Home, Blanco, 1952-53, 65-66; staff food dept. Blanco Mill Nursing Home, 1966—. County chmn. Am. Heart Assn., 1957-72, meml. and campaign mgr., 1957-72; bd. dirs. Blanco County unit Am. Cancer Soc., 1959-72, unit sec., 1971-74, 86—, pres., 1974-76; trustee Blanco Library, 1950-53, librarian, 1952-53; bd. dirs. Blanco County Tb Assn., 1951-53; sec. Council on Ministries, United Meth Ch., 1986—, sec. chancel choir, 1985-86, mem. nominating com., 1982—, parish com., 1986, Sunday Sch. tchr., 1949—, dir. Vacation Bible Sch., from 1968, asst. dir., 1986, chmn. children's dept., 1986—. Recipient Achievement citations Am. Heart Assn., 1970, 71, 73; citation Am. Cancer Soc., 1971, 25-yr. pin., 1985. Mem. Blanco C. of C. (sec. 1967-72, dir. 1967-71), Daus. of Nile, Wesleyan Service Guild (co-founder 1952, pres. 1968—), United Meth. Women (reporter 1986). Lodges: Daus. of Nile, Order Eastern Star (past matron; organist, sec. 1986—). Home: PO Box 246 Blanco TX 78606

BYE, JULIANNE, business executive; b. Mpls., Jan. 14, 1952; d. William D. and Margaret Jean (MacInnes) B. B.A., Mont. State U., 1974; M.B.A., Coll. St. Thomas, St. Paul, 1985. Adminstrv. researcher Billings and Yellowstone County study commns., Mont., 1975-77; sr. planner Hennepin County, Minn., 1978-82; assoc. dir. corp. devel. Naegele Outdoor Advt., Mpls., 1982-83; corp. treas. Hawaii Benefits, Eden Prairie, Minn., 1984—; exec. v.p. Nat. Benefits, Inc., Eden Prairie, 1983—. Mem. Mpls. Charter Commn., 1983, Mpls. Pay Equity Com., 1984, Eden Prairie Planning Commn., 1985. Mem. Eden Prairie C. of C. (chair edn. com. 1984), Minn. Women's Consortium, Minn. Assn. Woman in Housing (pres. 1980-82, program chair 1979). Avocations: travel; reading; hockey; skiing; walking. Office: Nat Benefits PO Box 444029 Eden Prairie MN 55344

BYE, ROSEANNE MARIE, restaurant research and product development executive; b. Chgo., Nov. 27, 1946; d. Paul David and Gwen Lucielle (Hipp) Forrester; B.S. in Foods and Nutrition, Western Ill. U., 1969; postgrad. in Mktg. and Mgmt., Calif. State U.-Irvine, Long Beach, and Los Angeles, 1970-78; m. Richard Wayne Bye, June 14, 1969. Test kitchen home economist Hunt-Wesson Foods, Inc., Fullerton, Calif., 1969-73; product and recipe devel. home economist Lawry's Foods, Inc., Los Angeles, 1973-74; mgr. research and product devel. Carl Karcher Enterprises, Anaheim, Calif., 1974-81; v.p. research and devel. Denny's Restaurants, La Mirada, Calif., 1981—; cons. new products, quality control, alcoholic beverage and licensing, others; participant mktg. research, seminars; panelist in field. Sec., publicity chmn. Orange County Music Center, Allegro chpt., 1979—; mem. Calif. Conf. on the Family, 1979—. Recipient Effie awards for new products, 1976, 78; Home Economist in Bus. awards of excellence, 1977, 78, 80; named Outstanding Home Economist in Bus. in Calif., 1977, 78. Mem. Am. Home Econs. Assn., Calif. Home Econs. Assn., Home Economists in Bus., Nat. Restaurant Assn., Women in Mgmt., Mktg. Research Assn., NOW, Soc. Advancement Food Service Research (bd. dirs. 1986—), Anaheim C. of C. (publicity chmn., 1977-78). Republican. Clubs: Soroptimist, Wine, Gourmet Dinner, Tennis and Swim. Mem. editorial council Internat. Foodservice; contbr. articles to Cotempo. Home: 5829 Valencia Dr Orange CA 92669 Office: 16700 Valley View Ave La Mirada CA 90637

BYER, SHERRY MARCIA PFEFFER, psychologist; b. Yonkers, N.Y., Nov. 6, 1946; d. Jack and Annette Gertrude (Sachs) Pfeffer; A.A., Dean Jr. Coll., 1966; B.A., Hofstra U., 1968; Ph.D., Ill. Inst. Tech., 1980; m. Lawrence Louis Byer, Feb. 24, 1979; children—David Robert Pfeffer, Stephen Craig. Clin. psychologist, intern Chgo. Read Mental Health Center, 1977-78; psychotherapist, sch. psychologist Maine Twp. High Schs., Park Ridge, Ill., 1978-79; sch. psychologist, Chgo. Public Schs., 1979-80; pvt. practice psychotherapy, Chgo., 1979—; psychologist Inst. for Health Maintenance, Chgo., 1980-84; clin. dir. Health Care Inst., 1984—; cons. behavioral medicine. Mem. Am. Psychol. Assn., Ill. Psychol. Assn., Gerontol Soc., Ill. Sch. Psychologist Assn., Chgo. Psychol. Assn., Am. Soc. for Clin. Hypnosis. Home: 1039 W Altgeld St Chicago IL 60614 Office: Suite 1428 666 Lake Shore Dr Chicago IL 60611

BYER EISENBERG, KAREN SUE, nurse; b. Bklyn., Mar. 11, 1954; d. Marvin and Florence (Beck) Byer; diploma nursing L.I. Coll. Hosp. Sch. Nursing, 1973; B.S. in Nursing, L.I. U., 1976, M.Profl. Studies, 1977; m. Howard Eisenberg, May 11, 1974. Nurse recovery room and surg. intensive care unit Downstate Med. Center, Bklyn., 1973-75; utilization rev. analyst Bezallel Health Related Facility, Far Rockaway, N.Y., 1975-76; utilization rev. analyst, R.N. supr. Seagirt Health Related Facility, Far Rockaway, 1976; staff nurse neurosurg. and rehab. nursing Downstate Med. Center, Bklyn., 1978, nurse intensive care unit, 1978-79, asst. nursing dir. pathology, clin. research asso. Research Found., 1979—. Mem. Oncology Nursing Soc., Am. Nurses Assn., N.Y. State Nurses Assn., N.Y. Acad. Scis., L.I. Coll. Hosp. Alumnae Assn. Contbr. articles to profl. jours. Office: 450 Clarkson Ave Box 25 Brooklyn NY 11203

BYERLY, JEAN MARIE, university administrator; b. Pitts., Dec. 29, 1958; d. Charles Edward and Nancy Jane (Early) B. B.A., Seton Hill Coll., Greensburg, Pa., 1980; M.A., George Washington U., 1983—; postgrad. in law, 1985—. Spl. project coordinator U.S. Dept. State, HHS, Washington, 1980-81; bilingual exec. sec. Citicorp Internat., Houston, 1981; adminstrv. asst. to dir. Nat. Orgn. for Victim Assistance, Washington, 1981-83; exec. assoc. to dean Sch. Pub. and Internat. Affairs, George Washington U., 1983—; dir. Campus Program Proposal, Washington. Vice pres. Com. on Western Hemispheric Relations, Washington, 1985; chmn. Grad. Student Forum Sch. Pub. and Internat. Affairs, 1984-85. Recipient Meritorious Service award U.S. Dept. State, 1980, Outstanding Service award U.S. Dept. HHS, 1981. Mem. Internat. Soc. Internat. Law, Inter-Am. Council, Nat. Orgn. Victim Assistance. Clubs: George Washington U., Catholic Alumni. Avocations: language study; reading; travel; camping; horseback riding. Home: 8274 Amity Circle Gaithersburg MD 20877 Office: Sch Pub and Internat Affairs 2013 G St NW Washington DC 20052

BYERS, RITA JEWELL, insurance company executive; b. Shelbyville, Ky., Oct. 30, 1947; d. Raymond M. and Wilma (Ragland) B.; student Western Ky. U., 1965-67; B.S., U. Louisville, 1980, postgrad. in bus. adminstrn., 1981—. Unit chief Commonwealth Life Ins. Co., Louisville, 1975-78, supr. policy values, 1978-79, supr. policy payments, 1979-81, mgr. office services and support, 1981—. Adviser, bd. dirs. Jr. Achievement. Fellow Life Mgmt. Inst.; mem. River City Bus. and Profl. Women, Assn. Records Mgrs. and Adminstrs., Bus. Forms Mgmt. Assn. (pres.), In-house Printing Mgrs. Assn., Internat. Info./Word Processing Assn., Smithsonian Assocs. Democrat. Baptist. Home: 224 Saint Joseph St Louisville KY 40203 Office: 4th St and Broadway Commonwealth Life Ins Co Louisville KY 40202

BYERS, SUSANNAH ANTOINETTE, nurse practitioner; b. Michigan City, Ind., Oct. 11, 1932; d. Edward and Henrietta Caroline (Schmidt) Pizarek; m. Jimmy D. Byers, Aug. 1, 1970; m. Ray E. Smeltzer, June 18, 1955 (div. Nov. 1968); children—Patrick John, Jean Marie, Thomas Edward. Diploma, Holy Cross Sch Nursing, South Bend, Ind., 1953; B.S.N., St. Mary's Coll., Notre Dame, Ind., 1954; cert. family nurse practitioner Ind. U.-N.W., 1978. Head nurse Beatty Meml. Hosp., Westville, Ind., 1954-55, adminstrv. supr., 1955-62, psychiat. nursing instr., 1962-71; news editor Westville Indicator, Ind., 1972-77; nurse practitioner Planned Parenthood N.W. Ind., Merrillville, Ind., 1979—. Pres., Town Bd. Trustees Westville, 1979; mem., 1977-80; mem. No. Ind. Regional Planning Comn., 1978-79. Mem. Nurses Assn. Am. Coll. Ob-Gyn (cert.) Nat. Assn. Nurse Practitioners in Family Planning, Ind. Assn. Nurse Practitioners in Family Planning (sec. 1985—), N.W. Ind. Council on Adolescent Pregnancy. Avocations: Sewing; quilting; stained glass window. Home: 156 Main St Westville IN 46391 Office: Planned Parenthood 8645 Connecticut Merrillville IN 46410

BYERS, TOMMIE MAE, financial analyst; b. Troutman, N.C., Sept. 8, 1949; d. Thomas Jefferson and Geraldine (McIntosh) B. B.A. in Acctg., Upsala Coll., East Orange, N.J., 1972; postgrad. N.J. Inst. Tech. Auditor, Ernst & Whinney, C.P.A.s, Newark, 1972-74; sr. budget accountant Supermarkets Gen., Woodbridge, N.J., 1974; mktg./budgeting analyst Airco Indsl. Gases, Murray Hill, N.J., 1974-78; fin. cons. Edwards Alexander & Assocs., Riverdale, N.J., 1978-80; auditor N.J. Dept. Labor, Paterson, 1980; fin. systems coordinator N.J. Dept. Energy, Newark, 1980-85; capital planner N.J. Office of Mgmt. and Budgeting, Trenton, 1985—; fin. adv. bd. People's Energy Coop., Inc., Newark, 1982-84. Vol. counselor Essex County Youth House, Newark, 1985—; lectr., vol. counselor N.J. Job Corp Ctr., Edison, 1986. Recipient Commendation from Gov. State N.J., 1983. Mem. Nat. Assn. Female Execs., Am. Soc. Pub. Adminstrn., N.J. Black Adminstrs. Network. Democrat. Avocation: reading. Office: NJ Office of Mgmt and Budgeting Div Planning 28 W State St Trenton NJ 08625

BYINGTON, KATHLEEN CORA, nurse, educator; b. Des Moines, July 16, 1952. B.S.N. Vanderbilt U., 1974, M.S.N., 1985. R.N., Tenn. Mem. nursing staff Vanderbilt Hosp., Nashville, 1972-79, 82-83, head nurse surg. pediatrics, 1976-79, pediatric clin. specialist, 1984—; instr. nursing Belmont Coll., Nashville, 1979-84. Mem. Sigma Theta Tau. Methodist. Office: Vanderbilt Hosp D2120 MCN Nashville TN 37232

BYNUM, BARBARA STEWART, health scientist administrator; b. Washington, June 13, 1936; d. Oliver Walton and Mabel (Easton) Stewart; m. Edward Bynum, Apr. 4, 1959; 1 son, Christian. B.A. in Chemistry, U. Pa., 1957; postgrad. in biochemistry, Georgetown U., 1958-60. Chemist Nat. Cancer Inst.-NIH, Bethesda, Md., 1958-71; adminstrv. asst., office assoc. dir. for adminstrn. NIH, Bethesda, 1971-72, sci. grants program specialist div. research grants, 1972-75, health scientist adminstr. div. research grants, 1975-78, asst. chief for spl. programs, sci. rev. br. div. research grants, 1978-81; dir. div. extramural activities Nat. Cancer Inst., Bethesda, 1981—; reviewer, cons.

AAAS, Washington, 1974—. Contbr. articles to profl. jours. Recipient Dirs. award NIH, 1980, Sr. Exec. Service Superior Performance award HHS, 1982. Mem. Am. Assn. Cancer Research, Am. Assn. Pathologists, AAAS, Biophys. Soc. Democrat. Roman Catholic. Office: Nat Cancer Inst 9000 Rockville Pike Bethesda MD 20892

BYNUM, ESTHER ANDERSON, art curator, gallery exec.; b. Henderson, Tex., Dec. 19, 1922; d. John Benton and Bertie Lee (Williams) Anderson; student So. Meth. U., Dallas, 1952, Tex. State U., Arlington, 1954; B.A., N.Tex. State U., 1965; M.A., U. Md., 1972, advanced grad. specialist in art edn. and secondary edn., 1973; postgrad. Western Md. U., 1975; m. James Louis Bynum, Mar. 7, 1942; children—James Lynn, John Michael, Marvin Anderson, Karen Melinda. Traveling art tchr. Montgomery County Public Schs., Rockville, Md., 1965-75, art coordinator, 1975-79; art curator, co-owner Four Oaks Gallery, Henderson, 1980—; artist-in-residence Longview Pub. Schs., 1985-86; art cons.; works exhibited juried shows: N.Y. Internat. Art Show, 1970, Laguna Beach (Calif.) Art Mus., 1973, Balt. Mus. Art, 1973-74, Jersey City Mus., 1974, Lowe Art Mus., Miami, Fla., 1975, Tex. Watercolor Soc., San Antonio, 1975-81. Vice pres. Concerned Citizens for Arts in Public Schs., 1973-75. Mem. AAUW, Am. Craft Council, Tex. Watercolor Soc., Henderson Art League, Delta Kappa Gamma, Methodist. Home: 711 Hwy 43 Henderson TX 75652 Office: 709 Hwy 43 Henderson TX 75652

BYRAM, BETTY JONES, accountant; b. Homer, La., Aug. 18, 1926; d. James Carl and Irene (Booth) Jones; B.A. in Econs., La. State U., 1947; postgrad. (acad. scholar), U. Ill., 1947-49; M.B.A., Lamar U., Beaumont, Tex., 1978; divorced; children—Beryl E. Byram Blankenship, Janet, Martha. Instr., researcher U. Ill., 1949; economist OPS, Shreveport, 1951-52; mgmt. analyst USAF, Barksdale AFB, La., 1953-54; sec.-treas. Universal Contractors, Inc., Beaumont, Tex., 1957-66; v.p. Byram-Swain Inc., Beaumont, 1966-73; partner Byram & Assos., C.P.A.s, Beaumont, 1979-84; instr. acctg. Lamar U., 1977—; v.p. Beaumont Housing Fin. Corp., 1980-82, pres., 1983-84; chmn. adv. council SBA, 1976-80. Commr., Beaumont Housing Authority, 1974-84; pres. Hospice, 1984-85; chmn. Beaumont Housing Appeals Bd., 1971—; mem. adminstrv. bd. Trinity United Methodist Ch., Beaumont, 1982, trustee, 1985—; chmn. makeup com. Nechos River Festival, 1985. C.P.A., Tex. Mem. Am. Inst. C.P.A.s, Am. Women's Soc. C.P.A.s, Tex. Soc. C.P.A.s, AAUW (chpt. treas. 1979-81), LWV (chpt. pres. 1961-63), Tex. Fedn. Republican Women (1st v.p. 1973-75), Beaumont Estate Planning Council (bd. dirs.), Tex. Gulf Coast Hist. Soc., Beaumont C. of C. (past chmn. econ. edn. com.). Home: 4550 Gladys Beaumont TX 77706 Office: PO Box 5208 Beaumont TX 77706

BYRD, HELEN MAE, ins. co. exec.; b. Durham, N.C., Feb. 9, 1930; d. Charlie Raymond and Olive Mae (Kelly) Byrd; student U. N.C., intermittently, 1955-65; m. Harry Richard Bray, Jr. With CIA, 1950-51; with Peoples Home Security Life Ins. Co., Durham, 1951—, sec. to pres., 1967-76, corp. sec., 1976—; dir. Home Security Fire and Casualty Ins. Co. Bd. dirs. Durham County Mental Health Assn., 1979-82. Cert. profl. sec. Fellow Life Mgmt. Inst.; mem. Nat. Secs. Assn. (local pres. 1968-69, internat. rules and bylaws com. 1975) Exec. Women Internat. Baptist. Club: Tobaccoland Civitan. Office: 505 W Chapel Hill St Durham NC 27701

BYRD, JACQUELINE PEARL, lawyer; b. Washington, July 16, 1946; d. Willie and Laura Marian (Richardson) Simon; divorced; children—Eric LeRoy, Keith William. B.S., D.C. Tchrs. Coll., 1974; J.D., Howard U., 1980. Bar: Md. 1981; notary pub., Md. Clk., U.S. Postal Service, Washington, 1964-81; asst. states atty. Prince George's County, Md., 1982—. Chairperson welfare com. U.S. Postal Service, Nat. Airport, Washington, 1979-80. Mem. Md. Bar Assn., Prince George's County Bar Assn., Assn. Trial Lawyers Am., J. Franklyn Bourne Law Club, Prince George's County Women's Caucus, Phi Delta Phi. Home: 3210 Dallas Dr Temple Hills MD 20748 Office: States Attys Office Courthouse Upper Marlboro MD 20772

BYRD, KATHLEEN MARY, state archeologist; b. Stamford, Conn., Feb. 2, 1949; s. Daniel Lester and Catherine Ruth (Byrne) Byrd; m. Robert Walter Neuman, May 4, 1980. B.A., Marquette U., 1971; M.A., La. State U., 1974; Ph.D., U. Fla., 1976. Archaeol. and zooarchaeol. cons. Baton Rouge, 1976-78; archaeologist II, State of La., Baton Rouge, 1978-79, state archaeologist, 1979—. Contbr. articles to profl. jours. Mem. La. Archaeol. Survey & Antiquities Commn., 1979—. Mem. Soc. Am. Archaeology, Soc. for Hist. Archaeology, La. Archaeol. Soc., Sigma Xi.

BYRD, MARQUITA LAVON, speech educator; b. Atlanta, Mar. 24, 1950; d. Robert David and Alma Ruth (Rowe) B.; 1 son from previous marriage, Henry Neal Wilbanks III. B.S., Central Mo. State U., Warrensburg, 1972; M.A., So. Ill. U., Edwardsville 1975; Ph.D., U. Mo.-Columbia, 1979. Asst. prof. U. So. Miss., Hattiesburg, 1978-81; asst. prof. U. Houston Downtown, 1981-83; asst. prof. speech S.E. Mo. State U., Cape Girardeau, 1983—. Mem. Speech Communication Assn. (v.p. black caucus 1982—), Alpha Kappa Alpha. Democrat. Methodist. Office: Dept Speech SE Mo State U Cape Girardeau MO 63701

BYRD, MARTHA GOODE, medical technologist; b. Denver, Aug. 30, 1943; d. William Law and Martha Catherine (Pate) Goode; B.S. in Biology, Furman U., 1965; diploma med. tech., Grady Meml. Hosp., Atlanta, 1965; m. Daniel English Byrd, Apr. 7, 1973; children—Susan Catherine, William English. Blood bank night supr. Grady Meml. Hosp., 1965-68, 71-73; research technologist, supr. histocompatibility lab. Emory U.-VA Hosp., Atlanta, 1968-71; sr. med. technologist, histocompatability lab. supr. Atlanta Regional Red Cross Blood Center, 1973-80; sr. med. technologist Pathology Services, Profl. Assoc., Tucker, Ga., 1980-83; research technologist Arthritis Found., Ctrs. for Disease Control, Atlanta, 1983—; lectr. in field. Mem. Am. Soc. Med. Tech., Am. Soc. Clin. Pathologists, Am. Assn. Blood Banks, Area Bloodbankers Orgn. (sec. 1972), Am. Assn. Clin. Histocompatability Testing. Democrat. Baptist. Home: 4055 Lake Erin Ct Tucker GA 30084 Office: 1600 Clifton Rd Atlanta GA 30033

BYRD, MARTHA JEAN, educational administrator; b. Heathman, Miss., Mar. 10, 1928; d. Gabe Edward and Lela Elizabeth (Ponder) Lee; m. William Earl Byrd, June 3, 1952; children—Beth, David, Neil. B.A. in Elem. Edn. and Music, Millsaps Coll., 1950; M.A. in Elem. Edn. and Sch. Adminstrn., Miss. Coll., 1970, specialist in elem. edn. and adminstrn., 1974. Cert. adminstr. elem. edn., Miss. Tchr. Indianola Sch., Miss., 1950-52, Yazoo City pub. schs., Miss., 1953-55, 64-69, Benton Sch., Miss., 1955-62, Bentonia Sch., Miss., 1962-64; tchr. Manchester Acad., Yazoo City, 1969-72, prin., 1972—; Bd. dirs. Yazoo Arts Council, 1978-84; founder, pres. Mozart Music Club, 1957—; organist First Baptist Ch., Indianola, 1946-52, Yazoo City, 1954-74. Mem. Miss. Pvt. Sch. Educators Assn. (officer 1969—), Miss. Pvt. Sch. Assn. (bd. dirs. 1985), Miss. Educators Assn. (state choral dir. 1963-64), Miss. Educators Assn., Yazoo City C. of C. Republican. Baptist. Avocations: traveling; music; sewing. Home: 2046 Fenwood Terr Yazoo City MS 39194 Office: Manchester Ednl Found PO Box 155 Yazoo City MS 39194

BYRD, MICHAELE ABNER, bus. temporary help company executive; b. Bklyn., June 22, 1949; d. Philip Russell and Yvonne Edythe (Dixon) Abner; student U. Pa., 1966-68, Marymount Coll., 1968-69; B.A., U. Pa., 1971; m. David Caulbert Byrd, III, July 24, 1976. Mktg. support rep. IBM, Washington, 1971-74, mktg. support rep. staff instr., Dallas, 1974-78, mktg. support mgr., McLean, Va., 1978-79, adminstrv. systems ops. mgr., Gaithersburg, Md., 1979-81, mktg. support rep. sch. tng. mgr., Dallas, 1981-82, office systems edn. specialist, 1982-84; info. systems mktg. cons., Bethesda, Md., 1984-85; nat. tng. mgr. Temporaries, Inc., Washington, 1985—. Mem. Big Bros. and Sisters Am. Mem. Am. Soc. Profl. and Exec. Women, Nat. Assn. Female Execs., Internat. Word Processing Assn., AAUW. Democrat. Roman Catholic. Home: 5523 Englishman Place Rockville MD 20852 Office: 3255 K St NW Washington DC 20007

BYRD, PATRICIA ROSE, educational administrator; b. Denver, Feb. 21, 1961; d. Robert Emmett and Germaine Agnes (Mueller) G.; m. Brian Douglas DePaul, June 10, 1979 (dec. Aug. 1981); m. Terry Lee Byrd, Sept. 28, 1984. A.A., Arapahoe Community Coll., 1982; B.A. in Organizational and Indsl. Communications, Met. State Coll., 1983—. Adult edn. tutor Arapahoe Community Coll., Littleton, Colo., 1981-82; art tchr. Landmark Christian Acad., Denver, 1982-83, art tchr., tutor, 1983-84, prin., 1984-85. Colo. Scholars scholar 1982. Republican. Avocations: writing; drawing; Bible study; camping; personal fitness. Home: 686 S Ogden Denver CO 80209 Office: Colo Housing Finance Authority 500 E 8th St Denver CO 80203

BYRNE, DIANE MARIE, statistical specialist; b. Detroit, Nov. 23, 1952; d. Romeo Fredrick and Patricia Ann (Murphy) Bernard; m. Larry Eugene Byrne, Aug. 20, 1971; children—Jennifer Leigh, Ryan Michael. B.S., U. Mich-Dearborn, 1981. Research assoc. laser technologist Sinia Hosp., Detroit, 1979-80; coordinator math. Nat. Inst. Tech., Livonia, Mich., 1981-83; cons., trainer Schoolcraft Coll., Livonia, 1983—, Argyle Assocs., Inc., New Canaan, Conn., 1983-85; adminstr. Quality Inst. Eaton Corp., 1985—. Mem. Am. Soc. Quality Control (regional counselor automotive div. 1985—), Am. Statis. Assn., Math. Assn. Am., Schoolcraft Coll. Found. Roman Catholic. Home: 10948 Edington St Livonia MI 48150

BYRNE, MARY BERNADETTE, television-film packaging company executive, communications consultant; b. N.Y.C.; d. Thomas Gorman and Maurica (Lloyd) B. Student Manhattanville Coll., U. Florence; B.A., U. Wash.; M.A., Middlebury Coll.; postgrad. Tchrs. Coll., Columbia U., Editor house organ Olivetti Corp. Am., N.Y.C., advt. specialist; publicity assoc. Time-Life Films, N.Y.C.; mgr. programming Visualscope TV div. Reeves Communications Corp., N.Y.C., dir. internat. div., v.p. parent co. in charge of Visualscope TV div., N.Y.C., officer parent co.; pres. Mary Byrne Assocs., N.Y.C., 1982—; media panelist N.Y. State Council on Arts, 1980-83. Mem. Nat. Acad. TV Arts and Scis., N.Y. Women in Film. Office: 30 W 60th St New York NY 10023

BYRNES, KATHLEEN MARY, machinery distribution company executive; b. West Chester, Pa., Mar. 12, 1942; d. Richard Timothy and Marion A. (Noe) B. B.A., Duquesne U., 1963; M.A., West Chester U., 1975. Copywriter Sudler & Hennessey, N.Y.C., 1963-65; med. writer Winthrop Labs., N.Y.C., 1966-68; sr. editor J.B. Lippincott, Phila., 1969-73; owner, exec. v.p., treas. Richard T. Byrnes Co., West Chester, 1973—. Mem. Woodworking Machinery Distbrs. Assn. (v.p.), Woodworking Machinery Importers Assn. (dir.). Avocations: reading, golf, travel. Home: 1102-17 Brinton Place Rd West Chester PA 19380 Office: Richard T Byrnes Co Inc 600 Hannum Ave West Chester PA 19382

BYRNES, MURIEL MARIE, research chemist; b. Chgo., Aug. 7, 1925; d. Edward David and Stella Ann (Courney) B.; B.S., Mt. Mary Coll., Milw., 1947. Chemist research labs. Quaker Oats Co., Chgo., 1947-52; dir. quality assurance Xttrium Labs., Chgo., 1952-70; sr. research scientist, sect. head Miles Labs., Chgo., 1970—. Recipient Alumnae award Mt. Mary Coll., 1977. Mem. Internat. Food Technologists, Am. Chem. Soc., Am. Oil Chemists Soc., Vitamin Chemists Soc. Roman Catholic. Home: 9717 S Keeler St Oak Lawn IL 60453

BYRON, ANN, clothing importer; b. Munich, W.Ger., Mar. 1, 1930; came to U.S., 1947; d. Balthasar and Anny (Mock) Wurmannstetter; m. Marvin C. Silver, July 24, 1976. Student Coll. of Puget Sound, 1948-50, Chenard Sch. Art, 1955-58. Designer, Danielle & Frolic Time, 1960-69; designer and mfr. handwoven ladies apparel, Ann Byron Handloomed Designs, Los Angeles, 1970-77; designer Picardo of Calif., Los Angeles, 1972-79; importer wearing apparel from W. Germany, Los Angeles, 1981—. Treas. Internat. com. Los Angeles Philharm., 1983-84. Mem. German Am. C. of C., Fashion Group, Westmac. Address: 1743 N Dillon St Los Angeles CA 90026

BYRON, BEVERLY BUTCHER, congresswoman; b. Balt., July 27, 1932; d. Harry C. and Ruth Butcher; student Hood Coll., 1962-64; m. Goodloe E. Byron, 1952 (dec.); children—Goodloe E. Jr., Barton Kimball, Mary McComas. Mem. 96th-99th Congresses from 6th Md. Dist. State treas. Md. Young Democrats, 1962, 65; bd. assos. Hood Coll.; bd. dirs. Frederick County chpt. ARC: sec. Frederick Heart Assn., 1974-79; chmn. Md. Phys. Fitness Commn.; mem. Frederick County Landmarks Found.; bd. dirs. Am. Hiking Soc.; bd. visitors Air Force Acad. Episcopalian. Office: 1216 Longworth House Office Bldg Washington DC 20515

BYRUM, MARNI ELAINE, lawyer; b. Warrenton, N.C., Apr. 16, 1955; d. Charles Curtis and Maxine (George) Byrum. B.A., Va. Poly. Inst. and State U., 1976; J.D., Pepperdine U., 1979. Bar: Va. 1979, U.S. Supreme Ct. 1983. Atty.-advisor Fed. Labor Relations Authority, Washington, 1979-82, exec. asst. to chmn. authority, 1982-83, asst. to chmn., 1983-84; pvt. practice, 1984—; arbitrator Better Bus. Bur., Washington, 1980—; . advisor Va. State Task Force on Missing and Abused Children. Recipient Spl. Achievement cert. Fed. Labor Relations Authority, 1983, 84. Mem. ABA (law student div. liaison 1978-79, Silver Key award 1978, 79), Va. State Bar, Va. Women's Attys. Assn., Women's Bar Assn., Phi Alpha Delta (dist. justice 1979—).

BYSIEWICZ, SHIRLEY RAISSI, lawyer; b. Enfield, Conn.; d. Kyriakos and Anna (Gavala) Raissi; B.A., J.D., M.S. L.S., U. Conn.; m. Stanley J. Bysiewicz, July 18, 1959; children—Susan, Walter John, Karen, Gail. Admitted to Conn. bar, 1954; mem. firm Raissi & Raissi, Enfield, 1954—; mem. faculty U. Conn. Sch. Law, Hartford, 1956— prof. law, 1965—, also law librarian. Mem. Permanent Commn. on Status Women for Conn., 1976-80, pres., 1978-79; mem. Conn. Law Library Adv. Com., 1976—; law revision commr. for Conn., 1980—. Mem. Bar Assn. Conn. (treas. 1975-78), Nat. Assn. Women Lawyers, ABA, Hartford County (exec. com.), Conn. (chmn. juvenile justice coms.) bar assns., Am. Bar Assn. Women Lawyers, Am. Assn. Law Schs. (co-presider sect. on status of women, sect. legal research 1974), Am. Assn. Law Librarians (law library jour. com., sec. 1980-83), U. Conn. Law Sch. Alumni Assn. (exec. sec. 1958-68), New Eng. Law Librarians (pres. 1970), Women's Equity Action League. Author: (with Max R. White) Forms of Town Government in Connecticut, 1954; Survey of County Law Libraries in Connecticut, 1967; Monarch's Dictionary of Legal Terms, 1983; co-author Selected Annotated Bibliography on Education for Professional Responsibility, 1968; (with Price & Bitner) Effective Legal Research, 1979. bus. mgr. Law Library Jour., 1968-72; co-editor Materials on Estate Planning, 1969; editor, compiler Juvenile Law Handbook, 1984. Contbr. law articles to profl. jours. Office: 65 Elizabeth St Hartford CT 06105

BYSTRYN, SARA WOLSKI, importer; b. Brest Litovsk, Russia; d. Charles and Louba (Prilouk) Wolski; student Sorbonne, Paris, 1930-33; m. Iser Bystryn, Dec. 23, 1930; children—Denise (Mrs. Eric Kandel), Jean-Claude. Came to U.S., 1949, naturalized, 1954. Owner, pres. Ibis Export Import Co., N.Y.C., 1951—. Active mem. French Resistance, 1942-44. Home: 800 West End Ave New York NY 10025 Office: 250 W 57th St New York NY 10019

CAADWAL-ILOTT, PAMELA, television executive, writer, consultant; b. Wales, United Kingdom; came to U.S., 1954. Writer, producer CBS, N.Y.C., 1954-55, dir. religious broadcasts, 1955-76, v.p. cultural and religious broadcasts, 1976—. Office: CBS Broadcast Group 524 W 57th St New York NY 10019

CABATIT-SEGAL, BETSY ROZELLS, educational administrator; b. Penang, Brit. Malaysia, Feb. 27, 1932; came to U.S., 1957, naturalized, 1969; d. Fructoso Ramos and Mathilda (Rozells) Cabatit; m. Marvin Segal, Dec. 17, 1974. B.S. in Nursing, U. Philippines, 1955; M.A. in Edn., U. Chgo., 1960. Instr. U. Philippines, Quezon City, 1955-56; chmn. med./surg. nursing U. Nueva Caceres, Philippines, 1956-57, Philippine Women's U., Manila, 1961-64; USA exchange vis. staff nurse Cook County Hosp., Chgo., 1957-60, instr., 1960-61, 64-65; instr. U. Ill., Chgo., 1965-68; dir. staff devel. Rush-Presbyterian St. Luke's Hosp., Chgo., 1968-69; instr. Coll. of DuPage, Glen Ellyn, Ill., 1970-74, asst. dean, 1970-78, assoc. dean health and public services, 1978—; mem. task force Coalition for Preservation Ill. Nurse Practice Act, 1986—. Mem. bd. dirs. Edn. Network for Older Adults, Chgo., 1980—, DuPage County Heart Assn., Ill., 1980—; cons. Excellence in Edn., Ill. Bd. Regents, 1986; mem. Ill. Community Coll. Pres.'s Council. Public Adminstrn. scholar, 1961. Mem. Am. Nurses' Assn., Ill. Nurses' Assn. (del. to Internat. Nurses Assn. conv. Chgo. 1978, 83, 85), Nat. League Nursing, Ill. League Nursing, Am. Soc. Allied Health Professions', Ill. Assn. Allied Health Professions' (treas. 1981-82), Health Edn. Resources Council for No. Ill. (pres. 1980-81), Philippine Nurses Assn. Chgo. (pres. 1967-68, 75-76), Am. Assn. Community and Jr. Colls. Women Adminstrs., Ill. Vocat. Assn. (mem. council of local adminstrs. 1980—). Democrat. Roman Catholic. Office: Main Campus Adminstrn Coll of DuPage 22d St and Lambert Rd Glen Ellyn IL 60137

CABBELL, PATRICIA, publicist; b. Phila., Aug. 10, 1945; d. Howard Edward and Vivian (Parks) Cabbell; m. John Andrew King III, July 27, 1963; 1 child, John Andrew IV. Student bus. Temple U., 1963, 79, 80; Assoc. degree, Charles Morris Price Sch. Journalism, Phila., 1975. Exec. asst. Phila. Tribune, 1968-72; publicity writer Rohm & Haas Co., Phila., 1972-75; assoc. dir. promotions Essence Mag., N.Y.C., 1975-77; assoc. dir. pub. affairs Sta. WHYV-TV, Phila., 1978-79; info. officer City of Phila., 1979-81; corp. mktg. and promotion rep. Southeastern Pa. Transp. Authority, Phila., 1981-85; rail promotion rep. Port Authority of N.Y. and N.J., 1985—. Active Pa. Coalition-100 Black Women, Phila., 1983—; co-chairperson communications task force Urban Coalition, Phila., 1974—; sec. adv. council Salvation Army, Phila., 1981—; cons. Phila. Film Festival, 1978—; campaign schedulor W.H. Gray for Re-Election to Congress, Phila., 1982; media coordinator Joe Rhodes for U.S. Senate, 1977. Mem. Pub. Relations Soc. Am., Phila. Pub. Relations Assn., Nat. Assn. Media Women (chpt. editor 1981-82). Democrat. Baptist. Office: One World Trade Ctr Suite 62W New York NY 10048

CABOT, ELAINE EVELYN, dietitian; b. Distant, Pa., June 14, 1924; d. Vincent Ray and Ella Sophia (Johnson) Hetrick; m. Ellsworth Sebastian Cabot, May 24, 1945; children—Pamela S. Zapf, Rochelle Dunn, Leslie E. B.S. in Dietetics, Pa. State U., 1944. Registered dietitian. Therapeutic dietitian Meml. Hosp., Wilmington, Del., 1944-45, Physicians Hosp., Plattsburgh, N.Y., 1947-48; teaching dietitian Crosue Irving Hosp., Syracuse, N.Y., 1950-53; out-patient dietitian Charity Hosp., New Orleans, 1954-55; chief dietitian St. John's Mercy Hosp., St. Louis, 1959-69; pres. Elaine E. Cabot Assocs., Inc., dietary cons., 1967—; mem. dietetic tech. adv. com. Florissant Valley Coll., 1978-79. Author: Handbook for Menu Makers, 1973; Contbg. editor Modern Nursing Home, 1968-74, Modern Hosp., 1969-73, Modern Health Care, 1974-77. Mem. Am. Dietetic Assn., Mo. Dietetic Assn., St. Louis Dietetic Assn., Beta Mu (local pres. 1943-44). Avocations: travel; symphony concerts. Address: 6 Quailways Dr Saint Louis MO 63141

CABRINETY, PATRICIA BUTLER, software executive; b. Earlville, N.Y., Sept. 4, 1932; d. Eugene Thomas and Helen Sylvester (Fulmer) Butler; m. Lawrence Paul Cabrinety, Aug. 20, 1955; children—Linda Anne Cabrinety, Margaret Marie Cabrinety, Stephen Michael Cabrinety. B.S. in Elem. Edn. and Music, SUNY-Potsdam, 1954. Cert. tchr. N.Y., Pa., Minn., Mass. Asst. music tchr. Hamilton Central Sch., N.Y., 1948-50; tchr. elem. schs. Cherry Lane Sch., Suffern, N.Y., 1954-56; music instr., Towanda, Pa., 1960-63, Sayre, Pa., 1963-79; pres. Superior Software Inc., Mpls., 1981—; poet and illustrator, Edina, Minn., 1981—; cons. in field. Composer, artist numerous compositions; inventor: Musical for Computer, 1981; author: Monthly Column on Boy Scouts, 1975-78. Recipient Golden Poet award World of Poetry, 1985; Poet of Month award All Season's Poetry, 1985. Mem. Nat. Assn. Female Execs., Nat. Writers Assn., DAR, AAUW, Pioneers, Legion of Mary, Third Order Carmelite, Mpls. Music Tchrs. Forum, Edina C. of C., Worcester County Music Assn., Worcester County Poetry Assn. Avocations: Hobbies; philately; art; needle craft; photography; outdoors. Home: 925 Pearl Hill Rd Fitchburg MA 01420 Office: Superior Software Inc PO Box 113 7074 Amundson Ave Minneapolis MN 55435

CACCAMISE, GENEVRA LOUISE BALL (MRS. ALFRED E. CACCAMISE), librarian; b. Mayville, N.Y., July 22, 1934; d. Herbert Oscar and Genevra (Green) Ball; B.A., Stetson U., DeLand, Fla., 1956; M.S. in L.S., Syracuse U., 1967; m. Alfred E. Caccamise, July 7, 1974. Tchr. grammar sch., Sanford, Fla., 1956-57, elem. sch., Longwood, Fla., 1957-58; tchr., librarian Enterprise (Fla.) Sch., 1958-63; librarian, media specialist Boston Ave. Sch., DeLand, 1963-82; head media specialist Blue Lake Sch., DeLand, 1982—; area dir. for Volusia County, Fla. Edn. Assn., 1963-65. Charter mem. West Volusia Meml. Hosp. aux., DeLand, 1962—; Girl Scout leader, 1955-56. Bd. dirs. Alhambra Villas Home Owners Assn., 1972-75; trustee, pres. DeLand Public Library. Mem. AAUW (2d v.p. chpt. 1965-67, rec. sec. 1961-65, 78-80, pres. 1980-82, parliamentarian 1982-84), Assn. Childhood Edn. (1st v.p. 1965-66, corr. sec. 1963-65), DAR (chpt. registrar 1969—; asst. chief page Continental Congress, Washington 1962-65), Bus. and Profl. Women's Club (corr. sec. DeLand 1968-71, 2d v.p. 1969-70), Stetson U. Alumni Assn. (class chmn. for ann. fund drive 1968), Volusia County Assn. Media in Edn. (treas.), Colonial Dames XVII Century, Magna Charta Dames, Soc. Mayflower Descs., Delta Kappa Gamma (pres. Beta Psi chpt.). Democrat. Episcopalian. An author Volusia County manual Instructing the Library Assistant, 1965. Home: PO Box 241 DeLand FL 32721 Office: 282 N Blue Lake Ave DeLand FL 32724

CACKOWSKI, IRENE KATHLEEN, librarian; b. Englewood, N.J., Sept. 9, 1946; d. Richard Jerome and Kathleen Elyse (Andrews) Dunphy; m. Leonard Francis Cackowski, July 11, 1970; children—Kathleen, Beth and Celia (twins). B.A., Coll. New Rochelle (N.Y.), 1968; M.L.S., L.I. U., Greenvale, N.Y., 1969. Cert. pub. librarian, ednl. media specialist, N.J. Library asst. New Rochelle Pub. Library, 1968-69, children's librarian, 1969; children's librarian Johnson Pub. Library, Hackensack, N.J., 1969-70; librarian South River High Sch. (N.J.), 1970-72; dir. South River Pub. Library, 1972—. Bd. dirs. Woodbridge Devel. Ctr., 1983; pres. bd. Literacy Vols. Middlesex County, N.J., 1981-86; sec. exec. bd. Regional Library Coop. Mem. ALA, N.J. Library Assn., Library Pub. Relations Council, Libraries of Middlesex (pres. 1983-84), South River Commerce Assn. Roman Catholic. Clubs: East Brunswick Women's, South River Woman's. Home: 15 Henry St East Brunswick NJ 08816 Office: South River Public Library 55 Appleby Ave South River NJ 08882

CACUCI, GABRIELA PARASCHIVA, lawyer; b. Bucharest, Romania, Oct. 14, 1953; came to U.S., 1975, naturalized, 1980; d. Luca C. and Elena-Livia (Papadopol) Mihailescu. Student Inst. Fine Arts, Bucharest, 1972-75; B.A. with honors in Polit. Sci., Barnard Coll., 1978; J.D., U. Va., 1981. Bar: Tenn. 1981. Law clk. U.S. Dist. Ct. (no. dist.) Ga., Atlanta, 1981-82; assoc. Wilson S. Ritchie Law Office, Knoxville, Tenn., 1982-83; assoc. firm Foglesong, Cruze, Dunaway, Shope & Harrell, Knoxville and LaFollette, Tenn., 1983-84, Shearman & Sterling, N.Y.C., 1984—. Mem. N.Y. State Bar Assn. Office: Shearman & Sterling 53 Wall St New York NY 10005

CADY, JANET ARLENE, association executive; b. Atlanta, Mich., Aug. 19, 1949; d. Arthur F. and Jean M. (Maanika) C.; student Oakland U., 1967-69; B.A. with high honors, Mich. State U., 1971; postgrad. Taiwan Normal U., 1972-74; M.A., U. Mich., 1975. Pub. relations officer Chinese Acupuncture Sci. Research Found., Taipei, Taiwan, 1972-74; project asst. Chinese econ. studies program U. Mich., 1975-77; program dir. internat. Asian studies program Yale-China Assn., New Haven, 1977-78; program dir. Nat. Com. U.S.-China Relations, N.Y.C., 1978—. Mem. Assn. Asian Studies, Nat. Assn. Fgn. Student Affairs, Yale-China Assn., Fgn. Policy Assn., Phi Beta Kappa, Phi Kappa Phi. Editor: Understanding China newsletter, 1974-75; (with E.A. Winckler) Urban Planning in China: Report of the U.S. Urban Planners Delegation to the People's Republic of China, 1980; Economic Reform in the People's Republic of China, 1985; author: Historic Preservation in the People's Republic of China, 1984; contbg. author: Urban Innovation Abroad: Problem Cities in Search of Solutions, 1984.

CADY, NELL GOODHUE, investment banker; b. Boston, May 10, 1961; d. Kendall Bingham Cady and Carol Helen (Conrad) Keyser. B.S., Cornell U., 1984, M.B.A., 1985. Intern trade fin. Continental Ill. Nat. Bank, Chgo., summer 1982; Intern Gt. Lakes dist. Mfrs. Hanover Trust, N.Y.C., summer 1984; trainee Bankers Trust Co., N.Y.C., 1985-86, assoc. leveraged buyouts, 1986—. Republican. Episcopalian. Avocations: sailing; scuba diving; public speaking; horseback riding. Office: Bankers Trust Co 280 Park Ave New York NY 10017

CAETANO, PATRICIA ANN, international lecturer, trainer, consultant; b. Portland, Oreg., Oct. 19, 1940; d. William Paul and Margaret Ann (MacLennan) Whaley; m. Richard James Caetano, Oct. 24, 1970; children—Elisabeth Anne, Kristyn Jennifer. B.S., U. Oreg., 1963. Owner, investor, real estate, Portland, 1964-70; trainer Nat. TV Studios, Tehran, Iran, 1974-77; exec. dir. China Study tours, San Francisco and San Diego, 1980-82; co-dir. Stratford Gallery, Del Mar, Calif., 1982-83; dir., owner Personal Devel. Ctr., San Diego, 1983—; trainer, lectr. Assn. Research and Therapy, Riverside, Calif., 1982—; cons., lectr. Kairos, Encinitas, Calif., 1982—; lectr. ACCESS, San Diego, 1981—. Contbr. articles to profl. jours. Writer, dir. stage plays, 1978-79, Pres. San Diego PTA, 1982, 83, v.p., 1977-82; chmn. area pub. relations San Diego Imperial council Girl Scouts U.S., 1981, 82; bd. dirs. Piruzi Pvt. Sch., Tehran, 1975-77. Recipient Hon. Service award PTA, 1983, Award of Merit, PTA, 1981; Award of Merit, Girl Scouts, 1982. Mem. Assn. Research and Therapy (editor newsletter 1984—, bd. dirs. 1984—), Calif. Assn. for Counseling and Devel., Friends of Jung. Republican. Office: Personal Devel Ctr 2435 San Diego Ave Suite A San Diego CA 92110

CAFFERATA, PATRICIA DILLON, state official; b. Albany, N.Y., Nov. 24, 1940; d. Kenneth Price and Barbara Farrell (Vucanovich) Dillon; student Mills Coll., 1958-61; B.A., Lewis and Clark Coll., 1963; m. H. Treat Cafferata, June

17, 1961; children—Elisa, Janet, Reynolds. Former mem. Nev. Assembly; now treas. State of Nev., Carson City. Former pres. Drs. Wives of Washoe County; bd. dirs. St. Mary's Hosp. Guild. Named Outstanding Freshman Legislator, Nev. Med. Assn., 1980. Mem. Nev. State Order Women Legislators (charter), Republican State Legislators Assn. Episcopalian. Club: Rep. Women's (Reno). Office: Office of Treasurer Capitol Complex Carson City NV 89710*

CAGGINS, RUTH PORTER, nurse, educator; b. Natchez, Miss., July 11, 1945; d. Henry Chappelle and Corinne Sadie (Baines) Porter; m. Don Randolph Caggins, July 1, 1978; children—Elva Rene, Don Randolph, Myles Thomas Chapelle. B.A., Dillard U., New Orleans, 1967; M.A., N.Y.U., 1973. Staff nurse Montefiore Hosp., Bronx, 1968-70, head nurse, 1970-72; nurse clinician Met. Hosp., N.Y.C., 1973-74, clin. supr., 1974-76; asst. prof. U. S.W. La., Lafayette, 1976-78, Prairie View A&M U. Coll. Nursing, Houston, 1978—. Mem., The Links Inc., Houston, 1982-86, Cultural Arts Council, Houston. Mem. Am. Nurses Assn., Am. Group Psychology Assn., A.K. Rice Inst., Houston Group Psychotherapy Soc., Sigma Theta Tau, Delta Sigma Theta. Democrat. Baptist. Avocations: Singing; sewing; traveling; aerobics; writing; teaching. Home: 5602 Goettee Circle Houston TX 77091 Office: Prairie View A&M U Coll Nursing 6436 Fannin Houston TX 77030

CAGNO, CAROL ANNE, registered nurse; b. Phila., Dec. 11, 1951; d. Daniel J. and Mary L. (Bronico) Cavaliere; m. Charles V. Cagno, July 22, 1972; 1 son, Charles V. R.N., Albert Einstein Hosp. Sch., Phila., 1971. Staff nurse clinic Community Nursing Service, Phila., 1972, staff nurse field, 1976-79; supr. Home Health Service of So. Phila., 1979-82; dir. profl. service Neighborhood Home Health Service, Phila., 1982-84, exec. dir., 1984—; pub. relations com. mem. Community Health Coordinators, Phila., 1982-83. Mem. Am. Nurses Assn., Pa. Nurses Assn. Republican. Roman Catholic.

CAHILL, LISA SOWLE, theology educator, author, lecturer; b. Phila., Mar. 27, 1948; d. Donald Edgar and Gretchen Elizabeth (MacRae) Sowle; m. Lawrence Robert Cahill, Mar. 25, 1972; children—Charlotte Mary, James Donald. B.A., U. Santa Clara, 1970; M.A. in Theology, U. Chgo., 1973, Ph.D. in Theology, 1976. Instr., Concordia Coll., Moorhead, Minn., 1976; asst. prof. theology Boston U., Chestnut Hill, Mass., 1976-82, assoc. prof., 1982—. Author: Between the Sexes: Toward a Christian Ethics of Sexuality, 1985. Assoc. editor Religious Studies Rev., 1981—; assoc. editor Jour. Religious Ethics, 1981—, mem. editorial bd., 1978-81; mem. editorial bd. Horizons, 1983—, mem. adv. bd., 1983—; mem. adv. bd. Jour. Law and Religion, 1983—. Contbr. articles to profl. jours. Mem. instl. rev. bd. Harvard Community Health Plan, 1979-85; mem. bioethics adv. com. March of Dimes, 1985—. Summer Research grantee Boston Coll., 1977. Mem. Am. Acad. Religion (ethics program com. 1979-82), Soc. Christian Ethics (bd. dirs. 1983-86) Cath. Theol. Soc. Am. (moral theology steering com. 1983—), Coll. Theology Soc., Hastings Inst. Democrat. Office: Theology Dept Boston Coll Chestnut Hill MA 02167

CAHILL, MARY FRAN, journalist; b. Milw.; d. Morgan Joseph and Claire Catherine (Warnimont) Cahill. B.A., M.A., Marquette U., cert in mgmt. Cert. emergency med. technician, Wis. Reporter, photographer News-Graphic, Inc., Cedarburg, Wis., 1965-67; picture editor Milw. Jour., 1967-76, feature writer, 1976-83, food writer, graphics specialist, 1983—, mem. unitholders' council, 1977-79, dir. Jour. Co., 1978-79, Newspapers Inc., 1978-79. Recipient Disting. Service award Milw. Fire Dept., 1972, 75, 77, 78, 79, 80; appreciation cert. USCG, 1975. Mem. Milw. Fire Hist. Soc. (dir. 1981-86, treas. 1981-83, sec. 1983-86), Zool. Soc. Milwaukee County, Zoo Pride, Wis. Emergency Med. Technicians Assn. (co-founder 1973), Wis. News Photographers Assn. (sec. 1972-74), Nat. Press Photographers Assn., Women in Communications, Nat. R.R. Hist. Soc., Les Amis du Vin, Am. Culinary Fedn., Sigma Delta Chi. Club: Milw. Press. Home: 6609 N Lake Dr Fox Point WI 53217 Office: Milwaukee Jour PO Box 661 Milwaukee WI 53216

CAHILL, PATRICIA DEAL, radio station executive; b. St. Louis, Oct. 9, 1947; d. Richard Joseph and Dorothy (Deal) C.; m. Stephen R. Crump, Apr. 22, 1978; children—Lindsay Cahill, Jessica Cahill Crump. B.A., U. Kans., 1969, M.A., 1971. Continuity dir. Sta. KANU-FM, Lawrence, Kans., 1970, audio reader dir., 1970-73; reporter Sta. KCUR-FM, Kansas City, Mo., 1973-75; news dir. Sta. KMUW-FM, Wichita, Kans., 1975, gen. mgr., 1976—; dir. Nat. Pub. Radio, 1982—. Chmn. Wichita Free U., 1979-81. Mem. Pub. Radio in Mid Am. (pres. 1979-80), Radio Research Consortium (bd. dirs. 1981—), Kans. Pub. Radio Assn. (bd. dirs. 1980—). Home: 1714 Park Pl Wichita KS 67203 Office: Sta KMUW 3317 E 17th St Wichita KS 67208

CAHILL, PHYLLIS HENDERSON, marketing executive, educator; b. Phila., Nov. 5, 1954; d. Phyllis Henderson Garofalo; m. Peter Joseph Cahill, Mar. 26, 1977 (div. June 1982). B.S. in Food Mktg., St. Joseph's Coll., Phila., 1976; student Carnegie Inst., 1982-83. Cert. Dale Carnegie course instr. Account rep. Quaker Oats Co., Cranford, N.Y., 1976-77; mktg. mgr. Lumex, Inc., Bayshore, N.Y., 1978, Foodmaker, Inc., Hauppauge, N.Y., 1979, Yorkshire Food Sales, New Hyde Park, N.Y., 1980-84, CutCo Industries, Jericho, N.Y., 1984-86; mgr. advt. and sales promotion Nutri/System, Willow Grove, Pa., 1986—. Home: 350 Hilltop #104 King of Prussia PA 19406 Office: Nutri/System 3901 Commerce Ave Willow Grove PA 19090

CAHNERS, HELENE RABB, civic worker; b. Boston, Nov. 29, 1920; d. Sidney R. and Esther (Cohn) Rabb; A.A., Westbrook Coll., 1940; student Mt. Holyoke Coll.; LL.D (hon.), Northeastern U., 1974; m. Norman L. Cahners, May 15, 1941; children—Robert Merrill, Andrew Philip, Nancy Lynne. Former mem. trust bd. 1st Nat. Bank Boston; dir. Boston Edison Co., Berkshire Mut. Life Ins. Co., SYR Corp. Pres. women's aux. Beth-Israel Hosp., Boston, 1959-61 (hon. life trustee hosp.); co-chmn. Council of Friends Boston Symphony Orch., 1962-68, chmn. bd. overseers Orch., 1980-82, also trustee; pres. women's div. Combined Jewish Philanthropies, Boston, 1965-67, asst. sec., 1967-69, v.p., 1969—; bd. dirs. ladies com. New Eng. Med. Center, Boston 1965, Children's Med. Center, Boston, 1961—; trustee Westbrook Coll. (Tower award 1966), chmn. bd., 1972-75; trustee Carroll Sch., 1971—, Boston Opera Assn., 1972—, Mt. Holyoke Coll., 1970-80, Women's Ednl. and Indsl. Union, Mus. Sci. Service League, World Affairs Council, Wang Ctr., Boston; mem. trust Boston Mus. Sci.; mem. adv. bd. Colby Coll. Art Mus., 1970—, Mayor's Office of Cultural Affairs; bd. dirs. WGBH-TV, Boston, also vice-chmn.; bd. dirs. United Community Planning Corp.; bd. visitors Boston U. Sch. Social Work; trustee, v.p. Boston Children's Service; mem. council on arts MIT; bd. visitors Sch. Social Work, Boston U. Recipient Tower Disting. Alumnae award Westbrook Coll., 1966; Ralph Lowell Disting. Citizen award, 1981. Home: 380 Beacon St Boston MA 02116

CAHOW, LINDA JEAN, asphalt paving company executive; b. Phila., Feb. 22, 1957; d. Raymond Randolph Cahow and Guri (Myreng) Ladestro. Student Prince George Community Coll.; B.A. in Law Enforcement, U. Md., 1979. Office mgr. Alldin Lamp Publs., Arlington, Va., 1979-80; sales rep. Certified Leasing Co., Washington, 1980; salesperson Rumors Restaurant, Washington, 1980-83; exec., owner, Asphalt Gen., Inc., College Park, Md., 1983—. Vol. Am. Cancer Soc., Washington, 1975-79, Am. Lung Assn., Md. chpt., 1977-79; mem. Animal Welfare League, Md., 1984-85. Mem. Nat. Assn. Female Execs., Nat. Asphalt Assn., Alpha Xi Delta (various offices 1975-79), Theta Chi, Sons of Norway. Club: U. Md. Fencing. Avocations: photography; sewing; water sports; cooking. Home: 7617 Fontainbleau Dr #2144 New Carrollton MD 20784

CAIN, CARLEN YVONNE, nurse; b. Hahn, Fed. Republic Germany, Sept. 30, 1956 (parents Am. citizens); d. James Richard, Jr. and Georgia (Yelverton) Cain. Assoc. Nursing, Jones County Jr. Coll., 1976; B.S. in Nursing, U. Miss., 1984; advanced cardiac life support tng., 1984. R.N., Miss.; cert. CPR instr. Surg. nurse Miss. Bapt. Med. Ctr., Jackson, 1976; med.-surg. nurse Smith County Hospital Raleigh, Miss., 1977-80; emergency room nurse, ambulance supr. Covington County Hosp., Collins, Miss., 1980-83; staff nurse, adult emergency room, mem. flight team Lifestar I. U. Miss. Med. Ctr., Jackson, 1983-84; staff nurse ICU/CCU, River Oaks Hosp., Flowood, Miss., 1984-86; nursing edn. instr. dept. hosp. edn. St. Dominic Jackson Meml. Hosp., 1986—. Mem. Am. Assn. Critical Care Nurses, S.H.A.R.E. Educators Assn., Jones County Jr. Coll. Alumni Assn., U. Miss. Sch. Nursing Alumni Assn., Am. Heart Assn., Miss. Heart Assn. Baptist. Home: 2945 Layfair Dr #315 Jackson MS 39208 Office: St Dominic Jackson Meml Hosp Lakeland Dr Jackson MS

CAIN, JANIS DEE, retired medical practice management consultant; b. Mesquite, Tex., Oct. 23, 1945; d. J.D. and Imogene Elizabeth (Smith) Duckworth; m. James William Cain, Oct. 23, 1965 (div. Mar. 1979). Grad. high sch., Forney, Tex. Sec., Trinity Universal Ins., Dallas, 1964-66; exec. sec. Blue Cross-Blue Shield, Dallas, 1966-71, supr., 1971-79, staff asst., 1979-80, payment and policy coordinator, 1980-82; cons. Harold Whittington & Assocs., Dallas, 1982-84, ret. Coach girl's basketball Spring Valley Athletic Assn., Richardson, Tex., 1980, Spl. Olympics and wheelchair sports Bachman Recreation Center, Dallas, 1983. Recipient Sportsmanship award Spring Valley Athletic Assn., Richardson, 1980. Democrat. Baptist. Home: Trenton FL 32693

CAIN, JOANNA MARY, physician, gynecologist-oncologist, educator; b. Yakima, Wash., July 11, 1950; d. Estill Virgil and Marguerite E. (Bottker) Cain; m. C. Norman Turrill, May 18, 1974. B.S., U. Wash., Seattle, 1973; M.D., Creighton U., Omaha, 1977. Diplomate Am. Bd. Ob-gyn. Resident in ob-gyn U. Washington, 1977-81; fellow in gyn.-oncology Meml. Sloan Kettering Cancer Ctr., N.Y.C., 1981-83; asst. attending physician, 1983-85; asst. prof. U. Wash., Seattle, 1985—. Contbr. articles to med. publs. Am. Cancer Soc. jr. clin. fellow, 1981-83; Am. Cancer Soc. faculty fellow, 1984-86. Mem. Am. Coll. Ob-Gyn (jr. fellow), N.Y. Acad. Sci. Office: RH-20 Div Gynecol Oncology U Wash Seattle WA 98195

CAIN, JULIE ANNE, former art gallery administrator; b. Houston, Sept. 21, 1956; d. Thomas Edward and Therese Catherine (Arnold) C. B.A., Vanderbilt U., 1978. Salesperson, Meinhard Galleries, Houston, 1978-81, dir. gallery, 1982-84; asst. dir. Office Spl. Projects, U. Houston, 1986—. Mem. Coll. Cabinet, Vanderbilt U., 1983. Mem. Phi Beta Kappa. Republican. Methodist.

CAIN, KELLY ANN, air force officer, administrator; b. Ironwood, Mich., Sept. 29, 1954; d. James Forrest and Mary Margaret (Smith) Rouse; m. Donald Morris Cain, Sept. 30, 1976; stepchildren—Cindy, Donald Morris. B.A. in Fgn. Langs., U. N.D., 1975; M.A. in Personnel Mgmt., Central Mich. U., 1979. Commd. 2d lt. U.S. Air Force, 1976, advanced through grades to capt., squadron intercept controller 615 Aircraft Control and Warning Squadron, Germany, 1976; squadron sect. comdr., exec. officer 89 Mil. Airlift Wing (Presdl. airlift), Md., 1976-79; chief publ. and exec. officer SAC, Omaha, 1979-82; air force exec. officer Joint U.S. Mil. Mission for Aid to Turkey, 1982-83; squadron sect. comdr. 1st Aircraft Generation Squadron, Hampton, Va., 1983-85; chief of protocol Hdqrs. Alaskan Air Command, Anchorage, 1985—. Foster parent, Nebr. Children's Home, Omaha, 1971; Big Sister, Big Bros./Big Sisters Am., Omaha, 1980-82; facilitator Daus. United, Hampton, 1984; mem. Anchorage Crime Commn., 1986. Mem. Air Force Assn. Republican. Roman Catholic. Club: Elmendorf Officers (adv. bd.). Avocations: Racquetball; skiing; chess. Office: Hdqrs Alaskan Air Command Chief of Protocol Elmendorf AFB AK 99506-5001

CAIN, LINDA CHARLOTTE, communications company executive, educator; b. Boston, Oct. 5, 1941; d. Charles Cummings Cain and Edna Augusta Cain Clark; B.A. in History and Govt., Boston U., 1963; M.Ed., Northeastern U., 1967. Admissions officer Children's Hosp. Med. Center, Boston, 1964-65; exec. asst. to mgr. Mass. Republican. State Com., 1965-67; tchr. Dover (Mass.) Public Schs., 1967-81; owner, mgr. Cain and Clark, Medfield, Mass., 1971—; pres. Beehive Communications, Inc., Medfield, 1982—; corp. clk., dir. Bay Shores Homeowners Assn., Inc., North Falmouth, Mass., 1978-82. Chairperson com. Sta. WGBH-TV Auction, 1973-76. Mem. NEA, Mass. Tchrs. Assn., Dover Sherborn Edn. Assn. (past pres.). Republican. Author: Blast-Off, 1973; author, developer mktg. and pub. service booklets. Home: 11 Pleasant St Medfield MA 02052

CAIN, MARCENA JEAN BEESLEY, retail store executive; b. Kingman, Kans., May 1, 1935; d. Albert Eugene and Stella Wanda (Ruthowski) Beesley; m. Kenneth B. Cain, Aug. 4, 1951; children—Kenneth Thomas, David Raymond. With AMVETS Thrift Stores, D.C., 1971—, asst. adminstr., 1971—; exec. adminstr. Amvets Value Village Thrift Stores, Balt.; ptnr. Bank St. Joint Venture Realty, Del-Mar Realty; pres. Family Thrift Center, Inc., Oakland Thrift Stores Inc.; sr. ptnr. Oakland Ctr. Partnership Ltd.; v.p. 4 corps. Mem. Bus. and Profl. Women's Club, Highlandtown Businessmen Assn., DAV Aux. (past nat. historian), Highlandtown Mchts. Assn. (pres. 1983-84), Govanstown Mchts. Assn. (rec. sec.), Affiliated Mchts. Assn. Balt. (pres.). Republican. Christian Scientist. Office: 3424 Eastern Ave Baltimore MD 21224

CAIN, MAY LYDIA, lawyer; b. Chgo., Feb. 13, 1956; d. William A. and Audrey (Rosin) C. Student U. Ill.-Champaign, 1973-74; B.A., Northwestern U., 1977; postgrad. in law U. Miami-Coral Gables, 1979-80; J.D., DePaul U., Chgo., 1980. Bar: Fla. 1980, U.S. Dist. Ct. (so. dist.) Fla. 1980, U.S. Ct. Appeals (5th and 11th cirs.) 1981. Ptnr., Cain and Cain, North Miami, Fla., 1980—. Recipient Am. Jurisprudence Book award in Labor Law U. Miami-Sch. Law, 1979; Pub. Interest Law Bank award, 1983. Mem. Fla. Assn. Women Lawyers (pres. Dade County chpt. 1983-84, editor newsletter 1984-85, pub. relations dir. 1984-85, sec. 1985-86), North Dade Bar Assn. (dir. 1981-82), Dade County Bar Assn. (staff writer Bull., chmn. lawyer referral service 1982-84), Fla. Bar (staff writer The Record 1983-84, editor Gen. Practice sect. newsletter 1984-86), Ill. State Bar Assn., Am. Judicature Soc., ABA, Nat. Assn. Women Lawyers. Mem. editorial bd. Fla. Bar Jour., vice chmn. editorial bd., 1986—. Office Cain and Cain 11755 Biscayne Blvd Suite 401 North Miami FL 33181

CAIN, VIRGINIA HARTIGAN, jud. orgn. exec., educator; b. Bklyn., May 1, 1922; d. James Gerard and H. Virginia (Williams) Hartigan; A.B., N.Y.U., 1943; M.Ed., U. Del., 1963; postgrad. U. Nev., 1972; m. Edmund Joseph Cain, Dec. 3, 1944; children—Edmund Joseph III, Mary Ellen Cain McMullen, James Michael. Personnel counselor Research and Devel. Labs., Ft. Monmouth, N.J., 1943-47; elem. and secondary tchr. and counselor, Reno, 1968-73; project dir. children in placement project Nat. Council Juvenile and Family Ct. Judges, Reno, 1974-76, curriculum dir., asst. tng. dir., 1976—; adj. asst. prof. U. Nev., Reno; mem. adv. bd. Com. To Aid Abused Women, Nat. Assn. Family Counselors in Juvenile Ct., 1981-82; del.-at-large White House Conf. on Families, 1980. Mem. Nev. Gov.'s Commn. on Status of Women, 1966-70, 72-81; del. Nat. Democratic Convs., 1970, 72, 80; Dem. chmn. Nev. chpt. ERA, 1980-82; mem. Dem. Nat. Com., 1980-82; mem. Platform Accountability Commn., 1982; 1st vice chmn. Nev. Dem. Com., 1980-82; mem. adv. bd. Mental Health Assn. Nev., 1966-72; mem. Nev. Gov.'s Commn. on Girl's Tng. Sch., 1972-76; mem. exec. com. Washoe County Dem. Central Comm., 1966-80; Nev. mem. Compliance Rev. Commn., 1972-76; mem. Nev. Charter Com., 1972-74; No. Nev. coordinator for Senator Edward Kennedy, 1979-80; active campaign worker for Adlai Stevenson, John F. Kennedy, Jimmy Carter; bd. dirs. United Way No. Nev., Planned Parenthood Nev.; mem. Nat. Com. for Support Pub. Schs.; mem. Sr. Citizens Adv. Bd. Washoe County; former chmn. early childhood edn. and legis. com. Del. PTA Bd.; former mem. adv. bd. Washoe Assn. for Mentally Retarded; co-program chmn. 21st Ann. South Pacific Regional Conf., Child Welfare League Am.-Nat. Council Juvenile Ct. Judges, 1976; numerous other civic and polit. activities. Recipient various service and profl. awards. Mem. Internat. Soc. Family Law, Children's Def. Fund, Women's Polit. Caucus, Nat. Assn. Counsel for Children, AAUW, LWV, Reno Bus. and Profl. Women (legis. chmn.), Nev. Art Gallery, Croesus Corp. Investment Club (pres.). Roman Catholic. Club: U. Nev. Faculty Wives. Home: 3710 Clover Way Reno NV 89509 Office: Box 8978 U Nev Reno NV 89507

CAIRNS, ROBERTA A. E., librarian; b. Waltham, Mass., Feb. 1, 1945; d. Robert H. and Elizabeth F. (Peck) C. B.A., Stonehill Coll., 1966; M.S., U. R.I., 1969. Librarian, Fiske Pub. Library, Wrentham, Mass., 1966-71; dir. Barrington Pub. Library (R.I.), 1971-79; dir. library services East Providence Pub. Library (R.I.), 1979—; adv. com. U. R.I. Grad. Library Sch., Kingston, 1983. Author: History of St. Mary's Church, 1978. Bd. dirs. Am Cancer Soc., East Providence, 1983; bd. dirs., v.p. East Providence C. of C., 1983—; bd. dirs. LWV, East Providence, 1983—, Bradley Hosp.; chairperson Citizens Adv. Commn. Cable TV, East Providence, 1983—; mem. Cable TV Statewide Adv. Council, 1984—. Named East Providence Woman of Yr., 1985. Mem. ALA, New Eng. Library Assn., R.I. Library Assn. (pres. 1986), Pub. Library Assn., East Providence Profl. Managerial and Tech. Employees Assn. (v.p.). Roman Catholic. Home: 1355 Wampanoag Trail East Providence RI 02915 Office: East Providence Pub Library 41 Grove Ave East Providence RI 02914

CAIRNS, SHIRLEY ANNE, financial planner; b. Hundred, W.Va., Sept. 26, 1937; d. John Martin and Thelma Irene Stiles; B.S., W.Va. U., 1959, M.A., 1964; cert. fin. planner; children—John Michael, Lyle Dennis, Glynis Ann. Tchr. public schs., Alliance, Ohio, 1958-60, Morgantown, W.Va., 1960-61; receptionist Strand Realty, Coronado, Calif., 1962-63; tchr., head bus. edn. dept. Sutherlin (Oreg.) High Sch., 1964-80; registered rep. IDS, Sutherlin, 1980-83; prin. Shirley A. Cairns & Assocs., 1983—. Mem. Democratic Central Com., 1980-85; Oreg. Dem. Platform Com., Oreg. Women's Polit. Caucus, Nat. Women's Polit. Caucus, Oreg. Dem. Women's Fedn.; sec. Calapoola Rural Fire Dist.; bd. dirs. March of Dimes. Mem. Internat. Assn. Fin. Planning, Inst. Cert. Fin. Planners, Am. Bus. Women's Assn., Roseburg C. of C. (dir.), AAUW, LWV, Umpqua Basin Life Underwriters Assn., Douglas County C. of C. (sec.). Home: Box 76 Oakland OR 97462 Office: 1012 SE Oak St Suite 330 Roseburg OR 97470

CALABIA, DAWN T., legislative staff consultant; b. Bklyn., May 22, 1941; d. Thomas Michael and Alice Brady (Diver) Tennant; B.A., St. John's U.; M.S.W., Fordham U., 1969; m. Florentine Calabia; children—Florentine Christopher, Theodore Rizal, Alison Maria Clara. Local area analyst N.Y.C. Planning Commn., 1967-68; urban planner Manoussoff Assos., 1969-72; fundraiser, cons. N.Y. State ADA, 1973-74; legis. asst. to Rep. Solarz (N.Y.), Washington 1978-84; staff cons. House Fgn. Affairs Com., 1984—. Mem. Nat. Assn. Social Workers, Ams. for Democratic Action (nat. bd. dirs.), St. John's U. Alumni Assn. (v.p.), Democratic Women Capitol Hill, NOW, Lambda Kappa Phi. Office: 707 House Annex I Washington DC 20515

CALCAGNI, MARIA MINGOLA, consultant, educator; b. New Bedford, Mass., Jan. 19, 1954; d. Bartholomew Canto and Lillian Ferreira (Belmarce) Mingola; B.S. in Biology, Simmons Coll., 1976; M.B.A. in Bus. Analysis, San Francisco State U., 1982; m. Dean E. Calcagni, June 26, 1976. Lectr. bus. math. San Francisco State U., 1980-83, also research cons. Kuehne, Rock & Mazour Options Mgmt. Co., San Francisco, 1981-83; lectr. math. U. Md., 1983—. Recipient Grad. Student Disting. Achievement award San Francisco State U., 1982. Mem. Beta Gamma Sigma. Home: Alte Rommelshauser Strasse 52 7050 Waiblingen West Germany Office: 5th Gen Hosp APO New York NY 09154

CALDEN, GERTRUDE BECKWITH, civic worker; b. Santa Paula, Calif., Apr. 18, 1909; d. Ralph Leslie and Bernice (Hart) Beckwith; grad. Woodbury Coll., 1928; postgrad. U. Calif., Santa Barbara, UCLA; m. Raymond A. MacMillan, Nov. 7, 1928 (div. 1948); 1 son, Thad C.; m. 2d Guy C. Calden, Jr., Dec. 16, 1961 (dec. 1967). Assoc. dir. Students Internat. Travel Assn., N.Y.C., 1949-51; lectr. on self-improvement to schs., colls., women's clubs So. Calif., 1951-54; cons., tchr., counselor Marymount Sch., Santa Barbara, 1953-54; adminstrv. asst. to pres. Resin Industries, Santa Barbara, Calif., 1954-58; adminstrv. asst. to corp. cons. Grant C. Ehrlich, Santa Barbara, 1958-61; treas. Wire Co. Am., Goleta, Calif., 1959-60; dir. Investors Research Fund. Inc., 1980—. Pres. Roosevelt Sch. PTA, 1944-46; sec. Jefferson Sch. PTA, 1941-42; chmn. tchr. recognition div. Santa Barbara County Selective Tchrs. Recruitment Council, 1960-61; mem. adv. com. to bd. govs. Calif. Community Colls., 1970; bd. dirs. community council Santa Barbara City Coll., 1956-82, pres., 1961-62; bd. dirs. U. Calif., Santa Barbara Affiliates, 1975, pres., 1978-80; trustee Found. for Santa Barbara City Coll., 1975-83, pres., 1977-79; emeritus bd. dirs., 1979—; trustee Found. for U. Calif., Santa Barbara, 1978-80; appropriations com. Santa Barbara Found., 1981-86; pres. Santa Barbara Citizens Adult Edn. Adv. Council; women's bd. Santa Barbara Mental Health Assn.; bd. dirs. Work Tng. Program, Inc., 1968—, Central Counties USO, 1969-71, Channel City Women's Forum, 1966—; mem. Citizens Commn. Civil Disorders U. Calif., Isla Vista, 1970-71; mem. Pres.'s Nat. Adv. Council on Adult Edn., 1974-80; mem. Am. Friends of Wilton Park, 1974—; bd. dirs. Rec. for Blind, Santa Barbara Unit, 1974-78, Alexander House, 1976-81; pres. bd. dirs. Friends for Hospice, Santa Barbara, 1981; pres. Montecito Republican Women's Club, 1963-65; bd. dirs. Santa Barbara Rep. Assembly, 1963-66, v.p., 1964; bd. dirs. Santa Barbara County Fedn. Rep. Women's Clubs, 1963-82, pres., 1966-69; bd. dirs. So. div. Calif. Fedn. Rep. Women, 1966-69; mem. 13th Congl. Dist. Rep. Com., 1965—; asso. mem. Calif. Rep. Central Com., 1967-68, mem., 1969-84; mem. Santa Barbara County central com., 1970-74, sec., 1971-74. Named Women of Yr., Greater Santa Barbara Area, 1974; fellow Wilton Park Internat. Conf., Sussex, Eng., 1972. Mem. Santa Barbara Personnel Assn. (sec. 1957-58), Santa Barbara C. of C. (edn. com. 1955, 57-61), Am. Assn. for UN, Family Service Agy., Am. Field Service, Mental Health Assn., Santa Barbara Hist. Soc., Citizens Planning Assn. of Santa Barbara County, St. Francis Hosp. Guild, LWV, Santa Barbara Council Women's Clubs, Calif. Hist. Soc., Univ. Affiliates U. Calif. Santa Barbara. Club: Zonta (pres. Santa Barbara 1956-57, 59-60, chmn. 18 dist. Amelia Earhart Scholarship com. 1957-58). Contbr. poems to anthology Gossamer Wings. Address: 819 E Pedregosa St Santa Barbara CA 93103

CALDER, JOAN MILLER, social worker; b. Syracuse, N.Y., Oct. 30, 1939; d. John Robert and Marjorie (Reid) Foreman Miller; m. George Donald Calder, June 24, 1961; children—Jeanette, George Donald. Student Russell Sage Coll., 1957-60; B.A., Bloomfield Coll., 1962; M.S.W., Fordham U., 1980. Cert. social worker, N.Y. Teenage program dir. YWCA, Elizabeth, N.J., 1962-65; adoption specialist, social worker Children's Aid and Adoption, Bogota, N.J., 1980-85; v.p. Family and Children's Service, Montclair, N.J., 1978-85; exec. dir. League for Family Service Bloomfield and Glen Ridge, N.J., 1985—. Task force chmn. state pub. affairs Jr. League N.J., 1976-77; community v.p. Montclair-Newark Jr. League, 1977-78; leader Girl Scouts U.S.A., 1970-82. Mem. Nat. Assn. Social Workers, Acad. Cert. Social Workers, Morris County Human Resource Assn. Home: 87 Douglas Rd Glen Ridge NJ 07028 Office: 29 Park St Bloomfield NJ 07003

CALDERON, LINDA CARON, nurse; b. N.J., Nov. 22, 1951; d. Arthur Donovan and Lillian Thomas; B.S.N., Calif. State U., Los Angeles, 1974, M.A., 1982; grad. nurse midwifery program, 1982; m. Rudy J. Calderon, May 3, 1975; children—Mikel Louis, John Matthew, Natalie Caron. Nurse, Huntington Meml. Hosp., Pasadena, Calif., 1975, nurse clinician, 1980, labor/delivery asst. head nurse, 1981-83; pvt. practice nurse midwife, 1983—. Mem. ACLU Found. Reproductive Project, 1981—. Mem. Calif. Perinatal Assn., Am. Coll. Nurse Midwives (assoc., chpt. treas.), Consortium for Nurse Midwives. Democrat. Roman Catholic. Home: 1145 Leonard St Pasadena CA 91107 Office: 620 S Pasadena Ave Pasadena CA 91105

CALDERONE, MARY STEICHEN, physician; b. N.Y.C., July 1, 1904; d. Edward J. and Clara (Smith) Steichen; m. Frank A. Calderone, Nov. 1941; children—Linda Steichen Hodes, Francesca Calderone-Steichen. Maria S. B.A., Vassar Coll., 1925; M.D., U. Rochester, 1939; M.P.H., Columbia U., 1942; D.Med. Sci. (hon.), Women's Med. Coll., 1967, L.H.D., Newark State Coll., 1971, Jersey City State Coll., 1982. Sc.D., Adelphi U., 1971, Worcester Found. Exptl. Biology, 1974, Brandeis U., 1975, Haverford Coll., 1978, Dickinson Coll., 1981; LL.D., Kenyon Coll., 1972; Ped.D. (hon.), Hofstra U., 1978, D. Hum., Bucknell U., 1982. Intern Bellevue Hosp., N.Y.C., 1939-40; med. dir. Planned Parenthood-World Population, 1953-64; co-founder, dir., pres. Sex Info. Edn. Council U.S., N.Y.C., 1964-82; adj. prof. program in humane sexuality NYU, N.Y.C., 1982—; lectr. human sexuality; 33d Lower lectr. Acad. Medicine and Cleve. Clinic. 1970; Rufus Jones lectr. Friends Gen. Conf., 1973; Hundley lectr. gynecology, Balt., 1973; president's disting. visitor Vassar Coll., 1983; 7th ann. Bronfman lectr. Am. Pub. Health Assn., 1968. Author: Release From Sexual Tensions, 1960; co-author: Family Book about Sexuality, 1981; author: Talking with Child about Sex, 1982; Editor: Abortion in U.S. 1958, Manual of Family Planning and Contraceptive Practice, 1964, rev. edit., 1970, Sexuality and Human Values, 1974; Contbr. articles to profl. jours., mags., textbooks, encys. Recipient 4th Ann. award for distinguished service to humanity Women's Aux. Albert Einstein Med. Center, Phila., 1966; Woman of the Conscience award Nat. Council Women, 1968; citation Merrill-Palmer Inst. Human Devel. and Family Life, Detroit, 1969; Woman of Achievement award Greater N.Y. chpt. women's div. Albert Einstein Coll. Medicine, Yeshiva U., 1969; Haven Emerson award N.Y.C. Public Health Assn., 1970; Ann. award Soc. Sci. Study of Sex, 1976; Elizabeth Blackwell award for disting. service to humanity Hobart and Wm. Smith Coll., 1977; Margaret Sanger award Planned Parenthood Fedn. Am., 1980; recipient Abram Sachar silver medal Brandeis U. Nat. Women's Com. 1983. Mcdonald House award Univ. Hosps. Women's Com., Cleve., 1983. Human Service award Mental Health Assn. New York and Bronx Counties, 1983, Lifetime Achievement award U., 1984, Jake Gimbel hon. lectr. award U. Calif. Sch. Medicine, 1984; named one of America's 75 Most Important Women Ladies Home Jour., 1971; one of 50 most influential women in U.S. Newspaper Enterprises Assn., 1975. Fellow Am. Public Health Assn. (Edward W. Browning award for prevention of disease 1980), Schlesinger Library Radcliffe Coll., 1983, Disting. Alumni award Columbia U., 1984, Jake Gimlad hon. lectr. award U. Calif. Sch. Medicine, 1984; named one of America's 75 Most Important Women Ladies Home Jour.,

1971; one of 50 most influential women in U.S. Newspaper Enterprises Assn., 1975. Fellow Am. Public Health Assn. (Edward W. Browning award for prevention of disease 1980), Soc. Sci. Study Sex (hon. life mem.); mem. Am. Coll. Sexologists, Am. Assn. Marriage and Family Counselors (hon. life mem.), Am. Assn. World Health, AMA (hon. life), Soc. Sex Therapy and Research, Alpha Omega Alpha. Quaker. Office: Dept Health Edn NYU 715 Broadway 2d Floor New York NY 10003

CALDWELL, CAROL GRAY, lawyer; b. Gadsden, Ala., Mar. 23, 1954; d. Jack Ernest and Jean Carol (Gillespie) Gray; m. Harry Edwin Caldwell, Jr., Jan. 7, 1984. A.B., U. Ala., 1976; J.D., Duke U., 1979. Bar: N.Y. 1980, Ala. 1984. Assoc., Dewey, Ballantine, Bushby, Palmer & Wood, N.Y.C., 1979-83; ptnr. Sirote, Permutt, Friend, Friedman, Held & Apolinsky, P.C., Birmingham, Ala., 1983—. Editor Duke Law Jour., 1978-79. Mem. ABA, New York County Bar Assn., Ala. Bar Assn., Birmingham Bar Assn. Methodist. Home: 2525 Brookwater Circle Birmingham AL 35243 Office: Sirote Permutt et al 2222 Arlington Ave S Birmingham AL 35255

CALDWELL, CHERYL NORMAN, marketing representative; b. Buffalo, Oct. 28, 1954; d. Franklin Leonard and Ruth Faverman (Norman) C. B.A. in Art, SUNY-Geneseo, 1977; M.B.A, N.C. Central U., 1981. Tchr., Durham City Schs. (N.C.), 1979-81; application programmer mktg. rep. IBM, N.Y.C., 1981—. Active Nat Alliance Bus.-Youth Motivation Task Force, Durham, 1981—. Mem. Women in Sales, Coalition 100 Black Women. Lutheran. Office: IBM 590 Madison Ave New York NY 10022

CALDWELL, DIANNE DEE, cosmetics executive; b. Youngstown, Ohio, Jan. 24, 1946; d. Leo William and June Marie (Gakel) Difford; B.S. in Edn., Kent (Ohio) State U., 1968; m. Thomas R. Caldwell, June 22, 1968; children—Ryan Thomas, Reed Jason. High sch. English tchr., Mogadore, Ohio, 1968-69; librarian Ann Arbor (Mich.) Public Schs., 1969-72; cons. Jafra Cosmetics, Inc.-Gillette, Saline, Mich., 1974-79, cons., mgr., 1977-79, regional dir., 1979-82; v.p. The Creative Circle, Saline, 1982—; div. sales mgr. Jafra Cosmetics, Inc., 1982—. Pres. Ann Arbor Police Wives Assn., 1971-75; mem. Republican Nat. Com.; mem. Saline Vocat. Edn. Adv. Com., 1979-80; spl. events chmn. Saline March of Dimes, 1973-75. Named Outstanding Mgr., Jafra Cosmetics, Inc.-Gillette, 1978; recipient Jan Day award, 1978, Saline Edn. Adv. award, 1979, 80. Mem. Nat. Assn. Female Execs., Nat. Ruffed Grouse Soc. Methodist. Office: 213 E Michigan Ave Saline MI 48176

CALDWELL, DOREEN CELESTE, real estate broker; b. Ketchikan, Alaska, May 21, 1938; d. Kenneth Loren and Anne Marie (Bram) Shrum; m. Robert George Caldwell, May 10, 1958; children—Douglas, Kim, Kenneth, Jeffrey, Jan, Anne. Cert. in real estate Chabot Coll., 1974; student Clatsop Coll., 1980-84. Lic. real estate broker, Oreg. Telephone operator Pacific N.W. Bell, Seattle, 1957-58, U.S. Army, Ketchikan, Alaska, 1957-58; service mgr. Sears Roebuck and Co., Ketchikan, 1962-66; real estate agt. Century 21, Hayward and Fremont, Calif., 1974-77, Seaside, Oreg., 1978-85; pres. Rainbird Realty Inc., Seaside, 1983—. Bd. dirs. Sunset Empire Parks and Recreation Dist., Seaside, 1980-83. Recipient Disting. Service award Seaside Jaycees, 1981; Very Important Person award Women's Council of Realtors, 1982. Mem. Clatsop County Bd. Realtors (Realtor of Yr. 1982, pres. 1983), Seaside Bus. and Profl. Women (sec. 1980), C. of C., Rebekah State F.L. Clubs Oreg. (state pres. 1984-85), Rebekah Assembly Oreg. (state officer 1982-84). Democrat. Lutheran. Club: Seaside Kids. Lodges: Soroptimist (charter mem.; treas. 1985), Rebekah (noble grand 1980), Lady Elks. Avocations: building and furnishing miniature houses; antiques; sewing; bowling. Home: 920 Oceanway Seaside OR 97138 Office: Rainbird Realty Inc 920 Oceanway Seaside OR 97138

CALDWELL, ELEANOR, artist; b. Kansas City, Mo., May 1, 1927; d. Earl Kendrick and Etta (Clark) C.; B.S. magna cum laude, in Edn., Southwest Mo. State U., 1948; M.A., Columbia U. Tchrs. Coll.,,1953, Ed.D. (Alumni fellow, Dow scholar 1958-59), 1959. Tchr. art high schs. in Mo. and Iowa, 1948-52; instr. art Southwest Mo. State U., 1953-54; asst. prof. Ft. Hays (Kans.) State U., 1954-57; instr. Columbia U. Tchrs. Coll., lectr. art edn. Queen's Coll., also supr. children's art carnival Mus. Modern Art, N.Y.C., 1957-59; prof., chmn. dept. art NW Mo. State Coll., Maryville, 1959-60; assoc. prof. Edinboro (Pa.) State Coll., 1960-62, Pa. State U., 1962-63; assoc. prof. No. Ill. U., DeKalb, 1963-64, prof. art, 1967-83; prof. emeritus, 1983—; assoc. prof. Ft. Hays State U., 1964-67; dir. Oakbrook (Ill.) Invitational Crafts Exhbn., 1968-84; cons., tchr. Arrowmont Sch. Arts and Crafts, Gatlinburg, Tenn., 1974-85; represented in permanent collections Denver Public Schs., Colo. Women's Coll., Denver, Ft. Hays State Coll., No. Ill. U., Sheldon Meml. Art Mus., Lincoln, Nebr., Arrowmont Sch. Arts and Crafts. Recipient Public Service award Ill. Sesquicentennial Commn., 1968; grantee No. Ill. U., 1968, 70, 74-80. Mem. Soc. N.Am. Goldsmiths, Am. Crafts Council, Artists Equity, AAUP, Ariz. Designer Craftsmen, Delta Kappa Gamma, Pi Lambda Theta, Kappa Delta Pi. Editor: Contemporary Jewelry, 1970.

CALDWELL, JOANNA GAYLE, medical auditor; b. Biloxi, Miss., Aug. 27, 1959; d. John Edward and Naomi June (McCarty) Rolen. Diploma, Washington Hosp. Ctr. Sch. Nursing, 1980. R.N., Md. Nurses aide Physicians Hosp., La Plata, Md., 1976-77; follow-up clk. Washington Hosp. Ctr. Tumor Registry, 1978, switchboard operator, 1978-79, follow-up clk. Washington Hosp. Ctr. Women's Clinic, 1978; R.N., So. Md. Hosp., Clinton, 1980-84; med. auditor Seafarers Welfare Plan, Camp Springs, Md., 1984—. Republican. Methodist. Avocations: gardening; needlework. Home: 876 Copley Ave Waldorf MD 20601 Office: Seafarers Welfare Plan 5201 Auth Way Camp Springs MD 20746

CALDWELL, MARJORIE ANNE, labor union administrator; b. Akron, Ohio, Mar. 21, 1937; d. Louis Andrew and Margaret (Teibel) Nemeth; m. Michael Phillips Caldwell, May 5, 1956 (div. 1967); children—Christopher Michael, William Martin, Daniel Patrick. Student pub. schs., Canoga Park, Calif. Adminstrv. asst. Local 1442, United Food and Comml. Workers Union, Santa Monica, Calif., 1976-80, sec.-treas., 1980-85, adminstrv. asst. Local 115, San Francisco, 1985—, mem. exec. bd. S.W. Regional Council, Sacramento, 1980-85; mem. exec. bd. Coalition Labor Union Women, Washington, 1978-80. Chairperson So. Calif. Democratic party, Los Angeles, 1983-85; mem. Dem. Nat. Com., Washington, 1985—. Mem. Nat. Women's Polit. Caucus, NOW, Consumer Fedn. Calif. (mem. policy bd.). Roman Catholic.

CALDWELL, MARY PERI, educator, counseling psychologist; b. Cleve., Aug. 21, 1935; d. Francesco and Gerlanda (Gagliano) Peri; m. Robert Joseph Caldwell, 1956 (div. 1962); children—Deborah Ann, Thomas Robert. B.S. in Edn., Kent State U., Ohio, 1961; M.A. in Counseling Psychology, Alfred Adler Inst., Chgo., 1981. Cert. clin. mental health counselor. Tchr. various sch. systems in Cleve. area, 1957-85; counseling psychologist in pvt. practice, Brunswick, Ohio, 1980—; mem. faculty, dir. Cleve. Inst. Adlerian Studies, 1983—, exec. sec., 1978-82, pres., 1982-84; lectr. U.S. and Can. Author workbook: Stress/Distress/Burnout: Resolving the Puzzle of Stress, 1983; editor: Adlerian Psychology Bull., 1983-86; contbr. articles to profl. jours. Leader various parent edn. groups, 1981—. Jennings Found. grantee, 1979; recipient Disting. Service award N.E. Ohio Tchrs. Assn., 1983. Mem. N.Am. Soc. Adlerian Psychology (clin. mem., assembly del., Outstanding Woman award 1980), Am. Assn. Counseling and Devel., Am. Mental Health Counselors Assn., Ohio Assn. Counseling and Devel., Ohio Sch. Counselors Assn., Gamma Phi Beta (pres. 1967-70). Avocations: tennis; travel; piano; watercolor painting. Home and Office: 88 Castle Ct Brunswick OH 44212

CALDWELL, PAULA DAY, telecommunications company executive; b. Colorado Springs, Colo., Nov. 11, 1954; d. Taylor Arnold and Constance Theo (Jenkins) Day Pearson; m. Michael Anthony Caldwell, Feb. 21, 1981. B.S., Lindenwood Colls., 1981; postgrad. bus. Dallas Bapt. U., 1982—. Exec. sec. Minority Econ. Devel. Agy., St. Louis, 1974-76; adminstrv. asst. New Age Fed. Savs. & Loan, St. Louis, 1976-78; bookkeeper Family Planning Council, 1978-81; account exec. AT&T, Dallas, 1981—. Bd. dirs. NAACP, Dallas, 1985-86. Recipient Eagle award AT&T, 1984. Mem. Nat. Assn. Female Execs., Assn. for Higher Edn. N. Tex. Democrat. Baptist. Home: PO Box 763845 Dallas TX 75376 Office: AT&T Communications 717 N Harwood St #2320 Dallas TX 75201

CALDWELL, RUBY MAY WINNINGHAM, artist; b. Porterville, Calif., Mar. 21, 1943; d. Jesse Clifton and Lena Frances (DuBose) Winningham; Kuhn; m. James Vernon Caldwell, Sept. 26, 1975 (dec.); m. Bert Acosta, Oct. 11, 1959 (div. Jan. 1970); children—Darlene Starr, Venus Dennise, Dawn Jeannine. Sec., receptionist, bookkeeper, various businesses, San Diego, 1964-72; sci. illustrator Research Inst. Scripps Clinic, LaJolla, Calif., 1979-81; mng. editor Monroe Tribune (Mich.), 1981-82; sci. illustrator LaJolla Cancer Research, 1983-85; owner, artist, sci. illustrator, Sci. Drafting, San Diego, 1973—; owner, artist, typesetter C.R. Type, San Diego, 1985—. Office mgr. Mexican Americans for Goldwater, 1964, Viva Nixon Campaign, 1968. Republican. Clubs: Am. Legion Aux. (treas. 1979-80). Home: 4226 Mt Voss Dr San Diego CA 92117

CALDWELL, SANDRA MARIE, accountant; b. Lexington, Ky., Apr. 11, 1959; d. Francis Mark and Frances Jane (Thomas) C. B.S. in Acctg., U. Ky., 1983; M.B.A., Xavier U., Cin., 1987. Record clk. Good Samaritan Hosp., Lexington, 1976-85; acctg. clk. Semicon Assocs., Lexington, 1985-86, acctg. analyst, 1986—. Mem. Nat. Assn. Accts., Nat. Assn. Female Execs. Democrat. Avocations: coin collecting; swimming. Office: Semicon Assocs Inc 1801 Old Frankfort Pike Lexington KY 40502

CALDWELL, SARAH, opera producer, condr.; b. Maryville, Mo.; student violin New Eng. Conservatory. Mem. faculty Tanglewood (Mass.) Sch. Music; created dept. of music theater at Boston U. and conducted Am. premiere of Hindemith's Mathis der Maler; founder, artistic dir., condr. Opera Co. of Boston which has produced 45 operas including Schoenberg's Moses and Aaron, 1966, Stravinsky's Rakes Progress, 1967, Mussorgsky's Boris Godunov, Offenbach's Voyage to the Moon, Berlioz' The Trojans, 1972 and Benvenuto Cellini, 1975, Prokofiev's War and Peace, 1974, Sessions' Montezuma, 1976, Tippett's Ice Break, 1979, Zimmermann's Die Soldaten, 1982; also former artistic dir. Am. Nat. Opera Co. presenting Falstaff, Tosca and Berg's Lulu in San Francisco, Chgo., Dallas and N.Y.C.; condr. La Traviata, Beijing, China, 1981. Address: care Opera Co Boston 539 Washington St Boston MA 02111*

CALDWELL, ZOE, actress, director; b. Hawthorn, Victoria, Australia, Sept. 14, 1933. Attended Methodist Ladies Coll., Melbourne, Australia; m. Robert Whitehead. Theater debut as mem. of Union Theatre Repertory Co., Melbourne, 1953; other appearances in "Colette", N.Y.C., 1970, "A. Bequest to the Nation", London, 1970, "The Creation of the World and Other Business", N.Y.C., 1972, "Love and Master Will", Washington, 1973, "The Dance of Death", N.Y.C., 1974, "Long Day's Journey Into Night", N.Y.C., Washington, 1976, "Medea", N.Y.C., 1982 (Tony award); plays directed include: An Almost Perfect Person, N.Y.C., 1977, "Richard II", Stratford, Ont., 1979, "These Men", N.Y. off-Broadway, 1980, "The Taming of the Shrew", Am. Shakespeare Theatre, 1985; appeared in The Madwoman of Chaillot, Goodman Theater, Chgo., 1964, repertory theater Stratford-on-Avon, 2 seasons, The Way of the World and The Caucasian Chalk Circle, Mpls., Slapstick Tragedy (Tony award for best supporting actress), N.Y.C., 1966; appeared in Antony and Cleopatra, Richard III and The Merry Wives of Windsor at Stratford, Ont. Shakespeare Festival, 1967; appeared in The Prime of Miss Jean Brodie (Tony award for best supporting actress 1968). Decorated Order Brit. Empire; recipient Word award, 1966. Address: care Whitehead-Stevens 1501 Broadway New York NY 10036

CALEY, KATHRYN H., respiratory therapist; b. Liberty, Miss., Dec. 22, 1922; d. Maude Rinner (Hammack) Tyler; m. Bruce Edward Caley, Jan. 24, 1942 (div. 1966); children—Larry Monette, Connie Joan, Alan Lee. A.A.S., Jefferson Community Coll., U. Ky., 1973; B.S., U. Louisville, 1977, M.Ed., 1979. Registered respiratory therapist, Ky. Respiratory therapy technician Jewish Hosp., Louisville, 1973-74; instr. Jefferson Community Coll., U. Ky, Louisville, 1974-76, asst. prof., 1976-79; critical care therapist Humana Hosp. U., Louisville, 1979-84, supr. respiratory therapy, 1984—; clin. evaluator Calif. Coll. Respiratory Therapy, 1978—. Am. Lung Assn. scholar U. Louisville, 1976. Democrat. Lutheran. Home: 3327 Breckinridge Ln Louisville KY 40220 Office: Humana Hosp U 530 S Jackson St Louisville KY 40202

CALHOUN, EVELYN WILLIAMS, social worker; b. Tyler, Tex., Sept. 12, 1921; d. James Stanley and Norma (Skelton) Williams; B.A., Baylor U., 1941; M.S.W., Worden Sch. Social Work, 1960; postgrad. U. Chgo., 1955-56; m. William Benjamin Calhoun, Jr., Mar. 15, 1942 (div. Mar. 1949); children—William Benjamin III, Anne Stanley (Mrs. Donald Elliot Loyd). Field worker Tex. Dept. Pub. Welfare, Tyler, 1953-55; field placement Salvation Army Family Service, Chgo., 1955-56; child welfare worker Tyler-Smith County Child Welfare Unit, 1957-59; field placement Tex. Inst. Rehab. and Research, Baylor U., Houston, 1959-60, med. social worker, 1960-64; research social worker pre-natal research project dept. obstetrics and gynecology U. Tex. Med. Br. at Galveston, 1964-66, supr. social service dept. obstetrics and gynecology, 1966-74, cons. satellite clinics, 1967-74, cons. family planning project, 1969-74, cons., supr. head and neck cancer service, ear, nose and throat, chest surgery and neurosurgery, 1974-78, cons., supr. plastic surgery and oral surgery service, 1975-78, supr. internal medicine services, otolaryngology, ophthalmology and dermatology, 1978-81; field instr. U. Houston Grad. Sch. Social Work, 1968-81. Bd. dirs. Galveston County Community Action Council, 1966-68, Galveston chpt. Am. Cancer Soc., 1974-81; trustee Houston Intergroup Assn., 1974-76. Lic. social psychotherapist, Tex.; cert. social worker, advanced clin. practitioner, Tex. Mem. Nat. Assn. Social Workers (chmn. research council San Jacinto chpt. 1963-64, dir. chpt. 1964-67, chmn. Galveston br. 1964-67, sec. 1967-68; group leader so. regional inst. 1966, alt. Tex. del. 1969-71, Tex. del. 1971-73, dir. 1969-73; alt. del. Tex. state council 1967), Acad. Cert. Social Workers, Galveston County Soc. Social Service Dirs. (sec. 1979-80), AAUW, Baylor Alumnae Assn., Daus. King (pres. 1976-78), Order De Moley, Delta Alpha Pi. Episcopalian. Toastmistress. Home: PO Box 893 Galveston TX 77550

CALHOUN, GLORIA LYNN, experimental psychologist; b. Mpls., Nov. 12, 1951; d. Robert Willard and Wilma Marie (Schmoock) Alrutz; B.A., Coll. Wooster, 1974; M.A., Wright State U., 1984; m. Kevin Paul Calhoun, Apr. 20, 1974 (div.); children—Mark Allan, Brian Patrick. Document research analyst Bunker Ramo Corp., Dayton, Ohio, 1974-75; human factors engr., Dayton, Ohio, 1975-81; research psychologist Systems Research Lab., Dayton, 1981-82; engring. research psychologist Armstrong Aerospace Med. Research Lab., Dayton, 1982—. Wright State U. scholar, 1980; NSF grantee, 1973. Recipient Leach Meml. prize in psychology Coll. Wooster, 1974. Mem. Human Factors Soc., Soc. Info. Display, Sigma Xi (asso.). Contbr. numerous articles to prof. publs. Home: 2814 Bahns Dr Beavercreek OH 45385 Office: AMRL/HEA Wright-Patterson AFB Dayton OH 45433

CALHOUN, NANCY BOLTON, gerontologist; b. South Orange, N.J., Nov. 12, 1935; d. John Hill and Sarah (Pierpont) Holton; B.A., Mt. Holyoke Coll., 1957; postgrad. Boston U. Sch. Theology, 1960-61; M.S.W., Syracuse U., 1973, cert. in gerontology, 1973; children—James, Elizabeth, Douglas, Kristin Bolton. Dir. religious edn. Parkway Community Ch., Milton, Mass., 1957-59; coordinator resident services and admissions Bernardine Apts., Syracuse, N.Y., 1973-75; coordinator admissions Loretto Geriatrics Center, Syracuse, 1974-76, supr. social services Intermediate Care Facility, 1975-77, dir. social work services, 1978—, v.p., dir. housing, 1984—; instr. Syracuse U. Sch. Social Work, 1974—; pvt. practitioner, 1977—. Mem. Nat. Assn. Social Workers (vice chmn. Central N.Y. 1975—), Acad. Cert. Social Workers, Am. Gerontol. Soc., Nat. Council Social Welfare, Coalition Social Workers in Long Term Care. Home: 876 Genesee St W Skaneateles NY 13152 Office: 700 Brighton Ave E Syracuse NY 13205

CALHOUN, SALLY HANSON, clinical psychologist, educator; b. Wauwatosa, Wis., July 7, 1939; d. Lee Delbert and Olive Elizabeth (Congdon) Hanson; B.A. with distinction in English, U. Mich., 1961, M.A. in English, 1963; M.A. (USPHS fellow), Northwestern U., 1967, Ph.D. in Clin. Psychology, 1970; m. David Redfearn Calhoun, Sept. 5, 1964; children—Douglas David, Julie Katherine. Clin. clk. Hines VA Hosp., 1964; psychologist Ill. State Psychiat. Inst., 1965-69; cons. Nelson Hall Pub. Co., 1972-78, also lectr. Northeastern Ill. U., 1972-77; with Assoc. Psychotherapists of Chgo., 1973-74; pvt. practice clin. psychology, Glenview, Ill., 1978—; asst. prof., core faculty Forest Inst. Profl. Psychology, 1979-85, assoc. prof., 1985—. Recipient awards for fiction Scholastic Mag., 1954, 56, Avery Hopwood writing award U. Mich., 1958. Mem. Am. Psychol. Assn., Ill. Psychol. Assn., Nat. Council Health Service Providers Psychology, Nat. Soc. Arts and Letters, Mortar Bd., Pi Beta Phi. Office: 1717 Glenview Rd Suite 200 Glenview IL 60025

CALI, BRENDA CHERYL, corporate recruiter; b. Vincennes, Ind., Apr. 6, 1949; d. James Leroy and Bonna Lee (Winemiller) Lasher; m. Joseph Anthony Cali, June 27, 1970 (div. 1980); m. John Joseph Zamorski, July 7, 1984. Cert. tech. tng. So. Ill. U., 1968. Singer, guitarist Carrie's and Village Inn, Carbondale, Ill., 1967-70; mgr. Elaine Powers Figure Salon, Carbondale, 1969-70; cosmetologist Don Roberts Salons, Hammond, Ind., 1970-72, Clarewood House, Houston, 1972-74; mgr. Vic Tanny Health Club, Milw., 1974-78; owner-operator Career Research, Inc., Oakfield, Wis., 1978—; cons. to health food chain and sr. ctr., Fond du Lac, Wis., 1985—. Author: Land That Job, 1979; writer folk song Country Eyes, 1983 (Ky. Fried Chicken award 1983). Recipient nat. sales, mktg. and promotion awards Vic Tanny Nat., 1975-78; winner Nashville amateur song writers contest, 1983. Mem. Nat. Assn. Exec. Women (cert. 1985), Nightingale-Conant Corp., Altrusa. Republican. Roman Catholic. Avocations: teaching exercise and positive metal attitude classes for elderly; oil painting; singing; writing poetry; tennis. Home: Route 1 Box 306 Oakfield WI 53065 Office: Career Research Inc Route 1 Box 306 Oakfield WI 53065

CALIMAFDE, PAULA ANNETTE, lawyer; b. N.Y.C., Oct. 14, 1951; d. John Michael and Annette (Walicki) C.; m. Alan S. Mark, Oct. 14, 1978; children—Ilana, Clifford. B.A., Swarthmore Coll., 1973; J.D., Catholic U. Am., 1976. Bar: Md. 1976, D.C. 1977. Prin., Paley, Rothman & Cooper, P.C., Chevy Chase, Md., 1976—; chmn., lectr. Practising Law Inst., 1983, 84. Lectr. Montgomery-Prince George's Continuing Legal Edn. Inst., Profl. Bus. Mgmt. Inst., ABA tax sect.; bd. dirs., v.p. Small Bus. Council Am., Inc., Washington; mem. White House Conf. on Small Bus., 1986. Author: Professional Corporations, 1981-84, Flexible Compensation Plans, 1983; contbr. articles to profl. jours., co-editor Annual Rev. Montgomery-Prince George's Continuing Legal Edn. Inst., Inc., 1982, 83, 84, 85. Mem. ABA (coms.), Md. State Bar Assn., Montgomery County Bar Assn. Democrat. Office: Paley Rothman & Cooper 5530 Wisconsin Ave Suite 1440 Chevy Chase MD 20815

CALKINS, JOANN RUBY, nursing administrator; b. Mich., June 28, 1934; d. William Russell and Imajean (Dunkle) Armentrout; A.S., Delta Coll., 1964; B.S., Central Mich. U., 1972, M.A., 1977; m. James W. Calkins, 1952; children—Russell, Jill, Cindy; m. W. Arthur Brindle, May 7, 1983. Staff nurse, L.P.N. clin. instr., asst. dir. Sch. Nursing, Midland (Mich.) Hosp., 1964-71; dir. nursing, dir. substance abuse unit Gladwin (Mich.) Hosp., 1972-76; prin. Calkins Profl. Counseling & Cons., Harrison, Mich., 1976-78, part-time, 1978-83; dir. nursing service Central Mich. Community Hosp., Mt. Pleasant, 1978-83; dir. nursing Oaklawn Hosp., Marshall, Mich., 1983—; part-time prin. W. Arthur and Assocs. Cons.; condr. workshops Mich. Dept. Public Health; Mich. Hosp. Assn.; exec. dir. Holistic Health Agy., 1977-82. Trustee, Mid-Mich. Community Coll. Recipient Murial A. Grimmason Nursing Scholarship award, 1962; Cert. nursing adminstr. Mem. Mich. Soc. Hosp. Nursing Adminstrs. (mem. steering com. 1979-80, dir., 14 county rep. 1980-83, pres. 1983-84, chmn. devel. com.), Mich. Nurses Assn., Am. Nurses Assn., Am. Orgn. Nurse Execs. Methodist. Lodge: Lioness Internat. (3d v.p. 1985). Home: 7480 Old 27 S Marshall MI 49068 Office: 200 N Madison Marshall MI 49068

CALKINS, VIRGINIA BRADY, physician; b. Balt., Oct. 8, 1924; d. Leo and Lucy (Jewett) Brady; m. Evan Calkins, Sept. 9, 1946; children—Sarah, Stephen, Lucy, Joan, Benjamin, Hugh, Ellen, Geoffrey, Timothy. Student Vassar Coll., 1942-43; B.A., U. Mich., 1945; M.D., Johns Hopkins U., 1949. Intern, John Hopkins Clinic, 1949-50; resident New Eng. Deaconess Hosp.; clin. physician McLean Hosp., Belmont, Mass., 1958-61, Gowanda Psychiat. Ctr., Hamburg, N.Y., 1962—. Delegate Republican Nat. Conv., Kansas City, 1976; trustee 4-H, Erie County, N.Y.; mem. Sch. Bd., Hamburg, 1977-83, pres., 1981-83. Presbyterian. Club: Vassar of Western N.Y. Home: 3799 Windover St Hamburg NY 14075

CALLAHAM, BETTY ELGIN, state librarian; b. Honea Path, S.C., Oct. 8, 1929; d. John Winfred and Alice (Dodson) Callaham; B.A., Duke U., 1950; M.A., Emory U., 1954, M.Librarianship, 1961. Tchr. public elem. and high schs., N.C., Ga. and S.C., 1950-60; field service librarian S.C. State Library, 1961-65, dir. field services, 1965-74, dep. librarian, 1974-79, state library dir., Columbia, 1979—; S.C. rep. White House Conf. on Library and Info. Services, 1979; conf. coordinator S.C. Gov.'s Conf. on Pub. Libraries, 1965, S.C. Pre-White House Conf. on Libraries and Info. Services, 1979. Mem. ALA (council 1977-80), S.C. Library Assn., (fed. relations coordinator 1976-80), Southeastern Library Assn., S.C. Women in Govt., Hist. Columbia Found., South Caroliniana Soc., Southeastern Library Network (trustee 1984—, vice chmn. 1985-86), Chief Officers State Library Agys. (chmn. liaison com. Library of Congress 1983-84, network com. 1984—). Baptist. Office: South Carolina State Library Box 11469 Columbia SC 29211

CALLAHAN, ELAINE SHAW, retail jeweler; b. Gilmer, Tex., July 14, 1926; d. Ellie Hugh and Emily Ethel (Campbell) Shaw; B.S. in Business, East Tex. Bapt. U., 1983; m. J. Carroll Callahan, Mar. 19, 1949; children—J. Kim, J. Elaine. Founder, 1953, since owner Carolane Co., jewelers, Longview, Tex.; owner Carolane Investment Co., 1953—, Carolane Fin. Co., 1953—. Active Piney Woods chpt. ARC. Mem. Longview Lawyers Wives, Longview Woman's Forum, Longview Fedn. Women's Clubs, Christian Women's Fellowship, Longview Symphony Guild, Henderson Woman's Forum, Phi Sigma Alpha (pres. Tex. Delta Mu). Mem. Christian Ch. (Disciples of Christ). Club: Order Eastern Star. Office: 1200 E Cotton St Longview TX 75602

CALLAHAN, MARILYN GAYLE, retail store official; b. Houston, Oct. 13, 1956; d. Selvin and Mary Beth (Barron) C. B.A., U. Houston, 1979. Student asst. U. Houston, 1975-79; asst. buyer Foley's, Houston, 1979-80, group sales mgr., 1980-82; area sales mgr. Joske's, Houston, 1982-83; control exec., 1982—. Mem. Am. Home Econs. Assn., Chemists and Colorists. Democrat. Baptist.

CALLAHAN, MARY CULLIPHER, insurance agency executive; b. Reydell, Ark., Jan. 27, 1932; d. John Edward and Pearl Terresa (Wood) Cullipher; m. Robert Leon Callahan, Dec. 4, 1949 (dec. Mar. 1982); children—C. Douglas, R. Dean. Office mgr., Ron Lusby Service Co., Pine Bluff, Ark., 1978-82; field rep. Fed. Crop Ins., Jackson, Miss., 1982-84; owner, mgr. Callahan Ins. Agy., Pine Bluff, 1984—. Justice of the Peace Jefferson County Quorum Ct., Pine Bluff, 1978-79; chmn. Jefferson County ARC, 1982. Mem. Am. Bus. Women's Assn. (pres. Bluff City chpt. 1981-83), Ark. Am. Bus. Womens Conv. (sec. treas. 1982), Ins. Women of S. Ark. (employee relations 1985-86). Democrat. Baptist. Home: Route 1 Box 139 Sherrill AR 72152 Office: Callahan Ins Agy 100 E 8th St 2301 Federal Bldg Pine Bluff AR 71611

CALLAHAN, MAUREEN, financial futures strategist; b. Ridley Park, Pa., Dec. 17, 1947; d. James W. and Honey J. (Taylor) Callahan; m. Edward Watts Morton Bever, Sept. 10, 1977; 1 son, Noah Callahan. A.B. cum laude, Rosemont Coll., 1976; M.A., Princeton U., 1978, Ph.D., 1981. Bond and note trader Morgan Bank, 1981-82; fin. futures strategist Morgan Futures Corp., N.Y.C., 1982-83; sr. v.p. Refco, Inc., 1984—. Princeton U. fellow, 1976-81. Mem. AAUW. Home: 65 Nassau St New York NY 10038 Office: Refco Inc 4 World Trade Center New York NY 10048

CALLAHAN, MAUREEN ANNE HAVIKEN, psychologist; b. N.Y.C., Feb. 12, 1939; d. Joseph Patrick and Catherine B. (Dunne) Haviken; B.A., Catholic U. Am., 1961; M.S., Hofstra U., Hempstead, N.Y., 1970; Ph.D., St. John's U., Jamaica, N.Y., 1978; m. Edward P. Callahan, June 30, 1962; children—Jennifer, Christina. Tchr. high and elem. schs.; also career counselor, sch. psychologist; ind. practice psychotherapy; mem. faculty C.W. Post Coll.; now assoc. prof. psychology Webster Coll., St. Louis. NDEA fellow. Mem. Am. Psychol. Assn., Mo. Psychol. Assn., St. Louis County Psychol. Assn., Orthopsychiat. Assn., Mo. Historic Soc. Address: 6 Fair Oaks St Saint Louis MO 63124

CALLAHAN, THELMA, pianist, educator; b. Sweetwater, Tenn., Feb. 2, 1908; d. Alvin S. and Ressa E. (Collins) Callahan; student Peabody Conservatory of Music, Balt., Eastman Sch. Music, Sherwood Music Sch., Chgo., N.Y.U.; studied with LaSalle Spier, Austin Conradi, James Friskin, Harold Bauer. Broadcast piano program, Washington radio stas. WRC, WJSV, WOL, WMAL, 1924-36; pvt. piano tchr., Washington, 1924—; D.C. chmn., adjudicator Nat. Piano Playing Auditions, 1948—; adjudicator broadcasting cos.; mem. extension faculty Sherwood Music Sch., 1936. Mem. Washington Piano Tchrs. Forum (past pres.), Nat. Fedn. Music Clubs, D.C. Fedn. Music Clubs (past pres.), Nat. Guild Piano Tchrs. (chmn. Washington chpt.), Washington Music Tchrs. Assn., Am. Coll. Musicians (nat. dir.). Methodist. Address: 3803 Ingomar St NW Washington DC 20015

CALLAN, CLAIR MARIE, physician, pharmaceutical director; b. Sleaford, Lincolnshire, Eng., May 18, 1940; d. Joseph Edward and Margaret Mary (Hart) Mills; m. John Patrick Callan, Apr. 4, 1964; children—Eoin, Grainne, Colm, Maeve. M.B., B.Surgery, B. in Art of Obstetrics, Univ. Coll., Dublin, Ireland, 1963. Intern Mater Hosp., Dublin, 1963-64, resident in anesthesia,

1964-65; staff physician State of Conn., Middletown, 1966-68; anesthesiologist St. Francis Hosp., Hartford, Conn., 1972-76; med. dir. Dept. of Income Maintenance, State of Conn., Hartford, 1978-84; dir. med. affairs Abbott Labs., Abbott Park, Ill., 1985—. Contbr. articles to profl. jours. Pres. PTA, Wethersfield, Conn., 1974, Capitol Region Assn. of Pvt. Swim Clubs, Hartford, 1978. Mem. Am. Med. Women's Assn. (pres. 1984-85, councillor 1981-83), AMA (pres. Conn. aux. 1979-81), Am. Acad. Med. Dirs. Republican. Roman Catholic. Avocations: tennis; golf; needlework. Home: 816 Paddock Ln Libertyville IL 60048 Office: Abbott Labs D970 Abbott Park IL 60061

CALLANAN, KATHLEEN JOAN, electrical engineer, airplane company executive; b. Detroit, Feb. 10, 1940; d. John Michael and Grace Marie (Kleehammer) C. B.S.E. in Physics, U. Mich., 1963; postgrad. in physics Northeastern U., 1963-65; M.S.E.E., U. Hawaii, 1971; diploma in Japanese lang. St. Joseph Inst. Japanese Studies, Tokyo, 1973; cert. in mgmt. Boeing Mil. Airplane Co. Employee Devel., 1985. Vis. scholar Sophia U., Tokyo, 1976-79; elec.-electronic components engr. Boeing Mil. Airplane Co., Wichita, Kans., 1979-83, instrumentation design engr., 1983-85, strategic planner for tech., 1985-86, research and engring. tech. supr., 1986—. Contbr. articles to profl. jours. Mem. Rose Hill Planning Commn., Kans., 1982-85; coordinator Boeing Employees Amateur Radio Soc., Wichita, 1982-83. Mem. Soc. Women Engrs. (sr. mem., sect. rep. 1981-83, sec. treas. 1985-86, regional bd. dirs. 1983-85), AIAA, Bus. and Profl. Women, Quarter Century Wireless Assn. (communications com. 1985-86). Lodge: Toastmasters (local pres. 1985-86, competent toastmaster 1985). Avocations: amateur radio; singing; bowling. Home: 1201 N West St Rose Hill KS 67133 Office: Boeing Mil Airplane Co 3810 S Oliver Wichita KS 67210

CALLAWAY, MARY MCDOWELL, lawyer, educator; b. Tallahassee, June 26, 1929; d. Charles G. and Mary M. (Hogan) McDowell; A.A., Pensacola Jr. Coll., 1972; B.A., U. West Fla., 1972; J.D., Fla. State U., 1974; LL.M., Emory U., 1981; children—Sara, Julia, Mark. Admitted to Fla. bar, 1975; asst. states atty. Fla. First Jud. Dist., Pensacola, 1975-76, chief asst. states atty., 1977-78; individual practice law, Pensacola, Fla., 1978—; asst. prof. dept. fin. and acctg. U. West Fla., Pensacola, 1978—; arbitrator Community Juvenile Arbitration Program for Escambia County. Mem. N.W. Fla. Creek Indian Council, 1981—, sec., 1983—; bd. dirs. Pensacola Mental Health Assn., 1985—. Mem. Am. Inst. C.P.A.s, Fla. Inst. C.P.A.s (pres. West. Fla. chpt.), ABA, Fla. Bar Assn., Escambia-Santa Rosa Bar Assn., Estate Planning Council N.W. Fla. (dir. 1985—), Fla. Women's Network, Network of Exec. Women (pres. 1983-84), Phi Delta Phi. Democrat. Methodist. Clubs: Pilot, VWF Women's, Panhandle Tiger Bay. Office: PO Box 3697 Pensacola FL 32506

CALLENDER, NORMA ANN, educator; b. Huntsville, Tex., May 10, 1933; d. Cleburn William Carswell and Nell Ruth (Collard) Hughes; m. Billy Gene Callender, July 13, 1951 (div. Mar. 1964); children—Teresa Elizabeth, Leslie Gemey, Shannah Hughes, Kelly Mari. B.S. in Edn., U. Houston, 1969; M.A., U. Houston at Clear Lake, 1977; postgrad. Lamar U., 1972-73, Tex. So. U., 1971, St. Thomas U., 1985, 86, Inst., NASA, Johnson Space Ctr., Summer 1986. Cert. reading specialist, Tex. Tchr., Houston Ind. Schs., 1969-70; co-counselor and instr. Ellington AFB, Houston, 1971; tchr. Clear Creek Schs., Seabrook, Tex., 1970-75; part-time instr. San Jacinto Coll., Pasadena, Tex., 1980-81; tchr. Clear Creek Schs., Webster, Tex., 1975—, mem. Prin.'s Council of Excellence, 1985, 86; owner, dir. Bay Area Tutoring and Reading Clinic, Clear Lake City, Tex., 1970—; mem. adv. bd. Clear Creek Ednl. Resource Ctr. Publ., League City, 1976-77; owner Bay Area Tng. Assocs., Webster, 1981—. Editor: A Prism of Prose and Poetry, 1983, 84, 85, 86; Basic Educational Teaching Aids, 1984, 85. Charter mem. Republican Presdl. Task Force, 1982; sustaining mem. Rep. Nat. Com., 1982—; state advisor U.S. Congl. Adv. Bd., 1985; charter mem. Clear Creek Assn. Retarded Citizens, Houston, 1982; bd. dirs. Ballet San Jacinto, 1985-86; mem. U.S. Senatorial Club, 1984—. Recipient Franklin award U. Houston, 1965-67; Delta Kappa Gamma/Beta Omicron scholar, 1967-68; PTA scholar, 1973; Berwin scholar, 1976; Mary Gibbs Jones scholar, 1976-77; Found. Econ. Edn. scholar, 1976. Mem. NEA, Tex. Tchrs. Assn., Clear Creek Educators Assn. (honorarium 1976, 77, 85), Tex. Classroom Tchrs. Assn., Internat. Reading Assn. (research com. chpt. 1976 77), U. Houston at Clear Lake Alumni Assn. (charter), Clear Lake Area C. of C. (leadership and edn. com. 1985), Gulf Coast Council Fgn. Affairs, Kappa Delta Pi. Mem. Pentecostal Ch. Home: 963 Seagate Ln Houston TX 77062 Office: Bay Area Tutoring and Reading Clinic PO Box 57345 Webster TX 77598

CALLIHAN, HARRIET K., medical society administrator; b. Chgo., Feb. 8, 1930; d. Harry Louis and Josephine (Olstad) Kohlman; B.A., U. Chgo., 1951, M.B.A., 1953; m. Clair Clifton Callihan, Dec. 17, 1955; 1 dau., Barbara Claire Eloy-Callihan. Personnel dir. Leo Burnett Co., Chgo., 1953-57, John Plain & Co., 1957-62, Follett Pub. Co., 1962-64, Needham, Harper & Steers, N.Y.C., 1966-68, Bell, Boyd, Lloyd, Haddad & Burns, 1964-66; Hume, Clement, Hume & Lee, 1968-70, owner, operator PersD, 1970-75; exec. dir. Inst. Medicine Chgo., from 1975, mng. editor ofcl. med. publ. Proceedings, from 1975; now pres. Am. Med. Writers, also Conf. Med. Soc. Execs.; sec.-treas. Interagy. Council on Smoking and Disease. Mem. Chgo. Soc. Assn. Execs., Conf. Med. Soc. Execs. Greater Chgo., Am. Med. Writers Assn., Profl. Conv. Mgrs. Assn., Women in Mgmt., Women in Health Care, Nat. Soc. Fund Raising Execs., Lincoln Park Zool. Soc., Field Mus. Natural History, Art Inst. Chgo., Chgo. Council Fgn. Relations, Execs. Club. Clubs: Westmoreland Country, Michigan Shores, Publicity of Chgo. Home: 422 Central Ave Wilmette IL 60091 Office: Inst. of Medicine of Chicago 332 S Michigan Ave Chicago IL 60604

CALLOWAY, CHERYL ANN, lawyer, musician; b. Cleve., Apr. 15, 1948; d. Willard Leland and Annie Willie (Young) Powell; m. Nathaniel Roy Calloway, June 6, 1970 (div. 1980); 1 child, Leland. B.S. in Music Edn., Case Western Res. U., 1970; J.D., Georgetown U., 1973. Bar: D.C. 1974. Atty., HEW, Washington, 1973-77, Dept. Interior, Washington, 1977-79, spl. asst. to Asst. Sec. for Fish, Wildlife and Parks, 1979-80; trial atty. FERC, Washington, 1980—. Composer various choral works, 1967—; co-editor 5 vols. Law Fellow's Manual, 1972. Choir dir. Met. Community Ch. of Washington, 1983-84; treas. Lincoln-Bethune Children's Ctr., Washington, 1982-83; vice chmn. bd. dirs. AN. CO., 1984, sec., 1985—. Summer intern awardee, HEW, 1972. Mem. ABA, Nat. Bar Assn., D.C. Bar Assn., Women's Bar Assn. of D.C., Pi Sigma Alpha, Kappa Beta Pi. Democrat. Home: 12502 Parkton St Fort Washington MD 20744

CALLOWAY, DORIS HOWES, educational administrator; b. Canton, Ohio, Feb. 14, 1923; d. Earl John and Lillian Ann (Roberts) Howes; B.S., Ohio State U., 1943; Ph.D., U. Chgo., 1947; m. Nathaniel O. Calloway, Feb. 14, 1946; children—David Karl, Candace Mary; m. 2d, Robert Olaf Nesheim, July 4, 1981. Researcher, Armed Forces Food and Container Inst., Chgo., 1951-61; chmn. dept. food sci. and nutrition Stanford U. Research Inst., Menlo Park, Calif., 1961-63; prof., chmn. dept. nutrition U. Calif.-Berkeley, 1962—; provost Profl. Schs. and Colls., 1981—; cons. FAO, 1974-75, Nat. Adv. Council on Aging, 1978-82; mem. expert adv. panel on nutrition WHO, 1972—; trustee Internat. Maize and Wheat Improvement Ctr., Mex., 1983—. Recipient Meritorious Civilian Service award Dept. Army, 1959. Mem. Am. Inst. Nutrition (pres. 1982-83, Conrad A. Elvehjem award 1986), Am. Dietetic Assn., Fedn. Am. Socs. Exptl. Biology (bd. dirs. 1985—). Author: Nutrition and Physical Fitness, 11th edit., 1984; contbr. articles to profl. jours. Office: 200 California Hall U Calif Berkeley CA 94720

CALLOWAY, FRANCES AMANDA, hotel executive; b. Birmingham, Ala., July 6, 1950; d. John Clyde and Nettye M. (Phillips) C.; student U. Ala., 1969-73, Hotel Sch., U. Houston, 1978. Mem. mgmt. staff Jolly Inns, Inc., Birmingham, 1971-72; gen. mgr. Airways Inn, Jackson, Miss., 1972-80; sec.-treas. Intergulf Motels Inc., Jackson, 1975-80, exec. ops. officer, 1980—; exec. v.p. Motor Hotel Investors Inc., Jackson, 1979-80, exec. ops. officer, 1980—; ptnr., ops. officer Inn Host Ltd., Jackson, 1980—; sr. v.p. hotel devels. Calco Assocs. Inc., Birmingham, Ala., 1984-85. Chmn., Miss. Tourist Promotion Com., 1978-79; mem. adv. bd. Travel South, 1979-80. Lic. real estate salesperson, Miss. Mem. Miss. Hotel/Motel Assn. (dir. 1978-79, v.p. 1979-80, pres. 1981—), Jackson Hotel/Motel Assn. (pres. 1979), Jackson C. of C. Democrat. Presbyterian. Club: The Club (Birmingham). Office: 1 Flowood Pl Jackson MS 39208

CALLOWAY, JANE GOODE, guidance counselor; b. Newark, Sept. 16, 1939; d. Harry Leonard and Marie (Cooper) Goode; 1 son, William Christian. B.M., New Eng. Conservatory Music, 1961; M.A. Music, Montclair State U., 1968, M.A. Pupil Personnel and Service, 1975; postgrad. Kean Coll., 1977-79, Rutgers U., 1978-80. Supr. elem. vocal music New Bedford Bd. Edn., Mass., 1961-64; vocal music tchr. Linden Bd. Edn., N.J., 1964-75, guidance counselor, 1975—; edn. cons. Youth Services Bur., Montclair, 1974-75; advisor Minorities in Engring. Program Union County Tech. Coll., Cranford, N.J., 1976—; community adv. bd. E.O.F., Fairleigh Dickinson U., 1976-80; advisor state funded program Linden Bd. Edn., 1977—. Sec. adminstrv. bd., dir. choirs St. John's United Meth. Ch., East Orange, 1956-72; trustee PTA Exec. Bd., Linden, 1977-80. Recipient Music awards Griffith Music Found., 1943-56, Bus. and Profl. Women, 1957; Service award Alpha Kappa Alpha, 1979. Mem. Delta Omicron (pres. 1960-61), Alpha Kappa Alpha (exec. bd. 1959-61). Democrat. Address: West Orange NJ 07052

CALMES, PHYLLIS JUNE, real estate executive; b. Normal, Ill., July 16, 1930; d. James Hess and Mary Ellen (Hess) Ellinger; m. Franklin Sutton Calmes, Oct. 15, 1949; children—Franklin, Gregory Scott. Student Berea Coll., 1947-49; B.A. in Edn., Ill. State U., 1968; Brokers lic., Ill. Central Coll., East Peoria, 1977; Grad., Realtor's Inst. Ill. Assn. Realtors, 1983. Cert. tchr., real estate broker, Ill. Office worker, Caterpillar Tractor Co., East Peoria, Ill., 1951-59; tchr. Creve Coeur Schs., Ill., 1960-64; tchr. Illini Bluffs, Glasford, Ill., 1964-78; broker, owner Exec. House Realty, Pekin, Ill., 1978—. Recipient Bicentennial award Hist. Soc. Pekin, 1978; named Woman of Yr., Am. Bus. Women Pekin, 1980. Mem. Am. Bus. Women's Assn. (chmn. com. 1978—), AAUW, Pekin Bd. Realtors (bd. dirs. 1979—, Realtor of Yr. 1985), Ill. Women's Council Realtors (bd. dirs. 1980-84; Woman of Yr.). Democrat. Baptist. Avocations: reading; gardening; crocheting; sewing. Home: 601 Washington St Pekin IL 61554 Office: Exec House Realty 1905 Willow St Pekin IL 61554

CALMESE, LINDA, computer training center executive, consultant; b. East St. Louis, Ill., June 3, 1947; d. Lonnie Daniel and Louise (Anderson) C. B.S., So. Ill. U., 1969, M.S., 1972, specialist in counselor edn., 1978. Tchr. bus. edn. St. Teresa Acad., East St. Louis, 1969-73, DODDS, Madrid, Spain, 1973-84; computer cons. Scott AFB, Ill., 1984-86; pres. Bits and Bytes Computer Tng. Ctr., Belleville, Ill., 1985—; instr. State Community Coll., East St. Louis, 1986; computer cons. Army Aviation Systems Command, St. Louis, 1986—. Mem. Nat. Assn. Female Execs., Delta Pi Epsilon, Pi Omega Pi. Democrat. Baptist. Avocations: traveling; computing; reading; aerobics. Office: Bits and Bytes Computer Tng Ctr 56 S 65th St Suite 1 Belleville IL 62223

CALTO, PENNY ANN, social studies educator; b. Chgo., Dec. 1, 1939; d. John Kerndt and Currency (Doty) Kerndt; m. Robert K. Calto, Apr. 16, 1966; children—John, James. B.A., Northeastern Ill. U., 1976, M.A., 1980. Primary tchr. St. Isaac Jogues, Niles, Ill., 1961-66; tchr. adult edn. Triton Coll., River Grove, Ill., 1968-70, Wright Jr. Coll., Chgo., 1970-74, YMCA, Niles, Ill., 1969-73; tchr. social studies St. Scholastica High Sch., Chgo., 1977—. Co-author: Curriculum Guide for Women's History, 1983. Bd. dirs. Ill. Women's Golf Assn., 1981—, Edgebrook Community Assn., Chgo., 1975-80; mem. Women for Peace, Chgo., 1983—. NEH grantee, 1982, 86, Ill. Council Humanities grantee, 1984; Fry Found. grantee, 1985; recipient Imelda Fischer award St. Scholastics High Sch. Alumnae Assn., 1982. Mem. NEA, Nat. Council Social Studies, U.S. Ski Assn., U.S. Triathlon Assn. Phi Alpha Theta.

CALVERT, NADIA RAE VENABLE, lawyer; b. Hope Hull, Ala., Aug. 7, 1930; d. Nathaniel Julian and Clara Gerald (Owen) Venable; m. Robert Wood Calvert, Dec. 15, 1956; children—Nadja Neuman, Winter Owen, Chadwell Spencer, Eric Brittain, Camille. B.A., Huntington Coll., 1953; M.A., Tulane U., 1958; J.D., S. Tex. Coll. Law, 1979. Bar: Tex. 1979, U.S. Supreme Ct. 1984. Instr. history Spring Hill Coll., Mobile, Ala., 1959-61, U. Ala., Huntsville, 1965-67, Coll. of the Mainland, Texas City, Tex., 1970-73; legal asst. Able & Coleman, Houston, 1973-79; assoc. Able, Barrow & Able Law Offices, Houston, 1979—. Contbr. articles in field to profl. jours. Tulane U. fellow, 1953-55; Huntington Coll. scholar, 1950; recipient Am. Jurisprudence award Bancroft-Whitney Pubs., 1977. Mem. ABA, Am. Trial Lawyers Assn., Tex. Trial Lawyers Assn., State Bar Tex. (mem. dist. com. on admissions 1983—), Houston Bar Assn., Houston Trial Lawyers Assn. Democrat. Home: PO Box 52681 Houston TX 77052 Office: Able Barrow & Able 909 Fannin #3450 Houston TX 77010

CALVERT, TERRI LEE, marketing specialist; b. Terre Haute, Ind., June 12, 1950; d. Clarence Edward and Cecelia Louise (Bridges) Jennings; m. Stephen Wayne Calvert, Mar. 11, 1971; 1 son, Aaron Michael. B.S. in English, Ind. State U., 1971; postgrad. in mktg. Webster U., 1981—. Tchr. English, St. Louis Pub. Schs., 1971-72; copywriter KATZ Radio, St. Louis, 1972-74; media service cons., Centralia, Ill., 1974-79; advt. proofreader Venture Stores, St. Louis, 1979-80; mktg. mgr. Gen. Bancshares Corp., St. Louis, 1980-81; mktg. specialist Fed. Intermediate Credit Bank of St. Louis, 1981—; cons. in mktg. Am. Solartron Corp., 1977-79. Producer slide show: The People Business, 1983, The Other Side of the Desk, 1984. Publicity dir. Am. Cancer Soc., Centralia, 1975-79. Mem. Am. Mktg. Assn., Internat. Assn. Bus. Communicators (Gold Quill award 1984). Democrat. Roman Catholic. Clubs: Advt. St. Louis, Newcomers (2d v.p. 1977). Office: Farm Credit Bank 1415 Olive St Box 431 Saint Louis MO 63166

CALVIN, DOROTHY VER STRATE, computer company executive; b. Grand Rapids, Mich., Dec. 22, 1929; d. Herman and Christina (Plakmyer) Ver Strate; m. Allen D. Calvin, Oct. 5, 1953; children—Jamie, Kris, Bufo, Scott. B.S. magna cum laude, Mich. State U., 1951. Mgr. data processing. Behavioral Research Labs., Menlo Park, Calif., 1972-75; dir. Mgmt. Info. Systems Inst. for Prof. Devel., San Jose, Calif. 1975-76; systems analyst, programmer Pacific Bell Info. Systems, San Francisco, 1976-81; staff mgr., 1981-84; mgr. applications devel. Data Architects Inc., San Francisco, 1984-86; pres. Ver Strate Press, San Francisco, 1986—. Instr., Downtown Community Coll., San Francisco, 1980-84; mem. computer curriculum adv. council San Francisco City Coll., 1982-84. Vice pres. LWV, Roanoke, Va., 1956-58; pres. Bulliss Purissima Parents Group, Los Altos, Calif., 1962-64; bd. dirs. Vols. for Israel, 1986—. Mem. Nat. Assn. Female Execs., Assn. Systems Mgmt., Assn. Women in Computing. Democrat. Avocations: computing; gardening; jogging; reading. Office: Ver Strate Press 1645 15th Ave San Francisco CA 94122

CAMACHO, ELENA VICTORIA, diversified goods company executive, consultant; b. Lausanne, Switzerland, Jan. 4, 1958; came to U.S., 1961; d. Jose Enrique and Ruth Mina (Waldman) C.; m. Barney Duncan Byrd, Apr. 8, 1985. B.A., U. Pa., 1979, M.S. in Edn., 1979; M.B.A., Northwestern U., 1983. Cert. tchr. secondary edn. Mktg. cons. R.W. Camacho Assocs., Bethesda, Md., 1976-79; asst. to dir. Sotheby's, Chgo., 1980; dir. ACI/Gallery Vaudoise, Washington, 1980-81; mktg. and sales rep. R.R. Donnelley & Sons, Chgo., 1983-85; pres. B&C Diversified, Nashville, 1985—. Author instruction module: Energy in Developing Nations, 1982. Mem. Vanderbilt Aid Soc., Nashville; mem. Friends of the Children's Hosp., Nashville, 1985—, Cheekwood Bot. Gardens & Fine Art Ctr., Nashville, 1985—. Mem. Nat. Assn. Female Execs., Md. Assn. Hispanic Bus. (exec. bd. dirs. 1985—, Assn. Women Entrepreneurs (Nashville founder, chmn.), NEA.

CAMARILLO, LINDA LOU, petroleum company executive; b. Chgo., Dec. 18, 1944; d. George Emry and Betty Jane (Carper) Jamison; student Calif. State U.-Bakersfield, 1981—; m. James Daniel Camarillo, Jan. 10, 1969; children—Daniel James, David Scott. With Tosco Corp., Bakersfield, Calif., 1974—, telecommunications mgr., 1983—. Clk., First Baptist Ch., Bakersfield, 1976, sec. long range planning com. and bldg council, 1973-76; life mem. Republican Nat. Com. Mem. Assn. Info. Systems Profls. (v.p. programs Bakersfield chpt. 1978-79, pres. 1979-80, 82-83, achievement award), Telecommunications Assn., Assn. Records Mgrs. and Adminstrs., Nat. Assn. Female Execs., Nat. Rifle Assn. Clubs: Safari Internat., Kern County Gun, South Valley Judo (adminst-r.). Home: 9910 Palm Ave Bakersfield CA 93308 Office: PO Box 2860 Bakersfield CA 93303

CAMERA, FRANCES ANN, banker; b. N.Y.C., Mar. 2, 1949; d. Anthony Joseph and Cecile Elizabeth (Merritt) C.; B.B.A., Pace U., 1977, postgrad. fin. mgmt., 1982—. Sec. to dean Sch. Edn. Pace U., N.Y.C., 1968-72; service asst. leasing div. Chem. Bank, N.Y.C., 1972-75, officer's asst., 1975-78, asst. mgr., 1978-81, asst. sec. mktg. officer, 1981-83, real estate officer, real estate div., 1983—. Recipient Outstanding Achievement award Republican Adv. Com., 1978. Mem. Concern, Inc., Nat. Assn. Female Execs., Phi Chi Theta. Office: 633 3d Ave New York NY 10017

CAMERON, BONNIE LONELLE, lawyer; b. Atlanta, Jan. 31, 1954; d. Weyman Henry and Lonelle (Brittain) C. B.A., Yale U., 1976; J.D., NYU, 1979. Bar: N.Y. 1979, Ga. 1985. Dist. counsel IRS, Newark, 1979-80, Atlanta, 1980—Recipient resolution of commendation Ga. Senate, 1980. Mem. ABA, N.Y. Bar Assn. Home: 1936 Trotti St NE Atlanta GA 30317 Office: Dist Counsel IRS 275 Peachtree St Atlanta GA 30370

CAMERON, CHARLOTTE ELAINE, financial administrator; b. Tucson, July 4, 1940; d. David Lee and Doris Arlene (Griffith) Burrows; student Consumnes River Community Coll., 1975, 76; m. David Paul Cameron III, Mar. 4, 1961; children—Judith Lynn, Barbara Anne. With Calif. State Dept. Edn., 1958-63, New Hope Sch. Dist., 1964-67, Calif. Canners & Growers, 1969-70, Beckman & Co., 1971; stenographer local environ. health services sect. Calif. Dept. Health Services, 1973-76; sec. to dir. residency tng. U. Calif. at Davis Med. Center, 1976-79; office mgr., fin. adminstr. Psychiat. Assocs. and Cons. of Sacramento Valley, Inc., 1979—. Mem. governing bd. New Hope Sch. Dist., 1975-85, pres., 1981-83. Mem. Calif. Sch. Bds. Assn., San Joaquin County Sch. Bd. Assn. Democrat. Home: 29280 N Cameron Rd Galt CA 95632 Office: 711 University Ave Sacramento CA 95825

CAMERON, DONNA WELK, real estate developer; b. Muscatine, Iowa, Nov. 9, 1943; d. Edward Reinholdt and Vera Madge (Bird) Welk; A.A., Muscatine Community Coll., 1963; B.S., B.A. in English, U. No. Iowa, 1965; M.S. in Vocat. Rehab. Counseling, Mankato (Minn.) State U., 1973. Instr. English, drama coach Frost (Minn.) High Sch., 1966-68; instr. English, Spanish, Writing Groves High Sch., Savannah High Sch., Savannah, Ga., 1968-70; reporter Daily Reporter, program developer Minorities Studies Center, Mankato State U., cons. Mankato High Sch., 1970-73; counselor, office supr., program developer Opportunities Industrialization Center of R.I., Providence; real estate buyer, 1975—; fin. cons., ins. and mut. funds sales N. D. Erickson & Assos., Providence, 1977-80, Barclay Douglas, Providence, 1980—, real estate developer; instr. R.I. Coll., 1971-73. Corp. mem. Newport County Community Mental Health Center, Inc., 1981—, Roger Williams Coll., Bristol, R.I., 1981; bd. dirs. Human Rights Commn., Mankato, 1974-75; mem. Family Service, Inc. bd., Providence, 1981—; appointee R.I. Bd. Internat. Women's Year, 1976; asso. mem. Jamestown Republican com.; mem. R.I. Rep. Leaders Council; mem. Rep. Senatorial Inner Circle. Mem. R.I. Builders Assn. Office: 22 Union St Jamestown RI 02835

CAMERON, IDA JANE, state government official; b. St. Paul, June 2, 1937; d. Bernis James and Elizabeth Mae Arcand; B.S., Eastern Mich. U., 1962; m. Don R. Cameron, Aug. 16, 1958; children—Amanda Marie, Benjamin David. Tchr., Mich. schs., 1962-76; exec. Fla. chpts. NOW, 1977-79; adminstrv. asst. State of Fla., 1979-80; exec. staff dir. Fla. Dept. Profl. Regulation, Tallahassee, 1978-81, div. dir. adminstrv. services, 1981-83; pres. I.J. Cameron, Mgmt. Consultants, Rockville, Md., 1984—. Chmn. Tallahassee Area ERA fundraising, 1978; mem. founding bd. Tallahassee Center Victims Spouse Abuse, 1979-80. Mem. NOW (chmn. Tallahassee chpt. 1977-79), Nat. Assn. Female Execs., AAUW. Home: 5830 Tudor Ln Rockville MD 20852

CAMERON, JUDITH ELAINE MOELLERING, marketing/public relations company executive; b. Eagle Grove, Iowa, May 26, 1943; d. Albert Edwin and Marion (Trask) Moellering; m. William Ewen Cameron, Aug. 13, 1966 (div. 1970). B.A., Drake U., 1965. Model, Younkers, Des Moines, 1962-65, asst. Harlan Miller, columnist, 1962-65; asst. buyer, copywriter, Younkers, 1965-66; personnel dir. 4th Northwestern Nat. Bank, Mpls., 1966; head copywriter SPF Advt., Mpls., 1966-68; dir. spl. projects program U. Minn., Mpls., 1968-70; pub. relations cons. Germany, Italy, Spain, 1970-71; mgr. Jetset Sportswear, Footville, Wis., 1971-72; artist, Almunecar, Spain, 1972-74; pub. relations dir. Topspin, Totalplan Sports Internat., A.G., Madrid, 1974-76, mng. dir., Madrid and London, 1976-80; European mgr. Siam Internat. Amalgamated Mfrs. Ltd., London, 1977-80; European rep. Siam Cement Trading Co., London, 1979-80; European mgr. Third Wave Electronics Co., Inc., London, 1980-82; exec. v.p., dir. Electronic Specialty Products, Inc., N.Y.C., 1983-84; pres. Comml. Brain, Inc., N.Y.C., 1984—, Rennert and Cameron, Inc., N.Y.C., 1985—. Mem. Republicans Abroad, Women Bus. Owners of N.Y., Nat. Assn. Female Execs., Iowa Soc. (founding mem.), Alpha Phi.

CAMERON, MARION A., metals company financial executive; b. Cork, Ireland, Nov. 8, 1950; came to U.S., 1970, naturalized, 1980, d. Sean S. and Siobhan P. (Foley) O'Leary; m. Michael J. Cameron, July 11, 1970; 1 child, Donald. Student Trinity Coll., Dublin, Ireland, 1968-70; B.B.A., Pace U., 1980, M.B.A., 1980. Treas., Amalgamet, Inc., N.Y.C., 1970-75, Bruxelles Lambert Group, N.Y.C., 1975-80; v.p. fin., treas. Sipi Metals Corp., Chgo., 1982—. Mem. The Copper Club, Mensa. Avocations: opera; theatre. Home: 301 Sheridan Rd Wilmette IL 60091 Office: Sipi Metals Corp 1720 Elston Ave Chicago IL 60622

CAMERON, PATRICIA SHEEHI, lawyer; b. Washington, Apr. 4, 1943; d. Wilbur and Jeanette (Saddic) Sheehi; children—David John, Anthony, Stephen. B.A. in Polit. Sci., Temple U., 1976, J.D., 1980. Bar: Pa. 1980. Mgr., Conestoga Vineyards, Lancaster, Pa., 1972-76; prosector Atty. Gen. State N.J., Trenton, 1981; sole practice, Phila., 1982—; assoc. prof. Temple U.; cons. Phila. Environ. Ctrs. Contbg. writer Lebanese Am. Jour. Panelist Nat. Soc. Student Social Workers, 1976; mem. White House Commn. on Ethnic Studies, 1976; adv. com. on pub. relations Lebanese Embassy. Mem. ABA, Fed. Bar Assn., Pa. Bar Assn., Phila. Bar Assn. Republican. Maronite Catholic. Office: 37 Franklin St Buffalo NY

CAMERON, SUZANNE HAYDEN, market analyst, securities and real estate broker; b. Newark, Ohio, Sept. 28, 1949; d. George Allen and Virginia (Scott) Hayden; B.A., (U. Rehab. scholar), Ohio State U., 1972, postgrad., 1976-78; postgrad. U. Chgo., 1973-78; 1 son, Allen. Orthodontic research Ohio State U., Columbus, 1972-76, Plikerd & Assos., Newark, 1973-77; barrier-free market research design, sales Sea Pines Plantation, Hilton Head Island, S.C., 1979-80, market research, developer coordination mktg., sales program Daufuskie Island, 1980; market research, developer, coordinator mktg. sales program Broad Creek Landing, A Sea Pines Co. Joint Venture, 1981—. Area chmn. United Appeal, Ohio, 1972; philanthropic chmn. Ohio State U., 1972; chmn. Easter Seals campaign, 1973. Mem. Am. Dental Hygienists Assn., Am. Land Devel. Assn., Alda-Timesharing Council, S.C. Bd. Realtors, Hilton Head Island Bd. Realtors, Ohio State U. Alumni Assn., Kappa Kappa Gamma. Republican. Presbyterian. Home: 2027 Sealoft St Hilton Head Island SC 29938 Office: PO Box 4890 Hilton Head Island SC 29938

CAMILLERI, GERALDINE, retail executive; b. Ogden, Utah, Dec. 22, 1919; d. Gerald Miller and Catherine Elizabeth (Pottiger) Steed; grad. high sch.; m. Robert Lee Behme, July 16, 1982; children by previous marriage—Jean Kay Crawford, Joan Faye, William Gi-more, Pauline Ross, Cheri Foley, Bruce Camilleri. With Los Gatos Aviaries (Calif.), 1944-50; presented bird shows, 1950-52; owner Andy's Pet Shop, San Jose, Calif., 1952—; mng. dir. Am. Pet Shows, Los Angeles and San Francisco, 1980—; bd. dirs. Pet Industry Joint Adv. Council, Washington, 1976—; mem. Animal Adv. Com. Santa Clara County, 1982—; bd. dirs. United Cerebral Palsy; mem. Calif. Pet Bird Adv. Com., 1974—; mem. Santa Clara County Task Force Humane Treatment of Animals, 1979-80; Named Woman of Yr., Am. Bus. Women's Assn., Palo Alto, Calif., 1980; recipient Edward B. Price award Western World Pet Supply Assn., 1981. Mem. San Jose Hist. Soc., San Jose Symphony Assn. Club: Soroptimists. Office: 1280 The Alameda San Jose CA 95126

CAMP, BARBARA ANN, municipal government official; b. Lancaster, Pa., Feb. 13, 1943; d. Linton Ferguson and Anna (Wills) Mennig; m. Nils Victor Anderson, Nov. 25, 1961 (div. 1972); children—Barbara Jean, Susan Michelle, Jennifer Eileen; m. Robert Tomlin Camp, Dec. 29, 1973. Registered mcpl. clk., N.J. Sec., Sun Oil Corp., Phila., 1960-61; sales clk. Thomas Jewelers, Ocean City, N.J., 1969-71; composite typist Avalon Herald, N.J., 1971-72; exec. sec. Publs. Press., Pleasantville, N.J., 1972-74; clk.-typist Twp. of Upper Tuckahoe, N.J., 1977-78, mcpl. clk., 1978—. Editor twp. calendar, 1984-86. Mem. Mcpl. Clks. Assn. of N.J. (asst. treas. 1985—), Internat. Inst. Mcpl. Clks., Cape May County Clks. Assn. (past sec., past v.p., past pres.), Assn. Twps. (sec.). Avocations: snow skiing; boating. Home: 223 Laurel Dr Marmora NJ 08223

CAMP, HAZEL LEE BURT, artist; b. Gainesville, Ga., Nov. 28, 1922; d. William Ernest and Annie Mae (Ramsey) Burt; student Md. Inst. Art, 1957-58, 62-63; m. William Oliver Camp, Jan. 24, 1942; children—William Oliver, David Byron. One-woman shows at Ga. Mus. Art, Rockville Art Mus., Coll. Notre Dame (Balt.), U. Md., Balt. Vertical Gallery, Cleveland Meml. Gallery (Balt.), Unicorn Gallery, 1982, Hampton Ctr. for Arts and Humanities (Va.), 1985, others; exhibited in juried shows at Peale Mus., Balt., Wilmington (Del.) Fine

Arts Center, Smithsonian Instn., Turner Gallery, Balt., City Hall Balt., Bendann Art Gallery, Balt., 1980, City Hall Gallery, Balt., 1982, Balt. Watercolor Soc., 1983, others; represented in permanent collections: Ga. Mus. Art, Peabody Inst. (Balt.), Rehoboth Art League, numerous pvt. collections. Recipient 1st prize Md. chpt. Artists' Equity, 1967; St. Marys County Art Assn., 1964, 67, 1st prize still life Cape May, N.J., 1969, Catonsville (Md.) Community Coll., 1969, St. John's Coll., 1969, Best in Show York (Pa.) Art Assn. Gallery, 1972, 2d award Md. Inst. Alumni Founding Chpt., Balt., 1976, Best in Show Three Arts Club, 1978, Watercolor award State Art Exhbt., Nat. League Am. Pen Women, 1979, 3d prize oil, 1966, Honorable Mention, Rehoboth Art League, 1983, Williamsburg Shopping Ctr. Art Jubilee, 1983, 84; Purchase award Juried showHampton (Va.) City Hall, 1985; Honorable Mention award Towsontown Festival, 1986. , others. Mem. Nat. League Am. Pen Women (pres. Carroll br. 1968-70, editor The Quill 1975-76, editor for Carroll br. 1982-83; rec. sec. nat. exec. bd. 1979-80; nat. nominating com. 1982; Md. art chmn. 1982), Artists' Equity, Rehoboth Art League, Md. Fedn. Art, Md. Inst. Alumni Assn., Balt. Watercolor Soc. (hon. mention 1982, sec. 1978-80), Va. Watercolor Soc., Peninsula Fine Arts Ctr. Democrat. Methodist. Contbr. illustrations to mags., booklets. Home: 2 Bayberry Dr Newport News VA 23601

CAMP, LAURIE SMITH, lawyer; b. Omaha, Nov. 28, 1953; d. Edson and Virginia Elizabeth (Abbott) Smith; m. Jon Allan Camp, May 12, 1975; 1 son, Jonathan Scott. B.A. with honors, Stanford U., 1974; J.D., U. Nebr., 1977. Bar: Nebr. 1977, Kans. 1979. In-house counsel 1st Nat. Bank, Lincoln, Nebr., 1977-78; assoc. Turner & Boisseau, Great Bend, Kans., 1978-80; gen. counsel Nebr. Dept. Correctional Services, Lincoln, 1980—; gen. ptnr., counsel Haymarket Historic Real Estate Rehab., Lincoln, 1982—. Editor-in-chief Nebr. Law Rev., 1976-77; contbr. articles to profl. jours. Mem. Nebr. Bar Assn., Kans. Bar Assn., Nebr. Correctional Assn. (pres. 1982-83). Office: Nebr Dept Correctional Services PO Box 94661 Lincoln NE 68509

CAMP, LEONA BERTINA, nurse; b. Seattle, Apr. 20, 1940; d. Dave M. and Selma (Jacobson) Dishaw; m. Gerald Marvin Camp, Dec. 15, 1959; children—David, Amy, Karen, Brenda. A.A. cum laude, De Anza Coll., 1973; B.S. cum laude in Nursing, Calif. State U.-Long Beach, 1985. R.N., Calif., cert. in pub. health. Scrub technician Union Meml. Hosp., Balt., 1959-61; asst. nurse Burham City, Ill., 1968, Valley Med. Ctr., San Jose, Calif., 1968-73; staff nurse Stanford U. Med. Ctr., Palo Alto, Calif., 1973—; staff nurse John Muir Meml. Hosp., Walnut Creek, Calif., 1980-84. Camp nurse Camp Beaverbrook, Cobb, Calif., 1975-83; emergency med. technician St. Thomas, 1979-80; nurse ARC, 1979-80. Mem. Sigma Theta Tau. Democrat. Episcopalian. Club: Future Nurses Assn. (pres. 1956). Lodge: Job's Daughters. Avocations: photography; traveling; hiking; swimming.

CAMP, ROSE ELIZABETH THOMAS, congressional administrator, legislative researcher; b. Lake Forest, Ill., Oct. 2, 1952; d. Gordon Ward and Rose Lorraine (Crossett) Thomas; m. Jack Tarpley Camp, Jr., Apr. 24, 1976; children—Thomas Henry, Sophia Rose. A.B., Sweet Briar Coll., 1974; J.D., Woodrow Wilson Coll. Law, 1981. Counselor, Ferry Hall Day Camp for Girls, Lake Forest, 1967-71; congl. intern Congressman Henry B. Gonzalez of Tex., San Antonio and Washington, 1973-74; legis. asst. Senator John L. McClellan of Ark., Washington, 1974-76; exec. asst. Glover and Davis, P.A., Newnan, Ga., 1976-78; office mgr. Congressman Newt Gingrich, Newnan, 1978-83, congl. adminstr., 1983—. Editor-in-chief Sweet Briar News, 1974; contbr., author to families history. Del. to Republican Conv., State of Ga., Atlanta, 1984, Sixth Dist., Newman, Ga., 1984; tour guide vol. Hist. Male Acad. Mus., Newnan, 1984; vol. ARC, Fort Sam Houston and Washington, 1972-76; mem. Rep. Women's Club, Newnan, 1979—. Served with USAR, 1973-74. Mem. LWV, DAR (page continental congress 1974), AAUW, Ga. Trust for Hist. Preservation, United Daughters of Confederacy (pres. Newnan 1981-83), Newnan-Coweta Hist. Soc., Nat. Soc. U.S. Daus., Colonial Dames of XVII Century, Daughters of the Am. Colonists, Sweet Briar Alumnae Assn. (class rep. 1974—). Presbyterian (deacon). Club: Driftwood Garden. Home: 1615 Handy Rd Newnan GA 30263 Office: Sixth Dist Congl Office (GA) US Congressman Newt Gingrich Suite E 6351 Jonesboro Rd Morrow GA 30260

CAMPANA, ANA ISABEL, architect; b. Banes, Oriente, Cuba, Jan. 16, 1934; came to U.S., 1967, naturalized, 1974; d. Abelardo Joaquin and Amparo (Cabrera) C. B.S., Instituto del Vedado, Havana, 1953; Architect, Havana U., 1962, postgrad., 1962; postgrad. Albany (N.Y.) Inst. History and Art, 1970. Architect, Ministry of Pub. Works, Havana, 1962-67; architect designer various firms, N.Y., 1967-74; sr. architect Gen. Electric Co., Schenectady, 1974—. Designer power plant bldgs., worldwide. Recipient 1st nat. award Nat. Mus. Com., Havana, 1948, 1st Province award, 1948. Mem. AIA (assoc.). Roman Catholic. Office: Gen Electric Co 1 River Rd Bldg 23 Room 301E Schenectady NY 12345

CAMPANARO, LAURA DOROTHY, quality control manager; b. Bridgeport, Conn., Aug. 7, 1935; d. Charles A. Urban and Veronica (Broadbrook) Urban Bernier; m. Robert Ernest Campanaro, Aug. 6, 1955; children—Robert, Anthony, Candace, Dean. Student Ashuntuck Community Coll., 1985—. Prodn. worker Remington Shaver, Milford, Conn., 1970-73; prodn. worker, quality insp. Owens Ill., Milford, 1974-79; quality insp. Am. Felt & Filter, Staffordville, Conn., 1980-84, quality control mgr., 1984—. Vol. worker Johnsons Meml. Hosp., Stafford, Conn., 1986. Mem. Am. Soc. for Quality Control. Office: Am Felt & Filter New City Rd Staffordville CT 06077

CAMPBELL, ANITA BELL, psychometrician; b. Lubbock, Tex., Mar. 6, 1949; d. Vernon Ellis and Ivean (Iler) B.; m. Robert James Campbell, June 4, 1983. B.A., Tex. Tech. U., 1971; M.S., Carnegie Mellon U., 1972; Ph.D., U. Ga., 1977. Asst. dir. dept. psychometrics Nat. Bd. Med. Examiners, Phila., 1975-78, asso. dir. dept. psychometrics, 1979-81, sr. psychometrician, 1981—. Elder, Old Pine St. Ch., Phila. Mem. Am. Ednl. Research Assn., Assn. Am. Med. Colls., Am. Psychol. Assn., Carnegie Mellon Alumni Clan, Tex. Tech Ex-Students Assn. (dist. rep.), Phi Mu. Democrat. Home: 5344 Lower Mountain Rd Box 151A RD 2 New Hope PA 18938 Office: 3930 Chestnut St Philadelphia PA 19104

CAMPBELL, CAROL CANDY, accountant; b. Vermillion, S.D., Mar. 12, 1948; d. Wyatt T. and Ruby G. (Drafhal) C.; grad. Barnes Sch. Commerce, Denver, 1971. Public acct., 1971—; pvt. practice acctg., Denver, 1979—. Mem. Nat. Soc. Enrolled Agts., Colo. Soc. Enrolled Agts. (sec. 1978-79), Nat. Soc. Public Accts., Colo. Soc. Public Accts., Nat. Assn. Female Execs. Episcopalian. Clubs: Women of St. John's, Pilot Internat. (dir. Denver 1980-81, corr. sec. 1984—), Pilot Bridge Marathon (S.W. dist. pilot coordinator for outreach div. 1983-84). Home: 2621 S Green Ct Denver CO 80219 Office: 4800 Happy Canyon Rd Suite 150 Denver CO 80237

CAMPBELL, CAROLINE KRAUSE, retail drug company executive; b. Praha, Tex., May 5, 1926; d. Charles Joseph and Mary Victoria (Havrde) Krause; student U. N.Mex.; diploma Alexander Hamilton Inst., N.Y.C., 1969; widow; children—Richard Elton, Don Michael, Scott Gary, Jonathan Miles, Candace Kay. Various secretarial positions, 1945-49; survey researcher Winona Research Co., Mpls., 1953-54; merchandiser, buyer Campbell Drug, Inc., Albuquerque, 1961-77, gen. mgr., 1978—, pres., 1978—, also dir. Active campaign Congressman Manuel Lujan; mem. dinner com. Nat. Jewish Hosp., Nat. Asthma Ctr., Albuquerque. Mem. Nat. Fedn. Ind. Bus., Nat. Assn. Retail Druggists, N.Mex. Pharm. Assn., Albuquerque Symphony Women's Assn., Albuquerque C. of C. (bd. dirs., congressional action com., state legis. com., city govt. com.), Albuquerque Rose Soc., Internat. Platform Assn., Assn. Commerce and Industry of N.Mex. (legis. com.). Republican. Clubs: Italian Cultural, Elks. Office: 8252 Menaul Blvd NE Albuquerque NM 87110

CAMPBELL, CAROLYN CLARK, lawyer; b. Washington, May 9, 1941; d. John Gary and Jewell Rochelle (Hill) Campbell; m. Joungwon Alexander Kim, July 1, 1960; 1 child, Elizabeth Mi-Li. B.A., Barnard Coll., 1970; J.D., Harvard Law Sch., 1973. Bar: N.Y. 1974, D.C. 1979, Pa. 1979, N.J. 1980. Assoc., Mudge, Rose, Guthrie & Alexander, N.Y.C., 1973-76; staff atty. U.S. Ct. Appeals (2d cir.), N.Y.C., 1977-79; ptnr. Campbell & Kim, N.Y.C., 1980—. Contbr. article to profl. jour. Mem. ABA, N.Y. Bar Assn., Pa. Bar Assn., D.C. Bar Assn., DAR (N.Y.C. chpt.). Home: 969 Park Ave New York NY 10028

CAMPBELL, CARY ELIZABETH, communication consultant; b. Dallas, Nov. 10, 1954; d. Jefferson Holland and Shelia Ann (Trapp) C.; B.A. in Humanities summa cum laude, Southwestern U., 1974; 1 son, Christopher Randolph. Editor, Southwestern Mag., Southwestern U., Georgetown, Tex., 1973-74; community resources specialist Tex. Research Inst. Mental Scis., Houston, 1974-77; editor Viva!, mag. for older adults, Houston, 1976-78, Wichita Falls (Tex.) Mag., 1979-80; editor-in-chief 8 Living Mags., Baker Publs., Dallas, 1980—; instr. art history St. Paul's Acad., 1976, St. Luke's Continuing Edn. program, Houston, 1975-76; instr. SW Writers Conf., Houston, and Fla. Suncoast Writers Conf., St. Petersburg, 1981-82, Fla. Mag. Assn., Tampa, 1982. Vice pres. Harris County Com. Aging, 1977, treas., 1976. Recipient Poetry award Southwestern Mag., 1972; Student Leadership award Southwestern U., 1974; Disting. Service award, Harris County Com. Aging, 1975; 1st Place Feature Writing, Tex. Press Women, 1981, Matrix award Women in Communication, 1982, 1st pl. advt. media award, 1982; Dist. 12 Advt. Fedn. award; 5 awards Colo. Press Women, 1983; 2 awards Nat. Fedn. Press Women. Mem. Tex. Press Women, Am. Soc. Mag. Editors, Nat. Writers Club, Nat. Assn. Real Estate Editors, Denver Advt. Fedn. Contbr. articles to various mags. Office: 6340 Marquita Dallas TX 75214 Office: PO Box 24035 Denver CO 80224

CAMPBELL, CLAIRE PATRICIA, nurse, educator; b. Jan. 10, 1933; d. Hugh Paul and Clara Louise (Bell) Campbell. Student So. Methodist U., 1956-57; B.S. in Nursing, U. Tex. Sch. Nursing-Galveston, 1959, Family Nurse Practitioner, 1979, cert., 1984; M.S. in Nursing, Tex. Woman's U. Sch. Nursing, 1971. Staff nurse Parkland Meml. Hosp., Dallas County Hosp. Dist., 1955-70, head nurse gen. surgery, chest surgery, neurosurgery, orthopedics, and internal medicine, until 1970; instr. nursing Tex. Woman's U. Sch. Nursing, Dallas, 1971-72; researcher nursing diagnosis, Dallas, 1972-77; family nurse practitioner Otis Engring. Health Service, Dallas, 1979—; adj. asst. prof. U. Tex. Sch. Nursing, Arlington, 1976—; cons. nursing diagnosis. Author: Nursing Diagnosis and Intervention in Nursing Practice, 1st edit., 1978, 2d edit., 1984. Mem. Am. Nurses Assn., Tex. Nurses Assn. - Dist. 4, North Am. Nursing Diagnosis Assn., Sigma Theta Tau. Roman Catholic.

CAMPBELL, DAWN MARIE, photo laboratory manager; b. Bradford, Pa., July 4, 1961; d. Ronald Harvey and Mary Alice (Ford) C. B.S., Rochester Inst. Tech., 1982. Salesman, Photogenesis, Rochester, N.Y., 1979-80; quality control technician Instant Photo, Rochester, 1980-82; quality assurance coordinator Berkey Photo, Cornwell Heights, Pa., 1982-84; ops. mgr. Instant Photo, Rochester, 1984—. Mem. Photographic Mktg. Assn., Nat. Assn. Female Execs., Alpha Sigma Alpha. Republican. Lutheran. Club: Hubbers Ski (Rochester). Home: 576A Greenleaf Meadows Rochester NY 14612 Office: Instant Photo 2771 W Henrietta Rd Rochester NY 14623

CAMPBELL, DIANA, writer, photographer; b. Winchester, Mass., Feb. 17, 1959; d. Thomas Joseph and Phyllis Theresa (Mahoney) Campbell. B.S. cum laude, Boston Coll., 1981. Fashion model, N.Y.C. and Boston, 1980-83; account exec. Polyform, Westboro, Mass., 1982-83; writer, pres. Campbell Assocs., Melrose, Mass., 1983—; writer MIT, Cambridge, Mass., 1981—; reporter Malden Publs. (Mass.), 1981—; fashion editor Boston Ledger, Brookline, Mass., 1983—. Mem. com. Boston 250th Jubilee Celebration, 1980; guest of honor Boston Tall Ships com., 1980. Melrose Victorian Day, 1980. Named Miss Mass., Miss Universe Contest, Inc., 1980; Diana Campbell Day, Mass. Ho. of Reps., 1980; named hon. citizen C. of C., Gulfport and Biloxi, Miss., 1980. Mem. Boston Coll. Alumni Assn., Advt. Club of Greater Boston. Home: 323 Washington St Melrose MA 02176

CAMPBELL, DORIS ELIZABETH, educator, librarian; b. Charlotte, N.C., Jan. 3, 1937; d. Albright and Mamie (Torrence) Holsey; m. Donald Russell Campbell, Aug. 21, 1960; children—Darren Gerrard, Derek Jerome. B.S., Barber-Scotia Coll., 1954-58; M.A., Ariz. State U., 1961-66. Tchr. nursery children Jones Community Ctr., Chicago Heights, Ill., 1958-59, girls social worker, 1959-82; tchr. elem. schs. Roosevelt Dist., Phoenix, 1959—, tchr. spl. edn. Valley View Sch., 1982-84, librarian, chpt. 1 resource tchr. Martin Luthern Sch., 1984—. Mem. sch. adv. council Martin Luther King Jr. Sch., Phoenix, 1984—; mem. Family Math Workshop, Tempe, Ariz., 1984—; mem. Ariz. Chpt. 1 Resource Pool, Phoenix, 1984—. Mem. Urban League, Urban League Guild, Phoenix, 1965—; mem. Ariz. Assn. Retarded Citizens, 1968—. Mem. NAACP, NEA, Ariz. Edn. Assn., Roosevelt Classroom Tchrs. Assn., Alpha Kappa Mu. Democrat. Presbyterian. Home: 1713 E Wier Ave Phoenix AZ 85040 Office: Martin Luther Jr Sch 4615 S 22d St Phoenix AZ 85040

CAMPBELL, ELAINE JOSEPHINE, writer, critic, educator; b. Phila., Aug. 6, 1932; d. William Maxwell and Anna Maria (Roller) Bauer; B.A. with maj. honors (Univ. scholar), U. Pa., 1954; M.A., Simmons Coll., 1973; Ph.D. (Univ. scholar), Brandeis U., 1981; m. John Bruce Campbell, Dec. 21, 1957; children—Jennifer Ann, Rebecca Ellen, Sabrina Frances. Soc. editor Main Line Times, Ardmore, Pa., 1954-55; adminstrv. asst. dean Sch. Nursing, U. Pa., 1955-57; teaching asst. dept. English and Am. lit. Brandeis U., 1974-80; lectr. English, Regis Coll., Weston, Mass., 1980-81, asst. prof. English, 1981-84, dir. freshman writing program, 1981-84; writer-editor The MITRE Corp., Bedford, Mass., 1984—; lectr. English, Boston U., 1985—. Author introduction: The Orchid House (P. Allfrey), 1982; co-editor: The Whistling Bird: Writing by West Indian Women; The Flamboyant Tree: Writing by Caribbean Women; contbr.: Fifty Caribbean Writers; Studies in Commonwealth Literature, A Double Colonozation; book reviewer Commonwealth Novel in English, Kunapipi; contbr. articles, revs., reports to profl. jours., U.S., Can., Jamaica, Denmark, India, Eng.; panelist at profl. meetings, convs. Mem. MLA, African Lit. Assn., Caribbean Studies Assn., Assn. Caribbean Studies (bd. dirs.), Assn. Commonwealth Lit. and Lang. Studies, Kappa Delta. Home: 63 Puritan Ln Sudbury MA 01776 also Havers care Gen Delivery Roadtown Tortola British Virgin Islands

CAMPBELL, ELLEN LOUISE, exploration geophysicist; b. Summit, N.J., Mar. 6, 1956; d. Douglas J. and Helen E. (Daggett) C. B.A., Colgate U., 1978. Processing geophysicist Houston Processors, Inc., 1978-80; exploration geophysicist ARCO Exploration, Houston, 1980—. Mem. Am. Assn. Petroleum Gologists, Soc. Exploration Geophysicists, Geophys. Soc. Houston, Assn. Women for Geoscis., Houston Geol. Soc. Office: ARCO Exploration PO Box 1346 Houston TX 77251

CAMPBELL, FRANCES HARVELL, member congressional staff; b. Goldston, N.C.; d. George Henry and Evelyn (Meggs) Harvell; m. John T. Campbell, Jr., Apr. 27, 1968 (div. Aug. 1973). B.S. magna cum laude, U. Md., 1982. Asst. to Congressman Claude Pepper, U.S. Ho. of Reps., 1968-80, staff dir., 1980—; exec. dir., curator Mildred and Claude Pepper Library. Author: Young America Speaks, 1957. Vice-pres. Democratic Women of Capitol Hill, 1982-83. Mem. Nat. Assn. Female Execs., Women in Govt. Relations, Adminstrv. Assts. Assn. Capitol Hill, Am. Mgmt. Assn., Nat. Dem. Club, Fla. State Soc. (dir. 1982—), Phi Kappa Phi, Alpha Sigma Lambda. Avocations: orchids; gourmet cooking; gardening. Home: 6222 Hardy Dr McLean VA 22101 Office: 2239 Rayburn House Office Bldg Washington DC 20515

CAMPBELL, HELEN ZOTT, writer, lectr.; b. Des Moines, Feb. 7, 1919; d. John Henry and Perna A. (Jones) Zott; student Fairmont Jr. Coll., 1938, Strayer Bus. Coll., 1939-40, George Washington U., 1943-45, Orgn. Mgmt. Inst., U. Del., 1973, Mgmt. Inst., Notre Dame U., 1978; m. Robert A. Campbell, Jr., Sept. 4, 1948; children—Karen Leigh, Debra Arlene. Acctg. clk. George Washington U., Washington, 1940-46; sec., bookkeeper NEA, Washington, 1946-47; sec., acct. W. E. Cumberland, Washington, 1947-52; acct. Am. Apparel Mfrs. Assn., Inc., Arlington, Va., 1967-72, asst. treas., 1972-79, dir. fin. services, 1973-79; free-lance artist, writer and lectr., 1979—. Jr. bd. George Washington U. Hosp., Washington, 1948-50, pres., 1950-52; bd. govs. English Speaking Union, Sydney, Australia, 1963-65. Recipient citation Philippine Govt., 1958, citation Children of Libya, 1963. Mem. Nat., Am., Washington socs. assn. execs., Nat. Assn. Execs. Clubs, Soc. Preservation Va. Antiquities, Assn. Fgn. Service Women, Arlington C. of C. (assn. council 1975-79), Zonta Internat., Kappa Delta. Republican. Presbyterian. Clubs: Capital Speakers, Washington, Nat. Press, Capitol Hill. Home: 5312 Westpath Way Fort Sumner Hills MD 20816

CAMPBELL, HOPE, author; b. Seattle, June 17; d. Howard R. and Genevieve E. (Talbot) McDonald; ed. Punahou Sch., Honolulu, Dominican Convent, Calif., Monticello Sch., Calif., John Marshall, Calif.; m. Charles Wallis (dec.); children—Christopher M., John Talbot. Actress, artist stage, radio and TV, Calif. and N.Y.; author: (plays) Fantasy of a Day in Court, 1980, Zekle's Wife, 1980, Why Not Join the Giraffes?, 1968, Mystery at Fire Island (adapted for CBS Children's Mystery Theater), 1981; books include: The Light of Lilith, 1961, Liza, 1965, Home to Hawaii, 1967, Why Not Join the Giraffes?, 1968, Meanwhile, Back at the Castle (adapted for ABC-TV, as the Almost Royal Family 1984) (Gold award Internat. Film Festival 1985), 1970, No More Trains to Tottenville, 1971, There's a Pizza Back in Cleveland (with Mary Anderson), 1972, Peter's Angel: A Story About Monsters, 1976, Mystery at Fire Island, 1978, Legend of Lost Earth, 1977, A Peak Beneath the Moon, 1979; co-creator War is the Enemy radio series. Served with USO. Mem. Authors Guild, Dramatists Guild, AFTRA, Actors Equity Assn.

CAMPBELL, JEANNE MARIE, government relations-public affairs company executive; b. Chgo.; d. John and Wilhelmina Evelyn (Powers) Kruzic; widowed; children—Keith Maclean, Scott McElroy. B.A., B.S., No. Ill. U., 1966; M.S. in Edn., 1971; M.A., Loyola U., Chgo., 1975; postgrad. Am. U., Washington. Mem. faculty Am. U., Washington, Loyola U., Chgo., 1973-77, George Washington U.; speechwriter Congressman Dan Rostenkowski, 1977-79; press sec. Congresswoman Margaret Heckler, 1979-80; v.p. New Eng. Council, Inc., Washington, 1981-85; sr. assoc. Martin Haley Cos., 1981-85; pres. Campbell-Raupe, Inc., Washington, 1985—. Vol. tutor Laubach Lit. Assn., Ill. and Washington, 1965—. Mem. Tax Coalition, Am. League Lobbyists (sec. 1983), Women in Govt. Relations. Avocation: writing. Home: 3806 N Richmond St Arlington VA 22207 Office: Campbell Raupe Inc 101515th St NW Washington DC 20005

CAMPBELL, JUDITH LOWE, child psychiatrist; b. Indpls., Jan. 21, 1946; d. Albert St. Clair and Adele V. (Lobraico) Lowe; B.S. in Zoology, Butler U., 1967; M.D., Ind. U., 1971; m. Robert Frank Campbell, Nov. 30, 1968; children—Christiaan Robert, Kevin Lowe, Geoffrey Ford. Resident in psychiatry Ind. U. Sch. Medicine, 1971-73, fellow in child psychiatry 1973-75; asst. dir. Riley Child Guidance Clinic, Indpls., 1975-79, dir. child psychiatry consultation, liaison service to pediatrics, 1975-79; dir. child psychiatry services Riley Hosp. for Children, 1979-85; pvt. practice child psychiatry, Indpls., 1985—; child psychiatry cons. Center for Mental Health of Madison County (Ind.), Anderson, 1975-77, Lutheran Child Welfare Assn., Indpls., 1974—, Lutherwood Children's Home, Indpls., 1974—, Jewish Family and Children's Services, 1983-84, child and adolescent div. Midtown Community Mental Health Center, 1983-85; instr. Ind. U. Sch. Medicine, Indpls., 1974-75, asst. prof. dept psychiatry, 1975—. Vol., Ind. State chpt. Cystic Fibrosis Found., 1977. Recipient Physician's Recognition award in Continuing Edn. AMA, 1974, 77; Helen McQuiston award in sci., 1967. Fellow Am. Psychiat. Assn., Ind. Psychiat. Soc. (councilor 1978-80, sec. 1981-83, editor newsletter 1981-83, chmn. com. women 1983-85), Am. Burn Assn., Am. Acad. Pediatrics (Ind. br.), Am. Med. Women's Assn., Am. Acad. Child Psychiatry, Am. Assn. Psychiat. Services for Children, Smithsonian Assocs., Field Mus. Natural History, Indpls. Mus. Art, Indpls. Zool. Soc., U. Psychiat. Assocs., Pi Beta Phi, Beta Sigma Phi. Clubs: Carmel Racquet, Eastern Star, Woodland Country. Contbr. articles on child psychiatry to profl. jours. Research on emotional aspects of burns in children, craniofacial anomalies in children, also sex differences in child and adolescent population groups. Office: 7250 Clearvista Dr Suite 345 Indianapolis IN 46256

CAMPBELL, JULIA WEIR, horsewoman, educator; b. Grand Junction, Colo., Apr. 2, 1939; d. John Stephen and Xenia (Marghetic) Casement; m. Kenneth Dale Campbell, Oct. 4, 1958 (div. 1978); children—Julie, Diana, Susan. Grad. Kent Sch., 1956; student Colo. State U., 1956, Denver U., 1957-58; Tchr. spl. edn. Los Lunas Hosp. (N.Mex.), 1964-66; owner, real estate broker Catnip Realty, Belen, N.Mex., 1967-83; with Farm Bur. Ins., Belen, 1981-83; owner, mgr. Catnip Farm, Belen, 1963-83; head horsemanship dept. North-East Colo. Jr. Coll., Sterling, 1983—. Mem. Valencia County Fair Bd. Recipient Silver award 4-H Club, Beber, N.Mex., 1969, Outstanding Citizen award Dist. Future Farmers Am., 1976. Mem. N.Mex. Horse Breeders Assn. (pub. relations and publicity com.), Am. Quarter Horse Assn., N.Mex. Quarter Horse Assn. (race com.), Rocky Mountain Quarter Horse Assn., Nat. Cutting Horse Assn. Republican. Episcopalian. Home: PO Box 1293 Sterling CO 80751

CAMPBELL, JUNE HERBST, educator, writer, inventor, business executive; b. Wilmington, Del., June 28, 1928; d. Ross Lyon and Mildred (Herbst) C. B.A., U. Del., 1950; M.A. in Edn., San Francisco State U., 1980. Tchr. physically handicapped, Media, Pa., 1967-77; tchr. Children's Hosp. Sch., Stanford, Calif., 1980-84; pres. Atlas Cold Baggie Co., Foster City, Calif., 1982—; resource specialist San Jose Unified Sch. Dist., Calif., 1984—. Author: Learning Through Art, 1975; The Money Book, 1978; It's Me Book, 1977; creator Time Bingo game, Money Bingo game; patentee insulated lunch bag, insulin pouch. Home: PO Box 4162 Foster City CA 94404

CAMPBELL, KARLYN KOHRS, educator; b. Blomkest, Minn., Apr. 16, 1937; d. Meinhard and Dorothy (Siegers) Kohrs; B.A., (Tozer scholar), Macalester Coll., 1958; M.A. (Tozer fellow), U. Minn., 1959, Ph.D., 1968; m. Paul Newell Campbell, Sept. 16, 1967. Asst. prof. SUNY, Brockport, 1959-63, Calif. State U., Los Angeles, 1966-71; asso. prof. SUNY, Binghamton, 1971-73, CUNY, 1973-74; prof. communication studies U. Kans., Lawrence, 1974-83, chairperson women's studies, 1983-86; prof. speech-communication U. Minn., Mpls., 1986—; Gladys Borchers lectr., U. Wis., Madison, 1974. Mem. Speech Communication Assn., Central States Speech Communication Assn., Nat. Womens Studies Assn., Phi Beta Kappa, Pi Phi Epsilon. Author: Critiques of Contemporary Rhetoric, 1972; Form and Genre, 1978; The Rhetorical Act, 1982; Interplay of Influence, 1983; editorial bd. Today's Speech, 1972-75, The Speech Teacher, 1973-75, Central States Speech Jour., 1977-79, Communication Monographs, 1978-80, Quarterly Jour. Speech, 1980-85; contbr. articles to profl. jours. Office: Dept Speech-Communication U Minn Minneapolis MN 55455

CAMPBELL, LUCINDRA, psychiatric nurse; b. New Brunswick, N.J., Sept. 13, 1954; d. Lawerance and Dinah Mae (Auld) Aiken; m. James Isaac Campbell; 1 dau., Cassandra Denise. Student Walterboro Sch. Nursing, Fayetteville State U., student Houston Bapt. U. Nurse, surg. nurse Colleton Hosp., Walterboro, S.C., 1968; nurse-therapist Oakwood Retirement Home, Walterboro, 1969-80; nurse Villa Rose Psychiat. Instn., San Antonio, 1980-81; nurse co-therapist Rosewood Gen. Hosp., Houston, 1981—. Mem. Nat. League Nursing, Hosp. Equities Inc., NAACP. Methodist (trustee 1978-79, Sunday sch. tchr. 1978-79). Home: 12614 A Mews Circle Houston TX 77082

CAMPBELL, MARGARET ANNE, education consultant; b. Denver, Nov. 13, 1917; d. Earl Ogilvie and Vera Elizabeth (Mallon) Linger; m. Leonard Earl Campbell, July 5, 1938; children—Margilee Campbell Saver, Beverly Campbell Fortin, Marilyn E. Campbell Waak. B.A., U. No. Colo., 1938; M.S., Wayne State Coll., 1959; Ed.D., U. Nebr., 1969; H.H.D. (hon.), Midland Coll., 1974, Doane Coll., 1983; L.H.D., Central Meth. Coll., Fayette, Mo., 1972. County supt. schs., Madison County, Madison, Nebr., 1955-63; dir. profl. services Nebr. Edn. Assn., Lincoln, 1963-65; adminstrv. asst., govt. services Lincoln Pub. Schs., 1965-72; dir. pub. affairs U. Nebr., Lincoln, 1972-74; commr. of edn. State of Nebr., Lincoln, 1975-82; edn. cons., Lincoln, 1983—; v.p. for edn. Nat. PTA, 1983-85; mem. Nat. Panel for Study of Am. High Schs., Carnegie Found., 1980-83; mem. Nat. Commn. for Excellence in Edn., 1981-85. Trustee Doane Coll., Crete, Nebr., 1972—; bd. dirs. Lincoln-Lancaster County Youth Service System, 1982—. Recipient Norman F. Thorpe Service award U. Nebr., Lincoln, 1979; Disting. Alumni award U. No. Colo., 1981; David H. Hutcheson award U. Nebr. Tchrs. Coll., 1982; Roscoe Shields award Nebr. Art Educators, 1982; Disting. Service award Concordia Coll., Seward, Nebr., 1984. Mem. Council of Chief State Sch. Officers (pres. 1979-80), Am. Assn. Sch. Adminstrs., Assn. for Supervision and Curriculum Devel., Assn. Tchr. Educators, Assn. Women Execs., AAUW (nat. pres. 1971-75), Bus. and Profl. Women, Lincoln C. of C. Republican. Presbyterian. Avocations: golf; cards. Home: 7500 South St Apt 8 Lincoln NE 68506

CAMPBELL, MARGARET SUE, medical technologist, business executive; b. Tyler, Tex., Oct. 18, 1953; d. Hugh and Martha Sue (Gassaway) McPhail; m. Bruce Howard Campbell, Jan. 8, 1983. B.A. in Biology, U. Tex.-Austin, 1977, B.S. in Med. Tech. Galveston, 1978. Cert. med. technologist Am. Soc. Clin. Pathologists. Sr. technologist Nat. Health Labs., Dallas, 1979-81; asst. supr. hematology Meth. Hosp., Dallas, 1981-82; med. technologist Rosewood Gen. Hosp., Houston, 1983—; chmn. Campbell Enterprises, Houston, 1983—. Active Jr. League Houston, 1983—; pres. Covenant Class Meml. Drive United Meth. Ch., Houston, 1983-84. Mem. Am. Soc. Med. Tech. Am. Soc. Clin. Pathologists, Amway Distbrs. Assn. U.S. Republican. Clubs: U. Tex. Ex-Students Assn. (Austin); Houston Directs Assn. Home: 1902 Marlberry St Houston TX 77084 Office: Rosewood Gen Hosp 9200 Westheimer St Houston TX 77063

CAMPBELL, MARY ANN, journalist; b. Portland, Oreg., Mar. 25, 1920; d. David Beasley and Margueritte (Dosch) C.; B.A., U. Oreg., 1943; M.S., Joseph Pulitzer Grad. Sch. Journalism, Columbia U., 1946. Reporter, Oreg. Jour., 1943-50; free-lance reporter, Portland, 1959; reporter Portland Reporter, 1960-64; editor Ontario (Oreg.) Argus-Observer, 1966-69; editor Polk Sun, Monmouth, Oreg., 1970-72; women's editor, reporter, feature writer Medford (Oreg.) Mail Tribune, 1972—, art, music critic, editor, feature writer, 1974—; tchr. Upward Bound Oreg. Prison Project, New Gate, 1965; del. Internat. Commn. on Monuments and Sites, UNESCO, Dresden, 1984. Mem. Oreg. Environ. Council, Sierra Club, Friends of the Earth, 1000 Friends of Oreg., Nat. Wildlife Fedn., Defenders of Wildlife, Nat. Trust. Hist. Preservation, Oreg. Hist. Soc., So. Oreg. Hist. Soc., So. Oreg. Humane Soc., Oreg. Humane Soc., Greenpeace, Amnesty Internat., Oreg. Wilderness Coalition, ACLU, Theta Sigma Phi, Sigma Delta Chi. Democrat. Office: PO Box 1108 Medford OR 97501

CAMPBELL, MARY BETH, reading educator, consultant; b. Muncie, Ind., Oct. 22, 1946; d. Carey Wallace and Mina Lucille (Shaffer) Opperman; m. Hugh Daniel Campbell; children—Heather J., Patrick H. B.A., Ball State U., 1968, M.A., 1971; Ph.D., U. Fla., 1981. Lifetime teaching cert. Calif. Elem. tchr. Santa Ana Unified Sch. Dist., Calif., 1968-71, Junction City Schs., Oreg., 1971-74, Alachua County Schs., Gainesville, Fla., 1974-75, P.K. Yonge Lab. Sch., Gainesville, 1975-79; asst. prof. U. Fla., Gainesville, 1981-82, dir. reading workshop, 1977; vis. asst. prof. La. State U., Baton Rouge, 1982; asst. prof. U. Nebr., Lincoln, 1982-83; cons., tchr. Belvidere Sch. Dist., Ill., 1986—; cons. testing State Dept. Edn., Gainesville, 1980-81; cons. reading Alachua County Reading Council, Gainesville, 1979; cons. creativity, Clearwater Exceptional Sch., Fla., 1978. Author monographs, articles in field. Recipient Mini Grant, State Dept. Edn., Fla., 1975-76, Star Grant in Reading, 1977-78, hon. mention Instructor Mag., 1979. Mem. Internat. Reading Assn., Kappa Delta Phi, Pi Lambda Theta. Avocation: reading. Office: Community Unit School Dist 100 1201 5th Ave Belvidere IL 61008

CAMPBELL, MARY KATHLEEN, mortgage banker; b. Torrance, Calif., Aug. 5, 1944; d. David F. and Katherine I. (Norton) Shields; m. John Alan Campbell, Aug. 19, 1963; children—Lisa Marie Campbell Mitchell, John Andrew. B.B.A. in Acctg., Nat. U., San Diego, 1984. Head cashier Navy Exchange, San Diego, 1968-69; customer relations mgr. J.M. Fields, Norfolk, Va., 1970-72; acct. Hart Enterprises, San Diego, 1973-76; asst. treas. Midwest Pacific Fin., Inc., San Diego, 1976-80, treas., 1980-84, v.p., treas., 1984—; asst. sec. Midwest Fed. Savs. of Eastern Iowa, Burlington, 1978—, asst. v.p., 1985—; treas., dir. Burlington Fin., San Diego, 1984—. Vol. worker Girl Scouts U.S.A., San Diego, 1970-77, Boy Scouts Am., San Diego, 1972-79, Am. Cancer Soc., San Diego, 1978-82; student-family liaison Am. Field Service, Poway, Calif., 1983—. Mem. Fin. Mgrs. Soc., Assn. for Profl. Mortgage Women, Am. Bus. Women's Assn. (treas. 1980-81, Woman of Yr. Poway 1982). Office: Midwest Pacific Financial Inc 7720 Cardinal Ct San Diego CA 92123

CAMPBELL, MARY KATHRYN, educator; b. Phila., Jan. 20, 1939; d. Henry Charles and Mary Kathryn (Horan) C.; A.B. in Chemistry, Rosemont Coll., 1960; Ph.D., Ind. U., 1965. Instr. Johns Hopkins U., 1965-68; asst. prof. chemistry Mt. Holyoke Coll., 1968-74, assoc. prof., 1974-81, prof., 1981—; vis. scholar U. Paris VIII, 1974-75, VII, 1977-79; vis. prof. U. Ariz., 1981-82; mem. panel on grad. fellowships NSF, 1980-81. Hon. Woodrow Wilson fellow, 1960, NSF fellow, 1960-64, NIH fellow, 1964-65; grantee in field. Mem. Am. Chem. Soc., AAAS, AAUP, AAUW, Sigma Xi. Contbr. articles to profl. jours. Office: Carr Laboratory Department of Chemistry Mount Holyoke College South Hadley MA 01075

CAMPBELL, MARY MARTHA GRIGGS, writer, public relations specialist; b. Chattanooga, June 12, 1946; d. Erick Earroll and Olive Josephine (Davis) Griggs; 1 dau., Martha Josephine. B.A., U. Tenn., 1971. Staff writer News-Free Press, Chattanooga, 1972-74; editor publs. Provident Life & Accident Ins. Co., Chattanooga, 1975-80; dir. pub. relations The McCallie Sch., Chattanooga, 1980-84; freelance writer and pub. relations cons., 1984—; pub. relations specialist, Chattanooga-Hamilton County Bicentennial Library, 1984—. Bd. dirs. Moccasin Bend Council Girl Scouts U.S.A., Chattanooga, 1978-83, Dance Theatre Workshop, Chattanooga, 1980-81, Chattanooga Ballet, 1985—, mem. pub. relations adv. com. Siskin Found., Chattanooga, 1983. Mem. Internat. Assn. Bus. Communicators (chpt. pres. 1981), Alpha Delta Pi. Office: 1001 Broad St Chattanooga TN 37402

CAMPBELL, NEVA TIPLEY, lawyer; b. LaGrande, Oreg., Oct. 21, 1933; d. Elmer Joseph Tipley and Lenore Evelyn (Combes) Herman; m. Zane Kay Campbell, Dec. 19, 1954; children—Blair T., Greggre Ann Campbell Adrian. B.A., Oreg. State U., 1955; J.D., Lewis & Clark Coll., 1973. Bar: Oreg. 1973, U.S. Dist. Ct. Oreg. 1974, U.S. Supreme Ct. 1984. Assoc., Schwabe, Williamson, Wyatt, Moore & Roberts, Portland, 1973-80, ptnr., 1981—. Commr. Oreg. State Lottery, 1985. Mem. ABA, Oreg. Bar Assn., Phi Kappa Phi. Home: 2320 SE Mulberry Dr Milwaukie OR 97267 Office: Schwabe Williamson Wyatt Moore & Roberts 1211 SW 5th St Suite 1800 Portland OR 97204

CAMPBELL, PATRICIA ANNE, handicrafts co. exec.; b. Pitts., Dec. 30; d. John A. and M. Lucille (Park) Campbell; B.S., Duquesne U., 1968; M.Ed., U. Pitts., 1969, Ph.D., 1974. Tchr., Avonworth Schs., 1968, Beaver County Community Coll., 1969, Northgate Schs., Pitts., 1974-75; mgmt. trainee Pitts. Nat. Bank, 1974-75; pres. Patpourri Enterprises, Sewickley, Pa., 1975—. Keiki concert chmn. Honolulu Symphony, 1978-80; mem. bd. Women's Symphony Assn., Honolulu, 1978-80; bd. dirs. women's guild Pitts. Ballet Theater, 1981-82. Recipient U. Pitts. Student Research award, 1974. Mem. Doctoral Assn. U. Pitts., AAUW, Pi Lambda Theta. Republican. Club: Pitts. Athletic Assn. Author: Prosocial Television Programming for Children: Expressions of Anger By Children During the Cognitive Revolution Period of development, 1974. Home: 216 Pine Rd Sewickley PA 15143

CAMPBELL, PATRICIA MARY, educational administrator, speech pathologist; b. San Diego, Oct. 17, 1948; d. Richard Robert and Mary Elizabeth (Keating) Harrison; m. Robert Campbell, Aug. 8, 1970; children—Blake David, Justin Richard. B.A., San Diego State U., 1971; M. Ed., 1981. Resource specialist Vista Unified, Calif., 1979-80, program specialist, 1980, dean students, 1980-83, asst. prin., 1983-84, prin., 1984—. Mem. Assn. Calif. Sch. Adminstrs. (pres. 1985—), Sigma Alpha Eta. Democrat. Roman Catholic. Avocations: jogging; aerobics. Home: 4902 Refugio Ave Carlsbad CA 92008 Office: Vista Unified Sch Dist 1575 Bonair Vista CA 92083

CAMPBELL, ROBERTA JUNE, auditor; b. Atlanta, Oct. 17, 1947; d. Robert Miles and Eunice (O'Neal) Saul; B.B.A. (Ga. Educators Assn. fellow), Ga. State U., 1970, M.Profl. Acctg. and Bus. Info. Sci. (Univ. fellow), 1978; m. Lloyd Ray Campbell; children—Michael, Sara, Brian. Cert. internal auditor (EDP), cert. quality analyst. Sr. acct. textile ops. Oxford Industries, Inc., Atlanta, 1969-71; corp. auditor U.S. Dept. Treasury, Atlanta, 1971-76; fin. systems dir. Indsl. Devel. Research Council, Atlanta, 1976-81; sr. EDP/fin. specialist Met. Atlanta Rapid Transit Authority, EDP auditor/specialist, 1981—; mem. adult edn. acctg. faculty Ga. U. System, 1972-76; cons., lectr. in field. Mem. Assoc. Info. Mgrs., Info. Industry Assn., Inst. Internal Auditors (EDP seminar chmn. 1985, chmn. seminars and research com.), Women's Transp. Seminar, EDP Auditors Assn. (gov. membership), Ga. State U. Alumni Assn. Co-author: Industrial Park Growth, 1979; New Industries of the Seventies, 1978, 2d edit. 1980; Composite Case History of New Facility Location-Utility Services, 1978; 5000 Growth Firms, 1981; Effective Auditing of Personnel, Payroll and Risk Management, 1983. Home: 2848 N Deshong Rd Stone Mountain GA 30087 Office: 401 W Peachtree St Suite 2000 Atlanta GA 30305

CAMPBELL, ROBIN CORWIN, lawyer; b. Bklyn., July 13, 1957; d. Eugene Joseph Corwin and Lorraine (Nadel) Minches; m. Les R. Campbell, July 1, 1978. B.A. in Internat. Affairs, Fla. State U., 1978; J.D. Nova Law Center, 1981. Bar: Fla. 1981, U.S. Dist. Ct. (so. dist.) Fla. 1981. Assoc. Capp, Reinstein, Kopelowitz & Atlas, P.A., Fort Lauderdale, Fla., 1981—. Mem. Nat. Counsel Jewish Women, Boca Raton, Fla., 1982-84. Mem. Assn. Trial Lawyers Am., Am. Judicature Soc., ABA, Broward County Bar Assn., Phi Beta Kappa, Phi Delta Phi (sec., treas. 1977-78). Democrat. Jewish. Office: Capp Reinstein Kopelowitz & Atlas 700 SE 3rd Ave Fort Lauderdale FL 33316

CAMPBELL, SALLY SIMMONS, magazine editor; b. Clearwater, Fla., Oct. 3, 1938; d. Stephen Emery and Clara Marie (Rugheimer) Simmons; m. Bruce Michael Campbell, Apr. 18, 1964; children—Stephen, Jamie. B.A., Duke U., 1960. Editor Houghton Mifflin Co., Boston, 1960-65; freelance writer, Wilton, Conn., 1978-83; editor Advisory Enterprises, Armonk, N.Y., 1983—. Contbr. articles to various publs. Recipient First Place award, Reader's Digest, 1979; Hon. mention Writing competition Writer's Digest Mag., 1983. Mem. Women in Communications (v.p. 1983-84; newsletter editor 1982-83, job bank chair. 1984-85).

CAMPBELL, SALLY WORTHINGTON, freelance writer, editor, public relations consultant; b. Pitts., Jan. 3, 1947; d. Aubrey Walter and Marie Ruth (Hennigsen) Worthington; B.A. in Journalism, Auburn U., 1968; m. John Jette Campbell, Aug. 31, 1968; children—Ashley, Heather, John Jette, Jr. Reporter-intern Montgomery, Ala. Jour., 1968; asst. editor Auburn (Ala.) Extension Service, 1968-69; tchr. lang. arts Nichols Jr. High Sch., Tuskegee, Ala., 1969-70; editor Where Mag., Houston, 1971-79, southwestern editorial supr., 1979; dir. public relations Austin (Tex.) Civic Ballet, 1980-82, v.p. Ballet Austin, 1983-84, also bd. dirs.; cons. public relations Retinitis Pigmentosa Found., Houston, 1979. Vice pres. Austin Jr. Forum, 1980-82; mem. Laguna Gloria Mus. Women's Art Guild, 1980—; writer for KTBC-TV 1st place award Region II public service announcement competition, Tex. Broadcasters Assn., 1981, Leadership Austin, 1983-84. Mem. Women in Communications, Alpha Omicron Pi. Republican. Presbyterian. Home and Office: 7705 Bramblewood Circle Austin TX 78731

CAMPBELL, STEPHANIE ANNE, television station executive; b. Kansas City, Mo., Dec. 17, 1948; d. Paul William and Annabelle (Pitcher) C.; m. Kirby William Sullivan, Aug. 23, 1975 (div. 1978). Student Western Md. Coll., 1966-67, Prairie State Coll., 1967-68. Prodn. asst. Needham, Harper and Steers, Chgo. 1968-70; traffic, ops. mgr. Sta. WTAF-TV, Phila., 1970-72; copywriter Cunningham and Walsh, Chgo., 1972-75, Batten, Barton, Durstin & Osborne, Chgo., 1975-76; writer, producer Shillito/Rike's Cin., 1976-79; prodn. supr. Procter and Gamble, Cin., 1979-80; ops. mgr. Sta. WDCA-TV, Washington, 1980-81, mgr. DCA Prodns., 1981-83, progrm. mgr., 1983—. Mem. Nat. Acad. TV Arts and Scis. (bd. govs. 1983—, pres. 1985—), Am. Women in Radio and TV. Republican. Methodist. Avocations: design needlepoint; tap dancing; jazz dancing; running. Home: 5301 Carlton St Bethesda MD 20816 Office: Sta WDCA-TV 5202 River Rd Washington DC 20816

CAMPBELL, SUSAN PANNILL, banker; b. Richmond, Va., May 28, 1947; d. Raymond Brodie and Lucie Courtice (McDonald) C. A.B., Coll. William and Mary, 1969; M.Ed., U. Va., 1970, postgrad., 1974-75; postgrad. Summer Inst. of Coll. Admissions, Harvard U., 1972. Counselor, instr. Thomas Nelson Community Coll., Hampton, Va., 1970-71; asst. dean admissions U. Va., Charlottesville, 1971-78; banking officer Tex. Commerce Bank, Houston, 1978-81, asst. v.p., 1981-82; asst. v.p. First City Nat. Bank, Houston, 1982-85, v.p., 1985—. Loaned exec. United Way, Houston, 1978; v.p. EnCorps, div. Houston Symphony League, 1981-82, pres., 1982-83, bd. dirs., 1983-85; bd. dirs. Houston Symphony League, 1982-83; bd. advisors Houston Symphony Soc., 1982-86; sec. tng. com. loaned execs. United Way, Houston, 1979-81. Honor award scholar Mary Baldwin Coll., Staunton, Va., 1965-66. Mem. Nat. Assn. Bank Women, Am. Symphony Orch. League (vol. council), Coll. William and Mary Alumni Assn. (dir. Houston chpt. 1981—), Kappa Alpha Theta. Democrat. Presbyterian. Office: First City Nat Bank Houston PO Box 2557 Houston TX 77252

CAMPBELL, SUZANN KAY, physical therapy educator; b. New London, Wis., Apr. 19, 1943; d. Martin J. and Virginia May (Schoenrock) Reetz; m. Richard T. Campbell, Feb. 6, 1965; children—Dianne Elizabeth, Deborah Carol. B.S. in Phys. Therapy, U. Wis., 1965, M.S., 1968, Ph.D. in Neurophysiology, 1973. Lic. phys. therapist; cert. neurodevelopmental therapist; cert. Brazelton instr. Staff therapist Central Wis. Colony, Madison, 1965-68; inst. U. Wis.-Madison, 1968-70; asst. prof. phys. therapy U. N.C., Chapel Hill, 1972-77, assoc. prof., 1977-84, prof., 1984—, Charles E. Culpeper fellow in med. scis., 1985—. research cons. Am. Occupational Therapy Assn., Washington, 1981—. Editor: Pediatric Neurologic Physical Therapy, 1984; editor Phys. and Occupational Therapy in Pediatrics jour., 1979—; mem. editorial adv. bd. Churchill Livingstone Pubs., N.Y.C., 1983—; contbr. articles to profl. jours. Mem. Am. Phys. Therapy Assn. (adv. council on phys. therapy edn. 1983-86, research fellow 1980, Golden Pen 1978, research award pediatrics sect. 1984), Wis. Phys. Therapy Assn. (pres. 1971-72), N.C. Phys. Therapy Assn. (treas. 1984-85), Chapel Hill Bird Club. Democrat. Office: Div Phys Therapy Wing E 222H U NC Sch Medicine Chapel Hill NC 27514

CAMPBELL, VERONICA MARIE, auditor, govt. ofcl.; b. Phila., Aug. 30, 1952; d. Charles F. and Virginia M. (Hibbits) C.; B.A., Barat Coll., Lake Forest, Ill., 1973. With Office Insp. Gen., Dept. Agr., 1973-82, auditor-in-charge fgn. ops. staff, Washingtion, 1979-82; supervisory auditor Office of Insp. Gen., U.S. Dept. Interior, 1982-84; asst. dir. Washington audit office Office Insp. Gen., Dept. Labor, 1984—. Mem. Assn. Govt. Accts., Delta Epsilon Sigma, Kappa Gamma Pi. Roman Catholic. Office: 601 D St NW Room 4100 Washington DC 20213

CAMPBELL-BELL, DOROTHY KATHRYN, lawyer; b. Mt. Clemens, Mich., Oct. 6, 1955; d. Bruce Hicks and Helen Joyce (Bailey) Campbell; m. Mark Joseph Bell, July 23, 1977. A.B. cum laude, Duke U., 1976; J.D., Vanderbilt U., 1980; student New Coll., Oxford (Eng.) U., 1976. Bar: Tenn. 1980, U.S. Dist. Ct. (mid. dist.) Tenn. 1981, U.S. Ct. Appeals (6th cir.) 1982. Inventory specialist Va. State Dept. Corrections, Richmond, Va., 1977; referral asst. Va. Lawyer Referral Service, Richmond, 1977; law clk. Chambers, Johnson, Brooks & Beckner, Nashville, 1979, Cross & Stiles, Nashville, 1979; clk. Ingraham, Corbett & Zinn, Nashville, 1978-79, 79-80, assoc., 1980-85, ptnr., 1986—. Vol., Friends of Children's Hosp., Nashville, 1981-83; tchr. St. George's Episcopal Ch., 1984-85; dir. Georgetown Homeowners Assn., Nashville, 1983-86; campaign vol. United Way, Nashville, 1981, 83; vol. instr. ARC Adapted Aquatics Program, 1981—, ARC Safety Services Com., 1985—, bd. dirs., 1986—. Angier B. Duke Meml. scholar, 1973. Mem. ABA, Tenn. Bar Assn., Nashville Bar Assn. (participant pro-bono program 1980—). Contbr. articles to profl. publ. Office: Ingraham Corbett & Zinn 2114 Parkway Towers Nashville TN 37219

CAMPBELL-GLENN, PATRICIA ANN, government official; b. Brandon, Miss., Dec. 15, 1942; d. James Alvin and Eunice Agnes (Finch) Campbell; children—Allison, Jennifer, Lee. B.S. in Edn., Ohio State U., 1971; postgrad. U. Ill., 1980—. Supr., investigator Civil Rights Commn., Columbus, Ohio, 1971-74; tchr. Columbus Bd. Edn., 1974-78; mediator, dep. dir. U.S. Dept. Justice, Chgo., 1979—. Contbr. articles to profl. jours. Tutor Nat. Literacy Campaign, 1985; commr. Boy Scouts Am., 1985-86; speaker Women's Bd., Ill., 1985-86. Recipient Humanitarian award Columbus Met. Action Community Action Orgn., 1980; Human Relations Spl. award Flint Human Relations Bd., Mich., 1985; Cert. of Appreciation, Kiwanis, Chgo., 1985. Mem. Nat. Council Negro Women, Nat. Assn. Female Execs., Soc. for Profls. in Dispute Resolution. A.M.E. Ch. (asst. supt. Bd. Christian Edn.) Club: VFW Ladies Aux. (pres. 1984-85). Home: 6231 Champlain Chicago IL 60637

CAMPO, SANDRA LUCY, university official; b. Detroit, Mar. 16, 1938; d. Norman Haire and Mary Catherine (McCorry) Sarvis; m. Alfredo Campo, Sept. 20, 1958; children—Kevin Frederick, Keith Charles. Ph.B., U. Detroit, 1962; M.Ed., Wayne State U., 1969. Tchr., Royal Oak (Mich.) Sch. System, 1960-63, Toms River (N.J.) Sch. System, 1976-79; gen. office supr. LUTC, Washington, 1979-81, exec. asst. to v.p., 1981; mgr. Ethics Resource Ctr., Washington, 1981-82; mgmt. trainee Southland, Alexandria, Va., 1982; adminstrv. asst. to dean Med. Sch., Georgetown U., 1982—; ednl. rep. NEA, Royal Oak, 1962. Sec., Welcome Wagon, Toms River, 1976; co-chmn. meeting Toms River Hawks Internat. Soc., 1978; trustee bd. Graeser Acres Plat III, St. Louis, 1973-75; founder Graeser Acres Self-Help Com., St. Louis, 1974; mem. Cath. Youth Orgn. bd. St. Mary's Catholic Ch., Alexandria, 1985—. Mem. AAUW (v.p. 1976-77, focus rep. 1982), Georgetown U. Women's Assn. (rec. sec. 1985-86, activities chmn. 1985—, pres. 1986—). Republican. Club: Fort Belvoir (Va.). Home: 3410 Ramsgate Terr Alexandria VA 22309

CAMPOS, WILMA FAY, computer consultant; b. Seymour, Ind., Feb. 8, 1954; d. William John and Sylvia Emma (Sweeney) Schlitzer; m. Steven Campos, Apr. 25, 1981. A.A.S., Pima Community Coll., 1978; student Academia Hispanoamericana, San Miguel de Allende, Guanajuato, Mex., 1979, Hogan Sch. Real Estate, 1982-83. Lic. real estate agt. Proof operator So. Ariz. Bank, Tucson, 1972-76; reconciler, Union Bank, Tucson, 1976-78; systems analyst City of Tucson 1978-80; programmer CF & I Steel Co., Pueblo, 1980-81; online specialist Colo. Nat. Bank, Denver, 1981; computer cons., Tucson, 1981—. Judge, Pima County Elections, Tucson, 1977, 78; election operator City of Tucson Elections, 1979. Avocations: travel; hiking; woodworking; photography. Home: 1640 W Dawn Dr Tucson AZ 85704 Office: Willy Campos Computer Cons 1640 W Dawn Dr Tucson AZ 85704

CAMRON, ROXANNE, editor; b. Los Angeles, May 16; d. S. Irving John and Roslyn (Weingerber) Spiro; m. Robert Camron, Sept. 28, 1969; children—Ashley Jennifer, Erin Jessica. B.A. in Journalism, U. So. Calif., 1967. West Coast fashion and beauty editor Teen mag., Los Angeles, 1969-70, sr. editor, 1972-73, editor, 1973—; pub. relation rep. Max Factor Co., 1970; asst. to creative dir. Polly Bergen Co., 1970-71; lectr. teen groups; freelance writer. Active Homeowners Assn. Mem. Women in Communications, Am. Soc. Exec. Women. Address: 8831 Sunset Blvd Los Angeles CA 90069

CANARINA, OPAL JEAN, nurse, administrator, educator, consultant, lecturer; b. Geneva County, Ala., Mar. 21, 1936; d. O. Lee and L. Ellen (Box) Peacock; m. Miles Steven Bajcar, June 27, 1953 (div.); children—Debra Lynn-Wilson; Wayne Steven; m. Arnold R. Canarina, June 19, 1965; children—Catherine Mary, Christopher John, Charles Benjamin. B.S.N. summa cum laude, George Mason U., Fairfax, Va., 1976, M.S.N., Vanderbilt U., 1981. R.N., Va., Tenn., Ky. Staff and charge nurse Georgetown U. Hosp., Washington, 1976; charge nurse ob-gyn Vanderbilt U. Hosp., Nashville, 1976-77; charge nurse labor and delivery service Baptist Hosp., Nashville, 1977-80; asst. prof. dept. baccalaureate nursing Austin Peay State U., Clarksville, Tenn., 1981-83; dir. nursing services Meml. Hosp., Guymon, Okla., 1983-85; dir. Women's Ctr./Maternal-Child Nursing, McKay-Dee Hosp. Ctr., Ogden, Utah, 1985—; cons. to middle Tenn. and No. Utah areas health and nursing issues. Recipient cert. of excellence R.N.s on campus George Mason U., 1976. Mem. Tenn. Nurses Assn. (legis. chmn. dist. 13, 1982—, pres. 1982), Va. Nurses Assn. (Student Nurse of Yr. award 1975), Am. Nurses Assn., Am. Nurses Found., Nurses Assn. Coll. Ob-Gyn, Sigma Theta Tau, Alpha Chi.

CANATSEY, SANDRA DAVIS, bldg. and devel. co. exec.; b. Trussville, Ala., Dec. 30, 1940; d. Samuel Robert and Beulah Gladys (Shook) Davis; B.S. in Edn., U. Kans., 1962; m. Steven Michael Canatsey, July 5, 1974; children—Kimberley, Kacee, Kevin, Kristine, Kip. Kindergarten tchr., Kansas City, Kans., 1962-64; elem. tchr. Larkspur Elem. Sch., Paradise Valley, Ariz., 1964-65; office mgr. Canatsey & Co., Tucson, 1976-78; sec., dir. Canatsey Bldg. & Devel. Co., Inc., Tucson, 1978—, Canlove Enterprises, Inc. Pres. Pathfinder Republican Women, 1980; mem. Five Star Rep. Women, 1982, pres., 1984—; exec. bd., treas. Tucson Symphony Women's Assn., 1981-83, pres., 1984—; mem. Tucson Med. Center Aux., 1973—; exec. com., sec. Ariz. Fedn. Rep. Women, 1981—; chmn. vols. Barry Goldwater for Senate, 1980. Life cert. substitute tchr., Ariz. Mem. So. Ariz. Home Builders Aux. (exec. com., v.p.), Alpha Phi Mothers Club. Home: 2520 Camino Principal Tucson AZ 85715 Office: 1625 N Alvernon Way Tucson AZ 85712

CANAVAN, ELLEN MCGEE, state legislator; b. San Antonio, Dec. 26, 1941; d. Edward Francis and Eleanor Mary (Mullen) McGee; B.A., Regis Coll., 1963; M.Ed., Boston Coll., 1975, C.A.E.S., 1978; M.P.A., Harvard U., 1985; m. M. Christopher Canavan, Jr., Apr. 18, 1965; children—Elizabeth Ann, Michael Edward. Personnel asst. Avco-Everett Research Lab., Everett, Mass., 1963-65; dir. rehab. Mass. Rehab. Commn., Chestnut Hill, 1977-78; dir. community edn. Norfolk Mental Health Assn., Norwood, Mass., 1978-80; mem. Mass. Ho. of Reps., 1980—, mem. coms. on banking, human services, elderly affairs. Mem. Gov.'s Spl. Commn. on Mental Health Facilities, Gov.'s Spl. Commn. on Violence Against Children, Spl. Commn. on Alcohol and Drug. Edn.; bd. dirs. YMCA; adv. bd. Glover Meml. Hosp., Mount Pleasant Hosp.; mem. Town Meeting, 1976—, chmn. spl. com. on mental health, 1976-77; mem. Needham (Mass.) Planning Bd., 1975-80. Mem. Nat. Fedn. Republican Women, Today's Women, Mass. Caucus Women Legislators, Mass. Legislators Assn., Boston Women, Nat. Conf. State Legislatures, Council State Govts., Women's Network (chmn.). Roman Catholic. Club: Brae Burn Country. Office: Room 22 State House Boston MA 02133

CANDELARIO, MELANIA, counselor; b. Toa Baja, P.R., Jan. 2, 1940; d. Irene Candelario and Victoria Santos Hernandez; m. Jose Antonio Cruz, May 17, 1974; children—Nancy Castillo, Madleine Melendez. B.S. in Psychology, Montclair State Coll., N.J., 1977. Ednl. aide Newark Bd. Edn., 1969-70, sch. clk., 1970-77, community coordinator, 1977-82, career counselor, 1982—. Mem., People United Better Sch., Newark, 1985, Nat. P.R. Congress, Phila., 1986. Named Mother of Yr., Pride Bowl, Newark, 1981. Mem. Nat. Assn. Female Execs., Am. Congress Real Estate, Hispanics in Higher Edn., P.R. Educators Assn. (sec. 1986—, Community Service award 1984), Parent Tchr. Students Assn. (v.p. 1984—). Roman Catholic. Home: 140 Roseville Ave #123 Newark NJ 07107 Office: Seton Hall U 400 S Orange Ave South Orange NJ 07079

CANDLER, ANN CLIFFORD, educator; b. Galveston, Tex., Sept. 23, 1947; d. Patrick Michael and Ellen Marie (Salmon) Clifford; B.S.Ed., Lamar U., 1970; M.Ed., U. Houston, 1976, Ed.D. (Am. Bus. Club Monterey chpt. grantee), 1981; 1 dau., Millicent. Spl. edn. tchr. Texas City (Tex.) Ind. Sch. Dist., 1970-72; research asst. Coll. Edn., U. Houston, 1974-76, assoc. prof. spl. edn. Tex. Tech. U., 1976—, acting asso. chairperson specializations area and chairperson spl. edn., 1980-81. Recipient award for teaching excellence Amoco, 1981; Tex. Tech. U. Coll. Edn. grantee, 1976-77, 78-79; Dept. Edn. Office Edn. for Handicapped grantee, 1979-81; Hogg Found. grantee, 1982-84; Tex. Instruments grantee, 1982-83. Mem. Council Exceptional Children, Assn. Children with Learning Disabilities, Assn. Severely Handicapped. Roman Catholic. Contbr. articles to profl. jours. Office: PO Box 4560 Lubbock TX 79409

CANE, MARILYN BLUMBERG, law educator; b. Rockville Centre, N.Y., Feb. 26, 1949; d. Howard G. and Lily (Goldberg) Blumberg; m. Edward Michael Cane, Dec. 24, 1970; children—Daniel Eric, Jonathan Marc Howard. B.A. magna cum laude, Cornell U., 1971; J.D. cum laude, Boston Coll., 1974. Bar: N.Y. 1975, Conn. 1977, Fla. 1981. Assoc. Reavis & McGrath, N.Y.C., 1975-77, Badger, Fisher, Cohen & Barnett, Greenwich, Conn., 1977-80; counsel corp. components Gen. Electric Co., Fairfield, Conn., 1980-81; assoc. Gunster, Yoakley Criser & Stewart, Palm Beach, Fla., 1981-83; prof. law Nova U. Law Ctr., Fort Lauderdale, Fla., 1983—; dir. Fairfield Health Plan, Stamford, Conn., 1978-80; mem. adv. com. banking dept. State of Conn., Hartford, 1977-80. Contbr. articles to legal jours. Bd. dirs., Jewish Community Day Sch., West Palm Beach, 1983-84, v.p., 1986—; alumnae interviewer Cornell U. secondary schs. com., 1972—. Woodrow Wilson fellow designate, 1971. Mem. ABA, Fla. Bar, Fla. Assn. Women Lawyers, Order of Coif. Home: 398 Knotty Wood Ln Wellington West Palm Beach FL 33414 Office: Nova U Ctr for Study of Law 3100 SW 9th Ave Fort Lauderdale FL 33315

CANFIELD, CAROL KATHRYN, horse breeder; b. Columbus, Ohio, July 29, 1929; d. Karl McKinley and Esther (Eileen (Enright) Koveleski; A.B., U. Chgo., 1951; postgrad. Purdue U., 1953-54; Ohio State U., Newark, 1962-65; m. Sheldon Arthur Canfield, Jan. 29, 1949; children—Karl Herbert, Peter Andreas, Benjamin Arthur. Statis. clk. Purdue Statis. Labs., Lafayette, Ind., 1951-52, draftsman, 1952-53, research asst., 1953-54; tchr. piano, organ Summers & Sons Piano Sales, Newark, Ohio, 1969-70; horsemaster Canfield Farm, Newark, 1971—. Violinist, Licking County Symphony Orch., 1956-59; active League of Women Voters. Mem. Ohio Horsemen's Council (pres. Licking County chpt. 1973—), Blazing Saddles Horse Club (sec. 1977-78, 80, pres. 1981). Clubs: Broken Arrow Riders, Flint Ridge, Sundowners Trail Riders (pres. 1985-86), Cutters (sec.-treas. 1970), Apache Trails Horse (sec. 1973—). Researcher status of horse trails in Ohio; promoter naming of Indian horse Cisco to Am. Indian Horse Registry Hall of Fame, 1984-85. Home: 2041 Hickman Rd NE Newark OH 43055

CANFIELD, HELEN J., utility company executive; b. Elmira, N.Y., Aug. 30, 1942; d. Ernest Harry and Julia Cora (Forker) Bowen; children—Tammy Austin, Timothy Canfield, Todd Canfield. Student Broome Community Coll. Nurses aide Corning Hosp., N.Y., 1960-65; office mgr. L.J. Graham, M.D., Corning, 1966-76; customer acctg. clk. N.Y. State Electric & Gas Corp., Corning, 1976-80, resdl. rep., Monticello, N.Y., 1981-82, staff analyst, Binghamton, 1982-85, customer accounts mgr., Oneonta, N.Y., 1985—, pres. Speakers Club, 1985-86, info. center coordinator, 1984-86. Mem. Nat. Assn. Female Execs. Republican. Clubs: Zonta, Civic of Binghamton. Avocations: flying; golf; swimming; tennis. Home: 45 Union St Sidney NY 13838 Office: New York State Electric and Gas 65 Country Club Rd Oneonta NY 13820

CANFIELD, JUDY OHLBAUM, psychologist; b. N.Y.C., May 15, 1947; d. Arthur and Ada Evelyn (Werner) Ohlbaum; B.A., Grinnell Coll., 1963; M.A., New Sch. Social Research, 1967; Ph.D., U.S. Internat. U., 1970; children—Oran David, Kyle Danya. Psychologist Mendocino State Hosp., Talmage, Calif., 1968-69, Douglas Coll., New Westminster, B.C., Can., 1971-72, Family and Childrens Clinic, Burnaby, B.C., 1971-72; tng. cons. VA Hosp., Northampton, Mass., 1972-75; dir. New Eng. Center, Amherst, Mass., 1972-76, Gateways, Lansdale, Pa., 1977-78; asst. prof. psychology Hahnemann Med. Coll., Phila., 1978—; pvt. practice psychology, Phila. and Bala-Cynwyd, Pa., 1977—; dir., pres. Inst. for Holistic Health, Phila., 1978—. Mem. Internat. Acad. Preventive Medicine, Am. Acad. Psychotherapists, Am. Psychol. Assn., Pa. Psychol. Assn., World Future Soc., Nat. Register of Health Service Providers in Psychology, Assn. Humanistic Psychology. Home and Office: 10 Marinita Ave San Rafael CA 94901

CANFIELD, LYNDA RAE, writer; b. Elmira, N.Y., June 15, 1947; d. Raymond Frank and Doris Rae (Kilbourne) C.; m. William U. Hensel, IV, Sept. 10, 1967 (div. Oct. 1975); children—Jason William, Aaron David. B.A., Albany State U., 1969; M.S., Pa. State U., 1972. Cert. psychologist, Wis. Psychologist, Madison Pub. Schs., 1972-77; realtor Lyons Romo Inc., Tucson, 1978-83; writer Bus. Publs., Tucson, 1983—. Contbr. articles on tourism, sci., bus. to mags. Pres. bd. Avra Water Coop., Avra Valley, Tucson, 1982—; pres. Picture Rocks Fire Aux., 1978-80. Recipient Merit award Met. Tucson C. of C. Rodeo Com., 1985. Democrat. Roman Catholic. Avocations: softball; banjo. Home: 9800 W Rudasill Rd Tucson AZ 85743 Office: Business Publs 3130 E Grant Rd Tucson AZ 85743

CANGUREL, SUSAN STONE, personnel executive; b. Madison, Wis., Sept. 11, 1946; d. John Mather and Lois Marie (Wiessinger) Murray; m. Melih Cangurel; children—Lora Rae, Julie Lynn. Student U. Wis., 1964-66, U. Wis., Milw., 1976-78, U. Tex., El Paso, 1981-84. Adminstrv. asst. Madison C. of C., 1967-72; mgr. processing dept. Kensington Mortgage & Fin. Corp., Milw., 1972-73, gen. mgr. adminstrn., 1973-75, asst. v.p., 1975-76, v.p., 1976-79; asst. v.p., internal auditor Mortgage Investment Co., El Paso, 1979-81, v.p. loan adminstrn., 1981-85; mgr. personnel services Summa Corp., Las Vegas, 1985—. Mem. Am. Soc. Personnel Adminstrs. Nat. Assn. Female Execs., Inst. Internal Auditors, Am. Mgmt. Assn. Author poems and short stories. Home: 2329 Mohigan Way Las Vegas NV 89109 Office: 4045 S Spencer St Las Vegas NV 89119

CANIA, LISA MAZZOLA, college public relations officer; b. Gloversville, N.Y., May 17, 1957; d. Frank D. and Louise Margaret (DiGiacomo) M.; m. Salvatore J. Cania, Jr., Dec. 29, 1978; 1 son, Salvatore J., III. B.A., Wells Coll., 1978; M.Ed., St. Lawrence U., 1982. Asst. mgr. Wells Coll. Store, Aurora, N.Y., 1975-78; adminstrv. asst. Music Theater N., Potsdam, N.Y., 1979; coordinator news services SUNY, Potsdam, 1980-83, dir. pub. info., 1983—. Editor Potsdam Coll. People, 1983—. Treas. Reachout of St. Lawrence County, Potsdam, 1984—. Recipient Disting. Service award Potsdam Coll., 1983. Mem. N.Y. Coll. Relations Council (pres. 1985—), SUNY Council on Univ. Affairs and Devel., Council for the Advancement and Support of Edn., Potsdam C. of C. (v.p. 1983—), Phi Beta Kappa. Roman Catholic. Avocations: ballet; reading; hiking; music; needlework. Home: Box 123 Hannawa Falls NY 13647 Office: SUNY Potsdam Potsdam NY 13676

CANN, SHARON LEE, health science librarian; b. Ft. Riley, Kans., Aug. 14, 1935; d. Roman S. and Cora Elon (George) Foote; m. Donald Clair Cann, May 16, 1964. Student Sophia U., Tokyo, 1955-57; B.A., Sacramento State U., 1959; M.S.L.S., Atlanta U., 1977. Cert. health scis. librarian. Recreation worker ARC, Korea, Morocco, France, 1960-64; shelflister Library Congress Washington, 1967-69; tchr. Lang. Ctr., Taipei, Taiwan, 1971-73; library tech. asst. Emory U., Atlanta, 1974-76; health sci. librarian Northside Hosp., Atlanta, 1977-85; library cons., 1985—; librarian area health edn. ctr., learning resource ctr. Morehouse Sch. Medicine, 1985—. Editor Update, publ. Ga. Health Scis. Library Assn., 1981; contbr. articles to publs. Chmn. Calif. Christian Youth in Govt Seminar, 1958. Named Alumni Top Twenty, Sacramento State U., 1959. Mem. ALA, Med. Library Assn., Spl. Library Assn. (dir. South Atlantic chpt. 1985), Ga. Library Assn. (spl. library div. chmn. 1983-85), Ga. Health Scis. Library Assn. (chmn. 1981-82), Atlanta Health Sci. Library (chmn. 1979), Am. Numis. Assn. Club: Toastmasters (Atlanta) sec.-treas. 1983-84). Home: 5520 Morning Creek Circle College Park GA 30349

CANNAVA, LUCILLE, alcoholism program specialist, consultant; b. Bklyn., Dec. 30, 1929; d. Patrick Michael and Anne Theresa (Conway) Casey; m. Robert Eugene Cannava, Nov. 11, 1950 (div. Dec. 1979); children—Judith, Robert C., Kevin R., Maureen V. A.A., Burlington County Coll., Pemberton, N.J., 1948; A.B., Notre Dame Coll., Balt., 1950. Cert. alcoholism counselor. Med. asst. H.H. Cohan M.D., Cinnaminson, N.J., 1963-70; alcoholism counselor Community Action, Burlington, N.J., 1970-72; supervising counselor U.S. Dept. Army, Ft. Dix., N.J., 1972-74; adminstr. Burlington County Alcohol Program, N.J., 1974-84; program evaluator N.J. Dept. Health Div. Alcoholism, Trenton, 1985—; pres. Comprehensive Alcoholism Recovery Programs, 1980-84; cons. drug info. edn. workshop Glassboro State Coll., N.J., 1974-82. Recipient Outstanding Achievement award U.S. Dept. Army, 1974; named Woman of Yr., Women and Alcohol Assn., 1981. Mem. Assn. Labor and Mgmt. Alcoholism Cons., So. N.J. Health Systems Agy. (bd. dirs. 1986), Task Force Women and Alcohol, Nat. Assn. Alcoholism Counselors (pres. 1986), Alpha Zeta. Avocations: horticulture; reading; aerobics. Home: 33 Myrtlewood Ln Willingboro NJ 08046 Office: NJ Div Alcoholism 129 E Hanover St Trenton NJ 08625

CANNON, CAROL SUE, state government agricultural laboratories director; b. Oklahoma City, July 23, 1942; d. Owen Henry and Violet L. (Hay) King; m. James A. Cannon, Apr. 14, 1961; children—James Alan, Randall O., Michael C. B.S. in Biology, Central State U., Okla., 1973. Typist clk. Okla. Dept. Agr., Oklahoma City, 1975-77, microbiologist, 1977-81, sr. microbiologist, 1981-83, dir. agr. labs., 1983—. Mem. Assn. Ofcl. Analytical Chemists. Democrat. Mem. Christian Ch. (Disciples of Christ). Avocations: snow skiing; water skiing; traveling. Office: Okla Dept Agr 2800 N Lincoln Blvd Oklahoma City OK 73105

CANNON, CORINNE BLANKS, lawyer; b. Columbia, S.C., July 7, 1947; d. Victor Gaston and Margaret Eloise (Weir) Blanks; m. John Douglas Cannon, May 5, 1973. B.A., Erskine Coll., 1969; J.D., U. S.C., 1972. Bar: S.C. 1972, U.S. Dist. Ct. S.C. 1973, U.S. Ct. Appeals (4th cir.) 1974. Atty., Kohn & Finkel, Columbia, 1972-77; ptnr. Cannon & Cannon, Clemson, S.C., 1977—. Treas., Clemson Area Youth Council, 1980—; pres. Old Ninety-Six Council Scouts U.S.A., Greenville, S.C., 1984—, Pickens Found. Econ. Devel., 1983—; exec. com. Oconee Country Democratic party, Walhalla, S.C., 1980—. Mem. Clemson C. of C. (pres. 1983), S.C. Bar Assn., S.C. Trial Lawyers Assn., ABA, Pickens and Oconee County Bar Assn., Phi Alpha Delta, Clubs: Assn. Profl. Women (v.p. 1980-81), AAUW (treas. 1980—). Democrat. Presbyterian. Office: PO Box 629 Clemson SC 29633

CANNON, PATRICIA A., social worker; b. N.Y.C., Jan. 12, 1940; d. Donald F. and Dorothy (Donovan) C. B.A., Marywood Coll., 1961; M.S.W., Fordham U., 1963. Social worker Cardinal McClockey Home, White Plains, N.Y., 1963-66, Bridgeport Bd. Edn. (Conn.), 1966-68, Cath. Charities, Bridgeport, 1968-72, Hall Neighborhood House, 1972-76; asst. dir. social work Bridgeport Hosp. (Conn.), 1976—. Fellow Orthopsychiat. Assn.; mem. Nat. Assn. Social Workers. Democrat. Roman Catholic. Home: 242 Sunwood Dr Huntington CT 06484 Office: Bridgeport Hosp 267 Grant St Bridgeport CT 06610

CANNONE, ROSALIE A(NTOINETTE), lawyer; b. Elizabeth, N.J., June 28, 1943; d. Nicola and Anna (LaMonica) C. B.A., Rutgers U., 1965; J.D., Seton Hall U., 1977. Bar: N.J. 1977, U.S. Dist. Ct. N.J. 1977, U.S. Supreme Ct. 1983. Employment interviewer N.J. State Dept. Labor and Industry, Elizabeth, 1965-66; tchr. St. Genevieve Sch., Elizabeth, 1966-68; tchr., supr., reading specialist Elizabeth Bd. Edn., 1968-77; atty. Office Gen. Counsel, Prentice-Hall, Inc., Englewood Cliffs, N.J., 1977-81; asst. gen. counsel Alfa-Laval, Inc., Ft. Lee, N.J., 1981-82, asst. gen. counsel, 1982—; sec. bd. dirs. Imo, Inc., Ft. Lee, 1984—, Stal Refrigeration, Ben Saleem, Pa., 1982-83; sec. bd. dirs. Celleco, Inc., Atlanta, 1982—; asst. sec. Alfa-Laval, Inc., Ft. Lee and subs., 1981—. Legal counsel Regular Democratic Orgn., Elizabeth, 1978—; mem. Rent Leveling and Control Bd. Elizabeth, 1977-79; mem. Putnam Manor Civic Assn., Union, N.J., 1979—, Union Dem. Club., 1979—. Mem. ABA, N.J. Bar Assn., Union County Bar Assn., Am. Arbitration Assn. (arbitrator). Office: Alfa-Laval Inc 2115 Linwood Ave Fort Lee NJ 07024

CANNON-HARRIS, SONDRA ENTRINA, personnel trainer; b. Abington, Pa., Aug. 31, 1950; d. Winfield Earl and Dorothy Louise (Luby) Cannon. B.S., Del. State Coll., 1972; postgrad. U. Del., 1973-75; M.A., Central Mich. U., 1980. Instr., New Castle County Schs., Wilmington, Del., 1975-78; tchr. Delcastle Tech. High Sch., Newport, Del., 1977-78; research asst. Prince George's Community Coll., Largo, Md., 1979; center rep. Central Mich. U., Mt. Pleasant, 1979-83; dir., course developer Charles County Community Coll., LaPlata, Md., 1983—, mem. affirmative action com., 1983-86. Co-chmn. So. Md. Childhood Conf., LaPlata, 1985; mem. Gov.'s Commn. on Status of Women, 1977-78. State of Del. fellow, 1972; recipient Found. award Bus. and Profl. Women Waldorf, Md., 1984. Mem. Nat. Assn. Female Execs., Nat. Soc. Internships and Experiential Edn., Phi Delta Kappa, Sigma Iota Epsilon, Alpha Kappa Mu. Democrat. Methodist. Avocations: designing and sewing; golf; writing; music. Home: 1210 Palmer Rd Apt 9 Fort Washington MD 20744 Office: Charles County Community Coll Box 910 Mitchell Rd LaPlata MD 20646

CANNY, PAULA KAY, lawyer; b. Washington, Mar. 8, 1955; d. Robert William and Catherine (Carlson) C. B.A. in Econs., Kirkland Coll., 1977; J.D., U. San Francisco, 1980. Bar: Calif. 1980, U.S. Ct. Appeals (9th cir.) 1980. Assoc., Wald, Brown & Knoll, Oakland, Calif., 1980-82; dep. dist. atty. Ventura County (Calif.), 1982-83, San Mateo (Calif.), 1983-84; ptnr. Ketchum and Canny, San Mateo, 1984—. Active NOW, Women's Sports Found. Mem. Assn. Trial Lawyers Am., U.S. Powerlifting Assn. Democrat. Office: 1450 Chapin Ave Burlingame CA 94010

CANTOR, ANNA RAE, artist, art educator; b. West New York, N.J., Dec. 9, 1914; d. Jacob Morris and Pauline (Horowitz) C. Student Art Students League; B.A., Hunter Coll., 1937; M.F.A., Rutgers U., 1966. Cert. tchr. N.J. Art tchr. Long Branch Bd. Edn., N.J., 1948-75. One woman shows include Little Gallery, New Brunswick, N.J., 1966, 79, The Garrett Red Bank, N.J., 1972, Caldwell Coll., N.J., 1979; exhibited in group shows at Guild Creative Arts, Shrewsbury, N.J., Nat. Gallery, N.Y.C., Lever House, N.Y.C., Summit Art Ctr., Summit, N.J., Hunterdon Art Ctr., Clinton, N.J., Montclair State Coll., N.J., Silvermine Guild Artists, New Canaan, Conn., Montclair Art Mus., N.J., Morris Mus. Arts and Scis., Morristown, N.J., Monmouth Mus., Lincroft, N.J., New Jersey State Mus., Trenton; represented in permanent collections Rutgers U., Hunterdon Art Ctr., N.J. State Mus., Monmouth Coll., Pfizer Corp., J&J Distbg. Corp., Jane Voorhees Zimmerli Art Mus. of Rutgers U. Mem. Bradley Beach Bd. Edn., N.J., 1981—. Mem. Nat. Assn. Women Artists, Artists Equity Assn. of N.J., Printmaking Council N.J.

CANTOR, ELEANOR WESCHLER, medical association executive; b. N.Y.C., Dec. 30, 1913; d. Samuel Peter and Anna (Rauchwerger) W.; m. Alfred Joseph Cantor, June 9, 1938; children—Pamela Corliss, Alfred Jay. B.A., Hunter Coll., N.Y.C., 1938. Producer radio quiz show CBS, N.Y.C., 1936-41; exec. officer Internat. Acad. Proctology, N.Y.C., 1948—, Internat. Bd. Proctology, 1950—; co-founder Acad. Psychosomatic Medicine, 1954.

CANTOR, JANE BRUSKIN, lawyer; b. Newark, Apr. 8, 1949; d. Harold Meyer and Bernice (Kaden) B.; m. Philip Seth Cantor, June 29, 1969; children—David, Mollie, Jennifer, Daniel. B.A., Douglass Coll., 1974; J.D., Rutgers U., 1980. Bar: N.J. 1980, N.Y. 1981. Law clk. Superior ct. N.J., New Brunswick, 1980-81; assoc. Heilbrunn, Finkelstein, et als., Old Bridge, N.J., 1981-82; ptnr. Garruto, Galex & Cantor, East Brunswick, N.J., 1982—. Mem. Condemnation Commn. Middlesex County, 1982—; mem. regional com. civil case mgmt. procedures N.J. State Cts., 1983-84. Officer, North Brunswick Hadassah, 1980; trustee Jewish Social Services Commn., 1982—; bd. dirs. Jewish Family Service Commn., East Brunswick, 1983. Mem. Women Lawyers Com. (pres. 1981-83), Middlesex County Trial Lawyers Assn. (treas. 1982-84, 2d v.p. 1985-86), Middlesex County Bar Assn., Am. Trial Lawyers Assn., ABA. Republican. Jewish. Office: Garruto Galex & Cantor 14 Old Bridge Turnpike East Brunswick NJ 08816

CANTOR, MURIEL G., sociologist, educator; b. Mpls., Mar. 2, 1923; d. Leo and Bess Goldsman; B.A., UCLA, 1964, M.A., 1966, Ph.D., 1969; m. Joel M. Cantor, Aug. 6, 1944; children—Murray Robert, Jane Cantor Shefler, James Leo. Lectr. dept. econs. and sociology Immaculate Heart Coll., Los Angeles, 1966-68; faculty Am. U., Washington, 1968—, instr., 1968-69, asst. prof. sociology, 1969-72, asso. prof., 1972-76, dept. chmn., 1973-75, 77-79, prof., 1976—; vis. prof. communications studies program UCLA, 1982; cons. Corp. Pub. Broadcasting, 1980; cons. agencies including NIMH. Bd. dirs. Population Inst., 1978-80; trustee WETA, 1972-76, NIMH grantee, 1979-81. Mem. Am. Sociol. Assn., D.C. Sociol. Soc. (pres. 1977-78), Sociologists for Women in Society, Eastern Sociol. Soc., So. Sociol. Soc. Author: The Hollywood TV Producer: His Work and His Audience, 1971; Prime Time Television: Content and Control, 1980; (with Phyllis L. Stewart) Varieties of Work Experience, 1974; Varieties of Work; 1982; (with Suzanne Pingree) The Soap Opera, 1983; (with Sandra Ball-Rokeach) Media, Audience, and Social Structure, 1986; mem. internat. panel advisors Internat. Ency. Communications. Home: 8408 Whitman Dr Bethesda MD 20817 Office: Dept Sociology American U Washington DC 20016

CANTOR, PAMELA CORLISS, clinical psychologist; b. N.Y.C., Apr. 23, 1944; d. Alfred Joseph and Eleanor (Weschler) Cantor; B.S. cum laude, Syracuse U., 1965; postgrad. (NIMH fellow), Johns Hopkins U. Med. Sch., 1969-70; Ph.D., Columbia U., 1972; postgrad. (clin. psychology fellow), Harvard U.-Children's Hosp. Med. Center, 1973-74; m. Howard Feldman, Sept. 11, 1969; children—Lauren Jaye, Jeffrey Lee. Instr., Radcliffe Inst., Harvard U., 1977-78; assoc. prof. Boston U., 1970-80; pvt. practice clin. psychology, Chestnut Hill, Mass., 1972—; assoc. dir. ctr. Study of Suicide Cambridge City Hosp. of Harvard U.; lectr. in field, TV and radio appearances. Mass. Gov.'s appointee Office for Children Statewide Adv. Bd., 1980—; adv. bd. Samaritans of Boston; co-chmn. Nat. Com. Prevention of Youth Suicide. Mem. Am. Psychol. Assn., Am. Assn. Suicidology (pres. 1985-86), Am. Orthopsychiat. Assn., Mass. Psychol. Assn., Am. Assn. Suicidology (dir.). Author: Understanding A Child's World—Readings in Infancy through Adolescence, 1977; cons. editor Suicide and Life-Threatening Behavior. Contbr. chpts to handbooks, numerous articles in field to profl. jours. Address: 80 Monadnock Rd Chestnut Hill MA 02167

CANTRELL, ANDREA, library administrator; b. Springfield, Mo., Jan. 1, 1948; d. A.J. Cantrell and Wilma (Snowden) Cave; m. James D. Hawkins, June 22, 1968 (div. 1977); m. Robert L. Clark, Jr., May 23, 1981 (div. 1985). B.A., Am. U., 1970; M.L.S., U. Md., College Park, 1971. Young adult services librarian Thomas Jefferson Regional Library, Jefferson City, Mo., 1971-72; reference librarian Springfield-Greene County Library (Mo.), 1972-74; coordinator Library resources Mo. State Library, Jefferson City, 1974-78; chief cons. service Wash. State Library, Olympia, 1978-79; dir. Joplin Pub. Library (Mo.), 1979-81; dir. library resources div. Okla. Hist. Soc., Oklahoma City, 1981-85; spl. collections librarian U. Ark., Fayetteville, 1985—. Contbr. articles to profl. jours. Mem. ALA (chmn. staff devel. com. 1977-78; genealogy com. 1983—), Assn. Specialized and Coop. Library Agys. (chmn. 1978-79), Mo. State Library Assn. (mem. various coms.), Zeta Tau Alpha. Lodge: Soroptimist Internat. Office: Spl Collections Dept U Ark Libraries Fayetteville AR 72701

CANTRELL, CLAIRE MARIE, nursing educator, therapeutic touch practitioner; b. Mt. Holly, N.J., Nov. 8, 1948; d. John Mowatt and Verna May (Rossell) C. R.N., Helene Fuld Sch. Nursing, Camden, N.J., 1969; B.S., S.W. Tex. State U., 1978, M.S., 1980. Pvt. duty nursing supr., San Antonio, 1973-80; nursing instr. Cancer Therapy and Research Ctr., San Antonio, 1978-80; research med. oncology, chemotherapy nurse U. Tex. Health Sci. Ctr., San Antonio, 1978-80, ednl. cons., 1980; staff nurse Nursefinders, San Antonio, 1981; instr. nursing Ancora Psychiat. Hosp., Hammonton, N.J., 1981-84; staff devel. coordinator St. Mary Hosp., Phila., 1984—; ednl., nursing cons. ednl./health sci., San Antonio, 1979-80. Asst. leader Girl Scouts U.S.A., Vineland, N.J., 1982-83. Served to 1st lt. AUS, 1970-71. Felix Fuld Found. scholar, 1966-69. Mem. Am. Nurses Assn., DAV, Oncology Nursing Soc., S.W. Tex. State U. Alumni Assn. Republican. Roman Catholic. Home: 922B Sutton Towers White Horse Pike and Collings Ave Collingswood NJ 08107 Office: St Mary Hosp Frankford and Palmer Sts Philadelphia PA

CANTRELL, COLEEN SHARON, nursing administrator; b. Williamsport, Pa., Feb. 8, 1952; d. William Francis and Natalie Elizabeth (Musser) Caldwell; 1 child; Christopher William Cantrell. B.S.N., Indiana U. of Pa., 1974. Commd. 1st lt. U.S. Army Nurse Corps, 1974, advanced through grades to capt., 1980; orthopedic staff nurse U.S. Army Nurse Corps, Fort Polk, La., Seoul, Korea, 1974-77, head nurse urology, Fort Bragg, N.C., 1977-78, evening, night supr., Fort Bragg, 1978-79, infection control nurse, 1979-80; head nurse urology St. John's Regional Med. Ctr., Joplin, Mo., 1981-84, staff nurse, 1980-81, dir. med. nursing service, 1984—. Asst. leader Explorer Scouts MoKan council Boy Scouts Am., 1984-85. Recipient U.S.A. Commendation award, 1977, 80, Cert. of award St. John's Regional Med. Ctr., 1983. Mem. Am. Nurses Assn., Internat. Urological Scis., Inc., Mo. Assn. Nursing Service Adminstrs., Res. Officer Assn. Lutheran. Avocations: playing piano, camping, reading. Office: St John's Regional Med Ctr 2727 McClelland Blvd Joplin MO 64801

CANTU, DARLENE MARIE, nursing educator; b. Butler, Pa., Apr. 3, 1951; d. George Richard and Mary Frances (Tomsey) Nebel; m. Charles Cantu, Jr., Sept. 3, 1977; 1 child, Francesca Michelle. B.S.N. magna cum laude, U. Pitts., 1974; M.S.N. summa cum laude, U. Tex. Sch. Biomed. Scis., San Antonio, 1979. Cert. neonatal intensive care nurse. Staff nurse Presbyn. Univ. Hosp., Pitts., 1974; staff, charge nurse, neonatal intensive care unit Brooke Army Med. Ctr., San Antonio, 1975-78; nursery coordinator Southwest Tex. Meth. Hosp., San Antonio, 1978-79; instr. Bapt. Meml. Hosp. Systems Sch. Nursing, San Antonio, 1979—, nurse instr. diploma nursing program, 1979—; clin. cons. maternal-newborn nursing, staff devel. dept. Bapt. Med. Ctr., San Antonio, 1980—. Vol. Children's Hosp., Pitts., 1973-74; instr. math. YMCA Pitts., 1972-73. Served to capt. Army Nurse Corps, 1974-78. Mem. Nurses Assn. of Am. Coll. Ob-Gyn, Nat. Assn. Neonatal Nurses, Explorer's Nursing Post, Sigma Theta Tau. Roman Catholic. Manuscript reviewer Brady Pub. Co., 1983—. Office: 111 Dallas St San Antonio TX 78286

CANTY, CARRIE REBECCA, clergywoman, educator; b. Sumter, S.C., Aug. 2, 1927; d. Frank Clifford and Marie (Willis) C. B.S., Morris Brown Coll., Atlanta, 1950; M.Ed., Temple U., 1970; Th.M. summa cum laude, Trinity Theol. Sem., Newburgh, Ind., 1982; Th.D. summa cum laude, Trinity U., Newburgh, 1983, Ph.D. summa cum laude, 1984. Ordained to ministry Fire Baptized Holiness Ch. of God of the Ams., 1965; cert. tchr., Pa., N.J.; cert. counselor, Pa., Ind. Tchr. Fuller Normal Indsl. Inst., Greenville, S.C., 1950-51, S.E. Delco Sch. Dist., Folcroft, Pa., 1955-74; instr. Youth Leadership, Greenville, 1971—; pastor Mt. Pleasant Ch., Phila., 1973-78, Mt. Finai Fire Baptized Holiness Ch., Mount Vernon, N.Y., 1979-82, Gethsemane Fire Baptized Holiness Ch., Phila., 1982—; instr. religious edn. dept. Pa. Dist., Phila., 1986—. Chairperson Be Ye Kind to One Another, Phila., 1974-78. Recipient Ambassador of Yr. award Young People Inst., 1972; Preservance award Religious Edn. Dept. of Pa. Dist., 1975; Bishop F.C. Canty award Religious Edn. Dept. of Pa. Dist., 1978; Leadership award Young People Inst., Pa. Dist., 1984. Mem. Ministerial Alliance (Pastor of Yr. 1983), Young People Inst. (coordinator 3 dists. fellowship 1982—), Nat. Assn. Female Execs. Democrat. Avocations: reading; basketball. Home: 5832 Webster St Philadelphia PA 19143 Office: Gethsemane Fire Baptized Holiness Ch 2629 W York St Philadelphia PA 19132

CANTY, GEORGIANNA TIPTON, electronics executive; b. Dallas, July 28, 1939; d. George B. and Georgia Lucile (Pringle) Torrance; m. Roy Allen Canty, Mar. 12, 1960 (div. 1977); children—Mitchell, Russell Blyth. Student So. Meth. U., 1959, San Jose City Coll., 1975, San Jose State U., 1978, Foothill Coll., 1965, 66. Vice-pres., Filipinas Micro-Circuits Internat., Santa Clara, Calif., 1983-84; mng. ptnr. Applied Software Products, Santa Clara, 1984—; propr., artist, restorer, appraiser Blue Pelican Gallery, San Jose, Calif., 1970-74; adminstrn. mgr. Toshiba Semiconductor, Santa Clara, 1975-80; v.p. co-founder, dir. Promptel, Inc., Santa Clara, 1980-83. Artist, illustrator: Pets and Poems, 1972. Bd. dirs. Youth Sci. Inst., San Jose, Calif., 1963; vol. VA, Palo Alto, Calif., 1964, Nat. Council Alcoholism, San Jose, 1983; mem. Republican Nat. Com., 1982. Mem. Am. Soc. Appraisers, Assn. Legal Adminstrs., ABA (assoc.), Profl. and Businesswomen's Assn. Home: PO Box 2844 Mission Sta Santa Clara CA 95055

CANTY, MARY LOUISE, pub. co. exec.; b. Somerville, Mass., Mar. 14, 1934; d. Cornelius Francis and Mary Ann (McCarthy) C.; With New Eng. Telephone Co., Boston, 1951-62; office mgr., purchasing agt. Cambridge Plating Co. (Mass.), 1962-65; with Shelby Pub. Corp., Wellesley, Mass., 1965—, now v.p., asst. treas., circulation mgr. John Liner Letter, also dir. Mem. Nat. Assn. Female Execs., Mass. Assn. Ins. Women, Nat. Assn. Ins. Women. Roman Catholic. Club: Irish Am. Office: 555 Washington St Wellesley MA 02181

CANZONETTA, CATHERINE MARIE, educational administrator; b. Wyandotte, Mich., May 14, 1954; d. Stanley Edward and Dolores Mary Ann (MacEachin) Krogol; m. Christopher Marino Canzonetta, June 21, 1975. B.B.A., Eastern Mich. U., 1979, M.Ed., 1986. Adminstrv. asst. Harper-Grace Hosps., Detroit, 1977-82; mgr. billing office Univ. Internists, Detroit, 1982; adminstrv. asst. Rose Med. Ctr., Denver, 1982-83; acting alumni dir. Eastern Mich. U., 1984, asst. alumni dir., 1983—, chair mem. and publicity Women's Assn., 1985—. Editor: (newsletter) Eastern Mich. U. Women's Assn., 1985-86; lectr. profl. confs. Mem. Council Advancement and Support of Edn., Mich. Advancement Council, Phi Delta Kappa. Democrat. Roman Catholic. Avocations: Travel; photography; needlework; hiking. Office: Eastern Mich U 202 McKenny Hall Ypsilanti MI 48124

CAPECELATRO, ANN JOSEPHINE (MRS. JOSEPH V. LEVENDUSKI), optometrist; b. West Haven, Conn., Jan. 11, 1925; d. Gennaro and Frances Mary (Cuzzocreo) Capecelatro; O.D., Pa. Coll. Optometry, 1946; m. Joseph V. Levenduski, June 12, 1954; children—David Joseph, Kathryn Frances. Practice optometry, New Haven, 1947—; mem. Conn. Bd. Examiners in Optometry. Trustee Cheshire Acad.; exec. com. bd. govs. U. New Haven. Mem. Conn., New Haven County optometric socs., New Eng. Council Optometrists, AAUW. Clubs: Women's Rep. of Orange, Grad. Home: 451 Prudden Ln Orange CT 06477 Office: 114 Sherman Ave New Haven CT 06511

CAPEHART, LYNNE CAROL, lawyer, educator; b. Ann Arbor, Mich., Dec. 3, 1941; d. Richard Gildart and Frances Miriam (Holmes) Fowler; m. Barney Lee Capehart, Sept. 2, 1961; children—Thomas David, Jeffrey Donald, Cynthia Diane. B.S. in Math., U. Okla., 1962; J.D., U. Fla., 1977. Bar: Fla., 1977. Computer analyst Air Force Cambridge Research Lab., Bedford, Mass., 1963-64; research assoc. U. Fla., Gainesville, 1978-81, instr. Law Sch., 1981-82, asst. dir. legal writing Law Sch., 1982—; Pro bono atty. Sierra Club, Gainesville, 1978—. Author: (with B.L. Capehart and J.F. Alexander) Florida's Electric Future, 1982; contbr. articles to various publs. Mem. governing bd. St. Johns River Water Mgmt. Dist., Palatka, Fla., 1979—, sec., 1981—; chmn. Oklawaha Basin Bd., 1985—; mem. Orange County Planning and Zoning Bd., Orange County, Fla., 1972; mem. bd. suprs. Alachua County Soil and Water Conservation Dist., Gainesville, 1979-80; mem. Gainesville Energy Conservation Adv. Commn., 1978-81, chmn., 1980-81. Recipient Fla. medal Fla. Sierra Club, 1982. Mem. ABA, Fla. Bar, Sierra Club (Fla. v.p. 1979-81), Phi Beta Kappa. Democrat.

CAPEN, JUDITH MEDORA, architect, educator; b. Cedar Rapids, Iowa, Oct. 3, 1949; d. Vernon Lewis and Maleta DeEtte (Marsteller) C.; m. Robert Alan Weinstein, Aug. 17, 1981; 1 child, Kirby Sarah Capen-Weinstein. B.Arch. cum laude, U. Cin., 1973; M.A. in Environ. Design, Yale U., 1978. Registered architect, Va., D.C., Md.; cert. Nat. Council Archtl. Registration Bds. Teaching asst. U. Cin., 1967, Yale U., 1977; assoc. Gunner Birkerts and Assocs., Birmingham, Mich., Dan Eytan Architecture and Planning, Tel Aviv, Model Cities Phys. Planning Program, Cin., AIA Research Corp., Washington, Imre and Anthony Halasz, Inc., Boston, 1967-76; co-founder, prin., corp. sec. architrave p.c. architects, Washington, 1976—; vis. asst. prof. U. Kans., Lawrence, 1979; vis. critic dept. architecture and planning Cath. U. Am., Washington, 1978-81, asst. prof., 1981—; cons., presenter at profl. seminars. Prin. works include Guaranty Bank & Trust Bldg., Merrifield, Va., N. Mex. House (featured in New Shelter Mag.), van Massenhove Addition (featured in Fine Homebldg. jour.), Pagio Coach House Restoration, Washington. Investigator, author Teaching Energy in Design proposal (2d place Assn. Collegiate Schs. Architecture competition 1983), 1982. Nat. Merit scholar, 1967-71; Yale U. scholar, 1976-77. Mem. AIA (Scholastic award 1977, Tchrs. Seminar scholar 1978, summer intern AIA Research Corp. 1977), Assn. Collegiate Schs. Architecture (bd. dirs. 1976-78, author article ann. meeting procs. 1980), Capitol Hill Restoration Soc. (landmarks com. 1980—), Nat. Trust Historic Preservation, Classical Am. Democrat. Office: architrave p c architects 918 F St NW Suite 200 Washington DC 20004

CAPLAN, DIANA LYNN, mortgage company executive; b. International Falls, Minn., July 19, 1948; d. Harold William and Marian Elizabeth (Carroll)

Carmody; m. Harvey Stephen Caplan, Sept. 3, 1966 (div. Nov. 1983); children—Staci, Stephanie. Student in polit. sci. Chico State U., 1966-67; real estate certs. U. Calif.-Santa Barbara; diploma in real estate counseling Chatham Ednl. Corp., Glendale, Calif., 1980. Broker-sales agt. Channel Island Realty, Santa Barbara, Calif., 1970-73; owner, broker Town 'n Country Realty, Santa Barbara, 1973-78, Pueblo Realty, Santa Barbara, 1978-80; pres. Sunset Mortgage Corp., Santa Barbara, 1980—. Recipient Gold award United Way Santa Barbara, 1980, Gold card Nat. Inst. Exchange Counselors, Calif., 1980. Mem. Santa Barbara Bd. Realtors (chmn. govt. relations 1980, chmn. multiple listing 1981, pres. 1982, Spl. Service award 1980, MLS award 1981, Presdl. award 1982), Women's Council Realtors (sec. Calif. 1982, legis. chmn. Calif. 1983), Calif. Assn. Realtors (dist. chmn. fin. and polit. affairs 1980-83), Nat. Assn. Realtors (fin. del. 1983, 84), Santa Barbara C. of C. (hon. bd. dirs. 1982), Futures Found., Calif. Scholarship Found. (life). Republican. Roman Catholic. Office: Sunset Mortgage Corp 109 S La Cumbre Ln Santa Barbara CA 93105

CAPLES, LOUISE SKINNER LEIGH, civic worker; b. Hertford, N.C., Nov. 5, 1915; d. Edward Augustus II and Mary Motley (Coke) Leigh; m. Delphin Delmas Caples, July 6, 1944; children—Pete L., Patricia Caples Greenwell, Richard J., Robert M. R.N. diploma, Franklin Sq. Hosp. Sch. Nursing, 1938; postgrad. in obstetrics Margaret Hague Maternity Hosp., 1939. Bd. dirs., 1st v.p. Franklin Sq. Hosp. Aux., 1947-49; leadership chmn. Md. Council of Hosp. Auxs., 1949-50, active recruitment nurses, 1950-60; mem. com. on careers Nat. League for Nursing, 1950-54; pres. Baltimore County Med. Aux., 1950-58, Med. and Chirurg. Faculty Md., 1959-60; organizing mem., 1st v.- Carroll County Hosp. Aux., 1961-62; state registrar Nat. Soc. DAR, Md., 1976-79; organizing state pres. Colonial Dames of XVII Century, Md., 1974-75; state rec. sec. Nat. Huguenot Soc., Md., 1980-82; nat. pres. Nat. Soc. Daus. Am. Colonists, 1985-88; vestryman All Saints Episcopal Ch., 1965-69. Served to 1st lt. Nurse Corps, U.S. Army, 1942-45; Middle East, ETO. Mem. Magna Charta Dames (life), Colonial Dames Am., Nat. Assn. Parliamentarians, Federated Women's Club Glyndon, Reisterstown C. of C., Owings Mills C. of C., Glyndon C. of C. Republican. Home: 1204 Nicodemus Rd Reisterstown MD 21136 Office: Nat Soc Daus Am Colonists 2205 Massachusetts Ave NW Washington DC 20008

CAPLIN, JO ANN, communications company executive; b. Indpls.; d. Irvin and Mildred Shirley (Brodsky) C. B.A., U. Mich.; M.A., Yale U., NYU. TV producer ABC News, N.Y.C., 1972-79, CBS News, N.Y.C. and Washington, 1979-85; pres. Caplin Communications, Inc., N.Y.C., 1986—; instr. New Sch. for Social Research, N.Y.C., 1980-81. Producer numerous TV shows, including: (documentary) Incest: The Best Kept Secret, 1979 (Emmy award 1980); (series) 30 Minutes, 1978-82 (Emmy award 1982), 20/20, CBS Mag., HBO Consumer Reports Spl. Bd. dirs. Nat. Found. for Advancement in the Arts, 1985—. Mem. Nat. Acad. TV Arts and Scis., Nat. Assn. Female Execs.

CAPOCCIA, ROSALIE LOUISE, retail store owner; b. Utica, N.Y., June 5, 1941; d. Julian Frank and Estelle (Sutkowski) Mikus; m. Andrew F. Capoccia, Aug. 18, 1968. B.A., Russell Sage Coll., 1979. Head sec. dept. radiology Meml. Hosp., Utica, N.Y., 1959-68; sec. dept. radiology Akron Gen. Hosp., Ohio, 1968, dept. polymer sci. U. Akron, 1968-70; adminstrv. asst. dept. radiology Meml. Hosp., Albany, N.Y., 1970-79; owner, operator Balloon Age, Latham, N.Y., 1980—; pres. Balloons Galore, Inc.; research asst. Nat. Inst. Dental Health, Akron, 1970-72. Bd. dirs., past pres. Meml. Hosp. Aux., Albany; founding mem., bd. dirs. Capital Women's Charity Found., Albany, 1981-85, pres., 1985—; bd. dirs. N.E. N.Y. March of Dimes, 1985—. Mem. AAUW, Albany C. of C., N.Y. State Women Bus. Owners, N.Y. State Corp. Vol. Council. Avocations: painting; interior decorating. Home: 56 Bentwood Ct Albany NY 12203 Office: 640 Loudon Rd Latham NY 12110

CAPODILUPO, ELIZABETH JEANNE HATTON, public relations director; b. McRae, Ga., May 3, 1940; d. Lewis Irby and Essee Elizabeth (Parker) Hatton; grad. Dale Carnegie Inst., 1976; m. Raphael S. Capodilupo, Jan. 21, 1967. Sec., A.R. Clark Acct., 1959; receptionist, girl Friday, Channel 13, Sta. WNDT-TV, N.Y.C., 1960-62, Coy Hunt and Co., N.Y.C., 1962-69; clk. Woodlawn Cemetery, Bronx, N.Y., 1969-71, historian, community affairs coordinator, 1971—, editor Woodlawn Cemetery News newsletter, 1979—, asst. to pres., 1986—, also dir. pub. relations; grad. asst. Dale Carnegie Inst., 1977-78. Chairwoman, Ann. Adm. Farragut Honor Ceremony, Bronx, 1976—; chmn. Nelly Bly Honor Ceremony, 1978, Toys for Needy Children, 1983-85; bd. dirs. Bronx Mus. Arts, 1981—, v.p. 1983-85; bd. dirs. Bronx Council on Arts, Bronx YMCA, Concerned Bronx Businessmen; mem. Bronx adv. bd. Salvation Army Recipient awards, including award citation VFW, 1976, Voice of Democracy Program judge's citation, 1980; cert. of appreciation Dale Carnegie Inst., 1977; Outstanding Citizenship award Bronx N.E. Kiwanis Club, 1981; YMCA Service to Youth award, 1983; citation Concerned Bronx Businessmen; proclamation for outstanding community service City of N.Y.; Woman of Yr. award Bronx YMCA, 1986. Mem. Women in Communication, Bronx County Hist. Soc., Network Orgn. Bronx Women, Bronx C. of C. (co-chmn. Indsl. Directory 1981). Methodist. Clubs: N.Y. Press, Women's City, Order Eastern Star. Researcher Woodlawn Cemetery's Hall of Fame. Office: The Woodlawn Cemetery PO Box 12 Bronx NY 10470

CAPONE, ANNETTE, editor. B.A., Pa. State U., 1966. Articles editor Seventeen mag., 1971-76; assoc. articles editor Ladies' Home Jour., 1979 81; assoc. editor Mademoiselle, 1981-83; editor-in-chief Redbook mag., 1983—. Mem. Women in Communications. Office: Redbook Mag Hearst Mags 224 W 57th St New York NY 10019*

CAPONE, MARGARET LYNCH, civic worker, parliamentarian; b. Wilkinsburg, Pa., May 21, 1907; d. John Edward and Anna Freda (Dunstrup) Lynch; m. Carmen R. Capone, July 21, 1936 (dec. May 1983); children—David Michael, Mary Ann Capone Sperling, Donald William. Student U. Pitts., 1925-33, 1949-53, Carnegie Inst. Tech., 1955-56. Parliamentarian Pa. Nurses Assn., 1960-68, Allegheny County Law Wives, Pa., 1975—; treas. Allegheny County LWV, 1965-69, v.p., 1969-73, pres., 1973-79, parliamentarian, 1979—, historian, 1980; parliamentarian St. Lucy Guild to Blind, Pitts., Allegheny County Lawyers Aux., Diocese Council Cath. Women, Marian Manor Guild; cons. parliamentarian. Author: So You've Joined A Club, 1954; Parliamentary Pointers, 1972. Editor Clea News, 1954-72. Named Woman of Yr., Clea News, 1973; Personality of Yr., Pitts. chpt. K.C., 1979. Mem. Nat. Assn. Parliamentarians (profl. registered parliamentarian, local pres. 1959-61, state pres. 1963-64, nat. v.p. 1977-79, chairperson rev. 1981—), Am. Inst. Parliamentarians (cert. profl. parliamentarian), Duquesne U. Women's Guild. Republican. Roman Catholic. Lodges: K.C. Women's Guild, Toastmistresses (pres. local club 1950-51, nat. bd. dirs. 1953-63, nat. sec. 1954-56, nat. v.p. 1956-57, editor Toastmistress Mag. 1958-62). Home: 6625 Woodwell St Pittsburgh PA 15217

CAPOOR, ASHA, wholesale book company executive; b. Ajmer, India, July 24, 1941 came to U.S., 1968, naturalized, 1982; d. Kailash C. and Jagrani (Khanna) Mehra; m. Madan Capoor, Jan. 10, 1964; children—Anjali, Vineeta. B.A., Savitri Coll., 1960; M.A., Govt. Coll., 1962; M.L.S., Pratt Inst., 1972. Research asst., N.Y.U., 1968-69, supr. R.R. Bowker Co., N.Y.C., 1973-76; mgr. Baker & Taylor co., div. of W.R. Grace Corp., Somerville, N.J., 1976-81, dir., 1981—. Research fellow Rajasthan Univ., India, 1963. Mem. ALA, N.J. Library Assn. (pres. 1981-83, tech. services), N.J. Assn. Info. Sci. (chmn., 1981-82 membership com.), Am. Assn. Info. Scis., Spl. Library Assn., Am. Nat. Standards Inst. (U.S. del. to China 1985). Home: 1741 Arrowbrook Dr Martinsville NJ 08836 Office: Baker and Taylor Co 6 Kirby Ave Somerville NJ 08876

CAPORALE, PATRICIA JEANE SENIOR, editor, reporter; b. Camden, N.J., Nov. 27, 1947; d. Cassius Floyd and Dorothy Amanda (Hauseman) Senior; m. Joseph Emil Caporale, May 28, 1968; children—Mark Andrew, Michael Charles, Lawrence Joseph. A.S. in Social Services, Camden County Coll., 1978. Asst. tchr. Archway Schs., Atco, N.J., 1978-80; freelance writer, N.J., 1978-81; assoc. editor Cam-Glo Newspapers, Clementon, N.J., 1979-80, mng. editor, Blackwood, N.J., 1981-82; editor Haddon Gazette, Haddonfield, N.J., 1982-83, Cherry Hill News (N.J.), 1983—. Author investigative articles (N.J. Press Assn. Enterprise award 1980), 1979, investigative series on housing industry (Bell Telephone Enterprise award 1981), 1980, health club regulations (award Sigma Delta Chi-Soc. Profl. Journalists), 1984. Twp. com. candidate Winslow Twp., 1976; fire commr. Fire Chief's Assn., Winslow Twp., 1983—. Named Outstanding Young Woman of Achievement, Camden County Council Girl Scouts U.S., 1983; recipient citation for representing World of People N.J. Gen. Assembly, 1983, ARC award, 1985, Phila. Press Assn. award, 1984, N.J. Press Assn., 1984. Mem. N.J. Press Assn. (award for gen. interest column 1980, awards 1984), Home and Sch. Assn. (v.p. 1977, pres. 1978), Internat. Platform Assn. Methodist. Home: 513 Steven Ave Berlin NJ 08009 Office: Cherry Hill News PO Box 5180 1111 Union Ave Cherry Hill NJ 08034

CAPP, IRENE M., manufacturing company official; b. Yonkers, N.Y., June 26, 1949; d. Harry and Anna (Chanas) Capp; B.A., U. Rochester, 1971; M.A., U. Chgo., 1974, M.B.A., 1976; m. Donald E. Kerr, Jr., Nov. 17, 1979; children—Mariel Ames, Ford Baker. With Booz Allen & Hamilton, Chgo., 1976-83, sr. assoc., 1979-83; mgr. strategic projects Abbott Labs., Abbott Park, Ill., 1983-84, bus. mgr. hosp. products div., 1983-85, dir. drugs and drug delivery systems; lectr., U. Chgo. Bus. Sch. Home: 1123 Chatfield Rd Winnetka IL 60093 Office: Abbott Labs Hosp Products Div Abbott Park IL 60064

CAPPELLO, EVE, behavior/business consultant; b. Sydney, Australia, Dec. 4, 1922; d. Nem and Ethel Shapira; came to U.S., 1940, naturalized, 1944; A.A., Santa Monica City Coll., 1972; B.A., Calif. State U.-Dominguez Hills, 1974; M.A., Pacific Western U., 1977, Ph.D., 1978; children—Frances Soskins, Alan Kazdin. Singer, pianist, Los Angeles, 1958-78; pvt. practice behavior and bus. cons., Los Angeles, 1976—; instr. Calif. State U. Extension, Dominguez Hills, 1977—; Mt. St. Mary's Coll., U. of Judaism, U. So. Calif.; founder, dir. A-C-T Inst.; former co-exec. dir. Total One Devel. Ctr. of Marina Del Rey; invited lectr. World Congress Behavior Therapy, Israel, U. Melbourne, Australia. Mem. Calif. State U.-Dominguez Hills Alumni Assn., Assn. Advancement Behavior Therapy, Assn. Behavioral Analysis, Orgnl. Bus. Mgmt. Assn., Wilshire Bus. and Profl. Women's Orgn., Women's Internat. Network (founder, pres.), Santa Monica C. of C., Alpha Gamma. Author: Let's Get Growing, 1979; The Professional Touch, 1983; Dr. Eve's Garden, 1984; Act, Don't React, 1985; The Game of the Name, 1985; newspaper columnist, 1976-79; contbr. articles to profl. jours. Home: 1271 Granville Ave Apt #202 Los Angeles CA 90025 Office: PO Box 25544 Los Angeles CA 90025

CAPPS, BARBARA LOUISE, respiratory therapist; b. Fresno, Calif., Dec. 11, 1933; d. Eugene Victor and Ruth (Lankford) Thalman; med. asst. diploma Fresno Tech. Coll., 1965; m. Ronald Dean Capps, Aug. 9, 1968; children—Rochelle Ruth Pope, Jeffra Lynn Pope, Karen Kay Pope, Jeannie Louise Briggs, Jay Eugene Pope, Ronald Lee Pope, Lisa Dianne Capps. From nurses aide to shift leader respiratory therapy Fresno Community Hosp., 1965-70; staff technician, then shift leader St. Agnes Hosp., Fresno, 1970-71; coordinator CuraCare Respiratory Therapy Services, Modesto, Calif., 1972-73, dist. mgr., 1973—; instr., trainer Am. Heart Assn. Mem. Republican Presdl. Task Force, 1982—. Mem. Am. Assn. Respiratory Therapy, Calif. Soc. Respiratory Therapy (chpt. membership chmn. 1972-73). Office: 1400 Lone Palm Dr Modesto CA 95353

CAPPS, LINDA GLOWRENE, radio station executive; b. Seattle, June 3, 1943; d. Andrew Waldamer Landin and Freida Glowrene (Robertson) Landin Smith; m. Jeffrey John Carlson, June 3, 1961 (div. 1972); children—Marabeth Estelle, Mia Arlene, Jeffrey John; m. George Lindel Capps, Jan. 19, 1979. Student Wanatchee Valley Coll., 1962, Spokane Community Coll., 1972. Owner, operator apple orchard, Okanogan, Wash., 1968-72; owner, operator pvt. prodn. co., 1972-75; disc jockey, sales rep., sales mgr. Sta. KRSC, Othello, Wash., 1977-80, gen. mgr., 1985—. Treas., pres. Okanogan PTA; v.p. County PTA Council; mem. Okanogan Electoral Bd., mem. White House Conf. Youth Moderation; active Juvenile Receiving House; sec., pres. Wenatchee YWCA; chmn. Wenatchee Handicapped Artists show; mem. Adams County (Wash.) Fair Bd., publicity chmn. fair and rodeo. Mem. Othello Bus. and Profl. Women (pres.), Dist. Bus. and Profl. Women (sec. treas.). Lodge: Altrusa. Avocations: fishing; needlework; quilting. Home: 3990 Scootney Rd Connell WA 99326 Office: Sta KRSC 180 E Main St Othello WA 99344

CAPPUCCILLI, DORIS JEAN, advertising agency executive; b. Ephrata, Pa., Dec. 13, 1942; d. Martin Jackson Charles and Grace (Jones) Delaney; m. James G. Goodeve, Apr. 5, 1960 (div. 1968); children—Sandra Lynn Goodeve Baker, Angela Rae, Jamie Gail; m. Alfred Cappuccilli, Nov. 21, 1973. Student in media design Chgo. Sch. Design, 1962-63. Sales rep. sta.-WOLF, Syracuse, N.Y., 1969-70; account exec. sta.-WFBL, Syracuse, 1970-75, WHEN-TV, Syracuse, 1975-77, sta.-WNDR, Syracuse, 1977-79; owner, pres. Broadcast Advt. Specialists, Syracuse, 1979—; lectr. Syracuse U., 1983-85. Advt. dir. polit. campaigns, Syracuse, 1981, 83; dir. St. Augustine's Ch. Bazaar, Baldwinsville, 1982; com. mem. St. Mary's Ch., Skaneateles, 1984-85. Recipient Exec. Sales award sta. WFBL, 1973, 74. Mem. LWV, Syracuse C. of C. Roman Catholic. Avocations: travel, tennis, boating, flower gardening. Office: Broadcast Advt Specialists 2010 W Genesee St Syracuse NY 13152

CARAM, DOROTHY FARRINGTON, educational consultant; b. McAllen, Tex., Jan. 14, 1933; d. Curtis Leon and Elena (Santander) Farrington; m. Pedro C. Caram, June 7, 1958; children—Pedro M., Juan D., Hector L., Jose M. B.A., Rice U., 1955, M.A., 1974; Ed.D. (fellow), U. Houston, 1982; postgrad. U. Madrid, 1957. Tchr., Houston Ind. Sch. Dist., 1955-56, 1956-60, St. Mark's Episcopal Sch., Houston, 1964-65; substitute tchr. St. Vincent De Paul Cath. Sch., Houston, 1965-68; mgr. med. office, Houston, 1983; dir. Fed. Home Loan Bank, Little Rock, 1976-82; pres. Inst. Hispanic Culture, Houston, 1983, Houston Ednl. Excellence Program, 1980; mem. task force Tex. Edn. Agy., 1981—; mem. adv. council Nat. Inst. Neurol. and Communicative Disorders and Health, 1972 76. Mem. council Miller Theater, Houston, 1976—, bd. dirs Houston Pops, 1983—; mem. Task Force Quality Integrated Edn., Houston, 1972; bd. dirs. Houston Lighthouse of Blind, 1982; mem. Civil Commn. Houston, 1983—. Mem. Houston Area Tchrs. Fgn. Lang., MLA, Southwestern Social Sci. Orgn., Southwestern Council Latin Am. Studies. Roman Catholic. Club: Cedars (pres. 1978) (Houston) Home: 3106 Aberdeen Way Houston TX 77025

CARAWAY, BETTY JONES, assistant to governor of Texas; b. Wichita Falls, Tex., Sept. 30, 1928; d. Ivey Lee and Lou (Jones) Sides; m. Charles E. Caraway (div. 1965); 1 child, Judith Caraway Buttrill. Student Mrs. Cuykendall Bus. Sch., summer 1944; diploma Hardin Jr. Coll., 1946; B.B.A., U. Tex., 1949; postgrad. Stanford U. Asst. to gen. counsel Library of Congress, Washington, 1967-68; asst. to dir. Pacific Missile Range, Dept. of Navy, Washington, 1968-69; asst. to sr. ptnr. Pittman, Lovett & Hennessee, Washington, 1969-77; asst. to campaign mgr. Church-Robb campaigns, Va.; asst. to campaign mgr. for Jimmy Carter, Washington; asst. to dir. Alcohol Fuels Dept., Dept. Energy, Washington, 1971-82; adminstrv. asst. to dir. Job Tng. Partnership Act program for Gov. White of Tex., Austin, 1983—. Social chmn. Houston Jr. Forum; chmn. Cherry Blossom Festival, Washington, 1977. Mem. U. Tex. Exes, Stanford Exes of Austin. Democrat. Methodist. Avocations: oil painting; scuba diving. Home: 2711 Friar Tuck Ln Austin TX 78704 Office: Office of Gov Adminstrn Asst to Dir JTPA 8317 Cross Park Dr Austin TX 78754

CARBERRY, DEIRDRE, ballerina; b. Manhasset, N.Y., Nov. 7, 1965; d. Larry P. and Marilyn (Monsour) Carberry. Student pub. schs., Fla., pvt. schs., Fla. and N.Y.C. Corps dancer Am. Ballet Theatre, N.Y.C., 1980-83, soloist, 1983—; prin. artist, U.S., Europe, Mid-East, S.Am., C.Am., 1979—; partners have included Mikhail Baryshnikov and Fernando Bujones; free lance model, 1975—. Recipient Silver medal, First U.S. Internat. Ballet Competition, Jackson, Miss., 1979; Harkness House scholar, 1978-79; N.Y. State Dance Summer program scholar, 1979, Sch. Am. Ballet scholar, 1979-80. Youngest person to join Am. Ballet Theatre; danced lead female role in World premier of The Little Ballet, created for her by Twyla Tharp. Office: Am Ballet Theatre 890 Broadway New York NY 10023

CARBINE, PATRICIA THERESA, editor, publisher; b. Villanova, Pa., Jan. 31, 1931; d. James T. and Margaret (Dee) Carbine; B.A. in English, Rosemont Coll., 1952. With Look mag., 1953-70, mng. editor, 1966-69, exec. editor, 1969-70; editor McCall's mag., 1970-72; pub., editor-in-chief Ms. mag., N.Y.C., 1972—; dir. N.Y. Life Ins. Co.; trustee Dry Dock Savs. Bank. Founder, bd. dirs. Ms. Found. for Women, Inc., 1972—, Ms. Found. for Communication and Edn., Inc., 1979—; trustee Rosemont Coll., 1972—. Mem. Am. Soc. Mag. Editors, Mag. Pubs. Assn. (dir. from 1973), Advt. Council (dir. 1975). Office: Ms Found for Edn and Communication Inc 119 W 40th St New York NY 10018*

CARBINE, SHARON, lawyer; b. Bryn Mawr, Pa., Feb. 14, 1950; d. Thomas Joseph and Mary Teresa (Loftus) Carbine. B.A., Temple U., 1972, J.D., 1974, LL.M. in Taxation, 1977. Bar: Pa. 1974, Tex. 1981; C.P.A., Tex. Atty., Altemose Cos., Center Square, Pa., 1973-75; law clk. presiding justice Ct. Common Pleas, Phila., summer, 1975; tax atty. Provident Mut. Life Ins. Co., Phila., 1975-77, Emhart Corp., Farmington, Conn., 1977-78; tax sr. Peat Marwick Mitchell & Co., Phila., 1978-79; legal counsel to gov.'s chief energy advisor Tex. Energy and Natural Resources Adv. Council, Austin, 1979-80; tax atty. Sun Co., Inc., Dallas, 1980-82; pvt. practice, Haverford, Pa., 1982-83; tax atty. Ebasco Services Inc., N.Y.C., 1983-84; pvt. practice law, King of Prussia, Pa., 1985—; dir. Quaker City Japanning and Enameling Co., Inc., Phila., Vol., Republican Party, 1964—; mem. Jaycees, Phila., 1978-79, Austin, Tex., 1979-80; bd. dirs. Republican Women of the Main Line, Bryn Mawr, Pa., 1983. Mem. Pa. Bar Assn., Montgomery Bar Assn., Delaware County Bar Assn., Phila. Bar Assn., Main Line Lawyers Forum, Delaware County Atty.-C.P.A. Forum, Brehon Law Soc., Delaware County Estate Planning Council, Main Line Women's Network, Main Line C. of C., C.P.A. Computer Users Group. Roman Catholic. Home: 110 Linwood Ave Ardmore PA 19003 Office: 120 S Warner Rd King of Prussia PA 19406

CARCHMAN, JOANN, museum executive; b. Albuquerque, Apr. 1, 1944; d. Harold Victor and Shirley Beatrice (Spiegleman) Gardenswartz; m. Philip Stanley Carchman, Sept. 5, 1966; children—Rebecca Maya, Jennifer Eve. B.F.A., U. Pa., 1966. Adminstr. Ednl. Testing Service, Princeton, N.J., 1966-68; dir. community relations The Art Mus., Princeton, 1978—. Mem. bd. Arts Council Princeton, 1978—. Mem. Am. Assn. Museums. Avocations: skiing; tennis; biking; gardening. Home: 4 Howe Circle Princeton NJ 08540 Office: The Art Mus Princeton U Princeton NJ 08544

CARDAMONE, MARGARET MARY, lawyer; b. Norristown, Pa., Apr. 15, 1949; d. Joseph J. and Camelia (Sirianni) C. B.A., U. Steubenville, 1971; J.D., U. Notre Dame, 1974. Bar: Pa. 1974. Law clk. to judge Ct. Common Pleas, Montgomery County, Norristown, 1974-75; asst. dist. atty. Berks County, Reading, Pa., 1976-77; staff atty. Criminal Procedural Rules Com., Phila., 1978-79; asst. regional counsel EPA, Phila., 1979—. Bd. dirs. Whitpain Hills Homeowners Assn., Center Square, Pa., 1982—. Mem. ABA, Montgomery County Bar Assn., Delta Zeta. Republican. Roman Catholic. Clubs: Wissahickon Skating, Notre Dame (Phila.). Home: 1750 Skippack Pike Townhouse 1313 Center Square PA 19422 Office: EPA 841 Chestnut Bldg Philadelphia PA 19107

CARDEN, EMMA ELIZABETH, artist, home design company executive; b. Memphis, Oct. 24, 1922; d. Joseph Neely and Myrtle Deacy Lee (Dover) Simons; m. Frank Jefferson Perry, Jan. 1939 (div. Mar. 1941); 1 child, Betty Lee; m. Hugh M. Carden, Sept. 2, 1943 (dec. June 1984); children—Dan Carle, Susan Darlene. Student pub. schs., Shelby County, Tenn. Pres. Sheld Inc., Paducah, Ky., 1984—; exhibited in group shows including Evansville Mus. Arts and Sci., 1967, 70, 73. Brook Meml. Art Gallery, Memphis, 1970, 72, 73, Parthenon of Nashville, 1971, 75; designer homes. Active The Woman's Club of Paducah, Gen. Fedn. Women's Clubs, including chmn. lit. and drama, 1981-83. Recipient Duchess of Paducah award Mayor of Paducah, 1976, also numerous awards for art, including First Place awards Paducah City Hall Exhbn., 1966, 67, 77 (2), So. Ill. Arts and Crafts Guild Fair, 1967, 68, 69, 70, 71 (3), Ky. Fedn. Women's Clubs, 1975, 77. Mem. Nat. Assn. Female Execs., Parents Without Ptnrs., Paducah Art Guild. Lodge: Order Eagles Aux. Avocations: hand crafts and art; petrology; astrology; archeology; metaphysics. Home and Studio: 404 Castleton Pike Paducah KY 42001

CARDEN, LINDA JACKSON, radio station executive; b. Franklin, Tenn., Sept. 30, 1950; d. Charles Robert and Eunice Rebecca (Tomlin) Jackson; m. Guy Dwain Carden, June 3, 1972; children—Guy Walker II, Robert Adams, Heather Elizabeth. Student Middle Tenn. State U., 1968-69. Office mgr. Sta. WIZO, Franklin, 1969-82, ops. mgr., 1982—. Vol. Am. Heart Assn., Franklin, 1983—, Mothers March of Dimes, Franklin, 1978—, United Way, Franklin, 1982—; active Williamson County Humane Assn., 1980—. Mem. Williamson County C. of C. (vol.). Republican. Mem. Ch. of Christ. Club: Franklin Bus. and Profl. Women's. Avocations: reading; arts and crafts. Office: Sta WIZO Radio Carters Creek Pike Box 249 Franklin TN 37065

CARDILLO, LAUREN FRANCESCA, writer, producer; b. New Rochelle, N.Y., Oct. 26, 1958; d. Anthony P. and Irene L. (Maruzzella) C. B.A. in Lit., Communications, Pace U., 1980; M.A. in Communication, Stanford U., 1982. Editor, ann. report Jr. Achievement, White Plains, N.Y., 1977-79, editor, newspaper Pace. U. New Morning, Pleasantville, 1979-80; producer, writer Elgen Long Prodn., San Mateo, Calif., 1981-82, Stanford U., Calif., 1981-82; freelance producer, writer, Calif. and N.Y., 1982 83; writer, assoc. producer NJSamoul and Co., Inc., N.Y.C., 1983-84; free lance writer, 1984—. Author: (documentary film) On a Wing and a Prayer, 1982 (1st place finalist Oakland Nat. Ednl. Film Festival 1983). Regents scholar N.Y. State, 1976, Trustees award, scholar Pace U., 1976; 80; Grad. fellow Stanford U., 1980. Mem. Women in Communications, Sigma Chi. Home: care 49 Eldredge Sq S Chatham MA 02633

CARDINALE, KATHLEEN CARMEL, medical center administrator; b. Donegal, Ireland, July 13, 1933; came to U.S., 1958, naturalized, 1966; d. Denis and Mary (Cannon) O'Boyle; R.N., Walton Hosp., Liverpool, Eng., 1955; B.A., Jersey City State Coll., 1971, M.A., 1973; m. Anthony Cardinale, Aug. 28, 1965. Staff nurse, acting-in-charge Manhattan Gen. Hosp., N.Y.C., 1958-59; charge nurse, acting-in-charge, Met. Hosp., N.Y.C., 1959-60; charge nurse, relief supr. Manhattan Gen. Hosp., N.Y.C., 1960-64, asst. dir. nursing, 1964-68, staffing coordinator, 1968-70; acting asso. dir. nursing Bernstein Inst., N.Y.C., 1970; clin. supr., clin. specialist Beth Israel Med. Center, N.Y.C., 1971-73; asst. dir. nursing Cabrini Med. Center, N.Y.C., 1974-77, assoc. dir. nursing, 1977-78, v.p. nursing services, 1978—. Mem. Am. Nurses Assn., Greater N.Y. Hosp. Assn. (mem. profl. affairs policy com.), Am. Hosp. Assn., Am. Soc. Nursing Service Adminstrs. Home: 545 E 14th St New York NY 10009 Office: 227 E 19th St New York NY 10003

CARDINALE, MARIAN FRANCES, medical technologist; b. Independence, La., June 21, 1933; d. Isadore Thomas and Rosalie Marretta Cardinale; B.S. in Zoology and Chemistry with honors, Southeastern La. U., 1955; M.B.A., U. New Orleans, 1977. Staff technologist Charity Hosp., New Orleans, 1955-56, chemistry supr., 1956-62; chemistry supr. Mercy Hosp., New Orleans, 1962-68; chief med. technologist Pendleton Meml. Meth. Hosp., New Orleans, 1968-81, lab. mgr., 1981-84, dir. lab., 1984-85, v.p. clin. services, 1985—. Trustee Blood Ctr. for S.E. La., 1986—. Mem. Am. Soc. Med. Tech. (bd. dirs. 1980-83, 85-86, pres. 1984-85), La. (pres. 1969-70), New Orleans socs. med. tech., Sierra Club. Democrat. Roman Catholic. Home: 2704 Whitney Pl #723 Metairie LA 70002 Office: Pendleton Meml Meth Hosp 5620 Read Blvd New Orleans LA 70127

CARDMAN, CECILIA, artist; b. Soveria Mannelli, Italy; d. Samuel and Maria (Mendicino) Cardman; B.F.A., U. Colo., 1934, B.A., 1934; student Instituto dei Belli Arte, Naples, Italy, 1921-23, Denver Art Mus., 1930-31, with Leon Kroll, Nat. Acad., 1945-46, others. Head dept. painting Mesa Coll., Grand Junction, Colo., 1930-40; one-man shows: Naples, Italy, Grist Mill Gallery, Chester, Vt., Bergdorf-Goodman, 1978, Jarvis Gallery, Sandwich, Mass., 1975, Elliott Mus., Stuart, Fla., Grand Junction, Colo., 1984; group shows include: Nat. Arts Club, 1975-76, Nat. Acad., 1945, Knickerbocker Artists, 1979, Nelson Gallery, 1937-38, Denver Art Mus., 1924-25, Nat. League Am. Pen Women, 1979, Grand Central Art Gallery, 1977, Am. Artist Profl. League, 1979-80. Recipient awards. Mem. Jackson Heights Art Club (1st prize 1982, 2d prize 1983), Coll. Women's Club, Salmagundi Club (dir., Lay Jury prize 1979), Nat. League Am. Pen Women (dir.; 1st v.p. N.Y.C. br.), Ky. Watercolor Soc., Sumi-e Soc. (award 1982), Artist Fellowship, Inc., Pen and Brush (dir.; Emily Hatch award 1982, 1st prize 1983), Knickerbocker Artists, Catherine Lorillard Wolfe Art Club (pres., dir., Best in Show award 1980), Am. Artists Profl. League (nat. dir.), Allied Artists Am. (dir. publicity), Nat. Acad. Western Art, Roman Catholic. Home: 34-06 81st St Penthouse Jackson Heights New York NY 11372

CARDONE, BONNIE JEAN, editor, author, photographer; b. Chgo., Feb. 21, 1942; d. Frederick Paul and Beverly Jean (Johnson) Rittschof; m. David Frederick Cardone, June 9, 1983 (div. Dec. 1978); children—Pamela Susan, Michael David. B.A. in Communication Arts, Mich. State U., 1963. Editorial asst. Jour. of Mich. State Dental Assn., Lansing, 1963-64, Nursing Home Adminstrn., Chgo., 1964-65; asst. editor Skin Diver, Los Angeles, 1976-77, sr. editor, 1977-81, exec. editor Skin Diver Mag., 1981—. Mem. Profl. Assn. Journalists. Clubs: Santa Monica Blue Fins (Calif.) (treas. 1976-77, pres. 1977-78, sec. 1985-86); Calif. Wreck Divers. Avocations: skiing; tennis. Office: Skin Diver Mag 8490 Sunset Blvd Los Angeles CA 90069

CARDONE, KATHLEEN, lawyer, judge; b. Medina, N.Y., Dec. 25, 1953; d. Vincent Dominic and Rose Elizabeth (Burgio) Cardone; m. Eduardo Ariel Rodriguez, June 20, 1980. Student U. Barcelona, 1973; student Andean Ctr., 1975; B.A., SUNY-Binghamton, 1976; J.D., St. Mary's Law Sch., San Antonio, 1979. Bar: Tex. 1979, U.S. Dist. Ct. (we. dist.) Tex. 19—. Sole practice, El Paso, Tex., 1982—; judge Mcpl. Ct. No. 5, El Paso, 1983—; legal cons. YWCA Women's Resource Ctr., El Paso., 1981—. Bd. dirs. YWCA, El Paso, 1981—; bd. dirs. El Paso del Norte Credit Union, 1983; steering com. mem. El Paso Community Devel., 1981; bd. dirs. El Paso Women's Employment and Edn., 1981. Mem. ABA, Tex. Bar Assn. Roman Catholic.

CARDOZA, ANNE, writer; b. N.Y.C., Nov. 18, 1941; d. Sara Nunez and Michael Cardoza. B.S. in Creative Writing, English, NYU, 1964; M.A. in Creative Writing, English, San Diego State U., 1979; diploma Hollywood Scriptwriting Inst., 1984. Author of 33 books including In The Chips: 101 Ways to Make Money with your Personal Computer, 1985; High Paying Jobs in Six Months or Less, 1984; Understanding Robotics, 1985; Careers in Robotics, 1985; Careers in Aerospace, 1985; author 28 books on contemporary urgent issues in the news and on self help such as Elderly Abuse, Teenage Pregnancy. Contbr. articles to various publs., film scripts, 2 novelettes and collections of short stories. Author of screenplay: Otherhood. Office: PO Box 4333 San Diego CA 92104

CARDOZO, ARLENE ROSSEN, author; b. Mpls., Jan. 12, 1938; d. Ralph and Beatrice (Cohen) Rossen; m. Richard Nunez Cardozo, June 29, 1959; children—Miriam, Rachel, Rebecca. B.A., U. Minn., 1958, M.A., 1982, postgrad., 1982—. Founder, dir. Writers Unlimited, Mpls., 1972-76, Woman at Home Workshops, Mpls., 1976-81; lectr. U. Minn. Summer Arts Study Center, 1982—; artist-in-residence Split Rock Arts Ctr., Duluth, Minn., 1985; cons. to woman at home, 1976—, manuscript and pub. industry. Author: Jewish Family Celebrations, 1982, Woman at Home, 1976; The Liberated Cookbook, 1972; contbr. essays, articles, reviews to Chgo. Sun Times, Mpls. Star/Tribune, Cleve. Plain Dealer, Newsday; L.J. Journalism Quar.; guest lectr. Harvard-Radcliffe U., 1982; others; guest appearances Today Show, Phil Donahue Show, radio and TV, U.S. and Can. Founder, Harvard Neighbors, Cambridge, 1963-64; vol. Mpls. pub. schs., 1972—. Mem. Authors Guild, Authors League Am., Nat. Book Critics Circle (charter), Minn. Press Club, Hadassah (life). Jewish. Home: 1955 East River Rd Minneapolis MN 55114

CARDUCCI, DIANE, hospital administrator; b. S.I., N.Y., Dec. 16; d. Geremia and Amelia (Mariano) C. A.A., S.I. Community Coll., 1967; B.S., Richmond Coll., 1970, M.S., 1972; postgrad. St. John's U., 1979-82. Tchr., librarian Our Lady of Mt. Carmel, S.I., 1967-72, St. Paul, S.I., 1972-81; tchr., prin. religious edn. Immaculate Conception, S.I., 1981-82; health care program planner Sea View Hosp. and Home, S.I., 1982-84, asst. dir. hosp., 1984-85, assoc. dir. hosp., 1986—. Editor Am. Com. on Italian Migration, 1983—. Chmn. bd. dirs. March of Dimes, S.I., 1985-86; bd. dirs. S.I. Hosp., 1985—; treas. N.Y.C. Community Bd. 1, S.I., 1975-80; sec. Northfield Local Devel. Corp., S.I., 1979-83, sec., 1982. Richmond County Bus. and Profl. Women scholar, 1982; recipient Outstanding Service Alumni Assn. Coll. of S.I., 1984; named Outstanding Italian Woman Coll. of S.I., 1985. Mem. Health Systems Agy., Am. Pub. Health Assn., N.Y. State Planning Assn., Am. Mgmt. Assn., Gateway Bus. and Profl. Women. Roman Catholic. Lodge: Lioness. Home: 4176 Richmond Ave Staten Island NY 10312

CARDULLO, MARIA ANN, educator; b. Boston, Apr. 11, 1942; d. Anthony Orlando and Rosina Margaret (Matthews) Cardullo; A.B. in Chemistry, Emmanuel Coll., 1963, A.B. in Biology, 1964; M.S., Boston Coll., 1967, Ph.D., 1971. Postdoctoral research assoc. in bacteriology and molecular biology Boston Coll., Chestnut Hill, Mass., 1971-77; chmn. dept. sci., tchr. biology and chemistry Christopher Columbus High Sch., Boston, 1977—. Recipient award for outstanding contbns. to secondary edn. NCEA, 1984. Mem. Am. Soc. Microbiology, Nat. Assn. Biology Tchrs., NEA, Sigma Xi. Roman Catholic. Contbr. articles to profl. jours. Office: 20 Tileston St Boston MA 02113

CARDWELL, SUE POOLE, environmental consultant; b. Clearfield, Pa., Oct. 31, 1952; d. Robert Thomas and Mary B. (Edwards) Poole; B.A., Transylvania U., Lexington, Ky., 1973; m. Charles Howard Cardwell, Nov. 26, 1979; children—Jonathan Aaron, Jacqueline Leigh. Chief clk.-typist Ky. Dept. Mines and Minerals, Lexington, 1974; sr. reclamation insp. div. reclamation Ky. Dept. Natural Resources, Madisonville, 1974-77; pres. Reclamation Services Unltd., Inc., Madisonville, 1977—; former mem. bd. dirs. West Ky. Coal Operators Assn.; chmn. West Ky. adv. group to Office Strip Mining, 1979-81; mem. exec. bd. Ann. Sedimentology Symposium, U. Ky., 1979—; mem. Ky. Adv. Com. on Strip Mining, 1979—; subcom. chmn. Mining and Reclamation Council Am., 1977—. Mem. exec. bd. Ky. Task Force on Missing and Exploited Children, 1983-84, sec. exec. bd., 1984—. Served with WAC, 1973-74. Mem. W.Va. Surface Mining and Relamation Assn., Profl. Reclamation Assn. (exec. bd. 1979-85), Soil Conservation Assn. Office: Reclamation Services Unltd Inc 12 Hartland Ave Madisonville KY 42431

CARELLI, GLORIA A., advertising agency executive; b. Bklyn., Jan. 20, 1932; m. John A. Carelli, 1953; children—John, Mark, Paul, Gina, Gail. Student Pratt Inst., Bklyn., 1950-52. Exec. v.p., prin. CGW Enterprises, Butler, N.J., 1969—. Trustee, Chilton Meml. Hosp., Pompton Plains, N.J., 1982—. Mem. Advt. Club No. Jersey (dir. 1982-83, 2d v.p. 1984—). Republican. Roman Catholic. Office: CGW Enterprises Inc 1250 Route 23 Butler NJ 07405

CARESS, JEANNETTE RAWSON, interior designer; b. Miller, S.D., Oct. 28, 1941; d. Fredrick and Alma F. (Dodd) Rawson; children—Jennifer L. Caress, Robert K. Caress. Student Riverside U., 1969. Apprentice, Greystone Builders, San Francisco, 1959-63; adminstrv. sec. San Francisco Pub. Health Service, 1964-68; owner J. Caress Interiors, Claremont, 1977—, Final Touch Drapery Room, Ontario, Calif., 1984—; tchr. Claremont Human Services, 1979—. Recipient West's Best 15, 1979. Club: Zonta. Office: J Caress Interiors 317 N Euclid Ave Ontario CA 91762

CAREY, ERNESTINE GILBRETH (MRS. CHARLES E. CAREY), author, lecturer; b. N.Y.C. Apr. 5, 1908; d. Frank Bunker and Lillian (Moller) Gilbreth; m. Charles Everett Carey, Sept. 13, 1930; children—Lillian Carey Clark, Charles Everett. B.A., Smith Coll., 1929. Buyer, R.H. Macy & Co., N.Y.C., 1930-44, James McCreery, N.Y.C., 1947-49; lectr., book reviewer, author syndicated newspaper articles, 1951; bd. dirs. Right to Read Inc., 1968—, co-chmn., 1967. Author: Jumping Jupiter, 1952; Rings Around Us, 1956; Giddy Moment, 1958; co-author: (with Frank B. Gilbreth Jr.) Cheaper By the Dozen, 1949; Belles on Their Toes, 1951. Contbr. articles to mags., book revs. and profl. jours. Trustee Manhasset Pub. Library, 1953-59, v.p., 1956-59; trustee Smith Coll., 1967-72. Co-recipient Prix Scarron French Internat. Humor award for Cheaper By the Dozen, 1951; (with Lillian Molter Gilbreth) McElligott medallion Assn. Marquette U. Women, 1966; Montgomery award Friends of Phoenix Pub. Library, 1981. Mem. Authors Guild Am. (life mem., guild council 1955-60), P.E.N., Coll. Conf. Council. Republican. Congregationalist. Clubs: Smith Coll. (asst. chmn. scholarship com. 1950-59) (L.I.), Smith College (Phoenix, vice chmn. scholarship com. 1967). Address: 6148 E Lincoln Dr Paradise Valley AZ 85253

CAREY, JANA THERESA HOWARD, lawyer; b. Huntsville, Ala., Apr. 20, 1945; d. Ernest Randall and Mary Regna (Baites) H.; B.S., Auburn U., 1967; M.S., Towson State Coll., 1973; J.D. summa cum laude, U. Balt., 1976. Admitted to Md. bar, 1976; home econs. tchr. Hampton High Sch., Melbourne, Australia, 1967; county ext. home economist U. Ga. Coop. Extension Services, Jefferson, 1967-70; state youth program devel. specialist U. Ga. Coop. Extension Service, Athens, 1970-72; state youth program devel. specialist U. Md. Coop. Extension Service, College Park, 1972-73; asso. law firm Venable, Baetjer & Howard, Balt., 1976-83, ptnr., 1983—; speaker, cons. Nat. Employment Law Inst., 1979—, Exec. Enterprises, Inc., 1978—, Profl. Seminar Assos., Inc., 1978-81, Antioch Sch. Law Center for Legal Studies, 1981. Mem. adv. com. Goucher Coll. Women's Mgmt. Devel. Project, 1979—; mem. Greater Balt. Com. Chamber Council, 1980—; pres., bd. dirs. Balt. New Directions for Women, 1980-81, bd. dirs., 1981—. Mem. Am. Judicature Soc., ABA (chmn. EEO subcom. programs), Bar Assn. Balt. City, Fed. Bar Assn., Md. Bar Assn. (spl. com. law and handicapped). Presbyterian. Club: Loophole Law Balt. Contbr. articles to profl. jours. Office: 1800 Mercantile Bank and Trust Bldg Two Hopkins Plaza Baltimore MD 21201

CAREY, KATHRYN ANN, corporate philanthropy, advertising and public relations executive, editor, consultant; b. Los Angeles, Oct. 18, 1949; d. Frank Randall and Evelyn Mae (Walmsley) C.; m. Richard Kenneth Sundt, Dec. 28, 1980. B.A. in Am. Studies with honors, Calif. State U.-Los Angeles, 1971. Tutor Calif. Dept. Vocat. Rehab., Los Angeles, 1970; teaching asst. U. So. Calif., 1974-75, UCLA, 1974-75; claims adjuster Auto Club So. Calif., San Gabriel, 1971-73; corp. pub. relations cons. Carnation Co., Los Angeles, 1973-78; pub. relations cons. Vivitar Corp., editor Vivitar Voice, Santa Monica, Calif., 1978; sr. advt. asst. Am. Honda Motor Co., Gardena, Calif., 1978-84; exec. dir. Am. Honda Found., 1984—; mgr. Honda Dealer Advt. Assns.; cons. advt., pub. relations, promotions. Cons., adminstr. Carnation Community Service award program. Calif. Life Scholarship Found. scholar, 1967. Mem. Advt. Club Los Angeles, Pub. Relations Soc. Am., So. Calif. Assn. Philanthropy, Council Founds. of Washington, Los Angeles Soc. for Prevention Cruelty to Animals, Green Peace, German Shepherd Dog Club Am., Am. Humane Assn., Elsa Wild Animal Appeal. Democrat. Methodist. Editor: Honda Views, 1978-84; Found. Focus; contbg. editor Mighty to Mini, 1978—. Office: 19603 S Vermont Ave Torrance CA 90502

CAREY, MARY VIRGINIA, writer; b. New Brighton, Cheshire, Eng., May 19, 1925; d. John Cornelius and Mary Alice (Hughes) Carey; B.S., Coll. of Mt. St. Vincent, 1946. Editorial asso. Coronet Mag., N.Y.C., 1948-55; asst. editor publs. Walt Disney Productions, Burbank, Calif., 1955-69; author: Mystery of the Flaming Footprints, 1971; Mystery of the Singing Serpent, 1972; Mystery of Monster Mountain, 1973; Secret of the Haunted Mirror, 1974; Mystery of the Invisible Dog, 1975; Mystery of Death Trap Mine, 1976; Mystery of the Magic Circle, 1978; Mystery of the Sinister Scarecrow, 1979; Mystery of the Scar-Faced Beggar, 1981; Mystery of the Blazing Cliffs, 1981; Love is Forever, 1975; Step-by-Step Candlemaking, 1972; Step-by-Step Winemaking, 1973; The Owl Who Loved Sunshine, 1977; Mystery of the Wandering Caveman, 1982; Mystery of the Missing Mermaid, 1983; Mystery of the Trail of Terror, 1984; The Gremlins Storybook, 1984; Mystery of the Creep-Show Crooks, 1985; A Place for Allie, 1985; editor: Grandmothers are Very Special People, 1977; author: (with George Sherman) A Compendium of Bunk, 1976. Mem. Author's Guild, Soc. Children's Book Writers, PEN. Roman Catholic. Address: 645 Hampshire Rd Apt 137 Westlake Village CA 91361

CAREY, NETTIE, health services administrator, dental hygienist; b. Balt., d. James Andrew and Emma (Johnson) C. Oral Hygiene cert., Howard U., 1959; B.S., U. D.C., 1978; M.B.P.A., Southeastern U., 1980. Dental hygiene counselor Dept. Human Services, D.C., 1960-80; chief dental dept. Constant Care Med. Center, Balt., 1980-83, asst. adminstr. health services, 1983—; chmn. bd. dirs. Social Hygiene Soc., Washington, 1982—. Recipient Alumni Achievement award Howard U. Coll. Dentistry, 1983. Mem. Am. Pub. Health Assn., Nat. Dental Hygienist Assn. (pres-elect 1983—), Bay Tri-State Dental Hygienists Assn. (pres. 1981—), Howard U. Dental Hygiene Alumni Assn. (com. chmn. 1972-82), Phi Delta Kappa. Baptist. Office: Constant Care Med Center 1501 Division St Baltimore MD 21217

CAREY, NORINE PATRICIA, golf club manufacturing company executive; b. Boston, Oct. 14, 1952; d. David Marsden and Eve (Casey) Carey. B.A. in Econs., Newton Coll. of Sacred Heart, Mass., 1974. Ins. salesperson Met. Life, N.Y.C., 1974-75; bank officer Chem. Bank, N.Y.C., 1975-80; pres. Pedersen Custom Golf Club, Co., Bridgeport, Conn., 1981—; dir. Bus. Women's Golf Assn., N.Y.C. Home: 211 E 70th St New York NY 10021 Office: Pedersen Custom Golf Club Co 312 Howard Ave Bridgeport CT 06605

CAREY, SARAH COLLINS, lawyer; b. N.Y.C., Aug. 12, 1938; d. Jerome Joseph and Susan (Atlee) Collins; m. James J. Carey, Aug. 28, 1962 (div. 1977); 1 child, Sasha; m. 2d John D. Reilly, Jan. 27, 1979; children—Sarah, Katherine. B.A., Radcliffe Coll., 1960; LL.B., Georgetown U., 1965. Bar: D.C. 1966, U.S. Supreme Ct. 1977. Soviet specialist USIA/U.S. Dept. State, 1961-65; asso. Arnold & Porter, Washington, 1965-68; asst. dir. Lawyers Com. for Civil Rights, Washington, 1968-73; ptnr. Adams Duque & Hazeltine and predecessor cos., Washington, 1973—; dir. HSB Internat.; cons. Ford Found., 1975-83, Carnegie Corp., 1984, Kettering Found., 1982—. Contbr. articles to profl. jours. Bd. dirs. New Transcentury Found., Washington, 1982—, Overseas Edn. Fund., 1982—, Inst. for Soviet-Am. Relations, 1983—, Georgetown U. Sch. Law Inst. for Pub. Representation, 1971-85, Am. Arbitration Assn., 1975-82, Vis. Nurses Assn., 1976-81. Mem. ABA (internat. law com.), D.C. Bar Assn. (sect. internat. law), Womens Bar Assn., Washington Internat. Trade Assn., others. Democrat. Office: Adams Duque & Hazeltine 1920 N St NW Suite 420 Washington DC 20036

CARGILE, DIANE J., educational administrator; b. Kelso, Wash., July 12, 1941; d. Robert L. and Kitty V. (Beverage) Young; m. Gary N. Cargile, Sept. 30, 1972; children—Larry Dean LeMaster, Ronald Cris Le Master. B.S.Ed., Mary Hardin-Baylor U., 1969; M.A.Ed., S.W. Tex. State U., 1975; Adminstr./Supt. Cert., 1976; Supervision Cert., Tarleton State U., 1980. Tchr. pub. sch. social studies and lang. arts, 1969-76; instr. Central Tex. Coll., 1971; asst. prin. Clarke Elem. Sch., Killeen, Tex., 1976-78, elem. and secondary curriculum cons., 1979-80, prin. Clarke Sch., 1981—; dir. Citizenship Curriculm Writing Project, 1979-80. Vol. presdl. campaign, 1980, city council campaign, 1980-81; del. Republican State Conv. N.Mex., 1964; elem. prin. rep. Curriculum Council, 1982-84, chmn. adminstrv. and tech. support com., 1982-84, tchr. adv. panel, 1974-76. Mem. Nat. Assn. Elem. Sch. Prins., Nat. Assn. Supervision and Curriculum Devel., Tex. Elem. Prins. and Suprs. Assn. Phi Delta Kappa, Delta Kappa Gamma. Baptist. Home: 734 Rattlesnake Rd Harker Heights TX 76543 Office: Comanche Rd Fort Hood TX 76544

CARIGNAN, DENNISE A., career counselor. Student San Francisco State U., 1977-78, Ron Bailie Sch. Broadcast, San Francisco, 1981-82. With Gibraltar Savs. & Loan Assn., San Francisco, 1972-74; pub. relations rep. Washington Bros. Distbg. Co., San Leandro, Calif., 1974-76; adminstrv. asst. Teleport Oil Co., San Francisco, 1977-79; case mgr. Project New Pride, ARC, San Francisco, 1980-83; intern news dept. Sta. KBLX-KRE Radio, Berkeley, 1983; career counselor Inner City Outpatient Services, San Francisco, 1983—. Mem., sec. audience devel. com. Oakland Symphony; mem. Chancel Choir; fundraiser S.C.A.R.E.; vol. ARC. Home: PO Box 10573 Oakland CA 94610

CARLE, DEIEDRE CATHERINE, health care administrator, corporate health consultant; b. Dayton, Ohio, June 7, 1951; d. Alonzo Roy and Catherine Vermell (Parker) C.; B.S., Central State U., 1978; M.S., U. Wis., 1980. Mem. faculty Bainbridge Christian Sch., Ga., 1972-73, Athens Christian Sch., Ga., 1973-74; phys. dir. YMCA of Greene County, Xenia, Ohio, 1974-76; exercise physiologist U. Wis.-LaCrosse, 1978-81; dir. cardiac rehab. Door County Med. Ctr., Sturgeon Bay, Wis., 1981-83; dir. cardiac rehab. St. Catherine Hosp., East Chicago, Ind., 1983—, exec. dir. corp. health services, 1983—; clin. cons. Skemp-Grandview Clinic and St. Francis Med. Ctr., LaCrosse, 1978-80; corp. health cons., Northwest Ind., Chgo., 1983—; cardiac rehab. cons., Midwestern region, 1983—; profl. tennis instr., Xenia, 1973-78. Contbr. articles to profl. jours. Race dir. Nat. Urban League, Gary, Ind., 1984. Central State U. scholar; coach of state champion varsity softball team, Athens, 1973, state champion basketball team, Bainbridge, 1974. Mem. Am. Coll. Sports Medicine (cert. exercise tech.), Am. Cardiology Techs. Assn. (registered), Assn. for Fitness in Bus., Lake County Master Gardener Assn. (master gardener). Club: Calumet Region Striders (Hammond). Avocations: gardening, running, canoeing, aquarium science, cycling. Office: St Catherine Hosp 4321 Fir St East Chicago IN 46323

CARLETON, MARY RUTH, television news anchorwoman, broadcasting educator; b. Sacramento, Feb. 2, 1948; d. Warren Alfred and Mary Gertrude (Clark) Case. B.A. in Polit. Sci., U. Calif.-Berkeley, 1970, M.J., 1974. Television news anchorwoman, reporter Sta. KXAS-TV, Ft. Worth, 1974-78, Sta. KING-TV, Seattle, 1978-80; TV news anchorwoman Sta. KOCO-TV, Oklahoma City, 1980-84; news anchor, reporter Sta. KTTV-TV, Los Angeles, 1984—; broadcast instr. U. Okla., 1981-82, Okla. Christian Coll., 1981-83. Trustee World Neighbors, 1983—; bd. dirs. Meadows Aux., 1982—, The Forum, 1982—. Named Communicator of Yr., Okla. Wildlife Fedn., 1983; Women in Communication Byliner, 1984; recipient Broadcasting award UPI, 1981; named Okla. Woman in News, Hospitality Club, 1981. Mem. Women in Communications (Clarion award 1981). Democrat. Episcopalian. Office: KTTV-TV 5746 Sunset Blvd Los Angeles CA 90028

CARLILE, OLGA GIZE, journalist; b. East Chicago, Ind., Jan. 9; d. Walter Edward and Emma Gize; B.A., Ind. U.; m. Robert Leslie Carlile, Aug. 24; children—Byron Thomas, Bradley Robert. Writer, Inland Steel Co., East Chicago; copy editor Freeport (Ill.) Jour. Standard, also soc. editor, women's editor, now asst. mng. editor. Bd. dirs. Am. Cancer Soc., Vis. Nurse Assn., Wa-tan-Ye Service Club, Community Chest, Community Concert Assn., YWCA; exec. bd. Boy Scouts Am.; v.p. Shakespeare Soc., 1975-76, bd. dirs. Jane Addamsland Park Bd. Recipient Silver Feather awards Ill. Women's Press Assn., 1974, 76, 77, 80, 81, 83, 84, 85; also awards Nat. Fedn. Press Women, UPI, AP; Sci. Writers award ADA. Mem. Nat. Fedn. Press Women (nat. bd.), Bus. and Profl. Women's Club (pres. 1960), Ill. Women's Press Assn. (v.p. 1978, 79, 80, pres. 1981—, Woman of Yr. 1981), AAUW, Women in Communications, Newspaper Food Editors and Writers Assn., PEO (v.p. 1980), LWV, Gamma Alpha Chi. Methodist. Author: Heritage Cookbook, 1976. Home: 1713 Manor Dr Freeport IL 61032 Office: 27 State Ave S Freeport IL 61033

CARLILE, PATRICIA ANN, executive search and management consultant; b. Waco, Tex., Jan. 8, 1941; d. Earl Dean Carlile and Lyndal Frances (Greer) Meadows. B.A. magna cum laude, Pace U., 1970. Asst. to pres. Patio Foods, Inc., San Antonio, 1958-60; asst. to treas. Phillips & Van Orden Co., San Francisco, 1963-67; cons. Arthur Young & Co., N.Y.C., Washington, 1970-73; staff asst. U.S. govt. agys., Washington, 1973-76; v.p. Leon A Farley Assocs., Washington, 1978-81; pres. Carlile Cons., Inc., Washington, 1981—; assoc. dir. The White House, Washington, 1981; acting exec. dir. Nat. Futures Assn., Chgo., 1982; cons. HEW, Washington, 1977, R.H. Perry & Assocs., Washington, 1978. Co-author: Executive Compensation, 1971. Recipient Superior Service award Fed. Energy Adminstrn., 1974. Mem. Greater Washington Bd. Trade, Nat. Assn. Corp. and Profl. Recruiters, Nat. Assn. Women Bus. Owners, AAUW. Republican. Avocations: tennis; theatre. Home: 4201 Cathedral Ave NW Washington DC 20036 Office: Carlile Cons Inc 1899 L St NW Suite 1001 Washington DC 20036

CARLINO, ROSE THERESE, nursing adminstr.; b. Bklyn., Oct. 3, 1928; d. Anthony and Clara (Bella) Carlino; R.N., St. Catherine's Hosp. Sch. Nursing, 1949; B.S. in Nursing, St. John's U., 1955, M.S. in Nursing Edn., 1960, M.A. in Sociology, 1976. Staff nurse St. Catherine's Hosp., 1949-51, asst. head nurse, 1951-52, head nurse, 1952-55, asst. clin. instr., supr. surgery, 1955-59, asst. dir. nursing service, 1959, asso. dir., 1959-64, dir., 1964-65; dir. nursing service Evangelical Deaconess Hosp., Bklyn., 1966-67; dir. nursing Deepdale Gen. Hosp., Little Neck, N.Y., 1967-69; asso. prof. Queensborough Community Coll., Bayside, N.Y., 1969-70, adj. prof. instl. research, 1971-73, adj. prof. community nursing and allied health curriculum devel., 1973—; asst. v.p. nursing Luth. Med. Center, Bklyn., 1970-75; v.p. and sec. bd. dirs. Queens Med. and Health Program, 1974-75; dir. nursing staff devel. St. Claire's Hosp., N.Y.C., 1978-79, cons. nursing service and edn., 1980—. Mem. N.Y. State Nurse's Assn., Nat. League for Nursing, Cath. Nurses' Assn., Am. Hosp. Assn. Soc. for Nursing Service Adminstrs., St. Catherine's Hosp. Sch. of Nursing Alumni Assn., St. John's U. Alumni Fedn., Nat. Council for Women, Bklyn. Lung Assn. (nursing adv. com.). Co-author: A Survey of Health Needs in Queens, 1971; Community Nursing, Clinical Associate, 1972. Home: 83-52 264th St Floral Park NY 11004

CARLISLE, JOHNNIE, educator; b. Wedowee, Ala., Sept. 14, 1921; d. John William and Hattie (Burrow) Carlisle; B.S., Ala. Coll., 1942; M.S., Columbia U., 1949; Ph.D., U. Tenn., 1975; m. Gordon Lee Carlisle, Oct. 15, 1950. Vocat. home econs. tchr. Gordo (Ala.) High Sch., 1942-43; supervisory tchr. vocat. home econs. Montevallo (Ala.) High Sch., 1943-45; supervisory tchr. home econs. and sci. Memphis State Tng. Sch., 1945-46; tchr. home econs. Miami Beach (Fla.) High Sch., 1946-50; asst. prof. home econs. Ala. Coll., Montevallo, 1950-57; tchr. Larrymore Elem. Sch., Norfolk, Va., 1958-59; substitute tchr. Oceanside (Calif.) Jr.-Sr. High Sch., 1960-61; tchr. biology, physics and gen. sci. Randolph County High Sch., Wedowee, Ala., 1961-62; asst. prof. home econs. U. Montevallo (Ala.), 1965—, assoc. prof., 1973-83, prof., 1983—; state advisor Coll. Home Econs. Clubs, 1954-55; mem. Ala. Nutrition Council, 1971-74, Birmingham Regional Nutrition Com., Inc., 1977-83; area worker March of Dimes, 1964-65. Recipient Disting. Service award for Grey Lady activities Kennedy Gen. Hosp., 1946; Nat. Teaching Fellowship grantee, 1967-68. Mem. Ala. Home Econs. Assn. (panel participant), Am. Home Econs. Assn., Nutrition Today Soc., Soc. for Nutrition Edn., Joint Legis. Council of Ala., Omicron Nu (nat. scholarship com. 1985—). Democrat. Baptist. Contbr. articles to profl. jours. Home: 365 Nabors St N Montevallo AL 35115 Office: 102 Bloch Hall Sta 101 Univ of Montevallo Montevallo AL 35115

CARLISLE, LILIAN MATAROSE BAKER (MRS. E. GRAFTON CARLISLE, JR.), author, lectr.; b. Meridian, Miss., Jan. 1, 1912; d. Joseph and Lilian (Flournoy) Baker; student Dickinson Coll., 1929-30, Pierce Coll. Bus. Adminstrn., 1930-31; B.A., U. Vt., 1981, M.A., 1986; m. E. Grafton Carlisle, Jr., Jan. 9, 1933; children—Mrs. E. S. Schwerdtle, Penelope. Legal sec. A. W. Sanson, Phila., 1931-35; adminstrv. sec. RAF Ferry Command, Montreal, Que., Can., 1942; exec. staff mem. in charge collections, research Shelburne (Vt.) Mus., 1951-61; exec. sec. Burlington Area Community Health Study, 1963, coordinator, 1964; asst. coordinator Vt. Mental Retardation Planning Project, 1965; project dir. 4-county Champlain Valley Medicare Alert, 1966; dir. public relations Champlain Valley Agrl. Fair, 1968-77; lectr. U. Vt. Elder Hostel program, 1976-77, mem. faculty Vacation Coll., 1980-83. Pres., Burlington Community Council for Social Welfare, 59-61, 71-73; chmn. bd. Interfaith Sr. Citizens, 1977-79; justice of peace, 1979-81; pres. Chittenden County Extension Adv. Com., 1977-78; lay mem. Gov.'s Conf. on Problems of Aging for White House Conf., 1960; chmn. publs. com. Vt. Bicentennial Commn., 1974-77; mem. Gov.'s Commn. on Mobile Homes, 1973—; mem. Vt. Ho. of Reps., 1968-70. Recipient Community Council Disting. Citizen award, 1978. Mem. Vt. (trustee, chmn. mus. com. 1967), N.Y. (faculty seminar) Chittenden (pres. 1969-72, editor Heritage Series of 10 books about Chittenden County towns 1972-76) hist. socs., Vt. Old Cemetery Assn., Vt. Folklore Soc., League Vt. Writers (dir. 1962; v.p., pres. 1967-69). Am. Pen Women (pres. Green Mountain br. 1980-82), Order Women Legislators (pres. Vt. br. 1972-74), Chi Omega. Conglist. (clk.). Club: Zonta (pres. 1964-65). Co-author: The Story of the Shelburne Museum, 1955; Profile of the Community, 1964; Environmental and Personal Health of the Community, 1964; Vermont Clock and Watchmakers, Silversmiths and Jewelers, 1970; also numerous catalogs on collections at Shelburne Mus.; editorial cons. Burlington Social Survey, 1967; contbr. articles to profl. jours. Home: 117 Lakeview Terr Burlington VT 05401

CARLISLE, LINDA SUE, oil company executive; b. Pinch, W.Va., Dec. 10, 1941; d. Dudley William and Agnes Marie (Osborne) C.; children—Cindy Lou Edds Cattell, David Earl Edds. Pres. Portraits by Ingels, 1970-82, Mineral Services, 1970-82, Ingels Realty, W.Va., 1978-82, Computer Mineral Brokerage, Inc., Bryan, Tex., 1982-83; chmn. bd. Ewing Oil of Dallas, Inc., 1983; chmn. bd., chief exec. officer, pres. First Internat. Oil and Gas, Inc., Denver, Newport Beach, Calif., Salt Lake City, Paris and London, 1983—; Bd. dirs. PASSAGES. Author: New Lady, 1977; The Mountains Speak, 1974; Traveling Heritage Road, 1973; Our Glorious Heritage, 1980; Reflections on the Ohio, 1981; Women in the 80's, 1982. Mem. CAP, SCORE/ACE, 1978-84. Mem. N. Tex. Oil and Gas Assn., Denver C. of C. Republican. Avocations: lecturing; writing; photography; fashion/jewelry designing; pilot. Office: First Internat Oil and Gas Inc 1380 Lawrence St Suite 700 Denver CO 80204

CARLSEN, DEBORAH EILEEN BETTRAY, data base analyst; b. Chgo., Nov. 6, 1956; d. Theodore Walter and Patricia Ann (Knorr) Bettray; m. Glen Carlsen, Apr. 26, 1981 (div. Dec. 1984); 1 child, Alana Lee. B.S. in Mgmt., Ill. Inst. Tech., 1978. Jr. systems analyst Milw. R.R., Chgo., 1978-79; programmer/analyst St. Paul Fed., Chgo., 1979-80; data base analyst Schwinn Bicycle, Chgo., 1980—. Mem. Nat. Assn. Female Execs. Roman Catholic. Home: 3124 N Lawndale Chicago IL 60618 Office: Schwinn Bicycle Co 1856 N Kostner Chicago IL 60639

CARLSEN, LINDA ANN, marketing executive; b. Emmetsburg, Iowa, Oct. 13, 1947; d. Axel Serenus and Artis Margaret (Henderson) C. B.A., U. Iowa, 1968; M.A., U. No. Iowa, 1975. Elem. tchr. pub. schs., Guttenberg, Iowa, 1969-71; secondary tchr. pub. schs., Andrew, Iowa, 1972-75; media specialist N.E. Iowa Tech. Inst., Dubuque, 1975-79; editorial asst. Brown Pub. Co., Dubuque, 1978-79; mktg. exec. Gemtastics, Garnavillo, Iowa, 1979—; vocat. instr. Pub. Schs. Garnavillo, 1980—. Mem. Iowa Ednl. Media Assn., NEA, Iowa State Edn. Assn. Republican. Mem. Ch. of Christ. Club: Christian Singles Assn. (Prairie du Chien Wis.). Office: Gemtastics 100 Main St Garnavillo IA 52049

CARLSON, BARBARA COIN, psychologist; b. Davenport, Iowa, July 27, 1927; d. William and Jule I. (Mulcahy) Coin; A.A., Los Angeles Valley Coll., 1964; B.S., Calif. State U., Los Angeles, 1969, M.A., 1975; Ph.D., U.S. Internat. U., San Diego, 1976; m. Douglas D. Carlson, May 8, 1948; children—Eric,

Matt, Kurt. Prof. nursing Cerritos Coll., Norwalk, Calif., 1972—; staff psychologist Spectrum Counseling Services, Arcadia, Calif., 1975—; pvt. practice clin. psychology, Rowland Heights, Calif., 1977—; pres. Profl. Assn. for Continuing Edn. Mem. Am. Psychol. Assn., Calif. Psychol. Assn., NEA, Calif. Tchrs. Assn., Am. Nurses Assn., Calif. Nurses Assn.

CARLSON, CAROLIN MCCORMICK FURST, civic worker; b. Williamsport, Pa., Apr. 20, 1934; d. S. Dale and Esther Caroline (McCormick) Furst O'Brien; B.A. cum laude, Smith Coll., 1955; m. Elton Frederic Carlson, Sept. 15, 1956 (dec. 1970); children—Eric Dale, Margaret Cora, Dwight Leonard. Caseworker, McKean County Child Welfare Services, Smethport, Pa., 1955-57; dir. First Nat. Bank of Port Allegany, Pa. Class fund sec. Abbot Acad., Phillips, Andover, 1951—; Jr. choir dir. Gethsemane Evangelical Lutheran Ch., Port Allegany, 1971-82, charter lay asst., 1972-74, 84—, congregational sec., 1973—, Theos chpt. exec. dir. and grief counselor, 1972-76, chmn. bicentennial celebration com., 1975-76, pres. Lutheran Ch. Women, 1959-61, treas., 1962-65, 84—, program chmn. 1976-80, 82—, sr. choir, 1983—, Emporium Ministerium grief counselor, 1984—; chmn. noon hour cultural series S.W. Smith Meml. Pub. Library, 1972-74, 77-78, bd. dirs., 1977—, v.p. spl. events, 1978-82, book selection, 1977—, pres. 1985; active Port Area Community TV, 1981—; den mother Allegheny Highland council Boy Scouts Am., Port Allegany, 1967-70, 76-79, sec., 1976-79, merit badge counselor, 1984—; asst. troop leader Keystone Tall Tree council Girl Scouts U.S.A., 1969-74; charter driver Meals on Wheels, 1972—; adv. bd. dirs. McKean County Children and Youth Services, 1980-83; v.p. Port Allegany High Sch. Band Boosters, 1982—; chmn. residential United Way, 1984, 85; bd. dirs. Port Allegheny Area Econ. Devel. Corp., 1984—. Recipient award Luth. Ch. Am., 1975. Mem. Smith Coll. Alumnae Assn., Abbot Acad. Alumnae Assn. Republican. Clubs: Indian Echo Country, Port Allegany Woman's (treas. 1957-60, 66-67, auditor 1965, 82, sec. 1963-65, 70-71, 2d v.p. 1967-68, 71-72, pres. 1977-79, chmn. new community pool 1977-79, choir 1961—), McKean County Women's (sec. 1958-60, 66-68, treas. 1970-72, 1st v.p. 1972-76), Coudersport Golf. Lodge: Order Eastern Star. Contbr. articles to weekly paper Reporter-Argus, 1961—. Home: 45 Church St Port Allegany PA 16743

CARLSON, DALE BICK, author; b. N.Y.C., May 24, 1935; d. Edgar M. and Estelle (Cohen) Bick; B.A., Wellesley Coll., 1957; m. Stanley Park, 1984; children—Daniel Carlson, Hannah Carlson. Author children's books, 1961—, including: Perkins the Brain, 1964; The House of Perkins, 1965; Miss Maloo, 1966; The Brainstormers; 1966; Frankenstein, 1968; Counting is Easy, 1969; Your Country, 1969; Arithmetic 1, 2, 3, 1969; The Electronic Teabowl, 1969; Warlord of the Genji, 1970; The Beggar King of China, 1971; The Mountain of Truth (Spring Festival Honor book), 1972; Good Morning Danny, 1972; Good Morning, Hannah, 1972; The Human Apes, 1973; Girls Are Equal Too, 1973; Baby Needs Shoes, 1974; Triple Boy, 1976; Where's Your Head?, 1977; The Plant People, 1977; The Wild Heart, 1977; The Shining Pool, 1979; Lovingsex for Both Sexes, 1979; Boys Have Feelings Too, 1980; Call Me Amanda, 1981; Manners that Matter, 1982; The Frog People, 1982; Charlie the Hero, 1983; 1984-85: The Jenny Dean Science Fiction Mysteries, The Mystery of the Shining Children; The Mystery of the Hidden Trap; The Secret of the Third Eye; The James Budd Mysteries; The Mystery of Galaxy Games; The Mystery of Operation Brain, 1984-85; others. Vice pres. Parents League of N.Y., editor-in-chief Parents League Bull., 1967-72. Mem. Authors League Am., Authors Guild. Address: 307 Neck Rd Madison CT 06443

CARLSON, FRANCES MARIE, data systems executive; b. Scranton, Pa., Feb. 11, 1947; d. Michael Jerome and Anne A. (Gaughan) Murphy; m. G. William Carlson, June 21, 1976; children—Jacqueline Anne, G. William Jr. B.A. in Psychology, Marywood Coll., Scranton, Pa., 1968. Asst. dir. personnel Pa. Hosp., Phila., 1968-72; personnel specialist ICI Am., Inc., Wilmington, Del., 1972-73; dir. corp. services ARA Services Inc., Phila., 1973-79; pres. Unified Data Systems, Inc., Phila., 1979—; chmn. bd., 1980—; dir. Automated Med. Systems, Inc., Phila. Bd. dirs. Pvt. Industry Council, Phila., 1983—; 1st pres. Forum Exec. Women, Phila., 1977-79. Office: Unified Data Systems Inc 841 Chestnut St Suite 1310 Philadelphia PA 19107

CARLSON, HELEN LOUISE, educator; b. Duluth, Minn., Oct. 20, 1940; d. Erling Emil and Ethel Florence (Lindberg) Nelson; B.S. summa cum laude, U. Minn., Duluth, 1961, M.A., 1975; Ph.D., U. Minn., Mpls., 1981; m. Gordon Jerome Carlson, Aug. 4, 1961; children—David J., Amy L., John D. Elem. tchr., pub. schs., Brockton, Mass., St. Paul and La Mesa, Calif., 1961-66, tchr. early child care provider, 1970-75; research asst. U. Minn., Duluth, 1975-77, instr., 1977-81, asst. prof. profl. edn., 1981—, head dept. child and family devel., 1984—; cons. St. Mary's Child Care Center, 1981-82, Midwest Regional Trainer Communication Model, 1982; bd. dirs. Duluth Early Childhood Consortium, 1981-82; mem. adv. bd. Duluth Community Schs. Parent and Family Life Programs, 1980-82, U. Minn. at Duluth Child Care Center, 1980-82; mem. edn. adv. bd. Duluth Head Start, 1979-80; adv. bd. Dean's Grant, U.S. Office Edn., Nat. Council Social Studies, Early Childhood, State history curriculum devel. project. Ednl. Devel. Program grantee, 1981-82, 82-83; lic. tchr., Minn. Mem. Nat. Assn. Edn. Young Children, Nat. Council Social Studies, Phi Delta Kappa (research grantee 1978; treas. chpt. 1978-81, v.p. chpt. 1981-82), Alpha Delta Kappa. Contbr. articles to profl. jours. Research in alt. service delivery models for learning disabled children, social interactions of infants and toddlers and their parents, 1982. Home: 4918 Jean Duluth Rd Duluth MN 55803 Office: 140 Montague Hall U Minn Duluth MN 55812

CARLSON, JEANNIE, writer; b. Bklyn., Jan. 13, 1955; d. Lloyd Arthur and Ruth Frances (Riley) Carlson; 1 child, Carl Philip. B.A., Randolph-Macon Woman's Coll., 1977. Mktg./editing rep. Harris Pub., White Plains, N.Y., 1982; adminstrv. asst. Ray Fried Assocs., Inc., Eastchester, N.Y., 1980-84; proofreader Nat. Pennysaver, Elmsford, N.Y., 1983-84; feature writer Asbury News, Crestwood, N.Y., 1983-84; chief writer P.R.S., St. Petersburg, Fla., 1984—; editor Children's Rights Am., Largo, Fla., 1984; pub. relations coordinator The Renaissance Cultural Ctr., Clearwater, Fla., 1985. Recipient Golden Poet award World of Poetry, 1985; World of Poetry award, 1983, 85; Recognition award Nat. Soc. Poets, 1979; poetry awards Internat. Publs., 1976-77. Mem. Nat. Writers Union, Nat. Assn. Female Execs. Methodist. Avocations: theatre; culinary arts.

CARLSON, JUDITH ELIZABETH, nurse; b. Penn Yan, N.Y., Aug. 26, 1946; d. Frank and Carmaletta (Wyman) Van De Mortel; R.N., Highland Hosp. Sch. Nursing, 1967; m. Dennis R. Carlson, June 3, 1967 (div.); children—Hope Stephanie, Christiaan Dennis. Staff nurse surg. unit Oceanside (Calif.) Community Hosp., 1967; staff nurse med. unit E.J. Noble Hosp., Canton, N.Y., 1968; staff nurse emergency room Corning (N.Y.) Community Hosp., 1968-70, New Hanover Meml. Hosp., Wilmington, N.C., 1972-75; staff nurse coronary care unit Duke U. Med. Center, Durham, N.C., 1975, head nurse urology clinic, supr. catheter audit team, 1976-83, head nurse dept. community and family medicine, 1983—; mem. faculty Travenol Labs., Inc., Deerfield, Ill., 1981. Co-leader, leader Girl Scouts, 1975-78. Mem. Am. Urology Allied Assn. Democrat. Methodist. Club: Duke Faculty (sec. bd. dirs. 1982-84). Home: 5604 Genesee Dr Durham NC 27712 Office: Box 3886 Duke U Med Center Durham NC 27710

CARLSON, M. SUSAN, lawyer; b. Lincoln, Nebr., Nov. 2, 1949; d. Arnold Emil and Mary (Lloyd) C.; m. Gerald Phillip Greiman, May 2, 1982; children—David Carlson Greiman, Nora Carlson Greiman. A.A., Cottey Coll., 1970; B.F.A. in Edn., U. Nebr., 1972; postgrad. Notre Dame in Japan, 1974; J.D., U. Nebr., 1976. Bar: Nebr. 1977, D.C. 1979. Tchr. history Stuart High Sch. (Nebr.), 1972-73; law clk. U.S. Ct. Appeals 8th Circuit, St. Louis, 1976-78; assoc. Kilcullen, Smith & Heenan, Washington, 1978-79; trial atty. U.S. Dept. Justice, Washington, 1980—, trial atty. land claims litigation, Guam, 1980-81. Founding dir. Nebr. Legal Research Service, Lincoln, 1975. Nebr. Bar Assn., D.C. Bar Assn., ABA, NOW.

CARLSON, NICOLA LOUISE, petroleum landman; b. Denver, July 27, 1955; d. John Joseph and Lillian Lucy (Cavarra) Gaudio; m. Gerald Duane Carlson, Oct. 27, 1979 (div. 1982); 1 son, Todd Clinton. B.A., U. Colo.-Denver, 1976. Mineral landman Exxon Minerals Co., Denver, 1977-81; petroleum landman TCPL Resources U.S.A. Ltd., Wessely Energy Corp., Dallas, 1981—. Mem. DALENPAC, 1982—. Mem. Am. Assn. Petroleum Landmen, Denver Assn. Petroleum Landmen, Dallas Assn. Petroleum Landmen, (treas. 1983-84, dir. 1984—), Rocky Mountain Assn. Mineral Landmen (treas. 1979-80, v.p. 1980-81, pres. 1981-82, service award 1982). Republican. Roman Catholic.

CARLSON, PRISCILLA MARTHA, publishing executive; b. New Haven, Aug. 20, 1951; d. Harold Oscar and Elizabeth Ann (Allen) C.; m. Peter Allen Benson, Aug. 2, 1980; 1 child, Jesse Allen. B.A., U. Conn., 1974. Prodn. editor Random House Ency., 1976-78; editor Random House Unabridged Dictionary, 1978-80; v.p., editorial and photog. services Research Publs., Inc., Woodbridge, Conn., 1981—. Mem. ALA (micropub. com.), Am. Nat. Standards Inst. (Z39 com.), Nat. Assn. Female Execs., Assn. Info. and Image Mgmt. Democrat. Roman Catholic. Address: Research Publications Inc 12 Lunar Dr Woodbridge CT 06565

CARLSON, RIA MARIE, public relations executive, writer; b. Los Angeles, Apr. 8, 1961; d. Erick Gustaf and Roberta Rae (Bandelin) C.; m. James Bradley Gerdts, May 19, 1985. B.A. cum laude, U. So. Calif., 1983. Assoc. producer NBC, Burbank, Calif., 1983-85; account exec. Kerr & Assocs. Pub. Relations, Huntington Beach, Calif., 1985—; free lance writer, 1985—. Scriptwriter award ceremony Latin Bus. Assn., 1985; author, editor newsletter Am. Sch. Food Service Assn. Bus. Report, 1985-86; contbr. articles to publs. Prodn. asst. Profiles in Pride, Black History Month, Burbank, 1985. Sealbearer Calif. Scholarship Fedn., 1983. Mem. Nat. Assn. Female Execs., Am. Film Inst., U. So. Calif. Alumni Assn., Blackstonians Pre-Law Hon. Soc. (life). Republican. Roman Catholic. Avocations: writing short stories; reading; skiing; softball; travel. Office: Kerr & Associates Inc 4911 Warner Ave Suite 208 Huntington Beach CA 92649

CARLSON, WILDA MAY, real estate sales agent; b. Rome, N.Y., Dec. 10, 1920; d. Percy Lloyd and Pearl Jessie (Huey) Bucklin; R.N., Buffalo Deaconess Hosp. Sch. Nursing, 1942; Public Health Nurse, SUNY, Buffalo, 1961; m. LeRoy E. Carlson, June 14, 1947; children—Nancy Carlson Stone, Carol Carlson Yannie. Admissions, supr. nurse W.C.A. Hosp., Jamestown, N.Y., 1942-45; indsl. nurse Proto Tool Co., Jamestown, 1963-65, 70-72, Marlin Rockwell div. TRW Corp., Falconer, N.Y., 1969-70; real estate saleswoman, 1973-74, 77—; dir. Fenton Park Nursing Home, 1965-67; nurse Chautauqua County Resource Center, Jamestown, 1981-82. Pres., Kiantone Mothers Club, Stillwater Ch.; Republican com. woman Kiantone Twp., 1950. Jamestown Vis. Nurse Assn. grantee, 1960-61. Mem. Chautauqua County Grad. Nurses Assn. Club: Women's Bus. and Profl. (Marvin) House. Home: 512 Barr St Jamestown NY 14701

CARLTON, BERTHA SUE, data processing executive; b. Bruce, Miss., Feb. 23, 1948; d. Ruby Marion Nichols and Virlon Levesta (Stacy) Nichols Goree; m. Charlie Lee Carlton, Nov. 9, 1968; 1 son, William Ben. B.S. in Bus. Tech. magna cum laude, U. Houston, 1983. Ops. supr. Aramco Services Co., Houston, 1978-82, analyst computer processing, 1982—. Recipient 1st Pl. Voice trophy Garland's Am. Guild Music, Houston, 1981, 82. Mem. Computer Security Inst. Baptist. Home: 1802 Sunny Dr Houston TX 77093 Office: Houston Lighting and Power Co 611 Walker St Houston TX 77002

CARLTON, LOIS BLOODGOOD, lawyer; b. Norfolk, Va., Jan. 30, 1942; d. Claude Frizzell and Margaret Belma (Howell) Bloodgood, Jr.; m. Thomas Clarence Carlton, June 10, 1967 (div. 1979); children—Thomas Clarence, Kathryn Howell. B.S., Barry Coll., 1978; J.D., Nova Law Sch., 1981. Bar: Fla. 1981. Sec.-typist U.S. Naval Air Sta., Norfolk, Va., 1960-64; sec. Comdr. Naval Forces, Iceland, 1964-66, NASA, Washington, 1966; sec. to chmn. bd. NUS Corp., Washington, 1966-67; law clk. to judge U.S. Cir. Ct., Ft. Lauderdale, Fla., 1980; ptnr. Scherer, Fishman & Carlton, Ft. Lauderdale, 1981—; spl. master apptd. by Judge Burnstein for supplementary hearing, Ft. Lauderdale, 1981—. Mem. Jr. Symphony Guild, Jr. League Ft. Lauderdale. Recipient Cert. of Merit, Nova Law Jour., 1979-80. Mem. ABA, Broward County Bar Assn., Broward County Women Lawyers Assn., Phi Alpha Delta. Republican. Episcopalian. Club: Quadrangle Tennis (Coral Springs, Fla.). Office: Scherer Fishman & Carlton 2734 E Oakland Park Blvd Ft Lauderdale FL 33306

CARLYSLE, SALLY JO, health services executive; b. Washington, Pa., Sept. 22, 1939; d. Donald Crawford and Bernice Meryl (Dowler) Ewing; m. Robert Wilkie, Aug. 9, 1986; children by previous marriage—Bonnie Vey, L. Craig. Student U. Pitts., Community Coll. of Allegheny County, LaSalle Extension U. Various secretarial positions U. Pitts. Grad. Sch. Public Health, 1957-65; fellowship sec. Indsl. Health Found., Pitts., 1965-67, asst. office mgr., 1967-71, office mgr. 1971-73, dir. office services, 1973-79, v.p. adminstrn., 1979—, also sec., trustee. Active Exec. Women's Council Greater Pitts. Mem. Am. Mgmt. Assn., Nat. Assn. Female Execs., Pitts. Bus. and Profl. Women's Club. Club, Order Eastern Star. Office: 34 Penn Circle W Pittsburgh PA 15206

CARMAN, IRENE HARRIET, home improvement drafting services company executive, consultant; b. Bklyn., July 12, 1924; d. Ralph and Clara Helen (Oster) Church; m. Raymond Oliver Carman, Sr., Apr. 19, 1942 (dec. 1976); children—Raymond Oliver, James Robert, Richard Thomas, Leah Rae, Ronald Lee, Irene Lynne, Russell Ray. Proof reader Marsh & McLennon Inc., N.Y.C., 1942; shipment researcher and tracer L.I.R.R., N.Y.C., 1945; building permit securer H. Reichheimer, Inc., Hicksville, N.Y., 1958-59; ptnr. R&H Drafting Corp., Hicksville and Levittown, 1959-64, owner, Levittown, 1964-72, pres., owner, 1972—. Dir. sr. citizens affairs Calvary Protestant Ch., Baldwin, N.Y., 1983—, bd. trustees, 1980—, recording sec., tchr., 1982—. Mem. Home Improvement Council, Levittown C. of C. (bd. dirs. 1977-81, pres., 1981-83). Republican. Avocations: collectibles, opera, literature, gardening, cooking, bowling. Office: R&H Drafting Corp 2900 Hempstead Turnpike Levittown NY 11756

CARMANY, KAREN MARIE, car rental company executive; b. Barberton, Ohio, July 15, 1941; d. Waitman Martin and Inez Marie (Gatts) Howell; m. James Paul Carmany, Aug. 20, 1960 (div. 1969); children—James David (dec.), Tawnya Marie Carmany-Smothermon; m. Ronald Julian Rudin, Apr. 20, 1985. B.A., Golden State U., 1982. Dir. patient services North Shore Hosp., Miami, Fla., 1971-76, Valley Hosp., Las Vegas, 1976-78; sales rep. L&N Uniform, Santa Ana, Calif., 1979-83; sales mgr. Avis Rent-A-Car, Las Vegas, 1983—. Bd. dirs. C. of C., Las Vegas, 1985-86, sec. to bd., 1986, membership chmn., 1985. Named semi-finalist Women of Achievement, C. of C. Women's Council, 1986; recipient Thomas A. First Humanitarian award Am. Hosp. Assn., 1973. Mem. Womens Convention Sales Assn. (pres. 1986—, treas. 1984), Hotel Sales Mktg. Assn. Club: Silver Key ITC (Las Vegas) (v.p. 1985-86). Avocations: reading, travel, fishing, backpacking. Home: 5113 Alpine Pl Las Vegas NV 89107 Office: Avis Rent-A-Car 5164 Rent Car Rd Las Vegas NV 89119

CARNAHAN, FRANCES MORRIS, magazine editor; b. Evergreen, Ala., Oct. 28, 1937; d. Houston DeLeon and Rene Vester (Bass) Morris; m. Peter Malott Carnahan, Feb. 13, 1960; children—Brian Morris, Edmund Malott. Student, U. Ala., 1956-58. With Mobile Press-Register, 1956-58, H.L. Green Co., N.Y.C., 1958-60, J.H. Lewis Advt. Agy., Mobile, 1960-61; with Early Am. Life mag., Hist. Times, Inc., Harrisburg, Pa., 1972—; editor Early Am. Life, 1975—. Costume designer, Harrisburg Community Theatre, 1961-71, Gov. Pa. Sch., 1976-77; Author articles. Mem. Am. Soc. Mag. Editors. Home: 1524 Greening Ln Harrisburg PA 17110 Office: Historical Times Inc 2245 Kohn Rd Harrisburg PA 17105

CARNES, LORRAINE, manufacturing company executive; b. Flint, Mich., Nov. 13, 1950; d. Lawrence and Johnnie Mae (Walls) Metcalfe; widowed; children—William Craig II. B.S., Central Mich. U., 1985. Sec. S.O.D.A.T., Flint, 1974-75; mortgage rep. Gen. Mortgage Co., Flint, 1974-75; labor relations staff BOC Metal Fab., Grand Blanc, Mich., 1983-84, supr. of hourly prodn., 1976-84, departmental planner, 1985—, quality of work life coordinator, 1983—. Mem. Ind. Bus. Girls Assn., Big Sisters Assn., Am. Mgmt. Assn., Nat. Assn. for Exec. Females. Democrat. Roman Catholic. Clubs: Flint Golferetts (sec. 1984—). Avocations: golf; bowling; swimming; sewing; reading; arts and crafts; karate; piano. Home: 1514 Wabash Ave Flint MI 48505 Office: BOC Metal Fabricating 10800 S Saginaw St Grand Blanc MI 48439

CARNESOLTAS, ANA-MARIA, lawyer; b. Havana, Cuba, Feb. 9, 1948; came to U.S., 1962; d. Manuel Ramon and Zenaida de las Mercedes (Enriquez) Carnesoltas. B.A., U. Calif.-Santa Barbara, 1970; J.D., Loyola Law Sch., Los Angeles, 1978. Bar: Calif. 1978, Fla. 1979. Dep probation officer Probation Dept., Santa Barbara, Calif., 1970-73; personnel analyst Dept. Personnel, Los Angeles, 1973-77; dep. dist. atty. Dist. Atty.'s Office, Los Angeles, 1978-80; asst. U.S. atty. U.S. Atty.'s Office, Miami, Fla., 1980-82; pvt. practice law, Miami, 1982-83; asst. city atty. City Atty.'s Office, Miami, 1983—; lectr. YMCA, Miami, 1983. Bd. dirs. Am. Heart Assn., Miami, 1983. Named Disting. Advocate, Loyola Law Sch., 1978. Mem. Calif. Probation Parole and Corrections Assn. (v.p. 1972-73), Cuban Am. Attys. Council, Cuban Am. Bar Assn. (dir. 1983, sec. 1984), Dade County Bar Assn., ABA, Fla. Assn. Women Lawyers, Assn. Trial Lawyers Am., Fed. Bar Assn. Democrat. Roman Catholic. Club: Latin Bus. and Profl. Women's (pres. 1984-85). Office: City Attys Office 169 E Flagler St Suite 1101 Miami FL 33131

CARNEVALE, FRANCA NELKEN, trade co. exec.; b. Rome, Feb. 10, 1937; came to U.S., 1968, naturalized, 1977; d. Leone Boris and Annita (Budin) Nelken; D. Pharm. cum laude, Rome U., 1959; m. Dario Carnevale, Feb. 28, 1959; children—Daniela, Flavia, Fulvia, Dario. Pharmacology tchr. Rome U., 1952-62; researcher on drugs, Suez Hosp., Egypt, 1963, Beirut (Lebanon) Italian Hosp., 1964-65; researcher children's allergies Bucharest Children's Hosp., 1966; internat. coordinator European lit. and publs. Pharmacology Inst. of Rome, Des Plaines, Ill., 1970; internat. coordinator S.Am. lit. and publs. Pharmacology Inst. of Bogota (Colombia), Miami, Fla., 1972; exec. v.p. Dafra Internat., Inc., Miami, 1978—; tchr., cons.; dir. Mem. Pharmacist Assn. Rome. Roman Catholic. Clubs: Ionosphere, B.A. Exec., Sons of Italy.

CARNEVALE, SALLY LONDON, textile marketing official; b. Newark, Mar. 17, 1954; d. Allen Jay and Elaine (Rose) London; m. Louis Michael Carnevale, May 25, 1980. B.S., U. Del., 1976; M.B.A., U. Wis., 1978. Cons., auditor Bus. Adv. Ctr., Wausau, Wis., 1977-78; market planner Celanese Fibers Mktg. Co., Celanese Corp., Charlotte, N.C., 1978-80, market research and planning analyst Celanese Fibers Ops., N.Y.C., 1980-82, fibers sales and merchandising rep., 1982-84; product mgr. home furnishings Collins & Aikman Corp., 1984-85, nat. sales mgr. home furnishings, 1985—. Mem. Big Bros./Big Sisters, Newark, Del., 1973-76, placement coordinator, Madison, Wis., 1976-78, big sister, Charlotte, N.C., 1978-81; vol. tutor dept. Social Services, various locations, 1975-80. Mem. Am. Mktg. Assn., Am. Field Service, Mu Kappa Tau. Club: Hadassah (life). Home: 253 E Palisade Ave Englewood NJ 07631 Office: 210 Madison Ave New York NY 10016

CARNEY, BARBARA JOYCE, executive search consultant; b. Chgo.; d. Maurice David and Celia (Baylen) Sachnoff; B.A. cum laude, UCLA, 1964; M.Ed., Nat. Coll. Edn., 1968; children—Michael, Michelle. Tchr., North Suburban Chgo. pub. schs., 1965-68; mfrs. rep. Shardon Mktg. Inc., Chgo., 1976-78; Midwestern regional sales mgr. Superscope, Inc., Chatsworth, Calif., 1977-80; nat. spl. markets sales mgr. Ronco, Inc., Elk Grove Village, Ill., 1980-81; exec. search cons. Womack & Assos., Inc., Chgo., 1982-85; prin. B. Carney & Assocs., 1985—. Bd. dirs. North Shore Mental Health Assn., 1975-76; chpt. v.p., chmn. LWV, 1968-76. Mem. Women in Mgmt., AAUW, Am. Soc. Profl. and Exec. Women, Nat. Assn. Female Execs. Office: 2020 Lincoln Park W Chicago IL 60614

CARNEY, KAY, actress, theater director, educator; b. Rice Lake, Wis., Aug. 2, 1933; d. Rexford Hugh and Margot Caroline (Haanstad) C.; B.S., U. Wis., 1955; M.A., Mt. Holyoke Coll., 1958; postgrad. Centre du Théâtre Nationale, 1970, Columbia U. and Case-Western Res. U., 1957-63; Creative Arts fellow U. Colo., 1963. Actress performing in London, Paris, Istanbul, Ankara, Tel Aviv and Nicosia, 1970-72, performing in Off Off-Broadway! An Anthology with Kay Carney, N.Y.C., Chgo., San Francisco, Vancouver, Balt., Phila., Boston and various U.S. colls., 1973—; performed Tongues, 1985, Camptown Ladies, 1986; dir. Mourning Pictures, Broadway and Lenox Arts Center, 1974, A Pretty Passion, Interart Theatre, N.Y.C., 1982, Quilt Pieces, Theatre of Open Eye, N.Y.C., 1983, Superwoman Bites the Dust, Playwright's Platform, Boston, 1984, numerous others; tchr. acting, directing and psychophys. work Hunter Coll., Henry St. Playhouse, SUNY, Purchase, U. Calif.-Santa Cruz, 1977-80; assoc. prof. dept. theatre Smith Coll., Northampton, Mass., 1980-82, Bklyn. Coll., 1983—; condr. workshops for profls. in U.S. and abroad; organizer, trainer La Mama theatre groups, Paris and Tel Aviv; bd. dirs. Bear Rep. Theatre, 1977-79; performed with Open Theater, 1965-67; seminarian with Jerzy Grotowski, 1970. Moratorium organizer, performer Angry Artists Against the War, 1966-70; mem. Performing Artists for Nuclear Disarmament, 1981—, St. Clements Arts in Religious Action Com., 1972-75; organizer Bay Area Women in Theatre Orgn., 1978-80. Kosciuszko Found. grantee, 1979; SUNY Research Found. grantee, 1976. Mem. Soc. Stage Dirs. and Choreographers, Actors Equity, AFTRA, East Central Theatre Conf., Am. Theatre Assn. (exec. com. women's program, presenter nat. convs.), League Profl. Theatre Women/N.Y. Democrat. Episcopalian. Contbr. articles to profl. jours. Office: Theatre Dept Bklyn College Brooklyn NY 11210

CARNEY, LORA ANNE, sales consultant; b. Sharon, Mass., July 15, 1951; d. Loring Woodbury and Ruth (Tompkins) C. B.A. magna cum laude in English, U. Mass., 1974; M.B.A. in Mktg., U. Tex.-Arlington, 1982. Stats. analyst Christian Sci. Pub. Soc., Boston, 1974-75; asst. dir. pub. info. Electric Council of New Eng., Bedford, Mass., 1975-77; programmer analyst Bell Helicopto Textron, Fort Worth, 1979-81; cons. intern Rath & Strong Systems Products Inc., Dallas, 1977-79, cons., 1981-83, sales cons., 1983—; cons. Barter Group, Arlington, 1981-83. Author of papers in field. Mem. Am. Prodn. and Inventory Control Soc., Soc. Tech. Communicators, Am. Nuclear Soc. (chmn. publs. com. 1975-76), Inst. Mgmt. Cons. Office: Rath & Strong Systems Products Inc 14901 Quorum Dr Suite 600 Dallas TX 75240

CARNEY, PAT, Canadian minister of energy, mines and resources, economist; b. Shanghai, China, May 26, 1935; d. John James and Dora (Sanders) C. B.A. in Econs. and Polit. Sci., U. B.C., 1960, M.A. in Regional Planning, 1977. Econ. journalist various publs. including Vancouver Sun, The Toronto Star, N.Y. Times, Times of London, 1955-70; owner, cons. Gemini North Ltd., Vancouver, B.C. and Yellowknife, Alta., Can., 1970-80; mem. Can. Ho. of Commons, from 1980; minister of energy, mines and resources, 1984—; project mgr. B.C. Ministry of Edn., 1977-78; project dir. B.C. Communications, Inc., 1979; asst. dir. gen. UN Human Settlements (HABITAT), 1976; Progressive Conservative critic Sec. of State, 1980, minister of state, 1981, minister of fin., 1983, minister of energy, mines and resources, 1983—. Writer TV spls. on fin. and econs., CBC. Recipient Can. Women's Press award, 1968, MacMillan Bloedel Ltd. awards (3). Mem. Assn. Profl. Economists of B.C., Can. Inst. Planners. Mem. Fed. Progressive Conservative Party. Club: Rideau (Ottawa). Office: Room 440-N Centre Block Parliament Bldgs Ottawa ON K1A 0A6 Canada

CARNEY, PHILLITA TOYIA, marketing communications management company executive; b. Chgo., Apr. 18, 1952; d. Phillip Leon Carney and Margaret Clarice (Ewing) Brown; m. John Andrus Davis, Mar. 4, 1985. Student, U. Utah, 1971-74; B.S. in Bus., Westminster Coll., 1976. Corp. tng. dir. U&I Sugar Corp., Salt Lake City, also Moses Lake, Wash., 1976-77; program coordinator Div. on Aging, Seattle, 1977-78; bus. devel. officer Del Green Assoc., Foster City, Calif., 1978-79; regional v.p. Equitec Fin. Group, San Francisco, Irvine and Oakland, Calif., 1979-84, United Resources, Oakland, 1984-86; owner, mgr. Carney & Assocs., Oakland, 1986—; dir. Total One, San Francisco, cons. in field. Moderator, creator pub. affairs radio program, 1975-76 (Best Pub. Affairs Program award Nat. Pub. Radio 1976). Del., White House Conf. on Small Bus., Washington, 1986. Recipient award Am. Legion, 1970; DAR, 1970. Mem. Internat. Assn. Fin. Planning, Women Entrepreneurs, Bus. and Profl. Women, Sales Mktg. Exec. Assn., Zonta Internat. (pres. 1985—). Avocations: jogging; swimming; reading; writing. Home: 1325 Alvarado Rd Berkeley CA 94705 Office: 580 Grand Ave Oakland CA 94610

CARNIE, MARY CATHERINE, TV station executive; b. Clayton, Ala., Oct. 25, 1938; d. Ories Kendall and Harriet Catherine (Scheffer) White; m. Gary Miles Carnie, Dec. 22, 1958 (div. May 1969); 1 child, Kendall Joanne. Cert. in Acting, Pasadena Playhouse Coll. Theatre Arts, 1959. Profl. actress Turn of the Century Cabaret Theatre, El Paso, Tex., 1962-73; continuity asst. KROD-TV, El Paso, 1968-69; drama critic El Paso Jour., 1977-78; continuity dir. KDBC-TV, El Paso, 1969—; continuity/promotion mgr. KDBC-TV, El Paso, 1982—; researcher Biog. Dictionary, Notable Women in Am. Theatre, 1982; scriptwriter Your Chamber and You, 1981, Your Zoo Needs You, 1973. Contbr. articles to profl. jours. Mem. task force Cultural Planning Project, El Paso, 1985; dir. edn. El Paso Zool. Soc. Bd., 1974; bd. dirs. Delta Day Care Ctr., 1973-78; mem. scholarship com., vocat. placement adv. com. El Paso/Ysleta Ind. Sch. Dist., 1979—; ruling elder Presbyn. Ch., 1971-77. Flat Rock Playhouse scholar, 1960. Mem. Actor's Fund Am. (life), Broadcasting Promotion and Mktg. Execs., Tex. Press Women (recording sec. 1983-85), Nat. Fedn. Press Women. Club: United Presbyn. Women. Avocations: reading; traveling. Home: 315 S Ascarate St El Paso TX 79905 Office: KDBC-TV 2201 Wyoming El Paso TX 79903

CARNS, SUSANNE, broadcasting executive, broadcaster; b. Ravenna, Ohio, Oct. 28, 1949; d. Stanley Benjamin and Betty (Carns) Gubanc. Grad. Conn. Sch. Broadcasting, 1977; student in theatre U. Akron, 1967-68, U. Mo.-Kansas City, 1968-69. Actress Longwharf Theatre, New Haven, 1973-74; news anchor Sta.-WIOF, Waterbury, Conn., 1974-75; air personality, newscaster Sta.-WSLR, Akron, Ohio, 1975-78; air personality Sta.-WSOY, Decatur, Ill., 1978-81; program dir., air personality Sta.-WMAY, Springfield, Ill., 1983—; songwriter; singer. Mem. Rd. Runners, Bicycle Club. Avocations: running; bicycling; biathlons; cooking music. Home: 1301 C Denison Dr Springfield IL 62704 Office: Sta-WMAY PO Box 460 Springfield IL 62705

CARON, VIVIENNE MARIE, educator, nun; b. Chathan, Ont., Can., Jan. 13, 1928; d. Adelard Joseph and Anne Rovina (Gamble) C. B. of Sacred Music, Pius X Sch. of Liturgical Music, Manhattanville Coll., 1967; B.A., U. Windsor, 1969. Joined Ursuline Sisters, Roman Catholic Ch., 1947. Tchr. Ont. Sch. Systems, 1951-63; dir. sisters formation Ursuline Sisters, Chatham, Ont., 1963-67, choir dir. Ursuline Sisters and Students, 1963-72; religious superior Ursuline Sisters, Toronto, Ont., 1973-78, Tecumseh, Ont., 1979-81; adminstr., religious superior Ursuline Sisters, Brescia Coll., London, Ont., 1981-85; tchr. French and world religions Brennan High Sch., Windsor, Ont., 1985—. Producer, dir. record Praise God, 1964. Chmn. religious assts. Young Christian Students, London diocese, 1960-66; mem. liturgical music commn., London, 1960-68.

CAROTHERS, JANE HOUGHTON, fine arts auction firm adminstr.; b. Corning, N.Y., Nov. 28, 1930; d. Arthur Amory and Jane Olmsted (McMillan) Houghton; grad. Foxcroft Sch., 1948, Katherine Gibbs Sch., 1950; student Wells Coll., 1948-49; children—Susan, Jane, Hope, Peter Hadley Exec. asst. Sotheby Parke Bernet, 1981—. Mem. women's com. N.Y. Public Library, 1958-60; mem. adv. com. Sawtooth Nat. Forest, 1971; chmn. Sun Valley Village Hosp. Emergency Room Aux., 1969-71; vol. pediatric recreation N.Y. Hosp., 1974-75; vol., mem. benefit com. Hosp. Spl. Surgery, 1974-75; mem. adv. bd. Exec. High Sch. Internships Am. Chmn., Vols. for Nixon-Lodge, Blaine County, Idaho, 1960; Republican precinct committeeman Blaine County, 1968-73; del. Idaho State Rep. Conv., 1968, 70; page Rep. Nat. Conv., 1968; chmn. Vols. for Nixon-Agnew, Blaine County, 1968; co-chmn. host com. Lt. Gov.'s Conv., 1971; Idaho chmn. Regional Women's Western States Conf., Phoenix, 1972; mem. N.Y. com. U.S. Ski Team. Trustee Blaine County Sch. Dist. 61; chmn. bd. trustees Corning (N.Y.) Public Library, 1957-60; bd. dirs Ketchum Community Library, 1965, chmn. bd. dirs., 1969, 70; trustee Sun Valley Ski Edn. Found., 1968-73, pres., 1969-73; trustee African-Am. Inst. (nominating com. 1975—, vol. 1975—, co-chmn. benefit com. 1977). Club: Sun Valley (Idaho) Ski (gov. 1969-73). Home: 320 E 46th St New York NY 10017 Office: 45 E 45th St New York NY 10017

CAROUSSO, DOROTHEE HUGHES, author, lecturer, genealogist; b. Winthrop, Mass., Oct. 4, 1909; d. Patrick Lawrence and Luella (Nowell) Hughes; student pub. schs., St. Agnes Acad., College Point, N.Y., Kurt's Bus. Sch., Los Angeles; L.H.D. (hon.), Combs Coll., 1968; m. Georges Carousso, Dec. 31, 1930; 1 dau., Dorothee Nowell (Mrs. George Neil McKinnon). Author: (fiction) Open Then the Door, 1942; Sports Afield, 1960; (TV plays) Climax, Studio One; also fiction, verse in Collier's, Household, All-Story, Gothic Stories, mags., Woman's Home Companion, Canadian Home Jour.; geneal. works have appeared in Geneal. Mag. N.J., Pa. Geneal. Mag., Nat. Geneal. Soc. Quar., Md. and Del. Genealogist, N.Y. Gen. and Biog. Record, New Eng. Hist. and Geneal. Register; book critic Bklyn. Eagle. Fellow Geneal. Soc. Pa. (hon. v.p.); mem. Hist. Soc. Pa., Nat. Geneal. Soc., Montgomery County (Pa.), Buck County (Pa.), hist socs., Nat. Soc. Colonial Dames Am., D.A.R., Descs. Colonial Clergy, Colonial Daus. 17th Century, Bucks County Writers Guild, New Eng. Historic Geneal. Soc., N.Y. Geneal. and Biog. Soc., Suffolk County Hist. Soc., Smithtown Hist. Soc., Daus. Utah Pioneers, Pa. Soc. New Eng. Women, Library Co. Phila. Address: 64 Cygnet Dr Smithtown NY 11787

CAROZZOLO, SHIRLEY JEAN, clergywoman; b. Buffalo, Nov. 21, 1935; d. Albert A. and Jean Louise (Hanna) La Chiusa; m. Vito A. Carozzolo, Sept. 17, 1966; children—Michael John Kurban, David Charles Kurban. Various secretarial positions, 1953-55, 68-74; office mgr. Haney Erection Services Inc., Tonawanda, N.Y., 1975-76, corp. sec., 1976-84, EEO officer, 1980-84; ordained minister of gospel Full Gospel Assemblies Internat.; corp. sec.-treas. New Covenant Evang. Ministries Inc., 1984—; fin. adminstr. World Outreach Conf., 1985; treas. New Covenant Tabernacle, 1985—. Mem. Niagara Frontier Subcontractors Assn. (membership chmn. 1978), Leadership Council Western N.Y. Am. Soc. Profl. and Exec. Women, Nat. Assn. Women in Constrn., Christian Ministries Assn. (1st v.p. 1985—), Nat. Assn. Ch. Bus. Adminstrs. Republican. Club: Kenmore Zonta (1st v.p. 1979-81, pres. 1981-82). Home: 426 Ashford Ave Tonawanda NY 14150 Office: One World Ministries Ctr PO Box 26 Buffalo NY 14223

CARPENTER, BETTE MARIE (MRS. HERBERT LARSON CARPENTER), Realtor, bldg. contractor; b. Hemet, Calif., Mar. 8, 1927; d. Scott William and Eugenia LeProhon (de Beaufert) Carl; student Oceanside Jr. Coll., 1943-45, UCLA, 1945-47; A.A., Rutledge Coll., 1982; postgrad. in law; m. Herbert Larson Carpenter, May 6, 1944; 1 dau., Carolyn Lee (Mrs. Kenneth Ray Dabbs). Propr., Bette M. Carpenter, Realtors, Carlsbad and Riverside, Calif., 1954-60; pres. Interstate Equities Corp., Carlsbad, 1960—; v.p., sec. LanInCo Corp. Nev., Las Vegas, 1964-72; v.p. mktg. Parkside Devel. Co., Santa Ana, Calif. Mem. Carlsbad Bd. Realtors (charter mem.), Calif. Real Estate Assn., Nat. Assn. Real Estate Bds., Nat. Inst. Real Estate Brokers, Urban Land Inst., Women Council Realtors, San Diego Assn. Legal Assts., Carlsbad C. of C. Republican. Office: San Jacinto CA and El Camino Real Carlsbad CA 92008

CARPENTER, CAROL SETTLE, banker; b. Schenectady, Oct. 22, 1953; d. Carl Oscar and Ursula Elsen (McEldowney) Settle; m. R. Jay Carpenter, May 4, 1985. B.S. in Bus. Adminstrn., Rochester Inst. Tech., 1975. Mgmt. trainee Lincoln First Bank, Rochester, N.Y., 1976-77; investment sec. Blyth Eastman Dillon, Scottsdale, Ariz., 1977-79; stockbroker E.F. Hutton, Scottsdale, 1979; stockbroker Rauscher Pierce Refsnes, Scottsdale, 1979-81; exec. v.p. RL Kotrozo Inc., Scottsdale, Ariz., 1981-85; trust officer United Bank Ariz., Phoenix, 1985—. Mem. Nat. Assn. Female Execs., Phi Gamma Nu. Republican. Presbyterian. Avocations: composing music; golf. Home: 374 E Verde Ln Phoenix AZ 85012 Office: 3300 N Central Ave Phoenix AZ 95012

CARPENTER, CINDY, university administrator; b. Memphis, Jan. 11, 1957; d. John William and Joyce Elizabeth (McDivitt) Carpenter. B.A., Union U., 1979. Asst. pub. relations dir. La. Coll., Pineville, 1979-80; prodn. coordinator Sta. WBBJ-TV, Jackson, Tenn., 1980-81; tour dir. Casey Jones Village, Jackson, 1981-82; membership mgr. C. of C., Jackson, 1982-83; dir. pub. relations Union U., Jackson, 1983—. Editor: The Unionite, 1983-85. Mem. com. Tenn. Homecoming '86 State of Tenn., 1985—. Mem. Baptist Pub. Relations Assn., Media Exchange Assn., Pub. Relations Soc. Am. Republican. Baptist. Avocations: reading; tennis; swimming; aerobics; antiques. Office: Union Univ Hwy 45 By-pass N Jackson TN 38305

CARPENTER, DOROTHY FULTON, state legislator; b. Ismay, Mont., Mar. 13, 1933; d. Daniel A. and Mary Ann (George) Fulton; B.A., Grinnell Coll., 1955; m. Thomas W. Carpenter, June 12, 1955; children—Mary Ione, James Thomas. Tchr. elem. schs., Houston, and Iowa City, 1955-58; mem. Iowa Ho. Reps., 1980—, asst. minority floor leader, 1982—. Pres. Planned Parenthood of Iowa, 1970; bd. dirs. Planned Parenthood Fedn. Am., 1977-80; fin. chmn. Episcopal Diocese of Iowa, 1979-80. Recipient Grinnell Coll. Alumni award, 1980. Mem. NOW, Common Cause. Republican.

CARPENTER, EDNA KEGLEY, dietitian; b. Newport News, Va., Apr. 28, 1945; d. Clarence Lee and Audrey Lee (Stephenson) Kegley; m. Robert P. Carpenter, Dec. 13, 1969 (dec. 1984); children—Andrew Scott, Jason Patrick. B.S., James Madison U., 1967; postgrad. Med. Coll. Va., 1968. Registered dietician, Va. Adminstrv. dietitian St. Joseph's Hosp., Syracuse, N.Y., 1969-72, Hampton Gen. Hosp., Va., 1973-76; cons. dietitian, Middlesex County, Va., 1976-77; food service dir. Gloucester Schs., Va., 1977-78, Rappahannock Hosp., Kilmarnock, Va., 1978-83, Charter Colonial Inst., Newport News, 1983—. Author: Diet Manual Hampton Gen. Hosp., 1973; Diet Manual Rappahannock Hospital, 1977; Diet Manual Charter Colonial Hospital, 1986. Mem. Tidewater Dietetic Assn. (treas. 1972-74, pres. 1975-76; Recognized Young Dietitian 1973), Va. Dietetic Assn. (Margaret McDonald scholar 1967, Disting. Dietitian award 1986; program chmn. 1973-74, treas. 1977-78, pres. 1980-81, chmn. by-laws com. 1981-83, state del. 1986—), Peninsula Nutrition Council, Am. Heart Assn. (nutrition com.), Nat. Assn. Female Execs. Avocations: music; reading; travel; Egyptology; ancient civilization. Office: Charter Colonial Inst 17579 Warwick Blvd Newport News VA 23603

CARPENTER, ELIZABETH SUTHERLAND, journalist, author; b. Salado, Tex., Sept. 1, 1920; d. Thomas Shelton and Mary Elizabeth (Robertson) Sutherland; B.J., U. Tex., 1942; m. Leslie Carpenter, June 17, 1944; children—Scott Sutherland, Christy. Reporter, United Press, Phila., 1944-45; propr. with husband Carpenter News Bur. representing nat. newspapers, Washington, 1945-61; exec. asst. to Vice Pres. Lyndon B. Johnson, 1961-63; pres. sec., staff dir. to Mrs. Johnson, 1963-69; v.p. Hill & Knowlton, Inc., Washington, 1972-76; cons. L.B.J. Library, Austin, Tex.; dir. United Bank, Austin, Salado Nat. Bank; co-chmn. ERAmerica, 1973-82. Recipient; Disting. Alumnae award U. Tex., 1974; award Ladies Home Jour., 1977. Mem. Nat. Women's Polit. Caucus (nat. policy council 1971—), Women's Nat. Press (pres. 1954-55), Alpha Phi, Theta Sigma Phi (Nat. Headliners award 1962). Author: Ruffles and Flourishes, 1970. Office: LBJ Library 2313 Red River Austin TX 78705 also 116 Skyline Dr Austin TX 28746

CARPENTER, GRACE HERRING, securities firm executive; b. Hazelton, W.Va., Aug. 19, 1935; d. Harold Clayton and Mabel Virginia (Niner) Herring; A.Bus., Davis & Elkins Coll., 1957; m. Norman Eugene Carpenter, Apr. 1, 1956. With acctg. dept. Davis Meml. Hosp., Elkins, W.Va., 1956-61; account exec. Wyllie & Thornhill, Inc., Charlottesville, Va., 1968-71, Mason & Lee, Charlottesville, 1971-76, Wheat First Securities, Charlottesville, 1976-79; v.p. Thomson McKinnon Securities, Charlottesville, 1979—, br. mgr., 1983—. Pres., Charlottesville Family Y., 1974-76; mem. adv. com. bus. tech. Piedmont Community Coll., 1978; sec.-treas. Greater Charlottesville Area Devel. Corp., 1980-84; v.p. Thomas Jefferson Area United Way, 1980-83, pres., 1986. Named Regional Mgr. of Year, Thomson McKinnon Securities, 1984. Mem. Charlottesville Albermarle C. of C. (v.p. 1980, chmn. 1982), Soc. Advancement Mgmt. (pres. 1977-78). Republican. Clubs: Order Eastern Star, White Shrine. Home: 670 Chapel Hill Rd Charlottesville VA 22901 Office: 401 E Water St Charlottesville VA 22902

CARPENTER, HELEN MCCRACKEN, history educator, author; b. Norwalk, Ohio, July 31, 1909; d. Irving and Myrtle Laura (McCracken) Carpenter. B.A., Ohio Wesleyan U., 1931; M.A., Columbia U., 1934, Ed.D., 1942. Cert. secondary tchr., Ohio. Tchr. pub. schs., Crestline, Ohio, 1931-33, Norwalk, 1934-36; instr. social studies edn. Ohio Wesleyan U., Delaware, 1936-38; instr. Tchrs. Coll. Columbia U., N.Y.C., 1940-42; asst. prof. Wilson Tchrs. Coll. (name now D.C. Tchrs. Coll.), Washington, 1942-43, R.I. State U., Kingston, 1943-44; prof. history Trenton (N.J.) State Coll., 1944-75, prof. emeritus, 1975—; edn. cons. U.S. Steel, N.Y.C., 1954-67, Inst. Life Ins., N.Y.C., 1964-66, Scholastic Internat., N.Y.C., 1972-74; social studies curriculum edn. cons. various sch. systems, 1964-75; cons. for publs. Am. Sch. Librarian Assn., field reader U.S. Office Edn., Washington, 1965-71. Author: Gateways to American History, 1942; Three Decades of Commitment to Education, 1978; (with others) Scribner Social Studies Series for Schools, 1948-62; author records: Leads to Listening, 1978; editor: Skills in Social Studies, 1953; Skill Development in Social Studies, 1963; contbr. articles to profl. jours. Bd. dirs. People-To-People chpt. Greater Trenton, 1972—, Vis. Nurses Assn., Trenton, 1975-80, Meals-on-Wheels, Trenton, 1976-80. Grace Dodge fellow Columbia U. Tchrs. Coll., 1938-39. Mem. Nat. Council for Social Studies (dir. 1951-52, 57-59, pres. 1956), N.J. Edn. Assn., Trenton Hist. Assn., LWV (state dir. 1951-52), Phi Beta Kappa, Delta Sigma Rho, Kappa Delta Pi (bd. dirs. greater Trenton alumni chpt. 1977—), Pi Lambda Theta, Delta Kappa Gamma (bd. dirs. Kappa chpt. Trenton 1975-79, 82-84), Phi Alpha Theta. Club: Zonta. Address: Ellwood 202 Pennswood Village Newton PA 18940

CARPENTER, LINDA BELMORE, hotel executive; b. Portland, Oreg., Apr. 29, 1950; d. Calvin C. and Dorothy B. (Belmore) Harper; m. David Gordon Carpenter, May 28, 1978 (div. Feb. 1986). Student Portland State U., 1968-72. With Hyatt Regency-New Orleans, 1975-77, catering sales dept. Hyatt-Regency-Capitol Hill, Washington, 1977-80, dir. catering Hyatt-Anaheim, Calif., 1980-83; mgr. Dockside Yacht Sales, Annapolis, Md., 1983-85; dir. sales and mktg. Annapolis Hotel, 1985—; ambassador State of Md., Annapolis, 1986—. Mem. Nat. Banquet Mgrs. Guild (founder Los Angeles chpt.), Nat. Assn. Female Execs. (area dir. 1985—), Annapolis C. of C. (ambassador 1985—), Greater Washington Soc. of Assn. Execs., Anne Arundel Trade Council, Md. Tourism Council (adv. bd.). Republican. Episcopalian. Avocations: sailing; travel; literature; calligraphy; ballet. Office: Annapolis Hotel 126 West St Annapolis MD 21401

CARPENTER, MARION PHYLLIS, govt. ofcl.; b. Seattle, Feb. 17, 1931; d. Kenneth Alden and Lora Catherine (Scott) Sprague; student U. Oreg., 1948-49; children—Linda Marie Hepler, Kenneth Frederick, Nancy Lynn. Receptionist, med. clk. Adult and Family Services, State of Oreg., McMinnville, 1964-68, assistance worker, 1968-73, supr., 1973-77, br. mgr., Florence, Oreg., 1977-86, Roseburg Adult and Family Services, 1986—. Mem. Florence Activity Center Bd., 1977-78; mem. McMinnville Planning Commn., 1975-77; asso. mother adviser Knowles Rainbow Girls, 1971-77; mem. Lane County Council Govt. Rural Transp. Com., 1981-84; vice chmn. Florence Area Coordinating Council, 1982-85, chmn., 1985-86; chmn. Florence Community Concert Assn., 1984-86; agy. bd. West Lane Hosp.'s Home Health, 1983—, chmn., 1983-86. Mem. Oreg. Mgmt. Assn., Nat. Assn. Female Execs., Am. Mgmt. Assn., Oreg. Gerontol. Assn., Oreg. Assn. Retarded Citizens. Republican. Presbyterian. Clubs: Soroptimists, Jr. Matrons, Eastern Star, Daus. of Nile. Home: PO Box 1166 Florence OR 97439 Office: PO Box 70 Roseburg OR 97470

CARPENTER, PHYLLIS MARIE ROSENAU, physician; b. Hastings, Nebr., Aug. 2, 1926; d. Alvin Benjamin and Sophia Helen (Schmidt) Rosenau; B.S., Hastings Coll., 1948; M.D., U. Nebr., 1951; cert. Gestalt Inst. Cleve., 1970; m. Charles Robert Carpenter, Mar. 24, 1956 (dec. Mar. 1972); children—Charles Robert, Carole Rose, Lucinda Joy. Intern, St. Luke's Hosp., Chgo., 1951-52; resident in pediatrics Children's Meml. Hosp., Chgo., 1952-54; asst. med. dir., clin. supr. EEG lab., Mcpl. Contagious Disease Hosp., Chgo., 1955-60; tchr. parenting; staff Well Baby Clinics, Infant Welfare, 1960-70; practice medicine specializing in Gestalt therapy preventive medicine and biofeedback Chgo. and Clarendon Hills, Ill., 1970—; founding fellow, mem. faculty Gestalt Inst. Chgo., 1970—, faculty chmn., 1981—; mem. faculty Coll. DuPage, 1975-79, No. Ill. U., 1979-80, George Williams Coll. Center Extended Programs, Chgo., 1979-85; therapist Martha Washington Alcoholic Rehab. Clinic, Chgo., 1969-75; staff Grant Hosp., Chgo., 1985—, Wholistic Health Ctr. of Hinsdale, Ill., 1986—. Organizer Community Presbyn. Ch. Nursery Sch., 65 1966. Mem. AAUW, Am. Assn. Biofeedback Clinicians (cert. clinician), Nat. Writers Club. Author articles in field. Contbg. editor Current Health Mag., 1981—. Home: 35 Norfolk St Clarendon Hills IL 60514 Office: 35 Norfolk St Clarendon Hills IL 60514 also 826 W Armitage Ave Chicago IL 60614

CARPENTER, SUSAN KAREN, lawyer; b. New Orleans, May 6, 1951; d. Donald Jack and Elise Ann (Diehl) C. B.A. in English magna cum laude, Smith Coll., 1973; J.D., Ind. U., 1976. Bar: Ind. 1976. Dep. pub. defender State of Ind., Indpls., 1976-81, pub. defender of Ind., 1981—; chief pub. defender Wayne County Pub. Defender Office, Richmond, Ind., 1981; mem. Criminal Code Study Commn., Indpls., 1981; mem. Ind. Supreme Ct. Records Mgmt. Com., 1983, Ind. Supreme Ct. Rules Subcom., 1983. Mem. Ind. State Bar Assn. (sec. criminal justice sect. 1983-84), Nat. Legal Aid and Defender Assn. (AMICUS com. 1984), Nat. Assn. Def. Lawyers, Ind. Lawyers Commn. (dir. 1984), Ind. Criminal Justice Inst. (trustee 1983—), Ind. Pub. Defender Council (dir. 1981—), Phi Beta Kappa. Office: Office of State Pub Defender 309 W Washington St Suite 501 Indianapolis IN 46204

CARPENTER, TERESA SUZANNE, journalist; b. Independence, Mo., Aug. 1, 1948; d. Rawlin Mack and Gloria Lee Harvey (Thompson) C. B.A., Graceland Coll., 1970; M.A. in Journalism, U. Mo., 1975. Sr. editor N.J. Monthly, Princeton, 1976-79; freelance journalist, N.Y.C., 1979-81; staff writer Village Voice, N.Y.C., 1981—. Fairchild fellow U. Mo., 1975-76; recipient Pulitzer prize for feature articles, 1981, Page One award N.Y. Newspaper Guild, 1981, Clarion award Women in Communications, 1982, 86, Front Page award N.Y. Newspaperwomen's Club, 1981. Democrat. Office: Village Voice 842 Broadway New York NY 10003

CARPENTER-MASON, BEVERLY NADINE, executive health care quality assurance nurse; b. Pitts., May 23, 1933; d. Frank Carpenter and Thelma Deresa (Williams) Smith; m. Sherman Robert Robinson, Jr., Dec. 26, 1953 (div. Jan. 1959); 1 child, Keith Michael; m. 2d, David Solomon Mason Jr., Sept. 10, 1960; 1 child, Tamara Nadina. R.N., Shadyside Hosp. Sch. Nursing, Pitts., 1954; B.S., St. Joseph's Coll., North Windham, Maine, 1979; M.S., So. Ill. U., 1981. Clinic mgr., clinician dermatol. services Malcolm Grow Med. Ctr., Camp Spring, Md., 1968-71; pediatric nurse practitioner Dept. Human Resources, Washington, 1971-73; asst. dir. nursing Glenn Dale Hosp., Md., 1973-81; nursing coordinator medicaid div. Forest Haven, Laurel, Md., 1981-83, spl. asst. to supr. for med. services, 1983-84; spl. asst. to supt. for quality assurance Burr. Habilitation Services, Laurel, 1984—; dir. ABQAURP, Inc., Mechanicsburg, Pa.; cons. in field; lectr. in field. Contbr. articles to profl. jours. Mem., donor ARC Blood Drive, Washington, Md., 1975—; chmn. nominations com. Prince Georges Nat. Council Negro Women, Md., 1984-85. Recipient award Dept. Air Force and D.C. Govt., 1966—; Della Robbia Gold medallion Am. Acad. Pediatrics, 1972. Mem. Am. Coll. Utilization Rev. Physicians, Am. Bd. Quality Assurance and Utilization Rev. (mem. editorial bd. jour. 1985—), Nat. Assn. Female Execs., Chi Eta Phi. Democrat. Baptist. Avocations: language study; travel; reading; writing; collecting antiques. Home: 11109 Winsford Ave Upper Marlboro MD 20772 Office: Bur Habilitation Services 3360 Center Ave Laurel MD 20707

CARPER, ANNA MARY, emerita librarian; b. Palmyra, Pa., Aug. 13, 1919; d. Frank S. and Ella M. (Ebersole) C.; A.B. cum laude, Elizabethtown (Pa.) Coll., 1941; M.S., Columbia U., 1951. Tchr., librarian Fredericksburg (Pa.) High Sch., 1941-47; tchr. South Lebanon (Pa.) Schs., 1947-50; head cataloger U. Md., College Park, 1951-60; dir. library Elizabethtown Coll., 1960-86, dir. emerita, 1986—. Hist. com. Ch. of the Brethren. Recipient award for service to Elizabethtown Coll., Elizabethtown Coll. Alumni, 1970. Mem. ALA, Pa. Library Assn., Lancaster County Library Assn., Delta Kappa Gamma. Home: 316 E Plum St Apt A Elizabethtown PA 17022

CARPER, GERTRUDE ESTHER, artist, marina owner; b. Jamestown, N.Y., Apr. 13, 1921; d. Zenas Mills and Virgie (Lytton) Hanks; m. J. Dennis Carper, Apr. 5, 1942; children—David Hanks, John Michael Dennis (dec. 1982). Fine Arts diploma Md. Inst. Art, 1950; voice student Frazier Gange, Peabody Inst. Music, 1952-55. Interior decorator O'Neill's (Importers), Balt., 1942-44; auditor Citizens Nat. Bank, Covington, Va., 1945-46; owner, developer Essex Yacht Harbor Marina, Balt., 1955—; St. Michael's Sanctuary, wildlife preserve, Balt., 1965—. Portrait artist, 1947—; exhibited one-woman shows Ferdinand Roter Gallery, Balt., 1963, Highfield Salon, Balt., 1967, Le Salon des Nations a Paris, 1985; exhibited group shows Md. Inst. Alumni Show, 1964, Essex Library, 1981, others. Author: Expressions for Children, 1985. Contbr. articles and poetry to ch. publs. and newspapers. Vol. tchr. of retarded persons, 1963—; leader Women's Circle at local Presbyterian chs., 1952—. Mem. Md. Inst. Art Alumni Assn. (life). Avocations: raising orchids, making tiny books, reading, poetry writing. Home: 4300 St Paul St Baltimore MD 21218 Office: Essex Yacht Harbour Marina 500 Sandalwood Rd Baltimore MD 21221

CARPER, GLENDA JOY, business executive; b. San Angelo, Tex., July 21, 1939; d. Sam Bruce and Lethia (McGilvray) Lambert; B.A., West Tex. State U., 1971; m. Donald Clayton Carper, July 29, 1956; children—LaDon, Kelli Lin. Billing clk. Gen. Telephone Co., San Angelo, 1957-59; bookkeeper Margarets, Lubbock, Tex., 1959-62; sec., treas. Bearings and Materials Handling Co., Inc., Amarillo, Tex., 1968—, Bamco of Amarillo, Bamco of Dumas, Bamco of Hereford; regional mgr. Kaman Bearing and Supply, 1985—; pres. Amarillo Credit Women Internat., 1980-81, dir., also mem. pres.'s task force com.; dir. Cert. Collectors, Inc. Second v.p. Lone Star Regional Council, 1981-82, pres. Region II 1983-84, 3d v.p. 1984-85. Named Credit Woman of Yr., State of Tex., 1985. Mem. Credit Women Internat. (v.p. 1980-81, treas. 1979-80, 2d v.p. Lone Star chpt. 1985-86, 1st v.p. 1986-87), Amarillo Assn. Credit Mgmt. (bd. dirs.). Republican. Presbyterian. Home: 3908 Eaton Dr Amarillo TX 79019 Office: 108 Crockett St Amarillo TX 79109

CARPIEN, JANNET SIEGLE, corporate executive, financial planner; b. Reading, Pa., Jan. 24, 1943; d. Robert Eugene and Helen (Jablonski) Siegle; m. Alan Hugh Carpien, Oct. 4, 1969; children—Juliette M., Seth M. B.S., Kutztown State U. (Pa.), 1964; postgrad. George Washington U., U. Madrid, San Diego State U. Tchr. Spanish and phys. edn. Holy Name High Sch., Rading, Pa., 1964-65; tchr. English, reading and speech Western High Sch., Washington, 1966-68; tchr. English Meml. Jr. High Sch., San Diego, 1968-70, Ballou High Sch., Washington, 1971-72; account exec. Johnston, Lemon & Co., Inc., Washington, 1976-84; corporate v.p., fin. planner Smith Barney Harris Upham & Co., 1984—; registered rep. N.Y. Stock Exchange, 1976—; mem. adj. faculty Coll. Fin. Planning George Washington U., Denver, 1983—. Contbr. articles to profl. jours. Chmn. com. on seminar Womens Nat. Bank Adv. Bd., Washington, 1979-80, 81-84; mem. bus. com. D.C. Commn. for Women, Washington, 1982—. Recipient Profl. Service award Washington Pub. Accts., 1979; Pres. Club Profl. Achievement award Johnston, Lemon & Co. Inc., 1983. Mem. Internat. Assn. Fin. Planning (sec. 1980-81, exec. v.p. 1985—), Stockbrokers Soc., Bond Club of Washington, Nat. Assn. Securities Dealers (broker). Democrat. Jewish. Office: Smith Barney Harris Upham & Co 1919 Pennsylvania Ave #610 Washington DC 20006*

CARR, ANNE ELIZABETH, real estate broker; b. Ithaca, N.Y., May 24, 1939; d. John Franklin II and Helen Louise (Ziegler) C.; m. Robert Kern Mansur, Sept. 7, 1980 (div. 1982). Student U. Rochester, 1957-60; B.A., U. Edinburgh, Scotland, 1962, M.A. in English Lit., 1962; postgrad. NYU, 1966, 77. Lic. real estate broker, Fla. With various advt. and pub. relations firms, N.Y.C., 1962-72; dir. communications Unishield, Inc., N.Y.C., 1972-74; dir. pub. relations Thermasol Ltd., N.Y.C., 1974-76; v.p., chief fin. officer Sports Mktg., Inc., N.Y.C., 1976-80; sales dir. Found. Investments, Highland Beach, Fla., 1980-85; dir. mktg. Concordia Properties, Highland Beach, 1985—. Author booklet. Mem. Nat. Assn. Realtors, Fla. Assn. Realtors, Delray Bd. Realtors, Mensa, Intertel, Women's Nat. Republican Club (dir. pub. relations N.Y.C., 1973), Goldwing Road Riders Assn., Women on Wheels. Avocations: motorcycling; scuba diving; pistol/rifle shooting. Home: 19523 Delaware Circle Boca Raton FL 33434

CARR, BERNADETTE PATRICIA (CARROZZA), editor, consultant; d. Francis and Elizabeth (O'Donnell) C.; B.A., In English Lt., Mercy Coll., Dobbs Ferry, N.Y., 1966; M.A. in Am. Lit., Fordham U., 1968. Mng. editor Photoplay mag., N.Y.C., 1969-70, editor, 1971-73; editor-in-chief MacFadden Fan Titles mag., N.Y.C., 1973-74; editor Weight Watchers mag., N.Y.C., 1975-80; editor-in-chief Everywoman mag., N.Y.C., 1980-82; dir. communications, assoc. pub., editor CPDA News, N.Y.C., 1982-84; asst. editor The Globe, N.Y.C., 1984-85; v.p. Rosnick Carr Issue Cons., Conn., 1985—. Mem. Sigma Phi Sigma. Home: 100 D Blachley Rd Stamford CT 06902

CARR, BESSIE, retired educator; b. Nathalie, Va., Oct. 10, 1920; d. Henry C. and Sirlena (Ewell) C. B.S., Elizabeth City Coll., N.C., 1942; M.A., Columbia U. Tchrs. Coll., 1948, P.D., 1950, Ed.D., 1952. Cert. adminstr., supr., tchr. Prin. pub. sch., Halifax, Va., 1942-47, Nathalie-Halifax County, Va., 1947-51; prof. edn. So. U., Baton Rouge, 1952-53; supr. schs. Lackland Schs., Cin., 1953-54; prof. edn. Wilberforce U., Ohio, 1954-55; tchr. Leland Sch., Pittsfield, Mass., 1956-60; chair math. dept., tchr. Lakeland Middle Sch., N.Y., 1961-83. Founder, organizer, sponsor 1st Math Bowl and Math Forum in area, 1970-76; founder Dr. Bessie Carr Award for high sch. honor grads. Halifax County Sr. High Sch., 1962. Mem. AAUW (auditor 1970-85), Delta Kappa Gamma (auditor internat. 1970-76), Assn. Suprs. of Math. (chair coordinating council 1976-80), Ret. Tchrs. Assn. Democrat. Avocations: travel; photography; souvenirs.

CARR, ELIZABETH, fine arts appraiser; b. Chgo., Sept. 24, 1922; d. Charles Columbus and Grace (Marlor) Zurick; grad. high sch., Chgo.; m. Peter J. Caracci, Jan. 29, 1944; children—Joann Caracci Pelka, Linda Caracci Lastowski. Tabulation operator U.S. Govt. IBM Tabulation Dept., Chgo., 1941-42; sec./dir. Caracci & Caracci Ins., Grand Western Currency Exchange; paralegal firm Arvey, Hodes, Costello, Burman, Chgo., 1971-74; appraiser fine arts, cons. in antiques, River Forest, Ill., 1962—; lectr. in field; instr. in antiques Loyola U. Chgo., 1978-80, St. Xavier Coll., 1980-82, Triton Coll., 1980-81. Served with WAVES, USN, 1943-44. Mem. Nat. Auctioneers Assn., Ill. State Auctioneers Assn., Victorian Soc., Internat. Wedgwood Soc., Hadji Baba Soc., Armenian Rug Soc., Chgo. Rug Soc. (sec. 1967-85), Old Lacers Soc., New Eng. Appraisers Assn., Internat. Soc. Fine Arts Appraisers (founder 1979, pres. 1978-82), Appraisers Ltd. (pres. 1978—), Nat. Assn. Female Execs., Nat. Home Based Women, Future Women, Nat. Women Bus. Owners, Bus. and Profl. Women's Assn. Roman Catholic. Contbr. articles to profl. jours.;

publisher, editor The Evaluator, 1979—. Office: PO Box 280 River Forest IL 60305

CARR, JUDITH ANN SAUNDERS, social worker; b. Charleston, W.Va., Apr. 26, 1942; d. James Allen and Grace Ann (Revels) Saunders; B.S. in Social Work, Eastern Mich. U., 1975, M.Guidance and Counseling, 1979; M.S.W., U. Mich., 1977, cert. specialist in gerontology, 1979; children—Marcia Arlene, Martin Anthony. With Ann Arbor (Mich.) Community Center, Inc., 1966—, dir. sr. citizen program, 1977—; field instr. U. Mich.; dir. Washtenaw County Area Agy. on Aging. Mem. Nat. Assn. Social Workers, Huron Valley Assn. Social Workers, Nat. Council on Aging. Home: 2918 Verle Ave Ann Arbor MI 48104 Office: 625 N Main St Ann Arbor MI 48104

CARR, RUTH ANNE, lawyer; b. Athens, Ga., July 22, 1947; d. James Fletcher and Bennie Lou (Blakely) C.; 1 child, Lisa Raye Rissmiller. A.B., U. Ga., 1966; J.D., Woodrow Wilson Coll., 1978. Bar: Ga. 1978. Sole practice, Atlanta, 1978-80; gen. mgr. Am. Seal and Stamp Co., Atlanta, 1980-81; sole practice, Atlanta, 1981-82; atty. State of Ga., Atlanta, 1982-86, adminstrv. law judge; legal services officer Ga. Div. Mental Health/Mental Retardation, 1986—; vis. tchr. Woodrow Wilson Coll., Atlanta, 1982; guest speaker DeKalb High Schs., Decatur, Ga., 1984. Bd. dirs. Terraces Condominium Assn., Atlanta, 1984. Mem. ABA, State Bar Ga., Ga. Trial Lawyers Assn., Atlanta Bar Assn. Home: 2527 Terrace Trail Decatur GA 30035 Office: Div Mental Health/Mental Retardation Room 306 878 Peachtree St Atlanta GA 30309

CARRAGHER, AUDREY ANN, state legislator; b. Jamaica Plain, Mass., Jan. 27, 1924; d. Daniel Joseph and Frances Louise (Wright) McLeod; R.N., Faulkner Hosp., 1945; postgrad. Northeastern U., 1968-76; B.Gen. Studies, U. N.H., 1978, postgrad., 1979; m. John C. Carragher, Nov. 11, 1947; children—John C., Janice, Daniel, Lawrence. Library trustee, mem. Bicentennial Commn., 1974; mem. New Eng. Bd. Library Trustees, 1975; chmn. Chelmsford Hist. Commn., 1975; mem. Growth Policy Commn., 1976; student rep. Lifelong Learning Council U. N.H., 1977; planner Nashua (N.H.) Human Services Council, 1978; mem. county Adv. Council on Aging, 1979; mem. N.H. Ho. of Reps., 1980—, mem. exec. dept. com., adminstrn. com., 1980-84, constl. revision com., 1980-82, subcom. chmn. for state reapportionment and for children and youth legislation, vice chmn. state instns. com., 1982-84, mem. joint com. on exec. reorgn., mem. policy com., Rep. floor leader, vice chairperson Health and human servs. com., 1984-86, mem. state/fed. relations com., 1984-86, vice chairperson joint com. on ann. sessions, 1985, elected del. N.H. Constitutional Conv., 1984-94; mem. health and human resources com. Nat. Conf. State Legislatures, 1984—. Pres., Chelmsford Friends of Library, 1973, Rep. Women's Club of Nashua, 1980-82; bd. dirs. N.H. Sch. Vols., 1980-85; mem. State Conf. on Aging-Social Services, 1981; pres. N.H. Fedn. Rep. Women, 1986—; mem. Nat. Fedn. Rep. Women, Nashua Fedn. Rep. Women; pres., founder Nashua Friends of Library, 1982-83; mem. planning bd. City of Nashua, 1984—, mem. long range master plan com. 1984-94; active ARC Blood Bank, 1970-82. Served with Cadet Nurses Corps, 1945. Mem. Nat. Order Women Legislators, N.H. Order Women Legislators. Roman Catholic. Clubs: Vesper Country, Women's Guild of Parish. Office: Legislative Office Bldg Concord NH 03301

CARRANTI, BARBARA MARIE, nurse; b. Syracuse, N.Y., Mar. 11, 1960; d. Pio Peter and Nancy Ann (Ryan) C. Diploma in nursing Crouse-Irving Meml. Hosp., 1981. R.N., N.Y. Nursing asst. Loreto Geriatric Ctr., Syracuse, N.Y., 1979; lic. practical nurse Crouse-Irving Meml. Hosp., Syracuse, 1980-81, R.N., 1981—, staff orientation nurse, 1981-84. Atlas Health Services scholar, 1984. Mem. Crouse Irving Alumni Assn., Nat. Student Nurses Assn. Democrat. Roman Catholic. Avocations: raquetball; crafts; reading. Home: 144 Hamden Dr Syracuse NY 13208 Office: Crouse Irving Meml Hosp 736 Irving Ave Syracuse NY 13210

CARRASCO, PATRICIA ANN, advertising, public relations manager; b. Staten Island, N.Y., July 24, 1949; d. Pasquale Carmine and Rosemarie Thomasina (Cash) Campanelli; m. Joseph Frank Carrasco, May 9, 1970; children—Stephanie, Pamela. Student Fordham U., 1976-78. Asst. v.p. Doremus & Co., N.Y.C., 1975-83, mgr. Casio Inc., Fairfield, N.J., 1983—. Mem. PTA, St. Rita's Sch., Staten Island, 1978—. Home: 3283 Victory Blvd Staten Island NY 10314 Office: Casio Inc 15 Gardner Rd Fairfield NJ 07006

CARRASCO, SHARON LEE, paper goods company executive; b. San Diego, May 18, 1947; d. Edward Michael Graham and Ida Mae (Kearney) McVady; m. Daniel Carrasco, Nov. 12, 1963 (div. 1972); children—Tina Marie Carrasco Peterson, Toni Lynne. A.A. in Bus. Mgmt., Cerritos Coll., 1976. Inventory mgr. Romanow Enterprises, Carson, Calif., 1972-77; nat. inventory and purchasing mgr. Kubota Tractor, Compton, Calif., 1977-82; materials mgr. Virco Mfg. Co., Gardena, Calif., 1982-84; purchasing mgr. Carter Precision, Commerce, Calif., 1984-85; purchasing and materials mgr. Universal Paper Goods Co., Los Angeles, 1985—; cons. small bus. ventures, Buena Park, Calif., 1983-85. Mem. Nat. Assn. Purchasing Mgmt. Democrat. Club: Kubota Mgmt. (activities coordinator 1979-81) (Compton). Avocations: computer analysis; book collecting. Office: Universal Paper Goods Inc 7171 Telegraph Rd Los Angeles CA 90040

CARRELL, CAROL ANN, nursing home administrator; b. Vallejo, Calif., June 17, 1946; d. Edward Gilbert Souza and Dorothy Mae (leach) Scott; m. George Arthur Kavorkian, Jr., Oct. 30, 1965 (div. Nov. 1973); children—George Arthur II, Timothy Brian. A.A. in Sci., Chabot Coll., Hayward, Calif., 1974; B.S. in Health Service Adminstrn., U. Phoenix, San Jose, Calif., 1982. Lic. nursing home adminstr., Calif. Ward clk. for med. records Washington Manor Convalescent Hosp., San Leandro, Calif., 1973-76; emergency room registration clk. Washington Twp. Hosp., Fremont, Calif., 1976; computer operator Yellow Freight and I.M.L., Hayward and San Leandro, 1976; adminstr. Park-Central Convalescent Hosp., Fremont, 1976-85, Park Place Convalescent Hosp., Pomona, Calif., 1985—; mem. adv. council Hayward Health Care, Kaiser, 1979—; mem. adv. bd. for handicapped adults Fremont Adult Sch., 1979-82; mem. adv. bd. dietetic asst. tng. program Merritt Coll., Oakland, Calif., 1980—; bd. dirs. So. Alameda County Com. on Aging, Hayward/Fremont, 1982-84; mem. adv. bd. on nursing edn. Ohlone Coll., Fremont, 1983; del. Calif. White House Conf. on Aging, Sacramento, 1981; lectr. in field. Co-founder Adult Day Care Ctr., Fremont, 1982. Mem. Calif. Assn. Health Facilities (corr. sec. East Bay chpt. 1981-82, chmn. consumer affairs 1981-82). Democrat. Home: 10145 Norwich St Cucamonga CA 91730 Office: Park Nursing Ctr 1550 N Park Ave Pomona CA 91730

CARRICK, PATRICIA MANNIES, educator; b. Peru, Ind., July 3, 1955; d. Oscar Harvey and Rachel Jane (Enyart) Mannies; m. Floyd Gregory Carrick, Nov. 27, 1982; 1 child, Jacqueline Michelle. B.S., Ball State U., 1977, M.S., 1980. Tchr. coach Marion Community Schs., Ind., 1977-78; grad. asst. Ball State U., Muncie, Ind., 1978-79; tchr., coach girls' track and field North Newton Schs., Morocco, Ind., 1979-80, Vigo County Sch. Corp., Terre Haute, Ind., 1980—; asst. coach girls' track Terre Haute Track Club, 1981—. Mem. Am. Fedn. Tchrs. Republican. Methodist. Club: Prairieton Young Homemakers. Avocations: running; needlecrafts. Office: South Vigo High Sch 3737 S 7th St Terre Haute IN 47802

CARRIERE, KATHLEEN MARIE, hotel company executive; b. New Orleans, Aug. 10, 1939; d. Marius Michael and Beatrice (Tiemann) C.; m. Robert J. Zito, Sept. 16, 1959 (dec. Mar. 1985); children—Allison Ann, Michael James, Marcella Marie. Student La. State U., Rutgers U. Travel mgr. Carefree Travel, Manahawkin, N.J., 1972-81, Love to Travel, Somers Point, N.J., 1982-83; hospitality instr., placement dir. Taylor Inst., Internat. Concierge Inst., Pomona, N.J., 1980-85; sales rep. Admiral Quarters, Atlantic City, 1985; tour and travel mgr. Claridge Casino Hotel, Atlantic City, 1985—; travel ops. cons. Horton Casino Mktg., Atlantic City, 1984; travel agts. tng. cons. Empress Travel, Pleasantville, N.J., 1984; trade show coordinator Travel and Industry Sales Mgrs. Assn., Atlantic City, Toronto, Ont., Can., 1985. Author: Vacation Cooking, 1979. Vice chairperson Salvation Army bd. advisors, Atlantic City, 1985, sec., 1983-84; edn. chairperson United Way, Atlantic City, 1985; sales rep. Explorer Scouts Boy Scouts Am., Atlantic City area, 1984-86; coordinator March of Dimes tennis tournament, Atlantic City, 1986. Mem. Bus. and Profl. Women, Inc. (program chmn., v.p. 1984-85, membership chmn. 1985-86, Pres.'s Appreciation award 1985), Travel Industry Sales Mgmt. Assn., Hotel Motel Assn. Sales Mktg., Am. Soc. Tng. and Devel., Womens C. of C., Manland C. of C. (arts chmn. 1983-84). Democrat. Roman Catholic. Avocations: cooking; dancing; writing; reading. Home: 445 N Harrisburg Ave Atlantic City NJ 08401 Office: Claridge Casino Hotel Park Pl Atlantic City NJ 08401

CARRILLO, SANDRA VIRGINIA, educator, realtor; b. N.Y.C., July 18, 1952; d. Carmen (Balleste) Quinones; m. Efrain Carrillo Sr., Nov. 16, 1974; children—Efrain Jr., Edwin. B.S. in Family and Consumer Studies, Herbert H. Lehman Coll., 1970-74. Cert. elem. tchr., N.Y., Pa. Rep. bus. office N.Y. Telephone Co., N.Y.C., 1974-76; dietitian Middletown Psychiat. Ctr., N.Y., 1979-80; food service adminstr. Hamilton Ave. Hosp., Monticello, N.Y., 1980-81; dietitian, supr. St. Anthony's Hosp., Warwick, N.Y., 1982-83; real estate sales assoc. Goldman Agy., Port Jervis, N.Y., 1985—; tchr. Hamilton Bicentennial Elem. Sch. Cuddebackville, N.Y., pres. PTA, 1984—. Mem. Deerpark Community Club (publicity chmn. 1984-85, photographer 1985—). Republican. Roman Catholic. Avocations: sewing; ceramics; crocheting; macrame; caligraphy. Office: Hamilton Bicentennial Elem Sch Route 209 Cuddebackville NY 12729

CARRINGTON, JANICE BRIDY, nurse; b. Richmond, Va., Jan. 17, 1956; d. John Norman and Catherine Amy (Gaines) Bridy; m. Bert Vonzell Edwards, Oct. 18, 1975 (div. Oct. 1984); children—Sabrina, Amy, Bertineilli, Bert Vonzell; m. Andrew Carrington, Jan. 24, 1986. Diploma Richmond Meml. Hosp. Sch. Nursing, 1981. R.N., Va. Nursing asst. I Richmond Meml. Hosp., 1979-80, nursing asst. II, 1980-81, nurse, 1981-83, asst. nurse mgr., 1983—; dist. nurse St. Mark Ch. of God in Christ, Richmond, 1984-85; nurse Miles Adult Home, New Kent county, Va., 1985, Helping Hand Adult Home, Richmond; blood pressure screening nurse ARC, Richmond, 1985. Mem. Ch. of God In Christ. Avocations: swimming; sewing; skating; bowling; baseball. Home: 1803 Brandonview Ave Richmond VA 23231 Office: Richmond Meml Hosp

CARROLL, AILEEN LORIS, educator; b. Anita, Pa., Dec. 20, 1911; d. John Scott and Bessie Ann (Ritter) Lester; m. Feb. 26, 1946; 1 son, John. Diploma, Buffalo Gen. Hosp. Sch. Nursing, 1934; B.S., U. Buffalo, 1945, M.S., 1951. Head nurse Buffalo Gen. Hosp., 1934-39, clin. instr., 1939-45, ednl. dir., 1946-47, dir. nurses service and Sch. Nursing, 1947-69, dean Sch. Nursing, 1969-77; sec. liaison bd. Millard Fillmore Suburban Hosp., Williamsville, N.Y., 1982—. Contbr. articles to profl. jours. Mem. Am. Heart Assn.; chmn. nurse disaster com. Buffalo chpt. ARC, 1958-80; mem. edn. com. Am Cancer Soc., 1975—; mem. nursing adv. com. Daemon Coll., Amherst, N.Y., 1975-76. Mem. AAUW (chmn. edn. found. 1981-82), Alumnae of U. Buffalo Sch. Nursing, Am. Nurses Assn., Amherst Mus., DAR (regent Buffalo 1982—), N.Y. State Nurses Assn. (pres. dist. 1, 1964-68) Republican. Presbyterian. Club: Amherst Garden (pres. 1980-81. Lodge: Order Eastern Star. Home: 210 Northledge Dr Snyder NY 14226

CARROLL, BARBARA ANNE, physician, educator; b. Beaumont, Tex., Oct. 20, 1945; d. Theron Demp and Annette Ione (Anderson) C. B.A., U. Tex., 1967; M.D., Stanford U., 1972. Intern, Stanford Hosp., Palo Alto, Calif., 1972, resident, 1973-76; research asst. Genetics Found., U. Tex.-Austin, 1963-67; teaching asst. NSF Summer Biology Workshop, Austin, 1967; clinician Planned Parenthood, Santa Clara, Calif., 1973-76; instr. extension div. U. Calif.-Santa Cruz, 1972-76; asst. prof. radiology Stanford U. Med. Sch., Palo Alto, 1977-84, assoc. prof. radiology, 1984-85; chief diagnostic ultrasound, 1977-85; assoc. prof. radiology Duke U., Durham, N.C., 1985—; cons. Searle, Santa Clara, 1977-78, Diasonics, Inc., Santa Clara, 1979-83, NIH, 1981-84, Acuson, 1984—, Contbr. articles to various publs.; reviewer numerous med. jours., 1982—. Bd. dirs. Planned Parenthood Santa Clara County, 1975-76. Agnes Axtell Moule Faculty scholar, 1979-84; recipient Cancer and Med. Research Found. award, 1980. Mem. Soc. Radiologists in Ultrasound, Am. Coll. Radiology, Am. Inst. Untrasound in Medicine, Assn. Women Radiologists, Assn. Univ. Radiologists, Phi Beta Kappa. Democrat. Episcopalian. Office: Dept Radiology Duke U Med Sch Box 3808 Durham NC 27710

CARROLL, DIAHANN, actress, singer; b. N.Y.C., July 17, 1935; d. John and Mabel (Faulk) Johnson. Student, N.Y. U. Began career as model; actress: motion pictures, including Claudine (Nominated for Acad. award as best actress by the Acad. Motion Picture Arts and Scis. 1974), Carmen Jones, Porgy and Bess, Hurry Sundown, Paris Blues; on Broadway in No Strings, House of Flowers; appeared in: play Same Time, Next Year; TV series Julia, 1968-71, Dynasty, 1984—. Author (with Ross Firestone) autobiography Diahann! Address: care Agy for Performing Arts 9000 Sunset Blvd Los Angeles CA 90069*

CARROLL, DIANA DEARING, home economics educator; b. Morristown, Tenn., Feb. 10, 1947; d. Ernest Calvin and Mary Leota (Purkey) Dearing; m. Michael David Carroll, June 3, 1972; children—David Calvin, Mary Lynn. B.S. in Home Econs. Edn., Carson-Newman Coll., 1969; M.S. in Housing, Mgmt. and Family Econs., U. Tenn., 1970; Ph.D. in Family Econs., Mgmt. and Housing, U. N.C.-Greensboro, 1982. Instr. home econs. East Carolina U., Greenville, N.C., 1970-71, 72-77; tchr. home econs. Morristown-Hamblen High Sch. W., Morristown, 1971-72; asst. prof. home econs. Carson-Newman Coll., Jefferson City, Tenn., 1977-85, assoc. prof., 1986—; mem. adv. bd. dept. home econs. Morristown-Hemblen High Sch., 1981-84, Jefferson County High Sch., Jefferson City, 1984-87. Author videotape and learning guide: Basic Family Financial Management, 1983. Recipient Outstanding Undergrad. Teaching award East Carolina U., 1976, Excellence in Advising award Carson-Newman Coll., 1985; named to Outstanding Young Women Am., U.S. Jaycees, 1978, 79, 82. Mem. Am. Home Econs. Assn., Tenn. Home Econs. Assn. (state scholarship chmn., Dist. Leadership award 1984), Am. Council on Consumer Interests, Am. Assn. Housing Educators (Teaching Idea award 1984), Kappa Omicron Phi (nat. v.p. program 1982-84), Delta Kappa Gamma (scholar 1981). Republican. Baptist. Avocations: playing piano; tennis; reading. Home: 1125 Keith Ln Morristown TN 37814 Office: Carson-Newman Coll Dept Home Econs Box 1880 Jefferson City TN 37760

CARROLL, DOROTHEA YVONNE BROWN, probation officer, social worker; b. N.Y.C., Nov. 16, 1946; d. James Carlton and Mildred Dorothea (Haynes) Brown; m. Jonathan Nathaniel Carroll (div. Dec. 1974); children—Rodney Lawrence, Erik Joseph, Tiffany Rayel. A.A., Tuoro Coll., N.Y.C., 1979, B.A., 1981. Youth counselor, Harlem Juvenile Div., N.Y.C., 1976-79; dental asst. Dr. Aaron Weiss, N.Y.C., 1980-81; legis. asst. to G.L. Daniels, N.Y. State Assembly, 1981; caseworker N.Y. Foundling Hosp., N.Y.C., 1981-83; case mgr. spl. services for children Dept. Human Resources, N.Y.C., 1983-85; adult supr. N.Y.C. Dept. Probation, N.Y.C., 1986—; research analyst MARCO Systems, N.Y.C., 1972-73. Bd. dirs. Golden Star Sr. Citizens, N.Y.C., 1968-80; den mother Greater N.Y. council Boy Scouts Am., N.Y.C., 1968-75; mem. county com. Martin Luther King Democratic Club, N.Y.C., 1980. Recipient Community Service award Martin Luther King Democratic Club, 1980. Mem. United Probation Officers Assn., Iota Phi Lambda. Episcopalian. Office: NYC Dept Probation Adult Supervision 215 E 161st St Bronx NY 10451

CARROLL, E. ELIZABETH JACKSON, educator, rancher; b. Mitchell, Oreg., Jan. 28, 1914; d. Martin Joseph and Mary Caroline (Stout) Jackson; m. Jesse Frank Carroll, July 8, 1942. Profl. degree, Oreg. Coll. Edn., 1934; B.S. in Edn., U. Oreg., 1947; M.A. in Adminstrn., Calif. State U.-Chico, 1952, M.A. in Counseling and Guidance, 1965; Ed.D., U. So. Calif., 1975. Cert. tchr. Calif., Oreg., Hawaii; cert. ombudsman, Calif. Tchr. State Pub. Schs., Oreg., 1934-42; acct., supr., U.S. Mil. Installation, Phoenix, 1943-45; tchr., educator Portland Pub. Schs., 1945-48; tchr., cons., supr. Calif. Pub. Schs., 1949-76; instr. Yuba Coll., Marysville, Calif., 1965-72; instr., asst. prof. Extended Learning div. Calif. State U.-Sacramento, 1968-85; mgr. Jackson Cattle Ranch, Mitchell Oreg., 1985—. Vol., Hist. Records Butte County Library, Calif., 1982-85; active Oroville Republican Women, 1960—, Hospice of Oroville. Mem. AAUW, Wheeler County Cattlemen Assn., U. So. Calif. Alumni Assn., U. Oreg. Alumni Assn., Calif. State U. Alumni Assn., Delta Kappa Gamma, Phi Delta Gamma, Psi Chi, Delta Epsilon, Omega Nu. Baptist. Lodge: Rebecca. Club: Mitchell Lioness.

CARROLL, FRANCES LAVERNE, educator; b. Scammon, Kans., Dec. 6, 1925; d. Robert Allen and Truda Hilda (Flanagan) Carroll; B.S., Kans. State Tchrs. Coll., 1948; M.A., U. Denver, 1956; postgrad. Western Res. U., 1957; Ph.D., U. Okla., 1970. Bank bookkeeper Baxter Springs Bank (Kans.), 1944; tchr. English and journalism high sch., Caney, Kans., 1947-49; librarian Field Kindley Meml. High Sch., Coffeyville, Kans., 1949-54; librarian Coffeyville Jr. Coll., 1954-62, supr. elem. sch. libraries, 1957-62; asst. prof. library sci. U. Okla., Norman, 1962-67, assoc. prof., 1971-75, prof., 1975—, acting dir. sch. library sci., 1974-75; head library studies Nedlands Coll. Advanced Edn. (formerly Western Australian Secondary Tchrs. Coll.), Perth, 1977-81; guest lectr. Drexel Inst. Tech., Phila., 1964, U. London, 1972, Pahlavi U., Shiraz, Iran, 1976; dir. U.S. Office Edn. Inst., 1966, 67, 69. U.S. Office Edn. grantee, 1969. Mem. AAUW, AAUP, ALA, Internat. Relations Round Table (chmn. membership 1970-74), Internat. Fedn. Library Assns. (chmn. sect. sch. libraries 1973-77), Okla. Library Assn., Delta Kappa Gamma, Phi Delta Kappa, Beta Phi Mu. Author: (with Mary Meacham) The Library at Mount Vernon, 1977, Books Kids Like, 1984; (with Pat Beilke) Guidelines for the Planning and Organization of School Library Media Centers, 1979; nat. series editor Reading for Young People, 1979—, Recent Advances in School Librarianship, 1981; contbr. articles to profl. jours. Office: 401 W Brooks St Norman OK 73019

CARROLL, JEANNE, public relations executive; b. Oak Park, Ill., May 20, 1929; d. John P. and Mary (Noonan) Carroll; B.A., U. London, 1950; M.A., Northwestern U., 1951; m. Harold M. Kass, Apr. 1966. Bus. girls editor Charm Mag., N.Y.C., 1951-53; pub. relations dir. Rosary Coll., River Forest, Ill., 1953-66; chmn. publicity Am. Cancer Soc., bd. dirs. W. and S.W. Suburban Unit, 1967—; med. adminstr., asst. to Dr. Harold Kass, Oak Park, Ill., 1969—. Pub. relations counselor in Midwest for Brown U., 1962; dir. pub. relations Mundelein Coll., 1968; producer radio show for teen-agers, Chgo., 1954; lectr. sci. devels. Bell Labs. for AT&T, 1954; participant annual Sun-Times seminars for coll. journalists MacMurray Coll., Jacksonville Ill. Chmn., March of Dimes campaign for Chgo., ednl. TV Channel 11, River Forest, 1963; trustee DePaul U., Chgo., chmn. Soc. Fellows dinner; chmn. Oak Park Hosp. Ben Din Dan, 1971-80; mem. com. library Internat. Relations, 1975-82; mem. bd. Arden Shores, sch. for boys, 1984—. Recipient Excellence award for coll. brochures Am. Coll. Pubs. Com., 1957; medal of recognition for work in pub. relations Bishop Fulton Sheen, 1960; Humanitarian award Performing Arts Ctr. and Citizens Com., Chgo., 1976. Mem. Ill. Assn. Coll. Admissions Counsellors (pres.), Assn. Coll. Pub. Relations Assn., Family Service Assn. Am. (past dir.), Acad. Hosp., Pub. Relations, Ill. (pres.), Chgo. (pub. relations dir.), med. soc. auxs., Oak Park Hosp. Aux. (pres. 1986), West Suburban Hosp. Med. Ctr. Aux. (life). Address: 712 Courtland Circle Springdale Western Springs IL 60558 Office: 715 Lake St Oak Park IL 60301

CARROLL, JUDY DEASON, human services executive; b. Oxford, Ala., Oct. 18, 1953; d. Charles Ben and Frances Leona (Hazel) Deason; m. Francis John Carroll, Jr., July 2, 1983; m. Ralph Lee Ambrose, June 6, 1970 (div. 1981); 1 child, Jennifer Anne. B.A. in History, Jacksonville State U., 1979; M.Urban Studies/Planning, U. Ala., 1982. Adminstrv. intern Birmingham (Ala.) City Council, 1981; program analyst, planner Area Agy. on Aging Dade County, Miami, Fla., 1981-82; sr. planner Area Agy. on Aging Broward County, Ft. Lauderdale, Fla., 1982-83; project dir. Council on Aging for Volusia Sr. Nutrition and Activities Program, Daytona Beach, Fla., 1983—; cons. Housing Coalition of Broward, Ft. Lauderdale, 1982-83; lectr., cons. Interfaith Council, Ft. Lauderdale, 1982-83; research fellow U. Ala., Birmingham, 1981. Mem. Fla. Council Aging, Fla. Assn. Service Providers, Nat. Assn. Sr. Centers, Nat. Assn. Nutrition and Activities Service Providers, Nat. Council on Aging, Phi Alpha Theta. Democrat. Mem. Ch. of Christ. Home: 384 Euclid Ave Daytona Beach FL 32018 Office: Senior Nutrition and Activities Program 524 S Beach St Daytona Beach FL 32014

CARROLL, KIM MARIE, nurse; b. Ottawa, Ill., Feb. 13, 1958; d. John J. and Charin E. (Reilley) Marmion; m. Thomas Christopher Carroll, Aug. 25, 1979; 1 child, Christopher John. B.S.N., U. Denver, 1983; diploma Copley Meml. Hosp. Sch. Nursing, Aurora, Ill., 1979. R.N., Ill., Colo.; critical care practitioner. Staff nurse Penrose Hosp., Colorado Springs, Colo., 1979-83, asst. head nurse cardiac floor, 1983-84; asst. dir. nurses Big Meadows Nursing Home, Savanna, Ill., 1985-86, dir. nurses, 1986—. Mem. Am. Assn. Critical Care Nurses, Nat. Assn. for Female Execs., Sigma Theta Tau. Roman Catholic. Avocation: skiing. Home: 112 3d St Savanna IL 61074 Office: Big Meadows Nursing Home 1000 Longmoor Ave Savanna IL 61074

CARROLL, LOIS MAE, nurse; b. Scranton, Pa., Oct. 29, 1929; d. Robert George and Mae Fietta (Richards) Fenstermacher; R.N., L.I. Sch. Nursing, Southampton, 1951; B.S. in Nursing, U. Ala., 1976, M.A., 1978; m. Joseph C. Carroll, Jan. 13, 1950; children—Joseph, Jeffrey, Robert. Staff nurse Crestwood Hosp., Huntsville, Ala., 1966-70; supr. occupational health Dunlop Tire & Rubber Co., Huntsville, 1970-78; student health coordinator No. Va. Community Coll., Manassas, 1978—, also adj. prof., chmn. coll. health and safety com.; CPR and first aid instr. Mem. Am. Assn. Occupational Health Nurses, Am. Coll. Health Assn., Bus. and Profl. Women's Club (dist. dir. 1973), Manassas Olde Town Assn., Alpha Lambda Delta. Republican. Unitarian. Home: 9301 Grant Ave Manassas VA 22110 Office: 6901 Sudley Rd Manassas VA 22110

CARROLL, NANCY LOUISE, public affairs specialist; b. Woodland, Calif., Jan. 4, 1944; d. Charles Harvin and Eleanore Elizabeth (Doty) Carroll; B.A., Golden Gate U., 1981; 1 son, Scott Kelly Morrison. With inventory, billing, mktg. depts. Ortho div. Chevron Chem. Co., San Francisco, 1970-73, field research, services, 1973-74, chem. buyer, purchasing, 1974-77, pub. affairs specialist youth and edn. Chevron U.S.A. Inc., San Francisco, 1977-83, pub. affairs counsel, Denver, 1983—. Chmn. nat. adv. bd. Distributive Edn. Clubs Am., 1982-83; bd. dirs. Nat. Soc. for Internships and Exptl. Edn., 1981-82; mem. nat. adv. council Future Bus. Leaders Am.; bd. dirs. Yolo County Sheltered Workshop, 1971-73, sec., 1972-73. Mem. Nat. Fedn. Bus. and Profl. Women's Clubs, Pub. Affairs Women, Pub. Relations Soc. Am., LWV, Phi Beta Lambda. Republican. Club: Commonwealth of Calif., Woodland Bus. and Profl. Women's (pres. 1973-74). Home: 6600 E Mississippi Ave #5 Denver CO 80224 Office: Chevron USA Inc 700 S Colorado Blvd Denver CO 80222

CARROLL, PATRICIA MARY, marketing and sales executive; b. N.Y.C., Dec. 5, 1939; d. Patrick Michael and Bridget Patricia (Ginnelly) Curran; m. Thomas Michael Carroll, Jan. 26, 1963; children—Matthew Thomas, Jeanne Anastasia. B.S., Fordham U., 1961; M.S., Coll. New Rochelle, 1975; postgrad. NYU, 1972, CUNY, 1983—. Cert. tchr. spl. edn. and English, N.Y. Exec. confidential sec. N.Y. Daily News, 1961-66; tchr. White Plains (N.Y.) Adult Edn. Ctr. and Westchester Devel. Ctr., 1975; asst. dir. nursing and allied health edn. March of Dimes Birth Defects Found., White Plains, 1976-84; product/mktg. mgr. Stoffel Seals Corp., Tuckahoe, N.Y., 1984—; copy editor Pergamon Press, Elmsford, N.Y., 1979; editor texts Appleton-Century-Crofts. Assoc. editor The First Six Hours of Life series, 1978-82, Prenatal Care series, 1978-82, 1978-85, Intrapartal Care series, 1980-82; editor: Concepts of Human Development (B. Raff and C. Windwer); assoc. editor The Birth Defects Original Article Series, 3 vols, 1984. Contbr. articles to profl. jours and newspapers. Legis. adv. com. N.Y. State Assembly, 1980-84; mem. Mamaroneck (N.Y.) Beautification Com., 1983, Coll. scholar, 1957. Mem. Women In Communications (program com. 1983-86), Women's Nat. Book Assn., AAUW. Roman Catholic. Home: 171 Maple Ave Mamaroneck NY 10543 Office: Stoffel Seals Corp 400 High Ave Nyack NY 10960

CARROLL, PATRICIA WHITEHEAD, computer company executive; b. Tallahassee, Fla., Oct. 20, 1954; d. Albert and Lucinda (Brown) Whitehead; m. Napoleon A. Carroll, May 28, 1979 (div. 1985). B.S. cum laude in Psychology, Bethune-Cookman Coll., 1977. Records supr. State Farm Ins. Co., Winter Haven, Fla., 1977-79; ins. agt. Pat Carroll Ins. Agy., Orlando, Fla., 1979-82; dir. mktg. Systems Support Corp., Washington, 1982-85, v.p., 1985—. Recipient Youth Day Appreciation award City of Titusville, 1976, Millionaire Club award State Farm Ins. Co., 1981, Million Dollar Round Table award State Farm Ins. Co., 1979, others. Mem. Nat. Assn. Female Execs., Am. Mgmt. Assn., Delta Sigma Theta. Democrat. Avocations: reading; coin and stamp collecting; outdoor sports. Office: Systems Support Corp 2100 M St NW #608 Washington DC 20036

CARROLL, RUDI YVONNE, personnel consultant; b. Camden, Ark., July 1, 1955; d. Rudolph Edison and Betty Zane (Everett) Peace; m. Mark Canby Carroll, Mar. 14, 1980. Grad. high sch., Little Rock. Lic. personnel cons., Ark. Exec. sec. State of Ark., Little Rock, 1973-77; cons. Dunhill Personnel, Little Rock, 1977-82; owner, operator Secretarial Search, Little Rock, 1982—. Mem. Ark. Personnel Assn., Little Rock C. of C. Methodist. Avocations: water skiing; camping; aerobics; horseback riding; cross-stitch. Home: 8 Ludington Cove Little Rock AR 72207 Office: Secretarial Search 7509 Cantrell St Suite 207B Little Rock AR 72207

CARROTT, ANN LOUISE, lawyer; b. Ft. Wayne, Ind., Aug. 4, 1952; d. John Theodore and Norma Lee (Boyle) C. B.A., Lawrence U., Appleton, Wis., 1973;

J.D., Hamline U., St. Paul, 1980. Bar: Minn. 1980, U.S. Dist. Ct. Minn. 1981. Head resident Albion Coll. (Mich.), 1973-75; detective Marshall Fiedl & Co., Schaumburg, Ill., 1975-77; asst. county atty. County of Morrison, Little Falls, Minn., 1980-83; atty. County of Douglas, Alexandria, Minn., 1984—. Chmn., founder Morrison County Child Protection Team, Little Falls, 1981-83; v.p. Devel. Achievement Ctr., Little Falls, 1983; v.p. LWV, Little Falls, 1983. Mem. ABA, Minn. Bar Assn., Minn. Women Lawyers. Democrat. Office: Douglas County Atty Office Douglas County Courthouse Alexandria MN 56308

CARR-RUFFINO, NORMA J., management consultant, business educator; b. Ft. Worth, Dec. 15, 1932; d. Robert Leroy and Lorene (Dickeson) Carr; B.B.A., Tex. Wesleyan U., 1968; M.B.E., North Tex. State U., 1969, Ph.D., 1973; m. Alfred Ruffino, Jan. 6, 1979; children by previous marriage—Randy, Brian, Carrie. Vice pres. Randy's, Inc., Ft. Worth, 1965-72; vocat. office educator coordinator Ft. Worth Public Schs., 1969-72; prof. bus. San Francisco State U., 1973—; mgmt. cons., 1972—; referee Calif. State Bar Ct., 1985—. Mem. Acad. Mgmt., Am. Bus. Communication Assn., Internat. Soc. Bus. Educators, Adminstrv. Mgmt. Soc., Internat. Communication Assn., Delta Pi Epsilon. Author: Theory Reinforcement and Skill Building, 2d edit., 1981; Writing Short Business Reports, 1980; The Promotable Woman, 1982, rev. edit., 1985. Editor Calif. Bus. Edn. Assn. Jour., 1975-76. Office: Sch of Business San Francisco State U 1600 Holloway St San Francisco CA 94132

CARRUTH, MARY GRACE, school administrator; b. Laurel, Miss., Dec. 3, 1924; d. Pink Clayton and Mary Elizabeth (Bethea) Morrison; m. Orville Malcolm Thomas, June 12, 1947 (div. Dec. 1964); children—Malcolm Morrison, Sarah Elizabeth; m. 2d, James Austin Carruth, Nov. 25, 1977. B.S., Miss. So. U., 1955; M.Ed., U. So. Miss., 1965. Cert. tchr., administrator, supr., spl. edn., Miss. Tchr., Petal Elem. Sch., Miss., 1959-65; elem. coordinator Am. Book Co., Atlanta, 1965-66; elem. and Title I coordinator Harrison County Sch., Gulfport, Miss., 1966-69; dist. reading supr. Pass Christian Sch., Miss., 1969-70; owner, dir. Gulf Coast Edn. Ctr., Gulfport, 1971—; propr. M.G.'s Specially for You Shop, 1985—. Probation vol. Harrison County Family Ct., 1973—. Recipient Cert. Appreciation Kiwanis Club, 1975. Fellow Assn. Children with Learning Disabilities; mem. Miss. Assn. Children with Learning Disabilities (bd. dirs. 1982-85), Assn. Proprietary Schs. and Colls. (bd. dirs. 1977-81), Miss. Council on Children, Chi Omega. Avocations: antiques; motorhome travel; reading; dancing; travel. Home: 219 Woodbine Dr Gulfport MS 39501 Office: Gulf Coast Edn Ctr 01025 Pass Rd Gulfport MS 39501 also 1920 24th Ave Gulfport MS 29501

CARSEY, MARCIA PETERSON, broadcasting company executive; b. South Weymouth, Mass., Nov. 21, 1944; d. John Edwin and Rebecca White (Simonds) Peterson; B.A. in English Lit., U. N.H., 1966; m. John Jay Carsey, Apr. 12, 1969; children—Rebecca P., John P. Prodn. asst. Tonight Show, NBC, N.Y.C., 1966-68; program supr. William Esty Advt., N.Y.C., 1968-69; exec. story editor Tomorrow Entertainment, Los Angeles, 1971-74; program exec. ABC, Los Angeles, 1974-76, v.p. comedy and variety programs, 1976-77, sr. v.p. comedy and variety programs, 1977-79, sr. v.p. prime time series, 1979-80; co-founder Carsey-Werner Co., West Los Angeles, TV series, film devel. and prodn., 1981—; exec. producer Oh Madeline, ABC, 1983, The Cosby Show, NBC, 1984—. Office: 10900 Wilshire Blvd Los Angeles CA 90024

CARSON, BONNIE L(OU), chemist; b. Kansas City, Kans., Aug. 11, 1940; d. Harold Lee and Lorene Marie (Draper) Bachert; student U. Kansas City, 1958-61; B.A. in Chemistry summa cum laude, U. N.H., 1963; M.S. in Organic Chemistry, Oreg. State U., 1966; m. David M. Carson, June, 1961 (div. 1973); 1 dau., Catherine (Katie) Leslie. Grad. teaching asst. Oreg. State U., 1963-66; organic chem. lab. instr. U. Waterloo, Ont., Can., 1968-69; asst. abstractor in macromolecular chemistry Chem. Abstracts Service, Columbus, Ohio, 1969-71; freelance Russian translator, 1971-73; asst. chemist Midwest Research Inst., Kansas City, Mo., 1973-75, asso. chemist, 1975-80, sr. chemist, 1980—. Mem. Am. Soc. Info. Sci., Am. Chem. Soc., Am. Inst. Chemists, N.Y. Acad. Sci., Soc. for Tech. Communication, Am. Translators Assn. (pres. Mid-Am. chpt. 1985), Author and Editor: (with others) Trace Metals in the Environment, 1977-81, Toxicology and Biological Monitoring of Metals, 1986; contbr. in field. Home: 5501 Holmes St Kansas City MO 64110 Office: 425 Volker Blvd Kansas City MO 64110

CARSON, CAROL S., economist; b. 1939. B.A., Coll. of Wooster, 1961; M.A., Fletcher Sch. Law and Diplomacy, Tufts U., 1962; Ph.D., George Washington U., 1971. Asst. to dir. Bur. Econ. Analysis, Commerce Dept., Washington, 1972-76, chief current bus. analysis, 1976-82, chief economist, 1982-83, dep. dir., 1985—; adj. asst. prof. Pace Coll. at Westchester, 1971-72. Address: Commerce Dept Bur Econ Analysis 1401 K St NW Washington DC 20230

CARSON, ELIZABETH HILL, civic worker; b. Des Moines, Apr. 21, 1928; d. Lee Forrest and Marian (Robbins) Hill; m. John Congleton Carson, Feb. 14, 1954; children—Elizabeth, John, Lee Hill, David, Barbara. B.A., Vassar Coll., 1950; J.D., U. Pa., 1953. Bar: Iowa 1953, U.S. Dist. Ct. (so. dist.) Iowa 1953. Atty., trust dept. Fidelity-Phila. Trust Co., Phila., 1954-55; pres. Jr. League San Diego, 1967-68, mem., 1960—; founding trustee U. Calif.-San Diego Med. Aux., 1967-70; mem. Vassar Club San Diego, 1960—, pres., 1962-64; mem. La Jolla High Sch. PTA, 1970-84, pres., 1973-75; pres. La Jolla Civic Ctr. Corp., 1977—; trustee Francis Parker Sch., 1969-84; trustee Children's Health Ctr., 1970-72, La Jolla Country Day Sch., 1982-85; bd. govs. San Diego Community Found., 1982—, corp. sec., 1982-84; founding dir. LEAD San Diego, 1980—; founding dir. EXCEL, 1983—; mem. State Calif. Judicial Selection Com. for San Diego County, 1966-74; mem. Las Patronas, 1970—; mem. child guidance adv. bd. Children's Health Ctr., 1969—; mem. bd. visitors U. San Diego Law Sch., 1974—; mem. acad. affairs com. U. San Diego; mem. task force on discipline San Diego Unified Sch. Dist., 1980-81, mem. task force on grad. requirements, 1981-84, mem. equity placement oversight com., 1985—; bd. dirs. San Diego chpt. ARC, 1985—. Mem. ABA, Iowa Bar Assn., San Diego County Bar Assn. Republican. Clubs Vassar (past pres.), La Jolla Beach and Tennis, Wednesday. Home: 1703 Soledad Ave La Jolla CA 92037

CARSON, HELEN SUE, chemical company executive; b. Stamford, Tex., June 24, 1943; d. George Rupert and Lottie Pearl (Hanson) Raley; B.S. in Chemistry and Math., Wayland Bapt. Coll., Plainview, Tex., 1971; postgrad. Eastern N.Mex. U.; children—William Wayne, Misti Beth. Lab. instr. chemistry Wayland Bapt. Coll., 1969-71; high sch. tchr., Dexter, N.Mex., 1971-72; chemist Champion Chem. Co., Houston, 1973; with Amoco Chem. Corp., Houston, 1974—, research chemist product devel. and tech. service, corrosion inhibitors, 1979-80, sr. research chemist corrosion inhibitors, 1981, product specialist internat. oil production chems., 1981, product specialist internat. oil chems., 1981-82, product mgr. inhibitors and biocides, 1982-84, sr. cons. prodn. chems., 1984—. Mem. Nat. Assn. Corrosion Engrs. (tech. coms.), Am. Bus. Women's Assn. (Bay Area Am. Bus. Woman of Yr. award 1980), Assn. Female Execs., Soc. Petroleum Engrs., Beta Sigma Phi (pres. 1975-76, Girl of Yr. award 1976). Republican. Author, patentee in field. Home: 207 Parliament St Houston TX 77034 Office: 5450 NW Central Dr Houston TX 77040

CARSON, JULIA M., state legislator; b. Louisville, July 8, 1938; 2 children. Ed. Ind. U., 1960-62, St. Mary of the Woods, 1976-78. Mem. In. Ho. of Reps., Indpls., 1972-76; mem. Ind. Senate, 1976—. Vice pres. Greater Indpls. Prog. Com.; nat. Democratic committeewoman; trustee YMCA; bd. dirs. Pub. Service Acad. Recipient Woman of Yr. Ind. award, 1974; Outstanding Leadership award AKA; Humanitarian award Christian Theol. Sem. Mem. NAACP, Urban League, Nat. Council Negro Women. Baptist. Office: Ind Senate State Capitol Indianapolis IN 46205*

CARSON, LILLIAN G., psychotherapist; b. N.Y.C., Mar. 22, 1933; d. Joseph and Helen E. (Tucker) Gershenson; B.A., UCLA, 1968, M.S.W., 1970, D.S.W., 1979; m. Ralph Carson, July 19, 1978 (dec. June 1983); children by previous marriage—Susan Gevirtz, Steven Gevirtz, Carrie Gevirtz; m. Sam T. Hurst, Dec. 11, 1984. Psychotherapist parent-infant consultation program, dept. child psychiatry Cedars Sinai Hosp., Los Angeles, 1970; dir. counseling Zahm Sch. Individual Edn., Los Angeles, 1970-72; dir. clinic Los Angeles Psychoanalytic Soc., 1972-82; pvt. practice psychotherapy, Los Angeles, 1970—; case supr. So. Calif. Counseling Center; instr. Calif. State Mental Health Tng. Center; cons. Santa Monica Child Devel. Centers; mem. exec. com., sec.-treas. Psychiat. Med. Group So. Calif., 1973-74; mem. profl. bd. Los Angeles County Mental Health Assn., 1974; bd. dirs. Friends of UCLA Child Care Services, 1981; mem. adv. council Los Angeles Child Devel. Center, 1981; staff mem. Westwood Psychiat. Hosp.; invited guest 20th birthday celebration meetings Hempstead Clinic, London, 1972, participant seminar by Anna Freud, 1978. Lic. clin. social worker, Calif. Fellow Calif. Soc. Clin. Social Work (nominating com. 1974-77), Am. Orthopsychiat. Assn.; mem. Center Improvement of Child Caring, Nat. Assn. Social Workers, Acad. Cert. Social Workers, Nat. Assn. Edn. of Young Children. Research in parenting and preschool children. Office: 803 Bramble Way Los Angeles CA 90049

CARSON, MARGARET MARIE, marketing director; b. Windber, Pa., Dec. 30, 1944; d. Peter and Margaret (Olenik) Buben; m. Claude Carson, Dec. 30, 1967 (div. 1974); m. Brian Charles Scruby, June 6, 1975; 1 stepchild, Debbie. B.A., U. Pitts., 1971; M.S. in Mgmt., Houston Bapt. U., 1985. Petroleum analyst Gulf Oil Co., Pitts., 1973-75, crude oil analyst, 1971-74, environ. coordinator, 1974-79, mgr. oil acquistition, Houston, 1980-84, mktg. dir., 1985—. Columnist The Collegian, 1984-85; contbr. to Cathedral Poets, 1976. Mem. Young Reps., Houston, 1980-85; sponsor Classical Guitar Soc., Houston; bd. dirs. Indiana U., Pa., 1980-81. Mem. Internat. Energy Analysts, Nat. Assn. Female Execs. Club: University. Office: Cabot Consulting 400 FM 1960 W Houston TX 77090

CARSON, MARY ANNETTE LUXFORD, manufacturing executive; b. Stockton, Calif., July 10, 1939; d. Robert G. and Hattie K. (Wilcox) Luxford; m. Thomas E. Carson, Oct. 17, 1958 (div. Jan. 1978); children—Deborah Ann Carson Tomlinson, Thomas Eric. Student Humphreys Coll., Stockton, 1959-60, Delta Coll., Stockton, 1962-64, Modesto Jr. Coll., 1971. Real estate lic., Calif. Office mgr. Souza's Meats, Tracy, Calif., 1970-72; adminstrv. sec. Owens Ill. Inc., Tracy, 1972-77; comml. artist Quantic Art Studio, Los Altos, Calif., 1977-78; personnel mgr. Oakwood Resort, Manteca, Calif., 1978-79; office mgr. Big Valley Sch., Modesto, 1979-84; owner, pres. Custom Nails, Inc., Modesto, 1983—. Mem. Sweet Adelines (dir. chpt. 1985), Am. Bus. Women's Assn. Republican. Mem. Grace Brethren Ch. Avocations: lecturing; reading; swimming. Home: PO Box 2869 Modesto CA 95351 Office: Custom Nails 217B Winmoore Way Modesto CA 95351

CARSON, VIRGINIA HILL, oil and gas executive; b. Los Angeles, Dec. 4, 1928; d. Percy Albert McCord and Flora May (Newking) Schultz; m. John Carson, Dec. 30, 1950 (dec.). B.A. in Internat. Relations, U. Calif.-Berkeley, 1949; postgrad. Stanford U., 1948, UCLA, 1951. Gen. office worker UN, San Francisco, 1949; ind. oil and gas profl., U.S., Can., Cuba, 1953-73; supr./specialist Sun Exploration & Prodn. Co., Dallas, 1978-83, profl. analyst, 1983—. Mem. Dallas Council World Affairs, 1984; mem. Dallas Downtown Republican Women, 1984; mem. Dallas Mus. Fine Arts, 1984, Make-a-Wish Found. Dallas, 1984. Nominated to Pres.'s Council Am. Inst. Mgmt., N.Y.C., 1974. Office: Sun Exploration Prodn Co PO Box 2880 Dallas TX 75221

CARSTEN, ARLENE DESMET, financial executive; b. Paterson, N.J., Dec. 5, 1937; d. Albert F. and Ann (Greutert) Desmet; student Alfred U., 1955-56; m. Alfred John Carsten, Feb. 11, 1956; children—Christopher Dale, Jonathan Glenn. Piano tchr., 1964-71; exec. dir. Inst. for Burn Medicine, San Diego, 1972-81, mem. adv. bd., 1981-84; chief fin. officer A.J. Carsten Co., San Diego, 1981—; dir. Nat. Burn Fedn., 1975-84. Organizer, mem. numerous community groups; chmn. San Diego County Mental Health Adv. Bd., 1972-74, mem., 1971-75; chmn. community relations subcom., mem. exec. com. Emergency Med. Services Com., San Diego, Riverside and Imperial Counties, 1973-75; pub. mem. psychology exam. com. Calif. Bd. Med. Quality Assurance, 1976-80, chmn., 1977; San Diego County Bd. Suprs. rep. Health Services Agy. Governing Body, 1980-81. Mem. Calif. Democratic State Central Com., 1968-74, exec. com., 1971-72, 73-74; mem. San Diego Dem. County Central Com., 1970-76, treas., 1972-74; chmn. edn. for legis. com. women's div. So. Calif. Dem. Com., 1972; dir. Muskie for Pres. Campaign, San Diego, 1972; councilwoman City of Del Mar, Calif., 1982-86, mayor pro tem, 1984, mayor, 1985. organizer, dir. numerous local campaigns. Bd. dirs. San Dieguito Family Service Assn., 1969-71, San Dieguito Dem. Club, 1965-71, San Diego Mental Health Assn., 1977-79. Recipient Key Woman award Dem. Party, 1968, 72, Spl. award of recognition San Diego Soc. Clin. Psychologists, 1975, 1st Ann. Community award Belles for Mental Health, San Diego County Mental Health Assn., 1974, Alfred U. Alumni Assn. citation, 1979, Spirit of Community Service award Inst. Burn Medicine, 1982. Mem. Republican Assos. Contbr. articles to profl. jours. Home: 1415 Via Alta Del Mar CA 92014 Office: 6711 Nancy Ridge Dr San Diego CA 92121

CART, PAULINE HARMON, Universology minister, educator; b. Jamestown, Ky., Nov. 3, 1914; d. Preston L. and Frances L. (Sullivan) Harmon; m. William C. Cart, July 3, 1936; children—Charles W., David N. B.S., Berea Coll., 1955; M.A., U. Mich.-Ann Arbor, 1957, postgrad., 1957; postgrad. Eastern Mich. U., 1957. Mgr., owner Gen. Store, Beattyville, Ky., 1936-41; def. worker Gen. Motors, Dayton, Ohio, 1941-46; tchr. Ann Arbor Pub. Schs., 1955-83, Leads Sch., Eng., 1963-64 miomassologist Coll. Natureopathic Physicians, St. Louis, 1959-84; minister, counselor Ch. of Universology, Ann Arbor, 1972—. Contbr. poems and short stories to mags. Instr. Touch for Health Found., Pasadena, Calif., 1972—, Ir. dology, Escondido, Calif., 1972—; mem. Conservative Caucus, Washington, 1973—. Mem. NEA (del. 1959), Am. Nutrition Counselors Am., Internat. Miomathetics Fedn. (sec. edn. 1985—), Assn. Mich. Myomassologists, Inc., Federated Organic Garden & Farming of Mich. (v.p. 1985-86), Delta Kappa Pi. Republican. Avocations: painting; quilting; crafts; writing; traveling. Home: 2564 Hawks Ave Ann Arbor MI 48104 Office: 2450 Hawks Ave Ann Arbor MI 48104

CARTE, SUZANNE LEWIS, educator; b. S. Charleston, W.Va., Nov. 16, 1943; d. Carson Richard and Thelma Lee (Dew) Lewis; m. John Herman Carte, Sept. 1, 1962; children—John Kevin, Jennifer Kristin, Samuel Jefferson. B.S., W.Va. State Coll., 1973; student W.Va. Coll. Grad. Studies, 1976-86. Tchr., Kanawha County Schs., Charleston, W.Va., 1978, tchr. history, 1979-81, tchr. intensive service unit, 1981, tchr. 6th grade, 1982—. Mem. Christian edn. commn. 1st Presbyterian Ch., St. Albans, W.Va., 1978. Mem. Kanawha Tchrs. Assn., AAUW, Phi Alpha Theta, Kappa Delta Pi, Alpha Delta Kappa. Democrat. Avocations: fishing; reading; traveling. Home: Rt 1 Box 762 Coal River Rd Saint Albans WV 25177 Office: Village Sch 1213 Village Dr South Charleston WV 25309

CARTER, BETSY L., magazine editor; b. N.Y.C., June 9, 1945; d. Rudy and Gerda Cohn; B.A., U. Mich., 1967. Editorial asst. McGraw Hill, 1967-68; editor co. mag. Am. Security & Trust Co., 1968-69; editorial asst. Atlantic Monthly, 1969-70; researcher Newsweek, N.Y.C., 1971-73, asst. editor, 1973-75, assoc. editor 1975-80; sr. editor Esquire Mag., N.Y.C., 1980-81, exec. editor, 1982-83, sr. exec. editor, 1983-84, editorial dir., 1984-86; editor, founder New York Woman mag., 1986—. freelance contbr. to Atlantic, Washington Post, Family Weekly. Office: 2 Park Ave New York NY 10016

CARTER, CAROLYN HOUCHIN, advertising agency executive; b. Louisville, Nov. 2, 1952; d. Paul Clayton and Georgia Houchin C.; B.S.J., Northwestern U., 1974, M.S.J., 1975. Asst. account exec. SSC&B Advt., Inc., N.Y.C., 1975-76, account exec., 1976-77; account exec. Grey Advt., Inc., N.Y.C., 1977-79, account supr., 1979-81, v.p., account supr., 1981-82, v.p., mgmt. supr., 1982-85, v.p., group mgmt. supr., 1985—; mem. Nat. Advt. Rev. Bd., 1983—. Mem. U.S. council World Communications Yr., 1983. Mem. March of Dimes Media Adv. Council, 1981-84, chmn., 1985—. Mem. Am. Mktg. Assn., N.Y. Women in Communications (pres. 1982-83, chmn. 1985 Matrix awards). Office: Grey Advt Inc 777 3d Ave New York NY 10017

CARTER, CHERYL MORDEN, child care administrator; b. Bismarck, N.D., Sept. 29, 1950; d. Ervin Carl and Vlasta Jeanette (Slavick) Hoesel; m. Craig Audley Morden, May 29, 1971 (div. 1979); 1 child, Brandt Anthony; m. David Michael Carter, Sept. 1, 1985; 1 child, James Davidson. B.S. in Elem. Edn., Eastern Mont. Coll., 1971; postgrad. Colo. State U., 1977, U. Colo., 1977, Community Coll. of Denver, 1979. Cert. child care adminstr. Asst. dir., tchr. Christ United Methodist Ch., Honolulu, 1972-73; owner, dir. Early Learners Presch., Billings, Mont., 1973-75; regional dir. LaPetite Acads., Denver, 1977-82, Children's World, Richmond, Va., 1982—. Mem. Nat. Assn. Female Execs., Nat. Assn. Edn. of Young Children, Va. Assn. for Early Childhood Edn. Methodist. Avocations: reading; decorating; fishing; camping; travel. Home: 12724 Old Country Ln Midlothian VA 23113 Office: Childrens World 10047 Midlothian Turnpike Richmond VA 23235

CARTER, DIANNA SUE, nurse; b. Lamesa, Tex., May 20, 1956; d. James Travis and Nellie Marie (Harrington) C. Diploma Meth. Hosp. Sch. Nursing, 1980. R.N., Tex. Staff nurse Meth. Hosp., Lubbock, Tex., 1980-81; staff nurse, asst. supr. Baylor Med. Ctr., Dallas, 1981-82; office mgr., nurse Robert Mathews, M.D., Dallas, 1982-83; float nurse St. Paul Hosp., Dallas, 1983; staff nurse Parkland Meml. Hosp., Dallas, 1981—. Vol. Dallas County Heritage Soc., 1982; active Jr. League, Dallas, 1983. Mem. Tex. Assn. Health Occupation Students (exec. council 1973-74), Nat. Nursing Student Assn., Tex. Nursing Students Assn. (dist. sec. 1979-80, local chmn. and conv. chmn. 1979-80; Outstanding Student award 1980, Leadership award 1979, Best OB Nurse award 1980), Nurses Assn. Ob-Gyn (chpt. chmn. 1983-84, conv. chmn. 1984). Mem. Christian Ch. Home: 2020 Tennessee Dallas TX 75224 Office: Parkland Meml Hosp 5959 Harry Hines Blvd Dallas TX 75235

CARTER, EDITH HOUSTON, statistician, educator; b. Charlotte, N.C., Oct. 12, 1936; d. Z. and Ellie (Hartsell) Houston; B.S., Appalachian State U., 1959, M.A., 1960; Ph.D., Va. Poly. Inst. and State U., 1976; m. Fletcher F. Carter, Apr. 2, 1961. Transcript analyst Fla. Dept. Edn., Tallahassee, 1961-65; instr. Radford U., 1969-70; prof. New River Community Coll., Dublin, Va., 1970—, dir. instl. research, 1974-78, asst. dean Coll. Arts and Scis., 1978-79, statistician, 1979-83. Violist Va. Poly. Inst. and State U. Orch., Radford U. Orch., S.W. Va. Opera Soc. Orch. Mem. Am. Ednl. Research Assn., Assn. Instl. Research (exec. bd. 1976-78), Southeastern Assn. Community Coll. Research (exec. bd. 1976-78, Outstanding Service award, Disting. Service award 1981), Nat. Council Research and Planning, Coll. Music Soc., Am. String Tchrs. Assn., Va. Fedn. Women's Clubs (dir. 1968-70). Methodist. Clubs: Radford Garden, Radford Jr. Woman's (pres. 1967-68). Editor Community Coll. Jour. Research and Planning, 1981—, Newsletter Southeastern Assn. Community Coll. Research, 1972—. Home: Box 5781 RU Radford VA 24142 Office: New River Community College Dublin VA 24084

CARTER, IMELDA SMITH, accountant; b. Picayune, Miss., Mar. 17, 1952; d. Richard Reginald and Helena Frances (Fuente) Smith; m. William Kemp Carter, May 25, 1974; 1 child, Richard William. B.S., U. So. Miss., 1973, M.S., 1974. Internal auditor Okla. State U., Stillwater, 1974-77, U. Va., Charlottesville, 1978-79, mgr. fin. reporting, 1979-85. Democrat. Roman Catholic. Avocations: needlecraft; sailing; water skiing. Home: 2675 Stowe Ct Charlottesville VA 22901 Office: Reporting and Control Univ Va Carruthers Hall Emmett St Charlottesville VA 22906

CARTER, IVA BROOKIN, educational administrator; b. Steelton, Pa., Aug. 30, 1935; d. Major Henry and Lela Mary (Shepherd) Brookin; m. James G. Carter, June 12, 1956 (div. 1963); m. Paul D. Gutwein, July 5, 1974. A.A., Central Pa. Bus. Coll., 1953; B.S., Elizabethtown Coll., 1959. Legal analyst Dept. Labor and Industry, Harrisburg, Pa., 1958-65; adminstr. Def. Intelligence Agy., Washington, 1965-69; head bus. dept. Janssen Inst., Washington, 1969-71; adminstr. Nat. Urban Coalition, Washington, 1971-72; pres., dir. Brook-Wein Bus. Inst., Washington, 1972—; cons. speaker Assn. Ind. Coll. and Schs., Las Vegas, Nev., 1981, Burmuda, 1980; co-founder, dir. Brook-Wein Bus. Inst., Washington, 1972—. Bd. dirs. D.C. Pvt. Industry Council, Washington, 1983-85, D.C. Rehab. Assn., 1980-83; mem. Nat. Rehab. Assn., Washington, Recipient Service award D.C. Rehab. Assn., 1982; Outstanding Service awards Assn. Ind. Colls. and Schs., 1980, 81; Pvt. Industry Council award City Mayor Washington, 1983. Mem. Nat. Assn. Women Bus. Owners, Nat. Assn. Female Execs., Nat. Bus. Edn. Assn., Eastern Bus. Edn. Assn., D.C. Bus. Edn. Assn. Democrat. Club: Vogue (chmn. activities com.) (Harrisburg, Pa.). Lodge: Elks (chmn. activities com. 1960-65). Office: Brook-Wein Bus Inst 2080 L St NW Washington DC 20036

CARTER, JANET HENSON, author, owner editorial agency; b. Dallas, Oct. 7, 1938; d. John Frank and Jean Maury (Greenwood) Henson; m. David M. Coker, 1958 (dec.); m. 2d. Richard A. Carter, 1966 (div. 1976); children—David Andrew, Christopher Allen, Richard Wesley; m. 3d Mickey C. Combs, 1980, (div. 1982). Student U. Tex., 1974-75; B.S., East Tex. State U., 1976. Owner Stitchendipitiy Art Needlework, Austin, 1966-75; writer, owner Literary Services Unlimited, Dallas, 1975—; owner The Resume Place, Dallas, 1982-83. Author: The Other Me, 1976; editor Forthcoming Mag., 1976-77; Henson Briefs, 1955-59; asst. editor: The Kangaroo Report, 1982; contbr. articles to various publs. Mem. Authors Guild/Authors League Am., Assn. Editorial Businesses, Romance Writers Am., Women in Communication. Methodist. Clubs: Hunt County Mothers of Twins (founder 1974) Mothers of Twins (Austin, Tex.); JayCettes (pres. 1962) (Greenville, Tex.). Home: 11426 Lanewood Circle Dallas TX 75218 Office: Literary Services Unlimited PO Box 38507 Dallas TX 75238

CARTER, JANICE ANN, association executive; b. Iowa City, Apr. 12, 1950; d. Howard R. and Lola Rae (Bartow) Carter. A.B., Smith Coll., 1972. Coordinator devel. Union of Ind. Colls. of Art, Kansas City, Mo., 1974-76; exec. dir. Rockford Arts Council, Ill., 1976-77; sr. cons. Lawrence-Leiter & Co., Kansas City, 1977-83; dir. mktg. Ashcraft, Inc., Kansas City, 1983-84; mgr., mem. services Am. Acad. Family Physicians, Kansas City, 1984—. Author: (with Price) Teleconferencing: A Guide for Associations, 1983. Pres. Met. chpt. Nat. Kidney Found., Kansas City, 1982-83; bd. dirs. Greater Kansas City Chpt. ARC, 1984—. Mem. Am. Mktg. Assn., Am. Soc. Assn. Execs. Club: Smith Coll. of Greater Kansas City (sec. 1981-83, treas. 1985—). Avocations: gardening; reading; photography. Home: 4517 State Line Rd Kansas City MO 64111 Office: Am Acad Family Physicians 1740 W 92nd St Kansas City MO 64114

CARTER, JOYCE ELAINE ARNDT, writer, editor, photographer; b. Bellevue, Ohio, Jan. 9, 1944; d. Bryce Leroy Arndt and Agnes Arline (Rudicel) Arndt Chellis; student Gonzaga U., 1962-63, Phoenix Coll., 1963-66, U. Wash., Seattle, 1966-67; m. Zane Hartson Carter, Jan. 16, 1965 (div. 1971). Editor de Paul Speaks mag., St. Vincent de Paul Parish, Phoenix, 1971-74; editor Ultreya internat. mag. Mt. Claret Cursillo Center, Phoenix, 1971-72; pub. info. photographer Phoenix Coll., 1972—; free lance writer. Mem. Nat. League Am. Pen Women, Poetry Soc. Democrat. Roman Catholic. Club: Phoenix Writers (pres. 1972-73). Contbr. poetry and fiction to nat. profl. and popular publs. Home: 1725 E Catalina Dr Phoenix AZ 85016

CARTER, LINDA SUSAN, broadcast journalist; b. Columbus, Ohio, Nov. 18, 1950; d. Edward Herman and Jane Lewis (Joseph) C.; m. Jerome Ronald Piasecki, June 5, 1976 (div. Feb. 1983); 1 dau., Amanda. B.A., Mich. State U., 1984. News dir. WAVZ-AM, New Haven, Conn., 1977-78, WABX-FM, Detroit, 1978—; news anchor WWJ-AM, Detroit, 1978-81; talk show host WXYZ-AM, Detroit, 1981-82; press sec. Office of the Gov., Lansing, Mich., 1982-83; news anchor WWJ-AM, Detroit, 1983-85; dir. pub. affairs Sta. WDIV-TV, Detroit, 1985-86, dir. editorials, 1986—. Vestrywoman, Cathedral Ch. of St. Paul, Detroit, 1982-83; mem. Rackman Symphony Choir. Mem. AFTRA (exec. bd. mem. 1982—). Episcopalian. Home: 1300 E Lafayette Blvd Apt 1009 Detroit MI 48207 Office: Sta UDIV-TV 550 W Lafayette Blvd Detroit MI 48231

CARTER, LISA JOYCE, paint manufacturing company executive; b. Galveston, Tex., June 1, 1959; d. Carlton and Dorothy Lee (McPeters) Pappas Kelly; m. Michael Page Carter, Aug. 19, 1978. Student N. Tex. State U., 1977, Richland Coll., 1978, U. Ark.-Little Rock, 1980, IBM Continuing Edn., 1981-82. Mktg. asst. Membership Services, Irving, Tex., 1978, tech. support asst., 1980; programmer, analyst Mail Mktg. Services, Little Rock, 1980-82; bus. broker VR Bus. Brokers, Longview, Tex., 1982-85; mgr., treas. Creative Coatings Inc., Kilgore, Tex., 1985—, also dir. Mem. Mothers Against Drunk Drivers, Longview, Tex., 1985-86. Mem. Data Processing Mgrs. Assn. Baptist. Avocations: skiing; traveling. Home: 110 E Hawkins Pkwy Apt 1102 Longview TX 75601 Office: Creative Coatings Inc 428 N Longview St Kilgore TX 75662

CARTER, MAE RIEDY, university official; b. Berkeley, Calif., May 20, 1921; d. Carl Joseph and Avis Blanche (Rhodehaver) Riedy; B.S., U. Calif., Berkeley, 1943; m. Robert C. Carter, Aug. 19, 1944; children—Catherine, Christin Ann. Ednl. adv., then program specialist div. continuing edn. U. Del., Newark, 1968-78, asst. provost for women's affairs, exec. dir. commn. status women Office Women's Affairs, 1978—; adv. bd. Rockefeller Family grant project, 1979-83. Regional v.p. Del. PTA, 1960-62; pres. Friends Newark Free Library, 1968-69; mem. fiscal planning com. Newark Spl. Sch. Dist., 1972. Recipient Outstanding Service award Women's Coordinating Council, 1977, 79; Spl. Recognition award, Nat. U. Extension Assn., 1977, award for credit programs, 1971, Creative Programming award, 1971; AAUW grantee, 1968; Fulbright grantee, 1976. Mem. AAUW (past br. pres.), Women's Equity Action League, Nat. Assn. Women Deans, Adminstrs. and Counselors, NOW, Women's Studies Assn. Republican. Author: (with Geis and Butler) Seeing and Evaluating People, 1982, Research on Seeing and Evaluating People; also papers, reports in field. Home: 604 Dallam Rd Newark DE 19711 Office: Office Women's Affairs Univ Del Newark DE 19711

CARTER, MARCÍA ELAINE COX, communications internal auditor; b. Washington, Jan. 25, 1959; d. James Richmond, Sr. and Gloria Elaine (Hansborough) C. B. cum laude in Bus., Ogelthorpe U., Atlanta, 1981. Asst. auditor Peat Marwick, Atlanta, 1981-83; asst. sr. auditor Cox Communications, Atlanta, 1983—. Campaign worker Andrew Young Campaign for Mayor, Atlanta, 1981-82, Andrew Young Re Election Campaign, Atlanta, 1985; vol. worker United Negro Coll. Fund, Atlanta, 1982-84. Nominated Outstanding Young Women of Am., 1983. Mem. Alpha Kappa Alpha (leadership fellow 1981), Omicron Delta Kappa (Leadership award 1978, inducted for outstanding leadership and contributions 1981), Nat. Assn. Black Accts., Atlanta Exchange Assn. Democrat. Baptist. Office: Cox Communications Inc 1400 Lake Hearn Dr Atlanta GA 30319

CARTER, MARTHA LOUISE, financial analyst; b. Chgo., Aug. 19, 1956; d. John Henry and Aurelia Celeste (Bernard) C. B.S. in Math., Purdue U., 1978, B.A. in French, 1978; M.B.A. in Fin., Wharton Sch., U. Pa., 1983. Systems analyst IBM, Gaithersburg, Md., 1978-81, fin. analyst, 1984—; investment analyst Am. Stock Exchange, N.Y.C., 1982; mgmt. cons. Touche Ross & Co., Chgo., 1983-84. Bd. dirs. Gaithersburg Guide Youth Services, 1985—. Mem. Assn. M.B.A. Execs., Nat. Assn. Female Execs., Bus. and Profl. Women, NOW, Nat. Women's Polit. Caucus (chpt. legis. com. 1986), LWV, Sierra Club, Nat. Geog. Soc., Phi Beta Kappa, Pi Delta Phi, Alpha Lambda Delta. Karate gold belt, 1985. Avocations: piano; singing; bike riding; hiking; reading. Office: IBM 100 Lake Forest Blvd Gaithersburg MD 20878

CARTER, MARY EDDIE, government official; b. Americus, Ga., Mar. 14, 1925; d. Walker G. and Mary Esther Stewart) C.; B.S., LaGrange (Ga.) Coll., 1946; M.S., U. Fla., Gainesville, 1949; Ph.D. (Rockefeller and Alex Cowan & Sons, Ltd. grantee), U. Edinburgh (Scotland), 1956. Microscopist, Callaway Mills, LaGrange, 1947-48; textile chemist So. Research Inst., Birmingham, Ala., 1949-51; chemist West Point Pepperel (Ga.), 1951-53; research asso. Am. Viscose div. FMC Corp., Phila., 1956-71; lab. chief textiles and clothing lab. Dept. Agr., Knoxville, Tenn., 1971-73, dir. So. Regional Research Center, 1973-80, assoc. adminstr. Agrl. Research Service, Washington, 1980—; prof. chemistry U. Tenn., Knoxville, 1971-73; instr. LaGrange Coll., 1946-47. Recipient Sr. Exec. Service Rank award, 1982. Mem. Am. Chem. Soc. (Herty award Ga. sect. 1979), Am. Assn. Textile Chemists and Colorists, Fiber Soc., Inter-Color Soc., Inst. Food Technologists, Am. Assn. Cereal Chemists, Fed. Exec. League, Fedn. Women, Fed. Exec. Inst., Sigma Xi. Author: Essential Fiber Chemistry, 1971; contbr. articles to tech. jours. Patentee in field. Office: USDA ARS OA Room 302A Administration Bldg Washington DC 20250

CARTER, MARY SLAUGHTER, education support adminstrator; b. Montgomery, Ala., Oct. 28, 1939; d. George Johnson and Julia Mae (Floyd) Franklin Johnson; m. Harold Brevard Franklin, Sr., Oct. 14, 1955 (dec. May 1970); children—Harold, Jr., Louis, Orlando Franklin, Javis Franklin-Wilson; m. Cecil James Carter, Jan. 6, 1979; 1 child, Kay Ann Carter-Corker. Bus. cert. Massey Draughon, 1968; student J.C. Calhoun Jr. Coll., Decatur, Ala., 1971-73; B.S. in Bus. Adminstrn., Troy State U., 1979. File clk. IBM, Huntsville, Ala., 1968-70, receptionist, 1970-71, sec., 1971-75, sec. specialist, Montgomery, Ala., 1975-80, edn. support adminstr., 1980—; substitute instr. Auburn U., Montgomery, 1981; vol. instr. Links Community Project, Montgomery, 1981; guest speaker Ala. State U., Montgomery, 1982. Deaconess Calvary Presbyterian Ch., Montgomery, 1980—, treas., 1983—; fgn. officer sponsorship, Maxwell AFB, Ala., 1979—; pres. Les Belle Amies Civic Orgn., Montgomery, 1982; spl. projects chairperson Continental Socs., Inc., Montgomery, 1983—; mem. Assn. Retarded Citizens, Montgomery, 1980—, Friends of Tarwater, Wetumpka, Ala., 1984—. Lupus Assn., Montgomery, 1983—, Kidney Found., Montgomery, 1981—; mem. Ala. Devel. Disabilities Planning Council, Montgomery, 1985-87. Recipient awards IBM, 1976-84. Mem. Phi Gamma Nu. Democrat. Club: Toastmasters (Montgomery, Ala.). Avocations: gardening; cooking. Home: 333 N Anton Dr Montgomery AL 36105 Office: IBM 4525 Executive Park Dr Montgomery AL 36111

CARTER, MELANIE SUE, lawyer; b. White Plains, N.Y., Jan. 2, 1957; d. Selden Booker and Shirley Emma (Abbott) C. A.B. with honors, Randolph-Macon Woman's Coll., 1978; J.D., Northwestern U., 1981. Bar: Ill. 1981. Assoc. Hoellen, Lukes & Halper, Chgo., 1981-86, ptnr., 1986—. Vol. tchr., adviser Chgo. Coalition for Legal Edn., 1984. Mem. ABA, Ill. Bar Assn., Chgo. Bar Assn. (legal com. for disabled 1983-84, probate com. 1984-85), Chgo. Council Fgn. Relations, Phi Beta Kappa. Baptist. Office: Hoellen Lukes & Halper 1940 W Irving Park Rd Chicago IL 60613

CARTER, MILDRED BROWN, communications company executive; b. Leo, S.C., Feb. 22, 1927; d. Eddie Washington and Hester Lessie Lee (Poston) Brown; m. Richard Bert Carter, Sept. 6, 1952; children—Paul, Mark, Janis, David. Student U. Wash., 1965. Sec. FBI, Washington, 1943-48, adminstrv. asst., 1948-51, adminstrv. asst. office of assoc. dir., 1952; on staff Bellevue Sch. Dist., Washington, 1965-70; sec., registrar Hyak Jr. High, Bellevue, 1971-75; asst. to exec. v.p. Bonneville Internat. Corp., Salt Lake City, 1975-83, exec. asst. to pres., 1983—. Mem. Beta Sigma Phi. Clubs: Woman's Century (Yakima, Wash.), Soc. Former FBI Women. Lodge: Soroptimists Internat. Home: 2180 Elaine Dr Bountiful UT 84010 Office: Bonneville Internat Corp Broadcast House Salt Lake City UT 84180

CARTER, PHYLLIS ELIZABETH, marriage and family therapist, educator; b. N.Y.C., June 28, 1941; d. Charlton and Rosetta (Davis) Stennett; m. Ronald H. Carter, Sept. 14, 1963; children—Tracy Lorette, Tanya Lynnette, Tina Louise, Tammy Lenore. B.S. in Sociology, Southeastern U., Greenville, S.C., 1978; M.S. in Counseling, St. John's U., 1983; advance cert. in marriage and family therapy Queens Coll., N.Y.C., 1984; M.Div., Nat. Theol. Sem., 1984. Pvt. practice marriage and family therapy, Uniondale, N.Y., 1984—; dir. counseling Refuge Ch., Freeport, N.Y., 1980—; instr. Blantan-Peale Grad. Inst., Forest Hills, N.Y., 1983—. Author: The Pastor's Rib and His Flock, 1979. Mem. Am. Assn. Marriage and Family Therapy, Am. Assn. Pastoral Counselors. Mem. Apostolic Ch. Avocations: writing, composing. Address: 815 Coleridge Rd Uniondale NY 11553

CARTER, REBECCA ANNE, nurse; b. Cairo, Ga., Nov. 2, 1955; d. Oscar Odysseus and Betty Lou (Scott) Sellars; m. James Edward Carter, Feb. 2, 1972; children—Calyn, Allison, Dustin. A.A., Albany Jr. Coll., 1980. Staff nurse Phoebe Putney Hosp., Albany, Ga., 1980-81, McLeod Regional Med. Ctr., Florence, S.C., 1981-82; charge nurse Palmyra Park Hosp., Albany, 1982—. Home: 1008 11th Ave Albany GA 31701 Office: Palmyra Park Hosp 2000 Palmyra Rd Albany GA 31701

CARTER, ROBERTA ECCLESTON, educator, therapist; b. Pitts.; d. Robert E. and Emily B. (Bucar) Carter; (div.); children—David Michael, Daniel Michael. Student Edinboro State U., 1962-63; B.S., California State U. of Pa., 1966; M.Ed., U. Pitts., 1969; postgrad. Rosebridge Grad. Sch., Walnut Creek, Calif., 1985—. Tchr., Bethel Park Sch. Dist., Pa., 1966-69; writer, media asst. Field Ednl. Pub., San Francisco, 1969-70; educator, counselor, specialist Alameda Unified Sch. Dist., Calif., 1970—; master trainer Calif. State Dept. Edn., Sacramento, 1984—; personal growth cons., Alameda, 1983—. Author: People, Places and Products, 1970, Teaching/Learning Units, 1969; co-author: Teacher's Manual Let's Read, 1968. Mem. AAUW, Calif. Fedn. Bus. and Profl. Women (legis. chair Alameda br. 1984-85, membership chair 1985), NEA, Calif. Edn. Assn., Alameda Edn. Assn., Charter Planetary Soc., Oakland Mus., Exploratorium, Big Bros. of East Bay, Alameda C. of C. (service award 1985). Republican. Avocations: aerobics; gardening; travel. Home: 1516 E Shore Dr Alameda CA 94501

CARTER, ROSALYNN SMITH, wife of former Pres. U.S.; b. nr. Plains, Ga., Aug. 18, 1927; d. Wilburn Edgar and Allethea (Murray) Smith; grad. Ga. Southwestern Coll., 1946; H.H.D. (hon.), Tift Coll., 1979; L.H.D. (hon.), Morehouse Coll., 1980; m. James Earl Carter, Jr., July 7, 1946; children—John William, James Earl III, Donnel Jeffrey, Amy Lynn. Past mem. Ga. Gov.'s Commn. to Improve Service for Mentally and Emotionally Handicapped; past hon. chmn. Ga. Spl. Olympics for Retarded Children; past hon. chmn. Pres.'s Commn. Mental Health. Recipient Merit award NOW; Vol. of Yr. award Southwestern Assn. Vol. Services; Vol. of Decade award Nat. Mental Health Assn., 1980; presdl. citation Am. Psychol. Assn., 1982. Baptist. Author: First Lady from Plains, 1984. Home: 75 Spring St SW Plains GA 31780

CARTER, RUTH B. (MRS. JOSEPH C. CARTER), association executive; b. Charlotte, Vt.; d. Ira E. and Sadie M. (Congdon) Burroughs; Ph.B., U. Vt., 1931; m. Joseph C. Carter, June 28, 1935. Prin., Newton Acad., Shoreham, Vt., 1931-35; substitute tchr. Spaulding High Sch., Barre, Vt., also Woodbury (Vt.) High Sch., 1935-36; tchr. Craftsbury Acad., Craftsbury Common, Vt., 1936-38; sales mgr., buyer Vt. Music Co., Barre, 1939-44; statistician Syracuse U., 1944-46; instr. English, Temple U., Phila., 1946-47; records clk. sec., 1947-56; tchr. English, Central High Sch., Phila., 1957, Springfield Twp. Sr. High Sch., Montgomery County, Pa., 1964-65; sec. Women's Univ. Club, Phila., 1961-64, treas., 1965-67; exec. dir. White-Williams Found., 1966-82, trustee, 1982—. Recipient Humanitarian award Chapel of Four Chaplains, 1981; city council citation City of Phila., 1982. Mem. AAUW (admissions chmn. 1959-61, treas. 1965-67), Women For Greater Phila., DAR (treas., historian, com. chmn., budget dir. Germantown chpt., regent 1983—), New Eng. Historic Geneal. Soc., Geneal. Soc. Vt., Soc. Mayflower Descs. (bd. dirs. 1983-84, sec. 1985—). Republican. Methodist. Clubs: Temple University Faculty Wives (pres. Center City group, sec. Old York Rd. group 1983—), Temple University Women's. Author: (with Joseph C. Carter) Anchors Aweigh Around the World with Ernest Vail Burroughs, 1960; Dixie Diary, 1965; Pilgrimage to the Lovely Lands of our Ancestors, 1984; Westward—Ho! And Home Again, 1985. Home: 40 W Mt Carmel Ave Glenside PA 19038

CARTER, SARALEE LESSMAN, immunologist, microbiologist; b. Chgo., Feb. 19, 1951; d. Julius A. and Ida (Oiring) Lessman; B.A., National Coll., 1971; m. John B. Carter, Oct. 7, 1979; 1 child, Robert Oiring. Supr. lab. immunology Weiss Meml. Hosp., Chgo., 1973-80; lab. immunology supr. Henrotin Hosp., Chgo., 1980-84; tech. dir. Lexington Med. Labs., West Columbia, S.C., 1984—; mem. nat. workshop faculty Am. Soc. Clin. Pathologists. Mem. Am. Soc. Clin. Pathologists (subspecialty cert. in microbiology and immunology, cert. med. technologist). Researcher Legionnaires Disease and mycoplasma pneumonia World Soc. Pathologists, Jerusalem, Israel, 1980. Contbr. articles to profl. jours. Office: 2720 Sunset Blvd W Columbia SC 29169

CARTER, SUE CLAUDELLE, chamber of commerce executive; b. Ellensburg, Wash., May 7, 1944; d. Claude H. and Elsie M. (Johnson) Norton; m. Frank A. Peter, June 14, 1969 (div. 1978); m. 2d James E. Carter, Sr., Nov. 23, 1980. A.A., Wenatchee Valley Coll., 1964. Mcpl. clk. City Kenai, Alaska, 1974-78; owner Concepts Unltd., Kenai, 1978-80; sales rep. Beluga Realty, Inc., Kenai, Alaska, 1980—; exec. dir., mgr. Greater Kenai Chamber of Commerce, Kenai, 1982—; dir., sec.-treas. Homer Electric Assn., 1980—. Sec. Pioneers Alaska, Aux. 16, Kenai, 1983; mem. CAP, Kenai, 1983—. Mem. Alaska State C. of C., Kenai Peninsula Bd. Realtors, Peninsula Council Chambers. Republican. Roman Catholic. Clubs: Twin Cities Soroptimist (charter, dir. 1981); Birch Ridge Country (Soldotna, Alaska) Lodge: Order Eastern Star. Home: 36875 Chinulna Dr Box 212 Kenai AK 99611 Office: Greater Kenai C of C Box 497 Kenai AK 99611

CARTER, VIRGINIA MILNER, financial management executive; b. Atlanta, July 1, 1919; d. Willis Justus and Virginia Amanda (Cohen) Milner; B.A., Agnes Scott Coll., 1940; student Smith Coll., 1943, Radcliffe Coll., 1944, So. Meth. U., 1959-60, Wharton Bus. Sch., 1978; children—Alverson, Ida Richards (Mrs. Joseph N. Consola, Jr.), Virginia Seixas, Robert Milner. Dist. mgr. Prestige Silver Co., Atlanta, Charlotte, N.C. and Richmond, Va., 1947-58; agt. Ga. Internat. Life Ins. Co. and predecessor co., Atlanta, 1959-61, agy. dir., 1961-69, asst. corp. sec., 1965-69; v.p. Employee Benefit Plans, Rome, Ga., 1969; acct. exec. Planned Equity, Atlanta, 1971; v.p. Profl. Investment Counselors, Atlanta, 1970; div. mgr. Waddell & Reed, Atlanta, 1972-76; nat. sales dir. A.L. Williams, Dulith, Dealer, Tucker, Ga., 1976—, also dir. A.L. Williams Corp.; former dir. Mario's Ristorantes, Inc., Nelco Enterprises. Bd. dirs. Atlanta YWCA, 1966-69; pres. bd. trustees Covenant Presbyn. Ch. Served to lt. USNR, 1942-45. Mem. AAUW, LWV, Bus. and Profl. Women, Internat. Assn. Fin. Planners, DAR, Nat. Assn. Life Underwriters, Cert. Fin. Planners. Republican. Club: Dunwoody Country. Home: 1786 Trapnall Dr Dunwoody GA 30338 Office: Al Williams 3120 Breckinridge Blvd Duluth GA 30199

CARTER, WANDA JOY, banker; b. Roxton, Tex., Mar. 19, 1932; d. Noble H. and Gertrude (Larkin) Weaver; m. Albert M. Carter, Jr., Sept. 3, 1955; children—Rickey K., Michael A. Student Tex. Tech. Coll., 1976, 78; grad. Am. Inst. Banking, Dallas, 1976; student U. Okla., 1980. With First Nat. Bank (now Republic Bank), Garland, Tex., 1957—, v.p., 1979—, loan officer, 1980—. Bd. dirs. Ptnrs. in Edn., Garland, 1986. Nat. Assn. Bank Women scholar, 1973. Mem. Am. Bus. Women Assn. (woman of yr. 1975, 86, past pres., now chmn. scholarship), Nat. Assn. Bank Women (sec. 1978-79). Republican. Baptist. Avocations: crochet; reading; needlepoint. Home: 1217 Travis St Garland TX 75040 Office: Republic Bank Garland PO Box 461228 Garland TX 75046

CARTER-BANE, SHARIE ELIZABETH, social service executive; b. Honolulu, July 18, 1958; d. Norman Lee and Betty C. (Lane) C.; m. Gregory Scott Bane, Oct. 20, 1979; children—Angel Kay, Adrienne Rae. Student Ill. State U., 1976-77, Danville Jr. Coll., 1977-78. Librarian asst. Hoopeston Jr. High Sch., Ill., 1975-76; dental asst., Hoopeston, 1977-78; reporter Danville Comml. News, Ill., 1978-79; exec. dir. Hoopeston Multi Agy., 1979—. Sec., Grant Twp. United Way, 1983-86; del. White House Conf. on Aging in Am., 1980; sec. Vermilion County Aging Adv. Com., 1985—. Mem. Vermilion Human Coalition, Nat. Alliance Info. and Referral, Nat. Assn. Female Execs. Democrat. Avocations: poetry; cooking; music; people. Home: 425 E Young St Hoopeston IL 60942 Office: 210 S Market St Suite 313 Hoopeston IL 60942

CARTIER, CELINE PAULE, librarian, administrator; b. Lacolle, Que., Can., May 10, 1930; d. Henri Rodolphe and Irene (Boudreau) Robitaille; m. Georges Cartier, Nov. 29, 1952; children—Nathalie, Guillaume. Diplome superieur en pedagogie, U. Montreal, 1948, certificats en litterature et linguistique, 1952; diplome de bibliothecaire-documentaliste, Inst. Catholique, Paris, 1962; maîtrise en adminstrn. publique, Ecole Nationale d'Adminstrn. Publique, 1976; maîtrise en bibliothéconomie, U. Montreal, 1982. Dir. Bibliotheque Centrale, Commn. des ecoles catholiques, Montreal, 1964-73; dir. spl. collections U. Quebec, 1973-76, dir. sector libraries, 1976-77; chief gen. library U. Laval, Que., 1977-78, gen. dir. libraries, 1978—. Contbr. articles to profl. jours. Mem. Corp. des Bibliothecaires Profs. de Quebec, Can. Library Assn., ALA, Fedn. Internat. des Assn. de Bibliothecaires et des Bibliotheques, Assn. pour l'avancement des Scis. et des techniques de la documentation. Office: Univ Laval Bibliotheque Cite Universitaire Ste Foy Quebec PQ G1K 7P4 Canada

CARTWRIGHT, CLAUDINE MELTON, former administrator; b. Winnsboro, La., May 14, 1933; d. Clyde Grafton and Lillian (Womack) Melton; m. Walter Clifford Cartwright, Sept. 6, 1951; 1 child, Sherri. Student La. Bus. Coll., Monroe, 1951-52, Fresno State Coll., 1955-56; B.A. in Psychology, Northeast La. U., 1976. Adminstr. La. Bus. Coll., 1976-81; area dir. Am. Heart Assn., Monroe, 1981-82; program dir. Monroe Area Guidance Ctr., 1982-83. Republican. Methodist. Home: 132 Hemlock Circle West Monroe LA 71291

CARTWRIGHT, MARY LOU, clinical laboratory scientist; b. Payette, Idaho, Apr. 5, 1923; d. Ray J. and Nellie Mae (Sherer) Decker; B.S., U. Houston, 1958; M.A., Central Mich. U., 1976; m. Chadwick Louis Cartwright, Sept. 13, 1947. Med. technologist Methodist Hosp., Houston, 1957-59, VA Hosp., Livermore, Calif., 1960-67, Kaiser Permanente Med. Center, Hayward, Calif., 1967-71, United Med. Lab., San Mateo, Calif., 1972-73; sr. med. technologist Oakland (Calif.) Hosp., 1974-86; cons. med. lab. tech. Oakland Pub. Schs. Chmn., Congressional Dist. 11 steering com. Common Cause, 1974-77; consumer mem. Alameda County (Calif.) Health Systems Agy., 1977-78. Served with USNR, 1945-53. Mem. Calif. Soc. Med. Tech., Calif. Assn. Med. Lab. Tech. (Technologist of Yr. award 1968, 78, Pres.'s award 1977, Service award chpt. 1978, 79), Am. Soc. Med. Tech. (by-laws chmn. 1981-83), Am. Bus. Women's Assn., Nat. Assn. Female Execs. Democrat. Home and Office: 231 Depot St #8 Grass Valley CA 95945

CARTWRIGHT, STEPHANIE (ZAVELL) (DOROTHEA COY), textile designer; b. N.Y.C., Feb. 18, 1914; d. James Joseph and Esther (McGrann) Coy; William K. Vanderbilt scholar, France and Italy, 1931; ed. Paris br. Parsons Sch. Design, N.Y. Sch. Fine and Applied Art, 1932, Columbia U.; m. Arnold Zavell, Feb. 15, 1946; children—Margot, A. Stephen. Designer window and interior displays Bonwit Teller; designer, stylist Susquehanna Silk Mills; pres. Fabrics by Cartwrights div. Roth Fabrics; v.p. Coutoure Fabrics, Ltd., 1945-54, pres., 1954—, also dir.; v.p., dir. Pavillon Fabrics Corp., Fabric Mart Corp.; lectr. textile design, overseer Parsons Sch. Design, Fashion Group Am. Career Course; design cons. Office aux. N.Y. Infirmary; asso. bd. dirs. Assn. Home; vice chmn. adv. council LaGuardia House Nursery; vol. painting class Yorkville Youth Council; past bd. govs. Boys and Girls Service League. Recipient Cover Design award Art et Inudstire, 1932; gold medal Calif. Fair Textile Expn., 1953-55; Mem. Parsons Alumni Assn. (council, pres. 1959), Republican Women in Industry and Professions (past pres. N.Y. chpt), Women's Nat. Fashion Group Am. (legis. com., past chmn. membershup com. N.Y.), Nat. Council Women, Internat. Platform Assn. Clubs: York; Univ. Womens (London). Contbr. chpt. to Your Future in Fashion Design, 1966.

CARTWRIGHT, TALULA ELIZABETH, writing educator, communication consultant; b. Asheville, N.C.; s. Ralph and Sarah Helen (Medford) C.; m. Edwin Byram Crabtree, May 23, 1976 (div.); children—Charity, Baxter. B.A., U. N.C., 1971, M.Ed., 1974, postgrad., 1975—. Instr. McDowell Tech. Inst., Marion, N.C., 1972-73, Guilford Tech. Community Coll., Jamestown, N.C., 1973—, Guilford Coll., Greensboro, N.C., 1982-84, U. N.C.-Greensboro, 1982—, N.C. A&T State U., Greensboro, 1984-85; cons. Communication Assocs., Greensboro, 1981—. Precinct chmn. Democratic Party, Greensboro, 1973-74. Winfield scholar U. N.C. at Greensboro, 1970; recipient Escheats award U. N.C.-Greensboro, 1971; Tchr. of Yr. award Greensboro Tech. Community Coll. Edn. Assn., 1982; Civitan Citizenship award, 1966. Mem. Internat. Assn. Bus. Communicators, Nat. Speakers Assn., Am. Soc. Tng. and Devel., Nat. Assn. Female Execs., Am. Mgmt. Assn. Seventh-Day Adventist.

CARUANA, MARY ELIZABETH, software development company executive; b. Chgo., July 27, 1950; d. Arthur Randall and Helen Louise (Jackman) Corwin; m. Roger James Caruana, June 10, 1972; 1 child, Jonathan. B.A., U. Ill., 1972; now postgrad. Rockford Coll. Pres. Caruana Computer Corp., Rockford, 1981—; spl. tech. asst. Ingersoll Milling Machine Co., Rockford, 1984-85. Home: 4107 Verde Ln Rockford IL 61111 Office: Caruana Computer Corp 4107 Verde Ln Rockford IL 61111

CARUS, MARIANNE, magazine editor; b. Dieringhausen, Germany, June 16, 1928; came to U.S., 1951, naturalized, 1956; d. Gunter Wilhelm Alexander and Elisabeth (Gesell) Sondermann; m. Milton Blouke Carus, Mar. 3, 1951; children—Andre, Christine, Inga. M.S., U. Freiburg, Fed. Republic Germany, 1951; postgrad. Sorbonne, U. Paris, U. Chgo. Editor, Open Court Publ. Co., La Salle, Ill., 1964-73; editor-in-chief Cricket Mag., La Salle, 1973—, gen. mgr., 1982—; v.p. Carus Corp., La Salle, 1975—; cons. editor Open Court Pub. Co., 1975—. Editor and compiler: (with Clifton Fadiman) Cricket's Choice, 1974. Bd. dirs. Ill. Valley Community Concert Assn., La Salle, 1960—. Mem. ALA (ALSC div., bd. dirs. 1982-85), Mag. Pubs. Assn., Friends of USBBY, Soc. of Children's Book Writers, Friends of the CCBC Inc., Children's Reading Roundtable Chgo. Clubs: Ill. Valley Garden (past pres.), La Salle Women's (La Salle). Avocations: reading; gardening; hiking; travel; music. Office: Cricket Mag 315 5th St Peru IL 61354

CARUSO, LINDA ANN, lawyer; b. Akron, Ohio, Sept. 22, 1940; d. Asbury Young and Gwyneth Maud (Stokes) Archer; m. Lawrence Robert Caruso; 1 son, Aaron Robert. B.A. cum laude in Polit. Sci., George Washington U., 1978, J.D., 1981. Bar: D.C. 1982, U.S. Dist. Ct. D.C. 1982, U.S. Ct. Appeals (D.C. cir.) 1982, U.S. Supreme Ct. 1985; cert. assoc. contract mgr. Vol. intern U.S. Senate Subcom. on Fed. Spending Practices and Open Govt., Washington, 1977; legal research asst. George Washington U. Law Sch. Govt. Contracts Program, 1979-81; assoc. Stassen, Kostos and Mason, Washington, 1981-82; ptnr. Caruso & Caruso, Washington, 1983—; lectr. Contbr. articles to profl. jours. Mem. Lawyers for Reagan and Bush, Women for Reagan and Bush. Mem. ABA, Fed. Bar Assn. (vice-chmn. com. space law), Am. Soc. Internat. Law, Washington Fgn. Law Soc., Women's Bar Assn. D.C., D.C. Bar Assn., Nat. Contract Mgmt. Assn., Nat. Assn. Women Bus. Owners, U.S. Senate Staff Club, Mortar Bd., Phi Delta Phi, Pi Sigma Alpha, Omicron Delta Kappa. Republican. Methodist. Club: Republican Women of Capitol Hill. Home: 6216 Goodview St Bethesda MD 20817-6102 Office: Caruso & Caruso Suite 727 Fed Bar Bldg 1815-H St NW Washington DC 20006

CARUSO, PATRICIA LOUISE, county official; b. Loring AFB, Maine, Nov. 28, 1954; d. John James and Geraldine Ruth (Sullivan) Geary; m. Stanley John Caruso, Oct. 23, 1976; children—Timothy, Sarah. B.A. magna cum laude, Lake Superior State Coll., 1975; Cert., U. Mich., 1977, M.A., 1978. Counselor Community Action Agy., Sault Saint Marie, Mich., 1975, employment and tng. coordinator, 1975-78; v.p. DMC Personnel Inc., Sault Saint Marie, 1978-79, pres., 1979-80; asst. to alumni dir. Lake Superior State Coll., Sault Saint Marie, 1983, mem. outstanding alumni selection com., 1982—; county controller Chippewa County, Sault Saint Marie, 1983—; cons. Mich. Dept. Edn., Sault Saint Marie, 1981. Mem. city master plan com. City of Sault Saint Marie, 1982—; bd. dirs. Religious Edn. Commn. on Nativity, Sault Saint Marie, 1984—; chairperson Chippewa County Democratic Party, Sault Saint Marie, 1982-83; campaign coordinator Dorrity for Congress, Sault Saint Marie, 1980, Irwin for State Senate, 1982. Named Local and Dist. Young Careerwoman, Bus. and Profl. Women, 1977, 84. Mem. Mich. Assn. County Adminstrv. Officers (bd dirs. 1985—) Govt. Fin. Officers Assn., Nat. Assn. County Adminstrv. Officers. Roman Catholic. Avocations: golf, skiing, running, reading, traveling. Office: Chippewa County 319 Court St Sault Saint Marie MI 49783

CARUTHERS, BARBARA SUE APGAR, physician, educator; b. Guthrie, Okla., Oct. 4, 1943; d. Wallace Duke and Gloria Jayne (Glover) McMillin; m. Charles George Caruthers, Apr. 1, 1976; 1 child, Larisa Ann. B.A. in Biology, Loretto Heights Coll., 1965; M.S. in Anatomy, U. Mich., 1968; M.D., Tex. Tech. Med. Sch., 1976. Diplomate Am. Bd. Family Practice, Am. Bd. Med. Examiners. Research asst. Parke Davis, Ann Arbor, Mich., 1965-66; research asst. Aerospace Med. Labs Wright-Patterson AFB, Ohio, 1968-70; instr. anatomy dept. Tex. Tech. U. Med. Sch., Lubbock, 1972-74, resident in family practice, 1976-79, clin. asst. prof., 1980-83; physician The Pavilion, Lubbock, 1981-83; sr. physician U. Mich. Hosp., dir. Gynecology Clinic, U. Mich. Health Service, health sci. instr. dept. family practice U. Mich., 1984—; former mem. staff St. Mary of the Plains Hosp.; mem. staff U. Mich. Hosp. Recipient Soroptomist resident tng. award, 1978, U. Mich. Outstanding Teaching Award, 1985. Mem. Am. Acad. Family Practice, Mich. State Med. Soc., Alpha Omega Alpha. Democrat. Mem. Ch. Latter Day Saints. Home: 884 Scio Meadow Ann Arbor MI 48103 Office: U Mich 207 Fletcher Ann Arbor MI 48109

CARVAINIS, MARIA, literary agent; b. Brisbane, Australia, Mar. 24, 1946; came to U.S., 1952, naturalized, 1965; d. Nicholas John and Edith Maude (Dent) Carvainis; B.A., CCNY, 1967; m. Ian Ross Jenkins, June 24, 1979. Editorial asst. MacMillan Inc., N.Y.C., 1967-69; interpreter, ITT, N.Y.C., 1969; asst. editor Basic Books, Inc., N.Y.C., 1970-72; freelance cons. to mags., book pubs., 1972-73; editor, spl. asst. to pub. Avon Books, Inc., N.Y.C., 1973-75; freelance author, editor, 1975-76; sr. editor Crown Pubs., Inc., N.Y.C., 1976-77; pres. Maria Carvainis Agy., Inc., N.Y.C., 1977—. N.Y. State Merit scholar, 1963-67. Mem. Authors Guild, Authors League Am., Writers Guild Am., Romance Writers Assn., Internat. Women's Writing Guild. Author: Crepes and Omelettes, 1976; co-author: Moustache, 1979. Address: 235 W End Ave New York NY 10023

CARVALHO, ANGELINA CHAVES AMERICA, physician, educator; b. Azores, Portugal, Sept. 26, 1938; came to U.S., 1968; d. Jose de Freitas and Maria dos Santos (Chaves) America; m. Jaime S. Carvalho, July 18, 1967; 1 son, Alexander A. B.S., U. Coimbra, 1962; M.D. (with honors), Lisbon Med. Sch., 1965. Resident in pathology and medicine Boston VA Hosp. (Mass.), 1967-70; clin. research fellow in medicine Mass. Gen. Hosp., Boston, 1971-73, head spl. coagulation lab., 1973-77; research assoc. MIT, Cambridge, 1971-73; instr. medicine Harvard U., Cambridge, 1973-77; head hemostasis lab. Meml. Hosp., Pawtucket, R.I., 1977-78; asst. prof. medicine Brown U., Providence, 1977-84, assoc. prof., 1984—; chief hematology sect. VA Med. Ctr., Providence, 1979—. Named NIH prin. investigator for grants. Mem. AAAS, Am. Med. Women's Assn., Am. Fedn. Clin. Research, Am. Heart Assn., Am. Soc. Hematology, Internat. Soc. Thrombosis and Haemostasis, Am. Thoracic Soc., Leukemia Soc. Am. (R.I. chpt.). Contbr. numerous articles to profl. jours. Home: 263 Powell St Stoughton MA 02072 Office: VA Med Ctr Davis Park Providence RI 02908

CARVER, ANITA KAY, educator, family counselor; b. Texarkana, Ark., May 9, 1948; d. David Henry and Johnnie Lee (Rochelle) Slaton; children—Eric Anthony, Jason Britt, Kera Gayle. B.S. with honors, Am. Tech. U., Killeen, Tex., 1975; M.S., E. Tex. State U., 1976. Cert. kindergarten and elem. tchr., counselor, Tex. Kindergarten tchr. Sheldon Ind. Sch. Dist., Houston, 1982—; alcoholism counselor Dowd House, Texarkana, Ark., 1976-78; dir. Child Devel. Ctr., Mt. Pleasant, Tex., 1978-80; tchr. Crandall (Tex.) Ind. Sch. Dist., 1980-82; children's counselor Parent-Child Resource Ctr., Texarkana, 1974-75;

co-developer Parent Survival Skills, Mt. Pleasant, 1978; counselor Info. Hot-Line, Texarkana, Tex., 1975-76; artist. Chmn. Nash chpt. Boy Scouts Am., 1974. Mem. Assn. Tex. Educators, Parent Tchr. Orgn., Nat. Assn. Edn. of Young Children, Psychodrama Soc. Am., Kappa Delta Phi. Republican. Methodist. Office: Sheldon Independent School District 8540 CE King Pkwy Houston TX 77044

CARVER, BARBARA ANN, temporary help service executive; b. Niagara Falls, Ont., Can.; came to U.S., 1955; d. Robert Leroy Housser and Rosemary (Waloshuk) Murdoch; m. John Rudy Carver, Nov. 21, 1964; children—Kevin, Christopher. Student Tarrant County Jr. Coll., Ft. Worth, 1969-71. Nurse various hosps., Tex., 1971-79; staff supr. Norrell Service, Houston, 1979-80, office mgr., 1980-81, ter. mgr., 1981-82, mgr. major accounts, 1982-83, br. mgr., 1983-84; br. mgr. Temps & Co., 1984—. Recipient Robert Gibson award Norrell Services, 1981, others. Office: Temps & Co 3707 FM 1960 W S-260 Houston TX 77068

CARVER, BLANCHE MCLERRAN, county government official; b. Hermitage Springs, Tenn., Mar. 5, 1920; d. Albert Harrison and Zona May (Caruthers) McLerran; m. Joseph Brown Carver, Aug. 7, 1940; children—Bobby Joe, Carmen Carver Matthews. Student Middle Tenn. State U., 1958. Supr. factory, Celina, Tenn., 1953-72; registrar at large Election Comm., Clay County, Celina, 1978—. Corr. county paper News and Views. Republican. Mem. Ch. of Christ. Avocation: travel. Home: Route 2 Box 189 Red Boiling Springs TN 37150 Office: Clay County Election Commn Courthouse Celina TN 38551

CARVER, JUANITA (NITA), plastic company executive; b. Indpls., Apr. 8, 1929; d. Willard H. and Golda M. Ashe; children—Daniel Charles, Robin Lewis, Scott Alan. Asst. librarian CAMSCO, 1962—; pres. Carver Corp., Phoenix, 1977—; chmn. bd. Mobius Corp., 1985—. Active PTA; den mother Cub Scouts; bd. dirs. Scottsdale Meml. Hosp. Aux., 1964-65, assoc. mem., 1980—. Republican. Methodist. Patentee Yarner latch hook rug yarn organizer. Home: 6255 E Avalon St Scottsdale AZ 85251

CARVER, JUDITH RAI, surgical supply company executive; b. Chgo., May 8, 1945; d. Raymond Edwin and Meri Frances (Petolick) Anderson; m. John H. Walters III, Sept. 9, 1967 (dec. 1971); m. Joseph Wayne Carver, May 23, 1981. Diploma in Nursing, Roseland Community Hosp., Chgo., 1966; B.S. in Health Sci., Chapman Coll., 1981. Asst. operating rm. supr. West Valley Community Hosp., Encino, Calif., 1977-79; sales rep. Xomed, Inc., Jacksonville, Fla., 1979, Chaston Inc., Dayville, Conn., 1979-80; regional sales mgr. Carapace, Inc., Tulsa, 1980-81; co-owner, sales exec. Western Surg. Specialities, Benicia, Calif., 1981—. Vol. Big Sister of Solano County, Calif., 1984; pres., bd. dirs. Big Bros.-Big Sisters of Napa and Solano Counties, 1986—. Home: 586 Capitol Dr. Benicia CA 94510 Office: Western Surg Specialities 940 Tyler St Suite 16 Benicia CA 94510

CARY, ARLENE D., hotel company sales executive; b. Chgo., Dec. 19, 1930; d. Seymour S. and Shirley L. (Land) C.; student U. Wis., 1949-52; B.A., U. Miami, 1953; m. Elliott D. Hagle, Dec. 30, 1972 (div.). Public relations account exec. Robert Howe & Co., 1953-55; sales mgr. Martin B. Iger & Co., 1955-57; sales mgr., gen. mgr. Sorrento Hotel, Miami Beach, Fla., 1957-59; gen. mgr. Mayflower Hotel, Manomet, Mass., 1959-60; various positions Aristocrat Inns of Am., 1960-72; v.p. sales, McCormick Ctr. Hotel, Chgo., 1972—. Active Nat. Women's Polit. Caucus, Internat. Orgn. Women Execs., membership promotion chmn., 1979-80, bd. dirs., 1980-81. Recipient disting. salesman award Sales and Mktg. Execs. Internat., 1977. Mem. Profl. Conv. Mgmt. Assn., Nat. Assn. Exposition Mgrs., Hotel Sales Mgmt. Assn., Meeting Planners Internat., Chgo. Soc. Assn. Execs. Jewish. Home: 1130 S Michigan Ave Apt 3203 Chicago IL 60605 Office: Mc Cormick Inn 23rd and Lake Shore Dr Chicago IL 60616

CARYER, JANE HATHEWAY, interior designer; b. Ottawa, Ill., Apr. 15, 1924; d. Elanathan P. and Vera (O'Connell) Hatheway; B.A., U. Wis., 1946; postgrad. Madison Bus. Coll., 1946-47. Sr. interior designer Hendrickson's, Inc., Madison, Wis., 1946-59; sr. interior designer, mgr., pres., treas. Jane H. Caryer, Inc., Madison, 1959-79; founder Caryer Interiors, Ltd., Madison, 1980—. Mem. Dane County Community Welfare Council, 1966-70; bd. dirs. Madison Westside YMCA, 1975-81; bd. dirs., pres. Madison Opportunity Center, Inc., 1966-73, 79-83; bd. dirs. Madison Civic Opera Guild, 1980—, v.p., 1982-83. Mem. Am. Soc. Interior Designers, U. Wis. Alumni Assn., Madison Art Assn., Aircraft Owners and Pilots Assn. Clubs: Altrusa Internat. (chpt. pres. 1966-68), Blackhawk Country (Madison). Home: Winchester Bay 102 Ferchland Pl Monona WI 53714 Office: PO Box 6054 4513 Monoma Dr Madison WI 53716

CASALE, MARIA L., foundation executive, communications consultant; b. N.Y.C., Apr. 26, 1948; d. Salvatore A. and Marie E. (Faga) Casale; m. John J. Kennedy, Sept. 18, 1976; 1 child, David Casale Kennedy. B.A., Coll. New Rochelle, 1969. Social worker Villa Loretto Sch., Peekskill, N.Y., 1970-75; editorial asst. Arno Press, N.Y.C., 1976-78; program coordinator Alicia Patterson Found., N.Y.C., 1978-82, v.p. bd. dirs., 1980—; cons. CB Communication, N.Y.C., 1983—. Mem. Women in Communications. Home: 574 West End Ave New York NY 10024 Office: CB Communication 120 E 56th St New York NY 10022

CASAREZ, NICOLE BREMNER, lawyer; b. Evanston, Ill., Apr. 11, 1956; d. John Edward and Eunice Grace (Miersch) Bremner; m. Rueben Charles Casarez, Nov. 13, 1982. B.J. with honors, U. Tex., 1976, J.D. with honors, 1979. Bar: Tex. 1979. Assoc. Crutcher, Hull, Ramsey & Jordan, Dallas, 1979-82, Vinson & Elkins, Houston, 1982—. Editor: Pocket Parts, 1983—. Mem. Lawyers Alliance for Nuclear Arms Control. Mem. ABA, State Bar Tex., Women in Communications, Houston Young Lawyers Assn. (chairperson communications com. 1983—, dir. 1984—). Lutheran. Club: Luth. Ch. Women (Houston). Office: Vinson & Elkins First City Tower Houston TX 77002

CASAS, LILLIAN, medical librarian; b. Cayey, P.R., Oct. 31, 1924; d. Guillermo and Maria (Llera) C.; B.A., U. P.R., 1951, M. Health Edn., 1973; M.S. in L.S., Syracuse U., 1958; m. Guillermo Lopez, May 3, 1956. Tchr. P.R. Dept. Edn. 1950; asst. librarian U. P.R. Sch. Medicine, San Juan, 1951-57, head cataloger, 1959-60, librarian, 1961-65, dir. Med. Scis. Campus Library, 1966-79; library cons., 1979—. Mem. P.R. Library Assn. (pres. 1964), Med. Library Assn. Home: 772 Gave Urb Lourdes Trujillo Alto PR 00760

CASAVANTES, RITA, computer company executive, industrial engineer; b. El Paso, Tex., Jan. 18, 1959; d. Luis and Nancy (Elliott) C. B.S.I.E., U. Tex.-El Paso, 1981. Indsl. engr. Tex. Instruments, Sherman, Tex., 1982-84, indsl. engring. supr., 1985—, also mem. library adv. council, 1985—. Editor Texoma Indsl. Newsletter, 1982-84 (Gold award 1984). Mem. Inst. Indsl. Engrs. (chpt. sec. 1982-84, chpt. v.p. 1984-85), Methods Time Measurement Assn., Am. Contract Bridge League. Republican. Roman Catholic. Avocations: bridge; needlework; boating. Home: 4401 Savannah Sherman TX 75090 Office: Tex Instruments Hwy 75 S MS 834 Sherman TX 75090

CASBURN, DEBORAH LYNN, trucking co. exec.; b. Lufkin, Tex., Jan. 28, 1951; d. Gervinus P. and Ella Bourrous; grad. Lufkin Secretarial and Bus. Coll., 1970; m. Archie Ronald Casburn, Mar. 9, 1979; 1 dau., Bridget Leah. Billing agt., Drs. Denman, Rowland & Smith, Assos., Lufkin, 1972-73; owner, Ronnie's Western Store, Lufkin, 1976-77; personnel asst. Louisiana Pacific Corp., Lufkin, 1978; v.p. G.P. Bourrous Trucking Co., Diboll, Tex., 1979—; sec., treas. New Waverly Truck & Trailer Inc., Diboll, 1979—. Mem. Women's Profl. Rodeo Assn., Am. Quarter Horse Assn., Nat. Assn. Female Execs. Methodist. Home: Route 1 Box 381 Diboll TX 75941 Office: 508 Burke St Diboll TX 75941

CASE, BARBARA SHARON, librarian; b. San Pedro, Calif., Nov. 21, 1946; d. Charles C. and Stella May (Pierce) Case; m. James V. Halloran III, Sept. 7, 1974. B.A., U. Calif.-Berkeley, 1969, M.L.S., 1970; postgrad. in bus. Harvard U., 1972-73. Catalog librarian U. Calif.-Santa Barbara, 1970-71; adminstrv. asst. to univ. librarian Calif. State U.-Los Angeles, 1973-76, head cataloging sect., 1976-82, mgr. cataloging services, 1982-83, coordinator library automation planning, 1982-83, asst. univ. librarian, 1984—; chairperson Calif. State U. Systemwide Bibliographic Standards Com., Long Beach, 1979-80, Systemwide Library Automation Standards Com., 1980-81, mem. Systemwide Online Pub. Access Catalog Evaluation Com., 1981—; chairperson info. resources mgmt. steering com. Calif. State U.-Los Angeles, 1986—. Mem. ALA, Calif. Library Assn., Calif. Acad. and Research Libraries. Home: 612 S Gertruda Ave Redondo Beach CA 90277 Office: Library Calif State U 5151 State University Dr Los Angeles CA 90032

CASE, ELIZABETH, artist, writer; b. Long Beach, Calif., July 24, 1930; d. Nelson and Sarah Lee (Odend'hal) Case; student French Inst., 1946, Art Students League, 1948-49, Elmira Coll., 1949-51, Syracuse U., 1951, Chaffey Jr. Coll., Ontario, Calif., Scripps Coll., Claremont, Calif., 1954; children—Walter J. Zwicker, Jr., Keith Allen Zwicker, Pat James Cioffi, Susan Karin Cioffi. Asst. animator Walt Disney Prodns., Burbank, Calif., 1956-58; faculty Lighthouse Art and Music Camp, 1961; faculty New Hope Art Sch. (Pa.), 1961; asst. promotion mgr., copywriter Reinhold Pub. Co., N.Y.C., 1962-63; copywriter Columbia U. Press, 1963; advt. coordinator Orbit Imperial Design Corp., 1964; prin. Gadfly Prodns., art, writing, promotions, 1969—; faculty Ft. Lee Adult Sch., 1975-83; sr. copywriter/designer spl. projects coll. textbook advt. Prentice-Hall, Inc., Englewood Cliffs, N.J., 1975-77; U.S. Navy combat artist, 1974—; with promotion and design dept. Rutherford Mus. (now Meadowlands Mus.), 1979—; sales promotion mgr. M. Grumbacher, Inc., N.Y.C., 1979-81; typographer, quality control Graphic Tech., Inc., N.Y.C.; one-man shows research library exhbn. facility Walt Disney Prodns., 1957-58, Swain's Gallery, New Hope, Pa., 1963, D'Alessio Gallery, 1963, Gallery 8, N.Y.C., 1969, Ft. Lee Pub. Library inaugural exhbns., 1975, Ridgefield Pub. Library, 1977, Old Bridge Pub. Library, 1978, Edgewater Nat. Bank, 1983, Lewis Hall Gallery, Eastern Va. Med. Sch. and Med. Authority, Norfolk, 1984, Edgewater Pub. Library, 1985; exhibited in group shows at Friends Central, Phila., 1960, Hist. Soc. Ann. Exhbn., Philips Mill, Pa., 1962-63, Englewood (N.J.) Armory Show, 1967, 68, Hadassah, Paramus, N.J., 1969, Bergen Community Coll., 1970; traveling exhbn. Bicentennial Am. Freedoms, Wilmington Opera House, Nat. Arts Club, 1975-76, Submarine Exhbn., Boat Show, Bergen County Mall, 1977, Bergen County Community Mus., 1984; represented in permanent collections at Washington Navy Yard Combat Art Collection, Ch. of Christ, Jersey City, Edgewater Pub. Library; executed murals at INSCON, San Dimas, Calif., 1956, Los Angeles County Hosp., 1958, Delaware Canal, New Hope, 1959; mural design Allegheny Airlines, Lumberville, Pa., 1960; mural corner Main and 202, New Hope, 1960, Lumberville Meth. Ch., 1961, swimming pool, Jerico Valley, Pa., 1961, Orbit Imperial Design Corp., N.Y.C., 1965, Fabric Shop, Ft. Lee, 1969, 72, Ch. of Good Shepherd, 1971, Palisadium restaurant Winston Towers Complex, Cliffside Park, N.J., 1974, Old Bridge Pub. Library, 1977, History of Children's Lit.; exterior frieze Met. Plant Exchange, Ft. Lee, N.J., 1979, History of Typography Graphic Tech. Inc.; group shows, Nat. Soc. of Mural Painters; Green Mountain Boys Vets. Home, 1981; illustrator cover Bucks County Life, Doylestown, Pa., 1961; Vanity Fair Books, 1962, Am. Scandinavian Rev., 1962, books Molecular Kinetic Theory, 1963, Theory of Lanthinides and Chemical Energy, 1963, Harle Publs., 1969-70, Programmed Algebra, Vols. 1 and 2, 1977, Vol. 3, 1980; designer, illus. What Do I Do with a Major In ... ?, (Malnig), 1984; Use and Misuse of Statistics, 1978; assignment paintings for USN, 1974—; lectr. Women of Brandeis U., 1964. Recipient spring concours award Art Students League, 1949, Outstanding Achievement award Elmira Coll., 1976, Merit award Edgewater (N.J.) Council, 1976, Edgewater Arts Council Festival, (1st and 2d prize), 1981. Mem. Navy League, Nat. Soc. Mural Painters (publicity chmn. 1973-75, sec. 1975, chmn. pub. relations 1980-81). Studio: PO Box 58 Edgewater NJ 07020*

CASE, KAREN ANN, lawyer; b. Milw., Apr. 7, 1944; d. Alfred F. and Hilda (Tomich) Case. B.S., Marquette U., J.D., 1966; LL.M. in Taxation, NYU, 1973. Bar: Wis. 1966. Tchr., Milw. Pub. Schs., 1968-72; ptnr. Meldman, Case & Weine Ltd., Milw., 1973-85, Meldman, Case & Weine div. Mulcahy & Wherry, S.C., 1985—; lectr. U. Wis.-Milw., 1974-78. Fellow Am. Acad. Matrimonial Lawyers; mem. Wis. Bar Assn. (bd. govs. 1981-84, 86—, bd. dirs. tax sect. 1981—), Milw. Bar Assn. (bd. dirs. 1985—), Wis. Bar Found. (bd. dirs. 1977—, treas. 1980—), Nat. Assn. Women Lawyers (Wis. del. 1982), Friends of Boerner Bot. Gardens (pres. 1984—), Milw. Rose Soc. (pres. 1981, bd. dirs. 1982), Park People Milw. (bd. dirs. 1982—, sec. 1983-84). Club: Profl. Dimensions (bd. dirs. 1985—), Tempo (sec. 1984-85) (Milw.). Home: 9803 Meadow Park Dr Hales Corners WI 53219 Office: Meldman Case & Weine Ltd 788 N Jefferson St Milwaukee WI 53202

CASE, MIMI (MARY LINDA), medical editor, writer; b. Oakland, Calif., Apr. 14, 1943; d. Robert Willis and Hilja (Hiltunen) C. B.A., San Francisco State U., 1966. Cert. tchr., Calif. Research asst. Schneider, Bernet & Hickman, Dallas, 1971-72; adminstrv. asst. Henry S. Miller Co., Dallas, 1972-73; mktg. sec. Crown Zellerbach Corp., San Francisco, 1973-76; ednl. rep. Year Book Med. Publishers, Chgo., 1976-79; office mgr. Orrick, Herrington & Sutcliffe, San Francisco, 1979-82; med. editor G.K. Hall & Co., Boston, 1982—. Author short stories. Campaign worker Republican Party, San Francisco, 1964-82. Mem. Boston Computer Soc. Office: G K Hall & Co 70 Lincoln St Boston MA 02111

CASE, SARAH LOUISE, nurse; b. Scranton, Pa., Feb. 20, 1955; d. William Earl and Sarah Evelyn (Moll) Dennis; m. Brian Lee Case, Dec. 16, 1978. R.N., Pa. Nursing coordinator Horsham Clinic, Ambler, Pa., 1979-83; dir. nursing Wyoming Valley Clinic, Wilkes-Barre, Pa., 1983-84; head nurse Pocono Hosp., East Stroudsburg, Pa., 1984—. Lutheran. Home: 401 S 9th St Leighton PA 18235 Office: Pocono Hosp East Stroudsburg PA 18301

CASEL, MARY LYNN, real estate broker; b. Carthage, N.Y., Jan. 16, 1943; d. Floyd Albert and Mary Frances (Schack) Neuroth; m. Ronald Anthony Casel, Nov. 28, 1963 (div. Nov. 1977); children—Mark, Steven, Glen. Grad. Harper Method, Rochester, N.Y., 1961. Lic. real estate broker. Owner M. L. Salon, Rochester, N.Y., 1962-72; specialty tchrs.-aide Broward County, Ft. Lauderdale, Fla., 1973-77; office mgr. Broward County Voter Registration, Margate, Fla., 1977-82; real estate salesperson Pelican Bay, Daytona Beach, Fla., 1982-84, broker, 1984-86, broker, sales mgr., 1986—. Mem. adv. bd. Democratic Club, Margate, Fla., 1977-82. Named Top Salesperson, Pelican Bay, Daytona Beach, 1982, Outstanding Achievement award, 1983. Mem. Nat. Assn. Realtors, Daytona Beach Bd. Realtors, Ft. Lauderdale Bd. Realtors. Avocations: travel; dancing; theater; real estate investments. Democrat. Roman Catholic. Home: 825 Pelican Bay Dr Daytona Beach FL 32019 Office: Horizon Communities Ltd 200 Forest Lake Blvd Daytona Beach FL 32019

CASEY, BEVERLY ANN, postmaster; b. Decaturville, Tenn., Aug. 6, 1949; d. Willie Hugh and Lillian Blanche (Ivy) Tillman; m. John Robert Casey, Jan. 19, 1969 (div. 1982); children—John Gary, Kimberly Jean. Student Jackson State Community Coll., 1982-84. Sec. State of Tenn., Western Institute, 1969-76; post office clk. U.S. Postal Service, Western Institute, 1977-82, postmaster, 1982-84; postmaster U.S. Postal Service, Pickwick Dam, Tenn., 1984—; officer-in-charge U.S. Postal Service, Michie, Tenn., 1984. Bd. dirs. Pickwick Med. Clinic, 1986; vol. Hardeman chpt. Saint Jude, Bolivar, Tenn., 1983; town chmn. Reelfoot council Girl Scouts U.S., 1980-84, activities chmn., 1980-84, recipient Appreciation award, 1983. Named Outstanding 3d Class Postmaster 380 area U.S. Postal Service, 1984; recipient Vol. Service award Cystic Fibrosis Found., Tenn. Chpt., 1982; Vol. Appreciation Cert. Western Mental Health, 1984. Mem. Nat. Assn. Postmasters of U.S., Nat. League of Postmasters (v.p. 1984-86), Toastmasters, Nat. Assn. Female Execs., 380 Postmasters Assn. (pres. 1983-84), U.S. Postal Service (bd. dirs. women's adv. council 1983—). Baptist. Club: Lioness. Avocations: walking; tennis. Home: PO Box 363 Pickwick Dam TN 38365 Office: US Postal Service Pickwick Dam TN 38365

CASEY, CATHERINE SUE, pediatrician, educator; b. Washington, Feb. 23, 1948; d. John Roland and Edna Hope (Batcheller) C. B.S., Coll. William and Mary, 1970; M.D., Med. Coll. Va., 1974. Diplomate Am. Bd. Pediatrics. Intern, Children's Hosp. Phila., 1974-75, resident, 1975-77; practice medicine specializing in pediatrics, Arlington, Va., 1977—; asst. clin. prof. pediatrics Georgetown U. Sch. Medicine, 1980—. Chmn. Project Santa Ana, humanitarian relief project, 1984—. Fellow Am. Acad. Pediatrics; mem. Am. Med. Women's Assn. (br. pres. 1983-84), Med. Soc. Va., No. Va. Pediatric Soc. (v.p. 1983-84, pres. 1984-85), Arlington County Med. Soc. (treas. 1984, sec. 1985, v.p. 1986). Democrat. Episcopalian. Office: 1715 N George Mason Dr Suite 205 Arlington VA 22205

CASEY, CHERRELYN ANN, technical communications specialist; b. Fairfield, Iowa, Sept. 16, 1944; d. Edward M. and Hazel Louise (Supalla) Chuck; B.A. in Math., U. Iowa, 1966; m. Donald Patrick Casey, Aug. 8, 1970; 1 son, Michael. With IBM Corp., 1966—, systems analyst, White Plains, N.Y., 1968-69, tech. writer, Boulder, Colo., 1970-74, project mgr. tech. writing, 1974-76, devel. mgr. info. planning and editing, 1976-78, devel. mgr. internal communications, 1978-80, adv. planner, 1981-83, mgr. font bus. planning and architecture, 1983—; lectr. in field.; speaker Internat. Tech. Communications Conf., 1982; pres. Concreative Contracting, Boulder, 1976—. Bd. editors Iowa State, Jour. Bus. and Tech. Communication, 1985—. Mem. communications com. St. John's Cath. Ch., 1980; trustee, sec. bd. Longmont Cable TV, 1983-85. Mem. Longmont C. of C. (edn. com. 1980), No. Colo. Home Builders Assn. Aux. (pres. 1980), Colo. Home Builders Assn. (legis. task force 1980), Soc. Tech. Communication, Young Execs. Inst., U. Iowa Alumni Assn., Women in Communications (v.p. programming 1980), Delta Delta Delta. Republican. Roman Catholic. Home: 1627 Twin Sisters Dr Longmont CO 80501 Office: PO Box 1900 Boulder CO 80302

CASEY, CONSTANCE ASTARITA, printer; b. New Orleans, June 9, 1938; d. John M. and Astarita (Zinsel) Laporte; m. Douglas L. Casey; children—Douglas Dale, Dawnell Constance. Student La. State U. Owner, operator Kwik Kopy Printing Co., Kenner, La., 1979—. Sponsor Jefferson Parish Women's softball championship team. Mem. Greater New Orleans Kwik Kopy Assn. (past v.p.), Kenner Bus. Assn. (past sec., treas. 2d v.p., 1st v.p., pres. 1986—), Jefferson Parish Pvt. Industry Council (bd. dirs.). Avocations: landscaping; interior decorating. Office: Kwik Kopy 2805 Williams Blvd Suite 4 Kenner LA 70062

CASEY, DEBORAH MARIE, contract administrator; b. Watertown, N.Y., Feb. 5, 1959; d. Walter Henry and Beverly Jean (Young) Cote; m. John Eugene Casey, Mar. 14, 1982. Student N. Nev. Community Coll., 1978. Office mgr. Air Service Co., Reno, Nev., 1979-81, Bridgerland Motors, Kemmerer, Wyo., 1981-82; dir. profit sharing Metalogic, Phoenix, 1982—, contract adminstr., 1982—; asst. dir. mktg. Novelogic, Phoenix, 1986—. Mem. Nat. Assn. Female Execs. Office: Metalogic 275 S Black Canyon Hwy Phoenix AZ 85009

CASEY, FAITH (FAYE) MARIE MYERS, marketing administrator; b. N.Y.C., Mar. 7, 1944; d. Mildred (Myers) Lake; m. Joseph Lawrence Casey, Jr., Apr. 16, 1966 (div. June 1971); 1 child, Kevin. A.A.S. in Engring. Scis., SUNY-Alfred, 1963; B.S. in Mgmt., Rochester Inst. Tech., 1977, M.B.A., 1980. Statis. analysis tech. Sylvania, Gen. Telephone & Electronics, Buffalo, 1963-66; mktg. statistician Hard Mfg. div. Sybron, Buffalo, 1969-72; mktg. research asst. Castle div. Sybron, Rochester, N.Y., 1972-77, mktg. research analyst, 1979-80, product mgr., 1980—; product specialist, Taylor Instrument div. Sybron, Rochester, N.Y., 1977-79. Bd. dirs. United Way Greater Rochester (N.Y.), 1981—, mem. planning com., 1982—; mem. mktg. and pub. relations com. Rochester-Monroe County chpt. ARC, 1984-85. Mem. Am. Mktg. Assn. (Rochester chpt., editor 1979-80, treas. 1980-81, pres. 1981-82, dir. 1982-84), Illuminating Engring Soc. (assoc.). Home: 6 Treetop Dr Fairport NY 14450 Office: Castle Div Sybron Corp PO Box 23077 Rochester NY 14692

CASEY, GLORIA JEAN, state official; b. Fresno, Calif., Dec. 30, 1946; d. Aide D. Ferris, Jr. and Maxine Clara (McMullen) Ferris Burner; m. William L.J. Casey, Jan. 25, 1964; children—Kimberley Jean, Montgomery Gene. A.A., Cosumnes River Coll., 1979; B.S. in Bus. Adminstrn., U. Redlands, 1980. Tng. officer Calif. Dept. Mental Hygiene, Sacramento, 1969-73, grants coordinator, 1973-78; contract mgr. Calif. Dept. Mental Health, Sacramento, 1978-84, personnel officer, 1984-85, health and safety officer, 1985—, mgr., cons. Employee Assistance Program, 1984—; co-owner Appliance Parts and Equipment Distbrs. La. cons. employee support resources Ctr. Active Psychology, Riverside, Calif., 1985. Writer Employee Assistance Newsletter, 1985—(Commendation award 1985); designer, decorator Creative Cakes by Gloria, 1975-76. Bd. dirs. Parkway Little League, Sacramento, 1977—, Valley Hi Community Assn., Sacramento, 1969-73; bd. dirs., leader Tierra del Oro council Girl Scouts U.S., 1970-75. Recipient awards country swing dance contests, 1985, 86. Mem. Assn. Labor, Mgmt. and Consultants on Alcoholism (spl. com. chmn. 1984-85), Employee Assistance Program Consultants, Calif. State Employees Assn., Pi Beta Phi Mothers Club. Republican. Club: Last Dancers (Sacramento). Lodge: Ind. Order Forresters. Avocations: cake decorating, country swing dancing and demo team, sports, sewing. Home: 6200 Gardenview Way Sacramento CA 95823 Office: State Dept of Mental Health 1600 9th St First Floor Sacramento CA 95814

CASEY, JULIA K., lawyer; b. Rochester, N.Y, Sept. 12, 1946; d. Henry and Jane (Palmer) Keller; m. David William Casey, June 10, 1966 (div. 1976); 1 son, Henry Keller. B.A., U. Wash., Seattle, 1968; J.D., U. Toledo, 1973. Bar: Ohio 1973, U.S. Dist. Ct. (we. dist.) N.Y. Assoc. Kaplan & Lehman, Toledo, 1973-75, Casey & Slaybod, Toledo, 1976—; chairperson Advocates Basic Legal Equality, Toledo, 1978-81, bd. dirs. 1981—; chairperson Juvenile Law Com., Toledo, 1983—; instr. advocates and guardians ad litem, Toledo, 1978—. Author: (poetry) Julia, 1978; singer, song writer When You Run, Mother Goose Blues, 1978. Recipient Am. Jurisprudence award Bancroft-Whitney Co., 1970, 72, 73. Mem. Ohio Bar Assn., Toledo Bar Assn., Women Involved in Toledo. Democrat.Baptist. Home: 2557 Greenway Toledo OH 43607 Office: Casey and Slaybod 420 Spitzer Bldg Toledo OH 43604

CASEY, KAREN ANNE, banker; b. Bklyn., Oct. 5, 1955; d. Stanley Joseph and Helen Katherine (Kosowski) Mozeleski; m. Dennis Joseph Casey, May 14, 1977. B.Bus.Adminstrn., Baruch Coll., CUNY, 1977. C.P.A., N.Y. Jr. acct. Coopers & Lybrand, N.Y.C., 1977-78, sr. acct., 1978-79, supr., 1979-81; asst. fin. controller Gulf Internat. Bank, N.Y.C., 1981-82, fin. controller, 1982; v.p., fin. controller Allied Irish Banks plc, N.Y.C., 1982—; bank rep. to Bank Adminstrn. Inst., 1983—, Inst. Fgn. Bankers, 1984—, Com. of Banking Insts. on Taxation, 1984—. Mem. Am. Inst. C.P.A.s, Am. Soc. Women Accts., N.Y. State Soc. C.P.A.s. Roman Catholic. Avocations: gardening; golf; tennis; reading. Office: Allied Irish Banks plc 405 Park Ave New York NY 10022

CASEY, KATHLEEN HEIRICH, lawyer; b. Chgo., Mar. 10, 1937; d. Bruneau Ernest and Kathleen Brennan (Grogan) Heirich; m. John Mannington Casey, Nov. 18, 1959 (div.); children—Sean, Kyle, Siobhan. A.B., Radcliffe Coll., 1959; J.D., St. John's U., 1974. Asst. corp. counsel Dept. of Law, N.Y.C., 1974-76, asst. atty. gen., 1977-79; appellate atty., asst. editor Bur. Prosecution and Def. Services, N.Y.C., 1976-78; sr. law clk. to presiding justice N.Y. State Supreme Ct., N.Y.C., 1979-81; atty. matrimonial law Colton Weissberg Hartnick Yamin & Sheresky, N.Y.C., 1981-83; atty. matrimonial law Milbank, Tweed, Hadley & McCloy, N.Y.C., 1983—; adj. faculty N.Y. Law Sch., 1983-84. Mem. county com. Dem. Party, Nassau County, 1971—. Fellow Am. Acad. Matrimonial Lawyers; mem. ABA (family law com.), Assn. Bar City N.Y. (matrimonial law com.), N.Y. State Women's Bar Assn. (officer 1985—), Am. Arbitration Assn. (family dispute resolution panel), Phi Delta Phi. Office: 1 Chase Manhattan Plaza New York NY 10005

CASEY, LADEANE OSLER, psychologist; b. Griswold, Iowa, May 27, 1926; d. Alonzo A. and Delia Emma (Sasse) Osler; B.A. cum laude, Grinnell Coll., 1947; M.A., Drake U., 1974; Ph.D. in Ednl. Psychology, Ariz. State U., 1977; m. Donald John Casey, June 21, 1947; children—Kent, Robert, Janice, Diane, Donna, Mark. Instr. physics lab. Grinnell (Iowa) Coll., 1947-48; tutor in chemistry and math. Iowa State U., 1954-58; behavior modification intern Center for Human Devel., Des Moines, 1973-74; instr. behavior modification practicum Ariz. State U., Tempe, 1974-75; instr. stats. dept. psychology Mesa (Ariz.) Community Coll., 1976-78; assoc. Human Resource Assocs., Tempe, Ariz., 1977-78; psychologist God's Little People, Mesa, 1977-79; clin. counselor Outreach Services, Inc., Mesa, 1977-79; pvt. practice counseling, Scottsdale, Ariz., 1978—; mem. staff Family Counseling and Psychol. Services, Scottsdale, 1979—; affiliate staff Scottsdale Meml. Hosp.; mem. staff Treatment Ctrs. of Am.; faculty advisor Columbia Pacific U. Exec. v.p. Lakota council Girl Scouts U.S.A., 1968-71. Recipient Outstanding Youth Leadership award Nat. Cath. Conf., 1971; lic. psychologist, Ariz. Mem. Am. Psychol. Assn., Scottsdale Psychol. Assn., Ariz. State Psychol. Assn., Maricopa Psychol. Assn., Soc. for Research in Child Devel., Nat. Soc. for Autistic Citizens, Am. Assn. of Sex Educators, Counselors and Therapists, Phi Beta Kappa, Iota Sigma Pi. Home: 5939 E Hummingbird Ln Paradise Valley AZ 85253 Office: 8300 N Hayden Rd Suite 112 Scottsdale AZ 85258

CASEY, MARIE C. (MRS. JOHN J. CASEY), mng. editor; b. New Haven, Jan. 13, 1917; d. James Edward and Mary (Lonergan) Coogan; B.A., Coll. New Rochelle, 1938; m. John J. Casey, Aug. 20, 1946; 1 dau., Eileen Mary. Advt. mgr. Brock-Hall Dairy, Hamden, Conn., 1946-53; mng. editor Am. Jour. Sci., Yale U., 1962—, assoc. mng. editor Radiocarbon. Sec., Rec. for the Blind, New Haven chpt., 1962-65; editor bull. ch. Women United of Conn., 1975-82. Mem. AAUW (corr. sec. Conn. div. 1963-69, past pres. local br., chmn. fellowships and scholarships coms. local br., v.p. program New Haven br. 1984—, former editor Conn. div. Nutmeg News), Am. Field Service (former chmn.). Roman Catholic. Home: 835 Grassy Hill Rd Orange CT 06477 Office: Yale Univ Kline Geology Lab New Haven CT 06511

CASEY, MARY LINDA, lawyer; b. Milan, Ind., Mar. 7, 1945; d. Russell and Loretta (Kline) Butt; m. John T. Casey, Apr. 13, 1974; 1 dau., Megan Elizabeth. B.A., Ind. U., 1967, J.D., 1970. Bar: Ind. 1970. Atty. estate tax IRS, Indpls., 1970-78; ptnr. Lucas, Clifford & Holcomb, Merrillville, Ind., 1978—; Fed. Women's program coordinator Indpls. dist. IRS, 1973-75; dir. Indpls. Council Fed. Agys., Indpls., 1975-76. Trustee Jasper County Library, Rensselaer, Ind., 1983—; bd. dirs. Merrillville Chamber Advancement Found., Inc., 1984—, v.p., 1984, pres., 1985. Recipient Pres.' award, Merrillville Chamber Advancement Found., Inc., 1984. Mem. Ind. Bar Assn., South Lake County Bar Assn., Ind. U. Alumni Assn. (exec. council 1980-83), Kappa Kappa Kappa. Methodist. Home: 51 Oak Tree Dr Rensselaer IN 47978 Office: Lucas Clifford & Holcomb 1000 E 80th Pl Merrillville IN 46410

CASEY, MILDRED STANCICK, insurance company executive; b. Quakertown, Pa., July 20, 1931; d. Stephen and Mary (Kerchmar) S.; m. Richard S. Casey; children—David S., Deborah M. Student Bethlehem Bus. Coll., 1949-51, Northampton County Area Community Coll., Moravian Coll. With Bethlehem Steel Corp. (Pa.), 1951-52; office sec. Fountain Hill Mills, Bethlehem, 1951-53; Ga. R.R. Bank & Trust Co., Augusta, 1953; receptionist, supr. Unionbank & Trust Co., Bethlehem, Pa., 1955-60, personnel asst., 1973-77; asst. v.p., personnel dir. Cement Nat. Bank, Northampton, Pa., 1977-85; human resources adminstr. Guardian Life Ins. Co., 1985—. Pres. Bethlehem Jaycee Wives, 1965-66; mem. Blue Shield Subscriber Adv. Council, Camp Hill, Pa., 1979—; bd. dirs. YWCA, Bethlehem, 1967-73, 84—, pres. bd., 1971-72; bd. dirs. United Fund, 1970-73; mem. Lehigh Valley Community Council, 1973. Mem. Am. Inst. Banking (state chmn. Lehigh Valley chpt. 1981-83, chpt. pres. 1980-81), Am. Soc. Personnel Adminstrs. (sec. 1983, pres. 1984). Democrat. Lutheran. Office: Guardian Life Ins Co 3900 Burgess Pl Bethlehem PA 18017

CASEY, PATRICIA MARIE, advertising executive; b. Chgo., June 9, 1951; d. William James and Mary Lou (Merrill) Mainzer; m. Francis James Casey, May 28, 1977 (div. Jan. 1985). B.A., So. Ill. U., 1973. Graphic artist Lawson Products, Des Plaines, Ill., 1975-78; advt. coordinator Diversey Chem. Co., Des Plaines, 1978-79; advt. mgr. ACCO Internat. Inc. USA, Wheeling, Ill., 1979-81; pres., owner Prism Communications, Inc., Des Plaines, 1982—; account exec. Images Photography, Des Plaines, 1982—. Tchr. Sunday Sch., Norwood Gospel Chapel, Chgo., 1977-80. Mem. Greater O'Hare Assn., Bus. Profl. Advt. Assn. Avocations: aerobics; running; body building; reading. Home: 1800 Palm Ct Mount Prospect IL 60056 Office: Prism Communications Inc 1225 Pond Rd Des Plaines IL 60016

CASEY, PATRICIA MARIE, management consultant; b. Framingham, Mass., Oct. 6, 1955; d. William Francis and Eileen Theresa (McCarthy) C.; B.S. cum laude in Mgmt., Northeastern U., 1978; M.B.A., Suffolk U., 1982. Head teller Framingham Trust Co. (Mass.), 1975-78; br. asst. Guaranty-First Trust Co., Waltham, Mass., 1978-79; payroll asst. Baybank Newton-Waltham Trust Co., Waltham, 1979; asst. controller The Dow Service Group, Boston, 1979-80; sr. auditor Multibank Fin. Corp., Quincy, Mass., 1980-84, audit supr., 1984-85; prin., mgmt. cons. AMC Cons. Services, 1985—. Recipient cert. of achievement Inst. Internal Auditors, 1980, 81. Mem. Nat. Assn. Female Execs., Inst. Internal Auditors, AAUW, Nat. Assn. Bank Women (audit chmn.), Nat. Assn. Accts. Democrat. Roman Catholic. Home and Office: 16 Paula Rd Milford MA 01757

CASH, SYLVIA LAMOUR, secretary; b. Durham, N.C., June 19, 1940; d. Benjamin Tyrus Cash and Flossie Irene (Addison) Cash Walker. Grad. secretarial sci. King's Bus. Coll., 1958. Cert. prof. sec. (CPS), 1969. Owner, mgr. Profl. Secretarial Service, Washington, 1969-72; sec. to Joseph Yablonski United Mine Workers, Washington, 1973-75; sec., office mgr. Yablonski Both and Edelman, Washington, 1975-77; exec. sec. to chief exec. officer Peabody Coal Co., St. Louis and Arlington, Va., 1978; sec. Van Ness Feldman Co., Washington, 1979, Latham Watkins & Hills Co., Washington, 1980—. Contbr. articles to profl. publs. Mem. N.C. Democratic Club Washington, 1966—; mem. Landlord-Tenant Relations Com., Alexandria, Va., 1970-71, Charter Change Rev. Com., Alexandria, 1971-72, No. Va. Criminal Justice Adv. Council, Fairfax, Va., 1979-80; chmn., trustee PSI Research and Ednl. Found., Kansas City, Mo., 1982-85; mem. Inst. for Certifying Secs., Kansas City, 1983-85; mem. adv. bd. Washington Bus. Sch., Tyson's Corner, Va., 1984—, Katharine Gibbs Sch., Rockville, Md., 1984—; chmn. Sec. Speakout '85, Albuquerque, 1985. Named to Washington Women of Yr., Washington Woman Mag., 1985. Mem. Nat. Assn. Parliamentarians, Va. Assn. Parliamentarians, CPS Assocs. (pres. 1976-77), Profl. Secs. Internat. (D.C. chpt. treas. 1971-73, v.p. 1973-74, pres. 1974-76, Del.-Md.-D.C. div. v.p. 1976-77, pres. 1977-79, internat. bd. dirs. S.E. div. 1979-81, 1st v.p. 1982-83, pres. elect 1983-84, pres. 1984-85). Democrat. Baptist. Club: NC Soc. Washington. Avocations: bridge; collecting depression glass. Home: 3245 Rio Dr Apt 712 Falls Church VA 22041 Office: Latham Watkins & Hills 1333 New Hampshire Ave NW Washington DC 20036

CASHELL, LOIS D., federal government administrator. Asst. sec. Fed. Energy Regulatory Commn., Dept. of Energy, Washington. Office: Dept of Energy Fed Energy Regulatory Commn 825 N Capitol St NE Washington DC 20426*

CASHMORE, PATSY JOY, editor, author, consultant, educator; b. Milw., July 20, 1943; d. Anthony J. and Eva Irene (Arseneau) Peters; m. Gary Roy Cashmore, July 5, 1963 (div. Feb. 1984); children—Jay Allen, Jeffery Scott. Student U. Ill.-Chgo., 1961-62, Inst. Broadcast Arts, Milw., 1966-67, U. Wis.-Milw., 1970, U. Wis.-Madison, 1971-76; student labor studies N.Y.C. Grad. Ctr., 1978. Copy writer H. Vincent Allen & Assocs., Chgo., 1961-63; asst. program coordinator Sta.-WRIT, Milw., 1967-69; asst. news assignment editor WITI-TV, Milw., 1969-72; pub. relations asst. Deaconess Hosp., Milw., 1972-73; asst. editor Milw. Labor Press, 1973-81, editor, 1981—; voice talent on radio and TV commls.; instr., mem. faculty adv. com. U. Wis. Extension-Sch. for Workers, Madison; panelist NEH; guest Israeli govt., 1976, Govt. W.Ger., 1980, pre-NATO talks Frederick Ebert Found., 1981, Peoples Republic of China, 1983, All Union Central Council of Trade Unions of Soviet Union, 1985. Contbr. articles to nat. publs. Chmn. communications com., treas. Milw. Council on Drug Abuse, 1981-83, bd. dirs., 1984-87; mem. community affairs com. United Way, 1983-86; active Variety Club, 1983-86; chmn. community adv. bd. Sta.-WVTV pub. TV, 1982-85; bd. dirs. Goals 2000 Communications Com., 1983. Mem. Internat. Labor Communications Assn. (v.p., Best Signed Column award 1973, Best Feature Story award 1975, award of Merit for best use of art 1982, Best Headline award 1982, First award for gen. excellence newspaper 1982, 83), Midwest Labor Press Assn. (pres.), Wis. Labor Press Assn. (treas.), Indsl. Relations Research Assn. (bd. dirs.), Milw. Jr. Acd. Club (past sec.-treas.). Nat. Assn. Female Execs., Sigma Delta Chi. Clubs: Wapatule Ski (newsletter editor 1984-85), Milw. Press (Milw.). Avocations: travel; skiing; golf; swimming. Office: Milwaukee County Labor Council 633 S Hawley Rd Milwaukee WI 53214

CASIANO, SONIA VALERA, hospital nursing administrator; b. Badoc, Ilocos Norte, Philippines, June 30, 1949; d. Felipe Malinit and Ester Valera (Balgos) Casiano; came to U.S., 1972; m. Peter Carl Herkrath, Dec. 31, 1980. B.S. in Nursing, U. Santo Tomas, Manila, 1970; M.A. in Nursing, Columbia U., 1979. R.N., N.Y., N.J., Calif.; registered critical care nurse; cert. emergency room nurse. Staff nurse Irvington Gen. Hosp. (N.J.), 1972-74, Flower and Fifth Ave. Hosp., N.Y.C., 1974; staff nurse, charge nurse Lenox Hill Hosp., N.Y.C., 1974-79, asst. dir. nursing, critical care nursing, 1979—; sr. instr. basic life support (cardio-pulmonary resuscitation) Lenox Hill Hosp., 1981—. Mem. Am. Assn. Critical Care Nurses. Roman Catholic. Home: PO Box 548 Lenox Hill Sta New York NY 10021 Office: Dept Nursing Lenox Hill Hosp 100 E 77th St New York NY 10021

CASON, GINETTE JANE, photographer; b. Cagny, France, Feb. 13, 1927; came to U.S., 1962, naturalized, 1978; d. Lucien and Suzanne (Dequen) Lequet; m. Michel Bourdy, Apr. 21, 1944 (div. 1958); children—Alain Joel, Patrick Lucien; m. Kenneth Glenn Cason, Mar. 26, 1970. B.A. in Bus. Mgmt., Caffin Coll., Surgeres, France, 1945; grad. Bonieux Photo Sch., Paris, 1952. Owner, mgr. Telecolor Studio, Albuquerque, 1969-74, Isle's Nat. Portraits, Hollywood, Calif., 1974-78, Cameo Family Portraits, Cerritos, Calif., 1978-81, Crown Family Portraits, Fountain Valley, Calif., 1980-83, Classic Photography, Torrance, Calif., 1983—; tng. dir. Telecolor Corp., Hollywood, 1969-74, Cameo Studio, 1974—. Recipient Achievement award Telecolor Corp., 1973. Mem. Nat. Assn. Female Execs., Torrance C. of C. Republican. Home: 8112 Holder St Buena Park CA 90620 Office: Classic Photographers 3220-A W Sepulveda Torrance CA 90505

CASPER, JACQUELINE ANN, banking official; b. Bridgeton, N.J., Aug. 30, 1938; d. Chester W. and Murial Mary (McLaughlin) Campbell; m. Kenneth E. Casper, Sept. 7, 1957; children—Todd K., Kimberly A. Teller Young Mens Savings & Loan, Bridgeton; customer service rep. United Jersey/Cumberland Nat. Bank, Bridgeton, 1979-80, adminstrv. asst., 1980-81, asst. branch mgr., 1981-86, branch mgr., asst. cashier, 1986—. Mem. Soroptimists Internat., Greater Bridgeton Bus. Assn., Am. Inst. Banking, N.J. Bankers Assn., Nat. Assn. Female Execs. Home: Route 5 Box 170 Bridgeton NJ 08302 Office: United Jersey/Cumberland Nat Bank PO Box 100 Bridgeton NJ 08302

CASPERSEN, BARBARA MORRIS, food company executive; b. Phila., Feb. 27, 1945; d. Samuel Wheeler and Eleanor May (Jones) Morris; B.A., Wellesley Coll., 1967; m. Finn M.W. Caspersen, June 17, 1967. Treas., dir. Westby Corp., Wilmington, Del., 1971—, Westby Mgmt. Inc., Andover, N.J., 1967—, Tri-Farms, Inc., Andover, 1967—; pres., dir. Clark Hill Sugary Inc., Canaan, N.H., 1971—. Bd. dirs. v.p. O.W. Caspersen Found., 1967—; trustee Hoosac Sch., 1968-76, Shipley Sch., 1980-84, Peck Sch., 1981—, Drew U., Groton Sch., N.J. Conservation Found., Gladstone Equestrian Assn.; trustee Hilltop Sch., 1974-83, pres., 1976-80, prin., 1980-81. Mem. English-Speaking Union U.S. (dir. 1972-73, dir. N.Y. chpt. 1970-75). Episcopalian. Club: Colony (N.Y.C.). Office: Westby Corp PO Box 800 Andover NJ 07821

CASSEL, CHRISTINE KAREN, physician; b. Mpls., Sept. 14, 1945; d. Charles Moore and Virginia Julia (Anderson) C.; A.B., U. Chgo., 1967; M.D., U. Mass., 1976. Intern, resident in internal medicine Children's Hosp., San Francisco, 1976-78; fellow in bioethics, Inst. Health Policy Studies, U. Calif., San Francisco, 1978-79; fellow geriatrics Portland (Oreg.) VA Hosp., 1979-81; asst. prof. medicine and public health U. Oreg. Health Scis. U., 1981-83; asst. prof. geriatrics and medicine Mt. Sinai Med. Ctr., N.Y.C., 1983-85; assoc. prof. medicine U. Chgo., 1985—. Woodrow Wilson fellow, 1967; Henry J. Kaiser Family Found. faculty scholar, 1982-85; diplomate Am. Bd. Internal Medicine. Fellow Am. Geriatrics Soc., ACP; mem. Physicians Social Responsibility (dir. 1983—), Soc. Health and Human Values (pres. 1986). Author: Ethical Dimensions in the Health Professions, 1981; Geriatric Medicine: Principles and Practice, 1984; Nuclear Weapons and Nuclear War: A Sourcebook for Health Professionals, 1984. Office: Sect Gen Internal Medicine Box 12 U Chgo Pritzker Sch Medicine Chicago IL 60637

CASSELL, CAROL ANNE, community educator; b. Buffalo, Apr. 25, 1936; d. A.J. and Dorothy (Diemert) Miller; m. Robert Edward Cassell, June 26, 1971; children by previous marriage—Don, Alisa, John, Michael Mendez; stepchildren—Lisa, Emily. B.A., U. N.Mex., 1970, M.P.A., 1976, Ph.D. with distinction, 1980. Dir. tng. J.B.A., Austin, Tex., 1976-79; dir. edn. Planned Parenthood Fedn. Am., N.Y.C., 1979-82; instr. U. N.Mex., 1974—; lectr. and cons. in field; cons. editor Jour. of Sex Edn. and Therapy, 1977—; invited scholar Soc. of Sci. Study of Sex, 1981; adv. bd. Nat. Family Life Edn. Network, 1981—. Author: Swept Away, 1984, Adolescent Straight From the Heart, 1986. Co-editor: A Sourcebook on Sexuality Education, 1987. Contbr. articles to textbooks and profl. jours. Mem. Albuquerque Task Force on Devel., 1985. Recipient Margaret Sanger award Inst. Family Research and Edn., 1979; Cert. of Recognition, Eta Sigma Gamma, 1982. Mem. Am. Assn. Sex Educators, Counselors and Therapists (pres. 1983-84), Authors Guild, Phi Kappa Phi. Democrat. Address: 7129 Edwina NE Albuquerque NM 87110

CASSELL, DANA KAY, communications company executive; b. Hornell, N.Y., Dec. 12, 1941; d. Robert William and Mayadell Louise (Reubens) Amacher; m. Don Cuddy, 1983; children—William, Denise, Jody, Robert. Copywriter Sta. WTOC-TV, Savannah, Ga., 1965-67; ins. agt. Liberty Nat. Life Ins. Co., Savannah, 1967-70; dist. mgr. LaSalle Extension U., Fla., 1972; mgr. Stuart Domestic Service (Fla.), 1974-75; pres. Cassell Communications Inc., Ft. Lauderdale, Fla., 1977—. Served with USAF, 1960-61. Mem. Internat. Bus. Writers, Nat. Writers Club, Fla. Freelance Writers Assn. (founder 1982, exec. dir. 1982—), Nat. Assn. Female Execs., Fla. Press Women, Women in Communications, Nat. Assn. Ind. Pubs. (bd. advisors), Fla. Pubs. Group, Fla. Mag. Assn. Mensa. Republican. Club: The Book Group. Author: How to Advertise and Promote Your Retail Store, 1983; Making Money With Your Home Computer, 1984; contbr. over 800 articles to various publs. Home: 3600 NW 34th St Lauderdale Lakes FL 33309 Office: PO Box 9844 Fort Lauderdale FL 33310

CASSELL, KAY ANN, association executive; b. Van Wert, Ohio, Sept. 24, 1941; d. Kenneth Miller and Pauline (Zimmerman) C. B.S., Carnegie Mellon U., 1963; M.L.S., Rutgers U., 1965; M.A., Bklyn. Coll., 1969. Reference librarian Bklyn. Coll. Library, 1965-68; adult services cons. N.J. State Library, Trenton, 1968-71; library cons.-vol. Peace Corps, Rabat, Morocco, 1971-73; adult services cons. Westchester Library System, White Plains, N.Y., 1973-75; dir. Bethlehem Pub. Library, Delmar, N.Y., 1975-81, Huntington (N.Y.) Pub. Library, 1981-85; exec. dir. Coordinating Council of Lit. Mags., N.Y.C., 1985—; adj. faculty mem. Grad. Sch. Library Sci., SUNY, Albany, 1976-78; chmn. community adv. com. Capital Dist. Humanities Program, Albany, 1980-81; bd. dirs. Literacy Vols. of Suffolk, Bellport, N.Y., 1981—. Active LWV, Huntington, 1982—. Mem. ALA (reference and adult services div. 1983-84), N.Y. Library Assn. (pres. reference and adult services sect. 1975-76), Suffolk County Library Assn., AAUW, Beta Phi Mu. Club: Bus. and Prof. Women's (Huntington). Office: Coordinating Council Lit Mags 666 Broadway New York NY 10012

CASSIDY, SUSAN OLEVIA, internist; b. Johnson City, N.Y., Jan. 18, 1953; d. Richard John and Joyce Grace (McMahon) C.; m. David Edmund Kapur, Apr. 29, 1983; children—Jennifer, David. B.S. in Zoology, U. Md., 1975; M.D., Vanderbilt U., 1979. Diplomate Nat. Bd. Med. Examiners. Intern Vanderbilt U., 1979-80; resident in internal medicine United Health Service, Johnson City, 1981-83, emergency room physician, 1980-81; specialist in internal medicine Assocs. in Internal Medicine, Endwell, N.Y., 1983—; faculty Upstate Med. Ctr./Coll. Medicine, SUNY-Binghamton, 1983—; cons. Am. Health Profiles, Nashville, 1975-80; chmn. med. standards com. Broome County Health Fair, Binghamton, N.Y., 1983. Bd. dirs. S.O.S. Shelter, Endicott, N.Y., 1980—. Mem. ACP, AMA, Broome County Med. Soc., Med. Soc. State N.Y., Bus. and Profl. Women's Orgn. Republican. Roman Catholic. Office: Assocs in Internal Medicine PC 333 Hooper Rd Endwell NY 13760

CASSTEVENS, FRANCES HARDING, medical researcher, genealogist; b. Winston-Salem, N.C., Sept. 9, 1936; d. Franklin Daniel Boone and Laura (Bowman) Harding; m. Gerald Royce Casstevens, Jan. 4, 1954; children—Gerald D., Caren J., Michael Lee, Tony Layne, Sandra K., Timothy T. Student Draughton Bus. Sch., 1954-55, Surry Community Coll., 1974-75; B.A. magna cum laude, U. N.C.-Greensboro, 1976, M.A., 1984. Clk.-typist McLean Trucking Co., Winston-Salem, 1956-58; postal clk. U.S. Post Office, Yadkinville, N.C., 1959-60; clk. Yadkin County Pub. Library, 1962-67; editorial asst. Bowman Gray Sch. Medicine, Wake Forest U., Winston-Salem, 1977-83, research asst., 1983—; ptnr. Casstevens Heraldic Arts, 1984—. Editor, author: Heritage of Yadkin County, 1981; author: (play) Retreat to Victory, 1976, Daniel Boone on the Yadkin, 1985; (poems) Beyond the Yadkin, The Battle of Shallow Ford, 1979; (geneal. history) The Descendants of Solomon Lineberry; Thomas Casteven: A Geneal. History, 1976. Leader 4-H Club, Yadkinville, 1970-72; pres. Yadkin County Hist. Soc., 1979-81, 86—, v.p., 1984-85. Mem. DAR (regent Henry Hampton chpt. 1967-72). Republican. Methodist. Home: Route 1 PO Box 99 Yadkinville NC 27055 Office: Bowman Gray Sch Medicine Wake Forest U 300 S Hawthorne Rd Winston-Salem NC 27103

CASTANEDA, IRMA SALINAS, labor association executive; b. Chihuahua, Mexico, Oct. 24, 1938; came to U.S., 1956; d. Elias E. and Adela (Acosta) Salinas; m. Carlos Castaneda, Mar. 4, 1961; children—Adella M., Carl A., Hector R. Student Colegio Palmore. Asst. bookkeeper Sec. Agr., Chihuahua, 1954-56; officer mgr. San Gabriel Valley Labor Assn., Cucamonga, Calif., 1956-78; gen. mgr. Corona Growers Inc., Corona, Calif., 1978—. Mem. Agrl. Personnel Mgmt. Assn., Corona Norco Safety Group, Employers Adv. Group, Farm Bur. Republican. Mem. Ch. of Nazarene. Lodge: Toastmistress Internat. Home: 952 W 17th St Upland CA 91786 Office: 211 N Pearl Corona CA 92786

CASTANO, ELVIRA PALMERIO, art historian, gallery dir.; b. Cin., July 23, 1929; d. John and Josephine Castano; B.A., Emerson Coll., Boston, 1950; postgrad. (Cardinal Spellman scholar), Pius XII Inst., Florence, Italy, 1954-55; m. Carlo Palmerio (dec.), June 1, 1958; 1 dau., Marina. Curator, Castano Art Gallery, Boston, 1965-78; dir. Castano Art Gallery, Needham, Mass., 1978—; Vatican translator; interpreter Italian art, specialist in Macchiaioli art; Italian lang. translator. Mem. Dante Alighieri Soc., Boston, Boston Mus. Fine Arts, Brockton (Mass.) Art Mus. (adv. bd.), Fogg Art Mus. of Harvard U., San Francisco Mus., Friends of Needham Library. Roman Catholic. Address: 245 Hunnewell St Needham MA 02194

CASTELLUCCI, DEBORAH TAIT, nursing educator; b. Reading, Pa., Nov. 27, 1948; d. Alexander MacIlreath and Dorothy Virginia (Tait) Dickson; m. Eugene Anthony Castellucci, June 13, 1970; children—Todd A., Sean A., Jed E. R.N., The Reading (Pa.) Hosp., 1969; B.S. in Edn., Millersville U., 1981, B.S. in Nursing, 1984; postgrad. U. Pa. Nurse, EENT dept. Reading Hosp., 1969-71, nurse ECU, 1971-76, 80-81; nurse educator Alvernia Coll., Reading, Pa., 1983—. Mem. Am. Nurses Assn., Pa. Nurses Assn., Reading Hosp. Alumni Assn., Delta Phi Eta. Democrat. Roman Catholic. Home: 900 Highwood Ave Reading PA 19607 Office: Alvernia Coll Reading PA 19607

CASTILLEJOS, MARIA ESTELA, ophthalmologist; b. Mexico City, Nov. 12, 1948; d. Santiago and Alicia (Rios) C.; m. Jose G. Hernandez, Dec. 26, 1971; 1 son, Santiago. Degree in Biochemistry magna cum laude, U. Mex., Mexico City, 1967, M.D., 1973. Intern, Moncton Hosp., (N.B., Can.), 1972-73; resident Jewish Hosp. and Med. Ctr., N.Y.C., 1973-75, resident in ophthalmology, 1975-78; fellow Harvard U. Med. Sch., Boston, 1979-80; chief retina service Mexican Inst. Health, Mexico City, 1980-82; practice medicine specializing in opthalmology (retina), San Diego, 1982—. Home: 3906 Ave San Miguel Bonita CA 92002 Office: 6699 Alvarado Rd Suite 2201 San Diego CA 92120

CASTILLO, MARY HELEN MÁRQUEZ, nurse; b. El Paso, May 27, 1936; d. José Anselmo and Irene María (Federico) Márquez; diploma St. Vincents Coll. Nursing, 1957; B.S.N., U. Tex., 1974, M.S.N., 1977; Ph.D., N.Mex. State U., 1983; m. William Richard Castillo, Dec. 28, 1957; children—Carole Angel, William Richard II, Cesar Orlando. Nurse, St. Vincents Hosp., Los Angeles, 1957; office nurse, staff nurse critical care, El Paso, 1958-61; nursing supr. Providence Meml. Hosp., El Paso, 1961-64, dir. edn. dept., 1964-65, dir. nursing services, 1965-76; assoc. prof. nursing U. Tex.-El Paso, 1976—; nursing services cons.; dir., officer, West Tex. Health Systems Agy., 1975—; mem. Profl. Adv. Council Life mgmt. Ctr. League United Latin Am. Citizens scholar, 1980. Mem. U.S.-Mex. Border Health Assn. (sec.), Dirs. of Nursing Services in El Paso (chmn. 1975), Tex. Nurses Assn. (v.p., pres.) Council Hosp. Nursing Tex. Hosp. Assn., Am. Hosp. Assn., Am. Nurses Assn., Tri Delta, Phi Delta Kappa, Sigma Theta Tau. Democrat. Roman Catholic. Clubs: U. Tex. Womens Aux., El Paso Womens. Contbr. articles to profl. jours. Home: 6544 Fiesta Dr El Paso TX 79912 Office: Coll Nursing U Tex El Paso TX 79902

CASTLE, BRENDA WAGNER, realtor; b. Kingsport, Tenn., Feb. 4, 1941; d. Fred Kelsie and Maxie Louise (Duff) Wagner; m. Norman Daniel Castle, May 30, 1966; children—Norman Daniel, John Eric. B.S., Berea Coll., 1963; M.Ed., Boston U., 1974. Salesman, J.C. Morgan Co., Fairmont, W.Va., 1976-77; ptnr. Century 21-Castle Morgan, Fairmont, 1977-78; owner, Century 21 Castle Realty, Fairmont, 1978-84, broker, 1984—. Mem. Fairmont Assn. Realtors (sec. 1978-79, 80-81), Tau Kappa Alpha. Democrat. Methodist. Home: 840 Hidden Valley Rd Kingsport TN 37663

CASTLE, SUE, author; b. Harrisburg, Pa., Feb. 2, 1940; d. Benjamin Louis and Sadye (Latt) Garonzik; m. Jay Sheldon Castle, Feb. 27, 1965; children—Jennifer, Bethany. B.A., Smith Coll., 1961; M.A., Tchrs. Coll., Columbia U., 1963. Research asst. Sloan Bus. Sch., MIT, Cambridge, 1961-62; systems designer Advanced Computer Techniques, N.Y.C., 1964-69; assoc. producer, head writer Mother's Minutes, ABC-TV, 1984-86, Mother's Day, Lifetime Cable, 1985-86. Author: The Complete Guide to Preparing Baby Foods, 1973; Face Talk, Hand Talk, Body Talk, 1976, The Complete New Guide to Preparing Baby Foods, 1981; (with L. Bocchicchio) Our Child's Medical Diary, 1982; Nutrition For Your Child's Most Important Years, 1984; (videocassette) Everything you Need to Know About your Newborn, 1986; Joan Lunden's Mother's Minutes, 1986. Bd. dirs. Ossining Childrens Ctr. (N.Y.), 1972-83. Mem. Sigma Xi. Democrat. Jewish. Clubs: Halloween Yacht (Stamford, Conn.); Smith (Westchester, N.Y.). Home: 23 Stephenson Terr Briarcliff Manor NY 10510

CASTOR, ELIZABETH B. (BETTY CASTOR), state legislator; b. Glassboro, N.J., May 11, 1941; d. Joseph L. and Gladys (Wright) Bowe; m. Donald F. Castor, 1966; children—Katherine, Karen, Frank. B.A., Glassboro State Coll., 1963; M.A., U. Miami, 1968. Mem. Fla. Senate, Tallahassee, 1976-78 and currently. Mem. Hillsborough County Bd. Commrs., Fla., 1972-76, chmn., 1975-76; mem. Hillsborough County Environ. Protection Commn., 1972-76, chmn., 1973-74; mem. exec. bd. Tampa Bay Regional Planning Council, 1972-76; mem. U. Fla. Ctr. for Govt. Responsibility, bd. dirs., 1977; mem. Hillsborough Hosp. and Welfare Bd., 1972-76, chmn., 1973-74; mem. council advisers U. South Fla. Recipient Good Govt. award Town 'N Country Jaycees, 1975, Outstanding Legislator of Yr. award FEA, 1977. Mem. LWV, Athena Soc. Democrat. Lutheran. Office: Fla Senate State Capitol Tallahassee FL 32301*

CASTRO, EDNA CARLENE, personnel executive; b. Twin Falls, Idaho, Mar. 25, 1942; d. Leo Walter and Joy Pauline (Rugh) Wright; A.A., Coll. So. Idaho, 1980; m. Robert G. Castro, Jr., June 30, 1971; children—R. Jeffrey, Leslie Joy. Personnel clk. Glendale div. Kellwood Corp., Twin Falls, 1969-71; office mgr. Snake River Area council Boy Scouts Am., Twin Falls, 1972-74; mgr. Nat. Car Rental Co., Twin Falls, 1974-78; personnel mgr. F. W. Woolworth Co., Twin Falls, 1978-84, E.F. Johnson Co., Twin Falls, 1984-85; dental asst. M.B. Dingman, D.D.S., P.A., 1986—; owner Edna's Gifts and Things, Twin Falls, 1985—; calligrapher, personnel cons.; vocat. instr. Coll. So. Idaho. Adv. bd. Distributive Edn. Club Am., 1980-84. Mem. Am. Soc. Personnel Adminstrn., Life Study Fellowship Republican. Mem. Ch. of Christ. Home: 207 Caswell Ave Twin Falls ID 83301

CASWELL, PATSY LOU, educational administrator; b. Priceville, Ky., June 7, 1938; d. Raymond and Orene Jane (Gibson) C.; B.S. in Phys. Edn., Western Ky. U., 1960; M.A. in Phys. Edn., No. Colo. U., 1966; postgrad. U. Louisville, 1975-77. Tchr. phys. edn. and health Pleasure Ridge Park High Sch., Louisville, 1960; tchr. swimming Wilson Jr. High Sch., Rockford, Ill., 1961-67; tchr. phys. edn., coach gymnastics Palo Verde High Sch., Tucson, 1967-68; tchr. phys. edn. Ahrens Trade Sch., 1968-70; chmn. dept. health and phys. edn., coach cross country and track, asst. athletic dir., then athletic dir. Thomas Jefferson High Sch., Louisville, 1970-79; Title IX compliance specialist Jefferson County Public Schs., Louisville, 1979-85; coordinator activities/athletics Durrett Edn. Ctr., Louisville, 1985—. Mem. Nat. Coalition for Sex Equity in Edn., AAUW, Women in Adminstrn., Jefferson County Adminstrs. Assn., Daus. of Am., Delta Kappa Gamma, Phi Delta Kappa. Democrat. Methodist. Home: 3509 Hanover Rd Louisville KY 40207 Office: Durrett Edn Ctr 4409 Preston Hwy Louisville KY 40213

CASWELL, PAULETTE REVA, lawyer; b. Chgo., June 8, 1951; d. Ben and Lillian (Cohen) Watstein; m. Michael Evidson, May 15, 1975 (div. Mar. 1979); 1 child, David Allan Philip; m. Charles Frank Caswell, III, Jan. 8, 1983. A.A., West Los Angeles Community Coll., 1971; B.A., Calif. State U.-Los Angeles, 1975; J.D., Whittier Coll., 1982; D.D. (hon.), St. Alban's Coll., San Francisco, 1974. Bar: Calif. 1982, U.S. Dist. Ct. (cen. dist.) Calif., 1983. Dir., Mensa of Los Angeles, 1977-83; sole practice, Los Angeles, 1982—; dir., founder Amicus, Los Angeles Area Ctr. Law and the Deaf; cons. Editor: Consumer Rights, 1982; author legal articles pamphlets, booklets. Legal adv. Ind. Living Ctrs.; adv. for deaf and visually-impaired. Mem. ABA, Los Angeles County Bar Assn., Legal Assistance Assn. Calif., State Bar Calif., Arts. Democrat. Jewish. Home: 645 N Gardner St Los Angeles CA 90036

CATALANO, MARIA ROSA, employment placement coordinator; b. Havana, Cuba, Dec. 21, 1955; came to U.S., 1962, naturalized, 1974; d. Jose Antonio and Aida (Oxamendi) Diaz; m. Carl Philip Catalano, Feb. 14, 1983. B.A. in Psychology, B.A. in Lit., Wellesley Coll., 1978; postgrad. in psychology Boston U., 1975. With Chelsea Pub. Library, Mass., summer 1976, Margaret Clapp Library, Wellesley Coll., Mass., 1975-78; asst. mgr. Burdine's Dept. Store, Hialeah, Fla., 1978; employment placement counselor Fla. State Employment

Office, Hialeah, 1979; radio announcer Sta. WINZ and Fla. State Employment Office, 1979; employment placement coordinator Catalano's Nurses Registry, Inc., Hialeah, 1979—. Benjamin and Norma P. Call scholar, 1974; scholar Wellesley Coll., 1974-78. Mem. Nat. Assn. for Female Execs., Chelsea Naval Hosp. Explorer's Club, Am. Soc. Notaries. Republican. Roman Catholic. Club: ANRI (Randolph, Mass.). Avocations: writing short stories and poems, collecting antiques, dolls, miniatures, paintings and prints. Home: 640 E 55th St Hialeah FL 33013 Office: Catalano's Nurses Registry Inc 555 W 49th St Hialeah FL 33012

CATALFO, BETTY MARIE, health service executive, nutritionist; b. N.Y.C., Nov. 2, 1942; d. Lawrence Santo and Gemma (Patrone) Lorefice; children—Anthony, Philip, Lawrence, Donna. Grad. Newtown High Sch., Elmhurst, N.Y., 1958. Sec., clk. ABC-TV, N.Y.C., 1957-60; lectr., nutritionist Weight Watchers, Manhasset, N.Y., 1976-75; founder, pres. Every-Bodys Diet, Inc. dba Stay Slim, Bronx, N.Y., 1976—; dir. in-home program N.Y. State Dept. Health, N.Y.C., 1985—; lectr. in field. Author: 101 Stay-Slim Recipes, 1983. Author, dir., producer: (video) Dancersize for Overweight, 1986; author, editor: (video) Eating Right For Life, 1985. Sponsor, lectr. St. Pauls Ctr., Bklyn., 1981—, Throgs Neck Assn. Retarded Children, Bronx, 1985—. Named Woman of Yr., Bayside Womens Club, N.Y., 1983; Merit award for Service Catholic Archdiocese of Bklyn., 1985. Mem. Nat. C. of C. for Women, Roundtable for Women in Food Service, Bus. and Profl. Women's Club, Pres. Council for Phys. Fitness, Nat. Assn. Female Execs. Democrat. Roman Catholic. Clubs: Mothers Sacred Heart Sch. (chairperson 1979-82); Democratic (campaign coordinator 1977-86). Avocations: reading; traveling; spending leisure time with my children. Home: 208-05 15th Rd Bayside NY 11360

CATCHINGS, YVONNE PARKS, artist, educator; b. Atlanta, Aug. 17; d. Andrew Walter and Hattie Marie (Brookins) Parks; A.B. in Art, Spelman Coll., 1955; M.A. in Art Edn., Columbia U., 1958; M.A. in Mus. Practice, U. Mich., 1970, Ph.D. in Edn., 1981; m. James A.A. Catchings, May 30, 1960; children—Andrea Yvonne Hunt Warner, Wanda Elaine Hunt McLean, James Albert A. Tchr. art Atlanta Bd. Edn., 1955-59; instr. in art spelman Coll., 1956-57; tchr. art Detroit Bd. Edn., 1959-75, art specialist, 1976—; lectr. Marygrove Coll., 1970-72; one-woman show: Black Artist South, Huntsville (Ala.) Mus., 1978; group shows: Forever Free: Art by African Am. Women, 1862-1980, traveling show, 1981; Fulbright-Hayes grantee for study, Zimbabwe, 1982; trustee Afro Am. Mus., 1970-72. Program chmn. Nat. Aux. to Nat. Dental Assn., 1966, chmn. art and craft, 1976; chmn. reception com. United Negro Coll. Fund, Detroit, 1980. Recipient Spirit of Detroit award Detroit Common Council, 1978, Mayor's award of Merit, City of Detroit, 1978; James D. Parks Art award Nat. Conf. Art, 1979. Mem. Nat. Art Edn. Assn., Nat. Conf. Artists, Your Heritage House Mus., Children's Mus., Mich. Art Therapist Assn., Phi Delta Kappa, Delta Sigma Theta (chmn. Founders Day 1965; nat. chmn. heritage and archives, mem. nat. exec. bd.). Clubs: The Links, The Moles, Smart Set, Carrousels. Author: You Ain't Free Yet Notes From a Black Woman, 1976; author geneal. publs. Home: 1306 Joliet Pl Detroit MI 48207

CATES, SHEILA MAE, library consultant; b. Hobart, Okla., Apr. 20, 1947; d. Arch B. and Bonnie Mae (Hayden) Alexander; m. Dennis Patrick Cates, Mar. 26, 1977; children—Patrick Alexander, Kristen Leigh. B.S. in Edn., Okla. State U., 1969; M.L.S., U. Okla., 1970. Jr. high sch. librarian Lawton Pub. Schs., Okla., 1969-70, high sch. librarian, 1970-73; library cons. Okla. Dept. Edn., Oklahoma City, 1974-77; cons. Madison Pub. Library, Wis., 1977-79; library cons. Office Pub. Instrn., Helena, Mont., 1981-85, Mont. State Library, Helena, 1985—. Contbr. to book: Elements of Computer Education, 1983; editor School/Public Library Cooperation, 1979; Curriculum Guide for Teaching Media Skills K-12, 1975. Active United Methodist Women, Helena, 1982—. Mem. Mont. Library Assn. (exec. bd. 1981—, conf. chmn. 1984), ALA, Nat. Assn. State Ednl. Media Profls. (sec. 1984-85). Democrat. Club: PEO (pres. 1979-80, 86-87, v.p. 1982-83). Home: 437 S Lamborn St Helena MT 59601 Office: Mont State Library 1515 E 6th Helena MT 59620

CATHCART, LINDA LOUISE, museum dir.; b. Lafayette, Ind., Oct. 20, 1947; d. Robert S. and Dolores J. Cathcart; B.A. in Fine Arts, Calif. State U., Fullerton, 1969; M.A. in Art History, Hunter Coll., City U. N.Y., 1972; Fulbright fellow Courtauld Art Inst., 1973-74. Curatorial asst. Whitney Mus. Am. Art, N.Y.C., 1971-73; instr. Sch. of Visual Arts, N.Y.C., 1971-73, 75; instr. Cambridge (Eng.) U., 1974; coordinator spl. programs Bklyn. Mus., 1974-75; curator Albright-Knox Art Gallery, Buffalo, 1975-79; dir. Contemporary Arts Mus., Houston, 1979—; adj. prof. SUNY, Buffalo, 1975-78. Mem. Am. Assn. Museums, Internat. Council Museums, Am. Assn. Mus. Dirs. Contbr. essays to catalogues in field. Office: Contemporary Arts Museum 5216 Montrose Blvd Houston TX 77006

CATHER, BETTY JOANNE, lawyer; b. Vancouver, Wash., May 26, 1956; d. Dick R. and Betty Ann (Grubb) Cather. B.A., U. Ariz., 1978, J.D., 1981. Bar: Ariz. 1981. Law clk. to trustee in bankruptcy U.S. Dept. Justice, Denver, summer 1980; staff atty. So. Ariz. Legal Aid, Ind., Tucson, 1982-83; sole practice, Tucson, 1983-84; geen. franchise counsel Ugly Duckling Rent-A-Car System, Inc., Tucson, 1984—; bd. advisors Dinnerware Artist' Coop. Mem. Pima County Bar Assn. (Pres.-elect young lawyers div.), Nat. Assn. Trial Lawyers. Democrat. Congregationalist. Office: Ugly Duckling Rent-A-Car System 6375 E Tanque Verde Suite 10 Tucson AZ 85715

CATHER, LETHA MAE, construction company executive; b. Stratford, Okla., May 2, 1941; d. Hollis Floyd and Lillie Lorene (Austin) Ford; diploma Draughons Sch. Bus., Oklahoma City, 1960; student Okla. State U., Okla. Bapt. U.; divorced. With Hartford Ins. Co., Oklahoma City, 1966-67; with Cowen Constrn., Inc., Tulsa, 1967—, head acctg., sec.-treas., dir., 1970—; sec.-treas., dir. Stevco Inc., Rock Ridge Devel. Co.; mem. adv. com. constrn. tech. dept. Tulsa Jr. Coll., 1977-81. Mem. Nat. Assn. Women in Constrn. (pres. Tulsa chpt. 1977-81, dist. dir. 1982-83). Democrat. Baptist. Office: 18 N Maybelle Ave Tulsa OK 74127

CATLIN, MARIAN WOOLSTON, physician; b. Seattle, Jan. 20, 1931; d. Howard Brown and Katharine Nichols (Dally) Woolston; B.A. cum laude, Vassar Coll., 1951; M.D. (Vassar fellow), Harvard U., 1955; m. Randolph Catlin, July 5, 1959; children—Laura Louise, Jennifer Woolston, Randolph III. Intern and resident pediatric medicine Children's Hosp., Boston, 1956; resident in psychiatry Mass. Mental Health Center, Boston, 1957-59, mem. staff children's unit, 1978-82; clin. fellow psychiatry Harvard U., 1957-59, Commonwealth fellow child psychiatry, 1975-78, clin. instr. psychiatry, 1975—; clin. instr. psychiatry Tufts U., 1957-59; pvt. practice child and adolescent psychiatry, Wellesley Hills, Mass., 1978—; speaker Rhodes House, Oxford (Eng.) U., 1961. Bd. dirs. preparatory div. New Eng. Conservatory Music, 1972-75, Parents and Children's Services. Mem. AMA, Mass. Med. Soc., Am. Acad. Child Psychiatry, Am. Psychiat. Assn., New Eng. Council Child Psychiatry (mem. chmn.), Mass. Psychiat. Soc. Episcopalian. Clubs: Vassar (mem. bd. 1963-75) (Boston); Board-Hills Garden (design cons. 1973-75) (Wellesley Hills, Mass.). Home: 314 North St Medfield MA 02052 Office: 316 Washington St Wellesley Hills MA 02181

CATOE, BETTE LORRINA, physician; b. Washington, Apr. 7, 1926; d. John Booker and Laura Beola (Adams) C.; B.S. cum laude, Howard U., 1948, M.D., 1951; m. Warren J. Strudwick, Sept. 17, 1949; children—Laura Christina, Warren J., William J. Intern, Freedmen's Hosp., Washington, 1951-52; pediatric resident Howard U. Freedman's Hosp., 1952-55; practice medicine specializing in pediatrics, Washington, 1956—; instr. bacteriology Howard U., 1955-57; mem. staff Providence Hosp., Cafritz Hosp., Columbia Hosp., Howard U. Hosp., Washington Hosp. Center; sch. health officer Dept. Health, Washington, 1960-64; clin. instr. Howard U., 1956—. Mem. D.C. Health Planning Adv. Council, 1967-77, chmn., 1973-77; chmn. D.C. Devel. Disabilities Adv. Council, 1970-74; mem. D.C. Mayor's Commn. on Food and Nutrition, 1971-72, Mayor's Commn. on Maternal and Child Health. 1978—; mem. D.C. Commn. Jud. Tenure and Disabilities, 1977—, chair, 1984—; bd. dirs. United Way of Nat. Capital Area, 1974-76, chmn. social planning com., 1974-75; bd. govs. St. Alban's Sch., 1978—; bd. dirs. D.C. Health and Welfare Council, 1968-73, pres., 1973-74; del. Democratic Nat. Conv., 1976; bd. dirs. Met. Washington Health and Welfare Council, 1970-72, Parent Council of Washington, 1974-75, Met. Med. Founds., Inc., Silver Spring YMCA, 1977-80. Mem. Am. Acad. Pediatrics, AMA, Nat. Med. Assn., D.C. Chirurg. Soc., D.C. Med. Soc., Am. Med. Women's Assn. (chmn. pediatric com. 1981-83), NAACP, Urban League, Am. Assn. Comprehensive Health Planners (dir. 1975-77), Women's Aux. Medico-Chirurg. Soc., Jack and Jill Am., Century Club of Nat. Assn. Negro Bus. and Profl. Women's Clubs (pres. 1985—), Alpha Kappa Alpha. Baptist. Clubs: Links, Carrousels, Women's Nat. Dem. Home: 1748 Sycamore St NW Washington DC 20012 Office: 5505 5th St Washington DC 20011

CATTANEO, JACQUELYN ANNETTE KAMMERER, artist, educator; b. Gallup, N.Mex., June 1, 1944; d. Ralph John and Gladys Agnes (O'Sullivan) Kammer; m. John Leo Cattaneo, Apr. 25, 1964; children—John Auro, Paul Anthony. Student Tex. Woman's U., 1962-64. Portrait artist, Gallup, 1972; one woman shows: Gallup Pub. Library, 1963, 66, 77, 78, 81, Gallup Lovelace Med. Clinic, Santa Fe Station Open House, 1981, Gallery 20, Farmington, N.Mex., 1985—; group shows include: Navajo Nation Library Invitational, 1978, Santa Fe Festival of Arts Invitational, 1979, N.Mex. State Fair, 1978, 79, 80, Catharine Lorillard Wolfe, N.Y.C., 1980, 81, 84, 85, 4th ann. exhbn. Salmagundi Club, 1984, 3d ann. Palm Beach Internat., New Orleans, 1984, Fine Arts Ctr. Taos, 1984, O'Brien's Art Emorium, 1986; represented in permanent collections: Zuni Arts and Crafts Ednl. Bldg., U. N.Mex., C.J. Wiemar Collection, Sunset Bank, Gallup, N.Mex., Civic Ctr., Las Cruces, N.Mex. represented by Lani Kyea Fine Arts Ctr. En Taos, also Roseborough Gallery, Farmington, N.Mex. Mem. Internat. Fine Arts Guild, Am. Portrait Soc. (permanent cert. 1985), Catharine Lorillard Wolfe Art Club of N.Y.C., Am. Portrait Soc. (cert.), Gallup Area Arts Council, Gallup C. of C. Club: Soroptimist (Gallup). Address: 210 E Green St Gallup NM 87301

CATTANI, MARYELLEN BILLETTE, diversified financial services company executive, lawyer; b. Bakersfield, Calif., Dec. 1, 1943; d. Arnold Theodore and Corinne Marilyn (Kovacevich) C.; m. Bernard Joseph Mikell, Jr., Apr. 1, 1978. A.B., Vassar Coll., 1965; J.D., U. Calif.-Berkeley, 1968. Bar: N.Y. 1969, Calif. 1969. Assoc., Davis Polk & Wardwell, N.Y.C., 1968-69; assoc. Orrick, Herrington & Sutcliffe, San Francisco, 1970-74, ptnr., 1975-81; v.p., gen. counsel Transamerica Corp., San Francisco, 1981-83, sr. v.p., gen. counsel, 1983—. Contbg. author: California Corporate Practice Guide, 1977; The Corporate Counsellor's Desk Book, 1982. Mem. vis. com. Golden Gate U. Sch. Law, San Francisco; trustee Vassar Coll.; mem. bd. regents St. Mary's Coll. of Calif.; bd. dirs. Legal Aid Soc. of San Francisco. Mem. State Bar Calif. (chmn. bus. law sec. 1980-81), State Bar N.Y., Calif. Women Lawyers, Bar Assn. San Francisco, ABA, San Francisco Downtown Women Lawyers Assn., Am. Corp. Counsel Assn. (dir.). Democrat. Roman Catholic. Club: Women's Forum West. Office: Transamerica Corp 600 Montgomery St San Francisco CA 94111

CATTERTON, DEIRDRE JEAN, engineering and defense consulting company executive; b. Washington, June 9, 1962; d. Edward Lee and Shirley Jean (Repass) C. B.A. in Govt. and Politics, George Mason U., 1983, postgrad., 1983—. Security systems analyst Info. Systems & Networks Corp., Chevy Chase, Md., 1984-85; systems analyst Dvaco Lion Internat. Inc., Rosslyn, Va., 1985; sales and mktg. rep. ARCO Corp., McLean, Va., 1986—. Mem., fundraising chmn. Loudoun County Republican Women's Club, Leesburg, 1982-83; mem. Va. Fedn. Rep. Women, Richmond, 1981—, Nat. Fedn. Rep. Women, Washington, 1981—; vol. Inaugural Com., Washington, 1984-85; mem. adv. council Richard Viguerie for Lt. Gov. Va., 1985; mem. choir Little River Baptist Ch., 1985—. Named Semi-finalist Miss Va.-U.S.A. Am. Pagents, Inc., 1984, Miss Metro Washington, 1984, 1985. Mem. Nat. Assn. Female Execs. Nat. Guild of Piano Tchrs., Nat. Frat. Student Musicians and Piano Hobbyists, Student Div. Am. Coll. Musicians. Office: ARCO Corp 1764 Old Meadows Ln McLean VA 22102

CATZ, ROCHELLE ZUKOR, lawyer; b. Providence, Aug. 21, 1945; d. Jerold and Frances (Konisky) Zukor; m. Robert Steven Catz, Apr. 28, 1968 (div. 1979); children—Shawn David, Jason Alan. A.B., U. So. Calif., 1968; M.S. in Edn., 1969; J.D., Antioch Sch. of Law, 1979. Tchr. Los Angeles Pub. Schs., 1968, Laguna Salada Union Sch. Dist., Pacifica, Calif., 1969-71, Omaha Pub. Schs., 1971-73; indexer/abstractor Eric Clearing House on Tchr. Edn., Washington, 1975-76; atty. Fla. Rural Legal Services, Ft. Myers, Fla., 1979-83; pvt. practice law, Ft. Myers, 1983—; mem. Fla. Legal Services, Pub. Benefits Work Group, Tallahassee, Fla., 1980-83; mem. Aging Network, Ft. Myers, Fla., 1983. Sec., Jewish Fedn. of Lee County, 1984-85. Mem. Pa. Bar Assn., Am. Bar Assn., Fla. Bar, Lee County Bar Assn. (treas. 1986-87), Nat. Orgn. Social Security Calimants Reps., Fla. Assn. Women Lawyers, Southwest Fla. Estate Planning Council. Democrat. Jewish. Clubs: Women's Network, Zonta (Ft. Myers, Fla.). Lodge: Order of Eastern Star. Office: 6363 McGregor Blvd Ft Myers FL 33907

CAUCUTT, AMY MEAD CARR, business administration educator; b. Christiansburg, Va., May 12, 1946; d. Francis Lewis and Miriam Mead (Arnold) Carr; m. Greg Caucutt; children—Mary A., Elizabeth M., George N. Student Wellesley Coll., 1964-65, Mich. State U., 1966, U. Wis.-Madison, 1967, U. Md., 1968-69, Rochester Community Coll., 1980-81; B.A. with honors, U. Wis.-Eau Claire, 1969; M.B.A., Winona State U., 1982. Instr. bus. adminstrn. Winona State U., Minn., 1982-84; asst. prof. Winona State U.-Rochester, Minn., 1984—; dir. Small Bus. Devel. Ctr., SBA, Winona, 1985—; cons. Olmsted Co., Rochester, 1982. Pub. mem. admissions com. Mayo Med. Sch., Rochester, 1979-82, Am. Assn. Med. Colls., Washington, 1982-83; bd. dirs., found. mem. Ability Bldg. Ctr., Inc., Rochester, 1984—; chmn., vice-chmn. Rochester Planning and Zoning Comm., 1983—; mem. Rochester Zoning Bd. Appeals, 1984, Recycling Task Force, Olmsted County, Minn., 1980-81; mem. housing com. Rochester- Olmsted Council of Govts., 1978-79; candidate for Olmsted County auditor, 1982; co-chmn. for state legis. campaign, precinct chmn., affirmative action officer Democratic Farmer Labor Party, Rochester, 1972—; active various coms., vol. Rochester Sch. Dist. 535, 1981—; mem. vestry, lay reader, Bible sch. dir., mem. various coms. St. Luke's Episcopal Ch., Rochester, 1970—. Mem. LWV (local pres. 1976-80, state sec. treas. 1980-82, mem. coms., League of Yr. 1982), Minn. Women's Network, Rochester C. of C., Minn. Edn. Assn. Home: 716 28th St NW Rochester MN 55901 Office: Winona State U-Rochester 2220 3d Ave SE Rochester MN 55904

CAUDILL, ELAINE HILL, psychiatric healthcare technician, college recruiter; b. Balt., June 9, 1942; d. Paul Berkley and Dora Eleanor (Brantley) Hill; m. Morrell Bertrand Shorter, Jr., Aug. 2, 1960 (Apr. 1978); children—David Alan (dec.), Susan Elaine Shorter Johnson; m. Roger Dean Caudill, Oct. 7, 1983. B.S.W., Ferrum Coll., 1982. Fed. employee VA Med. Ctr., Perry Point, Md., 1973-76, psychiat. nursing, Salem, Va., 1976-86; healthcare technician Psychiat. Service, 1986—; coll. recruiter Atalantis Corp., Roanoke, Va., 1985—. Editor newsletter: Am. Fedn. Govt. Employees. Vice pres. pub. relations S.E. Concerned Citizens Inc., Roanoke, 1970-80; mem. Democratic Congl. campaign com.; past leader Girl Scouts U.S.A., Md.; vol. Legal Aid Soc., sr. citizens and youth groups. Recipient Arthur S. Owens award, 1980, 81; Civic award S.E. Concerned Citizens, Inc., 1981. Mem. Nat. Assn. Female Execs., Nat. Assn. Social Workers. Democrat. Baptist. Club: Social Work. Lodge: Rose Mount Rebekah Lodge (conductor). Avocations: reading; swimming; volleyball; creweling; art; camping and fishing. Home: 658 Morrill Ave SE Roanoke VA 24013 Office: Salem VA Med Ctr Bldg 10 Room 105 Salem VA 24153

CAUGHLIN, STEPHENIE JANE, futures company executive, metals company executive; b. McAllen, Tex., July 23, 1948; d. James Daniel and Betty Jane (Warnock) C. B.A. in Family Econs., San Diego State U., 1972, M.Ed., 1973; M. in Psychology, U.S. Internat. U., San Diego, 1979. Cert. secondary life tchr., Calif. Owner, mgr. Minute Maid Service, San Diego, 1970-75; prin. Rainbow Fin. Services, San Diego, 1975-78; tchr. San Diego Unified Sch. Dist., 1973-80; mortgage broker Santa Fe Mortgage Co., San Diego, 1980-81; commodity broker Premex Commodities, San Diego, 1981-84; pres., owner Nationwide Futures Corp., San Diego, 1984—; owner, sec. Nationwide Metals Corp. Sec. Arroyo Sorrento Assn., Del Mar, Calif., 1978—. Mem. Nat. Futures Assn., Sierra Club. Republican. Avocations: horseback riding; swimming; skiing; gardening; raising domestic and exotic birds. Home: 3909 Arroyo Sorrento Rd San Diego CA 92130 Office: Nationwide Futures Corp PO Box 2177 La Jolla CA 92037

CAUSEY, KATHLEEN DIANE, probation and parole officer, tax accountant; b. Suffern, N.Y., Sept. 29, 1955; d. Robert Charles and Shirley Ann (Oakley) Conklin; m. Joseph Darius Causey, Nov. 17, 1976 (div. 1981); 1 child, Angela Diane. B.S. in Acctg., U. S.C., 1986. Asst. to merchandise mgr. Western Big Wheel, North Bergen, N.J., 1974-75; telecom supr. Dept. of Army, Fort Jackson, S.C., 1977-82; tax acct., Columbia, S.C., 1977—; asst. to dir. S.C. Sentencing Guidelines Commn., Columbia, 1982-86; probation and parole pub. service employment coordinator Parole and Community Corrections, Columbia, 1986—; data analysis staff S.C. Jail Commn., 1982-83, Gov.'s JJ Council, 1982-83, Sentencing Guidelines, 1982-83. Guardian-ad Litem Guardian-Ad-Litem Project, 1983—; choir dir. Incarnation Lutheran Ch., 1984-86; parents' adv. council Richland Sch. Dist. 1, 1984-85. Served with U.S. Army, 1975-77. Recipient Sustained Superior Performance award Dept. Army, 1981. Mem. Am. Correctional Assn., S.C. Correctional Assn., S.C. Victim Assistance Network, Nat. Assn. Female Execs., Am. Soc. Notaries, Am. Philatelic Soc. Republican. Avocation: professional singer. Home: 9 Upton Ct Columbia SC 29209 Office: SC Parole and Community Corrections 2221 Devine St Suite 612D Columbia SC 29205

CAUTHEN, DELORIS VAUGHAN, artist; b. Wilmington, N.C.; d. Robert S. and Margaret (Hurst) Vaughan; student U. S.C., 1950-52, Richland Art Sch., 1960-63, 75-76, Robert Brackman, Madison, Conn., 1976-77, Burnsville (N.C.) Painting in the Mountains Sch., 1980-86; student of Frank Allen, Rock Port, Mass., 1955; m. John Kelley Cauthen, Dec. 28, 1925 (dec. 1973); children—John Vaughan, Henry Jennings. One-woman shows of paintings and/or sculpture include: U. S.C., Florence, 1968, U. S.C., Aiken, 1970, Francis Marion Coll., Florence, 1980, S.C. Ednl. TV, Columbia, 1966, 70, Columbia (S.C.) Town Theater, 1960, Union County Library, Monroe, N.C., 1969, S.C. Fed. Savs. & Loan Assn., Columbia, 1979 Columbia Coll., 1981, Spring Mills, Ft. Mill, S.C., 1981, Columbia Coll., 1982: four 3 person shows Columbia Mus. Art (purchase award); numerous group shows including: Mint Mus. Art, Charlotte, N.C., 1962, 65, 66, Columbia Mus. Art, 1964, 70, 73, 77, Gibbs Art Gallery, Charleston, S.C., 1966, 67, 69, Telfair Acad. Art, Savannah, Ga., 1969, Beaufort (S.C.) Art Assn., 1969, S.C. State Fair, 1959 (blue ribbon), Columbia Coll.; represented in permanent collections: Mint Mus. Art, S.C. Nat. Bank, Columbia, U. S.C., Columbia, Columbia Mus. of Art, Columbia City Schs., Darlington (S.C.) City Schs., S.C. Gov.'s Mansion, Columbia, Banker's Trust, Columbia, others. Mem. S.C. Gov.'s Council of Advs. on Consumer Credit, 1974-78. Recipient S.C. Nat. Bank award, 1969-73, award Beaufort Art Assn., also numerous show awards including Judges Choice, Tel air Acad. Art, 1969 Mem. Columbia Artists Guild (top winner, hon. and merit awards), Guild S.C. Artists, Internat. Soc. Artists, Trenholm Artist Guild, Dutch Fork Artist Guild. Methodist. Address: 2407 Wheat St Columbia SC 29205

CAVALCANTE, CARI JO, association executive; b. Pitts., Apr. 21, 1959; d. Anthony and Mitzie LaVerne (Wunderley) C. B.S. in Broadcast and Film, Central Mo. State U., 1981. Pub. relations asst. Kansas City Kings, Mo., 1981-82; graphic artist Kansas City Area Transp. Authority, 1981-84, pub. relations coordinator, 1984-85; devel. specialist Mo. Spl. Olympics, Kansas City, 1985—; freelance graphic artist, 1981-84. Mem. pub. relations com. for spl. events Met. Orgn. to Counter Sexual Assault, Kansas City, 1986; prodn. coordinator for spl. event Marillac Ctr. for Children, Kansas City, 1985—. Club: Kansas City Field Hockey (pres. 1982-84). Avocations: sports; music. Office: Mo Spl Olympics Kansas City Area IV 12401 E 43d Suite 159 Independence MO 64055

CAVALLO, CAROL, oil company official; b. N.Y.C., Jan. 30, 1943; d. Gennaro Robert and Rose Immaculate (Migliore) Scrimo; m. Robert Eugene Cavallo, July 27, 1968 (div. 1983). B.S., Marymount Coll., 1983. With Texaco Inc., White Plains, N.Y., 1961—, staff asst. mktg., 1975-77, sr. personnel asst. ops., 1977-78, supr. employment services, 1978-80, supr. employment and adminstrn., 1980-82, coordinator planning and research, 1982-84, Western region employee relations rep., 1984—. Loaned exec. United Way of Westchester, White Plains, 1981; adv. bd. Office for Women, Westchester County, 1982-84, YWCA, White Plains, 1983-84. Mem. Westchester Personnel Mgmt. Assn. (pres. 1983, 84), Personnel Council White Plains C. of C. (co-chmn. 1981-82). Democrat. Roman Catholic. Office: Texaco Inc 3810 Wilshire Blvd Los Angeles CA 90010

CAVALLON, BETTY GABLER, interior designer; b. Waverly, N.Y., July 17, 1918; d. Wallace Frederick and Harriet (Heaton) Gabler; grad. Parisien Sch. Design, Detroit, 1939; m. Michel Francis Cavallon, Dec. 26, 1946 (dec. 1981); children—Claire, Carol (dec.); stepchildren—Michel, Mary; m. John W. Crist, Nov. 20, 1982 Fabric coordinator Montgomery Ward, 1940-46; interior designer Betty Cavallon Interiors Ltd., Stamford, Conn., 1946—. Mem. Am. Soc. Interior Designers (corp.). Republican. Episcopalian. Home and Office: 1369 Long Ridge Rd Stamford CT 06903

CAVANAUGH, ESTELLE DILG, adult educator, human resources development administrator; b. Tottenville, N.Y., May 12, 1923; d. Lynden Conrad and Ella Marie (Peterson) Dilg; m. Carl Edwin Klingler, Dec. 27, 1945 (div. Aug. 1957); children—Sally Ann Klingler Keele, Nancy Jean Klingler Shelley; m. Wallace J. Cavanaugh, June 1, 1985. B.S. in Bus. Adminstrn., U. So. Calif., 1968, M.B.A., 1972; Ed.D., UCLA, 1982. Cert. community coll. and adult edn. instr., Calif. Stenographer, supr. N.Y. Telephone Co., Albany, 1941-46; staff clk. Pacific Telephone, Los Angeles, 1947-51; exec. sec. TRW, Los Angeles, 1956-66, placement mgr., 1966-70, tng./orgn. devel. specialist, 1970-73; assoc. dir. dept. engr. sci. UCLA Extension, 1973—, instr. Grad. Sch. Edn., 1983. Contbr. in field. Patron Westchester YMCA, Los Angeles, 1949—, UCLA Child Care Ctr., 1980—; mem. edn. com. Westchester Methodist Ch., Los Angeles, 1984—. Served with USNR, 1942-45. Recipient Woman of Achievement award Bus. and Profl. Women, El Segundo, Calif., 1977; Edn. Achievement award Calif. Soc. Profl. Engrs., 1983. Fellow Inst. Advancement of Engring.; mem. Am. Soc. Engring. Edn. (chmn. continuing profl. devel. div. 1984-85), ASTD, Soc. Mfg. Engrs. (citation for Profl. Achievement 1977, Ednl. Achievement 1979), Nat. Univ. Continuing Edn. Assn., Adult and Continuing Edn. Assn., Bus. and Profl. Women Club (v.p. 1981-83). Republican. Club: Academic Women's Assn. UCLA. Lodge: Foresters. Office: UCLA Extension 10995 Le Conte Ave Los Angeles CA 90024

CAVANAUGH, LUCILLE, tax assessor; b. Oakdale, La.; d. John Williamson and Lulu Miranda (Williams) Gills; m. Ariel Bliss Cavanaugh, Dec. 24, 1936; children—Melva D., Judith K., Eugene W., Connie E., Corby L., Catherine A., Brenda G., Tina R., Kevin L. Student tax assessors seminars. Deputy tax assessor Parish of Vernon, Leesville, La., 1947-71, tax assessor, 1971-80. Pres. Leesville Pilot Club, La., 1976-77, 84-85. Democrat. Baptist. Lodge: Order of Eastern Star. Avocations: quilting; gardening. Home: 563 Alexandria Hwy Leesville LA 71446

CAVIEUX, LYDIA V(ANACORO), health center administrator, consultant; b. Bronx, N.Y., Sept. 5, 1954; d. Alfonso M. and Lelia D. (Adorno) Vanacoro; m. Peter James Cavieux, Aug. 14, 1976. B.A., Emerson Coll., 1976; M.P.A., NYU, 1980. Accredited records technician. Asst. clin. dir. Rye Psychiat. Hosp. (N.Y.), 1976-79; med. eval. mgr. Bergen County Profl. Standards Rev. Orgn., Hackensack, N.J., 1979-80; supr. utilization control Westchester Community Health Plan, White Plains, N.Y., 1980-81; dir. ops. So. Conn. Community Health Plan, Stamford, 1981; health ctrs. adminstr. Kaiser Found. Health Plan, White Plains, 1981—; cons. Rye Psychiatr. Hosp., 1979—. Fellow Group Health Assn.; mem. Am. Med. Records Assn., N.Y. State Quality Assurance Profls., Am. Soc. Personnel Adminstrn. Home: 1 Mundet Dr Ossining NY 10562 Office: Kaiser Found Health Plan 145 Westchester Ave White Plains NY 10601

CAVIN, RHONDA LYNN, lawyer; b. Loma Linda, Calif., Aug. 29, 1955; d. William James and M. Janece (Ridenhour) Cavin, Jr.; m. John Alexander Stewart, Aug. 29, 1981 (div. 1983). B.S., Loma Linda U., 1977; J.D., U. San Diego, 1980. Bar: Calif. 1982, Nev. 1983. Pvt. practice, San Diego, 1982; legal asst. Beckley, Singleton, DeLanoy & Jemison, Las Vegas, Nev., 1982-83; pvt. practice Hilbrecht & Assocs., Las Vegas, 1983—. Mem. ABA, Calif. Bar Assn., Nev. Bar Assn., Nev. Trial Lawyers Assn., So. Nev. Assn. Women Attys., Am. Trial Lawyers Assn., Las Vegas Bus. Women's Network, Phi Delta Phi. Democrat. Club: Renaissance Women (Las Vegas). Office: Hilbrecht & Assocs 723 Casino Center Blvd Las Vegas NV 89101

CAVNAR, MARGARET MARY (PEGGY), former state legislator, business executive, nurse; b. Buffalo, July 29, 1945; d. James John and Margaret Mary Murtha Nightengale; B.S. in Nursing, D'Youville Coll., 1967; m. Samuel M. Cavnar, 1977; children—Heather Anne, Heide Lynn, Dona Cavnar Hambly, Judy Cavnar Bentrim. Utilization rev. coordinator South Nev. Meml. Hosp., Las Vegas, 1975-77; v.p. Ranvac Publs., Las Vegas, 1976—; ptnr. Cavnar & Assocs., Reseda, Calif., 1976—, C & A Mgmt., Las Vegas, 1977—; pres. PS Computer Service, Las Vegas, 1978—. Mem. Clark County Republican Central Com., 1977—, Nev. Rep. Central Com., 1978-80; mem. Nev. Assembly, 1979-81; Rep. nominee for Nev. Senate, 1980; Rep. nominee for Congress from Nev. 1st dirs., 1982, 84; bd. dirs., treas. Nev. Med. Fed. Credit Union; v.p. Community Youth Activities Found., Inc., Civic Assn. Am.; mem. utilization rev. bd. Easter Seals; trustee Nev. Sch. Arts, 1980—; nat. adviser Project Prayer, 1978—; co-chmn. P.R.I.D.E. Com., 1983—; co-chmn. Tax Limitation Com., 1983, Personal Property Tax Elimination Com., 1979-82, Self-Help Against Food Tax Elimination Denial Com., 1980; mem. Nev. Profl. Standards Rev. Orgn., 1984; co-chmn. People Against Tax Hikes, 1983-84. Mem. Nev. Order Women Legislators (charter, parliamentarian 1980—), Sigma Theta Tau. Club: Cosmopolitanly Hers Info. (pres.). Office: PO Box 26073 Las Vegas NV 89126

CAWEIN, KATHRIN (MRS. SEABURY CONE MASTICK), artist; b. New London, Conn., May 9, 1895; d. Henry and Barbara (Franz) C.; M.A. (hon.), Oberlin Coll., 1966; D.F.A. (hon.), Pacific U., 1982; student Art Students League; m. Seabury Cone Mastick, Apr. 3, 1964. Music roll editor, music interpreter with various musicians, 1911-32; tchr. County Center Work Shop, 1935-36; owner studio for children, 1950-55; tchr. workshop Pacific U., Forest Grove, Oreg., 1983; one man shows: County Center, White Plains, N.Y., 1935, Village Art Center, N.Y.C., 1945, Town Hall, N.Y.C., 1950, 8th St. Playhouse, N.Y.C., 1953, Sarasota, Fla., 1973, U. Tampa (Fla.), 1973, Oberlin (Ohio) Coll., 1975, St. John's Ch., Pleasantville, N.Y., 1976, Berea (Ky.) Coll., 1977, Pacific U., 1979, 80, 81, 82, 85 (retrospective show 1985); exhibited group shows U.S., Eng., France, Italy, Ecuador, including Century of Progress, 1934, Tex. Centennial, 1937, World's Fair, 1939; represented in permanent collections at Met. Mus., Nat. Mus., Washington, Pa. State U., Tampa U., Oberlin Coll.; illuminated books St. Marks Ch., Van Nuys, Calif.; illuminated manuscripts Pacific U. Recipient Frank Talcott Non-Mem. prize Soc. Am. Etchers, 1936, prize for lithography Village Art Center, 1944, prize for etching Nat. Assn. Women Artists, 1947, prize for dry point Pleasantville Woman's Club, 1950, prize for etching, 1952, prize for dry point Westchester Fedn. Women's Clubs, 1951, others; Kathrin Cawein Gallery Art named in her honor Pacific U., 1985. Mem. Nat. Assn. Women Artists, Art Students League (life), Chgo. Soc. Etchers, Soc. Graphic Artists. Home and Studio: 35 Mountain Rd Pleasantville NY 10570

CAWS, MARY ANN, English, French and comparative literature educator, critic; b. Wilmington, N.C., Sept. 10, 1933; d. Harmon Chadbourn and Margaret Devereux (Lippitt) Rorison; B.A., Bryn Mawr Coll., 1954; M.A., Yale U., 1956, Ph.D., U. Kans., 1962; m. Peter Caws, June 2, 1956; children—Matthew, Hilary. Asst. instr. Romance langs. U. Kans., 1957-62, asst. editor univ. press, 1957-58, vis. asst. prof. spring 1963; lectr. Barnard Coll., 1962-63; mem. faculty Sarah Lawrence Coll., 1963-64; mem. faculty Hunter Coll., N.Y.C., 1966—, prof. 69—, Disting. prof. French and comparative lit., 1983—, prof. English, 1986—; exec. officer comparative lit. program CUNY Grad. Center, 1977-79, French program, 1979-86; Phi Beta Kappa vis. scholar, 1982-83. Fellow Guggenheim Found., 1972-73, Nat. Endowment Humanities, 1979-80; Fulbright travel fellow, 1972-73. Mem. MLA (exec. council 1973-77, v.p. 1982-83, pres. 1983-84), Am. Assn. Tchr. Frech, Internat. Assn. Philosophy and Lit. (exec. bd. 1982—), Am. Comparative Lit. Assn. (exec. com. 1981—), Acad. Lit. Studies (pres.1985). Author books in field; contbr. articles to profl. jours. Editor Dada/Surrealism, 1972, Le Siecle eclate, 1974; co-editor Dada/Surrealism and French Modernist series. Home: 140 E 81st St New York NY 10028 Office: CUNY Grad Center 33 W 42d St New York NY 10036

CAYLOR, SHIRLEY YVONNE, real estate consultant, accountant; b. Tampa, Fla., Aug. 12, 1949; d. Roy Pressley and Juanita Pearl (Hamm) Walker; m. William H. Curns III, Aug. 3, 1968 (div. Aug. 1976); m. Charles Stephen Caylor, July 7, 1979. B.S.B.A., Aquinas Coll., 1983; A.A., Miami-Dade Community Coll., 1976. Lic. real estate salesperson, Fla. Budget analyst ITT Communications Devel., Palm Coast, Fla., 1976-80; controller Bradford Scott Corp., Lansing, Mich., 1980-85; v.p., treas. Walker Enterprises, Sarasota, Fla., 1985—; ptnr. Walker & Assocs., Sarasota, 1985—. Mem. Nat. Assn. Female Execs., Nat. Assn. Realtors, Sarasota Bd. Realtors. Republican. Baptist. Home: 5407 Skyline Pl Sarasota FL 33582 Office: Walker Enterprises Inc Sarasota FL 33582

CAZALAS, MARY REBECCA WILLIAMS, retired lawyer, real estate executive; b. Atlanta, Nov. 11, 1927; d. George Edgar and Mary (Slappey) Williams; m. Albert Joseph Cazalas (dec. Feb. 1981). R.N., St. Joseph's Infirmary Sch. of Nursing, 1948; B.S., Oglethorpe U., 1954; M.S. in Anatomy, Emory U., 1960; J.D., Loyola U., New Orleans, 1967. Bar: La. 1967. Gen. duty nurse St. Joseph's Infirmary, Atlanta, 1948-50, Vanderbilt U. Hosp., Nashville, 1950-51, Johns Hopkins Hosp., Balt., 1953; instr. maternity nursing St. Joseph's Infirmay Sch. Nursing, Atlanta, 1954-59; med. researcher urology Tulane U. Sch. Medicine, New Orleans, 1961-65; legal researcher 4th Cir. Ct. Appeals, New Orleans, 1965-71; practice law, New Orleans, 1967-71; asst. U.S. atty., New Orleans, 1971-79; sr. trial atty. EEOC, 1979-85, ret., 1985; owner Cazalas Apts., 1968—; lectr. drug abuse So. U., New Orleans, 1972-78, Xavier U. Sch. Pharmacy, 1975-78; mem. bd. advisors Loyola U. Law School., New Orleans, 1974, v.p. adv. bd., 1975; mem. adv. bd. Loyola U., 1978; chmn. Women's com. Fed. Exec. Bd., 1974. Author textbook; contbr. articles to profl. jours. Adv. bd. Odyssey House, Inc., New Orleans, 1973; bd. dirs. Bethlehem House of Bread, 1975-79; mem. May of New Orleans Drug Abuse Adv. Com., 1976, mem. task force Area Agy. on Aging, 1976-80; mem. New Orleans Mus. Art, 1982—; mem. pres.' Council Loyola U., 1977—. Recipient Am. Jurisprudence award, 1963, 1st pl. for oil painting Fed. Bus. Assn., 1973; Superior Performance award U.S. Dept. Justice, 1974; cert. of appreciation Fed. Exec. Bd., 1975, 76, 77, 78; Outstanding Cardinal Key Rev. E.A. Doyle award, 1976; commendation Guam Legislature, 1977. Mem. Fed. Bar Assn. (dir. 1972-75, 1st v.p. 1973, nat. council 1974-78), Fed. Bar Assn. (chpt. dir. 1972, pres. 1974-75), Nat. Fed. Bar Assn. (chmn. drug abuse com. 1976, pres. adv. com. 1984—), Fed. Bus. Assn. (chmn. program com. 1974, v.p. 1976, pres. 1976-78), Am. Judicature Soc., La. Bar Assn., Nat. Assn. Women Lawyers, Nat. Health Lawyers Assn., DAR, New Orleans Art Assn., Sierra Club, Wilderness Soc., Am. Heart Assn.-La., Emory U. Alumni Assn., Oglethorpe U. Alumni Assn., Loyola U. Alumni Assn. (dir. 1974-75, v.p. 1976), Cardinal Key, Leconte, Phi Sigma, Alpha Epsilon Delta, Phi Delta Delta (mag. bus. mgr. 1968-70, v.p., treas. chpt. 1968-73, pres. chpt. 1970-72, province dir. 1970-72), Phi Alpha Delta (vice justice New Orleans 1974-76, justice 1976-78). Democrat. Roman Catholic. Home: 1116 City Park Ave New Orleans LA 70119

CAZALOT, ERNESTINE CARMEL PERRET, food company executive; b. New Orleans, Nov. 2, 1930; d. Ernest Benedict and Evelyn Anna (Arieux) Perret; m. Paul David Cazalot, May 17, 1951; children—Pamela Maria Cazalot Miller, Carol Ann. Student Chenet's Bus. Coll. Exec. sec. Benjamin Crump Real Estate, New Orleans, 1946-47, So. Cotton Oil Co., New Orleans, 1948-56, sec. to dist. mgr., exec. sec. to v.p. Blue Plate Foods, 1949—; credit mgr. D.H. Holmes Co., New Orleans, 1978—, mem. shrinkage com., 1980—, inventory desk control supr., 1981—. Recipient various awards. Mem. Inst. for Research on Women Execs., Nat. Assn. Female Execs. (cert. 1985). Democrat. Roman Catholic. Avocations: band; sewing; music; exercise; dancing; embroidery; art; crafts. Home: 519 State St New Orleans LA 70118

CAZAN, SYLVIA MARIE BUDAY (MRS. MATTHEW JOHN CAZAN), realtor; b. Youngstown, Ohio, Nov. 17, 1915; d. John J. and Sylvia (Grama) Buday; student U. Bucharest (Rumania), 1933-35, Youngstown Coll., 1936-38, Georgetown U. Inst. Langs. and Linguistics, 1950; m. Matthew John Cazan, July 14, 1935; 1 son, Matthew John G. Adminstrv. asst. statistics U.S. Dept. Def., 1941-52; spl. employee Dept. Justice, 1956-58; mgr. James L. Dixon & Co. Realtors, Falls Church, Va., 1959-70; mgr. Lewis & Silverman Inc., Chevy Chase, Md., 1970—. Mem. bd. examiners Georgetown U., 1950. Bd. dirs. Magnolia Internat. Debutante Ball. Recipient Commendation and Meritorious award Dept. Justice, 1958. Mem. Gen. Fedn. Women's Clubs (pres. 1955-56), Interscholastic Debating Soc., Washington, No. Va. real estate bds. Mem. Rumanian Orthodox Ch. Home: 6369 Lakeview Dr Lake Barcroft Estates Falls Church VA 22041 Office: 8401 Connecticut Ave Chevy Chase MD 20015

CEASE, JANE HARDY, state senator; b. Columbus, Miss., Jan. 23, 1936; m. Ron Cease, 1960; children—Allison, Abigail. B.F.A., Tulane U. State rep. Oreg. Legislature, Salem, 1979-85, state senator, 1985-89. Pres. Portland League Women Voters, 1971-73; chair Portland Area Women's Polit. Caucus, 1977-78, Met. Govts. Subcom. Local Govt. Com., Portland, 1979-83, Portland-Multnomah Commn. Aging Transp. Com., 1983-85; active Nat. Hwy. Safety Adv. Commn., 1980-83, Transp. and Communications Com. of Nat. Council State Legislatures, 1983-85, Oreg. Commn. Women, 1985—. Democrat. Clubs: Phoenix Rising, Parents United. Home: 2625 NE Hancock Portland OR 07212 Office: State Capitol Salem OR 97310

CEDERQUIST, DENA CAROLINE, former educator; b. Madrid, Iowa, Aug. 29, 1910; d. Clarence John and Clara (Bork) Cederquist; B.S., Iowa State Coll., 1931, M.S., 1935; Ph.D., U. Wis., 1945. Asst. dietitian Monmouth Meml. Hosp., Long Branch, N.J., 1932-33; instr. Kans. State Coll., Manhattan, 1937-41, U. Wis., 1941-42; with Mich. State U., 1944—, asst. prof., asso. prof., 1944-56, prof., head dept. foods and nutrition, 1956-71, prof. food sci. and nutrition, 1971-78, prof. emeritus, 1978—. Mem. Am. Dietetic Assn., Am. Home Econ. Assn., Sigma Xi, Omicron Nu, Phi Kappa Phi, Sigma Delta Epsilon. Home: 545 University Dr East Lansing MI 48823

CEKAN, JINDRA MONIQUE, investment banker; b. Rahway, N.J., July 5, 1961; d. Vaclav Jindrich and Helena Bozena (Blazek) C. B.A. in Econs., Gettysburg Coll., 1983, B.A. in Polit. Sci., 1983. Mgr. Wicker-With-Love, Linden, N.J., 1978-80; fin. analyst Salomon Bros., N.Y.C., 1984—. Mem. Met. Arts Soc., Alliance Francaise, Pi Lambda Sigma. Roman Catholic. Avocations: Czech; classical music; tennis; photography. Home: 17 Douglass St Brooklyn NY 11231 Office: Salomon Bros Inc 1 NY Plaza New York NY 10004

CELENTANO, LESLIE ZYTO, lawyer; b. N.Y.C., Aug. 12, 1954; d. Marcel Wolf and Muriel (Mankoff) Zyto; m. Domenick Anthony Celentano, Apr. 4, 1976. B.S., Montclair State Coll., 1975; J.D., N.Y. Law Sch., 1980. Bar: N.J. 1981, Fla. 1981; law clk. Slavitt et al, West Orange, N.J., 1978-81, assoc., 1981-83; asst. prosecutor Essex County Prosecutor's Office, Newark, 1984-85; treas. Celentano, Inc., Verona, N.J., 1980—. Mem. ABA, Fla. Bar Assn., N.J. Bar Assn., Essex County Bar Assn. Office: 354 Eisenhower Pkwy Livingston NJ 07039

CELLA, ELISA, management consultant, firm exec.; b. Paterson, N.J., May 23, 1944; d. Alexander and Frances (Biggio) C.; B.S., Fairleigh Dickinson U., 1960, postgrad., 1960-62; postgrad. N.Y. U., 1965-67. Controller, Rogers, Slade & Hill, Inc., cons. to mgmt., N.Y.C., 1962-72; corp. sec. Golightly-Internat., Inc., N.Y.C., 1972-84; dir. adminstrv. services Peat Marwick, N.Y.C., 1985—. Mem. Am. Mgmt. Assn. Home: 412 Pompton Ave Cedar Grove NJ 07009 Office: 345 Park Ave New York NY 10154

CELNIKER, AMY BERTRAM, public relations company executive; b. Phoenix, July 19, 1960; d. Richard Justin and Wilma Dorothy (Oetken) Bertram; m. Steven Israel Celniker, Mar. 27, 1982. B.S. magna cum laude in Telecommunications, Ariz. State U., 1981. Adminstrv. asst., jr. publicist Feltheimer/Knofsky Co., Los Angeles, 1981-82; jr. publicist Rogers & Cowan Pub. Relations, Beverly Hills, Calif., 1982-83, account exec. Lippin & Grant Pub. Relations Co., Los Angeles, 1983-86; account exec. Bozell, Jacobs, Kenyon and Eckhardt Pub. Relations, Los Angeles, 1986—. Chevron USA scholar, 1979-81. Mem. Hollywood Radio and TV Soc., Nat. Assn. Female Execs., Phi Kappa Phi. Avocations: ballet; jazz dancing; piano; snow skiing; weightlifting.

CENTER, INGRID GWYNNETH CATHERINE, county official; b. Farnham, Eng., Jan. 12, 1945; came to U.S., 1962; d. G.A. and V.G. (Jones) Bessette; student Carleton U., Ottawa, Ont., Can., 1960-61, U. Oslo, 1964; B.A., Cornell U., 1966, Assoc. in Risk Mgmt., 1981; m. Alfred M. Center, June 25, 1966. With Gen. Motors Corp., N.Y.C., 1967-68; faculty Meiji U., Tokyo, 1968-69, Gulf Tech. Coll., Bahrain, 1971-73; with Sony Corp. of Am., N.Y.C., 1976-78; budget analyst Barclays Bank of N.Y., N.Y.C., 1978-79, ins. analyst, 1980-82; risk mgr. City of Stamford, Conn., 1982-85; project dir., risk mgr. Ogden Corp., 1985-86; asst. budget dir., risk mgmt. County of Westchester, 1986—. Marguerite Bourgeois scholar, 1957-60; U. Oslo summer scholar, 1964. Mem. Bahrain Archaeol. Soc., Risk and Ins. Mgmt. Soc., Pub. Risk and Ins. Mgmt. Assn. Club: Awali Pony. Author: Batangas: The Holiday Province, 1975. Home: 97 Madison Ave Larchmont NY 10538

CENTERS, LOUISE VAN CORE, clinical psychologist, lawyer; b. Huntington Park, Calif.; B.A., U. So. Calif., 1953, Ph.D., 1958; J.D., Detroit Coll. Law, 1979. Bar: Mich. 1979, Fla. 1980. Chief clin. psychology sect. Sinai Hosp. of Detroit, 1970—; adj. asso. prof. psychology U. Windsor (Ont.); mem. Mich. State Bd. Psychology, 1975-80, chair, 1978, 79. Diplomate in clin. psychology Am. Bd. Profl. Psychology. Mem. Am. Psychol. Assn., Mich. Psychol. Assn. (past state pres., Disting. Psychologist award 1984), Mich. Soc. Lic. Psychologists (past state pres.), Mich. Interprofl. Assn. (pres. 1985), Nat. Women Lawyers Assn., Women Lawyers Mich., Kappa Delta. Contbr. articles profl. jours. Office: Dept of Psychiatry 14800 W McNichols Rd Detroit MI 48235

CEREGHETTI, SALLIE DYKMAN, cosmetics company executive; b. White Plains, N.Y., Nov. 11, 1936; d. Harry T. and Sallie (Dodson) Dykman; B.A., Ohio State U., 1958; m. C. Armand Cereghetti, May 7, 1960; children—Michelle Diane, Marc Armand. Account exec. James Seikses Co., N.Y.C., 1959-61; asst. prodn. mgr. Dreher Advt., N.Y.C., 1961-63, traffic mgr., 1963, account exec., 1965-68; with Bio-Pharma, Inc., Kansas City, Mo., after 1977, pub. edn. dir., 1980, nat. dir. pub. edn., after 1981; now pres. Dykman Assocs. Mem. AAUW, Fashion Group, Cosmetic Exec. Women. Republican. Christian Scientist. Home and Office: 9240 Riggs Ln Overland Park KS 66212

CERIA, CLEMENTINA DE VERA, nurse; b. Magsingal Ilocos Sur, Philippines, Jan. 22, 1959; came to U.S., 1970, naturalized, 1984; d. Hipolito Costales and Macaria (DeVera) C. B.S.N., U. Hawaii, 1982. R.N., Hawaii. Student helper Maluhia Hosp., Honolulu, 1979; nurse's aide St. Francis Hosp., Honolulu, 1982, nurse, 1982—. Catechism tchr. Our Lady of Mt. Catholic Ch., Honolulu, 1977, 78, 79, 82; vol. Beverly Manor Convalescent Ctr., Honolulu, 1977, 78, 79. Wallace Rider Farrington scholar Honolulu Star-Bull., 1978-82, Hans and Clara Zimmerman Found. scholar, 1979-80, Duty Free Shoppers Ltd. scholar, 1980-82. Mem. Hawaii Nurses' Assn., U.S.-Philippines Goodwill Found. (hon.), Jr. Filipino Cath. Club (pres. 1977-79, adv. 1980—). Avocations: reading; cooking; aerobics; Filipino folk dancing. Office: St Francis Hosp 2230 Liliha St Honolulu HI 96817

CERTAINE, EVELYN REBECCA, ret. social work adminstr.; b. Phila.; d. Lawrence and Sadie (Hall) C.; B.S. in Edn., Temple U., 1938, postgrad., 1960-63; M.S.W., U. Pa., 1965, postgrad., 1968. With Pa. Dept. Public Assistance, 1940-77, adminstrv. asst., until 1977; ret., 1977. Vol., Big Sisters, 1932-38, Armstrong Assn. (Urban League), 1932-36, ARC, USO, 1942-67; fund raiser for alumni Sch. Social Work, 1968-79; now pvt. social work practioner; active YWCA, various other community groups; bd. dirs. Dowingtown (Pa.) Indsl. and Agrl. Sch., 1977; fin. assoc. Temple U. Recipient Hon. citation for vol. work Chapel Four Chaplains, 1965; also plaques, awards, certs. USO, ARC, Dept. Army, Air Force. Mem. Nat. Assn. Social Workers, Nat. Acad. Cert. Social Workers, Otto Rank Psychoanalytical Soc., Alpha Kappa Alpha (sec. 1942-43, reporter 1945-46). Republican. Episcopalian. Club: Temple U. Mid-City Alumni.

CETEL, NANCY SUE, reproductive endocrinologist; b. N.Y.C., June 28, 1953; d. Ben and Clara Cetel; m. Joseph B. Weiss, June 10, 1979; children—Danielle, Jeremy. B.S. summa cum laude, SUNY-Stony Brook, 1974; M.D., NYU, 1978. Intern U. Calif. Med. Ctr., Irvine, 1978-79, resident, 1979-80; fellow in reproductive endocrinology, U. Calif.-San Diego, 1980-83; fellow U. So. Calif. Women's Hosp., 1983-84, clin. instr., 1980-83. NIH fellow; recipient Pacific Coast Fertility Soc. award, 1982. Mem. San Diego Women's Physicians Assn., Am. Fertility Soc., Calif. Med. Assn., Phi Beta Kappa. Contbr. articles to profl. jours. Office: Dept Reproductive Medicine U Calif-San Diego La Jolla CA 92037

CHABAN, MIRIAM, controller; b. Santiago de Cuba, Cuba, Nov. 26, 1952; came to U.S., 1962, naturalized, 1969; d. Armando and Ofelia (Alvarez) Chaban; m. Carlos Charles Ferreira, Dec. 30, 1983. B.S., St. John's U., Jamaica, N.Y., 1974. Eastern regional adminstrv. mgr. Sony Corp. Am., Park Ridge, N.J., 1974-81; fin. analyst Temco Service Industries, Inc., N.Y.C., 1981-86; controller Candid Prodns., Inc., 1986—.

CHABOT, JOYCE JENKINS, librarian; b. Roberts, Idaho, Mar. 6, 1924; d. Gordon Lorenzo Jenkins and Eva Parkinson (Packer) Jenkins Cordon; m. Ambrose Billy Chabot, Apr. 18, 1945; children—David Stephen, Terry Lynne, Jeane Annette, Robert Neal, Peggy Sue, Donna Joyce, Barbara Elaine, Debra Eve, Ambrose Brent. Sc.B., U. Idaho, 1944; B.A. in French, U. Wash., 1968, 5th yr. teaching credential, 1969, M.A. in Librarianship, 1971. Sec. St. Nicholas Sch., Seattle, 1968-69, Monson Real Estate, Provo, Utah, 1972-73; librarian Provo Pub. Library, 1973—; library dir., prof. Stevens Henager Coll. Bus., Provo, 1983—; book reviewer. Mem. Utah Library Assn., ALA, Utah Bus. Educators' Assn., Phi Kappa Phi, Beta Phi Mu, Lambda Delta Sigma. Mormon. Clubs: Etienne Literary, Squaw Peak Sam's (Provo); Sunburst Good Sam's (Orem, Utah). Office: Provo Pub Library 13 N 100 E Provo UT 84601

CHABROW, SHEILA SUE, English language educator; B.A., U. Miami (Fla.), 1961; student Harvard U., 1960-61, George Washington U., 1961-62, Va. Poly. Inst., 1972-74; M.S., Barry U., 1976. Writer, No. Va. Newspapers, Fairfax, 1969-73; dir. Olam Tikvah Sch., Fairfax, 1973-74; tchr. Palmetto Sr. High Sch., Miami, 1979-80; instr. psychology Barry U., Miami, 1980-81; instr. intensive English, U. Miami, Coral Gables, Fla., 1981—; Vice pres. Cutler Bay Estates, Miami, 1975-76; v.p. Parent Co-Op. Preschools Internat., 1972-73; pres. No. Va. Co-Op. Schs., 1969-70. Mem. Women in Communications, AAUW (sec. Annandale, Va. 1972), Theta Sigma Phi. Home: 13351 SW 57th Ct Miami FL 33156 Office: Dept Intensive English Univ Miami Coral Gables FL 33146

CHABY, DIANE BLOCK, public relations agy. exec.; b. N.Y.C., Oct. 2, 1935; d. Irving and Tillie Block; B.A. in English, N.Y. U., 1956, M.A. in English, 1968; postgrad. Yeshiva U. Grad. Center, 1972-73, John Clarke Acad., London, 1973; m. June 3, 1956 (div.); 1 son, Alan Seth. Free-lance columnist Westwood (N.J.) News, 1961-63; tchr., cons., trainer N.Y.C. Bd. Edn., 1966-78; free-lance writer and publicist, 1978; publicist, media specialist Peter Rothholz Assos., N.Y.C., 1979, dir. media relations, 1979-81; account group supr. Van Vechten & Assocs., N.Y.C., 1981-82; founder pres. Chaby Communications, N.Y.C., 1982—; free-lance mag. writer, 1981—; condr. career change workshops; tchr. trainer, lab. mgmt. cons. Right To Read; mem. Right To Read Task Force; cons. ednl. systems. Mem. Women in Communications, Bus. and Profl. Women. Office: 6 Peter Cooper Rd New York NY 10010

CHADWICK, DONNA MADDEN, music therapist, speech pathologist; b. Malden, Mass., May 17, 1947; d. John Richard and Miriam (Kelly) Madden; Mus.B., Anna Maria Coll., 1969; M.S., Emerson Coll., 1975. Music therapist Hogan Regional Center, Hathorne, Mass., 1969-74; dir. music therapy and speech pathologist North Shore Spl. Edn. Consortium, Salem, Mass., 1975-78; pvt. practice music therapy and speech pathology, Boston area, 1978—; instr. music therapy Northeastern U., Boston, 1978—, Anna Maria Coll., Paxton, Mass., 1979; dir. music therapy Dean Jr. Coll., Franklin, Mass., 1977-79; asst. prof., chmn. dept. music Emmanuel Coll., Boston, 1979—. HEW fellow, 1974-75. Lic. med. provider, lic. speech pathologist, Mass.; cert. music educator Mass. Mem. Am. Assn. Music Therapy (bd. dirs., nat. treas., exec. com., cert. music therapist), Nat. Assn. Music Therapy (New Eng. del., registered music therapist), Am. Speech and Hearing Assn. (cert. clin. competence, also state and local socs.), Mass. Music Therapy Alliance (co-founder 1980, exec. chmn. 1980-84, spl. projects chmn. 1984—), Am. Soc. Prevention Cruelty to Animals, Animal Betterment Citizens Action League, Defenders of Animal Rights, Friends of Animals. Roman Catholic. Author: (with Cynthia Clark) Clinically Adapted Instruments for the Multiply Handicapped), 1979; editorial bd. Music Therapy; contbr. articles to profl. jours.; work appears in documentary The Music Child. Home: 9 Sawmill Dr Westford MA 01886 Office: Emmanuel Coll 400 The Fenway Boston MA 02115

CHAFFEE, ESTHER RIDENOUR (MRS. THOMAS K. CHAFFEE), ch. organist; b. Lima, Ohio; d. Joshua Mechling and Jennie (Hitchcock) Ridenour; student Wittenberg U., 1929-30, Ball State U., 1956-57, Bluffton Coll., 1932-33, U. Mich., 1950-51; B.A. in Music Edn. Lawrence U., 1963; m. David R. Meily, May 23, 1934 (dec. 1972); children—Helen Adelia (Mrs. Melvin L. Bayer), Martha Frances (Mrs. Edward C. Senechal), Sara Elizabeth (Mrs. David C. Hayden); m. 2d, Thomas K. Chaffee, Jr., Aug. 1975. Elem. vocal music tchr., Lima, 1932-34, Morgan Sch., Appleton, Wis., 1963-75; substitute tchr., Washington, 1934-36, Pontiac and Birmingham, Mich., 1945-55; high sch. music tchr., Marion, Ind., 1955-58. Asst. organist Nat. City Christian Ch., Washington, 1934-36; organist, choir dir. First Bapt. Ch., Birmingham, 1950-53, All Sts. Episcopal Ch., Appleton, 1958-64, St. Thomas Episcopal Ch., Menasha, Wis., 1964-75; organist, choir master St. Albans Episcopal Ch., Olney, Ill., and St. Mary's Episcopal Ch., Robinson, Ill., 1975-77, St. Anne's Ch., De Pere, Wis., 1977—. Vol. tchr., programmer Children's Hosp., Detroit, 1950-54; dir. Civic Music Series, Marion, 1952; music tchr. Retarded Children's Sch., Marion, 1954-55; asst. music therapist Winnebago State Hosp., Oshkosh, Wis., 1967-71; music coordinator Opportunity Centers, SE Ill. Daycare Center. Mem. Organ Guild, Wis. Acad. Arts, Nat., Wis. music educators guilds, Am. Contract Bridge League (life master). Composer: St. Thomas and St. Anne Mass, other sacred works. Home and office: 2600 Riverside Dr Green Bay WI 54301

CHAFFEE, JEAN ANN, dental hygienist; b. Houston, Oct. 17, 1947; d. Claud and Georgia Lee (Wilson) Cochran; student DelMar Coll., 1965-67; certificate in dental hygiene, U. Tex., 1969; B.A., Dominican Coll., 1975; M.S.H.P., S.W. Tex. U., 1977; 1 son, Clinton Jared. Clin. coordinator Wharton (Tex.) Jr. Coll., 1975-76; dental hygienist J.R. Alexander, D.D.S., Austin, Tex., 1976-77; dental hygienist, coll. adminstr. St. Louis Community Coll., 1977—. Active Women's Commerce Assn., Arts and Edn. Council St. Louis, Mo. Bot. Garden. Mem. Greater St. Louis Dental Hygiene Soc., Mo. Dental Hygiene Assn., Am. Dental Hygiene Assn. Republican. Episcopalian. Address: 614 Valley Point Ln Saint Louis MO 63021

CHAGNON, LUCILLE TESSIER, career development firm executive, educational consultant; b. Gardner, Mass., June 1, 1936; d. Fred G. Tessier and Alfreda C. (Ross) Noel; m. Richard J. Chagnon, Sept. 16, 1978; children—Daniel, David. B.Mus., Rivier Coll., N.H., 1958; M.Ed., Boston Coll., 1972. Edn. specialist, N.H., 1960-76; internat. cons. Inst. Cultural Affairs, Chgo., 1973-79; staff tng. dir. CO-MHAR, Inc., Phila., 1979-81; pres., owner Chagnon Assocs. Exec. Career Mgmt., Inc., Collingswood, N.J., 1981—; sr. project staff Right Assocs., Phila., 1982—; adj. faculty dept. counseling psychology Temple U. Sch. Edn., Phila., 1985—. Author (with Richard J. Chagnon) The Best Is Yet to Be, 1985. Advisor, cons. Camden County Library Job and Career Info. Ctr., Voorhees, N.J., 1981—; mem. Collingswood Bd. Edn., 1985—. Mem. Am. Assn. for Counseling and Devel., Nat. Vocat. Guidance Assn., Assn. for Humanistic Edn. and Devel., New Horizons for Learning, Assn. Humanistic Edn., Career Planning and Adult Devel. Network, N.J. Assn. Women Bus. Owners (chmn. program com. 1983-84). Club: Mendelssohn of Phila. Home: 722 Linwood Ave Collingswood NJ 08108 Office: Chagnon Assocs Exec Career Mgmt Inc 722 Linwood Ave Collingswood NJ 08108

CHAIKIN, BONNIE PATRICIA, lawyer; b. N.Y.C., Apr. 4, 1953; d. Max and Paula (Blechman) Chaikin. Student Cornell U., 1970-73; B.A., Hofstra U., 1974; J.D., St. John's U., 1977. Law intern Queens Supreme Ct., 1977; admitted to N.Y. bar, 1978, Fla. bar, 1979, U.S. Customs Ct. bar, 1979, U.S. Tax Ct. bar, 1979, U.S. Dist. Ct. bar for Eastern and So. dists. N.Y., 1979, U.S. Ct. Customs and Patent Appeals bar, 1979; law asst. firm Weingold & Berman, N.Y.C., 1977-78; assoc. Dollinger, Gonski and Grossman, Carle Place, N.Y., 1978-79; mng. atty. firm Marsha Edelman, N.Y.C., 1979-80; individual practice law, Oceanside, N.Y., 1980—; dep. county atty. Nassau County, 1982—; profl. fashion model Other Dimensions, N.Y.C., 1980-82. Bd. dirs., counsel South Shore Planning Council. Mem. Fla. Bar Assn., N.Y. State Bar Assn., Nassau County Bar Assn. (sec. immigration law com.), Nassau-Suffolk Womens Bar Assn., Am. Immigration Lawyers, ABA, N.Y. State Juvenile Officers Assn. Office: One West St Mineola NY 11572

CHAIKOVSKA, MARTA MARIKA, manufacturing company executive, lawyer; b. Hartford, Conn., Oct. 6, 1951; d. Stephen Leo and Irene (Bandera) C.; m. Roman Nomitch, June 4, 1972 (div. 1980). B.A. in Polit. Sci., Vassar Coll., 1972; J.D., Boston U., 1974; J.D., Northwestern U., 1975; grad. Exec. Program, Bus. Sch. Stanford U., 1981. Bar: Ill. 1975. Assoc., McDermott Will & Emery Law Firm, Chgo., 1975-79; exec. v.p., dir., co-founder All Star Commutator, Inc., Elgin, Ill., 1980—; dir. spl. projects Parrot Corp., Ltd., Cwbran, Wales, U.K., 1984—; pres., dir. ASC Industries, London, 1985—; mng. ptnr. LBX Industries, Ltd., Chgo., 1985—; dir. Ked Corp., Miami. Mem. ABA. Club: Vassar. Avocations: climbing; golf; travel; tennis; cooking. Home: Catsash House Catsash Newport Gwent Wales United Kingdom Office: All Star Commutator Inc 370 Brook St Elgin IL also Parrot Corp Ltd Llantarnam Indsl Estate Gwent Cwmbran United Kingdom

CHALMERS, JEAN B., state legislator, lawyer; b. Madison, Wis., Oct. 20, 1927; d. William C. and Ruth V. C.; divorced; children—David Schwarz, Dina Schwarz Wenger, Jonathan Schwarz, Adam Schwarz. B.F.A., R.I. Sch. Design, 1950; J.D., U. Ga., 1968. Bar: Va. 1969, Maine 1972. Assoc. Corry & Corry, Richmond, Va., 1970-72, Knight & Cohen, Rockland, Maine, 1972-73; ptnr.

Knight, Chalmers & Brannan, and predecessor Knight & Chalmers, Rockland, 1974—; mem. Maine Senate, Augusta, 1985—; instr. Midcoast Community Coll. Mem. Maine Human Services Council, 1974-78; chmn. Rockland Charter Commn., 1978; councillor City of Rockland, from 1981; mem. exec. bd. Maine Dem. Party, from 1982; mem. Rockland and Knox County Dem. Com. Mem. ABA, Maine Bar Assn., Knox County Bar Assn., Assn. Maine Trial Lawyers, Mid-Coast C. of C. (bd. dirs.). Jewish. Office: Maine Senate State Capitol Augusta ME 04333*

CHAMALES, LINDA LORRAINE, lawyer; b. Crane, Tex., May 6, 1945; d. Douglas Franklin and Eunice LaVerne (Randolph) Chrane; m. Michael Hood Chamales, Aug. 19, 1967; children—Michael Scott, Michelynda. B.S. in Pharmacy, U. Tex.-Austin, 1968; J.D., Lewis and Clark Northwestern Law Sch., 1980. Bar: Oreg. 1980; registered pharmacist Tex. 1968, Okla. 1974, Oreg. 1975. Hosp. pharmacy supr. U. Tex. Med. Br. Hosp. Pharmacy, Galveston, 1968-74; mgr. Connie's RX Shop, Oklahoma City, 1974-75; hosp. pharmacist Forest Grove Community Hosp. (Oreg.), 1976-78; assoc. Williamson & Leineweber, St. Helens, Oreg., 1980-84; sole practice, divorce mediator, St. Helens, 1984—. Bd. dirs. Columbia County Legal Aide, St. Helens, 1982-83, Columbia County Women's Resource Ctr., St. Helens, 1984-85; den mother Boy Scouts Am., Warren, Oreg., 1978-79, council mem., 1979-80; team mother Scappoose Athletic Assn. (Oreg.), 1980-82. Recipient Outstanding Estate Planning Student award Lewis and Clark Law Sch., 1979. Mem. Columbia County Bar Assn. (sec. 1981-82), Am. Soc. Hosp. Pharmacists, Multnomah County Bar Assn., Am. Soc. Pharmacy Law, Oreg. Trial Lawyers Assn., AAUW. Office: Divorce Mediation Services PO Box 1101 Saint Helens OR 97051

CHAMBERLAIN, BARBARA ANN, social services administrator; b. Lansing, Mich. B.A. in Social Studies and Learning, Grand Valley State Colls., 1969; M.S.W. in Planning and Adminstrn., Western Mich. U., 1975. Dir., Day Care Ctr., Grand Rapids, Mich., 1969-71; regional mgr. adoption program Mich. Dept. Social Services, Kalamazoo, 1975-76, program specialist Children's Protective Services, 1976-79, spl. grants developer Office Planning, Budget and Evaluation, 1979-83; dir. devel. Crossroad/Ft. Wayne Children's Home (Ind.), 1983—; mgr. consortium White House Iniviative for Rural Devel., 1980-81. Home: 842 Beechlawn Ct East Lansing MI 48823 Office: Crossroad/Fort Wayne Children's Home 2525 Lake Ave Fort Wayne IN 46895

CHAMBERLAIN, CHARLOTTE APPEL, corporate officer; economist; b. N.Y.C., Apr. 30, 1946; d. Henry and Marie (Lugscheider) Appel. Ph.D. in Econs., Cornell U., 1971. Prof. econs. Northeastern U., Boston, 1971-73; br. chief forecasting and modeling U.S. Dept. Transp., Cambridge, Mass., 1973-79; v.p., mgr. dept. econs. Glendale Fed. Savs. and Loan Assn. (Calif.), 1979-81; dir. Office of Policy and Econ. Research, Fed. Home Loan Bank Bd., Washington, 1981-83; sr. v.p. asset liability mgmt. Glendale Fed. Savs. (Calif.), 1983-85, exec. v.p. strategic planning and mktg., 1985—. Bd. dirs. Real Estate Center, U. Calif., Berkeley. Lehman fellow. Mem. Am. Econ. Assn., Nat. Assn. Bus. Economists, Western Econs. Assn., Phi Beta Kappa, Phi Kappa Phi. Editor Jour. Housing Fin. Office: PO Box 1709 700 N Brand Blvd Glendale CA 91209

CHAMBERLAIN, JILL FRANCES, consulting company executive; b. Chgo., Mar. 25, 1954; d. Chester Emery and Mary Edythe (Hurd) C. B.A. in Math. with honors, Ill. State U., 1975; M.B.A., U. Chgo., 1981. Programmer, Arthur Andersen, Chgo., 1975-76; cons. Laventhol & Horwath, Chgo., 1976-77; fin. systems analyst U. Chgo. Hosp., 1978-80; v.p. CHI/COR Info. Mgmt., Inc., Chgo., 1980—; cons. RMS Bus. Systems, Chgo., 1976-77. Mem. Delaware Valley Disaster Recovery Info. Exchange Group. Libertarian. Methodist. Avocations: reading; traveling; needlework. Office: CHI/COR Info Mgmt Inc 6 Landmark Square 4th Floor Stamford CT 06901

CHAMBERLAIN, MONICA ANN, sales executive, medical technologist, microbiologist; b. San Diego, Mar. 18, 1956; d. Michael Aloysius and Martha Ann (Green) C. B.S. in Microbiology, San Diego State U., 1979. Lab. asst. San Diego State U., 1977-79, San Diego Health Dept., 1976-78; med. technologist intern El Centro Community Hosp., Calif., 1979-80; med. technologist Pioneer Meml. Hosp., Brauley, Calif., 1980-81, Sharp Meml. Hosp., San Diego, 1981-84; sales and service rep. 3M Diagnostic Systems, Mountain View, Calif., 1984—; cons. Nutri-Fact, Encinitas, Calif., 1984-85. Vol. research fellow San Diego Zoo, 1983; vol. Old Globe Theater, San Diego, 1982. Named Tech. Service Rep. of Yr., 3M Diagnostic Systems, 1985. Mem. Am. Soc. Clin. Pathologists, Nat. Assn. Female Execs., Am. Soc. Microbiology (pres. San Diego State U. chpt. 1978-79), Calif. Assn. Med. Lab. Technologists (treas. Desert chpt. 1980-81), San Diego State U. Microbiology Alumni Assn. (chmn. fundraiser 1984). Republican. Roman Catholic. Avocations: bicycling; racquetball; skiing; gourmet cuisine. Office: 3M Diagnostic Systems 1500 Salado Dr Mountain View CA 94043

CHAMBERLIN, JOAN KING, public affairs counselor, writer, lecturer; b. Los Angeles, Dec. 1, 1930; d. David Conacher Hutchon and Adelaide Arelia (Grillo) Cruit; m. William Theodore King, June 13, 1954 (div. 1973); children—Jonatha Helen, Patrice, Ted; m. Hugh Roberts Chamberlin, May 3, 1980; children—Doug, Candolyn. B.A. in English, Pa. State U., 1953; M.B.A. studies UCLA, 1982; Ph.D. in Govt., Claremont Grad. Sch., 1980. Field rep. U.S. Congressman Alphonso Bell, Los Angeles, 1968-74; assoc. prof. UCLA, 1973; adminstrv. coordinator Office of Mayor Tom Bradley, Los Angeles, 1974-76; public relations cons., assoc. The Wallace Jamie Resource Group, Inc., Los Angeles, 1976-78; spl. asst. Office U.S. Commr. on Edn., Washington, 1978-79; intern in govtl. ops. Arco Corp., Los Angeles, summer 1982; pres. Connections, Inc., Calif., Washington, 1980—; founder, pres. bd. trustees Rio Hondo Coll., Whittier, Calif., 1960-64; founding mem. Calif. Postsecondary Edn. Commn., 1972-74; v.p. bd. govs. Calif. Community Colls., 1969-75; founder, charge d'affaires The Five Ring Olympic Club, Los Angeles, 1984—. Author: Establishing the U.S. Dept. of Education in the Carter Administration, 1978-79, 1980. Mem. Duarte Unified Sch. Dist., 1972-73, Los Angeles Olympic Organizing Com. on Visitor Relations also dedicated host for Zord Ian Luke of Gt. Britain, chmn. fin. for Internat. Olympic Com.-Nat. Olympic Chmn. Confs.; mem. bd. counselors Coll. Continuing Edn. U. So. Calif. 1981-85; pres. Harvard Lawyers Wives, 1956, Women's Student Govt. Assn. Pa. State U., 1953 apptd. diplomatic rep. for Los Angeles World Affairs Council, 1973. Edn. Policy fellow Inst. for Ednl. Leadership, 1978-79; Carnegie Found. fellow, 1973; Danforth Found. fellow U. Oreg., 1954. Mem. Am. Polit. Sci. Assn., Domestic Policy Assn., Constitutional Rights Found., LWV, Coro Assocs. Christian Scientist. Avocations: swimming; sailing; tennis; aerobics; books; theatre. Home: 15534 Nalin Pl Los Angeles CA 90077 Office: Connections 2554 Lincoln Blvd PO Box 655 Marina del Rey CA 90291

CHAMBERLIN, MARGARET ELIZABETH, marketing executive; b. Denver, Oct. 3, 1952; d. Elmer John and Helen Claire (Kilday) Roth; m. Mark Hill Chamberlin, June 22, 1974. B.A. in Journalism, U. Okla., 1974; postgrad. in bus. adminstrn. Wichita State U., 1979-83. Account coordinator Advt. Concepts, Wichita, 1974-76; pub. relations dir. Wichita Symphony, 1976-77; dir. advt. Quik Print, Inc., 1977-78; account service copywriter Stephan Advt., Wichita, 1978-79; communications specialist KG and E, the Electric Co., Wichita, 1979-81; account exec. Lida Advt. Co., Wichita, 1981-84; dir. mktg. Union Nat. Bank of Wichita, 1984—. Recipient writing awards Kans. Press Women, 1978, 79, 81; Addy awards Wichita Advt. Club, 1980, 82, 83. Mem. Women in Communications (pres. Wichita chpt. 1978-79), Pub. Relations Soc. Am. (student liaison 1984-85), Kappa Delta. Republican. Congregationalist. Home: 157 N Edgemoor Dr Wichita KS 67208 Office: Union Nat Bank of Wichita PO Box 637 Wichita KS 67201

CHAMBERLIN, SHEILA ANN, auto manufacturing company public relations executive; b. Detroit, Feb. 25, 1953; d. Don Millard and Margaret (McLean) C. Student U. London, 1974; B.A., Hillsdale Coll., 1975; postgrad. Fairleigh Dickinson U., 1981-82, Villanova U., 1982-84. Radio announcer, producer WCSR-AM/FM, Hillsdale, Mich., 1972-75; field rep., lectr. Gen. Motors, Detroit, 1976-77, pub. relations coordinator Assembly div., Tarrytown, N.Y., 1977-80, regional rep., Hackensack, N.J., 1980-82, asst. regional mgr., Wayne, Pa., 1982-84, asst. mgr. pub. affairs, Flint, Mich., 1984—. Leader young writers workshop Marymount Coll., Tarrytown, N.Y., 1981, 82, 83. Solicitor, United Way Westchester, 1977-79; adviser Jr. Achievement Westchester, 1978-79. Recipient Merit award Gen. Motors, 1979. Mem. Public Relations Soc. Am., Women in Communications, GM Women's Club Phila. Republican. Office: 810 Mott Found Bldg Flint MI 48502

CHAMBERS, BETTE, association executive; b. Seattle, July 31, 1930; d. Ralph George and Edda Sommers Johnson; m. Charles M. Chambers, Sept. 19, 1949; children—Janice E. Chambers-Sharar, Martha J., Patrice L. Student U. Wash., 1946-52, Humboldt State U., Arcata, Calif., 1956-57, Sacramento State U., 1959-60, Eastern Wash. State U., 1966-67. Pres., Humanist Assn. Minn., 1961-64; bd. dirs. Am. Humanist Assn., Amherst, N.Y., 1968-82, pres., 1973-79, pres. emeritus, 1979—, exec. dir., 1978-79, 81-84; asst. to pres. Assn. Dr. Isaac Asimov, 1984—; co-founder Com. for Sci. Investigation of Claims of the Paranormal, 1976, fellow, 1976—; lectr., freelance writer. Recipient Humanist Merit award Am. Humanist Assn., 1979, Humanist Pioneer award, 1981; cert. sr. humanist counselor Am. Humanist Assn. Mem. AAAS, N.Y. Acad. Scis., ACLU, Planetary Soc. Democrat. Unitarian. Editorial bd. The Humanist, 1973—; editor Free Mind, Am. Humanist Assn. newsletter, 1975—; trustee Churchman mag., 1982—; contbr. articles to profl. jours. Home: 4116 Candlewood Dr SE Lacey WA 98503 Office: American Humanist Assn 7 Harwood Dr Amherst NY 14226

CHAMBERS, BEVERLY ZIVITSKI, graphics company manager, tax consultant; b. Middletown, Conn., July 31, 1952; d. Paul and Anne (Kost) Zivitski; divorced. A.A. in Liberal Arts, Daytona Beach Community Coll., 1977, A.S. in Tech. Illustration, 1978; B.S. in Art Adminstrn., U. Tampa, 1985. Artist, Eastern Graphics, Old Saybrook, Conn., 1973-74; sch. artist Inex, Daytona Beach, Fla., 1978; art dir. Daytona pub. and pvt. schs., Daytona Beach, 1979-80; artist Pearson & Clark, Lakeland, Fla., 1980-83; ops. mgr. Imperial Graphic, Largo, Fla., 1985—; tax preparer H & R Block, 1979-85. Recipient 1st prize Fla. Ad Council, 1979. Home: 9075 B 130th Ave N Largo FL 33543 Office: Imperial Graphics 9075 B 130th Ave N Largo FL 33543

CHAMBERS, ELIZABETH JANE, lawyer; b. Phila., Oct. 10, 1944; d. Frederic Worth and Margaretta (Minnick) C. B.A., West Chester U., 1966; M.A., Bryn Mawr Coll., 1970; J.D., Temple U., 1978. Bar: Pa. Supreme Ct. 1978, U.S. Dist. Ct. (ea. dist.) Pa. Instr., West Chester U., Pa., summer 1967; instr., asst. prof. Kutztown U., Pa., 1970-78; assoc. Sprague, Goldberg and Rubenstein, Phila., 1978-80; asst. dist. atty. Office Phila. Dist. Atty., 1980—. NDEA fellow, 1967-70. Mem. ABA, Pa. Dist. Atty.'s Assn., Lawyers Club Phila. Office: Philadelphia District Attorney 1300 Chestnut St Philadelphia PA 19102

CHAMBERS, IMOGENE KLUTTS, school administrator; b. Paden, Okla., Aug. 6, 1928; d. Odes and Lillie (Southard) Klutts; B.A., East Central State U., 1948; M.S., Okla. State U., 1974, Ed.D., 1980; m. Richard Lee Chambers, May 27, 1949. High sch. math. tchr. Marlow (Okla.) Sch. Dist., 1948-49; with Bartlesville (Okla.) Sch. Dist., 1950—, asst. supt. bus. affairs, treas. Ind. Sch. Dist. 30, 1977—; dir. Plaza Nat. Bank. Bd. dirs. Mutual Girls Club, 1981—. Mem. Am. Assn. Sch. Adminstrs., Okla. Assn. Sch. Bus. Ofcls., Assn. Sch. Bus. Ofcls. Internat., Assn. Sch. Bus. Ofcls. of U.S. and Can., Okla. Assn. Sch. Adminstrs., Okla. State U. Alumni Assn., Phi Delta Kappa. Democrat. Methodist. Home: 911 Greystone Place Bartlesville OK 74006 Office: Bartlesville Ind Sch Dist 301100 S Jennings St Bartlesville OK 74005

CHAMBERS, JOAN LOUISE, librarian, university administrator; b. Denver, Mar. 22, 1937; d. Joseph Harvey and Clara Elizabeth (Carleton) Baker; m. Donald Ray Chambers, Aug. 17, 1958. Student in English lit. U. Edinburgh, Scotland, 1957; B.A., U. No. Colo., 1958; M.S. in Library Sci., U. Calif.-Berkeley, 1970; M.S. in Systems Mgmt., U. So. Calif., 1985. Librarian U. Nev., Reno, 1970-79; asst. univ. librarian U. Calif.-San Diego, 1979-81; univ. librarian U. Calif.-Riverside, 1981-85; dir. libraries Colo. State U., Fort Collins, 1985—; mgmt. intern Duke U. Library, Durham, N.C., 1978-79; cons. tng. program Assn. Research Librarians, Washington, 1981; library cons. Calif. State U.-Sacramento, 1982. Active various soc. of friends groups. State of Nev. grantee U. Nev., 1976; U. Calif.-San Diego instl. improvement grantee, 1980-81; sr. fellow UCLA, summer 1982. Mem. ALA (councilor 1977-78), Assn. Coll. and Research Libraries (com. chairperson), Library Adminstrn. and Mgmt. Assn. of ALA, Library Info. Tech. Assn. of ALA, Sierra Club, Audubon Soc., SPUR, Beta Phi Mu, Phi lambda Theta, Kappa Delta Phi. Avocations: hiking; backpacking; downhill and cross-country skiing; tennis; local history. Office: Colo State U Univ Library Fort Collins CO 80521

CHAMBERS, LINDA DIANNE THOMPSON, social worker; b. Mexia, Tex., Apr. 21, 1953; d. Lee and Essie Mae (Hopes) Thompson; m. George Edward Chambers, Nov. 30, 1978; 1 child, Brandon. A.S. cum laude, Navarro Coll., Tex., 1974; B.S.W. magna cum laude, Tex. Woman's U., 1976; postgrad. Sam Houston U., 1982, U. Tex.-Arlington, 1986—. Mem. social work staff Dept. Human Resources, Ft. Worth, Tex., 1975, Children's Med. Ctr., Dallas, 1976, Mexia State Sch., Tex., 1976—. Pres., Raven Exquisites, Mexia, 1983-84, sec.-treas., 1984-85; mem. Tex. Hist. Found., Nat. Mus. Women in Arts, 1985—. Recipient numerous awards for scholarship and profl. excellence. Mem. Am. Sociol. Soc. (sec. 1975-76), Univ. Woman's Assn., Am. Childhood Edn. Internat., Nat. Assn. Social Workers, Nat. Assn. Female Execs., Am. Assn. Mental Deficiency, Nat. Assn. Future Women, Am. Soc. Profl. and Exec. Women, Nat. Assn. Negro Bus. and Profl. Women's Clubs, AAUW, Tex. Woman's U. Nat. Alumnae Assn., Mortar Bd. Honor Soc. (sec.-treas. 1975-76), Las Amigos, Phi Theta Kappa, Alpha Kappa Delta. Club: Young Democrats. Avocations: Reading; gardening; gourmet cooking. Home: 102 Hardin Mexia TX 76667

CHAMBERS, LOIS I., insurance agent, automation consultant; b. Omaha, Nov. 24, 1935; d. Edward J. and Evelyn B. (Davidson) Morrison; m. Frederick G. Chambers, Apr. 17, 1981; 1 son by previous marriage, Peter Edward Mscichowski. Ins. clk. Gross-Wilson Ins. Agy., 1955-57; ins. sec., bookkeeper Reed-Paulsen Ins. Agy., 1957-58; office mgr., asst. sec., agt. Don Biggs & Assocs., Vancouver, Wash., 1958—, Chambers & Assocs., Tualatin, Oreg. Mem. Citizens Com. Task Force, City of Vancouver, 1976, Block Grant Rev. Task Force, 1978—; chmn. adv. com. Clark Coll. Mem. Ins. Women of S.W. Wash., Nat. Assn. Ins. Women. Roman Catholic. Club: Soroptimist (Vancouver). Home: 8770 SW Umatilla St Tualatin OR 97062 Office: 916 Main St PO Box 189 Vancouver WA 98666

CHAMBERS, MARY PEYTON, state legislator; b. Poca, W.Va., Aug. 31, 1931; d. Henry Hanna and Hilda Claudia (Cary) Peyton; A.B., W.Va. Wesleyan Coll., 1952; M.A. in Spl. Edn., George Peabody Coll., 1955; m. Wilbert Franklin Chambers, July 6, 1957; children—Henry Peyton, James Erland, Jane Cary. Elem. tchr., W.Va. public schs., 1952-56; ednl. supr. Baird Childrens Center, Burlington, Vt., 1956-62; dir., counselor Upper Valley Adult Basic Edn., Lebanon, N.H., 1975—; mem. N.H. Ho. of Reps., 1972, dep. minority leader, 1974-84, minority leader, 1985—; chmn. Democratic Policy Com., 1975—. Office: New Hampshire State House Room 306 Concord NH 03301

CHAMBERS-MEYERS, TRESSA, consultant, writer; b. Lyon, Miss., Apr. 26, 1942; d. James W. and Anna L. (Dorsey) Chambers; m. Joseph R. Meyers, Mar. 18, 1961 (div. Apr. 1983); children—Monica Denise Meyers, Jon Raymond Meyers. B.A., Eastern Wash. U., 1965. Cert. sch. tchr., Calif. Tchr., San Francisco Unified Schs., 1969-75; freelance writer, San Francisco, 1975-81; writer-cons., 1981-83; founder, pres. Thought Motivation Inst., San Francisco, 1983—. Author: Balanced Living Program 1986; contbg. author: The Stress Strategists, 1986. Mem. Mayor's San Francisco Host Com., 1979—; mem. host. com. 1984 Democratic Conv., 1983; mem. Dem. Women's Forum, 1978—. Mem. Bus. Execs. for Nat. Security (charter), World Affairs Council No. Calif. (membership com.), Nat. Assn. Female Execs., Nat. Speakers Assn., Internat. Platform Assn., Assn. Continuing Higher Edn. Roman Catholic. Club: Circlets (v.p. 1978-84). Office: Thought Motivation Inst 2966 Diamond St Suite 151 San Francisco CA 94131

CHAMPA, JENNIE ANGELA, insurance and real estate broker; b. Fitchburg, Mass.; d. Sebastian and Maria (Rampulla) Cali; m. Anthony Joseph Champa, Oct. 4, 1941; children—Anthony Michael, Joyce Champa Suri, David S. Grad. high sch. Notary pub., 1942—; prin. Champa Ins. and Real Estate, Fitchburg, 1939—. Mem. Nat. Assn. Female Execs., Fitchburg Ind. Ins. Agts. Inc., Fitchburg C. of C., No. Worcester County Bd. Realtors (v.p. 1942-46), Women's Council Realtors. Home: 387 Water St Fitchburg MA 01420 Office: 377 Water St Fitchburg MA 01420

CHAMPAGNE, ANDRÉE, member Canadian House of Commons; b. 1939. Ed. Inst. Notre-Dame de Lorette, Saint-Hyacinthe. Active for 28 yrs. in communications, including radio, TV, theatre and film in prodn. and distbn., writing and pub. relations positions; Mem. Ho. of Commons, 1984—; minister Ministry of State for Youth, 1984—; sec. gen. Union des artistes, 1983-84; pres. Chez-nous des artistes, 1983-84; del. Internat. Fedn. Actors Conf., Moscow, 1984. Mem. Institut quebecois du cinema (bd. dirs.). Progressive Conservative. Office: Ministry of State for Youth Parliament Bldgs Ottawa ON K1A 0A2 Canada

CHAMPAGNE, MARIAN GROSBERG, lawyer; b. Schenectady, Dec. 17, 1915; d. Joseph E. and Rae Grosberg; m. Herbert Champagne, Aug. 18, 1940 (dec. May 1966); children—Emily, Margot J. B.A., Smith Coll., 1936; LL.B., Albany Law Sch., 1955, J.D., 1968. Bar: N.Y. 1956. Practice with Herbert Champagne, 1956-66; assoc. Wood Morris Sanford & Hatt, 1966-71. Mem. Fla. Mental Health Bd., 1975-78, Sarasota Mental Health Clinic, 1980-82. Mem. AAUW. Republican. Unitarian. Club: Smith Alumnae (Sarasota). Author: The Cauliflower Heart, 1944; Quimby and Son, 1962; Facing Life Alone, 1964; also pub. under names Elsa Gottlieb, Mary Jonathan, Kay Ottick, others. Home and Office: 3276 Pinecrest St Sarasota FL 33579

CHAMSON, SANDRA POTKORONY, psychologist; b. N.Y.C., Nov. 6, 1933; d. Daniel and Rose (Sukenik) Potkorony; m. Allan Chamson, Dec. 25, 1954 (div. 1978); children—Eugene, Amy. B.S. in Psychology, NYU, 1955; M.S. in Sch. Psychology, CCNY, 1957; Ph.D. in Psychology, Fla. Inst. Tech., Melbourne, 1983. Psychologist, Anne Arundel County Schs., Anapolis, Md., 1957-58, Bur. Child Guidance, N.Y.C., 1960-64, Region VI Dist., Bergen County, N.J., 1965-84; sole practice, N.Y.C., 1985—; psychol. cons. Ramaz Sch., N.Y.C., 1974-81. Mem. Am. Psychol. Assn., Nat. Assn. Sch. Psychologists, N.Y. Acad. Scis., Am. Orthopsychiat. Assn. Address: Apt 18-D 200 W 86th St New York NY 10024

CHAN, CAROLYN HONG, association executive; b. Greenville, Miss., Aug. 9, 1936; d. Chuck Kun and Mamie Goza (Wy) Hong; m. Tony Quong Chan, Aug. 1, 1958; children—Tony Russell, Mamie Cassandra. B.S., Miss. U. Women, 1958; postgrad. U. N.Mex., 1960-62, 70. Clk. typist U. Ill.-Chgo., 1958; tchr. pub. schs., Chgo., 1958-59, Albuquerque, 1959-63, 65-66; pres. N.Mex. Optometric Assn. Aux., 1965-66, membership chmn., 1966-67, scholarship chmn., 1967-68, state conv. chmn., pres. 1965-66; legis. chmn. Am. Optometric Assn. Aux., 1973-75, edn. research trustee, 1975-76, trustee bull. press, 1976-77, pres., 1978-79; pub. relations, bus. cons. CHC Enterprises, Albuquerque, 1983—. Mem. N.Mex. Arts and Crafts Fair Bd., 1968-69, Music Theatre Bd., 1965-70; treas. Albuquerque Chinese Sch., 1979-82; publicity dir. Music Theatre, 1965-67, mem. Bernalillo County Republican Central Com., 1977-78; mem. media com. N.Mex. Health Edn. Coalition, 1974-75; chmn. Nat. Adv. Council Bilingual Edn., U.S. Dept. Edn., 1982-83, mem., 1981-84. Mem. Santa Fe Opera Guild, Am. Optometric Assn., Optometric Editors Assn. (adv. bd. 1976-78), AAUW, Albuquerque Symphony Womens Assn., League Women Voters, N.Mex. Edn. Assn., NEA, Nat. Assn. Bilingual Edn., Phi Lamdba Theta, Epsilon Sigma Alpha. Unitarian. Home: 8515 La Sala Grande NE Albuquerque NM 87111

CHAN, GAYLE JOCELYN, lawyer, real estate broker; b. Happy Valley, Hong Kong, Nov. 5, 1949; came to U.S., 1966; d. Zuen Yuen and Julia Yan (Chu) Chen; m. Eric Hung Chen, June 18, 1977; children—Cary Hsian, Cory Hsian. B.A. in English, Simmons Coll., 1972, M.A. in English, 1973; M.S. in Pub. Relations, Boston U., 1974; A.M. in Edn., Stanford U., 1975; J.D., Hastings Coll., U. Calif.-San Francisco, 1977. Bar: Calif. 1977, U.S. Tax Ct. 1977, U.S. Supreme Ct. 1977. Vice-pres., counsel Grubb & Ellis Internat., San Francisco, 1977-78; atty. Gap Stores Inc., San Bruno, Calif., 1978-80; corp. counsel Wallpapers To Go and Gen. Mills, Inc., Hayward, Calif., 1980-82; ptnr. Ding, Ding & Chan, San Francisco, 1983—. Trustee Suicide Prevention and Crisis Ctr., Burlingame, Calif., sec. 1979-82; sec. Peninsula Assn. Chinese Ams., San Mateo, Calif., 1983; v.p. Asian Am. Community Council, San Mateo, 1980. Mem. Calif. Bar Assn., San Francisco Bar Assn., ABA, Asian Lawyers Bar Assn., Immigration Lawyers Bar Assn. Roman Catholic. Home: 1205 Canterbury Rd Hillsborough CA 94010 Office: Ding Ding & Chan 233 Sansome St #500 San Francisco CA 94104

CHAN, LINDA WAI SIM, fin. and investment analyst; b. Hong Kong, Aug. 20, 1945; came to U.S., 1970, naturalized, 1975; d. Lam K.C. and Fung Ming (Chan) Leung; B.S.S. in Econs. cum laude (Cheung Chun Shun scholar), Chinese U. of Hong Kong (United Coll.), 1967; M.A. in Econs., U. Colo., 1971; m. Shu Mui Chan, June 22, 1971. Chief research statistician Far Eastern Econ. Rev., 1967-70; sr. acct. C.R. Cushing & Co., Inc., 1972-76, 78-79; asst. controller Soros Assocs., N.Y.C., 1979—; project asst. Econ. Research Center of Hong Kong, 1964-65. Bd. deacons Broadway Presbyn. Ch., 1979-80; bd. elders Queens Chinese Presbyn. Ch., 1981—. Lic. ins. examiner N.Y. Mem. Econ. Soc. Hong Kong, Nat. Assn. Female Execs., Leadership Found. Republican. Editor Seedling, 1964-65.

CHANCY, VIVIAN ELIZABETH, state department manager; b. Boston, Mar. 28, 1925; d. Wesley and Mary Elizabeth (Wilson) Dixon; m. Francois Mondestin Chancy, Mar. 20, 1954; 1 child, Joette V. Chancy-Borden. A. in Bus. Adminstrn., U. Lowell, 1973; B.S. in Mgmt., Boston State Coll., 1977. Mgr. office Mass. Dept. Revenue, Brockton, 1983—. Treas. Ch. of All Nations, Boston, 1965-73, 78-80. Methodist. Club: Female Investment Venture (sec. 1978-82).

CHANDLER, BARBARA FARRAR, legal assistant; b. Charleston, W.Va., Mar. 19, 1934; d. Willie Baker and Francis Arbutus (Flowers) Farrar; m. Robert Kendall Chandler, Feb. 12, 1955 (div. 1978). Cert. Paralegal Inst., 1973; A.A., No. Va. Community Coll., 1977. Office mgr. Crickenberger & Moore, Fairfax, Va., 1971-75; instr. Paralegal Inst., McLean, Va., 1975-76; dir. support services Commonwealth's Atty., Arlington, Va., 1976—; dir. victim witness Assistance for Arlington County. Vol. Republican Party, Arlington, Democratic Party; mem. Williamsburg Civic Assn., Arlington, 1971—. Named Employer of Yr., No. Va. Community Coll., 1985. Mem. Nat. Dist. Attys. Assn., Nat. Capitol Area Paralegal Assn., Fraternal Order of Police. Episcopalian. Avocations: needlework, photography, volunteer social work. Home: 3312 N Pocomoke St Arlington VA 22207 Office: Commonwealth's Atty 1400 N Courthouse Rd Arlington VA 22201

CHANDLER, ELISABETH GORDON (MRS. LACI DE GERENDAY), sculptor, harpist; b. St. Louis, June 10, 1913; d. Henry Brace and Sara Ellen (Sallee) Gordon; grad. The Lenox School, 1931; pvt. study sculpture and harp; m. Robert Kirtland Chandler, May 27, 1946 (dec.); m. Laci de Gerenday, May 12, 1979. Exhibited sculptures N.A.D., National Sculpture Soc., Allied Artists Am., Nat. Arts Club, Pen and Brush, Lyme Art Assn., Mattatuck Museum, Catherine Lorillard Wolfe Art Club, Am. Artists Profl. League, Hudson Valley Art Assn., USIA, 1976-78, Lyme Art Center, 1979; represented in permanent collections Aircraft Carrier USS Forrestal, Gov. Dummer Acad., James Forrestal Research Center of Princeton U., Lenox Sch., James L. Collins Parochial Sch., Tex., Storm King Art Center, Columbia U., Forrestal Meml. Medal, Timoshenko Medal for Applied Mechanics, Benjamin Franklin Medal, Albert A. Michelson medal, Jonathan Edwards Medal, Shafto Broadcasting Award Medal, Woodrow Wilson Sch. of Princeton U., Georgia Pacific Bldg., Portland, Oreg., Messiah Coll., Grantham, Pa., Adlai E. Stevenson High Sch., Ill., Queen Anne's County, Md., Pace U., N.Y.C., Soc. Medalists, George Washington 250th Anniversary Medal, U.S. Capitol Hist. Soc., also represented in pvt. collections; performed as concert harpist on stage, radio, TV, 1933-45; mem. Mildred Dilling Harp Ensemble, 1934-46. instr. portrait sculpture Lyme Acad. Fine Arts, 1976—. Dir. Abbott Coin Counter Co., Inc., 1941-55. Chmn. Asso. Taxpayers Old Lyme, 1969-72. Trustee The Lenox Sch., 1953-55. Served with mus. therapy div. Am. Theatre Wing, 1942-45. Recipient 1st prize Bklyn. War Meml. competition, 1945; 1st prize sculpture Catherine Lorillard Wolfe Art Club, 1951, 58, 63; Founders prize Pen and Brush, 1954, 76, 78, Gold medal, 1957, 61, 63, 69, 74, Am. Heritage award, 1968, Solo Show award, 1961, 69, 75, Thomas R. Proctor prize N.A.D., 1956, Dessie Greer prize, 1960, 79, 85; sculpture prize Nat. Arts Club, 1959, 60, 62, Gold medal, 1971; Gold medal Am. Artists Profl. League, 1960, 73, 75, Anna Hyatt Huntington prize, 1970, 76, Harriet Mayer Meml. prize, 1961, sculpture prize, 1969; Gold medal Hudson Valley Art Assn., 1956, 69, 74, Mrs. John Newington award, 1976, 78; Lindsey Morris Meml. prize Allied Artists Am., 1973, Tallix Foundry award, 1978, Gold Medal, 1982; sculpture prize Acad. Artists, 1974; Sydney Taylor Meml. prize Knickerbocker Artists, 1975; New Netherlands D.A.R. Bicentennial medal, 1976; Tallix Foundry award, 1979, Nat. Sculpture Soc., 1979. N.A. Fellow Nat. Sculpture Soc. (council 1976-85, John Spring Founder award 1986), Am. Artists Profl. League (prize 1981), Internat. Inst. Arts and Letters; mem. Nat. Arts Club, Allied Artists of Am., Pen and Brush, Catherine Lorillard Wolfe Art Club, Lyme Art Assn. (pres. 1973-75), Council Am. Artist Socs. (dir. 1970-73), Am. Artists Profl. League (dir. 1970-73), Lyme Acad. Fine Arts (trustee 1976—, instr. 1976—). Home and Studio: 2 Mill Pond Ln Old Lyme CT 06371

CHANDLER, JOY KAZUE, elementary educator; b. Hanapepe, Hawaii, Dec. 22, 1946; d. Kazuto and Tokiko (Takenaka) Yoshioka; m. Robert Lloyd Chandler, Feb. 26, 1972; 1 child, Bobby Lloyd. B.A., Western Oreg. Coll., 1968, M.S., 1970. Elem. tchr., Salem, Oreg., 1968-70, Wahiawa, Hawaii, 1970-72; ESL adult tchr. Dept. Army, Ft. Dix, N.J., 1972-73; 6th-8th grade basic skills tchr. Haines Sch., Browns Mills, N.J., 1981-83; 2d-3d grade tchr. Marshall Sch., Ft. Ord, Calif., 1984; 1st grade tchr. Thomas Hayes Sch., Ft. Ord, 1984—. Parent rep. Marshall Sch. Sci. Found., 1984-85. Mem. Calif. Tchrs. Assn. Avocations: needlework, bicycling, gardening, painting. Home: 12 Julia Ave Salinas CA 93906 Office: Thomas Hayes Sch PO Box 1031 Monterey CA 93942

CHANDLER, RENIE TUCKER, correctional administrator; b. LaGrange, Ga., Dec. 22, 1940; d. William Brodie and Mamie Lucile (Howard) Tucker; m. David Eugene Watkins, July 25, 1959 (div. 1969); children—Richard, Crystal, David; m. B.J. Chandler, Aug. 30, 1982; 6 stepchildren. A.A., Am. River Coll., Sacramento 1967; B.A., Calif. State U.-Sacramento, 1971; M.A., Emory U., 1985. With Calif. Hwy. Patrol, 1969-71, Calif. Criminal Justice Agy., 1971-72, Ga. Crime Commn., 1972-73; with Ga. Prison System, Atlanta, 1973—, asst. dep. commr., 1980-83, exec. tng. adminstr., 1983—; instr., U. Ga., Decatur, 1985—. Ga. hearing officer, 1977—, peace officer, 1981—. Bd. dirs. Personal Prison Ministry, Inc., Atlanta, 1979—. Mem. Am. Correctional Assn., So. States Correctional Assn., Nat. Soc. Performance and Instrn., Nat. Assn. Female Execs., Ga. Council State Personnel Adminstrn., Beta Sigma Phi, Alpha Kappa Delta. Avocations: water sports. Office: Dept Corrections Martin luther King Jr Dr Atlanta GA 30334

CHANDLER, ROYLENE MCILHANEY, chamber of commerce executive; b. Waco, Tex., Dec. 7, 1938; d. James Roy and Hallie Jeanette (Sloan) McIlhaney; m. Lawrence Jerome Chandler, Nov. 2, 1957; children—Hamp, Chana Darlene. Grad. McCamey high sch., Tex. Radio announcer Sta. KCMR, McCamey, 1957-60; mgr. Western Union, 1961-63; mgr.-sec. McCamey C. of C., 1978—. Chmn. McCamey Sesquicentennial, 1984—; vice chmn. Upton County Hist. Commn., 1982—. Named 1st Lady McCamey's 50th Anniversary, McCamey Anniversary Com., 1975; recipient Outstanding Service award C. of C., 1978, True McCameyite award, 1984, Chamber Appreciation award, 1980. Mem. Permian Basin (com.), Planning Commn., Am. Legion Aux. (pres. 1978-82, dist. sgt. at arms 1981, dist. chaplain 1982—), Ladies Aux. Patriarch Militant. Baptist. Lodge: Rebekah (noble grand 1971, dist. dep. pres. 1977, recipient Decoration Chilvray, Tex., 1980, color bearer, 1979). Home: Box 955 McCamey TX 79752 Office: McCamey C of C Box 906 McCamey TX 79752

CHANDLER, VIRGINIA GOODMAN, occupational therapist; b. Evanston, Ill., Jan. 10, 1930; d. Daniel Guy and Helen (Schneider) Goodman; B.A. in Art and Psychology, So. Methodist U., 1951; postgrad. in occupational therapy Tex. Women's U., 1953; cert. ins. rehab. specialist; cert. in work adjustment and vocat. evaluation; children—Ron Lee, Chuck Lee. Occupational therapist Beverly Hills Sanitarium, Dallas, 1953-55; dir. occupational therapy Baylor U. Med. Center, Dallas, 1956-60, 68—, Fla. Sanitarium and Hosp., Orlando, 1962-65; staff therapist Parkland Mcml. Hosp., Dallas, 1965-68; cons. Arthritis Found., 1974—. Mem. coordinating bd. health adv. com. Tex. Coll. and Univ. System, 1980—; bd. dirs. Tex. Arthritis Found., chmn. patient services com., 1985—; bd. sponsors Kimball Art Mus. Named Tex. Occupational Therapist of Yr., 1985. Mem. Am. Occupational Therapy Assn. (del. Fla. 1964, Tex. 1980—), World Fedn. Occupational Therapists (participant 8th Internat. Congress, Hamburg, Germany, 1982, del. to 10th European Congress on Rheumatology, Moscow 1983), Am. Heart Assn., Chi Omega. Club: Boomerang (dir. 1971—). Author: (manual) Lightcast II Splints, 1976; Adult Visual Perceptual Evaluation, 1981; contbr. articles to profl. jours. Home: 11106 Shortmeadow Dallas TX 75218 Office: Baylor Univ Medical Center 3500 Gaston Ave Dallas TX 75246

CHANDOR, KAREN KAYSER, marketing executive; b. Los Angeles, Feb. 13, 1950; d. Ernest and Kathleen (Adams) Kayser; B.A., Wellesley Coll., 1970; M.B.A., Babson Coll., 1974, also postgrad. Vice pres. Tech. Steel Corp., Newton, Mass., 1971-73; asst. v.p. Thorndike, Doran, Paine & Lewis, Boston, 1973-76; v.p. Colonial Mgmt. Assos., Boston, 1976-77; v.p. mktg. Gardner and Preston Moss, Inc., Boston, 1977—. Mem. corp. Babson Coll., 1982—; trustee Mass. Eye and Ear Infirmary, 1985—. Cert. employee benefit specialist. Mem. Assn. Investment Mgmt. Sales Execs. (dir., past pres.), Internat. Found. Employee Benefits. Home: 28 Cartwright Rd Wellesley MA 02181 Office: One Winthrop Sq Boston MA 02110

CHANEY, EUNICE MCGUSTER, public relations specialist; b. Chgo., July 17; d. Leroy and Gladys (Greene) McGuster; m. Roy N. Chaney, June 30, 1957 (div. 1978); children—Karen, Mitchell. A.A., Wilson Jr. Coll., 1957. Fundraiser, Combined Jewish Appeal, Chgo., 1962-66; interviewer Cook County Bd. Edn., Chgo., 1966-68; account coordinator Chgo. Fedn., 1968-71; pub. relations, prodn. and adminstrv. asst. Jim Tilmon Prodns., Highland Park, Ill., 1971-74; asst. pub. affairs dir. Johnson Pub. Co., Chgo., 1974-78; communications account exec. Burrell Advt., Chgo., 1978—. Author: (with others) Chicago's Black Gold, 1983. Publicist, Mental Health Assn. Chgo., 1978-80, DuSable Mus., Chgo., 1976-79, Rumpelstiltskin and The Four of Us Social Group, Chgo., 1978-82. Mem. Black Pub. Relations Soc., Chgo. Advt. Club, Publicity Club Chgo., Pub. Relations Soc. Am. Office: Burrell Advt Inc 625 N Michigan Ave Chicago IL 60611

CHANG, SHIRLEY (HSIU-CHU) LIN, librarian; b. Chia-yi, Taiwan, June 22, 1937; came to U.S., 1962, naturalized, 1977; d. Tzu-kun and Ying (Chang) Lin; m. Parris H. Chang, Aug. 3, 1963; children—Yvette Y., Elaine Y., Bohdan P. B.A., Nat. Taiwan U., Taipei, 1960; postgrad. U. Wash., 1962-63, Pa. State U., 1976-77 M.L.S., Columbia U., 1967. Library asst. Yale U., New Haven, 1964, Columbia U., N.Y.C., 1964-67; asst. reference librarian Pa. State U., University Park, 1971-75; cataloguer Australian Nat. U., Canberra, 1978; catalog and reference librarian Lock Haven U. Pa., 1979—, asst. prof., 1982—. Mem. ALA, Chinese-Am. Librarians Assn. (chmn. awards com. 1982-83). Home: 1221 Edward St State College PA 16801 Office: Stevenson Library Lock Haven U of Pa Lock Haven PA 17745

CHANG, SUN-YUNG ALICE, mathematics educator; b. Li-an, China, Mar. 24, 1948; came to U.S., 1970; d. Fann Chang and Li-Ching Chern; m. Paul Chien-Ping Yang, Mar. 24, 1973; 1 son, Ray Yang. B.S., Nat. Taiwan U., 1970; Ph.D., U. Calif.-Berkeley, 1974. Asst. prof. math. U. Md., College Park, 1977-79; prof. UCLA, 1981—. Sloan Found. fellow, 1977, 78. Mem. Am. Math. Soc. Office: Dept Math UCLA Los Angeles CA 90024

CHANG, TOHSOOK PAIK, librarian; b. Seoul, Korea, Oct. 15, 1936; came to U.S., 1962, naturalized, 1974; d. Yong H. and Seok (Lee) Paik; m. Sang Ike Chang, July 18, 1964; children—Albert, Eugene. B.A., Ewha Womans U., 1959; M.L.S. SUNY-Albany, 1963; postgrad. Wash. State U., 1964-65. Asst. librarian Boston U. Library, 1963-64; librarian, instr., Alaska Meth. U., Anchorage, 1970-71; instr. Ewha Women's U., Seoul, 1971-72; librarian, assoc. prof., U. Alaska, Anchorage, 1972—; bd. dirs. Anchorage Korean Lang. Sch. Found., 1981—; mem. Anchorage Sch. Dist. Bilingual, Bicultural Edn. Adv. Com., 1980—, chmn., 1982-83. Active First Korean Presbyterian Ch., Korean Community Anchorage. Internat. fellow AAUW, 1962-63. Mem. ALA, Alaska Library Assn. Democrat. Home: 4112 Chess Dr Anchorage AK 99508 Office: U of Alaska 3211 Providence Dr Anchorage AK 99508

CHANGAR-SHAW, ILENE, county official; b. St. Louis, Feb. 20, 1937; d. Ely and Leona (Rosenblatt) Saphian; student U. Wis., Madison, 1956; B.A. summa cum laude, St. Louis U., 1977, M.A., Center Urban Programs, 1981, postgrad. in pub. policy analysis and adminstrn., 1981—; children—Cynthia Gay Changar, Michael David Changar, Daniel Ely Changar, Amy Beth Changar. Office mgr. Metro Housing Resources, St. Louis, 1973; adminstrv. asst. Community Behavioral Agys., St. Louis, 1974; supr. County Older Resident Program, St. Louis County (Mo.) Dept. Human Resources, 1975-78, mgr. field ops. County Older Resident Programs, 1978—; practicum instr. Washington U.; producer Accent on Age, Cable TV; mem. steering com. Operation Weather Survival, Metro St. Louis. Chmn. Univ. City House and Garden Tour, St. Louis, 1968-70; chmn. Congl. Action Fund, St. Louis, 1972; bd. dirs. New Democratic Coalition, St. Louis, 1972; mem. exec. com. Alliance for Community Togetherness, 1973; presenter Mid-Am. Congress on Aging, St. Louis, 1982. Recipient Achievement award Nat. Assn. Counties, 1978, 81, 83, Achievement award model community program Am. Can., 1985. Mem. Am. Planning Assn., Am. Soc. Public Adminstrn. (program chair 1983-84), Alumni Assn. St. Louis U. Author service handbooks, profl. papers. Home: 24 S Rock Hill Rd Saint Louis MO 63119 Office: 555 S Brentwood Saint Louis MO 63105

CHANT, DALE ANN, nurse; b. Woodbury, N.J., July 18, 1953; d. Howard Roy and Dale Ann (Moore) Verfaillie; A.A.S.N., Gloucester County Coll., 1978; B.S.N., Stockton State Coll., 1983; postgrad. Del. Law Sch., Widener U.; m. Frank Chant III, Apr. 11, 1969; children—Michael Frank, Bryan Scott. Nurse intensive care and coronary unit Our Lady of Lourdes Hosp., Camden, N.J., 1978-80; nurse Western Med. Services, Cherry Hill, N.J., 1980; dir. client services/continuing edn. Staff Builders Health Care Services, Mount Laurel, N.J., 1980-81; nurse emergency room Our Lady of Lourdes Hosp., Camden, 1981-84; cons. Staff Builders Health Care Services, 1981; instr. nursing Gloucester County Vocat. Sch., 1982-83; law clk. Ballen, Keiser & Gertel, 1984—. Mem. Nursing Edn. Com. Camden County, 1981. Mem. Am. Nurses Assn., N.J. Nurses Assn., Student Bar Assn., Sigma Theta Tau. Democrat. Methodist. Editor, contbg. editor Aspect, 1975. Home: 5 Hill Ln Woodbury NJ 08096

CHAPEL, DEBORAH COLLINS, nurse; b. Boston, Mar. 28, 1939; d. Richard and Jean (Chapman) Collins; m. Roger D. Bacon, Sept. 28, 1963 (div. Feb. 1979); 1 child, Richard Dale; m. John W. Chapel, June 8, 1984. B.S.N., Russell Sage Coll., N.Y., 1961; M.S. Spl. Edn., East Tex. State U., 1980. Cert. sch. nurse practitioner. Staff nurse, asst. head nurse Mass. Gen. Hosp., Boston, 1961-63; head nurse Twin Lakes Community Hosp., Folsom, Calif., 1964-66; staff nurse Dallas Ind. Sch. Dist., 1974-78, nurse-in-charge, 1978—. Vol., CPR and first aid instr. ARC, Dallas, 1978—. Mem. Nat. Assn. Sch. Nurses (pres. 1983-84), Am. Nurses Assn., Am. Sch. Health Assn., Classroom Tchrs. Dallas, Tex. State Tchrs. Assn., NEA, Tex. Sch. Health Assn. Republican. Episcopalian. Home: 7024 Freemont St Dallas TX 75231 Office: Hexter Elementary Sch 9720 Waterview Rd Dallas TX 75218

CHAPELLE, SUZANNE ELLERY, history educator; b. Phila., Sept. 21, 1942; d. John Channing and Jessie Horn (Myers) Ellery; m. Michael Thomas Greene, Sept. 15, 1972 (dec. 1973); 1 child, Jennifer; m. 2d Francis Oberlin Chapelle, Apr. 14, 1984. B.A., Harvard U., 1964; M.A., Johns Hopkins U., 1966, Ph.D., 1970. Asst. prof. Fed. City Coll., Washington, 1968-69; asst. prof. Am. history Towson State U., Balt., 1969-71; assoc. prof. Am. history Morgan State U., Balt., 1971-75, prof., 1975—. Author: Books for Pleasure, 1976; Baltimore: An Illustrated History, 1980; sr. author, editor: Maryland: A History of Its People, 1986. Mem. Am. Studies Assn., Popular Culture Assn. (mem. bd. 1980-82), Orgn. Am. Historians, Md. Hist. Soc., Mid-Atlantic Popular Culture Assn. (pres. 1977-80). Episcopalian. Home: 6021 Lakeview Rd Baltimore MD 21210 Office: History Dept Morgan State U Baltimore MD 21239

CHAPIN, DIANA DERBY, city official; b. St. Joseph, Mich., Nov. 15, 1942; d. David Norman and Gladys Ruth (Henke) Derby; B.A. cum laude (Woodrow Wilson fellow), U. Mich., 1964; M.A., Cornell U., 1966, Ph.D. (Woodrow Wilson dissertation fellow), 1971; m. James Burke Chapin, Mar. 16, 1968; children—James Derby, David Sheffield. Asst. prof. Queens Coll., N.Y.C., 1969-74; dist. adminstr. 8th Congl. Dist., N.Y.C., 1974-76; asst. commr. N.Y.C. Dept. Parks and Recreation, 1978-81, Queens Borough commr., 1981—; dep. commr. planning Dept. Parks and Recreation, N.Y.C., 1986—. Del. Democratic Nat. Conv., Miami, Fla., 1972; dist. leader 35th Assembly Dem. Dist., N.Y.C., 1972-78; mgr. various campaigns, 1977-78. Recipient ann. employee award N.Y.C. Dept. Parks and Recreation, 1982. Congregationalist. Contbr. articles to profl. publs. Home: 35-46 79th St Jackson Heights NY 11372 Office: 830 Fifth Ave New York NY 10021

CHAPIN, JULIE KURTZ, lawyer; b. Phila., Mar. 25, 1951; d. Louis Kurtz and Adele (Gersh) Greenfield; m. Thomas J. Chapin, May 18, 1986; 1 dau., Alexis Kate. Student Vassar Coll., 1968-69; B.A. and B.S. summa cum laude, U. Pa., 1971, J.D., 1974. Bar: Pa. 1974, U.S. Ct. Appeals (2d cir.) 1975, N.Y. 1976, U.S. Dist. Ct. (so. dist.) N.Y. 1976, U.S. Dist. Ct. (ea. dist.) N.Y. 1977, U.S. Ct. Appeals (D.C. cir.) 1978, D.C. 1978, U.S. Supreme Ct. 1979; cert. primary edn. Law clk. to Chief Justice Benjamin R. Jones, Pa. Supreme Ct., Phila., 1974-75; assoc. firm Hughes Hubbard & Reed, N.Y.C. and Washington, 1975-82; assoc. gen. counsel Celanese Corp., N.Y.C., 1982—, sec., legal advisor Celanese Corp. Polit. Action Com., 1984—; lectr. Am. Soc. Corp. Secs., N.Y.C., 1983-84; adviser com. on bankruptcy and corp. reorgn. Assn. Bar City of N.Y., 1976-77. Mem. ABA (sect. corp., banking and bus. law), Fed. Bar Assn., Phi Beta Kappa, Pi Lambda Theta. Home: 450 E 63d St Apt 5A New York NY 10021 Office: Celanese Corp 1211 Ave of Americas New York NY 10036

CHAPIN, PATRICIA MYERS, county official; b. Meadville, Pa., Aug. 24, 1941; d. Foster Myers and Ruth Florence (McClellan) Myers Jacoby; m. Thomas R. Chapin, Aug. 28, 1964; children—Tammy S., Thomas R. II, Timothy H. Grad. high sch., Oil City, Pa. Legal sec. McFate, McFate and McFate, Oil City, 1959-64, 66-72, Smathers and Thompson, Miami, Fla., 1964-65; exec. sec. Bedford County Planning, Pa., 1977-81; chief clk. Bedford County, 1981—. Republican. Office: Bedford County Commrs 203 S Juliana St Bedford PA 15522

CHAPMAN, CAROLYN, media exec.; b. Portsmouth, Ohio, Feb. 4, 1933; d. Roger Donald and Flowery Alice (Callaway) Carr; diploma Portsmouth Interstate Bus. Coll., 1954, S. Ohio Manpower Tng. Ctr., 1965; m. Edward J. Chapman, May 13, 1966; children—Cheryl, Roger, Lisa, Mark, Edmond, Sean. Dep. probation officer Scioto County Juvenile Ct., Portsmouth, 1960-63; coder II, Aid for Aged, Ohio Dept. Public Welfare, Columbus, 1964; clk. typist II, Bur. Vital Statistics, Dept. Health, Columbus, 1964, clk.-stenographer II, CD Div., 1966; clk.-stenographer ABC, Los Angeles, 1967, ops. coordinator, 1968-72, asso. dir., on-air dir., 1972—; cons. in video tape and TV prodn.; mem. negotiating com. Teamsters Union, Los Angeles, 1970. Ch. sec. Findlay St. Meth. Ch., Portsmouth, 1959-63, chmn. women's day program, 1962, chmn. commn. on missions, 1959-62, del. ann. conf., Cleve., 1963, sec. ofcl. bd., 1959-62; pres. local chpt. Ohio Republican Council, 1959-62, mem. state bd., 1962, del. from Scioto County to State Rep. Conv., Ohio, 1962; mem. film editing com. Social Health and Hygiene Assn., 1961-62; tribute com. for Tribute to Dorothy Arzner, 1975; Los Angeles Jr. C. of C., 1977. Mem. ABC Employees Assn. (pres. Hollywood branch, 1971-73), Dirs. Guild Am. (ad council 1981-82). Address: PO Box 43025 Los Angeles CA 90043

CHAPMAN, CLAUDIA GAYE, chiropractor; b. Trenton, Tenn., May 18, 1959; d. Thomas Iba and Tennie Ethel (French) Chapman. Student, U. Tenn., 1977-79; B.S. in Human Biology, Logan Coll. Chiropractic Medicine, Chesterfield, Mo., 1980, D.Chiropractic, 1982. Diplomate, Nat. Bd. Chiropractic Examiners. Assoc. doctor McCraw & Chapman, Memphis, 1982-85; assoc. doctor Morgan Chiropractic Ctr., Memphis, 1983-84; sole practice chiropractic medicine, Covington, Tenn., 1985—. Fund raiser Child Sexual Abuse Council, Memphis, 1986. Recipient 3d Place, Covington Amateur Armwrestling Championship, 1985. Mem. Am. Chiropractic Assn., Soroptimist Internat. (pres. Memphis 1984-86; Herberta Ann Leonardy Meml. award 1985), Nat. Assn. Female Execs., Women Doctors Club-Parker Chiropractic Research Found., Shelby County Chiropractic Assn. (pres. 1984-86; Hon. Plaque 1985). Avocations: writing; painting; weight-lifting; swimming. Home: Route 3 Box 174A Brighton TN 38011 Office: 420 Hwy 51 S Covington TN 38019

CHAPMAN, ELEANOR FINLEY, archaeological illustrator, lecturer; b. Macomb, Ill., Feb. 14, 1917; d. Charles William and Sylvia Mae (Fears) Finley; m. Carl Haley Chapman; children—Richard Carl, Stephen Finley. B.S. in Art Edn., N.J. State Tchrs. Coll., 1938; postgrad. in anthropology, U. N.Mex., 1941-42. Tchr. fine arts Bradley Park Sch., Neptune, N.J., 1938-41; free lance illustrator, 1946—. Co-author, illustrator: Indians and Archaeology of Missouri, 2d edit., 1983, Spiro Mound Copper, 1974; illustrator: The Archaeology of Missouri: I, 1975, The Archaeology of Missouri: II, 1980; slide lectures: Columbia Art League, 1977—. Recipient Blue Ribbon award for Original Doll United Fedn. Doll Clubs, 1975, 80. Mem. Mo. Archaeol. Soc. (art editor Mo. Archaeologist 1946-62, Memoir 1950—; service award 1961, hon. life membership 1984), Soc. Am. Archaeology, Kappa Delta Pi. Democrat. Unitarian. Clubs: Fortnightly (pres. 1964), Heritage Doll (pres. 1972-74), Mid-Mo. Doll (pres. 1975-77). Avocations: quilt designing; photography; doll making. Home: 211 Edgewood Ave Columbia MO 65203

CHAPMAN, ELEANOR HOWELLS, computer company executive; b. Durham, N.C., Feb. 19, 1938; d. John Lloyd and Callie Gertrude (Neighbors) Howells; student U. N.C.-Chapel Hill, 1960-61; div.; 1 child, Laura Ann. Bookkeeper, sec.-receptionist Ricca, Nelson and Gantt, C.P.A.s, Durham, N.C., 1958-60; legal sec. Haywood, Denny and Miller, Chapel Hill, 1961-62; sec. to dir. Cytology Lab. dept. pathology Duke U. Med. Center, Durham, 1962-63; sec. Noble Truck Leasing, Richmond, Va., 1963-64, Pitts. Plate Glass Co., Richmond, Va., 1964-65; sec. dept. biophysics Med. Coll. Va., Richmond, 1966-67, housestaff sec., 1967, departmental sec. dept. pathology, 1967-68; adminstrv. sec., asst. office mgr. Office of Chief Med. Examiner, State N.C., Chapel Hill, 1968-70; adminstrv. sec. dept. zoology U. N.C., Chapel Hill, 1970-73, adminstrv. asst. dept. chemistry, 1973-74; adminstrv. sec. div. neurology Duke U. Med. Center, Durham, N.C., 1974-77; acting adminstrv. asst. dept. neurology Baylor Coll. Medicine, 1977, adminstrv. asst., 1978-81, sr. adminstrv. asst., 1981-84; owner/operator ACE Computer Co., 1984—; part-time adminstrv. sec. Lipid Research Ctr., dept. medicine Baylor Coll. Medicine, 1985—; corp. sec. Diagnostic Cardiology of Houston, P.A. Vol., Houston Gulf Coast chpt. Muscular Dystrophy Assn., 1978—, mem. exec. com., 1978-84; bd. dirs. Houston Area Parkinson Disease Soc., 1981-84; sec. Neurology A Study Sect., NIH, 1979-82; vol. Camp Mission Possible, 1981. Mem. Am. Bus. Women's Assn., Nat. Assn. for Female Execs., Bellaire-S.W. Houston C. of C., Beta Sigma Phi. Office: 6475 Dawnridge Dr Houston TX 77035 also 7777 Southwest Freeway Suite 420 Houston TX 77074

CHAPMAN, ELSE MARTINUS, artist, sculptor, painter; b. Amsterdam, Netherlands, Nov. 8, 1930; came to U.S., 1952; d. Hendrik Jan and Elisabeth Petrolella (Broertjes) Martinus; m. Phillip Schleiffer, 1952 (div. 1958); m. Joseph M. Chapman, Mar. 1973. Grad Kunstnijverheids Sch., Amsterdam, 1949; postgrad. Ecole des Beaux Arts, Paris, 1949-51, Queens Coll., 1960; student Diane Kan, 1983-85, Helen Hu, 1982-85, Norman Carton, 1962-65. Pvt. cons., 1960-62; resettlement worker Ch. World Service, N.Y.C., 1962-66; prodn. mgr., spl. events coordinator Mus. Modern Art, N.Y.C., 1966-77; lectr. in field. Represented in permanent collections Madison Ave. Gallery, N.Y.C., Gemini Gallery, Palm Beach, Fla., Main St. Gallery, Nantucket, Mass., Boston, Duck Blind Ltd., Village of Duck, N.C., Munson Gallery, Santa Fe, HMS Fine Art, Martha's Vineyard, Mass.; represented in numerous pvt. collections. Mem. Oriental Brush Artists Guild (sec. 1980—), Sumi-e Soc. of U.S., Internat. Sculptors Soc., Netherlands Club. Avocations: weaving; swimming; yoga. Home and Studio: 175 Hurlbutt St Wilton CT 06897

CHAPMAN, ERNA MARTA RIEDEL (MRS. RAY F. CHAPMAN), home economist; b. Dresden, Germany, May 20, 1909 (brought to U.S. 1914, naturalized 1923); d. Joseph and Elsa (Mueller) Riedel; B.S., U. Md., 1934, M.S., 1936; postgrad. Ind. U., D.C. Tchrs. Coll., U. m. dean Coll. Home Econs., F. Chapman, Sept. 5, 1942. Sales, acting asst. buyer The Hecht Co., Washington, 1928-30; card punch operator Census Bur., 1930-31; grad. asst. U. Md. Coll. Home Econs., College Park, 1934-36; corr. editor Social Security Bd., Balt., 1936-38; vocat. home econs. tchr. D.C. public schs., Washington, 1938-56, state supr. home econs. edn., 1960-65; asst. prin. Roosevelt High Sch., Washington, 1956-60; state supr., supervising dir. home econs. edn. D.C. Public Schs., Washington, 1967-75; free lance home economist, farmer, 1975—; chmn. agrl. land preservation adv. bd. Anne Arundel County, Md., 1978-79; trustee Md. Agrl. Land Preservation Found., 1979-80, 84—; acting dean Coll. Home Econs., U. Md., College Park, 1965-67; mem. nat. adv. com. J.C. Penney Co., Inc. Family life cons. Teamwork Found.; mem. Gov.'s com. State of Md., Status of Women in Higher Edn., 1965-67; trustee U. Md. Alumni Assn.-Internat., 1973-84. Mem. NEA, Am. Vocat. Assn., Am. Home Econs. Assn., AAUW, Nat. Council Adminstrs. of Home Econs., Assn. Home Econs. Adminstrs., Nat. Assn. State Univs. and Land Grant Colls., D.C. Home Econs. Assn., Omicron Nu, Phi Kappa Phi, Phi Delta Gamma. Club: Research (D.C.). Contbr. articles to profl. jours. Home: 1660 Riedel Rd Gambrills MD 21054

CHAPMAN, EUGENIA SHELDON, political worker, former state legislator; b. Fairhope, Ala., Jan. 10, 1923; d. Chauncey Bailey and Rose (Donner) Sheldon; B.Ed., Chgo. State U., 1944; m. Gerald M. Chapman, Nov. 24, 1948; children—George, John, Katherine, Andrew. Tchr. public schs., Cicero, Ill., 1944-47, Chgo., 1947-51; mem. Ill. Ho. of Reps., 1964-83, minority whip, chmn. human resources com., standing com. on appropriations. Mem. Dist. 214 Bd. Edn., Cook County, Ill.; del. Dem. Nat. Nominating Convs., 1972, 80; mem. Cook County Dem. Central Com., 1982—, Ill. Dem. Central Com., 1984—; chief div. sr. citizens' advocacy Office Ill. Atty. Gen., 1983—. Named Best Legislator Independent Voters. Ill., 1966, 68, 70, 74, 76, 78, 80, 82. Mem. LWV (pres. Arlington Heights 1957-59), Bus. and Profl. Women's Club. Democrat. Address: 16 S Princeton Ct Arlington Heights IL 60005

CHAPMAN, FRANCES ELIZABETH CLAUSEN (MRS. WILLIAM JAMES CHAPMAN), civic worker; b. Atchison, Kans., Feb. 27, 1920; d. Erwin W. and Helen (Hackney) Clausen; B.A., Wellesley Coll., 1941; m. W. MacLean Johnson, Aug. 31, 1940 (dec. Nov. 1965); children—Stuart MacLean, Duncan Scott, Douglas Hamilton; m. 2d, William James Chapman, Dec. 5, 1970. Project dir. Women in Community Service, Inc., St. Louis, 1965-66; pres. Nursery Found., St. Louis, 1956-58, dir., 1953-59, 65-68; adv. com. Mo. State Children's Day Care, 1963—; chmn. day care com. Mo. Council Children and Youth, 1961, chmn. foster care sect., 1961-63, mem. steering com., 1967-69; spl. asst. to the pres. Webster Coll., 1966-68. Bd. dirs. New City Sch., 1967-69, Mid-County YMCA, 1967-70, St. Louis Conservatory and Sch. Arts, 1978—; trustee Jr. Coll. Dist., St. Louis-St. Louis County, 1968-80, pres. bd. trustees, 1971-73, 76-77; trustee John Burroughs Sch., 1973-79, Wellesley Coll., 1976-82; bd. dirs. Assn. Governing Bds. Univs. and Colls., 1970-80, v.p., 1977-78, chmn. bd., 1978-79, hon. trustee, 1982-85; bd. commrs. Nat. Commn. on Accrediting, 1971-72; bd. overseers Center for Research on Women in Higher Edn. and Professions, Wellesley, Mass., 1977-82; mem. Coordinating Bd. for Higher Edn. State of Mo., 1982—. Mem. Nat. Soc. Arts and Letters, Wellesley Coll. Alumnae Assn. (sec., dir. 1958-61). Club: Wellesley Coll. (pres. 1965-67). Home: 10 Overbrook Dr St Louis MO 63124

CHAPMAN, HOPE HORAN, psychologist; b. Chgo., Feb. 13, 1954; d. Theodore George and Idelle (Poll) H.; m. Stuart G. Chapman, Dec. 4, 1983. B.S. (Ill. State scholar), U. Ill., Champaign-Urbana, 1976; M.A. (research and teaching asst.), No. Ill. U., 1979. Recreational therapist Evanston (Ill.) Ridgeview Shelter Care Home, summer 1976; psychologist Glenwood (Iowa) State Hosp. Sch., 1979-83, Gov. Samuel Shapiro Devel. Ctr., 1985—; cons. Clarinda (Iowa) Mental Health Inst., 1980-83. Active Omaha Symphonic Chorus, 1981-83; mem. Omaha Public Schs. Citizens Adv. Com., 1980-81; mem. edn. com. Anti-Defamation League, 1980-84, chmn. com. anti-Semitism and Jewish youth, 1981-84. Mem. Am. Psychol. Assn., Am. Assn. Mental Deficiency, Midwest Psychol. Assn., Assn. Mental Health Affiliation with Israel. Phi Kappa Phi, Psi Chi. Jewish. Contbr. papers to profl. confs., jours.

CHAPMAN, JANICE CAROL, nursing educator; b. Wichita, Kans., June 4, 1952; d. Carl Eugene Sr. and Hazel Nadine (Luster) Headley; m. William Frank Chapman, Jr., July 9, 1976; children—Franklin Andrew, Jessica Pearl. Diploma in Nursing, Wesley Sch. Nursing, Wichita, Kans., 1973; B.S. in Nursing, Pittsburg State U., Kans., 1981; M.S. in Nursing, Wichita State U., 1986. R.N., Kans. Relief supr., charge nurse Labette County Med. Ctr., Parsons, Kans., 1977-78; from clinic nurse to asst. dir. Katy Meml. Hosp., Parsons, 1978-83; nursing instr. Labette Community Coll., Parsons, 1983—. Served to lt (j.g.) USN, 1973-76. Mem. Am. Nurses Assn., Kans. State Nurses Assn., NEA, Am. Diabetic Assn. (sec. 1980—). Democrat. Baptist. Avocations: sewing, sports, farming, gardening, bowling. Home: Route 1 Box 148 Mound Valley KS 67354 Office: Labette Community Coll 200 S 14th St Parsons KS 67357

CHAPMAN, JO ANN HOOVER, court administrator, consultant; b. El Paso, Tex., July 31, 1943; d. William Wesley Hoover and Edna (Wynans) Murdoch; div.; children—Jason Teague, William Justin. B.A., Tex. Western Coll., 1964; postgrad. U. Tex.-Austin, 1964-66, U. Tex.-El Paso, 1968-69. Cert. adminstr. in juvenile justice. French tchr. Austin Ind. Sch. Dist., 1966-67; tchr. modern dance, French, Spanish, El Paso Ind. Sch. Dist., Tex., 1968-70; project coordinator part time El Paso Drug Central, 1974; ct. adminstr. 327th Family Dist. Ct., El Paso, 1976-86; cons. Norfolk Juvenile Ct., Va., 1985. Author handbook; contbr. to profl. jour. Bd. Child Crisis Ctr. Nursery, El Paso, 1985-86; mem. U. Tex., El Paso, Profl. Women's Network, El Paso Commn. for Women. Recipient Outstanding Vol. award, Jr. League El Paso, 1972, Appreciation award, Miwanis Club of El Paso-NE, 1981; nominated Reach award, Young Women's Christian Assn., El Paso, 1981. Mem. Am. Bus. Women's Assn., Nat. Juvenile Ct. Services Assn. (v.p. 1983-85, faculty 1980—),

Nat. Council Juvenile and Family Ct. Judges (faculty 1980—), Tex. Coalition on Juvenile Justice (bd. 1985-86, faculty 1980—), W. Tex. Council Govts. (criminal adv. com. 1983—). Presbyterian. Club: Jr. League of El Paso (bd. 1971—). Avocations: Snow skiing; tennis; aerobics. Home: 8701 E Spanish Barb Trail Scottsdale AZ 85258

CHAPMAN, MARGARET (MARDI) ELLEN, telecommunications engineer; b. Port Huron, Mich., Feb. 5, 1943; d. Donald James and Margaret Helen (Wohlberg) Black; m. John Patrick Chapman, June 17, 1970 (div. Sept. 1980); 1 son, John Patrick III. B.S. in Edn., No. Mich. U., 1965; postgrad. Wayne State U., 1969, Eastern Mich. U., 1969-70, 84. Elem. tchr. Govt. Guam, Marianas Islands, 1966-68, pub. schs., Dearborn Heights, Mich., 1968-70, Omaha, 1970, Milw., 1976-78; regional dir. Conway Diet Inst., Milw., 1979-80; customer coordinator Nat. Telecom, Milw., 1980-81; ops. coordinator Gen. Dynamics, Oak Park, Mich., 1981-82; telecommunications engr. Auto Club Mich., Dearborn, 1982-84; telecommunications implementation project mgr. Electronic Data Systems, Southfield, Mich., 1985—; mem. ad hoc telecom com. Washtenaw Community Coll., Ypsilanti, Mich., 1983-85. Mem. Greater Detroit C. of C. (mktg. vol. 1983), Internat. Orgn. Women in Telecommunications (founder local chpt. 1981, pres. chpt. 1981-83, nat. bd. dirs. 1983—), Nat. Assn. Female Execs., Armed Forces Communications and Electronics Assn. (bd. dirs. 1986—). Club: GM Ski (Troy, Mich.). Home: 30072 Spring River Southfield MI 48076 Office: Electronic Data Systems Box 5121 Southfield MI 48086

CHAPMAN, MAXINE MARY, dance company administrator, choreographer; b. Vineland, N.J., Oct. 12, 1943; d. Max and Marie Louise (Procaccino) Bayuk; m. Philo Webster Chapman, Jr., Sept. 28, 1963; children—Denise Marie, Kimberly, Christopher. Student Trenton State Coll., Cumberland County Coll. Artistic dir. Vineland Regional Dance Co., 1980—. Choreographer (ballets) Nutcracker Ballet, 1976, Coppelia, 1977, Sleeping Beauty, 1982; choreographer, dir. (dance prodn.) An Evening with Gershwin, 1981, Miss Cumberland County Scholarship Pageant, 1975—. N.J. State Council on the Arts choreographic fellow, 1985. Mem. Dance Educators of Am., Nat. Assn. for Regional Ballet, Northeast Regional Ballet Assn. (asst. coordinator 1984—), Beta Sigma Phi (Woman of Yr. 1976-77). Avocations: jigsaw puzzles; boating; fishing; reading; music. Home: 2388 N East Ave Vineland NJ 08360

CHAPMAN, PAULA, non-commissioned army officer, counselor; b. Huntingburg, Ind., Oct. 27, 1950; d. Wilfred Edward and Gladys Virginia (Hall) Lottes; m. Jerry Lowell Jones, Nov. 1965 (div. Oct. 1976); m. Brian Charles Chapman, Oct. 7, 1976; 1 child, Jerrina Loraine. Tech. cert. Ind. Vocat. Tech. Coll., 1973; A.A., U. Md. European Campus, 1980; B.S., St. Thomas Aquinas Coll., 1983; M.S., C.W. Post Coll., L.I. U., 1985. Enlisted U.S. Army, 1973, advanced to staff sgt.-E6, 1982; with Reading and Study Skills Ctr., U.S. Mil. Acad., West Point, N.Y., 1981—, acting dir., 1984-86. Author: Reading Comprehension, 1980; author booklet: Study Skills, 1980. Editor workbook: Rapid Reading, 1981. Vol. Orange County Mental Health Assn., N.Y., 1986—. Decorated Army Achievement medal. Mem. Non-Commd. Officers Assn. (sec. 1985-86), Phi Kappa Phi. Club: Non-Commd. Officers (pres. 1985-86) (West Point). Avocations: raising pedigree poodles; travel; reading. Office: McLeod Young Weir One State Street Plaza New York NY 10004

CHAPMAN, TERRY PAYNE, veterinarian; b. Fairborn, Ohio, Aug. 11, 1956; d. John William and Maxine Ellen (McCullough) Payne; m. Gregory Charles Chapman, May 22, 1982; 1 child, Sarah Nicole. D.V.M., U. Mo., 1980. Veterinarian, Gallaway County Vet. Clinic, Fulton, Mo., 1981-82, Vet. Clinic, Inc., Mexico, Mo., 1982—. Bd. dirs. Audrain Humane Soc., Mexico, Mo., 1983—; active YMCA, 4-H orgn., Mexico. Mem. Am. Vet. Med. Assn., Am. Assn. Equine Practitioners, Mo. Vet. Med. Assn., Mexico Kennel Club; Phi Zeta (hon.), Gamma Sigma Delta (hon.), Phi Eta Sigma. Methodist. Home: Rt 2 Box 401 Mexico MO 65265 Office: Veterinary Clinic Inc Hwy 54E Mexico MO 65265

CHAPPELL, BARBARA KELLY, child welfare consultant; b. Columbia, S.C., Oct. 17, 1940; d. Arthur Lee and Katherine (Martin) Kelly; 1 child, Kelly Katherine. B.A. in English and Edn., U. S.C., 1962, M.S.W., 1974. Tchr. English, Dept. Edn., Honolulu, 1962-65, Alamo Heights High Sch., San Antonio, 1965-67; caseworker Dept. Social Services, Columbia, S.C., 1969-70; supr. Juvenile Placement and Aftercare, Columbia, 1970-72; child welfare cons. Edna McConnell Clark Found., N.Y.C., 1974-75; dir. Children's Foster Care Rev. Bd. System, Columbia, 1975-85; child welfare cons., 1985—; lectr. in field. Contbr. articles to profl. jours. Coordinator Child's Rights to Parents, Columbia, 1970-75. Episcopalian. Home and office: 3215 Girardeau Ave Columbia SC 29204

CHAPPELL, VANESSA AGNES, nurse; b. Jersey City, Jan. 21, 1958; d. Francis James and Agnes Margaret (Hermberg) Chappell. B.S.N., Wagner Coll., 1980; R.N., Holy Name Hosp. Sch. Nursing, 1978. Staff nurse Holy Name Hosp., Teaneck, N.J., 1978-80; staff nurse Christ Hosp., Jersey City, 1980-81; sr. charge nurse and preceptor Point Pleasant div. No. Ocean Hosp. System, N.J., 1982—, alt. rep. to procedure com., 1983—, mem. ednl. adv. com. for nursing, 1985—. Mem. Sigma Theta Tau. Roman Catholic.

CHARATAN, SHIRLEY CLARA real estate broker; b. Bklyn., Jan. 2, 1954; d. Joseph and Pauline (Margulies) C. B.S., B.A. in Psychology and Sociology, Queens Coll.-CUNY, 1975; student Fashion Inst. Textiles, 1975-76. Dietary aide Jewish Inst. for Geriatric Care, L.I., N.Y., 1972-73; med. auditor Interboro Hosp., Bklyn., 1973-74; store mgr. Butter Best Bake Shop, N.Y.C., 1968-74; office mgr. Syntex Fabrics/Kittenplan Assocs., N.Y.C., 1975-77; asst. v.p., br. mgr. Citicorp, N.A., N.Y.C., 1977-85; real estate broker, v.p. TSL Am., N.Y.C., 1985—. Active local politics, 1979-80, Lower Manhattan Region United Way, 1983; bd. dirs. Abraham Kazan Health Services Found., 1982—. Recipient Ptnr. in Edn. award N.Y.C. Pub. Schs., 1982-83, Friend of Distinction award Henry St. Settlement, N.Y.C., 1982-83; guest of honor Big Apple Health Fair, N.Y.C., 1983. Mem. Eastside C. of C. (bd. dirs., v.p. 1981—, chairperson ann. dinner 1984, co-chairperson ann. dinner 1986). Avocations: swimming, dancing, writing, community services, music. Home: 82-67 Austin St Apt 216 Kew Gardens NY 11415 Office: 29 E 10th St New York NY 10003

CHARBONNEAU, RHONA MAE, state legislator; b. Lowell, Mass., Feb. 20, 1928; d. Daniel Francis and Harriette (LaSalle) Shay; m. Claude Maurice Charbonneau, 1950; children—Claudia Charbonneau Dodds, Rhona Charbonneau Wollenhaupt, Richard, Mark, Alida. Ed. U. Lowell. Pres. Car Develop Corp., 1977—; sec. Continental Acad. Hair Design, Inc., 1981—, also dir.; mem. N.H. Ho. of Reps., 1982-84, N.H. Senate, 1984—. Mem. Hudson County Budget Com., N.H., 1983-85; trustee Hudson Library, 1984-85. Named Disting. Woman Leader, Nashua (N.H.) YWCA, 1985. Mem. Daus. Union Vets. Civil War (pres. 1949), Nat. Hairdressers and Cosmetologists Assn., N.H. Hairdressers and Cosmetologists Assn. (2d v.p. 1982-83), Hudson C. of C. (bd. dirs.). Republican. Lodge: Lionesses. Office: NH Senate State Capitol Concord NH 03301

CHARDIET, BERNICE KROLL, editor; b. N.Y.C., Nov. 12, 1930; d. Saul and Florence Kroll; B.A., Queens Coll., 1950; M.Ed., Hunter Coll., 1955; m. Oscar Chardiet, June 23, 1957; children—Simon Oscar, Jon Michel. Free lance writer, jazz pianist, rec. artist, 1950-55; tchr. English, DeWitt Clinton High Sch., 1955-59; promotion copywriter, promotion dir., book club editor Scholastic, Inc., N.Y.C., 1963-81, editorial dir., 1981—, producer, dir. Scholastic Records, 1967—; v.p. Scholastic Inc. Recipient award for rec. Jack and the Beanstalk, ALA, 1984. Mem. Author's Guild, Internat. Reading Assn., Nat. Council Tchrs. English, Soc. Children's Book Writers, ASCAP, Internat. Platform Assn., Direct Mail Mktg. Assn., P.E.N., Overseas Press Club. Author: C is for Circus, 1971; Juan BoBo and the Pig, 1973; The Monkeys and the Water Monster, 1974; Rapunzel Retold, 1980. Home: 500 E 77th St New York NY 10021 Office: 730 Broadway New York NY 10003

CHARKEY, CAROLYN LOUISE, newspaper executive; b. Cheyenne, Wyo., Nov. 23, 1939; d. John Frederick and Frances Louise (Riddell) LoSasso; ed. Colo. State U.; m. Norman Alan Charkey, Feb. 22, 1959 (dec. Sept. 1979); children—Mark Alan, Martin Todd. Freelance writer, public relations cons., 1958—; continuity dir. Sta. KCOL, Ft. Collins, 1964-65; reading tutor Ft. Collins Public Schs., 1965-69; owner, mgr. Carolyn's Interiors, Ft. Collins and Cheyenne, Wyo., 1970-77; sect. editor Wyo. Eagle, Cheyenne, 1972-74; info. officer State of Wyo., Cheyenne, 1974-77; dir. public relations programs Coors Distbg. Co., Tustin, Calif., 1978-82; mgr. community relations The Orange County Register, Santa Ana, 1982—; pres. The Register Charities Inc., 1982—. Bd. dirs. Leukemia Soc. Am. Inc., Orange County Community Relations Council, Indsl. League Orange County, Pacific Symphony, Master Chorale, Chariot Champions; pres. Orange County Sports Hall of Fame. Mem. Orange County C. of C. (dir.), Orange County Press Club, Internat. Assn. Bus. Communicators (accredited), Public Relations Soc. Am., Nat. Fedn. Press Women, So. Calif. Assn. Philanthropies. Republican. Office: 625 N Grand Ave Santa Ana CA 92711

CHARLES, FREDDIE ANN, health care marketing executive; b. La Grange, Tex., Jan. 9, 1943; d. Fred Leslie and Annette (Willman) Wallace; m. John Edward Charles, Dec. 23, 1965; children—Leslie Ann, John Andrew. B.S. in Home Econs., Southwest Tex. State U., 1965. Tchr. home econs. Harlandale Ind. Sch. Dist., San Antonio, 1965-68; computer operator Med. Clinic of Houston, 1972-75, data processing mgr., 1975-77, bus. office mgr., 1977-83, dir. mktg., 1984—; pvt. practice mktg. cons. Network 2000, Houston, 1986—. Mem. Nat. Assn. Female Execs., Meml. Exec. Club, Med. Adminstrs. of Tex., Med. Group Mgmt. Assn., Houston C. of C. (chmn.'s club) 1985-86). Republican. Methodist. Home: 5630 Portal Dr Houston TX 77096 Office: Med Clinic of Houston 1707 Sunset Blvd Houston TX 77005

CHARLES, MARGOT GRATZ, nurse; b. Phila., June 23, 1938; d. Earl Jay and Margaret Greil (Gerstley) Gratz; B.S.N., Cornell U., 1961; m. David Jay Charles, Aug. 29, 1965; children—Daniel Jay, Margery Gratz. Staff nurse Hosp. U. Pa., Phila., 1961-62; head nurse cardiopulmonary renal research unit Einstein No. Div., Phila., 1962-64; instr. Hosp. Sch. Nursing Temple U., 1964-65; part time positions, 1965-72; instr. Miami Dade Community Coll., 1972-74; nurse epidemiologist Coral Reef Gen. Hosp., Miami, Fla., 1974-77; instr. Jackson Meml. Hosp. Sch. Nursing, Miami, 1977-78; nurse epidemiologist Am. Hosp., Miami, 1978-84. Unit leader LWV, 1971-72, tel. chmn. Dade County, 1972; active Boy Scouts, Girl Scouts. Mem. Assn. Practitioners Infection Control (chmn. ways and means Dade County 1977, dir. Dade County chpt. 1982-83), Fla. Practitioners Infection Control (treas. 1981—), Beta Sigma Phi, Republican. Jewish. Home: 7701 Palmetto Ct Miami FL 33156

CHARLES-COBURN, NOEMI M. communications company executive; b. Palito Blanco, Tex., Nov. 6, 1955; d. Lauro Reyes and Stella Jasso (Charles) Nava; m. Steven Meredith Coburn, Jan. 9, 1981 (div. Apr. 1983). Student Trinity U., 1970-72; B.A. in Art and Math., U. Chgo., 1973. Freelance artist, Albuquerque, 1973-75; telephone installer Southwestern Bell Telephone Co., Alice and San Antonio, Tex., 1975-79; sr. engr. Communications Corp. Am., San Antonio, 1979-84, telecommunications cons. to USAF, Dallas, 1982-83; pres. Charles-Coburn & Assocs., Evanston, Ill., 1985—. Mem. Am. Soc. Profl./Exec. Women, Nat. Assn. for Female Execs. Democrat. Roman Catholic. Avocations: artwork, horseback riding, cooking. Home: PO Box 1414 Alice TX 78333 Office: Charles-Coburn & Assocs Inc 1900 Livingston St Evanston IL 60201

CHARLESWORTH, ALDA HESS, insurance agency manager; b. Ilion, N.Y., May 2, 1932; d. Harold Vaughan and Dorothy Mary (Dockstader) Hess; m. Edward Clay Page, Mar. 29, 1959 (div. 1967); children—Susan Leigh Terry, Lauren LeRoy Page. Sec. Chgo. Pneumatic Tool Co., Utica, N.Y., 1949-50, Gen. Electric Co., Utica, 1950-51; gen. office worker Peninsula Motor Club, Bradenton, Fla., 1957-60; gen. office worker Auto Club Utah, Ogden, 1962-64, mgr. Auto Club Ins. Agy., Salt Lake City, 1966—. Sec./treas. local dist. Republican party, Magna, Utah, 1980; sec. Central Ch. of Nazarene, Salt Lake City, 1981-83; bd. dirs. Alpha Omega Christian Sch., Salt Lake City, 1981-83. Mem. Ins. Women Salt Lake City (pres. 1976-78, Ins. Woman of Yr. 1977, 81), Ind. Ins. Agts. (dir. 1981-83), Profl. Ins. Agts., Nat. Assn. Ins. Women (regional legis. chmn. 1976-77, Regional Legis. award 1977, regional dir. region VIII 1980-81, You Make The Difference award 1977). Office: Auto Club Ins Agy Inc 560 E 500 S Salt Lake City UT 84102

CHARLTON, BETTY JO, state legislator; b. Reno County, Kans., June 15, 1923; d. Joseph and Elma (Johnson) Canning; B.A., U. Kans., 1970, M.A., 1976; m. Robert Sansom Charlton, Feb. 24, 1946; children—John Robert, Richard Bruce. Asst. instr. U. Kans., Lawrence, 1970-73; legis. adminstrv. services employee State of Kans., Topeka, 1977-78, legis. aide gov's. office, 1979; mem. Kans. Ho. of Reps., 1980—.

CHARLTON, MARGARET ELLEN JONSSON, civic worker; b. Dallas, Aug. 7, 1938; d. John Erik and Margaret Elizabeth (Fonde) Jonsson; student Skidmore Coll., 1956-57, So. Meth. U., 1957-60; m. George Volk Charlton, Jan. 23, 1960; children—Laura, Emily, Erik. Dir. KRLD radio, Dallas, 1970-74; 1st woman dir. First Nat. Bank Dallas, 1976-85, also vice-chmn. trust com. First woman trustee Meth. Hosp., 1972-83, mem. exec. com., 1977-81, mem. corp. bd., 1981-83; bd. dirs., chmn. exec. com. Lamplighter Sch., 1967—; bd. dirs. Winston Sch., 1973-84; bd. dirs., exec. com. Episcopal Sch. Dallas, 1976-83; mem. vis. com. Stanford U. Libraries, 1984—; bd. dirs. Found. for Callier Center for Communications Disorders, 1967—, v.p., 1974-85; mem. vis. com. dept. psychology M.I.T., 1978-84; past chmn. Crystal Charity Ball; bd. dirs. Susan G. Komen Found., 1983—; pres. The Jonsson Found.; past bd. dirs. Children's Med. Center, Hope Cottage, Children's Bur., Baylor Dental Sch., Dallas Health and Sci. Mus., Dallas YWCA, Dallas Day Nursery Assn. Margaret Jonsson Charlton Hosp. named in her honor, Dallas, 1973. Republican. Clubs: Dallas Woman's, University (bd. dirs.).

CHARLTON, MARJORIE BEVERLY, government official; b. Elgin, Ill., Feb. 27, 1925; d. Donald and Pauline (Hagelow) Beverly; B.S., Miami U., Oxford, Ohio, 1948; student U. Dubuque, 1942-43, Wright State U., 1959-60, 81, Air Force Inst., 1965—; m. Thomas E. Charlton, Dec. 15, 1961; 1 dau., Catherine; children from previous marriage—Lawrence Landaker, Peter Landaker; stepchildren—Russell, Carol, Bruce, Elizabeth. Advt. asst. McGraw Electric Co., Elgin, Ill., 1948-49; research asst. Ohio State U., 1950-52; With USAF, Ohio, 1960—; supervisory contract negotiator, 1967—. Bd. dirs. Buckeye Cabinets Inc., 1975—; v.p. Xenia Area Human Relations Council, 1970-73. Recipient spl. achievement and outstanding performance awards, USAF, Mem. Nat. Contract Mgmt. Assn., AAUW, Nat. Assn. Female Execs., DAR, Pi Beta Phi. Democrat. Presbyterian. Home: 425 Winding Trail Xenia OH 45385

CHARNEY, NANCY ELENA, chiropractor; b. Atlantic City, Oct. 29, 1951; d. Robert Rueben and Minnette (Sherman) C. B.S., U. Miami (Fla.), 1971; Dr.Chiropractic, Palmer Coll. Chiropractic, 1974. Gen. practice chiropractic medicine, Lafayette, Calif., 1974-76, Charney Chiropractic Office, Glendale, Calif., 1976-80; sr. mem. Charney Chiropractic Clinic, San Francisco, 1981—; dir. Los Angeles Coll. Chiropractic El Monte Clinic, 1979; asst. prof. Cleve. Coll. Chiropractic, 1980, chiropractic cons., 1980—. Diplomate Nat. Bd. Chiropractic Examiners. Recipient award in recognition of outstanding service to community, 1977-78; named Dr. of Yr. Mem. Calif. Chiropractic Assn., Am. Chiropractic Assn., Internat. Chiropractic Assn., San Francisco C. of C., Verdugo Hills Chiropractic Soc. (pres. 1979-80). Club: Bay Area Career Women. Lodge: Soroptimists (Glendale). Office: 4444 Geary Blvd San Francisco CA 94118

CHAROF, EILEEN JOAN, personnel services executive; b. Bronx, N.Y., July 2, 1947; d. Robert Gerard and Rosalie Fortuna (Nasta) Stickley; B.A. in Psychology, St. John's U., 1969; m. Alan I. Charof, Nov. 15, 1969. Regional adminstr. Am. Sign and Indicator Corp., N.Y.C., 1970-72; dir. adminstrn. Direct Mail Mktg. Assn., N.Y.C., 1972-74; mgr. Allied Temporary Service, N.Y.C., 1974-78; nat. ops. mgr. Temp Force, East Meadow, N.Y., 1978-80; v.p. Cyberway, N.Y.C., 1980-82; owner, pres. Astra Inc., 1983—. Mem., Nat. Assn. Temporary Services, Internat. Word Processing Assn. Office: 60 E 42d St New York NY 10165

CHARREN, GABRIELLE, dental technologist; b. Berlin, Germany, Nov. 15, 1937; came to U.S., 1959, naturalized, 1965; d. Hans Manfred and Margot (Kaufmann) Purucker; Masters degree cum laude in Dental Tech., Berufschule Hannover, W. Ger., 1959; postgrad., U. Madrid, 1970-71; 1 dau., Stefanie. Head ceramist Beverly Dental Ceramics, Beverly Hills, Calif., 1959-64; dept. mgr. Wolfsen Dental Lab., Los Angeles, 1964-66, Park Dental Lab., Inglewood, Calif., 1966-68; art. mgr., rep. artists J. Zuniga, Manolo, Coronado, Mallorca, Spain, 1968-70; disc jockey 3-lang. radio show, Mallorca, 1971-72; owner Oak Grove Dental Lab., Palo Alto, Calif., 1975-79; mgr. Capital City Dental Lab., Sacramento, 1980-81; owner Novadent Ceramics, Sacramento; condr. clinics in ceramic staining and anatomy. Pres., Parent Council, Keys Family Day Sch., Palo Alto, 1976-78; v.p. Parent Council Waldorf Sch., Sacramento, 1981—. Cert. dental technician, 1977. Mem. Nat. Assn. Dental Labs., Calif. Acad. for Dental Research and Edn., Calif. Dental Lab. Assts. (component pres. Sacramento 1983-84), Nat. Assn. Female Execs. Republican. Club: Arden Hills Swim and Tennis (Sacramento). Contbr. daily column Who's Who Daily Bull., English lang. newspaper, Mallorca, 1971-72; guest contbr. Spanish newspapers: Dairio Mallorca, Balleares, 1971-79. Home: 921 Castec Dr Sacramento CA 95825 Office: Novadent Ceramics 577 Arden Town Ct Sacramento CA 95825

CHARRON, ESTELLE IRMA, religious association executive; b. Duluth, Minn., Nov. 17, 1928; d. Harold Frederick and Amy Estelle (Hill) C. B.S. in Med. Tech., Marquette U., 1958; M.S. in Adminstrn., U. Notre Dame, 1984. Med. technologist Oconomowoc Meml. Hosp., Wis., 1962-69; mgr. printshop Coll. St. Scholastica, Duluth, Minn., 1973-74, mgr. bookstore, 1974-81; treas. Benedictine Sisters Benevolent Assn., Duluth, 1981—. Trustee St. Mary's Hosp., Duluth, 1981-87. Mem. Nat. Assn. Treasurers Religious Insts., Conf. Religious Treasurers. Roman Catholic. Avocations: backpacking; canoeing; scuba; painting. Home: St Scholastica Priory 1200 Kenwood Ave Duluth MN 55811

CHARTIER, JANELLEN OLSEN, airline inflight service coordinator; b. Chgo., Sept. 12, 1951; d. Roger Carl and Genevieve Ann (McCormick) Olsen; m. Lionel Pierre-Paul Chartier, Nov. 6, 1982. B.A. in French and Home Econs., U. Ill., 1973, M.A. in Teaching French, 1974; student U. Rouen (France), 1971-72. Cert. tchr., Ill. Flight attendant Delta Airlines, Atlanta, 1974—, French qualified, 1974—, Spanish qualified, 1977-82, German qualified, 1980—, in flight service coordinator, 1980—, European in flight service coordinator, 1983—, French examiner in-flight service dept., 1984—; interpreter Formax, Inc., Mokena, Ill., 1976-82. Bd. dirs. One Plus One Dance Co., Champaign, Ill., 1977-78. Mem. Alliance Maison Francaise de Chgo., Phi Delta Kappa, Alpha Lambda Delta. Roman Catholic. Home: 155 N Harbor Dr Apt 4306 Chicago IL 60601 Office: Delta Air Lines Hartsfield Internat Airport Atlanta GA 30320

CHASE, BARBARA LANDIS, educational administrator; b. Hershey, Pa., May 6, 1945; d. Floyd and Ruth (MacGee) Landis; m. David William Chase, June 10, 1967; children—Ashley Lawrence, Katherine Landis. A.B., Brown U., 1967. Tchr. Moses Brown Sch., Providence, 1967-68; tchr. dir. admission Wheeler Sch., Providence, 1973-80; headmistress Bryn Mawr Sch., Balt., 1980—; mem. bd. advisors Carney, Sandoe & Assocs., 1985—. Trustee Brown U., Providence, 1984—; bd. dirs. Balt. Project Black Students and Faculty, pres. bd., 1981-85. Mem. Assn. Ind. Md. Schs. (exec. bd. 1984—, Council women 1982-84), Nat. Assn. Ind. Schs. (admission com. 1981-83, sch. heads adv. com. 1982—, faculty advanced adminstrv. seminar 1985—). Avocations: reading; running; music; gardening. Home: 5613 Boxhill Ln Baltimore MD 21210 Office: Bryn Mawr Sch 109 W Melrose Ave Baltimore MD 21210

CHASE, DORIS TOTTEN, artist; b. Seattle, Apr. 29, 1923; d. William Phelps and Helen Mae (Feeney) Totten; student U. Wash., 1941-42; Ph.D. (hon.), U. Colo., 1974; div.; children—Gregary Totten Chase, Randall Totten Chase. Exhibited one-woman shows: Formes Gallery, Tokyo, 1970, Portland (Oreg.) Art Mus., 1976, 80, Mus. Modern Art, N.Y.C., 1978, 80, Hirschhorn Mus., Washington, 1974, 77, Wadsworth Atheneum, Hartford, Conn., 1973, U. Wash., Seattle, 1971, 78, 81, 82, Erica Williams/Ann Johnson Gallery, Seattle, 1980; represented in permanent collections: Mus. Fine Arts, Boston, Hudson River Mus., Yonkers, N.Y., Milw. Art Mus., Seattle Art Mus., Art Inst. Chgo., Mus. Modern Art, Kobe, Japan, Mus. Fine Arts, Houston, Smithsonian Instn., Washington, Pa. Acad. Fine Arts, Vancouver (Can.) Art Gallery, Nat. Collection Fine Arts, Washington, N.C. Mus. Art, Raleigh; monumental kinetic sculpture commns.: Expo 70, Osaka, Japan, Atlanta Sculpture Park, Kerry Park, Seattle, Lakeside Park, Anderson, Ind., Sculpture in the Park, N.Y.C., Open Eye Theatre, N.Y.C., Playground of Tomorrow, Los Angeles, Sculpture for Dance, Seattle, 1968, 69, Seattle Opera, 1972, Mus. Art, Montgomery, Ala.; guest lectures and presentations: Carpenter Center, Harvard U., 1975, SUNY, Purchase, 1978, UCLA, 1974, 80, 82, San Francisco State U., 1979, Winthrop (N.C.) Coll., 1978, CUNY, Bklyn., 1976, 77, 78, 84, N.Y. U., 1977, Fordham U., 1976, U. Cin., 1978, Sarah Lawrence Coll., 1977, U. Mich., 1977, 79, New Sch. Social Research, N.Y.C., 1979, Calif. Inst. Arts, 1976, 80, 82, MIT, 1976, Seattle Art Mus., 1972, 77, Lincoln Center Performing Arts Mus., N.Y.C., 1977, Brit. Film Inst., Cornell U., 1982, Steddeljck Mus., Amsterdam, 1982, Rutgers U., 1984; producer/dir. films and video including Table for One, 1984. Recipient awards, Mannheim, Ger., 1975, U. Mich., 1977, 78, 80, Ithaca, N.Y., 1978, 80, Chgo., 1977, 80, Bellevue, Wash., 1976, 77, 78, 80, Cannes, France, 1976, Deauville, France, Santa Clara, Calif., Northwestern U., Lille, France, N.Y. Film Festival, 1979, Am. Film Festival, N.Y.C., 1980, Doris Chase Dance Series, 1970-80, Doris Chase Concepts, 1980-83, Filmex, Los Angeles, 1981, numerous others. Mem. Women Artist Filmmakers, Whitney Mus., Mus. Modern Art, N.Y. Film Council, Assn. Ind. Video and Film. Home: 222 W 23d St New York NY 10011

CHASE, ELAINE RACO, author; b. Schenectady, Aug. 31, 1949; d. Ernest Salvatore and Helen Nancy (Scavia) Raco; m. Gary Dale Chase, Oct. 26, 1969; children—Marlayna, G. Marc II. Sec. Narcotic Addiction Control Commn., Albany, 1967-68; with WRGB-TV, Schenectady, 1968-70; copywriter Beckman Advt., Albany, 1970-72; tchr. creative writing, Casements Cultural Ctr., Ormond Beach, Fla., 1980-84; speaker, lectrs. Author: Rules of the Game, 1980; Tender Yearnings, 1981; A Dream Come True, 1982; Double Occupancy, 1982; Designing Woman, 1982; No Easy Way Out, 1982; Video Vixen, 1983; Best Laid Plans, 1983; Calculated Risk, 1983; Lady Be Bad, 1984; Special Delivery, 1984; Off the Wall; Eye of the Beholder, 1986. Mem. Romance Writers Am. (pres. Fla. chpt. 1980-84), Mystery Writers Am. Roman Catholic.

CHASE, JOYCE ELAINE, accountant, insurance company executive; b. Benton Harbor, Mich., Dec. 4, 1931; d. Richard I. and Evelyn Pauline (Hahn) Winney; student Mich. State Ins. Sch., 1974; grad. Sch. Nursing, Lake Mich. Coll., 1986; m. Ernest Arthur Chase, July 21, 1951; children—Ernest L., Arthur M., Robert J., William R., James R. Clk. Gillespie's Drug Store, Benton Harbor, 1945, WoolWorth's Store, Benton Harbor, 1946-47; bookkeeper Reeder's Bookkeeping Service, Benton Harbor, 1949; assembler VM Corp., Benton Harbor, 1950; telephone operator Mich. Bell Co., Benton Harbor, 1951; bookkeeper I & M Electric Co., Buchanan, Mich., 1952, Auto Specialties Co., St. Joseph, Mich., 1953; clk. Galien Drug Store, Galien, Mich., 1955; assembler Electro-Voice Corp., Buchanan, Mich., 1958-62; bookkeeper Chase Bookkeeping & Tax Service, Galien, Mich., 1963-67, sr. tax accountant, 1968—; ins. agt. Chase Ins. Service Center, Galien, Mich., 1974—; emergency med. technician and ambulance driver Galien Vol. Ambulance Service, 1974—. Cub. Scout den mother S.W. Mich. council Cub. Scouts Am., 1963-69; mem. Galien Twp. election bd., 1971-73; mem. Galien Sch. Election Bd., 1971—; pres. Galien Athletic Boosters, 1969; mem. Galien High Sch., PTA, 1966—, adv. com., 1965-68. Mem. Nat. Soc. Pub. Accountants, Mich. Emergency Services Health Council, Am. Legion Aux. Republican. Methodist. Home: US Route 12 East at Garwood Lake Galien MI 49113 Office: 112 N Main St Galien MI 49113

CHASE, LINDA JOANN, lawyer; b. Bklyn., July 1, 1948; d. Richard George and Jeannette (Mogilnicki) C.; m. Warren F. Luther, Oct. 6, 1973 (dec. 1977). B.A., SUNY-Albany, 1969; J.D., Fordham U., 1982. Bar: N.Y. 1983, U.S. Dist. Ct. (so. and ea. dists.) N.Y. 1983. Tchr., St. Kevin's Sch., Flushing, N.Y., 1970-73; program asst. Young Pres.'s Orgn., Inc., N.Y.C., 1973-75; paraprofl. Paul, Weiss, Rifkind, Wharton & Garrison, N.Y.C., 1976; program dir. Practising Law Inst., N.Y.C., 1977-82; assoc. Chadbourne, Parke, Whiteside & Wolff, N.Y.C., 1982-84, Phelan, Pope & John Ltd., Chgo., 1984—. Recipient U.S. Law award, U.S. Law Week, 1982. Mem. ABA, N.Y. State Bar Assn., Assn. Bar City N.Y., Women's Bar Assn. State of N.Y., N.Y. Women's Bar Assn. (bd. dirs. 1983-84). Democrat. Office: Phelan Pope & John Ltd 180 N Wacker Dr Chicago IL 60606

CHASE, LINDA KATHRYN, lawyer; b. Fredericksburg, Tex., Mar. 16, 1953; d. Dewey Lawrence and Vera Faye (Goode) C. B.S. in Chemistry and Biology, Hardin-Simmons U., 1975; M.A. in Biology, Baylor U., 1981, J.D., 1981. Bar: Tex. 1982, U.S. Dist. Ct. (so. dist.) Tex. 1982, U.S. Ct. Appeals (5th cir.) 1982, U.S. Ct. Customs. Sr. chemist Rexene Polyolefins Co., Pasadena, Tex., 1976-78; assoc. Parks and Moss, Houston, 1981-83; atty. Community Title Co., San Antonio, 1983—; sole practice, San Antonio, 1983—. Active San Antonio Home Builders Assn. Aux. Robert Welch Found. scholar in chem. research, 1974-75. Mem. Bexar County Women's Bar Assn., Women in Bus., Delta Theta Phi. Home: 15015 Enchanted Castle San Antonio TX 78247 Office: Community Title Co 2961 Mossrock Suite 208 San Antonio TX 78230

CHASE, LORIENE ECK, psychologist; b. Sacramento; d. Walter and Genevieve (Bennetts) Eck; A.B., U. So. Calif., 1948, M.A., 1949, Ph.D., 1953; m. Leo Goodman-Malamuth, 1946 (div. 1951); 1 son, Leo; m. 2d, Allen Chase, Mar. 4, 1960 (div.); m. 3d, Clifton W. King, 1974. Psychologist, Spastic Children's Found., Los Angeles, 1952-55, Inst. Group Psychotherapy, Beverly Hills, Calif., 1957-59; pvt. practice, 1953—; v.p. VSP Exec. Relocation Cons.; v.p. Chase-King Prodns. Condr., Dr. Loriene Chase Show, ABC-TV, Hollywood, Calif. 1966—; exec. producer Chase-King Prodns. Cons., Camarillo State Hosp.; bd. dirs., pres.'s circle U. So. Calif.; founding mem. Achievement Rewards for Coll. Scientists; bd. dirs. Chase-King Personal Devel. Center, Los Angeles; exec. bd. Cancer Research Center, Los Angeles. Writer syndicated newspaper column Casebook of Dr. Chase. Served with Waves World War II. Recipient Woman of Year in Psychology award Am. Mothers Com. Mem. Diadames, Assn. Media Psychologists, Les Dames de Champagne, Dame de Rotisseur, Nat. Art Assn., AFTRA, Screen Actors Guild, Internat. Platform Assn. Clubs: Regency, Lakeside Country. Author: The Human Miracle; columnist Westways mag. Address: 4925 Tarzana Woods Dr Tarzana CA 91356 also 375 Palomar Shell Beach CA

CHASE, MARY JANE, jewelry executive; b. Glouster, Ohio, July 16, 1938; d. Cecil Nelson and Juanita Marie (Anderson) McCafferty; grad. Andrews Sch., 1957; m. Robert Vincent Chase, Oct. 16, 1971; 1 child, Robert Vincent. Sec. to v.p. accessories div. TRW, Cleve., 1957-63; office mgr. Kaufman & Reynolds Constrn. Co., Sacramento, Calif., 1964-67; asst. to med. staff Roseville (Calif.) Community Hosp., 1967-69; asst. to v.p. ops. Intel Corp., Mountain View, Calif., 1969-70; exec. asst. to pres. Catamore Co., Inc., East Providence, R.I., 1971-74, dir. adminstrn., 1978-81, v.p. adminstrn., 1981-82; market dir. Johnson Matthey Jewelry Corp., East Providence, 1983-84, sr. mgr., 1984; v.p., sec. The Byfield Group, Inc., 1985—. Bd. dirs. Nat. Fedn. Republican Women, 1978-81, mem. nominating com., 1979; alt. del. Rep. Nat. Conv., 1976, 80; bd. dirs. East Providence unit Am. Cancer Soc., 1979-81; mem. Meml. Hosp. Aux., 1978—. Episcopalian. Home: 201 Wilson Ave Rumford RI 02916

CHASE, RENA LYNN, nurse, administrator; b. Saratoga Springs, N.Y., Sept. 29, 1949; d. Robert Francis Miller and June Estell (Schermerhorn) Miller Baumgardner; m. Leonard L. Chase, May 12, 1969 (dec. 1973); 1 child, Leonard W. A.S., Daytona Beach Community Coll., 1977. Nurse asst. Daytona Beach Gen. Hosp., Holly Hill, Fla., 1973-75, lic. practical nurse, 1976-77, staff and surg. R.N., 1977-79, R.N., intensive care unit supr., 1979-80, asst. dir. nurses, 1983—. Mem. Nat. League Nursing. Republican. Avocations: music; organ; swimming. Home: 430 Center St Ormond Beach FL 32074 Office: Daytona Beach Gen Hosp 1340 Ridgewood Ave Holly Hill FL 32074

CHASE, SHARON ELIZABETH, orthopedic research technician; b. New Berlin, N.Y., Sept. 7, 1947; d. Robert Low and Frances Louise (Parker) Chapin; m. Marcelle Edward Chase, Aug. 2, 1980; 1 child, Nicole Louise. Med. tech. diploma Northwest Inst., Mpls., 1966; B.S. in Biology, SUNY-Syracuse, B.S. in Life Scis., 1976. Clin. lab. technician Crouse-Irving Hosp., Syracuse, 1966-68; orthopedic research technician VA Hosp., Syracuse, 1968-81, Upstate Med. Ctr., Syracuse, 1981—. Contbr. articles to profl. jours. Exchange Student honor New Berlin Central Sch., Argentina Sch., 1964; recipient Good Citizenship award DAR, 1965, Bingham award, 1965, Danforth Found. award, 1965. Mem. Cousteau Soc. (founding mem.). Episcopalian. Avocations: walking, planting flowers. Home: 305 Hunt Dr Fayetteville NY 13066 Office: Upstate Med Ctr Dept of Orthopedic Surgery 750 E Adams St Syracuse NY 13210

CHASTANG, LINDA EARLEY, law educator, lawyer; b. Washington, Nov. 6, 1953; d. Charles Edward and LaVerne Cecelia (Mason) Earley; m. Mark J. Chastang, Aug. 30, 1980; children—Mark J., Rebecca. B.A., Sarah Lawrence Coll., 1974; J.D., Howard U., 1978; LL.M., Emory U., 1984. Bar: Fla., D.C. Legal asst. to dir. Inst. for Study of Ednl. Policy, Washington, 1977; asst. atty. gen. antitrust div. Fla. Atty. Gen.'s Office, 1978; atty. FTC, Atlanta, 1978-83; asst. prof. law Ga. State U. Coll. Law, Atlanta, 1982—; procurement appeals hearing officer City of Atlanta, 1984—. Mem. Fulton County Bd. Ethics, 1986—; sec. bd. dirs. Atlanta Neighborhood Housing Services, Inc., 1982-84, liaison mem. minority enrollment task force Law Sch. Admissions Council, 1982—; mem. regional devel. planning Council, Atlanta Regional Commn., 1980-83; mem. Sarah Lawrence Coll. Alumni Recruiters Network, 1978—; trustee Westview Neighborhood Housing Services, Inc., 1982-84. Named to Leadership Ga., 1985, Leadership Atlanta, 1986—. Mem. ABA (sects. antitrust, taxation and ethics), Gate City Bar Assn., Ga. Assn. Black Women Attys. Scholarship Found., Inc., Nat. Bar Assn. Nat. Trust Historic Preservation. Home: 808 Brookridge Dr NE Atlanta GA 30306 Office: Coll Law Ga State U University Plaza Atlanta GA 30303

CHATFIELD, CHERYL ANN, stock brokerage firm executive, writer; b. King's Park, N.Y., Jan. 24, 1946; d. William David and Mildred Ruth (King) C.; m. Gene Allen Chasser, Feb. 17, 1968 (div. 1979); m. James Bernard Arkebauer, Apr. 16, 1983. B.S., Central Conn. Coll., 1968, M.S., 1972; Ph.D., U. Conn., 1976. Cert. gen. prin. securities. Tchr. Bristol East High Sch., Conn., 1968-77; adminstr. New Britain Schs., Conn., 1977-79; prof. Ariz. State U., Phoenix, 1979; stockbroker J. Daniel Bell, Denver, 1980-83, Hyder and Co., Denver, 1983-84; stockbroker, pres. Denari Securities, Denver, 1984—; tchr. investment seminars Front Range Community Coll., Denver, 1984-86. Author: Low-Priced Riches, 1985, newspaper columns: For Women Investors, 1982-84, Commentary, 1985-86. Project bus. cons. Jr. Achievement, Denver, 1986; speaker women's groups, Denver, 1983-86. Mem. Nat. Assn. Female Execs., Aircraft Owners and Pilots Assn., Denver Security Traders Assn., AAUW, Colo. Venture Group (founding), Kappa Delta Pi. Republican. Roman Catholic. Avocation: flying. Office: Denari Securities Inc 1812 Market St Denver CO 80202

CHATFIELD-TAYLOR, ADELE, design administrator, historic preservationist; b. Washington, Jan. 29, 1945; d. Hobart Chatfield-Taylor and Mary Owen (Lyon) C.-T.; m. John Guare, May 20, 1981. B.A., Manhattanville Coll., 1966; M.S. in Historic Preservation, Columbia U., 1974; postgrad. (Loeb fellow), Harvard U., 1978-79. Archtl. historian Historic Am. Bldg. Survey, Washington, 1967; co-founder, dir. Urban Deadline Architects, Inc., 1968-73; landmarks preservation specialist N.Y.C. Landmarks Preservation Commn., 1973-74, asst. to chmn., 1974-79, dir. policy and programs, 1979-80; adj. prof. historic preservation program Grad. Sch. Architecture and Planning, Columbia U., 1976—; exec. dir. N.Y. Landmarks Preservation Found., 1980-84; dir. design arts program Nat. Endowment for Arts, 1984—; asst. dir. Neighborhood Conservation Conf. Nat. Endowment Arts, 1975; bd. dirs. Preservation ACTION, 1976-84, regional v.p., 1978-83, sec., 1983-84; trustee Ctr. for Bldg. Conservation, 1978-84; mem. U.S. del. to China, Women in Architecture, 1977, 80, U.S. del. to China, Historic Preservationists, 1982; mem. exec. com. U.S./Internat. Council on Monuments and Sites, 1979-84; mem. China adv. com. Nat. Endowment Arts, 1980—, vice chmn. design arts policy panel, 1978-82; bd. dirs. Nat. Alliance of Preservation Commns., 1983-84; trustee Tiber Island History Mus., 1983—; guest lectr. Harvard U., Mass. Inst. Tech., Columbia U., NYU, U. Va. Contbr. articles to profl. jours. Mem. restoration com. South Street Seaport Mus., 1975-84; mem. Nat. Com. on U.S.-China Relations, 1982—; mem. lawn adv. bd. U. Va., 1982-86; bd. dirs. Greenwich Village Trust for Historic Preservation, 1983-84. Archtl. fellow Ednl. Facilities Lab Acad. Ednl. Devel., 1982-83; Rome prize Am. Acad. in Rome, 1983-84; fellow N.Y. Inst. Humanities, 1983—. Mem. Archtl. League, Nat. Trust Historic Preservation, Friends of Cast Iron Architecture, Preservation League N.Y. State, Met. Mus. Art, Vernacular Architecture Soc., Decorative Arts Soc., Nat. Council of Preservation Execs. Office: Design Arts Program Nat Endowment for Arts 1100 Pennsylvania Ave NW Washington DC 20506

CHATWOOD, CONSTANCE JEAN, lawyer; b. Peoria, Ill., Sept. 26, 1953; d. Thomas Fletcher Chatwood and Arvilla Rose (Rakestraw) McGuire; m. Michael Bruce Hull, Sept. 3, 1983. B.A. summa cum laude, U. Nebr.-Omaha, 1974; J.D. magna cum laude, Creighton U., 1978. Bar: Nebr. 1978, D.C. 1979, U.S. Ct. Appeals (D.C. cir.) 1979, U.S. Supreme Ct. 1983. Tchr. secondary schs. Omaha Pub. Schs., 1975; law clk. Fitzgerald, Brown, Leahy, Strom, Schorr & Barmettler, Omaha, 1976, Kutak Rock & Huie, Omaha, 1977, 78; jud. clk. U.S. Ct. Appeals D.C. Cir., 1978-79; assoc. Covington & Burling, Washington, 1979—. Editor-in-chief Creighton Law Rev., 1977-78. Mem. ABA, D.C. Bar Assn., Alpha Lambda Delta, Phi Kappa Phi, Alpha Sigma Nu. Democrat. Roman Catholic. Office: Covington & Burling PO Box 7566 1201 Pennsylvania Ave Washington DC 20044

CHAVERS, RUBY MARGARETT, retail store administrator; b. Russellville, Ala., Nov. 21, 1956; d. Charlie Houston and Pauline (Hubbard) Nelson; m. John Willie Chavers, Jr., June 6, 1981; 1 child, Shannon Helene. B.S. in Acctg., Ala. A&M U., 1979. Internal auditor Cargill, Inc., Mpls., 1979-81, asst. acctg. mgr., 1981-82; internal auditor Target Stores, Mpls., 1982-84, cash mgr., 1984—. Mem. Twin Cities Cash Mgmt. Assn., Nat. Corp. Cash Mgmt. Assn., Inst. Internal Auditors, Nat. Assn. Black Accts., Nat. Assn. Female Execs., Delta Sigma Theta. Home: 3486 Pilgrim Ln N Plymouth MN 55441

CHAVEZ, CHRISTINA LINDA GARCIA, lawyer, state official; b. El Paso, Tex., Mar. 6, 1953; d. Raymond D. and Emma M. (Garcia) C. B.A., N.Mex. State U., 1975; J.D., Cath. U. Am., 1978. Bar: N.Mex. 1978, U.S. Dist. Ct. (N.Mex. dist.) 1978, U.S. Ct. Appeals (10th cir.) 1978. Equal employment opportunity specialist trainee Office Human Rights OEO, 1972-73; govt. intern equal employment div. N.Mex. State Planning Office, 1974; tutor, counselor Spl. Student Services, N.Mex. State U., 1973-75; summer intern The White House, Exec. Office of Pres., Washington, 1975, Dept. Labor, 1976; legal intern AYUDA para el Consumidor, Washington, 1977, Senator Pete Domenici, N.Mex., 1977; law clk. Dept. Labor, 1978; law clk., N.Mex. Supreme Ct., 1978-79; ptnr. Mitchell, Alley & Rubin, Santa Fe, 1979-83; supt. State N.Mex. Regulation and Licensing Dept., Santa Fe, 1983—. Trustee No. N.Mex. Legal Services, Santa Fe, 1980-81, St. Vincent's Hosp. Bd., Santa Fe, SP 1982-83, Santa Fe Group Homes, Inc., 1982-83; mem. N.Mex. Women's Polit. Caucus, 1975—. Recipient Spl. Achievement and Merit award Dept. of Labor, 1976; named Student of Yr., N.Mex. State U., 1975; Woman in 80's, N.Mex. Women's Polit. Caucus, 1980, other honors. Mem. Internat. Fedn. Women Lawyers, NOW, Mexican Am. Women Nat. Assn., N.Mex. Bar Assn. (mem. young lawyers div., women's legal rights sect.), First Judicial Dist. Bar Assn. (pres. 1984). Democrat. Roman Catholic. Office: Regulation and Licensing Dept Bataan Meml Bldg Santa Fe NM 87504

CHAVEZ, GRACIELA LECUBE, actress, writer; b. Buenos Aires, Argentina, Feb. 1, 1925; came to U.S., 1951; d. Mauricio and Maria Ana (Schmuckler) Wilensky; m. Eduardo P. Chavez, May 23, 1951; 1 child, Delfin E. Grad. Conservatorio Bellas Artes, 1941. Women's editor Hablemos Mag., Latin Am. countries, 1953-59; copywriter Avon Products, Inc., N.Y.C. for Latin Am. and Spain, 1959-85, copywriter cons., 1985—; Appeared in movies, stage plays, on radio, Buenos Aires, 1942-50. Author: For Editorial Concepts, 1986. Translator book and med. bull. Contbr. articles to mags. Recipient Best Actress awards, 1949, 50, 79, 80. Mem. Screen Actors Guild, Actors Equity Assn., AFTRA, Hispanic Orgn. Latin Actors. Home: 765 Riverside Dr 3-J New York NY 10032

CHAVEZ, LINDA, government official; b. Albuquerque, N.Mex., June 17, 1947; married; 3 children. B.A., U. Colo., 1970; postgrad. UCLA, 1970-72, U. Md., 1974-75. Mem. staff House Judiciary Subcom. on Civil and Constl. Rights, Washington, 1972-74; cons. civil rights sect. Office Mgmt. and Budget, Washington, 1977; editor Am. Educator mag., 1977-83; staff dir. U.S. Civil Rights Commn., 1983-85; dep. asst. to pres. and dir. Office Pub. Liaison, Exec. Office of Pres., 1985—. Office: Exec Office of the Pres Dept Communications 1600 Pennsylvania Ave NW Washington DC 20500*

CHAVEZ-SICHLER, PATRICIA JUNE, account development executive; b. Grants, N.Mex., Mar. 28, 1934; d. Joseph Epifanio and Mildred Elizabeth (Stull) Chavez; m. Terrance C. Newman, Mar. 4, 1953 (div. 1964); children—Robin Newman Langeliers, Laura Newman Smulktis; m. Ernest Frederick Sichler, Apr. 7, 1984. B.A., Ariz. State U., 1956; postgrad. Santa Fe Coll., 1986—. Project mgr. Carter Hawley Hale, Los Angeles, 1971-73; exec. Career Data, Los Angeles, 1973-75; systems analyst World Vision Inc., Monrovia, Calif., 1975-77, dir. vol. programs, 1977-79, mng. dir. World Vision Scandinavia, Stockholm, 1979-82, acct. devel. exec. World Vision Inc., 1982—; dir. Recovery Workshops, Los Lunas, N.Mex., 1979—; cons. PCS, Los Lunas, 1984—. Author: Picking Up the Pieces, 1980; (one-act play) Four Me; contbr. articles to profl. pubs. Mem. Nat. Assn. Female Execs., Data Processing Mgrs. Assn. Democrat. Lutheran. Avocations: music; tennis; horticulture. Home: 227 Sichler Dr Los Lunas NM 87031 Office: World Vision Inc 919 Huntington Dr Monrovia CA 91016

CHAVOOSHIAN, MARGE, artist, educator; b. N.Y.C., Jan. 8, 1925; d. Harry Mesrob and Anna (Tashjian) Kurkjian; m. Barkev Budd Chavooshian, Aug. 11, 1946; children—J. Dean, Nora Ann. Student Art Students League, 1943, Reginald Marsh, N.Y.C., 1943, Mario Cooper, N.Y.C., 1977. Designer Needlework Arts Co., N.Y.C., 1943-44; illustrator John David Men's Store, N.Y.C., 1944-45; illustrator, layout artist Fawcett Publs., N.Y.C., 1945-47; designer, illustrator Pa. State U., University Park, 1947-49; art tchr. Trenton pub. schs., N.J., 1958-68, art cons. Title One Program, 1968-74; painting instr. Princeton Art Assn., N.J., 1974-77, Jewish Community Ctr., Ewing, N.J., 1974-85, Contemporary Club, Trenton, 1974-85, YMCA, YWCA, Trent Ctr., Trenton, 1974—; artist-at-large Alliance For Arts Edn., N.J., 1979-80; adj. asst. prof. art instr. Mercer County Coll., West Windsor, N.J., 1985—. One woman shows include Rider Coll., 1974, Jersey City Mus., 1980, N.J. State Mus., 1981, Trenton City Mus., 1984; exhibited in group shows at Douglas Coll., N.J., 1977, Bergen Mus., Paramus, N.J., 1980, 81, 82, Hunterdon Art Ctr., Clinton, N.J., 1982, Morris Mus., Morristown, N.J., 1984, Oakside Cultural Ctr., Bloomfield, N.J., 1985; represented in permanent collections N.J. State Mus., Jersey City Mus., Trenton City Mus., Morris Mus., Rider Coll., Art Mus. San Lazarre, Italy. Recipient numerous awards Union Coll., Mercer County Cultural and Heritage Commn., Phillips Mill, Am. Watercolor Soc.; named Woman of Month Woman's Newspaper of Princeton, 1984. N.J. State Council Arts fellow, 1979. Mem. Nat. Assn. Women Artists (two yr. nat. travel award 1985), Am. Artists Profl. League (Am. Arts Council award 1973, Winsor Newton award 1980, others), Catherine Lorillard Wolfe Art Club (Bee Paper Co. award 1977, Anna Hyatt Huntington Bronze medal 1979), N.J. Watercolor Soc. (Newton Art Ctr. award 1972, Helen K. Bermel award 1984), Painters and Sculptors Soc. (Medal of Honor, Digby Chandler medal, others), Garden State Watercolor Soc. (Triangle Art Ctr. award 1976, Grumbacher Silver medal 1981, Merit award 1982), Midwest Watercolor Soc. Democrat. Mem. Apostolic Ch. Avocations: Piano; cooking; gardening. Home: 222 Morningside Dr Trenton NJ 08618

CHAWLA, GLORIA LYLES, information specialist; b. Shreveport, La., Feb. 6, 1946; d. Wilmer Merritt and Rose Lee (Sherman) Lyles; m. Manmohan Singh Chawla, Mar. 29, 1969; children—Andrew Lyle, Julie Christina. B.A. in History, La. State U.-Baton Rouge, 1969, M.A.L.S., 1970. Head librarian Brevard Community Coll., Melbourne, Fla., 1970-72; ref. librarian Carlsbad Library, Calif., 1972-73; head librarian Vista Library, Calif., 1973-75; info. specialist Houston, 1976—; pres. Bus. Research Services, 1981-84; info. specialist Rice U. Library, 1984—. La. State U. library grad. asistantship, 1969-70. Mem. ALA, Spl. Libraries Assn., Houston On-Line Users Group. Roman Catholic. Home: 3921 Bissonnet Houston TX 77005 Office: RICE Fondren Library Rice Univ PO Box 1892 Houston TX 77251-1892

CHEAIRS, CLAUDIA DENISE, data processing company official; b. Hamtramck, Mich., Apr. 21, 1951; d. Sidney Minrose and Rosa Eileen (McKinney) Jones; B.S., Mich. State U., East Lansing, 1973; m. John W. Cheairs, Sept. 15, 1979; children—Gianna Denise, Camille Dionne. With IBM Corp., Detroit, 1973—, staff asst., 1977-78, adminstrn. ops. mgr., 1978—; cons. in field. Mem. Brazeal Dennard Chorale, 1978—. Democrat. Methodist. Home: 14059 Grandmont St Detroit MI 48227 Office: 27800 Northwestern Hwy Southfield MI 48039

CHEATUM, BILLYE ANN, educator; b. Oklahoma City, Jan. 27, 1933; d. Leon Thomas and Agnes Mabel Cheatum, B.S., Okla. Coll. for Women, 1955; M.S., Smith Coll., 1957; Ph.D., Tex. Womans U., 1967. Tchr. phys. edn. U. Okla., Norman, 1957-60; instr. Syracuse U., 1960-61; instr., chmn. phys. edn. women Fla. So. Coll., 1961-63; mem. faculty Midwestern U. Wichita Falls, Tex., 1965-67; mem. faculty Western Mich. U., Kalamazoo, 1967—, prof. phys. edn., 1979—, coordinator spl. phys. edn., 1972—, chmn. dept. womens phys. edn., 1967-72, also adv. gerontology program; mem. nat. sport devel. com. U.S. Assn. for Blind Athletes. Nat. bd. dirs. Womens Equity Action League. Named to Alumnae Hall of Fame Mem. Am. Coll. Sport and Medicine, AAHPER, Am. Assn. Children with Learning Disabilities, AAUP, Nat. Wheelchair Athletic Assn., Mich. assn. Learning Disabilities. Democrat. Christian Ch. Author: Golf, 1969; Basketball-Five Player, 1972; contb. articles to profl. jours. Home: 2614 Taliesin St Kalamazoo MI 49008 Office: Phys Edn Dept Western Mich U Kalamazoo MI 49008

CHEATUM, LINDA ROSE, association administrator; b. San Antonio, July 3, 1943; d. Raoul Armand and Rosemarie (Cardenas) Berlanga; B.S. in Journalism, Tex. Woman's U., 1964; M.L.S., 1970; m. Dan Earl Cheatum, Apr. 23, 1966; children—Carole Diane, Candy Ann. Asst. editor Tex. Agrl. Experiment Station, Tex. A&M U., College Station, 1964-66; periodicals reference librarian Tex. Woman's U. Denton, 1970-73; acquisitions librarian Sci.-Engring. Library So. Meth. U., Dallas, Tex., 1973-75; librarian Am. Heart Assn. Nat. Center, Dallas, 1975-78, info. analyst div. research programs, 1978-82, chief data mgmt. Office of Research and Med. Programs, 1982-85, dir. data mgmt. and budget Office Sci. Affairs, 1985—. Active Richardson Assn. for Children with Learning Disabilities. Mem. Spl. Library Assn., Med. Library Assn., Tex. Library Assn. (mem. publs. com.), Dallas County Library Assn. (pres., v.p., editor newsletter), U.S. Figure Skating Assn. (low test figure judge), Palace Figure Skating Club (treas.). Editor Dallas-Tarrant County Health Sci. Consortia: Union List of Periodicals, 1979. Home: 3301 Shield Ln Garland TX 75042 Office: 7320 Greenville Ave Dallas TX 75231

CHEEVER, SUSAN LILEY, writer; b. N.Y.C., July 31, 1943; d. John and Mary Watson (Winternitz) C.; m. Robert Cowley, May, 1967 (div. 1975); m. Calvin Tomkins, II, Oct. 1, 1982; 1 child, Sarah Liley Cheever Tomkins. B.A., Brown U., 1965. Tchr., Colo. Rocky Mountain Sch., Colo., 1965-67, Scarborough Sch., N.Y., 1968-69; writer Westchester-Rockland Newspapers, N.Y., 1970-72; editor, writer Newsweek Mag., N.Y., 1974-78; free lance writer, N.Y., 1978—. Author: Looking for Work, 1980; A Handsome Man, 1981; The Cage, 1982; Home Before Dark, 1984. Guggenheim Found. fellow, 1984. Mem. Pen/Am. Ctr., Authors League. Democrat. Episcopalian.

CHELI, CAROL ANN, insurance agency executive; b. New Bedford, Mass., Feb. 28, 1942; d. Arthur August and Nova Billie (Lemire) Govoni; m. Michael Sylvia, Jan. 16, 1962 (div. Sept. 1973); 1 child, Wendy J.; m. Ronald L. Cheli, Mar. 19, 1977; 1 child, Ronald, Jr. Owner, Cheli Ins. Agy., Inc., Marshfield, Mass., 1982—, Plymouth, Mass., 1984—, Profl. Sch. Ins., Marshfield, 1982—, Ca-Ron Realty, Marshfield, 1984—; owner Cheli Rest Home of Brockton, Inc., 1985— of Wareham, Inc., Mass., 1986—. Vol. Marshfield Sch. System, 1984-85, mem. Mass. Ins. Adv. Com., 1983—; mem. Marshfield Capital Budget Com., 1985—. Mem. Mass. Assn. Ins. Women (adv. chmn. 1984-85), Nat. Assn. Female Execs. Republican. Roman Catholic. Lodge: Sons of Italy. Avocation: reading. Home: 61 Traveler Ln Marshfield MA 02050 Office: Cheli Ins Agy Inc 439 Plain St Marshfield MA 02050 also Cheli Rest Home 197 W Chestnut St Brockton MA 02401 also Cheli Rest Home of Wareham Inc 2 Depot St East Wareham MA 02538

CHELL, BEVERLY C., lawyer; b. Phila., Aug. 12, 1942; m. Robert M. Chell, June 21, 1964. B.A., U. Pa., 1964; J.D., N.Y. Law Sch., 1967; LL.M., NYU, 1973. Bar: N.Y. bar 1967. Asso. firm Polur & Polur, N.Y.C., 1967-68, Thomas V. Kingham, Esq., 1968-69; v.p., sec., asst. gen. counsel, dir. Athlone Industries, Inc., Parsippany, N.J., 1969-81; v.p., gen. counsel, sec. Macmillan, Inc., N.Y.C., 1981—. Mem. Assn. Bar City N.Y., Am. Soc. Corporate Secs. Clubs: U. Pa., N.Y. U. Home: 300 E 54th St New York NY Office: 866 3d Ave New York NY

CHELSTROM, MARILYN ANN, educational institution administrator; b. Mpls., Dec. 5; d. Arthur Rudolph and Signe (Johnson) C.; B.A., U. Minn., 1950; L.H.D., Oklahoma City U., 1981. Staff asst. Mpls. Citizens Com. Public Edn., 1950-57; coordinator, policies and procedures Lithium Corp. Am., Inc., Mpls., N.Y.C., 1957-62; exec. dir. The Robert A. Taft Inst. Govt., N.Y.C., 1962—, exec. v.p., 1977-78, pres., 1978—. Editor: Teaching the Excitement of Politics in America, 1984. Active LWV, Mpls., 1950-60, N.Y.C., 1972—; charter mem. Citizens League Greater Mpls., 1952-60; del. White House Conf. on Edn., 1955; vice chmn. Minn. Women for Humphrey, 1954. Recipient Cert. of Recognition for Service to Mpls. Public Schs., Mpls. Citizens Com., 1957; named Town Topper, Mpls. Star, 1958. Mem. Am. Polit. Sci. Assn., Minn. Alumni Assn. (gov. N.Y. 1963—, pres. 1971-73; nat. dir. 1971-75), Lutheran (treas. councilman). Club: Minn. Alumni (Mpls.). Home: 155 E 38th St New York NY 10016 Office: The Robert A Taft Inst Govt 420 Lexington Ave New York NY 10017

CHEN, CONCORDIA CHAO, mathematician; b. Peiping, China; came to U.S. 1955, naturalized 1969; d. Chun-fu and Kwie Hwa (Wong) Chao; B.A. in Bus. Adminstrn., Nat. Taiwan U., 1954; M.S. in Math., Marquette U., 1958; postgrad. Purdue U., 1958-60, M.I.T., 1961-62; m. Chin Chen, July 2, 1960; children—Marie Hui-mei, Albert Chao. Teaching asst. Purdue U., Lafayette, Ind., 1958-60; system analysis engr. electronic data processing div., Mpls.-Honeywell, Newton Highlands, Mass., 1960-63; mgmt. planning asst. Lederle Labs., Am. Cyanamid Co., Pearl River, N.Y., 1964-68, computer applications specialist, 1967, ops. analyst, 1967-68; staff programmer IBM, Sterling Forest, N.Y., 1968-78, adv. programmer, data processing mktg. group, Poughkeepsie, N.Y., 1978-80, mgr. systems programming and systems architecture, Princeton, N.J., 1980-82, sr. systems analyst, 1982-83, data processing mktg. cons., 1984—. Mem. edn. council MIT. Mem. Am. Math. Soc., Soc. Indsl. Applied Maths. Home: Mountain Pass Box 34 Route 6 Hopewell Junction NY 12533 Office: IBM China Br Office Gt Wall Hotel Room 430 Beijing People's Republic of China

CHEN, SOPHIE WU, investment company executive, consultant; b. Shanghai, China, Oct. 8, 1931; came to U.S., 1953, naturalized, 1961; d. Thomas M. and Yip-ching (Chow) Wu; m. Hughes Shi-Chih Chen, Nov. 30, 1957; children—Benjamin, Dexter, Theodore, Hugh. B.S., M.B.A., Boston U., 1957; student N.Y. Inst. Finance, 1976. Registered mutual fund dealer. Statistician United Nations, N.Y.C., 1957-60; chief treas., controller Air Am. Inc., Taipei, Taiwan, 1962-70; investment advisor Atalanta Forstman Leff, N.Y.C., 1971-76; fund adminstr. Drexel Burnham, N.Y.C., 1976-77; v.p., portfolio mgr., dir. ops. Unity Mgmt. Inc., N.Y.C., 1977—. Advisor fin. com. Christ Ch., Riverdale, N.Y., 1980—. Mem. Nat. Assn. Female Execs. Republican. Episcopalian. Avocations: travel, reading, music. Home: 248 W 256 St Riverdale NY 10471 Office: Unity Mgmt Inc 2001 Marcus Ave Lake Success NY 11042

CHENEY, NANCY A., oil company executive; b. Balt., July 12, 1944; d. Ralph Francis and Kathleen Margaret (Hunt) Cheney. B.A. in Liberal Arts, Mundelein Coll., 1966. Mgr., cons. Commonwealth Edison, N.Y.C., 1972-77; v.p., cons. Siegel & Gale, N.Y.C., 1977-78; mgr. tng. Citibank, N.Y.C., 1979; prin. Cheney Assocs., N.Y.C., 1978-81; dir. mktg. Hay Assocs., Phila., 1981-83; v.p. ops. Hydrocarbon Conversion, Inc., Dallas, 1983—; instr. bus. sch. NYU, 1975-78; guest lectr. Cornell U., Ithaca, N.Y., 1975. Mem. Am. Soc. Tng. Devel. (pres. N.Y. Met. chpt. 1977-79, Internat. award 1979, Nat. award 1978), Internat. Assn. Personnel Women. Office: Hydrocarbon Conversion Inc 14222 N Dallas Pkwy Suite 1059 Dallas TX 75240

CHENG, ANNA, real estate investment service company executive; b. Taipei, Taiwan, Oct. 15, 1954; came to U.S., 1973; d. Nunsai and Aisun Cheng; m. Ralph Jeffrey Cowing, Dec. 15, 1984. B.A. in Econs., Whitman Coll., 1976; M.B.A., U. Santa Clara, 1981. Fin. analyst Frontier Mgmt. Corp., Menlo Park, Calif., 1977-79; real estate exec. Fox & Carskadon Fin. Corp., San Mateo, Calif., 1980. Mem. Am. Mgmt. Assn., Fin. Mgmt. Assn., Am. Fin. Assn., Real Estate Securities and Syndication Inst., World Affairs Council, Center Democratic Instns., Asian Am. Theatre Co., San Francisco Mus. Modern Art, Smithsonian Instn., Signet Table, Mortar Bd. Contbr. articles to profl. publs. Office: 2755 Campus Dr San Mateo CA 94403

CHENG, VIRGINIA WAI, physician; b. Nanking, China, Jan. 1, 1944; d. Shu-Chuen and Min Fong (Liu) Cheng. B.A., Concordia Coll., 1965; B.S. in Medicine, U. N.D., 1967; M.D., Northwestern U., 1969. Intern Los Angeles County-U. So. Calif. Med. Center, Los Angeles, 1969-70, resident pediatrics, 1970-72, fellowship in pediatrics, adolescent medicine, 1972-73; mem. staff So. Calif. Permanente Group Medicine, Los Angeles, 1973—; asso. prof. clin. pediatrics U. So. Calif. Med. Sch., Los Angeles, 1978—. Diplomate Am. Bd. Pediatrics. Fellow Am. Acad. Pediatrics; mem. Los Angeles Pediatrics Soc. Office: Kaiser West LA 6041 Cadillac Ave Los Angeles CA 90034

CHENHALLS, ANNE MARIE, nurse, educator; b. Detroit, May 26, 1929; d. Peter and Beatrice Mary (Elliston) McLeod; m. Horacio Chenhalls, 1953 (dec.); children—Mark, Anne Marie Chenhalls Delamater. Student Detroit Conservatory Music, 1946-47; B. Vocat. Edn., B.S. in Nursing, Calif. State U.-Los Angeles, 1968; M.A., Calif. State U.-Long Beach, 1985. R.N., Calif. Nurse, Grace Hosp., Detroit, 1951-52; pvt. duty nurse, Mexico City, 1953-54; nurse St. Francis Hosp., Lynwood, Calif., 1957-63; assoc. prof. nursing

Compton Coll. (Calif.), 1964-72; health educator, sch. nurse Santa Ana Unified Sch. Dist. (Calif.), 1972-76, 79—; med. coordinator, internat. health cons. Agape Movement, San Bernardino, Calif., 1976-79; instr. community health, Uganda, 1982. Assoc. staff mem. Campus Crusade for Christ. U.S. govt. grantee, 1968. Mem. Calif. Sch. Nurses Assn., Calif. Tchrs. Assn., Internat. Platform Assn., Calif. Assn. Vocat. Educators. Democrat. Home: 12092-69 Sylvan River Fountain Valley CA 92708 Office: 1405 French St Santa Ana CA 92701

CHENNAULT, ANNA CHAN, business executive, author; b. Peking, China, June 23, 1925; d. Y.W. and Isabelle (Liao) Chan; B.A., Ling Nan U., Hong Kong, 1944; Litt.D., Chungang U., Seoul, Korea, 1967; LL.D., Lincoln U., 1970; H.H.D., Manahath Ednl. Center, 1970; m. Claire Lee Chennault, Dec. 21, 1947 (dec. July 1958); children—Claire Anna, Cynthia Louise. Came to U.S., 1948, naturalized, 1950. War corr. Central News Agy. (then located in Kunming, China and Shanghai, China), 1944-48, spl. Washington corr., 1965—; feature writer Hsin Ming Daily News, Shanghai, 1944-49; with Civil Air Transport, Taipei, Taiwan, 1946-57, editor bull., 1946-57, pub. relations officer, 1947-57; chief Chinese sect. Machine Translation Research Georgetown U., 1958-63; broadcaster Voice of Am. USIA, Washington, 1963-66; U.S. corr. Hsin Shen Daily News, Washington, 1958—; contbg. columnist Central News Agy., 1958—; columnist China Times, Taipei, 1977—; v.p. internat. affairs Flying Tiger Line, Inc., Washington, 1968-76; pres. TAC Internat. Inc., 1976—; dir. Sovran-D.C. Nat. Bank; lectr., writer, fashion designer, U.S. and Asia; aviation cons. adv. com. Fed. Energy Adminstrn. Mem. Pres.'s Adv. Com. on Arts, John F. Kennedy Center for Performing Arts; mem. U.S. Nat. Commn. for UNESCO; spl. rep. of Pres. to Philippine Aviation Week celebrations, 1973; spl. asst. to chmn. Asian-Pacific council Am. C. of C.; vice chmn. Pres.' Export Council, 1981—; mem. Commn. on Presdl. Scholars; co-chmn. U.S. Council S.E. Asian Trade and Investment, 1973—; mem. women's adv. com. on aviation Dept. Transp., 1982—; pres. Chinese Refugee Relief, Washington, 1962-74, Gen. Claire Lee Chennault Found., Washington, 1961-74; bd. govs. Am. Acad. Achievement, Dallas; trustee Center for Study of Presidency, Library Presdl. Papers; mem. Washington Republican Com., 1960—, mem. Nat. Rep. Fin. Com.; cons. heritage groups, nationalities div. on Asian affairs Rep. Nat. Com.; co-chmn. Fin. Com. to Re-elect Pres., 1972; chmn. Nat. Rep. Heritage Groups Council, 1979; chmn. U.S. Citizens in Asia to Re-elect Pres., 1972; del. Rep. Nat. Conv., 1972; bd. dirs. Washington Crossing Found., 1977—, USA-ROC Econ. Council, 1976—; trustee People to People Internat., 1976—; Recipient Woman of Distinction award Tex. Tech. Coll., Lubbock, 1966; Freedom award Order of Lafayette, Washington, 1966; Freedom award Free China Assn., Taipei, 1966, Golden Plate award Champion Democracy and Freedom Am. Acad. Achievement, 1967; Mother Gerard Phelan award Marymount Coll., 1985. Mem. Nat. Aero. Assn. (dir.), Overseas Press Club, Nat. Press Club, Nat. League Am. Pen Women, Writers Assn., Free China Writers Assn., 14th Air Force Assn. (chmn. awards), Fgn. Policy Assn. (nat. council), U.S. Air Force Wives Club, Flying Tiger Assn., Internat. Platform Assn., Am. Newspaper Women's Club, U.S. C. of C. (internat. policy com. 1978—, council trends and perspective 1976—), Nat. Mil. Families Assn. (chmn., founder), Theta Sigma Phi. Clubs: Army & Navy, 1925 F Street, International, Georgetown, Aero, Capitol Hill (Washington); Pisces. Author: Chennault and the Flying Tigers: Way of a Fighter, 1949, translated into Chinese, 1955; A Thousand Springs, 1962; Dictionary of New Simplified Chinese Characters, 1963; The Education of Anna, 1979; numerous books in Chinese including Song of Yesterday, 1961, M.E.E., 1963, My Two Worlds, 1965, The Other Half, 1966, Letters from U.S.A., 1967; author Chinese-English dictionaries. Home: 2510 Virginia Ave NW Washington DC 20037 Office: 1511 K St NW Washington DC 20005

CHENOWETH, ARLENE JOYCE, construction company executive; b. Cass City, Mich., Apr. 1, 1941; d. Robert Melvin and Geraldine Thelma (Bell) Milner; B.S., Olivet Nazarene Coll., Kankakee, Ill., 1963; postgrad. U. Mich., 1963-65; m. Robert R. Chenoweth, Sept. 1, 1962; children—Timothy, Eric, Gregg. Tchr. bus. edn. Swartz Creek (Mich.) Sr. High Sch., 1963-67, Flushing (Mich.) Sr. High Sch., 1969-74; pres., co-owner, exec. v.p. Chenoweth Constrn. Co., Inc., Fenton, Mich., 1974—; co-owner Chenoweth & Assos. Architects, Inc., Fenton, 1978—; v.p. A&B Enterprises; free-lance writer. Sunday sch. tchr.; lectr. on marriage and communication; mem. steering com. Vineyard Ladies Ministries, 1981-82; co-founder Fenton Christian Women's Breakfast Fellowship, 1981; dir. Eastern Mich. Dist. Women's Ministries, 1983—; mem. Eastern Mich. Dist. Bd. Christian Life, 1983—. Mem. Nat. Assn. Female Execs., Am. Mgmt. Assn., Fenton Area Bus. and Profl. Women's Club (charter mem., treas. 1979), Olivet Nazarene Coll. Alumni Assn. (dir. 1983—), Chenhen Flying Assn. Nazarene. Clubs: University (Flint, Mich.); Spring Meadows Country. Home: 12050 White Lake Rd Fenton MI 48430 Office: Chenoweth Constrn Co Inc 265 N Alloy Dr Fenton MI 48430

CHER, singer, actress; b. El Centro, Calif., May 20, 1946; d. Georgia and Gilbert LaPiere; student drama coach Jeff Corey; m. Sonny Bono, Oct. 27, 1964 (div.); 1 dau. Chastity; m. Gregg Allman (div.), June 1975; 1 son, Elijah Blue. Singer with husband as team Sonny and Cher, 1964-74; star TV show Cher, 1975-76, The Sonny and Cher Show, 1976-77; concert appearances with husband, 1977; numerous recs., TV, concert and benefit appearances with Sonny Bono; TV appearances ABC-TV, 1978; appearance with Sonny Bono in motion pictures Good Times, 1966, Chastity, 1969; Mask, 1985; appearances in films Come Back to the 5 & Dime, Jimmy Dean, Jimmy Dean, 1982, Silkwood, 1983; Broadway debut Come Back to the 5 & Dime, Jimmy Dean, Jimmy Dean, 1982; formed rock band Black Rose; recorded numerous albums. Address: care Katz-Gallin-Cleary Enterprises Inc 9255 Sunset Blvd Los Angeles CA 90069*

CHERNEKOFF, JILL, producer, talk show host; b. Phila., Sept. 8, 1955; d. Irving and Barbara C. B.S., U. Del.-Newark, 1977. News anchor Sta. WDEL-WSTW, Wilmington, Del., 1976-77; news anchor Sta. WPEN, Phila., 1978; news anchor Fairbanks Broadcasting, Phila., 1978-80; producer, host daily talk show Taft Broadcasting, Phila., 1980—; lectr. in field. Host: Telethon for United Cerebral Palsy (Outstanding Service award), 1982; Telethon for United Negro Coll. Fund, 1983. Recipient Outstanding Service award Lupus Found., 1981. Mem. Nat. Acad. TV Arts and Scis. (sec. 1984), Women in Communications, TV Radio Advt. Club Phila. Office: 330 Market St Philadelphia PA 19106

CHERNIACK, KAREN, advertising agency executive; b. London, Eng., Sept. 6, 1956; came to U.S., 1979; d. Reuben Mitchell and Edith Margaret (Gaspard) C. Student in Communications, Red River Coll., Winnipeg, Man., Can., 1976-78. Writer, researcher U. Man., Winnipeg, Can., summer 1978; dir. pub. relations Man. Heart Found., Winnipeg, 1979; writer Nat. Jewish Hosp., Denver, 1979; sr. account exec. Schenkein/Assocs., Englewood, Colo., 1980-82; pres. Marx Corp., Denver, 1982—. Vol. cons. Kyle Dudley Cancer Found., Denver, 1984-85. Recipient Alfie awards Denver Advt. Assn., 1982-83, Gold medals Art Dir.'s Club Denver 1982, Silver Medal, 1982, award of merit, 1982; Assoc. Exec. Achievement award, 1985, Theatre of the Mind Award, 1983, Andy awards Advt. Club of N.Y., 1983, 1984, Clio award, 1983, Best Logo award, 1983, 85, Best Sales Office over 500 Sq. Ft., 1985; Best in the West award Am. Advt. Fedn., 1985. Mem. Pub. Relations Soc. Am. (counselors acad., Gold Pick award 1982), One Club for Art and Copy, Denver Advt. Fedn. Avocations: breeding horses, riding cutting horses. Office: Marx Corp 535 16th St Suite 600 Denver CO 80202

CHERNOFF, ROSALIND RIVIN, advertising executive; b. Portsmouth, Va., Mar. 10, 1952; d. Bernard and Zelma (Goodman) Rivin; m. Carl Gary Chernoff, Apr. 4, 1982. B.A., Brandeis U., 1974; M.B.A., U. Va., 1977. Exec. trainee Mervyn's Dept. Store, Hayward, Calif., 1974-75; mktg. mgr. Fairchild Publs., N.Y.C., 1977-79; account exec. Grey Advt., N.Y.C., 1979-81; account supr. Leber Katz Ptnrs., N.Y.C., 1981—. Mem. Women in Communications. Office: Leber Katz Ptnrs 767 Fifth Ave New York NY 10153

CHEROSKE, JANICE MCKEEVER, educator; b. Los Angeles, July 28, 1929; s. Louis C. and Lela E. (Lewis) Schildwachter; B.A., Occidental Coll., 1948; M.A., Calif. State U., Dominguez Hills, 1974; postgrad. U. So. Calif., 1975-76; m. Kirk LeRoy McKeever, July 2, 1948 (dec. 1977); children—Kevin Miles, Wendelyn; m. Robert Husek Cheroske, Mar. 20, 1982. Asst. prin. Wadsworth Year Round Elementary Sch., Los Angeles; adminstr. Highly Gifted Magnet Ctr., 1983-84; personnel commr. City of Huntington Beach, Calif., 1984—. instr. Calif. State U., Dominguez, 1980—. Recipient Hon. Service award Avalon Council PTA, 1973; cert. reading specialist, Calif. Mem. Town Hall of Calif., World Affairs Council of Los Angeles, Kappa Kappa Iota. Author: The Orange County Appetizers Cookbook, 1980. Office: care Wendy Miles Enterprises PO Box 167 Sunset Beach CA 90742

CHERROFF, KATHLEEN PATRICIA, real estate company controller, accountant; b. Santa Monica, Calif., Apr. 2, 1948; d. Paul D. and Alice L. (Ward) Graney; m. Paul Gene Whaley, June 11, 1969 (div. 1974); m. Steven B. Cherroff, June 21, 1975. A.A. in Acctg., La Valley Coll., 1977; B.S. in Acctg., summa cum laude, Calif. State U.-Northridge, 1981. C.P.A., Calif. Staff acct. Maidy, Lederman & Co. C.P.A.s, Century City, Calif., 1977-80; sr. auditor Weber, Lipshie & Co. C.P.A.s, Beverly Hills, Calif., 1980-81; asst. controller Goldrich & Kest, Culver City, Calif., 1981-83, controller, 1983—; moderator, instr. Assn. HUD Mgmt. Agts. Seminar, Los Angeles, 1984-85. Vol., Edward Davis for Senator Campaign, Northridge, Calif., 1985. Mem. C.P.A.s Soc. of Calif. (mem. real estate com. 1981—), Am. Inst. C.P.A.s. Democrat. Avocations: photography; hiking; traveling. Home: 10854 Springfield Ave Northridge CA 91325-3055 Office: Goldrich & Kest 5150 Overland Ave Culver City CA 90231-3623

CHERRY, RONA BEATRICE, magazine editor, writer; b. N.Y.C., Apr. 26, 1948; d. Manuel M. and Sylvia Zelda Cherry. B.A., Am. U., 1968; M.S., Columbia U., 1971. Reporter, No. Va. Sun, Arlington, 1968, Akron Beacon Jour. (Ohio), 1969-70, Wall St. Jour., N.Y.C., 1971-72; assoc. editor Newsweek mag., N.Y.C., 1972-74; reporter N.Y. Times, N.Y.C., 1976-77; exec. editor Glamour mag., N.Y.C., 1977—; lectr. New Sch. for Social Research, 1978; lectr. Sch. Continuing Edn. NYU, 1980, faculty Summer Pub. Inst., 1981-83; faculty Reader's Digest writers' workshops. Co-author: The World of American Business, 1977; contbg. author: Woman in the Year 2000, 1974; contbr. articles to publs. including N.Y. Times Sunday mag., N.Y. Times Sunday Book Rev., Parade, Ms. mag., Christian Sci. Monitor. Nat. media adv. council March of Dimes, 1981—; mem. Nat. Mag. Awards Screening Com., 1980-82, research com. Internat. Women's Media Project. Recipient Media award Nat. Assn. Recycling Industries, 1973, Bus. Journalism award, U. Mo., 1977, writer's award, Am. Soc. Anesthesiologists, 1983, Maggie award Planned Parenthood Fedn. Am., 1986. Mem. Am. Soc. Mag. Editors, Women in Communications, Newswomen's Club N.Y. (v.p. 1985—), Internat. Platform Assn. Office: Glamour Mag 350 Madison Ave New York NY 10017

CHERRY, SANDRA WILSON, lawyer; b. Little Rock, Dec. 31, 1941; d. Berlin Alexander and Renna Glen (Barnes) Wilson; m. John Sandefur Cherry, Jr., Sept. 24, 1976; 1 child, Jane Wilson. B.A., U. Ark., 1962; J.D., U. Ark. Sch. Law, 1975. Bar: Ark., 1975, U.S. Dist. Ct. (ea. dist.) Ark., 1979, U.S. Ct. Appeals (8th cir.) 1980, U.S. Supreme Ct. 1979. Tchr. social studies Little Rock Sch. Dist., 1966-70; chmn. social studies dept. Horace Mann Jr. High Sch., Little Rock, 1970-72; asst. U.S. atty. Dept. Justice, Little Rock, 1975-81, 83—; commr. Ark. Pub. Service Commn., Little Rock, 1981-83; adj. instr. U. Ark. at Little Rock Sch. Law, Little Rock, 1980. Contbr. case note to Ark. Law Rev., 1975. Bd. dirs. Gaines House, Inc.; pres. U. Ark. at Little Rock Law Sch. Assn., 1980-81, bd. dirs., 1982. Mem. ABA, Ark. Bar Assn., (del. 1984—), Pulaski County Bar Assn., Ark. Women Lawyers Assn., Jr. League Little Rock (bd. dirs. 1974), Pi Beta Phi. Democrat. Presbyterian. Home: 4100 S Lookout St Little Rock AR 72205 Office: US Attys Office PO Box 1229 Little Rock AR 72203

CHERTOW, DORIS SALTZMAN, county official; b. N.Y.C., Apr. 23, 1925; d. Jacob and Ella Saltzman; m. Bernard Chertow, Feb. 2, 1947; children—Andrew Henry, Richard Philip, Marian Ruth, Douglas William, David Jacob. B.A., Hunter Coll., 1945; M.A., Radcliffe Coll., 1947; Ph.D., Syracuse U., 1968. Instr. Douglass Coll., New Brunswick, N.J., 1948-49; asst. to dir. inter univ. case program, Syracuse U., N.Y., 1963-64, grad. tchr., 1964-66; editor Pub. in Continuing Edn., Syracuse, 1968-77; county legislator Onondaga County, Syracuse, 1976—. Author numerous essays. Bd. dirs. Discovery Ctr., Syracuse, 1980—, Resolve Dispute Ctr., Syracuse, 1982-85, UN Assn., Syracuse, 1984—, Health Systems Agy., Syracuse, 1977-84, Legal Aid Soc., Syracuse, Assn. for Retarded, Syracuse, Literacy Vols., Syracuse; committee woman Democratic Party, Syracuse, 1952—. Grantee Office of Headstart OED, 1967. Mem. N.Y. State Suprs. and Legislators Assn., LWV, Nat. Orgn. Women. Jewish. Avocations: reading; swimming. Home: 139 Sunnyside Park Rd Syracuse NY 13214 Office: Onondaga County Legislature 407 Courthouse Syracuse NY 13202

CHERUNDOLO, MARY ANNE FRANCES, nurse; b. Taylor, Pa., May 24, 1944; d. Greno Paul and Nancy Madeline (Capalongo) Fumanti; m. Robert Francis Cherundolo, June 29, 1964; children—Jean Marie, Robert Francis, Joy Anne. Nursing diploma St. Joseph's Hosp., Balt., 1971. Cert. gerontol. nurse Am. Nurses Assn., 1984. Med.-surg. ICU nurse St. Joseph's Hosp., Balt., 1969-74; sch. health instr. Shrine Sacred Heart, Balt., 1972-74; supr. Anne Lynne Manor, Louisville, 1974, asst. dir. nursing, 1974-76; neighborhood dir. Cin. council Girl Scouts U.S.A., Aurora, Ind., 1976-78; office nurse V.J. Goel, Lawrenceberg, Ind., 1978; cardiac testing staff nurse J.C. Carter Co., Norwalk, Conn., 1979-80; staff nurse Courtland Gardens, Stamford, Conn., 1980, head nurse, 1981, asst. dir. nursing edn., 1981-83, dir. nursing, 1983—; cons. Homestead, Stamford, 1981-83. Pres., Home Sch. Assn., Shrine Sacred Heart, Balt., 1973; chmn. com. Central Catholic Home Sch., Norwalk, 1982-83; area chmn. Heart Fund Assn., Norwalk, 1981. Mem. Infection Control Nurses Fairfield County, Conn. Orgn. Gerontol. Nurse Educators, Dirs. of Nurse's Council Conn. Health Care Assn. Roman Catholic. Club: West Norwalk Community Guild (chmn. 1978-81). Home: 175 1/2 W Norwalk Rd Darien CT 06820

CHERWIN, LINDA YVONNE, travel executive; b. Plymouth, N.H., Dec. 15, 1948; d. Roger and Alice Mary (Theriault) Carignan; 1 child, M. Alison. Student Rivier Coll., Whittemore Sch. Bus. Asst. mgr. Travel New Horizons, Peterborough, N.H., 1972-76; mgr. Garnsey Bros. Travel, Sanford, Maine, 1976-77; gen. mgr. R-W Travel, Dover, N.H., 1977-84; pres., owner The Travel Pro, Somersworth, N.H., 84—. Sponsor, bd. dirs. Internat. Children's Festival, Somersworth, N.H., 1985-86. Mem. Am. Soc. Travel Agts., Am. Retail Travel Agts. Assn., C. of C. Republican. Address: The Travel Pro 396 High St Somersworth NH 03878

CHESLER, VICTORIA AIMEE, publishing executive, writer; b. N.Y.C., July 8, 1957; d. Bertram Arthur and Naomi (Aronson) C.; m. Matthew Robert Kovner, July 24, 1983. B.A. cum laude, Conn. Coll., 1979. Editorial asst. Biomedical Info. Corp., N.Y.C., 1979-80; editor Co-op West, N.Y.C., 1980-81; founder, pres. Manhattan Cooperator Publs., Inc., N.Y.C., 1981, mng. editor Manhattan Cooperator, 1981-82, exec. editor, 1982—; exec. editor The Apt. Buyer's Guide, N.Y.C., 1985—; free-lance writer, 1980—. Contbr. articles to Harper's Bazaar, Ski Mag., SAAVY, Redbook mag. Mem. NOW, Real Estate Bd. N.Y., Nat. Assn. Female Execs. Avocations: skiing; sailing; tennis; travel; drawing. Office: Manhattan Cooperator Publs Inc 23 Leonard St 3d Floor New York NY 10013

CHESNUT, CAROL FITTING, economist; b. Pecos, Tex., June 17, 1937; d. Ralph Ulf and Carol (Lowe) Fitting; B.A. magna cum laude, U. Colo., 1971; m. Dwayne A. Chesnut, Dec. 27, 1955; children—Carol Marie, Michelle, Mark Steven. Research asst. U. Colo., 1972; head quality controller Mathematica, Inc., Denver, 1973-74; cons. Mincome Manitoba (Can.), Winipeg, 1974; cons. economist Energy Cons. Assos. Inc., Denver, 1974-80, exec. v.p., 1979-80, also dir.; exec. v.p. ECA/Intercomp, 1980-81; mng. partner The Chesnut Consortium, Denver, 1981—; dir. Critical Resources, Inc.; on leave with staff Senator Gary Hart, 1978. Rep., Lakehurst Civic Assn., 1968. Precinct capt. Republican Party, 1960, 64; now committeewoman Dem. Precinct. Mem. Am. Mgmt. Assn., Soc. Petroleum Engrs., Assn. Women Geoscientists, Assn. Tng. and Devel., Opera Colo., ACLU, NOW, Phi Beta Kappa, Phi Chi Theta. Unitarian. Club: City of Denver, Friends of Phreatophytes. Office: 419 A Saint Paul Denver CO 80206

CHESNUTT, CAROLYN CRAWFORD, engineering consortium executive; b. Maryville, Tenn., Sept. 16, 1933; d. John Calvin Jr. and Emma Arey (Moore) Crawford; m. John Calvin Chesnutt, Sept. 7, 1955 (div. Feb. 1981); children—John Calvin, Thomas Walter, Margaret America, Carolyn Christian. B.A., Agnes Scott Coll., Decatur, Ga., 1955; M.Ed., U. S.C., 1972; M.S., Ga. Inst. Tech., 1979. Asst. librarian Hartsville Meml. Library, S.C., 1964-65; tchr. music Darlington Sch. System, S.C., 1965-68, tchr. math. and psychology, Hartsville, 1968-73; tchr. math. DeKalb County Sch. System, Clarkston, Ga., 1973-75; asst. to dean engring. Ga. Inst. Tech., Atlanta, 1975-77; exec. dir. Southeastern Consortium for Minorities in Engring., Inc., Atlanta, 1977—. Vice pres. Hartsville Arts Council, 1968-72; campaign chairperson Community Concert Assn., Hartsville, 1968-70, pres., 1970-72; pres. PTA, Hartsville, 1973, Class of 1955, Agnes Scott Coll., 1985—; mem. Atlanta Symphony Orch. Chorus; mem. com. to restructure bds. and agys. Presbyterian Ch. U.S., 1968-71, mem. gen. exec. bd., 1971-72. Grantee Alfred P. Sloan Found., 1977-81, NASA, 1982-85, Carnegie Corp., 1985-88, NSF, 1985-88. Mem. Nat. Assn. Precoll. Dirs. (charter, chairperson 1984-85), Soc. Women Engrs., Am. Soc. Engring. Edn., Am. Guild Oganists, NEA, S.C. Edn. Assn. Avocations: playing organ; travel; jogging. Home: 1166 Morningside Pl Atlanta GA 30306 Office: Southeastern Consortium for Minorities in Engring Inc care Ga Inst Tech Atlanta GA 30332

CHESTNUT, DONNA L. SHELNUT, photography laboratory executive; b. Birmingham, Ala., Sept. 16, 1952; d. J. O'Neal and Helen (Morrison) Shelnut; m. Hiram C. Stone, Jr., July 1972 (div. 1978); m. Peter John Chestnut, Jan. 26, 1980; children—Lisa R., Patricia L. Student Gadsden State Jr. Coll., Ala., 1971-72. Clk., dept. asst. mgr. Belk Hudson Co., Gadsden, 1970-71; bookkeeper, mgr. Waters Plumbing Co., Attalla, Ala., 1971-72; office mgr. Clean Rental Service, Gadsden, 1972-78, Photocraft Inc., Birmingham, Ala., 1978-79, Hallmark Constrn. Co., Birmingham, 1979-80; owner, sec.-treas. Chestnut Colour, Inc., Atlanta, 1980—. Mem. Assn. Profl. Color Labs. Republican. Baptist. Avocations: reading; running; sewing. Home: 4399 S Landing Dr Marietta GA 30066 Office: Chestnut Colour Inc 1436 Chattahoochee Ave Atlanta GA 30318

CHEVERS, WILDA ANITA YARDE (MRS. KENNETH CHEVERS), probation officer; b. N.Y.C.,; d. Wilsey Ivan and Herbertlee (Perry) Yarde; B.A., Hunter Coll., 1947; M.S.W., Columbia, 1959; Ph.D., N.Y.U., 1981; m. Kenneth Chevers, May 14, 1950; 1 dau., Pamela Anita. Probation officer, 1947-55; supr. probation officer, 1955-65; br. chief Office Probation for Cts. N.Y.C., 1965-72, asst. dir. probation, 1972-77, dep. commr. dept. probation, 1978—; conf. faculty mem. Nat. Council Juvenile and Family Ct. Judges; mem. faculty John Jay Coll. Criminal Justice, N.Y.C. Tech. Coll., Nat. Coll. Juvenile Justice; mem. adv. com. Family Ct., First Dept. Sec. Susan E. Wagner Adv. Bd., 1966-70. Sec., bd. dirs. Allen Community Day Care Center, 1971-75; bd. dirs. Allen Sr. Citizens Housing, Allen Christian Sch., Queensboro Soc. for Prevention Cruelty to Children. Named to Hunter Coll. Hall of Fame, 1983. Mem. ABA (assoc. criminal justice com.), N.Y. Bar Assn. (juvenile justice com.), Nat. Council on Crime and Delinquency, Nat. Assn. Social Workers, Acad. Cert. Social Workers. Middle Atlantic States Conf. Correction, Alumni Assn. Columbia Sch. Social Work, NAACP, Am. Soc. Pub. Adminstrn. (dir.), Counseliers, Delta Sigma Theta. Club: Hansel and Gretel (pres. 1967-69) (Queens, N.Y.). Home: 105-62 132d St Richmond Hill New York NY 11419 Office: NYC Dept Probation 115 Leonard St New York NY 10013

CHEW, PAT KENT, lawyer; b. El Paso, Tex., Sept. 30, 1950; d. Richard Chuck Lum and Lillian Gay (Ng) C.; m. Robert E. Kelley. A.B., Stanford U., 1972; M.Ed. in Psychology, U. Tex.-Austin, 1974, J.D., 1982. Bar: Ill. 1982, Calif. 1985. Placement dir. U. Tex., Austin, 1975-80; cons. Career Assos., Austin, 1979-80; assoc. Baker & McKenzie, Chgo., 1982-84, San Francisco, 1984-85; adj. prof. corp. law Hastings Coll. Law, U. Calif., 1984-85; asst. prof. corp. and internat. trade U. Pitts. Sch. Law, 1985—. Author: MBA, 1982; contbr. articles to publs. Recipient Contemporary Author award Gale Pub., 1982. Mem. ABA (council mem. gen. practice sect. 1983—, chmn. gen. practice sect. com. 1982-84, liaison standing com. on career devel. 1984), Phi Kappa Phi, Beta Gamma Sigma. Office: U Pitts Sch Law 3900 Forbes Ave Pittsburgh PA 15260

CHEWNING, GRACE ANN, city official; b. Chgo., Feb. 20, 1936; d. Henry Charles and Dorothy Caroline (Beese) Wendorff; m. Robert Kenneth Avera, July 2, 1952 (div. Mar. 1960); m. Robert Joseph Chewning, June 11, 1966. A.A., Valencia Community Coll., 1975; B.S., Rollins Coll., 1982. Council sec. City of Orlando, Fla., 1953-71, adminstrv. aide, 1971-74, dep. city clk., 1974-76, city clk., 1976—. Treas., past pres. Orlando Fed. Credit Union, 1960—; dir. Central Fla. Safety Council, Orlando, 1982—; sec., bd. dirs. Epilepsy Assn. Central Fla., Orlando, 1976—; founder, sec. Orlando Remembered, Inc., 1982—. Recipient Dedicated Service award Human Relations Commn., Orlando, 1972; Disting. Alumni award Rollins Coll., 1985; named to Fla. Women's Hall of Fame, Gov.'s Commn. on Status of Women, Tallahassee, 1982, 84. Mem. Internat. Inst. Municipal Clks., Fla. Assn. City Clks., Fla. Women in Govt. (pres. 1968-69), Women's Exec. Council (chmn. 1978—, outstanding woman in govt. 1981). Republican. Lutheran. Lodge: Amaranth (warden 1960-64). Avocations: reading; fishing; bowling; hypnosis. Home: 400 E Colonial Dr Apt 1303 Orlando FL 32803 Office: City of Orlando 400 S Orange Ave Orlando FL 32801

CHEZ, BONNIE FLOOD, nurse, health care consultant; b. Burlington, Vt., July 6, 1948; d. William Arthur Flood and Shirley (Smyle) F.; m. Ronald August Chez, Sept. 14, 1976. B.S.N., U. Vt., 1972; M.S.N., Cath. U., 1975. Staff nurse Georgetown U. Hosp., Washington, 1972-76; staff devel. instr. Prince George's Hosp., Cheverly, Md., 1976-78; perinatal outreach coordinator Pa. State U., Hershey, 1978-82; perinatal cons. Ind. practice Newark, 1982—; part time educator U. Medicine and Dentistry of N.J., Newark, 1983—; pres. Nursing Edn. Resources, Inc.; cons. Astra Pharm., Inc., Worchester, Mass., 1983—, Barnum Communications, Inc., N.Y.C., 1979-80, Sonicaid, Inc., Fredericksburg, Va., 1979, Corometrics, Inc., Wallingford, Conn., 1977—; Berkeley Bioengring., Inc. (Calif.), 1977; Med.-Legal Consulting Firm, Washington, 1977-78, Med. Research Group, Inc., Blue Bell, Pa., 1980—. Author: The Theory and Practice of Self Administered Medications in Family Centered Maternity Nursing, 1975; Preterm Labor-A Guide for You, 1983; (with R. Naeye) Factors That Predispose to Premature Rupture of the Fetal Membranes, 1983; contbr. articles to profl. jours.; producer videotapes, programmed slide shows. Mem. Am. Nurses' Assn., Nurses' Assn. Am. Coll. Obstetricians and Gynecologists (vice-chmn. Md. sect. 1974-76, chmn. Md. sect. 1976-78), Nat. Perinatal Assn., Nat. Assn. Female Execs. Home: 817 Harmon Cove Towers Secaucus NJ 07094 Office: Statewide Perinatal Ctr UH-F-250 U Medicine and Dentistry NJ 100 Bergen St Newark NJ 07103

CHI, LOTTA CHAI JUI, computer science executive; b. N.Y.C., Dec. 5, 1930; d. Chen Pien and Han Chih (Tang) Li; B.S., Heidelberg Coll., Tiffin, Ohio, 1953; M.S., Rutgers U., 1955; m. Michael Chi, June 15, 1957; children—Loretta Elizabeth, Maxwell Michael. Virologist, NIH, 1956-63; pres. L.C. Assocs., Arlington, Va., 1974—. Mem. N.Y. Acad. Scis., Am. Soc. Microbiologists, Nat. Assn. Women Bus. Owners, Am. Soc. Profl. and Exec. Women, Sigma Xi. Home: 2721 N 24th St Arlington VA 22207 Office: 2045 N 15th St Arlington VA 22201

CHIAPPERINI, PATRICIA BIGNOLI, real estate appraiser, consultant; b. N.Y.C., Jan. 16, 1946; d. Gennaro and Giovanna (Resburgo) Bignoli; m. Joseph M. Chiapperini, Dec. 14, 1968; B.B.A. in Acctg. and Econs., St. John's U., 1968; postgrad. U. Ala., 1968, Rutgers U., 1980, Am. Inst. Real Estate Appraisers, 1983. Staff Acct. Cleary, During & Co., N.Y.C., 1967-69; chief acct. Montgomery Bapt. Hosp. (Ala.), 1969-70; internal auditor Scottex Corp., N.Y.C., 1970-73; office mgr. Mid-Jersey Realty, East Brunswick, N.J., 1973-79; self-employed real estate appraiser, North Brunswick, N.J., 1979—; guest lect. Middlesex County Coll.; adj. prof. Jersey City State Coll. Chmn. Arts and Cultural Com., Milltown, N.J., 1979-83; active Am. Legion Aux., Milltown, 1973—. Recipient John Marshall award St. John's U., 1968. Mem. Nat. Assn. Ind. Fee Appraisers, Middlesex County Bd. Realtors, N.J. State Bd. Realtors, Central Jersey Ind. Fee Appraisers (treas. 1982-83, v.p. 1984), Am. Soc. Notaries, Nat. Assn. Ind. Fee Appraisers, Cert. Rev. Appraisers, Registered Mortgage Underwriters. Roman Catholic. Office: Patricia J Chiapperini Inc 735 Georges Rd North Brunswick NJ 08902

CHICAGO, JUDY, artist; b. Chgo., July 20, 1939; d. Arthur M. and May (Levenson) Cohen; B.A., UCLA, 1962, M.A., 1964. An organizer Feminist Studio Workshop, Los Angeles, 1970—; numerous one-artist exhbns., numerous group shows; The Dinner Party exhbn. at San Francisco Mus. Modern Art, 1979, U. Houston at Clear Lake City, 1980, Cyclorama Theater, Boston, 1980, Bklyn. Mus., 1980, Musée de l'Art Contemporain, Montreal, 1982, Glenbow Mus., Calgary, 1983, Edinburgh Festival Fringe, 1984, The Warehouse, London, 1985; The Birth Project exhbn. Art Mus. Santa Cruz, Calif., Vancouver Mus., Krannert Mus., Contemporary Arts Ctr., Santa Fe, Grant's Pass Mus. Art, Oreg., Phila. Art Alliance, R.H. Love Galleries, Chgo., others; represented in permanent collections. Recipient Mademoiselle Woman of Yr. award, 1973. Mem. Phi Beta Kappa. Author: Through the Flower, 1975; The Dinner Party: A Symbol of Our Heritage, 1979; Embroidering Our Heritage:

The Dinner Party Needlework, 1980; The Birth Project, 1985. Address: PO Box 834 Benicia CA 94510

CHICKLIS, BARBARA KAREN BURAK, computer company executive; b. Woonsocket, R.I., July 1, 1942; d. Steven and Stella Burak; B.S. in Math., Suffolk U., 1964; M.S.E.E. in Computer Sci., Northeastern U., 1974; m. William A. Gianopoulos, Apr. 3, 1981; children—Karen Barbara, Paul Steven. Systems programmer Raytheon Corp., Lexington, Mass., 1965-68, ITEK Corp., Lexington, 1968-71; project and staff leader Computation Center, Northeastern U., Boston, 1971-74; staff cons. Control Data Corp., Waltham, Mass., 1974-81, New Eng. mgr. for profl. services, mfg., 1981—. Recipient award Internat. Profl. Services Analyst Symposium, 1977, Outstanding Cons. Products Performance award for top performer in U.S., 1986. Mem. Assn. Computing Machinery. Republican. Office: Control Data 60 Hickory Dr Waltham MA 02154

CHICKOWSKY, CAROLL EVE, designer, consultant, educator; b. Detroit, Apr. 30, 1935; s. John and Constance Helen (Jastremsky) C. Student U. Mich., 1953-54; B.Indsl. Design, Pratt Inst., 1958; postgrad. U. Mo., 1979, Tex. Woman's U. Designer various cos., Detroit, Chgo., Calif., 1962-75; project mgr. Hosp. Bldg. and Equipment, St. Louis, 1975-79; dir. interiors Geren & Assocs., Ft. Worth, 1979-82; prin. Ergonomics Co., Ft. Worth, 1981—; cons. Henmi & Assoc., St. Louis, 1982—, Jaye Skaggs Designs, Fort Worth, 1985—, Growald Architects Interiors, 1984—; instr. Tex. Christian U., Ft. Worth, 1981-82, Washington U., St. Louis, 1982-83. Kate Maremont Found. grantee, 1964. Mem. Inst. Bus. Designers (profl.), AIA (assoc., appt. nat. bd., interiors com.), Illuminating Engring. Soc. Creator permanent exhibit Mus. Sci. and Industry, Chgo., 1964, TV/documentation on low income living quarters. Office: Ergonomics 612 N Bailey Fort Worth TX 76107

CHICOREL, S. MARIETTA, publishing executive; b. Vienna, Austria; came to U.S., 1939, naturalized, 1945; B.A., Wayne State U., 1952; M.A., U. Mich., 1960. Chief editor Ulrich's Internat. Periodicals Directory, R. R. Bowker Co., N.Y.C., 1966-68; project mgr. Info. Scis., Inc., Macmillan Pub. Co., Inc., N.Y.C., 1968-69; pres. Chicorel Library Pub. Corp., N.Y.C., 1969-79; prof. library sci. Queens Coll., 1971-72; pres. Am. Library Pub. Co., Inc., N.Y.C., 1979—; exec. council Library Resources and Tech. Services. Bd. govs. Booksellers League of N.Y., 1968-79. Mem. ALA (councilor), Am. Soc. Info. Scientists. Office: American Library Publishing Co Inc 275 Central Park W New York NY 10024

CHIDESTER, BARBARA MABBS, marketing executive; b. Evanston, Ill., Mar. 6, 1949; d. Ralph Renner and Barbara Ann (Birge) Mabbs. B.A., Northwestern U., 1971, postgrad., 1972. With Sears Roebuck and Co., 1971-75; mgr. merchandising services Samsonite Corp., Denver, 1976-78; v.p. mktg. Chidco Microsystems Corp., Denver, 1979-83; dir. mktg. Central City Opera House Assn., Denver, 1981; dir. mktg. services Nat. Demographics, Denver, 1982; prin./pres. BMC Mktg., Denver, 1982-85; account exec. Roger Williams Advt., Inc., Portland, Maine, 1985-86; product mgr. Agritech Systems, Inc., Portland, 1986—; dir. Pasta Via Internat., Denver, 1983. Loaned exec. Mile High United Way, Denver, 1978, mem. agy. relations com., 1979-80, vice chmn. agy. relations com., 1980; Republican del. 1980 Presdl./state elections, Denver County, 1980; spl. gifts Am. Cancer Soc., Denver, 1981; mktg. vol. Mile Hi Council on Alcoholism, Denver, 1983-84; chmn. mktg. task force Greater Portland United Way, 1985; chmn. pub. relations Maine Starlight Found., 1985. Recipient Graphics Gallery cert. excellence Strathmore Paper Co., 1977, Gold Key awards Bus. Profl. Advt. Assn. Colo., 1977. Mem. Am. Mktg. Assn., Women Bus. Owners Assn., Delta Delta Delta. Episcopalian. Club: Cherry Creek Sporting (Denver). Home: PO 303 DTS Portland ME 04112 Office: Agritech Systems 58 Fort St Portland ME 04101

CHIERCHIA, MADELINE CARMELLA, securities consulting company executive; b. Bklyn., Jan. 30, 1943; d. Lawrence Cataldo Carrozzo and Victoria Angel (Torchio) Carrozzo Petrisic; m. Jerry Chierchia, Oct. 3, 1959 (div. July 1975); children—Gertrude Chierchia Kraljic, Geraldine Rosalie Gorga. Student parochial schs. Bklyn. Personnel mgr. Argyle Personnel Agy., N.Y.C., 1976-77; clk. typist Atlantic Mut. Ins. Co., N.Y.C., 1977-78; sec. ARC, N.Y.C., 1978-82; mgr. D.F. King & Co. Inc. N.Y.C., 1982—. Mem. Proxy Div. Securities Industry Assn., Nat. Assn. Female Execs., Reorganization Securities Industry Assn. Democrat. Roman Catholic. Avocations: Bowling; chess; reading; old movies. Office: DF King & Co 60 Broad St New York NY 10004

CHILCUTT, DORTHE MARGARET, former educator, artist; b. Fond du Lac, Wis., Jan. 29, 1915; d. John William and Pearl Evelyn (Bernett) Trummer; B.S., U. Wis., 1940, M.S., 1952; postgrad. NYU, 1975-78, Instituto Allende, Mex., summer 1958, La Romita Sch. Art, Italy, 1978-82, Schohegan Sch. Painting and Sculpture, 1959; m. Booth Chilcutt, Feb. 14, 1942; children—Karen Chilcutt Hulett, Booth, Cindy Jo Chilcutt Underhill, Debra Ann Chilcutt-Flippo. Layout artist DeVry Corp., Chgo., 1941-42; tchr. art St. Louis pub. schs., 1931-33, Monroe County Schs., Key West, Fla., 1957-62, Okeechobee Jr. High Sch. (Fla.), 1963-84. One woman shows Little Gallery, Key West, 1960, Martello Gallery, Key West, 1963, Ft. Pierce Art Gallery (Fla.), 1970; exhibited in group shows Jacksonville Art Mus. (Fla.), 1959, Tampa Art Mus., 1960, Norton Art Gallery, West Palm Beach, Fla., 1960, Ft. Pierce Art Gallery, 1977—, St. Louis Art Mus., 1951, Wis. Salon of Art, Madison, 1947, Key West Art and Hist. Soc., 1957—, Key West Art Ctr., 1959; represented in permanent collections Ft. Pierce Art Gallery, Martello Galleries. Recipient Best of Show awards Fla. Fedn. Art, 1974, Ft. Pierce Art Gallery, 1977, Ybor City Ann. Fiesta Day, 1980, 1st pl. awards Highlands Art League 8th Ann., 1974, Jensen Beach Ann., Elliot Mus., 1974, 84, Ft. Pierce Scholarship Show, 1972-75, Four-County Art Show, Ft. Pierce, 1972-75, 82-86, others. Mem. Okeechobee Art League (pres. 1975-80), Fla. Watercolor Soc. (sec. 1974-84, bd. dirs. 1984-86), Gold Coast Water Color Soc., Nat. Art Edn. Assn., Fla. Art Edn. Assn., Miami Watercolor Soc., Key West Art and Hist. Soc. Democrat. Clubs: Ft. Pierce Art, Okeechobee Art. Contbr. articles to profl. jours. Home: 506 SW 15 St Okeechobee FL 33472

CHILD, JULIA MCWILLIAMS (MRS. PAUL CHILD), author, TV performer; b. Pasadena, Calif., Aug. 15, 1912; d. John and Julia Carolyn (Weston) McWilliams; B.A., Smith Coll., 1934; hon. degree Boston U., 1978, Bates Coll., 1983. m. Paul Child, Sept. 1, 1945. With advt. dept. W. & J. Sloane, N.Y.C., 1939-40; with OSS, Washington, Ceylon and China, 1941-45; condr. TV program The French Chef, WGBH-TV, Boston, 1962—, Julia Child & Co., 1978, Julia Child & More Co., 1980, PBS TV series Dinner at Julia's, 1983-84. Recipient Peabody award, 1964, Emmy award, 1966; decorated Ordre de Merite Agricole, Ordre National de Merite (France). Author: (with Simone Beck and Louisette Bertholle) Mastering the Art of French Cooking, 1961; The French Chef Cookbook, 1968; (with Simone Beck) Mastering the Art of French Cooking, Vol. II, 1970; From Julia Child's Kitchen, 1975; Julia Child & Company, 1978; Julia Child & More Company, 1979; monthly columnist From Julia Child's Kitchen, McCall's Mag., 1975-82; food editor Parade, 1982—; author (video cassettes) The Way to Cook, 1985. Weekly TV appearances ABC Good Morning Am., 1980—. Office: WGBH 125 Western Ave Boston MA 02134

CHILD, MARGARET SMILLIE, government official; b. Yonkers, N.Y., July 14, 1929; d. Harold Baxter and Marie (Maloney) Smillie; B.A., Mount Holyoke Coll., 1951; M.A., Cornell U., 1952; Ph.D., U. Md., 1972; m. James Robert Child, Dec. 30, 1955; children—Peter Truesdale, Elizabeth Baxter, Anne Margaret. Intelligence officer on Indonesia, CIA, Washington, 1952-61; editor, Monthly Indonesian Press Survey, Joint Publs. Research Service, Dept. Commerce, Washington, 1961-64; teaching asst. U. Md., College Park, 1964-68, instr. history, 1971-74; asst. prof. Am. U., Washington, 1973-75; asst. dir. div. research programs Nat. Endowment for the Humanities, Washington, 1974-82; asst. dir., chief research services Smithsonian Instn. Libraries, Washington, 1982—; cons. nat. paper preservation program Council on Library Resources, 1984-85. Office: Smithsonian Instn Libraries Washington DC

CHILDERS, NEIDA GENEIEVE, nurse; b. Chgo., Dec. 18, 1940; d. Louis Phillip and Phyllis Grace (Tutt) Bebo; student St. Bernard Coll., 1972-73; A.S., John C. Calhoun Jr. Coll., 1975; m. Bobby Childers, Feb. 28, 1959; children—Susan Ann, Bobby Ray, Betty Lynn. With Ill. Bell Telephone, Chgo., 1956-57, Western Electric, Chgo., 1965-66; patient care asst. Huntsville (Ala.) Hosp., 1974-75; staff nurse Pineview (Ala.) Hosp., 1975-78; dir. nursing Flint Nursing Home, Flint City, Ala., 1978-80; supr. Med. Park Convalescent Center, Decatur, Ala., 1980-85; staff nurse Pkwy. Med. Ctr., Decatur, 1985—. Mem. Am. Nurses Assn., Ala. Nurses Assn., Am. Heart Assn. Democrat. Baptist. Home: 600 Whispering Hills Circle Hartselle AL 35640 Office: 1306 14 Ave SE Decatur AL 35601

CHILDRES, MARY ROSE, wholesale distributor; b. Livingston, Ala., Apr. 13, 1936; d. Simon and Mary Magdalene (Sanders) Childress; A.S. in Secretarial Sci., U. Cin., 1973, B.S. in Adminstrv. Mgmt., 1976; M.B.A. in Mgmt. and Mktg., Columbia Pacific U., 1986; m. Robert W. Greene. Secretarial positions Hamilton County (Ohio) Welfare Dept., 1954-59, VA Hosp., Cin., 1959-63, Mut. Benefit Life Ins. Co., Cin., 1965-66, Ky. State U., Frankfort, 1966-68; nutrition program asst. W.Va. U., Charleston, 1969-70; with U. Cin., 1970-85, bus. adminstr., office of vice provost for continuing edn. and met. services 1978-85; pres. Rose's Gift Ideas, Cin., 1985—; fin. chmn. Nat. Univ. Continuing Edn. Conf., Cin., 1982. Chmn. Cornelius Van Jordan Scholarship Fund, U. Cin. Mem. Nat. Secs. Assn. (charter mem., co-founder Frankfort chpt.), AAUW, United Black Assn. of Faculty, Adminstrs. and Staff U. Cin. (treas.), Mid-Level Mgrs. Assn. U. Cin., Adminstrv. Women's Assn. U. Cin., Nat. Assn. Female Execs., Delta Tau Kappa. Mem. Ch. of God. Author: Handbook of Office Procedures, 1973, 75, Managing Funded Accounts Electronically. Home: 838 Crowden Dr Cincinnati OH 45224 Office: Rose's Gift Ideas 223 N Wayne Ave Cincinnati OH 45215

CHILDRESS, PHYLLIS ANN, construction executive; b. Fort Wayne, Ind., Feb. 28, 1937; d. Paschal J. and Pietrina M. (Ceccanese) Pallone; B.S. in Commerce, Internat. Coll., 1955; postgrad. Pima Community Coll., 1978-80; m. Kelly W. Childress, Aug. 24, 1973; children—Patricia, William, Jeffrey. Sec. to v.p. trust dept. Lincoln Nat. Bank, Ft. Wayne, Ind., 1955-57; sec. to pres. adminstrn. dept. Internat. Coll., Ft. Wayne, 1957-60; dir., sec. Lightning Homes, Inc., Homebuilders and Developers, Ft. Wayne, 1960-63; sec. to v.p., fin. dept., office mgr. fleet maintenance dept. N.Am. Van Lines, Inc., Ft. Wayne, 1963-71; asst. mktg. dir. ITT Electro-Optical Products, Ft. Wayne, 1972-76; asst. v.p. Empire West Builders, Inc., Tucson, 1977-80; staff constrn. mgmt. Akins Co., Tucson, 1981-82; with City of Tucson Archtl. Div., 1982-85; pres.-sec. Constrn. Techniques, Inc. Recipient Appreciation Cert. Nat. Assn. Women Constrn., 1978; named Sec. of yr. Tawasi chpt. Nat. Secs. Assn., 1967, recipient plaque for outstanding service, 1977. Mem. Internat. Tng. in Communication, Bus. and Profl. Women (pres. Cholla chpt.), Nat. Assn. Women in Constrn. (past chpt. pres.). Democrat. Baptist. Contbr. articles to various publs. Home: 2833 N Laurel Ave Tucson AZ 85712 Office: 2833 N Laurel Ave Tucson AZ 85712

CHILDS, ALTA VICTORIA, auto club administrator; b. Gunnison, Utah, Nov. 26, 1922; d. Lovell Lorenzo and Susan Almira (Swain) C.; student Latter Day Saints Bus. Coll. Bookkeeper, 9th Service Command, 1943-44, Lovinger Disinfectant Co., 1944-52; asst. corp. sec., bookkeeper Automobile Club of Utah, Salt Lake City, 1952—. Del., Republican State Conv., 1978, 79. Mem. Exec. Women Internat., Nat. Assn. Exec. Secs., Mormon. Home: 861 Downington Ave Salt Lake City UT 84105 Office: 560 E 5th St S Salt Lake City UT 84102

CHILDS, ERIN THERESE, psychotherapist; b. Redlands, Calif., Apr. 2, 1958; d. C. Russell and Maryann (Carpenter) C. B.A. cum laude, Loyola Marymount U., Los Angeles, 1979, M.A. magna cum laude, 1980; postgrad. Calif. Grad. Inst., 1982—. Lic. marriage, family and child therapist, Calif. Youth counselor II, Chino Youth Services (Calif.), 1979-81; counselor chem. dependency Behavioral Health Services, Gardena, Calif., 1981-83; pvt. practice psychotherapy, West Los Angeles, Calif., 1982—; psychotherapist, part-time cons. Thomas Aquinas Psychotherapy Clinic, Encino, Calif., 1982-84; clin. dir. Emergency Crisis Counseling, West Los Angeles, 1983; unit supr., dir. driving under the influence program Southbay unit. Behavioral Health Services, Gardena, Calif., 1984-86; treatment coordinator New Beginnings, Century City Hosp., Los Angeles, 1986—; instr. community services Pierce Jr. Coll., Woodland Hills, Calif., 1983, Santa Monica City Coll. (Calif.), 1984, West Los Angeles Community Coll., Culver City, Calif., 1984. Mem. Calif. Assn. Marriage and Family Therapists, ACLU, Psychologists for Social Responsibility, Psi Chi, Alpha Sigma Nu. Democrat. Roman Catholic. Office: 12304 Santa Monica Blvd Suite 108 West Los Angeles CA 90025

CHILDS, HARRIET ELIZABETH, publishing company official; b. New Rochelle, N.Y., Nov. 1, 1934; d. Henry Hebert and Pansy May (Guthrie) C. A.A.S., Westchester Community Coll., 1975; cert. Profl. Secs. Internat. Stenographer Southwestern Pub. Co., Pelham Manor, N.Y., 1953—, office supr., 1979—. Republican. Christian Scientist. Lodges: Soroptimists (corr. sec.); Lincoln Ct. Order of the Amaranth (White Plains, N.Y.); Order of Eastern Star (New Rochelle, N.Y.). Home: 60 Locust Ave Apt A115 New Rochelle NY 10801 Office: Southwestern Pub Co 925 Spring Rd Pelham Manor NY 10803

CHILDS, JOAN ELAYNE, clinical social worker, psychotherapist; b. Bronx, N.Y., Oct. 25, 1939; d. Morris Eugene and Mynn (Finkelstein) Gilbert; m. Paul S. Glassman, June 19, 1962 (div. 1975); children—Pamela Anne, Monica Lynne, Todd Daniel, Erika Paige, Aaron Gregory; m. Dennis Childs, Dec. 28, 1976 (div. Sept. 1985). B.Edn., U. Miami, 1961; M.S.W., Barry U., 1978. Lic. clin. social worker, Fla. Pvt. practice psychotherapy, Hallandale, Fla., 1978-80; psychotherapist Life Stress Ctr., Hallandale, 1980—; tchr., lectr. Dade City Broward Inst., Miami, 1978-80; social worker Home Health of U.S., Hallandale, 1978-80; lectr. Jewish Community Ctr., North Miami Beach, Fla., 1978-80, Tough Love, Miami, 1982. Informant, lectr. Broward Mental Health Assn. Recipient Health Fair award Hallandale Human Resource Dept., 1984. Mem. Fla. Assn. for Group Psychotherapy, Am. Assn. Marriage and Family Therapists, Nat. Assn. Social Workers, Acad. Cert. Social Workers, Nat. Council for Jewish Women. Democrat. Jewish. Avocations: accordionist; scuba diving; jogging; writing. Office: Life Stress Ctr 2500 E Hallandale Beach Blvd Hallandale FL 33009

CHILDS, MARGARETTA PRINGLE, archivist, reference librarian; b. Charleston, S.C., Sept. 29, 1912; d. Ernest Henry and Eleanor Thomas (McColl) Pringle; m. St. Julien Ravenel Childs, Sept. 18, 1935 (dec. Mar. 1983); children—Elisabeth, Ernest, Harriott, Eleanor. B.A., Wellesley Coll., 1932; Ph.D., Johns Hopkins U., 1940; M.Librarianship, Emory U., 1967. Librarian, Boulder Bluff Elem. Sch.; rare books cataloger Welch Med. Library, Balt., 1968-70, Pa. State U., 1970-74; archivist, curator rare books Coll. Charleston, 1974-78; archivist City of Charleston, 1974-77; field archivist S.C. Hist. Soc., Charleston, 1978—; mem. exec. com. Avery Inst. Afro-Am. History, 1981—. Contbr. revs. to profl. jours. Sec., exec. com. Charleston Interracial Com., 1947-58; bd. dirs. ACLU, State College, Pa., 1972-74, Charleston, 1976-82; co-founder, mem. Amnesty I, Charleston, 1978—. Mem. NAACP (mem. exec. com.). Democrat. Avocations: reading; travel; grandchildren. Office: SC Hist Soc Fireproof Bldg 100 Meeting St Charleston SC 29401

CHILDS, MARJORIE M., lawyer; b. N.Y.C., July 13, 1918; d. Charles William and Eva May (Tarrant) C.; student Hunter Coll., 1942-46; B.A., U. Calif., Berkeley, 1948; postgrad. Hastings Coll. Law, 1948-49; J.D., U. San Francisco, 1956; LL.D., Iowa Wesleyan Coll., 1973. Econ. research analyst Fgn. Service, U.S. Dept. State, Paris, 1949-50, Frankfurt, Germany, 1950-51; legal asst. Dept. Navy, San Francisco, 1956-60; admitted to Calif., bar, 1957, U.S. Supreme Ct. bar, 1969; practiced in San Francisco, 1962-64, 79—; asst. county counsel Humboldt County (Calif.), Eureka, 1960-62; mem. firm Berry, Childs & Berry, San Francisco, 1962-64; commr., referee, judge Juvenile Ct. San Francisco, 1964-79. Bd. govs. U. San Francisco, 1978-81. Recipient James Harlan award Iowa Wesleyan Coll., 1969. Fellow Am. Bar Found.; mem. Calif. State Bar (com. juvenile justice 1969-76, chmn. 1970-72, adviser 1972-76), Internat. (council 1975-76, del. 1978, 82), Am. (del. 1975-77, sec. family law sect. 1980-82), Fed. (pres. 1976-77) bar assns., Nat. Assn. Women Lawyers (pres. 1974-75), Queen's Bench (pres. 1967-68), AAUW (pres. br. 1970-72), Bar Assn. San Francisco. Club: Met. Contbr. articles to profl. jours. Home: 64 Turquoise Way San Francisco CA 94131 also PO Box 31430 San Francisco CA 94131 Office: 301 Junipero Serra Blvd Suite 260 San Francisco CA 94127

CHILDS, PAULA SUSAN, television reporter, producer; d. Ralph Harold and Doris N. (DiSaia) Childs; m. Dennis Charles Kauff, July 10, 1982; 1 child, Haley Childs Kauff. B.S. cum laude, Boston U. Anchor, reporter WSB-TV, Atlanta, 1981-82; reporter WBZ-TV, Boston, 1982-83; producer, reporter WGBH-TV, Boston, 1984, Ind. Network News, N.Y.C., 1985; TV reporter Entertainment Tonight, Los Angeles, 1985—. Mem. AFTRA. Advocations: tennis; sking; racketbail; running. Home: 320 Russett Rd Brookline MA 02167

CHILDS, SHIRLE MOONE, early childhood specialist; b. N.Y.C., Aug. 2, 1936; d. Harold McDaniel and Bessie Mary (Batts) Moone; student Queens Coll., 1953-55; B.S., U. Hartford, 1968, M.S., 1970; Ph.D. (Rockefeller fellow, Kettering Found. fellow), U. Conn., 1978; m. William Henri Childs, Sept. 5, 1971; children—Duane Kelby Milner, David Kent Milner. Claims rep. Travelers Ins. Co., Hartford, Conn., 1960-66; tchr. Hartford Public Schs., 1968-71, acting prin., 1973-76, coordinator early childhood edn., 1978—; asst. supt. div. instructional services East Orange Sch. Dist.; adj. prof., lectr. Eastern Conn. State Coll., Willimantic, 1974-76; bd. dirs. lang. readiness program U. Hartford Child Care Center; pres. bd. dirs. Women's League Day Care Center, 1982-84. Mem. Am. Assn. Sch. Adminstrs., Assn. Supervision and Curriculum Devel., Council Exceptional Children, Council Basic Edn., Conn. Assn. Suprs. and Instrs. Spl. Edn., Hartford Women's Network, Delta Sigma Theta (nat. sec.), Pi Lambda Theta (sec.), Phi Delta Kappa. Democrat. Methodist. Club: Eastern Star (officer). Research on affective and behavioral correlates of reading in urban primary classrooms. Home: 26 Regency Dr Windsor CT 06095 Office: 715 Park Ave East Orange NJ 07017

CHILKOV, DOROTHY TAYLOR, international business consultant; b. Pitts., Aug. 20, 1928; d. George Holiday and Frances K. (Klaman) Taylor; m. Samuel N. Chilkov, Oct. 14, 1951; children—Jill, Paul Jordan. Ed. Ariz. State U. TV, radio producer KABC/KLAC, Hollywood, Calif., 1949-64; fashion exec. Robinsons Dept. Stores, Beverly Hills, Calif., 1971-75; mgr. Beverly Hills C. of C.; and Visitors Bur., 1975-80; exec. v.p. Beverly Hills Bd. Realtors, 1980-85; cons. Four Seasons Hotels, Toronto, Ont., 1980—, Home Savs./Beverly Hills Savs., 1981-82; cons. marketing East West Network, Los Angeles, 1980; trustee ins. Calif. Assn. Realtors, Los Angeles, 1984—. Author: art catalogue African Makonde Sculpture, 1976; contbr. articles to various publs. Pres. Brentwood P.T.A., Los Angeles, 1964-65; edn. chmn. Los Angeles Dist. P.T.A., 1965; cons. Beverly Hills Taxpayers Assn., 1982-83; cons. Beverly Hills City CPR Program, 1983—; trustee U. West Los Angeles, 1984—. Recipient Mchts. award City Hope, Los Angeles, 1974; Am. Heart award, Am. Heart Assn., Los Angeles, 1967. Mem. Bus. and Profl. Women Los Angeles (chmn. 1981). Clubs: Friars (Beverly Hills); Sand and Sea (Santa Monica, Calif.). Office: Beverly Hills Bd of Realtors 405 S Beverly Dr Beverly Hills CA 90212

CHILTON, ALICE PLEASANCE HUNTER (MRS. ST. JOHN POINDEXTER CHILTON), former state ofcl., vocat. counselor; b. Boyce, La., Apr. 16, 1911; d. Albert Eugene and Maggie (Texada) Hunter; B.A., La. Coll., 1930; M.S., La. State U., 1934, Ph.D., 1982, Guidance Counselor certificate, 1954; m. St. John Poindexter Chilton, Mar. 2, 1935. Tchr. secondary sch., Glenmora, La., 1931-35; with La. Div. Employment Security and USES, Baton Rouge, 1937-74, employment interviewer and supr., 1937-43, personnel officer, 1943-46, ops. analyst, 1946-55, supr. counseling and tech. services, 1955-74. Vice pres., dir. LaPlace Enterprises, Inc., Belle Pointe Enterprises, Inc. Mem. curriculum study com. East Baton Rouge, Parish Sch. Bd., 1968; rec. sec. Quota Internat., Baton Rouge, 1961-62, 2d v.p., 1963-64. Bd. dirs. YWCO. Recipient certificate of merit La. Acad. Sci., 1960; certificate-35 years meritorious service La. Div. Employment Security, 1972. Mem. La. Personnel and Guidance Assn., Internat. Assn. Personnel in Employment Security, Nat. Trust Historic Preservation, La. Geneal. and Hist. Soc. (pres. 1957), La. Landmarks Soc., Found. for Hist. La., Kent Plantation House, Inc. (sec.), La. Preservation Alliance (dir. 1984-85). Clubs: Campus La. State U. (Faculty Wives). Methodist. Address: Route 2 Box 431 Boyce LA 71409

CHILTON, JOAN PATRICIA, personnel executive; b. Fairfax County, Va., Jan. 2, 1953; d. Frank McGloin and Sue (Stanford) C.; m. Trent Ray Richards, Apr. 12, 1986. B.S., Va. Poly. U., 1974. Interior designer Modern Design, Chevy Chase, Md., 1974-76; regional recruiter Steak & Ale Restaurants, Dallas, 1976-78; exec. recruiter Holiday Inns, Inc., Memphis, 1978-80, regional human resources dir., 1980—. Adviser Memphis Jr. Achievement, 1978. Mem. Young Profls. for Heart, Soc. Human Resource Profls. Avocations: aerobics, racquetball. Office: Holiday Inn Hotels 8340 W Bryn Mawr St Suite 600 Chicago IL 60631

CHILTON, JUDITH ANN, manufacturers representative; b. Columbia, Mo., Oct. 14, 1938; d. Otis Joseph and Lorraine (Mayol) Buchanan; m. Louis P. Hetlage, Sept. 8, 1973 (div. 1977); m. 2d Howard G. Chilton, Jr., Feb. 22, 1983. B.S. in Edn. and Speech Pathology, U. Mo., 1960; postgrad. Fla. Atlantic U., 1972. Speech pathologist Kern County Sch. Dist., Bakersfield, Calif., 1964-65; office adminstr., asst. Richard Karlson D.D.S., Pompano Beach, Fla., 1967-68; speech pathologist, area chairperson Broward County Sch. Dist., Ft. Lauderdale, Fla., 1968-73; Realtor, Century 21, Richardson, Tex., 1978; v.p. ops. Fain Sales Co., Dallas, 1978-84, pres., chief exec. officer, 1984—, also dir.; dir. Med. Specifics, Inc., Dallas, 1983—. Active Northwood Republican Women, Dallas, 1980. Mem. Am. Speech, Lang, and Hearing Assn. (clin. cert.), Tex. Assn. Realtors. Roman Catholic. Home: 6124 Southern Knoll Dr Dallas TX 75248 Office: Fain Sales Co 4418 Sunbelt Dr Dallas TX 75248

CHILTON, MELINDA LOU, advertising agency executive; b. Birmingham, Ala., Dec. 26, 1952; d. Henry and Marjorie Virginia (Carpenter) C. Student in Theatre Arts, Ala. Sch. Fine Arts, 1970, Columbia U., 1970-71, U. Ala., 1972-73. Tech. dir. Holiday Dinner Theatre, Birmingham, 1971-72; producer, writer Bonzo & Assocs. Advt., Birmingham, 1977-79; dir. Terra Advt., Birmingham, 1979-81; creative dir. Bentley, Huggins, & Lewis, Inc., Birmingham, 1981-85; advt. dir. Joe H. Brady & Assocs., 1985—; pub. relations and advt. cons. Birmingham-Jefferson Restaurant Assn., 1982-83. Vol., Planned Parenthood, Birmingham, 1983, Ben Erdreich for Congress Com., Birmingham, 1982; adv. dir. State of Ala. Ballet, Birmingham, 1983-85; bd. dirs. Friends Birmingham Pub. Library, 1982-84. Mem. Am. Advt. Fedn. (dir. Birmingham affiliate 1979-80, 80-81, 84-85), Birmingham Advt. Club (dir. 1979-81, 84-85, Addy awards 1982, 84, 85). Republican. Jewish. Home: 525 20th Ave S Birmingham AL 35205 Office: Joe H Brady & Assocs Inc 3029 3d Ave S Birmingham AL 35233

CHIN, CECILIA HUI-HSIN, art librarian; b. Tientsin, China, came to U.S., 1961; d. Yu-lin and Ti-yu (Fan) C. B.A., Nat. Taiwan U., Taipei, 1961; M.S.L.S., U. Ill., 1963. Cataloger, reference librarian Roosevelt U., Chgo., 1963; reference librarian, indexer Ryerson & Burnham Libraries, Chgo., 1963-70, head reference dept., indexer, 1970-75; acting dir. libraries Art Inst. Chgo., 1976-77, assoc. librarian, head reference dept., 1975-82; chief librarian Nat. Mus. Am. Art and Nat. Portrait Gallery, Smithsonian Instn., Washington, 1982—. Compiler: The Art Institute of Chicago Index to Art Periodicals, 1975. Recipient award Nat. Portrait Gallery, Smithsonian Instn., 1984. Mem. ALA, Spl. Libraries Assn., Art Libraries Soc., Coll. Art Assn., Washington Conservation Guild. Office: Nat Mus Am Art and Nat Portrait Gallery Smithsonian Instn Washington DC 20560

CHIN, JANET S., computer scientist; b. Hong Kong, July 27, 1949 (parents Am. citizens); d. Arthur Q. M. and Jenny N. C. (Loo) C.; B.S. in Math. with honors, U. Ill., 1970; M.S. in Computer Sci., U. Ill., Urbana, 1972. Computer scientist, research in secured operating systems group Lawrence Livermore (Calif.) Nat. Lab., 1972-75; applications programmer, laser research program, 1975-77, systems programmer, computer graphics group, 1977-79; project leader spl. projects unit Tymshare, Inc., Cupertino, Calif., 1979, mgr. computer graphics unit, 1979-83, mgr. system products sect., 1982-83; mgr. graphics Fortune Systems Corp., Redwood City, Calif., 1983-85; pres. Chin. Assocs., Computer Products Cons., 1985—; internat. rep., vice chmn. tech. com. on computer graphics Am. Nat. Standards Insts. Mem. Assn. Computing Machinery, Spl. Interest Group in Graphics, Spl. Interest Group in Human Interfaces, Nat. Computer Graphics Assn., World Computer Graphic Assn., Sigma Xi.

CHIN, JENNIFER YOUNG, public health educator; b. Honolulu, June 22, 1946; d. Michael W.T. and Sylvia (Ching) Young; B.A., San Francisco State Coll., 1969; M.P.H., U. Calif., Berkeley, 1971; m. Benny Chin, Nov. 16, 1975; children—Kenneth Michael, Lauren Marie, Catherine Rose. Edn. asst. Am. Cancer Soc., San Francisco, 1969-70; intern Lutheran Med. Center, Bklyn., 1971; community health educator Md. Dept. Health and Mental Hygiene, Balt., 1971-74; community health educator Northeast Med. Services, San Francisco, 1975; pub. health educator Child Health and Disability Prevention, San Francisco Public Health Dept., 1975—. USPHS grantee, 1970-71. Mem. Soc. No. Calif. Pub. Health Edn. (treas. 1976, 77), Am. Public Health Assn. Home: 1057 Holly St Alameda CA 94501

CHIN, SUE S. (SUCHIN), artist, photographer, community affairs activist; b. San Francisco; d. William W. and Soo-Up (Swebe) Chin; grad. Calif. Coll. Art,

Mpls. Art Inst., (scholar) Schaeffer Design Center; student Yasuo Kuniyoshi, Louis Hamon, Rico LeBrun. Photojournalist, All Together Now show, 1973, East-West News, Third World Newscasting, 1975-78, KNBC Sunday Show, Los Angeles, 1975, 76, Live on 4, 1981, Bay Area Scene, 1981; graphics printer, exhbns. include Kaiser Center, Zellerbach Plaza, Chinese Culture Center Galleries, Chinese Culture Center Galleries, Capricorn Asunder Art Commn. Gallery (all San Francisco), Newspace Galleries, New Coll. of Calif., Los Angeles County Mus. Art, Peace Plaza Japan Center, Calif. Mus. Sci. and Industry, Lucien Labaudt Gallery, Sacramento State Fair, AFL-CIO Labor Studies Center, Washington, Asian Women Artists (1st prize for conceptual painting, 1st prize photography), 1978; represented in permanent collections Los Angeles County Fedn. Labor, Calif. Mus. Sci. and Industry, AFL-CIO Labor Studies Center, Australian Trades Council, Hazeland and Co., also pvt. collections. Del. nat., state convs. Nat. Women's Polit. Caucus, 1977-83, San Francisco chpt. affirmative action chairperson, 1978-82, nat. conv. del., 1978-81, Calif. del., 1976-81. Recipient Honorarium AFL-CIO Labor Studies Center, Washington, 1975-76; award Centro Studi Ricerche delle Nazioni, Italy, 1985; bd. advisors Psycho Neurology Found. Bicentennial award Los Angeles County Mus. Art, 1976, 77, 78. Mem. Asian Women Artists (founding v.p., award 1978-79, 1st award in photography of Orient 1978-79), Calif. Chinese Artists (sec.-treas. 1978-81), Japanese Am. Art Council (chairperson 1978-84, dir.), San Francisco Women Artists, San Francisco Graphics Guild, Pacific/Asian Women Coalition Bay Area, Chinatown Council Performing and Visual Arts. Chmn., Full Moon Products; pres., dir. Aumni Oracle Inc. Featured in Calif. Living Mag., 1981; subject of documentary KGO-TV, 1982. Address: PO Box 1415 San Francisco CA 94101

CHING, CLARA YUEN, immunobiologist; b. Honolulu; m. Nathaniel P.H. Ching; 1 child, Natascha Wai Hung. B.S., U. Hawaii; M.S., U. Wis. Sch. Medicine-Madison; Ph.D., UCLA. Research microbiologist Pacific research sect. Nat. Inst. Allergies and Infectious Diseases, NIH, Honolulu, 1964-69; research assoc. Yale U. Sch. Medicine, New Haven, 1968-69; asst. prof. dept. tropical medicine U. Hawaii Sch. Medicine, Honolulu, 1969-70; research assoc. Meml. Sloan-Kettering Cancer Ctr., N.Y.C., 1976-79; instr. Cornell U. Med. Sch., N.Y.C., 1978; assoc. researcher U. Hawaii/Cancer Ctr. Hawaii, Honolulu, 1980-84, dept. medicine div. hematology-oncology U. Hawaii Sch. Medicine, 1984—, co-chair internat. symposium Natural Immunity and Biological Response Modifiers in Cancer and Other Diseases, Honolulu, 1985. Contbr. articles to med. and sci. jours. Trustee, Aux. Honolulu County Med. Soc., 1981, treas., 1982; mem. profl. edn. com. Pacific div. Am. Cancer Soc., 1980—; chmn. scholarship com. Assoc. Chinese Univ. Women, 1983, chmn. publicity com., 1984. NIH grantee, 1980-84, Nat. Cancer Inst. grantee, 1985-88. Mem. Health and Community Service Council Hawaii, Internat. Soc. Interferon Research (charter), N.Y. Acad. Sci., Tissue Culture Assn., Am. Soc. Microbiology (chpt. pres. 1984-85, pres.'s fellowship com.), Sigma Xi. Home: 2226 University Ave Honolulu HI 96822 Office: U Hawaii Sch Medicine Dept Medicine 2230 Liliha St Honolulu HI 98817

CHING, JENNIFER LYNNE, lawyer; b. Honolulu, Oct. 4, 1953; d. Edward Tim and Lillian (Ching) C.; m. G. Stephen Elisha, Apr. 21, 1983. B.A. cum laude, Lewis & Clark Coll., 1975, J.D., 1979. Bar: Hawaii 1979. Assoc. law firm Gill Park Park & Kim, Honolulu, 1979-80, Chun, Kerr & Dodd, Honolulu, 1981-82; dep. pros. atty. Dept. Pros. Atty., Honolulu, 1982—. Mem. ABA, Hawaii Bar Assn., Hawaii Women Lawyers, Assn. Trial Lawyers. Home: 1421 Alencastre St Honolulu HI 96816 Office: Dep Pros Atty 1164 Bishop St Honolulu HI 96813

CHINITZ, JODY ANNE KOLB, data processing officer; b. Bay City, Mich., July 8, 1953; d. Adam H. and Evelyn I. (Sylvester) Kolb; student Saginaw Valley State Coll., 1972, Bklyn. Coll., 1973-76; B.A. in Russian Lang. and Lit. summa cum laude, Hunter Coll., 1980; m. William A. Chinitz, Feb. 11, 1979. With personnel dept. N.Y. Life Ins. Co., N.Y.C., 1972-77, computer programmer, 1977-80; computer systems cons. Soroban Data Systems, Inc., N.Y.C., 1980-82; project leader Midlantic Nat. Bank, West Orange, N.J., 1982—. Mem. Am. Assn. Advancement of Slavic Studies. Home: 31 Norwood Ave Upper Montclair NJ 07043 Office: 95 Old Short Hills Rd West Orange NJ 07052

CHIPLEY, ANN WHITMIRE, state agency administrator; b. Greenville, S.C., Sept. 4, 1941; d. Henry Grady and Sara Elizabeth (Henderson) Whitmire Epperson Adair; m. Thomas Julian Chipley, Aug. 22, 1965; children—Kathleen Elizabeth, Carter Ann. B.A., Duke U., 1963. Tchr. pub. schs., Raleigh, N.C., 1963-66; women's editor Telegram, Rocky Mount, N.C., 1971-72; advocate planner City of Rocky Mount, 1976-77; co-owner, mgr. Chipley Assocs., Rocky Mount, 1978-83; exec. dir. N.C. Council on Status of Women, Raleigh, 1983—. Campaign mgr. N.C. United for ERA, 1982. Mem. AAUW (pres. N.C. div. 1980-82, nat. legis. com. 1982—). Democrat. Office: NC Council on Status of Women 526 N Wilmington St Raleigh NC 27604

CHISAKI, JANE MIEKO, librarian; b. Berkeley, Calif., June 9, 1958; d. Shunichi and Satoe (Shindo) C. A.B. in English, U. Calif.-Berkeley, 1980; M.L.S., San Jose State U., 1982. Student asst. San Jose State U. Library, 1981-82; media ctr. aide Orchard Sch., San Jose, 1982; librarian San Francisco Pub. Library, 1983; city children's librarian Alameda Free Library (Calif.), 1984—. Active Girl Scouts U.S.A., Berkeley, 1965—, Boy Scouts Am., 1983—. ALA, Calif. Library Assn., Assn. Children's Librarians (sec. 1985-86), Assn. for Library Services to Children. Democrat. Clubs: Mariner Scouts (skipper 1977—), Sea Exploring (skipper 1983—). Office: Alameda Free Library 1433 Oak St Alameda CA 94501

CHISAM, DONNA PRICE, industrial consultant; b. Sheffield, Ala., Oct. 24, 1946; d. Don C. and Bettie Ruth (Butler) Price; m. Phillip M. Chisam, Sept. 10, 1966; children—Richard, Stewart Michael. B.A., Northwestern State U., 1975. Various part-time positions and vol. work, 1964-75; adminstrv. asst. Bank of Am. Internat., Houston, 1975-76; personnel officer First Alabama Bank, Huntsville, 1976-78; organizational devel. officer ONAN Corp., Huntsville, 1978-80; indsl. cons., Huntsville, 1980—; cons. U. Ala., Huntsville, 1979-80. Mem. Am. Soc. Personnel Adminstrn. (pres. 1980-81; Merit award), Huntsville Roundtable. Republican. Baptist. Home: 11314 Mountaincrest Dr SE Huntsville AL 35803

CHISHOLM, JUNE FAYE, clinical psychologist; b. N.Y.C., Apr. 29, 1949; d. Wallace P. and Luretta (Brawley) Chisholm; B.A., Syracuse U., 1971; M.S., U. Mass., Ph.D., 1978. Asst. prof. psychology Fordham U., 1978-84, Pace U., 1986—; practice clin. psychology, N.Y.C., 1980—; sr. psychologist Harlem Hosp., 1982—; cons. N.Y.C. Bd. Edn. Mem. Am. Psychol. Assn., N.Y. State Psychol. Assn., N.Y. Soc. Clin. Psychologists, Chamber Music Assos. Office: 260 W 72 St Suite 1-B New York NY 10023

CHISHOLM, SUSAN MCBROOM, physical therapist; b. Jackson, Miss., Aug. 14, 1955; d. Robert Davis McBroom and Susan Ratcliff (Cabaniss) Culbertson; m. Charles Andrew Chisholm, Nov. 25, 1983. B.Phys. Therapy, U. Miss., 1978. Lic. phys. therapist, Miss., Tex. Staff phys. therapist Delta Med. Ctr., Greenville, Miss., 1978-79, St. Francis Hosp., Memphis, 1979-81; contract therapist Upjohn Co., Memphis, 1981-82; sr. phys. therapist Hermann Hosp., Houston, 1982-84, Houston Orthopaedic Assocs., 1984—. Republican. Episcopalian. Home: 8740 Westheimer Apt 64 Houston TX 77063 Office: Houston Orthopaedic Assocs 6601 Tarnef Suite 112 Houston TX 77074

CHISOLM, GRACE BUTLER, educational administrator, educational administration and interdisciplinary education educator; b. New Orleans; d. Washington R. Butler and Althea A. Landry; 1 child, Olethia Elise. B.S. in Music Edn., Xavier U., 1958; M.M. in Music Edn., Northwestern U., 1962; Sixth Yr. Cert. in Ednl. Adminstrn. and Supervision, Queens Coll., 1972; Ph.D., NYU, 1976. Tchr. instrumental music and English, Rivers Frederick Jr. High Sch., New Orleans, 1958-63, orchestral music N.Y.C. Bd. Edn., 1963-69; acting chairperson music dept. Jr. High Sch. 111, Bklyn., 1964-69; guest lectr. dept. edn. Bklyn. Coll., 1967-71; dir. coll. preparation and career program Title I Elem. and Secondary Edn. Act, Community Sch. Dist. 16, Bklyn., 1969-73; adj. lectr. dept. grad. programs in ednl. services Queens Coll., 1974-75; assoc. dir. Univ. Council for Ednl. Adminstrn., Columbus, Ohio, 1976-78; assoc. prof. ednl. adminstrn. North Tex. State U., 1978-83; prof. ednl. adminstrn. and interdisciplinary edn. Tex. A&M U., College Station, 1983—, asst. to pres., 1985—; for Women Deans, Adminstrs. and Counselors, Nat. Conf. of Profs. of Ednl. Adminstrn., Tex. Assn. for Supervision and Curriculum Devel., Tex. Profs. of Ednl. Adminstrn., Phi Delta Kappa (Henry Meissner Research award 1976), Delta Sigma Theta (pres. Bklyn. Alumnae Chpt. 1970-72, v.p. 1968-70). Office: Office of the President Tex A&M Univ College Station TX 77843

CHITTENDEN, MARGARET ROSALIND (ROSALIND CARSON), author: b. London, Jan. 31, 1933; came to U.S., 1958, naturalized, 1961; d. James Findlay and Mary Jane (Huthert) Barrass; m. James Carson Chittenden, Oct. 4, 1958; children—Stephen John, Sharon. Ed. in Eng. Author: When the Wild Ducks Come, 1972; Merrymaking in Great Britain, 1974; Findlay's Landing, 1975; Song of Dark Water, 1978; House of the Twilight Moon, 1979; The Other Child, 1979; The Face in the Mirror, 1980; Mystery of the Missing Pony, 1980; This Dark Enchantment, 1982; Song of Desire, 1982; Such Sweet Magic, 1983; Love Me Tomorrow, 1984; Lovespell, 1984; To Touch the Moon, 1985; also short stories. Mem. Romance Writers Am. Republican. Avocations: hiking dancing, travelling. Home and Office: 6101 Nyanza Park Dr Tacoma WA 98499

CHITTY, JUDY HUMISTON, banker; b. Glendale, Calif., Sept. 30, 1951; d. Donald Squier and Allene (McCall) Humiston; m. Louis Anthony Chitty, Jan. 7, 1977; (div. Nov. 1985); children—Amber Cecile, Erin Louise. B.A., U. Calif.-Berkeley, 1973; student U. Calif.-Santa Barbara, 1969-72. With Home Savs. of Am., Los Angeles, 1974—, mktg. research mgr., 1980-83, product devel. mgr., Irwindale, Calif., 1983-85, dir. consumer research, 1985-86, product mgr., 1986—. Mem. faculty U. So. Calif., 1984. Scholar, U. Calif. Santa Barbara-Berkeley, 1970-73; State Calif. scholar, 1969-70. Mem. Calif. Scholarship Fedn. (life), Am. Mktg. Assn., NOW (credit task force 1973), Common Cause. Democrat. Religious scientist. Home: 20262-E Arrow Hwy Covina CA 91724 Office: Home Savings of Am 4900 Rivergrade Rd Irwindale CA 91706

CHLAD, DOROTHY CLARA, safety education administrator; b. Cleve., Sept. 21, 1934; d. Stanley and Clara (Stebel) Krzynowek; m. Frank Ludwig Chlad, Sept. 1, 1956; children—Tammy Lynne, Lynne Marie. Student Georgetown U., 1970-71, U. Akron, 1972-73, others; D.H.L., Cedar Crest Coll., 1986. Asst. to fashion dir. Higbee's, Cleve., 1955-58; sec. Officers' Club, U.S. Army, Ft. Hood, Tex., 1958-60; tchr./dir. Safety Town, Bedford, Ohio, part-time 1964-74; co-owner nursery sch., Warrensville Heights, Ohio, 1973-74; dist. rep. Ohio Dept. Hwy. Safety, Columbus, 1972-74; founder, pres. Nat. Safety Town Ctr., Cleve., 1974—; mem. Hwy. Safety Conf., White House, 1976; mem. Nat. Conf. Safety Edn., Washington, 1978; cons. Sesame Street, 1979, state govts., 1974—; condr. workshops. Author instructional books, 10 child safety books. Pres. Jaycettes, Bedford, 1970-71; activeGreater Cleve. Growth Assn., 1976—; mem. bd. control Greater Cleve. Safety Council, 1976—. Named Activist of Yr., Nat. Ctr. Voluntary Action, 1977; Career Woman of Achievement, YWCA Cleve., 1979; recipient Pres.'s Vol. Action award Pres. U.S., 1983. Mem. Nat. Assn. Female Execs., Nat. Safety Council, Cleve. YWCA, Am. Driver/Traffic Safety Edn., Nat. Community Edn. Assn., Nat. Pedestrian Com., Vets. of Safety. Roman Catholic. Club: Jr. Women's. Home: 10169 Inlet Pointe E Aurora OH 44202 Office: PO Box 39312 Cleveland OH 44139

CHMIELEWSKI, MARY ANN CHRISTINE, nurse practitioner, primary health care consultant; b. Newark, Sept. 6, 1949; d. Stanley Thomas and Alexandria (Ananko) C. A.A.S., County Coll. Morris, Randolph, N.J., 1975; B.S.N., Seton Hall U., 1977, M.S.N., 1979. Cert. nurse practitioner. Nurse practitioner VA Med. Ctr., Wilkes-Barre, Pa., 1980-83; ind. nurse practitioner, Wilkes-Barre, 1983—; primary health care cons.; nurse clinician Nutritional Support Team, VA Med. Ctr., 1982-83. Robert Wood Johnson Found. trainee, 1978-79. Mem. Am. Assn. Critical Care Nurses, Am. Nurses Assn. (cert. adult nurse practitioner). Democrat. Roman Catholic. Home: 12B Beaver Ct Wilkes Barre PA 18702 Office: PO Box 2016 Wilkes Barre PA 18703

CHOI, SUSAN ELLEN, librarian, consultant; b. Duluth, Minn.; d. Abe O. and Ellen E. (Willppo) Martimo; m. Dan K. Choi, Mar. 28, 1970; children—Daniel, James, Joshua. B.A., Sacramento State Coll., 1970; M.A., San Jose State Coll., 1973. Library asst. San Mateo County Office Edn., Redwood City, Calif., 1970-71; supr. library services Santa Clara County Office Edn., San Jose, Calif., 1971—; cons.; mem. Calif. State Data Acquisition Adv. Com., 1977-80; reference adv. bd. Coop. Info. Network, 1977-80; copyright info. officer Santa Clara County Office Edn., 1980—. Editor: Guide to Resources for Improving Schools, 1979. Mem. Am. Assn. Ednl. Communications and Tech., Am. Ednl. Research Assn., ALA, Assn. Calif. Sch. Adminstrs., Am. Soc. Tng. and Devel., Calif. Media and Library Educators Assn. (pres. No. sect. 1982-83), Internat. Assn. Quality Control Circles, Nat. Assn. Female Execs., Nat. Sch. Pub. Relations Assn., Peninsula Media Adminstrs., Santa Clara County Sch. Librarians Assn., Women Leaders in Edn. of Santa Clara County (pres. 1981-82). Democrat. Lutheran. Home: 7494 Bayliss Ct San Jose CA 94139 Office: Santa Clara County Office of Education 100 Skyport Dr San Jose CA 95115

CHONG, DOROTHY BIERMA, trading and consulting company executive; b. Detroit, Mar. 27, 1925; d. Charles Allen and Jessica (Griffiths) Bierma; student Los Angeles City Coll., 1942-43, U. Mich., 1946-47; m. Richard Seng-Hoon Chong, Jan. 9, 1980; step-children—David C.S., Stephen C.L., Daniel C.Y. Adminstrv. asst. to plant mgr. Monsanto Co., Trenton, Mich., 1952-65; adminstrv. asst. to pres. Adache Assocs., Inc., Engrs., Cleve., 1965-69; credit mgr. Hawaiian Crane & Rigging, Ltd., Honolulu, 1969-70; adminstrv. mgr. East Central region Booz, Allen & Hamilton, Inc., Cleve., 1970-73; v.p. Amer-Asia Trading Co., Inc., Orlando, Fla., 1973—; broker, co-owner Sungold Realty Internat., Inc., Orlando, 1979—, Sungold Decor, Inc.; dir. Crown Savs. Assn. Mem. Chinese-Am. Assn. Central Fla. (sec., dir. 1980-81), World Trade Council for Central Fla., Nat. Assn. Realtors, Fla. Assn. Realtors, Orlando Area Bd. Realtors. Presbyterian. Club: Citrus. Home: 9652 Woodmont Pl Windermere FL 32786 Office: Amer-Asia Trading Co Inc Suite 112 7201 Lake Ellenor Dr Orlando FL 32809

CHONG, MARY DRUZILLEA, nurse; b. Fairview, Okla., Mar. 8, 1930; d. Charles Dewey and Viola Haddie (Ford) Crawford; A.A. (Bells scholarship), El Camino Jr. Coll., 1950; R.N., Los Angeles County Hosp. Sch. Nursing, 1953; B.S. in Nursing, Calif. State U.-Los Angeles, 1968; M. Nyuk Choy Chong, Aug. 24, 1952 (div. 1968); children—Anthony, Dorlinda. Staff nurse neurosurgery Los Angeles County Gen. Hosp., Los Angeles, 1957-58; staff nurse Harbor Gen. Hosp., Torrance, Calif., 1958-59, emergency room staff nurse, 1959-61, asst. head nurse, 1963-64, supr. neurosurgery intensive care unit, 1964-67, part-time relief nurse, 1967-69, head nurse chest medicine, 1969-72; tchr. YWCA Job Corps, 1972-74; emergency room staff nurse mobile intensive care nurse Victor Valley Hosp., Victorville, Calif., 1974-79; dir. nursing San Vicente Hosp., Los Angeles, 1980-82; dir. nursing Upjohn Healthcare Services, Los Angeles, 1982-85; dir. home health service Bear Valley Community Hosp. Home Health Agy., 1986—. Leader South Bay council Girl Scouts U.S.A., 1968. Mem. AAUW, Am. Gerontol Soc., Hosp. Discharge Planners Assn., Nat. Assn. Female Execs., Internat. Platform Assn., Calif. State U. Los Angeles Alumni Assn. Home: PO Box 697 Lucerne Valley CA 92356

CHONG, VANESSA YUKA, association executive; b.Honolulu, Apr. 9, 1955; d. Henry Akee and Beryl Leilani (Oue) C. B.S., U. Hawaii, 1977. Program counselor YWCA, Honolulu, 1977, program dir., 1980-81; program asst. Moiliili Community Ctr., Honolulu, 1978; housing coordinator Hawaii Commn. on Alcoholism, Honolulu, 1978-80; program dir. ACLU of Hawaii, Honolulu, 1981-84, exec. dir., 1984—. Mem. edn. com. Mental Health Assn., Honolulu, 1979-81; tutor YWCA Immigrant Program, Honolulu, 1976; camp counselor Camp Fire Girls, Inc., Honolulu, 1976, 77; case aide Dept. Social Services and Housing, Honolulu, 1975; bailiff aide Family Cts., Honolulu, 1973. Mem. Nat. Assn. Female Execs., ACLU. Avocations: hawaiian canoe paddling; playing piano; hiking.

CHOOKASIAN, LILI, contralto; b. Chgo.; student Philip Manuel, Chgo., Ludwig Donath, N.Y.C., Armen Boyajian, Paterson, N.J.; m. George Gavejian; 3 children. Voice tchr. Northwestern U.; debut La Cieca (Gioconda), Met. Opera, 1962; roles major cos., Argentina, Canada, Hamburg, Germany, Turin, Italy, Mexico City, Barcelona, Spain, Balt., Chgo., Cin., Dallas, Ft. Worth, Houston, Miami, N.Y. City Opera, Met. Opera, Phila. Lyric Opera, Portland, San Francisco Opera, Washington; rec. artist Deutsche Grammophon; appearances with symphony orchs.; coach repertoire. Office: care Thea Dispeker Artists Reps 59 E 54th St New York NY 10022*

CHOP, ROSE MARIE, nurse; b. Kans., Mar. 4, 1955; d. John and Helen Ann (Sachen) C.; B.S. Nursing, Fort Hays State U., 1978, postgrad. Kans. U. Med. Center, 1979-81; M.S. in Nursing, Wichita State U., 1983. With Providence-St. Margaret Health Center, Kansas City, Kans., 1973—, staff charge nurse pediatric, med.-surg. unit, 1981—; nursing supr. Lawrence Meml. Hosp. (Kans.), 1983—; staff faculty mem. Providence-St. Margaret's Health Center, 1980—; instr. CPR, 1981—; aerobic dance instr., 1981—. Mem. Am. Nurses Assn., Am. Heart Assn., Fort Hays State U. Alumni Assn. (life), Sigma Theta Tau. Democrat. Roman Catholic. Club: Croation Federal Union. Home: 3013 Bainbridge Circle Lawrence KS 66044 Office: Lawrence Meml Hosp 325 Maine Lawrence KS 66044

CHOPIN, SUSAN GARDINER, lawyer; b. Miami, Fla., Feb. 23, 1947; d. Maurice and Judith (Warden) Gardiner; m. L. Frank Chopin, Sept. 4, 1964; children—Philip, Alexandra, Christopher. B.B.A., Loyola U., New Orleans, 1966; J.D. cum laude, U. Miami, 1972; M.Litt. (Law), Oxford U., 1983. Bar: Fla. 1972, Iowa 1979. Sr. law clk. U.S. Dist. Ct. So. Dist. Fla., 1972-73; ptnr. Chopin & Chopin, Miami, 1973-77; assoc. prof. Drake U. Law Sch., 1979-80; sole practice, Palm Beach, Fla., 1981—. Editorial bd. Fla. Bar Jour., 1975—; contbr. articles to profl. jours., legal revs. Mem. Fla. Bar Assn., Iowa Bar Assn., Fed. Bar Assn., Fla. Assn. Women Lawyers, Internat. Bar Assn., ABA, Soc. Wig and Robe, Phi Kappa Phi, Phi Alpha Delta. Office: 2875 S Ocean Blvd Palm Beach FL 33480

CHORBA, MARY CATHERINE, account executive; b. Phila., Aug. 15, 1955; d. George Joseph and Mildred Mary (Hazinski) C.; B.A. in Sociology, Villanova U., 1977. Sales rep., fin. systems specialist TAB Products, N.J., 1977-78; personnel cons. Shaw & Shaw, Inc., Torrance, Calif., 1978-80; sales, mktg. recruitment cons., Torrance, 1980—; now account exec. AT&T Communications; cons. to bus. Mem. coordinating council City of Redondo Beach; mem. task forces Redondo Beach Sch. Bd. Recipient Pres.'s award Shaw & Shaw, Inc., 1979, Volt Info. Scis., N.Y.C.; cert. personnel cons., Calif. Mem. Nat. Assn. Female Execs., Calif. Assn. Personnel Cons., Women in Mgmt. South Bay, Women in Telecommunications, Nat. Assn. Bus. and Profl. Women, Torrance C. of C., Redondo Beach C. of C. Office: 32 Ave of Americas Suite 2432 New York NY 10013

CHOW, RITA KATHLEEN, government official; b. San Francisco, Aug. 19, 1926; d. Peter and May (Chan) C.; B.S., Stanford U., 1950, nursing diploma, 1950; B.I.S., George Mason U., 1983; M.S., Case Western Res. U., 1955; profl. diploma in nursing edn. adminstrn. Columbia U., 1961, Ed.D., 1968. Asst. in teaching Stanford (Calif.) U., 1951-52; instr., dir. student health Fresno (Calif.) Gen. Hosp. Sch. Nursing, 1952-54; instr. Wayne State U. Coll. Nursing, Detroit, 1957-58; research asso., project dir. cardiovascular nursing research Ohio State U., Columbus, 1965-68; spl. asst. to dep. dir. Nat. Center Health Services Research, Health Services and Mental Health Adminstrn., HEW, Rockville, Md., 1969-73; dep. dir. manpower utilization br., 1970-73, dep. dir. Office Long Term Care, dep. chief nurse officer USPHS, Rockville, 1973-77; chief quality assurance br. div. long-term care Office of Standards and Certification, Health Standards and Quality Bur., Health Care Fin. Adminstrn., HHS, 1977-82; dir. patient edn., asst. dir. nursing GWL Hansen's Disease Ctr., HRSA, HHS, Carrville, La., 1984—. Served with Nurse Corps, U.S. Army, 1954-57; commd. officer USPHS, 1968, advanced through grades to nurse dir., 1974. AAUW scholar, Nat. League Nursing fellow, 1959-61; recipient research grant Sigma Theta Tau, 1966; Fed. Nursing Service award Assn. Mil. Surgeons U.S., 1969; citation for outstanding contbn. to cardiovascular nursing Am. Heart Assn., 1972, 79, Nursing Edn. Alumni Assn. award for distinguished achievement in nursing research Columbia U. Tchrs. Coll., 1973; Meritorious Service medal USPHS, 1977; Disting. Alumnus award Case Western Res. U. Sch. Nursing, 1979. Author: Identifying Nursing Action with the Care of Cardiovascular Patients, 1967; Cardiosurgical Nursing Care: Understandings, Concepts, and Principles for Practice, 1975. Editorial bd. HPEER Am. Ednl. Research Assn., 1973-77; Contbr. to publs. in field. Address: USPHS GWL Hansen's Disease Ctr Carville LA 70721

CHOYKE, PHYLLIS MAY FORD, ceiling company executive, editor; b. Buffalo, Oct. 25, 1921; d. Thomas Cecil and Vera (Buchanan) Ford; B.S. summa cum laude (Bonbright scholar), Northwestern U., 1942; m. Arthur Davis Choyke, Jr., Aug. 18, 1945; children—Christopher Ford, Tyler Van. Reporter, City News Bur., Chgo., 1942-43; reporter met. sect. Chgo. Tribune, 1943-44; feature writer OWI, N.Y.C., 1944-45; sec. Artcrest Products Co. Inc., Chgo., 1951-63, v.p., 1963—; founder, dir. Harper Sq. Press, Chgo., 1967—. Mem. Chgo. Press Vets. Assn., Soc. Midland Authors, Phi Beta Kappa. Clubs: Arts (Chgo.), John Evans of Northwestern U. Editor: Gallery Series One/Poets, 1967; Gallery Series Two/Poets—Poems of the Inner World, 1968; Gallery Series Three/Poets (Levitations and Observations), 1970; Gallery Series Four/Poets—I Am Talking about Revolution, 1973; Gallery Series Five/Poets-To an Aging Nation (with occult overtones), 1977; (under name Phyllis Ford with J. Kachmar and H. Winter) Apertures to Anywhere (poems), 1979. Home: 29 E Division St Chicago IL 60610 Office: 401 W Ontario St Chicago IL 60610

CHRISCOE, CHRISTINE FAUST, industrial trainer; b. Atlanta, Oct. 29, 1950; d. Henry Charles and Shirley Faye (Birdwell) Faust; B.A., Spring Hill Coll., 1973; postgrad. Ga. State U., 1974—; m. Ralph D. Chriscoe, June 25, 1983. Trainer, Fed. Res. Bank, Atlanta, 1973-77; project mgr., tng. dept. Coca Cola U.S.A., Atlanta, 1977-79, sr. project mgr., 1979-81, mgr. tech. tng., 1981-84, mgr. sales, mgmt. and mktg. tng., 1984-85, mgr. bottler tng., 1984—. Mem. Internat. TV and Video Assn., Am. Soc. Tng. and Devel., Soc. Applied Learning Technologies. Bd. trustees Ga. Shakespeare Festival, 1986—. Roman Catholic. Office: PO Drawer 1734 Atlanta GA 30301

CHRIST, LINDA RUTH, voluntary services executive; b. Buffalo, Aug. 3, 1949; d. Albert Louis and Edna Frances (O'Connor) C. A.A., SUNY-Buffalo, 1979; B.A. with high distinction, 1981. Adminstrv. coordinator SUNY-Buffalo Urban Ctr., 1967-73; office mgr. E.J. Meyer Meml. Hosp., Buffalo, 1973-77; account auditor Office Erie County Comptroller, Buffalo, 1977-78; adminstrv. asst. Erie County Med. Ctr., Buffalo, 1978-82, coordinator vol. services, 1982-84; asst. dir. ret. sr. vol. program Erie County, 1984—. Author, producer audio-visual tape: Rehab. Medicine: A Multidiscipline Approach, 1979, Erie County Med. Ctr. Presents: Skilled Nursing Facility, 1984. Mem. Buffalo Sesquicentennial Com., 1982; co-chmn. div. United Way of Buffalo and Erie County, 1981-84; mem. adv. bd. Literacy Vols. Buffalo and Erie County, 1985-86. Mem. Buffalo Dental Assts. Soc. (hon.), Western N.Y. Dirs. Vol. Services, Vol. Adminstrs. of Western N.Y., Women in Communications (historian 1982-84, co-chmn. regional conf. 1983-85, dir., sec. 1984-86), Orgn. of Triangles (state officer N.Y. 1969-72). Lodge: Order of Eastern Star (worthy matron 1975, fin. com. 1983—, chmn. publicity 1983—). Office: Erie County Dept Sr Services 95 Franklin St Buffalo NY 14202

CHRISTATOS, ELIZABETH JANE, educational counselor; b. N.Y.C., Oct. 25, 1955; d. Michael and Edna C.; B.S. in Elem. Edn., St. Bonaventure U., 1977, M.S. in Edn., 1980. Elem. tchr., choral dir. St. Bonaventure Elem. Sch., Allegany, N.Y., 1977-78; kindergarten tchr. Castleberry Elem. Sch., Ft. Worth, 1978; tchr. St. Mary's Elem. Sch., Olean, N.Y., 1979, Belmont Central Sch., Belmont, N.Y., 1980, counselor Adult Edn. Program, 1980, counselor Guidepost, Olean, 1980-81; coordinating counselor Youth Employment Tng. Program, from 1981; now sch. counselor Seneca Nation of Indians; Hotline vol. Family Aid Crisis Tng. Program; active Olean (N.Y.) Community Theatre, 1981-84, Olean Community Orchestra, 1974-75 Olean Community Choir, 1980-82. chmn. dance Am. Cancer Soc., 1980. Recipient Pythian award, K.P., 1973. Mem. Am. Assn. Counseling and Devel., Nat. Audubon Soc., Olean Jaycees (Springboard program award). Lodge: Order of Amaranth. Home: 142 S 1st St Olean NY 14760 Office: Jefferson Elem Sch Salamanca NY 14779

CHRISTENSEN, BRENDA JAYNE, administrative assistant, consultant; b. Heber City, Utah, Nov. 1, 1954; d. William Joe Lee and Barbara Ann (Nyman) Applegate; m. Robert Neal Larsen, June 3, 1972 (div. 1974); 1 child, Kobi Jo; m. Gerald E. Christensen, July 21, 1983; 1 child, Megan Laska. Student Utah Tech. Coll., 1972, 83, Barbizon Modeling Inst., 1976-79, Steven Henager Coll., 1979-80, Intermountain Coll., 80-81. Legal sec., acct. Stanley Title Co., Heber City, Utah, 1972-76; exec. sec. Century Metals, Provo, Utah, 1976-79; profl. model Barbizon, Salt Lake City, 1976-79; v.p. Alpine Industries, Pleasant Grove, Utah, 1979-80; pres., mgr. BJL Secretarial Services, Orem, Utah, 1980-84; adminstrv. exec. AJ Perea & Assocs., Lindon, Utah, 1984—; exec. cons. Minority Contractors, Salt Lake City, 1984—; sr. cons. Satellite TV, Utah County, 1978-80. Editor: Micro-Visions Logo (Outstanding Logo award 1979), 1979. Ceramic instr. Srs. Over Sixty, 1972—; chmn. Mountainland Head Start, 1975. Served with USAR, 1974-75. Mem. Nat. Assn. Female Execs., Associated Gen. Contractors Am., Nat. Assn. Court Recorders. Republican. Mormon. Avocations: ceramics; tole painting; bowling. Office: AJ Perea & Assocs Inc 45 S Geneva Rd Lindon UT 84062

CHRISTENSEN, CAROLE CECILE PIGLER, social work educator; b. Bklyn., Mar. 14, 1939; d. Samuel and Georgia Mae (Williams) Pigler; B.A. in Sociology, Howard U., 1960; M.S.W., U. Mich., 1963; D.Ed. in Counseling Psychology, McGill U., 1980; m. Torkild Vejby Christensen, Sept. 21, 1963; children—Karin, Michael, Lisa. Instr. social work Danish Sch. Social Work, 1964-66; mental health counselor Danish Women's League Counseling Service, Copenhagen, 1964-68; lectr. social work McGill U., 1970-80, asst. prof., 1980—, mem. senate McGill U., 1983-86. Bd. dirs. Internat. YMCA, Montreal, Can.; bd. govs. McGill U. Fulbright fellow, 1960-61, Can. Council fellow, 1977-80. Recipient Outstanding Doctoral Dissertation Biennial award, 1981. Mem. Am. Psychol. Assn., Canadian Assn. Social Workers, Am. Assn. Marriage and Family Therapy (clin.), Internat. Soc. for Intercultural Edn., Tng. and Research (governing council), Nat. Congress Black Women (Montreal region), Am. Assn. Sex Educators Counselors and Therapists (cert.), Afro-Asian Assn. Can. (co-founder), Phi Beta Kappa, Phi Kappa Phi. Office: McGill University School of Social Work 3506 University St Montreal PQ H3A 2A7 Canada

CHRISTENSEN, ILA SNYDER, civic worker; b. Comstock, Nebr., June 22, 1914; d. Frank G. and Minnie M. (Knight) Snyder; m. James Myron Christensen, Feb. 3, 1940; children—James Gordon, Larry Dean. B.A. in Edn., Kearney State Tchrs. Coll., 1937. Life cert. tchr. Prin. and tchr. rural high schs., Loup City, Sweetwater and St. Paul, Nebr., 1938-41, high schs., Brayton and Farwell, Nebr., 1941, 44; high sch. tchr., Elba and Ericson, Nebr., 1944, 55-56; owner-operator Mode O'Day Shop, York, 1962-64. Editor-compiler: York Greenwood Cemetery, 1983; York County Cemeteries, 1985; Swanson Family History, 1985; others. Pres. York Women's Dept. Club, 1980-81, Am. Legion Aux., 1979-80, 84-85; mem. VFW Aux. mem. York Bus. and Profl. Women's Club, 1962-71. Recipient Service award Helping Hands of York Coll., 1983; cert. of appreciation ARC, 1983, Nebr. Vets. Home, 1985. Mem. Greater York Area Geneal. Soc. (pres. 1981-83; cert. of appreciation 1981), Nebr. State Geneal. Soc., Nebr. State His. Soc., York County Hist. Soc. (archivist), Sherman County Hist. Soc. Republican. Mem. Ch. of Christ. Lodge: Rebekah (dep. dist. pres. 1968-69, 71-72, noble grand 1967-68). Avocations: music; gardening; genealogical research. Home: 1801 Iowa St York NE 68467

CHRISTENSEN, SALLY H., government official; b. Washington, Apr. 25, 1935; d. Sharp Adolphus and Grayce Elizabeth (Long) Hayden; m. John William Christensen, Mar. 24, 1969; children—John Stephen, Donna Isabelle. Student Dunbarton Coll. of Holy Cross, 1953-54, Am. U., U. Va. Program asst. to dep. commr. U.S. Office Edn., Washington, 1957-62, chief higher edn. and elem. and secondary edn. br., 1962-68, dep. dir. budget and manpower div., 1968-72, chief budget rev. br., 1974-80; dep. asst. sec., U.S. Dept. Edn., Washington, 1980-81, acting asst. sec., 1981, dir. budget service, 1981—; cons. U.S. Office Edn., 1972-74. Author ann. report to Congress on developing instns., 1973-78. Mem. Com. of 100, Arlington, Va., 1982—; pres. Reed Elem. Sch., PTA, Arlington, 1979-80; mem., chmn. Adv. Council on Vol. Programs, Arlington Sch. Bd., 1977-80; sch. bd. rep. Reed Elem. Sch., 1977-79; vol. tchr. aide, 1975-79. Recipient Pres.'s Disting. Exec. award, 1982; Sr. Exec. Service Bonus award U.S. Dept. Edn., 1981-84; Spl. citations U.S. Sec. and Commr. of Edn., 1980, 81, others. Mem. Nat. Congress of Parents and Tchrs., U.S. Budget Officers Conf., Sr. Exec. Assn. Roman Catholic. Avocations: art history; philosophy; antiques; interior designing. Home: 5415 N 18th St Arlington VA 22205 Office: US Dept Edn 400 Maryland Ave Washington DC 20202

CHRISTENSON, EVELYN CAROL, writer, lecturer; b. Muskegon, Mich., Jan. 31, 1922; d. Edward F. and Edna B. Luhman; A.A., Bethel Coll., St. Paul; student Moody Bible Inst., Chgo.; m. Harold Christenson, Feb. 14, 1942; children—Jan Christenson Johnson, Nancy Christenson Thompson, Kurt. Sec. to pres. Bethel Coll. and Sem., 1946-50; founding pres. United Prayer Ministries, St. Paul, 1973, chmn. bd., 1976—; internat. lectr. Australia, N.Z., Eng., Ireland, Scotland, Taiwan, Japan, India; mem. com., lectr. Am. Festival of Evangelism, Kansas City, Mo., 1981; co-prayer chmn., lectr. Internat. Council Bibl. Inerrancy, San Diego, Calif., 1982; consultation com. Internat. Conf. Itinerant Evangelists, Amsterdam, 1983; a sponsor Yr. of the Bible, 1983; mem. U.S. Nat. Prayer Com., 1983—; coordinator women's workshops Internat. Prayer Assembly, Seoul, Korea, 1984, World Vision Annual Internat. Day of Prayer, 1985; prayer leader trainer Billy Graham's Crusade, Washington, 1985; writer; books include: What Happens When Women Pray (Top Ten list Christian Booksellers), 1975; Lord Change Me (Top Ten list Christian Booksellers), 1977, Gaining Through Losing (nat. devotional book of 1982 Evang. Christian Pubs. Assn.), 1980; teaching cons. colls. Mem. Prison Fellowship Bd. (Washington); adv. bd. Concerned Women of Am., Berean League of Minn. Named Pacesetter of Yr., Bethel Coll., 1976; books rated top two by woman author Booksellers Jour., 1979; named Churchwoman of Yr., Religious Heritage of Am., 1980. Mem. Alumni Assn. Bethel Coll., Bethel Coll. Aux., Sem. Wives Assn. Bethel Sem. Home and Office: 4265 Brigadoon Dr Saint Paul MN 55112

CHRISTENSON, FABIENNE FADELEY, jet engine mfg. co. exec.; b. Washington, June 20, 1951; d. James McNelledge and Catherine Shirley (Sweeney) Fadeley; B.S. cum laude, U. Md., 1976; M.B.A. with honors, Boston U., 1979; m. Gordon A. Christenson, Sept. 16, 1979. With Gen. Electric Aircraft Engine Group, Evendale, Ohio, 1979—, buyer, contract adminstr., foreman, prodn. control specialist, configuration control specialist; pres. Mfg. Tng. Program, 1980. Home: 3465 Principio Ave Cincinnati OH 45226 Office: Mail Drop A-182C Neumann Way Evendale OH 45215

CHRISTENSON, HELENE GOEHRING, retired accountant, auditor, budget analyst; b. Avon, S.D., May 24, 1912. B.S. in Bus. Adminstrn., U. Tulsa, 1957. Field auditor for various Honolulu C.P.A.s, 1958-64; adminstrv. asst. and fiduciary auditor Cooke Trust Ltd., 1965; auditor Naval Supply Ctr., 1967-69; acct., auditor Hdqrs. Fleet Marine Force, Pacific, 1969-81; budget and acctg. analyst Naval Constrn. Bns., Pearl Harbor, 1981-82, ret., 1982. Registered lobbyist for City, and County of Honolulu, Hawaii State Legislature 1981—; mem. Waikiki Neighborhood Bd., Honolulu, 1985; pres. Kalia, Inc., 1978—, Hawaii council Assns. Apt. Owners, 1985. Home: 425 Ena Rd Apt 906A Honolulu HI 96815

CHRISTIAENS, SHERRY, sales manager; b. Dallas, July 24, 1951; d. John Lee Kirby and Barbara Jane (Beary) Statton; m. Phillip Wayne Boston, Nov. 25, 1967 (div. Nov. 1977); 1 child, Chad Boston; m. 2d, Steven Leon Christiaens, Nov. 24, 1979; children—Cody, Bernae. Student U. Tex.-Dallas, Mt. San Antonio Coll., Calif. Asst. sales mgr. Dychem Internat., Dallas, 1978-80; asst. sales mgr., promotions mgr. Sta. KLIF, Dallas, 1974-78; regional sales mgr. Automatic Solar Covers, Inc., San Dimas, Calif., 1983—. Mem. NOW (chair chpt. media watch 1985, treas. chpt. 1984), Sales Profls. Los Angeles (founder, pres. 1983—), Nat. Assn. Female Execs. Avocations: English riding, horses. Home: 1306 Herring St West Covina CA 91790

CHRISTIAN, BETTY JO, lawyer; b. Temple, Tex., July 27, 1936; d. Joe and Mattie Manor (Brown) Wiest; m. Ernest S. Christian, Jr., Dec. 24, 1960. B.A. summa cum laude, U. Tex., 1957, LL.B., 1960. Bar: Tex. bar 1961, U.S. Supreme Ct. bar 1964, D.C. bar 1980. Law clk. Supreme Ct. Tex., 1960-61; atty. ICC, 1961-68, asst. gen. counsel, Washington, 1970-72, asso. gen. counsel, 1972-76, commr., 1976-79; partner firm Steptoe & Johnson, Washington, 1980—; atty. Labor Dept., Dallas, 1968-70. Mem. ABA, Fed. Bar Assn. (Younger Fed. Lawyer award 1964), Tex. Bar Assn., Am. Law Inst., Adminstrv. Conf. U.S., City Tavern Assn. Office: 1330 Connecticut Ave NW Washington DC 20036

CHRISTIAN, CAYE, advertising executive; b. Phila., June 11, 1922; d. Francis Samuel and Josephine (Buono) Bilotta; m. Granville Leo Hedgepeth, Oct. 16, 1943 (div. 1952); 1 son, Michael S. Hedgepeth. B.S., U. Pa., 1943. Producer, Sta. WNEW, N.Y.C., 1949-51; assoc. advt. dir. Gimbel Bros., Phila., 1951-55; advt. dir. Neiman Marcus, Dallas, 1955-57; v.p. Spiro & Assocs., Phila., 1957-70; sr. v.p. Lane Golden Phillips, Phila., 1970-81; exec. v.p., ptnr. Greenwald/Christian Advt. Inc., Phila., 1981—. Author films: To Your Credit, 1976; At Your Service, 1978. Mem. Bucks County (Pa.) Democratic Com., 1960. Mem. TV Radio and Advt. Club, Execs. Internat. (mktg. com. 1980—). Democrat. Roman Catholic. Home: 630 Kenilworth Mews Philadelphia PA 19147 Office: Greenwald Christian Advertising Inc 1760 Market St Philadelphia PA 19103

CHRISTIAN, DOLLY LEWIS, civic affairs administrator; b. N.Y.C.; d. Daniel Webster and Adeline (Walton) Lewis. Dir. civic affairs equal employment affirmative action program Sperry & Hutchinson Co., N.Y.C., 1968-84; program mgr. affirmative action programs IBM Corp., 1984—. Chmn. bd. N.Y. Urban League, 1977-78, pres., 1978-84; panel of arbitrators Am. Arbitration Assn., N.Y.C., 1973—; adv. com. master's degree program in fund raising mgmt. New Sch. for Social Research, N.Y.C., 1978—; mem. mgmt. assistance com. Greater N.Y. Fund United Way, 1983—; treas. Assoc. Black Charities, 1982-84; bd. dirs. Coalition of 100 Black Women, 1981. Recipient scroll of honor Nat. Council Negro Bus. and Profl. Women's Clubs, 1975, community service award, 1974, ombudswoman award, 1975; youth salute to black corp. execs. award Nat. Youth Movement, 1975, corp. recipient Mary McLeod Bethune award Nat. Council Negro Women, 1976; spl. corp. recognition award Met. Council of Brs., NAACP, 1981. Mem. Council Concerned Black Execs. (vice chmn. 1970-77), NAACP, N.Y. Personnel Mgmt. Assn., Edges Group (v.p. 1981), Nat. Urban Affairs Council (dir. 1977—). Home: Jamaica NY 11435 Office: IBM Corp 2000 Purchase St Purchase NY 10577

CHRISTIAN, KAREN DORTHEA HANSEN, legislative liaison, real estate broker, educator; b. Berkeley, Calif., Mar. 18, 1938; d. Kirby Walter and Isabel Jordan (Smith) Hansen; m. William Shannon Christian, Oct. 23, 1961 (div. Oct. 1975); children—Sarah Ann, Janet Jordan. Student U. Geneva, 1956; B.A., U. Calif.-Berkeley, 1959, teaching cert., 1960; postgrad. San Diego State Coll., 1960-62. Lic. real estate broker, Calif.; cert. tchr., Calif. Tchr., Carden Pvt. Sch., Fresno, Calif., 1974-75; tchr. music Fresno Unified Schs., 1975-76; salesman Brinker Real Estate, Fresno, 1975-78, Adanalian & Jackson Real Estate, Fresno, 1978-79, Bob Johansen Realty, Fresno, 1979-80; real estate broker Karen H. Christian, Realtor, Fresno, 1980—; legislative analyst Fresno Bd. Realtors, 1982-85, also dir., 1981-83. Mem. Republican Central Com., Fresno County, Calif., 1980-82; exec. dir. Taxpayers Assn. Fresno County, 1984—. Named Realtor-Assoc. of Year, 1979. Mem. Nat. Assn. Realtors, Calif. Assn. Realtors (dir. 1978-80, 82-84, dist. chmn. land use com. 1980-83), Fresno Area Mktg. Exchange (founder, sec. treas. 1978-79); U. Calif. Alumni Assn., LWV, Kappa Delta. Christian Scientist. Home and Office: 2539 W San Bruno Fresno CA 93711

CHRISTIAN, MAUREEN MAHER, clinical psychologist; b. Poughkeepsie, N.Y., Mar. 30, 1947; d. Thomas Francis and Linda Maher; B.A. (scholar), Trinity Coll., 1969; M.A., Am. U., 1971, Ph.D., 1979; m. James H. Christian, Aug. 8, 1970; 1 child, Justin Maher. Staff psychologist Youth Ctr. One, D.C. Dept. of Corrections, Lorton, Va., 1971-74, chief psychologist Youth Ctr. Two, 1974-80; clin. psychologist St. Elizabeth's Hosp., Washington, 1980-85, chief clin. psychologist, 1985—. Cons., bd. dirs. Isaiah House, Washington, 1979-80; bd. dirs. Shadowalk Home Assn., Fairfax Sta., Va., 1981-84, v.p., 1982-84; mem. reorgn. research task force D.C. Mental Health Service, 1985—; mem. exec. bd. Boy Scouts Am., 1982—; mem. Hospitalurde Psychology Adv. Council, 1985—. Recipient award of excellence D.C. Dept. Corrections, 1979, 80, St. Elizabeth's Hosp., 1984. Mem. Am. Psychol. Assn., D.C. Psychol. Assn., Med. Soc. St. Elizabeth's Hosp., Psi. Chi, Phi Kappa Phi. Contbr. articles to profl. publs. Office: St Elizabeths Hosp Mary O'Malley Div 2700 Martin Luther King Ave SE Washington DC 20032

CHRISTIAN, SHIRLEY ANN, journalist; b. Windsor, Mo., Jan. 16, 1938; d. Herbert Walsh and Minnie Lucille (Acker) C.; B.A., Pittsburg (Kans.) State U., 1960; M.A., Ohio State U., 1966; Nieman fellow, Harvard U., 1973-74. UN corr. AP, 1970-73, copy editor fgn. desk, N.Y.C., 1974-77, chief of bur., Santiago, Chile, 1977-79; Latin Am. corr. Miami (Fla.) Herald, 1979-84; fgn. affairs reporter in Washington, N.Y. Times, 1985—; adj. prof. journalism Columbia U., 1977. Author: Nicaragua: Revolution in the Family, 1985. Recipient Pulitzer prize for internat. reporting, 1981, George Polk Meml. award for fgn. reporting, 1981. Mem. Overseas Press Club. Congregationalist. Home: 4230 1/2 River Rd NW Washington DC 20016 Office: NY Times 1717 K St NW Washington DC 20036

CHRISTIANSON, KAREN MARIA ANNA, lawyer; b. Milw., Mar. 10, 1949; d. Donald Edwin and Maria (Kotelnikova) Jones; m. Gary Michael Christianson, June 26, 1971; 1 son, Michael. B.S., U. Wis., 1970; J.D., U. Oreg., 1979. Bar: Oreg. 1979, Wis. 1983. Tchr., S. Milw. Sch. Dist., 1970-71, Corvallis, Oreg., 1971-76; dep. dist. atty. Linn County, Albany, Oreg., 1979-83; city atty. West Bend (Wis.), 1984—. Mem. Planning Commn. Corvallis, 1980-83; active Benton County Democrats. Mem. Oreg. State Bar Assn., Wis. State Bar Assn., ABA, Phi Delta Phi. Club: PACE.

CHRISTIE, BARBARA LINETTE, lawyer; b. Phila., Sept. 28, 1947; d. James Snyder and Ingrid Wanda (Sommer) C. B.S., Chatham Coll., Pitts., 1969; J.D., Villanova U., 1972. Bar. Pa. 1972, U.S. Dist. Ct. (ea. dist.) Pa. 1973, U.S. Ct. Appeals (3d cir.) 1973, U.S. Supreme Ct. 1976. Asst. dist. atty. Phila. Dist. Atty.'s Office, 1972—, sr. trial asst. in homicide div., dist. atty., 1974—. Office: 1300 Chestnut St Philadelphia PA 19107

CHRISTIE, JEAN OGILVY, emerita history educator; b. Manila, Philippines, Feb. 8, 1912; d. Emerson Brewer and Clara Cecilia (Pray) C.; m. Robert Claus, June 27, 1938; children—Richard Alan, Peter. B.A., George Washington U., 1934; M.A., Fletcher Sch. Law and Diplomacy, Medford, Mass., 1935, Ph.D., Columbia U., 1963. Lectr. history Bklyn. Coll., 1955-60; instr. Hunter Coll., N.Y.C., 1960-62; instr., asst. prof., assoc. prof., prof. Fairleigh Dickinson U., Teaneck, N.J., 1963-77, prof. emerita, 1977—. Author: Morris Llewellyn Cooke, 1983. Co-editor: Decisions and Revisions, 1975, America Since World War II, 1976. Contbr. articles to hist. jours. Vice pres. Great Neck Reform Democratic Assn., N.Y., 1983—; mem. exec. bd. SANE, Great Neck, 1984—; chmn. book award com. Berkshire Conf., 1981-83; co-chmn. N.Y. Met. area coordinating conf. Women in Hist. Profession, 1985. Mem. Am. Hist. Assn., Orgn. Am. Historians, Conf. for Peace Research in History, Berkshire Conf. of Women Historians. Democrat. Avocations: hiking; piano; figure skating. Home: 34 Bellingham Ln Great Neck NY 11023

CHRISTIE, LAURIE POTTER, state agency administrator; b. Harvard, Ill., Sept. 20, 1956; d. Donald Eugene and Margurita Marie (Ferrero) Potter; m. Scott Graham Christie, Nov. 15, 1980. B.A., Ind. U., 1978. Constituent analyst Ind. State Senate, Indpls., 1979; exec. dir. Ind. State Election Bd., Indpls., 1981—; campaign cons. Ind. Republican State Com., 1978-81, Ind. State Senate, 1979. Author: Instruction Manual for Precinct Officials, 1982. Campus coordinator Myers for Congress Com., Bloomington, Ind., 1974; field campaign mgr. Ind. Rep. State Com., Indpls., 1978; campaign adviser Ind. State Legis. Coms., Indpls., 1978; dep. campaign mgr. Bob Orr for Gov. Coms., 1980; campaign advisor O'Laughlin for Clk. of Cts., 1982. Named Hon. Sec. of State, Ind. Sec. of State, 1979, Sagamore of Wabash, Gov. of Ind., 1981. Mem. Internat. Orgn. Election Ofcls., Nat. Assn. Secs. of State. Methodist. Club: Valley Riders Saddle. Office: Ind State Election Bd 850 N Meridian St Indianapolis IN 46204

CHRISTIN, VIOLET MARGUERITE, cons.; b. Chgo., Oct. 4, 1903; d. Charles A. and Eva M. (Bosse) C.; student Northwestern U., 1936-37, Am. Inst. Banking, 1955-75. With Nat. Bank of Austin, 1922-76, asst. sec., 1953-57, sec., 1957-65, sec., asst. v.p., 1965-76, sec. mktg. com., 1977-79; cons. Mem. Am. Inst. Banking, Ill. Bankers Assn. (50 year club), Assn. Chgo. Bank Women, Nat. Assn. Bank Women, Chgo. Fin. Advertisers (treas. 1964-65, 69-81, dir., treas. 1973-81, Eagle award 1977, First Lady Life Mem. 1981). Clubs: Chgo. Press, Execs., Chgo. Advt. Home: 805 N Grove Ave Oak Park IL 60302

CHRISTO-JAVACHEFF, JEANNE-CLAUDE, corporation executive; b. Morocco, June 13, 1935; d. Jacques Marie and Precilda Angela (Eton) de Guillebon; m. Christo Vladimirov Javacheff; 1 child, Cyril Christo. B.A. in Latin and Philosophy, U. Tunis, Paris, 1952. Dealer Christo's Works of Art, N.Y.C., 1958—, curator, registrar, 1958—; pres., treas. C.V.J. Corp., N.Y.C., 1970—. Author articles. Recipient Keys of City, Rifle, Colo., 1972, Kansas City, Mo., 1978, Miami, Fla., 1983. Cited by Calif. Legislature for Running Fence sculpture, 1976. Mem. Mus. Modern Art, Project Studios One, Archtl. League, Internat. Ctr. Photography. Avocation: photography. Address: CVJ Corp 48 Howard St New York NY 10013

CHRISTOLON, BLAIR KAY BIRKHOLZ, librarian; b. Oak Park, Ill., Oct. 1, 1947; d. William Howard and Evelyn Weinkauf (Mueller) Birkholz; B.A., U. Denver, 1969; M.L.S., Brigham Young U., Provo, Utah, 1976; m. Warren Kenneth Christolon, Aug. 12, 1972; children—Christopher Warren, Niklas Winston. Librarian, Johns Hopkins U., USIS, Bologna, Italy, 1972-73; tchr. Denver public schs., 1969-74; asst. dir. children's services Weber County Library, Ogden, Utah, 1975-77; dir. govt. library Overseas Pvt. Investment Corp., Washington, 1978; library cons. Dept. Edn., Washington, 1979-82; admissions dir. Alpha-Bet Sch., Manassas, Va., 1981-85, pres., 1984-85; librarian Prince William Library, Manassas, Va., 1985—. Mem. parent adv. com. Va. Coop. Extension, 1981—, editor newsletter, 1981—; cons. Parent Infant Handicapped Edn., 1979; v.p. Manassas Friends of Library, 1983—. Recipient Outstanding Woman award U. Denver, 1969. Mem. ALA, Delta Gamma. Home: 8396 Briarmont Ln Manassas VA 22111

CHRISTOPHER, DOLORES LEE, govt. ofcl.; b. N.Y.C., Feb. 5, 1940; d. Ernest Charles and Ethel Margrita (Cox) C.; A.A.S., Borough Manhattan Community Coll., 1970; B.A., Fordham U., 1978; M.B.A., N.Y. Inst. Tech., 1982. Various clerical positions, 1956-62; with U.S. Postal Service, 1965—, jr. acct. internat. accts. center, N.Y.C., 1976-77, supr. settle sect., 1977-81, mgr. center, 1981—, EEO counselor, 1977—; shop steward Am. Postal Workers Union, 1974-77. Bd. dirs. Manhattan Community Coll., 1964—, vice chmn., 1974; bd. dirs. Esplanade Gardens Coop., 1967-75, parlimentarian, vice chmn., treas., 1967-75. Recipient various service awards. Mem. Alumni Assn. Fordham U. Democrat. Roman Catholic. Home: 101-125 W 147th St New York NY 10039 Office: GPO Bldg Room 4519 New York NY 10099

CHRISTOPHER, MAURINE BROOKS, writer, editor; b. Three Springs, Tenn.; d. John Davis and Zula Pangle Brooks; B.A., Tusculum Coll., 1941; Litt.D. (hon.), St. John's U.; m. Milbourne Christopher, June 25, 1949. Reporter, entertainment editor Kingsport (Tenn.) Times, 1941-43; reporter, feature writer Balt. Sun, 1943-45; TV radio editor Advt. Age, 1947-51, sr. editor, head broadcast dept., 1951-77, dep. exec. editor, N.Y.C., 1977-79, dep. exec. editor, 1979-84, Videotech columnist, 1979—, roving editor, mem. editorial bd., 1984—. Mem. Am. Women in Radio and TV (past pres. N.Y.C. chpt., cert. of merit), Women in Communications, Assn. Study Afro-Am. Life and History. Author: America's Black Congressmen, 1971; Black Americans in Congress, 1976. Home: 333 Central Park W New York NY 10025 Office: 220 E 42d St New York NY 10017

CHRISTOPHER, SHERY ANN, indoor/outdoor recreation promoter, clothing designer; b. Baton Rouge, July 6, 1955; d. Joseph Aking Hochong and Jeannine Sanders. B.F.A., Met. State U., Denver, 1978. Cert. family counselor. Patient family counselor Children's Hosp., Denver, 1977-80; mktg. cons. Racom, Phoenix, 1981-83; Bibbins Rice, Lafayette, La., 1983-85; ptnr., dir. mktg. The Great Am. Adventure Game, Inc., New Orleans, 1985—; designer Designers, Inc., London, 1972-73; cons. Co-Med, Denver, 1979-80; advt. cons., 1981—. Author poetry: Here's To You, 1982. Researcher Greenpeace, Denver, 1979. Republican. Roman Catholic. Avocations: writing; fashion design; skiing; outdoor roller skating. Office: The Great Am Adventure Game Inc 2002 20th St Suite 4202 Kenner LA 70062

CHRISTY, AUDREY MEYER, public relations consultant; b. N.Y.C., Mar. 11, 1933; d. Mathias J. and Harriet Meyer; B.A., U. Buffalo, 1967; m. James R. Christy, Apr. 19, 1952; children—James R., III, Kathryn M., John T., Alysia A., William J. Public relations officer Turgeon Bros., Buffalo, 1968-69; mem. public relations staff Sch. Fine Arts, U. Nebr., Omaha, 1972; public relations exec. Mathews & Clark Advt., Sarasota, Fla., 1974-75; profiles editor Tampa Bay mag., Tampa, Fla., 1972; public relations cons. Bildex Corp., 1973-79; owner, operator Christy & Assocs., Venice, Fla., 1976—. Vice chmn. Erie County March of Dimes, 1970; bd. dirs. Sarasota chpt. Am. Cancer Soc.; mem. S.W. Fla. Ambulance Adv. Com., 1981; pres. Community Health Edn. Council. Recipient various advt. awards. Mem. Pub. Relations Soc. Am. (Outstanding Pub. Service award 1984), Fla. Hosp. Assn., Sarasota County C. of C. (v.p., bd. dirs., vice chmn. mktg. 1984-85), Sarasota Manatee Press Club, LWV (editor Sarasota publ. 1978-79). Home: 216 Bayshore Circle Venice FL Office: 609 S Tamiami Trail Venice FL

CHRONIC, BETTY MCWILLIAMS, state official, writer; b. Tulsa, June 24, 1925; d. Roland Forrest and Faye Catherine (Foster) McWilliams; m. William Lee Chronic, Apr. 7, 1945; children—Barbara, Jane, Katherine. Student U. Tulsa, 1943-46; B.A., U. Colo., 1950, postgrad., 1970, 74, 76. Cons., editor Mental Health Instns. Colo., 1955-59; mem. Colo. Bd. Health, Colo., 1963-68; field supr. U.S. Census, 1970; mem. Colo. Water Quality Control Commn., 1966-68, Boulder City-County Bd. Health, 1971-76; asst. county clk. and recorder Boulder County, 1973-74; elections officer Colo. Dept. State, Denver, 1976-77, dir. elections and licensing, 1977—; panelist regional seminars Fed. Election Commn., 1979, 83. Author: Colorado Year Book, 1964; editor Gov.'s Com. Report: What Are Your Responsibilities in Mental Health?, 1958. County vice-chmn., state sec. Colo. Republican Com., 1958-64; trustee 1st Presbyn. Ch., Boulder, 1973-78; bd. dirs. Boulder County United Way, 1967-77; neighborhood chmn. troop leader Girl Scouts U.S.A., 1965-76; presdl. elector Colo., 1960; vice chmn. Boulder Landmarks Adv. Bd., 1983—. Recipient Young Women of Achievement award Altrusa Club, 1967, Florence Sabin Health award Colo. Pub. Health Assn., 1976. Mem. Internat. Assn. Clks., Recorders, Elections Ofcls. and Treas., Phi Beta Kappa, Phi Alpha Theta. Republican. Home: 4705 Shawnee Pl Boulder CO 80303 Office: Dept of State 1575 Sherman St Room 214 Denver CO 80203

CHRONISTER, DONNA JEAN, mental health administrator; b. Kewanee, Ill., Sept. 3, 1943; d. Donald Lewis and Genevieve Marie (Mower) Marshall; m. William B. Chronister, Aug. 20, 1966 (div. May 1980). B.A., Park Coll., 1965; M.S.W., U. Ill., 1978. Stewardess TWA, Kansas City, Mo., 1965-66; casework supr. Mo. Div. Family Services, St. Louis, 1966-71; program dir. Champaign County Mental Health Ctr., Ill., 1972—; cons. Supportive Families of Mentally Ill, Champaign, 1983—, Bank of Ill., Champaign, 1982. Recipient Program of Yr. award Champaign Mental Health Assn., 1984; Community Support Systems grantee Ill. Dept. Mental Health, 1982, Residential Services grantee, 1984; transitional employment tng. grantee Ill. Dept. Rehab., 1985. Mem. Exec. Club Champaign County (pres. 1984-85, mem. founding bd. dirs. 1982-83), Ill. Assn. Community Mental Health Adminstrs. Avocations: golf, reading, travel. Home: 2705 Southwood St Champaign IL 61821 Office: Champaign County Mental Health Ctr Champaign IL 61820

CHRYSSICAS, VALERIE FOSTER, marketing and advertising agency executive; b. Newark, June 6, 1955; d. Robert Samuel and Adelaide J. (Nelson) Foster; m. Willie Alton Davis, III, June 14, 1974 (div. 1977); m. John Charles Chryssicas, Jr., Jan. 4, 1980; 1 child, Jason Christopher. Student Randolph-Macon Coll., 1973-75; B.A. in Spanish, Salisbury State Coll., 1977; M.S. in Sociolinguistics, Georgetown U., 1980. Account rep. List Am., Inc., Washington, 1980; account exec. Infomat, Inc., Rolling Hills Estates, Calif., 1981; pres. N.M.C., Inc., Newport Mktg., Irvine, Calif., 1982—. Libertarian. Office: NMC Inc dba Newport Mktg 1731 Kaiser Ave Irvine CA 92714

CHUMCHAL, PATRICIA ANNE, educational diagnostician, consultant; b. Edna, Tex., Nov. 26, 1938; d. William Conway and Laura Edith (Hessong) Scruggs; m. Rudy P. Chumchal, June 1, 1956; children—William R., Nancy G. Chumchal Mendieta. B.S., Southwest Tex. U., 1972; M.Ed., U. Houston, 1976. With Victoria Bank & Trust, Tex., 1959-61; salesperson Hoff Realty, Victoria, 1961-67; tchr. Presbyterian Day Sch., Victoria, 1965-67; tchr., supr. Devereux Found., Victoria, 1967-71; tchr. Mission Valley Ind. Sch. Dist., Tex., 1971-73; tchr., ednl. diagnostician Victoria Ind. Sch. Dist., Tex., 1973—. Developer curriculum for boys with severe emotional problems. Chairperson Crimestoppers, Victoria, 1985-86; del. Tex. Democratic Party, 1984. Mem. NEA (nat. del. 1983, 84, 85), Tex. State Tchrs. Assn., Victoria C. of C. (chmn. edn. awareness 1984-85, chmn. ptnrs. in learning 1984-85), Phi Delta Kappa, Kappa Delta Phi, Alpha Chi. Presbyterian. Clubs: Garden (pres. 1963), County Genealogical Soc. (pres. 1982-84). Avocations: reading; genealogical research; running; public speaking. Home: 705 Dundee St Victoria TX 77904

CHUN, CONNIE CASPE, state legislator; b. Iloilo City, Philippines, June 2, 1928; came to U.S., 1956, naturalized, 1962; R.N., Manila Sanitarium and Hosp., 1953; B.S. in Nursing, Loma Linda U., 1958; M.P.H. in Comprehensive Planning and Adminstrn., U. Hawaii, 1972, J.D., 1978; m. Hing Hua Chun, Apr. 10, 1970; children—May Lynne, Jerry, June, Hingson, Joy, Daven. Dir. nursing Golden Gate Hosp., San Francisco, 1962-68; asst. dir. nursing St. Francis Hosp., Honolulu, 1968-70; health planner Rehab. Hosp. of the Pacific, Honolulu, 1970-72; admitted to Hawaii bar, 1979; individual practice law, Honolulu, 1979; mem. Hawaii Ho. of Reps., 1980—, chmn. com. on public assistance and human services, 1980-82, mem. coms. on fin., human services, housing, state gen. planning, 1982—, vice chmn. com. on health, 1982—. Trustee sr. cardiovascular rehab. program Honolulu Med. Group, 1980-81, Filipino Garden, Inc., East-West Center, 1981—; chmn. Honolulu Police

Commn., 1979-80; v.p. Leeward Marathon Clinic, 1980; rev. bd. Mid Pacific Road Runners Club, 1980; mem. Women Democrats of Hawaii; adv. com. Pediatric Arthritis Ctr. of Hawaii. Fulbright scholar, 1956; R.N., Hawaii, Calif. Mem. Am. Bar Assn., Hawaii State Bar Assn., Hawaiian Women Lawyers, Am. Nurses Assn., Hawaii Nurses Assn., Am. Pub. Health Assn., Hawaii Pub. Health Assn., Filipino C. of C., U. Hawaii Law Sch. Alumni Assn., Bus. and Profl. Women's Club. Club: Filipino Women's. Co-author: Hawaii State Health Facilities Plan, 1975; Master Plan Rehabilitation Hospital of the Pacific, 1976; contbr. articles to legal jours. Office: State Capitol Room 433 Honolulu HI 96813

CHUN, WENDY SAU WAN, investment company executive; b. China, Oct. 17, 1951; came to U.S., 1975; d. Siu Kee and Lai Ching (Wong) C.; m. Wing Chiu Ng, Aug. 12, 1976. B.S., Hong Kong Bapt. Coll., 1973; postgrad. U. Hawaii-Manoa, 1975-77. Real estate saleswoman Tropic Shores Realty Co., Honolulu, 1977-80; pres., prin., broker Advance Realty Investment Co., Honolulu, 1980—; owner Video Fun Centre, Honolulu, 1981-83; v.p., immigration/fin. cons. Asia-Am. Investment, Inc., Honolulu, 1983—; co-owner, dir. H & N Tax, Honolulu, 1983—; internat. cons. Capital Investment of Hawaii, 1983—. Mem. Nat. Assn. Realtors. Avocations: singing; dancing; swimming; dramatic performances. Home: Apt 3302 2333 Kapiolani Blvd Honolulu HI 96826

CHUNG, JULIA, import and export company executive, management consultant; b. Kaohsiusg, Taiwan, Aug. 25, 1947; came to U.S., 1970, naturalized, 1984; d. Li-Chuan and Yu-King (Chiu) C. B.A., U. Chinese Culture, Taiwan, 1970; M.A., Loyola U., New Orleans, 1972. Owner, mgr. Chung Overseas Co., Hong Kong, China, 1978—, Taipei, Taiwan, 1978—, Portland, Oreg., 1980—. Avocations: tennis; swimming. Home: 1936 NW 143d Ave Apt 79 Portland OR 97229 Office: Chung Overseas Co PO Box 25622 Portland OR 97225

CHUPELA, DOLORES CAROLE, children's librarian; b. New Brunswick, N.J., Dec. 25, 1952; d. John Joseph and Cecilia Dolores (Pazdon) C. B.S., Douglass Coll., 1975; M.L.S., Rutgers U., 1984. Cert. tchr., N.J. Librarian, Edison Pub. Library (N.J.), 1979—. Speaker civic orgns. Named Tercentennial Citizen-of-Week, Middlesex County, N.J., New Brunswick, 1983; recipient Presdl. sports award in figure skating, 1980. Mem. ALA and Assn. Library Service to Children, N.J. Library Assn., Children's Book Council. Democrat. Roman Catholic. Club: Olde Monmouth Skating. Contbg. author 1984 Summer Reading Club Manual. Home: 51 Latonia St Edison NJ 08817 Office: Edison Pub Library 340 Plainfield Ave Edison NJ 08817

CHURCH, IRENE ZABOLY, personnel services co. exec.; b. Cleve., Feb. 18, 1947; d. Bela Paul and Irene Elizabeth (Chandas) Zaboly; student public schs.; children—Irene Elizabeth, Elizabeth Anne, Lauren Alexandria, John Dale. Personnel cons., Cleve., 1965; sec., Cleve., 1966-68; personnel cons., Cleve., 1968-70; owner, pres. Oxford Personnel, Euclid, Ohio, 1973—; pres. Oxford Temporaries, Inc., Euclid, 1979-81, chmn. bd., 1981—; guest lectr. in field; lectr. on work and family life. Fund raiser Better Bus. Bur., 1973; mem. council small enterprises Greater Cleve. Growth Assn., 1983—; chpt. leader Nat. Coalition on TV Violence, 1983—. Mem. Nat. Assn. Personnel Cons. (cert., co-chmn. ethics com. 1977-78), Ohio Assn. Personnel Cons. (trustee 1975-80, 1st v.p., chmn. bus. practices and ethics 1976-78), Greater Cleve. Assn. Personnel Cons. (1st v.p., chmn. bus. practices and ethics 1974-76, pres., recipient Vi Pender award 1976-77, adv., chmn. Vi Pender award 1977-78, bd. dirs., chmn. arbitration, chmn. fund raising 1980—, trustee 1985—), Euclid Chagrin Valley C. of C. Home: 8 Ridgecrest Dr Chagrin Falls OH 44022 Office: Exec Commons Suite 300 29425 Chagrin Blvd Pepper Pike OH 44122

CHURCH, JANICE MARIE, nurse; b. Mt. Vernon, Ohio, Jan. 18, 1949; d. Kenneth Merton Jacobs and Olga Victoria (Jessup) Jacobs Cohen; m. Danny Lee Parrott (div.); 1 child, Heatherlyn Elizabeth Viola Parrott; m. David Martin Church (div.); 1 child, Honahleigh Mercia Anne Church. R.N. Central Ohio Tech. Coll., Newark, 1978. Psychiat. nurse Mt. Vernon Developmental Center, 1978-80; aftercare coordinator Moundbuilders Guidance Center, Mt. Vernon, 1980—; vice chairperson Dist. 6 Aftercare Council, Columbus, Ohio, 1981—; bd. dirs. Kno-Ho-Co, Warsaw, Ohio, 1982—, vice chairperson, Mt. Vernon, 1983—. Bd. dirs. Family Planning Assn., Mt. Vernon, 1982—. Office: Moundbuilders Guidance Center 8402 Blackjack Rd Mount Vernon OH 43050

CHURCH, MARTHA ELEANOR, college president b. Pitts., Nov. 17, 1930; d. Walter Seward and Eleanor (Boyer) C.; B.A., Wellesley Coll., 1952; M.A., U. Pitts., 1954; Ph.D., U. Chgo., 1960; D.Sc. (hon.), Lake Erie Coll., 1975; D.Litt. (hon.), Houghton Coll., 1980; L.H.D. (hon.), Queen's Coll., N.C., 1981, Ursinus Coll., 1981, St. Joseph Coll., 1982, Towson State U., 1983. Lectr. geography Mt. Mercy Coll. (now Carlow Coll.), Pitts., 1953; instr. geology and geography Mt. Holyoke Coll., South Hadley, Mass., 1953-57; lectr. geography Ind. U. Gary Center, 1958; instr., then asst. prof. geography, Wellesley Coll., 1960-65; dean coll., prof. geography Wilson Coll., 1965-71; assoc. exec. sec. Commn. Higher Edn., Middle States Assn. Colls and Secondary Schs., 1971-75; pres. Hood Coll., 1975—; dir. Farmers and Mechanics Nat. Bank; vice-chmn. Am. Council on Edn., 1978-79; cons. for Choice: Books for College Libraries; adv. bd. Project Noncollegiate-Sponsored Instruction, 1974-77, HEW Fund for Improvement of Postsecondary Edn., 1976-79; mem. Sec. Navy's Adv. Bd. on Edn. and Tng., 1976-81. Bd. dirs. Four-Year Servicemen's Opportunity Project, 1973-75; chmn. Md. state adv. com. U.S. Commn. on Civil Rights, 1981-82; bd. dirs. Nat. Center Higher Edn. Mgmt. Systems, 1980-84, Inst. Edn. Leadership, 1982—; trustee Bradford Coll., 1982—, Peddie Sch., 1982—; mem. Higher Edn. Colloquium, 1981—, Edn. Commn. of the States, 1981—; mem. Md. Humanities Council, 1985—; pres. bd. dirs. Medici Found., 1985—. Recipient Christian R. and Mary F. Lindback Found. Disting. Teaching award Wilson Coll., 1971. Mem. Assn. Am. Colls. (steering com. baccalaureate degree project 1982-85), Md. Ind. Coll. and Univ. Assn. (pres. 1979-81), Am. Assn. Higher Edn. (pres. 1980-81), Am. Assn. Advancement Humanities (dir. 1979-83), Council Internat. Exchange of Scholars, AAUW, Am. Conf. Acad. Deans (sec., editor 1969-71), Am. Home Econs. Assn. (public mem. council profl. devel. 1981-83), Council Protestant Colls. and Univs. (dir. 1969-71), Sigma Delta Epsilon. Clubs: Cosmopolitan, Mount Vernon. Author: The Spatial Organization of Electric Power Territories in Massachusetts, 1960; contbg. author Opportunity in Adversity, 1985; co-editor: A Basic Geographical Library: A Selected and Annotated Book List for American Colleges, 1966; cons. editor Change Mag., 1980—. Home: President's House Hood Coll Frederick MD 21701

CHURCH, ROBERTA, retired government official; d. Robert R. Jr. and Sara (Johnson) Church; A.B., Northwestern U., 1935, M.A., 1937. Social worker Family and Child Welfare div. Chgo. Welfare Adminstrn., 1940-43, adoption div. Ill. Children's Home and Aid Soc., Chgo., 1943-53; cons. for minority groups U.S. Dept. Labor, 1953-61; cons. Rehab. Services Adminstrn., HEW, Washington, 1961-81, ret., 1981. Mem. Pres.'s Nat. Adv. Council on Adult Edn., 1970-75. Mem. Tenn. Republican Exec. Com., 1952-53, Shelby County Hist. Commn., 1982—. Recipient Certificate of Merit, Alpha Phi Alpha, 1956. Mem. Assn. for Study Negro Life and History (life), West Tenn. Hist. Soc., NAACP (life), Delta Sigma Theta. Republican. Episcopalian. Co-author: The Robert R. Churches of Memphis. Home: 99 N Main St Memphis TN 38103

CHURCH, SONIA JANE SHUTTER, librarian; b. York, Pa., Dec. 15, 1940; d. Robert Benjamin and Eva Alverta (Horn) Shutter; m. Ernest Layton Church, May 20, 1966; children—Robert Bruce, Jennifer Grace. B.S. in Edn., Millersville Coll. 1962; M.L.S., U. Pitts., 1978. Playground supr. York City Shepherd, Pa., 1961; officer USMC, 1962-66; children's librarian Prunedale br. Monterey County Library, Calif., 1978-79; youth services coordinator Monterey County Library, 1979-83, head librarian Prunedale br., 1983—; writer Book Beat Column for Fortnighter Newspaper, Salinas, 1983—. Editor pamphlet: What Will we Do with the Baby? a collection of nursery rhymes and finger plays, 1977. Mem. Deferred Comp. Task Force, Monterey County, 1983—, Mgmt. Comp. Commn., Monterey County, 1983—; chmn. adminstrv. com. Social Services Commn., 1983—, chmn. ad hoc com., 1983—; coordinating com. Boy Scouts Am., Salinas, 1983—; tchr. Sun. Sch., Luth. Ch. Good Shepherd, Salinas, 1982—. Served to capt., USMC 1962-66. Sico scholar, 1958-62. Mem. ALA, Assn. Library Service to Children, Calif. Library Assn., Assn. Children's Librarians of No. Calif., Sch. and Pub. Librarians Assn. Monterey Bay Area, Assn. Childhood Edn. Internat., Storytellers Unltd., Am. Legion (comdr. 1984-85), Women's Internat. Bowling Congress, Women's Bowling Assn., U. Pitts. Alumni Assn., Millersville Tchrs. Coll. Alumni Assn., Beta Phi Mu, Beta Sigma Phi. Democrat. Lutheran. Home: 17749 Pesante Rd Salinas CA 93907 Office: Prunedale Br Monterey County Library 8075 San Miguel Canyon Rd Salinas CA 92307

CHURCHVILLE, LIDA HOLLAND, librarian; b. Dallas, May 5, 1933; d. Norbert R. and Agnes J. (Buckley) Holland; B.A. in History, Russell Sage Coll., Troy, N.Y., 1965; M.L.S. (SUNY Library fellow 1966-67), SUNY, Albany, 1967; m. Joseph J. Churchville, Oct. 6, 1952 (dec. 1974); children—Lisa, Zoe, Anthony (dec.), Stephen. Legis. librarian Office Legis. Research, N.Y. Senate, Albany, 1967-75; chief law library U.S. Army Library, Washington, 1975-78; coordinator fed. women's program Dept. Defence, The Pentagon, 1976-78; chief library Nat. Archives and Records Services, 1978-81; reference and spl. project librarian Nat. Archives Library, 1981-83; spl. project librarian publs. unit Nat. Archives Trust Fund, 1983—. Mem. Women's Issues Task Force, 1981-83, Women's Nat. Democratic Club, 1981—. Recipient Outstanding Performance award The Pentagon, 1977. Mem. Am. Soc. Info. Sci., D.C. Library Assn., Law Librarians Soc. Washington, Soc. Am. Archivists, Nat. Women's Party, NOW, DC Online Users Group. Home: 5910 Cherrywood Terr Greenbelt MD 20770 Office: Room G7 Nat Archives 8th and Pennsylvania Ave NW Washington DC 20408

CHURGIN, HARRIET VIVIAN, retail company executive; b. Bklyn., Aug. 3, 1936; d. Peter and Sheila (Perlow) Robbins; m. Perry R. Churgin; children—Eileen Egbert, Heidi, Sterling. Student pub. schs., Bklyn. Owner Pretty Panties and Other Fine Lingerie, Brentwood, N.Y., 1981—. Leader Suffolk County Girl Scouts U.S.A., 1966-69; com. person Democratic Club, Islip, N.Y., 1984—. Mem. Nat. Assn. Female Execs. Jewish. Avocations: walking; camping; fishing; swimming. Home: 588 Grand Blvd Brentwood NY 11717

CHUSID, JUDITH FRANCINE (MARKS), psychologist, psychoanalyst; b. N.Y.C., Dec. 3, 1947; d. Harry and Phyllis A. Chusid; B.A., Queens Coll., 1971; M.A., NYU, 1974, Ph.D. (A.B.D.), 1981; P.D., St. John's U., 1978; grad. Manhattan Center for Psychoanalytic Studies; m. Dec. 12, 1982. Program supr. East N.Y. YM-YWHA, 1970; tchr. Lexington Sch. for Deaf, N.Y.C. Bd. Edn., 1971-76; instr. Adelphi U., Garden City, N.Y., 1976-80; pvt. practice psychoanalytic psychotherapy, Jackson Heights and N.Y.C., 1974—; founder, pres., chmn. bd. Positive Approaches to Sports Success Found., Jackson Heights, 1980—; faculty Ctr. Modern Psychoanalytic Studies; former mem. teaching faculty, tng. analyst Rockland Inst. for Psychoanalysis and Psychotherapy, Suffern, N.Y.; condr. workshops, lectr. field sports psychology. Co-founder, Actor's Voice, N.Y.C., 1982. Recipient Otto Klitgord award N.Y., 1967; cert. sch. psychologist, N.Y. State. Mem. Am. Psychol. Assn., Nat. Accreditation Assn. Psychoanalysis (cert.), Council Exceptional Children, AAUP, N.Y. State Assn. Sch. Psychologists, N.Y. State Educators Deaf, N.Y. State Tchrs. Emotionally Disturbed. Contbr. articles to profl. jours. Office: 220 E 26th St New York NY 10010

CHUTE, MARCHETTE, author; b. Wayzata, Minn., Aug. 16, 1909; d. William Young and Edith Mary (Pickburn) Chute; A.B., U. Minn., 1930; Litt.D., Western Coll. for Women, 1952, Carleton Coll., 1957, Dickinson Coll., 1964. Author: Rhymes About Ourselves, 1932; The Search for God, 1941; Rhymes About the Country, 1941; The Innocent Wayfaring, 1943; Geoffrey Chaucer of England, 1946; Rhymes About the City, 1946; The End of the Search, 1947; Shakespeare of London, 1950; An Introduction to Shakespeare, 1951; Ben Jonson of Westminster, 1953; The Wonderful Winter, 1954; Stories from Shakespeare, 1956; Around and About, 1957; Two Gentle Men: The Lives of George Herbert and Robert Herrick, 1959; Jesus of Israel, 1961; (with Ernestine Perrie) The Worlds of Shakespeare, 1963; The First Liberty: A History of the Right to Vote in America, 1619-1850, 1969; The Green Tree of Democracy, 1971; P.E.N. American Center: A History of the First Fifty Years, 1972; Rhymes About Us, 1974. Mem. exec. com. Nat. Book Com.; judge non-fiction Nat. Book Awards, 1952, 59. Recipient Author Meets the Critics award for best non-fiction of 1950; Chap-Book award Poetry Soc. Am., 1954; N.Y. Shakespeare Club award, 1954; Secondary Edn. Bd. book award, 1954; Oustanding Achievement award U. Minn., 1957. Fellow Royal Soc. Arts, Soc. Am. Historians; mem. Am. P.E.N. (pres. 1955-57), Am. Acad. Arts and Letters, Renaissance Soc. Am., Phi Beta Kappa. Home: 450 E 63d St New York NY 10021

CHUTIS, LAURIEANN LUCY, social worker; b. Detroit, Nov. 30, 1942; d. Paul J. and Helen Marie (Shilakes) C.; A.B., U. Mich., 1964, M.S.W., 1966. Community worker Tuskegee (Ala.) Inst., 1966; social worker Catholic Sch. Bd. Head Start, Chgo., 1966; community worker Cath. Charities, Chgo., 1966-70; asst. to dir. Ravenswood Hosp. Community Mental Health Center, Chgo., 1970-72, coordinator consultation and edn. dept., 1972, dir. consultation and edn. dept., 1972—; instr. Chgo. Bd. Edn., 1974—; guest lectr. various profl. assn. groups, 1975—; cons. NIMH, also various mental health centers, 1977—; pvt. practice individual group and family therapy; 1976—; region V coordinator Consultation-Edn. Conf., 1979-81; coordinator Nat. Consultation-Edn. Network, 1980—. Mem. Salvation Army Community Services Bd., 1978—. Mem. Nat. Assn. Social Work, Acad. Certified Social Work, World Fedn. Mental Health, Registry Clin. Social Workers, Nat. Council Community Mental Health Centers (council on Prevention 1976-79), Assn. Consultation-Edn. Service Providers (pres. 1978-79). Contbr. chpt. to To Your Good 1980; contbr. articles to profl. jours. Health, 1980. Office: 4550 N Winchester Chicago IL 60640

CHVANY, CATHERINE VAKAR, educator; b. Paris, Apr. 26, 1927; m. 1948; 3 children. B.A., Radcliffe Coll., 1963; Ph.D., Harvard U., 1970. Instr. Russian, Wellesley Coll., 1966-67; instr. MIT, 1967-70, lectr., 1970-71, asst. prof., 1971-74, assoc. prof. Russian, 1974-83, prof., 1983—; fellow Harvard Russian Research Ctr., 1979—. Lilly postdoctoral teaching award fellow MIT, 1975-76. Mem. Am. Assn. Advancement Slavic Studies, Linguistic Soc. Am., Am. Assn. Tchrs. Slavic and Eastern European Langs., Am. Council Teaching of Russian, Bulgarian Studies Assn. Author: On the Syntax of BE-Sentences in Russian, 1975. Co-editor: Slavic Transformational Syntax, 1974, Morphosyntax in Slavic, 1980, Gertruda Vakar. Stikhotvorenija, 1984; Mem. editorial adv. bd. SEEJ, Folica Slavica, RLJ, Essays in Poetics. Contbr. articles to profl. jours. Address: Dept Russian Room 14N MIT 77 Massachusetts Ave Cambridge MA 02139

CHVATAL, PATRICIA JOAN, lawyer; b. Walla Walla, Wash., July 6, 1950; d. Joseph J. and Mary R. (Doherty) C.; B.A. magna cum laude, Carroll Coll., 1972; J.D. cum laude, Gonzaga U., 1976. Admitted to Wash. bar., 1976; asso. firm Bennett and Carroll, Richland, Wash., 1976-78; jr. partner firm Bennett, Carroll and Chvatal, Richland, 1978-79; partner firm Carroll and Chvatal, Richland, 1979-81, Carroll, Chvatal and Heye, Richland, 1981—; lectr. seminars on law, State of Wash. Mem. Richland City Council Planning Commn.; bd. dirs. United Way, 1979-80, N.W. Women's Law Center, Seattle. Mem. Wash. State Bar Assn., Wash. Women Lawyers, Tri-City Women Lawyers (past pres.), AAUW, LWV, Cath. Daus. Am., Wash. Women United, Wash. Women's Polit. Caucus (pres. 1981), Altrusa. Democrat. Roman Catholic. Club: Bus. and Profl. Women's (pres. Richland chpt. 1977-79). Contbr. articles to legal jours. Home: 2120 Duportail Richland WA 99352 Office: PO Box 966 Richland WA 99352

CHWATSKY, ANN, photographer, educator; b. Phila., Jan. 11, 1942; d. Jules and Gladys (Coleman) Schneider; m. Robert Schulz, June 23, 1961 (div. 1964); 1 child, Marc; m. Howard Franklin Chwatsky, Nov. 2, 1965; 1 child, Julie. B.S. in Art Edn., Hofstra U., 1965, M.S., 1971; postgrad. L.I. U., 1973-74. Cert. tchr. Photography editor L.I. mag., 1976-80; instr. Internat. Ctr. Photography, N.Y.C., 1979-80, Parrish Art Mus., Southampton, N.Y., 1984—; mem. faculty L.I. U., Greenvale, N.Y., 1982—; coordinator master art workshop Southampton Coll., 1985; curator photo show East End Arts, Riverhead, N.Y., 1985; judge show Arts Guild, Rockville Centre, N.Y., 1985; dir. women's photography group C.W. Post Coll., 1977-78; photographer Newsweek, Newsday, Manchete, N.Y. Times, 1976—. One-person show: Post Gallery East, Westbury, N.Y., 1975; group shows include: L.I. Fine Arts Mus., 1984, Women's Interart Ctr., N.Y.C., 1976, 80, Parrish Art Mus., Southampton, 1979, Internat. Ctr. Photography, N.Y.C., 1980, 82, Nassau County Mus. Fine Arts, 1983, Soho 20 Gallery, N.Y.C., 1984, New Orleans World's Fair, 1984; represented in permanent collections: Forbes N.Y.C. Midtown YWCA, Nassau County Mus. Fine Arts, others. Active Lowenstein campaign; photographer Democratic vons.; bd. dirs. Rosa Lee Young Day Care Ctr., Rockville Centre, 1982-85. Recipient Estabrook Disting. Alumni award Hofstra U., 1984; Kodak Profl. Photographers award, 1984; Eastman Found. grantee, 1981-82; Polaroid grantee, 1980. Mem. Assn. Am. Mag. Profls., Picture Profls. Am., Profl. Women Photographers N.Y.C. Democrat. Jewish. Avocations: tennis; gardening; travel. Home: 85 Andover Rd Rockville Centre NY 11570

CHYTEN, ROSALYN HARRIET, medical management company executive; b. Boston, July 13, 1929; m. Max E. Lidman, Sept. 16, 1951 (div. Nov. 1981); 1 child, Kenneth L.; m. Edwin R. Chyten, May 11, 1983. Student Burdett Coll., 1948, Evening Coll. Arts, Scis. and Bus. Adminstrn., Boston Coll., 1970-78. Adminstr. A. J. Gorney, M.D., Boston, 1948-69, Boston Eye Assocs., P.C., Brookline, Mass., 1969-76; pres., founder Med. Practice Mgmt., Inc., Newton Centre, Mass., 1976—; cons. Polymer Tech. Corp., Wilmington, Mass., 1971-82, Bausch & Lomb, Rochester, N.Y., 1985—, Sports Medicine Systems, Wellesley Hills, Mass., 1985—. Mem. Congressman Barney Frank's Small Bus. Task Force, Waltham, Mass., 1982. Mem. Smaller Bus. Assn. New Eng., Med. Group Mgmt. Assn., Exec. Club New Eng. Women Bus. Owners, Mass. Computer Software Council. Avocations: travel; biking; skiing. Home: 250 Hammond Pond Pkwy 1202 N Chestnut Hill MA 02167 Office: Med Practice Mgmt Inc 10 Langley Rd Newton Centre MA 02159

CIACCIO, KARIN MCLAUGHLIN, lawyer; b. Galesburg, Ill., Feb. 9, 1947; d. Cleo Edward and Kathryn Louise (Payton) McLaughlin; m. Frederick Steven Ciaccio, May 4, 1968; children—John, Jennifer. B.S., So. Ill. U., 1969; postgrad. Law Sch. Temple U., 1971-72; J.D., DePaul U., 1975. Bar: Ill., U.S. Ct. Appeals (7th cir.); legal diplomate; cert. tchr. French. French tchr. Sherrard High Sch. (Ill.), 1969-70; law prof. U. Wis., Racine, 1975, Coll. of DuPage, Glen Ellyn, Ill., 1976; sole practice law, Lombard-Chgo., 1975-80, Woodhull-Galesburg, Ill., 1980—; city atty., Woodhull Village Bd., 1983—; speaker consumer laws, 1976—. Researcher legal textbook: Contracts to Make Wills, 1973. Zoning ofcl. Lombard Zoning Bd., 1978-80; mem. Alpha Cemetery Bd., Ill., 1980—; officer St. John's Cemetary Bd., Woodhull, 1983—; dir., officer Alwood Bus. Assn., Woodhull, 1984; mem. Republican Women Henry County, legis. chmn. 1981-83. Mem. ABA, Ill. Bar Assn., Henry County Bar Assn., Knox County Bar Assn., Phi Alpha Delta (sec. 1971-73). Club: Altrusa. Home: 545 Lake Dr Woodhull IL 61490 Office: 147 N Division Woodhull IL 61490

CIARDULLO, MARION DOROTHY, public relations specialist; b. Newport, R.I., Oct. 22, 1924; d. Benjamin and Fannie (Lack) Rudick; m. Michael Ciardullo, May 31, 1950; children—Robin Bruce, Frances Audrey. A.B., Hunter Coll., 1947; postgrad. Columbia U., 1950. Copywriter, gen. Asst. Vanguard Advt., N.Y.C., 1947-48; media specialist J. Walter Thompson, 1948-50; pub. relations coordinator Norden, United Technologies Corp., Norwalk, Conn., 1971-81; mgr. mktg. communications Safe Flight Instrument Corp., White Plains, N.Y., 1982-84; mgr. mktg. communications W.W. Gaertner Research, Inc., Norwalk, Conn., 1985—. Contbr. articles to profl. jours. Mem. Aviation/Space Writers Assn., Pub. Relations Soc. Am., Fairfield County Pub. Relations Soc., Internat. Assn. Bus. Communicators, Women in Communication. Democrat. Jewish. Home: 19 Dairy Farm Rd Norwalk CT 06851

CICERO, MARILYN BELLE, travel consultant; b. N.Y.C., July 16, 1931; d. Sam K. and Helen (Smith) Kass; m. Arthur Bennet Cicero, Jan. 27, 1952; children—Lori Cicero Boelig, Lois Cicero Woodbury. B.B.A., CCNY, 1953. Tchr. Burlington, Mass., Pub. Schs., 1965-69; mgr. Colpitts Travel Agy., Lexington, Mass., 1969-72, exec. v.p., 1972-80, pres., 1980—; pres. Colpitts Assocs., West Roxbury, Mass., 1975-78; pres. C and L Cons., Lexington, 1981—; v.p. Nova Assocs., Dallas, treas., 1985—; adv. bd. mem. Travel Edn. Ctr., Cambridge, Mass., Pan Am. World Airways, Boston; mem. Travel Agts. Adv. Bd. Active Women's Am. Ort. Lexington (founding pres., 1960-62). Mem. Inst. Cert. Travel Agts (life), Am. Soc. Travel Agts., Brit. Airways Travel Agts. (adv. bd. 1986), Soc. Travel Tourism Educators, Lexington C. of C. (dir., 1977—, fin. chmn., 1982—). Jewish. Home: 11 Cooke Rd Lexington MA 02173 Office: Colpitts Travel Ctr 1793 Massachusetts Ave Lexington MA 02173

CICHELLI, MARTHA JANE, software development company executive, programmer, analyst; b. Lewiston, Maine, Oct. 24, 1946; d. Robert Colton MacDuffee and Ida Jane (Sands) Downing; m. Richard J. Cichelli, May 18, 1968; 1 child, Sharon Jeanne. B.A., Temple U., 1968. Programmer, analyst E.I. duPont de Nemours, Wilmington, Del., 1968-71; systems programmer Pa. Power and Light, Allentown, 1971-75; owner, ptnr. Software Cons. Services, Nazareth, Pa., 1975—. Office: Software Consulting Services 3162 Bath Pike Nazareth PA 18064

CICHON, PAMELA DION, lawyer; b. Raleigh, N.C., Jan. 12, 1956; d. Wallace Martin and Corinne (Adams) C. B.A. with honors, U. Fla.-Gainesville, 1976; J.D., Stetson U., 1979. Bar: Fla. 1980. Tchr., Boca Ciega Sr. High St., St. Petersburg, Fla., 1979-80; uranium landman Amoco Minerals Co., Denver also Chadron, Nebr., 1980-81; petroleum landman Profl. Energy, Inc., Denver, 1981-82; atty. Cen. Fla. Legal Services, Daytona Beach, 1982; assoc. law firm Bosek & Sills, Daytona Beach, Fla., 1983—; assoc. law firm Foster, Ramos & Foster, Daytona Beach, Fla., 1984—; legal cons. Adams-Hillman & Assocs., Golden, Colo., 1982. Writer, editor newsletter Business Advisory Reports, 1980-81. Vol. lawyer Volusia County Vol. Lawyers Project, Daytona Beach, 1982—; clinic atty. Legal Advice Clinic, Daytona Beach, 1983-84. Mem. Fla. Assn. Women Lawyers, ABA, Fla. Bar Assn., Volusia County Bar Assn., Phi Delta Phi, Sigma Delta Tau. Office: Foster Ramos & Foster 315 S Palmetto Ave Daytona Beach FL 32014

CICHOSZ, MARY KAY PARRY, kitchen designer; b. Butte, Mont., Aug. 9, 1954; d. Sidney Colston Parry and Beverly Jean (Woodside) Parry Collins; m. Joseph Albert Cichosz, Aug. 21, 1976 (div. July 1984). B.A. in Design, Mont. State U., 1973; B.S. in Social Justice, 1980; cert. of completion edn. for Ministry by Corr., U. of the South. Sales clk. Phillips Bookstore, Bozeman, Mont., 1979-82; kitchen designer New Creation Cabinets, Bozeman, 1982-83, Decorator's Walk, Bozeman, 1983-86, Cabinet Specialist, Inc., Bozeman, 1986—. Recipient personal Progress award Dale Carnegie, 1985. Mem. Nat. Assn. Female Execs., Nat. Kitchen Bath Assn., Bus. and Profl. Women's Assn. Avocations: religious studies; art; athletics. Home: 1020 W Alderson PO Box 1824 Bozeman MT 59715 Office: Cabinet Specialists Inc 203 Haggerty Ln Bozeman MT 59715

CIELINSKI, AUDREY ANN, communications specialist, freelance writer, editor; b. Cleve., Sept. 10, 1957; d. Joseph and Dorothy Antoinette (Hanna) Cielinski. B.J. with high honors, U. Tex. at Austin, 1979. Reporter, writer Med. World News mag., N.Y.C., 1979, asst. copy chief, Houston, 1983-84; freelance writer, editor, 1984—; editorial asst. Jour Health and Social Behavior, Houston, 1980-81; sec. dept. psychiatry Baylor Coll. Medicine, Houston, 1980-81; procedures analyst, tech. writer, tech. librarian Harris County Data Processing Dept., Houston, 1981-83; communications specialist III, Office of Planning and Research, Houston Police Dept. Contbr. stories and articles to newspapers and mags. Vol. writer, graphic designer, office religious edn. St. Ambrose Roman Cath. Ch., Houston, 1983—; vol. editor newsletters Greater Houston area Am. Cancer Soc. and VGS, Inc. Mem. Women in Communications, Am. Med. Writers Assn., Soc. for Tech. Communication, Sigma Delta Chi, Phi Kappa Phi, Alpha Lambda Delta. Home: 4250 W 34th St Apt 70 Houston TX 77092 Office: Office of Planning and Research Houston Police Dept 33 Artesian Houston TX 77002

CIEMINSKI, LORRAINE NORMA, insurance agent, county commissioner; b. Arcadia, Wis., July 20, 1934; d. Ignatius Waldera and Helen D. (Kamrowski) Johnson; m. Richard J. Cieminski, Nov. 17, 1951; children—Nicholas, Nancy, Constance, Cathleen, Judy, Richard, Jr. Student in Bus. Adminstrn., Winona State U., 1969-71. Ins. agt. Markel & Assoc., Winona, Minn., 1969—; county commnr. Winona County, Minn., 1976—; ptnr. JonLee Maintenance, Winona, 1963—. Home: 309 E 4th St Winona MN 55987 Office: Winona County 3d and Washington Sts Winona MN 55987

CIENCIALA, ANNA MARIA, educator; b. Gdansk, Poland, Nov. 8, 1929; d. Andrew M. and Wanda M. (Waissmann) C.; came to U.S., 1965, naturalized, 1970; B.A., U. Liverpool, 1952; M.A., McGill U., 1955; Ph.D., Ind. U., 1962. Lectr. European history U. Ottawa, 1960-61, U. Toronto (Ont., Can.), 1961-65; asst. prof. history U. Kans., Lawrence, 1965-67, asso. prof., 1967-71, prof. history and Soviet and Eastern European area studies, 1971—. Recipient prize Pilsudski Inst. Am., 1968; Ford Found. fellow, 1958-60; Can. Council grantee, 1963; Fulbright-Hays fellow, 1968-69; U. Kans. gen. research grantee, 1965-75, 80-81; Am. Council Learned Socs. grantee, 1980, 83; Irex fellow, Poland, 1979-80. Mem. AAUP, AAUW, Am. Assn. Advancement Slavic Studies, Am. Hist. Assn., Kosciuszko Found., Pilsudski Inst. Am., Polish-Am. Inst. Arts and Scis., Polish-Am. Hist. Assn., Hist. Preservation. Author: Poland and the

Western Powers, 1938-39, 1968; From Versailles to Locarno, Keys to Polish Foreign Policy, 1919-25; editor: (with A. Headlam-Morley and R. Bryant) A Memoir of the Paris Peace Conference 1919, 1972; American Contributions to the Seventh International Congress of Slavists, 1973; contbr. articles to profl. jours. Home: 3045 Steven Dr Lawrence KS 66044 Office: Dept History U Kans Lawrence KS 60045

CINCIOTTA, LINDA ANN, lawyer; b. Washington, May 18, 1943; d. Nicholas Joseph and Laverne C. (Oakley) C.; m. John P. Olguin, Aug. 4, 1979. B.S., Georgetown U., 1965; J.D., George Washington U., 1970. Bar: D.C. 1970. Assoc., Arent, Fox, Plotkin & Kahn, Washington, 1970-77, ptnr., 1978-83; dir. Office of Atty. Personnel Mgmt., Dept. Justice, Washington, 1983—. Recipient U.S. Law Week award George Washington U. Nat. Law Ctr., 1970. Mem. Fed. Communications Bar Assn. (pres. 1980-81), Fed. Bar Assn., D.C. Bar Assn. Office: US Dept Justice Office of Attorney Personnel Mgmt 10th and Constitution Ave NW Washington DC 20530

CINIERO, PAULA MARIA, nurse; b. Washington, Oct. 12, 1961; d. O.A. Lin and Peggy Lou (Lanier) C. B.S. in Nursing, U. Md., 1984. Nursing asst. Montgomery Gen. Hosp., Olney, Md., 1983, U. Md. Hosp., Balt., 1983-84; staff nurse Duke U. Hosp., Durham, N.C., 1984-85; dir. profl. services Home Health Profls., Roxboro, N.C., 1985—. Mem. Am. Nurses Assn., N.C. Nurses Assn., Md. Assn. Nursing Students (pres. Balt. 1983-84). Democrat. Methodist. Lodges: Eastern Star, Order Rainbow Girls (adviser, 1985). Avocations: swimming; needlework; weightlifting; cooking. Home: 208 Pinegate Circle Apt 11 Chapel Hill NC 27514 Office: Duke U Hosp Erwin Rd Durham NC 27710

CINTRON, CARMEN DELIA, secretary; b. Las Piedres, P.R., Feb. 6, 1939; d. Bernardo and Juanita (Fernandez) C.; div.; children—Mario Ramirez, Humberto Jose Ramirez. A.A., Boricua Coll., 1983; postgrad. Baruch Coll., 1984. Sec. labor dept.-unemployment div. Office of Gov. P.R., Santurce, 1958-60; posting-machine operator Corona Brewer Corp., Santurce, 1960-62; consumer service rep. II Aqueduct and Sewer Authority, Rio Piedras, P.R., 1962-71; exec. sec. First Spanish Presbyn. Ch., Bklyn., 1975—; colloquim rep. Boricua Coll., Bklyn., 1983-84. Helper Presbyn. Sr. Citizens, Bklyn., 1975—; mem. Puerto Rican Traveling Theatre, 1983—, N.Y. Mus. Natural History, 1985. Mem. Am. Hort. Soc., Nature Conservancy, Citizens for Decency through Law, Am. Film Inst., Postal Commemorative Soc., Nat. Trust for Historic Preservation, People's Med. Soc., Nat. Health Fedn. Republican. Avocations: Reading; bicycling; walking. Home: 84-25 Elmhurst Ave Apt 1-I Elmhurst Queens NY 11373

CINTRON, EMMA VARGAS, clinical psychologist, educational counselor; b. Yauco, P.R., Aug. 8, 1926; d. Jose Vargas Bocheciampi and Maria Teresa Rivera de Vargas; B.A. in Sociology summa cum laude, Inter Am. U., San German, P.R., 1973, M.A. in Counseling and Guidance summa cum laude, 1974; postgrad. in psychology Centro Caribeno Estudios Postgraduados; Ph.D. in Counseling Psychology, Columbia Pacific U., 1985; m. Jorge N. Cintron, Feb. 14, 1948; children—Lisi C. Vazquez, Ileana C. Vazquez. Weekly columnist newspaper El Mundo, San Juan, P.R., 1979—; advisor for dormitories Inter Am. U., San German, P.R., 1978-79, part time prof. dept. edn., 1976-77, cons. orientation center, 1974-76; bus. mgr. U. P.R. Law Rev., Rio Piedras, 1963-71. Recipient award in journalism for newspaper work Puerto Rican Inst. Lit., 1984. Mem. P.R. Psychol. Assn., Nat. Hispanic Psychol. Assn. Am. Personnel and Guidance Assn., P.R. Guidance Assn., Phi Delta Kappa (editor Phi-De-Ka; Disting. Kappan of Yr. 1981). Methodist. Clubs: Lions (Domadoras; writing award 1985), Altrusa, Grandmothers, San German. Contbr. articles to newspapers including El Mundo, Impacto, El Leon, Revista Superate, Colinas, Puerto Rico Evangelico, Revista P.R. Profl., Revista El Intérprete. Home: Campus Inter Am U San German PR 00753 Office: Box 2547 San German PR 00753

CIOLLI, ANTOINETTE, librarian; b. N.Y.C., Aug. 20, 1915; d. Pietro and Mary (Palumbo) Ciolli; A.B., Bklyn. Coll., 1937, M.A., 1940; B.S. in L.S., Columbia U., 1943. Tchr. history and civics Bklyn. high schs., 1943-44; circulation librarian Bklyn. Coll. Library, 1944-46; instr. history Sch. Gen. Studies, Bklyn. Coll., 1944-50, asst. prof. library dept., 1965-72, asso. prof., 1973-81, prof. emerita, 1981—; reference librarian Bklyn. Coll. Library, 1947-59, chief sci. librarian, 1959-70, chief spl. collections div., 1970-81, hon. archivist, 1981—. Mem. ALA, Am. Hist. Assn., Spl. Libraries Assn. (museum group chpt. sec. 1950-51, 52-54), N.Y. Library Club, Beta Phi Mu. Author: (with Alexander L. Preminger and Lillian Lester) Urban Educator: Harry D. Gideonse, Brooklyn College and the City University of New York, 1970. Contbr. articles to profl. jours. Home: 1129 Bay Ridge Pkwy Brooklyn NY 11228

CIOMBOR, DEBORAH MCKEIGHAN, research scientist; b. Cleve., June 25, 1949; d. John Elmore and Harriette R. (Pinter) McKeighan; m. Stanley Fredrick Ciombor, Feb. 1, 1967; children—Kelly Jean, David Johnathon. A.B., Brown U., 1979. Research asst. dept. surgery R.I. Hosp., Providence, 1979-82, sr. research asst., dept. orthopaedics, 1982-84, research coordinator 1984—. Author: Surgical Clinics of North American, 1984. Contbr. articles to profl. jours. Grantee Am. Cancer Soc., 1983-84, R.I. Found., 1985. Mem. N.Y. Acad. Scis., East Coast Connective Tissue Soc., Am. Assn. Tissue Banks, Hastings Ctr., Inst. for Ethics and the Life Scis., Am. Council on Transplantation, Orthopaedic Research Soc., Bioelectric Repair and Growth Soc. Roman Catholic. Home: 9 Rosemary Ln Greenville RI 02828 Office: Rhode Island Hosp Dept Orthopaedics 593 Eddy St Providence RI 02902

CIOTOLA, LINDA ANN, fitness consultant; b. Balt., Sept. 17, 3996 d. Lawrence Andrew and Virginia (Wertley) Miller; B.A., Mt. St. Agnes Coll., 1969; M.Ed., Loyola Coll. of Balt., 1975; hon. broadcasting degree, Broadcasting Inst. Md., 1977; m. Joseph A. Ciotola, Jr., July 26, 1969; children—Joseph John, Alyson Marie. Tchr. English, public speaking Cath. High Sch., Balt., 1969-73; cons., editor textbooks, workbooks Local Union 24 Internat. Brotherhood Elec. Workers, Balt., 1973-75; tchr. English, Atholton High Sch., Howard County., Md., 1975-76; dir. activities and spl. events Villa Julie Coll., Stevenson, Md., 1976-79; cons., sec.-treas. Bus. Brokers Bldg. Maintenance & Mgmt., Inc., Ellicott City, Md., 1981—; founder The Fitness Movement, fitness evaluation and program design, Howard County, Md., 1983—; instr. fitness Howard County YMCA, 1981-82; lectr. in field; mem. faculty Broadcasting Inst. Md., 1976-77. Bd. dirs. Theatre Loyola Workshop, 1974-74, Theatre Incarnate, 1976—. Loyola Coll. grantee, 1974-75; Villa Julie Coll. grantee, 1977-78, 78-79. Mem. Nat. Wildlife Fedn., LWV, NOW, NEA, Ctr. Environ. Edn., Am. Inst. Cancer Research, Internat. Dance-Exercise Assn., Aerobic-Fitness Assn. Am., Animal Protection Inst., Sigma Phi Sigma. Address: 3986 View Top Rd Ellicott City MD 21043

CIPNIC, MONICA ROBIN, picture editor, writer, visual consultant; b. Poughkeepsie, N.Y., Sept. 12, 1950; d. Herman and Ruth (Rothberg) Cipnic. B.A., Skidmore Coll., 1972. Pub. relations asst., writer Empire State Coll., Saratoga Springs, N.Y., 1971-72; prodn. asst. Alden Films, New Orleans, 1972-77; asst. picture editor Popular Photography mag. Ziff-Davis Pub. Co., N.Y.C., 1973-75, assoc. picture editor Popular Photography and Photography Ann., 1975-80, picture editor, 1980—; photo editor CBS Pub. Group, 1985—; picture editor Camera Arts, N.Y.C., 1980-83; nat. adv. panel Scholastic Mag.-Kodak, 1982—; cons., judge NEA Fed. Design Program, Washington, 1980; judge photog. competitions, 1976—; mem. peer group selection com. Friends of Photography, Carmel, Calif., 1981—; lectr. on photography, various colls., 1977—. Contbr. articles, interviews to mags. Recipient Gold medal Art Dirs. Club, N.Y.C., 1981; Nat. Mag. award Am. Soc. Mag. Editors, N.Y.C., 1982; CBS Pres.'s award, 1985. Mem. Women in Communications, Am. Soc. Picture Profls., Soc. Photog. Educators. Home: 305 E 24th St New York NY 10010 Office: Popular Photography 1 Park Ave New York NY 10016

CIRILO, AMELIA MEDINA, chemistry educator, educational consultant; b. Parks, Tex., May 23, 1925; d. Constancio and Guadalupe (Guerra) C.; m. Arturo Medina, May 31, 1953 (div. June 1979); children—Dennis Glenn, Keith Allen, Sheryl Amelia, Jacqueline Kim. B.S. in Chemistry, North Tex. State U., 1950; M.Ed., U. Houston, 1954; Ph.D. in Edn. and Nuclear Engring., Tex. A&M U., 1975; cert. in radioisotope tech. Tex. Woman's U., Denton, 1962. Cert. in supervision, bilingual Spanish, Tex.; cert. permament profl. tchr., Tex. Tchr. sci., dept. head Starr County Schs., Rio Grande City, Tex., 1950-53; elem. tchr. San Benito-Brownsville, Tex., 1953-54, Kingsville (Tex.) Schs., 1954-56; tchr. sci., head dept. chem. physics LaJoya (Tex.) Pub. Schs., 1956-70; teaching asst. Tex. A&M U., College Station, 1970-74; instr. fire chemistry Del Mar Jr. Coll., Corpus Christi, Tex., 1974-75; exec. dir Hispanic Ednl. Research Mgmt. Analysis Nat. Assn., Inc., Corpus Christi, 1975-79; head dept. chem. physics San Isidro (Tex.) High Sch., 1979-82; tchr. chemistry W.H. Adamson High Sch., Dallas, 1982—, chmn. faculty adv. com., 1983-84; mem. core faculty Union Grad. Coll., Cin., P.R., Ft. Lauderdale, and San Diego, 1975-79; mathematician Well Instrument Devel. Co., Houston, summers 1950-54; panelist, program evaluator Dept. of Edn., Washington, 1977-79; program evaluator, Robstown, Tex., 1975-79; tchr. trainer Edn. 20 and 2 Region Ctrs., Corpus Christi and San Antonio, 1975-79; researcher, writer Coll. Edn. and Urban Studies, Harvard U., Cambridge, Mass., 1978-80; vis. prof. bilingual dept. East Tex. State Coll., Commerce, 1978; conf. presenter program evaluation, 1977-79. Author: Comparative Evaluation of Bilingual Programs (named one of best U.S. books), 1978; Reflections (poetry), 1983; contbr. chpt. to book. NSF grantee, 1963-65; bd. dirs. Meth. Home for Elderly, Weslaco, Tex., 1968, Am. Cancer Soc. fund drive, College Station, 1971-74; Brazos County advisor Tex. Constl. Revision Commn., 1973-74; sec. Goals for Corpus Christi Com. of 100; Corpus Christi rep. Southwestern Ednl. Authority, Edinburg, Tex., 1977-79; co-founder, dir. Women's Shelter, Corpus Christi, 1977-78; exec. bd. Nat. Com. Domestic Violence, 1978-80; pres. Elem. PTA, 1972-75; mem. Women's Polit. Caucus, Mex. Am. Democrats; Mem. Tex. Tchrs. Assn., NEA, Tex. Assn. Bilingual Educators, AAUW, Chem. Soc., Pan Am. Round Table, So. Sociol. Assn., Rocky Mountain Sociol. Assn., Metroplex Educators Sci. Assn., League United Latin Am. Citizens (pres. College Station 1973-74, past dist. dir. Corpus Christi). Home: 7121 Chinaberry Rd Dallas TX 75249 Office: Adamson High School 201 E 9th St Dallas TX 75203

CIRKER, BLANCHE, publisher; b. N.Y.C., Oct. 3, 1918; d. Frank and Tillie (Jager) Brodsky; B.A., Hunter Coll., 1939; M.S.W., U. Pa., 1941; m. Hayward Cirker, Aug. 11, 1939; children—Steven, Victoria. Family social worker intake office Jewish Child Care Assn., 1948-50; med. social worker Joint Disease Hosp., N.Y.C., 1950; book pub., 1950—; now v.p. Dover Publs., N.Y.C. Mem. Otto Rank Assn. (dir.). Author: Monograms and Alphabetic Devices, 1970; Dictionary of American Portraits, 1967; Golden Age of Poster, 1971; Book of Kells, 1982; Art Nouveau Postcards, 1983; Masterpieces of the Belle Epoch, 1983. Home: 199 Woodside Dr Hewlett Bay Park NY 11557 also 31 E 2d St Mineola NY 11501 Office: Dover Publications 180 Varick St New York NY 10014

CIRUTI, JOAN ESTELLE, Spanish educator; b. Ponchatoula, La., Aug. 8, 1930; d. Joseph Aloysius and Olga (Jordan) Ciruti; B.A., Southeastern La. Coll., 1950; M.A., U. Okla., 1954; Ph.D., Tulane U., 1959. Instr. modern langs. U. Okla., Norman, 1957-59, asst. prof., 1959-63; research asst. U.S. Office Edn., Washington, 1959-60; asst. prof. Spanish, Mt. Holyoke Coll., South Hadley, Mass., 1963-66, assoc. prof., 1966-71, chmn. dept. Spanish, 1965-71, prof., 1971—, now Helen Day Gould Found., dean of studies, 1971-74, chmn. dept. Spanish and Italian, 1975-81, 85-86, chmn. dept. German, 1976-79, 83-85. cons. Ednl. Testing Service, 1968-79. Named Distinguished Alumnus, Southeastern La. Coll., 1973. Mem. Am. Council on Teaching of Fgn. Langs., MLA (nomination, adv. com., 1962-64, nominating com. 1979-80, com. on acad. freedom 1980-83), Latin Am. Studies Assn. (mem. steering com. consortium Latin Am. studies programs 1969-72, com. on women 1973-74, nominating com. 1975), Am. Assn. Tchrs. Spanish and Portuguese, New Eng. Council on Latin Am. Studies, AAUP, AAUW, Phi Sigma Iota, Sigma Delta Pi. Co-author: Modern Spanish, 2d edit., 1966; Continuing Spanish, 1967. Contbg. editor: Handbook of Latin-American Studies, vol. 28, 1966, vol. 30, 1968, vol. 32, 1970. Home: 21 Jewett Ln South Hadley MA 01075

CISEK, CAROL MARIE, image and color consultant, writer; b. Syracuse, N.Y., Aug. 26, 1926; d. Fred Philip and Clara Elizabeth (Raupach) Kies; m. Richard M. Cisek, Sept. 15, 1956 (div. 1972); children—Michael, Melanie, Maria. B.A., Syracuse U., 1948; grad. Med. Technician, Buffalo Gen. Hosp., 1950. Cert. med. technician, Color Me Beautiful cons. Pub. relations dir. Minn. Dance Theatre, Mpls., 1968-71, Sci. Mus. Minn., St. Paul, 1975-76, Employers Overload, Mpls., 1977; ops. mgr. Gem Model and Talent Agy., Mpls., 1979-80; cons., owner Color Me Beautiful, Mpls., 1981—; dir. Wendy Ward program, Montgomery Ward Stores, 1973-75; contbr. fashion and beauty columns publs. Mpls., St. Paul. Bd. dirs. Minn. Dance Theatre, 1969-79, founder, bd. mem. Minn. Montessori Found. and Edina Montessori Sch., 1963-71; with pub. relations Democratic Farm Labor Feminist Caucus, Mpls., 1978-80. Mem. Fashion Group, Women in Communications (sec. Mpls. 1978-80), Minn. Press Club. Roman Catholic. Home: 1635 Oregon Ave S Minneapolis MN 55426 Office: Carol Cisek Color 1635 Oregon Ave Minneapolis MN 55426

CISNEY, MARCELLA, theatre director, administrator; b. Altoona, Pa.; d. Moses J. and Anne (Epstein) Abels; m. Robert C. Schnitzer, June 7, 1953. Student Am. Acad. Dramatic Arts, Bennington Sch. Arts, Neighborhood Playhouse Dirs. Seminar, NYU Radio-TV Workshop. Featured on Broadway in Girls in Uniform, Lady Precious Stream; dir. Off-Broadway and summer theatres; exec. dir. Jacksonville Civic Theatre (Fla.), 1942-45; producer-dir. Pasadena Playhouse (Calif.), 1946-48, Laguna Playhouse (Calif.), Las Palmas Theatre, Hollywood, 1948-49; head coach Warner Bros. Studio, 1948; network dir. for CBS-TV, N.Y., 1950-54; lectr. advanced theatre direction Columbia, 1955; adminstr. Rockefeller Found. project for Hungarian refugee artists, 1956; dir. N.Y.C. Opera, 1957-58; dir. all-star Skin of Our Teeth for Theatre Guild-State Dept. world tour, Latin Am. tour of Glass Menagerie, 1959-60; co-founder, artistic dir. Profl. Theatre Program, U. Mich., Ann Arbor, 1961-73; dir. premieres Child Buyer, 1963, An Evening's Frost, 1964, Wedding Band, 1965, Ivory Tower, 1966, Amazing Grace, 1967, The Castle, 1968, The Conjurer, 1969; dir. nat. tour An Evening's Frost, 1966, ACT West Coast premiere, 1968; producer Siamese Connections, 1971, Last Respects, 1972; theater chmn. Westport-Weston Arts Council, 1980-86; mem. bd. Westport Weston Arts Ctr., producer Works-in-Progress Series, 1980-86. arts cons. to pres. U. Bridgeport, 1974—; moderator seminars White Barn Theatre; 1st v.p. Westport Arts Council, 1978-81. Recipient Bronze medal Israeli Minister of Culture; Gold medal for Brussels Fair Program, Spl. Pres.'s citation U. Mich., 1972.

CITRIN, JUDITH, healer, counselor, artist, educator, sculptor; b. Chgo., May 29, 1934; d. Harvey and Estelle (Lieberman) Goldfeder; student Art Inst. Chgo., 1943, 47-48, U. Ill., 1951-53, Am. Acad. Art, 1953-54, Adler Inst., 1975, C.G. Jung 1979—, Esalen Inst., 1981; 1 son by previous marriage, Jeffrey Scott Levin. Asst. producer, researcher WTTW Channel 11, Chgo., 1963-68; freelance interior designer, jewelry designer, fabricator, clothing designer, 1963—; freelance painter and sculptor, 1968—; Reiki healer and transformational counselor, 1978—; group facilitator, tchr. Oasis Center, 1981—, Loyola U., 1984, 85, Fatima Ctr., Notre Dame, 1986, Interface, 1986; facilitator Healing Circle; artist in residency Cultural Ministry, Marrakech, Morocco, 1979-80; dir. Clearing House; works exhibited Musee des Oudaias, Rabat, Morocco, 1980, Art Inst. Chgo., 1973, 77, 81, Nat. Mus. Am. Art of Smithsonian Instn., 1982, Nat. Acad. Design, N.Y.C., 1982, Chgo. Cultural Center, 1979, Mus. Art of U. Okla., 1978. Ill. Arts Council grantee, 1977; Royal Air Maroc funding grantee, 1980-81. Mem. Assn. Holistic Health, Arts Club Chgo., Spiritual Emergency Network of Esalen Inst., Am. Reiki Assn., Inst. Noetic Scis. Contbg. writer to Under the Sign of Pisces, 1972; contbg. artist to Black Maria, 1972, Corona mag., 1986; contbg. editor The New Art Examiner, 1978, Corona mag., 1984. Home: 423 Greenleaf Ave Wilmette IL 60091 Office: The Clearing House 423 Greenleaf Ave Wilmette IL 60091

CITRON, DIANE, lawyer; b. Cin., Oct. 9, 1953; d. Carl and Georgia (Reid) C. B.A., Franklin and Marshall Coll., 1975; J.D., Case Western Res. U., 1978. Bar: D.C. 1978. Assoc., Wasserman, Orlow, Ginsberg & Rubin, Washington, 1978-80; staff atty. U.S. SEC, Washington, 1980-83; sr. counsel Freddie Mac, Washington, 1983—. Mem. Fed. Bar Assn., Women's Bar Assn. D.C., Bar Assn. D.C., Pi Gamma Mu. Democrat. Jewish. Office: Fed Home Loan Mortgage Corp 1776 G St NW Washington DC 20018

CIULLA, ROSALIE THERESA, marketing representative; b. Bklyn., Apr. 8, 1961; d. Thomas Salvatore and Mary Amelia (Della-Peruta) C. B.S., Dominican Coll. Blauvelt, N.Y., 1983; A.A.S. in Nursing, Coll. Mt. St. Vincent, 1981. Cert. personnel cons. Nurses aide Upjohn Health Care Services, West Nyack, N.Y., 1981—; personnel cons. Analysts Internat. Corp., N.Y.C., 1983-85; mktg. rep. Software Internat. Assocs., N.Y.C., 1985—. Vol. nurses's aide Sparkhill Sr. Citizen Ctr., N.Y., 1981—. Mem. Ind. Computing Cons. Assn., IBM User Group, Nat. Assn. Female Execs. Roman Catholic. Club: Mensa. Home: 42B W 23d St Bayonne NJ 07002 Office: Software Internat Assocs 150 Broadway Suite 1005 New York NY 10038

CLACK, DOUGLAS MAE, data base company executive, consultant; b. San Antonio, July 10, 1943; d. Douglas Campbell and Ida Mae (Norwood) King; m. Charles Leonard Clack, Aug. 6, 1966 (div. 1973); 1 son, Charles Leonard, Jr. B.A., U. Tex.-San Antonio, 1977; M.S., St. Mary's U., San Antonio, 1983. Engring. records clk. Southwestern Bell, San Antonio and Houston, 1970-72; clk., sec. Frost Bank, San Antonio, 1972-75; adminstr. San Antonio Independent Sch. Dist., 1977-84; owner, v.p. Diverse Data Systems, Inc., San Antonio, 1984—; cons. various profl. and ednl. agencies, 1980—; instr. Tex. Edn. Agy., Austin, 1980—, Alamo Community Coll. Dist., 1984—; speaker various Tex. sch. dists., 1980—. Contbr. articles to profl. jours. Sec. PTA, 1975-77, v.p., 1977-78; vol. ARC, 1978, Am. Cancer Soc., 1979; mem. adv. bd. Ella Austin Community Clinic, sec., 1981-84; vol. youth program New Mt. Pleasant Bapt. Ch.; mem. The Women's Coalition; mem. steering com. Women's Fair, 1985. Mem. Bus. and Profl. Women (corr. sec. 1983-85), LWV (local chair fin. com.), U. Tex. Alumni Assn., Am. Soc. Tng. and Devel., San Antonio Negro Bus. and Profl. Women, Greater Randolph Area C. of C., Alamo City C. of C., Bexar County Women's Ctr. Mentor's Program, Phillis Wheatley Alumni Assn. (charter mem., treas. 1984-85), Gamma Phi Lambda. Democrat. Club: Rising Star Internat. Tng. in Communications (charter mem.). Avocations: swimming; crafts; bicycling; exercising; reading; travel. Home: 12246 Brownstone St San Antonio TX 78233 Office: Diverse Data Systems Inc 1520 N Main Ave San Antonio TX 78212

CLAFLIN, CAROL ANN JEFFERS, management consultant; b. Hartford, Conn., Dec. 18, 1935; d. Jay Edward and Inda Anna (Hull) Jeffers; m. Herbert Edwin Claflin, June 15, 1957; 1 son, Craig Whitwood. B.S., Springfield Coll., 1957; postgrad. Lesley Coll., 1974-75, Nat. Tng. Labs. Inst. Applied Behavioral Scis., summers 1973, 74, 75, 79, 80. Mem. faculty Wapping Sch., South Windsor, Conn., 1957-58, Chamberlain Sch., New Britain, Conn., 1958-59, Gaffney Sch., New Britain, 1959-61; adj. assoc. prof. guidance and psychol. services Springfield (Mass.) Coll. Grad. Sch., 1979—; pres., dir. Devel. Bank, Acton, Mass., 1976—; regional cons., trainer, developer Nat. Ctr. Vol. Action, Washington, 1974-79; cons., trainer, developer Jr. League Boston, 1973-79; nat. staff recruiter Nat. Bd. YWCA, N.Y.C., 1968-71. Author: Group Decision Making, 1977; Leadership Development, 1976; Banker's Dining Guide to Downtown Boston, 1978. Bd. dirs. YWCA New Britain, 1968-71, pres., 1971, chmn. exec. com., 1971; bd. dirs. Concord/Weston Area Jr. League Boston, 1973-74, sustaining mem., 1978—; mem. governing bd. Berlin Congregational Ch. (Conn.), 1966-69, mem. bd. Christian edn., 1965-69, chmn., 1968-69; mem. nominating com. for governing bd. Trinitarian Congl. Ch., Concord, Mass., 1971-73; mem. nat. alumni bd. Springfield Coll., 1983—, nat. alumni fund bd., 1969-73, 80-81. Recipient Tarbell medallion Springfield Coll., 1984. Mem. Am. Soc. Tng. and Devel., Organizational Devel. Network. Republican. Club: Shuttle Meadow Country. Office: Development Bank 21 Nagog Hill Rd Acton MA 01720

CLAGETT, VIRGINIA MARIE, manufacturing company executive; b. Mesa, Ariz., Aug. 3, 1938; d. Westall Irwin and Elna Jeanne (Smith) Harmon; B.A., U. Ariz., 1959. Engring. aide numerical analysis lab. U. Ariz., Tucson, 1959-61; systems analyst Gen. Electric Co., Phoenix, 1961-70; project leader Honeywell Info. Systems, Inc., Phoenix, 1970-73, project engr., 1973-78, mgr. comml. compiler, 1978-81, mgr. software editing and control, 1982—. Mem. Am. Bus. Women's Assn., Nat. Assn. Female Execs., Epsilon Sigma Alpha (pres. Ariz. council 1979-80, corr. sec. internat. council 1984-85), credentials chmn. internat. council 1985-86). Republican. Episcopalian. Home: 3044 E Cannon Dr Phoenix AZ 85028 Office: PO Box 8000 Phoenix AZ 85066

CLAGETT, VIRGINIA PARKER, county official; b. Washington, July 18, 1943; d. William Merrick and Virginia (Lawrence) Parker; m. Brice McAdoo, Sept. 18, 1965; children—John Brice, Ann Brooke. Student U. Geneva, 1963-64; B.A., Smith Coll., 1965. Asst. reporter Triangle Stas., Phila., 1966-68; county councilwoman County of Anne Arundel, Annapolis, Md., 1974—, council chmn., 1984—. Vice chmn. Balt. Regional Planning Council, 1984—; trustee Hammond-Harwood House, 1978—, Chesapeake EPA, 1976—; mem. Alcohol and Drug Abuse Adv. Com., 1985—; mem. Anne Arundel County Agrl. Adv. Com., 1978—. Mem. Am. Bus. Womens Assn., Md. Assn. Counties (legis. com.). Democrat. Episcopalian. Avocations: tennis; gardening, horseback riding. Home: Ivy Neck West River MD 20778 Office: Anne Arundel County PO Box 1831 Annapolis MD 21404

CLAIBORNE, JOSIE KNOWLIN, lawyer; b. Florence, S.C., Sept. 13, 1948; d. Rufus and Correatha (Eaddy) Knowlin; m. Claudius B. Claiborne, May 15, 1969 (div. Mar. 1979); children—Claudia, Corrie, Abram Barrett. B.A., Duke U., 1971; J.D., U. N.C., 1979. Bar: N.C. 1979, S.C. 1980. Data processing asst. Hellmuth, Obata & Kassabuam, St. Louis, 1971-73; computer librarian Dartmouth Coll., Hanover, N.H., 1973-75; research asst. City of Charlotte (N.C.), 1975-76; gen. counsel Columbia Urban League (S.C.), 1980-82; atty. S.C. Electric & Gas Co., Columbia, 1982—. Legal counsel Carolina Sunshine for Children, Columbia, 1982—; mem. panel United Way of the Midlands, Columbia, 1981—. Fellow Inst. Creative Studies, Washington, 1969; Duke U. scholar, 1966-71. Mem. Am. Corp. Counsel Assn., ABA, S.C. Bar Assn., N.C. Bar Assn., Richland County Bar Assn. Methodist. Home: 513 Flora Dr Columbia SC 29204 Office: SC Electric and Gas Co PO Box 764 Columbia SC 29218

CLAIR, CAROLYN GREEN, civic worker; b. Boston, Sept. 18, 1909; d. James Maddocks and Marietta Cecelia (Foeley) Green; m. Miles Nelson Clair, June 16, 1928 (dec. 1981); children—Cynthia York Clair Norkin, Valerie DeLuce Clair Stelling, Ardith Monroe Clair Houghton. B.S., Boston U., 1930, postgrad., 1933. Treas. MNCC, Inc., 1977—; translator Am. Concrete Inst., Chgo., 1930-37. Regent Mass. Soc. DAR, 1933-35, page, 1932-36; pres. Mass. Soc. Children Am. Revolution, 1936-38, historian, 1937-39; v.p. Mass. chpt. Daus. Colonial Wars, 1969-71; active Salvation Army Aux., 1970—; active Assn. Country Women World, 1968—, lectr., 1972—, alt. to UN, 1974—; bd. dirs., mem. service league Boston Hosp. Women, 1966-76, officer, 1969-76; bd. overseers, 1974—, chmn. patient care adv. com., 1977—; pres. New Eng. Farm & Garden Assn., 1968-71, chmn. fellowship Woods Hole Oceanographic Instn.; assoc. Woods Hole Oceanographic Instn.; trustee Brigham & Women's Hosp. Boston, 1982—, mem. pathology com.; mem. Women's Rep. Club of N.Y.C., English-Speaking Union; Friend of Libraries of Boston U.; bd. dirs. Boston Morning Musicales, Tufts U., 1966-80; mem. council Boston Symphony Orch., 1969—; pres. Women's Nat. Farm Assn., 1972-74, chmn. adv. bd., 1974—; mem. corp. Affiliated Hosps. Ctr., Boston, 1975-76; mem. adv. bd. Nat. Arboretum, Washington, 1974-78; exec. bd. Country Women's Council, 1972-74; v.p. Mass. Hort. Soc., 1970—; lectr. environ. concerns. Recipient Brit. War Relief award, 1945. Mem. New Eng. Hist. Soc. (life), Mass. Hist. Soc., Pan Am. Soc., Internat. Platform Assn., People to People (translator), Boston Mus. Fine Arts, Internat. Womens Ednl. and Indsl. Union, Audubon Soc., Nat. Wildlife Fedn., Nat. Trust Historic Preservation, Bostonian Soc., Arnold Arboretum. Republican. Episcopalian. Home: Clair de Loon Box 63 Cataumet MA 02543

CLAIRE, COLLEEN MARION, lawyer; b. Tucson, Nov. 18, 1931; d. Fred William and M. Marion (Pennington) Koerner; m. Guy King Claire, July 15, 1955. B.S., U. So. Calif., 1952, LL.B., 1955. Bar: Calif. 1957. Assoc. Lawler, Felix & Hall, Los Angeles, 1956-65; ptnr. Rutan & Tucker, Santa Ana, Calif., 1965-76; sole practice, Newport Beach, Calif., 1976-79; assoc. Gibson, Dunn & Crutcher, Newport Beach, 1979-84; sole practice, Corona del Mar, Calif., 1984—. Mem. Orange County Performing Arts Endowment Com., Costa Mesa, Calif., 1983—; mem. Orange Coast Coll. Endowment Com., Costa Mesa, 1983—; mem. nat. com. Am. Ballet Com., N.Y.C., 1984—; bd. dirs. Music Ctr. Dance Presentations, 1985—. Recipient Better Bus. Girl award U. So. Calif. Sch. Commerce, 1952. Mem. Calif. State Bar Assn. (exec. com. Estate Planning, Trust, Probate Sect. 1973-82, chmn. 1980, advisor to exec. com. 1983-84), Orange County Bar Assn. (bd. dirs. 1973-77, mem. Estate Planning, Trust & Probate Law Sect. 1967—), ABA, Am. Coll. Probate Council, Internat. Acad. Estate & Trust Law, Beta Gamma Sigma. Clubs: Big Canyon Country, Balboa Bay, Newport Beach Country (Newport Beach). Author chpt. in book; lectr. ednl. programs.

CLAMAGE, SANDY, photographer; b. Chgo., Aug. 8, 1945; d. Robert and Elza Ann (Shapiro) C.; student Northwestern U., 1963-64, Laurence Merrick Studios, Hollywood, Calif., 1970-72, Los Angeles City Coll., 1975-76, Nikon Sch. Photography, 1976; 1 son, Eric Ray. Personal photographer to TV actor, Hollywood, Calif., 1975-76; ofcl. photographer Muscular Dystrophy Assn., Fresno, Calif., 1976-78; sports photographer All Am. Color, Culver City, Calif., spring 1979; sch. photographer Thompson Photography, Glendale,

Calif., fall 1979; staff photographer San Fernando Valley Fair Housing Council, Van Nuys, Calif., 1980; freelance photojournalist, 1979—; owner, mgr., photographer Reflections Photography, Diamond Springs, Calif., 1979—; exhibited works in Burbank Fine Arts Fedn. Multi-Media Exhibit, 1980; Central Library, Burbank, 1982, Calif. Hist. Soc., 1983. Recipient 3d Pl. award North Hollywood Arts and Crafts Show, 1977; 2d place award for color photo Celebration of the Arts show, 1983. Mem. Nat. Press Photographer's Assn., Women in Photography, Am. Soc. Picture Profls. Home: PO Box 313 Diamond Springs CA 95619 Office: PO Box 313 Diamond Springs CA 95619

CLAMAR, APHRODITE J., psychologist; b. Hartford, Conn., Sept. 26, 1933; d. James John and Georgia (Panas) C.; B.A., CCNY, 1953; M.A., Columbia U., 1955; Ph.D., N.Y. U., 1978; m. Richard Cohen, June 24, 1973. Mgmt. cons., psychologist Milla Alihan Assos., N.Y.C., 1957-62; research psychologist, coordinator Inst. Devel. Studies, N.Y. Med. Coll., 1964; intern psychologist Bellevue Psychiat. Hosp., N.Y.C., 1964-66; asso. prof. Fashion Inst. Tech., 1966-69; supervising psychologist Lifeline Center for Child Devel., N.Y.C., 1966-67; chief psychologist Beth Israel Med. Center, N.Y.C., 1967-70; dir. community-sch. mental health programs Soundview Community Services, Albert Einstein Coll. Medicine, Yeshiva U., 1970-73; dir. treatment program for ct.-related children, dept. child psychiatry Harlem Hosp. Med. Center, 1973-76; mem. faculty dept. psychiatry Columbia U., 1973-76; pvt. practice psychotherapy, N.Y.C., 1976—; cons. public health and mental health agys., 1976—; mem. faculty psychoanalytic psychotherapy tng. program Lenox Hill Hosp., N.Y.C., 1982—. Fellow AAAS; mem. Am. Psychol. Assn. (chair com. for women, div. psychotherapy 1980-82), Soc. for Psychoanalytic Psychotherapy, N.J. Psychol. Assn., Soc. Clin. and Exptl. Hypnosis, NOW, Assn. Women in Psychology. Democrat. Greek Orthodox. Author: (with Budd Hopkins) Missing Time, 1981; contbr. articles to profl. jours. and textbooks. Home: 162 E 80th St New York NY 10021 Office: 30 E 60th St New York NY 10022

CLAMPITT, AMY KATHLEEN, writer, editor; b. New Providence, Iowa, June 15, 1920; d. Roy Justin and Lutie Pauline (Felt) C. B.A. with honors in English, Grinnell Coll., 1941, D.H.L., 1984. Sec., writer Oxford Univ. Press, N.Y.C., 1943-51; reference librarian Nat. Audubon Soc., N.Y.C., 1952-59; free-lance writer, N.Y.C., 1960-77; editor E.P. Dutton, N.Y.C., 1977-82; writer-in-residence Coll. William & Mary, Williamsburg, Va., 1984-85. Author: (poetry) The Kingfisher, 1983; (poetry) What the Light Was Like, 1985. Guggenheim fellow, 1982-83; recipient Lit. award Am. Acad. Arts and Letters, 1984; fellow Acad. Am. Poets, 1984. Mem. PEN, Editorial Freelancers Assn. Democrat.

CLAMPITT, MARY O'BRIANT, government official; b. Connehatti, Miss., Feb. 18, 1931; d. Theron Russell and Ola Belle (Thompson) O'Briant; m. William Henry Clampitt, May 7, 1955; children—Russell, Henry, Amy, James. B.S., U. Md., 1978, M.A., 1982. Info. analyst FBI, Washington, 1951-56; editor Chief State Sch. Officers, NEA, Washington, 1976-77; editor, conf. mgr. Forum Officer, Nat. Acad. Sci., Washington, 1977-78; owner Clampitt Editorial Assocs., Chevy Chase, Md., 1970—; adminstrv. specialist White House Conf. on Aging, Washington, 1980-82; program analyst Office Insp. Gen., Health and Human Services, Washington, 1982-84; mgmt. analyst Food Safety Inspection Service, Washington, 1984—; Fed. women's program mgr. Food Safety Inspection Service, 1984—. Bibliographer: History of State Departments of Education, 1978. Pres. Lynnbrook Sch. PTA, Bethesda, Md., 1964; vol. Pres.'s Com. on Hiring Handicapped, 1985, Mothers Against Drunk Driving, 1985—. Mem. Federally Employed Women, Interagency Fed. Women's Program Mgrs., Phi Kappa Phi. Republican. Baptist. Clubs: Woman's Action Taskforce (bd. dirs.), Bus. and Profl. Women's. Avocations: hiking; biking; cooking; writing songs; entering and winning recipe contests. Home: 7114 Edgevale St Chevy Chase MD 20815 Office: Food Safety Inspection Service 14th and Independence Ave Washington DC 20815

CLANCE, PAULINE ROSE, psychology educator; b. Welch, W.Va., Oct. 19, 1938; d. George W. and Gladys (Riley) Rose; B.S. cum laude Lynchburg Coll., 1960; M.S., U. Ky., 1964, Ph.D., 1969; m. Lanier Clance, Dec. 14, 1959. Clin. psychologist G.B. Dinmick Child Guidance Clinic, Lexington, Ky., 1965; psychologist Univ. Hosp. Cleve., 1966-68, Brecksville VA Hosp., 1969-71; clin. psychologist Psychol. Services, Oberlin Coll., 1971-74; asst. prof. Oberlin Coll., 1971-74; prof. psychology Ga. State U., Atlanta, 1974—; pvt. practice clin. psychology, Atlanta, 1974—; cons. in field. Adv. bd. Odyssey Family Service, 1979—; mem. Com. on Minority and Poverty Groups, Coll. Entrance Examination Bd., 1972-75; peer reviewer grants nat. Endowment for Humanities, Washington, 1972—; reviewer curriculum materials Appalachian Center for Ednl. Equity, U. Tenn., 1978—. Oberlin Coll. leadership tng. grantee, 1973; Urban Life Center grantee, 1977; others. Mem. Southwestern Psychol. Assn. (pres. 1982-83), Am. Acad. Psychotherapists, AAUP, Assn. Women in Psychology, Am. Psychol. Assn. Co-author: The Teaching Sourcebook, 1980; author: The Imposter Phenomenon: Overcoming the Fear that Haunts Your Success, 1985; contbr. articles to profl. jours. Office: Dept Psychology Ga State U Atlanta GA 30303

CLANCY, CONSTANCE ALINE, librarian, consultant; b. Holyoke, Mass., May 2, 1934; d. Roberval Joseph and Yvonne Angelina (Berger) Hubert; m. Robert Elmer Clancy, Sept. 11, 1954; children—Robert Joseph, Michael Steven, Marguerite Aline. B.A., Am. Internat. Coll., 1970; M.S., Simmons Coll., 1974. Dept. head Springfield Monarch Ins. Co. (Mass.), 1959-61; library asst. South Hadley (Mass.) Pub. Library, 1961-68, head librarian, 1968-69, dir., 1969—; charter mem., users council Central/Western Mass. Automated Resource Sharing, Past On, 1982—; coordinator pub. access studio South Hadley Library System, 1977—. Hostess, moderator cable TV weekly program South Hadley Library Live, 1977—; cons., advisor video tape The Town Meeting Idea, 1977, I Remember South Hadley, 1977; bldg. cons., 1984—. Mem. town meeting Town of South Hadley, 1969—; chmn. South Hadley Arts Council, 1981—; treas. Mass. Extension Adv. Council, Mass. Coop. Extension, 1981—; vice-chmn. Hampshire County Extension Trustee Coop. Extension, Northampton, 1982—. Recipient Disting. Service award South Hadley Jaycees, 1981; Citizen of Yr. award Lions Club, 1984; grantee Mass. Bd. Library Commrs., 1971-79, Mass. Council Arts and Humanities, 1976-77, Mass. Arts Lottery Council, 1983-84. Mem. ALA, New Eng. Library Assn. (media com. 1979—), Mass. Library Assn. (pres. 1983-85), Western Mass. Library Club, Western Mass. Regional Library System (chmn. 1972-74, 77-79), South Hadley Hist. Soc. (pres. 1981-83). Republican. Roman Catholic. Clubs: Sohaywo (pres. 1959-61), Women's (pres. 1973-75) (South Hadley, Mass.); St. Patrick's Parish (chmn. council 1975-78); A Better Chance (pres. 1977-79). Home: 73 School St South Hadley MA 01075 Office: South Hadley Library System Bardwell St South Hadley MA 01075

CLANCY, ROSALIND LEE, modeling school administrator; b. Trenton, N.J., Oct. 1, 1948; d. Florindo Peter and Elsa (Lanzi) Manganelli; m. Joseph Michael Clancy, Jr., Apr. 15, 1973. A.A., Trenton Jr. Coll., 1969. Dir. Calif. Sch. Modeling and Charm, Trenton, N.J., 1972—; casting dir. Motion Picture Casting, N.Y.C., 1980—; mem. Miss Am. Scholarship Pageant, 1975—; chmn. Shamrock Specialties, Lawrenceville, N.J., 1983—; cons. Ladato Mgmt., N.Y.C., 1979— Cinema Liberty Prodns., Princeton, N.J., 1974—; judge Miss Am. Teenager, N.J., 1974—, Miss Teenage Am., N.J., 1975, preliminary Miss Universe, N.J., 1985. Recipient Profl. Excellence award Fermi Fedn., 1974. Republican. Lutheran. Clubs: Italian-Am. (Hamilton Twp., N.J.); Bordentown Yacht. Avocations: boating; sports. Home: 937 Brunswick Ave Trenton NJ 08638 Office: Calif Sch Modeling and Charm 937 Brunswick Ave Trenton NJ 08638

CLARK, ALICIA GARCIA, political party official; b. Vera Cruz, Mex., Jan. 13; came to U.S., 1970; d. Rafael Aully and Maria Luisa (Cobos) Garcia; m. Edward E. Clark, Oct. 20, 1970; 1 son, Edward E. M.S. in Chem. Engring., Nat. U. Mex., Mexico City, 1951. Chemist, Celanese Mexicana, Mexico City, 1951-53, lab. mgr., 1951-53, sales promotion mgr., 1958-65, sales promotion and advt. mgr., 1965-70. Nat. chmn. Libertarian Party, Houston, 1981-83; pres. San Marino (Calif.) Guild of Huntington Hosps., 1981-82, chmn. Celebrity Series, 1979—; Pres. Multiple Sclerosis Soc., San Gabriel Valley, Calif., 1977-78. Recipient award La Mujer de Hoy mag., 1969. Mem. Fashion Group (treas. 1969-70), Mex. Advt. Assn. (dir. 1969-70, award 1970). Club: San Marino Woman's (ways and means chmn. 1980).

CLARK, ANJA MARIA, lawyer; b. Vienna, Austria, Mar. 31, 1942; came to U.S., 1966, naturalized, 1982; d. Joseph and Josephine (Mokesch) Rernboeck; m. Robert Eugene Smith, Jan. 26, 1969 (div.); m. Donald Otis Clark, Nov. 5, 1983. B.A. summa cum laude in Sociology, Oglethorpe U., 1974; M.A. cum laude in Sociology, Ga. State U., 1977; J.D., John Marshall Law Sch., 1977. Bar: Ga. 1978. Paralegal asst., Atlanta, 1976-78; sole practice, Atlanta, 1978-84. Recipient Benjamin Parker Law award Oglethorpe U., 1974. Mem. Ga. Assn. Women Lawyers (sec.-treas. 1981-83), State Bar Ga., ABA, Bus. Council Ga. (internat. subcom. 1981-83), Women's Bar Assn. D.C. (dir. career opportunities 1984-85). Republican. Roman Catholic.

CLARK, BARBARA, auto club administrator; b. Santa Monica, Calif., Sept. 18, 1940; d. Cyrus Lowell and Anna Gretta (Mack) C. A.A., Santa Monica Coll., 1960; B.A., UCLA, 1962; M.A., Calif. State-U.-Los Angeles, 1982. Compensation asst. System Devel. Corp., Santa Monica, Calif., 1960-62, survey statistician, 1962-66, jr. compensation analyst, 1966-68, compensation analyst, 1968-70; compensation analyst Auto Club So. Calif. Los Angeles, 1970-72, research adminstr., 1972-73, compensation mgr., 1973—. Mem. Am. Compensation Assn. (western membership chmn. 1972), Nat. Assn. Female Execs., Caltech Mgmt. Discussion Group. Mem. Ch. Jesus Christ of Latter-day Saints. Home: 894 Commonwealth Ave Venice CA 90291

CLARK, BETTY JEAN, state legislator; b. Kansas City, Kans., Apr. 18, 1920; d. Raymond Carlisle and Mary Priscilla (Hunt) Walker; student Ft. Hays State U., 1937-38, U. Utah, 1939-40, U. Pacific, 1942-45, Garrett Evangelical Sem., 1948; m. Homer Orville Clark, Sept. 3, 1950; children—Peggy, Mark, Paul. Dir. student program Wesley Found., Ames, Iowa, 1948-51; dir. Christian edn. First United Meth. Ch., Mason City, Iowa, 1963-75; mem. Iowa Gen. Assembly, Des Moines, 1977—. Mem. Republican Women's Task Force. Mem. Bus. and Profl. Women, Women's Polit. Caucus, LWV, Fedn. Republican Women, P.E.O. Methodist. Clubs: Ch. Women United, Federated Women's Club, Older Women's League, United Meth. Women. Author: (with Harriet Ann Daffron) Nearer to Thee, 1956. Office: State Capitol Des Moines IA 50319

CLARK, BEVERLY ANN, lawyer; b. Davenport, Iowa, Dec. 9, 1944; d. F. Henry and Arlene F. (Meyer) C.; m. Richard Floss; children—Amy and Barry (twins). Student, Mich. State U., 1963-65; B.A., Calif. State U.-Fullerton, 1967; M.S.W., U. Iowa, 1975, J.D., 1980. Bar: Iowa 1980. Probation officer County of San Bernardino, San Bernardino, Calif., 1968, County of Riverside, Riverside, Calif., 1968-69; social worker Skiff Hosp., Newton, Iowa, 1971-73; social worker State of Iowa, Mitchellville, 1973-74, planner, Des Moines, 1976-77, law clk., Des Moines, 1980-81; instr. Des Moines Area Community Coll., Ankeny, Iowa, 1974-75; gen. counsel Pioneer Hi-Bred Internat., Inc., Des Moines, 1981—. Editor: Proceedings: Bicentennial Symposium on New Directions in Juvenile Justice, 1975. Founder Mothers of Twins Club, Newton, Iowa, 1971; co-chmn. Juvenile Justice Symposium, Des Moines, 1974-75; mem. Juvenile Justice Com., Des Moines, 1974-75; mem. Nat. Offender Based State Corrections Info. System Com., Ia. rep., 1976-78; incorporator, dir. Iowa Dance Theatre, Des Moines, 1981; mem. Pesticide User's Adv. Com., Fort Collins, Colo., 1981—. Mem. ABA (subcom. on docket. individual rights in work place, termination-at-will subcom.), Iowa Bar Assn., Polk County Bar Assn., Polk County Women Atty.'s Assn., Am. Trial Lawyers Assn., Am. Assn. Agrl. Lawyers. Home: Rural Route 1 Box 80 Baxter IA 50028 Office: Pioneer Hi-Bred International Inc 400 Locust St Suite 700 Des Moines IA 50309

CLARK, BONNIE HUFFMAN, nurse; b. Warrenton, Va., July 12, 1960; d. Jesse James and Lois J. (Gottschall) Huffman; m. Kim Steven Clark, Oct. 1, 1983. B.S. in Nursing, Radford U., 1983. R.N., Va. Nursing intern Hershey Med. Ctr., Pa., summer 1982; staff nurse Mary Washington Hosp., Fredricksburg, Va., summer 1983, Community Hosp., Roanoke, Va., 1983-85; nurse, rev. analyst Med. Soc. Va., Salem, 1985—. Mem. Va. Nurses Assn., Sigma Theta Tau. Methodist. Avocations: sewing; cross stitch. Home: 2519 10th St NW Roanoke VA 24012 Office: Med Soc Va 1626 Apperson Dr Salem VA 24153

CLARK, BRENDA VOGELSANG, radio station owner; b. Houston, Mar. 14, 1942; d. Gus Alexander and Marjorie (Balke) Vogelsang; children—Albert Reagan Jr., Clayton Clark, Julianne. B.S., U. Houston, 1979, M.A., 1982, Ph.D., 1983. Exec. dir. The Houstonian, Houston, 1982-83; pres., owner Brenda Clark & Assoc., Houston, 1983—; pres. Bay Broadcasters Ltd. dir. Tex. Capital Bank, Richmond, Civic Communications, Jackson, Miss., Austin Wholesale Grass Co., Tex. State chmn. vol. services Tex. Dept. Mental Health and Mental Retardation, Austin, 1980-83; county chmn. Fort Bend Democratic Party, Tex., 1984—; sec. Tex. Dem. County Chmn. Assn., Austin, 1984—. Recipient Commrs. award Tex. Dept. Mental Health-Mental Retardation, 1984, Govs. award State of Tex., 1984. Mem. Fort Bend Profl. Women. Methodist. Avocation: travel. Home: PO Box 385 Richmond TX 77469 Office: Brenda Clark & Assoc PO Box 1391 Bay City TX 77414

CLARK, CAROL CANDA, museum curator, art historian, educator; b. N.Y.C., July 21, 1947; d. Henry G. Canda and Dolores C. Adam; m. Jon D. Clark, May 24, 1969 (div. Apr. 1983). B.A. with distinction, U. Mich.-Ann Arbor, 1969, M.A., 1971; Ph.D., Case Western Res. U., Cleve., 1981. Registrar, U. Mich. Mus. Art, Ann Arbor, 1971-72; instr. Tex. Christian U., Ft. Worth, 1975-77; curator Amon Carter Mus. Ft. Worth, 1977-84; exec. prendergast fellow Williams Coll., Williamstown, Mass., 1984—, lectr. art history, 1984—; adj. prof. art history So. Methodist U., 1982-83; adj. curator of Am. Art, Clark Art Inst., Williamstown, Mass., 1984—; mem. art adv. panel IRS, Washington, 1983—. Author: Thomas Moran's Watercolors, 1980; (catalogue) American Impressionist and Realist Paintings, 1978. Mem. art and architecture adv. panel Tex. Commn. on the Arts, 1981-83. Kress Found. fellow, 1972-75. Mem. The Dunlap Soc. (mem. adv. council 1982—). Office: Williams Coll Mus Art Williamstown MA 01267

CLARK, CAROL LOIS, state consumer advocate, consultant; b. Salt Lake City, May 23, 1948; d. Norman W. and Lois Amanda (Colt) C. B.A. in English cum laude, U. Utah, 1970; M.Ed. in Secondary Edn., 1972, Ph.D. in Cultural Founds. of Edn., 1979; postgrad. Columbia U., summer 1980. Cert. profl. tchr., Utah, Mass. Tchr. Jordan Sch. dist., Sandy, Utah, 1972-78, 81-82; curriculum cons. Brigham Young U., Provo, 1978-79, cons., lectr., 1978—; program specialist Utah System Approach to Individualized Learning, Salt Lake City, 1980-81; consumer edn. specialist Utah Atty. Gen.'s Office, Salt Lake City, 1982-84; free-lance editor, curriculum developer Utah Office Edn., Salt Lake City, 1981-82; free-lance editor, cons. Dian Thomas Enterprises, Provo, 1981—; gov.'s adminstrv. asst. for edn. and communication; bd. dirs. Deseret Gymnasium, Salt Lake City, 1982—; mem. unproven med. practices com. Utah State Med. Assn., 1983-84; mem. Utah Ins. Consumer Action Com., 1983-84; mem. Utah Records Com., 1983-84; mem. Utah Gov.'s Securities Fraud Task Force, 1984; chmn. Utah Atty. Gen.'s Consumer Adv. Com., 1984. Author: A Singular Life, 1974; How to Avoid Getting Ripped Off: Essential But Hard-to-Find Consumer Facts for Women, 1985; co-author: Principles of Learning, 1981; contbr.: Consumer's Resource Handbook, 1986; consumer columnist Deseret News, 1982-84, Standard-Examiner, 1983-84, Golden Age, 1983-84, Cache County Citizen, 1984, Park Record, 1984, Sun Advocate, 1984, Richfield Reaper, 1984, Vernal Express, 1984, Color County Spectrum, 1984, Provo Daily Herald, 1984; contbr. articles, poetry to various publs.; editor: The Relief Society Magazine: A Legacy Remembered, 1914-1970, 1982. Mem. gen. bd. Relief Soc., Ch. of Jesus Christ of Latter-day Saints, Salt Lake City, 1973-84, state del., 1986; acting chmn. Republican Party Voting Dist., Salt Lake City, 1977, dist. vice chmn., 1984; mem. Utah Women's Legis. Council, 1977-79; mem. Denver region Ford Consumer Appeals Bd., 1983-84; mem. planning com. Utah Ednl. Seminar, 1985—. Recipient Tchr. of Yr. award Utah State Hist. Soc., 1975, Ann. Achievement award for best consumer publ. Nat. Assn. Consumer Agy. Adminstrs., 1983; named Outstanding Young Woman from Utah, 1982, Young Woman of Achievement, Nat. Council Women, 1984; Ch. of Jesus Christ of Latter-day Saints Historian's Office fellow, 1976. Mem. Salt Lake C. of C. (bus. in edn. com.), Nat. Futures Assn. (edn. adv. com. 1984—), Nat. Assn. Consumer Agy. Adminstrs., Profl. Rep. Women, Utah Women's Forum (founding mem.), Phi Kappa Phi, Alpha Xi Delta, Lambda Delta Sigma. Office: Utah Gov's Office 210 State Capital Bldg Salt Lake City UT 84114

CLARK, CAROLYN ARCHER, technologist, scientist; b. Leon County, Tex., Feb. 16, 1941; d. Ray Brooks and Dena Mae (Green) Archer; m. Frank Ray Clark, Nov. 20, 1960 (div. Oct. 1979); children—Frank Ray, Valerie Lynn, Bruce Layne. B.A., Sam Houston State U., 1961; M.S., Tex. A&M U., 1973, Ph.D., 1977. Supr., bookkeeper Republic Sewing Machine Distbrs., Dallas, 1961-65; door-to-door sales person Avon Products, Inc. Bryan, Tex., 1965-72; lectr. Tex. A&M Univ., College Station, Tex., 1977, research assoc., 1977-79; sr. sci. Lockheed Emsco., Houston, 1979-82, prin. scientist 1983-85; aerospace technologist phys. scientist Nat. Space Technology Lab., NASA, Miss., 1985—; cons. in field. Contbr. articles to profl. publs. Recipient Commendation for Outstanding Contbns. Lockheed, 1979-80, Commendation for Excellence, 1984; Cert. of Merit U.S. Dept. Agr. 1980; Grad. Research fellow Tex. A&M, 1975-76; NSF co-grantee Tex. A&M, 1976-77. Mem. Am. Soc. Plant Taxonomists, Bot. Soc. Am., Ecol. Soc. Am., Am. Soc. Photo-grammetry, Nat. Mgmt. Assn., Sigma Xi, Phi Sigma, Alpha Chi, Kappa Delta Pi. Republican. Avocations: sailing, scuba diving, tennis, piano. Office: NASA Earth Resources Lab Nat Space Tech Laboratory MS 39520

CLARK, CAROLYN LEIS, audiovisual specialist; b. Clairton, Pa., June 10, 1945; d. J. Clark and Aleda Marie (Blank) Leis; m. Richard M. Clark, 1965 (div. 1973); 1 son, Brian. Student Pa. State U., 1963-65; B.A. in Psychology with high honors, Rutgers U., 1972; cert. elem. edn. Kean Coll., 1974-75; postgrad. Hunter Coll., 1978. Art. therapist Rutkowski Sch., New Brunswick, N.J., 1968-69, tchr. emotionally impaired, 1969-73; edn. cons. AV Media Craftsman, Inc., N.Y.C., 1973, dir. creative services, 1974-79, v.p., 1980-82, pres., 1982—; audiovisual cons. J.C. Penney Co., N.Y.C., 1976-84; outside producer Pinkerton's, Inc., N.Y.C., 1979-84; cons. John Wiley & Sons, N.Y.C., 1979-84. Author, producer Consumer Edn., 1977-84; producer, dir. Mem. hon. bd. Jean Cocteau Theatre, N.Y.C., 1981-83. Recipient George Washington award Freedoms Found. at Valley Forge, 1977; Silver award Internat. Film and TV Festival, 1977; award of Merit, Soc. Tech. Communications, 1983; award of Achievement, Internat. Audio Visual Competition, 1983; award of Creative Excellence, U.S. Indsl. Film Festival, 1984; prize for security saety film Am. Soc. for Indsl. Security, 1985/ Mem. Nat. Assn. Female Execs., Wagner Internat. Soc., Screen Actors Guild, Motoric Devel. Program (asst. dir. 1971-74), Rutgers Alumni Assn., Assn. for Research and Enlightenment (N.Y. coordinator 1986), Delta Zeta. Presbyterian; mem. Unity Ch. Office: AV Media Craftsmen Inc 110 E 23rd St New York NY 10010

CLARK, CELIA RUE, lawyer; b. N.Y.C., Aug. 16, 1951; d. Edward Frank and Rosemary (Reddick) Clark, Jr.; m. Edgar Crawford Gentry, Jr., Aug. 11, 1979; 1 dau., Diana Marron. B.A. with distinction, U. Wis., 1974; J.D., U. Chgo., 1979. Bar: N.Y. 1980. Mng. editor Heldref Publs., Washington, 1974-78; assoc. Rogers & Wells, N.Y.C., 1979—. Contbg. author: Asset-Based Financing, 1984. Mem. ABA, N.Y. State Bar Assn., Nat. Assn. Female Execs., NOW. Democrat. Home: 22 Tudor Ln Yonkers NY 10701 Office: Rogers & Wells 200 Park Ave New York NY 10166

CLARK, CHARLENE KERNE, development and promotion coordinator, educator; b. Thibodaux, La., Apr. 15, 1947; d. Francis Lloyd and Ethel (Walker) Kerne; B.A., U. Southwestern La., 1969; M.A., U. Ark., 1970; Ph.D., La. State U., 1974; m. William B. Clark, Dec. 22, 1972; children—Mary Frances Lyons, Eleanor Kerne. Instr. in English, U. N.C., Greensboro, 1975-77; instr. bus. communication N.C. A&T State U., Greensboro, 1976-77; vis. asst. prof. English, Tex. A&M U., College Station, 1977-78; energy info. specialist Center Energy and Mineral Resources, Tex. A&M U., 1978-84; devel. and promotion coordinator Sterling C. Evans Library, Tex. A&M U., 1984—. Mem. ALA, Citizens Hist. Preservation, Internat. Assn. Bus. Communicators, Phi Kappa Phi. Roman Catholic. Home: 1009 Winter St Bryan TX 77801 Office: Sterling C Evans Library Tex A&M U College Station TX 77843

CLARK, CONNIE M., educator; b. Pound, Va., Mar. 8, 1948; d. Leonard Milton Mullins and Mildred (Cantrell) Rose; m. Marvin William Clark, Apr. 22, 1976. B.S. in English, Clinch Valley Coll., 1970; B.S. in Psychology, Va. Poly. Inst. and State U., 1974; M.A. in Edn., Union Coll., 1975; postgrad. U. R.I., 1978, U. Va., 1984. Sec. State Farm Ins., Pound, 1966-67; tchr. Wise County Sch. Bd., Wise, Va., 1970—; pres. Appalachian Edn. Lab., Charleston, W.Va., 1986. Precinct worker Democratic Party, Big Sonte Gap, 1977—. Mem. Nat. Council Tchrs. of English, Va. Edn. Assn. (pres. 1985, Appreciation award 1985, chmn. polit. action com. 1985), uniserv standards commn. 1982-85), Va. Bus. and Profl. Women (vice dir. Dist. I 1985-86), Wise County Edn. Assn. (legis. chmn. 1985-86), Bus. and Profl. Women (pres. Wise, Va. 1983-85), AAUW (legis. chmn. Big Stone Gap 1985). Baptist. Avocations: Reading; music; animals; outdoors. Home: 330 Pearl St Big Stone Gap VA 24219 Office: JJ Kelly High School PO Box 796 Wise VA 24293

CLARK, DARLENE ELISE PURNELL, title company officer; b. Phila., Dec. 25, 1956; d. Harry M. and Eola I. (Stanley) Purnell; m. Douglas Mark Clark, 1984. Student Am. U., 1973-77, U. Md., 1985—. Lic. in real estate sales, Md. Mortgage counselor Weaver Bros., Inc., Chevy Chase, Md., 1975-78; collection rep. Pennamco, Inc., Washington, 1979-80; receptionist Community Fed. Savs. & Loan Assn., Washington, 1980; escrow sec. Columbia Real Estate Title Ins. Co., Washington, 1980-82, escrow officer, br. mgr., 1983-86, asst. v.p., 1986—, tng. cons., 1985—. Democrat. Mem. Pentecostal Ch. Home: 5451 Morris Ave #4 Camp Springs MD 20746 Office: Columbia Real Estate Title Ins Co 1422 NW H St Washington DC 20005

CLARK, DEBORAH LYNN, financial executive; b. Pitts., Apr. 2, 1951; d. Clyde Wilson and Norma June (Glass) McCance; m. C. Richard Clark, Feb. 16, 1973. Grad. Computer Systems Inst., Pitts., 1970; student Point Park Coll. Office mgr. Pressure Chem. Co., Pitts., 1973-74, Budget Rent-a-Car, Pitts., 1974-75; acct. G.M.A.C. Fin., Pitts., 1975-79; sole propr. Clark Color Photography, Pitts., 1977-79; office mgr. McKeever, Varga & Assocs., C.P.A.s, Pitts., 1979-82; asst. controller Park Way Studios Internat. Inc., McKees Rocks, Pa., 1982-85, asst. sec.-treas., 1984—; prin. Clark Fin. Services, 1985—; pres. Pegasus Computer Corp., 1986—; controller several corps. Mem. Wedding Photographers Am., Assoc. Photographer Internat., Nat. Assn. Female Execs., Pa. Assn. Notaries. Club: Greater Pitts. Gun. Home: 3229 Faronia St Pittsburgh PA 15204 Office: Park Way Studios Internat Inc 825 Broadway McKees Rocks PA 15136

CLARK, DEBRA JEAN, nurse; b. Portsmouth, Ohio, Jan. 3, 1958; d. William Ivan Clark and Lillian Ruby (Ervin) Williamson. B.S. in Nursing, Berea Coll., Ky., 1981. Lic. R.N., Ohio, Ky. Staff charge nurse Mercy Hosp., Portsmouth, 1981-84, Berea Hosp., Inc., Ky., 1984—; nurse technician, team leader Mercy Hosp., Portsmouth, summer 1980. Author: (song) I'll Always Remember You, 1981; also book of illustrated poetry. Vol. student labor scheduling organizer Bloodmobile, Berea, 1976-81; donator St. Jude Children's Research Hosp., Memphis, Tenn., 1983-84, Cardinal Hill Rehab. Hosp., Lexington, 1981—, Berea Coll. Alumnae Assn., 1981—. Berea Coll. Nursing scholar, 1979-81. Democrat. Mem. Christian Ch. Club: Smithsonian Assn. (Washington). Avocations: reading; writing; photography; tennis; collecting music boxes. Home: Kentucky Towers Apt 7 Berea KY 40403

CLARK, DENISE LYNN, laboratory executive; b. Norristown, Pa., Oct. 14, 1954; d. James Carl and Rose Ann (DiNofrio) C. B.B.A., Ursinus Coll., Collegeville, Pa., 1985; postgrad. St. Joe's U., Phila. Customer service supr. Upjohn Co., King of Prussia, Pa., 1976-80; mgr. credit and collection SmithKline Clin. Lab., King of Prussia, 1980-85; mgr. nat. credit and collection SmithKline Bio-Sci. Labs., King of Prussia, 1986—. Mem. Nat. Assn. Female Execs., N.J. Assn. Credit Execs. Avocation: travel. Home: 2753 Apple Valley Ln Audubon PA 19403 Office: SmithKline Bio-Sci Labs 600 Allendale Rd King of Prussia PA 19406

CLARK, DONNA MAE, owner game farm; b. Shell Lake, Wis., Mar. 20, 1957; d. Vincent Ernest and Patricia Ann (Shannon) Bauer; m. James Frank Clark, Sept. 20, 1975; 1 child, Elizabeth Grace. Owner, operator Blonhaven Game Farm and Hunting Preserve, Milton, Wis., 1978—. Tchr. Sunday sch. Central Luth. Ch., Edgerton, Wis., 1983—. Mem. N.Am. Game Bird Assn., Nat. Poultry Improvement Plan, Wis. Game Preserve Assn. (editor 1983—), Wis. Hatcheries Assn., Pa. Gamebird Assn. Republican. Home: 362 N John Paul Rd Milton WI 53563 Office: Blonhaven PO Box 12 Route 2 Milton WI 53563

CLARK, DOROTHY JEAN, child devel. specialist; b. Portsmouth, Ohio, Feb. 5, 1926; d. Carl and Marguerite Anna (Ressinger) Warner; B.S. in Edn., Wittenberg Coll., 1950; M.Ed., Bowling Green State U., 1979; m. Edward Clark, Dec. 21, 1946 (dec.); children—Dawn, Roy Hamilton II, Scott Timothy, Eric Edward. Elem. sch. tchr., Springfield, Ohio, 1950-51, Yellow Springs, Ohio, 1970-72; presch. tchr. Community Children's Center, Yellow Springs, 1953-54, 59-60, 68-70, Antioch Sch., Yellow Springs, 1964-67; dir. Head Start, Greene County, Ohio, 1972-81; child devel. dir. Wright Patterson AFB, Ohio, 1981—; instr. Antioch Coll., Sinclair Coll.; child devel. cons. Mem. Nat. Assn. Edn. of Young Children, Mil. Early Childhood Alliance, Nat. Assn. Female Execs., Sigma Alpha Iota. Unitarian. Office: 2750 ABW SSRC Wright Patterson Air Force Base OH 45433

CLARK, ELEANOR, author; b. Los Angeles; d. Frederick Huntington and Eleanor (Phelps) C.; B.A., Vassar Coll.; m. Robert Penn Warren, Dec. 7, 1952; children—Rosanna, Gabriel Author: (novels) The Bitter Box, 1946; Baldur's Gate, 1971; Dr. Heart, A Novella, and Other Stories, 1975; Gloria Mundi, 1979; Camping Out, 1986; (for children) The Song of Roland, 1960; (non-fiction) Rome and a Villa, 1952, expanded edit., 1975; The Oysters of Locmariaquer, 1964; Eyes, Etc., A Memoir, 1977; Tamrant-13 Days in the Sahara, 1984; translator Dark Wedding (R. Sender), 1943; contbr. stories, essays and revs. to numerous publs. Mem. Corp. of Yaddo. Served with OSS, 1943-45. Guggenheim fellow, 1946-47, 49-50; recipient Nat. Book Award, 1965. Mem. Nat. Inst. Arts and Letters (award 1946). Address: 2495 Redding Rd Fairfield CT 06430

CLARK, ELOISE ELIZABETH, biologist, university official; b. Grundy, Va., Jan. 20, 1931; d. J. Francis Emmett and Ava Clayton (Harris) C.; B.A., U. Va., 1951; Ph.D. in Zoology, U. N.C., 1958; D.Sc., King Coll., 1976; postdoctoral research Washington U., St. Louis, 1957-58, U. Calif., Berkeley, 1958-59. Research asst., then instr. U. N.C., 1952-55; instr. physiology Marine Biol. Lab., Woods Hole, Mass., summers 1958-62; mem. faculty Columbia U., 1958-69, asso. prof. biol. sci., 1966-69; with NSF, Washington, 1969-83, head molecular biology, 1971-73, div. dir. biol. and med. scis., 1973-75, dep. asst. dir. biol., behavioral and social scis., 1975-76, asst. dir. biol., behavioral and social scis., 1976-83; v.p. acad. affairs, prof. biol. sci. Bowling Green State U. (Ohio), 1983—. Mem. alumnae bd. Mary Washington Coll., U. Va., 1967-70; bd. regents Nat. Library of Medicine, 1973-83; mem. policy group competitive grants program U.S. Dept. Agr.; mem. White House interdepartmental task force on women and interagy, 1978-80, task force for conf. on families, 1980; mem. com. on health and medicine, 1976-80; vice chmn. com. on food and renewable resources, 1977-80; mem. selective excellence task force Ohio Bd. Regents, 1984—; mem. Ohio Adv. Council for Coll. Prep. Edn., 1983—; mem. Ohio Inter-Univ. Council for Provosts, 1983—, chair, 1984-85. Named Disting. Alumnus, Mary Washington Coll., 1975; Wilson scholar, 1956; E.C. Drew scholar, 1956; USPHS postdoctoral fellow, 1957-59; recipient Disting. Service award NSF, 1978. Mem. Soc. Gen. Physiology (sec. 1965-67, council 1969-71), AAAS (council 1969-71, dir. 1978-82, com. on nominations 1984-85), Biophys. Soc. (council 1975-76), Am. Soc. Cell Biology (council 1972-75), Am. Inst. Biol. Scientists, Phi Beta Kappa (nat. com. on qualifications), Sigma Xi. Contbr. articles to profl. jours. Office: McFall Ctr Bowling Green State U Bowling Green OH 43403

CLARK, ESTHER FRANCES (MRS. JOHN H. CLARK, JR.), legal educator; b. Phila., Aug. 29, 1929; d. John and Lucy (Scapula) Giaccio; B.A., Temple U., 1950; J.D., Rutgers U., 1955; m. John H. Clark, Jr., June 12, 1954; 1 dau., Jacqueline. Admitted to Pa. bar, 1956, practiced in Chester, to 1976; prof. law Del. Law Sch., Widener U., Wilmington, 1976—. Bd. dirs. Taylor Hosp., Ridley Park, Pa., Lindsay Law Library. Fellow Am. Bar Found.; mem. Am., Pa. (chmn. com. legal edn. and bar admission, mem. ho. of dels.), Delaware County (pres. 1982) bar assns., Am. Trial Lawyers Assn., Delaware County Legal Assistance Assn. (dir. 1972-77, pres. bd. dirs. 1974-76). Club: Soroptimists. Roman Catholic. Asso. editor Rutgers U. Law Rev., 1954-55. Home: 207 Knoll Rd Wallingford PA 19086 Office: PO Box 7474 Wilmington DE 19803

CLARK, FAYE LOUISE, drama and speech educator; b. La., Oct. 9, 1936; student Centenary Coll., 1954-55; B.A. with honor, U. Southwestern La., 1962; M.A., U. Ga., 1966; m. Warren James Clark, Aug. 8, 1969; children—Roy, Kay Natalie. Tchr., Nova Exptl. Schs., Fort Lauderdale, Fla., 1963-65; faculty dept. drama and speech DeKalb Community Coll., Atlanta, 1967—, chmn. dept., 1977-81. Pres., Hawthorne Sch. PTA, 1983-84. Mem. Ga. Theatre Conf. (sec. 1968-69, rep. to Southeastern Theatre Conf. 1969), Ga. Psychol. Assn., Ga. Speech Assn., Atlanta Ballet Guild, Southeastern Theatre Conf., Atlanta Artists Club (sec. 1981-83, dir. 1983—), Young Women of Arts, High Mus. Art, Phi Kappa Phi, Pi Kappa Delta, Sigma Delta Pi, Kappa Delta Pi, Thalian-Blackfriars. Presbyterian. Club: Lake Lanier Sailing. Home: 2521 Melinda Dr NE Atlanta GA 30345 Office: Humanities Div DeKalb Community Coll North Campus Dunwoody GA 30338

CLARK, GLORIA JOY, government official; b. Fitchburg, Mass., Jan. 9, 1942; d. George Nicholas and Helen (Sakelarios) Maravell; m. John Michael Xifaras, Dec. 30, 1962 (div. 1969); m. 2d, Edward William Clark, Dec. 23, 1970; children—Rosa and James (twins). B.S., Wheelock Coll., 1963; M.Ed., Harvard U., 1969. Tchr. pub. schs., Dartmouth, Mass., 1963-64, Freedom Schs., Holly Springs, Miss., 1964-65; adminstrv. asst. Community Action Program, New Bedford, Mass., 1965-66; instr., counselor Job Corps, New Bedford, 1966-67; instr. sociology Community Coll., Fall River, Mass., 1969-70; Headstart dir. Community Action Program, Plymouth, Mass., 1970; dir. planning and evaluation Model Cities, New Bedford, Mass., 1971-72; research asst. Nuffield Coll., Oxford U. (Eng.), 1973; tchr. adult edn. Inner London Edn. Authority, 1975; community rep. Mass. Office for Children, New Bedford, 1976-79, regional dir., Lakeville, Mass., 1979-83, exec. dir., Boston, 1983—; incorporator Greater New Bedford (Mass.) Community Health Ctr., 1979, pres., 1979-83, bd. dirs., 1983—. Field coordinator The Dukakis Com. Southeastern Mass., 1982. Recipient Achievement award Greater New Bedford Community Health Ctr., 1983. Mem. NAACP (youth advisor 1965-68). Office: Mass Office for Children 150 Causeway St Boston MA 02114

CLARK, JANE COLBY, educator; b. Smith County, Kans., July 22, 1928; d. Noel Barclay and Velma Matilda (Helfinstine) Colby; B.S., Kans. State U., 1951; postgrad. Colo. State U., 1955-56, U. Colo., summers 1957-59; m. William Kline Clark, May 27, 1951; children—Courtney, Hilary. Tchr. rural sch., Smith County, 1946-47; sec., home service worker ARC, Boulder, Colo., 1952-55; tchr. public schs., Manhattan, Kans., 1956-59; temporary instr. in English, Kans. State U., 1968-74, instr., 1974—, asst. dir. writing lab. dept. English, 1974-84, dir. writing lab. dept. English, 1985—. Mem. Nat. Council Tchrs. English, Nat. Writing Centers Assn., Midwest Writing Centers Assn., Riley County Humane Soc., Mortar Bd. Alumnae, Phi Kappa Phi. Methodist. Contbr. book revs. to newspaper, Manhattan Mercury. Home: 2105 McDowell Ave Manhattan KS 66502 Office: 102 Denison Hall Kans State U Manhattan KS 66506

CLARK, JANET MORRISSEY, political scientist, educator; b. Kansas City, Kans., June 5, 1940; d. Edward Francis and Mildred Lois (Mack) Morrissey; A.A., Kansas City Community Coll., 1960; A.B., George Washington U., 1962, M.A. (Wolcott fellow 1963-64), 1964; Ph.D. (NDEA fellow 1967-70), U. Ill., 1973; m. Caleb Morgan Clark, Sept. 28, 1968; children—Emily Claire, Grace Ellen, Evelyn Adair. Social sci. research analyst Dept. Labor, Washington, 1962-64; instr. social sci. Kansas City Community Coll., 1964-67; instr. polit. sci. Parkland Coll., Champaign, Ill., 1970-71; asst. prof. govt. N.Mex. State U., Las Cruces, 1971-75, assoc. prof., 1975-81; assoc. prof. polit. sci. U. Wyo., Laramie, 1981-84, prof., 1984—. Recipient summer seminar stipend Nat. Endowment for Humanities, 1977. Mem. Am. Polit. Sci. Assn., Western Polit. Sci. Assn. (exec. council 1984-87), Western Social Sci. Assn. (pres. 1984-85), Women's Caucus for Polit. Sci. (treas. 1982-83), Phi Beta Kappa, Phi Kappa Phi, Beta Sigma Phi. Lutheran. Book rev. editor Social Sci. Jour., 1983—. Contbr. articles in field. Home: 519 S 12th St Laramie WY 82070

CLARK, JOAN BRYSON, accountant; b. N.Y.C., Nov. 19, 1940; d. William Harold and Mary (Reilly) Ingram; m. Henry Noel Bryson, Aug. 1, 1959 (div. 1969); 1 child, Christopher Bryson; m. Michael William Clark, Mar. 5, 1971; 1 child, Lauren. B.B.A., Baruch Coll., 1969. C.P.A., N.Y. Acct. Nenring Bros., N.Y.C., 1960-69; audit mgr. Main Hurdman, C.P.A.s, N.Y.C., 1969-73, 76-82; controller Hughes Hubbard & Reed, N.Y.C., 1982—. Mem. Am. Inst. C.P.A.s, N.Y. State Soc. C.P.A.s, Am. Woman's Soc. C.P.A.s, Am. Soc. Women Accts. (pres. N.Y. chpt. 1977-78), Nat. Assn. Female Execs. Democrat. Roman Catholic. Avocations: theater; opera; computers. Home: 500 Fort Washington Ave New York NY 10033 Office: Hughes Hubbard & Reed One Wall St New York NY 10005

CLARK, JOAN M., government official; b. Ridgefield Park, N.J., Mar. 27, 1922; attended Katherine Gibbs Sch., N.Y.C. With Fgn. Service, Dept. State, 1945—, clk., then adminstrv. asst., Berlin, beginning in 1945; econ. asst., London, 1951-53; adminstrv. asst., Belgrade, 1953-57; placement officer Dept. State, beginning in 1957, adminstrv. officer, to 1962; adminstrv. officer, Luxembourg, 1962-68; coordinator adminstrv. tng. Dept. State Sch. Profl. Studies, 1968-69; personnel officer, then adminstrv. officer Bur. Inter-Am. Affairs, Dept. State, 1969-71; dep. exec. dir., then exec. dir. Bur. European Affairs, 1971-77; dir. Office Mgmt. Ops., Dept. State, 1977-79; ambassador of Malta, 1979-81; dir. gen. Fgn. Service, Dept. State, 1981-83; asst. sec. state for consular affairs, 1983—. Office: Bur Consular Affairs 2201 C St NW Dept State Washington DC 20520

CLARK, JOYCE NAOMI JOHNSON, nurse; b. Corpus Christi, Oct. 4, 1936; d. Chester Fletcher and Ermal Olita (Bailey) Johnson; m. William Boyd Clark, Jan. 4, 1960; (div. 1967); 1 child, Sherene Joyce. R.N., Trinity U., 1958; student Corpus Christi State U., 1975-77. Staff nurse Van Nuys Community Hosp., Calif., 1963-64; U.S. Naval Hosp., Corpus Christi, 1964-68; asst. clin. coordinator surgery Meml. Med. Ctr., Corpus Christi, 1968—; cert. instrument flight instr. Corpus Christi, 1984—; flight instr. Stevenson Aircraft Supply, Brownsville, Tex., 1985—. Recipient Charles A. Mella award Meml. Med. Ctr., 1981; Paul E. Garber award CAP, 1986. Mem. Am. Assn. Operating Room Nurses (v.p. 1969), Aircraft Owners and Pilots Assn., USAF Aux. CAP Air Search and Rescue (comdr. 3d group, wing chief pilot; sr. mem. of yr. 1985). Avocation: flying. Home: 1310 Aswan St Corpus Christi TX 78412

CLARK, JUDITH REDMOND, editor, author; b. Mansfield, Ohio, Feb. 21, 1939; d. William Earl and Frances Marie (Frassrand) Redmond; m. Jack Palmer Clark, June 8, 1957; children—Robert Cornell, Julie Elizabeth, April Kelly, Stephanie Rachelle. Student U. Houston, 1964-68. Assoc. editor Universal News, Houston, 1977—; assoc. editor/writer Pipeline Digest, 1977—; freelance writer, photo journalist Mem. Women in Communications (v.p. Houston chpt. 1985-86), Soc. Profl. Journalists, 1960 Photog. Soc. Home: 11842 Hickory Hill Ln Cypress TX 77429 Office: Universal News 1840 Ridgecrest Houston TX 77055

CLARK, KAREN ELIZABETH, educator; b. Ft. Bragg, N.C., July 30, 1949; d. William Frederickson and Vada Madge (Gray) Gunkel; m. Michael Allen Clark, Aug. 20, 1970; 1 child, Elizabeth Jane. B.A. in Edn., Ariz. State U., 1980. Substitute tchr. Anchorage Sch. Dist., 1984—; staffing asst. Bur. Land Mgmt., Anchorage, 1980-82, land law examiner, 1982-83. Recipient award for outstanding performance, Bur. Land Mgmt., 1983. Mem. Internat. Platform Assn., Phi Alpha Theta. Democrat. Methodist. Avocations: reading. Home: 1324 Nelchina Anchorage AK 99501 Office: Anchorage Sch Dist 4600 Debarr Ave Anchorage AK 99508

CLARK, KAREN JUNE, English educator, political volunteer; b. Washington, June 23, 1938; d. Roy F. and Charlotte J. (Nicholson) Hendrickson; m. Wallace G. Clark, Jr., Oct. 16, 1959 (div. 1978); children—Dawn Elizabeth, Stephanie Ann. B.S. in Edn., Keene State Coll., 1961; M.A. in English, U. Wyo., 1970. Tchr. English Farmington Pub. Schs., N.M., 1961-63, U. Wyo., Laramie, 1963-64, Laramie Pub. Schs., 1964-65; instr. English St. Louis Community Coll., 1965-66, McClure Sr. High Sch., St. Louis, 1967-68, U. Kans., Lawrence, 1968-70, Lawrence High Sch., Kans., 1970—; speaker U. Kans., 1983; negotiator Lawrence Edn. Assn., 1980, 82, 83. Author: Comparative Mythology for High School Students, 1970; Teacher's Guide to Comparative Mythology, 1970. Editor: Readings in Philosophy for High School Seniors, 1983. Precinct committeewoman Douglas County Democratic Central Com., Lawrence, 1969; vice chmn. Douglas County Dem. Central Com., Lawrence, 1978; del. Kans. State Dem. Com., Topeka, 1978, 3d Dist. Dem. Com., Kansas City, 1978, 81, 2d Dist. Dem. Com., Topeka, 1982, Mid-Term Dem. Nat. Conf., Kansas City, 1974; chmn. John Simpson Campaign for U.S. Senate, Lawrence, Kans., 1980; chmn. 2d Dist. Resolutions Com., Topeka, 1983; co-ordinator Vols., Douglas County Dem. Central Com., Lawrence, 1978, 80, 82, 84; adviser, mgr. City Commn. on Election Campaigns and Sch. Bd. Election Campaigns, Lawrence, 1982, 85; co-ordinator Lawrence Edn. Assn., Sch. Referendum Campaign, 1978. Recipient cert. of Merit for outstanding devel. Extramural Ind. Study Ctr., U. Kans., Lawrence, 1970. Mem. Nat. Council Tchrs. English, NEA, Kans. Nat. Edn. Assn., Lawrence Edn. Assn., Phi Delta Kappa. Lutheran. Home: 1900 Camelback Dr Lawrence KS 66044

CLARK, LINDA CAULEY, lawyer; b. Opp, Ala., Oct. 8, 1926; d. Albert E. and Betty Lena (Woodham) Cauley; m. Clinton W. Clark, Apr. 18, 1945; 1 son, Jerome Clinton. B.S., Memphis State U., 1952, M.A., 1954; B.S., Glendale (Calif.) U., 1973, J.D., 1975. Bar: Calif. 1976. Sole practice, So. Calif., 1976-80, Tehachapi, Calif., 1980—. Mem. ABA, Calif. Bar Assn., Kern County Bar Assn., Kern County Women's Bar Assn., AAUW, Alumni Assn. Glendale Coll. Law (pres. 1977-80), Greater Tehachapi C. of C., Nat. Fedn. Bus. and Profl. Women's Clubs. Republican. Club: Los Angeles Athletic. Home: Bear Valley Springs CA 93561 Office: 102 S Robinson St Tehachapi CA 93561

CLARK, MARGARET, clergywoman; b. Miami, Fla., Feb. 15, 1949; d. George Earle and Margaret (Richards) Owen; m. Gerald Daniel Clark, Sept. 1, 1973. B.A. with honors, Ind. U., 1970; M.A., Columbia U., 1973, Union Theol. Sem., 1973; D. Min., N.Y. Theol. Sem., 1982. Ordained to ministry Christian Ch. Asst. minister Park Ave. Christian Ch., N.Y.C., 1971-74; asst. to pres. Nikko Ceramics, N.Y.C., 1974-77; assoc. minister Union Meml. Ch., Stamford, Conn., 1977-80; assoc. regional minister Northeast region Christian Ch., N.Y.C., 1980—; chmn. Ecumenical Ministries Higher Edn., N.Y.C., 1982-83, Com. Denominational Execs., N.Y.C., 1981-82. Author: Voices, 1982; contbr. to book: Go Quickly and Tell, 1966. Recipient Community Leadership Devel. award Stamford Council Chs., 1978. Mem. Council of Chs. City of N.Y. (bd. dirs.), Religion in Am. Life (bd. dirs.), Tri-State Media Ministry (pres., bd. dirs.), Council on Christian Unity (bd. dirs.). Home: 527 E 84th St New York NY 10028 Office: Christian Ch NE Region 132 W 31st St Suite 1541 New York NY 10001

CLARK, MARY ANNETTE, educator, guidance counselor; b. Ft. Worth, Mar. 31, 1914; d. Fred Eugene and Cora (Moody) Johnson; m. Eugene Clark, May 4, 1933 (dec. Mar. 1981); children—Mary Jean, Rosalind Kay. B.S., Prairie View A&M U., 1954; M.Ed., 1969; postgrad. U. Wis., 1972-73, Mich. State U., 1975. Beauty operator Coleman Beauty Sch., Dallas, 1933-36, cosmetology instr., 1936-42; owner Clark's Beauty Shop, Dallas, 1942-52; beauty tchr. Dallas Ind. Sch. Dist., 1952-69; guidance counselor Bishop Coll., Dallas, 1969-70; adminstr. Prairie View A&M U. (Tex.), 1970-80, asst. prof. edn., 1970-80, dean Cosmotology Inst., summers 1954-69; organizer, head cosmetology dept. Dallas Ind. Sch. Dis., 1952-69, organizer, sponsor Charm Club, 1952; head vocat. dept. Booker T. Washington High Sch., Dallas, 1960. Mgr., Miss Prairie View, Ft. Worth; mem. bd. Met. YWCA, Dallas, 1981—; mem. Motion Picture Classification Bd., Dallas, 1981-83; div. leader Maria Morgan br. YWCA, Dallas, 1981-84; mem. St. Phillips Community Adv. Council, Dallas, 1981-84; mem. Tex. Commn. on Status of Women, Austin, 1967, nat. del., Washington, 1968; mem. Goals for Dallas; bd. mem. St. Phillips Community Ctr., Dallas, 1961-62; mem. bishop's exec. council Diocese of Dallas. Named Woman of Yr., Nat. Beauty Culturalist League, Washington, 1970; recipient service awards, appreciation certs., citations, trophies. Mem. Nat. Beauty Culturalist League (v.p. 1951-63), Nat. Ret. Tchrs. Assn., Tex. Personnel and Guidance Assn., Tex. Beauty Culturalist League (state pres. 1947-69, pres. emeritus 1969—), Dallas Beautician Assn. (pres. 1942-45), Delta Sigma Theta, Phi Delta Kappa, Epsilon Pi Tau. Episcopalian. Home: 2923 Crest Ave Dallas TX 75216

CLARK, MARY HIGGINS, novelist. Chmn. bd. David J. Clark Enterprises, 1980—. Author: Aspire to the Heavens, 1969; Where Are the Children, 1975; A Stranger is Watching, 1978; The Cradle Will Fall, 1980; A Cry In the Night, 1982; Stillwatch, 1984; contbg. author anthology Best Post Stories, 1962. Address: 2508 Cleveland Ave Washington Township NJ 07675

CLARK, MARY SEAL, army officer; b. Montpelier, Miss.; d. Arthur Lee and Irene (Maze) Brownlee; m. David Lee, Apr. 23, 1973 (div. Mar. 1978); 1 child, Nykai Maria. B.S. in Health and Safety, U. Ill., 1976; postgrad. in edn. C.W. Post campus L. I.U., 1985—. Commd. 2d lt. U.S. Army, 1981, advanced through grades to capt.; mem. equal opportunity staff Mil. Police/Chem. Tng.Ctr., Ft. McClellan, Ala., 1981-83, co. comdr., 1983-84, sec. gen. staff, 1984; asst. dir. cadet activities U.S. Mil. Acad., West Point, N.Y., 1984—, tactical officer, 1986; cons. leadership and mgmt. devel. trainer Mil. Police and Chem. Sch. Tng. Ctr., Ft. McClellan, 1982-83. Recipient Meritorious Service medal Pres. of U.S., 1984. Avocations: jogging; weight training (nautilus). Home: PO Box 117 West Point NY 10996 Office: Directorate of Cadet Activities Attn Captain Clark Eisenhower Hall Bldg 655 West Point NY 10996

CLARK, MAXINE, retail exec.; b. Miami, Fla., Mar. 6, 1949; d. Kenneth and Anne (Lerch) Kasselman; B.A. in Journalism, U. Ga., 1971. Exec. trainee Hecht Co., Washington, 1971, hosiery buyer, 1971-72, misses sportswear buyer, 1972-76; mgr. mdse. planning and research May Dept. Stores Co., St. Louis, 1976-78, dir. mdse. devel., 1978-80, v.p. mktg. and sales promotion Venture Stores div., 1980-81, sr. v.p. mktg. and sales promotion, 1981—. Sec., Lafayette Sq. Restoration Com., 1978-79. Mem. Nat. Assn. Female Execs., St. Louis Women's Commerce Assn., St. Louis Forum, Advt. Club St. Louis, Advt. Fedn. St. Louis. Office: Venture Stores 615 Northwest Plaza Saint Ann MO 63074

CLARK, MOLLY ANN, high school administrator, educator; b. Ames, Iowa, June 7, 1952; d. Frank H. and Becky A. Flores; m. Gordon Fred Clark, Sept. 16, 1973; children—Cari Ann, Gordon Thomas. B.S., Iowa State U., 1973, M.S., 1982. Tchr., Lohrville Schs., Iowa, 1974-82; prin. Corwith-Wesley High Sch., Iowa, 1982—. Mem. Ednl. Adminstrs. Iowa, Nat. Assn. Secondary Schs. Prins., Iowa Women in Ednl. Leadership. Avocations: golf; reading; cards. Office: Corwith Wesley Community Sch Box 127 Corwith IA 50430

CLARK, NANCY RANDALL, state legislator; b. Portland, Maine, May 6, 1938; d. Willis Shaw and Marthajane (Lund) Randall; B.S., Husson Coll., 1962; M.Ed., U. Maine, 1968. Tchr. bus. edn. Scarborough High Sch., 1962-67, Freeport High Sch. Maine, 1968—; mem. Maine Ho. of Reps., 1972-78; mem. Maine Senate, 1978—. Mem. exec. com. Muscular Dystrophy Assn. Maine; bd. dirs. Arthritis Found., Maine chpt.; trustee Husson Coll., Freeport Conservation Trust; asst. majority leader New Eng. Bd. Higher Edn. Recipient Vets. Service award Am. Legion Maine, 1978; named Outstanding Legislator, 1977, Woman of Yr., Bus. and Profl. Women's Club, 1982. Mem. NEA, Nat. Order Women Legislators, LWV, AAUW, Maine Tchrs. Assn. (pres. 1974-75), Bus. Edn. Assn. Maine, New Eng. Bus. Educators Assn., Brunswick Bus. and Profl. Women's Club, Freeport Hist. Soc. Democrat. Congregationalist. Lodge: Order Eastern Star. Office: Maine Senate State Capitol Augusta ME 04333

CLARK, NANCY VECERA, public relations executive; b. Sealy, Tex., Aug. 18, 1953; d. Edwin Paul and Evelyn Francis (Rainosek) Vecera; m. Thomas Allan Clark, Nov. 11, 1981. B.S., U. Houston, 1974. Computer operator U. Houston, 1973-74; aptitude test adminstr. Ball Found., Houston, 1975-76; mgr., owner of office group Tex. Office Mgmt., Houston, 1977-79; devel. coordinator Hermann Hosp. Estate, Houston, 1979-86; v.p. Stricklin & Co., Houston, 1986—; cons. Devel. Support Groups, Houston, 1980—. Recipient Employee Honors award Hermann Hosp., 1981. Mem. Nat. Assn. Hosp. Devel., Nat. Soc. Fund Raising Execs. Club: Forum.

CLARK, PATRICIA ANN, law firm administrator, lawyers services firm executive; b. St. Louis, Mar. 10, 1943; d. Ernest Alonzo and Marguerite Bertha (Malone) Viveros; m. Russell G. Dorris, July 21, 1962 (div. 1977); children—Kathleen M. Dorris, Kristine S. Dorris, Keith M. Dorris; m. Richard Joseph Clark, May 28, 1982. Legal asst. cert. with honors, St. Louis Community Coll., 1984. Sec. Union Electric Co., St. Louis, 1961-65, legal asst./sec., 1977-82, also speaker Speakers Forum, 1980-82; jud. asst./sec. Mo. Ct. Appeals, St. Louis, 1982-84; legal adminstr., legal asst. Gray & Ritter, St. Louis, 1984—; pres., cons. Lawyers Service Ctr., St. Louis, 1984—. Mem. Assn. Legal Adminstrs., Nat. Assn. Women Bus. Owners, Nat. Assn. Female Execs., St. Louis Assn. Legal Assts., St. Louis Assn. Jud. Secs. (pres. 1983), Mo. Women in Energy (pres. 1980-82), Nat. Assn. Legal Secs., St. Louis Assn. Legal Secs. (speaker 1982-85), Women's Commerce Assn. Clubs: Francis Park Tennis (pres. 1985-87), South Hampshire Racquet Club (St. Louis). Avocations: sailing; tennis; scuba diving; skiing. Home: 15824 Newton Ridge Dr Chesterfield MO 63017 Office: Gray & Ritter 1015 Locust Suite 900 Saint Louis MO 63101

CLARK, RITA MARIE, nurse; b. Grand Island, Neb., Dec. 27, 1934; d. James M. and Edna M. (Sorensen) Dean Hill; m. Marlin D. Clark, 1951 (div. 1963); children—Lisa Anne Schultz, David M. Clark. B.S.N., U. Oreg., 1963; M.S. in Health Services, Columbia Pacific U., 1986. R.N., Calif., Oreg. Pub. health worker Multnomah County Pub. Health Dept., Portland, Oreg., 1968-71; psychiat. nurse VA Hosp., Portland, Oreg., 1971-73; supr. nursing Valley Migrant Clinic, Woodburn, Oreg., 1972-74; dir. nursing Silverton Hosp., Oreg., 1974-76; cardiology nurse USPHS Hosp., San Francisco, 1976-77; supr. pub. health Berkeley Health Dept., Calif., 1977-79; supr. pub. health nursing, Santa Cruz, Calif., 1979-80; nurse USPHS-Indian Hosp., Red Lake, Minn., 1980-81; nurse U.S. Army, 1981-84. Contbr. articles to profl. jours. Served as lt. comdr. USPHS, 1980-81; to maj. U.S. Army, 1981-84; mem. Res. Decorated U.S. Army Meritorious Service medal. Army, 1984. Mem. Assn. Mil. Surgeons U.S., Am. Assn. Female Execs., U.S. Res. Officers Assn. Democrat. Roman Catholic. Clubs: Officers (Presidio of San Francisco); Officers (Fort Sam Houston, Tex.). Avocations: fishing; camping; travel; grandchildren. Home: 1844 SW Custer St Portland OR 97219

CLARK, ROSANNE FAYE, magazine editor, journalist; b. Ashland, Ky., July 25, 1955; d. Ernest and Lucy Blema (Moss) C. B.A. in Journalism, U. Houston, 1977. Editorial asst. Tex. Assn. Bus., Houston, 1977-78, publs. mgr. Tex. Instruments, Houston, 1978-79; info. specialist U. Houston Office of Media Relations, 1979-80, asst. dir., 1980-81; asst. editor Houston mag., 1981-82, assoc. editor, 1982—; stringer Bus. Week, 1984. Co-editor: Rich Kids and Poor Kids: A More Personal Sociological Inquiry, 1982. Recipient George Kirksey Scholarship award, 1973; 1st place award Personality Profile, Women in Communications, 1983, 1st place award for feature series, 1983; 1st place award mag. feature Houston Press Club, 1984; Excellence in Media award Tex. Mental Health Assn., 1985, Mental Health Assn. Houston and Harris County 1985. Mem. Internat. Assn. Bus. Communications (award of merit 1983, awards of excellence 1984), Phi Kappa Phi. Democrat. Jewish. Office: Houston Mag 1100 Milam Bldg 25th Floor Houston TX 77002

CLARK, RUTH, personnel consultant; b. N.Y.C., Oct. 16, 1942; d. William B. and Pauline Cheek. Grad. George Washington High Sch. Mgr. data processing dept. Am. Express Co.; div. pres. Hour Power Temporary Agy., N.Y.C., 1972-74; founder, pres. Clark Unlimited Personnel, Inc., N.Y.C., 1974—, Clark Unlimited Placement, Inc., 1977—, CUP Stars, Inc., talent agy., 1977, downtown br. CUP, 1979—. Bd. dirs. Nat. March of Dimes, 1980—, Edwin Gould Services for Children, 1982—; mem. Democratic Nat. Com.; adv. bd. Nat. Minority Bus. Council; mem. entrepreneurship panel Harvard U. Recipient Role Model award New Future Found., 1979, Bus. Achievement award Black Action Retail Group, 1979; named Bus. Woman of Yr., also recipient Laurelton award Nat. Assn. Negro Bus. and Profl. Women's Clubs, 1978; recipient award Hunter Coll., 1979, Pacesetter award New Dawn Leadership for Women Assn., 1980, Cecelia C. Saunders award for outstanding entrepreneurship Harlem YWCA, 1982; Spl. Recognition award N.Y.C. Commn. on Status of Women, featured in commn. publ.: Conversations with Fifteen New Yorkers; Kizzy award, 1985; Econ. Devel. award Alpha Kappa Alpha. Mem. Nat. Assn. Temporary Services, Nat. Assn. Negro Bus. and Profl. Women's Club (Inaugural Crystal award 1984), Nat. Assn. Female Execs., Women's Forum, Women Bus. Owners of N.Y., Edges Group, Nat. Council Negro Women, NAACP (Roy Wilkins award 1986), Nat. Urban League (Seagram's Vanguard Achievement award 1986), N.Y. C. of C., N.Y.C. Commn. on Status of Women, Assn. Personnel Cons. of N.Y. State, Fin. Support Network (pres.), Nat. Assn. Black Women Entrepreneurs (award 1983), N.Y. Assn. Temporary Services (dir.), Women's Forum. Office: 2 W 45th St New York NY 10036

CLARK, SARA J., business executive; b. South Bend, Ind., Aug. 28, 1948; d. Robert F. and Maxine (Walker) Bennett; m. William H. Clark, Oct. 2, 1976; 1 child, Kristen Marie. Adminstrv. asst. Doherty Zable & Co., Chgo., 1975-77; gen. ptnr. Bennett Clark Co., Valparaiso, Ind., 1977—; mem. LaSalle St. Cashiers, Chgo., 1979-85, outing com. chmn., 1982. Mem. Am. Soc. Profl. Women. Republican. Presbyterian. Avocations: reading; travel; needlework.

CLARK, SHARON ANN, university public affairs administrator; b. Toledo, Jan. 14, 1939; d. Stanley Joseph and Anna Dorothy (Zulka) Gosik; B.A., U. Miami, 1974; m. John H. Clark, Aug. 23, 1961 (div. 1968); 1 dau., Tania Elizabeth. Staff writer U. Miami (Fla.), 1970-79; dir. News Bur., U. Miami, 1979-82, assoc. dir. pub. affairs, 1982-83; mus. adminstr., 1983—. Trustee, Dade Heritage Trust, 1979—; mem. Women's Com. of 100. Mem. Women in Communication, Public Relations Soc. Am., Beaux Arts. Roman Catholic. Club: Zonta. Home: 4712 SW 67th Ave Miami FL 33155 Office: 1301 Stanford Dr Coral Gables FL 33146

CLARK, SHERYL MARIE, nurse practitioner; b. Dallas, Nov. 12, 1944; d. William Stanford and Thelma Marie (Johnson) C.; B.S. in Nursing, U. Colo., 1967. Office nurse, supr. Dr. S.E. Wood, Charleston, S.C., 1970-72; staff nurse VA Hosp., Charleston, S.C., VA Hosp., Long Beach, Calif., 1972-73; family nurse practitioner Family Health Program, Long Beach, Calif., 1973-78; research nurse practitioner U. Calif., Irvine, 1978-79; mgr. health services

Martin-Marietta Aluminum Corp., Torrance, Calif., 1979-81; mgr. health services TRW, Redondo Beach, Calif., 1981—. Served with USNR, 1967-70. Mem. Calif. Nurses Assn. (pres. Region 1, Past chairperson interregional standing com. nurse practitioners), Am. Nurses Assn. (cert. family nurse practitioner), Am. Public Health Assn., Nat. Assn. Female Execs., Am. Assn. Occupational Health Nurses, Harbor Area Assn. Occupational Health Nurses (pres.). Republican. Home: 2313 Hungtington Ln Unit B Redondo Beach CA 90278 Office: One Space Park S/1459 Redondo Beach CA 90278

CLARK, SUSAN, actress; b. Sarnia, Ont., Can., Mar. 8, 1944; m. Alex Karras (2nd); 1 child, Katie. Studied at Royal Acad. of Dramatic Arts, Eng. Prof. theatre debut in "Silk Stockings", Michigan Summer Theatre; repertory work in England; motion picture debut in "Banning", 1967; other films include: Madigan, 1968, Coogan's Bluff, 1968, Tell Them Willie Boy is Here, 1970, Night Moves, 1975, Valdez is Coming, 1971, Airport 1975, 1974, Porky's, 1982, Nobody's Perfekt, 1981; appearing in TV series "Webster", 1983—, movies made for TV: Babe, 1975 (Emmy award), Amelia Earhart, 1976, Jimmie B and Andre, 1980, The Choice, 1981, The Astronaut, 1972. Address: care Kenneth Gross 8428 Melrose Place Suite C Los Angeles CA 90069*

CLARK, SYLVIA DOLORES, business educator; b. N.Y.C., June 5, 1959; d. Barna and Eva Anna (Beniczky-Gabriel) Csuros; m. Allen Lewis Spiegel, Aug. 19, 1984. B.B.A., Bernard Baruch Coll., CUNY, 1979; M.B.A., NYU, 1982. Research analyst Kornhauser and Colene and predecessor firm, N.Y.C., 1979-80; project coordinator Gen. Foods, Inc., White Plains, N.Y., 1980-82; research assoc. Lord, Geller, Federico, Einstein, Inc., N.Y.C., 1982-83; instr. Coll. of S.I., CUNY, 1984—. Recipient Becker Family Fund Scholarship award, 1978, Baruch Coll. Alumni Assn. Scholarship award, 1979. Mem. Am. Mktg. Assn., Am. Statis. Assn., Beta Gamma Sigma (past mem. exec. bd.). Home: 62 Renwick Ave Staten Island NY 10301 Office: Coll Staten Island 715 Ocean Terr Staten Island NY 10301

CLARK-BROOKS, BRONNIE DENISE, auditor, consultant; b. Washington, Dec. 13, 1954; d. Nathaniel Depriest Clark and Kay Frances (Grandy) Clark Joyner; m. John Francis Brooks, May 24, 1975; 1 child, Tynisha Asheba. A.A., Strayer Coll., Washington, 1980, B.S., 1982; with Riggs Nat. Bank, Washington, 1974-83; sr. EDP audit supr. First Am. Bank, Washington, 1983-85; systems acct. Fed. Home Loan Bank Bd./Fed. Savs. & Loan Ins. Corp./Fin. Assistance Div., Washington, 1985-86; EDP auditor Amtrak, Washington, 1986—. Mem. Apple Grove PTA and Citizens Assn., Fort Washington, Md., 1983. Mem. Strayer Coll. Alumni Assn., Washington Assn. Urban Bankers. Baptist. Avocations: modeling; designing; reading; dancing. Office: Amtrak-Nat RR Passenger Corp 400 N Capitol St NW Washington DC 20001

CLARKE, AMY POLAN, entertainment company executive; b. Bklyn., Nov. 16, 1950; d. Stanley Norton and Ella (Germain) Polan; m. Robert G. Clarke, Jr., Jan. 4, 1984. Student Monmouth Coll., 1968-69. Sec., reservationist Thomas Cook Travel Agy., Short Hills, N.J., 1970-72; sec. Monarch Entertainment Bur., Inc., Montclair, N.J., 1970-71, adminstrv. asst., 1971-75, v.p., 1975—, exec. v.p., gen. mgr., 1975—. Democrat. Jewish. Avocations: antique furniture; home designing; tennis. Office: Monarch Entertainment Bur Inc 7 N Mountain Ave Montclair NJ 07042

CLARKE, ANNE GREER, educator; b. Asheville, N.C., May 6, 1920; d. Allen M. and Betty H. Greer; m. Morris Clarke, Jan. 4, 1942; children—Morris Otis, George Allen, Betty Anne Clark Tinsley. B.S., NYU, 1961; grad. Columbus Coll., 1977. Tchr. Talbatton High Sch., Ga., 1941-43, Eddy High Sch., Milledgeville, Ga., 1943-45, Carver High Sch., Milledgeville, 1945-46, Risley High Sch., Brunswick, Ga., 1946-47, Carver High Sch., Douglas, Ga., 1947-50, Fifth Ave. Pub. Schs., Columbus, 1950-52, David Elem. Sch., Columbus, 1952-68, Winterfield Elem. Sch., Columbus, 1968-79. Bd. dirs. Girls Club, Columbus, Ga., Inc.; mem. Democratic Com. Recipient various certs. and plaques in field, Outstanding Tchr. award Winterfield Sch., 1979; named one of 100 Most Outstanding Tchrs. in Columbus Sch. Dist., 1979. Mem. NEA, Ga. Assn. Educators, Muscogee Edn. Assn., AAUW, Nat. Council Negro Women, Beth Salem United Presbyn. Women (pres.), Delta Sigma Theta. Presbyterian. Club: Phi Beta Sigma Shadows, Matrons. Home: 1483 Brazil Ave Columbus GA 31903

CLARKE, CAROLE SUE, psychologist; b. Washington, Dec. 25, 1946; d. Denzil Cope and Frances Louise (Hall) Bywaters; A.A.S., No. Va. Community Coll., 1972; B.A., Calif. State U., Los Angeles, 1974, M.A., 1976; Ph.D., U. So. Calif., 1978; m. Thomas D. Clarke, Dec. 18, 1971. Various secretarial and adminstrv. positions, Washington, 1964-71; counselor Am. Inst. Family Relations, Los Angeles, 1978-79; psychotherapist and seminar leader Transactional Analysis Inst. San Fernando Valley, 1978—; pres., chief exec. officer Assn. Women in Psychology, Counseling and Edn., Glendale, Calif., 1980-83, Assn. Women Psychotherapists and Counselors, 1983—; instr. U. La Verne. Mem. Glendale C. of C., Am. Psychol. Assn., Calif. Psychol. Assn., Nat. Bus. and Profl. Women's Assn., ASTD, Am. Personnel and Guidance Assn. Office: 611A E Glenoaks Blvd Glendale CA 91207

CLARKE, CHERYL PILGRIM, lawyer; b. Boston, July 31, 1948; d. Darnell Wilfred and Elizabeth (Pilgrim) Clarke. B.A., Simmons Coll., 1972; J.D., Suffolk U., 1975. Atty., hearing officer Cambridge Rent Control Bd., Mass., 1977-79; labor atty. NLRB, Boston, 1979-82; labor counsel Boston Sch. Commn., 1982—; trustee Cambridgeport Savs., Cambridge, 1983—; legal adv. to hon. consul Barbados, Boston, 1982—; bd. dirs. Legal Parent Protective Services, Inc., Cambridge, 1979—. Corp. mem. Cambridge Family YMCA, 1984—; trustee St. Paul African Meth. Episcopal Ch., Cambridge, 1982—. Mem. ABA, Mass. Bar Assn., Mass. Black Women Attys., Jr. League (provisional 1985—), Delta Sigma Theta (parliamentarian Boston alumni chpt. 1981-83). Democrat. Avocations: interior designing, needlepoint, real estate investing and management. Office: Boston Sch Com 26 Court St Boston MA 02108

CLARKE, GRETA FIELDS, dermatologist; b. Detroit; d. George William and Willa (Wright) Fields; B.S., U. Mich., 1962; M.D., Howard U., 1967; m. Robert Mines, May 6, 1979; 1 son, Richard Clement Clarke. Resident in dermatology NYU, 1969-72, clin. instr., 1972-77; practice medicine specializing in dermatology, N.Y.C., 1972-77; dermatologist Arlington Med. Group, Oakland, Calif., 1977-79; practice medicine specializing in dermatology, Berkeley, Calif., 1979—. Bd. dirs. Bay Area Black United Fund. Diplomate Am. Bd. Dermatology. Mem. Nat. Med. Assn. (chmn. council on concerns of women physicians), Golden State Med. Assn., Am. Acad. Dermatology, San Francisco Dermatol. Clubs: Jack and Jill Am. (chpt. pres. 1984-85), Alameda-Contra Costa Links. Office: 2500 Milvia St Berkeley CA 94704

CLARKE, HERMA BEATRICE MONTROSE, nutritionist, educator, health care consultant; b. East Coast, Demerara, Guyana, Jan. 14, 1943; came to U.S., 1964, naturalized, 1979; d. Milford Israel and Dulcie (Evadne) Montrose; m. Allan Daulman Clarke, June 29, 1961; children—Denise, Nigel, Simone. B.S., Morgan State Coll., 1968; M.S., Case Western Res. U., 1971; M.P.A., Rutgers U., 1982. Registered dietitian. Supr., then dietician Johns Hopkins Hosp., Balt., 1965-67; mgr. Govt. Services Inc., Washington, 1969; dietetic intern U. Hosps., Cleve., 1970; pub. health intern State Dept. Health, Columbus, Ohio, 1971; asst. mistress Dept. Edn., Guyana, 1960-64; dir. nutrition services Specialized Mgmt. Services, Orange, N.J., 1971-73; nutritionist U. Medicine and Dentistry, Newark, 1973—, mem. admissions com. Sch. Health Related Professions, 1986; nutritionist I, N.J. Med. Sch., Newark, 1975—, instr., 1974, asst. clin. prof., 1980-85, assoc. prof., 1985—; sole dir. Mid-Essex Nutrition Services, East Orange, N.J.; provider Crossroad Health Plan/Essex County Health Orgn., Inc., N.J., 1984—; advisor to dietetic interns Sch. Health Related Professions, U. Medicine and Dentistry, N.J. Med. Sch., 1984; health care cons. nursing homes and extended care facilities, Essex County, N.J., 1984—. Mem. acad. com. Rutgers U., Cook Coll., N.J., 1985. Fellow Internat. Inst. Edn., UN, N.Y., 1966, USPHS, Washington, 1972. Mem. Am. Dietetic Assn., Am. Soc. Pub. Adminstrn., Am. Coll. Nutrition, Am. Diabetes Assn., Am. Pub. Health Assn., Am. Soc. Hosp. Food Service Adminstrs., Am. Assn. Diabetic Educators, Soc. Nutrition Edn., Bus. and Profl. Women's Club. Roman Catholic. Clubs: Internat. Toastmasters (Essex County, N.J.). Avocations: music; reading; tennis; travel. Home: 31 Chelsea Pl East Orange NJ 07017 Office: Mid Essex Profl Bldg Suite 709 144 S Harrison St East Orange NJ 07018

CLARKE, INGRID GADWAY, academic ombudsman, consultant; b. Bad Homburg, Hesse, Fed. Republic Germany, Sept. 21, 1942; came to U.S., 1964, naturalized, 1982; d. Johann Kajetan and Irmgard (Schneider) Rebholz; m. David Scott Clarke, Dec. 24, 1984. B.A. equivalent, Johann Wolfgang Goethe Universität, Frankfurt, Fed. Republic Germany, 1964; M.A., Memphis State U., 1965; postgrad. Tulane U., 1965-69; Ph.D., So. Ill. U., 1984. Instr. So. Ill. U., Carbondale, 1969-74, univ. ombudsman, 1974—, also chairperson bd. dirs. students' legal assistance program, 1980—. Mem. Carbondale Human Relations Com., 1974-76; chairperson Carbondale Fair Housing Bd., 1978-82. Fulbright scholar, 1964-67. Mem. Fulbright Alumni Assn., Univ. and Coll. Ombudsman Assn. (pres. 1985-86), Soc. Profls. in Dispute Resolution, European Studies Council at Columbia U., Delta Phi Alpha. Avocations: opera; tennis; skiing. Office: So Ill U Office Univ Ombudsman Carbondale IL 62901

CLARKE, KIT HANSEN, radiologist; b. Louisville, May 24, 1944; d. Hans Peter and Katie (Jones) Hansen; A.B., Randolph-Macon Woman's Coll., 1966; M.D., U. Louisville, 1969; m. Dr. John M. Clarke, Feb. 14, 1976; children—Brett Bonnett, Blair Hansen, Brandon Chamberlain; stepchildren—Gray Campbell, Jeffrey William John M. Intern, Louisville Gen. Hosp., 1969-70; resident in internal medicine and radiology U. Tenn., Knoxville, 1970-73; resident in radiology U.S. Fla., Tampa, 1973-74; staff radiologist, chief spl. procedures Palms of Pasadena, Lake Seminole hosps., St. Petersburg, Fla., 1974—. Active Fla. Competitive Swim Assn. of AAU. Diplomate Am. Bd. Radiology. Fellow Am. Coll. Radiology; mem. Fla. West Coast Radiology Soc., Radiol. Soc. N.Am., AMA, Fla. Med. Assn., Pinellas County Med. Soc., Fla. Radiology Soc. Episcopalian. Home: 7171 9th St S Saint Petersburg FL 33705 Office: 1609 Pasadena Ave S Saint Petersburg FL 33707

CLARKE, LESLIE ANN, nurse; b. N.Y.C., Feb. 28, 1949; d. Robert Edward and Cecile Nevils (Payne) C.; m. Michael Alvin Maloy, Apr. 13, 1971 (div. Jan. 1981); children—Michael Akinwole, Nicole Chinyere. B.S.N., Boston U., 1970; M.S.N., U. Colo., 1980. Staff nurse Harlem Hosp., N.Y.C., 1970-71, Children's Hosp. of the King's Daus., Norfolk, Va., 1971-72, Children's Med. Ctr., Dallas, 1972-74; head nurse Med. City Dallas, 1974-76; community health nurse City of Dallas Health Dept., 1976-78; asst. dir. nursing Johns Hopkins Children's Ctr., Balt., 1980-85; v.p. nursing Rainbow Babies and Children's Hosp., Cleve., 1985—. Mem. Black Women's Polit. Caucus. Mem. Nat. Black Nurses Assn., MENSA, Alpha Kappa Alpha. Avocations: Sherlock Holmes; vegetable gardening; sewing. Office: Rainbow Babies and Children's Hosp 2101 Adelbert Rd Cleveland OH 44106

CLARKE, MARY ELIZABETH, retired army officer; b. Rochester, N.Y., Dec. 3, 1924; d. James M. and Lillian E. (Young) Kennedy; student U. Md., 1962; D.Mil.Sci., Norwich U., Northfield, Vt., 1978. Joined U.S. Army as pvt., 1945, advanced through grades to maj. gen., 1978; exec. asst. to Chief of Plans and Policies, Office of Econ. Opportunity, 1966-67; comdr. WAC Tng. Bn., 1967-68; office dep. chief of staff for personnel, 1968-71; WAC staff adviser 6th Army, 1971-72; comdr., comdt. U.S. Women's Army Corps Center and Sch., 1972-74; chief WAC Adv. Office, U.S. Army Mil. Personnel Center, Washington, 1974-75, dir. Women's Army Corps, Washington, 1975-78; comdr. U.S. Army Mil. Police and Chem. Sch. Tng. Center, Ft. McClellan, Ala., 1978-80; dir. human resources devel. Office of Dep. Chief of Staff for Personnel, Washington, 1980-81, ret., 1981; hon. prof. mil. sci. Jacksonville (Ala.) State U. Mem. Def. Adv. Com. on Women in the Services, 1984—, vice chmn., 1986—. Decorated D.S.M.; recipient Toastmasters Internat. award, 1984. Mem. Assn. of U.S. Army, United States Automobile Assn. (bd. dirs. 1978—), WAC Assn., WAC Mus. Found., Bus. and Profl. Women's Club. Address: 80 Fairway Dr Jacksonville AL 36265

CLARKE, MARY WHATLEY, writer; b. Palo Pinto, Tex., June 11, 1899; d. Cephas Vachel and Narcie Isabella (Abernathy) Whatley; student N.Mex. State Normal Sch., 1925; m. James Coltman Dunbar, Oct. 27, 1920 (dec. 1923); 1 dau., Mary Murray Dunbar Harper; m. Joe A. Clarke, Nov. 15, 1941 (dec. 1971). Owner, pub. Norwood (Man.) Press, 1924-26; advt. dept. Hudson's Bay Co., Winnipeg, Can., 1926-27; advt. mgr. Mineral Wells (Tex.) Daily Index, 1928-33, Breckenridge (Tex.) Am., 1939; pub. Palo Pinto (Tex.) County Star, 1933-44; writer; books include: The Palo Pinto Story, 1957; Life in the Saddle, 1963; David G. Burnet, First President of Texas Republic, 1969; Thomas J. Rusk: Soldier, Statesman, Patriot, 1971; John Chisum Jinglebob King of the Peros, 1984; Chief Bowles and the Texas Cherokees, 1971; The Swenson Saga and SMS Ranches, 1976; A Century of Cow Business, 1976; The Slaughter Ranches and Their Makers, 1979; contbr. numerous stories and articles to the Cattleman. Woman's bd. Ft. Worth Children's Hosp., pres., 1955-56. Mem. Lecture Found., Tarrant County Hist. Soc. (past pres., award), W. Tex. Press Assn. Presbyterian. Home: 3605 Bellaire Dr S Fort Worth TX 76109

CLARKE, URANA, writer, amateur astronomer, music educator; b. Wickliffe-on-the-Lake, Ohio, Sept. 8, 1902; d. Graham Warren and Grace Urana (Olsaver) Clarke. Artists and tchrs., diploma Mannes Music Sch., N.Y.C., 1925; Dalcroze cert. Sch. Music, N.Y.C., 1950; passed navigators exam. U.S. Power Squadron, 1943; student Pembroke Coll., Brown U.; B.S., Mont. State U., 1967, M.S., 1970. Mem. faculty Mannes Music Sch., 1922-49, Dalcroze Sch. Music, 1949-54; adv. editor in music The Book of Knowledge, 1949-61; v.p., dir. Saugatuck Circle Housing Devel., 1950-58; host Skies over the Big Sky Country, daily radio astronomy show, 1964-79, weekly radio programs Birds of Big Sky Country, 1972-79, Great Music of Religion, 1974-79; instr. continuing edn. Mont. State U.; guest lectr. celestial navigation, nautical astronomy, Hayden Planetarium, 1945; guest lectr. Roger Williams Planetarium, Providence, 1959-63. Adv. com. Nat. Rivers and Harbors Congresses, 1947-58; co-chmn. Barrington Town Blood Assurance Program, 1960-64; chmn. Park County chpt. ARC, 1965—, co-chmn. blood program, 1965—, 1st aid instr., 1941—, Red Cross first aid instr. trainer, 1969—, instr. cardio-pulmonary resuscitation, 1976—; vice chmn. Park County Local Govt. Study Commn., 1974-76; rep. Westport (Conn.) Town Meeting, 1955-57; treas. Park County Wilderness Coalition, 1977—; bd. dirs. Friends Livingston Library, 1978—; chmn. Park County Refugee Com., 1979—, Park County Local Govt. Rev. Commn., 1984-86. Mem. Music Library Assn., Royal Astron. Soc. Can., Inst. Nav., Maria Mitchell Soc. Nantucket, N.A. Yacht Racing Union, R.I. Meteor Research Orgn. (dir.), Internat. Soc. Mus. Research, Big Sky Astron. Soc. (dir.), Renaissance Soc., Am., Internat. musicological socs., Sierra Club, Trout Unltd., Mont. Wilderness Soc., Nature Conservancy, Am. Guild Organists. Lutheran. Club: Cedar Point Yacht. Author: The Heavens Are Telling (astronomy), 1951; Skies Over the Big Sky Country, 1965. Weekly newspaper columnist Big Skies; contbr. to mags. on music and astronomy. Pub. music elem. two-piano pieces, Five Chorale Preludes for Organ, 1975. Inventor, builder of Clarke adjustable piano stool. Address: Log-a-Rhythm 9th St Island Livingston MT 59047

CLARKE, VIRGINIA SEMBER, construction company executive; b. Sharon, Pa., Dec. 22, 1927; d. John Sember and Mary (Mickel) Sember; m. Able Phillip Clarke, Apr. 20, 1948; children—William, Clarissa. B.A., Youngstown Coll., 1950. Registered profl. builder. Clk., First Nat. Bank, Sharon, Pa., 1945-47; librarian Youngstown Pub. Library (Ohio), 1949-53; mgr. Women's div. Manpower Inc., St. Louis, 1953-55; designer children's clothes Johnston's Inc., Wylie, Tex., 1962-63; pres. V. Clarke Constrn. Inc., Dallas, 1977—. Chmn. bd. govs. Ursuline Acad., Dallas, 1974-76; vol. Republican Party, Dallas, 1968, 72-76, 80. Mem. Nat. Assn. Home Builders, Home Owners Warranty Corp., Home and Apt. Builders Assn. Met. Dallas. Republican. Episcopalian. Clubs: Newcomers (pres. 1956), Dallas Athletic, Country Dallas (dir. 1974-76), Soroptomist (charter). Home and Office: 2 Shepherds Way Heath TX 75087

CLARKSON, ELISABETH ANN HUDNUT, civic worker; b. Youngstown, Ohio, Apr. 20, 1925; d. Herbert Beecher and Edith (Schaaf) Hudnut; A.B., Wilson Coll., 1947; M.A., State U. N.Y., 1973, also postgrad.; LH.D. (hon.), Wilson Coll., 1985; m. William M.E. Clarkson, Sept. 23, 1950; children—Alison H., David B., Andrew E. With J.L. Hudson Co., Detroit, 1947-50; writer The Minute Parade, daily Sta. WGR, Detroit, 1948-50; trustee Wilson Coll., Chambersburg, Pa., 1970-83, chmn. bd. trustees, 1979-82; bd. dirs. Buffalo Mus. Sci., 1972—, bd. dirs., companion in charge Soc. Companion of the Holy Cross, 1986—; past chmn. jr. group Alright Knox Art Gallery; collector, curator Graphic Controls Corp. collection art, 1976-83; dir. Bischoff Clarkson Hudnut Corp., North Creek, N.Y., 1973-83; mem. Buffalo Art Commn., 1983—; mem. exec. bd. arts adv. council Southern U. Coll., Buffalo, 1985—; bd. dirs. N.Y. State Mus. Assoc., Albany. Recipient Trustee award for disting. service Wilson Coll., 1983. Episcopalian. Clubs: Garret, Buffalo Tennis and Squash. Author: You Can Always Tell a Freshman, 1949; also articles, dramatic presentations, archival materials Adirondack Mus., 1950-77. Home: 156 Bryant St Buffalo NY 14222 also Windover North Creek NY 12853

CLARKSON, SHIRLEY ANNE, educational administrator; b. Sterling, Ill., Sept. 14, 1934; d. Charles S. and Juliet (Darland) Long; m. June 14, 1957 (div.); 1 child, James M. B.A., U. Chgo., 1957. Adminstr. com. for comparative study of new nations, U. Chgo., 1960-64; dir. info. office. S.E. Asia Regional Council, Ann Arbor, Mich., 1969-72; program officer Am. Council Edn., Washington, 1972-75; assoc. dir. Council Internat. Cooperation in Higher Edn., Washington, 1976-79; staff Commn. Internat. Relations, Nat. Acad. Scis., Washington, 1979-80; asst. dir. research and devel. U. Mich., Ann Arbor, 1980—. Bd. dirs. Ann Arbor Community Ctr., 1985-87. Mem. Internat. Studies Assn., Council Advancement of Edn. Office: U Mich Ann Arbor MI 48109

CLARY, ROSALIE BRANDON STANTON, timber farm exec., civic worker; b. Evanston, Ill., Aug. 3, 1928; d. Frederick Charles Hite-Smith and Rose Cecile (Liebich) Stanton; B.S., Northwestern U., 1950, M.A., 1954; m. Virgil Vincent Clary, Oct. 17, 1959; children—Rosalie Marian, Frederick Stanton, Virgil Vincent, Kathleen Elizabeth. Tchr., Chgo. Public Schs., 1951-55, adjustment tchr., 1956-61; faculty Loyola U., Chgo., 1963; v.p. Stanton Enterprises, Inc., Adams County, Miss., 1971—; author Family History Record, genealogy record book, Kenilworth, Ill., 1977—. Leader, Girl Scouts, Winnetka, Ill., 1969-71, 78-82, Cub Scouts, 1972-77; badge counselor Boy Scouts Am., 1978—; election judge Republican party, 1977—. Mem. Nat. Soc. DAR (Ill. rec. sec. 1979-81, nat. vice chmn. program com. 1980-83, dir. Ill. 4th div. 1981-83, Ill. State chmn. sch. com. 1983-85, state vice regent 1986—), Am. Forestry Assn., Forest Farmers Assn., North Suburban Geneal. Soc. (v.p. 1979-82), Winnetka Hist. Soc. (governing bd. 1978—, pres. 1982-84), Delta Gamma (nat. cabinet 1985—). Roman Catholic. Home: 509 Elder Ln Winnetka IL 60093 Office: PO Box 401 Kenilworth IL 60043

CLASTER, JILL NADELL, educator, historian; d. Harry K. and Edith Lillian Nadell; B.A., N.Y. U., 1952; M.A., 1954; Ph.D., U. Pa., 1959; m. Millard L. Midonick, May 24, 1979; 1 dau. from previous marriage—Elizabeth Claster (dec.). Instr. history U. Pa., 1956-58; instr. ancient and medieval history U. Ky., Lexington, 1959-61, asst. prof., 1961-64; adj. asst. prof. classics N.Y. U., N.Y.C., 1964-65, asst. prof. history, 1965-68, asso. prof., 1968-83, prof., 1983—, acting undergrad. chmn. history, 1972-73, dir. M.A. in liberal studies program, 1976-78, asso. dean Washington Sq. and Univ. Coll., 1978; acting dean, 1978-79, dean, 1979—. Danforth grantee, 1966-68; Fulbright grantee, 1958-59. Mem. Am. Hist. Assn., Medieval Acad. Am., Archaeol. Inst. Am. Medieval Club N.Y. Author: Athenian Democracy: Triumph or Travesty, 1967; The Medieval Experience 300-1400, 1982; contbr. articles to profl. jours. Home: 32 Washington Sq W New York NY 10011 Office: NY Univ Washington Square and University Coll 910 Main Bldg New York NY 10003

CLAUS, CAROL JEAN, computer software company executive; b. Uniondale, N.Y., Dec. 17, 1959; d. Charles Joseph and Frances Meta (Fichter) C.; m. Armand Joseph Gasperetti, Jr., July 7, 1985. Student pub. schs., Uniondale. Asst. mgr. Record World, L.I., N.Y., 1977-82, mgr. Info. Builders Inc., N.Y.C., 1982—. Mem. Nat. Assn. Female Execs. Democrat. Roman Catholic.

CLAUSEL, NAN DONEY, communications executive; b. Houston, Aug. 24, 1926; d. Louden Charles and Mary Nan (Gaynor) Doney; student Mary Baldwin Coll., 1943-44, Barnard Coll., 1945-47; B.S., U. Houston, 1948; m. Calvin L. Clausel, Jr., Oct. 19, 1951 (div. 1965); children—Caroline Clausel Peter, David Louden. Public relations dir. Houston Soc. for Prevention Cruelty to Animals, 1965-66; promotion copy chief Houston Post, 1966-67; promotion copywriter St. Petersburg (Fla.) Times & Ind., 1967-69; asst. promotion mgr., promotion coordinator San Antonio Light, 1969-83, asst. dir. promotion and pub. affairs, 1983-85; owner Clausel & Co., Creative Services, San Antonio, 1985—; free-lance music reviewer, 1973-80. Active San Antonio Symphony Mastersingers, 1981—. Mem. Women in Communications, San Antonio Advt. Fedn. (dir. 1979-81), Mensa. Republican. Episcopalian. Home and office: 272 Emporia Blvd San Antonio TX 78209

CLAUSEN, BETTY JANE HANSEN, association executive; b. Brooklyn, Wis., Oct. 25, 1925; d. Arthur John and Kathryn (Hefty) Hansen; B.A., Beloit Coll., 1947; m. Henry Albert Clausen, Jan. 31, 1948 (div. 1976); 1 son, Scott Alyn. Psychometric sec., Vocat. Counseling Bur., Rockford (Ill.) Coll., 1947-48; classified ad-taker Beloit (Wis.) Daliy News, 1948-49; copy-writer WROK, Rockford, 1955-60; tchr. elementary schs., Rockford, Elmhurst, Ill., 1960-61; exec. mgr. Melrose Park (Ill.) C. of C., 1961-67; mng. dir. S.W. Sr. Center, Parma Heights, Ohio, 1967-77; exec. dir. Sr. Citizens, Inc., Hamilton, Ohio, 1977—. Founder, pres. Easter Seal Parents Group Rockford, 1957-60, project chmn. Villa Park, Ill., 1963-65; treas. Easter Seal Aux., 1965-66; treas. United Cerebral Palsy, Rockford, 1959-60, bd. dirs. Ill. Soc., 1959-60; co-chmn. 53-Minute March, Elmhurst, 1963; pres. Freeman Sch. PTA., Rockford, 1959-60; chmn. exceptional child PTA, Elmhurst, 1962-66; hon. life mem. Ill. PTA.; mem. S.W. Community Resource Council, 1968-77, Butler County Council on Aging, 1977-83; bd. dirs. Council Exceptional Children, New Neighbors League, S.W. Ceveland chpt., 1967; mem. council on aging Cin. Area Adv. Council, 1979-83. Named Citizen of Week, Elmhurst Press, 1966. Mem. Ill. C. of C., Ill. Assn. C. of C. Execs., West Suburban Council Chambers, Ohio Assn. Centers for Sr. Citizens, Delta Delta Delta. Club: Altrusa. Methodist. Home: 1224 Beissinger Rd Hamilton OH 45013 Office: 140 Ross Ave Hamilton OH 45013

CLAUSON, SHARYN FERNE, educator, consultant; b. Phila., Oct. 4, 1946; d. Eugene and Gertrud Jayn (Besser) C. B.A. in English, Temple U., 1968; M.Ed. in Psychology, Beaver Coll., 1979; M.B.A., Drexel U., 1982. Market analyst Epstein Research, Bala, Pa., 1967-69; cons. Ednl. Testing Service, Princeton, N.J., 1979-80; chief exec. officer CCX, Narberth, Pa., 1978-79; tchr. Cheltenham Twp. Sch. Dist., Elkins Park, Pa., 1969—; dir. Sharyn Clauson Bus. Communications, Narberth, Pa., 1975—; mem. adj. faculty Drexel U., Phila., 1979—; communications cons., 1975—. Editor: Curriculum for Optacon Music Reading, 1984. Mem. com. Women's Polit. Caucus, Phila., 1982. Mem. Am. Mktg. Assn., Businesswomen's Network, Nat. Speakers Assn. (chair), Nat. Assn. Profl. Saleswomen, Product Devel. and Mgmt. Assn., Nat. Council Tchrs. English, Delaware Valley Writing Council, Women Bus. Owners Greater Phila., Phi Delta Kappa. Home: 308 Oak Hill E Narberth PA 19072

CLAUSS, CHERRYL A., interior designer; b. Oswego, N.Y., July 13, 1942; d. George D. and Geraldine P. (Heimhilger) Arden; B.S., Syracuse U., 1964; postgrad. N.Y. Sch. Interior Design, 1979—; m. Karl J. Clauss, July 18, 1964; 1 dau., Jennifer A. Owner, The Designer's Touch, Warsaw, Ind., 1980-84; designer Freeman's Interiors, Ltd., Fayetteville, N.Y., 1984—. Pres., Washington Sch. Parent Tchrs. Orgn.; sec., mem. exec. bd. Humane Soc. Kosciusko County; mem. steering com. Friends of Mus.; active capital fund drive Community Gen. Hosp., Syracuse Stage, Syracuse Symphony. Mem. Internat. Soc. Interior Designers, Nat. Decorating Products Assn., AAUW (sec. Warsaw br.), Kappa Kappa, Kappa.

CLAUSSEN, SHARON LASKOWSKI, manufacturing company executive; b. Waterbury, Conn., Sept. 7, 1952; d. Edmund John and Frances (Bakinowski) Laskowski; m. William F. Claussen, June 25, 1983. B.S. in Mgmt. cum laude, Post Coll., 1984. Sr. adminstrv. clk. Picker Corp., Northford, Conn., 1973-77, prodn. planner, spare parts dept., 1979-80; sr. expeditor Corometrics Med. Systems, Wallingford, Conn., 1977-78; planner-scheduler battery chargers Chloride Systems, North Haven, Conn., 1978-79; data control adminstr.-supr. Emhart Industries, Berlin, Conn., 1980-84; prodn. planning supr. Skinner Valve, New Britain, Conn., 1984-85; prodn. control supr. Rex Precision Products, Wallingford, 1985—. Mem. Am. Prodn. and Inventory Control Soc. (asst. v.p. program 1980-81, cert. of recognition 1981). Episcopalian. Avocations: racquetball, cooking. Home: 81 Gale Ave Meriden CT 06450 Office: Rex Precision Products 46 Burnes Indsl Park Wallingford CT 06492

CLAVREUL, GENEVIEVE MARCELLINE, consulting firm executive; b. Paris, May 18, 1940; d. Marcel Henri and Emilie (Cauchois) Clavreul; came to U.S., 1959; children—Patricia, Christina, James E., Eric P. B.A. in Psychology, Calif. State U.-Bakersfield, 1976, M.Ed., 1977, M.P.A., 1979; Ph.D., Beverly Hills U., 1984. Head nurse Med. Ctr., Columbus, Ga., 1974-77; asst. dir. nursing Sioux Falls Hosp. (S.D.), 1977-78; dir. nursing San Joaquin Community Hosp., Bakersfield, 1978; qa coordinator Cedar-Sinai, Los Angeles, 1978; pres. Clavreul-Caviness Mgmt. Cons., Los Angeles, 1978—; cons. U. Calif.-Irvine, 1982, Stanford U., Palo Alto, Calif., 1982, State of N.J., Princeton, 1983. Author: Keep Those Nurses, 1982. Contbr. articles to profl. jours. Mem. polit. and pub. relations coms. Mcpl. Election Com. Los Angeles, 1982—; instr. and newsletter editor CPR Consortium, Los Angeles, 1982—. Recipient award for best grad. paper So. Sociol. Assn., 1975. Mem. Health Care Execs. Assn., Calif.

Hosp. Assn., Bus. and Profl. Assn. Los Angeles, Am. Soc. Healthcare Edn. (tng. sec. 1982), Hollywood C. of C. Democrat. Home: 4119 Los Feliz Blvd #9 Los Angeles CA 90027 Office: Catalyst-Concept Mgmt Cons 4119 Los Feliz Blvd Suite 10 Los Angeles CA 90027

CLAWSON, ROXANN ELOISE, college administrator, wordprocessing company executive; b. Dallas, Oct. 15, 1945; d. Robert Wellington Clawson and Jeannette Irene (Rodenhauser) Clawson Clayton. B.F.A., Mich. State U., 1968. Library asst. Cooper Union, N.Y.C., 1970-75, asst. librarian, 1976-82, asst. to dean, 1985—; pres. Standing By Wordprocessing, N.Y.C., 1982—; v.p. Word Group, N.Y.C., 1984—. Mem. Nat. Assn. Female Execs., N.Y. Personal Computer Group. Democrat. Lutheran. Avocation: interior decorating.

CLAXTON, HARRIETT MAROY JONES, educator; b. Dublin, Ga., Aug. 27, 1930; d. Paul Jackson and Maroy Athalia (Chappell) Jones; m. Edward B. Claxton, Jr., May 27, 1953; children—E. B. III, Paula Jones. A.A., Bethel Woman's Coll., 1949; A.B. magna cum laude, Mercer U., 1951; M.Ed., Ga. Coll., 1965. Social worker Laurens County Welfare Bd., Dublin, 1951-56; high sch. tchr., Dublin, 1961-66; instr. Middle Ga. Coll., Cochran, 1966-71, asst. prof. English, lit. and speech, 1971—. Contbr. articles to profl. jours. and newspapers. Pres. bd. Dublin Assn. Fine Arts, 1974-76, 82-84, Dublin Hist. Soc., 1976-78; mem. Laurens County Library Bd., 1960-68; chmn. Dublin Historic Rev. Bd., 1980-85. Named Woman of Yr., St. Patrick's Festival, Dublin, 1979; recipient Outstanding Service award Cancer Soc., Dublin, 1985. Mem. Ga. Assn. Edn. (sec. 1981—), DAR (regent, state, dist. and nat. awards), Sigma Mu. Democrat. Baptist. Clubs: Woman's Study (pres.), Erin Garden (pres.) (Dublin). Home: 101 Rosewood Dr Dublin GA 31021 Office: Middle Ga Coll Bellevue Ave Dublin GA 31021

CLAY, DONNA PAULETTE, lawyer; b. Houston, Jan. 2, 1950; d. Donald Eugene and Tommie Senior (Shackelford) C. B.A., UCLA, 1971; M.Ed., U. Nev.-Las Vegas, 1973; J.D., U. Calif.-Berkeley, 1980. Bar: Calif. 1980; cert. elem. edn., Calif. Elem. tchr. Oakland Unified Sch. Dist. (Calif.), 1973-76, resource instr., 1976-77; assoc. Pettit & Martin, San Francisco, 1980-82, Kornblum, Kelly & Herlihy, San Francisco, 1982—; mem. Sch. Instructional Strategy Council, Oakland, 1976-77; participant Hastings Coll. Advocacy, San Francisco, 1983. Assoc. editor Calif. Law Rev., 1978-80. Recipient Am. Jurisprudence award, 1978. Mem. ABA, Nat. Bar Assn., Charles Houston Bar Assn. (v.p. 1983—), Assn. Trial Lawyers Am., Alpha Kappa (grammateus Los Angeles 1969-70). Democrat. Office: Kornblum Kelly & Herlihy 445 Bush St 6th Floor San Francisco CA 94610

CLAY, LORI LEE GARBER, retailer; b. Gary, Ind., Mar. 19, 1957; d. Robert Samuel and Vivian May (Bray) Garber; m. Terry Dean Clay, Jan. 2, 1982; 1 stepdau., Melisa B. B.B.A. with honors, N.Mex. State U., 1980; M.B.A., Columbus Coll., Ga., 1985. Retail mgr. Army and Air Force Exchange Service, Ft. Bragg, N.C., 1980-81, Eglin AFB, Fla., 1981-82, Pope AFB, N.C., 1982-83; retail ops. mgr., Ft. Benning, Ga., 1983-84, retail sales and mdse. mgr., Ft. Benning, 1985—. Mem. Nat. Assn. Female Execs. Republican. Methodist. Avocations: water skiing, aerobics, poetry, reading. Home: 1438 Foxcroft Loop Columbus GA 31904 Office: Army Air Force Exchange Service Bldg 9230 Fort Benning GA 31995

CLAY, ROSALIND, compensation administrator; b. Selma, Ala., Nov. 22, 1954; d. Clarence Prentice and Claytonia (Robinson) C. B.S., U. South Fla., 1972; M.S., U. Ala., 1979. Social worker Birmingham Youth Inc. (Ala.), 1975-76; probation/parole officer Dept. Offender Rehab., Ocala, Fla., 1976-77; recruiter Rust Enging Co., Birmingham, Ala., 1977-79, mgr. benefits and coll. relations, 1979-81; mgr. compensation Rust Internat. Corp., 1981-84; supr. compensation adminstrn. M.W. Kellogg Co., 1984-85; compensation cons. Coca-Cola Foods, Houston, 1985-86, compensation mgr., 1986—. Mem. Am. Soc. Personnel Adminstrs., Am. Compensation Assn., Houston Personnel Assn., Houston Compensation Assn. t Office: Coca Cola Foods PO Box 2079 Houston TX 77252

CLAYBORNE, BRENDA LANE, city agency official, fraud investigator; b. N.Y.C., Dec. 24, 1950; d. James Walter and Ruth Richetta (Wellonc) Lane, divorced; children—James Byrd Clayborne, Crystal Jeaneen Betts. B.A. in Sociology, Norfolk State U., 1974; M.S.W., 1979. Asst. dir. placement service Norfolk State U., Va., 1978; social worker Norfolk Social Services, 1979-81, fraud investigator, 1981—; v.p., pub. relations coordinator Betts & Assocs., Virginia Beach, Va., 1985—; chairperson City Mgr.'s Employee Relations Com., Norfolk, 1983—. Vol. Am. Cancer Soc., Virginia Beach and Chesapeake, Va., 1982, 85, Sr. Citizen Olympics, Norfolk, 1985. Mem. Va. Council on Social Welfare, United Council on Welfare Fraud, Phi Beta Kappa. Baptist. Avocations: outdoor sports, especially football; cooking; creative writing. Home: 2015-D Brookland Dr Chesapeake VA 23324 Office: Betts & Assocs 1 Columbus Ctr Suite 626 Virginia Beach VA 23462

CLAYTON, DOROTHY RHODES, nurse; b. Jackson, Tenn., Dec. 31, 1926; d. Gleathus and Emma (White) Rhodes; m. John Richard Clayton, Oct. 9, 1957 (dec. Sept. 1960); children—Betsy Katherine, Mary Emily. A.A. in Nursing, Union U., Jackson Tenn., 1964. Cert. CPR instr., trainer, Tenn. Charge nurse Jackson Gen. Hosp. (Tenn.), 1965, pvt. duty nurse, 1965-84; coll. nurse Jackson State Community Coll., 1967—, State U. and Community Coll. System Tenn., 1967—; mem. counseling com. Jackson State Community Coll., mem. student personnel com. for instl. self-study program of commn. on colls., 1971, 83, coordinator program on drug abuse, developer health services brochure, Swine Flu Vaccine Program, Heart Day, health fairs, 1977-86, Diabetic Detection Week, First Aid for the Layman, planner, developer coll. health services, coordinator blood drives Lifeline Blood Vol. Program, 1974—; mem. crisis call ctr. com.; nurse, instr. ARC, 1973—; Mem. edn. com., bd. dirs. Am. Cancer Soc., 1979—; mem. Gov.'s Com. Employment for Handicapped in Madison County, 1982-86. Mem. Am. Nurses Assn., Tenn. Nurses Assn., Am. Coll. Health Assn., Mid-Am. Coll. Health Assn., West Tenn. Heart Assn., Altrusa of Jackson, (publicity chmn., rec. sec., treas., v.p., pres. various coms.), Baptist. Club: Jackson State Community Coll. Women's (pres., awards com., dinner theater com., nominating com.). Home: 86 Elmwood Dr Jackson TN 38305 Office: Jackson State Community Coll PO Box 2467 Jackson TN 38301

CLAYTON, EVELYN WILLIAMS, company executive; b. Durham, N.C., Feb. 11, 1951; d. Virge and Inez Florence (Jordan) Williams; m. Archie L. Clayton, Mar. 1, 1972 (div. May 1975); 1 child, Dorel. Student Durham Tech. Inst., 1969-71, Durham Bus. Coll., 1971-72, U. N.C.-Chapel Hill, 1977-81; A.B.A., Durham Tech. Inst., 1971. Fiscal officer Durham County Health Dept. (N.C.), 1974-82; dir. fin. MedVisit Inc., Butner, N.C., 1982—; exec. dir., pres. EC & Assocs., Durham, 1983—. Mem. Durham Com. on Affairs of Black People; cubmaster, Pack 442, Boy Scouts Am. Mem. N.C. Assn. Home Care (treas. 1980-83), N.C. Public Health Assn., NAACP, Durham C. of C., Better Bus. Bur. S.E. Democrat. Baptist. Home: 36 Burgess LnAve Durham NC 27707 Office: EC & Assocs 2514 University Dr Duram NC 27707

CLAYTON, JOAN BENNETT, real estate executive, writer; b. Chaleroi, Pa., Oct. 27, 1931; d. Frederick Calvin and Lena Margaret (Atkins) Bennett; m. Charles Winston Clayton, June 7, 1957; children—Charles Winston III, Clay Worthington, Cole Whitney, Elizabeth Hope. B.A., Rollins Coll., 1957. Pres. J.B.C. Corp., Winter Park, Fla., 1979-83; columnist Central Fla. Sun, Maitland, Fla., 1980-81; broker, salesman Clayton's Realty, Winter Park, 1981—. Author: Peas in a Pod, 1979; Unto You, 1982. Contbr. articles to profl. jours. Pres. Orlando Day Nursery, 1968-69; mem. exec. bd. Women of Fla. Symphony Soc.; pres. Winter Park Cotillion, 1973-74; pres. Fern Creek PTA, 1970-71; mem. central Fla. bd. Fellowship Christian Athletes, 1982-85, head adminstrv. com., 1984-85. Mem. Orlando Bd. Realtors, Christian Poetry Assn. Am., Phi Mu. Republican. Baptist. Home: Winter Park FL

CLAYTON, LINDA MAY, motel manager, plumbing company executive; b. Timmons, Ont., Can., Oct. 10, 1951; came to U.S., 1977, naturalized, June, 1984; d. William Cartwright and Mary (Hodgson) Cartwright Pringle; m. Zoltan Koleseri, Sept. 25, 1970 (div. Jan. 1977); m. M. Scott Clayton, Feb. 14, 1977; children—Katrina D., L. Denise. Office worker Clayton Realty, Englewood, Colo., 1976-77, Mountain Bell, Denver, 1978-79; controller, v.p. Buchanan Plumbing Co., Englewood, Colo., 1979—; gen. mgr. Penn Motel, Commerce City, 1981-85. Mem. Am. Hotel and Motel Assn. Republican. Avocations: swimming, water skiing, chess, cards. Home: 3201 S Franklin St Englewood CO 80110 Office: Buchanan Plumbing 2834 S Acoma St Englewood CO 80110

CLAYTON, SALLY JANE, lawyer; b. St. Louis, June 2, 1927; d. Harold Sylvester and Martha May (Sager) Pfeffer; m. Michel Ely Cressaty, Nov. 12, 1949 (div. 1956); m. Charles Frederick Clayton, May 30, 1956; children—Ann Harper, Thomas Henry. B.A., U. Ill., 1948; cert. U. Paris, 1949; J.D., St. Louis U., 1980. Bar: Ill. 1980. Receptionist, Ford Found., N.Y.C., 1953-54; asst. buyer Famous Barr Co., St. Louis, 1955-56; tchr. Sch. Dist. 9, Lebanon, Ill., 1956-77; assoc. Delmar O. Koebel, Lebanon, 1980—. Treas., Lebanon Edn. Assn., Sch. Dist. 9, 1974-75, Lebanon Citizens Assn., 1975; Republican candidate for state's atty., St. Clair County, Ill., 1984; bd. dirs. Call for Help Found., Belleville, Ill., 1984—. Recipient Disting. Service award in govt. and politics Clair County YWCA, 1985; French Govt. scholar, 1948. Mem. ABA, Ill. Bar Assn., St. Clair County Bar Assn., Metro East Women's Bar Assn., Assn. Trial Lawyers Am., Phi Beta Kappa, Phi Kappa Phi, Alpha Lambda Delta. Presbyterian. Home: 937 Belleville St Lebanon IL 62254 Office: Delmar O Koebel 109 W Saint Louis Lebanon IL 62254

CLAYTON, SHARON, publisher; b. Bunkerville, Nev., Jan. 26, 1935; d. Hyram and Edith (Bunker) Potter; m. Charles Carlton Clayton, Sept. 12, 1952; 1 son, James Brian. Student, E. Los Angeles Coll., 1952-53. Mgr. Olin-Mathieson Co., City of Commerce, Calif., 1960-62; gen. mgr. J & R Engring. Co., El Monte, Calif., 1962-65; comptroller, sec., treas. Cycle News Inc., Long Beach, Calif., 1965-73, pub., sec., treas., 1973—. Vice-pres. Kiefer Meml. Fund, found. sports medicine, 1979—. Recipient Rolf Tibbins award Motorcycle Industry Council, 1976. Mem. Am. Motorcycle Assn. (dirt track racing bd.). Republican. Club: Mormon. Office: Cycle News Inc Box 498 Long Beach CA 90801

CLAYTON, STUART DORTHEA, real estate executive; b. Berkeley, Calif., May 5, 1948; d. William F. and Sally D. Clayton; B.S., U. S.D., 1970; student Chapman Coll. World Campus Afloat, 1969, 72; grad. Realtors Inst., 1976; Tchr. Jefferson County Public Schs., 1970-72; liaison around the world cruises Orient Overseas Line, 1972-73; leasing agt. John Madden Co., Denver, 1974, Highline Med. Bldg., Denver, 1975; comml. leasing specialist Van Schaack & Co., Denver, 1975-80; mgr. Office Leasing div. Fuller & Co., Denver, 1980-85; speaker real estate workshops. Mem. Million Dollar Roundtable, 1975-84; named one of Colo.'s leading bus. women Colo. Bus. Mag., 1977. Lic. real estate broker, Colo. Mem. Colo. Assn. Realtors, Nat. Assn. Realtors. Denver C. of C. Contbr. articles on office bldgs. to profl. jours., newspapers; nat. speaker. Office: Frederick Ross Co 707 Seventeeth St Suite 2100 Denver CO 80202

CLAYTON, VERNA LEWIS, city official; b. Hamden, Ohio, Feb. 28, 1937; d. Matthews L. and Yail (Miller) Lewis; m. Frank R. Clayton, Feb. 4, 1956; children—Valerie Clayton Euneman, Barry L. Office mgr., Village of Buffalo Grove, Ill., 1972-78, village clk., 1971-79, village pres., 1979—. Mem. solid waste adv. com. Lake County, Ill., 1983—. Recipient Disting. Service award Amvets, 1981. Mem. Northwest Mcpl. Conf. (pres. 1983-84), Chgo. Area Transp. Study Council Mayors (vice chmn. 1981-83, chmn. 1985—), Mcpl. Clks. Ill. (treas. 1978-79), Mcpl. Clks. Lake County (pres. 1977-78), Ill. Mcpl. League (bd. dirs., v.p. 1985—). Republican. Methodist. Home: 911 Twisted Oak Ln Buffalo Grove IL 60090 Office: Village of Buffalo Grove 50 Raupp Blvd Buffalo Grove IL 60089

CLEAR, CAROLYN HILL, sales executive; b. Memphis, May 21, 1937; d. Owen Landale and Sylvia Mae (Walter) Hill; B.J., U. Mo., 1959; children—Stacey Alan, Sylvia Lee. Asst. to asst. advt. dir. MFA Ins. Cos., Columbia, Mo., 1958, 59-60; traffic director, copywriter, on-air announcer Sta. WENE, Endicott, N.Y., 1960-61; weekly columnist, advt. salesman Fort Bend Mirror, Stafford, Tex., 1970-71; advt. sales rep., promotion dir., nat. accounts mgr. Suburbia, Houston, 1972-76; dir. rep., advt. sales, mgr. directory sales Southwestern Bell, Houston, 1976-80, staff mgr. directory premise tng., 1981-83, div. sales mgr. Southwestern Bell Yellow Pages Inc., St. Louis, 1984-85, dir. sales and mktg. adminstrn., 1985—; dir. corp. tng. Southwestern Bell Publs., 1985—. Counselor, Youth Emergency Hot Line. Recipient Gold Key award Southwestern Bell, 1977. Republican. Presbyterian. Home: 2 Bitterfield Ct Ballwin MO 63011 Office: Room 520 112 N 4th St St Louis MO 63102

CLEARY, BEVERLY ATLEE, author; b. McMinnville, Oreg.; d. Chester Lloyd and Mable (Atlee) Bunn; B.A., U. Calif., 1938; B.A. in Librarianship, U. Wash., 1939; m. Clarence T. Cleary, Oct. 6, 1940, children—Marianne Elisabeth, Malcolm James. Children's librarian, Yakima, Wash., 1939-40; post librarian Regional Hosp., Oakland, Calif., 1942-45. Mem. Authors Guild of Authors League Am. Author: Henry Huggins, 1950; Ellen Tebbits, 1951; Henry and Beezus, 1952; Otis Spofford, 1953; Henry and Ribsy, 1954; Beezus and Ramona, 1955; Fifteen, 1956; Henry and the Paper Route, 1957; The Luckiest Girl, 1958; Jean and Johnny, 1959; The Real Hole, 1960; Hullabaloo ABC, 1960; Two Dog Biscuits, 1961; Emily's Runaway Imagination, 1961; Henry and the Clubhouse, 1962; Sister of the Bride, 1963; Ribsy, 1964; The Mouse and the Motorcycle, 1965; Mitch and Amy, 1967; Ramona the Pest (Georgia Children's Book award 1970), 1968; Runaway Ralph, 1970; Socks, 1973; Ramona the Brave, 1975; Ramona and her Father (Newbery Honor Book ALA 1978, Honor Book for U.S., Internat. Bd. and Books for Young People), 1977; Ramona and her Mother, 1979; Ramona Quimby, Age 8 (Newberry honor book 1982), 1981, Land of Enchantment (N.Mex. Library Assn. Children's book award 1981); Ralph S. Mouse, 1982; Dear Mr. Henshaw (Newberry award ALA 1984), 1983; Lucky Chuck, 1984; Ramona Forever, 1984. Recipient Young Reader's Choice award Pacific N.W. Library Assn., 1957, 60, 68, 71, 80; Dorothy Canfield Fisher Children's Book award Vt. Congress of Parents and Tchrs., 1958, 66, 85; Nene award Hawaii Assn. Sch. Librarians and Hawaii Library Assn., 1968, 69, 71, 72, 79; Sue Hefley award La. Assn. Sch. Librarians, 1973, William Allen White award Kans. Assn. Sch. Librarians and Kans. Tchrs. Assn., 1968, 75; Sequoyah Children's Book award Okla. Library Assn., 1971, 85; Charlie May Simon award Ark. Elem. Sch. Council, 1973, 84; Laura Ingalls Wilder award Children's Services div. ALA, 1975; Golden Archer award U. Wis., 1977; Newbery Honor Book, 1978; Regina medal Cath. Library Assn., 1980; Utah Children's Book award Children's Lit. Assn. Utah, 1980; Tenn. Children's Book award Tenn. Library Assn., 1980; Garden State award N.J. Library Assn., 1980, 84, 85; Tex. Bluebonnet award Tex. Library Assn. Tex. Assn. Sch. Librarians, 1981; Am. Book award, 1981; Golden Kite award Soc. Children's Book Writers, 1983; Christopher award, 1983; award Calif. Tchrs. of English, 1983; George C. Stone award Claremont Colls., 1983; Commonwealth Silver medal Commonwealth Club Calif., 1984; Young Readers award Mich. Council Tchrs. of English, 1984; Iowa Children's Choice award, 1984-85; Buckeye Children's Book award, 1985; Young Readers Choice award Ala. Library Assn., 1984; Mass. Children's Book award Salem State Coll., 1986. Address: care William Morrow 105 Madison Ave New York NY 10016

CLELAND, AUDRY JAYE, training administrator; b. Atmore, Ala., Aug. 13, 1932; d. Robert Lee and Minnie Lee (Sasser) Jaye; m. Vinson Oran Cleland, Jr., Apr. 10, 1953. A.A., Pensacola (Fla.) Jr. Coll., 1978; B.A., U. West Fla., 1981; M.S. in Pub. Adminstrn., Troy (Ala.) State U., 1983. Claims rep. Wash. State Employment Service, Colville, 1958-61; bookkeeper Jaye Trucking Co., Atmore, 1962-64; mgmt. asst. U.S. Air Force, Randolph AFB, Tex., 1964-68, Weisbaden AB, W.Ger., 1968-74; edn. technician DANTES (Def. Activity for Nontraditional Edn. Support), Pensacola, 1974-83; tng. adminstr. Navy Comptroller Standard Systems Activity, Pensacola, 1983—. Editor: Guide to External Degree Programs, 1982; Guide for Establishing and Operating an Adult Learning Center, 1983. Recipient Spl. Achievement award Def. Activity for Non-Traditional Edn. Support, 1983, hon. EEO award Naval Edn. and Tng. Program Devel. Ctr., 1981, Chief Naval Edn. and Tng., 1981. Mem. Am. Soc. Tng. and Devel. Republican. Baptist. Clubs: Spin Off Toastmistress (pres. 1979), Federally Employed Women (pres. Pensacola 1980). Lodge: Eastern Star.

CLELAND, JANIS LIVINGSTONE, veterinarian; b. Washington, June 25, 1950; d. Earl Leslie and Lillian Irene (Harris) Livingstone; m. William Paul Cleland, Jr., Aug. 24, 1974; 1 dau., Elisabeth Berchi. B.S. in Biology, George Mason U., 1972; D.V.M., U. Ga., 1976. Diplomate Am. Bd. Vet. Practitioners. Intern, U. Ga. Small Animal Clinic, Athens, 1976-77; veterinarian Mt. Park Animal Hosp., Lilburn, Ga., 1977—; clin. researcher Beecham Labs., Memphis, 1983—. Recipient Upjohn Clin. award, 1976; Faculty Scholastic award U. Ga., Phi Zeta, 1976. Mem. Am. Bd. Vet. Practitioners, AVMA, Ga. Vet. Med. Assn. (small animal com. 1984), Ga. Acad. Vet. Practice (sec.-treas. 1982), Greater Atlanta Vet. Med. Soc., Am. Animal Hosp. Assn., Gwinnett County C. of C., DAR. Methodist. Clubs: Gamma Sigma Delta, Phi Zeta. Home: 5285 Silver Creek Dr Lilburn GA 30247 Office: Mountain Park Animal Hosp 5324 Five Forks Trickum Rd Lilburn GA 30247

CLELAND, MARILYN ELAINE, rental company executive; b. Stockbridge, Mich., Nov. 2, 1942; d. Lee Harold and Phyllis Marie (King) Osborne; children—William Warren, Bruce Wayne Short. Acctg. office mgr. Stephens Co. of Houston, 1969-74; office mgr. Plaza Lincoln Mercury, Houston, 1974-75; data processing office mgr. Mort Hall Ford, Houston, 1975-79; bus. mgr. Joe Myers Rental, Houston, 1979—. Mem. Nat. Assn. Female Execs. Democrat. Methodist. Home: 14022 Walters Rd Lot 8084 Houston TX 77014 Office: Joe Myers Rental Inc 5707 Mitchelldale Houston TX 77092

CLEMENT, EVELYN GEER, library educator; b. Springfield, Mass., Sept. 1, 1926; d. Elihu and Helen (Schenck) Geer; m. J. R. Clement, Sept. 9, 1946 (div. 1972); children—James Randall, Timothy B., Susan Henson, Marc W., Audrey Ethriedge. B.A., with honors, U. Tulsa, 1965; M.L.S., U. Okla., 1966; Ph.D., Ind. U., 1975. Librarian Tulsa City-County Library, 1960-66; learning resources librarian Oral Roberts U., Tulsa, 1966-68; spl. instr. U. Okla., Norman, 1966-70; prof., chmn. library sci. Memphis State U., 1972-85, dir. Ctr. for Instructional Service and Research, 1985—, chmn. acad. senate, 1979-80, mem. faculty tenure and promotion appeals com., 1980-82, mem. standing univ. com. on libraries, 1975-80, chmn. women's task force, 1984-85. Editor: Bibliographic Control of Nonprint Media, 1972. Contbr. articles to profl. jours. Doctoral fellow U.S. Office Edn., Title II-B, Ind. U., 1968-71. Mem. ALA, Tenn. Library Assn., Memphis Library Council (chmn. 1974-75), Memphis Area Librarians' Assn. (vice chmn., chmn. elect 1985—), Memphis State U. Libraries Assn. (v.p., pres. elect 1985—), Pi Gamma Mu, Phi Alpha Theta, Beta Phi Mu. Republican. Avocations: microcomputer; needlepoint; exercise; reading. Home: 280 Patterson St Memphis TN 38111

CLEMENT, HOPE ELIZABETH ANNA, librarian; b. North Sydney, N.S., Can., Dec. 29, 1930; d. Harry Wells and Lana (Perkins) C.; B.A., U. of King's Coll., 1951; M.A., Dalhousie U., 1953; B.L.S., U. Toronto, 1955. With Nat. Library of Can., Ottawa, Ont., 1955—, chief nat. bibliography div., 1966-70, asst. dir. research and planning br., 1970-73, dir. research and planning br., 1973-77, asso. nat. librarian, 1977—. Mem. Can. Library Assn., Can. Assn. Info. Sci. Editor Canadiana, 1966-69. Office: Nat Library Can 395 Wellington St Ottawa ON K1A 0N4 Canada

CLEMENT, JACQUELINE PARKER, school administrator; b. Feb. 28, 1931; d. Donald C. Parker and Helen (Reininger) Parker Barnes; m. M.O. Clement. B.A., Mt. Holyoke Coll., 1952; postgrad. U. Calif.-Berkeley, 1953-56; M.Ed., Am. U., 1968; Ed.D., Harvard U., 1974; hon. degree, Lesley Coll., 1978. Dir., advisor Follow through Headstart, Lebanon, N.H., 1967-71; with div. adminstrn. N.H. State Dept. of Edn., Concord, 1971; asst. supt. Supervisory Union 22, Hanover, N.H., 1973-75; asst. supt. curriculum and instrn., Brookline, Mass., 1975-78; supt. schs., Lincoln, Mass., 1978-82; head The Winchester-Thurston Sch., Pitts., 1982—. Author: (with Mark Shedd) The Costs of Educational Innovation, 1972; Sex Bias in School Leadership, 1975; contbr. articles to profl. jours. Bd. dirs. Pitts. Youth Symphony, 1984; trustee Cambridge Sch., Weston, Mass., 1980. NEH fellow Stanford U., 1976; Dept. Econs. fellow U. Calif., 1953-54. Mem. Am. Assn. Sch. Adminstrs., Middle States Assn. Colls. and Schs. (adv. com.), Nat. Assn. Independent schs. (edn. issues commn.), Pa. Assn. of Independent Schs. (exec. com.), Pitts. Fund for Arts Edn. (bd. dirs.), Exec. Women's Council of Greater Pitts. Inc., Am. Ednl. Research Assn., Assn. for Supervison and Curriculum Devel., Cultural Edn. Collaborative (bd. dirs.). Office: The Winchester-Thurston Sch 555 Morewood Ave Pittsburgh PA

CLEMENT, JANICE FAYE, nursing administrator; b. Norfolk, Nebr., Aug. 19, 1946; d. Allen Edward and Hilda Bernice (Stange) Reeves; m. Roger Allen Clement, Oct. 6, 1968 (dec. July 1974). R.N., Meth. Sch. Nursing, Omaha, 1967; B.S. in Nursing, magna cum laude, Creighton U., 1978; M.S. in Nursing, U. Nebr., 1981. With Meth. Hosp., 1967-68, 70-83, asst. head nurse, 1974-77, staff devel. nurse, 1977-81, dir. staff adminstrv. services, 1981-83; pub. health nurse Wichita-Sedgwick County Health Dept., Wichita, Kans., 1970-72; dir. nursing Meth. Med. Ctr., St. Joseph, Mo., 1983-84, Broadlawns Med. Ctr., Des Moines, 1984—. Mem. adv. bd. Drake U. Nursing, Des Moines, 1984—, Tech. High Sch. Practical Nursing, 1984—. Mem. Am. Nurses Assn., Iowa Nurses Assn., Nat. League Nursing, Iowa League Nursing, Am. Orgn. Nurse Execs. (Iowa chpt.), Central Iowa Nursing Leadership Conf. (pres. 1985—), Colloquium Nursing Leaders Central Iowa, Am. Mgmt. Assn., Sigma Theta Tau. Republican. Methodist. Avocations: flying; sewing; golfing; walking; reading. Home: 4407 64th St Des Moines IA 50322 Office: Broadlawns Med Ctr 18th and Hickman Rd Des Moines IA 50314

CLEMENT, KATHERYN (KITTY), adoption agency director, consultant, trainer; b. Little Rock, Ark., Jan. 6, 1924; d. Louis Wangelin and Dorothy Louise (Butler) Fuess; m. William Crutcher Clement, July 28, 1945 (div. 1979); 4 sons, William, Louis, Peter, Richard. B.A., Tex. Women's U., Denton, 1945; M.S.S.W., U. Tex.-Arlington, 1971. Cert. social worker, Tex. Social worker Homes of St. Mark, Houston, 1967-69, Presbyn. Children's Home, Dallas, 1969-71; cons. therapist Child Study Ctr., Ft. Worth, 1971-74; supr. Harris County Child Welfare, Houston, 1974-79; field cons. Child Welfare League, N.Y.C., 1979-80; dir. Spaulding for Children, Houston, 1980—; trainer Dept. Human Resources State of Tex., 1981—. Co-author: Reaching Out, 1980; contbr. article to conf. Recipient Outstanding Woman award YWCA, Harris County, Tex., 1979; Dept. Health & Human Services grantee, 1982. Fellow N.Am. Ctr. Adoption, Child Welfare League Am., ACLU, Unitarian Universalist Women's Orgn., Tex. Abortion Rights Action League, Harris County Women's Polit. Caucus. Democrat. Unitarian. Club: Warwick Breakfast (sec., 1983-84) (Houston). Home: 3700 Wakeforest 91 Houston TX 77098 Office: Spaulding for Children 4219 Richmond Houston TX 77027

CLEMENT, SHIRLEY GEORGE, educational services company executive; b. El Paso, Tex., Feb. 14, 1926; d. Claude Samuel and Elizabeth Estelle (Mattice) Gillett; m. Paul Vincent Clement, Mar. 23, 1946; children—Brian Frank, Robert Vincent, Carol Elizabeth, Rosemary Adele. B.A. in English, Tex. Western Coll., 1963; postgrad. U. Tex.-El Paso, 1964, 65, N.Mex. State U., 1966, Sul Ross U., 1985—. Tchr. lang. arts Ysleta Ind. Schs., El Paso, 1960-62; tchr. adult edn., 1962-64, tchr. reading/lang. arts, 1964-77; owner, dir. Tutor House Learning Systems, El Paso, 1980—; dir. tutorial for sports teams U. Tex.-El Paso, 1984—; dir. continuing edn. program El Paso Community Coll., 1985—; mem. curriculum com. Ysleta Ind. Schs., El Paso, 1974; mem. Right to Read Task Force, 1975-77; mem. Bi-Centennial Steering Com., El Paso, 1975-76; lectr. on reading. Author: Beginning the Search, 1979; contbr. poems to Behold Texas, 1983. Treas. El Paso Republican Women, 1956; facilitator Goals for El Paso, 1975; mem. hospitality com. Sun Carnival, 1974, Cotton Festival, 1975. Mem. Internat. Reading Assn. (pres. El Paso County council 1973-74), Assn. Children with Learning Disabilities (tchr. 1980), Poetry Soc. Tex. (Panhandle Penwomen's first place award 1981), El Paso C. of C., Assn. Gifted and Talented, Chi Omega Alumnae (pres. 1952-53). Mem. Unity Sch. of Christianity. Avocations: dressmaking; tailoring; needlecraft; writing; singing. Home: 825 De Leon St El Paso TX 79912 Office: Tutor House 481 N Resler St D & E El Paso TX 79912

CLEMENT, YVONNE MADELINE, librarian; b. Tacoma, Wash., June 17, 1924; d. Cecil Edward and Madeline Edith (Wink) DeGuire; m. Ralph Louis Clement, Jr., June 25, 1949 (dec. Dec. 1969); children—Lawrence E., Catherine E. Gilbert, Mary Susan Clement Zimmerman, Michele Y. Clement Cates, David L. B.A., Holy Names Coll., Spokane, Wash., 1946; B.A.L.S., Rosary Coll., 1947. Asst. br. librarian Tacoma Pub. Library (Wash.), 1947-49; br. asst. Salt Lake County Library, Salt Lake City, 1967-69, br. librarian, 1969-71, assoc. dir., 1971—. Author: (with B.M. Hepworth) Utah Libraries: Heritage and Horizons, 1976. Bd. dirs. Utah council Camp Fire, Salt Lake City, 1983-84. Mem. ALA, Utah Library Assn., Mountain Plains Library Assn. Club: Zonta (Salt Lake City). Office: Salt Lake County Library System 2197 E 7000 S Salt Lake City UT 84121

CLEMENTS, PATRICIA SUE, media executive; b. Salt Lake City, July 8, 1958; d. James Madison and Barbara Boutwell (Jones) Bonds; m. Brian Lee Clements, Nov. 7, 1981. B.S. in Telecommunications cum laude, Oral Roberts U., 1980. TV prodn. asst. Oral Roberts U., Tulsa, 1976-79; film dir., audio engr. Sta. WMBB-TV, Panama City, Fla., 1981-82, continuty and pub. service announcement dir., 1982, program coordinator, 1982, program dir., 1982—. Author: (screenplay) Crying Wind, 1982. Mem. Humane Soc. Bay County, Panama City, 1984—; asst. tchr. adult Sunday sch. class Forest Park United

Meth. Ch., Panama City, 1983—. Mem. Nat. Assn. TV Program Execs., Fla. Assn. Broadcasters, Nat. Acad. TV Arts and Scis. Republican. Avocations: writing short stories, jazzercise, crocheting. Home: 2630 E 37th Plaza Panama City FL 32405 Office: Sta WMBB-TV 232 Harrison Ave Panama City FL 32401

CLEMENTS, SUSAN CHRISTINE, court reporter; b. Chgo., Oct. 11, 1957; d. Joseph Dominic and Betty E. (Kosowski) Milello; m. Michael Anthony Clements, Sept. 8, 1979; 1 child, Alexis Catherine. A.A.S., Mac Cormac Jr. Coll., Chgo., 1977. Court reporter F-M Reporting Service, Ltd., Chgo., 1977—, agy. owner, 1981—. Mem. Nat. Shorthand Reporters Assn., Ill. Shorthand Reporters Assn. Avocation: needlework crafts. Office: F-M Reporting Service Ltd 222 W Adams St Chicago IL 60606

CLEMMONS, FRANCES ANNE MANSELL (MRS. SLATON CLEMMONS), insurance company official; b. Camden, Miss., Dec. 21, 1915; d. Otho Franklin and Pearl (Dunlap) Mansell; B.S., Belhaven Coll., 1937, Mus.B., 1937; m. Rowe Sanders Crowder, Dec. 17, 1938 (div. Mar. 1954); children—Rowe Sanders, Frances Elizabeth; m. 2d, Slaton Clemmons, Nov. 21, 1965. Owner, operator Crowder Art Gallery, Jackson, Miss., 1946-50; dept. mgr., buyer Valley Dry Goods Co., Vicksburg, 1954-56; with Social Security Adminstrn., 1956-84, asst. dist. mgr., Rome, Ga., 1962-84; MEDICARE hearing officer Prudential Ins. Co. Am., 1984—. Charter mem. Citizens Adv. Council on Energy; mem. Rome Little Theatre, Rome Community Concert Assn., Rome Area C. of C., Interagy Council, Floyd County Merit Bd., Salvation Army Aux., Mayor's Com. Employment of Handicapped. Democrat. Presbyterian. Club: Quota Internat. (pres. Rome 1974-76, dist. 8 lt. gov. 1979-80, gov. 1980-82). Home: 412 E 3d Ave Rome GA 30161

CLEMMONS, PENNY, psychologist, educator; b. Chgo., Aug. 16, 1947; d. Trefin D. and Garnet Hope (Murray) Paganis; B.A., U. Ill., 1970; M.A., Roosevelt U., 1976; Ph.D., Calif. Grad. Inst., 1979. Tchr., Archdiocese of Chgo., 1967-69; outpatient treatment coordinator Grant Hosp., Chgo., 1969-74; marriage/family and child counselor, 1977—; clin. psychologist in pvt. practice, Los Angeles and Santa Barbara, 1981—; assoc. prof. psychology, dean admissions Calif. Grad. Inst., Los Angeles, 1979-82; asst. program dir. Fielding Inst., Santa Barbara, Calif., 1982-83; coordinator chem. dependency studies program Antioch U., 1983—; clin. dir. Inst. for Psychotherapy and Counseling, Los Angeles, 1980-83. Pres., bd. dirs. San Fernando Valley Counseling Center, 1978-80; v.p. bd. dirs. Ill. Alcoholism and Drug Dependence Assn., 1972-76; bd. dirs. Nat. Council on Alcoholism, Santa Barbara, v.p., 1984—. Recipient Pub. Service award, State of Ill., 1976; lic. clin. psychologist, Calif. Mem. Calif. Psychol. Assn., Santa Barbara Assn. Clin. Psychologists (sec.-treas.), Nat. Assn. Advancement Psychoanalysis, Assocs. for Interdisciplinary Studies, Acad. Psychosomatic Medicine. Contbr. articles to profl. jours. Office: 25 W Canon Perdido Suite D Santa Barbara CA 93101

CLENDANIEL, ANNE LUCILLE EVANS, communications consultant; b. Harrington, Del., Aug. 30, 1918; d. John Franklin and Bertha (Collison) Evans; student U. Del., 1936-37, spl. courses in writing, leadership and communications; m. Harry Edgar Clendaniel, Jr., Sept. 6, 1941 (div. 1985); children—Mary Catherine, John Evans. Exec. sec. Beacom Bus. Coll., 1939; legal sec., tax dept. duPont Co., 1939-45, Maguire, Voorhees & Wells, Orlando, Fla., 1943-45; vol., study group leader Great Books, 1945-61; legal sec. Young, Conaway, Stargatt, 1962-63; dir. communications Episcopal Diocese of Del., 1963-73; exec. dir. Del. chpt. Arthritis Found., Wilmington, 1974-84; bd. dirs. Del. Sr. Cons., 1984—. Mem. Del. Press Women, Profl. Staff Assn. Arthritis Found. Republican. Club: Wilmington Quota (pres. 1977-78), Contbr. poetry and verse, to newspapers, mags., anthologies, 1939-55; founder, writer Communion Diocesan paper, 1967-73; author The Arthritis Report, 1974-84; editor DSC newsletter.

CLERICI, RUTH HOUSEKNECHT, oil company executive; b. Jonesville, Mich., Dec. 12, 1913; d. George Benson and Annette (Wilcox) Davenport Houseknecht; m. Eugene Michael Clerici, Oct. 8, 1944; 1 child, Michael. Pres. Houseknecht Oil, Jonesville, Mich., 1970—; self-employed as oil producer, real estate, art, wood products, Jonesville, 1954—. Served with USN, 1944-45. Mem. Oil and Gas Assn. Avocations: creative writing; poetry; antique collecting; parapsychology; classical music. Home: 4811 Homer Rd Jonesville MI 49250 Office: Houseknecht Oil Producers Inc 1250 E Chicago Rd Jonesville MI 49250

CLEVELAND, ANNE C(ATHERINE), educator; B.S., Syracuse U., 1941; M.S., SUNY-Albany, 1947; postgrad. St. Rose Coll., 1954, Russell Sage Coll., 1968, Tex. Technol. U., 1969, Cornell U., 1964, Syracuse U., SUNY-Plattsburg. Tchr. various elem. schs., 1941-46, 47-51; tchr. Albany Pub. Schs., 1951-59; home econs. coordinator Glens Falls (N.Y.) City Schs., 1959-77. Chmn. vols. Adirondack br. ARC, 1985—. Mem. Home Econs. Tchrs. Assn. (numerous activities, including coordinator and founder Job Index Service 1977-79, N.Y. State pres. 1970-76, N.Y. State White Orchid award 1982), Am. Home Econs. Assn. (N.Y. State membership promotion chmn., state co-chmn. conv., pres. N.Y. State), N.Y. State Tchrs.' Assn. (chmn. ways and means, chmn. membership gen. chmn. chmn. zone conf. home econs. conf.), Nat. Assn. Vocat. Home Econs. Tchrs., AAUW (award 1977), Nat. Econs. Assn., Home Econs. Edn. Assn., N.Y. State Home Econs. Assn. (Service award 1982), DAR (sec. chpt.), Gen. Soc. Mayflower Descs. (corr. and rec. sec. local chpt.), Delta Kappa Gamma (numerous activities, including v.p. Alpha Epsilon chpt. pres. chpt. 2d v.p. state 1st v.p. state pres. state; Ruth Frasier scholar, Achievement award). Club: Catholic Daus. Am. (chmn. edn. 1966-79, 1st vice regent chpt. 1979-81, regent 1981-85). Address: 53 Sherman Ave Glens Falls NY 12801

CLEVELAND, HELEN BARTH, teaching cons., civic worker; b. Alliance, Ohio, Aug. 28, 1904; d. Luther Martin and Ella Mae (Forest) Barth; A.B., Mt. Union Coll., 1927; postgrad. Kent State U., 1929-32, Akron U., 1946-48, N.Y. U., 1950-53; M.A., Syracuse U., 1955, Ph.D., 1958; postgrad. London Acad. Arts, 1970, U. San Juan, 1972, Acad. Arts Honolulu, 1973; m. Harold J. Cleveland, Oct. 26, 1946; children—Carol, Ronald, Marilyn, George, Donald. Tchr., cons. Alliance Public Schs., 1927-74; instr. crafts Syracuse U., 1953-60; instr. art, Sierra Leone, 1963-64; pres., dir. Chautauqua (N.Y.) Art Gallery, 1963-76, pres. emeritus, bd. dirs., 1977—; chmn. bd. missions Christ United Methodist Ch., 1981-82; bd. dirs., cons. adminstr. Mabel Hartzel Mus., Alliance, 1974—; bd. dirs. Lighthouse Gallery, Tequesta, Fla., 1970-72, Canton (Ohio) Culture Center, 1970—; trustee Alliance Art Center, Wildwood Art Gallery; mem. Keating (Mich.) Antique Village. Recipient Bronze plaque Community Alliance Bi-Centennial Com., 1976, Community Service award Am. Legion Aux., 1975; named Outstanding Alumna, Alpha Delta Pi, 1981. Mem. AARP, (chpt. pres. 1981-82), Am. Fedn. Art, Ohio Fedn. Art; life mem. NEA, Ohio Edn. Assn. Republican. Methodist. Clubs: Mt. Union College Women, Alliance Woman, Chautauqua Woman, Univ. Women, Order Eastern Star, K.T. Ladies, Shrine Ladies, DeMolay-Rainbow (Mom of Year 1959). Author: Arts and Crafts, 1955; Art in Poetry, 1959; Creativity in Elementary Schools, 1963. Home: 1192 Parkside Dr Alliance OH 44601

CLEVELAND, JEANETTE NADINE, psychology educator; b. Oakland, Calif., Nov. 25, 1955; d. Robert Walter and Kathleen Marie (Terwilliger) C.; m. Kevin Richard Murphy, July 12, 1980. B.S. cum laude, Occidental Coll., 1977; Ph.D., Pa. State U., 1982. Asst. prof. Baruch Coll., CUNY, 1982-84; asst. prof. psychology Colo. State U., Ft. Collins, 1984—; cons. U.S. Navy, 1985-86. Editor: Performance Measurement and Theory, 1982. Colo. State U. faculty research grantee, 1984. Mem. Am. Psychol. Assn., Soc. for Indsl. Organizational Psychology, Soc. for Personality and Social Psychology, Acad. Mgmt., AAAS. Home: 1701 Tanglewood Dr Fort Collins CO 80525

CLEVELAND, LESLIE CLICK, lawyer; b. Corpus Christi, Tex., May 21, 1951; d. LaVar Donald and Patricia (McIlvaine) Click; 1 dau., Elizabeth Whitney. B.A. with distinction, U. Colo.-Boulder, 1973, J.D., 1976. Bar: Colo. 1976. Assoc. Clanahan, Tanner, Downing & Knowlton, Denver, 1976-78, Martin, Knapple, Humphrey & Tharp, Boulder, 1978-80; atty. J.C. Penney Co., Denver, 1980-82; assoc. Bourke & Jacobs, P.C., Denver, 1982-84; dir., sec. Click & Geddes Lumber Co., Denver, 1980—, Cleveland Mgmt., Inc., Denver, 1981-84. Vol., mgmt. cons. Tech. Assistance Ctr., Denver, 1984, 86; bd. dirs. Jr. League of Denver, 1982, Big Sisters Colo., Denver, 1984. Mem. Colo. Bar Assn., Denver Bar Assn., ABA, Colo. Women's Bar Assn. Republican. Episcopalian. Office: Bourke & Jacobs PC 4100 E Mississippi Ave Suite 1000 Denver CO 80222

CLEVELAND, MARCIA JOAN, lawyer; b. Holyoke, Mass., May 4, 1946; d. Arthur Burdett and Alice Marion (Craven) C.; m. Daniel W. Paul; children—Ingrid Kirsten, Aaron Samuel. B.A. with honors in History, Wellesley Coll., 1968; J.D., Yale U., 1971. Staff atty. Queens Legal Service, L.I., 1971-72; coordinating atty. Commn. Action for Legal Service, N.Y.C., 1972-74; sr. staff atty. Natural Resources Def. Counsel, N.Y.C., 1974-79; bur. chief Environ. Protection Bur., N.Y. Atty. Gen.'s Office, N.Y.C., 1979-84; asst. atty. gen. Maine Atty. Gen.'s office, 1985—; adj. prof. Columbia Sch. Pub. Health, N.Y.C., 1979-80, Rutgers Law Sch., Newark, N.J., 1982-84. Mem. exec. com. Ind. Neighborhood Democrats, Bklyn., 1969-76.

CLEVELAND, PATRICIA JEAN, nurse educator; b. Royston, Ga., Sept. 26, 1944; d. Hugh Dorsey and Doris Jean (Welborn) C. Lic. Practical Nurse diploma Lively Sch. Practical Nursing, Tallahassee, 1963; R.N., Birmingham Baptist Hosp. Sch. Nursing, 1967; B.S. Nursing, U. Ala., 1972, M.S.Nursing, 1975. Practical nurse Washington County Hosp., Chipley, Fla., 1963-64; doctor's office nurse, Chipley, 1964; nursing asst. Birmingham Bapt. Hosp., 1965-67, staff nurse, 1967-72; clin. assoc. U. Ala. Sch. Nursing, Birmingham, 1973-74, instr., 1975-77, asst. prof. nursing, 1977—. Mem. nursing services com. Birmingham chpt. ARC, 1983—, co-chmn., 1980-81, co-chmn. com. to plan activities for retarded adults, 1981—; sec. Concerned Citizens for Better Strip Mining Legislation, Morris, Ala., 1977-78. Mem. Am. Nurses Assn., Nat. League Nursing, Ala. Heart Assn., U. Ala. Sch. Nursing Alumni Assn. (dir. 1983—, chmn. newsletter com. 1975—). Democrat. Baptist. Office: U Ala Sch Nursing University Sta Birmingham AL 35294

CLEVELAND, PEGGY R., cytotechnologist; b. Cannelton, Ind., Dec. 9, 1929; d. —Pat— Clarence Francis and Alice Marie (Hall) Richey; cert. U. Louisville, 1956; B. Health Sci., U. Louisville, 1984; m. Peter Leslie Cleveland, Nov. 25, 1948 (dec. 1973); children—Pamela Cleveland Litch, Paula Cleveland Bertloff, Peter L. Cytotechnologist cancer survey project NIH, Louisville, 1956-59; chief cytotechnologist Parker Cytology Lab., Inc., Louisville, 1959-75; mgr. cytology dept. Am. Biomed. Corp., 1976-78, Nat. Health Labs., Inc., Louisville, 1978—; clin. instr. cytology Sch. Allied Health U. Louisville, 1980—, cytology adv. com., 1980-81, chmn., 1982, ednl. coordinator Nat. Health Labs., Inc. with cytology program U. Louisville; owner, operator Broke N. Bent Farm thoroughbred horse breeding and racing. Mem. Am. Soc. Clin. Pathologist (cert. cytotechnologist), Internat. Acad. Cytology (cert. cytotechnologist), Am. Soc. Cytology (pilot program continuing edn. certification), Horseman's Benevolent and Protective Assn. Democrat. Roman Catholic. Home: Route 1 Box 393 Lanesville IN 47136 Office: Nat Health Labs Inc 310 E Broadway Louisville KY 40202

CLEVELAND, SUSAN ELIZABETH, medical librarian; b. Plainfield, N.J., Mar. 14, 1946; d. Robert Astbury and Grace Ann (Long) Williamson; m. Stuart Craig Cleveland, Aug. 21, 1971; children—Heather Elizabeth, Catherine Elisa. B.A., Douglass Coll., 1968; M.L.S., Rutgers U., 1969. Cert. med. librarian. Acquisitions librarian Jefferson U., Phila., 1970-71; biomed. librarian VA Hosp., Hines, Ill., 1972; med. cataloger U. Ariz., Tucson, 1973-74; library dir. Univ. Hosp., Phila., 1974—; cons., Phila., 1974—. Recipient Legion of Honor, Chapel of 4 Chaplains, 1979; USPHS fellow, 1969-70. Mem. Med. Library Assn., Spl. Library Assn., Phila. Chpt. Med. Library Assn. (membership com.). Club: Caravan. Home: 612 N Hobart Dr Laurel Springs NJ 08021 Office: Hospital Univ Pa 3400 Spruce St Philadelphia PA 19104

CLEVENGER, PENELOPE, association executive; b. Denver, Dec. 6, 1940; d. Harold Friedland and Charlotte (Glatt) Friedland Beskin; m. Willie K. Clevenger, Oct. 15, 1961 (div.). A.A., Stephens Coll., 1960. Office mgr. Malcolm S. Gerald, Chgo., 1977-79; personnel mgr. Rolm/Midwest, Chgo., 1979-82; office adminstr. Nutech Engrs., Chgo., 1982-83; office mgr. Am. Acad. Orthopaedic Surgeons, Chgo., 1983-85; dir. adminstrn. U.S. Telecommunications Suppliers Assn., Chgo., 1985—. Bd. dirs. Ctr. Tng. and Rehab. of Disabled, Chgo., 1981-84; vol. Northwestern Meml. Hosp., 1985—. Mem. Am. Soc. Personnel Adminstrn. Democrat. Jewish. Home: 233 E Wacker Dr Apt 3913 Chicago IL 60601 Office: US Telecommunications Suppliers Assn Chicago IL

CLEVENGER, SANDRA KAY, educator; b. Grand Rapids, Mich., Aug. 24, 1947; d. Philip and Beverly Jane (Storz) Elve; A.A., Grand Rapids Jr. Coll., 1967; B.A., Mich. State U., 1973, M.A. in Spanish, 1974; Ph.D. candidate NYU, 1976—; children—Tracy Jo, Amy Sue; m. Charles Clevenger, May 27, 1983. Grad. asst. Mich. State U., 1973-75; instr. Calvin Coll., Grand Rapids, 1975-81, asst. prof., 1981-83, assoc. prof., 1983—. Mem. Am. Assn. Tchrs. Spanish and Portuguese. Home: 1981 South Shore Dr Holland MI 49423 Office: Spanish Dept Calvin College Grand Rapids MI 49506

CLEVENSON, DEENA, community activist, musician; b. Laconia, N.H., Aug. 21, 1947; d. Henry and Rita (Carpenter) Barrie C. M.A., U. N.H., 1970. Student dir. Syracuse (N.Y.) U., 1965-66; author, percussionist U. N.H., Durham, 1966-70, mus. dir., 1970-74; mus. dir. Theater-by-the-Sea, Portsmouth, N.H., 1974-78; courier Compucraft, South San Francisco, Calif., 1978-79; vol. coordinator San Francisco Women's Bldg., 1979—; cons. San Francisco Women's Ctrs., 1979-83, fundraiser, 1979-83, spl. events coordinator, 1979-83. Writer children's musicals. Mem. Alice B. Toklas Democratic Soc., San Francisco, 1983. Recipient Vol. award J. C. Penney, San Francisco, 1981, 82; Recognition of Outstanding Contbn. award Women's Found., San Francisco, 1982, 83. Office: San Francisco Women's Ctrs San Francisco CA

CLEVER, ELAINE COX, information services consultant; b. N.Y.C.; d. Russell Scarlott and Estelle Ruth (Gilliland) Cox; B.A., Pa. State U., 1944; M.S., Drexel U., 1961; Cert. IBM Systems Research Inst., 1962; postgrad. Drexel U., 1976-78; m. Fred E. Clever, Feb. 18, 1944; 1 son, Eric Conrad. Instr. reading Avon Sch., Barrington, N.J., 1954-59; librarian Woodland Sch. Barrington, 1959-63; librarian Haddon (N.J.) High Sch., 1963-64; head circulation dept. Temple U. Library, Phila., 1964-81; curator spl. collections WPVI-TV, 1981—; v.p. Berrywood Internat., Inc., 1984—; ptnr. Answers/Info. Brokers, 1982—. Office Edn. grantee, 1969-70. Mem. AAUP (membership chmn. 1979—, nat. council 1980-83, v.p. chpt.), Nat. Assn. Women Bus. Owners, Nat. Com. Pay Equity (collective bargaining and organizing com.), Nat. Librarians Assn. (cert. standards com.), Theta Sigma Phi, Beta Phi Mu. Mem. Society of Friends. Club: Engrs. (Phila.). Office: Answers/Info Brokers PO Box 2194 Haddonfield NJ 08033

CLEWIS, CHARLOTTE WRIGHT STAUB, educator; b. Pitts., Aug. 20, 1935; d. Schirmer Chalfant and Charlotte Wright (Rodgers) Staub; student Memphis State Coll., 1953-54, U. Wis., 1957-59; B.A., Newark State Coll., 1963; M.A.T., Loyola Marymount U., 1974; m. John Edward Clewis, Aug. 11, 1954; 1 dau., Charlotte Wright. Asst. to dir., housemother Leota Sch. and Camp, Evansville, Wis., 1957-59; tchr. math. Rahway Jr. High Sch. (N.J.), 1963-70; tchr. math. Torrance (Calif.) Unified Sch. Dist., 1970—, coordinator math. dept., 1977—, mem. math. steering com., 1978-83, 86—, mem. proficiency exam writing com., 1977—; mem. instructional materials rev. panel State of Calif., 1986. Sec., pres. Larga Vista Property Owners Assn., 1975-84; mem. Rolling Hills Estates City Celebration Com., 1975-81; treas. adult leaders YMCA, Metuchen, N.J., 1967-69; bd. dirs. Peninsula Symphony Assn., 1978-84; commr. Rolling Hills Estates Parks and Activities, 1981—, chmn., 1985. Named Tchr. of Year, Rahway Jr. High Sch., 1966; recipient Appreciation award PTA, 1984. Mem. Nat. Council Tchrs. Math., Calif. Math. Council. Club: Phidippides Track (sec. 1980-82, pres. 1982-83) (Los Angeles). Marathon runner. Home: 1 Gaucho Dr Rolling Hills Estates CA 90274 Office: 23751 Nancy Lee Ln Torrance CA 90505

CLIFFORD, ETH, author, editor; b. N.Y.C., Dec. 25, 1915; m. David Rosenberg, Oct. 18, 1941; 1 dau., Zipporah. Editor, David-Stewart Pub. Co., Indpls., 1961—; cons. editor, author Unified Coll. Press, Indpls., 1974—; lectr. on children's books. Author: (juveniles) Red is Never a Mouse, 1960; (with Willis Peterson) Wapiti, 1961; (with Raymond Carlson The Wind Has Scratchy Fingers, 1961; The Magnificent Myths of Man, 1972; The Year of the Three Legged Deer (Booklist award Friends of Am. Writers 1973), 1972; Search for the Crescent Moon, 1973; Burning Star, 1974; The Wild One, 1974; Show Me Missouri, 1975; The Cures of the Moonraker, 1977; The Rocking Chair Rebellion, 1978; Look at the Moon, Help I'm a Prisoner in the Library; The Killer Swan (Library of Congress Children's Book of Yr. 1980); The Dastardly Murder of Dirty Pete; (adult books) Go Fight City Hall (included in anthology), 1949; Uncle Julius and the Angel with Heartburn (included in anthology), 1951; contbg. editor and/or author spl. materials for ednl. books, encys., dictionaries. Mem. Authors Guild, Children's Reading Round Table, Soc. Children's Book Writers, Book Group of S. Fla. Address: care Scott Meredith Lit Agy 845 3d Ave New York NY 10022

CLIFFORD, GERALDINE JONCICH, educator, history researcher; b. San Pedro, Calif., Apr. 17, 1931; d. Marion and Geraldine Marie (Mustacich) Joncich; m. William F. Clifford, July 12, 1969. A.B., UCLA, 1954, M.Ed., 1957; Ed.D., Columbia U., 1961. Cert. tchr., Calif. Tchr. pub. schs., San Lorenzo, Calif., 1954-56, Escuela Bella Vista, Maracaibo, Venezuela, 1967-68; research asst. Inst. Lang. Arts, Tchrs. Coll., Columbia U., N.Y.C., 1959-61; lectr. U. Calif., Santa Barbara, 1961-62; asst. prof., assoc. prof. U. Calif., Berkeley, 1962-74, prof. sch. edn., 1974—, dept. chmn., 1978-81, acting dean sch. edn., 1980-81, 82. Author: The Sane Positivist: A Biography of Edward L. Thorndike, 1968, 83; The Shape of American Education, 1957. Fellow Guggenheim Found., 1965; humanities fellow Rockefeller Found., 1977; research grantee Spencer Found., 1974-77; recipient Radcliffe Coll. research award, 1982. Mem. History of Edn. Soc. (pres. 1976-77, bd. dirs. 1973-75), Am. Ednl. Research Assn. (v.p. 1973-75), Am. Hist. Assn., Am. Ednl. Studies Assn. Democrat. Office: Dept Edn Univ Calif Berkeley CA 94720

CLIFT, ULYSSINE GWENDOLYN GIBSON (MRS. JOSEPH WILLIAM CLIFT), social worker; b. Port Arthur, Tex., Aug. 12, 1937; d. Ulysses Grant and Matilda Louise (McShann) Gibson; B.A., Fisk U., 1958; M.A., U. Chgo., 1960; m. Joseph William Clift, Aug. 10, 1963; children—Kory Grant, Nathalie Louise-Gibson. Med. Social worker social service dept. U. Tex. Med. Br., Galveston, 1960-65; caseworker Family Service, Berkeley, Calif., 1965-67; dist. dir. Family and Childrens Service Assn., Dayton, Ohio, 1967-69; caseworker, field work supr. Family Service, Berkeley, Calif., 1969-72; field work supr. U. Calif., Berkeley, 1969-72; pvt. practice, 1972—Chmn. function and service com., Lincoln Center, Oakland; bd. dirs. Lincoln Child Fin. sec. No. Calif. Med., Dental and Pharm. Assn. Aux.; sec.), Sinkler-Miller Med. Assn. Aux.; vol. Samuel Merritt Hosp., Oakland, Am. Heart Assn. Lic. clin. social worker. Mem. Nat. Assn. Social Workers, Acad. Cert. Social Workers, No. Calif. Med., Dental, Pharm. Assn. Aux. (fin. sec.), Sinkler-Miller Med. Assn. Aux. (sec.), Alpha Kappa Delta, Alpha Kappa Alpha. Home: 14030 Broadway Terrace Oakland CA 94611 Office: 3300 Webster St Suite 308 Oakland CA 94609

CLIFTON, ANNE RUTENBER, psychotherapist; b. New Haven, Dec. 11, 1938; d. Ralph Dudley and Cleminette (Downing) Rutenber; B.A., Smith Coll., 1960, M.S.W., 1962; m. Roger Lambert Clifton, Sept. 9, 1961; 1 dau., Dawn Anne. Psychiat. case worker adult psychiatry unit Tufts-New Eng. Med. Center, Boston, 1962-68, supr. students, 1967-68; pvt. practice psychotherapy, Cambridge, Mass., 1966—; supr. med. students, staff social workers out-patient psychiatry Tufts New Eng. Med. Center, 1973—, also mem. exec. bd. Women's Resource Center, interim co-dir., 1986—. Lic. clin. social worker, Mass. asst. clin. prof. psychiatry Tufts U. Med. Sch., 1974—, research dept. psychiatry, 1966-68, 73, 77—. Mem. Acad. Cert. Social Workers, Nat. Assn. Social Workers, Phi Beta Kappa, Sigma Xi. Clubs: Cambridge Tennis, Mt. Auburn Tennis. Contbr. articles to profl. jours. Home: 126 Homer St Newton Center MA 02159 Office: 51 Brattle St Cambridge MA 02138

CLIFTON, CATHY MATTHEWS, printing company executive; b. St. Johns, Mich., Sept. 15, 1948; d. James Coffey and Jean (Crowell) Matthews; m. Ronald Lynne Clifton, Apr. 3, 1971 (div. Oct. 1977); m. Richard Douglas Hyman, Feb. 6, 1983. B.A., U. Ariz., 1971. Asst. pub. relations dir. C.W. Pine & Assocs., Phoenix, 1971-73; account exec. Morton & O'Shea, Phoenix, 1973-75; ptnr. Informative Image, Phoenix, 1975-77; account exec. Don Frank & Assocs., Marina Del Rey, Calif., 1977-79; sales rep. Forms Engring. Co., La Palma, Calif., 1979-81, mgr., San Francisco, 1981-84, v.p. sales mgr., 1983—, also dir.; chmn. San Francisco Direct Mktg. Seminar, 1982-83. Mem. NOW, San Francisco Advt. Club (dir. direct mktg. dept. 1982—, pres. direct mktg. dept. 1984-85, bd. dirs. 1986-87; Masters award 1983). Democrat. Club: Sierra. Home: 60 Olive Ave Larkspur CA 94939 Office: Forms Engring Co 300 Broadway St #23 San Francisco CA 94133

CLIFTON, JUDY RAELENE, assn. adminstr.; b. Safford, Ariz., Nov. 8, 1946; d. Ralph Newton and Fayrene (Goodner) Johnson; student Biola Coll., 1964-65; B.A. in Christian Edn., Southwestern Coll., 1970; m. Mar. 5, 1982. Editorial asst. Accent Publications, Denver, 1970-73; expediter Phelps Dodge Corp., Douglas, Ariz., 1974-78; exec. asst. So. Ariz. Internat. Livestock Assn., Inc., Tucson, 1978-80; supt.'s sec. Phelps Dodge Corp., 1981—; sec. exec. com. PAC, Phelps Dodge, 1985—. Mem. adv. bd. Ariz. Lung Assn.; leader 4-H, Douglas; mem. Republican Nat. Com., 1978—, Conservative Caucus, 1979—. Recipient Am. Legion Good Citizen award, 1964, DAR award, 1964. Mem. Nat. Assn. Female Execs., Inc., So. Ariz. Internat. Livestock Assn., AAUW, Eagle Forum, Freedom Found., N.Mex. Eagle Forum, Sigma Lamba Delta. Baptist. Clubs: Trunk & Tusk, Pima County Republican, Centre Ct., Westerners Internat., So. Ariz. Depression Glass, Tucson Tennis, Rep. Senatorial. Home: PO Box 301 Animas NM 88020

CLIFTON, PATRICIA DAVIS, educational administrator; b. Miami, Fla., Apr. 3, 1945; d. Roy Lee and Rachel Susan (Pinder) Davis; m. Ivery D. Clifton, May 28, 1967; 1 dau., Kalisa Nicole. B.S., Tuskegee Inst., 1967; M.Ed., U. Ill., 1975; Ed.S., U. Ga., 1979. Tchr., Petersburg Pub. Schs. (Va.), 1967-70, Prince Georges County Pub. Schs. (Md.), 1970-71, Urbana Sch. #116 (Ill.), 1972-75; dir. reading center Champaign Schs. (Ill.), 1975-76; reading supr. Clarke County Sch. (Ga.) Dist. 1976-80, coordinator elem. and middle schs., Athens, 1980-83, coordinator middle schs., 1982—. Mem. Internat. Reading Assn., Assn. Supervision and Curriculum Devel., Phi Delta Kappa, Phi Kappa Phi, Kappa Delta Pi, Delta Sigma Theta. Democrat. Methodist. Home: 305 Idylwood Dr Athens GA 30605 Office: Clarke County Sch Dist 500 College Ave Athens GA 30601

CLINE, CAROLYN JOAN, plastic and reconstructive surgeon; b. Boston; d. Paul S. and Elizabeth (Flom) Cline. B.A., Wellesley Coll., 1962; M.A., U. Cin., 1966; Ph.D., Washington U., 1970; diploma Washington Sch. Psychiatry, 1972; M.D., U. Miami (Fla.) 1975. Research asst. Harvard Dental Sch., Boston, 1962-64; research asst. physiology Laser Lab., Children's Hosp. Research Found., Cin., 1964, psychology dept. U. Cin., 1964-65; intern in clin. psychology St. Elizabeth's Hosp., Washington, 1966-67; psychologist Alexandria (Va.) Community Mental Health Ctr., 1967-68; research fellow NIH, Washington, 1968-69; chief psychologist Kingsbury Ctr. for Children, Washington, 1969-73; sole practice clin. psychology, Washington, 1970-73; assoc. Nat. Acad. Scis., 1974; intern internal medicine U. Wis. Hosps., Ctr. for Health Sci., Madison, 1975-76; resident in surgery Stanford U. Med. Ctr., 1976-78; fellow microvascular surgery dept. surgery U. Calif.-San Francisco, 1978-79; resident in plastic surgery St. Francis Hosp., San Francisco, 1979-82; practice medicine, specializing in plastic and reconstructive surgery, San Francisco, 1982—. Contbr. articles to profl. jours. Address: 450 Sutter St Suite 2432 San Francisco CA 94108

CLINE, CLEO RUTH, insurance consultant, broker; b. Hutchinson, Kans., Feb. 2, 1929; d. Earl Isaac and Lena (Little) Rounkles; m. Jack Byron Cline, Dec. 15, 1946. Grad. in ins. Am. Inst., 1977. Supr. Auto Club So. Calif., Los Angeles, 1947-54; underwriter Employees Mut. Des Moines, Wichita, Kans., 1954-56; various positions Crum Forster Co., Los Angeles, 1956-84; spl. acct. mgr. Indsl. Indemnity, Pasadena, Calif., 1979-84; ins. broker, instr., cons. Cleo Cline Cons., 1984—. Cons., contbr. to The Umbrella Book, 1978. Mem. fund-raising com. Blind Sports, San Francisco, 1977. Named Calif. Ins. Woman of Yr., Profl. Ins. Assn., Los Angeles, 1977. Mem. Nat. Soc. C.P.C.U.s (risk mgmt. sect., internat. ins. sect., officer San Gabriel chpt., coordinator 1st satellite teleconf. nat. seminar 1985, western regional bd. dirs. 1985—), Nat. Assn. Ins. Women, Internat. Soc. C.P.C.U.s (chmn. com. 1977-83). Republican. Office: 500 Shatto Pl Suite 510 Los Angeles CA 90020

CLINE, JOYCE NAN, sporting goods company executive; b. Raymondville, Mo., Feb. 13, 1929; d. Andy P. and Hazel Irene (Deweese) Johnson; m. Donald Holt White, Feb. 15, 1948 (dec. Sept. 1966); m. 2d, Harold Lloyd Cline, May 31, 1969. Diploma Draughons Bus. Coll., 1948. Gen. office staff Rawlings Sporting Goods, Willow Springs, Mo., 1956-57, office mgr., 1957-72, asst. plant mgr., 1972-82, personnel mgr., Fenton, Mo., 1982—. Bd. dirs. Willow Springs Ambulance Bd., 1970-74. Democrat. Methodist. Club: PEO. Lodge: Order of Rainbow (worthy advisor 1941-45). Avocations: hiking; wild flower enthusiast. Home: Route 1 Box 255 Willow Springs MO 65793 Office: Rawlings Sporting Goods Co 1859 Intertech Dr Fenton MO 63026

CLINE, JUDY ELIZABETH, writer, artist; b. Franklin, Ky., Dec. 24, 1944; d. Drew Saunders and Reba Mae (Webb) Gibson; student David Lipscomb

Coll., 1963-64, Western Ky. U., 1965-66; m. Oliver Lawson Cline, Jan. 7, 1967; 1 dau., Cheryl-renee. Adminstrv. asst. to purchasing mgr. Kendall Co., Chgo. div., 1964-65, adminstrv. asst. to mgr., Franklin, 1966-67; expeditor, asst. mgr. Malone and Hyde Distbn. Center, Franklin, 1976-81; with engring. dept. Sumner Mfg., Franklin, 1982—; writer, artist Whimsies Unltd., Franklin, 1975—; exhibited in group shows including Parthenon, Nashville, 1975-76, Berry Hill, Frankfort, Ky., 1978, Capitol Bldg., Carson City, Nev., 1979; cons. Right to Read Ednl Program., Franklin, 1971-81. Speaker, Ky. Democratic Conv., Frankfort, 1980; del. Dem. Nat. Conv., N.Y.C., 1980; alt. del. White House Conf. on Families, 1980; leader 4-H Club. Mem. Nat. Soc. Pub. Poets, So. Ky. Guild Artists and Craftsmen, Right to Life Orgn., Barren River Area Arts Commn. Mem. Ch. of Christ. Clubs: Ky. Extension Homemakers. Asst. editor Voices, 1965-66. Home and Office: 613 Sunnyside Dr Franklin KY 42134

CLINE, PAULINE M., educational administrator; b. Seattle, Aug. 25, 1947; d. Paul A. and Margaret V. (Reinhart) C. B.A. in Edn., Seattle U., 1969, M.Ed., 1975, Ed.D., 1983. Cert. tchr., prin., Wash. Tchr., Marysville High Sch., Wash., 1969-70; tchr./adminstr. Blanchet High Sch., Seattle, 1970-78; asst. prin. Edmonds High Sch., Wash., 1978-84; prin. College Place Middle Sch., Edmonds, 1984-85, Mountlake Terrace High Sch., Wash., 1985—; cons. Mem. Mountlake Terrace Centennial Commn., 1985—; chair Assumption Sch. Bd., Seattle, 1977. IDEA Kettering fellow, 1984, 86. Mem. South Snohomish County C. of C., Nat. Assn. Secondary Sch. Prins., Assn. Wash. Sch. Prins., Edmonds Prins. Assn., Assn. Supervision and Curriculum Devel., Phi Delta Kappa. Roman Catholic. Club: Women's University (Seattle). Avocations: skiing; kayaking; backpacking. Office: Mountlake Terrace High Sch 21801 44th Ave W Mountlake Terrace WA 98043

CLINE, RUTH ELEANOR HARWOOD, translator; b. Middletown, Conn., Oct. 31, 1946; d. Burton Henry and Eleanor May (Cash) Harwood; A.B., Smith Coll., 1968; M.A., Rutgers U., 1969; cert. translation from French, Georgetown U., 1978; m. William R. Cline, June 10, 1967; children—Alison, Marian. Translator, U.S. Dept. State, Washington, 1975—. Mem. Am. Translators Assn. (sec. accreditation com.), MLA, Internat. Arthurian Soc. Episcopalian. Translator English verse: Perceval; or the Story of the Grail (Chretien de Troyes), 1983; Yvain; or the Knight with the Lion, 1975. Home: 5315 Oakland Rd Chevy Chase MD 20815

CLINE, STARR, educator; b. Bklyn., Feb. 27, 1937; d. Albert and Any (Barocas) Funess; B.A. magna cum laude, Molloy Coll., 1974; postgrad. Hofstra U., 1977, Ed.D., Columbia U., 1985; m. Jerome Z. Cline, Apr. 27, 1957; children—Adam, Larry. Tchr., Oceanside (N.Y.) Public Schls., 1974-81, tchr. gifted elem. program, Herricks Public Schs., 1981—; coordinator Inst. on Gifted and Talented, Columbia U. for Three Village Sch. Dist., Setauket, L.I., 1978, asst. coordinator summer inst., 1978; field reader U.S. Dept. HEW, 1978; adj. instr. Molloy Coll., Hofstra U.; regional coordinator Advocacy for Gifted and Talented Edn., 1984; lectr., cons. in field. Pres., Ocean Lea Civic Assn., 1977; adv. com. N.Y.C. Gifted Ed., 1979. Winner 1st, 3d prizes Creative Problem Solving Inst., Buffalo, 1979; Pub. Service TV Tri-State award, N.Y., N.J., Conn., 1980, others. Mem. Advocacy Gifted and Talented Edn. (dir.), World Council Gifted and Talented Children, Nat. Assn. Gifted Children, L.I. Soc. Gifted and Talented, Assn. for Supervision and Curriculum Devel. Clubs: Kiwanettes (trustee 1982, pres. 1985). Contbr. articles to profl. jours.; author: Independent Study, 1980; Teaching for Talent, 1984. Home: 280 Concord Ave Oceanside NY 11572

CLINGERMAN, ARLENE MARIE NICK, service company official; b. Detroit, Feb. 13, 1944; d. James George and Irene Marie (Fisher) Nick; m. Richard Galen Clingerman, Mar. 12, 1969 (div. 1979); children—Nita, Linda, David, Jimmy, Tony. Student in nursing Mich. State U., 1962-63; B.A., Capitol U., 1983. Dir. clinic ops. Miami Valley Hosp., Ohio, 1973-74; dir. materials mgmt. Marion Gen. Hosp., Ind., 1974-79, Good Samaritan Hosp., Ohio, 1979-81; exec. dir. Womanline Inc., Ohio, 1981-83; exec. dir. ServiceMaster Industries Inc., Chgo., 1984-86; contracts administrator N.Y. Power Authority, 1986—; cons. and lectr. in field. Subject article in newspaper. Mem. Safe Homes Program, Mamaroneck, N.Y., 1985—, bd. dirs. Mamoroneck Pub. Schs., 1983—; bd. dirs. Tenant's Council, Mamoroneck, 1986—; nat. chmn. Helping Hand Program. Mem. Nat. Assn. Female Execs., Law and Mgmt. Club, Women's Bus. Orgn. Republican. Roman Catholic and Greek Orthodox. Avocations: Golf, reading, bicycling; sports; home restoration. Home: 518 Stanley Ave Mamaroneck NY 10543

CLINKSCALES, ANNA LEE JAMES, civic leader, public relations consultant; b. Balt., Aug. 8, 1931; d. Jesse and Margaret James; children—Alfred Jr., Angela, Antonio Jose. B.A., U. Md., 1973. Pres., Am. White House, Balt.; pres., founder Abraham Lincoln Reading and Tutoring Group, Balt.; founder, dir. Community Services Info Ctr., Balt.; owner Original Design by Anna (Swedish embroidery), Balt., 1976-77. Writer pilot program Stay In Sch. (Youth Opportunity award Pres. Lyndon B. Johnson, 1967). Convenor First Job Corps for Girls, Balt. (cited by OEC for outstanding service); chmn. first coordinating council Women in Community Service; former mem. steering com. Interracial and Interreligious Council W. Balt.; former bd. dirs. Balt. chpt. NAACP, Balt. Neighborhoods Inc., Greater Balt. Com., Allendale-Lynhurst Neighborhood Assn.; pres. Md., Nat. Council Negro Women. Recipient award Nat. Council Negro Women, 1967; honored by Pres. U.S., 1972, 73. Mem. Colonial and Indian Am. Cultures Internat. (coordinator, founder, dir. 1983), Colonial and Indian Am. Crafts Internat. (coordinator, founder, dir. 1983), Cultural Relations Internat. (coordinator 1983), Hobbies and Crafts Assn. (founder, dir.). Democrat. Roman Catholic.

CLINTON, LINDA PENELOPE HAMILTON, editor; b. Bklyn., Dec. 23, 1949; d. Alfred M. and Leona M. (Stokes) H.; A.A., Queensborough Community Coll., 1969; B.A., CCNY, 1971; m. Marcus Bethea Clinton, Mar. 3, 1973; children—Marcus Hamilton, John Christopher. Paralegal-adminstrv. asst. Simpson Thacher & Bartlett, N.Y.C., 1971-74; asst. editor McCall's Mag., N.Y.C., 1974-78; sr. editor Working Mother Mag., N.Y.C., 1978—. Mem. Am. Soc. Mag. Editors, Delta Sigma Theta. Office: 230 Park Ave New York NY 10169

CLIPSHAM, JACQUELINE ANN, artist; b. Welwyn Garden City, Hertfordshire, Eng. (parents Am. citizens), July 27, 1936; d. George Frederick and Helene Lucille (Lees) C.; B.A., Carleton Coll., 1958; postgrad. Universita per Stranieri, Perugia, Italy, 1959; M.A., Western Res. U., 1962. Mem. Clay Art Center, Port Chester, N.Y., 1963-66; dir. ceramics program and art workshop CORE Community Center, Sumter, S.C., 1965; mem. faculty Bklyn. Mus. Art Sch., 1968-79, Essex County Coll., Newark, 1979-80; mem. Atlantic Gallery, N.Y.C., 1974-83; mem. crafts task force Nat. Endowment for Arts, 1980; Culpeper Found. project coordinator, dept. community edn. Met. Mus. Art, N.Y.C., 1981-82; mem. grants panel for crafts N.J. State Council Arts, 1982; one-woman exhbn.: Willoughby (Ohio) Fine Arts Ctr., 1982; works exhibited: Cleve. Mus., Bklyn. Mus., Mus. Contemporary Crafts, N.Y.C., Butler Inst. Art, Youngstown, Ohio, Hunterdon Art Center, Clinton, N.J., Greenwich House Pottery, N.Y.C., Pratt Inst., Bklyn., Atlantic Gallery, N.Y.C., 1980, Webster Coll., St. Louis, 1981, Clay Art Ctr., Sound Shore Gallery, Port Chester, N.Y., 1983, Gemans Van Eck Gallery, N.Y.C., 1983, Thorpe Intermedia Gallery, Sparkill, N.Y., 1984, N.Y. Pub. Library, 1984; work loaned to Dept. Acad. Affairs, Met. Mus. Art, 1978; cons. dept. Am. art Met. Mus. Art, N.Y.C.; represented in permanent collections: Cleve. Mus. Art. Recipient awards for ceramics and sculpture Butler Inst. Am. Art, 1963, 64, 65, nat. merit award for ceramics Mus. Contemporary Crafts, 1966; N.Y. State Council Arts grantee, 1982-83. Mem. Coll. Art Assn., Am. Crafts Council, Women's Caucus for Art, Artists Equity N.Y., Alumni Assn. Cleve. Inst. Art, Empire State Crafts Alliance, N.J. Designer Craftsmen. Featured in Women Artists' Book, Women's Caucus for Art Exhbn., 1982, Artists' Books, From the Traditional to the Avant Garde, 1982, also govt. publ. on employment of disabled; reviewer NEA accessibility guidelines. Home: 4015 7th Ave Apt 5 Brooklyn NY 11232 Studio: PO Box 387 Califon NJ 07830

CLISBY, DORIANE LEIGH, accountant; b. Pitts., Sept. 6, 1958; d. Roosevelt and Constance (Boxley) Clisby, Jr. B.S. in Bus. Adminstrn., Clarion U., 1980. Fiduciary and estate tax acct. Pitts. Nat. Bank, 1980-82; staff acct. Houston Grand Opera, 1982-84; fund acct. AIM Mgmt., Houston, 1984—. Group leader Single Adult Ministry, Houston, 1983. Office: AIM Mgmt 11 Greenway Plaza Suite 1919 Houston TX 77046

CLIVER (KRIENKE), KENDRA-JEAN, art dealer, artist; b. Plainfield, N.J.; d. Edwin Kendall and Estelle (Blaine) C., m. Douglas Elliott Krienke, July 21, 1973. B.A., Drew U., postgrad. NAD. Freelance portrait painter, 1970-75; art restorer, 1970—; art framer, designer, 1974—; owner, mgr. Whistler Gallery, Inc., Basking Ridge, N.J., 1974—; arranger, cataloguer artist exhbns.; commd. Douglas Coll., U.S. Steel Co. Recipient Purchase award Drew U., 1968. Office: PO Box 362 Basking Ridge NJ 07920

CLOPINE, MARJORIE SHOWERS, librarian; b. N.Y.C., June 25, 1914; d. Ralph Walter and Angelina (Jackson) Showers; B.A., Pa. State U., 1935; M.S., Drexel U., 1936; M.S., Columbia U., 1949. Gen. asst. Library, Drexel U., Phila., 1937-42; asst. librarian Gen. Chem. Div., Allied Chem. Corp., Morristown, N.J., 1943-46; bibliographer U.S. Office Tech. Services, Washington, 1946; med. librarian VA Hosp., Washington, 1946-49; asst. librarian U.S. Naval Obs., Washington, 1949-52, librarian, 1952-63; asso. librarian Bethany (W.Va.) Coll., 1967-69; asso. librarian Marine Research Lab. Fla. Dept. Natural Resources, St. Petersburg, 1971-73; cons. in astronomy Dewey Decimal Classification Editorial Office, Library of Congress, Washington, 1956. Chmn., Community Improvement program, Fla. Dist. 14, Gen. Fedn. Women's Clubs, 1980-82; library cons. Garden Center, Oglebay Park, Wheeling, W.Va., 1965-69. Alice B. Kroeger Meml. scholar, 1935-36. Mem. AAUW, Nat. Assn. Ret. Fed. Employees, Spl. Libraries Assn., Beta Phi Mu. Clubs: Friends of the Arts and Scis., Internat. House, Woman's of Sarasota. Contbr. articles to profl. jours. Home and office: 8400 Vamo Rd Apt 1138 Sarasota FL 33581

CLOSE, ELIZABETH SCHEU, architect; b. Vienna, Austria, June 4, 1912 (came to U.S. 1932, naturalized 1938); d. Gustav and Helene (Riesz) C.; student Technische Hochschule, Vienna, 1931-32; B.Arch., Mass. Inst. Tech., 1934, M.Arch., 1935; m. Winston A. Close, Apr. 11, 1938; children—Anne Miriam (Mrs. Milton Ulmer), Roy Michel, Robert Arthur. Draftsman Oscar Stonorov, Architect, Phila., 1935-36; designer Magney & Tusler, Mpls., 1936-38; ptnr., architect Close & Scheu (name changed to Elizabeth and Winston Close 1941, to Close Assocs., Inc., 1969), Mpls., 1938—; instr. Mpls. Sch. Art, 1936-37; instr. design U. Minn. Sch. Arch., 1938-39. Mem. Gov.'s Commn. on Minn.'s Future. Bd. dirs. Civic Orch. Mpls., 1951-68; bd. dirs. Minn. Opera Co.; pres. New Friends Chamber Music, 1973-74. Recipient Honor award Pub. Housing Adminstrn., 1964; hon. mention F.D. Roosevelt Meml. competition, 1960; honor award Minn. Soc. Architects, 1975; YWCA outstanding achievement award, 1983. Fellow AIA (dir. Mpls. chpt., 1964-69); mem. Minn. Soc. Architects (v.p., pres. 1983). Prin. works include Garden City Devel., Brooklyn Center, Minn., 1957; Duff House, Wayzata, Minn., 1959; variety structures Met. Med. Center Complex, 1960—, Golden Age Homes, 1960, both Mpls.; Peavey Tech. Center, Chaska, Minn., 1970; Gray Freshwater Biological Institute, 1973; Windslope Housing Project, Eden Prairie, Minn., 1978; Family Practice Clinic, Vadnais Heights, Minn., 1979; Mus. Bldg., U. Minn. Home: 1588 Fulham St Saint Paul MN 55108 Office: Close Assocs Inc 3101 E Franklin Ave Minneapolis MN 55406

CLOSE, GLENN, actress, singer; b. Greenwich, Conn.; d. William C. and Bettine C.; m. Cabot Wade (div.); m. James Marlas, Sept. 1, 1984. Grad., Coll. of William and Mary, 1974. Theatre debut in "Love for Love" at Phoenix Theatre, N.Y., 1974; other N.Y.C. theatre roles include: The Real Thing, 1984 (Tony award), Benefactors, 1986, Childhood, 1985; film roles include: "The World According to Garp", 1982, "The Big Chill", 1983, "The Natural", 1984, "The Stone Boy", 1984, "Maxie", 1985, "Jagged Edge", 1985; TV movies include: The Orphan Train, 1979, Too Far to Go, 1979, Something About Amelia, 1984, The Elephant Man, 1982; appeared in theatre musical Barnum, 1980-81. Mem. Phi Beta Kappa. Address: care Creative Artists Agency Inc 1888 Century Park East Suite 1400 Los Angeles CA 90067*

CLOSE, KAREN ELIZABETH, marketing company executive, educator; b. Chgo., Oct. 5, 1951; d. Gordon Ralph and Ruth (Kernwein) C. B.F.A. cum laude, U. Ariz., 1973. Creative dir. Progressive Communications, Colorado Springs, Colo., 1976-78; art dir. PRACO Advt., Colorado Springs, 1978-80; creative dir. Erickson-Fuller Advt., Aspen, Colo., 1980-81; pres., owner Close Communications, Denver, 1982—; instr. evenings Colo. Inst. of Art, Denver, 1982—. Designer corp. identity packages. Big sister Big Sisters/Little Sisters, United Way, Denver, 1986. Mem. Nat. Safety Council, Denver C. of C., Kappa Alpha Theta (scholarship chmn.). Episcopalian. Club: Denver Athetic (medalist). Avocations: painting; play piano and guitar; skiing; tennis. Office: Close Communications 1250 14th St Denver CO 80202

CLOUDT, FLORENCE RICKER, architectural products company executive; b. Houston, July 12, 1925; d. Norman Hurd and Sallie Lee (St. Louis) Ricker; m. William Sandford Pottinger, Dec. 28, 1946 (div. Jan. 1975); children—Norman Sandford, Margaret Halliday; m. Frank Winfield Cloudt, Aug. 12, 1977 (div. May 1982). B.F.A., Sophie Newcomb Coll., 1946. Founder, pres. Florence Pottinger Nursery Sch., Atlanta, 1955-56; tchr. Montgomery County Schs., Md., 1956-60; master tchr. The Nat. Cathedral Sch., Washington, 1960-62; founder, pres. Florence Pottinger Interiors, Atlanta, 1962-78; co-founder, v.p. Focal Point, Inc., Atlanta, 1970-78, pres., 1978—; mem. decorative arts adv. bd. Nat. Trust for Hist. Preservation, Washington, 1985—. Producer pub. service TV program: Jr. League of Washington, 1957-62. Bd. dirs. Atlanta Landmarks, 1972—; sec. Roswell Hist. Soc., Ga., 1972-74; bd. advisors Atlanta Preservation Ctr., 1979, trustee, 1980—. Recipient Industry Found. award Am. Soc. Interior Designers, 1982; Outstanding Service award Atlanta Preservation Soc., 1983. Mem. Women Bus. Owners. Republican. Episcopalian. Club: Women Commerce (Atlanta). Avocations: painting; writing. Office: Focal Point Inc 2005 Marietta Rd NW Atlanta GA 30318

CLOVER, LOUISE SUZETTE, lawyer; b. Glendale, Calif., Mar. 11, 1954; d. Floyd Wesley and Sara Evelyn (Mulvehill) C. A.A., Glendale Community Coll., 1974; B.A., U. So. Calif., 1976; J.D., UCLA, 1979. Bar: Calif. 1979. Research asst. UCLA, 1978; law clk. to judges, Los Angeles, 1980-82; assoc. Adams, Duque & Hazeltine, Los Angeles, 1983—; prin. Clover Properties, Glendale, Calif., 1973—. recipient Am. Jurisprudence award Bancroft-Whitney Co., San Francisco, 1978. Mem. ABA, Los Angeles County Bar Assn. (coms.), Los Angeles Women Lawyers Assn. (bd. govs. 1981-82, appointive office 1982-83), Alpha Gamma Delta Alumnae Assn. (editor U. So. Calif. chpt. 1982-83). Democrat. Club: Altrusa. Home: 330 Lawson Pl Glendale CA 91202 Office: Adams Duque & Hazeltine 523 W 6th St Los Angeles CA 90014

CLOVIS, BARBARA FLIPSE, histopathologic technologist; b. Flushing, N.Y., Nov. 8, 1948; d. Robert Charles and Margaret Emily (Oehler) Flipse; H.T., N. Shore Hosp. Sch. Histologic Technique, 1968; student Eckerd Coll., 1970-71; m. Arnold J. Dazinis, June 3, 1978 (dec. 1980); stepchildren—Theresa Lee Dazinis, Denise Jeannette Dazinis; m. 2d, Ralph Clovis, Jan. 2, 1982; stepchildren—Ralph David, Suzanne Virginia. With Lane Bryant, Miami, Fla., 1966-67; histotechnologist N. Shore Hosp., Miami, 1967-70; mgr. thoroughbred breeding Kromor Farm, Reddick, Fla., 1971-73; histotechnologist, dir. Mid-Fla. Labs., Inc., Ocala, 1973-76; dir. Histopathology Lab., Marion Community Hosp., Ocala, 1976-80; mgr. comml. thoroughbred breeding facility Just-A-Farm, Dunnellon, Fla., 1980—; cons. dept. histopathology, Munroe Regional Med. Center, 1973-81. Youth coordinator, Holy Faith Episcopal Ch., 1981-83. Mem. Am. Soc. Clin. Pathologists, Nat. Soc. Histotechnology, Fla. Soc. Histotechnologists, Fla. Thoroughbred Breeders Assn. Republican. Episcopalian. Club: Elks (hon. mem.). Address: 11050 SW 140th Ave Dunnellon FL 32630

CLOW, MAURINE, emeritus psychology educator; b. Grafton, N.D., Sept. 30, 1908; d. Chester W. and Ellen C. (Terrill) C.; student U. N.D., 1926, 28-30; B.A., Stanford U., 1934, M.A., 1936, Ph.D., 1946; summer study Columbia U., 1942. Counselor, English tchr. Sarah Dix Hamlin Sch., San Francisco, 1935-36; resident asst. to dean of women Stanford U., 1936-38; dean women Whitman Coll., Walla Walla, Wash., 1938-46; assoc. dean students, prof. psychology U. Mont., Missoula, 1946-73, emeritus, 1973—. Recipient Matrix Table award Theta Sigma Phi, 1971. Mem. Am. Coll. Personnel Assn., Nat. Assn. Women Deans and Counselors (citation 1972), AAUW (pres. Walla Walla br., Wash. ednl. chmn. 1943-44), P.E.O., Mortar Board, Sigma Xi, Pi Lambda Theta, Psi Chi, Delta Gamma (Shield award 1972), Delta Kappa Gamma. Republican. Presbyterian (co-chmn. canvass program 1960, elder 1960—). Club: Order Eastern Star. Home: 23 Greenbrier Ln Missoula MT 59802

CLOWER, DONNA DARLENE, communications corporation executive; b. Loudon, Tenn., Jan. 23, 1956; d. Raymond Edward and Charlene Josephine (Pesterfield) C. B.B.A., Middle Tenn. State U., 1977, also postgrad, Cons., ACDS, Inc., Nashville, 1976; computer operator Rutherford Hosp., Murfreesboro, Tenn., 1976-78; cons. Earl Swensson Assocs., Nashville, 1978; personnel cons. Sanford Rose Assocs., Nashville, 1978-79; systems programmer South Central Bell Co., Nashville, 1979-84, staff mgr., 1984—. Vol., Telephone Pioneers Am., Nashville, 1979—, Spl. Olympics, Nashville, 1983—. Baptist. Home: PO Box 1771 Brentwood TN 37027 Office: South Central Bell Co PO Box 39 Nashville TN 37202

CLUTTER, MARY ELIZABETH, botanist, government official; b. Charleroi, Pa.; B.S., Allegheny Coll., 1953; M.S., U. Pitts., 1957, Ph.D. in Botany, 1960; Research assoc. Yale U., 1961-73, lectr. biology, 1965-78, sr. research assoc., 1973-78; program dir. NSF, Washington, 1976-81, sect. head, 1981-84, div. dir., 1984-85, staff dir., 1985—. Mem. AAAS, Am. Soc. Cell Biology, Am. Soc. Plant Physiologists, Soc. Devel. Biology, Assn. Women in Sci. Office: National Science Foundation 1800 G St NW Washington DC 20550

CLYBURN, ROSE MARY REED, marketing manager; b. New London, Conn., July 31, 1954; d. Raymond Morgan and Bernice Joan (Zaugg) Reed; B.S. in Zoology, U. R.I., 1976; M.B.A. in Fin., Northwe. U., 1984; m. Collins G. Clyburn, Aug. 14, 1982. Market research trainee PPG Industries Chems. Group, Pitts., 1976-77, field sales rep., Houston, 1977-78, sales rep. Chems. div., Chgo., 1978-80, sales devel. rep. splty. products unit, Chgo., 1980-83, market research assoc. Chems. Group, Pitts., 1983-86, product mgr. Chems. Group, 1986—. Advisor Pitts. Jr. Achievement, 1976-77. Mem. Soc. Plastic Engrs., Soc. Petroleum Engrs., Chem. Market Research Assn. Home: 2484 Corteland Dr Pittsburgh PA 15241 Office: One PPG Pl 35 N Pittsburgh PA 15272

COALTER AKERS, TERESA HELENA, boutique executive, radio station on-air personality; b. Olive Hill, Ky., Aug. 13, 1956; d. James Lawrence and Maude Evelyn (Burchett) Conley; m. Kyle Malcolm Coalter, Oct. 29, 1977 (div. Oct. 1984); m. Keith Akers, Apr. 4, 1985. Diploma Narrows High Sch. (Va.), 1974. Asst. mgr. Southland Corp., Falls Church, Va., 1974-76; electronic assembler Eagle Mine Corp., Narrows, 1978-79; laborer, Union steward Celeanese Corp., Narrows, 1979-82; salesperson Rest Haven Meml., Princeton, W.Va., 1977; supr. Princeton Mfg., 1976-77; salesperson, on-air personality Sta. WBDY, Bluefield, Va., 1982—; pres. New Image Boutique, Bluefield, 1984—. Active pub. relations ARC, Bluefield, 1984. Recipient Dedication award ARC 1984. Mem. Sales Exec. Club (award 1984), Nat. Assn. Female Execs. Republican. Baptist. Avocations: reading; biking; travel. Home: Glenview Estates #8 Princeton WV 24740 Office: Cherokee Bldg Suite 110 345 New St Kingsport TN 37660

COATES, DIANNE KAY, social worker; b. Adrian, Mich., Jan. 4, 1945; d. John Milton Yaw and Margaret Esther (Skinner) Yaw-Carpenter; m. Frederick Roy Coates, Nov. 22, 1975; 1 child by previous marriage, Cindi Kae McCarty. Student Jackson Bus. U., Mich., 1962-63; A.A. with honors, Macomb Community Coll., Warren, Mich., 1977; B.A. with high distinction, Madonna Coll., Livonia, Mich., 1979; M.S.W., Wayne State U., 1982; postgrad. Internat. Grad. Sch., St. Louis, 1984. Cert. social worker, Mich. Nat. service officer Mil. Order of the Purple Heart, Detroit, 1973-80; psychology technician VA Med. Ctr., Allen Park, Mich., 1980-84; clin. cons. HOMEBASE, Detroit, 1983—; clin. social worker Community Counseling Assocs., Adrian, Mich., 1983, Roseville, Mich., 1983—; group counselor Survivors of Homicide Detroit, 1981-82. Mem. Nat. Assn. Social Workers, Mich. Mental Health Assn., Social Work Assn. Madonna Coll. (co-founder), Mich. Alcohol and Addiction Assn., Wayne State U. Alumni Assn. Lodges: Ladies Aux. Mil. Order of Purple Heart (region 2 v.p. 1985-86), Ladies Aux. VFW, Ladies Aux. Disabled Am. Veterans. Home: 25214 Gratiot Box 50 Roseville MI 48066

COATES, JEAN PETTIJOHN, advertising agency executive; b. Portland, Oreg., Aug. 31, 1951; d. Elzo I. and Verona M. (McKittrick) Pettijohn; m. Michael Raymond Coates, Mar. 18, 1972; 1 child, Ashley Morgan. Student Oreg. State U., 1969-71; B.A., Portland State U., 1973. Art dir. J. Walter Thompson, San Francisco, 1975, Vicom Assocs., San Francisco, 1976-77; pres. Coates Advt. Inc., Portland, 1978—. Mem. Portland Advt. Fedn. (bd. dirs. 1983—, Rita Howard Trombly award 1980). Republican. Presbyterian. Lodge: Toastmasters. Avocation: interior design. Office: Coates Advt Inc 115 SW Ash Suite 323 Portland OR 97204

COATES, LESLIE NOFTSINGER, lawyer; b. Wilmington, Del., Aug. 3, 1954; d. Robert Benjamin and Alda Beryl (Marlin) Noftsinger; m. Raymond Davis Coates, Jr., Dec. 28, 1974; 1 dau., Lindsey Grozier. B.A., Goucher Coll., 1975; J.D., Del. Law Sch., 1979. Bar: Md. 1979. Ptnr. Coates, Coates, & Coates, P.A., Berlin, Md., 1979—. Mem. ABA, Md. Bar Assn., Worcester County Bar Assn. Democrat. Home: 9027 Ocean Pines Berlin MD 21811 Office: Coates Coates & Coates PA PO Box 366 Berlin MD 21811

COATS, MARCY ISNER, histologist; b. Kansas City, Mo., Jan. 19, 1953; d. Rennix Joseph and Margaret Mary (McCloskey) Isner; student Brevard Hosp. Sch. Histology, 1970-71; m. John Vincent Coats, Aug. 10, 1974. Histologist, Brevard Hosp., Melbourne, Fla., 1970-74, Fla. Hosp., Orlando, 1974-75, Pathology Assos., Tampa, Fla., 1975-77, Tampa Gen. Hosp., 1977-78, Women's Hosp., Tampa, 1978—. Mem. Am. Soc. Clin. Pathologists, Fla. Histology Soc. Home: Route 1 Box 2297 Sleepy Hollow Ln Plant City FL 33566 Office: 3030 W Buffalo Ave Tampa FL 33607

COBB, CAROLYN ANN, communications consultant; b. St. Louis, Feb. 21, 1950; d. Vincent Atlee and Margaret Elizabeth (Ottinger) Knopp; B.A., Harris Tchrs. Coll., 1973; M.A., Webster Coll., 1975; m. Richard Joseph Cobb, Aug. 7, 1976; 1 son, Richard Joseph. Tchr., St. Louis Public Schs. 1973-74; programmer Gen. Am. Life, 1974-75, Mercantile Trust Co., N.A. 1975-78; programmer/analyst Mo. Pacific R.R. 1979-81; data base adminstr, staff specialist Southwestern Bell, St. Louis 1981-84; cons. Cap Gemini Am., 1984—; participant leadership confs.; adv. bd. Ronald Winters Meml. Scholarship; fin. chmn. athletic com. St. Paul's United Ch. of Christ, Oakville, Mo., also coach volleyball and softball teams, mem. choir and adult fellowship; youth group leader Grace United Ch. of Christ; adviser Drop-In Ctr.; data processing adviser Explorer Post, Boy Scouts Am. Mem. Assn. Systems Mgmt., Data Processing Mgmt. Assn., Assn. Women in Computing (charter), Kappa Delta Pi. Republican. Editor: Fundamentals of Data Communications and Networking. Home and Office: 6520 Galewood Ct Saint Louis MO 63129

COBB, CARROLL, lawyer; b. Lamesa, Tex., June 18, 1926; d. George C. and Jewell F. (Forbes) Cobb; m. Glyn H. Cobb, Sept. 5, 1950; children—Carolynn, Martha. B.B.A., U. Tex., 1950, LL.B., 1955. Bar: Tex. Sole practice, Lubbock, Tex., 1955—. Mem. Tex. Ho. of Reps., Austin, 1953-57. Mem. ABA, Tex. Bar Assn. Democrat. Baptist. Home: 3302 55th St Lubbock TX 79413 Office: Carroll Cobb 1801 Ave Q Lubbock TX 79401

COBB, CHRISTINE MARIE, accountant; b. Hot Springs, Ark., Aug. 30, 1952; d. Louis Madison and Josephine Marie (Campagna) Cobb. B.S. B.A. with honors, U. Ark., 1974. C.P.A., Tex. Analyst, sr. analyst Gulf Oil, Houston, 1974-81, dir., 1981-83; owner Christine M. Cobb, C.P.A., Houston, 1983—; lectr. in field. Mem. Am. Inst. C.P.A.s, Tex. Soc. C.P.A.s, Houston C. of C., Alpha Chi Omega (pres. 1973-74). Republican. Methodist. Club: Ninety-Nines (treas.). Office: 2000 S Dairy Ashford Suite 660 Houston TX 77077

COBB, CORA ELEANOR, computer corporation executive; b. N.Y.C., Feb. 6, 1932; d. William Crosby and Margaret Elizabeth Rose (Haeseker) C.; m. John Daniel Hruza, June 21, 1958 (div. Dec. 1971); children—Steven Anton, Karl Andre, Eric Alan. A.B., Northeastern U., 1953; M.S., Simmons Coll., 1954; B.A., Met. State Coll., Denver, 1974; M.A., U. Colo., 1980. Cert. in data processing. Asst. librarian Social Library, Whitingsville, Mass., 1955; cataloguer Boston Coll. Law Sch. Library, Brighton, Mass., 1955-56; programmer Melpar, Inc., Boston, 1956-57, Internat. Computers Corp., Boston, 1957-58; statistician Liberty Mut. Ins. Co., Boston, 1958; assoc. engr. Douglas Aircraft Co., Santa Monica, Calif., 1958-59; fiscal cons. Colo. State Library, Denver, 1965-69; programmer Colo. div. Automated Data Processing, Denver, 1969-73; programmer/analyst Stearns-Roger Engring., Inc., Denver, 1974-77, City and County of Denver, 1977-79; sr. cons. EDS, Inc., Lakewood, Colo., 1979-80, AGS Computers, Denver, 1980-81, DASD Corp., Denver, 1981-82, Leardata, Inc., Denver, 1982-83; prin. computer systems designer Martin Marietta Data Systems, Englewood, Colo., 1983; pres., sr. analyst Empire Data Processing Corp., Denver, 1982—; cons. Mid-Continent Computer Services, Englewood, 1980, Nekoosa Envelopes, Inc., Englewood, 1980-81, Colo. Interstate Gas Co.,

Colorado Springs, 1982, Fischbach & Moore, Inc., Denver, 1982, Anschutz Corp., Denver, 1982-83, ICM Mortgage Corp., Denver, 1983, First Total Systems, Inc., Denver, 1983. Author, researcher monograph: Advanced Propulsion Systems for Interstellar Flight, 1959; ViewTek Screen Generator, 1984. Tchr., Mi Casa Women's Ctr., Denver, 1981; vol. Friends of Man, Denver, 1983-84. Mem. Data Processing Mgmt. Assn., Psi Chi (treas. 1973). Office: Empire Data Processing Corp 1230 S Bellaire St Apt 202 Denver CO 80222

COBB, RUTH, artist; b. Boston, Feb. 20, 1914; d. Charles Edward and Bessie (Cohen) C.; diploma, Mass. Coll. Art, 1935; m. Lawrence Kupferman, Apr. 29, 1937; children—Nancy Rose, David. One-woman shows: Shore Gallery, Boston, 1954, 58, 60, 63, 68, 70, 72, DeCordova Mus., Lincoln, Mass., 1955, Art Unlimited Gallery, San Francisco, 1961, Cober Gallery, N.Y.C., 1962, 65, 67, McNay Mus., San Antonio, 1966, Phila. Art Alliance, 1962, Galerie Moos, Montreal, Que., Can., 1969, Witte Mus., San Antonio, 1967, Harold Ernst Gallery, Boston, 1974, 75, 76, Midtown Gallery, N.Y.C., 1981, 82, Foster Harmon Gallery, Sarasota, Fla., 1984, Francesca Anderson Gallery, 1984; represented in permanent collections: Boston Mus. Fine Arts, Brandeis U., Butler Inst. Am. Art, Munson-Williams-Proctor Inst., Addison Gallery Am. Art, Va. Mus. Fine Arts, DeCordova Mus., Tufts U. Recipient awards Pa. Acad. Fine Arts, 1967, Allied Artists N.Y.C., 1966. Mem. Am. Watercolor Soc. (award), Boston Watercolor Soc. (award), Allied Artists Am. (award), NAD (award). Work featured in Am. Artist mag., 1979.

COBB, SUE MCCOURT, lawyer, educator; b. Los Angeles, Aug. 18, 1937; d. Benjamin Arnold and Ruth (Griffin) McCourt; m. Charles E. Cobb, Jr., Feb. 28, 1959; children—Christian McCourt, Tobin Templeton. B.A., Stanford U., 1959; J.D., U. Miami, 1978. Bar: Fla. 1978, U.S. Dist. Ct. (so. dist.) Fla. 1980. Tchr., Crystal Springs Sch. for Girls, Hillsborough, Calif., 1960-68; assoc. Greenberg, Traurig, Askew, Hoffman, Lipoff, Rosen & Quentel, P.A., Miami, Fla., 1978-83, ptnr., 1983—; chmn. bd. Fed. Res. Bank Atlanta, Miami br., 1984-86. Chmn., Dade County Super Bowl Authority, 1982-84; bd. dirs. Ransom-Everglades Sch., 1976—; Expo 500, Miami, 1982-84, United Way Dade County. Mem. ABA, Fla. Bar, Dade County Bar Assn., Nat. Assn. Bond Lawyers, Republican. Clubs: Boca Raton, Ocean Reef, Grove Isle, Indian Creek. Office: Greenberg Traurig et al 1401 Brickell Ave P H 1 Miami FL 33131

COBBIN MURPHY, EARLEAN, lawyer; b. Chgo., July 15, 1943; d. Eddie and Lucinda (Watts) Slaughter; A.A. with honors, Thornton Jr. Coll., 1969; B.S.Ed. cum laude (Legal Opportunities scholar, 1970), Chgo. State U., 1970; J.D., DePaul U., 1976; children—Kenneth, Alonzo, Charlean Renee, Twanda Lekecia. Sec., Samuel Miller & Co., Chgo., 1963-66, Sears Roebuck & Co., Chgo., 1966-68; tchr. Chgo. Vocat. High Sch., Chgo. Bd. Edn., 1971-75; bar: Ill. 1976; sole practice, Harvey, Ill., 1976-83; enforcement atty. securities div. Ill. Sec. of State, 1983—; part-time instr. Chgo. State U.; part time atty. Ill. Sec. of State. Mem. ABA, Nat. Bar Assn., Ill. Bar Assn., Cook County Bar Assn., Chgo. Bar Assn., Women's Bar Assn. Unitarian. Office: 180 N LaSalle Suite 418 Chicago IL 60602

COBBS, DOROTHY LEE, association official, educational consultant; b. Olive Branch, Ill., Dec. 6, 1946; d. Alvin and Willie Mae (Peck) James. B.A., U. Ill., 1971; M. Profl. Studies, Cornell U., 1975. Multihosp. systems specialist Am. Hosp. Assn., Chgo., 1976—; pres. Cobbs & Assocs., Chgo., 1983, Assoc. Mktg. Services, Chgo., 1982—. Author: Egyptian Diagram, 1975; newsletter editor Directory Multihosp. Systems, 1981, merit cert., 1982; contbr. articles on health care to profl. jours. Mem. Young Execs. in Politics, Chgo., 1983; mem. minority recruitment Com. Cornell U. Edmund J. James scholar, 1966. Mem. Nat. Assn. Health Services Execs., Nat. Assn. Female Execs., Internat. Platform Assn. Alpha Lambda Delta. Democrat. Club: Cornell U. (Chgo.). Home: 421 E 45th Pl Chicago IL 60653

COBEY, VIRGINIA BRANUM, interior designer, civic leader; b. Chgo.; d. Albert Marshall and Hope (Engelhard) B.; m. James Alexander Cobey, Aug. 1, 1942; children—Hope Cobey Batey, Christopher Earle, Lisa. A.A., Stephens Coll., 1939; B.F.A. in Drama, U. Iowa, 1941. Hostess, Stage Door Canteen, N.Y.C., 1942-43; mem. Am. Theatre Wing, N.Y.C., 1942-43; actress Little Theater of the Rockies, 1939-40; asst. buyer I. Magnin, Los Angeles, 1943-44; stylist Macy's, N.Y.C., 1945; owner, designer Virginia Cobey Art/Antiques, Pasadena, Calif., 1978—. Bd. dirs. Women's Council KCET-PBS, Los Angeles, 1968; v.p. Pasadena Art Alliance, 1971-73; chmn., bd. dirs. Friends of Occidental Coll., Los Angeles, 1975-76; patron Costume Council Los Angeles County Mus. Art, 1981-82, Friends of Vielles Maisons Françaises, Los Angeles, 1986—; bd. dirs. Internat. Student Ctr., UCLA, 1985—; organizer, chmn. Southwestern Affiliates Southwestern Sch. Law, 1983-85, recipient plaque, 1985. Ford Found. grantee, 1971—. Mem. Mus. Contemporary Art Los Angeles (patron), Beta Sigma Phi, Pi Beta Phi. Republican. Episcopalian. Club: Valley Hunt (Pasadena).

COBURN, MARJORIE FOSTER, psychologist; b. Salt Lake City, Feb. 28, 1939; d. Harlan Arnold and Alma (Ballinger) Polk; B.A. in Sociology, UCLA, 1960; asso. Montessori internat. diploma Washington Montessori Inst., 1968; M.A. in Psychology, U. No. Colo., 1979; Ph.D. in Psychology U. Denver, 1983; m. Robert Byron Coburn, July 2, 1977; children—Robert Scott, Polly Klea Foster, Matthew Ryan Foster, Kelly Anne. Lic. psychologist. Probation officer Alameda County (Calif.), 1960-62, Contra Costa County (Calif.), 1966, Fairfax County (Va.), 1967; dir. club for recovering mental patients Orange County (Fla.) Mental Health Assn., 1963-65; tchr. Va. Montessori Sch., Fairfax, Va., 1968-70; spl. edn. tchr. Leary Sch., Falls Church, Va., 1970-72, sch. adminstr., 1973-76; sch. adminstr. Aseltine Sch., San Diego, 1976-77, Coburn Montessori Sch., Colorado Springs, Colo., 1977-79; supervised pvt. practice psychotherapy, Colorado Springs, 1979-82; psychology intern U. Calif., San Diego, 1982-83; pvt. practice psychotherapy, La Jolla and Poway, Calif., 1983—; cons., condr. workshops in spl. edn.; bd. dirs. Calif. Assn. Pvt. Spl. Edn. Schs., 1976-77; mem. Leary Edn. Adv. Bd., 1977-80. Mem. Am. Orthopsychiat. Assn., Am. Psychol. Assn., Calif. Psychol. Assn., Acad. San Diego Psychologists, Phobia Soc., Council Exceptional Children, AAUW, NOW, Mensa Internat. Democrat. Episcopalian. Author: (with R. C. Orem) Montessori: Prescription for Children with Learning Disabilities, 1978. Home: 1633 Nautilus La Jolla CA 92037 Office: 836 Prospect Suite 201 La Jolla CA 92037

COCANOWER, LIANA CHERYL, lawyer; b. Salt Lake City, June 19, 1953; d. Elbert Ernest and Dorothy June (Smith) Miller; m. Michael A. Thiessen, Aug., 1973 (div. 1975); m. Michael Andrew Maher, Oct. 15, 1975 (div. Feb. 1981); m. David Lehman Cocanower, Sept. 21, 1983; children—Michael Whitten, Joseph Charles, Emily Elizabeth. B.E., Western Wash. State Coll., 1973; J.D., McGeorge Sch. Law, U. Pacific, 1979; LL.M. in Taxation, NYU, 1980. Bar: Calif. 1979, Ariz. 1980. Assoc. Lewis and Roca, Phoenix, 1980-85, ptnr., 1985—. Served with USAF, 1975-76. Mem. ABA (tax and real estate, probate and trust sects.), Calif. State Bar, Ariz. State Bar (tax sect.), Phi Delta Phi. Republican. Presbyterian. Home: 202 E McLellan Blvd Phoenix AZ 85012 Office: Lewis and Roca 100 W Washington 2200 Phoenix AZ 85003

COCCARI, BARBARA MOONEY, ednl. cons.; b. Greenburg, Pa., Sept. 28, 1946; d. Richard L. and Matilda M. (Barton) Mooney; student U. Ams., Mexico City, 1970; B.S., Calif. State Coll., 1966; M.A., N.Y. U., 1972; postgrad. U. Pitts., 1980—; m. David P. Coccari, May 26, 1973. Caseworker, N.Y.C. Dept. Social Service, 1966-70; community social worker N.Y.C. Human Resources Adminstrn., 1970-72; tchr., operator Adult Edn. Program, Intermediate Unit I, Waynesburg, Pa., 1975—; with Comoco Cons., Pine Bank, Pa., 1973—; counselor, social and community services Cath. Diocese of Pitts., 1980—; dir. Operation Outreach, Bowlby Public Library, Waynesburg, 1976-78. Treas., bd. dirs. Parents Anonymous of Greene County, 1979-80; sec. Health and Welfare Council, Greene County, 1980-81, pres., 1981-82; notary public, Pa. Recipient Golden Key award, Greene County. Democrat. Roman Catholic. Office: 243 E High St Waynesburg PA 15370

COCHRAN, CAROLYN, librarian; b. Tyler, Tex., July 13, 1934; d. Sidney Allen and Eudelle (Frazier) C.; m. Guy Milford Eley, June 1, 1963 (div.). B.A., Beaver Coll., 1956; M.A., U. Tex., 1960; M.L.S., Tex. Woman's U., 1970. Librarian, Canadian (Tex.) High Sch., 1970-71; rep. United Food Co., Amarillo, Tex., 1971-72; librarian Bishop Coll., Dallas, 1972-74; interviewer Tex. Employment Commn., Dallas, 1975-76; librarian St. Mary's Dominican, New Orleans, 1976-77; librarian DeVry Inst. Tech., Irving, Tex., 1978—; with Database Searching Handicapped Individuals, Irving, 1983—; vol. bibliographer Assn. Individuals with Disabilities, Dallas, 1982-85. Mem. Am. Coalition of Citizens with Disabilities, 1982—, Assn. Individuals with Disabilities, 1982—, Vols. in Tech. Assistance, 1985—, Radio Amateur Satellite Corp., 1985—. HEW fellow, 1967; honored Black History Collection, Dallas Morning News, Bishop Coll., Dallas, 1973. Mem. ALA, Spl. Library Assn. Club: Toastmistress (pres. 1982-83) (Irving). Reviewer Library Jour., 1974, Dallas Morning News, 1972-74, Amarillo Globe-News, 1970-71. Office: DeVry Inst Tech 4250 N Beltline Rd Irving TX 75038

COCHRAN, LEONA JEAN, consulting engineer; b. Gary, Ind., Nov. 2, 1936; d. Willie and Minnie Lee (Greer) Stroud; B.A., Mundelein Coll., 1981; M.S., Nat. Coll. Edn., 1982; m. Christopher C. Cochran Jr., Sept. 8, 1957; children—Karen Alise, Ronald Kevin. Exec. sec. to Dr. Brian Berry, U. Chgo., 1974; adminstrv. asst. Dr. John Sheaffer of Bauer, Sheaffer & Lear, Chgo., 1977; dir. adminstrn., treas., dir. Sheaffer & Roland, Inc., Chgo., 1976-84; pres. Synergistic Unltd., Chgo., 1984—; dir. Energy Harvest, Inc. Mem. Chgo. Bd. Edn., 1982—. Mem. Am. Mgmt. Assn. Mem. Evangelical Ch. Home: 8916 S Harper Chicago IL 60619 Office: Synergistic Unltd 180 N Michigan Ave Chicago IL 60601

COCHRAN, LYNNE ANN, educator, educational services administrator; b. Carroll, Iowa, Mar. 1, 1945; d. Norman North and Dorothy Mae (Dean) Hoft. B.A., Briar Cliff Coll., 1971; M.A. in Spl. Edn., Ariz. State U., 1979. Cert. elem. and spl. edn. tchr., Ariz. Tchr. St. Edward Sch., Waterloo, Iowa, 1968-70; tchr. Chino Valley Sch., Ariz., 1971-77, program developer, 1974-76; spl. edn. tchr. Tuba City Pub. Jr. High Sch., Ariz., 1978-82; spl. edn. tchr., dept. chmn. Tuba City High Sch., 1983—, curriculum developer, 1984-85; founder, pres. Unltd. Learning Enterprises, Inc., Tuba City, 1983-85. Probation aide Waterloo Juvenile Ct., 1970-71; vol. instr. Prescott Spl. Olympics 1977-78; local coordinator Tuba City Spl. Olympics, 1978-80. Mem. Council Exceptional Children, Assn. Children with Learning Disabilities, Ariz. Edn. Assn., NEA, Tuba City Unified Edn. Assn. (pres. 1985-86), Nat. Assn. Female Execs., Delta Kappa Gamma. Democrat. Avocations: reading; piano; camping; hiking; rafting. Office: Tuba City High Sch PO Box 67 Tuba City AZ 86045

COCHRAN, MARY LEFFLER, civic worker; b. Kansas City, Mo., May 4, 1921; d. Shepherd and Nora Elizabeth (McCaull) Leffler; B.S., Drake U., 1942; A.M. in T., Radcliffe Coll., 1947; m. John A. Cochran, July 10, 1943; children—Jacquelyn, Cynthia Cochran Johnston, Catherine Cochran Berg. Tchr. math. and history Anita (Iowa) High Sch.; 1942-43; timekeeper supr. Pratt-Whitney Aircraft, Kansas City, Mo., 1943-45; tchr. Ames (Iowa) High Sch., 1945-46; psychometrist Boston U. Counseling Service, 1947-49; pres. Delta Gamma Bldg. Corp., U. Ill., Urbana, 1953-56. Sec., U. Ill. Commerce Wives, 1955-56; pres. So. Ill. U. Women's Club, Carbondale, 1961-62, Newcomer's chmn., 1963-64; pres. Ariz. State U. Faculty Wives Club, Tempe, 1967-68; products chmn. Cactus-Pine council Girl Scouts U.S.A., 1967-68; pres. Salt River Panhellenic (Ariz.), 1973-75; sec. Ariz. State U. Lyric Opera Guild, 1973-76; bicentennial chmn. Salvation Army Aux., Tempe, 1975-76; asst. studio dir. Phoenix Studio Rec. for Blind, 1978-79. Recipient Bell Ringer award Salvation Army Aux., Tempe, 1976. Mem. Nat. Council State Garden Clubs (bd. dirs., personnel chmn. 1983-85, corr. sec. 1985—), Mortar Bd. (sr. adv. Ariz. State U. 1968-69), Kappa Delta Pi, Pi Kappa Delta, Pi Lambda Theta, Ariz. Fedn. Garden clubs (pres. 1981-83, rec. sec. 1976-79; Public Relations award 1979). Delta Gamma (chmn. Ariz. State U. adv. bd. 1965-67), P.E.O. Presbyterian. Clubs: Tempe Garden (pres. 1977-79), Desert Designers (pres. 1983-85). Editor calendar: The Gardener's Year for 1980, 81. Home: 116 E Greentree Dr Tempe AZ 85284

COCHRAN, OLIVE LEIGH MYATT (MRS. RAYMOND NEVITT COCHRAN), retired educational administrator; b. Monroe, La., Sept. 8, 1907; d. Webster Andrew and Martha Fidelia (Morton) Myatt; student La. State Normal Coll., 1923-25; kindergarten cert. Harris Tchrs. Coll., 1926; B.S. cum laude, La. State U., 1942; M.Ed., N.E. La. U., 1962; m. Raymond Nevitt Cochran, June 4, 1940; children—Kathleen, Susan (Mrs. Eric Mingledorff). Tchr. rural schs., Ouachita Parish, La., 1925-27, Georgia Tucker Elem. Sch., Monroe, 1927-43, 55-62; tchr., owner Cochran Nursery Sch., 1949-51; supr. elem. edn. Monroe Sch. System, 1962-67, dir. elem. curriculum, 1967-73; organizer first spl. edn. classes Monroe schs., 1964; supr. spl. edn. Monroe City schs., 1964-73; ret., 1973. Active CD. during World War II. Mem. Internat. Reading Assn. (dir. local unit 1970-73), Assn. Childhood Edn. Internat. (br. pres. 1967-71, treas. 1971-83), La. Assn. Childhood Edn. Internat., AAUW, Delta Kappa Gamma, Sigma Tau Delta. Republican. Baptist. Home: 1105 N 7th St Monroe LA 71201

COCHRAN, STEFANI DEIRDRE, psychotherapist; b. Manila, Philippines, Oct. 22, 1940; d. Robert Edgar and Susan Elizabeth (Jurika) Cecil; B.A., Stanford U., 1961; M.S.W., Cath. U. Am., 1975; m. Garrett Cochran, Dec. 22, 1962; children—Suzita, Heather; m. Daniel Couch, Nov. 6, 1976. Econ. analyst CIA, Langley, Va., 1961-66; social worker Fairfax County (Va.) Schs., 1975-79; exec. dir. Marriage and Family Clinic, Silver Spring, Md., 1979-80; pvt. practice Family Counseling and Evaluation Center, Oakton, Va., 1980—; dir. Remarriage Resources, 1983—; lectr. in field. Founder, No. Va. Stepfamily Assn., 1980; bd. dirs. Stepfamily Assn. Am., 1983-85. Carnegie Found. fellow, 1960. Mem. Nat. Assn. Social Workers, Acad. Cert. Social Workers, Am. Acad. Psychotherapists, Gestalt Inst. Cleve., Stepfamily Assn. Am., Soc. Clin. Social Work. Unitarian. Home: 2005 Cutwater Ct Reston VA 22091 Office: 2915 Hunter Mill Rd Suite 19 Oakton VA 22124

COCHRANE, LISA DIANE, advertising agency executive; b. Evanston, Ill., May 9, 1955; d. James Gordon and Ruth Diane (Leach) Hosfield; m. James Paul Blazevich, July 24, 1976 (div. Feb. 1982); m. 2d Cary Colby Cochrane, May 8, 1982; children—Christopher Corbin, Kate Diane. B.J. in Advt., U. Mo.-Columbia, 1976. Advt. trainee Marshall Field & Co., Chgo., 1976; media planner Ogilvy & Mather, Inc., Chgo., 1976-77, account exec., 1978-79, account supr., 1979—, v.p., 1982—. Mem. Chgo. Advt. Club, North Shore Alumnae Kappa Kappa Gamma (chmn. pub. relations 1980-81). Lutheran. Home: 2500 Hartzell St Evanston IL 60201

COCHRANE, PEGGY, architect, writer; b. Alhambra, Calif., July 9, 1926; d. E. Elliott and Gladys (Moran) C.; B.A., Scripps Coll., 1945; postgrad., U. So. Calif., 1951-52, Columbia U., 1954; m. Hugh Bowman, Nov. 24, 1954 (div.). Job capt. Kahn and Jacobs, N.Y.C., 1954-55; project architect Litchfield, Whiting, Panero & Severud, Teheran, Iran, 1956; archtl. designer Daniel, Mann, Johnson and Mendenhall, Los Angeles, 1956-59; individual practice architecture, Sherman Oaks, Calif., 1966—. Recipient Architecture prize Scripps Coll., 1945. Mem. Assn. Women in Architecture (life), Union Internationale des Femmes Architects. Republican. Episcopalian. Club: Dionysians (S. Pasadena). Author: (musical) Mayaland, 1979; (play) I Gave at the Office, 1980; The Witch Doctor's Manual; The Witch Doctor's Cookbook; mem. editorial bd. Los Angeles Architect, 1978—; contbr. to Contemporary Architects. Office: 14755 Ventura Blvd Suite 1-626 Sherman Oaks CA 91403

COCHRELL, SUE ANNE, owner child care center; b. Toledo; d. Garold William and Helena May (Layman) Roberts; m. Robert Clark Hunter, May 5, 1962 (div. Aug. 1972); children—Kevin, Kelli; m. Ronald Lee Cochrell, Dec. 4, 1976; stepchildren—Elizabeth, Cynthia, Kelly. B.S. in Edn., Bowling Green State U., 1964. Tchr. A Young World, Toledo, 1967-68, Hope Luth. Co-op, Toledo, 1968-70; on-air talent Romper Room, TV kindergarten, Toledo, 1970-78; developer-tchr. Ottawa River Pre-Kindergarten, Toledo, 1972-76; developer, dir. Happiness Is...Nursery Sch., Waterville, Ohio, 1974-82, Happiness Is...Child Care Center, Toledo, 1976—; mem. adv. bd. Woodward High Sch., Toledo, 1977—, Owens Tech. Coll., Oregon, Ohio, 1978—; mem. child care com. Toledo-Lucas County Council for Human Services, 1984—; mem. Ohio Day Care Adv. Com., 1979-81. Bd. dirs. Toledo Area Govtl. Research Assn., 1984—. Mem. Toledo Area Assn. for Edn. of Young Children. Republican. Methodist. Club: North Cape Yacht (LaSalle, Mich.). Avocations: boating; hiking; skiing. Home: 3130 Lambert Dr Toledo OH 43613 Office: Happiness Is Child Care Center 4549 Summit St Toledo OH 43611

COCKE, HILDA GIBSON, industrial engineer; b. Pittsylvania, Va., Apr. 16, 1931; d. Joseph Robert and Annie Doris (Gibson) Gibson; m. Frank Curtis Cocke, June 2, 1951 (div. 1980); children—Carol Anne, Frank, Jr., David. Student U. Va.-Danville, 1964-66, Danville Tech. Inst., 1966-70. Timekeeper Dan River, Inc., Danville, 1951-52, specification clk., 1952-59, office supr., 1959-73, dept. indsl. engr., 1973-80, mill mgr. indsl. engr., 1980-85, sr. indsl. engr., 1985—. Mem. Luncheon Bus. and Profl. Women's Club (pres. 1970-71; Woman of Yr. 1970), Internat. Mgmt. Club, Phi Sigma Alpha (pres. 1971-72; Woman of Yr. 1969). Club: Starwood Garden (pres. 1981-83). Avocations: arts, crafts. Home: 152 Woodberry Dr Danville VA 24540

COCKER, BARBARA JOAN, marine artist, interior designer; b. Uxbridge, Mass.; A.A., Becker Jr. Coll., 1943; student Mt. St. Mary Coll., 1944-45, Clark U., summer 1945, N.Y. Sch. Interior Design, 1965-67. Owner, operator Barbara J. Cocker, Interior Design, Rumson, N.J., 1966—; owner Barbara J. Cocker Paintings of the Sea Gallery, Nantucket, Mass., 1975—; tchr. adult edn. courses in interior design, 1965-68; artist, pvt. instr. marine art; pres. Maximus Praetorius Corp., Nantucket, Mass., 1979—; one-man shows marine paintings: Little Gallery, Barbizon, N.Y., 1971, Old Mill Assn., 1971, Pacem en Terris Gallery, N.Y.C., 1972, Central Jersey Bank & Trust Co., Rumson, 1971, 72, 74, 77, 79, Little Gallery, Nantucket Art Assn., 1975, 77, 79, 81, 84, Caravan House Galleries, N.Y.C., 1975, 79, Guild of Creative Art, Shrewsbury, N.J., 1976, 81, 85, IBM Corp., N.J., 1977, South St. Seaport Mus., N.Y., 1977, 80, Provident Nat. Bank, Phila., 1978, Gallery 100, Princeton, 1978, Bell Telephone Research Labs., 1982, 86, Art Alliance N.J., 1983, Gilpin House Gallery (Va.), Swain Art Gallery, N.J., 1984; group shows include: Burr Artists N.Y., Guild Creative Art N.J., Composers, Authors and Artists Am. NAD, Salmagundi Club N.Y.C., Monmouth Coll. Festival of Arts, Caravan House Galleries, Pen and Brush Club, N.Y.C., N.Y.C., Lever House Galleries, N.Y.C., Nat. Arts Club, N.Y.C., Ocean County Artists Guild, N.J. Mem. Burr Artists, Catharine Lorillard Wolfe Arts Club, Am. Artists Profl. League, N.Y. Guild Creative Arts, Nantucket Art Assn., Composers, Authors and Artists Am., Allied Artists Am., Monmouth Arts Found. (N.J.), So. Vt. Artists Inc., Pen and Brush Club (N.Y.C.). Address: 3 Rumson Rd Rumson NJ 07760 also Paintings Of Sea Gallery #16 Old South Wharf Nantucket MA 02554

COCKRELL, PEARL HAND, writer; b. Gadsden, Ala., Jan. 2, 1921; d. Arthur H. and May (Jones) Hand; m. Harold R. Cockrell, May 11, 1946; children—Pamela Cockrell White, Jan Cockrell Mitchell, Donis C. Schweizer. Student Massey Bus. Coll., Cleve. State Community Coll., Chattanooga State Community Coll. Author: poems Sing On, America, 1976; Of Men and Seasons, 1978. Contbr. to mags. including Sci. of Mind, Home Life, Modern Maturity, Music Ministry, Grit, Vol. Gardener, Tenn. Voices, The American, Ch. Musician, Progressive Farmer, Nat. Daffodil Jour., Missionary Messenger, Am. Camellia Jour., Poet's Monthly, Encore, Pen Woman, Old Hickory Rev., Pegasus, The Sampler, Prize poems Nat. Fedn. State Poetry Socs., Clover Collection Verses, Sandcutters, Rose Garden, Garden Prayers, Alalitcom, others. Weekly columnist So. Democrat, 1973-80. Recipient Tenn. Fedn. Garden Clubs, Inc. Poet Laureate award, 1973, 74, 75, 76, 77, Am. Legion award, 1974, Freedom Found. at Valley Forge award, 1976, 1st place poetry awards Nat. Fedn. State Poetry Socs., 1974 (2), 79, Authors and Artists Club Chattanooga, 1972, Ala. Writers Conclave Lit. Competition, 1975, 77, 78, Mid S. Poetry Festival, 1976, 77, 78 (2), 80, 81 (2), 84, Nat. Contest Ky. State Poetry Soc., 1976, Nat. Contest Utah State Poetry Soc., 1977, Deep S. Writers and Artists Assn., 1978, Dalton Creative Arts Guild, Ga., 1981, Nat. Contest Fla. State Poets Assn., 1985, 1st place prize Ann. Contest Poetry Soc. Tenn., 1986, numerous other awards. Mem. Nat. League Am. Pen Women (historian Chickasaw br., Tenn. State Letters awards 1975, 77, 81), Tenn. Writers Guild (past v.p.), Cleve. Creative Arts Guild (1st place awards 1973, 74 (2), 79, Catriona Dow plaque 1974). Home and Office: 916 62d St Ct W Bradenton FL 33529

COCO, MARY LEE, educational administrator, educational consultant; b. St. Louis, Feb. 21, 1933; d. Angelo Lee and Mary Rose (Venegoni) Genoni; m. Phillip Coco, May 9, 1953; children—Mary Ann, Donna, Catherine. Student Webster Coll., 1949-50, Fontbonne Coll., 1982-83. Lic. real estate broker. Tchr. Munson Sch. Music, St. Louis, 1965-67; mgr. Pettymark Inc., St. Louis, 1969-72; music studio mgr. Ludwig Aeolian Music, St. Louis, 1972-78; owner, adminstr. Suburban Music Sch., St. Louis, 1978—. Mem. Nat. Fedn. Music Clubs, Music Tchrs. Nat. Assn., Mid Am. Music Assn., Nat. Assn. Female Execs., Keyboard Amateur Musician Assn. (chmn. 1985—, dir. pub. relations 1985). Democrat. Roman Catholic. Avocations: embroidery; gardening. Office: Suburban Sch Music 716 Greeley Webster Groves MO 63119

COCO, SALLY HAHN, veterinarian; b. Corpus Christi, Tex., May 10, 1954; d. Roy Emmit and Mary Jo (Middleton) Hahn; m. Lambert Baldwin Coco, Jr., Dec. 18, 1977; 1 dau., Lindsay Bridges. Student Nicholls State U., 1971-73; D.V.M., La. State U., 1979. Lic. veterinarian, La., Tex. Veterinarian, owner Westside Vet. Clinic, De Ridder, La., 1979—; relief veterinarian, 1979-82; profl. commentator pet health series on local TV sta. Frequent guest speaker Beauregard Parish Schs.; mem. Nat. Rep. Com.; bd. dirs. Beauregard Meml. Hosp., Beauregard Community Concerns. Mem. Am. Vet. Assn. (sec. student chpt. 1977-78), AVMA, La. Vet. Med. Assn., Central La. Vet. Med. Assn., La. State U. Vet. Alumni Assn. (pres.-elect 1981-83, pres. 1983-85), Am. Assn. Women Veterinarians, Young Women's League (v.p. 1986). Republican. Baptist. Home: Star Route 1 Box 34 De Ridder LA 70634 Office: Westside Vet Clinic Star Route 1 Box 34 De Ridder LA 70634

CODER, RACHEL REED, social worker; b. Lexington, Ky., Oct. 17, 1940; B.A., Rollins Coll., 1962; M.S.W., Fordham U., 1965; married; 1 son. Social worker field placement Spence Chapin Adoption Agy., N.Y.C., 1962-64, obstet. unit St. Luke's Women's Hosp., N.Y.C., 1965-66; sr. social worker surg., orthopaedic and ENT units Lenox Hill Hosp., N.Y.C., 1966-70; dir social services Silver Hill Found., New Canaan, Conn., 1971-77, Bethesda Meml. Hosp., Boynton Beach, Fla., 1980-84; dir. social service Good Samaritan Hosp., West Palm Beach, Fla., 1984—; pvt. practice social work, New Canaan, 1985—; mem. faculty Grad. Sch. Social Work, U. Conn., 1975-76, Grad. Sch. Social Work, Barry U., 1981-82. Vol. group therapist USAFB, Glyfada, Athens, Greece, 1978-79; bd. dirs. Hospice of Boca Raton, Fla., 1980. Cert. social worker, N.Y.; lic. clin. social worker, Fla. Mem. Am. Hosp. Soc. for Dirs. Social Services, Nat. Assn. Social Work, Acad. Cert. Social Workers, Register Clin. Social Workers. Address: 6217 Celadon Circle Eastpointe Country Club Palm Beach Gardens FL 33410

CODINA, THELMA YAP, chemical engineer; b. Cebu City, Philippines, Oct. 9, 1942; d. Juan Escalona and Perpetua (Junio) Yap; m. Ricardo Codina; children—Nathaniel, Ricardo, Jr., Maria. B.S. in Chem. Engring., U. San Carlos, Philippines, 1964. Registered profl. engr., Ill. Quality control engr. Gen. Milling, Philippines, 1965-67; mem. faculty U. San Carlos, Philippines, 1967-74; process engr. Brown & Root, Naperville, Ill., 1978-85; lectr. hydraulics, 1984, chem. engr., U.S. EPA, Chgo., 1985—. Mem. Philippines Engrs. and Scientists Orgn. (sec. 1983-84), Am. Inst. Chem. Engrs., Ill. Soc. Profl. Engrs. Republican. Roman Catholic. Avocations: aerobic dancing; cooking; reading. Office: US EPA 230 S Dearborn Chicago IL 60604

CODY, JANE MERRIAM, classicist; b. Chgo., Oct. 20, 1941; d. John Henry and Charlotte (Orr) Merriam; A.B., Randolph-Macon Women's Coll., 1963; M.A., Bryn Mawr Coll., 1964, Ph.D., 1968; m. Bruce P. McNall; children—Erin Elizabeth, Thomas Edan, Katherine Anne, Bruce P.J. Instr., Pomona Coll., 1967-68; asst. prof. classics U. So. Calif., from 1968, assoc. prof., chmn. dept. classics, 1971-74, 80—; pres. Summa Galleries, Inc. Am. Council Learned Socs. fellow, 1975-76. Mem. Am. Philol. Assn., Archaeol. Inst. Am., Royal Numis. Soc., Am. Numis. Soc. Co-author: Wealth of the Ancient World, 1983; contbr. articles on Roman coins, history and lit. to profl. jours. Office: Taper Hall 224 U So Calif Los Angeles CA 90089

CODY, PAT(RICIA), designer, writer; b. Newport, Tenn., Aug. 16, 1943; d. James Donald and Martha Eva (Templin) Cody; m. 2d Jerry Ralph Pierce, Jan. 14, 1977. B.S., U. Tenn., 1966. Cert. home econs. tchr., Tenn. Mktg. home economist Tex. Electric Service Co., Ft. Worth, 1966-71; asst. dir. research Tarrant County Jr. Coll. Dist., Ft. Worth, 1971-75; writer, analyst Equitable Gen. Ins. Co., Ft. Worth, 1977; traffic mgr., copywriter Drawing Bd., Inc., Dallas, 1978-81; owner caliCO-DYsigns, Ft. Worth, 1981—. Author: Continuous Line Quilting Designs, 1984; also articles and designs in various crafts mags. Recipient 1st place award Block Design Contest award Fairfield Corp., 1981; Grand prize Block Design Contest, Ozark Mountains, 1982; 1st Place Wallhanging Design award Cabin Fever Calico, 1982; quilt accepted for display and book reprodn. Quilt Nat. Cultural Arts Ctr., Athens, Ohio, 1983. Mem. Internat. Quilt Assn., Nat. Quilting Assn., Trinity Valley Quilters Guild, Authors Guild. Republican Unitarian. Home and Office: caliCO-DYsigns 1561 Montclair Dr Fort Worth TX 76103

COE, ILSE G., lawyer, former banker; b. Koenigsberg, Germany, May 28, 1911; came to U.S., 1938, naturalized, 1946; Referendar, U. Koenigsberg, 1935, J.S.D., 1936; LL.B., Bklyn. Law Sch., 1946. Dir. econ. research Internat. Gen.

Electric Co., Berlin, 1936-38; asst. to sales promotion and advt. mgr. Ralph C. Coxhead Corp., N.Y.C., 1940-44; law clk. Mendes & Mount, N.Y.C., 1944-46; admitted to N.Y. bar, 1946; atty. Hill, Rivkins & Middleton, N.Y.C., 1946-50, McNutt, Longcope & Proctor, N.Y.C., 1950-52, Chadbourne, Hunt, Jaeckel & Brown, N.Y.C., 1952-54; asst. v.p., asst. trust officer Schroder Trust Co. and J. Henry Schroder Banking Corp., N.Y.C., 1954-76; dir., sec., editor Fgn. Tax Law Assn., Inc., L.I., N.Y., 1945-55; tchr. Drakes Bus. Sch., N.Y.C., 1946-49; lectr. on estate planning to ch., women and bar assn. groups, 1947—; tutor literacy vols., 1977-79; lectr. wills trusts and estates and photography Pace U.; exec. bd. Active Retirement Center, Pace U., 1977-79, v.p., 1980-81, pres., 1982-85, life ex-officio mem. exec. bd., 1985—. County com. woman Republican Party, 1948-50; former deacon, now ruling elder, chmn. investment com. 1st Presbyterian Ch., Bklyn. Recipient Human Relations award NCCJ, 1979. Mem. Bklyn. Women's Bar Assn. (past treas., sec., dir. 1960—), Protestant Lawyers Assn. of N.Y. Inc. (sec. 1960-75, 1st v.p. 1976-77, pres. 1978—), Internat. Fedn. Women Lawyers, Bklyn. Heights Assn., Bklyn. Hist. Soc. (investment com.), N.Y. Color Slide Club (by-laws chmn., dir. 1973-74), Bklyn. Mus., Bklyn. Bot. Garden, others. Home: 187 Hicks St Brooklyn Heights NY 11201

COELHO, JUDITH CAROL PRICE, medical technologist; b. Shelbyville, Ill., Aug. 20, 1942; d. Maurice Ray and Naomi Aileen (Milner) Price; B.S. in Med. Tech., Millikin U., 1970; cert. in med. tech. St. Mary's Sch. Med. Tech., 1969; m. Patrick S. Coelho, Jan. 16, 1971; children—Kawiki, Uilani. Lab. technician State of Ill. Dept. Agr., div. feeds, fertilizer and standards, 1961-63; lab. asst. Shelby County Meml. Hosp., Shelbyville, Ill., 1963-67, St. Mary's Hosp., Decatur, Ill., 1967-68, staff med. technologist, 1969-70; lab. supr. Molokai (Hawaii) Gen. Hosp., 1970-81; staff technologist Blood Bank of Hawaii, Honolulu, 1981-83; lab. supr. Pawaa Med. Lab., 1985—; instr. in field. Mem. infection control com. Molokai Gen. Hosp., sec., 1975-81, vice chairperson, mem. safety com., 1980-81; mem. safety com. Blood Bank of Hawaii, 1982; v.p. Kaunakakai Sch. PTA, 1979, pres., 1980-81; Cub Scouts leader, 1981—; tchr. Bible Sch., 1981-85, vol. tchr. asst., 1983-84; sec. Pearl Harbor Ch. of Christ, 1984-85. Mem. Am. Soc. Med. Tech., Hawaii Soc. Med. Tech. (scholarship chairperson 1977-78). Mem. Chs. of Christ. Clubs: Malia Alanon, Molokai Saddle (sec. 1981).

COFER, SUSAN JEANNIE, newspaper company manager; b. Gadsden, Ala., Aug. 18, 1953; d. Cholor Seldon Hughes and Beulah Ophelia (Causey) Nelson; m. Arthur Rutherford, Aug. 16, 1970 (div. Nov. 1983); children—Allyson Paige, Thomas Malcolm, Tamila Georgette; m. Michael Eugene Cofer, Feb. 21, 1985. Student G.C. Wallace Coll., Ala., 1980-81. Dist. sales rep. The Cullman Times, Ala., 1975-76, carrier, 1976-78, circulation supr., 1978-80, asst. circulation mgr., 1980-83; dist. mgr. Palm Beach Newspapers, West Palm Beach, Fla., 1984—. Designer clothing and interiors, toys. Foster parent, Cullman, 1974-80; fundraiser Cullman County Bd. Edn., 1979-83; pres. Cullman County Head Start, 1980-82. Democrat. Seventh-day Adventist. Avocations: crafts; reading; writing; horseback riding; swimming. Home: 2730 Hwy 441 8E RV 38 Okeechobee FL 33474 Office: Palm Beach Post 212 S Parrott Ave Okeechobee FL 33474

COFFEE, CHARLENE DAUGHERTY, accountant; b. Athens, Tenn., Feb. 3, 1943; d. Charles McGee and Alma (Millsaps) Daugherty; B.S., U. Tenn., Knoxville, 1964; m. Joe Donald Coffee, Apr. 9, 1966. Buyer trainee, Castner-Knott Co., Nashville, 1964-66; asst. buyer, buyer Harvey's, Nashville, 1966-67; mdse. control clk., supr. Sears Roebuck, Nashville, 1967-73, acctg. mgmt. trainee, 1973-74, mem. point of sale implementation team So. ter., 1974-77, controller acctg. and processing center, Atlanta, 1977-80, staff asst., field report consolidation, Chgo., 1980-81, staff asst. acctg. policy and procedure, 1981-83, sr. staff asst. acctg. services, 1983—. Mem. West dist. bd. dirs. Family Care Services Met. Chgo.; v.p. Ch. of Living Christ Congregation. Mem. DAR, AAUW, Delta Zeta. Lutheran. Home: 405 S Home Ave Unit #102 Oak Park IL 60302 Office: Sears Tower BSC 22-12 Chicago IL 60684

COFFEE, VIRGINIA CLAIRE, civic worker, former mayor; b. Alliance, Nebr., Dec. 8, 1920; d. James Maddigan and Adelaide Mary (Forde) Kennedy; B.S., Chadron State Coll., 1942; m. Bill Brown Coffee, June 21, 1942; children—Claire, Sara, Virginia Anne, Sue. High sch. prin., Whitman, Nebr., 1942; sec., bookkeeper Coffee & Son, Inc., Harrison, Nebr., 1965—, officer, 1967 ; mayor City of Harrison, 1970-80. Leader, Girl Scouts U.S.A., 1950-60, mem. Harrison Elem. Sch. bd., 1958-64; mem. liaison com. Chadron State Coll., 1975—; pub. relations chmn. Nebr. Cowbelles, 1968; sec. Northwest Stock Growers, 1971-73; corp. officer Ft. Robinson Centennial, 1973—; officer Gov.'s Fort Robinson Centennial Commn., 1973-75; hon. gov. Nebr. Centennial, 1967; chmn. Sioux County Bicentennial, 1973-77; trustee Nebr. State Hist. Soc. Found., 1975—, Village of Harrison, 1973-80. Mem. Nebr. State Hist. Soc. (dir. 1979-85, 2d v.p. 1982-84, 1st v.p. 1984-85, com. for marker to honor Harrison centennial 1985-86), Sioux County Hist. Soc. (dir. 1975-81, 83-84, past pres., Sioux county history book com. 1985-86), Wyo. Hist. Soc. Cardinal Key Honor Frat. Roman Catholic. Clubs: Sioux County Cowbelles, Nebr. Cowbells, Ladies Community, Harrison Community (dir. 1983—, officer 1984—), Contbr. articles to area newspapers; chmn. compilation com. book Sioux County Memoirs of Its Pioneers, 1967. Address: PO Box 336 Harrison NE 69346

COFFEY, BARBARA JORDAN, magazine editor, writer; Fashion editor Vogue Mag., N.Y.C., 1959-64; advt. writer Young & Rubicam, N.Y.C., 1965-67; writer Glamour Mag., N.Y.C., 1967-74, copy chief, 1974—, also mng. editor; books include: Glamour Health and Beauty Book, 1973; Glamour's Success Book, 1979; Beauty Begins at 40, 1984. Adv. bd. Women's Research and Edn. Inst., Washington. Mem. Am. Soc. Mag. Editors, Fashion Group, Women in Communication. Office: Glamour Magazine 350 Madison Ave New York NY 10017

COFFEY, HELEN ELIZABETH, physicist; b. Chelsea, Mass., Nov. 17, 1944; d. Timothy Patrick and Helen Williamina (Stevens) C. B.S., Merrimack Coll., 1966; M.S., U. Colo., 1969. Mem. staff M.I.T., Cambridge, 1969-70; physicist NOAA, Boulder, 1972—, br. chief solar and high atmosphere br., 1977—; sec. Internat. Ursigrams and World Days Service, 1981—. High Altitude Obs. Astrogeophysics fellow, 1966-67. Mem. Internat. Astronom. Union (commn. X working group internat. programs), Am. Geophys. Union (treas. Front Range br. 1985—), Am. Meteorol. Soc., Am. Astron. Soc., AAAS, Colo. Coordinating Council of Women's Orgns. (corr. sec. 1983-84), Sigma Xi (pres. chpt. 1985-86). Democrat. Roman Catholic. Club: Zonta of Boulder County (v.p. 1981-82, pres. 1983-84). Editor: Solar-Geophysical Data, 1977—; geomagnetic and solar data table Jour. Geophys. Research, 1981—. Home: 7659 Nikau Dr Longmont CO 80501 Office: World Data Center A Solar Terrestrial Physics NOAA E/GC2 325 Broadway Boulder CO 80303

COFFEY, MARY ELLEN, scientist; b. Cambridge, Mass., Sept. 19, 1943; d. Timothy Patrick and Helena Wilhelmina (Stevens) C. B.S., MIT, 1965; M.S., U. Colo., 1969; Sc.D., Harvard U., 1974. Asst. analyst EG&G Inc., Boston, 1966-67; project engr. AVCO, Lowell, Mass., 1969-70; sr. scientist, sect. mgr. NUS Corp., Rockville, Md., also Denver, 1973-82; sr. scientist Bechtel Group Inc., San Francisco, 1983—. Mem. Am. Meteorol. Soc., Am. Phys. Soc., Air Pollution Control Assn. Democrat. Roman Catholic. Club: Sierra. Avocations: hiking; tennis; reading. Home: 4408 Kearsarge Ct Concord CA 94518 Office: Bechtel Group Inc 50 Beale St San Francisco CA 94119

COFFEY, SUSANNE NORTON, issues analyst; b. Salinas, Calif., May 5, 1949; d. Richard Matthew Norton and Jacqueline Faye (Blaylock) Norton Kovach; m. Patrick Andrew Coffey, Mar. 9, 1969 (div. 1984); 1 child, Timothy Norton. Student Hartnell Coll., 1967-68, Monterey Peninsula Coll., 1973-74; B.A., San Diego State U., 1977; postgrad. in pub. adminstrn. Golden Gate U., 1985—. Pub. relations intern Mercy Hosp. and Med. Center, San Diego, 1977; editor publs. Alta Bates Hosp., Berkeley, Calif., 1977-79; editor Utility Reporter, Internat. Brotherhood Elec. Workers Local 1245, Walnut Creek, Calif., 1979-80; communications dir., 1980; news services rep. Pacific Gas & Electric Co., San Francisco, 1980-84, sr. issues analyst, 1984—. Parent vol. St. Paul's Sch., Oakland, Calif., 1982—; bd. dirs. St. Mark's Nursery Assn., Concord, Calif., 1979-80. Mem. Internat. Assn. Bus. Communicators (accredited; meetings coordinator San Francisco 1982-84), Internat. Labor Press Assn. (1st award for Gen. Excellence 1980). Democrat. Episcopalian. Home: 2373 Tiffin Rd Oakland CA 94602 Office: Pacific Gas & Electric Co 215 Market St Room 632 San Francisco CA 94106

COFFILL, MARJORIE LOUISE (MRS. WILLIAM CHARLES COFFILL), civic worker; b. Sonora, Calif., June 11, 1917; d. Eric J. and Pearl (Needham) Segerstrom; A.B. with distinction in Social Sci., Stanford, 1938, M.A. in Edn., 1941; m. William Charles Coffill, Jan. 25, 1948; children—William James, Eric John. Asst. mgr. Sonora Abstract & Title Co. (Calif.), 1938-39; mem. staff Dean of Women, Stanford, 1939-41; social dir. women's campus Pomona Coll., 1941-43, instr. psychology, 1941-43; asst. to field dir. ARC, Le Moore AFB, Calif., 1944-46; partner Riverbank Water Co., Riverbank Hughson, Calif., 1950-68; mem. Tuolumne County Mental Health Adv. Bd., 1963-69; mem. Central adv. council Supplementary Edn. Center, 1966-68; mem. Pres.'s adv. bd. Columbia Jr. Coll., chmn., 1972, 80, bd. dirs. found., 1973—; mem. Tuolumne County Bicentennial Com.; life mem. bd. dirs. Lung Assn. Valley Lode Counties; bd. dirs. Tuolumne County Salvation Army, 1974—; clk. bd. trustees Sonora Union High Sch., chmn. bd. trustees, 1969-71; pres. Tuolumne County Republican Women; asso. mem. Calif. Rep. Central Com., 1950; active PTA, ARC. Recipient Pi Lambda Theta award, 1940. Mem. AAUW (charter mem. Tuolumne County br., pres. Sonora br. 1965-68), Tuolumne County, Calif. hist. socs., Book Club Calif., Friends of Huntington Library, Friends Bancroft Library, Assoc. Stanford Libraries (adv. com. 1978-81), Oakland Mus. Episcopalian (sr. warden 1970-71, mem. vestry). Home: 376 E Summit Ave Sonora CA 95370

COFFIN, LINDA LEE, govt. ofcl.; b. Hutchinson, Kans.; d. Ralph B. and Virginia (Richards) L.; B.A., U. Calif., 1964; M.A., U. Okla., 1965. Mgmt. intern U.S. AEC, Richland, Wash., 1965-67, adminstrv. asst., 1967-68, contract adminstrn. asst., 1968-69, contract specialist, 1969-72; contract negotiator, acting chief Office Bus. Devel., SBA, Boston, 1972-74; sr. contract adminstr./negotiator Electric Power Research Inst., Palo Alto, Calif., 1974-76; contracting officer U.S. Geol. Survey, Menlo Park, Calif., 1976-78, nat. minority bus. officer and small bus. adviser, Reston, Va., 1978-79; dir. Office Small and Disadvantaged Bus., Dept. Treasury, Washington, 1979—; cons. Richland Flying Service, 1971-72. Bd. dirs. Campfire Girls, Richland Civic Light Opera. Mem. Am. Polit. Sci. Assn., Am. Acad. Arts and Scis., Nat. Contract Mgmt. Assn. (dir.), Calif. Alumni Assn., Wash. Pilots Assn. (dir.), Pi Sigma Alpha, Phi Alpha Theta, Zeta Tau Alpha. Home: 1965 Burnside Rd Sebastopol CA 95472 Office: Dept Treasury 15th and Pennsylvania Ave NW Suite 1320 Washington DC 20220

COFFMAN, EMILY JEANNE, marketing executive; b. Victoria, Tex., Nov. 5, 1953; d. Carl and Carrie W. (Brotherton) C. Cert. polit. studies Institut d'Etudes Politiques, Paris, 1974; B.A. in Polit. Sci. and French, Rice U., 1975; postgrad. U. Tex., 1975-76. Research asst. U. Tex. Ctr. Energy Studies, Austin, 1976-77; bilingual sec. Pullman Kellogg Co., Houston, 1978; adminstrv. asst. Golemon & Rolfe Assocs., Houston, 1978-80; Publs. coordinator CM, Inc., Houston, 1980-81; mktg. coordinator The Mayan Group Inc., Houston, 1981-84; mktg. coordinator Carter & Burgess, Inc., Houston, 1984—. Active Houston Area Women's Ctr. Mem. Women in Communications, Inc. (pres. 1984-85), Nat. Assn. Female Execs., Soc. Mktg. Profl. Services. Methodist. Clubs: Enterprise, Executive (Houston). Contbr. articles to profl. publs. Office: Carter & Burgess 6001 Savoy Suite 300 Houston TX 77036

COFFMAN, JUDY PENG, construction company executive, civic worker; b. Changsa, Hunan, China, May 16, 1943; came to U.S., 1965; d. Geoffrey Hwei and Janet (Young) Peng; children—Daniel, Sarah; m. William Henry Coffman, Oct. 15, 1977; 1 child, Rachel. Student Providence Coll., Taichung, Taiwan, 1964-65, East Los Angeles Coll., 1977. Asst. acct., Sun Moon Lake, Taichung, 1964-65; clk. Bank Am., Monterey Park, Calif., 1968-79; property mgr. B&J Investments, Rosemead, Calif., 1979-81; import agt. Caibao Co., San Gabriel, Calif., 1981-83; office mgr. Coffman Constrn., San Gabriel, 1983—. Dir. public relations Baptist Voice Children's Choir, Alhambra, Calif., 1981—; v.p. So. Calif. chpt. Chinese Am. PTA, 1983-85, pres., 1986—; mem. Consumer Affairs Adv. Commn. Los Angeles County, 1984—; co-chmn. Chinese Am. Republican Voters Assn., Monterey Park, 1984—, v.p. Los Angeles Asian Am. Rep. Women Federated, 1985—; com. mem. Calif. Rep. Central Com., 1985—. Home: 2516 W Las Flores St Alhambra CA 91803 Office: 230 E Valley Blvd San Gabriel CA 91776

COFFMAN, MARY ANNE B., lawyer; b. New Albany, Ind., Aug. 15, 1948; d. Donald O. and Mary Elizabeth (Wilkinson) Blankenburg; 1 son, Brian Anthony. B.S. in Bus., Ind. U., New Albany, 1973; M.Pub. Affairs, Ind. U., Bloomington, 1970, J.D., 1978. Bar: Ind. 1979, U.S. Dist. Ct. (so. dist.) Ind. 1979. Dep. pros. atty. State of Ind., Jeffersonville, 1978-81; sole practice, Jeffersonville, 1981—; law day coordinator Clark County Bar Assn., 1983. Bd. dirs. Ctr. for Lay Ministries, Jeffersonville, 1982, Boy Scouts Am., New Albany, 1981-83; stage crew mem. Clarksville Little Theatre, Ind., 1981—; big sister Big Bros./Big Sisters, Louisville, 1980—. Recipient Award of Merit, Clarksville Little Theatre, 1981; Leadership in the Community Appreciation award Sta. WXVW Radio, 1978. Mem. ABA, Ind. Bar Assn., Clark County Bar Assn., Phi Alpha Delta. Democrat. Episcopalian. Home: 512 Chippewa Dr Jeffersonville IN 47130 Office: Anne B Coffman 424 E Court Ave Jeffersonville IN 47130

COFONE, FRANCES JOANN, auditor; b. Newark, Dec. 15, 1961; d. Angelo Joseph and Antonietta (Via) C. B.A., Lafayette Coll., 1983. Asst. bookkeeper Del Enterprises, Livingston, N.J., 1981, inventory clk., Totowa, N.J., 1982; jr. tax acct. Prudential Ins. Co., Newark, 1983, acctg. reviewer, Roseland, N.J., 1983-84, asst. acctg. analyst, 1984-85, staff auditor, 1985—. Coach Lafayette Coll. Equestrian Team, Easton, Pa., 1986. Mem. Am. Women's Soc. C.P.A.s, Nat. Assn. Female Execs., Intercollegiate Horse Show Alumni Assn. (bd. dirs. 1985—, sec.-treas. 1984—). Home: 5 Freeman St Roseland NJ 07068 Office: Prudential Ins Co 56 N Livingston Ave Roseland NJ 07068

COGAN, ELAINE, writer, communications consultant; b. Bklyn., Sept. 24, 1932; d. Louis and Belle (Markowitz) Rosenberg; m. Arnold M. Cogan, Dec. 21, 1952; children—Mark, Suzanne, Leonard. Student journalism Portland State U., 1950-52; B.S. in Home Econs. with high honors, Oreg. State U., 1954. Weekly columnist Oreg. Jour. and Oregonian newspaper, Portland, 1970-85; ptnr. Cogan & Assocs., Portland, 1975-85, Cogan, Sharpe Cogan, 1985—, PACDO, Portland, 1984—; pres. Elaine's Tea Co., Portland, 1984—; commentator Radio Sta. KKSN, Portland, 1982—; cons. in communications to Multnomah County Dept. Corrections, U.S. Forest Service, Bonneville Power Adminstrn., Portland Devel. Commn., Women in Prodn., Am. Hosp. Assn., others. Author: (with Ben Padrow) You Can Talk to (Almost) Anyone about (Almost) Anything, 1984. Contbr. numerous articles to mags. and newspapers. Chairperson Providence Med. Ctr. Bd., Portland, 1985, Adv. Com. to Gov. Bob Straub, Salem, Oreg., 1978-80, Gov.'s Spl. Com. on Liquor Control, Salem, 1979, Task Force on Emergency Preparedness, Portland, 1982, Portland Devel. Commn., 1973-74; 1st woman pres. Congregation Neveh Shalom, 1978-80. Recipient Merit cert. Air Cargo Assn., Portland, 1985. Mem. LWV (pres. Portland 1969-71), Phi Kappa Phi, Omicron Nu. Democrat. Jewish. Avocations: sailing, reading, baking bread. Office: Cogan Sharpe Cogan 71 SW Oak St Portland OR 97204

COGAN, KATHERINE STILES, artist, writer; b. Camden, N.J., July 29, 1942; d. George Henry and Violet (Wiley) Stiles; children—Eileen Cogan, Cathleen, Kelleen. B.A. in Art Edn., Glassboro State Coll., 1973; cert. Pa. Acad. Fine Arts, 1984; postgrad. Tyler Sch. Art, 1974-75, Phila. Coll. Art, 1973-80, Temple U., 1975-76. Cert. art tchr., N.J. Tchr. art Cherry Hill High Sch., N.J., 1973-80; freelance photographer, writer, 1973—; adj. mem. art faculty Gloucester County Community Coll., Sewell, N.J., 1976; admissions asst. Pa. Acad. Fine Arts, Phila., 1985. Contbr. article series to Pa. Acad. Alumni Newsletter, 1984—, series of articles with photography and revs. on arts Art Matters mag., 1984—. One-woman show Kling Gallery, 1986, Muse Gallery, 1986; group shows include Pa. Acad. Fine Arts Student Ann., Phila., 1983-84, Temple U., Phila., 1984, Third St. Gallery, Phila., 1984, 1st Ann. Creative Artists Network Exhbn., Phila., 1984, Pa. Acad. Fine Arts 8th Ann. Fellowship Exhbn., Phila., 1985, Muse Gallery Anniversary Exhbn., Phila., 1985, Cheltenham 4th Ann. Juried Invitational Exhbn., Pa., 1985; represented in permanent collections MacDonalds Corp. Hdqrs., Ill., numerous pvt. collections Phila. Cresson travel scholar Pa. Acad. Fine Arts, 1983. Mem. Pa. Acad. Fine Arts Alumni Assn. Avocations: running; tennis; swimming; dance.

COGAN, MARY JO GLEBER GEORGE,, lawyer; b. Wilmington, Del., Aug. 13, 1954; d. Jacob Adam and Marilyn Roberta (Fox) Gleber; m. Julian N. Cogan; 1 child, Caitlin. B.A. in Polit. Sci., U. Del., 1978; J.D., U. San Diego, 1981. Bar: Calif. 1982. Assoc. Stebleton, Waters & May, El Cajon, Calif., 1982-83; ptnr. George & Allred, El Cajon, 1983-84; assoc. O'Dorisio, Wedell & Wade, San Diego, 1984-85; sole practice, San Diego, 1985—. Lillian Kratter Women's scholar U. San Diego, Law Sch., 1980-81. Mem. Calif. State Bar Assn., San Diego County Bar Assn., U. San Diego Law Sch. Alumni Assn. Democrat. Clubs: Theatergoers San Diego, Walkabout. Home: 7967 Westmore Rd San Diego CA 92126

COGGIN, CHARLOTTE JOAN, physician, educator; b. Takoma Park, Md., Aug. 6, 1928; d. Charles Benjamin and Nanette (McDonald) Coggin; B.A., Columbia Union Coll., 1948; M.D., Loma Linda U., 1952. Intern, Los Angeles County Gen. Hosp., 1952-53, resident in medicine, 1953-55; fellow in cardiology Children's Hosp. Los Angeles, White Meml. Hosp., Los Angeles, 1955-56, Hammersmith Hosp., London, 1956-57; resident in pediatrics, pediatric cardiology Hosp. for Sick Children, Toronto, Ont., Can., 1965-67; cardiologist, co-dir. heart surgery team Loma Linda (Calif.) U., 1963—, asst. prof. medicine 1961-73, assoc. prof. medicine, 1973—, asst. dean internat. programs, 1973-75, assoc. dean internat. programs, 1975—; pvt. practice medicine specializing in pediatric and adult cardiology, Los Angeles, 1957-67, Loma Linda, 1967—; mem. staff Loma Linda U. Med. Center; cardiologist, heart surgery mission to Pakistan and Asia, 1963, Greece, 1967-69, Saigon, Vietnam, 1974-75, Saudi Arabia, 1976—, China, 1984, 86, Hong Kong, 1985; trustee Tel-Med, Inc., 1972-80, pres., 1977-78. Mem. U.S. Pres.'s. Adv. Panel on Heart Disease, 1972—; gov.'s appointee Calif. Bd. Med. Quality Rev., dist. 12, 1976-79; bd. dirs. Versacare. Recipient awards for service in open heart surgery City of Karachi (Pakistan), 1963, Evangelismos Hosp., Athens, Greece, 1967-69; Golden Eagle Cine award Venice Film Festival for motion picture Arterial Septal Defect, 1964, 1st prize, 1964; named Outstanding Women of Yr. in Sci., Calif., Mus. Sci. and Industry, 1969; Gold medal of health Ministry of Health, Republic of Vietnam, 1974; Outstanding Woman award Gen. Conf. Seventh-day Adventists, 1975, Charles E. Weniger award for excellence, 1976; CASS grantee, 1974-83. Diplomate Am. Bd. Pediatrics. Mem. San Bernardino County Med. Soc. (vice chmn. communications com. 1974-75, chmn. communications com. 1975-76, editor 1975-76, chmn. travel com. 1984—, mem. hist. com.), Loma Linda U. Sch. Medicine Alumni Assn. (pres. 1978), AMA (mem. physicians adv. com. 1969—), Am. Acad. Pediatrics, Am., Calif. heart assns., Am. Med. Women's Assn., AAUP, Calif. Med. Assn. (com. on mem. services 1980-82, chmn. com. on med. schs. 1980-83), Am. Coll. Cardiology, Internat. Platform Assn., Democrat. Home: 11495 Benton St Loma Linda CA 92354 Office: Loma Linda U Med Center Loma Linda CA 92354

COHEN, ALISA BONNIE, health education administrator, medical illustrator, health consultant; b. Phila., Mar. 24, 1957; d. Carl and Vivian Edith (Landis) Bergman; m. Gregory Richard Cohen, Aug. 24, 1980. B.S. summa cum laude in Health Edn., U. Fla., 1978; cert. med. illustrator, Hahnemann Med. Coll., 1976. Asst. adminstr. Planned Parenthood, Gainesville, Fla., 1976-78; tchr. chemistry and biology Phila. Sch. Dist., 1979-81; freelance med. illustrator, Phila., 1976—; instr. health edn. Chippenham Hosp., Richmond, Va., 1981-83; dir. health edn. McGuire Clinic, Richmond, 1983—, also dir. city-wide wellness program, drug abuse program, smoking program, weight control program, all 1983—; dir. regional health edn. PruCare of Richmond, 1983—; Cons. self-def. for women Chippenham Hosp., 1983; cons. substance abuse/alcohol series St. John's Hosp., Richmond, 1983. Artist, TV presentation: Medical Illustrations, 1975; artist Jour. Blepharoplasty, 1980; contbr. articles to med. jours. Named Outstanding Artist Smithsonian Instn., 1974. Mem. Greater Richmond Area Inservice Council, Phi Beta Kappa, Eta Sigma Gamma (pres. 1977-78). Democrat. Jewish. Lodge: B'nai B'rith (pres. Phila. 1972-73). Home: 1243 Beacon St Penthouse A Brookline MA 02146 Office: McGuire Clinic Inc 7702 Parham Rd Richmond VA 23229

COHEN, ANNE SILBERSTEIN, psychotherapist, clinical social worker; b. Balt., Aug. 12, 1928; d. Louis M. and Marie Rita (Adlin) Silberstein; B.A., Goucher Coll., 1949; M.A., Montclair State Coll., 1974; M.S.W., Rutgers U., 1975; cert. N.J. Acad. Group Psychotherapy, 1976-78; postgrad. N.Y. Center for Psychoanalytic Tng., 1978—; m. Robert J. Cohen, Sept. 7, 1952; children—Laura Marjorie, Michael Louis. Social worker children's div. Dept. Public Welfare, Balt., 1950-53, Children's Protective Services, Pa. Soc. to Protect Children from Cruelty, Phila., 1953-56; mem. staff Social Work Family Life Improvement Project, Rutgers U. Grad. Sch., New Brunswick, N.J., 1964-68; social worker Catholic Family and Community Services, Paterson, N.J., 1974-75; psychotherapist, clin. social worker Essex County Guidance Center, East Orange, N.J., 1975-83; pvt. practice psychotherapy, marriage and family counseling, Livingston, N.J., 1980—. Mem. planning com. Mental Health Assn. N.J., 1980; bd. dirs. Community Psychiat. Inst. Inst., East Orange, N.J.; trustee Community Mental Health Ctr. of Oranges, Maplewood and Millburn, N.J., 1983—. Lic. marriage counselor, N.J. Fellow Am. Orthopsychiat. Assn., N.J. Soc. Clin. Social Work; mem. Acad. Cert. Social Workers, N.J. Acad. Group Psychotherapy, N.J. Soc. Clin. Social Work (dir., membership chairperson), Nat. Assn. Social Workers, Am. Assn. Marriage and Family Therapists, N.J. Assn. Women Therapists, N.J. Psychol. Assn., Soc. for Advancement Self-Psychology, Nat. Registry Health Care Providers, LWV, Nat. Council Jewish Women. Jewish. Office: Roosevelt Plaza Suite 305 2 W Northfield Rd Livingston NJ 07039

COHEN, AUDREY C., college president; b. May 14; d. Abe Cohen and Esther Cohen Morgan; children—Dawn Jennifer, Winifred Alisa. B.A. magna cum laude, U. Pitts., 1953; postgrad. in polit. sci. and edn. George Washington U., 1957-58. Founder, pres. Coll. Human Services, N.Y.C., 1964—, Am. Council Human Service, 1974—; exec. dir. Women's Talent Corps., 1964-68; founder, pres. Part-Time Research Assocs., 1958-64; lectr. in field; cons. Commn. Occupational Status Women in Nat. Vocat. Guidance Assn. Contbr. articles to profl. jours. Active subcom. higher edn. N.Y.C. Partnership; chmn. Com. on Yr. 2000, N.Y. World Future Soc.; nat. adv. com. Horizons-Bicentennial Commn.; mem. planning com. Hemispheric Congress Women, Miami, Fla., 1975-76; chmn. Nat. Task Force on Women, Edn. and Work, 1975; active Manhattan Borough Pres.'s Adv. Com. on Health Careers for Disadvantaged, Pub. Edn. Assn. Project for Restructured Edn. System N.Y.C. Recipient Stanley M. Isaacs award Am. Jewish Com., 1969; George Champion award Chase Manhattan Bank, 1970; Disting. Vis. prof. award U. Mass., 1975; Ednl. Devel. Cert. of Achievement award Atlantic Richfield Co., 1979; Otty award Our Town newspaper, 1981; Mina Shaughnessy scholarship award U.S. Office Edn., 1983; Empire State award, 1984-85; Outstanding Leadership in Higher Edn. award Commn. Ind. Colls. and Univs., 1984-85. Mem. Support Services Alliance, Inc. (bd. dirs.), Fin. Women's Assn., Am. Jewish Com. (exec. com., bd. dirs.), council Higher Ednl. Instns. Clubs: Economic, Harvard, Lotos, Women's Forum. Home: 37 E 67th St New York NY 10014 Office: Coll Human Services 345 Hudson St New York NY 10014

COHEN, CARLA LYNN, publisher; b. N.Y.C., Feb. 27, 1937; d. Barnet and Florence (Skolnick) Ellowis; children—Beth Diane, Jeffrey. Student Clark U., Adelphi U. Editor, Oceanside (N.Y.) Beacon, 1975-77; adminstrv. asst. pub. relations Bd. Suprs. Nassau County, 1977-78; pres. Carla Cohen Communications, Oceanside, N.Y., pres. Cotar Publs., Nassau Borders Papers, Floral Park, N.Y., 1981—; editor Voters Guide, Lawrence, N.Y., 1979-80. Grand Marshall Meml. Day parade, 1986. Recipient Patriotic Service award VFW, 1976; Outstanding Achievement award Am. Cancer Soc., 1976-77; Pub. Service award USAF, 1983; named Woman of Yr., B'nai B'rith, 1985, Sons of Italy, 1985. Mem. C. of C. (v.p. 1982—), LWV (v.p. 1979), Internat. Platform Assn. Republican. Jewish. Office: PO Box 155 Franklin Square NY 11010

COHEN, CLAUDIA, journalist; b. Englewood, N.J., Dec. 16, 1950; d. Robert B. and Harriet (Brandwein) C.; m. Ronald O. Perelman. B.A., U. Pa., 1972. Asst. editor More mag., N.Y.C., 1973-74, assoc. editor, 1974-76, mng. editor, 1976-77; reporter N.Y. Post, N.Y.C., 1977-78, editor Page Six, 1978-80; daily columnist N.Y. Daily News, N.Y.C., 1980-81; entertainment reporter Morning Show, Eyewitness News, WABC-TV, N.Y.C. lectr. New Sch. Office: 210 Central Park S New York NY 10019

COHEN, DIANE BERKOWITZ, lawyer; b. Vineland, N.J., June 11, 1938; d. Myer and Ida Mae (Subin) Berkowitz; m. Robert H. Cohen, June 11, 1958 (div. Dec. 1980); children—Ronald Jay, Stuart Daniel, Amy Suzanne; m. Samuel Gerstein, Aug. 5, 1984. A.A. magna cum laude, Fairleigh Dickinson U., 1958; B.A. summa cum laude, Glassboro State Coll., 1976; J.D. Temple U., 1979. Bar: Pa. 1979, U.S. Dist. Ct. N.J. 1979, U.S. Dist. Ct. (ea. dist.) Pa. 1979, N.J. 1980, U.S. Ct. Appeals (3d cir.) 1981. Assoc., Lewis Katz, Cherry Hill, N.J., 1979-81, Steven D. Weinstein, Cherry Hill, 1981-83; sole practice, Collingswood, N.J., 1983-85; ptnr. Gerstein, Cohen & Kurtzman, P.A., Haddonfield, N.J., 1985—; mem. ethics com. N.J. Supreme Ct. Vice chmn. Allied Jewish Appeal, Cherry Hill, 1968-72; v.p. Nat. Council Jewish Women, Haddonfield,

N.J., 1969-71; bd. dirs. Planned Parenthood Assn. Camden County, N.J., 1982—. Mem. Assn. Trial Lawyers Am., ABA, N.J. Bar Assn., Camden County Bar Assn. (chmn. women lawyers com., mem. jud. appointment com.). Office: Gerstein Cohen & Kurtzman PA 75 Haddon Ave Suite 200 Haddonfield NJ 08033

COHEN, DONNA EDEN, lawyer; b. Harlingen, Tex., Oct. 23, 1956; d. Gerald Myer and Annette Rose (Rodman) C. B.A., U. Mass., 1978; J.D., Suffolk U., 1981. Bar: Mass. 1981, U.S. Dist. Ct. Mass. 1982, U.S. Ct. Appeals (1st cir.) 1982. Assoc., Gilman-McLaughlin & Hanrahan, Boston, 1980—; lectr. Mass. Acad. Trial Attys., Boston, 1982—; mem. Gov.'s Com. Pre-paid Legal Services, 1983. Bd. dirs. Northeast Mass. chpt. Am. Heart Assn., Andover, 1982—. Mem. ABA, Mass. Bar Assn., Boston Bar Assn., Phi Delta Phi. Democrat. Jewish. Office: Gilman-McLaughlin & Hanrahan 470 Atlantic Ave Boston MA 02210

COHEN, EDITH MILLER, nutritionist; b. Bklyn., Apr. 8, 1923; d. Samuel and Hannah Miller; B.A., Hunter Coll., 1950; M.S. in Pub. Health, Tchrs. Coll., Columbia U., 1955; m. Marvin Cohen, Jan. 21, 1968. Dietitian Columbia Presbyterian Med. Center, N.Y.C., 1955-56; pub. health nutritionist, Bureau of Nutrition N.Y.C. Dept. of Health, N.Y.C., 1957-75; nutrition services cons. N.Y. State Dept. of Health, N.Y., 1975-82. Mem. Am. Dietetic Assn., Am. Pub. Health Assn. Home: 75 Henry St Apt 4E Brooklyn NY 11201

COHEN, FLORENCE EMERY, insurance executive; b. Paterson, N.J., Mar. 6, 1944; d. Claude John and Esther (Belber) Emery; m. Harvey H. Cohen, Sept. 5, 1965; children—John Aaron, Jason Matthew. A.B. in History, Temple U., 1965; M.A. in Social Scis., U. Chgo., 1970. Product planning mgr. Penn Mut. Ins. Co., Phila., 1970-77; dir. mktg. systems Prudential Co., Newark, 1978-80, v.p. mktg. analysis, 1980-82, v.p. tax adminstrn., 1983-84, v.p. market devel., 1984—; lectr. numerous industry assns. Mem. Friends of Handicapped, Mercer County, N.J., 1982—; exec. council Jersey City State Coll., N.J., 1985. Grad. Study fellow U. Del., 1965, Temple U., 1965, U. Chgo. 1970. Fellow Life Office Mgmt. Assn.; mem. Am. Soc. C.L.U.s, Sorotomists. Avocations: cooking, gardening, swimming. Home: 3 Stonelea Dr Princeton Junction NJ 08550 Office: Prudential Co 213 Washington St Newark NJ 07101

COHEN, GAIL PATRICIA, collectibles marketing company executive; b. N.Y.C., Dec. 12, 1942; d. Buddy and Helene (Weinsier) Taylor; m. Arthur Cohen, Nov. 2, 1963 (div. July 1968); children—Caren A., David H. A.A., Miami-Dade Community Coll., 1974; B.A. magna cum laude, Fla. Internat. U., 1976; postgrad. U. Miami, 1977; M.A., U. Ga., 1979. Tchr., vocat. counselor, coordinator summer teen employment program Rockway Jr. High Sch., Miami, Fla., 1974-79; adminstrv. asst., assoc. producer Sta. WICD-TV, Champaign, Ill., 1979-80; freelance reviewer social sci. books Library Jour., N.Y.C., 1979-81; with Bradford Exchange, Ltd., Chgo., 1980—, brokerage market analyst, 1983-84, sr. market analyst, 1984-85, communications and events mgr., 1985—; staff writer Daily Herald, 1984—; v.p. Photographers of Lake Zurich, Ill., 1985—. Contbr. articles and revs. to various publs. Active Democratic Presdl. campaigns. Miami-Dade Community Coll. scholar, 1974; Sociology/Anthropology scholar Fla. Internat. U., 1975; Hattie M. Strong Found. grantee, 1978. Mem. Profl. Photographers Am., Greenpeace, Women's Direct Response Group, Women Employed, Phi Theta Kappa. Office: Bradford Exchange Ltd 9333 Milwaukee Ave Niles IL 60648

COHEN, GLORIA ERNESTINE, educator, realtor; b. Bklyn., July 6, 1942; d. Victor George and Marion Theodosia (Roberts) C. B.S. in Edn., Wilberforce U., 1965; M.A. in Elem. Edn., Adelphi U., 1975; M.S. in Edn., Bklyn. Coll., 1986. Tchr. Bd. Edn., Bklyn., 1965—; case worker Dept. Welfare, Bklyn., 1965—. Mem. Northwest Civic Assn., Freeport, N.Y., 1973—, Roosevelt-Freeport Civic Assn., Freeport, 1984—. Mem. Assn. for Supervision and Curriculum Devel., Nat. Alliance of Black Sch. Educators, Inc., Bklyn. Reading Council of Internat. Reading Assn., N.Y. State Reading Assn., Assn. Black Educators of N.Y., Nat. Assn. Female Execs., Inc., Zeta Phi Beta, Kappa Delta Pi. Democrat. Roman Catholic. Clubs: FSO Internat. (Jamaica, N.Y.); Freeport Indoor Tennis. Avocations: tennis; skiing; swimming.

COHEN, HARRIET NEWMAN, lawyer; b. Providence, Dec. 8, 1932; d. Morris and Marion Newman; B.A. in Latin and Greek, Barnard Coll., 1952; M.A. in Latin and Greek (Tuition scholar), Bryn Mawr Coll., 1953; J.D. cum laude, Bklyn. Law Sch., 1974; 4 daus. Bar: N.Y. 1975. Assoc. Squadron, Gartenberg, Ellenoff & Plesent, N.Y.C., 1974-76, Phillips, Nizer, Benjamin, Krim & Ballon, N.Y.C., 1976-80, Golenbock & Barell, N.Y.C., 1980-83; ptnr. Golenbock and Barell, 1984—; tchr. domestic relations law Continuing Edn. div. CUNY, 1980—, adv. bd., 1982—; lectr. Assn. Bar City N.Y., 1982, N.Y. Women's Bar Assn., 1981, 82, N.Y. State Trial Lawyers Assn., 1981, 82. Mem. N.Y. Women's Bar Assn., (v.p. 1983-84), Assn. Bar City N.Y., N.Y. State Bar Assn., Bklyn. Law Rev. Alumni Assn. (trustee 1981—), Women's Bar Assn. State of N.Y. (dir. 1983-84). Office: 645 Fifth Ave 10th Floor New York NY 10022

COHEN, IDA BOGIN, export-import executive; b. Bklyn.; d. Joseph and Yetta (Harris) Bogin; student St. Johns U.; B.S., N.Y.U.; m. Barnet Gaster, June 26, 1941 (div. May 1955); m. 2d, Savin Cohen, Aug. 30, 1964. Sec.-treas. J. Gerber & Co., Inc., N.Y.C., 1942-54, v.p., dir., 1954-73; pres., dir. Austracan U.S.A., Inc., N.Y.C., 1960-73; v.p. Parts Warehouse, Inc., Woodside, N.Y., 1970-72, sec.-treas., 1972-84; also engaged in pvt. investments. Contbr. articles to South African Outspan, newspapers. Home: 12 Shorewood Dr Sands Point NY 11050

COHEN, IRENE, business executive; b. Berlin, July 14, 1936; d. Louis and Rita Nowikas; m. Seymour Cohen, Dec. 26, 1954; children—Diane, Steven. Student Syracuse U. Founder, owner Irene Cohen Personnel Services, Inc., N.Y.C., 1974—, Irene Cohen Temps, Inc., N.Y.C., 1977—, Word-Tex, Inc., N.Y.C., 1981—. Contbr. articles to profl. jours. Chairperson WBONY Adv. Bd.; adv. bd. Queens Coll. Bus. Program; active 100 Club, small bus. div. N.Y. C. of C. Recipient SBA award Women in Bus. Advocate; WBONY award for service industries; Entrepreneurial award Women Bus. Owners N.Y., 1984. Office: Irene Cohen Personnel Services Inc 475 Fifth Ave New York NY 10017*

COHEN, JEANETTE SCHEAR, artist; b. St. Louis, d. Morris and Pearl T. Schear; m. Kenneth Paul Cohen, Dec. 26, 1948; children—Matthew, Daryl, Claudia. B.F.A., Washington U., St. Louis, 1948. Life teaching credential, Calif. Free-lance artist St. Louis, 1950-57, Los Angeles, 1963-84, Olympia, Wash., 1984—; tchr. Pierce Coll., Woodland Hills, Calif., 1970-77, Los Angeles Valley Coll., Van Nuys, Calif., 1970-76; chief artist Blossom in the Cloud Co., Olympia and Woodland Hills, 1982—. Exhibited in group shows Cornucopia Gallery, Los Angeles, 1981, Palmer Gallery, Los Angeles, 1982, Pierce Art Gallery, Los Angeles, 1983. Designer: (stitchery sampler) No Space Like Home (commd. as gift to Apollo 14 astronauts and presented on nat. TV), 1971. Designer, artist various needlework projects contbd. to mags., books. Recipient numerous awards Orange County Fair, Laguna Beach Art Assn., others, 1964-84. Mem. Torana Art League (bd. dirs. 1968-70, awards), Orange County Art Assn. (awards), AAUW. Avocations: quiltmaking; sewing; metaphysical studies. Office: Blossom in the Cloud Co PO Box 6301 Olympia WA 98502

COHEN, JOYCE E., state legislator; d. Joseph and Evelyn (Sampson) Petik; divorced; children—Julia Jo, Aaron J. Grad. Coll. Med. Tech., Minn., 1955; student UCLA, 1957-58, Santa Ana Coll., 1961-62. Med. research technician dept. surgery U. Minn., 1955-58; med. research technician dept. tech. U. Calif., 1958-59, dept. bacteriology, 1959-61; med. research scientist Allergan Pharms., Santa Ana, Calif., 1961-70; ptnr. Co-Fo Investments, Lake Oswego, Oreg., 1978—; mem. Oreg. Ho. of Reps., 1979-81; chmn. legis. rules and ops. com., 1979-80, housing and urban devel. com. and judiciary subcom. 3; mem. jud. br. state energy policy rev. com., 1979; mem. Oreg. Senate, 1982—; chmn. com. on bus., housing and pub. fin.; chmn. joint com. trade and econ. devel. Mem. Assn. Family Conciliation Cts., Citizen's Council of Cts., Oreg. Environ. Council, Oreg. Women's Polit. Caucus, LWV. Democrat. Office: Oreg Senate State Capitol Salem OR 97310*

COHEN, KATE FRANK, interior design and visual consultant; b. Detroit, Jan. 15, 1947; d. Harold Leonard and Ruth Marie (Finley) Frank; m. Richard Henry Levey, Aug. 10, 1969 (div. 1975); 1 son, Jonah Shahn; m. 2d Steven Michael Cohen, Aug. 25, 1975; 1 son, Jedidiah Samuel. B.F.A., R.I. Sch. Design, 1969. Art tchr. Detroit Pub. Schs., 1969-70; instr. Ctr. for Creative Studies, Detroit, 1969-70, Lab. Sch. of Kingsbury Ctr. for Remedial Edn., Washington, 1970-72; retail mgr. Stangers Designs Unltd., Inc., Ann Arbor, Mich., 1974-75, Yvonne's Magasin de Cuisine & Tweeny's Cafe, Birmingham, Mich., 1981-82; dir. visual merchandising Thimbles div. BATUS Retail, N.Y.C., 1982-85; cons. Kate Frank Cohen Visual Merchandising & Design, Huntington Woods, Mich., 1979—; assoc. Ruth & Harold Frank Interiors, Inc., Bloomfield Hills, Mich., 1979—. Contbr. photographs to R.I. Sch. Design Portfolio, 1969, R.I. Sch. Design Alumni Bull., 1969, Modern Photography Mag., 1969, After Conviction, 1973; exhbns. include R.I. Sch. Design Photographers, Carr House Gallery, Providence, 1969, Hallmark Gallery, N.Y.C., 1969, Wayne State U., 1969, 831 Gallery, Birmingham, 1973, Detroit Artist Market, 1969-74, R.I. Sch. Design Alumni Exhbn., 1978, Huntington Woods Art Fair, 1979. Vol. VISTA, 1968, Detroit Artist Market, 1982—, Roeper City and Country Sch. Parent Council, Bloomfield Hills, 1980—, Gateway Montessori Sch. Parent Guild, Birmingham, 1979-85; alumni/admission rep. R.I. Sch. Design, 1983—. Mem. Detroit Inst. Arts Founders Soc., R.I. Sch. Design Alumni Assn., Nat. Assn. Female Execs., Detroit Artist Market. Democrat. Jewish. Home and Office: 3100 Sheridan Rd 4B Chicago IL 60657

COHEN, LUISA FAYE, educator, realtor; b. Pitts., Jan. 2, 1952; d. Emanuel and Mollie (Wise) Bucaresky; B.S. with highest honors, Pa. State U., 1973, M.S. magna cum laude, 1976; m. Howard I. Cohen, July 1, 1979. Tchr., Chartiers Valley Sch. Dist., Pitts., 1973—; with FFV Realty Inc., Mount Lebanon, Pa., 1986—. Mem. NEA, Pa. Edn. Assn., Pa. Assn. Supervision and Curriculum Devel., Chartiers Valley Edn. Assn., Pitts. Bd. Realtors, Phi Delta Kappa, Chi Omega. Jewish. Club: Mt. Lebanon Jr. Women's. Home: 253 Morrison Dr Pittsburgh PA 15216 Office: Chartiers Valley Sch Dist 2030 Swallow Hill Rd Pittsburgh PA 15220 also FFV Realty Inc 400 Cochran Rd Mount Lebanon PA 15228

COHEN, MARCELLA SUE, lawyer; b. Miami Beach, Fla., Nov. 24, 1952; m. Michael Bruce Cohen, Aug. 7, 1976; children—Steven, Stephanie. B.A., U. Miami (Fla.), 1973; J.D., Samford U., 1976; LL.M., NYU, 1978. Bar: Fla. 1978. Assoc. firm Tworoger & Asher, Ft. Lauderdale, Fla., 1978; spl. atty. organized crime and racketeering sect. U.S. Dept. Justice, Miami, Fla., 1979—. Office: Dept of Justice 77 SE 5th St Suite 401 Miami FL 33131

COHEN, MELANIE ROVNER, lawyer; b. Chgo., Aug. 9, 1944; d. Millard Jack and Sheila (Fox) Rovner; m. Arthur Wieber Cohen, Feb. 17, 1968; children—Mitchell Jay, Jennifer Sue. A.B., Brandeis U., 1965; J.D., DePaul U., 1977. Bar: Ill. 1977, U.S. Dist. Ct. (no. dist.) Ill., U.S. Ct. Appeals (7th cir.). Law clk. to justice U.S. Bankruptcy Ct., 1976-77; instr. secured and consumer transactions creditor-debtor law DePaul U., Chgo., 1980—; ptnr. Antonow & Fink, Chgo., 1977—. Mem. Supreme Ct. of Ill. Atty. Registration and Disciplinary Commn. Inquiry Bd., 1982—, hearing bd., 1986—. Panelist, speaker. Bd. dirs., v.p. Brandeis U. Nat. Alumni Assn., 1981—; life mem. Nat. Women's Com., 1975—, pres. Chgo. Chpt., 1975-82; mem. Glencoe Caucus (Ill.), 1977-80. Mem. ABA, Ill. State Bar Assn., Chgo. Bar Assn. (chmn. bankruptcy reorganization com. 1983—), Commenal Law League, Ill. Trial Lawyers Assn. Contbr. articles to profl. jours. Home: 167 Park Ave Glencoe IL 60022 Office: Antonow & Fink 111 E Wacker Dr Chicago IL 60601

COHEN, MICHELE DEBRA, publishing company sales executive; b. Bronx, N.Y., Jan. 29, 1959; d. Morton Herbert and Sally (Schwartz) C. Student Rutgers U., 1977, Charles Morris Price, 1980. Copy chief, account exec. 21 Century Mktg., Voorhees, N.J., 1981-82; sales. promotion mgr. North Am. Publishing, Phila., 1982-85; sales mgr. DBA Pub., Ft. Washington, Pa., 1985, JRG Communications, Haverford, Pa., 1985-86, Mc-Graw Hill Book Co., Delran, N.J., 1986—; copywriter, acct. exec. Michele Cohen Communications, Mt. Laurel, N.J., 1981—. Author poems, songs. Mem. NOW, Nat. Assn. Female Execs. Democrat. Avocations: sports, music, writing, politics. Home: 207 A Hastings Way Mount Laurel NJ 08054 Office: McGraw Hill Book Co 1835 Underwood Blvd Delran NJ 08075

COHEN, RACHELLE SHARON, journalist; b. Phila., Oct. 21, 1946; d. Hyman and Diane Doris (Schultz) Goldberg; m. Stanley Martin Cohen, June 22, 1968; 1 dau., Avril Heather. B.S., Temple U., Phila., 1968. Editor, Somerville Jour. (Mass.), 1968-70; reporter Lowell Sun (Mass.), 1970-72, AP, Boston, 1972-79; state house bur. chief Boston Herald Am., 1979-80, editorial page editor, 1980-82; editorial page editor Boston Herald, 1982—. Office: Boston Herald One Herald Sq Boston MA 02106

COHEN, RITA S., real estate broker; b. Montreal, Ont., Can., Jan. 11, 1934; came to U.S., 1959, naturalized, 1964; d. Meyer and Annie (Black) Friedman; ed. Grad. Realtors Inst.; m. Arthur Cohen, May 29, 1956; children—Mara Susan, Dana Sherril, Marcia Gayle. Vice pres., relocation dir. Robert Martin's Condo Mart Inc., Hartsdale, N.Y., 76-82; pres. Rita Cohen Realty Services Ltd., White Plains, N.Y., 1982—, Condos Plus, 1983—; tchr. condo and coop. course for real estate brokers Pace U. and Westchester County Realty Bd. and White Plains Adult Edn. Mem. Nat. Assn. Realtors, Westchester County Bd. Realtors, Women's Council Realtors, Hadassah (v.p. edn. 1978). Jewish. Home: 12 Ritchey Pl White Plains NY 10605 Office: 220 Westchester Ave White Plains NY 10604 also 152 S Highland Ave Ossining NY 10562

COHEN, ROBIN ELLEN, lawyer; b. N.Y.C., Aug. 23, 1955; d. Charles Solomon and Evelyn (Sweisky) C.; m. Peter T. Shapiro, June 23, 1985. J.D. cum laude, NYU, 1981; B.S., SUNY-Stony Brook, 1976; postgrad. Sloan Kettering Div. Cornell Grad. Sch. Med. Scis., 1976-77. Bar: N.Y. 1982, U.S. Dist. Ct. (ea. and so. dists.) N.Y. 1983. Assoc. atty. corp. dept. Rossman Colin Friend Lewis & Cohen, N.Y.C., 1981-84, Kramer Levin Nessen Kamlin & Frankel, N.Y.C., 1984—; clk. to presiding justice appellate div. 2d Dept., N.Y. State Supreme Ct., 1979. Mem. ABA, N.Y. Women's Bar Assn., N.Y. State Bar Assn., New York County Bar Assn., Bar Assn. City N.Y., Order of Coif. Democrat. Jewish. Home: 315 E 80th St New York NY 10021 Office: Kramer Levin et al 919 3d Ave New York NY 10022

COHEN, WENDY JO, advertising agency executive; b. N.Y.C., July 17, 1955; d. Stanley and Renee (Fierstein) C. B.A., SUNY-Binghamton, 1977. Adminstrv. asst. Ferber & Strauss Advt., N.Y.C., 1977-79; area mgr. Korvettes Dept. Store, Flushing, N.Y., 1979-80; adminstrv. asst. Merrill Lynch, N.Y.C., 1980; advt. asst. Deutsch, Shea & Evans, N.Y.C., 1980-81; asst. account exec. Bernard Schank Assocs., N.Y.C., 1981-82; account exec. Merling Marx & Seidman, N.Y.C., 1982—. Vol. big sister Jewish Bd. Family and Children's Services, N.Y.C., 1982. Mem. Am. Soc. Personnel Adminstrn. Home: 143-25 41 Ave Flushing NY 11355

COHEN, WILLA A., lawyer; b. Paterson, N.J., Apr. 27, 1954; d. Seymour and Anita (Sax) Cohen. B.S., U. Mich., 1975; M.A., Yale U., 1976; J.D., U. Pa., 1981. Bar: N.Y. 1982, N.J. 1983; asst. analyst Congressional Budget Office, Washington, 1976-78; asst. counsel/atty. Mfrs. Hanover Trust Co., N.Y.C., 1981-85; assoc. atty. Bank of Tokyo Trust Co., N.Y.C., 1985—. Mem. ABA, NOW, Women's Bar Assn. N.Y., Phi Beta Kappa. Home: 1374 Midland Ave #209 Bronxville NY 10708 Office: Bank of Tokyo Trust Co Legal Dept 100 Broadway New York NY 10005

COHEN-ADDAD, NICOLE ESTHER, pediatrician, neonatologist; b. Algiers, Algeria, Jan. 21, 1949; came to U.S., 1976, naturalized, 1981; d. Raoul and Alice (Aboucaya) Cohen-Addad. B.S., Lycée de Chantilly, France, 1966; prep. cert. med. studies, Paris, 1967; M.D., Univ. Med. Center, Pitié-Salpétrière, Paris, 1972. Intern, Beer-Sheva, Israel, 1973-74; resident pediatrics Wayne State U., Detroit, 1976-77, fellow in neonatology, 1978-80; teaching asst. pediatrics, resident pediatrics NYU, N.Y.C., 1977-78; instr. pediatrics Newark Beth Israel, 1981; instr. pediatrics Univ. Med. Sch. N.J., Newark, 1981-83, asst. prof. pediatrics, 1983—; dir. Fgn. Med. Grad. Workshop, Newark, 1983; faculty Fgn. Med. Grad. Workshop, Dearborn, Mich., 1983. Contbr. chpts. to books, articles to profl. jours. Active N.Y. County Democratic Com., 1983; vol. Village Vis. Neighbors, N.Y.C., 1983. Fellow Am. Acad. Pediatrics; mem. Am. Soc. Photobiology, Am. Med. Women's Assn., AAUW, AAUP, Am. Coll. Nutrition. Jewish. Home: 5 Charles St Apt 3F New York NY 10014 Office: Univ Med Sch NJ 100 Bergen St Newark NJ 07103

COHN, FRIEDA SELMA, librarian, acad. specialist; b. Princeton, Wis., Jan. 15, 1915; d. Hyman and Clara Louise (Feldman) Swed; B.S.Ed., U. Wis., 1935, M.A. in Math., 1936; m. Herbert E. Cohn, Mar. 17, 1946. Librarian, U. Wis., Madison, 1936-43, Forest Products Lab., Madison, 1943-48; librarian, acad. specialist, tutor U. Wis., Madison, 1948—. Bd. dirs. Temple Beth El. Recipient Spl. Achievement award Temple Beth El, 1972. Mem. Madison Area Library Council, Spl. Univ. Libraries Group, Assn. Computing Machinery. Clubs: Winged Foot (Tom Jones award 1978), Blue Line, Basketball Boosters, Hadassah. Home: 937 S Midvale Blvd Madison WI 53711 Office: 1210 W Dayton St Madison WI 53706

COHN, JUDITH R., lawyer; b. Phila., May 15, 1943; d. Mac and Evelyn (Greenbaum) Rutman; m. Marvin I. Cohn, June 23, 1963 (div. Aug. 1982); 1 son, Peter Laurence. B.A., Barnard Coll., 1964; J.D. magna cum laude, U. Pa., Law Sch., 1969. Bar: Pa., 1970, U.S. Ct. Appeals (3d cir.) 1970, U.S. Ct. Appeals (9th cir.) 1973, U.S. Ct. Appeals (8th cir.) 1973, U.S. Ct. Appeals (10th cir.) 1974, U.S. Supreme Ct. 1975. Law clk. to judge U.S. Ct. Appeals (3d Cir.), Phila., 1969-70; assoc. Wolf Block Schorr & Solis-Cohen, Phila., 1970-77, ptnr., 1977—; arbitrator Am. Arbitration Assn., U.S. Dist. Ct. (ea. dist.) Pa.; lectr. Wharton Sch., U. Pa., Phila., 1975-78; instr. appellate procedure U. Pa. Law Sch., Phila., 1978; speaker Kansas City Bar Assn. Franchise Review, 1982. Mem. ABA (moderator forum on franchising 1981), Pa. Bar Assn., Phila. Bar Assn., Lawyers Club Phila. Republican. Office: Wolf Block Schorr & Solis-Cohen 1200 Packard Bldg Philadelphia PA 19102

COHN, MILDRED, biochemist, educator; b. N.Y.C., July 12, 1913; d. Isidore M. and Bertha (Klein) Cohn; B.A., Hunter Coll., 1931, Sc.D. (hon.), 1984; M.A., Columbia U., 1932, Ph.D., 1938; Sc.D. (hon.), Women's Med. Coll., 1966, Radcliffe Coll., 1978, Washington U., St. Louis, 1981, Brandeis U., 1984, U. Pa., 1984, U. N.C., 1985; m. Henry Primakoff, May 31, 1938; children—Nina, Paul, Laura. Research asst. biochemistry George Washington U. Sch. Medicine, 1937-38; research assoc. Cornell U., 1938-46; research assoc. Washington U., 1946-50, 51-58, assoc. prof. biol. chemistry, 1958-60; assoc. prof. biophysics and phys. biochemistry U. Pa. Med. Sch., 1960-61, prof., 1961-78, Benjamin Rush prof. physiol. chemistry, 1978-82; sr. mem. Inst. Cancer Research, Phila., 1982—; Chancellor's disting. prof. biophysics U. Calif., Berkeley, spring 1981; vis. prof. biol. chemistry Johns Hopkins U. Med. Sch., 1985-86; research assoc. Harvard U., 1950-51; established investigator Am. Heart Assn., 1953-59, career investigator, 1964-78. Recipient Garvan medal; Cresson medal Franklin Inst., 1976; award Internat. Assn. Women Biochemists, 1979; Nat. Medal Sci., 1982. Mem. Am. Philos. Soc., Nat. Acad. Scis., Am. Chem. Soc., Harvey Soc., Am. Soc. Biol. Chemists, Am. Biophys. Soc., Am. Acad. Arts and Scis., Phi Beta Kappa, Sigma Xi. Editorial bd. jour. Biol. Chemistry, 1958-63, 67-72. Address: Inst Cancer Research 7701 Burholme Ave Fox Chase Philadelphia PA 19111

COHN, VIRGINIA S., public relations executive; b. Bklyn.; d. Lewis Henry and Beatrice Rita (Grouse) Saper; m. N. Burton Tretler, Feb. 7, 1940 (div. 1961); children—Amy Lynn Tretler Silverman, Richard Sterling; m. Julian M. Cohn, June 6, 1961 (dec. 1974). Grad. Ann-Reno Inst., N.Y.C., Bklyn. Coll. With various advt. agys., Miami, Fla., 1962-68; dir. advt., pub. relations Modernage, Miami, 1968-69, Bauder Coll., Miami and Ft. Lauderdale, Fla., 1970-84; owner, mgr. Two In Prodn., Miami, 1984-86; dir. pub. info. Hartford Easter Seal Rehab. Ctr., Conn., 1986—. Mem. Fashion Group Miami (treas. 1974-75), Internat. Soc. Interior Designers, Advt. Fedn. Greater Miami (pres. 1974-75, named Advt. Personality of Yr. 1975), Am. Acad. Advt., Nat. Home Fashions League, Miami C. of C. Republican. Jewish. Avocation: writing.

COHRT, CONSTANCE, financial planner; b. Orange, Calif., July 28, 1953; d. Theodore Frederick and Carrol Jean (Brinkerhoff) Cohrt. B.A., Colo. Coll., 1975. Adminstr. Springfield Life Ins. Co., Los Angeles, 1975-76; adminstr. Can. Life Assurance Co., Los Angeles, 1976-79; office mgr. Thomas Kline Assocs., Beverly Hills, Calif., 1979-80; assoc. Profl. Compensation Planners, Inc., N.Y.C., 1980—; v.p. Integrity, Inc., 1979-81. Named to Pres.' Club of Penn Mut. Life Ins. Co., 1982, also Top Club, 1982, 83, 84. Mem. Nat. Assn. Life Underwriters, Women's Life Underwriters Conf., Women Bus. Owners of N.Y., Greater Gotham Bus. Council (bd. dirs.), Cap and Gown, Phi Beta Kappa, Gamma Phi Beta. Episcopalian. Office: Profl Compensation Planners Inc 360 Lexington Ave New York NY 10017

COIGNEY, MARTHA WADSWORTH, theatre executive; b. N.Y.C., June 21, 1933; d. Charles and Martha Clay (Hollister) Wadsworth; m. Rodolphe Lucien Coigney, Dec. 27, 1969; 3 stepchildren. B.A., Vassar Coll., 1954. Exec. sec. Actors Studio, N.Y.C., 1956-59; asst. to pres. Teleprompter Corp., N.Y.C., 1960-61; adminstrv. and prodn. asst. to theatrical producer Roger L. Stevens (Nat. Endowment for Arts), 1962-65; asst. dir. Internat. Theatre Inst. U.S., N.Y.C., 1966-69, dir., 1969—, mem. internat. body exec. com., 1971—, v.p., 1981—. Mem. theatre panel N.Y. State Council of Arts, 1976-79, chmn., 1978-79; mem. internat. panel Nat. Endowment for Arts, 1979-80; bd. dirs. Theatre of Latin Am., 1973-79. Decorated officier Ordre des Arts et des Lettres (France), 1978. Mem. Nat. Theatre Conf. (pres. 1982-84). Club: Cosmopolitan. Contbr. articles to profl. publs. Home: 1200 Fifth Ave New York NY 10029 Office: 1860 Broadway New York NY 10023

COIN, SHEILA REGAN, management consultant; b. Columbus, Ohio, Feb. 17, 1942; d. James Daniel and Jean (Hodgson) Cook; m. Tasso H. Coin, Sept. 17, 1967; children—Tasso, Alison Regan. B.S., U. Iowa, 1964. R.N. Staff nurse VA Hosp., Boston, 1964-66; field rep. ARC, Chgo., 1966-67, adminstr., 1967; asst. div. dir. Am. Hosp. Assn., sec. Am. Soc. Hosp. Dirs. Nursing, Chgo., 1967-69; owner Coin & Assocs., Chgo., 1975-77; ptnr. Coin, Newell & Assocs., Chgo., 1977—; instr. dept. continuing edn. Loyola U., Chgo., 1975-77, Rock Valley Coll. Mgmt. Inst., Rockford, Ill., 1978-80, Ill. Central Coll. Inst. Personal and Profl. Devel., Peoria, 1979—, Triton Coll. Continuing Edn., River Grove, Ill., 1983-84, No. Ill. U. Continuing Edn., DeKalb, 1983—. Vol. Art Inst., Chgo., 1968-69; mem. Chgo. Beautiful Com., 1968-73; chmn. Mayor Daley's Chgo. Beautiful Awards Project, 1972; mem. jr. bd. Girl Scouts Assn., Chgo., 1975-76; mem. jr. governing bd. Chgo. Symphony Orch., 1971—, pres., 1977-78; governing mem. Orchestral Assn., Chgo., 1977-81; bd. dirs. Mid-Am. chpt. ARC, Chgo., 1979-81, bd. dirs. Chgo. dist., 1981—, chmn. fin. devel. com., 1982-85; dir. Com. for Thalossemia Chgo. Bd., 1981-82; mem. women's bd. Nat. Com. Prevention Child Abuse, Chgo., 1981-82. Mem. Am. Mgmt. Assn., Am. Soc. Tng. and Devel., Ill. Tng. and Devel. Assn. Democrat. Roman Catholic. Avocations: piano; tennis; national and international travel; spectator sports; family activities. Home: 1037 W North Shore Ave Chicago IL 60626 Office: Coin Newell & Assocs 919 N Michigan Ave Chicago IL 60611

COKER, CHARLOTTE NOEL, political activist; b. New Orleans, Dec. 28, 1930; d. Cecil Eugene and Esta Reed (Williams) Mahaffey; m. Rainey Morris Coker, Nov. 17, 1950; children—Patricia A. Coker Bracey, Carol J. Coker Johnson, Teresa J., Robert M. Student X-ray technician tng. St. Marys Hosp., Port Arthur, Tex., 1947-48, X-ray therapy, Emory U., 1949. Precinct committeewoman Spokane County Democratic Party, Spokane, Wash., 1970—, 6th legis. dist. leader, 1973-74, 77-78; state committeewoman Spokane County Dem. Central Com., 1975-76, 79-80, 81-82; vice chmn. Wash. State Dem. Com., Seattle, 1981; region 6 dir. Wash. State Fedn. Dem. Women's Clubs, 1979-80, state dir., 1981-85; tour guide Wash. Ho. of Reps., Olympia, 1975; aide Office of Gov. Dixy Lee Ray, Spokane, 1978-80. Mem. Spokane Quality of Life Council, 1975-77; mem. Spokane Task Force for Community Devel. Funds, 1978; Mem. Spokane Fedn. Women's Orgns. (pres. 1985—), Nat. Assn. Parliamentarians, Nat. Fedn. Dem. Women (parliamentarian 1985—), Gen. Fedn. Women's Clubs. Club: Jane Jefferson Dem. (v.p. 1979). Avocations: plate collecting; bridge; public affairs. Home: E 2215 45th Ave Spokane WA 99223

COKER, CLAUDIA GERMAINE, savings and loan examiner; b. Walnut Ridge, Ark., Jan. 6, 1953; d. Zack Tiley and Germaine Marie (Piantoni) C. B.S., Ark. State U., 1975. Cashier Harps Supermarket, Walnut Ridge, 1972-73, Rorex Supermarket Hoxie, Ark., 1973-74; office mgr. Higginbotham Burial Ins., Walnut Ridge, 1975; clk. typist Crane Co., Jonesboro, Ark., 1975-76; savs. and loan examiner Fed. Home Loan Bank Bd., Little Rock, 1976-85; Savs. and loan examiner Fed. Home Loan Bank, Dallas, 1985—. Recipient Civil Services Beta award Fed. Home Loan Bank Bd., 1978. Mem. Nat. Assn. Female Execs. Baptist. Clubs: Confederate Air Force (security detachment)(Harlingen, Tex.); Razorback Wing (security detachment)(Pine Bluff, Ark.). Avocations: counted cross stitch; knitting; needlepoint; reading; collecting depression glass. Home: 2723 C Greenbriar Dr Jonesboro AR 72401 Office: Fed Home Loan Bank-Examinations Div 1450 Tower Bldg Little Rock AR 72201

COKER, ELIZABETH BOATWRIGHT, author; b. Darlington, S.C., Apr. 21, 1909; d. Purvis Jenkins and Bessie (Heard) Boatwright; m. James Lide Coker, Sept. 27, 1930 (dec.); children—Penelope Hall, James Lide. A.B., Converse Coll., 1929; postgrad. Middlebury Coll., 1938. Assoc. prof. English,

Appalachian State U., Boone, N.C., 1971-72. Author: Daughter of Strangers, 1950; The Day of the Peacock, 1952; India Allan, 1953; The Big Drum, 1957; La Belle, 1959; Lady Rich, 1963; The Bees, 1968; Blood Red Roses, 1977; The Grasshopper King, 1981. Contbr. articles and poetry to lit. publs. Mem. Hartsville Sch. Bd., 1939-49; sec., bd. dirs. Blowing Rock Horse Show Assn., 1943-49; bd. dirs. United Cerebral Palsy of S.C.; nat. bd. dirs. Med. Coll. of Pa.; trustee Converse Coll., 1981—. Mem. Nat. Acad. Poets, Poetry Soc. Ga., AAUW, PEN, S.C. Poetry Soc., Authors Guild, Garden Club Am. Republican. Episcopalian. Clubs: Springdale Hall (Camden, S.C.); Hound Ears (Blowing Rock, N.C.).

COKER, JO ANN CHATHAM, real estate company executive; b. Dallas, Mar. 30, 1941; d. Chester and Winifred Lenora (Hervey) Chatham; m. Thomas Rudolph Coker, Dec. 21, 1957; children—Deborah LeNoir, Chester Thomas. Grad. Realtors Inst., Dallas, 1975; cert. resident specialist Realtors Nat. Mktg. Inst., Chgo., 1980. Lic. real estate broker, Tex. Bookkeeper Republic Nat. Bank, Dallas, 1958-60; retail sales Nat. Chain Stores, Tex., 1963-71; dir., trustee LWV of Tex., 1972-75; broker, mgr. Gene Tauzin Realtors, Garland, Tex., 1974-79; broker, owner Realty World Garland Assocs., Garland, 1979—; owner, cons. Metroplex Bus. Brokerage, Garland, 1985-86; cons. in field. Editor: (slide presentation) Constitutional Revision-Tex., 1972-73. Founder, organizer Garland Sch. Lunch program, 1969; juror Nat. Mcpl. League-All Am. Cities Jury, Dallas, 1974; dir. LWV Tex., 1971-74, pres. LWV of Garland, 1970-71; trustee LWV Edn. Fund, Tex., 1973-74; platform com. Tex. Democratic Conv., Houston, 1978; committeewoman Tex. Dem. Party 9th Senate Dist., 1980-82; pres. Garland Dem. Women, 1979; sec. Garland Area Dems., 1978-79, precinct chmn. Dallas County Dem. precincts 2201, 2301, Garland, 1980—; del. Tex. Dem. Conv., 1976, 78, 80, 82, 84, Nat. Dem. Conv., 1982; steering com. Krueger of Tex., 1983-84; pres. Garland Civic Theatre, 1982-84; dir. Tex. Non-profit Theatres, 1984—, treas., 1986-87; adminstrv. bd., sec. First United Methodist Ch., Garland, 1984, chmn. status of women, 1985—; com. mem. Dallas Area Rapid Transit Bd., Garland, 1983-84; mem. Charter Rev. Com., Garland, 1983-84, Bicentennial Steering com., Garland, 1975-76; chmn. Com. for Pub. Health, Garland, 1976-78. Mem. Garland Bd. Realtors (dir. 1982-85), Nat. Assn. Realtors, Tex. Assn. Realtors, Realty World N. Tex. Brokers Council (exec. sales club, 1978-84; trade group rep., 1984, treas. 1978, v.p. 1979, edn. com. 1981-84). Club: Am. Mensa. Avocations: travel; history; reading; swimming. Home: 2822 Green Oaks Garland TX 75040 Office: Realty World Garland Assocs 985 W Centerville Rd Garland TX 75041

COKER, KATHRYN ELAINE, district court clerk; b. Sutherland, Nebr., Oct. 6, 1936; d. Lloyd Harley and Doris Ella (Olson) Danielson; m. Zane Roger Coker Mar. 11, 1954; children—Lynda Kathryn Coker Lehl, Gregory Sherman. Grad. high sch. Sutherland. Dist. ct. clk., Ogallala, Nebr. Sec. Keith County Crimestoppers Program, Nebr.; sec., treas. Keith County Republican Central Com.; active Outreach Com., United Meth. Ch., Ogallala. Mem. Bus. and Profl. Women's Club (treas.), Keith-Perkins Legal Counties Secs. Assn. (sec.), Prophets Investment Club. (treas.). Home: Box 475 117 W 6th St Ogallala NE 69153 Office: Clk of Dist Ct Box 686 Ogallala NE 69153

COLABELLA, BETTY MARIE, engring. co. exec.; b. Mt. Carmel, Pa., May 27, 1925; d. Philip Christ and Edith Lavinia Wagner; student public schs. Mount Carmel, Pa.; m. Alfred V. Colabella, Jr., Aug. 28, 1945; children—Alfred V. III, Robert Clark, Edith Ann, Scott Michael. Sec.-treas. A.V. Colabella Engrs., Bordentown, N.J., 1955—, also dir. Mem. Bordentown Bd. Edn., 1965-75, pres., 1968-69, 73-74. Mem. Profl. Engrs. Soc. Mercer County Aux. (pres.), PTA Bordentown (pres.), Republican. Home: 19 Prince St Bordentown NJ 08505 Office: 138 Farnsworth Ave Bordentown NJ 08505

COLACHICO, JEANNE MARIE, lawyer; b. Medford, Mass., Mar. 1, 1951; d. Charles Anthony and Margaret Leona (Harvey) C.; B.A. magna cum laude, Regis Coll., Weston, Mass., 1973; M.Urban Affairs, Boston U., 1977; J.D., Suffolk U., Boston, 1981. Asst. to dir. consumer protection Office Atty. Gen. Mass., 1973-74; EEO specialist Def. Contract Adminstn., Boston region, 1974-81, EEO mgr. 1981-85; mgr. organizational devel., counsel for human resources Avco Systems Textron, Wilmington, Mass., 1985—; admitted to Mass. bar, 1981, Fed. Dist. Ct. bar, 1982, Ct. Appeals, 1982. Recipient numerous certs., service awards. Mem. ABA, Mass. Bar Assn., Mass. Assn. Women Lawyers, Nat. Assn. Female Execs., Boston Fed. Execs. Bd. (chmn. coms.), Federally Employed Women, Pan Am. Soc., Greater Boston Civil Rights Coalition, Phi Delta Phi. Author articles in field. Home: 109 Mitchell Ave Medford MA 02155 Office: 201 Lowell St Wilmington MA 01887

COLAGUORI, JUNE CAROL, marketing consultant; b. Pitts., Oct. 17, 1955; d. Julius Ceasar and Margaret (Haverlesko) Bilecky; m. Leo Colaguori, Apr. 1, 1978. Student U. Pitts, Forbes Tech. Sch., Pitts. Mktg. asst. Gen. Nutrition Corp., Pitts., 1981, mktg. mgr., 1982-83, promotions mgr., 1984, new product buyer, 1985, mgr. new bus. and product devel., 1986; mktg. cons., Los Angeles, 1986—. Mem. Nat. Assn. Female Execs., Pitts. Advt. Club, Personal Dynamics Inst. (cert.). Episcopalian. Office: 11039 Begonia Fountain Valley CA 92708

COLAMARINO, KATRIN BELENKY, lawyer; b. N.Y.C., Apr. 29, 1951; d. Allen Abram and Selma (Burwasser) Belenky Lang; m. Leonard J. Colamarino, Mar. 20, 1982; m. Barry E. Brenner, June 1, 1974 (div. June 1979); 1 dau., Rachel Erin. B.A., Vassar Coll., 1972; J.D., U. Richmond, 1976. Bar: Ohio 1976, U.S. Ct. Apls. (Fed. cir.), 1982. Staff atty. AM Internat. Inc., Cleve., 1976-78; atty. Lipkowitz & Plant, N.Y.C., 1980-81; atty. Docutel Olivetti Corp., Tarrytown, N.Y., 1981-84; atty. NYNEX Bus. Info. Systems, 1984-85; corp. counsel, sec. Logica Inc., N.Y.C., 1986—. Class agt. Fieldston Sch., N.Y.C., 1980—, exec. bd. Ethical Fieldston Alumni Assn., 1980—; alumnae council rep. Vassar Coll., 1982-86. Mem. Assn. Bar City N.Y., Customs and Trade Bar Assn., Westchester Fairfield Corp. Counsel Assn. Office: Logica Inc 666 3d Ave New York NY 10017

COLBERT, CLAUDETTE (LILY CHAUCHOIN), actress; b. Paris; came to U.S., 1910; d. Georges and Jeanne (Loew) Chauchoin; m. Norman Foster, Mar. 13, 1928; m. Joel Pressman, 1955. Grad., Washington Irving High Sch., 1923. Debut as Sibyl Blake in Wild Westcotts, Frazee Theatre, 1924; later appeared in plays including The Marionette Man, Leah Kleschna, High Stakes, The Kiss in a Taxi, the Ghost Train, Pearl of Great Price, Tin Pan Alley, See Naples and Die, Eugene O'Neill's Dynamo, A Talent for Murder; 1st appearance in London in the Barker, 1928; appeared in motion pictures, 1929—, including: the Lady Lies, Manslaughter, The Smiling Lieutenant, Sign of the Cross, Cleopatra, Private Worlds, Maid of Salem, It Happened One Night, The Gilded Lily, I Met Him in Paris, Bluebeard's Eighth Wife, Zaza Midnight, Drums Along the Mohawk, Skylark, Remember the Day, Palm Beach Story, No Time for Love, So Proudly We Hail, Parrish, Since You Went Away, Three Came Home, Bride for Sale, Arise My Live, Sleep My Love; starred in Broadway plays: Marriage-Go-Round, 1958-60, The Irregular Verb to Live, 1963, The Kingfisher, 1978; tour A Community of Two, 1973-74, Chgo. performances Marriage-Go-Round, 1976; appeared in Aren't We All at Theatre Royal Haymarket, London, 1984, N.Y., 1985. Appeared in TV spls. Best of Broadway, Including Royal Family, The Guardsman, Blythe Spirit, Private Worlds, 1954-56. Recipient Oscar award for best actress Nat. Acad. Motion Picture Arts and Scis., 1934.

COLBERT, LINDA ELAINE, nurse; b. Merced, Calif., Aug. 15, 1947; d. William Ralph and Elaine R. (Murray) Phelps; B.S., Calif. State U., Fresno, 1969, M.S.N., 1984. m. Gary Colbert, Aug. 24, 1968; children—Tamara, Rebecca, Valerie. Staff nurse Valley Med. Center, Fresno, Calif., 1969-72; night supr. Coalinga (Calif.) Dist. Hosp., 1973-75, dir. nurses, 1978-83; pvt. practice as family nurse practitioner, 1984—; coordinator med. assisting and emergency med. tech. program W. Hills Coll., 1975-78. Bd. trustees Coalinga Dist. Hosp., 1975-76.

COLBURN, JULIA KATHERINE LEE, educator; b. Columbus, Ohio, Feb. 8, 1927; d. Fred Merritt and Lillian May (Getrost) Lee; m. Joseph Linn Colburn, Sept. 5, 1947; children—Joseph Linn, Jr., David Laird, Andrew Lee, Julia LeeAnne. B.S. in Edn., Ohio State U., 1948. Library asst. Columbus Pub. Library, 1945-48, Ohio State U. Library, Columbus, 1945-47; life ins. acct. Nationwide Ins., Columbus, 1949-50; substitute tchr. Columbus Pub. Schs., 1965-69, 79-81; vol. resource person Columbus Pub. Schs., 1979—. Author: Ohio Daughters of 1812. Editor, compiler (state pub.) Star and Anchor, 1983-85 (nat. first award, 1984, 85). Presiding judge Franklin County Bd. Elections, Columbus, 1959—; pres. Linden Jr. Civic Club, Columbus, 1953, Rhapsody Unit, Columbus Symphony, 1975-77, Arlington Park PTA, Columbus, 1963-64, Linden-McKinley Jr.-Sr. High PTA, Columbus, 1964-66, Northland High PTA, Columbus, 1972-73; organizing pres. Lazarus Cancer Ray, Columbus, 1953; leader Northland council Girl Scouts U.S., 1968-70; vol. Vision Ctr., Columbus, 1969-72 (Named Vol. of Yr. 1971); v.p. Linden United Meth. Women, Columbus, 1965-66, pres. 1966-68, various coms. 1963—; pres. Meth. Youth Fellowship, Columbus, 1944-45; adminstrv. bd. Linden United Meth. Ch., Columbus, 1944-45, 52—, choir soloist, mem., 1945—, Sun. sch. tchr., 1959—, spl. membership awards 1971, 77; dist. chmn. Christian Global Concerns Columbus North Dist. United Meth. Women, 1973-77. Recipient Silver Good Citizenship medal Ohio Soc. SAR, 1978, Medal of Appreciation, Benjamin Franklin chpt., 1978. Mem. Ohio Geneal. Soc. (speakers staff 1978—), First Families of Ohio, DAR (Good Citizenship cert. 1945, state rec. sec. 1983-86, state vice regent 1986—, various offices and coms. 1976—), Children of Am. Revolution (sr. nat. rec. sec. 1982-84, various coms. 1974—; Ohio Service award, 1979, maj. benefactor 1986), U.S. Daus. of 1812 (parliamentarian, chmn. nat. membership 1985—, state pres. 1983-85), Colonial Dames XVII Century (state first v.p. 1985—), Daus. Colonial Wars (state historian 1984-86, nat. vice chmn. 1983-86), Women Desc. Ancient and Honorable Arty. Co. (state rec. sec. 1983-86, state pres. 1986—), Daus. Am. Colonists (Old Trails chpt. treas. 1981-85, vice regent 1985—), New Eng. Women (pres. Columbus colony 1984—), Colonial Daus. Seventeenth Century, Daus. Union Vets., Zeta Phi Eta. Republican. Club: Ohio Fedn. Women's (trustee, chmn. 1974-83). Lodges: Order of Eastern Star (star point 1961-62), Linden Lawanis (Kiwanis Aux. pres. 1964). Avocations: genealogy; music; writing. Home: 1887 Northcliff Dr Columbus OH 43229

COLBURN, NORMA ELAINE WHEELER, city official; b. St. Johnsbury, Vt., June 26, 1933; d. Clayton Wallace and Ida Minerva (Lang) Wheeler; student Burdett Coll., 1951, Rutgers U., 1968, 75; m. James Austin Colburn, Jan. 19, 1952; children—Candice Margaret, James Austin. Registered municipal clk., N.J. Exec. sec. Oswald L. Sanborn C.P.A.'s, Ridgewood, N.J., 1952; exec. sec. archtl. div. Am. Brakeshoe Co., Mahwah, N.J., 1952; postal clk. U.S. P.O., Lyndon Center, Vt., 1956-60; partner Colburn's Store, Lyndon Center, Vt., 1956-60; corr., feature writer Burlington (Vt.) Free Press, 1959-60; dep. borough clk., ct. clk., Allendale, N.J., 1968-70, sec. planning bd., dep. water collector, 1969-70, borough clk., 1970—, borough adminstr., 1972—. Active Girl Scouts U.S.A., 1965-66. Recipient Time Mag. Current Events award, 1950, 51. Mem. Municipal Clks. Assn. N.J., Bergen County Municipal Clks., Internat. Inst. Municipal Clks. Assn. Mem. Order Eastern Star. Home: 310 Brookside Av Allendale NJ 07401 Office: Office City Clk City Hall Allendale NJ 07401

COLBY, ANNE, psychologist; b. Galveston, Tex., Feb. 10, 1946; d. Malcolm Young and Emily Jane (Armacost) C.; m. William V.B. Damon; 1 dau., Caroline Colby. B.A., McGill U., 1968; Ph.D., Columbia U., 1972. Research assoc., lectr. Harvard U., Cambridge, Mass., 1972-80; dir. Henry A. Murray Research Center of Radcliffe Coll., Cambridge, 1980—; dir. research Clin. Devel. Inst. Lic. psychologist, Mass. Mem. Nat. Council for Research on Women (dir.). Author: The Measurement of Moral Judgment, 1986. Office: H A Murray Research Center Radcliffe Coll 10 Garden St Cambridge MA 02138

COLBY, LINDA SUSAN, safety executive, consultant; b. Los Angeles, Apr. 2, 1949; d. Lamar B. and Mary Ellen (Baggerly) LeDent; m. Dennis James Giguere, Nov. 11, 1972 (div. Oct. 1980); m. 2d, Barry Leland Colby, Oct. 18, 1980; (div. 1984); children—Andrea Leslie Giguere, Steven James Giguere. A.A., Cerritos Coll., 1975; B.A., Calif. State U.-Long Beach, 1978, B.S., 1972. Charge nurse Presbyn. Intercommunity Hosp., Whittier, Calif., 1975-77; charge nurse Anaheim Meml. Hosp. (Calif.), 1977-78; v.p. Pro-I-Zon, Long Beach, Calif., 1982—; benefits adminstr., occupational health nurse, Wilmington, Calif., 1979-84; safety supr. U.S. Borax and Chem. Corp., Wilmington, Calif., 1979—. Mem. Alpha Epsilon Phi. Office: US Borax & Chem Corp 300 Falcon St Wilmington CA 90744

COLBY, MARY ELIZABETH, antiques executive, specialist; b. Scottsburg, Ind., July 31, 1914; d. Clifford Lawson and Bessie (Weir) Reid; m. Edward Pendleton Colby, Apr. 6, 1954 (dec. 1983); m. Rudolf Myers, June 10, 1936 (dec.); 1 dau., Cheri Davis Langdell. A.B. cum laude, Ind. U., 1936. Asst. buyer, buyer dept. stores, Indpls., Los Angeles, Chgo., 1936-43, 46-54; v.p., sec. Port O'Call Pasadena Inc. stores, Calif., 1956-73; pres. Colby Antiques Inc., San Clemente, Calif., 1973—; pres. Mary Colby, Inc. (fine antiques appraisal firm), San Clemente, 1985—; lectr. antiques. Contbr. articles in field to publs. Chmn. San Clemente Beautification Com., 1975-76; Active, Rep. Party. Mem. Internat. Soc. Appraisers Inc. (charter mem.), Women in Communications, Phi Beta Kappa, Theta Sigma Phi. Methodist. Clubs: Town, Valley Hunt (Pasadena) Home: 1710 Calle de los Alamos San Clemente CA 92672 Office: Colby Antiques Inc 510 N El Camino Real San Clemente CA 92672

COLBY, TERRI LYNNE, marketing research manager; b. Lansing, Mich., Nov. 7, 1956; d. Donald F. and Dorothy (Smith) C.; m. Terry Dale Moore, Aug. 21, 1982. B.S., U. So. Calif., 1978, M.B.A., 1979. Mktg. research analyst Carnation Co., Los Angeles, 1980-82, sr. mktg. research analyst, 1982-83; sr. mktg. research analyst Kraft Co., Glenview, Ill., 1983-85, mktg. research mgr., 1985—. Mem. Am. Mktg. Assn., Delta Gamma. Office: Kraft Co Kraft Ct Glenview IL 60025

COLBY-HALL, ALICE MARY, Romance studies educator; b. Portland, Maine, Feb. 25, 1932; d. Frederick Eugene and Angie Fraser (Drown) Colby; B.A., Colby Coll., 1953; M.A., Middlebury Coll., 1954; Ph.D., Columbia, 1962; m. Robert A. Hall, Jr., May 8, 1976; stepchildren—Philip, Diana Hall Goodall, Carol Hall Erickson. Tchr. French, Latin Orono (Maine) High Sch., 1954-55; tchr. French Gould Acad., Bethel, Maine, 1955-57; lectr. French Columbia, 1959-60; instr. Romance lit. Cornell U., Ithaca, N.Y., 1962-63, asst. prof., 1963-66, assoc. prof., 1966-75, prof. Romance studies, 1975—Recipient Médaille des Amis d'Orange, 1985. Fulbright grantee, 1953-54; NEH fellow, 1984-85. Mem. Modern Lang. Assn., Medieval Acad. Am. (councillor 1983-86), Internat. Arthurian Soc., Societe Rencesvals, Académie de Vancluse, Phi Beta Kappa. Republican. Conglist. Author: The Portrait in Twelfth Century French Literature: An Example of the Stylistic Originality of Chretien de Troyes, 1965; also articles. Mem. editorial bd. Speculum, 1976-79, Olifant, 1974—. Home: 308 Cayuga Heights Rd Ithaca NY 14850 Office: Dept Romance Studies Cornell U Ithaca NY 14853

COLDIRON, KAREN SUE, banker; b. Greensburg, Ind., Mar. 16, 1940; d. Gordon Calvin and Ruth Helen (Anderson) Emly; m. James William Coldiron, Sept. 19, 1959; 1 child, Jeffrey William. Grad. Sch. of Banking, U. Wis., 1981. with Irwin Union Bank, Columbus, Ind., 1959—, v.p., 1982—; instr. Am. Inst. Banking., Columbus, Ind., 1976-79; dir. Ind. Clearing House, Indpls., 1983—. Bd. dirs. Barth County Hearth Assn., Columbus, Turning Point, Columbus, 1985—. Named Woman of Yr., Am. Bus. Women, 1977. Mem. Ind. Bankers Assn. (chmn. com.), Bus. and Profl. Women (state officer 1978, local pres. 1981-82), Nat. Assn. Bank Women (nat. bd. dirs., local, nat. officer 1979—, nat. sec. 1984-85), C. of C. Republican. Home: 2170 N Old S R 9 Columbus IN 47203 Office: Irwin Union Bank PO Box 929 500 Washington St Columbus IN 47201

COLDITZ, JUDY CAROL, hand rehabilitation center administrator, consultant; b. Livingston, Tenn., Oct. 10, 1949; d. Oscar Augustus and Leta Pauline (Smith) C. B.S. in Occupational Therapy, U. of Puget Sound, Tacoma, 1972. Lic. occupational therapist. Staff therapist UNC Hand Rehab. Ctr., Chapel Hill, N.C., 1972-74; hand therapist Raleigh Orthopaedic Clinic, N.C., 1979-82; dir. Occupational therapy Wake Med. Ctr., Raleigh, 1975-82; dir. Raleigh Hand Rehab. Ctr., 1982—. Author: (with others) Rehabilitation of the Hand, 1984; Manual on Management of Specific Hand Injuries, 1984; Bone Injuries, 1986. Contbr. articles to profl. jours. Editorial rev. bd. Am. Jour. Occupational Therapy, 1984-87. Adv. bd. dirs. N.C. Arthritis Found., Durham, N.C., 1981-83, N.C. Multiple Sclerosis Soc., Raleigh, 1981-82. Recipient Appreciation award City of Raleigh 1981, N.C. Arthritis Found., 1981. Mem. Am. Soc. Hand Therapists (founding, bd. dirs. 1980-82, treas. 1984-86), N.C. Occupational Therapy Assn. (legis. chair 1983-85, Scullin award 1981, Appreciation award 1984), Am. Occupational Therapy Assn. Club: Raleigh Ski and Outing. Avocations: whitewater canoeing, rennovating houses, sewing, weaving. Office: Raleigh Hand Rehab Ctr PO Box 30263 Raleigh NC 27622

COLE, ADELAIDE MEADOR, physical education educator; b. Hinton, W.Va., June 6, 1923; d. Vollmer Aden and Josephine Florence (Ratliff) Meador; A.B., Marshall Coll., 1946; M.A., Duke U., 1947; Ed.D., Columbia U., 1950; m. James Lewis Cole, Nov. 29, 1964; children—John, Alexandra, Mary Adelaide, Tanya Sean. Instr. phys. edn. Columbia U., 1950; prof. Cedarville (Ohio) Coll., 1951-52; asso. prof. Pan Am. Coll., Edinburg, Tex., 1953-60, Calif. Western U., San Diego, 1960-61, N.Mex. Highlands U., Las Vegas, 1961-65; prof. phys. edn. Ball State U., Muncie, Ind., 1967—, dir. grad. studies Sch. Phys. Edn., 1971-82, also adminstrv. asst. to chmn. sch., 1977-82. Recipient ARC Outstanding Service award, 1958. Mem. AAHPERD (Midwest chmn. research sect. 1981, Midwest chmn. resolutions com. 1984-86), Ind. Assn. for Health, Phys. Edn., Recreation and Dance (sec. 1981—, honor award 1985), LWV, DAR (regent Sarah Winston Henry chpt. 1983-85), Sigma Sigma Sigma, Phi Delta Kappa, Pi Lambda Theta. Democrat. Episcopalian. Clubs: Elks, Eagles, Rotarian women's auxs. Home: 968 Mary Lee Ave New Castle IN 47362 Office: Ball State U Muncie IN 47306

COLE, BETTY LOU MCDONEL SHELTON (MRS. DEWEY G. COLE JR.), judge; b. Elwood, Ind., June 5, 1926; d. Bernard Miller and Vee Marie (Robertson) McDonel; student Ind. U., 1947-50, LL.B., 1969; student Ball State U., 1964-65; m. Elbert Shelton, Dec. 13, 1944; children—Steven Elbert, Jeanette Louise; m. 2d, Dewey G. Cole, Jr., Dec. 24, 1975. Admitted to Ind. bar, 1969, Fed. Cts., 1969; practiced in Muncie, Ind., 1969—; pvt. practice Betty L. Shelton Law Office, 1970-78; sr. ptnr. firm Dunnuck, Cole, Rankin and Wyrick, Muncie, 1978-80; judge Delaware County Superior Ct., 1980—. Mem. Am., Ind., Muncie bar assns., Ind. Judges Assn., Am. Trial Lawyers, Ind. U. Law Alumni Assn., League Women Voters (league pres. 1963-64), Bus. and Profl. Women. Club: Delaware Country (Muncie). Office: 100 W Main St Delaware County Courthouse Muncie IN 47305

COLE, CAROLYN JO, brokerage company executive; b. Carmel, Calif., Apr. 22, 1943; d. Joseph Michael, Jr., and Dorothea Wagner (James) C.; A.B., Vassar Coll., 1965. Mgr. tech. services Aims Group, N.Y.C., 1965-67; editor Standard & Poor's Corp., N.Y.C., 1968-74; sr. v.p. PaineWebber, Inc., 1975—; guest lectr. Harvard U. Bus. Sch. Mem. N.Y.C. Commn. on Status of Women. Named to YWCA Acad. Women Achievers. Mem. N.Y. Soc. Security Analysts, Fin. Analysts Fedn., Soc. Fgn. Analysts, Fin. Women's Assn., Women's Econ. Roundtable, Econ. Club N.Y., NOW, DAR. Democrat. Episcopalian. Club: Vassar (N.Y.C.). Contbr. to Ency. Americana. Office: PaineWebber Inc 1285 Ave of Americas New York NY 10014

COLE, DIANE JACKSON, textile manufacturing company executive; b. Amesbury, Mass., Sept. 14, 1952; d. Robert Keith and Lois Elizabeth (Fogg) Jackson. B.F.A. cum laude, U. N.H., 1974; student U. London, Sir John Cass Coll. Art, London, Richmond Coll., Surrey, Eng. Owner Diane Jackson Cole Handweaving, Kennebunk, Maine, 1974—; pres. Kennebunk Weavers, Inc., 1981—. Contbr. articles to profl. jours., mags. Exhbns. include: Fiber Invitational, Milw., 1977, Currier Gallery Art, N.H., 1981, League N.H. Craftsmen, 1983. Mem. Profl. Crafts Orgn. Maine (newsletter editor 1978, sec. 1979, v.p. 1980), League N.H. Craftsmen, Nat. Bath, Bed and Linen Assn. Republican. Avocations: swimming, sailing, skiing, reading. Home: 9 Grove St Kennebunk ME 04043 Office: Kennebunk Weavers Inc Box A Canal St Suncook NH 03275

COLE, ELMA PHILLIPSON (MRS. JOHN STRICKLER COLE), social welfare executive; b. Piqua, Ohio, Aug. 9, 1909; d. Brice Leroy and Mabel (Gale) Phillipson; A.B., Berea Coll., 1930; M.A., U. Chgo., 1938; m. John Strickler Cole, Oct. 3., 1959. Various positions in social work, 1930-42; dir. social service dept. Children's Hosp. D.C., 1942-49; cons. public cooperation Midcentury White House Conf. Children and Youth, 1949-51; exec. sec. Nat. Midcentury Com. Children and Youth, 1951-53; cons. recruitment Am. Assn. Med. Social Workers, 1953; assoc. dir. Nat. Legal Aid and Defender Assn., 1953-56; exec. sec. Marshall Field Awards, Inc., 1956-57; dir. assoc. orgns. Nat. Assembly Social Policy and Devel., 1957-73; assoc. exec. dir. Nat. Assembly Nat. Vol. Health and Social Welfare Orgns., 1974; dir. edn. parenthood project Salvation Army, 1974-76, asst. sec. women's and children's social service dept., 1976-78, dir. research project devel. bur., social services dept., 1978—, also mem. Manhattan adv. bd., 1975—, sec., 1984—, hist. commn., 1978—; cons. nat. orgns. Golden Anniversary White House Conf. Children and Youth, 1959-60; mem. adv. council public service Nat. Assn. Life Underwriters and Inst. Life Ins.; mem. judges com. Louis I. Dublin Public Service awards, 1961-74; mem. com. public relations and fund raising Am. Found. for Blind Commn. on Accreditation, 1964-67; mem. adv. bd. sexuality edn. project Center for Population Options, 1977—; mem. task force vol. accreditation Council Nat. Orgns. for Adult Edn., 1974-78, v.p. Blue Ridge Inst. of So. Community Service Execs., 1977-79, exec. com., 1979-81; bd. dirs. Values and Human Sexuality Inst., 1980—; bd. dirs. James Lenox House and James Lenox House Assn., 1985—, sec., 1985—; mem. nat. adv. panel Planned Parenthood Fedn. Family Life Edn. Project, 1981; adv. bd. Nat. Family Life Edn. Network, 1982—. Mem. Public Relations Soc. Am. (accredited), Nat. Assn. Social Workers (accredited), Nat. Conf. Social Welfare (com. public relations 1961-66, 69-82; chmn. adminstrn. sect. 1966-67), Jr. League Washington, Pi Gamma Mu, Phi Kappa Phi. Club: Women's of N.Y. Contbr. articles to profl. jours., encys. Home: 19 Washington Sq N New York NY 10011 Office: 120 W 14th St New York NY 10011

COLE, EMMA CATHERINE, nurse; b. Spearville, Kans., Feb. 27, 1910; d. Nick and Mamie (Laudick) Arends; m. Allen Gilbert Cole, July 14, 1936; children—Gerald A., Floyd G., Catherine E., Larry L., Emmalee A., Alicia A. R.N., St. Rose's Hosp., Great Bend, Kans., 1932. Staff nurse Kearny County Hosp., Lakin, Kans., 1934-36, 56-66; night supr. Hamilton County Hosp., Syracuse, Kans., 1966-70, Prowers Med. Ctr., Lamar, Colo., 1970-74; night supr., staff nurse Mt. San Rafael Hosp., Trinidad, Colo., 1974-75; night supr. Kearny County Hosp., Lakin, 1975-79, Bent County Meml. Hosp., Las Animas, Colo., 1979—; farmer, rancher, Lakin, 1936-56; pvt. duty nurse, Kans., 1932-34. Mem. Kans. Registered Nurses, Colo. Registered Nurses. Democrat. Roman Catholic. Home: P0 Box 825 Lakin KS 67860 Office: Bent County Memorial Hospital Las Animas CO 81054

COLE, EVELYN MARIE, day care center owner, adminstr.; b. Alvon, W.Va., Sept. 14, 1928; d. Melvin Arthur and Lillie Mae (Fifer) Cole; student pub. schs.; m. Delford Lee Cole, Jan. 31, 1950; children—Karen Lee, Phillip Quinton, Jonathon Avery. Owner, adminstr. Evelyn's Home Away from Home Day Care, Roanoke, Va., 1975—; owner, adminstr. Foster Home and Shelter Home for State Va., Roanoke, 1969-72. Mem. Ch. of Christ. Home: 2122 Berkley Ave SW PO Box 4656 Roanoke VA 24015 Office: 1731 Grandin Rd SW Roanoke VA 24015

COLE, HELEN, state senator; b. Tishomingo, Okla., July 13, 1922; m. John Cole; 2 children. Mem. Okla. Ho. of Reps., 37-39th sessions; mem. Okla. Senate, 1984—. Active Cleveland County Republican Women's Club. Mem. Moore C. of C., Am. Legion Aux. Office: Okla Senate State Capitol Oklahoma City OK 73105*

COLE, JANE BAGBY, librarian; b. Tulsa, May 23, 1931; d. Walter James and Mary Frances (Eakin) Bagby; m. Bruce Herman Cole, June 7, 1953; children—Rosemary Neilsen, Dorothy Domrzalski, Robert Bagby, Frances. B.A., Grinnell Coll., 1953; M.A., U. Chgo., 1977. Library asst. Elem. Dist. 101, Western Springs, Ill., 1961-71, library aide, 1973-75; librarian Elem. Dist. 102, La Grange, Ill., 1975-77, River Forest Jr. High Sch., Ill., 1977-79; audio-visual dir. Elem. Dist. 7, Phoenix, 1980-83; library dir., curator Desert Bot. Garden, Phoenix, 1983—; discussion leader Gt. Books Found., Chgo., 1965-79, Phoenix, 1981—. Editor Saguaroland Bull., 1984—. Precinct worker senatorial campaign, Cook County, Ill., 1966-67, Maricopa County, Ariz., 1980. Mem. ALA, Spl. Libraries Assn., Ariz. Paper and Photograph Conservation Group, Council Bot. and Hort. Libraries. Office Desert Bot Garden 1201 N Galvin Pkwy Phoenix AZ 85008

COLE, JOAN HAYS, social worker, social clinical psychologist; b. Pitts., Sept. 4, 1929; d. Frank L. Wertheimer and Edith H. Einstein; B.A., Western Res. U., 1951; M.S. S.A. in Social Work, Case Western Res. U., 1962; Ph.D., Wright Inst., 1975; m. Robert M. Wendlinger, June 1984; children—Geoffrey F. Cole, Douglas R. Cole, Peter Hays Cole. Social group worker Alta House Settlement House, Cleve., 1958-59; housing dir. Cleve. Urban League, 1961-62; dir. Citizens for Safe Housing, Cleve., 1963; housing dir. United Planning Orgn., Washington, 1963-68; asst. prof. community orgn. U. Md., Balt., 1968-72; asso. prof. Lone Mountain Coll., San Francisco, 1975-78; psychotherapist, Berkeley, Calif., 1977—; cons. various public and vol. social welfare, health and housing agys., 1969—; mem. adj. faculty Union Grad. Sch. and Antioch West Coll., 1978-80; lectr. U. Calif. Sch. Social Welfare, Berkeley, 1980-84; mem. faculty Berkeley Psychotherapy Inst., 1981—, pres., 1983-85.

NIMH grantee, 1971-72, Sr. Social Work Career Devel. grantee, 1973-75. Fellow Soc. Clin. Social Work, Am. Orthopsychiat. Assn.; mem. Nat. Assn. Social Workers, Soc. Study of Social Issues, ACLU, NOW, Acad. Cert. Social Workers, Nat. Conf. on social Welfare and Psychotherapists for Social Responsibility. Home: 1377 Campus Dr Berkeley CA 94708 Office: 1905 Berkeley Way Berkeley CA 94704

COLE, JUNE ROBERTSON, psychotherapist; b. Dothan, Ala., Sept. 29, 1931; d. C. Pete and Mary (Danzey) Robertson; m. Robert Walker Cole, Jr., Feb. 11, 1956; children—Robert Pete, Mary Cathlyn. A.A., Del Mar Coll., 1974; B.A., Tex. A&I U., 1976; M.A., Corpus Christi State U., 1978; postgrad Fielding Inst., Santa Barbara, 1985—. Actress, singer, radio, films, TV, stage, 1933-55; rec. artist Gold Label Records, 1951-55; pres. Coastal Bend Security Co., corpus Christi, 1969-71; dir. Reality Therapy Ctr., Corpus Christi, 1975—; co dir. Counseling and Psychology Resource Ctr., Corpus Christi, 1984—; pvt. practice psychotherapy, 1976—. Bd. dirs. Coastal Bend Jazz Soc., 1978-79. Mem. Corpus Christi Council Women, NOW, Nueces County Psychol. Assn., Tex. Assn. Counseling and Devel., Gulf Coast Assn. Counseling and Devel., Tex. Mental Health Counselors Assn., Coastal Bend Marriage and Family Therapists Assn., Internat. Inst. Reality Therapists

COLE, KAREN LORRAINE, operating engineer; b. Norco, Calif., Apr. 12, 1954; d. William G. Willis and Lorraine Ruth (Buratti) Willis Beisner; children—Cirdon Brion, Vanna Alia. Apprentice, Trade Tech., Los Angeles, 1980-84, Journeyman Grad., 1984. Apprentice engr. Cushman & Wakefield, Los Angeles, 1980-83, Bank of Calif., 1983-84, chief operating engr., 1984—. Active Boy Scouts Am. Mem. Nat. Assn. Female Execs., Bldg. Owners and Mgrs. Assn., Local 501 Internat. Union. Avocations: design and construct stained-glass windows. Office: Cushman & Wakefield of California Inc 515 S Flower St Suite 2200 Los Angeles CA 90071

COLE, MERCEDES THERESE, med. technologist; b. Schenectady, Dec. 14, 1946; d. Ramon V. and Charlotte F. (Lachner) Azua; B.S. in Med. Tech., Gwynedd-Mercy Coll., 1969; M.S., Thomas Jefferson U., 1977; m. Richard L. Cole, Jr., Aug. 10, 1968; 1 dau., Maria Mercedes. With Clinica Samper, Bogota, Colombia, 1967; microbiologist Rolling Hill Hosp. and Diagnostic Center, Elkins Park, Pa., 1969-73, edn. coordinator for med. lab. technician program, 1973-75, program dir., 1976—, lab. mgr., 1983—; site surveyor/team mem. Nat. Accrediting Agy. for Clin. Lab. Scientists, 1978—. Mem. med. lab. technicians adv. com. Gwynedd-Mercy Coll., 1978—; chmn. Games June Fete, Abington Meml. Hosp., 1977-81; mem. emergency med. service adv. com. Abington Twp., 1977-78; chmn. ARC Bloodmobile, Rolling Hill, 1972-75, 77—. Mem. Am. Soc. Med. Technologists (student bowl coordinator regional playoffs 1978, 79), Pa. Soc. Med. Technologists (bd. dirs. 1982-84, chmn. ann. conv. 1981, 85), Thomas Jefferson U. Grad. Alumni (dir. 1982—, mem. nominating com. 1978-80). Home: 65 Shady Ln Philadelphia PA 19111 Office: 60 E Township Line Rd Elkins Park PA 19117

COLE, NANCY BERKEY, theater educator and director; b. Bklyn., July 9, 1936; d. Gerald Kirk and Jessie McMurray (Mincher) Berkey; m. Stephen R. Cole, May 17, 1958 (div.); children—Paula Murray and Leslie Jordan (twins). A.B. magna cum laude, Ind. U., 1959; M.F.A. in Acting, U. Iowa, 1964. Instr. English dept. U. Nebr., 1964-66; instr. theatre dept. Cornell U., Ithaca, N.Y., lectr./specialist music dept. Ithaca Coll., 1970-74; actress, dir. Ithaca Summer Repertory, Dartmouth Coll. Summer Repertory, Hanover, N.H., Front St. Theatre, Memphis, Ledges Playhouse, Grand Ledge, Mich. and Lincoln, Nebr., 1970-75; asst. prof. theatre Washington U., St. Louis, 1974-76; assoc. prof., chmn. dept. theatre U. South Fla., Tampa, 1976—, prof., 1982—, producer theatre, related programs, dance concerts, Coll. Fine Arts TV Series; dir. Hangar Theatre, Ithaca, N.Y., Cornell Savoyards, Ithaca, Palisades Theatre, St. Petersburg, Fla. Chief researcher Introduction to the Theatre (Oscar Brockett), 1962-63. Woodrow Wilson fellow, 1958-59; recipient nat., regional awards Am. Coll. Theatre Festival, 1979-80, 81-82; Washington U. research grantee, summer 1975. Mem. Am. Theatre Assn. (chmn. N.Y. conv. Women in Theatre 1982), Tampa Athena Soc., Dramatists Guild (assoc.), Phi Beta Kappa. Democrat. Episcopalian. Office: Dept Theatre U So Fla Tampa FL 33620

COLE, SHARLEVE MICHELLE, author, social anthropologist, consultant; b. Los Angeles, Aug. 21, 1940; d. Henry and Joyce (Raskin) Goldman; m. Laurence S. Cole, Aug. 30, 1959; 1 child, Jarett Evan. B.A., U. Calif.-Santa Barbara, 1960; postgrad. Sophie Newcomb U., 1961, Columbia U., 1961-64; Ed.D. (hon.), Franconia Coll., 1970. Asst. fashion editor Playboy Mag., N.Y.C., 1962-64; exec. dir. Lower Eastside Action Project, Inc., N.Y.C., 1964-75; dir. Inst. Juvenile Justice, N.Y.C., 1970-78; editorial cons.; childrens programming cons. Lamico Co., Los Angeles, 1976—. Author: Checking it Out, 1970; Violent Sheep, 1980; (with others) Anthology, 1972. Contbr. articles to profl. publs. Bd. dirs. E. Harlem Tenants Council, N.Y.C., 1964-73, Escuela Montessori Sch., N.Y.C., 1968-70; mem. Lower Eastside Coordinating Council, N.Y.C., 1964-78, Commn. for Sane Nuclear Policy, N.Y.C., 1970—, Human Factors Soc., 1975—. Norman Found. fellow, 1974; grantee Astor Found., 1972. Mem. Author's Guild. Jewish. Avocations: Computer applications to education; childrens films; architecture; antiques. Office: The Lamico Co 8033 Sunset Blvd #940 Los Angeles CA 90046

COLE, SUSIE CLEORA, government employee relations official; b. Bloomsburg, Pa.; d. Harry E. and Chloe Ann (McKinstry) Cole; m. Richard Edward Miller, July 31, 1959 (div. Aug. 1977); 1 child, Terri Lee Miller; m. Gerald Edward Nelson, Feb. 18, 1978 (div. June 1982). Student in history No. Va. Community Coll., 1982; also govt. courses. With Dept. Navy, Washington, 1957-74, Navy mil. pay regulations specialist, 1962-74; fiscal clk. Dept. State, Washington, 1975-77, sr. retirement claims examiner, 1977-83, employee relations officer, 1983—, also mgr. fed. health benefits program and mgr. fed. life ins. program, 1983—. Active Citizen's Band Radio Club, Fairfax, Va., 1974-82, Retarded Children's Ctr., Fairfax, 1981-82. Recipient various govt. awards, including Sustained Exceptional Achievement award Dept. State, 1983, 84, 85. Mem. Nat. Assn. Female Execs. Democrat. Avocations: reading; travel; history; music; art. Home: 4605 John Tyler Ct Apt 104 Annandale VA 22003 Office: US Dept State Office Employee Relations 2201 C St NW Washington DC 20520

COLE-ALEXANDER, LENORA, govt. ofcl.; b. Buffalo, Mar. 9, 1935; d. John L. and Susie L. (Stamper) Cole; B.S., SUNY Coll., Buffalo, 1957; M.Ed., SUNY, Buffalo, 1968, Ph.D., 1974; m. Theodore M. Alexander, June 22, 1975. Tchr. pub. schs., 1957-61; with Dept. Labor, now dir. Women's Bur., Washington. Former mem. D.C. Rental Accommodations Commn.; rep. to Orgn. for Econ. Cooperation and Devel., Paris, 1981; del. Internat. Commn. on Status of Women Conf., Cartegena, Columbia, 1982; mem. del. to Preparatory Conf. for Women World Conf., Vienna, Austria, 1983, UN Decade for Women World Conf., Nairobi, Kenya, 1985. Recipient Spl. Citation award Office of Gov., Puerto Rico, 1982, Salute for Contbrs. award Club Twenty, Washington, 1983, Disting. Am. and Humanitarian award Coahoma Jr. Coll. Alumni Assn. and Nat. Alumni Adv. Council and Found., 1983, Disting. Alumnus award SUNY-Buffalo, 1983, Disting. Service citation Nat. Black MBA Assn., 1984, others. Mem. Nat. Council Negro Women, Washington Opportunities for Women (past dir.), Legal Aid Soc. Washington (past trustee), Nat. Assn. Student Personnel Adminstrs. (past v.p.), Delta Sigma Theta. Office: Women's Bur Dept Labor 200 Constitution Ave NW Washington DC 20210

COLELLO, MARIANNE SCHWABA, manufacturing company controller; b. Chgo., Jan. 2, 1948; d. Thaddeus Jerome and Ann Marie (Hillmann) S.; m. James Edward Colello, Feb. 2, 1985. B.A. in Acctg., Northeastern Ill. U., 1980. C.P.A., Ill. Budget analyst Crane Packing Co., Morton Grove, Ill., 1976-80; controller CSC, Inc., Arlington Heights, Ill., 1980—. Mem. Ill. C.P.A. Soc. Avocations: drawing; painting. Home: 1442 Garden St Park Ridge IL 60068

COLEMAN, ANNE M., insurance executive; b. N.Y.C., Feb. 13, 1948; d. William Henry and Vivian (Noisette) Middleton; m. Darryl Leon Coleman, May 9, 1968 (div.); children—Tia Maria, Kenyth William, Dara Anne. B.S., CCNY, 1968. Lic. broker, N.Y. State. Sr. spl. accts. underwriter Hartford Ins. Co., N.Y.C., 1970-73; spl. risk underwriter Kemper Ins. Co., N.Y.C., 1973; large line underwriter Zurich Ins. Co., N.Y.C., 1973-75; mktg. rep. Schiff Terhune, N.Y.C., 1975-78; account mgr. Alexander & Alexander, Melville, N.Y., 1978-81; asst. v.p. Reed Stenhouse, N.Y.C., 1981-85; dir. ins. E.G. Bowman Co., 1985—. Mem. Islip Civic Assn., 1982; area rep. Girl Scouts U.S.A., Commack, N.Y., 1980-81; mem. NAACP, Port Jefferson, N.Y., 1979—; advisor Nassau-Suffolk Affirmative Action Program, Melville, 1980. Mem. Nat. Assn. Female Execs. Club: Drug and Chem. Home: 734 Cheryl Dr Iserlin NJ Office: EG Bowman Co Inc 97 Wall St New York NY 10005

COLEMAN, ANNETTE WILBOIS, biology educator; b. Des Moines, Iowa, Feb. 28, 1934; d. Fred J. and Agnes D. Wilbois; m. John R. Coleman, July 26, 1958; children—Alan, Benjamin, Suzanne. B.A., Columbia U., 1955; Ph.D., U. Ind., 1958. Postdoctoral fellow Johns Hopkins U., Balt., 1958-61; research associate U. Conn., 1961-63; research assoc. Brown U., Providence, 1964-72, asst. prof. biology research, 1972-76, asst. prof., 1976-80, assoc. prof., 1980-84, prof., 1984—, Stephen T. Olney prof. natural history, 1984—. NSF postdoctoral fellow, 1955-58, 58-60; Guggenheim fellow, 1983-84. Fellow N.Y. Acad. Scis.; mem. Bot. Soc. Am., Soc. Protozoologists, Phcol. Soc. Am. (pres. 1981-82). Office: Brown U Bio-Med Dept Providence RI 02912

COLEMAN, BEATRICE, clothing company executive; b. Jersey City, N.J., 1916. Grad. Barnard Coll., 1938. Chmn., pres., Maidenform, Inc., N.Y.C. Address: Maidenform Inc 90 Park Ave New York NY 10016

COLEMAN, BETHANY BALDWIN, insurance executive; b. Miami, Dec. 4, 1950; d. C. Jackson and Mary Susanne (Bonner) Baldwin; m. Carl Randolph Coleman, May 27, 1983. Student U. Ala., 1969-72. Lic. property and casualty ins. agt., life ins. agt., claims adjuster, Fla. Claims adjuster Liberty Mut. Ins. Co., Miami, 1973-75, Kemper Ins. Co., Miami, 1975-76; asst. to pres. Baldwin Ins. Agy., Miami, 1976—, also dir. Trustee Expo 500: 1992 Columbus Exposition, 1982—; Miami chairperson Nat. Family Bus. Council, 1983-84, bd. dirs., 1983; mem. citizens adv. bd. Bloomingdale's, So. Fla., 1984-85; mem. Orange Bowl Com., Miami, 1985—; mem. new tequestians com. Hist. Mus. of So. Fla., 1985—. Mem. Fla. Assn. Ind. Agts., Nat. Assn. Security Dealers, Ind. Ins. Agts. of Dade County, Greater Miami C. of C. (com. for United Way 1985), Phi Beta Phi, U. Ala. Alumni Assn. Clubs: Generation of Miami (pres. 1983-84, chmn. 1984-85), Riviera Country (Coral Gables, Fla.); Palm Bay, New World Ctr., U. Miami Hurricane (bd. dirs.), Bankers, (Miami). Home: 1532 Dorado Ave Coral Gables FL 33146 Office: Baldwin Ins Agy Inc 840 Biscayne Blvd Miami FL 33132

COLEMAN, CHRISTINE KAY, television producer; b. Jacksonville, Fla., Jan. 4, 1952; d. James Corbett and Ruth Edith (Christianson) Coleman. B.A. cum laude, Stephens Coll., Columbia, Mo., 1973. Assoc. producer news/public affairs Sta. WJXT-TV, Jacksonville, 1973; broadcast producer Gordon-Keitzman-Dennis, Inc. Mktg. and Pub. Relations, Oklahoma City, 1973-74; prodn. mgr., asst. creative dir. Young and Rubicam, West, San Diego, 1974-75; asst. promotion dir. Sta. KCST-TV, San Diego, 1976-80; spl. projects producer Sta. KCST-TV-Storer Broadcasting, Inc., San Diego, 1976-80; sr. producer, dir. Multi Image Prodns., San Diego, 1980-82; field producer The Animal Express for Prodns. for Entertainment and Learning, Inc., N.Y.C., 1982-84; producer Teleconfs., Hosp. Satellite Network, Los Angeles, 1984—; producer, host TV show You're On, 1976; producer, writer Old Globe Telethon (recipient Emmy for Spl. Events Category, 1980), 1979; producer, writer, host International Women's Year: Report to San Diego (recipient Emmy for Info./Documentary Spls. Category 1978), 1978. Office: 6430 Sunset Blvd Suite 918 Los Angeles CA 90028

COLEMAN, CLAIRE KOHN, public relations executive; b. New Castle, Pa., Nov. 19, 1924; d. Louis and Florence (Frank) K.; B.A., Pa. State U., 1945; m. Frederick H. Coleman, Mar. 10, 1957; children—Franklin, Elliot. Market editor Fairchild Publs., N.Y.C., 1945-48; asst. home editor N.Y. Times, 1949-50; public relations dir. United Wallpaper, Chgo., 1950-53; public relations dir. Asso. Am. Artists, N.Y.C., 1953-54; dir. Wallpaper Info. Bur., N.Y.C., 1954; dept. head Roy Bernard, Inc., N.Y.C., 1955-58; public relations dir. The Siesel Co., N.Y.C., 1972—, sr. v.p., 1981—. Mem. central steering com., Sch. Dist. Critical Assessments, New Rochelle, N.Y., 1969-71; bd. dirs., v.p. Beechmont Assn., 1960-74; mem. Mayor's Adv. Council on Aging, 1966; mem. Mayor's Adv. Com. on Bd. Edn. Appointments, 1969; v.p. Council of PTAs, 1969-70; chmn. women's div. United Jewish Appeal, New Rochelle, 1971. Fellow Nat. Home Fashions League (founder 1947, nat. treas. 1977-78, pres. 1980-81); mem. Public Relations Soc. Am., Women in Communications, Women Execs. in Public Relations (bd. dirs. 1983-84). Office: 845 3d Ave New York NY 10022

COLEMAN, CYNTHIA-LOU, educational administrator; b. Long Beach, Calif., July 4, 1953; d. Margaret Sue (Barnes) Conover; m. Martin H. Tusler, July 12, 1981; children—Megan Rose, Rachel Ferron. B.A., Hutchins Sch. Sonoma State U., 1975. Asst. Sonoma State U., Rohnert Park, Calif., 1973-76, Mendocino Coll., Ukiah, Calif., 1976-77; reporter Cotati Clarion, Rohnert Park, 1976; asst. Humboldt State U., Arcata, Calif., 1977-80, dir. pub. affairs, 1980—. Chmn. Planning Commn., City of Cotati, 1975-77. Recipient publs. award Nat. Schs. Pub. Relations Assn., 1975, 83. Mem. Am. Bus. Women's Assn., Internat. Assn. Bus. Communicators. Avocations: tennis, running, world travel, photography. Office: Humboldt State U Arcata CA 95521

COLEMAN, DIANN WALKER, lawyer; b. Taylor, La., Aug. 8, 1933; d. Curtis Odell and Rosalie (Whitton) Walker; m. William James Coleman, June 18, 1954 (div. Dec. 1977); children—Kathy Diann, Kevin James, Kent Walker, Kellye Susan. B.A. in Scoiology, La. Coll., 1954; J.D., U. Miss., 1978. Bar: Miss. 1978. Sole practice, Oxford, Miss., 1978—; pub. defender City of Oxford, County of Lafayette, 1980-84, city prosecutor, 1984—. Mem. long range planning com. Oxford-Univ. United Methodist Ch.; mem. pres.'s club La. Coll., Pineville; mem. adv. council U. Miss. Sch. Bus. Adminstrn.; mem. U. Miss. Loyalty Found.; co-dir. women's studies seminar U. Miss., 1972; bd. dirs. Beach House Condominium Corp., Gulf Shores, Ala.; patron, supporter numerous cultural and philanthropic projects. Mem. NOW, U. Miss. Alumni Assn., Ole Miss Rebel Tip-off Club, Miss. Bar Assn., Lafayette County Bar Assn., ABA, Am. Trial Lawyers Assn., Miss. Trial Lawyers Assn., Lamar Soc. Internat. Law, Alpha Chi, Phi Alpha Delta. Republican. Home: Rt 6 Box 245 Oxford MS 38655 Office: 1217 Jackson Ave Oxford MS 38655

COLEMAN, DONNA ANN, former state legislator; b. Sao Paulo, Brazil, Mar. 11, 1949; d. John M. and Donna (Hendricks) C.; B.S., U. Utah, 1974; postgrad. U. Mo.-St. Louis; M.B.A., Washington U., St. Louis, 1985. With Stanford Research Inst. (Calif.), 1975-76; corp. sec.-treas., dir., fin. officer Engineered Fire Protection, Inc., St. Louis, 1977—, bd. dirs., trustee employee profit sharing trust. Mem. Mo. Ho. of Reps., 1981-82, 83-84; dir. speakers bur. Mo. Citizens Council; del. Mo. Republican Conv., 1980, 84; mem. Mo. Rep. Platform Com., 1984; chmn. Mo. Ho. of Reps. Rep. Caucus Campaign Com., 1983-84. Mormon. Home: 2449 Baxton Way Chesterfield MO 63017

COLEMAN, ELISABETH CHARLOTTE, television producer; b. Woking, Surrey, Eng., May 26, 1945; came to U.S., 1949; d. David and Anne Lise (Bojesen) C.; m. Rock Brynner, Dec. 24, 1978 (div. Jan. 1984). B.A., Vassar Coll., 1966. Researcher, Newsweek Mag., N.Y.C., 1967-70, corr., San Francisco, 1970-73; reporter Newsroom KQED-TV, San Francisco, 1973; radio-TV reporter ABC News, N.Y.C., 1973-74; reporter KABC-TV News, Los Angeles, 1974-76; press sec. Gov. Edmund G. Brown, Jr., Sacramento, 1976-78; producer Inside Story, PBS series, N.Y.C., 1980-82, Jack Hilton Prodns., N.Y.C., 1982—. Contbr. articles to N.Y. Sunday Times Mag., Columbia Journalism Review, Family Weekly, N.Y. Daily News. Mem. Women in Communications, AFTRA. Home: 201 E 87th St Apt 14-L New York NY 10128 Office: Coleman Prodns Inc 201 E 87th St New York NY 10128

COLEMAN, FAYE EDWARDS, business executive, management consultant, educator; b. Boston, July 24, 1946; d. O'Ray and Rheable (McKinney) Edwards; m. Milton Richard Coleman, May 30, 1971; 1 child, Sekou Lumumba. B.S., Simmons Coll., 1968; M. Ed., U. Mass., 1973; Ph.D., U. Md., 1980. Program cons. Cornell U., Ithaca, N.Y., 1968-69; youth project coordinator United Orgns. Co. Community Improvement, Durham, N.C., 1969-70; child devel. specialist Prince George's County Model City Day Care (Md.), 1973-74; tng. coordinator Greater Mpls. Day Care Assn., 1974-76; project mgr. Children's First, Inc., Washington, 1976-78, Ctr. for Systems and Program Devel., Washington, 1978-80; sr. assoc. Creative Assocs., Washington, 1980-83; pres. Westover Corp., Washington, 1983—. Author: Status of Home-Based Effort within Head Start, 1977; Parent Involvement in Day Care, 1980; author/producer: slide-tape show-Through Our Eyes: Cultural Identity in Child Care, 1975. Conf. coordinator Spring Conf. Black Child Devel. Inst., Washington, 1980. Ford Found. fellow, 1972-73. Mem. Nat. Assn. Edn. Young Children, Black Child Devel. Inst., Nat. Assn. Female Execs., Am. Soc. Profl. Exec. Women, Creative Learning Inc. (v.p. 1981-83). Democrat. Office: Westover Cons Inc 3174 Westover Dr SE Washington DC 20020

COLEMAN, JANE CANDIA, writer, educator; b. Pitts., Jan. 9, 1939; d. Joseph R. and Sophia (Weyman) Candia; m. Bernard D. Coleman, Mar. 27, 1965; children—David A., Daniel N. B.A., U. Pitts., 1961. Tech. writer Biophysical Research Lab., Pitts., 1961-65; feature writer, arts critic Pitts. Sun, 1979-81; faculty dept. English, U. Pitts., 1981-82; writer-in-residence Carlow Coll., Pitts., 1981-84, dir. Women's Creative Writing Ctr., 1984—; lit. critic Sta. WYEP-FM, Pitts., 1981-82; lectr. Eastern Mont. Coll., 1985. Contbr. poetry to mags. including Yankee, Tar River Poetry, Backcountry, others; contbr. fiction to Crosscurrents, The Chowder Rev., Gila Rev. Recipient 1st prize for fiction The Plainswoman, 1983, Sewickley Mag., 1985; Pa. Mus. and Hist. Commn. grantee, 1985; Pa. Council for Arts grantee, 1986. Mem. Western Writers Am. (assoc.), Internat. Poetry Forum. Democrat. Roman Catholic. Avocations: horseback riding; playing harpsichord. Home: 400 Devonshire St Pittsburgh PA 15213 Office: Women's Creative Writing Ctr Carlow Coll 3333 5th Ave Pittsburgh PA 15213

COLEMAN, JANE DWIGHT DEXTER, communications executive; b. Boston, Aug. 24, 1942; d. Franklin and Mianne (Palfrey) Dexter; m. Peter S. Coleman, Aug. 18, 1969; 1 son, Dan C. A.B., Barnard Coll., 1965; M.Phil., Ph.D., Columbia U., 1976. Adj. lectr. Hunter Coll., 1974-75; mgr. program analysis CBS Broadcast Group, 1976-77, dir. program analysis, east, 1977-80; mgr. Sta. WINS, N.Y.C., 1980-81; v.p., gen. mgr. Sta. WIND, Chgo., 1981; pres. Oberland Prodns., N.Y.C., 1982-84; assoc. dir. adminstrn. Gannett Ctr. for Media Studies, 1985—. Mem. Nat. Acad. TV Arts and Scis., Internat. Radio and TV Soc. Office: Gannett Ctr for Media Studies Columbia U 2950 Broadway New York NY 10027

COLEMAN, JEAN BLACK, nurse; b. Sharon, Pa., Jan. 11, 1925; d. Charles B. and Sue E. (Dougherty) Black; m. Donald A. Coleman, July 3, 1946; children—Sue Ann Coleman Lynn, Donald Ashley. R.N., Spencer Hosp. Sch. Nursing, Meadville, Pa., 1945; student Vanderbilt U., 1952-54. Nurse, dir. nursing Bulloch Meml. Hosp., Statesboro, Ga., 1948-51, nurse supr. surgery, 1954-67, dir. nursing, 1967-71; physician's asst., 1951-52; physician's asst., nurse anesthetist to Robert H. Swint, Statesboro, 1971—. Named Woman of Year in Med. Field, Bus. and Profl. Women, 1980. Mem. Am. Nurses Assn., Ga. Nurses Assn., Am. Acad. Physicians Assts., Ga. Assn. Physicians Assts. (dir. 1975-79, v.p. 1979-80, pres. 1980-81). Democrat. Roman Catholic.

COLEMAN, JULIA KATHRYN, nurse; b. Greeley Colo., Apr. 25, 1953; d. Howell Roland Stone and Rose Mary (Herrick) Stone Peterson; m. Joseph Todd Coleman, Apr. 5, 1975; 1 child, Sarah Elizabeth. B.S. in Nursing, U. No. Colo., 1982. R.N., Colo. Staff nurse North Colo. Med. Ctr, Greeley, 1982-84; dir. nursing Yuma Dist. Hosp., Colo., 1984—. Served with USN, 1973-77. Mem. Colo. Soc. Nurse Execs., N.E. Dist. Dirs. of Nursing Orgn. Club: Tanda Women's (Yuma). Avocations: golf; camping; aerobics; bridge. Office: Yuma District Hosp 910 S Main St Yuma CO 80759

COLEMAN, LYNN DELL, fashion designer; b. Forrest City, Ark., Sept. 15, 1949; d. Carl D. and Mona Lee (Morris) Collingsworth; m. Bill D. Dover, June 12, 1970 (div. Sept. 1980); 1 child, Ashley Nicole; m. Ernest Robert Coleman, July 3, 1981. Student Stephens Coll., 1966-67; B.S.H.E., U. Ark., 1970. Asst. designer Bryan Industries, Tulsa, 1971, head designer, 1971—; cons. Gerico, Denver, 1980. Intern, Leadership Tulsa, 1982-83; mem. adv. com. Tulsa County Area Vo-Tech Sch., 1977-81; bd. dirs. Fort Smith Symphony, Ark., 1984-85, Old Fort Mus., 1985-86. Recipient Earnie award Childrenswear Mfrs. Assn, 1979, 80, 81, 83, 84, Hall of Fame, 1982, Mem. Fort Smith Republican Women. Baptist. Club: Quota (dir. 1980-83) (Tulsa). Avocations: water skiing; travel; gourmet cooking; reading. Home: 3001 Edgewater Cove Fort Smith AR 72903 Office: 1115 S Waldron #108 Fort Smith AR 72903

COLEMAN, MARILYN (ADAMS), poultry science consultant; b. Lancaster, S.C., Mar. 27, 1946; d. Coyte and Jill J.D. (Lyon) Adams; B.S. in Biology, U. S.C., 1968; Ph.D. in Physiology, Auburn U., 1976; postgrad. U. Va., summer, 1971, 72, Va. Poly. Inst., 1972; m. George Edward Coleman III, Jan. 27, 1968; children—Jill Ann Marie, George Edward IV. Teaching asst. U. S.C., 1967-68; research technician Va. Poly. Inst. and State U., Blacksburg, 1968, teaching asst. biology, 1970-72; tchr. biology and basketball coach Brunswick County (Va.) Pub. Schs., 1968-69; research asst. poultry sci. Auburn (Ala.) U., 1973-76; asst. prof. poultry sci. Ohio State U., Columbus, 1977-81, adj. asso. prof., 1982—; propr. MAC Assos., Columbus, Ohio, 1974—; cons. to poultry industry, 1974—. Pianist, New Cut Presbyn. Ch., Lancaster, 1960-64; tchr.'s aide Mountview Baptist Ch., Upper Arlington, Ohio, 1964. Nat. winner 4-H, 1964; NSF grantee, 1967, 71-72. Named Top 10 Young Execs., Esquire Mag., 1985. Mem. Poultry Sci. Assn., Am. Physiol. Assn., World Poultry Sci. Assn., Assn. of Southeastern Biologists, Auburn U. Alumni Assn., U. S.C. Alumni Assn., Sigma Xi, Phi Sigma. Republican. Contbr. numerous articles poultry sci. to profl. publs. Home and office: 2532 Zollinger Rd Columbus OH 43221

COLEMAN, MARY ANN, poet, educator; b. Marion, Ind., Jan. 3, 1928; d. William Henry and Helen Elizabeth (Jeffrey) Braunlin; m. Oliver McCarter Coleman, Jr., Mar. 4, 1955; children—Jeffrey Boyer, Christopher Braunlin. B.S. in Edn., Auburn U., 1950; postgrad. creative writing workshops, U. Iowa, 1954, Emory U., 1962, U. Ga., 1963, Breadloaf Writers Conf., Middlebury Coll., 1965. Tchr. pub. schs., Pompano Beach, Fla., 1951-52, East Point, Ga., 1953-55; welfare worker Atlanta Welfare Dept., 1952-53; tchr. creative writing DeKalb Coll., Atlanta, 1970, Emory-at-Oxford, Ga., 1973, Dixie Council of Authors and Journalists, St. Simon's Island, Ga., 1970, 71, 74, U. Ga., Athens, 1971—. Author: (poems) Disappearances, 1978. Contbr. poems to various publs. Mem. Poetry Soc. Am. (Consuelo Ford Meml. award for lyric poem 1974), Ga. State Poetry Soc. Episcopalian. Avocations: camping; photography; swimming; listening to music; singing. Home: 205 Sherwood Dr Athens GA 30606

COLEMAN, MARY LOUISE, medical laboratory administrator; b. Harrison, Miss., Dec. 1; d. Clyde and Mattie (Smith) Cadney; m. Clarence Ray Coleman, Feb. 12, 1972; 1 child, Shani Rashida. Student So. U., Baton Rouge, 1966-70; diploma in cytotech. Mount Sinai Hosp., Chgo., 1971. Registered Cytotechnologist. Cytotechnologist Pathology lab. Meml. Hosp., Gulfport, Miss., 1971-74, Meth. Hosp., Memphis, 1974-76, Mercy Hosp., Vicksburg, Miss., 1977-79; founder, lab. supr. So. Lab., Fayette, Miss., 1980—; asst. adminstr. Medgar Evers Home Health, Fayette, 1983-85. Trustee Copiah-Jefferson Regional Library, Fayette and Hazlehurst, 1985; campaign mgr. Sammy White for chancery clk. Jefferson County, 1983. Mem. So. Assn. Cytotechnologists, Miss. Soc. Cytopathologists, Am. Soc. Clin. Pathologists, Am. Entrepreneurs Assn., Am. Mgmt. Assn. Democrat. Roman Catholic. Avocations: tennis; dancing; traveling; sewing. Office: So Lab Inc 414 Rodney Rd Fayette MS 39069

COLEMAN, PAMELA, investment advisor; b. Wichita, Kans., July 17, 1938; d. Clarence William and Emry Regester (Ingraham) Coleman; student U. Okla., 1956-57, U. Mo., 1962-65, Wichita State U., 1972-73; children—Cristy Jeanne Coleman, Cathryn Coleman. Teller, Union Nat. Bank, Wichita, 1959, 1st Nat. Bank, Charleston, S.C., 1959-61, 1st Nat. Bank of New London (Conn.), 1961-62; acct., bookkeeper Greenbaum & Assos., Sydney, Australia, 1966-68; pres., chief exec. officer Sweet Peach Prodns. Pty., Ltd., Sydney, 1968-72; fin. mgr. Clarence Coleman Investments, Wichita, 1972-75, registered investment adv., office mgr., 1976—. Formerly active Project Bus. of Jr. Achievement; bd. dirs. Goodwill Industries of Wichita, 1978-80, sec., 1978-79, treas., 1979-80; active Angel Fire Guild of Santa Fe Opera, 1st v.p.; 1st v.p. The Guilds of Santa Fe Opera, Inc., 1984-85, pres. 1985-86. Mem. Eagle West C. of C. (treas. 1984-86), Midwest Hist. and Geneal. Soc., DAR, Soc. Mayflower Descs., Daus. Am. Colonists, Nat. Soc. Colonial Dames of Am. Club: Angel Fire Country. Office: 1005 Union Center Wichita KS 67202

COLEMAN, PATRICIA JOANNE, graphic designer; b. Mpls., June 25, 1941; d. Arthur Patrick and Catherine Ann (Janoweic) C.; B.A., Coll. St. Catherine, 1965; M.A., U. Minn., 1973; M.F.A., Va. Commonwealth U., 1985. Tchr. art secondary parochial schs., St. Paul, 1965-68; free lance graphic artist, St. Paul, 1968-71; tchr. art, arts area leader Edina (Minn.) Public Schs., 1969-78; free lance graphic designer/photographer Mpls., 1978-80; elem. art specialist Edina Public Schs., 1979-80; tchr. design Va. Commonwealth U., 1981-83; asst. profl. Calif. State U., Chico, 1984-85; graphic designer, 1986—. Mem. Graphic Artist Guild, ACM Spl. Interest Group Graphics, NOW, Am.

Inst. Graphic Artists, Art Dir. and Artist Club. Democrat. Home: 720 41st Ave #16 San Francisco CA 94121-3351

COLEMAN, SHIRLEY DIANN, Realtor, contractor; b. Candler County, Ga., May 1, 1935; d. Joseph Moye and Julia Alva (Lee) Hardee; m. Bennie Lewis Coleman, Nov. 24, 1955; 1 son, Mark Andrew. Student Huntingdon Coll., 1953-54, U. Ga., 1954-55, San Antonio Coll., 1961-62, Eastfield Coll., Dallas Richland Coll., Dallas, 1980-83. Lic. realtor, Tex. Clk. typist Cutter's Exchange, Atlanta, 1955-56, Union Nat. Bank, Little Rock, Ark., 1956-58; sec. Vandenberg Air Force Base, Lompoc, Calif., 1958-60; clk. Ft. Sam Houston, San Antonio, 1960-63; service rep. Social Security Adminstrn., Dallas, 1963-66; manpower devel. specialist U.S. Dept. Labor, Dallas, 1970-85; Realtor Re/Max Assocs., Dallas, 1985—. Tchr., youth leader East Grand Baptist Ch., Dallas, 1968-81, Casa View Baptist Ch., Dallas, 1981-83. Recipient Outstanding Performance award U.S. Army, 1962, Cash Performance award Dept. Labor, 1971, 72, 83. Democrat. Lodge: Rotary. Office: RE/Max Assocs Dallas 8614 Skillman St Dallas TX 75243

COLEMAN-FREELON, MARY DEAN, residential homes company executive, consultant; b. Mocksville, N.C., Oct. 3, 1930; d. George Wiley and Ollie (Hall) Smith; m. Lonzell Freelon, July 3, 1982; children—Sylvia King, Sam Michael. Student Winston-Salem Teacher's Coll., 1948-50; diploma Star Stenographic Sch. Bus., 1960. Pres., owner, exec. dir., adminstr. Coleman Homes Inc., Toledo, Ohio, 1973—; cons. Coleman Homes, 1973—; owner, mgr. Dean's Drive-In, Winston-Salem, N.C., 1966-68. Recipient Cert. of Participation, Role of Direct Care cert. State of Ohio Dept. Mental Health, Cert. of Participation Ohio Private Residential Assn. Mem. Nat. Assn. Exec. Women, Nat. Assn. of Persons with Severe Handicaps, Resort Condominium Internat. Democrat. Lodge: Ester-mi Chpt. Avocations: bowling, cooking, travel. Office: Coleman Homes Inc 1314 Indiana Toledo OH 43607

COLEN, HELEN SASS, plastic surgeon; b. Bytom, Poland, Jan. 9, 1947; came to U.S., 1963; d. Karl Julius and Sabina (Orgel) Sass; m. Stephen Robert Colen, Mar. 25, 1972; children—Kari, Michael. B.A., NYU, 1968, M.D., 1972. Diplomate Am. Bd. Surgery, Am. Bd. Plastic Surgery. Intern, Jefferson U. Hosp., 1972-74; gen. surgeon U. Colo., Denver, 1974-79; plastic surgeon U. Columbia St. Lukes, N.Y.C., 1979-81; microsurgeon Bellevue Hosp., N.Y.C., 1981-82; practice medicine specializing in plastic surgery, N.Y.C., 1982—. Mem. Phi Beta Kappa. Office: 784 Park Ave New York NY 10021

COLGAN, MARY CRESWELL, graphic artist; b. Augusta, Ga., Dec. 12, 1918; d. George Washington and Bennie George (Johnson) Summers; student Louisville Inst. Tech., 1937-40; m. Arthur Rudolf Colgan, July 6, 1953; 1 dau., Dorothy Anne (dec.). Adminstrv. asst., sec. to pres. S.D. Sch. Mines and Tech., Coll. of Engring. and Sci., 1949-54; exec. sec., office mgr. Dr. Joseph S. Knight, D.C., Hawthorne, Calif., 1970-73; ptnr. ARCI Enterprises, Palos Verdes, Calif., 1969-73; editor, artist MARCI originals for ARCI Assos., Rapid City, S.D., 1973—; sec.-treas. A.R. Colgan, Inc., Edgemont, 1964-82; dir., curator Colgan's Old Gen. Store Mus., Edgemont, 1968-78. Author: (with Arthur R. Colgaw) How to Earn Money with Cookbooks, 1986. Dist. chmn. Los Angeles County dist. 8, Am. Cancer Soc., 1965-66. Mem. Geneal. Soc. Pa. Republican. Home and Office: Spring Canyon Trail at Sheridan Lake Rd Box 2724 Rapid City SD 57709

COLGATE, DORIS ELEANOR, sailing school executive, retail store executive; b. Washington, May 12, 1941; d. Bernard Leonard and Frances Lillian (Goldstein) Horecker; m. Richard G. Buchanan, Sept. 6, 1959 (div. Aug. 1967); m. 2d, Stephen Colgate, Dec. 17, 1969. Student Antioch Coll., 1958-60, NYU, 1960-62. Research supr. Geyer Moyer Ballard, N.Y.C., 1962-64; adminstrv. asst. Yachting Mag., N.Y.C., 1964-68; v.p. Offshore Sailing Sch. Ltd., N.Y.C., 1968-78, pres., City Island, N.Y., 1978—; chief exec. officer On and Offshore, Inc., City Island, 1984—; v.p. Offshore Travel, Inc., City Island, 1978—. Author: The Bareboat Gourmet, 1983. Contbr. articles to profl. jours. Mem. Royal Ocean Racing Club, Am. Women's Econ. Devel. Corp. (adv. bd. 1980—). Club: Doubles (N.Y.C.). Avocations: sailing, photography, writing, cooking. Home: 400 E 54th St New York NY 10022 Office: Offshore Sailing Sch Ltd 190 E Schofield St City Island NY 10464

COLGLAZIER, RUTH CECILIA, business owner; b. Cheverly, Md., Feb. 27, 1950; d. Merle Lee and Ruth Elizabeth (Lusk) C. B.A. in History, U. Md., 1973. On board service attendant Nat. R.R. Passenger Orgn. (Amtrak), Washington, 1973-74, sec., 1975-76, ticket agt., 1976-77, consumer relations officer, 1977-79; bookkeeper Presbyterian Home of Washington, 1974-75; owner, mgr. Pleasure Chest, Ltd., Washington, 1979—; mem. Washington Better Bus. Bur. Designer, producer, coordinator fashion shows, 1980, 1982. Mem. Bus. and Profl. Assn. Georgetown, Pi Beta Phi (chmn. com. 1969-70). Democrat. Presbyterian. Office: Pleasure Chest Ltd 1063 Wisconsin Ave NW Washington DC 20007

COLIN, GEORGIA TALMEY, interior designer; b. Boston; d. George Nathan and Rose (Broad) Talmey; m. Ralph Frederick Colin, June 2, 1931; children—Ralph Frederick, Pamela Talmey Colin Harlech. Student Smith Coll., 1928, U. Genoble (France), 1927. Co-ptnr., Talmey Inc., Interior Designers, N.Y.C., 1928-34, pres., 1934—. Sec. Young Peoples Concert Com. of N.Y. Philharmonic Soc., 1940-49; mem. vis. com. Smith Coll. Mus. Art, 1951-70, chmn., 1954-57; bd. counselors Smith Coll., 1954-57. Profl. mem. Am. Inst. Interior Designers, Decorators Club, Nat. Soc. Interior Designers, Am. Soc. Interior Designers. Home: 941 Park Ave New York NY 10028 Office: Talmey Inc 941 Park Ave New York NY 10028

COLIN, VALERIE WHALIN, accountant; b. San Diego, Oct. 10, 1954; d. Louis D. and Jeannette (Pauls) Whalin; m. Philip M. Colin, Sept. 22, 1984. B.B.S. in Acctg., Loyola-Marymount U., Los Angeles, 1977. C.P.A., Calif. Staff acct. Milton J. Nenney, Los Angeles, 1977-78; mgr. Stonefield & Josephson, Los Angeles, 1978-85; ptnr. Savoy & Co., Los Angeles, 1985—. Mem. fund raising com. City of Hope-Professions & Fin. Assn., Los Angeles, 1985-86, Los Angeles County Mus. of Art, 1985-86. Mem. Am. Inst. C.P.A.s, Calif. Soc. C.P.A.s. Avocations: snow skiing; quilt making; decorating; piano. Office: Savoy & Co 11620 Wilshire 580 Los Angeles CA 90025

COLL, HELEN FRYE (MRS. ROBERT FRANCIS COLL), consultant, retired banker; b. nr. Lovettsville, Va., Dec. 2, 1921; d. Raymond C. and Minnie (Peters) Frye; grad. Wash. Sch. Secs., 1940, Sch. Financial Pub. Relations Northwestern U., 1963; grad. Stonier Grad. Sch. Banking Rutgers U., 1966; m. Lee Stanley Sherline, Sept. 1, 1942 (div. Feb. 1955); m. 2d, Robert Francis Coll, May 25, 1957 (dec. Apr. 1979). With Nat. Savs. & Trust Co. (now NS & T Bank, N.A.), Washington, from 1940, sec. to pres., 1948-51, asst. sec., 1951-55, sec., from 1955, v.p., from 1963, v.p., sec. bd., 1966-72, sr. v.p., sec. bd., from 1972, now ret.; now sr. citizen cons. Mem. Met. Bd. Trade. Club: City Tavern (Washington). Home: 1310 29th St Washington DC 20007 also Fantasy Farm Round Hill VA 22141

COLLART, MARIE ETHEL, association executive; b. Clarksburg, W.Va., Nov. 23, 1945; d. Richard C. and Ethel Collart; B.S., Ohio State U., 1967, M.S., 1970, Ph.D., 1979. Cert. fund-raising exec. Legis. agt., Ohio. Staff nurse Case Western Res. U. Hosp. Cleve., 1967-70; instr. Sch. Nursing Ohio State U., Columbus, 1971-72, dir. computer assisted instrn. program devel., 1972-73; dir. Ohio Thoracic Soc., 1973-81, dir. profl. edn. Ohio Lung Assn., 1973-81, pres., exec. dir. Central Ohio Lung Assn., 1981—; adj. asst. prof. Ohio State U. Allied Medicine div. Med. Coll., 1981—; mem. advanced faculty Creative Edn. Found. SUNY, Buffalo, 1975—; chmn. health medicine and safety category Columbus Internat. Film Festival, 1981—. Mem. City Upper Arlington Cultural Arts Com., 1971—; trustee Columbus Community Cable Access Bd.; judge Taft Broad-casting Jefferson Awards, 1986. Recipient Allied Health Profl. Educator award Am. Lung Assn., 1976, Chris Bronze plaque Columbus Internat. Film Festival, 1977. Mem. Am. Thoracic Soc., Assn. Ednl. Communication Technicians, Health Scis. Communications Assn., Nat. Soc. Fund Raising Execs., Upper Arlington C. of C., Phi Delta Kappa, Sigma Theta Tau. Republican. Club: Columbus Met. Photography: Nursing Care of Adults and Orthopedic Conditions (Leona Mourad), 1979. Home: 4063 Fairfax Dr Columbus OH 43220 Office: 1770 Arlingate Columbus OH 43228

COLLETON, VALENCIA DEANA, veterinarian; b. Birmingham, Ala., Dec. 19, 1958; d. Irvin Monroe and Marian (Hill) Smith; m. Curtis Alan Colleton, July 6, 1982. B.S., Tuskegee Inst., 1985, D.V.M., 1985. Pres. CEALDA Inc., Tuskegee, Ala., 1982-84; vet. med. officer U.S. Dept. Agr., San Juan, P.R., 1985—; owner Equkan Kennels, Tuskegee, 1983—. Active Washington Chapel AME Ch., 1982—, Caribe Kennel Club, Fort Buchanan Protestant Ch. Choir; youth dir. Protestant Youth Group Fort Buchanan. Recipient Acad. Excellence award U. Ala., 1976; Acad. Achievement award Tuskegee Inst., 1981. Mem. Nat. Assn. Female Execs., Am. Vet. Med. Assn., Am. Assn. Female Vets., Tuskegee Alumni Assn., Alpha Kappa Alpha. Avocations: drawing; aerobics; swimming; tennis; horseback riding; arts and crafts. Home: PO Box 34201 Fort Buchanan PR 00934 Office: US Dept Agr Animal and Plant Health Inspection Service GPO Call Box 71355 San Juan PR 00936

COLLETT, JOAN, librarian; b. St. Louis; d. Robert and Mary (Hoolan) C.; m. John E. Dustin, Nov. 19, 1983. B.A. magna cum laude, Maryville Coll., 1947; M.A., Washington U., St. Louis, 1950; M.S. in L.S., U. Ill., Urbana, 1954. Regional cons. W.Va. Library Commn., Spencer, W.Va., 1954-56; instr. Rosary Coll., River Forest, Ill., 1956-57; head extension dept. Gary (Ind.) Public Library, 1957-64; librarian Grailville Library, 1965; regional librarian USIA, Latin Am., Africa, 1966-78; exec. dir., librarian St. Louis Public Library, 1978—. Mem. ALA. Office: St Louis Pub Library Office of Dir 1301 Olive St Saint Louis MO 63103

COLLETTE, CAROLYN PENNEY, English educator; b. Boston, Aug. 2, 1945; d. George Kenneth and Mary (Takessian) Penney; m. David Raymond Collette, July 9, 1967; children—Matthew, Andrew. A.B., Mt. Holyoke Coll., 1967; M.A., U. Mass., 1969, Ph.D., 1971. With Mt. Holyoke Coll., South Hadley, Mass., 1970—, asst. prof., 1972-77, assoc. prof., 1977—. Contbr. articles to profl. jours. Woodrow Wilson fellow, 1967; NDEA fellow, 1969; NEH summer fellow, 1976. Mem. MLA, Medieval Acad. Am., William Morris Soc., Modern Humanities Research Assn., Phi Beta Kappa, Phi Kappa Phi. Episcopalian. Office: Mount Holyoke Coll Dept English South Hadley MA 01075

COLLETTE, FRANCES MADELYN, personnel and unemployment tax consultant, lawyer; b. Yonkers, N.Y., Aug. 5, 1947; d. Morris Aaron and Esther (Gang) Volbert; m. Roger Warren Collette, Dec. 25, 1971; 1 son, Darren Roger. B.Ed. summa cum laude, SUNY-Buffalo, 1969; J.D., cum laude, U. Miami, 1980. Bar: Fla. 1980. Employment counselor Fla. Bur. Employment Security, Miami, 1969-73; unemployment claims adjudicator Fla. Bur. Unemployment Claims, Miami, 1973-77; pres. Fla. unemployment tax and personnel cons. Unemployment Services Fla., Inc., Miami, 1977—. Mem. Printing Industry S. Fla., Fla. Pest Control Assn., Better Bus. Bur. S. Fla. (1st v.p. 1980—, bd. govs. 2d vice chmn. 1981-82), Nat. Assn. Women Bus. Owners. Jewish. Office: Unemployment Services Fla Inc 7220 SW 39th Terr Miami FL 33155

COLLIER, ALEXIS CHRISTINA, psychology educator; b. Norton, Va., July 10, 1951; d. S. Alexander and L. Belle (Robinett) Collier; B.S., Va. Poly. Inst. and State U., 1973; postgrad. Princeton U., 1973-74; Ph.D., U. Wash., 1976. Teaching and research asst. Princeton U., 1973-74, U. Wash., Seattle, 1974-76; asst. prof. psychology Ohio State U., Columbus, 1976-82, assoc. prof., 1982—; cons. to profl. jours. 1976—. NIMH grantee, 1980, mem. grant rev. com., 1981-84. Mem. Am. Psychol. Assn., Eastern Psychol. Assn., Midwestern Psychol. Assn., Psychonomic Soc., Internat. Soc. Developmental Psychobiology, NOW, Colony-Mortar Board, Alpha Lambda Delta, Phi Kappa Phi, Delta Zeta. Democrat. Baptist. Club: Columbus Met. Lodge: Order Eastern Star. Contbr. articles to jours. in psychology. Home: 5015 Hibbs Dr Columbus OH 43220 Office: 1885 Neil Ave Mall Columbus OH 43210

COLLIER, CANDACE, commercial real estate broker; b. Albuquerque, May 8, 1949; d. William Dickason and Betty June (Smith) Collier. Student U. N.Mex., 1969, Houston Community Coll., 1978. Owner, Collier Investments, Houston, 1974—; v.p. Wilson Investments, Houston, 1979-80, Am. Trust Co., Houston, 1982-83; broker assoc. Bice-Merrill Comml.; Houston, 1983—; gen. agt. mktg. Am. Fidelity Life Ins., Phoenix, 1983; mktg. cons. Energy Control Corp., Houston, 1983—. Vice-pres. Townhouse 84 Assn. Community Assn. Inst., Houston, 1983-84. Recipient Top Performance award Am. Fidelity Life, 1983; Sales and Mktg. award Am. Trust Co., 1983; Investment Specialist designee, 1983. Mem. Nat. Assn. Women in Comml. Real Estate, Women in Bus., Nat. Assn. Female Execs., Nat. Investment Soc., Am. Soc. Notaries, Am. Legion Aux. Clubs: University, River Oaks Women's Breakfast (Houston). Home: 9303 Hammerly TH 602 Houston TX 77080

COLLIER, CHARLOTTE MAE MEIER, publishing company executive; b. Wooster, Ohio, Sept. 24, 1947; d. Ferris Thorld and Sarah Edith (Johnson) Meier; m. John Edward Collier, Dec. 27, 1971; children—Elda Mae, John Icel. Student Case Western Res. U.; 1965-67; B.A., U. Mass., 1969, M.A., 1971, Ph.D., 1978. Project mgr. Chilton Research Services, Radnor, Pa., 1980-81; research mgr. Springhouse Corp., Pa., 1981-84, dir. research, 1984—; chair research com. Assn. Bus. Pubs., N.Y.C., 1985—; mem. Advt. Research Found., N.Y.C., 1984—. Contbr. articles and papers to profl. lit. Mem. Montgomery County Task Force on Older Adults, Pa., 1971-78, sec., 1977; cons. on aging programs Southeastern Pa. Lutheran Synod, Phila., 1980. Univ. fellow U. Mass., 1969-72; Gerontol. Soc. fellow, 1979-80. Mem. Am. Mktg. Assn., Am. Hosp. Assn., Nat. Assn. Home Care, Nat. Assn. Female Execs., Phi Beta Kappa. Democrat. Lutheran. Avocation: bicycling. Office: Springhouse Corp 1111 Bethlehem Pike Springhouse PA 19477

COLLIER, ELLEN CLODFELTER, foreign policy specialist; b. Lawrence, Kans., Oct. 19, 1927; d. Harve Malone and Martha June (Lambert) Clodfelter; B.A. cum laude with high distinction, Ohio State U., 1949; M.A., Am. U., 1951; grad. Nat. War Coll., 1978; m. Edwin Collier, May 25, 1951; children—Stephen Harve, Martha Lambert Collier Riva, Sarah Reiner, John Reiner, Catherine Clodfelter. U.S. fgn. policy analyst, fgn. affairs div. Congl. Research Service, Library of Congress, Washington, 1949-55, U.S. fgn. policy analyst, 1960-69, specialist, 1969—, head spl. project sect., 1972-75, head fgn. issues and nat. policy sect., 1975-76, head global issues sect., 1976-77. mem. staff subcom. on disarmament U.S. Senate Fgn. Relations Com., 1955-59. Mem. Internat. Studies Assn., Am. Soc. Internat. Law, Soc. Internat. Devel., Exec. Women in Govt., Phi Beta Kappa, Pi Sigma Alpha. Club: Potomac Pedalers. Author report. Editor: Congress and Foreign Policy, 1979-84. Office: Congressional Research Service Library of Congress Washington DC 20540

COLLIER, HELEN VANDIVORT, 1ounseling psychologist; b. Nagpur, India; d. William Boardley and Stephena Ruth (Hecker) C.; A.B., Ohio Wesleyan U.; M.Ed., Ed.D., U. Toledo; grad. San Diego Gestalt Tng. Center, Gestalt Inst. Cleve.; children—Keith Vandivort, Daniel Vandivort, Heidi Vandivort Childress; m. Gary J. Scrimgeour. Tchr. elem. schs., Itasca, Ill., 1951-54; ednl. cons. Toledo Bd. Edn., 1960-67; elem. counselor Toledo Public Schs., 1968; counseling psychologist, asst. prof. U. Toledo, 1968-74; asst. dir. adult counseling project Sch. Continuing Studies, Ind. U., Bloomington, 1975-76; dir. Human Devel. Assos., Bloomington, Ind., 1974-79, HVC Assos., Bloomington. cons. tng. and orgnl. devel., 1980—; part time faculty Nat. Jud. Coll., U. Nev., Reno, 1983—; organizational devel. analyst Harrah's Hotel Casino, Reno; pvt. practice psychotherapy. Lic. psychologist, Ohio; cert. marriage and family counselor, Nev. Mem. Am. Psychol. Assn., Am. Assn. Counseling and Devel., Nat. Vocat. Guidance Assn., Internat. Human Learning Resource Network. Co-editor: Meeting the Educational and Occupational Planning Needs of Adults, 1975; author: Freeing Ourselves: Removing Internal Barriers to Equality, 1979; Counseling Women: A Guide for Therapists, 1982; also articles. Office: PO Box 2809 Reno NV 89505

COLLIER, NORMA JEAN, public relations executive; b. Yankton, S.D.; d. Guy L. and Elizabeth J. (Donegan) Collier. Student George Washington U., Los Angeles City Coll., U. Md.-Seoul, Korea. Exec. sec. Universal Studios, Universal City, Calif., 1955-58, Leo Burnett Advt. Co., Hollywood, Calif., 1958-60; adminstrv. asst. Survey & Research Co., Seoul, 1960-63; exec. asst. John E. Horton Assocs., Washington, 1963-72; exec. asst. Doremus & Co., Washington, 1972-74; account exec. Doremus/West, Los Angeles, 1974-79, v.p., 1979—. Recipient Letter of Appreciation, Republic of Korea, 1963. Mem. Women in Communications (dir. chpt.). Republican. Roman Catholic. Club: Hollywood Studio (pres. 1957-58, house council). Home: 11147 Huston St North Hollywood CA 91601 Office: Doremus/West 10960 Wilshire Blvd Los Angeles CA 90024

COLLIER, RUBY JEAN, food products company executive; b. Nashville, Oct. 30, 1946; d. Ernest Herman and Edmonia (Betts) Collier. B.S., Tenn. State U., 1969; postgrad. U. Wis., 1983—. Substitute tchr. Met. Bd. Edn., Nashville, 1971-72; with J.C. Penney Co., Goodlettsville, Tenn., 1972; mgr. Gino's Inc., Clark, N.J., 1972-78; prodn. mgr. Carnation Instant Div., Oconomowoc, Wis., 1979—. Mem. Sigma Gamma Rho. Address: 2415 Pebble Valley Rd Apt 13 Waukesha WI 53186

COLLIER-ADAMS, JULIE, college dean; b. Hudson, N.Y., Nov. 16, 1940; d. Charles Armstrong and Marion Jane (Lasher) Collier; m. Peter Adams, Feb. 27, 1966 (div.); children—Melia, Emily. B.S. in Edn., Russell Sage Coll., 1962; M.Ed. in Higher Edn., U. Mass., 1974. Tchr. math. Rye Country Day Sch., N.Y., 1962-64; tchr. Iolani Sch., Honolulu, 1964-66, Fountain Valley Sch., Colorado Springs, Colo., 1968-69; head of residents U. Mass., Amherst, 1971-73, sr. head of residence, 1973-74; assoc. dean of student Colgate U., Hamilton, N.Y., 1974-76; dean of students Goucher Coll., Balt., 1976—; mem. Middle States Accreditation Assn., 1980—. Mem. Nat. Assn. for Women Deans, Adminstrs. and Counselors, Nat. Assn. Student Personnel Adminstrs., Eastern Assn. Coll. Deans and Advisers of Students. Office: Goucher Coll Towson MD 21204

COLLIER-EVANS, DEMETRA FRANCES, state government employment official; b. Nashville, Dec. 18, 1937; d. Oscar Collier and Earllee Elizabeth (Williams) Collier-Sheffield; m. Richard A. Gotha, Feb. 2, 1962 (div. Nov. 1965); m. George Perry Evans, Dec. 21, 1966; 1 child, Richard E. A.A., Solano Community Coll., 1974; B.A., Chapman Coll., 1981. Cert. tchr., Calif. Case responsible person Employment Devel. Dept., San Diego, 1975-82; vocat. tchr. San Diego Community Coll., 1982-83; job bank mgr. N.J. Job Service, Camden, 1985, placement specialist, 1984-85, 85—; cons. Bumble Bee Factory, San Diego, 1982. Developer: women's seminar Women's Opportunity Week, San Diego, 1982, network seminar Fed. Women's Week, Phila., 1985. Bd. dirs. Welfare Rights Orgn., San Diego, 1982. Served with USAF, 1956-59. Recipient Excellence cert. San Diego Employer Adv. Bd., San Diego, 1981, Leadership cert. Nat. U., San Diego, 1981. Mem. Black Advs. State Service (charter, corr. sec. 1979-81), Nat. Assn. Female Execs., AAUW, NAACP (life, rec. sec. San Diego 1982). Democrat. Avocations: calligraphy, sewing. Office: NJ Job Service 517 Federal Ave Camden NJ 08103

COLLINS, ANN ELIZABETH AVERITT (MRS. GALEN FRANKLIN COLLINS), civic leader; b. Peru, Ind., July 28, 1934; d. Robert Chancellor and Cleo (Hite) Averitt; B.A., Fla. Internat. U.; m. Galen Franklin Collins, Sept. 30, 1956; children—Galen Robert, Amelia Lynn, Scott Franklin, Daniel Chancellor. Co-soc. editor Elkhart (Ind.) Truth, 1955-56; mem. Elkhart Civic Theatre, 1957-60; mem. Chenango County Community Players, N.Y., 1960-63; co-founder Dogwood Playhouse, Bristol, Va.-Tenn., 1964, bd. dirs., 1964-69; co-founder Collero Puppets, Bristol, 1967; free lance writer, 1972—; dir. Christian edn. United Ch. Christ, Miami, 1978-82. Musical compositions include Why Am I Old; Little Boy, My Dear Son; Color; Willows; Soldier Boy; Is That Your Voice I Hear?. Home: 1431 Club Dr Lynchburg VA 24503

COLLINS, ANNE KRAMER, hospital patient advocate; b. Glen Cove, N.Y., Aug. 17, 1925; d. Matthew James and V. Marie (Murray) Kramer; m. Cornelius James Collins, Jr., June 20, 1945 (div. May 1967); children—Matthew Clint, Pati Marie. B.A., Manhattanville Coll., 1944; postgrad. C.W. Post Coll., 1978. Vice pres. Kramer Mortuary, Inc., Glen Cove, 1960-81; asst. dir. of pub. relations Nassau Library System, Garden City, N.Y., 1969-71; dir. patient relations, patient advocate Nassau County Med. Ctr., East Meadow, N.Y., 1971—, mem. quality assurance com., 1979—. Editor, hosp. newspaper At The Ctr., 1971-74. Mem. Am. Hosp. Assn., Soc. of Patient Reps. Roman Catholic. Clubs: Nassau Country, Manhattanville Coll. Alumni Assn., Women's Metro. Golf Assn. Avocations: golfing; tennis; bowling; writing; interior decorating. Home: Duck Pond Rd Glen Cove Long Island NY 11542 Office: Nassau County Med Ctr 2201 Hempstead Turnpike East Meadow NY 11554

COLLINS, BARBARA CLARK, retail company personnal executive; b. Orange, N.J., Oct. 2, 1953; d. John Anthony and Patricia O. (Horner) Clark; m. Richard Dwight Collins, Jan. 16, 1982. B.S. in Mgmt. Sci., Rutgers U. Coll., 1984. Exec. sec. to exec. v.p. Ronson Corp., Bridgewater, N.J., 1976-79; exec. asst. to pres. Egon Zehnder Internat., N.Y.C., 1979-80; personnel mgr. Adamas Carbide Corp., Kenilworth, N.J., 1980-84; v.p. human resources Van Heusen Factory Stores, Piscataway, N.J., 1984—. Mem. Internat. Assn. Personnel Women (bd., pres. elect 1986-87), Nat. Assn. Female Execs. Avocations: Horseback riding; skiing; reading; golf. Home: 33 Edgewood Terr Bridgewater NJ 08807 Office: Van Heusen Factory Stores PO Box 2206 New Brunswick NJ 08903

COLLINS, BRENDA ELAINE, automobile agency executive; b. Dec. 24, 1954, Tachikawa, Japan; came to U.S., 1955, naturalized, 1954; d. Charles William and Mary Evelyn (Stephens) Bassett; m. George Timothy Collins, June 29, 1974 (div. 1979). B.A., Calif. State U.-San Bernardino, 1979, cert. fin. mgmr., 1979. Supr. waitressing Marie Callendars, Redlands, Calif., 1977-79; subs. tchr. Redlands Unified Sch. Dist., Calif., 1979-81; salesperson L.J. Snow ford, Colton, Calif., 1981-82; sales adminstr. Theodore Robins Ford, Costa Mesa, Calif., 1983-85; fin. mgr. Campbell Porsche, Buena Park, Calif., 1985—. Vol. ARC, San Bernardino, 1972-73. Pythian scholar, 1972. Mem. Nat. Assn. Female Execs. Avocations: golf; tennis; bowling; interior decorating. Office: Campbell Porsche 6750 Manchester Blvd Buena Park CA 90621

COLLINS, CARDISS, congresswoman; b. St. Louis; d. Finley and Rosia Mary (Robertson) Robertson; certificate bus. Northwestern U., 1966, diploma in profl. accounting, 1967; m. George Collins (dec.); 1 son, B. Kevin. Stenographer, then sec. employment service Ill. Dept. Labor, 1950-58; sec., then revenue auditor Ill. Dept. Revenue, 1958-72; mem. 93-99th congresses from 7th Ill. Dist.; various offices Congl. Black Caucus. Vice pres. Lawndale Youth Commn., Chgo. Committeewoman 24th Ward Regular Democratic Orgn., Chgo.; adv. bd. Ill. Dem. Central Com. Office: 2264 Rayburn House Office Bldg Washington DC 20515

COLLINS, CLARICIE VISSER, university administrator; b. Hurley, S.D., Feb. 22, 1927; d. Leonard and Leta (Thompson) Visser; m. Gerald Morris Collins, Sept. 17, 1950 (div. Jan. 1981); children—Lowell Louise, Kimberly, G. Leonard, Alex, Andrea. B.A., U. S.D., 1949. Hostess Mid-Continent Airlines, Mpls., 1949-50; co-owner, operator Coyote Motel, Vermillion, S.D., 1951-62; exec. sec. U. S.D. Alumni Assn., Vermillion, 1967—; dir. alumni and pub. info. services U. S.D., Vermillion, 1983—. Editor: University of South Dakota 1967-1982, 1983; South Dakotan, 1967—. Bd. dirs. United Fund, Vermillion, 1963, Dakota Hosp. Assn., Vermillion, 1984—; vice-chairwoman Clay County Republican Central Com., Vermillion, 1963-66, chmn., 1968-71. Recipient Dakota Days Outstanding Service award U. S.D., 1974. Mem. Council for Advancement and Support Edn., (Disting. Service award 1985), S.D. Council for Advancement and Support Edn., Kappa Alpha Theta. Republican. Congregationalist. Club: PEO Sisterhood (pres. Vermillion 1963). Home: 812 Canby St Vermillion SD 57069 Office: U SD 414 E Clark St Vermillion SD 57069

COLLINS, DEBORAH DEANN, broadcasting executive; b. Houston, July 13, 1951; d. Carl James Nelson and Hattie Lucile (Ross) Massey; m. Alfonzia Collins, Jan. 8, 1977; 1 son, Alfonzia Collins. B.A., Tex. So. U., Houston, 1976. Anchor newscaster Sta. KTSU-FM, Houston, 1972-75, Sta. KCOH-AM, Houston, 1975, KYOK-AM, Houston, 1975-77; announcer music Sta. KLOL, Houston, 1976-77; news dir. Sta. KMJQ MAJIC-FM, 1977—, news and community affairs dir., talk show host, 1978—. Adv., Houston Prep. Sch., 1981; bd. dirs. Met. Ministries, 1981—, Kuumba House, 1982—; adv. Riverside Hosp., 1982; innovator Majic 102 Communications Scholarships, 1980; mem. Mayors Census Court; vol. Shape Community Ctr., 1980—, Clear Lake C. of C., 1980-81, all Houston. Recipient NAACP award for Community Work, 1982; Tex. So. U. Excellence in Communications award, 1983; Recognition award Adopt Black Children, 1982; Harvard U. Hon. Speaker's award, 1976; named Most Influential Black Woman in Houston, Black Experience Mag., 1983, 84; Am. Women in Radio and TV scholar, 1975. Mem. Delta Sigma Theta, Sigma Delta Chi. Mem. Penecostal Ch. Office: KMJQ 3100 Richmond Houston TX 77098

COLLINS, DIANA JOSEPHINE, psychologist; b. Potsdam, N.Y., Apr. 27, 1944; d. Philip Joseph and Janet Dorothy (Lynke) C.; grad. with high honors, SUNY; Psy.D., Mass. Sch. Profl. Psychology, 1981. Psychologist, N.H. Hosp., Concord, 1974-79; asst. dir. forensic unit, 1979-80; founder, dir. Victim/Witness Service County of Hillsborough, Manchester, N.H., 1980-84; pvt. practice, North Chelmsford, Mass.; adj. assoc. prof. U. N.H., 1974; adj. assoc. prof. Antioch Coll. of New Eng. Mem. AAUW, N.H. Psychol. Assn., Mass. Psychol. Assn., Eastern Psychol. Assn., Internat. Assn. Psychotherapists and

Counselors, Internat. Platform Assn., Am. Assn. Female Execs., Roman Catholic. Home: RFD 2 Contoocook NH 03229 Office: 85 Tyngsboro Rd Box 2036 North Chelmsford MA 01863

COLLINS, DOROTHY LANHAM, interior designer; b. Chgo., Sept. 26, 1926; d. Cecil Ray and Elizabeth (Billow) Lanham; children—Judith Collins Hunerberg, Tom, John, Patricia, Susan. Founder, owner, pres. Dorothy Collins Interiors, Inc., retail design studio, Edina, Minn., 1966—; mem. Burlington House Design Bd., Minn. Internat. Market Square Bd. Mem. Nat. Home Fashions League (nat. pres.), Fashion Group. Republican. Club: Calhoun Beach. Home: 6432 Red Fox Ct Edina MN 55436 Office: Dorothy Collins & Assocs 7010 France Ave S Edina MN 55435

COLLINS, DOROTHY (MRS. AKIBA EMANUEL), advertising and public relations agency executive; b. Salt Lake City; d. Joseph L. and Dorothy (Frey) Collins; A.B., U. Denver; m. Akiba Emanuel; 1 dau., Lynn Collins. Woman's page editor Rocky Mountain News, Denver; fashion editor NBC, N.Y.C.; pub. relations dir. Shwayder Bros., Denver; account exec. Ellington & Co., N.Y.C.; v.p. Infoplan, N.Y.C.; v.p., mgr. consumer group Burson-Marsteller, N.Y.C.; sr. v.p., chief exec. officer Public Relations div. Sam Lusky Assocs., Inc., Denver, 1981-83; sr. v.p., dir. consumer mktg. Burson-Marsteller, Denver, 1983—. Former nat. dir. women's activities Nat. Jewish Hosp., Denver; active Girl Scouts U.S.A.; trustee Spalding Rehab. Hosp., Marymount Coll., 1979-80. Mem. Nat. Home Fashions League (pres. N.Y. chpt. 1977-79), Women's Forum, Denver Fashion Group, Exec. Women in Pub. Relations. Clubs: Denver Women's Press, Denver Press. Home: 2950 Albion St Denver CO 80207

COLLINS, EILEEN LOUISE, economist; b. Chillicothe, Ohio, Dec. 15, 1942; d. Theodore Milton and Louise Alma (Suess) C.; B.A. (regional scholar), Bryn Mawr Coll., 1964; M.A., U. Wis., Madison, 1967, Ph.D., 1975. Lectr. dept. econs. U. Waterloo (Ont., Can.), 1971-73; asst. prof. dept. econs. Barnard Coll., N.Y.C., 1975-76; asst. prof. dept. econs. Fordham U., N.Y.C., 1976-78; economist NSF, Washington, 1978—. Editor: American Jobs and the Changing Industrial Base, 1984. Author papers and reports in field. Recipient NSF Outstanding Performance award, 1979, 81, 83, 84; NIMH fellow, 1969-71; Nat. Inst. Public Affairs fellow, 1966-67. Mem. Am. Econ. Assn., AAAS, Nat. Tax Assn., Washington Philos. Soc., Washington Women Economists. Club: Nat. Economists (v.p. elect seminars). Office: NSF 1800 G St NW Room 1229 Washington DC 20550

COLLINS, ELAINE DARNELL, medical technologist; b. New Orleans, Feb. 7, 1948; d. Lawrence and Gloria Catherine (Martin) C. B.S. in Med. Tech., Loyola U., New Orleans, 1970; M.A. in Mgmt. and Supervision, Central Mich. U., 1979, M.A. in Edn. candidate, 1984. Staff med. technologist Mercy Hosp., New Orleans, 1970-76, Robinson Med. Group, New Orleans, 1977-78; asst. supr. Tulane U. Med. Group, New Orleans, 1980-83, evening supr., 1983, edn. coordinator, 1983—; substitute tchr. Orleans Parish Sch. System. Mem. Urban League Greater New Orleans, New Orleans Sickle Cell Anemia Found., Contemporary Arts Ctr., Friends of the Audubon Zoo. J.T. Baker Chem. Co. scholar; grantee Hycel Co., Alpha Mu Tau. Mem. Am. Soc. Med. Tech., Am. Soc. Clin. Pathologists (affiliate), La. Soc. Med. Tech., New Orleans Soc. Med. Tech., La. Talent Bank of Women, Sigma Iota Epsilon. Democrat. Methodist.

COLLINS, GAIL PETTY, educator; b. Bronx, N.Y., June 11, 1947; d. Edward Joseph and Virginia (Lattmann) Petty; B.A., Mt. St. Mary Coll., 1969; M.S., Herbert H. Lehman Coll., 1973; postgrad. Cornell U., 1978. Tchr., Newburgh (N.Y.) City Sch. Dist., 1969-71; tchr. Clarkstown Central Sch. Dist., West Nyack, N.Y., 1971—. Commr. Rockland County Park Commn., Clarkstown, 1978-82, vice-chairperson, 1981; mem. Town of Clarkstown Bicentennial Commn., 1976; vol. Meals on Wheels; bd. dirs. Clarkstown United Way. Mem. Rockland County Tchrs. Assn. (dir. 1977-83, v.p. 1978-79, pres. 1979-82), N.Y. State United Tchrs. (alt. del., del. 1977-83), Am. Fedn. Tchrs. (alt. del., del. 1977-83), Rockland County Bldg. and Central Trades Council (del. 1976-83), Rockland County Hist. Soc., Coalition of Labor Union Women. Democrat. Home: 7-11 Lawrence Park Piermont NY 10968 Office: Lakewood Elem Sch 77 Lakeland Ave Congers NY 10920

COLLINS, GLADYS IRENE, university counselor; b. Dallas; d. Benjamin and Elizabeth (Banks) Thomas; m. Richard Conner Collins, Nov. 8, 1945 (dec. July 1970); 1 dau., Marrian Ruth Lacy. B.S., Prairie View U., 1939; M.Ed., U. Minn., 1960. Elem. art tchr. Dallas Ind. Sch. Dist., 1939-60, high sch. art tchr., 1960-65, high sch. adv. guidance counselor, 1965-79; career counselor So. Meth. U., Dallas, 1979, 84—; bldg. rep. J.W. Ray Sch., Dallas, 1941-45; sch. coordinator Project Upward Bound, Lincoln High Sch., Dallas, 1965-69, adv. guidance counselor, chmn. pupil personnel com., 1965-77; adv. guidance counselor, chmn. pupil personnel com. Arts Magnet Sch., Dallas, 1977-79. Trustee Dallas Mus. Art, 1980-1984, Mus. African-Am. Life and Culture, Dallas, 1978—; bd. dirs. Maria Morgan Br. YWCA; leader Girl Scouts U.S.A., 1940-45. Recipient Disting. Edn1. Service award Dallas Classroom Tchrs., 1967; Community Service award South Dallas Bus. and Profl. Women, 1968, Outstanding Tchr. of Yr. award Lincoln High Sch., Dallas, 1970; appreciation award Maria Morgan YWCA, Dallas, 1981, South Oak Cliff High Sch., Dallas, 1979. Mem. Dallas Negro Art Assn. (pres. 1943-46), Dallas Assn. Counselors (pres. 1966-68), Dallas Tchrs. Council (pres. 1952-66, appreciation award 1966), Delta Sigma Theta (past v.p.), Phi Delta Kappa (charter). Roman Catholic. Clubs: Wednesday Morning Study (pres.), Cedar Crest Civic (sec. 1980, rec. sec.) (Dallas).

COLLINS, JOAN HENRIETTA, actress; b. London, May 3, 1936; d. Joseph William and Elsa (Bessant) C.; m. Peter Holm, 1985; children from previous marriage—Tara Cynara Newley, Sacha Newley, Katie Kass. Films include: I Believe in You, Girl in the Red Velvet Swing, Rally Round the Flag Boys, Island in the Sun, Seven Thieves, Road to Hong Kong, Sunburn, The Stud, Game for Vultures, The Bitch, The Big Sleep; theatre appearance in The Last of Mrs. Cheyney; TV films include: The Man Who Came to Dinner, The Moneychanger, Paper Dolls, The Wild Women of Chastity Gulch; star TV series: Dynasty, 1981—; star, co-producer TV miniseries Sins, 1986; appeared in Hansel and Gretel, Faerie Tale Theatre, cable TV prodn. Author: Past Imperfect, 1978; Joan Collins Beauty Book, 1980; Katy: A Flight for Life, 1982. Office: Aaron Spelling Prodns 1041 N Formosa Los Angeles CA 90046

COLLINS, JOANNE ANITA, accounting educator; b. Chgo., Aug. 2, 1946; d. Elmer and Lucille Ann (Dombrowski) C. B.S. in Math., Ill. Inst. Tech., 1968, M.B.A., 1970; Ph.D. in Acctg., Northwestern U., 1976. C.P.A., Ill.; cert. mgmt. acct.; cert. cost analyst. Mem. staff EDP ops. Internat. Harvester, 1965-70; instr. Ill. Inst. Tech., Chgo., 1969-73; fin. analyst Continental Can Co., 1970-73; econ. analyst Sargent & Lundy, 1973; asst. prof. acctg. Wharton Sch., U. Pa., Phila., 1976-82; prof. acctg. Calif. State U., Los Angeles, 1982—; cons. in field. Contbr. articles to profl. jours. Recipient Alumni award Ill. Inst. Tech., 1968; Legion of Honor, Chapel of Four Chaplains, 1980. Mem. Am. Acctg. Assn., Am. Inst. C.P.A.s, Nat. Assn. Accts., Inst. Mgmt. Acctg., Am. Women's Soc. of C.P.A.s (charter mem. Los Angeles chpt.), Am. Soc. Women Accts., ACLU, Calif. Soc. C.P.A.s, Mensa. Democrat. Unitarian-Universalist. Home: 2550 S Garvey Ave #134 Alhambra CA 91803 Office: Calif State U 5151 State University Dr Los Angeles CA 90032

COLLINS, JUDITH NAN, economist; b. Melrose, Mass., Jan. 9, 1954; d. Ivor Winter and Shirley Nan (Rhea) C.; B.S. in Agrl. Econs., U. Wis., 1976, M.S. in Agrl. Econs. (Vilas fellow), 1978. Economist, Econ. Research Service, U.S. Dept. Agr., Washington, 1979-82; research assoc. United Way Am., Alexandria, Va., 1982-83, sr. research assoc., 1983—. Mem. Am. Agrl. Econs. Assn. Contbr. articles to profl. pubs. Home: 1138 Valley Dr Alexandria VA 22302 Office: 701 N Fairfax St Alexandria VA 22314

COLLINS, KAREN LYNN WISLER, psychologist; b. Oklahoma City, Mar. 25, 1949; d. Charles C. and Frances Joan (Higgins) Wisler; B.A. with honors, Stephen F. Austin State U., Nacogdoches, Tex., 1973; M.A., Tex. Christian U., 1978, Ph.D., 1979; m. David C. Eiland. Asst. prof. Dickinson (N.D.) State Coll., 1979-80; research asst. prof. psychiatry U. Tex. Med. Br., Galveston, 1980-81, asst. prof. dept. ob-gyn and sr. research asso. Office Ednl. Devel., 1981—. Mem. Am. Psychol. Assn., Southwestern Psychol. Assn., Am. Ednl. Research Assn., So. Soc. Philosophy and Psychology, Psi Chi, Alpha Kappa Delta, Alpha Chi, Delta Omicron, Phi Delta Kappa, Democrat. Methodist. Contbr. articles to profl. jours. Office: Dept Ob-Gyn U Tex Med Br Room 313 MW E-87 Galveston TX 77550

COLLINS, KAY GRAHAM, librarian; b. Omaha, Jan. 27, 1947; d. Henry and Helen (Graham) C. B.A., U. Ark., 1969; M.L.S., La. State U., 1978. Claims examiner U.S. R.R. Retirement Bd., Chgo., 1969-70, contact rep., Denver, 1970-75, Shreveport, La., 1975-77, claims examiner, Chgo., 1979-80, agy. librarian, 1980—. Mem. Am. Assn. Law Libraries, Chgo. Area Law Libraries, Fed. Mgrs. Assn., Richard III Soc. Presbyterian. Avocations: bowling; collecting antiquarian books on imperial Russia. Home: 525 W Deming St Apt 519 Chicago IL 60614 Office: US RR Retirement Bd 844 Rush St Room 800 Chicago IL 60611

COLLINS, MARCIA FREUCHTEL, materials engineer, chemist; b. Detroit, Apr. 19, 1948; d. Charles Andrew and Ethel Mary (Greig) Freuchtel. B.S. in Chemistry, U. Mich., 1969; M.S. in Material Sci. and Engring., Rutgers U., 1983. Instr. Allegheny Schs., Pa., 1970; research asst. Koppers Co., Monroeville, Pa., 1971; tech. dir. Liquid Crystal Ind., Turtle Creek, Pa., 1971-74; research scientist Alcoa Tech. Ctr., Alcoa Center, Pa., 1974-77; scientist Am. Hoechst, Somerville, N.J., 1978-83; materials engr. Teledyne Water Pik, Fort Collins, Colo., 1983—; cons. Liquid Crystal Ind., Turtle Creek, 1972-74; mem. affiliate faculty Colo. State U., Fort Collins, 1984-86. Contbr. articles to profl. jours. Patentee in field. Warden Town of Hampton, N.J., 1976; vice chmn. Homeowners Action Com., Hampton, 1976; dir. Amateur Astronomers, Clinton, N.J., 1978. Mem. Am. Chem. Soc., Soc. Plastics Engrs., Air Pollution Control Assn. (mem. com. 1984—), Nat. Assn. Environ. Professionals, Nat. Assn. Female Execs. Avocations: antiques; art; creative writing; show horses; photography. Office: Teledyne Water Pik 1730 E Prospect St Fort Collins CO 80524

COLLINS, MARGARET HELEN, pathologist; b. Bronx, N.Y., July 5, 1950; d. Michael Robert and Catherine (Murray) Collins. B.S. summa cum laude, Fordham U., 1972; M.D., Georgetown U., 1977. Diplomate Am. Bd. Pathology. Intern pathology Cornell U.-N.Y. Hosp., N.Y.C., 1977-78, resident in pathology, 1978-80; chief resident in pediatric pathology Columbia-Presbyn. Med. Ctr., N.Y.C., 1980-82, research resident in pediatric pathology, 1982-83, asst. prof. clin. pathology, 1983—. Contbr. research articles to med. jours. Research fellow N.Y. Lung Assn., 1983-85, Am. Lung Assn., 1985—. Mem. AMA, Am. Med. Women's Assn., Internat. Acad. Pathology, N.Y. Acad. Scis., AAAS, Am. Thoracic Soc., Women's Med. Assn. N.Y.C., Soc. Pediatric Pathology, Phi Beta Kappa. Democrat. Roman Catholic. Office: Dept Pathology Div Developmental Pathology Babies Hosp BHA-T12 3959 Broadway New York NY 10032

COLLINS, MARIE ESTES, lawyer, financial consultant; b. Pine Bluff, Ark., Aug. 14, 1940; d. Charles Clyde and Doris Marie (Ryburn) Estes; m. Larry Don Collins, Aug. 27, 1960 (div. 1983). Student Tex. Woman's U., 1958-60; B.S. in Math., U. Houston, 1962; M.Ed., Sam Houston U., 1969; postgrad. in Bus. Adminstrn., U. Tex., 1981, U. Houston-Clearlake, 1982; J.D., S. Tex. Coll. Law, 1986. Bar: Tex. Master educator math., physics. Math. tchr. San Jacinto Jr. High Sch., Pasadena, Tex., 1962-64, San Rayburn High Sch., Pasadena, 1964-81; math. instr. San Jacinto Coll., Houston, 1981-83; pvt. practice fin. cons., Houston, 1982—; securities instr. Wall St. Tng., Salt Lake City and Chgo., 1983; condr. seminars, Houston, 1982-85. Author curriculum guides, 1974. Dir. Pasadena Math. Contest, 1970; lectr. Nat. Assn. Tchrs. of Math., 1970-80; chmn. math. textbook com. Pasadena Schs., 1970-80; organizer, sponsor Mu Alpha Theta math. honor soc. San Rayburn High Sch., 1966-81; parade participant San Jacinto Coll. Founders Day Parade, 1981, 82. NSF grantee, 1965; named Tchr. of Yr. Pasadena C. of C., 1974. Mem. ABA, Tex. Bar Assn., Internat. Assn. Fin. Planners, Nat. Assn. Female Execs., Delta Kappa Gamma. Avocations: Skiing; bird watching; painting; hiking; dancing; aerobics. Home and Office: 20 Hideaway Dr Friendswood TX 77546

COLLINS, MARTHA LAYNE, governor Kentucky; b. Shelby County, Ky., Dec. 7, 1936; d. Everett Larkin and Mary Lorena (Taylor) Hall; student Lindenwood Coll.; B.S., U. Ky., 1959; m. Bill Collins, July 3, 1959; children—Stephen Louis, Marla Ann. Tchr., Fairdale High Sch., Louisville, Seneca High Sch., Louisville, Woodford County Jr. High Sch., Versailles, Ky., 1959-63, 67-71; lt. gov. of Ky., Frankfort, 1979-83, gov., 1983—; vice chmn. Nat. Conf. Lt. Govs., 1981-82, chmn., 1982-83; clk. Key. Supreme Ct., 1975. Exec. dir. Friendship Force, 1977—; chmn. Nat. Democratic Nominating Conv., 1984. Mem. Nat. Conf. Appellate Ct. Clks., Bus. and Profl. Womens Club, Ky. Commn. on Women, U. Ky. Alumni Assn., Chi Omega. Baptist. Club: Order of Eastern Star. Home: Exec Mansion Frankfort KY 40601 Office: Governor's Office State Capitol Frankfort KY 40601

COLLINS, MARVA DELOISE NETTLES, educational administrator, educator; b. Monroeville, Ala., Aug. 31, 1936; d. Alex L. and Bessie Maye (Knight) Nettles; m. Clarence Collins, Sept. 2, 1960; children—Patrick, Eric, Cynthia. B.A., Clark Coll., 1957, Howard U., 1980, D.H.L., Wilberforce U., 1980, Chgo. State U., 1981, D.Hum., Dartmouth Coll., 1981. Founder Westside Prep. Sch., 1975, tchr., 1975—. Subject of numerous publs.: including Marva Collins' Way, 1982; subject of: feature film Welcome to Success: The Marva Collins Story, 1981. Mem. Pres.'s Commn. on White House Fellowships, 1981—. Recipient numerous awards, including: Reading Found. Am. award, 1979; Soujourner Truth Nat. award, 1980; Tchr. of Yr. award Phi Delta Kappa, 1980; Am. Public Service award Am. Inst. for Public Service, 1981; Endow a Dream award, 1980; Educator of Yr. award Chgo. Urban League, 1980; Jefferson Nat. award, 1981. Mem. Alpha Kappa Alpha. Baptist. Club: Exec. Office: 4146 W Chicago Ave Chicago IL 60641

COLLINS, MARY ALICE, psychiatric social worker; b. Everett, Wash., Apr. 20, 1937; d. Harry Edward and Mary (Yates) Caton; B.A., Sociology, Seattle Pacific Coll., 1959; M.S.W., U. Mich., 1966; Ph.D., Mich. State U., 1974; m. Gerald C. Brocker, Mar. 24, 1980. Dir. teenage, adult and counseling depts. YWCA, Flint, Mich., 1959-64, 66-68; social worker Cath. Social Services, Flint, 1969-71, Ingham Med. Mental Health Center, Lansing, Mich., 1971-73; clin. social worker Genesee Psychiat. Center, Flint, 1974-84, Psychol. Evaluation and Treatment Ctr., East Lansing, 1982-84; pvt. practice, East Lansing, 1984—; instr. social work Lansing Community Coll. and Mich. State U., 1974; vis. prof. Hurley Med. Center, Flint, 1980-84; cons. Ingham County Dept. Social Services, 1971-73. Advisor human relations Youth League, Flint Council Chs., 1964-65; sec. Genesee County Young Democrats, 1960-61. Mem. Nat. Assn. Social Workers, Acad. Cert. Social Workers, Registry Clin. Social Workers, Registry Health Care Workers, Phi Kappa Phi, Alpha Kappa Sigma. Contbr. articles to profl. jours. Home: 5945 Round Lake Rd Laingsburg MI 48848 Office: 1451 East Lansing Dr East Lansing MI 48823

COLLINS, MARY BETH, association executive; b. Detroit, Jan. 3, 1925; d. James Edward and Mildred Ina (Barding) Hughes; B.A., Manhattanville Coll. Sacred Heart, 1947; M.A., Ariz. State U., 1970; m. Taber Loree Collins, Aug. 7, 1947; children—Louise Collins Alton, James, Suzanne, Mary Beth Collins Brenner, Mildred Collins Hittner, Marguerite Collins Zeller, Miriam Collins Huston, Frank, Jesse, Kathleen Collins Cheo, Martha DeVault. Community services coordinator Alcohol and Drug Abuse div. Ariz. Health Dept., Phoenix, 1967-68, acting dir., 1968-70; coordinator City of Phoenix Drug Control, 1970-73; exec. dir. Drug Action Coalition, Montgomery County, Md., 1973-74; exec. dir. Community Orgn. for Drug Abuse Control, 1974-76; adminstr. Office Substance Abuse Services, Mich. Dept. Pub. Health, Lansing, 1977-78; chmn. N.Y. State Commn. Prevention and Edn. of Alcohol and Substance Abuse, Albany, 1978-79; exec. dir. Internat. Assn. Prevention Programs, 1974—. Pres. Ariz. Family, Inc., 1970-71; bd. dirs. Community Orgn. for Drug Abuse Control, 1969-73; mem. adv. bd. Good Samaritan Hosp., Mental Health Services; mem. bd. Nat. Coordinating Council on Drug Edn., 1974-76. Mem. Internat. Council on Alcoholism and Addictions, Drugs, Alcohol and Women's Health Coalition (regional chmn.), Ariz. Alumnae of Sacred Heart (founding pres. 1963-64), Pi Lambda Theta. Home: PO Box 1825 Cave Creek AZ 85331 Office: PO Box 812 Carefree AZ 85377

COLLINS, MOIRA ANN, graphics and communications company executive, calligrapher; b. Washington, Dec. 16, 1942; d. Peter William and Louise (Carroll) Collins; m. Andrew Joseph Griffin, Aug. 21, 1965; children—Andrew Fitzgerald, Timothy Collins. B.A., U. Toronto (Ont., Can.), 1964; M.A. in Teaching, Northwestern U., 1965; M.Ed. in Urban Studies, Northeastern U., Chgo., 1968. Tchr., Chgo. Bd. Edn., 1965-68; apprentice to profl. calligraphers, scribes and illuminators, U.S. and Eng., 1971-75; freelance calligrapher, 1974-78; mem. publicity and promotional staff Swallow Press, Chgo., 1978-79; owner Letters, Chgo., 1979—. HEW fellow Northeastern U., 1967-68. Author, contbr.; Celebration: Anais Nin, 1975; contbr. to Goodfellow Rev. of Crafts, 1979. Calligrapher: Erotica, 1976, Chgo. Rev., 1978. Chmn. fund-raising Van Gorder Walden Sch., Chgo., 1979-80. Mem. Chgo. Calligraphy Collective (co-founder, chmn. 1976-77, pres. 1978-79, hon. mem.), Soc. Scribes N.Y., Soc. Calligraphers, Soc. Scribes and Illuminators (Eng.), Friends Calligraphy Calif., Gaming and Mfrs. Assn. Democrat. Roman Catholic. Home: 834 W Chalmers Pl Chicago IL 60614 Office: 429 W Ohio St Suite 555 Chicago IL 60610

COLLINS, MOLINDA MARTIN, nurse, health education educator, biology educator; b. Savannah, Tenn., Nov. 11, 1954; d. John Neal and Molina Opal (Gray) Martin; m. William Paul Collins, Jr., Mar. 16, 1974. A.A., Miss. County Community Coll., 1979; B.S. in Edn., U. Ark., 1982, Assoc. Sci. in Nursing, 1982. R.N. Sec., receptionist 1st Fed. Savs. & Loan Assn., Jackson, Tenn., 1973-76; adminstrv. asst. to acad. dean Union U., Jackson, 1976-77; personnel sec. Sears, Roebuck & Co., Fayetteville, Ark., 1980-82; R.N., Washington Regional Med. Ctr., Fayetteville, 1983—, mem. standards com., 1984—. Mem. N.W. Ark. Hunter Jumper Assn. (bd. dirs. 1984—), Kappi Delta Pi. Mem. Ch. of Christ. Avocations: riding, tennis, Nautilus training.

COLLINS, NANCY MARKSBERRY, lawyer; b. Owensboro, Ky., Aug. 11, 1953; d. William Hensley and Marion Louise (Bowman) M.; m. Paul Randall Collins, July 21, 1979; children—Rebecca Jane, Jonathan Patrick. B.Health Sci., U. Ky., 1975, J.D., 1978. Bar: Ky. 1978, U.S. Dist. Ct. (ea. and we. dists.) Ky. Atty., Hollon, Hollon & Hollon, Hazard, Ky., 1982—; asst. atty. gen. Commonwealth of Ky., Frankfort, 1978-82; asst. commonwealth atty., Hazard, 1982—. Vice-pres. Tri-County Democratic Woman's Club, Hazard, Ky., 1982—, Twin Counties Dem. Woman's Club, Hazard, 1984—; sec. Ky. Young Dems., Frankfort, 1975-76; pres. U. Ky. Young Dems., Lexington, 1974-75. Recipient Scholastic award Chi Omega, Lexington, Ky., 1975; named Outstanding Vol., Ky. Young Democrats, 1975. Mem. ABA, Am. Trial Lawyers Assn., Ky. Bar Assn., Ky. Acad. Trial Attys., Perry County Bar Assn., Mortar Bd., Phi Delta Phi, Chi Omega. Democrat. Baptist. Office: Hollon Hollon & Hollon PO Box 779 Hazard KY 41701

COLLINS, NANCY WHISNANT, medical foundation administrator; b. Charlotte, N.C., Dec. 20, 1933; d. Ward William and Marjorie Adele (Blackburn) Whisnant; student Queens Coll., Charlotte, 1951-53; A.B. in Journalism, U. N.C., 1955, M.S. in Personnel Adminstrn., 1967; postgrad. (fellow) Cornell U., 1955-56; m. James Q. Collins, Jr., Apr. 25, 1959; (div. 1974) children—James Quincy III, Charles Lowell, William Robey; m. 2d, Richard F. Chapman, May 29, 1982. Personnel asst. R.H. Macy & Co., Inc., N.Y.C., 1955; jr. exec. placement dir. Scofield Placement Agy., San Francisco, 1956-57; free-lance journalist, London, Paris, and Frankfort, W.Ger., 1957-59; program dir. Girl Scouts U.S., Hampton, Va., 1959-61; tour dir., Tokyo, Hong Kong, Singapore, 1965-66; asst. dir. Sloan Exec. Program, Stanford U., 1968-78; asst. dir. Hoover Instn., 1979-81; asst. to pres. Palo Alto (Calif.) Med. Found., 1981—; dir. Am. Healthway Systems. Mem. council Trinity Epsicopal Ch., Menlo Park Calif., 1975-80; fund raiser Cornell U., 1975-81; exec. council Stanford area council Boy Scouts Am., 1980-81; mem. San Mateo County Charter Rev. Com.; mem. personnel bd. City of Menlo Park, 1979—; mem. women's program bd. Coro Found.; trustee Pacific Grad. Sch. Psychology; sec. Chapman Research Fund; bd. dirs. Santa Clara County council Girl Scouts U.S. Richardson Found. grantee, 1967. Mem. AAUW, Am. Mgmt. Assn., Peninsula Profl. Women's Network (adv. council), Nat. Alliance Profl. and Exec. Women (speakers' bank), Catalyst, Kappa Delta. Episcopalian. Clubs: Overseas Press, Commonwealth. Author: Professional Women and their Mentors. Contbr. articles, short stories and poems to mags. and newspapers. Home: 1850 Oak Ave Menlo Park CA 94025 Office: Office of the Pres Palo Alto Med Found 400 Channing Ave Palo Alto CA 94301

COLLINS, SARAH FRENCH, librarian; b. Greensboro, N.C., Jan. 23, 1945; d. Merton Byron and Elizabeth Louise (Hale) French; m. Glenn Patrick Collins, Aug. 10, 1968; children—Brian Patrick, Alexander Hale. B.A., Grinnell Coll., 1967; M.S. with honors, Columbia U., 1978. Reference librarian Leonia Pub. Library (N.J.), 1978-80, asst. dir. 1980-86; dir. N.J. Hist. Soc. Library, 1986—. Mem. ALA, N.J. Library Assn., Mid-Atlantic Archives Conf. Beta Phi Mu. Home: 109 Gordonhurst Ave Upper Montclair NJ 07043 Office: NJ Hist Soc 230 Broadway Newark NJ 07104

COLLINS, SUSAN BALLANTYNE, health educator, consultant; b. Mineola, N.Y., Oct. 12, 1938; d. Howard Samuel and Bessie Eleanor (MacFarlane) Ballantyne; m. Richard J. Collins, July 12, 1962 (div. July 1978); children—Mark Richard, Matthew Howard. Diploma Roosevelt Hosp. Sch. Nursing, N.Y.C., 1959; B.S., Columbia U., 1963; M.Ed., U. Md., 1972. R.N.; cert. pub. health nurse, Calif. Staff nurse Roosevelt Hosp., N.Y.C., 1959-62, War Meml. Hosp., Saulte Ste. Marie, Mich., 1962; faculty Joseph Lawrence Sch. Nursing, New London, Conn., 1964-66; dir., founder Prince William County Sch. Practical Nursing, Manassas, Va., 1969-72; guest lectr. learning disabilities U. Va.-Reston, 1970-73; counselor, educator Woodbridge, Va., 1972-74; nurse counselor Golden Gate Regional Ctr., San Francisco, 1974-76; cons., Novato, Calif., 1976-77; dir. nurses Pacific Rehab. Ctr., Oakland, Calif., 1977-78; faculty continuing edn. dept. Sch. Nursing, U. Calif.-San Francisco, 1977-80, adult edn. dept. Coll. of Marin, Kentfield, Calif., 1981; instr., asst. dir. student services Samuel Merritt Hosp. Coll. Nursing, Oakland, 1978-81; adminstrv. nursing supr. Marin Gen. Hosp., San Rafael, Calif., 1980-84; faculty life long learning Dominican Coll., San Rafael, 1980-84; pres. Sue Collins & Assocs., Petaluma, Calif., 1985—; adminstrv. coordinator Petaluma Valley Hosp.; faculty extended edn. dept. Sonoma State U. Vestryperson, St. Francis Ch., Novato, 1977-80, commr., chair Commn. Status of Women, Sonoma County, Calif., 1979-83; mem. adv. bd. Dominican Coll. Mem. Calif. Nurses Assn., Am. Nurses Assn., Marin Aid Retarded Citizens, Redwood Empire Soc. Health Educators and Trainers, Am. Soc. Health Educators and Trainers, Redwood Empire Soc. Health Educators and Trainers, Calif. Health Resources, Inc. (pres. bd.). Republican. Episcopalian. Avocations: gardening, photography, herbs. Home and Office: Calif Health Resources Inc 1295 Ponderosa Dr Petaluma CA 94952

COLLINS, SUSAN ELLEN SONNEK, lawyer; b. Mobridge, S.D., Oct. 20, 1950; d. Frank and Muriel Elaine (Culp) Sonnek; m. Roy L. Collins, III, Feb. 14, 1980. B.A., U. S.D.-Vermillion, 1973, J.D., 1976; diploma Nat. Grad. Trust Sch., Evanston, Ill., 1981. Bar: S.D. 1976, Iowa 1976, Washington 1979, Tex. 1982; cert. in estate planning and probate Tex. Bd. Legal Specialization. Asst. trust officer Toy Nat. Bank, Sioux City, Iowa, 1976-79; trust officer Rainier Nat. Bank, Seattle, 1979-80; assoc. Finley, Kumble, Wagner, Heine, Underberg & Casey, Washington, 1980-81, Liddell, Sapp, Zivley & LaBoon, Houston, 1980—. Bd. dirs. Sioux City Vol. Bur., 1977-79, Sioux City Art Mus., 1977-79. Mem. ABA, Houston Estate & Fin. Forum, Eta Sigma Phi, Lambda Iota Tau. Episcopalian. Office: 3400 Texas Commerce Tower Houston TX 77002

COLLINSWORTH, FRANCES MARIANNE, cytotechnologist; b. Lay, Colo., July 17, 1921; d. Charles Howard and Mary Campbell (Brodie) Webb; B.S., Colo. State U., Ft. Collins, 1943; grad. Parkland Hosp. Sch. Cytotechnology, Dallas, 1969; m. J.D. Collinsworth, Aug. 4, 1945; 1 son, Ross Brian. Tchr. home econs. Sidney (Nebr.) High Sch., 1943-44; stewardness United Airlines, 1944-45; tchr. sci. Taipei Am. Assn. Sch., Tien Mou, Taiwan, 1959-61; chief cytotechnologist, sr. instr. Parkland Meml. Hosp., Dallas, 1969-70; supr. dept. cytology Damon Lab., Phoenix, 1982-84, Humana Hosp. Vol., ARC, 1959-65. Mem. Am. Soc. Cytology, Am. Soc. Clin. Pathologists, Am. Soc. Cytotechnology, Ariz. Cytology Assn., Colo. State U. Alumni Assn., Nat. Ret. Tchrs. Assn. Democrat. Episcopalian. Club: Delta Delta Delta. Home: 310 E Sharon Ave Phoenix AZ 85022 Office: 1947 E Thomas Rd Phoenix AZ 85016

COLLIS, KAY LYNN, banker, operations analyst; b. Dallas, July 15, 1958; d. Martin Edward and Norma June (Hall) Collis. A.A., Tyler Jr. Coll., 1978; B.B.A., Sam Houston State U., 1982. Mgr., World Finance Corp., Bryan, Tex., 1978-81; ops. analyst Republic Bank Dallas, 1983-85; officer, sect. mgr. MBank, Dallas, 1985—; cons. Collis Cons. Co., Sulphur Springs, Tex., 1983—. Mem. Nat. Assn. Female Execs., Am. Bus. Women's Assn., Nat. Assn. Bank Women, NOW. Republican. Episcopalian. Home: 8565 Parklane #1714 Dallas TX 75231 Office: MBank Dallas PO Box 225415 Dallas TX 75265

COLLOPY, ALICE FRANCES, lawyer; b. N.Y.C., Oct. 19, 1956; d. Edward Michael and Alice (Keegan) Collopy. A.B. magna cum laude, Georgetown U., 1978, J.D., 1981. Bar: N.Y. 1983. Atty., Burns, Hammer & Burns, N.Y.C., 1981-82; med. malpractice atty. Pegalis & Wachsman, Great Neck, N.Y., 1983—. Mem. Assn. Trial Lawyers of Am., ABA, N.Y. Bar Assn., Nassau County Bar Assn., Queens County Bar Assn., Phi Beta Kappa, Alpha Sigma Nu. Democrat. Roman Catholic. Home: 2457 Poplar St Bronx NY 10461 Office: Pegalis & Wachsman 175 E Shore Rd Great Neck NY 11023

COLMAR, JOYCE DEBRA, lawyer, social worker; b. Gloversville, N.Y., Aug. 29, 1947; d. Alan Remi Colmar and Martha (Kaplan) Carta. B.A. with honors, SUNY-Oswego, 1969; M.S.W., Fla. State U., 1971; J.D., Atlanta Law Sch., 1975. Bar: Ga. 1975; cert. social worker Acad. Cert. Social Workers, 1972. Social worker Child Welfare, Atlanta, 1971-74, Grady Meml. Hosp., Atlanta, 1974-81; sole practice, Atlanta, 1975—. Child welfare fellow, 1969. Mem. Ga. Bar Assn., Atlanta Bar Assn., ABA, Nat. Assn. Social Workers, Pi Gamma Mu, Phi Alpha Alpha, Ga. Assn. women Lawyers. Democrat. Jewish. Home: 662 Wendan Dr Decatur GA 30033 Office: 49 Waverly Way NE Atlanta GA 30307

COLOMBO, MARY JO, management consultant; b. Denver, Mar. 26, 1947; d. Arnold Melford and Coral (Bailiff) Sathre; A.D., Community Coll. Denver, 1973; B.S., Met. State Coll., 1978; m. Daniel Leonardo Colombo, July 4, 1966 (div. 1970); children—Michael Kevin, Jeffery Scott; m. Terry Gerrard, 1986. Staff nurse emergency room Beth Israel Hosp., Denver, 1973-79; adult nurse practitioner W.K. Podleski, M.D., Inc., Denver, 1979-80; pres. Rocky Mt. Stone Co., Denver, 1981—; v.p. Murphree-Palmer Adv. Group, Ltd., Denver, 1982—; dir., officer Mannering Oil Co., Novel Ideas, Inc., Murphree Palmer Adv. Group. Mem. Assn. Women Govt. Contractors, Women's Bus. Owners Assn., Nat. Assn. Female Execs., Colo. Nurses Assn. Democrat. Lutheran. Home: 5225 Kilmer Golden CO 80403

COLÓN, LYDIA M., banker; b. Santurce, P.R., June 2, 1947; d. Angel Luis and Lydia Maria (Pagán) Colon. B.A. magna cum laude, Marymount Manhattan Coll., 1978. Admissions office supr. NYU, N.Y.C., 1965-70; asst. v.p. Chem. Bank, N.Y.C., 1971-85; sr. assoc. First Washington Assocs., Arlington, Va., 1985—. Co-author: Innovations in Industrial Competitiveness at the State Level, 1985; Guide to State Capital Formation, 1984. Vice chmn. N.Y. State Adv. Council for Minority and Women-Owned Bus. Enterprise, 1984—; mem. ARC Minorities Initiative Task Force, 1985—, N.Y. Bus. Devel. Corp. Gov.'s Task Force N.Y., 1985; trustee Community Service Soc., N.Y., 1985—. Recipient Woman of the 80's award U.S. Dept. of Housing & Urban Devel., 1985; Polit. Sci. Gold medal Marymount Manhattan Coll., N.Y., 1978. Mem. Nat. Assn. Bank Women, Nat. Conf. Puerto Rican Women.

COLONEL, SHERI LYNN, advertising agency executive; b. Bklyn., Sept. 3, 1955; d. Irwin Murray Glaser and Rosalind (Mendelson) Krasik; m. Peter T. Colonel, Sept. 20, 1981. B.A. in Psychology, SUNY-Cortland, 1977. Account exec. Ted Bates Co., N.Y.C., 1978-80; account exec. SSC&B Advt., Inc., N.Y.C., 1980-82, account supr., 1982-83, v.p., 1983-84, sr. v.p., 1985—, mgmt. supr., 1983—. Jewish. Office: SSC&B Advt Inc 1 Dag Hammarskjold Plaza New York NY 10017

COLOSI, JENNIE LEE LAURA, engineering executive; b. Boston, Nov. 8, 1955; d. Anthony Leonard and Barbara Jean (Bouchie) C.; m. Garry Paul Balboni, Oct. 14, 1984. B.Civil Engring., Ga. Inst. Tech., 1977; M.B.A., Clark U., 1982. Registered profl. engr., Mass., Maine. Asst. supt. E.T. & L Constrn. Corp., Stow, Mass., 1977-80, civil engr., 1980-82, project engr., 1982-83, v.p. engring., 1983—; pres., treas., dir. Peachtree Constrn. Corp., Stow. Mem. Constrn. Industries Mass. (dir. 1984—), Nat. Assn. Women in Constrn. (pres. 1983-85, recruiter award 1984), Soc. Women Engrs. (publicity chmn. 1983-84), ASCE, Nat. Soc. Profl. Engrs., Aircraft Owners and Pilots Assn. Roman Catholic. Avocations: swimming; tennis; golf. Home: 55 Boxborough Rd Stow MA 01775 Office: E T & L Constrn Corp Route 117 and Delaney St Stow MA 01775

COLSON, DOROTHY KILGO, college administrator; b. Badin, N.C., Aug. 21, 1944; d. Charles Isom and Ruby (Gaines) Kilgo; m. Claude Colson, May 6, 1967; 1 child, Claude III. B.S., Livingstone Coll., 1966. Lab. technician J.P. Stevens Co., Greensboro, N.C., 1968; order entry clk. Cannon Mills Co., Kannapolis, N.C., 1968-71; sec., adminstrv. asst. Livingstone Coll., Salisbury, N.C., 1971-78, asst. dir., 1978-82, dir. devel., 1982—. Mem. Fair Housing Task Force, Salisbury, 1981—, Salisbury City Bd. Edn., 1983—; mem. Salisbury Recreation Adv. Bd., 1981-83; bd. dirs. Rowan County Hospice, Salisbury, 1983. Mem. Assn. Fund Raising Officers, Council Advancement and Support of Edn., Soc. Coll. and Univ. Planners, NAACP, Zeta Phi Beta. Democrat. Methodist. Avocations: reading; writing; walking. Home: 506 S Shaver St Salisbury NC 28144 Office: Livingstone Coll 701 W Monroe St Salisbury NC 28144

COLSON, PATRICIA LOUISE, educator, reading specialist; b. Waycross, Ga., Jan. 13, 1947; d. Lester Webster and Clara Juanita (Davis) McKee; m. Larry Walton Colson, Nov. 23, 1977; children—Rachel Colson, Allison Colson. B.S., Valdosta State Coll., 1968, M.Ed., 1972. Cert. reading specialist. Tchr. remedial reading West Gordon Elem. Sch., Valdosta; head Title I reading program tchrs. Valdosta City Sch. System, 1976-80, developer Title I reading materials, 1976—; presenter profl. in-service tng. programs; supr. edn. students in classroom Valdosta State Coll., guest lectr., 1976—; ednl. lobbyist; mem. Gov.'s Conf. Edn., 1976, 77, 78, 79, 80, 81, 82, 83, 84; rep. nat. ednl. conf. Nation At Risk, 1983. Mem. Valdosta Civic Roundtable, 1981—, Lowndes County for ERA, Lowndes County Dem. Party, 1980-84, Ga. State Dem. Party, 1982-84; vol. Cancer Crusade, 1979, 82, 84, 85; Commended by resolution Ga. Ho. Reps., 1982. Mem. Internat. Reading Assn. (presenter, presider, com. chmn., Ga. council) NEA (dist. 2 Ga. rep. to Congress), Ga. Assn. Educators (various state coms.), Pierce County Assn. Educators, Valdosta Assn. Educators (local legis. chmn. 1974—), AAUW (pres. 1981-83, legis. chmn. 1983—), Phi Delta Kappa, Delta Gamma. Clubs: Town and Country Garden; Jasmine Garden. Home: PO Box 2771 Valdosta GA Office: West Gorden Sch Valdosta GA

COLSTON, STEPHENIE WEBBER, mental health adminstrator; b. Odessa, Tex., Aug. 6, 1950; d. Selwyn Sanford and Rosamond Jack (Stephenson) Webber; 1 child, Kevin Todd. B.A., U. Okla., 1972, M.A., 1974, now postgrad. Cert. mental health adminstr. Sr. research analyst Okla. Legis. Council, Oklahoma City, 1975-79; coordinator research services Okla. Legis. Council, Oklahoma City, 1979-80; dir. fiscal and legal services Okla. State Senate, Oklahoma City, 1980-82; chief ops. Okla. Dept. Mental Health, Oklahoma City, 1982-85; exec. dir. Taliaferro Ctr., Lawton, Okla., 1985—. Mem. Assn. Mental Health Adminstrs. (pres. Okla. chpt. 1984), Am. Soc. Pub. Adminstrn. (mem. exec. council sect. on intergovtl. adminstrn. mgmt. 1984-87), Am. Mgmt. Assn., Nat. Assn. Female Execs., Lawton C. of C. Democrat. Avocations: racquetball; tennis; reading. Office: Taliaferro Ctr 602 SW 38th St Lawton OK 73505

COLT, JULIE GUION GEORGE HEWITT (MRS. S. BARCLAY COLT), civic worker; b. Princeton, N.J.; d. Charles Albert and Mary Leslie (Guion) George; student Vassar Coll., 1921-23; m. Edward Cooper Hewitt, June 11, 1927 (dec. Aug. 1966); children—Mary Leslie Guion (Mrs. David Waddell Bird), Edward Cooper, Jr.; m. 2d, Sackett Barclay Colt, Sept. 15, 1973. Social reporter, social editor Elizabeth (N.J.) Daily Jour., 1920-35, N.Y. Herald Tribune, 1925-37, Charm mag., Newark, 1928-33, Sportsman Mag., Summit, N.J., 1933-36, Newark Sunday Call, 1930-40, Newark Evening News, 1940-45; saleslady Morrell Studio Portraits, Plainfield, N.J., 1932-38. Vice pres. Elizabeth Dramatic Club, 1942-43; pres. Jr. League, Elizabeth, 1941-43; pres., exec. com. N.J. Jr. Leagues, 1943-45; trustee Vail Deane Sch., Elizabeth, N.J., 1967—, chmn. centennial com., 1967-69, pres. alumna assn., 1939-41; asso. vestry Trinity Ch., Elizabeth, 1968-83, vestry, 1983—; chmn. 1st ann. grandparents fund-raising com. Suffield (Conn.) Acad.; 4th Ward Republican committeewoman, Elizabeth, 1980—; chmn. Widows Dartmouth Coll. Class 1925, 1980-83. Named Alumna of Yr., Vail Deane Sch., 1981. Clubs: Jr. League of Elizabeth and Plainfield, Elizabeth Town and Country, Vassar (Essex County chpt.), Baltusrol Golf, Bay Head Yacht, Elizabethtown Cotillion, Monday Evening. Home: 50 Georgian Ct Elizabeth NJ 07208 also 634 East Ave Bay Head NJ 08742

COLVIN, CYNTHIA LOUISE, computer maintenance company executive; b. Oklahoma City, May 29, 1957; d. Robert Lee and Bettie Jo (Shahan) C. A.A. in Modern Language, San Jacinto Coll., Pasadena, Tex., 1978; B.A. in Journalism Tex. A & M U.-College Station, 1981. Pres. C.B. Systems, Pasadena, Tex., 1975-77; sales J.C. Penneys, Houston, 1977, Astroworld, Houston, 1978; sec. Talent Tree Temporary, Houston, 1981-83; escrow asst. Am. Title Co., Houston, 1981-83; escrow sec. Capital Title Co., Houston, 1983; dir. pub. relations and advt. Com-Tec Services, Inc., Houston, 1983—. Mem., music librarian Single Singers 1st Baptist Ch. Houston, 1981—; vol. Sta. KSBJ Radio, Houston, 1982. Mem. Sigma Delta Chi, Phi Theta Kappa (charter pres. 1979-80), Tex. State Phi Theta Kappa Alumni Assn. (pres. 1980-81). Home: 8503 Glenlea St Houston TX 77061 Office: Com-Tec Services Inc 1110 N Post Oak Rd Suite 340 Houston TX 77055

COLVIN, DIANE TREMMEL, lawyer; b. Sibley, Iowa, Jan. 15, 1944; d. Frank Carl and Lucile (Lenz) Tremmel; m. Harry J. Colvin, July 10, 1971. B.A., U. Iowa, 1965; M.A., U. Minn., 1966; J.D., U. Wis.-Madison, 1974. Bar: Wis. 1975, Washington 1975, Oreg. 1979, Alaska 1982. Research librarian Library of Congress, Washington, 1966-69; reference librarian U.S. Air Force Acad., Colo., 1970-71; staff counsel Senate Research Ctr., Olympia, Wash., 1975-76; staff counsel Nat. Ctr. State Cts., San Francisco, 1976-77; asst. city atty. City of Vancouver (Washington), 1980-81; asst. atty. gen. Alaska Dept. Law, Juneau, 1982-85; hearing examiner Alaska Dept. Revenue, Seattle, 1985—. Mem. ABA, Alaska Bar Assn., Oreg. Bar Assn., Washington Bar Assn., Wis. Bar Assn., Phi Beta Kappa, Beta Phi Mu.

COLVIN, MARILYN ANN, curriculum and instruction educator; b. Camden, Tex., Aug. 23, 1944; d. Clayton Kendrick and Aline (Kirkland) Berry; m. Walter Bishop Colvin, Aug. 12, 1967; children—Rachel Kirkland, Timothy Harper. B.B.A., U. Houston, 1966, B.S. in Edn., 1972, M.Ed., 1976, Ed.D., 1980. Provisional elem. teaching cert., Tex. Tchr. elem. schs. Aldine Ind. Sch. Dist., Houston, 1968-70; teaching fellow U. Houston, 1977-79; assoc. prof. curriculum and instrn. Houston Baptist U., 1979—. Contbr. chpt. to textbook; contbr. articles to profl. jours. Mem. Parent adv. council Parker Elem. Sch., Houston, 1982—; mem. alumni bd. U. Houston, 1983. Recipient Opal Goolsby Outstanding Tchr. award, Houston Baptist U., 1983, Outstanding Prof. award, Student Edn. Assn., 1983. Mem. Internat. Reading Assn. (mem. parents and reading com. Tex. State Council 1983—), Tex. Assn. Improvement of Reading (exec. com. U-Houston chpt. 1982-83), Greater Houston Area Reading Council (dir. 1981-83, rec. sec. 1983-84), Kappa Delta Pi (counselor Pi Eta chpt. Houston 1982—), Phi Delta Kappa, Delta Kappa Gamma, Delta Zeta. Methodist. Home: 5731 Spellman St Houston TX 77096 Office: Houston Baptist Univ 7502 Fondren Rd Houston TX 77074

COLWELL, RITA ROSSI, microbiologist, educator, university official; b. Beverly, Mass., Nov. 23, 1934; d. Louis and Louise G. (Di Palma) Rossi; B.S., Purdue U., 1956, M.S., 1958; Ph.D., U. Wash., 1961; m. Jack H. Colwell, May 31, 1956; children—Alison E.L., Stacie Anne. Research asst. U. Wash., 1957-58, predoctoral assoc. 1959-60, asst. research prof., 1961-64; guest scientist div. applied biology NRC Can., Ottawa, 1961-63; vis. asst. prof. biology Georgetown U., 1963-64, asst. prof. biology, 1964-66, assoc. prof., 1966-72; prof. microbiology U. Md., 1972—, dir. Sea Grant Coll. 1977-83, acting dir. Center Environ. and Estuarine Studies, 1980-81, v.p. acad. affairs U. Md. System, 1983—; mem. ad hoc com. on Klebsiella-Enterobacter-Hafnia-Serratia div. WHO, 1975—; mem. numerous coms. NSF, 1970—; mem. Nat. Sci. Bd., 1984—; bd. dirs. Upper Bay Survey, Md. Dept. Natural Resources, 1974-75; mem. Gov.'s Sci. Adv. Council, 1978—. Fellow Washington Acad. Sci. (bd. mgrs. 1976-79), AAAS, Am. Acad. Microbiology (bd. govs. 1979), Can. Coll. Microbiologists; mem. Am. Soc. Microbiology (pres. 1983-84; Fisher award 1985), Am. Type Culture Collection (trustee 1970-86, sec.-treas. 1971-78, vice chmn. 1978-80, chmn. 1980-81), Marine Tech. Soc. (exec. com. 1978—), Soc. Indsl. Microbiology (bd. govs. 1976-79), Am. Inst. Biol. Sci. (bd. gov. 1976-82), U.S. Fedn. Culture Collections (governing bd. 1978-84), Soc. Gen. Microbiology, Soc. Applied Bacteriology, Systematics Assn., Classification Soc., Soc. Invertebrate Pathology, Am. Soc. Limnology and Oceanography, Am. Oceanic Soc., Estuarine and Brackish Water Scis. Assn., Atlantic Estuarine Research Soc., Am. Littoral Assn., World Fedn. Culture Collections, Sigma Xi, Sigma Delta Epsilon, Phi Beta Kappa. Asso. editor Can. Jour. Microbiology, 1972-75, asst. editor, 1975-79; editorial bd. Microbiology Ecology, 1972—, Applied and Environ. Microbiology, 1969-81, Oil & Petrochem. Pollution, 1980—, Jour. Washington Acad. Sci., 1981—, Johns Hopkins U. Oceanographic Series, 1981-84, Revue de la Fondation Oceanographique Ricard, 1981—, J. Diarrheal Dis 1982—; editor-in-chief Marine Technol. Soc. Jour. contbr. chpts. to books and numerous articles to profl. jours. Office: Dept Microbiology U Md College Park Md 20742

COLY, LISETTE, foundation executive; b. N.Y.C., Apr. 6, 1950; d. Robert Raymond and Eileen (Lyttle-Garrett) C. B.A. cum laude, Hunter Coll., 1973. Sec., Parapsychology Found., Inc., N.Y.C., 1972-75, assoc. editor, 1975—, v.p., 1978—. Assoc. editor Parapsychology Rev. and Procs. Ann. Internat. Parapsychology Found. Confs., 1978—. Office: 1 Parapsychology Found Inc 228 E 71st St New York NY 10021

COMAS-DÍAZ, LILLIAN, psychologist; b. Chgo., July 18, 1950; d. Filiberto and Maria (Díaz) Comas; B.A., U. P.R., 1970, M.A., 1973; NIMH predoctoral psychology fellow, Yale U., 1979; Ph.D., U. Mass., 1979. Tchr. Yabucoa (P.R.) Public Sch., 1971-72; instr. psychology U. P.R., 1973; project dir. Clinica Hispana de Evaluación y Orientación, New Britain, Conn., 1976; psychologist Mental Health Clinic of New Britain Gen. Hosp., 1976-78; asst. prof. psychology Yale U., also asst. dir. Hill Mental Health Clinic, New Haven, 1979-83; dir. Hispanic Clinic, New Haven, 1983—. Recipient Humanitarian award Omega Psi Phi, 1981. Mem. Am. Psychol. Assn. (dir. ethnic minority affairs 1984—), Am. Orthopsychiat. Assn., Nat. Hispanic Psychol. Assn. Research and publs. on transcultural psychology, mental health services to ethnic minorities. Home: 1616 19th St NW Washington DC 20009 Office: 1200 17th St NW Washington DC 20036

COMBS, ANN RULEY, lawyer, nurse; b. Cin., Aug. 24, 1952; d. Louis Barnett and Carolyn Ann (Hayes) Ruley; m. Mark Edward Combs, June 24, 1978; children—Sarah Avery, Derek Edward. B.S. in Nursing, U. Mich., 1974; J.D., So. Meth. U., 1977. Bar: Ohio 1977; R.N., Ohio. Nurse Children's Hosp., Cin., 1977; assoc., Kohnen & Kohnen, Cin., 1977-78, 1982—; sole practice, Columbus, Ohio, 1978-81; lectr. Ohio Hosp. Assn., 1982, various Cin. hosps., 1982—, Tri State Perinatal Nurses Assn., Ohio, 1983, U. Cin. Sch. Law, 1984, Columbia Union Coll. Nursing, Palmer and Assocs., Inc., Creative Mgmt. Corp., Profl. Edn. Systems, Inc.; presenter mock depositions to area hosps., 1984—. Mem. ABA, Am. Nurse Attys. Assn., Ohio Bar Assn., Ohio Assn. Civil Trial Attys., U. Mich. Alumni Assn., Delta Theta Tau, Sigma Theta Tau, Chi Omega. Republican. Presbyterian. Home: 7650 Driftwind Ct Cincinnati OH 45242 Office: Kohnen & Kohnen 4500 Carew Tower 441 Vine St Cincinnati OH 45202

COMBS, BETTY JANE, educator; b. Nassau County, N.Y., Dec. 18, 1932; d. Raymond George and Elsie Jane Elliott; B.A., Pace U., 1972; M.A., Manhattanville Coll., 1976; M.S., Pace U., 1980; m. LeRoy Charles Combs, Mar. 22, 1952; children—Donald Charles, David Charles, James Robert, Jeffrey Raymond. Dir., Meml. Nursery Sch., White Plains, N.Y., 1959-68; substitute tchr., Westchester County, N.Y., 1968-72; dir. Lab Sch., asst. prof. early childhood edn. Pace U., Pleasantville, N.Y., 1972—. Vice pres. PTA, 1970-71; vice chmn. North Castle Republican Town Com., 1976—. Mem. Nat. Assn. Edn. Young Children, Assn. Supervision and Curriculum Devel., Nat. Assn. Early Childhood Educators, Phi Delta Kappa, Pi Lambda Theta (pres. 1985—). Methodist. Home: 23 Washington Pl North White Plains NY 10603 Office: Sch Edn Pace U Pleasantville NY 10570

COMBS, BRENDA CHRYSTEL, computer programmer; b. Fargo, N.D., Jan. 14, 1953; d. Virgil Booker T. and Eva Charles (Hooks) Combs; B.A. in Psychology, U. Redlands, 1975. Tchr., Monrovia (Calif.) High Sch., 1975-83; computer programmer So. Calif. Gas Co., Los Angeles, 1983—; minority relations rep. Calif. Tchrs. Assn., 1981-82; sch. rep. Monrovia Tchrs. Assn., 1980-81. Mem. Calif. Tchrs. Assn., Nat. Assn. Female Execs., Pi Lambda Theta. Home: PO Box 1916 Monrovia CA 91016 Office: Box 3249 Terminal Annex Los Angeles CA 90051

COMBS, JANET LOUISE, sales and advertising company executive; b. Houston, Jan. 13, 1959; d. James Lee and Mary Lynn (Woolley) Combs. B.S. in Bus. Adminstrn., U. Ark., 1981. With Exxon Chem. Co., Houston, 1981-82; asst. v.p. Promotional Products Co., Houston, 1982-86, v.p., 1986—. Active Greater Houston Young Republicans. Mem. Spring Branch Meml. C. of C., Houston C. of C, Girls' Cotillion, Mortar Bd., Blue Key, Kappa Alpha Theta (Founder's Meml. scholar 1980-81), Beta Gamma Sigma, Alpha Mu Alpha, Omicron Delta Kappa. Methodist. Home: 12611 Trail Hollow Houston TX 77024 Office: Promotional Products Co 1700 W Belt N Houston TX 77043

COMBS, JULIA ANN, educator, columnist; b. Dayton, Ohio, Aug. 19, 1931; d. Wilson Winton and Mary Martha (Miller) Tawney; m. Raymond Robert Combs, Dec. 5, 1953; children—Gregory Scott, Geoffrey Wilson, Robert Ashley, Leslie Ann, Clark Winton. B.A., Miami U., Oxford, Ohio, 1953; M.Ed., Wright State U., 1982; postgrad. U. Dayton, 1954, 83. Staff writer women's dept. Dayton Daily News, 1953-54; substitute tchr., Dayton, 1954-78; tchr. St. Luke's Sch., Beavercreek, Ohio, 1976-77; learning disabilities tutor Trotwood-Madison Schs., Trotwood, Ohio, 1978—; columnist, spl. writer Dayton Daily News, 1978—; area rep. Pacific Ednl. and Cultural Exchange, Westerville, Ohio, 1983—. Den mother Boy Scouts Am., Dayton; leader Girl Scouts U.S.A.; researcher South Park Hist. Dist. Recipient 1st place award for feature writing in newspaper category Cin. Editors' Assn. Publs. Contest, 1985. Mem. Women in Communications, Inc., Kappa Delta Pi. Republican. Lutheran. Home: 14 Patterson Rd Dayton OH 45419

COMBS, JULIA CAROLYN, oboist; b. Topeka, July 11, 1950; d. Joe Denton and Fay Magel (Meshew) C.; Mus.B., Memphis State U., 1972, Mus.M., 1974; D.M.A., North Tex. State U. Sch. Music, 1985; m. William Barney Stacy. Aug. 2, 1981. Oboist, solo English horn Memphis Opera Theater, 1971-74; 2d oboist Memphis Symphony, 1972-74; solo English horn Norfolk (Va.) Symphony, 1974-75; prin. oboe Norfolk Opera, 1974-75, U.S. Army Chamber Orch., 1975-78; assoc. prof. oboe U. Wyo., Laramie, 1978—; oboist New World Wind Quintet, 1978—; oboe and oboe d'amore soloist, 1976—. Served with U.S. Army, 1975-78. U. Wyo. grantee, 1981, 84; recipient John P. Ellbogen Meritorious Classroom Teaching award U. Wyo., 1983; Beatrice Gallatin Beuf Golden Apple teaching award U. Wyo. Mem. Internat. Double Reed Soc., Nat. Assn. Coll. Wind and Percussion Instrs., Women in the Arts (founding mem.), Music Educators Nat. Conf., DAR, Puppeteers Am., Union Internat. de la Marionnette, Sigma Alpha Iota, Pi Kappa Lambda, Phi Kappa Phi, Alpha Lambda Delta. Home: 1912 Custer Laramie WY 82070 Office: PO Box 3037 Univ Sta Music Dept U Wyo Laramie WY 82070

COMBS, MARILYN JEAN, aerobic exercise program executive; b. Louisville, Apr. 23, 1957; d. Alex Bertram and Betty Jane (Tucker) C. B.Applied Sci., U. Louisville, 1979. Mgr., European Health Spa, Louisville, 1977-81; owner, developer Shapenastics, Louisville, 1982—. Mem. adv. bd. Dance for Heart, Louisville, 1983—. Recipient Top Money Raiser awards Am. Heart Assn., Ky., 1983, 84. Mem. Internat. Dance Exercise Assn. Avocations: horseback riding, skiing, running.

COMBS, MARTHA LECIE SMITH, real estate broker; b. Bryan, Tex., Apr. 28, 1924; d. Robert E. Smith and M. Alline (Gidley) Smith Bell, and Thomas Lloyd Bell (stepfather); m. Joe Mac Walston, Aug. 3, 1944 (div. 1954); children—Terri Lee Walston Crow, Wendy M. Walston Howard; m. Jack R. Combs, Aug. 23, 1961. Student U. Tex., 1942-43. Vice pres. Circle 4 Ranches, Inc., Bryan, 1967—; pres. Combs and Combs Investments, Johnson City, Tex., 1969—, Fun-Tier Ranches, Inc., Johnson City, 1980—, Combs and Eastburn, Inc., Johnson City, 1980—. Mem. Nat. Assn. Realtors, Tex. Assn. Realtors, Longhorn Breeders Assn., South Tex. Longhorn Breeders Assn., Delta Delta Delta Alumnae. Republican. Episcopalian. Clubs: Austin Country, Headliners (Austin, Tex.); Johnson City Woman's, Community Garden (Johnson City). Avocations: golf; hunting; fishing. Home and office: Mountain Creek Ranch Route 1 Box 29 Johnson City TX 78636

COMBS, MARY JIM, educator; b. Carrollton, Ga., Dec. 13, 1933; d. Lewis Lee and Floy Burson Combs; B.S. in Home Econs., Ga. State Coll. for Women, 1955; M.Ed., U. Ga., 1963, Ed.S., 1967, Ed.D., 1974, m. Curtis E. Tate, Jr., Aug. 28, 1977; stepchildren—C. Emory, Milton O. Tchr., Cedartown (Ga.) High Sch., 1955-58, Carrollton (Ga.) High Sch., 1958-66; research asst. in vocat. edn. U. Ga., Athens, 1966-68, asst. prof., tchr. educator in home econs., 1968—. Mem. Ga. Assn. Future Homemakers Am. (hon.), Phoenix Soc., NEA, AAUP, Am. Home Econs. Assn., Ga. Home Econs. Assn., Am. Vocat. Assn., Ga. Vocat. Assn., Nat. Assn. Tchr. Educators for Vocat. Home Econs., Home Econs. Edn. Assn., Ga. Assn. Educators, Phi Upsilon Omicron, Phi Kappa Phi, Kappa Delta Pi, Delta Kappa Gamma. Contbr. articles to profl. publs. Home: 130 Wells Dr Athens GA 30606 Office: 624 Aderhold Hall U Ga Athens GA 30602

COMDEN, BETTY, writer, lyricist, performer; b. Bklyn., May 3, 1919; d. Leo and Rebecca (Sadvoransky) Comden; student Bklyn. Ethical Culture Sch., Erasmus Hall High Sch.; B.S., N.Y. U.; m. Steven Kyle, Jan. 4, 1942; children—Susanna, Alan. Performer, writer nightclub act Revuers. Writer book and lyrics (with Adolph Green) Broadway shows On the Town, 1944-45, Billion Dollar Baby, Two on the Aisle, Bells are Ringing, Fade-Out—Fade-In, Subways are for Sleeping, On the 20th Century (2 Tony awards), 1978, A Doll's Life, 1982; lyrics Wonderful Town, Peter Pan, Say, Darling, Do Re Mi, Hallelujah, Baby!; book for Applause; screen plays for Good News, Barkleys of Broadway, Band Wagon, Singing in the Rain, Auntie Mame; screenplay and lyrics for Bells are Ringing, On The Town, It's Always Fair Weather, What a Way to Go; A Party (performed with A. Green in show of their works), 1959, 77; also appeared in On the Town, 1972; lyricist, dir. (with Adolph Green) Lorelei, 1973. Recipient Donaldson award and Tony award for Wonderful Town, as co-lyricist best score, 1953; Tony award for Hallelujah, Baby, as co-writer best score, 1968; Tony award for Applause, 1970; Arts Achievement award City of N.Y.; Woman of Yr. Disting. Alumna, NYU; named to Theater Hall of Fame, Songwriters Hall of Fame. Mem. Dramatists Guild (council). Office: care The Dramatists Guild 234 W 44th St New York NY 10036

COMEAU, JOANNE HADFIELD, bank advertising executive; b. Providence, Mar. 12, 1952; d. Howard Vincent and Dorothy Anne (Griffin) Hadfield; m. Arthur Bill Comeau, Apr. 11, 1981. B.A. in Speech Communication, U. R.I., 1974. Procedure writer Liberty Mut. Ins. Co., Boston, 1974-76; account exec. Creamer Inc. Advt., Providence, 1977-82; dir. mktg. Notre Dame Hosp., Central Falls, R.I., 1983; asst. v.p. mktg. Fleet Nat. Bank, Providence, 1984—. Bd. dirs., chmn. pub. info. Am. Cancer Soc., Providence, 1984-86. Recipient Leonard E. Smith award Speech Dept. U. R.I., 1974; Unit of Yr. award for Pub. Info., R.I. div. Am. Cancer Soc., 1984. Mem. Nat. Assn. Female Execs., New Eng. Bank Mktg. Assn. Avocations: Racquetball; reading; acting/community theatre. Home: 221 Mountain Laurel Dr Cranston RI 02920 Office: Fleet National Bank 111 Westminster St Providence RI 02903

COMELLA, PATRICIA ANN EGAN, government official, consultant; b. N.Y.C., Jan. 26, 1941; d. John J. and Helen (Courtois) Egan; m. August John Comella, May 30, 1964; 1 son, Christopher. B.A., Hofstra U., 1962. Mathematician, NASA Goddard Space Flight Ctr., Greenbelt, Md., 1962-75; policy analyst Office of Policy Evaluation, U.S. Nuclear Regulatory Commn., Washington, 1975-79, br. chief Office of Standards Devel., 1979-81, dep. div. dir. Office Nuclear Regulatory Research, 1981-84; sr. regulatory assurance specialist Battelle Meml. Inst., Washington, 1984—. Office: Battelle Meml Inst 2030 M St NW Washington DC 20036

COMER, VIVIAN ADELIA, lawyer; b. Oak Ridge, June 11, 1954; d. Evan Philip and Mary Adelia (Blanc) C. Student Pa. State U., 1973-75; A.B., Brown U., 1978; J.D., U. Md.-Balt., 1981. Bar: Md. 1981, U.S. Ct. Appeals (2d cir.) 1982. Law clk. Md. Atty. Gen., Balt., 1979, U.S. atty., Balt., 1979, Commodity Futures Trading Commn., Washington, 1980-81, atty., 1981-82; atty. FDIC, Washington, 1982-84, sr. atty., 1985—, acting chief bankruptcy sect., 1985—; research editor Internat. Trade Law Jour., 1980-81. Mem. ABA, Md. Bar Assn., Democrat. Baptist. Home: 1330 New Hampshire Ave NW No 618 Washington DC 20036

COMET-EPSTEIN, SHARON, college administrator; b. Cleve., Oct. 25, 1950; d. Sol S. and Fay (Shochet) Comet; B.S. cum laude, Ohio State U., 1972; M.S., Case Western Res. U., 1974, Ph.D., 1985; m. Robert E. Epstein, Sept. 1, 1974; children—Adam Scott, Rachel. Instr., Columbus Jr. Theatre Arts, summer 1971; instr., designer allied health scis. Ohio State U., Columbus, 1971-72; ednl. project dir. Sch. Dentistry Case Western Res. U., Cleve., 1972-76, dir. ednl. resources and public affairs, 1976-85, asst. prof., 1986—; ednl. dir. Western Res. Geriatric Ctr., 1986—; mgmt. cons., 1982—. Recipient 2d place award Health Scis. Communications Assn., 1974. Mem. Women in Communications, Health Scis. Communications Assn., Am. Soc. Tng. and Devel., Am. Assn. Dental Schs., Pi Lambda Theta. Jewish. Clubs: Hasassah, ORT. Editor, Focus, 1975-77, Off The Cusp, 1976-78. Office: 2123 Abington Rd Cleveland OH 44106

COMPTON, ANN WOODRUFF, news correspondent; b. Chgo., Jan. 19, 1947; d. Charles Edward and Barbara (Ortlund) C.; B.A., Hollins (Va.) Coll., 1969; m. William Stevenson Hughes, Nov. 25, 1978; 4 children. Reporter, anchorwoman WDBJ-TV (CBS), Roanoke, Va., 1969-70, polit. reporter, state capitol bur. chief, Richmond, Va., 1971-73; fellow Washington Journalism Center, 1970; network radio anchorwoman ABC News, N.Y.C., 1973-74,

White House corr., Washington, 1974-79, congl. corr., Washington, 1979-81, 84— White House corr., 1981-84. Mem. adv. com. Gannett Ctr. Media Studies, Columbia U., 1984—. Mem. White House Corrs. Assn. (dir. 1977-79). Office: ABC News 1717 DeSales St NW Washington DC 20036

COMPTON, JULIA PORTER, nursing home administrator; b. Nashville, Dec. 4, 1944; d. William Claude and Julia Elise (McRory) Porter; m. Charles Jonathan Couey, May 24, 1963 (div. Feb. 1973); children—Elizabeth Dawn, Margaret Ann; m. 2d, Learon Winston Compton, Jan. 27, 1975; 1 dau., Kristy Lynn. Student Huntingdon Coll., 1962-63. Lic. nursing home adminstr., Ala. Activities supr. Marengo Nursing Home, Linden, Ala., 1970-72; adminstr. Phenix City Nursing Home (Ala.), 1973-74, Parkwood Health Facility, Phenix City, 1974-84, Canterbury Health Facility, Inc., Phenix City, 1984—; cons. activities, 1973—. Mem. health com. Russell County Extension Service, Phenix City. Mem. Am. Coll. Nursing Home Adminstrs., Phenix City C. of C. Baptist. Home: 1309 Thayer Dr Phenix City AL 36867 Office: Canterbury Health Facility Inc 1720 Knowles Rd Phenix City AL 36867

COMPTON, MARY BEATRICE BROWN (MRS. RALPH THEODORE COMPTON), public relations exec., writer; b. Washington, May 25, 1923; d. Robert James and Abie Eliza (Stone) Brown; grad. Thayer Acad., Chandler Sch., Leland Powers Sch. Radio, TV and Theatre, Boston, 1942; m. Ralph Theodore Compton, Mar. 18, 1961, step-children—Ralph Theodore, Patricia (Mrs. William R. Schnitzler). Radio program dir. Converse Co., Malden, Mass., 1942-45; radio continuity dept. Sta. WAAB, Yankee Network, Worcester, Mass., 1945-46; asst. dir. radio Leland Powers Sch. Radio, TV and Theatre, Boston, 1946-49, dir., 1949-51; program asst. Sta. KNBH, Hollywood, Calif., 1951-52; v.p. Acorn Film Co., Boston, 1953-54; dir. women's communications, editor Program Notes, radio interviewer NAM, 1954-61. Celebrities pub. relations Nat. Citizens for Nixon, 1968, Kennedy Ctr. Pub. Info., 1985—. Mem. Soc. Old Plymouth Colony Descs., Magna Carta Dames, Smithsonian Instn. Assos. Clubs: Congressional Country (Bethesda, Md.), Brooke Manor Country (Rockville, Md.). Home: 3428 Chiswick Ct Silver Spring MD 20906

COMPTON, NINA HELENE, business law educator, lawyer; b. Santa Fe, Oct. 21, 1950; d. Myron Hull and Helene (Dunn) Nickerson; m. Richard D. Adamson, Dec. 30, 1974 (div. 1980); m. 2d J. Douglas Compton, June 19, 1982. B.A., U. N.Mex.-Albuquerque, 1971, M.A., 1973; J.D., Del. Law Sch., 1978. Bar: N.Mex. 1979; Cert. tchr., N.Mex. Jud. law clk. Mcpl. Ct., Wilmington, Del., 1975-78; legal drafting staff Office of Gov., Santa Fe, 1979; assoc. Martin, Martin, Lutz & Cresswell, Las Cruces, N.Mex., 1979-81; asst. prof. bus. law N.Mex. State U., Las Cruces, 1981—, advisor Pre-Law Student Assn., 1981—; adj. faculty prof. bus. law, Ga. State U., 1982-83; pres. Latin Am. Studies Forum, Las Cruces, 1984—. Author: Study Guide to accompany The Legal Environment of Business (Kolasas), 1983; author research papers. Bd. dirs. and corp. council Amigos de las Americas Charity, Las Cruces, 1983; chmn. for univ. dept. United Way, Las Cruces, 1982-83; apptd. counselor to N.Mex. Border Commn., Santa Fe, 1981-83, mem. immigration subcom., 1983. Recipient Outstanding Tchr. award Coll. Bus. Adminstrn., N.Mex. State U., 1981, named Top Ten Campus-wide Faculty Mems., 1982; recipient cert. appreciation Office of Gov. N.Mex., 1982, 83. Mem. ABA, N.Mex. Bar Assn., Dona Ana County Bar Assn. sec. 1982—), Womens Trial Lawyers Caucus of Assn. Trial Lawyers Am., Am. Bus. Law Assn., Atlanta Bar Assn., Blue Key, Phi Gamma Nu (advisor 1982). Democrat. Episcopalian. Clubs: Las Cruces Jr. Womens, Faculty Womens. Home: 1073 Hillrise Ct Las Cruces NM 88001 Office: N Mex State Univ Dept Mktg and Gen Bus PO Box 5280 Las Cruces NM 88003

COMRAS, REMA, library director; b. N.Y.C., Oct. 26, 1936; d. Manuel and Zita (Kessel) C.; B.A., U. Fla., 1958; M.L.S., Syracuse (N.Y.) U., 1960; m. Jose Simonet, June 22, 1981. Librarian, Queensborough (N.Y.) Pub. Library, 1960-61, Spl. Services, U.S. Army, W.Ger. and France, 1962-64; asst. head librarian City of Hialeah (Fla.), 1964-73, library dir., 1973—. Mem. ALA, Fla. Library Assn., Dade County Library Assn., Beta Phi Mu. Office: 190 W 49th St Hialeah FL 33012

COMRIE, MILLICENT, physician, educator; b. Kingston, Jamaica, W.I., Aug. 6, 1948; came to U.S., 1969, naturalized, 1983; d. Daniel Ignatius and Myrtle Constantia (Williams) Ferguson; m. Frederick George Comrie, Aug. 26, 1972; children—Tamika A. Comrie, Sacha A. Comrie. B.S. in Chemistry, Howard U., 1972; M.D., SUNY-Bklyn., 1976; M.P.H., Columbia U., 1981. Resident, Long Island Coll. Hosp., Bklyn., 1976-80, chief adolescent gynecology, 1982—; clin. instr. Columbia U., N.Y.C., 1980-81; clin. asst. prof. Downstate Med. Ctr., Bklyn., 1983—, coordinator for med. students, 1982—. Mem. AMA, Am. Coll. Ob-Gyn (cert.), Bklyn. Gynecol. Soc. (Residents night award 1980). Avocations: music; dancing. Office: Long Island Coll Hosp 340 Henry St Brooklyn NY 11201

CONAGHAN, DOROTHY DELL, state legislator; b. Oklahoma City, Sept. 24, 1930; d. John Joseph and Wilhelmina Elizabeth (Boyer) Miller; student U. Okla., 1949-51; m. Brian Francis Conaghan, June 10, 1951 (dec. Apr. 1973); children—Joseph Lee, Charles Alan, Roger Lloyd. Mem. Okla. Ho. of Reps., 1973-86, minority caucus sec., 1977-82, asst. minority leader, 1983-86. Bd. dirs. Alpha II, Community Liaison Council Juvenile Services, Ponca City, Okla., Alcohol, Drug Abuse and Community Mental Health Planning and Coordinating Bd., Christian Found.; trustee Okla. chpt. Leukemia Soc. Am.; pres. Washington Sch. PTA, Tonkawa, 1965; vice chmn. Kay County Republican Com., 1960-64, 6th Dist. Congl. Rep. Com., 1967; del. Rep. Nat. Conv., 1968. Recipient Women Helping Women award Ponca City Soroptimist Club, 1975, hon. mem., 1978. Mem. Nat. Order Women Legislators, Am. Legis. Exchange Council (state dir.), Tonkawa C. of C., Am. Legion Aux., P.E.O., Beta Sigma Phi (hon.). Mem. Christian Ch. (Disciples of Christ). Clubs: Delphi Study, Order Eastern Star (past matron), Soroptomists Internat. of Ams. (hon.). Office: State Capitol Bldg Oklahoma City OK 73105

CONANT, DORIS KAPLAN, sculptor, civic worker, real estate developer; b. Phila., Apr. 28, 1925; d. Benjamin A. and Rae (Shander) Kaplan; B.A., U. Pa., 1945; postgrad. U. Havana, 1945, Art Inst. Chgo., 1962; m. Howard R. Conant, Dec. 14, 1947; children—Alison, Howard, Meredith Ann. One man shows Glenview Pub. Library, Northbrook Library,; exhibited in group shows Art Inst. Chgo. Sales and Rental Gallery, Design Unlimited, New Horizons in Sculpture, Old Orchard Art Fair, Lake Forest Coll. Exhbn. Sec. to consul Argentine Consulate, Phila., 1945-47; sec., dir. Interstate Steel Co., Des Plaines, Ill., 1948—; organizer proposed 1st Women's Bank Chgo.; dir. Upper Ave. Nat. Bank, Chgo., 1976-81; pres. Urban Innovations Ltd., Loftworks Two. First pres. ERA Ill.; mem. Chgo. Network. Recipient Glenview Brotherhood award, 1965; named one of outstanding women P.U.S.H., 1975. Club: Carlton. Home: 180 E Pearson St Chicago IL 60611 Office: 444 N Wells St Chicago IL 60610

CONANT, MARY PLACIDA, hosp. adminstr.; b. Modesto, Calif., Apr. 5, 1910; d. Daniel Frederick and Magdaleine Anne (Kaal) C.; grad. St. Mary's Coll. Nursing, San Francisco, 1931; B.S., San Francisco Coll. Women, 1936. Joined Sisters of Mercy, Roman Catholic Ch., 1931; nursing supr., instr. St Mary's Coll. Nursing, San Francisco, 1936-42, dir. nursing, 1942-52, receptionist, 1982—; adminstr. Notre Dame Hosp., San Francisco, 1952, St. Joseph's Hosp., Phoenix, 1953-65, Mercy Hosp. and Med. Center, San Diego, 1965-74, exec. dir., 1974-77; adminstr. Mercy Hosp., Bakersfield, Calif., 1976-82; bd dirs. Notre Dame Hosp., San Francisco, 1952-53; pres. bd. dirs. St. Joseph's Hosp., Phoenix, 1953-65, Mercy Hosp., San Diego, 1965-77, Mercy Hosp., Bakersfield, 1976-82. Recipient Disting. Pub. Service award Maricopa County (Ariz.) Med. Soc., 1962; Disting. Leadership and Service award NCCJ, 1972; Disting. Service award Comprehensive Health Planning Assn. San Diego and Imperial County, 1976; Cert. of Recognition Calif. State Legislature, 1977; Recognition award City of San Diego, 1977; registered nurse, Calif., Ariz. Fellow Am. Coll. Hosp. Adminstrs. Home: 3250 19th Ave San Francisco CA 94132

CONAWAY, JANE ELLEN, educator; b. Fostoria, Ohio, July 9, 1941; d. Robert and Virginia Conaway; B.A. in Elem. Edn., Mary Manse Coll., Toledo, 1966; M.Ed. in Elem. Edn., U. Ariz., 1969; postgrad. in reading, U. Toledo, 1975—. Tchr. Sandusky public schs., Ohio, 1966-67, Bellevue City Schs., Ohio, 1969-70; coordinator 1st grade small group instrn. program St. Marys Grade Sch., Sandusky, 1970-71; tchr. Chpt. I remedial reading Eastwood Local schs., Pemberville, Ohio, 1971—, also dist. dir. Right to Read program. Mem. NEA, Ohio Edn. Assn., Eastwood Edn. Assn., Ohio Reading Assn., Martha Weber Local Reading Assn., Ohio Assn. Gifted Children, Toledo Area Assn. for Gifted, Delta Kappa Gamma. Cert. as reading supr., reading tchr., Ohio; specialist in diagnostic and remedial reading. Home: 1302 Wexford Dr Waunakee WI 53597 Office: 4800 Sugar Ridge Rd Pemberville OH 43450

CONBOY, JANET ELIZABETH, developmental disabilities administrator; b. Birmingham, Ala., Apr. 8, 1947; d. Faris Lyndle and Thelma Maude (Bolin) Conboy. B.A., Birmingham So. coll., 1968; M.A., U. Mo., 1971, M.Ed., 1972. Tchr. English, speech Decatur City Schs. (Ala.), 1968-70; dir. guidance Rockport R-II Schs. (Mo.), 1972-77; br. office mgr. Albany Regional Ctr. Devel. Disabilities, Maryville, Mo., 1977-79, asst. dir., Albany, Mo., 1979-81, dir., 1981-83; chief community services div. mental retardation developmental disabilities Dept. Mental Health, Jefferson City, Mo., 1983-85, dep. dir. program devel. and client services div. mental retardation and devel. disabilities, 1985—. Mem. Mo. Planning Council Devel. Disabilities, 1984-85. Mem. AAUW, Mo. Women's Network, Am. Assn. Mental Deficiency (div. chmn. 1983-84), Am. Mgmt. Assn., Assn. Mental Health Adminstrs. Episcopalian. Home: 12-B Clarkson Rd Columbia MO 65201 Office: Dept Mental Health 2002 Missouri Blvd Jefferson City MO 65101

CONCEPCION, ISIS LILIBETH, anesthesiologist; b. Concepcion, Panama, July 4, 1955; came to U.S., 1956; d. Adam and Ismenia (Lezcano) Concepcion; m. Hermann Burgermeister, Sept. 13, 1980. M.D., Universidad Autonoma de Guadalajara, Mexico, 1975. Lic. physician/surgeon, N.Y., Calif., Mont. Rotating intern Regina Gen. Hosp. (Sask., Can.), 1976-77; community health physician Universidad Autonoma de Guadalajara (Mexico), 1977-78; rotating intern Moncton Hosp., New Brunswick, Can., 1978-79; resident in anesthesiology St. Vincent's Hosp., N.Y.C., 1980-82; fellow dept. anesthesiology and critical care medicine Meml. Sloan Kettering Cancer Ctr., N.Y.C., 1983—. Mem. AMA, N.Y. County Med. Soc., Am. Soc. Anesthesiologists, Internat. Anesthesia Research Soc., Nat. Assn. Residents and Interns. Seventh-Day Adventist. Home: 240 E 79th St New York NY 10021 Office: Meml Sloan Kettering Cancer Ctr 1275 York Ave New York NY 10021

CONDIE, CAROL JOY, anthropological consultant; b. Provo, Utah, Dec. 28, 1931; d. LeRoy and Thelma (Graff) Condie; m. M. Kent Stout, June 18, 1954; children—Carla Ann, Erik Roy, Paula Jane. B.A. in Anthropology, U. Utah, 1953; M.Ed., Cornell U., 1954; Ph.D. in Anthropology, U. N.Mex., 1973. Edn. coordinator Maxwell Mus. Anthropology, Albuquerque, 1973, dir. interpretation, 1974-77; asst. prof. anthropology U. N.Mex., Albuquerque, 1975-77; cons. anthropologist, Albuquerque, 1977-78; pres. Quivira Research Ctr., Albuquerque, 1978—; cons. ethnologist Navajo Social Studies Project, U. N.Mex., 1970-72; cons. archeologist Phillips Uranium, N.Mex., Colo., Ariz., 1979-81; cons. archeologist, ethnologist Bur. Land Mgmt., N.Mex., 1980-82; chmn. Albuquerque/Bernalillo County Archeol. Resources Adv. Com., 1985. Author: Quest for the Four Parrots, 1970; editor, author: Vocabulary of Apache—Collected by John G. Bourke in the 1870s and 1880s, 1980; The Cultural Resources of the Proposed New Mexico Generating Station, 1982; Anthropology in the Desert West: Essays in Honor of Jesse D. Jennings, 1985. Officer, Albuquerque PTA, 1964-82; mem. Downtown Core Area Schs. Com., Albuquerque, 1982; bd. dirs., treas. Maxwell Mus. Assn., 1980-83; mem. La Selva de Albuquerque Urban Forest Project, 1979—. Ford Found. fellow, 1953-54. Fellow Am. Anthrop. Assn.; mem. Soc. for Am. Archaeology (chmn. native Am. relations com. 1983—), N.Mex. Archeol. Council (pres. 1982-83), Am. Soc. for Ethnohistory, Sigma Xi, Democrat. Club: Las Aranas Spinners and Weavers Guild (pres. Las Aranas 1972). Home: 1809 Notre Dame NE Albuquerque NM 87106 Office: Quivira Research Ctr 3017 Commercial St NE Albuquerque NM 87107

CONDOS, BARBARA SEALE, real estate investment consultant, broker; b. Kenedy, Tex., Feb. 24, 1925; d. John Edgar and Bess Rochelle (Ainsworth) Seale; m. George James Condos, Dec. 24, 1955 (dec.); 1 child, James Alexander. Mus.B. magna cum laude, Incarnate Word Coll., San Antonio, 1946. Lic. real estate broker, Tex. Ptnr., chief exec. officer Mountain Top-V.I. Devel. Properties, V.I., 1977-85; ptnr. Condos & Rhame, San Antonio, 1976—, Investment Realty Co., San Antonio, 1978—; pres. Hallmark Realty, Inc., San Antonio, 1978—. Choreographer, dancer San Antonio Youth Concerts; actress San Antonio Little Theatre-Patio-Players 1948—; trustee San Antonio Little Theatre, 1953-76; trustee Incarnate Word Coll., San Antonio, 1977—, vice chmn., 1980-82; bd. dirs. San Antonio Performing Arts Assn., 1978—. Mem. Internat. Real Estate Fedn., Internat. Inst. of Valuers, Real Estate Securities and Syndication Inst., Tex. Assn. Realtors, San Antonio Bd. Realtors. Club: The Argyle (San Antonio). Avocation: painting. Home: 217 Geneseo Rd San Antonio TX 78209 Office: Investment Realty Co 1635 NE Loop 410 San Antonio TX 78209

CONDRA, NORMA LEE, newspaper publisher; b. Russell, Ky.; d. Pem Burton and Lottie Lee (Edleman) Kuhn; children—David, Cynthia Condra Snyder. Student U. Tenn. Pub. Country Hot Line News, Nashville, 1977-79, Wilson World, Lebanon, Tenn., 1979-80; founder, pub. Town & Country Courier, Nashville, 1981—, Hendersonville Free Press, Tenn., 1975—; dir. Nashville City Bank. Chmn. Hendersonville Arts Council, 1978-79. Mem. Suburban Newspapers of Am. (bd. dirs. 1981-85), Hendersonville C. of C. (bd. dirs., pres.-elect 1982). Republican. Methodist. Club: Tenn. Women's Golf Assn. (pres. 1980-82), Hillwood Country. Home: 106 Christopher St Nashville TN 37205 Office: Hendersonville Free Press 131 Sanders Ferry Rd Hendersonville TN 37075

CONDUIT, E. MARY, retired accountant; b. Broadford, Victoria, Australia, Feb. 12, 1923; d. William Robert and Ellen Mary (Logan) Hurley; m. Rupert Lyn Conduit, Oct. 9, 1943; children—William R., Alan John. Student Cath. Ladies Coll., 1935-39. Nurse various hosps., Australia, 1941-45; bookkeeper Great Am. Ins. Co., San Francisco, 1952-56, Cravens-Dargan Ins. Agy., 1956-58, Am. Home Gen. Agy., 1958-77; collections/investment mgr. Am. Internat. Marine, Oakland, Calif., 1977-84. Mem. Fairmont Hosp. Aux.; mem. Jerry Lewis Annual Telethon, Oakland; active Neighbor Watch, Heart Fund. Named to Ins. Women's Hall of Fame, 1980. Mem. Ins. Women of South Alameda County, Oakland Bus. and Profl. Women. Home: 4636 Kaphan Ave Oakland CA 94619

CONE, MARTHA CAROLINE, TV production company executive; b. Columbus, Ohio, Apr. 11, 1933; d. Francis Edward and Freda Katherine (Ehlers) Clymer; student Ohio State U., 1951-52; children—Denise Danielle Buyaky, David Douglas DeVoe. Asst. to program mgr. Sta. WLW-C-TV, Columbus, Ohio, 1952-53, Sta. WBNS-TV, Columbus, 1953-55; dir. women's programming Sta. WPTA-TV, Ft. Wayne, Ind., 1963-65; asst. to dir. press/publicity Sta. KNBC-TV, Los Angeles, 1965-69; comml. mgr. Lawrence Welk Show, Don Fedderson Prodns., Los Angeles, 1971-77; prodn. mgr.-syndication ops. West Coast, Goodson-Todman Prodns., Los Angeles, 1977—. Res. police officer City of Burbank (Calif.), 1979; vol. Burbank Community Hosp.; bd. dirs. Burbank Community Healthcare Found. Republican. Club: Foothill Civitan (Burbank, Calif.). Office: Goodson-Todman Prodns 6430 Sunset Blvd Los Angeles CA 90028

CONE, VIRGIE HORNE HYMAN, former educator, civic worker; b. Brooksville, Fla.; d. George G. and Virgie (Horne) Hyman; B.S., Fla. State Coll. Women, 1945; M.Ed., U. Fla., 1956; m. Edward Elbert Cone, Dec. 20, 1930 (dec. Feb. 1962); children—Molly Gentile, Edward Elbert. Tchr., Meml. Jr. High Sch., Hillsborough County, 1929-31; tchr. Duval County Robert E. Lee Sr. High Sch., Jacksonville, Fla., 1943-55, dean, 1955-70; prin. Lee High Sch. (1st woman secondary sch. prin. in county), 1971-74; owner Cone's Antiques. Chmn., ARC night vols. St. Vincent's Hosp., 1969-71; mem. task force Mayor's Community Planning Council, 1969; pres. Hamilton County unit Am. Cancer Soc., 1974-76; v.p. Hamilton County Meml. Hosp. Aux., 1975-76; mem. adv. council Health and Rehabilitative Services, Dist. 3, Fla.; dir. Area Agy. on Aging, 1977-82, bd. dirs., 1982—; del. White House Conf. on Aging, 1981; mem. adv. council Social Security; mem. adv. council State Civil Rights Commn.; pres. North Fla. Mental Health Bd., 1978-80; mem. Hamilton County Planning Council, Gov.'s Commn. on Status Women, 1978-80; mem. exec. bd. North Central Fla. Health Planning Council, 1979-80. Mem. Fla. Council Tchrs. Math. (curriculum chmn. 1952, sec. 1949), AAUW (Jacksonville v.p. 1953), Duval Tchrs. Assn. (chmn. profl. rights and responsibilities com. 1965-66), Jacksonville Panhellenic Assn. (pres. 1959-60, mem. scholarship com. 1963-68), Duval Personnel and Guidance Assn. (organizing chmn. 1966-69), Nat., Fla. assns. secondary prins., Hamilton Ret. Tchrs., Fla. Assn. Area Agy. Dirs. (pres.), Am. Assn. Ret. Persons (state legis. com.), Delta Kappa Gamma (chpt. pres. 1959-61), Sigma Kappa (nat. scholarship chmn. 1963-77). Clubs: Pilot of Jacksonville, Suwannee Valley Country (dir. 1978-80). Home: NW 3d St Jasper FL 32052

CONFINO, SHIRLEY ROSE LEWIS, interior designer; b. Albuquerque, Oct. 20, 1940; d. Benjamin Milton and Lena (Abrin) Lewis; B.A. magna cum laude, Queens Coll., 1977; diploma N.Y. Sch. Interior Design, 1973; div.; children—Steven Howard, Liza Beth Dara. With Aluminium Ltd., 1959-62; ind. artist, Queens, 1963-64; owner Ideas Unltd., Queens, 1970-79, Shirley Confino Interiors, Norfolk, Va., 1980—; tchr. Norfolk Vocat. High Sch. Bd. dirs. Tidewater Jewish Community Center, 1981-83, Cultural Experiences, 1981—, Norfolk Chamber Consort; co-founder L.I. chpt. Dysautonomia Found., 1972. Mem. Am. Soc. Interior Designers, Bus. and Profl. Women, Women in Constrn., Women's Forum, Norfolk C. of C. Club: Quota. Office: 819 W 21st St Norfolk VA 23517

CONFORTH, DIANA LYNN, marketing executive, telemarketing specialist; b. Paterson, N.J., July 12, 1953; d. James Anthony and Anne (Grassi) C. B.A., Montclair State Coll., 1975; M.A., Webster U., 1984. Sales assoc. Levitz Furniture, Fairfield, N.J., 1971-81; exec. search cons. Central EDP, Paramus, N.J., 1981-82; nat. telemktg. account rep. Greggs/McGraw-Hill, St. Louis, 1982-84; v.p. sales and mktg. RMR Inc., St. Louis, 1984-85; nat. telemktg. account rep. Greggs/McGraw-Hill, St. Louis, 1985—; telemktg. cons. Integrity Solutions, Denver, 1984, Tech. Careers, New Brunswick, N.J., 1984-85. Recipient Blue Blazer award McGraw-Hill, Manchester, Mo., 1983, Employee Suggestion award McGraw-Hill, Manchester, 1983. Mem. Am. Soc. Profl. and Exec. Women, Nat. Assn. Female Execs., Nat. Latin Honor Soc. Roman Catholic. Avocations: sports enthusiast; racquetball; softball; tennis. Home: 78 Weinmann Blvd Wayne NJ 07470 Office: McGraw-Hill Book Co 13955 Manchester Rd Manchester MO 63011

CONFORTI, JOANNE, advertising executive; b. N.Y.C., Apr. 17, 1944; d. Ralph and Josephine (Amico) C. Student, Bklyn. Coll., 1961-63. Trainee, Gen. Motors, N.Y.C., 1960-62, adminstrv. asst., 1962-66, personnel asst., 1966-70; staff asst. Bozell & Jacobs, Inc., N.Y.C., 1973-75, personnel and office mgr., 1975-77, personnel and office v.p., 1977-79, human resources dir., v.p., 1979-81, corp. human resources dir., sr. v.p., 1981—. Mem. Advt. Women of N.Y. Home: 252 E 61st St New York NY 10021 Office: Bozell & Jacobs 40 W 23d St New York NY 10010

CONGALTON, SUSAN TICHENOR, lawyer; b. Mount Vernon, N.Y., July 12, 1946; d. Arthur George and M. Marjorie (McDermott) Tichenor; m. Christopher W. Congalton, May 29, 1971. B.A. summa cum laude, Loretto Heights Coll., 1968; J.D., Georgetown U., 1971. Bar: N.Y. 1972. Assoc., Reavis & McGrath, N.Y.C., 1971-78, ptnr., 1978-85; v.p., gen. counsel Carson Pirie Scott's Co., 1985—. Mem. ABA, Assn. Bar City N.Y., N.Y. State Bar Assn. (com. corp. law, subcom. partnership law 1984-85), Fin. Women's Assn. Editor Georgetown Law Jour., 1969-71. Office: 36 S Wabash Suite 1301 Chicago IL 60603

CONGCO-MACAPINLAC, EVANGELINE GOZUN, internist, endocrinologist; b. Bacolor, Philippines; came to U.S., 1972; naturalized, 1980; d. Engracio D. and Rosario (Gozun) Congco; m. Efren L. Macapinlac, June 17, 1976; 1 child, Elaine Congco-Macapinlac. B.S. magna cum laude, U. Santo Tomas, Manila, 1966, M.D. cum laude, 1971. Intern in internal medicine U.Wis.-Milw., 1972-73; resident in internal medicine Wayne State U., Detroit, 1973-76; fellow in endocrinology U. Calif.-San Francisco, 1976-77; practice medicine specializing in internal medicine and endocrinology, Daly City, Calif., 19—; mem. staff Seton Med. Ctr., Daly City, 1980—, lectr. endocrinology, 1981—; acting med. dir. Guadalupe Health Ctr., Daly City, 1977-81; preceptor for lic. nurse practitioners San Francisco State U., 1978-81. Contbr. articles to med. jours. Recipient Ann. Humanitarian award No. San Mateo County, Cindy Smallwood Found., 1980. Mem. AMA, World Med. Assn., Nat. Assn. Female Execs. Avocations: hybrid tea roses; writing poems; travelling. Office: Westlake Med Bldg 48 Park Plaza Suite 306 Daly City CA 94015

CONGDON, MATTIE JOY ELLANORE, nurse practitioner, health educator, administrator; b. Freeman, S.D., June 17, 1940; d. John Samuel and Ada Irene (Andersen) C. Diploma Nursing Mounds-Midway Sch. Nursing, 1961; Cert. Multnomah Sch. Bible, 1965; B.S. in Nursing, U. Oreg. Health Scis. Ctr., 1966; postgrad. in linguistics U. Wash., 1967-68; Family Nurse Practitioner, U. Calif.-Davis, 1985. R.N. Operating room nurse St. John's Hosp., St. Paul, 1961-62, Emanuel Hosp., Portland, 1962-68; educator, instr. Tribe Med. Health Promoter Program, Wycliffe Bible Translators, Yarinacocha, Peru, S.Am., 1970-82, adminstr., coordinator, 1977-82, tribal med. coordinator Jungle area, Yarinacocha, 1981-82; adminstr. Jungle Out Patient Clinic, Yarinacocha, 1981-82; staff nurse Urgency Care Clinic Bess Kaiser Hosp., Portland, 1983; adminstr., med. provider Jungle Out Patient Clinic, Yarinacocha, Peru, 1985—. Republican. Baptist. Home: 1999 NE Division #33 Gresham OR 97030 Office: care Wycliffe Bible Translators Huntington Beach CA 92647

CONGER, MARY LANE, county official; b. Shelbyville, Tenn., July 1; d. Jacob Thomas and Grace (Howard) Lane; m. John Beall Conger, Apr. 14, 1940; children—John Beall, Jr., Malinda Conger Fyke. B.S., Middle Tenn. State U.; postgrad. U. Tenn.-Nashville, Peabody Coll., U. Tenn.-Knoxville. Classroom tchr. Bedford County Dept. Edn., Shelbyville, 1938-40; tchr. Lincoln County Dept. Edn., Fayetteville, Tenn., 1949-80, Headstart coordinator, 1965-70 (summers); commr. Lincoln County, Tenn., 1978—. Bd. dirs. Fayetteville-Lincoln County Library, 1978—, Lincoln County Cancer Soc., 1982—; sec. Lincoln County Law Enforcement Com., 1978-82, Lincoln County Solid Waste Com., 1982—, Lincoln County Fin. Com., 1982—; active Lincoln County Democratic Women, 1950—. Recipient Freedoms Found. of Valley Forge Nat. Classroom Tchr's. award, 1960. Mem. Lincoln County Ednl. Assn. (pres. 1977-78), NEA, Tenn. Retired Tchrs. Assn., Tenn. County Commrs. Assn., Lincoln County Farm Bur. (bd. dirs.), Mimosa Home Demonstration Club (v.p. 1983—), Round Dozen Lit. Club, Lincoln County Museum Assn. (bd. dirs. 1985—), Lincoln County Hist. Soc. (editor 4 editions of jour., 1983—, pres. 1985-86), Alpha Kappa Lit. Club (pres. 1948-50), Delta Kappa Gamma (chpt. pres. 1980-82). Methodist. Avocations: needlework; rug hooking; rug braiding; restoring family home. Home: Route 5 Box 338 Fayetteville TN 37334 Office: Lincoln County Seat Route 5 Box 338 Fayetteville TN 37334

CONIGLIARO, LAURA CLAIRE, securities analyst; b. N.Y.C., Oct. 24, 1945; d. Julius and Edna (Schechner) Gerber; m. Michael Gardham, June 9, 1968; children—Alison Leigh, Andrew Warren. B.A. summa cum laude, Boston U., 1966; M.B.A., Fairleigh Dickinson U., 1979. Intelligence analyst Nat. Security Agy., Fort Meade, Md., 1966-70; securities analyst Prudential-Bache Securities, Inc., N.Y.C., 1979—; venture capital and coverage of design and mfg. automation industries. Contbr. articles to profl. jours.; mem. adv. bd. Jour. Computer-Integrated Mfg., 1984. Mem. Robot Inst./Soc. Mfg. Engrs., Computer and Automated Systems Assn., Environ. Info. Ctr. Robotics (mem. adv. bd. 1984), Phi Beta Kappa. Office: Prudential-Bache Securities Inc One Seaport Plaza New York NY 10292

CONKLIN, CAROL MARIE, automotive executive, lawyer; b. Jamaica, N.Y., Dec. 7, 1931; s. Raymond Jerome and Caroline Veronica C.; student U. Detroit, 1949-51, LL.B., 1955. Admitted to Mich. bar, 1955; sr. title officer Lawyers Title Ins. Corp., 1972; dep. atty. in charge real estate for legal staff Gen. Motors Corp., 1974-77, sec., N.Y.C., 1978-83, legal staff real estate sect., Detroit, 1983—; sec. Gen. Motors Acceptance Corp., 1977. Honoree nat. bd. YWCA First Tribute to Women in Internat. Industry, 1978. Mem. ABA, Am. Soc. Corp. Secs., Inc., Mich. Bar Assn., Kappa Beta Pi. Office: Gen Motors Corp 3044 W Grand Blvd Room 4-144 Detroit MI 48202

CONKLIN, LYNN SUMMERS, computing company executive; b. Balt., Feb. 4, 1936; d. Harry Ricks and Doris Louise (Sturm) Summers; A.A., Valencia Community Coll., 1981; B. G.S., Rollins Coll., 1983; children—Vicky Lee, David Travis. Office mgr. Norrell Temporary Service, Winter Park, Fla., 1976-77, clerical div. mgr., 1977-79; office systems supr. Martin Marietta Data Systems, Orlando, Fla., 1979-80, office automation system adminstr., 1980-83; sr. customer rep. integrated office applications Harris Corp., Melbourne, Fla., 1983-85; sr. bus. systems designer Martin Marietta Data Systems, Orlando, Fla., 1985—; lectr. in field. Mem. Assn. Info. Systems Profls., Gamma Phi Beta. Home: 5324 Burning Tree Dr Orlando FL 32811 Office: PO Box 13385A Orlando FL 32859

CONKLIN, PATRICIA ANN, lawyer; b. Chester, Pa., Jan. 21, 1956; d. James Spencer and Elizabeth (Cauley) Conklin. B.A., Pa. State U., 1978; J.D., U. Pitts., 1981. Bar: Pa. 1982. Legal intern Pa. Mus. Commn., Harrisburg, 1979; law clk. Stonecipher, Cunningham Beard & Schmitt, Pitts., 1979-81; assoc. Broujos & Gilroy, Carlisle, Pa., 1981-82; pvt. practice law, Carlisle, Pa., 1982-83; atty. Hyatt Legal Services, Phila., 1983-84; assoc. Meneses & Dean, P.C., King of Prussia, 1984—; counselor dept. legal affairs Pa. State U., University Park, 1974-78; team mem. client counseling team U. Pitts., 1980; atty. Friends of Historic Rittenhousetown, Phila., Phila. Vol. Lawyers for Arts; Scholarship advisor Panhellenic Council, Pa. State U., University Park, 1978. Mem. ABA, Phila. Bar Assn., Allegheny County Bar Assn., Pa. Bar Assn., Montgomery County Bar Assn., Assn. Trial Lawyers Am., Omicron Delta Kappa, Kappa Kappa Gamma, Phi Alpha Delta. Democrat. Episcopalian. Home 329 Avon Dr Carlisle PA 17013 Office: 160 King of Prussia Plaza King of Prussia PA 19406

CONLEY, CAROLYN PATTON, accountant; b. Detroit, Mar. 5, 1944; d. Carl D and Roberta Jean (Kennedy) Patton; B.B.A., Wichita State U., 1966, M.S., 1967; m. Norman Eddy Conley, Nov. 19, 1967; 1 son, Sean Peter. Mem. audit staff Fox & Co., C.P.A.s, Wichita, 1967-69; controller Central Computing Inc., Wichita, 1969-70, Campus Activity Center, 1970-72, Inst. Logopedics, 1972-74; mgr. mgmt. services George U. Landis C.P.A., Wichita, 1974-76; tax analyst Dynatax div. Tymeshare, Wichita, 1976-78; pvt. practice acctg., Wichita, 1978—. Mem. Commn. Status of Women, 1975-81, pres., 1976; bd. dirs. Historic Wichita, 1981—, sec.-treas., 1982-83, v.p., 1983-84, pres., 1984-86; bd. dirs. YWCA, 1978—, treas., 1978—; campaign treas., local polit. campaigns; treas. Wichita Free U., 1981-84; participant Leadership 2000, 1983, Whitehouse Conf. on Small Bus., 1986. Mem. Nat. Assn. Women Bus. Owners (pres. 1982-83), Adminstrv. Mgmt. Soc. (membership chmn. 1981-82, v.p. fin. 1982-83), Nat. Assn. Accts., Am. Inst. C.P.A.s, Kans. Soc. C.P.A.s, Wichita Area C. of C. (seminar chmn. 1984). Clubs: Sports Car Am. (treas. dir.; Midwest div. Class A Rallye champion, 1974, 75, 76). Address: 2916 W 21st St Wichita KS 67203

CONLEY, CATHARINE ANASTASIA, molecular biologist; b. St. Albans, N.Y., May 24, 1938; d. Henry John and Catharine Anastasia (Wheeler) Smith; m. Charles Cameron Conley, Dec. 28, 1963 (dec. 1984); children—Charles Henry, Catharine Anastasia, John Alan. B.A., Coll. New Rochelle, 1960; postgrad. Johns Hopkins Sch. Medicine, 1960-61, U. Wis., 1964-65; M.S., Brown U., 1963. Hematology technician Grasslands Hosp., Valhalla, N.Y., 1961; bioassayist Cornell Med. Coll., N.Y.C., 1962; research technician McArdle Cancer Research Lab., Madison, Wis., 1980-84, U. Minn., St. Paul, 1985; research technician R&D Systems, Inc., Mpls., 1985—. Pres. Spring Harbor Sch. PTA, Madison, 1978-79; mem. parents adv. bd. Meml. High Sch., 1979-80; treas., den mother Blackhawk council Cub Scouts Am., Madison, 1977-78; docent Elvehjem Mus. Art, U. Wis.-Madison, 1972-80. Clubs: Indian Hills Garden (pres. 1973-75), Wisconsin State Garden (treas. Madison 1976-78). Office: R&D Systems Inc 614 McKinley Pl NE Minneapolis MN 55414

CONLEY, MARJORIE TAYLOR, construction company executive; b. Chgo., Nov. 14, 1920; d. Myron DeLoss and Margaret Elizabeth (Heppner) Taylor; grad. Walton Coll. Commerce, Chgo., 1939; m. Robert John Kostka, July 4, 1942 (div. 1963); children—Beverly Kostka Elk (dec.), Kent Allen, Kurt Stanton; m. 2d, George L. Conley, Jr., Mar. 13, 1964. Exec. sec. Jackson & Curtis and Boettcher & Co., Chgo., 1940-42; office mgr., asst. sec.-treas. Redwood Empire Savs. & Loan Assn., Petaluma, Calif., 1952-59; asst. indsl. advt. mgr. Fluor Corp., Santa Rosa, Calif., 1959-60; exec. v.p., mng. officer Bear Flag Builders Control Co., Santa Rosa, 1960-64; co-owner Conley Constrn. Co., Santa Rosa, 1964-75; sec.-treas. Conley Homes, Inc., Santa Rosa, 1975—. Mem. Women in Constrn. (charter pres.), Las Rosas Bus. and Profl. Women's Club (past pres.), Santa Rosa C. of C., Congress for Community Progress, Building Industry Assn. (bd. dirs.), Credit Women (past pres.), Psi Sigma Alpha. Republican. Clubs: Soroptimist Internat. (past pres. Santa Rosa; past regional gov., treas.; founder, region, fedn. treas., dir. Soroptimist Founds., Inc.). Order Eastern Star. Home: 3174 Blank Rd Sebastopol CA 95472 Office: 14 W 3d St Santa Rosa CA 95401

CONLIN, PATRICIA PETERS, banker; b. Santa Monica, Calif., Sept. 17, 1943; d. John Dennis and Dorothy Amanda (Tydeman) Peters; B.A. in econs. Magna Cum Laude, Cornell U., 1965; M.A. in econs., Stanford U., 1966. With Morgan Guaranty Trust Co. of N.Y., N.Y.C., 1966—, asst. treas., 1968-70, asst. v.p., 1970-73, v.p., 1973-84, sr. v.p., 1984—. Bd. dirs. Public Devel. Corp. City of N.Y. Mem. Phi Beta Kappa. Office: 23 Wall St New York NY 10015

CONLIN, ROXANNE BARTON, lawyer; b. Huron, S.D., June 30, 1944; d. Marion William and Alyce Muraine (Madden) Barton; B.A. (Readers Digest scholar), Drake U., 1964, J.D. (Fischer Found. scholar), 1966, M.P.A., 1979; m. James Clyde Conlin, Mar. 21, 1964; children—Deborah Ann, Douglas B., Jacalyn Rae, James Barton. Bar: Iowa 1966. Assoc. firm Davis, Huebner, Johnson & Burt, Des Moines, 1966-67; dep. indsl. commr. State of Iowa, Des Moines, 1967-68, asst. atty. gen., 1969-76; U.S. atty. for So. Dist. Iowa, Des Moines, 1977-81; now assoc. James & Galligan, P.C. Mem. Iowa Commn. on Status of Women, 1972-77. State chmn. Iowa Women's Polit. Caucus, Des Moines, 1973-76, del. nat. steering com. 1973-77; mem. adminstrv. com. Nat. Women's Polit. Caucus, 1975-77; nat. committeewoman Iowa Young Democrats, pres. Polk County Young Dems., 1965-66; pres. Drake U. Law Sch. Endowment Fund, 1985-86; del. Iowa Presdl. Conv., 1972; Dem. nominee for gov. of Iowa, 1982. Named to Iowa Women's Hall of Fame, 1981. Mem. ABA (mem. individual rights and responsibilities com. 1971-79), Iowa Bar Assn. (mem. career day panel 1971-76, mem. bar rev. com. 1972-73), Assn. Trail Lawyers Am. (chmn. consumer and victims coalition com.), Assn. Trial Lawyers Iowa (bd. dirs. 1984—), Women's Equity Action League, NOW (dir. 1969, bd. dirs. Legal Def. and Edn. Fund 1983—, gen. counsel 1985—), Phi Beta Kappa, Alpha Lambda Delta, Chi Omega (Social Service awards), Pi Alpha Delta. Office: 610 Equitable Bldg Des Moines IA 50309

CONLON, KATHRYN ANN, county official; b. Mankato, Minn., July 30, 1958; d. Ralph Raymond and Joan Margaret (Meyer) Walter; m. James Allan Conlon, Oct. 1, 1977; children—Jessica Marie, Brian Michael. Student Mankato Vocat. Sch. Teller Mankato Credit Union, 1977; clk. Nicollet County Credit Bur., Minn., 1977-78; abstractor Lorna Holmquist, St. Peter, Minn., 1978-82; dep. recorder, abstractor Nicollet County, 1982-84, county recorder, abstractor, 1984—, sec. to dept. heads, 1985, chmn. dept. heads, 1986. Mem. Spina Bifida Assn. Minn., 1981—, Spina Bifida Assn. Southwest Minn., 1983—; bd. dirs. Children's Central Child Care, 1985-87. Mem. Minn. Assn. County Recorders, VFW Aux., Am. Legion Aux. Avocations: handcrafting; camping; volleyball; racquet ball. Home: Route 4 Box 7 Saint Peter MN 56082 Office: Nicollet County Recorder PO Box 493 Saint Peter MN 56082

CONN, ELENOR DEBBIE, balloon company executive; b. Winnipeg, Man., Can., Aug. 11, 1944; came to U.S., 1982; d. Alan and Beatrice (Nusgart) Nozick; m. Sidney Harvey Conn, Dec. 1, 1963; children—Max, Lee, Nancy, Marla. B.A., U. Calgary, 1966; diploma edn. McGill U., 1968. Tchr., Calgary Bd. Edn., Alta., Can., 1969-75; mgr., owner Joy of Sound, Calgary, 1975-82; pres. Balloon Works, Statesville, N.C., 1982—. Pres. ladies aux. Temple Emanuel, 1985; dir. Nat. Balloon Rally, Statesville, 1983—; sec. Mulberry St. PTA, 1983—. Mem. Greater Statesville C. of C. (vice chair exec. women). Avocations: exercising, swimming. Home: 1 139 N Mulberry St Statesville NC 28677 Office: Balloon Works 810 Salisbury Rd Statesville NC 28677

CONNELL, ELSIE MAUREEN, medical office administrator; b. Kilgore, Tex., June 4, 1933; d. A. C. and Georgia Alice (Burton) McGraw; m. Gerald Davis Connell, Jan. 24, 1983; m. Dan Phillip Broadwater, May 5, 1954 (div. May 1980); children—Jack Phillip, Charles Wayne, Shelly Dee. Nurse, Gregg Meml. Hosp., Longview, Tex., 1958-59, Laird Meml. Hosp., Kilgore, 1959-70; receptionist Internal Medicine Assocs., Longview, 1970-71, ins. coordinator, purchasing agt., 1971-72, office mgr., 1972-76, bus. mgr., 1976—. Pres., Mathers Aux. Kilgore Baseball, 1970, 72; treas. bd. dirs. Kilgore Boys Baseball, 1972. Mem. Internal Medicine Adminstrs., Am. Coll. Med. Group Mgmt. Assn., Med. Group Mgmt. Assn., Med. Adminstrs. Tex. Republican. Baptist. Home: 708 Florey St Kilgore TX 75662 Office: Internal Medicine Assocs 701 N 6th St Longview TX 75601

CONNELL, JANICE, lawyer; b. Pa., Mar. 30, 1939; d. Louis John and Edna (Bonistall) Timchak; m. Edward F. Connell, Jr., Nov. 24, 1960; children—Elizabeth Ward, Edward F., III, William Troy. B.S.F.S., Georgetown U., 1961; M.Pub. and Internat. Affairs, U. Pitts., 1976; J.D., Duquesne U., 1979. Bar: Pa. 1979, U.S. Dist. Ct. (we. dist.) Pa. 1979, U.S. Ct. Appeals (3d cir.) 1979, U.S. Supreme Ct. 1983. Pres., Connell Leasing of Fla., Jacksonville, Fla., 1970-80, Regency Advt., Jacksonville, Fla., 1968-74; ptnr. Connell & Connell, Pitts., 1980—; v.p., sec. dir. Nat. Motor Leasing Inc., 1980-86; pres., dir. Internat. Motor Leasing Inc., 1986—; v.p., sec., dir. Transp. Lease Consultants Inc., 1986—. Sec., dir. Duquesne U. Women's Bd., Pitts., 1980—; emeritus bd. dirs. Wheeling (W.Va.) Coll. Charter Guild, 1984; bd. dirs. Wheeling Symphony Soc., 1967, Salvation Army, 1968, United Way, 1971, YWCA, 1972. Mem. ABA, Pa. Bar Assn., Allegheny County Bar Assn., N.Y. Stock Exchange (arbitrator), Nat. Assn. Securities Dealers (arbitrator), Am. Arbitration Assn., Assn. Junior Leagues (bd. dirs. Wheeling, W.Va. 1964-68, Jacksonville 1968-74, Pitts. 1974—). Home: 630 Academy Ave Sewickley PA 15143 Office: 107 Patton Dr Pittsburgh PA 15108

CONNELL, MARY JANE, lawyer; b. Pontiac, Mich., Mar. 11, 1947; d. Jerry J. and Louise (Newburg) Connell. B.A., U. Mich., 1969; M.A., Northwestern U., 1970; J.D. cum laude, Fordham U., 1982. Bar: N.Y. 1983. Tchr., South Middle Sch., Grand Rapids, Mich., 1970-72; exec. sec. Goodman Theatre, Chgo., 1972-74; legal asst., office sec. Weissberger & Harris, N.Y.C., 1974-81, Gottlieb, Schiff, Tickbin, Sternkler & Harris, N.Y.C., 1981-82; assoc. Cravath, Swaine & Moore, N.Y.C., 1982—. Mem. ABA, N.Y. State Bar Assn., Alpha Omicron Pi. Office: Cravath Swaine & Moore 1 Chase Manhattan Plaza New York NY 10005

CONNELL, SHIRLEY HUDGINS, public relations director; b. Washington, Oct. 5, 1946; d. Orville Thomas and Mary (Beran) H.; m. David Day Connell, Dec. 13, 1980 (div. 1985). B.A., U. R.I., 1968, M.A., 1970. Clk., editor MGM Studios, Culver City, Calif., 1970-72; scriptor, talent Monarch Records, Studio City, 1972-73; communications specialist U. So. Calif., Los Angeles, 1973-81; public relations dir. Six Flags Movieland, Buena Park, Calif., 1981-82, Donald J. Fager & Assocs., N.Y.C., 1982—; cons. Children's Television Workshop, N.Y.C., 1978. Contbr. articles to profl. jours. Mem. Greater Los Angeles Press Club, Nat. Assn. Female Execs. Clubs: Oceanic Soc. (bd. dirs. 1979-81), Marine Tech. Soc. (vice chmn. 1980-81). Avocations: photography; reading; swimming; wood finishing; writing; marine environmental science.

CONNELL, SUZANNE (SPARKS) MCLAURIN, retired librarian; b. Bennettsville, S.C., Sept. 12, 1917; d. John Bethea and Aleine (McLeod) McLaurin; A.B., Woman's Coll. of U. N.C., 1938; A.B. in L.S., U. N.C., 1940; 1 child, John Alexander (dec.). Library asst. Mt. Pleasant br. D.C. Public Library, Washington, 1940-41, post librarian Camp Sutton, N.C., 1943-44; post librarian McGuire Gen. Hosp., Richmond, Va., 1945-46, chief librarian McGuire VA Hosp., 1946-52, 59-62; chief librarian VA Hosp., Lake City, Fla., 1952-56; cataloger, chief books acquisitions, chief books circulation, asst. chief documents acquisitions Air U. Library, Maxwell AFB, Ala., 1956-59; head extension, head circulation Greensboro (N.C.) Public Library, 1962-63; reference librarian, asst. and acting base librarian Marine Corps Base, Camp Lejeune, N.C., 1963-66; part time cataloger Wilmington (N.C.) Public Library, 1967-75. Past vol., ARC, U.S. Naval Hosp., Marine Corps Base, Camp Lejeune, N.C., local hosp. and nursing home. Mem. ALA (pres. assn. hosp. and instn. libraries 1955-56), Phi Beta Kappa. Methodist. Contbr. articles to Brit. and Am. periodicals. Home: 249 E 11th St Apt 253-B Southport NC 28461

CONNELL, WESSIE GERTRUDE, library administrator; b. Cairo, Ga., Nov. 21, 1915; d. John H. and Gertrude (Pearce) C. Grad. high sch. Dir., Cairo Pub. Library (name changed to Roddenbery Meml. Library 1964), 1939—; cons., speaker to library and ednl. orgns. Contbg. author: Wonderful World of Books, 1952; Public Relations for Libraries, 1972; Journal and Essays, 1986. Library columnist Cairo Messenger. Advisor Grady County Courthouse Bldg. Com., 1983; pres. Wesleyan Service Guild, Methodist Ch., 1960-61. Recipient John Cotton Dana publicity awards, 1948, 49, 58, 59; Library Pub. Relations Council award, 1950; Garden Club Ga. Merit award, 1961; named Cairo Kiwanis Citizen of Yr., 1948; Woman of Yr., Rotary, Kiwanis and Lions clubs, 1959; plaque exemplary service Ga. Adult Edn. Assn., 1985. Mem. Ga. Library Assn., Southeastern Ga. Library Assn., ALA, Library Pub. Relations Council, Ga. Adult Edn. Council, Ga. Hist. Soc., Ga. Council Pub. Libraries (adv. council), Ga. Writers Assn., Oral History Council, Delta Kappa Gamma. Clubs: Cairo Women, Cairo Book (hon.), Camellia Garden (hon.). Home: 410 N Broad St Cairo GA 31728 Office: Roddenbery Memorial Library 320 N Broad St Cairo GA 31728

CONNELLY, DONNA MARIE, educational administrator; b. Mpls., Apr. 21, 1934; d. Thomas Reed and Helen Hope (Howard) James; children—Sharon, Mike, Cindy, Samantha, Lanna. A.A., Santa Monica City Coll., 1954; B.A., Calif. State U.-Fullerton, 1966, cert., 1967, M.S., 1974. Cert. tchr. learning and severely handicapped, Calif. Tchr. ednl. handicapped Brookhurst Jr. High Sch., Anaheim, Calif., 1967-68; tchr. severely emotionally disturbed State of Calif., Fullerton, 1970-72; asst. dir. Walden Sch., Anaheim, 1972-75; founder, dir. Claremont High Sch., Garden Grove, Calif., 1975—. Developer first educationally handicapped class, 1967, first severely educationally handicapped program for high sch. students in Calif. U.S. Govt. fellow, 1968. Mem. Garden Grove C. of C. Democrat. Home: 11241 Dallas Dr Garden Grove CA 92640 Office; Claremont High Sch 9821 Bixby PO Box 816 Garden Grove CA 92641

CONNELLY, LINDA LEE, college information specialist; b. Tacoma, Nov. 21, 1937; d. Norman J. and Dorothea Esther (Voorhies) Arrington; B.A., Western Wash. U., 1960, postgrad., 1980-82; m. Ralph Stanton Connelly, Dec. 26, 1959; children—Colleen Tracy, Jeffrey Wayne. Tchr., Port Orchard and Tacoma Schs., 1960-63; feature writer Tacoma Rev., 1973-74; coordinator Mother's March, Tacoma-Pierce County March of Dimes, 1974-75; info. asst. Ft. Steilacoom Community Coll., 1975-78, public info. officer, 1978—; community coll. adv. Dist. VIII Conf., Council for Advancement and Support Edn., 1979-80. Exec. bd. March of Dimes, Tacoma, 1975-77. Mem. Nat. Council for Community Relations (dist. trustee 1980-81, nat. sec. 1981-82, nat. v.p. 1982-83, pres. 1983-84), Wash. Assn. Community Coll. Public Info. Officers, Wash. State Info. Council, Tacoma C. of C. (edn. com., legis. com.). Clubs: Jr. Woman's of Tacoma (Clubwoman of Yr. 1973), Peninsula Fedn. Women's Clubs (dist. chmn. 1971-73), Bus. and Profl. Women's, Veleda Federated Woman's (v.p. 1974), Tacoma Outboard Assn. Office: 9401 Farwest Dr SW Tacoma WA 98498

CONNELLY, SHANNON, lawyer; b. Milw., Feb. 15, 1948; d. Lawrence and Harriet (Madsen) Parker; m. Stephen Dwight Connelly, July 9, 1968; children—Karen, Robert, Marianne. B.A., Northwestern U., 1970; J.D., Georgetown U., 1975. Bar: D.C. 1976, Ill. 1980. Assoc. Wheedon, Harris & Montgomery, Washington, 1976-80; mem. firm Sanderson & Majewski, Chgo., 1980-84; corp. counsel Beatrice Foods, Inc., Chgo., 1984—; lectr. Loyola U., Chgo., 1983-84. Active Girl Scouts U.S.A., 1981—. Mem. ABA, Ill. Bar Assn., Chgo. Bar Assn., Nat. Assn. Women Lawyers, Phi Beta Kappa. Democrat. Roman Catholic. Office: 200 E Ohio St Chicago IL 60611

CONNER, CINDY DIXON, publisher; b. Phila., Dec. 6, 1951; d. Robert Myatt and Maxine (Rivers) Dixon; m. Charles S. Conner, July 24, 1976; children—Robert Stockton, Jonathan Rivers. B.A., U. Miss., 1973; postgrad. Memphis State U., 1979. Asst. dir. univ. relations U. Tenn. Ctr. for Health Scis., Memphis, 1978-84; pub. Waterfowler's World, Germantown, Tenn., 1977—. Address: Water Fowl Publs Ltd PO Box 38306 Memphis TN 38183

CONNER, LINDA ANN, plant manager; b. County Jefferson, Iowa, June 18, 1941; d. Homer William and Helen Elizabeth (Edmund) Wiggins; m. Dwain H. Sutton, Sept. 26, 1955 (div. 1971); children—Larry D., Joel W., Bryan L.; m. 2d, C.D. Conner, Dec. 28, 1973; 1 stepdau., Cynthia. Student community coll., U. Iowa. Bookkeeper, sec. Am. Chain & Cable Co., 1963-69; office mgr. NML Ins. Co., Washington, Iowa, 1969-71; magistrate Keokuk County, Richland, Iowa, 1965-73; mgr. Pacemaker Bldgs. Co., Washington, Iowa, 1971-80; owner, mgr. Structural Components Corp., Washington, Iowa, 1978-80; plant mgr. Growmark Inc., Washington, Iowa, 1980—; controller 999 Corp., Washington, Iowa, 1980—. Author: Midwestern Meals in Minutes, 1983. Fin. chmn. Keokuk County Rep. Party, Siqourney, Iowa, 1983-85, mem. central com., 1965-73; sec. Richland Rep. Party, 1964—; former sec., den mother Boy Scouts Am., Richland; mem. SE Iowa Peace Officers, 1965-74; magistrate County of Keokuk, 1965-74. Mem. Washington (Iowa) C. of C. Methodist. Home: 209 Wasson St Richland IA 52585 Office: Growmark Inc Route 3 Box 17 Washington IA 52353

CONNER, SUSAN PUNZEL, history educator; b. Madison, Wis., Sept. 29, 1947; d. Ferdinand Frederick August and Mabel Katherine (Zellhoefer) Punzel; m. Ronald Joseph Conner, June 1, 1968. B.A. in History, Armstrong State U., 1969; M.A. in History, Fla. State U., 1974, Ph.D. in History, 1977. Instr., chmn. social sci. Calvary Day Sch., Savannah, Ga., 1969-72; instr. Ga. Tech. Inst., Atlanta, 1977-78; assoc. prof. history Tift Coll., Forsyth, Ga., 1978-82, prof. history, 1982—, Fuller E. Callaway prof. history, 1985—, chair social scis., 1978-85, chair div. arts and scis., 1985—, dir. archives, 1978—; cons. nat. register nominations, Forsyth, 1980—. Contbr. chpt. to books, articles to profl. jours. Bd. dirs. Middle Ga. Archives, Macon, 1983—; bd. dirs. Monroe Hist. Soc., Forsyth, 1983-85; sec.-treas. Monroe County C. of C., 1983-84, pres., 1984-85. Recipient NEH Newberry Summer Inst. award, 1978; Ga. Endowment to Humanities Semiquincentenary grantee, 1983; NEH travel grantee, 1985; Hist. Preservation Leadership award Ga. Clean Community Com., 1983. Mem. Ga. Assn. Historians (pres. 1981—), Am. Hist. Assn. Consortium on Revolutionary Europe, Soc. French Hist. Studies, Ga. Trust Historic Preservation, AAUW (grant honoree). Episcopalian. Club: Forsyth Woman's (pres. 1982-84). Home: 141 W Main St Forsyth GA 31029 Office: Tift Coll of Mercer U Tift College Dr Forsyth GA 31029

CONNERLY, DIANNA JEAN, business official; b. Urbana, Ill., June 7, 1947; d. Ellsworth Wayne and Imogene (Sundermeyer) Connerly; student Ill. Comml. Coll., 1967. Bookkeeper, Jerry Earl Pontiac, 1968-72; officer mgr. Jack Nicklaus Pontiac, 1972-76; office mgr. Simon Motors Inc., Palm Springs, Calif., 1977-83; bus. mgr., 1983—. Mem. Am. Bus. Women's Assn. (pub. relations dir. Trendsetter chpt. 1983—). Office: 78611 Highway 111 LaQuinta CA 92253

CONNERY, CAROL JEAN, marketing executive; b. Amarillo, Tex., Oct. 22, 1948; d. William Wayne and Joyce Jean (Forney) Connery; A.A., Christian Coll., 1969; B.J., U. Tex., Austin, 1971. Asst. dir. admissions Columbia (Mo.) Coll., 1971-80; exec. dir. nat. office Teenworld Scholarship Program, Overland Park, Kan., 1980-82; account exec. Mktg. Communications, Inc., Lenexa, Kans., 1983-86; account exec. Krupp/Taylor, Dallas, 1986—; cons. in field. Mem. Johnson County Bd. Realtors, Kans. Bd. Realtors, Mid-Am. Soc. Assn. Execs., Columbia Coll. Alumni Assn. Zeta Tau Alpha, Phi Theta Kappa (past nat. v.p.). Methodist. Home: Krupp-Taylor 545 E Carpenter Freeway Ste 1400 Irving TX 75062 Office: 545 E Carpenter Freeway Suite 1400 Irving TX 75062

CONN-LEVIN, NANCY BARBARA, health educator, writer, researcher; b. Newark, Mar. 16, 1952; d. Ralph Irving and Gertrude (Zacks) Conn; B.A., Sarah Lawrence Coll., 1974; postgrad. Princeton U., 1974-75; M.A., Goddard Coll., 1980; m. Eric M. Levin, Dec. 17, 1972; 1 dau., Amanda Conn-Levin. Cons. women's health, Manahawkin, N.J., 1976-80; cons. Ocean County Coll., CEA of Ocean County, Ocean County NOW, Women's Counseling and Community Services, Childbirth Edn. Assn. Ocean County, La Leche League of Tuckerton, 1977-80; dir. Health Info. Assocs., Inc., Plantation, Fla., 1982-85; adult educator Broward County Sch. Bd. (Fla.), 1983-85; adj. faculty Broward Community Coll., 1984-85; cons. Broward County Library; writer, researcher on health promotion, Ocean, N.J., 1986—; cons. on health info. Co-coordinator East Windsor (N.J.) NOW, 1974-75. Mem. Nat. Women's Health Network, Am. Public Health Assn., AAUW, Internat. Childbirth Edn. Assn., Am. Assn. for Counseling and Devel., Nat. Family Life Edn. Network. Compiler women's health info. and resources; developer, producer audio tape for relaxation tng. Wellness Through Relaxation, 1985. Home: 12 Cambridge Way Ocean NJ 07712 Office: Health Info Assocs PO Box 163 Oakhurst NJ 07755

CONNOLLY, LINDA LEE, insurance agent; b. Wichita, Kans., Dec. 31, 1946; d. Keith Leroy and Zada Mae (Carlson) England; student Wichita State U., 1965-67; grad. Wichita Bus. Coll., 1965, South Jersey Profl. Sch. Ins., 1979; student Comml. Lines Sch., U. Nev., 1981; m. Jan. 6, 1968; children—Robert, Michael. Asst. office supt. 3M Corp., Englewood, N.J., 1970-71; v.p. Heritage Ins. Agy., Vineland, N.J., 1974—. Mem. Ind. Agts. Assn., Profl. Agts. Assn., Mothers Against Drunk Driving. Methodist. Club: Vineland Jr. Soccer League. Home: 1609 Wills Pl Vineland NJ 08360 Office: 606 Landis Ave Vineland NJ 08360

CONNOLLY, MARGARET THERESA, real estate broker; b. County Monaghan, Ireland, Aug. 31, 1942; came to U.S., 1959, naturalized, 1966; d. Terrence and Elizabeth (McGivney) Clarke; m. Thady J. Connolly, Apr. 24, 1965; children—Francis J., Christine M. Grad. Diakin Sch. Real Estate, N.Y., 1976; cert. Empire Sch. Real Estate, 1983. Pres., Connolly Realty Co. doing bus. as Active Realty, Washingtonville, N.Y., 1976—. Mem. Internat. Assn. Real Estate Appraisers, Nat. Assn. Female Execs. Democrat. Roman Catholic. Avocations: painting; gardening. Home: MD 1-Rt 208 Washingtonville NY 10992 Office: Active Realty RD 2 Rt 208 Washingtonville NY 10992

CONNOLLY, MICHAELA, college administrator, nun; b. N.Y.C., Apr. 12, 1945; d. Michael James and Mary Bridget (Kiernan) C. B.S. in Edn., Dominican Coll., 1968; M.S. in Edn., Fordham U., 1973. Cert. elem. edn., N.Y.; joined Sisters of St. Dominic, Roman Catholic Ch., 1963. Tchr. Holy Spirit Sch., N.Y.C., 1967-68, St. Luke Sch., N.Y.C., 1968-72; dir. pub. relations Dominican Coll., Orangeburg, N.Y., 1972-73, dir. devel., 1973—; cons. Council Advancement Small Colls., 1975-77. Mem. Orangetown Cable TV Adv. Com., 1976—; mem. adv. bd. Rockland County Vicariate, 1979—. Named to Outstanding Young Women Am., U.S. Jaycees, 1977. Mem. Council Advancement and Support Edn., Rockland County Assn., Rockland Devel. Officers. Democrat. Home: 33 N Magnolia St Pearl River NY 10965 Office: Dominican Coll 10 Western Hwy Orangeburg NY 10962

CONNOLLY, PATRICIA MARY, accounting firm executive; b. Bronx, N.Y., Feb. 17, 1932; d. Eugene Joseph and Mary Catherine (Travers) C.; B.S., St. Joseph's U., Phila., 1963; M.S.W., Fordham U., 1965. With Catholic Social Services, Phila., 1954-63, 65-66; supr. homemaking services Bronx (N.Y.) Cath. Charities, 1966-68; dir. South Bronx Project, 1968-72; cons. Fedn. Protestant Welfare Agys., 1972-81; asst. to PIC Pub. Sector Practice; human resources coordinator Touche, Ross & Co., C.P.A.s, N.Y.C., 1981—; field instr. NYU; adj. lectr. Lehman Coll. Bd. mgrs. Citizens Advice Bur.; Sec. Bowery Planning Task Force, 1973-76, V.p., 1977-79; mem. community adv. bd. Montefiore Hosp., N.Y.C.; mem. Neighborhood Com. Asphalt Green, Carl Schurz Park Assn. Mem. Acad. Cert. Social Workers, Nat. Assn. Social Workers, Fordham U. Alumni Assn., Nat. Assn. Female Execs., Internat. Assn. Personnel Women, Am. Soc. Tng. and Devel., AAUW, Greater N.Y. Com. Women and Alcoholism, Regional Coalition on Services to Women with Drug and Alcohol Problems. Author manuals, chpts. in books. Home: 75 East End Ave Apt 5D New York NY 10028 Office: 1 World Trade Center 86th Floor New York NY 10048

CONNOR, BETTY JOYCE BAKER, nurse, educator; b. Philpot, Ky., May 3, 1937; d. George Henry and Frances Norma (Crutcher) Baker; m. Johnny Moore Connor, Nov. 23, 1975; children—Karen, Kimberly, Matthew. R.N., Owensboro-Daviess County Hosp. (Ky.) in assn. with Murray State U., 1959; B.S.N., U. Evansville, 1973, M.S.N. 1984; M.S., Murray State U., 1977. Staff nurse med. surg. unit Jewish Hosp., Louisville, 1959-60, CCU and ICU, 1967-69; supr. nursing staff McFarland Hosp., Lebanon, Tenn., 1960-61, instr. Sch. Practical Nursing, McFarland Hosp. in assn. with U. Tenn., 1961-62; staff nurse Lloyd Noland Hosp., Fairfield, Ala., team leader med.-surg. units, 1962-64; head nurse dept. urology Fresno Med. Group (Calif.), 1965, head nurse pediatric neurology dept., 1965-67; staff pub. health nurse family planning dept. Louisville—Jefferson County Health Dept., 1969-71; asst. prof.

nursing level I, U. Ky. Henderson Community Coll. Campus, 1973-75; asst. dir. nursing Our Lady of Mercy Hosp., Owensboro, Ky., 1975-76; instr. Owensboro Vocat. Sch., 1977; asst. prof. pathology dept. pub. health Palmer Coll., Davenport, Iowa, 1977-79; asst. prof. nursing level I, Ky. Wesleyan Coll., Owensboro, 1980-84. Mem. Nat. League Nursing Ky. League Nursing, Ky. Constituent League, AAUW, Wesleyan Women. Baptist. Club: Christian Women's. Home: 3848 S Griffith Ave Owensboro KY 42301

CONNOR, MARY ANNE, civic worker; b. Watertown, Wis., Aug. 18, 1930; d. Arthur Robert and Esther Florence (Mittag) Jaeger; student schs. Watertown; m. William Thomas Connor, Sept. 6, 1952; 1 dau., Mary Kay. Billing clk. Watertown Daily Times, 1955-72; machine operator, Owen Glove Lining, Watertown, 1973-75; office mgr. Feisst Liquor Co., Watertown, 1975-76; cook, Elks Club, Watertown, 1974-85. Sec., Watertown Municipal Band, 1950—; pres. local chpt. Am. Legion Aux., 1959-61, 77-79, county pres., 1960-62, dist. pres., 1965-67, dist. bowling chmn., 1966—, WALA state bowling dir., tournament mgr., 1979—; corr. sec. Watertown Meml. Hosp. Aux., 1980-81, membership chmn., 1978-79, chmn. fund raiser, 1981; active Watertown Hist. Soc., St. Mark's Ladies Aid; bd. dirs., blood bank chmn. ARC, 1977—; exec. sec. Watertown chpt. ARC, 1981—, also mem. speakers bur.; chmn. Jefferson County Govt. Day, 1972-83; sec.-treas. Fourth of July parade com., 1981—; vol. VA Hosp., Madison, Wis., sec.-treas., mem. exec. com., 1983—; bd. dirs. United Way, v.p., 1986—; hon. parade marshal, 1976. Recipient plaques Am. Legion, 1977, 78, 83. Mem. Watertown Women's Bowling Assn., Watertown VFW, Watertown Musicians Assn. Local 469 (rec. sec. 1977—), Amvets Aux. Lutheran. Clubs: Saturday, Elks Ladies, Wethonkitha, Turner Aux., Oconomowoc Band. Editor, The Overlook, 1980—. Home: 307 9th St Watertown WI 53094 Office: 314 Main St Watertown WI 53094

CONNOR, MARY KATHERINE, sales executive; b. Milw., Sept. 10, 1954; d. Robert Thomas and Dorothy Ann (Lipperer) Makie; m. Patrick James Connor, Oct. 11, 1975; children—Colin Robert, Kristy Ann. A.A., Coll. St. Benedict, 1972; student St. Cloud U., 1973; B.A., Western Ill. U., 1975; postgrad. St. Johns River Community Coll., 1981. Announcer WKAI, Macomb, Ill., 1974-75; talk show announcer KWJS, Arlington, Tex., 1976-77; news announcer KXOL, Fort Worth, 1977-79; news dir. WSUZ, East Palatka Fla., 1979-81; sales mgr. WIYD, Palatka, Fla., 1981—. Pres. Toys for Tots, Palatka, 1984; exec. dir. Arts Council Greater Palatka, 1981-83. Named Woman of Yr., Beta Sigma Phi, 1985. Democrat. Roman Catholic. Clubs: Pilot (pub. relations dir. 1982—), Garden (pres. 1982-85), Art League (pub. relations 1984-85), St. Johns River Community Coll. Women's (pres. 1979-81) (Palatka). Avocations: basket weaving; crafts. Office: WIYD 900 River St Palatka FL 32077

CONNOR, SUSAN SCHOLLE, lawyer; b. Detroit, Sept. 9, 1943; d. August and Kathleen (Jones) Scholle; m. John Thomas Connor, Jr., Dec. 18, 1965; children—Seanna, Marion, Josh. B.A., U. Mich., 1963; J.D., Harvard U., 1967; student U. Aix en Provence, 1962-63; postgrad. Law Sch. Moscow State U., 1974-76. Bar: N.J. 1968, D.C. 1972. Atty., Newark Legal Services Project, 1967-69; legis. counsel Gov. Richard Hughes, Trenton, 1970, Senator Philip A. Hart, Washington, 1973-74; adminstrv. officer UN Secretariat, N.Y.C., 1976-79; counsel Presl. Reorgn. Project, Office Mgmt. and Budget, Washington, 1979-81; counsel Pan Am. Health Orgn., Washington, 1981—. Bd. dirs. Women's Resource Devel. Group, Washington, 1983. Mem. ABA, Am. Soc. Internat. Law, Inter-Am. Bar Assn., Washington Fgn. Law Soc. (bd. dirs. 1983—). Phi Beta Kappa. Democrat. Episcopalian. Club: Chevy Chase (Md.). Home: 12 Primrose St Chevy Chase MD 20815 Office: Pan Am Health Orgn 525 23d St NW Washington DC 20037

CONNORS, DORSEY (MRS. JOHN E. FORBES), TV and radio commentator, newspaper columnist; b. Chgo.; d. William J. and Sara (MacLean) Connors; B.A. cum laude, U. Ill.; m. John E. Forbes; 1 dau., Stephanie. Appeared on Personality Profiles, Sta. WGN-TV, Chgo., 1948, Dorsey Connors Show, Sta. WMAQ-TV, Chgo., 1949-58, 61-63, Armchair Travels, Sta. WMAQ-TV, 1952-55, Home Show, NBC, 1954-57, Haute Couture Fashion Openings, NBC, Paris, France, 1954, 58, Dorsey Connors program, Sta. WGN, 1958-61, Tempo Nine, WGN-TV, 1961, Society in Chgo., Sta. WMAQ-TV, 1964; floor reporter Sta. WGN-TV, Republican Nat. Conv., Chgo., Democratic Nat. Conv., Los Angeles, 1960; writer column Hi! I'm Dorsey Connors, Chgo. Sun Times, 1965—. Founder Ill. Epilepsy League; mem. women's bd. USO; mem. woman's bd. Children's Home and Aid Soc. Mem. AFTRA, Screen Actor's Guild, Nat. Acad. TV Arts and Scis., Soc. Midland Authors, Guild of Chgo. Hist. Soc., Chi Omega. Roman Catholic. Author: Gadgets Galore, 1953; Save Time, Save Money, Save Yourself, 1972. Office: Chgo Sun Times 401 N Wabash Chicago IL 60611

CONOLEY, JOANN SHIPMAN, educational administrator; b. Bartlesville, Okla., July 19, 1931; d. Joe and Frances Loomis (Wall) Shipman; B.S. in English and Edn., Midwestern State U., Wichita Falls, Tex., 1968, M.S. in English and Edn., 1971; postgrad. Tex. A&M U., 1978—; m. Travis A. Conoley, Oct. 29, 1976; children by previous marriage—James F. Lane, Joe Scott Lane, Kimberly Diane Lane. Tchr. 3d grade Queen of Peace Sch., Wichita Falls, 1968-69; lang. arts team leader, jr. high sch. Wichita Falls Public Schs., 1969-74; fed. programs dir., reading coordinator Rockdale (Tex.) Public Schs., 1974-78, adminstrv. asst. to supt., 1978-79, asst. supt. adminstrn. and instrn., 1979—; reading cons. ALCOA, 1977—. Bd. dirs. Rockdale Public Library, 1975-79, pres., 1976-77; bd. dirs. Am. Cancer Soc. Cert. elem. and high sch. tchr., reading/lang. arts coordinator, reading cons., adminstr., Tex. Mem. NEA, Tex. State Tchrs. Assn., Nat. Council Tchrs. English, Internat. Reading Assn., Assn. Compensatory Edn. Tex. (exec. bd. 1977-83), Assn. Supervision and Curriculum Devel., Alpha Chi, Delta Kappa Gamma, Kappa Delta Pi. Home: 405 Bounds St Rockdale TX 76567 Office: Box 632 Rockdale TX 76567

CONOVER, NELLIE COBURN, retail furniture co. exec.; b. Lebanon, Ohio, Dec. 21, 1921; d. Frank C. and Isabel (Murphy) Coburn; student public schs.; m. Lawrence E. Conover, Jan. 11, 1941; children—Lawrence R., Carol, David C., Constance, Christina. Co-founder, 1949, since exec. sec.-treas. Larry Conover Furniture & Appliance, Inc., and predecessor, Milford, Ohio, also trustee co. pension fund. Mem. Milford C. of C., Cin. Hist. Soc., Milford Hist. Soc., DAR. Democrat. Roman Catholic. Address: 438 Main St Milford OH 45150

CONRAD, SALLY, state legislator. Mem. Vermont Senate, 1985—. Office: Vermont Senate State Capitol Montpelier VT 05602*

CONROY, PATRICIA FIORE, marketing and communications company executive, marketing consultant; b. Orange, N.J., Aug. 3, 1948; d. Nicholas S. and Julia (Picciuto) Fiore; m. David T. Conroy, Aug. 16, 1969 (div. Mar. 1978); 1 child, Kristin Marie. Student Fashion Inst. Tech., 1967; Assoc. Arts and Applied Sci., Fairleigh Dickinson U., 1973; student Parsons Sch. Design, 1977-78, Montclair State Coll., 1981-82. Designer Regal Knitwear, N.Y., S.C., 1967-69; buyer, fashion coordinator Brooks/Sealfon, N.J., 1969-76; prodn. coordinator H.G.O.-Walter Thompson, N.Y.C., 1976-77; assoc. pub., sr. research editor RAM Data Corp., N.Y.C., Chgo., 1977-80; mktg. mgr. Alba-Waldensian, N.Y.C., N.C., 1980-82; pres., owner P.C. Fiore & Assocs., Montclair, N.J., 1982—; cons. Kimberly-Clark, Neenah, Wis., 1984-85. Fellow North Jersey Advt. Club, Underfashion Club, C. of C. Montclair. Democrat. Roman Catholic. Avocations: aerobics; swimming; gormet cooking; sewing. Home: 23 Pease Ave Verona NJ 07044 Office: PC Fiore & Assocs Inc 215 Glen Ridge Ave Montclair NJ 07042

CONSIDINE, JILL, banker, state official Former pres., chief exec. officer The First Women's Bank, N.Y.C.; supt. banking dept. State of N.Y., N.Y.C., 1986—. Address: State of NY Banking Dept 2 Rector St New York NY 10006*

CONSIGNEY, JENNIFER ANN, personnel executive; b. Lake Charles, La., Apr. 18, 1947; d. Richard Joseph and Cathryn (Williams) Benton; m. Danny Charles Consigney, July 4, 1982; 1 son, Duc. Student, McNeese U., 1965-66. Personnel services coordinator So. Nev. Meml. Hosp., Las Vegas, 1971-80; dir. personnel Valley Hosp. Med. Ctr., Las Vegas, 1980—. Mem. Am. Soc. Personnel Adminstrn., Am. Soc. Hosp. Personnel Adminstrn. Democrat. Office: Valley Hosp Med Ctr 620 Shadow LN Las Vegas NV 89106

CONSTANT, PATRICIA REED, lawyer; b. Chandler, Ariz., Mar. 14, 1949; d. Charles William and Patricia (Elliott) Reed; m. Anthony F. Constant, Oct. 12, 1976 (div. 1981); children—Rebecca Kay, Jennifer Leigh. B.A. summa cum laude, Tex. A&I U., 1976; J.D., U. Tex., 1979. Bar: Tex. 1979, U.S. Dist. Ct. (so. dist.) Tex. 1980, U.S. Ct. Appeals (5th cir.) 1984. Assoc. Wood & Burney, Corpus Christi, Tex., 1979-85, ptnr., 1985—. Bd. dirs. Beautify Corpus Christi Assn., 1981-85; mem. Corpus Christi Bldg. Standards Rev. Bd., 1984—. Mem. ABA, Tex. Bar Assn., Nueces County Bar Assn. (sec. 1980-81), Nueces County Young Lawyers Assn. (dir. 1982-84, pres. 1984-85). Democrat. Episcopalian. Home: 3335 San Antonio Corpus Christi TX 78411 Office: Wood & Burney 1700 First City Tower II Corpus Christi TX 78478

CONSTANTINI, JOANN M., utility company administrator; b. Danbury, Conn., July 30, 1948; d. William Joseph and Mathilda Josephine (Ressler) C. B.A., Coll. White Plains, 1970; M. Orgnl. Behavior, U. Hartford, 19. Psychiat. social worker N.Y. State Dept Mental Hygiene, Wassaic, 1970-73; with Northeast Utilities Co., Hartford, Conn., 1973—, methods analyst, 1979-82, records adminstr., 1983—. Bd. dirs. Meriden YWCA, Conn., 1976-78, My Sister's Place shelter for women, Hartford, Conn., 1984—; vol. House of Bread soup kitchen, Hartford, 1984—. Mem. NOW (co-founder, pres. Meriden chpt. 1975-77), Assn. Records Mgrs. and Adminstrs. (dir., sec. 1984-85, fin. dir. 1985-86, nat. vice-chmn. public utilities industry action com. 1984-86), Electric Council New Eng. (chmn. records com. 1985-86), Assn. for Image and Info. Mgmt. (dir. 1984-86), Northeast Utilities Women's Forum (co-founder, treas. 1983-85), Coll. White Plains Alumnae Assn. Democrat. Roman Catholic. Avocations: bird-watching, antique collecting, cooking. Home: 12 Gaylord Ln Burlington CT 06013 Office: Northeast Utilities Co PO Box 270 Hartford CT 06141

CONSTANTS, DOROTHY MARIE, club woman; b. Newark, Feb. 5, 1928; d. Henry J. and Marie (McNamee) Trautfetter; m. Alfred C. Constants, Jr., July 14, 1951; children—Alfred C., III, David, Michael, Stephen. Student Drake Secretarial Sch., 1948, Traphagen Sch. Design, 1949. Exec. sec. Westinghouse Lamp Div., Bloomfield, N.J., 1945-51. Pres. Oakland Woman's Club, N.J., 1967-69, Don Bosco High Sch. Mothers Guild, Ramsey, N.J., 1971, Valley PTO, Oakland, N.J., 1972, Friends of Pub. Library, Oakland, 1982-84, N.J. State Fedn. Women's Clubs, New Brunswick, 1984-86. Named Woman of Yr., Women's Club of Oakland, 1975. Mem. Douglas Coll. Alumni Assn. (hon.). Roman Catholic. Avocations: cruising; reading; creative handiwork. Home: 168 Page Dr Oakland NJ 07436 Office: NJ State Fedn Women's Clubs 55 Clifton Ave New Brunswick NJ 08901

CONTARDO, BARBARA JOAN, market research officer; b. Everett, Mass., Mar. 15, 1943; d. Leonard and Rose Mary (Capuano) C. B.S. in Bus. Adminstrn., Boston U., 1964. Control analyst Am. Mut. Ins. Co., Wakefield, Mass., 1964-65; market research analyst H.P. Hood & Sons, Boston, 1965-67, with New Eng. Life Ins. Co., Boston, 1968—, sr. market research analyst, 1970—, research officer, 1983—. Mem. Am. Mktg. Assn. (pres. Boston chpt. 1976-77), Advt. Research Found., Life Ins. Market Research Assn., Assn. Consumer Research. Roman Catholic. Avocations: gardening; downhill skiing. Home: 77 Englewood Ave Everett MA 02149 Office: New Eng Life Ins Co 501 Boylston St Boston MA 02116

CONTI, DONNA LEE, nurse; b. Providence, June 20, 1956; d. Michael and Judith Rebecca (Altman) Umbriano; m. Richard Loreto Conti, July 15, 1975 (div. 1980). A.S., Community Coll. R.I., 1982. R.N., R.I. Lic. practical nurse Kent County Meml. Hosp., Warwick, R.I., 1978-82; nurse, St. Joseph's Hosp., Providence, R.I., 1982-83; admitting nurse Phoenix Bapt. Hosp., 1983—. Mem. Admitting Assn. Ariz. Democrat. Roman Catholic. Avocations: bicycling, reading, swimming, music. Home: 5022 W Beverly Ln Glendale AZ 85306 Office: 6025 N 20th Ave Phoenix AZ 85015

CONTRERAS-SWEET, MARIA, company executive; b. Guadaljara, Mex., Dec. 24, 1955; came to U.S., 1960; d. Rafael Quintero and Maria Guadalupe (Torres) Contreras; m. Raphael Raymond Sweet, Feb. 7, 1981; children—Rafael, Francesca. A.S. in Sec. Legal, Mt. San Antonio Coll., 1975; B.S. in Polit. Sci., Calif. State U.-Los Angeles, 1977. Field rep. Calif. State Speaker State Legis., Los Angeles, 1974-75; adminstrv. asst. Senator Joseph Montoya, Calif. State Senate, Los Angeles, 1975-79; dist. mgr. U.S. Census Bur., Dept. Commerce, Los Angeles, 1979-80; dir. pub. affairs 7up Bottling Co., Westinghouse Beverage Group, Los Angeles, 1980—. Bd. Mex.-Am. Opportunity Found., Los Angeles, 1982—, Rossi Youth Found., Los Angeles, 1978—; fund com. mem. E. Los Angeles Little Sisters, 1983—; adv. council Hispanic Women's Council, Los Angeles, 1982—; active Industry Environ. Council, Sacramento. Recipient Mother of Yr. award La Clinica Familiar del Barrio, Los Angeles, 1983; Humanitarian award Rossi Youth Found., 1983; Woman of Yr. award Mex.-Am. Opportunity Found., 1983. Mem. Internat. Assn. Bus. Communicators, Calif./Nev. Soft Drink Assn., RecyCal (fin. chair.). Democrat. Roman Catholic. Office: 7up Bottling Co 3220 E 26th St Vernon CA 90023

CONWAY, JANET VAIL, financial company executive; b. Washington, Aug. 6, 1952; d. Earle Leslie and Aida Elizabeth (Barnhart) Vail; m. James Edward Conway, Sept. 24, 1977. B.A., Maryville Coll., 1973; J.D., Franklin Pierce Law Ctr., 1976. Bar: N.H. 1979. Legis. bill drafter Legis. Reference Bur., Springfield, Ill., 1976-77; legis. atty. Office Legis. Services, Concord, N.H., 1978-80; rating analyst Standard & Poor's Corp., N.Y.C., 1980-81, rating specialist, 1981-82, rating officer, 1982-84, asst. v.p., 1984-85, v.p., 1986—. Bd. dirs. Maryville Coll., 1986—. Recipient Corp. Achievementaward for new product devel. McGraw-Hill, 1985. Mem. ABA, N.H. Bar Assn., Maryville Coll. Alumni Assn. (exec. bd. 1982-85). Episcopalian. Office: Standard & Poor's Corp 25 Broadway New York NY 10004

CONWAY, JILL KATHRYN KER, former college president; b. Hillston, New South Wales, Australia, Oct. 9, 1934; d. William Innis and Evelyn Mary (Adames) Ker; B.A., U. Sydney (Australia), 1958; Ph.D., Harvard U., 1969; hon. degrees: U. N.B., 1974, Mt. Holyoke Coll., 1975, Amherst Coll., 1976, York U., Toronto, 1977, U. N.H., 1977, Westfield State Coll., 1979, Mt. St. Vincent U., Halifax, N.S., 1980, Wesleyan U., 1980, U. Mass., Amherst, 1981, Williams Coll., 1982, U. Toronto, 1984, Queen's U., 1984, McGill U., 1985, SUNY, Potsdam, 1986; m. John James Conway, Dec. 22, 1962. Asst. prof. history U. Toronto (Ont., Can.), 1964-71, assoc. prof., 1971-75, v.p., 1973-75; pres. Smith Coll., Northampton, Mass., 1975-85; vis. scholar MIT, 1985-86; dir. Merrill Lynch & Co., Colgate-Palmolive, Arthur D. Little, Inc., Brascan Ltd. Trustee Hampshire Coll., 1976—, Clarke Sch. for Deaf, 1975-85, William H. Donner Found., 1976-86, Acad. Music, Northampton, 1975-85, Coll. Retirement Equities Fund; bd. overseers Harvard U., 1976-82; bd. dirs. Council Fin. Aid to Edn., Inc., 1981—; 2d v.p. New Eng. Colls. Fund, Inc., from 1981, pres., 1984-85; mem. Ind. Sector, Washington, 1981-85. Mem. Am. Antiquarian Soc., Mass. Hist. Soc., Am. Hist. Assn., Assn. Ind. Colls. and Univs. in Mass. (vice chmn. 1982-83, chmn. 1983-84). Research, numerous publs. on Am. social and intellectual history, history of family life and sex roles, history of edn.

CONWAY, KATHRYN LOUISE, university media administrator; b. Henry County, Va., Jan. 30, 1950; d. Richard Earl and Josephine Hope (Leftwich) C.; B.F.A., U. N.C., Chapel Hill, 1975, M.A. in Communications, 1985, cert. univ. mgmt. devel. program, 1981; cert. profl. mgmt. Young Execs. Inst., 1983. Advt. writer Sta. WTOB, Winston Salem, N.C., 1969; research asst. U. N.C., Chapel Hill, 1971, 73, photographer Photo Lab., 1974-75, assoc. dir. Media and Instructional Support Center, 1976—, dir. telecommunications devel., 1982-85; chairperson bd. Sta. WXYC-FM; mem. steering com., interim bd. dirs. N.C. Public Radio Assn.; lead actress Desperadoes, Pocket Theatre, off-off-Broadway, 1978, The Fate of my Joy teleplay Sta. WUNC-TV, Chapel Hill, 1978; mem. Chapel Hill Adv. Com. on Cable TV, 1979; mem. adv. com. on planning process U N.C., Chapel Hill Lectr. in field. Mem. Am. Mgmt. Assn. (cert. Fundamentals Data Communication), Am. Assn. Higher Edn., N.C. Ind. Film and Video Assn., N.C. Tech. Working Group in Communications (N.C. Microelectronics Ctr.), Functional Working Group in Video (N.C. Microelectronics Ctr.), Assn. Edni. Communications and Techs., U. N.C. Mgrs. Assn. (pres. 1983-86). Democrat. Home: Route 9 Box 361 Chapel Hill NC 27514 Office: PARS Bldg 312 208 N Columbia St Chapel Hill NC 27514

CONWAY, MAUREEN ANN, management consultant; b. Hoboken, N.J., July 25, 1945; d. Michael A. and Margaret (Spiegel) C.; B.A., William Paterson Coll., 1966; M.A., Montclair State Coll., 1971; M.B.A., Temple U., 1980. Tchr. math. high sch., Palisade Park, N.J., 1966-68; mem. tech. staff Bell Tel. Labs., Whippany, N.J., 1968-75; dir. info. systems IUIMC, Phila., 1975-83; dir. ops. CCA, Boston, 1983—. Bd. dirs. Penns Landing Sq. Condominium, 1977-83. Mem. IEEE, Assn. Computing Machinery, Am. Mgmt. Assn., Beta Gamma Sigma. Office: CCA Four Cambridge Ctr Cambridge MA 02142

CONWAY, PATRICIA MAUREEN, financial consultant; b. Ithaca, N.Y., Mar. 19, 1960; d. Donald Peter and Gladys Janet (Webster) Conway. B.S., Purdue U., 1982. Sr. fin. cons. Peterson & Co., N.Y.C., 1982—, recruiter, 1983—. Mem. Nat. Orgn. Female Execs. Republican. Roman Catholic. Home: 74 W 85th St Apt 1 New York NY 10024

CONWAY, SUSAN MARGARET, marketing executive, pension fund planner; b. Boston, May 1, 1958; d. Robert Thomas and Margaret Mary (Owen) C. A.B. in Econs., Mount Holyoke Coll., 1980; M.B.A., Harvard U., 1984. Analyst corp. fin. Smith Barney, N.Y.C., 1980-82; assoc. consumer markets Paine Webber, Inc., N.Y.C., 1984-85; mktg. mgr. expansion industries Am. Express, 1985—. Group leader Al-Anon, N.Y.C. and Boston, 1983—; big sister Big Sisters of N.Y., Bklyn., 1984—; class agt. fund raising Class of 1980 Mount Holyoke Coll., 1984—. Democrat. Roman Catholic. Avocations: tennis; skiing; running; art history; reading. Home: 18 Commonwealth Ave Dedham MA 02026 Office: Am Express World Fin Ctr New York NY 10285

CONWAY DE MACARIO, EVERLY, immunologist; b. Buenos Aires, Argentina, Apr. 20, 1939; came to U.S., 1974, naturalized, 1980; d. Delfin E. and Maria Gloria (Benatuil) Conway; Ph.D. in Pharmacy, Nat. U. Buenos Aires, 1960, Ph.D. in Biochemistry, 1962; m. Alberto J. L. Macario, Mar. 16, 1963; children—Alex, Everly. Research fellow Nat. Acad. Medicine Argentina, Buenos Aires, 1962-63; head lab. oncology and immunology Argentinian Assn. against Cancer, Buenos Aires, 1966-77; chief immunology Sch. Medicine, Buenos Aires, 1967-68; research fellow dept. tumor-biology Karolinska Inst., Stockholm, 1969-71; sr. research scientist Lab. Cell Biology, NRC Italy, Rome, 1971-73; vis. scientist Internat. Agy. Research on Cancer, WHO, Lyon, France, 1973-74; vis. scientist Brown U., Providence, 1974-76; research scientist Lab. Immunology, N.Y. State Dept. Health, Albany, 1976—; prof. Sch. Pub. Health Scis., 1986—, mem. admissions com., 1986—. Recipient Prof. J. M. Mezzadra award Nat. U. Buenos Aires, 1969; Travel award to Eng., 2d Internat. Immunology Congress, 1974; Gold medal Argentinian Soc. Biochemistry, 1980; Hans Osterman Found. grantee, Sweden, 1969; Sir Samuel Scott of Yews Trust grantee, Sweden, 1970; Winifred Cullis grantee Internat. Fedn. Univ. Women, 1972; NATO research grantee, 1975, 81; Dept. Energy grantee, 1981, 84; Travel awardee to China, 1985. Mem. Scandinavian Soc. Immunology, Italian Assn. Immunologists, French Soc. Immunology (travel award 1974), Am. Assn. Immunologists (chmn. com. on status of women 1980—, mem. edn. com. 1982-87, travel award to Australia 1977), Am. Soc. Microbiology. Co-editor: Monoclonal Antibodies Against Bacteria, 1985. Assoc. editor profl. jour., 1986—. Contbr. articles in field to profl. jours. Home: 18 Carriage Rd Delmar NY 12054 Office: Wadsworth Center Labs and Research Lab Immunology Empire State Plaza Albany NY 12201

CONWELL, ESTHER MARLY, physicist; b. N.Y.C., May 23, 1922; d. Charles and Ida (Korn) C.; B.A., Bklyn. Coll., 1942; M.S., U. Rochester, N.Y., 1945; Ph.D., U. Chgo., 1948; m. Abraham A. Rothberg, Sept. 30, 1945; 1 son, Lewis J. Instr., Bklyn. Coll., 1946-51; mem. tech. staff Bell Telephone Labs., 1951-52; physicist GTE Labs., Bayside, N.Y., 1952-61; mgr. dept. physics, 1961-72; Abby Rockefeller Mauze prof. M.I.T., 1972; prin. scientist Xerox Corp., Webster, N.Y., 1972-80, research fellow, 1981—; vis. prof. U. Paris, 1962-63; mem. adv. commn. engrng. NSF, 1978-81. Fellow IEEE, Am. Phys. Soc. Author: High Field Transport in Semiconductors, 1967; mem. editorial bd. Jour. Applied Physics, IEEE, Nat. Acad. Engrng.; contbr. numerous articles in field; patentee in field. Office: 800 Phillips Rd Webster NY 14580

CONWELL, THERESA GALLO, insurance company executive; b. Utica, N.Y., Mar. 6, 1947; d. Ernest and Anna (Caiazzo) Gallo; m. Charles Ray Conwell, Aug. 19, 1978. B.S.Ed., SUNY-Potsdam, 1968; M.A.Ed., SUNY-Cortland, 1978; Cert. tchr., N.Y.; C.L.U.; chartered fin. cons. Tchr. pub. schs., Clinton, N.Y., 1969-78, Portland, Conn., 1978-80; supr. mktg. services Phoenix Mut. Life Ins. Co., Hartford, Conn., 1980-82, assoc. mgr. agt. tng., 1982-84, mgr. agt. tng., 1984-85, dir. agt./mgmt. devel., 1985—; speaker to small bus. orgns., women's groups, N.Y., New Eng., 1986—. Mem. New Eng. Tng. Dir.'s Assn., Nat. Assn. Life Underwriters, Internat. Assn. Fin. Planners, Women's Life Underwriters Council, Nat. Assn. Female Execs., NOW. Democrat. Avocations: tennis; golf; swimming; aerobics; reading. Home: 7 Diane Dr Cromwell CT 06416 Office: Phoenix Mut Life Ins Co One American Row Hartford CT 06115

CONWELL, VIRGINIA DONLEY, librarian; b. Carlsbad, N.Mex., Jan. 3, 1921; d. William Guy and Frances Acree (Guthrie) Donley; m. Robert E.M. Conwell, Aug. 8, 1943 (dec. 1958); children—Elizabeth Conwell Shapiro, Virginia Conwell Hall. A.B., U. N.Mex., 1944; library credential U. So. Calif., 1962. Librarian, Montebello (Calif.) Unified Sch. Dist., 1962—. Files chmn. Downey Alumnae Panhellenic, 1978—. Mem. Calif. Media and Library Assn., Mortarboard, Chi Omega, Phi Alpha Theta. Democrat. Episcopalian. Clubs: Army Navy Country, Downey Alumnae Panhellenic. Address: 8132 Primrose Ln Downey CA 90240

COOK, ANN JENNALIE, English educator; b. Wewoka, Okla., Oct. 19, 1934; d. Arthur Holly and Bertha Maybelle (Stafford) C.; m. Howard Lee Harrod, Mar. 31, 1956 (div. 1971); children—Lee Ann, Amy Ceil; m. John Donelson Whalley, Sept. 10, 1975. B.A., U. Okla., 1956, M.A., 1959; Ph.D., Vanderbilt U., 1972. Tchr. English, drama, journalism pub. schs., N.C. and Conn., 1958-61, 64; instr. English, U. Okla., Norman, 1956-57, So. Conn. State Coll., New Haven, 1962-63; asst. prof. English, U. S.C., Columbia, 1972-74; exec. sec. Shakespeare Assn. Am., Nashville, 1975—; asst. prof. English, Vanderbilt U., Nashville, 1977-82, assoc. prof., 1982—; organizer world Shakespeare Congress, 1976, co-organizer 1981, 86; exec. com. Internat. Shakespeare Assn., 1981—; bd. dirs. Assn. Creative Theatre, Edn. and Research 1981—, Shakespeare Santa Cruz Festival, 1982—; trustee Folger Shakespeare Library, 1985—. Author: The Privileged Playgoers of Shakespeare's London, 1576-1640, 1981. Editor: Shakespeare Studies, 1973-80. Mem. editorial bd. Shakespeare Studies, 1980—, Shakespeare Quar., 1981—, Early English and Renaissance Drama, 1982—. Contbr. articles to profl. jours. Bd. dirs. Friends of Cheekwood, 1974-78, Symphony Guild, 1977-79, Ballet Soc., 1975-80, Ensemble Theater Co., 1978-79, Nashville. Fellow Danforth Found., 1967-72, Rockefeller Found., 1984, Guggenheim Found., 1985—. Mem. Nat. Lawyers Wives (rec. sec. 1981-82, bd. dirs. 1979—), Tenn. Bar aux. (pres. 1979-80), Shakespeare Inst. Birmingham U., Renaissance Soc. Am., MLA, South Atlantic MLA, Am. Soc. Theatre Research, Soc. Values in Higher Edn., Malone Soc. Episcopalian. Clubs: University, Hillwood Country (Nashville). Avocations: theater; reading; travel; gourmet cooking. Home: 91 Valley Forge St Nashville TN 37205 Office: Shakespeare Assn Am 6328 Vanderbilt Sta B Nashville TN 37235

COOK, APRIL BETH, retail store executive; b. Seattle, June 28, 1955; d. Donald Irvin and Sheila Beth (Buche) C.; m. Paul Victor Young, Mar. 23, 1975 (div. Aug. 1979). A.A. in Music Edn., Shoreline Community Coll., Seattle, 1973; cert. psychiat. nursing Baylor U., 1974; postgrad. in theology and psychology Concordia Coll., Milw., 1980—. With Tandy Leather Co., 1979—, store mgr., St. Petersburg, Fla., 1980-81, Tampa, Fla., 1981-83, product mgr., Fort Worth, 1983-85, warehouse supr., 1985-86, store mgr., Spokane, Wash., 1986—, also hazardous materials specialist, 1983—. Speaker Service-Youth Career Guidance, Tampa, 1981-83; sch. speaker Explorer Post, Longhorn council Boy Scouts Am., 1983-85. Served to pfc. U.S. Army, 1973-75. Recipient nat. sales awards Tandy Leather Co., 1979-83. Mem. Nat. Assn. Female Execs., Christian Bus. Women's Assn. Republican. Lutheran. Avocations: leathercraft; singing. Home: PO Box 7242 Spokane WA 99207 Office: Tandy Leather Co E 18 Indiana Ave Spokane WA 99207

COOK, BLANCHE WIESEN, history educator, journalist; b. N.Y.C., Apr. 20, 1941; d. David Theodore and Sadonia (Ecker) W. B.A., Hunter Coll., 1962; M.A. (fellow), Johns Hopkins U., 1964, Ph.D., 1970. Instr., Hampton Inst. (Va.), 1963, Stern Coll. for Women, Yeshiva U., N.Y.C., 1964-67; prof. history John Jay Coll., CUNY, 1968—; producer, broadcaster program stas. WBAI and KPFK, N.Y.C. and Los Angeles, 1978—; vis. prof. UCLA, 1982-83; syndicated journalist. Author: Crystal Eastman on Women and Revolution, 1978; Declassified Eisenhower, 1981; Biography of Eleanor Roosevelt, 1987; sr. editor: The Garland Library of War and Peace, 360 vols., 1970-80; contbr. articles to various publs. Faculty fellow CUNY, 1978, 82, 84. Mem. Orgn. Am. Historians (co-chair freedom of info. com.), Am. Hist. Assn., Coordinating Office Women in Hist. Profession (pres. N.Y.C. chpt. 1969-71), Berkshire

Women Historians, Soc. Historians Am. Fgn. Relations, Conf. on Peace Research in History (dir., v.p.), Women's Internat. League for Peace and Freedom, Pi Sigma Alpha, Phi Alpha Theta. Office: History Dept John Jay Coll CUNY 445 W 59th St New York NY 10019

COOK, DEBORAH ANN JENKINS, fiscal court magistrate; b. Stanford, Ky., Jan. 5, 1952; d. Earl Foster and Ines Margie (Owens) Jenkins; m. Jerry Randall Cook, Feb. 24, 1980; 1 child, Kristi Jo. B.A. in English with distinction, Eastern Ky. U., 1973. Staff writer Advocate-Messenger, Danville, Ky., 1973-78; staff writer Harrodsburg Herald, Ky., 1978-83, freelance columnist, 1983—; magistrate Boyle Fiscal Ct., Danville, Ky., 1978—. Named Ky. col., 1977; hon. state treas., Ky., 1979. Mem. Bluegrass Steam and Gas Engine Assn. Democrat. Baptist. Avocations: raising flowers; embroidery; reading; writing; crafts. Home: 616 Logan Ave Danville KY 40422

COOK, DIANE G(REFE), management consultant; b. Ft. Bragg, N.C., Aug. 13, 1943; d. Richard William and Marjorie Louise (Sine) G.; m. Gary M. Cook, Sept. 3, 1966; children—Christian M., Lauren S. B.A., Smith Coll., 1965. Program dir. N.Y.C. Commn. to UN and Consular Corps, 1968-70; exec. dir. Internat. Visitors Info. Service, Washington, 1971-74; v.p. Nat. Council for Internat. Visitors, Washington, 1981-83, pres., 1983-84; founder, officer of bd. Tulsa Council for Internat. Visitors, 1976-83; mem. exec. com. Meridian House Internat., Washington, 1983-84, counselor, 1984—; now mng. dir. Internat. Network Assocs.; nat. adv. council Experiment in Internat. Living, Brattleboro, Vt., 1979—. Speaker and writer in field. Pres. Assn. of Seven Colls. of Tulsa, 1978-80; chmn. Tulsa Humanities Com., 1980-82; mem. pub. sector Okla. Found. for Humanities, Oklahoma City, 1981-83; mem. Mayor's Com. on Internat. Visistors, Washington, 1972-74. Community internat. fellow USIA, 1981; recipient Commendation award U.S. Dept. State, 1974, Mayor's award, Washington, 1974. Mem. Denver Com. on Fgn. Relations, Am. Soc. Tng. and Devel., Am. Mgmt. Assn., Soc. Internat. Edn., Tng. and Research, Inst. Internat. Edn. Republican. Club: Smith Coll. (pres. Tulsa 1977-83). Office: Diane Cook Assocs 1692 S Sand Lily Dr Golden CO 80401

COOK, DORIS MARIE, accounting educator; b. Fayetteville, Ark., June 11, 1924; d. Ira and Mettie Jewell (Dorman) Cook; B.S. in Bus. Adminstrn., U. Ark., 1946, M.S., 1949; Ph.D., U. Tex., 1968; Staff acct. Haskins & Sells Tulsa, 1946-47; instr. acctg. U. Ark., Fayetteville, 1947-52, asst. prof., 1952-62, assoc. prof., 1962-69, prof., 1969—. C.P.A., Okla., Ark. Mem. Fayetteville Bus. and Profl. Womens Club (pres. 1973-74, 75-76, Woman of Yr. award 1977), Ark. Fedn. Bus. and Profl. Women's Clubs (chmn. found. com., 1975-77, treas. 1979-80), Ark. Soc. C.P.A.s (v.p., 1975-76, sec. student loan found. 1981-84, treas. 1984—), Am. Acctg. Assn., (chmn. Ark. membership com. 1981-82, 85-86, nat. chmn. membership com. 1982-83, chmn. Arthur Carter scholarship com. 1984-85), N.W. Ark. Chpt. C.P.A.s, (pres. 1980-81), Am. Inst. C.P.A.s, Am. Woman's Soc. C.P.A.s, Acad. Acctg. Historians (trustee 1985—), Mortar Board, Beta Gamma Sigma, Beta Alpha Psi (mem. nat. council 1973-80, editor newsletter 1973-77, nat. pres. 1977-78, dir. regional meetings 1978-79), Phi Gamma Nu, Alpha Lambda Delta, Delta Kappa Gamma (chpt. pres. 1978-80), Phi Kappa Phi. Editor newsletter Ozarks Econ. Assn., 1982-85. Contbr. profl. jours. Home: 1115 Leverett St Fayetteville AR 72701 Office: Dept Acctg Univ Ark Fayetteville AR 72701

COOK, ELEANOR BEATRICE, child care center executive; b. San Antonio, Sept. 15, 1939; d. Louis and Narvell Mary Jane (Warren) Jackson; m. James Robert Cook, June 28, 1958; children—Sheila Renee, James Robert III. A.A. St. Phillips Coll., San Antonio, 1958; A.A. San Antonio Coll., 1984; student Incarnate Word Coll., San Antonio, summer 1985. Dir., owner Sea Shell Child Care, San Antonio, 1969—, Grace Child Care, San Antonio, 1986—; minority adv. SBA, 1985. Recipient home econs. coop. Sam Houston High Sch., 1984, 85, home econs., Highland High Sch., 1984, 85, citation City of San Antonio, 1985. Mem. Alamo City C. of C. (Small Bus. Person of Yr. 1984, 85), Home Econs. Comparative Edn. Home: 4703 Lakewood Dr San Antonio TX 78220 Office: Sea Shell Child Care Ctr 207 S Gevers San Antonio TX 78203 also 1122 S WW White Rd San Antonio TX 78220

COOK, FRANCES D., ambassador; b. Charlestown, W.Va., Sept. 7, 1945, student Université d'Aix-Marseille, 1965-66; B.A., U. Va., 1967; M.P.A., Harvard U., 1978. With USIA (now ICA), Paris, 1967-69; spl. asst. to Ambassador Sargent Shriver, Jr., Paris, 1969-71; mem. U.S. del. to Vietnam treaty meetings, Paris; cultural affairs officer, Sydney, Australia, 1971-73, Dakar, 1973-75; fgn. service personnel officer, Washington, 1975-77; dir. Office of Public Affairs, Bur. African Affairs, U.S. Dept. State, 1978-80; apptd. fgn. service officer, 1980; U.S. ambassador to Burundi, 1980-83; consul gen., Alexandria, Egypt, 1983-86; dep. asst. Sec. of State Dept. State, Washington, 1986—. Club: Harvard. Office: Dept State Washington DC 20520*

COOK, HELGA GISELA, pharmaceuticals company official; b. Koenigsberg, E. Prussia, Ger., June 12, 1941; came to U.S., 1963, naturalized, 1974; d. Albert and Maria (Wunderlich) Woelk; bi-lingual bus. grad. in English and French, Vorbeck Lang. Inst., W.Ger., 1959; 1 son, Raymond J. Sec. EDP div. U.S. Army, Pirmasens, 1959-62, Internat. Leather Exhbn., Pirmasens, 1962-63; with comml. div. Honeywell, Pitts., 1966-70; with Mobay Chem. Corp., Pitts., 1970—, pricing clk., mktg., 1970-71, bilingual exec. sec., polyurethane div., 1971-74, exec. asst. to pres. and chief exec. officer, 1974-81, to chmn. and pres., 1981-86; exec. asst. to pres., chief exec. officer Bayer USA Inc., 1986—. Assoc. Merrick Art Gallery, New Brighton. Mem. Am. Soc. Profl. and Exec. Women, Nat. Assn. Female Execs., LWV of Beaver County (dir.). Office: Bayer USA Inc One Mellon Ctr Pittsburgh PA 15222

COOK, IVONNE JEANETTE, educator; b. San Francisco, Sept. 2, 1937; d. Ray Kenneth and Virginia Francis (Blim) Michaels; m. Robert Louis Cook, Nov. 23, 1969; 1 child, Dana Marie Maib Cook. Student MacMurray Coll. for Women, 1955-56, Colo. State U., 1956-57, B.Speech Arts, 1959; postgrad. U. Wyo., 1961-65, U. Colo., 1960, 72, 73, Brigham Young U., 1978. Dir. forensics Ft. Collins High Sch., Colo., 1959-61; speech instr. U. Wyo., Laramie, 1961-63; dir. speech drama Laramie High Sch., 1962-64; dir. speech, drama Ranum High Sch., Denver, 1964-68; dir. drama, speech Kelly Walsh High Sch., Casper, Wyo., 1968-69, Lander Valley High Sch., Wyo., 1969-70; tchr. speech, drama, English, Shoshoni Schs., Wyo., 1970-72; dir. drama, speech Rock Springs High Sch., Wyo., 1973-74; instr. speech, drama Western Wyo. Coll., Rock Springs, 1973-74; dir. speech, drama Green River High Sch., Wyo., 1974—; dir. children's theater workshop Wyo. State Dept. Edn., 1970-80; condr. workshops in field. Contbr. articles to profl. jours. Bd. dirs. Green River High Sch. Alumni Community Theatre, 1978—, Children's Theatre Creative Improvisation Workshops, 1970-80, Stage Crews Community Concerts and Fine Arts, 1974—; bd. dirs. Green River Community Fine Arts, 1975-80. Mem. NEA, Wyo. Edn. Assn., Green River Edn. Assn., Wyo. High Sch. Speech Assn., Wyo. High Sch. Theatre Assn., Nat. Forensic League, Delta Kappa Gamma, Alpha Delta Kappa, Beta Sigma Phi. Democrat. Episcopalian. Clubs: D.A.R., Job's Daus. Avocations: racing thoroughbred horses; writing poetry; play directing; speech coaching. Home: PO Box 936 Green River WY 82935 Office: Green River High Sch 300 Monroe Green River WY 82935

COOK, JOANN MARY, lawyer; b. Wichita, Kans., Aug. 13, 1953; d. Joseph Bruce and L. Anne (Klien) Cook; m. W. Brent Eilts, Aug. 10, 1974 (div. Jan. 1977). B.A. magna cum laude, Wichita State U., 1978; J.D., Washburn U., 1982. Bar: Kans. 1982. Research asst. Washburn Legal Research, Inc., Topeka, 1980-81, dir., 1981-82; assoc. Thad E. Nugent, Chartered, Overland Park, Kans., 1982—; dir. Research Advocate, Lawrence, Kans., 1982—. Vol., Big Sisters, Inc., Wichita, 1976-78; mem. vol. staff Women's Inc., Wichita, 1977-78, Rosebrook Ctr. for Domestic Violence Intervention, Kansas City, Mo., 1982-83. Mem. Am. Trial Lawyers Assn., Kans. Trial Lawyers Assn., ABA, Kans. Bar Assn., Johnson County Bar Assn. Democrat. Home: 6911 W 51st Pl Apt 2B Shawnee Mission KS 66202 Office: Thad E Nugent Chartered 10975 Grandview St Suite 145 Bldg 27 Overland Park KS 66210

COOK, JUDY ANN, nurse, clinical specialist, researcher; b. East St. Louis, Ill., Oct. 20, 1950; d. James Rufus and Thelma Louise (Levan) Hobbs; m. Rondal Earl Cook, Apr. 12, 1980; children—Laurie Beth, James Ronald. Diploma in nursing St. Luke's Hosp. Sch. Nursing, 1971; B.S. in Nursing, St. Louis U., 1975; M. Nursing Sci., U. Ark., 1977. Charge nurse Belleville Meml. Hosp., Ill., 1972-73; staff nurse St. Luke's Hosp., St. Louis, 1971-72, clin. instr., 1973-75; staff R.N. VA Hosp., St. Louis, 1975-76, surg. clin. specialist, Little Rock, 1976—; mem. faculty U. Ark., Little Rock, 1984—. Served to maj. U.S. Army Res., 1976—. Recipient Outstanding Young Woman award, 1984; Army Commendation medal, Army Achievement medal. Mem. Ark. Registry Allied Med. Specialists, Sigma Theta Tau, Delta Lambda. Mem. Ch. of Christ. Lodge: Order Eastern Star. Home: 67 Shoshoni Sherwood AR 72116 Office: Little Rock VA Med Ctr 4300 W 7th St Little Rock AR 72205

COOK, LYNN MAUREEN, public relations executive; b. Bremerton, Wash., Feb. 19, 1942; d. Hance and Frances Lucille (Teachout) Jacobson; student Olympic Coll.; B.F.A., U. Hawaii, 1972; m. David L. Cook, 1963 (div.); 1 dau., Elizabeth Louise. Asst. women's editor Bremerton Sun, Wash., 1966-68; display/advt. dir. Kramer's Men's Stores, Honolulu, 1971-74; public relations cons. Pacific Adminstrv. Devel. Corp., Honolulu, 1975-77; public relations asst. dir. Aloha United Way, Honolulu, 1977-79; v.p., dir. pub. relations Fawcett McDermott Cavanagh Brinck, Inc., Honolulu, 1979—. Exec. dir. Visitor Industry Edn. Council, 1979—, Bus. Communications Council, 1979-81; mem. Honolulu Neighborhood Bd. Council, 1977-79; bd. dirs. Honolulu Community Theatre, Aloha Liberty Found., Hawaii Theatre, Hawaii Heart Assn. Recipient Mayor's award, Artists of Hawaii, City of Honolulu, 1976, 77, 78. Mem. Public Relations Soc. Am., Women in Communications, Honolulu Advt. Fedn., Internat. Assn. Bus. Communicators, Honolulu Printmakers (pres. 1979-80), Honolulu Press Club, Theta Sigma Phi. Home: 1201 Wilder St Apt 801 Honolulu HI 96822 Office: Pauahi Tower Bishop Sq 23d Floor 1001 Bishop St Honolulu HI 96813

COOK, NANCY W., state legislator; b. May 11, 1936. Ed. U. Del. Mem. Del. Senate from 15th Dist. Democrat. Office: Del Senate State Capitol Dover DE 19901*

COOK, NORMA JEAN, hospital administrator; b. Porterdale, Ga., Oct. 23, 1948; d. Joseph C. and Margaret L. (McGiboney) C. B.S. in Nursing, Med. Coll. Ga., 1975; M.S. in Nursing, U. Ala., 1978. Staff nurse Ga. Warm Springs Hosp., 1976-77; staff nurse Spain Rehab. Ctr., Birmingham, Ala., 1977-78; nurse coordinator homebound program State Ala., Montgomery, 1978-81, state homebound coordinator, 1981-83; clin. nurse specialist Lakeshore Rehab., Birmingham, 1982-83; dir. rehab. nursing Roger C. Peace Rehab. Hosp., Greenville, S.C., 1983—; rehab. nurse cons. VA, Montgomery, 1980-83. Author: (with others) Rehabilitation Nursing: Concepts and Practices, 1981. Instr. ARC, Greenville, S.C., 1983—. Recipient Hope Chest award Nat. Multiple Sclerosis Soc., 1982. Mem. Am. Congress Rehab. Medicine, Assn. Rehab. Nurses, Nat. Head Injury Found. S.C. Home: 500 Wenwood Rd Apt 212 Greenville SC 29607 Office: Roger C Peace Rehab Hosp 701 Grove Rd Greenville SC 29605

COOK, PHYLLIS ANN, construction company executive; b. Monticello, Ky., May 19, 1947; d. Ray Waters and Nellie (Clark) Worley; m. Odus L. Cook, Nov. 20, 1971; children—Mona L., A Nichole. B.A., Ohio State U., 1980. Vice pres. Lisa Enterprises, Columbus, Ohio, 1979-84; owner, gen. contractor PRC Group, Columbus, 1984-85; constrn. mgr. McCormick Constrn. Co., Hunt Valley, Md., 1986—; cons. research, vocat. edn. Ohio State U., 1985. Facilitator women's entrepreneur group Met. Women's Ctr., 1984; bd. dirs. constrn. dept. Columbus Tech. Inst., 1983-86; vice chmn. adv. bd. Pvt. Industry Council for Columbus and Franklin County, 1983-85; participant Columbus City Council Study, 1985; mem. State of Ohio Apprenticeship Council, 1982-85; founder, bd. dirs. See What I Can Be program Columbus City Schs., 1983-85; v.p. Profl. Women's Forum, Columbus, 1984, pres., 1983-84; chmn. edn. com. YWCA, Columbus, 1984-85, chmn. Women of Achievement awards, 1984-85, bd. dirs., Balt.; v.p. fin. LWV, Columbus, 1984-85, bd. dirs., chmn. Women's Issues, Balt., 1986—. Home: 354 Ringold Valley Circle Cockeysville MD 21030 Office: McCormick Constrn 11011 McCormick Rd Hunt Valley MD 21031

COOK, REBECCA JOHNSON, lawyer, educator; A.B., Columbia U., 1970; M.A., Tufts U., 1972; M.P.A., Harvard U., 1973; J.D., Georgetown U., 1982. Bar: D.C. 1982. Dir. law program Internat. Planned Parenthood Fedn., London, 1973-78, legal adviser 1982—; assoc. firm Beveridge, Fairbanks and Diamond, 1980; cons. U.S. Congress, 1978-81; mem. legal counsel office The Upjohn Co., 1981-82; asst. prof. clin. pub. health Columbia U., N.Y.C., 1983—, staff atty. devel. law and policy program Ctr. for Population and Family Health, 1983—; dep. dir. Internat. Women's Rights Action Watch, 1986—. Contbr. articles to profl. jours. Bd. dirs. Operation Crossroads Africa, 1972-74, Pathfinder Fund, 1978—, Assn. for Vol. Surg. Contraception, 1982—, Internat. Projects Assistance Service, 1982—; mem. adv. com. on depo provera AID, 1978-80; mem. adv. bd. Program for Intro. and Adaptation of Contraceptive Tech., 1982—; U.S. del. 2d World Conf. on Nat. Parks, 1972; mem. Mass. Citizens Com. for Environ. Affairs 1972. Office: Ctr for Population and Family Health Columbia U 60 Haven Ave New York NY 10032

COOK, RUNETT HORTENSE, consultant, educator; b. Phila., Oct. 29, 1942; d. Henry T. and Helen L. (Herring) Cook. B.S., Cheyney Coll., 1964; M.A., Tchrs. Coll. N.Y.C., 1969; postgrad. Oxford U., 1973; Ph.D., Walden U., 1979. Social worker Women's Hosp., Phila., 1967-68; adminstr., supr. N.Y. Bd. Edn., N.Y.C., 1968—; prof. early childhood Columbia U., N.Y.C., 1972-74, CUNY, 1973-74, Coll. for Human Services, N.Y.C., 1973-74; lectr. Seton-Hall, Orange, N.J., 1971-72; founder, owner Swan, Inc., N.Y.C., 1978—. Author collection of poems Women of the 70's and 80's, 1982. Contbr. articles, paper to workshops. Founder, bd. dirs. More For Black Women, N.Y.C., 1978—. . Recipient Chapel of Four Chapels award Temple U., 1974. Mem. Doctorate Assn. N.Y., Black Women Female Network, Nat. Council Tchrs. English, Working Woman, Black Women's Polit. Orgn., Nova Polit. Orgn., Nat. Women's Polit. Caucus, Nat. Women's Health Network, Nat. Inst. Women of Color, Nat. Assn. Female Execs., Am. Women Econ. Devel. Orgn., Phi Delta Kappa, Epsilon Delta Chi. Democrat. Baptist. Clubs: Comdrs., Eagles. Lodges: Order of Eastern Star, Rose of Sharon. Home: 419 E 76th St Apt 5-A New York NY 10021

COOK, RUTH E., utilities commissioner, former state legislator; b. Berlin, Nov. 11, 1929; d. Samuel and Ilse (Meyer) Mohr; student N.Y. U.; m. John Oliver Cook, Oct. 31, 1954 (dec.); children—Roger Mohr, Judith Ellen. Exec. dir. State Council for Social Legis.; mem. N.C. Ho. of Reps., 1974-83, mem., chmn. appropriations base budget com. on human resources, vice-chmn. appropriations base budget com., vice-chmn. appropriations expansion budget com., vice-chmn. human resources com., vice-chmn. mental health com.; chmn. N.C. Housing Programs Study Commn., 1981-82; mem. Gov's Task Force on Sci. and Tech.; commr. N.C. Utilities Commn. 1983—. Bd. dirs. N.C. Housing Finance Agy., Women's Center Raleigh; chmn. N.C. Council for Hearing Impaired; exec. dir. State Council Social Legislation, 1966-74; charter mem. Raleigh Interch. Housing Corp., 1966-69. Mem N.C. Consumers Council (pres. 1977), Raleigh Wake LWV (past pres.), Women Execs. in State Govt. Office: NC Utilities Commn 430 N Salisbury St Raleigh NC 27602

COOK, SUSAN ALICE NEELEY, personnel administrator; b. Kane, Pa., Sept. 4, 1937; d. Leland Clyde and Cornelia Alice (Breitenbach) Neeley; m. Vernon Elijah Cook II, Sept. 6, 1958 (div. Jan. 1978); children—George Radford (dec. Mar. 1985), Bennett Austin. Student Smith Coll., 1955-58. With Liberty Nat. Bank & Trust Co., Oklahoma City, 1977—, v.p. employee relations, 1982-85, v.p. human resources planning, research and devel., 1985—. Vice pres. bd. trustees Westminster Day Sch., Oklahoma City, 1970-79, 85—; mem. adv. bd. St. Anthony Hosp., Oklahoma City, 1974—; mem. Energy Adv. Com. for Gov. Okla., 1973-74, Oklahoma City Transp. Survey Com., 1973-74, Okla. Arts Council, 1970-76; bd. dirs. Assn. Jr. Leagues, Inc., N.Y.C., 1974-76; mem. Nat. Task Force on Arts in Edn., 1975-76; mem. steering com. Okla. Task Force on Alcoholism, 1977-79; chmn. bus. div. United Way Campaign Cabinet, 1979, 81, 83; bd. dirs., mem. personnel com. Planned Parenthood, 1980-82; bd. dirs. ARC, 1980—, Child Care Connections, 1983-86. Fellow Am. Soc. for Tng. and Devel., The Forum (steering bd. 1978-80), Am. Soc. for Personnel Adminstrn., Oklahoma City Personnel Assn. Republican. Methodist. Club: Jr. League of Oklahoma City (treas. 1971-72, pres. 1972-73). Home: 1400 Glenbrook Terr Oklahoma City OK 73116 Office: Liberty Nat Bank & Trust Co PO Box 25848 Oklahoma City OK 73125

COOK, SUSAN VIRGINIA, lawyer; b. Oak Park, Ill., Jan. 25, 1947; d. Kenneth William and Virginia Susan (Snow) C.; m. Christopher Doucette, Aug. 12, 1983. B.A., U. Ariz., 1971; J.D., U. San Diego, 1974. Bar: Calif. 1974, U.S. Supreme Ct. 1981, U.S. Ct. Claims 1982, U.S. Ct. Appeals (D.C. cir.) 1981, U.S. Ct. Appeals (5th cir.) 1981, U.S. Ct. Appeals (9th cir.) 1983. Atty. Office Calif. Atty. Gen., San Diego, 1974-77, Office of San Diego City Atty., 1977-80; trial atty. Dept. Justice, Washington, 1980—; adj. prof. Western State Coll. Law, San Diego, 1978-80; v.p. Lawyers Club of San Diego, 1978-80. Mem. Calif. State Bar Com. on Computers and the Law, 1975-77; cons. San Diego Commn. on Status of Woman, 1977-79. U. San Diego Law Sch. scholar, 1972-73. Mem. Women's Bar Assn., Psi Chi. Avocations: skiing; travel. Office: Land and Natural Resources Div Dept Justice 10th and Constitution NW Washington DC 20530

COOK, SUZANNE B., designer; b. Macon, Ga., Nov. 19, 1934; d. William Lovejoy and Henrietta (Bonner) Baugheum; m. Dick Blydenstein, June 11, 1955 (div. Apr. 1969); m. 2d, Harvey Lionel Cook, Jan. 16, 1981. children—Lisa, Gerrit. B.A., Fla. Atlantic U., 1965. Dir. music Palm Beach Day Sch. (Fla.), 1969-74; pres., owner Haphazard Designs Inc., West Palm Beach, Fla., 1974—; mem. bd. mgrs. Flagler Nat. Bank, West Palm Beach, 1978—. Recipient awards Fla. State Bd. Edn., 1978, 80, 81, 83. Bd. govs. Big Bros. Big Sisters, 1980-83. Mem. Colonial Dames Am., Palm Beach Econ. Council (gov. 1981-83). Republican. Roman Catholic. Club: Breakers (Palm Beach).

COOK, SYBILLA POMEROY AVERY, librarian; b. Buffalo, Aug. 20, 1930; d. Edward Carrington and Elizabeth Amelia (Boorum) Avery; m. John D. Cook, June 12, 1951; children—Harold John, Robert Sherman, Raymond Avery. Student Smith Coll., 1948-50; B.S., Northwestern U.-Ill., 1951; M.A. in Library Sci., Rosary Coll., 1968; M.A. in Edn., U. Oreg., 1982. Librarian Sch. Dist. 103, Deerfield, Ill., 1968-69; media specialist Sch. Dist. 62, Des Plaines, Ill., 1969-76; librarian Sch. Dist. 116, Dillard, Oreg., 1976-78; library media specialist Sch. Dist. 12, Glide, Oreg., 1978—. Author: The Library Flipper, 1974; The Reference Flipper, 1983; (game) Referingo, 1982; (monograph) Instructional Design for Libraries, 1986; contbr. articles to profl. jours. Active Umpqua Valley Arts Assn., Roseburg, Community Concert Assn., Umpqua Symphony Assn. Named Glide Sch. Dist. Elem. Tchr. of Year, 1985; Oreg. Elem. Media Tchr. of Yr., 1984; U.S. Govt. fellow, 1967; State of Oreg. grantee, 1980. Mem. Soc. Children's Book Writers, ALA, Am. Assn. Sch. Libraries, Lane Douglas Regional Library Assn. (founding mem., pres. 1982-83), Oreg. Library Assn., Oreg. Edn. Media Assn. (legis. com. 1982-84, authors com. 1980-83; award 1984), Pacific Northwest Library Assn., Beta Phi Mu. Republican. Episcopalian. Club: Umpqua Velo. Home: 19 N River Dr Roseburg OR 97470 Office: Glide Elem Sch 1477 Glide Loop Rd Glide OR 97470

COOKE, BARBARA AYRES, association executive; b. Mpls., Dec. 4, 1936; d. Paul Revere and Mildred (Davidson) Ayres; m. Ralph F. Montgomery, Aug. 17, 1958 (div. 1969); m. James F. Cooke, May 14, 1975. B.S., Ind. U., 1959. Tchr., Indpls. Pub. Sch. System, 1959-61; found. exec. Continental Ill. Nat. Bank and Trust of Chgo., 1969-74; exec. dir. ARC, Berrien County, St. Joseph, Mich., 1975-77, Mid. Am., Chgo., 1977—; adj. prof. Aurora U., Ill., 1985—. Author: Leadership Portfolio, 1977. Mem. women's bd. Muncie Symphony, Ind., 1968; pres. Women's Aux. Ball Meml. Hosp., Muncie, 1968; bd. dirs. Thresholds, Chgo., 1973, Reading Is Fundamental, Chgo., 1973. Recipient Pelican award (2), Mid. Am. ARC, 1984, 85. Mem. Nat. Assn. Female Execs. Republican. Club: Women's Rep. of Chgo. Home: 46C 111 E Chestnut St Chicago IL 60611 Office: Mid Am Chpt ARC 43 East Ohio St Chicago IL 60611

COOKE, BARBARA LYNN, news production company executive; b. Mpls., May 22, 1956; d. Newell Orval and Jane Ann (Lobstein) Gaasedelen; m. Jeffrey Allen Cooke, Feb. 17, 1985. B.A., U. Minn., 1979; M.A., U. Kans., 1986. Sales acct. Modern Mdse., Mpls., 1979-83; media traffic coordinator Baxter Advt., Mpls., 1983-84; self-employed prodn. coordinator, Mpls., 1986—. Mem. Nat. Assn. Female Execs., Radio TV News Dirs. Assn., Alpha Phi. Avocation: flying; writing. Home and Office: 50 Groveland Terr #208 Minneapolis MN 55403

COOKE, CYNTHIA HUGHES, commercial real estate broker; b. Farmville, N.C., Oct. 18, 1959; d. Julius Leon and Ruby Jean (Murphrey) Hughes-Boros; m. Charles Edward Cooke, Jan. 6, 1978 (div. Oct. 1981); 1 child, William Bradley. Student Pitt Community Coll., 1980, Tenn. Coll., Memphis, 1980, Ariz. Sch. Real Estate, 1985. Lic. real estate broker, mortgage broker, Ariz. Agt., Cottonwood Real Estate, Litchfield Park, Ariz., 1981-83, DDI Properties, Phoenix, 1983; owner, pres. C&H Realty Resources, Phoenix, 1983—, Performance Mgmt., Phoenix, 1986—, owner, developer Blue Ridge Park, Raleigh, N.C., 1985—; owner, chmn. bd. Paragon Fin. Co., Phoenix, 1985—; cons. Arena & Son Constrn. Co., Phoenix, 1983—. Head soccer coach Ariz. Youth Soccer Orgn., 1984; tchr. pianist Advent Christian Ch., Farmville, 1975-80. Named One of 3 Outstanding Young Women of Phoenix, 1st Fed. Savs. and Phoenix Jaycees, 1985; recipient notice of achievement Ariz. Sec. of State, 1985. Mem. Phoenix C. of C., Nat. Assn. Realtors, Phoenix Bd. Realtors, (President's Round Table award for comml. sales 1982), Ariz. Assn. Realtors, Womens Council Realtors (v.p. 1981), Nat. Assn. Exec. Females, Better Bus. Bur., Nat. Assn. Realtors. Republican. Home: 166 Bahia Ln West Litchfield Park AZ 95340 Office: C&H Realty Resources 1990 W Camelback St Suite 205 Phoenix AZ 85015

COOKE, DOROTHY HELENA COSBY, mathematics educator, consultant, lecturer; b. Gloucester, Va., Jan. 8, 1941; d. Calvert Luchal and Pagie Florene (Dedmon) Cosby; m. Nathaniel Randolph Cooke, Sept. 2, 1961; 1 child, Nathaniel Randolph, Jr. B.S. in Math. Edn., Va. Union U., 1963; M.A. in Math. Edn., Hampton Inst., Va., 1970, M.A. in Guidance and Counseling, 1976; cert. Advanced Grad. Studies in Counselor Edn., Va. Poly. Inst. and State U., Blacksburg, 1981; D. Edn. in Counselor Edn. and Student Personnel Services, 1982. Secondary math. tchr. Va. pub. schs. 1963-71; instr. math. Rappahannock Community Coll., Glenns, Va., 1971-75, asst. prof. math. and counseling 1975-77, assoc. prof. math. and counseling, dir. student spl. services, 1977-82, prof. math. and counseling, dir. student spl. services, 1982—; cons., lectr. Rappahannock Community Coll., Glenns, 1971—, dir. spl. services, 1977—. Past mem. adv. com. Spl. Edn. Gloucester County Pub. Sch. System, Va.; bd. dirs. Gloucester chpt. ARC; mem. NAACP, non-resident mem. Lancaster and Northumberland Counties Devel. Services (Lands, Inc.), Kilmarnock, Va., past mem. local, state and nat. PTAs; past dir. Christian Edn. Bethel Bapt. Ch., Sassafras, Va.; mem. Gloucester County Sch. Bd. Selection Commn. Recipient Grad. Asst. for Minority Virginians Va. State Council Higher Edn. Mem. Am. Assn. Counseling and Devel., Va. Assn. Ednl. Opportunity Personnel, Mid-Eastern Assn. Ednl. Opportunity Personnel, Minority Affairs Coalition Va., Va. Counselors' Assn., Va. Assn. Non-White Concerns, So. Regional Council Black Am. Affairs, Assn. Community and Jr. Colls., Eastern Regional Counselors Adv. Council, Rappahannock Community Coll. Instl. Reps., Bd. Nat. Council Black Affairs, Am. Assn. Community and Jr. Colls., Kappa Delta Pi, Delta Psi Omega. Democrat. Avocations: singing, dramatic activities. Home: Route 5 Box 150 Gloucester VA 23061 Office: Rappahannock Community Coll Glenns VA 23149

COOKE, EVELYN KATHLEEN CHATMAN, educator; b. Jackson, Tenn.; d. Charles Elijah and Josie (Bond) Chatman; B.A. cum laude, Lane Coll., 1955; M.Ed., Xavier U.; m. James T. Cooke, Apr. 21, 1954 (div. Aug. 1970); 1 dau., Madelyn LaRene. Tchr. pub. schs., Chattanooga, 1957-67, Cin., 1967—; cons. career edn. Pub. Schs., Cin. Pres., Harriet Tubman's Black Women's Democratic Club; mem. upper grade sch study council. Mem. Fellowship United Meth. Musicians, NAACP, Council for Co-op Action, Am., Ohio, Cin. fedns. tchrs., Nat. Council Negro Women, Top Ladies of Distinction (nat. 2d v.p., dir. pub. relations), Sigma Gamma Rho, Gamma Theta, Sigma Rho Sigma, Epsilon Lambda Sigma. Methodist (dir. music ch.). Club: Top Ladies of Distinction, Inc. Home: 6748 Elwynne Dr Cincinnati OH 45236

COOKE, GLORIA DELL, social work administrator; b. Guthrie, Okla., Dec. 13, 1944; d. Al Bert and Audrey Deborah (Monroe) Prewitt; m. Alonzo Breon Cooke, July 25, 1970 (dec. Mar. 1983). B.A., Langston U., 1964; M.S.W., Atlanta U., 1966. Off. of class activities dir. Langston (Okla.) U., 1966-71; residence program dir. YWCA Residence, Houston, 1971-72; social worker Florence Crittenton Services, Houston, 1972-74, residence dir., 1974-76, project dir., 1976-79, dir. profl. services, 1979-83; program dir. maternity services DePelchin Faith Home, Houston, 1983—. Del. state conv. Democratic party, Houston, 1976. Recipient Citizenship award Langston chpt. NAACP, 1961; vocational rehab. grantee Atlanta U., 1964-66. Mem. Nat. Assn. Social Workers (program com. chmn. Houston chpt. 1974-75), Nat. Council Social Welfare, Nat. Coalition Black Women, Houston Assn. Concerned with Sch. Age Parents (vice-chmn. bd. 1978-79). Democrat. Baptist. Office: Crittenton Ctr of DePelchin 5107 Scotland St Houston TX 77007

COOKE, KAREN LUCILLE, commercial investigator; b. Bridgeport, Conn., Sept. 25, 1945; d. Gordon Woodrow and Mary Lucille (Kovach) C. Student Riverside City Coll. (Calif.). Owner, operator Fox Investigation, Phoenix, 1977—; personnel/security mgr. Arden Mayfair, Inc., Phoenix, 1972-83.

Named Spl. Dep. Maricopa County Sheriff's Dept., 1976. Mem. Am. Soc. Indsl. Security (dir. 1977-80, sec. 1979), Retail Grocers Ariz. (lottery com., adv. dir. 1983), Occupational Indsl Ctr. Ariz. (adv. dir. 1975-80), Ariz. Retail Investigators Assn. (pres. 1976, exec. dir. 1977-78), Phoenix Personnel Mgmt. Assn., 1st Ariz. Women's Town Hall. Democrat. Roman Catholic. Home: 1229 E Rowlands Ln Phoenix AZ 85022 Office: Fox Investigation 1777 W Camelback Rd A-109 Phoenix AZ 85015

COOKE-GLASNER, MARY KAY, nurse; b. Wichita, Kans., June 27, 1952; d. Bernard C. and Elnora M. (Osman) Van Arsdale; m. Dennis W. Cooke, June 3, 1972 (div. 1977); m. James Charles Glasner, May 14, 1983; 1 child, Jamie Kay Glasner. A.A., Butler County Community Coll., Kans., 1972; B.S.N., Wichita State U., 1986. Lic. critical care nurse, emergency nurse. Nurse asst. Susan B. Allen Hosp., El Dorado, Kans., 1966-72; staff nurse Wesley Med. Ctr., Wichita, 1972-74, head nurse, 1974-75; charge flight nurse Life Watch/ Wesley Med. Ctr., 1975-80, chief flight nurse, 1980—. Mem. Assn. Critical Care Nurses, Nat. Flight Nurses Assn. (liaison com. 1985-86). Club: Ashbeams (com. chair 1986). Office: Wesley Med Ctr 550 N Hillside Wichita KS 67214

COOKSEY, SALLY ANN, telephone company public relations official; b. Holdenville, Okla., Oct. 8, 1945; d. T.J. and Vesta (Sanders) C. B.A. in Radio and TV Broadcasting, U. Okla., 1967; student So. Meth. U., 1974-75, NYU, 1979-83. Asst. publicity dir. Sta. KRLD Radio, Dallas, 1967-68; media buyer, prodn. dir. John G. Burnett Advt., Dallas, 1968-69; promotion coordinator Dallas C. of C., 1969-73; sales promotion coordinator Bonanza Internat., Inc., Dallas, 1973-74; pub. affairs asst. Gen. Telephone Co. S.W., Dallas, 1974-75, pub. info. rep., 1975-76, pub. affairs mgr., Brownwood, Tex., 1976-80; communications mgr. Gen. Telephone Co. S.E., Durham, N.C., 1980-82; community affairs mgr. GTE Midwestern Telephone Ops., Westfield, Ind., 1982—; instr. Howard Payne U., Brownwood, 1978-79. Allocations com., New Horizons coordinator United Way Greater Indpls., 1983-84; exec. advisor Indpls. Jr. Achievement, 1984; advisor Explorer Scouts, Indpls., 1983-84; bd. dirs. United Way of Brownwood, 1978-79, Brown County Girl Scouts U.S.A., 1977-79. Named Most Outstanding Sr., U. Okla. Dept. Broadcasting, 1967. Mem. Dallas Advt. League (chmn. 1971-73), Dallas Press Club, San Angelo Press Club, Women in Communications, Durham C. of C. (beautification com.), Alpha Epsilon Rho. Baptist. Club: Brown County Democrats. Home: 785 High Dr Carmel IN 46032 Office: GTE Midwestern Telephone Operations PO Box 407 Westfield IN 46074

COOLIDGE, MARTHA, film director; b. New Haven, Aug. 17, 1946. Dir. films: Not a Pretty Picture, 1976, Valley Girl, 1983, The City Girl, 1983, National Lampoon's Joy of Sex, 1984, Real Genius, 1985, documentary David: Off and On, 1972; other documentary films directed include: More Than a School, 1973, Old Fashioned Woman, 1974, Not A Pretty Picture, 1976 (all 3 won Am. Film Festival awards). Address: care William Morris Agency 151 El Camino Beverly Hills CA 90212

COOMBS, C'CEAL PHELPS (MRS. BRUCE AVERY COOMBS), air company executive, civic worker; b. nr. Portland, Oreg.; d. Perry Edwin and Flora (Gowey) Phelps; B.S., U. Idaho, 1929; student Wash. State Coll., 1941; m. Bruce Avery Coombs, Nov. 28, 1929; children—Keith Avery, Glinda C'Ceal (Mrs. Nick E. Mason). Tchr. pub schs., Idaho, 1929-30; adminstrv. asst. Coombs West-Air Co. and Coombs Flying C Ranches, Yakima, Wash., 1945—; lobbyist for civic activities Wash. Legislature, 1947—; notary pub., Wash., 1960—. Del. White House Conf. on Children and Youth, 1960, Wash. State White House Conf. on Edn., 1955; mem. Wash. Citizens Council, Nat. Council on Crime and Delinquency, 1956—; bd. dirs., mem. exec. com. Wash. State Council Crime and Delinquency, 1956—, chmn., 1970-71, recipient Spl. State award, 1972, 76; mem. Allied Sch. Council Wash. 1951-53; mem. Western regional scholarship com. Ford Found., 1955-57; chmn. regional dist. Wash. Cities Legislation, 1960; chmn. Yakima County Sch. Bd., 1957-59; mem. Yakima County Health Dept., 1959-60; city councilwoman Yakima, 1959-61, asst. mayor, 1960; mem. Wash. Library Commn., 1960, 64-68, 72—, vice chmn., 1965-70, 75-76, recipient gov's. citation, 1976; del. UNESCO Conf. on Crime and Delinquency, Kyoto, Japan, 1970, Caracus, Venezuela, 1980; del. to Internat. Library Assn., Toronto, 1968, Washington, 1975, del. to worldwide seminar, Seoul, 1976, London, Brussels, 1977; del. Internat. Fedn. Libraries, Manila, 1980; trustee Wash. 4-H Found., 1960-79, chmn., 1969—, hon. trustee, 1979—; bd. mem. Wash. State Friends of Libraries, 1976, pres., 1977; mem. bd. Yakima County Law and Justice. Recipient Outstanding Citizen award Western Correctional Assn., 1974. Mem. Am. Library Trustee Assn. (regional dir. 1962—, pres. 1967-68), C. of C., Oreg., Idaho, Elmore County, Washington County, Calif. hist. socs., Windsor (Conn.) Hist. Assn. (life), Friends of Tewkesbury Abbey Eng. (life), Daus. Am. Colonists, Founders and Patriots, New Eng. Hist. Geneal. Soc., Conn. Hist. Soc., Dorchester (Mass.) Antiquarian and Hist. Soc., Conn. Soc. Genealogists, Ft. Simcoe Restoration Soc. (life), ALA (internat. trustee citation 1966, mem. bd. 1972—, council 1967-68, 71-72), Pacific N.W. (chmn. trustee sect. 1962-63), Wash. (chmn. 1960, trustee award 1967) library assns., Nat. Soc. Crown of Charlemagne, LWV, Allied Arts Council, Broadway Theatre League, Nat., Am., aviation assns., P.E.O., Federated Women, Colonial Dames (state rec. sec., pres. local chpt.), Altrusa, Nat. Soc. Magna Charta Dames, Descs. of Conqueror and His Companions, Friends of N.Y.C. Library. Home: Route 1 Box 1055 Yakima WA 98901

COOMBS, MARY BUTTERFIELD, maple sugar candy company executive; b. Jacksonville, Vt., Mar. 23, 1903; d. Marcius Augustine and Alice Lucretia (Dalrymple) Butterfield; m. Robert G. Coombs, Sept. 26, 1924 (dec. Mar. 1964); children—Anita Julia, Mary Ada, Robert G., Elaine Ruth, Joyce Emma. Student pub. schs., Brattleboro, Vt. Tchr. Brattleboro Elem. Sch., 1922-25; co-founder, worker Coombs Maple Products Inc., Jacksonville, Vt., 1925—, pres., 1964—. Past supt. Sunday sch., past chmn. ch. com. Jacksonville Community Ch.; past mem. bd. dirs., past v.p. Windham County Farm Bur., Vt. Voted Mother of Yr., State of Vt., 1977, Jacksonville Community Ch., 1978; recipient hon. award Internat. Maple Council, 1984. Mem. Jacksonville Home Makers Club (pres. 1953), DAR (chaplain Brattleboro chpt. 1980-85); hon. life mem. Nat. PTA, Aux. Am. Legion Jacksonville (chaplain), Vt. Sugar Makers Assn. (hon. award 1956). Republican. Home and Office: PO Box 229 Jacksonville VT 05342

COOMER, JOYCE MAE, graphic designer, bookkeeper; b. Danville, Ky., Apr. 26, 1954; d. Buford Carrington and Etwol (Thomas) Evans; m. Donald Marshall Overstreet, Sept. 8, 1971 (div. Dec. 1977); 1 child, Donald Keith; m. Gregory Foster, Dec. 23, 1977. Grad. high sch., Columbia, Ky. Proofreader Waggener-Walker Newspapers, Inc., Columbia, 1976-77, ad designer, 1977-79; graphic designer South Central Printing, Inc., Columbia, 1979-83; v.p. Printing Creations, Inc., Columbia, 1984—; coop. adviser Campbellsville Coll., Ky., 1985. Methodist. Avocations: reading; horseback riding; drawing and painting; writing; poetry. Office: Printing Creations Inc 201 Adams St Columbia KY 42728

COOMLER, RITA CAROL, health care services professional; b. Omaha, May 3, 1947; d. Edward Joseph and Wanda Ann (Siderewicz) Skorka; m. Robert John Coomler, Feb. 20, 1971; children—Karl, Karen, Jenny. Diploma St. Joseph's Sch. Nursing, Omaha, 1968; B.S.N. in Nursing, Calif. State U.-Los Angeles, 1977. Cert. emergency nurse. Head nurse family practice clinic U. Nebr. Med. Ctr., Omaha, 1968-71; mem. obstet. nursing staff Ventura County Med. Ctr., Calif., 1971; mem. emergency dept. staff, utilization rev. coordinator Santa Paula Hosp., Calif., 1976-81; chief quality assurance and utilization rev., risk mgmt. coordinator Our Lady of Lourdes Hosp., Pasco, Wash., 1981—. Mem. Emergency Nurses Assn. (chpt. pres. 1984-85). Republican. Roman Catholic. Avocation: swimming. Home: 207 E 45th Pl Kennewick WA 99337 Office: Our Lady of Lourdes Hosp 520 N 4th Ave Pasco WA 99301

COON, DOROTHY JEAN, city official; b. Little Rock, Aug. 18, 1927; d. James Clarence and Katie Mary (Johnson) Crawford; m. Howard E. Coon, Jr., July 24, 1947; children—Howard E. III, Dorothy Susan Coon Smith. Student pub. schs. Jackson and Byram, Miss. Clk.-typist City of Jackson, Miss., 1945, dep. clk., 1948-74, chief dept. city clk., 1974-83, asst. city clk., 1983-84, city clk., 1984—. Democrat. Lutheran. Home: PO Box 17 Jackson MS 39205 Office: City Clerk's Office PO Box 17 Jackson MS 39205

COONEY, BARBARA, illustrator, author; b. Bklyn., Aug. 6, 1917; d. Russell Schenck and Mae Evelyn (Bossert) C.; m. Guy Murchie, Dec. 1942 (div. Mar. 1947); children—Gretel, Barnaby; m. Charles T. Porter, July 16, 1949; children—Charles Talbot, Phoebe. B.A., Smith Coll., 1938; student, Art Students League, 1940. Author, illustrator children's books including: King of Wreck Island, 1941, The Kellyhorns, 1942, Captain Pottle's House, 1943, Christmas, 1967, Little Brother and Little Sister, 1982, Miss Rumphius, 1982; illustrator children's books: Wynken, Blynken & Nod, 1970, When the Sky is Like Lace, 1975, The Donkey Prince, 1977, I Am Cherry Alive, The Little Girl Sang, 1979, Ox-Cart Man, 1979, others. Recipient Caldecott medal for Chanticleer and the Fox, 1958, U. So. Miss. medal, 1975, Smith Coll. medal, 1976, Caldecott medal, 1980, Am. Book award, 1983. Home: Damariscotta ME 04543 Office: care Doubleday & Co 245 Park Ave New York NY 10167

COONEY, JOAN GANZ, television executive; b. Phoenix, Nov. 30, 1929; d. Sylvan C. and Pauline (Reardan) Ganz; B.A., U. Ariz., 1951, hon. degree, 1975; hon. degrees: Boston Coll., 1970, Hofstra U., Oberlin Coll., Ohio Wesleyan U., 1971, Princeton, 1973, Russell Sage Coll., 1974, Harvard, 1975, Allegheny Coll., 1976, Georgetown U., 1978, Notre Dame U., 1982, U. Miami, 1985; m. Timothy J. Cooney, Feb. 1964 (div.); m. 2d, Peter G. Peterson, Apr. 26, 1980. Reporter, Ariz. Republic, Phoenix, 1953-54; publicist NBC, N.Y.C., 1954-55; TV publicist U.S. Steel Hour, N.Y.C., 1955-62; producer pub. affairs documentaries Channel 13, WNET, N.Y.C., 1962-67; TV cons. Carnegie Corp. of N.Y., N.Y.C., 1967-68; exec. dir. Children's TV Workshop, producers Sesame St. and Electric Co., others, N.Y.C., 1968-70, pres., trustee, 1970—; dir. Xerox Corp., May Dept. Stores Co., Johnson & Johnson, Met. Life Ins. Co., Chase Manhattan Corp., Chase Manhattan Bank, N.A.; trustee Channel 13 (Ednl. Broadcasting Corp.), Nat. Child Labor Com., 1981—; mem. Pres.'s Commn. on Marihuana and Drug Abuse, 1971-73, Adv. Com. Trade Negotiations, 1978-80, Pres.'s Commn. for Nat. Agenda for Eighties, 1980. Recipient numerous awards for Electric Company, Sesame Street, other TV programs including Gold Key award Nat. Sch. Pub. Relations Assn.; Disting. Service medal Columbia Tchrs. Coll., Soc. for Family of Man; Gold medal Nat. Inst. Social Scis., Frederick Douglass award N.Y. Urban League, Quest medal, Friends of Edn. award NEA, Disting. Service award Nat. Assn. Ednl. Broadcasters, named Woman of Yr. in Edn., Ladies Home Jour., 1975; Woman of Decade award Ladies Home Jour., 1979. Mem. Nat. Acad. TV Arts and Scis., Council Fgn. Relations, Internat. Radio and TV Soc., Am. Women in Radio and TV, NOW, Nat. Inst. Social Scis. Office: President Children's TV Workshop 1 Lincoln Plaza New York NY 10023

COOPER, BRENDA JACQUELINE, court reporter, court reporting agency executive; b. London, June 23, 1946; came to U.S., 1967; d. Joseph and Effie (Nelson) Moss. Student Wimbledon Tech. Coll., Eng., 1963-65. Registered profl. ct. reporter, Fla. Sr. ct. reporter James Towell and Sons, London, 1970-73; trial ct. reporter N.Y. Supreme Ct., N.Y.C., 1973-75; sr. ct. reporter Raymond Reporting, West Palm Beach, Fla., 1975-79; owner, reporter Flagler Reporting Inc., West Palm Beach, 1979—. Mem. Royal Inst. Shorthand Writers (London), Nat. Shorthand Reporters Assn., Fla. Shorthand Reporters Assn. Republican. Avocations: interior decorating, horseback riding, oil painting, reading. Home: 1841 Abbey Rd West Palm Beach FL 33406 Office: Flagler Reporting Inc 2001 Palm Beach Lakes Blvd West Palm Beach FL 33409

COOPER, CAROL WILSON, college administrator, consultant; b. Inglewood, Calif., Nov. 3, 1941; d. Ralph Allen and Dorothy Angela (Stevens) Wilson; m. Harry E. Ghilarducci, June 19, 1971 (div. 1978); m. Kenneth William Cooper, Oct. 17, 1980. A.A., Los Angeles Harbor Coll., 1959; B.A., Calif. State U.-Sacramento, 1971, M.A., 1973, postgrad., 1974-84. Graphic artist Pacific Telephone, Sacramento, 1967-71; program coordinator City of Gilroy, Calif., 1971-74; children's librarian Santa Clara County Library, Gilroy, 1973-74; substitute tchr. Santa Clara County Office Edn., San Jose, Calif., 1973-74; instr. spl. edn., Gavilan Coll., Gilroy, 1973-74, cordinator spl. edn., 1972—; cons. Gilroy Unified Sch. Dist., 1982-83, Access for the Handicapped, 1984-85; commr. vocat. edn. Calif. Community and Jr. Coll. Assn., Sacramento, 1976-78; facilitator South County Interagy. Council, 1978. Editor, contbr. Ed-Lites Jour., 1983; developer, author of curriculum design for coll. program for handicapped, 1973-84, coll. program for retarded adults, 1973-84; developer logo Gilroy Recreation Dept., 1974. Campaign asst. Infelise for Assembly from 25th Dist., Gilroy,, 1982; mem. architecture and site com. Gilroy Planning Commn., 1980-83; chmn. bd. Gavilan Dist. Spl. Olympics, Gilroy, 1984—. Recipient resolution of appreciation Santa Clara County Commn. on Developmental Disabilities, 1978, cert. of appreciation Gavilan Dist. Spl. Olympics; named Employee of Yr. in Edn., Rotary Internat., 1978. Mem. Am. Assn. Women in Community and Jr. Colls., Calif. Assn. Postsecondary Educators of Disabled, Assn. for Developmentally Disabled (exec. bd. 1983—), Gilroy Literary Assn. (exec. bd. 1983-85), Gilroy C. of C. (Women in Chamber), Delta Kappa Gamma (exec. bd. 1982-84). Avocations: reading, walking, painting, quilt history. Office: Gavilan Coll 5055 Santa Theresa Blvd Gilroy CA 95020

COOPER, CHRISTINE ANN, insurance broker, consultant; b. Oakland, Calif., Aug. 5, 1952; d. Robert Earl and Jean Louise (Warren) C; m. Thomas E. Hawkins, July 14, 1974 (div. 1981). A.A., Diablo Valley Coll., 1972; B.A., U. Calif.-Davis, 1975. Rater, United Pacific Ins., Fresno, Calif., 1975-77; supr. Lundberg & Assoc., Fresno, 1977-81; office mgr. L.T. Petersen Ins., Fresno, 1981-83; account exec. Corroon & Black, Sacramento, 1983-85; owner, broker Christine A. Cooper Ins., Sacramento, 1985—; assoc. dir. All-Pro Team, Sacramento, 1986—. Editor Capitol News & Views newsletter, 1985—. Bd. dirs. Ins. Women of Sacramento, 1985-86; mem. Sacramento Women's Network, 1984—. Mem. C. of C., Profl. Ins. Agts. Democrat. Episcopalian. Avocations: creative writing, piano, sewing, softball, soccer, hiking, sailing, swimming, snorkeling, backpacking, camping, skiing. Home: 2800 Matheson Way Sacramento CA 95864 Office: Christine A Cooper Ins Services 1631 Executive Ct Sacramento CA 95864

COOPER, CLARINDA RYNN, retail company executive; b. Bloomington, Ind., Mar. 6, 1955; d. Dale Dallas and Catherine (Starbuck) C. B.A., Ind. U., 1978. Sales rep. Sears Roebuck & Co., Bloomington, Ind., 1974-80; asst. mgr. K-Mart, Speedway, Ind., 1980-81; salesperson FAS Auto Works, Bloomington, 1982; retail mgr. Deb Shops, Inc., Bloomington, 1982—; cons. Ind. U. Sch. Arts and Scis., Bloomington, 1985—. Mem. Nat. Assn. Female Execs., Career Track. Republican. Mem. Ch. of Christ. Avocations: music; reading; calligraphy; photography; fashion. Home: 612 W Allen Bloomington IN 47401 Office: Deb Shop #102 2866 E 3d Bloomington IN 47401

COOPER, DIANE ELIZABETH, home economist; b. Chgo., Feb. 2, 1942; d. Donald Howard and Margaret (Kingsley) C.; B.S. in Home Econs., U. Ariz., 1969. Home economist, research test kitchen supr. Sunbeam Appliance Co., Oak Brook, Ill., 1970-77; product devel. research home economist Ore-Ida Foods, Inc., Ontario, Oreg., 1977—. Mem. Am. Home Econs. Assn., Home Economists in Bus., Oreg. Home Econs. Assn. (dist. dir.), Treasure Valley Home Economists. Office: 175 NE 6th Ave Ontario OR 97914

COOPER, DIANNE LYNN, marketing executive; b. Columbus, Ohio, Aug. 9, 1950; d. Franklin Monroe and Katherine (Lochner) Frohnauer; m. Steven Lee Cooper, Sept. 24, 1974. B.S. in Mktg., Miami U., Oxford, Ohio, 1972. Project dir. Burgoyne, Inc., Cin., 1972-74; mgr. info. services Cin. C. of C., 1974-77; project dir. Burke Market Research, Cin., 1977-79; asst. mgr. research dept. Sive Assocs./Y & R, Cin., 1979-85; mgr. market research First Nat. Bank of Cin., 1985—. Recipient Mktg. Research award, 1986. Mem. Am. Mktg. Assn. (pres. Cin. chpt. 1985-86), Phi Beta Kappa. Republican. Lutheran. Office: First Nat Bank Cin 425 Walnut St Cincinnati OH 45202

COOPER, DONA HANKS, story analyst, consultant; b. Oklahoma City, Nov. 5, 1950; d. Charles William and Betty Hopkins (Cragen) C. B.A., Am. U., 1972; postgrad. U. Minn., 1972-73. Caseworker U.S. Senator Marlow W. Cook, Washington, 1973-74, U.S. Congressman Benjamin A. Gilman, Washington, 1974-75; artistic dir. Am. Soc. Theatre Arts, Washington, 1975-79; mng. dir. Ensemble Studio Theatre, Los Angeles, 1979-81; story analyst Metro Media, Hollywood, Calif., 1981-82, NBC, Burbank, Calif., 1982—, HBO, Los Angeles, 1984-85; dir. Oliver Hailey's Playwrighting Group, Los Angeles, 1982-85; radio drama cons. Radio Am., Washington, 1986; cons. Edgar Scherick Assocs., Los Angeles, 1985. Author plays: The Works of Lizzie Borden, 1981, California Calico, 1982, The Lone Star State, 1983, Rules of the House, 1984, Bosom Buddies, 1986. Sponsor Christian Children's Fund, 1983—. Mem. Nat. Assn. Female Execs., Dramatist Guild (assoc.), Phi Beta Phi. Democrat. Avocations: quilting; researching women's roles in Am. history. Home: 7029 Cozycroft Ave Canoga Park CA 91306

COOPER, DORIS JEAN, market research prodn. co. exec.; b. N.Y.C., Dec. 17, 1934; d. James N. and Georgina N. (Cassidy) Breslin; student Sch. of Commerce, N.Y. U., 1953-55, Hunter Coll., 1956-57; m. S. James Cooper, June 17, 1956; 1 son, David Austin. Asst. coding supr. Crossley S-D Surveys, N.Y.C., 1955-57; asst. field supr. Trendex, Inc., N.Y.C., 1957-59; coding dir. J. Walter Thompson Co., N.Y.C., 1960-63, Audits & Surveys, N.Y.C., 1964-65; pvt. practice cons., N.Y.C., 1965-73; pres. Cooper Services, Hastings-on-Hudson, N.Y., 1973—; cons. market research prodn. problems. Mem. Am. Mktg. Assn. (N.Y. chpt.), Nat. Bus. Women Owners Assn., Hastings C. of C. Republican. Episcopalian. Office: Cooper Services 419 Warburton Ave Hastings-on-Hudson NY 10706

COOPER, FREDDIE BELLE, mathematics and science educator; b. Mullins, S.C., May 29, 1939; d. Fred Douglas and Maxie Bell (Gilchrist) Phillips; m. Ulysses Cooper, Jan. 9, 1964; children—Michael Douglas, Myron David, Myles Duriel. B.S., Barber-Scotia Coll., 1961; M.S. in Natural Sci., N.Mex. Highlands U., 1966. Cert. secondary tchr. Sci. tchr. Menaul High Sch., Albuquerque, 1961-63; tchr., librarian Aynor Elem. Sch., S.C., 1966-67; sci. tchr. Knob Noster Jr. High Sch., Mo., 1969-71, East Jr. High Sch., Aurora, Colo., 1971-73; biology tchr. Judson High Sch., Converse, Tex., 1973-76; sci. tchr. Alessandro Jr. High Sch., Sunnymead, Calif., 1976-79, Dept. Def., Frankfurt, Fed. Republic Germany, 1979-81; math. tchr. Wahlquist Jr. High Sch., Ogden, Utah, 1982—. Writer curriculum guides. Publicity chairperson, bd. dirs. Pop Warner Little League Football Assn., March AFB, Calif., 1977-79; publicity chairperson Cub Scouts Am., Randolph AFB, Tex., 1975-76. Mem. NEA, Utah Edn. Assn., Weber Edn. Assn., Utah Council Tchrs. Math. Democrat. Lodges: Order Eastern Star (chpt. worthy matron 1975-76), Daus. of Isis (rec. sec. 1975-76). Avocations: gardening, softball, paino, sewing, walking. Home: 1307 W 200 N Clearfield UT 84015 Office: Wahlquist Jr High Sch Ogden UT 84015

COOPER, JANE TODD, poet, writer, educator; b. Bklyn., Dec. 24, 1943; d. John Curtis and Margaret E. (Johnston) C.; m. William Hudson Shoff; children—Donald Charles Taylor, Eamon Robert Taylor, Savannah Elizabeth Cooper-Ramsey. Student U. Pitts., 1965-68; B.A. in Lit., Duquesne U., 1965. Research asst. U. Pitts., 1966; instr. high sch., Pitts., 1967-73; ednl. dir. drug and alcohol treatment facility Pa. Dept. Corrections, Camp Hill, 1974-78; project trainer domiciliary care, dept. behavioral sci. Pa. State Coll. Medicine, Hershey, 1979-80; dir. primary health care projct Elizabethtown Hosp., Pa., 1980-81; mgr. personal care boarding home provider tng. project, dept. family and community medicine Pa. State Coll. Medicine, Hershey, 1982; cons. Pa. Dept. Aging, Pa. Dept. Pub. Welfare, Pa. Council on Arts, others, 1979—; copy writer, Harrisburg, Pa., 1979—; mem. steering com. Women in the Arts, Harrisburg, 1979-83; coordinator Eye Poets Reading Series, Lancaster, Pa., 1985—. Author: (poetry) Entering Pisces, 1985. Editor: ARTREACH, 1984; Home Management for Personal Care Boarding Home Providers, 1982. Poetry and prose pub. in lit. jours. and anthologies. Artist in residence N.J. State Arts Council, Pa. Council on the Arts, 1982—; Carroll scholar, 1964-65; Warner Lambert/Nat. Merit scholar, 1961-65. Mem. Poets and Writers, Acad. Am. Poets. Home: 3618 Centerfield Rd Harrisburg PA 17109

COOPER, JILL ZIMMERMAN, lawyer; b. Milw., Dec. 26, 1938; d. Jay V. and Bernice (Tucker) Z.; m. George Cooper, June 19, 1960 (div. 1974); 1 dau., Amanda; m. Thomas S. Udall, May 15, 1982. B.A., Wellesley Coll., 1960; M.A., Columbia U., 1967, J.D., 1973. Tchr., ednl. cons.; dep. atty. gen. State of N.Mex.; cultural affairs officer State of N.Mex.; sole practice law, Albuquerque. Home: 405 Laguna SW Albuquerque Santa Fe NM 87404

COOPER, JOSEPHINE SMITH, trade association executive; b. Raleigh, N.C., Aug. 2, 1945; d. Joseph W. and Marie (Peele) S.; B.A. in bus. and econs., Meredith Coll., Raleigh, 1967; M.S. in mgmt. Duke U., 1977. Program analyst Office of Air & Quality Planning and Standards EPA, Research Triangle Park, N.C., 1968-78, environ. profl. specialist Office of Research and Devel., Washington, 1978-80; mem. profl. staff majority leader Howard H. Baker, Jr., U.S. Senate Com. on Environ. and Public Works, Washington, 1980-83; asst. adminstr. for external affairs EPA, Washington, 1983-85; asst. v.p. for environ. and health program Am. Paper Inst., Washington, 1985-86; sr. v.p. for policy Synthetic Organic Chem. Mfrs. Assn., Washington, 1986—; treas. RTP Fed. Credit Union, 1969-72, pres., 1975. Congressional fellow, 1979-80. Mem. Federally Employed Women (treas., pres. 1972-77), Women in Govt. Relations. Mem. Disciples of Christ. Club: Cts. Royal Racquetball. Office: 1330 Connecticut Ave Suite 300 Washington DC 20036

COOPER, JUDY MIMS, judge; b. Dothan, Ala., Apr. 23, 1946; d. John L. and Dorothy (Trawick) Mims; m. Albert V. Cooper, Apr. 28, 1965; children—David V., James A. Clk.-typist Civil Service, Ft. Rucker, Ala., 1964-66, Athens, Ga., 1966-68; chief registrar Clay County, Fort Gaines, Ga., 1981—, magistrate judge, 1985-89; dep. clk., chief registrar Superior Ct. of Clay County, 1985—. Mem. Nat. Right to Work Com., Va., 1977; mem. Republican Nat. Com., Washington, 1980; mem. Nat. Rep. Congl. Com., Washington, 1982, Mothers Against Drunk Driving, 1982. Mem. Council Magistrate Judges, Voter Registrars Ga. Avocations: reading; cooking. Home: PO Box 158 Fort Gaines GA 31751 Office: Clay County Commrs S Washington St Fort Gaines GA 31751

COOPER, LIDA ELAINE, accountant; b. Goltry, Okla., May 18, 1932; d. Jesse Earl and Mildred Mabel (Secord) Wayman; m. Lloyd Gene Cooper, Aug. 4, 1956; children—Nancy Laine, Cammy Jean. A.A., Central Coll., 1952; B.A., Seattle Pacific U., 1954. C.P.A., Tex. Tchr. Sequim pub. schs., Wash., 1954-56; tax preparer J.T. Williams, Vacaville, Calif., 1967; pvt. practice acctg., Vacaville, 1968-70; prin. Cooper's Tax Service, Schertz, Tex., 1971—. Mem. Cibolo Valley C. of C. Republican. Presbyterian. Avocation: Painting. Home: 140 Cloverleaf Dr Schertz TX 78154 Office: Cooper's Tax Service 204 Mill St Schertz TX 78154

COOPER, MARIANNE (ABONYI), librarian, educator; b. Budapest, Hungary, Apr. 14, 1938; came to U.S., 1957, naturalized, 1962; d. Laszlo and Elisabeth (Lengyel) Abonyi; m. Herbert W. Cooper, June 11, 1961; children—Deborah S., Evelyn Ann. B.A., Syracuse U., 1960; M.L.S., Columbia U., 1961, D.L.S., 1980. Chemistry librarian Columbia U., N.Y.C., 1961-66; sr. info. scientist Am. Inst. Physics, N.Y.C., 1967-70; instr. Grad. Sch. Library and Info. Studies, Queens Coll., Flushing, N.Y., 1975-80, asst. prof., 1980—. Author: (with E. Terry) Secondary Services in Physics, 1969; (with C.W. Thayer) Primary Journal Literature of Physics, 1969; (with H.M. Watterson) Institutional Producers of Physics Literature, 1969; also articles and papers in info. sci. field. Editor: Secondary Information Services: Development and Future, 1982. Chmn. edn. com., mem. bd. dirs. West Birchwood Civic Assn., Jericho, N.Y., 1970-80. Mem. ALA, Am. Soc. for Info. Sci. (chpt. program chmn. 1981, chpt. rep. to nat. orgn. 1983-85, mem. and mktg. com. 1983-84, chmn. edn. com. 1985—), Assn. for Library and Info. Sci. Edn., Library Assn. CUNY, Spl. Libraries Assn., Phi Beta Kappa. Recipient George Virgil Fuller award Columbia U., 1972; Faculty-in-Residence award Queens Coll., 1982. Home: 17 St Lawrence Pl Jericho NY 11753 Office: Grad Sch of Library and Info Studies Queens Coll Flushing NY 11367

COOPER, MARY ADRIENNE, publishing company executive; b. Bklyn., Jan. 27, 1927; d. James H. and Helen (Hofeditz) C.; B.S., SUNY, Albany, 1948; postgrad. in bus. N.Y. U., 1949-50, Columbia U., 1976. With McGraw Hill, Inc., N.Y.C., 1953—, asst. v.p. fin. ops., 1973-75, v.p. adminstrv. services, 1976-84, sr. v.p. adminstrv. services, 1984—. Bd. dirs. McMahan Services for Children, N.Y.C., 1976—. Mem. Fin. Execs. Inst., Nat. Investor Relations Inst. Office: 1221 Ave of the Americas New York NY 10020

COOPER, MARY ELLEN, investment counsel executive; b. Mt. Clemens, Mich., Dec. 6, 1948; d. Irving Leroy and Lillian M. (Klockow) Cooper. B.S., Central Mich. U., 1971. Residence hall dir. Central Mich. U., Mt. Pleasant, 1972-78; asst. to pres. Video Enterprises, Los Angeles, 1978-80; life and disability agt. Pa. Life Ins. Co., Santa Monica, Calif., 1980; investment exec. Scudder, Stevens & Clark, Los Angeles, 1980—. Fellow Fin. Analysts Fedn., Los Angeles Soc. Fin. Analysts. Democrat. Lutheran. Home: 10620 Victory Blvd Apt 117 North Hollywood CA 91606 Office: Scudder Stevens & Clark 333 S Hope St 37th Floor Los Angeles CA 90071

COOPER, PATRICE O'HEGARTY COBB, business executive; b. Collooney, Sligo, Ireland, July 5, 1909; d. Timothy and Honorah E. (Scanlon) O'Hegarty; came to U.S., 1922, naturalized, 1943; student Bay State Inst. Commerce, 1926, St. Mary's Coll., 1927-29, Rutgers U. Sch. Bus. Adminstrn., 1944-45, Berkeley Secretarial Sch., 1951; m. Francis Cutter Cobb, Oct. 30, 1943 (dec. Jan. 1965); 1 dau., Patricia Cobb Oliver; m. 2d, J. Gilbert Cooper, Feb. 20, 1971. Fashion and beauty exec. Best and Co., N.Y.C., 1935-43; personnel mgmt. Heil Co., N.J., 1945-49; staff Lord and Taylor, 1950; fashion coordinator and commentator, Fla., 1957-69; fashion writer, soc. writer Pompano Beach (Fla.) Town News, Sun Sentinel, Pompano and Palm Beach Post Times, 1960-68; travel cons. Erin Gardner Travel, Boca Raton Fla., 1961—; pres., owner Irish Imports Galore, Ltd., Boca Raton, 1967—; co-owner Personnally Yours, public relations, 1962-64. Chmn., Community Concerts Assn., Short Hills, N.J., 1952-55; com. head Project Hope, Palm Beach and Broward Counties, 1961-62; mem. adv. bd. Ft. Lauderdale Forum, 1963-70; chmn. art exhibit Boca Raton Art Guild, 1967; life mem., past pres. North Broward Symphony Soc.; life mem. Ft. Lauderdale Symphony Soc., Debbie Rand Service League; charter, life mem. Fla. Atlantic Music Guild, Civic Ballet Ft. Lauderdale, Round Table Palm Beach; chmn. Le Premier Bal a Boca Raton, 1970, El Segundo Baile de Boca Raton, 1971; chmn. Symphony Ball, 1973, mem. com., 1974; chmn. Heart and Harness at Pompano Park, Heart Fund, 1972, mem. com., 1973; reservations chmn. Tiara Ball, Royal Dames, 1972; mem. Royal Dames Cancer Research; Gold Circle of Nova U.; founder-donor Caldwell Playhouse, Boca Raton, 1975; social chmn. Friends of Playhouse; founder Stars for Caldwell; founder, interim pres. Allegro Soc. Palm Beach; bd. dirs. South Fla. Symphony; founder Karen Slattery meml. scholarship fund Pope John Paul II High Sch., Boca Raton. Recipient Internat. award for individual achievement on behalf of Ireland, 1981; named Woman of Yr., Profl. Arts br. United League Am. Per Women, Boca Raton. Mem. Soc. of Ireland in Fla. (founder, past pres., hon. chmn.), Palm Beach Soc. 2d Life of U. Miami Transplantation (co-founder), Nat. Soc. Arts and Letters (life; ways and means chmn. Boca Raton chpt. 1981). Club: Boca Raton, Boca Pointe. Home: 1200 S Ocean Blvd Boca Raton FL 33432 Office: 403 Golf View Dr Boca Raton FL 33432

COOPER, PATRICIA ANN, journalist, educator, researcher, consultant; b. N.Y.C., Nov. 7, 1953; d. Leslie M. and Louise E. (Macklin) C.; m. James P. Nichols, Aug. 7, 1976 (div. Jan. 1980). Student CUNY, 1972-75; B.S. in Journalism and Edn., Long Island U., 1977; postgrad. Tchrs. Coll. Columbia U., 1979, Bank St. Coll. Edn., 1980. Community reporter, City Scene Newspaper, N.Y.C., 1977; research/editorial asst. Dun's Rev., N.Y.C., 1977-78; tchr. West Side Montessori Sch., N.Y.C., 1978-80; reporter The Pensacola Voice, Fla., 1980-81; adminstrv. asst. Signature Clothing Corp., N.Y.C., 1981; tchr. Langston Hughes Child Devel. Ctr. (now Morningside II Headstart Ctr.), N.Y.C., 1981-82; library inf. asst. Telephone Reference unit N.Y. Pub. Library, 1982-85; freelance writer, N.Y.C., 1985—; temporary perdiem tchr. N.Y.C. Bd. Edn., 1985—; temporary adminstrv. asst. Bread for the World, N.Y.C., 1986; edn. cons. Nat. Urban League, N.Y.C., 1986—. Author, assoc. editor BlackWorks Mag., 1977. Mem. Nat. Assn. Female Execs., Found. for Christian Living, Black Film Makers Found., Nat. Com. for Citizens in Edn. Baptist. Avocations: singing; painting; writing poetry; films; reading. Home: 209 W 104th St New York NY 10025

COOPER, PATRICIA DAWKINS, association executive; b. Houston, Feb. 5, 1944; d. Austin Eli and Sarah Lorraine (Rountree) Dawkins; B.A., Columbia Coll., 1965; children from previous marriage—Catherine Sloane, Sarah Riley, Patricia Daily. Appointments sec. to Congressman Tom Gettys, Washington, 1965; tchr. Lugoff (S.C.) Elem. Sch., 1967-68, Camden (S.C.) Elem. Sch., 1969-70; ombudsman State of S.C., 1970-73; asst. dir. Carolina Cup and Colonial Cup Internat., Camden, 1973—; adminstr. Camden Feed Co., 1973—; office mgr. Camden Tng. Center, thoroughbreds, 1973—; asst. sec. Mulberry Resources, Inc., 1980-82; sec.-treas. Equistar Products Co., 1980—. Bd. dirs. Kershaw County Fine Arts Center; sustaining mem. Camden Jr. Welfare League; bd. dirs. Kershaw County unit Am. Cancer Soc., 1980—; chmn. bd. dirs. Kershaw unit Am. Heart Assn., 1984—; bd. dirs. Palmetto Balloon Classic, 1983-86; mem. Kershaw County Tourism Adv. Com., 1986—. Mem. Nat. Steeplechase and Hunt Assn., Nat. Hay Assn., Greater Kershaw County C. of C. (v.p. pub. affairs 1983-86), Thoroughbred Assn. S.C. (sec.-treas. 1986—). Democrat. Methodist. Clubs: Camden Country, Sprindale Hall. Home: 409 Laurens Ct Camden SC 29020 Office: Knights Hill Rd Camden SC 29020

COOPER, PAULETTE MARCIA, author; b. Antwerp, Belgium, July 26, 1945; came to U.S., 1951; naturalized, 1951; d. Ted E. and Stella R. (Toepfer) C.; B.A. with honors, Brandeis U., 1964; M.A., CUNY, 1968. Free-lance writer, 1968—. Recipient Edgar Allan Poe spl. award Mystery Writers Am., 1975. Mem. Am. Soc. Journalists and Authors, N.Y. Press Club, Investigative Reporters and Editors, Nat. Acad. TV Arts & Scis., Travel Journalists Guild, Sigma Delta Chi. Author 6 books including: The Scandal of Scientology; The Medical Detectives; Growing Up Puerto Rican, also 500 articles. Address: 300 E 40th St New York NY 10016

COOPER, PHYLLIS YVONNE, secretary educator; b. Checotah, Okla., Oct. 6, 1949; d. Joseph Wilson and Edna Mae (Harris) C. A.A., Connors State U., Warner, Okla., 1969; B.S. in Bus. Edn., Northeastern State U., 1971, postgrad., 1979— . Sec. various depts. Muskogee Gen. Hosp., Okla., 1971-83; edn. sec., program asst. Muskogee Regional Med. Ctr., 1983—. Youth adviser Assembly of God Ch., Checotah, Okla., 1983—, sec.-treas., 1985—; sec. Lakewood Area Council Girl Scouts U.S., 1984—. Mem. Am. Bus. Women's Assn. (sec. 1983-84, pres. 1985-86; named Woman of Yr. 1985), Nat. Assn. Female Execs. Democrat. Avocations: singing, music, photography. Office: Muskogee Regional Med Ctr 300 Rockefeller Dr Muskogee OK 74401

COOPER, SUSAN CHALLEN, lawyer; b. Seattle, July 25, 1948; d. Herbert James and Virginia Lindsay (Wiese) Challen; 1 son, Jeffrey Challen Cooper. B.A., Stanford U., 1970; J.D. Boston Coll., 1977. Bar: Mass. 1977. Asst. editor Field Publs., Inc., Palo Alto, Calif., 1972-74; assoc. Bingham, Dana & Gould, Boston, 1977—. Contbr. articles to Boston Coll. Law Rev., 1975-76, articles editor, 1976-77. Bd. dirs. Wellesley Community Children's Ctr., 1983—. Nat. Merit scholar, 1966. Mem. ABA, Mass. Bar Assn., Boston Bar Assn., ACLU, Order of Coif. Democrat. Office: Bingham Dana & Gould 100 Federal St Boston MA 02110

COOPER, SUSAN LEE GENSEL, librarian; b. Los Angeles, May 2, 1941; d. John Pershing and Doris Olive (Tonk) Oder; m. William E. Gensel, Mar. 30, 1961 (div. Dec. 1981); children—Douglas, Robert; m. Robert E. Cooper, Sept. 21, 1985. B.A., U. Calif.-Riverside, 1964; M.S.L.S., U. So. Calif., 1971. Head serials tech. processing and automation U. Calif.-Riverside, 1964-70; head research librarian Cold Spring Harbor (N.Y.) Lab., 1972-77, dir. mktg. and libraries, 1978—; personal asst. Harry Chapin, folk-singer and composer, 1976-81; library cons. Performing Arts Found. L.I., 1975-80, sec. to bd. trustees, 1975-80; library cons. Otisville, Inc., N.Y., 1983-84. Compiler Cell Index, 1978; reviewer Med. Ref. Series Quar., 1982; spl. asst. Nobelist B. McClintock, 1983—. Mem. State Task Force on Planning Library Devel. on L.I., 1976-78; del. Gov.'s Conf. on Libraries, 1978; campaign chmn. Republicans for Sammis, Huntington, N.Y., 1983. Mem. Spl. Libraries Assn. (chpt. pres. 1976-77, div. pres. elect 1978-79), Med. Theatre N.Y. (dir. 1975-77), ALA, Suffolk County Library Assn., Nassau Library Assn., L.I. Library Resources Council (pres. 1975-77), Beta Phi Mu. Home: 37 Madison St Huntington NY 11743 Office: Cold Spring Harbor Library Box 100 Cold Spring Harbor NY 11724

COOPER, SUSAN M., insurance agent; b. Boston, Apr. 30, 1960; d. Saul and Sylvia Judith (Singer) Cooper. B.S.Ed., Keene State Coll., 1982. Ins. agt. Equitable Life Ins. Co., Wellesley, Mass., 1984—; teen counselor/health educator South Boston Community Health Ctr., 1982-84. Trustee Fox Run Condo Assn., Easton, Mass., 1985. Named Rookie of the Year, Women's Life Underwriters, Wellesley, 1984. Mem. Boston Life Underwriters, Life Underwriters Tng. Council, Million Dollar Round Table. Office: Equitable Life Assurance 45 Williams St Wellesley MA 02181

COOPER, THEODOSHIA SARAH MAE, rehab. social worker; b. Eudora, Ark., Mar. 26, 1925; d. James Weldon and Leola (Simon) Johnson; B.S. in Edn., Ark. Bapt. Coll., 1951; M.Ed., U. Ark., Fayetteville, 1980; m. J.V. Cooper, Apr. 12, 1944 (dec. Sept. 1980); children—Mary Louise, Patricia Ann. High sch. tchr., Ark., 1946-47; prin., tchr. Gravel Hill Elem. Sch., Benton, Ark., 1947-48; spl. edn. tchr. Children's Convalescent Center, Jacksonville, Ark., 1948-56; tchr., social worker Ark. Sch. Deaf, Little Rock, 1957-58; psychiat. social worker Ark. State Hosp., Little Rock, 1958-66, Easter Seal Agy., Little Rock, 1966-69; rehab. social worker, then supr. Ark. Rehab. Services, 1969-74, adminstr. facilities program, 1979—; Bd. dirs. Ark. Youth Planning Council; mem. Ark. Mental Health Adv. Bd.; bd. dirs. Little Rock YMCA; bd. dirs., sec. Little Rock Legal Aid Soc.; mem. Little Rock Community Concert Assn. Recipient award Ark. conf. Social Welfare, 1976, also numerous certs. and service awards; grantee Ark. Alcoholic Found., Yale U., Nat. Found. Infantile Paralysis, Eastern Mich. Coll., George Washington U. Mem. Nat. Rehab. Assn. (v.p. Ark. chpt. 1978), Ark. Assn. Mental Health (dir.), Ark. Rehab. Assn. (v.p. 1978), Am. Personnel and Guidance Assn., Am. Rehab. Counselor Assn., Nat. Rehab. Counseling Assn., Nat. Assn. Social Workers, Ark. Juvenile Correctional Assn. (past pres.), Ark. Council Social Welfare (past pres.), Am. Assn. Workers Blind, Am. Council Blind, Nat. Rehab. Adminstrn. Assn., Ark. Assn. Human Services, AAUW, Am. Public Welfare Assn., LWV. Baptist. Home: 1915 Battery St Little Rock AR 72202 Office: 1320-H Brookwood Dr Little Rock AR 72203

COOPERPERSON, ELLEN DONNA, university administrator, consultant; b. Bklyn., Mar. 28, 1946; d. Samuel and Eve (Satz) Bloom; m. Norman Cooperman, Nov. 24, 1965 (div. 1972); 1 child, Brian Cooperman. M.A. in Human Resource Devel. and Tng., Goddard grad. program Vt. Coll. at Norwich U., Montpelier, 1983. Prin. Beachbrook Sch., bklyn., 1970-72; br. mgr. Hershey Foods Corp., Farmingdale, N.Y., 1972-75; ops. mgr. Multi-Media Films, Babylon, N.Y., 1975-78; exec. dir. women's ednl. and counseling ctr. SUNY-Farmingdale, 1978—; cons. Human Resource Devel. and Tng. Ctr., Farmingdale, 1978—; mem. adj. faculty Cornell U., Farmingdale, N.Y., 1979-85; coordinator women's project C. W. Post Coll., Brentwood, N.Y., 1979-85. Producer/dir. films: Women Now, 1974; Yes Baby, She's My Sir, 1978. Del. NOW, N.Y., 1975-77, White House Commn., N.Y., 1978. Recipient Human Services award Office County Exec., Suffolk County, N.Y., 1983, proclamation Office County Exec., Nassau County, N.Y., 1984. Mem. L.I. Ctr. for Bus. and Profl. Women (bd. dirs. 1980-81), Am. Soc. Tng. and Devel., Internat. TV Assn. Office: SUNY Women's Ednl and Counseling Ctr Farmingdale NY 11735

COPE, ESTHER SIDNEY, history educator; b. West Chester, Pa., Sept. 10, 1942; d. Robert Wellington and Jane Davis (Stanton) Cope. B.A., Wilson Coll., 1964; M.A., U. Wis., 1965; Ph.D., Bryn Mawr Coll., 1969. Instr. history Ursinus Coll., Collegeville, Pa., 1968-70, asst. prof., 1970-75; asst. prof. of history U. Nebr., Lincoln, 1975-76, assoc. prof., 1976-81, prof., 1981—, chmn. dept., 1982-85. Author: Life of a Public Man, 1980; editor: Proceedings in Parliament, 1640, 1977; contbr. articles to profl. jours. Woodrow Wilson fellow, 1964; Woodrow Wilson dissertation fellow, 1967. Fellow Royal Hist. Soc.; mem. Am. Hist. Assn., Conf. on Brit. Studies, Internat. Commn. for History of Rep. and Parliamentary Instns., Phi Beta Kappa. Quaker. Office: Dept of History U Nebr Lincoln NE 68588

COPE, NANCY ELIZABETH, news producer; b. Woodbury, N.J., Dec. 4, 1952; d. William Fox and Kathryn Florence (Pime) C. B.S., U. Tenn., 1974. News reporter, editor Houston News Service, 1975-78; news assignment editor Sta. KHOU-TV, Houston, 1978-79; news producer Sta. KTRK-TV, Houston, 1979—. Mem. Soc. Profl. Journalists, NOW, Internat. Platform Assn. Office: KTRK-TV 3310 Bissonnet St Houston TX 77005

COPELAND, CAROLYN ABIGAIL, university dean; b. White Plains, N.Y., May 5, 1931; d. Robert Erford and Mary Terwilliger; B.A. (CEW scholar), U. Mich., 1973, M.A. (Rackham Grad. Student scholar), 1979; m. William E. Copeland, Aug. 16, 1964; children—Rob Cameron, Diana Elizabeth Bosworth. With dean's office Coll. Lit., Sci. and Arts, U. Mich., Ann Arbor, 1967—, asst. dean, 1980-84, assoc. dean, 1984—. Mem. Mortar Bd., Phi Beta Kappa (v.p. Alpha chpt. 1984—). Author: Tankas from the Koelz Collection, 1980; Walter Norman Koelz, A Biography, in progress. Research in Buddhist art history. Home: 520 Darwin Rd Pinckney MI 48169 Office: University of Michigan Ann Arbor MI 48109

COPELAND, KAREN LEE, TV executive; b. Chgo., Jan. 14, 1946; d. Hymen and Blanche (Feder) Cohen; m. Donald Copeland, May 30, 1974 (div. 1984). Student, Drake U., 1964-66; B.F.A., Columbia Coll., Chgo., 1968. Mem. prodn. staff WLS-TV, Chgo., 1967-69, exec. producer, 1969; freelance producer, dir., Los Angeles, 1969-73, programs include: The David Frost Show, The Della Reese Show, The Bob Hope Show, Christmas Around the World, 1970-71; staff producer WMAQ-TV, NBC, Chgo., 1973-81, mgr. programming, 1981; programs include: NBC Salutes Chic Chicago, Small World; dir. programming WNBC-TV, NBC, N.Y.C., 1981—, exec. producer spls.: Ask the Governors, Atomic High School, The Foxfire Glow, Town Meetings, Blacks: Present and Accounted For, Christmas in Rockefeller Center. Recipient Emmy award as producer Ask the Governors; Chgo. Emmy award for Best Spl. Event Program, NBC Salutes Chic Chicago. Mem. Directors Guild Am., Nat. Assn. TV Programming Execs., Internat. Radio and TV Soc. Address: Program Dir Sta WNBC-TV 30 Rockefeller Plaza New York NY 10020

COPELAND, TATIANA BRANDT, accountant, tax executive; b. Dresden, Germany; came to U.S., 1959, naturalized, 1967; d. Cyril Alexander and Maria (von Satin) Brandt; m. Gerret van Sweringen Copeland, May 12, 1979. B.S. summa cum laude, UCLA, 1964; M.B.A, U. Calif.-Berkeley, 1966. Sr. tax cons. Price Waterhouse & Co., Los Angeles, 1966-72; asst. tax mgr. Whittaker Corp., Los Angeles, 1972-75; mgr. internat. dept. E. I. Du Pont de Nemours, Wilmington, Del., 1975-80; pres. Tebec Assocs. Ltd., Wilmington, 1980—. Bd. dirs. Del. Symphony, Grand Opera House, N.Y.C. Opera, Nat. Symphony Orch., Washington; presdl. appointee Adv. Com. for Trade Negotiations, 1982—; mem. New Castle County Fin. Adv. Council, Del. Heritage Commn. Mem. Am. Inst. C.P.A.s, Calif. Soc. C.P.A.s, Del. Soc. C.P.A.s, Am. Woman's Soc. C.P.A.s, Am. Soc. Women Accts., World Affairs Council, Internat. Fiscal Assn., Internat. Assn. Fin. Planning, Wilmington Women in Bus., Phi Beta Kappa. Club: Rodney Square (dir.). Home: 175 Brecks Ln Wilmington DE 19807 Office: PO Box 3662 Wilmington DE 19807

COPESS, JOYCE TRAVIS, association executive; b. Lamar, Colo., Jan. 29, 1947; d. Morris Eugene and Mildred Marie (Neary) T.; m. Richard Dee Copess, Sept. 19, 1970. B.A., Colo. State U., 1969; postgrad. U. No. Colo., 1970-73, Ill. State U., 1976-81. Staff asst. in mgmt. communications State Farm Ins., Bloomington, Ill., 1969-81; staff v.p. edn. and communications Inst. Real Estate Mgmt. of Nat. Assn. Realtors, Chgo., 1981—; cons., lectr. in field. Mem. Pub. Relations Soc. Am., Internat. Bus. Communications, Women in Communications. Office: Inst Real Estate Mgmt 430 N Michigan Ave Chicago IL 60611

COPLEY, HELEN KINNEY, newspaper publisher; b. Cedar Rapids, Iowa, Nov. 28, 1922; d. Fred Everett and Margaret (Casey) Kinney; m. James S. Copley, Aug. 16, 1965 (dec.); 1 son, David Casey. Attended, Hunter Coll., N.Y.C., 1945. Assoc. The Copley Press, Inc., 1952—, chmn. exec. com., chmn. corp., dir., 1973—, chief exec. officer, sr. mgmt. bd., 1974—; chmn. bd. Copley News Service, San Diego, 1973—; chmn. editorial bd. Union-Tribune Pub. Co., 1973—; pub. San Diego Union and The Tribune, 1973—. Chmn. bd., trustee James S. Copley Found., 1973—; mem. Friends of Internat. Center, La Jolla. La Jolla Mus. Contemporary Art, La Jolla Town Council, Inc.; life patroness Makua Aux.; charter mem. San Diego Women's Council, Navy League; Life mem. San Diego Hall of Sci.; mem. San Diego Soc. Natural History; mem. women's com. San Diego Symphony Assn., Scripps Meml. Hosp. Aux., Social Service League of La Jolla; Life mem. Star of India Aux., Zool. Soc. San Diego; mem. YWCA; hon. chmn., bd. dirs. Washington Crossing Found.; trustee, bd. dirs. Freedoms Found. at Valley Forge; trustee, trustee devel. com. Scripps Clinic and Research Found.; trustee U. San Diego. Mem. Inter Am. Press Assn. (dir.), Calif. Press Assn., Am. Soc. Newspaper Editors, Am. Press Inst., Calif. Newspaper Pubs. Assn., Greater Los Angeles, Nat., San Diego, San Francisco press clubs, Nat. Newspaper Assn., Western Newspaper Found., Sigma Delta Chi. Republican. Roman Catholic. Clubs: Aurora (Ill.) Country; Cuyamaca, San Diego Yacht, Univ., U. San Diego Presidents (San Diego); De Anza Country (Borrego Springs, Calif.); La Jolla Beach and Tennis, La Jolla Country. Office: Copley Newspapers 7776 Ivanhoe Ave La Jolla CA 92038

COPLEY, SHARRON CAULK, educator; b. Columbia, Tenn., Oct. 2, 1947; d. Tom English and Beulah (Goodin) Caulk; children—Christopher, George English, Steffenee. B.A., George Peabody Coll. Tchrs., 1970; M.S., Vanderbilt U., 1980. Tchr., Ft. Campbell Jr. High Sch., Ky., 1970-71, Whitthorne Jr. High Sch., Columbia, Tenn., 1977—; chmn. edn. Homecoming '86 Maury County Schs., Columbia, 1984-86. Mem. Maury County Edn. Assn. (pres. 1983-84), Tenn. Edn. Assn., NEA, AAUW (pres. Tenn. div. 1983-85), Nat. Council Tchrs. English, Phi Delta Kappa. Mem. Ch. of Christ. Home: 1090 Rolling Fields Columbia TN 38401 Office: Whitthorne Jr High Sch 915 Experiment Ln Columbia TN 38401

COPOULOS, STACI GEORGE, nurse, health education coordinator; b. Sacramento, Mar. 8, 1957; d. George Ernest and JoAnna (Stilianos) C. B.S. in Nursing, B.A. in Sociology, U. Fla., 1981. R.N., Fla. Commd. 2d lt. U.S. Air Force, 1982; nurse intern U.S. Air Force Hosp., Wright Patterson AFB, Dayton, Ohio, 1982; staff nurse U.S. Air Force Hosp., Tinker AFB, Oklahoma City, 1982-85, health edn. coordinator, 1982-85; staff nurse David Grant Med. Ctr., Travis AFB, Calif., 1985—. Author booklet for diabetics, 1983. Republican. Greek Orthodox. Avocations: racquetball; swimming; horseback riding. Office: USAF Hosp David Grant Med Ctr Travis AFB CA

COPP, KATHRYN LYNN, advertising executive; b. Harlingen, Tex., Apr. 17, 1948; d. Clarence Charles and Frances Lucille (Adams) Adler; m. Dean Alfred Manson Mar. 16, 1974 (div. 1980); children—Troy Adler, Corey Bassett; m. Emmanuel Anthony Copp, June 18, 1983. B.B.A., U. Tex., 1970. Asst. v.p. Henry S. Miller Co., Dallas, 1970-75; buyer advt. Bozell & Jacobs, Dallas, 1976-81; v.p. Levenson & Levenson, Dallas, 1981—. Mem. Women's Guild, United Cerebral Palsy Assn., 1980—. Democrat. Roman Catholic. Home: 6614 Dartbrook Dallas TX 75240

COPP, LAUREL ARCHER, university dean; b. Sioux Falls, S.D., Nov. 12, 1931; B.S. in Nursing Edn., Dakota Wesleyan U., 1956; M. Nursing Edn., U. Pitts., 1960, Ph.D., 1967; cert. program health systems mgmt., Harvard U., 1974; m. John Dixon Copp. Asso. prof. Pa. State U., 1966-72; vis. prof. Thiel Coll., Greenville, Pa., 1969-75, also chief nursing research div. VA Central Office Dept. Medicine and Surgery, Washington, 1972-75; dean Sch. Nursing, prof. U. N.C., Chapel Hill, 1975—; vis. prof. Georgetown U., 1974, U. Tex., Arlington, 1985; mem. policy bd. Health Services Research Center; former chmn. Va./Carolinas' Doctoral Consortium; chair panel 55th NIH Consensus Conf. on Pain Mgmt., 1986. Named Alumnus of Yr., Dakota Wesleyan U., 1981, U. Pitts., 1982. Fellow Am. Acad. nursing; mem. Am. Assn. Colls. of Nursing, Am. Nurses Assn., Nat. League Nursing, Internat. Assn. Study of Pain, Sigma Theta Tau, Delta Kappa Gamma, Pi Lambda Theta. Editor: (with others) Recent Advances in Nursing (series); Perspectives on Pain, 1985; overseas mem. editorial bd. Jour. Advanced Nursing, London, Nursing and Health Care; asst. editor: Jour. Profl. Nursing; editorial bd. Scandinavian Jour. Caring Scis.; contbr. articles to profl. jours. Office: 107 Carrington Hall Chapel Hill NC 27514

COPPENHAVER, (CHARLOTTE) ANNE POWERS, school administrator, lecturer; b. Lebanon, Va., Sept. 6, 1945; d. Ralph Thomas and Charlotte Marie (Ayers) P.; m. Dorian H. Coppenhaver, Jan. 19, 1974. B.A., Duke U., 1967, M.A. in Edn., 1973, Ed.D., 1977. Cert. tchr., Tex. Curriculum developer, instr. Washington City Schs., 1967-70; cons. social studies N.C. Dept. Edn., Raleigh, 1970-73; instr. Bklyn. Coll., 1973-77; asst. prin. Dickinson High Sch., Tex., 1979-81, prin., 1981—; cons. Tex. Gulf Coast Schs.; lectr. U. Houston, Clear Lake City, 1982—. Mem. Nat. Assn. Secondary Sch. Prins., Tex. Assn. Secondary Sch. Prins., Dickinson C. of C., Delta Kappa Gamma. Lutheran. Avocations: playing piano; reading. Office: Dickinson High Sch 3800 Baker Dr Dickinson TX 77539

COPPERSMITH, MARIAN UNGAR, magazine publisher; b. Wilkes-Barre, Pa., June 11, 1933; d. Max H. and Tillie (Landau) Ungar; B.A., Pa. State U., 1953; m. Sy Barash, Jan. 31, 1954 (dec. Feb. 1975); children—Carol Lynn, Nan Ruth; m. 2d, W. Louis Coppersmith, Apr. 29, 1978. Tech. writer Kling Studios, Chgo., 1951; editorial dir. Daily Collegian, State College, Pa., 1953; grad. asst. dept. speech Pa. State U., State Coll., 1953-55; writer, salesman Friedman & Barash, State College, 1956-59; pub. State College Town-Gown, 1959—, pres., 1975—; cons. mktg. and public relations to various fin. instns.; instr. mktg. Pa. State U., University Park, 1973—. Chmn., Art Alliance Fund Campaign, 1971; mem. public relations com. Central Pa. Heart Assn., 1973; chmn. Cancer Crusade, State College, 1973-74; mem. Pa. Commn. for Women, 1980—; bd. govs. Pa. Free Enterprise Week, 1981—; vice chmn. bd. govs. Centre County Community Found., 1981—; pres. Nittany Council of Republican Women, 1960-61; bd. dirs. United Fund, 1965-70, asst. chmn., 1969; trustee Pa. State U., 1976—; bd. dirs. Pennsylvanians for Effective Govt., 1978; bd. dirs. United Way Pa., 1977—, treas., 1978; bd. dirs. Capital Blue Cross, 1978—, Women's Campaign Fund, 1982-85, Pa. Ben Franklin Partnership, 1983—, Mercy Hosp., Johnstown, 1983—. Recipient Kiwanis award, 1976, Small Businessperson of Year, 1981, Service to Soc. award Coll. Liberal Arts of Pa. State U., 1984. Mem. Nat. (public relations com. 1972-73), Pa. (public relations counsel 1967-75) cable TV assns., Women in Communications, C. of C. (dir. 1973-79, pres. 1974-75), Pa. C. of C. (dir. 1974—), Phi Sigma Sigma. Mem. B'nai B'rith (pres. 1956). Contbr. articles to profl. jours. Home: 620 Toftrees Ave Apt 359 State College PA 16803 also 900 Parkview Dr Johnstown PA 15905 Office: 403 S Allen St State College PA 16801

CORBETT, BARBARA LOUISE, advertising agency executive; b. Sioux City, Iowa, May 6, 1947; d. Bayliss and Shirley Louise (Wiese) Corbett; m. Henry F. Terbrueggen, Jr., Nov. 22, 1976. B.A. in Polit. Sci., Antioch Coll., 1969. Cert. bus. communicator. Copywriter, J.L. Hudson Co., Detroit, 1969-72, Patten Co., Southfield, Mich., 1972-73; copywriter/producer Campbell Ewald, Detroit, 1973-75; free lance writer, 1975-76; pres. Corbett Advt., Inc., Rochester, Mich., 1977—; tchr. Barbizon Sch., Southfield, 1979; prof. advt. Oakland Community Coll., 1980-82; judge Detroit News Scholastic Writing Awards competition, Detroit, 1979-80; lectr. in field. Recipient award for Ad of the Year, J.L. Hudson Co., 1971; Merit award Scklemian, 1971; Gold Award Creative Advt. Club of Detroit, 1974; others. Mem. Greater Rochester C. of C. (dir.), Indsl. Marketers of Detroit (past pres.), Mich. Advt. Agy. Council (past pres.), Midstates Agy. Network (past pres.), Adcraft. Republican. Unitarian. Home: 6175 Sheldon Rd Rochester MI 48063 Office: Corbett Advt Inc 800 W University Dr Suite F Rochester MI 48063

CORBETT, ELIZABETH MARIE, librarian; b. Paterson, N.J., Mar. 23, 1926; d. Alfred and Freda (Hartung) Crew; m. Edward Richard Corbett, Oct. 9, 1954. B.A., Wellesley Coll., 1947; M.L.S., Simmons Coll., 1969. With AT&T, N.Y.C., Pacific Telephone and Telegraph, San Francisco, New Eng. Telephone and Telegraph, Boston, 1947-68; circulation librarian Barnard Coll., N.Y.C., 1969-80, dir. library, 1980—; cons. Silliman U. Library, Dumaguete City, Philippines, 1977. Contbr. articles to profl. jours. Chair, China Libraries Commn. United Bd. Christian Higher Edn. in Asia, N.Y., 1978—. Mem. N.Y. Library Assn. (pres. acad. and spl. library sect. 1979-80), ALA. Office: Barnard Coll Library 3009 Broadway New York NY 10027

CORBETT, RUTH ALLEEN, artist, writer; b. Northville, Mich., Jan. 24, 1912; d. Howard James and Rhoda Alice (Fuller) Corbett; student Cranbrook Acad., 1932, Meinzinger Found. Art Sch., 1935-36, Famous Writer's Sch., 1967-69; m. Roy Brent, Feb. 23, 1958; children—Jana Loi Janczarek, Paton. Illustrator Simons-Michelson Advt. Co., Detroit, 1935-37, Bass-Luckoff, Inc., Detroit, 1937-39, Detroit Times, 1939-40, Canfield Assos., Detroit, 1947-53, Dow Chem Co., Midland, Mich., 1950-53, Creative Services, Detroit, 1953-56, Parke-Davis Pharm. Co., Detroit, 1954-56, H.J. Heinz Co., 1950, Mich. Bell Telephone Co., 1954-56, Detroit Edison Co., 1950-53, various automobile mfg. cos., 1947-53; advt. illustrator Universal Pictures Co., Universal City, Calif., 1956-74; tchr. art as pvt. tutor, also adult classes Pontiac (Mich.) High Sch., 1933-34; one woman show Freeman Gallery, Montrose, Calif., 1964; group shows Art Instrn., Mpls., 1935-65; exhibitor, lectr. on movie advt. art, writing books, 1979; columnist, cartoonist Sun City (Calif.) Times; executed mural Pontiac C. of C., 1934. Recipient Grand prize, numerous 1st prizes Art Instrn., Mpls., 1935-64, 1st, 2d, 3d prizes San Fernando Valley Club, 1961-63; Nonfiction Book award for Dying for a Cigarette?, Nat. Writers Club, 1976, Book award for Some Doctors Make Me Sick, 1980, Nat. Writers Club awards for Diary of a Hill Hugger, 1982, Some of My Best Friends Can Fly, 1983. Mem. Soc. Illustrators, Nat. Writers Club, Sun City Creative Writer's Group, Arts and Crafts Guild, Pontiac Sketch Club (pres. 1932-33), San Fernando Valley Art Club, Canyon Lake Art Assn. (2 awards for water color). Republican. Mem. Methodist-Episcopalian Ch. Author and illustrator: Daddy Danced the Charleston, 1970; Art as a Living, 1984; A Matter of Line; contbr. numerous articles on motion picture advt. to various mags. Home: 25681 Sun City Blvd Sun City CA 92381

CORBIN, KAREN SUE, management consulting company executive; b. N.Y.C., Dec. 12, 1945; d. Leonard and Claire Cynthia (Rothenberg) C.; B.S., N.Y.U., 1967, M.A., 1971. With Xerox Corp., 1973-86, mgr. office systems cons. program, Dallas, 1977-79, br. mgr., Chgo., 1979-81, mgr. dealer sales planning, Dallas, 1981-82, mgr. mktg. ops., 1982-83, nat. mgr. customer support and edn., 1983-84, nat. systems support mgr., 1985-86; pres. Advanced Resource Mgmt., Dallas, 1986—. Mem. Internat. Word Processing Assn., Nat.

Assn. Female Execs., Assn. Women Entrepreneurs Dallas, Phi Beta Kappa. Home and Office: 17659 Sun Meadow Dr Dallas TX 75252

CORBIN, KATRINA B., stockbroker, financial planner; b. Augusta, Ga., Sept. 4, 1952; d. James Foster and Margie (Hundley) Bowers; m. Wallace R. Land, June 21, 1973 (dec. 1978); m. William M. Corbin, Mar. 31, 1984. Student Wesleyan Coll., 1970-72, Augusta Coll., 1972-73, N.Y. Inst. Fin., 1981-82, Coll. Fin. Planning, 1985-86. With investment services Ga. Railroad Bank, Augusta, 1979-82; stockbroker Interstate Securities Corp., Augusta, 1982—; cons. New Horizons Investment Club, Augusta, 1983—, Heiress Investment Club, Augusta, 1983—, Augusta Woman's Club Investment Club, 1983—. Author newsletter, 1984. Active Augusta Woman's Club, 1984—. Mem. Internat. Assn. Fin. Planning, Inst. Cert. Fin. Planners, Nat. Assn. Female Execs., Network Augusta. Club: Toastmasters. Avocations: Aerobics; cross stitching. Home: 3318 Wheeler Rd Augusta GA 30909 Office: Interstate Securities Corp 699 Broad St Suite 1112 Augusta GA 30901

CORBIN, KRESTINE MARGARET, author, fashion designer, columnist; b. Reno, Apr. 24, 1937; d. Lawrence Albert and Judie Ellen (Johnston) Dickinson; B.S., U. Calif.-Davis, 1958; m. Lee D. Corbin, May 16, 1959 (div. 1982); children—Michelle Marie, Sheri Karin. Asst. prof. Bauder Coll., Sacramento, 1974—; columnist Sacramento Bee, 1976-81; owner Creative Sewing Co., Sacramento, 1976—; pres. Sierra Machinery Corp., Sparks, Nev., 1983—; nat. sales and promotion mgr. Westwood Retail Fabrics, N.Y.C., 1985—; cons. in field. Mem. Crocker Art Gallery Assn., 1960-78; mem. Republican Party election com., Sacramento, 1964, 68. Mem. Home Economists in Bus., Am. Home Econs. Assn., Internat. Fashion Group, Women's Fashion Fabrics Assn., Omicron Nu. Author: Suede Fabric Sewing Guide, 1973; Creative Sewing Book, 1978; (audio-visual) Fashions in the Making, 1974; producer: Cream of the Cream Collections (nat. show in 40 cities), 1978—; Style is What You Make It!, (nat. buyers show). Address: Westwood Inc. 1412 Broadway New York NY 10018

CORBIN, RORI COOPER, therapeutic recreation specialist, educator, consultant; b. N.Y.C., July 30, 1951; d. Charles Kneeland and Rose Elizabeth (Maggio) Cooper; m. William Ogden Corbin, Jr., Apr. 19, 1980; children—Drew Cooper, Laurel Foxworth. B.A., SUNY-Purchase, 1973; M.A., NYU, 1980. Cert. therapeutic recreation specialist. Sr. recreation therapist N.Y. State Letchworth, Thiells, 1975-86; cons. Corbin & Corbin Consulting, Monroe, N.Y., 1986—; mem. guest faculty Keane Coll., N.J., 1981; instr., trainer N.Y. Office Mental Retardation/Developmental Disabilities, 1981-82; instr. Orange County Community Coll., Middletown, N.Y., 1986. Writer, editor newsletter: The Fourth "r", 1983-85. NYU fellow, 1979-80; N.Y. State grantee, 1979-80. Mem. Nat. Recreation & Parks Assn., Nat. Assn. Female Execs. Republican. Roman Catholic. Avocations: gardening; bicycling; reading; camping. Home and Office: 61 Pine Tree Rd Monroe NY 10950

CORBITT, RUTH HARRIS, food company executive; b. Dehue, W.Va., Sept. 19, 1926; d. George T. and Lila Mae (Smith) Harris; widowed; children—Carol C. Harrison, David V. Student Mountain States Bus. Coll., Morris Harvey Coll. Exec. sec. Chattanooga Glass Co.; founder, owner, pres. Cobb Credit Bur., Mableton, Ga., 1962-65; sales rep., adminstr. Fla. Fish Distbrs. Inc., Jacksonville, Fla., 1965-68, pres., chief exec. officer, owner, 1968; lectr. bus. seminars. Trustee, Fla. Jr. Coll. Found., Jacksonville, 1981—; mem. campaign com. Bus. Women for Reagan-Bush, Washington, 1984. Fellow Southeastern Fisheries Assn.; mem. Jacksonville Women's Network, Fla. Women's Network, Women Bus. Owners of North Fla. (co-chmn. membership com. 1984—), Com. of 200 (rep. for Southeast Region, 1981—, co-chmn. membership com. 1984—). Avocation: painting. Office: Fla Fish Distbrs Inc 2318 Park St Jacksonville FL 32204

CORCORAN, ANN M., radio producer; b. Honesdale, Pa., Sept. 9, 1945; d. Gladys Alene (Collins); m. Stanley Mark Ericsson, May 15, 1971. Student public schs. Scranton, Pa. and N.Y. Revenue coordinator Am. Airlines, N.Y.C., 1963-67; supr. spl. sales, 1967-73, analyst budget and cost control, 1973-78; v.p. Americsson Enterprises, Hawley, Pa., Balt., 1979—; producer Balt. Women's News Mag., 1982-85, radio host, 1985—; mgmt. cons. Cellta Corp. Balt., 1984—. Chmn. Cable TV task force Balt. NOW, 1983—, treas., 1979-82; Md. rep. NOW, 1984—. Avocations: sailing; sewing; sketching. Office: Americksson Enterprises 116 W University Pky #110 Baltimore MD 21210

CORCORAN, KRISTINE DOROTHY, lawyer; b. Milw., Sept. 25, 1958; d. Ned W. Pack and Evelyn Dorothy Flach; m. James Webster Corcoran, May 28, 1983. B.A., Marquette U., 1979; J.D., Drake U., 1982. Bar: Iowa 1983, Nebr. 1983. Assoc., Robert E. Conley, P.C., Des Moines, Iowa, 1983, Harold J. Crawford & Assocs., Des Moines, 1983—. Mem. ABA, Nebr. Bar Assn., Iowa State Bar Assn., Polk County Bar Assn., Polk County Women's Attys., Phi Alpha Delta, Sigma Sigma Sigma, Pi Sigma Alpha, Phi Alpha Theta. Home: 536 43d St Apt 1 Des Moines IA 50312 Office: Harold J Crawford & Assocs 850 Insurance Exchange Bldg Des Moines IA 50309

CORCORAN, MARY BARBARA, educator; b. Pasadena, Calif., May 22, 1924; d. George Ernest and Ina Pearl (Thomas) Morrison; B.A., Wellesley Coll., 1946; M.A., Radcliffe Coll., 1949; postgrad. U. Munchen, 1949-50; Ph.D., Bryn Mawr Coll., 1958; m. James Leonard Corcoran, Dec. 22, 1956; children—Ann Morrison, Elizabeth Phippen. Translator, U.S. War Dept., Nurenberg, Germany, 1946-47; instr. German, Wellesley Coll., Mass., 1947-48; mem. faculty Vassar Coll., Poughkeepsie, N.Y., 1953—, prof., 1977—, chmn. German dept., 1977-83. Mem. Am. Assn. Tchrs. German, AAUP, MLA. Mem. United Ch. of Christ. Office: German Dept Vassar College Poughkeepsie NY 12601

CORCORAN, MAUREEN ELIZABETH, lawyer; b. Iowa City. B.A. cum laude, U. Iowa, 1966, M.A., 1967; J.D., Hastings Coll. Law, 1979. Bar: Calif. 1979. Assoc. Hassard, Bonnington Rogers & Huber, San Francisco, 1979-81; spl. asst. to gen. counsel HHS, Washington, 1981-82; spl. asst. U.S. atty. Dept. Justice, Washington, 1983; gen. counsel Dept. Edn., Washington, 1984-86. Mem. U.S. del. to UN Conf. on Women, Nairobi, Kenya, 1985. Mem. Fed. Bar Assn., ABA, San Francisco Bar Assn. Office: US Dept Edn Room 4087 400 Maryland Ave SW Washington DC 20202

CORCORAN, SHEILA MARGARET, lawyer; b. Evansville, Ind., Nov. 21, 1950; d. Patrick J.V. and Margaret Alice (Booth) Corcoran. B.A. cum laude, U. Evansville, 1972; J.D. cum laude, Ind. U., 1979. Bar: Ind., 1979. Asst. to dir. dept. health ins. AMA, Chgo., 1973-76; assoc. Berger and Berger, Evansville, 1979-83, ptnr., 1984—; Bd. dirs. Legal Aid Soc. Evansville, 1982—, Vanderburgh County CASA, Inc., Women's Alcoholic Halfway House, Evansville, 1982—; mem. adv. council Vanderburgh County Blood Services Council ARC, Evansville, 1982—; Troopleader Raintree Council Girl Scouts U.S., 1970-72, bd. dirs., 1972-73. Mem. Evansville Bar Assn. (continuing legal edn. com., 1985—), Ind. State Bar Assn., ABA. Roman Catholic. Home: 532 S Alvord Blvd Evansville IN 47714 Office: Berger and Berger 313 Main St Evansville IN 47708

CORD, VIRGINIA KIRK THARPE, radio station executive; b. Shreveport, La., Oct. 21, 1905; d. Edgar Allen and Rachel Virginia (Kirk) Tharpe; ed. UCLA, U. Nev.; m. Errett Lobban Cord, Jan. 3, 1931; children—Nancy Cord Phelps, Sally Cord Hummel, Susan Cord Pereira. Owner Sta. KCRL-TV, Reno, Nev. Recipient numerous citations for outstanding radio programming. Mem. Jr. League of Reno, DAR, Colonial Dames Am. Christian Scientist. Club: Reno Executives.

CORDER, BILLIE FARMER, clinical psychologist, artist; b. Dundee, Miss., Sept. 12, 1934; d. Lee Kennith and Jimmy Louise (Hawkins) Farmer; B.S., Memphis State U., 1957; M.A., Vanderbilt U., 1959; Ed.D., U. Ky., 1966; student Memphis Acad. Art, 1959, Sch. Design, N.C. State U., 1971-75; m. Robert Floyd Corder, July 11, 1961. Intern, U. Tenn. Sch. Medicine, Memphis, 1959; staff psychologist Eastern State Hosp., Lexington, Ky., 1960-65, Child Guidance Clinic, Lexington, 1965-67; asst. prof. psychology Inter-Am. U., P.R., 1967-68; dir. psychology adolescent day care Area Community Mental Health Center, Washington, 1968-70; dir. psychol. services Alcoholic Rehab. Center, Butner, N.C., 1970-71; co-dir. psychol. services in child psychiatry Dix Hosp., Raleigh, N.C., 1971—; mem. adv. bd. Raleigh Developmental Evaluation Clinic, 1976—; adj. faculty psychology dept. N.C. State U., Raleigh, 1975—, U. N.C. Sch. Medicine, 1975—. Mem. Wake County Youth Adv. Bd., 1979-80; mem. adv. com. Raleigh Arts Commn.; bd. dirs. Haven House for Children, Nazareth House for Children. Recipient best research award N.C. Dept. Mental Health, 1965, cert. of appreciation Washington Tchrs. Assn., 1969; numerous awards for art, including Purchase award N.C. Mus. Art, 1976, awards N.C. Watercolor Soc., 1978, 79; numerous research grants. Mem. Am. Psychol. Assn., Southeastern Psychol. Assn., N.C. Psychol. Assn., Am. Assn. Psychiat. Services for Children (program chmn. i976-77), Raleigh Artists Guild, Raleigh Fine Arts Soc., N.C. Art Soc., Women's Equity Action League. N.C. Women's Polit. Caucus, Durham Artists Guild, N.C. Watercolor Soc. (v.p.), AAUW. Democrat. Baptist. Club: Raleigh Racquet. Contbr. articles to profl. jours.; dir. editorial bd. N.C. Jour. Mental Health, 1974—; adj. editorial rev. bd. Hosp. and Community Psychiatry, Quar. Jour. Studies on Alcohol. Office: Child Psychiatry Clinic Dix Hospital Raleigh NC 27611

CORDES, LOVERNE CHRISTIAN, interior designer; b. Cleve., Feb. 13, 1927; d. Frank Andrew and Loverne (Brown) Christian; B.S., Purdue U., 1949; m. William Peter Cordes, Nov. 14, 1959; children—Christian Peter, Carey Pomeroy. Interior designer, buyer: Fred Epple Co., Cleve., 1949-67; owner Loverne Christian Cordes, Chagrin Falls, Ohio, 1967—, also mgr., buyer; faculty John Carroll U., Cleve., 1976-77; cons. Cleve. Mus. Art, Western Res. Hist. Soc. Bd. dirs. Dunham Tavern Mus., 1961-62; pres. Dunham Dames, 1971-72; mem. Soc. of Collectors, Western Res. Hist. Soc., Am. Furniture Collectors, Cleve. Mus. Art, Chagrin Falls Hist. Soc., Nat. Trust for Historic Preservation. Fellow Am. Soc. Interior Designers (nat. bd. dirs. 1969-75, nat. v.p. E. Central Region 1972-75, recipient first presdl. citation 1973, 74, 75, soc. rep. to first Russian design seminar 1975 and Internat. Fedn. Interior Design, Sweden 1975); mem. AIA (profl. affiliate), Nat. Home Fashions League (pres. Ohio chpt. 1962-63), Am. Inst. Interior Designers (pres. Ohio chpt. 1969-72), Internat. Platform Assn. Republican. Mem. United Church of Christ. Clubs: Chagrin Valley Country, Bowling Green (Milford, N.J.), Cleve. Garden Center, Audubon Soc., Arcadian Garden (pres. 1980-81), Dogwood Valley Garden, Kappa Kappa Gamma (pres. Cleve. alumni assn. 1966-68). Home and Office: 60 S Franklin St Chagrin Falls OH 44022

CORDINGLEY, MARY JEANETTE BOWLES (MRS. WILLIAM ANDREW CORDINGLEY), social worker, psychologist, artist; b. Des Moines, Jan. 1, 1918; d. William David and Florence (Spurrier) Bowles; student Stephens Coll., 1936; B.A., Carleton Coll., 1939; postgrad. U. Denver, 1944-45; M.A., U. Minn., 1948; grad. art student, 1963; M.A. in Psychology Pepperdine U.; m. William Andrew Cordingley, Mar. 17, 1942; children—William Andrew, Thomas Kent, Constance Louise. Co-pub. Univ. News, 1939-40; with U.S.O. Travelers Aid Service, 1942-44; mem. Jr. League, Des Moines, 1943, bd. dirs., sec. Mpls., 1951-56; clinic psychiat. social worker U. Minn. Hosp., 1947-48; social worker community service project neuropediatrics U. Minn., 1964-65; med. dir. med. sch. service Mont. Deaconess Hosp., 1970-74; instigator, pres. Original Pioneer Prints Notepaper Co.; paintings in variety of galleries and traveling shows; exhibited in numerous one man shows Chas. Russell Gallery, Mont., Student Union U. Minn., Nat. Biennial League Am. Pen Women, 1968, 70, U. Mont., 1974, Mont. Traveling Exhibit, 1966-67, Mus. of the Rockies hist. show, 1976, Bergen Art Guild, 1976-78, Russell Auction, 1977; graphic artist in metal etchings, represented Des Moines Art Center, other galleries; therapist Mental Health Center, 1977-82. Organizer, Hazeltine Nat. Golf Club Womens Assn., 1962-64, I. & R. Center, 1967; pres. adv. bd. Mont. State U.; past mem. bd. dirs. United Way, Youth Guidance Home. Recipient various awards. Mem. Nat. Assn. Social Workers, State Arts Council, Acad. Certified Social Workers. Co-author: Series on Mont. Instns. Home: 42 Prospect Dr Great Falls MT 59405

CORE, MARY CAROLYN W. PARSONS, radiologic technologist; b. Valparaiso, Fla., Dec. 8, 1949; d. Levi and Mary Etta (Elliott) Willey; m. Joel Kent Core, Aug. 3, 1979; 1 dau., Candace W. Parsons. Student Peninsula Gen. Hosp. Sch. Radiologic Tech., Salisbury, Md., 1969, U. Del. Extension, 1969-73, Del. Tech. Community Coll., 1973-79, St. Joseph's Coll., 1983-86. Technologist, Peninsula Gen. Hosp., Salisbury, 1967-72, tech. dir. edn. Sch. Radiologic Tech., 1973-75; technologist Johns Hopkins Hosp., 1972-73, Nanticoke Meml. Hosp., Seaford, Del., 1975-79; adminstrv. chief technologist, imaging depts. Shady Grove Adventist Hosp., Rockville, Md., 1979-81; dir. dept. radiol. scis., chief ops. officer Anne Arundel Diagnostics, Inc., and Anne Arundel MRI (Magnetic Resonance Imaging), Annapolis, Md., 1981—. Mem. Central Md. Council Girl Scouts U.S.A., Md. Soc. Radiologic Technologists (pres. 1980-81, sr. bd. mem. 1982-83, various awards including 1st Pl. Essay award 1974, 76, 84), Soc. Nuclear Medicine Technologists, Am. Hosp. Radiology Adminstrs. (v.p. 1984-85, chmn. by-laws com. 1984-85, statis. resources com. 1985-86), Am. Mgmt. Assn., Nat. Assn. Female Execs., Eastern Shore Dist. Radiologic Technologists (pres. 1976-78). Republican. Methodist. Home: 1907 Harcourt Ave Crofton MD 21114 Office: Franklin and Cathedral Sts Annapolis MD 21401

CORELL, BELLE OLIVER, educator, club and civic worker, writer; b. Suffolk, Va., July 30, 1902; d. Samuel Columbus and Eureka (Ashburn) Oliver; m. James Wesley Simmons, Apr. 27, 1926 (div. Apr. 1929); children—Belle Oliver (Mrs. Wm. E. Traver II), John Oliver; m. Harold Clifford Hart, Oct. 15, 1934 (dec. July 1937); m. Archibald Gerald Corell, Nov. 2, 1974 (dec. Aug. 1980). Student Mary Washington Coll., Fredericksburg, Va., 1920-22; A.B., George Washington U., 1944. Tchr., Martha Washington Coll., Abingdon, Va., 1922-23, Harpers Ferry (W.Va.) High Sch., 1923-24, Hopewell (Va.) High Sch., 1924-26, 28-29; asst. prin., Tenacre and Wellesley, Mass., 1938-39; asst. state service officer Dept. Public Welfare, Richmond, Va., 1929-31; adminstrv. asst. Dept. Justice, Washington, 1931-33; sec. NRA, Fed. Emergency Relief Adminstrn., U.S. Govt., 1933-34; nat. def. WPB, Washington, 1940-44; exec. sec. woman's aux. Episcopal Diocese Mass., Boston, 1945-48; asso. John M. Hancock, Lehman Bros., N.Y.C., 1948-54. Pres. Boston chpt. U.D.C., 1945-47, 58-59, rec. sec. gen., 1955-57; pres., Wellesley Council Ch. Women, 1958-60; mem. bd. Northfield League, 1955-64; bd. dirs. Mass. N.E. Grenfell Assn.; sec. Belleair Beach Property Owners Assn., 1965-68; dir. Belleair Beach Park Bd., 1978-79; dir. altar guild Calvary Episcopal Ch. Mem. DAR (regent Amos Mills chpt. Wellesley 1961-63), Mary Washington Coll. Alumnae Assn. (pres. 1941-44), AAUW, Belleair Beach Garden Club (pres. 1967-69), Federated Hills Garden Club (rec. sec. 1956, pres. 1961-62, sustaining mem.), Power Squadron of CAP. Episcopalian (dir. ch. altar guild). Clubs: Bath (St. Petersburg Beach, Fla.); No. Lake George Yacht. Author: Footprints—A History of the United Daughters of the Confederacy, 1959. Address: 117 5th St Belleair Beach FL 33535

COREY, JEAN, lawyer; b. Ronan, Mont., Sept. 16, 1953; d. Marion Thomas and Lora Mabel (Simard) Hedegaard; m. Lyle E. Corey, June 10, 1972 (div. 1976). Student Mont. State U., 1971-72, Calif. State U.-Los Angeles, 1976-78; J.D., Southwestern U., 1980. Bar: Calif. 1980. Assoc. Greene, O'Reilly, Agnew & Broillet, Los Angeles, 1981-82; sole practice, Los Angeles, 1982-84; assoc. Law Office of Al Schallau, Rancho Palos Verdes, Calif., 1984; sole practice, Santa Monica, Calif., 1985—. Mem. ABA, Assn. Trial Lawyers Am., Calif. Trial Lawyers Assn., Los Angeles Trial Lawyers Assn., Los Angeles County Bar Assn. Democrat. Office: 2801-B Ocean Park Blvd Suite L Santa Monica CA 90405

CORLETT, EMMA JEAN, social worker; b. Knox City, Tex., Aug. 4, 1926; d. LeRoy and Luella (Burns) Massey; B.A. in Secondary Edn. cum laude, N.W. Nazarene Coll., 1965; M.S.W. with honors, U. Utah, 1972; m. John Paul Corlett, Jan. 1, 1946 (dec. 1969); children—Jeanne Marie, Thomas Lee, Jan Louise. Feature writer Statesman Newspaper, Boise, Idaho, 1960-63; caseworker Idaho Dept. Pub. Assistance, Boise, 1965-68; mental health counselor Community Inst. Human Resources, Boise, 1969-70; dir. patient and family counseling Mercy Med. Center, Nampa, Idaho, 1972-75; edn. counselor U.S. Army, Seoul, S. Korea, 1975-76; med. social worker Kern Med. Center, Bakersfield, Calif., 1976-78, dir. med. social services, 1978-79; dir. med. social services Santa Barbara (Calif.) Cottage Hosp., 1979—. Named Mrs. Idaho, 1959; licensed clin. social worker, Calif. Mem. Nat. Assn. Social Workers, Acad. Certified Social Workers, Internat. Register Clin. Social Workers, AAUW, Soc. Hosp. Social Worker Dirs., Am. Hosp. Assn., U.S. Postal Clks. Aux. (nat. v.p. 1959-63). Phi Delta Lambda. Office: Santa Barbara Cottage Hosp Pueblo at Bath St Santa Barbara CA 93105

CORLEY, JOYCE, personnel executive; b. Schenectady, Jan. 10; d. J. Edmund and Jean (Hausman) C. Assoc. Sci., Harcum Jr. Coll., 1962; postgrad. Temple U. Med. asst. Bryn Mawr Med. & Diagnostic Clinic Ltd. (Pa.), 1962-66; sec. Calif. Computer Products, Bala Cynwya, Pa., 1966-70, Drexel Firestone, Phila., 1970-71; exec. sec. IU Internat., Phila., 1972-76; adminstrv. asst. Peat, Marwick Mitchell & Co., 1976-81, mgr. personnel services, 1981—. Mem. central allocations com. United Way, 1983-85, mem. sr. services rev. com., 1984-85. Mem. Nat. Assn. Female Execs., Internat. Assn. Personnel Women, Am. Soc. Personnel Adminstrs., Delaware Valley Corp. Travel Mgrs. Assn. Republican. Office: Peat Marwick Mitchell & Co 1600 Market St Philadelphia PA 19103

CORMIER, RAMONA THERESA, university administrator; b. Breaux Bridge, La., Jan. 21, 1923; d. Arthur Joseph and Florence Ann (Breaux) C. B.A. in Music Edn., U. Southwestern La., 1943; M.A. in Music, U. So. Calif., 1948; Ph.D., Tulane U., 1960. Music tchr. St. Martin Parish, Breaux Bridge, 1948-49; vocal music tchr. Ouachita Parish High Sch., Monroe, La., 1949-58; student tchr. supr. Northeast State Coll., 1956-58; instr. philosophy Newcomb Coll., Tulane U., New Orleans, 1960-61; instr., then asst. prof. U. Tenn., Knoxville, 1961-65; asst. prof., then prof. Bowling Green State U., Ohio, 1965—, assoc. provost, 1979-84, dean continuing edn. and summer programs, 1984—, assoc. dir. Philos. Documentation Ctr., 1969-73; cons., evaluator North Central Assn., 1982—. Author: (with J. Pallister) Waiting for Death: The Philosophical Significance of En attendant Godot, 1979; Editor: (with others) International Directory of Philosophy and Philosophers, 1978; Encounter: an Introduction to Philosophy, 1970; The Philosopher's Index, 1972. Contbr. articles to profl. jours. Served to ensign USN, 1943-46. Recipient Spl. Achievement award Bowling Green State U., 1975, Significant Contbns. award Women in Communication, 1976, Hollis A. Moore award Bowling Green State U., 1982, 83. Mem. Am. Philos. Assn., AAAS, Am. Soc. Aesthetics, Brit. Soc. Aesthetics, So. Soc. Philosophy and Psychology, Ohio Philos. Assn. (nat. v.p.), Am. Assn. Higher Edn., Nat. Univ. Continuing Edn. Assn., Ohio Continuing Higher Edn. Assn., Sigma Alpha Iota, Kappa Delta Pi, Phi Sigma Tau, Phi Kappa Phi. Democrat. Avocations: gardening; travel; photography. Home: 149 Baldwin St Bowling Green OH 43402 Office: Continuing Edn and Summer Programs Bowling Green State U Bowling Green OH 43403

CORN, JO ANN PHYLLIS, hospital administrator; b. Manomen, Minn., July 17, 1937; d. Joseph Jacob and Dorothy Claire (Oleson) Matysek; m. Poe Rolland, June 8, 1958 (div.); children—Poe David, Clayton Jay, Kelly Ann. Student Colo. State U., 1955-58; B.A., Adams State Coll., 1969; M.S.W., Our Lady of the Lake Coll., San Antonio, 1971; postgrad. U. Colo., 1973-75, U. No. Colo., 1980. Patient and family counselor St. Anthony Hosp., Denver, 1971-75, adminstrv. coordinator human resources, 1975-80, dir. human resources dept., 1980; dir. St. Anthony Hosp. North, Westminster, Colo., 1980—; dir. Internat. Banks, Engelwood, Denver, Wheatridge and Federal Heights, Colo.; bd. dirs. Central Colo. Health Planning Council, Denver, 1982-83; del. Denver Hosp. Liaison Com., 1982—. Mem. Adams County Econ. Devel. Council, 1982—; bd. dirs. Adams County ARC, 1983-84. Mem. Western Hosp. Assn. (del. 1982—), Colo. Hosp. Assn. (mem. task force on aging 1983—), Colo. Women's Forum for Health Care, Clear Creek Med. Soc., North Suburban Bus. and Profl. Women (bd. dirs. 1982-84, found. chmn. 1982-84), Met. Denver Hosp. Council (del. 1982—), Metro North C. of C., Broomfield C. of C., Lafayette C. of C., Louisville C. of C. Republican. Home: 2328 S Troy St Aurora CO 80014 Office: St Anthony North Hosp 2551 W 84th Ave Westminster CO 80030

CORN, LESLIE JOAN, producer, director, writer, programming executive; b. N.Y.C., Mar. 30, 1949; d. Peter and Jacqueline (DuVal) C. Student Northwestern U., 1966-68; B.A. in English, Finch Coll., 1970; M.A. in Psychology, New Sch. for Social Research, 1976. Radio interviewer Australian Broadcasting Commn., Sydney, 1970; asst. to writers Tonight Show, NBC-TV, N.Y.C., 1971, Burbank, Calif., 1971; assoc. producer Parent's Mag. Films, N.Y.C., 1972; asst. nationally syndicated show Living Easy with Dr. Joyce Brothers, N.Y.C., 1973; assoc. producer various TV commls., N.Y.C., 1974, RKO-TV documentary Inflation: A Few Answers, 1974; producer CARE's Internat. Children's Party, 1974; prodn. assoc. Money Maze, ABC-TV, N.Y.C., 1974-75; producer, dir. Miller-Brody Prodns., N.Y.C., 1975-78; dir. program and pub. services ABC Radio Network, N.Y.C., 1979-80, dir. program prodn., 1980-81; dir. programming CBS Radio Networks, 1981-83; pres., chief exec. officer Arielle Prodns. Internat., Ltd., N.Y.C., 1984—; producer, dir., writer Love Notes radio series, 1984—, Challenges radio feature series (in assn. with UNICEF), 1986—; producer, dir. Erma Bombeck in Motherhood: The Second Oldest Profession radio feature series, 1984—, Leo Buscaglia in Loving Each Other radio feature series, 1985—; dir., adapter books on tape for Warner Audio Publishing, including Rebecca (du Maurier), I the Jury (Spillane), Reflex (Francis), Brain (Cook), also dir. To Your Scattered Bodies Go (Farmer), Mosby's Memoirs (Bellow), Sweet Valley High (Pascal); dir., adapter books on tape for Bantam Audio Pub., Newman Communications, Listen for Pleasure; programming cons. Warner Communications, N.Y.C. and Columbus, Ohio, 1976-78; panelist Nat. Emmy awards, 1974-77, nominations panelist children's programming, 1977; vis. lectr. NYU Sr. Seminar, 1980, Spiritual Frontiers Fellowship, 1984, 85. Mem. Internat. Radio and TV Soc. (bd. govs. 1977-81), Nat. Acad. TV Arts and Scis., Nat. Acad. Rec. Arts and Scis., Mensa, Spiritual Frontiers Fellowship (programming com. 1984—), Delta Delta Delta. Office: Arielle Prodns Internat Ltd 265 E 66th St Suite 32-B New York NY 10021

CORN, MARILU ALDRICH, art gallery manager, portrait artist; b. Phila., Feb. 28, 1931; d. Truman H. and Helen-Mar (Gloninger) Aldrich; m. Robert A. Dauber, Feb. 28, 1953 (div. 1972); children—Craig Aldrich, Mark Christopher, Jeffrey Curtis (dec.), Anita Germaine; m. Donald J. Corn, Aug. 1972 (div. 1977). Student Phila. Bus. Coll., 1952. Sales cons. Center Art Galleries, Honolulu, 1976-81; asst. mgr. Vorpol Galleries, Laguna Beach, Calif., 1983; gallery mgr. Simic Galleries, Inc., Carmel Calif., 1984-86, LaJolla, Calif., 1986—. Vol., Humane Soc., Honolulu, 1980. Mem. Nat. Assn. Female Execs., Nat. Assn. Realtors, Hawaiian Malacol. Soc. Republican. Mem. Ch. of Religious Sci. Clubs: Kaneohe Yacht (Hawaii); Chandon (Yountville, Calif.). Avocations: shell collecting; scuba diving. Home: 3330-150 Caminito East Bluff LaJolla CA 92037 Office: Simic Galleries 7925 Girard Ave LaJolla CA 92037

CORN, WANDA MARIE, fine arts educator; b. New Haven, Nov. 13, 1940; d. Keith M. and Lydia M. (Fox) Jones; m. Joseph J. Corn, July 27, 1963. B.A., NYU, 1963, M.A., 1965, Ph.D., 1974. Instr. art history Washington Sq. Coll., NYU, 1965-66; lectr. U. Calif.-Berkeley, 1970, vis. asst. prof., 1976; lectr. Mills Coll., Oakland, Calif., 1970, vis. asst. prof., 1971, asst. prof., 1972-77, assoc. prof., 1977-80; assoc. prof. Stanford U., Calif., 1980—; vis. curator Fine Arts Mus., San Francisco, 1972, 73, 76; vis. curator Mpls. Inst. Arts, 1983-84, GrantWood travelling exhbn. to Whitney Mus. Am. Art, N.Y.C., Art Inst. Chgo., Fine Arts Mus. San Francisco; cons. Nat. Gallery Art, Washington, 1980; mem. adv. bd. Ctr. for Advanced Study in the Visual Arts, Nat. Gallery, 1986-89. Author: The Color of Mood, American Tonalism, 1880-1910, 1972; The Art of Andrew Wyeth, 1973; Grant Wood: The Regionalist Vision, 1983. Contbr. articles to profl. jours. Inst. of Fine Arts fellow, 1963-64; Ford Found. fellow, 1966-70; recipient Graves award 1974-75; Smithsonian fellow, 1978-79; Woodrow Wilson fellow, 1979-80; Stanford Humanities Ctr. fellow, 1982-83; Am. Council Learned Socs. grantee, 1982; research assoc. Smithsonian Instn., 1983—; Phi Beta Kappa scholar, 1984-85. Mem. Coll. Art Assn. (bd. dirs. 1970-73, 1980-84, editor Registry of Vis. Scholars and Artists, 1971-74, program chmn. ann. meeting, 1981, mem. numerous coms.), Women's Caucus for Art, Am. Studies Assn. (nat. council 1986-89), Assn. Historians of Am. Art. Office: Dept of Art Stanford U Stanford CA 94305

CORNACCHIONE, ANNE FRIEDLI, educator; b. Washington, Sept. 21, 1938; d. James John and Bertha Juliet (Friedli) Williams; m. Victor Emanuel Cornacchione, Nov. 19, 1971; 1 child by previous marriage, John Jay. A.A., Montgomery Coll., 1960; B.A., Am. U., 1961. Tchr. Fairfax County Pub. Schs., Fairfax, Va., 1961-69; exec. dir. Happy Time Sch., Alexandria, Va., 1977—; v.p. Maaco Auto Painting and Body Work, Vienna, Va., 1980—; pres. Embassy Schs., Arlington and Herndon, Va., 1983—. Mem. No. Va. Pvt. Sch. Assn. (treas. 1981—), Nat. Assn. for Edn. Young Children, Va. Assn. for Edn. Young Children, Nat. Assn. for Child Care Mgmt., So. Assn. for Children under Six. Republican. Lutheran. Club: Soroptimist (Fairfax, Va.). Avocations: reading, gourmet food.

CORNELIUS, LINDA LOUISE, advertising executive; b. Buffalo, Mar. 7, 1953; d. Adam Edward, Jr. and Virginia Elizabeth (Becker) Cornelius. B.A. summa cum laude, U. Pa., 1975, M.B.A., 1979. Asst. account exec. Ogilvy & Mather Advt., N.Y.C., 1979-80, account exec., 1980-82, account supr., 1982, v.p., account supr., 1983-84, v.p., mgmt. supr., 1984—. Mem. Phi Beta Kappa. Office: Ogilvy & Mather Advt 2 E 48th St New York NY 10017

CORNELIUS, OPAL F., physician placement executive, medical transcription company executive; b. Bankston, Ala., Oct. 12, 1941; d. Ervin Edward and

Lucille (Sanford) Freeman; m. E. R. Cornelius, Jr. Grad. high sch., Parrish, Ala. Med. transcriber State of Ala., Birmingham, 1961-63, St. Vincent's Hosp., Birmingham, 1963-64; exec. sec. Jefferson Health Found., Birmingham, 1965-78; owner, pres. Word Services, Inc., Morris, Ala., 1978—, Innovative Med. Search, Inc., Morris, 1981—; cons. Ala. Health Plan, Birmingham. Mem. bus. edn. com. Mortimer Jordan High Sch., Morris, 1983—, com. mem. Future Bus. Leaders Am., 1985 (cert. of appreciation 1985); bd. dirs. Morris Health Clinic, 1978-80. Baptist. Avocations: singing, water skiing, softball, gardening. Home: Cornelius Dr and Glenwood Rd Morris AL 35116 Office: Innovative Med Search Inc Cornelius Dr & Glenwood Rd PO Drawer 1 Morris AL 35116

CORNELL, DEBORAH ANN, university alumni relations administrator; b. Darby, Pa., Sept. 8, 1960; d. Lawrence William and Maryann Gertrude (Jenemann) C.; B.S. in Mktg. Mgmt., Drexel U., 1982, postgrad., 1985—. Rep. Lawrence S. Williams, Inc., Upper Darby, Pa., 1982-83; asst. dir. alumni relations Drexel U., Phila., 1983—; nat. fund raising exec. seminar speaker, 1985. Named Outstanding Young Woman of Am., 1986. W.W. Smith Found. grantee, 1980, 81, 82. Mem. Nat. Assn. Female Execs., Council for Advancement and Support of Edn., Nat. Soc. Fund Raising. Republican. Roman Catholic. Clubs: Drexel U. Faculty, Univ. Faculty (vice-chairperson bd. govs.). Office: 32d & Chestnut Sts Philadelphia PA 19104

CORNELL, DONNA MARIE, personnel company executive; b. Newburgh, N.Y., July 8, 1944; d. Salvatore and Frances Dorthea (Konkol) Decrosta; m. Richard H. Cornell, Apr. 7, 1966 (div. 1979); children—Daniel, Erica, Ryan; m. Jeffrey Russell Werner, June 3, 1984. Customer rep. Gen. Motors Acceptance, Middletown, N.Y., 1961-65; adminstrv. asst. Scott & Schechtmann, Esquires, Newburgh, 1965-69; mktg. rep. Orange County Police Benevolent Assn., Vails Gate, N.Y., 1971-73; mgr., owner Career Directions, Inc., Newburgh, 1975—; cons. Job Search Skills/Xicom Corp., Tuxedo, N.Y., 1980—. Bd. dirs. Orange Area United Fund, Newburgh, 1980—; mem. N.Y. State Bus. Council, Albany, 1982-84, Orange County Econ. Devel. Corp., Mid-Hudson Regional Econ. Devel. Council; bd. dirs. AMEN, Substance Abuse Program, Poughkeepsie, N.Y., 1983—, Mid Hudson Patterns for Progress. Named Jaycee of Yr., Newburgh chpt. N.Y. State Jaycees, 1974. Mem. Data Processing Mgmt. Assn., Am. Soc. Personnel Adminstrn. (past v.p.), Eastern Orange County Chamber (pres. 1982—), Women in Mgmt. Republican. Roman Catholic. Home: 11 Hinchcliffe Dr Newburgh NY 12550 Office: Career Directions Inc 280 Broadway Newburgh NY 12550

CORNETT, PATRICIA A., nurse, educator; b. Denver, Mar. 28, 1948; d. James A. and Florine Mae (Nemmers) C.; B.S., U. Colo., 1970; M.S., Tex. Womans U., 1976; postgrad. Rutgers U., 1983—; m. Harvey H. Latson III, June 6, 1970; children—Kimberly Marie, Keith Michael. Nurse, Cape Fear Valley Hosp., Fayetteville, N.C., 1970-71; instr. nursing Central Tex. Coll., Killeen, 1972-75; acting dir. nursing and inservice edn. St. Joseph's Hosp., Nogales, Ariz., 1976-77; ind. cons., community health nurse Army Regional Med. Center, Frankfurt, W.Ger., 1977-80, instr. U. Utah, Salt Lake City, 1980-82; pub. health nurse, dir. Sr. Citizens Health Screening Clinic, Tooele, Utah, 1981-82; asst. prof. Columbus Coll., Ga., 1985. Pack Health program cons. Boy Scouts Am., 1981-84, merit badge counselor, 1984—; troop leader Girl Scouts U.S., 1981-85. Mem. Am. Nurses Assn., Am. Assn. Critical Care Nurses, Utah Nurses Assn., Am. Public Health Assn., Nat. League Nursing, Am. Assn. Higher Edn., Sigma Theta Tau. Democrat. Roman Catholic Office: 104 Rainbow Ave Fort Benning GA 31905

CORNING, JOY COLE, state senator; b. Bridgewater, Iowa, Sept. 7, 1932; d. Perry Aaron and Ethel Marie (Sullivan) C.; m. Burton Eugene Corning, June 19, 1955; children—Carol, Claudia, Ann. B.A., U. No. Iowa, 1954. Cert. tchr. elem. edn., Iowa. Tchr. elem. sch. Greenfield Sch. Dist., Iowa, 1951-53, Waterloo Community Sch. Dist., Iowa, 1954-55; mem. Iowa State Senate from Cedar Falls, 1984—; Iowa Nat. Bankshares, dir. Midway Bank & Trust, Cedar Falls. Pres. Cedar Falls Sch. Bd., 1975-83; bd. dirs. Iowa Assn. Sch. Bds., Des Moines, 1983-84; state pres. Iowa Talented and Gifted, Des Moines, 1975-77; bd. dirs. Iowa Housing Fin. Authority, Des Moines, 1981-84; mem. Waterloo Theatre adv. bd., Cedar Arts Forum. Recipient Alumni Achievement award U. No. Iowa, 1985; named Citizen of Yr., Cedar Falls C. of C., 1984. Mem. AAUW, LWV, P.E.O., Delta Kappa Gamma. Republican. Mem. United Ch. of Christ. Home: 1017 Oak Park Blvd Cedar Falls IA 50613

CORPOLONGO, BARBARA JO, cartoonist; b. Des Moines, Aug. 17, 1944; d. Richard Spencer and Jo Anne (Nicholson) Spencer Clark; m. Heinz Georg Buschang, Apr. 1, 1967 (div. 1973); m. Donald Leroy Roberts, May 11, 1974 (div. 1976); m. John Dewey Corpolongo, May 20, 1978. B.F.A., U. Ariz., 1966, postgrad., 1966-68; postgrad. Stadelschule für Bildende Kunste, Frankfurt, Fed. Republic Germany, 1966. Tech. illustrator Dow Chem.-Rocky Flats, Golden, Colo., 1969-72; dir. advt. Learning Tree Pub. Co., Boulder, Colo., 1972-73; self employed cartoonist, free lance comml. artist, Jay, Okla., 1973—. Author: bjb Horsemanship, 1974; Horse Laffs for Trail Riders, 1983; monthly contbr. Western Horseman mag., under pen name bjb, 1970—. Physician's asst. Appaloosa Horse Club, Moscow, Idaho, 1978—. Address: Route 3 Box 234 Jay OK 74346

CORPORON, NANCY ANN, musician; b. Independence, Kans., Nov. 11, 1949; d. Lewis Leonard and Helen Maxine (Church) Corporon. B.M. in Music Performance, Oklahoma City U., 1971; M.B.A., NYU, 1985. French hornist; performer various orgns., Chgo. area, 1971-76, Broadway, N.Y.C. area, 1976—; contractor N.Y. Gilbert & Sullivan Players, Bklyn., 1978—, Bklyn. Philharmonic Community Concert Series, Bklyn., 1981—; performer Broadway musical prodns.; cons. Urban Bus. Assistance Corp., N.Y.C., 1981-83, v.p., 1983-84; music dir. N.Y Community Marching Band, N.Y.C., 1979-81; cons. S. Stre Seaport Tenants, N.Y.C., 1982-84; gen. mgr. New Amsterdam Symphony Orchestra, N.Y.C., 1977-78; founder, pres. Trimusicangle, Inc., N.Y.C., 1979-82. Recipient Cardinal Key, Oklahoma City U., 1971. Mem. NYU Bus. Forum, Sigma Alpha Iota (recipient Sword of Honor 1971), Pi Kappa Lambda. Office: 350 W 85th St Apt 57 New York NY 10024

CORR, ELEANOR NELSON, computer consultant; b. New Bedford, Mass., July 11, 1932; d. George Mark and Elsie Margaret (Vincent) Nelson; m. Rodman Elliot Taylor, May 24, 1951 (div. 1966); children—Rodman Elliot, Deborah, Clayton, Susan; m. Robert Leon Corr, June 24, 1967. A.A., Keystone Jr. Coll., 1976; postgrad. U. Scranton, Pa. State U. Asst. coordinator computers Keystone Jr. Coll., LaPlume, Pa., 1971-74, coordinator computer ctr., 1976-78, dir. data processing, 1978-84; computer cons. Encorr Cons., Clarks Summit, Pa., 1984—. Mem. Am. Mgmt. Assn., Data Processing Mgmt. Assn. (internat. dir. 1980—), Assn. Systems Mgmt., Women in Info. Processing, Abington Bus. and Profl. Assn. Republican. Episcopalian. Avocations: reading; swimming; racquetball, biking. Home: 218 Butternut Ln Clarks Summit PA 18411 Office: Encorr Cons PO Box 655 Clarks Summit PA 18411

CORRADO, CAROL JOAN, air force officer, nursing administrator; b. Utica, N.Y., Jan. 20, 1934; d. Peter Vincent and Nelda Katherine (Rosa) C. Diploma Crouse Irving Sch. Nursing, 1955; B.S.N., Syracuse U., 1963; M.S.N., U. Ala., 1973. Commd. 2d lt. Nurse Corps, U.S. Air Force, 1957, advanced through grades to col., 1980; operating room staff nurse 364th USAF Hosp., Laredo AFB, Tex., 1957-58, USAF Hosp., Wiesbaden, Fed. Republic Germany, 1958-59; operating room staff nurse, ward staff nurse USAFR, Griffiss AFB, N.Y., 1960-63; operating room staff nurse USAF Med. Ctr., Wright-Patterson AFB, Ohio, 1963-66; charge nurse metabolic research function, Sch. Aerospace Medicine, Brooks AFB, Tex., 1967-71; flight instr., In-Flight Med. Care OIC, 903d Aeromed. Evacuation Squadron, Cam Ranh Bay, Vietnam, 1971-72; charge nurse med. ward and aeromed. staging facility, DaNang AB, Vietnam, 1972; environ. health nurse, nurse epidemiologist USAF Hosp. Langley AFB, Va., 1973-76; adminstrv. nurse advisor to surgeon gen. Imperial Iranian Air Force, Tech. Assistance Field Team, Tehran, 1976-78; chief environ. medicine sect. USAF Hosp. Beale AFB, Calif., 1978-80; command nurse U.S. Air Force Logistics Command, Wright-Patterson AFB, Ohio, 1980—; cons., to U.S. Air Force Surgeon Gen. in nursing adminstrn., 1984—; leader workshops, instr. nursing courses. Decorated Air medal, Vietnam Cross of Gallantry. Mem. Am. Nurses Assn., Nat. League Nursing, Aerospace Med. Assn., Assn. Mil. Surgeons of U.S., Air Force Assn. (Tex. Nurse of Yr. 1968), Crouse Irving-Meml. Alumni Assn. Club: Wright Patterson Riding (pres. 1981-82). Avocations: equitation; Alpine skiing. Home: 3044 Village Green Dr Dayton OH 45432 Office: Hdqrs AFLC/SGN Wright-Patterson AFB OH 45433

CORREA, EILEEN ISRAEL, clinical psychologist; b. New Orleans, Sept. 26, 1950; d. Norman Charles and Jeannette (Simison) Israel; B.S., U. Southwestern La., 1972; M.S. (USPHS grantee 1973-75), U. Ga., 1975, Ph.D., 1977; m. John Henry Correa, Jan. 28, 1978; 1 child, John Bernard. Psychologist, Biloxi (Miss.) Gulfport VA Med. Center, 1977-79; acting chief psychology service New Orleans VA med. Center, 1980-81, clin. psychologist, 1979—, dir. psychology tng. program, 1981-83. Mem. Am. Psychol. Assn., Assn. Advancement Behavior Therapy, Southeastern Psychol. Assn. Democrat. Roman Catholic. Office: 1601 Perdido St New Orleans LA 70146

CORREA, ELSA ISABEL, psychiatrist; b. Guayaquil, Ecuador, Jan. 8, 1941; came to U.S., 1973; d. Telmo O. and Victoria L. (Franco) Abril; B.S., San Marcos U., Lima, Peru, 1964; M.D., 1971; m. Pelayo Correa, 1962; children—Patricia, Luz, Elsa, Fernando, Christopher, Jennifer. Intern, St. Mary of Nazareth Hosp., Chgo., 1974-75; resident Spring Group Hosp., Balt., 1975-77, Johns Hopkins Hosp., Balt., 1977-79; clin. and research fellow in psychiatry Johns Hopkins U. Sch. Medicine, Balt., 1977-81, asst. prof. psychiatry, 1981—; practice medicine specializing in psychiatry, Balt., 1977—; psychiatrist, mem. staff Johns Hopkins Hosp., Balt. City Hosp., 1977—; dir. acute psychiat unit Balt. City Hosp. (now Francis Scott Key Med. Ctr.), 1982—, asst. chief psychiatry, 1981—. Diplomate Am. Bd. Psychiatry and Neurology. Mem. Am. Psychiat. Assn., Md. Psychiat. Soc. Roman Catholic. Office: Dept Psy Francis Scott Key Med Ctr 4940 Eastern Ave Baltimore MD 21224

CORREA, LILLIAN, financial consultant; b. San Juan, P.R., May 16, 1951; d. Arnaldo Louis and Lillian (Anderson) C.; B.A., Emory U., 1973; Ed.M., Harvard U., 1974. Dir. tng. inst. Internat. Assn. Fin. Planning, Atlanta, 1974-80; mktg. cons. Golle and Homes Fin. Learning, Mpls., 1981-82; regional mgr. N.Y. Inst. Fin., N.Y.C., 1982-83; fin. cons. Robinson Humphrey, Am. Express, Inc., Atlanta, 1983—; lectr. in field. Contbr. articles to profl. jours. Mem. Nat. Network of Women in Sales, Atlanta Women's Commerce Club, Nat. Honor Soc., Eta Sigma Psi. Democrat. Avocations: travel; stamp collecting; swimming. Office: Robinson Humphrey Co 180 Interstate N Atlanta GA 30339

CORREA DA SILVA, GABRIELE B., child life specialist, educational specialist; b. Dessau, Germany; came to U.S., 1971; d. Georg and Karola Borchardt. Student U. Sao Paulo; B.A., U. Vienna, 1971; M.S. in Spl. Edn., So. Ill. U.-Carbondale, 1973; cert. advanced study U. Chgo., 1977. Cert. spl. edn. tchr. Spl. edn. tchr. Porter County Spl. Edn. Coop., Valparaiso, Ind., 1973-76; research asst. U. Chgo., 1976-77; pvt. practice ednl. specialist, Chgo., 1977-78; child life specialist Children's Meml. Hosp., Chgo., 1978—, supr. and trainer child life, 1978—; lectr. on child life various univs. Sao Paulo and Itu, Brazil, 19. Co-translator: The History of the Jews in Portugal, 1970; author, lectr. in field. So. Ill. U. rep. 10th and 11th Mohonk Cons. with Internat. Students, N.Y., 1973. Recipient Scholarship and Activity award, So. Ill. U., 1972; scholar U. Chgo., 1976-77. Mem. Assn. for Care of Children's Health (environ. com.), Phi Kappa Phi. Avocations: Literature; classical and Javanese music; arts. Office: Children's Memorial Hospital 2300 Children's Plaza Chicago IL 60614

CORRIGAN, CATHERINE MARY, market research analyst; b. Bronx, N.Y., Aug. 31, 1964; d. Edward and Bridget (Collins) C. Student in Mktg. NYU. Market research analyst Am. Internat. Group, N.Y.C., 1982—. Programmer, designer software. Mem. Nat. Assn. Female Execs. Avocations: horseback riding; softball; tennis; skiing; waterskiing. Home: 116 E 236th St Bronx NY 10470 Office: Am Internat Group 70 Pine St 8th Floor New York NY 10270

CORRIGAN, JANE MCGARA, veterinarian; b. Detroit, Dec. 2, 1946; d. Homer Joseph and Esther Lockwood (Skelding) McGara; A.B., Ind. U., 1968; D.V.M., Ohio State U., 1972; m. Lewis Corrigan, Apr. 8, 1972. Assoc. veterinarian Village Vet. Clinic, 1972-73; assoc. veterinarian Pacific Beach Vet. Clinic, San Diego, 1973-77; owner, mgr., 1977—. Mem. AVMA, Am. Animal Hosp. Assn., Calif. Vet. Med. Assn., San Diego County Vet. Med. Assn. (past membership chmn. and chmn. animal seminar, pres. 1981-82; past rep., sec., treas. Beach Mesa chpt.). Home: 2107 Calle Guaymas San Diego CA 92037 Office: 1362 Garnet Ave San Diego CA 92109

CORRIGAN, MAURA DENISE, lawyer; b. Cleve., June 14, 1948; d. Peter James and Mae Ardell (McCrone) C.; m. Joseph Dante Grano, July 11, 1976; children—Megan Elizabeth, Daniel Corrigan. B.A. with honors, Marygrove Coll., 1969; J.D. with honors, U. Detroit, 1973. Bar: Mich., 1974. Jud. clk. Mich. Ct. Appeals, Detroit, 1973-74; asst. prosecutor Wayne County, Mich., Detroit, 1974-79, asst. U.S. atty., Detroit, 1979-84, chief appellate div., 1979-86; chief asst. U.S. atty., 1986—; vice chmn. Mich. Com. To Formulate Rules of Criminal Procedure, Mich. Supreme Ct., 1982—; mem. com. on standard jury instrns. State Bar Mich., 1978-82; lectr. Mich. Jud. Inst., Inst. Continuing Legal Edn., ABA-Cin. Bar Litigation Sects., Dept. Justice Advocacy Inst. Contbr. chpt. to book, articles to legal rev. Vice chmn. Project Transition, Detroit, 1976—; mem. Citizens Adv. Council Lafayette Clinic, Detroit, 1979—; bd. dirs. Detroit Wayne County Criminal Advocacy Program, 1983-86. Recipient award of merit Detroit Commn. on Human Relations, 1974, Dir.'s award Dept. Justice, 1985. Mem. ABA, Women Lawyers Assn., Mich. Bar. Detroit Bar. Home: 1122 Balfour Rd Grosse Pointe Park MI 48230 Office: US Attry Eastern Dist Mich 920 Federal Bldg Detroit MI 48226

CORROTHERS, HELEN GLADYS, government criminal justice official; b. Montrose, Ark., Mar. 19, 1937; d. Thomas and Christene (Farley) Curl; m. Edward Corrothers, dec. 17, 1968 (div. Sept. 1983); 1 child, Michael Edward. A.A. in Liberal Arts magna cum laude, Ark. Bapt. Coll., 1955; B.S. in Bus. Adminstrn. Mgmt., Roosevelt U., 1965; grad. officer leadership sch. Women's Army Corps Sch., 1965; grad. Inst. Criminal Justice, Exec. Ctr. Continuing Edn., U. Chgo., 1973; postgrad. Calif. Coast U., 1981—. Commd. lt. U.S. Army, 1960, advanced through grades to capt., 1969; chief mil. personnel Hdqrs. and Hdqrs. Co., U.S. Army, Fort Myers, Va., 1965-67; dir. for housing Giessen Support Ctr., W.Ger., 1967-69; resigned, 1969; social interviewer Ark. Dept. Corrections, grady, 1970-71, supt. women's unit, Pine Bluff, 1971-83; mem. U.S. Parole Commn., Burlingame, Calif., 1983-85, U.S. Sentencing Commn., Washington, 1985—; instr. corrections U.Ark.-Pine Bluff, 1976-79; mem. bd. visitation Jefferson County Juvenile Ct., Pine Bluff, 1978-81; bd. dirs. Vols. in Cts., 1979-84, Vols. Am., 1985-88; mem. Am./Can. study team, Mexican penal system Am. Correctional Assn., Islas Marias, Mexico, summer 1981; mem. Ark. Commn. on Crimes and Law Enforcement, 1975-78. Mem. Ark. Commn. on Status of Women, 1976-78; bd. dirs. Com. Against Spouse Abuse, 1982-84. Decorated Army Commendation medal; recipient Ark. Woman of Achievement award Ark. Press Women's Assn., 1980, Human Relations award Ark. Edn. Assn., 1980, Outstanding Woman of Achievement award Sta.-KATV-TV, Little Rock, 1981, Disting. Service award, dir. and bd. corrections Ark. Dept. Corrections, 1983, Correctional Service award Vols. Am., 1984, William H. Hastie award Nat. Assn. Blacks in Criminal Justice, 1986. Mem. Am. Correctional Assn. (treas. 1980-86), N.Am. Assn. Wardens and Supts., Ark. Law Enforcement Assn., Nat. Assn. Female Execs., Nat. Council on Crime and Delinquency, Am. Soc. Criminology, Ark. Sheeriff's Assn. (hon.), Delta Sigma Theta (local sec. 1976-79, local parliamentarian 1983-84). Baptist. Avocations: reading; music. Office: US Sentencing Commn 1331 Pennsylvania Ave NW Washington DC 20004

CORSBERG, DOROTHY JEAN, humanities educator; b. Greeley, Colo., July 25, 1924; d. John Hermon and Inez Christine (Salberg) Corsberg; B.A., Colo. State Coll., 1946, M.A., 1952; postgrad. U. No. Colo., 60-81. Tchr., Oakesdale Consol. High Sch., Oakesdale, Wash., 1946-49; mem. faculty Northeastern Jr. Coll., Sterling, Colo., 1949—, dean women, 1949-62, chmn. humanities div., 1962-83, instructional dir. gen. studies, 1983—; critical reader/reviewer for ednl. materials; N.E. Colo. field cons. Colo. Humanities Program, 1982; mem. Colo. State Dept. Adv. Bd. Social Studies, 1966-68; chmn. Anna C. Petteys Scholarship Com., 1971-86; mem. rural libraries and humanities com. Colo. Planning and Resource Bd., 1982-83. Bd. dirs. Community Concert Assn., 1971-81. Named Outstanding Female Educator, U. No. Colo., 1968, Community Coll. Faculty Mem. of Yr., State Bd. Community Colls. and Occupational Edn. in Colo., 1981-82. Mem. NEA, Colo. Assn. Higher Edn. (program chmn., dir. 1965-67), Colo. Assn. Coll. Instructional Dirs., P.E.O. Democrat. Home: 1113 Beattie Dr Sterling CO 80751 Office: Northeastern Jr Coll Sterling CO 80751

CORSI, DEBORAH ERANDA, editor; b. McKeesport, Pa., May 6, 1953; d. Adolph J. and Francesca S. (D'Arliano) C. A.A.S., No. Va. Community Coll., 1980; B.A., Marymount Coll., 1984. Sec. Northwestern Mut. Life Ins. Co., Arlington, Va., 1971-72, adminstrv. asst., 1972-79; editorial asst. Smithsonian Mag., Washington, 1979-80; editorial and promotion asst. Smithsonian Instn. Press, 1981-83, editor, 1984-85; editor Jour. Alcohol Studies, 1986—. Roman Catholic. Address: 206 McFarlane Colonia NJ 07067

CORSO, JOHANNA MARY, technical writer; b. N.Y.C., Mar. 26, 1942; d. John Gerard and Helen Margaret (Romagnoli) Muccigrosso; m. Frank Anthony Corso, Apr. 24, 1965; children—Frank A. Jr., Christopher, Mark. B.S., Mt. St. Vincent Coll., Bronx, N.Y., 1963; M.A. Tchrs. Coll. Columbia U., 1964. Tchr. Albert Leonard Jr. High Sch., New Rochelle, N.Y., 1964-65; tchr. Monroe-Woodbury High Sch., Monroe, N.Y., 1965-66; mem. secretarial staff Rutgers U., 1975-79, mgr. info. div. for Packaging Engrs., 1981-85; asst. to tech. dir. Ctr. for Profl. Advancement, East Brunswick, N.J., 1979-81; tech. writer Carter-Wallace, Inc., 1986—. Author: Ency. Packaging Technology, 1986. Den mother Thomas A. Edison Council Boy Scouts Am. Milltown, 1976-79; mem. exec. com. for bond issue Joyce Kilmer Sch., Milltown, 1978. Mem. Am. Bus. Women's Assn. (corresponding sec. 1985-86; Woman of Year award 1982), The Packaging Inst. USA (chmn. basic edn. 1983-85). Roman Catholic. Club: Jr. Womens of Greater Brunswick Area.

CORSON, CLAIRE ELAINE, recreational vehicle company executive; b. Dallas, Aug. 25, 1954; d. Thomas Harold and Dorothy (Schneide) C. B.F.A., So. Meth. U., 1975; J.D., Notre Dame U., 1981; student Interlochen Ctr. for Arts, 1971. Bar: Ill. 1981, U.S. Dist. Ct. (no. dist.) Ill. 1981. Advt. account exec. DBG & H Ltd., Dallas, 1975-77; mgr. Shasta Industries, Inc., Dallas, 1977-78; lawyer McKenna, Storer, Rowe, White & Farrug, Chgo., 1981-83; v.p. advt. and pub. relations Coachmen Industries, Inc., Elkhart, Ind., 1983-84; v.p., gen. mgr. Coachmen Recreational Vehicle Co., Middlebury, Ind., 1985—. Dir., Interlochen Arts Acad. Alumni Bd., 1981, Elkhart Symphony, 1983, ARC, Elkhart, 1983. Mem. Internat. Assn. Bus. Communicators, Pub. Relations Soc. Am., Am. Mktg. Assn., ABA, Women in Communications, Inc., (v.p. 1977-78), Ill. Bar Assn. Republican. Office: Coachmen RV PO Box 30 Middlebury IN 46540

CORSON, HELEN BEARD, business owner, motivational consultant; b. Millville, N.J., Mary 27, 1935; d. Burley Columbus and Edna Kathleen (Moose) Beard; children—Robert Lore, Barbara, James Richard. B.A., Glassboro State Coll., 1971, M.A., 1973; registered records adminstr., U. Pa., 1955. Cert. transactional analyst, 1978. Tchr., Pub. Schs. Millville (N.J.), 1960-72; med. records cons. nursing homes, S. Jersey, 1963-84; counselor in pvt. practice, Pleasantville, N.J, 1978-82; dir. cons. and edn. Cumberland County Guidance Ctr., Millville, 1979-82; Mgmt. devel. cons. to bus. and individuals, South Jersey, 1978-82; owner Distributor for Success Motivation Inst., Atlanta, 1982. Author: Internal Dialogues, 1979; Does Your Diet Work, 1981; composer. Tchr., Sunday sch. Methodist Ch., Millville, 1958-63; choir leader, accompanist Presbyterian Ch., 1964-67. Recipient Builders award Success Motivation Inst., 1982, 83, Progressive Growth award, 1982, 83, First Degree Achiever award, 1983. Mem. Assn. Humanistic Psychology, N.J. Edn. Assn., Hillside Chapel and Internat. Truth Ctr., Am. Med. Records Assn., Internat. Transactional Analysis Assn. Club: Westminster (pres. 1953). Address: 6065 Roswell Rd NE Suite 528 Atlanta GA 30328

CORT, DIANA, social worker; b. N.Y.C., Oct. 27, 1934; d. Arthur and Augusta Deutsch; B.S., N.Y.U., 1955; M.S.W., Columbia U., 1957; m. Leonard Van Arsdale, Sept. 17, 1978; children by previous marriage—Hayley, Daniel. Clinician, Payne Whitney Clinic, N.Y. Hosp., N.Y.C., 1957-59, psychiat. clinic Jewish Bd. Guardians, N.Y.C., 1959-61; founder, pres. Big Six Towers Nursery Sch., N.Y.C., 1962-67; dir. intake and social service L.I. Consultation Center, Forest Hills, N.Y., 1966-84, clin. dir., coordinator clin. services, 1984—; supr., faculty mem. L.I. Inst. Mental Health, 1973—; cons. in social work Bergen Center for Child Devel., 1981—; dir. Seniors Option Service, Allendale, N.J., 1980—. Mem. Nat. Assn. Social Workers, N.Y. Soc. Clin. Social Workers. Address: 97 29 64th Rd Forest Hills NY 11374

CORTEZ, SANDRA RINEL, business executive; b. Tegucigalpa, Honduras, Dec. 21, 1949; came to U.S. 1965, naturalized, 1985; d. Samuel and Herminia (Ochoa) Quan; m. Emilio Cortez, Nov. 11, 1972; children—Daniel, Emilio, Claudia. Grad. Met. Bus. Coll., 1968. Exec. sec., interpreter Harza Engring. Co., Chgo., 1975-78; exec. sec. Eagle Internat. Mfg., Brownsville, Tex., 1979-80, Hunt Pan Am Aviation, Brownsville Internat. Airport, 1981-82; gen. mgr. Brownsville Communications, Tex., 1982-84; owner, gen. profl. mgr. Profl. Sectl. Services and Translation Bur., 1982—. Author: Manual for Telephone Operators, 1982—. Mem. Am. Heart Assn. (devel. chmn. Region 14), Ct. Interpreters and Translators, Nat. Assn. Female Execs., Bus. and Profl. Women. Republican. Roman Catholic. Avocations: reading; gourmet cooking; music. Home: 15 Corine Circle Brownsville TX 78521 Office: Professional Secretarial Services and Translation Bur 302 Kings Hwy Suite 210 Brownsville TX 78521

CORTEZ, YOLANDA, television administrator, programmer; b. Brownsville, Tex., Nov. 7, 1954; d. Jose and Maria de los Angeles (Capistran) Manzano; m. Alberto Cortez, Aug. 3, 1974; children—Vanessa, David. B.S., Pan Am. U., 1976. Cert. tchr., Tex. Tchr., Brownsville Sch. Dist., 1976-81; exec. sec. Valley Broadcasting Sta. KVEO-TV, Brownsville, 1981-82, program dir., 1982-83, adminstrv. asst., program dir., 1983—. Mem. exec. bd. Tex. Southmost Coll. Folklife Festival, 1983-84; mem. Pub. TV Community Adv. Com., 1985. Mem. Nat. Assn. TV Programming Execs. Democrat. Roman Catholic. Avocations: reading; jogging; swimming. Home: 175 Haggar Dr Brownsville TX 78521 Office: Valley Broadcasting Co KVEO-TV 394 N Expressway Brownsville TX 78521

CORTRIGHT, JOAN EISENBREY, market research executive; b. Phila., July 5, 1953; d. Nathan Dillingham and Eleanor (Beitler) C.; B.A. in Econs., Colo. Coll., 1977; M.B.A. (mktg. fellow), Keller Grad. Sch. Mgmt., Chgo., 1979. Owner, operator concession stand, Bryn Mawr, Pa., 1974-75; sr. research analyst Tech. Cons., Chgo., 1977-79; mktg. research analyst R.H. Donnelley Co., Chgo., 1979-81; mgr. market research Datacomp Corp., Phila., 1981-83; pres. The Research Asst., Wayne, Pa., 1984—. Mem. Am. Mktg. Assn., Nat. Assn. Female Execs., Pi Gamma Mu.

COSBY, LEIGH ANN, commercial property manager; b. Dallas, Aug. 19, 1952; d. Fred H. and Oneita F. (Needham) C. B.A., So. Meth. U., 1974. Lic. real estate broker, Tex.; cert. property mgr. Office mgr. Exec. Enterprises, Inc., Dallas, 1974-78; office mgr. Joe V. Hawn, Jr., Developer, Dallas, 1978-79; assoc. buyer Zale Corp., Dallas, 1979-81; property mgr., supr. Fults Mgmt. Co., Dallas, 1981-84; mgr. Plaza of the Americas, Wynne/Jackson Mgmt. Co., Dallas, 1984—. Mem., vol. Dallas Mus. League, 1981-85; mem. Children's Arts & Ideas Found., Dallas, 1985; mem. Dallas Ballet Women's Com. Mem. Inst. Real Estate Mgmt., Bldg. Owners & Mgrs. Assn., Comml. Real Estate Women, Greater Dallas Bd. Realtors. Republican. Mem. Unity Ch. Avocations: floral arranging; antique collections; music performances.

COSBY, MARY MARGARET, aircraft company executive, lawyer; b. Hattiesburg, Miss., Nov. 3, 1930; d. David Warren and Mary Lee (Hardin) Holmes; m. William Katrishen, Apr. 24, 1954 (div.); 1 child, Frances Antoinette; m. John Norman Cosby, Jan. 16, 1971. B.S., U. Miss., 1951; J.D., Villanova U., 1977. Bar: Pa. 1977, Miss. 1981. Adminstrv. asst. U.S. Congressman F. Smith, Washington, 1951-54; sec. U.S. Air Force, Tokyo, 1954-61; assoc. Duane, Morris Heckscher, Phila., 1977-81; gen. counsel S.E. Health Care, Baton Rouge, 1981—, dir., 1981—; pres. Bass Aviation, Fairhope, Ala., 1983—, Fairhope Aviation Services, Fairhope, 1983—; cons. Studebaker's of Am., Inc., Dallas, 1981-85. Pres. Mobile Gen. Hosp. Aux., Ala., 1968. Mem. ABA, Miss. Bar Assn., Def. Research Inst., LWV (v.p. Mobile 1967), Mortar Bd., Order of Coif, Pi Kappa Pi. Democrat. Episcopalian. Avocation: gardening. Home: 3603 Riviere Du Chien Rd Mobile AL 36609 Office: Fairhope Aviation Services Inc PO Box 925 Fairhope AL 36533

COSBY, SUSAN HENDRYSON, association executive, consultant; b. Denver, Apr. 22, 1946; d. Irvin Edward and Mary Elizabeth (Short) Henryson; m. Richard Wade Cosby, June 23, 1984. B.S., Ball State U., 1974; postgrad. Sangamon State U., 1980—. Cert. tchr., Tenn. Tchr., Chattanooga Pub. Schs., 1974-77, tchr. Title I, 1977-79; dir. communications Ill. State Dental Soc., Springfield, 1980-82; field service rep. ABA, Chgo., 1982-83, assoc. dir. planning, 1983—; bd. dirs., Am. Lawyers Aux., Chgo., 1984—; cons. gen. practice sect. ABA, 1983. Editor, author Ill. Dental Jour., 1980-82. Bd. dirs. Humane Animal League, Chattanooga, 1975-79; chmn. parade Lincoln Fest, Springfield, 1982. Mem. Chattanooga Edn. Assn. (pres. 1978-79), Women in Mgmt., Women in Communications, Am. Soc. Assn. Execs. Episcopalian. Home: 431 S Dearborn St Apt 606 Chicago IL 60604

COSCARELLO, BARBARA ANNE, municipal improvement corporation executive; b. Phila., July 22, 1941; d. Joseph A. and Carmela Mildred (Bossone) C.; B.A. with honors, Temple U., Phila., 1971; M.S., Drexel U., Phila., 1977. Mgr., Phila. Redevel. Authority, 1971-78; dir. Office Econ. Devel., City of York (Pa.), 1978-82; econ. devel. cons., 1982-84; exec. dir. Downtown Wilmington Improvement Corp., Inc.; ptnr. Devel. Cons.; bd. dirs. Pvt. Industry Council York County, York Rehab. and Industrialization Tng. Center, Del. Humanities Forum; mem. adv. council Salvation Army; bd. dirs., sec. York County Visitors and Tourist Bur.; instr. York Coll. Bd. dirs. Open, Inc., 1967-69, Older Ams. Center of Haddington, 1972-74. Mem. Nat. Council Urban Econ. Devel., Pa. Council Urban Econ. Devel. (Edward Deluca award 1981), Internat. Downtown Exec. Assn., Women's Network York. Author articles in field. Office: 618 Market St Mall Wilmington DE 19801

COSSIO-PINERO, ROSITA, psychotherapist; b. Havana, Cuba, Dec. 9, 1940; came to U.S., 1964, naturalized, 1970; d. Alejo and Rosa (Miralles) Cossio del Pino; B.A., Coll. of Sacred Heart, P.R., 1974; M.S., U. Bridgeport, 1976; postgrad. U. Miami (Fla.), 1977-79; m. Emilio R. Pinero, Feb. 11, 1966; children—Luis Alejo, Luis Orlando, Mayra Arrondo, Eileen B. Psychotherapist, Mentally Retarded Inst. of P.R., 1976-77, Miami (Fla.) Mental Health Center, 1978, aftercare clincian and psychotherapist, hypnotechnician, 1979—, day treatment program coordinator, info. specialist, 1979-80; profl. cons., chmn. fin. com. Adaptación. Vice pres. Coll. Engrs., Architects and Surveyors, San Juan, P.R., 1968-76; mem. Dem. Com. of P.R. of Nat. Dem. Party, 1968-76; active Am. Cancer Soc., 1975—; pres. Com. of Intellectuals and Writers of Freedom; pres. Assn. for Human Rights in Cuba; pres. Cuban Anti-defamation League, 1980—; dir. social services Tent City, Miami, 1980; asst. adminstr. Cuban Haitian Task Force, State Dept., 1980—. Mem. Am. Mental Health Counselors Assn., Am. Personnel and Guidance Assn., Am. Assn. Counselors. Democrat. Roman Catholic. Club: Dorado Beach (P.R.). Office: PO Box 651524 Miami FL 33165

COSTA, CATHERINE AURORA, state senator; b. Bklyn., Mar. 21, 1926; d. Salvatore and Matilde (Giumporcaro) Bravo; m. Joseph P. Costa, Sept. 7, 1946; children—Nicholas, Theodore, Nadine. Freeholder, Burlington County (N.J.), 1972-83; mem. N.J. Gen. Assembly, 1982-83; mem. N.J. Senate, 1984—. Founder, Willingboro Library (N.J.), 1959, trustee, 1962-66; bd. dirs., chmn. Willingboro Zoning Bd. Adjustment, 1969-73. Named N.J. Mother of Yr., 1976; Citizen of Yr., VFW, Willingboro, 1982; recipient Soil Conservation Supr. award N.J. Assn. Natural Resource Dists., 1973. Democrat. Roman Catholic. Home: 32 Twig Ln Willingboro NJ 08046 Office: Legislative Office 11 W Broad St Burlington NJ 08016

COSTA, DIANE MARIE, publishing company executive; b. Yonkers, N.Y., Oct. 31, 1944; d. Philip Eugene and Catherine Elaine (Brown) C. B.A., Mich. State U., 1966; postgrad. U. Kans.-Kansas City, 1979, 80. Tech. editor Bell Telephone Labs., Denver, 1969-72; mng. editor Plastic Machine, Industry Media, Denver, 1972-77; journalist Lear Siegler, Englewood, Colo., 1977-78; with Crothall-Am., Inc., 1978-84; prodn. supr. Rand McNally, Skokie, Ill., 1984—; dir. The Unsatisfied Man journalism rev., Denver, 1973-75. Dir., newsletter editor LWV, Denver, Lake Charles and Chgo., 1977-84; pres., treas. Condominium Owners Assn., Denver, 1976-78; dist. fin. chmn. Denver Democratic Party, 1977-78; polit. chmn. Colo. Women's Conf., 1977. Mem. Women in Communications (v.p. chpt. 1985—), Colo. Bus. Communicators, Women in Mgmt. (dir. chpt. 1984-85), Sigma Delta Chi. Club: Quota (Lake Charles). Office: Rand McNally 8255 N Central Park Skokie IL 60076

COSTA, MARY, soprano; b. Knoxville, Tenn.; student Los Angeles Conservatory of Music. Film voice of Sleeping Beauty by Walt Disney; appeared TV comms., 1955-57; debut Los Angeles Opera, 1958, in La Boheme, San Francisco Opera, 1959, as Violetta in La Traviata at Met. Opera, N.Y.C., 1964; appeared Glyndebourne Opera House, Royal Opera House Covent Garden, Teatro Nacional de San Carlos, Grand Theatre de Geneve, Vancouver, Lisbon, Kiev, Leningrad, Tbilisi, Boston, Cin., Hartford, Newark, Phila., San Antonio, Seattle; toured U.S. with Bernstein's Candide; appeared English prodn. Candide; revival Bernstein's Candide at John F. Kennedy Center for Performing Arts, 1971; tour Soviet Union, 1970; Bolshoi debut in La Traviatta, 1970; starring role motion picture The Great Waltz, 1972; appeared internat. recitals, orchs.; v.p. Hawaiian Fragrances, Honolulu, 1972. Vice pres. Calif. Inst. Arts. Named Woman of yr., Los Angeles, 1959; recipient DAR Honor medal, 1974; Mary Costa Scholarship established at U. Tenn., 1979. Address: care Calif Artists Mgmt 1182 Market St Suite 311 San Francisco CA 94102*

COSTANTINO, LORINE PROTZMAN, woodworking co. exec.; b. Chattanooga, Feb. 8, 1921; d. John Edgar and Rosa Jane (Ellis) McClelland; student U. Balt., U. Ill.; m. Conrad Protzman, 1937 (dec. 1958); children—Rosa Lorine, Charles Conrad, James Paul, Sharon Lee; m. 2d, Anthony A. Costantino, Feb. 27, 1960. With Conrad Protzman, Inc., Balt., 1954—, pres., chief exec., 1958—; developer apprenticeship programs for woodworking industry. Mem. Archtl. Woodworking Inst. (dir.), Bldg. Congress and Exchange Balt., Am. Sub-Contractors Assn., Nat. Assn. Women Bus. Owners, Iota Lambda Sigma (hon. mem. Nu chpt.). Republican. Roman Catholic. Club: Hillendale Country. Office: Conrad Protzman Inc 2325 Banger St Baltimore MD 21230

COSTELLO, ANNE MARIE, county government official; b. Salamanca, N.Y., June 23, 1936; d. Leo Edward and Marian Esther (Pavlock) Grabowski; m. William Raymond Costello, July 6, 1957; children—Celine Marie, Roger William. Student St. Bonaventure U., 1971-72. With Salamanca City Central Sch. Dist., N.Y., 1971—; county legislator Cattaraugus County, Little Valley, N.Y., 1976—, minority leader Dem. legislators, 1983; rep. to Upstate Council Elected Ofcls., 1982—; rep. to Western N.Y. Econ. Devel. Council, 1984—, chmn. subcom. tourism and trade, 1985—. Mem. U.S. Route 219 Assn., 1976—, Olean Bus. Inst. Adv. Bd., 1981—, Allegany Rehab. Ctr., 1985—. Mem. N.Y. State Assn. Counties (resolutions com. 1983—), Suprs. and Legislators Assn. N.Y. State (dir. 1985), Cattaraugus County Firemen's Aux., Kill Buck Firemen's Aux., Salamanca Rail Mus., Cattaraugus County Living Arts Assn., Am. Legion, Zonta Internat. Roman Catholic. Home: PO Box 24 Kill Buck NY 14748 Office: Cattaraugus County Courthouse Little Valley NY 14755

COSTELLO, JOAN, psychologist; b. Lawrence, Mass., Jan. 16, 1937; d. William Agustine and Helen Mary (Dolfe) C.; B.S., Boston Coll., 1959; M.S., Ill. Inst. Tech., 1963, Ph.D., 1967; 1 dau., Cathleen. Clin. psychologist Cath. Charities Chgo., 1960-70; research scientist Ill. Inst. Juvenile Research, 1964-70; asst. prof. Yale U., 1970-77; dean, Erikson Inst., Chgo., 1977-79; assoc. prof. Sch. Social Service Adminstrn., U. Chgo., 1979-85, dir. Chapin Hill Forum, 1985—; pvt. practice clin. psychology, 1985—; cons. U.S. Dept. Health and Human Services. Mem. Am. Psychol. Assn., Soc. Research Child Devel., Am. Orthopsychiat. Assn., AAAS. Office: 1535 Lake Cook Rd Suite 305 Northbrook IL 60025

COSTELLO, LORETTA ELIZABETH, realty firm executive; b. Jamaica, N.Y., Aug. 11, 1941; d. Peter F. and Loretta E. (McDermott) C. B.A., U. Md., 1963. Saleswoman, Lanier Bus. Products Co., N.Y.C., 1979-80; sales real estate N.K. Benjamin Realty Co., Forest Hills, N.Y.C., 1980-83; owner Town House Mgmt. Co., N.Y.C., 1982—; owner, broker Castleberry Realty Co., Rego Park, N.Y., 1984—, Forest Hills, N.Y., 1986—; residential apt. mgr. Recipient various realty awards. Mem. Nat. Assn. Female Execs., Nat. Assn. Realtors, N.Y. State Assn. Realtors, L.I. Bd. Realtors (appraisal div., mortgage/banking, profl. standards coms. 1985—), Electronic Realty Assn. (edn. com. 1986—), Forest Hills C. of C. Club: Marriot Hotel Health (Elmhurst, N.Y.). Office: Castleberry Realty Co 62-57 Woodhaven Blvd Rego Park NY 11374 also 117-16 Queens Blvd Forest Hills NY 11375

COSTELLO, MARIA THERESA, nurse; b. Lancaster, Pa., Oct. 21, 1957; d. Bruno Joel and Theresa Elizabeth (Covaleski) Barbacovi; m. James Joseph Costello, Aug. 5, 1978. B.S., Neumann Coll., Pa., 1980; M.S.N., Widener U., 1984. Nursing technician St. Luke's Meml. Hosp. Ctr., Utica, N.Y., 1978-79; staff nurse Riddle Meml. Hosp., Media, Pa., 1979-81, critical care staff nurse, 1979-80, charge nurse, 1981; staff nurse Brandywine Hosp., Coatesville, Pa., 1981—. Assoc. adv. Explorer Post, Boy Scouts Am., 1978-79. Roman Catholic. Home: RD 2 Box 365A Narvon PA 17555

COSTELLO, MARY, consulting company executive; b. Omaha, Oct. 25, 1940; d. Patrick Francis and Margaret Helen (Costello) Henry; m. Donald F. Costello, Sept. 2, 1961; children—Maureen, Rick, Dan, Peter, Tom, Ben, Meg. B.A. in Sociology, Duchesne Coll., 1964. Vice pres. Costello & Assocs., Lincoln, Nebr., 1970—; reporter, editor Sun Papers, Lincoln, 1970-80; editor Tafelspitz Mag., Vienna, Austria, 1981—; prof. job hunting skills Southeast Community Coll., Lincoln, 1985—. Author weekly column Over the Coffee Cup (1st place award Nat. Suburban Newspaper Assn., 1985, Nat. Press Women 1975—), 1968—. Bd. dirs. Cedars Found. Children's Home, Lincoln, 1984—, Madonna Care Facility Aux., Lincoln, 1985—. Mem. Nebr. Press Women (bd. dirs. 1978—), Nat. Press Women. Republican. Roman Catholic. Office: Costello & Assocs 5640 South St #3 Lincoln NE 68506

COSTELLO, MARY JANE, accountant; b. Ft. Worth, Aug. 22, 1956; d. Eugene Francis and Marie (Lawhon) Costello. B.B.A., U. Tex., 1979. C.P.A., Tex. Adminstrv. asst. M. David Lowe Personnel Services, Houston, summers 1974-76; sr. accountant Arthur Andersen & Co., Houston, 1979-84; controller Tex. Nat. Exploration Inc., Houston, 1984—. Vol. leader Young Life, Austin, 1975-78, Houston, 1980. Mem. Am. Inst. C.P.A.s, Petroleum Accts. Soc., Tex. Soc. C.P.A.S, U. Tex. Exes. Home: 12014 Mountain Ridge Rd Houston TX 77043 Office: Tex Nat Exploration Inc 1400 Post Oak Blvd Suite 1040 Houston TX 77056

COSTEN, MELVA WILSON, music and worship educator, consultant; b. Due West, S.C., May 29, 1933; d. John Theodore and Azzie Lee (Ellis) Wilson; m. James Hutten Costen, May 24, 1953; children—James Hutten, Craig Lamont, Cheryl Leatrice. A.B., Johnson C. Smith U., Charlotte, N.C., 1953; M.A., U. N.C., 1964; Ph.D., Ga. State U., 1978. Elem. tchr. pub. schs., Mecklenburg County, N.C., 1952-55; music tchr. pub. schs., Nash County, N.C., 1955-65; music enrichment tchr. Atlanta Pub. Schs., 1965-73; assoc. prof. music and worship Interdenominational Theol. Ctr., Atlanta, 1973—, chairperson curriculum revision, 1982-85. Composer Interdenominational Theol. Ctr. inauguration anthem, 1984. Chairperson Presbyn. Hymnbook Com., 1984-90. Mem. Alpha Kappa Alpha (dir. choir for albums 1978, 79, 84, Golden Dove award 1976). Democrat. Avocations: walking; Scrabble; social card games. Home: 3360 Laren Ln SW Atlanta GA 30311 Office: Interdenominational Theol Ctr 671 Beckwith St SW Atlanta GA 30314

COSTIGAN, MAUREEN, lawyer; b. Trenton, N.J., Nov. 7, 1956; d. Augustus John and Ellen (O'Connell) C.; m. John W. Van Schaik. B.A. magna cum laude, Cabrini Coll., 1978; J.D., Cath. U. Am., 1981; LL.M., Villanova U., 1984. Bar: D.C. 1981, N.J. 1982, U.S. Dist. Ct. N.J. 1982. Law clk. Arnold D. Berkeley Esq., Washington, 1980; assoc. Gerard E. Long Esq., Bridgewater, N.J., 1982-83, Malsbury & Armenante, Allentown, N.J., 1981-86, Law Offices Robert M. Adler, Washington, 1986—. Bruckman scholar, 1977-78. Mem. ABA, N.J. Bar Assn., D.C. Bar Assn. Home: 3600 Connecticut Ave NW Apt 307 Washington DC 20008 also 104 Carnegie Ctr Suite 105 Princeton NJ 08540

COTE, LAURA MARIE, hotel executive; b. Everett, Mass., Aug. 4, 1957; d. Arthur Paul Cote and Shirley Sally (Zichek) Cote Ray. Student Salem State Coll., 1976; cert. John Jay Coll., 1983; diploma U.S. Army Mil. Police Sch., 1978. Enlisted U.S. Army, 1978; mil. police investigator, Fort Monmouth, N.J., 1978-81; ret., 1981; chief security N.Y. Penta Hotel, N.Y.C., 1981-84; dir. security Lafayette Hotel, Boston, 1985—. Mem. Am. Soc. Indsl. Security, Greater Boston Security Dirs. Assn., Nat. Assn. Female Execs. Democrat. Avocations: theatre; sports; music. Home: 43 Wilbur St Everett MA 02149 Office: Lafayette Hotel 1 Ave de Lafayette Boston MA 02111

COTE-BEAUPRE, CAMILLE YVETTE, artist, educator; b. Worcester, Mass., May 21, 1926; d. Harvey and Blanche (Trahan) Cote; B.A. cum laude, Am. Internat. Coll., 1949; cert. in fine arts, Walker Studio Group, 1952; M.S., U. Bridgeport, 1967. Dir. arts and crafts South End Community Center, Springfield, Mass., 1955-58; art tchr. YWCA, Springfield, 1958-61; dir. workshops Hall Neighborhood House, Bridgeport, Conn., 1961-64, Jewish Community Center, Bridgeport, 1964-69; tchr., chmn. art dept. Notre Dame High Sch., Fairfield, Conn., 1970—; one man shows: Bridgeport Cath. Center, 1978, Creative Mind Gallery, Stratford, Conn., 1978, Burroughs Library, Bridgeport, 1979, Trumbull (Conn.) Library, 1981, St. Vincent's Hosp., Bridgeport, 1981, St. Joseph Manor, Trumbull, 1981; group shows include: Stamford (Conn.) Mus., 1977, Slade Mus., Norwich, Conn., 1975, Mus. Sci. and Industry, Bridgeport, 1974, Sacred Heart U., Bridgeport, 1979, Fairfield (Conn.) U., 1979, 56th grand nat. Am. Artists Profl. League, others; represented in permanent collections: Eastern Conn. State Coll., Trumbull Library Assn., St. Vincent's Hosp., St. Joseph's Manor. Mem. Conn. Classic Artists, Diocesan Bridgeport Edn. Assn., Newtown Soc. for Creative Arts, Am. Portrait Soc., Acad. Artists Assn., Nat. Arts Club. Home: 12 Melon Patch Ln Monroe CT 06468 Office: Notre Dame High School 220 Jefferson St Fairfield CT 06430

COTTOM-WINSLOW, MARGARET JEANNE, textbook author, painter, architectural designer; b. Mpls., Feb. 8, 1931; d. Robert Wayne and Zoe Anne (Williams) Cottom; m. Alan George Winslow, Aug. 22, 1954 (div. 1963); children—Curtis Matthew, Bradford Thomas. B.A., U. Calif.-Berkeley Coll. Architecture, 1955; M.F.A., Syracuse U., 1963. Archtl. designer (Peggy Winslow): Zachary Rosenfield, N.Y.C., 1963-64, Vollmer Assos., N.Y.C., 1964-65, Walter Dorwin Teague Assos., N.Y.C., 1965-67; contract author Harcourt Brace Jovanovich Inc., N.Y.C., 1968-79; dir. curriculum Internat. Center Ednl. Advancement, N.Y.C., 1976—; pvt. practice author and archtl. designer, N.Y.C., 1979—; cons. Margaret Cottom-Winslow Assocs.: Playground Clearing House, Inc., Phoenixville, Pa., 1979—, Talcott Mountain Sci. Center, Avon, Conn., 1982, Pratt Inst., Bklyn., 1979, others; keynote speaker symposium on Evolution of Ednl. Systems Cairo (Egypt) Book Fair, 1978. Author: (Margaret Cottom-Winslow) environ. text Care of a Small Planet The Humanities, 1980; co-author textbooks: Self Expression and Conduct the Humanities, 1978; Concepts in Science, 4th and 5th edits., 1975, 79; Expressions: Black Americans, 1972. Recipient purchase prize (painting) Univ. Coll., Syracuse, 1961. Mem. Nat. Council Tchrs. of English, Nat. Assn. Female Execs., AAUW, I.P.A., Archtl. Alliance. Democrat. Episcopalian. Home and Office: 501 E 87th St 5J New York NY 10128

COTTRELL, MARY-PATRICIA TROSS, banker; b. Seattle, Apr. 24, 1934; d. Alfred Carl and Alice-Grace (O'Neal) Tross; B.A. in Bus. Adminstrn., U. Wash., 1955; m. Richard Smith Cottrell, May 17, 1969. Systems service rep. IBM, Seattle, also Endicott, N.Y., 1955-58, customer edn. instr., Endicott, 1958-60, 62-65, edn. planning rep., San Jose, Calif. and Endicott, N.Y., 1960-62; cons. data processing, Stamford, Conn., 1965-66; asst. treas. Union Trust Co., Stamford, 1967-68, asst. v.p., 1969-76, v.p., 1976-78, v.p., head corp. services, 1978-83; v.p. corp. fin. services CityTrust, Bridgeport, Conn., 1983—. Bd. dirs. Family and Children's Aid of Greater Norwalk (Conn.), Gaylord Hosp. Mem. Electronic Funds Transfer Assn. (chmn. 1984-85, dir.), Fairfield County Bankers Assn. (dir., pres. 1984-85), West Norwalk Assn. (dir.). Republican. Roman Catholic. Club: Grad. Office: CityTrust 961 Main St Bridgeport CT 06601

COUCH, ALICE MAE, nursing home administrator, practical nurse; b. Genoa, Ohio, Jan. 22, 1936; d. Thomas William and Marie (Croston) Charlton; m. Earl Dean Couch, Oct. 16, 1954; children—George Gilbert, Andrew Dean, Larry William. Student W.Va. U., 1968, 70. Lic. practical nurse, W.Va.; lic. nursing home adminstr., W.Va. News reporter, Steubenville Herald, Ohio, 1953-55; clerical positions Valley Haven Rest Home, Wellsburg, W.Va., 1957-68, nurse, adminstr., 1968-72, owner, adminstr., 1972—; sec. W.Va. Health Care, Charleston, 1972-74, pres., 1974-76, 81-83, bd. dirs., 1983—; bd. dirs. New Martinsville Health Care, W.Va., 1982—, Lewis Wetzel Nursing Home, New Martinsville, 1980-83. Hon. bd. dirs. Brooke County Soc. Crippled Children and Adults, W.Va., 1984; mem. exec. com. Republican Party, Brooke County, 1979-80. Recipient Presdl. citation Am. Health Care Assn., 1976; Service award W.Va. Dept. Health, 1977; Better Life award W.Va. Health Care, 1977; Outstanding Service award W.Va. Health Care, 1980. Mem. W.Va. Health Systems Agy., W.Va. State Healthwide Coordinating Council, W.Va. Health Care Assn. Republican. Mem. Disciples of Christ Ch. Club: Wellsburg Jr. Woman's. Lodges: Women of Moose. Avocations: gardening; handicrafts; collecting English commemorative pieces. Home and Office: RD 3 Box 44 Wellsburg WV 26070

COUGHLAN, MARLEE TURNER, health resort executive, children's camp executive; b. Bronxville, N.Y., Feb. 16, 1933. B.A. in Polit. Sci., Stanford U., 1954. Elem. tchr. Palo Alto City Schs. (Calif.), 1954-56, Los Angeles City Schs., 1966-72; ptnr. CKT Assocs., Topanga, Calif., 1975—; co-owner, pres. No. Pines Health Resort Raymond, Maine, 1979—, also dir.; v.p., co-owner Kingsley Pines Camp, Raymond, 1983—, also dir. Vice pres. worship and spirituality com. Our Lady of Perpetual Help Ch.; pres. LWV of Maine. Home and Office: Route 85 Box 279 Raymond ME 04071

COUGHLIN, ELIZABETH ANN, union official, consultant; b. Americus, Ga., Oct. 1, 1945; d. Sammie Raymond and Ruth Willie (Missilidine) Simmons; m. Richard Paul Coughlin, Aug. 21, 1965. B.A. in Social Sci., St. Mary's Coll., 1978. Sr. med. abstractor Kaiser Hosp., Oakland, Calif., 1965-74; union rep. Office and Profl. Employees Union 29, Emeryville, Calif., 1974-76; cons. Nat. Council on Alcoholism, San Francisco, 1976-80, Simmons Coughlin Ltd., Oakland, 1980—; pres. Office and Profl. Employees Union 29, Emeryville, 1982—; mem. wage bd. State Calif. Indsl. Welfare Commn., Sacramento, 1976; co-chair Calif. Women's Commn. on Alcoholism, San Francisco, 1976-79; lectr., faculty mem. U. San Francisco, Duke U., U. Utah, Vista Coll., 1977-83; cons. State Calif., Sacramento, 1978-79. Prin. co-author: You Know You're a Peace Officer's Wife When, 1978. Editor The 29er, 1982-83. Mem. Friendship Force Internat., San Francisco, 1984-85. Recipient Past Pres. award Past Pres. Com. of Peace Officers' Wives' Club Affiliated Calif., 1978, Resolution of Spl. Pub. Honor and Highest Commendation, Calif. Legislature, 1980, Disting. Service award Nat. Council on Alcoholism, San Francisco, 1981; named Unionist of Yr., Alameda County Labor Council, Oakland, Calif., 1980. Mem. Assn. Labor/Mgmt. Adminstrs. and Cons. on Alcoholism, Problems of Alcoholism in Labor and Mgmt. (bd. dirs. 1984—). Avocations: world travel; reading. Home: 6121 Buenaventura Oakland CA 94605 Office: Office and Profl Employees Union 29 1475 Powell St Emeryville CA 94608

COUGHLIN, SISTER MAGDALEN, nun, coll. pres.; b. Wenatchee, Wash., Apr. 16, 1930; d. William J. and Cecilia (Diffley) C.; B.A. in History, Social Sci. Coll. of St. Catherine, St. Paul, 1952; postgrad. (Fulbright scholar), U. Nijmegen, The Netherlands, 1952-53; M.A. in Medieval History. Mt. St. Mary's Coll., Los Angeles, 1962; Ph.D. in Am. History (Haynes fellow). U. So. Calif., 1970. Tchr. history Alemany High Sch., San Fernando, Calif., 1960-61; tchr. history St. Mary's Acad., Los Angeles, 1961-63; asst. prof. history Mt. St. Mary's Coll., 1963-69, dean acad. devel., 1970-74, pres., 1976—; provincial councilor, regional superior Sisters of St. Joseph of Carondelet, Los Angeles, 1974-76. Mem. Am. Hist. Soc., Calif. Hist. Soc., Phi Alpha Theta, Pi Gamma Mu, Delta Epsilon Sigma, Kappa Gamma Pi, Lambda Iota Tau. Roman Catholic. Contbr. reviews and articles to profl. jours. Home and office: Mount St Mary's College 12001 Chalon Rd Los Angeles CA 90049*

COUGHLIN, MARYROSE, nurse; b. Springfield, Mass., Oct. 21, 1956; d. Robert William and Margaret Mildred C.; B.S.N. cum laude, Boston Coll., 1978. R.N., U. Va. Med. Center, Charlottesville, 1978-79; asst. head nurse Baystate Med. Center, Springfield, 1979-80, clin. supr. surg. nursing service, 1980-83, unit supr. telemetry unit, 1983-85, asst. dir., nurse recruiter, 1985—. Del., Democratic State Conv., 1982, 84, 86. Asso. mem. Dem. City Com. Mem. Am. Nurses Assn., Mass. Nurses Assn. (dir. chmn. legis. com., 2d v.p.), LWV, Nat. Assn. Health Care Recruiters, Sigma Theta Tau. Roman Catholic. Mem. editorial bd. Nursing Perspectives, 1981. Home: 20 Ashbrook St Springfield MA 01118 Office: Baystate Med Center Chestnut St Springfield MA 01107

COUKOS, CAROLYN COOK, lawyer, banker; b. Vinita, Okla., Apr. 15, 1941; d. Lloyd E. and Louise (Lester) Cook; m. James Stephen Coukos, June 11, 1966; children—Pamela Sue, Stephen James. B.A., U. Kans., 1964; J.D., Ind. U., 1976. Bar: Ind. 1976. Editorial asst. Time mag., N.Y.C., 1964-68; v.p. Am. Fletcher Nat. Bank & Trust Co., Indpls., 1976—. Contbr. articles to profl. jours. Republican precinct committeewoman, Indpls., 1982—; sec. Republican Women's Club, 1986; bd. dirs. Girls Clubs of Indpls., 1986; chair Fairness Coalition, 1985—. Mem. ABA (group editor taxation sect. newsletter 1983—), Ind. Bar Assn. (Best Article award 1977, mem. council probate, trust & real property sect. 1984), Indpls. Bar Assn. (founding chmn. com. on women and law 1977), Am. Assn. Bank Women, Network of Women in Bus., LWV, Nat. Fedn. Rep. Women, NOW. Methodist. Office: Am Fletcher Nat Bank & Trust Co 111 Monument Circle Indianapolis IN 46277

COULIS, KAREN MARIE, lawyer; b. Ann Arbor, Mich., Nov. 24, 1950; d. Charlton Thomas and Betty Lorraine (Kapanka) Campbell; m. Paul Thomas Coulis, Sept. 11, 1977; children—Thomas Charlton, Stephanie Dannielle. B.A., U. Dayton, 1973; J.D., Valparaiso U., 1976. Bar: Ind. 1976, U.S. Dist. Ct. (so. dist.) Ind. 1976, U.S. Dist. Ct. (no. dist.) Ind. 1978. Dep. prosecutor Porter County Prosecutor's Office, Valparaiso, Ind., 1976-78, Lake County Prosecutor's Office, Crown Point, Ind., 1979—; asst. bd. atty. Lake County Welfare Dept., Gary, Ind., 1978-79; liaison to Lake County Welfare Dept., Crown Point, 1979—; legis. chmn. Lake County Child Abuse Task Force, Griffith, Ind., 1981—; mem. Lake County Legal Issues Task Force, 1985—. Author: Tenant's Rights, 1972. 1st v.p. N.W. Ind. Symphony Women's Assn., Gary, 1981—. Recipient Brother Albert Rose award U. Dayton, 1973. Mem. ABA, Ind. Bar Assn., Phi Alpha Delta, Pi Sigma Alpha. Greek Orthodox. Home: 1330 Brookside Dr Munster IN 46321

COULTER, ELIZABETH JACKSON, biostatistician, economist, educator; b. Balt., Nov. 2, 1919; d. Waddie Pennington and Bessie (Gills) Jackson; A.B., Swarthmore (Pa.) Coll., 1941; A.M., Radcliffe Coll., 1946, Ph.D., 1948; m. Norman Arthur Coulter, Jr., June 23, 1951; 1 son, Robert Jackson. Asst. dir. health study Bur. Labor Stats., San Juan, P.R., 1946; research asst. Milbank Meml. Fund, N.Y.C., 1948-51; economist Office Def. Prodn., 1951-52; research analyst Children's Bur., HEW, 1952-53; statistician, then chief statistician Ohio Dept. Health, 1954-65; lectr. econs., then clin. asst. prof. preventive medicine Ohio State U., 1954-65; asst. clin. prof. biostats. U. Pitts. Sch. Public Health, 1958-62; asso. prof. biostats. U. N.C., Chapel Hill, 1965-72, prof., 1972—, asso. dean undergrad. public health studies, 1979—, asso. prof. econs., 1965-78; adj. asso. prof. hosp. adminstrn. Duke U., 1972-79. Mem. Am. Public Health Assn. (governing council 1970-72), Am. Econ. Assn., Am. Statis. Assn., Am. Acad. Polit. and Social Sci., AAAS, Biometric Soc., AAUP, Sigma Xi, Delta Omega. Methodist. Contbr. articles to profl. jours. Home: 1825 N Lake Shore Dr Chapel Hill NC 27514 Office: Sch Public Health U NC Chapel Hill NC 27514

COULTER, KYLE JANE, federal administrator; b. Brownwood, Tex., Oct. 1, 1937; d. Pat and Opal (Mitchell) Cagle; m. Gene Edward Coulter, Apr. 18, 1957 (div. 1967); children—Kimberly Shannon, Patrick Eugene, Katherine Venet. Student Iowa State U., 1955-57; B.S., Tex. Tech U., 1960, M.S., 1968, Ed.D., 1971; postgrad. Colo. State U., 1970, Mich. State U., 1971. Asst. prof. home econs. Tex. Tech U., Lubbock, 1971-76; asso. prof., assoc. dean home econs., 1976-80; dep. dir. Office of Higher Edn., Dept. Agr., Washington, 1980-82, dir., 1982—. Contbg. author to tech. publs., profl. jours. Recipient New Faculty Excellence in Teaching award Tex. Tech U., 1973; Dir.'s award Dept. Agr., 1980. Mem. Am. Council Consumer Interests (dissertation research award 1972), Am. Home Econs. Assn., Va. Home Econs. Assn., Sigma Xi, Phi Kappa Phi, Phi Upsilon Omicron. Methodist. Office: Higher Edn Programs Dept Agriculture 14th and Independence Ave Washington DC 20250

COULTER, LINDA NEWELL, office administrator; b. Hazlehurst, Miss., Dec. 24, 1948; d. Green B. and Iola (Morse) Newell; m. Larry B. Coulter, July 1, 1966; children—Lloyd B., Linsay Rose. B.A. in Bus. and Acctg., Copiah Lincoln Coll., 1966. Office mgr., exec. sec. Northwestern Mut. Life Ins. Co., Jackson, Miss., 1968-77; office mgr. Jordan & Assocs., Jackson, 1982—. Mem. Nat. Assn. Female Execs. Office: Jordan & Assocs 660 Lakeland E Dr PO Box 5346 Jackson MS 39216

COULTON, MARTHA JEAN GLASSCOE (MRS. MARTIN J. COULTON), librarian; b. Dayton, Ohio, Dec. 11, 1927; d. Lafayette Pierre and Gertrude Blanche (Miller) Glasscoe; student Dayton Art Inst., 1946-47; m. Martin J. Coulton, Sept. 6, 1947; children—Perry Jean, Martin John. Dir. Milton (Ohio) Union Pub. Library, 1968—. Active West Milton (Ohio) Cable TV Com. Recipient Outstanding Woman award Jaycees, 1979. Mem. ALA, Ohio Library Assn., Miami Valley Library Orgn. (sec. 1981, v.p. 1982, pres. 1983), Internat. Platform Assn., DAR. Home: 1910 N Mowry Rd Pleasant Hill OH 45359 Office: 560 S Main St West Milton OH 45383

COUNCE, AMY ELIZABETH, lawyer; b. Lafayette, La., Aug. 3, 1957; d. Harold J. and Lettie (Deas) Counce. B.A., La. State U., 1978, J.D., 1981. Bar: La. 1981. Ptnr., McKernan & Counce, Baton Rouge, 1981—. Mem. ABA, La. Bar Assn.; Assn. Trial Lawyers Am., La. Trial Lawyers Assn., Baton Rouge Bar Assn. Office: McKernan & Counce 5420 Corporate Blvd Suite 101 Baton Rouge LA 70808

COUNCIL, PAULINE CARTER, social services administrator; b. Camilla, Ga., Apr. 26, 1950; d. Willie Frank D., Sr., and Bernice (Brown) Carter; m. James F. Council, Jr., Jan. 26, 1980; children—Dawn Nichole, Kimberly Michelle, Ashley Monique, James F., III. B.A., Morris Brown Coll., 1972. Asst. planner Southwest Ga. Area Planning and Devel. Commn., Camilla, 1972-73, rev. coordinator, 1973-74, sr. planner, 1974-75; area agy. on aging coordinator S. Ga. Area Planning and Devel. Commn., Valdosta, 1975-77, area agy. on aging dir., 1977—. Chmn. Foster Grandparents, Valdosta, 1982-85, Dist. 8. Social Services Adv. Council Valdosta/Albany Area, 1985—; mem. Ga. Coalition of Black Women, Minority Affairs Com. Moody AFB, Valdosta, 1975-78; local rep. Martin Luther King, Jr. Ctr. for Non-violent Social Change, Atlanta, 1984-85; Brownie troop leader Flint River Council Girl Scouts U.S.A., Valdosta, 1982. Ga. Com. for Humanities grantee, 1977, 79; Ga. Dept. Human Resources grantee, 1977-85. Mem. Nat. Council on Aging, Nat. Assn. AAAs, Ga. Assn. AAAs. Democrat. Pentecostal. Home: Rt 10 Box 413 Valdosta GA 31601

COUNTEE, SANDRA FLOWERS, rehabilitation services administrator; b. Oklahoma City, Feb. 15, 1943; d. LeRoy and Minnie Ola Flowers; m. Harry J. McNeill. B.S., Kans. U., 1965; M.S., Columbia U., 1975; M.P.A., N.Y.U., 1979, A.B.D., 1983. Staff occupational therapist D.C. Gen. Hosp. Community Mental Health, 1965-68; supr. occupational therapy Columbia U.-Harlem Hosp. Center, N.Y.C., 1968-76, chief occupational therapy, 1976-78; asst. prof., dir. field work edn. Temple U., Phila., 1978-81; dist. mgr. N.Y. Commn. Blind and Visually Handicapped, N.Y. State Dept. Social Services, N.Y.C., 1981-82; dist. mgr. Office of Vocat. Rehab., N.Y. State Dept. Edn., White Plains, 1982—; clin. instr. rehab. medicine Columbia U., 1977-78; cons. Trinity Ch. and St. Margaret's House Devel., N.Y.C., 1979. Adv. bd. Community Home Health Services of Phila., 1980-81; mem. Westchester County Pvt. Industry Council, 1983—, Westchester County Council Disabled, 1983—; mem. bd. mgrs. Nyack YMCA, 1985—. Cert. social worker, N.Y.; lic. occupational therapist, N.Y. Mem. Am. Public Health Assn., Am. Soc. Pub. Adminstrn., Am. Occupational Therapy Assn. Home: 231 Treetop Circle Nanuet NY 10954

COURSHON, CAROL BIEL, civic worker; b. Cleve., Sept. 5, 1923; d. Maurice and Rita (Glueck) Biel; student Wesleyan Coll., Macon, Ga., 1941-42; m. Arthur Howard Courshon, Feb. 20, 1943; children—Barbara Mills, Deanne. With Washington Savs. & Loan Assn., Miami Beach, Fla., 1979-80, chmn. adv. bd., 1979-80, dir., 1980-82. Chmn. hotel-motel div. Mothers March Dimes, 1948-53; co-chmn. bus. div. Greater Miami Heart Fund campaign, 1977-78; bd. dirs. Children's Service Bur. of Dade County, 1960-70, Family Service Assn. Am., 1977-84, United Family and Children's Service (now Family Counseling Services), Dade County, 1970—; mem. adv. com. U. Miami-Jackson Meml. Children's Hosp. Ctr., 1983—; vol. tchrs. aide handicapped Dade County (Fla.) public schs., 1956-81; del. Democratic Nat. Conv., 1968; adv. bd. Jefferson Nat. Bank, Miami Beach, 1981—. Mem. Nat. Savs. and Loan League (exec. women's group 1979-83), Nat. Council Jewish Women (v.p. Bay div. 1953-55), Hadassah. Office: 301 41st St Miami Beach FL 33140

COURT, KATHRYN DIANA, publishing company executive; b. London, Dec. 23, 1948; came to U.S., 1976; d. Ian Howard and Elizabeth Irene (Freeman) Onslow; m. David Court, Feb. 1972; m. 2d, Jonathan Coleman, July 8, 1978. B.A. in English Lit. with honors, U. Leicester (Eng.), 1970. Editor, William Heinemann Ltd., London, 1971-76; editor Penguin Books, N.Y.C., 1977-79; editorial dir., 1979-83; editor-in-chief Viking Penguin, Inc., 1984—. Mem. Assn. Am. Pubs. (Freedom to Publish com.). Office: 40 W 23d St New York NY 10010

COURTENAY, IRENE DORIS, nursing consultant; b. Regina, Sask., Can., July 1, 1920; d. Thomas Greer and May Elizabeth (York) C.; R.N., Princess Alice Meml. Hosp., Eastbourne, Eng., 1942; B.S. in Nursing, U. Western Ont., 1956; M.P.H., U. Mich., 1957. Occupation health nurse Chrysler of Can., 1948-50, 52-55; cons. occupational health nursing N.C. Bd. Health, 1958-61; occupational health nursing specialist Nat. League for Nursing, 1961-64; cons. occupational health nursing Dept. Nat. Health and Welfare, Ottawa, Ont., Can., 1966-69; asst. prof., dir. grad. program occupational health nursing U. N.C., Chapel Hill, 1971-75; assoc. prof. occupational health N.Y. U., 1975-78; pvt. practice cons. occupational health nursing, 1978—. Mem. Am. Nurses Assn., Nat. League Nursing, Am. Assn. Occupational Health Nurses, Am. Bd. Occupational Health Nurses (dir.), Am. Indsl. Hygiene Assn. (asso.), Permanent Commn. and Internat. Assn. Occupational Health, AAUP, Am. Public Health Assn., Can. Council Occupational Health Nurses (dir., chmn. exam. com.). Mem. Anglican Ch. Author several publs. Home: 5110 Wyandotte St E #X14 Windsor ON N8S 1L2 Canada

COURTER, GAY ELEANOR, novelist, filmmaker; b. Pitts., Oct. 1, 1944; d. Leonard M. and Elsie (Spector) Weisman; m. Philip Ray Courter, Aug. 18, 1968; children—Blake Zachary, Joshua Forrest. B.A., Antioch Coll., 1966. Producer, writer ACI Films, N.Y.C., 1966-68, Courter Films, N.Y., Md., N.J., and Fla., 1969—. Author: The Beansprout Book, 1973; The Midwife, 1982; River of Dreams, 1984; Code Ezra, 1986. Film producer more than 100 ednl. and documentary film subjects. Recipient Blue Ribbon award Ednl. Film Library Assn.; Gold Eagle award Cine. Mem. Authors Guild, Writers Guild of Am. East, Internat. Childbirth Edn. Assn., Assn. for Psychoprophlyaxis in Obstetrics. Home: Route 4 Box 162 Crystal River FL 36269 Office: Courter Films and Assocs 121 NW Crystal St Crystal River FL 32629

COURTER, NINA KRONID, precast concrete products company executive; b. Vineland, N.J., Oct. 15, 1937; m. John Robert Courter; children—Elisabeth Anne, John Paul. B.S. in Bus. Adminstrn., Drexel Inst. Tech., 1960; postgrad. Glassboro State Coll., 1963, Rutgers U., 1982. Social worker Cumberland County Welfare, 1961-63; substitute tchr. Vineland Schs., N.J., 1965-70, homeside instr., 1970-72; instr. course YMCA, 1964-66; supr. volleyball and basketball programs Vineland Recreation Commn., 1968-72; owner Courter Co., Newfield, N.J., 1972—, pres., 1982—. Appointed Cumberland County Econ. Devel. Adv. Council; advisor Vocat. Indsl. Clubs Am., 1977-79; mem. gen. adv. com. Cumberland County Vocat. Sch., 1980—; mem. com. Holy Trinity Russian Orthodox Ch. of Vineland, N.J., 1981-84; mem. Cumberland Adv. Commn. on Women, 1984, 85. Mem. Nat. Assn. Women in Constrn., Nat. Precast Concrete Assn. Avocations: reading; music; traveling; antique jewelry. Home: 956 N Korff Dr Vineland NJ 08360 Office: Courter Co Rena St and Church St Newfield NJ 08344

COURTNEY, ELEANOR ELAINE, librarian; b. Beaver, Pa., Dec. 25, 1927; d. Robert Clarence and Geneva Mae (Oppelt) Stout; m. Paul Edwin Courtney, June 25, 1949; children—Christopher, Colleen, Julie. B.A. in Edn. cum laude, U. Pitts., 1948; M.L.S., U. Pitts., 1983. Cert. sch. librarian, tchr., Pa. English tchr. Beaver Falls High Sch. (Pa.), 1948-52; pvt. tutor, 1952-75; real estate salesperson PGH-FLA Realty, Verona, Pa., 1972-82; reference and young adult librarian Carnegie Free Library, Beaver Falls, 1983—. Former sec. Beaver Meml. Assn., citizens adv. com. Beaver Schs. Parents Adv. Council, aux. to Family Service Beaver County. Mem. ALA, Pa. Library Assn., Ch. and Synagogue Library Assn. (dir. 1983-84, book reviewer assn. mag.), Beaver Area Heritage Found., Beaver County Assn. Lawyers' Wives (organizer, pres. 1960-62). Club: Antiques (sec.-treas.) (Beaver). Methodist. Home: 115 Windy Ghoul Dr Beaver PA 15009 Office: Carnegie Free Library 1301 7th Ave Beaver Falls PA 15010

COURTNEY, NORMA ISABELLE, systems analyst; b. New Albany, Ind., Oct. 17, 1927; d. William and Mary Isabelle (Emery) Hagmann; B.S. in Computer Sci., Wright State U., Dayton, Ohio, 1975; M.B.A., U. Dayton, 1985; m. Robert Lee Courtney, Dec. 2, 1950; children—Deborah Lynn Courtney Smyth, Ellen Ann Courtney Irvin, Jennifer Lee Courtney Lightcap, Lisa Marie Courtney Blommel. With C.E., U.S. Army, Louisville, 1945-46, Ky. Actuarial Bur., Louisville, 1947-52; with NCR Corp., Dayton, 1976—, sr. prin. systems analyst, 1981—, project leader, 1983-85. Home: 615 Meadowview Dr Centerville OH 45459 Office: 3d Floor EMD Main and K Sts Dayton OH 45479

COURTOIS, CHRISTINE ANN, counseling psychologist; b. Providence, Aug. 29, 1949; d. Normand Albert and Dorice Irene (Dufort) Courtois; B.A. in History and Secondary Edn. (R.I. State scholar, Herbert Pell award), R.I. Coll., 1971; M.A. in Counseling (grad. asst., fellow), U. Md., 1973, Ph.D., 1979; m. Banks R. Chamberlain, Aug. 7, 1976. Asst. dir. Orientation Office, U. Md., 1975-77, counseling psychology intern Counseling Ctr., 1977-78, counselor, 1978-80; with Counseling and Testing Center, Cleve. State U., 1978-80; counseling psychologist U. Md., 1980-81, GAO, Washington, 1981-82, Women's Med. Center, 1981-83; pvt. practice counseling psychology, 1981—; adj. faculty George Mason U., 1982, U. Md., 1983—. Past mem. parish council St. Mathew's Roman Cath. Ch., Central Falls, R.I.; trustee Cleve. Rape Crisis Center, 1979-80; co-founder, dir. Univ. Women's Crisis Hotline, U. Md., 1972-76. Mem. Am. Psychol. Assn., D.C. Psychol. Assn., Am. Assn. Counseling and Devel., Am. Coll. Personnel Assn., Va. Counselor Assn., Nat. Orgn. Victim Assistance. Democrat. Author articles and chpts. in field. Office: 3 Washington Circle #206 Washington DC 20037

COURTOT, MARILYN EDITH, consultant; b. Plainfield, N.J., Mar. 17, 1943; d. Anthony Roland Hopcroft and Marion Edith (Schoenly) Hopcroft Rowen; m. George C. Courtot, Aug. 20, 1966 (div. Nov. 1981). B.A. in English, U. Md., 1965; M.S.L.S., Catholic U., 1972. Programmer, Prudential Ins. Co., Newark, 1965-66, Dept. Army, Lawton, Okla., 1966-68; systems analyst IBM Corp., Gaithersburg, Md., 1968-71; sr. systems analyst Library of Congress, Washington, 1971-73; adminstrv. dir. U.S. Senate, Washington, 1973-81, asst. sec., 1981-86; dir. standards and tech. Assn. Info. and Image Mgmt., Silver Spring, Md., 1986—. Editor: Glossary of Micrographics, 1982; contbr. articles to profl. jours. Recipient cert. of appreciation Nat. Micrographics Assn., 1973, 74, 77, 80, Pres.'s award Capitol chpt., 1978; award of merit Fed. Govt. Micrographics Council, 1977. Fellow Assn. for Info. and Image Mgmt.; mem. Continuing Library Edn. Network and Exchange, Info. Policy Discussion Group, Fed. ADP Users Group, Assn. Secs.-Gen. of Parliaments, White House Conf. on Libraries and Info. Service (adv. com. 1979), Nat. Commn. on Libraries and Info. Service (pub./pvt. sector task force 1979-81), Fed. Office Automation Conf. (adv. com. 1980-84). Office: Assn Info and Image Mgmt 1100 Wayne Ave Suite 1100 Silver Spring MD 20910

COUSINS, BERNICE BRIGANDO, educator, consultant; b. Flushing, N.Y., Nov. 2, 1937; d. August and Olympia (Tortora) Brigando; B.F.A. in Interior Design, Pratt Inst., 1955, postgrad. 1959; postgrad. City U. N.Y., 1966; children—David Bruce, Jason Bruce. Asst. to dir., tchr., Mus. Modern Art, Dept. Edn., N.Y.C., 1963-72; tchr. N.Y.C. Bd. Edn., 1966-73; with Am. Map Corp., N.Y.C., 1975-84, dir cartographic services, dir. mktg. services, also dir., 1979-84; lectr. in field. Curriculum Adv. Com., Public Sch. 85Q, 1976-77. Mem. Nat. Assn. Female Execs., Assn. for Research and Enlightment, Women Bus. Owners N.Y., Am. Space Found., High Frontier Soc., Am. Fedn. Astrologers. Contbr. articles to profl. jours.; researcher, compiler, editor: Nutritive Value of Common Foods, 1978; researcher, editor: Art Work: Schick-Colorprint Anatomy Charts, 1976—. Home: 41-19 23d Ave Astoria NY 11105 Office: PO Box 310 Flushing NY 11352

COUSINS, JANE CAMPBELL, real estate exec.; b. Camden, S.C., June 29, 1924; d. Herbert Allison and Mabel (Henning) Campbell; student Katherine Gibbs Sch., N.Y.C., 1945; m. James Lee Cousins, Dec. 19, 1949; children—Charles Henning, James Lee, Julie Elizabeth, Mary Allison. Field rep. ARC, 1943-44; stewardess Pan Am. Airways, 1947-49; engaged in real estate, 1964—; founder, 1967, pres., chief exec. officer Cousins Assos., Miami, Fla., 1967-81; pres. Merrill Lynch Realty/Cousins, Miami, 1981—; dir. Miami br. Fed. Res. Bank Atlanta, 1976-81; dir. Fed. Res. Bank Atlanta. Bd. dirs. Jr. Achievement Miami; trustee Fairchild Tropical Gardens, Bascom Palmer Eye Inst., Fla. Meml. Coll., South Miami Hosp., Boy Scouts Am., Fla. Lighthouse for Blind, Mailman Ctr. for Child Devel.; past pres. Beaux Arts of Lowe Gallery, U. Miami. Recipient Marketer of Yr. award Acad. Mktg. Sci., 1981. Mem. Nat. Assn. Real Estate Bds., Jr. League Miami, Greater Miami-Dade County C. of C., Fla. C. of C. (dir.). Republican. Episcopalian. Club: Bath (pres.) (Miami Beach). Office: 5830 SW 73d St Miami FL 33143

COUSINS, LINDA, publisher, editor, historical researcher, playwright; b. Knoxville, Tenn., Jan. 19, 1946; 1 child, Nadage Amia. B.S., U. Tenn., 1969. Pub., editor Universal Black Writer Press, N.Y.C., 1979—; pub. cons., Bklyn., 1985—; instr. English, writing and bus. skills Bklyn. YWCA, 1985—. Pub., editor: Black & In Brooklyn, 1983, Ancient Black Youth & Elders Reborn, 1985. Bd. dirs. Alonzo Players Theater, Bklyn., 1981-83; mem. adv. bd. Sisterhood of Black Single Mothers, Bklyn., 1985; founder Collective African-Am. Pubs., 1984—. Recipient Contbns. to Journalism award Bklyn. Coordinating Council, 1982; Contbns. to Journalism award West Indian Tribune Newspaper, 1982; Fannie Lou Hamer award Women's Ctr. Medgar Evers Coll., Bklyn., 1984. Mem. Com. of Small Mag. Editors and Pubs., Black Women in Pub., Poets & Writers, Inc., Coordinating Council Literary Mags. Mem. Unity Ch. Avocations: volunteer tutoring, historical reading. Office: Universal Black Writer Press PO Box 5 Radio City Sta New York NY 10101

COVER, EVA KATHERINE (NAST) TIMRUD, communications specialist; b. Kansas City, Mo., Apr. 7, 1946; d. Herbert Wilbur and Katherine Hall (Evans) Timrud; m. Thomas James Riley, Nov. 30, 1968 (div.); m. Jehu Fell Cover, May 23, 1982. B.J. in Advt., U. Mo., 1968. Editor, Waddell & Reed Inc., Kansas City, Mo., 1968-70; copywriter Berry World Travel, Kansas City, 1970-71, Western Auto, Kansas City, 1971-72; editor Nat. Sch. Supply and Equipment Assn., Arlington, Va., 1973-78, dir. communications, 1978-80; dir. communications Internat. Bus. Forms Industries, Inc., Arlington, 1980—. Author: The World of Business Forms, 1983. Pub. relations dir. Univ. Theatre, U. Mo., Columbia, 1966-67. Recipient Roy A. Roberts scholarship Kansas City Star, 1964-68; Curator's scholarship U. Mo., 1964-66, honors cert., 1966. Mem. Women in Communications, Inc. (dir. Washington profl. chpt. 1983-85), Internat. Assn. Bus. Communicators, Alpha Gamma Delta (1st v.p. 1966-67), Sigma Alpha Iota. Republican. Office: Internat Bus Forms Industries Inc 1730 N Lynn St Suite 501 Arlington VA 22209

COVEY, BETTY BENTON, financial planner; b. San Diego, Apr. 4, 1927; d. Frank Albert and Anna (Flenner) Benton; m. James V. Covey, Aug. 4, 1946 (dec. 1978); children—George Daniel, Kathleen Ann. Diploma Walter-Hartwell Bus. Coll., San Diego, 1946; M.B.A., LaJolla U., 1979. Asst. mgr. Lake Cove Growers, Finley, Calif., 1947-68; adminstrv. asst. Lakeport Schs., Calif., 1970-78; pvt. practice fin. planner, investment advisor, San Diego, 1980—. Contbr. articles to profl. jours. Recipient Lifetime award Lakeport PTA, 1970. Mem. Internat. Assn. Fin. Planning (sec. San Diego chpt. 1982, pres. 1983-85), Calif. Assn. Fin. Planning (bd. dirs. 1984—), Entrepreneur Club (Teamwork award 1984), Women in Mgmt. (Entrepreneur of Yr. 1983). Republican. Avocations: travel; dancing. Office: Kelley Duva Pendell Warschauer and Covey 1450 Frazee Rd Suite 407 San Diego CA 92108

COVEY, CHRISTINE COLETTE, lawyer; b. Cleve., Sept. 19, 1955; d. Eugene Joseph and Joanne (Liotta) C. B.A., Bowling Green State U., 1976; J.D., Cleve.-Marshall Law Sch., 1979. Bar: Ohio 1980. Assoc., Gillombardo & Eisenman, Cleve., 1979-81, Willacy & LoPresti, Cleve., 1981—. Recipient award Niagara Internat. Moot, Toronto, Can., 1978; award outstanding expository writing Nat. Assn. English Tchrs., 1972. Mem. Ohio State Bar Assn., ABA, Bar Assn. Greater Cleve., Order of Barristers. Republican. Roman Catholic. Office: Willacy & LoPresti 700 Western Reserve Bldg 1468 W 9th St Cleveland OH 44113

COVINGTON, EILEEN QUEEN, physical educator; b. Washington, May 25, 1946; d. Louis Edward and Evelyn (Travers) Q.; m. Norman Francis Covington, June 15, 1968; children—Norman, Marina, Deanna, Trena. B.S., D.C. Tchrs. Coll., 1971; postgrad. George Washington U., 1978-81. Tchr., coach Evan Jr. High Sch., D.C. Public Schs., 1971; tchr., coach Woodrow Wilson High Sch., Washington, 1971—, chmn. phys. edn. dept., 1971-75, 1977-81; cons. Coaches Assn., Washington, 1973-76. Named Coach of Yr., Eastern Bd. Ofcls., 1977, Nat. Coaches Assn. 2d Region, 1982, Winningest Coach Washington Coaches Assn., 1982; recipient Billie Jean King award Women Sports and Am. Fedn. Coaches, 1980-81. Mem. D.C. Coaches Assn. (v.p. volleyball 1981-83), D.C. Assn. Health, Phys. Edn. Athletics, D.C. High Sch. Coaches Club. Home: 7601 Ingrid Pl Landover MD 20785 Office: Woodrow Wilson High Sch Nebraska and Chesapeake Sts NW Washington DC 20016

COVINGTON, LOUISE MEMORY, genealogy researcher, educator; b. Whiteville, N.C., Jan. 14, 1913; d. Thomas Simms and Stella (Meredith) Memory; m. James Edwin Covington, Sept. 3, 1942 (dec. July 1967); 1 child, James Edwin. Student liberal arts George Washington U., 1931-34; cert. in genealogy U. N.C.-Wilmington, 1971. Dean New Hanover High Sch., Wilmington, 1934-41; legal sec. Stevens, Burgwin & Mintz, Wilmington, 1945-51, Mr. John Manning, Atty., Chapel Hill, N.C., 1961-65; instr. genealogy and local history Southeastern Community Coll., Whiteville, N.C., 1972—, Robeson Tech. Coll., Lumberton, N.C., 1985-86. Author: Memory and Kin, 1980; Thanks For the Memorys, 1983; History of First Baptist Church, 1983. Contbr. articles to various publs., 1965—. Pres. Whiteville Woman's Club, 1953-57, sec., 1957-60; clk. Selective Service System, Columbus County, N.C., 1953-60; sec. Whiteville Garden Club, 1954-58, pres., 1958-60; active ARC, Columbus County, 1952-61; trustee Columbus County Library, Whiteville, 1979—; librarian First Bapt. Ch., Whiteville, 1978—. Mem. DAR (various positions including sec. 1983—, regent 1977-79, 81-83), N.C. Geneal. Soc. Home: 113 W Oliver St Whiteville NC 28472

COVITZ, SHARON BAUM, college administrator; b. Cin., Mar. 13, 1946; d. Seymour Jack and Pauline Dorothy (Lutzky) Baum; m. Wesley Covitz, Aug. 4, 1968; children—Martha Illane, Seth Andrew, Dana Michelle. A.B., U. Cin., 1968, Ed.M., 1970; Ph.D., Boston Coll., 1979. Sec. Harvard U., Cambridge, Mass., 1970-71; asst. dir. alumni affairs U. Cin., 1972-73, speech instr., 1975-76; instr. Jefferson Community Coll., Louisville, 1975; asst. dir. continuing edn. Augusta Coll., Ga., 1976-79, dir. continuing edn., 1979—. Pres., mem. bd. dirs., founder Central Savannah River Area Family Counseling Ctr., Augusta, 1979-81; mem. nominating com. YWCA, Augusta, 1982-83; mem. budget panel United Way, Augusta, 1982-83; mem. exec. com. Davidson Fine Arts Sch. PTA, Augusta, 1984-85; founder, pres. Ronald McDonald House Augusta, 1982-84, bd. dirs., 1982-84, 85-86; hours chairperson, chaplain Augusta Jr. Woman's Club, 1981-85; bd. dirs. Augusta chpt. Hadassah, 1977-78, Adas Yeshuran Sisterhood, 1979-81, Univ. Hosp. Health Central, 1980-83, Augusta Opera Assn., 1981-82, Child Enrichment, Inc., Augusta, 1981-83, Augusta County Day Sch., Augusta, 1982-85, Augusta chpt. ARC, 1982-85. Recipient Good Citizenship award Augusta Jr. Woman's Club, 1983, Outstanding Citizen State of Ga. award Ga. Fedn. Women's Clubs, 1983. Mem. Augusta C. of C. (bd. dirs. Leadership Augusta 1980-81), Ga. Adult Edn. Assn. (editor newsletter and bd. dirs. 1984-86, Creative Programming award 1980), Nat. Univ. Continuing Edn. Assn. (bd. dirs. 1983-86), Central Savannah River Area Personnel Assn. (bd. dirs. 1982—), Profl. Women's Assn. (pres. 1980, sec. 1982), So. Assn. Colls. and Schs. (vis. com. 1982—). Jewish. Avocations: tennis; golf; needlepoint; painting. Home: 738 Ravenel Rd Augusta GA 30909 Office: Augusta Coll 2500 Walton Way Augusta GA 30910

COWAN, CHERRIE LORAINE, nurse, patient representative; b. Parkersburg, W.Va., Dec. 12, 1955; d. Harry J. and Betty M. (George) Fought; m. Vernon G. Cowan, Sept. 19, 1981; 1 child, Cassie Lynn; 1 stepchild, Jason Scott. Assoc. Applied Sci. in Nursing, Parkersburg Community Coll., 1977; student nursing W.Va. U., 1985—. R.N. (qualified critical care). Staff nurse pediatrics Camden-Clark Meml. Hosp., Parkersburg, 1977-80, critical care nurse, 1980-85, dir. patient advocate services, 1985—. Chairwoman Christian bd. edn. for presch., also coordinator pre-sch. nurseries Bethel Bapt. Ch., Parkersburg, 1982-85; supporter Assn. for Retarded Citizens, Parkersburg, 1984—, recipient Appreciation award, 1984. Mem. Am. Nurses Assn., W.Va. Nurses Assn., Nat. Assn. for Female Execs., Nat. Soc. Patient Reps., W.Va. Soc. Patient Reps., W.Va. PTA, Camden-Clark Meml. Hosp. Aux. Avocations: reading; swimming, aerobics. Home: Route 1 49 Wakefield Addition Washington WV 26181 Office: Camden-Clark Meml Hosp PO Box 718 Parkersburg WV 26102

COWAN, CINDY ANN, hotel executive, travel consultant; b. Fla., May 7, 1959; d. Irving and Marjorie (Friedland) Cowan. B.S., Tulane U., 1981. Counselor abused and foster children Methodist Children's Home, New Orleans, 1980-81; prodn. asst. Sta. WTVJ, Miami, Fla., 1981-82; dir. tour, activities and travel Diplomat Resort and Country Club, Hollywood, Fla., 1982—; phys. therapy asst. Meml. Hosp., Hollywood, 1977; conv. research dir. Diplomat Resort, 1981—; travel cons. Lawrence Travel and Diplomat Hotel, Hollywood, 1984—. Recipient World Champion Saddle-Bred Horseback Rider award Horse Back Riding Assn., 1970-77. Democrat. Jewish. Avocations: horseback riding; water skiing; snow skiing; boating. Office: Diplomat Resort and Country Club 3515 S Ocean Dr Hollywood FL 33019

COWAN, LOUISA KOSTICH, interior designer; b. Belgrade, Yugoslavia, June 15, 1927; came to U.S., 1949; d. Dushan Richard and Yovanka (Veselinov) K.; m. Eugene L. Cowan, Sept. 11, 1955. 1st Class Honors degree interior arch. and design, Acad. Applied Arts-Belgrade, 1949; 1st class honors degree Women's State Tchrs. Coll. of Applied Arts-Yugoslavia, summa cum laude, 1946. Interior designer, 1952-63; creative supr. Armstrong World Industries, Inc., Lancaster, Pa., 1964-71, asst. mgr., creative supr., 1972-75, creative dir., Residential Interior Design, 1976—; lectr. in field. Editorial designer, 1965—; contbr. articles to profl. jours. Recipient 1st prize award for total interior Upholstery Leather Group, Inc., 1956; Outstanding Performance award, Armstrong, 1983; Powerful Women of Lancaster, Intelligencer Jour., 1984. Mem. Am. Soc. Interior Designers, Historic Preservation Trust for Lancaster County, Smithsonian Inst., Lancaster Community Art Gallery. Republican. Lutheran. Club: Beta Sigma Phi. Office: Armstrong World Industries Inc Interior Design Ctr Lancaster PA 17603

COWARD, LOUISE PRETLOW, magazine editor; b. Harrisburg, Pa., May 1, 1944; d. William Jackman and Louise Giles (Holland) C. B.A., Mary Baldwin Coll., 1966. Personnel adminstr. U.S. News & World Report, Washington, 1969-77, asst. to exec. editor, 1977-79, adminstrv. editor, 1979—. Mem. Congressional Press Gallery. Republican. Episcopalian. Club: City Tavern. Home: 3411 Lowell St NW Washington DC 20016 Office: US News & World Report 2400 N St NW Washington DC 20037

COWDEN, JEAN WILLIAMS, food company executive; b. Lafayette, Ind., Aug. 12, 1943; d. Thomas Kyle and Clara (Williams) C. B.S., Cornell U., 1965; M.A., U. Mich., 1970. Tchr. San Diego Unified, 1965-70; mem. services dir. Nat. Rural Electric Coop. Assn., Washington, 1970-76; consumer affairs mgr. Oscar Mayer Foods Corp., Madison, Wis., 1976—; chmn. Nutrition Edn. with Industry Soc. Nat. Edn., 1985. Contbr. articles to profl. jours. Mem. Pub. Relations Soc. Am., Home Economists in Bus. (chmn. 1975-76), Soc. Consumer Affairs Profls., Soc. Nutrition Edn. Presbyterian. Club: Thinking Women (Madison). Office: Oscar Mayer Foods Corp 910 Mayer Ave Madison WI 53708

COWDEN, JULIANAN, steel company executive; craftsman; b. Midland, Tex.; d. Robert Edwin and Jett (Baker) Cowden; student Hockaday Jr. Coll., 1940-41; B.A., U. Tex., 1944. Rancher, oil investments JAL Co., Alvarado, Tex., 1950—, chmn. bd., 1970—; treas. J & M Steel Co., Inc., Ft. Worth, 1971—. Instr. jewelry and silversmith Ft. Worth Art Center, 1963-66; exhibited jewelry and sculpture in one-man shows at Simpson Gallery, Amarillo, 1969, Sq. House Mus., Panhandle, 1971; exhibited in group shows at Ft. Worth Art Center, Carlin Gallery, Mus. Internat. Folk Art, Santa Fe, Wichita Falls (Tex.) Art Mus., Tex. Tech U. Mus., Lubbock, Artist's Jamboree, San Antonio. Trustee, past pres. Tex. Sch. Bd. Assn.; mem. adv. com., mem. tech. and telecommunications systems adv. com. Tex State Bd. Edn.; mem. Fed. Relations Network; pres. Alvarado Ind. Sch. Dist. Bd., 1966-86; mem. Nat. Fedn. Republican Women; sustaining mem. Rep. Party, 1979—; mem. Rep. Senatorial Inner Circle; mem. Task Force Com. on Sch./Coll. Articulation; trustee Hockaday Sch., 1971-73; bd. dirs. Christian Heritage Found.; Mem. Nat. Sch. Bd. Assn., Tex. Designer Craftsmen, U. Tex. Ex-Students Assn. (life), Tex. Artists Craftsmen Guild (pres. 1970-72), S. W. Cattleraisers Assn., Ranch Heritage Assn., West Tex. C. of C. (dir.), Zeta Tau Alpha. Episcopalian. Clubs: Amarillo, Fort Worth. Home: PO Box 305-308 Alvarado TX 76009

COWDEN, SUSAN ELSBETH, engineering company executive; b. Chgo., Dec. 20, 1949; d. Robert B. and Billie Jo (Boland) Hacker; 1 dau., Jennifer. Draftsman, Dolan P. Williams P.E., Corpus Christi, Tex., 1968-69, Newman & Assocs., Corpus Christi, 1969-70, Southwestern Bell, Corpus Christi, 1970-71, Bernard Johnson, Inc., Houston, 1973-76; project coordinator, chief draftsman Landev Engrs., Inc., Houston, 1976—. Baptist. Home: 17019 Summer Dew Ln Houston TX 77095

COWEN, MILDRED L., association executive; b. St. Paul, Dec. 21, 1931; d. Charles and Dorothy (Greenstein) Locke; m. James G. Cowen, Oct. 21, 1956; children—Cari Lynn, James Louis, Jonathan Locke. Student U. Wis., 1949-52; B.A., U. Minn., 1953; postgrad. S.W. Inst. Fundraising, U. Tex., 1980. Assoc. dir. Jewish Nat. Fund, Houston, 1979-81, dir., 1981-82; dir. devel. and edn. Anti-Defamation League, B'nai B'rith, Houston, 1982-86; dist. adminstr. Office of Congressman, Houston, 1984; exec. v.p. Mental Health Assn. Houston and Harris County, 1985—. Bd. dirs. Jewish Family Service, 1979—; trustee Temple Emanu El, 1974—, sec., 1979, v.p. 1980—, v.p. bd. trustees, 1982, pres. sisterhood, 1974-76; pres. vol. services council Tex. Research Inst. Mental Scis., 1975-77; pres. Council Jewish Sisterhoods, 1976-77; bd. dirs. dist. 22, Nat. Fedn. Temple Sisterhoods, Interfaith Workshop; supr. music relgi religious sch.

Temple Emanu El, 1969-80; del.-at-large Nat. Women's Conf.; bd. dirs. Mental Health Assn., 1982—, sec. Houston/Harris County, 1983—; bd. dirs. S.W. region Anti Defamation League, 1985—, Commn. Jewish Edn.; mem. rev. panel United Way, 1984. Recipient Congregant of Yr. award Temple Emanu El, 1979. Composer children's music. Mem. Leadership Houston. Office: 4211 Southwest Freeway #209 Houston TX 77027

COWEN, SONIA SUE, university administrator; b. Wichita Falls, Tex., Sept. 30, 1952; d. Jackson Thompson and Shirley Isabel (Skerritt) C.; B.A. magna cum laude, East Wash. U., 1973; M.F.A. in Creative Writing, U. Mont., 1975; postgrad. U. Utah, 1981-82, Gonzaga U., 1983—. Grants adminstr. Eastern Wash. U., Cheney, 1978-81, 82, asst. to v.p. and provost, 1982-83, acad. projects adminstr., 1983—; registered ski instr., 1985-86; dir. Moving Ahead, 1985-86; mem. adj. faculty, 1979, exec. sec. N.W. Inst. for Advanced Study, 1978-81, 82—; teaching asst. U. Mont., Missoula, 1974-75; instr., head journalism program Coll. of Siskiyous, Weed, Calif., 1975-76; spl. asst. in adminstrn. Ednl. Service Dist. 101, Spokane, Wash., 1976-78; teaching fellow U. Utah, Salt Lake City, 1981-82; freelance writer; cons. grants and contracts to hosps. and state govts. Del. to Mont. State Land Use, 1974, Bend in the River Council, 1974-75; publicity chmn. Wash. State 4th Ann. Very Spl. Arts Festival for Handicapped Children and Adults, 1978, Nat. Theatre of Deaf Spokane Tour, 1978. Recipient Gov.'s Commendation, State of Wash., 1979, also named Outstanding Woman of Yr., 1979; recipient Leadership award YWCA, 1985; named Key Person, United Way of Spokane County, 1984; scholar Bread Loaf Writers Conf., 1973. Mem. Nat. Council Univ. Research Adminstrs., Nat. Assn. Coll. and Univ. Bus. Officers, Nat. Assn. Univ. Women Deans, Adminstrs. and Counselors, Am. Assn. State Colls. and Univs., LWV, Nat. Assn. Exec. Females (network dir. 1985—). Club: Panhandle Yacht, North Star Yacht (Coeur D'Alene, Idaho). Author: (with B. Mitchell and L. Triplett) Something About China, 1971; contbr. poems to various publs. Home: PO Box 172 Cheney WA 99004 Office: Eastern Washington U Cheney WA 99004

COWEN-MILLER, SANDRA LYNN, advt. and public relations agy. exec.; b. Mpls., July 26, 1944; d. Edward Thomas and Marie Elizabeth (Swank) Brandy; student pub. schs.; m. Robert S. Cowen, Oct. 11, 1965; 1 son, Jonathan David; m. 2d, Steven P. Miller, Apr. 28, 1978. Traffic mgr. Sta. KOOL, Phoenix, 1962; systems analyst Sta. KHJ, Los Angeles, 1965; media dir. Owens & Assos. Advt., Phoenix, 1966-69; part owner record distributorship ENDISCO, 1968-71; public relations dir. Owens & Assos. Advt., Phoenix, 1970-73; pres., owner Sandy Cowen Agy., Inc., Phoenix, 1973—; mem. Phoenix Media Adv. Bd.; speaker, lectr. in field. Vice pres. Samaritan Health Services Bd., Phoenix, 1980—; bd. dirs. Youth Eval. Treatment Centers 1981-82; mem. Tarp City Commn.; bd. dirs. Samaritan Health Services, 1983—; mem. Charter 100, 1982—, Clifton Flood Task Force. Recipient Pub. Relations award Nat. Hotel/Motel Assn., 1979. Mem. Am. Advt. Fedn., Retail Mktg. Group (past chmn.), Nat. Acad. TV Arts and Scis., Phoenix Advt. Club, Home Builders Assn. Central Ariz., Phoenix Press Club, Ariz. C. of C., Phoenix C. of C., Phoenix Better Bus. Bur. Home: 1809 N 13th Ave Phoenix AZ 85007 Office: 3003 N Central St Suite 2500 Phoenix AZ 85012

COWLES, MILLY, university dean; b. Ramer, Ala., May 29, 1932; d. Russell Fail and Sara (Mills) Cowles; B.S., Troy State U., 1952; M.A., U. Ala., 1958, Ph.D. (grad. fellow), 1962. Tchr. public schs., Montgomery, Ala., 1952-59; asst. then asso. prof. Grad. Sch. Edn., Rutgers U., 1962-66; assoc. prof. U. Ga., 1966-67; prof., dir. early childhood devel. and edn. Sch. Edn., U. S.C., Columbia, 1967-73; prof. U. Ala., Birmingham, 1973—, assoc. dean Sch. Edn., 1973-80, dean, 1980—. Dir. Williamsburg County Schs. Career Opportunity Program, 1970-73; cons. So. Edn. Found., Atlanta, Ga. Inst. Higher Edn. U. Ga., also numerous sch systems throughout Northeast and South. Bd. dirs. S.C. Assn. on Children Under Six, 1969-73. Recipient Outstanding Public Educator award Capstone Coll. Edn. Soc., U. Ala., 1977; Alumna of Yr. award Troy State U., 1981. Mem. Am. Ednl. Research Assn., Soc. for Research Child Devel., AAAS, AAUP, Nat. Council Tchrs. English, Internat. Reading Assn., Assn. for Supervision and Curriculum Devel. (mem. council on early childhood edn. 1969—, dir. 1978-82), Nat. Assn. for Edn. Young Children, Assn. for Childhood Devel. Internat., So. Assn. Children under Six (Ala. rep. to bd. dirs. 1985—), N.Y. Acad. Scis., Kappa Delta Pi (chpt. treas. 1964-66), Delta Kappa Gamma. Author: Taming the Young Savage, 1981; Developmental Discipline, 1982; editor, contbg. author: Perspectives in the Education of Disadvantaged Children, 1967. Research and publs. on psycholinguistic behaviors of rural children.

COWLEY, SHARRON SUE, association executive; b. Parkersburg, W.Va., Jan. 26, 1945; d. Harley Vernon and Stella Frances (Pearson) Fields; children—Bruce Wayne, James Gerard. Student W. Va. U., 1962, Ohio U., 1963, Ohio State U., 1975, U. Dayton, 1977. Social worker Montgomery County Juvenile Detention Ctr., Dayton, 1970-71; dir. sales Sheraton Corp., Dayton, 1971-75; exec. dir. Dayton Bar Assn., 1975—. Vol., Battered Wives, Dayton, 1980-81, Victim of Crimes, 1980—, Lawyers Assistance Com., Dayton, 1983—; lectr. in field. Mem. Nat. Assn. Bar Execs., Dayton Soc. Assn. Execs. (pres. 1978-79), Dayton Legal Secs. Assn. Republican. Avocations: home/house designing; tennis; reading; painting. Office: Dayton Bar Assn 120 W 2d St 1700 Hulman Bldg Dayton OH 45402

COWLISHAW, BONNIE CHERYL, talent agent, promoter; b. San Bernardino, Calif., May 5, 1947; d. Julian C. and Velma (Price) Beasley; m. Robert Jay Cowlishaw, Apr. 11, 1970; children—Terry Douglas, Tiffani Yvette. Student Valley Coll., San Bernardino, Calif., 1967. Lic. talent agt., mgr., promoter. Dancer, Los Angeles TV Stas., 1960-64; mgr. promotion, pub. relations Lansing (Mich.) Sound, 1980-82; owner Bonnie Cowlishaw Prodns., Grand Rapids, Mich., 1982—; cons. pub. relations Grand Rapids Wood Finishing Co., 1978—; promotional cons. WCUZ Radio, Grand Rapids, 1981—, Kellogg Ctr., Battle Creek, Mich., 1982—. Artist juried Art Shows, 1977-78; author: Friends-Family & Unicorns, 1982. Mem. St. Cecelia Music Soc., Literary Guild. Mem. Reformed Ch. Am. (pres. Reformed Ch. Women 1979). Office: Bonnie Cowlishaw Prodns 658 Cambridge Blvd East Grand Rapids MI 49506

COX, CAROL, retail human resource executive; b. Chgo., May 8, 1942; d. Raymond and Eunice (Diefendorf) C.; m. Koos Harm Schippers, Oct. 14, 1983. A.A., U. Bridgeport, 1960-62. Asst. personnel mgr. Genesco, Inc., N.Y.C., 1964-66; sr. v.p. personnel and communications Frederick Atkins, Inc., N.Y.C., 1966—; mem. fashion buying and merchandising dept. industry adv. bd. Fashion Inst. Tech.; lectr. Bd. dirs. Nat. Women's Employment and Edn., Inc., 1984—, co-chair N.Y. devel. com.; chmn. N.Y.C. Employment Council, 1983-84; adv. bd. Post Jr. Coll., 1976-83, Berkeley Sch., Westchester, N.Y., 1974-80; pres. co-op bd. Midtown Manor, Ltd. Mem. N.Y. Personnel Mgmt. Assn. (dir. 1976-79), Am. Soc. Personnel Adminstrn., Nat. Retail Mchts. Assn. (dir. 1972-80), Friend of N.Y.C. Commn. on Status of Women, N.Y. Bus. Group on Health (bd. dirs. 1985—, sec. 1986), N.Y. Personnel Mgmt. Assn. Democrat. Office: Frederick Atkins Inc 1515 Broadway New York NY 10036

COX, EILEEN FRANCES HINSHAW, foundation and business executive; b. Washington, Oct. 24, 1935; d. Max O. and Marguerite Mary (Wootton) Hinshaw; B.A. with honors, U. Md., 1967; M.A., Rutgers U., 1971; M.A., Columbia U., 1973; m. Robert Gene Cox, July 10, 1953; children—Ann Rebecca, Allan Robert. Staff asst. to dir. U.S./Mex. Border Devel. Commn., Exec. Office of Pres., Washington, 1967-68; asst. to Am. ambassador Conf. on Mex. Border Devel., San Diego, 1968; office mgr. Am. Acad. Cons., N.Y.C., 1971; devel. assoc. Found. Center, Inc., N.Y.C. and Cleve., 1975-78, cons., 1979; pres. Sloane & Hinshaw, Inc., N.Y.C., 1979-80, All Souls Music Soc., 1981—; cons. to bd. dirs. LeRoy Industries, Inc., 1985—; mem. U.S. del. U.S.-Mex. Trade Conf., Washington, 1967; Mem. N.Y.C. area council Unitarian Universalist Assn., 1979-80, mem. service com., 1979—; bd. dirs. Neighborhood Coalition for Shelter, Inc., 1983—; bd. mgrs. Soc. for Assistance of the Aging, 1985—. Mem. Met. Opera Guild, Center Inter-Am. Relations, Women's Econ. Round Table, Legal Aid Soc. N.Y., Pi Sigma Alpha, Phi Kappa Phi. Democrat. Home: 225 Central Park W Suite 1207 New York NY 10024

COX, ELEANOR VIRGINIA LEWIS, educational administrator; b. Little Rock, Oct. 19, 1944; d. William F. and Mildred M. (Johnson) Lewis; m. Vincent Teel Cox, Aug. 31, 1964; children—Marion Faith, Vincent Thomas. B.A., U. Ark., 1969; M.A., U. Ark.-Fayetteville, 1976, cert. in elem. edn., 1981. Tchr. elem sch., Little Rock, 1969-81, prin. Bale Elem. Sch., 1981—; instr. Principles for Effective Teaching, 1983—. Author: Berkeley Word Search, 1974. Bd. dirs. Vols. in Pub. Schs., Little Rock, 1982-84; bd. dirs. PTA, 1981-84, sec., 1984-85, vol. Drs. Hosp. Aux., 1985—. Peabody Coll. grantee, 1982-83. Mem. Nat. Assn. Elem. Prins., Ark. Assn. Elem. Prins., Prins. Roundtable. Democrat. Baptist. Club: Sophisticates (pres. 1977-78) (Little Rock). Avocations: ceramics; crewel work; writing children's books. Office: Gibbs Intermediate School 16th and Ringo St Little Rock AR 72202

COX, FLORENCE FAYE, educator, educational consultant; b. Marksville, La., Dec. 27, 1942; d. Russell and Louise (Jones) Barton; m. Irvin Nelson Cox, Dec. 7, 1985. B.S. in Edn., Prairie View A&M U., 1964; M.A. in Edn., Chgo. State U., 1977, M.S., 1980. Cert. tchr., adminstr., supr., Ill. Tchr., Pine Island Sch. Dist., Anahuac, Tex. 1964-65, Chester Sch. Dist., Tyler, Tex., 1965-66; tchr. Joliet Pub. Schs., Ill., 1966-76, ednl. cons., 1976—; ednl. cons. Marcourt Brace Jovonavich Pubs., Chgo., 1985-86; tchr. Nat. Coll. Edn., Evanston, Ill., 1980-82; adj. instr. Lewis U., Romeoville, Ill., 1984. Author: Curriculum Handbook, 1979; Operating the Apple Computer, 1982. Pres. Union Sch. Bd. Dist. 81, Joliet, Ill., 1979; mem. Joliet Community Access League, 1985. Mem. Bus. and Profl. Women (bd. dirs. 1985), Phi Delta Kappa, Alpha Kappa Alpha (Most Acad. Soror 1979, pres. 1984), Nat. Hook-up of Black Women. Roman Catholic. Avocations: song writing, piano, backgammon, swimming, modeling. Home: 1111 Karner Dr Joliet IL 60433 Office: Joliet Pub Sch Dist 86 420 N Raynor Ave Joliet IL 60435

COX, FRANCES LEWIS, retired university administrator; b. Pavo, Ga., Feb. 2, 1924; d. Dilborn Owen and Delia (Johnson) Lewis; m. William Franklin Cox, III, Oct. 22, 1942; children—William A., Virginia C., Susan C., Lewis Franklin, Elizabeth C. Student Extension Center, U. Ala., 1963-65. Asst. acctg. Bowman Gray Sch. of Medicine, Winston-Salem, N.C., 1960-63; research grants acctg. asst. U. Ala. Med. Center, Birmingham, 1963-65, asst. to chmn. dept. surgery, 1965-66, supr. grants acctg., 1966-67; budget, grants officer U. Ala. Hosps., Birmingham, 1967-72; asst. dir. budgets U. Ala., Birmingham, 1972-84. Mem. Nat. Assn. Accts. Republican. Baptist. Home: 308 Poinciana Dr Birmingham AL 35209

COX, GRACE BELDEN, retired clinical psychologist; b. Staunton, Ill., Dec. 8, 1906; d. Orville and Ida (Zimmerman) C.; B.Ed., Ill. State U., 1932; M.A., U. Ill., 1939; Ed.D., Temple U., 1958. Intern, Ill. Inst. Juvenile Research, Chgo., 1937-38, Moosehart (Ill.) Lab. Child Research, 1942-43; tchr. Public Schs. Springfield (Ill.), 1926-38, guidance counselor, 1938-42; psychologist Ill. Dept. Public Welfare, Springfield, 1942-43; dir. child study dept. Public Schs. Davenport (Iowa), 1943-46; psychologist Tri-County Child Guidance Center, Harrisburg, Pa., 1946-47; staff psychologist Pa. Dept. Welfare, Harrisburg, 1947-50, chief psychol. services, 1953-62; chief psychologist Ill. Dept. Public Instrn., Elgin, 1950-53; dir. psychology dept. Hamburg (Pa.) State Sch. and Hosp., 1962-72; pvt. practice cons., Hamburg, 1972—. Active Easter Seals. Title I grantee Hamburg State Sch., 1970-72; cert. psychologist, Ill., Pa.; diplomate Am. Bd. Profl. Psychologists; named Disting. Alumna, Ill. State U., 1977. Fellow Pa. Psychol. Assn.; mem. Am. Psychol. Assn., AAUW, Internat. Platform Assn., Pi Gamma Mu. Clubs: Woman's (Hamburg), Soroptomists, Order Eastern Star. Home and Office: Route 3 Box 168 Hamburg PA 19526

COX, ILO B., civic worker; b. Boone County, Ind., Nov. 22, 1911; d. Thomas W. and Golda F. (Staton) Bohannon; m. Le Roy Cox, June 27, 1930; children—Patsy Lee, Sally Elaine. Sec.-bookkeeper Hall-Neal Furnace Co., Indpls., 1929-34; officer mgr. Grand View Meml. Gardens, Grand Haven, Mich., 1957-61; sec. typist Clk. V.; Dept. Natural Resources, Lansing, Mich., 1961-71; dir. Nat. Safety Council, 1980-82, Broward chpt., Fla.; one of 15 citizens apptd. by mayor of Fort Lauderdale (Fla.) to plan Internat. Lethal Yellowing Conf. and 5 day conf.; beautification and bylaws chmn. Fort Lauderdale Hist. Soc., 1980-82, historian chmn., 1982-84; leader Girl Scouts U.S.A., 1949-55; assisted 32 orgns. of City of Fort Lauderdale plan and carry out Clean Up, Paint Up, Fix Up, 1979-81; registration chmn. Fort Lauderdale Fla. Woman's Club, 1973-75, treas., 1975-77, 2d v.p., 1978, pres., 1978-80; pres.'s aide and protocol chmn. Fla. Fedn. Women's Clubs, 1982-84, serving chmn., 1984-86, program chmn. free enterprise, 1986-88, Woman of the Yr., 1984; conservation chmn. Grand Haven Mich. Woman's Club, 1966-68. Republican. Presbyterian. Clubs: Spring Lake County (Mich.); Lehigh Country (Fla.); Toastmistress (Mich.) (pres.). Home: 1928 NE 7th Ct Fort Lauderdale FL 33304

COX, JOY DEAN, business executive; b. Oklahoma City, Sept. 13, 1940; d. Wordy John Neely and Ethel (Russell) Neely Biggs; m. Sidney Lee Johnson, Sept. 10, 1958 (div. 1963); m. Ronald Gene Cox, Sept. 22, 1964; children—Ronald D., Beverly Kay, Jeffrey Wilson. Student pub. schs., Oklahoma City. Long-distance operator S.W. Bell Telephone Co., Oklahoma City, 1958-59; clk. John Pilling Shoes Oklahoma City, 1960-62; cashier Dial Fin. Co., Houston, 1966; file clk., typist N. Am. Ins. Co., Oklahoma City, 1966-67; bookkeeper, co-owner farm and ranch operation, 1969—; co-owner/operator Apco Service Sta. and Bulk Fuel Plant, Taloga, Okla., 1972-75, D&R Service & Supply Co., Panola, Okla., 1979—; dealer/owner Cox Chevrolet, Wilburton, Okla., 1985—. Pres. Taloga Extension Homemakers, 1969-72, sec.-treas., 1973-75; entertainer Latimer County Rest Homes, Wilburton, 1978—; leader Latimer County 4-H, Wilburton, 1979—. Recipient Leadership award Latimer County 4-H, 1983. Democrat. Avocations: singing; swimming; skiing; motorcycling; reading. Office: D&R Service and Supply PO Box 55 Panola OK 74559

COX, JOY PHILPOT, accountant; b. Forrest City, Ark., Mar. 21, 1958; d. C.C. and Josephine Elizabeth (Herrod) Philpot; m. Steve Cox, May 24, 1980 (div.). B.S. in Acctg., Ark. State U., 1979. C.P.A., Ark. Internal auditor Memphis Light, Gas and Water Co., 1979-82; acct. Ark. Power and Light Co., Little Rock, 1983-85, internal auditor, 1985—. Adviser Memphis Jr. Achievement, 1981; mem. Little Rock Energy Polit. Action Com. Mem. Am. Inst. C.P.A.s, Ark. State Soc. C.P.A.s, Phi Mu, Alpha Kappa Psi. Baptist. Avocations: tennis; hiking; music; swimming. Home: 16 Flintwood St Little Rock AR 72207 Office: Ark Power and Light Co PO Box 551 Little Rock AR 72203

COX, JUANITA WILLIAMS, telephone answering service owner; b. Houston, Sept. 2, 1947; d. Nathaniel Frank and Ella (Kerr) Williams; children—Frank Wayne, John David. Student U. Houston, 1965-67, Howard Payne U., 1972-74. L. Para-legal James Bunnell, atty., Brownwood, Tex., 1972-81; para-legal, mgr. Brownwood Abstract, Brownwood, 1981-84; owner, operator Girl Friday Answering, Brownwood, 1974—, Yellow Cab Co., Brownwood, 1981—; owner operator Nita's Bail Bonds, 1984—, TurnKey Real Estate, 1984—; agt. Western Union, Brownwood, 1976—; para-legal Charles McCain, atty., Brownwood, 1984—. Co-author: Certified Legal Assistant, 1977. Chmn., mgr. Bunnell for County Judge campaign, Brownwood, 1979, Bunnell for Dist. Atty. camp, Brownwood, 1981; alt. del. Democratic party, Brownwood, 1984. Mem. Nat. Assn. Legal Secs., Nat. Policeman's Assn., Bounty Hunters Assn., Tex. Assn. Legal Assts., Tex. Assn. Legal Secs., Brownwood Legal Secs. Assn. (gov. 1980-84). Lutheran. Lodges: Eastern Star, Rebecca Sister. Avocations: swimming; ride horses; sewing; painting. Home: 902 Norwood St Brownwood TX 76801 Office: Personal Businesses 321 Brown St Brownwood TX 76801

COX, KATHRYN HONAKER, Salvation Army officer, clergyman; b. Beckley, W.Va., Mar. 22, 1924; d. William Wesley and Daisy Elizabeth (Lilly) Honaker; m. Lewis Kimber Cox, June 4, 1944; children—Mary Kathrine Cox Southwood, Lewis Kimber. Student Salvation Army Officers Tng., Atlanta, 1943-44; A.A. in Journalism and Psychology, Richland Coll., Dallas, 1974; B.S. in Criminal Justice, U. Tex.-Arlington, 1976, M.A. in Urban Affairs, 1977. Ordained minister, Salvation Army, 1944. Officer, Salvation Army, N.C., Ky., Tenn., Md., Ga., Fla., Va., Tex., 1944-84, assoc. dir. correctional services, Tex., 1972-81, ret., 1984, adminstrv. asst. property dept., Dallas, 1984—. Contbr. articles to Nat. War Cry. Kiest Found. scholar, Dallas, 1973; U. Tex.-Arlington scholar, 1975-76; Am. Bus Women scholar, 1977, recipient merit award, 1977. Vol., VA hosps. and mental instns. Mem. Ch. Women United (pres. Kingsport, Tenn. 1950's, sec.-treas. Waco 1970), Social Workers Assn. (sec. 1970), Bus. and Profl. Women (scholar, named Woman of Yr. 1970). Republican. Home: 6354 Velasco Ave Dallas TX 75214 Office: State Hdqrs The Salvation Army 500 N Ervay St Dallas TX 75214

COX, KAY LYNETTE, health careers occupation educator, development consultant; b. Great Bend, Kans., Aug. 24, 1939; d. Herbert L. and Donna Dorothy (De Vore) Priest; children—Dana Suzanne Pothier, Tod Matthew Stevens, Ryan Austin Cox. A.A. in Nursing, Mt. San Antonio Coll., Walnut, Calif., 1962; B.A. with distinction, U. Redlands, 1978, M.A. in Mgmt., 1986. R.N., Calif.; cert. in vocat. edn.; community coll. credential. Nurse, South Coast Med. Ctr., South Laguna, Calif., 1965-72; tng. coordinator Capistrano-Laguna Beach Regional Occupational Program, San Juan Capistrano, Calif., 1972—; cons. Calif. Dept. Edn., Sacramento, 1978—, tchr. health careers tchr. tng., 1983—, profl. devel. cons. for spl. projects and curriculum devel., 1985—; chmn. Calif. Health Careers Adv. Com., 1982—; legis. rep. Med. Assts. Alliance in Calif., 1984—. Author: Being a Health Unit Coordinator, 2d. edit., 1985 Pet Facilitated Therapy, 1985. Mem. Nat. Assn. Health Unit Coordinators (founding mem.; dir. edn. 1985—), Calif. Assn. Health Career Educators (chmn. med. assts. task force 1982—), Am. Vocat. Assn., Nat. Honor Soc. Avocations: animals; reading; collecting china and crystal. Office: Capistrano-Laguna Beach Regional Occupational Program 31522 El Camino Real San Juan Capistrano CA 92675

COX, L. SUSAN, association executive; b. Seoul, South Korea, July 8, 1952; came to U.S., 1956; d. Marvin Lebow and Martha Jane (Hutchings) Gourley; m. R. Mark Cox, Feb. 17, 1973; children—Michael, Kathleen. Student schs. Halsey, Oreg. With pub. relations, Oreg. State Fair, Salem, 1970-72; youth camp dir. Lane County 4-H, Eugene, Oreg., 1977; LaMaze instr. Albany Gen. Hosp., Oreg., 1976-81; pub. relations dept. N.W. Natural Gas Co., Albany, 1972-84; coordinator devel. Holt Internat. Childrens Services, Eugene, 1984-85, dir. devel., 1986—; mem. Refugee Child Welfare Com. Oreg., 1986—; dir. Korean Heritage Camps, Oreg. and N.J., 1986. Producer TV pub. service announcement, 1980-85; author articles in field. Communications dir. Linn County United Way, Oreg., 1983, bd. dirs., 1981—, loaned exec., 1981; bd. dirs. Linn County Assn. Retarded Citizens, 1976-78. Recipient Youth of Yr. award Senator Mark Hatfield, 1971; Nat. Report awards, Nat. 4-H Club Congress, 1970, Nat. 4-H Found., 1971; named Oreg. Dairy Princess, Nat. Dairy Commn., 1971. Mem. Joint Council on Internat. Childrens Services (program presenter 1986), N.Am. Council on Adoptable Children (faculty 1985), Coalition to End Racism (regional rep. 1985-86), Bus. and Profl. Women, Nat. Assn. Female Execs. Democrat. Methodist. Clubs: Parent (pres. Lebanon, Oreg. 1984), Zonta Internat. Avocations: Reading; sewing; camping. Home: 35554 Spicer Dr Lebanon OR 97355 Office: Holt International Childrens Services 1195 City View PO Box 2880 Eugene OR 97402

COX, LOUISE CAROL, nurse; b. Shreveport, La., Oct. 20, 1951; d. James Talley and Alice Louise (Tarver) C.; m. William John Piatnitza, Apr. 30, 1977 (div. June 1981). B.A., U. Tex.-Austin, 1972; B.S.N., Northwestern State U. La., Shreveport, 1975; M.S.N., U. Tex., Houston, 1979. R.N., Calif., Tex. Staff/charge nurse U.S. Naval Hosp., San Diego, 1975-77, Methodist Hosp., Houston, 1975, 78, St. Francis Hosp., Columbus, Ga., 1978; clin. nurse specialist M.D. Anderson Hosp., Houston, 1980-83, Johnson and Johnson Home Health Care, Houston, 1983-84; nursing services coordinator IMED Corp., San Diego, 1984—. Contbr. in field. Served to lt. U.S. Navy, 1975-77. Mem. Am. Cancer Soc., Am. Assn. Critical Care Nurses, Nat. Infusion Therapy Assn., Am. Soc. Parenteral and Enteral Nutrition, Sigma Theta Tau. Republican. Presbyterian. Club: San Diego Tennis and Racquet. Home: 11272 Promesa Dr San Diego CA 92124 Office: IMED 9925 Carroll Canyon Rd San Diego CA 92131

COX, MARLENE MILLICAN, nurse, rehabilitation consultant; b. Hanceville, Ala., July 8; d. Marl Maston and Mattie (Freeman) Millican; m. Robert Wimberly, II, July 24, 1982; children—Marla C. Dykes, Gena C. Reid. B.S.N., Samford U., 1975; A.D. Nursing Jefferson State Jr. Coll., 1968; cert. health care adminstrn. U. Ala.-Birmingham, 1974. Claims examiner Blue Cross Blue Shield Ala., Birmingham, 1955-60; R.N., East End Meml. Hosp., Birmingham, 1968-70, Bapt. Med. Ctr., 1970-72; coordinator ICU, Cooper Green Hosp., Birmingham, 1972-75; dist. mgr. Internat. Rehab., Birmingham, 1976-82; pres. Ind. Rehab. Cons., Birmingham, 1982—. Mem. Exec. Female Assn., Assn. Rehab. Nurses, Ala. Claims Assn., Pvt. Rehab. Suppliers Ga. Home: 5543 Circlestone Ln Stone Mountain GA 30088

COX, MARY JANE TRUESDELL, lawyer; b. LeMars, Iowa, Jan. 23, 1945; d. Myrle Edward and Jane (Steele) Truesdell; m. William N. Cox, Oct. 19, 1973; children—(Truman (dec.), Rebecca. stepchildren—Courtland, Kathleen. B.S., Mont State U., 1967, Masters degree, 1970; J.D., U. Denver, 1976. Bar: Colo. 1976. Clk., Office of Edn., Denver, 1967-68; caseworker Nev. State Welfare, Las Vegas, 1968-69; sec. Labor Finance Indsl. Bank, Denver, 1970-71; v.p. Denver Indsl. Bank, 1971-73; legal intern trust dept. Security Nat. Bank, Denver, 1973-74; assoc. Joyce S. Steinhardt, Englewood, Colo., 1976-77; sole practice, Denver, 1977-79, Littleton, Colo., 1979-80, Englewood, Colo., 1983-84, Littleton, Colo., 1984—; assoc. Robert T. Hinds, Littleton, 1980-83; real estate agt. Able & Co., Littleton, 1979-80. Editor Mo. Family Law Newsletter, 1979-81. Sunday sch. tchr., youth leader, Denver, 1978-84. Mem. ABA, Colo. Bar Assn. (chmn. family law sect. 1981-82, bd. govs. 1984-86, v.p. 1986-87), Arapahoe Bar Assn. (dir. 1981-84), Phi Kappa Phi. Office: 5601 S Broadway Suite 201 Littleton CO 80120

COX, MARY LINDA, paper distribution company executive; b. Alton, Ill., July 3, 1946; d. William M. and Helen (Winters) C. B.A., McKendree Coll., 1970; M.B.A., So. Ill. U., 1977; postgrad. date St. Louis U., 1984—. Exec. dir. Girl Scouts U.S.A., 1969-76; instr. So. Ill. U., Edwardsville, 1976-80; mgr. Smith-Scharff, St. Louis, 1980-81; account exec. AT&T, Tulsa, 1981-82; pres. Mo. Disposable Products, St. Louis, 1982—. Media specialist Tenn. Republican party, 1975; mem. fin. com. Greater St. Louis council Girl Scouts U.S.A.; mem. youth panel United Way St. Louis. Mem. Central Bus. Assn. (v.p. 1985), Beta Gamma Sigma (chpt. pres. 1978-79). Office: Mo Disposable Products 2649 Washington St Saint Louis MO 63103

COX, NANCY JANE, microbiologist; b. Emmetsburg, Iowa, July 21, 1948; d. Emmett Stanley and Verna Lucille (Olson) Cox; B.S. with honors, Iowa State U., 1970; Ph.D., Cambridge, (Eng.) U., 1975; m. M. Evan Lindsay, Apr. 11, 1981; 1 child, Julia Claire Lindsay. Postdoctoral fellow Muscular Dystrophy Assn., Balt. and Atlanta, 1975-77; staff fellow Centers for Disease Control, Atlanta, 1978-80, research chemist, 1980—. Recipient Marshall Scholarship for study abroad, 1970; postdoctoral fellow Muscular Dystrophy Assn. Am., 1975. Mem. AAAS, Am. Soc. Virology, Am. Soc. Microbiology, Sigma Xi. Methodist. Contbr. articles to profl. jours. and books. Office: Div Viral Diseases 7-111 Centers for Disease Control 1600 Clifton Rd Atlanta GA 30333

COX, SHARON DYER, banker; b. Waxahachie, Tex., Feb. 11, 1949; d. Ray and Betty (Hart) Williams Dyer; m. Charles E. Cox, Sept. 3, 1978. B.S. in History, U. Tex.-Arlington, 1970. Dealer cashier Paine, Webber, Jackson & Curtis, Dallas, 1971-73; sec.-interviewer Tex. Am. Bank, Dallas, 1973-76, asst. personnel dir., 1976-80, v.p., personnel dir., 1980-82, sr. v.p., 1982—, Dallas region human resources coordinator, 1983. Mem. Am. Soc. Personnel Adminstrs., Dallas Personnel Assn., Nat. Assn. Bank Women. Republican. Methodist. Office: Tex Am Bank of Dallas 100 Exchange Park Dallas TX 75235

COX, THELMA BANKS, educational consultant; b. Cambridge, Md., July 21, 1928; d. Charles Monroe and Ida Mae (Slacum) Banks; B.S., Morgan State U., 1948, M.S., 1972; Ph.D., Union Grad. Sch., Cin., 1980; m. Leonard Cox, June 25, 1949. Social caseworker Phila. Dept. Public Assistance, 1948-49; sci. tchr., Annapolis, Md., 1949-50; English tchr., Balt., 1950-65, reading tchr., 1965-66, dept. head, 1966-67, coordinator community schs., 1967-68, spl. projects coordinator, 1968-72, project mgr., 1972-73, regional supt., 1973-79, asst. supt. intergovtl. relations, 1980-83; mem. Md. Council Higher Edn., 1970-76, State Bd. Higher Edn., 1976-86. Pres., Girl Scouts of Central Md., 1982—. Named Woman of Year, Greyhound Bus Co., 1972. Mem. Am. Assn. Sch. Adminstrs., Nat. Assn. Black Sch. Educators, Delta Sigma Theta. Democrat. Editor: The Heritage of the Baltimore Chapter of Delta Sigma Theta, 1979. Home: 3344 Dolfield Ave Baltimore MD 21215

COX, WILMA BEATY, marketing and communications executive; b. Spokane, Wash., June 27, 1929; d. Robert Wilbur and Ruth Aseneth (Duran) Dudley; m. Robert S. Cox, Jr., Apr. 25, 1958 (div.); children—Charles Thomas, Leslee Ann Cox Stout, Robert Sayre, Nancy Elizabeth, Kristina Suzanne. B.A., San Jose State U., 1972, M.A., 1976. Cert. tchr., Calif. Asst. to dir. Crocker Art Gallery, Sacramento, 1973-74; dir. Pub. info. U. Calif.-Davis Sch. Medicine, 1974-76; dir. pub. affairs East Conn. State Coll., Willimantic, 1976-79; dir. pub. info. Bryn Mawr Coll., Pa., 1979-80; dir. pub. relations U. Puget Sound, Tacoma, Wash., 1980-83; dir. univ. communications U. Santa Clara (Calif.), 1983-85; dir. mktg. and communications Leisure Care, Inc., 1985—; cons. Hopkins Art Ctr., Dartmouth Coll., N.H., 1978; chairperson Com. on Publs. Standards, State of Conn., 1978-79. Author art catalogs. Bd. dirs. Crocker Art Gallery Assn., Sacramento, 1974-76; charter mem. communications group No. Calif. Cancer Program, Stanford, 1974-76; charter mem. bd. dirs. Sacramento Cancer Council, 1975-76; bd. dirs. San Jose State U. Art Alumni Assn., 1983—. Recipient Best Mus. Pub. award, Western Assn. Museums, 1976; Disting. Service award La Sangre Latina, Hispanic Soc. ECSC, 1979. Mem. Council Advancement and Support of Edn. (CASE, exceptional achievement award periodicals program 1983, exceptional achievement award total publs. program 1983; chairperson publs. track 1985, Gold medal individual recruiting, Gold medal program pubs. 1985), Women in Communications (sec. Tacoma-Olympia chpt. 1980-83), Internat. Bus. Communicators, Phila. Pub. Relations Assn. (mem. peer awards com. 1980), Phi Kappa Phi. Democrat. Home: 275-118th Ave SE Bellevue WA 98005

COYLE, BERTHA M., nurse; b. Galion, Ohio, Dec. 25, 1912; d. Edward E. and Blanche E. (Keiffer) Eichhorn; m. Charles W. Coyle, Oct. 5, 1946; children—Christine E. Coyle Snyder, Deborah A. Coyle Barron. diploma, Fairview Gen. Hosp., Sch. Nursing, 1933. Staff nurse Fairview Hosp., Cleve., 1933-35, Cleve. City Hosp., 1935-38; pvt. duty nurse Galion, Ohio, 1938-42; staff nurse Galion Hosp., 1947-66, coronary care head nurse, 1966-78; active nurse ARC, Galion, 1954-78; cons. in field. Chmn. Galion chpt., ARC, 1962, instr. prepared parenthood, 1954-78, mem. disaster program, blood bank, nursing service, 1954-78; counselor Girl Scouts U.S.A., Galion, 1956-65; Nurse Hope, Crawford County, Ohio unit Am. Cancer Soc., 1984-85; profl. edn. chmn. Am. Cancer Soc., 1986. Served to capt. U.S. Army, Nurses Corps, 1943-46. Decorated 3 overseas service bars, victory medal. Recipient commendation for Nursing Services, ARC, 1962; woman of yr. award, Business and Profl. Women's Club, 1962. Mem. ARC, Ohio, Nurses Assn., Am. Nurses Assn., Am. Heart Assn. Presbyterian (elder). Clubs: Am. Legion, Eastern Star. Address: 202 S Columbus St Galion OH 44833

COYNE, ELAINE ROBERTA, designer, metal sculptor; b. N.Y.C., Mar. 11, 1946; d. Albert Isadore and Ida (Cerin) Coyne; m. Lawrence Judson Starr, Oct. 19, 1946 (div. Jan. 1981); 1 child, Sheriden Shey. B.S., SUNY, Cortland, 1967; postgrad New Sch., N.Y.C., 1969, U. Allende, San Miguel, Mexico, 1972, Harvard U., 1973, Cornell U., 1971. Pres., Elaine Coyne Galleries, Boston, 1975-77, Atlanta, 1977—; commd. designer Vincent Motorcycle Club Am., Boston, Sherlock Holmes Club Am., N.Y.C., Atlas Copco, Atlanta, Atlanta High Mus. Art, Cobra Helicopter Marine Res., Atlanta designer fine art wearables, metals leathers, 1975—. Mem. 20th Century Soc., Accessories on Six. Republican. Jewish. Founder, pres., Children's Welcome child care ctr., N.Y.C., 1971. Avocations: swimming; tennis; sculpture. Office: Elaine Coyne Galleries 5269 Buford Hwy Atlanta GA 30340

COYNE, M(ARY) JEANNE, justice Minnesota Supreme Court; b. Mpls., Dec. 7, 1926; d. Vincent Mathias and Mae Lucille (Steinmetz) C. B.S., U. Minn.-Mpls., 1955, J.D., 1957. Bar: Minn. 1957, U.S. Dist. Ct. Minn. 1957, U.S. Ct. Appeals (8th cir.) 1958, U.S. Supreme Ct. 1964. Law clk. Minn. Supreme Ct., St. Paul, 1956-57; assoc. Meagher, Geer, Markham, Anderson & Flaskamp, Mpls., 1957-70, ptnr., 1970-82; assoc. justice Minn. Supreme Ct., St. Paul, 1982—, chmn. adv. com. rules of civil appellate procedure, 1982—; mem. Lawyers Profl. Responsibility Bd., 1982; instr. law U. Minn., 1964-68. Contbr. articles to legal jours. Mem. ABA, Minn. Bar Assn., Nat. Assn. Women Judges, Nat. Assn. Women Lawyers, Minn. Women Lawyers, U. Minn. Law Alumni Assn. (bd. dirs.), Order of Coif. Office: Minn Supreme Ct 230 State Capitol Saint Paul MN 55155

COYTE, CAROLINE R., writer; b. Panama C.Z., June 9, 1951; d. Hugh Wayne and Gloria (Scott) Randel; student Am. U., 1969-71, George Washington U., 1972-73; B.A. in Polit. Sci., U. Ariz., 1973; grad. Western State U. Coll. Law, 1984; m. Michael Alan Coyte, June 26, 1978; 1 child, Alistair Jeremy. Profl. staff/writer U.S. Senate Republican Policy Com., Washington, 1973-77; legis. asst./speechwriter U.S. Senator Cliff Hansen, Washington, 1977-78; dir. legislation Nat. Asphalt Pavement Assn., Washington, 1979-80; with Wickes Cos., San Diego, 1981-82, corp. govt. affairs analyst, 1982; with ICA Mortgage Corp., La Jolla, Calif., 1984—. Mem. Nat. Assn. Female Execs. Presbyterian.

COZENS, ROBERTA EATON, nursing educator; b. Gary, Ind., Apr. 1, 1943; d. Wayne Robert and Letha Jean (Trout) Eaton; m. George Deaves Cozens, Jr., May 18, 1960; children—Jennifer, Joanna. B.S., Columbia Union Coll., 1965; M.S., Cath. U. Am., 1981. Rehab. nurse Univ. Nursing Home, Silver Spring, Md., 1965; staff nurse Walter Reed Army Med. Ctr., Washington, 1965-67, Prince George's County Health Dept., Cheverly, Md., 1967-70, asst. supr., 1970-72, asst. dir. home health agy., 1972; asst. prof. nursing Prince George's Community Coll., Largo, Md., 1976—. Co-leader Girl Scout Council of Nation's Capital, Washington, 1983-84. Mem. Am. Nurses Assn., Nat. Student Nurses Assn., Md. Nurses Assn. (Dist. 6 dir. 1982-83, treas. 1969-73), Md. Assn. Nursing Students (outstanding dedication award 1983). Home: 11305 Sherrington Ct Upper Marlboro MD 20772 Office: Prince George's Community Coll 301 Largo Rd Largo MD 20772

CRABB, BARBARA BRANDRIFF, U.S. district judge; b. Green Bay, Wis., Mar. 17, 1939; d. Charles Edward and Mary (Forrest) Brandriff; A.B., U. Wis., 1960, J.D., 1962; m. Theodore E. Crabb, Jr., Aug. 29, 1959; children—Julia Forrest, Philip Elliott. Admitted to Wis. bar, 1963; asso. firm Roberts, Broadman, Suhr & Curry, Madison, 1962-64; research asst. U. Wis. Law Sch., 1968-70, Am. Bar Assn., Madison, 1970-71; U.S. magistrate, Madison, 1971-79; dist. judge U.S. Dist. Ct. Western Dist. Wis., Madison, 1979—, chief judge, 1980—; mem. Gov.'s Task Force Prison Reform, 1971-73. Membership chmn., v.p. Milw. LWV, 1966-68; mem. Milw. Jr. League, 1967-68. Mem. Nat. Council Fed. Magistrates, Nat. Assn. Women Judges, Dane County Bar Assn., U. Wis. Law Alumni Assn. Office: PO Box 591 Madison WI 53701

CRABS, YVONNE YOUNG, oil company executive; b. New Orleans, Mar. 3, 1955; d. Elo Joseph and Nola Marie (Lafleur) Young; m. Wyatt D. Crabs, Oct. 1, 1977. Student McNeese State U. Money room/credit J.C. Penneys, Lake Charles, La., 1973-77; sec. Conoco Inc., Ponca City, Okla., 1978-80, material analyst, 1980-85, publs. coordinator, 1985—. Democrat. Roman Catholic. Mem. Nat. Orgn. Female Execs. Club: St. Jude's Guild (Ponca City). Lodge: Women of Moose (guide 1983-84, 85-86, jr. regent 1984-85). Avocations: sewing; reading; arts and crafts. Home: 1217 Bradbary St Ponca City OK 74601 Office: Conoco Inc 1000 S Pine St PO Box 1267 Ponca City OK 74603

CRAFT, DIANA LEGAULT, publisher; b. Mt. Claire, N.J., June 25, 1948; d. Roger Maurice and Marie (Edwards) Legault; 1 son, Roger William. B.A., North Tex. State U., 1966, postgrad., 1970-71. Med. illustrator, designer U. Nebr. Med. Ctr., Omaha, 1971-72; asst. art dir. Bryne, Watts, Storey, New Orleans, 1973-74; owner Craft Illustrations, Dallas, 1975-78; pub., prin. Communicative Art Group, Richardson, Tex., 1978—; distbr., prin. Pub.'s Mktg. Group, Richardson, 1982—. Designer, illustrator: Kaye Johns Family Cookbook, 1982; The Beautiful You Cookbook, 1979; Your Proportions in Fashion, 1982; The Beautiful You Glamour Handbook, 1982. Address: Publishers Marketing Group 1343 Columbia St Suite 405 Richardson TX 75081

CRAFT, ELIZABETH ANN, educator; b. Lexington, Ky., Jan. 14, 1943; d. Richard P. and Beatrice (Coles) Harris; B.F.A. (Alumni Sesquicentennial scholar 1963-64, Univ. Upperclass scholar 1964-65), Ohio U., 1965; M.A., Ariz. State U., 1979; m. John Edward Craft, Dec. 18, 1965; children—Lauren Kelly, Jennifer Lavonia. Teaching asst. in speech Ohio U., 1964-65, in English, 1964-65; tchr. English, Steubenville (Ohio) High Sch., 1965, 68; debate coach, 1966-68; teaching asst. in communication Ariz. State U., 1978-79, faculty asso. in communication, 1980-82, instructional TV coordinator, 1982-85, dir. instructional TV, 1985—; speaker for civic orgns. Sec., Ariz. State Button Soc., 1980-82. Mem. Kappa Delta Pi. Mem. Christian Ch. (Disciples of Christ). Co-editor Ariz. State U. Faculty Wives Club newsletter, 1975-76. Home: 218 E Carter Dr Tempe AZ 85282 Office: Univ Media Systems Ariz State U Tempe AZ 85281

CRAFT, PEARL SARAH DIECK SERBUS, former editor; b. Riverdale, Ill.; d. Emil Edwin and Pearl (Kaiser) Dieck; m. Gerald Serbus, Jan. 26, 1946 (dec. Aug. 1969); children—Allan Lester, Bruce Alan, Curt Lyle; m. James E. Craft, Jan. 16, 1974 (dec. June 1984). Mem. home econs. staff, writer Chgo. Herald Examiner, 1934-39; operator test kitchen Household Sci. Inst., Mdse. Mart, Chgo., 1940-45; free-lance writer grocery chains, Chgo., 1945-49; Riv.-Dolton corr. Calumet Index, Chgo., 1953-58, editorial asst., 1958-60, asst. editor, 1960-68, editor, 1968-72; with Suburban Index, Chgo., 1959-72, editor, 1960-72; mng. editor Index Publs., 1972-74; free lance writer, 1974—. Public relations vol. New Hope Sch., 1959-67; bd. dirs. United Fund of Riverdale, Roseland Mental Health Assn., Thornton chpt. Am. Field Service. Recipient Disting. Service Meml. scroll PTA, 1959, Sch. Bell award Ill. Edn. Assn., 1965, Outstanding Citizen award Chgo. South C. of C., 1972. Named Outstanding Civic Leader Am. Mem. Ill. Woman's Press Assn. (past pres. Woman of Distinction 1968, recipient 46 state awards, 3 nat. awards), Nat. Fedn. Press Women (pres. parley past presidents 1981), Riverdale (v.p. 1966-68), Chgo. South (v.p., dir.) chambers commerce. Club: Women's Press of Ind. Home: 1421 N University Apt N-215 Little Rock AR 72207

CRAFTON-MASTERSON, ADRIENNE, real estate executive; b. Providence, Mar. 6, 1926; d. John Harold and Adrienne (Fitzgerald) Crafton; student No. Va. Community Coll., 1971-74; m. Francis T. Masterson, May 31, 1947 (div. Jan. 1977); children—Mary Victoria Masterson Bush, Kathleen Joan, John Andrew, Barbara Lynn Wickes. Mem. staff Senator T.F. Green of R.I., Washington, 1944-47, 54-60; mem. staff U.S. Senate Com. on Campaign Expenditures, 1944-45; asst. chief clk. Ho. Govt. Ops. Com., 1948-49, clk. Ho. Campaign Expenditures Com., 1950; asst. appointment sec. Office of Pres., 1951-53; with Hubbard Realty, Alexandria, Va., 1962-67; owner, mgr. Adrienne Investment Real Estate, Alexandria, 1968-83; pres. AIRE, Ltd., 1983—. Mem. No. Va. Bd. Realtors (chmn. comml. and indsl. com. 1981-82, community revitalization com. 1983-84), Nat. Assn. Realtors, Va. Assn. Realtors, Internat. Investment and Bus. Exchange, Urban Land Inst., Internat. Orgn. Real Estate Appraisers (sr.), Nat. Assn. Indsl. and Office Parks, Internat. Platform Assn., Alexandria C. of C., Friends of Kennedy Center (founding), Nat. Hist. Soc., Nat. Trust Hist. Preservation. Independent Democrat. Home: 1250 S Washington St Alexandria VA 22313 Office: 7925 Richman Hwy Alexandria VA 22306

CRAHAN, ELIZABETH SCHMIDT, medical association administrator; b. Cleve., Oct. 6, 1913; d. Edward and Margaret (Adams) Schmidt; student Wellesley Coll., 1931-32; B.Arch., U. So. Calif., 1937, M.L.S., 1960; m. Kenneth Acker, 1938 (div. 1968); children—Margaret Miller Johanningmeier, John Acker, Steven Acker, Charles Acker; m. 2d, Marcus E. Crahan, Dec. 16, 1968. Reference librarian Los Angeles County Med. Assn., 1960-61, head reference librarian, 1961-67, asst. librarian, 1967-78, dir. library services, 1978—. Founder, Med. Library Scholarship Found., 1967; pres. Friends of the UCLA Library, 1977-79. Mem. Spl. Libraries Assn., Med. Library Assn., Med. Library Group, So. Calif. and Ariz., Med. Mus. Assn., Am. Inst. Wine Food. Office: 634 S Westlake Ave Los Angeles CA 90057

CRAIG, DOROTHY LOUISE, publisher; b. San Antonio, Tex., Jan. 28, 1921; d. Henry P. and Henrietta B. (Michon) Ehrhardt; m. Roy M. Craig, 1941 (dec. 1979); children—Celeste, Bernadette, Jennifer; m. 2d, James C. Drain, Apr. 18, 1981. Grad San Antonio Vocat., Tech. Sch., 1937. Bookkeeper, Stamford Am. newspaper (Tex.), 1950-58, acct., buyer, 1958-62, advtg. acct., 1962-69; asst. to publisher, 1969-78, pub., pres., 1978—. Active Ind. Democratic party politics, 1977—. Mem. Tex. Press. Assn., West Tex. Pres. Assn. Mem. Disciples of Christ Chruch. Clubs: Pierian, Tex. Fedn. Women's (Stamford). Office: Stamford American 124 E Hamilton St Stamford TX 79552

CRAIG, KAREN LYNN, certified public accountant; b. Detroit, Mar. 17, 1959; d. John and Corinne (Legel) C.; m. Robert A. Steshetz, May 3, 1986. A. in Commerce, Henry Ford Community Coll., 1980; B.S. in Bus. and Acctg., Wayne State U., 1982. C.P.A., Mich. Cost and staff acct. Wilson Dairy Co., Detroit, 1982-83, sr. acct., 1983-84, acting controller, 1984; staff acct. Coopers & Lybrand, Detroit, 1984-85, sr. acct., 1986—. Mem. Mich. Assn. C.P.A.s, Nat. Assn. Female Execs. Avocations: music; photography; baseball. Office: Coopers & Lybrand 400 Tower Renaissance Ctr Detroit MI 48243

CRAIG, LEONE ERIN, government official; b. Sydney, Australia, May 10, 1945; came to U.S., 1946; d. James Robert and Iris Gralton (Adams) C. A.A. in Social Sci., Imperial Valley Coll., 1972. Letter carrier U.S. Postal Service, El Centro, Calif., 1966, clk., 1967-80, officer-in-charge, Winterhaven, Calif., 1978-79, postmaster, Westmorland, Calif., 1980-82, Calipatria, Calif., 1982—; com. mem. U.S. Postal Service Women's Program, Palm Springs, Calif., 1976-81, San Bernardino, Calif., 1981—. Bd. dirs. Imperial Valley Coll. Mus. Soc., El Centro, Calif., 1983-85, guide Michigan Artrain, El Centro, 1983; mem. planning commn. City of Calipatria. Mem. Nat. Assn. Postmasters U.S., Nat. League Postmasters U.S., Imperial County Postmasters' Assn. (pres. 1981-82, sec./treas. 1982—). Republican. Office: Postmaster US Postal Service 190 W Main St Calipatria CA 92233

CRAIG, LEXIE FERRELL, career vocational guidance counselor; b. Halls, Tenn., Dec. 12, 1921; d. Monroe Stancil and Hester May (Martin) Ferrell; m. Philip L. Craig, May 19, 1951; children—Douglas H., Laurie K., Barbara J. B.S. magna cum laude, George Peabody Coll., Vanderbilt U., 1944; M.A. with honors, Denver U., 1965; postgrad. Colo. U., 1972—, Colo. State U., 1964—, U. No. Colo., 1964—. Cert. local vocat. adminstr., vocat. guidance specialist, vocat. bus. specialist, vocat. home econs. specialist, reading specialist, nat. recreation dir. specialist. Danforth grad. fellow Mich. State U., East Lansing, 1944-46; nat. student counselor, field dir. student counseling dept. higher edn. Am. Bapt. Conv., summer service career projects dir. U.S. and Europe, 1946-51; coordinator religious and career activities counselor, Colo. U., 1951-52; tchr. home econs., phys. edn., counseling, dist. 96, Riverside, Ill., 1952-54; substitute tchr., psychometrist, reading specialist part time, Deerfield, Ill., 1956-59; substitute tchr. Littleton (Colo.) Dist. VI, 1961-63, guidance and career counselor Littleton Pub. Schs., 1963-67, 68—, now career vocat. counselor specialist, guidance counselor, Littleton High Sch., Dist. VI, also mem. vocat. needs and assessment com., career curriculum task force; dir., counselor YWCA Extension Program, Job Corps, Denver, 1967-68; tchr. adult edn. home econs. evenings, 1963-66; mem. Colo. Career Task Force, Lay conf. rep. Meth. Ch. Pastor/Parish Commn.; bd. dirs. Powell Careers Post Council Boy Scouts Am., also mem. Colo. Career Awareness Council; bd. dirs. So. Suburban Recreation, Littleton Community Arts Ctr.; bd. dirs., adv. council Powell PTO, Home Econs. in Homemaking; mem. local caucus com. Republican Party; mem. Dist. Environ. Sci. Council. Didcott scholar, 1942; Danforth home econs. and leadership scholar, 1943; Am. Leadership Camp Found. scholar, Shelby, Mich., 1942-45; Hildegarde Sweet Scholar, 1983; recipient Sullivan award and grant, named outstanding grad., 1944; named Littleton Mother of Year, 1977, Colo. Vocat. Counselor of Year, 1978; recipient plaque for recruiting and career guidance Navy and Air Force, 1980. Mem. NEA, AAUW, Colo. Edn. Assn., Littleton Edn. Assn., Am. Vocat. Assn., Colo. Vocat. Assn., Am. Personnel and Guidance Assn., Colo. Personnel and Guidance Assn. (pres., exec. bd.), Nat. Vocat. Guidance Assn. (Colo. rep.), Colo. Sch. Counselors Assn., Am. Field Service (pres. Littleton chpt.), Lit. Book Club Littleton Arts Ctr., Phi Delta Kappa, Delta Kappa Gamma Alpha Delta (chpt. pres.), Delta Pi Epsilon (past pres.), Pi Omega Pi (past pres.), Pi Gamma Mu (past pres.), Kappa Delta Pi (past pres.). Clubs: Order Eastern Star, Country Western Dance, Editor, pub. Join in a Song, 1949; editor The Church Follows Its Youth, 1950, curriculum units in consumer edn., home econs., careers, parenting classes.

CRAIG, MARIAN ELEANOR, social worker; b. N.Y.C., Feb. 24, 1948; d. Robert Stirling and Mary Elizabeth (Hobbie) C.; m. Charles M. Bicking, Oct. 13, 1985. B.A., Wells Coll., 1970; M.S.W., Boston U. Sch. Social Work, 1975. Social work asst. Odd Fellows' and Rebekah's Home for Aged, Lockport, N.Y., 1971-72; admissions coordinator Niagara Falls (N.Y.) Meml. Nursing Home, 1972-73; program dir. Don Orione Adult Day Health Center, East Boston, Mass., 1975-80; orgnl. cons. Project Homespun, Boston, 1981; dir. Greater Lynn (Mass.) Sr. Services Adult Day Health Centers, 1982—. Bd. dirs. Project Homespun; selective service counselor Draft Counseling Center, Buffalo, 1971-73. Mem. Acad. Cert. Social Workers, Nat. Assn. Social Workers, Mass. Audubon Soc., New Eng. Historic Geneal. Soc., Mass. Assn. Adult Day Health Services (v.p. 1984—). Office: Greater Lynn Services 90 Exchange St Lynn MA 01901

CRAIG, MARJORIE REED (MRS. JOHN THOMAS CROWLEY), physical therapist, author; b. Bangor, Maine, Mar. 9, 1912; d. Warren Everet and Harriet (Humphrey) C.; B.S. in Phys. Edn., Arnold Coll., 1932; postgrad. in phys. therapy Columbia, 1932-33; m. John Thomas Crowley, Sept. 9, 1935. Inst., Neurol. Inst., Columbia-Presbyn. Med. Center, 1935-42; supr. exercise Richard Hudnut Salon, N.Y.C., 1942-52, Elizabeth Arden Salon, N.Y.C., 1952-82. Author: Miss Craig's 21-Day Shape-Up Program; Miss Craig's Face-Saving Exercises; Miss Craig's Growing Up Exercise, 1973; Miss Craig's 10 Minute a Day Spot Reducing Program, 1979. Office: care Random House 201 E 50th St New York NY 10022

CRAIG, MYRITA PARKER, communications company executive; b. Joliet, Ill., Aug. 11, 1954; d. Kenneth P. and Myrita H. (Milligan) Parker; m. Alfred B. Craig, Aug. 8, 1981. B.A., U. Iowa, 1976. Account rep. AT&T, Cin., 1978-79, staff mgr. corp. planning, Chgo., 1980, ops. mgr., 1981, nat. account exec., Cin., 1981-82, nat. account mgr., 1982-85; asst. v.p. Cin. Bell Enterprises, 1985—. Author: Chapter Relations Handbook, 1977; Decolores, 1982. Pub. relations dir. Big Bros./Big Sisters, Joliet, Ill., 1977-78; com. chairperson Hyde Park Community United Methodist Ch., Cin., 1981-84; bd. dirs. Camp Fire Inc., Cin., 1984. Harry S. Bunker journalism scholar U. Iowa, Iowa City, 1975. Mem. Nat. Assn. Female Execs., Women in Communication, Am. Assn. Profl. and Exec. Women, Cin. C. of C., Delta Gamma (chpt. adviser 1981-84). Home: 338 Milton St Cincinnati OH 45210 Office: Cin Bell Enterprises 201 E 4th St Cincinnati OH 45202

CRAIG, SHARON ALANE, labor union official; b. Noblesville, Ind., Sept. 28, 1947; d. Ralph E. and Virginia K. Craig; student Ind. U., 1970-77; with Ind. Bell Telephone Co., Kokomo, 1968-77; with Communications Workers of Am., AFL-CIO, Indpls., 1977-80, Chgo., 1981—, staff rep., 1977—; mem. labor studies adv. com. Ind. U.; mem. Ind. AFL-CIO community services adv. com. NAACP, Indpls.; mem. union busters com. Ill. State AFL-CIO, 1981. Bd. dirs. City of Hope, 1977-80, Howard County Mental Health, 1973-76; mem. planning com. United Way of Howard County, 1976-77; sec. Citizens Action Coalition, 1980—; mem. Juvenile Justice Task Force; precinct committeeman Democratic Party, Kokomo, 1978; mem. CWA C.O.P.E. Quorum, 1977-84, CWA Platinum Quorum, 1985—. Recipient gold award United Way, 1978. Mem. Coalition of Labor Union Women, NOW, NARAL, CWA Concerned Women's Caucus, People for the Am. Way, Am. Assn. Ret. Citizens, Ill. Quality Worlife Council, Anti-Cruelty Soc. Episcopalian. Club: Ind. U. Alumni and Women's. Home: 1031 Maple Ln Elk Grove Village IL 60007 Office: 790 Busse Rd Elk Grove Village IL 60007

CRAIL, BONNIE WILKINS, magazine publisher, coordinator sporting events; b. Lodi, Calif., Oct. 31, 1948; d. James Benjamin Wilkins and Grace (Gross) Gammill. B.A., Ariz. State U., 1970, M.A., 1971. Gen. mgr. Consulate of France, Phoenix, 1967-73; asst. pub. relations dir. Praco Advt. and Pub. Relations, Colorado Springs, Colo., 1973-74; teaching fellow U. Utah, Salt Lake City, 1974-77; pub. mgr. Windsurfing Internat., Torrance, Calif., 1977-81; pub. Sail Boarder Mag., San Juan Capistrano, Calif., 1981—; dir. U.S. Boardsailing Assn., Oyster Bay, N.Y., 1983—; dir. sailing regattas Ocean Pacific Wave Classic, Honolulu, 1983, 85, Ocean Pacific Assn. World Cup, Honolulu, 1984, World Sailboard Mfrs. World Cup, San Francisco, 1983. Contbr. articles to profl. jours. Fgn. welcome asst. Utah Internat. Visitors Council, Salt Lake City, 1974-76, Ariz. World Affairs Council, Phoenix, 1967-73. Ariz. State U. Scholar 1969-70. Mem. Mensa, Brit. Soc., Brit. Californian Club, Western Publs. Assn., Profl. Sailboarders Assn. (sec. 1983—), Pub. Relations Soc. Am. Republican. Avocations: ballet; sailing; ice skating; skiing. Office: Surfer Publs Sail Boarder Mag 33046 Calle Aviador San Juan Capistrano CA 92675

CRAIN, LINDA EARGLE, educator; b. Columbia, S.C., Apr. 7, 1947; d. Oscar Lawrence and Betty Anne (Johnson) Eargle; B.A., U. S.C., 1969, M.Ed., 1979; 1 dau., Melanie Denise. With Credit Bur. of Columbia, 1965-67, with Sears Roebuck & Co., Columbia, 1967-69; tchr. Irmo (S.C.) Elem. Sch., 1969-72, 74-80; tchr. Nursery Rd. Elem. Sch., Columbia, 1980—. Named Tchr. of Yr., Nursery Rd. Elem. Sch., 1984. Mem. Irmo Chapin Edn. Assn. (past pres.), S.C. Edn. Assn., NEA. Democrat. Baptist. Home: 313 Conover Rd Columbia SC 29210 Office: Nursery Road Elem Sch 6706 Nursery Rd Columbia SC 29210

CRAIN, SHARON, management development company executive, lecturer and seminar presenter. B.S. in Exptl. Psychology; M.S. in Interpersonal Communications; Ph.D. in Ednl. Psychology. Mgmt. trainee World Hdqrs. Internat. Harvester Co., corp. mgr. employment opportunities, mgr. corp. communications; mktg. mgr. Bio-Dyne Corp., co-founder Nat. Migraine Found., dir. Women's Ctr. Exec. Devel., prin. Crain & Assocs., Boulder, Colo.; dir. mgmt. programs for Ednl. Sems. Inst.; TV and radio appearances on The Today Show, Good Morning America, Tomorrow with Tom Snyder, To Tell the Truth, Managing Your Mind; national speaker and sem. dir. on career devel. Author: How to Succeed in Business Without Ever Crying; Taking Stock: A Woman's Guide to Corporate Success (Macmillan Book Club Book of Month); Strategies to Relieve Business Stress, 1984. Author of several audio cassette programs; contbr. articles to various publs. Recipient Outstanding Achievement award in bus., Chgo.; Nat. Mag. Competition award for article in Chgo. Mag.; named one of top 10 bus. women in Chgo. Chicago Tribune. Office: Crain and Assocs Inc Sunburst Sunshine Canyon Boulder CO 80302

CRAMER, JANET MURIEL, retail company executive; b. St. Louis, Sept. 15, 1958; d. Eugene Stewart and Maxine Lucille (Graves) C. B.A., Calif. State U.-Fullerton, 1981. Market planner Harte-Hanks Communications, Brea, Calif., 1979-81; news reporter Sta. KOLO-TV, Reno, summer 1980; radio announcer Sta. KOCM-TV, Newport Beach, Calif., 1981-82; news reporter Sta. KTTC-TV, Rochester, Minn., 1982-83; advt. dir. Floor to Ceiling Stores, Inc., Rochester, 1983—. Recipient Home Ctr. of Yr. Advt. award of Merit Home Center Mag., 1986. Mem. Nat. Assn. Female Execs., Audit Bur. Circulations, Retail Advt. Council, Calif. Scholastic Fedn. Avocations: painting; writing; camping; skiing. Home: 3218 E River Rd NE Rochester MN 55904 Office: FCS Distbrs Inc 425 3d Ave SW Rochester MN 55902

CRAMER, MARGARET SULLIVAN, manufacturing company executive; b. Jackson County, Iowa, Nov. 3, 1933; d. Joseph M. and Margaret (Downey) Sullivan; B.S. in Bus. Adminstrn., N.Y. Inst. Tech., 1979, M.S., 1982; m. Robert E. Cramer, Feb. 14, 1953; children—Robert E., Laura Downey. With Chgo. Motor Club, Eastern Air Lines, Chgo., 1952-54, Robert F. Silverstein Agy., Midwest Steel Corp., Charleston, W.Va., 1956-60; with ILC Data Device Corp. subs. ILC Industries, Inc., Hicksville, N.Y., 1965-74, Bohemia, N.Y., 1974—, v.p. indsl. relations, 1978—. Treas., Cultural Arts Soc. Farmingdale, 1970-71, publicity chmn., 1971-72; mem. adv. council vocat. edn. adv. programs SUNY, Farmingdale, 1982—. Mem. L.I. Electronic Wage and Salary Council (pres. 1977-78, exec. com. 1978-79), Personnel Dirs. Council L.I. Assn., Electronic Industries Assn. (human resources council), Am. Electronics Assn., L.I. Human Resources Steering Group. Club: Nissequoque Golf. Office: 105 Wilbur Pl Bohemia NY 11716

CRAMER, ROXANNE HERRICK, educator; b. Albion, Mich., Apr. 24; d. Donald F. and Kathryn L. (Beery) Herrick; m. James Loveday Hofford, Jan. 29, 1955 (div.); children—William Herrick, Dana Webster, Paul Christopher; m. 2d Harold Leslie Cramer, Apr. 20, 1967. Student, U. Mich., 1952-55; B.A., U. Toledo, 1956; Ed.M., Harvard U., 1967; doctoral candidate Va. Poly. Inst. and State U., 1984—. Tchr. Wayland (Mass.) Pub. Schs., 1966-70, Fairfax County (Va.) Pub. Schs., 1970—; tchr./team leader Gifted/Talented program, 1975—; coordinating instr. Trinity Coll., Washington, 1978; nat. coordinator gifted children programs Am. Mensa, Ltd., 1981-84. Mem. Nat. Assn. Gifted Children, Am. Assn. Gifted Children, World Council Gifted and Talented Children, Va. Assn. Edn. Gifted, Intertel (mem. Hollingsworth award com. 1979—, now chmn.), Fairfax County Assn. Gifted, NEA, Va. Edn. Assn., Fairfax Edn. Assn., Mensa, Phi Delta Kappa. Club: Harvard (Washington). Contbr. articles to profl. jours. Home: PO Box 1145 Vienna VA 22180 Office: Louise Archer Gifted Ctr 324 Nutley St NW Vienna VA 22180

CRAMPTON, REBEKAH JEAN, lawyer, law educator; b. New Marlborough, Mass., Jan. 26, 1938; d. John and Marion Caroline (Jones) Somes; m. Harold W. Crampton, Jr., July 9, 1966; children—Kate, Gregory, Stephen. B.S. cum laude, U. Mass., 1959; J.D. magna cum laude, Western New Eng. Coll., 1978. Tchr., Apponequet High Sch., East Freetown, Mass., 1959-61, 65-66; dean, tchr. Amerikan Kiz Koleji, Izmir, Turkey, 1961-65; tchr. West Springfield High Sch. (Mass.), 1966-67; assoc. Walder & Pepyne, Greenfield, Mass., 1978-81; ptnr. Crampton, Dion & Johnston, P.C., Springfield, 1979—; adj. prof. Western New Eng. Coll. Sch. law, Springfield, 1980-85; spl. asst. atty. gen. sect. lead poisoning prevention Dept. Pub. Health, Commonwealth of Mass., 1981-84. Bd. dirs. Open Pantry Inc., Springfield, 1982—, Hampden County Civil Liberties Union, Springfield, 1983—. Mem. Hampden Young Lawyers Assn. (treas. 1981-82, asst. chmn. 1982-83, chmn. 1983-84), Mass. Bar Assn., ABA, Hampden Bar Assn. (exec. bd. 1983-84). Home: 192 Sunrise Terr Springfield MA 01119 Office: Crampton Dion & Johnston PC 260 Worthington St Springfield MA 01103

CRANDALL, PATRICIA IRENE, lawyer; b. Rhinelander, Wis., Apr. 28, 1945; d. John Edward and Irene Selma (Koskelin) Cerney; m. Jack Donald Brenton, Nov. 23, 1982; m. Thomas Dwane Crandall, Aug. 28, 1965 (div. 1976). B.S., Ind. U., 1969; M.S., U. Wis.,-Milw., 1973; J.D., Gonzaga U., 1977. Bar: Wash. 1977. Adminstrv. asst. U. Ind. Sch. Music, Bloomington, 1966-68; tchr. Notre Dame High Sch., Milw., 1970-71, Holy Rosary Sch., Milw., 1970-73; communications specialist Human Relations Council Greater Harrisburg (Pa.), 1973-74; assoc. Lukins & Annis, P.S., Spokane, 1977-78, prin., 1978—; adj. faculty Whitworth Coll., Spokane, 1986—. Mem. health edn. center adv. com. Holy Family Hosp., Spokane, 1983-85; bd. dirs. Profl. Resource Options, 1983—. Mem. ABA, Nat. Health Lawyers Assn., Spokane County Bar Assn. (trustee 1982-84) Wash. Bar Assn. (chair clients security funds com. 1983-84, chair code of profl. responsibility com. 1981-82), Wash. Soc. Hosp. Attys. (dir. 1983-84). Club: Spokane. Home: S 2424 Magnolia Spokane WA 99203 Office: Lukins & Annis PS 1600 Washington Trust Financial Center Spokane WA 99204

CRANDLEY, DONNA J., savings and loan executive; b. Milford, Conn., Dec. 30, 1955; d. Donald Lewis and Jeanne (Morin) Shaw. B.S. in Bus. Adminstrn. Providence Coll., 1978; programming cert. Computer Programming Inst., 1980. Staff acct. City of Milford (Conn.), 1978-80; staff acct. The Bank Mart, Bridgeport, Conn., 1980-81, acctg. mgr., 1981-82, asst. controller, 1982-83; v.p. Fin.Charter Fed. Savs. and Loan Assn., Stamford, Conn., 1983—; treas. Bedford Equities Corp., Stamford, 1984—; pres. BEC Devel. Corp., Stamford, 1985—; fin. cons. Charter Organizers, Stamford, 1983-84. Mem. Nat. Assn. Accts., Nat. Assn. Female Execs., Am. Soc. Woman Accts., Concerned Women Colls. Republican. Roman Catholic. Home: 198 Gulf St Milford CT 06460 Office: Charter Federal Savings and Loan Assn 612 Bedford St Stamford CT 06901

CRANE, BARBARA JOYCE, publishing company executive; b. Trenton, N.J., June 2, 1934; d. Herman and Elizabeth (Stein) Cohen; m. Stuart G. Crane, Aug. 27, 1956; children—Susan Jill, Patricia Lynne. B.A., Vassar Coll., 1956. Tchr., Trenton Public Schs., 1956-58; prin. Little People's Sch., Yardley, Pa., 1964-66; reading cons. Newtown Friends Sch., (Pa.), 1967-68; reading cons. Trenton State Coll., 1968-69; dir. demonstration sch., 1969-70; pres. Crane Pub. Co., Trenton, 1968—. Bd. dirs. Inst. for New World Archaeology, 1981—. Grantee Vassar Coll., 1967-68, Trenton State Coll., 1968-69, State N.J., 1968. Author: Crane Reading Systems. Mem. Internat. Reading Assn., Nat. Assn. Bilingual Edn. Clubs: Vassar Coll., Metedeconk River Yacht. Home: 1909 Yardley Rd Yardley PA 19067 Office: Crane Publ Co 1301 Hamilton Ave Trenton NJ 08629

CRANE, ELIZABETH ANN, educator; b. N.Y.C., Jan. 7, 1943; d. Clifford Murray, Jr. and Ruth Charlotte (Rieder) C.; B.A. in Biol. Scis., San Jose (Calif.) State U., 1966, M.A. in Early Childhood Edn., 1978. Tchr. 3d grade Moreland Sch. Dist., San Jose, 1967—; presider Asilomar Math. Conf., 1977, 78; mem. Moreland Dist. Adv. Com. Early Childhood Edn., 1975. Vice pres. Condo Homeowners Assn., 1984-85, pres., 1985-86. Mem. NEA, Nat. Council Tchrs. Math., Calif. Tchr. Assn., Moreland Sch. Dist. Assn., Home and Sch. Club (faculty rep. to bd. 1975-85), Calif. Math. Council (life), Santa Clara Valley Math. Assn. (rep. to exec. bd. 1979-84), Computer Using Educators, Santa Clara Reading Assn., San Jose State U. Alumni Assn. (life). Office: 4710 Campbell Ave San Jose CA 95130

CRANE, GLENDA PAULETTE, educator; b. Orlando, Fla., June 29, 1946; d. James Author and Elizabeth Lorine (Johnson) C.; A.A. in Edn., Orlando Jr. Coll., 1966; B.A. in Elem. Edn., U. S. Fla., 1967; postgrad. So. Bapt. Theol. Sem., 1970; M.Ed., Rollins Coll., 1985. Tchr., Orange County Schs., Orlando, 1967-70, 79-80, Lake Highland Prep. Sch., Orlando, 1981—; tchr. Belle Glade (Fla.) Christian Sch., 1970-79, asst. prin., 1970-74, prin., 1975-79. State treas. Fla. Rainbow Girls., 1964. Mem. NEA, Fla. Edn. Assn., Orange County Tchrs. Assn., Assn. Supervision and Curriculum Devel., Orange County Council Internat. Reading Assn., Fla. Reading Assn., Internat. Reading Assn., Alumni Assn. U. S. Fla., Alumni Assn. So. Bapt. Theol. Sem., Kappa Delta Pi. Democrat. Baptist. Clubs: Winter Park Pilot, Eastern Star, Winter Park Rainbow Girls. Home: 2406 S Bumby St Orlando FL 32806 Office: 901 N Highland Ave Orlando FL 32803

CRANE, JULIANNE GRANDIN, journalist; b. Charleston, W.Va., Mar. 29, 1943; d. James Franklin and Mary Frances (East) Grandin; B.J. (scholar), U. Tex., Austin, 1970, M.A., 1972. Communicator, journalist; freelance writer, broadcast reporter, producer, 1972—, media outlets include San Diego, Aspen, Colo., Omaha, Washington, and Seattle, 1973—; asst. promotion dir. Regional Shopping Center, San Diego, 1972-73; public info. dir. San Diego County Mental Health, 1973-77; instr. journalism and communication U. Nebr., Omaha, 1979-80; program dir., instr. journalism and mass media Highline Coll., Midway, Wash., 1980-83; spl. asst. to commr. pub. lands, Olympia, Wash., 1983—; media and mktg. cons.; mktg. cons. King County East Conn. and Visitors Bur., Seattle, 1981. Media cons. Center on Aging, San Diego, 1974; publicity dir. UN Week, San Diego, 1975; media relations v.p. NOW, San Diego, 1973-77; organizing com. Nat. Women's Polit. Caucus, San Diego, 1977; bd. dirs. Inst. Managerial and Profl. Women, Seattle, 1981-82. Recipient awards Nat. Press. Women, 1976, Calif. Press Women, 1976, San Diego Press Club, 1974, 75, 76; exemplary status award Wash. State Commn. Coll. Humanities Project, 1982. Mem. Women in Communications, Inc., LWV, Nat. Women's Polit. Caucus, Women's Inst. Freedom of the Press, Seattle Women's Network, Sigma Delta Chi. First woman reporter awarded credentials San Diego Padres Press Box, 1973. Home: PO Box 98263 Seattle WA 98188 Office: OW-21 Public Lands Bldg Olympia WA 98504

CRANE, KATHARINE ELIZABETH, editor, writer; b. Kenton, Ohio; d. George Edward and Kate (Rhodes) Crane; A.B., Smith Coll., 1916; Ph.D., U. Chgo., 1930. Tchr., St. Katherine's Sch., Davenport, Ia., 1916-17, Shippen Sch., Lancaster, Pa., 1920-22, Women's Coll., U. N.C., 1925-26; asst. editor Ency. Social Scis., 1929-30; asst. editor Dictionary Am. Biography, 1930-36, Social Studies and Social Edn., 1936-39; state supr., state guide, Va. Hist. Survey. Library Services, 1940-43; officer Dept. State, 1943-50; historian Mil. Air Transport Service, 1950-60; free-lance writer, 1960—. Author: Status of Countries in Relation to the War, 1944; Blair House, 1946; Mr. Carr of State, 1960. Contbr. articles to profl. jours. Home: 500 North Main St Kenton OH 43326

CRANE, MAIDA ROSENFELD, lawyer; b. Pitts. Mar. 14, 1955; d. David and Lois Jean (Blyler) Rosenfeld; m. Jon Crane, May 17, 1981. B.A. summa cum laude, U. Pa., 1976, J.D. cum laude, 1982. Bar: Pa. 1982. Customer services mgr. Counselor Films, Phila., 1977-79; summer assoc. Schnader, Harrison, Segal & Lewis, Phila., 1981, assoc., 1984—; law clk. U.S. Dist. Ct. for N.J., 1982-84. Mem. ABA, Pa. Bar Assn., Phila. Bar Assn., ACLU, Mortar Bd., Phi Beta Kappa. Democrat. Jewish. Home: 304A Windsor Ave Narberth PA 19072 Office: Schnader Harrison Segal & Lewis 1600 Market St Philadelphia PA

CRANE, PAULA LOUISE, owner data processing company; b. Akron, Ohio, Dec. 28, 1957; d. Anthony Barnum and Dolores Anne (Magusiak) C. B.S. in Systems Analysis, U. Miami, 1978; postgrad., 1982—. Programmer, analyst S.E. Data Processing, Miami, 1980-83; sr. fin. analyst S.E. Bank, N.A., Miami, 1983-84; info. ctr. cons. Metro Dade County, Miami, 1984; owner, dir. Crane Data Systems, Inc., (formerly Sabco, Inc.), Coral Gables, Fla., 1983—; owner, pres. Sabco of Miami, Inc., Coral Gables, 1984—. Mem. U. Miami Alumni, Delta Delta Delta Alumni (treas. Miami 1984—). Roman Catholic. Club: Progress. Avocations: dance; ballet; scuba diving; jogging. Home: 2180 Brickell Ave Apt 6 Miami FL 33129 Office: Crane Data Systems 4617 LeJeune Rd Coral Gables FL 33146 also care 1260 Clearmont St NE Suite 5 Palm Bay FL 32905

CRANE, PHYLLIS, artist; b. San Diego, Apr. 14, 1903; d. William Anderson and Mabel (Ray) C.; B.S., U. So. Calif., 1935, M.A., 1945; postgrad. Noyes (N.Y.) Sch. Rhythm and Creative Arts Studios, Portland, Conn., 1955. Tchr. schs. Pasadena, Calif., 1927-56, Peekskill, N.Y., 1958-60, Brewster, N.Y., 1960-62; co-program presenter Nature Moods to numerous clubs in N.Y.C. and Westchester County, 1979-84; one-woman shows: Contemporary Artists Gallery, Kingston, Jamaica, 1971, Dawson's Grist Mill Gallery, Chester Depot, Vt., 1974, 76, Port Chester (N.Y.) Library Gallery, 1975, Wood Pavalion Gallery, White Plains, N.Y., 1978; group shows include: Nat. Arts Club, 1965-79, Hansen Galleries, 1979, Pen and Brush Galleries, 1978-82, Sotheby Park Bernet Galleries, 1980, 81, Custom House Mus., World Trade Center, 1981, Lever House, 1980, 82, Salmagundi Club (all N.Y.C.), Burr Artists, Newhouse Galleries, Snug Harbor Cultural Ctr., S.I., N.Y., 1984, Am. Mus. Yorktown, Va., 1986; represented in permanent collections U.S., Europe; chmn. art shows No. Westchester, 1969-72, 77; co-chmn. art shows Hendrick Hudson Library, Montrose, N.Y., 1977; chmn. art show Lever House, N.Y.C., 1982. Bd. dirs. YWCA. Anglo-Am. Acad. hon. fellow, 1980. Mem. Pen and Brush (Emily Nichols Hatch award 1979, dir. 1980-85), Nat. League Am. Pen Women, Composers, Authors and Artists Am. (corr. sec. 1978-80), Burr Artists, Gotham Artists, DAR, Pi Beta Phi, Delta Kappa Gamma. Author: Fundamental Exercises Most Beneficial for Relaxation, 1943; contbr. articles in field to profl. jours. Home and studio: Boscobel Point Croton-On-Hudson NY 10520

CRANE, TREVA RAE, dental office manager, dental assistant; b. Princeton, Ill., Sept. 10, 1944; d. Raymond Hugh Buzard and Rose Elaine (Epperson) Stier; m. Larry Don Munz, Sept. 8, 1963 (dec. 1971); children—Shelley Rae, Brad Allen. A.A., Rockford Sch. Bus. Sec. Sterling Med. Group, Ill., 1962-63, Kraft Cheese Co., Milledgeville, Ill., 1963-64, Northwestern Steel Corp., Sterling, 1964; dist. sec. ARCO Corp., Deere Grove, Ill., 1970-71; office mgr. Dale E. Jacobson, D.D.S., Chetek, Wis., 1971—; con. Dental Soc. of Barron County. Editor numerous health articles. Chairperson Miss Chetek Pageant, 1976—. Mem. Chetek C. of C. (dir. 1978—, Service with Pageant award 1983, Service with Chamber award 1984). Club: Booster (dir. 1980-84, v.p. 1984-85). Avocations: water skiing; hiking; traveling; all sports. Home: PO Box 231 Chetek WI 54728 Office: Dale E Jacobson DDS 218 Douglas St Chetek WI 54728

CRANFORD, KAREN LAND, radio station owner; b. Brighton, Colo., May 6, 1954; d. Bernard William and Lola Lee (Hutsell) Land; m. Tony Alexander Cranford, Nov. 28, 1980. A.A., Northeastern Jr. Coll., 1976; Cert. Columbia Sch. Broadcasting, 1980; License, Kagy Real Estate Sch., 1977. Sec., Exxon Co. USA, Denver, 1973-74; sales mgr. Barbour & Co. Real Estate, Littleton, Colo., 1977-78; press aide Ted Strickland for Gov., Denver, 1978; adminstrv. asst. Frank Lee for U.S. Senate, Denver, 1979-80; owner, operator KCRT AM & FM Radio, Trinidad, Colo., 1981—. Producer, announcer newscasts, commls. Pres. Miss Colo. Scholarship Pageant, Denver, 1983—; fin. chmn. Trinidad Area Health Assn., 1984—; pub. relations chmn. Girl Scouts U.S.A., 1981—. Named Miss Colo., 1976; Young Career Woman, Bus. and Profl. Women, 1977, 81; Outstanding Scholar, Northeastern Jr. Coll., 1976. Mem. Colo. Broadcasters Assn., Nat. Broadcasters Assn., Colo. Realtors Assn., Bus. and Profl. Women, Xi Beta Chi, Beta Sigma Phi. Avocations: reading; stained glass; writing and arranging music; aerobics. Home: 1217 N Willow Trinidad CO 81082 Office: KCRT Radio 100 Fisher Dr Trinidad CO 81082

CRANK, RUTH ELIZABETH, financial planning executive, life insurance executive, manufacturing company executive, employment agency executive; b. Sidney, Ohio, Aug. 18, 1938; d. Charles Max Stephenson and Mildred Katherine (Hoover) Stephenson Foresythe; m. Robert G. Crank, Dec. 2, 1978; children—Rochelle, Roxanne, Troy, Juliana, Trent, Dominique. Dir. sch. project and ctr. U. Dayton, Father Phillip Hoelle, Ohio, 1971; field mgr. Avon Co., Cin., 1972-74; life ins. agt. N.Y. Life Ins. Co., Dayton, 1974—; pres. Crank & Crank, Dayton, 1982—; speaker in field; cons. in field. Leader Buckeye Trails council Girl Scouts U.S.A. lead Drill Team, Cheerleading Camps., 1964-74; founder Woodman Play Sch.; mem. Better Bus. Bur. Named Ace of Yr., N.Y. Life, 1975, Star & Exec. council, 1974-84, Centurim, 1974-1984; mem. Women's Million Dollar Round Table; first woman ins. agt. recognized by Dayton Gen. Mgmt. and Mgrs. Life Assn. for outstanding work, 1976. Mem. Dayton C. of C. Republican. Roman Catholic. Avocations: riding scooter, small motorcycle; playing organ; camping; swimming. Home and Office: Crank & Crank 4837 Kentfield Dr Dayton OH 45426

CRANMER-BRISKEY, KAREN SUE, editor; b. St. Joseph, Mich., Sept. 11, 1948; d. Raymond J. and Eris J. (Jacobsen) Piotroski; m. Jerry Burke Cranmer, Nov. 30, 1968 (div. Mar. 1981); 1 son, Colin Sean; m. Robert Joseph Briskey; July 28, 1984. Student Purdue U., 1966-68; B.S. cum laude, U. Minn.-Duluth, 1971. Cert. elem. tchr. Elem. tchr., Duluth, 1971-72; apt. mgr. Hallmark Village Apts., Clarksville, Ind., 1972-73; substitute tchr., Duluth, 1974-75; prodn. mgr. Harcourt Brace Jovanovich, Duluth, 1975-76, prodn. supr., 1976-79; mng. editor Hearing Instruments, 1979—. Author: Annual Survey of Hearing Aid Dispensing, 1980-85. Mem. Am. Auditory Soc. Home: 370 Ardmore Rd Des Plaines IL 60016 Office: 131 W 1st St Duluth MN 55802

CRAPER, JOAN PATRICIA, hospital administrator; b. Concord, N.H., May 7; d. William Edward and Dorothy May (Ormsbee) Jolin; m. Samuel Joseph Craper, Sept. 29, 1956; 1 child, Doreen Marie Craper Chelstowski. R.N. diploma cum laude, N.H. Sch. Nursing, 1954; cert. basic critical care Rutgers U., 1968; A.A.S. with honors, Fairleigh Dickinson U., 1973, B.A. in Sociology magna cum laude, 1976; cert. advanced critical care Hackensack Hosp., N.J., 1976; M.A. in Edn., Seton Hall U., 1979, postgrad. in edn. R.N., N.J. Head nurse St. Francis Hosp., Jersey City, 1954-55; operating room supr. Fairmount Hosp., Jersey City, 1955-57; recovery room charge nurse Christ Hosp., Jersey City, 1958-62; supr. and dir. inservice Saddle Brook Gen. Hosp., N.J., 1962-79, dir. nurses, 1979-80; asst. adminstr., dir. nursing services Kennedy Meml. Hosp. at Saddle Brook, 1980—. Mem. Bergen/Passaic Nurse Adminstrs. Group (chmn. 1980—), N.J. Soc. Nurse Adminstrs. (legis. com. 1982—), Am. Soc. Nurse Adminstrs., Doctoral Student Assn., Am. Nurses Assn. (continuing edn. council 1976-79), N.J. State Nurses Assn., Am. Hosp. Assn., N.J. Hosp. Assn., Critical Care Nurses Assn., Phi Omega Epsilon, Psi Chi. Roman Catholic. Home: 3-22 32d St Fair Lawn NJ 07410 Office: Kennedy Meml Hosps at Saddle Brook 300 Market St Saddle Brook NJ 07662

CRAPIVINSKY-JUTKOWITZ, BETTY, publishing executive; b. Santiago, Chile, May 20, 1936; came to U.S., 1967, naturalized, 1975; d. Benjamin and Clara (Meirovich-Henin) Crapivinsky-Huberman; student U. Chile, 1958-60; m. Joel M. Jutkowitz, July 22, 1966; children—Edward Andre, Monica Regina, Michael Steven. Pub., Benjamin Crapivinsky Publs. Ltd., Santiago, Chile, 1960-73; dir. publs. Inst. for Study of Human Issues, Phila., 1974—. Mem. research publs. rev. panel Nat. Endowment for Humanities, Washington, 1980-81. Nat. Endowment for Humanities grantee, 1979-82; NSF grantee, 1983-85. Mem. Phila. Publs. Group (founding mem. 1982). Democrat. Jewish. Home: 1420 Locust St Apt 12A Philadelphia PA 19102 Office: 210 S 13th St Philadelphia PA 19107

CRASWELL, ELLEN, state senator; b. Seattle, May 25, 1932; m. Bruce A. Craswell, 1953; children—Richard Bruce, James Arthur, Patricia Louise Craswell Johnson, Jill Ellen Craswell Solano. Student U. Wash. Mem. Wash. State Senate, pres. task force to sec. edn. Am. Legis. Exchange Council; dir. Gt. N.W. Fed. Savs. and Loan. Bd. dirs. Seattle Hearing and Speech Clinic. Republican. Methodist. Club: Altrusa. -1 Office: Senate of Wash State Capitol Olympia WA 98504*

CRATON, MARY ELIZABETH, consultant, nursing administrator, educator, lecturer; b. Audubon, N.J., Mar. 23, 1936; d. M. Norman and Mary F. (Seidner) Metzger; m. LeRoy K. Craton, Nov. 13, 1970. Nursing Diploma, Temple U., Phila., 1958, B.S., 1960; M.A., Calif. State U.-Los Angeles, 1968. Cert. nursing administr. Asst. dir. nursing Los Angeles County-U. So. Calif. Med. Ctr., 1967-69, dir. surg. specialties, 1969-75, dir. edn., 1975-81, dir. inst. continuing edn., nursing, 1977-81; cons., Los Angeles, 1981—; ptnr. DiMar Assocs., Santa Monica, Calif., 1983—. Contbr. articles to profl. jours. Artist, paintings. Fund raiser Bob Hope Cultural Ctr., Palm Desert, Calif., 1985. Recipient Laura H. Carnell award Temple U., 1958. Mem. Am. Assn. Neurosci. Nurses (pres. 1971-72), Inservice and Health Edn. Council Los Angeles (pres. 1983-84), Am. Nurses Assn. Republican. Roman Catholic. Clubs: Lakes Country, Scholl Canyon Ladies Golf (sec. 1983-84). Avocations: golf; skiing; swimming; tennis. Home: 281 Wild Horse Dr Palm Desert CA 92260 Office: DiMar Assocs 1341 Ocean Ave Suite 252 Santa Monica CA 90401

CRAWFORD, ALICE LOCICERO, psychologist; b. Paterson, N.J., Aug. 7, 1945; d. Thomas and Rose (Farah) Locicero; B.A., Coll. St. Elizabeth, 1966; Ph.D., Cath. U. Am., 1974; m. James Logan Crawford, Feb. 4, 1979; children—Emily Dawn, James Alexander. Tchr. public sch., Fair Lawn, N.J., 1966-69; intern in psychology Fairfax-Falls Church (Va.) Mental Health Center, 1972-73; postdoctoral intern in psychology Children's Hosp. and Judge Baker Guidance Center, Boston, 1973-74; coordinator mental health services for children Marth M. Eliot Health Center, Boston, 1974-75; supervising staff psychologist Judge Baker Guidance Center, Boston, 1975-76; psychologist in pvt. practice, 1976—; sr. staff psychologist Children's Hosp., Boston, and instr. psychology Harvard Med. Sch., Boston, 1976-80; cons. Day Care Service, U. Mass., Boston, 1974-75, Carroll Hall Sch., Lesley Coll., Cambridge, Mass., 1976-81, Roxbury Children's Service, Boston, 1978-80, Tri Cap Headstart, 1985—; instr. Northeastern U., Boston, 1974-76; lectr. Mass. Sch. Profl. Psychology, Newton, 1977-78, Simmons Coll., Boston, 1977-78. NDEA fellow, 1969-72; NIMH fellow, 1973-74. Mem. Am. Psychol. Assn., U.S. Orienteering Fedn., New Eng. Orienteering Club, Mass. Audubon Soc., Boston Children's Mus., Women's Action for Nuclear Disarmament, Children in Hosps., Caesarean Prevention Movement, La Leche League Internat., Mass. Friends of Midwives, Boston Mus. Sci., Mass. Assn. Psychoanalytic Psychologists. Research papers presented at profl. meetings. Address: 439 Huron Ave Cambridge MA 02138

CRAWFORD, ANN MACCOLLOM, journalist; b. Sterling, Mass., Apr. 8, 1927; d. Donald Bingham and Marjorie (Stiles) MacCollom; m. H. Vance Crawford, Jan. 24, 1948; children—Joel, Peter. B.A., Wellesley Coll., 1947. Corr., Sta. WAGM, Presque Isle, Maine, 1953-55; script writer Impcomation, Sterling Forest, N.Y., 1960-63; reporter Rockland Jour. News, Nyack, N.Y., 1965-67; reporter, editorial writer, columnist Bergen Record, Hackensack, N.J., 1963-65, 67-81, asst. editor, 1981—. Recipient Deadline Writing award Soc. of Silorians, N.Y.C., 1973. Mem. Sigma Delta Chi. Office: Bergen Record 150 River St Hackensack NJ 07602

CRAWFORD, BARBARA ANN, training adminstrator; b. Norfolk, Va., Nov. 23, 1944; d. Lillie (Alexander) Baldwin. B.A., Va. State U., 1966, M.S., East Tex. U., 1968; cert. in employment and tng. adminstrn. Harvard U., 1981. Tchr., DeKalb High Sch. (Tex.), 1966-68; counselor Norfolk State U. (Va.), 1968-70, devel. tng. program N.Y.C. Bd. Edn., 1970-71; asst. dir. Nat. Urban League, N.Y.C., 1971-75, confs. coordinator, 1975-78, mgr. tng. unit, 1978—. Mem. Christian Edn. Bd., Met. AME Ch., 1982—. Mem. Mid-Atlantic Assn. Tng. and Cons. (dir. 1983—), Soc. Co. Mgmt. Planners (dir. 1977-79), ASTD (Nat. awards com., 1983, award of Excellence, 1983, Appreciation award, minority network, 1983), Nat. Meeting Planners Assn., Nat. Assn. Female Execs., Coalition of 100 Black Women, Delta Sigma Theta (v.p., 1982). Democrat. Club: Norfolk (pres., 1982-83) (N.Y.C.). Home: 40 W 135th St Apt 14A New York NY 10037 Office: National Urban League Inc 500 E 62d St New York NY 10021

CRAWFORD, BUENA ELIZABETH, government agency analyst; b. Newport News, Va., Sept. 16, 1944; d. Fred Douglas and Lucille Louise (Watson) Moore, Sr.; m. Oscar Lee Crawford, Jr., Jan. 12, 1962; children—Michael, Anthony, Monica. B.S. in Bus. Adminstrn. and Acctg., Christopher Newport Coll., 1978; M.B.A., Hampton U., 1984—. Acct., Newport News Shipbldg./Tennco, 1978-81; program analyst NASA, Hampton, Va., 1981—. Chmn. Harris Family Circle, Hampton; mem. supervisory com. Langley Fed. Credit Union, Hampton, 1983—; mem. NASA Langley Exchange Council, Hampton, 1985—; mgmt. cons. NASA Langley Child Devel. Ctr., Hampton, 1985—. Recipient Spl. Achievement award NASA, 1982, Group Achievement award, 1983, Outstanding Performance award, 1984. Mem. Am. Soc. Mil. Comptrollers, Nat. Tech. Assn., Tidewater Real Estate Investors Group. Avocations: coin collecting; gardening; tennis; reading. Home: 5 Kings Point Dr Hampton VA 23669 Office: NASA Langley Research Ctr Hampton VA 23665

CRAWFORD, CAROL TALLMAN, government executive; b. Mt. Holly, N.J., Feb. 25, 1943; m. Ronald Crawford; children—Timothy, Jeffrey, Richard. B.A., Mt. Holyoke Coll., 1965; J.D. magna cum laude, Washington Coll. Law, Am. U., 1978. Bar: Va. 1978, D.C. 1979. Legis. asst. to Senator Bob Packwood, Washington, 1969-75, assoc. firm Collier, Shannon, Rill & Scott, Washington, 1979-81; exec. asst. to chmn. FTC, Washington, 1981-83, acting exec. dir., 1982, dir. Bur. Consumer Protection, from 1983; now dep. assoc. dir. econs. and govt. Office Mgmt. and Budget, 1983—; sr. advisor Reagan-Bush Transition Team, 1981. Trustee Barry Goldwater Chair of Am. Instns., Ariz. State U., Phoenix, 1983—. Mem. ABA, D.C. Bar Assn., Va. Bar Assn., Phi Delta Phi. Republican. Office: Office Mgmt and Budget Dept Econs and Govt Old Executive Office Bldg Washington DC 20500

CRAWFORD, CHRISTINA, author; b. Los Angeles, June 11, 1939; adopted dau. of Joan Crawford; B.A. in Communication magna cum laude, UCLA, 1974; M.A. in Communication Mgmt., U. So. Calif., 1975; m. C. David Koontz, Feb. 14, 1976. Actress, 1958-72; tchr., 1973-75; with corp. communications dept. Getty Oil Co., 1975-77; freelance author, 1978—; pres. Hermitage Co., Inc., 1978—; lectr., speaker in field; author: (non-fiction) Mommie Dearest, 1978; (fiction) Black Widow, 1982; also mag. articles. Rep., Annenberg Sch., 1975-77; trustee Christina Crawford Found., 1974—; pres. ICAN Assocs., 1979—; commr. Los Angeles County Dept. Children's Services, 1984—. Recipient various commendations and certs. of recognition. Mem. Writers Guild Am., Screen Actors Guild. Republican. Clubs: Braemar Country, Knights of Vine.

CRAWFORD, ELMA AISHA, biologist, researcher; b. Liberia, Aug. 17, 1959; came to U.S., 1980; d. Philip Francis Nathaniel and Florence K. (Rose) C. B.S.C., Claflin Coll., 1983; postgrad. S.C. State U., 1983-84, Georgetown U., 1984-85. Grad. teaching lab. asst. S.C. State Coll., Orangeburg, 1983-84; necropsy and histology technician Life Sci. Hazleton, Vienna, Va., 1985—; intern tchr. asst. Shriner's Hosp. Sch., 1980. Author monograph: How to Achieve Happiness in this World Full of Evil, 1981. Coordinator Young Christian for Global Justice, Orangeburg, S.C., 1982. Mem. Exec. Female. Methodist./Baptist.

CRAWFORD, FRANCES FREEMAN, musician, educator; b. Birmingham, Ala., Apr. 17, 1933; d. James Lewis and Flavia W. (DeVan) Freeman; B.Music Edn., U. Montevallo (Ala.), 1957; M.Mus., Fla. State U., 1963; m. Kenneth Herbert Crawford; children—James Freeman, Carolyn Redding, Kenneth DeVan. Tchr., Murphy High Sch., Mobile, 1954-61; mem. faculty Berea (Ky.) Coll., 1962-67; mem. faculty U. Ill. Sch. Music, Champaign-Urbana, 1967—, prof. voice, 1979—; recitalist, soloist with oratorio and orch., 1965—; maj. roles include Cio Cio San in Madame Butterfly, Donna Anna in Don Giovanni, Ariadne in Ariadne auf Naxos; judge, adjudicator, cons. in field, also tchr. master classes. Deacon, Univ. Pl. Christian Ch. (Disciples of Christ). Mem. Nat. Assn. Tchrs. Singing, Pi Kappa Lambda, Mu Phi Epsilon. Democrat. Home: 12 Golfview Ct Savoy IL 61874 Office: 200B Smith Music Hall Sch Music U Ill Urbana IL 61820

CRAWFORD, GAY JOHNSTON, communications executive; b. N.Y.C., Dec. 1, 1943; d. William Dickson and Jessianna Louise (Holmes) Johnston; m. Roy Patrick Crawford, June 11, 1966; children—David William, Katharine. Student U. Salzburg (Austria), 1962; A.A. with honors, Bradford Coll., 1963; A.B. with honors, U. Calif.-Berkeley, 1965. Reporter, club and fashion editor Berkeley (Calif.) Gazette, 1965; spl. asst. editor Oakland Tribune (Calif.), 1965; editorial asst., writer San Diego Mag., 1965-66; writer, pub. info. specialist U. Calif.-San Diego, La Jolla, 1966-68; free lance writer/editor, San Jose, Calif., 1968-69; community relations dir. KNTV, San Jose, 1969-85; pub. relations cons. Sta. KTEH, 1986—. Editor: Discovering Santa Clara Valley, 1973; Tailoring for Women, Step by Step, 1974. Bd. dirs., founder Hospice of the Valley, San Jose, 1979—; adv. bd. Children's Health Council, San Jose, 1982—, Coro Found., 1982—, Resource Ctr. for Women, 1984—; pres. bd. dirs. Santa Clara County unit Am. Cancer Soc., 1982-84; communications dir. United Way of Santa Clara County. Named Outstanding Women Journalism Student, Bay Area chpt. Theta Sigma Phi, 1965, Woman of Achievement, San Jose Mercury News, 1973, recipient Vol. Recognition award Midpeninsula Girls' Club, Palo Alto, 1977. Mem. Women in Communications (Woman of Achievement Far West region 1983), Pub. Relations Roundtable, Santa Clara County Broadcasters Assn. Republican. Episcopalian. Home: 14711 Aloha Ave Saratoga CA 95070

CRAWFORD, JEAN ANDRE, counselor; b. Chgo., Apr. 12, 1941; d. William Moses and Geneva Mae (Lacy) Jones; student Shimer Coll., 1959-60; B.A., Carthage Coll., 1966; M.Ed., Loyola U., Chgo., 1971; postgrad. Nat. Coll. Edn., Evanston, Ill., 1971-77, Northwestern U., 1976-83; m. John N. Crawford, Jr., June 28, 1969. Med. technologist, Chgo., 1960-62; primary and spl. edn. tchr. Chgo. Pub. Schs., 1966-71, counselor maladjusted children and their families, 1971—; counselor juvenile first-offenders, 1968—. Vol., Sta. WTTW-TV; vol. counselor deaf children and their families. Cert. elem. edn., spl. edn. and pupil personnel services, Ill. Mem. Ill. Assn. Counseling and Devel., Am., Ill. sch. counselors assns., Council Exceptional Children, Am. Assn. Counseling Devel., Coordinating Council Handicapped Children, Shimer Coll. Alumni

Assn. (sec. 1982-84), Phi Delta Kappa. Home: 601 E 32d St Chicago IL 60616 Office: 2131 W Monroe St Chicago IL 60612

CRAWFORD, LILLIAN FAY, insurance, realty executive; b. Ozona, Tex., July 18, 1940; d. Edward Leon (Tumlinson and Florine Alice (Elliott) Miller; m. Robert Dale Crawford, Sept. 12, 1955 (div. 1980); children—Robbie, Debra, Russel, Jeannie, Valerie; m. 2d, Robert R. Roller, Dec. 9, 1983; 1 stepson, Bryan Keith. Attended schs. in Tex. Lic. Group I life ins., real estate. Mgr. Pat Walker Figure Salon, Houston, 1974-76; owner, mgr. Crawford Ins., Port Lavaca, Tex., 1977—. Precinct chmn. Calhoun County, Port Lavaca, 1983. Baptist. Lodge: Eagles. Home: 115 Burnet Port Lavaca TX 77979 Office: Crawford Ins Real Estate Co 1620 W Main St Port Lavaca TX 77979

CRAWFORD, LINDA, novelist; b. Detroit, Aug. 2, 1938; d. Arthur Richard and Mary Elizabeth (Forshar) C. B.A., U. Mich., 1960, M.A., 1961. Author: In A Class By Herself, 1976; Something To Make Us Happy, 1978; Vanishing Acts, 1983; Ghost Of A Chance, 1985. Mem. Authors' Guild. Home and Office: 131 Prince St New York NY 10012

CRAWFORD, LORETTA FAYE, nurse; b. Alamosa, Colo., Mar. 22, 1951; d. Robert Max and Charlotte Mae (Alley) Winner; m. David Lee Crawford, Aug. 27, 1972; children—Kristina Lynn, Karry Lee. B.S.N., U. No. Colo., 1973, M.Nursing, 1984. R.N., Colo. Staff nurse Salem Gen. Hosp., Oreg., 1975-77; instr. psychiat. nursing San Juan Vo-Tech, Durango, Colo., 1983-84; staff nurse LaPlata Community Hosp., Durango, 1973-75, 78-80, shift supr., 1978-80, supr. med. unit, 1980-84, supr. psychiat. unit and cancer care coordinator, 1984—; speaker San Juan Hospice, Durango, 1984, vol. nurse, 1983—. Troop leader Chapparal council Girl Scouts Am., Durango, 1983—. U. No. Colo. scholar, 1970-73. Mem. Colo. Nurses Assn. (sec. 1975, v.p. 1982-83. Republican. Methodist. Avocations: sewing; camping; hiking; skiing. Home: 1924 Glenisle Durango CO 81301 Office: LaPlata Community Hosp 3801 Main Ave Durango CO 81301

CRAWFORD, MARTHA JEANNE, architectural interior designer; b. Rockford, Ill., June 25, 1925; d. Woodruff Lynden and LaVerna (Means) C. Student Vassar Coll., 1943-45, Rockford Coll., 1945, Parsons Sch. Design, 1945-48, Columbia U. Sch. Architecture, 1951-53. Asst. interior designer Eleanor LeMaire Assocs., N.Y.C., 1948-49; head color dept. Amos Parrish & Co., N.Y.C., 1950-52; contract interior designer Beeston and Patterson, N.Y.C., 1952-53, Welton Becket & Assocs., N.Y.C., 1952-53; cons. interior designer, N.Y.C., 1953-58; owner Martha Crawford and Assocs., comml. design co., N.Y.C., 1958-66; cons. interior designer Joseph Maxwell Assocs., Ft. Lauderdale, Fla., 1969-70, VVKR Partnership, Alexandria, Va., 1972-74, Design for Bus. Interiors, Washington, 1973-74; archtl. interior designer, Waukesha, Wis., 1975—; cons. color coordinator R.C.A. Rubber Co., Akron, Ohio, 1954-59, Timbertone Corp., N.Y.C., 1958-61; brochure cons. Rockcote Paints, Rockford, 1960-61. Contbr. to profl. publs. Vol. Inst. for Crippled and Disabled, N.Y.C., 1950-53; sec. Child Care Found., Fort Lauderdale, 1968-69; co-founder, coordinator Job Hunter's Network, Waukesha, 1982-86. Recipient hon. mention for outstanding interior of yr. S.M. Hexter Co., Cleve., 1959; 2d place award Dow Chem. Co., N.Y.C., 1960. Mem. Constrn. Specifications Inst. (bd. dirs. D.C. 1975, President's plaque 1975), AIA (assoc.), Archtl. League N.Y. (co-chmn. current work 1959-60). Club: Altrusa (pres. 1969-70) (Fort Lauderdale). Avocations: paint jazz pastels; listening to jazz; book discussion groups. Home and Office: W305 S4522 Brookhill Rd Waukesha WI 53188

CRAWFORD, MARY KAY, banker; b. Sacramento, Feb. 24, 1949; d. Sylvester Bernard and Dorothy Ellen (Kaliher) Novotny; m. William Edward Vanwinkle, Mar. 4, 1967; children—Anthony E., Daniel O.; m. Donald Ray Crawford, May 22, 1982; stepchildren—Donald R., Michelle K., Kelly. Student pub. schs., Elk Grove, Calif. Ops. supr. Crocker Nat. Bank, San Bernardino, Calif., 1978-80, ops. officer, Loma Linda, Calif., 1980-82, asst. v.p., ops. officer, San Bernardino, 1981-82, asst. v.p., operation support ctr. mgr., 1983-84, asst. v.p., br. mgr., 1984-85, asst. v.p., sales mgr., 1986—. Recipient Service award Crocker Nat. Bank, 1985. Mem. Better Bus. Bur., Mortgage Bankers Assn., San Bernardino C. of C. Republican. Baptist. Avocations: writing songs; singing; horseback riding. Home: PO Box 32 5966 Robin Oak Dr Angelus Oaks CA 92305 Office: Crocker Nat Bank 401 W 4th St San Bernardino CA 92401

CRAWFORD, MARY LOUISE PERRI, naval officer; b. Grand Haven, Mich.; d. Louis and Helen Marie (Buckley) Perri; m. Keith Eugene Crawford, Feb. 23, 1974; children—Matthew Perri, Michael Kirk. A.A., Muskegon County Community Coll., 1969; B.A., U. Mich., 1971. Commd. ensign U.S. Navy, 1971, advanced through grades to vice comdr., 1981; pub. affairs officer Naval Air Sta., Key West, Fla., 1974-77, adminstrv., personnel officer Naval Air Res. Detachment, Patuxent River, Md., 1977-78, adminstrn. br. head Strike Aircraft Test Directorate, Naval Air Test Ctr., Patuxent River, 1978-80, ops. watch officer Command Ctr., Comdr.-in-Chief Naval Forces Europe Staff, London, 1980-84, officer-in-charge Personnel Support Activity Detachment, Patuxent River, 1984-86; engring. officer Test and Evaluation Div., Strategic C3 Systems Directorate, Ctr. for Command, Control, and Communications, Def. Communications Agy., Washington, 1986—. Mem. AAUW, Women's Overseas Service League, U. Mich. Alumni Assn. Roman Catholic. Avocation: painting. Office: Defense Communications Agy Ctr Command Control Communications Test and Evaluation Div Washington DC 20305-2000

CRAWFORD, MIRIAM ISABEL, archivist, librarian; b. Bklyn., July 3, 1916; d. Joseph Irving and Rose (Harris) Wexner; m. William Henry Crawford, June 16, 1949; children—Fanny Jean, Douglass Barnes. B.A., Bklyn. Coll., 1937; B.S. in L.S., Columbia U., 1940, M.A. in Adult Edn., Tchrs. Coll., 1947. Cert. in archives adminstrn. Catalog asst. Bklyn. Pub. Library, 1937-39, br. asst., 1939-41, social sci. librarian, 1941-43; adult edn. dir. New Rochelle (N.Y.) Pub. Library, 1946-49; catalog asst. head Temple U. Library, Phila., 1958-65, univ. archivist, 1965—. Contbg. author: Affirmative Action...for Librarians, 1983, Archive-Library Relations, 1976; author articles in field. Served with WAC, 1943-46. Fellow Soc. Am. Archivists (coms. 1972-80); mem. ALA (councilor 1972-74, 78-82), Pa. Library Assn., Mid Atlantic Archives Conf., AAUP (treas. Temple U. chpt. 1984-85). Home: 4240 Parkside Ave Philadelphia PA 19104 Office: Temple University Libraries 13th and Berks Sts Philadelphia PA 19122

CRAWFORD, MURIEL LAURA, lawyer, author, educator; b. Bend, Oreg., Oct. 10, 1931; d. Mason Leland and Pauline Marie (DesIlets) Henderson; m. Barrett Matson Crawford, May 10, 1959; children—Laura Joanne, Janet Muriel, Barbara Elizabeth. Student, U. Calif., Berkeley, 1958-60, 67-69; B.A. with honors, U. Ill., 1973; J.D. with honors, Ill. Inst. Tech./Chgo.-Kent Coll. Law, 1977. Bar: Ill. 1977; C.L.U.; Chartered Fin. Cons. Atty., Washington Nat. Ins. Co., Evanston, Ill., 1977-80, sr. atty., 1980-81, asst. counsel, 1982-83, asst. gen. counsel, 1984—. Author: (with Greider and Beadles) Law and the Life Insurance Contract, 1984, also articles. Recipient Am. Jurisprudence award Lawyer's Coop. Pub. Co., 1975; 2d prize Internat. LeTourneau Student Med.-Legal Article contest, 1976; Bar and Gavel Soc. award Ill. Inst. Tech./Chgo.-Kent Student Bar Assn., 1977. Mem. ABA, Ill. Bar Assn., Chgo. Bar Assn., Am. Corporate Counsels Assn., Ill. Inst. Tech./Chgo.-Kent Alumni Assn. (dir. 1981—) Republican. Congregationalist. Office: Washington Nat Ins Co 1630 Chicago Ave Evanston IL 60201

CRAWFORD, PRISCILLA RUTH, social psychologist; b. Ferndale, Mich., Oct. 13, 1941; d. Ernest Henry and Ethel Ruth (Huth) Thomas; m. Thomas Earl Crawford, June 10, 1963 (div.). B.A., Butler U., 1962; postgrad. (Fulbright scholar) Goethe U., Ger., 1963; M.A. in Sociology (fellow), Ohio State U., 1965, Ph.D. (NIMH fellow), 1970. Mem. faculty sociology dept. Bklyn. Coll., 1966-67, Ind. U., Indpls., 1967-70; adj. faculty Roosevelt U., Chgo., 1974-77, Ind. U./Purdue U., Indpls., 1978—; research assoc. Gary (Ind.) Income Maintenance Expt., Ind. U. Northwest, 1970-73; cons. human resource and orgn. devel., Chgo., 1973-77; dir. human resource devel Ind. State Dept. Mental Health, Indpls., 1978-84, dir. edn. and tng., 1984—; vol. cons. numerous womens's groups, 1977—; cons. to state agys., So. Regional Edn. Bd., Nat. Orgn. Human Service Educators, NIMH, 1978—; mem. tng. adv. com. Ind. State Personnel Dept., 1983—; mem. adv. com. M.S. in Nursing degree program Ind. U. Sch. Nursing, 1982—; adv. com. Lic. Practical Nursing Initiative, 1981. Bd. dirs. Ind. Conf. Social Concerns, 1979-81; mem. Gov.'s Spl. Grant Com., Ind. Employment Tng. Council, 1981-82; mem. adv. bd. Program in Ind. Living, 1980-82; mem. adv. com. Indpls. Preschs., Inc., 1982—; bd. dirs. Women's Agenda for Action, 1981-83. Mem. Am. Sociol. Assn., Midwest Sociol. Soc., North Central Sociol. Assn., Am. Mgmt. Assn., Ohio Acad. Sci., Ind. Acad. Social Scis. (dir. 1978-81, 84—), AAUP, Phi Kappa Phi, Alpha Lambda Delta. Home: 1653 E Kessler Indianapolis IN 46220

CRAWFORD, RHONDALON, public relations executive, graphic designer; b. Rochester, Minn., Dec. 20, 1948; d. J. Norell and Barbara Katherine (Stindt) C.; m. Keith R. Herrmann, Aug. 11, 1984. B.F.A., U. Utah, 1983; A.Applied Scis., Utah Tech. Coll., 1978. Clk. typist SSS, Salt Lake City, 1968-70; exec. sec., bankard collector Walker Bank, Salt Lake City, 1970-76; freelance graphic designer, San Francisco, also Salt Lake City, 1976-80; graphic designer, owner Barlow/Crawford Design, Salt Lake City, 1980-84; investor relations specialist Profl. Communications, Ltd., Salt Lake City, 1985—; guest lectr. design Utah Tech. Coll. and U. Utah, Salt Lake City, 1981-83; judge graphic design state competition Vocat. and Indsl. Clubs Am., Ogden, Utah, 1983. Project coordinator Utah Arts Festival, Salt Lake City, 1983—; mem. Utah Council Vols., 1983-86, treas., 1985-86. Mem. Utah Advt. Fedn. (recipient Gold awards 1980-84, chmn. Gold awards com. 1983-85), Am. Advt. Fedn., Utah Assn. Women Bus. Owners (v.p. 1982), Women in Bus. Com. Avocations: travel, reading, cooking. Office: Profl Communications Ltd 4636 Highland Dr Salt Lake City UT 84117

CRAWFORD, SANDRA KAY, lawyer; b. Henderson, Tex., Sept. 23, 1934; d. Obie Lee and Zilpha Elizabeth (Ash) Stalcup; B.A., Wellesley Coll., 1957; LL.B., U. Tex., 1960; m. Dec. 21, 1968. Bar: Tex. 1960, Colo. 1967, Ill. 1974. Editor, research asst. to Herbert Hoover, 1961-62; trial atty. SEC, 1962-66; asst. v.p./legal Hamilton Mgmt. Corp., 1966-68; v.p., gen. counsel, sec. Transam. Fund Mgmt. Co., Los Angeles, 1968; cons. to law dept. Met. Life Ins. Co., N.Y.C., 1969-71; counsel Touche Ross & Co., Chgo., 1972-75; v.p., asso. gen. counsel Continental Ill. Nat. Bank and Trust Co. of Chgo., 1975-83; sr. div. counsel Motorola, Inc., Schaumberg, Ill., 1984; atty. Sears, Roebuck and Co., Chgo., 1985—. Mem. ABA, Ill. Bar Assn., Tex. Bar Assn., Colo. Bar Assn. Clubs: Saddle and Cycle, Carlton. Office: Sears Roebuck and Co Sears Tower BSC 41-2 Chicago IL 60684

CRAWFORD, SARA BROADDUS, nurse specialist, lecturer; b. Hong Kong, Nov. 21, 1931; came to U.S., 1945; d. Emmett L. and Margaret Cherry (Neal) Broaddus; m. Virgil Bruce Crawford, Jan. 1, 1951; children—David Bruce, Cheryl Anne. R.N., Norton Sch. Nursing, Louisville, 1952; B.S. in Nursing with distinction, Ind. U.-Indpls., 1972; M.S. in Edn. with great distinction, Ind. U. Southeast, Jeffersonville, 1979. R.N. Staff nurse/head nurse Norton Meml. Infirmary, Louisville 1952-55; office nurse, Sellersburg, Ind., 1958-68; instr. Norton Meml. Sch. Nursing, Louisville, 1972-75; nurse clinician Meth.-Evang. Hosp., Louisville, 1975-80, diabetes nurse specialist, 1980—; lectr. continuing edn., 1981—. Author ednl. game; editor-co-author manual: The Diabetics Reference Manual, 1983. Named Nurse of Yr., Glade, Louisville, 1982. Past pres. PTA, 1978-80. Mem. Am. Nurses Assn. (cert. in gerontology), Greater Louisville Assn. Diabetes Educators (founder, pres. 1981-83), Am. Diabetes Assn. (chpt. dir. 1983—), Am. Assn. Diabetes Educators (sect. editor 1983—, nat. bd. dirs. 1985—, award 1984), Ind. State Nurses Assn (dist. treas. 1982-84), Sigma Theta Tau. Republican. Baptist. Club: Lydia (Sellersburg, Ind.). Avocations: swimming; reading; painting. Home: 423 Cherry St Sellersburg IN 47172 Office: Methodist Hosp 315 E Broadway Louisville KY 40202

CRAWFORD, SUE ANN, office automation administrator; b. Concord, N.H., Aug. 21, 1955; d. Walter Richard and Sarah Jane (Chesley) Lampron; m. William George Crawford, June 4, 1977 (div. 1983); children—Trisha S., Beau D. A.A., Colby-Sawyer Coll., 1975; B.S. in Computer Sci., Franklin Pierce Coll., 1983. Research analyst N.H. Legis., Concord, 1976-84; office automation adminstr. IPC, Bristol, N.H., 1985—. Author article. Mem. Assn. Info. Systems Profls., Assn. for Computing Machinery. Republican. Roman Catholic. Avocations: skiing; reading; cooking; travel. Office: IPC PO Box B Bristol NH 03222

CRAWFORD, TWILA JEAN, mgmt., edn. and communications cons.; b. Sylvan Grove, Kans.; d. Walter W. and Irma J. (Ziegenbalg) Von Fange; B.A., Kans. State U., 1967, M.S., 1971; children—Rachel Shelle, Curtis Stanley. News dir. Sta. KMAN, Manhattan, Kans., 1961-69; corr. Topeka (Kans.) Daily Capital, 1964-69, instr. journalism Kans. State U., Manhattan, 1969-71, communications specialist Coop. Extension Service, 1971-77; mgmt., edn. and communications cons., Washington, 1977—. Bd. dirs. Lutheran Hosp. Assn., Manhattan, 1973-77, treas., 1974-77. Mem. Women in Communications, Agrl. Communicators in Edn., Nat. and Capitol Hill Women's Polit. Caucus. Washington Women's Network, Washington Ind. Writers, Sigma Delta Chi. Clubs: Nat. Press, Georgetown Women's. Home: 25 Farmington Dr Chevy Chase MD 20815

CRAWFORD-KUMMER, SONDRA, printing company executive; b. Balt., July 12, 1950; d. Donald Revere and Phyllis Edna (Finck) Crawford; m. Charles A. Kummer III, Mar. 17, 1979. Student Edinboro State Coll. Sec. RT&A Assocs., Balt., 1977-78; sec. Barton-Cotton, Inc., Balt., 1978-79, adminstrv. asst., 1979-81, mem. sales service staff, 1981-82, v.p. sales, 1982—, fund-raising cons., 1982—. Mem. Nat. Assn. Female Execs., Nat. Cath. Devel. Council. Republican. Presbyterian. Avocations: snow skiing; water skiing; basketball; yoga. Home: 6229 Gilston Park Rd Baltimore MD 21228 Office: Barton-Cotton Inc 1405 Parker Rd Baltimore MD 21227

CRAY, LINDA GARNETT, theological seminary administrator; b. Milo, Maine, Oct. 11, 1947; d. Hadley G. and Phyllis T. (Goodwin) Garnett; m. William A. Cray, Oct. 16, 1965; children—Amy L., Todd W. Diploma Beal Bus. Coll., 1966. Bookkeeper Hardy's Trailer Sales, Brewer, Maine, 1966-71; bookkeeper, dir. fin. aid Bangor Theol. Sem., Maine, 1974-82, bus. mgr., 1982—. Leader Abnaki council Girl Scouts U.S., 1974-76; co-chairperson Pioneer Girl Program, Calvary Bapt. Ch., Brewer, Maine, 1980-83, sec. Christian edn. com., 1983-84. Mem. Maine Student Fin. Aid Orgn. Club: Booster. Avocations: tennis; camping; biking. Office: Bangor Theol Sem 300 Union St Bangor ME 04401

CRAYNE, NANCY ANN, data processing consultant; b. Toledo, Aug. 27, 1942; d. Richard Vernor and Arlene Edna (Thull) Crayne; B.S., Bowling Green (Ohio) State U., 1964; postgrad. in bus. Oakland U., Rochester, Mich., 1983—. Analytical chemist Stauffer Chem. Co., Adrian, Mich., 1964-76; ind. computer programming cons., Westland, Mich., 1976-78; systems analyst Ford Motor Co., Dearborn, Mich., 1978-81; project mgr. Powderhorn Assocs., Hamtramck, Mich., 1981-82; computer cons. Mich. Cons. in Data Processing, Birmingham, Mich., 1982-84; computer cons. Charles Davis & Assocs., Detroit, 1984—. Mem. Nat. Assn. Female Execs., Mich. Profl. Women's Network (pres. 1981-82).

CREANY, CATHLEEN ANNETTE, television station executive; b. Johnstown, Pa., Jan. 14, 1950; d. Eugene Anthony and Winifred Nell (Sheridan) C. B.A. in Communication Arts, U. Notre Dame, 1972. Film editor Sta. KPHO-TV, Meredith Corp., Phoenix, 1976, promotion on-air specialist, 1977, comml. and documentary photographer, producer, 1978-80; news reporter, photographer Sta. WTVH-TV, Meredith Corp., Syracuse, N.Y., 1980, PM Mag. protographer, producer, 1980-81, PM Mag. exec. producer, 1981-82, program dir. 1982—. Recipient PM Mag. Nat. Reel award, 1980, 82, Best Photography award, 1982. Mem. N.Y. State Broadcasters, Nat. Assn. Program Execs. Avocations: running; tennis; skiing. Office: Sta WTVH-TV 980 James St Syracuse NY 13203

CREASON, NANCY STENCE, nurse; b. Elkader, Iowa, Aug. 7, 1938; d. Francis H. and Murrel (Cords) S.; B.S.N., U. Iowa, 1960; M.S.N., Wayne State U., 1964; Ph.D., U. Mich., 1977; children—James, Michael. Staff nurse, neurology-neurosurgery VA Hosp., Iowa City, 1960-61; rehab. field nurse Liberty Mut. Ins. Co., Chgo., 1961-63; instr., med. surg. nursing Coll. Nursing U. Ill., Chgo., 1965-66; instr., Sch. Nursing U. Mich., Ann Arbor, 1966-67, 69, asst. prof., 1973-74, asst. prof., chmn. fundamentals area instrn., 1975-77; asso. prof., asso. dean, dir. baccalaureate program Coll. Nursing U. Utah, Salt Lake City, 1977-78; asso. prof. nursing U. Ill., Urbana, 1978—, asst. dean Coll. Nursing, 1978—; mgmt. cons., 1978-81. Pres., Tiffin LWV, 1970-72; mem. Washtenaw County Commn. Status of Women, 1973-75; treas. troop Boy Scouts Am., 1979-82. Named to Central Community High Sch., 1982. Merit scholar U Iowa, 1955-57; U. Mich. fellow, 1974-75; Danforth asso., 1980—; USPHS grantee, 1981—; recipient Golden Apple award U. Ill., 1966; named to Central Community High Sch. Alumni Hall of Fame, 1982. Mem. Am. Nurses Assn. (council nurse researchers), Ill. Nurses Assn., Dist. 15 Nurses Assn. (dir.), State Nurses Active in Politics in Ill., Nurses Coalition for Action in Politics, Midwest Soc. Nurse Researchers, Sigma Theta Tau. Episcopalian. Contbr. articles to profl. jours. Home: 1820 Sadler Dr Champaign IL 61821 Office: 1115 1/2 W Oregon St Urbana IL 61801

CREASY, TONYA LEE, government agency administrator; b. Milford, Conn., Sept. 26, 1941; d. Chauncey Karl and Ruth Burdette (Smith) Lundberg; m. Le Roy John Matye (div. 1966); children—Bobby Lee, Chauncey Karl; m. Jack Kenneth Creasy, Dec. 22, 1975. B.S. in Bus. Adminstrn., Strayer Coll., 1976; postgrad. in Human Resource Mgmt., George Mason U., 1985—. Claims devel. clk. Social Security Adminstrn., Ft. Myers, Fla., 1965-70, service rep., Camp Springs, Md., 1970-73, tech. asst., Laurel, Md., 1973-74, claims rep., 1974-76, ops. supr., Richmond, Va., 1976-78, br. mgr., Upper Darby, Pa., 1978-80, Falls Church, Va., 1980-85, asst. dist. mgr., Camp Springs, 1985—. Facilitator, author, hostess cable TV spl. Social Security and Your Future, 1984. Creator, facilitator, producer cable TV series Women on the Move, 1986. Recipient several suggestion awards Social Security Adminstrn., 1969-71, Pub. Info. award Social Security Adminstrn., 1980. Active Fairfax YWCA, Va., 1982—. Mem. Pub. Employee Roundtable (bd. dirs., vice chmn. 1983—, Substained Service award 1985), Federally Employed Women (bd. dirs. 1985—, mem. exec. com., chmn. pub. relations com. 1985—), Social Security Mgrs. Assn. (Inspired Service award 1985), Nat. Assn. Ret. and Active Fed. Employees (1st v.p. 1985-86), Nat. Assn. Female Execs. Avocations: fishing; boating; crabing; antiques. Home: Gen Delivery Ophelia VA 22530

CREECH, SANDRA KAY, college administrator; b. San Antonio, Tex., Mar. 23, 1947; d. Bill G. and Frieda Maurine (Sanders) C.; 1 child, Colleen Dee Havican. B.S. in Math., U. Houston, 1972; M.P.A. in Govt. Info., Southwest Tex. State U., 1985. Adminstrv. asst. Dow Chem. Co., Houston, 1969-72; data processing dir. Jetero Constrn. Co., Houston, 1972-74; programmer-analyst Fannin Bank, Houston, 1974-75; sr. systems analyst Nat. Supply Co., Houston, 1975-79; dir. adminstrv. info. services Temple Jr. Coll., Tex., 1981—; cons.; presenter at profl. meetings. Mem. Edn. Planning Com., Hewitt, Tex., 1985-86. Mem. Tex. Jr. Coll. Tchrs. Assn., Assn. Studies in Higher Edn., Waco Hist. Found. Baha'i. Office: Temple Jr Coll 2600 S 1st St Temple TX 76643

CREED, JOYCE SUE, stockbroker; b. McLeansboro, Ill., Nov. 10, 1944; d. Vernon Jesse and Thelma Louise (Lowrey) Morris; m. Jack Stewart Wilding, July 4, 1970 (div. 1973); m. 2d, Thomas Richard Creed, Oct. 24, 1975. B.S., So. Ill. U., 1966; postgrad. U. Miami, Coral Gables, 1966-67. Cert. secondary and community coll. tchr., Calif. Tchr., Nat. Tchr. Corp., Ft. Lauderdale, 1966-67; tchr. Catalysts I, Peoria, Ill., 1972-73; registered asst. Davis, Skaggs & Co., San Francisco, 1975-80; stockbroker Birr, Wilson & Co., Paradise, Calif., 1982—; instr. Butte Community Coll., Oroville, 1985-86. Mem. Internat. Assn. Fin. Planners. Avocations: herbology; hiking. Office: Birr Wilson & Co 7030 A Skyway Paradise CA 95969

CREEDEN, CAROLINE HERRISE, banker; b. Monterrey, N.L., Mexico, Jan. 8, 1956; came to U.S., 1962; d. John James and Betty DeVere (Hodgin) C. B.A., U. Tex.-Austin, 1978; student CSBS Advanced Sch. for Bank Examiners, 1982. Distributive edn. student Alamo Heights Nat. Bank, San Antonio, 1973-74; bank examiner Tex. Banking Dept., Austin, Houston and San Antonio, Tex., 1979-82; asst. v.p. Tex. Commerce Bancshares, Inc., Houston, 1982-84, v.p., sect. mgr., 1984—. Mem. Zool. Soc. Houston, 1982-83, Longhorn Alumni Band, Austin, Tex., Houston, 1978—; sponsor Save a Child, Houston, 1982-83, Foster Parents Plan, 1985—. Recipient Arion award Alamo Heights High Sch., San Antonio, 1974. Mem. Am. Inst. Banking, Ex-Students Assn. U. Tex. (life), Tau Beta Sigma. Roman Catholic. Office: Tex Commerce Bancshares Inc 712 Main St Houston TX 77252

CREEL, BRENDA ROVENIA, accountant, computer consultant; b. Orlando, Fla., May 18, 1948; d. Harvel Alton Creel and Louise Wilma Joy (Michael) McKinney; m. Michael Keith Nations, Jan. 20, 1967 (div. 1978); children—James David, Michael, Melissa, Matthew, Mark. Student North Harris County Coll., 1978, Glendale Coll., 1983-84. Mgr. customer service Advanced Duplicating Co., Phoenix, 1982-83; acctg. cons. Titus Info. Systems, Phoenix, 1984-85; owner, mgr. Creel Bus. Cons., Glendale, Ariz., 1985—; acctg. cons. Sunvalco, Goodyear, Ariz., 1985—, R&S Enterprises, Glendale, 1984—; dir. Creel/Sanborn Investments, Phoenix. Supporter, Ariz. Action for Displaced Homemakers, Phoenix, 1982. Mem. Nat. Assn. Female Execs. Republican. Club: Soul Support (pres.) (Glendale). Office: Creel Bus Cons 5729 W Campo Bello Glendale AZ 85308

CRENSHAW, MARGARET PRICE, lawyer; b. Eugene, Oreg., Apr. 16, 1945; d. Warren Charles and Lillian Irene (Shidell) Price; B.A., Stanford U., 1967, M.A., 1968; J.D., Georgetown U., 1975; m. Albert Burford Crenshaw, Aug. 11, 1973; children—David Ollinger, Caroline Abbey. Bars: D.C. bar 1975, U.S. Ct. Appeals 1976, U.S. Ct. Claims 1976, U.S. Supreme Ct. 1983. Reporter Eugene Register-Guard, 1965, 66; press asst. Californians for Humphrey San Francisco, 1968, newswoman AP, New Haven, Conn., 1969; press asst. Rep. Jeffery Cohelan, Washington, 1969; research writer Congl. Quar., Washington, 1969-70; asst. editor Washington Post, 1970-72; law clerk firm Harrison, Lucey, Sagle & Solter, Washington, 1974-75; legis. counsel Senator Philip A. Hart, Washington, 1975-77; legis. counsel Senator Paul S. Sarbanes, Washington, 1977; asso. firm Brownstein, Zeidman & Schomer, Washington, 1977-79; counsel Senate Subcom. on Govt. Efficiency and the D.C., 1979-81, minority chief counsel, 1981-85, minority staff dir. Senate Com. on Govtl. Affairs, 1985—; adj. prof. journalism U. Md., College Park, 1975. Trustee Capitol Hill Day Sch., Washington. Ford Found. fellow, 1967-68. Mem. ABA, D.C. Bar Assn., Women's Bar Assn. D.C. Democrat. Episcopalian. Office: SD 346 Dirksen Senate Office Bldg Washington DC 20510

CRENSHAW, MARVA LOUISE, lawyer; b. DeFuniak Springs, Fla., Sept. 21, 1951; d. Lewis and Helen (Anderson) Crenshaw; m. Norman P. Campbell, Dec. 30, 1977; 1 dau., Kalinda I. B.S. in Polit. Sci. with honors, Tuskegee Inst., Ala., 1973; J.D., U. Fla., Gainesville, 1975. Bar: U.S. Dist. Ct. (mid. dist.) Fla., 1978, U.S. Ct. Appeals (11th cir.) 1978. Asst. state's atty. Dade County State's Atty. (Fla.), Miami, 1976-78; mng. atty. Bay Area Legal Services, Tampa, Fla., 1978-84, dep. dir., 1984—; cons. tng. adv. com. Fla. Legal Service, Tallahassee, 1982-84. Vice pres. bd. dirs. Suicide and Crises Ctr., Tampa, 1983-84, pres., 1984-85, also mem. Aux. Mem. ABA, Hillsborough County Bar Assn. (chmn. county ct. civil rules com. 1984-85), Fla. Bar Assn., George Edgecomb Bar Assn. Democrat. Baptist. Home: 14522 Wessex St Tampa FL 33625

CRENSHAW, TENA LULA, librarian; b. Coleman, Fla., Dec. 15, 1930; d. Herbert Joseph and Nellie Jackson (Wicker) Crenshaw; B.S., Fla. So. Coll., 1951; postgrad. U. Fla., 1952-55; M.L.S. (Univ. scholar), U. Okla., 1960. Tchr. pub. schs., Coleman, Fla., 1952-55, St. Petersburg, Fla., 1955-57, Houston, 1957-59; tech. librarian Army Rocket & Guided Missile Agy., Redstone Arsenal, Huntsville, Ala., 1960-61; acquisitions librarian Martin Marietta Corp., Orlando, Fla., 1961-64; reader services librarian John F. Kennedy Space Center, NASA, Fla., 1964-66; research information analyst, specialist, Lockheed Missiles and Space Co., Palo Alto, Calif., 1966-68; head services to pub. A.W. Calhoun Med. Library, Emory U., Atlanta, 1969-78; dep. dir. Louis Calder Meml. Library, U. Miami (Fla.) Sch. Medicine, 1979-80; head edn. library U. Fla., Gainesville, 1980-84; librarian Westinghouse Electric Corp., Orlando, 1984—; chmn. Fla. State Adv. Council on Libraries. Mem. Spl. Libraries Assn. (treas. S. Atlantic chpt. 1970-72, chmn. membership com. 1973, v.p. 1973-74, pres. 1974-75, mem. resolutions com. 1975-76, nominating com. biol. scis. div. 1974-75, chmn. 1977-78), Med. Library Assn. (mem. conf. planning com. So. regional group 1973-74, membership com. 1977-79 by laws rev. com. 1979-80), Southeastern (mem. new directions com. 1972-74, chmn. spl. libraries sect. 1974), Ga. (careers in librarianship com. 1974-77), Fla. library assns., D.A.R., Alpha Delta Pi, Kappa Delta Pi. Democrat. Episcopalian. Home: Vestavia Lake Apts Apt F 208 1100 S Delaney Ave Orlando FL 32806 Office: Westinghouse Electric Corp Library The Quadrangle Library MC-235 4400 Alafaya Trail Orlando FL 32826

CRESPIN, REGINE, soprano; b. Marseilles, Frace; d. Henri and Margherite (DiMeirone) C.; student Lycée Francais, Conservatoire de Paris. Appeared in numerous operas including Lohengrin, Mullhouse, France, 1950, Paris, 1951, N.Y.C., 1964, Tosca, Il Trovatore, Otello, Die Walkuere, Oberon, Fidelio, Der Rosenkavalier, Marseilles, Le Nozze di Figaro, Paris, 1956, Dialogues of the Carmelites, 1957, Parsifal, 1958, Ballo in Maschera, 1958, Fedra, Milan, Italy, 1959, Die Walkuere, Vienna, 1959, Der Rosenkavalier, Berlin, 1960, as the Marshallin, London, 1961, Les Troyens, Paris, 1961, Penelope, Buenos Aires, 1961, Otello, Ballo in Maschera, Die Walkuere, Der Rosenkavalier, Vienna, also Rosenkavalier, N.Y.C., 1962, Flying Dutchman, N.Y.C., 1962, Ballo in

Maschera, N.Y.C., 1962, La Vestale, N.Y.C., 1962, Herodiade, N.Y.C., 1963, Fidelio, Ballo in Maschera, Tannhauser, Fidelio, Chgo., 1963, Carnegie Hall, 1973, Met. Opera, 1973, Carmen, Met. Opera, 1975, Cavalleria Rusticana, San Francisco Opera, 1976, Dialogues of the Carmelites, Met. Opera, 1977, 78; soloist N.Y. Philharm., 1964-65; appeared in recital Hunter Coll., 1965. Office: Herbert H Breslin 119 W 57th St New York NY 10019*

CRESPO DE SOLIS, GLORIA, government administrator; b. Ponce, P.R., Apr. 1, 1930; d. Santiago and Gloria (Deodatti) Crespo; m. Hanny L. Solis, Oct. 12, 1955; children—Gloria, Giselle, Gianna, Glenda, Alan. B.A. in Edn., U. P.R., 1952. Tchr. Dept. Edn., Ponce, 1948-54; employment interviewer Dept. Labor, Ponce, 1955-57, placement officer and employer's relations rep., 1958-65, supr., 1965-68, work incentive program coordinator, 1968-77, adminstr., 1977—; mem. adv. council CETA, Ponce, Area Agy. of Aging, Ponce, 1982, 83, 84; EEO rep. Bur. Employment Security, Ponce, 1977-84; regional rep. for review of plans for foster children Social Service Agy., Ponce Area, 1984. Leader Caribe council Girl Scouts U.S.A., Ponce, 1949-53; trustee Consumers League, Ponce, 1983-84; mem. Catholic Daus. Am., Ponce, 1960-70. Mem. Am. Soc. Personnel Adminstrn. Nat. Fedn. Bus. and Profl. Women. Club: Lioness. Home: PO Box 763 Ponce PR 00733 Office: Dept Labor Bur Employment Security Box 991 Ponce PR 00733

CRESS, JEAN ELIZABETH, television executive; b. Sacramento, Calif., Nov. 10, 1951; d. Earl Sylvester Gimblin and Nancy Louise (Cress) Gimblin Steele. Student Sacramento City Coll., 1969-70, Calif. State U.-Sacramento, 1974-75. Pub. relations rep. BankAmericard, Sacramento, 1973-74; advance publicist Am. Freedom Train, Washington, 1976; publicity March of Dimes, Orlando, Fla., 1977; pre-promotion asst. Casablance Filmworks, Hollywood, Calif., 1977; prodn. asst. Merv Griffin Prodns., Hollywood, 1978-79; pub. affairs dir. Sta. KRTH, Los Angeles, 1978-79; promotion and advt. dir. Roaring Camp, Felton, Calif., 1981, news dir. Sta. KMFO Talkradio, Santa Cruz, Calif., 1981-82, program dir., 1982-84, gen. mgr. 1984-85; mktg. and sales mgr. Group W (Westinghouse) Cable TV, Santa Cruz, 1985—. Recipient Sam Seagull Advt. award Monterey Advt. Club, 1985. Home: 2939 Park Ave #4 Soquel CA 95073

CRESTA, CHERYL ANN, recreation therapist; b. Medford, Mass., Jan. 1, 1957; d. John Francis and Margaret Frances (Flynn) C. A.A., Merrimack Valley Coll. of U. N.H., 1981; B.S., U. N.H., 1983; Ed.M., Boston U., 1986. Cert. therapeutic recreation specialist. Med. records specialist Letterman Army Med. Ctr., Presidio of San Francisco, 1975-78; med. clk., typist VA Med. Ctr., Manchester, N.H., 1978-81, Palo Alto, Calif., 1981; recreation asst. VA Med. Ctr. and Nursing Home Care Units, Manchester, 1982-83; cert. therapeutic recreation therapist VA Med. Ctr. and Spinal Cord Injury Rehab. Ctr., West Roxbury, Mass., 1984—. Served with U.S. Army, 1975-78, with USAR, 1978-80. Mem. Nat. Recreation and Park Assn., Nat. Therapeutic Recreation Soc., Armed Forces Recreation Soc., N.H. Recreation and Park Soc., Am. Therapeutic Recreation Assn., New Eng. Therapeutic Recreation Consortium. Republican. Roman Catholic. Home: High St RFD #1 Candia NH 03034 Office: VA Med Ctr and Spinal Cord Injury Rehab Ctr 1400 VFW Pkwy West Roxbury MA 02132

CREVELING, JOANNE ROSS, public relations executive; b. Worcester, Mass., Jan. 27, 1935; d. John Ross and Joan Van Liew (Schenck) C.; m. Frank Lookstein, May 25, 1968; children—Robert Andrew, Thomas Schenck. B.A., Dickinson Coll., 1956; student N.Y. Sch. Interior Design, 1958. Owner, mgr. Joanne Creveling Inc., N.Y.C., 1974—; publicity dir. Henri Bendel Co., N.Y.C., 1969-74. Office: 30 E 60th St New York NY 10022

CREWS, RUTHELLEN, educator; b. McCaysville, Ga., July 3, 1927; d. Robert Harvey and Della P. (Mason) Crews; B.A., Maryville Coll., 1949; M.S., U. Tenn., Knoxville, 1959; Ed.D. (Delta Kappa Gamma Scholar), Tchrs. Coll., Columbia U., 1966. Tchr. English and speech Cradock High Sch., Portsmouth, Va., 1949-50; elementary tchr. Rose Sch., Morristown, Tenn., 1951-54; tchr. English and Speech Morristown High Sch., 1954-58; elementary sch. librarian Knox County Schs. Materials Center, Knoxville, Tenn., 1958-60; supr. of instrn. Knox County Schs., Knoxville, 1960-65; prof. edn. U. Fla., Gainesville, 1966—; cons. curriculum devel. in pub. schs.; lectr. in field. Mem. Nat. Council Tchrs. of English, Assn. for Supervision and Curriculum Devel., Internat. Reading Assn., Delta Kappa Gamma. Author: (with others) The World of Language, textbook series, 1970, rev. edit., 1973; (with others) Pathfinder, textbook series, 1978. Contbr. articles in field of edn. to profl. jours. Home: 1719-4B NW 23d Ave Gainesville FL 32605 Office: Coll of Edn U Fla Gainesville FL 32611

CRIDER, FRANCES CAROLYN, institute executive, educator; b. Dawson, Tex., Apr. 27, 1933; d. Robert Lee and Carrie (Lee) C.; B.S. in Edn., McMurry Coll., 1954; M.Ed. in Reading and Psychology, Eastern N.Mex. U., 1968, postgrad., 1969; Ed.S. in Elem. Edn. and Reading, U. Colo., 1973; Ed.D. in Reading and Multi Disciplinary Clinic Adminstrn., U. No. Colo., 1975; children—Catherine Dean, Elizabeth Gail. Instr. phys. edn. McMurry Coll., Abilene, Tex., 1954-55, Greiner Jr. High Sch., Dallas, 1955-56; tchr. Walker Elem. Sch., Roswell, N.Mex., 1965-67; grad. asst. Eastern N.Mex. U., Portales, 1967-68, teaching asst., 1968-69, coordinator reading edn., assoc. prof. edn., 1975-79; asst. prof. edn. Adams State Coll., Denver, 1969-70; instr. in reading, dir. Reading Services Clinic, Colo. State U., Ft. Collins, 1970-75; asst. prof. U. N.Mex., Albuquerque, 1979-80; pres. Dean Inst., Albuquerque, 1980-84; owner, dir. instrn. Sunset Mesa Schs., Albuquerque, 1982—; cons. Colo. Right-to-Read, Erie Community Unit, Title III, Colo. Migrant Edn., Portales Mcpl. Schs.; adj. faculty U. Portland, 1981-82; dir. Project ACT, Portland, 1980-82; panel mem. KENM-TV, 1976. Active sch. parents adv. bds., CAP, United Fund. Recipient merit award Eastern N.Mex. U., 1977. Mem. N.Mex., Internat., Portales, Western Coll. reading assns., Council Exceptional Children, Am. Council Univ. Faculty, Am. Soc. Curriculum and Devel., Nat. Ind. Pvt. Schs. Assn. (pres., bd. dirs.), N.Mex. Assn. Non-Pub. Schs. (bd. dirs.), AAUW, AAUP, Delta Kappa Gamma. Democrat. Presbyterian. Author: Foundations of Reading Syllabus, 1973-74; Study Skills Manual, 1973-74; Reading Clinic Manual, 1973-74. Home: 12800 Commanche St NE Albuquerque NM 87111 Office: Sunset Mesa Schs 3020 Morris St NE Albuquerque NM 87111

CRIDER, LOUISE ELAINE, accountant; b. Butler, Pa., Nov. 14, 1959; d. Charles Krenn and Ethel Myrtle (Bachman) C. B.S. in Bus. Adminstrn., Robert Morris Coll., 1981. Credit mgr. Reidbord Bros. Co., Pitts., 1982-85; plant acct. Penreco, Karns City, Pa., 1985—. Youth advisor Summit United Presbyn. Ch. Youth Group, Butler, Pa., 1984, 85. Mem. Phi Beta Lambda. Avocations: traveling; reading; swimming; hiking. Home: RD 4 Butrner Rd Butler PA 16001 Office: Penreco Karns City PA 16041

CRIGLER, SUSAN GUM, lawyer; b. Springfield, Mo., Sept. 8, 1954; d. R.P. and Pauline (Gum) Crigler. B.A., NE Mo. State U., 1976; J.D., U. Mo.-Columbia, 1979. Bar: Mo. 1979, U.S. Dist. Ct. (we. dist.) Mo. 1979. Legis. intern Mo. Ho. of Reps., Jefferson City, 1975-76; legal intern State of Mo. Securities Div., 1978; asst. city counselor City of Columbia, 1979—. Bd. dirs. Mid-Mo. br. Gateway chpt. Multiple Sclerosis Soc. J.J. Pershing scholar N.E. Mo. State U., 1973-76; Law Sch. Found. scholar U. Mo.-Columbia, 1976-79. Mem. Mo. Bar Assn., Boone County Bar Assn., Columbia C. of C. (women's network), Columbia Bus. and Profl. Women's Club. Democrat. Methodist. Office: City of Columbia PO Box N Columbia MO 65205

CRINER-WORMLEY, CHRISTINE CAROLYN, educational administrator; b. Galena Park, Tex., Aug. 23, 1949; d. Oscar Henry and Ogeal Carmen (Collins) Criner; m. Joel Allen Wormley, Nov. 27, 1970 (div. June 1984); children—Krystene Cholette, Deanna Dawn. B.A., Huston-Tillotson Coll., 1971; M.S., Pepperdine U., 1976. Tchr. Austin Ind. Sch. Dist., 1971-72, Compton Unified, Calif., 1972-73; tchr. Lynwood High Sch., Calif., 1973-79, dean students, 1979, asst. prin., 1979-82; prin. Vista High Sch., Lynwood, 1982—. Coordinator ednl. projects Black Am. Polit. Action Com., Lynwood, 1982-84. Mem. Nat. Assn. Secondary Sch. Prins., Consortium Advanced Leadership, Assault on Illiteracy Program, Calif. Consortium Ind. Study, Compton Community Coll. Found. Bd., Delta Sigma Theta. Democrat. Methodist. Avocations: jazz dance; swimming; tennis; skating. Home: 4264 Niland St Lynwood CA 90262 Office: Vista High Sch 11300 Wright Rd Lynwood CA 90262

CRIPPS, BARBARA ANN, accountant; b. Everett, Mass., Mar. 7, 1937; d. Francis Edward and Jessie May (Ward) Pleasant. B.S. in Acctg., Northeastern U., 1982, A.Bus., 1979; student Bentley Coll., 1960s, N.E. Sch. of Art, 1965-66. Supr. order and billing dept. Gillette, Boston, 1966-70; jr. acct. Sheraton Corp., Franchise Div., Boston, 1970-72, acct., 1972-73, mgr. acctg., 1973-80, mgr. account receivable and statis. analyses, 1980—. Portrait artist, exhibited in Sheraton Corp. Art Show. Active various polit. fund raising campaigns; trustee Ledgeview Estates, Quincy, Mass., 1984. Mem. Nat. Assn. Credit Execs., Nat. Assn. Female Credit Execs., Nat. Assn. Female Execs., Mass. Lic. Bd. Real Estate, Sigma Epsilon Rho. Democrat. Roman Catholic. Office: Sheraton Corp Franchise Div 60 State St Boston MA 02109-6002

CRIPPS, KATHY HICKEY, public relations company official; b. Bklyn., Feb. 2, 1951; d. Thomas Joseph and Maureen (Kane) Hickey; m. Robert F. Cripps, Jan. 16, 1971. B.A., Queens Coll., 1973; M.B.A., Fordham U., 1983. Sr. home economist Nestle Co., N.Y.C., 1974-76; dir. product info. Farberware, Bronx, 1976-82; v.p., client service mgr. Burson-Marsteller, N.Y.C., 1982—. Mem. Home Economists in Bus. (controller 1980-82, NE region adv. 1984-86), Women in Communications. Home: 50 Parkview Dr Bronxville NY 10708 Office: Burson-Marsteller 230 Park Ave New York NY 10003

CRIQUETTE, (RUTH DUBARRY MONTAGUE), artist, writer, lectr., educator; b. Paris; d. Roland Beauvais and Maria Violette (DuBarry) M.; student Ecole des Beaux Arts, pvt. ateliers, Paris, U. Nev., Lumis Art Acad., Prickett Sch. Painting, Ecole Marsan, Vernon, France. Dir. Prickett-Montague Studios of Painting, U.S.A., 1955-61; owner, dir. Montague Studio of Painting, New Orleans, 1962-63, Washington, 1964-69; asso. Ecole Marsan, 1970-72, Field Studio, Otter Rock, Oreg., 1974-76, Blue Ridge Mountains, Sterling, Va., 1976—; freelance writer, 1955—; tchr. oil painting, 1955—, color cons., 1955—. Recipient Lumis Art award, 1955; Golden Poet award World Poetry Press, 1985. Life fellow Internat. Inst. Arts and Letters (Switzerland); hon. mem. Int. Com. Centro Studi e Scambi Internat. (Rome), Internat. Acad. Leonardo da Vinci (Rome), Internat. Arts Guild (Monaco); charter mem. Women in the Arts Mus. Author: 100 monographs in oil painting, 1961—; author-illustrator travel chronicle Bahamian Ah-h-h, 1969, Prose Poems, Sunburst Anthology, 1972, Internat. Bouquet of Poems, 1972; contbr. to Today's Greatest Poems, 1983, World's Best Loved Poems, 1984. Exhibited paintings Le Salon des Nations a Paris, France, 1985. Home: Blue Ridge Studio PO Box 344 Sterling VA 22170

CRISCUOLO, WENDY LAURA, lawyer, interior design consultant; b. N.Y.C., Dec. 17, 1949; d. Joseph Andrew and Betty Jane (Jackson) C.; m. John Howard Price, Jr., Sept. 5, 1970 (div. Apr. 1981). B.A. with honors in Design, U. Calif.-Berkeley, 1973; J.D., U. San Francisco, 1982. Space planner GSA, San Francisco, 1973-79; sr. interior designer E. Lew & Assocs., San Francisco, 1979-80; design dir. Beier & Gunderson, Inc., Oakland, Calif., 1980-81; sr. interior designer Environ. Planning and Research, San Francisco, 1981-82; interior design cons., Mill Valley, 1982—; law clk. to Judge Spencer Williams, U.S. Dist. Ct., San Francisco, 1983-84; atty. Ciros Investments, Mill Valley, 1985—. Co-author: Guide to the Laws of Charitable Giving, 3d rev. edit., 1983; mem. U. San Francisco Law Rev., 1983. Bd. dirs. Morin Citizens for Energy Planning. Mem. State Bar Calif., Queen's Bench (San Francisco), Calif. Women Lawyers. Republican. Episcopalian. Club: Commonwealth (San Francisco). Avocation: creative writing.

CRISELL, KIMBERLY ANN, computer company executive, dancer; b. Los Angeles, Dec. 6, 1957; d. Robert Burton and Carolyn Joyce (Semko) C. B.A. with honors, U. Calif.-Santa Cruz, 1980. Instr., English Lang. Services, Oakland, Calif., 1980-81; freelance writer Gambit mag., New Orleans, 1981; instr. Tulane U., New Orleans, 1981; instr., editor Haitian-English Lang. Program, New Orleans, 1981-82; instr. Delgado Coll., New Orleans, 1982-83; instr., program coordinator Vietnamese Youth Ctr., San Francisco, 1984; dancer Khadra Internat. Folk Ballet, San Francisco, 1984—; dir. mktg. communications Centram Systems West, Inc., Berkeley, Calif., 1984—; communications coordinator Safeway Stores, Inc., Oakland, 1985. Writer shoppers guides, newsletter articles, press releases, brochures, users manuals. Vol. coordinator Friends of Haitians, 1981, editor, writer newsletter, 1981; dancer Komenka Ethnic Dance Ensemble, New Orleans, 1983; mem. Contemp. Art Ctr.'s Krewe of Clones, New Orleans, 1983, Californians for Nonsmokers Rights, Berkeley, 1985. Mem. Nat. Assn. Female Execs., Dance Action, Bay Area Dance Coalition. Democrat. Avocations: visual arts, travel, creative writing.

CRISMAN, JOANNE ELIZABETH, college administrator; b. Joliet, Ill., Mar. 15, 1929; d. Harvey James and Olive Joyce (Norton) Frick; m. Ronald E.W. Crisman, June 23, 1951; children—Jeffrey Thomas, Candace, Kevin James. B.A., Iowa Wesleyan U., 1950; M.A., Johnson State Coll., 1982. Mus. tchr. Iowa, Ill., Vt., 1959-73; alumni coordinator Johnson State Coll., Vt., 1982—. Contbr. articles to profl. jours. Mem. Gov.'s Commn. on Children and Youth, Montpelier, Vt., 1974-82, Gov's. Commn. on the Status of Women, Montpelier, 1983—; active Vt. Girl Scout Bd., 1975-78; bd. dirs. United Way, Washington County, Montpelier, 1981—. Mem. Nat. Identification Program for Women in Higher Edn., AAUW (pres. 1977-80). Republican. Unitarian. Home: 5 Liberty St Montpelier VT 05602

CRISMOND, LINDA FRY, librarian; b. Burbank, Calif., Mar. 1, 1943; d. Billy and Lois (Harding) Fry; 1 son, Dougal. B.S., U. Calif.-Santa Barbara, 1964, M.L.S., U. Calif.-Berkeley, 1965. Reference librarian San Francisco Pub. Library, 1965-72, head acquisitions, 1972-74; asst. univ. librarian U. So. Calif., Los Angeles, 1974-80; chief dep. county librarian Los Angeles County Pub. Library, 1980-81, county librarian, 1981—; bd. dirs. Productivity Ctr. of S.W., Los Angeles, 1984—; adv. bd. UCLA Sch. Library Mgmt., 1981—. Author: Directory of San Francisco Area Publishers, 1968. Bd. councillors U. So. Calif. Sch. Library and Info Mgmt., Los Angeles, 1980-84; chmn. bd. Los Angeles County Pub. Library Found., 1982—. Recipient Staff Mem. of Yr. award San Francisco Pub. Library. Mem. ALA (chmn. Percy Jury 1976-78, Gale Jury 1982-84, exec. com. resources sect.), Calif. Library Assn. (council 1980-82, fed. legis. coordinator 1983-84), Calif. County Librarians Assn. (pres. 1985). Office: Los Angeles County Pub Library 7400 E Imperial Hwy Downey CA 90241*

CRISP, RUTH HINTON, confectionary brokerage company executive; b. Winchester, Va., Sept. 11, 1944; d. Edward Raymond and Hazel Valene (Pyle) Payne; divorced; children—Teresa Anne Hinton, Paul Edward Hinton. Degree in interior design Fla. Sch. Art. Office worker Sea Cold Service, Atlanta, 1967-70; salesperson J. Reid Green Assocs., Atlanta, 1970-80; salesperson Richard Born Co., Atlanta, 1980-85, owner, pres. RCA Inc. doing bus. as Richard Born Co., Atlanta, 1986—; mem. broker adv. bd. Fleer Corp., 1983, Republic Tobacco Co., 1985. Named to honor roll Nat. Assn. Tobacco Distbrs., 1978. Mem. Nat. Candy Wholesale Assn. (Nat. Candy Ambassador award 1985), So. Tobacco and Candy Assn., So. Salesmen Club, Atlanta Candy and Tobacco Club (pres. 1982, Presdl. plaque 1983), Nat. Confectionary Salesmen (Ambassador award 1984, bd. dirs. 1985-86), Nat. Assn. Female Execs. Republican. Baptist. Avocations: reading; theater; golf; antiques. Office: RCA Inc doing bus as Richard Born Co 4289 Memorial Dr Suite I Decatur GA 30032

CRISP, WENDY, magazine editor. B.A. in English, Whitman Coll., 1965. Asst. editor Datamation, 1965-68, sr. editor, 1979-81; exec. editor Pasadena Action Center, 1969-73; mem. Crisp & Marley Advt., 1973-79; editor Small Systems World, 1975-79; editor-in-chief Savvy, 1981—. Bd. communications United Meth. Ch. Address: Savvy Magazine 3 Park Ave New York NY 10016

CRISPIN, MILDRED SWIFT (MRS. FREDERICK EATON CRISPIN), civic worker, writer; b. Branson, Mo.; d. Albert Duane and Anna (Harlan) Swift; student Galloway Woman's Coll., 1922-24; m. Herbert William Kochs, Dec. 1, 1928 (div. Mar. 1955); children—Susan Kochs Judevine (dec.), Herbert William, Judith Ann (Mrs. Nelson Shaw); m. 2d, George Walter King Snyder, Oct. 6, 1962 (dec. 1969); m. 3d, Frederick Eaton Crispin, May 20, 1972. Bd. dirs. Travelers Aid Soc., Chgo., 1936-68, nat. dir., 1948-71; bd. dirs. U.S.O., Chgo., 1944-65, nat. dir., 1951-57; bd. dirs. John Howard Assn., 1958-67, Community Fund Chgo., 1950-56, Welfare Council Met. Chgo., 1950-56; chmn. woman's div. Crusade of Mercy, Chgo., 1964. Mem. U.S. Women's Curling Assn. (co-founder 1947, pres. 1950, founder Indian Hill Women's Curling Club, Winnetka, Ill., 1945, chmn. 1945-46), DAR, Daus. Am. Colonists. Republican. Methodist. Clubs: Saddle and Cycle, Town and Country Arts (pres. 1957-58) (Chgo.); Everglades (Palm Beach, Fla.); Venice (Fla.) Yacht; Coral Ridge Yacht (Ft. Lauderdale, Fla.); Bird Key Yacht (Sarasota, Fla.). Home: Box 1098 Osprey FL 33559

CRIST, GERTRUDE H. (MRS. HOWARD G. CRIST, JR.), civic worker; b. Barnard, S.D.; d. Jacob H. and Lillian Belle (Freeman) Hartman; student S.D. State Coll., 1936-38; m. Howard Grafton Crist, Jr., Nov. 2, 1940; children—Howard Grafton III, Douglas Freeman. Owner, partner Farm and Home Service. Dir. Columbia Bank & Trust Co. Chmn., Westmoreland County chpt. ARC, 1946, sec., 1943-45, chmn. vol. spl. services, 1944-45; dist. chmn. Cancer drive Howard County; mem. Howard County Bd. Edn., 1953-70, pres., 1963-65; bd. dirs. Howard County Tb Assn.; adv. council Catonsville Community Coll.; chmn. Emergency Civil Def. Hosp. Howard County, 1961-62; sec. Community Action Council Howard County, 1965, dir., 1966; bd. dirs. Girl Scout Council Central Md., 1967-68; mem. Md. Council Higher Edn., 1968-76, State Bd. for Community Colls., 1968-77; trustee Howard Community Coll., 1966-71, v.p., 1969-70; bd. dirs. Howard County chpt. ARC, 1973—, v.p., 1976-77; mem. Md. Bd. for Higher Edn., 1977—, Howard County Commn. on Arts, 1975-77; v.p. Farm and Home Service, Inc., 1968-78. Mem. Md. Congress Parents and Tchrs. (life), Md. Assn. Bds. Edn. (pres. 1966, 67), Nat. Sch. Bds. Assn. (dir. 1968-71), W. Friendship PTA (sec. 1949-51), League Women Voters (county sec. 1957-59, dir. 1960-62, pres. 1959), Nat. Congress Parents and Tchrs. (hon. life mem.), Delta Kappa Gamma (hon. Alpha Beta State and Lambda chpts.). Episcopalian (vestryman; chmn. parish day sch. bd. 1970-73). Club: Cattail River Garden. Home: 13905 Burnt Woods Rd Sykesville MD 21784

CRIST, JUDITH (KLEIN), film and drama critic; b. N.Y.C., May 22, 1922; d. Solomon and Helen (Schoenberg) Klein; A.B., Hunter Coll., 1941; teaching fellow State Coll. Wash., 1942-43; M.Sc. in Journalism, Columbia U., 1945; m. William B. Crist, July 3, 1947; 1 son, Steven Gordon. Civilian instr. 3091st AAFBU, 1943-44; reporter N.Y. Herald Tribune, 1945-60, editor arts, 1960-63, assoc. theater critic, 1957-63, film critic, 1963-66; film, theater critic NBC-TV Today Show, 1963-73; film critic World Jour. Tribune, 1966-67; critic at large Ladies Home Jour., 1966-67; contbg. editor, film critic TV Guide, 1966—, N.Y. mag., 1968-75, The Washingtonian, 1970-72, Palm Springs Life, 1971-75; contbg. editor, film critic Saturday Rev., 1975-77, 80-84, N.Y. Post, 1977-78, MD/Mrs., 1977—, 50 Plus, 1978-83, L'Officiel/USA, 1979-80; arts critic Channel 9 News, Sta. WOR-TV, 1981—, Goodlife, 1985-86, Coming Attractions, 1985—; instr. journalism Hunter Coll., 1947, Sarah Lawrence Coll., 1958-59; assoc. journalism Columbia Grad. Sch. Journalism, 1959-62, lectr. journalism, 1962-64, adj. prof., 1964—. Trustee Anne O'Hare McCormick Scholarship Fund. Recipient Page One award N.Y. Newspaper Guild, 1955; George Polk award, 1961, N.Y. Newspaper Women Club awards, 1955, 59, 63, 65, 67, Edn. Writers Assn. award, 1952, Columbia Grad. Sch. Journalism Alumni award, 1961, named to 50th Anniversary Honors List, 1963; Centennial Pres.'s medal Hunter Coll., 1970; named to Hunter Alumni Hall of Fame, 1973. Mem. Columbia Journalism Alumni (pres. 1967-70), N.Y. Film Critics, Nat. Soc. Film Critic, Sigma Tau Delta. Author: The Private Eye, The Cowboy and the Very Naked Girl, 1968; Judith Crist's TV Guide to the Movies, 1974; Take 22: Moviemakers on Moviemaking, 1984; contbr. articles to mags. Office: 180 Riverside Dr New York NY 10024

CRISTO, DEBORA JO, holding company executive; b. Anadarko, Okla., June 15, 1954; d. Floyd Roger and Donna Jo (Manley) Hardesty; m. Constantine Gus Cristo, May 9, 1979; children—Paul Hardesty, Roger Alexander. B.A. in Sociology, Psychology, Anthropology, U. Tulsa, 1973. Mgr. multi-family leasing Hardesty Co., Tulsa, 1969-74, partnership adminstr., 1977-79; gen. mgr. Manley Co., Tulsa, 1974-76; exec. v.p. Resource Group Industries, Tulsa, 1979-81, Atlas Tower Corp., Vinita, Okla., 1981-83, Exomesa Corp., Tulsa, 1983—; pres. Athena Devel., Tulsa, 1982—; v.p., dir. Exomesa Financial Services, Inc., Tulsa, 1983—. Co-inventor Westower Technology, 1983-84; Co-designer Computerized Videotex Network System –Dax–; 1982-84. Recipient Cert. of Achievement Okla. senator, 1970; named Woman of Year, United Earth Found., 1973. Democrat. Greek Orthodox. Office: Exomesa Corp PO Box 52769 Tulsa OK 74152

CRITCHLOW, SUSAN MELISSA, public relations executive, graphic art consultant; b. Gainesville, Fla., Dec. 24, 1950; d. James Carlton and Mildred Estelle (Pringle) Barley; B.A., U. South Fla., 1972, M.A. in Speech Communication with honors, 1973; m. Warren Hartzell Critchlow, Jr., Aug. 18, 1973. Asst. dir. public relations Goodwill Industries of N. Fla., Inc., 1973-74; dir. public relations St. Luke's Hosp., Jacksonville, Fla., 1974; dir. informational services Greater Orange Park Community Hosp., Orange Park, Fla., 1974-82; pres. Susan Critchlow & Assocs., SC&A Pub. Co., Inc., Orange Park, 1976—, also Graphic Express, Inc. Bd. dirs. Childrens Haven. Named Northeast Fla. Bus. Communicator of Month, 1975, 78; recipient Addy awards, 1981, 82, 83, 84, 85. . Mem. Fla. Hosp. Assn. (bd. dirs. public relations council 1976-78, Gold award 1975, Silver award 1976), Jacksonville Hosp. Public Relations Council (chmn. 1975-77), Fla. Pub. Relations Assn. (Golden Image award 1975, 76, 77, 78, 79, 80, 81, 82), Pub. Relations Soc. Am., Jacksonville Advt. Fedn., Internat. Assn. Bus. Communicators. Democrat. Episcopalian. Home: 2309 Egremont Dr Orange Park FL 32073 Office: 2301 Park Ave Suite 305 Orange Park FL 32073

CRITTENDEN, LETA DAVIS, diagnostic sonographer, educator; b. Biloxi, Miss., Jan. 17, 1945; d. Alva Joseph Myers and Gloria (Gilbert) Baisden; m. James Lea Davis, Dec. 1, 1963 (div. 1977); children—James Lea, Gregory Matthew; m. Joseph Jay Crittenden, June 18, 1983; stepchildren—James J., Julie J., John J. Cert. Sacred Hearth Sch. Radiol. Tech., Pensacola, Fla., 1974; Cert. Diagnostic. Med. Sonography, U. Okla., 1975; A.A. in Diagnostic Med. Sonography, Pensacola Jr. Coll., 1979. Co-founder, owner Sch. Diagnostic Med. Sonography, West Fla. Regional Med. Ctr. Hosp., Pensacola, 1976—; adminstr., program dir. Fla. Inst. Ultrasound, 1979, instr., 1976-85; supr. ultrasound dept. Naval Aerospace Regional Med. Ctr., Pensacola, 1978—; cons., 1980—; dir. seminars; cons. Pensacola Jr. Coll., 1978. Vol. Am. Heart Assn., Mem. Am. Inst. Ultrasound in Medicine, Am. Soc. Diagnostic Med. Sonography, Am. Registry Radiol. Technologists, Escambia County Med. Soc. Aux., Fla. Med. Aux., AMA Aux., Pensacola C. of C. Republican. Baptist. Clubs: Pensacola Ski, Scenic Hills Country, Pensacola Country. Avocations: skiing, golf, tennis, reading. Home: 8909 Burning Tree St Pensacola FL 32514

CROAFF, MARVA J., marketing executive; b. Phoenix, May 19, 1950; d. Vernon B. and Velma L. (Love) Croaff; B.S. in Zoology, Ariz. State U., 1972; postgrad. San Francisco State U., 1973-75, Syracuse U., 1978, U. Wis.-Milw., 1976. Mgr. data control Health Application Systems, Burlingame, Calif., 1972-74, mgr. planning and evaluation, 1974-75; mgr. product devel. Blue Cross/Blue Shield, Milw., 1976-78, mgr. individual plans, Calif. Blue Cross, Oakland, 1978-79; ins. mktg. mgr. Durango Systems, Inc., San Jose, Calif., 1979-81; dir. mktg. Insurnet, Inc., Emeryville, Calif., 1981—. Chmn. corp. innovation task team Blue Cross/Blue Shield, Milw., 1977-78; participant in seminars on preventive health; solicitor, Milw. County Easter Seal Soc., 1977-78. Mem. Blue Cross/Blue Shield Assn. (nat. product adv. panel 1976-77, adv. panel worksite hypertension 1977-79), Faculty Assn. Sales and Mktg. Execs. Grad. Sch. Sales Mgmt. and Mktg., Sales and Mktg. Execs. Internat. Alumna, Sales and Mktg. Execs. Assn. San Francisco, Internat. Orgn. Women Execs. (dir. 1978-79), Am. Mktg. Assn., Am. Mgmt. Assn. Club: Commonwealth. Office: 1900 Powell St Emeryville CA 94608

CROCE, ARLENE LOUISE, dance critic; b. Providence, May 5, 1934; d. Michael Daniel and Louise Natalie (Pensa) C.; student U. N.C., 1951-53; B.A., Barnard Coll., 1955. Founder, editor Ballet Review, 1965-78; dance critic The New Yorker, N.Y.C., 1973—; dance panelist Nat. Endowment for Arts, 1977-80. Recipient Janeway Prize, Barnard Coll., 1955, Am. Acad. and Inst. Arts and Letters award, 1979, Arts and Culture award Mayor N.Y.C., 1979; Hodder fellow Princeton U., 1971; Guggenheim fellow, 1972, 85. Author: The Fred Astaire & Ginger Rogers Book, 1972; Afterimages, 1977; Going to the Dance, 1982. Office: 25 W 43d St New York NY 10036

CROCKER, MARILYN RUTH, marketing executive; b. Newton, Mass., Apr. 2, 1942; d. Sydney Rheinhalt Olaf and Ruth Rosamond (Wagner) Miller; m. Joseph Herbert Crocker, June 17, 1967; children—Joseph Benjamin, Jonathan Thomas. B.A., Smith Coll., 1963; M.A., Harvard U., 1964. English instr. Colby-Sawyer Coll., New London, N.H., 1965-67; instr. history Chgo. City Coll., 1967-69; internat. cons. Inst. Cultural Affairs, Chgo., Singapore and Bombay, 1969-78; v.p. Sumner Rahr & Co., Inc., Chgo., 1978-81; mgr. communications McDonald's Corp., Oak Brook, Ill., 1981-83; mktg. dir. Red Lobster Inns Am., Orlando, Fla., 1983-85, v.p., dir. mktg., 1985—; cons. Carl Jung Ctr., Evanston, Ill., 1980-81, Sumner Rahr & Co., Inc., Chgo., 1981-82, Horizons Unltd., Chgo., 1982-83, Lens Internat., Chgo., 1983—. Author: Socio-Economic Community Development, 1977. Vol., Ecumenical Inst.,

Chgo., 1967-75; vol. Am. Friends Service Com., Chapel Hill, N.C., 1965. Named Outstanding Woman in Bus., Sales and Mktg. Execs. of Orlando, 1985. Mem. Nat. Mktg. Assn., Pi Lambda Theta. Democrat. Methodist. Home: 2724 Lionheart Rd Winter Park FL 32792 Office: Red Lobster Inns Am 6770 Lake Ellenor Dr Orlando FL 32809

CROCKETT, CATHERINE GRAYSON, lawyer, divorce mediator; b. Norfolk, Va., Aug. 6, 1949; d. Douglas Harman and Mary Catherine (Sturgis) C.; m. Lafe Elkas Solomon, Aug. 25, 1979; children—Catherine Hannah, William David. B.A., Hollins Coll., 1971; M.A. (fellow), U. Americas-Puebla, Mex., 1973; J.D., Antioch Sch. Law, 1976. Bar: D.C. 1977, Md. 1981, U.S. Dist. Ct. D.C. 1980, U.S. Ct. Claims 1983. Adv. atty. NLRB, Washington, 1976-79; trial atty. EEOC, Washington, 1979-80; trainer divorce mediators Family Mediation Assn., Bethesda, Md., 1982-84; co-founder Nat. Center Mediation Edn., 1984; sole practice family law and divorce mediation, Bethesda, 1980—; instr. Cath. U. Am., Washington, 1984—; sec. bd. dirs. Family Mediation Assn., 1980-84; factfinder Montgomery County Md. Personnel Grievance System, 1982—; mem. family dispute panel Am. Arbitration Assn., 1983—. Mem. ABA, Women's Bar Assn. Md., Assn. Family and Conciliation Cts., Montgomery County Md. Bar Assn. (sec. family law sect. 1981-82). Democrat. Episcopalian. Contbg. author: Divorce Mediation: A Guide for Family Therapists, 1984; co-author: Starting Your Own Mediation Practice: A Workbook, 1985. Office: 4720 Montgomery Ln Suite 1000 Bethesda MD 20814

CROCKETT, ETHEL PUTNAM STACY, retired librarian; b. Mt. Vernon, N.Y., Jan. 19, 1915; d. Henry P. and Marian (Putnam) Stacy; B.A., Vassar Coll., 1936; M.A., San Jose State Coll., 1962; postgrad. U. Calif. at Berkeley, 1964-65, San Francisco State Coll., 1966; m. Clement Wirt Crockett, Aug. 17, 1936 (div. 1969); children—Patricia, Richard; m. 2d, Jack H. Aldridge, June 22, 1973. Children's librarian Corning (N.Y.) Meml. Library, 1958; gen. reference librarian San Jose (Calif.) City Coll., 1962-68; dir. library services City Coll. San Francisco, 1968-72; librarian State of Calif., Sacramento, 1972-80; dir. Inst. Tng. and Evaluation, San Francisco, 1971; vice chmn. Western Interstate Commn. on Higher Edn. Library Council, 1974-76; chmn. Calif. Intersegmental Task Force on Library Automation, 1974-76; chmn. Calif. Bd. Library Examiners, 1974-76; mem. adv. council edn. stats. Nat. Center Edn. Stats. 1975-79; adviser bd. Friends of Calif. Libraries; Adv. Com. on Libraries to Librarian of Congress, 1976-77. Mem. Sir Francis Drake Commn., Calif., 1974-80; mem. vis. com. Stanford U. Libraries, 1975-82, mem. adv. council, 1980—; mem. adv. bd. BALLOTS; adv. com. Ohio Coll. Library Center; adv. council Pacific SW Regional Med. Library Service, 1978-80; spl. events chmn. Pacific Hort. Found., 1983—; bd. dirs. Seadrift Property Owners Assn., 1980-84, Marin Income Property Owners Assn., 1980—; mem. adv. council Center for the Book, Library of Congress, 1980—. Mem. ALA, Calif. Library Assn. (chmn. library devel. standards com. 1970-71), Spl. Libraries Assn. (dir. 1970-72), Calif. Inst. Libraries (pres. 1973-74), Calif. Assn. Sch. Librarians (chmn. community coll. sect. 1966-67), Pvt. Libraries Assn. (Eng.), Chief Officers of State Library Agys. (chmn. 1974-77), Apt. House Consol. Assns., Calif. Media and Library Educators Assn., Book Club of Calif. (bd. dirs. 1981—, v.p. 1983—), Strybing Arboretum Soc., San Francisco Mus. Modern Art. Home: PO Box 457 Stinson Beach CA 94970

CROCKETT, LILLIAN GORDON, college administrator; b. Manchester, N.H.; d. Louis Jacob and Ida (Heifetz) Gordon; m. Maurice Harold Crockett, Aug. 7, 1944 (dec. July 1978); children—Philip Gordon, James David. B.S., N.H. Coll., 1984. Bursar N.H. Coll., Manchester, 1965-67, treas., 1967—; treas. gift shop Elliot Hosp., Manchester, 1968-70. Pres. Manchester Hadassah, 1965, Nat. Com. Brandeis, Manchester, 1967; bd. dirs. United Way Manchester, 1974-81, treas., 1977-78. Recipient Appreciation award United Way Manchester, 1981. Mem. Nat. Assn. Coll. and Univ. Bus. Officers, Am. Assn. Univ. Adminstrs. Office: NH Coll 2500 N River Rd Manchester NH 03104

CROCKETT-GALLO, BARBARA, dancer; b. Berkeley, Calif., Sept. 19, 1920; d. Earl Warner and Elsie Bliss (Kennedy) Wood; student public schs.; m. Deane Crockett, Dec. 7, 1941; children—Leslie Crockett Farrow, Allyson Deane Crockett Schwennesen; m. 2d, Albert Gallo, Nov. 23, 1978. Dancer, San Francisco Ballet, 1938-43; artistic dir., instr. Crockett Dance Studio, Sacramento, 1945—; founder, 1965, since prin. dancer, artistic dir. Sacramento Ballet; bd. dirs. Sacramento Regional Arts Council, 1974-77; mem. dance panel Calif. Arts Council, 1981, 82, 85. Recipient Community Service award Sacramento Regional Arts Council. Mem. Nat. Assn. Regional Ballet (pres. 1972-74, dir. 1974-85), Pacific Regional Ballet Assn. (co-founder 1966, pres. 1975). Office: 4050 Manzanita Ave Carmichael CA 95608

CROFFORD, HELEN LOIS, accountant; b. Mesa, Ariz., Sept. 1, 1932; d. Elmer Earl and Lillian Irene (Williams) C.; grad. Lamson Bus. Coll., Phoenix, 1952. Acct., Bob Fisher Enterprises, Inc., Holbrook, Ariz., 1964-78; office mgr. for physician, Holbrook, 1978-79; office mgr. Trans Western Services, Inc., Holbrook, 1979; acct., Northland Pioneer Coll., Holbrook, 1980—. Squadron comdr. CAP, 1965-67, mission coordinator, 1970-79, group comdr., 1972-77, mem. regional staff, 1977-79, wing. historian, 1984—; mem. Navajo Fair Commn., 1966-75; mem. Navajo County Natural Resource Conservation Dist., 1970—, sec.-treas., 1971-81, chairperson, 1981-85; chmn. Navajo County Emergency Service Council, 1984-85. Mem. Ariz. Assn. Conservation Dists. (exec. bd. 1977-78, sec., 1979-80, v.p. 1981-82, pres. 1983-84, past pres. 1985), Nat. Assn. Conservation Dists. (edn. and youth com. 1984), Nat. Assn. Female Execs., D.A.R. Democrat. Home: Box 36 Woodruff AZ 85942 Office: 1200 E Hermosa Dr Holbrook AZ 86025

CROFOOT, REBECCA JANE, caseworker; b. Omaha, June 2, 1942; d. Daniel Milton and Margaret Faith (Spearman) Seibold; m. James Peter Crofoot, June 18, 1977; children—Thomas James, Elizabeth Katharine. B.A., U. Nebr., 1965. Field dir., day camp dir. Wagon Wheel council Girl Scouts Am., Colorado Springs, Colo., 1966-67; caseworker Nebr. Children's Home Soc., Omaha, 1968-80, 81—. Mem. adv. com. Family Service, Omaha, 1983—; mem. choir St. Pauls United Meth. Ch., 1968—; pres. Friends of Library, Papillion, Nebr., 1984—; trustee Papillion Pub. Library, 1979-83; mem. Bd. Adjustment Sharpy County, Nebr.; mem. missions com. St. Paul's United Meth. Ch., 1984—. Office: Nebr Childrens Home Soc 3549 Fontenelle Blvd Omaha NE 68104

CROMARTIE, LILLIAN BAIRD, environmental health specialist; b. Statesville, N.C., Feb. 8, 1953; d. Clay Gilbert and Frances Sudderth Baird; m. Robert A. Cromartie, Nov. 2, 1974 (div. Apr. 1984); children—Alex, Bevin. B.A., Lenoir Rhyne Coll., 1974. Owner, Cromartie Farms, Ocala, Fla., 1976-84; vocat. rehab. counselor Health and Rehab. Services, St. Petersburg, Fla., 1975-76, environ. health specialist, 1984—. Mem. Fla. Environ. Health Assn. Republican. Methodist. Avocations: film; sailing; dancing; cooking. Home: 1917 NE 7th St Ocala FL 32670 Office: Marion County Pub Health PO Box 2408 Ocala FL 32678

CROMWELL, FLORENCE STEVENS, occupational therapist; b. Lewistown, Pa., May 14, 1922; d. William Andrew and Florence (Stevens) Cromwell; B.S. in Edn. (Kappa Kappa Gamma scholar), Miami U., Oxford, Ohio, 1943; B.S. in Occupational Therapy, Washington U., St. Louis, 1949; M.A., U. So. Calif., 1952; certificate in Health Facility Adminstrn., UCLA, 1978. Mem. staff, then supervising therapist Los Angeles County Gen. Hosp., 1949-53; occupational therapist Goodwill Industries, Los Angeles, 1954-55; staff therapist Vis. Nurse Assn., Phila., 1955-56; research therapist United Cerebral Palsy Assn., Los Angeles, 1956-60; dir. occupational therapy Orthopaedic Hosp., Los Angeles, 1961-67; part-time instr., cons. U. So. Calif. occupational therapy dept., 1952-53, 58-60, 65-67, asso. prof., 1970-76, acting chmn. dept. 1973-76, occupational therapy coordinator Research and Tng. Ctr., Sch. Medicine, 1967-70, mem. adv. bd. Project SEARCH, Sch. Medicine, 1969-72; asso. dir. Los Angeles Job Corps Center, 1977-78, cons. in edn. and program devel., 1976—. Mem. scholarship com. Los Angeles March of Dimes, 1963-70. Bd. dirs. Am. Occupational Therapy Found., 1965-69, v.p., 1966-69; bd. dirs. Nat. Health Council, 1975-78. Served to lt. (j.g.) WAVES, 1943-46. Recipient Disting. Alumni award Washington U., 1978. FellowAm. Occupational Therapy Assn. (pres. 1967-73); mem. Inst. Medicine of Nat. Acad. Scis., So. Calif. Occupational Therapy Assn. (pres. 1950-51), Coalition Ind. Health Professions (chmn. 1973-74), Assn. Schs. Allied Health Professions (dir. 1973-74), World Fedn. Occupational Therapists, Cwen, Mortar Bd., Kappa Delta Pi, Kappa Kappa Gamma. Author: Manual for Basic Skills Assessment, 1960; also articles; editor Occupational Therapy in Health Care, 1984—. Home: Pasadena CA 91103

CRONHOLM, BEBRA TIDWELL, author, advertising and public relations consultant; b. Albertville, Ala., Nov. 6, 1952; d. Ollis Cleveland and DeMile Yvonne Tidwell. B.A. in Journalism and English, U. Ala., 1974. Continuity dir. Sta. KAUM, ABC, Houston, 1976-77; copy supr. Point Communications, Houston, 1977-81, Popejoy & Fischel Advt., Dallas, 1980; account exec. Tracy-Locke/BBDO, Dallas, 1981; owner Bebra/Writer, Dallas, 1982—. Contbr. articles to jours. in field. Recipient 1st place in Grand Prix award Houston Ad Club, 1977; hon. mention Houston Art Dirs. Club, 1978. Mem. Women in Communications, Dallas Ad League (Silver Tops award 1983, 84). Republican. Home: 9912 Silvertree Dallas TX 75243

CRONIN, KATHLEEN JUNE, college administrator; b. Spokane, June 4, 1930; d. Leo and Ruth Frances (Eva) C. A.S., Coll. Great Falls, 1954; B.A., U. Portland, 1957; M.A., Mt. St. Mary's Coll., 1968; M.S., Boston U., 1970, Ed.D., 1974; postgrad. Loyola U., New Orleans, 1976. Joined Sisters of Providence, 1948. Tchr. elem. schs. Missoula and Great Falls, Mont., 1954-56, high schs., Missoula, Great Falls, Mont. and Walla Walla, Wash., 1956-65; asst. to pres. Coll. Great Falls, 1965-68, dir. pub. relations, 1979—, dir. Guild, 1979—, dir. Speakers Bur., 1979—; ednl. TV dir. cons. Catholic Communications N.W., Seattle, 1975-79. Contbr. articles to profl. jours. Opportunities chmn. Big Sky council Girl Scouts U.S.A., 1981—; chmn. Great Falls Centennial Commn., 1982-84; mem. Great Falls Community Concert Bd., 1982—; chmn. pub. relations Salvation Army Bd., 1984—; mem. publicity/communication com. United Way of Great Falls, 1985—. Named Freedom Found. tchr. Nat. Freedom's Found., 1959, Woman of Yr. Great Falls Soroptimists, 1984, Great Falls Bus. & Profl. Women, 1985. Mem. Mont. Am. Women in Radio and TV (sec. v.p. 1982—), Great Falls Advt. Fedn., Am. Council on Edn., AAUW, Am. Bus. Women, Cascade County Hist. Soc., Mont. Hist. Soc., Coll. Great Falls Alumni Assn. (dir. 1979—), Zonta (v.p.), Pi Lambda Theta, Delta Epsilon Sigma, Tau Mu Epsilon, Delta Kappa Gamma, Alpha Delta Kappa. Democrat. Avocations: organist; music; photography; cooking; sewing. Home: 1301 20th St S Great Falls MT 59405 Office: Coll Freat Falls Great Falls MT 59405

CROOKSHANKS, BETTY DORSEY, state legislator; b. Rainelle, W.Va., Oct. 27, 1944; d. Talmage Lee and Gilda Marie (Sovine) Dorsey; B.A., W.Va. Inst. Tech., 1968; M.A., W.Va. U., 1973; m. Donald Eugene Crookshanks, Sept. 1, 1972. Sec., NIH, 1965-66; tchr., coach Fayette County Bd. Edn., Meadow Bridge, W.Va., 1968-78; life underwriter Farm Family Life Ins. Co., 1979-82; tchr. Greenbrier (W.Va.) West High Sch., 1981-84; mgr. Sta. WYKM, 1984—; mem. W.Va. Ho. of Dels., 1977—. Mem. adv. bd. W.Va. Woman's Commn., 1977—, Greenbrier Valley Domestic Violence Com.; treas. Rupert Community Library, 1977—; bd. dirs. Seneca Mental Health/Mental Retardation Council, 1978-82, treas., 1979-80, pres., 1980-82; bd. dirs. W.Va. Health Systems Agy., 1980-82; bd. dirs. W.Va. div. Am. Cancer Soc., 1981-83; pres. Greenbrier County Cancer Soc., 1981-82; treas. Big Clear Creek Baptist Ch., 1982-85. Recipient meritorious award W.Va. div. Isaac Walton League of Am., 1978; Disting. Service award W.Va. Osteo. Sch. Medicine, 1982; named Outstanding Young Woman of W.Va., 1980. Mem. Order of Women Legislators, Farm Bur., Rainelle Bus. and Profl. Women's Club (treas. 1982-85, pres. 1986-87), Delta Kappa Gamma (sec. 1980-82, 1st v.p. 1982-85). Democrat. Clubs: Quota (bd. dirs. 1981-83), Rupert Woman's (pres. 1979-80), Order of Eastern Star, White Shrine, Rebekah.

CRORY, ELIZABETH L., state legislator; b. Gardner, Mass., Sept. 12, 1932; d. James Quaiel and Mary (Reilly) Lupien; m. Frederick E. Crory, Aug. 21, 1954; children—Thomas, David, Ellen, Ann, Edward, Stephen. A.B., U. Mass., 1954; M.A.L.S., Dartmouth Coll., 1975. Tchr., Amherst (Mass.) Schs., 1954, Lyme (N.H.) Schs., 1972-76; mem. N.H. Ho. of Reps., 1977—, mem. commerce/consumer affairs com., 1977-84, mem. spl. com. on med. malpractice, 1984. Mem. N.H. Democratic State Com., to 1984; treas. Grafton County Dem. Com., Hanover, N.H., 1980-84; chair Women's Vote '84 Task Force, Manchester, 1984. Roman Catholic. Home: 40 Rip Rd Hanover NH 03755*

CROSBY, CHRISTINE CURRIER, office equipment mktg. co. exec.; b. Utica, Aug. 3, 1945; d. Wayne Arthur and Bernadette (Townley) Currier; student King Coll., 1976-80; children—Michele, Tiffany. With Delta Bus. Systems, Inc., Orlando, Fla., 1976—, exec. v.p., 1980—; pres. Currier Davis Pub., Inc., Orlando. Mem. Sales and Mktg. Execs. Assn., Exec. Women Internat., Women's Network, Fla. C. of C. Republican. Home: 101 Red Cedar Dr Longwood FL 32750 Office: 4601 Parkway Commerce Blvd Orlando FL 32804

CROSBY, LAVON KEHOE STUART, civic leader; b. Hastings, Nebr., Apr. 25, 1924; d. Charles William and Kathryn Marie (Farrell) Kehoe; m. Lester Stuart, Oct. 9, 1948 (dec. 1970); children—Mary Stuart Bolin, Michael, Timothy, Frederick Stuart. Student U. Nebr. U. Asst. to pres. Hastings Tribune Corp., Nebr., 1941-68; mem. staff U.S. Senator Roman Hruska, Washington, 1968-71. Chmn. music com. Cathedral of Risen Christ Choir, Lincoln, Nebr.; pres. Lincoln Community Playhouse Guild; bd. dirs., chmn. membership com. Lincoln Community Playhouse; v.p., bd. dirs. Lincoln Symphony Guild; bd. dirs. Lincoln Symphony Orch. Assn., 1972-82; founder Nebr. Found. for Humanities; mem. Lincoln Symphony Found. Bd., 1984—; bd. dirs. Friends of Ctr. for Great Plains Studies, 1984—; vice chmn. Nebr. Arts Council, 1981-82, chmn., 1982-85; past mem. and sec. Pershing Auditorium Bd.; pres. Nebr. Legis. Ladies League, 1977-78; adv. bd. Cath. social Services Bur.; budget chmn. Nebr. Mother's Assn.; chmn. legis. affairs Diocesan Council Cath. Women; v.p. Heritage League, Lincoln, 1985—; pres. Cornhusker Republican Women, 1974-75. Recipient Mayor's Arts award, Lincoln, 1985; Gov.'s Arts award, Nebr., 1986. Club: University (Lincoln). Home: 3720 S 40th St Lincoln NE 68506

CROSBY, SUSAN MARY, medical instrument company executive; b. Jersey City, Feb. 8, 1954; d. Vincent G. and Joan L. (Shanley) Raine; m. Edward J. Crosby, Sept. 6, 1975 (div. 1982); children—Edward J., Kathryn. R.N., Muhlenberg Hosp. Sch. Nursing, 1975; Assoc. Sci., Union Coll., 1975. Nurse, Bayshore Hosp., Holmdel, N.J., 1975-76; oncology nurse Monmouth Med. Ctr., Long Branch, N.J., 1976-78; emergency room nurse Riverview Hosp., Red Bank, N.J., 1978-82; saleswoman surg. instruments Aesculap Instrument Corp., Burlingame, Calif., 1982—, Eastern regional sales trainer, 1986—; group instr. Dale Carnegie Course, 1985—. Recipient Human Relations award Dale Carnegie, 1985. Mem. Nat. Assn. Profl. Saleswomen, Nat. Assn. Female Execs. Republican. Roman Catholic. Club: ATA Fitness Ctr. (Middletown). Home: 1101 Knollwood Dr Middletown NJ 07748 Office: Aesculap Instruments Corp 875 Stanton Rd Burlingame CA 94010

CROSS, BRENDA KAY, business executive; b. Takoma Park, Md., Jan. 21, 1956; d. Douglas W. and Sara V. (Criddle) Cross. B.B.A., Ohio U., 1979. Freight claims analyst Honolulu Freight Service, 1979-80; salesperson Houston Export Crating, 1980-81; owner-pres. Cross Enterprises, Houston, 1981-83, 20/20 Enterprises, Chattanooga, 1983—. Mem. Advt. Splty. Inst. Avocations: travel; reading; sailing. Office: 20/20 Enterprises PO Box 21009 Chattanooga TN 37421

CROSS, CONSTANCE JOAN, public information executive; b. Chgo., June 11, 1946; d. Alfred Hollis and Mildred Frances (Haggerty) Horrabin; m. Thomas Edward Cross, June 7, 1969; children—Jason Nathaniel, Aaron Jacob. A.A. in Liberal Arts, Ottumwa Heights Jr. Coll., 1966; B.A. in English, Creighton U., 1968. Tchr. English, Waterloo Community Schs., Iowa, 1969-72, substitute tchr., 1972-75; tchr. English, human relations Hawkeye Inst. Tech., Waterloo, 1975-79; admissions com. coordinator Coll. St. Benedict, St. Joseph, Minn., 1979-81, dir. pub. info., 1981—; ballet instr. Waterloo Recreation Ctr., 1972-79; speaker marriage preparation St. Cloud Diocese, St. Cloud, Minn., 1979—. Div. chair United Way, St. Cloud, 1984-85; bd. dirs. St. Cloud Civic Orchestra, 1982—. Mem. AAUW, Forum Exec. Women, Minn. Women's Network, St. Cloud C. of C. (chair tri-coll. 1983-84), Beta Sigma Phi (v.p. 1982-83). Avocations: ballet; cross country skiing; biking. Home: 640 Roosevelt Rd Saint Cloud MN 56301 Office: Coll St Benedict College Ave Saint Joseph MN 56374

CROSS, DOLORES E., educational adminstrator; b. Newark, Aug. 29, 1937; d. Charles and Ozie (Johnson) Tucker; children from previous marriage—Thomas E., Jane E. B.S., Seton Hall U., 1963; M.S., Hofstra U. 1968; Ph.D., U. Mich. 1971. LL.D., Marymount Coll., N.Y.C. 1984. Asst. prof. edn. Northwestern U., Evanston, Ill. 1971-74; assoc. prof. Claremont Grad. Sch., Calif., 1974-78; vice chancellor CUNY, 1978-81; pres. N.Y. State Higher Edn. Service Corp., Albany, 1981—. Bd. dirs. 100 Black Women, Albany, 1983-84; bd. dirs. Nat. Council Higher Edn. Loan Program, Washington, 1982—. Editor: Teaching in a Multicultural Society, 1978. Mem. Am. Edn. Research Assn., Am. Council on Edn., Women Execs. in State Govt. (founding), Nat. Scholarship Services and Fund for Negro Studies (bd. dirs., chmn. 1983). Avocations: hiking; cycling; theater; writing. Home: 300 1st Ave #4G New York NY 10009

CROSS, DOROTHY ABIGAIL, librarian; b. Bangor, Mich., Sept. 9, 1924; d. John Laird and Alice Estelle (Wilcox) C.; B.A., Wayne State U., 1956; M.A. in Library Sci., U. Mich., 1957. Jr. librarian Detroit Public Library, 1957-59; adminstrv. librarian U.S. Army, Braconne, France, 1959-61, Poitiers, France, 1961-63; area library supr., 1963, asst. command librarian, Kaiserslautern, Germany, 1963-67, acquisitions librarian, Aschaffenburg, Germany, 1967, Munich, Germany, 1967-69, sr. staff library specialist, Munich, 1969-72, command librarian, Stuttgart, Germany, 1972-75, dep. staff librarian, Heidelberg, Germany, 1975-77; chief librarian 18th Airborne Corps and Ft. Bragg (N.C.), 1977-79; chief ADP sect. Pentagon Library, Washington, 1979-80, chief readers services br., 1980-83, dir., 1983—. Mem. ALA, Spl. Libraries Assn., U. Mich. Alumni assn., Delta Omicron. Methodist. Home: 6008 Old Landing Way Burke VA 22015 Office: Pentagon Library Room 1A526 Pentagon Washington DC 20310-6000

CROSS, JANIS ALEXANDER, lawyer; b. Plainview, Tex., Sept. 8, 1954; d. James Robert Alexander and Virginia May (Etter) Rech; m. Stephen Douglas Cross, Aug. 19, 1978; children—Beau Austin, Katherine Elizabeth. B.A., Tex. Tech. U., 1976, J.D., 1979. Bar: Tex. 1979. Sole practice, Amarillo, Tex., 1979-81; staff atty. Pioneer Corp., Amarillo, 1981-84; corp. atty. Cabot Corp., Amarillo, 1984—; instr. paralegal edn. West Tex. State U., Canyon, 1982—. Dir. Amarillo Women's Network, 1980-82, Amarillo March of Dimes, 1980-82, Campfire Girls, 1980-82, Plemmons-Eackle Neighborhood Assn., 1981-2. Mem. Fed. Energy Bar Assn., Amarillo Bar Assn., ABA, LWV, AAUW, Gamma Phi Beta. Republican. Baptist. Office: Cabot Corp PO Box 9901 Amarillo TX 79105

CROSS, JOAN ROBERTSON, psychologist; b. Denver, Mar. 26, 1938; d. Jack Rolf and Lois Faye (Griffin) Robertson; m. John Raymond Cross, Jr., Sept. 19, 1956; children—Chrisa Juliette, Jamie Jacqueline. B.A., UCLA, 1962; M.Ed., N. Tex. State U., 1972; Ed.D., E. Tex. State U., 1978. Tchr., Lubbock (Tex.) Ind. Sch. Dist., 1967-68, Plano (Tex.) Ind. Sch. Dist., 1968-72; counselor L.D. Bell High Sch., Hurst, Tex., 1972-75; prof. Eastfield Coll., Dallas, 1975-79; pvt. practice psychology, Dallas, 1979—; owner Reflection Pubs., Dallas, 1982—; lectr. in field. Author: Characteristics of Select Married Women Who Have Male Friends, 1978; For Male Therapists: Treating the Female Patient, 1981; The Role of Innovative Woman and Her Positive Impact on Family Life, 1981; The Woman of the 80's, 1982; Understanding Mom: A Teenage Daughter's Guide, 1982; Your Mom, Your Man and You, 1983; The Mother's Touch, 1983; Premenstrual Syndrome: A Family Affair, 1984; Portraits of the Mother Daughter Bond, 1984. Mem. Am. Psychol. Assn., Tex. Psychol. Assn., Dallas Psychol. Assn., Am. Assn. Marriage and Family Therapists, Tex. Assn. Marriage and Family Therapists, Dallas Assn. Marriage and Family Therapists, Am. Soc. Clin. Hypnosis, NOW, LWV, Psi Chi. Home: 1517 Westridge Dr Plano TX 75075 Office: 4825 LBJ Freeway Suite 167 Dallas TX 75234

CROSS, JUDITH ANN, lawyer; b. Balt., Sept. 23, 1949; d. Joseph William and Ruth Marie (Pratt) Ortman; m. Kris Roger Cross, Nov. 15, 1969. A.A., Villa Julie, 1969; B.A. magna cum laude, U. Balt., 1980, J.D. magna cum laude, 1983. Bar: Md. 1983, U.S. Dist. Ct. Md. 1983, U.S. Ct. Appeals (4th cir.) 1983. Legal sec. various firms, Balt., 1970-72; pretrial release officer Dist. Ct. Md., Balt., 1972-78; fiscal officer, legal. asst. Office Atty. Gen., Balt., 1978-80; law clk. House Counsel Liberty Mut. Ins. Co., Balt., 1980-83; intern, student prosecutor State's Atty. Office, Balt., summer 1982; trial atty. Law Offices Eugene A. Edgett, Jr., Balt., 1983—. Contbr. articles to legal jours. Mem. jud. evaluation team Sheppard and Enoch Pratt Hosp., Balt., 1972-78; mem. Ednor Gardens Community Assn., 1975—. Mem. ABA, Md. Bar Assn., Balt. City Bar Assn., Women's Bar Assn. Home: 3627 Rexmere Rd Baltimore MD 21218 Office: Law Office of Eugene A Edgett Jr 400 Charles Ctr South 36 S Charles St Baltimore MD 21201

CROSS, JULIA BAUMGARDNER, government official; b. Bristol, Tenn., Aug. 28, 1923; d. John Dixon and Bessie Gertrude (Kegley) Baumgardner; student Va. Intermont Coll., 1941-43; B.S., U. Tenn., 1946; m. Ralph Edgar Cross, Sept. 3, 1949 (dec.); children—William Mitchell (dec.), Charles Duane, Julianne (dec.). Sec. to pres. Va. Intermont Coll., Bristol, 1946-49; sec. to editor Methodist Pub. House, Nashville, 1966-68, editorial asst., 1968-69; dep. clk. U.S. Dist. Ct., Nashville, 1969-73, courtroom dep. clk., 1973-78, chief dep. clk., 1978, clk., 1978—. Active Tenn. Performing Arts Center, Tenn. State Mus., Nashville Symphony Assn.; chmn. ch. chpt. Episcopal Ch. Mem. Mental Health Assn. Nashville, Fed. Ct. Clks. Assn. (host clk. nat. nat. conv. 1984), Assn. of Records Mgrs. and Adminstrs. (legis. com.), Middle Tenn. Fed. Exec. Assn. (policy com.), Phi Mu (life). Office: 800 US Courthouse 801 Broadway Nashville TN 37203

CROSS, JUNE VICTORIA, news producer/correspondent; b. N.Y.C., Jan. 5, 1954; d. James and Norma Cross; B.A. Harvard U., 1975. Reporter various newspapers, Mass., 1973-76; asst. dir., prodn. mgr. Sta. WGBH-TV, Boston, 1977-78; reporter MacNeil/Lehrer Report, WNET-TV, N.Y.C., 1978-81, WETA-TV Shirlington, Va., 1981-84; producer/corr. MacNeil-Lehrer News Hour, 1985—. Recipient Emmy for disting. coverage of breaking news story, 1983; award for disting. reporting on def. issues Air Force Assn., 1984; Sch. Urban and Pub. Affairs fellow Carnegie-Mellon U., 1981. Mem. Am. Film Inst., Nat. Assn. Black Journalists, Coalition of One Hundred Black Women, Council on Fgn. Relations, Assn. Black Harvard Alumni (dir. 1980-81). Club: Radcliffe. Writer, producer Simple's Harlem, 1975. Home: 1614 G St SE Washington DC 20003 Office: 3620 27th St S Shirlington VA 22206

CROSS, LAURA ELIZABETH, lawyer; b. Lathrop, Mo.; d. Pross T. and Nina (Peel) C.; A.B., Lindenwood Coll., 1923; B.Litt., Columbia Sch. Journalism, 1925; J.D., George Washington U., 1939. Bibliog. research Library of Congress, Washington, 1931-42; admitted to D.C. bar, 1940; atty. Office Chief of Engrs., U.S. Army, 1942-73; practiced in Washington, 1973—. Mem. ABA, Fed., D.C. bar assns., Am. Judicature Soc., Women in Communications, Kappa Beta Pi, Theta Sigma Phi. Home and Office: 2500 Wisconsin Ave NW Washington DC 20007

CROSS, LOUISE PORTLOCK, manufacturing company executive; b. Norfolk, Va., Jan. 20, 1907; d. William Seth and Mary Louise (Fanshow) Portlock; m. James Byron Cross, July 17, 1929; 1 child, Blanche Louise. Grad. high sch. With J.B. Cross Inc., Norfolk, 1952—, exec. pres., 1959-60, then pres., chief exec. officer, from 1960, now pres., treas., agt. Lodges: Order Eastern Star, Ladies Oriental Shrine N.Am. Home: Mayflower Seaside Towers 205-34th St Virginia Beach VA 23451 Office: 3797 Progress Rd Norfolk VA 23502

CROSS, LULACLAY (LU) HAYES, data collector; b. Greenville, Ala., Aug. 3, 1946; d. Willis Clay and Mary Lucille (Luckie) Hayes; m. Duane Wesley Cross, Mar. 2, 1974; 1 child, Luane Michelle. B.S., Troy State U., 1967, M.S., 1971. Asst. principal Laurens County Sch. Bd., Dublin, Ga., 1977-79; curriculum coordinator Cemericus Sch. System, Americus, Ga., 1979-81; tng. specialist Greenville Scounty Sch. Dist., S.C., 1981-83, asst. principal., 1983-84; cons. Digital Equip. Corp., Atlanta, 1984-85; data collector Metro-CESA, Atlanta, 1985—. Researcher, developer statewide program for staff development. Mem. Nat. Assn. Female Execs., ASTD, Kappa Pi. Baptist. Club: Princeton West-Meadow Chase Garden (Marietta, Ga.) (pres. 1986—). Avocations: piano; painting; crafts; dance. Office: M-CESA Regional Devel Ctr 2268 Adams St NW 30318

CROSS, STEPHANIE LEE, computer hardware company executive; b. Sioux City, Iowa, Dec. 11, 1942; d. Ralph William and Bessie Mae (Baugh) McSwain; m. Anthony Lucero, 1962 (div. 1966); children—Maria, Jennifer; m. Keith Curtis Cobell, 1968 (dec. June 1978); children—Keith, Christopher; m. Gerry Lane Cross, July 27, 1981. Student Woodbury Coll., 1960-61, UCLA, 1961-70. Personnel adminstr. Daconics Corp., Sunnyvale, Calif., 1972-73; owner, operator Daisy Electric and Refrigeration Co., Marysville, Calif., 1974-80; adminstrv. asst. Space Command, U.S. Air Force, Colorado Springs, Colo., 1982-83; gen. mgr. SAE Research and Devel. Lab., Colorado Springs, 1983-85; adminstrv. mgr. Sperry Corp., Colorado Springs, 1985—. Author short stories. Group leader Bay Area council Girl Scouts U.S., 1971-73; community leader

4-H, Marysville, Calif., 1974-78; ind. hospice caregiver, Colo., Calif., 1978—. Recipient letter of commendation Gov. Calif., 1964. Mem. Nat. Assn. Female Execs. Democrat. Avocations: writing; public speaking; hunting; Tahitian dancing. Home: 11945 Columbine Hills Rd Colorado Springs CO 80908

CROSSLAND, HARRIET KENT, portrait painter; b. Cleve., Sept. 8, 1902; d. Carl and Harriet Emily (Bacon) Dueringer; pupil of Margaret McDonald Phillips; m. Paul Marion Crossland, Sept. 20, 1959. Portrait painter, 1952—; freelance editor med. papers, 1953-70; represented in permanent collection John F. Kennedy Library, Boston. Fund raiser Am. Cancer Soc.; mem. fund raising com. Vol. Action Bur.; mem. Santa Rosa Symphony League; mem. visual arts com. Luther Burbank Center for the Arts, Santa Rosa, 1982—. Recipient award of merit Am. Cancer Soc., 1979, 84. Mem. Artists Round Table, Sonoma County Med. Assn. Aux., Am. Med. Women's Assn. (friend), Am. Cancer Soc., DAR, Stanford U. Alumni Assn. Clubs: Ret. Officers Wives, Sonoma County Press, Sat. Afternoon. Editor, illustrator: X-Rays and Radium in Treatment of Diseases of the Skin, 1967. Prin. donor Crossland Lab. for Audiovisual Learning in Dermatology, Stanford U. Sch. Medicine. Address: 2247 Sunrise Dr Santa Rosa CA 95405

CROSSLIN, LOUISE, real estate broker; b. Sallisaw, Okla., May 29, 1927; d. Alvon A. and Maye M. (Burton) Diffee; student Oklahoma City U., 1949, 50; m. Paul L. Crosslin, July 18, 1943; children—Alvon Paul, Norman Randy. With CRE, Tahlequah, Okla., 1952—, owner, broker, 1955—; supr. Mr. Quik Stores. Mem. Rural Water Dist., Tahlequah, 1972-75. Mem. C. of C. (sec. 1952-82), Home Builders Assn., Okla. Real Estate Commn., Am. Legion Aux., VFW Aux., Beta Sigma Phi. Democrat. Baptist. Club: Sportsmen Acres Devel. Co. (pres. 1970-82). Home: PO Box 164 Tahlequah OK 74464 Office: 400 S Muskogee Tahlequah OK 74464

CROSSWELL, CAROL MCCORMICK, lawyer; b. Buffalo, Dec. 21, 1928; d. Albert L.L. and Helen (McDowell) McCormick; student Radcliffe Coll.; LL.B. cum laude, U. Buffalo, 1948; postgrad. Columbia U., 1960, (fellow) Harvard U. Sch. Internat. Law, 1961; m. William J. Crosswell (dec.); m. 2d, Gilbert Wheatland Smith, Feb. 2, 1952 (div. Feb. 1972); children—Carol, Linda. Bar: N.Y. 1948, D.C. 1953, Fla. 1967. Mem. legal staff UN, 1948-51; mem. U.S. Govt. Psychol. Strategy Bd., 1951-53; U.S. del. Inter Am. Council Jurists, Santiago, Chile, 1960; practiced in N.Y.C., 1950—, Palm Beach, Fla., 1967—; mem. firm Weidon and Crosswell, 1950-66, Winkle Sims Kenny & Crosswell, 1979—; prof. internat. bus. transactions Nova Law Sch. Mem. Fla. Marine Commn., 1968—; bd. dirs. Jr. League, Millard Fillmore Hosp., Buffalo, Save the Children Fedn., Gebbie Found. Inst.; bd. govs. Nova U. Law Center. Mem. Soc. Women Geographers, Fellows of Harvard. Clubs: Indian Harbor Yacht (Greenwich, Conn.); Buffalo Country; N.Y. Skating, Olcott Yacht (N.Y.C.); Palm Beach Yacht, Sail Fish, Beach (Palm Beach, Fla.); Royal Can. Yacht (Toronto, Ont.). Author: Protection of International Personnel, 1956; Financing Foreign Investment, 1962; International Business Techniques, 1963; International Business Law and Knowhow, 1980. Home: 123 Australian Ave Palm Beach FL 33480 also Cherrycroft Burt NY Office: South County Rd Palm Beach FL 33480 also Pan Am Bldg 200 Park Ave New York NY

CROTTY, KATHLEEN, writer, journalist, reporter, editor; b. Chgo., Nov. 28, 1938; d. William Allen and Loretto Claire (O'Hayer) Crotty; children—Terrence, Lisabeth, Bradford, Lance. A.S., U. Detroit, 1956-57; postgrad. Wayne State U., 1957-58, Baylor U., 1963-64, U. Houston, 1965-68. Airline hostess Capital Airlines, Washington, 1959-60; asst. to producer The Jam Handy Corp., Detroit, 1960, The Nancy Ames Show, Houston, 1972; corr. Suburbia-Reporter Newspapers, Houston, 1978-80; sr. editor, cont. writer Pioneer Publs., Houston, 1980-83; free-lance writer, journalist. Author/editor: The Story of The American Oil Industry-Brine to Bonanza, 1981, Houston: A History of Its Business, Industry & Port, 1982; editor: Our Mother's Pearls (book of poetry), 1983. Mem. Rice Bus. and Profl. Women's Assn. Roman Catholic. Club: Clipt Wings (past pres.). Avocations: reading; writing; needlepoint; phys. fitness.

CROUCH, DANEE MILLER, writer; b. Abilene, Tex., Jan. 15, 1935; d. Alex Jefferson and Alma (Phillips) Miller; m. David M. Crouch, Dec. 26, 1957; children—Kathy, Cindy, Mary Claire, John. B.Journalism, U. Tex.-Austin, 1957; postgrad. Trinity U., San Antonio, 1982-83. Mag. asst. editor Pipe Line Industry, Houston, 1957; reporter Galveston Tribune (Tex.), 1957-58; tchr. Ball High Sch., Galveston, 1958-69; faculty Our Lady of the Lake U., San Antonio, 1963-64; free lance writer, author articles, newsletters, orgn. publicity, 1968—; author, producer children's TV show, 1981. Elder, Covenant Presbyterian Ch., San Antonio, 1982-84; mem. PTA bds., 1968-80 (3 service awards); bd. dirs. San Antonio Urban Council, 1984. Winner short story contest SW Writers' Conf., 1975. Mem. Women in Communication, San Antonio Calligraphers' Guild, San Antonio Symphony League, Tex. Med. Assn. Aux. (state com. chmn. 1982-83), Bexar County Med. Soc. Aux. Republican. Home: 304 Happy Trail San Antonio TX 78231

CROUCH, DOROTHY RUTH, publishing company executive; b. Bridgeport, Conn., Nov. 28, 1940; d. William M. and Dorothy R. (Miller) C. A.A., Stephens Coll., 1959; B.S., Miami U., Oxford, Ohio, 1961. Expediter customer service Equity Paper Co., Bridgeport, 1961-63; adminstrv. trainee Gen. Dynamics Electronics, Rochester, N.Y., 1963; sr. prodn. editor Prentice-Hall, Inc., Englewood Cliffs, N.J., 1964-70; mng. editor Warner Books, Inc., N.Y.C., 1970-73, v.p. prodn., 1973-74, v.p., gen. mgr., 1974—, dir. internat. mktg. Warner Publisher Services, Inc., v.p. internat., 1980—. Mem. NOW (past officer N.Y.C. chpt.), Am. Arbitration Assn., Assn. Am. Pubs. (past officer, 1974-78), Republican. Episcopalian. Club: Saint Anthony's (N.Y.C.). Contbr. articles to popular mags. Office: Warner Publishing Inc 666 Fifth Ave New York NY 10103

CROUCH, EVELYN, nurse, educator; b. Ponce, P.R., May 18, 1945; d. Everett Irvin and Juanita Victoria (Ruiz) C.; diploma St. Luke's Epis. Sch. Nursing, 1966; B.S.N. cum laude, Cath. U. P.R., 1972; M.S.N., U. Tex., Austin, 1978, postgrad., 1981—; m. Julio M. Rivera, Aug. 8, 1970; children—Evelyn Aixa, Julio Irvin, Alex Raul. Staff clin. nurse St. Luke's Episcopal Hosp., Ponce, P.R., 1966-67; clin. nurse Columbia Presbyn. Med. Center, N.Y.C., 1967-69; pvt. duty nurse, Ponce, 1969-72; nursing instr. Cath. U. P.R., Ponce, 1972-80, prof. Grad. Sch. Nursing, 1983—; clin. nurse USPHS Hosp., Houston, 1980-81; asst. instr. U. Tex., Austin, 1981-82; cons. labor and delivery Castaner (P.R.) Hosp., Damas Hosp., Ponce, P.R., 1978-80; dir. cultural and social activities Delicias, Ponce, P.R., 1980; chmn. recruitment Coll. Profl. Nurses, Ponce, 1979-80; coordinator Assoc. Degree Nursing Program, Regional Coll., Ponce, 1980. Mem. Nat. League Nursing, Assn. Nurses Grad. Sch. (research rep.), Coll. Profl. Nurses P.R. Democrat. Episcopalian. Home: BE-33 4th St Urb Las Delicias Ponce PR 00731 Office: Cath Univ PR Dept Nursing Ave Las Americas Ponce PR

CROUCH, JANICE MARIE, nurse; b. Akron, Ohio, July 31, 1931; d. Richard Munford and Grace (Highwarden) Munford Williams; m. Eric Jason Crouch (div. Oct. 1979). Diploma Columbia Hosp. (S.C.), 1952; student U. D.C., 1960—. R.N., S.C., Pa., D.C. Supr. operating room Spartanburg Gen. Hosp. (S.C.), 1952-53; charge nurse Montifore Hosp., Pitts., 1953-56; asst. head nurse Washington Hosp. Ctr., 1957-63; tchr. D.C. Pub. Schs., 1963-80, nursing coordinator, 1980—; mem. D.C. Statewide Health Coordinating Council, 1981-82. Recipient Mary McLeod Bethune Centennial award Nat. Council Negro Women. Mem. Nat. Black, Nurses Assn. (D.C. chpt. organizer 1978), Nat. Assn. Practical Nurses (sec. educators' council 1983-84), D.C. Vocat. Assn. (sec. 1978—), Columbia Hosp. Alumnae of S.C. (founder, pres. D.C. chpt.), Coalition of Health Advocates, Chi Eta Phi (chpt. Sisterhood award 1977). Office: DC Pub Sch 27 O St NW Washington DC 20020

CROUCH, MADGE LOUISE, government official; b. Winston-Salem, N.C., Sept. 21, 1919; d. Amos C. and Emma Jane (Griffith) C. Diploma Bklyn. Meth. Hosp. Sch. Nursing, 1941; B.S., Columbia U., 1947; M.A., George Washington U., 1961. Mem. faculty Meth. Hosp. Sch. Nursing, Bklyn., 1941-43, 47-48; asst. dir., nat. dir. nursing blood program ARC, Washington, 1948-65; br. dir. blood and blood products, dept. dir. div. biologics evaluation Bur. Biologics, FDA, Washington, 1965-82, dept. dir. Office Biologics, Center Drugs and Biologics, 1982—. Served with USNR, 1943-46. Recipient Commendable awards FDA, 1974, 77, Pfizer Meml. award, 1961; Legis. fellow, 1982. Mem. Internat. Soc. Blood Transfusion. Office: 8800 Rockville Pike Bethesda MD 20892

CROUCH, NANCY LOUISE, janitorial service company executive; b. Dallas, Sept. 19, 1942; d. Herman Edward and Virginia Lee (Nichols) Canada; m. Ben Michael Crouch, June 4, 1965; children—Caren Elaine, Amy Lynn. B.A., Baylor U., 1965; M.A., So. Ill. U., 1971. Cert. tchr. secondary sch., Tex. Tchr. English, Latin University High Sch., Waco, Tex., 1965-66; tchr. English Monterey High Sch., Lubbock, Tex., 1966-68; teaching asst. So. Ill. U., Carbondale, 1968-72; instr. composition Tex. A&M U., College Station, 1973-77, Blinn Coll., Bryan, Tex., 1977-80; pres. Celerity, Inc., College Station, 1977—; editor, cons. Brazosland Realty, Bryan, 1977-82, Tex. Water Resources Inst., College Station, 1978-84. Chmn. Mother's March on Birth Defects, Bryan and College Station, 1983, Small Bus. Council, Bryan and College Station, 1983; mem. Brazos Beautiful, 1984—, Better Bus. Bur., 1984—. Mem. Bldg. Services Contractors Assn., Am. Bus. Women's Assn. (pres., 1979-80, rec. sec. 1981-82; named Woman of Yr. 1983), Bryan and College Station C. of C. (comml. v.p. 1984, treas. 1985), Brazos Valley Art League (pres. 1974). Club: TAMU Women's Social (v.p. 1972-73, sec. 1973-74) (College Station). Home: 8700 Appomattox College Station TX 77840 Office: Home Care Services 109 Cooner College Station TX 77840

CROUCH, SOFIA CASTRO, state official, consultant, researcher; b. Lingayen, Philippines, May 11, 1931; d. Ignacio Asara-Cruz and Maria Consolacion (Bravo) Castro; came to U.S., 1951; m. Harvey Jesse Crouch, Sept. 27, 1972. B.S., Ga. State Coll. for Women, 1952; M.Ed., U. Ga., 1953, D.Ed., 1965. Dean of edn. Visayan Central Coll., Iloilo City, Philippines, 1954-63; supr. Glynn County Bd. Edn., Brunswick, Ga., 1966-68; coordinator research 9th Dist. Services Ctr., Cleveland, Ga., 1968-73; researcher Atlanta Bd. Edn., 1973-75; grant project dir. Ga. Dept. Human Resources, Atlanta, 1977—. Vol. United Way, Atlanta, 1973-76, Wyche Fowler Campaign Com., Atlanta, 1974-82, Joe Frank Harris for Gov. Com., Atlanta, 1982; del. Internat. Assembly, Williamsburg, Va., 1964. Mem. Ga. Assn. Educators (pub. relations com. 1969-71), Ga. Council Adminstrs. Spl. Edn., Assn. Suprs. and Curriculum Dirs., Atlanta Bd. Realtors, Phi Kappa Phi, Kappa Delta. Democrat. Roman Catholic. Club: Homemakers (Sandy Springs, Ga.). Lodges: Rotary Internat. (scholar 1951-53), Sandy Springs Rotary (named Lady of Yr. 1981). Home: 16755 Morris Rd Alpharetta GA 30201 Office: Profl Services Ga Retardation Ctr 4770 N Peachtree Rd Atlanta GA 30338

CROUSE, JEANNE CLARE, general contractor; b. Hartford, Conn., July 1, 1949; d. Murray Stuart and Dorothy Marie (Miller) Crouse; children—Jennifer, Michael. B.A., Goucher Coll., 1971; M.F.A., U. Ky., 1972. Adminstrv. asst. L.B. Swan & Assocs., West Hartford, Conn., 1974-76; project mgr. W.T. Whale Co., Wethersfield, Conn., 1976-81; founder, pres. Merit Constrn., Inc. West Hartford, 1981—. Mem. Assn. Builders and Contractors, Bldg. Owners and Mgrs. Assn., Constrn. Specifications Inst., Assn. Entrepreneurial Women. Club: Goucher Coll. Alumnae (pres.). Avocations: sailing; traveling.

CROUT, ELEANOR MUECKE (MRS. G. STANLEY CROUT), civic worker; d. Berthold Muecke, Jr. and Eleanor B. Thalmann; B.A., Mt. Holyoke Coll., 1959; M.A., Columbia, 1960; children—Alexandra Lynn, Stephen Andrew, Charles Merrill. Tchr., Walnut Hill Sch., Natick, Mass., 1960; DeWitt Clinton High Sch., Bronx, N.Y.C., 1961-62. Mem. Jr. Welfare Assn., Santa Fe, 1962-68, program chmn., 1963-64, treas., 1964-65, pres., 1965-66, pub. relations chmn., 1967-68; chmn. Community Christmas Store, Santa Fe, 1965; co-chmn. ticket sales Heart Fund Benefit, 1969; active March of Dimes drive, 1964, Heart Fund, 1965, Am. Cancer Soc. Drive, 1969, United Way, 1983-85; mem. St. Vincent Hosp. Aux., 1967-68, chmn. com., benefit, 1965, 69; mem. Santa Fe Council Internat. Relations, 1968-80; chmn. Girl Scout Expn., 1972. Bd. dirs. Jr. Welfare Assn., 1964-68, Girl's Club, 1965-66, 79-86, Shelter Care for Youth, 1982-84; bd. dirs., chmn. personnel services Sangre de Cristo council Girl Scouts U.S.A., 1972-75; bd. dirs. St. Michael's High Sch., Santa Fe, 1975-77; coordinator City Elementary Sch. Competitive Swimming Program, 1973-79. Mem. Mt. Holyoke Alumnae Assn., Delta Kappa Pi, Phi Lambda Theta. Club: Santa Fe Garden (co-chmn. house and garden tours 1972, sec. 1974-75, dir. 1972-76, publicity chmn. 1974-76). Episcopalian. Address: 32 Old Arroya Chamisa Rd Santa Fe NM 875051

CROW, ELIZABETH SMITH, editor; b. N.Y.C., July 29, 1946; d. Harrison Venture and Marlis (deGreve) Smith; B.A., Mills Coll., 1968; postgrad. Brown U., 1969-70; m. Charles P. Crow, Mar. 2, 1974; children—Samuel Harrison, Rachel Venture. Editorial asst. New Yorker mag., N.Y.C., 1968-69; exec. editor New York mag., N.Y.C., 1970-78; editor-in-chief Parents mag., N.Y.C., 1978—; v.p., co-founder Editors' Organizing Com.; screener Nat. Mag. Awards, 1981—; freelance book reviewer Washington Post, N.Y. Times; video and computer software reviewer Video Rev. Mag., 1983—. Mem. Am. Soc. Mag. Editors (mem. exec. com. 1984—), Womens Media Group. Democrat. Club: Cosmopolitan. Office: Parents Magazine 685 3d Ave New York NY 10017

CROW, ROBERTA W., retail human resources administrator, consultant; b. Long View, Tex., Oct. 31, 1950; d. George Clifford and Marie (Mitchell) C. Student U. Ala., 1968-70; A.A.S. in Fine Arts-Drama, Music, Am. Musical & Dramatic Acad., N.Y.C., 1972. Cert. personnel cons., Nat. Assn. Personnel Cons. Exec. trainee/retail merchandising and mgmt. Bergdorf-Goodman, N.Y.C.; account exec., cons. Lawrence Agy., N.Y.C., 1974-77; store mgr., dist. sales mgr. Career House, Bensalem, Pa. and N.Y.C., 1977-82; dir. research and recruting Retail Recruiters, Internat., N.Y.C., 1982-83; dir. exec. search/retail and mfg. Lloyd Cons., Inc., N.Y.C. and Chgo., 1983-85; dir. human resources R.P. McCoy Apparel, Ltd. dba Labels for Less, N.Y.C., 1985—; pvt. practice venture capital and human resources consulting, N.Y.C., 1985—; ind. cons. Donaldson, Lufkin & Jenrette, N.Y.C., 1985; guest lectr. Lab. Inst. Tech., N.Y.C., 1985—. Mem. Nat. Assn. Female Execs., Nat. Assn. Personnel Cons., Am. Mgmt. Assn. Democrat. Episcopalian. Avocations: attending theatre and concerts; internat. traveling; study of foreign cultures and languages.

CROW, SHERRY RUTH, librarian; b. WaKeeney, Kans., July 31, 1957; d. Robert Lester and Rosemary (Noah) Hillman; m. Steven Charles Crow, Dec. 17, 1977. B.S. in Elem. Edn. summa cum laude, Ft. Hays State U., 1977; M.L.S., Brigham Young U., 1983. Cert. tchr., Utah, Kans., pub. librarian, N.J. Head children's dept. Hays Pub. Library (Kans.), 1978-82; library intern Farrer Jr. High Sch., Provo, Utah, 1982-83; young adult-adult librarian West Milford Twp. Library (N.J.), 1983—; instr. Ft. Hays State U., Hays, Kans., 1980-82. Mem. ALA, Kans. Library Assn. (sec.-treas. jr. mems. roundtable 1981-82, pres. children's sect. 1982), Beta Phi Mu. Mem. Ch. of Nazarene. Home: Rural Route 6 Box 393 Sussex NJ 07461 Office: West Milford Twp Library Union Valley Rd West Milford NJ 07480

CROWDER, BARBARA LYNN, lawyer; b. Mattoon, Ill., Feb. 3, 1956; d. Robert Dale and Martha Elizabeth (Harrison) C.; m. Lawrence Owen Taliana, Apr. 17, 1982; children—Paul Joseph, Robert Lawrence. B.A., U. Ill., 1978, J.D., 1981. Bar: Ill. 1981. Assoc., Louis E. Olivero, Peru, Ill., 1981-82; asst. state's atty. Madison County (Ill.), Edwardsville, 1982-84; ptnr. Robbins & Crowder, 1985—. Mem. Edwardsville Plan Commn., Edwardsville Zoning Bd. Appeals. Named Best Oral Advocate, Moot Ct. Bd., 1979; recipient Parliamentary Debate award U. Ill., 1978; named Outstanding Sr., Phi Alpha Delta, 1981. Mem. Ill. Bar Assn., ABA, Am. Trial Lawyers Assn., Women Lawyers Assn. Metro-East (v.p. 1985), Edwardsville Bus. and Profl. Women. Democrat. Home: 982 Surrey Dr Edwardsville IL 62025 Office: 1538-D Troy Rd Edwardsville IL 62025

CROWDER, MARIE ANN, systems analyst, accountant; b. Pensacola, Fla., Sept. 27, 1948; d. Walter Eugene and Loraine (Bryant) Mitchell; m. J. Elliott Crowder; children—Sedrick Wales, Roslyn Nicole. A.A., Pensacola Jr. Coll., 1977; B.A., U. W. Fla., 1979, M.B.A., 1981. Mfg. asst. Monsanto Co., Pensacola, Fla., 1970-73, purchasing asst., 1974-76, gen. acctg. clk., 1977-78, cost acctg. clk., 1979-80, process systems analyst, 1981-82, adminstrv. systems analyst, 1983—. Advisor, Jr. Achievement of N.W. Fla., Pensacola, 1983, cons., 1985. Mem. Data Processing Mgmt. Assn., Am. Mgmt. Assn., Nat. Assn. Female Execs., Am. Soc. Women Accts. (dir. 1983-85, program com. chmn. 1986-87), Alpha Kappa Alpha (fin. sec. 1986); Alpha Wives Assn. Avocations: reading; tennis; interior decorating. Home: 8329 Pilgrim Rd Pensacola FL 32514 Office: Monsanto Co PO Box 12830 Pensacola FL 32575

CROWE, KAREN LYNN, rental car executive; b. Atlanta, Aug. 18, 1956; d. Dan Franklin and Sara Amanda (Huggins) Fowler; m. Joseph Timothy Crowe, July 22, 1978. B.S., Ga. Southwestern U., 1974. Resident advisor Ga. South Western Coll., Americus, 1975-77; intern Ga. State Dept. Human Resources, Americus, 1977; registrar, instr. Gupton Jones Coll., Atlanta, 1978; rental rep. Hertz, Atlanta, 1979, stolen conversion adminstr., 1979-80, fleet adminstr., 1981-85, spl. projects mgr., 1986—. Baptist. Club: Atlanta Track. Home: PO Box 1073 Fayetteville GA 30214 Office: Hertz Rent A Car 3420 Normanberry Dr Atlanta GA 30354

CROWELL, PEARL TROUTZ, summer resort exec.; b. Clay County, Mo., Nov. 7, 1908; d. James Walter and Carrie Lottie Rose (Vanderhoef) Troutz; student William Jewell Coll., 1926-27, Kansas City Art Inst., 1927-29, Purdue U. seminars, 1941-60; m. Wilbur Gale Crowell, Feb. 10, 1934 (dec. 1977); children—Gayle Ann Crowell Boyer, James Elliott. Owner-operator Crestwood Flowers, Kansas City, Mo., 1934-42; farmer, 1942-82; owner-operator Big Chief Lodge, Monticello, Ind., 1957—; real estate salesperson, Burnettsville and Monticello. Democratic precinct committeeman, 1948-72; bd. dirs. White County Hosp. Aux., 1954—. Mem. Monticello C. of C. (dir. 1970-82). Mem. Ch. of Christ. Clubs: Adams Home Econs. (past pres.), Bus. and Profl., Monticello Women of Moose, Twin Lakes Senior Citizen, Carroll County Democratic Women's. Address: Big Chief Lodge 207 Indiana Beach Rd Monticello IN 47960 also Rural Route 1 Burnettsville IN 47926

CROWLEY, CASSANDRA ANN, ballet company administrator, choreographer; b. Tacoma, Wash., Nov. 3, 1949; d. James Lewis and Ann (Bossert) C. B.A. in Comparative Arts, U. Puget Sound., 1976; M.A. in Dance, Butler U., 1977. Dancer Ljubljana Ballet, Yugoslavia, 1971-74; acting artistic dir. Wilkes-Barre Ballet Theatre, Pa., 1978-79; ballet mistress Lexington Ballet, Ky., 1979-80; sch. dir. Canton Ballet, Ohio, 1980-81, artistic dir., 1981—. Mem. Nat. Assn. for Regional Ballet (bd. dirs. 1984—), Northeast Regional Ballet Assn. (coordinator 1984—), Dance Ohio, Canton Art Inst., Palace Theater Assn. Republican. Avocations: foreign languages; thoroughbred industry; travel; Slavic countries. Office: Canton Ballet 1001 Market Ave N Canton OH 44702

CROWLEY, MARY JO (HUME), newspaper librarian; b. Owosso, Mich., Jan. 19, 1944; d. Robert Arthur and Mary Helen (Iverson) Hume; m. James Michael Crowley, Aug. 20, 1971 (div. Aug. 1985); children—David Michael, Benjamin Thomas. B.A., Mich. State U., 1966; M.L.S., U. Mich., 1971. Librarian, Emmons Jr. High Sch., Mishawaka, Ind., 1971-72, St. Francis High Sch., S.I., 1972-75, 78, 79; reference librarian St. John's U., S.I., N.Y., 1980-81; library dir. Phila. Newspaper Inc., 1983—. Pres., Children's Harbor Parent Cooperative Preschool, 1979-80; pres., bd. dirs. Greene Towne Montessori Preschool, Phila., 1982-83. Mem. Spl. Library Assn., World Affairs Council Phila., Assn. for Info. and Image Mgmt., U. Mich. Library Alumni Assn., Youth for Understanding. Roman Catholic. Office: Philadelphia Newspapers Inc 400 N Broad St Philadelphia PA 19101

CROWLEY, SUSAN, public affairs executive; b. Bayonne, N.J., Dec. 19, 1947; d. Robert Richard and June Margaret (Mulhearn) Bauman; m. Patrick Riley Crowley, June 6, 1970. B.A., Rollins Coll., 1969. Buyer, Allied Stores Corp., N.Y.C., 1971-73; assoc. editor Clothes Mag., N.Y.C., 1973-75; asst. to planning mgr. Citibank, Caracas, Venezuela, 1975-76; sr. editor Retail Week Mag., N.Y.C., 1977-81; mgr. pub. affairs analysis Merck & Co., Inc., Rahway, N.J., 1981—. Republican. Office: Merck & Co Inc PO Box 2000 Bldg 32 51 Rahway NJ 07052

CROWN, ROBERTA, artist, educator; b. N.Y.C., Sept. 9, 1946; d. Louis and Sophia (Siegal) C. B.A., Queens Coll., M.A., 1970. Art tchr. N.Y. Bd. Edn., N.Y.C., 1969—. Group shows include: Air Naval Res. Show (1st prize oils, 3d prize watercolors), 1969, Citibank, N.Y.C., 1976, Bklyn. Coll. (2d prize oils), 1978, Women in the Arts Gallery, N.Y.C., 1979, Contemporary Arts Ctr., New Orleans, 1980, Parnassus Gallery, Woodstock, N.Y., 1980, Gallery 14, Copenhagen 1980, Internat. Women's Art Festival, Copenhagen, 1980, Newhouse Gallery, S.I., N.Y., 1981, Garcia Gallery, Bronx, N.Y., 1983, Cork Gallery, N.Y.C., 1984, City Gallery, N.Y.C., 1984, Franklin Furnace, N.Y.C., 1984, Queens Mus., Flushing, N.Y., 1984; one-woman show: Andalusia Arts, Inc. Gallery, N.Y.C., 1974. Mem. Women in the Arts Found., Inc. (exec. coordinator 1980—), Women Caucus in Art, N.Y. State Assn. Tchrs. Art.

CROWNINGSHIELD, SHARON KAY, savings and loan executive; b. Cedar Rapids, Iowa, Dec. 1, 1948; d. Marvin John Henry and Maxine Harriet (Barlow) Rathje; student in acctg. Mesa Jr. Coll., 1974-75; m. Gary Crowningshield, Sept. 9, 1967; children—Scott, Vicki. With Home Fed. Savs. & Loan Assn., San Diego, 1968—, mgr., 1974—, v.p., 1980—, asst. controller, 1980-83, mem. polit. action coms. for fed. and state, 1980—. Mem. Fin. Mgrs. Soc. for Savs. and Loan Assn. (chpt. pres. 1985-86). Office: 5565 Morehouse Dr San Diego CA 92121

CROWSON, BONNIE LOU, dental assisting educator; b. St. John's, Mich., July 9, 1949; d. Forest Charles and Dorothy Kathleene (Williams) Kremer; m. Walter Collon Crowson, Nov. 30, 1974; 1 stepchild, Jony Collon. A.A.S., Ferris State Coll., 1969; B.S., U. Mich., 1979; M. Secondary Sch. Adminstrn., Mich. State U., 1983. Registered dental asst., Mich. Supr. dental aux. utilization program U. Mich., Ann Arbor, 1969-71; dental asst. educator Northwest Oakland Vocat. Ctr., Clarkston, Mich., 1971-82, Southeast Oakland Vocat. Ctr., Royal Oak, Mich., 1982—; cons. Warren Consol. Schs., Mich., 1973-74, Livonia Pub. Schs., Mich., 1976-77. Author: (with others) State Performance Objectives for Secondary Dental Asst. Programs, 1973, Dental Glossary Workbook, 1973, Guidelines for Dental Asst., 1974. Mem. Am. Dental Assts. Assn. (treas. 1971, sec. 1972, pres. elect 1973, pres. 1974). Health Occupations Educators, Mich. Edn. Assn., NEA. Republican. Methodist. Clubs: Birmingham Power Squadron, Detroit Boat. Home: 1970 Graefield St Birmingham MI 48008

CROXFORD, LYNNE LOUISE, social services adminstr.; b. Schenectady, N.Y., Nov. 9, 1947; d. Frederick William and Elizabeth Elger (Irish) C.; B.A., Kalamazoo Coll., 1969; M.P.A., Wayne State U., 1975; m. Daniel Roderick Talhelm; 2 children, Alan Frederick, Thomas Arthur. Caseworker dept. social service County of Calhoun, Battle Creek, Mich., 1969-70; caseworker, supr. County of Oakland, Pontiac, Mich., 1970-76; program specialist Mich. Dept. Social Services, Lansing, 1976-78; exec. coordinator for programming Mich. State Planning Council for Devel. Disabilities, 1978-79; staff coordinator Gov. Com. on Unification of Public Mental Health System, Lansing, 1979-80; dir. dept. social service County of Ingham, Lansing, 1980—; adv. Mich. Assn. Non-Profit Residential Facilities, 1976-78. Trustee, Unitarian Universalist Ch. of Greater Lansing, 1979-82, v.p., 1980-82; bd. dirs. Council for Prevention Child Abuse and Neglect, 1980-83; mem. Lansing Tri-County Pvt. Industry Council, 1980—. Mem. Am. Soc. Public Adminstrn. (nat. council 1986—), Am. Pub. Welfare Assn., Michigan County Social Services Assn. Club: Zonta (charter Mich. Capitol area). Contbr. in field. Home: 531 Gainsborough Dr East Lansing MI 48823 Office: 5303 S Cedar St Lansing MI 48910

CROYLE, BARBARA ANN, transportation/service company executive; b. Knoxville, Tenn., Oct. 22, 1949; d. Charles Evans and Myrtle Elizabeth (Kellam) C.; B.A. cum laude in Sociology, Coll. William and Mary, 1971; cert. corp. tax and securities law Inst. Paralegal Tng., 1971; J.D., U. Colo., 1975; cert. program mgmt. devel. Colo. Women's Coll., 1980; M.B.A., U. Denver, 1983. Bar: Colo. 1976. Paralegal firm Holland & Hart, Denver, 1972-73; law clk. Colo. Ct. Appeals, Denver, summer 1976; assoc. firm Shaw Spangler & Roth, Denver, 1976-77; with Petro-Lewis Corp., Denver, after 1977, mgr. acquisitions/lands; now mgr. strategic planning Westinghouse, Transp. Div. tchr. oil and gas law Colo. Paralegal Inst., 1978, 79; arbitrator Am. Arbitration Assn.; vol. arbitrator Better Bus. Bur. Bd. dirs., vol. mediator Denver Center Dispute Resolution; bd. dirs. Women and Bus. Enterprises, Inc.; vol. Legal Info. Center, YWCA-Colo. Women's Bar. Recipient Community Services award Petro-Lewis Corp., 1981. Mem. Am. Bar Assn., Colo. Bar Assn., Denver Bar Assn., Colo. Women's Bar Assn., Exec. and Profl. Women's Council, Denver Assn. Petroleum Landmen, Nat. Assn. Female Execs. Home: PO Box 128 Verona PA 15147 Office: 1501 Lebanon Church Rd Pittsburgh PA 15147

CROZIER, PRUDENCE SLITOR, economist; b. Boston, Oct. 27, 1940; d. Richard Eaton and Louise (Bean) S.; m. William Marshall Crozier, Jr., June 20, 1964; children—Matthew Eaton, Abigail Parsons, Patience Wells. B.A. with honors, Wellesley Coll., 1962; M.A. in Econs., Yale U., 1963; Ph.D. in Econs., Harvard U., 1971. Research asst. Fed. Reserve Bank, Boston, 1963-64; teaching fellow-tutor Harvard U., Cambridge, Mass., 1966-69; instr. Wellesley Coll., Mass., 1969-70; sr. economist Data Resources Inc., Lexington, Mass., 1973-74; bd. dirs. Mass. Health and Ednl. Facilities Authority, 1985—, Omega Fund, 1984—. Contbr. article to profl. jour. Trustee Newton Wellesley Hosp., Mass., 1978—; overseer Center Research on Women, Wellesley, 1982-83;

trustee Wellesley Coll., 1980—. Mem. Am. Econ. Assn., Boston Econ. Club, Phi Beta Kappa. Home: 41 Ridge Hill Farm Rd Wellesley MA 02181

CRUIKSHANK, KAREN LOUISE, department store executive; b. Detroit, Nov. 24, 1946; d. Gilbert Wesley and Daisy Elizabeth (Bateman) Jacobson. B.S., Western Mich. U., 1968. Asst. buyer Hudson's, Detroit, 1968-71, div. sales mgr., 1971-73, buyer, 1973-81, mgr. exec. placement, 1981-84, dir. exec. placement and devel., 1984—. Mem. Am. Soc. Tng. and Devel. Republican. Presbyterian. Avocation: horses. Home: 8901 Allen Rd PO Box 249 Clarkston MI 48016 Office: Hudsons 1206 Woodward Detroit MI 48226

CRULL, ANNA WELCH, technical consultant, business analysis; b. Centerville, Miss., Oct. 30, 1934; d. George A. and Marian J. Welch; B.S., U. Miss., 1955; M.S., U. Mo., 1959; m. Carroll Marshall Crull, Dec. 18, 1954; children—Frank, Wayne. Mem. research and devel. staff Redstone Arsenal and instr. U. Ala., Huntsville, 1959-69; pres. Chem. Tech. Cons., Houston, 1970—; tech. and bus. cons. in separation sci. and membrane tech. Mem. Am. Chem. Soc., Soc. Petroleum Engrs., Am. Inst. Chem. Engrs., Nat. Water Supply Improvement Assn., Sigma Xi. Methodist. Author tech. and mktg. reports for chem. process industry; mng. editor newsletter Applied Genetic News, membrane/Separation Tech. News, Battery/EV Tech. News, Enhanced Energy Recovery News.

CRUM, KAY MCDONALD, marketing consultant; b. Greeneville, Tenn., Sept. 16, 1935; d. John Kidwell and Ina Frances (Reeser) McDonald; student Hiwassee Coll., 1954, Steed Bus. Coll., 1955, E. Tenn. State U., 1970-71, U. Tenn., 1977; m. Daniel R. Crum, Aug. 18, 1956; children—Debra Kay, Darren Russell, David Michael. Lic. in real estate and property mgmt. counselor, Tenn., N.C. With Formex div. Huyck Corp., Greeneville, 1961-81, mktg. communications mgr., 1977-79, mktg. communications mgr. forming and drying div., 1978-81; pres., owner CEI Mktg. Cons., cons. for bus. and fin., Greeneville, Tenn., 1981—; lectr. in field. Contbr. articles to profl. jours.

CRUM, NANCY L., credit union executive; b. Araphoe, Okla., July 22, 1918; d. Chester A. and Gertrude A. (Smith) Walker; m. Lee David Crum, Feb. 9, 1940 (dec. Jan. 1980); children—Robert L., Thomas R., Lana Dee Crum Berry, William I. Student Mooberry Sch. Bus., Brownsville, Tex., 1947-49. Sec. to prin. Brownsville High Sch., Tex., 1960-68; employee Tchrs.' Credit Union, Brownsville, 1968-73, pres., 1973—. Mem. Tex. Credit Union League (adv. dir. 1979—), Magic Valley Chpt. Credit Unions (pres. 1974-79), Pan Am. Round Table II (bd. dirs. 1972-76), Brownsville C. of C. Republican. Mem. Ch. of Christ. Office: Brownsville Tchrs Credit Union 2455 Price Rd Brownsville TX 78521

CRUMBAKER, MARY KATHRYN (MRS. WILLIAM GOODMAN WILLIAMSON), business educator; b. Gt. Falls, Mont.; d. Calvin and Kathryn Elizabeth (Harbaugh) Crumbaker; student U. Mont., 1939, Southwestern U. at Memphis, 1942-43, Whitman Coll., 1939-41; B.S., U. Oreg., 1946; postgrad. Hochschule for Music, Vienna, Austria, 1947-48; M.Ed., Oreg. State U., 1966; Ph.D., Nat. Christian U. Dallas, 1974; m. William Goodman Williamson, Dec. 17, 1941 (dec. Oct. 1970); children—James Calvin, Albert Jerome, Kathryn Erilda. Sec., exec. sec. Granada (Miss.) Elem. Sch., also U.S. C.E., 1941-44; substitute sec. U. Oreg., 1944-46; head comml. studies Internat. Trade Coll., Chgo., 1948-51; tchr. Mich. Dept. Rehab., Am. Legion Tb Hosp., Battle Creek, 1952-53; tchr. U.S. Army, Kokura, Japan, 1954-56; tchr. Clark Bus. Coll., Topeka, 1956-58; charm sch. dir., dir. tng. Eugene (Oreg.) Bus. Coll. 1959-70, mgr., corp. sec.-treas., 1970—, pres., 1974-85, prof. emeritus, 1986—; prof. bus. Eugene Coll. Bus. and Tech., 1985—; lectr., Am. econ. system and music Austro-Am. Soc., Vienna, 1946-48. Mem. exec. bd. S.W. Oreg. Mus. Sci. and Industry, 1972-75; den mother Oreg. Trail council Boy Scouts Am., 1959-69; chmn. West Univ. Neighborhood, 1981, 82; mem. Neighborhood Leaders Council, 1981; treas. Eugene WCTU, 1980-82; precinct committeeman Republican party, 1960—; pres. Central Lane Rep. Women, 1970; chmn. constn. and bylaws Lane County Council Orgns., 1985—; pres. Lane County WCTU, 1985—. Named Troop Mother of Yr. Boy Scouts Am., 1971. Mem. Nat. Fedn. Bus. and Profl. Women's Clubs, Oreg. Fedn. Bus. and Profl. Women (found. chmn. 1986—), Am. Bus. Women, Am. Inst. Profl. Cons., Rubicon Soc., Eugene Bus. and Profl. Women's Club (pres. 1966, 79), DAR, Daus. of Nile, Am. Forestry Assn., Nat. Rifle Assn., PEO (treas. chpt. H, 1986-87), AAUW, Beta Gamma Sigma, Mu Phi Epsilon. Clubs: Eugene City (life mem.), Zonta (pub. Newsletter 1984—), Dial (pres. Eugene 1973-74). Lodges: Order Eastern Star (musician), White Shrine of Jerusalem (musician), Order of Amaranth (musician; condr. 1982-83, royal matron 1984-85). Kiwanis (hon.). Author: Typing with Less Than 2 Hands, 1962. Home: 1031 Mill St Eugene OR 97401 Office: 383 E 11th St Eugene OR 97401

CRUMBO, MINISA, artist; b. Tulsa, Sept. 2, 1942: d. Woodrow and Lillian (Hogue) C.; student Tex. Western U., El Paso, 1961-62, U. Colo., Boulder, 1970-71, Taos (N.Mex.) Acad. Fine Arts, 1972-74, Sch. Visual Arts, N.Y.C., 1974-75, Wasatch (Utah) Acad.; children—Woody Carter, Chris Carter. One-woman shows: Gilcrease Inst. Am. History and Art, Tulsa, 1976, Tulsey Town Gallery, Tulsa, 1975, USSR, 1978-79, Roy Clark Ranch Party-TV Spl., 1976, Pottawatomie Agrl. and Cultural Center, Shawnee, Okla., 1977, Okla. Gov.'s Spl. Showing, 1976, Adobe Gallery, Las Vegas, 1977, traveling exhbn. Indian Art Show, U. Oreg., 1977; other exhbns.; Pushkin Mus., Moscow, Montreux (Switzerland) Jazz Festival, 1979, Harwelden, Tulsa, 1979, Oklahoma City U., 1981, Independence (Kans.) Community Coll., 1981, Native Am. Women in Art, Kans. Mus. History, 1984, Native Am. Women Show, Indian Ter. Gallery, Sapulpa, Okla., 1985; represented in permanent collections at Heard Mus., Phoenix, Gilcrease Inst. Am. History and Art, Philbrook Art Center, Tulsa, U. Tulsa Art Center, Pushkin Mus., Moscow, Wasatch Acad., Oklahoma City U., Baker U., Baldwin, Kans., Independence (Kans.) Community Coll., also pvt. collections in U.S. and Europe; guest artist instr. Taos Pueblo Day Sch. Center; designer, instr. Native Am. Studies program Wasatch Acad., Utah. Recipient Graphics award for pencil drawing Creek Woman, 29th Am. Indian Exhbn. at Philbrook Art Center; Disting. Alumni award Wasatch Acad., 1980; Disting. Service award Baker U., 1982. Mem. Native Am. Ch. Home: 515 N 2d St Independence KS 67301 Office: PO Box 4003 Beverly Hills CA 90213

CRUM DE GROOT, SUSAN LOUISE, school neuropsychologist; b. Queens, N.Y., Mar. 16, 1953; d. James Robert and Louise Madeline (Yaeger) Crum; B.S. in Psychology and Religion, Evangel Coll., 1975; M.A. in Psychology, Montclair State Coll., 1978; Ph.D., Rutgers U., 1986; cert. sch. psychologist, N.Y., N.J.; m. Bruce Anthony De Groot, Aug. 11, 1973; 1 son, Ross Hamilton. Vol. counselor, instr. Good Samaritan Boys Ranch, Springfield, N.J., 1975; income maintenance worker Passaic County (N.J.) Welfare Bd., 1975-76; grad. asst. psychology dept. Montclair (N.J.) State Coll., 1976-77, acting dir. second careers program, 1977; adj. Kean Coll., Union, N.J., 1978; devel. counselor Counseling Services, Nutley, N.J., 1977-78; coordinator career decision program Bergen Community Coll., Paramus, 1978-80; spl. agt. Prudential, Wayne, N.J., 1980-84; owner Oxford Ins. Agy., 1982-84; psychology intern Bergen Pines Hosp., Paramus, N.J., 1984-85; neuropsychology intern Warwick Valley Sch. Dist., Warwick, N.Y., 1985-86; school neuropsychologist Janet Lockwood Sch., Orange County Cerebral Palsy Assn., Goshen, N.Y., 1986—. Pres., Opponents of Hunger, 1970-71; patient companion Essex County Mental Hosp., 1971-72; vol. child aide St. Mary's Hosp., Passaic, N.J., 1976-77; vol. psychology intern Mt. Carmel Guild Outpatient Clinic, Newark. Mem. Am. Psychol. Assn. (assoc.), N.J. Coll. and Univ. Coalition Women's Edn., Assn. Adult Edn. N.J., Psi Chi. Mem. Assembly of God Ch. Home: 8 Mountainside Rd Ext Warwick NY 10990 Office: Janet Lockwood Sch Erie St Goshen NY

CRUMP, GEORGIA NELL, lawyer; b. Clarksville, Tex., Apr. 18, 1953; d. Givens Lindsay and Elza Murl (Hutchinson) C. A.B., Muhlenberg Coll., 1975; J.D., Baylor U., 1978; postgrad. U. London, 1974. Bar: Tex. 1978. Asst. city atty. City of McAllen, (Tex.), 1978-80; assoc. Ewers, Toothaker, McAllen, 1980-81; city atty. City of Edinburg (Tex.), 1981—. Vice pres. Rio Grande Valley Chorale, Edinburg, 1983-84, pres., 1984-85; founding mem. McAllen Organized for Pub. Service, 1981-83; block capt. Olde Town Neighborhood Assn., McAllen, 1981-84. Mem. ABA, State Bar Tex., Tex. City Attys. Assn., Nat. Inst. Mcpl. Law Officers, Hidalgo County Bar Assn. (dir. 1983-85, treas. 1982-83), Hidalgo County Young Lawyers Assn. Democrat. Clubs: Sierra, Audubon Soc. Home: 1208 Nyssa McAllen TX 78501 Office: City of Edinburg PO Box 1079 Edinburg TX 78540

CRUMP, SARAH DERRICK, advertising agency financial executive; b. Converse, La., Aug. 23, 1919; d. Samuel Holiday and Mable (Pearson) Derrick; m. Curtis Buren Crump, Dec. 24, 1936; 1 son, Lewis Buren (dec.). Student Tyler Comml. Coll., 1936-38, U. Wash.-Seattle, 1944-45. Co-owner franchise Gen. Foods Corp., Dallas, 1959-71; accountant Blalock Ins. Co., Shreveport, La., 1971-73; comptroller Robert K. Butcher Assocs., Inc., Shreveport, La., 1973—. Democrat. Southern Baptist.

CRUSE, IRMA BELLE RUSSELL, writer; b. Hackneyville, Ala., May 3, 1911; d. Charles Henry and Nellie Dunn (Ledbetter) Russell; student Birmingham-So. Coll., 1927-28; corr. student U. Chgo., U. Wis., U. Minn., intermittently 1958-68; A.B., U. Ala., 1976; M.A. in English, Samford U., M.A. in History, 1984; m. Jesse Clyde Cruse, Dec. 22, 1931; children—Allan Baird, Howard Russell. With So. Bell and successor South Central Bell, Birmingham, Ala., 1928-44, 54-76, pub. relations supr., 1965-68, rate supr., 1968-76; free lance writer, 1956—. Bd. dirs. Festival of Arts, Birmingham, 1970-73, Birmingham Council Christian Edn.; v.p. Birmingham Council Clubs, 1973-74; pres. Jefferson County Radio and TV Council, 1971-72; mem. Gov.'s Commn. Employment of Handicapped. Recipient numerous awards including Freedoms Found. award, 1967-69; named Beautiful Activist, 1972; nominated Women of Yr., Birmingham, 1971, 72, 74-76, 82, Woman of Achievement Met. Bus. and Profl. Women's Club, 1970-71. Mem. Birmingham Bus. Communicators, Ala. Writers' Conclave (pres. 1973-74), Birmingham Bus. and Profl. Women (pres. 1970-71), Women in Communications (pres. 1970-71), Birmingham Bus. Communicators (pres. 1968-69), Telephone Pioneers Am. (editor newsletter 1970-74), Ala. State Poetry Soc. (program chmn. 1972-74, editor newsletter 1976-78), Women's C. of C. (2d v.p. 1978—), Ala. Bapt. Hist. Commn., Freedoms Found. of Valley Forge, Birmingham Geneal. Soc., Salvation Army Women's Aux., Women's C. of C., Nat. Soc. Am. Pen Women, Sigma Tau Delta, Phi Kappa Phi, Phi Alpha Theta. Club: Quota of Birmingham (pres. 1976-77). Contbr. articles to various publs. Home: 136 Memory Ct Birmingham AL 35213

CRUTCHER, PAMELA PADWICK, advertising executive, public relations specialist; b. Columbus, Ohio, June 13, 1943; d. James William and Tiami Judith (Leighton) Bampton; m. Ryder Edwards McNeal, Oct. 16, 1965 (div.); children—Ryder Padwick, Darby Edwards; m. Walter Thomas Crutcher, Aug. 9, 1975; 1 child, Thomas Baber III. A.A., Dean Jr. Coll., 1963. Asst. dir. Louisville Central Area, 1973-76; dir. pub. relations and fund raising Louisville Sch. Art, 1976-78; owner, sec. Crutcher, Kelly and Assocs., Louisville, 1978-82, Translation Co., Louisville, 1980-82; owner, pres. TechniGraphics Inc., Louisville, 1983—. Bd. dirs. Art Ctr. Assn., Louisville, 1979-81; pub. relations cons. Ky. Opera Assn., Louisville, 1979-80. Mem. Jr. League Louisville, Am. Women in Radio and TV, Advt. Club Louisville. Democrat. Episcopalian. Club: Jefferson (Louisville). Avocations: sailing; snow skiing; antique collecting. Home: 501 Club Ln Louisville KY 40207 Office: TechniGraphics Inc 161 Chenoweth Ln Louisville KY 40207

CRUZ, ROSA ILEANA, physician, researcher; b. San Juan, P.R., Dec. 24, 1955; d. Carlos Daniel and Emilia Cruz. B.S. magna cum laude, U. P.R., 1976, M.D., 1980. Diplomate Am. Bd. Ob-Gyn. Intern ob-gyn U. P.R. Med. Scis. Campus, 1980-81, resident, 1981-84; reproductive endocrinology fellow dept. ob-gyn, Univ. Medicine and Dentistry, Rutgers Med. Sch., New Brunswick, N.J., 1984-85, reproductive endocrinology fellow and adj. instr., 1985—; cons. physician RESOLVE of Central N.J., 1984—; lectr. in field. Contbr. articles to profl. jours. Mem. Image: World St. chpt., 1985—. Mem. Am. Assn. Sexual Educators, Therapists & Counselors (P.R. chpt.), Am. Fertility Soc. (assoc.), Am. Coll. Ob-Gyn (jr. fellow), AMA, N.Y. Acad. Scis., Assn. Ex-Alumni of U. P.R. Med. Scis. Campus. Avocations: fishing; sailing; bowling; jogging; manual crafts. Home: 589 Trinidata St Bayamon Puerto Rico 00619 Office: UMDNJ-Rutgers Med Sch Acad Health Sci Ctr CN-19 New Brunswick NJ 08903

CSEH, ROSEMARY ANN, editor, writer; b. Akron, Ohio, May 27, 1952; d. John Augustus and Rose Sue (Zeller) Cseh. Cert., Instituto Tecnológico de Estudios Sudamericanos y Occidentales, Guadalajara, Mex., 1972; B.A., U. Akron, 1974; M.A., 1976. Freelance writer, Europe and U.S., 1977-78; editor, adminstrv. asst. Volair Ltd., Kent, Ohio, 1978-80; account exec. Flehinger Mktg., Akron, 1981, Threshold Advt., Akron, 1981-82; editor, writer Bill Communications, Akron, 1982—; freelance cons., Akron, 1978—. Contbr. articles to bus. publs. Mem. Women in Communications, Phi Sigma Alpha. Democrat. Office: Bill Communications Inc 110 N Miller Rd Akron OH 44313

CSENCSITS, CARLA M(ALACHOWSKI), investment company executive; b. Southington, Conn., Nov. 26, 1953; d. Carl Raymond and Jeanette Ann (Zoni) Malachowski; m. Frank J. Csencsits, Mar. 20, 1982; A.A., Endicott Jr. Coll., 1973; B.A. in History, Newton Coll./Boston Coll., 1975. Admissions rep. Katharine Gibbs Sch., Boston, 1977-79, cons., 1981; mgr. sales tng. and devel. Katharine Gibbs Sch. subs. Macmillan Inc., N.Y.C., 1979-81; mgr. mgmt. info. systems Fidelity Investments, Boston, 1982-85, dir. market mgmt., 1985—; speaker, panelist profl. assn. Mem. Am. Soc. Tng. and Devel., Nat. Assn. Securities Dealers. Office: Fidelity Investments 82 Devonshire St I7B Boston MA 02109

CSERESZNYE, GEORGINA MARIE, ednl. adminstr.; b. Detroit, June 27, 1944; d. George Armand and Dorothy Elizabeth (McKee) Daubresse; B.A., Eastern Mich. U., 1966, M.A., 1969; Ed.D., Wayne State U., Detroit, 1980; children—Lisa Marie, Renee Lynn. Mem. staff Wayne-Westland (Mich.) Community Schs., 1966-84, co-prin. P.D. Graham Elementary Sch., 1978-80, exec. asst. to supt. schs., 1980-84; asst. supt. instrn. Phoenix Union High Sch. Dist. (Ariz.), 1984—. Bd. dirs. Wayne-Westland Found.; v.p. Wayne-Westland Arts Assn., 1981-82. Mem. Nat. Assn. Sch. Prins., Mich. Assn. Sch. Adminstrs., Mich. Elementary and Middle Sch. Prins. Assn., Mich. Council Women Ednl. Adminstrn., Wayne C. of C., Alpha Delta Kappa, Phi Delta Kappa. Roman Catholic. Contbr. articles to profl. jours. Home: 4725 E LeMarche Ave Phoenix AZ 85032 Office: 2526 W Osborn Rd Phoenix AZ 85017

CUADRA, DOROTHY ELIZABETH, lawyer; b. Washington County, Kans., Dec. 5, 1932; d. Gilbert H. and Nan Ellen (Smith) Stanbrough; m. Emilio L. Cuadra, 1957 (div.); 1 dau., Dione Catherine. B.S. in Engring., UCLA, 1959, M.S. in Engring., 1965; J.D., U. Va., 1977. Bar: Alaska 1977, D.C. 1977, Va. 1977. Research engr. Marquardt Corp., Van Nuys, Calif., 1959-63; research engr. Boeing Co., Seattle, 1965-66; sr. research engr., cons. Wyle Labs., El Segundo, Calif., 1966-71; dep. for program devel. Office of Noise Control EPA, Washington, 1971-74; assoc. Robertson, Monagle & Eastaugh, P.C., Juneau, Alaska, 1977-84, bd. dirs., 1985—. Mem. Sci. Adv. Com. Alaska Eskimo Whaling Commn., 1980-82; pres. LWV, Juneau, 1981-82; bd. dirs. LWV, Alaska, 1984-85. Amelia Earhart Grad. fellow. Mem. ABA, Acoustical Soc. Am. (regional coordinator Alaska 1977-85), Alaska Bar Assn. Democrat. Jewish. Office: Robertson Monagle & Eastaugh PO Box 1211 Juneau AK 99802

CUDDY, MARIAN PAGE, editor; b. Covington, Ky., Aug. 23, 1943; d. Clyde R. and Marian G. (von Beushausen) Tipton; B.A., Ohio State U., 1962. Dir. subs. rights G.P. Putnam's Sons, N.Y.C., 1972-75; editor-in-chief, exec. v.p. Berkley Pub. Co., N.Y.C., 1975-78; asst. pub. Simon & Schuster, N.Y.C., 1978-79; sr. editor Avon Books, N.Y.C., 1979-82, v.p., editorial dirs., 1982—. Mem. Women's Media Group. Home: 34 Perry St New York NY 10014 Office: 1790 Broadway New York NY 10019

CUDLIPP, ALICE VERNER, health care executive; b. Richmond, Va., Nov. 1, 1941; d. Joseph Henry and Irene (Mills) C. B.A., Bridgewater Coll., Va., 1962; M.A., U. Richmond, 1968. Tchr., dept. head Chesterfield Pub. Schs., Va., 1967-71, Nansemond County Pub. Schs., Va., 1962-67; lectr. in residence U. Va., 1973-74; exec. v.p. Smithdeal Massey Coll., Richmond, 1975-78; asst. v.p. Columbia Hosp., Milw., 1982-84; pres., chief exec. officer Med. Placement Services Inc., Milw., 1984—; gen. ptnr. Courtland Ltd., Richmond, 1981—; cons. and lectr. in field. DuPont fellow U. Va., 1966; NSF grantee Longwood Coll., 1964. Mem. Columbia Coll. Nursing Alumni Assn. (chmn. 1984-85), Nat. League Nursing, Am. Mgmt. Assn., Phi Delta Epsilon, Alpha Psi Omega, Delta Kappa Gamma. Presbyterian. Club: YMCA (Brown Deer, Wis.). Office: Med Placement Services Inc 710 N Plankington Ave Milwaukee WI 53203

CULBERT, SANDRA KAY, interior designer, public relations consultant; b. Robinson, Ill., July 27, 1945; d. David Crockett and Alice Mae (Harmon) Carruth; m. James Richard Culbert, Dec. 29, 1976; children—Kimberlee Mae, Jennifer Lynn, Jami Rene. Student Ariz. State U., Tempe, 1970-73. Exec. sec., jr. acct. McDonald's Hamburgers, San Jose, Calif., 1965-69; office mgr. N.Y. Life Ins. Co., Scottsdale, Ariz., 1970-74; Realtor, relocation dir. Century 21 Real Estate, Scottsdale, 1974-76; owner, operator Badgeman 1978-82, SKC Designs, Mission Viejo, Calif., 1982—; adminstrv. dir., bus. cons., dir. Mr. Build, San Diego, 1983-85; public relations cons. Localpro Service corps, San Diego, 1985—. Leader Girl Scouts U.S.A., 10 yrs.; vol. worker Assn. for Retarded, San Diego, Human Soc., San Diego. Mem. Nat. Assn. Female Execs., Internat. Montessori Soc., LWV. Republican. Avocations: skeet shooting; tennis; horseback riding; travel. Home: 1627 Citrus Hills Ln Escondido CA 92027 Office: Localpro Service Corps 935 Pennsylvania Ave Escondico CA 92027

CULBERTSON, KATHERYN CAMPBELL, lawyer; b. Tom's Creek, Va., Aug. 14, 1920; d. Robert Fugate and Mary E.V. Campbell (Leonard) C.; B.S., E. Tenn. State U., 1940; B.S. in Library Sci., George Peabody Library Sch., 1942; J.D., YMCA Night Law Sch., 1968. Librarian, Bur. Ships Tech. Library, U.S. Navy Dept., Washington, 1945-49, 51-53; librarian Lincoln Elem. Sch., Kingsport, Tenn., 1949-50, 50-51; librarian Regional Library, Tenn. State Library and Archives, Johnson City, 1953-61; dir. extension services library Met. Govt. Nashville and Davidson County, 1961-71; Tenn. state librarian and archivist, 1972-82; admitted to Tenn. bar, 1969; since practiced in Nashville. Mem. library com. Pres.'s Com. Employment of Handicapped, 1966—; mem. library com. Nat. Bus. and Profl. Women's Found., 1968-70; pres. Tenn. Fedn. Bus. and Profl. Women's Clubs, Inc., 1974-75. Mem. Lawyers Assn. for Women, Tenn. Bar Assn., ALA, Southeastern Library Assn., Tenn. Library Assn., DAR. Republican. Club: Bus. and Profl. Women's (pres. Nashville 1970-71). Contbr. to Ency. of Edn. Office: 1506 Church St Suite 4 Nashville TN 37203

CULBREATH, ELIZABETH JOSEPHINE, chemical cleaning company executive; b. Portland, Tenn., Jan. 7, 1927; d. John Garnett and Ola (Hardin) White; student Vol. Community Coll., 1980-82; m. Bob R. Culbreath, Oct. 21, 1944; children—Georgia, Robert, Elizabeth Ann. Sec., A&P Tea Co., 1944-50; exec. sec. Indpls. Morris Plan, 1950-56; bookkeeper Whittington Fabricating Co., 1956-59; bookkeeper Imperial Fabricating Co., Portland, Tenn., 1964, sec.-treas., 1964—; sec.-treas. Imperial Chem. Cleaning, Inc., Portland, 1978—; partner, bookkeeper Culbreath Dairy Farms, Cottontown, Tenn., 1979—; acct. Fleet Design & Engring., Inc., Portland, 1980—; owner, operator E. J. C. Real Estate, Portland, 1981—; owner-ptnr. So. Fin. Resources, 1982—. Mem. civic adv. bd. Highland Hosp. Mem. Nat. Assn. Exec. Secs., Sumner County Bd. Realtors. Baptist. Clubs: Blue Grass Country, Silver Springs Country, Order Eastern Star. Home: Rural Route 2 Cottontown TN 37048 Office: PO Box 429 Portland TN 37148

CULL, BARBARA GOLDSTEIN, educational administrator, special education researcher; b. Los Angeles, Dec. 14, 1940; d. David and Miriam Pearl (Harmell) Goldstein; m. Gordon Bailey Cull, Apr. 6, 1964; children—Elizabeth, Jason. B.E., UCLA, 1964, M.Ed., 1975. Cert. elem. tchr., Calif.; cert. reading specialist, learning handicapped tchr., sch. adminstr. Ednl. therapist, Los Angeles, 1970-72; dir. ednl. therapy, adminstr., instr. Fernald Sch., UCLA, 1972-77; tchr. educator Grad. Sch. Edn., UCLA, 1977; adj. prof. Pepperdine U., Los Angeles, 1977-78; exec. dir. Ednl. Resource and Services Ctr., Beverly Hills, Calif., 1978—; mem. Calif. Spl. Edn. Commn., 1980-81. Mem. Calif. Assn. Ednl. Therapists, Calif. Assn. Neurologically Handicapped Children (pres. 1980-81), Beverly Hills C. of C., Phi Delta Kappa, Phi Lambda Theta. Democrat. Jewish. Avocations: collecting children's books and toys; reading; travel. Office: ERAS Ctr 9261 W 3d St Beverly Hills CA 90210

CULLEN, KARON NUNNALLY, public relations executive; b. Richmond, Va., Jan. 27, 1947; d. Moses Washington and Alice Maude (Emory) Nunnally; B.A., Mary Baldwin Coll., 1968; postgrad Radcliffe Coll. Pub. Sch., 1968. Dir. publicity Americana Hotels, Inc., N.Y.C., 1970-71; dir. public relations Princess Hotels Internat., N.Y.C., 1971-74; chmn. Cullen and Taylor, Ltd., N.Y.C., 1974-82; pres. Cullen and Casey, Ltd., N.Y.C., 1982-85; exec. v.p. Good Relations, Inc., N.Y.C., 1985—. Bd. dirs. Irvington House for Med. Research, N.Y.C.; co-chmn. spl. com. Manhattan Theatre Club, N.Y.C. Mem. Public Relations Soc. Am., Soc. Am. Travel Writers (sec. N.Y.C. chpt.), Pride and Alarm (public relations corp. leaders N.Y.C.). Club. Doubles (N.Y.C.). Office: Good Relations Inc 185 Madison Ave New York NY 10016

CULLEN, MARY RUTH, lawyer; b. Flagler, Colo., Dec. 9, 1954; d. Wiliam A. and Anna Lucy (Reed) Cullen. B.A. in History, U. Colo., 1978; J.D., U. Mich., 1981. Bar: Colo. 1982, U.S. Dist. Ct. Colo. 1982. Law clk. Hon. Richard C. McLean, 20th Jud. Dist., Boulder, Colo., 1982-83; assoc. firm Scates & Assocs., P.C., Aurora, Colo., 1984—. Mem. Phi Beta Kappa. Democrat. Office: Scates & Assocs PC 3025 S Parker Rd #229 Aurora CO 80014

CULLEN-RISKIN, BONNIE MAUREEN, advertising film company executive; b. Mineola, N.Y., Aug. 8, 1942; d. William Joseph and Sylvia Ethel (Tuomola) Cullen. B.A., Bucknell U., 1964; student N.Y. Sch. Interior Design, 1969-71. Mem. staff Radio/TV Traffic, Grey Advt. Co., N.Y.C., 1964-65; radio/TV traffic mgr. Carl Ally Advt. Co., N.Y.C., 1965-67; radio/TV bus. mgr. Scali, McCabe, Sloves, N.Y.C., 1967-73; sec.-treas., ptnr. Jerry Bender Editorial, N.Y.C., 1973—.

CULLINAN, PHYLLIS ANN, city clerk; b. Ottumwa, Iowa, Dec. 22, 1946; d. Donald Robert and Lois Levita (Saulsbury) McInerney; m. David Lee Cullinan, Sept. 14, 1968 (div. May 1975); children—Chris Robert, Hollie Ann. A.A., Ottumwa Heights Jr. Coll., 1967; cert. mcpl. clk. Internat. Inst. Mcpl. Clks., 1981. Clk. I City of Ottumwa, 1967-73, city clk., 1974—. Mem. Internat. Inst. Mcpl. Clks. Democrat. Roman Catholic. Avocation: sewing. Home: 1306 Locust Ottumwa IA 52501 Office: City of Ottumwa 105 E 3d St Ottumwa IA 52501

CULLINANE, MARILYN CORBETT, college administrator, consultant; b. N.Y.C., Nov. 28, 1930; d. John Joseph and Jean Frances (Kenny) Corbett; m. John William Cullinane, May 12, 1951; children—Jacqueline, Brian, Jeanne. B.A., Empire State Coll., 1976; M.A., L.I. U., 1978; M.A., M. Ed., Columbia U., 1981, 83, Ed.D., 1985. Interior designer, New City, N.Y., 1960-76; instr. psychology Mercy Coll., Dobbs Ferry, N.Y., 1978-82; psychol. counselor Rockland Community Coll., Suffern, N.Y., 1979-81, dir. life mgmt. skills, 1982-86, asst. dean, 1985—; cons. Krisland Group, Knoxville, Tenn., 1984-86, Inst. for Life Coping Skills, Inc., N.Y.C., 1981—; mentor Empire State Coll., Lower Hudson Div., 1980-86, Author program devel.: Your Evolving Self, 1985; (with others) Adkins Life Sklls Career Development Series, 1985. Recipient Profl. Contbr. award Ctr. for the Study of Higher Edn., Memphis State U., 1983. Mem. Am. Psychol. Assn., Am. Soc. Tng. and Devel., N.Y. State Assn. Two-Yr. Colls., Bus. and Profl. Women's Club, Avocations: antique collecting; gardening. Home: 26 Park Terr New City NY 10956 Office: Rockland Community Coll 105 Colege Rd Suffern NY 10901

CULLINGFORD, HATICE S., chemical engineer; b. Konya, Turkey, June 10, 1945; came to U.S., 1966, naturalized, 1971; d. Ahmet and Emine (Kadayifcioglu) Harmanci. Student Middle East Tech. U., 1962-66; B.S. with high honors, N.C. State U., 1969, Ph.D., 1974. Statis. clk. Research Triangle Inst., 1966; reactor engr. AEC, Washington, 1973-75; spl. asst. ERDA, Washington, 1975; mech. engr. Dept. Energy, Washington, 1975-78; staff mem. Los Alamos Nat. Lab., 1978-82; sci. cons., Houston, 1982-84; ECLSS test bed mgr. Johnson Space Ctr., NASA, Houston, 1984-85, sr. project engr. advanced tech. dept., 1985—; developer services or products; mem. internal adv. com. Ctr. for Nonlinear Studies Los Alamos Nat. Lab., 1981; organizer tech. workshops, sessions at society meetings; lectr. in field. Mem. U. N.Mex., Los Alamos curriculum review com., 1980. Recipient Woman's Badge, Tau Beta Pi, 1968, ERDA Spl. Achievement award, 1976; Inventor award Los Alamos Nat. Lab., 1982; Cities Service fellow, 1969-72. Mem. Am. Nuclear Soc. (sec.-treas. fusion energy div. 1982-84, vice chmn. South Tex. sect. 1984-86), Am. Inst. Chem. Engrs. (organizer, 1st chmn. No. N.Mex. club 1980-81, chmn. low-pressure processes and tech. 1981—), Am. Chem. Soc., Comml. Devel. Assn., Assn. Energy Engrs., Fusion Power Assocs., Internat. Assn. Hydrogen Energy, AIAA, Nat. Soc. Profl. Engrs., Soc. for Risk Analysis, Engrs. Council Houston (councilor, sec. energy com.), Sierra Club, Phi Kappa Phi, Pi Mu Epsilon. Club: No. N.Mex. Chem. Engrs. Club: Houston Orienteering. Editor, author tech. reports; contbr. articles to profl. jours.; inventor in field.

CULLOM, DELORES MAE, histologist; b. Denton, Tex., Apr. 9, 1935; d. Noval P. and Gracie Mae (Oliver) Roach; student Tex. Christian U., 1959-62; m. Thomas Edward Cullom, Feb. 18, 1972; children—Juanita Hamilton, Aletha Ballenger. Histologist, Harris Hosp., Ft. Worth, 1956-66, Tex. Med.

Labs., Ft. Worth, 1966-71, Ft. Worth Med. Lab., 1971-75; chief histologist Tex. Coll. Osteo., Ft. Worth, 1975—. Mem. N. Tex. Soc. Histologists, Am. Soc. Clin. Pathologists, Nat. Soc. Histologists, N. Tex. Soc. Histotechnologists. Home: 3050 Bird St Fort Worth TX 76111 Office: Camp Bowie at Montgomery Fort Worth TX 76111

CULOTTA, WINIFRED IMOGENE (JEANNE) RICHARDSON (MRS. JAMES J. CULOTTA), civic-philanthropic worker; b. Midway, Ala. Mar. 11, 1922; d. James Fred and Sybil Irene (Tucker) Richardson; grad. Draughons Bus. Coll., 1939-40; m. James Joseph Culotta, Apr. 18, 1942; children—James Joseph II, Sybil Richelle. Exec. sec., Hartford Life and Accident Ins. Co., Montgomery, Ala., 1940-41; exec. sec., personnel dept. Michoud USAF, New Orleans, 1943; pres. Home Builders Assn. Greater New Orleans Aux., 1954, 55, bd. dirs., 1953—; pres. Nat. Assn. Home Builders Women's Aux., 1966, bd. dirs., 1955, 62-82; pres. Lit. Study Group, 1975, Crippled Children's Hosp. Guild, 1974-75, The Pontalbans, 1976-78, Workers of Magnolia Sch. for Retarded, 1977-78, Les Quarante Ecolieres, 1982-83; organizing pres., bd. dirs. East Jefferson Gen. Hosp. Aux., 1972—; bd. dirs. Goodwill Industries Vol. Services, 1972—, pres., 1980-81; bd. dirs. Crippled Children's Hosp. Guild, 1969-84, Lit. Study Group, 1972-81, St. Mary's Dominican Coll. Assos., 1975-79, Archbishop's Community Appeal, 1975—, Women's Aux. Eye and Ear Inst. La., 1975-79, corr. sec., 1979-80; bd. dirs. Sara Mayo Hosp. Guild, 1976-78, St. Charles Gen. Hosp. Aux., 1977, 80, East Jefferson Gen. Hosp. Found., 1977—, Friends of Inst. Human Understanding, 1979-85, Sophie Gumbel Guild, 1979-84, Les Quarante Ecolieres, 1979-82, Friends of Ronald McDonald House, 1983-86, v.p., 1984, La. chpt. Juvenile Diabetes Found. Internat., 1985—; fund raising chmn. Ten Outstanding Persons of 1982 Gala, Celebrity Ball and Pro-Celebrity Tennis Classic, La. chpt. Juvenile Diabetes Found. Internat., 1984. Recipient ABC Radio community service award, 1966; Jefferson Parish Outstanding Woman award 1971, Great Lady award, 1977; named to Town & Country's Nationwide Honor Roll Vol. Women, 1979, Vol. Activist, 1980, one of Ten Outstanding Persons in Greater New Orleans, 1981; Sertoma Service to Mankind award, 1984. Republican. Roman Catholic. Club: Metairie Woman's (dir. 1952-58, 67-72, 74-81, 74-81, 84—, pres. 1968-69).

CULP, MARILYN MARGARET WAGNER, sociologist; b. Milw., Jan. 1, 1945; d. Charles Gustave and Evelyn Eve Wagner; B.A. cum laude, Baldwin Wallace Coll., 1967; M.A. with honors, Bowling Green State U., 1969; m. Ronald Edward Culp, Aug. 9, 1969. Asst. prof. sociology Cuyahoga Community Coll., Parma, Ohio, 1969-75; pvt. practice marriage counseling, 1971—; dir. victims assistance programs Multnomah County Dist. Atty.'s Office, Portland, Oreg., 1975—; instr. Bur. Police Standards and Tng.; speaker in field. Mem. Task Force on Domestic Violence, Task Force on Victims; chairperson Tri County Community Council Safety Com.; bd. dirs. Crime Victims Assistance Network, City County Pub. Safety Commn., Crime Victims United. Named Outstanding Female Prof., Cuyahoga Community Coll., 1969-75; recipient Margery Fry award for outstanding practitioner in victim services, 1983. Mem. Am. Sociol. Assn., Am., Oreg. (dir.) assns. marriage and family therapists, Am. Assn. Marriage and Family Therapists. Club: Baldwin Wallace Women's. Home: 12245 NW Maple Hill Ln Portland OR 97229 Office: 1021 SW 4th St Portland OR 97204

CULPEPPER, DOROTHY JUNE, retired aviation executive; b. San Angelo, Tex., Aug. 30, 1933; d. James Ross and Mary Lena (Hooper) C.; student U. Miami; children—J. Michael Miller, Matthew T. Miller, Richard E. Miller. Sec. to junket masters Dunes Hotel, Las Vegas, Nev., 1971-72; asst. to Howard Hughes staff Summa Corp., Miami, Freeport, Bahamas, 1972-76; adminstrn. mgr. aviation div. Resorts Internat., North Miami, Fla., 1976-84. Vol. counselor stroke victims. Recipient Spl. award FAA, 1980. Mem. Nat. Assn. Female Execs., Am. Bus. Women's Assn., Internat. Platform Assn. Democrat. Baptist. Home: 5830 SW 94th Ct Miami FL 33173 Office: 915 NE 125th St North Miami FL 33161

CULVER, BOBBYE JO, real estate company executive; b. Runge, Tex., Jan. 8, 1926; d. Walter Herman and Lydia Ella (Fricke) von Rosenberg; 1 child, David Eric. B.A. with honors, Southwest Tex. State U., 1946; postgrad. Columbia U., 1948, Am. Coll. Real Estate, 1978. Lic. real estate broker. Tchr. Bay City High Sch., Tex., 1948-52; publicity dir. La Mesa Park Race Track, Raton, N.Mex., 1966-73; rancher, Kenedy, Tex., 1973-77; sales mgr., broker Century 21 Norris, Canyon Lake, Tex., 1977—; mem. Turf Publicists Am., Raton, 1966-73; pres. Camp Warnecke Estates Homeowner's Assn., New Braunfels, Tex., 1984, v.p., 1985. Recipient Million Dollar Sales award Century 21 Real Estate, 1977, 83. Mem. New Braunfels C. of C., Nat. Assn. Realtors, Tex. Assn. Realtors, New Braunfels Bd. Realtors. Republican. Episcopalian. Avocations: photography; golf. Office: Century 21 Norris Realty Inc Hwy 2673 PO Box 2168 Canyon Lake TX 78130

CULVER, MARIE LOUISE, nurse; b. Milw., Dec. 7, 1961; d. Leon Gordon and Rachael Elizabeth (Romanowski) C. R.N., Columbia Coll. Nursing, Milw., 1984; postgrad. Columbia/Carroll Coll. Nursing. Crew trainer McDonald's Restaurant, Milw., 1978-79; nursing asst. Lakewood Care Ctr., Milw., 1981-82; supply clk. Columbia Hosp., Milw., 1982-84; library asst. Columbia Coll. Nursing, Milw., 1982-84; nurse Columbia Hosp., Milw., 1984-85; nurse, supr. Med. Placement Services, Inc., Milw., 1985—. Mem. Columbia Alumni Assn., John Birch Soc. Republican. Roman Catholic. Avocations: biking; camping; hiking; badminton; reading. Home: 2521N Downer Ave Apt B Milwaukee WI 53211 Office: Med Placement Services Inc 710 N Plankinton Ave Milwaukee WI 53203

CUMBERLAND, MARY ELIZABETH, securities trader; b. Crockett County, Tenn., Nov. 9, 1948; d. Clint Charles and Hazel Elizabeth (Reasons) Warren; m. Jerry Dean Cumberland, Apr. 19, 1968; children—David Corey, Christian Elise. Student West Tenn. Bus. Coll. Mcpl. underwriter UMIC, Inc., Memphis, 1968-71, Cammack & Pera, Inc., Memphis, 1971-74; govt. securities trader G. Weeks & Co., Inc., Memphis, 1974-77; govt. securities trader, v.p. Trans Am. Securities, Memphis, 1977-79; govt. securities trader, exec. v.p. Carty & Co., Inc., Memphis, 1979-85; govt. securities trader, office mgr., dir. M.G.S.I., Inc., Memphis, 1985—, also dir.; expert witness SEC, Atlanta, 1984, Union Planters Nat. Bank, Memphis, 1984. Active Lakeland Civic Club, Tenn.; charter mem. Republican Presdl. Task Force, Washington, 1982-86; sub-chmn. deaconess task force Decatur Trinity Christian Ch., Memphis, 1986. Mem. Nat. Assn. Female Execs. Avocations: reading; travel; swimming; horseback riding; fishing. Home: 10323 Memphis Arlington Rd Lakeland TN 38002

CUMMIN, SYLVIA ESTHER, educator; b. N.Y.C., Mar. 15; d. Harry and Sarah (Josephson) Smolok; B.S., N.Y. U., 1946, M.A., 1947; m. Alfred S. Cummin, Mar. 24, 1946; 1 dau., Cynthia Katherine. Mktg. adminstr. Ayerst Labs. div. Am. Home Products, N.Y.C., 1946-55; tchr. Queensbury (N.Y.) High Sch., 1955-57, Corfu (N.Y.) Central Sch., 1957-59, Brookline (Mass.) High Sch., 1959-63; tchr. bus. Westfield (N.J.) Secondary Sch., 1963—. Active, Westfield PTA, 1963—, YWCA, 1966—; sponsor, committeewoman Nat. Debutante Assembly, N.Y.C., 1972—, Internat. Debutante Ball, N.Y.C., 1973—, Debutante Cotillion, Washington, 1973—, Ball of the Silver Rose, Vienna, Austria, 1973—; Cert. tchr., Mass., N.Y., N.J. Mem. NEA, N.J. Edn. Assn., Mass. Tchrs. Assn., N.Y. Educators Assn., Eastern Bus. Tchrs. Assn., Nat. Bus. Edn. Assn., N.Y. U. Alumni Assn., N.Y. U. Faculty Wives Assn., Am. Platform Assn. Clubs: Westfield Coll. Women's, Glens Falls Country, Garden. Contbr. articles to profl. jours. Home: 2 Naworth Pass Westfield NJ 07090 Office: Edison Jr High Sch Rahway Ave Westfield NJ 07090

CUMMING, JEAN, librarian, missionary; b. Houston, Aug. 17, 1950; d. Louis Anton and Annie Kamila (Slansky) Navratil; m. Colin Cumming, July 1, 1982. A.A., Wharton County Jr. Coll., 1970; B.A., Tex. Woman's U., 1972; postgrad. Unification Theol. Sem., 1980—. Library technician Project Job, U.S. Civil Service Commn., Dallas, 1972; clk.-typist Menasco, Fort Worth, 1972-73; fin. mgr. Internat. Exchange Press, San Francisco, 1974-75; library clk., adminstrv. clk. Bechtel Power Corp., San Francisco, 1974-75; exec. sec. Internat. Cultural Found., N.Y.C., 1975-80; cataloguer Unification Theol. Sem., Barrytown, N.Y., 1981-83, dir. tech. services, 1984—. Vol. community work Unification Ch. Home Ch. Program Harlem, N.Y., 1976-80. Mem. ALA, Internat. Cultural Found. Confs. (exec. sec.). Home: CPO Box 1401 7 Wiltwyck #1C Kingston NY 12401 Office: Unification Theol Sem Library 10 Dock Rd Barrytown NY 12507

CUMMINGS, ANA GUERRERO, lawyer; b. Mexico, Jan. 13, 1941; d. Geromimo S. and Rebecca (Reta) Guerrero; m. Jerry P. Cummings, Oct. 25, 1975. B.B.A., U. Tex., 1963; J.D., U. Houston, 1978. Acct. Am. Airco, Houston, 1963-66; revenue agt. IRS, Houston, 1966-74, appeals officer, 1974-80, atty. to Chief Counsel, Houston, 1980—. Nat. bd. dirs. YWCA, 1968-72; chmn. local parish council, 1981-83; exec. v.p. Met. Orgn., Houston, 1982-85. Named Fed. Employee of Yr., 1981; recipient Spl. Merit award, 1983. Roman Catholic. Home: PO Box 61633 Houston TX 77208

CUMMINGS, ANGELA LUCIA, jewelry designer; b. Jan. 22, 1944; Austria; came to U.S., 1947, naturalized, 1956; d. Adolf and Erika (Behrends) Baeumker; m. Bruce W. Cummings, Feb. 8, 1970; Grad. Zeichenakademie, Germany, 1968. Jewelry designer Tiffany & Co., N.Y.C., 1968-83; owner, jewelry designer Angela Cummings, Inc., N.Y.C., 1983—, Angela Cummings Studio, Wilton, Conn., 1983—. Avocation: gardening. Office: Angela Cummings Inc 730 Fifth Ave New York NY 10019

CUMMINGS, CHARMAINE JO, nursing educator, nurse; b. Chgo., June 7, 1948; d. Joseph Leo and Romaine J. (Ziegler) Metzl; m. P. Dann Cummings, June 14, 1969; children—Brian, Carrie Ann. Student St. Petersburg Jr. Coll., Clearwater, Fla., 1966-67, U. Fla.-Gainesville, 1967-69; B.S. in Nursing, U. Cin., 1971; M.S., Wagner Coll., S.I., 1982; postgrad. NYU, 1982—. Asst. head nurse Jewish Hosp., Cin., 1971-72; instr. Christ Hosp., Cin., 1972-73; instr. nursing Deaconess Hosp., Cin., 1973; staff nurse J.F. Kennedy Hosp., Edison, N.J., 1977; allergy nurse practitioner Dr. F.A. Schulaner, Westfield, N.J., 1977-81; instr. nursing Bloomfield Coll. (N.J.), 1981-85; nurse educator NIH, 1985—; speaker in field. Chmn. hospitality Friends of the Westfield Library, 1980; leader Washington Rock council Girl Scouts U.S.A., Westfield, 1982, 83. Mem. Am. Nurses Assn., AAUP, Md. Nurses Assn., Am. Acad. Scis., Am. Assn. Neurosci. Nurses (program chmn. Greater Washington Area chpt.), , Sigma Theta Tau. Republican. Congregationalist. Clubs: Plainfield Country (jr. golf chmn. 1984) (Plainfield, N.J.); Newcomers (chmn. hospitality 1972-73) (Westfield). Home: 11740 Lone Tree Ct Columbia MD 21044 Office: NIH Bldg 10 Room 70-55 9000 Rockville Pike Bethesda MD 20205

CUMMINGS, CONSTANCE, actress; b. Seattle; d. Dallas Vernon and Kate Logan (Cummings) Halverstadt; m. Benn Wolfe Levy, 1933 (dec.); children—Jonathan, Jemina. Chmn., Young People's Theatre Panel; mem. Arts Council, 1963-69. Broadway debut Treasure Girl, 1928; London debut Sour Grapes, Repertory Players, 1934; film debut Movie Crazy, 1932; appeared on radio, TV, films, theatre; joined Nat. Theatre Co., 1971; appeared in London stage prodns.: Madame Bovary, 1937; Romeo and Juliet, 1939, Saint Joan, 1939, The Petrified Forest, 1942, Return to Tyass, 1950, Lysistrata, 1957, The Rape of the Belt, 1957, Who's Afraid of Virginia Woolf?, 1964, Justice is a Woman, 1966, Fallen Angel, 1967, Nat. Theatre Co., A Long Day's Journey Into Night, 1972, The Cherry Orchard, 1973, The Circle, 1975, Mrs. Warren's Profession, Vienna, 1976, 82, Wings, U.S., 1978, London, 1979, Hay Fever, 1980, The Golden Age, 1981, The Chalk Garden, N.Y.C., 1982, Eve, 1984, The Glass Menagerie, U.S., London, 1985; performed in: Claudel-Honnegar oratorio St. Joan at the Stake, Albert Hall, London, 1949, Peter and the Wolf, Albert Hall, 1955, Wings on Am. pub. TV; dir., Royal Ct. Theatre. Recipient Tony award for Wings, 1979, Obie award, 1979, Drama Desk award, 1979; decorated comdr. Order Brit. Empire. Mem. Brit. Actors Equity (mem. council), Royal Soc. for Encouragement of Arts and Commerce. Mem. Labour Party. Club: Chelsea Arts. Office: 68 Old Church St London SW 3 England

CUMMINGS, CONSTANCE PENNY, public relations executive; b. Morristown, N.J., Feb. 12, 1948; d. Renwick Speer and Juliana Diane (Novotny) C.; B.A., U. Md., 1970. With Kaiser Aluminum, Washington, 1970-71, Manning, Selvage & Lee, pub. relations, Washington, 1971-77; dir. pub. relations Sheraton Washington Hotel, 1977-82, area dir. pub. relations Sheraton Corp., Washington, 1982-84, dir. pub. relations N.Am., 1984—. Recipient Sheraton Corp. Pres. award, 1978, Pub. Relations award, 1981, 82. Bd. dirs. Big Sisters of Met. Washington, 1984. Mem. Am. News Women's Club (pres. 1982-83), Am. Women in Radio and TV (pres. chpt. 1976), Pub. Relations Soc. Am. (dir. 1977). Contbr. articles in field. Office: Sheraton Corp 2660 Woodley Rd NW Washington DC 20008

CUMMINGS, JEANETTE GLENN, gerontologist, social worker, nursing home administrator; b. Cyrene, Ga., Aug. 11, 1949; d. Asbery and Euzera (Humphrey) Glenn; B.S., Tuskegee Inst., 1972; M.S.W. (Univ. fellow), Atlanta U., 1973; gerontology leadership cert. Ga. State U., 1983; m. Jesse Cummings, Dec. 30, 1978. Dir. resident services Wesley Homes Inc., Atlanta, 1973-78; sr. citizen planner/coordinator Central Savannah River Area Planning Commn., Augusta, Ga., 1979, dir. Area Agy. on Aging, 1979—; cons. on group work with elderly, organizing social service programs. Mem. Mental Health/Mental Retardation Assn., Augusta; chairperson Mental Health/Mental Retardation Adv. Council; mem. exec. bd. Leadership Augusta; participant Leadership Ga.; mem. Sr. Enrichment Assn., Augusta. Elected Employee of Yr., Central Savannal River Area Planning Commn., 1980; named Social Worker of Yr. Augusta unit Nat. Assn. Social Workers, 1982; Citizen of Yr. Sr. Enrichment Assn., 1982. Mem. Nat. Assn. Social Workers, Acad. Cert. Social Workers, Ga. Gerontology Soc., Southeastern Assn. Area Agy. on Aging Dirs., Nat. Assn. Found. Execs., Delta Sigma Theta. Democrat. Mem. Unity Ch. Club: Tuskegee Alumni. Home: 2715 Vernon Dr. W Augusta GA 30906 Office: 2123 Wrightsboro Rd Augusta GA 30904

CUMMINGS, KATHLEEN, medical systems administrator; b. Oak Park, Ill., July 16, 1947; d. Mark Joseph and Margaret (Lamping) C.; m. Thomas James Knight, Jr., May 2, 1970 (div. Jan. 1982); children—Brandy Lynn, Thomas James III; m. Alvin L. Jones, Nov. 23, 1983. B.F.A., Quincy Coll., 1969. Service rep. Ill. Bell Telephone Co., Chgo., 1970-73; collection mgr. Gen. Telephone Answering Service, Chgo., 1973-75; sr. collector Children's Meml. Hosp., Chgo., 1975-80; bus. officer mgr. Seton Med. Ctr., St. Joseph's Hosp., Chgo., 1981-83; sr. legal investigator Hayt, Hayt, & Landau, Evanston, Ill., 1983-84; office mgr. Shared Med. System, Oak Park, Ill., 1985—. Campaign vol. Democratic Party, Chgo., 1982. Roman Catholic. Avocations: jogging; photography. Home: 2607 E 73d St Chicago IL 60649 Office: Shared Med System Oak Park IL 60302

CUMMINGS, MARY JANE, wholesale material company executive; b. Bogard, Mo., Oct. 24, 1934; d. Claude and Nellie Evelyn (Brock) Ellis; m. George Litchfield, Aug. 6, 1952; children—Timmothy Claude, George Litchfield, Cynthia Jane. Student Kansas City Kans. Community Coll., 1973-75, 77-78, 80-81, Rockhurst U., 1975. Bookkeeper, Am. Bldg. Materials, Kansas City, 1969-71; bookkeeper Arrowhead Bldg., Kansas City, 1971-76; credit mgr., controller Rew Materials, Inc., Kansas City, 1976—. Mem. Nat. Assn. Credit Mgmt. (dir. 1985—), Kansas City Wholesale Credit Assn. (dir. 1982-84; Credit Woman of Yr., 1977-78, 78-79, 81-82, Boss of Yr., 1985), Constrn. Fin. Mgmt. Assn. Avocations: volleyball; walking; cooking. Home: 2215 N 115th Kansas City KS 66109 Office: Rew Materials Inc 1136 Southwest Blvd Kansas City KS 66103

CUNANAN, MELISA SORIAO, nurse; b. Naga City, Philippines, July 11, 1959; came to U.S., 1982; d. Amado Mopera and Benny (Soriao) C.; 1 child, Mark. B.S. in Nursing, U. Nueva Caceres, Naga City, Philippines, 1980. Staff nurse Makati Med. Ctr., Makati, Manila, Philippines, 1981-82, Luth. Gen. Hosp., San Antonio, 1982-84; staff nurse Rio Grande Regional Hosp., McAllen, Tex., 1984-85, charge nurse, 1985—. Mem. Red Cross Youth Orgn., Manila, Philippines, 1980. Roman Catholic.

CUNLIFFE, DIANE, mortgage corporation executive; b. Gloucester, N.J., May 23, 1942; d. John V. and Helen (Pratt) Danella; student schs., Gloucester; m. Eric Cunliffe, Nov. 28, 1973; children—James, Kenneth. Sr. processor Jefferson Mortgage Co., Cherry Hill, N.J., 1969-74; asst. v.p., owner Provident Mortgage Corp., Haddonfield, N.J., 1974-78, U.S. Mortgage Corp., Cherry Hill, 1978—; owner Antiques & Bygones, 1979—, Main St. Antiques, Medford, N.J. Loan underwriter Fed. Nat. Mortgage Assn. Mem. N.J. Bd. Realtors, Camden County Bd. Realtors, Gloucester County Bd. Realtors, Women's Credit Mgrs. League. Republican. Home: 155 W Centennial Dr Medford NJ 08055 Office: 216 Haddon Ave Westmont NJ 08108

CUNNIFF, MARY TERESA, business executive; b. Boston, Nov. 16, 1950; d. John Patrick and Marie-Theresa (Riccelli) Rose; m. James Walter Cunniff, Nov. 21, 1971; children—Ann-Marie, Teresa Jean, Sean James. Treas., J.W. Cunniff Co., 1971-81; pres., treas. Berniff Industries, Inc., Stoughton, Mass., 1983—, chmn. bd., 1983—, also dir. Dir. vols. Goddard Hosp., Stoughton, 1969-71. Mem. C. of C. (dir.). Democrat. Roman Catholic. Address: 309 Morton St Stoughton MA 02072

CUNNINGHAM, ALICE WELT, lawyer, educator; b. Washington, Aug. 18, 1949; d. Samuel Louis and Beatrice (Boxer) Welt; m. Daniel Paul Cunningham, Aug. 10, 1975; 1 child, Samuel Paul. B.A. summa cum laude, Yale Coll., 1971; J.D., Harvard U., 1974. Bar: N.Y. 1975, Calif. 1975. Assoc. Shearman & Sterling, N.Y.C., 1974-75, Heller, Ehrman, White & McAuliffe, San Francisco, 1975-78, Debevoise & Plimpton, N.Y.C., 1978-83; assoc. prof. N.Y. Law Sch., N.Y.C., 1983—. Contbr. articles to profl. jours. Mem. ABA (subcom. U.S. activities foreigners, tax treaties of taxation sect.), N.Y. State Bar Assn., N.Y.C. Bar Assn. (taxation com. 1979-82). Home: 1172 Park Ave Apt 12-C New York NY 10128 Office: NY Law Sch 57 Worth St New York NY 10013

CUNNINGHAM, CECELIA GORDON, early childhood educator, consultant; b. Charleston, S.C., Mar. 30, 1942; d. Clarence James and Flossie (White) Gordon; m. Herbert N. Cunningham, Aug. 9, 1961; children—Ardmease Dietra, Tamara Yvette, Bernateen W. Camille. B.S. in Elem. Edn., Coll. of Charleston, 1975, M.A. in Early Childhood, 1983. Early childhood tchr. Sanders-Clyde Sch., Charleston, 1975—; cons., tchr. Migrant Educator, Charleston, 1980—. Mem., actress Charleston Ebony Ensemble, 1983—; mem. YWCA, Charleston, 1985—; bd. dir. Sickle Cell Anemia, Charleston, 1985—. Recipient Upward Mobility Tchr. award City of Charleston, 1980; Tchr. of Yr. award Sanders-Clyde Sch., 1976, 85. Mem. Charleston chpt. Links, Inc. (chmn. arts com. 1984—), Heart Fund Assn. (fund raising chmn., Outstanding Service award 1984-85), Alpha Kappa Alpha. Democrat. Mem. African Methodist Episcopal Ch. Home: 3 Glenwood Ave Charleston SC 29403 Office: Sanders-Clyde Elem Sch 805 Morrison Dr Charleston SC 29403

CUNNINGHAM, DOROTHY RUTH, savings and loan executive; b. Ashland, Ky., Nov. 23, 1951; d. Clayton Allen and Jamie Sue (Rogers) Cunningham; m. Dennis Michael Cline, Dec. 14, 1969 (div. 1976). B.S. in Acctg. magna cum laude, U. Balt., 1981, postgrad., 1985—. C.P.A., Md. Word processing supr. R.M. Towill Corp., Honolulu, 1971-73; real estate reviewer Prudential Ins. Co., Balt., 1973-78; real estate investment analyst Equitable Life Assurance Soc. U.S., Balt., Washington, 1978-83; v.p. Chevy Chase Savs. and Loan, Md., 1983—. Vol. Nat. Aquarium in Balt., 1982—. Mem. Comml. Real Estate Women Balt. (pres. 1985-86), Am. Inst. C.P.A.s, Mortgage Bankers Assn., Nat. Assn. Indsl. and Office Parks, Urban Land Inst., Am. Inst. Real Estate Appraisers. Avocations: home renovation; racquetball; reading; computers. Home: 19 E Henrietta St Baltimore MD 21230 Office: Chevy Chase S & L 8401 Connecticut Ave Suite 101 Chevy Chase MD 20815

CUNNINGHAM, JEAN WOODEN, lawyer, educator, statae legislator; b. Hampton, Va., June 28, 1946; d. Roger Omly and Norville (King) Wooden; m. John Henry Cunningham, Jr., Sept. 9, 1967 (dec. Nov. 13, 1984). children—Brooke, Justin, Bradford. B.A., Va. State U., 1968; J.D., Howard U., 1974. Bar: Mich. 1975, Va. 1978. Tchr., Prince George County, Va., 1968; tech. writer IBM, Poughkeepsie, N.Y., 1968-71; intern Exec. Office of Pres., Washington, summer 1972; labor atty. Reynolds Metals Co., Richmond, Va., 1977-78, 81—, Ford Motor Co., Detroit, 1974-77; ptnr. Chambliss, Cunningham, Hughes and Macbeth, Richmond, 1979-81; prof. Va. Commonwealth U., Richmond, 1978-81; mem. Ho. of Dels., Va. Gen. Assembly, 1986—. Mem. Va. State Bd. Social Services, 1982-86, Richmond Renaissance, 1982-85, Indsl. Devel. Authority Richmond, 1980-84; bd. visitors Va. State U., 1984-86. Mem. Va. Assn. Black Women Attys. (sec.-treas. 1980-82, v.p. 1982-84), Old Dominion Bar Assn. (sec.-treas. 1979-83), Nat. Alumni Assn. Va. State U. (pres. 1981—), Delta Sigma Theta. Democrat. Baptist. Club: Links. Home: 2607 E Grace St Richmond VA 23223

CUNNINGHAM, MARGARET HOWELL, civic worker, educator; b. Bartlesville, Okla., Aug. 21, 1938; d. Herbert Leon and Maude May (Love) Howell; m. James Lee Cunningham, June 26, 1959; children—Amy Love, Christopher Howell. Student Lindenwood Coll., 1956-57; student U. Okla., 1957-59, B.A. in History, 1962; student U. Md.-Aberdeen, 1959-60, U. Colo., summer 1958. European tour leader Americans Abroad, Mpls., 1962; tchr. social studies and French, high sch. Midwest City, Okla., 1962-63. Pres. Channel 6 Vols., sta. KRMA-TV, Denver, 1974-78, Council for Pub. TV, 1978-82, chmn. strategic planning, 1983—, on-air spokesperson, 1976—, lay rep. to Pub. Broadcasting service, mem. nominating com. for bd. dirs., 1984-85, also cons.; lay del. to Nat. Assn. Pub. TV Stas.; bd. dirs. Pub. Broadcasting Service, Washington, 1978-84, task force pub. TV and pvt. sector, 1983-84, bd. liaison to program advisory com., 1983-84; part-time employee Exec. Relocation Services, Inc. Bd. dirs., nominating chmn. Colo. Jud. Inst., Denver, 1982—; trustee, pres. Sewall Rehab. Ctr., Denver, 1977-78; pres. Symphony Debs, 1981-82; trustee Denver Symphony, 1981-82. Recipient award of excellence Pacific Mountain Network, 1984. Mem. Denver Press Club, Alpha Lambda Delta, Kappa Alpha Theta. Republican. Presbyterian. Home: 7 Village Rd Englewood CO 80110 Office: KRMA-TV 1261 Glenarm Pl Denver CO 80204

CUNNINGHAM, MARY ELIZABETH, venture capital company executive; b. Portland, Maine, Sept. 1, 1951; d. Shirley (Sears) C.; m. William Joseph Agee, June 5, 1982. B.A., Wellesley Coll., 1973; M.B.A., Harvard U., 1979; postgrad. Trinity Coll., Dublin, 1972; D.H.L. (hon.), Franklin Pierce Coll., 1983. Asst. treas. Chase Manhattan Bank, N.Y.C., 1974-77; corp. v.p. strategic planning Bendix Corp., Southfield, Mich., 1979-80; exec. v.p. planning, corp. v.p. strategic planning Joseph Seagram & Sons, N.Y.C., 1981-84; pres., chief operating officer Semper Enterprises, Inc., Osterville, Mass., 1982—; cons. Uniform Software Systems, Santa Monica, Calif., 1983; dir. Cyborex Labs., Phoenix, 1984; cons. Forest Fuels, Inc., East Swanzey, N.H., 1983. Author: Powerplay, 1984; contbr. articles to profl. jours. Bd. dirs. Franklin Pierce Coll., Rindge, N.H., 1983—, Marymount Manhattan Coll., N.Y.C., 1983—, Myasthenia Gravis Found., N.Y.C., 1983—, Blueberry Ctr. for Emotionally Disturbed Children, N.Y.C., 1983—; bd. advisors Jour. Bus. Strategy; mem. strategic planning com. The Conf. Bd.; mem. United Negro Coll. Fund, Women's Equity Action League; mem. women's forum, nat. corporate adv. bd. NOW Legal Def. and Edn. Fund; mem. adv. com. Com. for Nat. Security; chmn.'s advisor U.S. Congl. Adv. Bd. Recipient Econ. Equity award Women's Equity Action League, N.Y.C., 1982; named to YWCA's Acad. Women Achievers, 1980. Mem. Am. Mgmt. Assn., Phi Beta Kappa. Roman Catholic. Clubs: Commonwealth of Calif. (San Francisco); Economic (N.Y.C.); Women's Economic (Detroit). Home: Oyster Harbors Osterville MA 02655 Office: Semper Enterprises Inc PO Box 2001 Oyster Harbors Osterville MA 02655

CUNNINGHAM, PATRICIA MARIE REEDY, nurse; b. Scranton, Pa., Nov. 9, 1940; d. John Walter and Mary Zita (Dempsey) Reedy; R.N., Highland Hosp. Sch. Nursing, 1963; B.S., Chapman Coll., 1980, postgrad. 1980-83; m. Harold W. Cunningham, Oct. 30, 1971; children—Marie, David, Wayne, Deborah. Indsl. nurse Walt Disney World, Lake Buena Vista, Fla., 1973-74; staff charge nurse Mercy Hosp., Orlando, Fla., 1972-73, asst. head nurse emergency room, 1974-76; nursing services supr. Kaiser Found. Hosp., Hayward, Calif., 1976-78, asst. nursing adminstr., 1978-84; nursing adminstr. St. James Mercy Hosp., Hornell, N.Y., 1984—. Lic. nurse, Fla., N.Y., Calif. Mem. Am. Nurses Assn., N.Y. State Nurses Assn., N.Y. State Dist. 3 Nurses Assn. Democrat. Roman Catholic. Clubs: Shaklee Salesman, Diamite Distbr. Home: 24 W Main St Canisteo NY 14823 Office: 411 Canisteo St Hornell NY 14843

CUNNINGHAM, SUSAN EILEEN, pilot; b. Mishawaka, Ind., Aug. 3, 1959; d. Dale Lakeene and Willa Lou (Wilcoxon) C. B.A., Ind. State U., 1980. Flight instr. Brown Flying Sch., Terre Haute, Ind., 1980-81; charter pilot Air Travel Charter, Bowling Green, Ind., 1981-82; chief instr. Four Flags Aviation, Niles, Mich., 1982-84, chief pilot, 1984; charter pilot SBN Aviation Inc., South Bend, Ind., 1984; first officer Simmons Airlines, Inc., Marquette, Mich., 1984-85, capt., 1985—. Recipient Jeff Hardaway Meml. scholarship Aerospace Tech. Dept., Ind. State U., 1979. Mem. Alpha Eta Rho (sec. 1978-79, v.p. 1979-80). Methodist. Avocations: softball; music; sports; travel.

CUPIT, DAWN ALICE, government official, consultant; b. Spring Valley, Wis., Jan. 21, 1938; d. George Lester and Alice Marie (Adank) Lancaster; m. Robert Henry Cupit, May 20, 1960; children—Joseph Randall, Roberta Joan, Cynthia Ann. Assoc. Acctg., Richland Coll., Dallas, 1980. Acct. Dept. Def., Patuxent River, Md., 1969-76; auditor Def. Contract Audit Agy., Dept. Def., Dallas, 1976-79; auditor Dept. Energy, Dallas, 1979-82; contract analyst Def. Logistics Agy., Dept. Def., Dallas, 1982—. Author computer software revs., statis. sampling articles. Named Auditor of Yr., Def. Contract Audit Agy., 1978; recipient Superior Performance award Def. Logistics Agy., 1983, Commendable Service award, 1984, other performance awards. Mem. Assn.

Govt. Accts. (dir. 1980), Mensa (job bank chmn. 1984). Avocations: books/collectibles; computers. Home: 1441 Sequoia St Plano TX 75023

CUPP, ANETA JOAN, educator; b. Bonham, Tex., Dec. 30, 1940; d. Emmett Morgan and Hattie Fay (Taylor) Northcutt; m. Charles Daniel Cupp, Mar. 8, 1980; 1 son, Daniel Emmett, B.Mus., North Tex. State U., 1963; M.Ed., U. Houston, 1983. Sec. health workshop North Tex. State U., Denton summer 1963; recreation music dir. Parks and Recreation Dept. Houston, summers 1964, 65, 66, 68; tchr. elem. itinerant music Houston Ind. Sch. Dist., 1963-80; elem. music tchr. Luther Burbank Elem. Magnet Sch., Houston, 1980—. Program dir. PTA, 1963-80, program cons., 1980-84. Jim Collins scholar Corsicana Sr. High Sch., 1959. Named Tchr. of Year, Houston Ind. Sch. Dist., 1976, named to Hall of Honor, 1984. Mem. Houston Music Educators, Houston Tchrs. Assn., Congress Houston Tchrs., Tex. State Tchrs. Assn. Mem. Ch. Jesus Christ of Latter-day Saints (Sunday School bd.). Home: 1237 Althea Houston TX 77018 Office: Burbank Elementary Sch 216 Tidwell Houston TX 77022

CUPPLES, JANET CUMMINGS, business executive; b. Burnsville, Miss., Dec. 22, 1942; d. James E. and Juanita (Hale) Cummings; m. David C. Linton, May 21, 1961 (div. 1984); 1 child, Jeffory Mark; m. Thomas Gilbert Cupples, Mar. 5, 1984. Student N.E. Miss. Jr. Coll., 1960-61, Memphis State U., 1975-76, Sheffield Tech. Ctr., Memphis, 1984-85. Property owner, Burnsville, 1974—. Chair bus. adv. com. Sheffield Tech. Ctr., 1986—; exec. com. Bldg. Bridges for A Better Memphis, 1985—; founder, chair Memphis Women's Com. on Crime, 1985—; donor Women of Achievement, Inc., Memphis, 1986; pub. info. officer Bldg. Bridges for A Better Memphis, 1985—; mem., vol. Memphis Brooks Mus. Art, 1980—; mem. Friends of Shelby County Library, 1986—. Contbr. articles to newspapers. Mem. Nat. Assn. Female Execs., NOW, Network Profl. Women's Orgn., NCCJ, Republican Career Women, Memphis Peace and Justice Ctr. Methodist. Avocations: community service; writing; teaching. Office: 3021 Eagle Dr Memphis TN 38115

CURCURUTO-ROSE, FELICIA ELVIRA, consultant; b. N.Y.C., Dec. 12, 1951; d. Philip and Jane Amy (Monroe) Curcuruto; m. Kari Olavi Nieminen, July 27, 1974 (div. Oct. 1981); m. Michael Dale Rose, Jan. 10, 1982; 1 child, Breana Munro. Student Pierce Jr. Coll., 1972; B.A. in Drama, U. So. Calif., 1975. Bookkeeper, sec. Philip Curcuruto Chiropractic Corp., Van Nuys, Calif., 1972-77; freelance performer, Hollywood, Calif., 1968-77; assoc. producer Headshop, Kaiser Broadcasting, Hollywood, 1970-72; pub. relations, producer, writer Saquirius Prodns., Century City, Calif., 1977-80; freelance pub. relations, Los Angeles, 1981; property mgr. Middlegate Corp., San Francisco, 1982; cons. Dalicia Enterprises, Inc., Los Angeles, 1983—; propr. Firewind, Healdsburg, Calif., 1986—. Producer, actress: Viva! Felicia!, 1969. Author: I'll Be Missing You, 1984, Daughter of a God, 1986. Mem. Nat. Assn. Female Execs., Am. Fedn. TV and Radio Artists, Am. Film Inst., Ind. Feature Project, DAR (past regent), U. So. Calif. Alumni Assn. Republican. Unitarian. Club: Clan Munro Assn. Avocations: hiking; dancing; needlepoint; latchhooking; tapestries; crocheting; knitting; reading.

CURÉ, DENESE, financial corporation executive; b. June 16, 1938; d. Sidney Madison and Dorothea Aimee (Von Winter) C. B.A. summa cum laude, Vol. Coll., Gallatin, Tenn., C.F.P. Owner, operator Communications, Nashville, 1971-81; owner, pres. Fin. Strategies, Inc., Nashville, 1981—. Author numerous poems. Contbr. articles to profl. publ. Profl. counselor Rape and Sexual Abuse Ctr., Nashville, 1979—. Mem. Sales and Mktg. Execs. Republican. Avocations: running; nutrition; politics; economics. Office: Fin Strategies Inc 2400 Crestmoor Suite 317 Nashville TN 37215

CURIE, EVE, author, lcturer; b. Paris, Dec. 6, 1904; d. Pierre (Nobel prize winner for work in radium 1903) and Marie (Skiodowska) (Nobel prize winner in radio-active substances, 1903, in chemistry 1911) Curie; B.S., Ph.B., Sevigne Coll.; D.H.L. (hon.), Mills Coll., 1939, Russell Sage Coll., 1941; Litt.D. (hon.), U. Rochester, 1941; Hartwick Coll., 1983; m. Henry Richardson Labouisse, Nov. 19, 1954. Took up study of music and gave first concert as pianist, Paris, 1925, later concerts in France and Belgium; mus. critic for Candide (weekly jour.) for several years; also wrote articles on motion pictures and the theater; made first visit to U.S. with mother, 1921; on 2d visit lectured in 10 U.S. cities (speaks English, French and Polish), 1939; witnessed fall of France, 1940, went to London to work for cause of Free France; came to U.S., 1941, lectured on war in France and Eng.; because of pro ally activities deprived of French citizenship by Vichy Govt., 1941. Served in Europe with Fighting French as officer in Women's div. of army; one of pubs. Paris Presse (daily), resigned to return to ind. writing, 1949. Spl. adviser Sec. Gen., NATO, 1952-54. Decorated Chevalier Legion of Honor (France), 1939; Polonia Restituta (Poland), 1939; Croix de Guerre (France), 1944. Author: Madame Curie (selection of Lit. Guild, Jr. Guild, Book-of-the-Month Club, Scientific Book of the month; Nat. book award for non-fiction), 1937; Journey Among Warriors (Lit. Guild Selection), 1943. Home: 1 Sutton Pl S New York NY 10022

CURL, LOUISE GERALDINE, college administrator; b. Allegan, Mich., June 24, 1935; d. Edgar J. and Blanche (Smith) Munroe; m. Harrold Twain Curl; children—David, Colleen Curl Warner, Steven. B.S. in Elem. Edn., Olivet Nazarene Coll., Kankakee, Ill., 1959; M.A. in Elem. Edn., Boise State U., 1974; M.B.A., Baldwin Wallace Coll., 1983. Elem. sch. tchr., Ill., Oreg. and Idaho, 1959-71; resource tchr./cons. Nampa (Idaho) Pub. Schs., 1971-74; elem. sch. prin., 1974-78; prof. tchr. edn. Mt. Vernon Nazarene Coll. (Ohio), 1978-81, dir. adminstrv. services, Title III coordinator, purchasing dir., 1981—; curriculum cons. Ch. of the Nazarene, Kansas City, Mo., 1978-80; organizer Kokosing Valley Reading Council, Mt. Vernon, 1979. Mem. Idaho Assn. Elem. Sch. Prins. (pres.-elect 1977-78), Nat. Assn. Elem. Sch. Prins., Internat. Reading Assn. (pres. local council 1976-77, state bd. 1976-78; State Outstanding Field Service award 1978), Coll. and Univ. Personnel Assn., Nat. Assn. Coll/Univ. Bus. Officers, Nat. Council Accreditation of Tchr. Edn. (on-site coll./univ. evaluator Northwestern states and Calif. 1974-78), NEA, Nampa Edn. Assn. (sec.-treas. 1972-73), AAUW (chpt. pres. 1969), Phi Delta Kappa, Delta Mu Delta. Home: 20 McIntosh Ct Howard OH 43028 Office: 800 Martinsburg Rd Mount Vernon OH 43050

CURLEE, DOROTHY SUMNER, social worker; b. Coleman, Tex., July 31, 1921; d. Thaddeus Pickett and Lena (Pierson) Sumner; B.A., Howard Payne Coll., 1942; postgrad. Tulane U., 1944; M.S. in Social Work, Columbia U., 1963; 1 child, Lenae. Supr. child welfare Tex. Dept. Human Resources, 1944-54, 59-60; dir. adoptions Hope Cottage Children's Bur., Dallas, 1961-69; cons. Adoption Resource Exchange N.Am., Child Welfare League Am., 1969-70; asso. dir. Children's Home Soc. N.C., Greensboro, 1970-72; med. psychiat. social worker Tex. Dept. Mental Health and Mental Retardation, Denton, 1972-78; program mgr. crippled children's div. Tex. Dept. Health, Abilene, 1978—; field instr. social work U. Tex., 1950-52, 69, 86. Mem. Acad. Cert. Social Workers, Nat. Assn. Social Workers, Tex. Assn. Mental Health (dir. 1957-59), Daus. Republic Tex. Home: PO Box 3643 Abilene TX 79604 Office: Commerce Abilene TX 79605

CURLER, (MARY) BERNICE (MRS. ALBERT ELMER CURLER), writer; b. Los Angeles, Dec. 4, 1915; d. Charles Ether and Josephine Babetta (Meier) Davis; student Woodbury Coll., 1934-35; m. Albert Elmer Curler, Apr. 10, 1938; children—Daniel Jay, Dawna Dee. Freelance writer of short stories and articles for various nat. mags. including McCalls, Parents Mag., Modern Maturity, Success Unlimited, Progressive Women, Christian Sci. Moniter, Small World, Ladys Circle, Chevron USA, Writer's Digest, National Enquirer, 1957—; author: (play) Mazle's Red Garter, 1962; Story of a Medal, 1976; contbg. author: Creative Congregations, 1972. Instr. article writing Cosumnes River Evening Coll., Sacramento, 1971-82; asst. dir. Sierra Writing Camp; condr. writing seminars. Recipient Achievement award Sacramento Regional Arts Council. Mem. Calif. Writers Club (pres. 1960-61, dir. 1960—, Jack London award 1981), Am. Soc. Journalists and Authors. Home and Office: 8156 Waikiki Dr Fair Oaks CA 95628

CURNUTT, BARBARA SUE, youth consultant; b. San Antonio, Mar. 25, 1950; d. Harry O. and Esther (Clark) C. B.S. in Edn., Tex. Tech. U., 1972; M.A. in Religious Edn., Southwest Bapt. Semr, 1976. Cert. tchr., Tex. Tchr., Northside Ind. Sch. Dist., San Antonio, 1972-74; cons. Bapt. Gen. Conv. Tex., Dallas, 1977—; trainer, cons. Tex. Leadership Tng. Conf., Waco, 1977—, Nat. Youth Ministers Conf., 1982, nat. Acteens Conf., 1979. Vol., Dallas County Juvenile Dept., 1981—; vol. Republican nat. conv. and Dallas County hdqrs., 1984. So. Baptist. Contbr. articles to profl. jours. Office: Baptist General Convention of Texas 511 N Akard St Suite 1130 Dallas TX 75201

CURRAN, BARBARA A., state official, lawyer. Degree with honors in Journalism (Alumnae Leadership medal), St. Mary of the Woods Coll.; M.A., Syracuse U.; J.D., Seton Hall U., 1977. Bar: N.J. 1977. Ptnr., Publs. Ltd.; editor Rahway News-Record, Clark Patriot; served in Gen. Assembly, 1974-80; pres. Bd. Pub. Utilities, Newark, 1980—; asst. to dean Seton Hall Sch. Law Contbr. articles to profl. jours. Exec. dir. N.J. Republican party; rep. Am. Council Young Polit. Leaders in Romania, Belgium and Eng. Named Woman of Yr., N.J. Fedn. of Rep. Women, 1979. Mem. Nat. Acad. TV Arts and Scis. (officer). Address: Pub Utilities Bd 101 Commerce St Newark NJ 07102

CURRAN, CAROL ANNE, commercial real estate company official; b. San Francisco, Nov. 2, 1943; d. Andrew Joseph and Verna Maude (Woodman) Geiser; A.A. in Bus., City Coll. San Francisco; A.A. in Bus. Adminstrn., Foothill Coll.; B.S. in Bus. Adminstrn., San Jose State U., M.B.A., 1978; teaching credential Calif. Community Coll. System, 1980. Employee recruiter, employment rep., asst. mgr. Pacific Telephone Co., San Francisco, 1962-65; with Stanford U., 1965-68; with mktg. dept. Varian Assocs., Palo Alto, Calif., 1968-71; with Michael C. Fields, Menlo Park, Calif., 1971-72; adminstrv. asst., editor co. newsletter Time/Data Corp., Palo Alto, Calif., 1972-74; ind. cons. Olson Labs., Anaheim, Calif., 1977-78; office bldg. specialist, sr. sales cons. Coldwell Banker Comml. Real Estate Services, San Jose, Calif., 1978—. Trustee Music and Arts Found. Santa Clara County 1984-85; mem. City of San Jose Mayor's Econ. Devel./Image Bd., 1986—. Named Office Bldg. Broker of Yr., San Jose C. of C., 1982; named to Comml. Real Estate Hall of Fame, City of San Jose, 1985. Mem. Peninsula Profl. Women's Network, Assn. South Bay Brokers (dir. 1981), World Affairs Council No. Calif. Office: 226 Airport Pkwy Suite 150 San Jose CA 95110

CURRAN, CATHERINE MOORE, lawyer; b. Jersey City, June 25, 1948; d. Harold Joseph and Mary Kathleen (Mindrup) Moore; m. Patrick M. Curran, Jan. 25, 1969; children—Patrick Michael, Mark Andrew. A.B., Douglass Coll., 1973; J.D., Seton Hall U., 1978. Bar: N.J. 1978, U.S. Dist. Ct. N.J. 1978, U.S. Ct. Appeals (3d cir.) 1980. Law clk. to justice Supreme Ct. N.J., Morristown, 1978-79; assoc. Lum, Biunno & Tompkins, Newark, 1979-83, Lum, Hoens, Abeles, Conant & Danzis, Newark, 1984-85; litigation atty. Sea-Land Corp., 1985—; mem. spl. com. on admission to bar Supreme Ct., Newark, 1980-81, adv. com. on admission to bar, 1981—. Mem. ABA, N.J. Bar Assn., Morris County Bar Assn. Home: 4 Jessica Ct Chatham NJ 07928 Office: Sea-Land Corp Law Dept 10 Parsonage Rd Edison NJ 08837

CURRAN, HILDA PATRICIA, social worker; b. Patterson, N.J., Jan. 15, 1938; d. James Patrick and Hilda Lucille (Walsh) C.; A.B., Hiram Coll., 1959; M.S.W., Ohio State U., 1963; m. Robert S. Kennon, Nov. 1980. Tchr., Cin. Bd. Edn., 1960; caseworker Franklin County Welfare Dept., Columbus, Ohio, 1960-61; mem. relocation staff Springfield (Mass.) Redevel. Authority, 1963-64; neighborhood organizer Community Council Greater Springfield, 1964-65; mem. program devel. staff United Community Centers, Bklyn., 1965-67; facilities devel. specialist in vocat. rehab. Mich. Dept. Edn., Lansing, 1967-70; program devel. specialist Bur. Community Services, Mich. Dept. Labor, Lansing, 1970-78, dir. Office Women and Work, 1978—. Mem. Ingham County Housing Commn., 1977-79, Ingham County Social Services Bd., 1979-82; bd. dirs., officer Big Bros.-Big Sisters Greater Lansing, 1968-82; charter mem. bd., officer Big Bros.-Big Sisters Am., 1977—, Big Sisters Internat., 1973-77, pres. 1976-77; trustee Hiram Coll., 1985—. Recipient Diana award in govt. YWCA, 1977; ann. award for outstanding achievement Hiram Coll., 1980. Mem. Nat. Assn. Social Workers (mem. del. assembly 1977, 81, 84, fin. com. 1985—pres. Lansing-Jackson chpt. 1978-80, named Lansing-Jackson Social Worker of Yr. 1977), Acad. Cert. Social Workers, AAUW (women as agent of change award 1981), Phi Kappa Phi (life). Clubs: Zonta, Torch (pres. 1979-80) (Lansing). Home: 415 McPherson Lansing MI 48915 Office: 309 N Washington St Lansing MI 48909

CURRAN, JEANNE KNOX, sociology educator, researcher; b. Houston, Oct. 16, 1935; d. Roy Raymond and Catherine Theresa (Curran) Knox; m. Robert Seidner, 1967 (div. 1972); m. Arnold M. Notkoff, Aug. 22, 1976; 1 child, Tanya Alexis. B.A., Newcomb Coll., 1957; M.A., UCLA, 1967, J.D., 1985; Ph.D., U. So. Calif., 1971. Prof. sociology Calif. State U.-Dominguez Hills, Carson, 1972—, dept. chmn., 1981-82. Author; Boring Academic Research Made Fun, 1978; Up the Job Market, 1980. Alternate rep. Democratic County Council, Los Angeles, 1972-74; pres. Manhattan Beach Dem. Club (Calif.), 1972-73; docent Frank Lloyd Wright's Hollyhock House, Los Angeles, 1981-82. Recipient nomination Disting. Teaching award Calif. State U., 1984, 85, Service to Campus Community honor City Council of Carson, 1985. Mem. ABA, Am. Sociol. Assn., Phi Alpha Delta, Phi Kappa Phi. Democrat. Jewish. Avocations: drawing; painting; clothes design. Office: Calif State U Dominguez Hills 1000 E Victoria Carson CA 90747

CURRAN, KATHRYN, pub relations exec.; b. N.Y.C., Oct. 7, 1941; d. George A. and Dorothy A. (Stillwell) McKeon; B.A., N.Y.U., 1961; postgrad. Russian Inst., Fordham U.; m. William H. Curran, Oct. 1, 1962. Account exec., pub. relations B.B.D.O., 1969-71; v.p. pub. relations Wisser & Sanchez, Inc., N.Y.C., 1971-75; v.p. BritAm Promotions, N.Y.C., 1975-78; exec. v.p. Inter Americas Advt., N.Y.C., 1978—, cons. in field. Mem. Am. Women in Radio and TV, N.Y. Women in Communications, Am. Platform Assn. Republican. Club: Publicity (N.Y.C.). Home: Plains and Town Rds Moodus CT 06469 Office: 200 Madison Ave New York NY 10016

CURRIE, BARBARA FLYNN, state legislator; b. LaCrosse, Wis., May 3, 1940; d. Frank T. and Elsie R. (Gobel) Flynn; A.B. cum laude, U. Chgo., 1968, A.M., 1973; m. David P. Currie, Dec. 29, 1959; children—Stephen Francis, Margaret Rose. Asst. study dir. Nat. Opinion Research Center, Chgo., 1973-77; part time instr. polit. sci. DePaul U., Chgo., 1973-74; mem. Ill. Ho. of Reps., 1979—, chmn. House Democratic Study Group, 1981-83, House Select Com. on World's Fair, co-chmn. House Spl. Com. Investigating McCormick Pl.; vice chmn. House Revenue Com., House Appropriations Com. Mem. adv. bd. Harriet Harris YWCA; v.p. Chgo. LWV, 1965-69; mem. ACLU, Hyde Park-Kenwood Community Conf., South Shore Commn., South Shore Hist. Soc., Ind. Voters of Ill.-Ind. Precinct Orgn., Hyde Park Coop. Soc., Ams. for Dem. Action. Named best legislator Ind. Voters of Ill., 1980, 82, 84 Ethel Parker award, 1982, best legislator Ill. Credit Union League; recipient Ill. Environ. Council award, Ill. Community Action Agys. award, Ill. Women's Polit. Caucus Lottie Holman O'Neill award; Susan B. Anthony award, honor award Nat. Trust Historic Preservation; awards Welfare Rights Coalition of Orgns., Ill. Pub. Action Council, Chgo. Heart Assn., ACLU, DAV, Delta Kappa Gamma; named Legislator of Yr., Ill. Nurses Assn., 1984, Nat. Assn. Social Workers, 1984, Ill. Women's Substance Abuse Coalition, 1984. Mem. Ill. Conf. Women Legislators, Nat. Order Women Legislators. Contbr. article to publ. Office: 2107 Stratton Office Bldg Springfield IL 62706

CURRIE, REBECCA ELAINE, builder, broker, realtor; b. Atlanta, Sept. 24, 1952; d. William M. Currie and Beverly (Barton) Collins; m. Walter Butch Metcalf, May 28, 1978 (div. 1985); 1 child, Rachel D. Ridling. Sales assoc. Century 21 Bouvette, Riverdale, Ga., 1981-82, Re-Max Assocs., Jonesboro, Ga., 1982-83; builder, broker Rebecca Properties, Inc., Jonesboro, 1983—. Mem. Bd. Realtors. Clubs: Presidents, Executive, Century 21 Million Dollar, Century 21 2 Million Dollar. Home: 9858 Currie's Crossing Jonesboro GA 30236

CURRIE, SISTER EILEEN, college president. Pres. Cabrini Coll., Radnor, Pa. Office: Cabrini Coll Eagle and King of Prussia Rds Radnor PA 19087*

CURRIN, ELLEN CAROLE, lawyer; b. Raleigh, N.C., Feb. 24, 1955; d. Elvin Thomas and Pansy Diora (Jonas) Currin. A.B. summa cum laude, U. N.C., 1976; J.D., U. Miss., 1981. Bar: Miss. 1981. Dir. orgn. Nat. Teen Age Republican hdqrs., Manassas, Va., 1976-78; asst. to chmn. urban and regional planning dept. George Washington U., Washington, 1978; atty. Pacific Legal Found., Washington, 1981-83; atty. Office Gen. Counsel U.S. Dept. Energy, Washington, 1983—; lectr. land use law to profl. orgns., 1982-83. Contbr. articles to profl. jours. Docent boyhood home of Robert E. Lee, Alexandria, Va., 1977-78, 82—. Fellow Coll. Pub. Interest Law-Pacific Legal Found., Washington, 1981; grantee criminal law trial practice program U. Miss., 1981. Mem. ABA, Miss. Bar Assn., U. N.C. Alumni Assn. (life mem.), U. Miss. Alumni Assn., DAR (com. chmn. Raleigh 1975-81), Phi Delta Phi. Republican. Baptist. Club: Jr. League (Washington). Office: US Dept Energy 1000 Independence Ave SW Washington DC 20585

CURRY, CONSTANCE WINIFRED, community affairs administrator, lawyer; b. Paterson, N.J., July 19, 1933; d. Ernest and Constance Hazelton (Richmond) C. B.A., Agnes Scott Coll., 1955; postgrad. U. Bordeaux, France, 1955-56; J.D., Woodrow Wilson Coll. Law, 1983. Bar: Ga. 1983. Field sec. Coll. Council for UN, N.Y.C., 1957-59; dir. so. region U.S. Nat. Student Assn., Atlanta, 1959-64; rep. so. field Am. Friends Service Com., Atlanta, 1964-75; dir. human services dept., City of Atlanta, 1975—; mem. task force on homeless, Atlanta, 1982-85, on disabilities, Atlanta, 1982-85. Bd. dirs. Community Friendship Housing, Atlanta, 1985, Radio Free Ga., Atlanta, 1982-85, Mem. Ga. Women Lawyers Assn., Am. Judicature Soc., Southerners for Econ. Justice (bd. dirs. 1975-85), Ga. Civil Liberties Union (bd. dirs. 1980-85), Ga. Legal Services (bd. dirs. 1983-85), Phi Beta Kappa. Democrat. Presbyterian. Avocation: studying French. Home: 930 Myrtle St NE Atlanta GA 30309 Office: OCCA City Atlanta 68 Mitchell St SW Atlanta GA 30335

CURRY, ELAINE JANICE, chemical manufacturing company executive; b. Springfield, Vt., Apr. 30, 1943; d. Maynard Joseph and Jeanette (Lacasse) Sirotka; m. Arthur E. Curry, Oct. 20, 1973; 1 dau., Marianne Elizabeth. A.S., Colby Sawyer Coll., 1963. Exec. sec. Essexbank, Peabody, Mass., 1968-71, sr. programmer analyst, 1971-76; sr. programmer analyst LFE Corp., Waltham, Mass., 1977-78; supr. systems programming Bostik div. Emhart Corp., Middleton, Mass., 1978-81, mgr. systems programming 1981-83, mgr. info. systems, 1983—. Adviser, Jr. Achievement, Lynn, Mass., 1971. Mem. Am. Mgmt. Assn., Assn. Systems Mgmt. Republican. Roman Catholic. Home: 148 North Rd Bedford MA 01730 Office: Bostik Div Emhart Corp Boston St Middleton MA 01949

CURRY, ELEANOR LOU, lawyer, educator; b. Charleston, W.Va., Oct. 21, 1942; d. Chester Hatfield and Jessie Eleanor (Williams) C. B.S., W.Va. U., 1963; J.D., St. Mary's U., 1970; LL.M., Emory U., 1975. Bar: Tex. 1971. Atty., U.S. Treasury Dept., Atlanta, 1972-75; assoc. prof. taxation U. Tex.-San Antonio, 1975—; cons. tax planning and audit. Served to capt. USAF, 1964-68. Mem. ABA, Tex. Bar Assn. Office: E Lou Curry Atty PO Box 29006 San Antonio TX 78229

CURRY, KAREN ANN, dietetic technician; b. N.Y.C., June 28, 1955; d. William and Veronica (Boylan) Galante; m. Brian Micheal Curry, May 7, 1977; children—Rachel Marie, Amanda Lynn. A.A.S., Suffolk County Community Coll. Eastern Campus, 1981. Diet clk. Brookhaven Meml. Hosp., East Patchogue, N.Y., 1972-80, supr., 1980-81; supr. United Presbyterian Residence, Woodbury, N.Y., 1981-82; tech. asst. Suffolk Community Coll., Riverhead, N.Y., 1984—, also mem. adv. com. for dietetic technicians, 1985—. North Shore asst. campaign mgr. Democratic campaign to re-elect John Randolph, N.Y., 1977. Mem. Am. Dietetic Assn. Office: Suffolk County Community Coll Ea Campus Speonk-Riverhead Rd Riverhead NY 11901

CURRY, MARGARET ANN, nurse educator; b. Dallas, Dec. 15, 1926; d. Curtis Herbert and Jetty Bell (Moreland) Gourley; A.A. in Natural Scis., Victor Valley Coll., 1970; B.S.N., Calif. State U., 1972; M.Nursing, UCLA, 1974; postgrad. Tchrs. Coll. Columbia U., summers 1976-79; Ph.D., Kans. State U., 1983; m. Earl Dean Curry, Dec. 25, 1970. Office nurse, Houston, 1947-49; psychiat. technician Wash. State Hosp., 1958-59; physician asst., Spokane, Wash., 1959-65; camp nurse Wash. Summer Camp, Medical Lake, 1962-64; office nurse, Sacramento, 1965-69; psychiat. nurse Neuro-Psychiat. Inst., Los Angeles, 1973; asst. prof. nursing Kans. State U., 1974-75; asst. prof. Radford U., 1975-76, 78-79; asst. prof. U. Tex., 1976-77, 77-78; asso. prof. St. Mary of the Plains Coll., 1979; asst. prof. Pittsburg (Kans.) State U., 1980; asst. prof. nursing Wichita State U., 1980-83; assoc. prof., adminstr. Coll. Nursing, U. Southwestern La., Lafayette, 1983—; ARC nurse, Va., Tex., and Kans., 1974—. Mem. NEA, AAUP, Am. Nurses Assn., Nat. League Nursing, Internat. Transactional Analysis Assn., Am. Assn. Mental Deficiency, Kans. State Nurses Assn., UCLA Nurses Alumni, Tex. Nurses Assn., AAUW, Sigma Theta Tau, Phi Delta Kappa, Nat. Council Family Relations. Democrat. Contbr. in field. Office: Coll Nursing Box 42490 Univ Southwestern La Lafayette LA 70504

CURRY, NANCY ELLEN, educator; b. Brockway, Pa., Jan. 26, 1931; d. George R. and Mary F. (Covert) C.; B.A., Grove City Coll., 1952; M.Ed., U. Pitts., 1956, Ph.D., 1972. Tchr. public schs., East Brady and Oakmont, Pa., 1952-55; presch. demonstration tchr. Arsenal Family and Children's Center, U. Pitts., 1953-79, asso. dir., 1971-79; instr. Sch. of Health Related Professions, U. Pitts., 1956-61, asst. prof., 1961-72, asso. prof., 1972-75, prof., 1975—, acting chmn. dept. child devel./child care, 1972-73, chmn. dept., 1973—; asso. Pitts. Psychoanalytic Inst., 1974—; Fulbright exchange tchr. North Oxford Nursery Sch., Oxford, Eng., 1957-58; asso. dir. early childhood project Edn. Professions Devel. Act, U.S. Office Edn., 1970-74; cons. in field. Lic. psychologist, Pa. Mem. AAUP, Assn. for Care of Children in Hosps., Nat. Assn. for Edn. of Young Children, Am. Psychol. Assn., Am. Psychoanalytic Assn. Producer child devel. films, also articles in field. Office: 213 Pennsylvania Hall U Pitts Pittsburgh PA 15261

CURRY, SANDRA MORRIS, teacher, coordinator, entrepreneur; b. Alexandria, Va., Mar. 24, 1948; d. Bruce Brawner and Mary Eloise (Hitt) Morris; m. John Brooks Curry II, Nov. 25, 1971; children—Amanda Brooks, Rachael Abigail. B.S. in Retailing and Bus., Va. Commonwealth U., 1970. Lic. secondary tchr. Asst. buyer Woodward & Lothrop, Washington, 1970-71, Thalhimer's Dept. Store, Richmond, Va., 1971-72; sec. Memphis City Sch. System, Va., 1972-73, elem. tchr., 1973-75, reading tchr. Valley Elem., Hot Springs, Va., 1975-76; mktg. tchr., coordinator Bath County High Sch., Hot Springs, 1976-77, Covington High Sch., Va., 1980—; owner Secretarial Services Unltd., Covington, 1985—. Mem. Alleghany Highlands Arts and Crafts Ctr., Inc., Covington, 1984—, Friends of Library, Covington, 1983—; Covington high sch. rep. Supt.'s Adv. Council, 1984—; sponsor Distributive Edn. Clubs Am., Bath County High Sch., 1976-77, Covington, 1980—. Named Vocat. Tchr. of Yr., Bath County High Sch., 1977. Mem. Va. Assn. Distributive Edn. Tchrs. Republican. Methodist. Club: Mountain River Garden. Avocations: arts, crafts, bike riding, music appreciation. Home: Route 5 Box 32 Clearwater Park Covington VA 24426 Office: Covington High Sch 531 S Lexington Ave Covington VA 24426

CURTIN, CATHERINE MARIE, footwear manufacturing company executive; b. Portland, Oreg., July 3, 1951; d. Edmond and Olive Joan (Schrantz) C. B.A., U. Portland, 1973; B.A., Univ. Coll., Cork, Ireland, 1976, M.A., 1976. Freelance cons., researcher, lectr., Pacific N.W., 1976—; historian Archdiocese of Portland, 1976-78; market research devel. Property Mgmt. Services Inc., Vancouver, Wash., 1978-80; adj. instr. history U. Portland, 1981—; dir. contbns. Nike, Inc., Beaverton, Oreg., 1981-84, research asst. to chmn., 1984—; assoc. Oreg. Grad. Ctr., Beaverton, 1983-84. Contbr. chpt. to book. Vol., Oreg. Hist. Soc., 1980-81, Spl. Olympics, Portland, 1981—; bd. dirs. Oreg. Spl. Olympics; assoc. Oreg. Symphony Soc., Portland, 1985—. Mem. Am. Com. on Irish Studies, All Ireland Cultural Soc., U.S.-China Peoples Friendship Assn., N.W. China Council. Democrat. Club: Oreg. Road Runners (Portland). Avocations: early 20th century Chinese history, Chinese lang./writing, running. Office: Nike Inc 3900 S W Murray Rd Beaverton OR 97005

CURTIN, JANE THERESE, actress, writer; b. Cambridge, Mass., Sept. 6, 1947; d. John Joseph and Mary Constance (Farrell) C.; m. Patrick F. Lynch, Apr. 31, 1975. A.A., Elizabeth Seton Jr. Coll., 1967; student, Northeastern U., 1967-68. Appeared in plays The Proposition, Cambridge and N.Y.C., 1968-72, Last of the Red Hot Lovers touring co., 1973; Broadway debut: Candida, 1981; author, actress: Off-Broadway mus. rev. Pretzels, 1974-75; appeared TV series NBC Saturday Night Live, 1975-79, Kate & Allie, 1984—; appeared: in films Mr. Mike's Mondo Video, 1979, How to Beat the High Cost of Living, 1980; TV films include Divorce Wars-A Love Story, 1982. Recipient Emmy awards for outstanding lead actress in a comedy series, 1984, 85. Mem. Screen Actors Guild, Actors Equity, AFTRA. Office: care Creative Artists Agy 1888 Century Park E Suite 1400 Los Angeles CA 90067*

CURTIS, AGNES RARITY, association administrator; b. White Plains, N.Y., May 18, 1935; d. David and Madeline Beatrice (Newman) Rarity; m. Alexander Rodman Curtis, June 29, 1957; children—Jenifer Anne, Lauren Agnes, Mary Madeline. R.N., Newport Hosp. Sch. Nursing, 1955; B.S. in Nursing, Salve Regina Coll., 1975, M.A., 1979. Pediatric nurse Newport Hosp., R.I., 1955-57; nurse Project Head Start, Newport, 1968-74; home and hosp. teaching coordinator Newport Sch. Dept., 1975-76; founder, dir. Young Parents Program, Newport, 1977—. Author: How to Start a Young Parents Program in Your Town, 1984. Trustee, Newport Hosp., 1984—; bd. dirs. Self-Help,

Riverside, R.I., 1985—. Recipient Service award Permanent Adv. Commn. on Women, 1980. Mem. LWV, AAUW, Nurses Assn. Am. Coll. Obstetricians and Gynecologists, Coalition of Adolescent Health Services and Edn. (co-founder; chmn. 1978-79), Nat. Assn. Female Execs. Roman Catholic. Avocations: walking; gardening; reading. Home: Eastnor Ct Newport RI 02840 Office: Young Parents Program RI 135 Pelham St Newport RI 02840

CURTIS, ALVA MARSH, artist; b. N.Y.C., June 15, 1911; d. Charles Johan and Elizabeth (Hagstrom) Berg; student Art Students League, N.Y.C., 1928-29, Grand Central Art Sch., 1934-36, N.Y. Sch. Fine Arts, 1930-31, Nat. Acad., N.Y.C., 1934-35, Columbia U., 1943-44, Yale U., 1969-70; m. Terrill Belknap Marsh, Nov. 3, 1932; children—Owen Thayer, Charles Ames, Ronald Belknap; m. Russell G. Curtis, Aug. 11, 1979; children—Russell G. Jr., William E. One woman shows: Scranton Meml. Library, Madison, Conn., 1969, Phippsburg (Maine) Library, 1964, Town and County Club, Hartford, Conn., 1976, Conn. Bank & Trust Co., Madison, 1977, 1st Fed. Savs. & Loan, Madison, 1977; group shows include: The Mariner's Mus., Newport News, Va., Va. Salmagundi Club, N.Y.C., Smithsonian Inst., Washington, 1964, 66, Internat. Maritime Art Award Show (Sculpture award), 1981, Nat. League Am. Penwomen Art Show (Sculpture award), Atlanta, 1982, Arnold Gallery, Newport, R.I., 1984, Copley Gallery, Boston, 1986, Candlewood Gallery (Sculpture award 1986), New Milford, Conn., 1986; represented in permanent collections: Swedish Club, Chgo., Conn. Bank & Trust Co., Windsor, Phippsburg Library, also pvt. collections; partner, art dir. Terrill Belknap Marsh, Assos., N.Y.C., 1934-69; lectr. in field. Vice chmn. Madison Inland Wetlands Agy., 1974-84. Mem. Am. Soc. Marine Artists, New Eng. Sculpture Assn., Nat. Arts Club, Nat. League Am. Penwomen (pres. 1978—, Greenwich br. 1958). Republican. Episcopalian. Clubs: Lyme Art Assn., Madison Winter, Garden Madison. Home: 12 Dogwood Ln Madison CT 06443

CURTIS, CYNTHIA GRIMSLEY, cattle producer; b. Greensboro, N.C., Mar. 2, 1924; d. Harry Barnette and Lucy Dix (Estes) Grimsley; m. Richard Brice Curtis, Dec. 31, 1943 (dec. Mar. 1967); children—Richard Brice, Cynthia Curtis Lewis, William Harry (dec.), Lucy Curtis Ogletree, M. Elizabeth Curtis Crumbley, Thomas Russell. Student U. N.C.-Greensboro, 1940-43, U. Ga., 1967, 76-78. Owner, operator Curtis Cattle Co., Watkinsville, Ga., 1972—; bd. dirs. Nat. Livestock and Meat Bd., 1984—; mem. beef commodity com. Ga. Farm Bur., 1986. Bd. dirs. Greene County Hosp. Authority, Greensboro, Ga., 1983—; vice chmn., 1985-86; mem. county com. Farmers Home Adminstrn., Greensboro, Ga., 1983-86, chmn., 1985-86; mem. adv. bd. Greene County Cancer Soc., 1980—. Mem. Ga. Cattlemen's Assn. (exec. dir. 1978-80, treas. 1980-82, regional v.p. 1982-85, Most Valuable Mem. 1979), Am. Nat. Cattlewomen, Inc. (exec. com. 1980-82, regional coordinator 1979, 83; Sioux City Stockyards award 1985), Ga. Cattlewomen's Assn. (pres. 1978-80, 82-83, bd. dirs. 1986), Nat. Cattlemen's Assn. Republican. Episcopalian. Home and Office: Route 3 Box 248 Watkinsville GA 30677

CURTIS, DONNA ROBASON, librarian; b. Brownwood, Tex., July 3, 1943; d. Don Todd and Frances Virginia (Carter) Robason; m. Robert L. Curtis, Aug. 12, 1967 (div. Oct. 1974); children—Kaaren Leigh, Robin Lynne. B.A., McMurry Coll., Abilene, Tex., 1965; M.A., U. Denver, 1977. Tchr., Roswell Mcpl. Schs. (N.Mex.), 1965-66; community organizer, head start program coordinator Chaves County Community Action Program, Roswell, 1966-67; tchr. Lake Arthur Schs. (N.Mex.), 1967-68; dir. student activities N.Mex. Jr. Coll., Hobbs, 1969-71; cataloger Library Processing Ctr. Hobbs Mcpl. Schs., 1974, coordinator elem. libraries, 1982—; owner Kit 'n' Kaboodle Needlework, Hobbs, 1974; serials librarian U. Denver, 1975, adminstrv. sec. Sch. Social Work, 1975-77; legal asst./librarian Reynolds, Bryan & Francoeur, Hobbs, 1978-80, Cox, Imke and Proctor, P.A., Hobbs, 1980-82; pres. Library Services, Ltd., Hobbs, 1982—. Mem. ALA, Assn. for Library Service to Children, Am. Assn. Sch. Librarians, Children's Literature Assn., Internat. Reading Assn., N.Mex. Library Assn., AAUW (project RENEW grantee 1975), Alpha Delta Kappa. Democrat. Methodist. Home: 1109 Grayson St Hobbs NM 88240 Office: Hobbs Mcpl Schs PO Box 1040 Hobbs NM 88240

CURTIS, FRANCES JO, real estate broker-developer; b. Winnepeg, Man., Can., Oct. 17, 1923; d. William and Anna (Strelecki) Curnell; brought to U.S., 1925, naturalized, 1951; student U. Detroit, 1952-54, Oakland U., 1974-76; grad. Specs Howard Sch. Broadcast Arts, 1979; children—Carol (Mrs. Bill Lowery), Dennis Curtis, Bradley. Founder, prin. Troy Realty (Mich.), 1954—; founder, pub. Tri-City Messenger, Troy, 1956-61; owner Meadowbrook Realty & Mortgage, 1976—; owner, host radio program Sta. WTIQ (radio), 1982—. Sec. of Incorporation, City of Troy, 1955; founding mem. Indsl. Com. Troy, 1957-62, Library Com., 1959-65, Sewer Com., 1958-62, Civic Center Com., 1960-65 (all Troy); mem. Crittenton Hosp. Com., Rochester, Mich., 1958-62. Mem. Coast Guard Aux., 1980. Lic. broadcaster, ham operator. Mem. Troy C. of C. (founder 1959), Air Force Assn. (Mich. aerospace chmn., state 3d v.p.), Internat. Platform Assn. Clubs: Houston Press, Nat. Press. Home: 1039 N Woodward PO Box 475 Birmingham MI 48012 Office: 2820 W Maple Troy MI 48084

CURTIS, JANE GAYLE, market research analyst; b. Springfield, Ky.; d. Harold Richmond and Louise (Bohannon) C. A.A., Eastern Ky. U., 1971; B.S. in Commerce, U. Louisville, 1977, M.B.A., 1982. Adminstrv. asst. Union Trust, Inc., Louisville, 1973-76; credit analyst Brown-Forman Distillers, Louisville, 1976-78, market analyst, 1979-82; sales analyst Brown & Williamson Tobacco Co., Louisville, 1982-83, market research analyst, 1983-84, sr. research analyst, 1984—; owner, operator Curtis & Co., discount buying, Louisville, 1982—. Mem. Am. Mktg. Assn. (v.p.-treas. Louisville 1983-84).

CURTIS, KATHY MARIA, nurse; b. Wiesbaden, Germany, Nov. 15, 1951; d. Aleck George and Gladys Louise (Campbell) Alexander; m. Terry Lee Curtis, Nov. 23, 1975; children—Jennifer, Seth. A.A., Diablo Valley Community Coll., 1971; B.S. in Nursing, Calif. State U.-Chico, 1974. R.N., Calif.; cert. pub. health nurse, Calif. Staff nurse Carson Tahoe Hosp., Carson City, Nev., 1981; relief supr., staff nurse pulmonary ICU Loma Linda U. Med. Ctr., Calif., 1981-83; asst. dir. nursing pro-tem Lassen Community Hosp., Susanville, Calif., 1982-83, dir. ICU, CCU, 1983-84. Bd. dirs. Susanville Seventh Day Adventist Elem. Sch., 1985—. Avocations: sewing; hiking; back packing. Home: 699-425 Marilyn Way Susanville CA 96130

CURTIS, LINDA LEE, writer; b. Stafford, Kans., Apr. 18, 1950; d. Robert Lee and Donna Leatrice (Joy) Herren. A.A., Barton County Community Coll., Great Bend, Kans., 1978. Staff poet Chronicles, Phoenix, 1982-83, Soundboard mag., Phoenix, 1983—. Author: Midnight Echoes, 1976; More Than My Share, 1979, Intermission, 1982; Money-Making Ideas for Poets, 1984. Named Poet of Yr., Soundboard mag., 1984. Democrat. Avocations: painting; batik.

CURTIS, MACHELLE MCKINLEY, telemarketing consulting company executive; b. Racine, Wis., Mar. 22, 1948; d. Wilbert Leon and Alma Jean (Baird) McKinley; m. William Childs Curtis, Aug. 23, 1980. Student U. Wis.-LaCrosse, 1966-68; B.S., No. Ill. U., 1971; M.S. Emerson Coll., 1974. Cert. speech and lang. pathology, Mass. Pathologist speech and lang. Bd. Edn., Lincoln, Mass., 1974-79; v.p. Mitterling Method, Inc., Boston, 1980-82; pres. Tele-Connections, Aurora, Colo., 1983—; lectr. in field. Author: (with others) Winning Words: A New Approach to Developing Effective Speaking Skills. Emerson Coll. fellow, 1972; Racine Environ. Com. grantee, 1968, 69. Mem. Rocky Mountain Telemktg. Assn., Am. Soc. Tng. and Devel. Office: Tele-Connections PO Box 440025 Aurora CO 80044

CURTIS, MARY PACIFICO, advertising agency executive; b. Chgo., Feb. 22, 1953; d. Louis Enrico Pacifico and Margaret (Geneva) Peterson; m. Douglas Reid Curtis, Jan. 2, 1982. B.S., Northwestern U., 1973. Assoc. producer Panorama Prodns., Santa Clara, Calif., 1975-76; copy chief Moorhead Mktg., San Francisco, 1976-77; pres. Pacifico & Assocs. Inc., San Jose, Calif., 1977—; founder Silicon Valley Bank, San Jose, 1984—. Bd. dirs. Childrens Counseling Ctr., Santa Clara, 1980—, pres.; bd. dirs. San Jose Symphony Assn., 1984-85. Recipient San Francisco Cable Car award San Francisco Ad Club, 1978; Best in the West awards of merit, 1979, 80; Maggie award, 1980; Addy award, 1984; Joey award, 1984; Murphy award, 1984. Mem. San Jose Ad Club, Peninsula Women in Advt., San Jose Women in Advt., Western States Ad Agys. Assn., Am. Mktg. Assn. Roman Catholic. Avocations: photography; tennis; skiing. Office: Pacifico & Assocs Inc 2145 The Alameda San Jose CA 95126

CURTIS, ODESSA COLENE, public health nurse; b. Royalton, Ill., Jan. 29, 1924; d. Forrest Houston and Martha Magdalene (Crane) Johnson; m. Dean Daniel Curtis, June 18, 1945; children—Joseph A., Jon M. R.N., Mo. Bapt. Hosp. Sch., St. Louis, 1942; B.S.N., Sacred Heart Dominican Coll., Houston, 1964; postgrad. nursing Tex. Women's U., 1974-75. R.N., Mo., Tex. Staff nurse labor and delivery St. Mary's Hosp., Mpls., 1947-48; staff nurse U. Tex. M.D. Anderson Hosp., Houston, 1961-63; charge nurse labor and delivery Meml. Bapt. Hosp. Southwest, Houston, 1963-65; nursing supr. City of Houston Dept. Pub. Health, 1965—; commentator Am. Pub. Health Conv., New Orleans, 1974. Del., 13th Sen. Dist. Republican Party, Houston, 1980; vol., United Way, 1983; den mother Boy Scouts Am. pack 535, 1958. Mem. Sacred Heart Dominican Coll. Alumni Assn., St. Thomas U. Alumni Assn., Am. Nurses Assn., Tex. Nurse Assn. Dist. 9, Tex. Pub. Health Assn., ARC. Office: City of Houston Dept Health 1115 N McGregor Houston TX 77030

CURTIS, PATRICIA DOLORES, building products company executive; b. Oak Park, Ill., Nov. 21, 1927; d. Richard Peter and Viola Delores (Meyer) Heckmann; m. Howard M. Curtis, Sept. 22, 1945; children—Terry, Suzanne, Paul. Sec., treas. Heckmann Bldg. Products, Inc., Chgo., 1950-60, pres., 1960—. Office: 4015 W Carroll Ave Chicago IL 60624

CURTIS, SHIRLEY ANN, educator; b. Nauvoo, Ala., Sept. 25, 1943; d. Edward Herbert and Grace (Roden) C.; B.A. in English and Speech, U. S.Fla., Tampa, 1964, M.A. in English, 1969; Ph.D. in Higher Edn., Fla. State U., 1979; m. Frederick Cameron Sumner, Dec. 16, 1972 (div.); 1 son, Matthew Frederick Curtis; m. Edwin Charles Carlson, May 3, 1983 (div.); 1 dau., Kathryn Curtis Carlson. Jr. and sr. high sch. tchr., Fla. and Calif., 1965-67; resident counselor, instr. English, U. South Fla., 1967-70; prof. communications and humanities Polk Community Coll., Winter Haven, Fla., 1970—, pres. faculty senate, 1982-83. Vice pres., program chmn. Unitarian-Universalist Fellowship, Lakeland, Fla., 1980-82, pres., 1982-84; del. Fla. Democratic Conv., 1978; co-founder Cinema Six, 1972-74; pres. Fla. dist. Unitarian-Universalist Assn., 1983-85. Mem. Internat. Transactional Analysis Assn., Nat. Assn. Bus. and Profl. Women, Fla. Women's Network, Nat. Assn. Female Execs., NOW, Fla. Assn. Community Colls., Sierra Club. Democrat. Office: Dept Communication and Fine Arts Polk Community Coll 999 Ave H NE Winter Haven FL 33881

CURTIS-LOPEZ, DONNA, social worker and supervisor, cleaning products distributing company executive; b. Evanston, Ill., Sept. 4, 1944; d. Don Frederic and Bernardina (Lopez) C.; m. Norman Neal Davis, III, Nov. 22, 1970 (div. May 1980); 1 child, Samantha Alma. A.A., Joliet Jr. Coll., 1965; postgrad. Western Mich. U., 1972-74. Sec., various cos., Chgo., 1967-69; sec. Kalamazoo Child Guidance, Mich., 1969-70; social worker Mich. Dept. Social Services, Kalamazoo, 1970-77, supr. social work, Battle Creek and Albion, Mich., 1977—; owner Dreams, Kalamazoo, Mich., 1983—; vol. probation officer Kalamazoo County Juvenile Ct., 1985—. Bd. dirs. East Side Community Ctr., Kalamazoo, 1972. Mem. Mich. Council Social Service Workers. Democrat. Roman Catholic. Lodge: Lioness (Battle Creek) (2d v.p. 1985—). Avocations: reading; swimming; cycling; movies; ceramics. Home: 920 Albert Kalamazoo MI 49001 Office: Calhoun County Dept Social Services 101 N Albion St Albion MI 49224

CURTISS, FLORENCE MARIE, retired nurse; b. Flushing, Ohio, June 7, 1922; d. John William and Sara Bell (Anderson) Evans; R.N., Ohio Valley Gen. Hosp. Sch. Nursing, 1943; B.S. in Nursing, Ohio State U., 1948; m. John Stuart Curtiss, Dec. 4, 1949; children—Sandra Lynn, Philip Evan, Alan Stuart. Supr., VA Hosp., Battle Creek, Mich., 1949-51, instr., 1958-82; trustee VA Employees Credit Union, 1977—. Chmn. bd. dirs. McKay Library, Augusta, Mich., 1967—; chmn. Bicentennial Com., 1976; sec. Augusta Sesquicentennial Com., 1984-85; treas. Augusta Mus. Served with Nurse Corps, USN, 1944-46. Mem. Mich. Library Assn. Republican. Methodist. Home: 412 N Augusta Dr Augusta MI 49012

CURTRIGHT, GLADYS STEELE, real estate broker; b. Evansville, Wis., May 13, 1904; d. Robert L. and Mamie L. (Haley) Steele; student Rockford (Ill.) Coll., Beloit (Wis.) Coll.; m. Walter L. Curtright, Dec. 22, 1923; children—Lois Rae Curtright Henderson, Jay B. Cosmotologist, Cin., 1922-28; agt. Prudential Ins. Co., Beloit, 1930-33; various acctg. positions, 1942-50; owner refail gift shop and real estate office, Beloit, 1950-64; broker, salesman J.R. Schuster Agy., Beloit, 1964-72, Exec. Services, Sanibel, Fla., 1974-78; v.p., broker Bluebill Properties, Inc., Sanibel Island, 1978—; past pres. Beloit Bd. Realtors. Mem. Nat. Assn. Relators, Fla. Assn. Realtors, Ft. Myers Bd. Realtors, Naples Area Bd. Realtors. Methodist. Home: 896 Angel Wing Dr Sanibel Island FL 33597 Office: 2422 Periwinkle Way Sanibel Island FL 33957

CURVIN, KENYA JOYCE, energy executive, composer; b. Oklahoma City, June 15, 1938; d. T. Clinton and A. Jean (Coulter) Wallace; student Belhaven Coll., Jackson, Miss., 1957, Oklahoma City U., 1958, Okla. U., 1976-78; m. James Daniel Curvin, June 9, 1977; 1 child, Cimarron Trace Anthony Curvin; children by previous marriage—Derek Jerome Sanderson, Gina Rachelle Sanderson. New accounts rep. Fidelity Bank N.A., Oklahoma City, 1964-68; geol. asst. G.B.K. Co., Oklahoma City, 1968-72; psychiat. unit mgr. Queens Hosp., Honolulu, 1972-74; exec. officer Standard of Wewoka, Inc., Oklahoma City, 1974—, also dir.; naturalist Okla. Tourism and Recreation Dept., 1977-78; pres., dir. Wildcat Mapping, Inc., Oklahoma City, 1979—; owner M.W. Galaxy Music, Norman, Okla., 1981—; v.p. Scissortail Oil Corp., 1982—; asst. v.p. G.B.K. Co., 1982; drafting coordinator GADSCO, Inc.; ecology and conservation lectr. Mem. Nat. Assn. Female Execs. (network dir.), Okla. Petroleum Drafting Assn., Internat. Platform Assn., Better Bus. Bur., Canadian River Park Assn. (life). Democrat. Author: Manna-Mana (poetry), 1977; composer: Redland (musical play), 1980 (Okla. Heritage award 1982); Milky Way Galaxy, 1981; ballads; photographer. Office: 1343 First National Center W Oklahoma City OK 73102

CUSACK, MARY JOSEPHINE, lawyer; b. Canton, Ohio, Mar. 3, 1935; d. Edward Thomas and Mary (O'Meara) Cusack; A.B, Marquette U., 1957; J.D., Ohio State U., 1959. Admitted to Ohio bar, 1959, U.S. Supreme Ct. bar, 1962; mem. firm Cotruvo and Cusack, Columbus, Ohio; atty. for Indsl. Commn. Ohio, Columbus, 1960-61, Office Tax Commr., Columbus, 1961-65. Pres., E.T. Cusack, Inc., Canton, 1963-64, dir., 1960-64; spl. counsel to Atty. Gen. William J. Brown. Mem. Ohio Commn. on Status of Women. Mem. Am. Bar Assn., Ohio Bar Assn. (past chmn. workmen's compensation com., mem. council dels.), Columbus Bar Assn. (profl. ethics com., adv. com. fees, workmen's compensation, Women Lawyers Club Columbus (past pres.), Ohio Acad. Trial Lawyers (workmen's compensation com.), Franklin County Trial Lawyers (sec.), Nat. Assn. Women Lawyers (rec. sec.), Ohio Assn. Attys. Gen. (past pres.), Am. Arbitration Assn. (nat. panel arbitrators), Thomas More Soc., Kappa Beta Pi (past internat. pres., del. Profl. Frat. Assn.), Theta Phi Alpha. Clubs: Columbus Toastmistress (past pres.), Columbus Met. Home: 229 W Southington Ave Worthington OH 43085 Office: 50 W Broad St Columbus OH 43215

CUSHING, KAY SMITH, public relations executive; b. Pitts., Feb. 21, 1944; d. George Byron and Margaret Elizabeth (Smith) C.; m. Kenneth Neuhausen, May 16, 1981. B.A., Lindenwood Coll., 1965. Gen. mgr. Pitts. Ballet Theatre, 1975-78; account supr. Ketchum Pub. Relations, Pitts., 1978-79, v.p., 1979-82, group mgr., 1982-84, sr. v.p., 1984—Mem. strategic planning com. United Way of Allegheny County. Recipient Matrix award Women in Communications, Pitts., 1983, 84. Mem. Pub. Relations Soc. Am. (pres.) Pitts. chpt. 1985, Vic Barkman award (1984), Fedn. Girls Sch. Socs. Republican. Roman Catholic. Clubs: Altrusa, Carnegie 100, Concordia (Pitts.). Office: Ketchum Pub Relations 6 PPG Pl Pittsburgh PA 15222

CUSHMAN, HELEN BAKER, cons., historian; b. Perth Amboy, N.J.; d. Ivan Franklin and Lucile (Atkinson) Baker; B.A., Barnard Coll.; postgrad. N.Y. U.; m. Robert Arnold Cushman, June 2, 1945; children—Lucinda, Robert. Route analyst Air Transport Command, Washington, 1942-44; personnel asst. Gen. Cable Corp., N.Y.C., 1944-45; sr. staff asst. to chmn. Trans World Airline, Inc., N.Y.C., 1946-50; mng. assoc. H. M. Baker Assocs., Westfield, N.J., 1958—; cons. to various corps., 1958—. Pres. Barnard Coll. Club North Central, N.J., 1962-64; pres. PTA, 1964-65. Recipient Literary award Am. Records Mgmt. Assn. 1972. Mem. N.J. Hist. Soc., Soc. Am. Archivists. Club: PEO. Office: Box 363 Westfield NJ 07090

CUSHMAN, MARY SUSAN LIVINGSTONE, university dean; b. Detroit, Jan. 7, 1932; d. T.W. Palmer and Elizabeth Trowbridge (Wilkins) Livingstone; m. Joseph David Cushman, Jr., July 16, 1955; children—David Knight Livingstone, William Claybrook. A.B., Wellesley Coll., 1953; Ed.M., Harvard U., 1954. Tchr., Brevard County Pub. Schs., Cocoa, Fla., 1954-57, Fla. State U. Sch., Tallahassee, 1957-61, Sewanee Nursery Sch. and Kindergarten, 1968-69; prin. Sewanee Pub. Sch., 1969-71; dean of women U. of South, Sewanee, 1971—. Trustee St. Andrew's-Sewanee Sch., St. Andrew's, Tenn., 1981—. Mem. Nat. Assn. Student Personnel Adminstrs., NOW. Democrat. Episcopalian. Home: Box 128 Sewanee TN 37375 Office: Univ of South Sewanee TN 37375

CUSHMAN, ORIS MILDRED, nurse, hospital education administrator; b. Springfield, Mass., Nov. 22, 1931; d. Wesley Austin and Alice Mildred (Vaile) Stockwell; m. Laurence Arnold Cushman, Apr. 16, 1955; children—Lynn Ann Cushman Crandall, Laurence Arnold III. Diploma in nursing Hartford Hosp. Sch. Nursing (Conn.), 1953; B.S., Western Mich. U., 1978, M.A., 1980. Staff nurse Wesson Maternal Hosp., Springfield, 1953-54, acting supr., 1954-55; staff nurse Hartford Hosp., 1955-56, head nurse, 1956, staff nurse, 1957-59; staff nurse, charge nurse Reed City Hosp. (Mich.), 1961-67; supr. Meml. Hosp., St. Joseph, Mich., 1967-75, clin. supr. maternal/child health, 1975-77, dir. maternal/child health 1977-80; dir. edn. Pawating Hosp., Niles, Mich., 1980—. Sec. Women's aux. Reed City Hosp., 1964-65, v.p., 1965-66, pres., 1966-67; mem. adv. bd. on family life edn. St. Joseph Sch. Bd. (Mich.), 1979-80. Mem. Nurses Assn. Am. Coll. Obstetricians and Gynecologists, Perinatal Assn. Mich., S.W. Mich. Perinatal Assn. (founding; v.p. 1979-80, pres. 1980), S.W. Mich. Healthcare Edn. Council (sec. 1983-85), Tri-County Continuing Edn. Council Southwestern Mich. (founding, chairperson 1983-84), Mich. Soc. Healthcare Edn. and Tng. (sec. 1985-86), Am. Soc. Healthcare Edn. and Tng., Mich. Health Council. Republican. Office: Pawating Hosp 31 N Saint Joseph Ave Niles MI 49120

CUSICK, ANDREA COONEY, sales executive; b. Woodstock, Ill., June 19, 1954; d. James H. and Karlen (Hecht) Cooney; m. Robert W. Cusick, Nov. 27, 1976. B.S. in Advt., U. Ill., 1976. Traffic-continuity dir. Sta. WDBR-FM, Springfield, Ill., 1976-77, account rep., 1977-80, sales mgr., 1980—; participant Ill. Broadcasters Assn. Edn. Panels, Ill. univs., 1981—. Mem. Ill. Broadcasters Assn., Springfield Advt. and Pub. Relations Fedn. (pres. 1982-83). Office: WDBR-FM 712 S Dirksen Pkwy Springfield IL 62703

CUSICK, PATRICIA DAULTON, insurance company executive; b. N.Y.C., Aug. 21, 1938; d. Marion Daulton and Francine (Hermansen) Martin; m. Kenneth S. Evans, June 8, 1955 (dec. 1979); 1 son, Randall Lee; m. 2d, Thomas Patrick Cusick, May 9, 1980. Personnel asst. European Exchange Service, Fontainebleau, France, 1961-64, City Water Bd., San Antonio, 1964-69; interviewer United Services Automobile Assn., San Antonio, 1969-75, EEO coordinator, 1975-83, dir. counseling and affirmative action, 1983—. Mem. Am. Soc. Personnel Adminstrs., San Antonio Personnel and Mgmt. Assn. (v.p. adminstrn. 1983, pres.-elect 1984). Republican. Office: United Services Automobile Assn USAA Bldg San Antonio TX 78288

CUSTER, MARY JO, university official; b. Cortland, N.Y., Aug. 1, 1955; d. Edward Daniel and Nancy Janet (Burdick) Dwyer; m. James Robert Custer, Aug. 1, 1980; 1 dau., Jessica Lynn. Student, Nazareth Coll., Rochester, N.Y., 1973-75; B.S. in Nursing, Syracuse U., 1978, B.S. in Psychology, 1978. Cert. in sanitation and tng. Nat. Inst. Foodservice Industry. Service supr. dining services Syracuse U. (N.Y.), 1978-79, asst. mgr. dining services, 1979-81, dir. sanitation and tng. dining services, 1981-82, asst. to v.p. instnl. services, 1983-85, asst. to sr v.p. for student services, 1985—; lectr. in field. Contbr. articles to profl. jours. Mem. United Methodist Women's Aux., 1980—, Firemen's Aux., Cuyler, N.Y., 1980—; sec. Tioughnioga Lake Assn., 1972-80. Recipient award for disting. service Nat. Inst. Foodservice Industry, 1983. Mem. Nat. Assn. Coll. and Univ. Food Services (Meritorious Service award 1983), Nat. Restaurant Assn., Am. Mgmt. Assn., Internat. Assn. Milk, Food and Environ. Sanitarians, Assn. Coll. and Univ. Housing Officers-Internat. Republican. Roman Catholic. Home: 4539 Route 13 Truxton NY 13158 Office: 606 University Ave Syracuse NY 13210

CUTHBERTSON, MRS. GEORGE RAYMOND, club woman; b. Liberty, Mo., Apr. 2, 1911; d. Edgar and Mary Jane (Anderson) Archer; student William Jewell Coll., 1929-31; m. George Raymond Cuthbertson, Sept. 3, 1931. Dist. capt. Mothers' March of Dimes, 1959-60; mem. Bergen County Panhellenic Council 1957-60; mem. woman's com. William Jewell Coll. Mem. Mo. Hist. Soc., Clay County Hist. Soc., DAR, Huguenot Soc. S.C., Clay County Mus. Assn., Geneal. Soc. Liberty (Mo.), Alpha Delta Pi. Baptist. Clubs: Liberty Hills Country, Fortnightly, P.E.O. Home: 8 College Pl W Liberty MO 64068

CUTHBERTSON, IDA DIENER, government agency official; b. Cleve.; d. Gottlieb John and Tess Diener. Student Ohio State U., Va. Poly. Inst. and State U. Community planner, pub. participation coordinator Soil Conservation Service, Washington; statistician Ohio Dept. Health, Columbus; research asst. Research Analysis Co., McLean, Va.; grad. research asst. Va. Poly. Inst. and State U., Reston; congl. fellow U.S. Dept. Agr., Washington, 1984. Recipient Superior Performance award Soil Conservation Service, Washington, 1978; Commendation award Office Mgmt. and Budget, 1979; Cert. of Achievement, Pres. of U.S., 1980; Spl. Act award Sec. Agr., 1983. Mem. Orgn. Profl. Employment of USDA (exec. v.p. 1982-85), Am. Inst. Cert. Planners (charter mem.), Soil Conservation Soc. Am. (chpt. sec. 1977), World Future Soc. Office: Soil Conservation Service USDA 14 & Independence Ave SW Washington DC 20250

CUTLER, BESS, art gallery dealer; b. Salem, Mass., Dec. 13, 1949; d. Joseph George and Deborah Willard (Roud) Cutler. B.A., Brandeis U., 1971; M.F.A., Tufts U., 1976. Co-dir. Cutler/Stavaridis Gallery, Boston, 1978-83; owner, dir. Bess Cutler Gallery, N.Y.C., 1983—; instr. DeCordova Mus., Lincoln, Mass., 1976-80; painter. Visitor Sch. Mus. Fine Arts, Boston, 1983—. Democrat. Jewish. Office: Bess Cutler Gallery 164 Mercer St New York NY 10012

CUTLER, BEVERLY WINSLOW, judge; b. Washington, Sept. 10, 1949; d. Lloyd Norton and Louise Winslow (Howe) Cutler; m. Mark Andrew Weaver, Sept. 22, 1977; children—Lucia Mary, Andrew Thaddeus. B.A., Stanford U., 1971; J.D., Yale U., 1974. Bar: Alaska 1975. Research atty. Alaska Jud. Council, Anchorage, 1974-75; atty. Alaska Pub. Defender Agy., Anchorage, 1975-77; judge Alaska Dist. Ct., Anchorage, 1977-82, Alaska Superior Ct., Palmer, 1982—. Mem. ABA, Alaska Bar Assn., Anchorage Assn. Women Lawyers, Nat. Assn. Women Judges, Nat. Assn. Women in Criminal Justice. Home: Edgerton Park Rd Palmer AK 99645 Office: Alaska Court System 268 E Firewood Ln Palmer AK 99645

CUTLER, MARTHA MARIE EMERY, publishing executive; b. Lodi, Calif., Sept. 15, 1939; d. Wallace Haile and Elizabeth Dorothy Emery; m. David H. Cutler, Dec. 6, 1959; children—Geoffrey Horton, Gregory Abbott. B.A. in Elem. Edn., Calif. State U.-Los Angeles, 1965. Corp. v.p. Merchant Mag., Inc., Newport Beach, Calif., 1965—, also dir.; corp. v.p. Cutler Pub., Inc., Newport Beach, 1981—, also dir. Mem. Jr. League Newport Harbor. Recipient award for vol. hours given to Huntington Meml. Hosp., Huntington Meml. Clinic Aux., Pasadena, Calif., 1972. Republican. Episcopalian. Clubs: Newport Beach & Tennis, Seaview Swim and Tennis. Home: 2011 Yacht Vindex Newport Beach CA 92660 Office: 4500 Campus Dr Suite 480 Newport Beach CA 92660

CUTLER, PHYLLIS L., librarian; b. Boston, Mar. 31, 1928; d. Louis and Sadie (Ginsberg) Nanes; m. Maxwell Cutler, Dec. 23, 1948; children—Lewis Howard, Neal David, Jonathan Dana. A.B., Harvard U., 1962; M.L.S., Simmons Coll., 1966. Adminstrv. asst. Morrill Meml. Library, Norwood,

Mass., 1968-71; asst. univ. librarian Brandeis U., Waltham, Mass., 1971-82; coll. librarian Williams Coll., Willimstown, Mass., 1982—; lectr. in field. Mem. ALA, Spl. Libraries Assn. (sec. 1973-74), New Eng. Library Assn. (chmn. coll. libraries sect. 1978), Simmons Coll. Alumni Assn. (pres. chpt. 1982-83, governing bd. 1976—). Office: Williams College Sawyer Library Williamstown MA 01267

CUTLER, RUTH ELLEN LEMON, publisher; b. York, Nebr., Feb. 26, 1928; d. Harry Oliver and Ruby Elizabeth (Hartgrave) Lemon; student Latter-day Saints Bus. Coll., 1946; m. Harold Max Cutler, Nov. 17, 1944 (div. 1971); children—Sheryl, Harold Max, Pamela. Sec., photostat operator IRS, Salt Lake City, 1951-54; sec. Purdue U. Sch. Civil Engring., West Lafayette, Ind. and engring. firms, 1954-60; exec. sec. Rico Argentine Mining Co., Salt Lake City and Rico, Colo., 1960-63; exec., legal sec. Manpower, Inc., Salt Lake City, 1959-71; owner, operator Mountain View Motel and Country Club Motel, Salt Lake City, 1963-64; exec. sec., adminstrv. asst. to clin. psychologist in pvt. practice, Salt Lake City, 1964-70; legal sec., head office staff Watkins & Faber, attys., Salt Lake City, 1971-73; adminstrv. sec. F-15 Radar div. Hughes Aircraft Co., Culver City, Calif., 1973—; dir., v.p., sec. Cutler Enterprises, Inc., Salt Lake City, 1963-71; founder, pres., pub. Gallant House Inc., Heber City, Utah, 1983—. State del. Utah Republican party, 1967-69; active various community drives. Mem. League Utah Writers. Home: RFD Box 289 Heber City UT 84032

CUTLER, SEENA NORMA, psychiatric social worker; b. N.Y.C., Apr. 18, 1928; d. Nat and Rose S. Schwartz; B.A., N.Y. U., Washington Sq. Coll., 1951; M.S.W., Columbia U., 1955; m. B. Robert Cutler, Nov. 24, 1954; children—Andrew Neale, Matthew Steven. Social worker Bklyn. VA Hosp., 1955-59, Roosevelt Hosp., N.Y.C., 1974-77; sr. social worker, supr. Community Health Program, Queens-Nassau, Inc., New Hyde Park, N.Y., 1977—; pvt. practice therapist; cons. VA Div. of Handicapped, Kansas City, Kans., 1976; guest lectr. Nassau County Dept. Sr. Citizens Affairs, 1980-81, Am. Cancer Soc., 1981, Am. Coll. Obstetrics and Gynecology; group therapist, various groups, 1979-81, 83-84. Bd. dirs. and com. mem. Temple Emanuel of Gt. Neck, N.Y., 1965-76, v.p. Sisterhood, 1969-71; com. mem. Gt. Neck Public Schs., 1964-79. Recipient award, Bklyn. VA Hosp., 1959; cert. social worker. Mem. Nat. Assn. Social Workers. Democrat. Home: 48 Berkshire Rd Great Neck NY 11023 Office: 410 Lakeville Rd New Hyde Park NY 11042

CUTRONE, PAMELA F., real estate executive; b. Greenwich, Conn., Dec. 6, 1954; d. Edwin Dewey, Jr. and Margaret (Cantello) Frost; m. Patsy Cutrone, Jr., Sept. 10, 1983; children—Leann, Susan. Grad. Katherine Gibbs Sch., 1976, Conn. Real Estate Inst., 1980. Mgr. adminstrn. Hyers/Smith, Inc., Norwalk, Conn., 1978-85, corp. sec., 1984—; Realtor, Diversified Realty Assocs., Norwalk, 1985—. Bd. dirs. Conn. Arthritis Found., vol. Wethersfield, 1983—; chmn. Norwalk Arthritis Support Group, Norwalk Hosp., 1984—; fin. dir. St. Paul's Choir Guild, Norwalk, 1986. Mem. Norwalk Bd. Realtors, Darien Bd. Realtors, Nat. Assn. Female Execs. Clubs: Women's of Norwalk, Women's Aux. of South Norwalk Boat Club. Office: Diversified Realty Assocs 178 Connecticut Ave Norwalk CT 06854

CUTTING, MARY DOROTHEA, audio and audio-visual communications company executive; b. N.Y.C., Feb. 20, 1943; d. Elliotte Robinson and Mary Dorothea (Clarke) Little; m. James H. B. Cutting, July 18, 1964; children—Gwendolyn Louise, Laura Elizabeth. Student Whitman Coll., 1960-62; B.A. in English Lit., U. Wash., 1964. Tchr. English, Severna Park High Sch., Md., 1965-66; remedial reading substitute tchr. St. Patrick's Day Sch., Washington, 1976-77; v.p. mktg. The Cutting Corp., Washington, 1978—, also dir. Editor children's cassettes: Fisher-Price Toys Spellbinder Series, 1983 (Consumer Com. of Ams. for Democratic Action award for being one of nation's 6 best toys for under $5 1983). Vol. chmn., bd. dirs. Washington Assn. for TV and Children, 1977. Mem. Internat. Assn. Bus. Communicators, Jr. League Washington (bd. dirs. 1977). Republican. Episcopalian. Office: The Cutting Corp 4200 Wisconsin Ave Suite 523 Washington DC 20016

CYN, T.G., writer; b. Hollywood, Calif., Feb. 29, 1948; d. Edwin Whitfield and Virginia Lou (Newcomb) McKinley; m. Gerald J. Harvey, June 28, 1970 (div. 1976); m. 2d, Stanley John Maleski, Jr., Oct. 21, 1979 (div. 1984). Student Riverside City Coll., 1965-67, Orange Coast Coll., 1967-68. Editor Al buraag mag., 1979; freelance writer, editor Profl. Horseman, Equine Practitioner, Small Animal Practitioner, The Consultant, Arabian Horse Mktg. and Bus. Rev., Washington, 1980-82; dir. publs. Am. Horse Council, Washington, 1982-84; cons. Haifa Arabians, Diamond Bar, Calif., 1983—, Khemosabi Syndicate, Diamond Bar, 1983—; pres. T. G. Cyn & Co. Author: Tangled Mane, 1983; Gardner Bloodstock Consultant, 1980; Resilient Heart Cowards, 1985, Tangled Mane Volume, II, 1986; The Lonesome Pony, 1986. Mem. Women in Communications, Internat. Arabian Horse Assn., Arabian Horse Registry Am., Am. Horse Shows Assn.

CYWINSKI, DONNA LEEDS, lawyer; b. Miami, Fla., Apr. 26, 1955; d. Donald Rexon and Loma Catherine (Rafferty) Leeds; m. Richard Anthony Cywinski, Jan. 3, 1976. B.A., Villanova U., 1978; J.D., U. Houston, 1982. Bar: Tex. 1982. Briefing atty. 1st Ct. Appeals Tex., Houston, 1982-83; assoc. Harvill and Hardy, Houston, 1983—. Mem. ABA, Tex. State Bar Assn., Houston Bar Assn., Houston Young Lawyers Assn., Houston Trial Lawyers Assn., Assn. Women Attys., Order of Barristers, Phi Kappa Phi, Phi Alpha Theta. Home: 17127 Park Lodge Dr Spring TX 77279 Office: Harvill & Hardy 500 Two Houston Ctr Houston TX 77002

CZARSTY, JUDITH BRANCH, government official, accountant; b. Newport News, Va., Feb. 24, 1944; d. Alexander Newsome and Iris Fern (Patchell) Branch; m. Steven Lawrence Czarsty, Aug. 10, 1974; 1 child, Steven L. Jr. B.S. cum laude, George Mason U., 1974. Staff auditor GAO, Washington, 1974-78, chief adminstr. fin., 1978-80, dep. chief, fin. mgmt. br., 1980-83, supervisory acct./auditor, 1983—. Recipient cert. Merit, GAO, 1977, Div. Dir.'s award, 1979, GAO Meritorious Service award, 1980. Mem. Am. Acctg. Assn., Am. Inst. for Decision Scis., Altrusa Internat. (chpt. treas. 1982-85), Mary Washington Coll. Alumni, Beta Epsilon Phi (chpt. pres. 1972-73), Alpha Chi. Club: Faculty Wives (Mary Washington Coll., Fredericksburg, Va.). Avocations: recreational vehicle camping; tennis. Home: PO Box 1494 Fredericksburg VA 22402 Office: US Gen Accounting Office 1111 18th St Washington DC 20548

CZAYA, MARY THERESA, educational administrator; b. Carteret, N.J., June 2, 1917; d. Francis and Theresa (Mezglewski) Dylag; B.S., N.J. State Tchrs. Coll., 1947; M.Ed., Rutgers U., 1957; postgrad. U. Mexico, 1958; m. Francis Czaya, June 22, 1946; 1 son, Paul. Tchr., Nathan Hale Sch., Carteret, N.J., 1940-46, Columbus Sch., Carteret, 1946-61, prin., 1961-70; prin. Washington & Cleveland Schs., Carteret, 1970-79, Minue Sch., Carteret, 1979-83. Trustee Carteret Public Library, 1972-78; mem. Middlesex County Mental Health Bd., 1961-66, Carteret Juvenile Delinquency Bd., 1974-75; trustee Middlesex County Coll., 1972—, bd. sec., 1978-81, bd. v.p., 1981—. Recipient cert. of merit VFW Aux., 1978. Mem. N.J. Congress Parents and Tchrs. (life), Nat. Elem. Prins. Assn., N.J. Elem. Prins. Assn., Kappa Delta Phi. Home: 75 Edgar St Carteret NJ 07008

CZERWIEC, ELOISE IRENE, nursing educator; b. Plymouth, Ind., Nov. 14, 1946; d. Francis William and Irene Marie (Pickavet) Xaver; m. Anthony John Czerwiec, Jr., May 29, 1971; children—Laura Louise, Anthony John, III. A.A., Ancilla Coll., 1967; B.S. in Nursing, DePaul U., 1970. Registered nurse. Med. surg. and nursery staff nurse Presbyn.-St. Lukes Hosp., Chgo., 1970-72; nursery charge nurse Holy Cross Hosp., Chgo., 1972-74; tchr. practical nursing program Chgo. Pub. Schs., 1974—. Leader, Chgo. Council 4-H, 1983. Mem. Nat. League Nursing, Ill. League Nursing, Chgo. Tchrs. Union, DePaul U. Nursing Alumni Assn., Goebel Collectors Club. Democrat. Roman Catholic. Office Practical Nursing Program Chicago Pub Schs 2131 W Monroe St Chicago IL 60612

CZNARTY, DONNA MAE, educator; b. Bridgeport, Conn., Aug. 17, 1950; d. Richard W. and Dorothy Mae (Kosturko (Oefinger); m. William C. Cole, Jr., July 11, 1970; 1 child, Michael William Cole; m. Thomas Robert Cznarty, Apr. 29, 1983. B.S. in Edn., So. Conn. State U., 1973, M.S. in Edn., 1977. Lang. arts tchr. Shelton Bd. Edn., Conn., 1973-82; English tchr. Millbrook Bd. Edn., N.Y., 1985—. Mem. Mid-Hudson Reading Council, Internat. Reading Assn., Nat. Assn. Female Execs. Republican. Roman Catholic. Avocations: Interior design; fashion; travel Home: 71 Hibernia Heights Dr Salt Point NY 12578 Office: Millbrook High Sch Alden Pl Millbrook NY 12545

DAANE, JEANETTE KALOUS, librarian; b. Fond du Lac, Wis., June 7, 1929; d. Frank Otto and Adela Henrietta (Hirsig) Kalous; m. Calvin John Daane, Dec. 19, 1948; children—Jean Ghose, Pieter Daane, Elizabeth Daane Stolle. B.A., Rockford Coll., 1952; M.S., Ind. U., 1956; M.L.S., U. Hawaii, 1969; M.A., Ariz. State U., 1979. Elementary tchr. Grosse Pointe Public Schs. (Mich.), 1952, St. Claire Shores Public Schs. (Mich.), 1952-53, Bedford Public Schs. (Ind.), 1953-55, Dade County Public Schs., Miami, 1955-56; librarian Tempe Public Schs. (Ariz.), 1963-68, Mesa Community Coll. (Ariz.), 1969—, instr. humanities, 1983—, instr. library tech., 1969—. Pres., Democratic Women, Tempe, 1963. Title II-B fellow, 1968-69. Mem. Ariz. Library Assn. (treas. 1982-84, Disting. Service award 1984), ALA. Democrat. Episcopalian. Home: 2123 S Paseo Loma Mesa AZ 95202 Office: Mesa Community Coll 1833 W Southern Ave Mesa AZ 95202

DABNEY, JUNE BOSLEY, educator, singer; b. St. Louis, Apr. 13, 1935; d. Preston Tyler and Alma Jean (Thompson) Bosley; B.M.E., Lincoln U., 1956; postgrad. Harris-Stowe State Coll., summers 1964-68, St. Louis U., summer, 1964, Webster Coll., 1980—; children—Diane Charisse Hawkins, Dellarese Carmen Hawkins, Marion P. Hawkins, Raphael Franklin Dabney. Tchr. vocal music and voice S.W. High Sch., 1976-77; tchr. vocal music, founder Honors Concert Choir, Visual and Performing Arts High Sch., St. Louis, 1977-80; tchr. vocal music, dir. student activities, Honors Music High Sch., 1980-82; music dir. Peacock Alley Cultural Art Center Workshops, St. Louis, 1982—; band dir. Cleveland High Sch., St. Louis, 1983-84; performing concert artist. Democratic committeewoman 1st Ward, St. Louis, 1974-76. Met. Opera audition winner, 1966; Ted Mack Original Amateur Hour winner, 1966-67; Recipient service award Chick Finney Assocs., 1970, Meritorious award in music St. Louis Silhouettes, 1967, Black Women of Unity award, 1974, Key to City and Gateway, Mayor A.J. Cervantes, 1975; Sumner High Sch. Alumni soloist 30th Anniversary, 1980; recipient Katz Radio Service award, 1966, service award Honors Music High Sch., 1982. Mem. Nat. Assn. Female Execs., Clarence Wilson Music Guild, Delta Sigma Theta. Club: St. Louis Div. Devel. Treatment Center Parents. Home: 5024 Durant Ave Saint Louis MO 63115

DABOLL, EVELYN LOUISE KENYON, tax and fin., real estate cons.; b. Old Mystic, Conn., Feb. 22, 1927; d. Anson Surber and L. Maude (Tinker) Kenyon; student Jackson (Miss.) Sch. Law, 1954; m. H. Merle Witt, Oct. 29, 1945 (div. Apr. 1956); m. 2d, Frederick A. Daboll, Feb. 9, 1962. Instr. traffic dept. So. New Eng. Telephone Co., New Britain, Conn. and Mystic, Conn., 1943-45; residential designer Frank Kincannon, AIA, Tupelo, Miss., 1949-51; chief dep. Chancery clk. Chancery Clk's Office, Tupelo, 1951-54; jr. partner Sadler Oil Co., Jackson, Miss., 1954-61; owner, operator Witt Enterprises, bookkeeping and secretarial services, 1961-62; adminstr. asst. Copp, Brenneman & Tighe, attys., New London, Conn., 1961-62; owner, operator Daboll Enterprises, Noank, Conn., 1963—. Moderator, Town of Groton Rep. Town Meeting, 1969-70, rep., 1968-70; mem. Bd. Selectmen Groton, 1980-81. Mem. New London Bd. Realtors, VFW Aux. Democrat. Baptist. Address: 206 Seneca Dr Noank CT 06340

DACEY, EILEEN M., lawyer; b. N.Y.C., Dec. 15, 1948; d. Gabriel A. and Mary (Breen) D.; m. Kinchen C. Bizzell, Jan. 1, 1984 B.A. in Sociology, SUNY-Stony Brook, 1970; J.D., St. John's U., 1975. Assoc. Mendes & Mount, N.Y.C., 1976-80, jr. ptnr., 1980—. Mem. Vol. Lawyers for the Arts. Mem. ABA, Assn. Bar City N.Y., (com. on ins. law). Republican. Home: 208 E 35th St New York NY 10016 Office: Mendes & Mount 3 Park Ave New York NY 10016

DACEY, KATHLEEN RYAN, judge; b. Boston; A.B. with honors, Emmanuel Coll., 1941; M.S. in L.S. (Mass. Library Assn. scholar), Simmons Coll., 1942; LL.B., Northeastern U., 1945, J.D., 1945; postgrad. Boston U. Law Sch., 1945-46. Admitted to Mass. bar, 1945, U.S. Supreme Ct. bar, 1957; law clk. to justices Mass. Supreme Jud. Ct., 1945-47; practiced in Boston, 1947-75; asst. atty. gen., chief civil bur. Mass. Dep. Atty. Gen., Boston, 1975-77; U.S. Adminstrv. law judge, 1977—; auditor, master Commonwealth of Mass., 1972-75, Suffolk and Norfolk Counties (Mass.), 1972-75; asst. dist. atty. Suffolk County, 1971-72, mem. panel def. counsel for indigent persons U.S. Dist. Ct., Dist. Mass.; lectr., speaker in field. Bd. dirs. Mission United Neighborhood Improvement Team, Boston; mem. Boston Sch. Com., 1945-46, chmn., 1946-47. Recipient Oratorical Contest prize Am. Legion; Silver Shingle award Boston U. Sch. Law, 1980; named Alumnae Woman of Year Northeastern U. Law Sch. Alumni Assn., 1976. Mem. Internat. Bar Assn., Am. Bar Assn. (ho. of dels. 1981—), Mass. Bar Assn., Boston Bar Assn., Norfolk Bar Assn., Middlesex Bar Assn., Am. Trial Lawyers Assn., Mass. Trial Lawyers Assn., Nat. Assn. Women Lawyers (pres.), Mass. Assn. Women Lawyers, Internat. Fedn. Women Lawyers, Boston U. Law Sch. Alumni Assn. (corr. sec. 1974-76), Boston U. Nat. Alumni Council. Contbr. articles to legal jours. Office: Health and Human Services Bur Hearings and Appeals 55 Summer St Boston MA 02110

DADURKA, VICKI, business consultant; b. Shamokin, Pa.; d. Edward and Florence (Pilarski) Dadurka. Student Santa Monica Coll. (Calif.), 1973-74; J.D., U. San Fernando, 1979; cert. fin. mgmt., NYU, 1982. Bar: Calif. 1980. Legal, exec. secretarial and adminstrv. positions, Calif. and Pa., 1965-75; paralegal Pratter & Young, Beverly Hills, Calif., 1976-78; legal asst. Gibson, Dunn & Crutcher, Century City, Calif., 1978-79; sole practice, Los Angeles, 1980-84; project coordinator Los Angeles Olympic Organizing Com., Los Angeles, 1984. Treas., Dauphin County Young Democrats, Harrisburg, Pa., 1971, exec. bd. dirs., 1971-72. Recipient Am. Jurisprudence award Bancroft-Whitney Co., 1978; Spl. Community Service award Dauphin County Young Democrats., 1971. Mem. ABA, Los Angeles County Bar Assn., Women Lawyers Assn. of Los Angeles, Nat. Assn. Female Execs. Office: PO Box 25778 Los Angeles CA 90025

DAFFIN, CAROL FARWELL, manufacturing company executive; b. Harrison, N.Y., Oct. 21, 1953; d. Edward B. and Frances R. (Brown) Farwell; student Chesapeake Coll., 1981, U. Md., 1976-77; m. Ronald Wayne Daffin, July 9, 1977; children—Jenny Alice, Kate Frances, Paul Edward. Salesman, Easton (Md.) Pub. Co., 1973-74; sales mgr. Chesapeake Products, Inc., Easton, 1974-75; v.p. Helm Distbrs., Inc., Easton, 1975-78, now dir.; pres. Daffin Disposables, Inc., Secretary, Md., 1977—, also dir.; dir. Daffin Corp., Secretary. Recipient Md. tng. grant, 1980, 83. Mem. NOW, Nat. Safety Council, Nat. Assn. Women in Bus., Safety Equipment Mfrs. Assn., Nat. Safety Equipment Dealers Assn., Am. Nuclear Soc., Am. Apparel Mfrs. Assn., Indsl. Safety Equipment Assn., Talbot County Bd. Realtors, Nat. Assn. Bus. and Profl. Women (Young Career Woman award 1982), Internat. Non-Woven Dealers Assn., Talbot County C. of C., Dorchester County C. of C. Republican. Office: 1 Daffin Square Secretary MD 21664

DAFOE, ARDITH JEANNE, lawyer; b. Zeeland, Mich., Nov. 11, 1938; d. Clarence H. and Ann (Goodyke) Brower; m. Darrell Duane DaFoe, Sept. 15, 1962 (div. Aug. 1977); children—Rachelle Anne, Chad Matthew. B.A., Hope Coll., 1960; M.A., Mich. State U., 1976; J.D., Thomas M. Cooley Law Sch., Lansing, Mich., 1982. Bar: Mich. 1982, U.S. Dist. Ct. (ea. and we. dists.) Mich. 1982, U.S. Ct. Appeals (6th cir.) 1985, U.S. Supreme Ct. 1986. Policewoman, Lansing Police Dept., 1960-63; social worker Ingham County Probate Ct., Lansing, 1963-66; exec. dir. Big Sisters of Lansing, Inc., 1967-73, Big Bros./Big Sisters of Greater Lansing, Inc., 1973-80; assoc. Hankins & Assocs., P.C., Okemos, Mich., 1982-84; sole practice, Lansing, 1984-85, Office of Criminal Justice, 1985—. Editorial bd. Law Rev. Thomas M. Cooley Law Sch., 1980-81. Recipient award Big Sisters Internat., Inc., Big Bros./Big Sisters Am., Inc., 1976. Mem. ABA, Mich. Bar Assn., Ingham County Bar Assn., Assn. Trial Lawyers Am., Mich. Trial Lawyers Assn. Office: PO Box 30026 Lansing MI 48909

DAGG, DIANE MARIE, information processing specialist; b. Wichita, Kans., May 1, 1953; d. Ronald Martin and Bonnie Mae (Lyons) Gray; m. Adam LeRoy Dagg, Dec. 11, 1982. Student Kans. Wesleyan U., 1971-74; B.B.A. in Econs., Washburn U., 1977. Adminstrv. asst. The Villages, Inc., Topeka, 1975-81; office support mgr. Office Automation Systems of Topeka, Inc., Topeka, 1981—. Actress Topeka Civic Theatre, 1975—; dancer Topeka Ballet Co., 1978; bd. dirs. Dance Arts Topeka, 1979-81, v.p.-membership, 1980-81. Named Best Actress, Alpha Psi Omega, Kans. Wesleyan U., 1972, 75; recipient Renna Hunter awards (2) Topeka Civic Theatre, 1984-85. Democrat. Presbyterian. Office: Office Automation Systems Topeka Inc 3124 SW 29th St Suite 1 Topeka KS 66614

DAGGETT, MARSHA LEA, home economist, educator; b. Ft. Stockton, Tex., Feb. 10, 1917; d. Marsh and Artie (McLeod) Lea; B.S., Tex. Women's U., 1938; M.Ed., Sam Houston State U., 1957; Ph.D., Tex. Woman's U., 1972; m. Walter M. Daggett, June 19, 1938 (div. 1964); 1 son, Merrell. Tchr. sci. Calvert (Tex.) High Sch., 1954-57; tchr. vocat. home econs. Bremond (Tex.) High Sch., 1960-61; instr. home econs. Sam Houston State U., Huntsville, 1962-63, Stephen F. Austin State U., Nacogdoches, Tex., 1963-64; instr. to asst. prof. home econs. Lamar U., Beaumont, Tex., 1964-71; asst. to asso. prof. home econs. S.W. Tex. State U., San Marcos, 1972-77. Recipient teaching excellence award S.W. Tex. State U., 1975. Mem. Am., Tex. (exec. council 1966-72, 77—) home econs. assns., Jefferson, Tex. hist. assns., Internat. Nutrition Congress, Internat. Fedn. Home Econs., Internat., Am. dietetic assns., AAUP, AAUW, Inst. Food Technologists, Soc. Nutrition Edn., Nutrition Today, Tex. Nutrition Council (exec. council 1965-72), Internat. Gem Finders Soc., Ft. Stockton Hist. Soc. (dir. 1978-86, pres. 1980-82), Tex. Sheep and Goat Raisers Assn., Pecos County Livestock Show Assn., Pecos County Hist. Com., Tex. Womans U. Alumnae Assn., Nat. Wildlife Fedn. (world asso. mem.), Kappa Lambda Kappa (Tchr. of Yr. 1974, Appreciation award 1977), Delta Kappa Gamma, Kappa Omicron Phi, Phi Epsilon Omicron. Presbyn. Club: Pioneer (pres. 1978-79) (Ft. Stockton), Fort Stockton Lit. (pres. 1984-85). Editor Pecos County History, 1978-84. Home: Box 1545 Fort Stockton TX 79735

D'AGNESE, HELEN JEAN (MRS. JOHN J. D'AGNESE), artist; b. N.Y.C.; d. Leonardo and Rose (Redavid) De Santis; student CUNY, 1940-42, Oakland Art Inst., 1954-56; m. John J. D'Agnese, Oct. 29, 1942; children—John, Linda, Diane, Michele, Helen, Gina, Paul. One-man shows: Maude Sullivan Gallery, El Paso, 1964, John Wanamaker Gallery, Phila., 1966, U. N.Mex., 1967, Karo Manducci Gallery, San Francisco, 1968, Tuskegee Inst. Carver Mus., 1968, Lord & Taylor Gallery, N.Y.C., 1969, Harmon Gallery, Naples, Fla., 1970, Fountainbleau, Miami, 1970, Reflections Gallery, Atlanta, 1972, Williams Gallery, Atlanta, 1973, Americana Gallery, Mineola, Tex., 1977, E. M. Howard Gallery, Amelia Island, Fla., 1978, Haitian Primitives Gallery, 1981, others; group shows: Musseo des Artes, Juárez, México, 1968, Benedictine Art Show, N.Y.C., 1967, Southeast Contemporary Art Show, Atlanta, 1968, Atlanta U., 1969, Red Piano Gallery, Hilton Head, S.C., Terrace Gallery, Atlanta, Ann. Bible Heritage Art Exhibit, Marietta, Ga., 1976, Nat. Judaic Theme Exhbn., Atlanta, 1976, Crystal Britton Gallery, Atlanta; represented in permanent collections: Pres. Jimmy Carter, Juarez (Mexico) Art Mus., Vatican Mus., Rome, Atlanta Art Gallery. Judge art show Mt. Loretto Acad., El Paso, 1967; commd., executed sculpture of Bob Marley in Limestone, 1985; art demonstration and lectr. Margaret Harris Sch., Atlanta, 1970; artist-in-residence Montessori Sch., Atlanta, 1978-79. Recipient Gold medal Accademia Italia delle Arti, Italy, 1979; 1st place sculpture award Tybee Island Art Festival, 1982. Mem. Atlanta Lawn Tennis Assn. Club: Tennis (Atlanta). Address: 1683 Knob Hill Ct NE Atlanta GA 30329

DAGUANO, KAREN MARTHA, educational administrator, consultant; b. Jersey City, Mar. 15, 1950; d. Albert and Helen Therese (Zelenty) Daguano. B.A., Jersey City State Coll., 1972; M.Ed., U. Va., 1973, Ed.D., 1981. Tchr. spl. edn. Virginia Beach City Schs. (Va.), 1973-77; asst. dir. instnl. research SUNY-New Paltz, 1981-83, dir. instnl. research, 1983-85; dir. instnl. research and planning Glassboro State Coll., N.J., 1985—. Mem. Am. Ednl. Research Assn., Assn. Instnl. Research, SUNY Assn. Instl. Research and Planning Officers, Advancement Women in Higher Edn. Adminstrn. Democrat. Roman Catholic. Office: Office Instnl Research and Planning Glassboro State Coll Glassboro NJ 08028

D'AGUSTO, KAREN ROSE, lawyer; b. Phila., Jan. 4, 1952; d. Les and Anne (Masciarelli) Heilenman; m. Stephen Joseph Bernasconi, Aug. 21, 1976; 1 dau., Lesley Anne D'Agusto. B.A. in History cum laude, Immaculata Coll., 1974; J.D., U. San Diego, 1977; postgrad. U. So. Calif., 1983—. Bar: Conn. 1977, Hawaii 1978. Tng. coordinator Protection and Advocacy, Honolulu, 1978, advocacy coordinator, 1979, staff atty., 1980-81, assoc. dir., 1982, project dir., 1983—; pvt. practice law, Mililani, Hawaii, 1980—; instr. Hawaii Pacific Coll., Honolulu, 1982; atty. Mil. Montessori Sch., Honolulu, 1982-84; dir. Harmon-Johnson Inst., Honolulu, 1983—. Author: Legal Rights of Handicapped, 1980. Author, editor curriculum Vol. Guardians Ad. Litem, 1982. Pres. Central Oahu Mental Health Center, Pearl City, Hawaii, 1981-82. Mem. Nat. Assn. Female Execs., Am. Bar Assn., Hawaii State Bar Assn., Hawaii Lawyers Care, Am. Assn. Counsel for Children Counsel. Office: Protection and Advocacy 1580 Makaloa Ave Honolulu HI 96789

DAHBANY, AVIVAH, psychologist; b. Bklyn., Jan. 3, 1951; d. Hyman and Esther (Levy) D.; B.A., CCNY, 1974, M.S., 1978. Fellow in Clin. Psychology Albert Einstein Coll. Medicine, 1976-77; psychologist Adams Sch., N.Y.C., 1977-78; dir. spl. edn., psychologist Dov Revel Yeshiva, Forest Hills, N.Y., 1978-79; psychologist Franklin Twp. Public Schs., Somerset, N.J., 1979—; adj. lectr. CCNY, 1977-78; adj. instr. Monmouth Coll., 1981; psychol. cons. Middlesex Gen. U. Hosp., Laurie Devel. Inst., Child Evaluation Ctr., 1985—. Mem. N.Y. Assn. Sch. Psychologists (chairperson student certification task force 1977-78), Am. Psychol. Assn., Nat. Assn. Sch. Psychologists, NEA. Home: 1425H Oak Tree Dr North Brunswick NJ 08902 Office: Pupil Personnel Services 761 Hamilton St Somerset NJ 08873

DAHIR, CAROL ANN, arts and educational administrator, consultant; b. Bklyn., Jan. 1, 1950; d. Mitchell Najeeb and Laura Bernice (Abrams) D. B.A., SUNY-Stony Brook, 1971, M.A., 1972; postgrad. C. W. Post Coll., Greenvale, N.Y., 1972-77, 85—, NYU, 1983-84. Cert. elem. and secondary counselor, sch. dist. adminstr., N.Y. Tchr. Middle Country Schs., Centereach, N.Y., 1971-75, counselor, 1976—; exec. dir. Kids for Kids Prodns., Inc., Centereach, 1977—; cons. arts adminstrn. and devel., Long Island, N.Y.C., 1980—. Mem. alumni bd. Stony Brook Alumni, 1972-75. Recipient Jenkins award PTA, 1982, Harold award Three Village Newspaper, 1985. Mem. Am. Theatre Assn., Children's Theatre Assn., Nat. Assn. Female Execs., AAUW, N.Y. State Tchr.'s Assn. Avocations: theatre; museums; skiing; tennis; reading.

DAHL, ARLENE, actress, author, fashion designer; b. Mpls., Aug. 11, 1928; d. Rudolph and Idelle (Swan) Dahl; student (1st, 2d, 3d scholastic prizes for fashion designs) U. Minn., Mpls. Inst. Art, Mpls. Coll. Music, Mpls. Bus. Coll.; m. Marc A. Rosen, 1984; children by previous marriage—Lorenzo Lamas, Carole Christine Holmes, Stephen Schaum. Broadway appearances include Mr. Strauss Goes to Boston, 1946, Cyrano de Bergerac, 1953, Applause, 1972; 28 motion pictures include My Wild Irish Rose, 1947, Three Little Words, 1950, Sangaree, 1953, Woman's World, 1954, Journey to the Center of the Earth, 1959, Kisses for My President, 1963, The Land Raiders, 1969; TV series: Arlene Dahl's Beauty Spot, ABC-TV, 1965-66, Arlene Dahl's Starscope, 1979-80 H.B.O. and Arlene Dahl's Lovescopes, ABC, 1982, 83; guest appearances Jig Saw John, Burke's Law, Chrysler Theater, Love Boat, Fantasy Island, One Life To Live, also nat. talk and quiz shows; syndicated beauty columnist Chgo. Tribune—N.Y. News Syndicate, 1950-71; designer sleepwear A. N. Saab & Co., 1951-57; v.p. Kenyon & Eckhardt Advt. Agy., Inc., 1967-72, pres. woman's world div., 1967-72; nat. beauty and health dir. Sears, Roebuck & Co., 1970-75; pres. Arlene Dahl Enterprises, 1965-75, Dahlia Parfums, Inc., 1975—, Dahlia Prodns., Inc., 1978—, Dahlmark Prodns. Internat., 1981—; designer Vogue Patterns, 1980-85; Hon. life mem. Father Flanagan's Boys Town, Hollywood Mus.; bd. dirs. Pearl Buck Found; ambassadress City of Hope. Decorated comdr. Order de Bontemps de Bordeaux; named Woman of Yr. in Communications, N.Y. Advt. Club, 1969; Mother of Yr., 1980; Heads of Fame award, 1982; Bronze Halo award, 1983—; Todays Woman, 1981; winner 8 Laurel box office awards for motion pictures. Mem. Acad. Motion Picture Arts and Scis., Nat. Acad. TV Arts and Scis., Authors League, Acad. TV Arts and Scis. Author: Always Ask a Man, 1965; 12 Beautyscopes, 1968, rev. edit., 1978, Secrets of Hair Care, 1970; Secrets of Skin Care, 1970; Beyond Beauty, 1980; Arlene Dahl's Lovescopes, 1983. Address: PO Box 911 Beverly Hills CA 90213

DAHLBERG, ELIZABETH LUNDQUIST, consulting radio engineer; b. N.Y.C., Apr. 2, 1918; d. Otto William and Eleanor (Van Twisk) Lundquist; m. Gustav I. Dahlberg, Oct. 12, 1946; children—Mariane Diaz, William G. Dahlberg. B.A., Hunter Coll., 1940; postgrad. George Washington U., 1945. Registered profl. engr., D.C. Cons. engr. Raymond Wilmotte Inc., Washington, 1945-47, Frank McIntosh & Assocs., Washington, 1947-56; cons. engr., ptnr. Lohnes & Culver, Washington, 1956—. Mem. Assn. Fed. Communications Cons. Engrs. (pres. 1973-74), Broadcast Pioneers (award for disting. service to broadcasting 1984). Roman Catholic. Lodge: Vasa Order of Am. Home: 6204 Winnebago Rd Bethesda MD 20816 Office: Lohnes & Culver 1156 15 St NW Washington DC 20005

DAHLBERG, JOYCE KAREN, communications consultant; b. Mpls., Sept. 30, 1943; d. Elon Clinton and Adelynne Elizabeth (Mitchell) Tuttle; m. Curtis Leroy Dahlberg, Dec. 23, 1967; children—Eric Curtis, Curtis Elon. B.A. cum laude, Hamline U., 1965; postgrad. U. Minn., community colls., 1965—. Tchr. English, Ind. Sch. Dist. 281, Robbinsdale, Minn., 1965-68; patient fin. rep. Univ. Hosps., U. Minn., Mpls., 1968-70; space analyst health scis. U. Minn., Mpls., 1970-71; freelance photographer, writer, editor for bus. communications, magazines, newspapers, Mpls., 1975—; newsletter editor Fridley Council for High Potential Children, 1981—, sec., 1981-82, pres., 1985-87; newsletter editor Minn. Park Suprs. Assn., 1980-86; writer ednl. videotapes Osseo TV/Media Prodns., 1978-81 (Upper Miss. Ednl. Videotape Competition award for excellence 1979); writer pub. relations materials, software manuals, other tech. manuals, poetry, photography, children's stories, bus. videotapes. Active United Methodist Ch., Fridley, Minn., 1978—, coordinator Year of Child, 1979; YWCA Program Council, 1975-78, No. Suburban YWCA, Mpls.; vol. tchr. OMNIBUS, Fridley Schs., 1982, community edn. tchr., 1985-86, others. Mem. Women in Communications (continuing edn. com., 1984-86), Minn. Council on Gifted and Talented (pres. Fridley chpt.), Nat. Assn. Gifted Children, Fridley Council for High Potential Children, Freelance Communicators Network, Minn. Women's Network. Methodist. Address: 205 Rice Creek Blvd NE Minneapolis MN 55432

DAHLBERG, NANCY LEE, religious executive; b Phila., May 21, 1946; d. Arthur Henderson and Mary Jane (Ringgold) Dunham; m. Dennis H. Dahlberg, June 3, 1965 (div. 1984); children—Kimberly Beth, Erik Todd. Student San Francisco State U., 1965-66, West Chester U., 1982-84, Edison U., 1984—. Mem. field staff San Francisco Bay council Girl Scouts U.S.A., Brisbane, Calif., 1972-73; fund raiser United Way, San Francisco, 1973-74; asst. dir. mktg. Barclays Bank of Calif., 1974-76; freelance research writer, Thousand Oaks, Calif., 1979-80, dir. pub. relations Nat. Ministries, Valley Forge, Pa., 1980—. Mem. Am. Bapt. Pub. Relations Assn., Internat. Communication Assn., Internat. Assn. Bus. Communicators, Women in Communication, Religious Pub. Relations Council. Democrat. Baptist. Office: Am Bapt Chs Nat Ministries PO Box 851 Valley Forge PA 19482

DAHLBERG, SOPHIA FLORANCE, insurance agent, writer; b. Tulsa, Sept. 4, 1928; d. Hayes Louis Little Bear and Lorraine Mary Ivers; student Okla. Coll. Liberal Arts, 1973; m. W. N. Overton, Dec. 30, 1944; children—Mickie Chouteau, Hayes Neil, Roger Dean, Michael Anthony, Nakomis Ann; m. 2d, Gilbert Harry Dahlberg, Oct. 29, 1960. With Smoot-Holman, Inglewood, Calif., 1950-51, N.Am. Aviation, Compton, Calif., 1959-60; restaurant mgr. Catalina Island, Calif., 1964-66; mgr. Authentic Am. Indian Singers and Dancers, 1961-64; dancer, 1944-81; bail bondsman Stuyvesant Ins., Davenport, Iowa, 1977-80; life ins. agt., Duncan, Okla., 1984—; lectr. in field. Mem. Stephens County Hist. Soc., Duncan, Okla., 1972-82. Mem. Am. Legion Aux., Okla. Hist. Soc. Democrat. Roman Catholic. Clubs: Klash-Kah-she Indian Woman's, Cher-O-Kan Gateway Soc., others. Author: The Adventures of Nakomis, 1964; Osage Indian Neosho Agency in Kansas, 1983; The Enumeration of the Osage Tribe of Indians in Oklahoma, 1983; Those Illustrious Frenchmen, 1985; A Personal Experience, 1984; author children's stories. Contbr. biographies to hist. soc. publs., articles to profl. jours.

DAHLIN, ELIZABETH CARLSON, university administrator; b. Worcester, Mass., July 26, 1931; d. Alden Gustaf and Elizabeth Christine (Peterson) Carlson; B.A., Wellesley Coll., 1953; postgrad. Harvard U., 1953, 64; M.A., George Washington U., 1971; m. Douglas Gordon Dahlin, June 27, 1953; children—Christine Elizabeth, Cynthia Jean, Constance May. Substitute tchr. Fairfax County, Va., 1958-77; asst. folklife specialist, concessions mgr. Smithsonian Instn., Washington, 1976-77; asst. to exec. dir. Nat. Sch. Vol. Program, Alexandria, Va., 1978-80; asst. to v.p. devel. George Mason U., Fairfax, Va., 1980-83, dir. devel., 1983—; exec. dir. George Mason U. Found., 1983—. Treas., bd. dirs. Nation's Capital Council Girl Scouts U.S., 1972-78, award, 1978; chief election judge Fairfax County Electoral Bd., 1967-75; chmn. Belle Haven precinct Mount Vernon dist. Fairfax County Democratic Com.; bd. dirs. Alexandria Symphony, 1983—; deacon United Ch. of Christ; mem. alumni council Wellesley Coll., 1970, 81. Brown U. grad. fellow, 1953. Mem. Va. Women's Polit. Caucus, Council Advancement and Support Edn., Profl. Women's Network, Textile Mus., Smithsonian Assos., Nat. Aviation Club, AAUW, George Washington U. Alumni Council (edn. council), Arlington C. of C. (bd. dirs. 1984—), Phi Delta Kappa. Clubs: Wellesley (bd. dirs. 1969—, treas. 1978-80, pres. 1980-82), Harvard (Washington); Fort Myer Officer's. Home: 6041 Edgewood Terr Alexandria VA 22307 Office: Devel House George Mason U 4400 University Dr Fairfax VA 22030

DAI, JING LING, medical writer, researcher, research and medical affairs consultant; b. Tacoma; d. Yunan and Yet Sze Ling; m. Shenyu Dai (div.); children—Alexander M., Benjamin M. Student Temple U., 1960-63; B.A. in Journalism, Calif. State U.-Long Beach, 1968; M.P.H., UCLA, 1977; C.M.E., U. So. Calif., 1984. Exec. editor Bearing & Transmission Specialist, 1971-72; dir. publs. City of Hope Nat. Med. Ctr., Duarte, Calif., 1972-74; sr. proposal engr., writer, subcontractor for aerospace cos., 1965-66, 79-82, 86—; med. affairs research cons., Gravity Guidance, Inc., Pasadena, Calif., 1982—; freelance writer, cons.; research cons. Musculo-Skeletal Clinic, Pasadena, 1982—. Did pilot study in U.S. on premarital rubella vaccination, analyzed effectiveness of Calif. state legislation, 1977; contbr. articles to profl. jours. Bd. dirs., v.p. Bouggless-White Scholarship Found., Long Beach, 1967-71; publicity adviser Am. Cancer Soc., Los Angeles, 1975; adv. Metric Cert. Specialist Bd., U.S. Metric Assn., 1981—. USPHS grantee, UCLA, 1975-77. Mem. Women in Communications (chmn. careers conf., Los Angeles, 1975, award 1975), Am. Med. Writers Assn., Am. Pub. Health Assn., Nat. Assn. Female Execs., Assn. Health Services Research, Soc. Tech. Communication (chmn. ways/means, internat. tech. com. conf. 1978), Council Biology Editors. Home: 320 S Gramercy Place Los Angeles CA 90020

DAIGNEAULT, MARILYN YVONNE, meeting planner, consultant; b. Atlanta, Apr. 18, 1935; d. Charles Frederick and Gaynell Edith (Teem) Eichwurtzle; m. William Lawrence Stephenson, June 17, 1955 (div. 1960); children—Beverly, Mark, Douglas; m. George Arthur Daigneault, Jan. 21, 1962; children—Ruth, Susan, Joseph, David; stepchildren—Rachelle, Michael. B.A. in Journalism, Maine U., 1957. Adminstrv. asst. H.B. Atkinson Co., Washington, 1963-66; free lance proofreader, Washington, 1970-75; meeting and incentive planner, cons. assns. and corps., Washington, 1975—; dir. D&D Assocs, Rockville, 1982—. Active Nat. Fedn. Republican Women, 1983-86; sponsor GOP Victory Fund, 1984-86. Mem. Nat. Assn. Female Execs. (network dir. 1985-86), Am. Assn. Writers, Nat. Assn. Women Bus. Owners, Am. Assn. Profl. Cons., Epsilon Delta Chi. Republican. Club: Rockville Women's. Avocations: writing; research; teaching meeting planning; traveling; helping young people. Office: D&D Assocs 11404 Hounds Way Rockville MD 20852

DAIL, SHIRLEY ANN, plan service and printing company executive; b. Parkers Prairie, Minn., Oct. 9, 1933; d. Reuben Merle and Hattie Teresa (Gadow) Baumann; m. Harrison Fred Dail, Nov. 27, 1965; children—Kevin, Dwayne, Anthony Curtis, Robin Denise, Harrison Fred III. Student U.S. Naval Storekeeping Sch., 1953. Office mgr. Plan Service, Tucson, 1962-82, Builders Plan Service, Tucson, 1982—. Commr. Bobby Sox Softball, Tucson, 1980—. Served with USN, 1952-56. Mem. Associated Gen. Contractors, Constrn. Specifications Inst. (Outstanding Service award Tucson chpt. 1980), Women in Constrn. (sec. 1983-84, v.p. 1969-70), Tucson Masonry Assn., Am. Bus. Women, Altrusa Bus. Women (bd. dirs.). Republican. Lutheran. Lodges: Sertoma (local pres. 1969-70, 74-75, local gov. 1976-78, 86—), Woodman of World (local sec. 1975—, state sec. 1980-84, state pres.). Home: 8061 E 2d St Tucson AZ 85719 Office: Shirley's Plan Service Inc 425 S Plumer Tucson AZ 85719

DAILEY, ANGELA ZIZZI, investment company executive, marketing executive; b. N.Y.C., July 1, 1948; d. Peter and Ada F. (Cilento) Zizzi; m. Joseph P. Dailey, Sept. 14, 1979. B.A., Trinity Coll., Washington, 1970. Fundraiser, Arthritis Found., N.Y.C., 1970-71, pub. relations Whitney Mus., N.Y.C., 1972; dir. corp. communications Drexel Brunham Lambert, N.Y.C., 1972—. Bd. dirs. YWCA, N.Y.C., 1982—, Acad. of Women Achievers, 1980—. Mem. Women Execs. in Pub. Relations (dir. 1980-83). Office: Drexel Burnham Lambert 60 Broad St New York NY 10004

DAILY, NANCY KENNER, aviation services company executive; b. Winston-Salem, N.C., Aug. 11, 1941; s. Burl Thomas and Lettie (Jester) Kenner; m. James Aldrich Daily, Mar. 21, 1964; children—Heather, Stacey, Tracey. B.S., East Carolina U., 1963; M.A., Villanova U., 1967. Tchr. Guilford County Schs., Greensboro, N.C., 1963-66; pres. Athens Air, Inc., Tenn., 1977—; agt. Aviation Underwriting Agy., Greensboro, 1981—; instr. Tenn. Wesleyan Coll., Athens, 1981—. Republican. Roman Catholic. Home: 3575 Edgewood Circle Cleveland TN 37311 Office: Box 405 Athens TN 37303

DA KAY, THERESA ELIZABETH, optometrist; b. East Stroudsburg, Pa., Oct. 18, 1953; d. Howard Alexander and Mamie (Martino) Da K.; m. Stephen R. Stimson, Sept. 10, 1983; 1 child, Alexander Matthew. B.S. Lebanon Valley Coll., 1976; B.S., O.D., Pa. Coll. Optometry, 1980. Lic. optometrist, Pa., N.J. Pvt. practice optometry, Wind Gap, Pa., 1980—; staff optometrist Easton Hosp. Eye Clinic, Pa., 1980—; speaker in field. Mem. Am. Optometric Assn., Pa. Optometric Assn., Lehigh Valley Optometric Soc. Republican. Roman Catholic. Avocations: reading; cooking; gardening; physical fitness. Office: 16 S Broadway Wind Gap PA 18091

DALE, PATRICIA, public relations executive; b. N.Y.C., Nov. 19, 1947; d. William D'Arcy and Doris (Rothback) Cayton; m. Paul Goldstein, June 16, 1985. B.A. in English, Finch Coll., 1969. Adminstrv. asst. McCaffrey McCall Advt., N.Y.C., 1969-70; asst. to head casting J. Walter Thompson Agy., N.Y.C., 1970-71; publicity dir. The Big Fights, N.Y.C., 1971-72; account exec. N.Am. Precis Syndicate, N.Y.C., 1973-79, exec. v.p., 1980—, ptnr., 1977—. Mem. exec. adv. com. Bowery Residence Com., N.Y.C., 1983—; active Nat. Anti-Abortion campaign, Nat. Rights Action League; bd. dirs. Center for Hyperactive Children, 1983—, The Hope Program, 1985; pub. relations vol. Vera Inst., 1984—. Mem. Women in Communications (publicity work 1979—). Home: 300 E 40th St New York NY 10016 Office: N Am Precis Syndicate 201 E 42d St New York NY 10017

DALECKI, CHRISTINE MARIE, nurse, cancer information guidance center executive; b. Salt Lake City, Jan. 10, 1953; d. H.W. and Carole Ann (Thatcher) Cagle; m. Robert Edward Dalecki, Aug. 11, 1984; children—Aaron Matthew, Sean Robert. Student U. Houston, 1971-72; A.A., Central Tex. Coll., 1974; student Temple Jr. Coll., 1975-77, U. Tex., 1977. R.N., Tex. Staff nurse, Olin E. Teague VA Hosp., 1974-76, unit inservice coordinator, 1976-77; co-leader and developer cancer support, VA Med. Ctr., Temple, 1977-80; inservice and staff nurse Rosewood Hosp., Houston, 1981; sr. sales rep., nursing cons., U.H.I. Corp., Houston, Los Angelos, 1982-84; assoc. dir. Cancer Info. Guidance Ctr., Spring, Tex., 1984—. Mem. Am. Cancer Soc. (vol. 1978-80, nurses com. 1984—), Oncology Nursing Soc., Northwest Oncology Spl. Interest Group. Avocations: swimming; tennis; reading; sewing; camping. Home and Office: 21411 Oak Bridge Ln Spring TX 77388

D'ALENE, ALIXANDRIA FRANCES, management consultant; b. Buffalo, Oct. 21, 1951; d. Fern (Hill) D'A.; B.A., Canisius Coll., Buffalo, 1973, M.S., 1975, M.B.A., 1980. Tchr., Buffalo public schs., 1973-76; personnel cons. Sanford Rose Assos., Williamsville, N.Y., 1976-78; mgr. benefits adminstrn. Service Systems Corp., Clarence, N.Y., 1978-80; mgr. employee relations Del Monte Corp., Walnut Creek, Calif., 1980-82; human resource mgmt. cons. H.R.S., Inc., Winston-Salem, N.C., 1982—. Mem. Assn. Personnel Adminstrs., Indsl. Personnel Soc., Phi Alpha Theta. Episcopalian. Home: 15 Colony Park Kernersville NC 27284

D'ALESSIO, KITTY, cosmetic and clothing co. exec.; b. Sea Girt, N.J., 1929; B.A., Upsala Coll., 1948; Formerly with B. Altman and Co., N.Y.C.; fashion cons. NBC/TV, N.Y.C.; sr. v.p., dir. Norman, Craig, and Hummel, until 1979; pres. Chanel, Inc., N.Y.C., 1979—. Office: Chanel Inc 9 W 57th St New York NY 10019

D'ALFONSO, MARYANN MAZZAFRO, college administrator, poet; b. Phila., Aug. 6, 1957; d. Daniel Charles and Geraldine Conchetta (Salvitti) Mazzafro; m. Ronald Michael, June 21, 1985. B.A., Holy Family Coll., 1979; M.A., U. Pa., 1981. Instr. speech Holy Family Coll., Phila., 1982, acting dir. Alumni Assn., 1981-82, pub. relations asst., 1982-83, dir. pub. relations, 1983—. Author: (poems) Mask, 1973 (Spl. award Am. Collegiate Poets 1979), Augue; Seared Memory, White Lace of Triumph (award of Merit World of Poetry 1982). Scholar U. Pa., 1979-81. Mem. TV Radio and Advt. Club Phila., Council Advancement and Support of Edn., Delta Tau Kappa. Roman Catholic. Avocations: writing; playing piano and guitar; sewing; free style exercise. Office: Holy Family Coll Grant and Frankford Ave Philadelphia PA 19114

DALLAS, DOROTHY BENZ, painter, printmaker; b. N.Y.C.; d. John Jacob and Elsie Bertha (Bruns) Benz; m. Donald Peter Dallas, Sept. 1, 1952; children—Diana, Bruce, Linda, Andrew. Cert. interior design Pratt Inst., 1950, B.F.A., 1979, M.F.A., 1981. Interior designer Voorhees, Walker, Smith, Smith, Haines, N.Y.C., 1950-55; self-employed interior designer, N.Y.C., 1955-63. One-woman shows: Old Church Cultural Ctr., Demarest, N.J., 1983, Interchurch Ctr., N.Y.C., 1983, Dwight/Englewood Sch., 1981, Pratt Inst., Bklyn., 1981; group shows include: Nat. Assn. Women Artists, Bergen Mus., Paramus, N.J., 1983, Monmouth Mus., 1982, Nat. Arts Club, N.Y.C., 1984, Summit Art Ctr., 1981. Active St. Luke's Hosp. Aux., N.Y.C., 1978—. Recipient 3d prize Painter and Sculptors Soc., 1982, 3d prize Garden State Water Color Soc., 1984. Mem. Nat. Assn. Women Artists (2d prize 1984), Catherine Lorillard Wolfe Art Club (bd. dirs. 1982—), N.J. Water Color Soc. (membership chmn. 1981—, Members Show 1st prize 1981), Art Ctr. Water Color Affiliates (founder, sec. 1978-84), Salagundi Club. Republican. Lutheran. Avocations: gardening; sailing; snorkling. Home and Studio: 378 Eastwood Ct Englewood NJ 07631

DALLAS, LYNNE LOUISE, lawyer; b. Holden, Mass., May 18, 1950. B.A., U. Rochester, 1972; J.D., Harvard U., 1975. Bar: N.Y. 1977, U.S. Dist. Ct. (ea. and so. dists.) N.Y. 1977, Supreme Ct. U.S. 1983. Instr. U. Miami Sch. Law (Fla.), 1975-76; assoc. Sullivan & Cromwell, N.Y.C., 1976-84; assoc. prof. law Am. U., Washington, 1984—. Mem. ABA, Phi Beta Kappa. Home: 1531 W Falkland Ln Apt 139 Silver Spring MD 20910

DALLI, KATHRYN MARY, lawyer; b. Syosset, N.Y., Dec. 20, 1956; d. Frank Joseph and Gloria (Donato) Dalli. B.A. cum laude, State U. Coll., Fredonia, 1979; J.D., Southwestern U. Sch. of Law, 1982. Bar: N.Y., 1983, U.S. Dist. Ct. (ea. and so. dists.) N.Y. 1985. Counselor Battered Women's Legal Counseling Clinic, Los Angeles, 1980; law clk. Arnett, Hatten & Clo, Los Angeles, 1981-82; atty. Portnoy & Rubin, Huntington, N.Y., 1983-84, Friedman, Friedman, Levy & Bottiglieri, P.C., N.Y.C., 1984—. Mem. ACLU, N.Y. State Bar Assn., Assn. Trial Lawyers Am., ABA, N.Y. State Trial Lawyers Assn., NOW. Democrat. Office: Friedman Friedman Levy & Bottiglieri PC 250 W 57th St New York NY 10107

DALLY, ALICE GERTRUDE GHERKE, author, educator; b. Defiance, Ohio, Feb. 18, 1910; d. William Ernest and Emma Amelia Ort Gherke; student Wausau Coll., 1927-29, U. Wis., 1930-38, Bryan Stenotype Coll., 1965-66, San Bernardino Valley Coll., 1960-79, Chaffey Coll., 1965-66, U. Calif., Riverside, 1966; Ph.D., Golden State U., 1981; m. John Wesley Dally, Sept. 17, 1938 (dec.). Ct. reporter; asst. credit mgr., interviewer U. Wis.; acct. State of Wis.; sr. interviewer, investigator fed. govt.; mgr. kennel; legal sec.; clk. of ct.; med. sec.; legal sec. to dist. atty.; exec. sec.; adminstr.; univ. tchr., coll. tchr.; tchr. adult edn.; substitute tchr. Mem. Nat. Ret. Tchrs. Assn., Polish Am. Hist. Assn., Calif. Tchrs. Assn. (life), Calif. Ret. Tchrs. Assn., NEA (life), Nat. Assn. Female Execs. U. Wis. Alumni Assn. (life). Club: San Bernardino Coin. Author: Suzanne's Family; Suzanne's Merry Chase; also poetry.

DALLY, BEVERLY JEAN, legal assistant, executive; b. Akron, Ohio, Nov. 2, 1935; d. George Tilman and Julia Mae (McClure) Willoughby; m. Don I. Dally, July 10, 1955 (div. 1981); children—Bruce, Alan, Jack. Student, Hilbert Coll., Hamburg, N.Y., 1975-76, SUNY-Buffalo, 1972-75. Legal asst. Cowen & Swados, Buffalo, 1977-78, Eikenburg & Stiles, Houston, 1978-79; Foreman & Dyess, Houston, 1979-84, Michael G. Page, Atty.-at-Law, The Woodlands, Tex., 1984-85, Fulbright & Jaworski, Houston, 1985-86, Granada Corp., Houston, 1986—. Contbr. article to legal publ. Mem. Houston Legal Assts. Assn. (chmn. com. 1980), Nat. Assn. Female Execs. (Houston). Republican. Methodist. Office: Granada Corp 10900 Richmond Ave Houston TX 77042

DALLY, REBECCA POLSTON, lawyer; b. Columbus, Ga., Dec. 4, 1955; d. James Olon and Lottie Myrl (Woodham) Polston; m. Hal W. Dally, June 28, 1980; children—Patrick William, Melissa Leigh. Student Mercer U., 1973-75; B.A. cum laude, Ga. State U., 1976; J.D., U. Ga., 1979. Bar: Ga. 1979. Asst. loan coordinator Transam. Real Estate Tax Service, Atlanta, 1975-77; sole practice law, Social Circle, Ga., 1981—; spl. asst. dist. atty. Alcovy Jud. Circuit, Monroe and Covington, Ga., 1982-84; spl. asst. atty. gen., 1984—. Bd. dirs. Social Circle Hist. Preservation Soc., 1982—; trustee Walton County Arts Council, 1983—, Hist. Soc. Walton Council, 1984—; mem. fin. com. Social Circle Pub. Library; vol. ARC, Social Circle Nursing Home, 1980-81. Mem. ABA, Ga. Trial Lawyers Assn., Alcovy Jud. Circuit Bar Assn. (v.p. 1983-84, pres. 1984-85), Walton County Bar Assn. (v.p. 1982-83, pres. 1983-84), State Bar Ga., Social Circle Mcht. and Trade Assn., Walton County C. of C., Phi Alpha Delta. Baptist. Home: PO Box 745 Social Circle GA 30279 Office: 137 E Hightower Trail Social Circle GA 30279

DALPES, LINDA FRANCES, management firm executive; b. New Orleans, Jan. 3, 1938; d. Walter James and Frances Katherine (Jordan) Fountain. A.A., Stephens Coll., 1957; B.A., U. Hawaii, 1959. Cert. dental asst. Sr. claims analyst Am. Gen. Life Inc. Co., Houston, 1960-64; mgr. claims Southwest region Calif. Western States Life Ins. Co., Houston, 1964-68; mgmt. cons. Met. Agy., Houston, 1968-70; clinic adminstr. Harris & Adams, Inc., Houston, 1970-75; founder, pres. Team Coordinators, Houston, 1975—; clinician major dental meetings; internat. lectr., cons. south, southwest univs.; internat. lectr.; exec. sec. Tex. Dental Hygienists Assn., 1972-75. Mem. LWV, Am. Mgmt. Assn., AAUW, Nat. Assn. Women Bus. Owners, Nat. Assn. Female Execs. Republican. Episcopalian. Home: 120 E Fork Rd Cleveland TX 77327 Office: PO Box 60744 Houston TX 77205

DALRYMPLE, JEAN, theatre producer-director; b. Morristown, N.J., Sept. 2, 1910; d. George Hull and Elizabeth Van Kirk (Collins) D.; educated privately; m. Ward Morehouse, Mar. 31, 1932 (dec.); m. 2d, P. D. Ginder, Nov. 1951 (dec.). Producer, dir. numerous plays, musicals and operas, 1939—; mgr., publicist various stage personalities, singers, 1933—; impressario publicity dir./mgr. concert and opera stars including pianist José Iturbi, violinist Nathan Milstein, conductor Leopold Stokowski, sopranos Grace Moore, Lily Pons, Zinka Milanov, Natalie Bodanya, Bidu Sayao, others, 1939-79; dir. Am. Theatre, Brussels World's Fair, 1958; tour of Latin Am. with Teahouse of August Moon in Spanish for Dept. State, 1956; dir. N.Y.C. Ctr. Drama and Musicals, 1943-69; a founder N.Y.C. Opera, 1944, N.Y.C. Ctr. of Music and Drama, 1943, N.Y.C. Ballet, 1948; apptd. by Pres. Johnson to Nat. Council on the Arts, 1963-69; mem. NEA opera panel, 1971-72, theatre panel, 1973-74; publicity dir., mgr. Berlin Arts Festival, Dept. State, 1951; pres. Light Opera Manhattan, Friends Theatre Collection, Mus. City of N.Y.; bd. dirs. New Dramatists, Soldiers', Sailors' and Airmens' Club. Decorated Order Crown Belgium; recipient 5 citations, proclamation City of N.Y. Mem. Am. Theatre Wing (dir.), ANTA (dir.). Presbyterian. Club: Silver Spring Country (Ridgefield, Conn.). Author: September Child, 1963; Careers and Opportunities in the Theatre, 1968; Dalrymple's Pinafore Farm Cookbook, 1970; From The Last Row, 1976; The Complete Handbook for Community Theatres, 1979; co-author: The Folklore and Facts of Natural Nutrition, 1974. Home and Office: 150 W 55th St New York NY 10019

DAL SANTO, DIANE, judge; b. East Chicago, Ind., Sept. 20, 1949; d. John Quentin Dal Santo and Helen (Koval) D. B.A., U. N. Mex., 1971; cert. Inst. Internat. and Comparative Law, Guadalajara, Mex., 1978; J.D., U. San Diego, 1980. Bar: N.Mex. 1980, U.S. Dist. Ct. N.Mex. 1980. Ct. planner Met. Criminal Justice Coordinating Council, Albuquerque, 1973-75; planning coordinator Dist. Atty.'s Office, Albuquerque, 1975-76, exec. asst. to dist. atty., 1976-77, asst dist. atty. for violent crimes, 1980-82; chief dep. city atty. City of Albuquerque, 1983; assoc. firm T.B. Keleher & Assocs., 1983-84; judge Met. Ct., 1985—. Bd. dirs. Nat. Council Alcoholism, 1984, S.W. Ballet Co., Albuquerque, 1982-83; mem. Mayor's Task Force on Alcoholism and Crime. Recipient Woman of Yr. award Duke City Bus. and Profl. Women, 1985; U. San Diego scholar, 1978-79. Mem, ABA, N.Mex. Bar Assn., Albuquerque Bar Assn., Nat. Assn. Women Judges, LWV, N.Mex. Council on Crime and Delinquency. Democrat. Office: Met Ct PO Box 133 Albuquerque NM 87103

DALTON, PHYLLIS IRENE, library consultant; b. Marietta, Kans., Sept. 25, 1909; d. Benjamin Reuben and Pearl (Travelute) Bull; m. Jack Mason Dalton, Feb. 13, 1950. B.S., U. Nebr., 1931, M.A., 1941; M.A., U. Denver, 1942. Tchr. city schs., Marysville, Kans., 1931-40; reference librarian Lincoln Pub. Library, Nebr.; librarian U. Nebr., Lincoln, 1941-48; librarian Calif. State Library, Sacramento, 1948-57, asst. state librarian, 1957-72; pvt. library cons., Las Vegas, 1972—. Author: Library Service to the Deaf and Hearing Impaired, 1985 (Pres's Com. Employment of Handicapped award 1985). Contbr. chpt., articles, reports to books and publs. in field. Mem. exec. bd. So. Nev. Hist. Soc., Las Vegas, 1983-84; mem. So. Nev. Com. on Employment of Handicapped, 1980—; mem. adv. com. Nat. Orgn. on Disability, 1982—; bd. dirs. Friends of So. Nev. Libraries; trustee Univ. Library Soc., U. Nev.-Las Vegas. Mem. Allied Arts Council. Recipient Libraria Sodalitas, U. So. Calif., 1972, Alumni Achievement award U. Denver, 1977, Alumni Achievement award U. Nebr., Lincoln, 1983. Mem. ALA (councilor 1963-64, exceptional service award 1981), Assn. State Libraries (pres. 1964-65), Calif. Library Assn. (pres. 1969), Nev. Library Assn. (hon.), Internat. Fedn. Library Assns. and Instns. (chair working group on library service to prisons), LWV, AAUW. Republican. Presbyterian. Club: Pilot (parliamentarian). Home: 205 E Harmon Ave Apt 801 Las Vegas NV 89109

DALY, DOROTHY JOAN, educational administrator; b. Bklyn., Jan. 18, 1926; d. George James and Genevieve (Canning) Basso; m. Richard Arthur Daly, June 21, 1970. B.A., St. Johns U., 1950; M.S.W., Fordham U., 1951; cert. in ednl. adminstrn. Hofstra U., 1972. Founding adminstr. Good Samaritan Hosp., West Islip, N.Y., 1959-65; U.S. dir. Daus. of Wisdom, Islip, 1965-68; social worker, dir. state demonstration early intervention program Bd. Coop. Ednl. Services, Patchogue, N.Y., 1968-76, dir. planning, program devel., 1976—, designer, dir. 1st regional employee assistance program, 1982—. Pres., Suffolk Community Council, Smithtown, N.Y., 1980-83, bd. dirs., 1983—; bd. dirs. The Ministries, Coram, N.Y., 1983—; mem. social services adv. com. to county exec., 1978; mem. Suffolk County Blue Ribbon Com. on Teen Pregnancy, 1979. Mem. Nat. Assn. Social Workers, Nat. Assn. Social Workers, Nat. Conf. Social Welfare, Internat. Conf. Social Welfare, Phi Delta Kappa. Home: 222 Captain's Way Bay Shore NY 11706 Office: Bd Coop Ednl Services 201 Sunrise Hwy Patchogue NY 11772

DALY, JANE MARIE, public relations executive, college administrator; b. Burlington, Iowa, Feb. 20, 1956; d. James Clement and Mary Elizabeth (Kassmeyer) D. B.A., Clarke Coll., 1978. Reporter, bus. editor Garden City Telegram, Harris Newspapers, Kans., 1978-80; Sunday editor The Hawk Eye, Harris Newspapers, Burlington, Iowa, 1980-83; dir. pub. relations, faculty, instr. communication Clarke Coll., Dubuque, Iowa, 1983—. Doctrine tchr. St. Dominic Parish, Garden City, Kans., 1979; officer St. Patrick Parish Council, Burlington, 1981-83; state del. Iowa Democratic Conv., 1984. Recipient 3d Place award feature writing Kans. AP, 1978, Golden Quill award for edn. reporting Kans. NEA, 1979, 1st Place award for spl. edits. Kans. Press Women, 1979, 3d Place award for editorial writing Kans. Press Women, 1979, 2d Place award for editorial pages Iowa Newspaper Assn., 1982, 2d Place award for editorial pages Harris Newspapers, Iowa, Kans., Calif., 1982, 2d Place award for spl. issue Iowa Newspaper Assn., 1983, 1st Place award for editorial pages Harris Newspapers, Iowa, Kans., Calif., 1983. Mem. Council for Advancement, Support for Edn. (silver medal 1984-85), Dubuque Area C. of C. (bd. mem. 1984). Roman Catholic. Avocations: photography; calligraphy; outdoor recreation; the arts. Home: 529 Fenelon Pl Dubuque IA 52001 Office: Clarke Coll 1550 Clarke Dr Dubuque IA 52001

DALY, MARY F., theologian, feminist philosopher. A.B., Coll. of St. Rose, Albany, N.Y.; A.M., Cath. U.; S.T.L., S.T.D., Ph.D., U. Fribourg. Assoc. prof. dept. theology Boston Coll. Author: The Church and the Second Sex; Beyond God the Father, 1973, 2nd edit. rev. 1985; Gyn/Ecology, Pure Lust, 1984. Address: Boston College Dept Theology Chestnut Hill MA 02167

DALY, PATRICIA HIGHLEYMAN, horse breeder, realtor; b. San Diego, Dec. 16, 1942; d. Daly and Elisabeth (Johnson) Highleyman; m. Jack Tripp Cline, 1966 (div. 1973); children—Elisabeth, Katharine, Johnson (Daly); m. Charles Allen Daugherty, Aug. 1983 (div. Jan. 1985). Cert., U. Catholique de Louvain, 1962; B.A., Vassar Coll., 1980; postgrad. Calif. State U.-Dominguez Hills, 1986—. Owner, trainer Amber Farm, Rolling Hills, Calif., 1973—, Greenwich, Conn., 1977-79, Bedford, N.Y., 1979-82, Charlottesville, Va., 1985—; realtor Kirtley Realty, Charlottesvile, 1986—. Active Pegasus, Greenwich, 1977-79; chmn. golf tournament Children's Home Soc., Los Angeles, 1984; docent Point Vicente Interpretive Ctr., Rancho Palos Verdes,

Calif., 1984-85. Recipient many ribbons, trophies for riding, breeding horses; cert. U.S. Coast Guard Aux., Redondo Beach, Calif., 1984. Mem. Calif. Thoroughbred Breeders Assn., Nat. Assn. Female Execs. Republican. Episcopalian. Clubs: Farmington Hunt (Charlottesville, Va.); Jockey (N.Y.); Flintridge Hunt (Calif.); OxRidge Hunt (Darien, Conn.). Avocations: oil painting; sailing; skiing; riding. Home: 3570 Brinnington Rd Charlottesville VA 22901 Office: Kirtley Realty 250 West Charlottesville VA 22901

DALY, TYNE, actress; b. Madison, Wis., Feb. 21, 1947; d. James D. and Hope Newell; m. Georg Stanford Brown; 3 children. Student Brandeis U., Am. Music and Dramatic Acad., N.Y.C. Films include John and Mary, 1969, Play It as It Lays, 1972, The Entertainer, 1976, The Enforcer, 1976, Zoot Swit, 1981; star TV series: Cagney and Lacey (Emmy awards for best actress in drama series 1983, 84, 85), 1982—; movies for TV include In Search of America, 1971, A Howling in the Woods, 1971, Heat of Anger, 1972, The Women's Room, 1980. Recipient 1985 Disting. Artist award, Club 100 of the Los Angeles Music Ctr. Address: care The Balke-Glenn Agency Ltd 409 N Camden Dr Suite 202 Beverly Hills CA 90210*

D'AMBROSIO, MADELEINE B., insurance company executive; b. N.Y.C., Jan. 18, 1950; d. Patrick James and Madeleine Rheta (LaSalle) Maccaronei. B.A., Manhattanville Coll., N.Y., 1971. Cert. employee benefit specialist. With Mut. of Am., N.Y.C., 1972-75; benefit plan counselor Tchrs. Ins. and Annuity Assn.-Coll. Retirement Equities Fund, N.Y.C., 1975-79, asst. adv. officer, 1979-81, adv. officer, 1981-84, regional mgr. instl. counseling, 1983, asst. v.p., 1984-86, 2d v.p., 1986—. Mem. Internat. Soc. Cert. Employee Benefit Specialists (bd. dirs. N.Y. chpt.), Nat. Assn. Female Execs., AAUW, Nat. Orgn. Italian Am. Women. Home: 30 Waterside Plaza New York NY 10010 Office: TIAA-CREF 730 3d Ave New York NY 10017

DAMERON, MABEL MARIE (SANDY), insurance broker; b. Springfield, Ohio, Dec. 1, 1934; d. William Edward and Eva Lutishia (Minton) Whipp; m. Charles Richard Dameron, Dec. 3, 1966 (div. 1972). Student American River Coll., 1967. Cert. profl. ins. woman. Sec. various cos., Springfield, Ohio and Norfolk, Va., 1952-54; sec. McCleary-Jones, Inc., Springfield, 1954-58, Dale E. Miller Ins., Springfield, 1958-64; underwriter Nat. Union Ins., Sacramento, Calif., 1964-68; ins. agt., broker Sims & Grupe/Imco, Stockton, Calif. and San Francisco, 1968-74; ins. agt. Foster Miller Ins., Springfield, 1974-79; asst. v.p., broker Imco Ins. Mgmt. Corp., Pleasant Hill, Calif., 1980—. Mem. Ins. Women's Club Sacramento, Ins. Women of Springfield (past pres.), San Francisco Ins. Women's Assn. (mem. exec. bd.), Nat. Assn. Ins. Women. Republican. Home: 2737 Polk St Apt 6 San Francisco CA 94109 Office: Imco Ins Mgmt Corp 2255 Contra Costa Blvd Suite 202 Pleasant Hill CA 94523

DAMERY, CAROLYN, health maintenance organization executive; b. Chgo., Oct. 16, 1948; d. Ellsworth Elmer and Martha (Rees) Kimmel; m. Michael Damery, Aug. 20, 1970 (div. 1979); 1 child, Christopher Noble. B.A., Purdue U., 1972; M.P.H., U. N.C., 1975; postgrad. Bradley U., 1979-81. Research asst. St. Louis County Dept. Health, 1970-74; adjudicator Ill. Dept.. Labor, Peoria, 1975-77; dir. planning and devel. Ill. Central Health Systems Agy., Peoria, 1977-82; dir. profl. services Health Plan Central Ill., Inc., Peoria, 1982—. Bd. dirs. Heart of Ill. United Way, Peoria, 1985—, Morton Jr. Women's Assn., 1978-79, social services adv. council Tri-County Regional Planning Commn., Peoria, 1978-82. Mem. Group Health Assn. Am., Am. Pub. Health Assn., Ill. Pub. Health Assn. Avocations: gardening, gourmet cooking, reading. Office: Health Plan Central Ill Inc 207 Main St Peoria IL 61602

DAMES, KATERI K. BRANDON, writer; b. N.Y.C., Mar. 21, 1946; d. John A. and Dorothy A. (Cullinan) Krannawitter; m. Robert L. Dames, May 28, 1966 (div. June 1971); 1 child, Damien; m. 2d Earl Kenneth Carr, May 18, 1978 (dec. June 1983); 1 stepchild, Jac. Drama student St. Louis U., 1964-66; B.A. in Behavioral Scis., Ohio State U., 1975; M.S. in Corrections, Xavier U., 1977; M.A. in Journalism Ohio State U., 1985. Acting arts and crafts dir. Ellsworth AFB (S.D.), 1967-68; choreographer S.D. Sch. Mines, Rapid City, 1971; asst. costumer, actress Nauman Films, Custer, S.D., 1971; copywriter Cable TV, Rapid City, 1971; cottage dir. Rosemont Sch., Columbus, 1975-76; legis. aide Ohio Ho. of Reps., Columbus, 1977-78; work adjustment counselor Vision Center, Columbus, 1977-79, mem. adj. faculty social work Ohio State U., Columbus, 1978-85, mem. univ. press bd., 1981-85; coordinator info. Action for Children, Columbus, 1979-84; owner Fairy Godmother Ltd., children's parties and photography, Columbus, 1982-84; promotion dir. Kelton Ho. Mus., Columbus, 1983-84; contbr., producer Sta. WOSU morning edition, 1981-85; media cons., 1985—. Author: Action for Children: A Child's Resource Guide to Columbus, 1983; Job Seeking Skills for the Blind, 1979; contbr. articles to Day Care and Early Edn., Reader's Digest, others. Mem. emergency assistance task force Columbus City Council, 1982-85; negotiator United Way, Columbus, 1977-85; bd. dirs., sec. Rosemont Sch., Columbus, 1979-85; bd. dirs. Downtown Playsch., Columbus, 1982-85. Recipient English award United Way Columbus, 1984. Mem. Women in Communications, Am. Soc. for Tng. and Devel. Prescott Women's Network (v.p. 1985-86), Prescott Art Docents, Prescott Symphony Assn., Alpha Phi. Roman Catholic. Club: Jr. League of Columbus (asst. editor news mag. 1982—). Home: 1925 Rock Castle Prescott AZ 86301

DAMIANO, DOROTHY JEANNE, nurse, consultant; b. North Adams, Mass., Aug. 14, 1928; d. Patrick and Angelina (Irace) Laino; m. Apr. 25, 1955 (div. 1957). Diploma St. Luke's Hosp. Sch. Nursing, 1949. Staff nurse, North Adams, Mass., 1949-51; staff nurse VA Hosp., Albany, N.Y., 1951-52, insulin therapy nurse, 1952-54, head nurse psychiat. unit, 1954-66, coordinator Day Treatment Ctr. Psychiat. unit, 1966-83; mem. instl. review bd. regarding ethical issues for patients Albany Med. Ctr., 1970-83; nursing cons. VA Med. Ctr., Albany, 1983-85. Recipient Florence Nightingale award VA Med. Ctr., 1955, 65. Roman Catholic. Home: 92 Yorkshire Dr East Greenbush NY 12061

D'AMICO, FRANCES CLARE, physical education educator; b. Queens, N.Y., June 5, 1943; d. Frank and Theresa (Pavone) D'A. B.A., Hunter Coll., N.Y.C., 1964; M.S., Bklyn. Coll., 1968; Ph.D., NYU, 1982. Tchr., Jr. High Sch. 73, Queens, N.Y., 1964-67, New Hyde Park Meml. High Sch., 1967-70; prof. phys. edn. Queensborough Community Coll., Bayside, N.Y., 1970—, dir. acad. advisement, 1979-82. Mem. Am. Assn. Higher Edn., Am. Ednl. Research Assn. Office: Queensborough Community College Bayside NY 11364

D'AMICO, JOANN RITA, steel construction company executive, medical evaluator; b. Phila., Jan. 21, 1939; d. Angelo and Eleanor Margaret (Morrone) Rinaldi; m. Albert Michael D'Amico, Jan. 28, 1961; children—Albert, Angelique, Lisa, Christopher, Blythe. Sec., Prudential Ins. Co., Phila., 1957-61; med. sec. Phila. Coll. Pharmacy and Sci., 1969-71; med. evaluator Inst. for Applied Pharm. Research, Phila., 1971—; owner, pres. Mitchell Bar Placement, Phila., 1974—; trustee apprentice fund Ironworkers Local #405, Phila., 1978—, trustee severance annuity fund, 1978—. Judge of elections Republican Party, 1981—; mem. Presdl. Task Force, 1982—, U.S. Senatorial Club, 1984—; notary pub. Mem. Internat. Found. Employee Benefit Plans. Roman Catholic. Avocations: gardening, collecting antiques; outdoor pursuits. Home: 2254 S Bonsall St Philadelphia PA 19145

D'AMICO, NANCY JUNE, systems analyst; b. Ellwood City, Pa., Feb. 1, 1961; d. Frank D'Amico and Margaret Mary Christy. B.S., U. Pitts., 1983. Grad. programmer analyst NCR Corp., Cambridge, Ohio, 1983-84, assoc. programmer analyst, 1984-85, programmer, analyst, 1985—. Mem. Nat. Assn. Female Execs. (network dir.), IEEE Computer Soc. Roman Catholic. Avocations: snow skiing; water skiing; cooking. Office: NCR Corp PO Box 728 Cambridge OH 43725

D'AMICO, VIRGINIA ANN, fund raiser; b. Youngstown, Ohio, Apr. 26, 1948; d. Samuel and Ann T. (DeCola) D'Amico; student Notre Dame Coll., Cleve., 1966; B.A., Youngstown U., 1970; postgrad. U. Hawaii, 1971; M.Ed., Boston U., 1975; m. Larry D. Myer, Jan. 8, 1977 (div.). Health and phys. edn. instr. St. Mary's High Sch., Sandusky, Ohio, 1970-73; teaching asst. Boston U., 1973-74; instr. psychology Newbury Jr. Coll., Boston, 1974; Kellogg fellow, planning assoc. United Way, Louisville, and United Way of Wichita, Kans., 1975, asst. campaign dir., Wichita, 1976-78, campaign dir., 1979-82; asst. campaign dir. United Way of Tex. Gulf Coast, Houston, 1982-84, assoc. campaign dir. mktg. ops., 1985, v.p. resource devel., 1986—. Bd. dirs. Maize Community Bldg., Kans., 1980-81; ARC vol., 1967-70, water safety instr., 1967-70, emergency social service com., 1977-82. Mem. Am. Mgmt. Assn., Kappa Delta Pi, Sigma Sigma Sigma. Republican. Roman Catholic. Office: 1010 Waugh Dr Houston TX 77019

DAMON, CLAUDIA CORDS, lawyer; b. Heidelberg, Ger., Aug. 11, 1946; d. Helmuth and Jutta (Sorge) Cords; m. Edward Neilson Damon, Aug. 25, 1973; children—Caroline Cords, Samuel Cords. B.A., Wellesley Coll., 1967; M.A., Boston U., 1968, J.D., 1974. Bar: N.H. 1974. Tchr. history MacDuffie Sch. for Girls, Springfield, Mass., 1968-69; research asst. Princeton U., 1969-71; assoc. Sheehan, Phinney, Bass & Green, P.A., Manchester, N.H., 1974-78, shareholder, 1979—; mem. N.H. Bd. Bar Examiners, 1980—. Bd. dirs. Merrimack Valley Day Care Services, Concord, N.H., 1983—; chmn. Boscawen Zoning Bd. Adjustment (N.H.), 1976—; bd. dirs. Girls Club Manchester, 1975-80, Manchester YMCA, 1986—; mem. steering com. N.H. Bus. Com. Arts. Mem. ABA, N.H. Trial Lawyers Assn., Assn. Trial Lawyers Am., N.H. Bar Assn. Office: Sheehan Phinney Bass & Green 1000 Elm St Manchester NH 03101

DAMRON, EVAUNE ELIZABETH, insurance company executive; b. Firth, Idaho, Nov. 12, 1927; d. Robert E. and Mary Irene (Johnsen) Dye; m. Wesley Glenn Damron, Mar. 4, 1947; children—Kathleen Damron Galloway, Barton G. (dec.). Delivery supr. Western Union Tel. Co., Pocatello, Ida., 1952-65; fire ins. coder Farm Bur. Ins., Pocatello, Idaho, 1966-70, comml. underwriter, 1970-75, comml. underwriting supr., 1975-82, comml. lines research and devel. mgr., 1982—. Mem. Nat. Assn. C.P.C.U.s, Nat. Assn. Ins. Women, Ins. Women of Pocatello (tchr. ins. classes 1977-78), CPCU Soc. Idaho. Mem. Ch. of Jesus Christ of Latter-day Saints. Home: 533 Richland St Pocatello ID 83201 Office: Farm Bur Ins 845 W Center St Pocatello ID 83201

DAMRON, HAZEL BRANHAM, radio station executive; b. Fort Gay, W.Va., Oct. 28, 1928; d. Arbie and Ruth (Perry) Branham; m. Cecil P. Damron, Sept. 27, 1947; 1 child, Frederick Cecil. Student various community service courses. Exec. sec. Packaging Corp. Am., Rittman, Ohio, 1947-65; city clk. City of Rittman, 1965-66; exec. sec. Mc-Cormack Advt., Huntington, W.Va., 1969-70; receptionist Wayne County Health Dept., W.Va., 1970-71; field facilitator Urban/Rural Program, Washington, 1971-75; sec., program dir. Sta.-WFGH-Pub. Radio, Fort Gay, 1979—; sec.-treas. Community Broadcasters Assn., Fort Gay, 1979—; mem. Mountain Heritage Com., Fort Gay, 1982. Sec. Rittman C. of C., 1963; field facilitator Urban/Rural Devel. Program Fort Gay, 1971; sec. Sch. Community Council, Fort Gay, 1972. Democrat. Baptist. Avocations: crocheting; reading; gospel music; gardening. Home: Route 2 Box 414 Fort Gay WV 25514 Office: Sta-WFGH Fort Gay High Sch Court St Fort Gay WV 25514

DAMSBO, ANN MARIE, psychologist, clinic administrator; b. Cortland, N.Y., July 7, 1931; d. Jorgen Einer and Agatha Irene (Schenck) D.; B.S., San Diego State Coll., 1952; M.A., U.S. Internat. U., 1974, Ph.D., 1975; 6 foster children. Commd. 2d lt. U.S. Army, 1952, advanced through grades to capt., 1957; staff therapist Letterman Army Hosp., San Francisco, 1953-54, 56-58, 61-62, Ft. Devers, Mass., 1955-56, Walter Reed Army Hosp., Washington, 1958-59, Tripler Army Hosp., Hosp., Hawaii, 1959-61, Ft. Benning, Ga., 1962-64; chief therapist U.S. Army Hosp., Ft. McPherson, Ga., 1964-67, ret., 1967; med. missionary So. Presbyterian Ch., Taiwan, 1968-70; psychology intern, burn center Univ. Hosp., San Diego, 1975; pre-doctoral intern Naval Regional Med. Center, San Diego, 1975-76, postdoctoral intern, 1975-76, chief, founder pain clinic, 1976—; cons. on forensic hypnosis, fed. investigation agys.; lectr. in field, U.S., Can., Eng., France, Australia. Fellow Am. Soc. Clin. Hypnosis (faculty); mem. San Diego Soc. Clin. Hypnosis (pres. 1980), Am. Psychol. Assn., Am. Phys. Therapy Assn., Calif. Soc. Clin. Hypnosis (bd. govs.), Internat. Platform Assn., Internat. Soc. Clin. and Exptl. Hypnosis, N.Y. Acad. Sci., AAAS. Republican. Methodist. Club: Job's Daus. Contbr. articles to profl. publs.; also chpt. in book. Home: 1062 W 5th Ave Escondido CA 92025 Office: Chief Pain Clinic Naval Regional Med Center San Diego CA 92134

DAMSKER, BECA, clinical microbiologist; b. Jassy, Romania, Jan. 15, 1923; came to U.S., 1969, naturalized, 1974; d. Jacques and Rose Grünspan; M.D., Bucharest U., 1950; M.Sc., U. Montreal (Que., Can.), 1969; m. Mircea Damsker, May 11, 1944. Intern, resident and fellow, Bucharest, 1950-59; specialist physician, clin. lab. Hosp. Extrapulmonary Tb, Bucharest, 1959-63; research physician Hadassah Hebrew U., 1964-66; dir. clin. lab., Jerusalem, 1966-67; clin. lab. supr., asst. dir. Mt. Sinai Hosp., N.Y.C., 1969-80, assoc. dir. microbiology, 1980—; instr., then asst. prof. Mt. Sinai Med. Sch., 1970—. Recipient Physicians Recognition award AMA, 1971, 81, 84. Mem. Am. Soc. Microbiology, AMA, N.Y. Film Soc., Met. Mus. Contbr. articles on mycobacteriology to profl. jours. Office: 1 Gustave Levy Pl New York NY 10029

DANAHER, MALLORY MILLETT-JONES, actress, photographer; b. St. Paul; d. James Albert and Helen Rose (Feely) Millett; B.A., U. Minn.; m. Thomas C. Danaher, Mar. 1985; 1 child by previous marriage, Kristen Vigard. Active with N.Y. Theatre, 1971-84, mem. original cos. of Annie and The Best Little Whorehouse in Texas, 1977; appeared in Dodsworth, Berkshire Theatre Festival, 1978; also on Love of Life, CBS-TV, 1978-79, NBC Movie of the Week, Eischied: Only the Pretty Girls Die, 1979; Edward Albee's Everything in the Garden (dir. Shelley Winters), Actors' Studio, 1980—, also Another World, NBC, New Line Cinema: Alone in the Dark; appeared in House of Blue Leaves, Berkshire Theatre Festival, 1981, Tootsie, Columbia Pictures, Tornado, Lincoln Ctr. Library Theatre, Stella, N.Y.C.; Cocteau's one-character play The Human Voice at Deutsches-Haes, NYU, Full Moon and High Tide, Actors Studio; off-Broadway prodn. Loose Connections, Judith Anderson Theatre; exhibitor of photography: Third Eye Gallery, N.Y.C., 1974-75, Modernage Discovery Gallery, N.Y.C., 1976-79, Gallery of St. Clement's, N.Y.C., 1979; author: Fatherless Child.

DANBURG, DEBRA, state legislator; b. Houston, Sept. 25, 1951; d. Stanley and Barbara Jean (Hamilton) D.; B.A., U. Houston, 1974, J.D., 1979. Asst. dir., lobbyist Texans for ERA, 1974-75; atty. pvt. practice, Houston, 1979—; mem. Tex. Ho. of Reps., 1981—; del. Democratic Nat. Convention, 1984; co-chmn. Gary Hart for Pres. campaign, 1984; Tex. rep. Am. Council of Young Polit. Leaders, 1982. Mem. Harris County Democratic Exec. Com., 1976-80, bilateral adv. com. Cultural Exchange The Netherlands-USA, 1986. Named Outstanding feminist NOW, 1975, best legistlator Houston mag., 1981, vol. of yr. KS/AIDS Found., 1984; recipient spl. presdl. award Houston Apt. Assn., 1985. Mem. Tex. Bar Assn., Gulf Coast Conservation Assn., Ducks Unlimited Inc., Houston Bar Assn. Office: Texas House of Representatives State Capitol Austin TX 78769

DANCA, SARAH ELIZABETH, construction company executive, advisor; b. Boston, Nov. 15, 1942; d. Arthur Francis and Elizabeth (Cusack) McGeown; m. John Joseph Danca; children—Sarah E., John J., Susan M. Diploma Sharon High Sch. Lic. constrn. supr. Mass. Office worker, New England Telephone Co., Boston, 1960-64; constrn. mgr. Danca Co., Sharon, Mass., 1976-78; pres., chief exec. officer Danca Corp., Sharon, 1978—, also dir. Parent advisor New Eng. Conservatory Prep., Boston, 1975; mem. parent bd. Newton Country Day Sch., Mass., 1984. Mem. Nat. Assn. Women in Constrn. (co-chmn. 1984), Mass. Associated Gen. Contractors, Women Constrn. Owners and Execs. Avocations: walking; gardening. Home: 248 Mansfield St Sharon MA 02067 Office: Danca Corp 248 Mansfield St Sharon MA 02067

DANCE, GLORIA FENDERSON, dance studio executive, ballet administrator; b. Portsmouth, Va., Mar. 10, 1932; d. Charles Bourrell and Ottillia Lavinia (Korn) Fenderson; m. Walter Forrest Dance III, June 4, 1951; children—Walter Forrest IV, Jon Marlon, Gloria Cherie. Student pub. schs., Petersburg. Cert. promotional dir., modeling/finishing and charm sch., cosmotologist. Assoc. tchr. Boyer/Traylor Dance Acad., Richmond, Va., 1952-60; founder, owner, dir. Gloria F. Dance Sch. Dancing, Petersburg, 1960—; artistic dir. Petersburg Ballet, Inc., 1984—. Block leader Ind. Voters, Walnut Hill, 1955—; chairwoman Jr. Woman's Club, Petersburg; Va. chairwoman Petersburg Dance Festival, White House Performance, Aug. 1984; chairwoman 1985 July 4 Festival, Petersburg. Recipient hon. award Optimist Club, Colonial Heights, Va., 1950-63, Va. Hon. award Va. Nat. Dance Week, 1984, Petersburg Pub. Service award Alumni Gloria F. Dance Sch., 1980, award Best Actress-Actress/Dancer, Liot, South Pacific, Mosque, Richmond, 1950; named Miss Virginia in Miss Am. Pageant, Altantic City, Sept. 1950; prin. judge Miss America Preliminaries, Va., Md., N.C., Tenn., 1950's-80's; Dance Library Dedication (Gloria F. Dance Collection), Petersburg Pub. Library. Mem. Dance Educators of Am., Profl. Dance Tchrs., Miss America Sorority (life). Presbyterian. Clubs: Petersburg Country; Ft. Lee Country (Va.); Battlefield Park and Racquet. Avocations: boating; swimming; snow skiing; dancing. Home: 1806 Brandon Ave Petersburg VA 23805 Office: Gloria F Dance Studios and Petersburg Ballet Inc 44 Goodwich Ave Petersburg VA 23805

DANCO, KATHARINE LECK, educator; b. Wilton, Conn., June 11, 1929; d. Walter Charles and Katharine (Elmendorf) Leck; m. Leon A. Danco, Aug. 25, 1951; children—Suzanne, Walter. R.N., Roosevelt Hosp. Sch. Nursing, 1950, R.N., N.Y., Ohio. Vice pres., treas. Univ. Services Inst., Cleve., 1968—, v.p., treas. Center for Family Bus., Cleve., 1973—, faculty, 1970—, seminar dir., 1971—; also dir. syndicated columnist numerous trade mags., 1978—, The Family in Bus., Cleve., 1978—. Author: From the Other Side of the Bed, 1980; contbr. articles to profl. jours. Bd. dirs. Julie Billiart Sch., Cleve., 1976—. Episcopalian. Home: 28230 Cedar Rd Pepper Pike OH 44122 Office: PO Box 24268 Center for Family Bus Cleveland OH 44124

DANCY, BONITA JOYCE, lawyer; b. Balt., Jan. 21, 1946; d. Homer Benson and Joyce Harper) Dancy; m. Theron Napoleon Whitaker, July 10, 1982. B.A., Morgan U., Balt., 1967; M.Social Work, U. Md.-Balt., 1971; J.D., 1981. cert. in advanced group therapy U. Chgo., 1972. Bar: Md. 1981; cert. social worker. Family service supr. Dept. Social Service Balt., 1967-72; assoc. prof. sociology Coppin State Coll., Balt., 1973-75; adminstr. N.W. Youth Services, Balt., 1972-81; adj. prof. Morgan State Coll., Balt., 1975-81; atty. advisor to gen. counsel HHS, Balt., 1981-82; master in chancery Cir. Ct. Balt. City, 1982—; mem. Md. Gov.'s Landlord Tenant Law Commn., 1975—; v.p. Md. Pre-trial Diversion Program, Balt., 1974-80; tng. cons. U. Md. Sch. Social Work, Balt., 1974-75. Bd. dirs., v.p. Mental Health Assn. Balt., 1983; exec. bd. Balt. Urban League, 1974-80, bd. dirs., 1981-82; mem. Balt. Urban League Leaguettes, Balt., 1968—, also past pres. Named Vol. of Yr., Balt. Urban League, 1983. Mem. ABA, Md. Bar Assn., Balt. City Bar Assn., Monumental City Bar Assn., Nat. Bar Assn., Phi Alpha Theta, Alpha Kappa Alpha. Office: Circuit Ct Baltimore City 111 N Calvert St Baltimore MD 21202

D'ANDREA, JENNIFER, engineering company administrator; b. Elizabeth, N.J., Sept. 23, 1951; d. Anthony Michael and Minnie Francis (Tiesi) Merullo; m. Charles D'Andrea, Aug. 26, 1973. B.S., Rutgers U., 1973; M.B.A., 1979. Benefits cons. William M. Mercer, Inc., N.Y.C., 1973-79; mgr. employee benefits Stone & Webster Inc., N.Y.C., 1979—. Roman Catholic. Avocations: running; skiing; hiking; biking. Home: 520 Pottersville Rd Gladstone NJ 07934 Office: Stone & Webster Inc 250 W 34th St New York NY 10019

DANDRY, TONIA MARIE, lawyer; b. New Orleans, Mar. 1, 1956; d. Anthony Joseph and Shirley Ann (Jumonville) Dandry. B.S.N., La. State U., 1978; J.D., Loyola Law Sch.-New Orleans, 1982. Registered nurse, La.; bar: La. Nurse, W. Jefferson Gen. Hosp., Marrero, La., 1974-81; law clk. Herman, Herman & Katz, New Orleans, 1980-82, assoc., 1982—. Decennial scholar, 1974-75. Mem. Assn. for Women Attys. (employment chmn.), New Orleans Bar Assn., Assn. Trial Lawyers Am., La. Trial Lawyers Assn., Am. Assn. Nurse Attys., Am. Council for Career Women, Am. Soc. Law and Medicine. Clubs: Altrusa, New Orleans Bus. and Profl. Women's. Office: Herman Herman & Katz 8200 O'Keefe New Orleans LA 70113

DANEK, MARITA MCKENNA, educational administrator; b. Garden City, N.Y., June 7, 1942; d. James A. and Mary Rita (Noble) McKenna; B.A., Catholic U., 1964; M.Ed., U. Md., 1970, Ph.D., 1979; m. Joseph Gerard Danek, June 18, 1966; children—Joseph, Jennifer, Geoffrey. Vocat. rehab. counselor State of Md., Bladensburg, 1966-70; counselor Model Secondary Sch. for Deaf, Washington, 1970-73; asst. prof. rehab. counseling Dept. Counseling, Gallaudet Coll., Washington, 1979-83, assoc. prof., 1983—, dir. rehab. counseling (deafness) program, 1981—. Rehab. Services Adminstrn. fellow, 1976-78, D.C. Services for Independent Living grantee, 1982; Women's Ednl. Equity Act grantee, 1982; Nat. Inst. Handicapped Research grantee, 1984; Switzer scholar, 1985. Mem. Am. Psychol. Assn., Nat. Rehab. Assn., Am. Personnel and Guidance Assn., Am. Deafness and Rehab. Assn., Am. Ednl. Research Assn. Contbr. articles to profl. publs. Office: Gallaudet Coll 113 Fowler Hall Washington DC 20002

DANFORD, ARDATH ANNE, retired library director; b. Lima, Ohio, Feb. 11, 1930; d. Howard Gorby and Grace Rose (Klug) D.; B.A., Fla. State U., 1951, M.A., 1952. Head tech. services Lima Public Library, 1956-60; librarian Way Public Library, Perrysburg, Ohio, 1960-70; asst. dir. Toledo-Lucas County Public Library, 1971-77, dir., from 1977, now ret., bd. dirs OHIONET. Recipient Toledo Headliner award Women in Communication, 1978, Boss of Yr. award PerRoMa chpt. Am. Bus. Women's Assn., 1978. Mem. ALA, Ohio Library Assn., League Women Voters, Maumee Valley Hist. Soc. Methodist. Club. Zonta (pres. club 1975-76) (Toledo). Author: The Perrysburg Story, 1966. Home: 2025 Sandringham St Toledo OH 43615

DANFORTH, FRANCES MUELLER (MRS. WILLIAM PAUL DANFORTH), civic worker; b. Austin, Tex., Mar. 23, 1914; d. Rudolph George and Laura Emma (Von Boeckmann) Mueller; B.J., U. Tex., 1935, B.A., 1936; M.S., Columbia U., 1938; m. William Paul Danforth, Aug. 16, 1942; children—William Paul, Douglas Mueller, Donald Lee. Grader dept. journalism U. Tex., Austin, 1934; asst. dir. Interscholastic League Press Bur., U. Tex., 1936-37; asst. editor Alcade, monthly alumni mag., 1936-37, 38-42; editor Star Points, nat. papers Delta Delta Delta Chgo., 1968-70; now buyer, bookkeeper Danforth's Antiques and Gifts, Austin. Pres. Austin Symphony League, 1967-68; state v.p. Tex. Women's Assn. Symphony Orchs., 1970; pres. Austin Vol. Bur., 1966-68; bd. dirs., sec. USO, 1971-72; bd. dirs. Symphony Orch. Soc.; bd. dirs., sec. Cen-Tex. chpt. ARC, pres. Altenheim, 1961-62. Mem. Women in Communications, Mortar Board (Austin alumna pres. 1978—) Delta Delta Delta, Lutheran (pres. ch. women 1972-74). Clubs: Settlement, Lawyers Wives (mem. bd., sec. 1973-74), Woman's (sec. 1972-74, v.p. 1977-79) (all Austin). Home: 1400 West Ave Austin TX 78701

DANGOT, GILDA ROSE, training executive, management consultant; b. N.Y.C., Aug. 18, 1952; d. Alter and Paula (Mentlik) Dangot. B.A., CCNY, 1973; cert. in tng. and devel., NYU, 1973; postgrad. in law Syracuse Coll. Law, 1973-74. Cert. tchr. N.Y. Mgmt. intern Dept. Consumer Affairs, N.Y.C., 1973; tchr. N.Y.C. Bd. Edn., 1974-75; community cons. N.Y.C. Human Rights Commn., 1975-78, spl. projects cons., 1978-79, dir. info. and resource devel., 1979-80, dir. tng., 1980—; mgmt. cons. Dynamic Devel., N.Y.C., 1980—, Am. Airlines, N.Y.C., 1984—, Kings Auto, N.Y.C., 1982-83, El Al Airlines, 1984—, Sheraton Corp., 1984, Bank Hapoalim, 1985—, World Trade Inst., 1984—; lectr. N.Y. Network for Learning, 1980-82, Westwinds Learning Ctr., N.Y.C., 1982—; adj. instr. Queens Coll., N.Y.C., 1984. Author: ABCs of Getting Help, 1976; So Your Organization Needs Money, 1978; How to Negotiate Anything, 1983. Founder Little Red Sch. House Community and Cultural Ctr., Inc., N.Y.C., 1978; pres. B'Nai Hashoah: Children of Holocaust Survivors, N.Y.C., 1979; founder, bd. dirs. internat. Network of Children of Survivors, N.Y.C., 1981. Recipient Gov.'s cert. for excellence in govt., 1969, Mayor's Scholarship, N.Y.C., 1983. Mem. Am. Soc. Tng. and Devel., Inter-Govt. Tgn. Council, Nat. Soc. Fund-Raising Execs. (cert. of recognition 1982), The Bus. Initiatives, Ind. Cons. Spl. Interest Group (chmn. program com.), Orgn. Devel. Network, Phi Beta Kappa, Pi Sigma Alpha, Kappa Delta Pi.

DANIEL, CECILE MARGARET, township official; b. New Bedford, Mass., Mar. 28, 1956; d. Romeo Alfred and Leona Blanch (Lemiuex) D.; m. George Walter Waterman, III, Aug. 4, 1984. B.A. in Polit. Sci., U. Mass., 1978; M.A. in Pub. Adminstrn., Pa. State U., 1981. Twp. mgr. Towamencin Twp., Pa., 1981—. Mem. Pa. Assn. Mcpl. Mgrs., S.E. Pa. Mgrs. Assn., Montgomery Assn. Twp. Ofcls. (sec. 1983), Pa. Mgr's. Ednl. Com. Republican. Roman Catholic. Avocations: reading; running; tennis. Home: 1133 Black Rock Rd RD #1 Phoenixville PA 19460 Office: Township Office Towamencin PA 19443

DANIEL, ELEANOR SAUER, economist, real estate executive; b. N.Y.C., Feb. 8, 1917; d. Charles Peter and Elsie Edna (Dommer) Sauer; B.A. magna cum laude (Bardwell fellow), Mt. Holyoke Coll., 1936; M.A. (Perkins fellow), Columbia U., 1937; m. John Carl Daniel, Dec. 31, 1952; children—Victoria Ann, Charles Timothy. Economist, U.S. Steel Co., N.Y.C., 1938; lectr. econs. Bklyn. Coll., 1939-40; with Mut. Life Ins. Co. N.Y., N.Y.C., 1940-74, asst. v.p., 1972-74, sr. econ. adviser, 1972-74; economist Fed. Home Loan Bank, N.Y.C., 1974-75; v.p., dir. Daniel Realty Cos., N.Y.C., 1975—; dir., chmn. fin. com. Atlantic City Electric Co.; former mem. bd. mgrs. U.S. Savs. Bank Newark; mem. Pres's. Task Force Fed. Credit Programs, 1968-69; mem. N.J. Gov.'s Econ. Recovery Com., 1975-76; mem. econ. adv. bd. U.S. Sec. Commerce, 1971-73; mem. bus. research adv. council U.S. Bur. Labor Statistics, 1966—; former trustee Blue Shield of N.J. Past trustee Mt. Holyoke Coll., also vice chmn., mem. fin. com. Mem. Am. Econ. Assn., Am. Fin. Assn. (past dir.), Phi Beta Kappa. Author: (with J.J. O'Leary and S.F. Foster) Our National Debt and Our Savings; contbr. articles to profl. jours. Home: 34 North Dr East Brunswick NJ 08816

DANIEL, EVELYN H(OPE), educator, educational administrator, consultant; b. Whitefield, Maine, Nov. 23, 1933; d. George Snowdeal and Evelyn Lura (Cole) Cunningham; m. Alfred Eugene Foulkes, Mar. 30, 1951 (div. 1956); m. 2d Harold Clifford Daniel, Jan. 1, 1957 (div. 1974); children—Jeffrey Martin, Dawn Hope; adopted children—Nancy Karen, George Warren. A.B. magna cum laude, U. N.C.-Wilmington, 1968; M.L.S., U. Md., 1969, Ph.D., 1974. Asst. prof. U. Ky., 1972-74; asst. prof. grad. library sch. U. R.I., 1974-76; assoc. prof., asst. dean Sch. Info. Studies, Syracuse U. (N.Y.), 1976-81, dean and prof., 1981-85; dean, prof. Sch. Library Sci., U. N.C., Chapel Hill, 1985—; cons. Edn. Radio and TV, Tehran, Iran, 1976-77, Millersville State Coll. (Pa.), 1983, Fgn. Service Inst. U.S. Dept. State, Washington, 1983-85, U.S. Dept. Edn. Accreditation Study, 1985-86. Co-author: Media and Microcomputers in the Library, 1984; contbr. articles to profl. jours.; mem. editorial bd. Library Research, 1979—. NDEA fellow, 1968-69. Mem. ALA (chmn. standing com. on edn. 1980-84, coordinator Library Edn. Assembly, 1980—, vice chmn. N.Y. Statewide Continuing Library Edn. Adv. Com. 1982-85). Assn. for Library and Edn. Sci. Educators (chmn. Council of Deans and Dirs. 1983-84). Home: 100 Cathy Rd Carrboro NC 27510 Office: 100 Manning Hall (026A) Univ NC Chapel Hill NC 27514

DANIEL, JUDY JACKSON, construction company executive; b. Tupelo, Miss., Jan. 4, 1952; d. Alfred Knox and Martha Lucille (Grantham) Jackson; m. Joseph Richard Daniel, Sept. 12, 1979 (div. 1982); 1 child, Richard Kirkpatrick. B.A. in English, U. Miss., 1974; M.A. in History, Memphis State U., 1980, M.C.R.P. in Urban Planning, 1984. Mktg. adminstr. Elkington & Keltner, Memphis, 1982-85; mrs. rep. Knox Jackson Assoc., Memphis, 1985-86; market devel. rep. Rentenbach Constrn., Memphis, 1986—. Membership chmn. 3d tier Symphony Support Group, Memphis, 1984-86; bd. dirs. Memphis Heritage Historic Preservation Soc., 1983-84. Episcopalian.

DANIEL, LYNN (LINDA) MARIE, microbiologist; b. Abilene, Tex., Aug. 19, 1944; d. James Marcus and Mary Marie (Hill) Daniel; B.S., U. Tex., 1969. Microbiologist, instr., Good Samaritan Hosp., Phoenix, 1967-70; supr., ednl. coordinator Desert Samaritan Hosp., Mesa, Ariz., 1970-73; surveyor/cons. Ariz. Dept. Health, Phoenix, 1973-76; owner, cons. Lab. Cons., Ltd., Tempe, Ariz., 1976-77; owner, pres., supr. Mobile Microbiology Services, Inc., Tempe, 1977-85; owner Microlab Spltys., 1983-85; dir. infectious disease dept. Nat. Health Labs., Phoenix, 1985—; tchr. Maricopa County Jr. Colls., 1972-73; cons. in field; lectr. in field. Mem. Nat. Registry of Microbiologists, Am. Soc. Microbiology, Am. Soc. Med. Technologists. Home: 507 W Manhatton Dr Tempe AZ 85282 Office: 1225 S 23d St Phoenix AZ 85034

DANIEL, SHARON REBECCA ROSE, educational administrator; b. Detroit, Aug. 28, 1955; d. James Edward and Wilma Jo (Thacker) D. A.B. in Edn., Marion Coll., Ind., 1976; M.A. in Edn., Ball State U., 1983. Cert. tchr., Ind. Tchr., dept. head Westside Christian Sch. and Noah's Ark Day Care Ctr., Marion, Ind., 1980-82, asst. dir., 1982-84, adminstrv. dir., 1984—; pvt. music tchr. Band dir. Am. Legion Hoosier Girl's State, Marion, 1982. Mem. Christian Instrumental Dirs. Assn., Assn. Supervision and Curriculum Devel. Republican. Mem. Assemblies of God. Avocations: music, travel. Home: 906 S Norton St Marion IN 46953 Office: Westside Christian Sch 2011 W 10th St Marion IN 46953

DANIEL-DREYFUS, SUSAN B. RUSSE, civic worker; b. St. Louis, May 30, 1940; d. Frederick William and Suzanne (Mackay) Russe; m. Don B. Faerber, Nov. 27, 1962 (div. Nov. 1968); 1 dau., Suzanne Mackay; m. Marc Andre Daniel-Dreyfus, Aug. 9, 1969. Student Smith Coll., 1958-60, Corcoran Sch. Fine Arts, 1960-61, Washington U., St. Louis, 1961-62. Mng. ptnr. Communications, Inc., 1980-82. Mem. St. Louis-St. Louis County White House Conf. on Edn., 1966-68; mem. Mo. 1st Gov.'s Conf. on Edn., 1966, 2d Conf., 1968; bd. dirs. St. Louis Smith Coll.; hon. bd. dirs. New Music Circle; mem. woman's bd. dirs. Washington U., New Music Circle, 1963-67; mem. woman's bd. Mo. Hist. Soc.; bd. dirs. Non-Partisan Ct. Plan for Mo., Young Audiences Inc., 1967-69; bd. dirs. Childrens Art Bazaar, 1968-70; founder St. Louis Opera Theater; chmn. Art. Mus. Bond Issue election St. Louis, 1966; jr. bd. dirs. St. Louis Symphony, 1966-68, Opportunities Indsl. Center, Boston; legis. chmn. bd. dirs. Boston LWV, 1969-72; mem. council, bd. dirs. Jr. League Boston, 1970-72, 74-76, Family Counseling-Region West, Boston, 1979—; pres. Family Counseling Bd., Brookline, Mass.; bd. govs. Tunbridge Sch.; trustee Chestnut Hill Sch., Boston, Brookline Friendly Soc.; mem. steering com. ann. fund Boston Children's Hosp. Med. Center, 1980-84; v.p. Nat. Friends Bd., Joslin Diabetes Found., 1980-83; mem. corp. bd. Joslin Diabetes Center; v.p. bd. dirs. Boston Center Internat. Visitors, 1979-82; Boston bd. dirs. Mass. Soc. Prevention of Cruelty to Children, 1980-84; exec. v.p. Ctr. for Middle East Bus., 1978-82; asst. dir. Harvard Bus. Sch. Fund, 1982—; pres. bd. Brookline Community Fund. Mem. Colonial Dames, Soc. Art Historians. Clubs: Women's City (dir.) (Boston); Vincent (dir.). Home: 120 Middlesex Rd Chestnut Hill MA 02167

DANIELS, ANNIE BELLE, beauty school executive; b. Grove Hill, Ala.; d. Jack and Ledester (Pugh) Guin; m. Charles E. Daniels, Sept. 20, 1955; children—Thomas, Gerald. Grad. Inst. Cosmetology, 1967, 1968, Assoc. Doctorate, 1979. Registered profl. hairdresser, Va. Directress, owner Madam Daniels' Sch. Beauty Culture, Newport News, Va., 1959—; mem. local curriculum adv. com. on cosmetology Thomas Nelson Community Coll., Newport News. Life mem., mem. nat. exec. bd. NAACP, active Newport News chpt.; YWCA, Newport News - Hampton Chpt. Continental Socs., Inc., Nat. Council Negro Women, Hampton Rds. Boys Club, Matilda Tents #131, Newport News Women's Democratic Club. Recipient Freedom Fund Pennant award NAACP, 1966, Life Membership Dr. award, 1969, Outstanding Service award Va. State Conf. Freedom Fund, 1969, 72; Sammy Davis, Jr. Life Membership award, 1970; Kivie Kaplan's award, 1971, Outstanding Service award Hampton Rds. Boy's Club, 1971-72; Community Service award Thomas Nelson Community Coll., 1972-73; achievement award Am. Tobacco Co., 1974; Outstanding Service award Medic-Home Health Ctr., Newport News, 1975; Citation for Outstanding Community Service, Sarah B. Hudgins Regional Ctr. and Peninsula Assn. for Retarded Children, 1977; Invincible Woman award Phyllis Wheatley YWCA, 1977; service award Va. Dept. Welfare, 1979; Bigger and Better Bus. award Phi Beta Sigma, 1982; Outstanding Work award Beauty Land Ltd., 1985; named Citizen of Yr., Alpha Alpha chpt. Psi Psi Fraternity, Inc., Newport News, 1979, to Blue Book of Tidewater, 1981. Mem. Nat. Beauty Culture League, Inc. (exec. bd., instr. wig styling, bldg. com. for research ctr., named Queen 1972, service award 1979), Va. State Beauticians Assn., Inc. (Outstanding Service award 1968, 73, trophy 1973), Dist. Cosmetology Assn. (Outstanding Service award 1974), Peninsula C. of C., Theta Mu Sigma, Psi Phi Frat. (Alpha Alpha chpt.). Club: Toppers. Lodge: Order Eastern Star. Home: 943 12th St Newport News VA 23607 Office: Madam Daniels' Sch Beauty Culture 2905 Chestnut Ave Newport News VA 23607

DANIELS, ARLENE KAPLAN, sociologist, educator; b. N.Y.C., Dec. 10, 1930; d. Jacob and Elizabeth (Rathstein) Kaplan; B.A. with honors in English; U. Calif.-Berkeley, 1952; M.A. in Sociology, 1954, Ph.D. in Sociology, 1960; m. Richard Rene Daniels, June 9, 1956. Instr. dept. speech U. Calif., Berkeley, 1959-61; research assoc. Mental Research Inst., Palo Alto, Calif., 1961-66; assoc. prof. sociology San Francisco State Coll., 1966-70; chief Center for Study Women in Soc., Inst. Sci. Analysis, San Francisco, 1970-77; dir. program on women Northwestern U., Evanston, Ill., 1975-80, prof. dept. sociology, 1975—; cons. NIMH, 1971-73, NEH, 1975-80, Nat. Inst. Edn., 1978-80. Trustee Bus. and Profl. Women's Research Found. Bd., 1980-85, Women's Equity Action League Legal and Ednl. Def. Bd., 1979-81; mem. Chgo. Research Assos. Bd., 1981—. Recipient Social Sci. Research Council Faculty Research award, 1970-71; Ford Found. Faculty fellow, 1975-76; grantee Nat. Inst. Edn., 1978-79, 79-82, NSF, 1974-75, NIMH, 1973-74. Mem. Sociologists Women in Soc. (pres. 1975-76), Am. Sociology Assn. (council 1979-82), Soc. Study Social Problems (v.p. 1981-82, pres. 1987), Soc. Study Symbolic Inter-Action. Editor: (with Rachel Kahn-Hut) Academics on the Line 1970; co-editor: Hearth and Home: Images of Women in the Mass Media, 1978, Education: Straightjacket or Opportunity?, 1979, Women and Work, 1982; Women and Trade Unions in Eleven Industrialized Countries, 1984; co-author: Working in Foundations, 1985. Editor Jour. Social Problems, 1974-78; assoc. editor Contemporary Sociology, 1980-82, Symbolic Interaction, 1979-82. Home: 3404 Lodge Dr Belmont CA 94002 Office: Dept of Sociology Northwestern University 1810 Chicago Ave Evanston IL 60201

DANIELS, DOROTHY, writer; b. Waterbury, Conn., July 1, 1915; d. Judson Richard and Mary (Guilfoile) Smith; student Central Conn. State Coll., 1932-36; m., Oct. 7, 1937. Tng. tchr., New Britain, Conn., 1937-39; actress, 1939-40. Author 132 books under name Dorothy Daniels, 1962—, most recent including: House of Silence, 1980, Nicola, 1980, Monte Carlo, 1981, Sisters of Valcour, 1981, For Love and Valcour, 1983; seven books under name Suzanne Somers, 1961-73, including: The Caduceus Tree, 1961, Image of Truth, 1963, Romany Curse, 1971, House on Thunder Hill, 1973; Crisis at Valcour, 1985; other books under names Cynthia Cavanaugh, Angela Gray, Daniella Dorsett. Active Citizens Adv. Com. Ventura Sch., Calif. Youth Authority, Republican Women's Club. Mem. Nat. League Am. Pen Women (nat. hon.), Authors Guild, Ventura County Writers' Club.

DANIELS, ELISABETH ANN MICHAEL, mayor; b. Kansas City, Mo., Oct. 12, 1944; d. Archie Washigton and Elizabeth Virginia (Moreland) Michael; student Central Mo. State U., Warrensburg, 1963-66, Ottawa U., Overland Park, Kans., 1984—; m. Joseph Ames Daniels, Sept 1, 1963; children—Jeffrey Michael, Christopher Ames. Adminstrv. sec., dean women Central Mo. State U., 1966-68; minister youth and music First Baptist Ch., Carrollton, Mo., 1970-73; propr. Ann's Catering Service, Carrollton, 1973—; mayor Town of Carrollton, 1977—; v.p., bd. govs. Area II Health Systems Agy., 1979—; exec. com., v.p., chmn. personnel com. Mo. Valley Regional Planning Commn., 1977-84, exec. dir., 1984—; chmn. Sub Area Health Council, 1980—, Regional Manpower Adv. Council, 1981—; mem. Mo. Older Adults Transp. Bd., 1981—; pres. bd. dirs. OATS, Inc., 1982—, acting exec. dir., 1985—. Pres. community adv. bd. Sta. KMOS-TV, 1980—. Mem. Mo. Mcpl. League, PEO, Federated Woman's Club, Beta Sigma Phi., Home: 1112 Hilltop Dr Carrollton MO 64633 Office: 201 W Benton St Carrollton MO 64633

DANIELS, ELLEN PAPPAS, communications executive, consultant; b. Cleve., Dec. 5, 1956; d. Leonard Gust and Effie Violet (Vamis) Pappas; m. Thomas Campbell Daniels, July 28, 1979. B.Music, Baldwin-Wallace Coll., 1979; postgrad. Kent State U., 1982—. Pub. relations staff Baldwin-Wallace Coll., Berea, Ohio, 1977-79; prodn. mgr. Loos, Edwards & Sexauer Advt., Akron, Ohio, 1979-81; communications exec. Kent State U., Canton, Ohio, 1981-85; mgr. advt. Harshaw/Filtrol Corp., Cleve., 1985—; cons. Carson/Dellosa Pub., Akron, 1980, MARS, Akron, 1982-83, SCI Communications, Inc., Canton, 1983—. Mem. Coll. Com. of Cultural Ctr., Canton, 1983. Mem. Women in Communications, Inc. (v.p. 1982-85, pres.-elect 1985-86), Women Adminstrs. of Kent (pres. 1984-85). Home: 5203 Stow Rd Stow OH 44224 Office: Harshaw/Filtrol Corp Cleveland OH

DANIELS, GERALDINE B., radiologist; b. Jersey City, Apr. 17, 1943; d. August J. and Loretta A. Daniels. B.A., Rutgers U., 1964; M.D., N.Y. Med. Coll., 1968. Diplomate Am. Bd. Radiology (diagnostic radiology). Intern, S.I. Hosp. (N.Y.), 1968-69; resident diagnostic radiology Bronx VA Hosp. (N.Y.), 1969-72; radiologist VA Hosp., Newington, Conn., 1972-74; asst. radiologist St. Joseph's Hosp., Stamford, Conn., 1974-75; radiologist, co-dir. ultra div. Maimonides Med. Ctr., Bklyn., 1975-79; dir. ultrasound dept. St. John's Riverside Hosp., Yonkers, N.Y., 1979-80; practice diagnostic ultrasound, Yonkers, 1980—; asst. prof. clin. radiology Downstate Med. Sch., 1979-80; instr. radiology U. Conn., Farmington, 1972-74. Vol., ASPCA, 1982, N.Y.C. Opera Guild, 1981-82. Recipient Physician's Recognition award AMA, 1982—. Mem. Am. Inst. Ultrasound in Medicine (sr.; (ultra tech. sch. survey team), Am. Coll. Radiology, Med. Soc. State N.Y., N.Y. County Med. Soc., Westchester County Med. Soc. (assoc.), Yonkers Acad. Medicine, Radiol. Soc. N.Am., Nat. Trust Hist. Preservation, Met. Opera Guild, N.Y. Zool. Soc. Cooper-Hewit Mus. Office: Diagnostic Ultrasound 1022 N Broadway Yonkers NY 10701

DANIELS, JANE EVANGELINE, nurse, educator; b. Goodhue County, Minn., Nov. 12, 1931; d. Elmer Wilfred and Grace Evangeline (Johnson) Anderson; grad. Kahler Hosp. Sch. Nursing, Rochester, Minn., 1954; m. Owen R. Daniels, May 19, 1953; children—Jon Stewart, Christine Grace, Peter Ray. Head nurse gynecology and hematology Rochester (Minn.) Methodist Hosp., 1954-56, staff nurse dermatology, 1958-69, head nurse dermatology, 1969-74, dermatology nurse specialist, instr. Rochester Meth. Hosp.-Mayo Clinic Dermatologic Nursing Program, Rochester, Minn., 1974—; cons. in field; instr. nursing edn. programs, patient teaching programs related to dermatology. Registered nurse, Minn. Mem. Am. Nurses' Assn., Methodist-Kahler Alumni Assn. Lutheran. Developer curriculum, coordinator 1st nursing program devoted entirely to dermatology, offered to registered nurses nationally 1975—. Home: 1521 8th Ave NE Rochester MN 55904 Office: 201 W Center St Rochester MN 55902

DANIELS, JANET VICTORIA, management analyst; b. Bay City, Mich., Apr. 19, 1943. A.A., Delta Coll., Mich., 1968; C.dA. U. Grenoble, France, 1969; B.S. cum laude, Mich. State U., 1971; M.S., So. Ill. U., 1975. Compliance officer U.S. Dept. Interior, Washington, 1972-77, program evaluation specialist Bur. Land Mgmt., 1978-79, spl. asst. Office of Asst. Sec., 1979-80, staff specialist for Alaska programs, 1980-81, mineral leasing specialist Bur. Land Mgmt., 1981-83; mgmt. analyst Nat. Park Service, Lakewood, Colo., 1984—; instr. Presdl. Classroom for Young Ams., 1976. Editor: Guide to Wind Cave National Park, 1984; author articles. Active Savs. Bonds campaigns. Mem. Nat. Trust Hist. Preservation (assoc.), Denver Art Mus. (assoc.), Historic Denver Soc., Natural History Assn. (life), Nat. Assn. Female Execs. Democrat. Avocations: sailing; golf; tennis; English saddle riding; antiques; gourmet cooking. Office: Nat Park Service Regional Office 655 Parfet St PO Box 25287 Lakewood CO 80225

DANIELS, LESLIE BETH, city ofcl.; b. Kansas City, Mo., July 14, 1951; d. Charles Lee and Helen Atanasoff D.; B.A., U. Ariz., 1972; M.A., U. Phoenix, 1981; postgrad. U. Okla. Econ. Devel. Inst., 1983. Copywriter public relations, Tucson, 1972-74, graphic artist/electronic typesetter, 1974-75, polit. campaign mgr., 1972-77; adminstrv. asst. City Mgrs. Office, City of Tucson, 1978-85; transit coordinator City of Tucson Transp. Dept., 1985—. Editor, State Republican Com. newspaper, 1975-76; chmn. Pima County Young Rep. League, 1973-74; dist. 9 chmn. Pima County Rep. Central Com., 1974. Mem. Ariz. Assn. Indsl. Developers, Kappa Tau Alpha, Delta Sigma Pi. Republican. Methodist. Club: Pima County Trunk 'n Tusk (publicity chmn. 1974-77). Home: 7369 E 20th St Tucson AZ 85710 Office: PO Box 27210 Tucson AZ 85726

DANIELS, MADELINE MARIE, psychotherapist, author; b. Newark, Oct. 14, 1948; d. William and Dorothy Barlow; B.A. cum laude, CCNY, 1971; Ph.D., Union Grad. Sch., Yellow Springs, Ohio, 1975; m. Peter W. Daniels, Oct. 18, 1976; children—Jonathan, Jedediah, Jeremiah. Lectr., Westchester Community Coll., also Bronx Community Coll., 1973-74; mem. adj. faculty SUNY, Purchase, 1974-76; data processing coordinator GTE Internat., 1976-78; lectr. div. continuing edn. U. N.H., 1979—; exec. dir. Crossroads Center Human Integration, East Kingston, N.H., 1979—; psychotherapist, lectr., cons. in field. Cert. ind. biofeedback practitioner. Mem. Am. Psychol. Assn., Biofeedback Soc. Am., Soc. Psychol. Athropology, N.H. Psychol. Orgn., NOW, Phi Beta Kappa. Author: Realistic Leadership, 1983; Living Your Religion in the Real World, 1985. Office: Crossroads Center East Kingston NH 03827

DANIELS, MARIAN FAYE, clerk of court; b. Blairsburg, Iowa, May 7, 1926; d. Menno J. and Anna (Boyenga) Isebrands; m. Harry Merton Daniels, May 15, 1954; children—Faye Ann, Robert Charles, Doris Jean. B.S.C., U. Iowa, 1946. Licensed real estate broker. Real estate closer Quinlan & Tyson, Inc., Evanston, Ill., 1946-52; prodn. sec., mgr. Rand McNally, Skokie, Ill., 1952-54; real estate broker, Webster City, Iowa, 1960-68; legal sec. Karr, Karr & Karr, P.C., Webster City, 1968-72; dep. clk. ct. Hamilton County, Webster City, 1972-79, clk. dist. ct., 1979—, registrar vital stats., 1979—. Chmn. Republican Precinct 3B, Webster City, 1973—; mem. Hamilton County Rep. Central Com., Webster City, 1974—; precinct chmn. Central Com., Iowa Republicans, 1980—; mem. adv. council Iowa Central Adult Edn., Webster City, 1968-70; chmn. bd. dirs. Rainbow for Girls, Webster City, 1972; chmn. Webster City Planning Commn., Iowa, 1978. Mem. Iowa State Clks. Assn. (pres. dist. 1 1980—, service award 1981-84), Bus. Profl. Women (pres. 1968-69), U. Iowa Alumni Assn. (life), U. Iowa Bus. Adminstrn. Constituent Assn. (life), Am. Legion Aux., VFW. Congregationalist. Club: Bridge (Webster City). Lodges: Women of the Moose, Order of Eastern Star. Avocations: biking; sewing; grandparenting. Home: 1612 Sunset Dr Webster City IA 50595 Office: 2500 Superior St Webster City IA 50595

DANIELS, MARLENE D., lawyer; b. Englewood, N.J., Mar. 11, 1941; d. Joseph H. and Eleanor (Seifert) D. Grad. Conn. Coll. for Women, 1963; J.D., Fordham U., 1966. Bar: N.Y. 1966. Assoc. Hill, Betts & Nash, N.Y.C., 1967-73, ptnr., 1973—. Bd. editors Jour. Maritime Law and Commerce, 1979—. Mem. ABA (com. on marine financing 1980), Am. Arbitration Assn. (nat. panel of arbitrators), Assn. Bar City of N.Y. (admiralty com.), Internat. Bar Assn., Norwegian Am. C. of C. (bd. dirs.), Maritime Law Assn. U.S. (subcom. on maritime fin. 1979). Office: Suite 5215 World Trade Center New York NY 10048

DANIELS, NORMA L., state legislator. Mem. Kans Senate. Democrat. Office: Kans Senate State Capitol Topeka KS 66612*

DANIELS, PEARL GRAY, business educator; b. Montgomery, Ala., Sept. 10, 1926; d. Abraham Harrison and Nancy (Jones) Gray; m. Simon Duval Daniels, Oct. 20, 1974; children—Valerie G. Wheeler, Nathan G. Wheeler. A.A., Stillman Coll., 1947; B.S., Ala. State U., 1952; Ed.M., Tuskegee U., 1958. Tchr. bus. Dallas County Bd. Edn., Selma, Ala., 1951-52; sec. Tuskegee U., Ala., 1955-56, 1957-58; tchr. bus. Macon County Tng. Sch., Roba, Ala., 1955-56; sec. Howard U., Washington, 1960, U. D.C., Washington, 1961; bus. tchr. D.C. Bd. Edn., Washington, 1962-72; asst. prin. Cardozo Adult Evening Sch., Washington, 1972-73; asst. prof. Ala. State U., Montgomery, 1974—. Author: Portrait of Fred D. Gray, 1975; Freshman Orientation Study Guide Manual, 1976; Test Taking Techniques, 1986. Recipient Cert. Merit Ala. Dem. Conf. 1983, Disting. Educator and Alumni award Stillman Coll. Alumni Assn., 1985; named Outstanding Woman of Yr. 1984. Fellow Inst. Devel. Ednl. Activities, 1973—, NDEA 1965. Mem. NAACP, Nat. Bus. Edn. Assn., Ala. Assn. Tchr. Educators, Kappa Delta Pi, Iota Phi Lambda, Sigma Gamma Rho. Democrat. Clubs: Montgomery City Fedn. Women's and Youth (corr. sec. 1983-85, 2d v.p. 1985—), Nancy Gray Arms Federated (pres. 1980—) (Montgomery). Home: 2585 Westwood Dr Montgomery AL 36108 Office: Ala State U 915 S Jackson St Montgomery AL 36195

DANIELS, SUSAN BARBARA, librarian; b. Buffalo, Apr. 30, 1941; d. Anthony and Barbara Winslow (Hulen) DiFilippo. B.S. in L.S., SUNY-Geneseo, 1968; M.S. in L.S., Syracuse U., 1969. Cert. pub. librarian, N.Y. Sch. librarian Frontier Sch. Dist., Hamburg, N.Y., 1969-70; head librarian Cheektowaga Pub. Library (N.Y.), 1970-74; asst. librarian Aurora Town Pub. Library, East Aurora, N.Y., 1974-76, acting library dir., 1977, library dir., 1977-82; dir. Hamburg Pub. Library, 1982—; mem. various coms. Buffalo and Erie County Pub. Library System, 1980—; instr. continuing edn. workshop SUNY-Buffalo, summer 1982. Chmn. sr. citizen adv. com. Town of Aurora, 1980-81; bd. dirs. East Aurora Boys Club, 1981—. Mem. Hamburg C. of C., Grosvenor Soc., ALA, N.Y. Library Assn., Librarian's Assn., Staff Assn. Buffalo and Erie County Pub. Library (pres. 1983-84), Bus. and Profl. Women's Club, Kappa Delta Pi. Episcopalian. Club: Zonta (dir. Aurora 1979-80). Home: 38 Kathryn Dr Orchard Park NY 14127 Office: Hamburg Pub Library 102 Buffalo St Hamburg NY 14075

DANIELS, SUZANNE MADELEINE, med. technologist; b. Worcester, Mass., July 23, 1941; d. George Edward and Ruth Bernadette (St. Martin) Brodeur; student Central New Eng. Coll. Tech., 1959-62; M.T., Worcester City Hosp. Sch. Med. Tech., 1962; m. Charles Daniels; children—Edward, Jennifer. Flight exam technician Pratt & Whitney, E. Hartford, Conn., 1962-63; sect. head chemistry/radioisotopes Mt. Sinai Hosp., Hartford, Conn., 1963-65; gen. technician Meml. Hosp., Worcester, 1965-69; blood bank supr. Milford-Whitinsville Regional Hosp., Milford, Mass., 1969-70; asst. clin. supr., sect. head chemistry Worcester Hahnemann Hosp., 1970-75; lab. supr. Weeks Meml. Hosp., Lancaster, N.H., 1975—; clin. teaching staff Vt. Coll. Sch. Med. Lab. Technicians, 1975—. Mem. Am. Soc. Clin. Pathologists, Clin. Lab. Mgmt. Assn. Roman Catholic. Clubs: Twin Mt. Snowmobile, Bethlehem Country. Home: PO Box H Twin Mountain NH 03595 Office: Middle St Lancaster NH 03584

DANIELSON, PATRICIA ROCHELLE FRANK, urban planner; b. Manhattan, N.Y., Dec. 22, 1941; d. Maxwell and Theresa (Kleckner) Frank; m. Michael Nils Danielson, Sept. 8, 1979; m. Seymour B. Fingerhood, Sept. 15, 1963 (div. Dec. 1978); children—Karl John, Louisa Laura. A.A., Thomas Edison State Coll., 1973; M.U.P., Princeton U., 1976. policy planner Gov's Office, Trenton, 1978-80; program devel. specialist N.J. Dept. Community Affairs, Trenton, 1980-82; sr. planner Eggers Group, N.Y.C., 1982-85; pvt. research and public affairs cons., Princeton, N.J., 1985—. Chmn. bd. trustees Thomas A. Edison State Coll., Trenton, 1984—, trustee, 1978—. Mem. Princeton Research Forum, N.J. State Coll. Gov. Bd. Assn., Am. Soc. Public Adminstrs. Avocations: creative writing; folk music.

DANIELSON, PHYLLIS I., art school administrator, tapestry artist; b. Marion, Ind. B.A. in Art, Ball State U., 1953; M.A., Mich. State U., 1960, Ed.S., 1966; Ed.D., Ind. U., 1968. One-person shows: Jewish Community Ctr., Indpls., 1972, Eye-Opener Gallery, Cin., 1972, Mint Mus. Art, 1974, Herron Art Gallery, Indpls., 1974, Sloane O'Stickey Gallery, Cleve., 1974, Women in Art, West Bend, Wis., 1976; group exhbns. include: Weatherspoon Gallery, Greensboro, N.C., 1969, 70, Stichery, Pa., 1971, Iowa, 1975; Matrix Gallery, Bloomington, Ind., 1972; pres. Kendall Sch. Design, Grand Rapids, Mich., 1976—; asst. prof. art Ball State U., Muncie, Ind., 1966-67; asst. prof. art edn. U. N.C., Greensboro, 1968-70; assoc. prof. edn. and art Herron Sch. Art, Indpls., 1970-76. Contbr. articles to profl. jours. Mem. Nat. Art Edn. Assn., Nat. Council Art Adminstrs., Nat. Assn. Sch. Art, Coll. Art Assn. Address: Kendall School of Design 1110 College Ave NE Grand Rapids MI 49503

DANIELS-SHORT, JOYCE A., career development director, cosmetologist; b. Mounds, Ill., Apr. 7, 1946; d. Roy Lee Daniels and Louise (Austin) Patterson; m. James L. Short, Jr., Feb. 29, 1964 (div. 1971); children—Sheila, Mario, JaKeema, Neali. B.A. in Sociology, DePaul U., 1979; postgrad. in urban planning U. Ill., Chgo., 1986—. Lic. cosmetologist. Machine operator J.L. Clark Mfg. Co., Chgo., 1966-69; store mgr. U.S. Hair of Ill., Chgo., 1970-73; employment specialist Midwest Women's Ctr., Chgo., 1979-84; dir. career devel. S. Suburban YWCA Met. Chgo., 1984—. Founding bd. mem. Ill. Minority Women's Caucus, Chgo., 1980—, pub. relations chmn., 1985—; poll watcher, canvasser Women's Network, 1983. Mem. Nat. Assn. Female Execs., Nat. Hook-up of Black Women. Democrat. Avocations: Singing; dancing; cooking. Office: Chicago Met YWCA Suburban Center 3612 W Lincoln Hwy Olympia Fields IL 60471

DANIS, JULIE MARIE, snack food company executive; b. Dayton, Ohio, Aug. 19, 1955; d. Charles Wheaton and Elizabeth Jane (Sliter) D. B.S., Northwestern U., 1977; A.M., U. Chgo., 1979, M.B.A., 1984. Juvenile justice planner Ill. Law Enforcement Commn., Chgo., 1979-80; prin. budget analyst City of Chgo., 1980-82; account mgmt. intern Foote, Cone & Belding, Chgo., 1983; assoc. product mgr. Frito-Lay, Inc., Dallas, 1984—. Cons. United Way of Chgo., 1980. Mem. Nat. Assn. Female Execs., Pi Beta Phi. Democrat. Roman Catholic. Clubs: 500, Inc., Backstagers, Jr. League. Avocations: theater and dance patron; aerobics; tennis; travel. Home: 5859 Frankford Rd #509 Dallas TX 75252 Office: Frito-Lay Inc 7701 Carpenter Rd Plano TX 75024

DANKO, HELEN ELIZABETH, educator; b. Detroit, Apr. 16, 1928; d. John and Elizabeth (Miskolczi) Bohan; m. Stephen Paul Danko, Aug. 3, 1957; 1 child, John Paul Stephen. Ph.B., U. Detroit, 1950; M.A., Wayne State U., 1954; specialists tng. Eastern Mich. U., 1964-68. Cert. elem. and high sch. tchr., Mich. with Lincoln Park Sch. Dist., head English dept. Lincoln Park High Sch., 1982—; curriculum and textbook cons. Wyandotte Pub. Schs., Mich., 1978—. Officer Wyandotte Bd. Edn., 1977-85; sec. Wayne County Assn. Sch. Bds., 1983-85, program chmn., 1984—; mem. Down River League Catholic Women, LWV, Jr. Altar Soc.; active coach, officer and vol. with numerous youth athletic programs. Recipient Disting. Service award Mich. Parent-Tchr.-Student Assn., 1985; named Tchr. of Yr., Mich. Parent-Tchr.-Student Assn., 1985. Mem. Lincoln Park Bus. and Profl. Women (former officer, Woman of Yr. 1963), Nat. Council English Tchrs., Am. Bus. Women, AAUW. Republican. Roman Catholic. Lodges: Daus. Isabella; William Penn Ladies Auxiliary. Avocations: theatre; ethnic dancing and culture; creative writing. Office: Lincoln Park High Sch 1701 Champaign St Lincoln Park MI 48146

DANKO, PAT ST. JOHN, visual artist, writer; b. Orange, Tex., Aug. 7, 1944; d. George Milton and Rebecca Alice (McCoppin) Solomon; m. Jim Danko, Aug. 19, 1973 (dec. 1983). B.A., Dominican Coll., Houston, 1965; B.F.A., U. Houston, 1979; postgrad. Mus. Fine Arts Sch., Houston, U. Ibero-Americana, Mexico, Mich. State U. Teaching asst. Mich. State U., East Lansing, 1966; vol. Peace Corps, Chile, 1966-69; silkscreen apprentice, printer Atelier Zárate, Buenos Aires, 1970; tchr. high sch. Orange Ind. Sch. Dist. (Tex.), 1971, Houston Ind. Sch. Dist., 1973; instr. English, English Lang. Services, Houston, 1973-75; instr. English, Spanish, Inlingua Lang. Schs., 1976; instr. Art League Houston, 1978-81; performance art writer Houston Art Scene, 1979—, editor, 1981—, mng. editor, 1982-83, exec. editor, 1983—; acting Tex. editor New Art Examiner, 1985-86; contbg. editor Tex. New Art Examiner, 1986—; ind. art hist. researcher, writer; freelance writer; visual artist, pub. collections: N.Y. Feminist Art Inst.; Equinox Theatre, Houston; Chomo Uri Collective, U. Mass.; McGlothlin Ins. Agy., Houston; Cameron Petroleum Co., Houston. Sculpture, artist, designer numerous artistic performances; exhbns. of artistic work to numerous museums and cultural instns. throughout Tex. Jesse H. Jones Found. fellow, 1961-65; recipient Presdl. Commendation by Pres. Johnson for Service to U.S. and Chile, 1970; named Outstanding Young Woman of Am., OYWA Press, Chgo., 1972; Commonwealth of Mass. Council on Arts and Humanities grantee, 1978-79; Coordinating Council of Literary Magazines grantee, 1978-79; Cultural Arts Council of Houston, Sum Arts grantee for sculpture The Matriarch as Phoenix, 1982; Shell Found. grantee for performance of Thanatopsis, 1983. Mem. Artists Equity Assn., Contemporary Arts Mus. (Houston). Roman Catholic. Address: 2112 Dunlavy Houston TX 77006

DANN, EMILY, chemical company executive; b. Albany, Ga., July 26, 1932; d. Jesse Lyman and Evelyn (Calhoun) Dann; m. Christian A. Hansen, June 7, 1977; children—Leslie Montgomery Eagan, Ann Montgomery. B.A., Huntingdon Coll., 1954; M.S. in Math., U. Houston, 1964; Ed.D., Rutgers U., 1976. Instr., Lee Coll., Baytown, Tex., 1965-67; prof. Middlesex County Coll., Edison, N.J., 1967-81; dir. human resources LCP Chem. & Plastics Co., Edison, 1981—; cons. Title I math. program Bedminster (N.J.) Pub. Sch., 1976-77; mem. co-adj. faculty Grad. Sch. Edn., Rutgers U., 1976-81, Kean Coll., 1980-81. Contbr. articles to profl. jours. Mem. Acad. Mgmt., Orgn. Devel. Network, Am. Soc. Tng. and Devel., Am. Math. Assn., Jean Piaget Soc. Home: 1 Scenic Dr Highlands NJ 07732 Office: LCP Chem & Plastics Co Raritan Plaza II Edison NJ 08837

DANNEMAN, REBECCA BROWN, nursing adminstrator; b. Hanover, Pa., June 4, 1951; d. William Henry and Geneva Kathleen (Caples) Brown; m. Donald James Danneman, Aug. 16, 1981. A.A., Howard Community Coll., 1976. Staff nurse Montgomery Gen. Hosp., Olney, Md., 1976-79, charge nurse, 1979-80; staff nurse Seneca House, Poolesville, Md., 1980-82, dir. nursing, 1982—; instr. Office Edn. and Tng. for Addiction Services, Balt., 1983—; cons. North Arundel Hosp., Glen Burnie, Dd., 1981, George Washington Hosp., Washington, 1982, Sam Shoemaker House, Westminster, Md., 1982, Meadows Recovery, Gambrils, Md., 1983. Mem. citizen's adv. council Sam Shoemaker House, 1982—. Mem. Md. Nurses Assn. (monitor impaired nurse com. 1982-85), Drug and Alcohol Nurses Assn., Carroll County Bus. and Profl. Women's Assn. Office: Seneca House 13025 Riley's Lock Rd Poolesville MD 20837

DANNER, PAMELA BECK, lawyer; b. Shelbyville, Ind., Dec. 2, 1948; d. Raymond F. and Lorna (Thomas) Beck; m. David L. Danner, Sept. 30, 1972; children—Constance Lynne and Laurel Beck. B.A., Purdue U., 1971; M.A., Am. U., 1973; J.D., Georgetown U., 1977. Bar: Ind. 1977, D.C. 1978, Va. 1985. Cert. secondary tchr. Md. Tchr. Montgomery County (Md.,) Pub. Schs., Rockville, 1972-74; law clk. HUD, Washington, 1976-77, atty., 1977-79, dir. office manufactured housing and regulatory functions, 1982-84; sole practice, Washington, 1979-82, 84—; dir. Ideamatics Inc., Washington, 1976—; grad. research asst. Am. U., 1971-72. Editor Georgetown Internat. Law Jour., 1976-77. Trustee, rec. sec., 2d v.p. Barney Neighborhood House, Washington, 1982—; mem. D.C. Bldg. Code Adv. Com. Named an Outstanding Young Women Am., U.S. Jr. C. of C. Internat., 1982. Mem. D.C. Inter-Am. Council, ABA, D.C. Bar Assn., Ind. Bar Assn., Va. State Bar. Clubs: Ind. State Soc., Wis. State Soc.

DANNER, REGINA GAIL, nursing home administrator; b. Chgo., Aug. 14, 1944; d. Reginald Guy and Emily Ann (Cox) Foster. R.N., Touro Hosp., New Orleans, 1978. Nurse, Charity Hosp., New Orleans, 1969-70; Montelepre Hosp., 1970-75, Metairie Healthcare Nursing Home, 1975-79; adminstr. Waldon Healthcare, Kenner, La., 1979-84, Montelepre Nursing Ctr., Hammond, La., 1985—. Contbr. articles to profl. jours. Fellow Am. Coll. Healthcare Adminstrs. (nat. membership com. 1985-87); mem. La. Healthcare Assn. (legis. pub. relations, edn., peer rev. 1982-84), Kenner Bus. Assn., Nat. League Nursing, Nat. Assn. Female Execs., Jefferson Council Aging, Nat. Assn. Practical Nursing. Office: Montelepre Nursing Ctr 1300 Derek Dr Hammond LA 70403

DANSER, ELLEN SPENCER, publishing co. exec.; b. Mancelona, Mich., Mar. 15, 1922; d. Edward C. and Emma (Maffitt) Shafer; student Bliss Bus. Coll., 1939-43; m. Harold W. Danser, Jr., June 22, 1969. Treas. SSS Corp., North Adams, Mass., 1950-63; v.p., treas. Paper Service Co., Holyoke, Mass., 1963-69; nat. sales mgr. F. Weber Co., Phila., 1969-71; cons. sales promotion Wall St. Transcript, N.Y.C., 1970-72; owner, pres., treas. Elan Pub. Co., Inc. and Elan Products, Meredith, N.H., 1972—. Treas., First Congl. Ch. of Meredith, 1978—; pres. Community Garden Club, 1975. Republican. Home: Oak Island Meredith NH 03253 Office: PO Box 683 Meredith NH 03253

D'ANTONIO, ANN ROSE, cost accountant; b. Lucca, Italy, Sept. 28, 1941; came to U.S., 1952; d. Frank and Lilia (Marchetti) Marcheschi; m. Louis D'Antonio, Sept. 12, 1959; children—LouAnn, Joseph, Joanne, MaryAnn, Frank, Mario. A.A., Moraine Valley Coll., 1985; student Govs. State U., 1985—. Keypunch operator Reserve Ins. Co., Chgo., 1959-60; sales rep. Queen's Way, Chgo., 1967-68; housekeeping supr. St. Francis Hosp., Blue Island, Ill., 1968-69; timekeeper Borg & Beck div. Borg-Warner Corp., Chgo., 1969-80; cost acct. Borg-Warner Automotive, Chgo., 1980—. Bookkeeper, treas. Eckankar Ctr., Chgo., 1982-83; co-founder, sec. Citizens for a Better Blue Island, 1985-86; costume designer Blue Island Community Theater, 1975-76. Democrat. Avocations: gardening; costume design; sewing; personal computers; soul travel. Home: 2617 W Walnut St Blue Island IL 60406 Office: 5950 W 66th St Chicago IL 60638

DANZEISEN, KATHRYN ELIZABETH, lawyer; b. Orange, N.J., Sept. 16, 1950; d. Henry Francis and Elizabeth (Fisher) Cox; m. David Paul Danzeisen, Apr. 23, 1983. B.S., Villanova U., 1972; M.B.A., St. Joseph's U., 1978; J.D., Pace U., 1981. Bar: N.Y. 1981. Sr. chemist Am. Cyanamid, Clifton, N.J., 1974-77; cons. Shaklee Corp., San Francisco, 1978; law intern in human rights State of N.Y., N.Y.C., 1980; assoc. atty. Seaman & Ashley, N.Y.C., 1981-82; sole practice, Armonk, N.Y., 1982—; corp. counsel Vangard Tours, Inc., Ossining, N.Y., 1983—. Com. mem. Hudson River Waterfront Commn., Ossining, 1983. Sun Oil Corp. chem. engring. scholar, 1968. Mem. ABA, N.Y. State Bar Assn., Women's Westchester Bar Assn., Women's Farm Bur., Women's Bar Assn. of State of N.Y. Roman Catholic. Home: 77 Whippoorwill Rd Armonk NY 10504

DANZIG, JOAN, newspaper editor; b. Elmira, N.Y., Mar. 3, 1929; d. George Hamilton and Estelle (Saqui) Danzig; m. Joseph Krasner; children—Susan, Karin. B.A., Empire State Coll., 1975; student Elmira Coll., 1946-47; B.A., Empire State Coll., 1975. Asst. feature editor Buffalo News, 1952-60; reporter, society editor Evening Times, Sayre, Pa., 1948-51; editor Lifestyles Sect., fashion editor Buffalo News, 1960—. Recipient Page One award Buffalo Newspaper Guild, 1957, 64, Pa. Women's Press Assn., 1949, Outstanding Woman award Community Adv. Council, SUNY-Buffalo. Mem. Am. Newspaper Guild, Bus. and Profl. Women (charter pres. 1948-50), AAUW, Sigma Delta Chi. Address: The Buffalo News 1 News Plaza Buffalo NY 14240

DANZIGER, GERTRUDE, metal fabricating mfg. co. exec.; b. Chgo., Oct. 24, 1919; d. Isidor and Clara (Fuchs) Seelig; student Northwestern U., 1937-40, U. Wis., 1945; m. Sigmund H. Danziger (dec.); children—Robert, Steven, James, Charles. Sec., Homak Mfg. Co., Chgo. 1955-78, pres., 1979—, also dir. Patentee mech. and design process. Office: 4433 S Springfield St Chicago IL 60032

DANZIGER, JOAN, sculptor; b. N.Y.C., June 17, 1934; d. Emanuel and Martha (Kaplan) Schwartz; m. Martin Danziger, June 17, 1958. B.F.A., Cornell U., 1954; B.F.A. (hon.), Acad. Fine Art, Rome, 1958. One woman exhbns. include: Corcoran Gallery, Washington, 1975, Calif. Mus. Sci. and Industry, Los Angeles, 1977, Muckenthal Cultural Ctr., Los Angeles, 1977, SUNY-Albany, 1978, Jacksonville Mus. Art and Sci. (Fla.), 1979, Fendrick Gallery, Washington, 1979, Terry Dintenfass Gallery, N.Y.C., 1980, Joy Horwich Gallery, Chgo., N.J. State Mus., Trenton, 1982, Benjamin Mangel Gallery, Phila., Louisiana World Expn., New Orleans, 1984, Textile Mus., Washington, 1985. vis. artist, lectr. Smithsonian Instn., 1980-82; artist-in-residence AFL-CIO Labor Studies Ctr., 1975; visual arts panelist D.C. Commn. Arts and Humanities, 1974-79, 84-85; scuepture panelist N.J. State Council Arts, 1982. Commd. by Nat. Mus. Am. Art, Jacksonville Mus. Arts and Scis., Columbia Hosp., Washington, Frostburg State Coll. (Md.), George Meany Labor Studies Ctr., New Orleans Mus. Art, D.C. Conv. Ctr., Nat. Mus. Women in Arts, N.J. State Mus., Nat. Endowment Arts grantee, 1975. Mem. Artists Equity, Washington Sculptors Group (bd. dirs.), New Art. Home: 2909 Brandywine St NW Washington DC 20008

DAPELO, MARIE CLAIRE, credit company financial representative; b. San Francisco, May 11, 1961; d. Louis George and Claire Virginia (Morris) D.; 1 child, Daniel Louis. B.S., Calif. State U.-Hayward, 1985. Restaurant mgr. Foodmaker Inc., Hayward, Calif., 1978-85; account exec. Transworld Systems, Sacramento, 1985-86; fin. rep. Credithrift of Am. Fair Oaks, Calif., 1986—. Mem. NOW, Nat. Assn. Female Execs. Mem. Sierra Club. Democrat. Roman Catholic. Home: 8508 Cherry Crest C Elkgrove CA 95624 Office: Credithrift and Loan Inc 1418 K St 1 Sacramento CA 95814

DARAKANANDA, CHONGRAKSA, bus. exec.; b. Nakhon Srithammaraj, Thailand, Dec. 21, 1933; came to U.S., 1977, permanent resident, 1979; d. Hen Jen Lim and Francim Wen; 10th grade cert. Sukit Coll. Sch., 1954; 12th grade cert. Triam-Udom Prep. Sch., 1956; m. Damri Darakananda, Aug. 10, 1957; children—Chutindhon, Aksornprasit, Pinipjporn, Bovornrat, Vacharaphong. Bus. woman, mgr., exec. various trading and mfg. cos., Thailand, 1956-77; dir., treas. Saha-Union Internat. (U.S.A.) Inc., San Francisco, 1977-78, pres., Daly City, Calif., 1978—, exec. dir. fin. and personnel Saha-Union Corp. Ltd., Bangkok, Thailand, 1972—, guest lectr. middle mgmt., supr. tng. of group, chmn. com. for grievances of group. Mem. Personnel Mgmt. Assn. Thailand (life), Thai Mgmt. Assn. (corp.), Am. Mgmt. Assn. Thailand Chpt. (corp.). Buddhist. Club: Royal Bangkok Sports. Home: 455 37th Ave San Francisco CA 94121 Office: 419 Allan St Daly City CA 94014

DARASZ, MARIA, hospital patient account manager, medical financial consultant firm executive; b. Springfield, Mass., Sept. 10, 1954; d. Stanislaw and Hildegard (Grzenia) D.; 1 child, Rosemarie. B.Hosp. Adminstrn., U. Mass., 1985, postgrad. in Hosp. Adminstrn., 1985—. Collector, Credit Bur. Western Mass., Springfield, 1971-78; with Wing Meml. Hosp., Palmer, Mass., 1978—, bus. office supr., 1978-79, data processing mgr., 1979-80, patient account mgr., 1980-85, dir. patient finances, 1985—; cons. Palmer Ambulance Soc., 1982—, Podiatry Assocs., Westfield, Mass., 1985—, Dr. Peter Kelly, Palmer, 1985—. Artist pen and ink drawings (awards Soc. Am. Artists 1977). Mem. Hosp. Fin. Mgrs. Assn., Mass. Assn. Patient Account Mgrs., New Eng. Assn. Patient Account Mgrs., Nat. Assn. Female Execs., Am. Guild Patient Account Mgrs., Soc. N.Am. Artists. Roman Catholic. Avocation: Art. Home: 40 Scott St Springfield MA 01108 Office: Wing Health Systems Inc Wing Memorial Hospital Wright St Palmer MA 01069

DARBY, DONNA JEAN, executive relocation and public relations company executive; b. Ft. Wayne, Ind., May 14, 1934; d. Leonard Christian and Eleanor Leone (Battenberg) Roebel, m. Keith Anderson Darby, July 27, 1957; children—Diana Lynn, Ellen Kimberly. B.A., Mich. State U., 1955; M.S., Ind. U.-Bloomington, 1957. Lic. tchr. Tchr. English, Smart Jr. High Sch., Ft. Wayne, 1955-56, South Side High Sch., Ft. Wayne, 1956-60, Chattanooga High Sch., 1960-62, U. Chattanooga, 1960-62; pres. Contacts, Inc., Ft. Wayne, 1976—; pub. info. dir. East Allen County Schs., New Haven, Ind., 1982—; cons. Colwell-Van Riper County Sch., Ft. Wayne, 1983, Executive Relocation, Austin, Tex., 1983, Kalamazoo, 1983, Kansas City, Mo., 1984. Exec. dir. Leadership Ft. Wayne, 1982—; chmn. bd. dirs. Historic River Cruises, 1979-83; pres.-elect United Way of Allen County, 1984; v.p. United Way of Ind., 1984; v.p Conv. and Visitors Bur. Ft. Wayne, 1983; bd. dirs. United Way Lower Eastern Shore, 1985—; mem. jr. bd. Peninsula Gen. Hosp. Mem. Women in Communications Inc. (chmn. 1984), Pub. Relations Soc. Am., Women Bus. Owners' Assn., Ind. Tourism Council, Kappa Kappa Kappa (Woman of Year 1978). Republican. Clubs: Rivergreenway, Fort Wayne Futures. Home: 2005 Nithsdale Dr Salisbury MD 21801 Office: Leadership Fort Wayne 2101 Coliseum Blvd E Fort Wayne IN 46805

DARDEN, MARY DUNLAP, management consultant; b. Richmond, Va., Aug. 10, 1952; d. Oscar Bruton and Ann Wingfield (Johnson) D.; B.S. in Math. and Edn., Va. Poly. Inst. and State U., 1974; M.B.A., U. Richmond, 1984. Mktg. rep. IBM, Richmond, 1974-78; territorial saleswoman Swan, Inc., Richmond, 1978, dir. ops., 1978-83; pres. Cygnet, Inc., mgmt. cons., 1980—. Bd. dirs., sec.-treas. Va. Small Bus. Financing Authority, 1984-86; Va. del. White House Conf. on Small Bus., 1986. Named to 100 Percent Club, IBM, 1976, 77. Mem. St. Mary's Hosp. Aux., Richmond Assn. Women Bus. Owners (sec. 1983-84, pres. 1984-85). Presbyterian. Home: 2435 Crowncrest Pl Richmond VA 23229 Office: Cygnet Inc PO Box 29768 Richmond VA 23229

DARDEN, SUE EAGLES, librarian; b. Miami, Fla., Aug. 13, 1943; d. Archie Yelverton and Bobbie (Jones) Eagles; m. Paul Fisher Darden, Jr., Aug. 24, 1969 (dec. June 1978). B.A., Atlantic Christian Coll., 1965; M.L.S., U. Tex., Austin, 1970. Instr. Chowan Coll., Murfreesboro, N.C., 1966-68; librarian asst. Albemarle Regional Library, Winston, N.C., 1968-69; br. librarian Multnomah County Pub. Library, Portland, Oreg., 1971-72; asst. dir. Stanly County Pub. Library, Albemarle, N.C., 1973-76, dir., 1976-80; asst. dir. Norfolk Pub. Library (Va.), 1980-83, dir., 1983—. Mem. ALA (friends, vols. and advocates com. pub. relations sect. 1985-87), Southeastern Library Assn. (sec. pub. library sect. 1982-84), Va. Library Assn. (chmn. conf. program 1984, mem. council 1984-86). Office: Norfolk Public Library 301 E City Hall Ave Norfolk VA 23510

DARIN, DIANE ELIZABETH, tool and die company executive; b. Wyandotte, Mich., July 26, 1940; d. William F. and Della J. (Shell) Darin. Computer and wire machining degree Oak Ridge Assoc. Univs., 1980. Researcher, Detroit News, 1959-60; with pub. relations dept. Gen. Motors Tech. Ctr., Warren, Mich., 1960-75; v.p. Alignment Engring., Knoxville, Tenn., 1975-83, pres., owner, 1983—; pres., owner Aggressive Tool and Machine, Oak Ridge, 1983—, Aristocrat Stamping & Mfg. Co., Inc., 1985—. Office: Alignment Engring 6000 Industrial Heights Dr Knoxville TN 37919

DARITY, EVANGELINE ROYALL, educator, dean; b. Wilson, N.C., June 16, 1927; B.Sc. in Religious Edn., Barber-Scotia Coll., Concord, N.C., 1949; M.Ed., Smith Coll., 1969; Ed.D., U. Mass., Amherst, 1978; m. William A. Darity; children—William, Janki Evangelia. Various YWCA positions 1949-53; tchr., Egypt, N.C. and Mass., 1953-67; asst. to class deans Smith Coll., Northampton, Mass., 1968-75; v.p. student affairs Barber-Scotia Coll., 1978-79; exec. dir. YWCA, Holyoke, Mass., 1979-81; assoc. dean studies, assoc. dean 3d world affairs Mt. Holyoke Coll., South Hadley, Mass., 1981—; corp. mem. Community Savs. Bank, Holyoke. Mem. Amherst Town Meeting, 1971-80; mem. adv. bd. Community Adolescent Resource and Edn. Ctr.; trustee Barber-Scotia Coll., Concord, N.C. Mem. AAUW (br. pres. 1971-74, 86-88), Am. Assn. Counseling and Devel., Nat. Assn. Women Deans, Counselors and Adminstrs., LWV, Alpha Kappa Alpha, Phi Delta Kappa. Home: 105 Heatherstone Rd Amherst MA 01002 Office: Mount Holyoke College South Hadley MA 01075

DARKIS, MILDRED LEE MORRIS (MRS. FREDERICK RANDOLPH DARKIS), civic worker; b. nr. Salisbury, Md.; d. Elisha Purnell and Martha Florence (Bailey) Morris; A.B., U. Md., 1924; m. Frederick Randolph Darkis, Oct. 6, 1928; children—Frederick Randolph, Thomas Morris, Barbara Lee (Mrs. James Frederick Blake). Tchr. English and Am. history high sch., Pittsville, Md., 1924-25, Salisbury, 1925-28. Pres. Durram Parent-Tchr. Council, 1945-47, Hope Valley Garden Club, 1962-64; bd. dirs. Durham YWCA, 1946-48, v.p., 1948; bd. dirs. Durham Child Guidance Clinic, 1945-47, Girl Scout Council, 1944-48; chmn. woman's div. Community Chest, Durham, 1946-47. Mem. D.A.R. (N.C. chmn. nat. honor roll 1961-64, chpt. regent 1968-70), Phi Kappa Phi, Alpha Omicron Pi. Republican. Methodist (tchr. adult Bible class, v.p. Durham dist. Woman's Div. Christian Service 1957-59, steward 1960, bd. stewards 1972—). Club: Hope Valley Country. Address: 3010 Surrey Rd Durham NC 27707

DARKOVICH, SHARON MARIE, nurse; b. Ft. Wayne, Ind., Dec. 10, 1949; d. Gerald Antone LaCanne and Ida Eileen (Bowman) LaCanne Cutler; m. Robert Eliot Ness, July 17, 1971 (dec. Aug. 1976); m. Paul Darkovich, Jan. 23, 1981; 1 child, Amy Elizabeth. B.S. in Nursing, Case Western Res. U., 1973, B.A. in Psychology, 1978. R.N., Ohio. Staff nurse Univ. Hosps., Cleve., 1973, asst. head nurse, 1973-76; quality assurance coordinator St. Luke's Hosp., Cleve., 1976-83, 84—, dir. nursing, 1983-84. Mem. Am. Nurses Assn., Greater Cleve. Nurses Assn. (mem. dist. council on practice, 1982-84), Sigma Theta Tau. Avocations: reading; needlework; sewing; camping.

DARLING, ALBERTA STATKUS, art museum executive; b. Hammond, Ind., Apr. 28, 1944; d. Albert William and Helen Anne (Vaicunas) Statkus; m. William Anthony Darling, Aug. 12, 1967; children—Elizabeth Suzanne, William Anthony. B.S., U. Wis., 1967. English tchr. Nathan Hale High Sch., West Allis, Wis., 1967-69, Castle Rock High Sch., Colo., 1969-71; community vol. work, Milw., 1971—; cons. orgn. devel., Milw., 1982—; dir. mktg. and communications Milw. Art Mus., 1983—. A founder Goals for Greater Milw. 2000, 1980-84; co-chair Action 2000, 1984-86; bd. dirs., exec. com. United Way, Milw., 1982—, chair project 1985, 1984-85; founder Today's Girls/Tomorrow's Women, Milw., 1982—; pres. Jr. League Milw., 1980-82, Planned Parenthood Milw., 1982-84, Future Milw., 1983-85. Recipient Vol. Action award Milw. Civic Alliance, 1984, Community Service award United Way, 1984, Leader of Future award Milw. Mag., 1985. Mem. Greater Milw. Com., TEMPO Profl. Women, Am. Mktg. Assn. (Marketer of Yr. 1984), Pub. Relations Soc. Am., Internat. Assn. Bus. Communicators. Republican. Avocations: travel, art history, contemporary American literature, golf, tennis. Home: 1325 W Dean Rd Milwaukee WI 53217 Office: Milw Art Mus 750 N Lincoln Memorial Dr Milwaukee WI 53217

DARLING, MARYLIN BALKCOM, dance educator, choreographer; b. Montgomery, Ala., Sept. 20, 1944; d. Toland and Martha Letita (Balkcom) Barfield; m. Michael Patrick Darling, June 24, 1972; 1 child, Michael Patrick, Jr. B.S. in Home Econs. and Dance, Fla. State U., 1966, Mus.M. in Dance, 1970; Ph.D. in Ednl. Adminstrn., Ga. State U., 1986. Customer rep. Xerox Corp., Jacksonville, Fla., 1967-68; prof. dance Agnes Scott Coll., Decatur, Ga., 1971—; mem. adv. bd. Dance Atlanta, 1973-76; mem. bd. artists in schs. panel Ga. Council for Arts, Atlanta, 1981; bd. dirs. DeKalb Council for Arts, Decatur, 1981—. Choreographer numerous works. Publicity chmn. Dance Coalition of Met. Atlanta, 1981—; mem. Nat. Soc. Colonial Dames, Macon, Ga., 1981—, Alden Soc. Am., Duxbury, Mass., 1982—. Summer fellow Agnes Scott Coll., 1981-86; nominated for Epic award Cable Dekalb for Media Presentation of So. Comfort, 1983. Mem. Ga. Assn. Phys. Edn. Recreation and Dance (pres. dance sect. 1985—, v.p. dance div. 1985—), Nat. Dance Assn. (regional coordinator 1986). Methodist. Office: Agnes Scott Coll East College Ave Decatur GA 30030

DARLINGTON, ELEANOR MERRITT, artist, educator; b. N.Y.C., Aug. 17, 1933; d. Wilbert Alexander and Lynet (Hyman) Lipsett; m. Lorenzo Merritt, June 26, 1954 (div. Apr. 1974); children—Lori, Lisa; m. W. H. Chris Darlington, July 26, 1980. B.A., Bklyn. Coll., 1955, M.A., 1958. Art tchr. jr. high sch., N.Y.C., 1955-58, Westbury Jr. High Sch., N.Y., 1960-70; chmn. art dept. dist.-wide Westbury Sch. Dist., 1970-82. One-woman shows: Nassau County Cultural Mus., Hempstead, N.Y., 1974, Am. Internat. Coll., Springfield, Mass., 1975, 81, The Craftery Gallery, Hartford, Conn., 1976. Illustrator articles. Vice-pres. bd. dirs. Greater Westbury Arts Council, N.Y., 1969-72; treas. Friends of Emily Lane Gallery, Hofstra U., Hempstead, N.Y., 1975; pres. L.I. Black Artists Assn., Hempstead, 1974-78, mem. Supts. Conf. Planning Com. on Arts and Humanities, Westbury, 1975; mem. adv. bd. Faculty of Art Workshop Gallery, Roosevelt, N.Y., 1972-76. Recipient First Prize Graphics, Tanglewood Preserve Outdoor Show, Lakeview, N.Y., 1974, Best in Show L.I. Art Tchrs. Assn., Town Hall, Hempstead, 1980. Mem. Sarasota Art Assn., Manatee Art League.

DARLOW, JULIA DONOVAN, lawyer; b. Detroit, Sept. 18, 1941; d. Frank William and Helen Adele (Turner) Donovan; m. George Anthony Gratton Darlow; 1 child, Gillian; m. John Corbett O'Meara. A.B., Vassar Coll., 1963; postgrad. Columbia U. Law Sch., 1964-65; J.D. cum laude, Wayne State U., 1971. Bar: Mich. 1971, U.S. Dist. Ct. 1971. Adj. prof. Wayen State U., Detroit, 1974-75, assoc. Dickinson, Wright, Moon, Van Dusen & Freeman, Detroit, 1971-78, ptnr., 1978—. Bd. dirs., trustee Detroit Grand Opera Assn., Detroit, 1978—trustee Hutzel Hosp., 1984—. Fellow Am. Bar Found.; mem. State Bar Mich. (commr. 1977—, exec. com. 1979-83, sec. 1980-81, pres.-elect 1985—), Mich. Women Lawyers Assn. (pres. 1977-78), Detroit Bar Assn. Found. (trustee 1982-85, treas. 1984-85), Am. Judicature Soc. (dir. 1985—). Club: Renaissance (Detroit). Office: Dickinson Wright Moon Van Dusen & Freeman 800 First National Bldg Detroit MI 48226

DARMAN, LESLEY PATRICIA, multi-media company executive; b. Providence, Aug. 3, 1939; d. Frank Joseph and Frances (Goldstein) Darman; m. Howard Louis Kirschenbaum, Apr. 6, 1982. Student, Boston U., 1958-59; A.S., Garland Jr. Coll., 1959; postgrad. U. Florence-Italy, 1961-62. Tchr. kindergarten Ethical Culture Sch., N.Y.C., 1959-60; promotion dir. Evelyn Schless Shoe Co., N.Y.C., 1966—; floral designer Home Design, 1972-76; promotion Jim Sant'andrea Multi-Media Prodns., N.Y.C., 1972-76, v.p., 1979—. Tchr. flower arrangement Lighthouse for the Blind, 1972-76. Home: 118 E 18th St New York NY 10003

DARNALL, ROBERTA MORROW, university official; b. Kemmerer, Wyo., May 18, 1949; d. C. Dale and Eugenia Stayner (Christmas) Morrow; B.S., U. Wyo., Laramie, 1972; m. Leslie A. Darnall, Sept. 3, 1977. Tariff sec., ins. adminstr. Wyo. Trucking Assn., Casper, 1973-75; asst. clerical supr. Wyo. Legislature, Cheyenne, 1972-77; congl. campaign press aide, 1974; pub. relations dir. in Casper, Wyo. Republican Central Com., 1976-77; asst. dir. alumni relations U. Wyo., 1977-81, dir. of alumni, 1981—; exec. com. Higher Edn. Assn. Rockies. Mem. Council Advancement and Support Edn. (membership com.), Higher Edn. Assn. Rockies, Am. Soc. Assn. Execs., Laramie C. of C. (pizzazz and acad. instns. com.), PEO (courtesy com.), Sigma Delta Chi. Republican. Episcopalian. Home: 1172 Frontera Dr Laramie WY 82070 Office: Box 3137 Univ Station Laramie WY 82071

DARNEILLE, SARAH ANN, oil and gas company executive; b. Houston, May 26, 1950; d. George Joseph and Roberta Shepherd (Higgins) Darneille; B.A., U. Colo., 1972; M.B.A., U. Houston, 1980. Various mktg. positions, to 1976; sec.-treas. Westates-Italo Co., 1977—, also dir.; Westates Petroleum Co. Liquidating Trust, 1976—. Episcopalian. Home: 4237 S Judson St West University Houston TX 77005 Office: One Houston Center Suite 1504 Houston TX 77010 also Via Napo Torriani 29 20124 Milan Italy

DARNELL, PATRICIA ANN, nurse; b. Liberal, Kans., Aug. 22, 1954; d. Bobby Joe and Elberta Lea (Edwards) D. B.S. in Nursing, Ft. Hays State U., Kans., 1981. R.N., Kans., Okla. Nursing asst. S.W. Med. Ctr., Liberal, Kans., 1972-76, Good Samaritan Ctr., Dodge City, Kans., 1977; practical nurse Southwest Med. Ctr., 1977-78, operating room staff nurse, 1982-83; practical nurse St. Anthony Hosp., Hays, Kans., 1979, 81; operating room staff nurse Bapt. Med. Ctr. Okla., Oklahoma City, 1983—; nursing supr. Internat. Mission, July, 1986. Vol. with local Girl Scouts U.S.A. Mem. Assn. Operating Room Nurses. Presbyterian. Avocations: sailing; camping; hiking; needlepoint; travel. Home: 3136 Northwest Expressway #127 Oklahoma City OK 73112 Office: Bapt Med Ctr Dept Surgery 3300 Northwest Expressway Oklahoma City OK 73112

D'ARRIGO, ENID, principal, consultant; b. Bklyn., Oct. 26, 1944; d. Jonah Kahn and Irene (Brody) K.; m. James Richard D'Arrigo, Jan. 23, 1964; children—Jennifer, Dana. B.S., Bklyn. Coll., 1965, M.S., 1967; C.A.S., Hofstra U., 1977. Cert. elem. tchr., ednl. adminstr. Tchr. N.Y.C. Pub. Schs., Bklyn., 1965-68; tchr. Oceanside Pub. Sch., N.Y., 1968, 77-81, adminstrv. intern, 1981-83, project dir., 1983-84, prin., 1984—; con. in-service edn. L.I. Sch. Dist.,

1982—. Mem. Nassau-Suffolk Council Adminstrv. Women Edn., Nassau County Math. Tchrs., Kappa Delta Pi, Phi Delta Kappa. Avocations: tennis; reading; cooking. Home: 3795 Carrel Blvd Oceanside NY 11572 Office: Oceanside Middle Sch Alice and Beatrice Aves Oceanside NY 11572

DARSAW, SHARON YVONNE, freight transportation company executive; b. Jersey City, Feb. 6, 1952; d. Israel Thomas and Bernice (Youngblood) Shields; m. Larry Darsaw, June 30, 1970 (div. July 24, 1985); 1 child, Jonathan Vincent. Student Jersey City State Coll., Acad. Advanced Traffic Newark, 1984—, Bus. Womens' Tng. Inst, Newark, 1986. Endorsement clk. N.Y. Property Ins., N.Y.C., 1971-73; exec. sec. Clopay Corp., Bayonne, N.J., 1973-79; freight dispatcher R&N Western Enterprises, South Kearny, N.J., 1980-85; exec. officer Western Industries Inc., South Kearny, N.J., 1985—. Mem. Tranp. Brokers Conf. Am., Nat. Assn. Female Execs., Am. Bus. Womens Assn., NAACP. Instr. children. N.J. Assn. Gen. Baptist Conv. Democrat. Avocation: Reading. Home: 2220 Arlington Ave Jersey City NJ 07305 Office: Western Industries Inc 1 Hackensack Ave Suite 9 South Kearny NJ 02032

DART, CAROL ANNE, consulting company executive, lobbyist; b. Bloomfield, Mo., July 21, 1950; d. Frank M. and Rita (Decelis) Hodge; B.A., Sangamon State U., 1982; m. William Edward Dart, June 28, 1974. Asst. to program dir. WICS-TV, NBC, Springfield, Ill., 1973-75; adminstrv. asst. Air Time, Inc., Chgo., 1975-76; v.p. Dart & Assocs., Springfield, 1976-78; pres. C. Dart, Cons., 1979—; govt. affairs cons./lobbyist Juvenile Diabetes Found. 1980-81. Mem. Atty. Gen.'s Task Force on Hazardous Waste in Ill., Ill. Diabetes Adv. Council; chair 20th Congressional Dist. Mem. Am. Soc. Assn. Execs., Chgo. Soc. Assn. Execs., Women in Mgmt., Inc. (Capital City area chpt. founder 1982, nat. pres. 1984-86, dir.), Ill. Soc. Assn. Execs. (exec. dir.), Citizens for Am., Springfield C. of C. (govt. action com.). Roman Catholic. Office: PO Box 1964 Springfield IL 62705

DARTING, EDITH ANNE, pharmaceutical company supervisor; b. Hillsboro, Kans., Jan. 1, 1945; d. Sammuel E. and Carrie (Swehla) Jewett; m. John Ronald Darting, Aug. 8, 1979; children—Theresa Michelle, Lloyd L. Grad., Emporia State Tchrs. Coll., 1963-65. Materials insp. Sterling Drug Inc., McPherson, Kans., 1977-78, auditor, 1978-82, coordinator, 1982—. Mem. Nat. Assn. Female Execs., Am. Soc. Quality Control. Republican. Methodist. Home: 320 N Birch St Hillsboro KS 67063 Office: Sterling Drug Inc Box 1048 McPherson KS 67460

DARWIN, SUSAN MARIE, radio station executive; b. Boston, May 17, 1957; d. Richard Michael and Dorothy Alice (Carey) D. Student Bridgewater State Coll., 1975-77; B.S. in Communication and Journalism, Suffolk U., 1978-79. News editor Sta. WBZ, Boston, 1979-80; news dir. Sta. WDLW, Waltham, Mass., 1980-83, Sta. WBOS-FM, Boston, 1983-84, 84—; freelance journalist, eastern Mass., 1984; sec. AP Mass., 1984-85. Writer, editor, producer, anchor Who's Running, 1982 (AP Pub. Affairs First Place award 1981). Mem. vol. crisis staff, outreach com., fin. com. Transition House, Cambridge, Mass., 1981—. Avocations: swimming; skiing; white water rafting; dancing; Office: Sta-WBOS-FM 160 N Washington St Boston MA 02114

DASHER, CHARLOTTE ANN, rehabilitation counselor; b. Nashville, Ga., Sept. 11, 1948; d. Johnny Vestus and Alma Lee (Griner) Dasher. A.A., DeKalb Jr. Coll., 1972; B.S., Ga. State U., 1974; M.Ed., U. Ga., 1977. Encode operator 1st Nat. Bank, Atlanta, 1966-67; stenographer II, State Dept. Edn., Atlanta, 1967-70, stenographer III, 1970-71; rehab. intern State Dept. Human Resources, Augusta, Ga., 1974-76, counselor I, Tifton, Ga., 1976-80, sr. rehab. counselor, 1980—; mem. Spl. Edn. Adv. Council, Tifton, 1976—, Adv. Com. for Handicapped, Fitzgerald, Ga., 1979—, Vocat. Edn. Adv. Com., Tifton, 1983—; pres.-elect Council for Exceptional Children, Tifton, 1983-84. Bd. dirs. Tift County Assn. for Retarded Citizens, 1979—; projects chmn. Tiftarea Civitan, 1981—; Sunday Sch. tchr. 1st Bapt. Ch., Tifton, 1982—; Spl. Olympics coordinator Tift County, 1982—. Recipient Service awards Tiftarea Civitan, 1982-83, Honor Key, 1983; nominated for Handicapped Profl. Woman of Yr., Tifton Jaycettes, 1981. Mem. Ga. Rehab. Counseling Assn. (sec.-treas. 1983-84, pres. SW Dist. chpt. 1980-81, Currie Counselor of Yr. award 1982), Ga. Rehab. Assn., Nat. Rehab. Assn., Am. Soc. Personnel Adminstrs. Democrat. Baptist. Office: Div Rehab Services PO Box 1629 Room 314 Tifton GA 31793

DASSANCE, MARY ALICE, library staff member; b. Grand Ledge, Mich., Sept. 4, 1933; d. Howard Leslie and Alice Angeline (Egleston) Green; m. Laurence Lee Dassance, Mar. 8, 1952 (dec. 1983); children—Leslie, Nadine, Charles, Debra. A.A., Lansing Community Coll., 1979; postgrad. Western Mich. U. Cert. library technician, Mich. Tech. asst. Lansing Community Coll. (Mich.), 1975—. Co-author article in profl. jour. Mem. Mich. Library Assn., Spl. Libraries Assn. (mem. nominating com. Western Mich. chpt. 1983, sec.-elect 1984-85). Methodist. Clubs: Extension (Grand Ledge); Women's Internat. Bowling Assn. (local league pres.). Lodge: Order Eastern Star (worthy matron 1959-60). Office: Arts and Sci Library Lansing Community Coll PO Box 40010 Lansing MI 48901

DASTÉ, KATHRYN LOUISE, management consultant; b. Los Angeles, Sept. 28, 1951; d. Richard Leonard Kater and June (Yale) Kater Hooten; m. John Cary Dasté, July 24, 1973 (div. Apr. 1978). Student music Calif. State U.-Northridge; 1969-72; B.A. in Mgmt., U. Redlands, 1985. Lic. minister Universal Ch. of the Master, 1979; cert. in human resources, 1982. Asst. buyer Bullock's Wilshire, Los Angeles, 1973-76; corp. mgr. recruiting and tng. Robinson's Dept. Store, Los Angeles, 1976-80, buyer, 1977-80; regional personnel mgr. Gen. Nutrition Ctrs., Los Angeles, 1980-82; personnel mgr. Carnation Co., Los Angeles, 1982-84; owner, pres. Profitivity Inc., mgmt. cons., Los Angeles, 1983—; cons. Ariz. Shoe Corp., Phoenix, 1983—, Security Pacific Nat. Bank, Los Angeles, 1984—, Cousin's Home Furnishings, San Diego, 1983—, Law Office of Ron Supancic, Los Angeles, 1983—. Author: Great Sales Strategy, 1982; Are You Hiring the Smile?, 1984; Focused Feedback, 1985. Practitioner, Encino (Calif.) Community Ch. (Calif.), 1978; counselor Universal Ch. of New Age, Santa Monica, Calif., 1980. Mem. Am. Soc. for Tng. and Devel., Western Coll. Placement Assn., Western Shoe Assocs. Democrat.

DASTRUP, LANIS BLAUER, educator, realtor; b. Logan, Utah, Aug. 17, 1935; d. Ernest Richard and Rose (Parker) Blauer; m. Bernard Curtis Dastrup, Dec. 20, 1957; children—Julie, Michael Curtis, Kelly Richard. B.S., Brigham Young U., 1957. Tchr. numerous schs., Utah, 1957—, Roosevelt Jr. High Sch., 1985—; real estate salesman Four-D Realty, Roosevelt, 1980—. Pres. Altrus, Roosevelt, 1983-84; sec. Dist. Republicans, Duchesne, Utah, 1985—. Mem. NEA, Duchesne Edn. Assn., Socialette Club Federated (pres. 1976-78). Mormon. Lodge: Lady Lions (pres. 1962-63). Avocations: handwork; singing; gardening. Home: Route 2 Box 2065 Roosevelt UT 84066 Office: Roosevelt Jr High Sch Drawer 160 Roosevelt UT 84066

DATTA, GOURI, psychiatrist; b. Varanasi, India, May 15, 1949; d. Birendra Nath and Gita (Sen) Das-Gupta; B.Sc.I., Chandradhari Mithila Coll., 1965; M.B.B.S., Darbhanga Med. Coll., 1971; m. Sanjay Datta, Mar. 15, 1973; 1 dau., Nandini. Intern, Beverly (Mass.) Hosp., 1974-75; resident St. Elizabeth's Hosp., Brighton, Mass., 1976-79; practice medicine specializing in psychiatry, Georgetown and Newton, Mass., 1979—; mem. staffs St. Elizabeths Hosp., Baldpate Hosp.; clin. instr. psychiatry Tufts Med. Sch., Boston. Diplomate Am. Bd. Psychiatry and Neurology. Mem. AMA, Am. Psychiat. Assn., Mass. Med. Soc., Mass. Psychiat. Soc. Hindu. Author book of poems (in Bengali). Office: Baldpate Hosp Georgetown MA 01833

DATTA, LOIS-ELLIN, government administrator; b. Paterson, N.J., June 12, 1932; d. Gerald Gershon and Martha Rose (Cohen) G.; m. Padma Rag Datta, Dec. 20, 1953; children—Tane Mohan, Eric Raman. B.A., W.Va. U., 1952, M.A., 1956; M.A., Bryn Mawr Coll., 1957, Ph.D., 1961. Researcher Gen. Electric Co., Valley Forge, Pa., 1961-63; research fellow NIH, Bethesda, Md., 1963-68; chief early childhood research U.S. Dept. HEW, Washington, 1968-72; assoc. dir. Nat. Inst. Edn., Washington, 1972-82, U.S. GAO, Washington, 1982—. Recipient Myrdal award Evaluation Research Soc. Office: GAO Room 5741 441 G St NW Washington DC 20548

DATZ, RUTH ELIZABETH, educator, musician; b. Greensburg, Pa., June 10, 1936; d. Robert Albert and Ruth Elizabeth (Bates) Datz; B.A., Indiana (Pa.) U., 1958; M.A., NYU, 1961; postgrad Pa. State U., 1962-63, U. Colo., 1971, SUNY-Potsdam, 1978. Tchr. music pub. schs., Middletown Twp., N.J., 1958-61, Tyrone, Pa., 1961-65, Ann Arbor, Mich., 1965—; counselor, recreation dir., dir. jr. girls div. Interlochen (Mich.) Nat. Music Camp, 1956-69; head womens counselor New Eng. Music Camp, Maine, 1970, 72; flutist, pit orchestras, N.Y.C., 1959-61; conductor spl. chorus. Mem. Republican. Com., Tyrone, 1962-65. Mem. Music Educators Nat. Conf., Mich. Music Educators Assn., Mich. Sch. Vocal Assn., Am. Choral Dirs. Assn., Nat. Assn. Humanities Edn., NEA, Mich. Edn. Assn., Delta Omicron, Delta Zeta. Mem. United Ch. of Christ. Clubs: Ann Arbor Dog Tng., Eastern Star, Job's Daughters. Home: 1564 Barrington Pl Ann Arbor MI 48103 Office: 2727 Fuller Rd Ann Arbor MI 48105

DAUBENAS, JEAN DOROTHY TENBRINCK, librarian; b. N.Y.C., Apr. 4, 1940; d. Eduard J.A. and Margaret Dorothy (Schaffner) Tenbrinck; A.B., Barnard Coll., 1962; grad. Am. Acad. Dramatic Arts, 1963; M.A., N.Y. U., 1965; M.L.S., U. Ariz., 1972; postgrad U. Utah, 1975—; m. Joseph Anthony Daubenas, May 29, 1965. Tchr., Beth Jacob Tchrs. Sem. Am., Bronx, 1965-66; caseworker, Dept. Social Services, N.Y.C., 1966-67; actress Boothbay (Maine) Playhouse, others, 1967-70; reference librarian Ariz. State U., Tempe, 1972-75; asst. librarian, asst. prof. library sci. Avila Coll., Kansas City, Mo., 1979-83; periodicals librarian, assoc. prof. St. John's U., Jamaica, N.Y., 1983—. N.Y. State Regents scholar, 1958-62; U. Ariz. scholar, 1971-72. Mem. ALA, Actors Equity Assn., AAUP, Beta Phi Mu, Phi Kappa Phi. Roman Catholic. Home: 175-39 Dalny Rd Apt 6B Jamaica Estates NY 11432 Office: Library St John's Univ Grand Central and Utopia Pkwys Jamaica NY 11439

DAVENPORT, DEBORAH ANNE, training company executive; b. Port Jefferson, N.Y., July 2, 1948; d. Francis M., Jr., and Nell Sperry (Brown) D.; A.B., Ind. U., 1970; M.B.A., Cleve. State U., 1981. Mktg. services mgr. Premier Indsl. Corp., Cleve., 1974-75, prodn. mgr., 1975-76, distbn. sales ops. mgr., 1976-78; dir. planning services Mr. Wiggs Dept. Stores, Inc. (SDC Inc.), Beachwood, Ohio, 1978-79, asst. v.p. planning and info. services, 1979-82, v.p., 1982-83; dir. planning and analysis SCOA Industries, Inc., Columbus, Ohio, 1983-85; exec. v.p. Mentor Techs., Columbus, 1985—. guest lectr. Cleve. State U. Trustee, Opera/Columbus. Mem. Planning Forum (pres. Cleve. 1983-84), Assn. M.B.A. Execs., Beta Gamma Sigma. Club: Lakeside Yacht (Cleve.). Software designer. Office: 33 N High St Columbus OH 43215

DAVENPORT, FLORENCE ANN MARIE, non-profit agency administrator; b. Phila., Oct. 24, 1947; d. John and Helene Marie (Lesniak) D. A.A., Pierce Jr. Coll., Calif., 1968; B.S., San Fernando Valley State Coll., 1970; cert. fundraising U. So. Calif., 1984. Program dir. recreation services Dept. Army, Bayreuth, Ger., 1971-73; asst. dir. Bob Hope USO Club, Hollywood, Calif., 1974-77; exec. dir. Frankfurt USO, Ger., 1977-80, Keflavik USO, Iceland, 1980-82; fund raiser/adminstrv. asst. Washoe Assn. Retarded Citizens, Reno, Nev., 1984-85; devel. programmer Salvation Army, Reno, 1985—; cons. Corpus Christie USO, Tex., 1982. Recipient cert. of appreciation Marine Corps Gen. Megan, 1977, Army Col. Chikalla, 1978, Gen. Kroesen, 1980. Mem. Calif. Park and Recreation Soc., Nat. Recreation and Park Assn., Armed Forces Recreation Soc., Nat. Assn. Female Execs., Nat. Soc. Fund Raising Execs. Republican. Roman Catholic. Clubs: Reno Bus. and Profl. Women's, Truckee Meadows Quilters (Reno). Avocations: quilting; photography; travel. Home: 2228 Cannonball Rd Sparks NV 89431 Office: Salvation Army 180 W 5th St Reno NV 89431

DAVENPORT, JOANNA, physical education educator; b. Salem, Mass., Jan. 17, 1933; d. Carleton and Virginia (Price) D.; B.S., Skidmore Coll., 1954; M.S., Smith Coll., 1958; Ph.D., Ohio State U., 1966. Instr., Mt. Holyoke Coll., South Hadley, Mass., 1954-56; tchr. public schs., Colo. and Maine, 1956-59; instr. U. Vt., Burlington, 1959-62, Colo. State U., Ft. Collins, 1962-63, Ohio State U., Columbus, 1963-65; asst. prof., chmn. dept. U. Vt., Burlington, 1965-67; assoc. prof. U. Ill., Urbana, 1967-76; assoc. prof., women's athletic dir. Auburn (Ala.) U., 1976-85; prof., dir. athletics, phys. edn., recreation SUNY, Plattsburgh, 1985—; vis. prof., cons. phys. edn. and athletics U.S. Mil. Acad., West Point, N.Y., 1968-79; coordinator U.S. delegation to Internat. Olympic Acad., 1981; mem. Edn. Council of U.S. Olympic Com., 1977—; U.S. del. Republic of China Olympic Acad., 1983; lectr. Internat. Olympic Acad., 1986. Sec. Class of 1954 Skidmore Coll. Recipient 2d prize internat. writing contest Internat. Olympic Com., 1981. Mem. Nat. Assn. Girls and Women in Sport (pres. 1976-77), N.Am. Soc. Sport History, Nat. Assn. Sport and Phys. Edn. (pres. history acad. 1982-83), Nat. Assn. Phys. Edn. in Higher Edn. (necrologist), So. Assn. Phys. Edn. of Coll. Women, AAHPERD. Contbr. chpts. in books, articles in encys. Home: 86 Park Ave W Plattsburgh NY 12901 Office: Memorial Hall State University NY Plattsburgh NY 12901

DAVENPORT, LUCINDA DIANE, mass communications educator, public relations consultant; b. Texas City, Tex., Apr. 23, 1957; d. Gordon Elliott and Frances Jean (Ellis) D. B.A., Baylor U., 1979; M.A., U. Iowa, 1984. Asst. producer Sta. KWBU-FM, Waco, Tex., 1977-78, news dir., 1978-79; pub. relations asst. Tex. State Tech. Inst., Waco, 1978-79; pub. relations ofcl. Gordon Jewelry Corp., Houston, 1979-80; personnel and mgmt. systems analyst Am. Gen. Life Ins. Co., Houston, 1980-81; instr. mass communications U. Iowa, Iowa City, 1981-84, Ohio U., Athens, 1984—; pub. relations cons., Houston, 1979-84; videotex cons.; lectr. women's studies; freelance writer, editor. Writer, producer radio documentaries, 1977-79; contbr. articles to newspapers; contbr. photographs to newspapers and in-house publs. Recipient Portrait Photography award Am. Gen. Life Ins. Co., 1981. Mem. Women in Communications, Internat. Assn. Bus. Communicators, Pub. Relations Soc. Am., AAUW, Assn. Educators in Journalism and Mass Communication, Kappa Tau Alpha. Sigma Delta Chi, Alpha Epsilon Rho, Kappa Alpha Theta. Presbyterian. Club: Baylor U. Alumna. Home: 6 Coulson Ave Athens OH 45701 Office: Sch Journalism and Mass Communications Ohio U Athens OH 45701

DAVIAS, NERY GONZALEZ, business executive; b. Buffalo, Oct. 18, 1952; d. Concepcion Gonzalez and Rosita (Leon) Glosek; m. Erico Estrondos DaVias, June 6, 1978; children—Jason, Layla, Erico Jr., Joshua. B.A. in Sociology, Empire State Coll., 1979. Rep., DaVias Enterprises, Buffalo, 1977-81; organizer, dir. pub. relations Fireside Theatre Group/United Theatre Artist Group, Milw., 1986—. Active Rich for Poor Fundraisers, Milw., 1985; mem. Republican Nat. Com. Recipient Pub. Relations award Fireside Theatre Group, 1986. Avocation: performing arts. Office: Fireside Theatre Group/United Theatre Artist Group PO Box 92563 Milwaukee WI 53202

DAVID, JOANNE, insurance agent; b. N.Y.C., Mar. 18, 1955; d. John and Vanetta (Johnson) Chapple; m. Vernon David, June 26, 1982. B.A. in Sociology, Colby Coll., Waterville, Maine, 1977. Asst. dir. communication Harper & Row, Publishers, N.Y.C., 1979-82; agt. Equitable Life of N.Y., N.Y.C., 1982—. Mem. Nat. Assn. Female Execs., Nat. Assn. Life Underwriters. Avocations: photography; modern dance; reading. Office: Equitable Life Assurance Soc of US 1 Penn Plaza Suite 4315 New York NY 10119

DAVID, JOYCE BALABAN, lawyer; b. Bklyn., Aug. 18, 1949; d. Asher and Selma (Weinberger) Balaban; children—Laura Renee, Jonathan Eric David. B.A., NYU, 1972; J.D., Bklyn. Law Sch., 1977. Bar: N.Y. 1978, U.S. Supreme Ct. 1982, U.S. Dist. Ct. (ea. and so. dists.) N.Y. 1983, Trial atty. Legal Aid, Bklyn., 1977-83; sole practice law, Bklyn., 1983—. Acting vice chmn. for communications Bklyn. Women's Polit. Caucus, 1984. Mem. Kings County Criminal Bar Assn. (v.p. 1984—), Bklyn. Bar Assn., Bklyn. Council Women Lawyers (exec. com. 1983—), Women in Communications (speakers bur. N.Y. 1984). Democrat. Jewish. Home: 1615 Ave I Brooklyn NY 11230 Office: 16 Court St Brooklyn NY 11241

DAVID, JUDY BREINER, advertising and promotion consultant, writer, producer; b. Milw., May 26, 1938; d. James Mirko and Fannie (Apple) Breiner; divorced; children—Rod Alan, Donna Lyn. Student Washington U., St. Louis, 1956-58. Dir./producer amateur theatricals Empire Producing Co., Kansas City, Mo., 1959; supr. pub. relations, tours, producer and host interview show Sta. KETC-TV, St. Louis, 1959-60; freelance pub. relations writer, St. Louis, 1966-69; copywriter George Johnson Advt., Inc., St. Louis, 1968, Ridgeway Advt., St. Louis, 1969; copywriter, producer Gardner/Wells, Rich, Greene, Inc., St. Louis, 1970-74; sr. writer, producer McCann-Erickson, Inc., Atlanta, 1974-77; freelance writer, producer, promotions, cons., doing bus. as A Functional Literate, Atlanta, 1977—; judge CLIO Awards, 1982, 84, 86, ADDY Awards, 1980, 81, 83, 84, 86, Hollywood Radio and TV Internat. Broadcast awards, 1984; panelist, lectr. Ga. State U., DeKalb Coll., Portfolio Ctr.; radio and stage performer, cartoonist, comedy writer, product designer. Author: Moonlighter's Guide to Success, 1978, Vol., Atlanta Soc. for Blind, 1975, 76, 77, Ga. Press Assn. Gridiron, 1978, 79, 80, 81, Jewish Vocat. Services, 1982, others; mem. communications adv. bd. Atlanta Jewish Fedn., 1985, 86, Interfaith Shelters for Homeless, 1984, 85, 86. Named to ADWEEK All Am. Creative Team, 1982; recipient Addy awards, 1974, 75, 77, 80-85, Phoenix award, 1974, 75, 76, 78, 81, 82, Andy awards, 1976, 78, 80-83, CLIO, 1975, 81, 85, Maxi award, 1982, 83, Cable Mktg. award, 1983, Telly award, 1985, Hollywood Radio & TV Internat. Broadcast award, 1983, Internat. Radio Festival of N.Y. award, 1985, Silver Microphone awards, 1984, 86. Mem. Atlanta Soc. Communication Artists (dir. 1974-75), Women Bus. Owners, High Mus. Soc., Sierra Club, Greenpeace, Zool. Soc., Bot. Soc., Am. Film Inst. Address: 2324 Bry-Mar Dr Atlanta GA 30345

DAVIDSON, ANNE STOWELL, lawyer; b. Rye, N.Y., Feb. 24, 1949; d. Robert Harold and Anne (Breeding) Davidson. B.A. magna cum laude, Smith Coll., 1971; J.D. cum laude, George Washington U., 1974. Bar: D.C. 1975, U.S. Supreme Ct. 1980. Asst. gen. counsel FDA, Rockville, Md., 1974-78; counsel Abbott Labs., North Chicago, Ill., 1978-79; counsel U.S. Pharm. Ops. Schering-Plough Corp., Kenilworth, N.J., 1979-83; sr. counsel Sandoz, Inc., E. Hanover, N.J., 1983—. Trustee, N.J. Pops Orch. Recipient Dawes Prize Smith Coll., 1971. Mem. ABA, Pharm. Mfrs. Assn., Food and Drug Law Inst., Proprietary Assn. (govt. affairs com.). Republican. Presbyterian. Club: Smith Coll. (pres. 1981-82). Contbr. articles to profl. jours. Office: Sandoz Inc 59 Route 10 East Hanover NJ 07936

DAVIDSON, BARBARA JEAN, association executive; b. Los Angeles, Aug. 9, 1943; d. Henry Frank Bloomfield and Beverly Claire (Malnick) Bloomfield Fiori; m. George Merrill Straw, June 26, 1964 (div.); children—Cynthia Tranter Straw Davidson, George Michael Straw Davidson; m. Mark Kelly Davidson, Aug. 13, 1973. A.A. in Sociology, Pierce Jr. Coll., 1964; B.A. in Sociology, UCLA, 1983. Vol. Project Caring, Los Angeles, 1978-80; ombudsman program problem solver Los Angeles City Ombudsman, 1980-85; exec. dir., founder Action for Seniors, Inc., Agouri Hills, Calif., 1983—; v.p. West San Fernando Valley Sr. Concerns, Los Angeles, 1984-86; chmn. Central San Fernando Valley Sr. Concerns, 1986. Contbr. articles to newspapers. Organizer, sponsor Sr. Health and Info. Fair, 1984, Sr. Job and Info. Fair, 1984-86. Recipient Proclamation award Mayor Carol Sahm of Agoura Hills, 1984, Mayor Tom Bradley of Los Angeles, 1985; commendation award Supr. Michael Antonivich of Los Angeles, 1985; cert. of recognition Senator Ed Davis, 1985. Mem. Advocacy Allaince for Aging Patients (bd. dirs.), Advocate for Elder Abuse/Project Caring (cert. of appreciation 1977, 78, 79), Los Angeles Affiliated Coms. on Aging (recognition award 1984). Republican. Jewish. Avocations: boating; fishing; theater; cooking. Office: Goebel Sr Ctr Action for Srs Inc 110 S Conejo Sch Rd Thousand Oaks CA 91362

DAVIDSON, GRACE EVELYN, nursing educator, consultant; b. Wabash, Ind., Aug. 2, 1920; d. William Alexander and Jennie Lavinia (Baker) Davidson. Diploma Columbia Presbyn. Sch. Nursing, 1942; B.S., U. Minn., 1948; M.A., Tchrs. Coll. Columbia U., 1954, postgrad. 1963-64. Instr., Sch. Nursing, Columbia U., N.Y.C., 1948-51; assoc. prof. Skidmore Coll., Saratoga Springs, N.Y., 1954-66; asst. adminstr., dir. nursing Univ. Hosp., NYU Med. Center, 1966-79, assoc. prof. part-time, 1977-79, prof. 1979—; cons. nursing service adminstrn., N.Y.C., 1980—. Served to maj. Army Nurse Corps, 1943-46, 51-53; WWII, Korea. Recipient Alumni Fedn. medal Columbia U., 1981; Plaque for leadership in nursing NYU Med. Ctr., 1983. Mem. Nursing Edn. Alumnae Assn. Tchrs. Coll. Columbia U. (achievement award 1977), Nat. Assn. Female Execs., Inc., Am. Nurses Assn., Nat. League Nursing, Columbia U.-Presbyn. Hosp. Sch. Nursing Alumnae Assn. (pres. 1970-76, Disting. Alumnae award 1981), Ret. Officers Assn., LWV. Republican. Presbyterian. Contbr. articles to profl. jours. Home: 67 Chestnut St Dumont NJ 07628

DAVIDSON, JESSICA URSULA, music educator; b. Rome, N.Y., Jan. 10, 1914; d. Jay Sidney and Lucy Adelaide (Clarke) Brown; grad. Potsdam State Coll., 1934; B.Mus. in Music Edn., U. Del., 1972, M.Ed. in Music Edn., West Chester State Coll., 1973; Ph.D. in Secondary Edn.-Music Edn., U. Md., 1978; m. Alexander Clyde Davidson, June 8, 1936; children—Shirley Anne, Nancy Jeannette. Tchr. music Adams Center High Sch., 1934-36, 42-43; dir. music Ave. Methodist Ch., Del. 1946-75; dir. Student Nurses Choir, Del., 1965-75; tchr. piano, organ Kimball Music Co., 1967-69; tchr. music Milford Spl. Dist., Del., 1969-70; tchr. music New Castle County (Del.) Sch. Dist., 1970-77, 78-79; tchr. music edn. U. Md., 1977-78; dir. music edn. and area music program for Council on Aging Multi-Disciplinary Center for Research in Gerontology, U. Ky., 1979—. Class rep. U. Del., 1977—. Mem. Music Educators Nat. Conf., Ky. State Music Edn. Assn., Nat. Ret. Tchrs. Assn., Am. Assn. Ret. Persons, Delta Kappa Gamma (chmn. music com. Newcastle, Del 1975-77, mem. program com. Lexington 1980). Republican. Methodist. Clubs: Order Eastern Star (matron 1942), Univ. Composer: Christmas Cantata: The Birth of Christ According to Saint Luke, 1970, The Night the Christ Child Came to Earth, 1965, The Greatest of These Is Love, 1973 Mothers of the World, 1965, Christmas in Kentucky, 1980. Home: 1043 Cross Keys Rd Lexington KY 40504 Office: Ligon House University of Kentucky Lexington KY 40506

DAVIDSON, KATHLYN ROSE, business owner; b. Oakland, Calif., Feb. 3, 1942; d. Alfred G. Ware and Betty A. (Ferrara) McGlade; m. Phillip S. Davidson, Mar. 23, 1968; children—Diana S., David S., Dana L. Grad. high sch. Advt. mgr. Morning News, San Leandro, Calif., 1966-68; traffic sec. Standard Register, Oakland, Calif., 1969-71; owner Castro Valley Appliances, Calif. 1971-73, Creative Workshop, Ukiah, Calif., 1976—; instr. Mendocino Coll., Ukiah, 1980-82; cons. Mendocino County Schs., 1984-85. Active Muscular Dystrophy Assn., bd. dirs. Project Sanctuary, Ukiah, 1983—. Mem. Bus. and Profl. Women (pres. 1985—; Employer of Yr. Ukiah 1982), Nat. Assn. Quick Printers, Ukiah C. of C., Mendocino County C. of C. (dir. 1983—), LWV. Democrat. Club: Toastmasters (Ukiah). Avocations: boating; fishing; swimming; travel; speaking. Office: Creative Workshop 759 S State St Ukiah CA 95482

DAVIDSON, PHYLLIS JEANNETTE, real estate investor; b. Forest, Ohio, Dec. 28, 1935; d. Jesse Gail Davidson and Cleora Fern (Wise) Davidson Barger; m. David Kassab, May 30, 1956 (div. Aug. 1968); children—Jay, Daniel, Lance, Cynthia. Student real estate and contract law Valley State Coll., Van Nuys, Calif., 1974-75, apt. house mgmt. Adult Sch., Hollywood, Calif., 1975. Lic. real estate agt. Long distance operator Ohio Bell Telephone Co., Findlay, 1952-54; service rep. Pacific Bell Telephone Co., Hollywood, 1954-56; pvt. real estate investor, Encino, Calif., 1956-69, Beverly Hills, Calif., also Houston, 1970—; property dir., fin. v.p. Royal Hawaiian Mgmt. Co., Beverly Hills, 1969-70; ptnr. Investment Futures; dir. Woodlake Forest III, Houston. Mem. New Eng. Backgammon Club, Bayou Backgammon Club, Exec. Forum Houston. Democrat. Methodist. Club: P.I.P.S. (Los Angeles). Home: 25 Bayou Pointe Houston TX 77063

DAVIDSON, SHARON MARIE, educator; b. Bronx, N.Y., May 6, 1955; d. Robert Eugene and Lillie Jane Rowe Davidson; B.S. in Early Childhood Edn., D.C. Tchrs. Coll., 1977; M.A., Trinity Coll., Washington, 1978. Dir. Parent-Child Center, D.C. Public Schs., 1978-80; tng. coordinator parenting and employability skills for teenage parents D.C. Dept. Labor, also Asso. for Renewal in Edn., 1979; cons. St. Ann's Infant and Maternity Home, Hyattsville, Md., 1980; tng. coordinator, early childhood devel. specialist Parent Focus, Assos. Renewal in Edn., 1980; coordinating instr. Trinity Coll., 1980-81; dir. The Children's Center, early childhood devel. specialist Arlington (Va.) Hosp., 1981-82; tchr. D.C. Pub. Schs., 1982—; mem. D.C. Task Force Adolescent Sexuality and Parenting, 1978—; mem. D.C. Mayor's Task Force Internat. Yr. of Child, 1978—. Recipient certs. and plaques of recognition. Mem. Assn. Childhood Edn. Internat., Coalition Children and Youth, Day Care and Child Devel. Council Am., Nat. Assn. Edn. Young Children, Nat. Black Child Devel. Inst., Council Exceptional Children, Com. Internat. Profl. Women, Nat. Center Clin. Infant Programs, AAUW Kappa Delta Pi, Phi Delta Kappa. Democrat. Roman Catholic.

DAVIDSON, SHERRILL IDELLE, lawyer; b. Alexandria, La., Dec. 28, 1956; d. Barbara Jordan (Evans) D. B.S., La. Tech. U., 1978; J.D., La. State U., 1981; postgrad. Universite de Paris-L'Institute Catholique, 1980. Bar: La. 1981. Asst. head resident Highland Dormitory, La. State U., Baton Rouge, 1978-79; clk. Sklar, Nachman, Schmidt and Dowsher, attys. of law, 1980-81; assoc. Gold, Little, Simon, Weems, and Bruser, attys. of law, 1981-82; staff atty. 3d party liability sect., Dept. Health and Human Resources, Baton Rouge, 1982—. La. Tech. U. scholar, 1975, La. debate scholar, 1975. Mem. ABA, La. State Bar Assn., Pi Kappa Delta, Phi Beta, Omicron Delta Kappa, Gamma Beta Phi. Democrat. Roman Catholic. Home: 450 Cloud Dr Apt 11 Baton Rouge LA 70806 Office: PO Box 1133 Baton Rouge LA 70821

DAVIES, DONNA STEWART, hospital administrator; b. Sharon, Pa., Aug. 19, 1931; d. Donald Aubrey and Virginia Maxine (Howard) Stewart Vessella; m. Walter O. Davies, Mar. 22, 1974. Diploma nursing Jameson Meml. Hosp., New Castle, Pa., 1952; B.S.N., Pitts. U., 1956; M.Ed., Duquesne U., 1960. Instr. nursing Duquesne U., Pitts., 1956-60, asst. prof., 1960-63, assoc. prof., chmn. R.N. program, 1963-67; dir. nursing edn. Jameson Meml. Hosp. New Castle, Pa., 1967-77, dir. nursing affairs, 1977-79, v.p. patient services, 1979—. Cons. Crouse Irving Hosp. Sch. Nursing, Syracuse, 1968; chmn. nursing program adv. com. Sippery Rock State Coll. (Pa.), 1976-80; co-chmn. nursing edn. com. Mahoning Shenango Health Edn. Network, Youngstown, Ohio, 1974—. Mem. Mental Health/Retardation Bd., New Castle, 1970-74, mem. adv. bd. YWCA, New Castle, 1969-72; bd. dirs. Lawrence County Vis. Nurse Assn., 1980-83, pres., 1983-84. Mem. Nat. League Nursing, Pa. League Nursing, Pa. Soc. Nurse Ecuators (chmn. program com. 1979-80), Am. Coll. Hosp. Adminstrs., Bus. and Profl. Women New Castle (com. chmn. 1977), Sigma Theta Tau. Republican. Presbyterian. Clubs: Lions (pres. 1983—), Eastern Star, Soroptimist (pres. 1976-77). Office: Jameson Meml Hosp W Leasure Ave New Castle PA 16105

DAVIES, JANE B. (MRS. LYN DAVIES), archtitectural historian; b. Amboy, Ill., Sept. 9, 1913; d. Henry Harold and Clara May (Heermans) Badger; B.A., Wellesley Coll., 1935; M.A., Columbia U., 1942, B.S. in L.S. with high honors, 1944; postgrad. U. Mich., summer 1936, U. Wis., summers 1937, 38; m. Lyn Davies, July 18, 1942. Tchr. Monticello Prep. Sch., Godfrey, Ill., 1935-37, Kent Sch. Girls, Denver, 1937-41, Halsted Sch., Yonkers, N.Y., 1942-43; reference librarian Columbia Univ. Libraries, 1944-50, rare book cataloger, 1951-77; cons. Nat. Trust Historic Preservation, 1965, Smithsonian Inst., 1967, Greensboro (N.C.) Preservation Soc., 1967-70, Historic Green Springs, 1970-73, 82, Llewellyn Park Hist. Dist., 1982-84, Sleepy Hollow restorations; lectr. on Am. archtl. history. Am. Council Learned Socs. grantee, 1970, Am. Philos. Soc. grantee, 1970-71; Nat. Endowment for Humanities fellow, 1978. Mem. Soc. Archtl. Historians (sec.-treas. N.Y. chpt. 1959-67), Victorian Soc. Am. (adv. com. 1966-76), Nat. Trust Historic Preservation, Friends of Lyndhurst, N.Y. Hist. Soc., Archtl. League N.Y., Preservation League N.Y. State, Greensboro Preservation Soc. (hon.), Phi Beta Kappa, Beta Phi Mu. Presbyn. Author intro. Houston Mus. Fine Arts: The Gothic Revival Style in America, 1830-1870, 1976; Alexander Jackson Davis: Rural Residences (1837), 1980. Editorial asst. Jour. Soc. Archtl. Historians, 1964-65. Contbr. articles on Am. archtl. history to mags., jours. and Macmillan Ency. of Architects. Home: 549 W 123d St New York NY 10027

DAVIES, LOIS SHILLING, civic worker, writer; b. Troy, Ohio, June 5, 1909; d. Harry Ernest and Clara (Prugh) Shilling; m. Alfred W. Davies, June 14, 1932 (dec.); children—A. Robert, Thomas J., Matthew H. B.A., Ohio Wesleyan U., 1932. Y-Teen dir. YWCA, Piqua, Ohio, 1951-54; tchr. Miami County Schs., Ohio, 1949, 61; dir. Miami County Children's Services, 1965; exec. dir. Am. Heart Assn. Miami County, 1966-75; founder, leader, bd. dirs. Troy council Girl Scouts U.S., 1930-48; tchr. water safety ARC, 1930-48; mem. Miami County Central Democratic Com., 1970-80; bd. dirs. United Fund, Troy, 1977-81; chmn. Bd. Archtl. Rev., Troy, 1984-85. Author, interviewer oral history: Troy 1913 Flood, 1976; co-author: Some Self-Evident Truths, 1980; local history columnist Troy Daily News, 1983-85. Recipient Woman of Yr. award Troy Bus. and Profl. Women's Club, 1980; Charles A. Glatt award Ohio Edn. Assn., 1982-83, Troy C. of C. (instr. Leadership Troy 1984-85, Outstanding contbns. award 1980). Mem. AAUW (bd. positions 1965-80), Troy Hist. Soc. (pres. 1977-79). Methodist. Avocations: researching and documenting local history; Ohio Senior Olympics; Volksmarch. Home and Office: 113 N Market St Troy OH 45373

DAVIES, MARIE LOUISE, business executive; b. Oakland, Calif., Apr. 19, 1949; d. Edward Henry and Louise (Colombo) D. B.A. in Behavioral Sci., Calif. State U.-San Jose, 1972. Order processing supr. Altex Sci. Co., Berkeley, Calif., 1976-78, material planner, 1978-80; traffic supr. Smithkline Beckman, Inc., Berkeley, 1980-82, distbn. supr., 1982-84, column prodn. mgr., 1986—, XBMS project mgr., San Ramon, Calif., 1984-86. Mem. Bay Area Consumer Action, San Francisco, 1976. Recipient Cost Reduction Suggestion award Beckman Instruments, 1983. Mem. Am. Prodn. and Inventory Control Soc., Nat. Council Phys. Distbn. Mgmt., Am. Soc. Transp. and Logistics, Sierra Club. Democrat. Roman Catholic. Club: Lakeridge (El Sobrante, Calif.). Avocations: tennis; skiing; golf; travel; fishing.

DAVIES, OLGA G., insurance executive; b. Ukraine, Dec. 26, 1927; came to U.S., 19; d. Michael and Mary (Lohinska) Gabrysz; m. William David Davies, Nov. 12, 1950; children—Nancy, Barbara, William. Student Rutgers U., 1975; cert. Stockton State Coll., 1976; cert. of ins. Ins. Inst. Am., 1977. Ins. underwriter Tifft, Laver & Co., Atlantic City, 1948-51; office mgr., corp. sec., ins. agt. C.J. Adams Co., Ins. Inc., Atlantic City, 1952—. Mem. Nat. Assn. Ins. Women, Ins. Women Atlantic County (pres. 1977-79). Republican. Presbyterian. Home: 112 Pennsylvania Ave Absecon NJ 08201 Office: CJ Adams Co Ins Inc 20 S Tennessee Ave PO Box 1047 Atlantic City NJ 08404

DAVIES-TILLEY, LAURA FRANCES, lawyer; b. Burlington, Vt., Apr. 3, 1951; d. Robert Isaac and Olive May (Morris) Davies; m. James R. Deveney II, June 9, 1973 (div. Dec. 1981); m. 2d Douglas Gilbert Tilley, II, Sept. 5, 1982. B.A., U. Vt., 1973; J.D., Georgetown U., 1976. Bar: Md. 1976. Law clk. Pub. Defender, Annapolis, Md., 1975-76; legis. drafter Md. Legislature, Annapolis, 1977; corp. counsel Easco Corp., Balt., 1977-79; counsel Comml. Credit Corp., Balt., 1979—. Mem. ABA, Conf. Personal Fin. Law, Phi Beta Kappa. Unitarian. Home: 7 N Cherry Grove Ave Annapolis MD 21401 Office: Comml Credit Corp 300 Saint Paul Pl Baltimore MD 21202

DAVILA-JOHNSTON, RUTH MARIE, computer programmer/analyst; b. Honolulu, Oct. 11, 1960; d. Daniel and Sally (Yunson) Davila; m. Johnnie Dean Johnston, Sept. 15, 1984. B.S., Southwest Mo. State U., Springfield, 1982. Computer programmer/analyst Marine Corps Fin. Ctr., Kansas City, Mo., 1983—. Mem. Nat. Assn. Female Execs., Southwest Mo. State U. Alumni Assn., Delta Sigma Pi. Roman Catholic. Avocations: shopping craft shows; swimming; dancing; reading. Home: 7 Belmo St Belton MO 64012 Office: Marine Corps Fin Ctr 1500 E 95th St Kansas City MO 64197

DAVIS, (ALICE) DIANE WILCOX, retail buyer, consultant; b. Chgo., Jan. 10, 1937; d. Charles Albert and Alice-Diane (Kjellander) Wilcox; m. James Barnhart Lohr, Sept. 1, 1956 (div. 1971); m. Jean-Pierre Alexandre Radley, Aug. 30, 1973 (div. 1981); m. Richard Manchester Davis, Nov. 24, 1982; children—Alice-Diane Wilcox Lohr, Valerie Barnhart Lohr. Student Brown U., 1954-56. Asst. buyer couture, Gidding-Jenny Stores, Cin., 1968-69, buyer, 1969-71; buyer couture, Neiman-Marcus Stores, Dallas, 1971-73, Saks Fifth Ave., N.Y.C., 1973-78; v.p. wholesale-retail and pub. relations, Julio Stores, N.Y.C., 1978-79; mgmt. cons., San Miguel De Allende, Mexico, 1979—. Bd. dirs., chmn. endowment fund Centro De Crecimiento, San Miguel de Allende, 1984-85; pres. bd. dirs. La Fiesta Internacional de San Miguel Allende; chmn. La Fiesta 86, San Miguel Ednl. Found. Mem. Brown U. Alumni Assn. (v.p. Cin. chpt. 1968-71). Avocations: bridge, skiing. Address: APDO 418 San Miguel de Allende Guanajuato Mexico 37700

DAVIS, ALICE ELIZA MORSE (MRS. GEORGE ARTHUR DAVIS), club woman; b. Milo, Maine; d. John Willis and Mabel (Martin) Morse; student U. Maine, 1919-21; grad. Gilman Comml. Sch., Bangor, Maine, 1936; m. Maynard Havey, Dec. 22, 1921 (dec. Dec. 1930); 1 dau., Gloria (Mrs. Lee Baker); m. 2d, George Arthur Davis, Aug. 18, 1947 (dec. Jan. 1969). Tchr. public schs. Maine, 1922-25; sec. Agrl. Mktg. Service, USDA, Washington, 1936-46; mem. community adv. com. Maine Hwy. Safety Com., 1962-64; mem. adv. council Maine Civil War Centennial Commn., 1961-65; mem. nat. adv. bd. Am. Security Council, Washington, 1971—; charter mem. Security and Intelligence Fund, Washington, 1977—; Maine chmn. nat. def. com. D.A.R., 1958-65, resolutions com., 1958-75, regent chpt., 1962-64, 72-76, area rep. speakers staff com., 1968-74; nat. vice chmn. Northeastern div. Americanism and D.A.R. Manual for Citizenship Com., 1965-68; Maine pres. Daus. Colonial Wars, 1965-68, nat. vice chmn. program com. 1st div. states, 1968-71, mem. Nat. Officers Club, 1966—; nat. chmn. Am. def. and legislation, Nat. Soc. New Eng. Women, 1966-69, nat. vice chmn. resolutions com., 1966-69, v.p. Augusta Colony, Maine, 1966-72; pres. 1972-75, registrar, 1979-81; nat. mem. Smithsonian Assn., 1977-85; sustaining mem. Republican Nat. Com.; mem. Nat. Travel Club, Soc. Mayflower Descs., Nat. Rifle Assn.; charter mem. Mason (N.H.) Hist. Soc., 1969—; mem. Pine Tree Soc. for Crippled Children and Adults, 1975—; mem. Ret. Officers Assn., 1977—; mem. Republican Presdl. Task Force, 1985-86. Mem. Order Eastern Star (life). Home: Harbor Rd Winter Harbor ME 04693 Mailing address: PO Box 264 Winter Harbor ME 04693

DAVIS, ALICE J., municipal employee; b. Galveston, Tex., Aug. 4, 1929; d. Joseph Edward Reagan and Gertrude Bertha Reagan Zeller; m. Bob J. Davis, Oct. 22, 1948; 1 child, Paula Lynn Davis Baughman. A.A., San Jacinto Coll., 1966; B.S., Western Ill. U., 1976. With office staff various automobile dealerships, Houston, 1951-68, Yeast Printing Co., Macomb, Ill., 1974-77; clk. Office of City Clk., City of Macomb, 1977—. Youth program leader 1st Meth. Ch., Pasadena, Tex., 1960-63; mem. choir Wesley United Meth. Ch., Macomb, 1968—; area chmn. Macomb United Way, 1970-71, program chmn., 1984-85. Mem. Univ. Faculty Women, Macomb Home Econs. Assn. (pres. 1981-82), Kappa Omicron Phi, Phi Kappa Phi, Beta Sigma Phi, Xi Epsilon Rho (pres. 1981-82, 86-87). Lodges: Eastern Star, White Shrine, Deer. Office: Office of City Clerk City of Macomb Macomb IL 61455

DAVIS, ALICE VIRGINIA GUNN, piano educator; b. Daingerfield, Tex., July 24, 1918; d. Walter Harrison and Lena Belle (Porter) Gunn; student pub. schs., Daingerfield; m. Joseph Marion Davis, Dec. 25, 1938; children—Joe Lane, Jerrol Porter. Pvt. instr. piano, Omaha, Tex., 1962—; organist Meth. Ch., 1965—, dir. children's music, tchr. Sunday Sch., Bible study leader. Mem. Nat. Guild Piano Tchrs. (sr. collegiate diploma, hall of fame), Nat. Music Tchrs. Assn. (officer), N.E. Tex. Music Tchrs. Assn. Am. Assn. Ret. Persons (program Chmn. local chpt. 5 yrs). Contbr. articles to newspapers. Home and Office: Route 1 Box 57 Omaha TX 75571

DAVIS, ANN GOUGER, lawyer; b. New Castle, Pa., Oct. 14, 1939; d. Matthew Martin and Mary Louise (Goehring) Gouger; m. George Humphries Davis, June 17, 1961; children—Matthew Miller, Catherine Powell. A.B., Vassar Coll., 1961; M.A.T., U. Chgo., 1963; J.D. cum laude, Ind. U., Indpls., 1978. Bar: Ind. 1979, U.S. Dist. Ct. (no. and so. dists.) Ind. Tchr., Homewood-Flossmoor High Sch., Flossmoor, Ill., 1962-66, Purdue U., West Lafayette, Ind., 1966-68; atty. Vaughan, Vaughan & Layden, Lafayette, Ind., 1979-83; atty., mgr. Women's Legal Clinic, Indpls., 1983-84; ptnr. Holder & Davis, Lafayette, 1985—. Bd. dirs. LWV Montgomery County, Crawfordsville, Ind., 1968-75, Planned Parenthood, Lafayette; bd. dirs., pres., sec.-treas. Youth Service Bur., Montgomery County, Crawfordsville, 1971-74, 79; pres. Ind. Symphony Soc., Crawfordsville unit, 1972; vestry St. John's Episcopal Ch., Crawfordsville, 1974-75; local chmn. United Fund, Crawfordsville, 1975; chmn. Crawfordsville Commn. on Status of Women, 1979-80. Mem. ABA, Ind. State Bar Assn., Indpls. Bar Assn., Tippecanoe Bar Assn. Episcopalian. Club: The Athenian (membership chmn. 1977) (Crawfordsville). Office: Holder & Davis 700 Bank One Bldg Lafayette IN

DAVIS, ANN GRAY, nurse, consultant; b. Phila., Jan. 18, 1932; d. Joseph Edward and Elaine (Wheaton) Gray; m. Herbert Paul Davis, Oct. 21, 1950 (div. June 1976); children—Debra Gianni, Paul, Derek, Megan. B.S., Roberts Wesleyan Coll., 1974; M.N., Emory U., 1978. Cert. clin. specialist adult Psychiatric mental health nursing. Nurse, St. John's Home, Rochester, N.Y., 1974-75; instr. nursing Roberts Wesleyan Coll., Rochester, 1975-77; instr. nursing Lenoir-Rhyne Coll., Hickory, N.C., 1978-79, acting chmn. dept. nursing, 1979-80; psychiat. nurse clinician Glenn R. Frye Hosp., Hickory, N.C., 1980-81, dir. staff devel., 1981-82, asst. dir. nursing cons., assessment, research and evaluation, 1982-84, clin. specialist psychiatry, 1984—; guest faculty Lenoir-Rhyne Coll. and Northstate Acad., 1981—; adj. faculty N.C. U., Greensboro, 1985—; psychiat. nursing cons. Sec. treas. Catawba Valley Health Planning Council, 1978-82; mem. adv. council Health Occupations Edn., 1981-82; mem. Task Force on Edn., Catawba County, 1982—; mem. Family Life Task Force, Catawba County, 1982—; mem. Rape Task Force, N.C. Council on Status of Women, 1981—. NIMH grantee, 1977-78. Mem. Am. Nurses' Assn. (cert. clin. specialist in adult psychiat. nursing, mem. council specialists in psychiat/mental health nursing), N.C. State Nurses' Assn., Catawba Valley Assn. Clin. Therapists, Catawba County C. of C. (health com. 1986—), Sigma Theta Tau, Alpha Kappa Sigma. Democrat. Episcopalian. Office: 420 N Center St Psychiatry Glenn R Frye Regional Med Ctr Hickory NC 28601

DAVIS, ARBELIA, department store buyer; b. McZenzie, Tenn., Oct. 17, 1946; d. Henry and Josephine (Taylor) Holmes; m. Garland Davis, Jr., June 23, 1974 (dec. Dec. 1979). Student Iowa State U., 1974, Ellsworth Community Coll., Iowa, 1977, Kirkwood Community Coll., Cedar Rapids, Iowa, 1977-79. Salesperson Armstrong Dept. Store, Cedar Rapids, 1965-67, buyer, 1971--. Bd. dirs. YMCA, Cedar Rapids, 1977-79, Linn County Cancer Soc., 1980--, Family Service, Cedar Rapids, 1983--, Cedar Rapids Arts Council, 1985--; vol. Mercy Hosp., Cedar Rapids, 1979-84. Mem. Am. Bus. Women's Assn. (Woman of Yr. award Cedar Rapids 1976), Cedar Rapids C. of C. (ambassador 1982--), Symphony Guild (life mem.), Beyond Rubies, Cedar Rapids Jr. League. Club: Elmcrest Country (Cedar Rapids). Avocations: travel; cooking. Home: 1420 7th Ave SE Cedar Rapids IA 52404 Office: Armstrong Dept Store 222 3d Ave SE Cedar Rapids IA 52401

DAVIS, AUDREY BLYMAN, medical sciences curator, author; b. Hicksville, N.Y., Nov. 9, 1934; d. George William Blyman and Helen Rosalie Usewack; m. Miles Davis, Aug. 6, 1960; children—Laura Helen, Allan Watson. B.S., Adelphi U., Garden City, N.Y., 1952-56; Ph.D., John Hopkins U., 1969. Sci. tchr. Sewanhaka High Sch., Floral Park, N.Y., 1956-58, Saugus (Mass.) High Sch., 1959-60; cons. Sci. Service, Washington, 1966-70; curator med. scis. Smithsonian Instn., Washington, 1967—; mus. cons. U.S. Armed Forces Inst. Pathology, Washington, 1983-84; Muetter Mus., Phila., 1979-80; cons. N.J. Med. Sch., New Brunswick, 1982; Kate Hurd Mead lectr., 1985; Keynote speaker Buffalo Vis. Nursing Assn., 1985. Author: Medicine and Its Technology (Choice award for outstanding acad. book 1983), 1981; Bloodletting Instruments in the NMAH, 1979; The Circulation of the Blood and Medical Chemistry in England, 1650-1680, 1974; contbr. articles, monographs in field to publs. Recipient Excellence Award as chairperson, editor newsletter Smithsonian Instn. Women's Council, 1982. Mem. Hist. Sci. Soc. (sec. 1982-85, council 1975-78), Am. Assn. Hist. Medicine (council 1976-79), Am. Hist. Assn., Am. Council Learned Socs, Conf. Secs. Democrat. Roman Catholic. Club: Bolton Swim, Tennis (Balt.) (former tennis chmn.) Office: Smithsonian Instn NMAH 5000 Washington DC 20560

DAVIS, BARBARA AVENT, government official; b. Durham, N.C., Sept. 22, 1935; d. Dallas Gaston and Elsie Amelia (Baugh) Avent; B.S. magna cum laude in Bus. Adminstrn., U. Tenn., Chattanooga, 1979, M.B.A., 1981; m. Jack Davis, May 30, 1953; 1 son, David Jack. Various secretarial positions, 1953-65; with TVA, Chattanooga, 1973—, mgmt. asst., 1979-82, supr. records, sales and adminstrn., 1982-85, land mgmt. specialist, 1985—. Pres. Brainerd United Methodist Women, Chattanooga, 1972-74, trustee ch., 1980-83. Mem. Nat. Mgmt. Assn., Chattanooga Symphony Guild, U. Tenn. Chattanooga Alumni Council (treas.), Alpha Soc. Home: 4604 Rocky River Rd Chattanooga TN 37416 Office: 464 Lupton Bldg Chattanooga TN 37401

DAVIS, BARBARA JANE, medical technologist; b. New Britain, Conn., Sept. 30, 1937; d. Anthony Joseph and Mary Ann (Nargi) Fallo; cert. med. tech. New Britain Gen. Hosp. Sch. Med. Tech., 1958; A.S., Galveston Coll., 1978; B.S. in Marine Sci., Tex. A&M U., 1981; m. George D. Davis, Sept. 12, 1959; children—Peter Anthony, George Dewey, Sandra Louise. Med. technologist Rancho Los Amigos Hosp., Downey, Calif., 1959-63, Lawrence and Meml. Hosps., New London, Conn., 1963-65, Bapt. Hosp., Pensacola, Fla., 1965-66, Hollywood (Fla.) Meml. Hosp., 1966, Bay Harbor Hosp., Harbor City, Calif., 1971-73, Miami Dade Gen. Hosp. (Coral Reef Gen. Hosp.), Miami, Fla., 1975-77, U. Tex. Med. br. Galveston, 1977, County of Galveston 4c's Clinic, 1981-82, U. South Ala. Family Practice Ctr., Mobile, 1983—. Lic. med. technologist, Calif., Fla. Recipient of appreciation Elks Lodge 126, 1982. Mem. Am. Soc. Clin. Pathologists (cert. med. technologist), Delta Zeta, Gamma Chi Rho. Home: 6421 Princeton Woods Dr N Mobile AL 36618 also 419 Anderson Dr Destin FL 32541

DAVIS, BARBARA JEAN SIEMENS, service company executive; b. Louisville, Nov. 12, 1931; d. Gustav Adolph Siemens and Alberta Jeanette (McAdams) Simon; m. Donald Elmore Davis, Aug. 4, 1950; children—Dale Montgomery, Gale Sue Davis Beaty. Mktg. and personnel mgr. Kelly Services, Louisville, 1962-65; tchr. asst. TV English, Jefferson County Schs., Louisville, 1960-70; wedding and floral designer Wedding Ring, Louisville, 1971-73; owner, designer Nook Flowers and Gifts, Memphis, 1973-75; cons. pub. relations Dixie Rents, Memphis, 1975-79; div. mgr. pres. Party Concepts, Inc., Memphis, 1980—. Author: Wedding Workshop Brides Work Book, 1984. Mem. Sales and Mktg. Execs., Am. Rental Assn. (mem. party council 1985—), Nat. Assn. Wedding Cons. (pres. 1983—). Republican. Presbyterian. Home: 2200 Admington Pl Cordova TN 38018

DAVIS, BARBARA LOUISE, electronics company executive; b. North Adams, Mass., Aug. 25, 1955; d. Louis John and Shirley Antoinette (David) Davis. Student acctg. North Adams State Coll., 1977—. With Sprague Electric Co., North Adams, 1973—, research sec. customs dept., 1977-80, corp. mgr. customs dept., 1980—. Mem. Electronic Industries Assn. (customs adv. group 1982—). Roman Catholic. Home: PO Box 629 Lanesboro MA 01237 Office: Sprague Electric Co 41 Hampden Rd Mansfield MA 02048

DAVIS, BARBARA M(AE), librarian; b. Cranston, R.I., Dec. 23, 1926; d. Harrie S. and Marguerite M. (Cameron) D.; Sc.B. in Chemistry, Brown U., 1948; M.S. in L.S., Simmons Coll., 1956. Asst. research librarian research and devel. dept. Cabot Corp., Cambridge, Mass., 1948-57, research librarian, 1957-61, research librarian Billerica (Mass.) Research Center, 1961-68, head tech. info. services, 1968-81, mgr. tech. info. center, 1981—. Dir. Cabot Boston Credit Union, 1956-59, 61-64, 72-78, clk., 1961-64, 72-77, v.p., 1977-78; chmn. research com. Greater Boston Young Republican Club, 1959-61. Mem. Am. Chem. Soc. (sec. div. chem. lit. 1961-65), Spl. Libraries Assn. (chmn. Boston chpt. 1965-66, chmn. chemistry div. 1971-72), Simmons Coll. Library Sch. Alumni (v.p. 1965-66). Home: 37 Drummer Boy Way Lexington MA 02173 Office: Cabot Corp Concord Rd Billerica MA 01821

DAVIS, BEATRICE ANNA KIMSEY, educator, civic worker; b. Oklahoma City, June 23, 1917; d. Carl Cleveland and Beatrice Mary (Rudersdorf) Kimsey; grad. Ward-Belmont Coll., 1938; B.A., Vanderbilt U., 1940; M.Ed., Lamar U., 1973; m. Bruce A. Davis, Jan. 22, 1942; children—Belinda Anne Davis Pillow, Beatrice Annette Davis Orynawka, Beverly Anna Davis Steckler. Personnel interviewer Ft. Sam Houston, San Antonio, 1942-43; advisor Jr. Achievement, 1974-80; asst. instr. drama Watkins Night Sch., Nashville, 1939-40; substitute tchr. Port Arthur (Tex.) Ind. Sch. Dist., 1950-64; high sch. English tchr. South Park Ind. Sch. Dist., 1964—, head English dept., 1982-85; tchr. Nederland (Tex.) Ind. Sch. Dist., 1948-50. Pres. Port Arthur Family Services Am., 1979-81 Women's Orgn. 1st Presbyn. Ch.; v.p. Jefferson High Sch. PTA; mem. bd. Hughen Sch. for Crippled Children, Gates Meml. Library, PTA of Tyrell Elem. Sch., Port Arthur, Parliamentarians of Port Arthur, Story League of Port Arthur; trustee, membership com., tchr. Presbyn. Ch. of Covenant; mem. Beaumont Art Mus., Community Concert Assn. Port Arthur; docent McFaddin-Ward Home, Beaumont, Tex.; mem. Women's Commn. S.E. Tex., 1985—. Served as ensign USNR, 1942-43; lt. comdr. Res. Recipient numerous awards for outstanding civic service, various ednl. stipends and grants; named Tchr. of Yr. for South Park High Sch., Tex. A&M U., 1981-82. Mem. NEA, All Tchrs. Assn. Beaumont, Nat. Council Reading Tchrs., S.E. Tex. Council Reading Tchrs., Tex. Assn. for Specialists in Group Work, Sabine-Neches Personnel and Guidance Assn. AAUW (past pres. Port Arthur), Federated Women's Club (past pres. bd. Port Arthur), Rosehill Bd. (past pres.), Panhellenic Assn. (past pres. Port Arthur), Women's Orgn. Symphony Club (pres pres.). Choral Club (past pres.). Thalian Drama Group (past v.p.), Heritage Soc., Hist. Soc., Reading, Knights of Neches Aux., DAR, United Daus. Confederacy, English-Speaking Union U.S., Key Club, Sigma Kappa Alumni, Phi Lambda Phi, Phi Delta Kappa Republican. Clubs: Port Arthur Country (past pres.), Port Arthur Country Club Women's Aux. (pres.). Co-author Curriculum Guides for Reading, 1973, 81, for English, 1980; contbr. articles to mags. Home: 2816 35th St Port Arthur TX 77640

DAVIS, BERTHA GERMIZE, artist; b. Vilno, Lithuania; came to U.S., 1940, naturalized, 1941; d. Abraham and Dvora Germaize; student Stewart Van Orden, Pan Am. Coll., 1960-61, Fred Samualson and James Pinco, Art Inst. of San Migual Allende, Mex., 1965, Harold Phenix, 1972-73, Ed Whitney, 1973-74, Bud Shackelford, 1976, Zoltan Szabo, 1977, Morris Shubin, 1977; children—Sylvia Davis Caplan, Doryn Davis Chervin. Owner, operator art gallery, Houston, 1969-72; asst. mgr. Art Internat., Houston, 1972-75; asst. mgr. Kirt Niven Gallery, Dallas, 1977-78; one woman shows: Pan Am. Coll., 1960, Jewish Community Center, Houston, McAllen State Bank, 1974, La Ciudadela, Monterey, Mex., Houston Public Library, U. Tex. Health Sci. Center, Dallas, 1979, Gallery of Discovery, Dallas, 1981, Channel 13 TV Gallery, Dallas, 1981, Sol Del Rio Gallery, San Antonio, 1982, Wichita Falls, Tex., 1985, Jewish Community Ctr., 1986, also others; group shows include: Watercolor Soc. Houston, S.W. Watercolor Soc., Am. Painters in Paris, Cooperstown Art Exhibit, Issac Delgado Mus. Art, New Orleans, Corpus Christi Art Found., Salmagundi Club Art Show, N.Y.C., 1979, Dallas, Laguna Gloria Mus., Austin, Tex., 1979, 84, Catharine Lorillard Wolfe Art Club, N.Y.C., 1980, Houshangs Gallery, Dallas, 1980, Nimbus Gallery, Dallas; showings in Marsha London Gallery, N.Y.C., Nat. Design Center, N.Y.C., Fonteinbleau Gallery of N.Y., Deportive Israelita de México, Paige Gallery, 1984, Dallas S.L. Gallery, 1984; represented in permanent collection: Shell Oil Co., Houston, Transco Tower, Arthur Anderson Acctg. Co. Mem. Tex. Fine Art Assn., S.W. Watercolor Assn., Richardson Civic Art Assn., Artist Sculptors Contemporary Assn., Art League Houston, Houston Art Assn. Prin. illustrator: Open Dallas, 1976; works reproduced in various publs. Home: 8803 Jackwood St Houston TX 77036

DAVIS, BETTE RUTH ELIZABETH, actress; b. Lowell, Mass., Apr. 5, 1908; d. Harlow Morrell and Ruth (Favor) D.; ed. Cushing Acad., Ashburnham, Mass.; m. Harmon Oscar Nelson, Jr., Aug. 18, 1932 (div.); m. Arthur Farnsworth, Dec. 1940 (dec. Aug. 25, 1943); m. William Grant Sherry, Nov. 30, 1945; 1 dau., Barbara Davis; m. Gary Merrill, Aug. 1950 (div.); adopted children—Margot, Michael. Began as motion picture actress, 1931; leading pictures include Of Human Bondage, Bordertown, Dangerous (Acad. award Best Actress 1935), The Petrified Forest, Jezebel (Acad. award Best Actress 1938), Dark Victory, Juarez, The Old Maid, The Private Lives of Elizabeth and Essex, The Great Lie, The Bride Came C.O.D., All About Eve, 1950, Payment on Demand, 1951, Phone Call from a Stranger, 1952, The Star, 1953, The Virgin Queen, 1955, Storm Center, The Catered Affair, 1956, John Paul Jones, 1959, The Scapegoat, 1959, What Ever Happened to Baby Jane, Dead Ringer, Painted Canvas, 1963, Where Love Has Gone, Hush, Hush, Sweet Charlotte, 1964, The Nanny, 1965, The Anniversary, 1967, Connecting Rooms, 1969, Bunny O'Hare, 1970, Madam Sin, 1971, The Game, 1972, Burnt Offerings, 1977, Death on the Nile, 1979, Watcher in the Woods, 1979; TV movies Sister Aimee, 1977, Miniseries The Dark Secret of Harvest Home, 1978, Strangers (Emmy award), 1979, White Momma, 1980, Skyward, 1980, Family Reunion, 1981, A Piano for Mrs. Cimino, 1982; Little Gloria Happy At Last, 1982; Right of Way, 1983; (play) The Night of the Iguana. Recipient Am. Film Inst. Life Achievement award, 1977; Am. Acad. Arts award, 1983; Disting. Pub. Service medal Dept. Def., 1983; Crystal award Women in Films, 1983. Author: The Lonely Life, 1962; co-author: Mother Goddam, 1974. Office: care Gottlieb Schiff Ticktin Sternklar and Harris 555 Fifth Ave New York NY 10017*

DAVIS, BETTY JEAN BOURBONIA, real estate investment executive; b. Ft. Bayard, N.Mex., Mar. 12, 1931; d. John Alexander and Ora M. (Caudill) Bourbonia; B.S. in Elem. Edn., U. N.Mex., 1954; children—Janice Ann Cox Plagge, Elizabeth Ora Cox. Gen. partner BJD Realty Co., Albuquerque, 1977—. Bd. dirs. Albuquerque Opera Guild, 1977-79, 81-83, 85-86, membership co-chmn., 1977-79; mem. Friends of Art, 1978—, Friends of Little Theatre, 1973—, Mus. N.Mex. Found. Recipient Matrix award for journalism Jr. League. Mem. Albuquerque Mus. Assn., N.M. Hist. Soc., Albuquerque Symphony Women Assn., Jr. League Albuquerque, Alumni Assn. U. N.Mex. (dir. 1973-76), Mus. N.Mex. Found., Alpha Chi Omega. Republican. Methodist. Clubs: Alpha Chi Omega Mother's, Tanoan Country, Internat., Century (U. N.Mex.), Order Eastern Star, Order Rainbow for Girls (past grand worthy adv. N.Mex., past mother adv. Friendship Assembly 50), Alpha Chi Omega (chpt. adv. 1958 building corp. 1962-77). Home: 7816 Vista Del Arroyo NE Albuquerque NM 87109

DAVIS, BILLIE JOHNSTON, school counselor; b. Charleston, W.Va., Sept. 24, 1933; d. William Andrew, Jr. and Garnet Macil (Johnston) D.; B.S., Morris Harvey Coll., Charleston, W.Va., 1954; M.A., W.Va. U., 1957. Tchr. math. Kanawha County schs., Charleston, 1954-59, counselor, 1959—; mem. public edn. study commn. W.Va. Legislature, 1980; mem. W.Va. Commn. on Juvenile Law, 1982—; bd. dirs. W.Va. Com. for Prevention Child Abuse, W.Va. Sch. Health Adv. Com. Recipient anne Maynard award W.Va. Sch. Counselor assn., 1986. Mem. Am. Assn. Counseling and Devel., W.Va. Assn. Counseling and Devel. (pres. 1964-66, legis. chmn., 1974—; spl. award legis. services 1981), W.Va. Edn. Assn. (past legis. chmn.), Kanawha County Sch. Counselors Assn.

(pres., legis. chmn. 1974—), Alpha Delta Kappa (past chpt. pres.), Phi Delta Kappa. Democrat. Baptist. Home: 915 Breezemont Dr Charleston WV 25302 Office: Dunbar Jr High Sch 1300 Myers Ave Dunbar WV 25064

DAVIS, BONITA CAROLE, social worker, state grants officer; b. Spartanburg, S.C., July 12, 1941; d. Calvin, Jr. and Johnnie Maude (Jones) D.; B.A., Bennett Coll., Greensboro, N.C., 1966; M.S.W., Adelphi U., Garden City, N.Y., 1972. Successively caseworker, supr., adoption coordinator, adoption div. N.Y.C. Dept. Social Services, 1966-70, 72-73; dir. edn. and career hdqrs. N.Y. Community Tng. Inst., 1973-79; part-time lectr. Adelphi U. Sch. Social Work, 1974-80; mgr. gov.'s discretionary grant program N.Y. State Dept. Labor, Albany, 1980-83, assoc. dir. spl. employee services, 1983-84, employment and tng. adminstr., 1984—; cons. career and organizational devel. Bd. dirs. 21st Century Polit. Action Com. United Negro Coll. Fund scholar, 1959-60. Mem. Nat. Assn. Black Social Workers, Assn. Non-White Concerns, Nat. Women's Referral Network, NAACP, Urban League, Public Employees Fedn. Club: Order Eastern Star. Home: 8 Hall Pl Albany NY 12210 Office: Bldg 12 State Campus Albany NY 12240

DAVIS, BONNIE CHRISTELL, lawyer; b. Petersburg, Va., July 13, 1949; d. Robert Madison and Margaret Elizabeth (Collier) D. B.A., Longwood Coll., 1971; J.D., U. Richmond, 1980. Bar: Va. 1980, U.S. Dist. Ct. 1980, U.S. Ct. Appeals (4th cir.) 1982. Tchr., Chesterfield County Schs. (Va.), 1971-77; sole practice law, Chesterfield, Va., 1980-83; asst. commonwealth atty. Chesterfield County, 1983—. Adviser, Youth Services Commn., Chesterfield, 1983—; cons. Task Force on Child Abuse, 1983—, Met. Richmond Multi-Discipline Team on Spouse Abuse, 1983—; mem. nat. adv. com. for prodn. on missing and runaway children Theatre IV. Mem. Va. Bar Assn., Chesterfield Colonial Heights Bar Assn., Va. Commonwealth's Attys. Assn. Baptist. Club: Quota. Home: 14 Marshall St Petersburg VA 23803 Office: Office Commonwealth's Atty Courthouse Sq Chesterfield VA 23832

DAVIS, CAROL, market research services company executive; b. N.Y.C., July 8, 1939; d. A. Leonidas and Margaret Trotta; m. William A. Davis, Jr., May 22, 1965; children—William A. III, Robert C. B.A., Marymount Coll., 1961; M.S., NYU, 1962. Buyer Assoc. Merchandising Corp., N.Y.C., 1962-69; pres. Davis Market Research Services, Inc., Calabasas, Calif., 1969—. Mem. Market Research Assn. (nat. sec. 1985—, pres. So. Calif. chpt. 1985—), Am. Mktg. Assn. Office: Davis Market Research Services Inc 23801 Calabasas Rd Calabasas CA 91302

DAVIS, CAROL LYN, historic research consultant; b. West Palm Beach, Fla., Oct. 22, 1953; d. Robert Lee and Barbara Jean (Collett) D.; B.F.A., Tex. Christian U., Ft. Worth, 1975, M.A. in Am. Studies, 1977. Research and devel. product line designer Am. Handicrafts/Meribee Needlearts, Ft. Worth, 1977-81; ceramics/china sales cons. Dillard's, Ft. Worth, 1981-82, dept. mgr., 1981; dept. mgr. Stripling-Cox, Ft. Worth, 1982-83; freelance ceramic and string art designer, 1982-83; with phase III IV, V historic sites inventory of Tarrant County for Historic Preservation Council for Tarrant County (Tex.) and Page, Anderson & Turnbull, Inc., San Francisco, 1983-86. Mem. mgmt. adv. panel Chem. Week, 1981. Mem. Nat. Trust Historic Preservation, Ft. Worth Opera Assn., Royal Oak Found., Wiltshire Family History Soc. (Eng.). Democrat. Episcopalian. Contbr. pamphlets in field. Home: 7800 Garza Ave Fort Worth TX 76116 Office: Historic Preservation Council 215A S Jennings Ave Fort Worth TX 76104

DAVIS, CAROLE ANN, speech/language and hearing pathologist; b. Bklyn., Oct. 6, 1946; d. Benjamin and Elsie (Steinberg) Honigman; student Emerson Coll., 1965-66; L.I. U., 1966-68; M.S., Bklyn. Coll., 1972; postgrad. City U. N.Y., 1971-72, Adelphi U., 1978-79, Hofstra U., 1983-84; m. Mark George Davis, Sept. 1, 1968; children—Rachel, Buffy. Speech tchr. Bur. for Speech Improvement, Bklyn., 1968-71; cons. to devel. clinic L.I. U., 1971; supr. speech and hearing pediatric unit Suffolk Devel. Center, 1972-75, coordinator outpatient clinic, mem. admissions com., 1972-75; cons. Assn. for Down's Syndrome Children, West Islip, N.Y., 1975-76; cons. Port Jefferson Nursing Home and Health Related Facility, 1976; tchr. speech and hearing impaired BOCES 3, James E. Allen Learning Center, Melville, N.Y., 1977-81; speech/lang. pathologist in spl. edn. Half Hollow Hills Sch. Dist. 5, 1982—. Vice pres. Dix Hills Hadassah Fundraiser, 1976, Brandeis U. Nat. Women's Com. Fundraiser, 1978. CUNY Clin. fellow, 1971. Mem. L.I. Speech and Hearing Assn. (2d v.p.), N.Y. State Speech, Hearing, Lang. Assn., Am. Speech and Hearing Assn., Assn. Supervision and Curriculum Devel., Nassau-Suffolk Council Adminstrv. Women in Edn. Jewish. Home: 21 Ground Pine Ct Dix Hills NY 11746 Office: Half Hollow Hills Sch Dist 5 Melville NY 11746

DAVIS, CAROLYNE KAHLE, health care adminstrator; b. Penn Yan, N.Y., Jan. 31, 1932; d. Paul Frederick and Alice Edgerton (Cargill) Kahle; m. Ott Howard Davis, June 28, 1953; 1 son, Richard Ott. B.S., Johns Hopkins U., 1954; M.S., Syracuse U., 1965, Ph.D., 1972; LL.D., Georgetown U., 1982; D.Sc. (hon.), U. Evansville, 1982, U. Medicine and Dentistry N.J., 1984. Chairperson baccalaureate nursing program Syracuse U. (N.Y.), 1969-73; dean Sch. Nursing, U. Mich., Ann Arbor, 1973-75, prof. nursing and edn., 1973-81, assoc. v.p. acad. affairs, 1975-81; adminstr. Health Care Fin. Adminstrn., Washington, 1981—; mem. Commn. for Leadership Devel., Am. Council Edn., Mich., 1977-80. Contbr. articles to profl. jours. Bd. dirs. Mich. Heart Assn., 1973-81; mem. Sch. Bd., Fayetteville-Manlius System, N.Y., 1971-73; chmn. Mich. Health Data Corp., 1978-80; trustee Johns Hopkins U., Balt., 1979-81; bd. dirs. Am. Assn. Higher Edn., Washington, 1980-81; mem. task force on health manpower planning Assn. Acad. Health Ctrs., 1980-81. Recipient Cullen Prize Adminstrn., Johns Hopkins U., 1954; Bronze medallion Dept. Health and Human Services, Washington, 1983. Fellow Am. Acad. Nursing; mem. Nat. League Nursing (bd. dirs. 1979-81), Phi Delta Kappa, Sigma Theta Tau. Republican. Office: Dept Health and Human Services Room 314-G Humphrey Bldg Health Care Fin Adminstrn 200 Independence Ave SW Washington DC 20201

DAVIS, CELESTIA BRANNEN, reading cons.; b. Swenson, Tex., June 20, 1915; d. Calvin Ernest and Iva (Galloway) Brannen; B. Religious Edn., Southwestern Baptist Sem., 1946; M. Ed., Eastern N. Mex. U., 1965, edn. specialist, 1968; Ed.D., Tex. Woman's U., 1976; m. Paul Wendelin Davis, Oct. 6, 1935; one dau., Wendelin Ann (Mrs. William Arden Taylor). Prin. Stonewall County Sch., Aspermont, Tex., 1932-34; head tchr. Sacaton (Ariz.) Pub. Sch., 1953-59; elem. tchr. Carlsbad, N. Mex., 1962-63; remedial reading tchr. Marton, Tex., 1963-67; reading cons. Tex. Edn. Agency, Austin, 1968—, edn. grantee, 1976-77. Mem. Assn. State English and Reading Suprs. (pres. 1975-76), Internat. Reading Assn. (state orgn. chmn. 1968-76, Founders award Tex. council 1976), DAR, Tex. State Council Reading and Supervision, Tex. Council Lang. Arts Suprs., Nat. Council Tchrs. English (cons. to CEE commn. on supervision and curriculum devel. 1982—), Delta Kappa Gamma. Democrat. Baptist. Contbr. articles to profl. publs. Home: 9610 Covey Ridge Ln Austin TX 78758 Office: 201 E 11th St Austin TX 78701

DAVIS, CHERYL MARIE, computer company executive; b. Winona, Minn., Dec. 30, 1945; d. George W. and Beverly F. (Cieminski) Wos; A.B. in English with honors in humanities, Stanford U., 1968; postgrad. Ga. State U., 1974-75, U. Tex., Austin, 1975-81; m. John Nicholas Davis, Aug. 24, 1985; children by previous marriage—David Austin Russell, Timothy Francis George Russell, Cristi Lynn Traver, Pamela Cindy Traver. Programmer Fairchild Semiconductor, Mountain View, Calif., 1966-67; programming mgr. adminstrn. computing Stanford (Calif.) U., 1969-74; mgmt. info. systems dir. Ga. State U., Atlanta, 1974-75; software engrng. mgr. INTEL, Austin, Tex., 1976-81, product mktg. mgr., 1982-84; bus. mgr. Wollongong Group, Palo Alto, Calif., 1985—; bd. dirs. Coll. and Univ. Systems Exchange, 1974-76, Info. Success Systems, 1972. Tchr. religious edn. St. Theresa Sch., 1976-78, St. Thomas More Sch., 1978-79, mem. fin. com. St. Thomas More, 1978-79. Recipient Bausch & Lomb award, 1964, Nat. Sci. Fair award, 1964. Mem. Phi Kappa Phi. Republican. Roman Catholic. Club: Stanford Alumni. Contbr. papers to profl. publs. and confs. Home: 930 Damian Way Los Altos CA 94022 Office: Wollongong Group 1129 San Antonio Rd Palo Alto CA 94303

DAVIS, CLARA MAE, travel service executive; b. Saginaw, Mich., Feb. 27, 1922; d. Clifford Wallace and Nellie Catharine (Young) Caldwell; m. John Alfred Davis, May 2, 1942; children—Jonelle Adair, Cherry Margaret, Deborah Catharine. Student Flint Jr. Coll., 1940-41. Sec. Norwalk Truck Line, Chgo., 1949-56; exec. sec. Ford Motor Co., Chicago Heights, Ill., 1956-59; owner, founder Davis Temporaries, Chicago Heights, 1960, cons., 1975—; pres., mgr. Davis Travel Service, Chicago Heights, 1975—; cons. Prairie State Coll., Chicago Heights. Mem. Inst. Cert. Travel Agents. Republican. Lodge: Altrusa (pres. Chicago Heights 1969-71). Avocations: breeding and raising thoroughbred horses. Home: Rural Route 3 Box 1234 Crete IL 60417 Office: Davis Travel Service Inc 353 W Lincoln Hwy Chicago Heights IL 60411

DAVIS, COLEEN COCKERILL, educator; b. Pampa, Tex., Sept. 20, 1930; d. Charles Clifford and Myrtle Edith (Harris) Cockerill; m. (div. Dec. 1984); David Christopher, Denis Benjamin (dec. 1979). B.S., U. Okla., 1951; M.S., UCLA, 1952; postgrad. U.So. Calif., Whittier Coll., UCLA. Cert. tchr., Calif. Chmn, dept. home econs., tchr. Whittier Union High Sch. Dist., Calif., 1952-85; substitute tchr., 1985—; home tchr., 1985—, cons. 1986—; co-host America's Bed & Breakfast, Whittier, 1983—, also founder, pres., exec. dir. Contbr. articles to newspapers. Founder Children of Murdered Parents, Whittier, 1984, Coalition of Orgns. and People, Whittier, 1984, Whistle, Ltd., Whittier, 1984; chpt. leader Parents of Murdered Children, Whittier. Mem. Calif. Tchrs. Assn., NEA, Whittier C. of C. (ambassador). Republican. Episcopalian. Avocation: volunteer worker. Office: PO Box 9302 Whittier CA 90608

DAVIS, CONNIE E., nurse, administrator; b. Klamath Falls, Oreg., Mar. 30, 1954; d. Gilbert Dean and Ruth Nadine (Hall) Davis. B.S. maxima cum laude in Nursing, U. Portland, Oreg., 1977; M.S. in Nursing, Loma Linda (Calif.) U., 1980. R.N. Calif., Oreg. Charge nurse intensive treatment Kellogg Psychiat. Hosp., Corona, Calif., 1977-78; staff nurse psychiat. dept. St. Antonio Community Hosp., Upland, Calif., 1978-79, head nurse psychiatric adult unit St. Mary's Hosp-McAuley, San Francisco, 1979; charge nurse So. Humbold Dist. Hosp., Gaberville, Calif., 1979-80; intensive coronary care nurse Redwood Meml. Hosp., Fortana, Calif., 1980-81; instr. nursing Central Oreg. Community Coll., Bend Oreg., 1981-84; nursing supr. Alta Vista Chem. Dependency Recovery Hosp., Bakersfield, Calif., 1984—; trainer, crises counselor Central Oreg. Battering, Rape orgn., Bend, Oreg., 1983; crises counselor Central Oreg. Crises Service, Bend, 1983. Recipient Pres.'s Award U. Portland, 1977. Mem. Oreg. Council Assoc. Degree Programs (bd. dirs. exec. com. treas. 1983-84), Kern R.N. Soc. Republican. Home: 4700 Nordic Dr #G Bakersfield CA 93309 Office: Alta Vista Chem Dependency Recovery Hosp Bakersfield CA 93309

DAVIS, CONNIE WATERS, public relations and marketing executive, fashion consultant; b. Gainesville, Ga., July 3, 1948; d. Starling Randolph and Evelyn Jeanette (Bonds) Waters; m. John W. Davis, Jr., Sept. 24, 1971; 1 son, John Christopher. A.A., Gainesville Jr. Coll., 1968; student Evaluation Inst. of Washington, 1970, Brenau Coll., 1972, U. Ga., 1972-73, 1985—. Project evaluator Model Cities Program, Gainesville, 1970-74; personnel dir. Lanier Park Hosp., Gainesville, 1977-79; asst. dir. Ga. Mountains Ctr., Gainesville, 1979-83; owner, chief exec. officer Models by Davis and Davis, Gainesville, 1979—; dir. pub. relations and sales Ramada Hotel, Gainesville, 1985—; dir. Fashion Works, Gainesville. Contbr. articles to mags. and newsletters. Publicity chmn. Cancer Soc., 1982, 83, 85, Heart Assn., 1984; mem. Theatre Wings and Arts Council; bd. dirs., mem. mktg. com. Gainesville Jr. Coll., 1985—; bd. dirs. ARC, 1978-79. Recipient Peach award Lions Club, 1979; Vol. award ARC, 1978; various modeling awards So. Models Assn., 1983; named Best Dressed Woman, Fashion Tour Group, 1984. Mem. Gainesville C. of C., Tourism & Conv. Bur. (chmn. 1983-84), Northeast Ga. Advt. Club, Personnel Adminstrs. Group, Ga. Hospitality and Travel Assn., Phoenix Soc., Beta Sigma Phi. Democrat. Baptist. Club: Fashion (bd. dirs.). Avocations: exercising; skiing; boating; jogging; writing. Home: 1085 Longview Dr Gainesville GA 30501 Office: Ramada Hotel PO Box 2176 Gainesville GA 30503 and Models by Davis & Davis Inc PO Box 2635 Gainesville GA 30503

DAVIS, CORALIE GUARINO, librarian; b. New Orleans, Nov. 13, 1926; d. Anthony and Florence Olivia (Ducros) Guarino; m. George Warren Davis, Jr., June 13, 1953 (dec. 1966); 1 son, Mark Jefferson. B.F.A., Tulane U., 1947; M.Ed., U. New Orleans, 1975; M.L.S., La. State U., 1980. Library asst. New Orleans Pub. Library, 1949-50; draftsman Shell Oil Co., New Orleans, 1950-54; library asst., then librarian U. New Orleans, 1967—. Author: Index to New Orleans Magazine, 1982; (pamphlet) Selected Bibliography of Works of James Dakin, 1981; (pamphlet) Folk Architecture of Louisiana, a Selected Bibliography. Contbr. articles to profl. jour. Treas. Chalmette Nat. Hist. Park Assn., New Orleans, 1978—; corr. sec. Geneal. Research Soc. New Orleans, 1983-84; treas. La. Colonials (Founders chpt.), New Orleans, 1977-79, bd. dirs., chmn. La. history award, 1984—; mem. New Orleans Mus. Art; treas. Friends of U. New Orleans Library, 1977—. Mem. La. Hist. Soc., St. Bernard Hist. Soc., La. Landmarks Soc., Friends of Cabildo, Dames of Ct. of Honor La., Am. Legion Aux., Descs. of Founders of New Orleans, Tulane Alumni Assn., Newcomb Alumni Assn., U. New Orleans Alumni Assn., U.S. Daus. of 1812 (hon. v.p. nat. life 1981—, pres. Officers Nat. Club 1981-84, nat. historian 1979-81, 1st v.p. nat. 1976-79, chmn. nat. jr. membership 1973-76, nat. chmn. pub. relations 1970-73), La. State Soc. Daus. of 1812 (pres. 1971-73, registrar 1960-83), DAR (treas. Spirit of '76 chpt. 1974-76), Phi Kappa Phi, Phi Delta Kappa, Beta Phi Mu. Democrat. Roman Catholic. Home: 5030 Touro St New Orleans LA 70122 Office: U New Orleans Library Lakefront Dr New Orleans LA 70148

DAVIS, CYNTHIA GAIL, physician, naval officer; b. Cleve., Jan. 13, 1956; d. Donald B. and Joyce (Walters) Robertson; m. Martin Alex Davis, Apr. 10, 1980. B.A., UCLA, 1978; M.D., Uniformed Services U., 1982. Commd. ensign U.S. Navy, 1978, advanced through grades to lt., 1982; staff physician Br. Hosp., U.S. Marine Corps, Twenty Nine Palms, Calif., 1983-84; med./surg. intern U.S. Naval Hosp., San Diego, 1982-83, postdoctoral tng. in head and neck surgery, 1984—; med. officer Clinic/Hdqrs. Bn., U.S. Marine Corps Air Ground Combat Ctr., 1983-84; organizer, com. mem. biology of cancer program UCLA, 1978; vol. Cystic Fibrosis Clinic, UCLA, 1977-78. Latter Day Saints Hosp. research fellow, 1977. Mem. AMA, Assn. Mil. Surgeons U.S., Am. Acad. Otolaryngology, Am. Acad. Facial Plastic and Reconstructive Surgery, Alpha Phi. Democrat. Presbyterian. Home: 2377 Ron Way San Diego CA 92123 Office: Dept Otolaryngology US Naval Hosp San Diego CA 92134

DAVIS, DAISY SIDNEY, educator; b. Bay City, Tex., Nov. 7, 1944; d. Alex. C. and Alice M. (Edison) Sidney; m. John Dee Davis, Apr. 17, 1968; children—Anaca Michelle, Lowell Kent. B.S., Bishop Coll., 1966; M.S., East Tex. State U., 1971; M. Ed., Prairie View Agrl. and Mech., 1980. Lifetime profl. tchr. cert., Tex., 1979. Tchr., Dallas pub. schs., 1966—. Coordinator, Get Out the Vote campaign, Dallas, 1972, 1980-1984. Recipient Outstanding Tchr. award Dallas pub. schs., 1980; Jack Lowe award for ednl. excellence, 1982; named to Hall of Fame, Holmes Acad., 1979. Mem. NEA, Tex. State Tchrs. Assn., Classroom Tchrs. Dallas (faculty rep. 1971-77), Dallas County History Tchrs., Afro-Am. Daus. Republic of Tex. (founder), Zeta Phi Beta. Democrat. Baptist. Club: Jack & Jill, (Dallas). Home: 1302 Mill Stream Dr Dallas TX 75232 Office: 4747 Veterans Dr Dallas TX 75216

DAVIS, DEBORAH LEIGH, nurse; b. Washington, Feb. 11, 1951; d. Clifford Davis and Ruth Anne (Werber) Davis Murphy; m. Louis William Solomon, May 31, 1978 (div.). B.S.N., Emory U., 1973. Clin. instr. Md. Inst. Emergency Medicine, Balt., 1976-81; field nurse Med. Personnel Pool, Balt., 1982—, clin. dir. Nurse Bank, Homecare div., 1984—. Home: 3521 Meadowside Rd Baltimore MD 21207

DAVIS, DIANNE JAMES, lawyer; b. Montgomery, Ala., Nov. 24, 1953; d. Wilbur Lowery and Ruth (Tucker) James; m. Timothy Bledsoe Davis, Jan. 19, 1980. B.A., Huntingdon U., 1976; M.B.A., Auburn U., 1978; J.D., Jones Law Inst., 1981. Bar: Ala. 1982. Practice Law, Alexander City, Ala., 1982—. Mem. ABA, Assn. Trial Lawyers Am., Ala. Bar Assn., Ala. Assn. Criminal Lawyers, Pi Sigma Alpha. Home: 212 Clubview Dr Alexander City AL 35010 Office: PO Box 823 Alexander City AL 35010

DAVIS, DORINNE SUE TAYLOR LOVAS, audiologist; b. East Orange, N.J., Mar. 29, 1949; d. William Henry and Evelyn Doris (Thorp) Taylor; B.A., Montclair State Coll., 1971, M.A., 1973; m. Warren B. Davis, Jr., Aug. 10, 1985; children—Larissa Louise, Peter Alexander. Ednl. audiologist Morris County Coll., Dover, N.J., 1974-75, Kinnelon (N.J.) Bd. Edn., 1972—, Inst. for Career Advancement, Inc., 1980-82, Dover Gen. Hosp., 1984—. Cert. tchr. of hearing impaired, speech correctionist, tchr. speech and drama N.J. Dept. Edn.; nursery sch. endorsement. Mem. Am. Speech and Hearing Assn. (cert. of clin. competence in audiology), N.J. Speech and Hearing Assn., Morris County Speech and Hearing Assn., NEA, N.J. Edn. Assn., Morris County Edn. Assn., Kinnelon Edn. Assn., Self Help for the Hard of Hearing, Ednl. Audiology Assn. (pres. elect). Methodist. Home: 4 Musconetcong Ave Stanhope NJ 07874 Office: Spl Services Kinnelon Bd Edn Kiel Ave Kinnelon NJ 07405

DAVIS, DOROTHY COMSTOCK, civic worker; b. West Hartford, Conn., Sept. 25, 1913; d. John Chenevard and Gladys Nell (Kibbe) Comstock; m. George W. Davis, Feb. 10, 1934 (dec. 1964); 1 child, John C. Student Larson Secretarial Sch., 1932. Br. sec. Society for Savings, Hartford, 1959-76; mem. adv. bd. New England Bank and Trust Co., Enfield, Conn.; justice of peace, 1973—, notary public, 1963—. Treas. Somers Hist. Soc., 1964—; hon. mem. Republican Town Com., Somers, 1981, mem. 1964-81, past sec., past vice chmn.; mem., sec. Somers Bd. Edn., 1943-47; corporator Johnson Meml. Hosp., Stafford Springs, Conn., 1973-78, trustee, exec. bd. dirs., 1978—, treas. exec. bd., 1979-80, v.p. exec. bd. 1980-82, pres. exec. bd. 1982-83. Congregationalist. Avocations: interior decorating; traveling. Home: 73 Plymouth Rd Somers CT 06071

DAVIS, EDNA PAULINE, educational administrator, educator; b. Houston, Jan. 23; d. Thomas Jefferson and Pinkie Clara (Vaughns) D. B.A., B.S., Tex. So. U., 1953, M.A. summa cum laude, 1960; Ed.D., Madison State U., 1977. Cert. tchr. Classroom tchr., Houston, 1955-84; asst. prin. Blackshear Sch., Houston, 1980—tchr. under-achievers, 1984—; cons. Xerox Corp., Zaner-Blaser Co. A founder 3d Ward Civic Club, Neighborhood Charity Club; active ARC, United Fund; pres. women's dept. S. Houston Dist. Church of God in Christ. Recipient Appreciation award Tex. So. U., 1979, Sam award Houston Ind. Sch. Dist., 1979. Mem. Nat. Tchrs. Assn., Tex. Tchrs. Assn., Houston Tchrs. Assn. (sec. 1972-75), YWCA (life), Sigma Gamma Rho, Alpha Kappa Mu. Democrat. Lodges: Eastern Star, Courts of Calanthe.

DAVIS, EDNA W., lawyer; b. Northridge, Calif., Aug. 7, 1958; d. Lawrence Emery and Joan Frances (Berry) D. A.B., Calif. State U.-Northridge, 1980; J.D., U. Calif.-San Francisco, 1983. Bar: Calif. 1983. Assoc. Horner, Gordon & Skelley, San Francisco, 1983—. Active local Democratic polit. campaigns. Mem. ALA, State Bar Calif., San Francisco Bar Assn., Nat. Assn. Women Attys., Mensa. Lutheran. Club: San Francisco Tennis. Address: Werik Complex 24 California St Room 312 San Francisco CA 94111

DAVIS, ELAINE RITA, data processor; b. Washington, Oct. 27, 1946; d. Sidney Lawrence Davidson and Lillian Leibovitch; B.S. in Math., U. Md., 1968; m. Edward A. Davis, Oct. 26, 1969. Systems engr. IBM, Arlington, Va., 1968-70; mgr. computer planning Irving Trust Co., N.Y.C., 1970-78; sr. mgmt. cons. Touche Ross & Co., C.P.A.s, Newark, 1978-81; mgr. tech. services Dell Pub. Co., Pine Brook, N.J., 1981—. Mem. Exec. Women N.J. (a founder, pres.), Nat. Council Jewish Women (dir.). Office: Dell Pub Co 6 Regent St Livingston NJ 07039

DAVIS, ELAINE ROLLINS, health facility adminstr.; b. Rome, Ga., Feb. 3, 1948; d. James R. and Doris M. Rollins; student, DeKalb Community Coll., 1972-74; children—Kelline, Robert, Tamara. With, Hirschfield & Assos., Atlanta, 1975-79; owner, pres. Am. Home Health Care of Ga., Inc., Decatur, 1979—; pres. Continuum of Care, Inc.; chmn. bd. dirs. Supplemental Staffing, Inc., Home Clin. Services, Inc., Provider Services, Inc., Provider Communications, Inc. Mem. Am. Fedn. Home Health Agencies, Ga. Assn. Home Health Agencies. Republican. Home: Route 3 Loganville GA 30249 Office: American Home Health Care of Georgia Inc 3250 Memorial Dr PO Box 36300 Decatur GA 30032

DAVIS, ELISE MILLER (MRS. LEO M. DAVIS), author; b. Corsicana, Tex., Oct. 12, 1915; d. Moses Myre and Rachelle (Daniels) Miller; student U. Tex., 1930-31; m. Jay Albert Davis, June 27, 1937 (dec. June 1973); 1 dau., Rayna Miller (Mrs. Michael Edwin Loeb); m. 2d, Leo M. Davis, Aug. 23, 1974. Freelance writer, 1945—; merchandiser and dir. Jay Davis, Inc., Amarillo, Tex., 1956-73; instr. mag. writing U. Tex., Dallas, 1978; lectr. creative writing Baylor U., Waco, Tex., 1980, 81, 83. Mem. Am. Soc. Journalists and Authors (bd. dirs. 1985—). Author: The Answer Is God, 1955; articles to periodicals including Reader's Digest, Woman's Day, Nation's Business, others. Home: 3906 Old Mill Rd Waco TX 76710

DAVIS, ELIZABETH ANN, city official; b. Kansas City, Mo., Jan. 16, 1941; d. Samuel Wyatt and Maurita Bell (Irick) Driggers, Jr.; m. Roy Edward Davis, Jr., July 1, 1957; children—Scott Edward, Catherine Elizabeth, Christopher Kelly, Sean Wyatt. Cert. mcpl. clk., Tex. Sec. First Nat. Bank, Fort Worth, 1966-69; office mgr. City of Luling, Tex., 1972-73; adminstrv. sec. State of Tex., Austin, 1973-74; office coordinator City of Arlington, Tex., 1974-77; city sec. City of Granbury, Tex., 1977-83, City of Bedford, Tex., 1983—; adv. mem. mcpl. records project Tex. State Library, Austin, 1984—. Mem. Assn. City Clks. and Secs. of Tex., Internat. Inst. Mcpl. Clks. (profl. status com., 1984—, fed. legis. com., 1985—; cert.), North Central Tex. City Secs. Assn. (sec. treas. 1985), Assn. City Clks. and Secs. of Tex. (chmn. resolutions com. 1984, retirement com. 1985), Tex. Assn. for Ct. Adminstrn. Republican. Methodist. Avocations: music; gardening; reading; tennis; cooking. Home: 7720 Aubrey Ln North Richland Hills TX 76180 Office: City of Bedford PO Box 157 Bedford TX 76021

DAVIS, ELIZABETH BROOKS, corporate executive; b. Bonham, Tex., May 25, 1953; d. James Walter and Ruth Alice (Borland) D. B.A., So. Meth. U., 1975; M.A., Georgetown U., 1977. Dir. personnel INSLAW, Inc., Washington, 1978—; adminstrv. officer PCI, Washington, 1977-78. Internat. outreach com. St. Alban's Episcopal Ch., Washington, 1980-82. Mem. Nat. Assn. Female Execs., AAUW, Am. Assn. Personnel Adminstrn., Mortar Bd. Democrat. Office: INSLAW Inc 1125 15th St NW Suite 600 Washington DC 20005

DAVIS, ELIZABETH EMILY LOUISE THORPE, visual psychophysicist; b. Grosse Pointe Farms, Mich., Aug. 11, 1948; d. Jack and Mary Alvina (McCarron) Thorpe; student U. Calif.-Irvine, 1966-69; B.S., U. Ala., 1972; M.A., Columbia U., 1975, M.Phil., 1976, Ph.D., 1979; m. Ronald Wilson Davis, May 16, 1969. Lectr. Am. Lit. and English composition Nei Ming Inst., Lamtin, Hong Kong, 1969-71; research fellow Columbia U., 1973-77; research assoc., N.Y.U., 1979-81, adj. asst. prof., 1981; prof. exptl. psychology Oberlin (Ohio) Coll., 1981-82; research asst. prof., mem. grad. faculty SUNY Coll. Optometry, 1983—. Recipient Nat. Research Services award; fellow Hertz Found., 1983; NIH grantee, 1979-81, 84—; grantee Sigma Xi, 1979, Oberlin Coll., 1981. Mem. AAAS, Am. Psychol. Assn., Assn. Research Vision and Ophthalmology, Soc. Neurosci., Optical Soc. Am., N.Y. Acad. Scis., Sigma Xi, Pi Mu Epsilon. Author papers in field. Office: SUNY Coll Optometry 100 E 24th St New York NY 10010

DAVIS, ELIZABETH STOUT, retired educator, writer; b. Salem, Ind., Mar. 12, 1907; d. Arthur Lindley and Bettye Collier (Wilson) Stout; m. James Brown Davis, Nov. 14, 1931 (dec. 1977); 1 child, Elizabeth Jane. Student Ogontz Jr. Coll., 1922-26. Mem. staff, reporter Fortune mag., N.Y.C., 1929-32; pres. Mary & Alexander Laughlin Children's Ctr., Sewickley, Pa., 1955-58. Author: (poems) Excuse for Singing, 1951. Pres. Allegheny County Garden Club, Pitts., 1962-64, regent Kenmore Nat. Shrine, Fredericksburg, Va., 1972—. Recipient citation ARC, 1943-46. Mem. Nat. Soc. Colonial Dames (chmn. Pitts. com.). Republican. Episcopalian. Club: Naples Yacht. Home: 1900 Gulf Shore Blvd N Apt 506 Naples FL 33940

DAVIS, ELLA JEAN, English educator, educational consultant; b. Lake, Miss., Mar. 30, 1949; d. Aaron Norris and Ora Lee (Riley) Mayers; m. Wade K. Davis, Sept. 7, 1974; children—Devin, Aqua-Raven, Kinton. B.S. in Speech/English, Jackson State U., 1971; M.A. in Speech Communication, Wayne State U., 1973, M.A. in English, 1977. Cert. tchr., Mich. Tchr., Detroit Inst. Tech., 1974-80; tchr., Wayne County Community Coll., Detroit, 1973—; dir. programs, sr. pub. and community relations specialist Wayne State U., 1980—; cons. Creative Ednl. Concepts, Detroit, 1978—, Lang. and Learning Program, N.Y.C., 1981-83. Mem. Women's Conf. of Concern, Detroit, 1985. Fellow U. Mich., 1985, Wayne State U., 1986. Mem. Nat. Council Tchrs. English, Nat. Council Black Studies, Mich. Coll. English Assn., Zeta Phi Beta. Democrat. Congregationalist. Club: Top Ladies of Distinction. Office: Ctr for Black Studies Wayne State Univ Detroit MI 48202

DAVIS, ELLEN BEAR, cultural and education institution executive; b. Orlando, Fla., Sept. 20, 1944; d. Gustave Samuel and Corene (Berman) Bear; m. Peter Davis, Jan. 7, 1967; children—Andrew Scott, Jonathan Michael. B.A., Smith Coll., 1965; M.S., London Sch. Econs., 1966. Dir. student tchr. activities World Affairs Council, Phila., 1967-70; sr. author Mexican Nat. Textbooks, Mexico City, 1971-75; program dir. Internat. House of Phila., 1976-80, v.p., 1980-81, pres., 1981—. Trustee Greater Phila. Cultural Assn., West Phila. Partnership, West Phila. C. of C. Home: 508 Manor Rd Wynnewood PA 19096

DAVIS, EVELYN MARGUERITE B., educator; b. Springfield, Mo.; d. Philip Edward and Della Jane (Morris) Bailey; student public schs., Springfield; m. James Harvey Davis, Sept. 22, 1946. Bible tchr., pianist East Ave. Bapt. Ch., Springfield, Mo., 1934-46; tchr., Bible, organist, pianist, vocal soloist and dir. youth choir Bible Bapt. Ch., Maplewood, Mo., 1956-69; pvt. instr. piano and organ, Affton, Mo., 1960-71, St. Charles, Mo., 1971—; Bible instr. 3d Bapt. Ch., St. Louis, 1948-54; pianist, soloist, Bible tchr. Temple Bapt. Ch., Kirkwood, Mo., 1969-71; dir. youth orch., music arranger, organist, pianist, vocal soloist, tchr. Bible, Bible Bapt. Ch., St. Charles, Mo., 1971-78, Faith Missionary Bapt. Ch., 1978-82; asst. organist-pianist, vocal soloist, tchr. Bible, Bible Ch., Arnold, Mo., 1969—, also harpist and composer; organist, vocal soloist, floral arranger Bellview Bapt. Ch., Springfield, 1984—; faculty St. Charles Bible Bapt. Christian Sch., 1976-77; interior decorator and floral arranger; tchr. piano-organ, voice. Fellow Am. Biog. Assn. (life); mem. Am. Guild Organists, Nat. Guild Piano Tchrs., Internat. Platform Assn. Executed mural in oils Bible Bapt. Ch., Maplewood (now in Arnold, Mo. Bible Ch.); composer cantata, psalms, other sacred works. Home: RFD 2 Box 405 Rogersville MO 65742

DAVIS, FRANCES M., lawyer, corp. exec.; b. 1925; grad. U. Calif., Los Angeles, 1946; J.D., U. Calif., Berkeley, 1953. Partner firm LeProhn & LeProhn, 1960-67; asst. dean Earl Warren Legal Center, Calif. Coll. Trial Judges, 1968-72; assoc. firm Pillsbury, Madison & Sutro, 1972-75; v.p., gen. counsel Potlatch Corp., San Francisco, 1975—. Bd. overseers U. Calif., San Francisco; mem. adv. bd. KOIT, San Francisco. Office: Potlatch Corp 1 Maritime Plaza PO Box 3591 San Francisco CA 94119

DAVIS, HARRIET PARMENTER, brokerage account executive; b. Ipswich, Mass., Mar. 27, 1942; d. Charles William and Marjorie Alice (Parmenter) D.; A.B., Wheaton Coll., Norton, Mass., 1963; student Sweet Briar Coll. Jr. Yr. in France, 1961-62; M.A., Boston U., 1967; M.B.A., Simmons Coll., 1975. Instr. French, Chamberlayne Jr. Coll., Boston, 1967-71; research asso. Boston Globe, 1973-74; sr. fin. cons., tax shelter specialist Merrill Lynch, Pierce, Fenner & Smith, Boston, 1976—. Steering com. Wheaton Coll. Ann. Fund; trustee Cambridge (Mass.) YWCA. Mem. Boston Stockbrokers Club. Republican. Episcopalian. Club: Myopia Hunt. Home: 19 Chauncy St Cambridge MA 02138 Office: Merrill Lynch Copley Pl Boston MA 02116

DAVIS, HELEN GORDON, state legislator; b. N.Y.C., Dec. 25; d. Harry Gordon and Doree Gordon; B.A., Bklyn. Coll.; postgrad. U. South Fla., 1967-70; m. Gene Davis; children—Stephanie, Karen, Gordon. Tchr., High Sch. Commerce, N.Y.C., Hillsborough High Sch., Tampa, Fla.; grad. asst. U. South Fla., 1968; mem. Fla. Ho. of Reps., 1974—, vice chmn. appropriations com., chmn. state employee pay and benefits com. Jud. chmn. Local Govt. Study Commn. Hillsborough County (Fla.), 1964; mem. Tampa Commn. on Juvenile Delinquency, 1966-69, Mayor's Citizens Adv. Com., 1966-69, Quality Edn. Commn., 1966-68, Gov.'s Citizen Com. for Ct. Reform, 1972, Hillsborough County Planning Commn., 1973-74; mem. Gov.'s Commn. on Jud. Reform, 1976; mem. employment com. Commn. Community Relations, 1966-69; by-laws chmn. Arts Council Tampa, 1971-74; 1st v.p. Tampa Symphony Guild, 1974; bd. dirs. U. South Fla. Found., 1968-74, Stop Rape, 1973-74; founder Women's Survival Center, Tampa, 1978. Recipient U. South Fla. Young Democrats Humanitarian award, 1974; Diana award NOW, 1975; Woman of Achievement in Arts award Tampa, 1975; Tampa Human Relations award, 1976; Hannah G. Solomon Citizen of Yr. award, 1980; St. Petersburg Times/Fla. Civil Liberties award, 1980. Mem. LWV (pres. Hillsborough County 1966-69, lobbyist, Fla. adminstrn. of justice chmn. 1969-74), PTA (past pres.), Temple Guild Sisterhood (past pres.), Am. Arbitration Assn. Home: 45 Adalia Ave Tampa FL 33606 Office: 178 E Davis Blvd Tampa FL 33602

DAVIS, HELEN NANCY MATSON (MRS. CHAUNCEY D. DAVIS), real estate broker, civic worker; b. Zanesville, Ohio, Nov. 18, 1905; d. Austin F. and Georgianna (Hale) Matson; grad. high sch.; m. Chauncey D. Davis, May 1, 1924; children—James Harvey, Robert Lee. Real estate broker, South Bend, Wash., 1964—. Exec. sec. Pacific County Tb League, 1936-62; chmn. Park Bd., South Bend, 1955—; ofcl. Pacific County Bicentennial Pageant; trustee Pacific County Hist. Soc. Named Woman of Yr. Pacific County C. of C., 1949, 61. Mem. Nat. League Am. Pen Women, Dramatists Guild Inc., Propaelaeum Study Club, Chinook Indian Tribe (hon.), Delta Kappa Gamma. Republican. Methodist. Rebekah. Club: Garden (South Bend). Composer: Washington, My Home (ofcl. state song Wash.), 1959; Eliza and the Lumberjack (mus. play). Home: 606 W 2d St South Bend WA 98586 Office: 705 Robert Bush Dr South Bend WA 98586

DAVIS, JACQUELINE MARIE VINCENT (MRS. LOUIS REID DAVIS), educator; b. Birmingham, Ala.; d. Jud Fred and Marie (Yates) Vincent; A.B. cum laude, Birmingham-So. Coll., 1943; M.A., Columbia U., 1950; M.S., U. Ala., 1958, Ed.D., 1961; postgrad. U. Va., George Washington U.; m. Louis Reid Davis, July 17, 1943. Tchr., Fork Union (Va.) Mil. Acad., 1943-46, Ft. Belvoir, Va., 1946-48; tchr., adminstrv. asst., supr. Quantico (Va.) Post Schs., 1950-52; instr., prof. dept. child devel. and family life U. Ala. Sch. Home Econs., 1952-57, asso. prof., 1957-67, prof. child devel., dir. Child Devel. Center, 1967—, mem. grad. council, adminstr. head start tng. program; dir. Ala. Presch. Inst., 1964—; mem. NASA scholarship selection bd. U. Ala., 1966; mem. Gov.'s Adv. Com. on Day Care, 1963-66; mem. State Adv. Com. on Children and Youth, 1960—; coordinator Head Start supplementary tng. programs State of Ala. Adviser, mem. selection com. Tombigbee council Girl Scouts U.S.A., 1961-66; cons. Tuscaloosa Community Action Program, 1965-66. Mem. Nat. Assn. Edn. of Young Children (planning bd. 1963-64), U.S. Nat. Com. Early Childhood Edn., World Orgn. Early Childhood Edn., Southeastern Council Family Relations, So. (pres. 1961, mem. exec. bd. 1961—, chmn. 19th ann. conf.), Ala. (pres. 1963-64) assns. children under six, Ala. Home Econs. Assn. (chmn. profl. sect. family life and child devel. 1963—, v.p., mem. governing bd. 1969-70), Comparative Edn. Soc., NEA, Am. Home Econs. Assn., Phi Beta Kappa, Kappa Delta Pi, Kappa Delta Epsilon. Methodist. Contbr. articles to profl. jours. Home: 47 Guilds Wood Tuscaloosa AL 35401 Office: PO Box 1211 University AL 35486

DAVIS, JAN, former educator; b. Corpus Christi, Tex., June 29, 1943; d. Reuben T. and Ruby (Englert) Pattillo; A.A., Del Mar Coll., 1963; B.A., U. Houston, 1965; teaching cert. S.W. Tex. State U., 1971; m. William A. Davis, Dec. 26, 1964; children—William A., Wade. Tchr., Edna (Tex.) Jr. High Sch., 1966-67, counselor, 1967-68; tchr. Pleasanton (Tex.) High Sch., 1972-85; mem. Pleasanton Public Schs. Supt.'s Com., 1975-77, 78-79; chmn. social studies dept. Pleasanton Public Schs., 1976-85. Leader 4-H, 1978—. Mem. Tex. Classroom Tchrs. Assn. (Tchr. of Year 1979), Pleasanton Classroom Tchrs. Assn. Roman Catholic. Clubs: Pleasanton Jr. Woman's (1st v.p. 1976, pres. 1977), A&M Women's of Atascosa County (Tex.) (pres. 1978-80). Home: 112 Tallwood Dr Georgetown TX 78628

DAVIS, JANICE MARIE, secretary, staff administrator; b. Atlantic, Va., Feb. 22, 1956; d. Robert and Helen Shirley (Harmon) D.; B.S., Del. State Coll., Dover, 1978. Legal sec. firm Dell, Craighill, Fentress & Benton, Washington, 1980; staff adminstr. MCI Telecommunications, Sherman Oaks, Calif., 1980—. Mem. NAACP. Democrat. Baptist. Avocations: reading, tennis, biking, bowling. Home: 17808 Sherman Way Apt 313 Reseda CA 91335 Office: MCI Telecommunications Corp 15303 Ventura Blvd Suite 300 Sherman Oaks CA 91403

DAVIS, JOANNE HERRING, foreign service officer, consultant; b. San Antonio; d. W. Dunlap and Maelan McGill (Johnson); m. Robert R. Herring (dec.); children—Beau S. King, Robin D. King, Ed., U. Tex. TV talk show hostess, editor Sta. KHOU TV, Houston, 1963-72, Sta. KPRC-TV, Houston, 1973-75; hon. consul gen. Pakistan and Morocco, Houston, 1973—; cons. LTV, WEDTECH, CONTRAVES; bd. dirs. First Bank Houston, Coronado Oil Co., Kittinger Furniture, Internat. Films Prodns. Inc.; hostess numerous fgn. ministers, princes, ambassadors including Kings of Sweden, Jordan, Morocco, Pres. of Egypt, Pres. of Pakistan, Shah of Iran, Prime Minister of Belgium, Houston. Knighted, King of Belgium; Decorated, Pres. Pakistan. Bd. dirs. Lindbergh Fund, Moroccan Am. Found., Houston Ballet, Houston Youth Symphony. Republican. Presbyterian. Clubs: Lyford Cay; Met. (N.Y.C.); Rivers Oaks Country, Ramada, Houston.

DAVIS, JOSEPHINE FRANCES, nurse; b. Fort Sill, Okla., Nov. 15, 1946; d. Josephine (James) King; m. Theodore Davis, Nov. 17, 1979; 1 child, Jennifer. Student Hampton Inst., Va., 1964-65, Northeastern U., 1968. R.N., Mass. Mgr. Central Sterile Supply Lahey Clinic Med. Ctr., Burlington, Mass., 1979-81; mgr. central processing dept. New Eng. Med. Ctr., Boston, 1981-83; asst. dir. materials mgmt. Cedars Sinai Med Ctr., Los Angeles, 1983-84; nurse cons. Pilling Co., Ft. Washington, Pa., 1981—; bd. dirs. Dimock Vocat. Health Program, Boston, 1983. Contbr. articles to profl. jours. Mem. Assn. Operating Room Nurses, Am. Hosp. Assn. Central Supply Personnel, Internat. Assn. Central Supply Mgmt., Health Care Material Mgmt. Soc. Democrat. Episcopalian. Avocations: sewing; painting; aerobics. Office: Cedars Sinai Med Ctr 8700 Beverly Blvd Los Angeles CA 90048

DAVIS, JOYCE CORALIE, manufacturing company executive; b. N.Y.C., Jan. 7, 1925; d. Samuel Stanley and Florence Lenore (Hay) D.; B.A. in Bus. Adminstrn., St. John's U., Jamaica, N.Y., 1946; postgrad. Katherine Gibbs Sch.; m. Paul L. Roberts, Oct. 5, 1966 (div. 1979); children—Paula Lenore, Bruce Linwood, Valerie Elizabeth. Sec., St. Philip's Episcopal Ch., N.Y.C., 1946-57; with Union Carbide Corp., 1958—, mgr. office and clerical staff, chems. and plastics div., N.Y.C., 1973-76, mgr. profl. recruiting, EEO, agrl. products div., 1976, mgr. compensation, 1976—. Mem. Corp. Women's Network, Assn. Female Execs., Nat. Assn. Negro Women, Gamma Phi Delta (past chpt. pres.). Democrat. Episcopalian. Office: Union Carbide Corp Old Ridgebury Rd Danbury CT 06817

DAVIS, JOYCE LUAYNE, educator of mentally retarded; b. Vallejo, Calif., Oct. 5, 1918; d. Wayne Ignatius and Lucy Dow (Brewer) Weeks; m. James Lowell Davis, Jan. 3, 1948 (div. Jan. 1963); children—Jessica, Jeffrey, Jill, Jan. Student San Francisco Jr. Coll., 1935-37; B.A. in Psychology, U. Calif.-Berkeley, 1940; postgrad. in spl. edn. San Francisco State U., 1948-49. Accredited adult edn. tchr., Calif. Dir., co-founder Lucinda Weeks Sch. for Handicapped Children, San Francisco, 1938-68; dir. Hoberg's Sugar Pine Ranch and Sch., Cobb, Calif., 1972-74; Galassi Residential Care Home, Finley, Calif., 1974-76; dir. Lucinda Weeks Opportunity House, Lakeport, Calif., 1976-84, qualified mental retardation profl., 1984—; co-founder Advs. for Ind. Living, 1980; founder Weeks/Davis, Inc., 1983. Home: 2520 Hartley Rd Lakeport CA 95453 Office: Lucinda Weeks Opportunity House 2520 Hartley Rd Lakeport CA 95453

DAVIS, JUNE FIKSDAL, recovery centre administrator, designer; b. Alexandria, Minn., June 18, 1944; d. Mads and Gladys Lillian Katherine (Engstrom) Fiksdal; m. Merrill Nathaniel Davis III, June 20, 1971; adopted children—Kim Geoffrey, Marc Lee. Cert. with highest honors, Am. Sch. Floral Arts, Chgo., 1965. Floral designer Fiksdal Flowers, Rochester, Minn., 1960-70; prin. floral designer, nat. design tchr. Retail Florists, Kansas City, Mo., also Houston, 1970-81; pres. owner, founder The Gables Found., Inc., Rochester, 1982—; floral designer, 1981—. Author: Floral Design (Am. Inst. Floral Design award 1974), 1973. Cellist Rochester Symphony Orch., 1960-69; bd. dirs., fin. planner United Way, 1974; real estate placement Riverplace Devel., 1980; bd. dirs. Rochester Ballet, 1975; mem. Rochester PTA; chair Symphony Ball, Rochester Symphony, 1975; coordinator music program, new pipe organ, harpsichord Unitarian Ch., 1975-81 (Outstanding Service award 1977), project pres. Walden Hill Bach Soc., 1975-82. Mem. Am. Inst. Floral Design, Bus. and Profl. Women, P.E.O. Avocations: gourmet cooking, water sports, winter sports, skiing, European travel, camping, music. Office: Gables Found Inc 300 3d Ave SE Rochester MN 55904

DAVIS, JUNE WATKINS, advertising executive; b. Anchorage, Alaska, Apr. 18, 1953; d. Donald Spencely and Martha Ruth (Smith) Watkins; m. Paul Edwin Davis, Aug. 11, 1984. B.A., U. W. Fla., 1980. Agt., Northwestern Mut. Co., Pensacola, 1978-80; account exec. WEAR TV, Pensacola, 1980-82; account asst. E.W. Bullock Mktg. Co., Pensacola, 1982-83; media dir., 1983-84; v.p., ptnr. Bullock Watkins Assocs., 1984—. DuPont Found. scholar, 1978-79. Mem. W. Fla. Advt. Council, Am. Assn. Advt. Agys., C. of C. Pensacola, W. Fla. Advt. Council (bd. dirs. 1983-84; v.p. 1985—), Phi Theta Kappa, Alpha Mu Gamma, Am. Advt. Fedn. (chmn. Addy awards Pensacola 1985). Republican. Episcopalian. Avocations: travel; banjo. Office: Bullock Watkins Assocs Mktg Communications Inc 730 Bayfront Pkwy Suite V Pensacola FL 32501

DAVIS, KAREN PADGETT, economist, educator; b. Blackwell, Okla., Nov. 14, 1942; d. Walter Dwight and Thelma Louise (Kohler) Padgett; B.A. (Univ. fellow), Rice U., 1965, Ph.D., 1969; 1 child, Kelly Denise. Asst. prof. econs. Rice U., 1969-70; econ. policy fellow Social Security Adminstrn. at Brookings Instn., Washington, 1970-71, research asso. Brookings Instn., 1971-74, sr. fellow, 1974-77; dep. asst. sec. for planning and evaluation/health HEW, Washington, 1977-80; adminstr. health resources adminstrn. USPHS, 1980-81; prof. Johns Hopkins U., 1981—; chmn., 1983—; vis. lectr. Harvard U., 1974-75. Recipient John W. Gardner dissertation award Rice U., 1969. Mem. Inst. Medicine, Am. Econs. Assn., Phi Beta Kappa. Author: National Health Insurance: Benefits, Costs and Consequences, 1975; Health and the War on Poverty, 1978; Medicare Policy: New Directions for Health and Long-Term Care, 1986; asso. editor Milbank Meml. Fund Quar., Health and Soc., 1972-77. Home: 10537 Farnham Dr Bethesda MD 20814 Office: Johns Hopkins U Sch Hygiene and Public Health Dept Health Policy and Mgmt 624 N Broadway Baltimore MD 21205

DAVIS, KATHLEEN VIRGINIA VIRGILIO, college administrator; b. Camden, N.J., Mar. 3, 1950; d. Nicholas James Virgilio and Concetta Virginia (Startare) Virgilio Biebel; m. James Gordon Davis, Aug. 13, 1977. B.S., St. Francis Coll., 1972; M.A., Glassboro State Coll., 1981. Tchr., Camden City pub. schs., 1972-81; asst. dean continuing edn. Orangeburg Calhoun Tech. Coll., S.C., 1981-84; job. tng. div. coordinator Orangeburg Calhoun Tech. Coll., 1984—. Mem. Orangeburg C. of C., Am. Assn. Women in Community and Jr. Colls., S.C. Tech. Edn. Assn., S.C. Network Women in Higher Edn. Adminstrn. Republican. Roman Catholic. Home: 3129 Landing Way Orangeburg SC 29115 Office: Orangeburg Calhoun Tech Coll 3250 St Matthews Rd NE Orangeburg SC 29115

DAVIS, LAURA ARLENE, foundation administrator; b. Battle Creek, Mich., Apr. 14, 1935; d. Paul Bennett and Daisy E. (Coston) Borgard; m. John R. Davis, Aug. 7, 1955; children—Scott Judson, Cynthia Ann Davis Welker. B.S., Central Mich. U., 1986. Sec., Mich. Loan Co., Battle Creek, 1952-56; legal sec. Ryan, Sullivan & Hamilton, Battle Creek, 1957-64; exec. sec. W.K. Kellogg Found., Battle Creek, 1965-76, adminstrn./program asst., 1976, fellowship dir., 1977, asst. v.p. adminstrn., asst. corp. sec., 1978-84; v.p. adminstrn., corp. sec., 1984—. Mem. word processing adv. com. Kellogg Community Coll., Battle Creek, 1982—; v.p. bd. dirs. State Tech. Inst. and Rehab. Ctr., Delton, Mich., 1983-84; pres. bd. dirs. Charitable Union, Battle Creek, 1983-85; mem. allocations panel United Way of Battle Creek, 1983; trustee Binder Park 200. Mem. Adminstrv. Mgmt. Soc. (pres. chpt. 1982-83), Soc. Office Automation Profls., Am. Mgmt. Assn. Home: 131 Hanson Dr Battle Creek MI 49017 Office: WK Kellogg Foundation 400 North Ave Battle Creek MI 49016

DAVIS, LORRAINE JENSEN, magazine editor; b. Omaha, Apr. 2, 1924; d. Theron R. and L. Mildred (Henkel) Jensen; B.A., U. Denver, 1946; m. Richard Morris Davis, Apr. 4, 1959; 1 dau., Laura Jensen. Copywriter, Glamour mag., N.Y.C., 1946-54, prodn. editor, 1954-61; prodn. editor Vogue Children mag., N.Y.C., 1963-66; writer, assoc. features editor Vogue mag., N.Y.C., 1966-77, mng. editor, writer women's news column, 1977—; editor Vogue Living and Food Guide, 1975, editorial cons. Vogue Beauty and Health Guide, 1979-81. Recipient Disting. Citizen award Alpha Gamma Delta, 1981. Mem. NOW, Am. Soc. Mag. Editors. Democrat. Episcopalian. Editor: Cooking with Colette (by Colette Rossant), 1975; Fairchild Dictionary of Fashion (by Charlotte Calasibetta), 1975; English translation Paul Bocuse's French Cooking, 1977. Home: 425 E 63d St W3J New York NY 10021 Office: Vogue 350 Madison Ave New York NY 10017

DAVIS, LOUISE SPIERS, educator; b. Malden, Mass., Jan. 11, 1911; d. Thomas H. and Elizabeth (Sullivan) Spiers; m. Frank L. Davis, June 24, 1939 (dec. Oct. 1952); children—Elizabeth Davis Littleton, Jane F. Davis-Gavin. A.B., Boston U., 1932, M.A., 1965; Ed.M., Tufts U., 1962; student U. London, 1966, Goldsmith Coll. London, 1966. Cert. secondary tchr., Mass. Tchr., Malden Pub. Schs., Mass., 1932-39; with Bedford Pub. Schs., 1953-73, tchr. emeritus, cons., 1973—; tchr. adult edn. program Hanscom AFB, Bedford, Mass., 1973-84; lectr., cons. in field; mem. Mass. Dept. Edn. Nat. Council Social Studies, 1960-73; Mass. rep. Nat. Educators Conf. on Fgn. Policy, Dept. of State, Washington, 1967; Author pamplet; contbr. articles to profl. jours. Editor: Mass. Industry, 1966-67. Demonstration tchr., lectr. Newsweek Mag., 1970-73. Co-chmn. Bedford Democratic Town Com., 1976-78, coordinator, 1972-84, assoc. mem., 1984. advisor Human Relations Council, 1962-63; del. Dem. State Conv., Springfield, Mass., 1982; class agt. ann. fund raising Boston U., Tufts U. Recipient Disting. Service Tchrs. medal Freedoms Found., 1970; State Citation, Dept. Edn., 1962, 63, 64, State Citation in field of human relations, Mass., 1962, 63; Coe fellow; Louise S. Davis Ann. Citizenship scholar. Mem. Mem. NEA, Mass. Tchrs. Assn., Nat. Council Social Studies, New Eng. History Tchrs. Assn., AAUW (pres. Housatonic Br. 1947-49), Tufts Alumni Assn., Boston U. Alumni Assn. Roman Catholic. Clubs: Hyannisport Yacht, Hyannis Yacht (assoc.); Boston U. of Cape Cod, Tufts U. of Cape Cod; Bedfords Woman's Community (com. chmn. 1965-70), Bedford Hist. Assn., Theta Phi Alpha, Delta Sigma Rho. Home: 36 Craigville Beach Rd PO Box 171 Hyannis Port MA 02647

DAVIS, LOURIE IRENE BELL, computer systems specialist; b. Las Vegas, N.Mex., Apr. 8, 1930; d. Currie Oscar and Minnie I. (Rodgers) Bell; m. Robert Eugene Davis, Aug. 21, 1950; children—Judith Anne, Robert Patrick. B.S., West Tex. U., 1959; student Eastern N.Mex. U., 1947-49. Cert. systems profl.; cert. data processing profl. Programmer/analyst Blue Cross/Blue Shield Okla., Tulsa, 1972-75, mgr. systems, 1977-81, dir. info. systems, 1981-82, mgr. project control, 1982-83, mgr. info. ctr., 1984-85, mgr. profl. cons. and tng., 1985—; systems curriculum coordinator Tulsa Jr. Coll., 1975-76, mem. computer sci. adv. bd., 1976-83; mem. steering com. U.S. Senate Bus. Adv. Bd., 1981; cons. Mem. budget panel United Way Tulsa, 1981—; mem. Pres.'s Task Force, 1982—. Mem. Assn. Systems Mgmt. (regional dir. 1985—, chpt. membership chair 1982-84; internat. awards 1980, 84), AAUW, Tulsa Area Systems Edn. Assn. (recorder 1980-81), Alpha Chi, Mensa, Intertel (nat. acceptance com. chair 1978). Republican. Presbyterian. Home: 2403 W Oklahoma Tulsa OK 74127 Office: Blue Cross 1215 S Boulder Box 3283 Tulsa OK 74102

DAVIS, MARGARET BRYAN, paleoecology researcher, educator; b. Boston, Oct. 23, 1931. A.B., Radcliffe Coll., 1953; Ph.D. in Biology, Harvard U., 1957. Fellow dept. biology Harvard U., Cambridge, Mass., 1957-58, dept. geosci. Calif. Inst. Tech., Pasadena, 1959-60; research fellow dept. zoology Yale U., New Haven, 1960-61; research assoc. dept. botany U. Mich., Ann Arbor, 1961-64, assoc. research biologist Gt. Lakes Research div., 1964-70, assoc. prof. dept. zoology, 1966-70, research biologist, prof. zoology, 1970-73; prof. ecology dept. biology Yale U., 1973-76; head dept. ecology and behavioral biology U. Minn., Mpls., 1976-81, prof. ecology, 1976-82, Regents prof. ecology, 1982—; vis. prof. Quaternary Research Ctr., U. Wash., 1973; vis. investigator Environ. Studies Program U. Calif.-Santa Barbara, 1981-82. Fellow Geol. Soc. Am.; mem. Ecol. Soc. Am., AAAS, Am. Quaternary Assn. (councillor 1969-70, 72-76, pres. 1978-80), Am. Soc. Limnology and Oceanography, Nat. Acad. Scis., Phi Beta Kappa, Sigma Xi. Address: 107 Zool Bldg U Minn 318 Church St Minneapolis MN 55455

DAVIS, MARGARET MONTEITH, school administrator; b. Grenada, Miss.; d. Joe and Vera (Hughes) Monteith; m. Hiram Davis, Feb. 6, 1982; stepchildren—Hiram III, Carol. A.A., Holmes Jr. Coll., 1966; B.S., Miss. State U., 1968; M.Ed., U. Miss., 1972, Ed.S., 1980. Cert. tchr., adminstr., Miss. Tchr. Huntsville Pub. Schs., Ala., 1968-69, Batesville Pub. Schs., Miss., 1969-74; tchr. Grenada Pub. Schs., Miss., 1974-78, prin. Lizzie Horn Sch., 1978-82, prin. Grenada Jr. High Sch., 1982—. Mem. Miss. Assn. Sch. Adminstrs., U. Miss. Sch. Edn. Alumni Assn. (bd. dirs. 1984—), Miss. Assn. Supervision and Curriculum. Avocations: needlepoint; reading; traveling. Office: Grenada Jr High Sch Jones Rd Grenada MS 38901

DAVIS, MARIAN BELLE, former museum curator, educator; b. St. Louis County, Mo., Sept. 24, 1911; d. John William and Frances Edith (Walters) D.; A.B., Washington U., St. Louis, 1932, M.A., 1935, postgrad., 1935-36; M.A., Radcliffe Coll., 1939, Ph.D., 1948. Mus. instr. Worcester (Mass.) Art Mus., 1941-44; instr. U. Tex., Austin, 1944-45, asst. prof. art, 1946-50, asso. prof., 1950-60, prof., 1960-78, prof. emeritus, 1978—, chief curator Univ. Art. Mus., 1963-78. Alice Longfellow fellow, 1940-41; U. Tex. at Austin grantee, 1951. Mem. Renaissance Soc., Coll. Art Assn. (editorial advisory bd. Coll. Art Jour., 1953-60, dir., 1951-55), Soc. Archtl. Historians, Archeol. Inst. Am., Nat. Trust, Phi Beta Kappa. Unitarian. Contbr. numerous articles, book and exhbn. revs. to art and hist. jours., to catalogues. Home: 2701 Wooldridge Dr Austin TX 78703*

DAVIS, MARION PEASE (MRS. PAUL DAVIS), social work administrator; b. Derby, Conn., Oct. 9, 1918; d. John Wood and Myrtle Stowe (Humphrey) Pease; B.A. in Psychology, U. Bridgeport (Conn.), 1964, M.S.W., U. Conn., 1969; m. Paul Davis, Oct. 15, 1938; children—Linda Davis Payne, Robert, Richard. Caseworker, Conn. Welfare Dept., Bridgeport, 1964-65, social worker protective service dept., 1965-67, supr. protective service unit, 1969-73, sr. psychiat. social worker, 1973-75, supervisory psychiat. social worker, 1975-78; dir. psychiat. social workers Greater Bridgeport Community Mental Health Center, 1973-82, chmn. housing com., 1974-78, mem. accreditation com., 1974-78, chmn., 1978-81, psychiat. social work chief, 1978-82; pvt. practice, 1982—; owner Winning Combinations, 1983—. Mem. Nat. Assn. Social Workers (exec. com. 1974-75, editorial com. 1975-77), Am. Assn. Marriage Family Counsellors (asso.), Huxley Inst. Biosocial Research (v.p., dir. 1978-81), Conn. Assn. Human Services, Mental Health Services Coordinating Com. (rec. sec., exec. com. 1975-82, corr. sec. 1978-82), LWV (bd. dirs. 1985—), Nat. Assn. Social Work Register Clin. Social Workers. Home: Sunset Ln Washington CT 06794

DAVIS, MARJORIE ALICE, city official; b. Newton, Mass., July 1, 1917; d. Herbert Francis and Harriet Cole (Dodge) Parmenter; A.B., Wellesley Coll., 1939; spl. grad. student Radcliffe Coll., 1941; cert. Harvard U., 1940; spl. courses in social work Boston U., 1961-62; m. Charles William Davis, Aug. 31, 1940 (dec.); children—Harriet Parmenter, Charles Edwin II. Exec. dir. Mid-Essex Area council Girl Scouts U.S.A., South Hamilton, Mass., 1952-59, Greater Lynn council, 1959-63, Merrimack River council, Andover, Mass., 1963-80; mem. Wenham Bd. Selectmen, 1972—, chmn., 1977—. Mem. Met. Area Planning Council, 1975—, sec., 1984—, mem. regional orgn. com., mem. exec. com.; mem. Mass. Com. Criminal Justice, 1974; exec. dir. Essex County Greenbelt Assn., 1980; mem. Lynn (Mass.) Area Pvt. Industry Council, 1982—, bd. dirs. North Shore Family Planning Council, 1981, treas., 1982-83; v.p., 1983—, pres., 1986—; mem. ct./Community Relations Com. for Essex County, 1975; pres. Hamilton-Wenham Community Service, 1970-80, bd. dirs., 1983—; sec. United Fund of Central North Shore, 1969-84; mem. exec. com. Essex County Adv. Bd., 1983—, sec., 1984—; pres. Hamilton-Wenham Vis. Nurses Assn., 1963-73, Bay area dir., 1983—; v.p. Mass. chpt. Children Am. Revolution, 1944; mem. Republican Town Com. Mem. Mass. Selectmen's Assn., Essex County Selectmen's Assn. (pres. 1984-85, bd. dirs.), Women Elected Mcpl. Ofcls., Mass. Mcpl. Assn. (bd. dirs.). Episcopalian. Clubs: Harvard (Boston); Singing Beach (Manchester, Mass.). Home: 143 Grapevine Rd Wenham MA 01984

DAVIS, MARVA ALEXIS KENON, lawyer; b. Quincy, Fla., May 26, 1952; d. Harold Kenon and Thelma L. Robinson; m. Calvin C. Davis, Sept. 2, 1973. B.A. in Polit. Sci., Lincoln U., Pa., 1974; J.D., Fla. State U., 1977. Bar: Fla. 1977. Sole practice, Quincy, 1981-82; ptnr. Travis & Davis, P.A., Quincy, 1982—; asst. gen. counsel Fla. Commn. Human Relations, Tallahassee, 1979-81; asst. pub. defender Office Pub. Defender, Tallahassee, 1977-79; gen. counsel Community Econ. Devel. Orgn., 1982—, Midway Community Council, 1978—; dir. Legal Services North Fla., 1981—. Mem. Barristers Assn. (pres. 1982-84), Fla. Bar Assn., ABA, Assn. Trial Lawyers Am., Acad. Fla. Trial Lawyers, Nat. Bar Assn. Democrat. Mem. Worldwide Ch. of God. Home: Route 1 Box 3045 Havana FL 32333 Office: Travis & Davis PA 229 E Washington St Quincy FL 32351

DAVIS, MARY ALICE, political worker; b. Lorman, Miss., June 13, 1955; d. Robert Lee and Alice (Reed) D.; 1 child, Carltrelle. Student U. Wis.-Milw., Sawyer Bus. Inst., Control Data Inst., H&R Block Corp., M.A.T.C. Sec. O.C. White Soul Club, Milw., 1972-84, asst. to dir., 1985—; mem. adv. bd. Minority C. of C., Milw., 1985—. Coordinator Hal Jackson Talented Teens, Milw., 1978—, Democratic Presidential Campaign, Milw., 1980, Mike McGhee for Alderman Campaign, Milw., 1985, Ronald P. Britton for Municipal Judge, Milw., 1986, Hair in Motion Fund Raiser, Milw., 1983-85; advisory mem. United Negro Coll. Walk/Run, Milw., 1985—; co-chmn. NAACP Midwest Region III Conf., Milw., 1986; com. mem. cancer and the Black American, Am. Cancer Soc., Milw., 1984-85. Nominated to Outstanding Young Woman of Am., 1982; recipient WEB Dubois award NAACP, 1985, Cancer Soc. award Am. Cancer Soc., 1984, 85. Mem. Nat. Assn. Female Execs., NAACP (bd. dirs. 1982—, sec.). Democrat. Baptist. Home: 4031 N Elmhurst Rd Milwaukee WI

53216 Office: O C White Soul Club Inc 2212 N Martin Luther King Dr Milwaukee WI 53212

DAVIS, MATILDA SUTTON, association executive; b. Washington, Sept. 1, 1945; d. Alphonso Lafayette and Alice Beatrice (Covington) Sutton; B.A., Antioch Coll., 1977; 1 son, Eric Davis; foster children—Billy Carpenter, Mary Carpenter, Melissa Carpenter. Coordinator program services Liberation for Ex-Offenders Through Employment Opportunities, Washington, 1978-79; client rep. Dist. Line Fin. Center, Washington, 1972—; dir. adminstrv. services Am. Nurses' Assn., Washington, 1980—; prin. Mattie Davis, cons., Washington. Active Washington chpt. People United To Save Humanity. Mem. Nat. Assn. Female Execs., Am. Soc. Profl. and Exec. Women. Club: Met. Women's Dem. (Washington). Home: 1673 Columbia Rd NW Apt 204 Washington DC 20009 Office: 1101 14th St NW Suite 200 Washington DC 20005

DAVIS, MICHELE STAR, educator; b. Auburn, Ind., Dec. 31, 1946; d. Robert Emmett and April Dawn (Bowser) Davis; B.A. summa cum laude, St. Francis Coll., 1970; M.A., Purdue U., 1972, Ph.D., 1979; m. Richard D. Watman, Sept. 13, 1981. Teaching asst. Purdue U., West Lafayette, Ind., 1970-72, grad. instr., 1973-77; lectr. Ohio State U., Columbus, 1979-80, instr., 1980-83, program asst. Office of Hispanic Student Programs, 1983—, faculty adv. La Hermandad Latina (club for Hispanic students), founder, dir. Teatro Unidad, dir. Ohio State U. summer Spanish Lang. Camp, 1982; leader seminars, workshops Office Hispanic Student Programs, 1979-82. Leader cultural presentations to elem., jr. high and high sch. students through Internat. Council of Mid Ohio. Recipient Hermandad Latina and MECHA award, Ohio State U., 1981. Mem. Am. Assn. Tchrs. of Spanish and Portuguese, Ohio Theatre Affiliation, Ohio Community Theatre Assn., Am. Council of Tchrs. of Fgn. Lang., MLA. Author: A Dramatist and His Characters, 1982; Un Don Juan del Siglo XX: El Conquistador Conquistado, 1981; Del Realismo a la Vanguardia en Tres Dramaturgos Hispanoamericanos, 1981; Dreams and Reflections: The Cycle of Human Existence. Two Plays by Dantes and Giovaninetti; contbr. articles to profl. jours. Home: 23201 Rapp Dean Rd Raymond OH 43067 Office: Room 347 Ohio Union 1739 N High St Columbus OH 43210

DAVIS, MINNIE DELORES, consultant; b. Laurens, S.C., Oct. 27, 1945; d. John Ed and Minnie Florie (Watts) Davis. B.A., No. Ill. U., 1967; M.B.A., U. Chgo., 1973. Tchr., Chgo. Bd. Edn., 1967-72; internal auditor Container Corp. Am., Chgo., 1973-74; sr. corp. auditor NCR Corp., Dayton, Ohio, 1974-76; mgmt. project specialist J.I. Case Co., Racine, Wis., 1976-79, sr. fin. analyst, 1979-81; dir. strategic planning Peoples Natural Gas Co., Council Bluffs, Iowa, 1981-84; sr. cons. Arthur D. Little, Inc., Washington, 1984—; vis. prof. Black Exec. Exchange Program, Nat. Urban League, 1978-82, 84—; mem. bus. program adv. bd. Ft. Valley State Coll., Ga., 1979-82. Chmn. family services allocations Midlands United Way, Omaha, 1983-84; mem. Foster Care Rev. Bd., Racine, Wis., 1979-80, Nat. Council Negro Women, Omaha, 1983-84; bd. dirs. Racine Area United Way, 1979-81. Mem. N. Am. Soc. Corp. Planners, Strategic Mgmt. Soc., Nat. Black M.B.A. Assn., Nat. Hook Up of Black Women. Club: Southwestern Service (v.p. 1979-80). Office: Arthur D Little Inc 600 Maryland Ave SW 8th Floor Washington DC 20024

DAVIS, NADYNE EVELYN, nursing educator; b. Yakima, Wash., June 19, 1936; d. Ted and Alene Gwendolyn (Kincaid) Haubrich; m. James Wesley Davis, Jr., Apr. 12, 1958; children—James Wesley, Theodore Alan, Wendy Marie, Keily Ann. B.S.N., U. Wash., 1963; postgrad. Central Wash. State Coll., 1966, Eastern Wash. U., 1969-70; M.Ed., Gonzaga U., 1971; postgrad. Witworth Coll., 1976. R.N., Wash. Staff nurse St. Elizabeth Hosp., Yakima, 1963-64, staff devel. nurse, 1964, asst. dir. Sch. Nursing, 1965-68; mem. nursing faculty Deaconness Hosp. Sch. Nursing, Spokane, Wash., 1969; con. curriculum devel. Spokane Community Coll., 1971, nursing educator, 1971—. Area chmn. heart drive Am. Heart Assn., Spokane, 1975-79; mem. task force Planned Parenthood edn., Spokane, 1981-85; bd. dirs. Politically United Nurses for Consumer Health, Seattle, 1981-83, Wash. State Nurses Found., 1983—; mem. adv. com. Women's Health Care, 1985—. Mem. Assn. Higher Edn., Am. Nurses Assn., Wash. State Nurses Assn. (1st v.p. 1983-85, dir. 1979-83, state legis. com. 1983-85, state bd. rep. to emergency dept., nurses assn. coordinating council 1979-83), Wash. State League Nursing (treas. 1966-68), Inland Empire Nurses Assn. (dir. 1975-79, pres. 1977-79, Outstanding Nurse award 1985), Sigma Theta Tau, Alpha Gamma Delta (pres. alumni assn. 1981-82, 85-86 1st v.p. 1982-83). Republican. Roman Catholic. Club: Spokane. Home: E 11811 Glenview Circle Spokane WA 99206 Office: Spokane Community Coll N 1810 Greene Spokane WA 99207

DAVIS, NATALIE ZEMON, educator; b. Detroit, Nov. 8, 1928; m. 1948, 3 children. B.A., Smith Coll., 1949, D.H.L., 1977; M.A., Radcliffe Coll., 1950; Ph.D. in History, U. Mich., 1959; D.H.L., Northwestern U.,1983, Lawrence U., 1984, U. Rochester, 1986, others; D.L., Wesleyan U., 1984. Lectr. history Brown U., 1959-61, asst. prof., 1961-63; asst. prof. econs. U. Toronto, 1964-67, assoc. prof. history, 1967-71; vis. assoc. prof. U. Calif.-Berkeley, 1968, prof., 1971-77; prof. history Princeton U., 1977—, Henry Charles Lea prof., 1981—. Social Sci. Research Council fellow, 1962-63. Recipient William Koren Jr. prize Soc. Hist. Studies, 1968, 71; Howard T. Behrman award, 1983, Outstanding Achievement award U. Mich., 1975; Radcliffe Grad. Soc. medal for disting, achievement, 1983, others; NEH fellow, 1981-82; Guggenheim fellow, 1985—. Fellow Am. Acad. Arts and Scis.; mem. Am. Soc. Reformation Research, Am. Hist. Assn. (pres. 1987), Soc. For Hist. Studies, Renaissance Soc. Am. Author: Society and Culture in Early Modern France, 1975; The Return of Martin Guerre, 1983. Contbr. articles to profl. jours. Address: Dept History Princeton U Princeton NJ 08540

DAVIS, OLIVE MCFATE, trade show executive; b. Oakland, Calif., Nov. 16, 1922; d. Thomas Albert and Leana Jewel (Combs) McFate; student Inst. Orgnl. Mgmt., 1980-82, 84-86; m. Warren L. Davis, Jan. 18, 1942 (dec. 1976); children—Jean, Patricia, Larry, Allan, Bonnie. Partner with husband in farming, Calif., 1943-69; newspaper corr. Stockton (Calif.) Record, 1968-73; urban 4-H coordinator, San Joaquin County, Stockton, 1973; writer-researcher S.T. & E. R.R., Stockton, 1974-76; coordinator Central Valley Agrl. Expo, Stockton, 1976-77; trade show exec. Stockton C. of C., 1976—. Chmn. Stockton Cultural Heritage Bd., 1981-82; regional dir. Am. Field Service, 1970-73; pres. 4-H Leaders Council, 1956; bd. dirs. Linden Devel. Commn., 1975, Linden Peters C. of C., 1974-77. Named Citizen of Year, Linden Lions, 1973. Mem. Nat. League Am. Pen Women, Nat. Assn. Agrl. Mktg., San Joaquin County Hist. Soc. (pres. 1981-82), Calif. Hist. Soc. Club: Linden Garden. Author: Slow Tired & Easy Railroad, 1976; Stockton Sunrise Port on the San Joaquine, 1984. Office: 445 W Weber Ave Suite 220 Stockton CA 95203

DAVIS, OLIVIA ANNE CARR (MRS. TOM LUCIAN DAVIS), author; b. Leeds, Eng., Dec. 4, 1922; d. Henry Marvell and Olive Frances Kate (Rumble) Carr; student pvt. sch., pvt. tutors; m. Tom Lucian Davis, Oct. 13, 1943; children—Sebastian, Miranda, Penelope. Came to U.S., 1951, naturalized, 1956. Sec., Mil. Intelligence, War Office, London and Oxford, Eng., 1941-44. Recipient Emily Clark Balch award Va. Quar. Rev., 1969. Mem. Authors Guild, Smithsonian Resident Assos., Nat. Trust Historic Preservation, Audubon Soc. Author: The Last of the Greeks, 1968; The Steps of the Sun, 1972; The Scent of Apples, 1973; contbr. short stories to lit. quars. and anthologies in U.S. and abroad. Home: 6828 Floyd Ave Springfield VA 22150 Office: care Curtis Brown Ltd 575 Madison Ave New York NY 10022

DAVIS, PEGGY COOPER, law educator; b. Hamilton, Ohio, Feb. 19, 1943; d. George Clinton and Margaret (Gillespie) Cooper; m. Gordon Jamison Davis, Aug. 24, 1968; 1 dau., Elizabeth Cooper. B.A., Western Coll. for Women, 1963; student Barnard Coll., 1963-64; J.D., Harvard U., 1968; student N.Y. Soc. for Freudian Psychologists, 1972-73. Bar: N.Y., 1969, U.S. Supreme Ct., 1976. Law clk. to judge U.S. Dist. Ct., N.Y.C., 1972-73; asst. counsel capital punishment project NAACP Legal Def., N.Y.C., 1973-77; assoc. prof. Rutgers U., Sch. Law, N.J., 1977-78, NYU Sch. Law, 1983—; dep. criminal justice coordinator City of N.Y., 1979-80; judge Family Ct. State of N.Y., 1980-83. Contbr. articles to profl. jours. Bd. dirs. Vera Inst., N.Y.C., Com. for Modern Cts., Child Welfare Reform Com., N.Y.C., 1985. Fellow N.Y. Inst. for Humanities. Office: NYU Sch Law 40 Washington Sq New York NY 10012

DAVIS, PENNY ANN, lawyer, educator; b. Kennedy, Ala., Feb. 14, 1952; d. John William and Mary Evelyn (Keenum) Davis; m. Eugene B. Williams, May 10, 1984; 1 child, Lance Christopher Williams. B.S., U. Ala., 1973, M.A., 1974, J.D., 1978. Assoc. dean women Wingate (N.C.) Coll., 1974-75; dormitory dir. U. Ala., University, 1975-78; law clk. to Judge Walter Galwin, 5th Circuit Ct. Appeals, Tuscaloosa, Ala., 1978-79; assoc. dir. Ala. Law Inst., University, 1979—; instr. Shelton State Coll., Tuscaloosa, 1982—; adj. faculty U. Ala. Sch. Law, 1984-85. Author: (with McCurley) Alabama Divorce, Alimony and Child Custody, 1982, Land Laws of Alabama, 4th edit., 1984; editor: Handbook for Alabama Tax Assessors, Tax Collectors, and Lisense Commissioners, 2nd edit., 1981, co-editor 3d edit., 1985. Mem. Ala. Victim/Witness Resources Task Force, 1981-82, Ala. Domestic Violence Com., 1981-82, state Jail Standards Citizens Adv. Com., 1981. Mem. ABA (mem. com.), Ala. Bar Assn., Tuscaloosa County Bar Assn. Baptist. Home: 21 Englewood Dr Tuscaloosa AL 35405 Office: Ala Law Inst PO Box 1425 University AL 35486

DAVIS, RACHEL LEE, advertising executive; b. Arkadelphia, Ark., Sept. 8, 1952; d. James Lawrence and Dorothy Marie (Diamond) Mostert; m. Richard Lawrence Davis, Nov. 17, 1979. B.S. in Advt., U. Tex., 1975. Account exec. DBG&H Unlimited, Inc., Dallas, 1975-76, sr. account exec., 1976-78, v.p., 1979-80; co-owner Oldfield Davis, Inc., Dallas, 1980—; bd. dirs. Sales and Mktg. Council Dallas, 1978-80. Recipient Silver Tops award Dallas Advt. League, 1981. Mem. Dallas C. of C., Dallas Advt. League, Kappa Kappa Gamma. Presbyterian. Clubs: Cotillion, Slipper (Dallas). Office: 3811 Turtle Creek Blvd Suite 400 Dallas TX 75219

DAVIS, REBECCA ANN HENRY, public adminstration executive; b. Ruston, La., Sept. 11, 1948; d. George Wayne and Vina (Greer) Henry; m. Michael P. Brown, Nov. 29, 1968 (div. June 1974); children—Christopher Douglas; m. James Harry Davis, May 12, 1976. B.A., La. Tech. U., 1969; M.A., U. Okla., 1976. Regional alcoholism and drug abuse coordinator Nortex Regional Planning Commn., Wichita Falls, Tex., 1975-79; adminstrv. asst. to exec. dir. Tex. Commn. on Alcoholism (now Tex. Commn. Alcohol and Drug Abuse), Austin, 1979-81, dep. dir., 1982—. Mem. Wichita Mental Health Assn., Wichita Falls, Tex., 1976-79; coordinator Silent Friends Benefit Com., Wichita Falls, 1976-79; chair, vice-chair Citizens Traffic Safety Council, Wichita Falls, 1976-79; mem. Austin Council on Fgn. Affairs, 1984-86. Mem. Human Relations Assn., Women in Tex. Govt., Beta Sigma Phi. Democrat. Baptist. Office: Tex Commn on Alcohol and Drug Abuse 1705 Guadalupe Austin TX 78701

DAVIS, REBECCA WING, accountant; b. Provo, Utah, Apr. 23, 1953; d. Sherman William and Martha Elayne (Hinckley) W.; m. Michael Whitaker Davis, Aug. 11, 1983; children—Joseph Michael, Margaret Jeanne. Student Brigham Young U., 1971-72; B.S., U. Utah, 1976, M.B.A., 1982. Typist, pool supr. Haskins & Sells, Salt Lake City, 1977-78; real estate salesperson Ken Mayne Inc., Salt Lake City, 1978-79; exec. sec. Eimco PMD, Salt Lake City, 1979-80; legal sec. Richard G. Cook, P.C., Salt Lake City, 1980; fin. analyst E-Systems, Inc., Salt Lake City, 1982-83; acct. U. Utah, Salt Lake City, 1983—. Campaign worker Frances Farley for Congress, Salt Lake City, 1982. Mem. Women in Communications. Democrat.

DAVIS, RUTH ANN, interior designer; b. Centralia, Ill., Aug. 14, 1940; d. Emerson Howard and Olga (Hugo) D.; B.A. in Interior Design, U. Nebr., Omaha, 1970; M.A., Iowa State U., 1972; pupil of M. Alain Leisuitre, Paris. Pres. Ruth Ann Davis Interior Design Inc., Omaha, 1973—; vis. instr. contract interiors and hist. interiors U. Nebr., 1974—; guest lectr. U. Nebr., Iowa State U., U. Iowa; speaker on art deco; bd. dirs. Landmarks, Inc., Met. Arts Council Omaha; hon. bd. dirs., guest lectr. Miami Beach (Fla.) Design Preservation League; mem. Save the Astro Theater City Commn., Save WOW Bldg. Com. Mem. Am. Soc. Interior Designers (pres. Nebr./Iowa chpt. 1980-81, regional v.p. 1982-83, chmn. Peace Corps Initiative 1983-84, chmn. ASID Ednl. Found. 1984), Nat. Trust Historic Preservation. Address: 1113 Harvey St Omaha NE 68102

DAVIS, RUTH ELENOR, nurse writer, photographer; b. Johnstown, Pa., Oct. 3, 1925; d. Callen and Lenora W. (Morse) Weimer; m. Francis E. Davis, 1948 (div., 1981); children—Edward L., Christopher J. R.N., Conemaugh Valley Meml. Hosp. Sch. Nursing, 1947. Staff nurse, Conemaugh Valley Meml. Hosp., Johnstown, Pa., 1947-49, Phila. Gen. Hosp., 1949-50, So. Balt. Gen. Hosp., 1951-52; staff nurse Phila. Coll. Osteopathy, 1954-58, night supr., 1959-71; operating room supr. Meml. Hosp., York, Pa., 1971-74; freelance photojournalist, York, 1975—. Contbr. numerous articles to profl. jours. Founding pres. Folk Heritage Inst., York, Nursing Archives Found., cofounder York Nursing Mus. Mem. Women in Communications (sec., 1980). Republican. Methodist. Home and Office: 36 N Russell St York PA 17402

DAVIS, SANDRA KAY, advertising agency executive; b. Lawrence, Kans., Nov. 15, 1951; d. Clifford Turl and Josephine Margaret (Votaw) Davis. B.A., U. Kans., 1974; M.A., NYU, 1981. Acct. exec. The DR Group, N.Y.C., 1974—; cons. Artist's Space, N.Y.C., 1979. Mem. WDRG Women's Direct Response Group. Home: 31 Bedford St New York NY 10014 Office: The DR Group 522 Fifth Ave New York NY 10036

DAVIS, SARA JANE, utility company official; b. Jackson, Mich., Feb. 24, 1948; d. Leonard William and Margery Barbara (Smith) Lashley; A.A. in Bus. Mgmt. and Data Processing, Lansing Community Coll., 1978; B.A., Spring Arbor Coll., 1984. Computer programmer Consumers Power Co., Jackson, 1968-79, computer analyst, 1979-82, supr. software services, 1982-83, supr. energy supply systems support, 1984-85, project mgr. customer communications, 1986—. Mem. mktg. com. United Way; mem. steering com. Employees for Better Govt. PAC. Mem. Assn. for Systems Mgmt. (chpt. dir.). Club: Nat. Fedn. Bus. and Profl. Women (v.p.). Office: Consumers Power Co 1945 Parnall Rd Jackson MI 49201

DAVIS, SHARRON KAY, credit reporting company executive; b. Lubbock, Tex., Mar. 27, 1953; d. Cleon Elmer and Wilma (Dawson) D.; m. (div. Sept. 1977). Diploma in fashion merchandising and bus. Bauder Fashion Coll., Arlington, Tex., 1972. Dist. sec. Gen. Electric Credit Corp., Lubbock, 1973-77; asst. to mgr. Equico Lessors, Lubbock, 1977-78; loan processor Nat. Mortgage Co., San Antonio, 1978-79; gen. mgr. Chilton Credit Reporting, Lubbock, 1979—. Local vol. worker Am. Cancer Soc., 1982—, March of Dimes, 1985. Named Mgr. of Yr., Chilton Credit Reporting, 1983. Mem. Credit Women Internat. (Boss of Yr. award 1985). Republican. Home: 4609 62d St Lubbock TX 79414 Office: Chilton Credit Reporting 6502 Slide Rd Suite 203 Lubbock TX 79416

DAVIS, SHIRLEY CAROL SPENCE, nurse; b. Drexel Hill, Pa., Sept. 8, 1938; d. William Lloyd and Hilda Irene (Marshall) Spence; m. Davis Louis Davis, Feb. 6, 1960 (dec. May 1979); 1 son, David Louis. Diploma in nursing Orange Meml. Hosp., 1959; student in nursing Lake Superior State Coll., 1977-78; B.S. in Nursing, U. South Fla., 1981, M.S. in Nursing, 1985. Operating room nurse Eastern Maine Gen. Hosp., Bangor, 1960-62, S. Community Hosp., Oklahoma City, 1972-75; staff nurse recovery room float team Doctors Hosp., Shreveport, La., 1969-70; infectious care unit nurse Bayfront Med. Ctr., St. Petersburg, Fla., 1970-71, staff nurse float team to med./surg./neurol. units, 1978-85, James A. Haley VA Hosp., Tampa, Fla., 1985—. Vol., Family Services, Scott AFB, Ill., 1975-77, ARC, Scott AFB, Ill., 1975-77. Mem. Am. Nurses Assn., Fla. Nurses Assn., Am. Heart Assn., Sigma Theta Tau. Republican. Methodist. Clubs: Squadron Wives (Barksdale AFB) (treas. 1965-66), Officers' Wives. Home: 30 Sycamore Ct Palm Harbor FL 33563 Office: James A Haley VA Hosp 13000 Bruce B Downs Blvd Tampa FL 33612

DAVIS, SUSAN MARIE, graphic arts consultant; b. Lynwood, Calif., Nov. 10, 1951; d. Richard P. and Mary L. Davis; student Cypress (Calif.) City Coll., 1969-71; m. Lawrence A. Sherwin, Feb. 26, 1980. From office mgr. to v.p., sales mgr. Quality Graphics, Santa Ana, Calif. 1974-81; pres. Susan Davis Graphic Services, Inc., Tustin, Calif., 1981—; seminar leader, 1979—. Mem. Printing Industries Assn. (treas., dir. So. Calif. chpt. 1978-83). Address: 14751 Plaza Dr Suite E Tustin CA 92680

DAVIS, TERRY SERFASS, psychologist; b. Los Angeles, Nov. 6, 1942; d. George Donald and Mriam Allen (Baisden) Serfass; B.A. with distinction, U. Redlands, 1966; Ph.D. in Clin. Psychology (USPHS fellow 1966-68), U. So. Calif., 1973; children—Sheryl Ann Barak, Janet Lee Barak. Field placement supr. psychology dept. UCLA, 1973-76, dir. family rehab. coordinator project, extension dept., 1976-81; out-patient counselor alcoholism, recovery service San Pedro (Calif.) Peninsula Hosp., 1979-80; lectr. health and safety Calif. State U., Los Angeles, 1975-78; pvt. practice psychology, Torrance, Calif., 1978—; dir clin. services addictive disease unit Charter Pacific Hosp., Torrance, 1981-83; coordinator alcohol/drug tng. programs, extension dept. UCLA, 1978—; faculty Antioch U.-West, 1981-82, instr. grad. program, 1985; clin. supr. South Bay Human Services, Torrance, 1985-86; cons. in field. Bd. dirs. CLARE Found., 1977-80, pres., 1979-80; bd. dirs. Felicity House, 1974-80, pres., 1977-78, 79-80; bd. dirs. Valley Women's Center, 1978-79. Mem. Calif. Assn. Alcoholic Recovery Homes (pres. Los Angeles chpt. 1979-80), Am. Psychol. Assn., Western Psychol. Assn., Calif. Psychol. Assn., Assn. Women in Psychology, Alcohol and Drug Problems Assn., Calif. Women's Commn. Alcoholism, Sierra Club. Office: 3246 N Sepulveda Blvd Suite 204 Torrance CA 90505

DAVIS, THELMA LORRAINE FAULKNER, retired educator, political worker; b. Columbus, Ga., June 20, 1906; d. John Asa and Amanda Louise (Hill) Faulkner; m. Lewis Herschel Davis, Mar. 21, 1926 (dec. 1970); 1 child, Lisa Erline. A.B., Mercer U., 1953, M.Ed., 1959. Cert. elem. tchr., Ga., supervising student tchrs., Ga., reading specialist, Ga. Tchr., Ga. Pub. Schs., until 1982; reading specialist, Griffin-Spalding County, Ga., 1966-73; conv. del. World Confederation of Orgns. of Teaching Profession, various locations internationally, 6 yrs., 1963-76. Contbr. articles to profl. jours. Life mem. Ga. Congress of Parents and Tchrs., 1950-74; mem. Educators for Johnson and Humphrey, 1964-65; alt. to Democratic Nat. Conv., 1964; speaker on edn. Okla. Senate and Ho. of Reps., 1964; speaker on compulsary edn. law, tchrs.' salaries Senate and Ho. of Reps., 49 states; speaker Gov.'s Conf. on Edn., 1965; pres. LWV, Griffin, 1980-81. Recipient Outstanding Service award Va., 1972, La., 1974, S.C., 1976, Gov. of Ga. Vol. award, 1982. Mem. Griffin-Spalding Assn. Educators (pres. 1956-58, award for 35 yrs. of appreciated services, 1974), Ga. Assn. Educators (pres. dept. classroom tchrs. 1960-62, ann. service award 1954, award for strengthening human relationships 1982), NEA (life mem., pres. dept. classroom tchrs. 1964-65, disting. service award 1966-71, Trentholm award for human relations 1970, M.Communications for advancement of Edn. in Am. 1971), Am. Assn. Sch. Adminstrs. (hon., life), AAUW (community leadership award 1982, pres. Griffin chpt. 1982-84, sec. 1984—, Griffin rep. to Council on Aging Ret. Tchrs. Assn., Delta Kappa Gamma. Baptist. Avocations: tutoring, visiting nursing homes. Home: 19 Terracedale Ct Griffin GA 30223

DAVIS, ULILLAH ELMORE, pharmacist; b. Ashland, Miss., Mar. 15, 1932; d. Hayse and Graftee (McKenzie) Elmore; m. Edward Davis, Jr., Dec. 5, 1959; children—Karen Lynn, Keith Edward. B.S. in Pharmacy, Xavier U., New Orleans, 1955. Registered pharmacist, La., Ohio. Instr. chemistry, biology, dean of women. Miss. Indsl. Coll., Holly Spring, 1956-57; asst. mgr. Shauter Drug Co., Cleve., 1958-59; staff pharmacist Highland View Hosp., Warrensville, Ohio, 1960-70, asst. dir. pharmacy, 1971-78; sr. staff pharmacist Cleve. Met. Gen. Hosp., 1979; dir. pharmacy Kenneth W. Clement Ctr., Cleve., 1980-85; dir. pharmacy Sunny Acres Skilled Nursing Facility, Warrensville, 1986—. Trustee Lee Seville Ch., 1985. Recipient Super Achievement award Highland View Hosp, 1975. Mem. Cleve. Soc. Hosp. Pharmacists, Ohio Soc. Hosp. Pharmacists, Am. Soc. Hosp. Pharmacists, Nat. Pharm. Assn., Cleve. Pharm. Assn. (sec. 1984—), Xavier Alumni Assn., Cleve. Tots and Teens (v.p. 1973-75, Super Performance award 1979), East End Settle Coop. (pres. 1975-78), NAACP, Nat. Council Negro Women, Phillis Wheatley Aux., Alpha Kappa Alpha Achievement award 1982). Democrat. Baptist. Avocations: gourmet cooking; jogging. Home: 20150 S Woodland Rd Shaker Heights OH 44122 Office: Sunny Acres Nursing Facility 4310 Richmond Rd Warrensville OH 44122

DAVIS, VICTORIA, real estate development and property management company executive; b. Memphis, June 3, 1943; d. Willie and Queen Victoria (Cook) Alexander; m. Nathaniel R. Davis, Sr., Jan. 6, 1976; children—Nathaniel, Mikal, Peridot, Malik. B.S., Spelman Coll., 1965; M. Pub. Adminstrn., U. Minn., 1970. Service rep. Social Security Adminstrn., Memphis, 1965-68; housing specialist Urban East Cons., Atlanta, 1970-71; property mgr. Shelter Devel. Corp., Bloomington, Minn., 1971-72; chief loan mgmt. br. HUD, St. Paul-Mpls., 1972-77; program adminstr. Minn. Community Devel. Corp., St. Paul, 1978-79; exec. dir. Minn. Bus. League, St. Paul-Mpls., 1979-82; gen. ptnr. BNV Properties, St. Paul, 1982—, also dir. Commr., Small Bus. Commn., State Minn., 1981-82, Fin. Bonding Commn., City of St. Paul, 1985—; chmn. bd. Benjamin E. Mays Fundamental Sch., St. Paul, 1981—; mem. Set-Aside Adv. Com., Minn., 1982—; chmn. budget com. St. Paul Sch. Dist. #625, 1982-83; bd. dirs. Citizens for Excellence in Edn., St. Paul, 1983—; mem. Gov. Mfg. Growth Council, State of Minn., 1984—; mem. Dist. 8 Community Planning Council, St. Paul, 1985. Adminstrn. Aging grantee, 1968; Ford fellow, 1970; recipient Performance award HUD, 1974, Affirmative Action award HUD, 1975, Appreciation award Minn. Bus. League, 1981, 82, Vol. award United Negro Coll. Fund, 1977. Mem. St. Paul Black Women's Network (pres. 1984—), NAACP (exec. bd. 1981—), Sigma Theta. Democrat. Baptist. Avocations: swimming; bargain shopping. Office: BNV Properties 586 W Central Ave St Paul MN 55103

DAVIS, VIDA AVERY, accountant; b. Nashville, Sept. 6, 1962; d. Parnell Napolean and Gloria (Reid) Avery; m. Christopher Raphael Davis, June 23, 1984. B.A. in Econs., Spelman Coll., 1984. Mgr. trainee United Labs. Am., Marietta, Ga., 1984-85; fin. coordinator Tempa Temporaries, Atlanta, 1985-86; staff acct. Turner Assocs., Atlanta, 1986—. Democrat. Presbyterian.

DAVIS, VIRGINIA KESLER, fire equipment company executive; b. Pecos, Tex., Oct. 2, 1912; d. Isaac Terrel and Caroline Edna (Bates) Kesler; m. Steve A. Davis, Aug. 17, 1938 (dec. Apr. 22, 1984); children—Steve A., Jr., Ronald E., Carolyn (dec. 1967), Roberta Janel. Ed. Lippert's Bus. Coll. Plainview, Tex. Mgr. Portales Bottling Co., N.Mex., 1936-38; mgr. Artesia Fire Equipment Co., N.Mex., 1954—. Pres. Central PTA, Artesia, 1955-56. Clubs: Altrusa (pres. 1977-78) (Artesia); Woman (Portales, N.Mex.). Home: 1011 S 2d St PO Box 469 Artesia NM 88210 Office: Artesia Fire Equipment Inc 1014 S 1st St Artesia NM 88210

DAVIS, WANDA ROSE, lawyer; b. Lampasas, Tex., Oct. 4, 1937; d. Ellis DeWitt and Julia Doris (Rose) Cockrell; m. Richard Andrew Fulcher, May 9, 1959 (div. 1969); 1 son, Greg Ellis; m. Edwin Leon Davis, Jan. 14, 1973 (div. 1985). B.B.A., U. Tex., 1959, J.D., 1971. Bar: Tex. 1971, Colo. 1981, U.S. Dist. Ct. (no. dist.) Tex. 1972, U.S. Dist. Ct. Colo. 1981, U.S. Ct. Appeals (10th cir. 1981, U.S. Supreme Ct. 1976. Atty. Atlantic Richfield Co., Dallas, 1971; assoc. firm Crocker & Murphy, Dallas, 1971-72; prin. Wanda Davis, Atty. at Law, Dallas, 1972-73; ptnr. firm Davis & Davis Inc., Dallas, 1973-75; atty. adviser HUD, Dallas, 1974-75, Air Force Acctg. and Fin. Ctr., Denver, 1976—; co-chmn. regional Profl. Devel. Inst., Am. Soc. Mil. Comptrollers, Colorado Springs, Colo., 1982; chmn. Lowry AFB Noontime Edn. Program, Exercise Program, Denver, 1977-83; mem. speakers bur. Colo. Women's Bar, 1982-83, Lowry AFB, 1981-83; mem. fed. ct. liaison com. U.S. Dist. Ct. Colo., 1983. Contbr. numerous articles to profl. jours. Bd. dirs. Pres.'s Council Met. Denver, 1981-83; mem. Lowry AFB Alcohol Abuse Exec. Com., 1981-84. Recipient Spl. Achievement award USAF, 1978, 3 Suggestion awards; Upward Mobility award Fed. Profl. and Adminstrv. Women, Denver, 1979. Mem. Fed. Bar Assn. (pres. Colo. 1982-83, mem. nat. council 1984—, 2d v.p. for 10th cir., Earl W. Kintner Disting. Service award 1983, v.p. 10th cir. 1986), Colo. Trial Lawyers Assn., Bus. and Profl. Women's Club (dist. IV East dir. 1983-84, Colo. v.p. 1986), Am. Soc. Mil. Comptrollers (pres. 1984-85), Denver South Met. Bus. and Profl. Women's Club (pres. 1982-83, dist. dir. 1983-84, state 2d v.p. 1985-86), Denver Silver Spruce Am. Bus. Women's Assn. (pres. 1981-82; Woman of Yr. award 1982), Colo. Jud. Inst., Colo. Concerned Lawyers, Profl. Mgrs. Assn., Fed. Women's Program (v.p. Denver 1980), Dallas Bar Assn., Tex. Bar Assn., Denver Bar Assn., Altrusa, Zonta, Denver Nancy Langhorn Federally Employed Women. (pres. 1979-80). Christian. Office: Air Force Acctg and Fin Ctr AFAFC/JAL Denver CO 80279

DAVIS, WENDY MOIRA, construction company executive; b. London, Dec. 9, 1929; came to U.S., 1969, naturalized, 1978; d. Bruce John and Rosemary Whyl (Abrahams) Baron; student pvt. schs., Sussex, Eng.; m. William John Davis, Oct. 20, 1951; children—Faith Ilda, William Baron and Waverley Rowena (twins), Kyle Micheal. Code enforcement officer City of Treasure Isle (Fla.), 1976-77; spl. codes insp. Pinellas County (Fla.) Bldg. Dept., 1977-79; plan review analyst City of Dunedin (Fla.), 1979-80, acting bldg. ofcl., 1980-81; sales mgr. Sunstyle Homes of Citrus County, Inverness, Fla., 1982-85; pres. Damason Constrn. Corp., Citrus County, Inverness, 1985—. Chmn. adv. bd. Largo (Fla.) High Sch., 1972-77; mem. adv. bd. Boy Scouts Am., Rainbow Girls. Served with Women's RAF, 1948-51. Mem. Nat. Inst. Bldg. Scis. (pres. Fla. consultative council 1981-84), Elec. Council Fla. (state dir., state pres., chmn. edn.), So. Bldg. Code Congress (v.p. West Coast chpt.), Citrus County

Builders Assn. (chmn. legis. com.). Democrat. Clubs: University, Order Eastern Star. Contbr. articles to profl. jours. Home: 1055 N Lyle Ave Crystal River FL 32629 Office: 115 S Croft Ave Inverness FL 32650

DAVIS, WILMA JEAN, nursing home adminstr.; b. Goodland, Mo., Apr. 24, 1931; d. Sherman L. and Bessie Keith; cert. housing mgmt., Community Sch. Practical Nursing, Columbia U., 1977, cert. activity dir., 1977, med. records cert., 1978; m. Billy Davis, Mar. 15, 1968; children—Jackie, David, Joey, Kelly. Colonial Nursing Home, Bismarck, Mo., 1958—, Lone Pine Congregate Center, Ironton, Mo., 1977—, Belleview (Mo.) Nursing Home, 1956—. Mem. Am. Health Care Assn., Mo. Assn. Lic. Practical Nurses, Mo. Health Care Assn., Activity Dirs. Assn. Mo. Methodist. Club: Order Eastern Star. Address: Box 24 Star Route Belleview MO 63623

DAVIS, WILMA JOYCE, insurance company operations center manager; b. Bells, Tenn., Feb. 24, 1951; d. Wilmer Franklin and Thelma (Fears) Davis; 1 dau., Jillian. B.S., Lambuth Coll., 1971. Claims field asst. Hartford Ins. Group, Hartford, Conn., 1971-73; ops. supr. Allstate Ins. Co., Farmington, Conn., 1973-75, ops. tech. specialist, Murray Hill, N.J., 1975-76, ops. div. mgr., Long Island, N.Y. and Murray Hill, 1976-80, ops. dept. mgr., Rochester, N.Y., 1980-81, project dir., Northbrook, Ill., 1981-82, regional ops ctr. mgr., Murray Hill, 1982—. Named Woman Achiever of Yr., N.Y. YWCA, 1983. Baptist. Office: Allstate Ins Co Mountain Ave Murray Hill NJ 07094

DAVIS-LOFTON, DEBRA ANN, speech pathologist; b. Houston, Sept. 2, 1955; d. Walter and Lucille (Cornish) Davis; m. Lionel Anderson Lofton, June 12, 1982. B.S., Baylor U., 1977; M.A., U. Houston, 1983. Billing clk. Triangle Refineries, Houston, 1977; speech pathologist, spl. edn. tchr. Houston Ind. Sch. Dist., 1977—; cons. Lofton Enterprises, 1982—. Pianist, dir. ch. choir South Union Bapt. Ch., 1977—. Mem. Tex. Speech and Hearing Assn., Council for Exceptional Children, Nat. Speech, Hearing and Lang. Assn., Houston Fedn. Tchrs. Democrat. Baptist. Home: 6732 Goforth St Houston TX 77021

DAVISON, BETSY JANE, training consultant; b. Cleve., Dec. 22, 1921; d. Alexander Stuart and Helen Eva (Chapman) D.; student Albion (Mich.) Coll., 1941-43; B.A., U. Chgo., 1943; M.A., Tchrs. Coll., Columbia U., 1952. Civilian recreation dir. U.S. Army and Air Force Overseas, 1945-55; command recreation dir. Hdqrs. U.S. Air Forces in Europe, Ger., 1956-58; coordinator student activities Kean (N.J.) Coll., 1959-66; cons. edn. and tng. Assn. Jr. Leagues, N.Y.C., 1966-70; dir. tng. Mental Health Materials Center, N.Y.C., 1971-76; tng. cons. APC Skills Co., N.Y.C., 1977-78; dir. tng. and confs. Child Welfare League Am., N.Y.C., 1979-83; tng. cons., 1983—. Mem. Am. Soc. Tng. and Devel., Am. Adult Edn. Assn., Kappa Delta Pi, Pi Lambda Theta, Delta Sigma Rho, Alpha Lambda Delta. Author tng. manuals. Home and Office: 333 E 43d St New York NY 10017

DAVISON, DOROTHY, urban planner; b. Boston, June 22, 1925; d. Israel and Tillie (Bloom) Goldstein; student Chaffey Coll., 1947, Ind. U., 1948-50, Harvard U., 1952-55, Contra Costa Coll., 1956-59, U. Calif., Berkeley, 1960; B.A. in Urban Studies-Community Devel., San Francisco State U., 1968; postgrad. in basic indsl. devel. Tex. A&M U., 1982; postgrad. Econ. Devel. Inst., U. Okla., 1982-84; m. Sol Davison, Feb. 3, 1945; children—Scott J., Mark G. With CSC, Mass., Calif., Tex. and Fla., 1942-46; apptd. to Mayor's Citizen Adv. Com., Richmond Urban Renewal Agy., Assn. Bay Area Govts. and Richmond (Calif.) Model Cities, 1956-72; chief planner Harris County Community Devel. Agy., Houston, 1975-82, asst. dir., 1982-84, dir. research and devel., 1984-85; exec. dir. Harris County Housing Authority and Harris County Community Devel. Agy., 1985—. Cons. Tex. A&M U. Agrl. Extension Resource Council; Gulf Coast regional econ. devel. com. Houston/Galveston Area Council; nat. del. White House Conf. on Aging, 1981; Tex. del. Gov.'s Conf. Aging, 1981; chmn. housing for elderly Houston/Harris County Area Agy. Aging, 1981. Cert. housing mgr.; specialist in sr. citizen housing; recipient cert. merit City of Richmond, 1969, Women in Govt. cert. U. Houston, 1978, ct. resolution Harris County Commrs., 1981; lic. real estate broker, Tex. Mem. Am. Planning Assn., Nat. Assn. Housing and Redevel. Ofcls. (internat. com.), Tex. Indsl. Devel. Council, Nat. Assn. Home Builders (srs. housing com. 1984—), Nat. Inst. Sr. Housing (del. council 1985—). Home: 11919 Pebble Rock Dr Houston TX 77077 Office: 3100 Timmons Ln Suite 202 Houston TX 77027

DAWKINS, MARVA PHYLLIS, psychologist; b. Jacksonville, Fla., Apr. 12, 1948; d. Ralph and Altamese (Padgett) D.; student U. Freiburg (W.Ger.), 1969-70; B.S., Stetson U., 1971; M.S., Fla. State U., 1972, Ph.D., 1975. Research asst. Fla. State U., Tallahassee, 1970-72; clin. intern, psychology dept. Presbyn.-St. Luke's Med. Center and mental health dept. Mile Square Health Center, Chgo., 1973-74; staff psychologist, dir. aftercare treatment program, mental health dept. Mile Square Health Center, Chgo., 1974-75, staff psychologist, coordinator devel. disabilities program, 1976-79; asst. prof. psychology U. North Fla., Jacksonville, 1975-76, Rush U.-Presbyn. St. Luke's Med. Center, Chgo., 1976—; pvt. practice clin. psychology, 1977—; exec. dir. Inst. for Community Mental Health, 1979—. Registered psychologist, Ill. Mem. Am. Psychol. Assn., Assn. Black Psychologists. Office: PO Box 49474 Chicago IL 60649

DAWLEY, PATRICIA KELLY, bank executive; b. Seattle, July 27, 1937; d. Gail W. and Edith Kelly; B.A., U. Wash., 1959; M.B.A., N.Y. U., 1979. Exec. v.p., sec. Anchor Savs. Bank, N.Y.C., 1978—. Mem. Nat. Assn. Bank Women, AAUW, Delta Gamma. Club: Zonta. Office: New York NY

DAWSON, CYNTHIA FORESMAN, oil company financial executive; b. Greenville, Miss., Nov. 11, 1954; d. David Laird and Evelyn Virginia (Bush) Foresman; m. Michael R. Dawson, Jan. 31, 1981. B.S., Miss. State U., 1976, M.B.A., 1978. Acct., Shell Oil Co., New Orleans, 1978-81, acctg. supr., Houston, 1981; acctg. mgr. Elf Aquitaine Petroleum, Houston, 1981—. Methodist. Office: 1000 Louisiana Allied Bank Plaza Suite 3800 Houston TX 77002

DAWSON, JUDITH M SHEEHAN, educational administrator; b. Honolulu, Nov. 3, 1939; d. Wade Edmund and Barbara Montague (Guard) Sheehan; m. Donald D. Dawson, Apr. 4, 1964 (div. Aug. 1979); children—Mark Lynn, Starr Montague. Student Wellesley Coll., 1957-59; B.A., U. Calif.-Berkeley, 1962; M.A., U. Hawaii, 1977. Exec. sec. Halekulani Hotel, Honolulu, 1962-64; reservations mgr. Waikiki Grand Hotel, Honolulu, 1964-65; community relations officer East-West Ctr., Honolulu, 1965-66; dir. devel. Punahou Sch., Honolulu, 1978—. Bd. dirs. Boys Club Am., Honolulu, 1982—; trustee, v.p. Atherton Family Found., Honolulu, 1980—; trustee Hawaiian Mission Childrens Soc., 1982—, pres., 1986—. Mem. Hawaii Soc. Fund-Raising Execs. (trustee, bd. dirs. 1983—), Oriental Art Soc. (bd. dirs. 1979—). Republican. Episcopalian. Club: Oahu Country (Honolulu). Home: 3155 Kaohinani Dr Honolulu HI 96817 Office: Punahou Sch 1601 Punahou St Honolulu HI 96822

DAWSON, KATHLEEN MARIE, personnel executive; b. Nagoya, Japan, Nov. 15, 1956; d. Owen Lafayette and Mary Eunice (Paul) Dawson; m. Serge O. Pieters, Aug. 19, 1982. B.B.A., Midwestern State U., 1977; M.B.A., 1981. Personnel clk. Mental Health/Mental Retardation Ctr., Wichita Falls, Tex., 1978-79; personnel asst. Ingersoll-Rand, Wichita Falls, Tex., 1979-80; employment mgr. Howmet Turbine, Wichita Falls, Tex., 1980-81, personnel mgr., 1981—; cons. in field. Loaned exec. United Way, Wichita Falls, 1983, vol., 1981-82; mem. Alcoholism Adv. Council, 1983, Child Care Task Force/Community Council, 1982; active Beacon Lighthouse for Blind, 1981-82. Named Young Career Woman, Bus. and Profl. Women's Club, 1983. Mem. Tex.-Okla. Personnel Assn. (pres.), Bus. and Profl. Women's Club, Am. Soc. Personnel Adminstrn., Tex. Assn. Bus. (corp. mem.), Indsl. Forum. Home: 1013 Preston Rd Burkburnett TX 76354 Office: PO Box 1616 6200 Central Freeway Wichita Falls TX 76354

DAWSON, MARY ANN WEYFORTH, federal commissioner; b. St. Louis, Aug. 31, 1944; d. Francis Griffin and Jeanne Gething Weyforth; A.B. in Govt., Washington U., St. Louis, 1966; m. Rhett B. Dawson, Jan. 15, 1976; 1 child, Elizabeth Stuart. Legis. asst. Rep. James Symington, Mo., 1969-72; legis. asst., press sec. Rep. Richard Ichord, Mo., 1973; press sec. Senator Packwood, 1973-75, legis. dir., 1975-76, adminstrv. asst., chief of staff, 1976-81; commr. FCC, Washington, 1981—. Mem. Am. Council Young Polit. Leaders (sec.-gen. Atlantic assn.), Washington U. Alumni Assn. Republican. Roman Catholic. Office: FCC 1919 M St NW Washington DC 20554

DAWSON, SARAH ELIZABETH, data processing professional; b. Houston, Dec. 3, 1942; d. James Thomas Sr. and Lester (Barnes) D. B.B.A., Stephen F. Austin State U., 1964, M.B.A., 1972. Computer operator Stephen F. Austin State U., Nacogdoches, Tex., 1964-65; computer operator Southland Paper Mills, Lufkin, Tex., 1965-67, jr. programmer, 1967-69; programmer Am. Gen. Ins. Co., Houston, 1969-71; dir. data processing Mother Frances Hosp., Tyler, Tex., 1972-76; sr. analyst, cons. Lone Star Gas Co., Dallas, 1976-80; sr. product analyst Uccel Corp. (formerly Univ. Computing Co.), Dallas, 1980—; product cons. Global Software Inc., 1986—. Tchr. local ch., Cushing, Tex., 1960—; pres. Dist. Women's Missionary Soc., East Tex., 1978-82; v.p. High Sch. Ex-Students Assn., Cushing, 1981; pres. Dist. Ch. Fellowship, East Tex. Recipient Uccel achievement award, 1984, Chmn. Bd. award for excellence, 1985. Mem. Assn. M.B.A.s, Nat. Assn. Female Execs., AAUW. Democrat. Congregational Methodist.

DAWSON, VELORIA JEAN, accountant; b. Portland, Oreg., Feb. 1, 1953; d. Lee and Maxine (James) Nanze; m. Alfred Earl Dawson, June 5, 1976. B.A. in Acctg., Tex. Luth. Coll., Seguin, 1974; student Texarkana Community Coll. (Tex.), 1971, 72, 74, East Tex. State U., Texarkana, 1973. Acctg. asst. Exxon Chem., Houston, 1977-79; auditor Blue Cross-Blue Shield, Houston, 1979-81, sr. auditor, 1981; reimbursement cons. Lifemark Corp., Houston, 1981-83, sr. reimbursement cons., 1983—. Mem. Healthcare Fin. Mgmt. Assn., Nat. Assn. Black Accts. Democrat. Office: Lifemark Corp 3800 Buffalo Speedway Houston TX 77098

DAY, BEVERLY JEAN, state insurance examiner; b. Tacoma, Wash., July 29, 1942; d. Therial Etheon and Georgia Ykema (Fisher) Wright; A.A., Riverside City Coll., 1962; B.A., U. Md., 1969; M.B.A., U. Utah, 1975; m. Dallas Glenn Day, June 13, 1964; 1 child, Linda Gayle. Cert. fin. examiner Acct., Toledo Scale Corp., Riverside, Calif., 1962-64, Dikeou Bros., Denver, 1964-65, Redlands (Calif.) Community Hosp., 1965-66, Titan Constrn. Co., Denver, 1969-72; med. record technician U.S. Air Force Hosp., RAF Lakenheath, England, 1973-76; insurance examiner State of Colo. Ins. Div., Denver, 1977—, now sr. ins. examiner. Recipient scholarship Am. Soc. Women Accountants, 1961. Mem. Soc. Fin. Examiners (state chmn.) Assn. M.B.A. Execs., Nat. Assn. Female Execs., Inc., Am. Med. Record Assn., AAUW. Republican. Methodist. Home: 10330 W Burgundy Ave Littleton CO 80127 Office: Div Ins State of Colo First Western Plaza Bldg 303 W Colfax Ave 5th Floor Denver CO 80204

DAY, DEBRA-LYNN GENDUSO, biomedical research company executive. B.A., Harvard U., 1975; M.S. in Pharmacology, NYU, Sackler Inst. Grad. Biomed. Scis., 1979; Ph.D. in Pharmacology, NYU, 1982; M.D., Case Western Res. U., 1986. Chief technician dept. pathology, Div. Immunochemistry, Englewood Hosp., N.J., 1970-71; troupe mem. Bucks County Playhouse, New Hope, Pa., 1971; chief technician dept. pathology, Div. Immunochemistry, Englewood Hosp.; lab. technician dept. pediatric hematology Flower and Fifth Ave. Hosp. and Met. City Hosp., N.Y.C., 1974; lab. technician dept. preventive medicine N.J. Coll. Medicine and Dentistry, Newark, 1975; research asst. depts. pharmacology and medicine Div. Human Genetics, NYU Med. Ctr., N.Y.C., 1977-78; health services cons. Hudson Regional Health Commn., Jersey City, 1977-78; grad. fellow faculty appointee dept. pharmacology NYU Med. Ctr., N.Y.C., 1978-79; sr. research asst. dept. medicine Case Western Res. U., Cleve., 1979-82, research assoc. dept. molecular biology and microbiology, 1982-84; exec. v.p. biomed. research Lysantian Mgt., Inc., Cleve., 1984—. Contbr. articles to profl. jours. Uniti scholar; Am. Heart Assn. research fellow; recipient Letter of Recognition for excellence in teaching Dean of Undergrad. Studies and Western Res. Coll.'s Class of 1984. Mem. Internat. Thespian Soc., Ohio Med. Soc., N.Y. Acad. Sci., AAAS, AMA, Am. Soc. Cell Biology. Avocations: repertory theatre; classical ballet; theatre dance; choreography; travel; modeling.

DAY, GENA THERESE, income tax preparation executive; b. Fort Knox, Ky., Apr. 22, 1954; d. James Francis and Frances Ann (Shotts) Fritz; m. Dan Ronald Day, July 8, 1972; children—Brandie Lee, Daniel James. Student pub. schs. Income tax preparer H&R Block, Inc., Pontiac, Mich., 1974-75, checker, 1975-77, seasonal adminstrv. asst., 1977-79, asst. adminstr., Madison Heights, Mich., 1979-80, dist. mgr., Detroit, 1980—. Mem. Nat. Assn. Female Execs. Home: 51 Parakeet Hill Pontiac MI 48055 Office: H&R Block Inc 14311 W McNichols Detroit MI 48235

DAY, GRACE ANNE, violinist; b. Tondo, Belgian Congo, Jan. 4, 1933, (parents Am. citizens); d. George Wesley and Ellen Irene (Peckham) Westcott; B.M., Eastman Sch. Music, 1957; m. Bernard Hoffer, June 1957; children—Kara Hoffer Day, Gilbert Hoffer; m. 2d, Robert Day, Feb. 8, 1972; adopted children—Ronald Day, Robin Day. Violinist, Rochester (N.Y.) Philharmo. Orch., 1953-58, orch. Radio City Music Hall, N.Y.C., 1964-65, N.J. Symphony, Newark, 1965-66, Toledo Symphony, 1966-67, Indpls. Symphony Orch., 1967—, Suzuki and Friends Chamber Orch., Indpls., 1980—; mem. faculty Am. U., 1961; pvt. tchr. violin. Mem. Matinee Musical. Home: 903 W 54th St Indianapolis IN 46208

DAY, JANICE ELDREDGE, cosmetic company executive; b. New Bedford, Mass., Sept. 26, 1919; d. Wendell Tripp and Lucy Forbush (Houghton) Eldredge, B.A. in English, Middlebury Coll., 1941; m. Frank Perrett, Apr. 22, 1949; 1 dau., Janna. Publicity writer A.H. Handley, Boston, 1941-42; sec. media Ladies Home Jour., Boston, 1942-45, McCann, Erickson, N.Y.C., 1945; sec. Cambridge U. Press, MacMillan Co., N.Y.C., 1945-46; exec. sec. Fort Monroe, Va., 1946-47, Stone & Webster Engrg., 1947-49; mgr. sales Collier Co., San Francisco, 1947-48; unit mgr. Stanley Home Products, Los Angeles, 1949-51; dist. sales mgr. Beauty Creators Cosmetics, Los Angeles, 1951-56; co-founder, v.p. sales and mktg. Jafra Cosmetics, Inc., Malibu, Calif., 1956-76, chmn. bd., 1976—. Recipient Alumni Achievement award Middlebury Coll., 1983. Mem. Direct Selling Assn. (dir.). Republican. Episcopalian. Home: Box 1085 Malibu CA 90265 Office: Jafra Cosmetics Inc Westlake Village CA 91361

DAY, JENNIE D., state legislator. Mem. R.I. Senate, 1985—. Democrat. Office: RI Senate State Capitol Providence RI 02903*

DAY, JULIA FRANCES, lawyer; b. Atlanta, Feb. 23, 1947; d. Thomas Thorne and Julia (Gemes) Flagler; m. Stephen Joseph Day, May 1, 1970; 1 dau., Ashley Elizabeth. A.B., U. Ga., 1968; J.D., Lincoln U., 1979. Bar: Calif. 1979. Paralegal Ericksen, Arbuthnot, McCarthy, Kearny & Walsh, San Francisco, 1978-79, assoc., 1979-83, ptnr., office mgr., San Jose, Calif., 1983—. Mem. ABA, Calif. Bar Assn., Santa Clara Bar Assn., No. Calif. Def. Counsel, Calif. Trial Lawyers Assn., San Jose C. of C., Republican. Episcopalian. Club: Commerce (San Francisco); U. Ga. Alumni. Home: 35 Elston Ct San Carlos CA 94070 Office: Ericksen Arbuthnot McCarthy Kearny & Walsh 351 Miller St San Jose CA 95110

DAY, MARY, ballet company executive; b. Washington, Student ballet with Lisa Gardinier. Mem. Washington Nat. Ballet, 1937-39; co-founder Washington Sch. of Ballet, 1944; co-founder Washington Ballet, 1956, now artistic dir. Address: Washington Ballet 3515 Wisconsin Ave NW Washington DC 20016*

DAY, MARYLOUISE MULDOON (MRS. RICHARD DAYTON DAY), appraiser; b. St. Louis; d. Joseph A. and Dorothy (Lang) Muldoon; A.B., Washington U., St. Louis, 1940; postgrad. Air U., 1958, George Washington U., 1963-64; grad. Real Estate Inst. Md., 1972; m. Richard Dayton Day, Aug. 15, 1959. Intelligence specialist U.S. Air Force, Washington, 1947-60; program officer, spl. asst. to dir. project devel. VISTA, OEO, 1965-67; v.p. Culpeper Corp., Wilmington, Del., 1955-65; with Joint Intelligence Bur., London, Eng., 1953; appraiser, cons. on antiques, fine arts, 1969—; pres. Agts. For Sales Ltd., 1974—, Marylouise M. Day, Inc., 1978—. Recipient citation U.S. Air Force, 1960. Fellow Inc. Soc. Valuers and Auctioneers (London), Am. Soc. Appraisers (chpt. 1st v.p. 1977-78, pres. 1978-79, chmn. fine arts forum 1976-78, gov. Region 3 1980-82, internat. sec. 1982-84); mem. Appraisers Assn. Am., Irish Georgian Soc., Winterthur Guild, Assn. Former Intelligence Officers, Delta Gamma. Club: Kenwood Golf and Country (Washington). Home: 4928 Sentinel Dr Bethesda MD 20816

DAY, VICKI JEANETTE, art director; b. Odessa, Tex., Jan. 27, 1951; d. Bobby Brower and Norma Jean (Richey) Smith; m. Larry Stephen Day, Apr. 18, 1972. Student, Comml. Coll. Odessa, 1970-71, So. Meth. U., 1982. Office clk. TG&Y, Odessa, 1970-72; buyer's asst. Stripling's, Ft. Worth, 1972-73, Monnig's Dept. Store, Ft. Worth, 1973-74; paste-up artist Ft. Worth Shopper/Observer, 1974-78, asst. prodn. foreman, 1978-79; art dir. Paint Horse Jour., Ft. Worth, 1979—. Recipient outstanding student award Adult Urban Project, Ft. Worth, 1974; Excellence awards Livestock Publs. Council, 1979, 80, 83, Am. Horse Council, 1981, 82, 84. Democrat.

DAYANI, ELIZABETH LOUISE, nurse executive; b. Birmingham, Ala., Apr. 28, 1950; d. Jon Killough and Flora L. (Worthington) Crow; m. John Hassan Dayani, June 13, 1970; 1 child, John Hassan. B.S.N. cum laude, Vanderbilt U., 1971, M.S.N., 1972. Cert. family nurse practitioner. Instr., Vanderbilt U., Nashville, 1972-74; dir./practitioner Moore County Primary Care Ctr., Lynchburg, Tenn., 1974-75; family nurse practitioner Nashville Met. Health Dept., 1975-76; asst. prof. Wayne State U. Sch. Nursing, Detroit, 1976-77, U. Kans. Sch. Nursing, Kansas City, 1977-81, asso. prof., 1981-82, adj. prof., 1983—; co-owner, corp. adminstr. Am. Nursing Resources, Inc., Kansas City, Mo., 1982—; affiliated faculty U. Mo. Sch. Nursing, 1985—; cons. in field, Co-author: The Nurse Entrepreneur, 1984; assoc. editor Nursing Econs., 1985; contbg. editor The Nurse Practitioner, 1979-82; editorial bd. The Kans. Nurse, 1983; contbr. articles to profl. jours. Recipient Service award Moore County, 1975; others. Mem. Am. Nurses Assn., Nat. League Nursing, Nat. Assn. Women Bus. Owners, Nat. Assn. Home Care, Nurse Cons. Assn., Kans. Nurses Found., Sigma Theta Tau. Republican. Presbyterian. Clubs: Central Exchange, Soroptimists (Kansas City, Mo.). Avocations: reading; travel; jogging. Office: Am Nursing Resources Inc 3100 Broadway Suite 111 Kansas City MO 64111

DAYTON, PATRICIA COCHRAN, banker; b. Balt., June 4, 1940; d. Elmer Stephen and Catherine (Miller) Cochran; m. James Elton Baughman, Sept. 28, 1963 (div. June 1971); 1 son, James Dean; m. Edson Burton Dayton, Apr. 13, 1973. A.A., Villa Julie Coll., 1960; B.S. in Fin., U. Balt., 1975, M.B.A., 1977. Assoc. dean U. Balt., 1977-78, asst. prof., 1977-81; mktg. research officer First Nat. Bank of Md., Balt., 1978-81; asst. v.p. Merc.-Safe Deposit and Trust Co., Balt., 1981-83; tng. officer Sun Banks of Fla., Inc., Orlando, 1983-84, corp. cash mgmt. customer service officer, 1984-85, asst. v.p., 1985—; mktg. cons., Orlando, 1983—; co-founder, women's grad. program in mgmt. U. Balt., 1976; career counselor Continuing Edn. for Women, Valencia Community Coll., 1984—. Mem. Baltimore County Commn. for Women, 1979-81. Mem. Am. Mktg. Assn., Nat. Assn. Bank Women, Bank Mktg. Assn., Beta Alpha. Office: Sun Banks of Fla PO Box 3833 200 S Orange Ave Orlando FL 32897

DEA, MARGARET MARY, wholesale school supplies company executive; b. St. Albans, Vt., Feb. 8, 1946; s. Ralph Homer and Irene Mae (Trombly) Wilson; m. Eugene Michael Dea, Aug. 26, 1967; children—Francesca Meredith, Vanessa Laurel. B.A., U. Vt., 1967; student Art Students League, 1972-77, Sch. Visual Arts, 1975-77. Tchr. French, Hun Sch., Princeton, N.J., 1968-70; tchr. French, Spanish, Newark Acad., Short Hills, N.J., 1970-71; dir. reading, research and edn. Park Sch., Indpls., summers, 1968-71; exec. tng. personnel Bloomingdale's, N.Y.C., 1972-74; commn. portrait artist, Englewood, N.J., Lake Forest, Ill., 1974-79; pres. Service Plus, Inc., Fort Myers, Fla., 1979—, United So., Inc., 1983—; graphic designer E.M. Dea & Assocs., Fort Myers, 1984—, v.p., 1985—. Editor, author Bloomingdale's employee mag. Faces, 1972-74. Mem. Portrait Soc. Am., Nat. Assn. Female Execs., Portrait Inst., Womens Network, Lee County Alliance Arts. Republican. Roman Catholic. Club: Jr. League Bergen County. Avocations: piano; needlework; drawing; photography. Office: Service Plus Inc 30 Mildred Dr Fort Myers FL 33901

DEAL, JOANNE BAKER, freelance writer, publicity consultant; b. Long Beach, Calif., July 17, 1955; d. Richard Gene and Grace Lorraine (Thomas) Baker; m. Thomas Everett Deal, Aug. 18, 1979; 1 dau., Sarah Joy. A.A., Long Beach City Coll., 1975; B.A. Speech Communication, U. So. Calif., 1977; postgrad. Calif. State U.-Fullerton, 1978-79. Office mgr., research asst. U. So. Calif., Los Angeles, 1975-77; layout typist, copy editor McDonnell Douglas Corp., Long Beach, Calif., 1977-78; creative asst. K. Esterly & Assocs., La Habra, Calif., 1978; grad. asst. Calif. State U., Fullerton, 1978-79; asst. editor, publicity asst. Globe Pequot Press, Chester, Conn., 1980-82; free lance writer, Ivoryton, Conn., 1982—; multi-media cons./asst. Twentyone-hundred Prodns., Madison, Wis., 1977, Karl Karcher Entr., Anaheim, Calif., 1978; research cons., asst. Orange County chpt. Pub. Relations Soc. Am., 1978. Contbr. articles to various publs.; editor: Great New England Churches, 1982; Factory Store Guide to All New England, 1981; The Bluefish Cookbook, 1981. Advisor publicity/fundraising Refugee Resettlement Projects, Interfaith Council Old Saybrook, 1980, Lower Valley chpt. Pro-Life Council Conn., 1980—; newsletter editor Clinton Bapt. Ch., Conn., 1983—. Mem. Women in Communications, Phi Beta Kappa, Phi Kappa Phi. Republican. Baptist. Address: 68 Mares Hill Rd Ivoryton CT 06442

DEAL, PATRICIA LOU EISENBISE, educational administrator; b. Reading, Pa., Mar. 25, 1932; d. Jasper Paul and Mae (Rozycki) Eisenbise; B.S., Albright Coll., 1954; M.A., Pacific Lutheran U., 1978; m. Robert Lee Deal, May 31, 1955; children—Robert Lee Jr., David Alan, James Edward. Tchr. aide instr.-coordinator Clover Park Vocat.-Tech. Inst., Tacoma, Wash., 1970-78, asst. to program supr. of secondary vocat. edn., 1979, career edn. asst., fed. and spl. projects asst., 1979-81, asst. dir. Elective High Sch., 1981-82, dir., 1982-84, 85, dir. Elective High Sch. and Adult Edn., 1985-86; dir. Singletree Estates, Yelm, Wash., 1981-84, 85. Recipient Community Service award United Way, 1980; honoree Clover Park Found., 1984, 85, 86. Mem. Wash. Vocat. Assn. (pres. Clover Park local unit 1981-82, legis. chmn. 1980-81, exec. bd. local chpt. 1985-86), Wash. Assn. Career Edn. (mem. exec. bd. 1980-81), Am. Vocat. Assn., C. of C., Pierce County Adminstrv. Women in Edn., South Sound Women's Network, Nat. Council Local Adminstrs., Wash. Assn. Vocat. Adminstrs. Home: 8401 Woodlawn Ave SW Tacoma WA 98499 Office: 4500 Steilacoom Blvd SW Tacoma WA 98499

DEALMEIDA, MARCELLA J., banker; d. Floyd Francis and Ruth Elma (Cox) Craig; grad. Sch. Consumer Banking, U. Va., 1973; children—Steven Craig and Victor James (twins). Fashion model, 1941-42; tchr. of voice, piano and organ, 1943-53; with First Nat. Bank & Trust Co., Joplin, Mo., 1953-81, v.p., 1976-81; sr. v.p. Centerre Bank of Springfield (Mo.), 1981—; condr. TV program on banking and fin., 1974-75, workshops for Am. Bankers Assn., 1974-75; speaker in field. Bd. dirs. S.W. Mo. Health Systems Agy., 1975-79; mem. Gov. Mo. Adv. Council, 1971-74; exec. com. Jasper County Devel. Assn., 1969-72; vice chmn. Mo. Health Planning Council, 1976; mem. adv. council U. Mo. Health Services Research Center, U. Mo. Spl. Emphasis Health Care Tech. Center. Named to Hall of Honor, Joplin Ann. Celebration Commn., 1973. Mem. Nat. Assn. Bank Women (past chmn. Ozark group), Mo. (past chmn., dir. women's div.), Am. (adv. bd. installment loan div. 1973-79) bankers assns., Am. Inst. Banking (div. dir., bd. govs.), Joplin C. of C. (chmn. red carpet com. 1970-79). Baptist. Clubs: Briarbrook Golf and Country, Mid-Am. Press (dir. 1975—). Home: Route 2 Fair Grove MO 65648 Office: 300 S Jefferson St PO Box 1745SSS Springfield MO 65806

DEAN, DEAREST (LORENE GLOSUP), songwriter; b. Volin, S.D., Oct. 4, 1911; d. John Henry and Bessie Marie Donnelly Peterson; m. Eddie Glosup, Sept. 11, 1931; children—Donna Lee Knorr, Edgar Glosup II. Student public schs. Yankton, S.D. Composer songs including: One Has My Name, 1948; The Lonely Hours, 1970, 1501 Miles of Heaven, 1970, Walk Beside Me, 1980. Sec., ARC, Burbank, Calif., 1943. Bd. dirs. Acad. Country Music, Hollywood, 1960-62. Mem. ASCAP. Republican. Roman Catholic. Avocation: golf.

DEAN, DEBORAH GORE, government agency administrator; b. N.Y.C., Nov. 30, 1954; d. Gordon Evans and Mary (Gore) D. B.S., Georgetown U., 1980. Mng. editor Encore Mag., Washington, 1978-79; publisher City Life Mag., Washington, 1979-81; dir. pub. relations Global Research Internat., Washington, 1981; spl. asst. to asst. sec. U.S. Dept. Energy, Washington, 1981-82; spl. asst. to sec., dir. exec. secretariat U.S. Dept. HUD, Washington, 1982-84, exec. asst. to sec., 1984—; mem. planning group Nat. Urban Coalition, Washington, 1985; rep. Indemnity Council Nat. Endowments of Arts, Washington, 1983—, adv. bd. on child abuse and neglect Dept. HHS, Washington, 1985; chmn. Nat. Campaign of Pub./Private Partnerships for Fair Housing, Washington, 1983—. Editor: The Georgetowner mag., 1978. Fundraiser, The Textile Mus., Washington, 1984; vol. Reagan-Bush '80, Rockville, Md., 1979-80; speechwriter Gore for Gov. Campaigns, Rockville, 1974, 78, Leadership Found., Washington, 1972, 73. Named Outstanding Young Women of Am., 1984, Woman of Yr. N.Y. Black Rep. Council, 1984; recipient Key to City Deborah Gore Dean Day, Providence, 1984. Mem. Nat. Press Club, Nat. Strategy Info. Ctr. Roman Catholic. Home: 4201 Cathedral Ave NW #1201-E Washington DC 20016 Office: US Dept HUD 451 7th St SW Room 10000 Washington DC 20410

DEAN, DONNA RAE, employment administrator; b. Oak Ridge, Sept. 30, 1945; d. Lloyd Ray and Connie Victoria (Chappell) Bryson; m. Donald William Dean, Apr. 20, 1974; 1 stepson, Donald Mark. A.A., Rollins Coll., 1978, B.S., 1979. Adminstrv. sec. Martin Marietta Aerospace, Cape Canaveral, Fla., 1972-74, exec. sec., 1974, asso. analyst personnel, 1974-76, personnel adminstrn. specialist, 1976-79, sr. specialist personnel adminstrn., 1979-82, adminstr. employment, 1982—. Campaign mgr. Lori Wilson for county commr., Cocoa Beach, Fla., 1970, for state senate, Merritt Island, 1972, Cocoa Beach, 1974. Recipient Vice Pres.'s award Martin Marietta Aerospace, 1978, 81, Titan Gold Medallion, 1979, Titan III Double Check award, 1976. Mem. Brevard Personnel Assn. (past dir., sec.), Am. Soc. Personnel Adminstrn. Republican. Baptist. Clubs: Martin Marietta Mgmt. (dir. 1974-75), Young Republicans. Home: 600 Milford Point Merritt Island FL 32952 Office: Martin Marietta Aerospace PO Box 1399 Cocoa Beach FL 32931

DEAN, ELIZABETH NATIONS, banker, lawyer; b. Orange, Tex., Aug. 25, 1951; d. Charles Wayne and Frances (Forsythe) D.; children by previous marriage—Sterling Pierce Jeffries, Travis Clark Jeffries. B.A. in Fine Arts, U. N.Mex., 1975, J.D., 1978. Bar: N.Mex. 1978. Trust officer, corp. trust mgr. Sunwest Bank of Albuquerque, 1979—. Mem. N.Mex. Bar Assn. Office: Sunwest Bank of Albuquerque PO Box 1344 Albuquerque NM 87110

DEAN, FRANCES CHILDERS, educator; b. Lipan, Tex., Apr. 20, 1930; 1 dau., Deborah Jane. B.S., Tex. Woman's U., 1959, M.L.S., 1962; postgrad. U. Md., 1963-68, U. Va., 1979-83. Elem. librarian pub. schs., Dallas, 1959-62, Fairfax, Va., 1963; secondary librarian Montgomery County, Rockville, Md., 1963-69, tchr. specialist, 1969-72, coordinator div. instructional materials, 1976-80, dir. dept. instructional resources, 1980—. Author: American Assn. Sch. Librarians Yearbook, 1978; contbr. articles to profl. jours. Trustee Freedom To Read Found., 1974-76, 78. Recipient outstanding service award D.C. Sch. Librarians, 1978. Mem. Am. Assn. Sch. Librarians (dir. 1972-74, pres. 1977-78, 1st Intellectual Freedom award 1982), ALA (chmn. intellectual freedom com. 1978-80), Ednl. Film Library Assn. (dir. 1979), Soc. Sch. Librarians Internat. (pres. 1986), Beta Phi Mu, Assn. Supervision and Curriculum Devel., Children's Book Guild Washington. Home: 528 Meadow Hall Dr Rockville MD 20851 Office: Montgomery County Pub Schs 850 Hungerford Dr Rockville MD 20851

DEAN, JUANITA MARIE (NITA), writer; b. Columbus, Ohio, Sept. 14, 1948; d. John Harold Burger and Theresa Alice (Parzinger) Burger Chainey; m. James Lynn Dean, Mar. 15, 1969; 1 child, Terrel Joanna. B.S. in Communication, Ohio U., 1970. News reporter Sta. WATH-Radio, Athens, Ohio, 1972-73; film editor, floor dir. Sta. WCMH-TV, Columbus, 1974-77; orientation specialist CETA, Hamilton, Ohio, 1977-78; exec. dir. Louisville Zoo Soc., 1978-82; pub. relations assoc. Louisville Baptist Hosps., 1982-83; freelance writer, contbg. to publs. including Louisville Times/Courier Jour., 1983—; cons. Whittenberg Photog., Louisville, 1982; writer, performer radio spots Jefferson Mall, Louisville, 1979—; assoc. dir. communications and mktg. United Way of Franklin County. Leader council Girl Scouts U.S., Jeffersontown, 1983—. Honored with resolution Butler County Bd. Commrs., Hamilton, 1978. Mem. Assn. Zool. Parks and Aquariums, Women in Communications, Pub. Relations Soc. Am., Internat. Assn. Bus. Communicators, Mortar Board. Roman Catholic. Home: 1133 Forest Rise Dr Westerville OH 43081 Office: United Way of Franklin County 360 S 3d St Columbus OH 43215

DEAN, KATHLEEN IOVINE, telephone company employee; b. Syracuse, N.Y., Mar. 28, 1951; d. Dominick Albert and Mary Elizabeth (Jenner) Iovine; m. Roy Franklin Dean, June 20, 1970; 1 child, Kevin James. A.S. magna cum laude in Bus. Mgmt., Maria Regina Coll., 1986. Directory assistance operator N.Y. Telephone Co., Syracuse, 1969-72, drafter, 1972—; center mgr. Jr. Achievement, Liverpool, N.Y., 1981—, nat. conf. workshop leader, Bloomington, Ind., 1976-79, conf. coordinator, Liverpool, N.Y., 1977-86. Advisor Jr. Achievement, Syracuse, 1976-81; daycare adv. Parents for Onondaga County Daycare, Syracuse, 1974; vol. Discovery Ctr. Sci. Mus., Syracuse, 1985; art show coordinator N.Y. Telephone, 1986; vol. worker Nat. Kidney Found., U.S. Olympic Telethon, 1976, U.S. Olympic Com., 1984. Recipient 6-Yr. Vol. award Jr. Achievement, 1981. Mem. Nat. Assn. Female Execs., Am. Inst. Parliamentarians, Future Telephone Pioneers of Am., Alpha Sigma Lambda. Democrat. Roman Catholic. Lodge: Ladies Aux. of VFW (conductress 1973-74). Avocations: reading; travel; gourmet cooking; resume writing. Home: 201 Craigie St Syracuse NY 13206 Office: New York Telephone Co Customer Services-Engring 500 S Salina St 6th Floor Syracuse NY 13202

DEAN, LINDA BARSOM, special education educator, writer; b. Biloxi, Miss., Oct. 29, 1950; d. George Kasper and Judith Buel (Reed) Barsom; m. John Edward Dean, June 15, 1974; children—Justin Ryan, Jeffrey Taylor. B.S., Fla. State U., 1972; postgrad. Valdosta State Coll., 1973-74; M.Ed., U. New Orleans, 1976; student Inst. Children's Lit., 1982-83. Cert. spl. edn. tchr., Ala. Tchr. for multi-handicapped Ochlocknee Children's Ctr., 1972-73; tchr. for emotionally disturbed North Andrews Gardens Elem. Sch., Ft. Lauderdale, Fla., 1973-75; dir. program for devel. delayed DePaul Hosp., New Orleans, 1975-76; free-lance writer children's stories and books, Mobile, Ala., 1983—; mem. core staff First Chance Project, Ochlocknee Children's Ctr., 1972-74, mem. curriculum devel. staff, 1973-74, coordinator Climax Children's Ctr., 1973-74; del. Internat. Council for Exceptional Children Conv. from Fla. State U., 1972, Southwest Ga., 1973. Sec., bd. dirs. Mobile area LWV, 1984-86, chmn. War Vets. Study, 1985—; v.p., co-founder Mobilians for Better Nutrition, 1982; active LaLeche League, 1977-81; tchr. confraternity on Christian doctrine St. Clements Ch., Ft. Lauderdale, 1974-75, St. Joan of Arc Ch., Mobile, 1981—; tutor learning disabled children Rotary Rehab. Ctr., 1984-85, Old Dauphin Way Sch., 1985-86. Named Tchr. of Yr. of Exceptional Children for Southwest Ga., Ga. Fedn. Council for Exceptional Children 1974. Mem. Nat. Trust for Hist. Preservation, Hist. Mobile Preservation Soc., Aircraft Owners and Pilots Assn., Oakleigh Garden Soc., Spring Hill Food Coop., Zeta Tau Alpha. Republican. Roman Catholic. Club: Port City Pacers Road Runners (Mobile).

DEAN, LOUISE DANFORTH, educator; b. St. Louis, May 1, 1933; d. Carlton Miles and Christine Alice (Danforth) D.; B.A., Calif. State U., Northridge, 1971, M.A. with honors, 1974; Ed.D., Nova U., 1980; children—Deborah Louise, Lee E., Linda Gail, Laura Dean. Dir., Congl. Presch., Chatsworth, Calif., 1971-74; dir. campus child devel. ctr. Los Angeles Valley Coll., Moorpark, Calif., 1974-75, instr. child devel., 1975—; prof. Los Angeles Valley Coll., chmn. dept. family and cons. studies, 1979-86; assoc. prof. Calif. State U., Northridge, 1977; pres., past public policy chair Valley chpt. So. Calif. Edn. Young Children; bd. dirs. Child Care Consortium of San Fernando Valley, 1975-84; mem. accreditation com. Western Assn. Schs. and Colls., 1986; presenter Nat. Adv. Council on Women Hearings, 1979. Named Outstanding Calif. Home Econs. Prof. of Yr., 1984. Mem. Assn. Supervision and Curriculum Devel., Nat. Assn. Edn. of Young Children (nat. presenter 1977), Calif. Assn. Edn. Young Children (bd. dirs. 1982—), So. Calif. Assn. Edn. of Young Children (editor newsletter, pres. 1984), Child Care Consortium San Fernando Valley, NOW, Phi Kappa Phi, Kappa Kappa Gamma. Presbyterian. Home: 17808 Lemarsh St Northridge CA 91325 Office: 5800 Fulton Ave Van Nuys CA 91401

DEAN, LYDIA MARGARET CARTER (MRS. HALSEY ALBERT DEAN), food and nutrition consultant; educator, author; b. Bedford, Va., July 11, 1919; d. Christopher C. and Hettie (Gross) Carter; grad. Averett Coll.; B.S., Madison Coll., 1941; M.S., Va. Poly. Inst. and State U., 1951; U. Va.; Ph.D., Mich. State U.; Sc.D., UCLA, 1985; m. Halsey Albert Dean, Dec. 24, 1941; children—Halsey Albert, John Carter, Lydia Margerae. Dietetic intern, therapeutic dietitian St. Vincent de Paul Hosp., Norfolk, 1942, physicist, U.S. Naval Operating Base, Norfolk, Va., 1943-45; clin. dietitian, instr. Roanoke Meml. Hosps., 1946-51; asso. prof. nutrition Va. Poly. Inst. and State U., 1951-53; community nutritionist and supr. sch. lunch program Roanoke (Va.) Public Schs., 1953-60; dir. dept. dietetics and nutrition Southwestern Med. Center, Roanoke, 1960-67; food and nutrition cons. Nat. hdqrs. ARC, Washington, 1967-79, vol. food and nutrition cons., 1973-82; nutrition cons. U.S. Dept. Agr., Dept. Army, Washington, ARC, 1973—; dir. coordinated undergrad. degree program U. Hawaii, 1974; cons. Am. Dietetic Assn., 1969—, dir. communications, 1975—; mem. task force White House Conf. Food and Nutrition, 1969—; chmn. fed. com. Interagy. Com. on Nutrition Edn., 1970-71; tech. rep. to AID and Dept. State; chmn. Crusade for Nutrition Edn., Washington, 1970—; food cons. internat. tng. Dept. Agr., 1973; cons., participant U.S. Senatorial Nat. Nutrition Policy Conf., 1974. Fellow Am. Pub. Health Assn.; mem. Am. Dietetic Assn. (dir. communications ann. meeting program and publs. 1975—), Bus. and Profl. Women's Clubs U.S.A. (cons. 1970—, pres.-elect 1980-81, pres. 1981-82); Woman of Year 1982), Am. Home Econs. Assn. (rep. and treas. Joint Congressional Com.), AAUW, Inst. Food Technologists, Soc. for Nutrition Edn., Soc. for Nutrition Today (charter). Author: (with Virginia McMasters) Community Emergency Feeding, 1972; (with Stanton and Hatfield) Help! My Child Won't Eat Right, 1973; The Gourmet Nutrition Cookbook, 1978, rev. edit., 1980; Stress Food Book, 1980, rev. edit., 1981; The Stress Foodbook, 1982; Your Personal Health Book, 1982. Contbr. articles to profl. jours. Home: 7816 Birnam Wood Dr McLean VA 22102

DEAN, MARGARET GENEVIEVE, lawyer; b. Bklyn., Dec. 30, 1943; d. Richard Gerard and Pearl Dorothy (Olson) D.; B.A., Hunter Coll., 1967; J.D., U. Conn., 1980; m. Norman Dean, Apr. 3, 1966; children—Peter, Richard, Dean. Bar: Conn. 1980. Research asst. dept. pediatric psychiatry Bklyn. Jewish Med. Center, 1965-66; research asst. dept. internal medicine Yale U. Med. Sch., 1974; assoc. Hartford, Conn., 1978-81; pvt. practice employment rights and labor law, New Haven, 1982—; chmn. bd. RESPOND, New Haven, 1984—; mem. women's adv. panel Sta.-WTNH-TV, New Haven, 1975-78; commentator Sta. WELI, 1976—. Mem. employment task force NOW, Tucson, 1970-71, founder New Haven chpt., 1973, cons. coordinator employment task force, 1973-77, mem. nat. ins. task force, 1976-77; co-founder Ariz. Women's Polit. Caucus, 1972; mem. public edn. com. Conn. div. Am. Cancer Soc., 1973-74; mem. citizens' adv. bd. Conn. State Police and Sex Crimes Adv. Bd., 1974-75; mem. Orange (Conn.) Democratic Town Com.; bd. dirs., chmn. legis. and by-laws com. Griffin Hosp. Aux., Derby, Conn. Mem. New Haven Bar Assn., Conn. Bar Assn., Unitarian. Home: 888 Indian Hill Rd Orange CT 06477 Office: 29 Whitney Ave New Haven CT 06510

DEAN, MARGO, artistic director; b. Fort Worth, Dec. 9, 1930; d. Arthur Augustus and Margaret (Holliday) Webster; m. Beale Dean, Sept. 3, 1948; children—Webster Beale, Giselle Liseanne. B.F.A., Ward-Belmont Coll., 1947; postgrad. Tex. Christian U., 1948. Ballet appearances, Louisville, 1948, Dallas, 1947; prin. dancer, choreographer Fort Worth Opera Ballet, 1955-60; dir. Fort Worth Ballet Assn., 1961; artistic dir. Ballet Concerto, Fort Worth, 1969—. Bd. dirs. Fort Worth Symphony Orch. Mem. Southwestern Regional Ballet Assn. (pres. 1985—, bd. dirs. 1985—), Nat. Assn. Regional Ballet. Republican. Presbyterian. Clubs: Fort Worth, Fort Worth Boat, Ridglea Country. Office: 3803 Camp Bowie St Fort Worth TX 76107

DEAN, MARY T., realty company executive; b. Washington, Oct. 28, 1942; d. John Joseph and Lillian Joyce (Phillips) Dean. Student, U. Md., 1970's, Montgomery Coll., 1981-82, Am. U., Washington, D.C., 1983. Sec., U.S. Treasury Dept., 1960-67; adminstrv. asst. Arthur Andersen & Co., Washington, 1967-69, Leisure Time Industries, Inc., Washington, 1969-70, Ringling Bros. Circus, Washington, 1970-77; exec. adminstrv. officer Washington REIT, Bethesda, Md., 1977—; dir., sec. Boardwalk One Owners Assn., Ocean City, Md., 1982—. Mem. Nat. Assn. Secs., Nat. Assn. Female Execs., Notary Assn. Democrat. Roman Catholic. Home: 19028 Quail Valley Blvd Gaithersburg MD 20879 Office: Washington Real Estate Investment Trust 4936 Fairmont Ave Bethesda MD 20814

DEAN, NANCY LEONA, educational administrator; b. N.Y.C., July 16, 1934; d. Stephan Dimitri and Mary Ann (Styga) Bondarenko; A.B., Coll. Mount St. Vincent, 1956; M.S., U. So. Calif., 1963; Ed.D., Brigham Young U., 1975; m. Marshall F. Sisca, Apr. 12, 1958; m. Robert C. Dean, Jan. 10, 1984. Prin., Fernald Sch., UCLA, 1971-72, 15th St. Sch., San Pedro, Calif., 1973-74; prin. Gulf Ave. Elem. Sch., Wilmington, Calif., 1974-84, Laurel Sch., 1985—. Vice pres. Wilmington Coordinating Council, 1975-83, pres., 1983-84. Mem. Assn. Adminstrs. Los Angeles, Assn. Calif. Sch. Adminstrs., Assn. Supervision and Curriculum Devel., Town Hall, Women in Ednl. Leadership, Delta Kappa Gamma, Phi Delta Kappa. Independent. Roman Catholic. Home: 2700 Via Elevado Palos Verdes Estates CA 90274 Office: Laurel Sch 925 N Hayworth Ave Los Angeles CA 90046

DEAN, PAMELA LOUISE, real estate broker, diet bakery owner; b. Greenville, Ohio, Jan. 7, 1943; d. Robert Lee and Edith Elizabeth (Wood) Cook; B.A. in Sociology, U. Wash., 1972, postgrad., 1974; 1 son, Bret Ronald Wright. Lic. real estate broker. Parole counselor, Pasco, Wash., 1972; owner Thunderhead Turquoise & Silver Co., Seattle, 1973-75; realtor, div. mgr., broker, Sherwood & Roberts Inc., Seattle, 1975-80; owner So-Low Sweet Shops, diet bakeries, Seattle, 1980—; designated broker, sec. Found. and Omega Corp., Mountlake Terrace, Wash., 1984; mng. broker Windermere Real Estate, Inc., 1984—; speaker in field. Active United Good Neighbor Fund, 1980. Mem. Bus. and Profl. Women's Assn., Bus. Women's Network, Nat. Assn. Female Execs. Home: 3229 115th Ave NE 241 Bellevue WA 98004 Office: 2420 2d Ave Seattle WA 98121

DEAN, PAMELA RADCLIFFE, nursing service executive; b. Northampton, Mass., Dec. 20, 1946; d. Raymond James and Claire (Racicot) Radcliffe; m. Alfred Joseph Dean, Feb. 28, 1969; children—Jennifer Radcliffe, Jessica Claire. Student Smith Sch. Practical Nursing, Northampton, Mass., 1967; student in bus. adminstrn. Springfield/Community Coll. (Mass.), 1980-82. Lic. practical nurse, Mass. Staff nurse Cooley Dickinson Hosp., Northampton, 1967-69; service dir. Kelly Health Care, Springfield, 1974-80; regional dir. Olsten Health Care Services, Springfield, 1980-81; pres. Hampden County Nursing Services, Springfield, 1981—, pres. Hampden County Home Care Services, 1983—, Hampshire County Nursing Services, Northampton, 1984—. Mem. Springfield Women Bus. Owners; Springfield C. of C. Office: Hampden County Nursing Services 96 Industry Ave Springfield MA

DE ANGELIS, DEBORAH ANN AYARS, university athletics official; b. San Diego, July 2, 1948; d. Charles Orvil and Janet Isabel (Glithero) A.; m. David C. De Angelis, Sept. 29, 1984. B.A., U. Calif.-Santa Barbara, 1970, Certificate in Social Services, 1972; M.S., U. Mass., 1979. Eligibility worker County Welfare Dept., Santa Barbara, Calif., 1970-73; women's crew coach Northeastern U., Boston, 1979-83, bus. mgr. women's athletics, 1983—; com. mem. Women's Olympic Rowing Com., 1976-84; life trustee Nat. Rowing Found., 1984; life mem. selection com. Southland Saving Hall of Fame, 1984—; rowing mgr. Women's Olympic Team, 1976, 80; head mgr. U.S. Olympic Festival, Syracuse, N.Y., 1981, coach, Indpls., 1982, Colorado Springs, Colo., 1983. Mem. Nat. Women's Rowing Assn. (Woman of Yr. award 1983), Nat. Assn. Amateur Oarsmen, Fedn. Sociétés d'Aviron (women's commn. 1978—), U.S. Rowing Assn. (bd. dirs. 1985-87, co-chmn. internat. div., co-chmn. events div.; women's v.p. 1985—). Club: ZLAC Rowing. Office: Northeastern U Women's Athletics 360 Huntington Ave Boston MA 02115

DEANGELIS, SUSAN PENNY, jewelry manufacturing company executive; b. N.Y.C., Nov. 20, 1950; s. Milton Abraham and Anne Pearl (Fleischer) Zwilling; m. Ivo DeAngelis, July 25, 1971 (div. Feb. 1982); m. Benjamin H. Pfeffer, May 17, 1985. B.A. cum laude, Bklyn. Coll., 1971. Spl. projects coordinator, customer service rep. N.Y. Property Ins. Underwriting Assocs., N.Y.C., 1971-72; office mgr. Pyramid Personnel Agy., N.Y.C., 1972-73; dir. human resources Feature Enterprises Inc., N.Y.C., 1973—; cons. JWJ Enterprises, Inc., N.Y.C., 1984-85. N.Y. State Bd. Regents scholar, 1967. Mem. Nat. Assn. Female Execs., N.Y. Assn. New Ams. (pvt. sector adv. com. 1985-86). Jewish. Avocations: photography, calligraphy, painting. Home: 2258 E 27th St Brooklyn NY 11229 Office: Feature Enterprises Inc 130 W 46th St New York NY 10036

DEAREN, DENISE ANN, advertising executive; b. Danville, Ky., Oct. 16, 1952; d. William Henson and Clara Jenelle (Oakley) Dearen. B.A., Tex. Christian U., 1977. Pub. relations asst. Fairmont Hotel, Dallas, 1978-79; account exec., copywriter NCH Corp., Irving, Tex., 1979-83, sr. account exec., 1983—. Mem. Women in Communications (editor 1983-84, Over Achiever award 1981, 83), Internat. Assn. Bus. Communicators. Home: 2707 W Royal Ln #503 Irving TX 75063 Office: NCH Corp 2727 Chemsearch Blvd Irving TX 75062

DEARMENT, LINDA MERRIMAN, civic worker; b. Meadville, Pa., Aug. 25, 1947; d. William J. and Autumn (Smith) Merriman; m. William Stuart DeArment, Aug. 23, 1969; children—Joan S., Jonathan, S., Ryan W. B.S., Slippery Rock State U., 1969. Cert. secondary edn. tchr., Pa. Tchr. Crawford Central Sch., Meadville, Pa., 1969-72. Treas. City Hosp. Aux., Meadeville, 1974-75, pres., 1976-77; chmn. Friends of Library, Meadville, 1979-80; campaign chmn. United Way, Meadville, 1983; bd. dirs. YWCA, Meadville, 1973-76; sec. bd. dirs. Sta. WQLN-TV, Erie, Pa., 1984—; deacon First Presbyn. Ch., 1983-85; pres. United Presbyn. Women, First Presbyn. Ch., 1985—; health promotion chmn. Meadville Med. Ctr., 1986-87; chmn. Chamelloch, Inc., Centennial Celebration, 1986. Mem. Meadville Garden Club (program chmn.), Woman's Literary Club (pres. 1985-86). Republican. Avocations: reading; needlepoint; golf.

DEAS, ALBERTA D., educator, educational administrator; b. Charleston, S.C., Mar. 15, 1934; d. Michael and Carrie Lee (Waring) D.; m. Joe Major Williford, Dec. 19, 1957 (div. Oct. 1964); children—Joel Major, Jon Michael. B.S., S.C. State Coll., 1956; M.Ed., U. Mass., 1975, Ed.D., 1978. Gen. mgr. Sta. WMOZ, Mobile, Ala., 1959-62; chmn. bus. edn. dept. Carver Tech., Mobile, 1962-68; project dir. Westfield State Coll., Mass., 1975-77; asst. prof. S.C. State Coll., Orangeburg, 1977-82; gen. mgr. Sta. WLGI-FM, Hemingway, S.C., 1982-84; sch. adminstr. Louis Gregary Inst., Hemingway, 1980-85; owner, dir. Tiny Tot Presch., Mobile, 1961-65; adminstr. Ind. State U., Terre Haute, 1968-69; owner Garden of Eden, Orangeburg, S.C.; program analyst Office of Econ. Opportunities, Charleston, 1969-71; adminstr. Baha'i Regional Office, Goose Creek, S.C., 1971-74; del UN Internat. Women's Conf., Nairobi, Kenya. Author: (filmstrip) Parenting: Early Childhood, 1980; (manual) Exchange Student/Australia, 1976. Mem. Children Defense Fund, Washington, 1985—. Mem. Nat. Council of Women, Nat. Spiritual Assembly of Baha'is of U.S., Phi Delta Kappa (Coll. Tchr. Yr. 1979). Avocations: health and fitness; dancing; travel; reading. Home: PO Box 2152 Orangeburg SC 29115 Office: Garden of Eden 389 Russell St Orangeburg SC 29115

DEASY, THERESA, law firm financial executive; b. N.Y.C., May 19, 1958; d. Thomas Edward Deasy and Dorothy Beatrice (Federico) Deasy Cox; m. Dennis James Stanton, May 29, 1983. B.S. in Commerce, Depaul U., 1981. Acctg. clk. Kirkland & Ellis, Chgo., 1979-80; fin. div. clk. Talman Home Fed. Savs. & Loan, Chgo., 1980-81; staff acctg. Sachnoff Weaver & Rubenstien, Chgo., 1981-83, asst. controller, 1984—; dir. The Commons of Evanston. Vol. leader Ravenswood Hosp. Mental Health Ctr., Chgo., 1984—. Mem. Am. Soc. Women Accts., Nat. Assn. Female Execs., Notaries Assn. Ill. Avocations: travel; photography; skiing; racquetball. Home: 308 Main St Evanston IL 60202 Office: Sachnoff Weaver & Rubenstein Ltd 30 S Wacker Dr 29th Floor Chicago IL 60606

DEATON, JACKLYN KAY, relocation specialist, real estate consultant; b. Saint Louis, Apr. 18, 1939; d. E. Carleton and Nelle L. (Wilson) Spinney; m. Mason Scott Thomas, Oct. 28, 1958 (div. 1968); 1 dau., Toy Michelle Thomas Evans. Student U. Denver, 1962, 1967-68. Credit mgr. Info. Handling Services, Denver, 1964-66; real estate agt., Denver, 1966-68; chpt. dir. Am. Express Club Continental, Denver, 1968-70; relocation dir. Koelbel & Co., Denver, 1977-80; dir. HomeSearch, Van Relco, Inc., Denver, 1980-84; East Coast mktg. cons. VanRelco Relocation Mgmt., 1984-85. Active Am. Med. Ctr. Mem. Denver Art Mus., Urban Land Inst., Nat. Assn. Corp. Real Estate Execs., Am. Soc. Personnel Adminstrs., Am. Soc. Home Inspectors, Am. Econ. Developers Council, Econ. Developers Council Colo., Am. Mensa. Clubs: English Speaking Union (Denver), Ports of Call, Rocky Mountain Jaguar (Denver), ToastMasters Internat. (Colo. finalist 1967). Home: PO Box 3004 Brookland-ville MD 21022

DEBOE, MARGARET ANNE, accountant, financial consultant; b. Marfa, Tex., Nov. 19, 1944; d. John George and Margaret Amalia (Bjornstad) Hofbauer; m. Joel Augustus DeBoe, Sept. 6, 1969; children—Jason Everett, Jeremy Dean. A.B., Coll. William and Mary, 1967, M.B.A., 1968. C.P.A., Tex., D.C. Staff acct. Smulkin, Barsky, Hoffman & Denton, Washington, 1968; fin. mgmt. trainee Chrysler Corp., Detroit, 1969; staff acct. Main Lafrentz & Co., El Paso, Tex., 1970-71; staff acct., mgr. Fox & Co., Washington, 1971-79, ptnr., 1979-83; self-employed acct. and cons., Arlington, Va., 1984—. Mem. steering com. The Network, Washington, 1979-84. Mem. Nat. Assn. Women Bus. Owners, Am. Inst. C.P.A.s (nonprofit com. 1982-85), D.C. Inst. C.P.A.s (dir. 1981—, pres. 1984-85, outstanding chmn. 1979, 80, 81). Home: 3605 Bent Branch Ct Falls Church VA 22041 Office: DeBoe & Stone CPAs 2009 N 14th St Suite 612 Arlington VA 22201

DEBOER, DAWN, magazine-newspaper editor; b. New Orleans, Aug. 28, 1953; d. Herman and June Catherine (Selzer) deBoer. B.Jour., U. Tex., 1979. Prodn. specialist TEPSA, Austin, Tex., 1978-79; sr. editor, mng. editor Backpacker & Ski X-C, N.Y.C., 1979-81; spl. sect. editor Houston Chronicle, 1981-83; features dir., mag. editor Sunday mag. Texarkana Gazette, Tex., 1983—. Contbr. articles to profl. jours. Charter contbr. Statue of Liberty Found., 1985; distbr. Texarkana Gazette Cheer Fund, 1985; line bearer Hands Across America, 1986. Recipient Cert. of Recognition, Texarkana Gazette, 1985. Mem. Nat. Assn. Female Execs., Am. Assn. Sunday and Feature Editors, Cousteau Soc., Smithsonian Assocs. Democrat. Avocations: photography; painting; drawing; piano; sailing; hiking; backpacking.

DEBORDE, LINDA PLAYER, real estate broker, Realtor; b. Chester, S.C., June 20, 1939; d. Clyde Louis and Mary Janet (Gulledge) Player; m. Robert A. Wingate, Nov. 21, 1954 (dec. Apr. 1970); children—Cynthia, Tyna Lynn, Janetta; m. 2d Charles Norman DeBorde, Dec. 16, 1971. Student Daytona Community Coll., 1977-79; cert. Grad. Realtors Inst., 1980. Teller Bank of Warwick, Va., 1957-60; cashier Food Town, Salisbury, N.C., 1963-64; cashier, asst. mgr. 7-11 store, New Smyrna Beach, Fla., 1970-72; sec., ins. clk. Max Kreis Agy., New Smyrna Beach, 1975-77; salesman, mgr., appraiser Indian River Real Estate, New Smyrna Beach, 1977-79; broker-owner Nu-Day Realty, Inc., New Smyrna Beach, 1979—. Pres. New Smyrna Jr. High PTA, 1972, Chisholm Sch. PTA, New Smyrna Beach, 1973; treas. New Smyrna High Band Parents, 1973-75. Named to Million Dollar Circle, Nat. Assn. Home Builders, 1978; Fla. Assn. Realtors, Grad. Realtors Inst. scholar, 1981. Mem. New Smyrna Bd. Realtors (bd. dirs. 1978—, v.p. 1981-82, pres. 1982-83, Realtor of Yr. 1982), Fla. Assn. Realtors (bd. dirs. 1981-83), Nat. Assn. Realtors, Am. Bus. Women's Assn. (sec. 1978-79, treas. 1979-80, Woman of Yr. 1981), Nat. Home Builders Assn. (bd. dirs. Edgewater chpt. 1985—), New Smyrna C. of C. (bd. dirs. 1984—), Beta Sigma Phi (corr. sec. 1977-78). Lodge: Elks Ladies (corr. sec. lodge 1974-75). Office: Nu-Day Realty Inc 406 N Orange St New Smyrna Beach FL 32069

DE BRUN, SHAUNA DOYLE, investment banker; b. Boston, June 3, 1956; d. John Justin and Marie Therese (Carey) Doyle; m. Seamus Christopher de Brun, July 24, 1982. B.A., Mt. Holyoke Coll., 1978; student U. Salzburg, 1974-75; postgrad. Harvard U., 1981-82; M. Internat. Affairs Columbia U., 1984. Assoc., Salomon Brothers, N.Y.C., 1978; research assoc. Kennedy Sch. Govt., Cambridge, Mass., 1979-80; faculty assoc. Harvard Bus. Sch., 1980-81; fgn. expert Beijing Normal U., Peoples Republic China, 1981-82; assoc. dir. N.Y. Capital Resources, N.Y.C., 1984-85; ptnr. Eppler & Co., Denver, 1985—. Contract cons. Booz, Allen & Hamilton, N.Y.C., 1981-82. Columbia U. Internat. fellow, 1982; Sarah Williston scholar Mt. Holyoke Coll., 1975. Mem. Nat. Assn. Female Execs., Soc. Internat. Devel., Phi Beta Kappa. Club: Harvard. Avocations: piano; horseback riding. Office: Eppler & Co 1660 Lincoln St Suite 2800 Denver CO 80264

DEBUONO, LAUREEN, lawyer; b. N.Y.C., July 24, 1957; d. Richard and Catherine (Brutto) DeB. B.A. summa cum laude, Duke U., 1977; M.A., Stanford U., 1978; J.D., NYU, 1981. Bar: Calif. 1982, U.S. Dist. Ct. (no. dist.) 1982. Assoc. Bronson, Bronson & McKinnon, San Francisco, 1981-83, Heller, Ehrman, White & McAuliffe, San Francisco, 1983—. Mem. ABA, Calif. Women Lawyers, Legal Aid Soc. San Francisco, Phi Beta Kappa, Pi Sigma Alpha. Roman Catholic. Home: 2058 Vallejo St Apt 2 San Francisco CA 94123 Office: Heller Ehrman White & McAuliffe 44 Montgomery St San Francisco CA 94104

DEBUS, ELEANOR VIOLA, business management company executive; b. Buffalo, May 19, 1920; d. Arthur Adam and Viola Charlotte (Pohl) D.; student Chown Bus. Sch., 1939. Sec., Buffalo Wire Works, 1939-45; home talent producer Empire Producing Co., Kansas City, Mo., sec. Owens Corning Fiberglass, Buffalo; public relations and publicity Niagara Falls Theatre, Ont., Can.; pub. relations dir. Woman's Internat. Bowling Congress, Columbus, Ohio, 1957-59; publicist, sec. Ice Capades, Hollywood, Calif., 1961-63; sec. to controller Rexall Drug Co., Los Angeles, 1963-67; bus. mgmt. acct. Samuel Berke & Co., Beverly Hills, Calif., 1967-75; Gadbois Mgmt. Co., Beverly Hills, 1975-76; sec., treas. Sasha Corp., Los Angeles, 1976—; bus. mgr. Dean Martin and Shirley MacLaine; pres. Tempo Co., Los Angeles, 1976—. Mem. Nat. Assn. Female Execs., Nat. Notary Assn., Nat. Film Soc., Am. Film Inst.

Republican. Lodge: Order Eastern Star. Contbr. articles to various mags. Office: Tempo Co 1900 Ave of Stars #1230 Los Angeles CA 90067

DEBUS, JAYNE VONFORELL, real estate agency executive; b. Wheatland, Wyo., July 18, 1952; d. Gordon Earl von Forell and Mary Lee (Grissom) Bowen; m. Bruce Edward Debus, Aug. 9, 1975. certificate in fashion merchandising Parks Sch. Bus., Denver, 1970-71; student in gen. bus. U. Wyo., 1972-73. Designated broker, 1979. Sec. AT&T, Denver, 1971-72; legal sec. Porter, Stanley, Platte and Arthur, Columbus, Ohio, 1973-74; market asst. Investors Mgmt. Scis., Inc., Littleton, Colo., 1974-76; legal sec. Dunmire and Blessing, Attys., Hastings, Nebr., 1976-77; sec. Mid-Nebraska Mental Retardation Services, Hastings, 1977-78; owner, broker Century 21 Properties Unltd., 1977—. Active membership drive United Way, Hastings, 1979-82; bd. dirs. YMCA, Hastings, 1984—; adv. bd. mem. Devel. Services Corp., Hastings, 1981—. Named Bus. Woman of Week, First Savs. Co., 1982. Mem. Bus. and Profl. Women, Nat. Assn. Realtors, Nebr. Assn. Realtors, Hastings Bd. of Realtors (activities chmn. 1979-82, dir. 1981—), Hastings C. of C., Altrusa. Republican. Congregationalist. Lodges: Jobs Daughters, Order of Eastern Star. Home: 1213 Westridge Dr Hastings NE 68901 Office: Century 21 Properties Unltd 322 N Minnesota St Hastings NE 68901

DECAIR, SHEILA MARIE COOK, automotive company executive, public relations consultant; b. Washington; d. Edward Joseph and Maxine Olivia (Waters) C.; m. Leonard George Cook, Jr., Aug. 31, 1974 (div. June 1977); children—Edward Joseph II, Eileen Maxine; m. 2d, Thomas Palmer DeCair, Aug. 28, 1984. B.S., U. Ariz.; Master Dance, Dance Masters Assn. Am., 1971. Lighting designer Eastern Seaboard, 1973-76; cons. Holiday U./U.S. Health and Recreation, Washington, 1976-77; pres. Cook Assocs. Advt., Inc., Washington, 1977-83; cons. U.S. Health and Recreation, Washington, 1972-73, 1977-83; cons. pub. relations Toyota Motor Co., Silver Spring, Md., 1983, Ford Motor Co., Silver Spring, 1983-85; asst. gen. mgr. Martens Subaru, Annapolis, Md., 1984; dir. pub. relations Met. Mchts. Assn., Washington, 1980-82. Editor: Metropolitan Merchants Directory, 1980, 82. Assoc., Friends of the Nat. Zoo, Washington, 19-7, 78, 79; player N. Mex. State Softball Team, Congl. League, Washington, 1979-84; fundraiser U. Mex. State Office, Washington, 1976-77. Recipient Sales Excellence award Toyota Motor Co., 1983. Mem. Nat. Assn. Female Execs. (nat. dir. 1983), Dance Masters Assn. Am. (soloist 1969-71). Republican. Home: 3925 Benton St NW Washington DC 20007

DE CHAMPLAIN, VERA CHOPAK, artist, painter; b. Kulmbach, Germany, Jan. 26, 1928; Am. citizen; d. Nathaniel and Selma (Stiefel) Florsheim; m. Albert Chopak de Champlain, 1948. Student, Art Students League, N.Y.C., 1950-60; spl. studies with Edwin Dickinson, 1962-64. Art dir., tchr. Emanuel Ctr., N.Y.C., 1967—. One person show Consulate Fed. Republic of Germany, N.Y.C., 1986; exhibited group shows including Munich, W. Ger., 1966, Rudolph Gallery, Woodstock, N.Y., 1967, Fusco Gallery, N.Y.C., 1969, 70, Artists Equity Gallery, N.Y.C., 1970-77, Lever House, N.Y.C., 1974, 80, 85; Avery Fisher Hall-Cork Gallery, N.Y.C., 1979, 82, 83, 84, Fontainebleau Gallery, N.Y.C., 1972, 73, 74, NYU, 1978, Met. Mus., 1979, B. Altman Gallery, N.Y.C., 1982, Muriel Karasik Gallery, Westhampton Beach, N.Y., 1980, Lever House, N.Y., 1985; represented in permanent collections Butler Inst. Am. Art, Youngstown, Ohio, Ga. Mus. Art, Athens, Slater Mus., Norwich, Conn., Webster Coll., St. Louis, Evansville Mus. Arts and Sci. (Ind.), Smithsonian Instn., Archives Am. Art, Washington. Recipient award in portrait painting, Hainesfalls, N.Y., 1965; subject of TV interview, 1984. Fellow Royal Soc. Arts (London); mem. Artists Equity Assn. N.Y., Arts Students League (life), Nat. Soc. Arts and Letters (art chmn. 1969—), Kappa Pi (life). Clubs: Woman Pays, Liederkranz City of N.Y. (trustee 1979—). Home: 230 Riverside Dr New York NY 10025

DECICCO, ANNE LOMMEL, association executive; b. N.Y.C., Sept. 27, 1950; d. Richard Arthur and Nancy (Robertson) Lommel; m. Bruce A. Hydo; children—Geoffrey Lommel, Melanie Paige, Benjamin Bruce. Vice pres. human resources and mgmt. practices N.J. Hosp. Assn., 1981-84, v.p. corp. and strategic planning, 1984, asst. to pres. for health affairs, 1982—, corp. v.p. strategic planning and human resources, 1985—; trustee Somerset Med. Ctr., Somerville, N.J., dir. Chemocare Inc. Mem. Am. Mgmt. Assn., N.J. Assn. Soc. Execs., Internat. Hosp. Fedn. Home: 358 2d St Dunellen NJ 08812 Office: Center Health Affairs 760 Alexander Rd Princeton NJ 08540

DECK, LAURA MAYME, advertising agency executive; b. Gary, Ind., Mar. 10, 1952; d. George Henry and Barbara Ann (Wilkins) Deck. B.A. magna cum laude, Denison U., 1974; M.A., Ohio State U., 1978. Copywriter, Caldwell-VanRiper, Inc., Indpls., 1974-76; advt. mgr. Ind. Dept. Commerce, Indpls., 1979; copywriter Carlson & Co., Inc., Indpls., 1979, account exec., 1981—, v.p., 1982—; advt. cons. Ind. Gov.'s Council on Fitness, Indpls., 1981; mem. assoc. faculty Ind. U.-Purdue U., Indpls., 1979—. Named Sagamore of Wabash, 1984; scholar Internat. Grad. Summer Sch., Oxford (Eng.) U., 1977; media grantee NEH, 1978. Mem. Art Dirs. Club Ind. (dir. 1983, excellence awards 1976, 82, 83, 84), Indpls. Advt. Club (Addi awards 1977, 80, 82, 84), Ind. Tchrs. Writing, Denison Alumni Club (pres. Indpls. chpt. 1980—). Club: Indy Runners (Indpls.). Office: Carlson & Co Inc 9292 N Meridian St Indianapolis IN 46260

DECKER, BARBARA QUIJANO, personnel manager; b. Des Moines, Nov. 26, 1949; d. Frank A. and Mary Virginia (Beltrame) Quijano; m. Kent Charles Decker, Aug. 10, 1974; 1 child, Casey Charles. B.A., Drake U., 1972, M. Pub. Adminstrn., 1983. Cert. secondary tchr., Iowa. Tchr. high sch. Marshalltown Bd. Edn. (Iowa), 1973-74; personnel adminstr. Des Moines Register & Tribune, 1975-78; personnel mgr. Syntex Agribus., Des Moines, 1978—. Adviser Des Moines Community Coll., Ankeny, Iowa, 1981-84; mem. sch. bd. Christ the King Parish and Sch., Des Moines, 1984—. Mem. Am. Assn. Personnel Adminstrs. (program mem. 1983-84, sec. 1984—), Am. Soc. Tng. and Devel., Des Moines Equal Opportunity-Affirmative Action Adminstrs., Assn. Human Resource Systems Profls., Phi Beta Kappa, Pi Alpha Alpha. Roman Catholic. Office: Syntex Agribus Inc 2538 SE 43d St Des Moines IA 50317

DECKER, DEBRA ELNORA, librarian; b. Williamsport, Pa., Oct. 25, 1946; d. Herman Thomas and Harriett Lucina (Mullen) Palmer; B.S., Lock Haven State Coll., 1968; M.Ed., West Chester State Coll., 1971; M.S. in Library Sci., Clarion State Coll., 1981; m. Sept. 7, 1969; 1 dau., Moana Kai. Tchr., Owen J. Roberts Sch. Dist., Pottstown, Pa., 1968-73; instr., Becker Research Learning Center, Clarion (Pa.) State Coll., 1976-80, librarian instr., Instructional Materials Center, 1980-84, serials coordinator Carlson Library, 1984—. Neighborhood chmn. Brookville Council Girls Scouts U.S., 1976-82; bd. dirs. Brookville Area United Fund, 1980-83; officer Zion United Methodist Ch., 1977—. Mem. NEA, ALA, Pa. Library Assn., Pa. Edn. Assn., Assn. Pa. State Coll. and Univ. Faculties, Phi Delta Kappa. Democrat. Home: RD 4 Box 250 Brookville PA 15825 Office: Carlson Library Clarion State Coll Clarion PA 16214

DECKER, JEAN CAMPBELL, retired financial executive; b. Chgo., Mar. 10, 1915; d. Dm and Bertha (Campbell) Decker; B.A. in Bus. Adminstrn., U. Chgo., 1937. Notary pub., Ill. With Calco Mfg. Co., Addison, Ill., 1950-85, treas., 1969-81, plan adminstr., dir. pension plan, 1976-82, cons., 1981—; treas. Gustafson Enterprises, Inc., Addison, Ill., 1971-85, dir., 1971-78, 82-85; treas. Environ, Inc., Haines City, Fla., 1971-72. Mem. U. Chgo. Alumni Assn., Phi Delta Upsilon. Republican. Home: 885 Smith St Glen Ellyn IL 60137

DECKER, JOSEPHINE L., clinic administrator; b. Barling, Ark., May 24, 1933; d. Ralph and Ada A. (Claborn) Snider; student public schs., Muldrow, Okla.; m. William Arlen Decker, Feb. 4, 1952; 1 son, Peter A. With Southwestern Bell Telephone Co., Ft. Smith, Ark., 1951-52; with Holt Krock Clinic, Ft. Smith, 1952—, bus. adminstr., 1970—. Bd. dirs. Sparks Credit Union, Adv. Council Northside and Southside high schs., Ft. Smith, Ft. Smith Girls Shelter, Ft. Smith Credit Bur. Mem. Credit Women Internat., Soc. Cert. Consumer Credit Execs. Office: Holt Krock Clinic 1500 Dodson Ave Fort Smith AR 72901

DECKER, MARY TERESA, athlete; b. Bunnvale, N.J., Aug. 4, 1958; d. John and Jacqueline Decker; m. Ron Tabb (div. 1983); m. Richard Slaney, June 1, 1985; 1 child, Ashley Lynn. Student U. Colo., 1977-78. Amateur runner, 1969—; holder several world track and field records, 1980—; winner 2 gold medals at 1500 and 3000 meter World Track and Field Championship, Helsinki, Finland, 1983; mem. U.S. Olympic teams, 1980, 84; cons. to CBS Records, Timex, Eastman Kodak. Recipient Jesse Owens Internat. Amateur Athlete award, 1982, AAU Sullivan award, 1982; named Amateur Sportswoman of the Year, Women's Sports Found, 1982, 83; Top Sportswoman A.P. Europe, 1985. Address: Athletics West 3968 W 13th St Eugene OR 97402*

DECKER, NANCY MARIE CRAIG, nurse; b. West Palm Beach, Fla., Mar. 9, 1948; d. Hoyt Burl and Dorothy Louise (Harvey) Craig; m. Roger Wilbur Decker, Apr. 6, 1967; 1 son, Hoyt. A.S., Indian River Community Coll., 1978. Cert. surg. tech.; cert. electrocardiography technician; R.N. Ward sec. St. Mary's Hosp., West Palm Beach, Fla., 1966-68; head depts. EEG and EKG, Palm Beach Gardens Hosp. (Fla.), 1968-75; relief charge nurse, staff nurse Palm Beach Martin County Med. Center, Jupiter, Fla., 1979-81; head nurse, inservice dir. Lakeside Health Center, West Palm Beach, 1982-83, asst. dir. nursing, 1983-84; dir. nursing Royal Manor, Royal Palm Beach, Fla., 1984—. Mem. continuing edn. com. Am. Cancer Soc., 1983—; vol. ARC, 1964—; instr. CPR, Am. Heart Assn., 1981—. Moose Women scholar, 1978. Mem. Am. Cancer Soc., Inservice Dirs. Palm Beach County (library com. chmn. 1983—), VFW (dist. 3 conductress 1983-84, dist. 3 guard 1982-83, dist. 3 chaplain 1984-85, jr. v.p. 1985-86, sr. v.p. 1985-86; local chaplain 1982-83, local pres. 1985-86, aide to Fla. pres. 1985-86), Beta Sigma Phi (corr. sec. 1983-84), extension officer 1985-86). Lodge: Women of Moose (sr. regent 1975-76, coll. regents degree 1978, star recorder degree 1983).

DE COOK, GRACE, government official; b. Clark County, Ind., Oct. 27, 1930; d. Jacob and Grace (Whitesides) de C. M.S., West Coast U., 1978. Staff asst. to dir. space div. Air Force (Minuteman Program), Cocoa Beach, Fla. and Los Angeles, 1955-58; mgmt. asst. to dir. NASA, Santa Monica, Calif., 1960-68; vocat. counselor VA, Los Angeles, 1969-73; dir. Los Angeles Fed. Exec. Bd., 1973—. Recipient Outstanding Service in Edn. award Calif. State U.-Los Angeles, 1976, Calif. State U.-Dominguez Hills, 1978. Mem. Am. Soc. Profl. Adminstrs. (policy mem. 1974—), Coll. Fed. Council So. Calif., Town Hall Calif., Los Angeles World Affairs Council, Los Angeles County Mus. Art, DAR, Hancock Park Hist. Soc., AAUW. Home: PO Box 24214 Los Angeles CA 90024 Office: PO Box 1109 Los Angeles CA 90053

DECOTIS, DEBORAH ANNE, investment banker; b. Salem, Mass., Nov. 13, 1952; d. John and Marie (Mahoney) DeC. B.A., Smith Coll., 1974; M.B.A. (Miller scholar), Stanford U., 1978. Analyst, Morgan Stanley & Co., Inc., N.Y.C., 1974-76, assoc., 1978-82, v.p., London, 1983-84, prin., N.Y.C., 1985—. Office: Morgan Stanley & Co Inc 1251 Ave of Americas New York NY 10020

DECOURSEY, EILEEN MARIE, industrial manufacturing company executive; b. East Orange, N.J., Sept. 20, 1932; d. Andrew A. and Mildred H. (Shields) DeC.; m. Sidney Jack McDuff, Aug. 21, 1976. B.S. in Edn. and Speech, Kean Coll., 1954; postgrad. NYU, 1960-61. Personnel asst. Warner-Lambert Co., Morris Plains, N.J., 1956-59; research assoc. Handy Assoc., N.Y.C., 1959-60; jr. account exec. Johnson and Higgins, N.Y.C., 1960-64; personnel supr. Time Inc., N.Y.C., 1964-66; mgr. employee benefits Bristol-Myers Co., N.Y.C., 1966-71; v.p., exec. asst. to chmn. Squibb Corp., N.Y.C., 1971-75; v.p. employee relations Manville Corp., Denver, 1975-85; pres. Exec. Research Assocs., 1985—; dir. First Colo. Bank and Trust Co., Denver; membership chmn. Personnel Round Table, 1982-83, chmn. program, 1983-84, chmn., 1984-85, chmn. emeritus, 1985—; one of founders Human Resources Roundtable Group, 1980—. Bd. dirs. Mile High United Way, Denver, 1976-78; trustee Loretto Heights Coll., Denver, 1977—. Mem. Mgmt. and Personnel Research Council of Conf. Bd., Am. Soc. Personnel Adminstrs. (bd. dirs. 1972-78), Am. Mgmt. Assn. (human resources council 1972-78), Denver C. of C. Republican. Club: Denver Country; Garden of Gods (Colorado Springs).

DE COUX, JANET, sculptor; b. Niles, Mich., Oct. 4, 1904; d. John Charles and Bertha (Wright) de C. Former student, Carnegie Inst. Tech., N.Y. Sch. Design, R.I. Sch. Design, Chgo. Art Inst. Apprentice C.P. Jennewein, N.Y.C., 1927-29, James Earl Fraser, Westport, Conn., 1932-35; apprentice to others; resident instr. Cranbrook Acad. Art, Birmingham, Mich., 1942-45; self-employed sculptor, Gibsonia, Pa., 1945—. Sculptures include Deborah Song, 1942 (Widener medal 1942), Heroic Portrait William Penn, State Capitol Pa., Harrisburgh, 1967. Fellow Tiffany Found., 1927, Guggenheim Found., 1939-42; grantee Am. Acad.-Nat. Inst. Art and Letters, 1945. Fellow Nat. Sculpture Soc. (Lindsay Meml. prize 1940); academician mem. Nat. Acad. Design. Democrat. Episcopalian.

DECROW, KAREN, lawyer, author, lecturer; b. Chgo., Dec. 18, 1937; d. Samuel Meyer and Juliette (Abt) Lipschultz; B.S., Northwestern U., 1959; J.D., Syracuse U., 1972; m. Alexander Allen Kolben, 1960 (div. 1965); m. 2d, Roger Edward DeCrow, 1965 (div. 1972). Resort editor Golf Digest mag., Evanston, Ill., 1959-60; editor Am. Soc. Planning Ofcls., Chgo., 1960-61; writer Center for Study Liberal Edn. for Adults, Chgo., 1961-64; editor Holt, Rinehart, Winston, Inc., N.Y.C., 1965; editor L.W. Singer, Syracuse, N.Y., 1965-66; writer Eastern Regional Inst. for Edn., Syracuse, 1967-69; nat. bd. mem. NOW 1968-77, nat. pres., 1974-77, also nat. politics task force chairperson; admitted to N.Y. State bar; legal practice specializing in constl. law, lit. and entertainment law, also gender discrimination law; cons. on affirmative action; lectr. colls. and univs., U.S., Can., Mex., Greece, USSR, Finland, Radio Free Europe; adv. council dept. sociology Princeton U. Trustee Elizabeth Cady Stanton Found.; a nat. coordinator Women's Strike for Equality, 1970; legis. specialist N.Y. Women's Bar Assn.; mem. ad hoc com. Women for Human Rights; bd. advisers Working Women's Inst. Candidate for mayor Syracuse, 1969; bd. dirs. Schs. for Candidates; mem. chancellor's affirmative action com. Syracuse U.; mem. Dist. Atty.'s Adv. Council. Recipient Kharas award N.Y. Civil Liberties Union, 1985. Mem. Am. Arbitration Assn., Yale Polit. Union (hon. life), ACLU. Author: (with Roger DeCrow) University Adult Education: A Selected Bibliography, 1967; The Young Woman's Guide to Liberation, 1971; Sexist Justice, 1974; (with Robert Seidenberg) Women Who Marry Houses: Panic and Protest in Agoraphobia, 1983; editor: The Pregnant Teenager (Howard Osofsky), 1968; Corporate Wives, Coporate Casualities (Robert Seidenberg), 1973; columnist Syracuse New Times; contbr. articles to newspapers including N.Y. Times, Los Angeles Times, Chgo. Sun-Times, Miami Herald, Boston Globe, USA Today, Internat. Herald Tribune, Newsday, Houston Chronicle, also to mags. including Mademoiselle, Vogue, Penthouse, The Civil Rights Quar. Address: 7 Fir Tree Ln Jamesville NY 13078

DE CUENCA, PILAR AURORA, librarian, children's book translator; b. Camaguey, Cuba, July 1, 1931; came to U.S., 1966, naturalized, 1972; d. Miguel and Sara (Garcia) de Cuenca. Ed.D., U. Havana, Cuba, 1955; M.L.S., Queens Coll., 1971. Cert. bilingual tchr., N.Y., media specialist, N.Y. Bilingual tchr., community relations liaison Pub. Sch. 32, Bklyn., 1968-69; sch. librarian Sch. Dist. 7, Bronx, N.Y., 1969-74; 80—; library supr. Regional Bilingual Resource Ctr., Bd. Edn., N.Y.C., 1974-80; Compiler bibliographies of bilingual materials; translator children's books; contbr. articles to profl. jours. Mem. ALA, United Fed. Tchrs. Home: 61-27 232 St Bayside NY 11364

DE CUEVAS, ELIZABETH, sculptor; b. St. Germain en Laye, France, Jan. 22, 1929 (Am. citizen); d. George and Margaret (Strong) De C.; student Vassar Coll., 1946-48; A.B., Sarah Lawrence Coll., 1952; student John Hovannes, Art Students League, N.Y.C., 1963-68; 1 dau., Deborah Carmichael. One-woman shows Lee Ault Gallery, N.Y.C., 1977, 78, Tower Gallery, Southampton, N.Y., 1980, Iolas-Jackson Gallery, N.Y.C., 1983-85, Guild Hall Mus., East Hampton, N.Y., 1985; exhibited in group shows Guild Hall, East Hampton, N.Y., 1980, Art Students League of N.Y., 1982, Bruce Mus., Greenwich, Conn., 1984, 85, Tower Gallery, N.Y.C., 1984, Andre Zarre Gallery, N.Y.C., 1985, Kouros Gallery, N.Y.C. and Ridgefield, Conn., 1985, Susan Blanchard Gallery, N.Y.C., 1985-86; represented in pvt. collections. Club: Vassar of N.Y.

DECYK, ROXANNE JEAN, manufacturing company executive, lawyer; b. Chgo., Nov. 5, 1952; d. Walter and Tillie (Kuzma) D.; m. William C. Young, Sept. 1, 1973; m. David Shute, Oct. 1, 1977. A.B., U. Ill., J.D., Marquette U. Bar: Wis. 1977, Ill. 1981. Pres. Penta Advt., Champaign, Ill., 1972-73; staff journalist Coll. Medicine U. Ill., 1973-74; assoc. Foley & Lardner, Milw., 1977-79; pres. Corp. Legal Communications, Milw., 1980-81; v.p., sec., asst. to chmn. Internat. Harvester Co. (now Navistar Internat. Corp.), Chgo., 1981-83, v.p. adminstrn., sec., from 1983, now sr. v.p. for corp. relations; dir. Lincoln Nat. Pension, Ft. Wayne, Ind., First Trust, Chgo. Bd. dirs. YWCA, Greater Milw., 1980, Jr. Achievement, Chgo., 1982—. Recipient Nat. Merit Scholar award Outboard Marine Corp., 1970. Mem. Econ. Club Chgo., ABA, State Bar Wis., Ill. State Bar Assn., Am. Soc. Corp. Secs., Chgo. Network, Phi Beta Kappa. Club: Women's Athletic (Chgo.). Office: Internat Harvester Co 401 N Michigan Ave Chicago IL 60611

DEDIOT, LILIANE CHRISTINE, transportation executive; b. Havana, Cuba, Apr. 15, 1950; came to U.S., 1960, naturalized, 1968; d. Luis Gregorio and Christina (Saladrigas) D.; B.S. magna cum laude, Fla. Internat. U., 1975; M.B.A., Embry-Riddle Aero. U., 1978. Flight attendant Pan Am. World Airways, 1971-78, in-flight supr., 1974, flight attendant instr., 1973-74, 76; indsl. engr. Eastern Airlines, Inc., Miami, Fla., 1978-79, sr. analyst in-flight service programs, 1979-81, mgr. passenger services, 1981-83; dir. reservations and group sales Norwegian Caribbean Lines, Miami, 1983—. Mem. Am. Inst. Indsl. Engrs., World Wings Internat., Travel Industry Assn. Fla., Leukemia Soc. Am. (exec. com. so. Fla. chmpt.), Alpha Eta Rho. Republican. Roman Catholic. Home: 1910 SW 5th Ave Miami FL 33129 Office: One Biscayne Tower Miami FL 33131

DEDMAN, BOBBYE GRISWOLD, business education educator; b. Morrison, Tenn., Nov. 13, 1928; d. Winfred Anderson and Thelma Margaret (Snipes) Griswold; m. Harold Curtis Dedman, Aug. 29, 1948; children—James Curtis, Robert Scott, William Griswold. B.S., George Peabody Coll., Nashville, 1949, M.A., 1950. Cert. tchr. Tenn. Tchr. bus. edn. Demonstration Sch., George Peabody Coll., Nashville, 1949-50, Davidson County Schs., Nashville, 1950-51, Chattanooga City Schs., Tenn., 1954-60, Hamilton County Schs., Chattanooga, 1961—; adj. instr. bus. edn. U. Tenn., Chattanooga, 1970—, Chattanooga State Community Coll., 1974-77; Tenn. Career Ladder III tchr., 1985—; cons. and lectr. in field. Mem. adv. bd. Pub. Access Channel 2, Chattanooga, 1983—; steering com. Gov.'s Homecoming Celebration, Red Bank, Tenn., 1983—. George Peabody Coll. fellow, 1949; recipient Community Service award City of Chattanooga Human Services Dept., 1985. Mem. NEA, Nat. Bus. Edn. Assn., Tenn. Bus. Edn. Assn. (pres. 1974-75), Chattanooga C. of C. (work-learn scholar 1982), Delta Pi Epsilon, Aplha Delta Kappa (pres. state orgn. 1974-76). Republican. Methodist. Avocations: bridge; photography; travel; socialwork. Home: 3801 Sliger Cir Chattanooga TN 37415 Office: Red Bank High Sch Morrison Springs Rd Chattanooga TN 37415

DEDOMINIC, PATTY LEE, personnel service executive; b. Glendale, Calif., Mar. 5, 1951; d. Harold and Eleanor Margaret Timm; m. John DeDominic, Mar. 7, 1969 (div. 1984); children—Eric, Chris, Nicholas. Mgr., Task Force, Los Angeles, 1972-75; dist. sales mgr. Avon Products, Pasadena, Calif., 1975-78; pres., founder PDQ Personnel Services, Inc., Los Angeles, 1979—. Contbr. articles to bus. mags. Bd. dirs. Los Angeles Women's Campaign Fund, 1984-85; mem. small bus. adv. council Calif. Senate and Calif. Assembly, 1984—; mem. nat. adv. council SBA, 1984—. Named Woman of Yr., Women in Mgmt., 1984, Women's Bus. Advocate, SBA, 1983. Mem. Women in Mgmt. (pres. 1981-82), Nat. Assn. Women Bus. Owners (pres. 1983-84), Town Hall. Office: PDQ Personnel Services Inc 5900 Wilshire Blvd Suite 700 Los Angeles CA 90036

DEEL, FRANCES QUINN, air force librarian; b. Pottsville, Pa., Mar. 9, 1939; d. Charles Joseph and Carrie Miriam (Ketner) Q.; m. Ronald Eugene Deel, Feb. 5, 1983. B.S., Millersville State Coll., 1960; M.L.S., Rutgers U., 1964; M.P.A., U. West Fla., 1981. Post librarian U.S. Army Armor (Desert Tng. Ctr.), Ft. Irwin, Calif., 1964-66; staff librarian Mil. Dist. of Washington, 1966-67; supervisory librarian 1st Logistical Command, APO San Francisco, 1967-68; tech. process specialist Naval Edn. and Tng. Supervisory Command, Washington, 1968-77, Pensacola, Fla., 1968-77; chief tech. library USAF Armament Lab., Eglin AFB, Fla., 1977-81; dir. command libraries Air Force Systems Command (Andrews AFB), Washington, 1981—; mem. exec. adv. council Fed. Library and Info. Network, Washington, 1983-86. Mem. AIA (dir.-at-large armed forces libraries sect. Chgo. 1983—), Spl. Libraries Assn., D.C. Library Assn. Roman Catholic. Home: 9225 Forest Haven Dr Alexandria VA 22309 Office: Air Force Systems Command HQ AFSC Andrews AFB Washington DC 20334

DEEM, JANE ANN, graphic artist; b. Dayton, Ohio, Aug. 25, 1954; d. Francis Elbert and Mary Jane (Melling) D. B.F.A., Ohio U., 1976. Substitute art tchr. Kettering Sch. Dist., Ohio, 1976-77; prodn. supr. Subia, Inc., Hawthorne, Calif., 1977-80; prodn. mgr. Lienett Co., Inc., Los Alamitos, Calif., 1980-81; v.p., ptnr. Comml. Graffix, Playa Del Rey, Calif., 1981—. Democrat. Mem. Christian Ch. Avocations: music; decorating; sewing; pets; computers. Office: Commercial Graffix 200 E Culver Blvd Playa Del Rey CA 90293

DEEMER, JANET ANN, business executive; b. Pitts., June 29, 1953; d. Harry Richard and Marion Elizabeth (James) D.; student Kent State U., 1971-73; A.S., Duluth Bus. U., 1975; student in bus. adminstrn. Nat. U. Adminstrv. asst. to v.p. sales and promotions Ringling Bros., Barnum & Bailey Circus World, Orlando, Fla., 1977-78; media and spl. events dir. DuQuoin (Ill.) State Fairgrounds, 1979; dir. ops., spl. assignment ETS Promotional Mktg., San Diego, 1981; bus. mgr., dir. Thorntree Group, Inc., Solana Beach, Calif., 1981—; bus. mgr. Ira Katz Cons.; dir. Samantha One, Inc.; mem. adv. bd. TLZ, Inc. Mem. Am. Mktg. Assn., Nat. Assn. Female Execs. Office: 1025 Prospect Suite 310 La Jolla CA 92037

DEEN, EDITH ALDERMAN, author; b. Weatherford, Tex., Feb. 28, 1905; d. James Harris and Sara (Scheuber) Alderman; student Tex. U., 1922-23, Tex. Christian U., 1923-24, Columbia U., 1926; B.A., Tex. Woman's U., 1953, Litt.D., 1959, M.A., 1960; Litt.D., Tex. Christian U., 1972; m. Edgar Deen, Dec. 30, 1945 (dec.). Woman's editor Daily columnist Fort Worth Evening Press, 1924-54. Mem. Fort Worth City Council, 1965-67; mem. bd. regents Tex. Woman's Univ., 1951-63. Named Exec. Woman of Year, Zonta Club, 1983; recipient First Lady award Altrusa Club, 1949, Headliner award Women in Communications, 1963, Disting. Sr. Citizen award Women's Civic Club, 1974. Mem. Tex. Inst. Letters, Women in Communications. Author: All of the Women of the Bible, 1955; Great Women of the Christian Faith, 1959; Family Living in the Bible, 1963; The Bible's Legacy for Womanhood, 1970; All the Bible's Men of Hope, 1974; Wisdom from Women in the Bible, 1978. Home and Office: 2420 Refugio St Fort Worth TX 76106

DEEN, NANCY NEWLAND, dairy farm executive; b. Los Angeles, Jan. 19, 1923; d. Edward Harvey Newland and Joyce Abbott (Percey) Fluhr; m. Jack Egbert Deen, Jan. 22, 1946 (dec. Aug. 1976); children—Margaret, Jacqueline, John, George, Nancy, Patricia, Robert, Richard. Student UCLA, 1941-44; B.B.A., East Tex. State U., 1981. Mgr., pres. Deen Agri-Service, Inc., Wills Point, Tex., 1976—; acct. First Bapt. Learning Ctr., Wills Point, 1982—. Sec., bd. dirs. First Bapt. Learning Ctr., 1982—. Named Dairyman of Yr., Van Zandt Farm & Ranch, 1983. Avocations: sewing; cooking; cross stitch. Home and Office: Route 5 Box 530 Wills Point TX 75169

DEERING, CHERYL ANN, advertising executive; b. Quantico, Va., Oct. 1, 1950; d. Claude Elliott and Carolyn Ida (Costa) D.; student U. No. Colo., 1968-72. Prodn. mgr. Sidaris Co., Los Angeles, 1972-74; owner, mgr. The Precious Point, Los Angeles, 1974-76; advt. coordinator Hartfield Zodys Inc., Los Angeles, 1976-77; dir. advt. The Federated Group, City of Commerce, Calif., 1977-80; account mgr. W. B. Doner & Co., Advt., Detroit, 1980-81; pres. Deering & Holmes, Inc., advt., N.Y.C., 1981-83. Mem. Advt. Club Los Angeles. Home: 1365 York Ave New York NY 10021 Office: 360 Lexington Ave New York NY 10017

DEES, SALLY BICE, research microbiologist; b. Montgomery, Ala., July 5, 1933; d. Stoughton Nathaniel and Sibyl Carolyn (Simpson) Bice; children—Deborah Diane Samuels, Laura Carolyn Wood, Marza Katherine Samuels. B.A., Huntingdon Coll., 1955; M.S., Ga. State U., 1970. Cert. specialist in pub. health and med. lab. microbiology. Microbiologist Ala. State Health Dept., Montgomery, 1955-57, Ga. State Health Dept., Atlanta, 1957-61; research microbiologist Ctr. for Disease Control, Atlanta, 1961-85; research microbiologist Emory U. Med. Sch., 1985—. Lectr. in field. Contbr. articles to profl. publs. Trainer, scheduler Contact Teleministries, 24-Hour Crisis Line, 1977-78. Mem. Am. Soc. Microbiology, Sigma Xi. Mem. Hotlanta Hoedowners Clogging Team. Office: Microbiology Dept Woodruff Bldg Emory U Med Sch Atlanta GA 30322

DEES, SANDRA KAY MARTIN, school psychologist; b. Omaha, Apr. 18, 1944; d. Leslie B. and Ruth Lillian (May) Martin; m. Doyce B. Dees; B.A. magna cum laude, Tex. Christian U., 1965, M.A., 1972; postgrad. Washington U., St. Louis. Adminstrv. asst./research coordinator Hosp. Improvement Project, Wichita Falls (Tex.) State Hosp., 1968-69; caseworker adoptions Edna Gladney Home, Ft. Worth, Tex., 1970-71; psychologist Mexia (Tex.) State Sch., 1971-72; sch. psychologist Ft. Worth Ind. Sch. Dist., 1971-78, spl. edn. evaluator, 1978-86; pvt. counselor, 1986—; project mgr. Growth Center Project, 1975-77, lectr. in field. Founder, leader Alateen Group, Wichita Falls,

1969. Dallas Tex. Christian U. Women's Club creative writing scholar, 1962-64, Virginia Alpha scholar, 1963; NASA research asst., 1965-67; USPHS trainee, 1967-68; cert. Am. Montessori Soc., 1977. Mem. Ft. Worth Public Schs. Adminstrs. Assn., Mental Health Assn., Mortar Bd., Mensa, Alpha Chi, Phi Alpha Theta, Psi Chi, Phi Delta Kappa. Contbr. articles to profl. publs. Home: 29 Bounty Rd W Fort Worth TX 76132 Office: 3210 W Lancaster St Ft Worth TX 76107

DEES, SUSAN COONS, physician, educator; b. Hancock, Mich., May 26, 1909; d. George Herbert and Myrta Amanda (Vogel) Coons; m. John Essary Dees, Jan. 7, 1935; children—Elizabeth, John Essary, Nancy, Susan. B.A., Goucher Coll., 1930; M.D., Johns Hopkins U., 1934; M.S., U. Minn., 1938. Diplomate Am. Bd. Pediatrics, Am. Bd. Allery and Immunology. Intern Johns Hopkins Hosp., Balt., 1934-35; asst. resident in medicine U. Rochester, N.Y., 1935-36; fellow in allergy and pediatrics U. Minn., Mpls., 1936-37; from assoc. prof. to prof. Duke U., Durham, N.C., 1939-79, prof. emeritus, allergy cons. Duke U. Med. Ctr., 1979—; chief div. pediatric allergy Duke U. Med. Ctr., 1940-79. Contbr. ariticles to profl. jours. Recipient Von Pirquet award Georgetown U., 1977. Fellow Am. Acad. Allergy (v.p. 1973, B. Ratner award 1971), Am. Coll. Allergists (2nd v.p. 1978, Bela Schick award 1972); mem. N.C. Pediatric Soc. (pres. 1960). Democrat. Episcopalian. Office: Duke U Med Ctr Dept Pediatrics Durham NC 27710

DE FAZIO, LYNETTE STEVENS, dancer, choreographer, educator, chiropractor; b. Berkeley, Calif., Sept. 29; d. Honore and Mabel J. (Estavan) Stevens; student U. Calif., Berkeley, 1950-55, San Francisco State Coll., 1950-51; D.Chiropractic, Life-West Chiropractic Coll., San Lorenzo, Calif., 1983; B.A., New Coll. Calif., 1986. Contract child dancer Monogram Movie Studio, Hollywood, Calif., 1938-40; dancer, instr. San Francisco Ballet, 1953-64; performer San Francisco Opera Ring, 1960-67; performer, choreographer Oakland Civic Light Opera, 1963-70; owner, dir. Ballet Arts Studio, Oakland, 1960—; instr. Peralta Community Coll. Dist., Laney Campus, Grove St. Campus, 1971—, chmn. dance dept., 1985—; teaching specialist Oakland Unified Sch. Dist.-Childrens Center, 1968—; fgn. exchange dance dir. Academie de Danses, Paris, France, 1966; cons., instr. U. Calif. at Los Angeles Edn. Extension, Fresno State Coll., Calif. Childrens Centers Dirs. and Suprs. Assn., Fed. Projects Office Pittsburg Unified Sch. Dist., Tulare City Sch. Dist., 1971-73; researcher HEW Ednl. Testing Service, Berkeley, 1974; resident choreographer San Francisco Children's Opera, 1970—; ballet mistress Dimensions Dance Theater, Oakland, 1977-79; cons. Gianchetta Sch. of Dance, San Francisco and Concord, Calif., Robicheau Boston Ballet, TV series Patchwork Family, CBS, N.Y.C. Recipient credential of eminence in dance edn., life credential Calif. Community Colls., standard services credential, childrens centers credential all from Calif. Dept. Edn.; Notable Ams. award, 1976-77. Mem. Profl. Dance Tchrs. Assn. Am. Author: Basic Music Outlines for Dance Classes, 1960, rev., 1968; Teaching Techniques and Choreography for Advanced Dancers, 1965; Basic Music Outlines for Dance Classes, 1965; A Teacher's Guide for Ballet Techniques, 1970; Principle Procedures in Basic Curriculum, 1974; Objectives and Standards of Performance for Physical Development, 1975. Asso. music composer, lyricist The Ballet of Mother Goose, 1968. Asso. music arranger Le Ballet du Cirque, 1964; Techniques of a Ballet School, 1970, rev. edit., 1974. Choreographer Ravel's "Valses Nobles Et Sentimentales", 1976, Pachelbel's Cannon in D for Strings and Continuo, 1979, The Opera Ballets, 1986. Home and Office: 4923 Harbord Dr Oakland CA 94618

DE FILIPPO, RITA MARCELLA, budget analyst; b. N.Y.C.; d. Sal and Margaret (Jaeger) DeF.; student Los Angeles City Coll., 1957, City Coll. San Francisco, 1975, U. San Francisco, 1976; cert. acctg., LaSalle U., 1968. Asst. advt. dir. Gump's, Inc., San Francisco, 1959; research statistician Honig-Cooper & Harrington, advt. agy., San Francisco, 1960-61; salesperson Landau Realty, San Francisco, 1962-63; mgmt. analyst Oakland Army Base (Calif.), 1978-80; budget analyst Dept. Army, San Francisco, 1980—. Recipient Outstanding Performance award Fed. Govt., 1979. Mem. Am. Bus. Women's Assn. (treas. 1978-79), Am. Soc. Mil. Comptrollers, Assn. Women in Sci., Assn. U.S. Army, Nat. Fedn. Fed. Employees (trustee 1972), World Affairs Council. Club: Sierra. Office: Presidio of San Francisco San Francisco CA 94129

DE FOOR, MARJORIE KEEN, food company executive; b. West Palm Beach, Fla., Oct. 31, 1929; d. Stephen Wesley and Ada Mae Keen; student Stetson U., 1947; A.A., Stephens Coll., Mo., 1948; B.S., U. Ala., 1949; children—James Allison, Stephen Charles, Sheila Keen Monaco. With Keen Fruit Corp., Frostproof, Fla., 1956—, v.p., 1980-82, pres., 1982—, also dir. Republican. Episcopalian. Club: Tower (Tampa, Fla.). Home: 1402 Olivia St Key West FL 33040

DEFOREST, JUNE, violinist; b. Pitts., June 30, 1939; d. William Edward and Isabel (Nameth) DeF.; m. Daniel R. Morganstern, June 19, 1966. Student Carnegie-Mellon U., 1957-60; B.Mus., Manhattan Sch. Music, N.Y.C., 1963, M.Mus., 1974. Violinist, concertmaster Joffrey Ballet, N.Y.C., Can. Opera Co. Toronto, Ont., 1968; asst. concertmaster Am. Ballet Theater, N.Y.C., 1967-70, violinist, 1971—; violinist Chgo. Lyric Opera, 1969—; violinist Am. Chamber Trio, 1975—. Mem. Internat. Congress of Symphony and Opera Musicians (del. 1983, 84, 85), Coll. Music Soc., Chamber Music Am., Am. Chamber Concerts. Address: 890 West End Ave New York NY 10025

DEFRANCES, ARLENE LAWRENCE, manufacturing company executive; b. Greensburg, Pa., Aug. 18, 1937; d. John James and Josephine Ann (Kirn) Lawrence; m. Wayne Louis DeFrnces, Apr. 16, 1955; children—Monte Lawrence, Cory Lawrence, Marie Colltte. Student Westmoreland County Community Coll. Sec., Pa. Guernsey Breeders Assn., Greensburg, 1955-57; sec. U.S. Army Combat Devel., Fort Benning, Ga., 1957-58; sec., exec. sec. Union Carbide Corp., Export, Pa., 1959-72, adminstrv. asst., 1972-80, employee relations adminstr., 1980—. Bus. adviser, INROADS, Inc., Pitts., 1983—; inplant coordinator United Way, 1981—; in plant chmn. blood drive ARc, Greensburg, 1980—., chmn. community publicity, 1980—. Mem. Pitts. Personnel Assn., Nat. Fedn. Bus. Profl. Women (sec. 1985—, exec. bd. 1985—), Nat. Assn. Female Execs., Salem Crossroads Hist. Restoration Soc. Democrat. Roman Catholic. Avocations: Farmhouse restoration; oil and acrylic painting; jazz. Home: RD 1 Box 328 Export PA 15632 Office: Union Carbide Corp RD 4 Mellon Rd Bushy Run Research Ctr Export PA 15632

DEFRANCIS, PAMELLA HEBSON, communications executive; b. Evanston, Ill., Mar. 19, 1947; d. George C. and Helen M. (Lampe) Hebson; m. Peter Joseph DeFrancis, Nov. 11, 1978; 1 dau. B.A., U. Pa., 1969. Advt. mgr. Am. Express Co., N.Y.C., 1970-76, dept. store mktg. mgr., 1976-78, communications dir., 1978-79. dir. market devel., 1979-80, dir. industry mktg., 1980-83; assoc. v.p. Prudential Bache Securities Inc., N.Y.C., 1983-85; v.p., mgmt. supr. Wunderman, Ricotta & Kline, Inc., N.Y.C., 1985—. Mem. N.Y. Direct Mktg. Assn., Fin. Women's Assn. Episcopalian. Office: Wunderman Ricotta & Kline Inc 575 Madison Ave New York NY 10021

DE GAMARRA, AHNAL MARYNIKA CRIEGO, educator; b. Calcutta, India, Oct. 19, 1947; d. Giovani and Ahnal Nadija (Patni) Criego; m. Jorge Edmundo Llanos, Jan. 25, 1975. A.A., Los Angeles, Community Coll., 1968; B.A., Calif. State U., Los Angeles, 1976, M.A., 1981; postgrad. U.S. Internat. U., 1986—. Medicare supr. Occidental Life Ins. Co., Los Angeles, 1967-76; tchr. Los Angeles Unified Sch. Dist., 1974-81, adult educator, 1978—; adult educator Compton Unified Sch. Dist., Calif., 1978—; prof. Calif. State U., Los Angeles, 1980-85; pvt. instrn., 1963-76; ednl. cons. Harlan L. Polsky Assocs., Los Angeles, 1980; literacy cons. State of Calif., 1979—. Names Tchr. of Yr., Compton Unified Sch. Dist., 1981-82. Mem. Adult Edn. Assn. Los Angeles, Calif. Adult Basic Edn. League, Council Exceptional Children, Calif. Council Adult Edn., Calif. Tchrs. Assn., NEA, Nat. Literacy Council, Kappa Delta Pi, Pi Delta Theta. Democrat. Avocations: reading; foreign languages. Office: PO Box 36371 Los Angeles CA 90036

DEGENHART, PEARL C., artist, educator; b. Phillipsburg, Mont., Feb. 25; d. L.C. and Ellen (O'Neill) Degenhart; A.B., U. Mont., 1923; A.M., Columbia, 1928. Tchr. art Arcata (Calif.) Union High Sci., 1928—. One-man shows Stafford Inn, Scotia, Calif., 1954, Humboldt State Coll., 1951, 75, Humboldt Fed. Bldg., 1975, Ramada Inn, 1975, Corta Maderia Art Gallery, 1975; exhibited group shows San Francisco Art Assn., 1932, 37, 40, Contemporary Arts Gallery, N.Y.C., 1939, Denver, 1938, Humboldt State Coll., 1935, 45, 54, Spokane Wash., 1948, Oakland Art Gallery, 1948, Humboldt Fed. Gallery, 1966, Eureka Courthouse, 1968, Trinidad (Calif) Art Show, 1974-75, Redwood Art Assn., 1982, 83, 84; author children's book, 1982, 84. Mem. Bus. and Profl. Women's Club. Nat. League Am. Pen Women, Alpha Xi Delta, Delta Phi Delta. Contbr. to art, juvenile mags. Address: Box 142 Trinidad CA 95570

DEGNAN, JANE HEALY, university administrator; b. Albany, N.Y.; d. John Francis and Ruth Elizabeth (Hughes) Healy; m. Michael J. Degnan; children—Diana, Laura, Deborah. B.A. in English, Coll. St. Elizabeth, Madison, N.J., 1962; M.A. in English, Montclair State Coll., 1973. Tchr. English, Lincoln Jr. High Sch., West Orange, N.J., 1976-81; dir., program developer Westfall Film Prodns., Madison, N.J., 1981-83; coordinator pub. relations Seton Hall U., South Orange, N.J., 1983—; pres., cons. Connor Martin Agy., West Orange, 1981—; host radio talk show Viewpoint, 1985—. Author film scripts, articles, children's stories. Democrat. Roman Catholic.

DEGOTHSEIR, LINDA MARIE, nurse; b. Westchester, Pa., Oct. 16, 1959; d. Lowell Albert and K. Joan (Connor) Toenniessen; m. William Gerard DeGothseir, Oct. 24, 1981; 1 son, William Michael. B.S. in Nursing, Villanova U., 1981; postgrad. in oncology Widener U. R.N., Pa. Nurses aide St. Francis Hosp., Darby, Pa., 1976-80; nurses aide Delaware County Meml. Hosp., Drexel Hill, Pa., 1979-81, nurse oncology unit, 1981—. Recipient Meritorious Civilian award Policemen's Benevolent Assn., Cape May, N.J., 1985. Mem. Oncology Nurses Soc., Democrat. Roman Catholic. Avocation: ceramics. Office: Delaware County Meml Hosp Lansdowne Ave Drexel Hill PA 19026

DE GRAFFENRIED, VELDA MAE CAMP (MRS. THOMAS P. DEGRAFFENRIED), clinical laboratory executive; b. Kirwin, Kans.; d. George Robert and Laura (Woodward) Camp; student No. Ill. U., 1959-60; m. Thomas P. deGraffenried, May 23, 1942; children—Donna Rae McCaffrey, Albert Lawrence II, Nicholas Thomas. Office mgr. deGraffenried & Fisher Clin. Labs., DeKalb, Ill., 1957-64, exec. sec., 1964—, dir. pub. affairs until 1985; dir. public affairs deGraffenried Med. Cons. Service, Inc. Vice pres. Haish Sch. PTA, DeKalb, 1958-59; den mother cub scouts Chief Shabbona council Boy Scouts Am., 1957-60; supr. Teen Age Club, Louisville, 1949-50; county crusade chmn. Am. Cancer Soc., 1965, mem. exec. bd. DeKalb County, 1964—, dir. public affairs, 1970—, chmn. bd., 1978-80, chmn. Radiothon, 1972-82, 83-87, sec. DeKalb County Soc., 1969—, mem. state bd. Ill. div., 1985—. Recipient commendations Am. Cancer Soc., 1965, 74, Boy Scouts Am., 1955. Mem. DeKalb County Med. Soc. Aux. (sec. 1959-60, 76—, pres. 1973-74), DeKalb Hosp. Aux. Methodist. Home: 1208 Sunnymeade Trail DeKalb IL 60115

DEGRAW, FRANCES LEE DISHMAN, lawyer, banker; b. Newport News, Va., Oct. 26, 1936; d. Robert Ernest and Charlotte Elizabeth (Bishop) Dishman; m. Edward Carleton Hurman, June 19, 1955 (div. 1965) children—Bobbi C. Kesnig, Bonni G. Sandt, Johanna L. Hurman; m. 2d Donald Xavier DeGraw, Apr. 4, 1965. B.S. B.A. with honors, Christopher Newport Coll., 1974; J.D., Marshall Wythe Law Sch., Williamsburg, Va., 1976. Bar: Va. 1977, Fla. 1977, U.S. Tax Ct. 1977, U.S. Dist. Ct. (so. dist.) Fla. 1977. Tax specialist Coopers & Lybrand, Miami, Fla., 1977-78; assoc. Bruce Scheiner P.A., Ft. Myers, Fla., 1978-79; trust officer, v.p. Flagship Bank of Tampa, Punta Gorda, Fla., 1979-83; v.p. Fla. Nat. Bank, Punta Gorda, 1984-85, Orlando, 1985—; dir. Solar Pool Heaters, Inc., 1983-84; dir. fin., instr. Fla. Inst. for Legal Assts., 1986—. Columnist Estate Advisor weekly newspaper, 1983-85; announcer daily radio program on estate advice, 1980-81. Trustee St. Joseph Hosp., Port Charlotte, Fla., 1981-85, treas., 1983-85; bd. dirs. Wesleyan Coll.-SW Fla., Port Charlotte, 1983-85, Am. Cancer Soc., Charlotte County, Fla., 1980. Mem. ABA, Va. Bar Assn., Fla. Bar Assn., Orange County Bar Assn., Charlotte County Bar Assn., Central Fla. Assn. Women Lawyers, Central Fla. Estate Planning Council. Democrat. Episcopalian. Home: 329 Gilbert Rd Orlando FL 32792-4310 Office: Fla Nat Bank 801 N Orange Ave Orlando FL 32802-3593

DEGROOTE, DEIRDRE SABINE, farm manager; b. Melbourne, Australia, Oct. 21, 1942; d. Herbert Charles and Mulaika (Barclay Stone) Corben; m. John Shaw Sabine, IV, Aug. 21, 1961 (dec. 1966); 1 child, John Sabine; m. John Webster DeGroote, Jan. 28, 1969; children—Jessica, Jerusha; 1 stepchild, Thomas. B.A., Miss. State U., 1962; M.Ed., Auburn U., 1968; Ph.D., U. Ala., 1972. Counselor Lawson State Jr. Coll., Birmingham, Ala., 1969-71; asst. to med. dean U. Ala. Sch. Medicine, Birmingham, 1971-73; mgr. med. services Ingalls Shipbldg., Pascagoula, Miss., 1973-77; farm mgr. Ceres Farms, Hurley, Miss., 1977—. Contbr. articles to jours. Sec. Jackson County Citizens for Tax Reform, 1985. Recipient Restoration award Jackson County Hist. Soc., 1982. Mem. Internat. Arabian Horse Assn. (chmn. drugs and medications 1979-84, chmn. research and medicine 1985), Miss. Arabian Horse Assn. (pres. 1976-77), Dixie Gulf Arabian Horse Assn. (pres. 1981-82), World Arabian Horse Assn., Am. Horse Shows Assn. Avocations: cooking, interior decoration. Home: PO Box 167 Hurley MS 39555

DEGUIRE, KATHRYN SILBER, psychologist; b. Mankato, Minn., Nov. 16, 1932; d. Ernest Albert and Anna (John) Silber; Mus.B., Eastman Sch. Music U. Rochester, 1954; postgrad. Akademie fur Musik und Darstellende Kunst, Vienna, 1954-55, Upsala Coll., 1966-69; M.A., Fordham U., 1971, Ph.D., 1974; m. John Diaz, Aug. 22, 1981; 1 dau., Lise Kathryn. Pianist, organist, instr. piano, 1955-66; clin. asst. psychologist Meml. Sloan Kettering Cancer Center, N.Y.C., 1974-83; pvt. practice, N.Y.C. and Fairfield, N.J., 1976—; lectr. Upsala Coll., East Orange, N.J., 1971-72, 78-81. Fulbright scholar, Vienna, 1954-55; USPHS grantee, 1969-71. Mem. Am. Psychol. Assn., N.J. Psychol. Assn., Soc. Psychologists in Pvt. Practice (pres. 1986—). Rec. artist: Orion. Home: 26 Sand Rd Fairfield NJ 07006 Office: 120 E 34th St Suite 2L New York NY 10016

DE HAAN-PULS, JOYCE ELAINE, sales representative; b. Grand Rapids, Mich., Dec. 22, 1941; d. Harry Herman and Dorothy Elaine (Kikstra) DeHaan; student Calvin Coll., 1960-61; B.S. with honors, Grand Valley State Colls., 1978; postgrad. U. Sarajevo, Yugoslavia, 1978, Grad. Inst., Siedman Grad. Coll., 1979—; children—Bruce Todd, Daniel Lane, Cristy-Ann Sara Elizabeth Puls. Owner, operator Joyce Elaine's Beauty Parlor, Grandville, Mich., 1960-64; asst. assessor City of Hudsonville, Mich., 1978; dir. displaced homemaker program Women's Resource Center, Grand Rapids, 1979-81; visual products rep. 3M Corp., Grand Rapids, 1982-85, sr. account rep., Detroit, 1985—; mem. Ottawa County (Mich.) CETA Adv. Bd. Bd. dirs. Downtown Day Care Center, Grand Rapids, 1972. Recipient cert. of appreciation Bishop of Saigon, Vietnam, 1969; Top Sales rep. 3M/US, 1983, VIP, 1983, 84, 85; Phillip Morris scholar, 1975. Mem. Nat. Assn. Fgn. Students, Nat. Assn. for Female Execs., Grand Rapids Council on World Affairs, Am. Soc. Public Adminstrn. Republican. Home: 1824 Hampton Rd Grosse Pointe Woods MI 48236 Office: 2225 Oak Industrial Dr Grand Rapids MI 49505

DEHNEL, MARGARET ANNE LEWIS, psychologist; b. Ottawa County, Ohio, Apr. 24, 1915; d. Charles Edward and Lulu Ann (Kamke) Lewis; B.Ed., U. Toledo, 1939, M.Ed., 1960; postgrad. George Washington U., U. Mich., Wayne State U.; m. John E.E. Dehnel (div.). Instr. U. Toledo, 1945-47; chief sch. psychologist Bedford Pub. Schs., Temperance, Mich., 1960-67; chief psychol. services Project PUPIL, Fremont, Ohio, 1967-70; dir. Child Study Auglaize County (Ohio) Schs., Wapakoneta, 1970-79; coordinator regional assessment project W. Central Ohio Schs., 1979-80; dir. spl. edn. Wapakoneta City Schs., 1980-85; individual practice psychologist, Temperance, also Toledo, 1965-70, now Wapakoneta; U.S. del. Internat. Assn. Spl. Edn., London, Eng., 1966. Bd. dirs. Regional Spl. Edn. Center. Served as officer USNR, 1943-45. Mem. Nat. (charter), Ohio (program com.) sch. psychologists assns., Council on Mental Retardation (charter), Council on Children with Learning Disorders (charter), Council for Exceptional Children, Ohio Assn. Children with Learning Disabilities (state legislative com.), Council Adminstrs. Spl. Edn., AAUW, Toledo Mus. Art, Phi Kappa Phi, Kappa Delta. Congregationalist. Club: Soroptimists (bd. dirs.). Home: 326 Stinebaugh Dr Apt 1 Wapakoneta OH 45895 Office: 326 Stinebaugh Wapakoneta OH 45895

DEIANA, MELINDA LEE, newspaper account executive; b. Port Arthur, Tex., Nov. 16, 1958; d. Milton Glenn and Barbara Jane (Sharp) Smith; m. Jeffrey Francis Deiana, May 1, 1982. B.S. in Fine Arts, Lamar U., 1981; B.S. in Home Econs., 1981. Promotion, pub. service trainee Sta. KFDM-TV, Beaumont, Tex., 1981-82, promotion mgr., 1982-85; account exec. Middlesex News, Framingham, Mass., 1985—. Mem. panel Coordinating Bd. Tex. Coll. and Univ. Systems, Edn. Info. Ctrs. Program, Austin, 1979; bd. dirs. Baby Redbird Day Sch., Lamar U., 1979. Sabine area Home Econs. Assn. scholar, 1980, Beaumont Home Econs. Assn. scholar, 1978. Mem. Broadcast Promotion and Mktg. Execs., Tex. State Nutrition Council (exec. bd. 1979-80), Cap and Gown Hon. Soc., Alpha Chi Omega (asst. treas. 1980), Kappa Omicron Phi. Avocations: travel; gourmet cooking; dress designing; swimming; volleyball. Office: Middlesex News 33 New York Ave Framingham MA 01070

DEIBLER, BARBARA ELLEN, librarian; b. Pottsville, Pa., Aug. 11, 1943; d. Samuel Elwood and Miriam Elizabeth (Houser) D.; B.A., Pa. State U., 1965; M.S., Drexel U., 1966. Cataloger, State Library Pa., Harrisburg, 1966-82, head cataloger, 1972-82, rare book librarian, 1980—, asst. coordinator collection mgmt., 1982—. Librarian, Hist. Soc. Schuylkill County, 1971-77. Mem. Am. Acad. Polit. and Social Scis., Acad. Polit. Sci., Schuylkill County Allied Artists (dir. 1976-77), Pa. Library Assn., Hist. Soc. Pa. Baptist. Clubs: Pilot of Pottsville (rec. sec. 1974-75, dir. 1975-77), Pilot of Harrisburg (pres. 1979-81, treas. 1978-79, dir. 1981-83, sec. 1983-85, v.p. 1985—). Author: Pennsylvania German Barn Signs: For Protection or Just for Nice, 1978; Simplified Cataloging for Libraries, 1978; The State Library of Pennsylvania: The Philadelphia Years, 1982; Books of State: A Peripatetic Collection, 1983; A Treasure Trove of Books, 1986. Home: 2285 W Norwegian St Pottsville PA 17901 Office: Box 1601 Harrisburg PA 17105

DEIBLER, MARIE PHILLIPS, media relations specialist, university official, author; b. Gary, W. Va., May 20; d. George Monroe and Lura (Watson) Phillips; m. William Dan Deibler, Apr. 10, 1944 (dec.); 1 dau., Deborah Deibler Steele. A.B., Marshall U., 1943; postgrad. George Washington U., U. South Fla. Writer Washington Post, Washington, 1940-41, 43-44; staff writer/reporter A.P., Jacksonville, Fla., 1944-47; editor Que Pasa in Puerto Rico, San Juan, 1951-54; asst. editor U.S. Lady mag., Washington, 1961-65; editor U. Tampa mag. (Fla.), 1966-71; writer/media specialist U. South Fla., Tampa, 1972—. Author: What Every Military Kid Should Know, 1969; contbr. articles to mags. and newspapers. Bd. dirs. Hillsborough Polit. Caucus, Tampa, 1983—; bd. dirs., v.p. Friends of Temple Terrace Library (Fla.), 1978—; mem. citizens adv. com. Met. Planning, Orgn., Tampa, 1986—. Recipient Best Mag. in Category award Fla. Mag. Assn., 1968. Mem. Am. News Women Club, Women in Communications. Democrat. Episcopalian. Club: Tiger Bay (Tampa). Office: Office of Media Relations U South Fla Tampa FL 33620

DEISTER, CHRISTINE ROSEMARY, airline executive; b. Lowestoft, Eng., Apr. 16, 1949; came to U.S., 1973; d. Douglas Stephen and Vera (Mears) Smith; m. Terrence Leonard Deister, Aug. 28, 1976; 1 dau., Nicole Stephanie. Gen. cert. in edn. U. London. Supr. revenue acctg. Trans World Airlines, London, 1967-73, supr. air freight systems and acctg., Kansas City, Mo., 1973-79, mgr. credit ops., Kansas City, 1979-81, mgr. disbursements, Kansas City, 1981-85, dir. cash ops., 1985—; treas., corp. officer Duncourt & Assocs., Kansas City, Mo. Bus. coordinator Heart of Am. United Way, 1981. Recipient Charles C. Tillinghast award; named Employee of Yr., Controller's Dept. TWA, 1978. Mem. Internat. Concerns Com. for Children. Home: R R 27 PO Box 277D Parkville MO 64152 Office: TWA 11500 NW Ambassador Dr Kansas City MO 64153

DEITSCH, MARIAN MIMI, writer, editor; b. Scranton, Pa., Apr. 9, 1933; d. David T. and Florence V. (Chait) Rubin; m. Thomas A. Deitsch, Oct. 16, 1955 (dec. Nov. 1983); children—Lisa Ellen, Thomas Alan. A.B., Barnard Coll., 1954; postgrad. NYU, 1956-57, William Paterson Coll., Wayne, N.J., 1982-83. Writer, Scranton Times, 1954; asst. economist Fed. Res. Bank N.Y., N.Y.C., 1955-60; mktg. rep. Welcome Wagon Internat., Memphis, 1974-79; writer Jewish News, East Orange, N.J., 1979; editor C.H. Kline & Co., Inc., Fairfield, N.J., 1979-84, sr. cons., 1984—. Author: (with others) Guide to Energy, 1981; editor: Guide to Plastics Industry, 1982; Guide to Packaging Industry, 1980; Entering Livingston, 1963; contbr. articles to profl. jours. Bd. dirs. Hemlock Farms Community Assn., Lords Valley, Pa., 1977-78, 83-85; mem. various coms., 1977—; pres. Livingston (N.J.) LWV, 1969-71; chmn. Livingston Ednl. Liaison Com., 1968-69. Mem. Women in Communications. Home: 21 Coddington Terr Livingston NJ 07039 Office: Charles H Kline & Co 330 Passaic Ave Fairfield NJ 07006

DEITZ, SUSAN ROSE, newspaper advice columnist; b. Far Rockaway, N.Y., Mar. 21, 1934; d. Emanuel and Florence Jean (Goodstein) Davis; m. Morris J. Mandelker, Nov. 29, 1975; 1 son, Scott Richard; m. Richard Alan Deitz, Dec. 22, 1958 (dec. 1967). Student Smith Coll., Barnard Coll., N.Y.C., Art Students League, N.Y.C., Stella Adler Theater Studio. Syndicated advice columnist Los Angeles Times Syndicate, 1975—; mem. faculty New Sch., N.Y.C., 1977-79; radio personality. Author: (novel) Valency Girl, 1976. Mem. Women in Communications (Outstanding Mem. award 1984), Authors Guild. Club: Smith Coll.

DEJACIMO, ALEXANDRIA WELZIEN, social service agency administrator, management consultant; b. Chgo., June 4, 1951; d. Michael J. and Alexandria (Babel) Welzien; m. John R. DeJacimo, Sr., Dec. 27, 1975; children—Angelina, John R., Matthew. B.A., George Williams Coll., 1972; M.P.A., Roosevelt U., 1980. Community youth worker Omni-House, Wheeling, Ill., 1972-73; dir. bus. and fin. Omni Youth Services, Wheeling, 1972-86; assoc. exec. dir. Maine Ctr. Mental Health, 1986—; cons. Synergistic Office Systems, Libertyville, 1973—. Contbr. articles to various publs. Mem. Inst. Cert. Profl. Mgrs. (cert. mgr.), Internat. Mgmt. Council YMCA (chpt. pres. 1983-85, div. pres. 1985-86, mem. nat. exec. com. 1984, 86). Roman Catholic. Office: Maine Ctr Mental Health 832 Busse Hwy Park Ridge IL 60068

DÉJAH, LINDA SCHWEBER, clinical audiologist; b. N.Y.C., May 24, 1949; d. Nathan Louis and Barbara (Bernstein) Schweber; m. Raymond Dejah, Apr. 21, 1974 (div. 1978). B.A., L.I. U., 1971; M.A., Hofstra U., 1973. Lic. audiologist, N.Y. Audiologist, Floating Hosp., N.Y.C., 1973; asst. dir. audiology N.Y. Eye and Ear Infirmary, N.Y.C., 1973—; cons. Margaret Tietz Nursing Home, Queens, N.Y., 1979—. Mem. Am. Speech and Hearing Assn., Sigma Pi. Club: Vertical (N.Y.C.). Home: 300 E 33d St New York NY 10016 Office: New York Eye and Ear Infirmary 310 E 14th St New York NY 10003

DE JESUS-MCCARTHY, FE TERESA, physician; b. Samar, Philippines, Dec. 31, 1942; came to U.S., naturalized, 1978; d. Felicisimo V. and Baslia E. de J.; M.D., U. Philippines, 1966; m. Thomas J. McCarthy, Mar. 3, 1973; children—Amour Fe, Vida Linda. Practice medicine specializing in ob-gyn, Schenectady; mem. staff Bellevue Maternity Hosp. Mem. AMA, Am. Med. Women's Assn., Am. Fertility Soc., Am. Coll. Ob-Gyn, Am. Assn. Gynecol. Laparoscopists, N.Y. State Med. Soc., Med. Soc. of Schenectady County. Home: 1261 Hempstead Rd Schenectady NY 12309 Office: PO Box 1030 2210 Troy Rd Schenectady NY 12301*

DEJMEK, LUDMILA MARIE, architect; b. Prague, Czechoslovakia, Jan. 19, 1941; d. Sava and Edita (Sedlackova) Sedlacek; grad. Czech Tech. U., 1962; postgrad. Charles IV U. of Prague, 1963; grad. Acad. of Fine Arts, 1967; postgrad. L'Universite de Paris, La Sorbonne, L'Institute d'Urbanisme, 1964, L'Institute Catholique a Paris, 1967-68; M.Arch., Nova Scotia Tech. Coll., 1971; children—Mark, Andrea. Constrn. supr. Steel Corp. of Kladno, Czechoslovakia, 1962-63; designer Krushen & Dailey, Waterloo, Ont., also Donald Skinner, Architect, 1967-72; architect Centrel Mortgage & Housing Corp., Hamilton, Ont., 1972-74, program mgr., 1974-76; prin. firm Ludmila Dejmek, architects and engrs., Cambridge, Ont., Can., 1976—. NRC Can. grantee, 1970-71; recipient 2000 Kcs award, City Hall, Czechoslovakia, 1967, 3000 Kcs award CSSR Embassy, New Delhi, India, 1966. Mem. Ont. Assn. Architects, Profl. Engrs. Ont., Canadian Fedn. Univ. Women. Club: Chicopee Ski. Address: 126 Park Ave Cambridge ON N1S 2S6 Canada

DE JOIA, RUTH ANN, county official; b. Meadville, Pa., Aug. 16, 1927; continuing edn. student Pa. State U., 1976—; m. Joseph F.A. De Joia, June 28, 1947; children—John F., Joanne Marie De Joia Winans. Sec. various lawyers Meadville, Pa., 1945-56; clk.-typist Crawford County Assessment Office, 1956-59, sec. to chief adult and juvenile probation officer, 1959-65; sec. Holiday Inn of Meadville, 1965-66, asst. innkeeper, 1966-68; exec. sec. Crawford County Tourist Assn., 1970-71; with Domestic Relations Sect., Ct. Common Pleas of Crawford County, Meadville, 1971—, adminstrv. asst., 1976, asst. dir., 1977, dir., 1978—. Past officer PTA; mem. Crawford County Mental Health Assn., 1970-83, Crawford County Community Council, 1978—, Child Adv. Council Pa., 1979-80; mem. Women's resource group Crawford County Drug and Alcohol Commn., 1980. Mem. Domestic Relations Assn. Pa. (dir. 1978-81, sec. 1980-81), Nat. Reciprocal and Family Support Enforcement Assn., Eastern Regional Reciprocal and Family Support Enforcement Assn., Eastern Regional Council on Welfare Fraud. Mem. United Ch. of Christ. Home: PO Box 248 Meadville PA 16335 Office: PO Box 385 Meadville PA 16335

DEJOIE, CAROLYN BARNES MILANES, educator; b. New Orleans, Apr. 17; d. Edward Franklin and Alice Philomene (Milanes) Barnes; children—Deirdre, Prudhomme III, Duan. M.A., Universidad Nacional de Mexico, Mexico City, 1962; M.S.W., U. Wis., 1970; Ph.D., Union U., Cin., 1976. Cert. psychotherapist, Wis. Instr. So. U., Baton Rouge, 1962-63; asst. prof. Va. State Coll., Norfolk, 1963-66; asst. to pres. U. Wis. System, Madison, 1970-73, prof. adult edn. U. Wis., Madison, 1973—; fgn. lang cons., Mexico City, 1960-62; pvt. practice psychotherapy, 1980—; exec. dir. Organizacion Hispana Americana, 1974-75; spl. con. on crime prevention, Nassau, Bahamas, 1985. Mem. adv. editorial bd. Jour. of Negro Edn., 1985. Editor: Readings from a Black Perspective, 1984. Research on views of death, racism, sexism; author book of poetry: Just Me, 1980. Mem. adv. bd. Madison Met. Schs. Human Relations Council, 1975-85; mem. exec. bd. Madison chpt. ACLU, 1978-80, Council Minority Pub. Adminstrs., Madison, 1980-82; bd. dirs. Dane County Mental Health (Wis.), 1980-82; Recipient Recognition award Va. State Coll., 1962, Outstanding Woman award Zeta Phi Beta, 1975; Black Women: Achievements Against the Odds award Wis. Humanities Com., 1983, Gov.'s Spl award State of Wis., 1984, Appreciation award Madison Metro Sch. Dist., 1984, Outstanding Contbn. to Soc. award Alpha Kappa Alpha, 1984; Fulbright scholar, 1966-67. Mem. AAUP, AAUW, Nat. Assn. Media Women, Nat. Assn. Social Workers. Home: 5322 Fairway Dr Madison WI 53711 Office: 610 Langdon St Madison WI 53706

DE KOONING, ELAINE, artist; b. N.Y.C., Mar. 12, 1920; d. Charles Frank and Mary Ellen (O'Brien) Fried; hon. degree Western Coll. Women, Oxford, Ohio, 1964; D.F.A., Moore Coll. Art, Phila., 1972; L.H.D., Adelphi U., 1985; m. William de Kooning, Dec. 9, 1943. One-woman shows include Stable Gallery, N.Y.C., 1954, 56, Tibor de Nagy Gallery, N.Y.C. 1957, Graham Gallery, N.Y.C. 1960, 61, 63, 65. U. N.Mex., 1957, Mus. N.Mex., Santa Fe, 1959, Gump's, San Francisco, 1959, Washington Gallery Modern Art (presdl. portraits), 1964, Lyman Allen Mus., New London, Conn., (retrospective), 1959, Montclair (N.J.) Art Mus., 1973, Benson Gallery, Bridgehampton, N.Y., 1973, Ill. Wesleyan U., Bloomington, 1975, Coll. St. Catherine, St. Paul, 1975, Tampa Bay Arts Center, 1975, Image Gallery, U. Ga., 1977, Lauren Rogers Mus. Art, Miss., 1979, Grimaldis Gallery, Balt., 1980, Spectrum Fine Arts Ltd., N.Y.C., 1981, Ruth Schaffner Gallery, Santa Barbara, Calif., 1981, Himmelfarb Gallery, Water Mill, N.Y., 1981, Phoenix II Gallery, Washington, 1982, Greenberg Gallery, St. Louis, 1982, Port Washington (N.Y.) Library, 1982, Gruenebaum Gallery, N.Y.C., 1982, Guild Hall Mus., East Hampton, N.Y., 1983, Arts Club of Chgo., 1983; Adelphi U. Ctr. Gallery, 1984, Vered Gallery, East Hampton, 1984, Grimaldis Gallery, Balt., 1985; represented in permanent collections Mus. Modern Art. Loeb Center, N.Y.C., Kennedy Library, Cambridge, Mass., Truman Library, Independence, Mo., Elmira (N.Y.) Coll., Ark. Arts Center, Little Rock, Jewish Community Center, Bayonne, N.J., Montclair (N.J.) Art Mus., CIBA-Geigy Corp., Ardsley, N.Y., Neuberger Mus., Purchase, N.Y., Washington Gallery Modern Art, also pvt. collections; tchr. U. N.Mex., 1959, Pa. State U., 1960, Contemporary Art Assn., Houston, 1952, U. Calif. at Davis, 1963-64, Yale U., 1967, Carnegie-Mellon U., 1969-70, U. Pa., 1970-72, Wagner Coll., 1970, U. Pa., 1971—, N.Y. Studio Sch., Paris, France, 1974—, Parsons Sch. Fine Art, 1974-76; Lamar Dodd chair U. Ga., Athens, 1976-78, Hilton and Sally Avery Chair Bard Coll., 1982. Office: care Gruenebaum Gallery 38 E 57th St New York NY 10022

DELACATO, JANICE ELAINE, learning consultant; b. Bklyn., June 6, 1926; d. Frode Siegfried and Vilma (Riis) Fernstrom; m. Carl Henry Delacato, June 20, 1951; children—Elizabeth Delacato Putnam, Carl Henry, David Fernstrom. A.B., Bryn Mawr Coll., 1948. Tchr., Rydal Hall, Ogontz Sch., Pa., 1948-49, The Spence Sch., N.Y.C., 1949-50, Chestnut Hill Acad., Phila., 1950-52; co-dir. The Chestnut Hill Reading Clinic, Phila., 1951-65, Delacato & Delacato, Cons. in Learning, Phila., 1972—; mgr. Morton (Pa.) Book Store, 1972—; co-dir. The Delacato & Delacato Conf. on Autism and Learning Disabilities, 1979—. Chmn. fund-raising com. Springside Sch., 1969-71; treas. Main St. Fair Antiques Booth, Chestnut Hill Hosp., 1965-77. Recipient Main St. Fair award Chestnut Hill Hosp., 1972. Mem. AAUW. Republican. Unitarian. Club: Phila. Cricket. Editor newsletter Temple U. Med. Center Women's Aux., Phila., 1953-65; class editor Bryn Mawr Coll. Alumnae Bull., 1966-79. Home: "The Glen" Thomas Rd at Northwestern Ave Philadelphia PA 19118 Office: Delacato and Delacato Suite 107 Plymouth Plaza Plymouth Meeting PA 19462

DELACERDA, MELISSA GRINER, lawyer; b. St. Petersburg, Fla., Mar. 17, 1952; d. Joseph Henry and Dorothy Jean (Stephens) G.; m. Fred G. DeLacerda, June 17, 1972. B.S., Memphis State U., 1973; J.D., U. Tulsa, 1979. Bar: Okla. 1979. Tchr., elem. sch., Crowley, La., 1974-75; sports reporter Daily Advertiser, Lafayette, La., 1974-75; assoc. firm Bird & Hochderffer, Stillwater, Okla., 1979-80; sole practice law, Stillwater, 1980—. Bd. dirs. Alcoholism Council Area Okla., 1981-82, Stillwater Domestic Violence Services, 1979—. Mem. Okla. Bar Assn., Payne County Bar Assn. (sec. 1984), Am. Trial Lawyers Assn., Bus. and Profl. Women Stillwater (pres. 1975), Stillwater C. of C. (ambassador 1982-84). Office: 720 S Husband St Suite 5 Stillwater OK 74074

DELAMAR, GLORIA, author, writer; married; 5 children. B.S. in Early Childhood Edn., U. Pitts., 1951, postgrad., 1952. Tchr. kindergarten Pitts. Pub. Schs., 1951-55; substitute tchr. kindergarten, pub. schs., Richmond, Va., 1967-70; freelance market research supr. and interviewer, Richmond, 1970-76; free-lance pub. relations writer, 1976—; tchr. writing Nat. League Am. Pen Women, Richmon, 1975, 76, Gloria Dei Creative Arts Ctr., Phila., 1977—, Unitarian Soc. Germantown's Community Enrichment Classes, Phila., 1977-81, Elkins Park Library Summer Reading and Writing Club, 1979-80, parent-sponsored pvt. classes during sch. strike, 1981; lectr. in field to adults, children. Author: Play Aesop, 1971; Children's Counting-Out Rhymes, Fingerplays, Jump-Rope and Bounce-Ball Chants and Other Rhythms: A Comprehensive English Language Reference, 1983; Rounds for Voices and Simple Instruments: A Comprehensive English Language Reference. Co-editor, contbg. author: Voices. Contbr. articles, fillers, verses to various mags., newspapers, 1968—. Bd. dirs. Better Films and TV Council Pitts., 1963-67, Richmond Pub. Forum, Inc., 1968-76. Mem. Nat. League Am. Pen Women (pres. Richmond br. 1974-76, pres. Phila. br. 1978-80, pres. Pa. 1978-80, 80-82), Soc. Children's Books Writers, Phila. Children's Reading Round Table, Phila. Writers' Conf. (pres. 1981-82), Pi Lambda Theta. Office: 7303 Sharpless Rd Melrose Park PA 19126

DELAMIELLEURE, DEBORAH ANN, nurse; b. Detroit, Feb. 16, 1953; d. Gerald Charles and Ann (Gera) Selke; m. Gary Stanley Delamielleure, Nov. 23, 1973; children—Robin Lynn, Megan Marie. Diploma in nursing, Providence Hosp. Sch. Nursing, 1973. Staff nurse Flint Osteo. Hosp. (Mich.), 1973, Bi-County Community Hosp., Warren, Mich., 1974-75; charge nurse Bay Osteo. Hosp., Bay City, Mich., 1977-78; office nurse J.C. Gromada D.O., Bay City, 1981-85, Larry J. Ross, Jr., M.D., Peoria, Ill., 1985—; vol. Shriners Mich. Mini-Clinic, 1981-84. Roman Catholic. Home: 1200 S Lafayette Bartonville IL 61607

DELAND, DIANE O. AMMONS, business executive; b. Redding, Calif., Jan. 3, 1940; d. Mark T. and Lucille I. (Wissert) Ammons; m. Maurice Graham DeLand, Feb. 19, 1966 (div. 1974); 1 child, Charles Maurice DeLand. B.A., U. Calif.-Berkeley, 1961; Cert., Goethe Inst., Berlin, 1961; postgrad. Am. U., 1969-71. Economist, AID, U.S. Dept. State, Washington, 1962-70; sr. economist U.S. EPA, Washington, 1970-73, PBGC, Washington, 1974-76; rep. U.S. Govt. Inter-Agy. Task Force, Washington, 1978; dir. tech. programs Pension Benefit Guaranty, Washington, 1976-79; pres. Pension Corp., Los Angeles, 1979—; cons. and lectr. in field. Co-author: (tech. booklet) Guidelines on Plan Termination, 1977; Syllabus on Pension Plans, 1981. Headmaster council Indian Mountain Sch., Conn., 1984—. Named Life mem. Calif. Scholastic Soc., 1957, U.S. Pres.'s Govt. exchange scholar, 1978-79. Mem. Women in Bus., Nat. Assn. Female Execs., Am. Soc. Pension Actuaries (assoc.), Jr. League. Avocations: Painting; reading; skiing; tennis; travel. Office: Pension Corp 429 Santa Monica Blvd Suite 320 Santa Monica CA 90401

DELANEY, CATHY EILEEN, state ofcl.; b. Binghamton, N.Y., Apr. 5, 1947; d. Martin Frank and Beverly Carolyn (Hamlin) Piza; B.A., Harpur Coll., Binghamton, 1968; M.S.W., Syracuse (N.Y.) U., 1976; m. Frank L. Delaney, June 28, 1969. Public assistance caseworker Seneca County Dept. Social Services, Seneca Falls, N.Y., 1968; psychiat. social worker Willard (N.Y.) Psychiat. Center, 1968-73, Broome Devel. Center, Binghamton, 1973-74, 76; congl. legis. aide, 1975; asst. dir. bur. program and fiscal audits N.Y. State Office Mental Retardation and Devel. Disabilities, Albany, 1976-80, statewide coordinator intermediate care facilities for developmentally disabled, 1980, cert. coordinator Western County service group, 1980-83, Upstate unit dir. Bur. Cert. Control, 1983—, also mem. office human relations com.; adj. instr. SUNY Sch. Social Welfare, Albany, 1982-83. Grantee HEW, 1975-76. Mem. Upstate Assn. Psychiat. Social Workers in State Schs. and Hosps. (sec. 1970), Am. Soc. Public Adminstrn., Am. Assn. Mental Deficiency, Nat. Assn. Social Workers. Office: PO Box 3153 Albany NY 12203

DELANEY, ELEANOR CECILIA COUGHLIN, educator; b. Elizabeth, N.J.; d. John C. and Eleanor C. (Fadde) Coughlin; B.S., Sch. Edn. Rutgers U., 1930, M.A., 1939; Ph.D., Columbia U., 1954; 1 son, John. Tchr. public schs., Elizabeth, N.J., 1927; prin. Woodrow Wilson Sch., Elizabeth, 1941-55; prof. Grad. Sch. Edn., Rutgers U., New Brunswick, N.J., 1955—, chmn. dept. ednl. adminstrn. and supervision, 1974—; vis. prof. William and Mary Coll., U. Mex., Columbia U.; ednl. cons. sch. systems, N.J., N.Y., Va., 1950—. Mem. Elizabeth Charter Commn., 1960-61; chmn. Mayor's Adv. Commn. on Urban Devel., 1962-64, Elizabeth Human Relations Commn., 1968-75; mem. Elizabeth Bd. Edn., 1972-79, pres., 1973-76; mem. exec. bd. Union County chpt. ARC; mem. exec. bd. Vis. Nurse and Health Assn., 1977—; pres., 1981-85. Mem. AAUW, Nat., N.J. edn. assns., Dept. Elem. Sch. Prins., AAUP, AAAS, Am. Ednl. Research Assn., Kappa Delta Pi, Pi Lambda Theta, Phi Delta Kappa. Author: Spanish Gold, Lands of Middle America, Our Friends in South America, Science-Life Series, Book 4; Persistent Problems in Education. Contbr. articles to profl. mags. Home: 220 W Jersey St Elizabeth NJ 07202

DE LANGE, VICTORIA PUIG, editor; b. Guayaquil, Ecuador, Dec. 3, 1919; d. Carlos Puig Vilazar and Rosa Marie (Parada) Puig; student U. Catolica, Chile, 1955; children—Luis C. Aguirre, Barbara Pereira, Christian Lange. Attache, Embassies of Washington and Chile, 1946-60; consul gen. of Ecuador, Fla., 1962-64; adviser State of Fla., 1964-65; Latin Am. syndicated columnist, 1972—; editor-in-chief Spanish lang. edit. Harper's Bazaar, 1984—; pres. Ideas Plus Internat.; also free lance writer; fashion cons. Founder People to People Com., 1963; mem. Council for Internat. Visitors, 1964-77; mem. Customers Adv. Bd., Burdines, 1975; mem. bd. Summer Star Theatre, 1974; mem. spl. adv. bd. Germaine Monteil Non Stop Achievers. Recipient Keys of Dade County, Fla., and Miami, Medal of Merit, Govt. Ecuador, 1967, Most Outstanding Ecuador born journalist in internat. field medal, 1982; named Hon. Citizen, State Fla., 1966, Woman of Year, Ecuador, 1975. Mem. Internat. Soc. Arts (dir. 1977). Roman Catholic. Clubs: Turnberry, Jockey (Miami), Bay Internat. Office: 1450 Coral Way Suite 12 Miami FL 33145

DELANO, DOROTHY ANN, typesetting, graphics and printing administrator; b. Jamaica, N.Y., Nov. 17, 1926; d. George Allston and Viola (Teller) Savage; m. Russell Standish Delano, Dec. 25, 1969; m. Harrison Dearing Gordon, Dec. 17, 1948 (dec. 1967); children—Tracey Ann, Gordon. B.A., Tufts U. 1949. Copywriter, H.B. Humphrey Co., Boston, 1949-51; freelance copywriter, Boston, 1952-60; founder, pres., chief exec. officer Girl Friday Services, Inc., Braintree, Mass., 1960—. Trustee, bd. of investment Weymouth Savs. Bank, Mass., 1976—. Mem. South Shore C. of C. (past bd. dirs.). Republican. Avocations: Writing; travel; painting; designing. Office: Girl Friday Services Inc 22 River St Braintree MA 02184

DELANO, LINDA CHRISTINE, physical education educator, coach; b. Chgo., June 6, 1953; d. William Stevens and Louise Catherine (Uccello) D. B.S.E., No. Ill. U., 1975, M.S.E., 1980. Tchr. phys. edn. Libertyville (Ill.) High Sch., 1975—, head volleyball coach, head softball coach, 1975—; basketball assignment chmn. North Suburban Conf., Lake County, Ill., 1983-84. Contbr. articles to profl. jours. Named Athlete of Yr., Ind. Register, Vernon Hills, Ill., 1982; sec.-treas. sr. girls league No. Ill. Sr. and Jr. Fast Pitch Softball Leagues, 1981, 82, 83. Mem. U.S. Field Hockey Assn. (chmn. north central sect. 1980-82, 83-85, chmn. membership com. 1982-83), Ill. Assn. Health, Phys. Edn. and Recreation (Lake County rep. 1976-81, award 1982), AAHPERD (life), Ill. Coaches Assn. for Girls' and Women's Sports (pres. softball coaches assn. 1980-81). Roman Catholic. Home: 504 Arlington Ct Vernon Hills IL 60061 Office: Libertyville High Sch 708 W Park Ave Libertyville IL 60048

DE LARROCHA, ALICIA DE LA CALLE, concert pianist; b. Barcelona, Spain, May 23, 1923; d. Eduardo and Teresa (De La Calle) de L.; grad. (prize extraordinary, Gold medal), Acad. Marshall, Barcelona; m. Juan Torra, June 21, 1950; children—Juan, Alicia. Debut, Barcelona, 1927; solo recitalist, concert pianist major orchs. in Europe, U.S., Can., Central and S. Am., S. Africa, N.Z., Australia, Japan; dir. Acad. Marshall, 1959—; rec. artist Hispavox, CBS, Decca-London, records. Recipient Harriet Cohen Internat. Music award, 1968; Paderewski Meml. medal, 1961; Grand prix du Disque Acad. Charles Cros, 1960, 74; Edison award, 1968; Grammy award, 1974, 75; 1st Gold medal Merito a la Vocacion, 1972; decorated Order Civil Merit, Order Isabel la Catolica (Spain). Mem. Musica en Compostela (dir.), Hispanic Soc. Am. (corr.), Internat. Piano Archives (hon. pres.) Address: 119 W 57th St New York NY 10019*

DE LA TORRE, BLANCA BIANCHI, lawyer; b. Florida, Cuba, Sept. 25, 1948; came to U.S., 1962, naturalized, 1970; d. Ricardo and Josefina (Arias) Bianchi; m. Raul de la Torre, Dec. 21, 1974; children—Carina, Adriana. B.A. magna cum laude in Social Scis., U. P.R., 1971, J.D. cum laude, 1974. Bar: P.R. 1975, Ind. 1978, D.C. 1978, U.S. Supreme Ct. 1979. Hearing examiner Consumer Affairs Dept., Santurce, P.R., 1974-77; supervising atty. Legal Services Program, Gary, Ind., 1977-81; ptnr. Rivera, Schlesinger & de la Torre, East Chicago, Ind., 1981-85; sole practice, East Chicago, 1985—. Mem. U. P.R. Law Rev., 1974. Sec. bd. trustees Lake Area United Way, 1983, treas., 1985; pres. Lake Area Energy Assistance Program, 1983, St. Patrick's Parish Council, Chesterton, Ind., 1983-85; sec. St. Patrick's Home and Sch. Assn., 1985-86. Mem. Colegio de Abogados de Puerto Rico, ABA, E. Chicago Bar Assn., Hispanic Bar Assn., Nat. Assn. Social Security Claimants' Reps. Republican. Roman Catholic. Office: 525 W Chicago Ave East Chicago IN 46312

DELATTRE, CHRISTINE, glass company executive; b. Bouake, Ivory Coast, May 1, 1949; d. Robert and Simone D.; m. Dominique Bourgeade, Dec. 22, 1980; 1 child, Benjamin. M.B.A., Institut d'Etudes Politiques de Paris, 1970. Econ. surveyor Saint Gobain en Ballage, Paris, 1977-80, mktg. mgr., 1980-82; mktg. dir. Saint Gobain Desjonqueres, Paris, 1982-84; pres., chief exec. officer Saint Gobain Desjonqueres USA, N.Y.C., 1984—. Home: 300 E 75th St New York NY 10021 Office: SGD Glass Co 600 Madison Ave New York NY 10022

DELAVAL, NANCY DUNN, science and technology author, publicity consultant; b. Brantley, Ala., Oct. 7, 1936; d. George W. and Lucy (McDaniel) Dunn; children—Lucy, Molly. Student George Washington U., 1957; B.S. in Journalism, Ohio U., 1961, M.A. in Creative Writing, 1965. Novelist and short story writer, Athens, Ohio, 1960-68; edn. specialist U.S. Navy, Pensacola, Fla., 1974-79, sci. and tech. writer Naval Civil Engring. Lab., Port Hueneme, Calif., 1979—. Author: If the Dead Rise Not, 1965; short stories and poetry; contbr. articles to profl. jours. Served with USN, 1954-58. Mem. Women in Communications, Nat. Assn. Govt. Communicators, NOW. Club: Toastmistress (pres. 1978-79). Office: Pub Affairs Dept Naval Civil Engring Lab Port Hueneme CA 93043

DE LA VEGA, DIANNE WINIFRED DEMARINIS (MRS. JORGE DE LA VEGA), government official; b. Cleve.; d. Gerald M. and Dorothy (Philp) DeMarinis; student Case Western Res. U., 1948-50, M.A., 1969; B.A., U. Am., 1952; Ph.D. in Psychology, Internat. Coll., Los Angeles, 1977; M.A., Goddard Coll., 1978; m. Jorge Alejandro de la Vega, July 19, 1952; children—Constance, Francisco Javier, Alexandra. Faculty, Western Res. U., Cleve., 1961-62; instr. Instituto Mexicano-Norteamericano de Relaciones Culturales, Mexico, 1967; supr. fgn. press Mexican Olympic Organizing Com., Mexico, 1968; asst. to producer Producciones Ojo, Canal 8 TV, Mexico, 1969; exec. asst. Internat. Exec. Service Corps, Mexico City, 1969-70; asst. to dir. U.S. Internat. U. Mexico, Mexico City, 1970-75; family planning evaluator for Latin Am., AID, 1976; with dept. spl. edn. region IX Nat. Center on Child Abuse and Neglect, Children's Bur., Office Child Devel., HEW, Calif. State U., 1977—. Chmn. Puppet's Jr. League, Mexico City, 1967, chmn. ways and means, 1968; sec. Tlaxcala-Okla. Partner's of Alliance for Progress, 1967—; bd. dirs. Hot Line of Mexico City; mem. Los Angeles adv. com. 1984 Olympics. Lic. marriage and family counselor. Mem. Inst. Bioenergetic Analysis, Flying Samaritans, Pro Salud Maternal, Transactional Analysis Assn., Club: Jr. League (Los Angeles). Home: 130 Alta Ave D Santa Monica CA 90402

DE LAY, DOROTHY (MRS. EDWARD NEWHOUSE), violinist, educator; b. Medicine Lodge, Kans., Mar. 31, 1917; d. Glenn Adney and Cecile (Osborn) DeLay; student Oberlin Coll., 1933-34, D.Music (hon.), 1981; B.A., Mich. State U., 1937; Artists diploma, Juilliard Grad. Sch. Music, 1941; m. Edward Newhouse, Mar. 5, 1941; children—Jeffrey H., Alison Dinsmore. Solo, chamber music performances in U.S., Can. S.Am., 1937—; violinist, founder Stuyvesant Trio, 1940-42; mem. faculty Juilliard Sch. Music, N.Y.C., 1947—, Sarah Lawrence Coll., 1948—, Meadowmount Summer Sch. Music, Westport, N.Y., 1948-70, Aspen Summer Music Sch., 1971—; Starling prof. violin U. Cin., 1974—; vis. prof. violin Phila. Coll. Performing Arts, 1977-83, New Eng. Conservatory, 1978—; condr. master classes univs. and conservatories in U.S., Europe, Asia, Africa, Near East. Recipient Outstanding Artist-Tchr. award Am. String Tchrs Assn., 1975; Highest Honors citation Nat. Fedn. Music Clubs, 1982; Outstanding Alumna award Mich. State U., 1984; King Solomon award Am.-Israel Cultural Fedn., 1985; Dorothy De Lay Day proclaimed by Gov. Kans., 1982. Mem. Mu Phi Epsilon. Contbr. articles on violins, violinists to various encys. Home: 349 N Broadway Upper Nyack NY 10960

DE LEON, CIRA JANE, psychiatrist; b. Havana, Cuba, Dec. 27, 1949; d. Frank and Cira I. (De Leon) De Leon. B.S. magna cum laude, St. Thomas U., Houston, 1972; M.D., U. Tex. Med. Br., Galveston, 1976. Resident in psychiatry Timberlawn Hosp., Dallas, 1976-79; physician emergency room John Peter Smith Hosp., Ft. Worth, 1977-79; clin. dir. Mental Health Clinic, Houston, 1979-83; practice medicine specializing in psychiatry, Houston, 1979—; program med. dir. chem. dependency unit Belle Park Hosp., Houston, 1983-84, pres. med. staff, 1985, program med. dir. Psychiat. ICU, 1985—; med. dir. Inst. Motivational Devel., 1983—; psychiat. cons. for other physicians, attys., 1979—. Mem. Am. Med. Polit. Action Com., 1982-85, Houston Hispanic Forum, 1986—. St. Thomas U. scholar, 1968-72, Alliance Français scholar, Tours, France, 1970. Mem. AMA, Am. Psychiat. Assn., Am. Med. Women's Assn., Tex. Med. Assn., Houston Psychiat. Soc., Harris County Med. Soc. Republican. Roman Catholic. Office: 7500 Beechnut St Suite 330 Houston TX 77074

DE LEON, LIDIA M(ARIA), magazine editor; b. Havana, Cuba, Sept. 10, 1957; came to U.S., 1959; d. Leon J. and Lydia (Diaz Cruz) deL. B.A. in Communications cum laude, U. Miami, Coral Gables, Fla., 1979. Staff writer Miami Herald, Fla., 1978-79; editorial asst. Halsey Pub. Co., Miami, 1980-81, assoc. editor, 1981, editor, 1981—; editor Delta SKY Mag., 1983—. Mem. Am. Soc. Mag. Editors, Fla. Mag. Assn. Clubs: Jockey, Cricket (Miami). Avocation: tennis. Office: Halsey Pub Co 12955 Biscayne Blvd North Miami FL 33181

DE LEON, MARIA MAGDALENA, language educator; b. Mathis, Tex., July 22, 1944; d. Santiago and Maria Consuelo (Silva) Vallejo; m. Guadalupe H. De Leon, Mar. 29, 1963; children—Barbara, Ismael, Leonzo, Vanita, Primitivo. A.A., Bee County Coll., 1974; B.S., Tex. A&I U., 1976, M.S., 1982. Cert. tchr., Tex. Tchr. aide Mathis Community Action, Tex., 1968-72; tchr. Adult Basic Edn., Mathis, 1972-75, Mathis Ind. Sch. Dist., 1976—; tax return preparer, Mathis, 1975—. Mem. Mennonite Bd. Edn., 1983—, Mathis Bank Boosters, 1985—; tchr., mem. Tabernaculo de Fe Mennotie Ch., Mathis, 1985—; del. S. Tex. Mennonite Central Conf., Mathis, 1986; sponsor Tabernaculo De Fe Mennonite Youth Fellowship, 1986; sec. Community Action Com., Mathis, 1978. Mem. Tex. State Tchr. Assn., Nat. Assn. Female Execs., Concilio Naiconal de Iglesias Menonitas Hispanas (com. adminstrv. 1982-84), Phi Theta Kappa, Gamma Lambda, Sigma Delta Pi. Democrat. Avocations: reading; sewing; working with youth. Home: 713 E Stone St Mathis TX 78268

DELGADO, YOLANDA YVETTE, business educator; b. N.Y.C., May 28, 1954; d. Francisca Delgado; children—Nichol F.L. Crooks, Jazmin N. Campbell. B.A., Herbert H. Lehman Coll., 1984. Bilingual instr. Herbert H. Lehman Coll., Bronx, N.Y., 1980-81; corp. tchr. Career Blazers Word Processing Ctr., N.Y.C., 1983-84; bus. instr. Girls Club N.Y., Bronx, 1984-85; instr. Am. Bus. Inst., Bronx, 1985—. Mem. Nat. Assn. Female Execs., Bus. Edn. Assn. Avocation: devel. of tests, manual and instrn. materials. Home: 1555 Grand Concourse Bronx NY 10452 Office: Am Bus Inst 2432 Grand Concourse Bronx NY 10456

DELGADO SMITH, ASCENSION, educational administrator; b. Seville, Spain, Mar. 19, 1934; came to U.S., 1962, naturalized, 1966; d. Vicente Delgado and Asuncion Arias (Domimguez) Gonzalez; children—Jerome, Frank. B.S., Seville Coll., 1954; B.A., Centenary Coll., 1969; M.Ed., La. State U., 1972; postgrad., La. Tech. U., 1974. Sci. and Spanish tchr. St. Vincent Acad., Shreveport, La., 1962-69; sci. tchr. Captain Shreve High Sch., Shreveport, 1969-74, sci. coordinator, 1974-78; sci. supr. Secondary Sch. Caddo Parish, Shreveport, 1978-79; founder, 1st prin. Caddo Magnet High Sch., Shreveport, 1979—. Writing team La. Energy Conservation Guide, Baton Rouge, 1979. Named Educator of Distinction, La. PTA 1981, Hon. Senator La. 1979. Mem. Parent/Tchr. Sch. Assn., La. Assn. Educators, Caddo Assn. Educators, NEA, Assn. Supervision and Curriculum Devel., La. Assn. Prins., Nat. Assn. Secondary Sch. Prins., Phi Kappa Phi, Lambda Iota Tau, Delta Kappa Gamma. Republican. Roman Catholic. Home: 4627 Orchid Shreveport LA 71105 Office: Caddo Parish Magnet High Sch 1601 Viking Dr Shreveport LA 71101

DELIBES, CLAUDE BLANCHE, communications company executive; b. Paris, Sept. 20, 1932; d. Andre Jean and Simone (Barou) Seligmann; came to U.S., 1940; naturalized, 1954; B.A., Sorbonne U., Paris, 1953; m. Maurice Delibes, Dec. 31, 1961; 1 son by previous marriage, Roger Schwartz; 1 dau., Jacqueline Delibes. Editor Fairchild Publications, N.Y.C., 1961-65; pub. relations dir. West Point Pepperell Corp., N.Y.C., 1968-72; sr. account supr. The Siesel Co., N.Y.C., 1972-75; pres. Delibes Communications, Ltd., N.Y.C., 1975—. Mem. Women Execs. in Pub. Relations, Fashion Group, Advt. Women of N.Y., French-Am. C. of C. Home: 1601 3d Ave New York NY 10028 Office: 200 W 57th St New York NY 10019

DELK, DIANE DAWSON, oil company executive; b. San Antonio, Mar. 11, 1951; d. Joseph Turner and Melba Louise (Bruno) Dawson; m. Aug. 19, 1972 (div. Oct. 1983); children—Colin Dawson Davis, Brian Sanders Davis, Justin Randolph Davis; m. Thomas Michael Delk, June 22, 1984. B.Mus. cum laude, Baylor U., 1973; postgrad. Peabody Coll., 1973-74, Corpus Christi State U., 1983. Freelance pianist, Waco and Corpus Christi, 1975-79; pvt. music tchr., Waco, Tex., 1976-79; land mgr. Joseph T. Dawson, Oil Operator, Corpus Christi, 1983—. Bd. dirs. Jr. League of Corpus Christi, 1979-82, chmn. drug awareness com. Texans War on Drugs, 1981-82; chmn. Bayfest Drinks Concession Fundraiser, Corpus Christi, 1982. Recipient Outstanding Active Vol. of Yr. award Jr. League Corpus Christi, 1982. Avocations: snow skiing; scuba diving; hunting; gardening, horseback riding. Home: 2407 Amistad Portland TX 78374 Office: Joseph T Dawson Oil Operator 630 Petroleum Tower Corpus Christi TX 78474

DELLA-GIUSTINA, MARSHA ANN, TV news producer, educator; b. Springfield, Mass., Jan. 27, 1947; d. Joseph Augustus and Jennie Delores (Subotin) Della-G.; B.A. in English, Russell Sage Coll., Troy, N.Y., 1968; M.S. in Broadcast Journalism, Boston U., 1974, Ed.D. in Media and Tech., 1985; m. John R. Wetmiller, Aug. 26, 1972. Jr. high sch. tchr., Agawam and Westfield, Mass., 1968-72; radio public affairs host-producer sta. WBZ-FM, Boston, 1973-74; TV news producer-writer sta. WCVB-TV, Boston, 1976-85; journalism program dir., asso. prof. broadcast journalism Emerson Coll., Boston, 1976—; owner, producer Giustina Prodns., Arlington, Mass., 1979—; co-chmn. Freedom of Info. Act Symposium, 1982; cons. in field. Commr., Agawam Youth Commn., 1970-72; mem. Agawam Town Meeting, 1970-72; co-chmn. reunion com. Russell Sage Coll. Alumni Class 1968, 1978-83; mem. media com. Mass. ERA Referendum Com., 1974-76; lobbyist NOW, 1973-76. Recipient Emmy award, 1977, 81, award for disting. achievement in broadcast journalism edn., 1983. Mem. Am. Women Radio and TV, Nat. Acad. TV Arts and Scis., Boston Women's Media Network, Assn. Edn. in Journalism, Internat. Radio and TV Soc., Russell Sage Coll. Alumni Assn., Sigma Delta Chi. Democrat. Home: 113 Gray St Arlington MA 02174 Office: Emerson Coll 100 Beacon St Boston MA 02116

DELLING, IRIS BEE, mfg. co. contract adminstr.; b. Kansas City, Mo., Mar. 3, 1925; d. Ross B. and Margaret E. (Briley) Smithson; B.Fgn. Service, U. So. Calif., 1948, M.Liberal Arts, 1976; 1 son, Anthony Ross Delling. With Fgn. Service, Dept. State, Washington, 1949-52; sec. Pacific div. Bendix Corp., Burbank, Calif., 1955-64; sec. Librascope div. Singer Co., Glendale, Calif., 1964-73, job control coordinator, 1973-77, contract adminstr., 1977—. Served with USMC, 1945-46. Mem. Phi Beta Kappa, Phi Kappa Phi, Pi Sigma Alpha, Alpha Xi Delta. Clubs: Marine Corps League, NOW, Sierra, Women Marines Assn.

DELLINGER, ANN COLVARD, publishing company executive; b. Gastonia, N.C., Feb. 11, 1948; d. Eulas Phillip and Pansy Patrick (Moten) Colvard; m. C. Frank Dellinger, July 29, 1966; children—Candace, Phillip, Patti. Student Belmont Abbey Coll., 1984—, cert. mgmt./communications, 19. Office mgr. food services Belmont Abbey Coll., Belmont, N.C., 1979-80, asst. dir. food services, 1980-81; adminstrv. asst. to chmn. bd. Good Will (Pubs.), Inc., Gastonia, N.C., 1981-83, co-author, asst. editor, 1982—, mgr. incentive program, 1983-84, sales promotion mgr., 1984—. Co-author: The Way to Go, 1985, Be the Best You Can Be, 1985. Chmn. ways and means com. Parkland Elem. Sch., Rockester, N.Y., 1976-77; bd. dirs. Belmont Abbey Coll. Athletic Found., 1981—, v.p. bd., 1982—, dir. coll. cheer leaders, 1981-85; co-pres. Sacred Heart Home Sch. Assn., Belmont, 1983-85. Recipient Appreciation award Belmont Abbey Coll. Student Body, 1981; named Pacemaker of Piedmont, Gastonia Gazette, 1984. Mem. Nat. Assn. Female Execs., Am. Mgmt. Assn., Am. Mktg. Assn., Charlotte Soc. Communicating Arts, Smithsonian Assocs. Roman Catholic. Club: Gastonia Newcomers (social dir. 1980-81). Home: 305 Amity Circle Belmont NC 28012 Office: Good Will (Pubs) Inc 1520 S York Rd Gastonia NC 28052

DELLINGER, SUSAN JEAN, computer software engineer, consultant; b. Piqua, Ohio, Jan. 29, 1951; d. Joseph Cecil and Betty Jean (Hayman) Dellinger; m. Thomas Warren Lawhorn, Mar. 8, 1975 (div.); m. 2d, Richard Lee Spieker, June 28, 1980; 1 dau., Emily Dawn; stepchildren—Kimberly Ann, Tamara Lee, Erick Glen. B.S. in Applied Sci., Miami U., Oxford, Ohio, 1973. Programmer, Control Data Corp., Arden Hills, Minn., 1973-74; programmer analyst System Devel. Corp., Colorado Springs, Colo., 1974-75; assoc. engr. Ford Aerospace and Communications Corp., Colorado Springs, 1975-77; asst. project mgr. Informatics, Inc., Colorado Springs, 1977-79; program tech. support mgr. Inco, Inc., subs. McDonnell Douglas Corp., Colorado Springs, 1979—; co-owner, cons. Custom Computer Systems, Colorado Springs, 1982—. Mem. Women in Info. Processing (pres. Colorado Springs forum 1982), Assn. Computing Machinery. Republican. Presbyterian. Office: INCO Inc Space Tech Div 4146 E Bijou St Colorado Springs CO 80909

DELLOBUONO, PATRICIA, businesswoman; b. Long Branch, N.J., Aug. 4, 1942; m. William DelloBuono, Feb. 26, 1963; 3 children. Student Monmouth Coll., 1960-61, Fairleigh Dickinson U., 1961-62, Palm Beach Jr. Coll., 1980. Legal sec., 1961-77; founder, pres. Legal Courier Services, Inc., and Action Courier, West Palm Beach, Fla., 1977—; arbitrator Better Bus. Bur. Mem. spl. action com. YWCA, 1982-83. Recipient 1983 Small Bus. Person of Yr. award, C. of C. of Palm Beaches; 1983 Golden Girl award, Individual Career Achievement Thru Networking, 1983. Mem. C. of C. Palm Beaches (dir.). Avocations: scuba diving; bible study. Home: 5165 El Claro Dr W West Palm Beach FL 33415 Office: 423 Clematis St West Palm Beach FL 33401

DELMAN, JOY LEDA, law educator, lawyer; b. Phila., Feb. 5, 1954; d. Jacob and Esther (Polan) D.; m. Howard R. Schiffman, June 29, 1975; 1 child, Jesse Sayre Delman Schiffman. B.A. with honors, U. Pa., 1975; J.D., Georgetown U., 1978. Bar: Pa. 1979, U.S. Dist. Ct. (ea. dist.) Pa. 1979, Calif. 1983, U.S. Dist. Ct. (so. dist.) Calif. 1982, U.S. Ct. Appeals (9th cir.) 1985. Jud. law clk. Hon. Murray C. Goldman, Phila., 1979-80; assoc. Obermayer, Rebmann, Maxwell & Hippel, Phila., 1980-81; assoc. Gray, Cary, Ames & Frye, San Diego, 1981-83; prof. law Western State U., San Diego, 1983—, faculty advisor Criminal Justice Jour.; mem. adv. bd. Lawyers Alliance for Nuclear Arms Control; lectr. Am. Law Inst., ABA, Harcourt Brace Jovanovich Law Group. Editor Am. Criminal Law Rev., 1978. Mem. ABA, San Diego County Bar Assn., Calif. Trial Lawyers Assn., San Diego Trial Lawyers Assn., San Diego Med. Legal Soc. Office: Western State Univ Sch Law 2121 San Diego Ave San Diego CA 92110

DELMAR-MCCLURE, NELLIE, psychologist, educator; b. San Antonio, Tex., Sept. 25, 1940; d. Eduardo and Maria (Lopez-Bravo) Delmar; m. Robert E. McClure, June 30, 1962; children—David Robert, Michael Robert. B.A., Pepperdine U., 1962, M.A., 1966; Ph.D., U.S. Internat. U., San Diego, 1974. Lic. psychologist, Calif. Instr. psychology Pepperdine U., Los Angeles, 1966-69, Rio Hondo Coll., Whittier, Calif., 1968-72; instr., research assoc. dept. health care planning So. Ill. U. Sch. Medicine, Springfield, 1973-74; prof. psychology U. Autonoma de Guadalajara, Mex., 1974-75; asst. clin. prof. dept. pediatrics U. Calif.-Irvine, 1982-84; asst. prof. Fuller Grad. Sch. Psychology, Pasadena, 1983-85; psychologist Los Angeles Psychol. Ctr., 1966-67, Rancho Los Amigos Hosp., Downey, Calif., 1966-67, pvt. practice, 1974—; clin. prof. family medicine U. Calif.-Irvine, 1986—; lectr. on parent-child issues, 1966-72. Spina bifida grantee Nat. Found., 1980; recipient Pollygramatic award for psychology, 1961, Zeta Kappa award for psychology, 1961, Phi Beta award, 1961. Mem. Am. Psychol. Assn., Calif. Psychol. Assn., Psi Chi. Democrat. Presbyterian. Home: Yorba Linda CA Office: Med Ctr 500 S Anaheim Hills Rd Anaheim Hills CA 92807

DELMERICO, FRANCES EUGENIA, retired music educator, piano teacher; b. Battle Creek, Mich., Feb. 17, 1918; d. Frank and Laura Theodosia (Adams) Minges; m. George Gregory Delmerico, June 16, 1946 (dec. 1958); children—Daniel Adams, Bruce Eugene deMedici. B.Music in Music Edn., Mich. State Coll., 1939; postgrad. Mich. State U., Western Mich. U. Cert. tchr., Mich. Music tchr. Quincy Pub. Schs., Mich., 1939-40, Fraser Pub. Schs., Mich., 1940-42, Lakeview Consul. Schs., Battle Creek, 1942-44, Harper Creek Community Sch., Battle Creek, 1964-73, Battle Creek Pub. Sch., 1973-80; piano tchr., Battle Creek, Mich., 1980—; writer program notes Battle Creek Symphony Orchestra, 1980-85. Active Lakeview Sch. Dist. Citizens' Com., Battle Creek, 1980-81, Battle Creek Hist. Soc.; bd. dirs. Battle Creek Area United Arts Council, 1980-83, Battle Creek Community Concert Assn., 1979-83; pres. ch. council First Congregational Ch., 1983-85, v.p. Women's fellowship, 1985—. Mem. Battle Creek Area Music Tchrs. Assn. (v.p. 1981-83, pres. 1983-85), Mich. Music Tchrs. Assn., Music Tchrs. Nat. Assn., Area and State Ret. Sch. Personnel Assn., Battle Creek Morning Musical Club (2d v.p. 1982-83, sec. 1983-85), Battle Creek Woman's Club (v.p. 1984-85, pres. 1985—), AAUW, Delta Kappa Gamma (mem. state music com. 1976-78, 2d v.p. 1984—, Outstanding Service cert. 1983). Avocations: bridge; golf; assisting with music related student activities. Home: 160 S Minges Rd Battle Creek MI 49017

DELOACH, MARION VIRGINIA, school principal; b. Hinesville, Ga., Sept. 11, 1933; d. Ralph Howard and Betty Armatha (Todd) Groover; m. James Mondell DeLoach, May 25, 1951; children—Eddie Wayne, Pamela Kay, James M. Jr., Patty Gail. Student Draughon's Bus. Sch., Savannah, 1950; M.Elem-.Edn., Armstrong State Coll., 1970; Edn. Specialist, Ga. So. Coll., 1980. Bookkeeper, Pittsburg Plate Co., Savannah, 1951-52; substitute tchr. Mercer Middle Sch., Savannah, 1966-67, prin., 1977—; 6th grade tchr. Haynes Elem. Sch., Savannah, 1970-73, curriculum specialist, 1973-77. Sunday Sch. tchr. First Baptist Ch., Garden City, Ga., 1956—; pres. local PTA, 1965-67, life mem., since 1967—. Named Garden City Mother of Yr., Garden City Jaycees, 1965; Chatham County Family of Yr., Savannah, 1982. Fellow Ga. Assn. Middle Sch. Prins.; mem. Nat. Assn. Secondary Sch. Prins., Alpha Delta Kappa. Avocations: playing softball, reading, camping. Home: 204 Byck Ave Garden City GA 31408 Office: Mercer Middle Sch 201 Rommel Ave Garden City GA 31408

DELOFFI, AUDREY YOUNG, social worker; b. Portland, Maine, Apr. 9, 1947; d. William G. and Elcye M. (Ross) Y.; B.A., U. N.H., Durham, 1969; M.S.W., Boston Coll., Chestnut Hill, 1974. Social worker Children's Protective Services, Worcester, Mass., 1969-73, Salem, Mass., 1974-77; social work intern McLean Hosp., Belmont, Mass., 1973-74; prin. clin. social worker Danvers State Hosp., Hathorne, Mass., 1977-78, clin. social work supr., 1978-79; crisis team worker Project RAP, Beverly, Mass., 1977-81; vis. lectr. Salem State Coll., 1976—; mental health coordinator Dept. Mental Health, Lynn, Mass., 1979-81; asso. area dir. Dept. Mental Health, Lynn, Mass., 1981-83, area dir., 1983-85; chief operating officer Met. State Hosp., Waltham Dept. Mental Health, Mass., 1985—; mem. Greater Lynn Sr. Services Adv. Bd., 1982—; also cons. Mem. alumni bd. dirs. Boston Coll. Sch. Social Work, 1976-68, 80-82; bd. dirs. Social Advocates for Youth, 1975-79, pres. 1977-79; bd. dirs. Melrose Hickory Hawks Ski Club, 1976-78, sec., 1977-78; bd. dirs. Project Rap, Beverly; clk. Tabernacle Ch., Salem, Mass., 1985—. Recipient Outstanding Service award Social Advocates for Youth, 1979; lic. ind. clin. social worker, Mass. Mem. Nat. Assn. Social Workers (dir. N.E. region steering com. 1977-81, vice chmn. 1978-80), Acad. Cert. Social Workers (lic. ind. clin. social worker). Protestant. Home: 7 Laurent Rd Salem MA 01970 Office: 475 Trapelo Rd Waltham MA 02254

DELONEY, BERNICE BEARD, business executive, county training administrator; b. Jackson, Tenn., Apr. 29, 1934; d. Joe Walter and Emma (Greene) Beard; m. Carl E. Deloney, Aug. 13, 1950 (dec. May 1982); children—William, Carl E., James Walter, Lisa Ann. B.S. in Food and Nutrition, Tenn. State U., 1958; postgrad. in edn. U. Ill.-Chgo., 1966-67; postgrad. in nutrition Purdue U., 1968-69. Dietetic intern Cook County Hosp., Chgo., 1958-59, therapeutic and adminstrv. dietitian, 1959-63; therapeutic and adminstrv. dietitian Michael Reese Hosp., Chgo., 1963-66; tchr. Chgo. Bd. Edn., 1966-69; cons. dietitian to health care facility, Chgo., 1969-79; tchr. nutrition Central YMCA Community Coll., Chgo., 1979-82; founder, owner, operator VOTEC Catering Co., Gary, Ind., and Chgo., 1982—; co-founder, owner, operator, proposal writer VOTEC, Inc., Gary, 1982—; program operator Lake County Job Tng. Coop., Ind., 1982—; cons. dietitian Cons. in Health Care Facilities, Chgo., 1981. Named Woman of Yr., Tenn. State U., 1983; subject of resolution by mayor and Gary Common Council, 1983. Mem. Am. Dietetic Assn., Ill. Dietetic Assn. (chmn. nominating com. 1959), South Suburban Dietetic Assn., Cons. Dietitians/Health Care Facilities (chmn. 1980-81), Dietitians in Pvt. Practice, Tenn. State Alumni Assn. (local sec. 1981-83, local program chmn. 1984), Du Sable Mus. (trustee), Alpha Kappa Alpha. Democrat. Mem. Christian Ch. (disciples of Christ). Club: Links, Inc. (chmn. fund raiser 1984) (Chgo.). Avocations: travel; boating; interior decorating; gourmet cooking. Home: 8400 S Saint Lawrence Ave Chicago IL 60619 Office: VOTEC Inc 4742 Broadway Suite A Gary IN 46408

DELONG, DEBORAH, lawyer; b. Louisville, Sept. 5, 1950; d. Henry F. and Lois Jean (Stepp) DeL.; m. John William Hust, Dec. 22, 1973 (div.); m. 2d, Michael A. Marrero, Jan. 12, 1981; 1 dau., Amelie DeLong. B.A., Vanderbilt U., 1972; J.D., U. Cin., 1975. Bar: Ohio. Assoc., Paxton & Seasongood, Cin., 1975-83, ptnr., 1983—. Contbr. articles to profl. jours. Officer Jr. League Cin., 1979—; bd. dirs. Displaced Homemakers, Cin., 1983—; bd. dirs., officer Children's Psychat. Ctr., Cin., 1979—. Mem. ABA, Cin. Bar Assn., Ohio Bar Assn. Republican. Episcopalian. Home: 14 Arcadia Pl Cincinnati OH 45208 Office: Paxton & Seasongood 1700 Central Trust Tower 1 W 4th St Cincinnati OH 45202

DELONG, NANCY GLYN, journalist, public relations and communications cons.; b. Columbus, Ohio, Oct. 2, 1946; d. Glen A. and Reba Z. (Pope) DeL.; B.A. in Journalism and English, Ohio State U., 1969. Exec. dir. Tri-County Dental Health Council, Detroit, 1971-76, reporter The Detroit News, 1970-71, The Columbus (Ohio) Dispatch, 1965-68; editorial photographer, contbg. editor Amusement Bus., 1968-73; producer The Oz of Prevention, Detroit, 1971-74; partner Real to Reel 1973-77; pres. project promotion Glyn Prodn. Ltd., 1977-79; pres. N. Glynn & Assocs., Inc., Southfield, Mich., 1979-82; bus. cons., 1976—; interior designer, 1976—; assoc. Walt Peabody Advt. Service Inc., Ft. Lauderdale, Fla.; beauty cons. Mary Kay Cosmetics, Inc., Dallas, 1982-85; dir. employee assistance programs and pub. relations Shepherd Hill, Newark, Ohio, 1985—. Profl. boxing judge, State of Mich. Contbr. articles to various mags.; contbg. editor Downbeat, 1966-68, Billboard, 1968-73; producer ednl. films on health and rehab.; producer, dir. Super Party '82. Address: 4779 Musket Way Columbus OH 43228

DELORENZO, SUSAN SMITH, insurance company executive; b. Boston, June 8, 1945; d. W. Arthur and Jane (Cowan) Smith; m. Arthur E. DeLorenzo, June 26, 1965 (div. June 1973); children—Arthur E., Jr., Dana Leigh. A.A.S., Green Mountain Coll., 1965; student Onondaga Community Coll., 1968, 76, Syracus U., 1976-78, Rochester Inst. Tech., 1978-80. Lic. ins. rep. Paralegal, legal sec. Frank E. Visco, Cortland, N.Y., 1971-76; exec. sec. trust and investment Lincoln 1st Bank N.A., Syracuse, N.Y., 1976-78; personnel asst. Brewer-Titchener Corp., Cortland, 1978-80; regional life adminstr. U.S. Life Ins. Co., Syracuse, 1980-81; regional sales adminstr. Nat. Benefit Life Ins. Co., White Plains, N.Y., 1981-82, nat. dir. regional sales adminstrn., N.Y.C., 1982-84, asst. v.p., nat. dir. sales adminstrn., 1984-85; v.p. opns. Nat. Fin. Corp., 1985—. Mem. Nat. Assn. Female Execs., Nat. Assn. Life Underwriters, Women's Life Underwriters Conf., Life Suprs. Assn. N.Y., Fairfield Network Exec. Women, Women in Mgmt., NOW. Home: RD 1 Barrett Hill Rd Mahopac NY 10541 Office: Nat Fin Corp Stamford CT 06901

DE LOS REYES, LEVIS VIRGINIA, nurse; b. Jacksonville, Ill., Sept. 3, 1919; d. Dio Kyle and Eleanor Gertrude (Dyer) Duke; m. Joseph Manuel de los Reyes, Mar. 10, 1972. R.N., Our Saviours Hosp. Sch. Nursing. Staff nurse, bus. mgr. Surgeons Clinic, Los Angeles, 1945—. Aux. mem. Direct Relief Found., Santa Barbara, Calif., 1975—; mem. Calif. Med. Ctr. Guild Cancer Ctr., also treas., 1975-77. Mem. Internat. Therapists Assn., Internat. Coll. of Surgeons (aux. mem.), Pan-Pacific Surg. Soc. (aux. mem.). Republican. Roman Catholic. Lodge: Shriners (aux. mem.). Avocations: antique collecting; oil painting. Office: J M de los Reyes MD 2010 Wilshire Blvd Los Angeles CA 90057

DELOUGHERY, GRACE LEONA, nursing educator; b. Allison, Iowa, Jan. 17, 1933; d. Ed F. and Alma K. (Kampman) Meinen; B.S., U. Minn., 1955, M.P.H., 1960; Ph.D., Claremont Grad. Sch., 1966; m. Henry O. Deloughery, Nov. 30, 1962; children—Paul Edward, Michael, Kathleen. Staff nurse Mpls. Dept. Pub. Health, 1955-59; research fellow U. Minn. Sch. Pub. Health, 1960-63; sch. nurse Val Verde Sch. Dist., Perris, Calif., part-time 1963-66; community coordinator, nurse in Title I pilot project in San Jacinto, Riverside (Calif.) County Schs., 1966, cons. Title I, 1966-67; assoc. prof. U. N.C. Coll. Nursing, 1967-68; asst. prof. U. Calif. Sch. Nursing, Los Angeles, 1968-72; dean Center Nursing Edn., Spokane, 1972-74; prof., head dept. nursing Winona (Minn.) State U., 1975-77; adminstr. Deloughery Home Sr. Adults, 1977-84; assoc. prof. Ind. U., New Albany, 1984—; participant seminars, condr. workshops, cons. in field. Recipient award for research Calif. Edn. Research and Guidance Assn., 1967. Fellow Am. Pub. Health Assn., Am. Assn. Social Psychiatry (treas. 1974-78); mem. Am. Nurses Assn., Nat. League Nursing, Am. Sch. Health Assn., Internat. Mental Health Fedn., Wash. Pub. Health Assn., Acad. Polit. and Social Sci., Acad. Polit. Sci., Pi Lambda Theta. Lutheran. Club: Winona Country. Contbr. to profl. jours. Home: Route 2 Box 402 Georgetown IN 47122 Office: Ind U 4201 Grantline Rd New Albany IN 47150

DELOZIER, CHARLOTTE BEELER, electronics company executive; b. Oak Ridge, Dec. 22, 1951; d. William Don and Dorothy (Wells) Beeler; m. Martin William DeLozier, Aug. 21, 1972; 1 child, Ashley Michele. B.S. with honors in Edn., U. Tenn., 1972. Tchr. pub. schs., Knoxville, Tenn., 1973-82; owner, pres. MAC-1 Electronics, Knoxville, 1981—. Mem. Knoxville Adminstrn. Bd., 1984-86, Knoxville Council on Ministries, 1984-86; leader Youth Council, Knoxville, 1984-86. Mem. Knoxville Assn. Women Execs. (chmn. profl. devel. com. 1986), Nat. Assn. Women Execs., East Tenn. Minority Supplier Devel. Council (bd. dirs.), Nat. Fedn. Ind. Bus., Knoxville C. of C. (small bus. com.), Republican. Methodist. Avocations: sports; travel; fashion. Home: 10737 Yarnell Rd Knoxville TN 37922 Office: MAC-1 Electronics 201 Center Park Dr Knoxville TN 37922

DELTON, FREDA, real estate broker; b. N.Y.C., June 10, 1931; d. Harry and Minnie (Rosenbaum) Eckhaus; m. David Delton, June 27, 1954; children—Carol, Mark. Student NYU. Lic. real estate broker, N.Y. Asst. personnel dir. Franklin Simon, N.Y.C., 1950-57; mem. sales staff Ron Herbst Real Estate, Tarrytown, N.Y., 1969-72; real estate broker, office mgr. Frank Carretta, Inc., Briarcliff, N.Y., 1973-83; broker Lois Seiden Real Estate, Briarcliff, 1983—. Organizer, leader Group Against Garbage, Briarcliff Manor, 1981-83; vol. worker pre-sch. vision screening program Lighthouse, 1981—; village trustee Briarcliff Manor, 1983—. Mem. Westchester County Bd. Realtors (mem. fin. com. 1983—), Westchester County Builders Inst. Home: 193 Larch Rd Briarcliff Manor NY 10510 Office: Lois Seiden Real Estate 1238 Pleasantville Rd Briarcliff Manor NY 10510

DELU, CHRISTINA HUURNINK, association executive; b. Lochem, Gelderland, Netherlands, Feb. 22, 1936; came to U.S. 1956, naturalized, 1967; d. Johan and Berendina Willemina (Beumkes) Huurnink; children—Winifred Bernice, Michael John, Dietrich John, Jennette Christina. Student Music-school-Arnhem, Holland, 1951-54, Conservatory, The Hague, Holland, 1954-56, Bibleschool, Calgary, Alta., Can., 1958, Christian Tng. Ctr. Ordained to ministry, Assemblies of God, 1977. Pianist/harpist Europe, Can., U.S.A., 1954-65; usher/worker The Kathryn Kuhlman Found., Pitts., 1972-76; radio broadcaster various stas., Va., Ala., N.C., W.Va., 1974—; pub. speaker in field. Interpreter ARC, Norfolk, Va., 1976—; active Women in Leadership, Norfolk, 1984, 85, pres., 85; mem. Women in Crisis, 1985. Author: The Holy Spirit, 1980, Inspiration, 1981, How to Feel Loved Again, 1982; composer/writer songs; writer/perform radio talks. Evangelist Christina Delu Found., 1973—. Mem. NAACP. Democrat. Dutch Reformed Ch. Avocations: piano playing; reading; writing; singing. Office: Christina Delu Found Inc PO Box 14236 2080 Colane Rd Norfolk VA 23518

DE LUCCIA, EILEEN DOROTHY, day care center director, consultant; b. Paterson, N.J., Oct. 26, 1943; d. John Arthur and Dorothy Julia (Muzio) Van Vliet; m. Nicholas Sabatino De Luccia, May 19, 1974. B.A., William Paterson Coll., 1966. Certified tchr. Tchr. fifth grade North Haledon Bd. Edn., N.J., 1966-69, Wayne Bd. Edn., N.J., 1969-73; spl. edn. tchr. Oakland Bd. Edn., N.J., 1973-75; dir. Gingerbread Castle Day Sch., Oakland, 1977—; cons., Oakland, 1983—. Bd. dirs. Ramapo Bergen Animal Rescue, Inc., Oakland, 1981-82. Mem. Oakland C. of C. Avocations: animal rescues; behaviorism; shelter work; tutoring; gardening. Home: 40 Venna Ave North Haledon NJ 07508 Office: Gingerbread Castle Day Sch Ramapo Valley Rd Oakland NJ 07436

DEL VALLE, HELEN CYNTHIA, artist, designer; b. Chgo., Sept. 22, 1933; d. Andrew Jack and Mary Texanna (Cohen) Del Valle; B.F.A., Pa. Acad. Fine Arts, 1952; B.J., Northwestern U., 1960; diploma in profl. modeling Patricia Stevens Sch., Chgo., 1963. Tchr., Bay Hill Sch., Bushnell, Fla., 1952-54; creative artist House of Baldwin Galleries, Chgo., 1954-59; freelance artist, designer, Chgo., 1960—; paintings pub. newspaper Brighton Park Life, Chgo., 1973, Artists/USA, 1974; exhibited in group shows Navy Pier, Chgo., 1982, 909 N. Michigan Ave., Chgo., 1982; one-woman shows Balzekas Mus., Chgo., Chgo. Pub. Library, 1971-74, Combined Ins. Co., 1970-73, 75, also Spain, Italy, London, Israel, Austria; part-time hand, foot model for fashion mags., 1960—. Recipient 1st place award in portraiture N.Y. Profl. Art Show, N.Y.C., 1968; 1971, 3d award for watercolor. Ill. State Art Show, 1981; honorable mention award in still life Mcpl. Art League of Chgo., 1973; Silver plaque Am. Soc. Artists, 1974, 1st place award for Clipper Ship, N.H., 1983, other awards. Mem. Nat. League Am. Pen Women (Dingle Meml. award Chgo. chpt. 1971, 1st award for landscape 1973, 2d award in traditional painting 1971, 1st place painting award ann. exhibit 1979, 3d place award for watercolor ann. show 1980, 3d place award for watercolor state exhibit 1981; mem. art. com. Chgo. chpt. 1982-84), Mcpl. Art League Chgo., Am. Soc. Artists (v.p., membership chmn.), Internat. Poetry Soc. (Eng.), Poets and Patrons, Citizens Republic, Tax Limitation Com., Internat. Platform Assn., Renaissance Soc. of U. Chgo. Club: The Cordon. Contbr. poems to New Voices in Am. Poetry (prize for Autumn, 1973). Office: PO Box 958 Chicago IL 60690

DELVENTHAL, PRISCILLA JANE, histologist; b. Chgo., July 29, 1938; d. Ralph Daniel and Geneva Mae (Walden) Esterly; student No. Ill. U., So. Ill. U.; diploma histology, St. Anthony's Hosp., Rockford, Ill., 1961; m. LeRoy Earl Delventhal, Sept. 3, 1966; children—Kathryn Lee, Lane Aaron, Daniel Albert. Tchr., Rockford, Ill., 1960-61; asst. supr. surg. pathology-histology lab. U. Colo. Med. Sch., Denver, 1961-64; head histology Lutheran Hosp., Wheatridge, Colo., 1964-65; asst. head histology Colo. State U., Ft. Collins, 1966-68; head histology lab. Pathology Lab. Assocs., Lander, Wyo., 1977-84; supr. histologist portamedic services Hooper Homes, 1978—; supr. histology and cytology labs. Lander Valley Regional Med. Ctr., 1984—. Active local Boy Scout Am.; dir. jr. choir Trinity Luth. Ch., Riverton, Wy. 1978-81, St. Johns Luth. Ch., Ft. Collins, Colo. 1967-67. Mem. Am. Soc. Clin. Pathologists (assoc.), Colo. Soc. Histotech. (charter). Home: 829 Sheryl Sue Dr Riverton WY 82501 Office: 906 Main St Lander WY 82520

DELYON, JOHANNA EVE, editor; b. Ansbach, W. Ger., Mar. 11, 1957; came to U.S., 1957; d. Joseph Victor DeLyon and Johanna Elizabeth Zahn. B.S. in Comml. Arts, Calif. Poly. U.-Pomona, 1979. Editor, Highlander Publs., Hacienda Heights, Calif., 1980-81; staff reporter San Gabriel Valley Tribune, West Covina, Calif., 1981-83; assoc. editor Teaching, Learning and Computing mag. Seldin Publs., Placentia, Calif., 1983-84; sr. editor Automotive Age mag. Freed-Crown-Lee Pubs., Inc. 1984—; editor newsletter Youth for Christ, Covina, 1983—. Mem. Evang. Free Ch., Fullerton, Calif., 1981. Mem. So. Calif. Press Club. Office: Freed-Crown-Lee Pub Inc 6931 Van Nuys Blvd Van Nuys CA 91405

DE MAIO, MARIE ROSE, educator; b. Newark, July 23, 1940; d. Rocco and Carmelina (Goione) De M. B.A., Newark State Coll., 1962, M.A., 1966; M.A. in Adminstrn. and Supervision, Kean Coll., 1978. Tchr. elem. sch., West Orange, N.J., 1962—, tchr. summer exptl. learning lab., 1968-69, counselor Newark Dept. Recreation Summer Playground Program, 1966; speech correctionist Newark State Coll. Speech Clinic, 1962-66; asst. tchr. Kean Coll., summer, 1977. Chairperson fundraising Cancer and Heart Funds, Essex County Civic Assn. Ladies Aux., 1968-77. Mem. NEA, N.J. Edn. Assn., Essex County Edn. Assn., West Orange Edn. Assn. (co-chairperson negotiations com. 1976—, bldg. rep. 1963-68, chairperson tchr. edn. and profl. standards com. 1973, membership sec. 1968-72, sec. 1974-80, v.p. 1979—), Bloomfield Fedn. Music (v.p. bd. trustees 1979—), Anthony Gallo Athletic Assn. (pres. 1983-85), Assn. for Supervision and Curriculum Devel. Roman Catholic.

DEMARCO, DIANE LYNN, contractor; b. Fort Worth, June 4, 1958; d. Ronald Charles and Rita Bernice (Davis) DeMarco. B.S., U. Fla., 1981. Cert. gen. contractor, Fla. Vice pres. DeMarco Homes, Boca Raton, Fla., 1981—. Project coordiantor Boca Raton Hist. Soc., 1983-85; cons. historic Palm Beach County Preservation bd., 1984-85; bd. dirs. St. Joan of Arc Catholic Ch. Constrn. Bd., Boca Raton, 1985; restorationist Old Town Hall, 1983-85, Raulerson House, 1986; bd. dirs. City Boca Raton Preservation Bd., 1984—. Recipient Spl. Achievement award Fa. Trust for Historic Preservation, 1985, Fed. Restoration grant Fla. Dept. Stte, 1984, Leadership 84 award Boca Raton C. of C., 1984. Mem. Boca Raton C. of C. (com. chmn. 1985), Boca Raton Hist. Soc., Nat. Asn. Women in Constrn., Nat. Bldg. Mus., Fellowship Single Profls. (pres. 1984-85), Nat. Assn. Miniature Enthusiasts, Sigma Lambda Chi. Republican. Avocations: doll and miniature collecting; camping; quilting. Office: DeMarco Homes Inc 4260 NW 1st Ave #50 Boca Raton FL 33431

DEMARCO, DIANNE LOUISE, insurance broker; b. Plainfield, N.J., Nov. 28, 1944; d. Robert Douglas and Mildred Verna (Little) Hanna; m. Ronald J. Lemmermad, May 1963 (div. 1968); m.2d Joseph L. DeMarco, Jr., Aug. 28, 1970; children—Joseph L. III, (dec.), Dawn S. Grad. high sch., Collingswood, N.J. Lic. ins. broker. Sec., Smolens-Landgraf, Westmont, N.J., 1962-64, Anderson-Jackson-Metts, Camden, N.J., 1964, John Damiani, Camden, 1965, Penthouse, Merchantville, N.J., 1965-66, Landmore, Westmont, 1966-68; broker, owner PRIORITY Corp., Audubon, N.J., 1968—. Organizer Camden County chpt. Compassionate Friends, 1979—, cons., 1983. Mem. Profl. Ins. Agts., Ind. Ins. Agts. N.J., Audubon Ind. Bus. and Profl. Assn., Nat. Assn. Ins. Women (treas. Cherry Hill 1983-84). Club: Medford Village Country (sec. 1981, asst. tournament chmn. 1983). Home: 113 E Kings Hwy Audubon NJ 08106 Office: PRIORITY Corp 240 S White House Pike Audubon NJ 08106

DEMARCO, GERALDINE SAYLOR, bookbinder, restorer; b. Santa Monica, Calif., Sept. 15, 1934; d. Al V. and Florence Amelia (Imschweiler) Saylor; m. Louis Earl DeMarco, Oct. 23, 1950; children—Jeri, Edward, Carrie, Joni, Christina, Wendy, Alan, Mark, Curtis, Josie, Lia, Gregory. A.A., Skagit Valley Coll., Mt. Vernon, Wash., 1970. Library technician I, Skagit Valley Coll., Mt. Vernon, 1970-71; br. librarian Whatcom County Library, Bellingham, Wash., 1980-83; book restorer Western Wash. U., Bellingham, 1983—; book restoring Assumption Sch. Bellingham, 1980-82, Fairhaven Middle Sch., Bellingham, 1982-83. Com. mem. Sudden Valley Community Assn., Bellingham, 1970-83; leader Totem council Girl Scouts U.S., 1970-76; com. mem. cub scout pack 21 Mt. Baker council Boy Scouts Am., 1980-83; religion tchr. Sacred Heart Ch., Bellingham, 1983-85. Mem. Nat. Geneal. Soc., Geneal. Soc. Harlan County, Ky. Democrat. Roman Catholic. Avocations: swimming; needlework; genealogy. Home: 203 Sudden Valley Bellingham WA 98226

DEMARCO, RITA LOUISE, market research administrator, consultant; b. Cleve., Oct. 26, 1949; d. Anthony Joseph and Lillian Mary (Koeth) D. B.S. in Edn., Baldwin-Wallace Coll., 1970, M.B.A., 1977. Tchr. Highland Local Schs., Cleve., 1972-77, mng. editor-Am. machinist tng. programs Beckwith & Assocs. subs. McGraw Hill, Cleve., 1977-79; mgr. ind. research and devel. and bus. devel. Gould Inc., Rolling Meadows, Ill., 1979-82; mgr. market research and planning Master Builders div. Sandoz, Cleve., 1982—; prof. William Rainey Harper Coll., Chgo., 1980-81; pres., cons. Profl. Individualized Tng. Systems, Cleve., 1982—. Author/editor: Upper Engine Rebuild, 1978. Contbr. articles to Bridge Repair Markets, 1983. Baldwin Wallace Coll. scholar, 1967-70. Mem. Am. Mktg. Assn. (newsletter chmn. 1980-81), Planning Execs. Inst., Am. Soc. for Tng. and Devel., Kappa Delta Pi. Democrat. Roman Catholic. Club:

Masque and Staff (Chgo.). Office: Master Builders div Martin Marietta 23700 Chagrin Blvd Beachwood OH 44122

DEMAREE, BETTY, artist, educator; b. Denver, Oct. 19, 1918; d. Nathaniel and Margaret Elizabeth (Sanderson) Wolfson; m. Dean Clay DeMaree, Jan. 15, 1962; 1 stepchild. Student Cooper Union Sch. Art, 1938-41. Textile designer Am. Textile Co., N.Y.C., 1940-43; self-employed greeting card designer, Los Angeles, 1945-48; self-employed designer, Bolivia, S.Am., 1948-53; self-employed custom ceramics designer, Denver, 1954-65; self-employed painter, tchr., Denver, 1967—; condr. numerous workshops; judge various art shows; bd. dirs. Rocky Mountain Nat. Watermedia Soc. ann. exhbn. Exhibited in group shows at Southwestern Watercolor Soc., Dallas, 1968-84, Am. Watercolor Soc., N.Y.C., 1976-84, Allied Artists Am., N.Y.C., 1977-78; Rocky Mountain Nat. Watermedia Exhbn., 1975, 77, Gallery A, Taos, N.Mex., Cason Gallery, Helena, Mont., Oregon Trail, Casper, Wyo., Driscol Gallery Ltd., Vail, Colo.; represented in permanent collections Los Alamos Nat. Lab., United Banks Colo., Mason, Reuler and Peake, Denver, Central Bank and Trust, Denver, James Ins. Co., Denver, Thorson Corp., Littleton, Colo., Colo. State U., Fort Collins, Rocky Mountain Energy Corp., Broomfield, Colo., Combs-Gates Airport, Denver, Harris Bank and Trust, Scottsdale, Ariz., Utah State U., Logan, others. Recipient Strathmore Paper award, 1984, Catherine Lorillard Wolfe Art Club award, 1984. Mem. Southwestern Watercolor Soc. (named Best of Show 1969, selected for travelling show 1969), Am. Watercolor Soc. (Emily Lowe Meml. award 1976), Allied Artists Am. (John Young-Hunter award 1977, Winsor Newton award for watercolor 1978), Audubon Artists Am., Rocky Mountain Nat. Watermedia Soc., Colo. Watercolor Soc. Denver Artists Guild, Colo. Artist Assn. (award 1981). Republican. Christian Scientist. Home and Office: Betty DeMaree Studio 4725 W Quincy Ave Denver CO 80236

DEMAREE, DENA ELIZABETH, nurse educator; b. Seymour, Ind., Mar. 4, 1944; d. George Diedrick and Mabel Harriet (Brackemyre) Miller; m. David Thomas Demaree, June 18, 1966; children—Meredith Anne, Matthew David. Diploma, Methodist Hosp. Sch. Nursing, Indpls., 1965; B.S.N., Ind. U.-Indpls., 1972; M.S.N., U. Ky., 1977. R.N., Ky. Staff nurse coronary care, supr. Methodist Hosp., Indpls., 1966-74; nurse epidemiologist St. Joseph Hosp., Lexington, 1974-77; asst. prof. nursing Eastern Ky. U., Richmond, 1977—; exec. coordinator Hospice Boyle County Inc., Danville, Ky., 1983-85, bd. dirs., 1982—; cons. Collins, Kubal & Miles, edn. unit, 1983—; on-call staff ICU, Ephraim McDowell Hosp., Danville, 1981—. Mem. Republican County Exec. Bd., Boyle County, Ky., 1981-83, Arthritis Found. Louisville; mem. Women's Health Forum III, Danville, planning com., 1982; pres. United Meth. Women, Danville, 1982. HEW grantee, 1971, 76. Mem. Am. Nurse Assn., Ky. Nurse Assn. (pub. relations membership com. chmn. 1981-82, dist. 9 v.p. 1978-81, sec. 1981-82, program chmn. 1982—), Sigma Theta Tau. Office: Rowlett 223 Eastern Kentucky U Eastern Bypass Richmond KY 40475

DEMAREST, SYLVIA M., lawyer; b. Lake Charles, La., Aug. 16, 1944; d. Edmund and Emily (Meyers) D.; m. James A. Johnston, Jr., Oct. 31, 1975 (div. Dec. 1979). Student U. S.W. La., 1963-66; J.D., U. Tex., 1969. Bar: Tex. 1969, U.S. Supreme Ct. 1973, U.S. Ct. Appeals (5th cir.) 1970, U.S. Ct. Appeals (7th cir.) 1979, U.S. Ct. Appeals (11th cir.) 1980, U.S. Dist. Ct. (no. dist.) Tex. 1970, U.S. Dist. Ct. (ea. dist.) Tex. 1970, U.S. Dist. Ct. (so. dist.) Tex. 1972. Reginald H. Smith Community Lawyer fellow, Corpus Christi and Dallas, 1969-71; house counsel Tex. Inst. Ednl. Devel., San Antonio, 1972-73; staff atty. Dallas Legal Services Found., Inc., 1973, exec. dir., 1973-76; sole practice, Dallas, 1977-78; mgr. product litigation, dir. Windle Turley, P.C., Dallas, 1978-83; sole practice, 1983-85; ptnr. Demarest & Smith, 1985—; mem. faculty trial advocacy program So. Meth. U. Law Sch., 1984; lectr. Mem. State Bar Tex., ABA, Am. Trial Lawyers Assn., Dallas Bar Assn., Tex. Trial Lawyers Assn., Dallas Trial Lawyers Assn. (past pres.). Democrat. Roman Catholic. Home: 1812 Atlantic St Dallas TX 75208 Office: 1150 St Paul Pl 750 N St Paul St Dallas TX 75201

DEMARIS, SHIRLEY HANSEN, engineering consultant; b. Lakeview, Oreg., Oct. 7, 1945; d. Frank L. and Bonnie Jean (Follett) Hansen; m. Roger Lewis DeMaris, Aug. 24, 1968; children—Frank, Cynthia. B.A.E.E., Oreg. State U., 1968. Registered profl. engr., Oreg. Elec. engr. Rural Electrification, Washington, 1968-71, Bonneville Power, Portland, Oreg., 1971-76, Ctr. 4 Engring., Redmond, Oreg., 1980-82; engring. cons., Bend, Oreg., 1982—; mem. speakers bur., women's adv. group Bonneville Power, Portland, 1977—. Coordinator Tumalo Elem. Sch., Bend, 1984, 85, coach Sisters Little League, Tumalo, 1983-85. Mem. Soc. Women Engrs., IEEE, Central Oreg. Architects and Engrs. (pres. 1982-83). Democrat. Baptist.

DEMARR, MARY JEAN, educator; b. Champaign, Ill., Sept. 20, 1932; d. William Fleming and Laura Alice (Shauman) Bailey; B.A., Lawrence Coll., 1954; M.A., U. Ill., 1957, Ph.D., 1963; postgrad. Universitaet Tuebingen, 1954-55, Moscow State U., 1961-62. Asst. prof. English, Willamette U., 1964-65; asst. prof. English, Ind. State U., 1965-70, asso. prof., 1970-75, prof., 1975—. Recipient Fulbright assistantship, 1954-55. Mem. MLA, Modern Humanities Research Assn., AAUP, Nat. Council Tchrs. of English, ACLU, Phi Beta Kappa, Phi Kappa Phi. Presbyterian. Co-author: Adolescent Female Portraits in the American Novel 1961-1981: An Annotated Bibliography, 1983; Am. editor: Annual Bibliography of English Language and Literature, 1974—. Home: 2841 Mariposa Dr Terre Haute IN 47803 Office: Dept English Ind State U Terre Haute IN 47809

DEMAS, TULA ANN, librarian, marriage, child and family counselor; b. San Bernardino, Calif., Apr. 7, 1941; d. James and Loraine (Candelaria) D. B.A., Calif. State U.-San Bernardino, 1971, M.Ed. in Sch. Counseling, 1972; M.S. in L.S., U. So. Calif., 1971; M.A. in Family and Child Counseling, Chapman Coll., 1975. Lic. marriage, family and child counselor. Librarian technician San Bernardino Valley Coll., 1962-76; librarian Mt. San Antonio Community Coll., Walnut, Calif., 1976—; instr. marriage, family and child counseling Chapman Coll., Orange, Calif., 1979—; pvt. practice marriage, child and family counseling, San Bernardino, 1979—; leader workshops for state confs., 1981—. Mem. Affirmative Action Com., 1976—, pres., 1978-79. Mem. Marriage, Family and Child Counselors (state oral examiner 1983), La Raza (pres. 1976-78, Pres.'s award 1977), Marriage Family and Child Therapists (treas. Inland Empire chpt. 1980-83, prs. elect 1983-84), San Bernardino Humane Soc. (life). Democrat. Roman Catholic. Home: 2854 N Arrowhead Ave San Bernardino CA 92405

DEMATTEIS, MARY JO, advertising and public relations executive; b. Washington, Jan. 13, 1946; d. M.A. and Josephine (Iavasile) Dematteis. B.S., U. Md., 1967, postgrad. 1971-73. Editor employee publs., tng. specialist Marriott Corp., Washington, 1972-76; pub. relations dir. McDonalds Corp., Vienna, Va., 1976-78; advt. mgr. First Tenn. Bank, Memphis, 1978-81; v.p. mktg. Merrill Lynch Realty, Dallas, 1981-82; account exec. DBG&H Advt., Dallas, 1982-83; exec. account mgr. Dedie Leahy & Co., Dallas, 1983—; guest lectr. Cornell U., 1974. Hospitality chmn. Assn. Tex. Broadcast Execs., Dallas, 1981—; publicity com. Friends of Suicide Prevention Ctr., Dallas., 1982-83; pub. relations chmn. D.C. Spl. Olympics, 1976-78; publicity chmn. Wheelchair Basketball Assn., Memphis, 1981, Germantown Charity Horseshow, Memphis, 1978-81; mem. Tex. Sesquicentennial Com., 1984-86. Named Outstanding Employee, McDonald's Corp., 1977. Mem. Nat. Press Club. Roman Catholic. Clubs: Hunter's Creek Sportman's Country, Chimaris. Home: 16400 Ledgemont #805 Dallas TX 75248 Office: Dedie Leahy & Co 3100 Carlisle Suite 224 Dallas TX 75204

DEMAYO, DOROTHY ELAINE, modeling school executive; b. Roxbury, Mass., Nov. 3, 1922; d. William Charles and Florence Mae (Cribby) Falke; m. Armand Joseph DeMayo, Aug. 9, 1940; (dec. June 1979); children—Joan Frances, Beverly Jean, Armand Joseph, Wendy Mae, Brooks June. Cert. sch. operator, Mass. Owner, operator Dot DeMayo Sch. Charm and Modeling, Attleboro, Mass., 1968-80, Dot DeMayo Modeling Agy., Attleboro; instr. modeling; dir., commentator fashion shows; mem. adv. bd. World Modeling Assn. Am., N.Y.C. Chairwoman Am. Cancer Soc., Mass., 1969-70, Heart Assn., Attleboro. Recipient Fashion Inst. Tech. award, 1974, Heart Found. award, 1979. Mem. Internat. Platform Assn., Internat. Model's Soc. (founder), World Modeling Assn. (state dir., 5 awards 1968-80). Avocations: designing clothes; collecting clocks and mirrors. Office: 42 Prairie Ave Attleboro MA 02703

DEMBIAK, DOROTHY ANN, recreational association executive, financial executive; b. Passaic, N.J., Oct. 17, 1946; d. Stanley Dembiak and Florence Czaikoski. Grad. The Kimberley Sch., Montclair, N.J.; B.S., Fairleigh Dickinson U., 1968, B.A. in Edn., 1974. Tchr. cert. N.J. Tchr. reading and math., jr. high sch., 1976-78; staff acct. Melnor Industries, Moonachie, N.J., 1968-75; acctg. rep., office mgr. Sedata Systems, Ft. Lauderdale, Fla., 1979-81; controller Capital America, Ft. Lauderdale, 1981-83; controller Nat. Golf Found., North Palm Beach, Fla., 1983—. Mem. Nat. Assn. Accts. Office: Nat Golf Found 200 Castlewood Dr North Palm Beach FL 33408

DEMBSKI, BARBARA, newspaper editor; b. Chgo., Aug. 23, 1951; d. Anthony and Angeline (Komperda) D.; m. Carl William Schwartz, Aug. 21, 1971; 1 son. Student U. Ill.-Champaign, 1969-71, U. Wis.-Milw., 1973. Reporter, Milw. Jour., 1972-82, asst. Lifestyle editor, 1982, lifestyle editor, 1982—; participant Am. Press Inst., Reston, Va., 1983. Mem. Sigma Delta Chi (dir. 1977-79), Milw. Press Club (best feature award 1980), Wis. Press Assn. (Best Lifestyle sect. award 1982, 83, 84). Roman Catholic. Office: Milw Jour 333 W State St Milwaukee WI 53201

DEMBSKI, BARBRA JEAN, industrial safety administrator, consultant; b. Chgo., Oct. 26, 1950; d. M.V.J. and Lauretta Barbara (Adamski) D. Student Loyola U., Chgo., 1970-72; A.A., Triton Coll., 1976; cert. Ga. Inst. Tech., 1984. Registered beauty culturist, Ill. Safety dir. Village of Franklin Park, Ill., 1974-78; mktg. specialist Nat. Loss Control Service Corp., Long Grove, Ill., 1978-79, cons., 1980—; indsl. safety adminstr. Nat. Safety Council, Chgo., 1980—. Editor: Industrial Safety, 1977-78 (award 1978-79), Industrial Safety, 1978-79 (award 1979). Contbr. articles to profl. jours., texts, manuals; producer safety tng. programs. Recipient Raymond Lascoe award Nat. Safety Council, 1978, William H. Cameron award, 1978-79, cert. Appreciation, 1979; named Young Career Woman of Yr., Nat. Bus. and Profl. Women's Assn., 1977-78, Hon. Citizen City of New Orleans, 1984. Mem. Nat. Assn. Female Execs., Nat. Cosmetologists Assn., Chgo. Cosmetologists Assn.

DEMCHAK, IRENE, educator; b. Carbondale, Pa., Sept. 25, 1944; d. Peter and Pauline (Costello) Semonick; B.S. in Home Econs. Edn., Marywood Coll., Scranton, Pa., 1966, M.S. in Edn., 1969; postgrad. in home econs. edn. Pa. State U., summers 1969-71. Asst. home economist Lackawanna County (Pa.), summer, 1966; tchr. home econs., chairperson dept. home econs. Mountain View High Sch., Kingsley, Pa., 1966—; resource person for nutrition edn. tng.; adv. Future Homemakers Am.; sec. local negotiations team; co-adv. sch. Youth Edn. Club; panelist, local coll., 1979—; participant Pa. Profl. Standards and Practices Comm. Task Force, 1979—; mem. Nat. Council for Accreditation of Tchr. Edn., Title 4-C and Pa. Dept. Edn. Evaluator Pool, 1980—; judge fashion shows, county fairs, 1975-82. Leader 4-H Club, Mayfield, Pa., 1963—, also active county, state levels; active Democratic Party of Lackawanna County; tchr. folk dancing, 1978- 80. Dept. Agr. grantee, 1981-82, 84; Pa. Dept. Edn. grantee, 1979-81. Mem. Pa. Home Econs. Assn., Am. Home Econs. Assn., Internat. Home Econs. Assn., Pa. State Edn. Assn., NEA, Pa. Vocat. Assn., Am. Vocat. Assn., Fed. Russian Orthodox Clubs Am., Marywood Coll. Alumni Assn., Omicron Nu, Pi Lambda Theta. Home: 327 Delaware St Mayfield PA 18433 Office: Mountain View High Sch Kingsley PA 18826

DEMENT, SANDRA HELENE, lawyer; b. Tokyo, Apr. 15, 1949; came to U.S., 1950; d. Russell O. and Charlotte (Krupa) DeM.; m. Victor S. Sterling, Feb. 12, 1972 (div. 1978); m. 2d David Arthur Deuter, Aug. 28, 1982. B.A., Whitman Coll., 1970; J.D., George Washington U., 1978. Bar: D.C., Ill. Program dir. Youth Citizenship Fund, Washington, 1971-72; assoc. Citizen Action Group, Washington, 1972-73; exec. dir. Nat. Resource Ctr., Washington, 1974-79; v.p. ops. Banker Legal Service Corp., Chgo., 1979-80; pres. DeMent & Deuter Assocs., Chgo., 1980-81; dir. legal plans Hyatt Legal Services, Kansas City, Mo., 1981—; adv. bd. on delivery systems study Legal Service Corp., Washington, 1978-80; bd. dirs. Am. Prepaid Legal Services Inst., Chgo., 1975-80, Am. Arbitration Assn., N.Y.C., 1980—, Nat. Bd. Trial Advocacy, Washington, 1979—. Editor: Group Legal Service Plans, 1981; author report. Mem. ABA (commn. on lawyer advt. 1977-80), D.C. Bar, Ill. Bar Assn. Democrat. 1401 W 50th Terr Kansas City MO 64112 Office: Hyatt Legal Services 4410 Main St Kansas City MO 64111

DE MERE-DWYER, LEONA, medical artist; b. Memphis, May 1, 1928; d. Clifton and Leona (McCarthy) De Mere; B.A., Southwestern U., Memphis, 1949; M.Sc., Memphis State U., 1984; m. John Thomas Dwyer, May 10, 1952; children—John, DeMere, Patrice, Brian, Anne-Clifton DeMere Dwyer, McCarthy-DeMere Dwyer. Med. artist for McCarthy DeMere, Memphis, 1950-80; pres. Aesthetic Med. & Forensic Art, 1984—; speech therapist, Memphis, 1950-82; lic. embalmer, funeral dir., 1981; lectr. on med. art univs., conf., assns.; cons. in prostheses Vocat. Rehab. Services; bereavement counselor. Organizer Ladies of St. Jude, Memphis, 1960; active Brooks Art Gallery League of Memphis; leader Confraternity of Christian Doctrine, St. Louis Cath. Ch., 1966-67; vice dir. Tellico Hist. Found., 1980-80; mem. exec. bd. Chickasaw council Boy Scouts Am.; active Republican campaign coms. Lic. Fedn. Internationale de'Automobile, (internat. car racing), 1972; recipient Disting. Service award Gupton-Jones Coll. Mortuary Sci., 1981; Silver Sons of the Am. Revolution medal, 1985. Mem. Assn. Med. Illustrators, Am. Assn. Med. Assts., Emergency Dept. Nurses Assn., Am. Physicians Nurses Assn., Am. Soc. Plastic and Reconstructive Surgeons Found. (guest mem., cons.), Women in Law (chmn. assos.), FORUM, Nat. Death Edn. Soc., Exec. Women Am., Brandeis U. Women, DAR (1st v.p. regent 1980), UDC (pres. Nathan Bedford Forrest chpt.), Cotton Carnival Assn. (chairperson children's ct. 1968-70), Pi Sigma Eta, Kappa Delta (adv.), Kappa Delta Pi. Clubs: Tennessee, Royal Matron Amaranth (Faith Ct.), Sertoma (1st female mem. Memphis, 1st female life mem. Sertoma Internat.) (Memphis). Contbr. articles to profl. jours. Home: 660 W Suggs Dr Memphis TN 38119

DEMERS, JUDY LEE, university dean, state legislator; b. Grand Forks, N.D., June 27, 1944; d. Robert L. and V. Margaret (Harming) Prosser; m. Donald E. DeMers, Oct. 3, 1964 (div. Oct. 1971); 1 son, Robert M.; m. Joseph M. Murphy, Mar. 5, 1977 (div. Oct. 1983). B.S.N., U. N.D., 1966; M.Ed., U. Wash., 1973, postgrad., 1973-75. Pub. health nurse Govt. D.C., 1966-68, Combined Nursing Service, Mpls., 1968-69; instr. pub. health nursing U. N.D. Coll. Nursing, Grand Forks, 1969-71, assoc. dir. Medex program Sch. Medicine, 1970-72, dir., family nurse practitioner program, 1977-82, assoc. dir. rural health, 1982—, dir. undergrad. med. edn., 1982-83, assoc. dean, 1983—; research assoc. U. Wash., Seattle, 1973-76; mem. N.D. Ho. of Reps., 1982—; cons. Health Manpower Devel. Staff, Honolulu, 1975-81, Assn. Physician Asst. Programs, Washington, 1979-82; site visitor, cons. AMA-Com. Allied Health Edn. Accreditation, Chgo., 1979-81. Author: Educating New Health Practitioners, 1976; editorial bd. P.A. Jour., 1976-78; contbr. articles to profl. jours. Sec., bd. dirs. Valley Family Planning and Edn. Ctr., Grand Forks, N.D., 1982—; exec. com., bd. dirs. Agassiz Health Systems Agy., Grand Forks, 1982—; mem. N.D. State Daycare Adv. Com., 1983—, Mayor's Adv. Com. on Police Policy, Grand Forks, 1983-85, N.D. State Foster Care Adv. Com., 1985—, N.D. State Hypertension Adv. Com., 1983-85, Gov.'s Com. on DUI and Traffic Safety, 1985—, statewide adv. com. on AIDS, 1985—; mem. N.D. Ho. of Reps., 1982—. Recipient award Alpha Lambda Delta, 1963; Pub. Citizen of Yr. award N.D. chpt. Nat. Assn. Social Workers, 1986; U. Wash. regional med. program service fellow, 1972-73; U. Wash. Kellogg Allied health fellow, 1972; named N.D. Nurse of Yr., N.D. State Nurses Assn., Bismarck, 1983. Mem. Am. Nurses Assn., Am. Pub. Health Assn., Am. Ednl. Research Assn., N.D. Pub. Health Assn., N.D. Mental Health Assn., Assn. for Retarded Citizens, N.D. Nurses Assn. (cabinet on edn. and practice 1982-86), Pi Lambda Theta, Sigma Theta Tau, NOW, ACLU, LWV. Democrat. Home: 1826 Lewis Blvd Grand Forks ND 58201 Office: U ND Sch Medicine 500 Columbia Rd Grand Forks ND 58201

DEMERY, HAZEL GURLEY, nurse; b. Lexington, Tenn., Sept. 20, 1922; d. Marshall Tilliman and Effie (Beecham) Gurley; m. James B. Demery, July 18, 1942 (div. 1973); 1 child, Martha Ann. Student pub. schs., Blytheville, Ark. Head nurse Robinson Clinic, Manila, Ark., 1941-42, Congers Clinic, Lexington, 1942-43, Dickerson Clinic, Hartford, Ky., 1949-50; supt. nurses Blytheville Hosp., 1943-45, chief surg. nurse, 1945-46; office nurse M.H. Moseley, Eddyville, Ky., 1953-59, W.H. England, Grand Rivers, Ky., 1967—; indsl. nurse Reed Crushed Stone, Co., Inc., Grand Rivers, 1972—. Mem. bd. Community Mental Health, Mayfield, Ky., 1975-76, Livington County Hosp., Salem, Ky., 1975-76, Nashville Regional Red Cross Blood Program, 1976-79. Pres. Grand Rivers PTA, 1967-68; chmn. Livingston County Blood Program, 1961—; hon. clk. Ct. of Appeals, 1975; county chmn. Democratic party. Mem. Ch. of Christ. Club: Lake City Homemakers (pres. 1960-61) (Grand Rivers). Lodge: Eastern Star (worthy matron 1958-59). Home: Lake City Grand Rivers KY 42045 Office: Dr WH Englands Clinic Main St Box 158 Grand Rivers KY 42045

DEMETRIADES, DESPINA GUS, real estate executive, writer; b. Gastonia, N.C.; d. Gus George and Athena (Leventis) D.; B.A. in Psychology, Columbia U., 1966; M.A. in Counselor Edn., Appalachian State U., Boone, N.C., 1967. Instr., Lynchburg (Va.) Coll., 1967-69; dir. inservice edn. Gastonia Meml. Hosp., 1970-77; edn. coordinator Catawba/Wateree Health Edn. Consortium, Lancaster, S.C., 1977-78; pres., devel. analyst Profl. Devel. Systems, Gastonia, 1978-82; edn. dir. Wesley Long Community Hosp., Greensboro, N.C., 1982-84; sales/tech. freelance writer, Greensboro, 1984—; real estate appraiser. Mem. Women's Forum of N.C., LWV. Greek Orthodox. Home: 4314 Big Tree Way Greensboro NC 27409 Office: PO Box 18311 Greensboro NC 27419

DEMETRIUS, ANABEL STAFFORD, association executive, trainer; b. Chgo., July 2, 1941; d. Philip Truesdale and Joanna Bartlett (Rogers) Stafford; m. Kris Demetrius, Feb. 2, 1970 (div. 1978); 1 child, Rebecca Bartlett. B.A. in Edn., U. N.Mex., 1967; M.P.A., Ind. U., 1983. Personnel officer City of Los Angeles Community Redevel. Agy., 1970-73; cons. supr. Houston-Harris County Community action Assn., 1966-69; U.S. Peace Corps vol., Philippines, 1962-64; Exec. dir. Santa Barbara Community Action Assn., Calif., 1974-78; dir. community devel. tng. Santa Barbara County Schs., 1978-81; asst. exec. dir. Ind. Health Care Assn., Indpls., 1983-84; exec. dir. Pi Lambda Theta, Bloomington, Ind., 1984—; instr. Santa Barbara City Coll., 1978-81; participation trainer Ind. U., Bloomington, 1982—. Author: Job Hunter's Guide, 1973. Chmn. Adult Day Health Care Planning Com., Santa Barbara, 1976; pres. sub-area council Health Systems Agy., Santa Barbara, 1979; precinct committeeman Monroe County Democratic Party, Ind., 1982; chmn. social concerns com. Unitarian Ch., Santa Barbara, 1978; bd. dirs. Santa Barbara Dem. League, 1977-79. Named to Outstanding Young Women Am., U.S. Jaycees, 1965. Mem. Am. Soc. Assn. Execs., Sch. Pub. and Environ. Affairs Alumni Assn. of Ind. U. (bd. dirs.), Central Ind. Assn. Tng. and Devel., Nat. Assn. Female Execs., Spurs (chpt. pres. 1960-61), Pi Lambda Theta, Phi Kappa Phi. Club: Alpine Ski (Bloomington). Avocations: skiing; ski racing; real estate; art; politics. Home: 6636 E State Rd 46 Bloomington IN 47401 Office: Pi Lambda Theta 4104 E Third Bloomington IN 47401

DEMHARTER, CHERYL ANN MARIE, association administrator; b. New Orleans, May 20, 1955; d. Anton Irwin and Liliane Irene (Auger) D.; B.A. magna cum laude, U. New Orleans, 1975; M.A., Tulane U., 1978, Ph.D., 1981. Grad. teaching asst. Tulane U., New Orleans, 1977-80, vis. instr. French, 1980-81; asst. prof. French, U. Tex., Austin, 1981-86; asst. dir. fgn. lang. programs MLA, N.Y.C., 1986—. Recipient summer stipends U. Tex. Research Inst., 1982, 85, Nat. Endowment for Humanities, 1982; faculty enrichment grantee Canadian Govt., 1984, faculty research grantee, 1985. Mem. MLA, Am. Assn. Tchrs. French, Internat. Soc. Phonetic Scis., Am. Council Teaching Fgn. Langs., Rocky Mountain Modern Lang. Assn., N.E. MLA, Council Devel. Assn. Can. Studies in the U.S., Northeast Council Que. Studies, So. Council Francophone Studies (2d v.p. 1985-86), Phi Kappa Phi. Office: Fgn Lang Programs MLA 10 Astor Place New York NY 10003

DEMIK, ANITA LORRAINE, legal secretary, assistant; b. Aurora, Ill., Oct. 11, 1945; d. Thorsten Oscar and Emily Kristine (Sorensen) Ostergren; m. Robert A. DeMik, Sept. 11, 1965; children—Thor Arnold, Michael James, Todd Arthur. Cert. profl. sec. Legal sec. McDermott, Will & Emery, Chgo., 1977-81; adminstrv. asst. Sch. Social Service, U. Chgo., 1981-82; legal sec., dept. coordinator Kirkland & Ellis, Chgo., 1982-84; legal sec., legal asst. Bell, Boyd & Lloyd, Chgo., 1984—; v.p., sec. Atina, Inc., Park Forest, Ill., 1984—. Author papers on secretarial professionalism and ethics. Guest speaker EPA, Chgo., 1984-85; guest instr. Catherine Bus. Coll., Chgo., 1985; speaker Archdiocese Carousel of Learning, Chgo., 1985. Mem. Profl. Secs. Internat. (sec. 1982-83, v.p. 1983-84, pres. 1984-85, membership chmn. 1985-86, Chgo. chpt.; chmn. retirement ctrs. trust ctr., Ill. div., 1986—; del. internat. conv. Toronto 1964, alt. internat. conv. Louisville 1965), Nat. Assn. for Exec. Women. Democrat. Lutheran. Club: Will County Extension (pres. 1972-73) (Beecher, Ill.). Avocations: computers; writing. Home: 439 Homan Ave Park Forest IL 60466 Office: Bell Boyd & Lloyd 70 W Madison #3200 Chicago IL 60602

DEMILLION, JULIANNE, personal health fitness trainer, therapeutic rehabilitation consultant; b. Monessen, Pa., Dec. 20, 1955; d. William Vincent and Enise Mary (Tocci) DeM. B.A., B.S., U. Pitts., 1977; cert. massage therapist Phoenix Therapeutic Massage Coll., 1985. Mgr. program devel. Exclusively Women Spas, Scottsdale, 1977-81; self-employed exercise therapist, Scottsdale, 1981-83, self-employed personal trainer, Scottsdale, 1983—; cons. in field, City of Phoenix, 1981—. Mem. Scottsdale Ctr. for the Arts Assn., 1984. Mem. Am. Massage Therapy Assn., Ariz. Massage Therapy Assn. (sec.-treas. 1986—), Internat. Dance and Exercise Assn., Nat. Assn. Female Execs., Circulo-Systems Ltd., Am. Coll. Sports Medicine. Scottsdale AZ

DEMIRJIAN, ARLENE, social worker; b. Bridgeport, Conn., Mar. 1, 1941; d. John and Sara (Andrikian) D.; B.A., Clark U., 1962; M.S.W. (scholar), Boston U., 1965; cert. in psychoanalytic psychotherapy Inst. for Study of Psychotherapy, 1975. Social worker Bellevue Psychiat. Hosp., N.Y.C., 1965-69, founder pilot program for heroin addicts, 1969; pvt. practice psychotherapy, N.Y.C., 1974—; cons. N.Y. State Div. Substance Abuse Services, 1974—, U.S. Dept. State, 1982. Cert. social worker, N.Y. Mem. Nat. Assn. Social Workers, Armenian Gen. Benevolent Union. Contbr. articles on heroin abuse and on Soviet psychiatry to publs. Home: 308 E 79th St New York NY 10021 Office: 425 E 86th St New York NY 10028

DEMLER, LINDA KASS, insurance company administrator; b. Pocatello, Idaho, Feb. 17, 1954; d. Theodore Edwin and Pauline Therese (Gaudreau) Kass; m. Frederick Russel Demler, Aug. 26, 1976; 1 child, Todd Frederick. B.S. cum laude in Psychology, Pa. State U., 1976. Dining mgr. Holiday Inn, State College, Pa., 1976-77; restaurant mgr. Corner Room, State College, 1977-78; acctg. mgr. Heim, Heckendorn & Bruce, State College, 1978-80; div. mgr. N.Y. Life Ins. Co., N.Y.C., 1980—. Active Republican Nat. Com., Washington, 1985—. Mem. Nat. Assn. Female Execs., Am. Mgmt. Assn., Psi Chi, Alpha Lambda Delta. Home: 4 Effingham Rd Yardley PA 19067

DEMONG, PHYLLIS, painter, writer, illustrator; b. Washington, Mar. 3, 1920; d. Frank Elliott and Minne Belle (White) Hickman; m. Francis L. Demong, Mar. 24, 1941; children—Peter, Geoffrey, Thomas, Sarah. B.F.A., Syracuse U., 1940. One woman shows: Wood Mus., Montpelier, Vt., The Munson Gallery, New Haven, Conn., The Peel Gallery, Danby, Vt., Middlebury Coll., Gallery Two, Woodstock, Vt., Munson Gallery, Chatham, Mass., St. Pauls Cathedral, Burlington, Vt.; group shows include: Everson Mus., Syracuse, N.Y., Meml. Gallery, Rochester, N.Y., Roberson Mus. Biennial, Binghamton, N.Y., Stratton (Vt.) Arts Festivals; represented in permanent collections: Munson Williams Proctor Inst., Utica, N.Y., Everson Mus., Marine Midland Trust Co., Syracuse, Cooperstown Art Assn. (N.Y.), Central Presbyn. Ch., Rochester, N.Y., Vt. Fed. Savs., Burlington, Vt. Author, illustrator: Celebearties & Other Bears, 1979; It's A Pig World Out There, 1980; Rare & Undone Saints, 1981; designer: Bakery Lane Soup Bowl, 1978. Recipient Artist of N.Y. Purchase award Munson Williams Proctor Inst., 1966; Purchase award Marine Midland Everson Mus., 1967; George Arents medal Syracuse U., 1974; Vt. Artists 1st prize Norwich U., 1978. Mem. So. Vt. Artists, No. Vt. Artists, Cooperstown N.Y. Art Assn., Associated Artists of Syracuse (Gordon Steele Meml. medal), Provincetown Art Assn. Democrat. Episcopalian. Home: PO Box 70 Middlebury VT 05753

DEMPSEY, PATRICIA LOUISE, social worker; b. Waterbury, Conn., Sept. 20, 1947; d. James Louis and Phyllis Virginia (Reid) D.; B.A., Fordham U., 1973; M.S. (Mott fellow), Columbia U., 1975. Dir. Youth Services System, East Side Settlement House, Bronx, N.Y., 1975-76; dep. dir. food stamp alert Community Council Greater N.Y., 1976-77; dir. youth services United Neighborhood Houses of N.Y., 1977-78; program dir. Harlem br. YMCA Greater N.Y., 1978-80, dir. spl. projects, 1980-83; asst. to commr. N.Y.C. Human Resources Adminstrn., 1985—; mem. faculty Adelphi U. Sch. Social Work, 1978—; asst. prof. Hunter Sch. Social Work, CUNY, 1985—; cons. Cornell U.; cons. Nat. Council Negro Women. Mem. Bronx Council for Advocacy of Children and Youth, 1975—, mem. edn., child abuse and juvenile justice task forces, 1978—; bd. dirs. Juvenile Justice Coalition of N.Y., Spofford Juvenile Detention Ctr. Cert. social worker. Mem. Nat. Assn. Social Workers, Nat. Assn. Black Social Workers, Riverdale Mental Health Assn., Assn. Profl.

Dirs. YMCA Greater N.Y., Columbia U. Alumni Assn. Office: 180 W 135th St New York NY 10030

DEMUTH, NINA LEWIS, chemical air sterilization company executive; b. Benton, Ill., July 14, 1921; d. William Henry and Agnes Clara (Landreth) Lewis; student Nassau Coll., 1976—; m. Herbert Willard Demuth, Feb. 16, 1947; 1 dau., Nina Dale (dec.). With Barbour Co., Inc., St. Louis, 1939-47, v.p., 1943-47; pres. Demuth Co., Garden City, N.Y., 1948—, Demuth Service Corp., Garden City, 1955—, Demuth Devel. Corp., Garden City, 1958. Mem. Parenteral Drug Assn. (dir. 1977-79), Parenteral Drug Assn. Found. for Pharm. Scis. (incorporator 1979, pres. 1979-83, dir. 1979-85, treas. 1984—), Huguenot Soc. Methodist. Contbr. articles in field to profl. publs. Office: PO Box 242 Garden City NY 11530

DEMYAN, JEANNE RAUCH, veterinarian; b. Columbia, S.C., Nov. 1, 1951; d. Jacob Elton and Edna Mae (Long) Rauch; m. John Edward Demyan, Sept. 1, 1976. B.S. with honors, Clemson U., 1972; D.V.M., U. Ga., 1976. Assoc. veterinarian Johnson McKee Animal Hosp., Salisbury, Md., 1976; zoo veterinarian Riverbanks Zoo, Columbia, S.C., 1976; research assoc. Squibb Inst. Med. Research, New Brunswick, N.J., 1976-78, dir. lab. animal medicine, Princeton, N.J., 1978; owner Travelers Rest (S.C.) Animal Hosp., 1979—; mem. adv. council North Greenville Hosp., Travelers Rest, 1981-83; co. mem. Greenville Concert Ballet. Mem. AVMA, Greenville Vet. Med. Assn., Am. Holistic Veterinary Med. Assn., Internat. Veterinary Acupuncture Soc., NOW (convenor 1st S.C. chpt. 1971, pres. 1972). Episcopalian. Office: Travelers Rest Animal Hosp 409 Old Buncombe Rd Travelers Rest SC 29690

DENATALE, CAROLE EGAN, lawyer; b. Buffalo, Dec. 10, 1954; d. John Lloyd and Dorothy (Nigro) Egan; m. Richard Grimes, Aug. 18, 1979. B.A. magna cum laude, Mt. Holyoke Coll., 1976; J.D., SUNY-Buffalo, 1979. Bar: N.Y., 1980, Ariz., 1980. Law clk. Diebold & Millonzi, Buffalo, 1978-79; assoc. John Lloyd Egan, Buffalo, 1979-80, Cates & Roediger, Phoenix, 1980-81, Kuhn, Muller & Bazerman, N.Y.C., 1982-84, Kane, Dalsimer, Kane, Sullivan & Kurucz, N.Y.C., 1984—. Sarah Williston scholar, Mt. Holyoke Coll., 1973; Mary Lyon Scholar, 1976. Recipient Jessie Goodwin Spaulding Prize, Mt. Holyoke Coll., 1974, Cornelia Catlin Coulter Prize, 1975, Jean Renneisen Toub Prize, 1976. Mem. ABA, N.Y. State Bar Assn., State Bar Ariz., N.Y. Patent Law Assn., Jr. League, Phi Beta Kappa. Office: Kane Dalsimer Kane Sullivan & Kurucz 420 Lexington Ave New York NY 10170

DENEAULT, MAUREEN ISDEPSKI, art educator, puppeteer; b. Acushnet, Mass., Mar. 4, 1942; d. Frank James and Mary Elizabeth (Soltys) Isdepski; m. Louis A.L. Deneault, June 13, 1970; 1 son, Ethan Albert Nathan. B.F.A., Southeastern Mass. U., 1969, M.F.A., 1971; M.Ed., Bridgewater State Coll., 1972, postgrad., 1982—. Cert. spl. subject tchr. (art), librarian. Library aide, Southeastern Mass. U., North Dartmouth, 1968-69, teaching asst. graphic arts, 1969-71; tech. illustrator Raytheon, Inc., Newport, R.I., 1969; graphic designer MI Studio Graphics, New Bedford, Mass., 1969—; sch. librarian Joseph H. Martin Sch., Taunton Pub. Schs., East Taunton, Mass., 1973-81, set designer music dept., 1975-81, elem. art tchr. Taunton Pub. Schs., Taunton, Mass., 1983—; dir., puppeteer, puppet designer, instr. Puppetree Playhouse, New Bedford, 1981—; teaching asst. library sci. Bridgewater State Coll. (Mass.), 1982-83; set designer Taunton Children's Theatre, 1979; instr. puppetry, Southeastern Mass. U., 1982. Author/illustrator: Regenesis: 1971, Wandering..., 1969, Lowicz-Style Wedding Design, 1973 (spl. award), Nicolas Copernicus, 1973 (hon. mention); instructional manuals: Puppetry Titles: The Basic Mouth Puppet, The Basic Hand Puppet, 1981, The Priest's Vestments, 1983, The Bishop's Vestments, 1984, The Deacon's Vestments, 1984. Advt. designer. co-chmn. Internat. Fair segment of Whaling City Festival, New Bedford, 1973. City of New Bedford scholar, 1965-69. Mem. ALA, Puppeteers Am., New Eng. Ednl. Media Assn., EEA, Mass. Tchrs. Assn., Taunton Educators Assn. Episcopalian. Club: Polish Women's Bus. and Profl. rec. sec. New Bedford 1972-73). Office: Puppetree Playhouse 87 Harvard St New Bedford MA 02746

DENEHIE, LINDA SUE, nursing adminstrator; b. Beaumont, Tex., Nov. 21, 1950; d. William Hillman and Evelyn Doris (Cole) Hosey; m. Frank Edward Spring, Jr., Sept. 13, 1969 (div. Mar. 1978); children—Frank Edward Spring III, Deanna Michele; m. 2d, Douglas Eric Denehie, Apr. 11, 1981. Diploma nursing, Mastin Sch. Nursing, 1972. Staff R.N., Mobile (Ala.) Gen. Hosp., 1972-76; head nurse ICU, Ocean Springs (Miss.) Hosp., 1976-79; staff nurse Community Home Health Care Agy., Ocean Springs, 1979-83, dir. nursing, 1983—. Mem. Am. Nurses Assn., Miss. Nurses Assn. Democrat. Roman Catholic. Home: 5 Forest Hills Dr Ocean Springs MS 39564 Office: Community Home Health Inc 2999 Bienville Blvd Ocean Springs MS 39564

DENHAM, MARY GRAY, business woman; b. Albion, Pa., Sept. 6, 1929; d. Delmer E. and Ruth Audeen (Gray) Beatty; m. Gene E. Denham, Dec. 12, 1969 (dec.); children—Mary Ruth, Susan, 1 step dau., Wendy Koivisto. Catalog writer Gen. Electric, Erie, Pa., 1953-61; with Sperry-Rand Corp., Phoenix, 1961-69; with Motorola, Inc., Scottsdale, Ariz., 1969-79, supr. drafting and data control, 1975-79; configuration/document control supr. ADDA Corp., Campbell, Calif., 1979-83; supr. release documents ESL, Sunnyvale, Calif., 1983—. Mem. Am. Bus. Women (past pres.), Nat. Assn. Female Execs., La Societe de Femme (past v.p.), Clowns of Am. (past pres. Clown Alley 7). 5514 N 61 St Lane Glendale AZ 85301 Home: 1261 Newhall St San Jose CA 95126 Office: 495 Java Dr Sunnyvale CA 94088

DENK, RUTH ERNA SCHREYER, business executive; b. Wiesbaden, Hessen, Germany, Jan. 29, 1934; d. Edward Richard Schreyer and Erna Elsa (Weidenfeller) Horner; came to U.S., 1950; m. Horst George Denk, Sept. 12, 1953; 1 dau., Suzanne Romy Thelen. B.S., NYU, 1977. Cert. mgmt. and indsl. relations. Exec. supr. central reservation Hilton Hotels, N.Y.C., 1954-60; v.p., treas. Denk Baking Corp., Bklyn., 1971, sr. v.p., 1977-83, pres., 1984-85, chmn., chief exec. officer, 1985—; pres. DBC Enterprises, Charleston, S.C., 1984-85, pres., chmn., chief exec. officer, 1985—. Mem. fin. com. Easter Seal Society, N.Y., 1970-74; dir. devel., auditions eastern region Nat. Council of Met. Opera Co., 1982—; bd. dirs. Third Street Music Sch. Settlement, N.Y.C., 1982—; commr. Presdl. Commn. German-Am. Tricentennial, 1983-84. Decorated officer's cross order of Merit (W.Ger.). Mem. Ind. Bakers Assn. (young pres.' council, nat. affairs com., polit. edn. com., 1980, bd. dirs. Washington 1982—), Newcomen Soc. Lutheran. Office: Denk Baking Corp 495 Flatbush Ave Brooklyn NY 11225

DENMAN, ALEXANDRA, lawyer; b. Oklahoma City, June 22, 1947; d. Dale and Norma Jean (Warmack) Denman; m. Benjamin J. Stein, Sept. 7, 1977. B.A., Vassar Coll., 1969; student Yale Coll., 1968-69; J.D., George Washington U., 1973. Bar: D.C. 1973, Calif. 1978. Assoc. Donovan Leisure Newton & Irvine, Washington, 1973-77, Overton, Lyman & Prince, Los Angeles, 1977-78; atty. motion picture div. Paramount Pictures Corp., Los Angeles, 1982-85; v.p.-legal and theatrical United Artists Corp., Beverly Hills, Calif., 1986—. Researcher books: Moneypower, 1981, Manhattan Gambit, 1983. Mem. ABA, Attys. for Animal Rights, Bar Assn. County Los Angeles. Republican. Presbyterian. Office: United Artists Corp 450 N Roxbury Dr Beverly Hills CA 90210

DENNARD, GWENDOLYN DORTHELIA, physician; b. Detroit, May 19, 1945; d. Willis Melvin and Bealer (Williams) Dennard. B.S. in Med. Tech., U. Nebr., 1967; M.D., Wayne State U., 1975. Intern, Wayne State U. Affiliated Hosps., Detroit, 1975-76; resident Hutzel Hosp., Detroit, 1976-78; pvt. practice internal medicine, Detroit, 1978-82, Sacramento, 1983—, Galt, Calif., 1985—; staff Sutter Community Hosps., Sacramento, 1983—; clin. assoc., in internal medicine U. Calif., Davis and Davis Med. Ctr., Sacramento, 1984—; cons. internist Sobriety Brings a Change, Sacramento, 1983—; staff Sutter Community Hosp., Mercy Gen. Hosp., Sacramento, Lodi Meml. Hosp., Lodi Community Hosp., Calif. Bd. dirs. YWCA, Detroit, 1980-82, Mich. Cancer Found., Detroit, 1981-82; organizer dist. campaign, pres. Detroit City Council, 1981-82; mem. com. on program edn. Sacramento br. Am. Cancer Soc. Served to capt. USAR, 1983—. Mem. AMA, Am. Med. Women's Assn. (bd. dirs. Sacramento chpt. 1983—), Am. Soc. Internal Medicine, Calif. Soc. Internal Medicine. Baptist. Office: St Lukes Med Bldg 2600 Capitol Ave Suite 311 Sacramento CA 95816 also Galt Profl Plaza 425 Pine St Suite 3 Galt CA 95632

DENNER, VALERIE LOUISE DAINO, nurse; b. N.Y.C., July 21, 1952; d. Albert and Violet Louise (Acanfora) Daino; m. Alan Matthew Denner, May 29, 1976; 1 child, Tami Danielle. Diploma in nursing YWCA/Bklyn.-Cumberland Med. Ctr., 1972; A.A. Sci., Genesee Community Coll., 1975; B.A., SUNY-Albany, 1980; M.S., Quinnipeac Coll., 1986. Staff nurse Albany Med. Ctr., N.Y., 1972-73, Hosp. of St. Raphael, New Haven, 1976-77; nursing instr. Quinnipeac Coll., Hamden, Conn., 1977-79; nurse Med-Staff, Boston, 1979-81; br. adminstr. Nurse World, Inc./Home Care Am. div. of Cosmopolitan Care Corp. Amex, Orlando, 1981-86, corp. v.p., 1985-86; mem. med. adv. bd. Hospice of Central Fla., Orlando, 1984-85, Kimberly Clark Corp., Balt., 1986—; lectr. LPN Assn. of Orlando, 1986; founder, gen. ptnr. Home Med. Suppliers, 1984; founder, v.p. B. Daino Constrn., 1983, Investiclaim, Inc., 1986; founder, pres. Respiratory Therapy Inc., 1985. Asst. producer CBS 60 Minutes program, Sharon, Mass., 1980-81. Founder Hosp. of St. Raphael Physician Spouse Assn., 1976-79; pres., founder Citizens Action Group for Protection of Buyers of Newly Constructed Homes, 1979-81. Mem. Orlando C. of C., Am. Nurses Assn., Fla. Nurses Assn. (del. 1983), Nat. Assn. Female Execs., Nat. Assn. for Notary Publics, Orange County Med. Aux. Republican. Avocations: designing and building houses; numismatics; skiing; swimming. Home: 9162 Kilgore Rd Orlando FL 32819 Office: Nurse World/Home Care Am 1950 Lee Rd Orlando FL 32789

DENNEY, NANCY CHASTEEN, energy education specialist; b. Griffin, Ga., Feb. 18, 1944; d. James Wilson and Sara Margaret (Hollingsworth) Chasteen; m. Woodrow Wilson Denney, Jr., Apr. 12, 1968; children—Courtney Leigh, Austin Kirk. B.S., U. Ga., 1967. Tchr. home econs. Newton County Bd. Edn., Covington, Ga., 1967; tchr., sci., home econs. Clayton County Bd. Edn., Forest Park, Ga., 1967-69; home economist Pub. Service Co. N.C., Durham, 1969-73; freelance home economist 1973-81; energy edn. specialist U. Ga., Athens, 1981—. Co-editor monthly newsletter Energy News, 1981-85. Officer, aux. Am. Cancer Soc., 1976—. Decorated Order Long Leaf Pine, N.C., 1971; recipient Nat. Energy award U.S. Dept Energy, 1984. Mem. Ga. Home Econs. Assn. (state chmn. Home Economist in Homemaking 1980-82, treas. 1982-84, chmn. pub. relations 1984-85), Am. Home Econs. Assn., U. Ga. Coll. Home Econs. Alumni Assn. (treas. 1980-82). Clubs: Jr. Womens, Cedar Creek Garden. Avocations: Photography; genealogy. Office: Ga Ctr for Continuing Edn U Ga Athens GA 30602

DENNIS, DONNA, sculptor; b. Springfield, Ohio, 1942; One-person exhbns.: Hotels, West Broadway Gallery, N.Y.C., 1973; Donna Dennis, Wilcox Gallery, Swarthmore Coll., Pa., 1974; Subway Stations and Tourist Cabins, Holly Solomon Gallery, N.Y.C., 1976; City Station and Country Stops, JFK Ctr. Performing Arts, Washington, 1977; Maquettes and Drawings, Adler Gallery, Los Angeles, 1978; Donna Dennis, Holly Solomon Gallery, N.Y.C., 1978; Three Sculptures by Donna Dennis, Contemporary Arts Ctr., Cin., 1979; Donna Dennis, Sullivant Gallery, Ohio State U., Columbus, 1980; Drawings and Maquettes, Holly Solomon Gallery, N.Y.C., 1980; N.Y. and N.J., Holly Solomon Gallery, 1980; Maquettes and Drawings, Locus Solus Gallery, Genoa, Italy, 1981; Mad River Tunnel, Entrance and Exit, Dayton, 1981; Holly Solomon Gallery, N.Y.C., 1983; Abe Adler Gallery, Los Angeles, 1983; Moccasin Creek Cabins, Outdoor Installation, Moccasin Creek, Aberdeen, S.D., 1983; Night Stops, Neuberger Mus. SUNY-Purchase, 1985, Deep Stas., U. Mass.-Amherst, 1985; group exhbns. include: numerous galleries, N.Y.C., 1972, 73, 74, 75; most recent: Venice Bienale, Italy, 1984, numerous others. Set Design: Midsummer's Night Dream, 1973. TV Interviews: Gulliver's Travels series, 1979; CBS Cable Network, 1981; Manhattan Cable TV, 1986. N.Y. State Creative Artists Pub. Service grantee, 1975; NEA fellow, 1977; Guggenheim fellow, 1979; NEA fellow, 1980; N.Y. State Creative Artists Pub. Service grantee, 1981; Am. Acad. and Inst. Arts and Letters grantee, 1984; N.Y. Found. Arts. pub. service grantee, 1985. Address: 131 Duane St New York NY 10013

DENNIS, DOROTHY ELIZABETH, industrial coatings manufacturing company executive; b. Tipton, Ind., July 3, 1918; d. Glenn Cleo and Lucy Lenore (Woods) McCorkle; m. John R. Dennis, Sept. 12, 1943 (dec. Sept. 1981); 1 child, Jane Lynn Dennis Weir. A.A., Stephens Coll., 1938; B.S., Northwestern U., 1940. Cert. tchr. English and speech, Pa. Speech therapist J.W. Riley Hosp., Indpls., 1940-43, Borden Gen. Hosp., Chickasha, Okla., 1945-46; tchr. English, Bethel Park Sch. Dist., Pa., 1959-80; pres., chmn. bd. Densco Inc., Bethel Park, 1981—. Exec. sec. Tipton County chpt. ARC, Ind., 1944. Trustee Bethel Park Library Bd., 1975-81. Mem. Countryside Book Club, Presbyn. Women's Assn. (pres. 1953-55), Pitts. Symphony Soc. Avocations: sailing; swimming; canoeing; book reviewing.

DENNIS, GOLDA NAN, accountant; b. Baird, Tex., Nov. 18, 1938; d. John Leroy and Juanita H. (Holloway) Thornton; grad. Twin City Bus. Coll., 1963; m. James D. Dennis, Sept. 14, 1979; children by previous marriage—Ida Anita, Tena Mari, Benjamin Franklin, Michaelle Lenae. Controller, Authentic Furniture Products, Dallas, 1972-75; data processing mgr., asst. controller, treas. Hart Graphics, Inc., Austin, Tex., 1977-79; credit mgr. Western Mktg., Inc., Abilene, Tex., 1979-80; tax acct. Lajet, Inc., Abilene, 1980-83; acct. Smith, Nolen CPA Co., 1983—. Mem. U.S. Congl. Adv. Bd., 1982-84. Mem. Nat. Accts. Assn. (dir. recruits 1982-83), Female Execs. Assn. Democrat. Baptist. Home: 926 Ballinger Abilene TX 79605 Office: Smith Nolen Co 4400 Buffalo Gap Rd Suite 3000 Abilene TX 79606

DENNIS, IVANETTE JONES, editor, writer; b. Elk City, Okla., Sept. 30, 1940; d. Carroll Noel and Mary Nadine (Childress) Jones; m. Glenn Ray Dennis, Feb. 6, 1965; children—Suzanne Kaye, Cynthia Elizabeth. A.A., Stephens Coll., 1960; B.A., U. Okla., 1963. Editor Hallmark Cards, Kansas City, Mo., 1963-67; freelance editor/writer, Mpls., 1967-68, Balt., 1968-72, Richardson, Tex., 1972—; co-chmn. Tex. Experience, 1981-83, editor, 1981—. Editor: New Comic Limericks, 1967; (cookbook) The Texas Experience, 1982; contbr. articles to newspapers and mags. Mem. adminstrv. bd. 1st United Methodist Ch., Richardson, 1984—; chmn. Jr. Gt. Books, Richardson, 1976-81. Recipient Vol. Service award Girl Scouts U.S.A., Richardson, 1978. Mem. Women in Communications (scholar 1981), AAUW (membership award 1980). Republican. Clubs: Richardson Reviewers (sec. 1977-78), Newcomers (chairperson 1973-75), Richardson Woman's (pres. 1984). Home: 1305 Comanche Richardson TX 75080

DENNIS, JUANITA, microbiologist; b. New Orleans, June 2, 1929; d. Lawrence Alphonse and Brunetta (Williams) Dennis; B.A., Dillard U., 1951; Cert. in Med. Tech., U. Calif., San Francisco, 1954; Med. technologist Kaiser Found. Hosp., Oakland, Calif., 1954-55; microbiologist virology Viral and Rickettsial Diseases Lab., State Dept. Health Services, Berkeley, Calif., 1955—, supr., 1981—. Mem. Am. Soc. Microbiology, No. Calif. Assn. Am. Soc. Microbiologists, No. Calif. Assn. Public Health Microbiologists, Profl. Photographers of Am., Calif. Inventors Council. Contbr. articles to profl. jours. Patentee in field. Home: 1225 Derby St Berkeley CA 94702 Office: 2151 Berkeley Way Berkeley CA 94704

DENNIS, LOUISE AMANDA-COOK, food service company executive; b. Tallahassee, July 23, 1943; d. Appie and Addie (Patrick) Cook; B.S. in Instn. Mgmt., Fla. A&M U., 1967; M.S. in Nutrition, Howard U., 1972; postgrad. Howard U., 1973; m. Solomon Dennis, Dec. 31, 1961; children—Deborah, Darrick. Therapeutic dietitian Jacobi Hosp., N.Y.C., 1967-68; food service mgr. Howard U., 1968-74; food service dir. Saga Food Corp., Washington Crossing, Pa., 1974-80, also affirmative action rep.; spl. asst. to pres. Food Mgmt. Concepts, Atlanta, 1980-83, exec. v.p., 1983—; pres. Quality Food Service Inc., Atlanta, 1984—. Mem. Am. Dietetic Assn., Omicron Nu. Mem. African Methodist Episcopal Ch. Home: 3940 Andrews Crossings Roswell GA 30075 Office: PO Box 18580 Atlanta GA 30326

DENNIS, LYNETTE COLLEEN, contract administrator; b. Des Moines, Aug. 27, 1946; d. Benjamin W. and Vernette L. (Ronnenberg) D.; children—Eric Marshall, Jason Robert. B.S., N.W. Mo. State U., 1968; M.A., Antioch Sch. Law, Washington, 1985. Notary public. Ct. services Fairfax County sheriff, Va., 1978-80; adminstrv. mgr. Tech. Applications, Falls Church, Va., 1980-81; contract adminstr. Advanced Tech., Reston, Va., 1981-83; sr. contract analyst Maxfield Assocs. Ltd., Arlington, Va., 1983-85; sr. contract planner Wheeler Industries, Arlington, 1985—. Adminstr., Glenside Counseling Ctr., Glendale Heights, Ill., 1976-77. Mem. Profl. Women's Network, Innsiders, AAUW. Avocations: furniture and house restoration; investments. Home: 10201 Commonwealth Blvd Fairfax VA 22032

DENNIS, SHIRLEY MAE, state official; b. Omaha, Feb. 26, 1938; d. Millard and Iantha (Hall) Haynes; m. William D. C. Dennis, Dec. 28, 1968; children—Pamela, Robin, Sherrie. Student Cheyney (Pa.) State Coll., 1955-56, Real Estate Inst., Phila., 1959, Am. Inst. Planners, 1970; A.S. in Bus. Adminstrn., Temple U., 1985; LL.D., Lincoln U., 1986. Sales and office mgr. Tucker & Tucker, Phila., 1961-67; equal opportunity specialist Redevel. Authority, Phila., 1967-68; housing dir. Urban League Phila., 1968-71; mng. dir. Housing Assn. Delaware Valley, Phila., 1971-79; exec. dep. sec. Pa. Dept. Community Affairs, Harrisburg, 1979, sec., 1979—; chairperson Pa. Housing Fin. Agy., Harrisburg, Pa., 1979—; mem. exec. bd. council State Community Affairs, Washington, 1980—; exec. com. Nat. State Housing Fin., Washington, 1982—; co-chairperson Phila. Housing Task Force, 1978. Mem. Coalition of 100 Black Women, Phila., 1982, Abington (Pa.) Meml. Hosp., 1982; bd. mem. Abington Health Care Corp., 1983; mem. Phila. Tribune Charities, 1978; mem. Nat. Leadership Conf./Women in State Govt., 1983—; mem. Gov.'s Econ. Devel. Com. of Cabinet, 1980—; chmn. Pa. Martin Luther King, Jr. Holiday Commn.; mem. Gov.'s Human Resources Com., 1980—; mem. Pa. Indsl. Devel. Authority, 1979—. Recipient Community Service award Nat. Assn. Negro Bus. and Profl. Women, 1981; Pub. Service award Pa. Fedn. Bus. and Profl. Women's Club, 1980; Leadership award Phila. Tribune Charities, 1977. Republican. Baptist. Club: Couples (Willow Grove, Pa.) (treas. 1980-82). Home: 1656 Easton Rd Willow Grove PA 19090 Office: Dept Community Affairs Room 317 Forum Bldg Harrisburg PA 17120

DENNISTON, MARJORIE MCGEORGE, educator, travel slide lecturer; b. Coraopolis, Pa., Mar. 21, 1913; d. Chauncey Kirk and Elsie (George) McGeorge; m. Delbert Dicks Denniston, Dec. 25, 1942 (dec. 1973); 1 child, Robert Bruce. Student Ohio U., 1931-33; B.A., Westminster Coll., 1936; postgrad. U. Kans., 1959, Western Ill. U., 1962, 64. Elem. tchr. county schs., West Pittsburg, Pa., 1936-42, New Castle Sch. System, Pa., 1942, 51-78; vol. aid Pa. Assn. Retarded Children, Jameson Hosp., Law County Home, 1983—. Mem. AAUW, Delta Kappa Gamma. Republican. Presbyterian. Club: Woman's (parliamentarian 1984—). Avocations: photography; coin and rock collecting. Home: 331 Laurel Blvd New Castle PA 16101

DENNISTON, PAMELA BOGGS, financial consultant; b. San Diego, Feb. 15, 1948; d. Warren Leo and Edna Mae (Hippensteel) Boggs; m. John Henry Cynkar, July 26, 1969 (div. 1973); m. Warren Kent Denniston Jr., Mar. 20, 1980; step children—Julie, Warren, Edward, Scott. A.A., Coll. DuPage, 1984; B.A. in Applied Behavioral Sci., Nat. Coll. Edn., 1985. Sales cons. ARA Services, Des Plaines, Ill., 1977-78; regional sales mgr. Canteen Corp., Chgo., 1978-79; nat. mktg. mgr. Borg-Warner Leasing, Schaumburg, Ill., 1979-81; owner, cons. Adv. Mgmt. Systems, Downers Grove, Ill., 1981—; vol. Borg-Warner, Schaumburg, 1981—; owner, mgr. Boggs Homemade Ice Cream Shoppe, Downers Grove, 1980—. Cons. Downers Grove C. of C., 1981—; mem. planning Commn. Village of Downers Grove, 1984—; vol. Indian Boundary YMCA, Downers Grove, 1981—. Republican. Club: Downers Grove Republican Women. Avocations: travel; sailing; camping; hiking. Home: 234 4th St Downers Grove IL 60515 Office: Adv Mgmt Systems 52 N Fullerton Glendale Heights IL 60139

DENNO, ZETTA LEE, social services administrator; b. Pueblo, Colo., Apr. 22, 1943; d. Clarence Loyd P. and Myrtle Louise (McFerren) Bewley; m. Robert E. Everhart, Feb. 13, 1965 (div. 1975); children—Tod Alan, Shelly Anne, Karen Marie; m. Roy Joseph Denno, Aug. 12, 1977; stepchildren—Roy Scott, Randy Michael. Student Columbia Pacific U. Youth dir. Rochester YWCA, N.Y., 1972-81; youth employment specialist Genesee Settlement House, Rochester, 1981-82, family services coordinator, 1982—. Bd. dirs. Twelve Corners Day Care Ctr., Rochester, 1978—, Parents Anonymous of Rochester; co-chmn. adv. com. Monroe County Blue Cross, 1983—. Mem. Nat. Assn. Female Execs., Nat. Assn. Edn. Young Children. Club: Altrusa. Home: 930 Garden Ln Webster NY 14580 Office: Genesee Settlement House Inc 10 Dake St Rochester NY 14605

DENNY, BONNIE ELIZABETH, banker; b. Shelby County, Ind., May 16, 1935; d. James Albert and Valeria Ethel (Gregory) Kelley; student public schs.; m. Billy Denny, Sept. 25, 1953. With State Bank of Waldron (Ind.), 1953-85, asst. cashier, 1974-78, asst. v.p., 1978-85; asst. v.p. Central Ind. Bank N.A., 1985—. Democrat. Baptist. Home: Box 92 Waldron IN 46182 Office: Box 7 Waldron IN 46182

DENNY, JUDITH ANN, lawyer; b. Lamar, Mo., Sept. 18, 1946; d. Lee Livingston and Genevieve Adelpha (Falke) D.; B.A., La. Tech. U., 1968; J.D., George Washington U., 1972; m. Thomas M. Lenard, May 29, 1976; children—Julia Lee, Michael William. Bar: D.C. 1973. Asst. spl. prosecutor Watergate Spl. Prosecution Office, Washington, 1973-75; pros. atty. U.S. Dept. Justice, 1975-78; dir. div. compliance U.S. Office Edn., HEW, 1978-80; acting asst. insp. gen. for investigations U.S. Dept. Edn., 1980; dep. dir. policy and compliance, office of revenue sharing U.S. Dept. Treasury, Washington, 1980-83, counselor to gen. counsel, 1983—. Mem. D.C. Bar Assn., Fed. Bar Assn. (dep. chmn. com. on fed. liaison for law enforcement agys. 1984). Home: 3214 Porter St NW Washington DC 20008 Office: 15th and Pennsylvania Ave NW Washington DC 20220

DENNY, SANDRA LEE, account executive; b. Pensacola, Fla., Aug. 13, 1945; d. Ceylon Edwin and Marjorie (Stilphen) Harry; m. Bill Elderkin, June 6, 1965 (div. Apr. 1978); children—Pamela, Angela, Amy; m. 2d, Clark Allen Denny, Apr. 11, 1980. Student pub. schs., Niagara Falls, N.Y. Owner, Reeds Sporting Goods Co., Kalispell, Mont., 1968-74; br. mgr. Mont. Auto Assn., Kalispell, 1974-76; asst. br. mgr. Budget Fin. Co., Kalispell, 1976-78; br. bank mgr. Credithrift, Denver, 1978-83; account exec. Citicorp, Denver, 1983—; real estate and multi-lines ins. broker, 1983—. Leader, Girl Scouts U.S.A., Colo., 1968-80; bd. dirs. March of Dimes, Kalispell, 1973-78; sec. Bus. and Profl. Women, Golden, Colo., 1979-80. Republican. Home: 317 Ford St Golden CO 80401 Office: Citicorp 1675 Larimer Denver CO 80202

DENNY, SUANNE EMILY, medical technologist; b. Rochester, N.Y., Feb. 27, 1947; d. Crawford Alfred and Doris Catherine (Coventry) D.; A.A.S., Rochester Int. Tech., 1967, B.S., 1969; cert. med. tech. St. Mary's Sch. Med. Tech., 1969; postgrad. U. Rochester Med. Sch., 1972, 74, 76, 80. Staff technologist St. Mary's Hosp., Rochester, 1969-70; technologist Soldiers and Sailors Meml. Hosp., Penn Yan, N.Y., 1970-78, sr. technologist, 1978-80, supr. hematology and blood bank dept., asst. lab. supr., 1980-84; technologist, sr. hematologist Animal Reference Labs., Houston, 1984—; instr. Finger Lakes Shared Edn. and Tng. Program; cons. technologist Rushville Community Clinic; instr. Keuka Coll. Active Career Day programs Penn Yan Acad., 1976-80; mem. youth com. Penn Yan Area Council of Chs., 1974; deacon 1st Presbyn. Ch., Penn Yan, 1977-80, ruling elder, 1983-84. Mem. Am. Soc. Med. Tech., Tex. State Soc. Med. Tech., Am. Soc. Clin. Pathologists (registered med. technologist, specialist in hematology), World Wildlife Fund (charter mem.), Animal Protection Inst. Am., Defenders of Wildlife, Greenpeace, Seal and Whale Rescue Funds, Nat. Humane Edn. Soc., Internat. Fund Animal Welfare, African Wildlife Leadership Fund, Center for Environ. Edn., Nat. Cert. Agy. for Med. Lab. Personnel, Alpha Sigma Alpha. Democrat. Home: 1011 S Kansas La Porte TX 77571 Office: 722 W 19th St Houston Tx

DENSMORE, ANN, writer, speech pathologist/audiologist, fundraiser; b. Los Angeles, Nov. 24, 1941; d. Ray B. and Margaret M. (Walsh) D.; B.S. cum laude, UCLA, 1963; M.A. in Communicative Disorders, Calif. State U., 1975; student Cape Cod Conservatory of Arts, 1977-79, Harvard U./Radcliffe Coll. graphics-architecture program, 1980—; children—Kristin Ann, Jennifer Ann. Tchr., Santa Monica (Calif.) Unified Sch. Dist., 1973-74; speech pathologist Kennedy Child Study Center, 1975-76; audiologist VA Hosp. Sepulveda, Calif., 1976-77, New Eng. Rehab. Hosp., Woburn, Mass., 1978; audiology cons. Wellesley (Mass.) Public Schs., 1979; speech pathologist Framingham (Mass.) Public Schs., 1979; speech pathologist and audiologist The Learning Center for Deaf Children, Framingham, 1978-80; dir. ann. fund Babson Coll., 1981-83;

asst. dir. devel. Lakey Clinic Med. Ctr., 1984-86; assoc. dir. corp. relations Harvard Med. Sch., 1986—; free-lance photographer, 1979—; exhibited photographs Copley Soc. of Boston, 1979-80. Lic. speech pathologist and audiologist Calif. Mem. Am. Speech and Hearing Assn. (cert. speech pathologist-audiologist), Artists Assn. of Nantucket, Copley Soc. of Boston. Episcopalian. Home: 9 Roanoke Wellesley MA 02181 Office: 4 Mall Rd Burlington MA 01805

DENSON, WAVA LUCENE, newspaper pub., comml. printer; b. Seiling, Okla., June 2, 1920; d. William Frederick and Edith Woodward (Clark) Spies; student Seiling public schs.; m. W.W. Denson, Feb. 12, 1939; 1 son, Jerry Lynn. With Gage (Okla.) Record, 1939—, co-owner, pub., 1946-74, owner, pub., 1974-82; co-owner, pub. Ellis County Capital, 1953-74, owner, pub., 1974-82; reporter Ellis County election news Daily Oklahoman, 1975-82. Recipient cert. of appreciation for community service Young Jaycees, 1975, cert. Okla. State Election Bds., 1978. Mem. Okla. Press Assn., Gage Women's Research Club (pres. 1947-48), Am. Legion Aux. Democrat. Mem. Ch. of Christ. Home: 115 N Madison St Arnett OK 73832 Office: 323 E Renfrow St Arnett OK 73832

DENTON, EMMA MANEY, banker; b. Hiawassee, Ga., Nov. 25, 1905; d. Milton M. and Missouri (Eller) Maney; student pvt. schs., Hiawassee; m. James Young Denton, May 20, 1920 (dec. Jan. 1982); children—J.C., Evelyn Isabel Denton Groves, Ruth Elois Denton Anderson, J. William, Emma Jean Denton Anderson. Assoc. cashier Bank of Hiawassee, 1936-70, cashier, 1970—, dir., 1950—. Chmn. county drive Am. Cancer Soc., 1944-60; flower show judge. Recipient Service award Am. Cancer Soc., 1977; Emma Denton Day, Bank of Hiawassee, 1979; awards flower shows. Mem. DAR, Friendship Community Club, Hiawassee Garden Club (charter mem., pres. 1960—), State Garden Club Ga. (hon. life), Nat. Council Garden Clubs (life). Baptist. Address: Bank of Hiawassee Main St Hiawassee GA 30546

DENTON, SUSAN ANN, environmental laboratory executive, chemist; b. Hot Springs, Ark., June 29, 1956; d. James Webster and Anna Laura (Phillips) Kendall; m. James Fredrick Denton, Nov. 30, 1973. Student Garland County Community Coll., 1977-79. Lab. dir. Weyerhaeuser Co., Hot Springs, Ark., 1980-86, Entek Labs., Hot Springs, 1986—. Resource vol. Nat. Park Service, Hot Springs, 1983—. Mem. Am. Chem. Soc., Assn. Ofcl. Analytical Chemists, Nat. Assn. Female Execs. Democrat. Avocations: motorcycles; cats; water sports. Home: Route 7 Box 27 Hot Springs National park AR 71901 Office: Entek Labs 875 Park Ave Hot Springs National park AR 71901

DENVER, EILEEN ANN, magazine editor; b. N.Y.C., Nov. 16, 1942; d. Daniel Joseph and Katherine Agnes (Boland) D.; B.A., Coll. New Rochelle, 1964; M.A., Ind. U., 1967. Asst. prof. English, St. Peter's Coll., Jersey City, 1967-70; asst. copy editor Am. Home Mag., N.Y.C., 1970-75; asst. editor Consumer Reports Mag., Mt. Vernon, N.Y., 1975-78, asst. mng. editor, 1978-79, mng. editor, 1979—. Mem. NOW. Office: Consumer Reports Magazine 256 Washington St Mount Vernon NY 10553

DEOGNY, B. LYNN, research biologist, laboratory executive; b. Fayetteville, N.C., May 26, 1939; d. George Woodrow and Dorothy Calleen (Phillips) Stephens; m. Donald Lee DeOgny, Feb. 8, 1961 (div. 1984); children—Stephanie Lynn, Melanie Donn, Kerri Leigh. Cytology cert. U. Okla., 1961; B.S. in Sci., Central State U., Edmond, Okla., 1966. Research biologist Okla. Med. Research Found., Oklahoma City, 1967-74, Calif. Inst. Tech., Pasadena, 1975-81; research assoc. AMGEN, Thousand Oaks, Calif., 1981-83, DNAX, Palo Alto, Calif., 1983-85; v.p. OCS Labs., Inc., Denton, Tex., 1985—; research biologist Howard Hughes Med. Inst., Dallas, 1985—; cons. pharm. cos. and labs. Contbr. article to Clinica Chemica Acta, 1974. Mem. Nat. Assn. Female Execs. Republican. Baptist. Avocations: swimming; painting; sewing; crocheting. Office: Howard Hughes Med Inst 5323 Harry Hines Blvd Dallas TX 75235

DE OLARTE, GLORIA ACOSTA, plastic surgeon; b. Cali, Colombia, July 28, 1948 (came to U.S., 1973); d. Marco T. and Blanca (Perez) Acosta; m. Felipe Olarte, May 26, 1973; 1 dau., Natalia. M.D., U. Antioquia, 1971. Diplomate: Am. Bd. Plastic Surgeons, 1980. Intern Bapt. Meml. Hosp., Houston, 1973-74; resident gen. surgery, Albany (N.Y.) Med. Ctr., 1974-77, plastic surgery, 1977-79; staff microsurgery Ralph Davis Med. Ctr., San Francisco, 1979; craniofacial Hosp. Enfants Malades, Paris, 1979-80; pvt. practice plastic surgery, Pasadena, Calif., 1981—. Mem. Am. Med. Women's Assn., Am. Soc. Plastic and Reconstructive Surgery, AMA, Calif. Med. Assn. Contbr. article to profl. jours. Office: 63 N Madison Ave Suite 606 Pasadena CA 91101

DEOLIVEIRA, LOUISE MARY ANN, market research executive; b. Bklyn., Apr. 23, 1939; d. Antonio and Carmela (Fioto) DeOliveira; m. George H. Taylor, Nov. 30, 1972; (div. 1984); m. 2d, Edmund P. Klein, 1984. B.A., NYU, 1960, M.A., 1962. Field dept. supr. Trendex, Inc., N.Y.C., 1960-62; field dir. N.T. Fouriezos & Assocs., N.Y.C., 1962-70; exec. v.p. Market Facts, Inc., N.Y.C., 1970—. Mem. Am. Mktg. Assn. Democrat. Roman Catholic. Office: Market Facts Inc 605 3d Ave New York NY 10158

D'EOR-HYNES, DANIELLE DEBORAH, employment agency executive, day care firm executive; b. Watertown, N.Y., Aug. 10, 1953; d. Miles Delosse Wright and Marie Anne Jeanette (Aubin) Wright Aubin; m. Keith Crayton, Aug. 10, 1976 (div. Oct. 1980); m. Mark Francis Hynes, Jan. 3, 1981; children—Nicole Marie Hynes, Greta Colette Hynes. Student Monroe Community Coll., 1977-78, Canisius Coll., 1979-80. Lic. day care dir., Maine. Sales and repair mgr. Auto City of Buffalo, 1979-80; adminstrv. asst. Nissho-Iwai Am. Corp., N.Y.C., 1980-81, House of Three Real Estate Devel., Portsmouth, N.H., 1984-85; owner, operator FreeLance Temps-Network, Cape Neddick, Maine, 1983—, Nippersinker Licensed Day Care, Neddick, 1985—; active mem. Maine Food Program, Augusta, 1985—. Author picture book: Mommy Works, Daddy Works, 1985. Editor, mixer cassette/picture book: The Story of Whistles, 1986. Leader Rochester council Girl Scouts U.S., 1979. Mem. Nat. Assn. Female Execs. Lutheran. Avocations: rading; writing; skiing. Home and Office: Box 419 Rural Route 1 Cape Neddick ME 03902

DEPAOLIS, MARY V., health care administrator; b. Sewickley, Pa., May 12, 1944; d. Leo F. and Joanna (Loria) DePaolis; R.N. diploma Mercy Hosp., 1965; B.S. in Biology and Edn., U. Pitts., 1974, M.Ed., 1978, postgrad. 1980-82. Cert. R.N. anesthetist. Staff nurse anesthetist Children's Hosp., Pitts., 1968-72; nurse anesthetist various hosps., Pitts., 1972-74; anesthesia instr., nurse anesthetist Eye and Ear Hosp., Pitts., 1974-75; dir. U. Health Center of Pitts. Sch. of Anesthesia, 1975—; clin. asst. prof. U. Pitts. Sch. of Medicine, 1975—; vis. lectr. anesthesia and health care various nursing orgns., 1975—. Mem. adv. com. Allegheny County Bldg. Better Boards Project, 1982—; mem. Allegheny County Drug and Alcohol Planning Council, 1982-84. Recipient HEW Public Health Service award, 1974. Mem. Am. Soc. Tng. and Devel., Am. Assn. Nurse Anesthetists (edn. cons. 1981—), Pa. Assn. of Nurse Anesthetists (trustee 1975-77, mem. govt. relations com. 1981-83, pres. 1984-85), Assn. for Supervision and Curriculum Devel., Soc. of Neurosurg. Anesthesia. Contbr. articles on anesthesiology to profl. jours. Home: 2936 Strachan Ave Pittsburgh PA 15216 Office: University Health Center of Pittsburgh School of Anesthesia 3459 5th Ave Pittsburgh PA 15213

DEPAUW, LINDA GRANT, historian, educator; b. N.Y.C., Jan 19, 1940; d. Phillip and Ruth Grant; B.A., Swarthmore Coll., 1961; Ph.D., Johns Hopkins U., 1964. Asst. prof. history George Mason Coll., U. Va., Fairfax, 1964-65; spl. asst. to archivist U.S., Nat. Archives, Washington, 1965-66; asst. prof. history George Washington U., Washington, 1966-69, assoc. prof., 1969-75, prof. Am. history, 1975—; editor-in-chief, project dir. Documentary History of the First Fed. Congress, 1965-84. Woodrow Wilson fellow, 1961. Mem. Am. Hist. Assn. (Beveridge award 1964) Am. Mil. Inst., Assn. Documentary Editing, Authors Guild, Coordinating Com. on Women in the Hist. Profession, Inter-Univ. Seminar on Armed Forces and Soc., Nat. Women's Studies Assn., Orgn. Am. Historians, So. Hist. Assn., U.S. Naval Inst. Author: The Eleventh Pillar: New York State and the Federal Constitution, 1966; Founding Mothers: Women of America in the Revolutionary Era, 1975; Remember the Ladies, 1976; Seafaring Women, 1982; editor, pub. Minerva: Quar. Report on Women and the Military, 1983—. Home: 1101 S Arlington Ridge Rd Arlington VA 22202 Office: Dept History George Washington U Washington DC 20052

DEPAUW, MARY ELIZABETH, psychologist; b. Chgo., Dec. 2, 1948; d. Charles Anton and Beata Marie (Gough) Janovsky; B.S., Loyola U., Chgo., 1970; M.Ed., U. Mo.-Columbia, 1977, Ph.D., 1980; m. A. Philip DePauw, III, Sept. 6, 1969; children—A. Philip, Elizabeth B. Fin. aid asst. U. Chgo. Grad. Sch. Bus., 1972-75; student personnel intern Center for Student Life, U. Mo., Columbia, 1977-78, counselor intern Counseling Services, 1978-80; dir. counseling and career devel. St. Mary's Coll., Notre Dame, Ind., 1980—, adj. asst. prof. psychology, 1981—. Mem. Women's Assn. of S. Bend (Ind.) Symphony, 1981—; mem. aux. St. Joseph County Med. Soc., 1980—; bd. dirs. St. Joseph County Mental Health Assn., 1982—, v.p. adminstrn., 1984—; mem. bd. edn. St. Joseph High Sch., 1985—; dir. tng. Abuse Assault and Rape Crisis Center, Columbia, 1978-79. Mem. Am. Psychol. Assn., Ind. Psychol. Assn., Am. Assn. Counseling and Devel., Am. Coll. Personnel Assn., AAUW, Phi Delta Kappa, Phi Mu., U. Mo. Alumni Assn. Roman Catholic. Author: (with Robert Callis, Sharon K. Pope) Ethical Standards Casebook, 3rd edit., 1982. Contbr. articles to profl. jours. Home: 52817 Brookdale Dr South Bend IN 46637 Office: 165 LeMans Hall Saint Marys Coll Notre Dame IN 46556

DEPETRIS, JACQUIE KAYE, security supervisor, consultant; b. Pasco, Wash., July 1, 1951; d. Steven Albert Babick and Doris Maxine (Harlan) Merriman; m. Brian Copeland McDonald, Dec. 7, 1970 (div. 1972); m. Michael Lyn Mashburn, Apr. 6, 1978 (div. 1984); 1 child, Kara Nadine; m. Dana Preston DePetris, Aug. 4, 1984. Student Foothill Coll., U. San Francisco, 1981—, DeAnza Coll. Microfilm/audit clerk Wash. Pub. Supply System, Richland, 1978-80; personnel sec. Crystal Technology, Inc., Palo Alto, Calif., 1980-82; office sec./receptionist Skyles Elec. Works, Mt. View, Calif., 1982; adminstrv. aide security GTE Communications, Mountain View, 1982-84; security supr. Systems Control Technology, Inc., Palo Alto, 1984—; indsl. specialist A&J Cons., Palo Alto, 1984—. Team mgr. Bay Area Womens Soccer League, 1982-83. Mem. Nat. Classification Mgmt. Soc., Nat. Assn. Female Execs. Democrat. Avocation: soccer. Office: Systems Control Technology Inc 1801 Page Mill Rd PO Box 10180 Palo Alto CA 94303

DE PÍNERO, EUROPA GONZÁLEZ GARRIGA (MRS. JOSE A. DE PINERO), educator; b. Aguadilla, P.R., Feb. 1, 1918; d. Juan C. Gonzalez Giocoechea and Maria Garriga Chacon; B.A. in Edn., U. P.R., 1938, profl. diploma, 1954; M.A. in Edn., N.Y.U., 1956, Ed.D., 1965; J.D., Inter-Am. U. P.R., 1978; m. Jose A. de Pinero, Dec. 23, 1939 (dec.); children—Jose Juan, Luis Roberto, Europa Maria de Pínero del Valle, Imgard L. Tchr. elementary, jr. and high schs., prin. P.R. Dept. Pub. Instrn., 1938-58, asst. supt., supt. schs., 1960-65; instr. edn., supr. students U. P.R., 1958-60; prof., chmn. dept. edn. Inter Am. U. P.R., Hato Rey, 1966-70, dean acad. affairs, 1970-73, prof. grad. studies Sch. Edn., 1974—. Mem. cons. com. for devel. vocat. and tech. edn. P.R. Dept. Edn.; cons. P.R. Dept. Sch. Prins., 1968—; mem. sch. bd., pres. acad. com. Caribbean Consol. Schs. P.R., 1967-69. Recipient awards for outstanding edni. work. Mem. Am. Assn. Colls. Tchr. Edn. (Distinguished Achievement award 1969), Assn. for Supervision and Curriculum Devel., Assn. for Childhood Edn. Internat., Am. Assn. for Higher Edn., Nat. Inst. for Advanced Study in Teaching Disadvantaged, Nat. Assn. for Edn. Young Children, Nat. Home Study Council, Am. Acad. Polit. and Social Sci., NEA (life), Tchrs. Assn. P.R., Am. Assn. U. Profs., N.Y. U. Alumni Assn. P.R. (past pres.). Author: Tendencias Ideas Pedagogicas: Su Aplicacion en Puerto Rico, 1971; Accountability and Change in Education, 1972; Schools in Transition, 1973; El Director de las Escuelas Publicas de Puerto Rico; Sus Problemas, Intereses y Necesidades, 1973; Del Quehacer Educativo Puertorriqueno, 1974; Evaluación del Maestro, Sistema de Mérito: Relación con el Derecho Administrativo, 1978; contbr. articles to ednl. jours. Home: 372 R Lamar St Hato Rey PR 00918

DEPTULA, ELAINE SHIRLEY, computer software company executive; b. Chgo., June 25, 1941; d. Thaddeus Augusta Dabrowski and Charlotte Mary (Drake) Dabrowski Gaiauskas; m. Leonard Francis Deptula, Nov. 26, 1960 (div. May 1975); children—Renee, Gina, Leonard. Student Moraine Valley Coll., 1980—. Cert. ins. broker, real estate agt., notary pub., Ill. Agt. Van Dale Realty, other real estate firms, Chgo. area, 1974—; loan asst. Bridgeview Bank & Trust Co. (Ill.), 1975-76; exec. sec. Evans Products, Chgo., also Oak Brook, Ill., 1976-79; exec. sec. Pansophic Systems, Oak Brook, 1979-80, nat. accounts coordinator, 1980-82, publs. supr., 1982—. Mem. Soc. for Tech. Communications. Republican. Roman Catholic. Office: Pansophic Systems Inc 709 Enterprise Dr Oak Brook IL 60521

DEPUE, BOBBIE LEE, soft drink company executive, consultant; b. Cooper, Tex., July 22, 1938; d. Carl Benson and Mary Mozelle (Gatlin) Hewitt; m. Ronald Earl DePue, Nov. 12, 1954; children—Michael Allen, David Anthony, Gregory Scott. B.A. in Bus. Mgmt., Prescott Coll., Ariz., 1985. Food service sales mgr. Pepsi Cola Bottling Group, Phoenix, 1978-79; dist. sales mgr. Pepsi Cola Co., Ariz., N.Mex., Nev., West Tex., 1979-82, div. devel. mgr., western div., Phoenix, 1982—. Mem. Corp. Bus. and Profl. Women, Nat. Assn. Female Execs. Republican. Home and Office: 326 E Paradise Ln Phoenix AZ 85022

DERBY, ANNE RAFTERMAN, biomedical engineer; b. N.Y.C., Feb. 1, 1949; d. Nathan Joseph and Phyllis Fannie (Kerner) Rafterman; A.B., Barnard Coll., 1969; M.S., Columbia U. Sch. Engring. and Applied Scis., 1971; m. Jeffrey Haskell Derby, Sept. 13, 1970; children—Nina Rafterman, Suzanne Rafterman. Clin. engr. dept. surgery Bronx (N.Y.) VA Hosp., 1971-75; chief bio-med. engring. Bronx VA Med. Center, 1975-81; dep. dir. facilities engring. service Nat. Insts. Environ. Health Scis., NIH, Research Triangle Park, N.C., 1981-84; dir. hosp. computer info. services Rex Hosp., Raleigh, N.C., 1984-85; product mgr. Atwork Corp., Chapel Hill, N.C., 1986—; asst. in surgery Mt. Sinai Sch. Medicine, CUNY, 1973-82; cons. hosp. planning, biomed. engring. Adv. council Girl Scouts U.S.A. NSF fellow, 1964-65; VA research fellow, 1973-76. Mem. N.Y. Acad. Scis., IEEE, Assn. Advancement Med. Instrumentation. Democrat. Jewish. Contbr. articles to profl. jours., 1972—. Office: Atwork Corp 700 Eastowne Dr Chapel Hill NC 27514

DERBYSHIRE, G. LOUISE, histotechnologist; b. Lowell, Mass., Apr. 6, 1925; d. William W. and Gerturde (Sherlock) Greene; m. Frederick Merrill Derbyshire (dec. Oct. 1981); 1 child, Leslie Lake; 1 stepdau., Nancy Chase. Cert., New Eng. Sch. Art, 1948, Mass. Sch. Physiotherapy, 1945; B.A., Rivier Coll., N.H., 1973. Med. technologist Hale Hops., Haverhill, Mass., 1945-46, St. John's Hosp., Lowell, 1946-48; med. tech. supr. Cushing VA Hosp., Framingham, Mass., 1948-52; histotechnologist and supr. St. John's Hosp., 1955—; real estate assoc. Foster & Foster, Chelmsford, Mass., part-time, 1985—. Mem. Tyngsboro-Dunstable Hist. Soc., Am. Soc. Clin. Pathologist, Nat. Soc. Histotechnologists (charter), Mass. Soc. Histotechnologists (charter), Greater Lowell Bd. Realtors. Republican. Episcopalian. Clubs: Samaritins. Avocations: quilting; sewing; color and design. Office: St John's Hosp Lowell MA 01852

DERDARIAN, CHRISTINE ANNE, lawyer; b. Highland Park, Mich., Aug. 30, 1948; d. Samuel and Mae Margaret (Mikjian) D. B.A. in Sociology, U. Mich., 1970; J.D., Detroit Coll. Law, 1973. Bar: Mich. 1973. Sole practice, Detroit, 1974; asst. atty. gen. Mich. Dept. Atty. Gen., Lansing, 1974-80, sr. specialist, asst. atty. gen., Detroit, 1980-85, asst. in charge labor div., Lansing, 1985—. Bd. dirs. Internat. Inst. Met. Detroit, 1980—, v.p., 1984-86, pres., 1986—. Mem. ABA, Am. Trial Lawyers Assn., Young Lawyers Council, State Bar Mich. (dir. 1981-83, communications com. 1982—), Mich. Women's Forum. Democrat. Club: Women's Econ. of Detroit (pres. 1984-85). Home: 6952 Sandalwood Dr Birmingham MI 48010 Office: Mich Dept Atty Gen 1st Floor Plaza One Bldg Lansing MI 48913

DEREBERY, VIRGINIA JANE, occupational medicine physician; b. San Angelo, Tex., Jan. 9, 1953; d. Jean Carlat and Jacqueline (Nodler) D.; m. William Hershey Tullis, Feb. 28, 1982. Student U. Okla., 1974, M.D., 1978. Diplomate Nat. Bd. Med. Examiners. Intern, Mercy Med. Ctr., Denver; resident in occupational medicine U. Cin. Sch. Medicine; dir. Holly Health Services, Denver, 1979-82; dir. occupational medicine dept. Merced County Med. Ctr., Calif., 1982—; med. dir. Phoenix Alcohol Treatment Unit, Merced, 1983—; council mem. Commn. Pub. Health, Denver Med. Soc., 1981-82; bd. dirs. St. Joseph Hosp. Occupational Med. Council, 1981-82. Contbr. articles to profl. jours. Mem. Am. Occupational Medicine Assn., Western Occupational Med. Assn. (del. 1983), Merced County Med. Soc. Republican. Home: 3906 Glengarry Austin TX 78731 Office: Merced Community Med Center 301 E 13th St Merced CA 95340

DE RIEMER, JANE THOMPSON, market research company owner, consultant; b. York, Pa., Apr. 27, 1919; d. Theodore Gregg and Gladys Ruth (Dickey) Thompson; m. James Dorman Carty, Sept. 30, 1944 (dec. Oct. 1945); m. 2d, William Breckinridge DeRiemer, May 26, 1956; children—Lysbet True, Jan Gregg, Peter Breckinridge. B.S., Drexel U., 1941. Owner, analyst J. DeRiemer Assocs., Inc., Wilmington, Del., 1969—. Bd. dirs., chmn. pub. relations Mental Health Assocs., Wilmington; bd. dirs., co-founder, state coordinator Reach to Recovery, Am. Cancer Soc. Del., recipient Terese Lasser award, 1982. Mem. Am. Mktg. Assn., Mktg. Research Assn., Wilmington Women in Bus. (chmn. 1983—). Republican. Episcopalian. Clubs: Country, Rodney Square (Wilmington). Home: Box 187 RD 3 Hockossin DE 19707 Office: Jane DeRiemer Assocs Inc 4003 Kennett Pike Wilmington DE 19807

DERINGER, MARIA AGUILA, real estate executive, accountant; b. Havana, Cuba, July 6, 1954; arrived in U.S., 1960, naturalized, 1968; d. Rafael Aguila and Gloria (Azcuy) Fisher; m. Delio Diaz, Nov. 16, 1973 (div.); m. Don Deringer, Dec. 23, 1983. B.B.A., U. Miami, 1974. Controller, Adminstrv. Planning Group, Inc., Miami, 1974-75; sr. acct. Hurdman & Cranstoun C.P.A., Miami, 1975-77, Arazoza, Gravier & Co., PA, Coral Gables, Fla., 1978-80; controller, treas. Cobra Internat. N.V., Inc., Pompano Beach, Fla., 1981—; pres. D&M Investment Group Inc., Pompano Beach, 1983—. Mem. Nat. Assn. Female Execs. Democrat. Roman Catholic. Office: Cobra International NV Inc 4933 NW 11th Ave Pompano Beach FL 33064

DERIVERA, DOROTHY PEARL BEHM, librarian; b. Libertyville, Ill., Mar. 1, 1922; d. Michael L. and Erma Cora (Dryer) Behm; B.A., Mundelein Coll., 1946; M.Ed., Northeastern Ill. U., 1970; postgrad. U. Americas, Mexico City, 1955, U. Ariz., 1957, Tex. Western U., 1961, Northeastern N.Mex. U., 1962; m. James Enriquez de Rivera, Apr. 22, 1946; children—Sue Anne DeRivera Foss, Charles, Michael, James, John. Owner gift shop, Libertyville, 1944-48; story lady, sta. mgr. KNOG, Nogales, Ariz., 1953-55; producer, master of ceremonies Internat. Variety Show, KOPO-TV, Tucson, 1954-55; radio and TV columnist Nogales Herald, 1954-55; tchr. elem. sch., Nogales, 1956-59, El Paso, Tex., 1959-62, Walker AFB, Roswell, N.Mex., 1962-63, Deerfield, Ill., 1963-68; elem. sch. librarian, audiovisual coordinator Deerfield Pub. Schs., 1968-74, Cadwell Elem. Sch., Deerfield, 1968-76, Maplewood Elem. Sch., Deerfield, 1976—. Mem. NEA (life), Ill. Edn. Assn., Nat. Council Tchrs. English, Internat. Reading Assn., ALA, Chgo.-Suburban Audiovisual Roundtable, Chgo. Council Fgn. Relations, Ill. Librarians Assn., Ill. Assn. Sch. Librarians, Ill. Audiovisual Assn. for Ednl. Communications, Deerfield Hist. Soc. (dir. 1969-72), Deerfield Tchrs. Assn. (charter mem., pres. 1967-68, dir. 1963-67, social chmn. 1972-73), United Ostomy Assn. (exec. bd. Highland Park chpt. 1978—, newsletter editor 1978—, v.p. 1980-81, pres. 1981-82), Mundelein Coll. Alumnae Assn. (mem. governing bd. 1971-74, rep. to Internat. Fedn. Cath. Alumnae 1973-74), Alpha Tau Omega Parents Assn. at U. Iowa (pres. 1970-71), Cath. Daus. Am., Alpha Delta Kappa. Roman Catholic. Home: 509 Willow Ave Deerfield IL 60015 Office: 1321 Wilmot Rd Deerfield IL 60015

DERKSEN, CHARLOTTE RUTH MEYNINK, earth sciences librarian; b. Newberg, Oreg., Mar. 15, 1944; d. John Philip and Wanda Marie (Rohrbough) Meynink; m. Roy Arthur Derksen, Dec. 27, 1966; children—Kathryn Marie Lesedi, Elizabeth Charlotte. B.S. in Geology, Wheaton Coll.-(Ill.), 1966; M.A. in Geology, U. Oreg., 1968, M.L.S., 1973. Faculty and librarian Moeding Coll., Ootse Botswana, 1968-70, head history dept., 1970-71; tchr. Jackson Pub. High Sch. (Minn.), 1975-77; sci. librarian U. Wis., Oshkosh, 1977-80; librarian and bibliographer Stanford U., 1980—, acting chief scis., 1985—. Author articles. Mem. ALA, Spl. Library Assn., Western Assn. Map Librarians, Geosci. Info. Soc., Cartographic Users Adv. Council (ALA rep. 1983-85, GIS rep. 1985—). Republican. Lutheran. Home: 2161 Clarke Ave East Palo Alto CA 94303 Office: Branner Earth Sciences Library Stanford U Stanford CA 94305

DEROIN, JAN ELIZABETH, lawyer; b. Beatrice, Nebr., Feb. 11, 1952; d. Glenn W. and Mary Jane (Fry) Plucknett; m. David DeRoin, Aug. 27, 1977; children—David A., Erik W. B.A. in Polit. Sci., U. Nebr., 1974; J.D., Creighton U., 1977. Bar: Nebr. 1977. Assoc. firm Mitchell & Demerath, Omaha, 1977-80; asst. trust officer First Nat. Bank Omaha, 1981—. Mem. Am. Inst. Banking, ABA, Nebr. Bar Assn., Omaha Bar Assn., Omaha Estate Planning Council. Republican. Office: First National Bank Omaha One First National Ctr Omaha NE 68102

DEROSA, MARY CATHERINE, obstetrician-gynecologist, educator; b. Utica, N.Y., Dec. 13, 1952; d. Humbert Francis and Anne Theresa (Cavallo) DeRosa. B.A. summa cum laude, Western Md. Coll., 1974; M.D., SUNY Syracuse, 1978. Resident U. Rochester (N.Y.), 1978-82. Attending physician ob-gyn Genesee Hosp., Rochester, 1982—; clin. instr. ob-gyn. Strong Meml. Hosp., U. Rochester, 1982—; cons., mem. Therapeutic Alternatives Social Abuse, Rochester, 1983; lectr. Jewish Family Services, Rochester, 1982-83. Mem. Med. Soc. State N.Y., Monroe County Med. Soc., Beta Beta Beta, Alpha Omega Alpha. Roman Catholic. Office: 220 Alexander St Rochester NY 14607

DEROSA, SUSAN JANE, trucking firm executive; b. N.Y.C., Aug. 22, 1946; d. Francis Gerard and Rita Barbara (Stegman) Reiss; m. John Anthony DeRosa, June 17, 1935; children—John, Robin. Student, Queens Coll., 1984. Electronic data processing tape librarian DeCoppet & Doremus, N.Y.C., 1963-67, Eastman Dillon Union Securities Corp., N.Y.C., 1967-70; adminstrv. asst. Barry Joel Warehouse Corp., Maspeth, N.Y., 1978—. Pres., Friendly Acres Owners Assn., Pike County, Pa., 1979-85; dir. social affairs Queens Coll., 1984—, ACE Student Assn., Flushing, N.Y., 1985—. Mem. Our Lady of the Miraculous Medal Home and Sch. Assn. Democrat. Roman Catholic. Club: Xavier High Sch. Mothers (N.Y.C.).

DEROS-DAWSON, ROSEMARY GRACE, medical malpractice investigator, nurse; b. Belfast, Ireland, Feb. 21, 1947; came to U.S., 1968, naturalized, 1980; d. Donald James Cranston and Harriet Anna (Lannon) D. S.R.N., Royal Victoria Hosp., Belfast, 1968; R.N., U.S.A.; pvt. investigator, N.Y. Staff nurse Royal Victoria Hosp., Belfast, 1968; charge nurse United Hosp., Port Chester, N.Y., 1968-71; charge nurse neurology/neurosurgery Sloan Kettering Inst., N.Y.C., 1972-78; dir. med. malpractice unit/trial preparation Compass Assocs., White Plains, N.Y., 1978-85; pres. Regency Investigations Inc., Scarsdale, N.Y., 1985—; cons. in field of med. malpractice for numerous def. law firms; guest lectr. claims dept. ins. cos. Mem. Royal Coll. Nursing, N.Y. State Nurses Assn., Am. Nurses Assn., Albany Claims Assn. Republican. Presbyterian. Home: 700 Scarsdale Ave Scarsdale NY 10583 Office: PO Box 58 H Scarsdale NY 10503

DERRICK, DEBRA LYNN, sales executive; b. Greenville, S.C., Nov. 28, 1960; d. Claude Roland and Ruth Ann (Black) D. A.A. in Fashion Merchandising, Anderson Coll., 1981; B.S. in Bus. Adminstrn., Lander Coll., 1984. Sales rep. Carolina Microfilm, Greenville, S.C., 1984-86; area sales mgr. Liberty Life Ins. Co., Greenville, 1986—. Mem. Va. League Savs. Instns. Home: 3302B Forest Edge Ct Richmond VA 23229

DERSH, RHODA E., management consultant; b. Phila., Sept. 10, 1934; d. Maurice S. and Kay (Weiner) Eisman; B.A., U. Pa., 1955; M.A., Fletcher Sch. Law and Diplomacy, Tufts U., 1956; M.B.A., Manhattan Coll., 1980; m. Jerome Dersh, Dec. 23, 1956; children—Debra Lori, Jeffrey Jonathan. Interpreter, Consul of Chile, Phila., 1954-57; teaching and staff positions Albright Coll., Reading, Pa., Mt. Holyoke Coll., Amherst Coll., 1957-64; cons., systems designer non-profit, ednl., bus. and profl. orgns., Reading, 1965—; pres., chief exec. officer Pace Inst., 1982—, Pace Mgmt., Inc., 1984—, Wordserv, Inc., 1985—; exec. dir. Public Sch. Budget Study Project, Reading, 1975-79, cons. dir., 1979—; pres., chief exec. officer Profl. Practice Mgmt. Assocs., Reading, 1977—; founder, dir. Pace Inst., Reading; chmn. Public Service Cons. Project, 1980—; writer, lectr. exec. com. Inst. Community Affairs, 1975—; chairperson Community Plan Task Force for City of Reading, 1973-75; chmn. budget allocations panel United Way, 1974-76; del. White House Conf. on Children, 1970; co-founder, pres. World Affairs Council of Reading and Berks, 1963-65; chmn. Berks County Children and Youth Com., 1958-72; bd. dirs. United Way, 1984—; chmn. program com. Leadership Berks, 1985—; active AAUW, LWV. Recipient project grant AAUW Ednl. Found., 1975-76, Outstanding Women's award Jr. League of Reading, 1974. Mem. Am. Mgmt. Assn., Am. Acad. Ind. Consultants (dir., accredited ind. cons.), Nat. Com. Citizens in Edn., Nat. Assn. Female Execs., LWV, AAUW, Berks County C. of C. (chmn. edn. com.), Pa. C. of C. (edn. com.), Am. Acad. Polit. and Social Scis., Author: The School Budget Is Your Business, 1976; Business Management for Professional Offices, 1977; The School Budget: It's Your Money, 1979; Part Time Professionals and Managers, 1979; contbr. articles to periodicals. Office: Profl Practice Mgmt Assos Suite 305 606 Court St Reading PA 19601

DE RUVO, CLAIRE CHARLOTTE KINGSBURY, university official; b. Jersey City, Feb. 18, 1930; d. Owen John, Sr. and May Gertrude (Theurer) Kingsbury; student Fresno (Calif.) City Coll., 1970-72, SUNY, Binghamton,

1979-80; children—Deborah Ann, Frederick Philip, Jr. Adminstrv. asst. Valley Regional Tng. Center, Fresno; personnel interviewer Fresno Community Hosp.; adminstrv. asst. to exec. dir. univ. aux. services SUNY, Binghamton, 1974-81, asst. to exec. dir. for adminstrv. ops., 1981—; notary public. Mem. Nat. Assn. Coll. and Univ. Food Services, Internat. Platform Assn., Am. Mgmt. Assns., Am. Soc. Public Adminstrn. (Central Valley chpt.), Nat. Assn. Coll. Aux. Services, Broome County C. of C., Nat. Restaurant Assn., N.Y. State Restaurant Assn., SUNY Aux. Service Assn. Republican. Baptist. Home: RD 1 Box 158 Harpursville NY 13788 Office: Auxiliary Campus Enterprises State U NY at Binghamton Vestal Pkwy E Binghamton NY 13901

DE SALVO, LORRAINE CONSTANCE, univ. ofcl.; b. N.Y.C., June 15, 1950; d. William Joseph and Elizabeth Agnes De S.; B.S., U. Md., 1972, para-legal cert., 1978. Personnel officer, classification analyst U. Md., College Park, 1974-75, asst. employment mgr., 1975-76, asst. benefits officer, 1976-77, asst. employment mgr., 1977-78, adminstr. personnel and facilities dept. physics and astronomy, 1978—. Mem. Shih Tzu Fanciers Greater Balt. (v.p., program chmn.), Alumni Assn. U. Md., Alpha Xi Delta Alumnae. Clubs: Nat. Capital Area Shih-Tzu, Am. Shih Tsu (ways and means com.). Editor: Palace Scrolls newsletter, 1981. Office: Dept Physics and Astronomy U Md College Park MD 20742

DESANTIS, JUDITH MARIAN, army officer; b. Hoboken, N.J., June 14, 1956; d. Irmo Mario and Julia Marie (Gialanella) DeS.; m. Kenneth John Hlavac, Sept. 5, 1976 (div. Feb. 1985); m. Harold Richard Jones, Aug. 31, 1985. Student Canisius Coll., Buffalo, 1974-76; B.S., Columbus Coll., Ga., 1979; M.B.A., Fla. Inst. Tech., 1986. Commd. 2d lt. U.S. Army, 1979; advanced through grades to capt., 1983; adjutant 3d Infantry div. Arty., Kitzingen, Ger., 1980-82; adjutant U.S.A. Trasana, White Sands Missile Range, N.Mex., 1982-84, co. comdr., White Sands Missile Range, 1984-85, adjutant logistics officer Recruiting Bn., Ft. Monmouth, N.J., 1985—. Decorated Commendation medal, Achievement medal, Parachute Wings. Mem. Assn. U.S. Army, Nat. Assn. Female execs. Democrat. Roman Catholic. Avocations: needlepoint; reading; tennis; basketball; softball. Home: 542 Shrewsbury Ave Red Bank NJ 07701 Office: US Army Recruiting Bn Bldg 295 Fort Monmouth NJ 07703

DESAUTELS, ANNE CATHERINE, market communications executive; b. Balt., Sept. 9, 1956; d. Paul Ernest and Lenora Catherine (Brennan) Desautels. B.A. cum laude, U. Md., 1978; student Goucher Coll., 1974-75; artist-in-residence Wolftrap/Am. U. Summer Acad., 1973. Supr., mdse. adjustments Woodward & Lothrop, Washington, 1979-81; officer mgr., researcher Paul Stafford Assocs., Washington, 1981-82; grad. recruiting adminstr. Strategic Planning Assocs., Washington, 1982-84; contract adminstr. Citcom Systems, Inc., Herndon, Va., 1984-85, market communications mgr., 1985—; pub. relations specialist Peabody Devel. Corp., Washington, 1985—. Com. mem. Internat. Trade Assn. No. Va., 1985—; panelist U.S. Sml. Bus. Adminstrn. Mktg. Edn. Service, 1986. Mem. C. of C. (com. mem.), Phi Beta Kappa, Phi Kappa Phi, Delta Phi Alpha. Republican. Roman Catholic. Avocations: cross country cycling; jazz; dancing; music. Home: 1 Scott Cir NW Washington DC 20036 Office: Citcom Systems Inc 13505 Dulles Technology Dr Herndon VA 22071

DESCH, CAROL ANN, librarian; b. Albany, N.Y., Oct. 11, 1952; d. Charles Orth and Viola May (Bathrick) D.; m. Paul Silverstein, July 31, 1982. B.S. in Edn., SUNY-Oneonta, 1974; M.L.S., SUNY-Albany, 1977. Reference librarian Bethlehem Pub. Library, Delmar, N.Y., 1977-79, head reference and info. services, 1979-84; asst. in library services N.Y. State Library, Albany, 1984—; cons. N.Y. State Edn. Info. Ctr. Program, Albany, 1982; advisor Regents External Degree Program, Albany, 1979-84. Contbr. articles to profl. jours. Chmn. exec. com. Capital Dist. Humanities Program, Albany, 1981-84. Margaret E. Martigoni grantee N.Y. Library Assn., 1978. Mem. ALA (alternative edn. programs sect. chmn. 1980-82, v.p. 1982-83, pres. 1983-84, PLA orgn. com. chmn. 1984-85, dir. at large exec. bd. 1985—), N.Y. Library Assn., Beta Phi Mu. Office: Bur Library Devel NY State Library State Edn Dept Cultural Edn Ctr 10th Floor Albany NY 12230

DESCHAINE, BARBARA RALPH, real estate broker; b. Syracuse, N.Y., Feb. 16, 1930; d. George John and Dora Belle (Manchester) Ralph; B.A., St. Lawrence U., 1952; postgrad. Pa. State U., 1969-72; grad. Pa. Realtors Inst., 1973; student Realtors Nat. Mktg. Inst., 1974-75; children—Olav Bernt Kollevoll, Kristan George Kollevoll, Eric John Kollevoll; m. 2d, Bernard Richard Deschaine, May 23, 1981. Salesman, Brose Realty, Easton, Pa., 1967-72, assoc. broker/mgr., 1973, broker, owner, 1974—; mem. Pa. Real Estate Polit. Edn. Com. Bd. dirs. Easton Area C. of C., 1973-79, v.p. organizational improvement, 1975-76, v.p. econ. devel., 1976-77, pres., 1977-78; mem. Greater Easton Corp. Strategy Group, 1977-78; mem. Northampton County Revenue Appeals Bd., 1984—; trustee Easton YMCA, 1984—; Mem. Eastern Northampton County Bd. Realtors (dir. 1973—, sec. 1977, v.p. 1980-81, Realtor of Yr. 1978), Bethlehem Bd. Realtors, Pa. Assn. Realtors, Nat. Assn. Realtors, Realtors Nat. Mktg. Inst., Homes for Living Network (state chmn. 1980), Nat. Assn. Female Execs., Sales and Mktg. Execs. (dir. Easton area chpt. 1976—, Disting. Sales award 1982), Phi Beta Kappa. Republican. Presbyterian. Home: 330 Paxinosa Rd W Easton PA 18042 Office: 131-133 N 4th St Easton PA 18042

DESELM, MARY ELIZABETH (BEE), county official; b. Columbus, Ohio, June 1, 1925; d. Lincoln Henry and Inez (Fultz) Hersee; m. Henry Rawie DeSelm, June 11, 1948; children—Diane DeSelm Overcast, Richard Lowell. B.S. in Nursing, Ohio State U., 1946, B.S. in Edn., 1948. Head nurse obstetrics Ohio State U. Hosp., Columbus, 1948-49; tchr. obstetrical nursing White Cross Hosp., Columbus, 1949-52; violinist Knoxville Symphony Orch., 1956-65; religious edn. dir. Tenn. Valley Unitarian Ch., Knoxville, 1965-75; squire County of Knox, Tenn., 1976-80, commr., 1980—. Pres., fin. chmn. LWV, Knoxville, 1960—; mem. Met. Planning Commn., Knox County, Tenn., 1976-80; mem. adv. com. Knoxville Women's Ctr., 1978—; mem., sec. Hist. Zoning Commn., Knox County, 1980—; mem. adv. com. Knoxville Job Corps, 1980—, Agape (Alcoholic Women), Knoxville, 1981—; pres. elect Tenn. Valley Unitarian Ch., 1985—. Recipient Annie Selwyn award Knoxville Women's Ctr., 1985. Mem. Tenn. County Commrs. Assn. (sec. 1985—). Republican. Club: Music Study (sec. 1975-76). Avocations: music; swimming; walking. Home: 424 Hillvale Turn W Knoxville TN 37919 Office: City County Bldg 400 W Main Ave Knoxville TN 37902

DE SERIO, JOSEPHINE, electronic office equipment company executive, consultant; b. Matewan, W.Va., Feb. 6, 1942; d. Arthur and Ruth (Justus) Charles; m. George Raymond DeSerio, June 15, 1963; 1 child, Sheila Ann. Gen. office clk. Twentieth Century, Norfolk, Va., summer 1959; invoice clk. J.C. Penney Co., Norfolk, 1963-65, catalog mgr., Charleston, W.Va., 1968-72; corp. sec. APD, Inc., Stanton, Calif., 1973-75; pres. DSJ Bus. Systems, Fountain Valley, Calif., 1975—. Mem. Nat. Office Machine Dealer Assn., Fountain Valley C. of C. Office: DSJ Bus Systems 11577 C Slater Ave Fountain Valley CA 92708

DESFOSSES, HELEN ROBERTA, political scientist, university official; b. Dover, N.H., Apr. 24, 1945; d. Robert Louis and Agnes Mary (Mater) D.; B.A., Mount Holyoke Coll., 1965; M.A., Harvard U., 1967; Ph.D., Boston U., 1971; 1 son, Adam Robsohn Cohn. Chmn., Soviet and East European Studies, Boston U., 1970-72; chmn. dept. govt. Emmanuel Coll., Boston, 1972-74; research fellow Harvard U. Russian Research Center, 1974-76; asso. dean Coll. Arts, Scis. and Letters, U. Mich., Dearborn, 1976-78; dean undergrad. studies and asst. v.p. acad. affairs SUNY, Albany, 1978-82, asso. v.p. research and ednl. devel., 1982-83, dir. pub. policy program, 1983-84, chmn. dept. pub. affairs and policy, 1984—; cons. Internat. Communications Agy., Fgn. Service Inst., Refugee Policy Group, Roosevelt Ctr. for Policy Studies, Forum Inst.; mem. exec. com. and bd. dir. Center for Women in Govt., 1979-83. Bd., dirs. Detroit Urban League, 1977-78, Washington Park Theatre Co., 1984—; chmn. Commn. on Peace and Justice, Diocese of Albany, 1981-85; active Albany YWCA, 1985—; bd. dirs. Mercy House, 1985—; trustee Albany Pub. Library, 1986—. NDEA fellow, 1967-70, Coretta Scott King fellow AAUW, 1969-70, Population Council fellow, 1974-75, Nat. Acad. Scis. exchange scholar, 1975, Ford Found. fellow, 1975-76, Andrew W. Mellon Found. fellow, 1980. Mem. Am. Polit. Sci. Assn., African Studies Assn., Am. Assn. Advancement Slavic Studies, ACLU (state bd. Mich. 1977-78), NAACP (legal redress com. Albany 1979-85). Democrat. Roman Catholic. Author: Soviet Policy Toward Black Africa, 1972; Socialism in the Third World, 1975; Soviet Population Policy, 1981. Office: SUNY Milne 107 135 Western Ave Albany NY 12222

DE SHAW, LINDA LEE, application specialist; b. Abington, Pa., Dec. 1, 1945; d. Roy Gilbert and Marjorie Marie (Hammer) De Shaw; m. Henry Edmund Ford, May 27, 1965 (div. 1973); m. 2d Clemens Alvin Meyer, Aug. 29, 1973 (div. 1977); m. 3d James Everett Funk, Nov. 23, 1977. B.F.A., Tulane U., 1966. Computer programmer IBM Corp., White Plains, N.Y., 1967-69, Raleigh, N.C., 1970-73, Gaithersburg, Md., 1974-76, Raleigh, 1977-80, systems engr., 1981-84, industry application specialist, 1985—; founder, mem. Triangle Area Info. Ctr. Users Group, Raleigh-Durham, N.C., 1983—. Designer, printer, illustrator: Butterflies and Boats: A Book of Poems for Children, 1966. Mem. Artspace, Inc., Raleigh, 1983-84. Mem. Nat. Fedn. Bus. and Profl. Women, Raleigh Bus. and Profl. Women's Club (chmn. young career women com. 1981, chmn. membership com. 1982), Nat. Assn. Female Execs., Alpha Delta Pi (pledge advisor 1972-73). Republican. Episcopalian. Home: Route 1 Box 149-M Youngsville NC 27596

DESHON, DIANNE ADELE, retail executive; company executive; b. Boston, Aug. 13; d. Albert Francis and Celia Adella (Fredette) D. B.S. in Bus. Adminstrn., Suffolk U., 1977, M.B.A., 1982. Mil. sales mgr. Green Shoe Mfg. Co., Boston, 1969-70; adminstrv. asst. Norfolk Corp., North Quincy, Mass., 1970-75; asst. sec. to dean bus. sch. Suffolk U., Boston, 1975-77; sr. systems analyst Boston Gas Co., 1977-84; systems devel. project mgr. Stop to Shop Cos., Inc., North Quincy, 1984—. Mem. Phi Chi Theta (v.p. profl. devel. 1978-84) Club: Altrusa. Avocations: tennis; golf; piano. Home: 14 Carruth St Quincy MA 02170 Office: Stop 6 Shop Cos Inc 1776 Heritage Dr North Quincy MA 02171

DESMOND, MURDINA MACFARGUHAP, pediatrics educator, researcher; b. Isle of Lewis, Scotland, Nov. 14, 1916; came to U.S., 1925; d. Alexander and Margaret Muir (Graham) MacFarguhan; m. James Lewis Desmond, July 10, 1948; children—Margaret Graham, James Alexander. B.A., Smith Coll., 1938; M.D., Temple U. Coll. Medicine, 1942. Diplomate Am. Bd. Pediatrics. Neonatology fellow George Washington U. Sch. Medicine, Washington, 1947-48; instr. pediatrics Baylor Coll. Medicine, Houston, 1948-53, asst. prof., 1952-62, head sect. newborn care, 1953-72, prof. pediatrics and community medicine, 1962—, dir. Meyer Ctr. for Devel. Pediatrics, 1972—. Served to lt. USNR, 1943-46. Recipient Wyeth award for pediatric research Wyeth Co., Baylor Alumnae Teaching award, 1973, S. Kalisky award Tex. Pediatric Soc., 1981. Mem. Am. Acad. Pediatrics, Am. Pediat. Soc., Soc. Pediat. Research. Office: Meyer Ctr for Devel Pediatrics Tex Childrens Hosp Tex Med Ctr Houston TX 77030

DESOMOGYI, AILEEN ADA, retired librarian; b. London, Nov. 26, 1911; d. Harry Alfred and Ada Amelia (Ponten) Taylor; immigrated to Can., 1966; B.A., Royal Holloway Coll., U. London, 1936, M.A., 1938; M.L.S., U. Western Ont., 1971; m. Leslie Kuti, Nov. 22, 1958; m. 2d, Joseph DeSomogyi, July 8, 1966. Librarian in spl. and public libraries, Eng., 1943-66; sr. instr. Nat. Coal Bd., 1957; charge regional collection S.W. Ont., Lawson Library, U. Western Ont., 1966-71; cataloger Coop. Book Centre Can., 1971; mem. staff E. York (Ont.) Public Library, 1971-74; librarian Ont. Ministry Govt. Services Mgmt. and Info. Services Library, 1975-78, Sperry-Univac Computer Systems, Toronto (Ont.) Central Library, 1980-81. Mem. ALA, Internat. Platform Assn., English Speaking Union, Canadian Orgn. for Devel. Through Edn., Royal Canadian Geog. Soc., Consumers Assn. of Can., Canadian Wildlife Fedn., Ont. Humane Soc., Internat. Fund Animal Welfare, Royal Holloway Coll. Assn., Am. Biog. Inst. (contbg. mem. nat. bd. advisors), Am. Biog. Inst. Research Assn. (dep. gov. 1986). Roman Catholic. Contbr. articles to profl. jours. Home: 9 Bonnie Brae Blvd Toronto ON M4J 4N3 Canada

DESPRES, GINA HELEN, lawyer; b. Sydney, Australia, Sept. 28, 1941; came to U.S., 1964, naturalized, 1972; d. George Alfred and Winifred Florence (Bush) Eviston; B.A. with honors (Commonwealth scholar 1960-64), U. Sydney, 1964; postgrad. (NDEA fellow 1966-68), U. Calif., Berkeley, 1965-70; J.D., UCLA, 1974; m. John Despres, Sept. 23, 1964; children—Sarah, Naomi. Bar: Calif. 1974, D.C. 1976. Atty. firm Irell & Manella, Los Angeles, 1974-75; mem. firm Caplin & Drysdale, Washington, 1976-77; with Dept. Energy, 1977-79, dir. internat. energy and energy security policy, 1978-79; counsel, tax and internat. affairs U.S. Senator Bradley of N.J., 1979—. Bd. editors UCLA Law Rev. 1973-74. Mem. D.C. Bar Assn. Author articles in field. Office: 731 Hart Senate Office Bldg Washington DC 20515

DESSASO, DEBORAH ANN, association administrative specialist, freelance writer; b. Washington, Feb. 6, 1952; d. Coleman and Virginia Beatrice (Taylor) D.; student public schs., Washington, Clk.-stenographer FTC, Washington, 1969-70; sec. NEA, Washington, 1970-72; sec. Nat. Ret. Tchrs. Assn./Am. Assn. Ret. Persons, Washington, 1972-79, assoc. adminstrv. specialist, 1979-80, adminstrv. specialist, 1980—; founding mem., sec. Andrus Fed. Credit Union, 1980. Mem. Nat. Assn. Female Execs. Mem. Worldwide Ch. of God. Home: 3052 Stanton Rd SE Washington DC 20020 Office: 1909 K St NW Washington DC 20049

DESTEIN, BEVERLEE JEAN, government official; b. Beverly, Mass., Nov. 27, 1950; d. S. Robert and Doris L. (Bennett) DeStein. B.A., Gordon Coll. summa cum laude, 1978; J.D., Vt. Law Sch., 1981; student Grove City Coll., 1969-71. Bar: Pa. 1981. TV talk show host WYTV-TV, Youngstown, Ohio, 1971-73; spl. events coordinator Strouss Dept. Stores, Youngstown, 1973-75; TV producer/dir. WPSX-TV, University Park, Pa., 1975-77; trial atty. Office of Allegheny Pub. Defender, 1981-82; TV legal contbr. WTAE-TV, Pitts., 1981-85; city magistrate City of Pitts., 1982-85; spl. asst. to dir. pub. affairs U.S. Dept. Justice, 1986—; lectr. in field. Creator, TV-Law Promotion, Law 4 You, 1984. Bd. advisors, bd. dirs. The Alcohol Recovery Ctr., Pitts., 1983-84. Mem. ABA, Pa. Bar Assn., Pa. Assn. Dist. Justices, Allegheny County Bar Assn. (pub. relations com.), AFTRA. Republican. Presbyterian. Office: US Dept Justice Office Pub Affairs Room 1213 Washington DC 20530

DETAMORE, RUTH A., personnel management specialist; b. Marion, Ind., Nov. 20, 1946; d. Ruth May Virginia (Sherman) Henderson; A.A., Ball State U., 1979, B.S. (Cecil Lagle Meml. scholar), 1982. Clk.-stenographer, FDA, HEW, Washington, 1964; sec. Lincoln Nat. Life Ins. Co., Ft. Wayne, Ind., 1964-65; clk.-stenographer ward adminstrn. VA Med. Center, Marion, 1965-69, asst. chief ward adminstrn., 1969-73, ward mgr., 1973-74, chief ambulatory care and processing, 1974-77, personnel mgmt. specialist, 1977—; mem. adv. bd. Marion Occupational Devel. Center, 1982; chmn. supervisory com. Fed. Employees Credit Union, 1981-82. Recipient profl. awards. Mem. Women in Communication, Am. Bus. Women's Assn., Female Execs. Assn., Soc. Advancement of Mgmt., Ind. State Hosp. Personnel Assn., VA Employees Assn., YWCA. Home: 112 E North H St Gas City IN 46933

DETERMAN, SHERI MAE, marketing manager; b. Dallas, June 13, 1954; d. Bruce Herbert and Norma Mae (Schumer) Verran; m. Ronald Howard Determan, Sept. 29, 1979. B.S. in Bus. Adminstrn., Calif. State U.-Northridge, 1979; M.S. in Bus. Adminstrn. and Mktg., 1982. Advt. coordinator Action Industries, Los Angeles, 1978-79; account mgr. NCR Corp., Los Angeles, 1979-82; mktg. mgr. M/D Systems, Inc., Encino, Calif., 1982—; profl. ice skater Ice Follies, toured U.S., Can., 1972-74. Recipient Wall St. Jour. award, 1979; Arco Acad. Excellence award, 1981. Mem. Beta Gamma Sigma.

DETERT-MORIARTY, JUDITH ANNE, civic worker, graphic artist; b. Portage, Wis., July 10, 1952; d. Duane Harlan and Ann Jane (Devine) Detert; m. Patrick Edward Moriarty, July 22, 1978; children—Colin Edward, Eleanor Grace. Student U. Wis.-Madison, 1970-73, U. Wis.-Green Bay, 1984—. Legis. sec., messenger State of Wis. Assembly, Madison, 1972, 74-76; casualty-property div. clk. Capitol Indemnity Corp., Madison, 1976-77; sec./credit clk. comml. credit div. Affiliated Bank of Madison, 1977-78; word processor consumer protection div. Wis. Dept. Agr., Madison, 1978; part time graphics arts composing specialist Moraine Park Tech. Inst., Fond du Lac, Wis., 1978-79; free lance artist Picas, Pictures and Promotion (formerly Detert Graphics), 1978—; prodn. asst. West Bend News, 1980-83; devel. assoc. Riveredge Nature Ctr., Inc., Newburg, Wis., 1983-84; dir. fund-raising and program devel. part time, Voluntary Action Ctr. of Washington County, West Bend, 1984-86; devel. cons. West Bend Hospice Program, 1985. Vol. activities include: Dane County vol. Udall for Pres., 1976; Washington County campaign coordinator Nat. Unity Campaign for John Anderson for Pres., 1980; Washington County ward coordinator Earl for G v., 1982; Washington County campaign chmn. Peg Leutenschlager (state senate), Washington County ward coordinator Mondale/Ferraro, 1984; publicity coordinator Wis. Intellectual Freedom. Coalition, 1981; founding exec. bd. mem., newsletter editor Moral Alternatives, Catholics for a Free Choice Wis. community contact; bd. dirs., v.p. Wis. Pro-Choice Conf., 1981-82; pres., founder People of Washington County United for Choice, 1981-83; bd. pres. Planned Parenthood of Washington County, 1984-85, newsletter editor, mem. coms., 1980-85; bd. mem. Montessori Children's House, West Bend, 1983-85, newsletter editor, com. chmn.; artist LWV Washington County, 1984-86; newsletter artist, artist Friends of Battered Women, West Bend, 1983-86. Mem. Nat. Assn. Female Execs., Women in Communications, Wis. Women's Network, Dem. Party Wis., Population Inst., NOW (newsletter editor Dane County 1977-78, coordinator Wis. state reproductive rights task force 1982-84, coordinator reproductive rights task force North Suburban Chpt., 1981-84). Avocations: Reading; hand spinning and knitting; world wide correspondence. Home: 929 Citrus Ln Cleveland WI 53015

DETJEN, NANCY, university official; b. Los Angeles, May 1, 1937; d. Claggett and Vivien V. (Gatz) Offutt; m. Ronald Dean Detjen, July 11, 1964; children—Camille, Lara, Ronald, Nicole. B.A. magna cum laude, U. So. Calif., 1958; M.A., Calif. State U.-Los Angeles, 1971; Ph.D., U. Minn., 1976. Tchr., Punahou Sch., Honolulu, 1960-61, Los Angeles City Schs., 1963-72; adminstr. Dist. 623, Roseville, Minn., 1972-78; prin. Palos Verdes High Sch., Calif., 1978-85; coordinator adminstrv. services credential program Calif. State U., Dominguez Hills, 1985—; cons. Contbr. articles to profl. jours. Trustee Little Co. of Mary Hosp., Torrance, Calif., 1984; deacon St. Peter's Presbyn. Ch., Rancho Palos Verdes, 1980-81; mem. Republican Women; mem. adv. council Calif. State U.-Dominguez Hills, 1982-85; mem. San Pedro Peninsula Wellness Adv. Council, 1980-84. Bush fellow, 1974-75; named South Bay Woman of Yr., Torrance YWCA, 1985. Mem. Nat. Assn. Secondary Sch. Prins., Palos Verdes Adminstrs. Assn. (pres.-elect 1985), Phi Beta Kappa, Phi Kappa Phi. Avocations: reading; tennis. Home: 29010 Covecrest Dr Rancho Palos Verdes CA 90274

DE TREVILLE, BRENDA CARTER, hospital marketing administrator, consultant; b. Sanford, Fla., Jan. 21, 1950; d. Jesse William and Ruby Dean (Brewer) Carter; m. Richard Haskell de Treville, June 16, 1979. A.A., U. Fla., 1970; B.A. in Communications, U. Central Fla., 1972. Sr. publicist, Walt Disney World Co., Lake Buena Vista, Fla., 1971-76; dir. pub. relations Ringling Bros. Circus World, Haines City, Fla., 1976-78; dir. corp. communications Fla. Cypress Gardens, Winter Haven, Fla., 1978-81; dir. mktg. Six Flags Stars Hall of Fame, Orlando, Fla., 1981-83; mktg. cons. Six Flags Atlantis, Hollywood, Fla., 1983; chief mktg. officer, asst. adminstr. AMI Brookwood Community Hosp. & Univ. Community Hosp., Orlando, 1983—; co-owner Image Mrkt. Group, Inc., Orlando, 1983-84; cons. in field. Contbr. articles to profl. jours. Bd. dirs. Am. Diabetes Assn., Orlando, 1984-85, Police Athletic League, Orlando, 1984-86; bd. trustees Central Fla. Leukemia Assn., Orlando, 1985, v.p., 1986—. Mem. Fla. Pub. Relations Assn. (Golden Image awards 1980, 84, 85), Am. Mktg. Assn. (v.p. 1983-85, pres. 1986—). Pub. Relations Soc. Am., Orlando C. of C. (bd. dirs. Project 2000 1984-85), Zeta Tau Alpha. Democrat. Methodist. Lodges: Order Eastern Star. Home: 8227 Tansy Dr Orlando FL 32819 Office: AMI Brookwood Community Hosp 1800 Mercy Dr Orlando FL 32808

DETTERMAN, DEBORAH ALLYNN, accountant; b. Bklyn., Oct. 3, 1951; d. Herbert Allen and Mary Eleanor (Van Ness) Wortmann.; m. Paul Eric Detterman, Oct. 26, 1985. B.S., Fairleigh Dickinson U., 1984. Actuarial supr. Bankers Nat. Life Ins. Co., Parsippany, N.J., 1969-76; staff acct. Bobst Champlain, Inc., Roseland, N.J., 1976-82; staff acct., controller Blonder-Tongue Labs., Inc., Old Bridge, N.J., 1982—. Treas., North Jersey Walk for Mankind, West Caldwell, N.J., 1980-81. Dir. youth choir Presbyn. Ch. West Caldwell, 1980-82. N.J. Soc. C.P.A.s scholar, 1982. Mem. Nat. Assn. Female Execs., Delta Mu Delta, Phi Omega Epsilon. Presbyterian. Office: Blonder Tongue Labs Inc 1 Jake Brown Rd Old Bridge NJ 08857

DETWILER, CHARLOTTE JANE, acct.; b. Cleve., Oct. 27, 1920; d. Homer and Agnes Ellen Breyley; student Bob Jones U., 1947, Western Res. U., 1953; m. Erving Detwiler, Nov. 26, 1958; children—Joel, John, David. Exec. sec. to pres. Fed. Reserve Bank, Cleve., exec. sec. to pres. Alloys & Chems., Cleve., 1952-55; personnel dir. Carlon Products, Aurora, Ohio, 1956-66; bus. mgr., treas. Cooper Chevrolet, Aurora, 1966-73; bus. mgr. Haydocy Pontiac, Akron, 1973-77; controller, treas. Aubrey McDonald Creations (and predecessor co.), Akron, 1977—, also dir. Served with USAAF, 1942-45. Mem. Credit Women's Internat. (v.P. 1980-81), Nat. Assn. Accts., Akron Credit Women's Internat. Baptist. Office: Aubrey McDonald Creations 565 Wolf Ledges Pkwy Akron OH 44311

DEUMAN, LEANNE BARNES, lawyer; b. Sault Ste. Marie, Mich., Oct. 7, 1951; d. Wayne Gordon and Anne (Welsh) Barnes; m. Gary Wayne Deuman, Apr. 25, 1981. B.A. cum laude in English Lang. and Lit., Lake Superior State Coll., 1975; J.D. cum laude, Thomas M. Cooley Law Sch., 1982. Bar: Mich. 1982. Bus. mgr. E.U.P. Mental Health Bd., Sault Ste. Marie, Mich., 1976-79; assoc. Thomas J. Veum, P.C., Sault Ste. Marie, 1982—. Trustee, First United Presbyn. Ch., 1984—. Recipient Disting. Student Alumni award T.M. Cooley Law Sch., 1982; Ga. Emery Scholar, Mich. Fedn. Bus. and Profl. Women's Club, 1979-82. Mem. Mich. Bar Assn., Mich. Trial Lawyers Assn., Women Lawyers Assn. Mich., 51st Jud. Dist. Bar Assn., NOW, Chippewa Baroque Soc., Bus. and Profl. Women's Club. Presbyterian. Address: Thomas J Veum PC 216 Ashman St Sault Ste Marie MI 49783

DEUSS, JEAN, retired librarian; b. Chgo., Dec. 6, 1922; d. Edward Louis and Harriet (Goodwin) D. B.A., U. Wis., 1944; M.S., Columbia U., 1959. Cataloger library N.Y.C. Council Fgn. Relations, 1959-61; head cataloger research library Fed. Res. Bank N.Y., N.Y.C., 1961-68, asst. chief librarian, 1969-70, chief librarian, 1970-85, ret., 1985. Book reviewer Library Jour., 1961—. Bd. dirs. U. Wis. Found., 1983—. Mem. Spl. Libraries Assn. (assoc. treas. 1967-70, pres. N.Y. chpt. 1971-72, dir. 1972-76). Episcopalian. Clubs: N.Y. Library, Archons of Colophon. Guest editor: Banking and Finance Collections, Special Collections, vol. 2, no. 3. Home: 260 W 12th St New York NY 10014

DEUTSCH, BARBARA SUSAN, cable television executive; b. Newark, Nov. 27, 1940; d. Abe and Sophia Elizabeth (Nehemkis) D.; B.A., U. Mich., 1961; M.Ed., Boston U., 1962. Head resident SUNY, Geneseo, 1962-63; asst. dean students SUNY, Cortland, 1963-65; asst. dean students U. Calif., Santa Barbara, 1965-72, adviser for sororities and fraternities, 1972-84; exec. asst. Cox Cable Santa Barbara, Goleta, Calif., 1984—; adviser Western Regional Interfrat. and Panhellenic Conf., 1979-83; cons. leadership tng. and group devel. Mem. Santa Barbara County Affirmative Action Commn., 1978-80. Mem. Assn. Frat. Advisors (exec. com., Western regional rep. 1980; v.p. projects 1981), Nat. Assn. Student Personnel Adminstrs., Order Omega, Delta Phi Epsilon (internat. exec. council), Pi Lambda Theta. Club: U. Mich. of Santa Barbara (pres., treas., sec.). Office: Cox Cable Santa Barbara 22 S Fairview St Goleta CA 93117

DEUTSCH, ELLEN SUE, lawyer,; b. Bklyn., Nov. 2, 1942; d. Norman and Betty (Newman) Kaplan; m. John G. Williams, Jan. 2, 1984; children—Scott, Adam. B.A., Antioch Coll., Yellow Springs, Ohio, 1975; J.D., Cath. U., 1977. Atty., Office of Telecommunication Policy, Exec. Office of the Pres., Washington, 1975-77, FCC, Washington, 1977-78; dir. policy analysis Dept. of Commerce, Washington, 1978-82; cons., assoc. Irwin & Deutsch, Washington, 1982-84; ptnr. Kadison, Pfaelzer, Woodard, Quinn & Rossi, 1986—; dir. fed. regulation Bell Communications Research, Inc., Washington, 1984—; cons. Telecommunications Cons. Group, Washington, 1982-85. Mem. ABA, Fed. Communications Bar Assn., D.C. Bar Assn. Office: Fletcher Heald & Hildreth 1225 Connecticut Ave NW Washington DC 20036

DEUTSCH, FLORENCE ELAYNE GOODILL, nursing administrator; b. San Diego, Aug. 1, 1923; d. George Ehrlich and Beatrice Marie (Urick) Goodill; m. Edward Thomas Deutsch, June 27, 1953 (dec.); 1 son, George Edward. B.S.N., Villa Maria Coll., 1948; diploma in nursing Evanston Hosp., Northwestern U., 1947; M.Ed., Edinboro U., 1961. Staff nurse St. Vincent Hosp., Erie, Pa., 1947; clin. instr.-supr. Hamot Med. Ctr., Erie, 1948-58, dir. edn., 1958-62, dir. Sch. Nursing, 1962-66, 69-73; exec. dir. Florence Crittenton Home, Erie, 1966-69; asst. adminstr., dir. nursing Capitol Hill Hosp., Washington, 1974-79; assoc. adminstr. profl. services Millcreek Community Hosp., 1980-82; v.p. nursing East Liverpool City Hosp. (Ohio), 1982—; lectr., cons. on nursing and nursing law. Bd. dirs., sec. Columbiana County Cancer Soc.; bd. dirs. Ohio Valley Home Health Services, 1986—. Served with USNR, 1948-53. Named Most Outstanding Nurse Erie County, 1969. Mem. Nat. League Nursing, Am. Orgn. Nurse Execs., Am. Soc. Law and Medicine, Northeast Ohio Nursing Service Adminstrs. (chmn. 1986-87), East Liverpool

C. of C., Sigma Theta Tau, Delta Kappa Gamma. Republican. Presbyterian. Editor: Penn League News, 1968-70; contbr. articles to profl. jours. Address: 13623 Ingles Ave East Liverpool OH 43920

DEUTSCH, JACKIE MERRILL, marketing communications consultant; b. N.J., June 21, 1948; d. Kenneth and Bea Demner; B.A., Upsala Coll., 1970; m. Leonard B. Deutsch, Dec. 26, 1972. Copywriter, Lennen & Newell, Advt., N.Y.C., 1970-72; copy dir. R R Advt. and Pub. Relations, Springfield, N.J., 1972-74; cotbg. editor Apt. Life mag., Des Moines, Iowa, 1974-76; pub. relations writer, Promotion Resources, N.Y.C., 1976-79; writer, producer Burson-Marsteller, N.Y.C., 1979-80; propr., creative dir. JDW &P Communications, N.Y.C., 1980-84; founder Network Resources Group, N.Y.C., 1982—; promotion mgr. Four Winds Travel, Inc., N.Y.C., 1984-86; mgr. promotion devel. Dun & Bradstreet Bus. Edn. Services, N.Y.C., 1986—. Recipient Golden Reel of Excellence award ITVA, 1982; Silver Screen award U.S. Indsl. Film, 1982. Mem. Nat. Assn. Female Execs., NOW. Address: 345 E 80th St Apt 27J New York NY 10021

DEUTSCH, NINA, concert pianist, actress; b. San Antonio, Mar. 15; d. Irvin and Freda D.; B.S., Juilliard Sch. Music; M.M.A., Yale U., 1973. Concert pianist, 1958—; rec. artist Vox Prodns.; only woman to record complete solo piano music of Charles Ives, 1976; recs. include: piano arrangement of Variations on America (Ives); freelance writer on music for N.Y. Times, UPI and mags., 1974—; music cons. Joe Franklin Show, WOR-TV, 1975—; exec. v.p. Internat. Symphony. Bd. dirs. Metzner Found. for Overseas Relief; Ft. Lee coordinator Channel 13, 1974. NEA grantee, 1977; Tanglewood fellow, 1966; recipient award for Am. music Nat. Fedn. Music Clubs, 1975; Oberlin Coll. scholar. Mem. Music Critics Assn., Author: Portrait of Clara Wreck Schumann. Home: 410 Hazlitt Ave Leonia NJ 07605

DEUTSCH, SYLVIA, municipal official; b. Bklyn., July 9, 1924; d. Nathan and Dora Schatz; m. Leon Deutsch, Dec. 21, 1946; children—Jack, Nathaniel Mark, Jeremy Joseph. A.B. cum laude, Bklyn. Coll., 1947. Exec. dir. Proportional Representation Ednl. Project, 1969-70; dir. N.Y. Met. Council, 1972-78; edn. cons. Am. Jewish Congress, 1972-78, nat. dir. field ops. and membership, 1978-81; mem. N.Y.C. Planning Commn., 1972-81, chmn. N.Y.C. Bd. Standards and Appeals, N.Y.C., 1981—. Mem. Mayor's Commn. Taxi Regulatory Issues, 1981-82; v.p., chmn. legis. com. United Parents Assns., 1967-72, chmn. orgn. dept. and high schs., 1962-67; mem. Citizens Commn. City U., 1969-71; co-founder, exec. v.p. Com. for Pub. Higher Edn., 1966-74; mem. Mayor's Commn. Status of Women, 1976-79. Named Alumna of Yr. Bklyn. Coll., 1974; recipient Community Service award NCCJ, 1976. Jewish. Office: Bd of Standards and Appeals 161 Ave of Americas New York NY 10013

DEUTZ, NATALIE RUBINSTEIN, consultant; b. Plymouth, Mass., Sept. 26; d. Louis and Lillian Rubinstein; student Simmons Coll., 1937, Modern Sch. Applied Art, 1938-40; m. Nov. 29, 1947 (dec.). Fashion buyer Wm. Filene's Sons Co., Boston, 1940-47; asst. to corp. pres. Columbia Textiles, Inc., N.Y.C., 1956-68; dir. John Robert Powers Sch., N.Y.C., 1968-72; v.p., nat. dir. fashion merchandising, dir. advt. workshop Barbizon Internat., Inc., N.Y.C., 1972-83; cons., 1983—. Mem. Fashion Group, Nat. Acad. TV Arts and Scis., Screen Actors Guild, AFTRA.

DEVEREAUX, CHARITA LEE, home economist; b. Cleve., Sept. 28, 1947; d. John F. and Elizabeth A. (Shatto) Page; B.S. in Applied Sci., Miami U., Oxford, Ohio, 1968; m. Terence H. Devereaux, May 1, 1976; children—Mary Charita, Donovan Terence. Dietitian, State of N.J., 1968-69; home economist Ohio Edison Co., 1969-77; freelance home economist, substitute tchr., Cleve., 1979—; lectr. Cuyahoga Community Coll., 1984. instr. Cuyahoga Community Coll., 1984—. Mem. Home Economists in Homemaking, Am. Econs. Assn. Home: 1514 Mayview Ave Cleveland OH 44109

DEVEREAUX, MARILYN, real estate investor and developer; b. Sewickley, Pa., Mar. 6, 1941; d. Walter Greene and Marion Margaret (Mucha) D. B.A., UCLA, 1966; M.A., U. Calif., Berkeley, 1968. Instr. Russian lang. U. Calif., Berkeley and U. Calif., Davis, 1970-73; real estate salesperson Fred Sands Realtors, Los Angeles, 1973-76; sr. v.p. constrn. Solender & Co., Inc., Los Angeles, 1977-81; ops. mgr. Merrill-Lynch Comml. Services, Los Angeles, 1981-82; real estate broker Merrill Lynch, Los Angeles, 1982—. Mem. Los Angeles Bd. Realtors, Beverly Hills Bd. Realtors, Phi Beta Kappa. Republican. Club: Los Angeles Athletic. Office: Merrill Lynch Realty 11020 San Vicente Blvd Los Angeles CA 90049

DEVERICK, BARBARA HOLSCLAW, utility ofcl.; b. Lenoir, N.C., July 20, 1924; d. Oscar H. and Mayna (Tuttle) Holsclaw; A.A. in Acctg., Nat. Sch. Commerce, 1942; student U. N.C., 1961-62, U. Mich., 1966; m. Percy Fontz Deverick, Oct. 13, 1944. With Blue Ridge Electric Membership Corp., Lenoir, 1946—, acct., 1956-59, office mgr., 1949-60, adminstrv. asst., 1960-64, mgr. organizational planning and personnel services, 1964—; interviewer Vets. Office, W.Va. U., Morgantown, 1945-46; participant central com. meeting Internat. Co-op Alliance, Copenhagen, 1978; mgmt. cons. to Jamaica Public Service Co., Kingston, 1979-80. Chmn. United Fund, Lenoir-Caldwell County, N.C., 1964-65; pres. Rural Electric Women's Task Force, 1971-73; mem. Caldwell County Bd. Edn., 1968-76, chmn., 1972-76, bd. dirs. ARC, 1963—, pres., 1968-72; bd. dirs. 4-H Devel. Assn., 1966-72, pres., 1968-70; bd. dirs. Western Piedmont Symphony, 1975-79, N.C. Agrl. Found., 1973-76; bd. dirs. Keep N.C. Beautiful, Inc., 1973—, pres., 1981-83; bd. dirs. N.C. Sch. Bd. Assn., 1973-76; trustee Caldwell Community Coll., 1964-73, sec., 1964-73; mem. central com. Internat. Coop. Alliance, 1976-80; mem. exec. com. Coop. League U.S.A., 1978-80, v.p., 1982—. Recipient Advanced Mgmt. Achievement award Nat. Rural Electric Co-op Assn., 1960, L.A. Dysart Citizenship award Lenoir-Caldwell County C. of C., 1964, State of N.C. 4-H Alumni award, 1970; named N.C. Career Woman of Yr., 1981. Mem. Am. Mgmt. Assn., Nat. Assn. Accts., Adminstrv. Mgmt. Soc., Lenoir Bus. and Profl. Womens Club. Republican. Mem. Advent Christian Ch. Contbr. numerous articles on personnel mgmt. to various profl. mags., also articles to religious publs. Home: 128 Echo Dr PO Box 522 Lenoir NC 28645 Office: 1216 Blowing Rock Blvd NE Lenoir NC 28645

DEVILLERS, JUDITH ANNE, site development company executive, interior designer; b. Columbus, Ohio, Feb. 24, 1936; d. Edmund Joseph and Rose (Renard) DeVillers. B.S., Ohio State U., 1958. Interior designer F&R Lazarus Co., Columbus, 1958-76, Keenan & Keenan, 1976-78, Environ. Designers, Inc., 1978-85; pres. Exco Co., Columbus, 1983—, INDEC Inc., 1985—. Mem. Am. Soc. Interior Designers, Builders Exchange Central Ohio. Republican. Roman Catholic. Home: 5707 Strathmore Ln Dublin OH 43017 Office: Exco Co 2047 Leonard Ave PO Box 2642 Columbus OH 43216 also INDEC Inc PO Box 16335 Columbus OH 43216

DEVINE, SHARON JEAN, lawyer; b. Milw., Feb. 27, 1948; d. George John Devine and Ethel May (Langworthy) Devine Chase; m. Curtiss Coughlin; children—Devin Curtiss, Katharine Langworthy. B.S. in Linguistics, Georgetown U., 1970; J.D., Boston U., 1975. Bar: Ohio, Colo. Staff atty. FTC, Cleve., 1975-79; asst. regional dir., Denver, 1979-82; atty. Mountain Bell, Denver, 1982-84, U.S. West Direct, 1984-85; assoc. gen. counsel U.S. West Direct, 1985—; dir. Denver Consortium, 1982-83, Ctr. for Applied Prevention, Boulder, Colo., 1982—. Contbr. article to law rev. Mem. Colo. Bar Assn., Denver Bar Assn., Colo. Women's Bar Assn. Club: Jr. League of Denver. Office: US West Direct 2500 S Havana Aurora CO 80014

DEVLIN, MARTHA RACHAL, advertising company executive; b. New Orleans, Jan. 2, 1942; d. Thomas Edward and Mary Evangeline (Carson) Rachal; m. Michael Coles Devlin, Aug. 11, 1966 (div. Nov. 1979); 1 child, Jennifer Elaine. Student Spring Hill Coll. Adminstrv. asst. to dir. blood bank, Mt. Sinai Hosp., N.Y.C., 1966-68; sec. Laury Girls, N.Y.C., 1970-72; exec. sec. to sr. v.p., gen. mgr. internat. div. Grey Advt., N.Y.C., 1972-74; exec. sec. dist. sales office Xerox Corp., Ft. Lauderdale, Fla., 1975-76; asst. and coach to singer Michael Devlin, 1976-78; adminstrv. asst. to exec. creative dir. Ted Bates Advt., N.Y.C., 1978-86, bus. devel. coordinator, 1986—. Office: Ted Bates Advt/New York 1515 Broadway New York NY 10036

DEVOE, VIOLET ANN, systems analyst; b. Chgo., Sept. 27, 1940; d. Lambert Fred and Jean Mary (O'Hagan) Craemer; B.A. in Math., Mt. St. Mary's Coll., 1962; postgrad. in bus. adminstrn. San Diego State U.; m. Daniel Franklin Devoe, Dec. 29, 1962; children—Debra Jean, Alan Daniel, Lambert Theodore. Cert. data processor. Research asst. RAND Corp., Santa Monica, Calif., 1962-63; sci. programmer Litton Industries, Canoga Park, Calif., 1964; programmer analyst Lockheed-Calif. Co., Burbank, Calif., 1965-66, 69-72; sr. systems analyst County of San Diego (Calif.), 1972-80; sr. systems analyst Acctg. Corp. Am., San Diego, 1980-84; v.p. Presidio Components Inc., 1984—. Mem. Data Processing Mgmt. Assn., Assn. Systems Mgmt., Coronado Schs. Found., Am. Mensa Ltd. Republican. Roman Catholic. Club: Soroptimists (Coronado, Calif.). Home: 610 1st St Coronado CA 92118 Office: 1929 1st St San Diego CA 92101

DE VORE, DENISE ELLEN, marine biologist, researcher; b. N.Y.C., May 2, 1955; d. Bert and Laura Esther (Borrego) De V. B.S. in Biology and French, Coll. Mt. St. Vincent, 1977; M.S. in Biology, Adelphi U., 1979; postgrad. in Marine Scis., U. P.R., 1980—. Teaching asst. dept. biology Adelphi U., 1977-79; research assoc. U. Md., 1979; research asst. Ctr. Energy and Environ. Research Dept. Marine Scis. U. P.R., Mayaguez, 1980-81, 83—; profl. chem. cons. Mayaguez Water Treatment, 1980-81. Contbr. articles to profl. jours. Vol. tutor for high sch. students in Sci. Fair 1981—. NSF trainee, 1981-83; Slocum-Lunz Found. grantee, 1983. Mem. AAAS, Internat. Soc. Toxinology, Internat. Soc. Chem. Ecology, Sigma Xi, Alpha Mu Gamma, Beta Beta Beta. Home: 326 Tejas St San Gerardo Rio Piedras PR 00926 Office: U PR Dept Marine Scis RUM Mayaguez PR 00708

DEVORE, KIMBERLY K., health care executive; b. Louisville, June 19, 1947; d. Wendell O. and Shirley F. DeV.; student (Florence Allen Scholar), Xavier U., 1972-76; A.A., Coll. Mt. St. Joseph, 1979. Patient registration supr. St. Francis Hosp., Cin., 1974-76; cons., bus. mgr. Family Health Care Found., Cin., 1976-77; exec. dir. Hospice of Cin., Inc., 1977-80; pres. Micro Med., 1979—; v.p. Sycamore Profl. Assn., 1979—; ptnr. Enchanted House, 1979-86, sec., 1979-80, treas., 1980-81; bd. dirs. Nat. Hospice Org., 1979-82, Hospice of the Miami Valley, Inc., 1982-86; chmn. personnel, by laws com., mem. service and rehab. com. Hamilton County Unit Am. Cancer Soc., 1977-78; chmn. long term planning com., fin. com., annual meeting com. Nat. Hospice Org., 1979-82; co-founder, pres., state chmn. Ohio Hospice Orgn., 1978-83, Nat. League for Nursing, Ohio Hosp. Assn., Greater Cin. Soc. of Fund Raisers, Better Housing League, Nat., Ohio, fedns. bus. and profl. women's clubs, Cin. Bus. and Profl. Women's Club (pres. 1973-75).

DE VRIES, JANET MARGARET, clergywoman; b. Chgo., Feb. 24, 1950; d. Calvin Thomas and Janet May (Clark) DeV.; B.A., Hope Coll., Holland, Mich., 1972; M.Div., Union Theol. Sem., N.Y.C., 1978; m. William J. Cowfer, Sept. 6, 1980; stepchildren—David E., Jonathan C., Stephanie L. Ordained to ministry United Presbyterian Ch., U.S.A., 1977; coordinator tng. Support Agy., United Presbyn. Ch., N.Y.C., 1980-83, mng. dir. div. stewardship/tng. support agy., program specialist vols. in mission, Program Agy., N.Y.C., 1973-78, coordinator communication and ch. support Synod S. Calif., Los Angeles, 1973-80; instr. Claremont (Calif.) Sch. Theology, 1979. Gannett Newspaper scholar, 1967. Mem. UN Assn., Religious Public Relations Council. Author: Learning the Pacific Way: A Guide for All Ages, 1982; also articles. Office: Room 921 475 Riverside Dr New York NY 10115

DE VRIES, MARGARET GARRITSEN, economist; b. Detroit, Feb. 11, 1922; d. John Edward and Margaret Florence (Ruggles) Garritsen; B.A. in Econs. with honors (AAUW scholar 1939-42, Univ. scholar 1942), U. Mich., 1943; Ph.D. in Econs. (Inst. fellow), Mass. Inst. Tech., 1946; m. Barend A. de Vries, 1952; children—Christine, Barton. With Internat. Monetary Fund, Washington, 1946—, asst. chief multiple currency practices div., 1953-57, chief Far Eastern div., 1957-59, econ. cons., 1963-73, historian, 1973—; profl. lectr. econs. George Washington U., 1946-49, 1958-63. Recipient Disting. Alumni award U. Mich., 1980. Ford Found. grantee, 1959-62. Mem. Am. Econ. Assn., Internat. Studies Assn., Washington Women Economists Assn., Phi Beta Kappa, Phi Kappa Phi (Nat. Fellowship award 1943). Author: (with Irving S. Friedman) Postwar Foreign Economic Policy of the United States, 1947; (with J. Keith Horsefield) The International Monetary Fund, 1945-1965; Twenty Years of International Monetary Cooperation, 3 vols., 1969; The International Monetary Fund, 1966-71, 1972-78; The System under Stress, 2 vols. 1977; Cooperation on Trial, 3 vols., 1985; The IMF In a Changing World, 1945-1985, 1986; contbr. articles to profl. jours. Home: 10018 Woodhil Rd Bethesda MD 20817

DEW, CAROL ANN, state official; b. Springfield, Ill., Nov. 30, 1942; d. Jerome Dewitt Colby and Viviam Maxine (Johnson) Irwin; 1 son, Paul William Sandefur. With Ill. Dept. Rev., Springfield, 1962-66; comml. artist Spl. Services, Bamberg, Germany, 1966-68; disbursement clk. Pillsbury Co., Springfield, 1968-69; data processing analyst, programmer Ill. Dept. Registration, Springfield, 1969-74; self employed mgmt. cons., Springfield, 1974-76; sales rep. Xerox Corp., Springfield, 1976-77; adminstrv. asst. Ill. Dept. Conservation, Springfield, 1977-80; data processing analyst Ill. Dept. Pub. Aid, Springfield, 1980-81; info. systems exec. Ill. Depts. Commerce and Community Affairs and Adminstrv. Services, Springfield, 1981-82; dep. dir. acctg. revenue Office of Sec. State Ill., Springfield, 1982-83. Mem. Springfield Human Relations Commn.; mem. Springfield Citizens Adv. Com. to Mayor; mem. New Horizons Housing Task Force; mem. Springfield Water, Light and Power Utility Adv. Bd.; mem. Springfield Tourism and Conv. Commn.; mem. Springfield Housing Devel. Corp. Mem. Nat. Assn. Female Execs., Nat. Assn. Bus. and Profl. Women. Republican. Baptist.

DEW, JOAN KING, author; b. Columbus, Ga., June 24, 1932; d. Henry Grady and Vivian Pauline (Cook) King; m. Clifford Dew (div.); children—Clifford L., Jr., Michael David; m. 2d. Albert Schmitt (div.); children—Christopher, Thomas. Student, Fla. State U., 1949-51; reporter, feature writer Fort Lauderdale (Fla.) Daily News, 1950-56; editor Nassau (Bahamas) Guardian, 1956-58; stringer UPI, Bahamas, 1956-58; copy chief Art and Publicity, Ltd., Kingston, Jamaica, 1958-60; feature writer, author column Male Call, Valley Times Today, North Hollywood, Calif., 1960-66; freelance writer, Hollywood, Calif., 1966-77, Nashville, 1977—. Author: Singers and Sweethearts: The Women in Country Music, 1977; Stand By Your Man: The Autobiography of Tammy Wynette, 1978; Minnie Pearl, The Autobiography of Minnie Pearl, 1980; Ruby Dawn, 1985; contbr. numerous articles to nat. mags. Office: PO Box 150904 Nashville TN 37215

DEWALD, GRETTA MOLL, county official; b. Kutztown, Pa., Oct. 26, 1929; d. Lloyd A. and Olga (Wuchter) M.; m. Charles Frederick DeWald, Dec. 20, 1951; children—Michael S., Jonathon G., Henry L., Janie P., Joseph C. B.A., Agnes Scott Coll., 1950. Tchr. secondary schs. Eastman City Schs., Ga., 1950-51, Bass High Sch., Atlanta, 1951-52; project exec. sec. Appalachian project Day Care and Child Devel. Council Am., Atlanta, 1971-73; researcher Ga. Senate, Atlanta, 1973-74; community relations officer Met. Atlanta Rapid Transit Authority, 1976-77, bd. dirs., 1977; dir. women's div. Democratic Nat. Com., Washington, 1977-80; exec. asst. to chief exec. officer and bd. commrs. DeKalb County, Decatur, Ga., 1981—. Aide to commr. DeKalb Bd. Commrs., 1974-77. Mem. Ga. Commn. on Volunteerism, 1970-74, Ga. Women's Adv. Com., 1972-74, Nat. Adv. Com. of Women, 1977-80. Chmn., DeKalb County Dem. Com., 1972-74, 4th Congl. Dist. Ga. Com., 1974-76; campaigner, Peanut Brigade, N.H., Vt., Md., Ohio, Wi., Fla., Pa., 1976; del. Dem. Nat. Conv., 1972, 74, 76, 80; mem. adv. bd. Ga. Women's Polit. Caucus, 1983—; So. regional coordinator Dem. Task Force, Nat. Women's Polit. Caucus, 1983-85; mem. adv. bd. DeKalb Women's Network, 1983—; bd. dirs. DeKalb Library System, 1981—; sec. bd. dirs. DeKalb Humane Soc. Mem. Nat. Assn. County Adminstrs., Ga. Council County Adminstrs. (v.p. 1986—), Nat. Assn. Counties (steering com. intergovtl. relations 1981—), Women's Council Nat. Assn. Counties. Presbyterian. Home: 1096 DeLeon Ct Clarkston GA 30021 Office: New Court House 9th Floor Commn Office 456 N McDonough St Decatur GA 30030

DEWAR, DEBRA ANN, electrical sales representative; b. Denver, July 23, 1954; d. Louis Mac and Wilma Jean (Stidham) Perry; 1 child, Mark David Dewar. With warehouse sales dept. Gen. Electric Co., Denver, 1978-81; purchasing agt. Gash Electric Co., Wheatridge, Colo., 1981-82; lighting quotations salesman Hendrie-Bolthoff, Denver, 1982-84; sales rep. Westinghouse Elec. Sales, Denver, 1984—. Office: Westinghouse Elec Supply Co 1661 W 3d Ave Denver CO 80223

DEWAR, MILDRED (JO) ELLER (MRS. DONALD NORMAN DEWAR), librarian; b. Wilkesboro, N.C., Nov. 9, 1925; d. Charles Franklin and Golda (Velt) Eller; student Brevard Coll., 1942-44; diploma Jr. Coll., 1944; A.B., Berea Coll., 1946; B.S.L.S., U. N.C., 1948; postgrad. Barry Coll., U. Fla., U. Miami; m. Donald Norman Dewar, Mar. 6, 1954; 1 dau., Heather. Tchr., librarian Mountain View High Sch., Hays, N.C., 1946-47; chief librarian Tenn. Wesleyan Coll., Athens, 1948-50; dept. head U. Tex. Library, Austin, 1951; librarian U.S. Army Spl. Services, Ft. Jackson, S.C., 1951-52; chief post library system, Ft. Stewart, Ga., 1952-54; librarian Olsen Jr. High Sch., Dania, Fla., 1955-56, Lauderdale Manors Sch., Ft. Lauderdale, Fla., 1956-63; head reader's services Miami-Dade Community Coll. Library, Miami, Fla., 1963-70, library dir. South Campus, 1970—; vis. instr. U. Ga., summer 1967; co-exec. dir. Nat. Library Week in Fla., 1965-66; mem. Fla. learning resources standing com. Council on Instructional Affairs. Mem. AAUW (past br. v.p.), ALA, Fla. Library Assn., Am., Fla. (past pres.) assns. sch. librarians, SE Fla. Ednl. Consortium (library task force), Delta Kappa Gamma. Contbr. articles to profl. jours.; mem. editorial bd. Community and Jr. Coll. Libraries. Home: 3520 Crystal View Ct Coconut Grove FL 33133 Office: 11011 SW 104th St Miami FL 33176

DEWARE, MABEL MARGARET, Canadian government official; b. Moncton, N.B., Aug. 9, 1926; d. Hugh Fraser and Mary Elizabeth Ann (Adams) Keiver; m. Ralph Baxter Deware, Aug. 1, 1945; children—Kimberly Jon, Peter Thomas, Michael Hugh, Joanne Christine. Student Moncton schs. Minister of continuing edn., Fredricton, N.B., 1982—; minister labour and manpower N.B., 1978-82; mgr. Keeware Mgmt. Ltd.; elected M.L.A. for Moncton West province g.e., 1978. Conservative. Baptist. Office: PO Box 6000 Chestnut Complex 416 York St Fredricton NB E3B 5H1 Canada*

DEWBERRY, CLAIRE DEARMENT, engineering librarian; b. Youngstown, Ohio, Oct. 12, 1937; d. Eugene Howard and Ruth (Bright) DeA.; m. Carl R. Meinstereifel, 1956 (div. 1964, 79); children—Paul, Dawn; m. Olin Jerry Dewberry, Jr., 1974 (div.). B.S., Clarion State U., 1967; M.L.S., Ga. State U., 1977. Cert. library media specialist, Ga. Librarian Henry County, Stockbridge, Ga., 1967-69; head librarian Russell High Sch., East Point, Ga., 1969-84; engrng. librarian Rockwell Internat., Duluth, Ga., 1984—; rep. GIDEP, Corona, Calif., 1984—. Author newsletter: Blueline. Mem. Spl. Libraries Assn., Mensa, AIAA. Democrat. Avocations: computers; flea market selling; dollhouse accessories. Home 5623 Cobb Meadow Norcross GA 30093 Office: Rockwell Internat Corp 1800 Satellite Blvd Duluth GA 30136

DEWEY, ANNE ELIZABETH MARIE, lawyer; b. Balt., Mar. 16, 1951; d. George Daniel and Elizabeth Patricia (Mohan) D.; m. Peter Michael Barnett, Aug. 27, 1977; children—Brendan M., Andrew P. B.A., Mich. State U., 1972; J.D., U. Chgo., 1975; postgrad. Stonier Grad. Sch. Banking, 1983. Bar: D.C. 1976. Atty., FTC, Washington, 1975-78; atty. enforcement and compliance div. U.S. Comptroller of Currency, Washington, 1978-81, sr. atty. Office Legis. Counsel, 1981-83, sr. atty. Dallas Dist. Office, 1983-86, sr. atty. legal adv. services div., Washington, 1986—; dir. Women in Housing and Fin., Washington, 1982-83. Recipient award for superior performance Comptroller of Currency, 1979. Mem. ABA (sect. on corp. banking and bus. law.) Home: 833 Fontaine St Alexandria VA 22302 Office: Comptroller of Currency 490 L'Enfant Plaza Washington DC 20219

DEWEY, DOLORES (DOLLY) GAY, sheet metal company executive, nurse, consultant; b. Buffalo, Nov. 2, 1932; d. Joseph Stanley and Jeannette (Pachla) Gay; m. John William Dewey, Aug. 23, 1958 (div. 1982); children—Mari Lynn, Karen Ann. B.S. in Nursing Niagara U., 1954; postgrad. Canisius Coll., Buffalo, 1955-56. R.N. Head nurse Mt. St. Mary's Hosp., Niagara Falls, 1955-58; pres. Gay Sheet Metal Dies, Buffalo, 1964—; exec. bd. Medical Care Adv. Commn., Raleigh, N.C., 1975-77; cons. speaker Ostomy Orgn., N.C., 1977—. Chmn. N.C. Republican 4th Congl. Dist., Wake, 1977-81; chmn. County Rep. Party, 1975-77; exec. bd. Capital Health Systems Agy., Durham, N.C., 1976-81; corr. sec. AAUW, Raleigh, Named Woman of Yr., Wake County Rep. Womens Club, 1975. Mem. Nat. Fedn. Ind. Bus., N.C. Nurses Assn., Nat. Assn. Female Execs. Roman Catholic. Club: U.S. Senatorial. Avocations: painting; water skiing; ice skating; travelling. Home: PO Box 17604 Raleigh NC 27619 Office: Gay Sheet Metal Dies 301 Hinman Ave Buffalo NY 14216

DEWEY, PAT PARKER, radio station executive, composer; b. Berkeley, Calif., Jan. 27, 1923; d. George and Mildred (Johnston) Parker; student Sullins Jr. Coll., 1940-41; Mus.B., U. Miss., 1943; m. Grayson Headley, Dec. 30, 1946 (dec. 1961); m. 2d, M. Lee Williams, Dec. 18, 1964 (div.); 1 son, Philip Lee Williams; m. Ralph B. Dewey, Dec. 26, 1976. Woman's dir. radio sta. WNNT, Warsaw, Va., commentator daily women's program, Chat with Pat, 1957-60, now owner, pres. radio station WNNT AM-FM; partner WKWI-FM, Kilmarnock, Va.; asst. soc. editor Jackson Daily News, 1943-44. Composer: concerto for piano and orch., Rhapsody of Youth, performed by Nat. Air Force Symphony, Washington, Lisner Auditorium, 1947, guest pianist with Nat. Air Force Symphony, 1964, 75; (song) Cotton Picking Blues, featured in several musicals in Miss., Washington; (song) Maid of Cotton, used as theme song Nat. Cotton Council, 1945-51; (song) Lucky X, ofcl. song Chi Omega. Chmn., Red Cross water safety program, Lancaster County, Va., 1950-56; mem. exec. com. Jr. Assembly, Washington; jr. chmn. Home Hospitality Com., Washington, 1943-46; jr. chmn. UN Club activities, Washington, 1943-48; chmn. Fountain of Flowers Ball, 1981, Somerville Circle, Florence Crittenton Home; radio-TV publicity chmn. Washington Antiques Show, 1982, Landon Azalea Festival, 1978, 80, 82, 85, Washington Home Benefit, 1984. Mem. Am. Women in Radio and Television (dir. Va. 1962-65), Va. Assn. Broadcasters. Internat. Platform Assn., Nat. Assn. Am. Composers and Conductors, Women's Com. for Nat. Symphony Orch., Chi Omega, Delta Beta Sigma, Sigma Alpha Iota, Alpha Psi Omega. Episcopalian. Clubs: Friday Morning Music; Debutante of Miss., Women's (chmn. music div. Lancaster County, Va. 1956-60); Washington, Congl. Country (Washington); Kenwood Golf and Country; Kenwood Garden; Tides Inn Chesapeake; Congl. Golf; Pisces; Indian Creek Yacht and Country, Windmill Point Yacht. Home: 6211 Garnett Dr Chevy Chase MD 20815 also Steamboat Landing Irvington VA Office: Radio Sta WNNT Warsaw VA 22572

DEWEY, PAULINE T., newspaper publisher, editor; b. Lyons, Kans., Aug. 2, 1913; d. Ivan L. and Betty Maude (Dalton) Stone; student Kans. State Coll., 1931-32, U. So. Calif., 1943; m. J. Sterling Thomas, Feb. 15, 1938 (dec.); children—Betty Claire (dec.), Anthony Thomas (dec.); m. 2d, Franklin Noah Dewey, Jr., Nov. 24, 1952 (dec. June 1968). Editor, Airview News, Douglas Aircraft, Santa Monica, Calif., 1942-45; pub. relations mgr. Calif. Intelligence Bur., Los Angeles, 1945-48; owner Thomas & Assos., realtors, Los Angeles, also Palm Springs, Calif., 1948-52; editor, pub. Nev. Times, Las Vegas, 1960—. Former chmn. local Heart Fund drive; mem. Gov.'s Com. Mobile Homes and Travel Trailers, 1973-75, Citizens' Group Project 701 for City's Master Plan, 1973-75, Commn. Manufactured Housing Div., Nevada; former trustee Clark County Library, Las Vegas; past chmn. bd. R.S.V.P. Recipient Boise Cascade Woman of Year award Los Angeles br. Boise Cascade Co., 1971, Gov.'s citation, 1971, certificates of appreciation from various local orgns. Mem. So. Nev. Park Operators Assn. (hon.), North Las Vegas C. of C. (former dir.), Better Bus. Bur., Army Athletic Assn., Am. Assn. Ret. Persons, LWV. Clubs: Am. Penwomen's (v.p. internat.), Internat. Toastmistress. Address: PO Box 4142 North Las Vegas NV 89030

DE WINDT, HERMA ILEAN, retail credit executive; b. N.Y.C.; d. Ernold G. and Benjamina (Jackson) Sewell. B.S., CUNY, 1982; M.A., New Sch. Social Research, 1985. Staff supr., R.H. Macy's & Co., Inc., 1967-68, jr. exec., 1968-73, alternate exec., 1971-73, asst. to dept. mgr., 1973-74, credit exec., 1974-81, credit fraud exec., 1981—. Fellow, Am. Mgmt. Assn.; mem. Am. Mktg. Assn., Am. Soc. Personnel Adminstrn., AAUW, Am. Assn. Female Execs., Sigma Iota Epsilon, Sigma Alpha Delta. Democrat. Episcopalian. Office: Credit Dept R H Macy's & Co Inc 151 W 34th St New York NY 10001

DEWITT, BEVERLY WHANN, riding club administrator, packaging consultant and designer; b. Los Angeles, Feb. 14, 1926; d. Jesse Pluve and Lillian Marguerite (Voss) Whann; m. Eugene Thomas Vandergrift, Jan. 1, 1948 (div. Mar. 1968); m. Woodrow Wilson DeWitt, Mar. 30, 1968. Student, U. So. Calif., 1959-61, Chouinard Art Inst., 1961-63. Artist, Standard Paper Box, Los Angeles, 1945-48; ceramic designer Vande Ceramics, Pasadena, Calif., 1965-68; art dir. Standard Graphic Arts, Los Angeles, 1968-72; interior/graphic designer DeWitt Design, Glendale, Calif., 1972-83; mgr. Rancho Bernardo Riding Club, San Diego, 1983—. Designed logo DeWitt Freight Forwarding, 1974, Royal Hawaiian Movers, 1981, Oakmont Country Club, 1982, Rainbow Vet. Hosp., 1984, San Diego Appaloosa Assn., Alert Telephone Answering Service. Republican. Clubs: Oakmont Country (Glendale, Calif.) (v.p. 1971, pres. 1972-73); Appaloosa Horse (Moscow, Idaho); Cal-Western Appaloosa (alt. show dir.) (Clovis, Calif.). Avocations: horseback riding; horse showmanship; golf; painting watercolors; tapestry needlework. Office: Rancho Bernardo Riding Club 18009 Pomerado Rd San Diego CA 92128

DEWITT, SANDRA LOU, fin. exec.; b. Bremerton, Wash., Feb. 2, 1944; d. Miles Eugene and Billie Elizabeth (McLean) Hurley; student public schs., Garden Grove, Calif.; m. William Albert DeWitt, Dec. 30, 1961; children—Rebecca Sue, William Albert. Sec., claims examiner RIMCO, Dallas, 1972-73; casualty claims supr. Am. PetroFina Co. of Tex., Dallas, 1973-77; dir. ins. and risk mgmt. Ramada Inns, Inc., Phoenix, 1977—. Bd. dirs., sec. Ramada Inn Employee Credit Union, 1980—. Mem. Risk and Ins. Mgmt. Soc. (chpt. v.p. 1981-82, pres. 1982—), Am. Bus. Women's Assn., Am. Soc. Profl. and Exec. Women, Nat. Assn. Female Execs., Ariz. Assn. Ins. Adjusters. Republican. Methodist. Club: Order Eastern Star. Home: 5034 E Columbine Dr Scottsdale AZ 85254 Office: 3838 E Van Buren St Phoenix AZ 85001

DEWITT, SYLVIA N., financial planning and investment brokerage executive, financial columnist; b. Brantford, Ont., Can., Aug. 18, 1950; d. Michael and Phyllis (Carridy) Nancoff. B.S. in Fin., Iowa State U., 1979, B.S. in Econs., 1979. Registered fin. planner. Stockbroker Piper, Jaffray & Hopwood, Inc., Des Moines, 1979-81; personnel mgmt. Presdl. Transition Team, Washington, 1980-81; pres. DeWitt Fin. Planning Services, Inc., Des Moines, 1982—. Columnist Lee Town News/West Des Moines Express, 1983—; contbr. articles to mags., profl. jours. Co-chmn. Polk County Reagan Election Com., Des Moines, 1980. Recipient Century Club award Integrated Resources Equity Corp., 1985. Mem. Iowa Mgmt. Assn., Am. Bus. Women's Assn., Nat. Assn. Profl. Saleswomen, Entrepreneurs Network (steering com. 1984), Des Moines C. of C. Republican. Lutheran. Clubs: Sports Car Club Am. (Des Moines); Porsche Am. Lodge: Soroptimist Internat. Office: DeWitt Fin Planning Services Inc 310-8th St Des Moines IA 50309

DEXTER, CAROLYN R., management and marketing educator; b. Washington; d. Harris E. and Florence Isbell Dexter. B.S., St. Lawrence U., 1948; M.A., Columbia U., 1959, Ph.D., 1967. Mgr. safe deposit dept. 1st Nat. Bank & Trust Co. Poughkeepsie, N.Y., 1948-53; dir. research and stats. Girl Scouts U.S.A., N.Y.C., 1960-65; cons. mktg. and strategic planning, N.Y.C., 1965-67; corp. sociologist John Hancock Mut. Life Ins. Co. Boston, 1967-69; assoc. prof. mktg. and mgmt. Pa. State U., Middletown, 1969—, acting head bus. adminstrn., 1984—. Mem. mktg. adv. com. St. Joseph's Hosp., Lancaster, Pa., 1985. Contbr. articles to profl. jours.; assoc. editor Marketplace Exchange, 1984—, Sociol. Perspective, 1981—, Social. Welfare, Social Planning/Policy and Social Development: An International Data Base, 1981—. Treas., Jr. League, 1955-56. Mem. Harrisburg Hist. Assn., Acad. Mgmt. (bd. govs. 1981-84, chmn. status on women com. 1985—, Eastern Acad. Mgmt. (pres. elect 1985-86, bd. govs. 1984—), Am. Mktg. Assn. (pres. Central Pa. chpt. 1974), Am. Sociol. Assn. (bd. dirs. 1978-83), Eastern Sociol. Soc., Nat. Council State Sociol. Assns. (pres. 1979), Internat. Sociol. Assn., Inst. Internationale de Sociologie, North Central Sociol. Assn., Sociologists for Women in Society (bd. dirs. 1973-79), So. Acad. Mgmt., Southwestern Acad. Mgmt., Am. Inst. Decision Scis. Club: Univ. Womens (London). Office: Pa State U Dept Bus Adminstrn Middletown PA 17057

DEXTER, DALLAS-LEE, insurance executive, consultant; b. Rockville Center, N.Y., Nov. 30, 1950; d. David D. and Jane (Nexbitt) D.; m. Leonard Eugene Carter, Nov. 6, 1975 (div. 1982). Student numerous dance courses; B.S., Mills Coll., 1972; M.A., Tchrs. Coll. Columbia U., 1974; postgrad. Nat. U. Mex., 1974, Lesley Coll., 1974, Fgn. Service Inst., 1977, Johns Hopkins Sch. Advanced Internat. Studies, 1982, Middle East Inst., 1982-83. Cert. ins., securities, teaching. Tchr. Am. Sch., Hawalli, Kuwait, 1975-76, Copenhagen Internat. Sch., 1977-79, Rygaards Internat. Sch., Hellerup, Denmark, 1980-81; cons. Mark V Assocs., Inc., N.Y.C., 1982—; sales rep. First Investors Corp., Arlington, Va., 1985-86; assoc. Potomac Ins. and Fin. Planning Group, Rockville, Md., 1985—; dancer Twyla Tharp Dance Co., 1969-70, James Cunningham Co., 1970, others; cons. Resources Planning Systems, McLean, Va., 1983-85, Mgmt. Engring. Affiliates, Calabasas, Calif., 1984, Success, Inc., Palm Beach, Fla., 1985—, Aerojet General, Washington, 1983. Campaign worker Reagan-Bush, Washington, 1983-84; active Rock Creek Women's Republican Club, Chevy Chase Women's Rep. Club, Montgomery County Rep. Club, Nat. Fedn. Rep. Women; mem. women's com. Nat. Symphony Orch.; charter mem., sponsor Assn. of Friends of Mus. Modern Art of Latin Am. Mem. Nat. Assn. Life Underwriters, U.S. C. of C., D.C. Life Underwriters Assn., Nat. Assn. Female Execs. (network dir. 1985—), Am. Fed. Preparedness Assn., Air Force Assn., AAUW, Phi Delta Kappa. Unitarian. Club: Renaissance Women. Avocations: Travel; treatre; music; dance; painting; drawing. Home: 1280 21st St NW Washington DC 20036 Office: Potomac Insurance and Financial Planning Group 6244 Montrose Rd Rockville MD 20852

DEXTER, VIVIAN ANN, electronic manufacturing company executive; b. Rochester, N.Y., Feb. 19, 1942; d. Holmer Alvin and Tina Laura (Monroe) Fry; m. William Deville Dexter, May 25, 1962 (div. June 1975); 1 child, Vivian Ann II. B.A., Elmira Coll., 1978; M.A., N.C. State U., 1983. Engaged in staff mgmt. Corning Glass Works (N.Y.), 1960-77, mfg. mgmt., Raleigh, N.C., 1977-80; instr. V.I. Coll., St. Thomas, 1980-81; sr. foreman AVX Corp., Myrtle Beach, S.C., 1981-82, employment mgr., 1982-83, quality circle facilitator, 1983—. Mem. Leadership Grand Strand III, Myrtle Beach, 1983, United Way Horry County, Myrtle Beach, 1983-84; bd. dirs. Citizens Against Spouse Abuse, Myrtle Beach, 1982-84. Recipient 1st place award Indsl. Safety Commn., Raleigh, 1979. Mem. Internat. Assn. Quality Circles (cert.), Organizational Dynamics Making Things Better (cert.), Am. Personnel Assn., Word Processing Assn. Democrat. Home: PO Box 1942 Myrtle Beach SC 29577 Office: AVX Corp PO Box 867 Myrtle Beach SC 29577

DEXTRAS, MARY LOU, religious organization coordinator; b. Youngstown, Ohio, Sept. 20, 1922; d. Guido and Catherine (Spagnola) Bernard; m. Albert Raymond Dextras, Feb. 9, 1946; children—Suzanne, Paul A., Cathie, Mary Alice, Dee Anne. Student Youngstown Bus. Sch., Wichita State U., 1984—. Exec. sec. U.S. Air Force, Kadena, Okinawa, 1957-62; youth dir. McConnell AFB, Wichita, Kans., 1963-64; real estate agt. Egan Realtors, Derby, Kans., 1965-80; coordinator Congregation Sisters of St. Joseph Coordinated Services, Wichita, 1980—. Served to sgt. USMCWR, 1942-45. Mem. Derby Arts Council, Kans. Named Mother of Yr., Bergstrom AFB, Austin, 1956; recipient Koza Shi Fujenkai award Women's Fedn., Okinawa, 1960; People-to-People award Pres. Eisenhower, 1961. Mem. Derby Bd. Edn., pres., 1978-79, 84-85. Democrat. Roman Catholic. Lodges: Soroptimists, K.C. Aux. (Derby, Kans.). Avocations: Tap dancing; piano. Office: Congregation of Sisters of St Joseph Coordinated Services 3720 E Bayley Wichita KS 67218

DEYOUNG, KAREN JEAN, journalist; b. Chgo., Jan. 4, 1949; d. Edward Leonard and Jeanette K. (Clausen) DeY.; B.S. cum laude in Journalism and Communication, U. Fla., 1971. Features writer St. Petersburg (Fla.) Times, 1972-74; freelance reporter, Western Africa, 1974-75; Latin Am. corr. Washington Post, 1977-80, dep. fgn. editor, 1980-81, fgn. editor, 1981-85, London Bur. chief, 1985—. Recipient Disting. Service award fgn. reporting Sigma Delta Chi, 1979, Fgn. Corr. award Inter-Am. Press Assn., 1979; Maria Moors Cabot award Columbia U., 1981. Address: 1150 15th St NW Washington DC 20071

DEYOUNG, LILLIAN JEANETTE, nurse educator; R.N., Thomas Dee Hosp., Utah, 1947; B.S. in Nursing Edn., U. Utah, 1950, M.S. in Ednl. Adminstrn., 1955, Ph.D. in Ednl. Adminstrn., 1975. Assoc. dir. nursing edn. Latter Day Saints Hosp., Salt Lake City, 1954-55; dir. Sch. Nursing St. Luke's Hosp., Denver, 1955-72; assoc. prof., curriculum coordinator Intercollegiate Center for Nursing Edn., Spokane, 1972-73; asst. dir. nursing service U. Utah Med. Center, Salt Lake City, 1973-75; prof. nursing U. Akron, Ohio, 1975—, also dean; mem. council deans Ohio Bd. Regents; mem. State of Ohio Bd. Nursing Edn. and Nurse Registration, 1979-83, v.p. 1980-82, pres., 1982-83; dir. Huntington Nat. Bank, Akron. Trustee Akron Gen. Med. Center, 1978—. Mem. Ohio League Nursing, Midwest Alliance in Nursing, Am. Nurses Assn., Ohio Nurses Assn., Nat. League Nursing (exec. com. council baccalaureate and higher degree program 1981-83, task force on structure 1982-83), ARC, Am. Assn. Higher Edn., Sigma Theta Tau. Author: Foundations of Nursing as Conceived, Learned, and Practiced in Professional Nursing, 1966, 72, 76; Dynamics of Nursing, 1981, 5th edit., 1985. Home: 711 Lafayette Dr Akron OH 44303 Office: 101B Mary Gladwin Hall Akron OH 44325

D'HARNONCOURT, ANNE, museum director; b. Washington, Sept. 7, 1943; d. René and Sarah (Carr) d'Harnoncourt; B.A., Radcliffe Coll., 1965; M.A. with distinction, Courtauld Inst. Art, U. London, 1967; m. Joseph J. Rishel, June 19, 1971. Curatorial asst. Phila. Mus. Art, 1967-69; asst. curator 20th Century Art, Art Inst. Chgo., 1969-71; curator 20th Century Art, Phila. Mus. Art, 1971—. Mem. Phi Beta Kappa. Exhibitions organized: John Cage: Scores and Prints (with Patterson Sims), 1982; Futurism and the Internat. Avant-Garde, 1980; Eight Artists, 1978; Violet Oakley (with Ann Percy), 1979; Philadelphia: Three Centuries of Am. Art (with other collaborators), 1976; Marcel Duchamp (with Kynaston McShine), 1973-74. Author: The Cubist Cockatoo: Preliminary Exploration of Joseph Cornell's Hommages to Juan Gris, 1978; Etant Donnes . . . Reflections on a New Work by Marcel Duchamp (with Walter Hopps), 1969. Office: Phila Mus of Art PO Box 7646 Philadelphia PA 19101-7646

DHOLAKIA, RUBY ROY, management educator; b. Calcutta, India, Feb. 16, 1948; came to U.S. 1963; d. Somendra Nath and Saila Rani Roy; B.S. in Bus. Adminstrn., U. Calif., Berkeley, 1967, M.B.A., 1969; Ph.D., Northwestern U., 1976; m. Nikhilesh Dholakia, Aug. 30, 1974; 1 son, Ritik. Mktg. analyst Wells Fargo Bank, San Francisco 1969; asst. prof. Indian Inst. Mgmt., Calcutta 1970-73, 76-78; vis. faculty Indian Inst. Mgmt., Ahmedabad, 1977-79; assoc. prof. Kans. State U., 1979-81; assoc. prof. U. R.I., 1981-84, prof., 1984—; cons. in field of consumer research. Am. Mgmt. Assn. fellow, 1975; AAAA fellow 1982. Mem. Am. Mktg. Assn., Assn. Consumer Research. Contbr. articles in field to profl. jours. Office: PO Box 279 Kingston RI 02881 also Ballentine Hall University of Rhode Island Kingston RI 02881

DIAL, ELEANORE MAXWELL, educator; b. Norwich, Conn., Feb. 21, 1929; d. Joseph Walter and Irene (Beetham) Maxwell; B.A., U. Bridgeport (Conn.), 1951; M.A. in Spanish, Mexico City Coll., 1955; Ph.D., U. Mo., 1968; m. John E. Dial, Aug. 27, 1959. Mem. faculty U. Wisc.-Milw., 1968-75, Ind. State U., Terre Haute, 1975-78, Bowling Green (Ohio) State U., 1978-79; assoc. prof. dept. fgn. langs. and lits. Iowa State U., Ames, 1979—; cons. pub. co.; participant workshops; del. 1st World Congress Women Journalists and Writers, Mex., 1975, also mem. edn. commn. NDEA grantee, 1967; Center Latin Am. grantee, 1972; NEH summer seminar UCLA, 1982, U. Calif.-Santa Barbara, 1984. Mem. Am. Assn. Tchrs. Spanish and Portuguese, Midwest MLA, MLA, N. Central Council Latin Americanists, Midwest Assn. Latin Am. Studies, Caribbean Studies Assn., European Assn. Profs. of Spanish, Feministus Unidas, Phi Sigma Iota, Sigma Delta Pi. Contbr. articles and revs. to scholarly jours. Home: 921 Burnett Ave Ames IA 50010 Office: Iowa State U Ames IA 50010

DIAMANT, BETSY MARIA, librarian; b. Stamford, Conn., June 2, 1957; d. Philip E. and Shirley F. (Dichter) Diamant; m. Murray F. Spiegel, June 21, 1981 (div. 1985). Student Hebrew U., Jerusalem, 1978-79; B.A. magna cum laude with high honors in sociology, Brandeis U., 1980; M.L.S., Rutgers U., 1983; grad. Simmons Coll., 1981. Children's librarian Ocean Twp. Library, Oakhurst, N.J., 1982; sch. librarian Solomon Schechter Day Sch. of Marlboro (N.J.), 1982-83, library cons., 1983-85; children's librarian East Brunswick Pub. Library (N.J.), 1983-85; dept. head children's services Metuchen Pub. Library, N.J., 1985—. Editor Hamagshimim Jour., 1976-78; mem. editorial bd. Focus mag., 1978-80. Jr./intermediate adviser New Eng. Young Judaea, 1979-80; pres. Nat. Young Judea, 1974-75; organizer Soviet Jewry activities, 1981—. Recipient Human Rights Achievement award Brandeis U. Nat. Women's Com., 1984. Conn. State scholar, 1975; Polaroid Honors Community Research grantee, 1979. Mem. ALA, N.J. Library Assn., Am. Jewish Librarians Assn., N.J. Jewish Librarians Assn., Tale Weavers Storytelling Group. Democrat. Jewish. Club: Israeli Folkdance (Tenafly, N.J.). Office: Metuchen Public Library 480 Middlesex Ave Metuchen NJ 08840

DIAMOND, ADELINA, writer; b. Chgo., Oct. 9, 1927; d. Herbert C. and Jennie (Friedman) Lust; A.B., U. Chgo., 1947; M.P.A., N.Y. U., 1972, postgrad., 1981; m. Edwin Diamond, Dec. 5, 1948; children—Ellen, Franna, Louise. Sportswear buyer Mandel Bros., Chgo., 1947-49, advt. copywriter, 1949-50; fashion reporter Womens Wear Daily, Chgo., 1950-52; editor Hyde Park Herald, Chgo., 1953-56; v.p. Edwin and Adelina Diamond Assos., communications and pub. affairs, N.Y.C., 1969—; assoc. Center for Housing Partnerships, N.Y.C., 1970-72; Eastern public affairs rep. U. Chgo., 1972-78; dir. public relations Carnegie Council on Children, 1978-81; cons. Children's Def. Fund, 1978-81; founding mem. Women U.S.A., Friends of NOW, N.Y.C.; founder, chairperson Friends of ERA. Home: 20 Waterside Plaza New York NY 10010

DIAMOND, DOROTHY BLUM, author, editor; b. N.Y.C., Sept. 7, 1919; d. Asher and Lily (Williams) Blum; m. Walter H. Diamond, June 15, 1947. B.A. with highest honors, Wellesley Coll., 1940; M.S., Columbia U., 1941. Reporter, Newark Star-Ledger, 1941; assoc. editor Young Am. mag., N.Y.C., 1941-42; sr. editor, columnist Tide mag., N.Y.C., 1942-47, 55-59; columnist Printers Ink, N.Y.C., 1959-61, Modern Floor Coverings, N.Y.C., 1958-63; author: Tax Havens of the World, 1974; Tax-Free Trade Zones of the World, 1976; International Tax Treaties of All Nations, 1976; Capital Formation and Investment Incentives Around the World, 1983, also supplements; contbr. articles to mags. and newspapers. Mem. Merchandising Execs. Club (award 1958), World Trade Writers Assn., Phi Beta Kappa. Club: Wellesley-in-Westchester (past bd. dirs.). Home: 9 Old Farm Ln Hartsdale NY 10530 Office: Overseas Press & Cons 9 Old Farm Lane Hartsdale NY 10530

DIAMOND, HARRIET LYNN, human resource development consultant, freelance writer; b. Newark, Apr. 22, 1941; d. Fred and Pauline (Kantorwitz) Hillman; m. Michael Diamond, Dec. 27, 1964; children—Ellen, Linda. Student Douglass Coll., 1959-61; B.A. in English, Rutgers U., 1963; M.A. in Adminstrn. and Supervision, Kean Coll., 1980. Cert. tchr. English, prin., supr., N.J. Asst. pub. relations dir. Newark Mus., 1963-64; asst. dir. internal pub. Bamberger's, Newark, 1964; English and reading instr. Union County Regional Adult Sch., Kenilworth, N.J., 1970-73; dir. Union County Regional Adult Learning Ctr., Kenilworth, 1973-83; adminstr. Seton Hall U., South Orange, N.J., 1983-84; pres. Diamond Assocs., Westfield, N.J., 1984—. Author: GED Test 3 Science, 1976, 2d edit., 1985; English the Easy Way, 1982; Writing the Easy Way, 1985; Grammar - In Plain English, 1977; also articles in profl. jours. and newspapers. Editor The Adult Educator, 1983-85, Jour. Lifelong Learning, 1985. Recipient N.J. Author award Alumni Assn. N.J. Inst. Tech., 1986; citation for contbns. to adult edn. N.J. Senate, 1983. Mem. Assn. for Adult Edn. N.J. (legis. chmn. 1980-83, Leadership award 1983), N.J. Assn. for Lifelong Learning (pres. 1985-86), Am. Assn. for Adult and Continuing Edn. N.J. Women Bus. Owners, N.J. Bus. and Industry Assn., Am. Soc. for Tng. and Devel. Home: 490 Otisco Dr Westfield NJ 07090 Office: Diamond Assocs 490 Otisco Dr Westfield NJ 07090

DIAMOND, KAREN WALTZER, fitness teacher trainer, consultant; b. Bronx, N.Y., May 20, 1939; d. Bernard and Blanche (Zwillenberg) Waltzer; m. George N. Diamond, Aug. 20, 1960; children—Gary, Deena, Adam. B.A., Am. U., 1961. Area dir. Eve Nelson Cosmetics, Washington, 1961-62; performer, dancer Library Theatre, Washington, 1972; creative dir. Karen Diamond Sch. Exercise, 1973-84, Karen Diamond Studio, 1981-84; dir. Karen Diamond Method Fitness, Bethesda, Md., 1985—; performer, resident fitness expert ABC TV, Washington, 1976-79, NBC TV, 1976; mem. cert. com. IDEA Found., San Diego, 1984—; mem. music revue bd. Music In Motion, Alameda, Calif., 1985—; mem. Md. Gov.'s Commn. on Fitness and Sports, 1979-83. Contbr. articles to mags.; author, performer fitness audio cassette, 1976. Chmn. dance com. Jewish Community Ctr. Greater D.C. Area, 1968-73, bd. dirs., 1972-75; bd. dirs. Brandeis Women's Com., Washington, 1971-76; mem. Brandeis Women's Com. Fellow Am. Coll. Sports Medicine; mem. Met. Dance Assn., Internat. Dance Exercise Assn., Nat. Assn. Women Bus. Owners. Avocations: knitting; crocheting; cooking; travel; walking; gardening. Home and Office: 5203 Ridgefield Rd Bethesda MD 20816

DIAMOND, LAUREN HEIDEN, lawyer; b. Bklyn., Oct. 2, 1958; d. Harry Leon and Barbara (Brenin) H.; m. Brian Louis Diamond, Mar. 27, 1982. B.A. in Psychology, SUNY-Stony Brook, 1979; J.D., Bklyn. Law Sch., 1982. Bar: N.Y. 1983. Law clk. Schneider, Kleinick & Weitz, N.Y.C., 1980-81, Young & Young, N.Y.C., 1981; student law clk. Hon. Jacob D. Fuchsberg, N.Y.C., 1981; intern Kings County Dist. Atty.'s Office, Bklyn., 1981-82; assoc. law firm William A. Prinsell, Esq., N.Y.C., 1982-83; assoc. law firm Lanzone & Kramer, N.Y.C., 1983—. Mem. Bklyn. Bar Assn., ABA, N.Y. State Trial Lawyers Assn., Bklyn. Law Sch. Alumni Assn., Phi Beta Kappa. Jewish. Office: Lanzone & Kramer 26 Broadway New York NY 10004

DIAMOND, LINDA BARBARA, information systems director, consultant; b. Queens, N.Y., Feb. 18, 1943; d. Irving Jerome and Sylvia (Heiser) Klein; m. Barry S. Diamond, Dec. 24, 1962; children—Brian, Robert, Sean. B.A. in Edn. and Math., Queens Coll., 1964. Tchr., Patchoque, L.I., N.Y., 1964-66; programmer Capac, Ridgefield, Conn., 1975-77; sr. tech. rep. Gen. Electric Info. Services, Stamford, Conn., 1977-80, sr. account mgr., 1980-82; sr. systems engr. Datapoint Corp., Stamford, 1982-85; dir. info. systems Direct Mktg. Assn., N.Y.C., 1985—; cons. Micro Systems, Trumbull, Conn., 1986—, N.Y./Conn. Fin. Planning, Bridgeport, Conn., 1984—. Mem. Assn. Info. Systems Profls., Nat. Assn. Exec. Females, Direct Mktg. Computer Assn., Conn. Edn. Assn. Jewish. Home: 4 Harwood Terr Trumbull CT 06611 Office: Direct Mktg Assn 6 E 43rd St New York NY 10017

DIAMOND, LOUISA TORREZ, educator; b. N.Y.C., July 13, 1930; d. Max T. and Emma (Meshoulam) Tassler; student Universidad de las Americas, Pueblo, Mexico, 1954-55, 63-64; A.A., Los Angeles Pierce Coll., 1970-72; B.A. summa cum laude, Calif. State U., 1976; postgrad. U. So. Calif., 1976-79; m. Donald A. Diamond, Aug. 1, 1965; 1 dau., Maxine R. Diamond; children by previous marriage—Fortuna Israel, Emily Israel. Tchr., Lang. Acad., Universidad Autonoma Mexico, Mexico City, 1959-63; owner, mgr. Creaciones Fortuna S.A., Mexico City, 1963-65; tchr. English as second language, Spanish Community Adult Sch. Area 8 In-Service, Los Angeles Unified Sch. Dist., 1971-78; tchr. Grant High Sch., 1982—, Reseda Community Adult Sch., 1982—; instr. Calif. State U., Northridge, 1976-78. Recipient Outstanding Ednl. Leadership award Los Angeles Unified Sch. Dist., 1980, First Pl. award for abstract oil painting Northridge Cultural Arts and Hist. Assn., 1970. Mem. United Tchrs. Los Angeles. Clubs: Latin Am. (Los Angeles); City of Hope. Home: 18284 Karen Dr Tarzana CA 91356 Office: 13000 Oxnard St Van Nuys CA 91401

DIAMOND, ROBIN GAY, publishing company official; b. Cleve., Sept. 21, 1944; d. Albert E. Winston and Miriam J. Mandell; student Calif. State U., Northridge, 1962-63, 81-82, Santa Monica City Coll., 1966-67, Pierce Community Coll., 1974-75; grad. exec. program UCLA Grad. Sch. Mgmt., 1985; m. Stephen E. Diamond, Dec. 27, 1981; children by previous marriage—Lisa Michelle Erickson, Stephanie Diane Erickson. Exec. sec. with Dean Witter, Reynolds, Encino, Calif., 1976-77; adminstrv. asst. Paine Webber, Encino, 1977-79; supr. personnel and adminstrn. NILS Pub. Co., Chatsworth, Calif., 1979-81, mgr. adminstrn., 1981-83, dir. sales and adminstrn., 1983—. Mem. Nat. Assn. Female Execs., NOW, Nat. Notary Assn., ABC Employees Assn. (bd. dirs., 1980). Office: 21625 Prairie St Chatsworth CA 91311

DIAMOND, STELLA, lawyer; b. Wilmington, Del., July 18, 1948; d. John Anthony and Mary (Cooper) D. B.A., U. Del.-Newark, 1970; student U. Madrid, 1969; J.D., Vanderbilt U., 1977. Bar: Fla. 1977. Tchr. langs. Montgomery County Pub. Schs., Silver Spring, Md., 1970-73; ptnr. Diamond & Diamond P.A., Ft. Myers, Fla., 1977—. Bd. dirs. Fla. Rural Legal Services, Bartow, 1983—. Mem. ABA, Assn. Trial Lawyers Am., Fla. Bar Assn., Lee County Bar Assn., Nat. Assn. Women Lawyers, Fla. Assn. Women Lawyers. Democrat. Greek Orthodox. Home: 6300 S Point Blvd # 452 Fort Myers FL 33907 Office: PO Drawer 2590 2036 McGregor Blvd Fort Myers FL 33902

DIAMOND, SUSAN Z., management consultant; b. Okla., Aug. 20, 1949; d. Louis Edward and Henrietta (Wood) D.; A.B. (Nat. Merit scholar, GRTS scholar), U. Chgo., 1970; M.B.A., DePaul U., 1979; m. Allan T. Devitt, July 27, 1974. Dir. study guide prodn. Am. Sch. Co., Chgo., 1972-75; publs. supr. Allied Van Lines, Broadview, Ill., 1975-78, sr. account services rep., 1978-79; pres. Diamond Assocs. Ltd., Melrose Park, Ill., 1978—; condr. seminars Am. Mgmt. Assn. Author mag. articles in field. Mem. Assn. Info. and Image Mgmt., Nat. Assn. Accts., Internat. Records Mgmt. Council, Records Mgmt. Soc. Gt. Britain, Adminstrv. Mgmt. Soc., Assn. Records Mgrs. and Adminstrs., Bus. Forms Mgmt. Assn., Delta Mu Delta. Author: How to Talk More Effectively, 1972; Preparing Administrative Manuals, 1981; How to Manage Administrative Operations, 1981; How to be an Effective Secretary in the Modern Office, 1982; 1982; Records Management: A Practical Guide, 1983; co-author: Finance Without Fear, 1984; editor Mobility Trends, 1975-78. Office: 2851 N Pearl St Melrose Park IL 60160

DIAMOND ROVNER, ILANA KARA, United States district judge; b. Riga, Latvia, Aug. 21, 1938; came to U.S., 1939, naturalized, 1954; d. Stanley and Ronny (Medalje) Diamond; m. Richard Nyles Rovner, Mar. 9, 1963; 1 child, Maxwell Rabson. A.B., Bryn Mawr Coll., 1960; postgrad. Oxford U., 1960, Kings Coll. U., London, 1960-61, Georgetown U., 1961-64, NYU, 1962; J.D., Chgo. Kent Coll. Law, 1966. Bar: Ill. 1972; U.S. Dist. Ct. (no. dist. Ill.) 1972, U.S. Ct. Appeals (7th cir.) 1977, U.S. Supreme Ct. 1981. Legal researcher Phelan, Pope and John Ltd., Chgo., 1971; law clk. to former chief judge U.S. Dist. Ct. No. Dist. Ill., Chgo., 1972-73; asst. U.S. atty. U.S. Atty's Office, No. Dist. Ill., Chgo., 1973-77, dep. chief, pub. protection unit, 1975-76, chief pub. protection unit, 1976-77, U.S. dist. judge, 1984—; dep. gov. for Chgo. and legal counsel Gov.'s Office, State of Ill., Chgo., 1977-84. Trustee Bryn Mawr Coll., Pa., 1983—; mem. bd. overseers Ill. Inst. Tech., Chgo. Kent Coll. Law, 1983. Recipient Ann. Guardian Police award 1977; U.S. Dept. Justice Spl. Achievement award, 1976; Annual Nat. Law and Social Justice Leadership award, 1975; Spl. Commendation award U.S. Dept. Justice, 1975; named Chgo. Woman of Yr., 1985. Mem. Fed. Bar Assn. (treas. 1978-79, sec. 1979-80, 2d v.p. Chgo. chpt. 1980-81, v.p. 1981-82, pres. 1982-83, 7th cir. 2d v.p. 1983-84, v.p. 1984—). Republican. Jewish. Office: US Dist Ct for No Dist Ill 219 S Dearborn St Chicago IL 60604

DIANTO, LINDA CHRISTINE, therapeutic activities coordinator; b. Bklyn., Dec. 11, 1949; d. Salvatore and Josephine (Battaglia) Lore; m. Nicholas L. Dianto, June 26, 1971. A.A. in Psychology, Staten Island Community Coll., 1969; B.A., Richmond Coll., Staten Island, 1971, M.S. in Edn., 1974; postgrad. NYU, 1984—. Cert. tchr., N.Y.; lic. recreation adminstr., N.J. Tchr. St. Mary's Sch., Staten Island, 1971-74; staff Vacation Day Camp, N.Y.C. Bd. Edn., 1973-75; dir. activities and vols. Golden Gate Health Care Ctr., Staten Island, 1974—; recreation cons. Princeton Nursing Home, N.J., 1980-81, Sheepshead Nursing Home, Bklyn., 1984—; lectr., seminar presenter. Treas. Deborah Heart Found., Staten Island, 1985—; mem. scholarship com. Chiropractic Edn. Found., Inc., Albany, N.Y., 1985—. Recipient Worker's Pin, Deborah Hosp. Found., Browns Mills, N.J., 1984; Disting. Service award N.Y. State Chiropractic Assn. Dist. 5, 1985. Mem. N.Y. State Parks and Recreation Soc., Nat. Recreation and Parks Assn., Nat. Therapeutic Recreation Soc., Staten Island Activities Dirs. Assn. (treas. 1984—), Women's Aux. N.Y. State Chiropractic Assn. (dist. pres. 1981-84, state treas. 1984-85). Republican. Roman Catholic. Avocations: travel; interior decorating; playing piano; sewing; antiquing.

DIAS, JACQUELINE LYNN, management consultant; b. Burbank, Calif., Nov. 30, 1960; d. Lyndon Carroll and Beth Luine (Pierce) Rains; m. Michael John Dias, July 28, 1984. A.A. cum laude, La. Valley Jr. Coll., 1979; B.A. magna cum laude, Calif. State U.-Northridge, 1981; M.B.A., Pepperdine U. Office mgr. sales Val Corp./Am. Energy Savs., Northridge, Calif., 1980-81, Harold Ring & Assocs., Encino, Calif., 1981-82; energy services sales specialist Honeywell, Inc., Commerce, Calif., 1982-84; supr. Exec. Life, West Los Angeles, Calif., 1984-85; owner, mgmt. cons. Mgmt. Trends, Los Angeles, 1984—; cons. Tiger Enterprises, Los Angeles, 1983—, Hope Chapel, Venice, Calif., 1984—, Channel One Video, Venice, 1985. Campaign worker Mondale/Ferraro, Van Nuys, Calif., 1983, Jimmy Carter/Walter Mondale, Van Nuys, 1979. Mem. Adminstrv. Mgmt. Soc. (Speaker award 1985), Nat. Assn. Female Execs., Calif. Assn. Sch. Transp. ofcls. Democrat. Avocations: singing; acting; dancing; racquetball; swimming. Office: care Mgmt Trends 3814 Sawtelle Blvd Suite 8 Los Angeles CA 90066

DIAZ, ELENA, lawyer; b. Kingsville, Tex., Nov. 1, 1955; s. David and Dalia Isaura (Garza) D. B.A. with high honors (scholar), U. Tex.-Austin, 1977, J.D., 1980. Bar: Tex. 1980; lic. counselor. Law clk. U. Tex.-Austin, 1978-79, student atty. Criminal Def. Clinic, 1980; intern, student atty. Office Dist. Atty., Brownsville, Tex., 1979; jr. atty. IRS, Washington, 1980-81, assoc. atty., Dallas, 1981—. Voter registrar S.W. Voter Registration Project, Dallas, 1983-84; pro bono atty. Pvt. Bar Involvement, Dallas, 1984; return preparer Vol. Income Tax Assistance, Washington and Dallas, 1981, 84. Mem. ABA, Fed. Bar Assn., Mexican Am. Bar Assn. Dallas (sec. 1983-84), Hispanic C. of C., Phi Beta Kappa, Alpha Lambda Delta, Phi Kappa Phi. Democrat. Catholic. Clubs: Mexican Am. Bus. and Profl. Women's (dir. Dallas 1983-84), Hispanic Orgn. Women (Dallas). Home: 4721 Coles Manor Pl Apt 426 Dallas TX 75204 Office: Dist Counsel Office IRS 1100 Commerce Room 12A24 Dallas TX 75242

DIAZ, MAGNA M., librarian, educator; b. N.Y.C., Mar. 20, 1951; d. Jose Enrique Rodriguez and Juanita (Diaz) Rodriguez Garcia; m. Ramon A. Diaz, Jr., May 1, 1976. 1 dau., Joana Marie. B.A., U. P.R., 1972; postgrad. Community Coll. Phila., 1978, Temple U., summer 1979, 80; M.L.S., Rutgers U., 1980. Tchr. English Pub. Sch. Bd., P.R., 1972-76; bilingual cataloger Temple U., Merit Ctr., Phila., 1980; bilingual librarian Camden Free Pub. Library (N.J.), 1980-81; children's librarian Free Library Phila., 1981-82, bilingual librarian, 1983—; reference librarian Community Coll. Phila., 1982; chairperson Spanish com. Free Library Phila. Recipient HEW scholarship, 1980. Mem. ALA. Democrat. Lutheran. Home: 5243 Horrocks St Philadelphia PA 19124 Office: Free Library Phila 6th & Lehigh Ave Philadelphia PA 19133

DIAZ-DIAZ, MARIA TERESA, planner; b. Havana, Cuba, Aug. 27, 1939; came to U.S., 1961, naturalized, 1981; d. Armando and Rosario Diaz; m. Manuel Garcia-Avila, Jan. 28, 1967; children—Ileana E., Manolin, Daniel. Student, Havana U., 1959-61; B.B.A. in Fin. with high honors, U. P.R., 1981; B.B.A. in Acctg., Fla. U., 1980. Acct., Colon Fuste Diaz & Assocs., P.R., 1968-75; acct. Ocala Sunshine Co., Miami, Fla., 1979-80, v.p., 1984; profl. planner New Eng. Mut. Life Ins. Co., Miami, 1985—; pres. Mid & Assocs., Miami, 1986—. Contbr. poems, essays to lit. mag., 1967-69. Mem. Cuban Acct. Assn., Nat. Assn. Female Execs., New Eng. Life Leaders Assn. Presbyterian. Avocation: organ. Office: New Eng Life Ins Co 7270 NW 12th St Suite 200 Miami FL 33126

DI BIETZ, ERICA MARGRETHE, state mental health official; b. N.Y.C., Nov. 2, 1935; d. August and Elizabeth (Hutka) DiBietz; B.A., Columbia U., 1955; M.S.W. (John F. Kennedy fellow), U. Md., 1976, now postgrad.; children—Regina Antunes, Lisette Antunes, Alexander Antunes. Asst. to sec. for trust and estate law Trust div. N.Y. State Bankers Assn., N.Y.C., 1956-59; tchr. child life, counselor Johns Hopkins Hosp., Balt., 1973-74, mem. women's bd., 1966—; med. social worker John F. Kennedy Inst. Habilitation of Children, Balt., 1974-75; dir. spl. programs Md. Dept. Health and Mental Hygiene, Springfield Hosp. Center, Sykesville, Md., 1977-85, co-founder, Family support group in state hosp., 1979-82, dir. spl. population programs, chmn. staff devel. com., 1978-79, spl. asst. to asst. secretariat, 1985—, mem. patient adv. coms. Md. Atty. Gen.'s Office, 1979-83; mem. continuing edn. com. U. Md., 1978-80; coordinator human rights adv. com. Springfield Hosp., chmn. unit for deaf psychiat. patients steering com. Mem. women's com. Balt. Symphony Orch., 1965-69; founder Dulaney Symphony Soc., 1968; del. public edn. nominating conv. Baltimore County Bd. Edn., 1977-78. HEW grantee, 1974; Mem. Am. Psychol. Assn., Md. Psychol. Assn., Am. Hosp. Assn., Am. Assn. Mental Deficiency, Nat. Alliance for Mentally Ill. (edn. and curriculum com.). Episcopalian. Author works in field. Home: 2309 Foxley Rd Timonium MD 21093 Office: Md State Dept Health and Mental Hygiene 201 W Preston St Baltimore MD 21201

DIBLIN, PATTI KAY, software development company administrator; b. Fresno, Calif., Dec. 28, 1956; d. Donald Edward and Frances Mae (Samson) D. B.S. in Acctg., Calif. Poly. U., 1982. Acct., Coopers & Lybrand, Los Angeles, 1982-83, Lear-Seigler Inc., Santa Monica, Calif., 1983-85; contract adminstr. LOGICON Inc., San Pedro, Calif., 1985—; speaker aerospace Women's Employment Options Conf., Los Angeles, 1985. Mem. selection com. YWCA, Los Angeles, 1985. Mem. Nat. Contract Mgmt. Assn., Nat. Assn. Female Execs. Republican. Mem. Ch. of Religious Science. Avocations: running. Home: 550 Orange Ave 120 Long Beach CA 90802

DI CARLO, ELLA MERKEL, newspaper columnist, historian; b. Plauen, Germany, July 11, 1919; came to U.S., 1927; d. Paul Albin and Martha Frieda (Paeltz) Merkel; m. Joseph Anthony Di Carlo Dec. 27, 1939; children—Sandra, Joseph, Donna Maria, Jeffrey. Student Smith Coll., 1966-67, Holyoke Community Coll., 1967-68, Am. Internat. Coll., 1974. Lay preacher Conn. Valley Unitarian-Universal Assn., Conn. and Mass., 1966—; reporter Transcript-Telegram, Holyoke, Mass., 1968-70, news and wire editor, 1970-73, columnist, 1970—, editorial page editor, 1973-80, asst. to editor and pub., 1973-84; corporator Peoples' Savs. Bank, Holyoke, 1980—; hist. cons. Holyoke Heritage Park, 1984—; Author: Keep Your Meter Running, 1964; The Black Community in Holyoke, 1979; Holyoke-Chicopee: A Perspective, 1982; contbr. articles, stories and poems to mags. and newspapers. Treas. Holyoke Republican City Com., 1968-82; bd. dirs. Holyoke chpt. NCCJ, 1967—, Urban Ministry, Holyoke, 1978-81; charter mem. Friends of Holyoke Mus., sec. 1959-63; mem. Mayor's Com. on Power Proposal, 1964; chmn. Ecumenical Centennial Com., 1972; mem pub. relations com. Mental Health Bd., 1969-71. Recipient Human Relations award NCCJ, 1972; award for editorial writing Northeastern Assn. Press Execs. Assn., 1980; named Woman of Yr., Italian Progressive Soc., 1985. Mem. LWV. Clubs: Holyoke Women's (pres. 1962-63), Wistariahurst Mus. (v.p. 1981-82). Home: Main Poland Rd Conway MA 01341

DICENSO, MELANIE SUE, financial planner; b. Flint, Mich., Feb. 21, 1955; d. Jean Lolah (Cash) Hemming; m. Gregory DiCenso, Dec. 27, 1975 (div. Dec. 1980). Student savs. adminstrn. Inst. Fin. Edn., Salt Lake City, 1977-78. Lic. in securities and ins., Mich.; cert. fin. planner. With Prudential Fed. Savs. & Loan, Salt Lake City, 1976-78, First Citizens Bank, Troy, Mich., 1978-80, Rockwell Internat. Credit Union, Troy, 1980-84, Van Arnem Fin. Services, Birmingham, Mich., 1984; registered rep., individual and corp. fin. planning Mariner Fin. Services, Plymouth, Mich., 1984—. Vol. worker Big Sisters/Big Bros. Assn., Detroit, 1982. Mem. Internat. Assn. Fin. Planners. Club: Zonta Internat., Women's Club Troy (house ways and means com. 1985—). Avocations: skiing; hang-gliding. Home: 27306 Parkview Blvd Suite 7311 Warren MI 48092 Office: Mariner Fin Services 42209 Ann Arbor Rd Plymouth MI 48170

DICK, FLORENE FAYE, writer/photographer; b. Los Angeles, Jan. 18, 1922; d. Joseph and Wilhelmina Faye (Vivial) Harwich; student Los Angeles City Coll., 1939-41; m. George Oliver Perkins, Mar. 15, 1941 (dec. Apr. 1945); m. 2d, Ernest Lee Dick, Feb. 4, 1946; children—Virginia Faye Perkins Paschke, Barbara Lee Dick Enfield, Frank Joseph. Research librarian Wallace & Tiernan, Monrovia, Calif., 1955-57; editor/proofreader Stanford Research Inst., Menlo Park, Calif., 1959-61; tech. editor ElectroData Corp., Pasadena, Calif., 1961, Aerojet ElectroSystems Co., Azusa, Calif., 1961, 65-67, 78; lit. search editor Jet Propulsion Lab., Pasadena, 1962; sec. to Dr. Linus Pauling, Calif. Inst. Tech., Pasadena, 1963-64; med. sec. Childrens Hosp., Los Angeles, 1964; people editor, then editor Azusa Herald, 1967-73; news writer Citrus Coll., Azusa, 1973-74; freelance writer/photographer, 1972—; publs./news editor Pomona Coll., Claremont, Calif., 1974-76, 79-80; co-owner E.L. Dick Machine Shop, Upland, Calif., 1974—; staff writer/photographer West End Guide (now Night and Day Guide), Upland, Calif., 1980—; vol. proofreader Aid to Visually Handicapped, Pasadena, 1961-64. Bd. dirs. Calif. Clinic Sch., Puente, 1968-70; charter mem. aux. Foothill Presbyn. Hosp., Glendora, Calif., 1968; mem. prodn. com. Miss Azusa Pageant, also chaperone to Miss Calif. Pageant, Santa Cruz, Calif., 1967-72. Recipient various certs. merit. Mem. Press Club So. Calif. (charter), Nat. Fedn. Press Women, Calif. Press Women (1st pl. editor award 1973). Home: PO Box 1407 Upland CA 91786 Office: Night and Day Guide 1153 W 9th St Upland CA 91786

DICK, NANCY E., lieutenant governor Colorado; b. Detroit, July 22, 1930; B.A. in Bus. Adminstrn., Mich. State U.; m. Stephen Barnett; children—Margot, Timber, Justin. Mem. Colo. Gen. Assembly, 1974-79, vice chmn. transp. and energy com., 1975-76; lt. gov. of Colo., 1979—; chmn. Colo. Rural Council; mem. U.S. steering com. Inst. Cultural Affairs Internat. Expn. Rural Devel., 1983. Chmn., Colo. Council Indian Affairs; exec. bd. Gov.'s Interstate Indian Council, 1981-83; leader trade mission to Hunan Province, China, 1983. Named Disting. Alumna, Mich. State, U., 1981. Democrat. Office: Office of Lt Gov State Capitol Bldg Room 144 Denver CO 80203

DICK, SHERYL LYNN, lawyer; b. Kansas City, Mo., Apr. 9, 1954; d. Robert Dean and Margaret Louise (Adamson) D. B.S., U. Kans.-Lawrence, 1976; J.D., Washburn U., 1983. Bar: Kans. 1983. Tchr., Shawnee Mission (Kans.) Pub. Schs., 1977-80; atty. Mut. Benefit Life Ins. Co., Kansas City, Mo., 1984—. Contbr. Washburn Law Jour., 1982, tech. editor, 1982-83. Mem. ABA, Kans. Bar Assn., Phi Delta Phi (vice magister 1981-82). Office: Mut Benefit Life Ins Co 2323 Grand Ave Kansas City MO 64108

DICKEMANN, MILDRED, anthropology educator; b. Seattle, Oct. 12, 1929; d. Charles Theodore and Mildred Ione (Rogers) D. A.B., U. Mich., 1950; Ph.D., U. Calif.-Berkeley, 1958. Instr. Merritt Coll., Oakland, Calif., 1960-64; asst. prof. U. Kans., Lawrence, 1964-67; assoc. prof. Sonoma State U., Rohnert Park, Calif., 1968-72, prof., 1972—. Contbr. articles to profl publs. Fellow NSF, Harry F. Guggenheim Found. Fellow Am. Anthrop. Assn., Sigma Xi; mem. Council of Anthropology and Edn., Soc. Med. Anthropology. Democrat. Clubs: East Bay Lesbian and Gay. Home: 1728 Allston Way Berkeley CA 94703 Office: Sonoma State U Dept Anthropology 1801 E Cotati Ave Rohnert Park CA 94928

DICKENS, ALICE MOSS, educational administrator; b. Newark, Nov. 5, 1940; d. Eugene Labon and Lillian (Knowles) Moss; m. Clarence Albert Dickens, Aug. 10, 1968 (div.); 1 child, Nicole Pearlene. B.A., Newark State Coll., 1962; M.A., 1973; Ed.D., Rutgers U., 1984. Tchr. Newark Bd. Edn., 1962-71, asst. to prin., 1971-74, vice prin., 1974-79, acting prin., 1979-80, prin., 1980—; free-lance lectr. pub. speaker, No. N.J., 1980-85. Author: How Little is Little, 1979; author, editor: I Want, 1980. Dist. leader East Orange Democratic Orgn., N.J., 1970-72, first ward chairlady, 1970-72, sec. com., 1970-72. Recipient Outstanding Service award Newark Vice Prins. Assn., 1976, 77, 78. Mem. City Adminstrs. and Suprs. Assn., Assn. Supervision and Curriculum Devel., N.E. Coalition Ednl. Leaders, Newark Prins. Assn., Kappa Delta Pi, Iota Phi Lambda (sec. 1983-84). Roman Catholic. Avocations: tennis; swimming; reading. Office: Warren St Sch 200 Warren St Newark NJ 07103

DICKENS, DORIS LEE (MRS. AUSTIN LECOUNT FICKLING), psychiatrist; b. Roxboro, N.C., Oct. 12; d. Lee Edward and Delma Ernestine (Hester) Dickens; B.S. magna cum laude, Va. Union U., 1960; M.D., Howard U., 1966; m. Austin LeCount Fickling, Oct. 15, 1975. Intern, St. Elizabeth's Hosp., Washington, 1966-67, resident, 1967-70; staff psychiatrist, dir. Mental Health Program for Deaf, St. Elizabeth's Hosp., Washington, after 1970, now chief program; cons. NIMH. Bd. dirs. Nat. Health Care Found. for Deaf. Recipient Dorothea Lynde Dix award, 1980; diplomate Nat. Bd. Med. Examiners. Mem. Am. Psychiat. Assn., Washington Psychiat. Soc., Alpha Kappa Mu, Beta Kappa Chi. Author: How and When Psychiatry Can Help You, 1972; You and Your Doctor; contbg. author: Hearing and Hearing Impairment, 1979; contbg. author Counseling Deaf People, Research and Practice. Home: 12308 Surrey Circle Tantallon MD 20022 Office: 2700 Martin L King Ave Washington DC 20032

DICKENS, VERA JOSIE, beauty supply company executive; b. Dixon, Mo., Nov. 27, 1933; d. Thomas Leddel and Lydia Louise (Tackett) Bacon; m. Harold Freddie Dickens, June 4, 1949; children—Harold Joseph, William Lee. Br. mgr. Midwest Beauty Supply, Jonesboro, Ark., 1964-76; mgr. Cache Beauty Supply, Jonesboro, 1976-83, corp. pres., 1983—. Mem. Beauty and Barber Supply Inst. Mem. Christian Ch. Lodge: Eastern Star. Office: Cache Beauty Supply Inc 2826 E Highland Dr Jonesboro AR 72401

DICKER, DAWN ELANA, broadcasting executive; b. Balt., Dec. 24, 1958; d. Herbert Harry and Anne Merle (Knowles) Hochhalter; m. Ron. J. Dicker, June 14, 1980. B.A. in English and Creative Writing, Towson State U., 1979. Pub. relations asst. Savs. Bank Balt., 1979-82; announcer Sta.-WTOW, Towson, Md., 1979-82; announcer-pub. service Sta.-WABS, Arlington, Va., 1982-83, asst. program dir., 1983-85, program dir., 1985—. Contbr. articles to local newspapers, 1979-82, album revs. to CCM Mag., 1984. Mem. Lambda Iota Tau. Republican. Office: Sta WABS 5545 Lee Hwy Arlington VA 22207

DICKERSON, BETTY JEAN, nurse; b. Cotton Plant, Ark., Dec. 16, 1936; d. Laurence Von and LaVerne Roddy; A.A. in Nursing, Ind. U., 1971; B.S. Nursing, Purdue U., 1976; M.S. in Restorative Nursing Govs. State U., 1980; m. Robert E. Dickerson, Jan. 8, 1954; children—Carolyn, Edward, Monteena. Staff nurse Our Lady of Mercy Hosp., Dyer, Ind., 1971; staff nurse pediatrics St. Mary Med. Center, Gary, Ind., 1971-75, asst. dir. nursing service, 1975-83, asst. adminstr. nursing services, 1983—, instr. heart-lung assessment, 1977-79; instr. med. secs. Marion Bus. Coll., 1973-74; clin. nurse instr. Ind. U. N.W., 1980-81. Bd. dirs. Ind. U. N.W., 1981—, v.p., 1985-86, pres., 1986-87; bd. dirs. Hospice N.W. Ind., 1981—, 3d v.p., 1985-86, 86-87. Recipient Outstanding Nurse of Yr. award Ind. U., 1971, Very Spl. Person award Ind. U. N.W. Sch. Nursing, 1984. Mem. Ind. State, Am. nurses assns., Nat. League Nursing, Ind. U., Purdue U., Govs. State U. alumni assns., Ind. U. Nurses Soc. (alumni), Young Women's Christian Council. Author hosp. pediatrics teaching manual, 1974. Home: Gary IN 46404

DICKERSON, LAUREL, data processing executive; b. Erie, Pa., Sept. 2, 1943; d. Norman Kingston and Jayne Lucille (Willits) D. B.A., Park Coll., 1967; M.A., Mich. State U., 1973, Ph.D., 1977. Vol. Peace Corps, Columbia, S.Am., 1964-66; mgmt. specialist U.S. Dept. Army, Washington, 1967-70; edn. specialist U.S. Office Edn., Washington, 1970-72; faculty U. Md., Balt., 1976-77, U. Fla., Gainesville, 1977-83; tech. audit coordinator Data Gen. Corp., Milford, Mass., 1983-85; mgr. CAI/CAVI devel. Data Gen. Corp., 1985—; cons. in field. Author: The Management of Reading Instruction, 1983. Bd. dirs. Women's Half-Way House, Gainesville, 1980-82. Mem. Women in Instructional Tech. (founder, coordinator), Assn. for Edn. Communications and Tech. (div. pres. 1980-81, dir. 1979-80), Assn. for Ednl. Communications and Tech. Avocations: motorcycling; roller skating; reading. Home: 6 Highwood Dr Franklin MA 02038 Office: Data Gen Corp 50 Maple St Milford MA 01757

DICKERSON, NANCY HANSCHMAN, television producer, journalist; b. Milw.; d. Frederick R. and Florence (Conners) Hanschman; student Clarke Coll., Dubuque, Iowa; grad. U. Wis., 1948; postgrad. Harvard U.; H.H.D., Am. Internat. Coll., Springfield, Mass.; m. Claude Wyatt Dickerson, Feb. 24, 1962 (div. 1983); children—Elizabeth, Ann, Jane, Michael, John. Sch. tchr., Milw.; staff asst. Senate Fgn. Relations Com., Washington; prod. CBS News, 1956-60. 1st woman news corr., 1960-63; news corr. NBC, 1963-70; news analyst Inside Washington, syndicated nationally for TV stas., 1971—; producer spl. syndicated TV programs, pres. Dickerson Co., 1971—; founder, exec. producer TV Corp. Am., 1980—; polit. commentator Newsweek Broadcasting Service; reporter Pres. Kennedy's funeral, Republican and Democratic convs., Civil Rights March on Washington, Kennedy, Johnson and Nixon inaugurations; represented Pub. Broadcasting Corp. on all-network Conversation with Pres. Nixon, 1970; lectr. Trustee, Am. U. Recipient Collegian award LaSalle Coll., Phila.; Spirit of Achievement award Albert Einstein Coll., Yeshiva U.; Sigma Delta Chi award Boston U.; Pioneer award New Eng. Women's Press Assn.; Peabody award and ABA Silver Gavel award for 1982 TV program on Watergate; assoc. fellow Pierson Coll., Yale U., 1972—. Mem. Radio-TV News Analysts. Clubs: Washington Press (past v.p.), Federal City. Author: Among Those Present, 1976. Office: 1811 Kalorama Sq Washington DC 20008

DICKERSON, PAMELA MAY, writer; b. Orange, Calif., June 6, 1961; d. Joseph Beattie, III and Norma May (Miller) D. B.A. in Bus. Adminstrn., B.A. in English summa cum laude, Chapman Coll., 1980. Free-lance writer, editor, Garden Grove, Calif., 1980-84; documentation mgr. Am. Data Industries, Irvine, Calif., 1984—. Contbr. miscellaneous articles to newspapers. Mem. Nat. Assn. for Female Execs., Soc. for Tech. Communication, Islamic Computer Soc., Orange County Islamic Soc. (mem. publs. com. 1982—), Smithsonian Assocs. Republican. Muslim. Avocations: reading; theater.

DICKEY, CHERYL, financial services company executive; b. Lynwood, Calif., Nov. 13, 1959; d. Elmer Daniel and Jacquelyn Joan (Myers) D. A.A., Fullerton Coll., 1982; student Calif. Poly. Inst.-Pomona, 1982-85; Owner, operator Self-Services, Santa Ana, Calif., 1978-84; account exec. Dun & Bradstreet, Los Angeles, 1985—. Republican. Avocations: classical piano; skiing; writing. Home: 1213 Vega Circle LaVerne CA 92701

DICKEY, JULIA EDWARDS, librarian, management and organizational consultant; b. Sioux Falls, S.D., Mar. 6, 1940; d. John Keith and Henrietta Barbara (Zerell) Edwards; student DePauw U., 1958-59; A.B., Ind. U., 1962, M.L.S., 1967, postgrad., 1967; m. Joseph E. Dickey, June 18, 1959; children—Joseph E., John Edwards. Asst. acquisitions librarian Ind. U. Regional Campus Libraries, 1965-67; head tech. services Bartholomew County Library, Columbus, Ind., 1967-74; reference dir. Southeastern Ind. Area Library Services Authority, 1974-78, dir., 1978-80; pres. Pea Patch Airlines div. Jedco Enterprises, 1981—; pres. Ind. EAA Council, 1982—; pres. Human Services, Inc., 1976-78, sec. 1975, v.p., 1977; legis. strategy chmn. Ind. Library Coop. Devel., 1975. Mem. Columbus exec. bd. Mayor's Task Force on Status of Women, 1973—; del. Ind. Sch. Nominating Assembly, 1973-75, 75-77; mem. adv. council Ind./Nat. Network Study, 1977-79; bd. dirs. Columbus Women's Center; precinct coordinator Vols. For Bayh, 1974; treas. Hayes for State Rep. Com., 1978, 82, 84—; sheriff Columbus 1st precinct, 1975, clk., 1976-77, insp., 1978, judge, 1980, 82. Mem. ALA, Ind. Library Assn. (dist. chmn. 1972-73, pres. library edn. div. 1980-81; legis. com. jointly with Ind. Library Trustees Assn. 1978-81), Library Assts. and Technicians Round Table (chmn. 1968-69), Tech. Services Round Table (chmn. 1971-72, sec. library planning com. jointly with Ind. Library Trustees Assn. 1969-72), AAUW (pres. 1973-75), Bartholomew County Library Staff Assn. (pres. 1975-76), Internat. Exptl. Aircraft Assn. (founding pres. Columbus chpt. 1981, pres. state orgn. 1982—, major achievement award for service to Sport aviation 1983), Psi Iota Xi (v.p.). Clubs: Zonta (newsletter editor 1981-84, rec. sec. 1984-85), First Tuesday Forum (Columbus). Home and Office: 511 Terrace Lake Rd Columbus IN 47201

DICKEY, MARY PATRICK, communications executive; b. Birmingham, Ala., July 3, 1946; d. John T. and Kathryn (Ahearn) Byrnes; m. David E. Pavlick, Sept. 13, 1975 (div. June 1981); m. 2d, Alan Ford Dickey, June 21, 1981; 1 son, John Bartlett. A.A., Marymount Coll., 1966; B.A., Duquesne U., 1968. Editor, Am. Express, N.Y.C., 1969-72; editor/promotion writer Ziff-Davis Pub. Co., N.Y.C., 1972-75, Penthouse Internat., N.Y.C., 1975-76; copywriter Home Box Office, N.Y.C., 1979-80, mgr. creative services, 1980-82, dir. creative services, 1982—. Contbr. articles to profl. jours. Mem. AAUW, Nat. Acad. TV Arts and Scis., Women in Cable, N.Y. Women in Communications. Democrat. Congregationalist. Home: 61 Hawthorne Pl Summit NJ 07901 Office: Home Box Office 1271 6th Ave New York NY 10020

DICKINSON, CATHERINE SCHATZ, microbiologist; b. Cin., Jan. 6, 1927; d. Ralph Marvin and Mabel (Dare) Schatz; student U. Cin., 1944-46, postgrad. 1952; A.B., Miami U., Oxford, Ohio, 1948; m. Willard C. Dickinson, Jr., June 23, 1956; children—Kellie Dare, Bradley Clark. Supr., Bacteriology Lab., Children's Hosp., Cin., 1948-53; supr., sect. head Microbiology Lab., Ochsner Found. Hosp., New Orleans, 1953—; lectr. in field. Mem. New Orleans Area Soc. for Microbiology (pres. 1979), Am. Soc. Microbiology, Am. Soc. Clin. Pathologists (specialist in microbiology), New Orleans Soc. Microbiology, Nat. Registry for Microbiologists, Delta Zeta. Episcopalian. Club: Order Eastern Star. Home: 10001 Hyde Pl River Ridge LA 70123 Office: 1516 Jefferson Hwy New Orleans LA 70121

DICKINSON, DANA LYNNE, engineer; b. Dayton, Ohio, Oct. 6, 1951; d. John David and Hertha Doris (Whitford) D. S.B., S.M., MIT, 1974. Cons. engr. Arthur D. Little, Inc., Cambridge, Mass., 1975-76; sr. engr. Gen. Electric Knolls Atomic Power Lab., Schenectady, N.Y., 1976—; free lance computer programmer, 1983—. Avocations: bicycling, piano, bridge, volleyball. Home: Box 1198 Saratoga Springs NY 12866 Office: Gen Electric Knolls Atomic Power Lab Box 1072 Schenectady NY 12301

DICKINSON, JANE W. (MRS. E.F. SHERWOOD DICKINSON), club woman; b. Kalamazoo, Sept. 27, 1919; d. Charles Herman and Rachel (Whaler) Wagner; student Hollins Coll., 1938-39; B.A., Duke U., 1941; M.Ed., Goucher Coll., 1965; m. E.F. Sherwood Dickinson, Oct. 23, 1943; children—Diane Jane Gray Clem, Carolyn Dickinson Vane. Exec. sec. Petroleum Industry Com., Balt., 1941-43; exec. sec. Sherwood Feed Mills Inc., Balt., 1943-79. Mem. exec. com. Children's Aid Md., 1960-61; mem. bd. women's aux. Balt. Symphony Orch., 1958-60; dist. chmn. Balt. Cancer Drive, 1958; dist. chmn. Balt. Mental Health Drive, 1957; co-chmn. Balt. United Appeal, 1968; bd. mgrs. Pickersgill Retirement Home. Mem. Alpha Delta Phi. Republican. Episcopalian. Clubs: Three Arts (sec. 1958-60, bd. govs. 1960-64, 67—, pres. 1970-72) (Balt.); Women's (bd. govs. 1960-64) (Roland Park); Cliff Dwellers Garden. Home: 1003 Bellemore Rd Baltimore MD 21210

DICKINSON, JUNE MCWADE, foundation administrator; b. Rochester, N.Y., June 26, 1924; d. Howard L. and Esther G. (Benz) McWade; privately educated; M.F.A., Internat. U.; L.H.D. (hon.), Calif. Christian U., D.D., 1980; m. Edward Dickinson, May 3, 1946 (dec. 1975). Cert. lay profl. Episcopal Ch. Founder, 1949, since pres. Schumann Meml. Found.; registered music therapist; dir. Casterbridge Village Fine Arts, Conesus, N.Y., 1963——; owner Ink Pen Beacon, weekly newspaper, Conesus, 1962—, Livingston Enterprises, Lakeville, N.Y.; grantsman, pres. Casterbridge Village Devel. Corp.; mem. adj. faculty Calif. Christian U., Internat. U., also Univ. Insts. depts. City Temple Programs; dir. pub. relations St. Michael's Epis. Ch., Geneseo, N.Y. Mem. panel for women's ednl. equity program HEW; bd. dirs. Western Region Bishopric of Ecumenical Religion and Gen. Edn.; mem. steering com. Com. for Whole Ministry of Episcopal Ch., Diocese of Rochester, chairperson Episcopal Women's History Project. Recipient Community Leader of Am. award, 1969; decorated knight's cross Order Merit (Fed. Republic Ger.); named Rochester Citizen of Day (2), Livingston County Citizen of Week. Fellow Internat. Biog. Assn.; mem. Women in Founds./Corporate Philanthropy, ASCAP, Coll. Music Soc., League of Women Composers, Advs. for the Arts, Livingston County C. of C., Internat. Platform Assn., Rochester Women's Network, Episcopal Communicators, Confraternity of Blessed Sacrament, Compeer, Thomas Hardy Soc. (Dorchester, Eng.). Clubs: Conesus Lake Sportsmen, Conesus Lake Water Ski (founder, adviser, sr. mem.); Rochester. Composer: Love's Wine, Sunset Through the Rain, Old Valentines, Glass Balls on a Christmas Tree, High School Memories, My Hand in God's, Happy Pilgrims, My Irish Coleen, In a Bavarian Garden. Address: 2904 E Lake Rd Livonia NY 14487

DICKINSON, LAURA ANN, lawyer; b. Aberdeen, S.D., Oct. 31, 1956; d. Pierre Owen and Beatrice Ann (Irmen) D.; m. Thomas J. Lee, Apr. 28, 1984. B.S., U. S.D., 1979; J.D., U. Notre Dame, 1982. Bar: Ill. 1982. Corporate atty. McDonald's Corp., Oak Brook, Ill., 1982—. Univ. scholar U. S.D., Vermillion, 1979. Mem. ABA (bus. law sect. 1982—), Ill. State Bar Assn. (pub. relations com. 1983—, young lawyer's div. sect. council 1983—), Phi Beta Kappa, Phi Alpha Theta. Democrat. Roman Catholic. Home: 2754 Hampden Ct Apt 1705 Chicago IL 60614 Office: McDonald's Corp One McDonald's Plaza Oak Brook IL 60521

DICKINSON, SUZANNE MARY, neurologist; b. Montreal, Que., Can., Sept. 17, 1943; came to U.S., 1975; d. Jerome Joseph and Helen Mary (Hyman) Kelly; m. Jack A. Goldberg, Mar. 5, 1978. B.S., Simmons Coll., Boston, 1968; M.S., Boston U., 1970; M.D., McMaster U., Hamilton, Ont., Can., 1973. Intern, McMaster U., 1974-75; resident Montefiore Hosp., Bronx, N.Y., 1975-76; resident and chief resident in neurology Mt. Sinai Hosp., N.Y.C., 1977-80; practice medicine specializing in neurology, N.Y.C., 1980—; cons. neurologist Gracie Square Hosp., N.Y.C., 1980—. Mem. Coll. Physicians and Surgeons Ont., Am. Acad. Neurology, N.Y. Acad. Scis., AMA. Office: 2 E 77th St New York NY 10021

DICKLIN, JACKIE MARIE, nutrition educator; b. Milw., Sept. 23, 1954; m. John Edward Dicklin, July 26, 1980. B.S. in Dietetics, U. Wis., 1978. Asst. dietitian Mequon Care Ctr., Wis., 1978-79; food service mgr. Scottsdale Nursing Ctr., Ariz., 1979; nutritionist Mesa Unified Sch. Dist., Ariz., 1979-81; nutrition edn. specialist Ariz. Dept. Edn. and U. Ariz., 1981-82; dir. Focus: Nutrition 2, Inc., Phoenix, 1982—; instr. Ariz. Dept. Edn., 1982-83, Ariz. State U., Tempe, 1981; day care home insp. Recipient Citation of Merit, Gov. Ariz., 1982. Mem. Soc. for Nutrition Edn., Educators in Industry. Roman Catholic. Avocations: sports; racquetball; aerobics. Address: 13035 N 68th St Phoenix AZ 85254

DICKMAN, CYNTHIA MARLENE, stockbroker; b. Auburn, Ind., Jan. 19, 1953; d. Burtis Lee and Elsie Caroline (Baughman) Dickman; m. Thomas Michael Fisher, June 7, 1980 (div. Jan. 1982). B.A. in Math., Ind. U., 1976. Mktg. rep. IBM Corp., Ft. Wayne, Ind., 1975-77; account rep. Office Interiors, Inc., Ft. Wayne, 1977-79; stockbroker Merrill Lynch, Ft. Wayne, 1979-80, Dallas, 1982—; owner Fisher Products, Mt. Zion, Ill., 1980-82. Mem. Network Profl. Women, 500 Inc. Republican. Mem. Disciples of Christ. Club: University (Dallas). Home: 4050 Frankford Rd Unit 502 Dallas TX 75252 Office: Merrill Lynch 5580 LBJ Freeway Dallas TX 75252

DICKMAN, DONNA MCCORD, audiologist; b. Colon, Panama, Jan. 19, 1942; d. William Oree and Irene (Dimmer) McCord; m. Robert Neil Dickman, Apr. 22, 1967; 1 child, Eric McCord. B.A., Mary Washington Coll., 1963; M.Ed., U. Va., 1965; Ph.D., U. Md., 1973. Cert. in audioloby and speech pathology. Audiologist Children's Med. Center, Washington, 1965-68, VA Hosp., Washington, 1968-72; dir. hearing conservation program Washington Hearing Soc., 1973-75; dir. environ. noise program Council of Govts., Washington, 1975-81; dir. tng. services Nat. Energy Ctr., Washington, 1981-82; dir. confs. and convs. Alexander Graham Bell Assn. for Deaf, Washington, 1983—. Author: Sounds Alive, 1979; Preparing for a Quieter Tomorrow, 1979. Founding mem. Friends of Kennedy Ctr., Washington, 1967. Recipient award U.S. EPA, 1981. Mem. Am. Speech and Hearing Assn., Acoustical Soc. Am.,

Nat. Assn. Noise Control Ofcls. (bd. dirs. 1979-80). Home: 2623 O St NW Washington DC 20007 Office: Alexander Graham Bell Assn 3417 Volta Pl Washington DC 20007

DICKMAN, VIRGINIA MYERS (MRS. RONALD), legal secretary; b. Tampa, Fla., Oct. 1, 1940; d. Thomas B. and Virginia Kathryn (Robinson) Kirby; student public schs. Sec. to Walter Burnside, Jr., Tampa, 1958-61; sec. Hughes Aircraft Co., Newport News, Va., 1961-62; sec. Lifsey & Johnston, Attys., Tampa, 1962-66, Shackleford, Farrior, Stallings & Evans, Tampa, 1966—. Named Legal Sec. of Yr. Tampa Legal Secs. Assn., 1977-78. Mem. Nat. Assn. Legal Secs., Fla. Assn. Legal Secs. (del. state conv. 1979-81, 84, ways and means chmn. 1980-81, corr. sec. 1981-82), Tampa Legal Secs. Assn. (pres. 1978-79, gov. 1979-81, legal edn. co-chmn. 1980-81, historian 1982, 85, public relations chmn., parliamentarian 1981-84, fundraiser chmn. 1982-85), Presbyterian. Home: 121 Floral Dr Tampa FL 33613 Office: Shackleford Farrior Stallings & Evans PO Box 3324 Tampa FL 33601

DICKSON, BARBARA GAIL, bank trust executive; b. Oakland, Calif., May 7, 1951; d. Edward H. and Elizabeth C. (Clark) D.; m. Edward Everett Smiley, Jan. 14, 1984. B.A., Tulane U., 1973; M.S. in Fin., U. Tex., Dallas, 1985. Acctg. clk. Sunmark Co., St. Louis, 1974-75; research asst. 1st Nat. Bank, Palm Beach, Fla., 1973-74; research asst. Republic Bank, Dallas, 1975-78, statis. analyst, 1978-80, portfolio mgr., asst. v.p. and trust officer, 1980—. Sunday sch. tchr. Saint Michael's and All Angels Episcopal. Chs., Dallas, 1982—. Mem. Fin. Analysts Fedn., U. Tex. Fin. Club, Kappa Alpha Theta. Republican. Club: Tulane Alumni (Dallas). Home: 7207 Marquette St Dallas TX 75225 Office: Republic Bank PO Box 241 Dallas TX 75221

DICKSON, CAROL ANNE, educator, consultant; b. Greenville, S.C. B.A., U. N.C.-Greensboro; M.A., Wake Forest Coll., Winston-Salem, N.C.; B.S., Fontbonne Coll., St. Louis, 1973; M.S., Ohio State U., 1975, Ph.D., 1979. Cons., C.A. Dickson Cons., Colorado Springs, Colo., 1979-81; asst. prof. U. Hawaii-Manoa, Honolulu, 19821—; dir. Fashion Group, Inc., Honolulu, Fashion Guild of Hawaii, Honolulu; cons. in field. Contbr. articles to profl. jours. Campaign mgr. Susie Shear, Mo. Ho. of Reps., St. Louis, 1973. Research grantee Ohio State U., 1978, Coll. Tropical Agr., 1983-85. Mem. Assn. Coll. Profs. Textiles and Clothing (jour. mktg. 1984—), Fashion Group Honolulu (program chmn. 1984-86), Internat. Fedn. Home Econs., Costume Soc. Am., Am. Home Econs. Assn., Am. Collegiate Retailing Assn. Roman Catholic. Avocations: flying; reading; creating in stained glass; gardening. Home: 1025 Wilder Ave 6A Honolulu HI 96822 Office: U Hawaii Dept Human Resources 2515 Campus Rd Honolulu HI 96822

DICKSON, EVA MAE, credit bureau executive; b. Clarion, Iowa, Jan. 16, 1922; d. James and Ivah Blanche (Breckenridge) D. Grad. Interstate Bus. Coll., Klamath Falls, Oreg., 1943. Reporter, Mchts. Credit Service, Klamath Falls, 1941, mgr., 1973—; credit dept. Montgomery Ward, Klamath Falls, 1941-42; bookkeeper Heilbronner Fuel Co., Klamath Falls, 1942; stenographer City of Klamath Falls, 1943, bookkeeper, office mgr., 1943-52; owner, operator All Star Bus. Service, Klamath Falls, 1953-58, Ace Mimeo Service, Klamath Falls, 1958-73. Bd. dirs. United Way, Klamath Falls, 1980—; sec. Klamath Community Concert Assn., 1956—; treas., memls. chmn. Klamath County chpt. Am. Cancer Soc.; bd. dirs., treas. Hope in Crisis; mem. Klamath County Centennial Com., 1982, Unification for Progress Joint Planning Com., 1985; mem. nursing adv. com. Oreg. Inst. Tech., 1982—; mem. Klamath Employment Tng. Adv. Com., 1983-86; bd. dirs., sec., treas. Klamath Consumer Council; sec. Unified City for Progress Task Force, 1983-84, Snowflake, Winter Festival, 1984-85. Recipient Bronze Leadership award Assoc. Credit Burs., Inc., 1976. Mem. Consumer Credit Assn. Oreg. (pres. 1984-85), Credit Women Internat. (treas. dist. 10 1984-85), Assoc. Credit Bur. Pacific N.W. (pres. 1981-82), Assoc. Credit Bur. Oreg. (pres. 1978-80), Klamath Basin Credit Women-Internat. (pres. 1976-78), Soc. Cert. Consumer Credit Exec., Internat. Consumer Credit Assn., Klamath County C. of C. (pres. 1979, ambassadors com. 1980—). Republican. Presbyterian. Club: Quota (pres. 1958-59, dist. gov. 1969-70). Avocations: painting, traveling. Office: Merchants Credit Service Inc 724 Main Room 200 Klamath Falls OR 97601

DICKSON, FLORA SPECTOR, govt. ofcl.; b. Buenos Aires, Argentina; d. Goodman Max and Rose C. (Herzlich) Spector; came to U.S., 1950, naturalized, 1960; student Columbia U., 1950; A.A., Miami Dade Community Coll., 1963; B.A., U. Miami, 1965; M.A., 1968, postgrad., 1968-69; children—Glenn, Errol, Robert. Teaching fellow U. Miami, 1967-68; instr. Spanish, Miami Dade Community Coll., 1968-69; social worker, public assistance eligibility specialist Fla. Dept. Health and Rehab. Services, Coral Gables, 1969-80, dist. XI staff adv. council rep., 1977-78, sec., 1979, adminstrv. asst. for client relations, 1980-82, residential placement coordinator for dist. program Office Devel. Services, Miami, 1982-84, human services program analyst Adult Congregate Living Facilities, 1984—. Sec., Temple Zamora, Coral Gables, Fla., 1974; pres. Friends Unlimited, Temple Beth Am. South Miami, Fla., 1975; facilitator Solo Center Dade County Mental Health Assn., 1977—; vol. Cedars of Lebanon Health Care Center; active various community drives. NDEA/HEW fellow, U. Miami, 1965. Mem. Friends Hispanic Am. Lit., AAUW, Sigma Delta Pi, Iota Tau Alpha. Democrat. Jewish. Office: 1320 S Dixie Hwy Coral Gables FL 33146

DICKSON, PEGGY SUE, realty executive; b. Oklahoma City, June 1, 1936; d. Henry L. and Dixie (Martin) Lyle; m. Herbert R. Dickson, Feb. 4, 1969 (div. Sept. 1979); children—Sally Kathleen, Garrett Guillory. B.A. magna cum laude, Lamar U., 1966. Tchr., Dallas Ind. Sch. Dist., 1967-68; sales Charles Freeman Realtors, Dallas, 1969-79; pres., relocation dir. Hank Dickerson Relocation Services, Inc., Dallas, 1979—; speaker in field. Mem. Nat. Bd. Realtors, Tex. Bd. Realtors, Tex. Relocation Council, Dallas Relocation Council, Relocation Dirs. Council, Phi Kappa Phi. Club: Exec. Women Dallas. Home: 5531 Boca Raton St Dallas TX 75230 Office: Hank Dickerson Realtors 17370 Preston Rd Dallas TX 75252

DICKSON-PORTER, CLAUDIA BLAIR, librarian; b. Memphis, Oct. 22, 1925; d. Walton Avery and Annie Laurie (Tate) Tucker; B.S., U. Nebr., Omaha, 1964; M.L.S., N. Tex. State U., Denton, 1971, Ph.D., 1979; m. Benjamin A. Dickson, June 5, 1945 (div.); children—Susan Dickson Morrison, Andrea Dickson Darby, Donna Dickson Stephens, Reid W., Bryan A.; m. 2d, William G. Porter, Feb. 8, 1978. Tchrs. schs. in Nebr. and Hawaii, 1964-71; librarian Nat. Assn. Retarded Citizens, Arlington, Tex., from 1971; dir. Regional Office TAS VI, Research and Tng Center in Mental Retardation Tex. Tech. U.; dir. planning Tex. Planning Council for Devel. Disabilities, Tex. Dept. Mental Health/Mental Retardation, 1979-80; program specialist Office of Devel. Disabilities, Office of Human Devel., Fed. Region VI, Dallas, 1980-82, grants mgmt. specialist Office of Fiscal Ops., 1982-83; Head Start Community rep. Adminstrn. for Children, Youth and Families, 1983-84; program specialist So. Region Adminstrn. on Developmental Disabilities, Fed. Region VI, 1984—; tchr. community services courses El Centro Jr. Coll., Dallas Recipient Disting. Alumnus award North Tex. State U., 1984. Mem. Spl. Libraries Assn., Southwestern, Tex. library assns., Am. Assn. Mental Deficiency, Council Exceptional Children, Soc. S.W. Archivists, Local History Soc., Phi Delta Kappa. Author, compiler in field. Home: 2413 Lakeside Dr Arlington TX 76013 Office: 1200 Main Tower Dallas TX 75202

DIDION, JOAN, author; b. Sacramento, Dec. 5, 1934; d. Frank Reese and Eduene (Jerrett) Didion; B.A., U. Calif., Berkeley, 1956; m. John Gregory Dunne, Jan. 1964; 1 dau., Quintana. Assoc. feature editor Vogue mag., 1956-63; former columnist Saturday Evening Post; former contbg. editor National Review; now freelance writer; novels: Run River, 1963, Play It As It Lays, 1971, A Book of Common Prayer, 1977, Democracy: A Novel, 1984; author books of essays Slouching Towards Bethlehem, 1969, The White Album, 1979, (non-fiction) Salvador, 1983; co-author screenplays for films The Panic in Needle Park, 1971, A Star Is Born, 1976. Recipient 1st prize Vogue's Prix de Paris, 1956; Breadloaf Writers Conf. fellow, 1963; Morton Dauwen Zabel fellow AAAL, 1978. Office: care Simon and Schuster Inc 1230 Ave of Americas New York NY 10020*

DIDOMENICO, DOROTHY ANN, cytotechnologist; b. Blossburg, Pa., Aug. 19, 1941; d. George Houk Gurnsey and Ann (Mahosky) Gurnsey Verdolini; children—Monica Angela Cole, Damien Anthony. Cert., Sch. Cytotech., Thomas Jefferson Med. Coll., 1960; student Va. Commonwealth U., evenings 1972-84. Cytotechnologist, Thomas Jefferson Med. Coll., Phila., 1960-61, 66-68; chief cytotechnologist Mercy Cath. Med. Ctr., Darby, Pa., 1968-70, St. Luke's Hosp., Richmond, Va., 1970-73; supr. cytology dept. Physician's Pathology Lab., Richmond, 1971-76, Retreat Hosp., Richmond, 1973-85; owner, mgr. DiDomenico Cytological Service, Inc., Richmond, 1976-85; sect. chief, cytology dept. Henrico Doctors Hosp., Richmond, 1985—; mem. profl. edn. com. Va. div. Am. Cancer Soc., 1976-78. Contbr. articles to mags. Am. Cancer Soc. scholar, 1959. Mem. Va. Soc. Cytology (mem. founding com., exec. com., 1st pres. 1976-77, chmn. bd. dirs. 1976-78, pres.-elect 1986-87), Internat. Acad. Cytology, Am. Soc. Clin. Pathologists, Am. Soc. Cytology, Am. Soc. for Cytotech. (regional dir. 1986-87), So. Assn. Cytotechnologists, Richmond Assn. Women Bus. Owners. Avocations: reading, swimming, cross stitch. Office: Henrico Doctors Hosp Cytology Dept 8921-23 Three Chopt Rd Richmond VA 23229

DIDRICKSON, LOLETA ANDERSON, state legislator; b. Chgo., May 22, 1941; d. J. Henning and Ruth (Anderson) Anderson; m. Charles E. Didrickson, June 17, 1961; children—Abby, Charles E., John. Student U. Ill., 1958-61; B.A., Governors State U., 1974. Legis. aide state senator 1979-82; gen. mgr. Titan Jack Mfg., Chicago Heights, 1981-82; mem. Ill. Ho. of Reps., 1983—. Mem. Jr. League Am., Rockford; pres. Homewood-Flossmoor High Sch. Parents Bd., Flossmoor, Ill., 1981; v.p., bd. dirs. Prairie State Coll. Found., Chicago Heights, 1982-83; precinct capt., area chmn. Rich Twp. Republicans, Cook County, 1978—; alt. del.-at-large Rep. nat. conv., 1984. Mem. Taylor Inst., South Suburban Assn. Commerce, LWV. Roman Catholic. Home: 1111 Brassie Ave Flossmoor IL 60422 Office: State Rep 18154 Harwood Ave Homewood IL 60430

DIE, ANN MARIE HAYES, psychologist, educator; b. Baytown, Tex., Aug. 15, 1944; d. Robert L. and Dorothy Ann (Cooke) Hayes; B.S. with highest honors, Lamar U., 1962; M.Ed., U. Houston, 1969; Ph.D., Tex. A&M U., 1977; m. Jerome Glynn Die, June 5, 1971; 1 dau., Meredith Anne. Tchr., Deepwater Elem. Sch., Deer Park, Tex., 1966-69, team leader, tchr., 1969-71; tchr. Lansdowne Elem. Sch., Lexington, Ky., 1971-73; asst. prof. dept. psychology Lamar U., 1977-82, assoc. prof., dir. Psychol. Clinic, 1982—, dir. grad. programs in psychology, 1981—, pres. Faculty Senate, 1985-86; adminstr. adolescent residential unit Mental Health Mental Retardation of S.E. Tex., 1979-80; pvt. practice clin. psychology, Beaumont, Tex., 1979—; mem. community adv. com. Beaumont State Center Human Devel., 1981—, Mental Health/Mental Retardation S.E. Tex., 1980—; participant Nat. Identification Program for Women, Am. Council on Edn., 1985; cons. in field. Group leader Juvenile Justice Workshop, Beaumont; bd. dirs. Beaumont Civic Opera, Lamar U. Meth. Student Ctr. Cert. tchr., psychologist, Tex. Recipient Regents Merit award, 1979; Coll. Health and Behavioral Sci. Merit award, 1982. Mem. Am. Psychol. Assn., Southwestern Psychol. Assn., Tex. Psychol. Assn., S.E. Tex. Psychol. Assn. (treas. 1978-79, 79-80, pres. 1983), Tex. Council Family Relations, Nat. Council Family Relations, Mental Health Assn. Jefferson County, Nat. Register Health Service Providers in Psychology, Beaumont Art Mus. Methodist. Club: Port Arthur Yacht. Contbr. articles to profl. jours. Home: 855 Belvedere Dr Beaumont TX 77706 Office: PO Box 10036 Lamar U Beaumont TX 77710

DIEBENOW, ANITA RUTH, nurse; b. San Antonio, Jan. 30, 1946; d. Roland Paul and Ruth (Kunkel) Wiederaenders; diploma Luth. Hosp. Sch. Nursing, St. Louis, 1967; B.S.N., U. Tex., 1975; M.S., Tex. Woman's U., 1977; m. Peter Diebenow, July 1, 1967; children—Steven, Nathan. Staff nurse Moline (Ill.) Luth. Hosp., 1967-68, St. Louis Children's Hosp., 1968-69; asst. head nurse Ft. Worth Children's Hosp., 1970; office nurse W. B. Scroggie, M.D., Ft. Worth, 1971-75; supr. N. Central Tex. Home Health Agy., Ft. Worth, 1975; instr. U. Tex. at Arlington Sch. Nursing, 1976-80; asst. prof. nursing U. Miami, 1981-82; clin. coordinator maternal-child services Broward Gen. Med. Center, Ft. Lauderdale, Fla., 1982-84, dir. maternal-child nursing, 1984—; parent cons. Parenting Guidance Center, Ft. Worth, 1979-81. Mem. Life Issues Task Force, Circle T council Girl Scouts U.S.A., 1979-80. Mem. Am. Nurses' Assn., Nat. League Nursing, Internat. Childbirth Edn. Assn., LeLeche League Internat., Nurses' Assn. of Am. Coll. Ob-Gyn., Sigma Theta Tau. Lutheran. Office: 1600 S Andrews Ave Fort Lauderdale FL 33316

DIEBOLT, JUDITH KAREN, journalist; b. Atchison, Kans., Oct. 6, 1948; d. George Edward and Mary Lou (Hill) D. B.S.J., U. Kans., 1970. Reporter, Detroit Free Press, 1970-81, columnist, 1981—, asst. city editor, 1983—. Recipient Pub. Service award Mich. AP, 1979. Mem. Newspaper Guild (treas. local 22 1974-75, rep. assembly 1984). Roman Catholic. Clubs: University, Detroit Press. Office: Detroit Free Press 321 W Lafayette St Detroit MI 48213

DIEHL, JUDITH RUHE, county commissioner; b. Allentown, Pa., July 3, 1926; d. Percy Bott and Amy Catherine (Sieger) Ruhe; m. William Edward Diehl, June 12, 1948; children—Shelley, William Allan, Georgia, Jennifer. B.S., U. Pa., 1949. Field rep. Pa. Program for Women and Girl Offenders, Inc., Phila., 1976-77; field coordinator The Pa. Prison Soc., Phila., 1979-80; county commr. County of Lehigh, Allentown, 1980—; dir. Pa. Blue Shield, Camp Hill, 1985—; trustee Muhlenberg Coll., Allentown, 1985—. Author: A Woman's Place: Equal Partnership in Daily Ministry, 1985. Alternate del. Democratic Nat. Conv., Nashville, 1978. Recipient Human Services award Allentown Human Relations Commn., 1979. Mem. AAUW, LWV. Lutheran. Avocations: singing; knitting. Office: Commrs Lehigh County Courthouse Box 1548 Allentown PA 18105

DIEHL, MARY JANE ELLSWORTH, educator; b. Denville, N.J.; d. Robert George and Angennetta (Keeffe) Ellsworth; B.A., Montclair State Coll., 1940, M.A., 1960; Ed.D., Rutgers U., 1967; m. Edwin D. Diehl, Jan. 14, 1940 (dec. Aug. 1962); children—Digby, Michael. Dir. edn. Middlesex County Health League, New Brunswick, N.J., 1946-49; vice prin., tchr. Montville Twp. Sch., Montville, N.J., 1953-59; team tchr. Mountain Lakes (N.J.) High Sch., 1960-61; profl. asst. adv. services Ednl. Testing Service, Princeton, N.J., 1962-67; prof. Monmouth Coll., West Long Branch, N.J., 1967-85, prof. emeritus, 1985—, regional coordinator Project Head Start Tng. Program, 1968-69; asst. dir. Project Head Start Tng. Program, Rutgers U., summer 1967. Mem. Assn. for Supervision and Curriculum Devel. (nat. bd. mem. 1967-80), AAUW (fellowship chmn. Princeton br. 1968—), N.J. Assn. Supervision and Curriculum Devel., World Council on Curriculum and Instrn. Home: Poor Farm Rd Harbourton NJ 08534 Office: Monmouth Coll West Long Branch NJ 07764

DIEMER, JUDY LYNN, utility company official; b Victoria, Tex., Apr. 30, 1949; d. Forrest C. and Prebble R. (Weir) D.; m. Raymond E. Laube, Jr. B.B.A., Tex. A&I U., 1971. Lic. real estate broker, Tex. Mktg. rep. IBM, Dallas, 1973-77; realtor Lively Real Estate Co., Dallas, 1978-79; cons. Arthur Young & Co., Dallas, 1979-80; adminstrv. mgr. Mary Kay Cosmetics, Dallas, 1980-81; v.p., cons. Micronet Inc., Dallas, 1981; adminstrv. mgr. Central & SW Services, Dallas, 1981—. Mem., past officer Women's Ctr. Dallas. Mem. Adminstrv. Mgmt. Soc. (officer), Internat. Facilities Mgmt. Assn., Dallas Mus. Fine Art. Republican. Baptist. Home: 4511 N Hall St Dallas TX 75219 Office: Central and South West Services Co 2121 San Jacinto St Suite 2500 Dallas TX 75202

DIENER, BETTY JANE, marketing educator; b. Washington, Sept. 15, 1940; d. Edward George and Minnie (Feild) D. A.B., Wellesley Coll., 1962; M.B.A., Harvard U., 1964, D.B.A., 1974. Account exec. Young & Rubicam, Inc., N.Y.C., 1964-70; product mgr. Am. Cyanamid Co., Wayne, N.J., 1970-72; asst. dean Sch. Bus., Case Western Res. U., Cleve., 1974-79; dean Sch. Bus. Adminstrn., Old Dominion U., Norfolk, Va., 1979-82; sec. commerce and resources Commonwealth of Va., Richmond, 1982-86; prof. mktg. Old Dominion U., Norfolk, Va., 1986—. Contbr. articles to profl. publs. Commr. Norfolk Indsl. Devel. Authority, 1979-82; mem. Citizens Council for Chesapeake Bay, 1986—; bd. dirs. Norfolk Conv. and Visitors Bur., 1979-82, Va. Orch. Group, 1982—, Karamu House, 1975-79, Womenspace, 1975-79, Rapid Recovery, 1975-79, Woodruff Hosp., 1975-79; adviser Jr. Achievement, 1963-64, Plans for Progress, 1968-70, Leadership Met. Richmond, 1980-82. Named Outstanding Working Woman, Glamour Mag., 1979, One of 10 Outstanding Career Women of Decade, Glamour Mag., 1984; recipient Honor award Soil Conservation Soc., 1984. Mem. Norfolk C. of C. (bd. dirs. 1979-82). Democrat. Clubs: Women's City of Cleve. (bd. dirs. 1976-79); Harbor, Town Point (Norfolk); Ocean Reef (Key Largo, Fla.). Home: 3288 Page Ave Virginia Beach VA 23451 Office: Old Dominion U Richmond VA

DIENER, MARY ELEANOR MCMATH, business devel., mktg. research and mktg. services exec., metric transition specialist; b. Washington, July 20, 1929; d. Mercer Bailey and Margaret Therese (Chase) McMath; student Internat. Coll. Tokyo, 1947-48; B.A., Manhattanville Coll., 1951; M.S. in Human Service Adminstrn., Antioch U., 1978; m. William Harrison Diener, Sept. 3, 1951; children—Eric, Paul, Lawrence, Valerie. Mem. econ. analysis staff, reporter co. mag. The World, Gen. Motors of Brazil, Sao Paulo, 1951-52; asst. to Am. dir. Cultural Union of Brazil-U.S., Sao Paulo, 1953-54; dir.-mgr. shopping service research, Sao Paulo, 1956-62; feature writer, columnist Brazil Herald, C. of C. and Brazilian Bus., Sao Paulo, 1961-65; pres. Assitencia Social de Vila Alpina, Sao Paulo, 1956-62; editor, display advt. mgr. The Citizen, weekly newspaper, Sarasota, Fla., 1966-67; account rep. Center for Mktg. and Research, Sarasota, 1969-71; pres. Diener & Assos., Inc., bus. devel., mktg. research and mktg. services firm, Research Triangle Park, N.C., 1972—. mem. adv. council to U.S. Senate Com. on Small Bus.; mem. N.C. Gov.'s Advocacy Council on Small Bus.; chmn. N.C. del. White House Conf. on Small Bus.; woman advocate for small bus. SBA, 1981. Recipient Outstanding Am. award Brazilian govt., 1964, Addy award, 1972; cert. of appreciation White House Conf. on Small Bus. Fellow Internat. Poetry Soc., Internat. Acad. Poets; mem. U.S. Metric Assn. (regional dir.), Nat. Assn. Women Bus. Owners (pres. N.C. chpt., dir. nat. orgn., cert. of appreciation), Am. Mktg. Assn., Nat. League Am. Pen Women (local pres. 1972-74), Am. Advt. Fedn., Women in Communications, Am. Assn. Public Opinion Research, Am. Mgmt. Assn., U.S. C. of C. Republican. Roman Catholic. Co-author: Economics Survey of Brazil 1952-53; author: (poetry) When The Sun Goes Down, 1969; Let's Make It Work, 1979; Have You Come a Long Way, Baby?; contbr. poems to anthologies, numerous articles and position papers to bus. and fin. publs. Address: PO Box 12052 200 Park Bldg Suite 111 Research Triangle Park NC 27709

DIERS, DONNA KAYE, nurse, educator; b. Sheridan, Wyo., May 11, 1938; d. Don C. and Ilene H. Diers; B.S. in Nursing, U. Denver, 1960; M.S.N., Yale U., 1964. Psychiat. staff nurse Yale Psychiat. Inst., New Haven, 1960-62; mem. faculty Yale U. Sch. Nursing, 1964—, dean, 1972—, prof. 1978—; mem. Inst. Medicine, Nat. Acad. Scis.; mem. adv. com. advanced tng. grants, div. nursing Dept. Health and Human Services, 1978—; mem. peer rev. com. Nat. Center Health Services Research, 1982; bd. dirs. Community Health Care Plan, Yale Health Plan. Fellow Am. Acad. Nursing; mem. Am. Nurses Assn., Am. Assn. Colls. Nursing, Sigma Theta Tau (chpt. charter mem.). Author: Research in Nursing Practice, 1979, also articles, monographs, chpts. in books. Mem. editorial adv. bds. Nursing Outlook, Cancer Nursing, Image. Office: 855 Howard Ave PO Box 3333 New Haven CT 05610

DIESTELKAMP, DAWN L., medical laboratory administrator; b. Fresno, Calif., Apr. 23, 1954; d. Don A. and Joy L. (Davis) D. B.S. in Microbiology, Calif. State U., Fresno, 1976, M.P.A., 1983. Lic. clin. lab. technologist. Clin. lab. technologist Valley Med. Ctr. Lab., Fresno, 1977-83, quality control coordinator, 1983-85, data processing coordinator, 1985—; cons. Valley Children's Hosp., Fresno, Calif. Assn. for Physically Handicapped, Fresno; lectr. chemistry Calif. State U.-Fresno, 1985. Mem. Nat. Assn. Female Execs. Democrat. Avocation: reading. Office: Valley Med Ctr Lab 445 S Cedar Ave Fresno CA 93702

DIETRICH, DEBORAH SUE, financial planner; b. Paducah, Ky., Sept. 16, 1950; d. Robert Arnold and Willie Mae (Lester) Fields; m. James Irvin Dietrich, Apr. 3, 1976 (div. Nov. 1983). A.A., Paducah Community Coll., 1970; B.A., Murray State U., 1973. Asst. v.p. Deem Cabinets, Inc., Largo, Fla., 1974-82; salesman, agt., fin. planner trainee Thomas Levy & Assocs Inc., Tampa, Fla., 1982-84; fin. planner Deborah Dietrich & Assocs., Largo, 1984—; account exec. Tampa Bay Health Plan, St. Petersburg, Fla., 1985—. Campaign mgr. Largo City Commn. Seat 3, 1985; mem. Citizen's Adv. com. to Pinellas County Met. Planning Orgn., Fla., 1984—. Named Hon. Conch and Citizen of the Fabulous Fla. Keys, W. G. Harvey, Mayor, Monroe County, Fla., 1985. Mem. Greater Largo C. of C. (chmn. membership com. 1984-85), Alpha Sigma Alpha (mem. constn. com. 1984-86, ad hoc com. to Nat. Panhellenic Council Conv. 1985, pres. Tri City Fla. alumnae chpt. 1980-85). Republican. Home: 12908 124th Ave N Largo FL 33544

DIETRICH, MARTHA JANE (SHULTZ), genealogist; b. Brazil, Ind., Aug. 19, 1916; d. Charles Russell and Florence Delilah (McIntire) Shultz; grad. Ind. State U.; m. E(arl) Donald Dietrich, June 17, 1939; children—Florence Ann Dietrich Harris, Jean Carol Dietrich Litterst, Charles Donald. Clk., CSC, Washington, 1937-43; personnel officer Armed Forces Med. Library, Washington, 1948-54; personnel staffing specialist, Washington, 1954-70, ret., 1970; profl. free lance genealogist, College Park, Md., 1970—. Cert. Am. lineage specialist; authorized Bd. Cert. of Genealogists, Washington. Mem. Ky. Hist. Soc. (life), Md. Hist. Soc., Md. Geneal. Soc., Ind. Hist. Soc., Conn. Geneal. Soc., Va. Geneal. Soc., Wabash Valley (Ind.) Geneal. Soc., Clay County (Ind.) Geneal. Soc., Adams County (Ohio) Geneal. Soc., Berks County (Pa.) Geneal. Soc., Somerset County (Pa.) Geneal. Soc., Geneal. Soc. Pa., Prince George's County (Md.) Geneal. Soc., DAR, Nat. Officers Club, DAR, (state registrar 1973-76, state vice regent 1976-79), Md. DAR (state regent 1979-82, hon. state regent 1982—), Md. State DAR Officers Club, Colonial Dames XVII Century Nat. Officers Club (registrar gen. 1974-79), Daus. Am. Colonists (state chmn. 1977-79), Daus. Colonial Wars, UDC, Daus. of 1812, Sons and Daus. of Pilgrims, Magna Charta Dames, Order Crown of Charlemagne (registrar gen. 1982—), Soc. Ind. Pioneers, Order Ky. Cols., Clan MacIntyre Assn. (genealogist 1978-84), Daus. Barons of Runnymede, Colonial Dames XVII Century (state pres. D.C. state soc. 1975-77, acting registrar gen. 1974-75, registrar gen. 1975-79, service awards 1977, 78), Soc. Ky. Pioneers, Colonial Daus. Seventeenth Century, Flagon and Trencher, Kappa Kappa, Kappa Kappa Kappa (Ind.). Episcopalian. Home and Office: 4616 Guilford Rd College Park MD 20740

DIETRICH, SUZANNE CLAIRE, instructional designer; b. Granite City, Ill., Apr. 9, 1937; d. Charles Daniel and Evelyn Blanche (Waters) D.; B.S. in Speech, Northwestern U., 1958; M.S. in Pub. Communication, Boston U., 1967; postgrad. So. Ill. U., 1973—. Intern, prodn. staff Sta. WGBH-TV, Boston, 1958-59, asst. dir., 1962-64, asst. dir. program Invitation to Art, 1958; cons. producer dir. dept. instructional TV radio Ill. Office Supt. Pub. Instruction, Springfield, 1969-70; dir. program prodn. and distbn., 1970-72; instr. faculty call staff, speech dept. Sch. Fine Arts So. Ill. U., Edwardsville, 1972—, grad. asst. for doctoral program office of dean Sch. Edn., 1975-78; research asst. Ill. public telecommunications study for Ill. Public Broadcasting Council, 1979-80; cons. and research in communications, 1980—; exec. producer, dir. TV programs Con-Con Countdown, 1970, The Flag Speaks, 1971. Roman Catholic. Home: 1011 Minnesota Ave Edwardsville IL 62025

DIETZ, JANIS CAMILLE, manufacturing company executive; b. Washington, May 26, 1950; d. Albert and Joan Mildred (MacMullen) Weinstein; m. John William Dietz, Apr. 10, 1981. B.A., U. R.I., 1971; M.B.A., Calif. Poly. U., Pomona, 1984. Customer service trainer People's Bank, Providence, 1974-76; salesman, food broker Bradshaw Co., Los Angeles, 1976-78; salesman Johnson & Johnson, Los Angeles, 1978-79, Gen. Electric Co., Los Angeles, 1979-82; regional sales mgr. Leviton Co., Los Angeles, 1982-85; nat. sales mgr. Jensen Gen. div. Nortek Co., Los Angeles, 1985—; sales trainer, Upland, Calif., 1985—. Dir. pub. relations Jr. Achievement, Providence, 1975-76. Recipient Sector Service award Gen. Electric Co., Fairfield, Conn., 1980. Mem. Nat. Assn. Female Execs., Sales Profls. Los Angeles (v.p. 1984-86). Unitarian. Club: Toastmasters (adminstrv. v.p. 1985). Avocations: sewing; running. Office: Jensen Gen 1946 E 46th St Los Angeles CA 90058

DIETZ, MARGARET JANE, public information official; b. Omaha, Apr. 15, 1924; d. Lawrence Louis and Jeanette Amalia (Meile) Neumann; m. Richard Henry Dietz, May 30, 1949 (dec. July 1971); children—Henry Louis, Frederick Richard, Susan Margaret, John Lawrence (dec.). B.A., U. Nebr., 1946; M.S., Columbia U., 1949. Wire editor Kearney (Nebr.) Daily Hub, 1946-47; state society editor Omaha World-Herald, 1947-48; library aide Akron (Ohio) Pub. Library, 1963-66, publicity and display dir., 1966-74, editor Owlet, 1966-74; pub. info. officer Northeastern Ohio Univs. Coll. Medicine, Rootstown, 1974-85, dir. Office of Communications, 1985—. Mem. culture and entertainment com. Goals for Greater Akron, 1976; pres. bd. Weathervane Community Playhouse, Akron, 1982-85. Mem. Pub. Relations Soc. Am., Women in Communications, Assn. Am. Med. Schs. Group on Pub. Relations, LWV (newsletter editor Akron 1957-60). Clubs: College, Press, Akron Woman's City. Home: 887 Canyon Trail Akron OH 44303 Office: Northeastern Ohio Univs Coll Medicine 4209 State Rt 44 Rootstown OH 44272

DIETZ-BORMAN, MARY ROSSWELL, book co. exec.; b. Knoxville, Tenn.; d. Rosswell Bryan and Alice Beatrice (Fitzgerald) D.; B.A., UCLA, 1952; m. R.C. Borman, Dec. 13, 1980. Mgr. textbook personnel UCLA Student Store, 1952-54; inventory control mgr. Tech. Book Co., Los Angeles, 1954-69;

acquisitions mgr., sales service mgr. Stacey div. Brodart Inc., San Francisco, 1970-72; dir. mktg. library service div. College Book Co., Los Angeles, 1972-76; owner Dietz Book Co., 1976—. Active Sunset Young Republican Clubs, 1961-62; chmn. Los Angeles County Delegation; recording sec., 1963; v.p., 1964; mem. bd. dirs., 1965-74. Mem. Nat. Women's Book Assn., Spl. Libraries Assn., Med. Library Group., Calif. Library Assn., Assn. of Western Hosps., Catholic Alumni Clubs Internat. (Los Angeles, San Francisco chpts.). Roman Catholic. Clubs: Valley Artist Guild. One woman art show Ont. Pub. Library, 1965; represented in Hollywood Bowl's Festival of Music and Art, 1966, 67. Home: 13360 Maxella Ave Apt 10 Marina del Rey CA 90291

DIFATE, HELEN KESSLER, architect; b. Mt. Vernon, N.Y., Jan. 23, 1942; d. Lawrence Victor and Helen de Forestal (McKernan) Kessler; B.A., Coll. of New Rochelle, 1963; B.Arch., Cooper Union, 1968; m. Victor George DiFate, Jr., June 5, 1966; children—Eric Victor, Kristen Helen. Designer, Bro. Cajetan J.B. Baumann O.F.M. Architect, FAIA, N.Y.C., 1962-70; project dir. Philip J. Wilker Architect & Assos., Bronxville, N.Y., 1970-71; designer Robert A. Green & Philip G. McIntosh AIA, Architects, N. Tarrytown, N.Y., 1971-72; architect Fleagle and Kaeyer, Architects, Yonkers, N.Y., 1972-74, Anselevicius/Rupe/Assos., St. Louis, 1974-75; architect Helen Kessler DiFate AIA Architect, St. Louis, 1971—; part time faculty engr. div., archtl. option, St. Louis Community Coll. Meramec, 1975-76, also mem. drafting and design tech. adv. com.; mem. Women's Assn. of St. Louis Symphony Soc., Friends of St. Louis Art Mus., Friends of St. Louis Sci. Mus. Registered architect, N.Y., Mo., Ill.; certified Nat. Council Archtl. Registration Bds. Mem. AIA (corporate mem.; dir. Westchester, N.Y., chpt., 1974, officer St. Louis chpt. 1984, 85), Mo. Council Architects, Alliance of Women in Architecture, Clayton (Mo.) C. of C. Roman Catholic. Archtl. project published in books: Buildings Reborn: New Uses, Old Places (Barbaralee Diamonstein), 1978, The Building Art in St. Louis: Two Centuries (George McCue), 1981. Office: 131 N Bemiston Ave Saint Louis MO 63105

DI FILIPPO, FRANCES, business executive; b. Jersey City, Oct. 4, 1935; d. James and Maria (Figurelli) Di F. Student Fordham U., 1973-77. System analyst NCR, Dayton, Ohio, 1963-69; system analyst Bambergers, Newark, N.J., 1969-72; v.p. Citicorp, Miami, 1972-86; pres. FDF Exec. Services, Inc., Plantation, Fla., 1986—. Mem. Nat. Assn. Female Execs. Avocations: stained glass; tennis. Home: 10160 Torchwood Ave Plantation FL 33324

DIGENNARO, JOANN PASQUALE, foundation executive, lawyer; b. Logansport, Ind., Sept. 2, 1942; d. Thomas Charles and Mary Lucy (D'Andrea) Pasquale; m. Myles Ruaul DiGennaro, July 7, 1967. B.A. in Humanities, Purdue U., 1965; postgrad. U. Rome, 1966; M.S. in Textile Econs., U. Md., 1976; postgrad. in law (scholar) Oxford U., 1978; J.D., George Mason U., 1979. Bar: Va. 1980. With Raleigh's Stores, Washington, 1967-73; instr. U. Md.-College Park, 1974-75; atty./advisor Gen Counsel's Office, Washington, 1980-81; pres. Ctr. for Excellence in Edn., McLean, Va., 1982—; cons. Apparel Industry mag., Los Angeles, 1980-81. Author: Textile Trade, 1980; contbr. articles to profl. jours. Legis. chmn. Greater McLean Republican Women, 1970; coordinator Gerald Ford Presdl. Campaign No. Va., 1976; mem. exec. bd. Mental Health Assn. No. Va., 1976-77; mem. Va. State Bd. Corrections, 1977, vice-chair, 1981; chair Library Bd. Trustees, Fairfax, Va., 1978-79. Named Outstanding Alumnus George Mason U., 1982. Mem. ABA, Va. State Bar. Roman Catholic. Home: 11740 Quay Rd Oakton VA 22124 Office: Ctr for Excellence in Edn 7710 Old Springhouse McLean VA 22102

DIGERONIMO, SUZANNE KAY, architect; b. Berwick, Pa., Mar. 27, 1947; d. George and Eleanor (Kapsak) Marcincavage; m. Louis Anthony DiGeronimo, Sept. 19, 1969; children—Marcello, Luciano. B.Arch., Cooper Union, 1971, Assoc. Applied Sci., Fashion Inst. Tech., N.Y.C., 1967; student Pratt Inst., 1967-68, Columbia U., 1968-70. Registered architect, N.J., N.Y., Mich., Calif., N.H., Conn. Pres. Architects DiGeronimo, Paramus, N.J., 1969—. Mem. exec. women's council C. of C. and Industry, Hackensack, N.J., 1984-85, mem. legis. com., 1984-85; trustee N.J. Inst. Tech., Newark, 1984—; dir. Pvt. Enterprise Polit. Action Com., Hackensack, 1985. Mem. Soc. Am. Mil. Engrs., AIA, Am. Arbitration Assn., N.J. Soc. Architects, Architects League No. N.J. Roman Catholic. Home: 16 Beekman Pl Fair Lawn NJ 07410 Office: Architects DiGeronimo 12 Sunflower Ave Paramus NJ 07652

DIGGINS, RUTH LOIS, music teacher; b. Rhodes, Iowa, Nov. 10, 1900; d. Charles and Bertha Roberts; m. Mace Edson Diggins, Aug. 12, 1920; 1 son, Dean R. Student Drake U., 1918-19; grad. Palmer Sch. Chiropractic, Davenport, Iowa, 1922. Gen. practice chiropractic medicine, Iowa, 1924-73; music (piano, vocal, violin, guitar) tchr., 1915—, Hampton, Iowa, 1924—; dir. ch. choirs Ch. of Christ, Hampton, 1952-60, Congl. Ch., Hampton, 1948-72; owner, mgr. Diggins Dance Sch., Mason City, Iowa, Hampton Dance Sch. Mem. Bus. and Profl. Women's Club. Clubs: Women's, E.C.D., Treble Clef Music (Hampton) (pres.). Home: 4 2d Ave NE Hampton IA 50441

DIGGS, CAROL BETH, marketing executive; b. Lubbock, Tex., Feb. 26, 1949; d. Billy Horace and Adele Frieda (Krueger) Diggs; m. Aloy Louis Ruland Jr., Oct. 10, 1981. B.A. with honors, Okla. U., 1970; M.A., George Washington U., 1974; postgrad. Johns Hopkins U., 1974-76. Tchr. Norman (Okla.) Pub. Schs., 1970-71; promotion asst. Johns Hopkins U. Press, Balt., 1976-77; tng. asst. 1st Nat. Bank Md., Balt., 1977-78, mktg coordinator, 1978-79, br. adminstrn. officer, exec., 1979-83, product mgmt. exec., 1983-84, sr. product mgmt. exec., 1985—. Contbr. poetry Anthology of Modern Poets, 1969. Mem. Balt. Symphony Chorus, 1976-83, bd. dirs., 1979-81; ch. promotion coordinator Md. Bicentenniel Fund, Balt., 1983; editor The Tower, Ch. of the Messiah, Balt., 1982-84; mem. adv. bd. Md. Ch. News, 1984—, The Claggett Com., 1985—. Eastern Star scholar, Okla. U., 1967, E.K. Gaylord scholar, 1967, 69; fellow George Washington U., 1972-74, Johns Hopkins U., 1974-76. Mem. MLA, Nat. Assn. Bank Women, Alpha Lambda Delta, Sigma Delta Pi (treas. 1973-74). Republican. Home: 2118 Oak Lodge Rd Baltimore MD 21228 Office: 1st Nat Bank Maryland 25 S Charles St Baltimore MD 21203

DIGIOVANNI, ELEANOR ELMA, scaffold installation company executive; b. Long Island City, N.Y., May 14, 1944; d. Charles and Josephine (Laureni) DiG. Student Queensboro Coll. Collector Atlas/Re/Sun Ins. Co., N.Y.C., 1965-69; instr. Oak Manor Equitation, Weyers Cave, Va., 1970-76; dispatcher, salesperson Safway Steel Products, Long Island City, N.Y., 1977-83; ops. mgr. York Scaffold, Long Island City, 1983—. Democrat. Roman Catholic. Home: 14-34 30th Rd Astoria NY 11102 Office: York Scaffold Equipment Corp 37-20 12th St Long Island City NY 11101

DIGMAN, KATARINA CERNOZUBOV, psychologist; b. Belgrade, Yugoslavia, Sept. 5, 1941; came to U.S., 1967, naturalized, 1974; d. Konstantin N. and Leonila (Yourschenko) Cernozubov; A.B. in Psychology, U. Belgrade, 1964; M.A. in Psychology, U. Hawaii, 1968, Ph.D., 1970; m. John M. Digman, Jan. 23, 1971; 1 dau., Maria-Anna. Teaching asst. dept. psychology U. Belgrade, 1963-64; field asst. Inst. Internat. Studies, U. Calif., Berkeley, 1965, research asst. dept. anthropology, 1965; intern Neuropsychiat. Clinic, U. Belgrade, 1963-66; chief dept. psychology Neuropsychiat. Clinic, U. Novi Sad Med. Sch., Vojvodina, Yugoslavia, 1966-67; grad. asst. dept. psychology U. Hawaii, Honolulu, 1967-70, lectr., 1969, asst. researcher, 1974-78, mem. grad. faculty, 1977-79, asst. prof. women's studies program, 1975-77; cons. psychologist Hawaii State Hosp., 1967-70, clin. psychologist, 1970-71; mem. grad. faculty Outreach program Antioch Coll., Honolulu, 1975-79, Outreach program U. No. Colo., Honolulu, 1975—; founder, dir. Women's Counseling Clinic and Resource Center, Honolulu, 1977—; publisher Everywoman, 1978—; participant archeol. excavation expdn. pre-Colombian sites, 1976-81. Recipient Best Student award Philos. U. Belgrade, 1964. Mem. Am. Psychol. Assn., Hawaii Psychol. Assn., Western Psychol. Assn., Internat. Assn. Applied Psychology, Soc. for Life History Research, Nat. Register of Health Providers, Nat. Wildlife Fedn., Friends of Animals, Am. Mus. Natural History, Hawaii Horse Show Assn., N.Am. Riding for Handicapped Assn. (dir. operating ctr. 1981, regional chmn. 1985—), Am. Horse Show Assn., Maya Study Club. Contbr. numerous articles on psychopathology, social psychology and exptl. psychology to profl. jours. Office: 1314 S King St Suite 708 Honolulu HI 96814

DI GREGORIO, DEBRA GWEN, communications company executive, editor, writer; b. Louisville, Ky.; d. Francois and Dorli Maltilde (Hoenigsburg) Di G. Certificate, U. Nice, France, 1975; B.A. in Contemporary Arts, Ramapo Coll. N.J., Mahwah, 1978. Pub. relations dir. Bergen Community Mus., Paramus, N.J., 1980-81; writer The Record, Hackensack, N.J., 1981-82; asst. editor Am. Health Mag., N.Y.C., 1982-83; freelance writer, editor, Ridgewood, N.J., 1983-85; pres., owner Camares Communications, Ridgewood, 1985—. Author cover stories Family Computing Mag., 1984, 85. Independent Democrat. Avocations: cross country skiing; kite flying; writing; acting. Home: 136 Union St Ridgewood NJ 07450 Office: Camares Communications 4 Franklin Ave Ridgewood NJ 07450

DI GREGORIO, WENDY WEBER, social services administrator; b. Bryn Mawr, Pa., Sept. 8, 1953; d. Harry Grover and Dorothy Muriel (Currier) Weber; m. Frank Joseph DiGregorio, Apr. 8, 1978. B.A. in Sociology, Rider Coll., Lawrenceville, N.J., 1976, M.A. in Counseling, 1978; M.S. in Health Adminstrn. L.I. U., 1985. Clin. specialist Bonnie Brae Farm for Boys, Millington, N.J., 1978; unit coordinator Greer-Woodycrest Children's Services, Inc., Pomona, N.Y., 1978-80; intermediate care facility residence supr. Contemporary Guidance Services, N.Y.C., 1980-81; intermediate care facility residence dir. Venture Inn, Inc., Nanuet, N.Y., 1981-83, program dir., 1982-83; assoc. dir. Spectrum for Living, Closter, N.J., 1983-85; clin. coordinator dept. psychiatry Bronx-Lebanon Hosp. Ctr., N.Y., 1985—. Mem. Am. Assn. Mental Deficiency, Tourette Syndrome Assn., Moblzn. for Animals, Animal Welfare League of Westchester, Alpha Beta Kappa. Republican. Club: Westchester Cat. Home: 53 Kisco Park Dr Mount Kisco NY 10549 Office: Inpatient Psychiatry Unit Bronx-Lebanon Hosp Ctr 1276 Fulton Ave Bronx NY 10456

DILKS, ELIZABETH THOMAS S., poet, clubwoman; b. North Merion, Bryn Mawr, Pa., July 21, 1917; d. Benjamin and Elizabeth Jones (Thomas) Shank; student Louis Shenk Voice Studios, Phila., 1939-42, Pison Acad. of Appreciation of Arts, Phila., 1941-43, Taylor Coll., Phila., 1943-45; m. John Henry Dilks. Restorer antique furniture and old farmhouses, Paoli, Pa., 1947-52, Malvern, Pa., 1952-62, Md., 1962—. Recipient Soc. Am. Citizens award; poem hung at Christian C. Sanderson Mus. Fellow Internat. Acad. Poets, Anglo Am. Acad. (hon.); mem. Acad. Am. Poets, Poets and Writers, Poets and Writers, Inc., Fedn. Women's Clubs, Christian C. Sanderson Mus. (life), Internat. Platform Assn., Clubs: Whitford Country (Exton, Pa.); Miles River Yacht (St. Michaels, Md.). Author, illustrator: Poetry-His and Hers, 1976; A Drop in the Bucket; contbr. poetry to mags. and newspapers, anthologies.

DILL, ANNE HOLDEN, educator; b. Poplarville, Miss., Mar. 7, 1920; d. James Houston and Florence Elizabeth (Henley) Holden; B.S., U. Ala., 1954, M.A., 1955, Ed.S., 1970; m. Elmer Dill, Jan. 25, 1941; children—Winston Elmer, Jane Anne, Caroll Elizabeth Dill Norman. High sch. tchr. in Ga., 1958-65; instr. Western world lit. U. Ga. Center, Dublin, 1965-66; instr. English, Gadsden (Ala.) Jr. Coll., 1966-83. Mem. Nat. Council Tchrs. English, NEA, AAUW, S.Central MLA, Southeastern Conf. English in Two-Year Colls., Conf. Coll. Composition and Communication, Ala. Coll. English Tchrs. Assn., Ala. Council Tchrs. English, Ala. Jr. Coll. Assn., Ala. Edn. Assn., DAR (regent James Gadsden chpt. 1983—), Children of Am. Revolution, Princess Noccalula Soc. (sr. organizing pres.). Democrat. Baptist. Clubs: Gadsden Woman's, Gadsden Music. Home: 850 Walnut St Gadsden AL 35901

DILLARD, ANNIE, author; b. Pitts., Apr. 30, 1945; d. Frank and Pam (Lambert) Doak; m. Gary Clevidence, 1979; 1 dau., Rosie. B.A., Hollins Coll., 1967, M.A., 1968. Columnist, The Living Wilderness, Wilderness Soc., 1973-75; contbg. editor Harper's mag., N.Y.C., 1973—; scholar-in-residence Western Wash. U., Bellingham, 1975-78; disting. vis. prof. Wesleyan U., 1979-80, adj. prof., 1981—. Mem. Nat. Com. on U.S.-China Relations. Recipient, award N.Y. Press Club, 1974, Wash. Gov.'s award for contbn. to lit., 1978. Mem. Poetry Soc. Am., Authors Guild, Nat. Citizens for Pub. Libraries, Phi Beta Kappa. Author: (poetry) Tickets For A Prayer Wheel, 1974; Pilgrim at Tinker Creek (Pulitzer prize for gen. non-fiction 1974), 1974; Holy the Firm, 1977; Living by Fiction, 1982; Teaching a Stone to Talk, 1982; Encounters with Chinese Writers, 1984. Address: care Blanche Gregory 2 Tudor City Pl New York NY 10017

DILLARD, JOAN HELEN, financial executive; b. Balt., June 12, 1951; d. Anthony Joseph and Frances Helen (Waclawski) Bartynski; m. Gordon Earl Dillard, Apr. 21, 1984; 1 child, Valerie Kay. A.A., Anne Arundel Community Coll., Md., 1973; B.A., U. Md., 1977; M.B.A., U. Balt., 1984. Instr. music Acad. Music, Glen Burnie, Md., 1972-77; cash mgr. Johns Hopkins Hosp., Balt., 1979-83, Md. Casualty Co., Balt., 1983-85; 2d v.p., asst. treas. Am. Gen. Corp., Houston, 1985—. Mem. Nat. Corp. Cash Mgmt. Assn., Houston Cash Mgmt. Assn. (v.p. 1986). Office: Am Gen Corp 2929 Allen Pkwy Houston TX 77019

DILLEHAY, PAMELA ANN, marketing communications professional; b. Berkeley, Calif., Feb. 2, 1957; s. Ronald Clifford and Valerie Ruth (Sherborne) D. B.A., U. Calif.-Santa Cruz, 1980. Translator/writer/counselor Choice Med. Clinic, Santa Cruz, Calif., 1980-82; writer KSCO Radio, Santa Cruz, 1982; mktg. programs analyst Cygnet Tech., Inc., Sunnyvale, Calif., 1983-86; public relations specialist Borland Internat., Scotts Valley, Calif., 1986—. Counselor Planned Parenthood, Santa Cruz, 1977-80; peer advisor U. Calif.-Santa Cruz, 1980. Undergrad. research grantee U. Calif.-Santa Cruz, 1979. Avocations: scuba diving; stained glass; volleyball. Home: 1056 Audrey Ave Campbell CA 95008 Office: Borland Internat 4585 Scotts Valley Dr Scotts Valley CA 95066

DILLINGHAM, MARJORIE CARTER, foreign language educator; b. Bicknell, Ind., Aug. 20, 1915; Ph.D. in Spanish (Delta Kappa Gamma scholar and fellow), Fla. State U., 1970; m. William Pyrle Dillingham, (dec. 1981); children—William Pyrle (dec.), Robert Carter, Sharon Dillingham Martin. High sch. tchr., Fla.; former instr. St. George's Sch., Havana; former mem. faculty Panama Canal Zone Coll., Fla. State U., U. Ga., Duke U.; dir. traveling Spanish conversation classes. U.S. rep. (with husband) Hemispheric Conf. on Taxation, Rosario, Argentina. Mem. Am. Assn. Tchrs. Spanish and Portuguese (past pres. Fla. chpt.), Fla. Edn. Assn. (past pres. fgn. lang. div.), La Sociedad Honoraria Hispanica (past nat. pres.), Fgn. Lang. Tchrs. Leon County, Fla. (pres.), Delta Kappa Gamma (pres.), Phi Kappa Phi, Sigma Delta Pi, Beta Pi Theta, Kappa Delta Pi, Alpha Omicron Pi, Delta Kappa Gamma. Home: 2109 Trescott Dr Tallahassee FL 32312

DILLINGOFSKI, MARY SUE, film company executive; b. Madison, Wis., Dec. 27, 1944; d. Albert F. and Camille M. (Blott) D. B.A., Lawrence U., 1967; M.S., U. Wis., 1970, Ph.D., 1980. Tchr. English, Madison Pub. Schs. (Wis.), 1967-70; tchr. reading Niles Pub. Schs. (Ill.), 1971-72, Kamehameha Schs., Honolulu, 1972-77; lectr. U. Wis., Madison, 1977-80; cons. Scott, Foresman & Co., Glenview, Ill., 1980-81, mktg. mgr., 1981-86; dir. mkgt. Films Inc., Chgo., 1986—; cons. diagnostician Univ. Hosp. Learning Disability Clinic, Madison, Wis., 1977-80; ednl. cons. Kalihi Palama Adult Edn. Ctr., Honolulu, 1973-75; Author: Nonprint Media and Reading, 1979; Sociolinguistics and Reading (W.S. Gray Research award 1980), 1978; also articles in profl. jours. Active Apollo Chorus, Chgo., 1983—, Friends of Sta. WHA, Madison, 1978-80, Mem. Bus. Vols. for Arts, Art Deco Soc. Chgo. Office: Films Inc 5547 N Ravenswood Chicago IL 60640

DILLMAN, LINDA WILSON, marketing executive; b. Boston, Aug. 3, 1940; d. Francis Stone and Edith (Tuttle) Wilson; m. David McKnight Dillman, Feb. 8, 1964 (div. 1982); children—Jennifer Cox Dillman, Edith Stone Dillman. B.S., Northwestern U., 1963. Writer, Sta. WGN Radio & TV, Chgo., 1963-65; press info. dir. Sta. WBBM Radio, Chgo., 1965-67; devel. officer Spertus Coll. Judaica, Chgo., 1975-76; dir. pub. relations North Suburban Blood Ctr., Glenview, Ill., 1976-81, North Suburban Health Resources, Glenview, 1976-78; dir. mktg. Blood Ctr. No. Ill., Glenview, 1981—; cons. and lectr. in field. Contbr. articles to profl. jours. Bd. dirs. First Congregational Ch., Wilmette, Ill., 1980—; mem. community adv. com. Northwestern Program on Women, Evanston, Ill., 1982—. Mem. Women in Communications (pres.-elect 1981-82, pres. 1982-83, del., mem. coms.), Assn. Blood Donor Recruiters, Northwest Press Club (pres. 1980-82), Ill. Hosp. Pub. Relations Soc., Chgo. Hosp. Council Pub. Relations Soc. Avocations: writing; photography; figure skating; travel. Office: Blood Ctr No Ill 1255 N Milwaukee Ave Glenview IL 60025

DILLON, ANN MAZYCK, telephone company executive; b. Winston-Salem, N.C., Sept. 26, 1949; d. Edward Harleston and June (Carroll) M.; B.A., U. N.C., Greensboro, 1971; postgrad. Wake Forest U. Babcock Sch. Mgmt., 1973, Rutgers U., 1976. Tech. publs. editor Western Electric Co., Winston-Salem, 1971-75; mktg. asst. AT&T, Morristown, N.J., 1975-76, Basking Ridge, N.J., 1976-78, mktg. assoc., 1978-79, mgr. tng. So. Bell Telephone Co., Atlanta, 1979-82, staff mgr., 1982—. Vol. asst. Forsyth County (N.C.) Pub. Library, 1974; active LWV, 1980-83, Cobb Women's Polit. Alliance, 1982-83; choir pres. St. Luke's Episcopal Ch., 1982-83, mem. steering com. Ch. Fellowship Orgn., 1981—; dep. registrar Cobb County, 1982-83; mem. Cobb Dem. Exec. Steering Com., 1982-84, rep. to state Dem. Conv., 1982; gubernatorial campaign vol., 1981-82; team leader fund raising campaign Atlanta Symphony Orch., 1985. Mem. Soc. Consumer Affairs Profls. Democrat. Office: So Bell Telephone Co 675 W Peachtree St NE Atlanta GA 30375

DILLON, CASSANDRA GADDIS, lawyer; b. Hattiesburg, Miss., Nov. 22, 1939; d. Roy L. and Hazel (Byrd) Gaddis; m. William J. Dillon, Sept. 30, 1960; 1 dau., Sondra Leigh. A.S., Gulf Coast Jr. Coll., 1971; studies under Lester C. Franklin. Bar: Miss. 1979. Legal asst. Ben C. Moore, Pascagoula, Miss., 1965-79, assoc., 1979-82; sole practice, Pascagoula, 1983—. Mem. Home Builders Assn., Bd. Realtors, State Bar Assn. Miss., ABA, Jackson County Bar Assn. Home: 808 W Grant Ave Pascagoula MS 30567 Office: PO Box 1482 605 Delmas Ave Suite 103 Pascagoula MS 39567

DILLON, LINDA MARIE, state education administrator; b. Albany, N.Y., Oct. 17, 1949; d. Joseph John and Anna Marie (Porcello) Sgambelluri; m. William E. Dillon, Jr., Oct. 27, 1973; children—Christopher Matthew, Stephanie Lyn. B.S. in Acctg., Russell Sage Coll., Albany, 1985. Sr. personnel adminstr. N.Y. State Higher Edn. Service Corp., Albany, 1980—; oral examiner N.Y. State Dept. Civil Service, Albany, 1983—. Mem. Internat. Personnel Mgmt. Assn., Omicron Delta Epsilon. Democrat. Roman Catholic. Avocations: photography; travel. Home: 541 Park Ave Albany NY 12208

DILLON, LINDA SCHNULLE, vocational educator; b. Berwyn, Ill., Aug. 11, 1948; d. Robert and Alvanell (Riddle) Schnulle; m. David Austin Dillon, May 15, 1979. B.S., Iowa State U., 1970; M.S., U. N.C., 1976; Ph.D., Ohio State U., 1979. Distributive edn. coordinator West Charlotte High Sch., Charlotte, N.C., 1974-76; acad. adviser Ohio State U., Columbus, 1976-78; grad. research assoc. Nat. Ctr. for Research in Vocat. Edn., Columbus, 1978-79; assoc. prof. occupational edn. N.C. State U., Raleigh, 1979—; dir. sex equity grant N.C. Dept. Community Colls., 1980-82; dir. Labor Market Info. grant, Raleigh, 1982. Editor: (with LeVene Olson) Highlights from the VocEd Journal, 1983. Contbr. articles to profl. jours. Fellow N.C. Japan Ctr.; mem. Am. Soc. for Tng. and Devel. (Nathaniel Hill research award Research Triangle chpt. 1982, chpt. treas. 1983—, governing bd. 1984), Am. Vocat. Edn. Personnel Devel. Assn. (nat. treas. 1983-85, pres.-elect 1986), Am. Vocat. Assn. (life), N.C. Council Vocat. Tchr. Educators (gov. 1981-85). Office: NC State U 502 Poe Hall Raleigh NC 27695

DILORENZO, KATHLEEN MARY, lawyer; b. Phila., June 21, 1955; d. John Daniel and Marion Ann (Sanuck) Nagurny; m. Nicholas Leonard DiLorenzo, July 30, 1983. B.S. in Journalism, Temple U., 1975, J.D., 1980, LL.M. in Taxation, 1984. Bar: Pa., U.S. Dist. Ct. (ea. dist.) Pa., U.S. Ct. Appeals (3d cir.). Law clk. Office Gen. Counsel, HHS, Phila., 1978-79, U.S. Dept. Labor, Phila., 1979-80; atty. U.S. Ry. Assn., Phila., 1980-81; atty., environ. specialist U.S. EPA, Phila., 1980-81; asst. David L. White, Esq., 1981—; sole practice law, Phila., 1981—; claims atty. Pa. Mfrs. Assn. Ins. Co., Phila., 1981-82, corp. counsel, 1982—. Author articles in books and jours. Herman M. Ellis scholar, 1975. Mem. ABA, Pa. Bar Assn., Phila. Bar Assn. (speakers bur. 1984—, atty. reference bur. 1984—, workers' compensation com. 1982—). Republican. Ukrainian Catholic. Office: Pa Mfrs Assn Ins Co Inc 925 Chestnut St Philadelphia PA 19107*

DILWORTH, LINDA GAIL, systems administrator, consultant; b. Ocala, Fla., June 2, 1954; d. Lawrence E. and Pauline (Nelson) Parkey; m. Jerome G. Dilworth, Aug. 16, 1975; 1 child, J. Glendon II. B.S., Fla. A&M U., 1975; M.P.A., Fla. State U., 1978, postgrad., 1981—. Fiscal asst. State of Fla., Tallahassee, 1979-80, mgmt. analyst, 1980-82, mgmt. analyst supr., 1982-84, systems project coordinator, 1984-85, systems project adminstr., 1985—; office systems cons., 1982—. Chmn. bd. Bond Community Ventures, 1983; sec. Nat. Council Negro Women, 1985. Recipient Woman of Yr. award Am. Bus. Women's Assn., 1985. Mem. Am. Soc. Pub. Adminstrn. Democrat. Baptist. Clubs: Am. Bus. Women's Assn. (pres. 1984-85), Delta Sigma Theta. Avocations: sewing; reading; chess. Office: Office State Comptroller Div Info Systems The Capitol Tallahassee FL 32301

DIMAIO, VIRGINIA SUE, gallery owner; b. Houston, July 6, 1921; d. Jesse Lee and Gabriella Sue (Norris) Chambers; A.B., U. Redlands, 1943; student U. So. Calif., 1943-45, Scripps Coll., 1943, Pomona Coll., 1945; m. James V. DiMaio, 1955 (div. 1968); children—Victoria, James V. Owner, Capistrano Trading Post, San Juan Capistrano, Calif., 1946—; owner, dir. Galeria Capistrano, 1979—; owner LaPinata Mexican Restaurant, 1979—; cons., appraiser Southwestern and Am. Indian Handcrafts; established ann. Helen Hardin Meml. scholarship for woman artist grad. Inst. Am. Indian Art, Santa Fe, also ann. Helen Hardin award for outstanding woman artist at Indian Market, SW Assn. on Indian Affairs, Santa Fe. Mem. Indian Arts and Crafts Assn., Southwest Assn. Indian Affairs, Heard Mus., San Juan Capistano C. of C. Republican. Roman Catholic. Office: 31741 Camino Capistrano San Juan Capistrano CA 92675

DIMERY, SHARON MARCIA, science educator; b. Wilmington, Del., Feb. 21, 1960; d. Robert John and Betty Jean (Harris) Wisniewski; m. Rudolph Charles Dimery, Jr., Feb. 18, 1980; 1 dau., Lauren Marie. B.A. in Biology, U. Calif.-Riverside, 1983, M.A. in Ednl. Adminstrn., 1986. Cert. tchr., adminstrv. services credential, Calif. Sci. tchr. Jurupa Unified Sch. Dist., Rubidoux, Calif., 1984—. Mem. Nat. Sci. Tchrs. Assn., Nat. Assn. Female Execs., Assn. Calif. Sch. Adminstrs. (student mem.). Democrat. Roman Catholic. Avocations: reading; bird-watching. Office: Rubidoux High Sch 4250 Opal St Rubidoux CA 92505

DIMERY, WILLIE JACQULYN, funeral home executive, educator; b. Kingstree, S.C., May 26, 1930; d. Ezra Moody and Coree (Postell) Kinder; m. James F. Dimery, June 6, 1955; children—Esther Dimery Furman, Johnny R., Virgil L., Walter, Kevin, Carolyn Elaine. B.A., U. S.C., 1984; postgrad. Clayton U. Ptnr., operator Domery Rogers Funeral Home, Hemingway, S.C.; substitute tchr. pub. schs., 1972-75, 85—. Mem. Nat. Funeral Dirs. and Morticians Assn., Epsilon Delta Chi. Methodist. Club: Democratic (Hemingway). Lodge: Order Eastern Star. Home: PO Box 41 Hemingway SC 29554

DIMICK, NINA GRACE, software company executive, educator; b. Richmond, Vt., Sept. 3, 1949; d. Howard Alboro and Marion Kate (Dike) D.; m. Earle William Hill, Jan. 17, 1972 (div. Apr. 1976); children—Janet Lea, Stephen Howard, B.A., Johnson State Coll., 1983; M.Acctg. Info. Systems, U. West Fla., 1984. Computer lab. mgr. Johnson State Coll., Vt., 1982-83; tchr. Coastal Tng. Inst., Pensacola, Fla., 1983-84, Community Coll. Vt., Barre, 1984—; mgr. quality control Datamann, Inc., Wilder, Vt., 1984—. Author: How to Choose a Computer for Small Business, 1984. Editor: Guide to JSC Computer Room, 1983. Named Pres. of Yr., Vt. VFW Aux., 1980, 81; recipient Second Highest Chmn. award Nat. VFW Aux., 1981. Mem. Nat. Assn. Female Execs., Assn. Masters Bus. Arts, Data Processing Mgmt. Assn. (pres. 1981-83; Golden Past Pin 1983). Republican. Mennonite. Avocations: painting with watercolors; horseback riding. Home: NCR 35 Box 146 Woodstock VT 05091 Office: Datamann Inc Wilder VT 05088

DIMINO, MARY JANE, real estate broker, investment exec.; b. Norristown, Pa., June 21, 1942; d. Elwood Smith and Mary Ellen (Delaney) Horning; grad. Am. Inst. Banking, 1964, Va. Realtors Inst. at U. Va., 1975; student No. Va. Community Coll., 1976—; m. John M. Dimino, Aug. 8, 1964(div. 1982); children—John, Andrew, Mary Teresa, Gregory. Various secretarial positions, 1960-69; sales asso. House & Home Real Estate Corp., Manassas, Va., 1973-74; asso. broker Panorama Real Estate, Manassas, 1974-75, Long & Foster Real Estate, 1975-76; asso. broker Century 21 Capital Realty, Manassas, 1976—, mgr. Fairfax (Va.) Office, 1977, part-owner, sec.-treas., Manassas, 1981—; owner Income Growth Assos. Named to Million Dollar Sales Club, Century 21, 1977, 79, 80, 81; lic. real estate broker. Mem. No. Va. Bd. Realtors, Prince William Bd. Realtors (Million Dollar Sales Club 1977, 80), Nat. Assn. Realtors, Va. Assn. Realtors, Realtors Nat. Mktg. Inst. (cert. residential specialist), Century 21 Investment Soc., Nat. Assn. Female Execs., Real Estate Exchange Group. Office: 8803 Sudley Rd Manassas VA 22110

DIMMETTE, WENDY, writer, educator; b. Dexter, Tex., Nov. 8, 1924; d. Wilburn Hill and Willie Mae (McKenzie) Wendt; m. Jack Ray Lindsey, Dec. 18, 1948 (dec. 1956); m. James Edwin Dimmette, Jan. 18, 1960; children—Ramsey Lindsey, Thomas Lindsey, Hillary Lindsey, Susan Lindsey, Wendy. B.A., So. Meth. U., 1975, M.A., 1980. Med. sec. James E. Dimmette, M.D., Dallas, 1961—; profl. writer, 1980—; poetry tchr. in community colls., Dallas,

1983—; condr. poetry workshops, Dallas, 1980—; poetry reader pub. and pvt. high schs., Dallas, 1980—; story teller elem. schs., Dallas, 1980—. Author: Taking Moonlight (poetry), 1980. Children's books include: Obie the Owl, 1982, How Deep Is the Dark, 1982, Other Faces, 1982, The List, 1982, Journey from A to Z, 1982, Ptumpi and B'Zings, 1983. Contbr. poetry to mags. and anthologies. Mem. Poetry Soc. Tex., Dallas Mus. Fine Arts. Republican. Episcopalian. Home: 3207 Wendy Ln Dallas TX 75214

DIMMICK, CAROLYN REABER, U.S. District Court judge; b. Seattle, Oct. 24, 1929; d. Maurice Clifford and Margaret (Taylor) Reaber; B.A., U. Wash., 1951; J.D., 1953; LL.D., Gonzaga U., 1982; m. Cyrus A. Dimmick, Sept. 10, 1955; children—Taylor, Dana. Admitted to Wash. bar, 1953; asst. atty. gen. State of Wash., 1953-54; dep. pros. atty. King County, Wash., 1955-62; individual practice law, Seattle, 1959-60, 62-65; judge dist. ct., 1965-75, judge superior ct., 1976-81; justice Wash. Supreme Ct., Olympia, 1981-85; judge U.S. Dist. Ct. Wash., Seattle, 1985—. Named Alumni of Yr. John B. Allen Sch., 1978; recipient award World Plan Execs. Council, 1981; recipient Matrix Table award, 1981. Mem. Am. Bar Assn., Am. Judicature Soc., Am. Judges Assn., Nat. Assn. Women Judges, World Assn. of Judges, Wash. State Bar Assn. Clubs: Wash. Athletic, Wing Point Golf. Office: US Dist Courthouse Seattle WA 98104

DIMONACO, JANIS SUSAN, social service adminstr., social worker, cons.; b. Springfield, Mass., Apr. 20, 1951; d. Vincent and Conchetta Rachel (Lombard) DiM.; A.A., Holyoke Community Coll., 1972; B.A., Westfield State Coll., 1974; M.Ed., C.A.S., Springfield Coll., 1976; Ph.D., Calif. Western U., 1979; m. Henry J. Sobinski, May 2, 1981; 1 stepdau., Andrea Sobinski. Sr. vocat. counselor C&ROP, Inc., Chicopee, Mass., 1975-76, dir. employment and tng., program, 1976-78; founder, exec. dir. Hampden County Women's Center, Inc., Springfield, Mass., 1978—; co-founder, pres. Valley Mental Health Assos., Inc., Springfield, 1978—; prin. Dr. Janis S. DiMonaco & Assos., Springfield, 1980—; founder, pres. Health Mgmt. Center, Inc., 1981; mem. adj. faculty Springfield Tech. Community Coll., Bay State Med. Center, Western New Eng. Coll.; bd. dirs. Community Care Mental Health Center; cons. in field; lectr. violence against women, wellness health promotion programs; mem. Mass. Employment and Tng. Council, 1978—; chairperson Mass. Community Action Programs Dirs. Assn. on Manpower/Youth, 1978. Named Outstanding Young Woman of Yr., U.S. Jaycees, 1977; lic. ind. clin. social worker; cert. vocat./ednl. counselor; cert. secondary sch. guidance counselor, Mass. Mem. Am. Personnel and Guidance Assn., Am. Assn. Sex Educators, Counselors and Therapists, Am. Vocat. Guidance Assn., Am. Assn. Student Personnel, Am. Assn. Marriage and Family Therapists (clin.). Home: 14 Browngate LN Simsbury CT 06070 Office: 88 Appleton St Springfield MA 01108

DINALE, MARGHERITA SILVI, educator; b. Pisa, Italy, Oct. 20, 1928; came to U.S., 1957, naturalized, 1961; d. Luigi and Adelia (Savelli) Silvi; Dottore in Lettere, Universita Firenze, Florence, Italy, 1949; m. Franco Dinale, June 18, 1955; children—Martina, Silvia. Instr., Smith Coll., 1955-58; assoc. prof. Italian, 1968—, chmn. dept. Italian, 1976—, dir. Sch. In Italy, 1957, 68, 75, 82-84; research scholar Radcliffe Coll., 1958-59; lectr. Wellesley Coll., 1959, Boston U., 1960; lectr. Middlebury Summer Sch. Langs., 1956, 58, 61. Mem. Dante Soc. Am., Am. Assn. Tchrs. Italian, Dante Alighieri Soc. (Rome). Author: Tutti i luoghi che ho visto, 1977; contbr. poetry to Paragone-Letterature, Alfabeta, Erba d'Arno, articles to Il Mondo. Home: 20 Round Hill Rd Northampton MA 01060 Office: Wright Hall Smith Coll Northampton MA 01063

DINARDO, LUELLA KAY, special events coordinator; b. Montrose, Colo., May 3, 1948; d. William Edgar and Evelyn Ruth (Carlson) Bray; m. Monte Talbot, Aug. 22, 1970 (div. May 1972); m. John Nicholas DiNardo, Sept. 25, 1976; 1 child, Nicholas John. B.S., Colo. State U., 1970. With accounts payable and receivable dept. Beaver Mesa Exploration, Denver, 1976-79; self-employed bookkeeper, Denver, 1979-86; pres. Planned Occasions Unltd., Inc., Denver, 1986—. Charter mem. Republican Presdl. Task Force, 1981—; mem. Nat. Fedn. Rep. Women, 1983—. Served to 2d lt. USAF, 1973-75. Mem. Nat. Assn. Female Execs., Beta Epsilon. Congregationalist. Avocations: reading; aerobic dance. Home and Office: 3921 S Narcissus Way Denver CO 80237

DINEGAR, CAROLINE ADELAIDE, political scientist, university adminstrator; b. N.Y.C., Oct. 9, 1923; d. Robert Henry Fales and Carrie Fulton (Hudson) D.; A.B., Cornell U., 1945; M.A., Columbia U., 1949, Ph.D., 1960. With U.S. Dept. State Mission to UN, N.Y.C., 1948-53; research officer, mem. del. U.S. to 3d sess. Gen. Assembly UN Paris, 1948, fgn. affairs officer, mem. del. U.S. to 6th sess. Gen. Assembly UN, Paris, 1951; instr. U. Conn., Hartford, 1956-64; asst. prof., U. Conn., Storrs, 1964-65; asst. prof. San Fernando Valley State Coll., Northridge, Calif., 1964-66; asst. prof. Woodrow Wilson dept. govt., fgn. affairs, U. Va., Charlottesville, 1967-70; prof., chmn. dept. polit. sci. U. New Haven, 1970-72, 75—, now asst. provost; vis. prof. internat. strategy Naval War Coll., Newport, R.I., 1980-81; dir. U.S. Peace Corps, Malaysia, 1972-75. HEW grantee East Asian Inst. Columbia U., 1966-67. Contbr. articles to profl. jours. Home: 246 Colony Rd New Haven CT 06511 Office: U New Haven PO Box 1307 New Haven CT 06505

DINEZZA, JANICE HELEN, TV media research executive; b. Buffalo, Mar. 21, 1953; d. Gregory Joseph and Helen Genevieve (Hermon) DiNezza; student Erie Community Coll., 1971-72; B.A., Southwestern U., Tucson, 1983. Office mgr. R. H. Stark Co., Buffalo, 1974-76; media dept. mgr. Healy Schutte & Comstock, Ltd., Buffalo, 1976-80; v.p., dir. media Tavco Mktg. and Media, Buffalo, 1980; media research dir. Cable Time Network, Inc., Buffalo, 1980-82; pres. DiNezza Media Services, Buffalo, 1982-83; group media supr. Healy-Schutte & Comstock Advt., Ltd., Buffalo, 1983—. Pub. service advt. coordinator Erie County Citizens Com. Sexual Assault, 1979—; writer, producer, numerous tv commls. and radio announcements on program services and needs of Vol. Supportive Advocate Program, 1979—; mem. Committees' Speakers Bur., 1980—; solicitor trainer, retail div. United Way Campaign Buffalo and Erie County, 1981-82. Mem. Women in Communications (pres. 1981-84, nat. dir., v.p. region 1984—), Nat. Orgn. Italian Am. Women, Women in Touch, C. of C. (vice chmn. com.), Center for Women in Mgmt., Women in Cable. Democrat. Roman Catholic. Home: 22 Tomcyn Ln Williamsville NY 14221 Office: 564 Franklin St Buffalo NY 14202

DINKEL, JUNE MCCARTY, nurse; b. Hillsdale, Ind., Apr. 2, 1923; d. Bartholomew H. and Della (Seid) McCarty; grad. St. Anthony Hosp. Sch. Nursing, Terre Haute, Ind., 1944; m. Ralph R. Dinkel, May 30, 1944; children—Ralph Michael, Margaret Susan. Pvt. duty nursing Terre Haute, 1944-60; office nurse, Terre Haute, 1960-62; staff nurse Student Health Center, Ind. State U., Terre Haute, 1962-68, dir. nurses, 1968—. Mem. Am. Coll. Health Assn., Mid-Am. Coll. Health Assn. Roman Catholic. Home: 1932 S 30th St Terre Haute IN 47803 Office: 567 N 5th St Terre Haute IN 47809

DINKINS, CAROL EGGERT, lawyer, former government official; b. Corpus Christi, Tex., Nov. 9, 1945; d. Edgar H., Jr. and Evelyn S. (Scheel) Eggert; m. O. Theodore Dinkins, Jr., July 2, 1966; children—Anne, Amy. B.S., U. Tex, 1968; J.D., U. Houston, 1971. Bar: Tex. 1971. Adj. asst. prof. law U. Houston Coll. Law, also prin. asso. Tex. Law Inst. Coastal and Marine Resources, U. Houston, 1971-73; asso., then partner firm Vinson & Elkins, Houston, 1973-81, 83—; asst. atty. gen. land and natural resources Dept. Justice, 1981-83, U.S. dep. atty.-gen., 1984-85; chmn. Pres.'s Task Force on Legal Equity for Women, 1981-83; mem. Hawaiian Native Study Commn., 1981-83; dir. Nat. Consumer Coop. Banks Bd., 1981. Author articles in field. Chmn. Tex. Gov.'s Task Force Coast Mgmt., 1979, Tex. Gov.'s Flood Control Action Group, 1980-81. Mem. ABA, State Bar Tex., Houston Bar Assn., Tex. Water Conservation Assn., Houston Law Rev. Assn. (dir. 1978—). Republican. Lutheran. Office: Vinson & Elkins 3300 First City Tower 1001 Fannin Houston TX 77002*

DINKINS, JANE POLING, software quality assurance consultant; b. Van Wert, Ohio, Oct. 11, 1928; d. Doyt Carl and Kathryn (Sawyer) Poling; B.B.A., So. Methodist U., 1974. Stewardess instr., chief stewardess Am. Airlines, 1946-50; exec. sec., adminstrv. asst. Southland Royalty Co., Ft. Worth, 1956-63; exec. sec. Charles E. Seay, Inc. and C.W. Goyer, Jr., Dallas, 1963-68; systems analyst, programmer Southland Life Ins. Co., Dallas, 1968-69, 1st Nat. Bank, Dallas, 1969-72, Occidental Life Ins. Co., Los Angeles, 1972-73; systems analyst, programmer Pacific Mut. Life Ins. Co., Newport Beach, Calif., 1973-74, mgr. mut. fund subs., 1975; systems analyst, programmer Info. Services div. TRW, Orange, Calif., 1975-79; EDP auditor Union Bank, Los Angeles, 1979; sr. EDP auditor Security Pacific Nat. Bank, Glendale, Calif., 1979-80, asst. v.p., 1981; mgmt. cons. Automation Program Office, Fed. Res. Bank, Dallas, 1982-85; pres. Poling & Assocs., Inc., 1985—. Mem. Am. Mgmt. Assn., EDP Auditors Assn., Quality Assurance Inst. (cert. quality analyst), Bachelors Etc., Sigma Kappa. Republican. Methodist. Club: Univ. (Dallas). Home and Office: 4820 Westgrove Dr Apt #606 Dallas TX 75248

DINKINS, LINDA DIANNE, jewelry company executive; b. Kyle, W. Va., Oct. 3, 1949; d. David Tenneras and Remona Lee (Dalton) Fuller; m. Baynard Juan Dinkins, Jr., Aug. 16, 1969; 1 child, Tanya. Student Wayne County Coll., Halmark Bus. Sch. Keypunch operator Detroit Edison, 1970-71; evaluator Northeastern High Sch., Detroit, 1971-72; med. records mgr. Total Health Care, Detroit, 1972-79; v.p., part-owner, nat. sales trainer Classique Creations, Dallas, 1979—; part-owner Fifth Ave. Jewelry Designs Inc.; motivation speaker. Active Southeastern Little League, Detroit, 1982. Recipient Nat. Trainer award Classique Creations, 1979, 82, Top Orgn. award 1982, 84. Mem. Internat. Platform Assn. Baptist. Club: Quette. Office: Fifth Ave Designs Inc PO Box 35388 Detroit MI 48235-0388

DINNERSTEIN, MYRA, university official; b. Phila., Apr. 19, 1934; d. Ben and Kathryn (Sharp) Rosenberg; m. Leonard Dinnerstein, Aug. 20, 1961; children—Andrew, Julie. A.B., U. Pa., 1956; M.A., Columbia U., 1963, Ph.D., 1971. Assoc. editor Ency. Yearbook, Grolier Pub. Co., N.Y.C., 1960-63; dir. women's studies U. Ariz., Tucson, 1975—, dir. S.W. Inst. for Research on Women, 1979—; mem. Ariz. Council on Humanities, Phoenix, 1975-80, 83—; Ariz. state coordinator Am. Council on Edn., Washington, 1978-80; dir. Nat. Council for Research on Women, N.Y.C., 1982—. Editor: Changing Perspectives on Menopause, 1982; contbr. articles to profl. jours. Pres. nat. adv. bd. New Directions for Young Women, Tucson, 1981. Recipient Faculty Achievement award U. Ariz. Alumni Assn., 1980; citation award Mortar Bd. U. Ariz., 1981; Faculty Recognition award Tucson Trade Bur., 1982; named to Mortar Bd. Hall of Fame, U. Ariz., 1985. Mem. Nat. Women's Studies Assn., Am. Hist. Assn., Phi Beta Kappa. Democrat. Jewish. Office: 269 Modern Languages Bldg Univ Ariz Tucson AZ 85711

DINOFSKY, LILLIAN RUSHINK, school principal; b. Jersey City, July 8, 1926; d. Abraham and Gussie F. (Konskowolski) Rushink; B.S., Bklyn. Coll., 1947; M.A., N.Y. U., 1949; Ed.D., Nova U., 1975; m. Nat Dinofsky, Aug. 26, 1945; 1 son, Adam C. Tchr. elem. pub. schs., N.Y.C., 1948-59, asst. prin. elem. sch., Bklyn., 1959-64, aux. prin., 1968-70, prin., 1970—. Mem. Nat. Assn. Elem. Sch. Prins., N.Y. Soc. Adminstrv. Women in Edn., Elem. Sch. Sci. Assn. N.Y., Nat. Reading Soc., N.Y.C. Elem. Sch. Prins. Assn., Amateur Astronomers Assn. Jewish. Author: Adapting and Implementing a Pilot Television-Reading-Language Arts Program, 1975. Office: 1970 Homecrest Ave Brooklyn NY 11229

DINSMORE, IRIS JEAN, oil field tools company executive; b. Profitt, Tex., Sept. 3, 1922; d. William Weslie and Pearl Estell (Thomas) Cole; m. James William Dinsmore, Apr. 18, 1942; children—Jimmie Lea, Carolyn Sue. Student N. Tex. State Tchrs. Coll., 1939-40. Vice pres. Star Tool Co., Hobbs, N.Mex., 1961-82, pres., dir., 1982—; pres. Testers, Inc., Hobbs, 1961-75; v.p., dir. B & B Machine Shop, Inc., Hobbs, 1983—, Crown Inspection, Inc., Hobbs, 1985; dir. Moncor Bank, Hobbs; adv. Desk & Derrick Club, Hobbs, 1983—. Girl scout leader Girl Scouts U.S.; city co-chmn. March of Dimes, Hobbs, 1961, 65. Democrat. Methodist. Office: Star Tool Co PO Box 2008 Hobbs NM 88240

DINWIDDIE, JANIS ELIZABETH, museum official; b. San Gabriel, Calif., Mar. 2, 1948; d. Redfield Towers and Eileen Hilma (Hamilton) D.; m. Charles Lindsay Steenrod, Dec. 23, 1976. Student U. Calif.-Irvine, 1965-66; B.A. in Art, Calif. State U.-Fullerton, 1971. Freelance graphic designer, Costa Mesa and Leucadia, Calif., 1972-75; office mgr. Environ. Research Assocs., Del Mar, Calif., 1974-76; bus. mgr. U. Calif.-San Diego Ext., 1976-79, conf. mgr., 1979-82; dir. spl. events Los Angeles County Mus. Art, 1982—. Mem. visitor relations adv. commn. Los Angeles Olympic Organizing Com., 1980-84. Mem. Women in Design. Office: 5905 Wilshire Blvd Los Angeles CA 90036

DION, NANCY LOGAN, health care administrator, management consultant; b. Bayonne, N.J., July 15, 1941; d. Walter Parker and Ethel B. (Kreiss) Logan; 1 son, Kenneth W. Diploma in nursing Bayonne Hosp., 1961; B.S., Fla. Internat. U., 1974, M.S. in Mgmt., 1976; postgrad. in bus. adminstrn. Nova U., 1980. Indsl. nurse AT&T, N.Y.C., 1966; pvt. duty nurse, Miami, Fla., 1967-69; dir. nursing Long Term Care Facility, Miami, 1969-72; nursing supr. Jackson Meml. Hosp., Miami, 1972-75, asst. adminstr., 1975-79; patient services dir. South Fla. State Hosp., Hollywood, 1979-85, adminstr., 1985—; adj. prof. Fla. Internat. U., Miami, 1979-81, Nova U., Ft. Lauderdale, Fla., 1980-82; mgmt. cons. U. Miami Hosp., 1979—; textbook resource cons.. Mem. Acad. Mgmt., Nat. Assn. Quality Assurance Profls., Fla. Assn. Quality Assurance Profls. (v.p. 1985-86), Dade County Assn. Quality Assurance Profls. (v.p. 1983-84, pres. 1984-86), Am. Coll. Hosp. Adminstrs. Roman Catholic. Home: 11401 NE 8th Ave Miami FL 33161

DIOSEGY, ARLENE JAYNE, lawyer; b. Pitts., Sept. 13, 1949; d. William Cornelius and Rosemarie Arlene (Voivoda) D.; m. Charles Richard Mansfield, Apr. 11, 1981; 1 dau., Corey Redling. B.A., Allegheny Coll., 1971; J.D., Temple U., 1974. Bar: Pa. 1974, Colo. 1981, N.C. 1982. Assoc., Smith & Roberts, Harrisburg, Pa., 1974-75; asst. atty. gen. Commonwealth of Pa., Harrisburg, 1975-77; chief counsel Gov.'s Council on Drug and Alcohol Abuse, Harrisburg, 1977-80; dir. legal affairs and risk mgmt. U. Colo. Health Scis. Ctr., Denver, 1980-81; asst. univ. counsel, adj. asst. prof. Duke U., Durham, N.C., 1981-85; cons. Colo. Dept. Health, 1980-81; v.p. legal services Coastal Group, Inc. Mem. ABA, N.C. Bar Assn. (vice chmn. health law sect. 1985-86, chmn. 1986-87), N.C. Soc. Health Care Attys. (bd. dirs. 1985), Am. Coll. Legal Medicine, Nat. Health Care Lawyers Assn. Office: Coastal Group Inc PO Box 3079 Durham NC 27705

DI OTTAVIO, ROSE SCHOLASTICA, acquisition consultant; b. West Chester, Pa., July 11, 1950; d. Carlo Arthur and Lena Rose (Mammarella) Di O. B.S., U. Pitts., 1971, M.S., 1972. Research asst. Regional Comprehensive Health Planning Council, Inc., Phila., 1973-75, planning assoc., 1975-77; sr. planning assoc. Health Systems Agy. S.E. Pa., Inc., Phila., 1977, dep. dir., 1977-81; cons. Plante & Moran, Southfield, Mich., 1981-83; v.p. devel. Horsham Psychiat. Group, Ambler, Pa., 1983-84; exec. v.p., dir. Capital Home Care Group, North Wales, Pa., 1984-86; regulatory cons. Albert Einstein Med. Ctr., Phila., 1984-86; acquisition cons. Venture Investment Profls., 1986—; founder, pres. Health Ventures Ltd., 1986—. Chairwoman Met. Home Health Services, Inc., Horsham, Pa., 1985-86. Senatorial scholar, 1969-71. Mem. U. Pitts. Alumni Assn., Assn. Research and Enlightenment, Amnesty Internat., Nat. Assn. Female Execs., Found. Health Care Mgmt., Am. Soc. Profl. and Exec. Women, Career Guild. Office: Health Ventures Ltd 9 E Moreland Ave Philadelphia PA 19118

DIPALMA, BARBARA ANN, certified financial planner; b. N.Y.C., July 24, 1939; d. Walter Strockbine and Marion Arlene (Lenz) Schuessler; m. Alphonse G. DiPalma, Nov. 21, 1959; children—Christopher G., Dina A. Student Orange County Community Coll., Coll. for Fin. Planning; cert. fin. planner, Adelphi U., 1985. Radio announcer Sta. WTBQ-Radio, Warwick, N.Y., 1973-77; news reporter Advertizer Photo News, Monroe and Warwick, N.Y., 1970-77; sec. Chemtrol Lawn Service, Fla. and N.Y., 1977-78; v.p. Gary Goldberg & Co Inc., Suffern, N.Y., 1978—. Bd. elections Woodbury Republican Club, N.Y., 1970-77; chmn. Woodbury Archtl. Rev. Bd., 1974-80; bd. dirs. Am. Cancer Soc., Orange County, N.Y., 1978-80, Pengiun Repertory Co., StonyPoint, N.Y., 1984-86; sec. Woodbury Republicans, 1974-76. Recipient Service award Monroe Lions Club, 1976, Woodbury BiCentennial, 1976, K.C., 1977, Congl. cert. Rep. Congl. Campaign, 1984. Mem. Internat. Assn. Fin. Planners, Inst. Cert. Fin. Planners, Nat. Assn. Female Execs., Adelphi U. Soc. Fin. Planners. Club: Women of Woodbury (pres. 1973-74). Avocations: travel; slimnastics; working out. Home: PO Box 404 Overlook Dr Highland Mills NY 10930 Office: Gary Goldberg & Co Inc 75 Montebello Rd Suffern NY 10901

DI PRIMA, STEPHANIE MARIE, educational administrator; b. Chgo., Aug. 29, 1952; d. Joseph and Ann Marie (Albate) DiP. B.A., Rosary Coll., 1973; M.Ed., Loyola U., Chgo., 1978. Tchr., St. Vincent Ferrer Sch., River Forest, Ill., 1974-78; prin. Our Lady of Hope Sch., Rosemont, Ill., 1978-81, Sacred Heart Sch., Winnetka, Ill., 1981-84, St. Monica Sch., Chgo., 1984—. Mem. Nat. Cath. Educators Assn., Nat. Assn. Elem. Sch. Prins., Assn. Supervision and Curriculum Devel., Women in Mgmt., Prins. Coalition for Arts, Prins. Support Group, Adminstrs. Growth Group, Archdiocesan Prins. Assn. Office: 5115 N Montclare Ave Chicago IL 60656

DIRK, LISA, executive assistant; b. Washington, Oct. 5, 1956; d. Robert Anthony and Elsi Mae (Updyke) Brenkworth; m. Douglas Michael Dirk, June 12, 1976; children—Robert Anthony, Adam Michael. B.A. in Criminal Justice, Moorhead State U., 1981; postgrad. N.D. State U., 1981. Sec. Harmon Glass Co., Fargo, N.D., 1976-78, N.D. State U., Fargo, 1978-81; owner Handloader Heaven, Fargo, 1981-83; exec. asst. Fargo Glass & Paint Co., 1983—. Mem. Nat. Assn. Female Execs. Methodist. Avocations: reading; needlepoint.

DIRKSEN, CYNTHIA RAYE, financial sales and management executive; b. Omaha, Mar. 7, 1953; d. Raymond John and Cecilia Agnes (Wiesen) Stovie; m. Samuel Allen Dirksen, June 4, 1977; children—Dustin Allen, Misty Raye. B.A. in Elem. and Spl. Edn., U. No. Iowa, 1974, Coaching endorsement, 1975. Spl. edn. tchr. Webster City Community Schs., Iowa, 1975-77; multi-categorical resource instr. Hampton Community Schs., Iowa, 1977-79; real estate broker Barnes Ins. & Realty, Hampton, 1978-85; real estate broker Dirksen & Assocs., 1985—; registered rep. IDS, Hampton, 1979-82; dist. mgr. IDS/Am. Express, Hampton, 1982-84; mgr. francise assoc. FSC Securities, Hampton, 1984—; bus. ins. designate Life Underwriter Tng. Council, Washington, 1982—; qualified fin. correlator IDS/Am. Express, Mpls., 1981-84. Mem. Hampton Community Devel., 1985—; v.p. St. Patrick's Bd. Edn., Hampton, 1985—; speaker natural family planning. Named Outstanding Young Religious Leader, Hampton Jaycees, 1978, Outstanding Young Woman, Referrals-Hampton, 1979. Mem. Hampton C. of C., Pride and Joy Mother's Club (treas. 1985—), Toastmasters, N. Iowa Touring Club. Roman Catholic. Avocations: swimming, bicycling (cycled across U.S. 1976, 78), cross-country skiing, reading. Home: Rural Route 1 Box 106D Hampton IA 50441 Office: FSC Securities 21 Federal N Hampton IA 50441

DISALLE-LINDSKOLD, BARBARA JOAN, lawyer; b. Toledo, July 18, 1932; d. Michael Vincent and Myrtle Eugene (England) DiSalle; m. John Eric Lindskold, July 22, 1961 (div. July 1982); children—Jayne, Ann, Graydon, Susan. B.S., St. Mary's Coll., 1954; J.D., Howard U., 1979. Bar: D.C. 1980, D.C. Ct. Appeals 1980, U.S. Ct. Appeals D.C. Cir. 1981. Conf. asst. dept. sec. legislation HHS, Washington, 1979-80; staff atty. United Planning Orgn., Washington, 1980-81; sole practice, Washington, 1982—. Mem. Women's Bar Assn., ABA, Trial Lawyers Assn. (sec. family div.). Democrat. Roman Catholic. Home: 4723 Oak Rd Shadyside MD 20764 Office: 2444 39th Pl NW #1 Washington DC 20007

DISALVATORE, ROANNE, banker; b. Frankfurt, W. Ger., May 29, 1950; d. William James and Virginia Frances D.; A.A., U. Md., Munich, 1970; A.B., Wellesley Coll., 1972; M.B.A., U. Mich., 1974. Intern, Citibank, N.A., N.Y.C., 1973; exec. trainee, acct. officer Irving Trust Co., N.Y.C., 1974-78; v.p. internat. corp. banking, credit rev. Southeast Bank N.A., 1979—. Mem. Nat. Assn. Female Execs., Nat. Assn. Bank Women, U. Mich. Alumni Assn., Miami Wellesley Club. Office: 1 Southeast Fin Ctr 100 S Biscayne Blvd Miami FL 33131

DI SANTO, GRACE JOHANNE DEMARCO (MRS. FRANK MICHAEL DI SANTO), poet; b. Derby, Conn., July 12, 1924; d. Richard and Fannie (DeMarco) De Marco; student N.Y.U. Sch. Journalism, 1941-43; A.B. in English, Belmont Abbey Coll., 1974; m. Frank Michael DiSanto, Aug. 30, 1946; children—Frank Richard, Bernadette Mary, Roxanne Judith. Newswriter, Australian Asso. Press, N.Y.C., 1942-43; staff reporter Ansonia Sentinel, Derby, 1943-45; feature writer, drama critic Bridgeport Herald, New Haven, 1945-46; editor monthly bull. Pa. State Coll. Optometry, Phila., 1947-48; free-lance writer, 1949-54; founder, pres. bd. Investors Ltd., Morganton, N.C., 1966-67. Pres., Burke County chpt. N.C. Symphony Soc., 1968-70; mem. exec. bd. Community Concerts Assn., 1962-71; trustee N.C. Symphony Soc., 1965-68, 69-70, North State Acad., Hickory, N.C., 1974—; bd. dirs. Belmont Abbey Coll., 1986—. Recipient Oscar Arnold Young Meml. award, 1982. Republican. Roman Catholic. Clubs: Grandfather Golf and Country (Linville, N.C.); Mimosa Hills Golf. Author: (poetry) The Eye is Single; Portrait of the Port as Teacher: James Dickey; contbr. The Dream Book: An Anthology of Writings by Italian-Am. Women. Address: 218 Riverside Dr Morganton NC 28655 also Grandfather Golf And Country Club Linville NC 28646

DISENHAUS, HELEN ELIZABETH, lawyer; b. Washington, Nov. 2, 1948; d. Nathan and Henrietta (Weiss) Disenhaus; m. Brian Girard Driscoll, Sept. 11, 1977; children—Daniel Benjamin, David Michael. A.B., Mt. Holyoke Coll., 1970; M.A.T., Wesleyan U., Conn., 1972; J.D., Yale U., 1977. Bar: D.C. 1977. Tchr. English, Glastonbury (Conn.) High Sch., 1971-74; atty. law firm Dow, Lohnes & Albertson, Washington, 1977—; pres. D.C. chpt. Am. Women in Radio and TV, 1982-83, bd. dirs., 1983-84, nat. v.p. govt. industry affairs, 1984-86, sec.-treas., 1986—; mem. exec. com. Yale Law Sch., 1983-84. Sarah Williston scholar, 1968. Mem. D.C. Bar Assn., Women's Bar Assn. D.C., Fed. Communications Bar Assn., ABA, Yale Law Sch. Assn. D.C. (pres. 1982-83), Phi Beta Kappa. Jewish. Club: Yale (N.Y.), Mt. Holyoke Club (Washington). Office: Dow Lohnes & Albertson 1255 23rd St NW Ste 500 Washington DC 20037

DISENHOUSE, PATRICIA ANN, medical microbiology technologist; b. Kansas City, Kans., June 29, 1948; d. Robert Edward and Bonnie Lynn (Pittman) Woeppel; m. Harvey Alan Disenhouse, May 31, 1970; children—Rebecca, Daniel, Joshua. B.A., Emporia State U., 1969; Diploma in Med. Tech. U. Iowa, 1970. Technologist, phlebotomist VA Hosp., Iowa City, 1969-70; med. technologist U. Hosps., Iowa City, 1970-71, Davis County Hosp., Bloomfield, Iowa, 1971-75, Southeast Iowa Blood Bank, Ottumwa, Iowa, 1975, Lab Control, Ottumwa, 1978—. Leader Moingona Council Girl Scouts U.S., 1980—. Mem. Am. Soc. Clin. Pathologists. Jewish. Avocation: working with children. Home: 1340 Bladensburg Rd Ottumwa IA 52501

DISHMAN, PATRICIA LOUISE, public relations executive; b. Ft. Worth, Oct. 20, 1939; d. Hubert Clinton and Cora Ophelia (Wood) D. B.S., Hardin Simmons U., 1962; M.A., U. Okla., 1969. Asst. editor So. Bapt. Radio-TV Commn., Ft. Worth, 1962-63; adult program and pub. relations dir. Midland YMCA, Midland, 1964-68; dir. pub. relations and devel. Midland Meml. Hosp., 1969-81; editor, pub. Petro plex Focus Mag., Midland, 1983-85; owner, mgr. Write Communications, Midland, 1981-86, dir. pub. relations St. Joseph's Hosp. and Health Ctr., Paris, Tex., 1986—. Author: Ten Who Overcame, 1966; contbr. articles to profl. jours. Mem. Tex. Pub. Relations Assn., Indian Arts and Crafts Assn., Midland C. of C., Projecto Huasteco Sonrisa Alegre Internat. Republican. Baptist. Avocations: photography; camping.

DISMUKES, CAROL DELORES, county official; b. Giddings, Tex., July 17, 1938; d. Herbert Emil and Ruby (Alexander) Jaehne; m. Harold Charles Schumann, Feb. 7, 1959 (div. May 1970); children—Timothy, Michael, Keith, Gregory; m. Milton Brown Dismukes, Mar. 19, 1971. Student Tex. Lutheran Coll., 1958. Dep. Lee County Clk., Giddings, Tex., 1970-74, chief dep., 1975-77; accounts receivable clk. Invader Inc., Giddings, 1977-79; prodn. sec. Humble Exploration, Giddings, 1979-80; county clk. Lee County, Giddings, 1980—. Mem., Dime Box Ind. Sch. Dist. Trustees, Tex., 1972-80, pres., 1977-80; v.p. St. Johns Lutheran Ch. Council, 1982-84; chmn. Dime Box Homecoming and Mini-Marathon, 1978—. Mem. County and Dist. Clks Assn. Tex. Democrat. Avocations: reading; sewing. Office: County Clk Lee County PO Box 419 Giddings TX 78942

DISMUKES, KAREN ELROD, women's apparel stores executive; b. Rutherford County, Murfreesboro, Tenn., Jan. 4, 1943; d. Elrod Cecil and Elrod Betty (Garmany) Henson; student Fla. So. Coll., 1965-68, Middle Tenn. State U., 1968-69, U. Tenn., 1978; m. James R. Dismukes, July 14, 1969; children—Tara Elizabeth, Karen A., James Russell. Owner, The Village Sq., Murfreesboro, Tenn., 1965—, Magazin I, The French Shop, Nashville, 1985—; sec.-treas. Dismukes, Inc., investment co.; poetry editor Murfreesboro Daily News Jour., 1969-70; lectr. on ladies' apparel. Bd. dirs. Charity Circle, Murfreesboro, 1968; trustee, youth chmn. Monteagle Sunday Sch. Assembly, 1981-82; others. Recipient MAZE award Murfreesboro Archtl. and Zoning Commn., 1978.

Mem. Nashville C. of C., Alpha Delta Kappa (founder). Club: Stone River Country. Methodist. Contbr. poetry to newspapers. Home: 434 E Main St Murfreesboro TN 37130 also 419 Jackson Blvd Nashville TN 37205 Office: 105 Public Sq Murfreesboro TN 37130 also Village Sq Top Coventry Ct Nashville TN 37215 also Magazin I The French Shop 1820 WestEnd Ave Nashville TN 37203

DISTENFELD, YVONNE SCHLAFSTEIN, lawyer; b. Washington, Dec. 23, 1956; d. Rachmill and Beverly Ann (Levy) Schlafstein; m. Jeffrey Steven Distenfeld, Aug. 3, 1980. B.S., Cornell U., 1978; J.D., Georgetown U., 1981. Bar: D.C. 1981. Legis. intern Com. on Labor and Pub. Welfare, Washington, summer 1976; law clk. Lainof, Cohen, Weinstein & Poretz, Alexandria, Va., summers 1979, 80; law clk. Satellite TV Corp., Washington, 1981, atty., 1981-84, asst. corp. sec., 1983-84; assoc. gen. counsel C.R.I., Inc., Rockville, Md., 1984—, asst. corp. sec., 1984—. Editor law and policy in internat. bus. Georgetown U. Law Ctr., 1979-81. Mem. ABA, D.C. Bar Assn., Fed. Communications Bar Assn., Omicron Nu. Democrat. Jewish. Club: Cornell (interviewer secondary schs. com.) (Washington). Office: CRI Inc 11300 Rockville Pike Rockville MD 20852

DITHRIDGE, BETTY, civic worker; b. Los Angeles, Sept. 11, 1920; d. Thomas Edward and Louise (Miles) Mitchell; m. Andrew Morrison Dithridge, May 11, 1940; 1 child, Andrew Morrison Jr. Student, UCLA, 1937-39. Boy scout and cub scout leader Los Angeles Orphan's Home Soc., 1952-69, sec. extension com., 1959-61, chmn., 1966-68; vol. worker USO; mem. Los Angeles Jr. Philharmonic Com., 1949—; active Symphonies for Youth Concerts, 1958-59; founder, chmn. San Marino Protection Com., 1971-72; sec. Los Angeles County Grand Jury, 1974-75; bd. dirs. Pasadena chpt. ARC, 1961-62, Vol. Service Bur. Pasadena; bd. dirs., treas. Wilshire Community Police Council, 1979-81; mem. citizens adv. com. Los Angeles Olympics Organizing Com., 1982-84. Recipient awards for work with local youth groups. Mem. Wilshire C. of C. (chmn. women's bur. 1957-59), Los Angeles C. of C. Assocs. Los Angeles City Coll., Orange County Marine Inst., Friends of Huntington Library, D.A.R., Friends of San Juan Capistrano Library, Los Angeles Grand Jurors Assn., Alpha Phi, Sigma Alpha Iota. Clubs: Los Angeles Tennis, Wilshire Country. Home: 35411 Beach Rd Capistrano Beach CA 92624

DITTERT, DINAH LEE, broadcasting executive; b. Gassville, Ark., Oct. 8, 1934; d. William Mack and Helen Rosalea (Showalter) Van Sandt; m. J. Lee Dittert, Jr., July 10, 1955; children—Theresa Ann, Diana Lynn, Christopher Lee, Johanna Marie. Student Sam Houston U., 1952-53, U. Tex.-Austin, 1953-55. Stringer, Houston Post, 1972—; columnist Belleville Times, 1973—; co-owner Ad-Lib Advt. Agy., Bellville, 1973—; mgr. communications KACO-AM, Belleville, gen. mgr., co-owner, 1974—. Chmn., Austin County Fair Parade, 1965-75; organizer Democratic Women's Club Austin County, 1967; del. Tex. Dem. Conv., Dallas, 1967-68; campaign mgr. Judge Lee Dittert, 1967-74; organizer St. Mary's Episcopal Day Sch., 1965. Named Citizen of Yr., Bellville Lions, 1975. Mem. Nat. Assn. Female Execs., C. of C. (bd. dirs. 1975), Alpha Epsilon Rho, Tex. Ex-Students Assn. (life). Club: Women's Golf Assn. Avocations: rock collecting; jazz. Office: KACO-AM 238 W Main St Bellville TX 77418

DITTO, TANYA BRADY, telephone co. adminstr.; b. Thibodaux, La., Aug. 21, 1934; d. John Ansel and Irene Marie (Landry) Brady; B.S. in English, Speech Edn., La. State U., 1956; m. William Harold Ditto, May 26, 1956; children—Steven, Diana, Susan. Librarian, Del Rio (Tex.) High Sch., 1957-58, Ins. Library, Atlanta, 1958-59; tchr. South Lafourche High Sch., Galliano, La., 1960-63, 67-69; dir. personnel, public, community relations Lafourche Telephone Co., Larose, 1969—; sec.-treas. Latelco. Leader, service unit chmn., area coordinator, mem. pres.'s cabinet S.E. La. council Girl Scouts U.S.A., 1969-79; den mother Plantation dist. Boy Scouts Am., Larose, 1970-72; pres. Larose Elem. Sch. PTA, 1972-73; bd. dirs. Assn. La. Arts and Artists. Recipient Thanks Badge, Girl Scouts U.S.A., 1974. Mem. Ind. Telephone Pioneer Assn., Orgn. Protection and Advancement of Small Telephone Cos., La. Telephone Assn. Republican. Roman Catholic. Author: The Longest Street, A Story of Lafourche Parish and Grand Isle. Home: 122 W 9th St Larose LA 70373 Office: 112 W 10th St Larose LA 70373

DITTON, DELORES ELAINE, formerinsurance agent; b. Bedford, Ind., Apr. 6, 1934; d. Haase John and Beulah Glen (Guthrie) Benzel; m. Louis George Ditton, Nov. 8, 1950; children—Cynthia, Ryan. R.N., Lutheran Hosp., Ft. Wayne, 1957; B.S. in Health Arts, Coll. of St. Francis, Joliet, 1980; grad. Bill Miller Sch. Real Estate, 1981, Midwest Ins. Sch., 1983, Ft. Wayne Ground Sch., 1978. Lic. nurse, real estate, ins., Ind.; lic. pvt. pilot. Nurse, surg., coronary, critical care areas, Ft. Wayne, Ind., 1957-83; head nurse geriatric facility, Ft. Wayne, 1983; sales rep. New Era Mfg. Co. energy efficient homes. Sci. Fair judge Aerospace Edn. Council, 1983, 84, 85. 86. Mem. Ninety Nines (co-founder Three Rivers chpt., sec. 1983-86, membership chmn.), Aircraft Owners and Pilots Assn., Cherokee Pilots Assn., Fort Wayne Aviation Assn. Active Ft. Wayne area flotilla Coast Guard Aux. Home: 5417 Inland Trail Fort Wayne IN 46825

DITZION, GRACE, artist, playwright, songwriter; b. Montreal, Que., Can.; B.A., Hunter Coll.; M.A., NYU; children—Lynn Shaw, Bruce. Tchr., N.Y.C. Bd. Edn., 1937-74; exhibited in one woman shows at Mus. of the Air (Cable TV), 1977, Nat. Arts Club, 1977, Westchester Community Coll., 1977, Salmagundi Club (award for sculpture), 1977, 1st Fed. Savs. Bank, 1979; group shows include Nat. Acad., Allied Artists of Am., Springfield Mus., Ponce Mus., P.R., Pittsfield Mus., Hudson Valley Art Assn., Chung-Cheng Cultural Center, St. John's U., Lincoln Center Cork Gallery, others; represented in permanent collections at Milford (Conn.) Fine Arts Council, Auburn (N.Y.) Community Coll., City U. Grad. Center, U. Hawaii; mem. awards jury Washington Sq. Outdoor Art Exhibit, 1977-79, NCCJ, 1977; vice-chmn. awards jury Salmagundi Art Club, 1978, 79, 80; cons. Womanart Gallery, 1976-78; TV appearances The Price Is Right, Mid-day Live Show, Richard Roffman Focus Show, 1977, 78. Recipient numerous art awards including 1st prizes, Gold medal, Purchase prize, Award of Excellence, Council Am. Artists Socs. award, Award of Merit. Mem. Am. Artists Profl. League, Artists Fellowship, Inc., Am. Portrait Soc., Nat. Arts Club, Internat. Beaux Arts Club of Performing Arts, Internat. Soc. Artists, Women's Press Club of N.Y.C. Important works include portrait of author on dust jacket of book, Club, 1974; (plays) A Moment of Truth, The Decision, A Dream Within a Dream, Sliding on a Rainbow. Home and Studio: 3635 Johnson Ave New York NY 10463

DI VENERE, CATHERINE LENA, TV official; b. Chgo., Oct. 6, 1941; d. Joseph and Josephine (Zucchero) Di V. Ed. pub. schs., continuing edn., spl. courses exec. program Drake U., 1985, Am. Mgmt. Assn., 1984. From sales asst. to asst. sales mgr. Blair TV, Chgo., 1961-69, sales asst. to v.p., Midwest sales mgr., 1969-74, adminstrv. asst. to pres. TV Market div., 1974-76, adminstrv. mgr., Chgo., 1976-80, v.p., mgr. office adminstrn., 1980—. Mem. Joint Civic Com. Italian-Ams., 1983, edn. com., 1985. Mem. Nat. Assn. Female Execs., Apostolate of Women, Am. Women in Radio and TV, Park Ridge Ct. Devel. Assn. (pres.). Democrat. Roman Catholic. Office: John Blair & Co 645 N Michigan Ave Chicago IL 60611

DIXON, ANN MARIE, cheese company executive; b. Binghamton, N.Y., Aug. 30, 1941; d. Carl Hugo and Alice Marie (Arvidson) Jacobson; m. John Paul Dixon, Dec. 20, 1975; stepchildren—Peter, Sam, Sarah; 1 child, Amanda B.A., St. Lawrence U., 1963. High sch. English tchr., N.Y., Mass., Vt., 1964-78; operator family farm, Guilford, Vt., 1980-84; founder, owner, pres. Guilford Cheese Co., 1984—. Mem. Am. Cheese Soc. (bd. dirs. 1983-86), Vt. Splty. Food Producers Assn. (bd. dirs., v.p. 1985), Am. Inst. Wine and Food, Women's Culinary Guild. Lutheran. Avocations: skiing; tennis. Home: RD 2 Box 182 Guilford VT 05301 Office: Guilford Cheese Co Inc RD 2 Box 182 Guilford VT 05301

DIXON, CAROLE, merchandise mart director; b. Gainsville, Tex., Mar. 21, 1943; d. George C. and Ann C. (Wistrand) Dixon; ed. Keuka Coll., Penn Yan, N.Y., N.Y. U. Real Estate Inst.; children—Kristin, Shaun. Real estate sales No. Westchester Land Co., Pound Ridge, N.Y., 1970-76; exec. dir. N.Y. Mdse. Mart, N.Y.C., 1979—; dir. N.Y. Tabletop Assn. Bd. dirs. 23d St. Assn. Mem. Nat. Home Fashions League, World Assn. Mart Mgrs. Contbr. articles to profl. jours. Home: 25 W 81st St New York NY 10024 Office: 41 Madison Ave New York NY 10010

DIXON, EVA CRAWFORD JOHNSON, librarian; b. Evinston, Fla., Aug. 28, 1909; d. William Alpheus and Willie (Crawford) Johnson; A.B. with honors in Edn., U. Fla., 1937, M.A., 1948; postgrad. Fla. State U., 1950, Appalachian State Tchrs. Coll., 1955; m. Thomas Gordon Dixon, Dec. 14, 1935 (div. 1944). Tchr. English, librarian Jefferson High Sch., Monticello, Fla., 1945-47; audio-visual dir. Jefferson County Schs., 1948-50; tchr. English, librarian Meigs (Ga.) High Sch., 1954-55; librarian Chipola Jr. Coll., Marianna, Fla., 1955-57, dir. library services, 1958-80, emeritus, 1980—, chmn. student aid and scholarship com., 1961-65; parliamentarian Fla. Gov.'s on Library on Info. Services, 1977-78; parliamentary workshop Tchr., Crystal River, Gainsville and Inverness, Fla., 1984-86. Elder, 1st Presbyterian Ch. Marianna, 1976—, chmn. witness/evangelism com., 1978-80, parliamentarian Fla. Presbytery, 1979-82. Recipient DAR Honor medal, 1984; prof. registered parliamentarian, 1985. Mem. Jefferson County Edn. Assn. (pres. 1948-50), Fla. Edn. Assn. Honor Socs. (chmn. 1950-51), Bus. and Profl. Women's Club (pres. 1958-59, 62-63), Fla. Fedn. Bus. Profl. and Women's Clubs (dist. dir. 1962-63), Women of 1st Presbyn. Ch. (pres. 1962-65), Nat. Assn. Parliamentarians (tchr., 1983—, v.p., program chmn. Jacksonville Mace unit 1983-84), Am. Inst. Parliamentarians (sec. Jacksonville area 1984), Kappa Delta Pi. Contbr. articles to profl. jours. Home: 6621 Shindler Dr Jacksonville FL 32222

DIXON, HELEN NAOMI, social worker, nurse; b. Sarasota, Fla., Aug. 8, 1936; d. Charlie Jones and Willie Mae King; m. Harold Eugene Dixon, Aug. 16, 1953 (dec. 1954); children—Linda Renee Burrell, Charlette Treacer Oliver. A.S. in Med. Records, Essex City Coll., 1972; B.A. in Behavioral Sci., Shaw U., 1974; postgrad. Rutgers U., 1974-76. Unit mgr. Orange Meml. Hosp., N.J., 1960-66, sr. record clk., 1966-70; med. asst. Dr. Phillip Stewart, Newark, 1971-73; pharm. sec. St. Michael's Hosp., Newark, 1973-74; social worker Essex County Welfare, Newark, 1974-82; nurse asst. Med. Personnel Poole, Sarasota, 1982—. Parent friend Child Protective Team, Sarasota, 1984-85; vol. transp. Sr. Citizens, Sarasota, 1984-85; poll insp. Voters Adminstrn. Office, Sarasota, 1982-85. Recipient Appreciation for Dedication award 1st Baptist Ch. Sunday Sch., N.J., 1982; grantee VA, Essex Coll. Democrat. Clubs: Cosmopolitan Women's (N.J.) (publicity com. 1970-75), Shaw U. Alumni (N.C.) (exec. sec. 1975-80). Lodge: Eastern Star (program chmn. 1972-83). Avocation: community counseling. Address: 1741 34th St Charlie Jones St Sarasota FL 33580

DIXON, JOYCE ELLEN, program director, news administrator; b. Savannah, Ga., Dec. 24, 1956; d. Ralph A. and Ruth H. (Sane) D. B.A. in Edn., U. S.C., 1980. Cert. secondary tchr., Ga. Tchr. English, Westfield Sch., Pery, Ga., 1980-82; news, music program dir. sta. WCLA-AM-FM, Claxton, Ga., 1982—. Mem. pub. relations com. Miss Altamaha Scholarship Pageant, Claxton, Ga., 1984—; pub. info. dir. Evans Cancer Soc., Claxton, 1984—; mem. pub. info. com. Evans chpt. ARC, Claxton, 1984; mem. survey com. Community Strategy Com., Claxton, 1985. Mem. Sigma Delta Chi, Delta Zeta (2d v.p. 1979). Republican. Methodist. Avocations: cross stitch, quilting, video collection. Home: PO Box 122 7 W Liberty St Claxton GA 30417 Office: WCLA AM-FM 316 N River St Claxton GA 30417

DIXON, JUDY BARKER, health club executive; b. Montclair, N.J., Aug. 16, 1949; d. Arthur Wood and Elizabeth (Massey) D.; children—Selin, Marian. B.S., U. So. Calif., 1973. Sports commentator PBS-TV, 1974-79; coordinator women's athletics, Yale U., New Haven, 1973-77; promotion mgr. Bancroft Sporting Goods, Woonsocket, R.I., 1977-79; market mgr. Dennison Nat., Holyoke, Mass., 1979-83; owner, mgr. Amherst Racquet and Fitness Ctr., Mass., 1984—. Intake chairperson Am. Cancer Soc., Hampshire, Country. Nominee for Emmy award Acad. TV Arts and Scis., 1975. Democrat. Office: Amherst Racquet & Fitness Ctr Route 166 Sunderland MA 01375

DIXON, LORRAINE VALLERAND, educator, retailer; b. Waterbury, Conn., Oct. 8, 1934; d. Walter and Dorothy (Pelletier) Vallerand; m. Alfred M. Dixon, May 14, 1955; children—Michael, Thomas, Robert. B.S. in Edn., So. Conn. State U., 1971, M.S. in Spl. Edn., 1975, postgrad., 1983. Tchr. of handicapped Title III Project, Oxford, Conn., 1971-74; coordinator, tchr. Wattertown Bd. Edn., Conn., 1974—; co-owner, mgr. Town & Country, Oakville, Conn., 1976—. Mem. Democratic Town Com., Prospect, Conn., 1963-75; recording clk. Prospect Planning and Zoning Commn., 1964-67, Prospect Town Council, 1967-71. Mem. Adminstrn. and Supervision Assn. So. Conn. U. (sec. 1985—), Watertown Fedn. Tchrs. (negotiator 1981-82), Prospect C. of C., Phi Delta Kappa. Roman Catholic. Avocation: baseball fan. Home: 5 Hemlock Rd Prospect CT 06712

DIXON, RITA HURT, educational administrator; b. Harlan, Ky., Mar. 21, 1938. B.A., Georgetown Coll., 1960; M.Ed., Xavier U., 1967; postgrad. Va. Poly. Inst. and State U., Radford U., James Madison U. Tchr. French, Oakwood High Sch., Dayton, Ohio, 1960-61, Worthington High Sch., Ohio, 1961; mem. personnel staff Kimberly Clark Corp., West Carrollton, Ohio, 1962-64; French and English tchr. West Carrollton High Sch., 1964-67, counselor, 1967-69; coordinator counseling and testing New River Community Coll., Dublin, Va., 1975-83, dir. student devel., 1983—; presenter workshops, seminars in field; rep. for New River Community Coll. to Nat. Identification Program in Higher Edn.; chmn. bd. dirs. Community Coll. Ministries, 1985—. Mem. Va. Personnel and Guidance Assn., New River Personnel and Guidance Assn. (pres. 1980), Va. Counselors Assn. (dir. grant project), Am. Personnel and Guidance Assn., New River Community Coll. Women's Orgn. (pres. 1979-80), Wytheville Community Coll. Faculty Wives (pres. 1979-80), Nat. Assn. Female Execs., Phi Delta Kappa. Home: 880 Mountain View Dr Wytheville VA 24382

DIXON, SHERRIE ROSEN, banker; b. N.Y.C., Oct. 14, 1955; d. Irving and Gertrude (Chernick) Rosen; m. James T. Dixon, June 26, 1976; 1 child, Alexandra J. B.S., Northwestern U., Evanston, Ill., 1972-76; J.D. Loyola U., Chgo., 1979. Bar: Ill. 1979. Asst. tax counsel No. Trust, Chgo., 1979-80; asst. trust officer Chemical Bank, N.Y.C., 1981-83, trust officer, 1984—. Mem. ABA, Westchester County Bar Assn., Westchester Women's Bar Assn., Westchester Estate Planning Council, Jr. League of West Chester on the Ground. Democrat. Jewish. Home: 96 N Chatsworth Ave Larchmont NY 10538 Office: Chemical Bank Trust Dept 30 Rockefeller Plaza New York NY 10112

DIXON, SHIRLEY JUANITA, restaurant owner; b. Canton, N.C., June 29, 1935; d. Willard Luther and Bessie Eugenia (Scroggs) Clark; m. Clinton Matthew Dixon, Jan. 3, 1953; children—Elizabeth Secrest, Hugh Monroe III, Cynthia Owen, Sharon Fouts. B.S., Wayne State U., 1956; postgrad. Mary Baldwin Coll., 1958, U. N.C., 1977. Acct., Standard Oil Co., Detroit, 1955-57; asst. door mgr. Statler Hilton, Detroit, 1958-60; bookkeeper Osborne Lumber Co., Canton, N.C., 1960-61; bus. owner, pres. Dixon's Restaurant, Canton, 1961—; judge N.C. Assn. Distributive Edn. Assn., state and dist., 1982—. Membership chair Haywood County Assn. Retarded Citizens Bd., 1985—; bd. commrs. Haywood Vocationals Opportunities, 1985—; dist. dir. 11th Congl. Dist. Democratic Women, 1982—; state Teen-Dem. advisor State Dem. party, 1985—; alderwoman Town of Canton, N.C.; vice-chair Gov.'s Adv. Council on Aging, State N.C., 1982—; 2d v.p. crime prevention Community Watch Bd., State N.C., 1985—; mem. Criminal Justice Bd., N.C. Assembly on Women and the Economy; chair. Western N.C. Epilipsey Assn.; bd. dirs. Canton Recreation Dept. Recipient Outstanding Service award Crime Prevention from Gov., 1982, Gov.'s Spl. Vol. award, 1983, Outstanding Service award N.C. Community Watch Assn., 1984, Community Service award to Handicapped, 1983-84; named Employer of Yr. for Hiring Handicapped N.C. Assn. for Retarded Citizens, 1985. Mem. NOW, Women's Polit. Caucus, Nat. Assn. Female Execs., Women's Forum N.C., Canton Bus. and Profl. Women's Club (pres. 1974-79; Woman of Yr. 1984). Democrat. Episcopalian. Club: Altrusa. Avocation: softball club. Home: 104 Skyland Terrace Canton NC 28716 Office: Dixon's Restaurant 30 N Main St Canton NC 28716

DIXON, THELMA CHAPMAN, diversified business executive; b. Jack, Ala., Dec. 13, 1907; d. William Clanton and Etta Elizabeth (Dawkins) Chapman; m. Charles Dixon, Apr. 30, 1930 (dec. Oct. 1976); children—Catherine Dixon Roland, Marjorie Dixon Vick (dec.). Student pub. schs. Ptnr., Charles Dixon & Co., Andalusia, Ala., 1931-76, owner, 1976—; sec.-treas. Turpentine Producers, Inc., Chickasaw, Ala., 1939-44; ptnr. Dixon Industries, Andalusia, 1934-38, Dixon Lumber Co., Andalusia, 1941-52; v.p. Dixon Lumber Co., Inc., 1952-69, chmn. bd., 1976-78; vice chmn. D & G Devel. Pty., Ltd., Perth, Australia, 1967-76, chmn. bd., 1976—; sec.-treas. D-C Constrn., Inc., Andalusia, 1952-63; ptnr. Dixon Investment Co., Andalusia, 1952-76; exec. com. Citibanc of Andalusia, 1979-83, SouthTrust Bank of Andalusia, 1983-85; dir. So. Nat. Corp., Covington County Bank, Andalusia. Active East Three Notch Sch. PTA, 1942-48, pres., 1945; mem. adminstrv. bd. First United Meth. Ch., Andalusia, 1977; founder Thelma Dixon Found., Andalusia, 1981; active Andalusia Hist. Soc., 1983—; trustee Andalusia Pub. Library, 1985—. Recipient Benefactor award Am. Library Trustees Assn., 1978; elected Hall of Honor Huntingdon Coll. for Endowed Scholarship, Montgomery, Ala., 1979. Mem. Forest Farmers Assn., Am. Forest Assn., U.S. C. of C., Ala. C. of C., Andalusia C. of C., Am. Legion Aux., Nat. Soc. Magna Charta Dames Phila., DAR, Nat. Soc. Colonial Dames IVII Century. Clubs: Fleur de Lis Garden (pres. 1967-69), Mentor (Andalusia). Avocations: fishing; gardening; needlework. Office: Charles Dixon & Co 900 S Three Notche St PO Box 908 Andalusia AL 36420

DIXON-LABRIE, GLORIA DEAN, government administrator; b. Texarkana, Tex., Sept. 6, 1942; d. Prentice Rolland and Eunice Rolland Dixon; children by previous marriage—Tony Fritz, Pamela Fritz; m. Kenneth John LaBrie; 1 child, J. Kipp LaBrie; 1 stepchild, Angela N. LaBrie. B.B.A., Avila Coll., Kansas City, Mo., 1976. Office mgr. Fed. Hwy. Adminstrn., Kansas City, Mo., 1973-78, fin. specialist, Topeka, 1978-79, fed. women's program mgr., Kansas City, 1979-83; regional dir. civil rights Urban Mass Transp. Adminstrn., Dept. Transp., Kansas City, Mo., 1983—. Active NAACP, IMAGE, Hispanic Employment Council, Mo. Black Leadership Assn.; pres. United Way Women's Council; mem. citizen rev. Heart of Am. United Way; spl. advocate Jackson County Juvenile Ct.; mem. voluntary action com. Fed. Exec. Bd., 1974-76, chmn., 1975-76; past vice chmn. Greater Kansas City Equal Opportunity Com.; judge youth awards B'nai B'rith; past vice chmn. St. Joseph/Kansas City Diocesan Sch. Bd.; mem. exec. bd. Greater Kansas City Urban League; past corp. bd. mem. Human Resources Commn. Recipient various awards, including Spl. award Fed. Exec. Bd., 1974, Spl. Service award, 1976; Outstanding Achievement award Affirmative Action Com., 1980; Adminstr.'s award of Merit, Urban Mass. Transp. Adminstrn., 1982, Sec.'s award for vol. service Dept. Transp., 1984; scholar Kansas City Jr. Coll., Kans., 1960. Mem. Federally Employed Women (Greater Kansas City chpt.) (charter mem., past v.p.), Federally Employed Women (Central Plains chpt.) (organizer chpt., past pres.), Delta Sigma Theta (Kansas City, Mo., Alumnae chpt.) (social action chmn.). Roman Catholic. Avocations: reading; camping; needlework. Home: 615 E 79th Terr Kansas City MO 64131 Office: Dept Transp Urban Mass Transp Adminstrn 6301 Rockhill Rd Room 100 Kansas City MO 64131

DIXSON, KERMET MARIA, educational administrator; b. Los Angeles, Feb. 11, 1950; d. Blanchard and Sally (Terry) Smith; m. Ronald Elliott Dixson, June 20, 1968 (div. 1972); 1 child, Ronda Elaine. B.A., UCLA, 1971; M.Ed., Calif. State U., 1974. Tchr. Compton Unified Sch. Dist., Calif., 1972-73; tchr. Inglewood Unified Sch. Dist., Calif., 1973-74, adminstr., 1974-78, dir. spl. projects, 1978—, grants writer, 1972—; cons. Council Black Nurses, Los Angeles, 1975; univ. lectr. Dominguez U., Calif., 1977-78; state program reviewer State Dept. Edn., Calif., 1978—. Author: Educational Project Blossoms, 1982. Editor: Educational Project Flores, 1983. Recipient Award of Recognition Cert. for Leadership Devel., 1983. Mem. EDUCARE, 100 Black Profl. Women's Assn., NAACP, UCLA Black Alumni Assn., Assn. Calif. Sch. Adminstrs., Black Sch. Educators, Inglewood Mgmt. Assn. Democrat. Baptist. Avocations: tennis, reading, writing. Home: 3220 W 82d St Inglewood CA 90305 Office: Inglewood Unified Sch Dist 401 S Inglewood Ave Inglewood CA 90301

DIYANNI, SUSAN CLARE, lawyer, educator; b. Denville, N.J., Jan. 1, 1955; d. Edward Salvatore and Lena (Derrico) DiY.; m. Robert R. Lanning, Oct. 2, 1982. B.A., Muhlenberg Coll., Allentown, Pa., 1977; postgrad. U. Pa., 1980-81; J.D., Harvard U., 1981. Bar: N.J. 1981, N.Y. 1982, Pa. 1982. Law clk. U.S. Dist. Ct., Phila., 1980; with IBM, 1981—, atty. Nat. Distbn. div., Princeton, N.J., 1983—; instr. bus. law Rider Coll., 1983—, IBM, 1982—, Berkeley Sch., White Plains, N.Y., 1982; hearing officer Rutgers U., New Brunswick, N.J., 1983—. Mem. Del-Aware, environ. orgn., 1983—, Bucks Alliance Nuclear Disarmament, 1983—; nominee Falls Twp. (Pa.) Planning Bd. and Environ. Commn., 1984—. Recipient Informal Contbn. award IBM, 1983; Nat. Merit scholar, 1973-77. Mem. N.J. Bar Assn., N.Y. Bar Assn., Pa. Bar Assn., Nat. Assn. Female Execs., Phi Beta Kappa. Democrat. Roman Catholic. Home: 844 N Lafayette Ave Morrisville PA 19067 Office: IBM 590 Madison Ave New York NY 10022

DJERF, ANNE VICTORIA, insurance company executive; b. Denver, Feb. 12, 1945; d. Nicholas John and Estelle Ann (Sullivan) Fowler; m. Karl Ero Djerf, Dec. 14, 1968. Student Marymount Manhattan Coll., 1982—. With Midland Ins. Co., N.Y.C., 1971—, v.p., 1984—. Mem. Am. Soc. Personnel Adminstrs., Ins. Women N.Y., Atlantic Highlands Hist. Soc. Democrat. Presbyterian. Office: Midland Insurance Co 160 Water St New York NY 10038

DLUGACZ, JUDITH ANN, recording company executive; b. Queens, N.Y., Mar. 2, 1952; d. Jason S. and Dorothy (Hack) D. B.A., U. Mich., 1972. Electrician apprentice, Washington, 1972-73; tchr. spl. edn., Washington, 1973-75; founder, pres. Olivia Records, Washington, 1973—; cons. in field. Exec. producer 25 albums, 1973—. Mem. Nat. Acad. Rec. Arts and Scis. Jewish. Avocations: golf; photography. Office: Olivia Records Inc 4400 Market Oakland CA 94608

DMYTRYSHAK, CAROLE ANN, banker; b. Altoona, Pa., Mar. 16, 1942; d. Michael and Dorothy Bernice (Garman) D.; B.S. in Math., Drexel U., Phila., 1965; M.S. in Computer Sci., Pratt Inst., 1974. With Bankers Trust Co., N.Y.C., 1967-85, now sr. v.p. in charge mktg. and research ops. European Am. Bank; cons. in field. Mem. Bank Mktg. Assn., N.Y. Map Soc., NOW. Home: 118 E 19th St New York NY 10003 Office: European Am Bank 10 Hanover Sq New York NY 10015

DOAK, JANICE ASKEW, banker; b. Houston, Jan. 18, 1925; d. Andrew Miller and Cleo Elizabeth Askew; B.B.A., U. Tex., Austin, 1944; m. Ira Kennedy Doak, Dec. 9, 1944; children—Barbara Sue, Carolyn M. With Bank of Houston, 1949—, cashier, 1960-62, v.p., cashier, 1962-74, v.p., 1974-86, sr. v.p., 1986—. Vol. worker St. Luke's Episcopal Hosp., 1973—; docent Harris County Heritage Soc. Mem. Nat. Assn. Bank Women, Am. Inst. Banking (past dir. Houston chpt.), Credit Women Internat. (pres. Lone Star council 1986), Credit Reps. Assn. Greater Houston Banks (bd. dirs.), Houston Credit Women (pres. 1977-78, 84-85), Am. Bus. Women's Assn. (pres. Houston charter chpt. 1980-81), Fedn. Houston Profl. Women (v.p. 1982-83, honoree) Alpha Chi Omega. Episcopalian. Clubs: Altrusa (pres. 1967-68) (Houston), Order Eastern Star (worthy matron). Office: Bank of Houston 5115 Main St Houston TX 77002

DOAN, NANCY NHAN, dealer credit analyst; b. Saigon, Vietnam; Jan. 6, 1960; came to U.S., 1975; d. Ho Van and Vinh Hoang (Thi) D. B.A., Calif. State U.-Fullerton, 1983. Fin. services officer Bank of Am., Whittier, Calif., 1978-85; loan officer Bank of San Pedro, Long Beach, Calif., 1985; dealer credit analyst Toyota Motor Credit Corp., Torrance, Calif., 1985—. Mem. Nat. Assn. Female Execs. Republican. Baptist. Avocation: travel. Home: 14009 E Dunton Dr Whittier CA 90605

DOBELIS, INGE NACHMAN, book editor; b. Würzburg, Germany, Nov. 16, 1933; came to U.S., 1938, naturalized, 1951; d. Rudolf Hugo and Resi (Hamburger) Nachman; B.A. in English, U. Ga., 1956; m. Miervaldis C. Dobelis, May 4, 1969; 1 son, Arthur N. Editorial positions Buttenheim Publs. and Crowell-Collier, 1956-64; copy editor Gen. Book div. Readers Digest, N.Y.C., 1965-72, asso. editor, 1973-79, sr. editor, 1979-85, sr. staff editor, 1985—. Exec. bd., officer Murray Hill Democratic Club, 1968-74; exec. bd. Community Bd. No. 6, N.Y.C., 1973-78, sec., 1976, chmn. health and hosps. com., 1974-78; trustee, officer Brotherhood Synagogue, 1983—; mem. N.Y. Dem. County Com., 1967-74. Mem. Phi Beta Kappa. Assoc. editor: Reader's Digest Family Encyclopedia of American History, 1975; Reader's Digest Family Health Guide and Medical Encyclopedia, 1976; Reader's Digest Illustrated Guide to Gardening, 1978; editor: Readers Digest Family Legal Guide, 1981; Quick and Thrifty Cooking, 1984; Magic and Medicine of Plants, 1986. Home: 201 E 17th St New York NY 10003 Office: 750 3d Ave New York NY 10016

DOBELLE, GLADYS KLEINMAN, public affairs executive; b. N.Y.C., Feb. 15, 1943; d. Irving and Sally Kleinman; m. William H. Dobelle, Dec. 31, 1972. B.A. with honors, Hunter Coll., 1964; postgrad. Harvard Inst. Arts Adminstrn., 1971. Mem. faculty Cambridge Ctr. for Adult Edn. (Mass.), Boston Ctr. for Adult Edn., 1968-72; asst. to pub. Boston After Dark, 1968-69; asst. to dir. Newport Romantic Music Festival (R.I.), summer 1969; exec. dir. Harvard Ind. newspaper, Cambridge, 1969-70; pub. relations dir. Boston Ctr.

for Arts, 1970-72, Ballet West, Salt Lake City, 1973, San Francisco Opera, 1974, San Francisco Symphony, 1975; pres. Glad Tidings, pub. affairs cons., N.Y.C., 1976—; mem. faculty New Sch. Social Research, N.Y.C., 1977-80, NYU, 1979-81; cons. Boston Globe, Harvard Inst. Arts Adminstrn., Fine Arts Devel., America's Cup Races, 1970; chmn. Dialogue: A Working Woman's Seminar, 1977-79. Mem. Citizen's Com. for N.Y.C., Assn. for a Better N.Y. Mem. Pub. Relations Soc. Am., Regional Plan Assn., Am. Women in Radio and TV, LWV, Central Park Community Council, Jewish Community Relations Council, others. Jewish. Editor: Getting into Ink and Print and On the Air, 1971. Clubs: City of N.Y., Women's City. Home: One Lincoln Plaza New York NY 10023 Office: Glad Tidings 20 W 64th St New York NY 10023

DOBIE, SHIRLEY IMOGENE, psychologist; b. Grosse Pointe Park, Mich., Jan. 30, 1930; d. Joseph L. and Gwendolyn Kemp; B.A., Wayne State U., 1954, M.A., 1956, Ph.D., 1959; m. Victor Bloom, June 30, 1973; children—Dorcas, Gordon, Elizabeth. Intern, Lafayette Clinic, Detroit, 1957; adj. asst. prof. Wayne State U., 1960-63, adj. asso. prof., 1964—; staff psychologist Lafayette Clinic, 1959-64, chief psychologist adult out-patient dept., 1964-66, acting head dept. psychology, 1968-69, dir. clin. psychology tng. program, 1967-76, dir. psychiat. edn., 1976-78, cons. in individual and group psychotherapy, 1978—; cons. psychologist U. Mich., 1969-71; psychol. cons. Harper Hosp., 1970-78; pvt. practice supervision of psychologists, social workers and psychiatrists in individual and group psychotherapy, 1978—. Recipient Sigma Xi research award, 1959; cert. cons. psychologist, Mich.; diplomate Am. Bd. Profl. Psychology. Mem. Am. Group Psychotherapy Assn. (cert. 1976), Am. Psychol. Assn., Mich. Group Psychotherapy Assn., Mich. Psychol. Assn., Wolverine State Group Psychotherapy Soc. (pres.). Contbr. articles to profl. jours. Home and Office: 1007 Three Mile Dr Grosse Pointe Park MI 48230

DOBLER, NORMA (MRS. CLIFFORD DOBLER), state legislator, civic worker; b. Haines, Oreg., May 2, 1917; d. Lester and Bessie (Bircket) Woodhouse; student U. Cin., 1935-37; B.S. in Bus., U. Idaho, 1939; m. Clifford Dobler, June 14, 1941; children—Sharon Louise Dobler Vega, Carol Marie Dobler Harris, Terry Lee. Sec. to registrar U. Idaho, 1939-41; sec. to judge, Caldwell, Idaho, 1945; sec. Am. Express Co., Seattle, 1943; lab. technician U. Idaho Coll. Forestry, Moscow, 1963-69; mem. Idaho Ho. of Reps., 1973-77, Idaho Senate, 1977—; mem. health and human services com. Nat. Conf. State Legislators; mem. Idaho Job Tng. Coordinating Council; mem. Idaho Developmental Disabilities Adv. Council, 1977-81; chairperson Gov.'s Task Force Independence, alternative nursing homes; mem. Commn. on Nursing and Nursing Edn.; mem. State Edn. Equity Com., 1986—, State Adv. Council on Aging, 1986—. Mem. LWV, 1951—, bd. dirs. Moscow, 1953-68, pres. Idaho, 1968-71; county adv. bd. trustee Moscow Sch. Dist., 1963-69, vice chmn., 1966-69; bd. dirs. Idaho Sch. Trustees Assn., 1969; leader 4-H Club, 1951-64; pres. Moscow PTA, 1958-59, life mem. Recipient Service award Idaho Home Economists, 1979; Conservation Legislator of Yr. award Idaho Wildlife Fedn., 1984; named Citizen of Yr. Nat. Assn. Social Workers, Idaho chpt., 1980; Outstanding Alumna award dept. home econs. U. Idaho, 1984; Conservation Legislator of Yr. award Idaho Wildlife Fedn., 1984. Mem. AAUW (hon.), Delta Kappa Gamma (hon.). Methodist (pres. Woman's Soc. Christian Service 1972, supt. ch. sch. 1953-65, mem. ofcl. bd. 1953-67, 72). Home: 1401 Alpowa St Moscow ID 83843

DODD, DARLENE MAE, nurse, air force officer; b. Dowagiac, Mich., Oct. 11, 1935; d. Charles B. and Lila H. Dodd; diploma in nursing Borgess Hosp. Sch. Nursing, Kalamazoo, 1957; grad. U.S. Air Force Flight Nurse Course, 1959, U.S. Air Force Squadron Officers Sch., 1963, Air Command and Staff Coll., 1973; student So. Oreg. State Coll. Commd. 2d lt. U.S. Air Force, 1959, advanced through grades to lt. col., 1975; staff nurse, Randolph AFB, Tex., 1959-60, Ladd AFB, Alaska, 1960-62, Selfridge AFB, Mich., 1962-63; Cam Rahn Bay Air Base, Vietnam, 1966-67, Seymour Johnson AFB, N.C., 1967-69, Air Force Acad., 1971-72; flight nurse 22d Aeromed. Evacuation, Tex., 1963-66; chief nurse Danang AFB, Vietnam, 1967; flight nurse Yokotu AFB, Japan, 1969-71; clin. coordinator ob/gyn and flight nurse, Elmendorf AFB, Alaska, 1973-76; clin. nurse coordinator obstetrics-gynecology and pediatric services USAF Med. Center, Keesler AFB, Miss., 1976-79, ret., 1979. Decorated Bronze Star, Meritorious Service medal, Air Force Commendation medal (3). Mem. So. Oreg. Hist. Soc., DAV, Ret. Officers Assn., Vietnam Vets. Am., VFW, Uniformed Services Disabled Retirees, Smithsonian Instn. Assocs., Psy Chi, Phi Kappa Phi. Clubs: Psychology, Women of Moose. Home: 712 W 1st St Phoenix OR 97535

DODD, PATRICIA ANN, publisher, editor; b. San Angelo, Tex., Sept. 14, 1950; d. Dale Francis and Mary Frances (Wright) D. A.A., Eastern N.Mex. U., 1971. Legal sec. Richard E. Hartman, Denver, 1971-72; exec. sec. MDC, Denver, 1972-75, Kissinger Petroleum Co., Denver, 1975-76; assoc. pub., mng. editor Denver Living Mag., Baker Publs., Denver, 1976—. Recipient Innovation award Baker Publs., Inc., 1983, Editorial Excellence award, 1981. Mem. Colo. Apt. Assn., Colo. Press Women (1st pl. award for editing 1983, 84), Nat. Fedn. Press Women (2d pl. award for editing 1983), Home Builders Assn. Met. Denver, Women in Communications. Republican. Roman Catholic. Home: 14602 E 2d Ave Apt C103 Aurora CO 80111 Office: Baker Publications Denver Living Mag 13693 E Iliff Ave Suite 230 Aurora CO 80014

DODERER, MINNETTE FRERICHS, state legislator; b. Holland, Iowa, May 16, 1923; d. John A. and Sophie S. Frerichs; B.A., U. Iowa, 1948; m. Fred H. Doderer, Aug. 5, 1944; children—Dennis, Kay Lynn. Mem. Iowa Ho. of Reps. 1964-69, 80—, minority whip, 1967-68, chairperson ways and means com., 1983—; mem. Iowa Senate, 1969-79, pres. pro tem, 1975-76; vis. prof. Stephens Coll., Iowa State Coll. (both 1979); vice-chairwoman Iowa Interstate Cooperation Commn., 1965-66; Vice-chairwoman Democratic Party Johnson County, 1957-60; mem. Dem. Nat. Com., 1968-70, Dem. Nat. Policy Council Elected Ofcls., 1973-76; chairwoman Iowa del. Internat. Women's Del. Bd. fellows Iowa Sch. Religion. Recipient Disting. Service award Iowa Edn. Assn., 1969; mem. Iowa Women's Hall of Fame, 1978. Mem. LWV, Delta Kappa Gamma (hon.). Democrat. Methodist.

DODGE, MADELINE RUTH WHEELAN, learning center administrator; b. Pueblo, Colo., July 24, 1929; d. Theodore Charles and Ruth Madeline (Caulfield) Wheelan; m. James E. Dodge, Feb. 21, 1952; children—Arlene, Kathleen, James, Jr., Thomas. Student Wash. State U., 1947-49; B.A., U. Wash., 1970. Asst. tchr. U. Wash., Seattle, 1965-67, head tchr., 1967-70, supr., 1970-71, dir., 1971-76, cons., 1979-80; instr. North Seattle Community Coll., 1978; dir., owner Christopher Robin Learning Ctr., 1976—; cons. Model Cities Seattle U., 1971-75, various colls., univs., head start programs. Contbr. articles to profl. jours. Vol. Juvenile Ct., King County Guardian Ad Litem Program, 1978—. Office: Christopher Robin Learning Ctr 7016 35th NE Seattle WA 98115

DODSON, JOANN HODGMAN, nursing educator; b. Detroit, Aug. 8, 1937; d. Charles Edwin and Elizabeth (Ranck) Hodgman; m. Leslie Dodson, Sept. 9, 1961; children—Charles, Jeffrey. B.S. in Nursing, U. Mich., 1959; M.S. in Nursing, Wayne State U., 1980. Cert. pub. health U. Calif.-San Francisco, 1960. Instr. Bronson Sch., Kalamazoo, 1963-65; staff nurse Hurley Hosp., Flint, Mich., 1966-73; instr. Mott Community Coll., Flint, 1972; staff nurse Bronson Hosp., Kalamazoo, 1974-79; instr. nursing Nazareth (Mich.) Coll., 1979—; mem. nursing adv. bd. ARC, Kalamazoo, 1980—. Bd. dirs. Hospice Greater Kalamazoo, 1980—; mem. Kalamazoo County Commn. on Aging, 1983—. Mem. Nat. League for Nursing, AAUW, Sigma Theta Tau. Office: Nazareth College Nazareth MI 49074

DOEHRING, CLAUDIA GAIL, insurance company executive; b. Mt. Pleasant, Mich., Jan. 5, 1950; d. Wilton Robert and Mary Ann (Dunn) Doehring. Student, Mich. State U., 1968-69. C.L.U.; chartered fin. cons. Asst. mgr. Equitable Life, Detroit, 1974-75, N.Y.C., 1975-76, project mgr., 1976-77, adminstrv. mgr., 1977-78, mgr. profl. devel., 1978-83, product mgr., 1983—. Contbr. articles to profl. jours. Project mgr. United Way campaign, N.Y.C., 1983, Productivity Com., N.Y.C., 1982-83. Mem. Am. Soc. C.L.U.'s. Home: 108 N Passaic Ave Chatham NJ 07928 Office: Equitable Life Assurance Soc US 2 Penn Plaza 21st Floor New York NY 10001

DOERING, JOANNE, legislative aide, management analyst; b. N.Y.C., Aug. 10, 1949; d. Gilbert Guthrey and Grace Josephine (Grossholtz) Everly; m. Robert Edgar Doering, Mar. 21, 1968 (div. 1983); children—Tammy Lyn, Robert Henry. B.S., N.Y. Inst. Tech., 1979. Mgmt. analyst Suffolk County Exec. Office, Hauppauge, N.Y., 1980-84; legis. aide Suffolk County Legislature, Hauppauge, 1984—, mem. exec. task force on emergency housing, 1981-82, legis. task force on affordable housing, 1984-85. Bd. mem. R.A.P. Enrichment Program, Southold, N.Y., 1974-77; mem. Chairman's Club, West Islip, N.Y., 1984—. Recipient Sociology award for 1980, N.Y. Inst. Tech. Mem. Am. Soc. Pub. Adminstrs., Nu Upsilon Tau. Republican. Club: Mensa. Avocations: Real estate investment; bridge; piano; travel. Home: 260 Highwood Rd Southold NY 11971 Office: Suffolk County Legislature Veterans Memorial Hwy Hauppauge NY 11787

DOERNER, MAUREEN ANNE, lawyer; b. Bridgeport, Conn., Oct. 8, 1951; d. William James and Anne Marie (Carey) Doerner; m. Thomas Anthony Singarella, May 17, 1971 (div. 1983). B.A., So. Conn. State Coll., 1973; J.D., Creighton U., 1981. Bar: Nebr. 1981, U.S. Dist. Ct. Nebr. 1981. Psychiat. security treatment aide Whiting Forensic Inst., Middletown, Conn., 1973-74; income maintenance technician Douglas County Social Services, Omaha, 1975-76; child support worker Douglas County Child Support Enforcement, Omaha, 1976-78; law clk. Wall, Wintroub & Weiner, Omaha, 1979-81, assoc., 1981-82; staff atty. Legal Aid Soc., Inc., Omaha, 1982—; client and counseling competition judge Creighton U. Law Sch., 1982, 83. Editor: Creighton Law Rev., 1980-81. Winthrop and Frances Lane Found. scholar, 1980-81. Mem. Nebr. State Bar Assn. (panel 1982), ABA, Omaha Bar Assn. Democrat. Home: 608 N 50th St Apt 103 Omaha NE 68132 Office: Legal Aid Soc Inc 500 S 18th St Omaha NE 68102

DOERNER, SALLY ROSEMARY, lawyer; b. Washington, May 25, 1951; d. Fred William and Rosemary (Glomb) Doerner. B.A., Boston U., 1974; J.D., U. Miami, 1977. Bar: Fla. 1978; assoc., research asst. Richard M. Gale, Miami, Fla., 1979-81; law clk. Chief Judge Alan R. Schwartz, Fla. 3rd Dist. Ct. Appeal, 1981-82; assoc. Walton, Lantaff, Schroeder & Carson, 1982—. Adj. prof. legal research and writing U. Miami, Coral Gables, Fla., 1983—. Mem. Fla. Bar Assn., Fla. Assn. Women Lawyers, Dade County Bar Assn. Office: Walton Lantaff Schroeder & Carson 900 Alfred I duPont Bldg Miami FL 33131

DOEZEMA, MARIANNE, art historian; b. Grand Rapids, Mich., Sept. 8, 1950; d. Charles William and Geraldine Frances (Slopsema) D.; m. Michael Andrew Marlais, Dec. 29, 1977. B.A., Mich. State U., 1973; M.A., U. Mich., 1975. Instr. dept. art history and edn. Cleve. Mus. Art, 1976-79, asst. curator, 1980-81; curator of edn. Ga. Mus. Art, Athens, 1981-83, assoc. dir., 1983—. Author: American Realism and the Industrial Age, 1980. Contbr. articles to profl. jours. Presdl. U. Grad. fellow Boston U., 1985—. Mem. Coll. Art Assn. Am. Office: Ga Mus Art U Ga Jackson St Athens GA 30602

DOGAN, SHIRLEY BARRON, industrial engineer; b. Ft. Pierce, Fla., Jan. 17, 1955; d. Charlie and Mable Elizabeth (Yeartie) Barron. B.S., Fla. State U., 1976. Indsl. engr., Milliken & Co., Pacolet/Union, S.C., 1977-80, E.I. DuPont & Co., Florence, S.C., 1980—. State judge Jr. Engr. and Tech. Soc., Florence, 1982; chmn. publicity United Way of Florence, 1983; asst. troop leader Pee Dee council Girl Scouts U.S.A., Florence, 1983. Mem. Nat. Assn. Female Execs. Baptist. Avocations: jogging; gardening.

DOHERTY, ANNA MARIE, mag. editor; b. Baldwin, N.Y., Oct. 28, 1929; d. Dennis James and Helen Elizabeth (Koch) D.; A.A., Immaculata Coll., 1949; cert. Traphagen Sch. Interior Design, 1950. Assoc. food editor This Week mag., N.Y.C., 1952-66, N.Y. Herald Tribune, 1952-66; acting food editor N.Y. World Jour. Tribune, 1966-67; food editor, columnist Suffolk Sun, L.I., N.Y., 1967-69; with Family Circle mag. (N.Y. Times Co.), N.Y.C., 1970—, sr. editor, dir. editorial services, 1971-79, women's service editor, 1979—; editor Cashing in on the Next Three Weeks column, 1980—; author, editor Family Circle's 429 Great Gifts to Make, 1976; Food industry cons., 1965—; freelance food writer, 1966—; contbr. articles to profl. jours. Mem. Internat. Fund for Monuments (Venice com.), Nat. Trust Historic Preservation, Met. Opera Guild, Met. Mus. Art, Smithsonian Instn. Club: Newswomen's (dir. N.Y.C. 1970-72). Home: 154 E 61st St New York NY 10021 also 4080 Peconic Bay Blvd Laurel NY 11948 Office: 488 Madison Ave New York NY 10022

DOHERTY, EILEEN PATRICIA, university administrator, educator; b. Astoria, N.Y., Aug. 21, 1952; d. Joseph John and Joan Ellen (Conway) D. B.A., St. John's U., 1974, M.B.A., 1978; M.A., Columbia U., 1976, Ed.M., 1985. Asst. to dean admissions St. John's U., Jamaica, N.Y., 1974-75, asst. to dir. instnl. research, 1975-76, asst. dean Evening & Weekend Coll., 1976-80, asst. dean Coll. Bus. Adminstrn., 1980-81, assoc. dean St. Vincent's Coll., dir. Evening and Weekend sessions, 1981—, adj. prof. econs., 1978—. Hosp. vol. ARC, N.Y.C., 1967; rep. of city comptroller Steinway Bus. Improvement Dist., Astoria, N.Y., 1982—; mem. Queens Community Planning Bd., 1980-83. Mem. Am. Assn. Higher Edn., Am. Econ. Assn., Am. Mktg. Assn., Am. Fin. Assn., Am. Soc. for Tng. and Devel., Phi Delta Kappa, Psi Chi, Kappa Delta Pi, Pres. Soc. Alumni Assn. (rec. sec. 1983—). Roman Catholic. Office: St Johns U 113 Bent Hall Jamaica NY 11439

DOHERTY, JOSEPHINE VARLEY, computer company executive; b. N.Y.C., Mar. 1, 1940; d. Michael and Elizabeth (O'Donnell) Varley; B.A. (N.Y. State Regents scholar 1958-62), Marymount Manhattan Coll., 1962; M.A., St. John's U., 1970; m. William G. Doherty, Aug. 15, 1970; children—Katherine Varley, Andrew Attwood. English tchr. St. Catherine Acad., Bronx, 1962-67; English dept. adminstr. Christ the King High Sch., boys' div., Queens, N.Y., 1967-72; KEN-MAC div. mgr. Aspen Systems Corp., N.Y.C., 1977-80; dir. procedures and tng. Am. Legal Systems, N.Y.C., 1980-82, mgr. computerized projects, 1982, regional mgr., 1982-85, corp. services mgr., 1985—. Lic. English tchr., N.Y. Mem. Nat. Assn. Female Execs, Am. Mgmt. Assn. Office: 475 Park Ave New York NY 10016

DOHERTY, MARY CUSHING, lawyer; b. Evanston, Ill., Apr. 22, 1953; d. F. John and Margaret Louise (Wolf) Cushing; m. James Francis Doherty, Aug. 20, 1977; children—John Francis, Margaret Rose. B.A., U. Del., 1975; J.D., Villanova U., 1978. Bar: Pa. 1978, N.J., 1978, U.S. Dist. Ct. (ea. dist.) Pa. 1978, U.S. Dist. Ct. N.J. 1978. Assoc. Abrahams and Loewenstein, Phila., 1979—; also lectr., course planner Pa. Bar Inst., Pa. Bar Assn., others. Contbr. articles to Pa. Law Jour., 1981. Mem. staff Pre-Cana Counselling, Roman Cath. Chs., 1981—; counselor UNITE of Jeanes Hosp., Phila., 1984, bd. dirs., 1985-86, v.p., 1986—. Minerva Schultz Found. grantee, 1978. Fellow Am. Acad. Matrimonial Lawyers; mem. Phila. Bar Assn. (chmn. family law sect. 1985, del. bd. govs. 1986), ABA, N.J. Bar Assn., Hidden Meadow Community Assn., Bus. Women's Network. Roman Catholic. Office: Abrahams & Loewenstein 1430 Land Title Bldg Philadelphia PA 19110

DOHERTY, MARYANNE, lawyer, retail company executive; b. Brockton, Mass., Aug. 2, 1954; d. Robert O. and Therese (Mack) D. B.B.A., Providence Coll., 1976; J.D., Suffolk U., 1981. Bar: Mass. 1981; C.P.A., Mass. Auditor, Meahl, McNamara & Co., Boston, 1976-78; fin. analyst Lechmere Dayton Hudson, Woburn, Mass., 1978-81; sr. tax accountant Price Waterhouse, Boston, 1981-83; tax mgr. The Stop & Shop Cos. Inc., Boston, 1983—. Mem. ABA, Mass. Soc. C.P.A.s. Roman Catholic. Home: 21 Phillips St Quincy MA 02170 Office: The Stop & Shop Cos Inc Box 369 Boston MA 02101

DOHMAN, GLORIA ANN, librarian; b. Vermillion, S.D., June 19, 1949; d. Marlyn Doyle and Dorothy Marie (Peterson) Edman; student Ball State U., 1973; B.A., Sioux Falls Coll., 1971; M.S., Tri-Coll. U., 1984; m. Terry L. Dohman, Aug. 16, 1970; children—Robb Quincy, Kristin LeeAnn. Librarian/audio visual coordinator U.S. Dependent Schs., Hahn AFB, W.Ger., 1973-74; library coordinator/dir. Wahpeton (N.D.) Public Schs. and Leach Public Library, Wahpeton, 1974-76; periodicals/media librarian N.D. State Sch. Sci., Wahpeton, 1976—; del. White House Conf. Libraries and Info. Services, 1979; del. N.D. Gov.'s Conf. on Libraries and Info. Services, 1978. Trustee, Leach Public Library, 1977-83, chmn. bd., 1978-80. Mem. ALA, N.D. Library Assn. (sec. acad. sect. 1981-83), LWV (chpt. dir. 1977-79), Mountain Plains Library Assn., AAUW. Lutheran. Home: 1631 N 5th St Wahpeton ND 58075 Office: ND State Sch Sci Wahpeton ND 58075

DOI, MARY MARGARET, lawyer; b. Santa Fe, N.Mex., Feb. 1, 1956; d. James Isao and Mary Masako (Yamashita) Doi. B.A. cum laude, Yale Coll., 1977; J.D., Harvard U., 1980; student Sorbonne, Paris, summer 1975. Bar: N.Y. 1981. Intern to Congressman Frank Horton, Washington, 1976, intern Selection Com. Mem., Rochester, N.Y., 1977-78; assoc. Milbank, Tweed, Hadley & McCloy, N.Y.C., 1980-82; assoc. Young & Rubicam, Inc., N.Y.C., 1982-83; assoc. Harris, Beach, Wilcox, Rubin and Levey, Rochester, 1983—; dancer Claravita Coolshoes Dance Co., N.Y.C., 1983-84. Editor Civil Rights Civil Liberties Law Rev., Cambridge, Mass., 1979-80. Bd. dirs. Community Child Care Ctr., Rochester, 1983—, Urban League of Rochester, 1984—. Mem. ABA, N.Y. State Bar Assn., Council of N.Y. Law Assn. Buddhist. Office: Harris Beach Wilcox Rubin and Levey Two State St Rochester NY 14614

DOLAN, KAREN ELLIOTT, marketing company executive; b. Columbus, Ohio, Jan. 12, 1943; d. William Elliott and Ethelyne Marie (Winland) Stoyle; student Ohio U., 1960-63; m. Joseph A. Dolan, Jan. 14, 1967; children—Kelly Annette, Joseph Andrew. Office mgr. Westside Newspapers, Inc., Cleve., 1963-67; with Dial Am. Mktg., Inc., Cleve., 1973—, asst. br. mgr., 1976-78, br. mgr., 1978—; vol. arbitrator Better Bus. Bur. Leader Girl Scouts U.S.A., 1975-79; mem. Rep. Task Force, sec., 1985, 86. Named Mgr. of Yr., Dial Am. Mktg. Inc., 1980. Mem. Greater Cleve. Growth Assn., Northcoast Exec. Women's Network, Northeast Ohio Direct Mail and Mktg. Assn., Sales and Mktg. Club, Nat. Assn. Female Execs. Republican. Roman Catholic. Clubs: Sailing, Edgewater Yacht (sec. 1985, 86). Home: 1251 Edwards Ave Lakewood OH 44107 Office: 20800 Center Ridge #415 Rocky River OH 44116

DOLAN, MARYANNE MCLORN, writer, educator, lecturer; b. N.Y.C., July 14, 1924; d. Frederick Joseph and Kathryn Cecilia (Carroll) McLorn; m. John Francis Dolan, Oct. 6, 1951; children—John Carroll, James Francis McLorn, William Brennan. B.A., San Francisco State U., 1978, M.A., 1981. Tchr. classes and seminars in antiques and collectibles U. Calif.-Berkeley, U. Calif.-Davis, U. Calif.-Santa Cruz, Coll. of Marin, Kentfield, Calif., Mills Coll., Oakland, Calif., St. Mary's Coll., Moraga, Calif., 1969—; tchr. writing Dolan Sch., 1978—; owner antique shop, Benicia, Calif., 1970—. Author: Vintage Clothing, 1880-1960, 1983; Collecting Rhinestone Jewelry, 1984; weekly columnist The Collector, 1979—; contbr. articles to profl. jours. Mem. AAUW, Internat. Soc. Appraisers, Calif. Writers Club, Internat. Platform Assn. Republican. Roman Catholic. Home: 138 Belle Ave Pleasant Hill CA 94523 Office: 191 West J St Benicia CA 94510

DOLAN, PATRICIA, foundation executive; b. Devon, Pa., Mar. 17, 1935; d. Roger Joseph and Anna Mary (De Cecco) Napoletano; B.J., Temple U., 1957; postgrad. Pa. State U., 1966; children—G. Donald, Cheryl A. Mgr. communications/community relations Gen. Electric Co., Valley Forge, Pa., 1960-81; dir. communications Soc. Holy Child Jesus, 1981-82; co-owner/dir. Meetings Plus, cons., Wayne, Pa., 1982-85; dir. corp. communications Devercux Found., 1985—; cons. in field. Chmn. St. Agnes Med. Center, Phila., 1982-83, trustee, 1976—; trustee Burn Found. Greater Del. Valley, 1976—; mem. Nat. Teen Adv. Com., 1978-81; adv. com. OIC's of Am., 1974-80. Recipient Profl. Recognition Program award, Gen. Electric, 1970; Public Service award, OIC, 1976. Mem. Phila. Public Relations Assn., Nat. Assn. Female Execs., Sons of Italy. Republican. Roman Catholic. Contbr. articles to profl. jours. Home: 239 S Gulph Rd King of Prussia PA 19406 Office: 19 S Waterloo Rd Devon PA 19333

DOLE, ELIZABETH HANFORD, secretary U.S. Department Transportation, former commr. FTC; b. Salisbury, N.C., July 29, 1936; d. John Van and Mary Ella (Cathey) Hanford; B.A. with honors in Polit. Sci., Duke U., 1958; postgrad. Oxford (Eng.) U., summer 1959; M.A. in Edn., Harvard U., 1960, J.D., 1965; m. Robert Joseph Dole (U.S. Senator from Kans.), Dec. 6, 1975. Admitted to D.C. bar, 1966; staff asst. to asst. sec. for edn. HEW, Washington, 1966-67; practiced in Washington, 1967-68; asso. dir. legis. affairs, then exec. dir. Pres.'s Com. for Consumer Interests, Washington, 1968-71; dep. dir. Office Consumer Affairs, The White House, Washington, 1971-73; commr. FTC, Washington, 1973-79; chmn. Voters for Reagan-Bush, 1980; dir. Human Services Group, Office of Exec. Br. Mgmt., Office of Pres.-Elect, 1980; asst. to pres. for public liaison, 1981-83; sec. U.S. Dept. Transp., 1983—. Trustee, Duke U., 1974—, also mem. bd. advisors Bus. Sch.; trustee Washington Opera; bd. dirs. Am. Council on Young Polit. Leaders; mem. overseers com. to visit J.F. Kennedy Sch. Govt., Harvard U.; mem. council Harvard U. Law Sch. Assos. Recipient Arthur S. Flemming award U.S. Govt., 1972; named one of Am.'s 200 Young Leaders, Time mag., 1974. Office: 400 7th St SW Washington DC 20590

DOLE, GRACE FULLER, librarian, artist; b. Cambridge, Mass., Sept. 20; d. John Soper and Margaret Fernald Dole; m. Paul E. Kohler, Jan. 22, 1944; (div. May 1946); 1 dau., Margaret K. Nicholson. B.A., Bryn Mawr Coll., 1944; M.L.S., Columbia U., 1954. Library cert., N.Y. Tchr. French, librarian Low-Heywood Sch., Stamford, Conn., 1948-50; sch. librarian Greenwich Library (Conn.), 1950-53; librarian reference dept. N.Y. Pub. Library, N.Y.C., 1954-56; asst. librarian, then librarian Benton & Bowles, Inc., N.Y.C., 1956-62; reference librarian Ferguson Library, Stamford, 1962-64; librarian U. Conn. Library, Stamford, 1964-75, library specialist, 1975—; mem. Library Adminstrs. group Fairfield County (Conn.), 1974-75; exhibited Chinese brushwork in various shows. Mem. Assn. Coll. and Research Libraries, ALA, Spl. Libraries Assn. (treas. Hudson Valley chpt. 1984-86), English Speaking Union, Pen and Brush. Clubs: Catharine Loriallard Wolfe Art (bd. dirs. 1975-78), Margret Fernald Dole Contemporary Art (pres. 1975—); Nat. Arts, Pen and Brush (N.Y.C.); Indian Harbor Yacht (Greenwich). Home: 503 W Lyon Farm Dr Greenwich CT 06830 Office: U Conn Scofieldtown Rd Stamford CT 06903

DOLEZILEK, PAMELA K., mentally handicapped program administrator; b. Topeka, Nov. 11, 1953; d. Harold Hubert and Norma Jean (Crites) D. B.A. in Sociology, Washburn U., Topeka, 1978; Student, Paralegal Inst., Phoenix, 1984. Proof operator Commerce Bank & Trust, Topeka, 1974-78; research analyst State of Kans., Hays, 1978-81, pub. health educator, 1981-83; computer operator Jeter & Larson, Hays, 1983-85; apt. living coordinator Devel. Services of N.W. Kans., Hays, 1985—. Active, Assembly of God Ch. Avocations: racquetball; tennis; swimming; bicycling; latchhook; macrame. Home: 1326 Felten Hays KS 67601

DOLJACK, BARBARA LYNN, publishing company executive; b. Cleve., Mar. 14, 1942; d. Rudolph Frank and Mary Jean Doljack; student Ohio Dominican Coll., 1960-62, Tobe-Coburn Sch. Fashion Careers, N.Y.C., 1963. With Bloomingdale's, N.Y.C., 1963-66, asst. fashion dir., 1964-66; sr. merchandising coordinator Seventeen Mag., N.Y.C., 1966-69, merchandising editor, 1969-71, merchandising dir., 1971-76; dir. promotion services Seventeen mag., 1976-82, mktg. dir. direct merchandising, pub. relations, promotion, composing and buy-by-mail depts., 1982—; dir. promotion services Panorama mag., 1979-81. Mem. exec. alumnae com. The Tobe-Coburn Sch., 1976-79, also mem. industry adv. com.; mem. various coms. The Floating Hosp., 1978—; pres. exec. com. Friends of Henry St. Settlement, 1976-78, adv. com., 1979—. Recipient Mehitabel award, 1979; The T award Tobe-Coburn Sch., 1968. Mem. N.Y. Jr. League, Mktg. Communications Execs. Internat. (chpt. bd. dirs. 1977-79), Advt. Women of N.Y., Nat. Home Fashions League, Women in Communications, The Fashion Group (v.p. bd. govs. 1981-83). Club: Gardiner's Bay Country. Home: 310 E 70 St New York NY 10021 Office: 850 3d Ave New York NY 10022

DOLLAR, SANDRA MARIE, marketing and communication executive; b. Phila., Feb. 10, 1949; d. Francis William and Marion Beatrice (Gross) D.; B.A., Bryn Mawr Coll., 1971. Asst. to advt. mgr. Theodore Presser Co., Bryn Mawr, Pa., 1971-72; freelance writer, 1972-73; editor, publicity coordinator AMP Spl. Industries, Valley Forge, Pa., 1973-75; public info. coordinator Peirce Jr. Coll., Phila., 1975-76; Vistas editor Roswell (N.Mex.) Daily Record, 1977-78; publs. coordinator Penn Mut. Life Ins. Co., Phila., 1979-80; mgr. editorial services CIGNA Corp., Phila., 1980-84; dir. mktg. and communication Huggins Fin. Services, Inc., Phila., 1984—. Mem. pub. relations com., co. communications subcom. United Way S.E. Pa., 1983. Recipient Mary Swindler award, Mary Windsor award Bryn Mawr Coll., 1969, Media award N.Mex. div. Am. Cancer

Soc., 1977, Guy Rader award N.Mex. Med. Soc., 1977, Communicators award United Way Am. and SE Pa., 1980, 81, 82, Bell Ringer award Bus./Profl. Advt. Assn., 1981. Bryn Mawr Coll. alumnae regional scholar, 1967-71; Pa. State scholar, 1967-70. Mem. Internat. Assn. Bus. Communicators (program chmn. 1982-84). Office: 229 S 18th St Philadelphia PA 19103

DOLMAN, VIOLA ELIZABETH, realtor; b. Ellsworth, Kans., Dec. 9, 1922; m. Baird Dolman (div.); children—David, Laura. B.S., Kans. State U., 1944; M.S., Stanford U., 1948. Pres., Owner Dolman Assocs., Inc., Honolulu, 1970—. Bd. dirs. Hawaii chpt. ARC, 1985—, Aloha United Way, 1985—; trustee Acad. Pacific, Honolulu, 1985—. Mem. Nat. Assn. Realtors (bd. dirs.), Hawaii Assn. Realtors (bd. dirs., pres. 1982-83, Realtor of Yr. 1983), Honolulu Bd. Realtors (pres. 1978-79, bd. dirs. 1985—, Realtor of Yr. 1976). Club: Zonta. Office: Dolman Assocs Inc 210 Ward Ave Suite 100 Honolulu HI 96814

DOLSON, BARBARA STRANDBURG, media marketing research executive; b. Mt. Kisco, N.Y., Apr. 28, 1958; d. Lewis Arnold and Barbara Lois (Conroy) Strandburg; m. Timothy Edward Dolson, Mar. 23, 1985. B.A. in Mktg. magna cum laude, U. South Fla., 1980. Media project dir. A.C. Nielsen Co., Dunedin, Fla., 1980—. Mem. Am. Mktg. Assn. (communications dir. 1983-84, hospitality dir. 1984-85, sec. 1985-86), Cable TV Adminstrn. and Mktg., Beta Gamma Sigma. Republican. Roman Catholic. Avocations: tennis.

DOLSON, VIVIAN ANTOINETTE, sales executive; b. Chgo., July 17, 1925; d. Werner Henry and Lillian Rose (Ghilardi) Steger; student DePaul U., 1943-46; m. Sept. 10, 1948 (div.); children—Bill, David. Asst. registrar DePaul U., 1952-55, exec. sec., 1955-58; asst. personnel dir. Stat. Tabulating Co., Chgo., 1958-61; owner, operator Dolson Market Research, Chgo., 1961-75; dist. sales mgr. for Ill. and Wis., Borroughs/Lear Siegler Co., Chgo., 1975-78, asst. nat. sales mgr., Kalamazoo, 1978-81; nat. sales mgr. Marvel Metal Products, Chgo., 1981-84; pres. Dolson Associates, Inc., Honolulu, 1984—; career cons. Triton Jr. Coll. Mem. Am. Market Research Assn., Nat. Office Products Assn. Am. Mgmt. Assn., Mfr. Assocs. Nat. Assn. Club: Soroptomists Internat. Home: 3138 Waialae Ave Apt 218 Honolulu HI 96816

DOLTON, MARY L. (LU), telephone company personnel executive; b. Grand Island, Nebr., June 4, 1951; d. Fred Peter and Maryanne (Wardyn) Matulka. Student NE Nebr. Tech.-Community Coll., 1976-77. With NW Bell Telephone Co., 1969—, instr. customer services, Grand Island, Nebr., 1974-75, supr. customer services, Norfolk, Nebr., 1975-76, mgr. operator services, Norfolk, 1976-78, staff mgr. of mgmt. devel., Omaha, 1978-83, dir. product sales, 1983-84, staff mgr. personnel planning bd. mem. EEO council, 1983-85, mgr. corp. adminstrn. and utilization, 1985—. Master of ceremonies for Nebr. Ednl. TV fundraisers, 1977-86; loaned exec. United Way, 1978-80. Named Young Career Woman of Yr., Bus. and Profl. Women, Norfolk, 1977. Mem. Am. Soc. Tng. and Devel., Bus. and Profl. Women (chpt. pres. 1977-78), C. of C. (pres. elect women's div. 1977-78). Roman Catholic. Clubs: Porsche (treas. 1982—, membership chmn. 1984) (Omaha), Omaha Ski (trip treas. 1979-81). Office: NW Bell Telephone Co 100 S 19th St Omaha NE 68102

DOMANN, PHYLLIS SUE, human resources educator; b. Mexico, Mo., Oct. 12, 1947; d. Albert Henry Theodore and Mildred (Crawford) D. B.S. Ed., N.E. Mo. State U., 1969; M.S., Okla. State U., 1979; postgrad. U. Ark., 1979, North Tex. State U., 1982—. Dist. advisor Heart of Mo. council Girl Scouts, Jefferson City, Mo., 1969-74; exec. dir., camp dir. Dogwood Tails council Girl Scouts U.S., Springfield, Mo., 1974-77; instr. U. Ark., Fayetteville, 1978-79; instr. S.W. Mo. State U., Springfield, 1979-82; asst. prof. personnel adminstrn. Western Ill. U., Macomb, 1983—. Bd. dirs. Dogwood Trails council Girl Scouts, 1980-82, sec. bd. Two Rivers council, 1984—; instr. ARC, Jefferson City, Mo., 1970-74. Mem. AAUW, Am. soc. Personnel Adminstrn., Am. Soc. tng. and Devel., Assn. Vol. Adminstrn., Nat. Assn. Female Execs., Delta Pi Epsilon. Club: Westerwinds Athletic (bd. dirs. 1986—). Avocations: canoeing; whitewater rafting; camping; gardening; reading. Home: 205 N Lamoine St Macomb IL 61455 Office: Western Ill U Coll Bus Macomb IL 61455

DOMASH, DIANNE JOY, psychologist, nutritional consultant; b. N.Y.C., July 30, 1959; d. Norman and Zelda (Senft) D. B.S., C.W. Post Coll., 1979, profl. diploma, 1986; M.S., Hofstra U., 1980, Ph.D., U.S. Internat. U., San Diego, 1983. Lic. psychologist; cert. nutritional cons.; cert. paramedic. Psychologist, U.S. Internat. U., 1980-82, San Diego City Schs., 1981-83, Sachem Central Sch. Dist., Holbrook, N.Y., 1984; exec. dir. LIFE, Great Neck, N.Y., 1984—. Firefighter, paramedic Port Washington Fire Dept., N.Y., 1985—; instr. CPR Great Neck United Community Fund; vol. North Shore Univ. Hosp., Manhasset, N.Y. Mem. Am. Psychol. Assn., N.Y. State Psychol. Assn., Nassau County Psychol. Assn. (mem. exec. bd. 1984-85), Fire Fighters Benevolent Assn. Avocation: photography. Home: PO Box 4289 Great Neck NY 11027

DOMBRO, MARCIA WINTERS, nurse, ednl. adminstr.; b. Clinton, Minn., Dec. 14, 1940; d. Benton Jay and Thelma Elizabeth (Roth) Winters; B.S.N., U. Wash., 1963; M.S. in Adult Edn., Fla. Internat. U., 1976; m. Roy S. Dombro, Sept. 10, 1967; children—Rayna Lisette, Meryl Elana. Public health nurse Seattle-King County Health Dept., 1964-66, N.Y.C. Dept. Health Bur. Nursing, 1966-67; head nurse home care unit Bellevue Hosp., N.Y.C., 1967-68; asst. clin. instr. in obstetrics City Hosp. at Elmhurst, N.Y.C., 1968; clin. instr. obstetrics Miami-Dade Community Coll., 1973-74; instr. U. Miami Sch. Nursing, 1976-80; dir. dept. nursing edn. Baptist Hosp. Miami (Fla.), 1980—; adj. faculty U. Miami Sch. Nursing, 1984—; tchr. sex edn. for schs., civic groups, parent edn. groups. Active ERA, NOW, Miami. Mem. Nurses Assn.-Am. Coll. Ob-Gyn. (sec.-treas. Dade County 1985), Am. Nurses' Assn., Nat. League for Nursing, Am. Soc. Psychoprophylaxis in Obstetrics (cert. childbirth instr. 1970, coordinator South Fla. 1976-81), Am. Soc. Health Edn. and Tng. Jewish. Author: Post Partum for the Childbirth Educator-A Programmed Text, 1976; contb. articles to profl. jours.; co-producer audiovisual kit: Born Sexy, 1976. Home: 9841 SW 123d St Miami FL 33176 Office: 8900 N Kendall Dr Miami FL 33176

DOMBROWSKI, PARIS LYNNE, businesswoman; b. Bloomington, Ind., July 26, 1950; d. Robert Eugene and Harriet Mae (Curtis) Cox; m. Ronald Bernard Hayduk, Aug. 3, 1972 (dec. 1979); children—Veronica Elizabeth, Ronald Bernard (dec. 1978); m. J. Louis Dombrowski, Dec. 11, 1982; children—Douglas, Kathy, Nancy. Student Wayne State U., 1976-77. Silk screen engr. Burroughs Inc., Plymouth, Mich., 1967-69; mgr. The Match Box, Wyandotte, Mich., 1969-72; apprentice chef various restaurants, Detroit, 1972-77; owner, operator Lioness & Her Cub, Canton, Mich., 1980-81; pres. Parties by Paris, Inc., Bethesda, Md., 1984—, Oui Cater & More, Rockville, Md., 1984—. Cons. Six Schs., Inc., Washington, 1983—. Mem. Women's Bus. Orgn., Nat. Assn. Catering Execs., Rockville C. of C. Home: 7207 Thomas Branch Dr Bethesda MD 20817 Office: Oui Cater and More Suite 226 12140 Parklawn Dr Rockville MD 20852

DOMER, EVRON JEAN, nurse; b. Stockton, Calif., June 24, 1933; d. Thomas Jefferson and Nella Myrthen (Heard) Markey; m. Barry Willis Domer, May 25, 1958; children—Wendy Louise, Cara Renell Domer Overman, Susan Gayle, Thomas Andrew. A.A., U. Calif.-Berkeley, 1952; B.S., U. Calif.-San Francisco, 1955. Registered nurse, Calif.; life teaching credential, Calif. Staff nurse San Joaquin Local Health Dist., Stockton, 1955-59, 70-72; mem. faculty Delta Coll., Stockton, 1965-66; tchr. Lodi Children's Ctr., Calif., 1966-68; head nurse med.-surg Lodi Meml. Hosp., 1969-70; staff nurse med.-surg. St. Joseph's Hosp., Stockton, part-time, 1972-77, asst. organizer, supr. home health care, 1977-78; inservice dir. Gross Convalescent Hosp., Lodi, 1979-82; staff nurse Dameron Hosp., Stockton, 1983—; clin. instr. San Joaquin Delta Coll., Stockton, part-time, 1980-84. Mem. Cath. Social Services Bd., Stockton, 1971-73. Named Woman of Yr., Tokay Jr. Woman's Club, Lodi, 1967. Mem. Am. Nurses Assn., AAUW, Scleraderma Assn. Republican. Episcopalian. Avocations: trailering; traveling; refinishing and upholstering furniture; gardening. Home: 4580 Winding River Circle Stockton CA 95207 Office: Dameron Hosp 525 W Acacia St Stockton CA 95203

DOMINIAK, GERALDINE FLORENCE, accountant; b. Detroit, Sept. 28, 1934; d. Benjamin Vincent and Geraldine Esther (Davey) D.; B.S., U. Detroit, 1954, M.B.A., 1956; Ph.D., Mich. State U., 1966. Audit supr. Coopers & Lybrand, 1958-63; asst. prof. U. Detroit, 1965-68; assoc. prof. Mich. State U., 1968-69; prof. acctg. Tex. Christian U., Ft. Worth, 1969—, chmn. dept., 1974-82; Arthur Young prof. acctg. Fla. A&M U., 1977. Ford Found. fellow, 1964-65; C.P.A., Mich. Mem. Am. Inst. C.P.A.s, Am. Acctg. Assn., Assn. Govt. Accts., Nat. Assn. Accts., Am. Woman's Soc. C.P.A.s, Tex. Soc. C.P.A.s, AAUP, ACLU, Beta Alpha Psi, Beta Gamma Sigma. Roman Catholic. Author: (with J. Edwards and T. Hedges) Interim Financial Reporting, 1972; (with J. Louderback) Managerial Accounting, 1975, 2d edit., 1978, 3d edit., 1982, 4th edit., 1985. Home: 4401 Cardiff St Fort Worth TX 76133 Office: Sch Bus Tex Christian U Fort Worth TX 76129

DOMINIQUE, LISE MARIE, broadcasting executive, air personality; b. Lake Forest, Ill., Mar. 5, 1956; d. Nazaire Louis and Eleanor (Steffin) D. B.S. in Radio and TV, U. Ill., 1978. Sales rep. Staffbuilders, San Jose, Calif., 1979-80; account exec. Marquez-Ramirez Advt., San Jose, 1980; morning disc jockey Sta.-KRVE, Los Gatos, Calif., 1981-83; evening air personality Sta.-KHTT, San Jose, 1983-85, news dir., 1983-85, news dir. Stas.-KSJO/KHTT, 1984-85; weekend morning air personality Sta. KEEN-AM, San Jose, 1985; relief news asst. Sta. KSAN-FM, Oakland, Calif., 1985; relief weather person Sta. KICU-TV, San Jose, 1985; traffic reporter for KCBS-San Francisco Traffic Central, Hayward, Calif., 1985—. Mem. Radio-TV New Dirs. Assn. Home: 1279 Curtiss Ave San Jose CA 95125

DOMKE, DAWN MARIE, insurance company executive; b. Plymouth, Ind., Nov. 6, 1953; d. Rollo Glenn Ringer and Dorothy Louise (Beyler) Morgan; m. Wihart Bryan Bell, June 30, 1973 (div. May 1982); children—Michael Bryan, Jameson Bradley; m. Alan Martin Domke, Mar. 5, 1983; children—Trishcia Dawn, Alan Martin. Student Bethel Coll., 1973, Sir Wilfrid Laurier U., 1974-76, Dominion Assurance Sch. Bus., 1979-80. Voice tchr. Emmanuel Coll., Kitchener, Ont., Can., 1973-80; ins. rep. Dominion Life Assurance Co., Kitchener, 1979-80; dir. Good Health Med. Ctr., Mishawaka, Ind., 1982-83, Nutri-System Weight Loss Med. Ctrs., Chgo. and South Bend, Ind., 1980-82; sec., South Bend, 1984-85; ins. supr. Bankers Life & ICH Co., Mishawaka, 1985—. Ella Leeper Found. scholar, 1972; recipient Am. Legion award, 1973, Dominion Life Sales Leader award, 1980, Bankers Life sales campaign plaque, 1985. Mem. Nat. Assn. Female Execs. Avocations: teaching-performing voice/piano. Home: 1048 Diamond Ave South Bend IN 46628 Office: Bankers Life Ins Co Suite 1-A 4609 Grape Rd Mishawaka IN 46545

DOMM, ALICE, lawyer; b. Phila., May 22, 1954; d. William Donald and Alice Frances (Day) D. B.A., Gettysburg Coll. (Pa.), 1976; J.D., Rutgers U., 1981. Bar: N.J. 1981, Pa. 1981. Atty., juvenile sect. chief Office of the Pub. Defender, New Brunswick, N.J., 1982—; assoc. prof. Glassboro Coll. (N.J.), 1980-81; mem. exec. com. Young Lawyers, Middlesex County, N.J. Bd. dirs. Police Athletic League, New Brunswick, 1982-85; mem. Middlesex County Youth Services Commn., New Brunswick; mem. Gov.'s Council on Child Abuse and Neglect, Middlesex County; mem. Criminal Justice Planning Com. Middlesex County. Mem. ABA, N.J. Bar Assn., Middlesex County Bar Assn. (trustee; chmn. young lawyers com.), Middlesex County Women's Bar Assn. (steering com., treas.), Assn. Criminal Def. Lawyers N.J. Office: Office of the Public Defender 172 New St New Brunswick NJ 08903

DOMMEL, DARLENE HURST, writer; b. Charles City, Iowa, July 11, 1940; d. Roy and Elsie (Hopkes) Hurst; B.S. with high distinction, U. Minn., 1963, M.S., 1965, grad. exec. program Grad. Sch. Bus. Adminstrn., 1972; postgrad. So. Meth. U., 1976-77; m. James H. Dommel, Oct. 15, 1961; children—Diann, Christine, David. Pub. health nurse Combined Nursing Service, Mpls., 1963-64; contbr. articles on pottery to various collectors and antiques mags., 1967—; organizer, exhibitor of art pottery display touring fin. instns. in upper midwest, 1976—; lectr. and cons. health care, antiques, journalism; health care specialist Health Services Research Center, St. Louis Park Med. Center, 1978-79; instr. Augsburg Coll., 1979-81. Mem. Minn. Adv. Task Force on Epilepsy, 1981-83, State Council for Handicapped, 1982-84, Dept. Pub. Welfare Adv. Council on Mental Retardation and Phys. Disabilities, 1982-84; mem. profl. adv. com. Epilepsy Found. Minn., 1984—. Mem. Mpls. Inst. Arts. USPHS trainee, 1964-65; Sigma Theta Tau scholar, 1962-63; Martha Ripley scholar, 1961-62; U. Minn. Sch. Nursing Found. scholar, 1962. Mem. AAUW, U. Minn. Alumni Assn., Nat. Writers Club, Nat. League for Nursing, Minn. League for Nursing (pres. 1983-85), Minn. Coalition on Health Care Cost, Minn. Regional Assembly Constituent Leagues for Nursing (exec. com. 1985—). Gethsemane Luth. Ch. Women, Minn. Women in Higher Edn., Minn. Women's Polit. Caucus, Sigma Theta Tau, Delta Delta Delta. Lutheran. Home: 510 Westwood Dr N Golden Valley MN 55422

DOMROE, BARBARA, artist, printmaker; b. N.Y.C., July 27, 1939; d. Emanuel and Elsie (Zarefsa) Domroe; m. George Wesley Wecklein, Sept. 9, 1964; children—Christopher, Meredith. B.F.A., Pratt Inst., 1961. Comml. artist, N.Y.C., 1961-68; artist, N.Y., N.J., 1969-76; etcher and printmaker Domroe Art, Bermond Ltd., N.Y., 1975—, also Art Spectrum N.Y. Pratt Inst. scholar 1957. Recipient Soc. Illustrators award 1957. Mem. Nat. Assn. Women Artists (France Lieber Meml. prize 1982). Democrat. Avocations: reading; music. Home and Office: 10 Chatham Rd Commack NY 11725

DONAHOE, RITA LOUISE, Realtor; b. Boston, Jan. 16, 1930; d. Franklin Augustine and Barbara Rita (Coyne) Bannister; student Boston Coll., 1948-51; m. Robert Francis Donahoe, June 15, 1957; children—Steven Francis, Christopher John. Asst. clk. Suffolk Superior Criminal Ct., Boston, 1948-57; v.p., treas. D&G Constrn. Co., Inc., Merrimack, N.H., 1964-68; broker Fisher Assos., real estate, Nashua, N.H., 1968-71; propr. R. Donahoe Assos., Bedford, N.H., 1971—. Mem. Nashua (v.p. 1975, pres. 1976, Realtor of Year 1977), Manchester bds. Realtors, So. N.H., (v.p. 1975—, award 1973), Greater Manchester multiple listing services, Women's Council Realtors (chpt. pres. 1974), Nat., N.H. (dir. exec. com. 1976—) assns. Realtors, Realtors Nat. Mktg. Inst., Manchester C. of C. Club: Manchester Country. Home: Davis Rd Merrimack NH 03054

DONAHUE, KATHLEEN ANN, lawyer; b. Yonkers, N.Y., May 7, 1947; d. James P. and Margaret E. (O'Brien) D. B.A., Albertus Magnus Coll., New Haven, 1969; J.D., Suffolk U., 1978. Bar: Mass. 1979. Law clk. to judge U.S. Ct. Appeals 1st Circuit, Boston, 1979-80; assoc. Oteri & Weinberg, Boston, 1980-81; sole practice, Cohasset, Mass., 1981—. Polit advisor to nat. polit. candidates, 1968-70. Pettingill Law scholar, 1976-78. Mem. ABA, Norfolk County Bar Assn., Mass. Bar Assn., Plymouth County Bar Assn., Quincy Bar Assn., Phi Delta Phi. Democrat. Club: Cohasset Drama. Home: 28 Whitcomb Rd Minot MA 02055 Office: Box 421 Cohasset MA 02025

DONAHUE, LAURA KENT, state senator; b. Quincy, Ill., Apr. 22, 1949; d. Laurence S. and Mary Lou (McFarland) Kent; m. Michael A. Donahue, July 16, 1983. B.S., Stephens Coll., 1971. Mem. Ill. State Senate, Quincy, 1981. Mem. Lincoln Club of Adams County, Ill. Fedn. Republican Women. Mem. P.E.O. Lodge: Altrusa. Office: State Senator Laura Donahue 400 Maine St Quincy IL 62301

DONAHUE, MARY CATHERINE, magazine advertising executive; b. N.Y.C., May 3, 1954; d. Daniel Patrick and Rosemary Ann (DePhillips) D. B.A., Coll. Holy Cross, Worcester, Mass., 1976; postgrad. in Bus. Adminstrn., NYU. Media buyer William Esty, N.Y.C., 1976-77; media planner Benton & Bowles, N.Y.C., 1977-78; sr. media planner N.W. Ayer, N.Y.C., 1978-79; mktg. dir. Cosmopolitan Mag., N.Y.C., 1979-80, account exec., sales, 1980-81; account mgr. Family Weekly Mag. (div. CBS), N.Y.C., 1981—. Mem. Advt. Women of N.Y., Coll. of Holy Cross Alumni/Alumnae Club N.Y. (sec. 1977-79, v.p. 1980-82, pres. 1984). Roman Catholic. Home: 12 E 86th St New York NY 10028 Office: 1515 Broadway New York NY 10036

DONAHUE, MARY KATHERINE, librarian; b. Dallas, Jan. 14, 1942; d. Joseph W. and Ellen (Onan) D.; B.A., Our Lady of the Lake U., 1963; M.L.S., U. Calif., Berkeley, 1965; M.A., Tex. A&M U., 1983; m. John Patrick Hooker, July 29, 1976. Librarian, Dallas Public Library, 1963-64, 65; 1st asst. Lubbock (Tex.) City-County Libraries, 1965-69, asst. dir., 1966-68; librarian U. Tex., Arlington, 1969; corp. librarian Univ. Computing Co., Dallas, 1969-72; sr. librarian Corpus Christi (Tex.) Public Libraries, 1973-75, adminstrv. coordinator, 1975-76; coordinator Hidalgo County (Tex.) Library System, McAllen, 1976-80; asst. prof. Tex. A&M U., College Station, 1981-84; cons. in field. Mem. Hidalgo County Hist. Commn., 1978-81, Brazos County Hist. Commn., 1982—, Rio Grande Valley Council for Arts, 1977-81. Recipient Disting. Service award Tex. Hist. Commn. Mem. ALA, Tex. Library Assn., Alpha Chi.

DONAHUE, ROSANNE FRANCES, university administrator; b. Brookline, Mass., Jan. 8, 1953; d. John Francis and Alice Helena (Kirby) Fraine; m. Robert James Donahue, Mar. 9, 1969 (div. Mar. 1979). B.A. in English, U. Mass.-Boston, 1983, postgrad. Sec. grad. studies U. Mass., Boston, 1975-78, asst. instl. planning, 1978-82, adminstrv. asst., 1982—, mem. dean's search, 1983. Recipient Disting. Service award U. Mass.-Boston, 1984, Pride in Performance award Gov. Dukakis of Mass., 1985. Avocation: coach girls' softball team. Home: 22 Westford St Allston MA 02134 Office: U Mass at Boston Harbor Campus Boston MA 02125

DONALD, CLARA PHILLIPS, educator; b. Nashville; d. Ezra and Lucy (King) Phillips; m. Grady H. Donald, June 21, 1953; children—Grady H., Jr., Michael T., Angelyn Yvonne. B.S., Tenn. State U., 1956; M.A., Columbia U., 1974. Missionary advisor, tchr. religion, Jamaica, 1954; tchr., Holloway High Sch., Murfreesboro, Tenn.; 1954-55; tchr. Nashville Pub. Sch., 1959-66; tchr. Pub. Sch. Dist. 8, Bronx, N.Y., 1966—; exptl. tchr. Peabody Coll.; Head Start dir. summer programs, Bronx, 1966, 67; head tchr. Pre-Sch. program Pub. Sch. 140, Bronx, 1969-71; Chmn. Consumer Affairs Com., Bronx Planning Bd. 4, 1978; pres. missionary soc. mem. Deaconess bd. Greater Victory Bapt. Ch. Mem. United Fedn. Tchrs. (chmn. sch. chpt.), Baptist Ministers Wives Assn., Nat. Edn. Assn., Alpha Kappa Alpha. Avocations: Bible study; reading; traveling.

DONALDSON, MARCELINE MALICA, consulting company executive; b. New Orleans, Oct. 25, 1937; d. Maurice and Doris Gaynelle (Taylor) D.; grad. N.Y.C.; grad. Program for Mgmt. Devel., Harvard, m. Robert A. Bennett; children—Elise Karen Leon, Malica Aronowitz, Michelle, Jacqueline Aronowitz. Owner, Ma-Li-Kai, Inc., Mpls., 1965-69; stock broker Dain, Kalman & Quail, Inc., Mpls., 1969-71; sales and mktg. with Pillsbury Co., Mpls., 1972-73; owner, pres. Donaldson & Assocs., Inc., Wayzata, Minn., 1973-77; sales/mktg. IBM, after 1977; pres. cons. firm. Precinct chmn. Republican Party, 1974-79; mem. nat. fund raising com. Black Women's Community Devel. Found.; nat. bd. NOW, 1973-75; fund raiser legal def. fund NAACP. Mem. Acad. Mgmt., Needlework Guild Minn., Cin. Art Mus., Harvard Bus. Sch. Club Cin. (v.p.). Republican. Episcopalian. Home: 49 Hawthorne St Cambridge MA 02138

DONATH, THERESE (PHYLLIS THERESE FREEMAN), artist, writer; b. Hammond, Ind., Dec. 14, 1928; d. Arthur Max and Lillian Louise (Donath) Helfer; student Monticello Coll., 1946-47; B.F.A., St. Joseph's Coll., 1975; additional study Oxbow Summer Sch. Painting, Immaculate Heart Coll., Hollywood, Calif., Monticello Coll., Alton, Ill., Penland, N.C., Haystack, Maine; children—Mark, Alex, Kim. Interviewer, producer Viewpoint, Sta. WLNR-FM, Lansing, Ill., 1963-64; reporter, columnist N.W. Ind. Sentinel, 1965; freelance writer Monterey Peninsula Herald, 1981-85; contbg. author Monterey Life mag. 1981-84; asst. dir. Michael Karolyi Meml. Found., Vence, France, 1979; one-woman shows include: Ill. Inst. Tech., Chgo., 1971; group shows include: Palos Verdes (Calif.) Mus., 1974, Los Angeles Inst. Contemporary Art, 1978, Mus. Contemporary Art, Chgo., 1975, Calif. State U., Fullerton, 1973, No. Ill. U., DeKalb, 1971; represented in permanent collections including Kennedy Gallery, N.Y.C., also pvt. collections; creative cons. Asian Tours and Travel, 1983-85; instr., lectr. Penland, N.C., 1970, Haystack Mountain Sch., Deer Isle, Maine, 1974, Sheffield Poly., Eng., 1978. Bd. dirs., sec. Mental Health Soc. Greater Chgo., 1963-64; exec. dir. Lansing (Ill.) Mental Health Soc., 1963-64. Recipient awards No. Ind. Art Mus., 1966, 70, 71, 73; grantee Ragdale Found., Lake Forest, Ill., 1982. Represented in The Mirror Book, 1978; author: Before I Die; contbr. articles to profl. jours., newspapers; illustrator: Run Computer Run, 1983. Office: Mixed Media Route 3 Box 74 Vashon Island WA 98070

DONATO, LORETTA ANN, advertising executive; b. Scotch Plains, N.J., Aug. 7, 1947; d. Albert Samuel and Frances Janet (Dello-Russo) D. B.A., Marquette U., 1969. Dir. continuity Sta. WPAT, Patterson, N.J., 1969-72; asst. dir. legal clearance Grey Advt., Inc., N.Y.C., 1972-80, dir. legal clearance, 1980-82, v.p., 1982—. Vol., Am. Mus. Natural History, N.Y.C., 1982—, N.Y. Philharm. Orch., 1984—. Office: Grey Advt Inc 777 3d Ave New York NY 10017

DONEGAN, JANE BAUER, history educator, author; b. Bklyn., Sept. 24, 1933; d. Henry William and Mary E. (Barlow) Bauer; m. Denis I. Donegan, Jan. 16, 1956 (div.); children—Stuart Barlow, Jennifer Barlow; m. Robert A. Huff, Mar. 6, 1981. B.A., Syracuse U., 1954, M.A., 1959, Ph.D., 1972. Grad. asst. Syracuse U., Maxwell Sch., 1955; tchr., chair Fabius (N.Y.) Central Sch., 1955-59, 60-62; tchr. Deposit (N.Y.) Central Sch., 1959-60; prof. history, coordinator women's studies Onondaga Community Coll., Syracuse, N.Y., 1962—; reviewer NEH pub. programs, Washington, 1979-82; panelist NEH Edn. Programs, Washington, 1980, NEH Profl. Nominating, Washington, 1980; mem. SUNY Commn. on Hon. Degrees, Albany, 1983-86. Author: Women and Men Midwives, 1978; Hydropathic Highway to Happiness, 1986. Contbr. articles to profl. jours. NEH research fellow, Washington, 1980-81; NEH grantee, Washington, summer 1977; faculty research fellow SUNY Research Found., Albany, 1978; recipient trustees' recognition award Onondaga Community Coll., 1980. Mem. Orgn. Am. Historians, Am. Assn. for History of Medicine, Soc. for Social History of Medicine, Am. Hist. Soc., Upstate N.Y. Women's History Conf. Office: Dept Social Scis Onondaga Community Coll Syracuse NY 13215

DONELSON, ANGIE FIELDS CANTRELL MERRITT, real estate executive; b. Hermitage, Tenn., Dec. 2, 1914; d. Dempsey Weaver and Nora (Johnson) Cantrell; student public and pvt. schs., Hermitage, Nashville; m. Gilbert Stroud Merritt, Dec. 15, 1934 (dec.); 1 son, Gilbert Stroud; m. 2d, John Donelson, Jr., VII, Apr. 23, 1966 (dec.); step-children—John, Agnes Donelson Williams (dec.), William Stockley. Pres., So. Woodenware Co., Nashville, 1955-61, So. Properties, Inc., Hermitage, 1961—. Chmn. comml. flower exhibits Tenn. State Fair, 1951; committeewoman and v.p. Davidson County Agrl. Soil and Conservation Community Com., 1959-60; bd. mem. Nashville Symphony Assn., 1961-64, regional council mem., 1977-79; chmn. bd. Nashville Presbyn. Neighborhood Settlement House; founding bd. mem. Davidson County Cancer Soc.; bd. mem. Nashville Vis. Nurse Service; dist. chmn., speakers bur. Am. Red Cross. Mem. Vanderbilt U. Aid, Peabody Coll. Aid, Tenn. Hist. Soc., Descs. of Ft. Nashboro Pioneers (bd. dirs.), English Speaking Union. Presbyterian. Clubs: Ladies Hermitage Assn. (dir. 1949—), DAR, (chpt. regent 1941), Lebanon Rd. Garden Club (pres. 1947), Horticulture Soc. Davidson County (v.p. 1949). Clubs: Ravenwood Country, Centennial, Belle Meade. Contbr. to books and mags. on history of Tenn. Home: Stone Hall Stones River Rd Hermitage TN 37076 Office: Lebanon Rd Hermitage TN 37076

DONIGAN, CLARA VIRGINIA, social worker; b. Denver, Oct. 6, 1920; d. Anton Theodore and Leah Ann (Dibble) Pape; A.A., A.F.A., Colo. Woman's Coll., 1940; B.S., U. Ill., 1942; M.S.W., U. Wash., 1957; lic. clin. social worker; m. Thomas Pattison Donigan, May 19, 1955; children—Thomas P. II (dec.), Mark Lockwood. Hosp. social worker ARC, 1945-51; social worker Assoc. Luth. Welfare, 1955-56; acting supr. child therapy Santa Maria Mental Health Clinic, Calif., 1963-66; instr. Brevard Community Coll., Cocoa, Fla., 1967-70; dir. social work Wuesthoff Meml. Hosp., Rockledge, Fla., 1970-76; sub-dist. adminstr. Dept. Health and Rehab. Services, Rockledge, 1976—. Vice chmn. Brevard Status of Children Com.; mem. Brevard Council on Children and Youth. Mem. Nat. Assn. Social Workers, Council So. Social Service Execs. Inst., Health Systems Agy. East Central Fla. (charter), Soc. Hosp. Social Service Dirs. (co-founder Fla. chpt.), Council Social Service Execs. Brevard County (charter pres.). Episcopalian. Home: 215 Antigua Dr Cocoa Beach FL 32931 Office: 705 Avocado St Cocoa FL 32922

DONISTHORPE, CHRISTINE ANN, state senator; b. Christina, Mont., May 31, 1932; d. Lambert A. and Ludmilla (Hruska) Benes; m. Oscar Lloyd Donisthorpe, 1951; children—Paul, Karen, Bruce, Brian. Student U. Mont., 1951-53, San Juan Coll., N.Mex. Real Estate Sch., 1958-70. Pres. Bd. of Edn., Bloomfield, N.Mex., 1975-81; mem. N.Mex. State Senate, 1979—, mem. edn. com., 1979, fin. com., 1980, edn. study com., 1981; mem. Bd. Realtors San Juan County, 1978-81. Adv. bd. Salvation Army, 1970-75; active C. of C. Recipient U.S. Soil and Water Conservation award, 1967; Hon. State Future Farmers Adv. award, 1975. Mem. N.Mex. Hay Growers Assn. Republican. Methodist. Address: PO Box 746 Bloomfield NM 87413•

DONLEVY, COLLEEN THERESA, sales executive; b. Paterson, N.J., Apr. 29, 1954; d. John William and Anne Marie (Field) D.; student Marymount Coll., 1974; B.A. in Psychology, Manhattanville Coll., 1975; M.B.A., U. Miami, 1978. Mdse. mgr. J.C. Penney, Miami, Fla., 1978-80; exec. v.p., v.p., sales/mktg. dir. King Cola Fla. and Carolinas Corp., Miami Beach, 1980—; terr. mgr. Kellogg Co., 1981—. Mem. Crime Patrol. Mem. AAUW. Republican. Roman Catholic. Home and Office: 7380 NW 1st St Apt 202 Plantation FL 33317

DONLEY, BARBARA ELLEN, nurse anesthetist; b. Burlington, Wis., Sept. 1, 1932; d. Arthur W. and Lillian C. (Luhn) Juranek; R.N., St. Francis Sch. Nursing, 1953; cert. registered nurse anesthetist St. Francis Sch. Anesthesia, 1954; B.A., Redlands U., 1976; M.Sci. Health Care Mgmt., Calif. State U., Los Angeles, 1980; m. Clifford A. Donley, June 15, 1963; children—Timothy A., Jennifer A. Staff nurse anesthetist Misericordia Hosp., Milw., 1954-62, Kaiser Permanente, Los Angeles, 1962-65, Bellflower, Calif., 1965-70, chief nurse anesthetist, 1970-80, dept. adminstr., 1980—; clin. supr., didactic lectr. Kaiser Permanente Sch. Anesthesia, 1972-75; instr. CPR, 1975-77. Tchr. religious edn. jr. high level St. Cyprian Catholic Ch., Long Beach, Calif., 1977-84. Mem. Am. Assn. Nurse Anesthetists, Calif. Assn. Nurse Anesthetists, Greater Los Angeles Heart Assn., Nat. Assn. Female Execs. Republican. Roman Catholic.

DONLEY, BETTIE LOUX, publishing executive; b. Drexel Hill, Pa., Nov. 5, 1931; d. Frank Turner and Elizabeth Ida (Kauffman) Loux; B.S., Pa. State U., 1953. Prodn. coordinator, editorial research Nat. Geog. Soc., Washington, 1959-69; editor World Traveler mag., dir. publs. Alexander Graham Bell Assn. for Deaf, Washington, 1969-76; mng. editor The Magnificent Foragers, A Zoo for All Seasons (Smithsonian Exposition Books); contbr. Our 50 States, Our World (Nat. Geog. Soc.); mng. editor Health Care for Women Internat., Issues in Comprehensive Nursing, Issues in Mental Health Nursing, Sociol. Spectrum, editor Fundamentals of Aquatic Toxicology, Occupational Hazards, Numerical Heat Transfer, 1983-84. Mem. forum White House Conf. Children, 1970. Recipient award for picture story Ednl. Press Assn. Am., 1970, award for layout, 1971, award for one-theme issue, 1973, Eleanor Fishburn award for outstanding contbn. to internat. understanding among readers, 1971. Mem. Washington Book Publishers, Washington Ind. Writers, Women in Communications, Ednl. Press Assn. Am., Alpha Gamma Delta, Smithsonian Assos. Democrat. Episcopalian. Club: Silver Spring (Md.) Garden (v.p. 1970-71). Editor Grace Ch. Messenger, 1971-82. Home: 1217 Woodside Pkwy Silver Spring MD 20910

DONLEY, PEGGY O'NEILL, lawyer; b. Dallas, May 11, 1950; d. Donald C. and Verna (Mirgain) O'Neill; m. Richard Wayne Donley, July 31, 1976. B.A., East Tex. State U., 1971; J.D., South Tex. Coll. Law, 1980; postgrad. Loyola U., New Orleans, 1981-83, Corpus Christi State U., 1984. Bar: Tex. 1980, La. 1981; cert. protection profl. Police officer, detective Houston Police Dept., 1972-76; spl. agt. Exxon Co., U.S.A., Houston, 1976-80, New Orleans, 1980-83, Corpus Christi, Tex., 1983-84, asst. trial atty. litigation dept., Houston, 1984—. Mem. ABA, Tex. Bar Assn., La. Bar Assn., Houston Bar Assn., Internat. Platform Assn., Am. Soc. for Indsl. Security (sec. New Orleans chpt. 1982, vice chmn. 1983). Democrat. Methodist. Office: Exxon Co USA PO Box 2180 Houston TX 77752

DONNALLY, PATRICIA BRODERICK, fashion editor; b. Cheverly, Md., Mar. 11, 1955; d. James Duane and Olga Frances (Duenas) Broderick; m. Robert Andrew Donnally, Dec. 30, 1977. B.S., U. Md., 1977. Fashion editor The Washington Times (D.C.), 1983—, The San Francisco Chronicle, 1985—. Recipient Atrium 33 award, 1984; Lulu award, 1985. Mem. Washington Fashion Group, Inc. Home: 2838 Jessup Rd Jessup MD 20794 Office: The San Francisco Chronicle 901 Mission St San Francisco CA 94103

DONNELL, LORETTA, educator; b. Dallas; d. Claude Raymond and Lottie (Watts) Wilson; m. Stanley Joe Donnell, Dec. 27, 1958 (dec. May 1977); children—Joseph Bradford, Lori Beth. B.S. in Edn., North Tex. State U., 1959; postgrad. in edn. East Tex. State U., 1978; postgrad. in acctg. and bus. U. Tex.-Dallas, 1980-82. Elem. tchr. Dallas Ind. Schs., 1959, El Paso (Tex.) Ind. Schs., 1959-60, Austin (Tex.) Ind. Schs., 1960-65; owner, bookkeeper Medicine Cabinet Pharmacy, Dallas, 1976-77; tchr. 2d grade Garland (Tex.) Ind. Schs., 1977—, acad. coach computer literacy classes, curriculum writer, summer sch. tchr. Project B.E.S.T., 1983—. Mem. edn. com. Highlands Christian Ch., Dallas, 1983—. Mem. Kappa Delta. Republican. Office: Parkcrest Elem Sch 2232 Parkcrest St Garland TX 75240

DONNELL, SANDRA DI BELLA, county official; b. Newark, Nov. 25, 1944; d. Anthony Robert and Camille (De Rose) Di Bella; m. James M. Donnell, Sept. 18, 1965; children—Danielle Di Bella, Philip Anthony. Student Cumberland Coll., 1962-66, U. Tenn., 1967. Owner, buyer Donnell's LaFemme, Lebanon, Tenn., 1970—; lobbyist Tenn. Home Health Assn., Nashville, 1982-83; owner, operator Donnell Diversified Investments, Mt. Juliet, Tenn., 1967—; owner, operator D and A Hawaii Co., Old Hickory, Tenn., 1984—; county commr. Wilson County, Tenn., 1979—; Contbr. articles, poetry to profl. jours. Pres. Wilson County Cancer Soc., 1982-84; chmn. Tenn. Easter Seal Camp, Nashville, 1985; active Tenn. Gifted Children's Assn., Am. Cancer Soc.; fundraiser chmn. St. Stephens Catholic Ch., Mt. Juliet, 1984—. Mem. Women in Politics, Tenn. County Commrs. Assn., Tenn. Federated Womens' Club (publicity chmn.). Democrat. Avocations: aerobics; nutrition; travel; tennis; swimming. Home: 5328 Vanderbilt Rd Mount Juliet TN 37122 Office: Wilson County Seat Route 5 Vanderbilt Rd Mount Juliet TN 37122

DONNELLY, BARBARA SCHETTLER, med. technologist; b. Sweetwater, Tenn., Dec. 2, 1933; d. Clarence G. and Irene Elizabeth (Brown) Schettler; A.A., Tenn. Wesleyan Coll., 1952; B.S., U. Tenn., 1954; cert. med. tech., Erlanger Hosp. Sch. Med. Tech., 1954; postgrad. So. Meth. U., 1980-81; children—Linda Ann, Richard Michael. Med. technologist Erlanger Hosp., Chattanooga, 1953-57, St. Luke's Episcopal Hosp., Tex. Med. Center, Houston, 1957-58, 1962; engring. research and devel. SCI Systems Inc., Huntsville, Ala., 1974-76; cons. hematology systems Abbott Labs., Dallas, 1976-77, hematology specialist, Dallas, Irving, Tex., 1977-81, tech. specialist microbiology systems, Irving, 1981-82, tech. service coordinator microbiology, bio-chemistry, and hematology systems, 1982—. Recipient 5-Yr. Service award, Abbott Labs. Mem. Am. Soc. Clin. Pathologists (cert. med. technologist), Am. Soc. Microbiology. Contbr. articles on cytology to profl. jours. Home: 204 Greenbriar Ln Bedford TX 76021 Office: 1921 Hurd St Irving TX 75061

DONNELLY, MARY ELIZABETH, advertising agency executive; b. Detroit, Aug. 15, 1957; d. Arthur Frederick and Agnes Margaret (Connelly) Donnelly. B.S., Kans. State U., 1980. Account exec. Atwood Advt., Prairie Village, Kans., 1981-82, Bloom Agy., Dallas, 1982-84, The Sherrill Co., Dallas, 1984—. Mem. Women in Communications, Pub. Relations Soc. Am. Republican. Roman Catholic. Office: Sherrill Co 5115 McKinney Ave Dallas TX 75205

DONNELLY, PHYLLIS BESWICK, reading consultant; b. Elk Point, Alta., Can., Nov. 19, 1939; naturalized, 1966; d. Colin Alfred John and Ruby Ellen (Gudwer) Beswick; student U. Alta., 1957-58, Northwestern U., 1961-62, Ind. U., 1962-63, M.S. in Edn., 1967 B.S. in Edn., Bethel Coll., Mishawaka, Ind., 1964; m. John Vincent Donnelly, Nov. 28, 1975; children—Deirdre, Sean, Patrick. Elem. tchr. Strathearn Elem. Sch., Edmonton, Alta., Can., 1958-61, Harris Sch., Chgo., 1961-62, Culver (Ind.) Community Schs., 1964-66; reading cons., curriculum writer Cleveland Hts.-University Hts. Bd. of Edn., Cleveland Heights, Ohio, 1967—, program dir. Right-to-Read, 1974—; grad. prof. N.S. Summer Sch. Tchrs., Dalhousie U., Halifax, 1968. Pres. Judson Park Evening Aux. Vols. Mem. Internat. Reading Assn., Mary C. Austin Reading Council, Am. Fedn. Tchrs., Ohio Fedn. Tchrs., Cleveland Hts.-University Hts. Fedn. Tchrs., AAUW (elected to Ohio Roster of Women 1977), LWV. Democrat. Club: City. Author: Reading Evaluation, 1974, Primary Reading Writing and Listening Skills, 1977; co-author: Developmental Reading Guides, vols. 1, 2, 1975, vol. 3, 1976. Home: 10494 Lake Shore Blvd Cleveland OH 44108 Office: 2155 Miramar Blvd Cleveland Heights OH 44118

DONNELLY, ROSE ANN, educator; b. Bklyn., Feb. 21, 1925; d. James John and Madeline Lillian (La Tuga) Garone; m. Albert Joseph Donnelly, July 16, 1955. B.A., Barnard Coll., 1948; M.A., Columbia U., 1949, Ed.D., 1957. Tchr., Bklyn. Public Schs., 1950-56, tchr. in charge, 1956-57, asst. prin., 1958-67, prin., 1967-85, dir. funded and spl. programs, 1985—. Served with WAC, 1945-46. Mem. Assn. Supervision and Curriculum Devel., N.Y.C. Elem. Sch. Prins. Assn., Nat. Council Adminstrv. Women in Edn., Council Suprs. and Adminstrs. (dist. 21 treas.), N.Y.C. Assn. Supervision and Curriculum Devel., Bklyn. Reading Council. Club: Barnard Coll. (L.I.). Contbr. articles to profl. jours. Home: 149 Beach 141 St Belle Harbor NY 11694 Office: 345 Van Sicklen St Brooklyn NY 11223

DONNEM, SARAH LUND, civic worker; b. St. Louis, Apr. 10, 1936; d. Joel Y. and Erle Hall (Harsh) Lund; B.A., Vassar Coll., 1958; m. Roland W. Donnem, Feb. 18, 1961; children—Elizabeth Prince, Sarah Madison. Tech. aide Bell Labs., Whippany, N.J., 1959-60; chmn. placement vol. opportunities N.Y. Jr. League, 1972-73, asst. treas. 1974-75, chmn. urban problems relating to mental health, 1967-69, mem. project research com., 1967-71, chmn., 1973-74 bd. mgrs., 1973-74; chmn. community research D.C. Jr. League, 1970-71, mem. bd. mgrs., 1970-71; bd. dirs. East Side Settlement House, Bronx, N.Y., 1972—, v.p., 1975-76; bd. dirs. Stanley M. Isaacs Neighborhood Center, N.Y.C., 1973-76, v.p., 1975-76; bd. dirs. Presbyterian Home for Aged Women, N.Y.C., 1974-76, v.p., 1976; mem. exec. bd. N.Y. Aux. of Blue Ridge Sch., 1971-75, sec., 1965-67, pres., 1973-75; budget and benevolence com. Brick Presbyn. Ch., N.Y.C., 1973-76, mem. social service com., 1973-74, chmn. fgn. students com., 1963-64; mem. community life council Fairmount Presbyn. Ch., 1982—, mem. emergency needs com., 1983—; mem. women's com. Cleve. Orch., 1979—, trustee, 1985—; bd. dirs. Search and Care, N.Y.C., 1973-76, Project LEARN, Cleve., 1978-82, Council on Older Persons, Fedn. Community Planning, Cleve., 1978-82; bd. dirs. Commn. on Social Concerns, 1981, rev. com., 1982-83; trustee Cleve. Ballet '80, exec. com., 1981-82, fin. com. 1982—; trustee Golden Age Centers Greater Cleve., 1978, 1st v.p., 1980, pres., 1981—, exec. bd. Women's Council, 1978—; bd. advisors Ret. Sr. Vol. Program, 1982, trustee, 1983—; mem. strategic planning com. Cleve. United Way, 1985—; chmn. Yale Ball, 1982, 83. Named Vol. of Yr., N.Y. Jr. League, 1975. Mem. Nat. Inst. Social Scis. (mem. membership com. 1972—, trustee 1984—), Nat. Soc. of Colonial Dames, Western Res. Hist. Soc. (mem. women's adv. council 1977—; corr. sec. 1978; chmn. Antique Show 1979, 80). Republican. Presbyterian. Clubs: Colony (N.Y.C.); Chevy Chase (Washington); Intown, Kirtland, Cleve. Vassar (sec. 1980-82, v.p. 1983, pres. 1984—) (Cleve.). Address: 2945 Fontenay Rd Shaker Heights OH 44120

DONNER, ALICE WILKINSON, social worker; b. Phila., July 5, 1922; d. William MacIlhenny and Mary (Yost) Wilkinson; B.S. in Edn., U. Pa., 1944; M.A., Villanova (Pa.) U., 1975; M.S.W., Temple U., Phila., 1977; m. William T. Donner, Apr. 12, 1946; children—William W., Marda Elisa, Mary Alice, Margot Ramona. Elementary sch. tchr., 1944-50; renal social worker Abington (Pa.) Meml. Hosp., 1977—. Bd. dirs. Jenkintown Day Nursery, 1966-75, treas., 1969-71, v.p., 1972-74; bd. dirs. Montgonery County Homemaker Home Health Aide, 1965-74, v.p., 1970-72. Mem. Nat. Assn. Social Workers, Acad. Cert. Social Workers, Council Nephrology Social Workers. Home: 314 Wellington Terr Jenkintown PA 19046 Office: Abington Meml Hosp Abington PA 19001

DONNER, JOANNE, writer, former fashion model; b. Cleve., Feb. 25, 1947; d. Morris and Bess (Newmark) Jaffa; m. Sheldon J. Donner, Dec. 21, 1968; 1 son, M. Brooks. B.S. with honors, Kent State U., 1970. Tchr., Warrensville Heights (Ohio) City Schs., 1970-71; free-lance fashion model, Atlanta, 1979-84; free-lance writer, Atlanta, 1980—; S.E. corr. BMT Publs., N.Y.C., 1981-85; seminar speaker on fashion and retailing topics, 1985— . Contbg. editor Apparel Industry Mag., 1982—, Atlanta Mag., 1983—, Bus. Atlanta, 1985—; contbr. non-fiction articles to mags. Winner 1st place award unpub. category Reader's Digest/U.S.C. Writers' Workshop, 1984; Atrium award, 1984. Mem. Atlanta Women's Network, Mem. Soc. Profl. Journalists, Women in Communications, Fashion Group. Club: Press (Atlanta). Home: 2380 Kings Point Dr Atlanta GA 30338 Office: PO Box 80134 Atlanta GA 30366

DONOGHUE, ANN LAWSON, retired secretary; b. Chgo., Jan. 18, 1922; d. Lawrence Joseph and Elizabeth Frances (McCarthy) Lawson; m. John Joseph Donoghue, Sept. 4, 1943 (dec. Feb. 1968); 1 child, Michael. A.A.S. in Bus., Watson Bus. Coll., 1943; student in Art, Hyde Park Art Ctr., 1961-64. Sec., Chgo. Bd. Edn., 1960-82, ret., 1982; interior decorating cons. Ryder Sch., Chgo., 1969. Byford Sch., 1974. Trustee, Acorn Pub. Library Dist., Oak Forest, Ill., 1980—, pres., 1982-85. Mem. ALA, Am. Library Trustee Assn. (sec. nat. com. on legislation 1985—, edn. of library nat. com. 1985-86), Ill. Library Assn., Ill. Library Trustee Assn. Roman Catholic. Avocations: reading; sculpture; oil painting; china painting; traveling. Home: 15411 Betty Ann Ln Oak Forest IL 60452

DONOGHUE, ELIZABETH MARION MACMAHON (MRS. FLORENCE JOSEPH DONOGHUE), emerita museum curator; b. Castleisland, Kerry, Ireland, Nov. 9, 1896 (parents Am. citizens); d. James and Johanna Mary (Brosnan) MacMahon; B.A., Calvin Coolidge Coll., 1955, M.A., 1956; m. Florence Joseph Donoghue, Apr. 17, 1963 (dec. July 1970). Acct., Boston Wool Trade, 1914-33; tchr. Everett (Mass.) High Sch., 1934-63; trustee Wenham (Mass.) Hist. Assn. and Mus., Inc., 1956—, curator dolls, 1960-82. Driver, Red Cross Motor Corps, Boston, 1939-41, Civilian Def. Motor Corps, Everett, 1941-43. Mem. Antique Toy Collectors Am., Doll Club Gt. Britain, Doll Collectors Am., Emerald Isle, L.I., Ginny doll clubs, League Cath. Women, Mus. Fine Arts Boston, Nat. Ret. Tchrs. Assn., United Fedn. Doll Clubs, Am. Irish Hist. Soc. (life), Christ Child Soc. (life), Soc. Preservation N.E. Antiquities (life), Yesteryears Doll Mus. (life), Eire Soc. Boston (life, editor Bull. 1954-64), Worcester Art Mus., Boston U. Alumni Assn. Contbr. articles to profl. jours. Home: 86 Bradford St Everett MA 02149

DONOGHUE, MILDRED RANSDORF, educator; Ed.D., UCLA, 1962; J.D., Western State U., 1979; m. Charles K. Donoghue (dec.); children—Kathleen, James. Instr. Immaculate Heart Coll., Los Angeles, 1961-62; asst. prof. edn. Calif. State U., Fullerton, 1962-66, assoc. prof., 1966-71, prof., 1971—. Cons. various sch. dists. Mem. Nat. Council Tchrs. English, Am. Dialect Soc., Am. Council on Tchrs. of Fgn. Langs., Am. Ednl. Research Assn., AAUP, Nat. Soc. for Study Edn., Am. Assn. Tchrs. Spanish and Portuguese, Internat. Reading Assn., Nat. Assn. for Edn. of Young Children, Orange County Med. Assn., Los Angeles County Med. Assn. Women's Aux., Phi Beta Kappa, Phi Kappa Phi, Pi Lambda Theta. Author: Foreign Languages and the Schools, 1967; Foreign Languages and the Elementary School Child, 1968; The Child and the English Language Arts, 1971, 75, 79, 85. Second Languages in Primary Education, 1979. Contbr. articles to profl. jours. Office: Dept Elem Edn Calif State U Fullerton CA 92634

DONOHUE, EDITH M., continuing education coordinator, consultant; b. Balt., Nov. 10, 1938; d. Edward Anthony and Beatrice (Jones) McParland; m. Salvatore R. Donohue, Aug. 23, 1960; children—Kathleen, Deborah. B.A., Coll. Notre Dame, Balt., 1960; M.S., Johns Hopkins U., 1981, CASE, 1985. Dir. pub. relations Coll. Notre Dame, Balt., 1970-71, asst. dir. continuing edn., 1978-81, dir. continuing edn., 1981-86; coordinator program bus. and industry Catonsville Community Coll., Baltimore County, Md., 1986—. Co-editor, contbg. author career devel. workshop manual, 1985. Pres. Cathedral Sch. Parents Assn., 1972-74; asst. treas., treas. Md. Gen. Hosp. Aux., 1975-78; dir. Homeland Assn., 1978-81; regional rep., leader Girl Scouts Central Md., 1975-76; dir. sect. Exec. Women's Network, Balt., 1983-85; adv. bd. Mayor's Com. on Aging, 1981—; dir. Md. Assn. Higher Edn., 1985—. Recipient Mayor's Citation, City of Balt. Council, 1985. Mem. Am. Assn. Tng. and Devel., Am. Assn. Counseling and Devel., Am. Assn. Adult and Continuing Edn., AAUW (dir., v.p. 1980-83), Chi Sigma Iota, Phi Delta Kappa. Democrat. Roman Catholic. Lodge: Order Sons of Italy in Am. Avocations: tennis; theatre; aerobics; handcrafts; symphony; opera. Home: 5420 Springlake Way Baltimore MD 21212 Office: Catonsville Community College 800 S Rolling Rd Baltimore MD 21228

DONOHUE, ELEANOR M., lawyer; b. N.Y.C., June 15, 1935; d. Patrick Joseph and Beatrice Anne (Bligh) Donohue; m. Harry Foster Smith, Feb. 15, 1958 (div. June 1978); children—Elizabeth, Jennifer, H. Foster, Pamela, Edwin Malachy, Andrea. A.B. in Math., Mt. St. Vincent Coll., 1956; J.D., U. Santa Clara, 1984, M.A. in Counseling, 1985. Bars: Calif. Computer specialist IBM, N.Y.C., 1956-58; real estate salesperson Shannon & Luchs, Wheaton, Md., 1967-68; tchr. Cupertino Union Sch. Dist., Calif., 1974-81; sole practice, San Jose, Calif., 1985—; dir. SCS Office Concepts. Founder, St. Michael's Montessori Sch., N.Y.C. Democrat. Roman Catholic. Home: 20797 Granada Ct Saratoga CA 95070

DONOHUE, HELEN SHAY, speech pathologist, audiologist; b. Ansonia, Conn., Jan. 26; d. Thomas Francis and Margaret (Buckley) Shay; B.S., So. Conn. State Coll., 1948; M.A., Columbia U., 1958; profl. diploma U. Bridgeport, 1961; m. Thomas C. Donahue, Dec. 7, 1943. Speech and hearing therapist New Haven Public Schs., 1958-68; pvt. practice speech pathology, audiology, Boca Raton, Fla., 1969—; cons. in field. Bd. dirs. Riviera Civic Assn., 1975. Mem. Am. Speech and Hearing Assn. (cert. clin. competence), AAAS, AAUW, Pi Lambda Theta. Home: 25 College St #3 Clinton CT 06413

DONOHUE, MARGARET ANNE, retail company executive; b. Bronxville, N.Y., Aug. 13, 1953; d. James Patrick and Marie Elizabeth (Strack) Donohue. A.A.S. in Merchandising, Fashion Inst. Tech., N.Y.C., 1973, A.A.S. in Textile Tech., 1976; B.S. in Mktg., SUNY, 1978. Asst. buyer Sears, Roebuck & Co., N.Y.C., 1973-79; asst. to pres., gen. mgr. Lonia Designs, Inc., N.Y.C., 1979—. Roman Catholic. Home: 285 Ave C Apt 8E New York NY 10009 Office: Lonia Designs Inc 55 W 55th St New York NY 10019

DONOHUE, MARY HORROCKS, public relations professional; b. Lansdowne, Pa., Jan. 20, 1948; d. Charles A. and Augusta M. (Fox) Horrocks; m. John Dean Loughlin, Jr., Oct. 29, 1970 (div. 1979); 1 son, Charles Raymond; m. 2d Douglas Jay Donohue, Nov. 28, 1981. B.A. in Humanities cum laude, West Chester U., 1970. Staff writer Tribune-Rev., Bethany, Okla., 1974-79; tchr. Keystone Sch., Oklahoma City, 1975-78; corres. West Branch Citizen, West Chester, Pa., 1979-81, East Branch Citizen, Downington, Pa., 1979-81; tchr. Concept Sch., Westtown, Pa., 1979-80; info. and mktg. specialist The Devereux Found., Devon, Pa., 1980-85; copy writer Nat. Liberty Corp., Frazer, Pa., 1985; communications coordinator Elwyn Insts., Pa., 1985—; writing cons. Sunbeam Family Services, Inc., Oklahoma City, 1978, Exton-Frazer Rotary Club, 1986. Contbr. articles to profl. jours. Mem. adv. bd. Exceptional Craftsmen, Frazer, Pa., 1982-85; jr. troop leader Girl Scouts U.S.A., Havertown, 1969; pub. relations officer Boy Scouts Am., Westtown, Pa., 1980. Mem. Oklahoma City Writers Club, Del. County Press Club, Women in Communication, Am. Mktg. Assn., Am. Soc. Hosp. Pub. Relations of Am. Hosp. Assn., Phila. Advt. Women. Republican. Roman Catholic. Home: 1309 Pottstown Pike West Chester PA 19380 Office: Elwyn Insts Elwyn PA 19063

DONOVAN, CHRISTINE ANNE, writer, producer; b. Passaic, N.J., May 1, 1950; d. Frank A. and Frances Catherine (Grady) D. Student Cypress Coll., 1968-70; B.Mus., U. Calif.-Fullerton, 1976; postgrad. U. Calif.-Irvine, 1978-81. Profl. singer/actress, 1966-80; mem. ops. staff Disneyland, Anaheim, Calif., 1968-77, editor internal communications, 1977-78; writer WED Enterprises, Glendale, Calif., 1978-79; supr. internal communications Disneyland, 1980-82, writer/producer Disneyland/Disney World, Anaheim, Orlando, 1982—; host TV mag. Reel to Reel, Orlando, 1984—; cons. UCLA Med. Ctr., 1981. Spl. events coordinator United Way Orange County, 1982. Mem. Women in Communications, Internat. Assn. Bus. Communicators, Toastmistress Internat. Roman Catholic (cantor/mem. ch. choir). Office: Media Prodn Epcot Ctr PO Box 40 Lake Buena Vista FL 32830

DONOVAN, MARGARET ANN, educator; b. Detroit, Aug. 6, 1939; d. Edward Grove and Jean C. Donovan; B.A., U. Detroit, 1961; M.A., Eastern Mich. U., 1969; Ed.D., U. Hawaii, 1977. Elementary sch. tchr., Mich., 1961-69, Hawaii, 1969—; ednl. specialist for lang. arts, testing and edn., pub. relations Leeward Dist. Office, Waipahu, 1978—; part-time instr. curriculum and instrn. U. Hawaii, 1975—; mem. Title IV Adv. Council, Gifted and Talented Adv. Council. Mem Internat. Reading Assn., Nat. Council Tchrs. English, Council Exceptional Children, Assn. Supervision and Curriculum Devel., Am. Ednl. Research Assn., Pi Lambda Theta, Delta Kappa Gamma Club: Zonta. (pres. 1984-1986). Home: 2185 Aha Niu Pl Honolulu HI 96821 Office: Dept Edn Honolulu Dist Office 4967 Kilauea Ave Honolulu HI 96821

DONOVAN, MARGARET HENDERLITE, pianist, educator; b. Baird, Tex., May 6, 1925; d. Peter Baxter and Jessie (Newton) Henderlite; A.A., Tarleton State U., 1943; B.Music cum laude (T scholar), Am. Conservatory of Music, 1945, M.Music cum laude, 1953, postgrad., 1953; m. Russell J. Donovan, Sept. 4, 1949; children—Russell John, Peter Henderlite, Rachel Lynn, Margaret Newton, Tammy Jayne. Duo pianist with Charles W. Froh, Tex. State U., Stephenville, 1939-43; pianist, accompanist New Trier High Sch., Winnetka, Ill., 1945-47, Am. Conservatory of Music, Chgo., 1943-53, mem. faculty, 1954—; mem. faculty piano Park Forest (Ill.) Conservatory of Music, 1958—; pvt. piano instr., 1954—; profl. accompianist; adjudicator Nat. Guild of Piano Playing Auditions, 1960—, Soc. of Am. Musicians, 1962, Ill. Fedn. Music Clubs and Auditions, Chgo., 1962—. Organist, pianist United Ch. of Christ, Sauk Village, Ill. Recipient Hattstaedt Gold medal Piano award, 1945. Mem. Lakeview Mus. Soc., Cordon Club, Nat. Soc. Lit. and Arts, Am. Coll. Musicians, Soc. Am. Music, Music Tchrs. Nat. Assn., Internat. Platform Assn., Sigma Alpha Iota. Presbyn. Home: 1872 Reichert Ave Sauk Village IL 60411

DONOVAN, NANCY HEFFNER, travel agency executive; b. Columbus, Ohio, July 23, 1949; d. William Bennett and Janet Ann (Pease) Heffner; m. Stephen P. Donovan, Jr., Sept. 24, 1983. A.B., Bradford Jr. Coll., 1969; B.A., Trinity Coll., 1971. Travel agt. Provident Travel, Cin., 1972-76, v.p., 1976-79, exec. v.p., 1979-83; pres. Ames Travel, Cin., 1983—. Trustee Cin. May Festival, 1982—; active Cin. Jr. League. Republican. Presbyterian. Avocations: singing; swimming; reading; traveling. Home: 1271 Ida St Cincinnati OH 45202 Office: Ames Travel Service 604 Carew Tower Cincinnati OH 45202

DOODY, BARBARA PETTETT, computer specialist; b. Cin., Sept. 18, 1938; d. Philip Wayne and Virginia Bird (Handley) P.; student Sinclair Coll., Tulane U.; 1 son, Daniel Frederick Reasor, Jr. Owner, mgr. Honeysuckle Pet Shop, Tipp City, Ohio, 1970-76; office mgr. Doody & Doody, C.P.A.s, New Orleans, 1976-77, computer ops. mgr., 1979—; office mgr. San Diego Yacht Club, 1977-79. Mem. DECUSERS Assn., DAR, UDC. Republican. Lutheran. Home: 16 Cypress Covington LA 70433 Office: 1160 Commerce Bldg New Orleans LA 70112

DOODY, MARGARET ANNE, English language educator; b. St. John, N.B., Can., Sept. 21, 1939; d. Hubert and Anne Ruth (Cornwall) D.; came to U.S., 1976; B.A., Dalhousie U., Can., 1960; B.A. with 1st class hons., Lady Margaret Hall, Oxford (Eng.) U., 1962, M.A., D.Phil. (Can. Council fellow 1964-65, Imperial Oil fellow 1965-68), 1968. Instr. in English, U. Victoria (B.C., Can.), 1962-64, asst. prof. English, 1968-69; lectr. Univ. Coll. Swansea (Wales), 1969-76; asso. prof. English, U. Calif., Berkeley, 1976-80; prof. English dept. Princeton (N.J.) U., 1980—. Guggenheim postdoctoral fellow, 1979. Anglican (Episcopalian). Author: A Natural Passion: A Study of the Novels of Samuel Richardson, 1974; Aristotle Detective, 1978; (novel) The Alchemists, 1980; (with F. Stuber) Clarissa: A Theater Work, Part I, 1984; The Daring Muse: Augustan Poetry Reconsidered, 1985. Office: English Dept Princeton U Princeton NJ 08544

DOOLEY, JO ANN CATHERINE, publishing company executive; b. Cin., Nov. 24, 1930; d. Joseph Frank and Margaret Mary (Flynn) Dooley; ed. U. Cin., 1966. Clk., Castellini Co., Cin., 1949-52; IBM operator Kroger Co., Cin., 1952; asst. acct. Gardner Publs., Inc., Cin., 1953-67, treas., sec., 1967—, dir., 1983—, v.p. fin., 1986—, also trustee employees profit sharing trust, trustee retirement trust. Mem. Am. Soc. Women Accts. (advt. mgr. Woman CPA 1979-81, nat. pres. 1982-83, treas. 1984—, trustee Ednl. Found.), Am. Mgmt. Assn., Cin. Women's Forum, Nat. Assn. Female Execs. Roman Catholic. Office: 6600 Clough Pike Cincinnati OH 45244

DOOLEY, MARY AGNES, college president; b. Sommerville, Mass., Mar. 5, 1923; d. Richard and Mary A. (O'Neill) D.; B.A., Elms Coll., 1944; M.A., Assumption Coll., 1960, L.H.D. (hon.), 1982; Doctorat d'Université, U. Paris, 1968; LL.D. (hon.) Am. Internat. Coll., 1981; D.Ministry, St. Louis U. Aquinas Inst., 1983; Litt.D. (hon.), Fitchburg State Coll., 1985. Joined Congregation of the Sisters of St. Joseph, 1944; tchr. St. Joseph's High Sch., North Adams, Mass., 1946-65; chmn. lang. dept. Elms Coll., Chicopee, Mass., 1968-70, pres., 1979—; pres. Leadership Conf. Women Religious U.S., Washington, 1978-79; pres. Congregation Sisters of St. Joseph, Springfield, Mass., 1971-79; corporator Community Savs. Bank, Holyoke, Mass., trustee, 1984—. Recipient Disting. Alumna award Elms Coll., 1979; decorated chevalier dans l'Ordre des Palmes Academiques (France), 1981; named Woman of Yr., Chicopee Bus. and Profl. Women's Club. Mem. Assn. Cath. Colls. and Univs. (dir. 1980-85), Leadership Conf. Women Religious, Delta Epsilon Sigma. Roman Catholic. Contbr. articles in field to profl. jours.

DOOLEY, WANDA MARIE, retail buyer; b. Kansas City, Kans., Jan. 29, 1952; d. Richard Burton and Bette Ann (McClure) D. B.S., Kans. State U., 1974; M.A., N.Y. U., 1982. Saleswoman, bookkeeper Internat. Boutique, N.Y.C., 1974-75; asst. buyer Mercantile Buying Office, N.Y.C., 1975-78, children's wear buyer, 1978—. Mem. Black Retail Action Group (Buyer Achievement award 1982), Alpha Kappa Alpha. Democrat. Methodist. Home: 225 Central Park W Apt 1109 New York NY 10024

DOPLER, ROSEMARY, computer graphics technical consultant; b. Fairfax, Va. July 10, 1955; d. Kenyon Lee and Mary Louise (Mattingly) Demory; m. Alvin Bernard Dopler, Jr., Nov. 22, 1980. B.A., U. Ala.-Huntsville, 1979; M.Adminstrv. Sci., 1982. Sr. systems engr. Integraph Corp., Huntsville, Ala., 1979—. U. Ala. Acad. Achievement scholar, 1978. Mem. Psi Chi. Republican. Roman Catholic. Avocations: jogging; cycling; reading; cooking. Office: Integraph Corp 1 Madison Industrial Park Huntsville AL 35807

DOPP, ALICE FLORENCE, librarian; b. Detroit, Oct. 28, 1931; d. Kenneth Wilton and Florence Caroline (Gabriel) Marsh; m. James Wellington Dopp, Jr., Aug. 1, 1969; m. Harold Lewis Allen, Aug. 1, 1953 (div. July 1960); 1 child, Laurie Jeanne. B.A., Wayne State U., 1965; M.L.S., U. Mich., 1967. Reference librarian Detroit Pub. Library, 1967-69; cataloger San Luis Obispo (Calif.) City Library, 1970-73; head tech. services San Luis Obispo City/County Library, 1973-78; head tech. services Las Vegas-Clark County Library Dist., 1981—; cons. San Luis Obispo Friends of Library, 1975-78; organizer, cons. Second Edit. Book Store, Las Vegas, 1982-83. Art tchr. local 500, United Auto Workers, Detroit, 1964; bd. mem. Detroit Pub. Library Staff Credit Union, Detroit, 1968; chmn. Internat. Inst. Supper Club, Detroit, 1967. Mem. ALA, Mich. Library Assn., Calif. Library Assn., Nev. Library Assn. (chmn. S.O.U.P. 1983-84), Black Gold Tech. Services Com. (chmn. 1977-78), AAUW. Democrat. Lutheran. Club: Silver Queens Investment (acctg. ptnr. 1981-83) (Las Vegas). Office: Las Vegas-Clark County Library Dist 1401 E Flamingo Rd Las Vegas NV 89119

DORA, JOAN TERESA, municipal clerk; b. Jersey City, Jan. 7, 1935; d. Samuel Francis and Helen Elizabeth (Curry) Kaminsky; m. Ewald Dora, Feb. 6, 1960; children—Deborah Ann, Walter John. Student County Coll. Morris-Randolph, N.J., 1970-73, Rutgers U., 1978—. Cert. mcpl. clk., N.J. Bookkeeper, office mgr. Lake Hopatcong Water Corp., High Ridge Water Co./High Ridge Sewer Co., N.J., 1970-77; acct. Lieberman & Co., Newton, N.J., 1977-78; mcpl. clk. Borough of Hopatcong, N.J., 1978—. Trustee, corp. sec. U.S. Land & Utilities, N.Y.C., 1973-77. Recipient Merit award Rotary Club, 1982, Citizenship award, Rotary Club, 1985. Mem. Hopatcong C. of C. (pres. 1982-84), N.J. Fedn. Bus. and Profl. Women (asst. treas. 1982-83), Sussex County Mcpl. Clks. Assn. (pres. 1981-82), Mcpl. Clks. Assn., Internat. Inst. Mcpl. Clks. Clubs: Hopatcong Women's, N.W. Morris Bus. and Profl. Women's (pres. 1982-83), Deborah Hosp. Found. (1st v.p. 1982-83). Avocations: walking; golf. Home: PO Box 112 Hopatcong NJ 07843 Office: Borough Hopatcong Mcpl Bldg River Styx Rd Hopatcong NJ 07843

DORAN, DORIS JEANNE, librarian; b. Chambersburg, Pa., July 19, 1932; d. John Franklin and Kathleen Elmira (Cooke) Fraker; B.S., Wilson Coll., 1954; M.L.S., U. Md., 1970, postgrad., 1976-77; m. Francis Joseph Doran, Feb. 5, 1955; children—Brenda Lou, Polly Ann. Asst. buyer Joseph Horne Co., Pitts., 1955-56; dir. research library Sears Roebuck & Co., Chgo., 1956-58; project officer contracts John I. Thompson Co., Washington, 1967-69, staff asst. to v.p. info. sci. div., 1969-70; program officer grants div. Nat. Library of Medicine, Bethesda, Md., 1970-79, program analyst Office of Dir., 1980-82; project dir. Nat. Med. Audiovisual Center, 1979; asst. for network devel. VA, Washington, 1982-84; co-owner, treas., gen. mgr. Gilran Lighting Products, Springfield, Va., 1969—. Mem. Med. Library Assn., Health Scis. Communications Assn. Home: 4816 Cloister Dr Rockville MD 20852 Office: 7518H Fullerton Rd Springfield VA 22153

DORAN, KAREN CATO, lawyer, clinical social worker; b. Tucson, May 26, 1952; d. Benjamin Ralph and Wilma Lucille (Roberts) Cato; m. James Peter Doran, Dec. 29, 1975; children—Paul Tyler, Timothy James. B.A., Duke U., 1974; M.S.W., Boston Coll., 1976; J.D., U. Va., 1983. Bar: Va. 1983. Clin. social worker Denver State Sch., Taunton, Mass., 1976-77; asst. dir. Danville-Pittsylvania Mental Health Ctr., Danville, Va., 1977-79, clin. dir., 1979-80; instr. Averett Coll., Danville, 1979; assoc. Christian, Barton, Epps, Brent & Chappell, Richmond, Va., 1983-84; sole practice law, Richmond, 1984—; examiner Va. Licensing Bd., Richmond, 1980-82. Columnist Danville register, 1979-80. Youth counselor First United Meth. Ch., Danville, 1978-80; v.p. Va. Law Women, Charlottesville, 1980-83. Recipient NIMH award Boston Coll., 1975-76; Outstanding Young Women Am. award Jaycees, 1979, Dillard fellow U. Va., 1981-83. Mem. Nat. Assn. Social Workers, Acad. Cert. Social Workers, Va. State Bar Assn., Va. Bar Assn., ABA, Richmond Bar Assn., Met. Richmond Women's Bar Assn., Duke U. Alumni, Delta Delta Delta. Home: 524 Williamsdale Dr Richmond VA 23235

DORE, ANITA WILKES, English educator; b. N.Y.C., Dec. 16, 1914; d. Abraham P. and Rose (Hirsch) Wilkes; m. Robert M. Dore, June 26, 1938; children—Marjorie Dore Allen, Elizabeth. B.A., Vassar Coll., 1935; M.A. with honors, Columbia U., 1937. Cert. English tchr., N.Y. Tchr. high sch. English, Bd. Edn., N.Y.C., 1937-41, 56-59, TV broadcaster, producer, 1961-65, coordinator English jr. high sch. div., 1959-61, chairperson English dept., 1965-67, asst. dir. English, 1967-73, dir. English, N.Y.C. schs., 1973-83, cons., 1983—; cons. Young Playwrights Dramatists Guild, N.Y.C., 1983—. Author: Premier Book of Major Poets, 1970, Emerging Woman, 1974; co-author: Distrust of Authority, 1981; also articles. Pres., bd. dirs. Sch. Settlement House, Bklyn., 1951-53; mem. edn. com. NOW, N.Y.C., 1972-75; chairperson Child Study Children's Book Com. Bank St. Coll., 1983—; bd. dirs. Westport-Weston Arts Council, Conn., 1983—; trustee Westport Library, Conn.; 1985—. Recipient Elizabeth Dana prize in English, Vassar Coll., 1934. Fellow N.Y. State English Council (v.p. 1970-75); mem. Nat. Council Tchrs. English Lit. Commn., N.Y.C. Assn. Tchrs. English (v.p. 1962-70). Democrat. Avocations: theatre; traveling. Home: 36 E 36th St New York NY 10016

DORE-DUFFY, PAULA, immunologist, educator; b. Hyannis, Mass., Feb. 23, 1948; d. Paul and Doris J. (Hochu) Dore; B.S., Simmons Coll,. 1972; Ph.D., La. State U. Sch. Medicine, 1976; m. Michael Charles Duffy, Dec. 27, 1972. Research asst. dept. microbiology and molecular genetics Harvard Med. Sch., Boston, 1970-71; research asso. La. State U. Med. Sch., New Orleans, 1972-76, lab. instr., 1974; fellow U. Conn. Sch. Medicine, Farmington, 1976-77, asst. prof. medicine div. rheumatic diseases, 1978—, asst. prof. neurology, 1979-82, assoc. prof. neurology, 1982—, chief div. neuroimmunology, 1982—; dir. Multiple Sclerosis Center, 1982—. Fellow Nat. Multiple Sclerosis Soc. (bd. dirs. Conn. Valley br. 1980—, Spl. award 1981); mem. Am. Assn. Immunologists, Am. Soc. Microbiology, Am. Fedn. Clin. Research, Union of Concerned Scientists, AAAS, N.Y. Acad. Scis. Contbr. clin. studies on neuroimmunology to sci. jours. Home: St Andrews Dr Farmington CT 06032 Office: Dept Neurology Univ Conn Health Center Farmington Ave 06032

DOREMUS, CHERIE BELLE DEPIETRO, public relations executive; b. Columbus, Ohio, Oct. 20, 1943; d. Charles James and Margaret Irene (Littlewood) DePietro; student Citrus Coll., 1961-63; m. Rick Doremus; children—Sean, Shannon Drake. Copywriter for homebuilding co., 1969-71; founding mem. The Groundlings, improvisational comedy group, Los Angeles, 1973-74; with Martin Advt., Tustin, Calif., 1971-74; freelance publicist, writer, 1974-78; founder, pres. Kerr & Assocs., pub. relations, Huntington Beach, Calif., 1978—; tchr. improvisational comedy to adults and children; founder Kerr Comedy Co. Winner 1st place Top 40 Lyric Competition in Music City Song Festival, 1985. Mem. Calif. Press Women's Assn. Office: 4911 Warner Ave Suite 208 Huntington Beach CA 92649

DORFMAN, KAREN K., corporate consultant, lecturer; b. Indpls., Mar. 3, 1950; d. John and Margie King; B.A., U. Tex., 1972; M.A., Ind. U., 1976. Sales rep. John H. Harland Co., 1977—; guest lectr. Ind. U.-Purdue U., Mem. various clubs. Home: 5678 N Meridian Indianapolis IN 46208

DORIAN, NANCY CURRIER, linguist, educator; b. New Brunswick, N.J., Nov. 5, 1936; d. Donald Clayton and Edith (McEwen) Dorian; B.A. summa cum laude, Conn. Coll. for Women, 1958; postgrad. Yale U., 1959-60; M.A., U. Mich., 1961, Ph.D. (Rackham fellow), 1965. Lectr., Bryn Mawr (Pa.) Coll., 1965-66, asst. prof., 1966-72, asso. prof., 1972-78, prof. linguistics in German and anthropology, 1978—, William R. Kenan, Jr. prof., 1980-85; vis. lectr. U. Pa., 1966, 70, U. Kiel, 1967-68. Fulbright scholar to Germany, 1958-59; NSF research grantee, 1978-79. Mem. Linguistic Soc. Am., Internat. Linguistic Assn., N.E. Folklore Soc., Eastern States Celtic Assn., Scottish Oral History Group, An Comunn Gaidhealach, Phi Beta Kappa. Democrat. Unitarian. Author: East Sutherland Gaelic, 1978; Language Death, 1981; The Tyranny of Tide, 1985; contbr. articles to profl. jours. Office: Bryn Mawr Coll Bryn Mawr PA 19010

DORMAN, HATTIE LAWRENCE, management consultant, former government agency official; b. Cleve., July 22, 1932; d. J. Lyman and Claire A. (Lenoir) Lawrence; m. James L. Dorman, May 16, 1959; children—Lydia, Lynda, James Lawrence. Student Fenn Coll. (Cleve. State U.), part time 1950-58, D.C. Tchrs. Coll., 1960-64, Dept. Agr. Grad. Sch., 1968-69. Clk., tax specialist, mgmt. analyst, supr., staff advisor IRS, Washington, 1954-79; spl. asst. to dep. asst. sec. adminstrn. Dept. Treasury, Washington, 1978-79; dep. dir. Interagency Com. on Women's Bus. Enterprise, SBA; Task Force on EEO, Dept. Treasury 1978-79; mem. Pres.'s Task Force on Women Bus. Owners, from 1979, now ret.; trainer and speaker in field. Sec. Linton Hall Guild, 1978-80; chmn. trainer, cons., leader Girl Scout Service Unit, 1971-80; ofcl. observer Nat. Women's Conf., Houston, 1977; bd. dirs. YWCA, 1957-62; mem. planning com. Black Women's Summit, 1981; mem. Vestry Register, St. Paul's Episcopal Ch., 1981—. Recipient spl. achievement award Commr. IRS, 1978, thanks badge Girl Scout Nation's Capital, 1977, recognition cert. for work in Christian edn. St. Paul's Episcopal Ch., 1976, Mary McLeod Bethune Centennial award Nat. Council Negro Women, 1975, other awards and certs. of appreciation. Mem. Am. Soc. Public Adminstrs., Federally Employed Women, Alumni Fed. Exec. Inst. Club: Delta Sigma Theta. Journalist Neighbor's Inc., 1969-71.

DORMAN, MARY ANN, educational administrator; b. Taylor, Tex., Aug. 12, 1948; d. Martin Oscar and Alice Boja (Blom) Hackemesser; m. Preston Charles Dorman, Apr. 20, 1972 (div. 1977). B.S., U. Houston, 1970; M.Ed., Tex. A & M, 1977. Cert. adminstr., supr., tchr. physics, math., phys. sci. With coop. program NASA, Houston, 1968-70; tchr. Aldine Ind. Sch. Dist., Houston, 1971-74; tchr. Fort Bend Ind. Sch. Dist., Sugarland, Tex., 1974-80, prin., 1980-84, dir. staff devel., 1984—. Author: Lab Experiments for Physical Science (book-manual), 1979. Participant, co-author expts. in sci. NSF, 1980. Recipient Tchr. of Yr. award Fort Bend Ind. Sch. Dist., 1980. Mem. Nat. Sci. Tchrs. Assn., Tex. Assn. Secondary Sch. Prins., Phi Delta Kappa. Democrat. Lutheran. Home: 6601 Sands Point #60 Houston TX 77074 Office: Fort Bend Ind Sch Dist PO Box 1004 Sugarland TX 77478

DORMAN-SEIDEN, HARRIET, financial services company executive; b. N.Y.C., Nov. 20, 1946; d. Bernard and Evelyn (Stone) Dorman; m. Gary Matthew Seiden, Jan. 16, 1977 (div. Sept. 1983); 1 dau., Lauren. Student Syracuse U., 1966-68; B.S. in Edn. and Spanish, NYU, 1968; postgrad. Universidad de las Americas, 1967; M.A. in Ednl. Psychology, NYU, 1972. Cert. tchr., N.Y. Broker asst. Goldman Sachs & Co., N.Y.C., 1968-70; tchr. N.Y.C. Bd. Edn., 1970-72; cons. Yale Ednl. Services, Portchester, N.Y., 1973-74; personnel asst. Dun & Bradstreet, N.Y.C., 1974-77; mgr. personnel services, 1977-80; dir. human resources Moody's Investors Services, N.Y.C., 1980—; dir. Word-Tex, N.Y.C., 1982—; mem. Sr. Employment Adv. Council, N.Y.C. Dept. Aging, 1982—. Mem. Am. Soc. Personnel Adminstrn. (legis. liaison 1983-85, dir. 1985-86, chmn. profl. devel. seminars 1985-86). Republican. Home: 170 E 77th St New York NY 10021 Office: Moodys Investors Service 99 Church St New York NY 10007

DORMIRE, SHARON LEE, nurse, nursing educator; b. Clearfield, Pa., July 4, 1954; d. Paul Bruce and Gertrude Mae (Livergood) Kyler; m. Rodman Lisle Dormire, May 21, 1977. Diploma Williamport (Pa.) Hosp. Sch. Nursing, 1975; B.S. in Nursing magna cum laude, Indiana U. of Pa., 1982; postgrad. Va. Commonwealth U., 1984—. R.N., Pa. Staff nurse, prenatal instr. Maple Avenue Hosp., DuBois, Pa., 1975-76, Sacred Heart Hosp., Cumberland, Md., 1976-78; inservice instr. Meml. Hosp., Cumberland, 1979-80; staff nurse Latrobe (Pa.) Hosp., 1980-81; nursing instr. St. Margaret Hosp., Pitts., 1982-84. Recipient Leadership award Williamsport Hosp. Sch. Nursing, 1975. Mem. Nat. League Nursing, Am. Nurses Assn., Sigma Theta Tau, Epsilon Sigma Alpha (pres. Alpha Delta chpt. 1982-84, treas. Md. council 1983-84, pres. 1984-85, Girl of Yr. award 1983). Home: 1545-E Honey Grove Dr Richmond VA 23229

DORN, JENNIFER LYNN, government official; b. Grande Island, Nebr., Dec. 7, 1950; d. Harold Clarence and Ethel Agnes D.; m. David James Oldfield (div. 1980). B.A., Oreg. State U., 1973, M.F.A., U. Conn., 1977. Account exec. J.R. Tendler Assocs., Woodbridge, Conn., 1974-75; legis. asst. to Senator Mark Hatfield, Washington, 1977-81; mem. staff Senate Appropriations Com., Washington, 1981-83; spl. asst. to Sec. Dept. Transp., Washington, 1983-84; dir. Comml. Space Transp., Washington, 1984-85; assoc. dep. sec. U.S. Dept. Transp., 1985—. Mem. Washington Women's Network (bd. dirs. 1982-85), Nat. Space Club (bd. dirs. 1985—), Women's Transp. Seminar, Oreg. Women's Forum, Astrolaw Adv. Com. Republican. Lutheran. Home: 2248 Washington Ave Apt 103 Silver Spring MD 20910

DORN, MARIAN MARGARET, educator, sports management administrator; b. North Chicago, Ill., Sept. 25, 1931; d. John and Marian (Petkovsek) Jelovsek; m. Eugene G. Dorn, Aug. 2, 1952 (div. 1975); 1 child, Bradford Jay. B.S., U. Ill., 1953; M.S., U. So. Calif., 1961. Tchr., North Chicago Community High Sch., 1954-56; tchr., advisor activities, high sch., Pico-Rivera, Calif., 1956-62; tchr., coach Calif. High Sch., Whittier, 1962-65, prof. phys. edn., chmn. dept., coach, asst. chmn. div. women's athletic dir. Cypress (Calif.) Coll., 1966 ; mgr. Billie Jean King Tennis Ctr., Long Beach, Calif., 1982-86, founder King-Dorn Golf Schs., Long Beach, 1984; staff mem. FMS Assocs., Long Beach; pres. So. Calif. Athletic Conf., 1981. Recipient cert. of merit Cypress Elem. Sch. Dist., 1976; Outstanding Service award Cypress Coll., 1986. Mem. Calif. (v.p. So. dist.), San Gabriel Valley (pres.) assns. health, phys. edn. and recreation, So. Calif. Community Coll. Athletic Council (sec., dir. pub. relations), NEA, Calif. Tchrs. Assn., AAHPER, Ladies Profl. Golf Assn. Republican. Conglist. Author: Bowling Manual, 1974. Home: 21321 Norwalk #146 Hawaiian Gardens CA 90716 Office: 9200 Valley View Cypress CA 90630

DORNER, IRENE MARIE-THERESE, medical technologist; b. Los Angeles, Jan. 6, 1934; d. Otto Urban and Erna Johanna (Schüle) Wilhelm; m. Robert W. Dorner, June 27, 1954 (div. 1977); children—Samuel Robert, Jessica Anne. B.A. in Bacteriology, UCLA, 1957. Cert., lic. med. technologist, Calif. Med. technologist Riverside Community Hosp. (Calif.), 1957-58; sr. med. technologist hematology San Bernardino Community Hosp. (Calif.), 1958-62; supr. blood bank Jewish Hosp., St. Louis, 1962-64; supr. blood bank Barnes Hosp., St. Louis, 1965-79, instr. Sch. Anesthesiology, 1970-79; instr. blood bank specialist program Washington U. Med. Ctr., St. Louis, 1968-79; clin. instr. dept. allied health service St. Louis U., 1968, dept. pathology, 1980—; mgr. lab. services Hosp. Div. City of St. Louis, 1980—; lectr. profl. assns., workshops, seminars. Contbr. articles to publs. in field. Cub master St. Louis council Boy Scouts Am., St. Louis, 1978-79; mem. Soc. for Preservation of Health, St. Louis, 1983—. Recipient L. Jean Stubbins award S. Central Assn. Blood Banks, 1975. Mem. Am. Assn. Clin. Pathologists, Am. Assn. Blood Banks (insp. 1975-80), Heart of Am. Assn. Blood Banks (pres. 1969-70, v.p. 1982-83), Clin. Lab. Mgmt. Assn., ARC (med. adv. bd. 1973-79, tech. adv. bd. 1974-79). Republican. Roman Catholic. Home: 42 Aberdeen Pl Clayton MO 63105 Office: Snodgras Lab 1606 Grattan Saint Louis MO 63104

DORNER, SHARON A. HADDON, educator; b. Morristown, N.J., Nov. 3, 1943; d. William P. and Eleanor (Dygert) Haddon; B.A. in Bus. Edn., Montclair State Coll., 1965, M.A. in Bus. Edn., 1970, M.A. in Guidance and Counseling, 1978; Ed.D. in Vocat.-Tech. Edn., Adminstrn. and Supervision, Rutgers U., 1982; children—Wendy, Meridith. Tchr., Morris Knolls High Sch., 1965-70; tchr. Katherine Gibbs Sec. Sch., Montclair, N.J., 1973-74; tchr. Leonia (N.J.) High Sch., 1974-75; tchr. bus. Woodcliff Sch., Woodcliff Lake, N.J., 1976—, adminstrv. intern to supt., 1980—; tchr. adult sch. Sussex Vocat. Sch., County Coll. Morris, Randolph, N.J. Judge, Election Bd., Montclair, 1972-82. Mem. Assn. Supervision and Curriculum Devel., Am. Vocat. Assn., Am. Vocat. Research Assn., N.J. Vocat. Assn., NEA, N.J. Edn. Assn., Bergen County Edn. Assn., Woodcliff Lake Edn. Assn. (sec. 1976—), N.J. Bus. Edn. Assn., Nat. Bus. Edn. Assn., Eastern Bus. Tchrs. Assn., Consumers League (dir. 1979—), N.J. Coalition Ednl. Leaders (treas. 1983—, Northeastern regional rep. 1982-83), Northeast Coalition Ednl. Leaders, Delta Pi Epsilon (pres. Beta Phi chpt. 1979-80, v.p. 1978-79, sec. 1976-78, newsletter editor 1974-76, nat. com. 1980-84, nat. council rep. 1981—, chmn. nat. com. 1982-84), Sigma Kappa (nat. alumnae province officer 1977-81, nat. alumnae dist. dir. 1981—), Phi Delta Kappa (pres. 1980-82 treas. 1975-79, 82—, council del. 1977-80), Omicron Tau Theta. Clubs: Daus. of Nile, N.J. Eastern Star. Mem. adv. bd. Today's Sec., 1981-82. Home: 28 College Ave Upper Montclair NJ 07043 Office: 134 Woodcliff Ave Woodcliff Lake NJ 07675

DORO, MARION ELIZABETH, political scientist, educator; b. Miami, Fla., Oct. 9, 1928; d. George and Alma (Carram) D.; B.A., Fla. State U., 1951, M.A., 1952; Ph.D. (Bennett fellow), U. Pa., 1959. Instr. polit. sci. Wheaton Coll., Norton, Mass., 1958-60; Ford Found. Area Studies fellow U. London, Kenya, Africa, 1960-62; asst. prof. Conn. Coll., New London, 1962-65, assoc. prof., 1965-70, prof., 1970—, now Lucy Marsh Haskell prof., dir. grad. studies, 1975-79, chmn. dept. govt., 1981—; Fulbright fellow Makerere U., Kampala, Uganda, 1963-64; vis. research fellow, Am. Philos. Soc. grantee East Africa Inst. Social Sci. Research, 1971-72; sr. research fellow Radcliffe Inst., Cambridge, Mass., 1968-69; sr. assoc. St. Anthony's Coll., Oxford U., 1977-78; vis. faculty Africa Research Program, Yale U., 1984-85. AAUW Am. fellow, 1977-78. Mem. Am., New Eng. (chmn. status women com. 1972-75, exec. council 1973-75), Northeast (exec. council 1974-76, 82-84) polit. sci. assns., African Studies Assn. (dir. program nat. meetings 1976), AAUP, AAUW, Soc. Fellows Bunting Inst. of Radcliffe Coll. (exec. bd., co-chairperson), Phi Beta Kappa, Phi Kappa Phi, Pi Sigma Alpha. Editor: (with N. Stultz) Governing in Black Africa, 1970, 2d edit., 1986; Rhodesia/Zimbabwe: A Bibliographic Guide to the Nationalist Period, 1984; mem. editorial bd. African Studies Rev.; contbr. articles and book revs. to profl. jours. Office: Conn Coll Box 1457 New London CT 06320

DOROUGH, ALLIE CLAIRE COOPER, club woman; b. Columbiana, Ala., Jan. 19, 1929; d. Boling Zachariah and Amy Mae (Brunson) Cooper; m. Talmadge Jackson Dorough, Apr. 14, 1950; children—Larry Jack, Kerrye Claire. B.S., Stamford U., 1950. Geneal. researcher, complier histories Brunson, Blanchard, DuBose, Cooper, Looney, Pinckney, Brooks, Clark, and Dorough families; mem. Ala. Hist. Commn., 1978—, Jefferson County Republican Women's Club, 1960—. Mem. Magna Charta Dames, Daus. Am. Colonies (chpt. chmn.), DAR (organizing regent Josiah Brunson chpt. 1974, state chmn. 1979—, pres. Jefferson County regents council 1975), Ala. DAR Officers Club, Ala. Soc. Children Am. Revolution (sr. 1st v.p.), UDC (officer Ala. div. 1981-83, organizing pres. Johnny Reb chpt., dist. dir., 1981-84, 1st v.p.), Officers Club Ala. Div. UDC, Children of Confederacy (organizing dir. Johnny Reb chpt. 1981—), U.S. Daus. 1812 (1st v.p. Ala. soc., treas. Ala. soc. officers club, pres. Ala. charter chpt. 1982-85), Huguenot Soc. of Colony of Manakin in Colony of Va. (hon. pres. Ala. br. 1978—), Dames Ct. of Honor (hon. pres. Ala. soc. 1981-83), Sons and Daus. Pilgrims (gov. Ala. br. 1981-84), Nat. Soc. So. Dames Am. (pres. Ala. soc. 1984—), Daus. Founders and Patriots Am. (treas. Ala. chpt.), Huguenot Soc. Ala. (treas. 1983-85), Birmingham Geneal. Soc. (officer 1981), Colonial Dames XVII Century (pres. George Maris chpt. 1983-85), Ala. Soc. Colonial Dames XII Century Officers Club, Trussville Hist. Soc. (an organizer), Shelby County Hist. Soc., Jefferson County Pharm. Assn. Aux. (past pres.), Ala. Pharm. Assn. Aux. (state chmn.), Nat. Assn. Retail Druggists Aux., Garden Club (officer), Phi Mu. Methodist. Home: 831 Rose Dr Birmingham AL 35235

DORR, LORNA BITGOOD, librarian; b. New London, Conn., May 2, 1941; d. Royal Earl and Frances Allen (Minson) Bitgood; m. Darwin Dorr, Apr. 25, 1964 (div. Mar. 1984); children—Benjamin Paul, Christopher Joseph. B.A., Alfred U., 1963; postgrad. U. Coll., Washington U., St. Louis, 1973-74, Mars Hill Coll., 1980-82; M.L.S., U.S.C., 1985. Elem. music tchr., Newburgh (N.Y.) Public Schs., 1963-65; library asst. R. M. Strozier Library, Fla. State U., 1965-67, acting head circulation div., 1968-69; book orderer dept. ind. study U. Minn., 1967-68; swimming instr. Asheville (N.C.) YWCA, 1978; circulation supr. Meml. Library, Mars Hill Coll., 1979-82; chief reference asst. Ramsey Library U. N.C., Asheville, 1982-85; reference librarian Western Carolina U., 1986—. Mem. Brevard (N.C.) Chamber Orch., 1979-84; mem. Asheville Symphony, 1981-83; former mem. bd. dirs., com. chmn. Community Center for Arts, Asheville. Mem. ALA, N.C. Library Assn., Western N.C. Library Assn. Episcopalian. Home: 54 Briarwood Rd Asheville NC 28804

DORSCH, ROBERTA FUNK, association executive; b. Balt., July 9, 1943; d. Edward Joseph and Roberta E. (Harris) Funk; student U. Md., 1961-63; cert. Johns Hopkins Hosp. Sch. Cytotechnology, 1967; m. Dennis Edward Dorsch, Apr. 26, 1969; 1 dau., Brenda Jean. Staff cytotechnologist Johns Hopkins Hosp., Balt., 1962-69, Meml. Hosp. Easton (Md.), 1969-71; sr. cytotechnologist Johns Hopkins Hosp., 1971-75, VA Hosp., Balt., 1975-78, Sacred Heart Hosp., Cumberland, Md., 1978-80; field dir. Shawnee Girl Scout Council, Martinsburg, W.Va., 1981—; tchr. swimming Cash Valley Sch., La Vale, Md., 1981—; tchr. water ballet Cumberland Dept. Parks and Recreation, 1980-82, Frostburg Dept. Recreation, 1983—. Bd. dirs. Allegany County unit Am. Cancer Soc., 1979-81, 82—, mem. pub. edn. com. Md. div., 1984—; exec. com. PTA, Cash Valley Elem. Sch., 1980-82; mem. rev. bd. selections com. Allegany/Garrett County Foster Care, 1986—; active youth activities Ellerslie United Meth. Ch., 1979— mem. Allegany County Children's Council, 1984—, pres., 1985-86; active Allegany County Chem. People, 1983-85, Md. Alcohol Drug Resource Team of Allegany County, 1985—. Mem. Am. Soc. Cytology, Md. Assn. Cytotechnologists (pres. 1974-76), Am. Soc. Clin. Pathologists, Am. Soc. Cytotechnologists. Clubs: Frostburg Badminton (v.p. 1981-82). Republican. Roman Catholic. Contbr. articles to profl. jours. Address: PO Box 358 Ellerslie MD 21529

DORSETT, CORA MATHENY, librarian; b. Camden, Ark., July 15, 1921; d. Walter Stanton and Cora (Smith) Matheny; B.S. in Edn. summa cum laude, Centenary Coll. La., 1963; M.S. in L.S. (Grad. fellow), U. Miss., 1965, Ph.D., 1972; postgrad. U. Okla., 1973. Tchr. pub. schs., Shreveport, La., 1963-64; dir. Pine Bluff and Jefferson County Pub. Library, Pine Bluff, Ark., 1965—. Bd. dirs. Pine Bluff Community Art Center, 1966-67; mem. steering com. Pine Bluff-Jefferson County Am. Revolution Bicentennial Celebration, 1975-76. Recipient Social Sci. award Chi Omega, 1963. Mem. Am., Ark., Southeastern library assns., Jefferson County Hist. Assn., Kappa Delta Pi, Phi Delta Kappa, Alpha Chi. Episcopalian. Home: 1305 W 35th Ave Pine Bluff AR 71603 Office: 200 E 8th Ave Pine Bluff AR 71601

DORSEY, DOROTHY JEAN, hospital official; b. Orange, Tex., Feb. 3, 1947; d. Richard Joshua Dorsey and Rosa Mary (Williams) Dorsey Alex. B.S., Grambling U., 1969; postgrad. in bus. adminstrn. Century U., Beverly Hills, Calif., 1985—. Dietary interviewer research div. Children's Hosp., Columbus, Ohio, 1969-70; supervising dietitian Rockland Psychiat. Ctr., Orangeburg, N.Y., 1970-74; dir. food service Community Gen. Hosp. of Sullivan County, Monticello, N.Y., 1974-78; asst. mgr. Gino's Restaurant, Caldwell, N.J., 1978-80; asst. dir. food service St. Mary's Hosp., Passaic, N.J., 1980—. Del. Young Democrats Assn., Monticello, 1974-78. Mem. Am. Dietetic Assn., Nutrition Today Soc., Am. Soc. Food Service Adminstrs. Democrat. Baptist. Home: PO Box 221 Clifton NJ 07011

DORSEY, NINA CLAIRE TABOR, banker, business executive; b. Arabi, Ga., Feb. 26, 1917; d. Fred Cox and Irene (Tuck) Tabor; m. James B. Dorsey, Oct. 10, 1937 (dec. Dec. 1959); children—James Elliot, Alec Glenn. A.B., Wesleyan Coll., Macon, Ga., 1937. Lic. funeral dir., Ga.; lic. tchr., Ga. Funeral dir. Dorsey Funeral Home, Abbeville, Ga., 1937-57; owner, operator Dorsey Realty, Wilcox & Crisp Counties, Ga., 1938—; self-employed ins. agt., Abbeville, 1950—; pres., chmn. bd., cashier Dorsey State Bank, Abbeville, 1957-86, ret.; oil jobber Phillips Petroleum Co., Dorsey Oil Co. Inc., Abbeville, 1959—. Pres. Abbeville Woman's Club; active Abbeville PTA, including pres.; active various community fundraising drives; v.p. Woman's Missionary Soc., Abbeville, including; treas. Little River Bapt. Assn., Wilcox County, Ga. Recipient Community Service award Phillips Petroleum Co.; Wilcox County Woman of Yr., 1985. Mem. Ga. Bankers Assn. (chmn. women's div. dist.), Ga. Pvt. bankers Assn. (sec.), Ind. Bankers Assn., Nat. Bankers Assn., Ga. Oilmen's Assn., Nat. Oilmen's Assn., Nat. Fedn. Ind. Bus. (dist. chmn.). Democrat. Lodge: Lionesses (bd. dirs., fin. chmn. local club, v.p. 1985-86). Avocation: sports. Home: PO Box 338 Abbeville GA 31001 Office: Dorsey State Bank Abbeville GA 31001

DORSEY, OLIVIA BETTY, purchasing executive; b. Pitts., Sept. 13, 1948; d. Lenwood and Lillian Allise (Bailey) Washington Robinson; m. Jimmy Dorsey, Dec. 29, 1970; children—Eric Lee, James Starlin, Chad Demonn. Student Allegheny Community Coll., 1966-67, Coll. of DuPage, 1969-70, Robert Moser Bus. Sch., 1969, Harper Coll., 1979-80. Sec., Internat. Harvester Co., Schaumburg, Ill., 1974-75, inventory control clk., 1975-76, adminstrv. asst., 1976-77, employee relations, 1977-79, material scheduler, 1979-81, corp. buyer, 1981—. Steward J.W. James Meml. A.M.E. Ch., 1982—, ofcl. bd. 1981—, pres. choir, 1982—. Mem. Nat. Assn. Female Execs. Office: Internat Harvester Co 600 Woodfield Schaumburg IL 60196

DORSEY, RHODA MARY, college president; b. Dorchester, Mass., Sept. 9, 1927; d. Thomas Francis and Hedwig (Hoge) D.; B.A., Smith Coll., 1949, LL.D., 1979; B.A., Newnham Coll., Cambridge, 1951, M.A., 1954; Ph.D., U. Minn., 1956; LL.D., Nazareth Coll. of Rochester, 1970; D.H.L. (hon.), Mt. St. Mary's Coll., 1976, Mt. Vernon Coll., 1979, Coll. St. Catherine, 1983; L.H.D., Johns Hopkins U., 1986. Teaching asst. U. Minn., 1951-53; faculty Goucher Coll., Towson, Md., 1954—, asst. prof., 1957-62, assoc. prof., 1962-65, prof., 1965—, asst. dean, 1962-65, dean and v.p., 1968-74, acting pres., 1973-74, pres., 1974—; vis. lectr. Monash U. and Australian Nat. U., 1966-67; mem. Middle Atlantic Dist. Com. of Selection for Rhodes Scholarship; dir. U.S. Fidelity and Guaranty Co., Chesapeake & Potomac Telephone Co., Noxell Corp., First Nat. Bank Md. Del. House of the Good Shepherd, Balt.; bd. dirs. Am. Friends of Cambridge U., 1978—, Gen. German Aged People's Home, Balt., 1984—, Greater Balt. Com. Leadership Program, 1985; trustee Ind. Coll. Funds Am., 1985—; del. UN Decade for Women Conf., 1985. Boston Globe fellow, 1949-50; Fulbright fellow, 1949-51; Fulbright-Hayes grantee, 1966-67; Outstanding Achievement award U. Minn. Alumni Assn., 1984; Outstanding Woman Mgr. of 1984, Balt. Women's Program in Mgmt. and WMAR-TV; Andrew White medal Loyola Coll. of Balt., 1985. Mem. AAUP, AAUW (fellow, 1954-55), Middle State Assn. Colls. and Schs. (pres. 1984), Md. Ind. Coll. and Univ. Assn. (chmn.), Phi Beta Kappa. Clubs: Smith of Balt., Hamilton St. (Balt.), Cosmopolitan of N.Y. Office: Goucher Coll Towson MD 21204

DORSHER, STEPHANIE ANN, editor; b. Beach, N.D., Mar. 11, 1955; d. Edmund Francis and Doris Mae (Elston) Kukowski; m. Charles David Dorsher, June 5, 1976; children: Stella Annastatia, Delilah Mae, Madonna Danielle. B.S. in Edn., U. N.D., 1978. Elem. music tchr. Visitation Convent Sch., St. Paul, 1978-79; asst. product librarian Comserv Corp., Mendota Heights, Minn., 1979-80, tech. librarian, Eagan, Minn., 1980-82, corp. librarian, 1982-85, tech. editor, 1985—. Cons., vol. Holy Trinity Sch., St. Paul, 1983—. Mem. Minn. On-Line User's Group (membership chmn. 1983—), Spl. Libraries Assn. Republican. Roman Catholic. Office: Comserv Corp 3400 Comserv Dr Eagan MN 55122

DOSER, JANICE MARIE, nurse; b. Yankton, S.D., Nov. 27, 1941; d. Harold Henry and Loretta Agnes (Engle) Sonnenfield; B.S. in Nursing, Coll. St. Teresa, Winona, Minn., 1963; postgrad. U. Wis., LaCrosse, summers 1974, 75; m. Robert Francis Doser, Aug. 23, 1969; children—Andrew, Laura, James, Thomas, Sara. Staff nurse St. Mary's Hosp., Rochester, Minn., 1963-64, head nurse, 1964-66, instr. psychiat. nursing, 1966-69; asst. instr. nursing U. Utah, 1969-72; asst. instr. psychiat. nursing Viterbo Coll., LaCrosse, 1973-76; public health nurse State of Wyo., 1976-77; part-time staff nurse Sweetwater Meml. Hosp., Rock Springs, Wyo., 1978-79, 81-83; instr. extended degree program registered nurses U. Wyo., 1979-85. Mem. Am. Nurses Assn., Wyo. Nurses Assn., Dist. 6 Nurses Assn. (treas.). Democrat. Roman Catholic. Club: Rock Springs Swim (sec.). Home: 1108 Hilltop Dr Rock Springs WY 82901

DOSS, DONNA SUE, software engineer; b. Dearborn, Mich., June 18, 1961; d. Norman Eugene and Carolyn Ann (Weber) Caldwell; m. Robert James Doss, May 22, 1982. B.S., Eastern Mich. U., 1984. Computer programmer Morgan Electric, Inc., Southfield, Mich., 1984-85; software engr. Volvo Automated Systems, Sterling Heights, Mich., 1985—. Mem. Nat. Assn. Female Execs., Inc., Golden Key, Phi Kappa Phi. Presbyterian. Avocations: tennis; reading. Home: 7962 Harding St Taylor MI 48180 Office: Volvo Automated Systems 7000 Nineteen Mile Rd Sterling Heights MI 48078

DOSS, JUDITH HARRIS, country club executive; b. Memphis, Dec. 7, 1934; d. Wiley Chasteen and Irene Randle (Hodges) Harris; student Memphis State U., 1952-53, seminars U. Tenn., Nashville, 1971-76, Tenn. State U., 1978-81, Vanderbilt U., 1982, Gourmet's Oxford (Eng.) Center for Mgmt. Studies, 1982, Lo Scaldavivande Cooking Sch., Rome, 1983; m. Leslie Doss, Jr., 1953 (div. 1973); children—Leslie Walter III, Randle Elizabeth. Sec., receptionist James W. Stewart, investor, Dixie Oil Co., 1971-75; food service dir. The Webb Sch., Bell Buckle, Tenn., 1976-83; mgr. Plantation Country Club, Pharr, Tex., 1983—; mem. 3d Nat. Conf. Nutrition, 1980, Nat. Food Policy Conf., Washington, 1982. Pres. Hillwood Presbyn. Ch. Women, Nashville, 1968-70; mem. Nashville Symphony Guild. Mem. Colonial Dames Am. (chpt. dir. 1981-83), Ladies Hermitage Assn. (life), Cheekwood Fine Arts Center, Assn. Tenn. Antiquities, Nat. Assn. Female Execs., Club Mgrs. Assn. Am., Pharr C. of C., Tex. Restaurant Assn., Orgn. Women Execs. (v.p. 1986-87), DAR, Alpha Gamma Delta. Clubs: Shelbyville Women's, Zonta (chpt. bd. dirs. 1986—). Contbr. to The Webb Cookbook, 1977, 79. Home: 2729 Ashley Ct Pharr TX 78577 Office: Plantation Country Club 2503 Palmer Dr Pharr TX 78577

DOSSETT, BETTY JO, retired government official; b. Laurel, Miss., Sept. 14, 1931; d. James Daniel and Mary Allen (Ishee) Mooney; B.S., U. So. Miss., 1953, M.Ed., 1972; m. James Roland Dossett, Apr. 5, 1952 (div. Apr. 1974); children—Linda Gail, Mark Richard. Social ins. rep. Social Security Adminstrn., Hattiesburg, Miss., 1960-66, Holiday, Fla., 1976-78, Dallas, 1978-83, ret., 1983; bus. cons. to Paul Stephen Lee, concert organist, 1976-81. Tchr., coordinator high sch. Sunday sch. Main St. Baptist Ch., Hattiesburg, 1962-66, 69-71; bd. dirs. aux. So. Bapt. Women's Missionary Union, Whitehaven Bapt. Ch., Memphis, 1966-67. Recipient Fed. Employee Recognition award Tampa Bay Fed. Exec. Assn., 1977, 15-Yrs. Service award Social Security Adminstrn., 1979, Presdl. Achievement award, 1982. Mem. U. So. Miss. Alumni Assn. Home: 209 S 24th Ave Hattiesburg MS 39401

DOSSETT, SANDRA NEWMAN, nurse; b. Henderson, Ky., Oct. 10, 1954; d. William Houston and Lyda Mae (Duncan) Newman; m. John Beverly Dossett, Mar. 28, 1975. A.S. in Nursing, Henderson Community Coll., 1974; B.S. in Nursing, U. Evansville, 1982, M.S. in Nursing, 1985. Cert. operating room nurse. With Community Methodist Hosp., Henderson, 1975—, asst. supr. surgery, 1977-82, diabetic educator, 1982-85, quality assurance coordinator, 1985—; instr. CPR. Robert H. English scholar Henderson Community Coll., 1972. Mem. Am. Assn. Diabetic Educators, N.Y. Acad. Scis., Nat. Assn. Quality Assurance Profls., Sigma Theta Tau. Democrat. Baptist. Home: 2243 Melwood Dr Henderson KY 42420 Office: Community Methodist Hosp 1305 N Elm St Henderson KY 42420

DOTSON, CHERYL LANIER, accountant, city official; b. Houston, July 7, 1954; d. Samuel W. and Elise (Nobles) Dotson. B.B.A. magna cum laude, U. Houston, 1976. Mgr. mgmt. cons. dept. Peat, Marwick, Mitchell & Co., Houston, 1976-84; dir. fiscal affairs Houston Police Dept., 1984—. Bd. dirs. fin. com. Vocat. Guidance Service, Houston, 1980; vice chmn. bd. dirs., 1982-83; mem. City Houston Ethics Com., 1982-84; lectr. Blacks and Math., Houston, 1981-84. Mem. Tex. Soc. C.P.A.s, Am. Inst. C.P.A.s, Nat. Assn. Black Accts., Delta Sigma Theta, Phi Kappa Phi. Democrat. Baptist. Lodge: Mem. Order Eastern Star. Home: 206 Plaza Verde Dr Condo E-32 Houston TX 77038 Office: City of Houston 61 Reisner St Houston TX 77002

DOTSON, LINDA DELORISE, radio station executive; b. Toccoa, Ga., May 12, 1942; d. Roy L. Keller and Minnie Lee P. (Hunter) K. m. Vaughn Franlin Dotson, Nov. 11, 1961; children—Kertina Lynn, Tammy Louise. Student Brenau Coll., 1984-85. With The Times, Gainesville, Ga., 1963-66; with advt. dept. Sta. WGGA, Gainesville, 1967-77, advt. mgr., 1977-78; ptnr., gen. mgr. WLBA Radio, Gainesville, 1978—; tchr. broadcast mgmt. Brenau Coll., 1986. Group leader Camp Fire Orgn., Gainesville, 1968-76, dir., 1977-78; mem. publicity com. Emmanuel Bapt. Ch., 1976-85, Sunday Sch. tchr., 1978-85. Mem. N.E. Ga. Advt. Club, Women in Communications, Ga. Assn. Broadcasters. Democrat. Clubs: Oakwood Booster. Avocations: decorating; sewing; gardening; landscaping; remodeling. Address: WLBA 303 W Washington St Gainesville GA 30501

DOTY, DELLA CORRINE, financial consultant; b. Marshalltown, Iowa, Apr. 12, 1945; d. Edwin Francis and Della Edna (Keller) Mack; B.S.B.A. in Acctg., Drake U., 1967; m. Philip Edward Doty, Dec. 23, 1967; children—Sarah Corrine, Anne Elizabeth. Audit staff Alexander Grant & Co., C.P.A.s, Denver, 1967-71; controller Valley View Hosp. and Med. Center, Denver, 1971-75; rate rev. specialist Colo. Hosp. Assn., Denver, 1975-79; pvt. fin. cons., Littleton, Colo., 1979—; lectr. in field. Dir., asst. treas. YWCA of Metro Denver, 1972-74; dir. Colo. Heart Assn., 1974-82; active Jr. League of Denver, 1979—, v.p. mktg., 1985-86; sec. Littleton Pub. Schs. Bldg. Authority, 1983-86; active various charitable orgns.; v.p. fin. and housing Alpha Phi Internat., 1974-78, trustee, 1980—; dir., treas. Alpha Phi Found., 1978—. Recipient Founders Merit award Healthcare Fin. Mgmt. Assn., 1976, 83, Outstanding Vol. award Jr. League of Denver, 1984; C.P.A., Colo. Mem. Am. Inst. C.P.A.s, Colo. Soc. C.P.A.s, Hosp. Fin. Mgmt. Assn., Alpha Phi (Ursa Major award 1980). Republican. Baptist. Contbr. articles to profl. jours. Address: 5981 S Coventry Ln W Littleton CO 80123

DOTY, KATHLYN ELAINE, university official; b. Oak Park, Ill., Jan. 12, 1948; d. Paul Stephen and Helen May (Henderson) Mackey; M.B.A., U. Chgo., 1979; m. Richard Lee Doty, Nov. 27, 1973. Programmer trainee Time-Life, Inc., Chgo., 1967-68; jr. systems analyst Aldens Inc., Chgo., 1968-69, sr. systems analyst, 1969-71, project mgr., 1971-76; self-employed data processing cons., Chgo., 1976-78; dir. systems devel. Loyola U. Chgo., 1978—, bd. dirs., chmn. membership and edn. com. Loyola U. Employees' Fed. Credit Union, 1979—. Mem. Coll. and Univ. Systems Exchange (dir. 1984—), Nat. Assn. Female Execs., Assn. Systems Mgmt., Assn. Women in Computing (v.p. Chgo. chpt. 1981-82, pres. 1983-84), Assn. Computer Users. Home: PO Box 919 Oak Park IL 60303 Office: 2160 S 1st Ave Maywood IL 60153

DOUGHERTY, BONNIE JOAN, property management company executive; b. Newark, Dec. 20, 1950; d. William Martin and Alice Ella (Campbell) D. B.A. in Psychology, Maonmouth Coll., 1971. Lic. real estate broker, Colo., N.Mex.; lic. real estate salesman, Ariz. Asst. mgr. Viewmont Village Apts., Scranton, Pa., 1972-74; resident mgr. Levering & Reid, Houston, 1976-78; v.p. Allen Assocs., Denver, 1978-83; v.p. adminstrn. Arthur Assocs., Albuquerque, 1983; regional property mgr. Empire West Cos., Tucson, 1984; property supr. Evans Withycombe, Tucson, 1985—; instr. Nat. Apt. Assn., Denver, 1981-83, El Paso, Tex., 1984. Pres., Pier Point Homeowners Assn., Aurora, Colo., 1982. Mem. Nat. Assn. Female Execs., Ariz. Multi Housing Assn., Nat. Apt. Assn., Inst. Real Estate Mgmt. (cert. property mgr. 1983). Lodge: Eastern Star. Avocations: swimming; collecting Southwest Indian Art. Office: Evans Withycombe 1580 N Kolb #210 Tucson AZ 85715

DOUGHERTY, ELEANOR CARTON, farming and real estate development owner, educator, writer; b. Chgo., July 17, 1947; d. William Holmes and Eleanor Jane (Simons) D.; m. Michael Marion Kostiuk, Oct. 14, 1972 (div. 1984); 1 child, Damian. B.A. in Spanish, U. Colo., 1969; M.S. in Adult Literacy, U. Pa., 1983. Tchr. Town Sch. for Boys, San Francisco, 1970-72, St. Mark's Sch. Tex., Dallas, 1973-75; founder, asst. dir. Esperanza Sch., Houston, 1977-79; instr. Community Coll. Phila., 1980-82; lectr. Drexel U., Phila., 1982-85; owner farming and real estate devel., Santa Fe, N.Mex., 1985—; bus. ptnr. Christina Bergh Tapestries and Textiles, Santa Fe, 1986—; also writer; cons. writing Phila. area businesses, 1981-85; staff dir. bus. writing dept. humanities and communications Drexel U., 1983-85; reviewer tech. and acad. jour., publs., 1984—; cons. edn. various adult community services, Phila., 1981-85. Author: Texas Anthology of Poetry, 1976. Journalist, corr. Am. Photographer Mag., 1978-79; curator photography exhibit T.V. Robinson Gallery, Inc., 1979. Mem. Women In Family Owned Businesses (charter mem.), U. Pa. Grad. Sch. Edn. Alumnae Assn. (bd. dirs. 1983-85), Nat. Council Tchrs. English, Kappa Delta Pi. Democrat. Avocations: photography, painting, collecting American works of art. Home: 630 E Alameda St Santa Fe NM 87501

DOUGHERTY, JUNE EILEEN, librarian; b. Union City, N.J., Mar. 27, 1929; d. Robert John and Jane Veronica (Smith) Beyrer; B.A. in Edn., Paterson State Coll., 1967; postgrad. Rutgers U. Sch. Library Sci., 1959-69; m. Donald E. Dougherty, Dec. 2, 1946; 1 son, Glen Allan. With A. B. Dumont, Paterson, N.J., 1950-54; sch. librarian St. Paul's Elementary Sch., Prospect Park, N.J., 1957—; dir. North Haledon (N.J.) Free Pub. Library, 1957—; sec.-treas. Dougherty & Dougherty, Inc., North Haledon, 1968—. Den mother Boy Scouts Am., 1954-57; mem. Gov. N.J.'s Tercentenary Com., 1962-64. Mem. Am., N.J., N. Haledon library assns., Cath. Library Assn., N.J. Libraries Roundtable, Bergen-Passaic Library Club, Friends N. Haledon Library. Roman Catholic. Club: St. Paul's Social. Home: 155 Westervelt Ave North Haledon NJ 07508 Office: 129 Overlook Ave North Haledon NJ 07508

DOUGHERTY, LINDA SELLERS, insurance company executive; b. Wilmington, N.C., Feb. 26, 1949; d. William Rhydell and Ruby (Suggs) Sellers; m. James Macon Michaux, Aug. 17, 1968 (div. 1972); 1 child, Jessica Elizabeth Michaux; m. Patrick Michael Dougherty, Apr. 23, 1983. B.S. in Acctg., U. N. Fla., 1982. With acctg. dept. Peninsular Life Ins. Co., Jacksonville, Fla., 1966-74; acctg. mgr. GW Life Ins. Co., Jacksonville, 1974-76; asst. treas. Peninsular Title Ins. Co., Jacksonville, 1976-78; fin. dept. mgr. Sun Life Group, Atlanta, 1978-82; v.p., controller Nat. Benefit Life, N.Y.C., 1982-85; v.p. acctg. Empire Blue Cross/Blue Shield, N.Y.C., 1985—. Mem. N.Y. Ins. Accts., Am. Bus. Women's Assn., Nat. Assn. Female Execs., Soc. of Ins. Accts., Ins. Acctg. & Stats. Assn. Republican. Roman Catholic.

DOUGHERTY, MAUREEN PATRICIA, lawyer; b. Vineland, N.J., May 30, 1948; d. John Francis and Kathryn Evelyn (Mattioli) D.; m. Walter G. Scheuerman III, Aug. 21, 1971 (div. 1984); children—Kathleen Meghan, Christian Michael. B.A., Rosemont Coll., 1970; J.D., Seton Hall U., 1979; LL.M. in Taxation, NYU, 1986. Bar: N.J. 1979. With Sudler Real Estate, Chgo., 1971-73; mgr. Arlen Realty, Chgo., 1973-75; assoc. Lawrence Levitt, Esq., Millburn, N.J., 1980-82, Gutkin Miller Shapiro & Selesner, Milburn, 1982-85, Waters, McPherson, McNeill P.A., Secaucus, N.J., 1985—; asst. prof. acctg. Fairleigh Dickinson U., Madison, N.J., 1986—. Author: Testamentary Trusts, N.J. Trans. Guide, 1986. Mem. Jr. League Oranges and Short Hills, 1978-81. Mem. ABA, N.J. Bar Assn., Essex County Bar Assn. Roman Catholic. Home: 9 Essex Dr Mendham NJ 07945 Office: Waters McPherson McNeill 400 Plaza Dr Secaucus NJ 07945

DOUGHERTY, MOLLY IRELAND, organization executive; b. Austin, Tex., Oct. 3, 1949; d. John Chrysostom and Mary Ireland (Graves) D. Student Stanford U., 1968-71, Grad. Theol. Union, Berkeley, 1976; B.A., Antioch U. W., 1979. Tchr., fundraiser Oakland Community Sch., Calif., 1973-77; assoc. producer, asst. editor film Nicaragua: These Same Hands, Palo Alto, Calif., 1980; free lance journalist, translator, Nicaragua, 1981; edn1. programs dir. Found. for Open Co., Berkeley, 1982-83; assoc. producer, film: Short Circuit: Inside the Death Squads; exec. dir. Vecinos, A Tex. Inter-Am. Initiative, Austin, Tex., 1984—. Bd. dirs. Nat. Immigration Refugee and Citizenship Forum, Washington, 1985—. Home: 506 W 33d St Austin TX 78705 Office: Vecinos A Tex Inter-Am Initiative PO Box 4562 Austin TX 78765

DOUGHERTY, URSEL THIELBEULE, communications, marketing executive; b. Rotenburg, W. Ger., July 30, 1942; naturalized U.S. citizen, 1965; d. Hugo and Margarete (Marquardt) Thielbeule; B.A. summa cum laude in Polit. Sci., Cleve. State U., 1971; M.A. in Polit. Sci., U. Wis., 1972; M.B.A. in Fin., Case Western Res., 1982; m. Erich A. Eichhorn, Jan. 3, 1979. Journalist maj. daily, women's mag., Germany, 1962-66; assoc. editor Farm Chems., 1967; publs. mgr. Trabon Systems, 1967-68; research analyst Legis. Council, State of Wis., 1972; pub. relations adminstr. to mgr. pub. info. Eaton Corp., Cleve., 1972-84; dir. pub. affairs Freightliner/Mercedes-Benz Truck Co., 1984—; cons. small bus. Trustee, Lake Erie council Girl Scouts U.S.A., 1975-82, Sr. Citizen Resources, 1978-81; ambassador Jr. Achievement, 1979; steering com. YWCA Career Women of Achievement, 1981; adv. bd. Women's Career Networking, 1980-84; trustee, chmn. fin. com. Young Audience Greater Cleve., 1982-84. Mem. Women in Communications, Sales and Mktg. Execs. Cleve., Public Relations Soc. Am., Detroit Press Club, Cleve. Inst. Art, Am. Exec. Women, Pub. Affairs Council. Home: 1510 Crest Rd Cleveland Heights OH 44121 Office: Freightliner Corp PO Box 3849 Portland OR 97208

DOUGLAS, ARE'WANDA WILLIAMS, occupational therapist; b. Bossier City, La., Mar. 19, 1956; d. Charlie and Pearline (Robinson) Williams; m. William Hamilton Douglas, Mar. 9, 1985. B.S. in Occupational Therapy N.E. La. U., 1982; student La. State U., 1974-79. Staff occupational therapist Central La. State Hosp., Pineville, 1982-85; occupational therapy supr. E. La. State Hosp., Jackson, 1985; occupational therapist Our Lady of the Lake Med. Ctr., Baton Rouge, 1985—. Sec., Rapides Parish Voters League, 1984. Mem. Nat. Assn. Female Execs., La. Occupational Therapy Assn. (nominating com. 1983, 84), Am. Occupational Therapy Assn., Delta Sigma Theta (regional rep. 1980-82, exec. bd. 1980-82, membership com. 1984). Democrat. Baptist. Avocations: flute; bicycling. Home: 7221 Plank Rd PO Box 73768 Baton Rouge LA 73768 Office: 5000 Hennessy Blvd Baton Rouge LA 70831

DOUGLAS, BERNARDINE DAPHYNE, broadcasting company executive; b. Danville, Ky., Mar. 28, 1941; d. Bernard Taft and Leona (Smith) D.; m. Anthony Keith Martignon, June 19, 1978 (div. Sept. 1979); 1 dau., Tracy Leona. Student, U. Cin., 1959-62. Community affairs/news dir. Sta. WXIX-TV, Cin., 1973-74, traffic mgr., 1974; account exec. Sta. KPLR-TV, St. Louis, 1974-76, sales mgr., 1976-78; dir. sales research and spl. projects, 1978; account exec. Sta. KXOK, St. Louis, 1979-81; regional/nat. sales mgr. Sta. KMJM-FM, St. Louis, 1981-83; gen. mgr. Sta. KATZ-WZEN-FM, St. Louis, 1983—; mem. adv. bd. Black Cultural Prodns., Cin., 1973-74. Exec. producer TV program Panorama: Abortion, 1973. Mem. 1st Women's Task Force United Appeal, Cin., 1974; mem. adv. bd. Our Lady's Inn, St. Louis, 1982—. Recipient Sarah Deutsch award City of Hope, Cin., 1974. Mem. Am. Women Radio and TV (sec. 1972-74), Black Media Assn. (dir. 1973-74), Regional Commerce and Growth Assn. Office: Unity Broadcasting Network-Mo Inc 1139 Olive St Suite 303 Saint Louis MO 63101

DOUGLAS, CAMILLE MARGRETHE JENSEN, real estate development and finance executive; b. N.Y.C., Sept. 24, 1951; d. Frode and Camille (McLean (Anderson) Jensen; m. Peter R. Douglas, Mar. 10, 1984. B.A., Smith Coll., 1973; M.C.P., Harvard U., 1977. With N.Y.C. Mayor's Office of Lower Manhattan Devel., 1973-74, Arthur Erickson Architects, Vancouver, B.C., 1974-75; teaching asst. Grad. Sch. Design, Harvard U., Cambridge, Mass., 1976-77; with Morgan Stanley Realty/Brooks Harvey & Co., N.Y.C., 1977-82; corp. sr. v.p. Olympia & York Properties, N.Y.C., 1982—; lectr. Grad. Sch. Bus., Columbia U., 1980, 81, 82, Federation Internationale des Administrateurs de Biens Conseils Immobiliers Congress, 1982, Grad. Sch. Bus., Harvard U., 1983, Urban Land Inst., 1985; with Bedford Stuyvesant Restoration Corp., N.Y.C., summer 1976. Founding trustee and treas. Jordan Soc. Mem. Urban Land Inst., Real Estate Bd. N.Y. Club: Harvard of N.Y. Contbr. article to Shopping Centers Today. Office: 237 Park Ave New York NY 10117

DOUGLAS, CAROLYN JOHNSON, educator; b. Phila., June 13, 1942; d. Stephen Francis and Alberta Mays Johnson; m. Willie Turner Douglas, Oct. 10, 1970. B.S., Cheyney U., 1968; M.Edn., Antioch U., 1981. Tchr. Phila. Bd. Edn., 1970—, creator, chairperson Black History Program. Fellow Black Women's Ednl. Alliance. Democrat. Mem. African Methodist Episcopal Ch. Club: Philly Jewel (Phila.). Avocations: interior decorating; modeling. Home: 1089 Cooper Ct Voorhees NJ 08043 Office: William D Kelley Sch 28th and Oxford Sts Philadelphia PA 19121

DOUGLAS, CORINNE B., university personnel official; b. Bklyn., Mar. 11, 1935; d. Michael M. and Sylvia (Cohen) Savitt; m. Jeffrey Douglas, June 17, 1973; 1 child, Mindy. B.A. in Psychology, Marymount Manhattan Coll., 1985. Cert. alcohol counselor, employee relations. Placement counselor Snelling & Snelling, N.Y.C., 1960-66; employment mgr. Am. Heart Assn., N.Y.C., 1966-73; employment mgr. Cornell U. Med. Coll., N.Y.C., 1975-85, mgr. employment and employee relations, 1985-86, asst. personnel dir., 1986—; trainer, seminar leader pvt. practice, N.Y.C., 1983—; adv. council Katie Gibbs for N.Y.C. Dept. on Aging, 1985-86. Columnist, Corinne's Kitchen Corner, Bklyn. Graphic, 1973-75. Mem. Am. Bus. Woman's Assn. (pres. N.Y.C. chpt. 1985-86, Friendship award 1985), N.Y. Personnel Mgrs. Assn., Employment Mgrs. Assn. Democrat. Avocation: Cooking. Office: Cornell Univ Medical College 445 E 69th St New York NY 10021

DOUGLAS, CYNTHIA LYNN, pathologist; b. Appleton, Wis., Oct. 7, 1952; d. Richard Richard and Shirley Ann (Cole) Douglas. B.A. summa cum laude, Central Wash. State U., Ellensburg, 1975; M.D., U. Wash., 1978. Resident U. Wash. Med. Ctr., Seattle, 1978-82; co-dir. lab. Twin Cities Community Hosp., Templeton, Calif., 1983-85, dir., 1985—; locum tenens coroner Chelan County Coroner office, Wenatchee, Wash., 1982-83; locum tenens lab. dir. Northwest Med. Lab., Seattle, 1982-83; labs. insp. Coll. Am. Pathologists, 1982; lectr. U. Wash., high schools and community groups. Fellow Coll. Am. Pathologists; mem. Calif. Med. Assn., Am. Soc. Clin. Pathologists, Oreg. Pathology Soc., AMA, San Luis Obispo County Med. Soc., San Luis Obispo Pathology Soc., Women's Med. Soc. (utilization rev. chmn. 1985, tissue and transfusion 1983—), Templeton C. of C. Clubs: Cousteau Soc., Greenpeace. Home: 932 Walnut Dr Paso Robles CA 93446 Office: Twin Cities Community Hosp-Lab 1100 Las Tablas Rd Templeton CA 93465

DOUGLAS, JOAN COYKENDALL, financial planning agency executive; b. Torrance, Calif., Jan. 3, 1943; d. James Dan Coykendall and Helen M. (Clark) Grinnell; m. Bill Douglas Tabor, Nov. 7, 1964 (div. 1975); children—Kara Lisa, Paige Ayson; m. Francis Clark Douglas, July 24, 1976. B.A. with honors, Tex. Tech. U., 1964; M.A., N. Tex. State U., 1978; Fin. Planner, Coll. Fin. Planning, Denver, 1984. Cert. fin. planner, speech pathologist; cert-clin. competence. Secondary tchr., pub. and pvt. schs., Irving, Lubbock and Corpus Christi, Tex., 1964-67; budget analyst U.S. P.O. Dept., Washington, 1967-69; dir. pvt. sch. WestBros., DeRidder, La., 1969-72; teaching fellow N. Tex. State U., Denton, 1973-76; speech pathologist Dallas Ind. Schs., 1979-82, dist. cons., tchr., 1981-82; fin. planner Fin. Strategies, Dallas, 1982-85, Pace Fin. Group, 1985—; speaker fin. planning seminars, various civic groups. Pres., PTA, DeRidder, 1971; creator mealtime program for severely handicapped, 1980, recipient award ARC, 1981; vol. State Bd. Mental Health, Dallas, 1982. Mem. Internat. Assn. Fin. Planners (bd. dirs.), Inst. for Cert. Fin. Planners (bd. dirs.), Am. Speech and Hearing Assn., Kappa Kappa Gamma Alumnae, Phi Kappa Phi, Sigma Tau Delta. Republican. Episcopalian. Club: Young Women of Arts. Lodge: Women of Rotary. Home: 6839 Truxton Dallas TX 75231 Office: Pace Fin Group Two Lincoln Centre 5420 LBJ Freeway Suite 710 Dallas TX 75240

DOUGLAS, MARION JOAN, labor negotiator; b. Jersey City, May 29, 1940; d. Walter Stanley and Sophie Francis (Zysk) Binaski; children—Jane Dee, Alex Jay. B.A., Mich. State U., 1962; M.S.W., Sacramento State Coll., 1971; M.P.A., Calif. State U.-Sacramento, 1981. Owner, mgr. Linkletter-Totten Dance Studios, Sacramento, 1962-68, Young World of Discovery, Sacramento, 1965-68; welfare worker Sacramento County, 1964-67, welfare supr., 1968-72, child welfare supr., 1972-75, sr. personnel analyst, 1976-78, personnel program mgr., 1978-81, labor relations rep., 1981—; cons. State Dept. Health, Sacramento, 1975-76; cons. in field. Author/editor newsletter Thursday's Child, 1972-74. Presiding officer Community Resource Orgn., Fair Oaks, Calif., 1970-72; exec. bd. Foster Parent's Assn., Sacramento, 1972-75; organizer Foster Care Sch. Dist. liaison programs, 1973-75; rep. Calif. Welfare Dirs. Assn., 1975-76; county staff advisor Joint Powers Authority, Sacramento, 1978-81; mem. Mgmt. Devel. Com., Sacramento, 1979-80; vol., auctioneer KVIE Pub. TV, Sacramento, 1970-84; adv. bd. Job and Info. Resource Ctr., 1976-77; spl. adv. task force coordinator Sacramento Employment and Tng. Adv. Council, 1980-81; vol. leader Am. Lung Assn., Sacramento, 1983-86 Calif. Dept. Social Welfare ednl. stipend, 1967-68, County of Sacramento ednl. stipend, 1969-70; recipient Achievement award Nat. Assn. Counties, 1981. Mem. Mgmt. Women's Forum, Indsl. Relations Assn. No. Calif., Nat. Assn. Female Execs., Mensa. Republican. Avocations: real estate; nutrition. Home: 7812 Palmyra Dr Fair Oaks CA 95628 Office: County of Sacramento Dept Personnel Mgmt 700 H St 5th Fl Sacramento CA 95814

DOUGLAS, PAMELA JO, journalist; b. Athens, Ohio, Dec. 12, 1954; d. Charles Henry and Clara Louise (Withers) D. B.J., Ohio U., 1977. Intern news reporter Athens Messenger (Ohio), 1976, Logan (Ohio) Daily News, 1977; news reporter, photographer Parkersburg (W.Va.) Sentinel, 1977—. Provisional mem. Jr. League Parkersburg, 1984; mem. Custody Rev. Council, Dept. Human Services, Parkersburg, 1981-82; pub. relations chmn., hotline chmn., sec. Domestic Violence Coalition of Parkersburg, 1981-84; mem. pub. affairs com. YWCA. Mem. Ohio Valley Press Club (sec. 1984), Sigma Delta Chi. Home: 1202-A Lockwood St Belpre OH 45714

DOUGLAS-HAMILTON, NATALIE WALES (LADY MALCOLM DOUGLAS-HAMILTON), civic, patriotic orgn. exec.; b. Cohasset, Mass., Aug. 8, 1909; d. Nathaniel and Enid Mariner (Scarritt) Wales; student pvt. schs., N.Y.C.; Dr. Humanities (hon.), Rollins Coll., 1942; m. Kenelm Winslow, 1929; children—Natalie Winslow Burnett, Mary Chilton Winslow Mead; m. 2d, Edward Latham, 1937; m. 3d, Edward Bragg Paine, 1947 (dec. 1950); m. 4th, Lord Malcolm Douglas-Hamilton, 1953 (dec. 1964). Founder, pres. Bundles for Britain, 1939-42, Bundles For Am., 1939-42, Bundles for Bluejackets, 1939-42; asst. to publisher N.Y. Times, 1942-47; founder, pres. Common Cause, Inc., 1947-51; founder Citizens for Freedom, Inc., 1956; founder House of Good Taste exhibit N.Y. World's Fair, 1962-64; founder, pres. Center of Am. Living, Inc., 1966-71; pres. Am.-Scottish Found., Inc., N.Y.C., 1965—; founder, pres. Com. to United Am., Inc., 1971—. Decorated Comdr. British Empire. Mem. DAR. Republican. Episcopalian. Home: 174 E 74th St New York NY 10021 Office: PO Box 537 Lenox Hill Station New York NY 10021

DOUGLASS, DONNA NIKSCH, business executive; b. Joplin, Mo., Aug. 4, 1945; d. Donald Edward and Ruth Angelus (Nagel) D.; B.S., Ind. U., 1969, M.S., 1971; postgrad. Emory U., 1972-73, Ga. State U., 1974-75; m. Merrill E. Douglass, June 5, 1971; 2 daus., Jennifer Ruth, Kathryn Victoria. Teaching asst. N. Ga. Coll., 1974, 75; assoc. dir. Time Mgmt. Center, Grandville, Mich., 1971—, v.p., 1980—; tchr., cons. on time mgmt. Mem. Nat. Speakers Assn. Author: Manage Your Time, Manage Your Work, Manage Yourself, 1980; Choice & Compromise: A Woman's Guide to Balancing Family and Career, 1983; Time Tips for Today's Busy Women, 1984; editor-in-chief Time Talk, monthly newsletter, 1978—; columnist on time mgmt. Office: Time Mgmt Center PO Box 5 Grandville MI 49418

DOUGLASS, ENID HART, mayor, oral historian; b. Los Angeles, Oct. 23, 1926; d. Frank Roland and Enid (Lewis) Hart; m. Malcolm P. Douglass, Aug. 28, 1948; children—Malcolm Paul, John Aubrey, Susan Enid. B.A., Pomona Coll., 1948; M.A., Claremont Grad. Sch., 1959. Research asst. World Book Ency., Palo Alto, Calif., 1953-54; exec. sec., asst. dir. oral history program Claremont Grad. Sch., Calif., 1963-71, dir. oral history program, 1971—, lectr. history, 1977—, assoc. editor Papers of Salmon P. Chase; mem. Calif. Heritage Preservation Commn., 1977-85, chmn., 1983-85. Contbr. articles to profl. jours. Mayor, City of Claremont, 1982—, mayor-pro-tem, 1980-82, mem. city council, 1978—; mem. founding bd. Claremont Heritage, Inc., 1977-80; mem. Gov.'s Office of Planning and Research Adv. Council, Calif., 1977-82. Named Disting. Alumna, Claremont Grad. Sch., 1981. Mem. Oral History Assn. (pres. 1979-80), S.W. Oral History Assn., Nat. Council on Pub. History, LWV, Phi Beta Kappa. Democrat. Avocations; tennis. Home: 1195 Berkeley Ave Claremont CA 91711 Office: Claremont Grad Sch Oral History Program 900 N College Ave Claremont CA 91711

DOUGLASS, EVA ROSE, bookkeeper; b. Reynolds, Ind., Apr. 16, 1936; d. Kenneth and Marie (Burnett) Firth; A.A., Bellevue (Wash.) Community Coll., 1973; m. Robert E. Douglass, July 8, 1955; children—Robert E., June E., Michele E. Acct., owner Douglass Bus. Services, Inc., Bellevue, 1974—; acct. Tom Locks & Assocs., Mercer Island, Wash., 1974, Carmar Steel, Inc., Bellevue, 1973-74. Mem. adv. bd., acctg. dept. Bellevue Community Coll. Mem. Wash. Assn. Accts. (chpt. sec.-treas. 1977-78, co-chmn. editorial and publs. com. 1979-80, chpt. v.p. 1981-82, pres.-elect 1982-83, pres. 1983-84, state treas. 1982-85), Am. Soc. Women Accts., Nat. Soc. Public Accts. Office: 13219 Northrup Way Suite 212 Bellevue WA 98008-2020

DOUMLELE, RUTH HAILEY, communications company executive, broadcast accounting consultant; b. Charlotte County, Va., Nov. 6, 1925; d. Clarrie Robert Hailey and Virginia Susan (Slaughter) Ferguson; m. John Antony Doumlele, May 8, 1943; children—John Antony, Suzanne Denise Doumlele Owen. Cert. in commerce, U. Richmond, 1968; B.A., Mary Baldwin Coll., 1982. Sta. acct. WLEE-Radio, Richmond, Va., 1965-67, bus. mgr., 1967-73; area bus. mgr. Nationwide Communications Inc., Richmond, 1973-75; corp. bus. mgr. Neighborhood Communications Corp., Richmond, 1978—; owner Broadcast Acctg. Cons., Midlothian, Va., 1986—; treas., dir. Guests of Honor, Ltd., Richmond, 1984—. Contbr. articles to profl. jours. Mem. editorial rev. bd. The Woman C.P.A., 1980—. Mem. Am. Soc. Women Accts. (chpt. pres. 1974-76), Broadcast Fin. Mgmt. Assn., Nat. League Am. Pen Women (br. pres. 1984-86), Am. Fedn. Astrologers. Episcopalian. Avocations: salt water fishing; civil war history; travel; astrology. Home: 2510 Chastain Ln Midlothian VA 23113 Office: Neighborhood Communications Corp 629 E Main St Richmond VA 23206

DOUNIS, GEORGETTE DIANE, nurse; b. Washington, July 9, 1958; d. Peter George and Demetra (Pavlos) D. B.A. in Nursing, Jamestown Coll., 1980; M.S. in Nursing, Cath. U. Am., 1985. R.N.; cert. adult nurse practitioner, emergency nurse. Nurse, Leland Meml. Hosp., Riverdale, Md., 1980, Prince Georges Gen. Hosp., Cheverly, Md., 1981-83, Shady Grove Adventist Hosp., Rockville, Md., 1983—; staff and charge nurse Health Care Network, Washington Conv. Center, 1983-84, D.C. Armory, 1983—, R.F.K. Stadium, 1984—. Mem. Emergency Nurses Assn., Nurse Practitioners Assn. D.C. Greek Orthodox. Home: 4802 Rockford Dr Hyattsville MD 20784 Office: Emergency Dept Shady Grove Adventist Hosp 9901 Medical Center Dr Rockville MD 20850

DOUTHIT, AUDREY HOLZER, social worker; b. Cin., May 2, 1925; d. William Frederick and Emma Elizabeth Holzer; B.A., U. Cin., 1946; M.A., U. Chgo., 1948; m. Harold Henry Douthit, July 17, 1948; 1 dau., Susan Emily Douthit Hollinberger. Social worker Presbyn. Hosp., Chgo., 1948-50; dir. social service dept. Drake Meml. Hosp., Cin., 1952-56; intake supr. Marion County Assn. Retarded Citizens, Indpls., 1966-78; dir. admissions New Hope Found. of Ind., Indpls., 1978-85; grad. student supr. Ind. U. Pres., So. Club of Indpls., 1976; mem. North Group Indpls. Symphony, Indpls. Mus. of Art, Second Presbyn. Ch. Mem. Nat. Assn. Social Workers, Clin. Register Social Workers, Acad. Cert. Social Workers, Republican. Club: Kappa Alpha Theta. Home: 8120 N Brent Ave Indianapolis IN 42640

DOUTHIT, DOROTHY BALFE, administrator; b. Faribault, Minn., Nov. 1, 1937; d. James A. and Irene A. (Miller) Balfe; div.; children—James, Susan. B.A., Wayne State U., 1960; M.A., U. Tex., 1965, Ph.D., 1967; M.A., Central Mich. U., 1974. Prin., dir. Kalihi Palama Edn. Ctr., Honolulu, 1970-75; pres., prin. Acad. of Pacific, Honolulu, 1975—; co-founder Hale Mahala Sch., 1970; curriculum specialist U. Hawaii, Honolulu, 1968-70; vis. asst. prof. German, 1967-68. Author: Samoan Demonstration Project, 1973, 74. Trustee Hawaii Loa Coll., 1984—, Hawaii Child Ctrs., Oahu, 1984—; mem. Hawaii Com. for Humanities, 1976-82, dir., 1980-82; chair citizens adv. bd. Pub. Radio, 1982—; chair humanities com. Community Scholarship Program, 1982—; mem. Miss Hawaii Scholarship Com., 1981—, chair, 1983-84; mem. nominating com. Girl Scouts U.S.A., 1982—, chair, 1982-83; mem. Friends of East West Ctr., Historic Hawaii. Mem. Hawaii Assn. Ind. Schs. (chair 1981-82). Avocations: swimming; choral music. Home: 903 Alewa Dr Honolulu HI 96817 Office: 913 Alewa Dr Honolulu HI 96817

DOVE, PATRICIA HOLLY, business/marketing consultant, housekeeping company executive; b. Mineola, N.Y., Dec. 27, 1949; d. Ronald Garrett and Ruth (Clarke) D.; stepdau. E. Lois Dove; student Forbes Trail Tech. Inst., 1967; B.S. in Chemistry cum laude, City U. N.Y., 1974; M.B.A., Babson Coll., 1981; m. George M. Patton, Feb. 7, 1970 (div. 1979). Research chemist, product mgr. Collaborative Research, Inc., Waltham, Mass., 1974-78; asst. to dir. corp. devel. Thiokol Corp., Newtown, Pa., 1979; asst. to comptroller Vac Hyd Processing Co., Woburn, Mass., 1979; nat. accounts sales rep. Millipore Corp., Bedford, Mass., 1980-81; sales and mktg. cons., Acton, Mass., 1981, Piedmont Calif., 1982-83; life ins. rep., service mgr. COPA/ITT Life Ins. Co., San Mateo, Calif., 1983; mktg. mgr. Strata GM Corp., Santa Clara, Calif., 1983-84; owner P.H. Dove Enterprises, Santa Clara, 1984—. Mem. Bus. and Profl. Women Boston (Nike award 1980), Am. Soc. Profl. and Exec. Women, Nat. Assn. Female Execs. Address: 1809 Joan Way Apt 10 Santa Clara CA 95050

DOVRING, KARIN ELSA INGEBORG, author, playwright; b. Stenstorp, Sweden, Dec. 5, 1919; came to U.S., 1953, naturalized, 1968; grad. Coll. Commerce, Gothenburg, Sweden, 1936; M.A., Lund (Sweden) U., 1943, Ph.D., 1951; Phil. Licentiate, Gothenburg U., 1947; m. Folke Dovring, May 30, 1943. Journalist several Swedish daily newspapers and weekly mags., 1940-60; tchr. Swedish colls.; research assoc. Yale U., New Haven, 1953-60; fgn. corr. Swedish newspapers, Italy, Switzerland, France and Germany, 1956-60; vis. prof. Internat. U., Rome, 1958-60, Gottingen (W.Ger.) U., 1962; lectr. numerous univs. including Yale U., U. Wis., McGill U., U. Iowa; research assoc. U. Ill., Urbana, 1968-69; free-lance writer, journalist, 1960—; radio and TV interviews; books include Songs of Zion, 1951, Land Reform as a Propaganda Theme, 3d edit. 1965, Road of Propaganda, 1959, Optional Society, 1972; Frontiers of Communication, 1975, (short stories) No Parking This Side of Heaven, 1982; Harold D. Lasswell: His Communication with a Future, 1986; contbr. numerous articles to mags.; writer Ill. Alliance to Prevent Nuclear War, radio theater. Recipient Swedish Nat. award for short stories Bonniers Pub. House Stockholm, 1951; lit. awards Internat. Acad. Leonardo da Vinci, Rome, 1982-83. Mem. NOW, Société Jean Jacques Rousseau (hon. life), Inst. Freedom of Press (life asso.). Democrat. Address: 613 W Vermont Ave Urbana IL 61801

DOW, MARY ALEXIS, accountant; b. South Amboy, N.J., Feb. 19, 1949; d. Alexander and Elizabeth Anne (Reilly) Pawlowski; m. Russell Alfred Dow, June 19, 1971. B.S. with honors, U. R.I., 1971. C.P.A., Oreg. Staff acct. Deloitte, Haskins & Sells, Boston, 1971-74; sr. acct. Price Waterhouse, Portland, Oreg., 1974-77, mgr., 1977-81, sr. mgr., 1981-84; chief fin. officer Copeland Lumber Yards Inc., Portland, 1984—. Mem. fin. com. Oreg. Mus. Sci. and Industry; mem. bd., treas. Legal Advocacy for Women Inc., 1977-80; mem. NOW, treas. Portland chpt., 1976-77. Mem. Am. Inst. C.P.A.s, Oreg. Soc. C.P.A.s, Am. Women's Soc. C.P.A.s, Portland Retail Controllers Group (dir., past pres.). Roman Catholic. Clubs: City (bd. govs.), University (Portland). Contbr. articles to profl. publs. Office: 901 NE Glisan St Portland OR 97232

DOWBEN, CARLA LURIE, lawyer, educator; b. Chgo., Jan. 22, 1932; d. Harold H. and Gertrude (Geitner) Lurie; m. Robert Dowben, June 20, 1950; children—Peter Arnold, Jonathan Stuart, Susan Laurie. A.B., U. Chgo., 1950; J.D., Temple U., 1955; postgrad. cert., Brandeis U., 1968. Bar: Ill. 1957, Mass. 1963, Tex. 1974, fed. cts., 1957, U.S. Supreme Ct., 1974. Assoc. Conrad and Verges, Chgo., 1957-62; exec. officer MIT, Cambridge, Mass., 1963-64; legal planner, Mass. Health Planning Project, Boston, 1964-69; assoc. prof. Life Scis. Inst., Brown U., Providence, 1970-72; asst. prof. health law U. Tex. Health Sci. Ctr., Dallas, 1973-78, assoc. prof., 1978—; mem. Brice and Mankoff, Dallas; cons. Bd. dirs. Mental Health Assn., 1958—, Ft. Worth Assn. Retarded Citizens, 1980—, Advocacy, Inc., 1981—. Mem. ABA, Tex. Bar Assn., Dallas Bar Assn., Nat. Health Lawyers Assn., Hastings Inst. Ethics, Tex. Family Planning Assn. Quaker. Contbr. articles to profl. jours.; active in drafting health, mental health legislation, agency regulations in several state, local govts. Home: 7150 Eudora Dr Dallas TX 75230 Office: Brice and Mankoff 300 Crescent Ct Dallas TX 75201-1841

DOWD, DAWN KURTZ, chemical company executive; b. Harrisburg, Pa., Aug. 11, 1948; d. Oran Sylvester and Aubrey Elizabeth (Howard) Kurtz; m. Joseph Raymond Dowd, June 20, 1971; children—Bernie Jospeh, Katrena Aubrey, B.S., U. N.C.-Greensboro, 1970, M.S., 1976. Site benefits mgr. CIBA-GEIGY Corp., Greensboro, N.C., 1973-80, mgr. human resources dyestuffs and chems., 1980-84, dir. human resources, 1985—. Bd. dirs. Family and Children's Services, 1981-85. Mem. Am. Soc. Personnel Adminstrs., Am. Compensation Assn., N.C. Placement Assn., Personnel Assn. Greensboro, Women's Profl. Forum. Democrat. Methodist. Office: CIBA-GEIGY Corp PO Box 18300 Greensboro NC 27419

DOWD, SUSAN ELIZABETH, computer consultant; b. Boston, Apr. 13, 1950; d. John Francis and Annette Patricia (Breen) D.; 1 child, Julia Michelle Rish. B.A. in English, Regis Coll., Weston, Mass., 1972; postgrad. NYU, 1972-73. Advt. mgr. 3M/Linolex, North Billerica, Mass., 1974-76; mktg. rep. Digital Equipment Corp., N.Y.C., 1976-78; pvt. practice computer cons., 1978-80; word processing/personal computer cons. Nat. Freelancers Inc., N.Y.C., 1981-85; pres. User Friendly Forces, 1985—. Contbr. articles to profl. jours.; contbr. poetry to mags. Mem. Ind. Computer Cons. Assn., Assn. Info. Systems Profls., N.Y. Amateur Computer Club, Nat. Assn. Female Execs. Office: User Friendly Forces 310 Madison Ave New York NY 10017

DOWDEY, DIANE, English educator; b. Fort Worth, Feb. 11, 1955; d. Ernest Hoyt and Rosalie (Chapman) Dowdey; m. Lawrence Richard Caruso, Aug. 18, 1984. B.A., Tex. Christian U., 1976; M.A., U. Mo., 1977; Ph.D., U. Wis.-Madison, 1984. Adj. prof. Tarrant County Jr. Coll., Hurst, Tex., 1979-80; instr. U. Tex., Arlington, 1980; asst. prof. Tex. A&M, College Station, 1984—. Contbr. poems to profl. publs. Del., Tex. State Democratic Conv., 1976, del., floor leader, 1980. Master's fellow U. Mo., 1976-77, travel fellow U. Wis., 1982. Mem. MLA, Nat. Council Tchrs. English, Conf. Coll. Composition and Communication, Internat. Soc. for History Rhetoric, Phi Beta Kappa. Mem. Christian Ch. (Disciples of Christ). Office: Tex A&M Dept English College Station TX 77843

DOWDLE, JOAN GATES, educator, school principal; b. Helena, Ala., Jan. 2, 1934; d. John and Hattie (Cook) Gates; m. Joseph Clyde Dowdle, Aug. 26, 1956; children—Barbara Jan, Jeanne Olive, Joanna Gates. B.S., Ala. Coll. Women, 1954; M.A., U. Ala.-Tuscaloosa, 1973, Ed.D., 1980. Cert. adminstr. Ala. Tchr. Montgomery Schs., Ala., 1954-56, Auburn Schs., Ala., 1956-57, Raleigh Pub. Schs., N.C., 1958-62; tchr., staff developer Huntsville City Schs., Ala., 1967-74, prin., 1974-85; prin. Tuscaloosa City Schs., Ala., 1985—; adj. prof. U. Ala., 1984—; cons., Ala., 1980—, chmn., cons. So. Assn. Colls. and Schs., Ala., 1978—. Grade level author: New Zaner Blosser 7th Grade Spelling Book, 1983. Officer, Community Ballet Assn., Huntsville, 1964-67; bd. dirs. Multiple Sclerosis Soc., Huntsville, 1970-75. Recipient Savs. Bond award Raleigh Kiwanis Club 1960, Leadership award Ala. Council Sch. Adminstrs. 1981, Prin. of Year Nomination award Ala. State PTA 1980. Mem. Nat. Assn. Middle Schs., Nat. Assn. Elem. Prins., Nat. Assn. Secondary Prins., Delta Kappa Gamma (sec. 1982), Phi Delta Kappa. Baptist. Club: U. Women's (pres. Huntsville 1980-81, Tuscaloosa). Lodge: Soroptomists. Avocations: reading; cooking. Home: Tuscaloosa AL 35401 Office: Tuscaloosa Middle Sch 1210 21st Ave Tuscaloosa AL 35401

DOWDLE, JUDITH LINDQUIST, lawyer; b. Elmhurst, Ill., Sept. 30, 1949; d. John Axel and Ethel Linea (Johnson) Lindquist; m. John Anthony Dowdle, June 26, 1970; children—John Erick, Andrew Ryden, Lindsay Julia, Claire Linea. B.S., U. Ill., 1971; J.D., U. Chgo., 1974. Bar: Minn. 1974; cert. math. tchr., Ill. Atty., researcher Ill. Legis. Investigating Commn., Chgo., summer 1972; atty., shareholder Fredrikson & Byron Law Firm, Mpls., 1974-84; of counsel firm Gray, Plant, Mooty, Mooty & Bennett, P.A., Mpls., 1984—; lectr. for Am. Law Inst., ABA, Minn. Continuing Legal Edn. Legal cons. Mpls. Mayor's Task Force on City Employee Pensions, 1976-77; cons., advisor, mem. Gov.'s Small Bus. Innovation Research Grant Commn., Mpls., 1983—; cons., advisor, mem. Gov.'s Council on Entrepreneurship and Innovation, 1984. Bd. dirs., v.p. Southside Family Nurturing Center, Mpls., 1978-85; trustee Minn. Pub. Employees Retirement Assn., 1985—. Mem. Minn. Bar Assn. (chairperson employee benefits sect. 1983-84), ABA (tax sect.), Mpls. Pension Council, Midwest Pension Conf., Nat. Assn. Women Bus. Owners, Order Coif, Phi Beta Kappa, Phi Kappa Phi. Home: 295 Woodlawn Ave Saint Paul MN 55105 Office: Gray Plant Mooty et al 3400 City Ctr 33 S 6th St Minneapolis MN 55402

DOWDY, CHARLENE YOUNTS, county official; b. Portsmouth, Va., Jan. 12, 1945; d. Charles Edward Sr. and Julia (Briggs) Younts; m. Jerry Thomas Dowdy, Apr. 3, 1965; children—Sonya Constance, Tonya Van Pelt. X-ray asst. Albemarle Hosp., Elizabeth City, N.C., 1965-67; dep. register of deeds Currituck County, N.C., 1975-81, register of deeds, 1981—; sec. 1st Dist. Register of Deeds, Currituck, 1983-84, v.p., 1984—. Rep. Democratic Assn. Currituck, 1985; pianist Powells Point Bapt. Ch., 1969-70; pres. Kilmarlic Home Demonstration, N.C., 1974-75; leader 4-H Club. Mem. DAR. Lodge: Order of Eastern Star (worthy matron 1974). Avocations: dancing; gardening; reading. Office: Register of Deeds PO Box 71 Currituck NC 27966

DOWDY, HELEN MARIE, educational administrator; b. Macon, Ga., Mar. 10, 1930; d. Manly Calvin and Eriel Marie (Merriman) Britt; m. Lemuel Stroud Dowdy, Sept. 5, 1953; children—Lemuel David, Donald Manly. A.A., Mars Hill Coll., 1950. Cert., N.C. Pub. Mgr. Program. Sec. First Citizens Bank, Raleigh, N.C., 1950-53, N.C. State U., Raleigh, 1953-55; adminstrv. asst. N.C. Dept. Curriculum Study, Raleigh, 1959-63; adminstrv. asst. N.C. Dept. Community Colls., Raleigh, 1963-77, spl. asst. to pres., 1977—; cons. N.C. Employees Tng. Ctr., Raleigh, 1974-76; mem. adv. com. N.C. Employee Suggestion System, 1978—. Vice pres. Cary Jr. Woman's Club (N.C.), 1964. Mem. N.C. Assn. Ednl. Office Personnel (pres. dist. 10, 1977-78, scholarship fund named in her honor 1979), Am. Bus. Womens Assn. (chmn. edn. com. Cary chpt. 1979-80). Democrat. Lutheran. Office: NC Dept Community Colls 114 W Edenton St Raleigh NC 27611

DOWELL, CATHERINE ELIZABETH, insurance agency executive; b. Jersey City, May 23, 1925; d. Nicholas Louis and Emily Amelia (Nelson) De Lear; m. Sidney Fred Dowell, Apr. 5, 1947; children—Kenneth Alan, Patricia Dowell Montferret. B.A., Newark Coll. Engring., 1945. Sec., Fed. Storage Co., Newark, 1942-49; exec. sec. Allen B. DeMont Labs., Clifton, N.J., 1952-57; mgr., v.p. Montclair Assocs., ins. agy., Fairfield, N.J., 1961-76; pres., prin. Leone Agy., Inc., doing bus. as Dowell Ins. Assocs., Fair Lawn, N.J., 1976—; rep. Hanover Agy. Council, Piscataway, N.J., 1982-85, Crum & Forster Agy. Council, Parsippany, N.J., 1982-84. Sunday Sch. tchr. Totowa Union Methodist Ch., 1962-73. Mem. Profl. Ins. Assn., Ind. Agts. Assn. Lodge: Order Eastern Star (worthy matron 1973-74, treas. 1974—). Avocations: swimming, ice skating, sewing, decorating, gourmet cooking. Home: 761 Alps Rd Wayne NJ 07470 Office: Dowell Ins Assocs 4-14 Saddle River Rd Fair Lawn NJ 07410

DOWLING, DOROTHY RITA, communications company executive; b. Bklyn., Oct. 4, 1944; d. Leonard Thomas and Dorothy Mary Dowling; m. James O'Neill. B.A., Montclair State Coll., 1966; postgrad. AT&T exec. M.S. program Pace U., 1967-69. Researcher, Ogilvy & Mather, N.Y.C., 1969-73; dir. research Einstein Assos., N.Y.C., 1973-75; bus. analyst Xerox, Rochester, N.Y., 1975-76; industry analyst EFTS, AT&T, Morristown, N.J., 1975-76, market mgr., 1976, market mgr. systems mktg. Morris Plains, N.J., 1977-79, market mgr. product and services delivery, 1979-81, dist. mgr. bus. mktg. ops., 1980-82, mgr. services delivery, 1982-84; mgr. advt. promotions NYNEX Corp., White Plains, N.Y., 1984—. Mem. Women in Communications. Home: 308 Glenbrook Rd Stamford CT 06906 Office: 70 W Red Oak Ln White Plains NY

DOWLING, JACQUES MACCUISTON, sculptor, painter, writer; b. Texarkana, Tex., Oct. 19, 1906; d. Charles Edward and Viola John (Estes) MacCuiston; Tchrs. Certificate, Coll. Marshall, 1923; studied art Loyola U., Frolich's Sch. Fine Art, Los Angeles, NAD, Art Students League, N.Y.C.; Ph.D., Colo. State Christian Coll. One man shows include: Fedn. Dallas Artists, 1950, 52, Rush Gallery, 1958, Sartor's Gallery, 1958, Sheraton-Dallas Hotel, 1960, Dallas Meml. Auditorium, 1960; exhibited in group shows at Dallas Mus. Fine Arts, Mus. of N.Mex., Fedn. Dallas Artists, Sartor's Galleries, Ney Art Mus., Oak Cliff Soc. of Fine Arts, Sartor's Gallery, Shuttles Gallery, Sheraton-Park Internat. Platform Assn., 1966-68, Phillips Mills Art Assn., 1967-74, Yardley Ann. Exhbn., 1968-73, Tinicum Art Festival, 1968, Woodmere Art Gallery (life mem.), 1972-74, others; selected sculpture 1st S.W. ann. show Mus. N.Mex., 1958; represented in permanent collections several corps., many pvt. homes. Recipient 1st Sculpture Fedn. Dallas Artists, 1950-54, pinned (all awards jewels), 1961; Hon. Cert. award Dallas Fed. Bus. Assn., 1964; two 1st awards N.J. Fedn. Womens Clubs, 1972, two 1st award, 1974, 1st and 2d award 1975, Gold medal Accademia Italia, 1979, Golden Centaur award Accademia Italia, 1982, Gold medal Internat. Parliament (U.S.A.) of Safety and Peace, 1983, Statue of Victory, Centro Studi e Ricerche delle Nazioni, Parma, Italy, 1983; Oscar d' Italia, Accademia Italia, 1985; named Cavalier of Arts, Accademia Bedriacense, 1985, many others, including 3 awards for journalism, 1962-63; Golden Flame award World Parliament (U.S.A.), 1986. Fellow Internat. Inst. Arts and Letters (life); mem. Cousteau Soc. (founding), U.S. Chess Fedn., Am. Contract Bridge League, Am. Assn. Ret. Persons, Internat. Acad. Lit., Arts and Sci. (hon. life mem., Tommaso Campanello with gold medal award 1972), C. of C. South Hunterdon (charter). Republican. Episcopalian. Mem. Order Eastern Star (past grand officer; past matron). Address: 723 Tam O'Shanter Ave Sun City Center FL 33570

DOWLING, JEANNINE MARIE, manufacturing company executive; b. N.Y.C., Nov. 19, 1952; d. William Donald and Jeanne Dolores (Millet) Dowling; student Mich. State U., 1970-71, Harpur Coll., 1971-72; B.A., cum laude, SUNY, 1974; m. Michael E. Twomey, Sept. 20, 1980; 2 children. Dir. pub. info. N.Y. State Div. Human Rights, N.Y.C., 1975-78; mgr. pub. affairs programs Philip Morris, Inc., N.Y.C., 1978—. Dep. press sec. N.Y. State Carter Presdl. Campaign, 1974-75; mem. N.Y.C. Commn. on Status of Women, 1979—. Recipient Industry award Nat. Conf. Puerto Rican Women, 1981. Mem. Women in Communications (chmn. Matrix com. 1983), Public Relations Soc. Am., Women in Govt. Relations, N.Y. Public Affairs Profls., Nat. Women's Polit. Caucus, Lifelong Learning Council, Women's Econ. Round Table, Internat. Assn. Bus. Communicators, Women's Equity Action League. Office: Philip Morris 120 Park Ave New York NY 10017

DOWLING, LONA BUCHANAN, nurse; b. Washingon, Feb. 7, 1950; d. Aaron Ernie and Louise Katherine (Willis) Buchanan; m. Frankie Lee Dowling, Sept. 18, 1976; children—David Lee, Allison Lynn. Diploma in nursing Washington Hosp. Ctr., 1971. Staff nurse Prince George Gen. Hosp., Cheverly, Md., 1971-72, asst. head nurse emergency room, 1972-74, head nurse, 1974-75; asst. head nurse emergency room Doctors Hosp., Lanham, Md., 1975-79; staff nurse Ashland Dist. Hosp., Kans., 1979-81; community health nurse, county school nurse Comanche County, Coldwater, Kans., 1981—. Organizer 1st SADD chpt. in Southwest Kans., 1984; ednl. chmn. Comanche County Cancer Soc., 1984—; ednl. co-chmn. South Central Coalition for Health Services, Kans., 1983-84; CPR instr. ARC, Wichita, Kans., 1982—, bd. dirs. Iroquois Ctr. Human Devel. Mem. Kans. Pub. Health Assn., Kans. Assn. Local Health Depts., Bus. and Profl. Women's Club (corr. sec. 1983). Republican. Clubs: Twin Hills Extension Homemaker Unit, Mothers Advancement Protection. Avocations, photography; needlework; horses; entertaining; fishing. Home: HC 72 Box 45 Coldwater KS 67029-9725 Office: Comanche County Health Dept PO Box 433 Courthouse Coldwater KS 67029-0433

DOWLING, RUBY HEATH, pianist; b. Robinson, Ill., Mar. 26, 1898; d. Lawrence Seymour and Clara Ella (Frye) Heath; B.Mus., Am. Conservatory of Music, Chgo., 1925; studied with Carl Friedberg, Madame Samaroff, Silvio Scionti, Chgo., 1923-35, Rudolph Ganz, Maurice Dumcznil, Paris, 1928; postgrad. Ind. U., 1973-76. Instr. piano and music theory Kansas City Conservatory, 1938-42; studied with Herbert Kuebler, Lincoln Trail Coll., Robinson, Ill., 1971—; recs. include: Piano Music of the Romantic Era, 1976, Piano Music By Bach, Mozart, and Chopin, 1978; dir. L.S. Heath & Sons, Inc., 1946—. Mem. Mu Phi Epsilon. Address: 412 Heath Ln Robinson IL 62454

DOWNER, SUSAN QUINETTE OLSCHNER, lawyer; b. St. Louis, July 18, 1950; d. Paul Quinette and Rena (Wolfe) Olschner; m. Philip Stuart Downer, Aug. 7, 1971; children—Abigail Liane, Paul Quinette. B.A., So. Meth. U., 1972; J.D., Emory U., 1975. Bar: Ga. 1975, U.S. Dist. Ct. for mid. and so. dists. Fla., no. dist. Ga., ea. dist. La., Mass., so. dist. N.Y., no. and so. dists. Tex., U.S. Ct. Appeals for 11th and 5th cirs. Atty. Delta Air Lines, Inc., Atlanta, 1975-80, asst. sec., atty., 1979-80, asst. sec., sr. atty., 1980—; asst. sec. Delta Air Lines Found., 1980—; dir. Research Atlanta. Bd. dirs. Atlanta Care Ctr., 1983—. Mem. Am. Soc. Corp. Secs. (adv. dir. South Eastern Regional Group; 1981—), ABA (EEO com. labor employment law sect. 1984), Ga. Bar Assn., Atlanta Bar Assn. Home: 804 Edgewood Ave NE Atlanta GA 30307 Office: Law Dept Delta Air Lines Inc Hartsfield Atlanta Internat Airport Atlanta GA 30320

DOWNIE, CAROL MARCIA, health care information systems executive, consultant; b. Fonddulac, Wis., Aug. 4, 1941; d. Julien Joseph and Marcia Harriet (Fadner) Arpin; m. Edward Blake Downie, III, Aug. 4, 1962 (div. July 1980); children—Eve Marcia, Alice Dorothy. B.A. in Psychology, U. Ark., 1961; postgrad. in arts lit. Ga. So. Coll., 1964-65. Lang. arts tchr. Perryton Pub. Schs., Tex., 1961-62; sci. computer programmer Collins Radio, Cedar Rapids, Iowa, 1962-64; systems programmer So. Ry., Atlanta, 1965-68; info. systems mgr. Blue Cross and Blue Shield, Little Rock, 1973-76, Mayo Clinic, Rochester, Minn., 1979—; staff analyst Standard Oil of Ind., Chgo., 1976-79; dir. Guide Internat., Chgo.; cons. Am. Hosp. Assn., Chgo. Author: (with others) Clinical Laboratory Annual, 1984. Contbr. articles to profl. publs. Editor newsletters Medical Computing, 1979-84. Pres. Lincoln Sch. Parents Assn., Rochester, 1981-83; mem. fin. com., choir, vol. 1st Presbyn. Ch., Rochester, 1982-84; med. program coordinator River Trails council Girl Scouts U.S., 1983—. Mem. Community Health Computing Users Group (pres. 1981-83). Avocations: music, books, gardening, kids, extramural profl. speaking and writing. Home: 610 SW 11 St Rochester MN 55902 Office: Mayo Clinic 200 SW 1 St Rochester MN 55905

DOWNING, JEANNE MARIE, real estate firm executive; b. Ann Arbor, Mich., Apr. 26, 1943; d. W. Jack and Margaret Ann (Quermbach) D.; m. William T. Owesney, Sept. 6, 1975. B.S. in Chemistry, U. Mich., 1966. Real estate agt. Hopper Realty, Falls Church, Va., 1972-75; pres. Jeanne M. Downing, Inc., Springfield, Va., 1975-82, Real Estate Exchange, Inc., Florence, S.C., 1982—; sec. S.C. Real Estate Mktg. and Exchange Council, Inc., 1983—. Bd. dirs. Big Sisters S.C., Florence, 1984—. Named Exchangor of Yr., Met. Washington Real Estate Exchangors, 1978. Mem. Florence Bd. Realtors (edn. com. 1985—). Republican. Avocation: gardening. Office: Real Estate Exchange Inc 1807 W Cherokee Suite 101 Florence SC 29501

DOWNING, MARGARET MARY, newspaper editor; b. Altoona, Pa., June 3, 1952; d. Irvine William and Iva Ann (Regan) D. B.A. magna cum laude, Tex. Christian U., 1974. Reporting intern Corpus Christi Caller Times, summer 1973; reporter, bur. chief Beaumont Enterprise & Jour. (Tex.), 1974-76, Dallas Times Herald, 1976-80; reporter, asst. city editor Houston Post, 1980—. Mem. Pumas A Soccer Team, Houston. Mem. Press Club of Houston (pres. 1984, bd. dirs. 1982-85), Greater Houston Hunter-Jumper Assn., Sigma Delta Chi. Episcopalian. Home: 6216 Community Dr Houston TX 77005 Office: Houston Post 4747 SW Freeway Houston TX 77001

DOWNS, BRANDI ELIZABETH, artist; b. McComb, Miss., Aug. 11, 1932; d. Jack Denson and Martha Ethel (Bornman) Hammack; B.F.A., Miss. State Coll. Women, 1955; m. William K. Douglas, Dec. 23, 1956; children—Martha Anne, William K., Christine Rachel. Artist, WLBT-TV, Jackson, Miss., 1955, Gorden Marks Advt., Jackson, 1955-57, Dallas Times Herald, 1957-58, Whaley Studio, Dallas, 1958; art dir. Jiffy Printing, Dallas, 1958-59; tchr. art Dallas Public Schs., 1959-62; one-man shows Municipal Art Gallery, Jackson, 1955, French Quarter Gallery, New Orleans, 1967—71, Sheraton Gallery, San Juan, P.R., 1968, La Concia Gallery, San Juan, 1972, Our Lady of Holy Cross, 1971, San Geronimo Gallery, San Juan, 1973, French Quarter Design, New Orleans, 1974-75, Symmetry Gallery, New Orleans, 1976-77; exhibited in group shows Norfolk (Va.) Mus., 1953, Nat. Kappa Pi Exhbn., 1954. Recipient 1st prize Colonial Dames Art award, Columbus Miss., 1954; 1st prize Allison Wells, 1955; silver medal Tommaso Campanella Soc., Rome, 1970, Gold medal, 1972. Mem. Am. Artist Profl. League, Soc. N.Am. Artists. Home: Route 1 Box 29 Mount Croghan SC 29727 Office: 832 Orleans Ave New Orleans LA 70116

DOWNS, MARILYN WILSON, brush company executive; b. New Orleans, Nov. 21, 1930; d. Mixon Howard and Zita Philomene (Bergeron) Wilson; children—Roxie Regan, Matt Daniel Regan. Student U. Mich., 1973-74. Adminstrv. asst. R. O. Rush, Baton Rouge, 1952-60, C. F. Gravel, Alexandria, La., 1960-62, Gov. Jimmie Davis, Baton Rouge, 1962-64, Gov. J. McKeithen, Baton Rouge, 1964-72; exec. asst. mgr. B. R. Hilton Hotel, Baton Rouge, 1973-77; dir. personnel/adminstrn. Kirby Bldg. Systems, Houston, 1977-80; exec. v.p., gen. mgr. Worcester Brush Co., Mass., 1980—; treas., corp. sec. R. F. Richard Corp., Worcester Brush Co., 1980—. Mem. Worcester Indsl. Devel. Financing Authority, 1984—. Democrat. Methodist. Home: 80 Salisbury St Suite 703 Worcester MA 01609 Office: Worcester Brush Co 38 Austin St PO Box 658 Worcester MA 01601

DOWNS, NANCY JANE, child center executive; b. Lansing, Mich., July 12, 1936; d. George Melville and Gertrude Irene (Foster) Whitson-Fisher; m. Jerry Lane Downs, Sept. 7, 1956 (div. 1971); children—Daniel Lane, Debra Louise. A.A., Christian Coll. for Women (now Columbia Coll.), Mo., 1956; B.S. in Elem. Edn., Washington U., St. Louis, 1961; M.A. in Teaching, Webster U., St. Louis, 1975. Cert. tchr. Mo. Tchr. reading pub. schs., Calif., N.Mex., 1961-67, Ferguson-Florissant Dist., St. Louis, 1967-69; tchr. 2d grade Parkway Sch. Dist., St. Louis, 1971-72; tchr. pre-sch. Children's Chalet, St. Louis, 1973-74; dir., developer Personalized Preschool, St. Louis, 1974-80; pres., exec. dir. Personalized Way Child Ctr. Inc., St. Louis, 1980—. Author: (program) Personalized Educational Preschool Program, 1974; (booklets) Me Here and Now, 1974. Mem., St. Louis Regional Commerce and Growth Assn., St. Louis, 1983-86. Mem. Internat. Assn. Edn. Young Children, Child Day Care Assn., C. of C. (Mo.), St. Louis Assn. Edn. Young Children (treas. 1984-86). Democrat. Ch. Religious Science. Club: St. Louis Ski. Avocations: sailing; skiing; golfing; reading. Office: Personalized Way Child Ctr 1915 Ross Ave Saint Louis MO 63146

DOWNS-JACOBS, EILEEN MARGARET, former educator; b. Chgo., Aug. 22, 1942; d. John Preston and Eileen Mary (Sheehan) Downs; B.S. in Speech and Hearing Therapy, B.S. in Speech and Drama K-12, Nazareth Coll. Ky., 1964; M.S. in Spl. Edn. K-12, Portland (Oreg.) State U., 1974, postgrad., 1977-78; m. Owen Jacobs, Sept. 19, 1975; children—Shannon (dec.), Kevin. Speech tchr. and therapist schs. in Mich., Colo., Col., Idaho and Oreg., 1964-74; itinerant specialist, mem. ednl. support personnel team Portland Public Schs., 1974-76; Title I specialist Baker (Oreg.) Public Schs., 1976-79, dir. fed./vocat. and testing programs, 1978-82; workshop leader, cons. in field. Chmn. bd. dirs. Crossroads Creative and Performing Arts Center, 1976-80; pres. Cystic Fibrosis Assn. Portland, Boise and Denver, 1968-76; com. chmn. Baker Disaster Relief fund raising, 1980; bd. dirs. Uinta County Mental Health Assn., coordinator secondary sch. for spl. edn. Mem. Am. Soc. Profl. and Exec. Women, Nat. Assn. Female Execs., Oreg. Assn. Vocat. Adminstrs., N.W. Women in Ednl. Adminstrn., AAUW, Council for Exceptional Children, Blue Mountain Quarter Horse Assn., Oreg. Cowbelle Assn., Baker County Cowbelle Assn. Democrat. Roman Catholic. Author handbook. Home: PO Box 1004 Evanston WY 82930

DOXTATOR, RUTH ELANORA ROTHSCHILD, automotive company executive, art consultant; b. N.Y.C., Aug. 5, 1944; d. Guy and Madiline Rothschild; m. A.R. Spiconardi, Feb. 12, 1960 (dec. Feb. 1980); children—Robert L., Vincent E., Kennith A., Joseph A.; m. Robert H. Doxtator, Feb. 13, 1981; 1 stepchild, Donald. A.S., Manhattanville Coll., 1958; B.A., CCNY, 1962; cert. art tchr. New Paltz Coll., N.Y., 1976. Adviser N.Y. Telephone Co., N.Y.C., 1958-61; art adviser Barraccini Corp., N.Y.C., 1961-63; asst. adminstr. Phelps Meml. Hosp., Tarrytown, N.Y., 1963-70; pres., owner, mgr. Beaver Constrn. Co., Wappingers, N.Y., 1976-81; co-owner, v.p. R.R. & Sons Constrn. Co., Hopewell, N.Y., 1981-83; v.p., mgr. Car World Inc., Poughkeepsie, N.Y., 1983-86. Art dir. Republican campaign, Poughkeepsie, 1978-79. Mem. Nat. Assn. Female Execs. Roman Catholic. Club: Amirita (Poughkeepsie). Avocations: art; gardening; music; reading. Home: 38 Stephens Dr Hopewell Junction NY 12533

DOYLE, CONSTANCE TALCOTT JOHNSTON, physician; b. Mansfield, Ohio, July 8, 1945; d. Frederick Lyman IV and Nancy Jean Bushnell (Johnston) Talcott; B.S., Ohio U., 1967; M.D., Ohio State U., 1971; m. Alan Jerome Demsky, June 13, 1976; children—Ian Frederick Demsky, Zachary Adam Demsky. Intern, Riverside Hosp., Columbus, Ohio, 1971-72; resident in internal medicine Hurley Hosp. and U. Mich., Flint, 1972-74, emergency physician Oakwood Hosp., Dearborn, Mich., 1974-76, Jackson County (Mich.) Emergency Services, Jackson, 1975—; disaster cons., co-chmn. emergency med. services disaster com. Region II EMS, 1978-79; course dir. advanced cardiac life support and chmn. advanced life support com. W.A. Foote Meml. Hosp., Jackson, 1979—, others; clin. instr. emergency services, dept. surgery U. Mich., 1981—, flight physician survival flight, 1983—; instr. Jackson County Emergency Med. Technician refresher courses, Jackson Community Coll. Bd. dirs. Jackson County Heart Assn., 1979—. Mem. Am. Med. Women's Assn., Am. Coll. Emergency Physicians (Mich. disaster com., dir. Mich. 1979-85, chmn. Mich. disaster com. 1979—, treas. Mich. 1984-85, pres.-elect 1985—, nat. ad hoc disaster com. 1982-83, nat. disaster com. 1983—; cons. Fed. Emergency Mgmt. Agy. disaster mgmt. course 1982—), World Assn. Emergency and Disaster Medicine (Club of Maine, lctr. Brighton, Eng. 1985), ACP, Mich. Assn. Emergency Med. Technicians (dir. 1979-80), Mich. State, Jackson County med. socs., Sierra Club. Jewish. Contbg. author: Clinical Approach to Poisoning and Toxicology, 1983; contbr. article to profl. jour. Home: 1665 Lansdowne Rd Ann Arbor MI 48105 Office: WA Foote Hospital East Emergency Dept Jackson MI 49201

DOYLE, DOROTHY ANGELA, consulting firm executive, writer; b. Orange, N.J., Aug. 22, 1935; d. Michael Edward and Angelina (Battista) Palmieri; m. William J. Doyle, Oct. 3, 1953; children—Lisa, Jeffrey. A.A., Broward Community Coll., Davie, Fla., 1971; B.A. in English, Fla. Atlantic U., 1974. Substitute tchr. Broward County Schs., Ft. Lauderdale, Fla., 1974-75; freelance writer, Miramar, Fla., 1977—; owner, mgr. Dorothy Doyle, Pembroke Pines, Fla., 1982; v.p. communications Mfrs. Support Services Corp., Atlanta, 1983—. Contbr. articles to mags. Organizer, communications coordinator Alzheimer's and Related Disorders Assn., Ft. Lauderdale, 1980, now mem. Ga. chpt.; troop organizer Girl Scouts U.S.A., Broward County, 1969. Mem. Nat. Writers Club, Women in Communications, Phi Theta Kappa. Republican. Roman Catholic. Club: Hollywood (Fla.) Toastmasters (ednl. v.p. 1978). Home: Alpharetta GA Office: Manufacturers Support Services Corp 600 Houze Way Suite 2D Roswell GA 30076

DOYLE, IRENE ELIZABETH, electronic sales executive, nurse; b. West Point, Iowa, Oct. 5, 1920; d. Joseph Deidrich and Mary Adelaide (Groene) Schulte; m. William Joseph Doyle, Feb. 3, 1956. R.N., Mercy Hosp., 1941. Courier nurse Santa Fe R.R., Chgo., 1947-50; indsl. nurse Montgomery Ward, Chgo., 1950-54; rep. Hornblower & Weeks, Chgo., 1954-56; v.p. William J. Doyle Co., Chgo., 1956-80, Ormond Beach, Fla., 1980—. Served with M.C., U.S. Army, 1942-46. Mem. Electronic Reps. Assn. Republican. Roman Catholic. Club: Oceanside Country (Ormond Beach).

DOYLE, JANE COLBY GOODNOW, nursing educator; b. Fitchburg, Mass., Apr. 17, 1941; d. Donald Ray and Mary (Lane) Goodnow; m. Lawrence Joseph Doyle, Oct. 9, 1976. B.S.N., Skidmore Coll., 1963; M.S.N., Boston U., 1976; M.B.A., Western New Eng. Coll., 1984. Staff nurse Meml. Hosp., N.Y.C., 1963-66, Meml. Hosp., Springfield, Vt., 1968-69; staff educator Windham Hosp., Willimantic, Conn., 1970-71; instr. Leominster Hosp. Sch. Nursing (Mass.), 1971—; adviser Mass. Senate of Student Nurses, 1972-73. Author: (video tape script) Hosp. Productivity, 1983. Bd. dirs. Hickory Hills Landowners Assn., Lunenburg, Mass., 1983, Leominster Vis. Nurses Assn., 1980—; mem. Leominster Hosp. Guild, 1978—. Mem. Am. Nurses Assn., Leominster Hosp. Nurses Assn. (chmn. 1975-81), Nat. League Nursing, Concern for Dying, Kidney Transplant/Dialysis Assn., Sigma Theta Tau (Beta Epsilon chpt.). Home: 36 Hemlock Dr Lunenburg MA 01462 Office: Leominster Hosp Sch Nursing Hospital Rd Leominster MA 01453

DOYLE, JUDITH MANLEY, marriage and family therapist, consultant; b. Los Angeles, Aug. 18, 1943; d. Raymond Ross Manley and Sarah Virginia (Pletcher) Manley Flint; 1 child, Brennan Corey. B.A., Calif. State U.-Long Beach, 1975, M.S., 1977. Counselor Calif. State U., Long Beach, 1976-78; case mgmt. supr. Bridge/Boys Club, Wilmington, Calif., 1978-80, ElMonte Sr. Citizens Ctr., Calif., 1979-81; dir. counseling services Gay/Lesbian Community Service Ctr., Orange County, Calif., 1985—; owner, therapist Judith M. Doyle MFCC, Long Beach, 1978—; cons. Aids Response Program, Garden Grove, Calif., 1985—; med. adv. bd. Aids Service Found., Costa Mesa, Calif., 1985—. Golden mem. Long Beach Lambda Democratic Club, 1980—; chmn. So. Calif. Women for Understanding, Los Angeles, 1981-85; pres., bd. dirs. Long Beach Lesbian and Gay Pride, Inc., 1983—; apptd. mem. Calif. State Commn. Econ. Devel. Task Force, 1984-85. Recipient Woman of Yr. award Lambda Democratic Club, 1981, Christopher Street W., 1986; Spl. Person award Press/Telegram, 1985; Myra Riddell Service award So. Calif. Women for Understanding. Mem. Calif. Assn. Marriage and Family Therapists (bd. dirs. 1981-85, pres. 1985-86), Am. Assn. Counseling and Devel., Nat. Assn. Female Execs., ACLU, Greenpeace, People for the Am. Way, Nat. Mus. Women in the Arts (charter), Mus. Contemporary Art (charter), Calypso Soc. Avocations: dancing; theatre; volleyball; softball. Office: Judith M Doyle MFCC 4041 E 4th St Long Beach CA

DOYLE, JUDITH STOVALL, real estate executive; b. Dothan, Ala., Apr. 19, 1940; d. E.H. and Justine (Knowles) Stovall; m. John P. Doyle, Aug. 22, 1964; children—John Patrick III, Michael D., Julie A. B.S., Miss. U. for Women, 1961. Tchr. math., jr. high sch., Gulfport, Miss., 1961-62; with dept. pub. relations SUNY-Buffalo, 1962-64; tchr. math., jr. high schs., Alexandria, Va., 1964-65, Auburn, N.Y., 1970-71; Realtor, assoc. Mosher Real Estate, Auburn, 1972-80; owner, mgr. real estate property, Auburn, 1977—. Active, past pres. Mercy Aux., Auburn; mem. Owasco Bd. Assessment Rev., N.Y., 1976—; v.p. Sacred Heart Parish Council, Auburn, 1985-86; bd. dirs. Unity House, Auburn, 1985-88. Democrat. Roman Catholic. Lodge: Ancient Order Hibernians (charter mem. Ladies Aux. 2).

DOYLE, PHYLLIS D'AGOSTINO, educational administrator; b. Buffalo, July 15, 1931; d. Michael and Rose (Rea) D'A.; m. David Doyle, Sept. 1, 1970; children—Rosalind, Rock. B.S., Canisius Coll., 1964; M.S.W., U. Buffalo, 1966. Social worker supr. West Seneca Devel. Ctr., 1966-76; instr. D'Youville Coll., 1966-69, Erie Community Coll., Buffalo, 1979—; team leader JNA Devel. Ctr., Perrysburg, N.Y., 1976—. Vice-chmn. Adv. Bd. for Lovejoy Youth and Elderly, 1977—. NIMH grantee, 1964-66. Mem. Am. Acad. Social Workers, Am. Acad. Mental Deficiency, N.Y. State Cert. Social Workers. Home: 151 Atlantic Ave Sloan NY 14212

DOYLE, THERESA LIPARI, real estate marketing executive, public relations specialist; b. Long Beach, Calif., Aug. 27, 1957; d. Joseph and Joyce Lorraine (Wagle) Lipari; m. Timothy Xavier Doyle, June 26, 1982. B.A., Calif. State U.-Fullerton, 1980. Fundraising asst. Am. Heart Assn., Santa Ana, Calif., 1980; account exec. Kerr & Assocs. Pub. Relations, Huntington Beach, Calif., 1980-83; dir. mktg. Covington Homes, Fullerton, Calif., 1983—; pub. relations cons. Am. Heart Assn., 1980-84, Family Crisis Ctr., Orange County, Calif., 1980-83. Recipient Outstanding Pub. Relations award Publicity Club Los Angeles, 1980. Mem. Women in Communications, Inc. (Outstanding Mag. Article award 1980, Outstanding Pub. Relations award 1980), Sales and Mktg. Council of Bldg. Industry Assn., Nat. Assn. Female Execs., Southern Calif. Women in Advertising, Calif. State U.-Fullerton Alumni Assn. Republican. Roman Catholic. Office: Covington Homes 2451 E Orangethorpe Ave Fullerton CA 92806

DOYLE, VERLA DOHERTY (MRS. JACOBS H. DOYLE), club woman; b. Franklin, Pa., Aug. 12, 1912; d. Wilbur Felix and Walza (Magee) Doherty; A.B., St. Francis Xavier Coll. Women, 1936; m. Jacobs H. Doyle, Nov. 10, 1951. Case worker Pa. Dept. Pub. Assistance, Franklin, 1937-41; with U.S.O., Nat. Catholic Community Service, 1941-47, successively asst. club dir., club dir., rep. Tenn. maneuvers, 1943-44, traveling dir. S.E. region U.S., 1944-46; exec. sec. Cath. Youth Orgn., Nashville, 1949-51; bd. dirs. Nashville Diocesan Council Cath. Women, 1951—, sec., 1955-57, pres., 1959-61; nat. youth chmn. Nat. Council Cath. Women, 1958-62; del. Pres.'s White House Conf. Children and Youth, Washington, 1960; bd. dirs. Cath. Youth Orgn., Nashville, 1951-55, Nat. Multiple Sclerosis Soc., Nashville chpt., 1963-64. Alternate del. Democratic Conv. from Tenn., 1952, 56. Mem. Cath. Daus. Am., Cheekwood Cultural Center, St. Xavier Coll. Alumnae, Tenn., Nashville bar auxs. Clubs: Richland Country, Newman (dir. 1963-64), Colonna (treas. 1956, pres. 1958-60) (Nashville). Address: 6117 Robin Hill Rd Nashville TN 37205

DRABEK, DONNA MARIE, nurse; b. Hartford, Conn., Dec. 19, 1952; d. Thomas Francis and Helen Margurite (Cersoil) Cutarelli; m. Charles Lee Drabek, Nov. 24, 1973. L.P.N., Robert Morris Jr. Coll., 1973; B.S.N., U. Bridgeport, 1982. Lic. practical nurse Elaine Boyd Creshe Nursing Home, Bloomingdale, Ill., 1974-77, Derby (Conn.) Nursing Home, 1977-80; nurse Griffin Hosp., Derby, 1982—. Mem. Quality Assurance (recognition award 1983). Roman Catholic. Home: 52 Old Sentinel Hill Derby CT 06418 Office: Griffin Hosp 130 Division St Derby CT 06418

DRAGE, HELEN LILLIAN, retired accountant; b. Calgary, Alta., Can., Dec. 26, 1925; d. Eugene Ernest and Clara Elizabeth (Patch) Palmer; student LaSalle Extension U., 1971; m. Cecil Drage May 25, 1944; children—Donna, Gary, David, Julie Ann. Bookkeeper, Drage Trucking Hwy. Constrn., 1947-49, 50-51, 56-60, Drage Trucking Gypsum Quarry, 1952-55, Drage Trucking. Log Haul, 1962-74; acct. Jade Logging Ltd., 1975-85; Yoga instr. Bd. dirs. Golden Hosp. (B.C., Can.); pres. Donald Home & Sch. Assn. Clubs: Golden Light Horse, Golden Figure Skating (dir. 1972-74). Home: Birch Crescent Golden BC V0A 1H Canada

DRAGO, LINDA SUSAN, law librarian, lawyer; b. Pitts., June 16, 1950; d. Paul Francis and Cecilia (Wojciechowski) Fink; m. Carl Michael Drago, Sept. 4, 1976. B.A., Duquesne U., 1972; M.L.S., U. Pitts., 1973, J.D., 1983. Bar: Pa. 1983. Br. librarian Carnegie Library Pitts., 1973-80; legal researcher Legal Dept. Diocese Pitts., 1981-83; assoc. dir. law library U. Pitts. Law Sch., 1983-84; assoc. Cauley, Conflenti & Latella, Pitts., 1984—; legal researcher Legal Dept Diocese Pitts., 1980—. Legal researcher Church Property, Finances & Related Corporations: A Conon Law Handbook, 1983. Mem. Pa. Bar Assn., Allegheny County Bar Assn., ABA, Pa. Trial Lawyers Assn., Am. Assn. Law Libraries, St. Thomas More Soc., Beta Phi Mu. Democrat. Roman Catholic. Home: 4653 Homeridge Dr Munhall PA 15120 Office: 1212 Manor Bldg Pittsburgh PA 15219

DRAKE, DONNA MARIE, investment company executive; b. Washington, Oct. 19, 1953; d. James Edward and Geraldine Gloria (Williamson) D. B.A. cum laude, Wesleyan U., Middletown, Conn., 1975. With Merrill Lynch, N.Y.C., 1975—, sr. exec. recruiter, 1979-80, career devel. adminstr., 1980-83, human resources specialist, 1983—, asst. v.p., 1983—. Cons. personnel D.C. Rape Crisis Ctr., 1982. Johnston scholar, 1972. Mem. Career Planning and Adult Devel. Network, Internat. Assn. Personnel Women, Kappa Delta Pi. Home: 6 Deerberry Ln Monmouth Junction NJ 08852 Office: Merrill Lynch Pierce Fenner & Smith One Liberty Plaza New York NY 10080

DRAKE, GRACE L., state senator, photographer; b. New London, Conn., May 25, 1926; d. Daniel Harvey and Marion Gertrude (Wiech) Driscoll; m. William Lee Drake, June 9, 1946; children—Sandra DeNobile Drake. Student Williams Meml. Inst. Portrait photographer Am. Photographic Corp., N.Y.C., 1944-72, studio mgr., 1958-66, studio troubleshooter, 1966-72; senator State of Ohio, Columbus, 1984—. Mem. Carmelite Guild of Cleve., 1973—; v.p. Briar Lake Assn., Solon, Ohio, 1983-86; pres. Western Res. Women's Republican Club, 1983-85; mem. state screening com. Reagan-Bush, 1984; co-chmn. Cuyahoga County Rep. Voter Registration, 1984; ward leader, Rep. Party, Solon, 1978-84, del. for George Bush, 22nd dist., 1980; pres. Solon Rep. Cub, 1978-83; mem. Ohio Fedn. Republican Women, Nat. Fedn. Rep. Women; exec. com. Cuyahoga County Rep. Orgn.; active various campaigns. Recipient Outstanding Woman award, Nat. Fedn. Rep. Women, 1984. Mem. Nat. Conf. State Legislators. Roman Catholic. Avocations: bridge; golf. Home: 5954 Briardale Ln Solon OH 43068 Office: Ohio Senate Statehouse Columbus OH 43216-4209

DRAKE, JANE BROIDA, former marketing executive; b. St. Louis, Nov. 12, 1927; d. Max and Jennie (Cohen) Broida; m. Arnold Gooze, Dec. 10, 1945 (div. 1955); children—Mitchell Eric, Keith Edward (dec.); m. 2d, Orval Leroy Drake, Dec. 26, 1982. Bookkeeper's asst. Herman Lieberman Acctg. Firm, Los Angeles, 1947; office mgr. Video Tape Products, Santa Monica, Calif., 1973-77; ops. officer Pacific Audio Mktg. Corp., Marina Del Rey, Calif., 1981-82; v.p. ops. and adminstrn. Cambridge Corp., Santa Monica, 1982-84; v.p. ops. and adminstrn. Century Concepts, Inc. and Cambridge Corp., Santa Monica, 1982-84. Jewish.

DRAKE, LYNN ANNETTE, physician; b. Albuquerque, Aug. 4, 1945; d. Olen Lester and Lucille Susan (Henry) Drake; B.A., Adams State Coll., 1966, M.A., 1967; M.D., U. Tenn., 1971. Instr. math. Adams State Coll., Alamosa, Colo., 1966-67; intern City of Memphis Hosp., 1971-72, resident in dermatology, 1972-75, chief resident, 1974-75; mem. faculty dept. medicine, div. dermatology U. Tenn. Center Health Scis., also Med. Practice Group, Inc.; asst. prof. dermatology Emory U., Atlanta; chief dermatology VA Med. Center, Atlanta; chmn. chemosurgery tag group VA; instr. advanced cardiac life support Am. Heart Assn.; mem. emergency room com. St. Joseph Hosp. Vol., Am. Cancer Soc., 1973-75. Diplomate Am. Bd. Dermatology (chmn. com. health care quality assurance 1984—). Robert Wood Johnson Health Policy fellow, 1986-87. Fellow Am. Acad. Dermatology; mem. Soc. for Investigative Dermatology, Am. Acad. Dermatology (com. on health planning), Women's Med. Assn., ACP, Ga. Dermatology Soc., Atlanta Dermatology Soc. (program chmn.), Am. Assn. Med. Colls., Council Acad. Scis., Women's Dermatology Soc. (housestaff liaison com., nominating com., pres. 1984-86). Dermatology Found. Home: 1670 Clairmont Rd Atlanta GA 30033 Office: Emory U Clinic 1365 Clifton Rd NE Atlanta GA 30322

DRAKE, SHEILA JO, teacher educator; b. Terre Haute, Ind., Dec. 26, 1944; d. Lloyd Black and Pearl (Baker) Cusick; m. James M. Drake; 1 child, Christy. B.S., Ind. State U., 1966; M.Ed., North Tex. State U., 1971; Ph.D., Ind. State U., 1978. Tchr. elem. schs., Vigo County Sch. Dist., Terre Haute, 1966-67; tchr. N.W. Ind. Sch. Dist., Justin, Tex., 1967-69, supr. spl. services, 1970-74; assoc. prof. edn. Kans. Wesleyan U., Salina, 1978—, dir. summer enrichment series gifted students, 1981—; adviser to bd. Occupational Ctr. for Central Kans., 1985. project leader 4H, 1983-84. Mem. Assn. Tchr. Educators (state bd. dirs.), Delta Kappa Gamma (pres. Salinas coordinating council, also pres. Beta Nu chpt.), Phi Delta Kappa (past pres.), Beta Sigma Phi (past pres.). Avocations: reading; collecting depression glass; traveling. Home: 1845 Valley View Dr Salina KS 67401 Office: Kans Wesleyan U 101 E Clifflin St Salina KS 67401

DRAUCKER, JO ANNE, business executive; b. Atlantic City, Aug. 14, 1948; d. James Snowden and Mary Rose (Sacco) Wade; m. Albert Dewey Draucker, May 25, 1980. Student Va. Commonwealth U., 1966-69. Instr. Richmond Dept. Recreation and Parks, Va., 1966-69; adminstrv. asst. United Va. Bank, Richmond, 1969-74; owner Premiere Inc., Richmond, 1974—, Ellman's Inc., Richmond, 1981—; instr. Va. Commonwealth U., 1980—. Performer Va. Mus. Theatre, 1963-69, Swift Creek Mill Playhouse, 1973-77, Barksdale Theatre, 1973-77, others. Mem. Blvd. Civic Assn., 1980-85. Mem. Retail Mchts. Greater Richmond, Richmond C. of C. Carytown Mchts./Bus. Assn. (treas. 1981, pres. 1982-84, 1st v.p. 1985-86). Roman Catholic. Avocations: theatre; dance. Office: Premiere Inc 3339 W Cary St Richmond VA 23221

DRAZIN, LISA, real estate investment banker, financial consultant; b. Washington, Nov. 26, 1953; d. Sidney and Bernice Ann (Jeweler) D. A.B. with honors, Wellesley Coll., 1976; M.B.A., George Washington U., 1980. Securities analyst Geico, Inc., Chevy Chase, Md., 1982; mng. prin. Jefferson Securities Ltd., Bethesda, Md., 1983; chmn., chief exec. officer Drazin & Co., Inc., Bethesda, 1985—, Drazin Properties, Inc., Bethesda, 1985—, Drazin Securities, Inc., Bethesda, 1985—; affiliate Montgomery County Bd. Realtors. Founder, Ivy Connection, Washington, 1982; mem. Nat. Trust for Historic Preservation. Mem. Beta Gamma Sigma. Club: Wellesley (interns coordinator, recent grads. rep. 1981-84) (Washington). Office: Drazin & Co Inc 6403 Kirby Rd Bethesda MD 20817

DREIER, BERNICE, advertising executive; b. Springfield, Mass., Apr. 3, 1925; d. Ely and Sarah Deena (Hurwitz) Slotnick; m. Robert Edward Dreier, June 30, 1946; children—Cindy, Eric. B.A., Am. Internat. Coll., 1946; M.S., Western Conn. State Coll., 1968. Substitute tchr. Stamford (Conn.) Pub. Schs., 1958-67; bookkeeper Manpower, Stamford, 1967-68, Knudsen-Moore, Stamford, 1968-71; media dir. Knudsen Moore, Norwalk, Conn., 1971-83, Knudsen Moore Schropfer, Stamford, 1983—. Home: 17 Putter Dr Stamford CT 06907

DRENKHAHN, BETTY J.T., former university publications manager, editor, writer; b. Attica, Ind., Apr. 24, 1922; d. Clinton J. and Elizabeth J. (Oakley) Tinsman; m. Andrew O. Drenkhahn, May 22, 1954 (div. Apr. 1956); 1 child, Elizabeth Wellman. B.A., U. Wis., 1943; M.A., Northwestern U., 1958. Editor, Agrl. Info., Purdue U., West Lafayette, Ind., 1961-67, info. specialist, editor-in-chief, 1975-80, univ. publs. mgr., 1980-85; ret., 1985; editor Rowman & Littlefield, N.Y.C., 1967-68; mng. editor No. Ill. U. Press, DeKalb, 1968-71; librarian/researcher Irwin Mgmt. Co., Columbus, Ind., 1972-75. Case and recreation worker Am. Red Cross-Service to Mil. Hosps., Germany and U.S., 1951-53. Awarded master cert. in music, Mozarteum, Salzburg, Austria, 1950. Mem. Women in Communications, Inc., Agrl. Communicators in Edn. Home: 3605 Steck Ave Apt 1077 Austin TX 78759

DRENNAN, MARIE CATHERINE, freelance journalist; b. Ft. Wayne, Ind., Feb. 5, 1934; d. Matthew Christopher and Marie Katherine (Sommers) D.; student Ft. Wayne Art Sch., 1942-43. Announcer, Radio Ft. Wayne, WANE, 1950-56; traffic mgr. 1952-56, copywriter, 1951-56; hostess Transworld Airlines, Kansas City, Mo., Detroit, 1956-58; co-owner, v.p. Tops 'n' Talent, Detroit, 1959-67; writer, editor, coordinator spl. promotions Ross Roy, Inc., Detroit, 1969-73; writer, editor, coordinator promotion, spl. projects, mktg. services and sales devel. Detroit Free Press, 1975-83; freelance writer, coordinator spl. projects, 1984—. Recipient awards for Night Flight radio program as benefit to State tourist industry Mich. Ho. of Reps., 1971, Gov. William G. Milliken, 1972. Mem. Founders Soc. of Detroit Inst. Arts, Nat. Hist. Soc., Nat. Humane Soc., Nat. Writers Club, Nat. Assn. Female Execs., Detroit Press Club, Adcrafters. Roman Catholic. Home: 8900 E Jefferson St Apt 304 Detroit MI 48214

DRESCHER, JOAN E., author, illustrator; b. N.Y.C., Mar. 6, 1939; d. Joseph Manley and Elizabeth (Straub) McIntosh; m. Kenneth W. Drescher, June 11, 1960; children—Lisa, Kimberly, Kenneth. Student, Rochester Inst. Tech., 1958-59, Parsons Sch. Design, 1960-63, Art Students League, 1964. Tchr. writing Cambridge Ctr. for Adult Edn. (Mass.), Cambridge Art Assn., 1973-78, Mass. Coll. Art, Boston, 1975-76, Art Inst. Boston, 1977-79, Lesley Coll., Cambridge, 1979-81; artist-in-residence Hingham Pub. Schs., 1984, Kingston and Milton pub schs., 1982-83, China Trade Mus., Milton, Mass., 1983; lectr. in field. Author, illustrator: Max and Rufus, 1982; I'm in Charge, 1981; The Marvelous Mess, 1980; Your Family, My Family, 1980; Tell Me Grandma/Tell Me Grandpa, 1979; What Are Daisies for, 1975; My Mother's Getting Married, 1985; Your Doctor, My Doctor, 1985; illustrator: Horrible Hannah, 1980; Follow that Ghost, 1979; Bubbles and Soap Films, 1979; The Other Place, 1978; Nonna, 1975, others; murals executed Parents and Childrens Services, Boston, 1982, The Children's Hosp., 1983-84, St. Anne's Hosp., Fall River, Mass., Meml.-Sloan Kettering Hosp., N.Y.C. Recipient Illustration award N.Y. Acad. Sci., 1980; Social Studies award, 1980. Mem. Soc. Illustrators, Soc. Childrens' Book Writers, Authors Guild. Address: 23 Cedar St Hingham MA 02043

DRESCHER, SUSAN LYNN, lawyer; b. Bklyn., Feb. 24, 1948; d. Sol and Esther Marion (Siegal) D.; m. Victor Elliot Penan, Aug. 16, 1970 (div. Dec. 1979). B.A. cum laude Tufts U., 1970; J.D. summa cum laude, Am. U., 1982. Bar: U.S. Ct. Appeals (D.C. Ctr.) 1982, U.S. Dist. Ct. Md. 1983, U.S. Ct.

Appeals (4th cir.) 1983. Interior designer Susan (Drescher) Penan Designs, Miami, Fla. and Bethesda, Md., 1972-79; law clk. U.S. Dist. Ct. Md., Balt., 1982-83; assoc. Skadden, Arps, Slate, Meagher & Flom, Washington, 1983—. Co-designer landscape architecture, Washington (Grand award for Landscape Architecture 1974); mng. editor Washington Coll. of Law Law Rev., 1981-82. Mem. ABA, D.C. Bar Assn., Phi Delta Phi. Democrat. Office: Skadden Arps Slate Meagher & Flom 919 18th St NW Washington DC 20006

DRESDALE, MARCELLA LILLY, retail company executive; b. Detroit, May 22, 1959; d. John Richard and Marcella (Seymour) Lilly; m. Richard Conrad Dresdale, Aug. 3, 1984. B.A., Trinity Coll., Washington, 1981. Mdse. asst. Elizabeth Arden, N.Y.C., 1981-83; sales mgr. R.H. Macy & Co., N.Y.C., 1983-84, asst. buyer, 1984-86; assoc. merchandising product mgr. sleepwear Associated Merchandising Corp., N.Y.C., 1986—. Avocations: sailing; travel; art. Home: 420 E 80th Apt 11A New York NY 10021 Office: Associated Merchandising Corp 1440 Broadway New York NY 10018

DRESSELHAUS, MILDRED SPIEWAK, electrical engineering educator; b. Bklyn., Nov. 11, 1930; d. Meyer and Ethel (Teichteil) Spiewak; A.B., Hunter Coll., 1951; Fulbright fellow Cambridge U. (Eng.), 1951-52; A.M., Radcliffe Coll., 1953; Ph.D. in Physics, U. Chgo., 1958; D.Eng. (hon.), Worcester Poly. Inst., 1976; D.Sc. (hon.), Smith Coll., 1980, Hunter Coll., 1982, Newark Inst. Tech., 1984; m. Gene F. Dresselhaus, May 25, 1958; children—Marianne, Carl Eric, Paul David, Eliot Michael. NSF postdoctoral fellow Cornell U., 1958-60; mem. staff Lincoln Lab., MIT, 1960-67, Abby Rockefeller Mauze vis. prof. MIT, 1967-68, prof. elec. engring., 1968—, prof. physics, 1983—, assoc. head dept. elec. engring., 1972-74, Abby Rockefeller Mauze chair, 1973-85, Inst. prof., 1985—; dir. Center Materials Sci. and Engring., 1977-83, also vis. scientist Francis Bitter Nat. Magnet Lab.; vis. prof. Campinas U., Brazil, summer 1971, Israel Inst. Tech., Technion, summer 1972, also Tokyo, 1973, Caracas, Venezuela, 1977; Chancellor's vis. prof. U. Calif.-Berkeley, 1985; chmn. evaluation panels Nat. Bur. Standards, 1978-83; Graffin lectr. Am. Carbon Soc., 1982, mem. sci. adv. com. Allied Corp., 1980-84; mem. Energy Research Adv. Bd., 1983—; dir. Chem. Fund, 1983—, Rogers Corp., 1986—. Recipient Hunter Coll. Hall of Fame award, 1972, Radcliffe Coll. Alumni medal, 1973, MIT Killian award, 1986. Fellow Am. Phys. Soc. (chmn. nominating com. 1975-76, Buckley prize com. 1976-77, chmn. 1977-78, new materials prize com. 1980, v.p. 1982, pres.-elect 1983, pres. 1984), IEEE (publs. bd., press bd., long range planning com.), AAAS (governing bd. 1985—); mem. Soc. Women Engrs. (achievement award 1977), Nat. Acad. Engring. (council 1981—), Nat. Acad. Scis., Am. Acad. Arts and Scis., Nat. Acad. Scis., Asso. Harvard Alumni (dir. 1974-76), Brazilian Acad. Sci. (corr.). Contbr. articles to profl. jours. Home: 147 Jason St Arlington MA 02174 Office: Mass Inst Tech Cambridge MA 02139

DRESSER, ROBERTA LEAZENBY, microbiologist; b. Fayette, Mo., Sept. 30, 1940; d. James Daniel and Mary Ann (Bates) Leazenby; B.A., U. Mo., 1961, B.Med.Sci., 1963, M.S. in Med. Microbiology, 1968; m. Steven T. Dresser, Dec. 17, 1959 (dec. Aug. 1973); children—Sara, Steven M., Todd, Thomas; m. 2d, Louis A. Kaufman, Dec. 30, 1977. Various clin. lab. positions with U.S. Army, USPHS and VA hosps., 1963-74; commnd. officer USPHS, 1974—; microbiologist div. in vitro diagnostic device standards Bur. Med. Devices, FDA, 1974-80, supervisory program analyst Office Asso. Dir. Standards, 1980-82, spl. asst. for regulatory analysis, 1982-83, analyst, div. planning and evaluation Ctr. for Devices and Radiol. Health, 1983—. Mem. vestry All Saints Episcopal Ch., San Francisco, 1973-74. Mem. Am. Soc. Microbiology, Am. Soc. Clin. Pathologists, Federally Employed Women, Commd. Officers Assn., Nat. Assn. Female Execs., Children Am. Revolution (officer 1980—). Democrat. Home: 2128 Edgewater Pkwy Silver Spring MD 20903 Office: 5600 Fishers Ln Rockville MD 20857

DREVES, DEBORAH ANN, television station promotion manager; b. Chgo., Apr. 23, 1959; d. Billy Jack and Hannelore (Walter) Tidmore; m. Richard Arthur Dreves, Dec. 14, 1979. B.A. in Communicative Disorders, U. Central Fla., 1979. Traffic mgr. Sta. WRCC FM, Cape Coral, Fla., 1980; promotion mgr. Sta. WLEQ FM, Bonita Springs, Fla., 1981; promotion mgr. Sta. WINK-TV, Ft. Myers, Fla., 1981—. Mem. Advt. Fedn. Southwest Fla. (chairperson com. 1983—), Assn. Broadcast Promotion and Mktg. Execs. (Gold medallion 1982, 84). Republican. Avocations: horticulture, bird watching. Office: WINK-TV PO Box 1060 Fort Myers FL 33902

DREW, BETTY BERG, parliamentarian, civic worker; b. Green Bay, Wis., May 27, 1929; d. Walter Richard and Viola Marion (Holz) Berg; m. Dale Robert Drew, June 3, 1950; children—Laura Jane, John Robert, Thomas Richard, James Berg. Diploma in Nursing, Wesley Meml. Hosp. Sch. Nursing, 1950. Registered profl. parliamentarian, Mich. Judge for high sch. parliamentary competitions, local, state and nat. levels, Mich., 1978—; organizer coalition of State Organ Donor Agencies, Ann Arbor, Mich., 1982—; lectr. for parliamentary unit Oakland-Birmingham, Mich., 1983-86. Officer PTO, Bloomfield Hills, Mich., 1970, 77; mem. Bloomfield Republican Women's Club. Mem. AMA Aux. (speaker of house 1984-86), Mich. State Assn. Parliamentarians (sec. 1983-86), Nat. Assn. Parliamentarians, Mich. State Med. Soc. Aux. (pres. 1983-84), Women's Nat. Farm and Garden Assn. (Vernor br. pres. 1977-78), P.E.O. (pres. chpt. 1985-87). Republican. Congregationalist. Avocations: Golf; knitting; sewing; bridge; piano. Home: 4454 Barchester Dr Bloomfield Hills MI 48013

DREW, ELIZABETH, journalist; b. Cin., Nov. 16, 1935; d. William J. and Estelle Jacobs Brenner; B.A., Wellesley Coll., 1957; D.H.L. (hon.), Hood Coll., 1976, D.H.L., Yale U., 1976, Trinity Coll., 1978, Reed Coll., 1979, William, Coll., 1981; LL.D. (hon.), Georgetown U., 1981; m. J. Patterson Drew, Apr. 11, 1964 (dec. Sept. 1970); m. 2d David Webster, Sept. 26, 1981. Writer, Congressional Quar., 1959-64; Washington editor Atlantic Monthly, 1967-73; host TV interview program Thirty Minutes With, 1971-73; commentator Agronsky & Co., Post Newsweek TV and radio stas., nationally syndicated, 1973—; writer New Yorker Mag., Washington, 1973—. Recipient award Soc. Mag. Writers, 1971; Achievement award Wellesley Alumnae, 1973; DuPont award, 1973; Mo. medal, 1979; Sidney Hillman award, 1983. Author: Washington Journal, 1975; American Journal, 1977; Senator, 1979; Portrait of an Election, 1981; Politics and Money, 1983; Campaign Journal, 1985. Office: 1700 K St NW Washington DC 20006

DREW, KATHERINE FISCHER, historian, educator; b. Houston, Sept. 24, 1923; d. Herbert H. and Martha Fischer; B.A., Rice Inst., 1944, M.A., 1945; Ph.D., Cornell U., 1950; m. Ronald F. Drew, July 21, 1951; Asst. prof. history Rice U., Houston, 1950-57, assoc. prof., 1957-64, prof., 1964—, Harris Masterson Jr. prof. history, 1982-84, Lynette S. Autrey prof., 1984—, chmn. dept. history, 1970-80. Guggenheim fellow, 1959, NEH sr. fellow, 1974-75. Fellow Mediaeval Acad. Am.; mem. Am. Hist. Assn., Am. Soc. Legal History, Phi Beta Kappa. Author: The Burgundian Code, 1949; A Study of Lombard Laws, 1956; Barbarian Invasions, 1970; The Lombard Laws, 1974. Editor: Rice Studies, 1966-81. Office: Dept History Rice U Houston TX 77251

DREW, NADINE WRIGHT, college official; b. Timmonsville, S.C., Sept. 11, 1954; d. Norman P. and Maxine (Wilson) Wright; m. Antonius M.A. Drew, Nov. 24, 1979; children—Andre Marcus, LaKesha Alaina, Lenneice Antonia. B.S. in Bus. Adminstrn., Barry U., 1976, B.S. in Mktg./Mgmt., 1976. Legis. asst. to Senator Bob Graham, Miami, Fla., 1976-78; adminstrv. asst. Hunt/Meyer Community Relations, Miami, 1978-80; dir. pub. affairs and publs. Fla. Meml. Coll., Miami, 1980—; pub. relations dir. Nat. Speakers Bur., 1984—. Mem. Internat. Bus. Assn. Communicators, Women in Communications (2d v.p.), Pub. Relations Soc. Am. Democrat. Mem. Ch. of God. Home: 552 NW 45th St Miami FL 33127 Office: Fla Meml Coll 15800 NW 42nd Ave Miami FL 33127

DREW, SALLY LOUISE, health maintenance company executive; b. Ashtabula, Ohio, July 13, 1953; d. Robert Leo and Sally Louise (Peck) Downes; m. Steven Richard Drew, Aug. 25, 1984; 1 child, Sarah Melissa. B.S. in Bus. Adminstrn., Rollins Coll., 1984. Joined U.S. Air Force, 1971, advanced through grades to tech. sgt., 1984; inventory mgr., many different locations, 1971-78; basic tng. instr. 3743 basic mil. training squadron, Lackland AFB, Tex., 1978-81; logistics mgr. equal opportunities mgmt. inst., Dept. Def., Patrick AFB, Fla., 1981-84; purchasing agt. Health Am. Corp. Tex., San Antonio, 1984-85, material mgr., 1985, dir. support service, 1985—. Brownies leader, local Girl Scouts U.S.A., 1983; runner 10 miles for United Way, Melbourne, Fla., 1983, for Am. Heart Assn., Orlando, Fla., 1983. Named Non-Commissioned Officer in Charge Technician of Yr., SAC Supply Squadron, Wurtsmith AFB, Mich., 1977, Instr. of Month, 3743 basic mil. training squadron, Lackland AFB, Mar. 1979. Mem. Purchasing Mgmt. Assn. (profl. devel. chmn. San Antonio 1985—), Tex. Hosp. Assn. Club: Randolph AFB Officers Wives. Avocations: running road races; cooking. Office: Health Am Corp of Tex 610 Lanark St Suite 203A San Antonio TX 78218

DREW-FRIAS, PRISCILLA ANN, career consultant, real estate agent, emergency medical technician; b. Chgo., Oct. 1, 1945; d. Russell Paul and Helen Joan (Giambone) Drew; m. Carl Nicholas Blacker, Sept. 8, 1962 (div. Aug. 1967); children—Lisa Blacker, Laura L. Duggan; m. 2d, Jorge H. Frias, Dec. 13, 1973 (div. Oct. 1978). Student, Triton Coll., River Grove, Ill., 1981-84. Nationally registered emergency med. technician. Office adminstr. Space/Mgmt. Program, Chgo., 1977-78; gen. mgr. Show 'n Sell Jewels, Schiller Park, Ill., 1979-80; personnel mgr. Wesbon Internat., Chgo., 1980-81; asst. personnel dir. Amco Engring., Schiller Park, 1981—; pres. Drew & Assocs., Harwood Heights, Ill., 1983—, also lectr. and workshop leader; lectr., workshop leader Triton Coll., 1981—. Mem. Triton Coll. Employers Adv. Bd., 1983-84. Mem. Nat. Assn. Future Women (chmn. membership com. and job referral com. North Suburban chpt. 1983-84), Nat. Assn. for Female Execs., Schiller Park C. of C. (sec. 1985—). Clubs: Triton Coll. Small Bus. Owners Assn. Office: Drew & Assocs PO Box 381 Des Plaines IL 60016

DREWRY, IRENE VELA, Spanish educator; b. Bartlesville, Okla., Apr. 22, 1929; d. Fidel and Clara Wilma (Kohler) Vela; m. Robert E. Drewry, Mar. 1, 1952; children—Leigh Ann, David Paul. B.A., U. Wash., 1973, teaching credential, 1975, 5th yr., 1981. Tchr. migrant edn. Yakima Sch. Dist., Wash., 1977-78; tchr. Spanish, Northshore Sch. Dist., Bothell, Wash., 1978-79, Bellevue Sch. Dist., 1983-84; substitute tchr., 1980-83; tchr. Spanish, Mercer Island Sch. Dist., Wash., 1984—; tchr. English as a Second Lang., Bellevue Community Coll., 1984—. Active Eastside Mental Health, Bellevue, 1980—. Mem. NEA, Wash. Assn. Fgn. Lang. Tchrs., Wash. Assn. Educators Speakers Other Langs., Mercer Island Edn. Assn. Democrat. Roman Catholic. Avocations: art; antique collecting; theatre; travel. Home: 102 Cedar Crest Ln Bellevue WA 98004 Office: Mercer Island Sch Dist 9100 SE 42d St Mercer Island WA 98040

DREY, EDNA W., business executive; b. Joplin, Mo., Apr. 5, 1955; d. Charles R. and Agnes Sarah (Bullfinch) Jones; m. Kenneth John Drey, Sept. 9, 1982. A.A., Joplin Jr. Coll., 1975; B.A., N.W. Mo. State Tchrs. Coll., 1977. Tchr. rural schs., Mo. and Ill., 1977-82; owner, mgr. Manchester Apt. Mgrs. Ltd., St. Louis, 1985—. Mem. Indsl. Mgmt. Assn., Nat. Assn. Female Execs., Mensa. Address: Werik Apts 9641 Manchester Rd Saint Louis MO 63119

DRIES, ANN NORBERTA, home economist, consumer advisor; b. N.Y.C., Dec. 11, 1925; d. George Andrew and Rose Miriam (Cunningham) D.; A.B. (Borden scholar), Hunter Coll., 1948, M.A., 1950. Tchr. home econs., jr. high sch., Mt. Vernon, N.Y., 1948-49; instr. home econs. Hunter Coll., N.Y.C., 1949-53; writer, star singing kitchen TV show, WOR-TV, N.Y.C., 1952-53; pub. relations home economist Aluminum Co. of Am., N.Y.C., 1953-67; dir. home econs., Doyle, Dane, Bernbach Advt. Agy., N.Y.C., 1967-70; dir. home econs., consumer services Nestle Co., Inc., White Plains, N.Y., 1970—. Named ten-yr. outstanding grad. Hunter Coll., 1958. Mem. Am., N.Y. State home econs. assns., Nat., N.Y.C. home economists in bus., Am. Women in Radio and TV, Nat. Home Fashion League, Advt. Women of N.Y., Electrical Women's Round Table, Soc. Consumer Affairs Profls., Am. Council on Consumer Interests, Conf. of Consumer Orgns., Phi Upsilon Omicron, Omicron Nu. Home: 39-11 210th St New York NY 11361 Office: 100 Bloomingdale Rd White Plains NY 10605

DRIGGS, MARGARET, journalist, public relations executive; b. Kansas City, Kans., June 30, 1909; d. William Foster and Lillie (Landers) Brazier; A.B., U. Kans., 1930; postgrad. Hofstra Coll., 1960, Pratt Inst. Sch. Library Sci., 1964-65; m. Jack Weems Quarrier, Nov. 26, 1933 (div. July 1945); children—John Chilton II, Philip Harrington, Camille Elizabeth; m. 2d, Howard R. Driggs, Sept. 26, 1948. Corr., Kansas City (Mo.-Kans.) Star, 1930-33; adminstrv. asst. to sec. and dir. public relations Hofstra Coll., 1956-61; asst. to nat. pres. Am. Pioneer Trails Assn., N.Y.C., 1948-63; dir. public relations, yearbook adv., Cathedral Sch. of St. Mary, Garden City, N.Y., 1969-73, librarian, 1972-74; chmn. Morven Guides for lectures and tours of Gov.'s Mansion, Princeton, N.J., 1975-82; chmn. of docents N.J. Hist. Soc. Mus., Princeton, 1982—; installed Duchess of Richelieu Collection, St. Mary's Library, 1972; exhibitor Driggs Collection of Americana; speaker on Indians. Active in acquisition of funds for scholarships in univs., Med. Center Princeton, 1975—. Recipient medal Am. Yearbook Co., 1970, Columbia Scholastic Press Assn., 1970. Mem. N.Y.U. Faculty Club (hon.), Nat. Council Coll. Publs. Advs., Internat. Platform Assn., U.S. Com. for UNICEF, Assn. Coll. and Research Libraries, Friends of Princeton U. Library, Hist. Soc. Princeton, N.J. Hist. Soc. (women's bd.), Nat. Trust Hist. Preservation, Smithsonian Assocs., Pi Delta Epsilon (Gold Key 1958). Episcopalian. Clubs: Present Day, Women's Coll. Princeton (chmn. 65th Ann. luncheon and benefit 1981), U. Kans. Gold Medal (citation and pin 1980). Photographer-editor: Vive Rochambeau, Vive Washington: the Bicentennial Celebration in Princeton, 1981 (French-Am. Alliance medal 1981). Home: 135 Princeton Arms S Cranbury NJ 08512

DRILL, BARBARA ANN, music educator; b. Duncan, Okla., Nov. 11, 1933; d. John Knox and Lula Ann (Hatley) Bowling; m. Lewis Stewart Drill, June 12, 1971; children by previous marriage—Daniel Knox Kiniry, John Michael Kiniry. B.Mus., So. Meth. U., 1955. Tchr. music Dallas Ind. Schs., 1955-58, 67-70; pvt. tchr. piano and organ, Dallas, 1955—; organist Casa View Christian Ch., Dallas, 1978—; accompanist Dallas Girls Chorus, 1982—; tchr. music Hockaday Sch., Dallas, 1983—; dir. children's choir Cara View Christian Ch., 1982—; accompanist various festivals, recitals, 1955—; organist/accompanist Tex. Ch. Choir Chorale European Tour, 1985. Recipient Recognition for outstanding contbn. to program for talented and gifted, Dallas Ind. Sch., 1977. Mem. Dallas Music Tchrs. Assn., Tex. Music Tchrs. Assn., Music Tchrs. Nat. Assn., Choristers Guild, Assn. Disciple Musicians, Tex. Music Educators Assn., Am. Guild Organists, Gamma Phi Beta. Republican. Home: 8635 Hackney Ln Dallas TX 75238 Office: Hockaday Preparatory Sch 11600 Welch Rd Dallas TX 75229

DRILL, VIRGINIA GRAHAM, bank personnel executive; b. Durham, N.C., July 28, 1947; d. John Borden and Ruby McKay (Barrett) Graham; m. Zachary Caleb Drill, Nov. 2, 1975; 1 child, Catherine Camille. B.A. in History, U. N.C., 1968; postgrad. Yale U., 1969. City personnel mgr. Northwestern Bank, Durham, 1981-83, Triangle area personnel adminstr., Raleigh, N.C., 1983-85; consumer bank services mgr. First Union Nat. Bank, Raleigh, 1986—. Loaned exec. United Way Durham County, 1981. Mem. Durham-Triangle Personnel Assn., Raleigh-Wake Personnel Assn., Am. Soc. Personnel Adminstrs., Phi Beta Kappa. Office: Northwestern Bank Fayetteville St Mall Raleigh NC 27602

DRISCOLL, CONSTANCE FITZGERALD, educator, author; b. Lawrence, Mass., Mar. 29, 1926; d. John James and Mary Anne (Leecock) Fitzgerald; A.B., Radcliffe Coll., 1946; postgrad. Harvard U., U. Hartford (Conn.), U. Bridgeport (Conn.), Worcester (Mass.) State Coll.; m. Francis George Driscoll, Aug. 21, 1948; children—Frances Mary, Martha Anne, Sara Helene, Maribeth Lee. Secondary sch. tchr., North Andover, Mass., 1946-48; book reviewer N.Y.C. and Boston pubs., 1955-64; asst. conf. edn. dir. U. Hartford, 1964-68; lectr. Pace U., N.Y.C., 1973-74; edn. commentary Radio WVOX, New Rochelle, N.Y., 1974-75; asst. edn. adv. Nat. Girl Scouts, 1972-74; pres., owner, dir. Open Corridor Schs. Cons., Inc., Bronxville, N.Y., 1972—, pres., dir. Open Corridor Schs., Inc., Oxford, Mass., 1984—; assoc. Worcester State Coll. (Mass.) 1984—. Author curriculum materials. Home: 338 Main St Oxford MA 01540 Office: Box 433 Bronxville NY 10708

DRISCOLL, DAWN-MARIE, lawyer; b. Framingham, Mass., Nov. 5, 1946; d. Paul Francis and Wanda Louise (Haznar) D.; m. Norman S. Marcus, Apr. 8, 1978; 1 son, Christopher. B.A., Regis Coll., 1968; J.D., Suffolk U., 1973. Bar: Mass., 1973, Mass. grad. legis. fellow, 1969; lectr. Law Sch., Boston Coll., 1975, Law Sch., Suffolk U., Boston, 1975; asst. counsel Mass. Senate, Boston, 1973-78; counsel, Filene's, Boston, 1978-80, v.p., counsel, 1980—; dir. exec. com. Boston Mcpl. Research Bur. Bd. dirs. New Eng. Legal Found., Boston, Boston Better Bus. Bur., United Community Planning Corp., Roxburg Community Coll. Found. Contbr. articles to law rev. and newspapers. Trustee, Regis Coll., 1984; mem. Gov.'s commn. on Mature Industries, Gov.'s Adv. Com. on Massbank. Mem. ABA, Mass. Bar Assn., Boston Bar Assn. (council 1981-84). Clubs: Boston, Union, Boston Study Group. Office: Filene's Exec Offices 426 Washington St Boston MA 02101

DRISCOLL, GENEVIEVE (JEANNE) BOSSON, mgmt. and orgn. devel. cons.; b. Pitts., Mar. 26, 1937; d. George August and Emma Haling Bleichner; B.S. cum laude, Fla. State U., 1959; postgrad. program for specialists in orgn. devel. Nat. Tng. Labs., 1970. m. John Edwin Bosson, June 17, 1959; 1 son, Matthew Edwin; m. 2d Frederick Driscoll, Oct. 7, 1972; stepchildren—Jennifer Locke, Cynthia Hall, Molly Davis, Julie Ann. Planning asst. Center for Planning and Innovation, Dept. Edn. State of N.Y., 1967-71, planning cons. So. Tier Regional Office for Ednl. Planning, Elmira, N.Y., 1971-72; tng. dir. Neusteters, Inc., Denver, 1973-74; orgn. devel. specialist CONNECT, Inc., N.Y.C., 1975-77; cons. Robert H. Schaffer & Assos., Stamford, Conn., 1977-80; partner Driscoll Cons. Group, Williamstown, Mass., 1980—; sales tng. mgr. Sheaffer Eaton div. Textron Inc., Pittsfield, Mass.; cons. in field. Office: 24 Lee Terr Williamstown MA 01267

DRISCOLL, JOSEPHINE MARGARET, state official; b. East Helena, Mont., July 7, 1923; d. George and Josephine (Masonovich) Nick; m. William J. Driscoll, Sept. 6, 1953 (div. 1967); children—Sara Kathleen, Maureen Elaine. With Fireman's Fund Group, Helena, Mont., 1940-53, Wolfstone & Co., Seattle, 1953-57, 59-62; supr. rates and forms Mont. Ins. Dept., Helena, 1966-74, asst. chief dep., 1974-77, chief dep. ins. commr., 1977-81; asst. commr. State Oreg. Dept. Commerce, Salem, 1981, ins. commr., 1981—. Named Woman of Yr., Ins. Women's Assn., Helena, Mont., 1978. Mem. Am. Bus. Women's Assn. (pres. chpt.; Woman of Yr. 1980), Nat. Assn. Ins. Commrs. (pres. 1986). Republican. Serbian Orthodox. Office: Ins Div Dept Commerce 158 12th St NE Salem OR 97310

DRISCOLL, SANDRA MAY, educational administrator; b. Framingham, Mass., Sept. 1, 1936; d. William and Elsie (Nelson) Hammond; m. Donald Driscoll, June 28, 1958; children—Theresa, Michael, Kevin, Marianne. B.A., Kean Coll., 1976; M. Edn., West Ga. Coll., 1979; Edn. Specialist, Jaxonville State Coll., 1984. Tchr., media specialist Maplewood-South Orange, N.J., 1972-77; media specialist Rome City Schs., Ga., 1977-81; prin. West End Elem. Sch., Rome City Schs., 1981—; Mem. adv. council Juvenile Ct., Community Com. Fight Against Drugs and Alcohol in Teenagers. Recipient Elem. Sch. Bell award Ga. Assn. Educators 1984. Mem. Nat. Elem. Sch. Prins. Assn., Ga. Assn. Elem. Sch. Prins., Assn. Supervision and Curriculum Devel., Phi Delta Kappa, Kappa Delta Pi, Phi Kappa Phi. Roman Catholic. Avocations: reading; swimming; sports. Home: 26 Orchard Spring Rd Rome GA 30161 Office: West End Elem Sch Brown Fox Dr Rome GA 30161

DRISCOLL, SHIRLEY GRIFFITH, pathologist, educator; b. Pittston, Pa., Feb. 8, 1923; d. William Edmund and Margaret Helen (Underwood) Griffith; m. John J. Driscoll, Sept. 18, 1948. A.B., U. Pa., 1945, M.D., 1949. Intern, Mt. Auburn Hosp., Cambridge, Mass., 1949-50; pathologist Boston Lying in Hosp., 1958-65, pathologist Boston Hosp. for Women, 1965-78, pathologist in chief 1978-81, instr., asst. prof., assoc. prof. Harvard U., 1958-75, prof., 1975—, dir. women's and perinatal div. of pathology Brigham and Womens Hosp., Boston, 1981—. Author: (with Benirschke) Pathology of Human Placenta, 1967. Mem. AAAS, Teratology Soc., New Eng. Pediatric Pathology Group, Soc. Pediatric Pathology, Obstet. Soc. Boston, Mass. Med. Soc., New Eng. Soc. Pathology Mass. Soc. Pathology, Am. Soc. Clin. Pathologists, Internat. Acad. Pathology. Office: 75 Francis St Boston MA 02115

DRIVER, PAMELA JEAN, management consultant; b. Louisville, June 30, 1957; d. Stanley L. and Dorothy (Meador) K.; m. Jesse E. Driver, June 18, 1976; children—Clifford Dewayne, Jennifer Michele. B.S., U. Tenn., 1978, M.S., 1982. Dietary supr. Fort Sanders Presbyn. Hosp., Knoxville, Tenn., 1977-78; nutrition edn. project dir. Loudon County Schs., Loudon, Tenn., 1980-82, foodservice supr., 1980-83; pres., owner Driver & Assocs., Philadelphia, Tenn., 1982—; seminar, tng. presenter; editor, pub. foodservice newsletter. Chmn. March of Dimes, Heart Fund drives. Recipient 4-H Leader award Loudon County 4-H, 1981, 82, 83; Tenn. Nutrition edn. grantee, 1980-82. Mem. Nat. Restaurant Assn., Soc. Nutrition Edn. (membership coordinator Tenn. 1980-83), Am. Home Econs. Assn. (area pres. Tenn. conv. com.), Tenn. Sch. Food Service Assn. (resolutions chmn. conv. com. 1982-83), Am. Sch. Food Service Assn., Tenn. Home Econs. Assn. (conv. com.), Am. Mgmt. Assn., Omicron Nu. Baptist. Home: Route 1 Philadelphia TN 37846 Office: Driver and Assocs PO Box 139 Philadelphia TN 37846

DROGUETT, GLORIA IRENE, television prodn. co. exec.; b. New Orleans, Feb. 13, 1934; d. Wade Alfred and Naomi Bernice (Nelson) Gremillion; student Burroughs Bus. Sch., 1953; m. Rudy Droguett, Dec. 12, 1953; children—Lawrence Allen, Darrell Alan. Sales mgr. Western Steel Craft, Ingelwood, Calif., 1953-63; sec.-treas. Calif. Toiletries Reps., Los Angeles, 1964-74; sales mgr., sec.-treas., chief fin. officer Syntar Prodns., Los Angeles, 1975-79; v.p., chief fin. officer Fenestra Prodns., Inc., 1979—; bus. cons. Dalar Pub. Corp., 1978—. Mem. Research Inst. Am., Soc. Preservation of Variety and Performing Arts, Ebell of Los Angeles, Nat. Assistance League Am., Girls Club Aux. of Los Angeles Assistance League. Republican. Christian Scientist. Club: Job's Daus. (past honored queen). Home: 2329 Kenilworth Ave Los Angeles CA 90039

DRONET, VIRGIE MAE, educator; b. Kaplan, La., Mar. 17, 1941; d. Percy Joseph and Zula Mae (Harrington) D.; B.S., U. Southwestern La., 1963, M.Ed., 1970; Ed.S., McNeese State U., 1976; Ed.D., E. Tex. State U., 1979. Tchr. sci.-math., Lake Arthur, La., 1962-77; asst. instr. Center Ednl. Media and Tech., E. Tex. State U., 1977-78; with photog. prodn. lab., 1977-78; chmn. secondary level sci. com. Jefferson Davis Parish, Lake Arthur, 1976—; tchr. physics, chemistry, biology, algebra, computer scis. Lake Arthur High Sch.; vis. lectr. McNeese State U.; mem. Internat. Scholarship Com., 1980-81. Delta Kappa Gamma scholar, 1973, 77; NSF grantee, 1967. Mem. NEA, Assn. Ednl. Communications and Tech., Nat. Council Tchrs. Math., Assn. Supervision and Curriculum Devel., La. Assn. Educators, La. Assn. Ednl. Communications and Tech., La. Assn. Supervision and Curriculum Devel., Jefferson Davis Assn. Educators, Catholic Daus. Am., Delta Kappa Gamma (participant leadership seminar Baylor U. 1982), Phi Delta Kappa, Kappa Delta Pi, Kappa Mu Epsilon, Alpha Omega. Democrat. Author articles in field; editor La. Deltian, 1981. Home: PO Box 674 Lake Arthur LA 70549 Office: PO Drawer AP Lake Arthur LA 70549

DROZDA, HELEN DOROTHY, psychiatric social worker; b. Omaha, Mar. 21, 1924; d. Joseph J. and Mary E. (Sabatka) D.; B.S., U. Nebr., 1955; M.S., So. Ill. U., 1965; postgrad. Tex. Tech U., 1969, Midwestern U., 1968-69; Ph.D., Colo. State Christian Coll., 1973. Supervising group counselor San Diego Probation Dept., 1956-57; health edn. dir. YWCA, Omaha, 1954-56; Y-teen dir. YWCA, Alton, Bloomington and Peoria, Ill., 1958-62; guidance dir. Acad. of Our Lady, Peoria, 1962-64, St. Teresa Acad., East St. Louis, Ill., 1964-67, Knox County Pub. Schs., Benjamin, Tex., 1967-69; guidance dir. Wilbarger County Pub. Schs., Vernon, Tex., 1969-70; exec. dir. Burk Guidance and Counseling Services, Burkburnett, Tex., 1970-86; social service supr. Western unit Wichita Falls State Hosp., Tex. Cert. rehab. counselor; named Social Worker of Yr., 1984. Mem. Am. Legion, Air Force Assn., Am. Guidance and Personnel Assn., Nat. Assn. Social Workers (chmn. Red River unit), Midwest Soc. Individual Psychology, Tex. Pub. Employees Assn., Tex. Social Psychotherapy Assn., Acad. Certified Social Workers, Nat. Rifle Assn., Am. Assn. Ret. Persons. Home: 820 Sheppard Rd Burkburnett TX 76354 Office: Burk Guidance and Counseling Burkburnett TX 76354

DRUCKER, CHRISTINE MARIE, lawyer; b. Sioux City, Iowa, Apr. 16, 1947; d. Sigmund James and Paula Frances (Riedmann) Kulawik; m. John Joseph Drucker, Jr., June 19, 1971; children—Emily Catherine, Jeremy David. B.A., Webster Coll., 1969; J.D., St. Louis U., 1972. Bar: Mo. 1972, Ill. 1973, Minn. 1977. Law clk. Mo. Ct. Appeals, St. Louis, 1972-73; assoc. law firm Walsh, Case & Coale, Chgo., 1973-74; atty. Ill. States Atty.'s Assn., Elgin, Ill., 1974-76; atty.-advisor U.S. Dept. Interior, Mpls., 1979-81; sole practice law, Mpls., 1983—; legal counsel Task Force on Cable TV of Minn. Women's Consortium, 1983-84. Mem. DFL Feminist Caucus, 1982—. Mem. ABA, Minn. Bar Assn., Minn. Women's Lawyers (mem. legis. action com. 1984), Hennepin County Bar Assn. (mem. coms.), Minn. Women's Network (bd. dirs.). Democrat. Roman Catholic (mem. fin. com. 1980-82, chmn. reception com. 1979-80). Home: 5121 Bryant Ave S Minneapolis MN 55419 Office: 580 Lumber Exchange Bldg 10 S 5th St Minneapolis MN 55402

DRUCKER, VITA CLARICE, data processing systems consultant; b. Los Angeles, Jan. 1, 1949; d. Henry and Rose (Kaplan) Drucker. B.A. cum laude in Math., UCLA, 1970, M.A.T. in Math., 1972. Cert. secondary tchr., Calif. Mathematician, Fed. Hwy. Adminstrn., Washington, 1970; mgmt. analyst

FAA, Washington, 1972; teaching asst. dept. math. UCLA, 1970-72; sr. systems analyst Bank of Am., San Francisco, 1973-79; tech. rep. Nat. CSS, Inc., San Francisco, 1979-81; cons., San Francisco, 1981-84, Hong Kong, 1984—. Founder, Soc. Sociol. Devel. of Growth and Expression of Body, Mind, Spirit, Annandale, Va. and San Francisco, 1977. Mem. Nat. Assn. Female Execs., Ind. Computer Consultants Assn., UCLA Alumni Assn., Alpha Lambda Delta. Club: Commonwealth (San Francisco).

DRUM, JOAN MCCASKIE, domestic engineer, consultant; b. Paterson, N.J., Oct. 14, 1942; d. Prestley Edgar and Martha Bearce (Cleavinger) McCaskie; m. Brian Drum, Sept. 20, 1969; children—Adam Cass, Carly McCaskie. B.A., St. Lawrence U., Canton, N.Y., 1964. Adminstrv. asst. J. Henry Schroder, London, 1964-65; account exec. Equitable Life, N.Y.C., 1965-68; owner, operator Green House, Milburn, N.J., 1974-78; cons. Drum Assocs., N.Y.C., 1969—. Bd. dirs. CLEAN, Milburn, 1982-84, Planned Parenthood, Milburn, 1982-84, Prospect House, East Orange, N.J., 1982; exec. bd. Milburn PTAs, 1977—; mem. consumer adv. bd. Kings Supermarket, 1984-86; bd. dirs. Wyo. Civic Assn., Milburn, 1985, LWV, Milburn and Short Hills, N.J., 1985; campaign mgr. Twp. Com. candidates, 1974, 79, 82, 84, County Exec. candidates, Milburn, 1978, 82, gubernatorial candidates, Milburn, 1981, 85; county committeeperson Essex County Com., Milburn, 1974-85, exec. bd., 1978-85; co-chmn. Democratic Club, Milburn and Short Hills, 1982—; vice chmn. Community Mental Health Ctr. of the Oranges, Maplewood and Milburn, 1982-85, treas., 1985-87. Clubs: Lake Naomi and Timber Trails (bd. govs. 1983-87, recreation chair), Maplewood Tennis. Avocation: tennis.

DRUM, SARA RUTH, nursing administrator; b. Evanston, Ill., Aug. 6, 1929; d. Raymond Borland and Ruth Armstrong (Pettit) D.; R.N., Ch. Home and Hosp. Sch. Nursing, 1955; postgrad. in gerontology and nursing adminstrn. U. Ariz., Weber State Coll., UCLA, U. So. Calif., U. Calif.-Northridge; Dir. nursing Colonial Convalescent Hosp., Santa Ana, 1967-68; supr. Rio Hondo Meml. Hosp., Downey, Calif., 1968-69; dir. nursing Intercommunity Convalescent Hosp., Norwalk, Calif., 1969-76, Southland Geriatric Ctr., Norwalk, 1976-85, Calif. Convalescent Hosp., Long Beach, 1985-86. Mem. assoc. degree nursing adv. com. Cerritos Coll.; adv. bd. baccalaureate degree nurse program Biola Coll.; mem. occupational adv. com. nursing Whittier Union High Sch. Dist. Democrat. Home: 4200 Blue Heron Circle Anacortes WA 98221

DRUMHELLER, D.D. THOMPSON micro-computer consultant; b. Northfield, N.J., Oct. 2, 1946; d. Paul Jones and Evelyn Louise (Paschall) Thompson; m. C. Edwin Drumheller, Feb. 12, 1972; stepchildren—Robert, James. B.B.A., U. N.Mex., 1968. Dir. Acad. Devel. Corp., N.Y.C., 1969-71, CBS Inc., N.Y.C., 1971-73; pvt. practice mgmt. cons., N.Y.C., 1973-75; legal adminstr. Greenbaum, Wolff & Ernst, N.Y.C., 1975-80, Paul & Thomson, Miami, 1980-83; pres. D'Lynn Bus. Services, North Miami, 1984—. Mem. ABA, Assn. Legal Adminstrs. (pres. chpt. 1982-83), Bus. Council, North Miami C. of C. Home: The Reef Club 4B 16565 NE 26th Ave North Miami Beach FL 33160 Office: D'Lynn Business Services North Miami FL 33181

DRUMMOND, GILLIAN M., home furnishings company executive; b. Haywardsheath, Eng., Apr. 3, 1943; came to U.S., 1951; d. Bernard Gilbert and Margaret (Soot Hutcheson) D. Cert. N.Y. Sch. Interior Design, 1965; student U. Geneva, 1961-62. Asst. designer B. Altman & Co., N.Y.C., 1966-68; interior designer Tate & Hall, N.Y.C., 1968-72; Practice interior design, N.Y.C., 1972-75; mgr. customer relations Marcel Dekker Inc., N.Y.C., 1975-78; exec. dir. S.M. Hexter, N.Y.C., 1978-80; exec. dir. East Coast Winfield Design Assocs., N.Y.C., 1980-82; home furnishings cons., N.Y.C., 1982-85; pres. Gillian Drummond Inc., Wilmington N.C., 1985—. Conservative candidate N.Y. Congress, 1974; bd. dirs. Arts Council Lower Cape Fear; program chmn. St. Thomas Celebration of Arts. Mem. Decorative Fabrics Assn. (membership chmn. 1982-84), Nat. Home Fashions League, Nat. Assn. Female Execs., Nat. Trust Historic Preservation, Historic Wilmington Found. Republican. Address: 7 N 23d St Wilmington NC 28405 Office: 3 Ann St Wilmington NC 28401

DRUMMOND, PAULA GRIER, lawyer; b. Fort Lauderdale, Fla., Dec. 8, 1950; d. John Perkins and Jeanne (Bottomley) Grier; m. Michael A. Fruchey, Aug. 30, 1968 (div. Oct. 1972); 1 child, Cecily N.; m. Richard Wayne Drummond, June 17, 1978; 1 child, John Edward. A.A. with honors, Brevard Community Coll., 1973; B.A. summa cum laude, U. Central Fla., 1975; J.D., Fla. State U., 1978. Bar: Fla. 1978, U.S. Dist. Ct. (no. dist.) Fla. 1978, U.S. Supreme Ct. 1984. Law clk. U.S. Magistrate, No. Dist. Fla., Pensacola, 1978-80; asst. county atty. Escambia County, Fla., Pensacola, 1980-82, county atty., 1982-83; sole practice, Pensacola, 1983—. Bd. dirs. YWCA, Pensacola, 1985. Mem. ABA, Fla. Bar Assn. (exec. council local govt. law sect. 1982-83), Escambia-Santa Rosa Bar Assn. (exec. com. 1984-85, chmn. bar found. com. 1984-85), Pensacola Network Exec. Women (v.p. 1985-86). Clubs: Panhandle Tiger Bay, Gulf Coast Econs. (Pensacola). Office: PO Box 9253 15 W La Rua St Pensacola FL 32513-9253

DRURY, DEBORAH ANN, business owner; b. Pasadena, Tex., Oct. 8, 1956; d. Joseph H. and Shirley E. (Calk) Yerkes; m. Brian Michael Spires, July 12, 1974 (div. Mar. 1984) children—Brian Michael, Bailey Ann. m. James Bailey, Drury, III, Nov. 10, 1984. Student San Jacinto Coll., 1974-77. Sec., gen. mgr. Cryo-Therm Fabrications, Houston, 1974-78; sales mgr. Extol div. Childres Corp., Houston, 1978-80; pres., owner Arrow Insulation, Inc., Houston, 1980—. Area dir. Muscular Dystrophy Assn., Pasadena, 1982-83; mem. com. Houston and Pasadena Livestock Show and Rodeo, 1982, 83; entertainment chair Strawberry Festival, Pasadena, 1983; Mem. S.W. Insulation Contractors Assn., Houston Bus. Council (coms.). Avocations: skiing; sports. Home: 3954 Salvador Pasadena TX 77504 Office: 5828 Cheswood Houston TX 77087

DRYDEN, JUDY CANADAY, government official; b. Elkhart, Kans., Dec. 14, 1930; d. Lieu Pierce and Eva Maudie (Caler) Canaday; m. Donald W. Dryden, May 6, 1949; children—Donald Wayne, Mary Anne, John Robert. Student, Iola Jr. Coll., Kans., 1947-49, Northwestern State U., Natchitoches, La., 1974. Clk.-typist spl. services U.S. Army, Ft. Polk, La., 1962-66, mil. personnel clk. testing, 1966-67, computer operator, data processing, 1967-70, computer systems analyst Mgmt. Info. Systems Office, Ft. Polk, La., 1970-74, computer specialist, Ft. Dix, N.J., 1974-76, computer specialist Hdqrs. Tng. and Doctrine Command, Info. Mgmt. Div., Ft. Monroe, Va., 1976-82, chief customer services br., Data Processing Field Office, 1982, chief customer support div., 1982-83, chief office automation and mgmt. br., 1983-85, chief accountability, acquisition and contracting, 1985—. Mem. fin. com. Phoebus Baptist Ch., Hampton, Va., 1982-85, chmn., 1983, ch. clk., 1983-86. Recipient Sustained Superior Performance award Dept. of Army, 1979, Outstanding Performance award 1981. Mem. Nat. Assn. Female Execs., Leadership Found., Assn. U.S. Army, Smithsonian Assocs., Internat. Platform Assn., Nat. Trust for Hist. Preservation. Democrat. Baptist. Home: 9 Pavilion Pl Hampton VA 23664 Office: Data Processing Field Office Bldg 117 Fort Monroe VA 23651

DRYDEN, MARY ELIZABETH, legal librarian, writer, actress; b. Chgo., Oct. 18, 1949; d. James Heard and Hazel Anne (Potts) Rule; m. Ian Dryden, Nov. 22, 1975. Student, U. London, 1969, Bath U., 1970; B.A., Scripps Coll., 1971; postgrad. U. Edinburgh, 1971-74. Head librarian Hahn, Cazier & Leff, San Diego, 1980, Fredman, Silverberg & Lewis, San Diego, 1980-83, Riordan & McKinzie, Los Angeles, 1983—. Theatrical appearances include Antony and Cleopatra, McOwen Theatre, London, 1984, Table Manners, Los Angeles, 1985, Harliquinade, Los Angeles, 1985. Freelance photog. model, 1973—. Book critic Los Angeles Times; contbr. articles to newspapers. Mem. Soc. Calif. Soc. Law Librarians, Am. Film Inst., Theatre Palisades, Mensa, Phi Beta Kappa. Avocations: photography; wine; architecture; fine art; languages; music. Office: Riordan & McKinzie 29th Floor 300 S Grand Ave Los Angeles CA 90071

DRYER, DOROTHEA MERRILL (MRS. EDWIN JASON DRYER), lawyer; b. Salt Lake City; d. George Edmund and Lillian (Chapman) Merrill; A.B., Stanford, 1936; LL.B., Yale, 1940; m. Edwin Jason Dryer, Feb. 28, 1942; children—Diana Claire Dryer Wright, Faith Ellen. Admitted to Utah bar, 1941, U.S. Supreme Ct. bar, U.S. Ct. Mil. Appeals; clk. to Chief Justice Wolfe, Utah Supreme Ct., 1941; atty. Bur. Immigration, Dept. Justice, Washington, 1941-42; practiced in Salt Lake City, 1943-47, Washington, 1948—; dep. county atty., Salt Lake City, 1947-48. Fellow Am. Assn. Criminology; mem. Am., Fed., Utah bar assns., Nat. Assn. Women Lawyers, Am. Judicature Soc., Nat. Assn. for Gifted Children, Assn. for Gifted, Internat. Platform Assn., Oral History Assn., Kappa Kappa Gamma. Unitarian. Clubs: Jr. League Washington; Potomac Bus. and Profl. Women's; Nat. Lawyers. Home: 5126 Palisade Ln NW Washington DC 20016 Office: Farm Running Brook Farm Route 1 Bentonville VA 22610

DRYNAN, MARGARET ISOBEL, music teacher, retired consultant; b. Toronto, Ont., Can., Dec. 10, 1915; d. William James and Ellen (Rowney) Brown; Mus.B., U. Toronto, 1943; m. George Drynan, July 3, 1940; children—Judith, John, James. Mem. nat. exec. bd. Royal Can. Coll. after 1951, nat. 1st v.p., 1980-82, nat. pres., 1982-84; pres. Oshawa Council for the Arts, Ont., Can., 1972-74; dir. Canterbury Singers, Oshawa, 1952-69; music supr., cons. Durham Bd. Edn., 1960-80; bd. dirs. Oshawa Symphony, 1960-80, 1st v.p., 1984-86, pres., 1986—, percussionist. Recipient award Royal Conservatory Toronto, 1975, other awards. Hon. fellow Royal Can. Coll. Organists; mem. Fedn. Women Tchrs., Can. Fedn. Adjudicators, Registered Music Tchrs. (past pres.). Anglican. Compositions include: Songs for Judith, Why do the bells?, Including Me, Missa Brevis in F, The Fate of Gilbert Gim, The Canada Goose (operetta). Home: 589 Pinewood St Oshawa ON L1G 2S2 Canada

DUAFALA, MARY ELAINE, pharmacist; b. Sewickly, Pa., Feb. 25, 1951; d. Edward and Julia Rose (Telesz) D. B.S. in Pharmacy, U. Pitts., 1973; M.S., Ohio State U., 1975. Registered pharmacist, Pa., Ohio, N.Y. Drug info. and research pharmacist Grant Hosp., Columbus, Ohio, 1975-78, asst. dir. pharmacy, 1978-82, assoc. dir. pharmacy, 1982; chief pharmacy services Gaston Meml. Hosp., Gastonia, N.C., 1982-85; assoc. dir. pharmacy services Meml. Sloan-Kettering Cancer Ctr., N.Y.C., 1985—; clin. instr. Ohio State U., Columbus, 1976-82, mem. pharmacy practice adv. com., 1977-82; chmn. pharmacy com. Columbus Community Clin. Oncology Program, 1982. Author research writings, 1975 (Roche Research award). Mem. Am. Soc. Hosp. Pharmacists, Am. Pharm. Assn., N.Y. State Council Hosp. Pharmacists, Rho Chi. Home: 375 Shunpike Rd Chatham NJ 07928 Office: Memorial Sloan-Kettering Cancer Center 1275 York Ave New York NY 10021

DUARTE, BONITA KATHLEEN BOWMAN, temporary help company executive; b. Hagerstown, Md., Jan. 26, 1947; d. John Edward and Ruth Kathleen (Harrison) Boward; m. Wiliam Patrick FitzGerald Duarte, June 30, 1979. Student, U. Nebr., 1969-70, U. Md., 1972, 74. Dep. planner Lincoln Action Program, Lincoln, Nebr., 1968-70; asst. adminstr. Howrey & Simon, Washington, 1970-76; adminstr. Bergson, Borkland et al, Washington, 1977-78; asst. adminstr. Steptoe & Johnson, Washington, 1978-79; adminstr. Pendleton & Sabian, Denver, 1979-80; v.p., chief fin. officer Temporary Profls. Inc., Denver, 1983—. Dir., Give Thanks Found. Inc., Denver, 1983—. Mem. Nat. Assn. Temporary Services, Nat. Assn. Female Execs., Colo. Assn. Temporary Services, Denver C. of C. Avocation: tailor. Office: Temporary Profls Inc 1600 Stout St Denver CO 80202

DUBAY, SANDRA LOUISE, author; b. Battle Creek, Mich., Oct. 6, 1954; d. Harry Andrew and Reatha Lenore (Bingham) DuBay. A.A., Wastenaw Community Coll., Ann Arbor, Mich., 1974; B.A. in Psychology, U. Mich., 1976. Freelance writer, 1978—; owner Just Books. Author: Mistress of the Sun King, 1980; Flame of Fidelity, 1981; The Claverleigh Curse, 1982; Fidelity's Flight, 1983; Whispers of Passion, 1984; In Passion's Shadow, 1984; Crimson Conquest, 1984; Where Passion Dwells, 1985; By Love Beguiled, 1986. Methodist. Home: 801 Bradfield St Bay City MI 48706

DUBELL, JAN GALEY, real estate broker; b. Omaha, June 9, 1951; d. David Ola and Minaruth (McWhirter) Galey; children—Stephen, Rachel. Student B.C. Coll., Pemberton, N.J., 1978-80, Am. Inst. Banking, 1982-84, Northlake Coll., Irving, Tex., 1984-86. Licensed real estate broker. Cons., Dallas, 1982-83; office trainee Guaranty Bank, Dallas, 1981-82; mktg. officer First Bank/Las Colinas, Irving, Tex., 1983-84; realtor assoc. Henry S Miller Co., Irving, 1984—. Named Million Dollar Producer, Women's Council Realtors, Irving, 1985, Million Dollar Club, Henry S Miller Co., Irving, 1985, 86. Mem. Nat. Assn. Realtors, Tex. Assn. Realtors, Irving Bd. Realtors, Dallas Bd. Realtors, N.E. Tarrant County Bd. Realtors, Irving C. of C. (com. mem. women's div. 1984-86), Las Colinas Women's Assn. (com. mem. 1985-86). Episcopalian. Avocations: horseback riding; aerobics. Office: Henry S Miller Co 4950 N O'Connor Suite 195 Irving TX 75062

DUBIN, E. BEVERLY, photographer, graphic artist, designer; b. Los Angeles, Dec. 11, 1945; d. Beatrice Winograd. Student U. Miami, Fla., 1963-64, Emerson Coll., 1964-66, New Sch. for Social Research, 1966-67; B.F.A., San Francisco Art Acad., 1971; M.A. in Art, Lone Mountain Coll., 1973; postgrad. U. Calif., Extension Ctr., 1971-73, Screen Printing Acad., 1973. One woman shows: Circle Gallery, San Francisco, 1972, Old Ways Gallery, Oakland, Calif., 1973; group shows include: Renaissance Pleasure Faire, 1970-80, Wonder Fair, Oakland, 1970, Gt. Himalaya Cookie Co., San Francisco, 1974, Squaw Valley (Calif.) Art Ctr., 1984; books include: Roll Your Own, 1973; Water Squatters, 1975; Show and Tell (poetry and photographs), 1985; photographs appeared in following jours. and newspapers: San Francisco Examiner/Chronicle, 1973, Oakland Telegraph, 1973, Clear Creek mag., 1972, Bookpaper, 1975; guest lectr. in field. Office: PO Box 189 San Anselmo CA 94960

DUBIN, ELLEN ZAWEL, management consultant; b. N.Y.C., Oct. 20, 1938; d. Joseph and Leona (Snitkoff) Richman; B.A., City U. N.Y., 1970; postgrad. Yeshiva U., 1972, A. K. Rice Inst. Group Dynamics, 1974; m. Howard S. Dubin, Sept. 17, 1978; children by previous marriage—Alyssa Zawel, Leigh Zawel, Reva Zawel, Joshua Zawel. Community advocate, 1961-73; consumer ombudsperson Washington supermarket div. Greenbelt Consumer Services, Silver Spring, Md., 1974-76; founding pres. Nat. Consumers Congress, Washington, 1973-76; pres. Zawel Assos., Inc., Harrington Park, N.J., 1976-78; v.p. external affairs The Stop and Shop Cos., Inc., Boston, 1978-83; pres. E.Z. Dubin Assocs., Sharon, Mass., 1983—; bd. dirs. Nat. Consumer Resource Center, 1976-80. Bd. dirs. Mass. Assn. Mental Health. Mem. Food Mktg. Inst., Public Relations Soc. Am., Am. Nat. Metric Council, Soc. Consumer Affairs Profls., Pi Sigma Alpha. Office: EZ Dubin Assocs Sharon MA 02067

DUBLIN, ELVIE WILSON, clinical psychologist; b. Athens, Greece, May 18, 1937; d. Anthony I. and Rosa (Protecdicos) Nicolopoulos; B.A., Ind. U., 1966, Ph.D., 1972; m. John Wilson, Oct. 29, 1958 (div. 1967); children—David, Toni; m. 2d, James Dublin, Dec. 21, 1973 (div. 1978). Cons., Hospitality House Nursing Home, Bedford, Ind., 1972-73; psychotherapist Choice, Inc., 1973-79, sec.-treas., 1973-79; pres. Studentworld, Inc., 1978-81; pvt. practice psychology, Bloomington, Ind., 1979—; Arabian horse breeder, founder, owner Tall Oaks Arabians, 1980—; chmn. advt. com. Samtyr Syndicate; bd. dirs. Midwestern Psychotherapy Inst., 1977. NSF trainee, 1965-67; USPHS trainee, 1967-70. Mem. Am. Psychol. Assn., Ind. Psychol. Assn., Assn. Advancement Psychology, Internat. Arabian Horse Assn., Am. Horse Show Assn., Ind. Arabian Horse Club; assoc. mem. Arabian Horse Registry of Am., Phi Beta Kappa. Clubs: Arabian Jockey, Ind. Arabian Horse (racing com. 1986—). Home: 9401 E St Rd 46 Bloomington IN 47401 Office: 4151 E 3d St Bloomington IN 47401

DUBOFF, DIANE GAIL, accessory manufacturing company executive, designer; b. N.Y.C., Aug. 3, 1947; d. Jack and Roslyn Mildred (Eichner) Gumenick; m. Michael Harold DuBoff, July 29, 1972; children—Jill Bonnie, Robert Evan. B.A., Adelphia U., 1970. Media buyer, Wunderman, Ricotta & Kline, N.Y.C., 1970-72; with dept. pub. relations Club Med, Inc., N.Y.C., 1972-74; owner, pres. Granny's Girl, Ltd., Mamaroneck, N.Y., 1978-80, Diane's Designs, Mamaroneck, 1980—, Silly Goose Enterprises Inc., Mamaroneck, 1983—; cons. Doe Spun, Inc., N.Y.C. Vice pres. PTA, Mamaroneck, 1981-83; mem. Westchester Council for the Arts, 1980—. Mem. Am. Women's Econ. Devel. Democrat. Jewish. Avocation: tennis. Home: 7 McKenna Pl Mamaroneck NY 10543

DUBOFSKY, JEAN EBERHART, justice Colorado Supreme Court; b. 1942; B.A., Stanford U., 1964; LL.B., Harvard U., 1967; m. Frank N. Dubofsky; children—Joshua, Matthew. Admitted to Colo. bar, 1967; legis. asst. to U.S. Senator Walter F. Mondale, 1967-69; atty. Colo. Rural Legal Services, Boulder, 1969-72, Legal Aid Soc. Met. Denver, 1972-73; ptnr. Kelly, Dubofsky, Haglund & Garnsey, Denver, 1973-75; dep. atty. gen. Colo., 1975-77; counsel Kelly, Haglund, Garnsey & Kahn, 1977-79; justice Colo. Supreme Ct., Denver, 1979—. Office: 465 State Judicial Bldg 2 E 14th Ave Denver CO 80203*

DUBOSE, ALETA GAYLE, pharmaceutical company executive; b. Liberty, Tex., Oct. 1, 1949; d. Prentice and Jewel Victoria (Turner) Odom; m. David LeRoy DuBose Aug. 9, 1969 (div. 1983); 1 child, Prentice Russell. B.A. magna cum laude, Sam Houston U., 1971. Cert. secondary tchr., Tex. Secondary tchr. Dayton pub. schs., Tex., 1971-77; sales rep. Pfizer Labs., Houston, 1977-82, asst. to regional mgr., Atlanta, 1982-83, dist. mgr., New Orleans, 1983-85, sr. med. rep., 1985—. Recipient Tchr. of Yr. award Dayton Ind. Sch. Dist., 1972; Pacesetter award Pfizer Labs., 1981. Mem. Nat. Assn. Female Execs., Tex. State Tchrs. Assn. (life), Alpha Chi, Kappa Delta Phi. Methodist. Clubs: 100 (New Orleans); Smithsonian (Washington). Avocations: stained glass; water sports; reading; running; aerobics. Home and Office: 207 Lorelei Circle Slidell LA 70458

DUBROFF, DIANA D., lawyer, TV producer; b. N.Y.C., Mar. 4, 1909; d. Meyer and Gussie (Ginsburg) Leibow; B.S., Hunter Coll., 1928; J.D., Bklyn. Law Sch., 1931; m. Alexander DuBroff (dec.); children—Elinor, William. Tchr. young children, 1928-61; sole practice law, N.Y.C., 1961—; founder, dean Practising Justice Inst., 1961-86; producer cable TV series Practical Justice by a Creative Lawyer. Columnist Let's Look at the Law. Designer concept of divorce and homemaker ins.; organizer groups to insure child support; developer personalized affordable settlement strategies. Home and Office: 12 W 72d St New York NY 10023

DUBROW, JOYCE CAROL, report processor, purchasing agent consultant; b. Detroit, Oct. 27, 1928; d. Harvey and Ruth (Levien) Melvin; m. Samuel Rupert Kramer, July 12, 1951 (div. 1957); children—Roberta Anne, Jeffrey Mark; m. Leonard Dubrow, Jan. 20, 1959 (div.); 1 son, John Steven. Student, UCLA, 1948. Self-employed mcht., Kramer's of Honolulu, 1951-57; bookkeeper J. A. Cappuccilli, Syracuse, N.Y., 1960-66, G. H. Miner Co., Syracuse, 1967-70; report processor, purchasing agt. Ernest & Whinney Syracuse, 1970—; self-employed builder J. C. & Assocs., Syracuse, 1983—; cons. internat. duty drawback D&D Assocs., Syracuse and Boston, 1981—; actress film South Pacific, 1957. Aide to disabled Home Aides Central N.Y., Inc., Syracuse, 1974—; campaign mgr. Town Dewitt Bd. Nominee, Syracuse, 1980-81. Served as hon. capt. to maj. ROTC, 1943-44. Democrat. Jewish.

DUBROW, MARSHA ANN, high technology company executive, composer; b. Newark, Dec. 27, 1948; d. Leo and Rose (Haberman) Dubrow; m. Daniel Leon Chaykin, Jan. 17, 1970 (div. 1985); 1 son, Alexander. B.A. cum laude, U. Pa., 1970; M.A., NYU, 1975; M.F.A., Princeton U., 1977, postgrad., 1977-78, 81-82. Prodn. coordinator Children's TV Workshop, N.Y.C., 1970-73; instr. Princeton U., 1976-78; mgr. mktg. communications, cons. AT&T/Techs., Inc., Morristown, N.J., 1978-80; dir. mktg. and ops. Acadia Communications, N.Y.C., 1980-83; dir. planning and mktg. Access Methods, Inc., N.Y.C., 1984—; pres. Techolog, Inc., Montclair, N.J., 1985—. Mem. YWCA, Montclair, N.J., 1980—; mem. program com. bus. and profl. group Nat. Council Jewish Women, Essex County, N.J., 1983—. Recipient Theodore Presser award U. Pa., 1970; William C. Langley fellow NYU, 1974; Josephine de Karman fellow Aerojet-Gen. Corp., 1981. Mem. Am. Guild Authors and Composers, Am. Mgmt. Assn., Nat. Assn. Female Execs. Home: 34 Marion Rd Upper Montclair NJ 07043

DUBRULE, HARRIET ANN, household products company executive; b. Manchester, N.H., July 16, 1935; d. Carroll Frank and Elizabeth (Libbey) Dodge; m. Richard Paul Dubrule, June 20, 1954; children—Karen, Deborah, Barry, Dawn. Student Worcester State Tchrs. Coll., 1953-54. Mgr. Tupperware Home Parties, Orlando, Fla., 1965-73, exec. v.p. Emerald Sales, Escondido, Calif., 1973—; tng. counselor Emerald Sales, Inc., Escondido, 1973—. Mem. Nat. Assn. Female Execs.

DUBUC, MARY ELLEN, educator; b. N.Y.C. July 20, 1950; d. Patrick Joseph and Catherine (McKenna) Reynolds; B.A. cum laude (scholar), Marymount Manhattan Coll., 1972; M.A., Columbia U., 1973; cert. advanced grad. studies R.I. Coll., 1985; m. Leo Dennis Dubuc, Jr., Sept. 9, 1978; children—Brian Robert, Kimberly Ann. Spl. edn. tchr. Cardinal Cushing Sch., Hanover, Mass., 1973-76, Ferncliff Manor Sch., Yonkers, N.Y., 1976-77; program coordinator Bronx Devel. Services, 1977-78; dir. edn. R.I. Assn. Retarded, Woonsocket, 1978-84, spl. edn. cons., 1984—. Fed. trainee, 1971, 72. Mem. Assn. Severely Handicapped, R.I. Assn. Retarded Citizens, Nat. Assn. Female Execs., R.I. Assn. Adult and Continuing Edn. (v.p. pub. relations 1986-87). Office: 80 Fabien St Woonsocket RI 02895

DUCA, DENISE JEAN, personnel executive; b. N.Y.C., Sept. 24, 1951; d. Joseph Robert and Grace (Giannino) Duca. B.P.S., Pace U., 1983; M.Ed., Columbia U., 1984—. Personnel sec. Bendix Internat., N.Y.C., 1971-74; employment rep. Kennecott Corp., Stamford, Conn., 1974-80; mgr. employment Viacom Internat., N.Y.C., 1980-82; mgr. hdqrs. personnel Colgate Palmolive Co., N.Y.C., 1982—. Mem. task force Pace U., 1983. Mem. Am. Soc. Personnel Adminstrn., Pace U. Alumni Assn. (bd. dirs.). Address: Colgate Palmolive Co 300 Park Ave New York NY 10022

DUCKETT, CHLOE ZELLA, foreign service staff officer; b. Akron, Ohio, June 25, 1925; d. Owen C. and Audrey Z. (Brown) Sandefur; m. Lee L. Duckett, Apr. 30, 1949 (div.); children—Lee L., Theo Duckett Pierce. B.A. in Psychology, U. Ariz., 1949; M.Ed., 1982. Office mgr. Marsh Aviation, Tucson, 1946-48; real estate saleswoman James C. Grant Realty, Tucson, 1950-51; asst. office mgr. aircraft overhaul Grand Central Aircraft, Tucson, 1952-54; asst. to mgr. Tucson Airport Authority, 1957-74; commd. fgn. service officer Dept. State, 1974; staff officer, Mozambique, 1974-75, Swaziland, 1975-76, Martinique, 1976-78, France, 1979-80, Yemen, 1980-81, San Salvador, El Salvador, 1982-84, London, 1984—. Nav. instr. CAP, Tucson, 1946-51. Mem. Am. Personnel and Guidance Assn., Am. Assn. Airport Execs., Am. Fgn. Service Assn., Internat. Platform Assn., Mensa. Club: Altrusa (pres. Tucson 1973-74). Co-author concept requiring apprentices to complete basic first aid tng. program before receiving journeyman cert., adopted by AFL/CIO nationwide, 1964. Home: 2124 E 1st St Tucson AZ 85719 Office: Am Embassy London Box 40 FPO New York NY 09510

DUCKETT, EVELYN FELTZS, system analyst, methods analyst; b. San Bernardino, Calif., May 25, 1946; d. Tyree and Nancy Evelyn (Baker) Feltzs; m. John Amoureux Duckett, June 21, 1969; children—Nicole, Kyle, Ryan. B.A. in Speech, UCLA, 1967; M.A. in Communicative Disorders, U. So. Calif., 1969; M.B.A. with honors, U. Houston, 1983. Cert. clin. competence, speech pathologist, tchr., Calif.; lic. med. examiner. Social worker Los Angeles County, 1967-69; speech pathologist Dubnoff Sch., Los Angeles County, 1969-75, Princeton Med. Ctr., N.J., 1976-77; pvt. practice speech pathology Princeton nursing homes; methods analyst GRT So. Life Ins. Co., Houston, 1983-84; cons. Princeton Nursing Homes, 1976-77. Mem. Nat. Black M.B.A. Assn., Am. Speech and Hearing Assn., Delta Sigma Theta (pres. 1965-66). Democrat. Clubs: Petroleum Women's (treas. 1978-80), Am. Women's (Oslo, Norway); St. John Vianney Bridge (pres. 1981, 83); Yanbu, Saudi Arabia Women's.Avocations: painting; bridge; tennis; reading.

DUCKOR, ANITA SPERRY, energy services manager; b. Pine City, Minn., Dec. 3, 1945; d. Thomas E. and Marjory Cowling (Stuck) Sperry; m. Michael John Duckor, Oct. 11, 1963 (div. Oct. 1980); 1 son, Brent Michael; m. Richard R. Pollick, Sept. 11, 1982. B.S. in Bus. with highest honors and distinction (Outstanding Grad. award), San Diego State U., 1979. Residential mktg. coordinator San Diego Gas & Electric Co., 1979-80, comml./indsl. mktg. coordinator, 1981-82; conservation planning analyst/project leader No. States Power Co., Mpls., 1982-83; mgr. energy services NORENCO Corp., Mpls., 1983—. Mem. Nat. Assn. Energy Services Cos. (bd. dirs. 1983—, v.p. 1985—), Am. Mgmt. Assn., Am. Mktg. Assn., Twin Cities Energy Engrs., Minn. Women's Network (bd. dirs. 1985—, exec. mem.), NOW, Phi Kappa Phi, Beta Gamma Sigma, Sigma Iota Epsilon. Office: PO Box 1396 Minneapolis MN 55440

DUCO, JOSEPHINE DIANE, title insurance executive; b. Detroit, Apr. 28, 1947; d. Henry Leopold and Antoinette (Bono) D. B.A. in Sociology, U. Mich., 1969; M.B.A. with distinction in Acctg., L.I. U., 1981. Head teller Am. Savs. Bank, N.Y.C., 1975-77, customer service rep., 1977-78, acct., 1978-79; staff acct. Radio City Music Hall, N.Y.C., 1980; chief acct. Northeast region Am. Title Ins. Co., N.Y.C., 1980-81, asst. regional controller, 1981-83, regional controller, 1983—, v.p., 1984—, asst. sec., 1986—. Mem. Nat. Assn. Accts., Nat. Assn. Female Execs., AAUW, LWV. Office: Am Title Ins Co 675 3d Ave New York NY 10017

DUCY, PATRICIA CORNELIA, computer software consulting company executive; b. Bklyn., July 17, 1945; d. Clement Ambrose and Ellen Catherine (O'Brien) D. Student Ottumwa Heights Jr. Coll., 1963-64, George Washington

U., 1967-69, No. Va. Community Coll., 1980—, U.S. Dept. Agr. Grad. Sch., Washington, 1983—. Staffing mgr. audit dept. Arthur Andersen & Co., Washington, 1973-75; comptroller The Co. Inkwell, Arlington, Va., 1976-78; registrar Antioch Sch. Law, Washington, 1978-79; dir. fin. and adminstrn. SRA Corp., Arlington, Va., 1979-81; mem. staff com. govt.-univ. relations Nat. Acad. Scis., Washington, 1981-83; dir. fin. and adminstrn. Advanced Systems Devel. Inc., Silver Spring, Md., 1983—; cons. in field. Vol. J.F. Kennedy Campaign, Bethesda, Md., 1960, Georgetown U. Hosp., Washington, 1960-63; sec. D.C. chpt. Am. Jr. Red Cross, 1962; prodn. coordinator Am. Light Opera Co., Washington, 1964-67. Recipient 500-hour award Georgetown U. Hosp., 1961, Mem. Am. Mgmt. Assn., Nat. Contracts Mgmt. Assn., Tech. Mktg. Soc. Am. Democrat. Roman Catholic. Office: Advanced Systems Devel Inc 1701 N Ft Myer Dr Suite 1101 Arlington VA 22209

DUDARYK, SHARON DIANN, educator; b. Detroit, Aug. 29, 1945; d. Marion and Nettie (Shishka) Slimak; piano student Detroit Conservatory of Music, 1965—; M.Ed. in Counseling, Wayne State U., 1971; postgrad. in chemistry, physics, astronomy Oakland Community Coll.; m. Peter Dudaryk, Sept. 1, 1965 (div., 1975); children—Jeffrey Michael Dudaryk, Linda Helen Dudaryk, Patricia Marie Kelly. Vol. remedial tchr. Royal Oak Twp., 1966; elem. tchr., Detroit, 1967—, kindergarten tchr. Van Zile Elem. Sch., 1978—, adult edn. tchr. Osborn High Sch., 1977, bilingual edn. Arabic/English, Greenfield Union Elem. Sch., 1984-85; counselor Stellwager Elem. Sch., 1984. Active family workshops, PTA, Founders Soc. Detroit Inst. of Art, LWV, 1978-79; v.p. Bovenschen Sch. PTO, 1983-84; leader Oakland County 4-H. Served as career counselor M.C., USNR, 1979—. Mem. Detroit Fedn. Tchrs. Met. Detroit Reading Council, Detroit Guidance Assn., Nat. Assn. Children with Learning Disabilities, Birmingham Bloomfield Art Assn., Interlocken Assn. Creative and Talented, Warren Assn. Gifted and Talented, Wayne State U. Alumni Assn., Navy League, AAUW, Nat. Pilots Assn., Nat. Ret. Tchrs. Assn., Mich. Farm Bur., Nat. Fedn. Rep. Women. Eastern Orthodox. Club: Federated Russian Orthodox. Condr. research in field of nutrition. Home: 2725 Saratoga Troy MI 48084 Office: 2915 E Outer Dr Detroit MI 48234

DUDICS, SUSAN ELAINE, interior designer; b. Perth Amboy, N.J., Oct. 22, 1950; d. Theodore W. and Joyce M. (Ryals) D. B.S. in Sociology, W.Va. U., 1972; postgrad. Rutgers U., 1975-78, U. Calif.-Irvine, 1979-81, Can. Coll., 1981—. Programmer Prudential Life, Newark, 1972-73; sr. systems analyst Johnson & Johnson, New Brunswick, N.J., 1973-78, Sperry Univac, Irvine, Calif., 1978-80; sr. systems analyst, project leader Robert A. McNeil, San Mateo, Calif., 1981-83; design dir. TransDesigns, Woodstock, Ga., 1982—. High sch. mentor Directions, San Francisco, 1985-86. Mem. Women Entrepreneurs (membership com., treas. 1983—), Central N.J. Alumni Assn. (assoc. sec., founder, pres.), Delta Gamma. Recipient awards TransDesigns, Woodstock, Ga., 1984, 85. Club: Leads. Avocations: skiing; sewing; scuba diving; ballet; hand crafts.

DUDINSKY, VIRGINIA KAY, newspaper editor; b. Warren, Ohio, Nov. 3, 1949; d. Calvin Coolidge and Doris Marie (Owen) Patchin; m. Stephen John Dudinsky, Oct. 7, 1967 (div. Apr. 1979); children—Thomas Allen, Stephanie Lynn. Student Kent State U., 1976-77; Cosmotologist, Isabelle Sch. Beauty, 1969. Office mgr. sales White Real Estate, Munson, Ohio, 1977-78; editor's asst. The Valley News, Orwell, Ohio, 1979-81, editor, 1981—; real estate assoc. Steve J. Jozsa Realty, Orwell, 1979—; cons., East Orwell, Ohio, 1975—. Mem. Ohio Newspaper Assn., Grand Valley C. of C. Democrat. Roman Catholic. Home: 666 Windsor Rd East Orwell OH 44034 Office: The Valley News 9 S Maple St Orwell OH 44076

DUDKOWSKI, LAURA ANN, accountant; b. Chgo., July 31, 1950; d. Vincent Joseph and Wanda Ann (Buda) D. A.A., Wilbur Wright Coll., Chgo., 1970; B.S.B.A., Roosevelt U., Chgo., 1980. Asst. credit mgr. Stange Co., Chgo., 1977-81; auditor, acct. Thomas Havey C.P.A., Chgo., 1981; auditor, staff acct. Fields & Fields, C.P.A.s, Chgo., 1982; owner, operator Laura A. Dudkowski, acctg., bookkeeping service, Bolingbrook, Ill., 1982-83, Comprehensive Acctg. Services, Bolingbrook, 1983-85; controller/warehouse mgr. Stuart Hale Co., 1985—. Mem. Broadview Concert Band; treas., sec. Chgo. Met. Symphony Orch. Mem. Am. Bus. Women's Assn. (pres. Pathways chpt.), Southwest Suburban Bus. and Profl. Women's Assn. (treas. chpt.), Am. Mgmt. Assn. Home: 204 N Monterey Dr Bolingbrook IL 60439

DUDLEY, MARGARET SUSAN, insurance company executive; b. Waterloo, Iowa, Dec. 9, 1951; d. Everett Thomas and Helen Clare (Mooney) Griffin; 1 child, Christopher Jason. B.S.W., Mars Hill Coll., 1981. Head admitting Sampson Meml. Hosp., Clinton, N.C., 1973-74; bank teller Wachovia Bank & Trust, Washington, N.C., 1974-76, 78; substitute tchr. Madison High Sch., Marshall, N.C., 1977; receptionist, sec. Edwards Oil Co., Mars Hill, N.C., 1979-81; Tupperware mgr. Blue Ridge Party Sales, Arden, N.C., 1981-83; sales assoc. Paul Revere Ins., Asheville, N.C., 1984—. Co-chmn. Cookie Drive, Girl Scouts, Madison County, 1979; co-founder Neighbors-in-Need, Madison County, 1981; membership chmn. P.T.A., Ira B. Jones Elementary Sch., 1986. Named VIP Mgr., Tupperware Home Parties, Norfolk, Va., 1983. Mem. Nat. Assn. Female Execs., Nat. Assn. Health Underwriters, YWCA. Democrat. Episcopalian. Club: Friendship Force (Asheville, N.C.), Bus. and Profl. Women. Avocations: swimming; piano; reading; travel. Home: 25 Melrose Ave Asheville NC 28804 Office: Paul Revere Ins Co Suite 500 NW Plaza Asheville NC 28801

DUDLEY, MARY CATHERINE, marketing executive; b. Wausau, Wis., Jan. 27, 1953; d. Richard David and Eileen (Deneen) Dudley; B.A., Tex. Christian U., 1975; m. William David Stotesbery, June 21, 1975. Reporter, Austin (Tex.) Am.-Statesman, 1975-78; polit. columnist Tex. Woman Mag., Austin, 1978-80; media cons., mktg. mgr. Austin Conv. Bur., Austin C. of C., 1980-82; sr. promotion specialist Bausch & Lomb, Austin, 1982-84, mktg. promotion mgr. Houston Instrument div., 1984—; cons. in field. Bd. dirs. Center for Battered Women, Austin, 1981-83; vol. coordinator Austin Symphony Sq., 1980-81, mem., 1980—; mem. Austin Commn. on Status of Women, 1978-79. Recipient Med. Reporting award Tex. Med. Assn., 1977. Mem. Women in Communications (chpt. bd. dirs. 1979-80), Tex. Soc. Assn. Execs., Austin Sister City Assn. Roman Catholic. Office: 8500 Cameron Rd Austin TX 78753

DUDLEY, MARY HEWITT, microcomputer systems consultant; b. Glendale, Ariz., Sept. 7, 1955; d. Veryl C. and Geraldine (McConnell) Hewitt; m. Robert Warren Dudley, Apr. 5, 1980. B.A., U. Ill., 1977; M.A., Am. Grad. Sch. Internat. Mgmt., 1979. Cons. Booz, Allen & Hamilton, Chgo., 1979-80; mktg. mgr. Flexibox, Inc., Houston, 1980-82; stategic planning assoc. N.L. Baroid, 1982-83; mgr. product planning Compaq Computer Corp., Houston, 1983-85; cons. Abtex Computer Systems Ltd., Aberdeen, Scotland, 1985—. Mem. Am. Mktg. Assn. Home: Clifton Cottage Banchoey-Devenick Aberdeen AB1 5YD Scotland Office: Abtex Computer Systems Ltd 58-60 Carden Pl Aberdeen AB1 1UP Scotland

DUDLEY, MIRIAM SUE, librarian; b. Minot, N.D., Dec. 25, 1924; d. Henry Phillips and Geta Lea (Feldman) Fine; m. Norman Houston Dudley, Aug. 23, 1952; children—Noah, Seth. B.A., UCLA, 1945; M.S. in L.S., U. So. Calif., 1949. Bibliographer UCLA, 1949-56, reference librarian Coll. Library, 1968-82; cons. Ednl. Bd. of NEH, Washington. Author: Library Instructional Skills, 1968, rev., through 1980; contbr. articles to library jours. Mem. Hollywood Coordinating Council, Los Angeles, 1971, Hollywood High Adv. Council, 1971. Mem. Assn. Coll. and Research Libraries (div. ALA; founder bibliographic instrn. sect., chmn. 1978-79, ann. award for excellence given in name 1984—). Democrat. Jewish. Home: 15455 Glenoaks Blvd #301 Sylmar CA 91342

DUEMLING, LOUISA COPELAND, farmer, chemical company executive; b. Phila., Apr. 20, 1936; d. Lammot duPont and Pamela (Cunningham) Copeland; m. Robert Werner Duemling, May 15, 1982; children by previous marriage—Letitia Biddle Blitzer, Pamela C. Biddle, James C. Biddle. B.S., Cornell U., 1958. Owner, Andelot Farm, Worton, Md., 1984—; dir. E.I. duPont de Nemours & Co., Wilmington, Del. Pres. bd. Miss Porter's Sch., Farmington, Conn., 1974-79; trustee Corcoran Gallery Art, Washington, 1978—, Winterthur Mus., Wilmington, 1979—, Md. chpt. Nature Conservancy, 1984—; bd. dirs. Nat. Parks Found., 1980—. Republican. Episcopalian. Clubs: Chevy Chase, Colony. Avocations: gardening; tennis; travel. Home: 3027 N St NW Washington DC 20007 Office: Andelot Farm PO Box 338 Worton MD 21678

DUER, ELLEN ANN, physician; b. Balt., Feb. 3, 1936; d. Emmett Paul and Annie (Sollers) Dagon; A.B., George Washington U., 1959; M.D., U. Md., 1964; postgrad. Johns Hopkins U., 1965-68; children—Lyle JordanMillan V, Elizabeth Lyle Millan, Ann Sheridan Worthington Millan; m. T. Marshall Duer, Jr., Aug. 23, 1985. Intern Union Meml. Hosp., Balt., 1964-65; resident anesthesiology Johns Hopkins Hosp., Balt., 1965-68; fellow dept. surgery Johns Hopkins, 1965-68; practice medicine specializing in anesthesiology, Balt., 1968—; attending staff Union Meml. Hosp., Church Home and Hosp., Franklin Sq. Hosp., Children's Hosp., Mercy Hosp. (all Balt.), 1982—; attending staff James Lawrence Kernan Hosp., Balt., 1982—, co-chief dept. anesthesiology, 1984—, mem. quality assurance com., 1984—; mem. faculty Church Home and Hosp., Balt., 1969-74, affiliate cons. emergency room, 1969-74, chief emergency dept., 1973; faculty dept. anesthesiology U. Md. Sch. Med., 1975-78; attending staff Univ. Hosp., 1975-78; cons. anesthesiologist Md. Penitentiary, cons. Utilisations Rev. Md., 1973-82; mem. med. audit com. Mercy Hosp., 1979—; fellow critical care medicine U. Md. Inst. Emergency Medicine, 1975. Mem. AMA, Am., Md. Socs. anesthesiologists, Md.-D.C. Soc. Anesthesiologists (legis. com. 1984-85), Balt. City Med. and Chirurgical Soc., Internat. Congress Anesthesiologists, Am. Coll. Emergency Physicians, Met. Emergency Dept Heads, Am. Med. Polit. Action Com., Am. Horse Show Assn., Md. Horse Show Assn., Pony Breeders Assn., Chesapeake Bay Yacht Racing Assn., Potapskut Sailing Assn., Chesapeake Bay Found., Md. Hist. Soc., Md. Maritime Mus. Episcopalian. Clubs: Annapolis Yacht, Sailing of Chesapeake; L'Hirondelle (Ruxton, Md.); Bachelor's Cotillion (Balt.). Address: 1011 Wagner Rd Baltimore MD 21204

DUER, ELLEN ANN DAGON (MRS. T. MARSHALL DUER, JR.), physician; b. Balt., Feb. 3, 1936; d. Emmett Paul and Annie (Sollers) Dagon; A.B., George Washington U., 1959; M.D., U. Md., 1964; postgrad. Johns Hopkins U., 1965-68; m. Lyle Jordan Millan IV, Dec. 21, 1963; children—Lyle Jordan V, Elizabeth Lyle, Ann Sheridan Worthington.; m. T. Marshall Duer, Jr., Aug. 23, 1985. Intern, Union Meml. Hosp., Balt., 1964-65; resident anesthesiology Johns Hopkins Hosp., Balt., 1965-68, fellow in surgery, 1965-68; practice medicine specializing in anesthesiology, Balt., 1968—; attending staff Union Meml. Hosp., Church Home and Hosp., Franklin Sq. Hosp., Children's Hosp., James Lawrence Kernan Hosp., Balt., 1982—; faculty Church Home and Hosp., Balt., 1969—, affiliate cons. emergency room, 1969—, mem. med. audit and utilizations com., 1970-72, mem. emergency and ambulatory care com., 1973-74, chief emergency dept., 1973-74; cons. anesthesiologist Md. State Penitentiary, 1971; fellow in critical care medicine Md. Inst. Emergency Medicine, 1975-76; mem. infection control com. U. Md. Hosp., 1975—; instr. anesthesiology U. Md. Sch. Medicine, 1975—; staff anesthesiologist Mercy Hosp., 1978—, audit com., 1979-80, 82. Mem. AMA, Am. Coll. Emergency Physicians, Met. Emergency Dept. Heads, Am., Md. socs. anaesthesiologists, Balt. City Med. and Chirurgical Soc., Internat. Congress Anaesthesiologists, Internat. Anaesthesia Research Soc., Am., Md. horse shows assns. Magotha River Sailing Assn., U.S. Yacht Racing Union, Chesapeake Bay Yacht Racing Assn. Episcopalian. Address: PO Box 76 Brooklandville MD 21022

DUER, SHIRLEY POWELL, state legislator; b. Meigs County, Tenn., Dec. 20, 1935; d. John Scott and Dean Sherrill Stanton; student Huntingdon Coll., 1952-55; B.S., Tenn. Tech. U., 1977; m. Carl T. Duer, Sept. 10, 1955; children—Michelle, Elizabeth, Carl Thomas. Tchr., Walker County, Ga., 1955-57; research chemist U. Tenn. Med. Units, Memphis, 1960-65; field rep. Gov's. Office, Cookeville, Tenn., 1979; mem. Tenn. Ho. of Reps., 1980—, Republican whip, 1985—; mem. State Adv. Council Vocat. Edn., 1981—. Mem. Tenn. Commn. for Humanities; sec. Tenn. Conservation Commn., 1970-76; mem. Cumberland County Beautiful Assn. Mem. Nat. Republican Legislators Assn., Am. Legislative Exchange Council, Orgn. Women Legislators, C. of C., Am. Legion Aux., Phi Kappa Phi, Phi Alpha Theta. Republican. Congregationalist. Home: Route 9 Box 53 Holiday Dr Crossville TN 38555 Office: Room 115 War Memorial Bldg Nashville TN 37219

DUERR-LEVINE, DIANE, marketing executive; b. Tulsa, Mar. 8, 1938; d. Arthur and Reta (Reeves) Duerr; B.A. in Math., U. Mich., 1960; M.B.A., Columbia U., 1963; m. Matthew A. Levine, June 9, 1963; 1 child, Arielle. Systems engr. Xerox Corp., N.Y.C., 1963-64; products mgr. Lever Bros. Corp., N.Y.C., 1964-68; sr. br. mgr. Am. Home Products Corp., N.Y.C., 1968-71; account supr. Honig-Cooper Herrington (now Foote Cone/Honig), San Francisco, 1971-72; v.p. advt. and sales promotion Continental Airlines, Los Angeles, 1973-76, dir. mktg. and communications San Francisco Bay Area Transit Dist., 1976-78; pres., founder Inst. Health Mgmt., San Francisco, 1978—; prof. San Francisco State U., 1982-85. Bd. dirs. Greybridge, Palo Alto, Calif., Pacific Select Corp., San Francisco; mem. bus. adv. bd. San Francisco State U., chmn. membership com.; cons. Solar Energy Research Inst., No. Calif. Coalition for ERA. Mem. Columbia U. Grad. Sch. Bus. Alumni Assn., Kappa Kappa Gamma, Beta Gamma Sigma. Recipient numerous mktg. and advt. awards. Democrat. Mem. Soc. of Friends. Author: Executive Edge, 1981; Vital Living after Fifty, 1982. Office: 101 Lansdale Ave San Francisco CA 94127

DUFAULT, MARY LOUISE SELKER, lawyer, educator; b. Clarion, Pa., May 9, 1937; d. Ambrose John and Mary Elizabeth (Meisinger) Selker; m. Larry Bernard Dufault, June 22, 1963; children—Michael, Jacqueline. B.S., Ind. State Tchrs. Coll., 1959; M.S., Pa. State U., 1962; M.A., U. Conn., 1974; J.D., Franklin Pierce Law Ctr., 1980. Tchr., Carlisle Pub. Schs., Pa., 1959-61; asst. prof. Juniata Coll., Huntingdon, Pa., 1962-69, Colby Coll., New London, N.H., 1975-77; ptnr. Dufault & Dufault, New London, 1980—. Trustee New London Hosp., 1983—; mem. stewardship com. St. Andrew's Ch., New London, 1982-84, budget com. Town of New London, 1982-86. Ind. State Tchrs. Coll. scholar, 1955-59. Mem. ABA, N.H. Bar Assn. (econs. of law com. 1984—), New London Bar Assn. (co-pres. 1984), New London C. of C. (dir. 1981—), LWV, NOW, Kappa Delta Pi, Kappa Omicron Phi. Democrat. Episcopalian. Clubs: Lake Sunapee Yacht, New London Garden, New London Outing. Home: Woodland Way New London NH 03257 Office: Dufault & Dufault Box 306 New London NH 03257

DUFF, MARGARET KAPP, author, librarian; b. Walton, Ind., Jan. 4; d. Harvey Edward and Dulcie Marie (Crim) Kapp; m. Cloyd Edgar Duff, Oct. 26, 1940; children—Jonathan Kapp, Barbara Duff Flack. B.A., Butler U., 1937; M.L.S., Case Western Res. U., 1966. Children's librarian Cuyahoga County Library, Cleve., 1966-70, dir. Puppet Ctr., 1970-81; author children's books, 1972—. Author: Rum Pum Pum, 1978, Princess & Pumpkin, 1980, Dancing Turtle, 1982. Trustee women's com. Cleve. Orch., 1960-65; trustee women's com. Cleve. Inst. of Mus., 1964-68. Recipient 2d prize for ceramic sculpture Cleve. Mus. Art, 1957; Puppet performance Cleve. Orch. Key Concerts, 1979. Mem. ALA (1984 Caldecott Com. for 1985 award), Internat. Bd. on Books for Young People.

DUFF, RUTH ELEANOR, college dean; b. Alexander County, Ill., Dec. 19, 1934; d. Richard Ernest and Ruth Ethel (Dickerson) D.; B.S. in Edn., S.E. Mo. State Coll., 1961; M.S. in Edn., So. Ill. U., 1968, Ph.D. (Coll. Edn. dissertation fellow 1972), 1973. Primary and elem. sch. tchr., Ill., 1954-65; dir. demonstration presch. program Alexander County Sch. Dist. I, 1965-68; instr., Head Start regional tng. officer So. Ill. U., 1968-70, instr., dir. Head Start supplementary tng., 1970-72; asso. prof. early childhood edn. U. S.C., Columbia, 1973-74, coordinator early childhood edn., 1974-79, asst. dean acad. affairs, 1979-80, asst. dean students and programs Coll. Edn., 1980-82, asst. dean tchr. edn., 1982-83, assoc. dean, 1983—, prof., 1981-82; sec. Midlands Human Resources Devel. Commn., 1980—; mem. Gov. S.C. Interagy. Coordinating Council Early Childhood Devel. and Edn., 1981—, Gov. S.C. Adv. Com. Early Childhood Devel. and Edn., 1980—. Fellow, tchr. tng. for disadvantaged, summer 1970. Mem. Assn. Childhood Edn. Internat., U.S. Nat. Com. Early Childhood Edn., Organization Mondiale pour l'Education Prescolaire, Nat. Assn. Edn. Young Children, So. Assn. Children Under Six, S.C. Assn. Children Under Six, Soc. Research Child Devel., Phi Delta Kappa. Co-author: The Parent-Teacher Bond: Relating, Responding, Rewarding, 1978; Early Childhood Education, 1980; others. Contbr. articles to profl. jours., chpts. to books. Home: 2612 Monroe St Columbia SC 29205 Office: Booker T Washington Children's Center USC Columbia SC 29208

DUFFEE, BEVERLY ANN, educator; b. Sharon, Pa., Apr. 18, 1946; d. Kenneth Ira and Edith Belle (Farringer) Duffee; B.A., Roberts Wesleyan Coll., 1968; M.A., Calif. State U., 1973. Personnel adminstr./programmer Newport Electronics, Santa Ana, Calif., 1973-77; personnel counselor Dennis & Dennis Personnel Services, Santa Ana, 1978; sales sec. Gould Inc., Auto. Battery Div., Irvine, Calif., 1979-81; chmn. dept. English, tchr. Leffingwell Christian Jr./Sr. High Sch., Norwalk, Calif., 1981—; instr. English, Biola U., La Mirada, Calif., 1984-85. Mem. World Gospel Mission, Alpha Kappa Sigma. Republican. Methodist. Home: 8811 Park St Space 98 Bellflower CA 90706 Office: 11032 Leffingwell Rd Norwalk CA 90650

DUFFEY, RONNIE, insurance executive; b. Bronx, N.Y., Apr. 7, 1947; d. Harold and Julianne (Bradley) Silverman; m. Robert Andrew Duffey, Aug. 11, 1968; 1 child, Jonathan Andrew. A.A., Bronx Community Coll., 1965; student Hunter Coll., 1965. Sr. v.p. Presdl. Life Ins. Co., Nyack, N.Y., 1972—, also dir.; ednl. rep. Life Office Mgmt. Assn., Atlanta, 1977—. Treas. local cub scout pack Boy Scouts Am., 1980-81. Mem. CAPSCO Users Group (sec.-treas. 1983-85, chmn. 1985—). Republican. Lutheran. Avocations: skiing, flying, reading. Home: 179 Treetop Circle Nanuet NY 10954 Office: Presdl Life Ins Co 69 Lydecker St Nyack NY 10960

DUFFY, CAROLINE ELIZABETH, sales executive; b. Columbus, Ohio, Feb. 22, 1962; d. Robert Young and Harriett Lou (Smalley) D. B.A., Ind. U., 1984. Intern Arthur Andersen & Co., Chgo., 1983; sales rep. R. R. Donnelley & Sons Co., N.Y.C., 1984-86, Oak Brook, Ill., 1986—. Author: Anthology of High School Poetry, 1978. Reporter, copy editor Ind. Daily Student, 1981; feature writer Dayton Daily News, 1982. Mem. Women in Prodn., Delta Gamma Alumnae. Democrat. Roman Catholic. Avocation: jogging. Office: R R Donnelley & Sons Co 2122 S York Rd Suite 300 Oak Brook IL 60521

DUFFY, ESTHER RODGERS (MRS. ROGER FRANCIS DUFFY), librarian; b. Pitts., Aug. 14, 1911; d. Arthur Gregory and Charlotte Catherine (Nagle) Rodgers; B. Music and B.S. in Music Edn., Seton Hill Coll., 1932; postgrad. U. Pitts., 1933, Carnegie Inst., 1935, Simmons Coll., 1941-42; m. Roger Francis Duffy, Nov. 14, 1945; children—Katherine, Mary Anne, Roger. Instr. music Coll. Misericordia, Dallas, Pa., 1932-37; music librarian Cornell U., Ithaca, N.Y., 1937-41; asst. music librarian Columbia U., N.Y.C., 1942-43; research librarian OSS, State Dept., 1943-44, Balkans outpost rep. Office War Info., 1944-46, Balkans regional rep. USIS, 1946; asst. to pres. Juilliard Sch. Music, N.Y.C., 1947-49; asst. to mng. dir. U.S. Internat. Book Assn., N.Y.C., 1945-47; librarian fine arts Greenwich (Conn.) Library, 1961-81. Mem. adv. com. Greenwich Sr. Center; trustee Greenwich Center for Chamber Music. Mem. Greenwich Arts Council. Mem. Schubert Club, AAUW, Kappa Gamma Pi. Home: 2 Peters Rd Riverside CT 06878

DUFFY, EVELYN GROENKE, clinical nurse specialist, consultant; b. London, Mar. 30, 1953; came to U.S., 1953; d. John Herman and Marcella Irene (Engelman) Groenke; m. Mark Elton Duffy, Aug. 7, 1976; 1 child, Patrick Sean. B.S., Baylor U., 1975; M.S., U. Wis.-Madison, 1981. R.N., Ohio, Wis., Tex.; cert. geriatric nurse practitioner. Staff nurse Ohio State U. Hosp., Columbus, 1975-76; team leader Vis. Nurse Service, Madison, Wis., 1976-79; nurse practitioner William S. Middleton Meml. VA Hosp., Madison, 1981-84; clin. nurse specialist VA Med. Ctr., Cleve., 1985—; clin. preceptor U. Wis.-Madison, 1981-84. Bd. dirs. Calvary Luth. Chapel, Madison, 1977-78, sec. Calvary Luth. Women, 1980-81. Recipient Performance award VA, 1982. HEW traineeship, 1979-81. Mem. Am. Nurses Assn., Gerontol. Soc. Am., Madison Dist. Nurses Assn. (chmn. pub. relations com., 1983-84), Wis. Nurses Assn. (bd. dirs. nurse practitioner council 1981-83), Vis. Nurse Service Staff Assn. (sec. 1978-79). Sigma Theta Tau. Avocations: stained glass; running; sailing; cross country skiing; gourmet cooking. Office: VA Med Ctr 10701 East Blvd Cleveland OH 44106

DUFFY, MARY BROCK, physician, county official; b. Meadville, Pa., Feb. 8, 1920; d. George Harrison and Mary Belle (Gibson) Brock; m. Richard N. Duffy, Jr., Feb. 13, 1949 (dec. 1973); children—Mary Gibson Duffy Andrews, Richard N., III, Randolph Brock, John Chapman. A.B., Allegheny Coll., 1941; M.D., U. Pa., 1944; M.P.H., U. N.C., 1962. Diplomate Am. Bd. Preventive Medicine. Intern Phila. Gen. Hosp., 1944-45; resident Children's Hosp. Phila., 1945-46, Babies Hosp., Wilmington, N.C., 1946-47; practice medicine specializing in pediatrics, New Bern, N.C., 1947-51; asst. dir. Knox County Health Dept., Knoxville, Tenn., 1962-67, dir., 1967—; regional dir. Knoxville-Knox County Region, Tenn., Dept. Health and Environment, Knoxville, 1984—, lectr. on health adminstrn. U. Tenn., 1968-78; preceptor, family practice residency program U. Tenn. Meml. Hosp., Knoxville, 1968—. Mem. planning council United Way, Knoxville, 1965-71, 1975-81; bd. dirs. Smokey Mountain br. Arthritis Found, 1981—, Planned Parenthood, Knoxville, 1964-74, Knox Clean Air League, 1962-68; med. advisor Knoxville-Knox County Headstart Program, 1965—; mem. community action com. Knoxville-Knox County, 1968—. Recipient Outstanding Tenn. womens award U. Tenn. Panhellenic Council, 1974, Chancellors' award U. Tenn., 1978; Gold citation for outstanding achievement Allegheny Coll., 1981; Disting. Service award Tenn. Pub. Health Assn., 1981. Mem. Am. Assn. Pub. Health Physicians, (pres. 1980-81), U.S. Conf. Local Health Officers (pres. 1985-86), So. Health Assn. (governing council 1980-85, exec. com. 1984—), Tenn. Pub. Health Assn. (pres. 1977-78, exec. com. 1969-84), Nat. Assn. county health Officers, Knoxville Acad. Medicine, Tenn. Med. Assn., AMA, Phi Beta Kappa, Alpha Chi Omega; fellow Am. Coll. Preventive Medicine, Am. Pub. Health Assn. (gov. council 1975-83, 1985—). Presbyterian. Club: Leconte (Knoxville). Office: Knox County Health Dept Cleveland Pl Knoxville TN 37917

DUFFY, MARY PATRICIA, fashion executive; b. N.Y.C., Mar. 6, 1945; d. Morton Peter and Miriam V. (Tracy) D. B.A., Mt. Holyoke Coll., 1966. Asst. buyer Jordan Marsh, Boston, 1966-68; counselor Snelling & Snelling, Boston, 1968-72; adjudicator Commonwealth of Mass., Boston, 1973-75; mgr. Sheraton Gallery, Boston, 1975-79; pres. Big Beauties/Little Women Models, N.Y.C., 1979—; spokeswoman L'Eggs Pantyhose, 1983—, Amy Adams, 1984—, Gitano, 1985-86; commentator fashion shows; numerous TV appearances. Mem. N.Y. Jr. League, 1972—, St. Barts Community Club, 1983—. Mem. N.Y. Fashion Group, Internat. Model Mgmt. Assn., N.Y.C. C. of C., Better Bus. Bur., Mt. Holyoke Alumni Assn. Republican. Roman Catholic. Club: Downtown Athletic (N.Y.C.). Office: BB/LW, Inc 159 Madison 7C New York NY 10016

DUFFY, R. LORETT, advertising and public relations executive; b. Scranton, Pa., May 23, 1936; d. John R. and Loretta (Walsh) Williams; divorced; children—Kathleen, Patrick, Noreen, Sharon, Irene. Adminstrv. asst. Decair Helicopters, Inc., Spring Valley, N.Y., 1970-76; controller asst. Lone Star Industries, Inc., West Nyack, N.Y., 1977-80; pub. relations, advt. sales rep. Broward Cablevision, Davie, Fla., 1980—. Mem. adv. bd. ARC. Recipient Media award Davie Democratic Club. Mem. Dovie-Cooper City C. of C., Davie C. of C. (dir., v.p. 1985-86, Extraordinary Service award), Movie Picture and TV Industry Assn., Advt. Fedn. Greater Ft. Lauderdale, Ft. Lauderdale C. of C. Democrat. Roman Catholic. Club: Soroptimist Internat. (corresponding sec., bd. dirs.). Home: 3150 W Rolling Hill Circle Apt 505 Davie FL 33328 Office: 5001 S University Dr Davie FL 33314

DUGAL, ELIZABETH ANN, lawyer; b. Opelousas, La., Aug. 28, 1954; d. George Louis and Elizabeth Ann (Thoms) D.; student U. Southwestern La., 1971-74; B.A., La. State U., 1977, J.D., 1977. Bar: La. 1977. Legal research asst., expropriation div. La. Dept. Hwys., Baton Rouge, 1976-77; sole practice law, Lafayette, La., 1977—; hostess monthly TV program Sta. KLFY; tchr. courses, workshops. Mem. Acadiana Women's Polit. Caucus; mem. Lafayette Regional Planning Commn., chmn., 1984; mem. Lafayette Parish Planning Commn., 1981—, chmn., 1986; vice chmn. Talent Bank of Lafayette, 1982-83, chmn., 1984—; mem. Lafayette Mayor's Commn. on Needs of Women, 1984—, pres.-elect, 1986—. Mem. ABA, La. Bar Assn., La. Trial Lawyers Assn., Lafayette Parish Bar Assn., AAUW (legis. chmn. 1979-80), UDC, Alpha Lambda Delta, Phi Gamma Mu, Phi Kappa Phi, Phi Alpha Delta. Republican. Roman Catholic. Clubs: Zonta, Lafayette Bus. and Profl. Women (Outstanding Woman 1985). Author publs. in field. Office: 1207 Lafayette St Lafayette LA 70501

DUGAN, DIXIE LOUISE, social worker; b. Lebanon, Ind., Apr. 11, 1949; d. James Chapman and Carol (Kelly) D.; m. Harold Jones, June 20, 1976 (div. 1978); 1 child, Kelly; m. John Carter Truax, Nov. 23, 1984. Student Ind. U., 1981—. Sec. Dept. Def. Communications, Pentagon, Arlington, Va., 1967-69; br. office mgr. NASA-Goddard Space Flight Ctr., Greenbelt, Md., 1969-71; librarian Putnam County Pub. Library, Greencastle, Ind., 1973-74; food co-op coordinator Ozark Area Community Action, Bolivar, Mo., 1974-75; outreach worker Agy. on Aging, Spencer, Ind., 1978-79; spl. projects coordinator South Central Community Action Program, Inc., Bloomington, Ind., 1979—; bd. dirs. Area 10 Nutrition Project, Bloomington, 1980-83; pres. bd. dirs. Hoosier

Hills Food Bank, Bloomington, 1984—. Mem. Monroe County Social Workers Assn. (Social Worker of Yr. 1984), Gray Panthers of Bloomington, Golden Key. Democrat. Avocations: folklore; weightlifting; bicycling; reading; gardening. Home: Campus View 220 Bloomington IN 47401 Office: South Central Community Action 907 E 2d St Bloomington IN 47401

DUGAN, KIMIKO HATTA (MRS. WAYNE ALEXANDER DUGAN), anatomist, educator; b. Kyoto City, Japan, Oct. 21, 1924; came to U.S., 1948, naturalized, 1956; d. Shinzo and Sano (Hatta) Hatta; student U. Md., 1957-58; B.A., Okla. Coll. Women, 1961; M.S., U. Okla., 1965, Ph.D., 1970; m. Wayne Alexander Dugan, Aug. 18, 1947 (dec. Aug. 1971). Grad. fellow dept. anatomy Sch. Medicine, U. Okla., Oklahoma City, 1964-69, instr. dept. anat. sci. Coll. Medicine, 1969-71, asst. prof., 1971-78, asso. prof., 1978—. Recipient Undergrad. Chemistry Achievement award Okla. Coll. Women, 1960; elected to U. Sci. and Arts Okla. (formerly Okla. Coll. Women) Alumni Hall of Fame, 1977. Mem. Am. Assn. Anatomists, AAAS, AAUW, Okla. Acad. Sci., Am. Chem. Soc., Am. Soc. Zoologists, Electron Microscopy Soc. Am., N.Y. Acad. Sci., Internat. Soc. Developmental Comparatvie Immunology, Sigma Xi. Episcopalian. Home: 1139 NW 63d St Oklahoma City OK 73116 Office: Dept Anat Scis Coll Medicine U Okla Health Scis Center PO Box 26901 Oklahoma City OK 73190

DUGGAN, CAROL COOK, researcher; b. Conway, S.C., May 25, 1946; d. Pierce Embree and Lillian Watkins (Eller) Cook; m. Kevin Duggan, Dec. 29, 1973. B.A., Columbia Coll., 1968; M.S., U. Ky., 1970. Reference asst. Richland County Pub. Library, Columbia, S.C., 1968-69, asst. to dir., 1970, chief adult services, 1971-82; dir. Maris Research, Columbia, 1982—. Mem. Friends of Richland County Pub. Library, 1977—, Greater Columbia (S.C.) Literacy Council, 1973—. Recipient Sternheimer award, 1968. Mem. ALA (councilor 1980-82, chmn. state membership com. 1979-83), S.C. Library Assn. (sec. 1976, exec. bd. 1976, 78-82), S.C. Pub. Library Assn. (pres. 1980-81), Beta Phi Mu. Methodist (exec. bd. United Methodist Women 1983—). Club: PEO (pres. 1985—, chmn. amendments and recommendations com. 1985—), Columbia Coll. Afternoon of S.C. Home: 2101 Woodmere Dr Columbia SC 29204

DUGGAN, CATHERINE MARIE, investment advisory services company executive; b. St. Louis, June 15, 1949; d. William Joseph and Fern Beatrice (Dodson) D.; 1 child, Christina Jennifer. Lic. real estate assoc., Calif.; registered mortgage underwriter. Salesperson, Schauer Realty, Los Angeles, 1975-76; sales mgr. Property Store, Los Angeles, 1976-77; cons. Expert Realtor, Los Angeles, 1977-79; ptnr. Duggan, Ruggieri & Co., Los Angeles, 1979-82; v.p. Am Cal Co., Los Angeles, 1982—. Mem. Apt. Owners Assn., Nat. Assn. Female Execs., Calif. Mortgage Bankers Assn., Young Mortgage Bankers, Nat. Assn. Rev. Appraisers and Mortgage Underwriters. Roman Catholic. Avocation: Tang Soo Do karate. Office: Am Cal Co 4730 Woodman St Suite 220 Sherman Oaks CA 91423

DUGGAN, MAUREEN, government health administrator; b. Salamanca, N.Y., Feb. 17, 1945; d. William B. and Rita L. (Haley) D.; B.A. (U.S. Office Edn. trainee), SUNY, Albany, 1966, M.A., 1967; postgrad. Temple U., 1967, Union Coll., 1972, U. Md., 1977. With N.Y. State Dept. Health, 1968—, asso. med. care adminstr. Syracuse Area Office, 1978, hosp. program dir., 1978-79, standards unit chief, Albany, 1979-82, dir. bur. health care analysis, 1982—; vis. lectr. Syracuse U., 1978. Weekly vol. Big Bros./Big Sisters Am., Albany, 1978—; mem. affirmative action adv. com. Dept. Health, Center for Women in Govt., Albany, 1979. Recipient Commr.'s Recognition award, 1984. Mem. Am. Public Health Assn., Nat. Assn. Female Execs., N.Y. State Women Mgrs. Network. Home: 283 Woodlawn Ave Albany NY 12208 Office: Tower Bldg Empire Plaza Albany NY 12237

DUGGER, MARY ELIZABETH, personnel administrator, public information officer; b. Borger, Tex., June 6, 1953; d. Wayne Loyd Norman Sr. and M. Virginia (Bond) Yell; m. Brendan Patrick Davidson, June 17, 1972 (div.); m. William Albert Dugger II, July 9, 1979; 1 son, Sean William Albert III. Student McMurry Coll., 1971-72, Regis Coll., 1979-81. Adminstrv. clk. Colo. Housing Fin. Authority, Denver, 1980-81, adminstrv. asst., 1982-83, adminstrv. officer, 1983—. Served with USAF, 1972-80. Decorated Commendation medal, Meritorious Service medal (USAF); recipient Internat. Yr. of Woman award U.S. Dept. Army, 1975. Mem. Am. Soc. Personnel Adminstrs. Home: 3721 S Espana Way Aurora CO 80013 Office: Colo Housing Fin Authority 500 E 8th Ave Denver CO 80013

DUGICK, ANGELA EVA MARIE, banker; b. Luneburg, W. Ger., Aug. 9, 1949; d. Erwin Richard and Maria Aloysia (Fucik) Kruse; came to U.S., 1953, naturalized, 1960; student Case Western Res. U., 1967-70; B.A. in Econs., U. Alaska, 1977; m. Joseph Dugick, July 11, 1970; 1 child, J. Paul. Econs. researcher Cook Inlet Region, Inc., an Alaska native corp., Anchorage, 1976, mgr. research and analysis, 1976-79, spl. projects coordinator, 1979-81; devel. mgr. Quadrant Devel. Co., Anchorage, 1981-84; v.p. income property Alaska Mut. Bank, 1984-86; asst. v.p. income property Banner Banc, Dallas, 1986—. Bd. dirs. Overall Econ. Devel. Commn., Mat-Su Borough, 1977-80; chmn. zoning subcom. Anchorage Land Use Task Force; mem. Anchorage Econ. Devel. Commn., 1985-86. Mem. Nat. Assn. Bus. Economists, Anchorage Bd. Realtors (bd. dirs. 1983—), Alaska Mortgage Bankers Assn., Dallas Mortgage Bankers Assn. Republican. Roman Catholic. Home: 2305 Covington Lane Plano TX 75023 Office: 12770 Coit Rd Suite 226 Dallas TX 75251

DUHIG, VIVIAN IRENE, educator; b. Henrietta, Okla., Oct. 12, 1922; d. Jesse Lawrence and Bessie Devon (Martin) Chesshir; student So. Tex. Jr. Coll., 1954; B.A. (scholar), Rice U., 1961; postgrad McNeese State U., 1976-77; m. William Gordon Duhig, Jan. 18, 1952; children—Michael Lee and Margaret Louise (adopted twins). High sch. English and math. tchr., Houston, 1961-70; asst. dir. community relations St. Patrick Hosp., Lake Charles, La., 1974-77; adminstrv. asst. architect, Sulphur, La., 1977-79; owner Public Relations Secretarial Service, Lake Charles, 1979-82; tchr. English, history and civics Houston Ind. Sch. Dist., 1982—; free lance secretarial service, Houston, 1982—; field ops. supr. for 12-parish dist., 1980 census, Lake Charles; Parish exec. com. Rep. Party, 1977-79; active polit. campaigns; pres. 7th Dist. Republican Women Club, 1977-79, del. nat. convs., 1977, 79, 83, del. state conv., 1984; mem. Women in Support of Pres., Houston chpt.; charter mem., organizing com. La. Preservation Alliance, chmn. public relations com.; pres. Calcasieu Hist. Preservation Soc., 1977-79; chmn. home show, 1975, 76; mem. La. Assn. for Retarded Citizens, 1970-79; vol. St. Patrick Hosp. Aux.; active La. Women Opposed to ERA. Mem. Am. Bus. Women's Assn., C. of C. (legis. affairs and red carpet coms.), Rice Alumni Assn. Mem. Church of Christ. Club: Toastmasters Internat. Contbr. research, hist., news articles to pubs. Home: 8578 Ariel Houston TX 77074

DUKE, BETTE MARIE, design firm executive; b. Yakima, Wash., Jan. 5, 1942; d. Ernest G. and Alma F. (Gerriets) Boos; m. Lawrence W. Duke, July 4, 1965 (div. 1968). Student Calif. Coll Arts and Crafts, 1960-61; B.A. in Indsl. Design, Art Ctr. Coll. Design, 1964, Designer, E.J. Krause and Assocs., Los Angeles, 1965-65; design asst. Nicolas Disjakov, San Francisco, 1966-68; freelance designer Bette Duke Graphics, San Francisco, 1968-81; art dir. Food & Wine mag., Am. Express Pub. Co., N.Y.C., 1981-84; pres. Focus on Food, design firm, 1985—; design instr. San Francisco City Coll., 1976-78, Acad. Art Coll., San Francisco, 1978-80. Recipient Gold medal San Francisco Soc. Communicating Arts, 1980; awards of Merit, Art Dir. Clubs, N.Y., San Francisco, Los Angeles, 1968-80, Mem. San Francisco Profl. Food Soc. (past sec.), Am. Inst. Graphic Arts, Art designer: The Best of Food and Wine, 1983; Good Food Fast, 1985. Home: 1675 York St 24-H New York NY 10128 Office: 134 Fifth Ave New York NY 10011

DUKE, CAROL MICHIELS, real estate broker; b. Alexandria, La., Sept. 2, 1944; d. Leo A., Sr. and Elva L. (Wilson) Michiels; m. M. Carey Duke, Jr., Apr. 23, 1971; 1 child, Perrianne. Student in personnel mgmt. Nichols State U., 1974-77; grad. Dale Carnegie Inst. Cert. resdl. broker Realtors Inst., La. Realtors Assn.; lic. real estate broker, Tex.; lic. notary pub., Tex. Office mgr. Bayou Constrn. Co., Houma, La., 1974-76; realtor, mgr. Glynn & Assoc. Realtors, Houma, La., 1976-79; owner, broker Century 21 Real Estate One, Houma, 1979-81; regional v.p. Century 21 of Tex. and La., Houston, 1981-82; v.p., gen. mgr. Doyle Stuckey Realtors, Houston, 1982-83; broker/mgr. Gary Greene Realtors, Better Homes & Gardens, Houston, 1983-85; regional mgr. Better Homes & Gardens Real Estate Service, Des Moines, 1985—; com. mem. Farm and Land Inst., Austin, 1972—; seminar condr.; chmn. conv. booth Realtors Nat. Home Builders, Houston, 1983. Editor Training and Policy Manual, 1982. Local chmn. Easter Seal Soc., Houma, 1979. Recipient Top Listing award, numerous Top Quarterly awards La. Dist. of Century 21, 1980, Yearly Top Goal award, Yearly Bottom Line award, Top Prodn. award, numerous Top Quarterly awards, Better Homes & Gardens, Houston, 1983, 84. Mem. Houston Bd. Realtors (edn. com. 1984-85), Tex. Assn. Realtors (realtor/builder, sec. 1983-86), Nat. Assn. Realtors, Realtors Nat. Mktg. Inst., West Houston C. of C., Jaycee Jaynes (state bd. dirs. 1976-77, sec. 1977-78). Democrat. Roman Catholic. Home: 13807 Aspen Hollow Houston TX 77082 Office: Better Homes & Gardens Real Estate Service 13807 Aspen Hollow Houston TX 77082

DUKE, ELLEN KAY, computer marketing executive, community activist; b. Indpls., June 7, 1952; d. Richard Thomas and Ruby Mae (Wright) D. Student Chapman Coll., Orange, Calif., 1972; B.S. in Pub. Affairs, Ind. U.-Bloomington, 1975; postgrad. Portland State U., 1980-81. News reporter, Salem Statesman, Corvallis, Oreg., 1976-78; com. adminstr. Oreg. State Legislature, Salem, 1979-80; pub. involvement coordinator Met. Regional Service Dist., Portland, 1981-82; account mgr. Thunder & Visions, Portland, 1982-83; project asst. Amdahl Corp., Sunnyvale, Calif., 1983-84; spl. project coordinator Computerland Corp., Hayward, Calif., 1984—; producer, lead facilitator Sage, Inc., Walnut Creek, Calif., 1982—. Co-author: (ednl. film) Communication Skills, 1975. Chairperson Corvallis Budget Commn., Oreg., 1978; commr. Hayward Library, Calif., 1985—, Alameda County Consumer Affairs, Oakland, 1985; rep. Nat. Democratic Conv., N.Y.C., 1982. Named Able Toastmaster Toastmasters Internat., 1981. Mem. Nat. Assn. Female Execs., Am. Mktg. Assn. Club: Sierra, (San Francisco). Office: Computerland 2750 Sydney Way Hayward CA 94546

DUKE, JUDITH SILVERMAN, author; b. Portchester, N.Y., Mar. 27, 1934; d. Herbert Francis and Fannye (Cohen) Silverman; B.A., Cornell U., 1955; postgrad. N.Y.U. Sch. Bus. Adminstrn.; m. Alan Duke, Mar. 2, 1968; 1 dau., Sharon. Research asst. Boni Watkins, Jason & Co., N.Y.C., 1955; statistician Nat. Footwear Mfrs. Assn., Washington, 1956-59; head research dept. Lefcourt Realty Corp., N.Y.C., 1959-60; asst. to dir. market research Life mag., 1960-70; abstracter-indexer Morningside Assos., Pleasantville, N.Y., 1973-75; free-lance writer, 1976—; author: The Children's Literature Market, 1977-82, 1977; The Religious Communications Market, 1978-1983, 1978; The Business Information Markets, 1979-1984, 1979; Children's Books and Mags., 1979; Religious Publishing and Communications, 1981; The Technical, Scientific and Medical Publishing Market, 1981-86, 1981, rev., 1985; editor: The Knowledge Industry 200, 1983; mng. editor: U.S. Book Publishing Yearbook and Directory, 1981-82, 1982; assoc. editor Advanced Tech. Libraries, Data Base Alert, 1983—. Address: 6 Carriage Hill Millwood NY 10546

DUKE, VERONICA MURRAY, social worker; b. Cape May, N.J., Sept. 28, 1931; d. Thomas Patrick and Cora Beatrice (Davies) Murray; student U. Tampa, 1949-51; B.S., U. Fla., 1953; M.S.W., U. Mo., 1959; m. Alvah G. Heideman, Jr., 1955 (div. 1976); children—Alvah G. III, Sara Elizabeth; m. 2d, George Duke, Jr., 1979. Caseworker, Hillsborough County, Tampa, Fla., 1954-56; caseworker State of Mo., Fulton, 1956-59; chief social worker Mo. State Sch., 1959-60; psychiat. social worker State of Alaska, Anchorage, 1970-72; chief social worker Alaska Psychiat. Inst., U. Alaska, Anchorage, 1972—; field instr. U. Wash.-Yeshiva U. Republican Committeewoman, Anchorage, Mo., 1969; pres. Camp Fire Girls Council, 1969-70. Served as ensign USNR, 1953-54: Korea. Mem. Nat. Assn. Social Workers, Soc. Dirs. Hosp. Social Work, Acad. Cert. Social Workers, U.S. Ski Assn., Mo. Alumni Assn., Clin. Social Work Registry, Circle of Friends, U. Pacific. Republican. Episcopalian. Clubs: Soroptimists, Women's of Am. Home: 1710 Eastridge Dr Anchorage AK 99501 Office: 2900 Providence Rd Anchorage AK 99508

DUKERT, BETTY COLE, television producer; b. Muskogee, Okla., May 9, 1927; d. Irvan Dill and Ione (Bowman) Cole; m. Joseph M. Dukert, May 19, 1968. Student Lindenwood Coll., St. Charles, Mo., 1945-46, Drury Coll., Springfield, Mo., 1946-47; B.J., U. Mo., 1949. With Sta. KICK, Springfield, Mo., 1949-50; adminstrv. asst. Juvenile Office, Green County, Mo., 1950-52; with Sta. WRC-TV/NBC, Washington, 1952-56; assoc. producer Meet the Press, NBC, Washington, 1956-75, producer, 1975—; mem. Robert F. Kennedy Journalism Awards Com., 1978-82. Trustee Drury Coll., Springfield, Mo., 1984—. Recipient Disting. Alumna award Drury Coll., 1975; Disting. Alumni award U. Mo., 1978; Ted Yates award Washington chpt. Nat. Acad. TV Arts and Scis., 1979; Pub. Relations award for pub. service Am. Legion Nat. Comdrs., 1981. Mem. Am. Women in Radio and TV, Am. News Women's Club, Radio/TV Corrs. Assn., Women's Forum Washington, Soc. Profl. Journalists (dir. 1983-84). Club: Nat. Press. Office: NBC News 4001 Nebraska Ave NW Washington DC 20016

DULAJ, NANCE LILLIAN IRENE KOPER, public health administrator; b. Chgo., Nov. 5; d. John Florian and Anastasia Nancy (Borowa) Koper; m. John Dulaj, Feb. 23, 1952 (div. 1972); children—George John, Glenard Ray, Gloria Janine (dec.). A.A., Bogan Coll., Chgo., 1962; B.A., St. Xavier Coll., Chgo., 1970, 82; Diploma, John Robert Powers Sch., Chgo., 1984. Cert. tchr. Ill. Tchr. numerous schs. in Ill.; sec. to exec. v.p. and patent counsel Velsicol Chem. Corp., Chgo., 1973-77; evening reservations mgr. Drake Hotel, Chgo., 1973-75, Ritz-Carlton Hotel, Chgo., 1976-79; adminstrv. asst. to sr. ptnr., tax dept. mgr. Thomas Havey & Co., C.P.A.s, Chgo., 1977-80; paralegal, sec. to main ptnr. Maher & Newman Ltd., Chgo., 1980; adminstrv. asst. to commr. of health Bur. of Labs., Chgo., 1980—; evening reservations mgr. Park-Hyatt Hotel, Chgo., 1981. Weekly contbr. Southwest News Herald, The Territory Times; contbr. numerous articles to profl. pubs. Capt., ARC Blood Drive, 1983; mem. spl. project bd. St. Xavier Coll., Chgo., 1984; mem. Chgo. Plan Commn.; participant numerous civic and cultural activities. Mem. Chgo. Hist. Soc., Chgo. Council Fgn. Relations, 20th Century R.R. Club, Am-European Student Union, Nature Conservancy, Polish Arts Club, Polish Nat. Alliance, Coalition Polish-Am. Women, Queen's Guild, Troubadours Drama Group, Nat. Assn. Female Execs., Nat. Assn. Legal Secs., Women in Communications, Ill. Assn. Legal Secs., Chgo. Assn. Legal Secs. (asst. treas. 1983, chmn. Law Week 1984), Galena C. of C., St. Xavier Coll. Alumni Assn., Epsilon Eta Phi, Phi Chi Theta. Home: 7235 S Avers Ave Chicago IL 60629 Office: Suite LL-169 Daley Civic Ctr 50 W Washington St Chicago IL 60602

DULANY, ELIZABETH GJELSNESS, university press administrator; b. Charleston, S.C., Mar. 11, 1931; d. Rudolph Hjalmar and Ruth Elizabeth (Weaver) Gjelsness; m. Donelson Edwin Dulany, Mar. 19, 1955; 1 child, Christopher Daniel. B.A., Bryn Mawr Coll., 1952. Proofreader, editor Books in Print, R.R. Bowker Co., N.Y.C., summers 1948-51, mng. editor, summer 1952; med. sec., editor dept. pediatrics U. Mich. Hosp., Ann Arbor, 1953-54; editorial asst. E.P. Dutton & Co., N.Y.C., 1954-55; editorial asst. U. Ill. Press, Champaign, 1956-59, asst. to editor, 1959-60, asst. editor, 1960-67, assoc. editor, 1967-72, mng. editor, 1972—, asst. dir., 1983—. Democrat. Episcopalian. Home: 73 Greencroft Champaign IL 61820 Office: U Ill Press 54 E Gregory St Champaign IL 61820

DULA-WILSON, CAROLYN ROSETTA, autoleasing specialist; b. Lenoir, N.C., Mar. 24, 1956; d. Charles Barber and Gertrude (Felder) Dula; m. Darryel Ray Wilson, June 29, 1984. B.S., N.C. A&T State U., 1978. Customer service rep. So. Bell, Greensboro, N.C., 1978-79; waitress, hostess Coco's Hamburgers, Atlanta, 1979-81; mgr. Pizza Hut, Inc., Decatur, Ga., 1981-83, Wendy's Internat., Atlanta, 1983-84; auto leasing specialist Autolease Atlanta, 1984—. Sec. Know-Your-Neighbor Club, Atlanta, 1982. Recipient T. Austin Finch scholarship Thomasville Industries, N.C., 1974. Mem. Intown Bus. Assocs., Nat. Assn. Female Execs.

DULLIEN, STARLEY BEATRIX, entertainment company executive; b. Wiesbaden, Hessen, W. Ger., July 26, 1951; d. Milan Nicholas and Martha Henriette (Zwinkau) Drakulich; m. Thomas Klaus-Dieter Dullien, Jan. 2, 1975; 1 son, Daniel Claudio Didier. B.A., U. Utah, 1974; Teaching Cert. in Multilingual/Multicultural Edn., U. Utah, 1976. Conf. dir. Nat. Network for Bilingual Edn., Salt Lake City, 1976-77; assoc. tchr. U. Utah, Salt Lake City, 1974-79; transfer agt. Western Capital and Securities, Salt Lake City, 1979-82; promotion dir. Saltair Resort, Salt Lake City, 1982-83; sec., treas. Starbar, Inc., Salt Lake City, 1982-83; pres. Stardust, Inc., Salt Lake City, 1983—; dir. Les Chic Orgn., Salt Lake City, 1977-79, Jazzin' Dance Co., Salt Lake City, 1982-83; title VII curriculum coordinator Nat. Network for Bilingual Bicultural Edn., Salt Lake City, 1976. Performance grantee Utah Arts Council, 1982. Mem. Phoenix Conv. Bur., Salt Lake Conv. Bur., Utah Advt. Fedn., Women's Info. Network. Democrat. Office: 161 W 6th South Suite 142 Salt Lake City UT 84101

DUMAS, ELNORA JEANETTE, psychotherapist; b. Elmira, N.Y., Oct. 24, 1938; d. Henry and Ira Mae (Lewis) D.; B.S., Howard U., 1960, M.S.W., 1962; postgrad. New Sch. Social Research, 1979-80. Supr., Bronx (N.Y.) State Hosp., 1968-71; asst. dir., then dir. Project Teen Aid, Bklyn., 1967-68; supr. N.Y.C. Soc. Meth. Ch., Headstart Program/Foster Home Care Div., Bur. Child Welfare, 1964-67; cons. Pre-Kindergarten Headstart, N.Y.C., 1969-71, Maternal and Infant Care Family Planning Project, N.Y.C., 1963-64; caseworker Community Service Soc./Warwick State Tng. Sch., 1962-63; pvt. practice psychotherapy, Bklyn., 1971—; cons. Reed & DiSalvo Assos., N.Y.C., 1971; sec. Psychiat. Outpatient Clinics Am., 1971; asst. sec. Bklyn. Psychiat. Centers, 1974—; pres. Bushwick Mental Health Clinic, 1974—; supr. prison health service N.Y. Dept. Health, Jr. League Bklyn . Den mother Boy Scouts Am., Bklyn., 1975; vol. Internat. Center Fgn. Students and Businessmen, Bklyn., 1977, Vol. Literacy Program, 1980—; transp. hostess Nat. Dem. Conv., 1976. Cert. social worker, N.Y. State. Mem. Nat. Assn. Social Workers, Jr. League of Bklyn., Bklyn. Women's Polit. Caucus, Acad. Cert. Social Workers, Nat. Assn. Black Social Workers, Coalition of 100 Black Women, NAACP, Lambda Kappa Mu (Gamma chpt.). Democrat. Roman Catholic. Club: KC Aux. Home: 361 Clinton Ave Brooklyn NY 11238

DUMAS, SANDRA LEE, personnel executive, personnel consultant; b. Malone, N.Y., Mar. 27, 1957; d. Leonard James and Myrtle Lucille (Beverlin) Dumas. A.S., NYU-Canton, 1976; student Tunxis Community Coll., 1977-79. Receptionist N.W. Enterprises, Malone, 1972; receptionist, sec. Wasley Products, Inc., Plainville, Conn., 1973, time study estimator, 1974-76; prodn. control clk., 1976-77, personnel asst., 1977-79, asst. personnel mgr., 1979-82, personnel mgr., 1982—; cons. Wasley Lighting, Essex, Conn., 1982—, Precision Molding, New Britain, Conn., 1985—. Bd. dirs. United Way of Plainville, 1985-88, Wheeler Clinic, Inc., Plainville, 1984—; trustee UAW Internat. Union Welfare Fund, Hartford, Conn., 1984-88; crisis intervention counselor Help Line, Plainville, 1983-84; rape crisis counselor YWCA, New Britain, Conn., 1984-85; Strike Back Against Crime rep. Strike Back, New Haven, 1984—; cons. Jr. Achievement Project Bus., Plainville, 1986; advisor Coop. Work Experience, Bristol Eastern High Sch., 1982-85. Recipient Outstanding Young Woman award Jaycee Women, Bristol, Conn., 1984, Conn. Outstanding Young Citizens award WFSB Channel 3, Conn. Jaycees, 1985, Proclamation, Mayor City of Bristol, 1985. Mem. Nat. Assn. Female Execs., Am. Soc. Personnel Adminstrn., Internat. Found. Employee Benefit Plans, Nat. Safety Council, Mfrs. Hartford County, Conn. Bus. and Industry Assn. Democrat. Roman Catholic. Club: Jr Women's (co-chmn. health and safety 1977-78) (Bristol). Avocations: bowling; swimming. Office: Wasley Products Inc Plainville Indsl Park Plainville CT 06062

DUMMETT, JOCELYN ANGELA, physician; b. Leicester, Eng., Sept. 15, 1956; came to U.S. 1966; d. Kenneth John and Sheila Amanda (Waterman) Dummett. M. Biology, Bklyn. Coll., 1976; M.D., Howard U., 1980. Diplomate Nat. Bd. Med. Examiners. Intern St. Vincent's Hosp., N.Y.C., 1980; resident Kings County Hosp. Ctr., Downstate Med. Ctr., Brooklyn, 1981-83, clin. instr., 1983-85, clin. asst. prof., 1985—; attending pediatrician 50 Greene Med. Ctr., Bklyn., 1983-84; vol. child life program Downstate Med. Ctr., 1974-75, preceptor L.B. Johnson sch. health program, 1985—. Recipient Excellence in Pediatrics, Howard U. Coll. Medicine, Washington, 1980. Fellow Am. Acad. Pediatrics; mem. Nat. Assn. Residents and Interns, Provident Clin. Soc., Kings County Med. Soc., Nat. Med. Assn., Bklyn. Pediatric Soc. Democrat. Office: 156 E 37th St Brooklyn NY 11203

DUMOND, MARY MARQUIS, newspaper editor, writer, educator; b. Mpls., Feb. 5, 1925; d. Harry Stanton and Mary Alexa (Whitmire) Marquis. B.J., U. Mo., 1947; M.English, No. Ariz. U., 1969. Instr. journalism No. Ariz. U., Flagstaff, 1969-73; editor Tribune, LaCrosse, Wis., 1973-74; owner Have Broom, Sedona, Ariz., 1974-75; writer News-Sun, Sun City, Ariz., 1975—, co-editor, 1983—. Author: Birds of Arizona, 1953; editor newspaper sect. View, 1980—, Sun Living, 1954-57. Pub. relations advisor Citizens for Better Flagstaff, 1972-73. Mem. Ariz. Authors Assn., Ariz. Press Club, Sigma Delta Chi, Theta Sigma Phi (chmn. 1964-68). Democrat. Address: 12643 N 113th Ave Youngtown AZ 85363

DUMONT, VIRGINIA PETERSON, educator, writer; b. Salt Lake City, Jan. 19, 1918; d. Frederick L. and Florence Julie (Carpenter) Peterson; B.A. with honors in English, Mills Coll., 1938; postgrad. (grad. scholar), Bryn Mawr Coll., 1938-39, (spl. fellow), 1939-40; m. R. Peaslee DuMont, Aug. 5, 1940; children—Virginia Patricia DuMont Kelly, Peaslee Frederick, Jayne Louise DuMont Mack, Julia Blanche, Peter Bruce, Lorna Elizabeth DuMont Shinkle, Edward Carroll. Home tchr. Piedmont (Calif.) High Sch., 1970-73; pvt. tutor in English and reading skills, 1970—. Mem. adv. com. on ednl. philosophy Piedmont Unified Sch. Dist., 1967-68; mem. Friends of Oakland Library; mem. Piedmont bd. Am. Field Service, 1965-69. Mem. Mills Coll. Alumnae Assn. (chmn. continuing ednl. pilot study 1957-59, nat. gov. 1958-59, dir. Phila. br. 1939, pres. Washington br. 1946-47, pres. Oakland, Calif. br. 1969-70, v.p. program 1983-84), Calif. Writers Club, LWV (v.p. Piedmont 1978-83), Oakland Mus. Assn., San Francisco Mus. Soc., Phi Beta Kappa. Contbr. poetry and articles to profl. books; editorial bd. Mills Coll. Alumnae Quar., 1978—. Address: 212 Carmel Ave Piedmont CA 94611

DUNAGAN, CAROL LEE, insurance specialist; b. Bessemer, Mich., Nov. 12, 1946; d. William Franklin and Jean Carol (Berling) Dunagan; m. Henry Wallace Haug, Aug. 12, 1965 (div. 1971); children—Betsy Kaye, Matthew Paul; m. Darwin W. Smith, Oct. 27, 1979 (div. 1984). Student pub. schs. Receptionist, Waite & Co., Bozeman, Mont., 1975-77; claims, clerical supr. Ranger Ins., Phoenix and Denver, 1977-79; office mgr. State Farm Ins., Bozeman, 1979-85; adjuster Frontier Adjusters Cheyenne, Wyo., 1985—. Actress Loft Community Theatre, Bozeman, 1975-83, pres., mem. bd., 1984; actress Cheyenne Little Theatre Players, 1985-86; campaign mgr. local city commn. candidate, Bozeman, 1981; youth leader Bozeman United Methodist Ch., 1982. Named Bozeman Ins. Woman of Year, 1984. Mem. Nat. Assn. Ins. Women (chpt. pres. 1982-83).

DUNAIEF, LEAH S., newspaper editor, publisher, writer; b. N.Y.C., Aug. 21, 1940; d. Rudolph and Mollie (Rosenthal) Salmansohn; m. Ivan F. Dunaief, Feb. 24, 1963; children—Joshua, Daniel, David. B.A., Barnard Coll., 1962; M.B.A., Columbia U., 1982. Writer, researcher Time, Inc., N.Y.C., 1963-67; founder editor, pub. Village Times, Setauket, N.Y., 1976—, pres., chmn. bd. Village Times, Inc. Contbr., New York Times; contbr., researcher Time Life Sci. Library. Mem. Speaker Stanley Fink's Small Bus. Commn. for L.I.; mem. Congessman Mrazek's Women's Issues Com.; assoc. trustee Dowling Coll., Oakdale, N.Y. Recipient numerous media awards from state and nat. press assns. Mem. N.Y. Press Assn. (pres. 1984-85), Nat. Newspaper Assn. (state chmn. 1982—; 1st place for investigative reporting, weeklies and small dailies 1985). Office: Village Times 185 Route 25A Box VT Setauket NY 11733

DUNAWAY, FAYE, actress; b. Bascom, Fla., Jan. 14, 1941; student U. Fla., Boston U.; m. Peter Wolf, 1974 (div. 1979); m. Terry O'Neill; 1 child, Liam. An original mem. Lincoln Center Repertory Co.; appeared in Hogan's Goat, off-Broadway, Curse of an Aching Heart, Broadway, 1982; played Bonnie in motion picture Bonnie and Clyde, 1967; appeared in motion pictures The Happening, 1966, Hurry Sundown, 1966, Extraordinary Seaman, 1967, The Thomas Crown Affair, 1968, A Place for Lovers, 1968 The Arrangement, 1969, Puzzle of a Downfall Child, 1970, Little Big Man, 1970, Doc, 1971, Oklahoma Crude, 1972, Three Musketeers, 1973, Four Musketeers, 1973, Towering Inferno, 1974, Chinatown, 1974, Three Days of the Condor, 1975, Network (Acad. award for best actress), 1976, The Voyage of the Dammed, 1976 Eyes of Laura Mars, 1978, The Champ, 1978, First Deadly Sin, 1980, Mommie Dearest, 1981, The Wicked Lady, 1983, Ordeal by Innocence, 1984, Supergirl, 1984; appeared on TV in After the Fall, Duchess of Windsor, Disappearance of Sister Aimee, Evita and the Country Girl, Agatha Christie's 13 at Dinner, 1985, Beverly Hills Madam, 1986, TV miniseries Ellis Island, 1984, Christopher Columbus, 1985. Recipient Most Promising Newcomer Award Brit. Film Acad., 1968. Address: care Creative Artists Agy Inc 1888 Century Park E Suite 1400 Los Angeles CA 90067*

DUNBAR, (ISOBEL) MOIRA, glaciologist; b. Edinburgh, Scotland, Feb. 3, 1918; d. William and Elizabeth Mary (Robertson) D. Grad. Cranley Sch. for Girls, Edinburgh, 1935; B.A., Oxford U., Eng., 1939, M.A., 1948; postgrad. in Russian, U.S. Army Lang. Sch., 1958. Joined Arctic Research sect. Def. Research Bd. (later div. earth scis.), 1947, acting dir. earth scis., 1975-77; mem. del. studying icebreaker ops. in USSR, 1964; mem. com. on glaciology Polar Research Bd., U.S. NRC, 1976-80; mem. Can. Environ. Adv. Council, 1972-78.

Author: (with K.R. Greenaway) Arctic Canada from the Air, 1956; also numerous sci. papers on sea ice research. Recipient Centennial award Can. Meteorol. Service, 1971; Massey medal, 1972. Fellow Arctic Inst. N.Am. (bd. govs. 1966-69), Royal Can. Geog. Soc. (bd. dirs. 1974—), Internat. Glaciology Soc.; mem. Royal Soc. Can. Anglican. Avocations: horseback riding; theatre; music; Arctic history. Office: Rural Route 1 Dunrobin ON K0A 1T0 Canada

DUNBAR, KATHY BAILEY, nursing administrator, educator; b. Adrian, Mich., May 31, 1951; d. George Herbert and Mary Lois (Chrisman) Barrows; m. Gary Hal Dunbar, May 1, 1984; children by a previous marriage—Jennifer Marie Bailey, Jessica Leilani Bailey, Joshua Wade Bailey. R.N., Hackley Hosp. Sch. Nursing, 1974; B.S.N. magna cum laude, U. Mich., 1985. R.N., Mich. Pvt. duty nurse, Lenawee County, Mich., summer 1974; staff nurse G.N. Wilcox Meml. Hosp., Lihue, Kauai, Hawaii, 1974-75; coordinator inservice edn. Herrick Hosp., Tecumseh, Mich., 1976-82, asst. adminstr. nursing, 1983—; staff nurse emergency room and CCU Saline Community Hosp., Mich., 1979-82; coordinator, instr. Jackson Community Coll., Mich., 1980-81; mem. health occupations adv. com. Lenawee Area VoTech Ctr., Adrian, Mich., 1982-84; lectr. in field. Mem. Lenawee County Mgrs' Club. Republican. Lutheran. Avocations: reading; writing poetry; gardening; swimming. Office: Herrick Meml Hosp 500 F Pottawatamie St Tecumseh MI 49286

DUNBAR, KORA LOUISE, educational administrator; b. Dunnell, La., Oct. 14, 1938; d. Percy Melvin and Esther Beatrice (McCoully) Travallion; m. Donald Carlye Wade, 1957; children—Karla Rene (Mrs. B. Johnson), Donald Carlye; m. Eddie James Dunbar, 1977; stepchildren—Vivian, Alleyne, Stephanie. B.S., Grambling Coll., 1965; M.A., N.E. La. U., 1971, Ed. Spec., 1973; M.A., San Diego State U., 1976; Ed.D., Northern Ariz. U., 1979. Sec. to prin. Ouachita Parish Sch. Dist., Myles High Sch., Sterlington, La., 1960-64; mem. faculty Carroll Jr. High Sch., Monroe, La., 1965-73; tchr. adult edn., English, speech, and social studies Monroe City Sch. Bd., 1970-72; guidance counselor Wossman High Sch., Monroe, 1973; tchr., counselor, adminstrv. intern Sweetwater Union High Sch. Dist., Imperial Beach, Calif., 1973-76; multicultural curriculum writer, resource tchr. Sweetwater Union High Sch., Chula Vista, Calif., 1976-78; dean students Poway Unified Sch. Dist., Meadowbrook Middle Sch., Calif., 1978-79; asst. prin. Mt. Carmel High Sch., San Diego, 1979-81; prin. Poway Unified Sch. Dist., Los Penasquitos Elem. Sch., San Diego, 1981-85; prin.-in-residence, adminstr. Tng. Ctr., San Diego County Office of Edn., 1985—; adj. prof. No. Ariz. U., Flagstaff, 1983-84; Nat. U., 1984—; condr. numerous inservice workshops, 1973—. Author: (Susan Van Zant) Parent Effectiveness Program, 1983; author reports and monographs in field. Carnegie fellow San Diego State U., 1975-76. Mem. Assn. Calif. Sch. Adminstrs., Assn. Poway Sch. Mgrs. (pres. 1981-82), Southwest Personnel and Guidance Assn., Black Child Devel. Inst., Visible Black Educators San Diego County (co-founder). Phi Delta Kappa, Delta Kappa Gamma. Baptist. Office: 6401 Linda Vista Road San Diego CA 92111-7399

DUNCAN, ANN HUBERTY, university administrator; b. Sacramento, Sept. 21, 1933; d. Martin R. and Gertrude (Turner) Huberty; m. John B. Duncan, June 30, 1957 (div. July 1971); children—Robert Martin, Kenneth Ross. B.A., U. Calif.-Berkeley, 1956; M.A., Calif. State U.-Hayward, 1977; postgrad. Pepperdine U., 1984—. Cert. tchr. Personnel dir. Calif. Sch. Employees Assn., 1974-75; assoc. personnel analyst City of Oakland, Calif., 1975-76; dir. employer-employee relations City of Livermore, Calif., 1976-80; pres. Duncan & Assocs., Los Angeles and Castro Valley, Calif., 1980-84; asst. dir. Ctr. Ednl. Leadership, Pepperdine U., Los Angeles, 1984—; prof. Grad. Sch. Pub. Adminstrn., J.F.K., Orinda, Calif., 1979-83; lectr. career devel. San Jose State U., 1974-84. Mem. Hayward Zoning Commn., 1970-71; trustee Chabot Coll., Hayward, 1971-84; pres. bd., 1975, 79. Recipient Pub. Service award Alameda County Sch. Bd. Assn., 1975, 79, Calif. Community Coll. Trustees Assn., 1984. Mem. Calif. Elected Women's Assn. for Ednl. Research (charter, state bd. dirs.), U.S.-China Peoples Friendship Assn., LWV (chpt. pres. 1968-70), No. Calif. Personnel and Employee Relations Assn., Calif. Community Coll. Trustees Assn. Republican. Avocations: politics; travel. Home: 1250 Monaco Pacific Palisades CA 90272 Office: 3415 Sepulveda Blvd Los Angeles CA 90034

DUNCAN, DEIDRA RENEE, accountant; b. Tullahoma, Tenn., Sept. 21, 1954; d. Ernest J. and Gladys M. (Yokley) Duncan; student Blair Sch. Music, Vanderbilt U., 1966-71; B.B.A., Middle Tenn. State U., 1976, M.B.A., 1978. Pvt. practice acctg., Manchester, Tenn.; mag. writer. Mem. Am. Inst. C.P.A.s, Tenn. Soc. C.P.A.s, Internat. Platform Assn., Mensa. Republican. Anglican. Club: Tullahoma Junior Woman's. Home: Deerfield Estates Route 68 Box 8808 Manchester TN 37355

DUNCAN, ELIZABETH CHARLOTTE, educational therapist, educator, psychologist, author, lecturer; b. Los Angeles, Mar. 10, 1919; d. Frederick John de St. Vrain and Nellie Mae (Goucher) Schwankovsky; m. William McConnell Duncan, Oct. 12, 1941 (div. 1949); 1 child, Susan Elizabeth Duncan Sturges. B.A., Calif. U.-Long Beach, 1953; M.A., U. Calif.-Los Angeles, 1962; Ph.D., Internat. Coll., 1984. Dir. gifted program Palos Verdes Sch. Dist., Calif., 1958-64; TV tchr., participant ednl. films Los Angeles County, 1961-64; dir. U. So. Calif. Presch., Los Angeles, 1965-69; cons. Western Kennedy U., Agoura Hills, Calif., 1984-86; ednl. therapist pvt. practice, Malibu and Thousand Oaks, Calif., 1979—; mem. Research Inst. of Scripps Clinic, La Jolla, Calif.; charter mem. Inst. Behav. Med., Santa Barbara, Calif.; TV performer: (documentary) The Other Side, 1985. Author: Persephond's Child, 1984. Active Chryalis Ctr., Los Angeles, 1984-86, Ventura County Mental Health Adv. Bd., Calif., 1985-86, United Way, Los Angeles, 1985-86. Recipient Emmy award for best documentary Am. TV Arts and Scis., 1976. Mem. Transpersonal Psychol. Assn., Am. Counseling and Devel. Assn., Calif. State Orgn. Gifted Edn. (sec. 1962-64). Democrat. Avocations: swimming; plays; concerts; boating; political issues, especially women and child abuse. Office: 86 Long Ct Thousand Oaks CA 91360

DUNCAN, FRANCES MURPHY, teacher educator; b. Utica, N.Y., June 23, 1920; d. Edward Simon and Elizabeth Myers (Stack) Murphy; B.A., Barnard Coll., Columbia U., 1942; M.Ed., Auburn U., 1963, Ed.D., 1969; m. Lee C. Duncan, June 23, 1947 (div. June 1969); children—Lee C., Edward M., Paul H., Elizabeth B., Nancy R., Richard L. Head sci. dept. Arnold Jr. High Sch., Columbus, Ga., 1960-63; tchr. physiology, Spanish, Jordan High Sch., Columbus, 1963-64; tchr. spl. edn. mentally retarded Muscogee County Sch. System, Columbus, 1964-65; instr. spl. edn. Auburn (Ala.) U., 1966-69; asso. dir. Douglas Sch. for Learning Disabilities, Columbus, 1969-70; prof. edn. and spl. edn. Columbus Coll., 1970-85; ret., 1985; dir. Columbus Specialized Presch. Past sec. exec. bd. Muscular Dystrophy Assn., 1968-70; 73-74; mem. Gov.'s Commn. on Disabled Georgians; past trustee Listening Eyes Sch. for Deaf; mem. adv. bd. Columbus Health Dept. Tng. Centers; chmn. Consumer Adv. Bd. Vocat. Rehab., Mayor's Com. on Handicapped; mem. team for evaluation and placement of exceptional children Columbus Public Schs. Fellow Am. Assn. Mental Deficiency; mem. AAUP, AAUW (pres. 1973-75, div. rec. sec. 1975—), Council Exceptional Children (legis. chmn. 1973-74), Kappa Delta Pi, Psi Chi, Delta Kappa Gamma, Phi Delta Kappa. Roman Catholic. Home: 1811 Alta Vista Dr Columbus GA 31907

DUNCAN, JOHANNA MONICA, child development center administrator, statistical researcher; b. N.Y.C., Oct. 25, 1955; d. Gilbert Hoffman and Johanna Margarete (Sauer) D. B.A., CUNY, 1974, M.P.A., 1981; cert. advanced mgmt. and leadership devel. Atlanta U., 1981. Dir. career devel. Bronx Community Coll., CUNY, 1975-77, dir. spl. programs York Coll., 1977-80; dep. dir. Inst. Family and Community Life, Queens Coll., CUNY and N.Y.C. Bd. Edn., 1980-81; dir. evaluation R&D, Ctr. Labor and Urban Programs, Research and Analysis, Queens Coll., 1981-85; dir. adminstrn. Northside Ctr. for Child Devel., Inc., 1985—; cons. pres.'s office on devel. Employment and Tng. Research Ctr., 1980-81; seminar instr. Aviation Devel. Council and York Coll., 1977-78, Aviation Devel. Council and Queens Coll., 1980-81. Co-author: When a College Works with a Public School, 1984. Mem. Assn. Equality and Excellence in Edn. (v.p. chpt. 1979-81). Democrat.

DUNCAN, KAY ANN, nursing educator; b. Bloomsburg, Pa., Feb. 3, 1948; d. Harry Leroy and Florence (Valencik) Loreman; m. William W. Duncan II, Nov. 27, 1976; 1 child, Eric David. B.S.Nursing cum laude, U. Del., 1972; postgrad. Bloomsburg U., 1983—. Staff nurse ICU, Bon Secours Hosp., Methuen, Mass., 1972-74; psychiat. staff nurse Outlook Hosp., Hampstead, N.H., 1974-75, dir. nurses, 1975-76; psychiat. staff nurse Geisinger Med. Ctr., Danville, Pa., 1976-79, instr. psychiat. nursing Sch. Nursing, 1979—, team coordinator psychiat. nursing team, 1984—. Mem. Sigma Theta Tau, Phi Kappa Phi. Democrat. Roman Catholic. Office: Geisinger Med Ctr Sch Nursing Academy Ave Danville PA 17822

DUNCAN, KIT, social worker; b. Anderson, Ind., Jan. 1, 1956; s. Leo and Theda (Robinson) Craig; A.A., Freed-Hardeman Coll., 1975; B.A., Lubbock Christian Coll., 1978; M.S. in Social Work, U. Tex., 1985. Caseworker Smithlawn Maternity Home, Lubbock, Tex., 1978-79; campus caseworker Christ's Haven for Children, Keller, Tex., 1979-82; VA, Temple, Tex., 1982-83; dir. family services AGAPE of N.C., Inc., 1983-85; program dir. Luth. Family Services, Jonesville, N.C., 1985—. Recipient Psychology/Sociology award Lubbock Christian Coll., 1978-79. Mem. Nat. Assn. Social Workers. Mem. Ch. of Christ. Office: PO Box 282 Jonesville NC 28642

DUNCAN, LINDA LEE, government personnel administrator; b. Balt., Dec. 31, 1949; d. Ervin Ryland and Betty Marie (Jones) Taylor, Jr.; m. Ray D. Charron, Oct., 1975 (div. 1979); 1 child, Jennifer Lorraine Watkins; m. Edgar D. Duncan, May 25, 1985. B.A. in Human Resources, St. Leo Coll., 1983. Employee relations specialist Dobbins AFB, Marietta, Ga., 1978-80, chief labor employee relations, EEO, and tng., 1980-82, personnel officer, 1982—; chief labor and employee relations, 1982-83, employee relations specialist, 1983-85; instr. Gunter Air Force Sch., Montgomery, Ala., 1985, 86. Sec., Northeast Cobb Jaycee Women, Marietta, 1984, external dir., 1985, sec., 1986; pres. Cobb Christmas, Inc. Marietta, 1985. Recipient numerous awards U.S. Air Force, 1982—. Mem. Nat. Assn. Female Execs., Federally Employed Women. Home: 2713 Macby Ave Marietta GA 30066 Office: Dobbins AFB 94 CSG/DPCE Dobbins AFB Marietta GA 30069

DUNCAN, MARGARET DUNSMORE (MRS. WILLIAM FOWLER DUNCAN), civic worker; b. Summit, N.J., Sept. 9, 1920; d. James and Margaret (Montgomery) Dunsmore; student Fresno State Coll., 1941; m. William Fowler Duncan, June 17, 1940; children—William Fowler, Laird Douglas, Fraser Scott. Gray lady A.R.C., Oahu, Hawaii, from 1959, chmn. vols. Langley AFB; active Heart Fund and Neuromuscular Disease drives; mem. Los Ninos Guild, Childrens Hosp. Orange County; vol. San Clemente Gen. Hosp. (Calif.); program chmn. United Presbyn. Women. Mem. Fairfax Hosp. Aux., Clans of Scotland, U.S.A., Scribe, Internat. Platform Assn., Order of Diana, League Women Voters, Beta Sigma Phi (past chpt. pres.). Republican. Presbyterian. (chmn. missionary edn. women's assn., mariner, fellowship chmn. 1973, 74, ordained deacon 1974). Clubs: Ikebana, Air Force Officers Wives (Washington); Neighborhood Garden; Wheeler AFB Officers Woman's (1st v.p. 1960) (Oahu, Hawaii); Langley Officers Wives, Langley Yacht, Langley Golf; San Clemente Garden, San Clemente Women's; Am. Wives, Am. Officers' Wives, NATO Wives. Home: 502 Calle DeSoto San Clemente CA 92672

DUNCAN, PATTI LOU, lawyer; b. Altus, Okla., July 22, 1953; d. Robert Allen and Erma Lou (Parks) Duncan; m. Richard A. Capshaw, July 3, 1981; 1 son, Christopher Sean. B.S. in Econs., U. Okla., 1976, J.D. with honors, 1980. Bar: Tex. 1980. Assoc. Johnson & Swanson, Dallas, 1980—. Contbr. articles to profl. jours. Arthur E. Lippold Scholar, 1977; Brown Oil and Gas award, U. Okla., 1980. Mem. Tex. Bar Assn., Order of Coif. Democrat.

DUNCAN, SHARON ELAINE, publishing company executive, researcher psycholinguistics; b. Durand, Mich., Mar. 21, 1936; d. James Emerson and Marion Gertrude (Mu Maugh) D.; m. Gene R, Watts, Dec. 31, 1981; 1 child, Sabrina Maria Duncan. B.A., Mich. State U., 1961, M.A., 1963; postgrad. Universidad Autónoma de Mex., 1962, U. Calif.-Berkeley, 1963-65; Ph.D., Union Grad. Sch., 1979. Instr. Spanish, Meredith Coll., Raleigh, N.C., 1963-64; grad. asst. comparative lit. U. Calif.-Berkeley, 1964-65; lectr. fgn. langs. San Francisco State U., 1965-68; acct. mgr. Latin Am. div. Compton Advt., Inc., San Francisco, 1969-71; dir. program devel. Bilingual Children's TV, Oakland, Calif., 1972-76; pres. DeAvila, Duncan and Assocs., Inc., San Rafael, Calif., 1978—; cons. materials devel. Linguametrics Group, San Rafael, 1975—; dir. Delta Squared, Inc., San Rafael, 1980—; ptnr. Delta/3, Oakland, 1984. Translator: On Creating a New Attitude, 1968; co-author: (film) Let There Be Light, 19794; (test) Language Assessment Scales, 1976; book A Convergent Approach to Oral Language Assessment, 1982; A Survival Guide to Remodeling, 1983, author: Bilingualism and Cognitive Functioning, 1979; Selfish Shellfish Sellers, 1980; Jugando Hablamos, 1980; Autolas: Computerized Data Management for Language Proficiency Data, 1982; After the Final No: A Book of Poetry, 1984; contbr. articles to profl. jours. Mem. Nat. Assn. Bilingual Educators (editorial bd. 1981-84), Am. Consortium on Teaching of Fgn. Langs., Latin Am. Parents Assn. Democrat. Congregationalist. Club: Bienvenidos Los Niños. Office: De Avila Duncan and Associates Inc PO Box 3495 San Rafael CA 94912

DUNCAN, VICKY STUMBO, personnel service company executive; b. War, W.Va., Sept. 3, 1936; d. John Henry and Hazel Margaret (Gross) Stumbo; student Lamar U., Beaumont, Tex., 1974-75, Orange Coast Coll., Costa Mesa CA, 1982-85; m. Bill Duncan, June 2, 1956; children—Christopher Wayne, William Edward, Kimberly Lynn. Bookkeeper, Security Pacific Bank, Hollywood, Calif., 1955-56; teller Bank of Hawaii, Oahu, 1958-59; credit/collection clk. Montgomery Ward & Co., Houston, 1964-68; counselor mgr. Snelling & Snelling, Beaumont, 1972-75; dir. agy. tng., mem. corp. staff Am. Bus. Service Corp., Newport Beach, Calif., 1971-82. Mem. Am. Mgmt. Assn., Am. Employment Assn., Adminstrv. Mgmt. Soc., Bus. and Profl. Women, Am. Bus. Women, Calif. Assn. Personnel Cons., Beta Sigma Phi. Republican. Home: 1202 Genoa St Santa Ana CA 92704

DUNCAN, VIRGINIA BAUER, power corporation executive, television producer, director; b. Lansing, Mich., June 9, 1929; d. Theodore Irving and Maurine Virginia (Foote) Bauer; B.A., U. Mich., 1951; m. Bruce G. Duncan, Oct. 27, 1956; children—John C., Michael G., Timothy B. Producer, dir. KQED-TV, San Francisco, 1960-75; pres. Candide Prodns., Inc., San Francisco, 1966—; corp. exec. Bechtel Power Corp.; dir. Corp. for Public Broadcasting, Washington, 1975-79, First Interstate Bank of Calif., 1979—. Bd. dirs. Town Sch. for Boys, San Francisco, 1966-70; pres., Parents Assn. Marin Parents Assn. Marin County Day Sch., Corte Madera, Calif., 1971-72; mem. public media panel Nat. Endowment for Arts, Washington, 1973-79; chmn. bd. dirs. Yosemite Inst., 1974-84; trustee Katharine Branson/Mt. Tamalpais High Sch., Ross, Calif., 1975-82; assoc. council Mills Coll., Oakland, Calif., 1975—; mem. Carnegie Commn. on Future of Public Broadcasting, 1977-79; mem. Council for Arts, M.I.T., 1977-80; bd. dirs. James Irvine Found., 1979—. Recipient Edward W McQuade award for disting. programming in field of social justice, 1964; NET award for excellence for individual contbn. to outstanding television programming, 1966; Readers Digest Found. award, 1969; CINE Golden Eagle award, 1970; Emmy award Nat. Acad., TV Arts and Scis., 1971. Office: Box 18222 San Francisco CA 94118

DUNCAN, VIRGINIA IRWIN, lawyer; b. Parker Dam, Calif., May 7, 1949; d. George Gothic and Virginia E. (Dick) Irwin; m. Richard Vaughn Duncan, Jan. 25, 1971; 1 dau., Jessica Von. B.S. in Spl. Edn., No. Ariz. U., 1972, B.S. in Elem. Edn., 1972, M.A. in Spl. Edn., 1978; J.D., U. Ariz., 1983. Cert. tchr. elem. edn., spl. edn., learning disabled, gifted, mentally retarded, blind, Ariz.; bar: Ariz. 1983. Dir., instr. spl. edn. program Beaver Creek Sch. Dist., Rimrock, Ariz., 1975-78; instr. Yavapai Community Coll., Verde Campus, Ariz., 1977-78; tchr. Verde Valley Sch., Sedona, Ariz., 1978, Beaver Creek Sch., Rimrock, 1972-79; assoc. Joyce & Frankel, P.A., Sedona, 1983—. Recipient Am. Jurisprudence award Lawyers Coop. Pub. Co. and Bancroft-Whitney Co., 1982, Samuel M. Fegtly award U. Ariz., 1982; Am. Field Service exchange student, 1966. Mem. ABA, Ariz. Bar Assn., Phi Kappa Phi, Phi Delta Phi. Democrat. Home: PO Box 3275 Sedona AZ 86340 Office: Joyce & Frankel PA PO Box 3984 Sedona AZ 86340

DUNCAN, YVONNE VERONICA, public relations executive; b. Kingston, Jamaica, Aug. 27, 1948; came to U.S., 1977; d. Ivan Lloyd and Myrtle C. (Bell) D. Diploma in Radio-TV Arts, Ryerson Poly. Inst., Toronto, Ont., Can., 1969. Pub. relations officer Jamaica Tourist Bd., Kingston, 1972-74; dir. broadcast prodn. Dunlop, Corbin, Compton Advt., Kingston, 1974-77; account exec. broadcast Peter Martin Assocs. Inc., Pub. Relations, N.Y.C., 1977-81; exec. v.p., account group supr. Van Vechten & Assocs. Pub. Relations, N.Y.C., 1981—. Mem. Caribbean Tourism Assn., Caribbean Hotel Assn., Publicity Club N.Y., Nat. Assn. Female Execs. Office: Van Vechten Assocs 427 E 74th St New York NY 10021

DUNCAN-TREVIRANUS, ANN, counselor, consultant, minister; b. Phila., June 27, 1935; d. William Howard and Mildredgrace (DeFerbrache) Duncan; m. William Anthony Crimmins, Aug. 21, 1954 (div.); children—Catherine, Tom, John, Hugh, Paul, Eve; m. 2d, Hamish Henry Alexandar Stewart Treviranus, Dec. 26, 1983. A.D., U. Maine, 1980; ecumenical minister studies, 1983. Registered nurse, Maine, Va. Pres., filmmaker Noumena, Inc., N.Y.C., Europe, USSR 1971-73; staff nurse Eastern Maine Med. Ctr., Bangor, Maine, 1979-80; family counselor, pvt. practice hypnotherapist, Camden, Maine, 1980-82; network mem. Holistic Health/USA-Asia-Europe for Maine Holistic Health Network, Portland, 1982-83; counselor, cons. Vortex, Inc., Washington, 1982—; founder-dir. Internat. Inst. Transpersonal Diplomacy, 1985—; dir. Rev. Elizabeth Ann Bogert Meml. Fund for Study and Practice Christian Mysticism, Phila., 1983-84; dir. U.S. Assocs. for Cultural Triangle of Sri Lanka, Washington, 1983-84. Originator, nat. bd. dirs. Camden/Nuwara Eliya Sister Cities Project, 1982—; mem. Crime Watch, Camden, 1982-83; spl. cons. U.S. Ambassador to Sri Lanka, Colombo, 1982-83; mem. Maine State Soc., Washington, 1982-86. Mem. Am. Holistic Nurse's Assn. (charter), Internat. Transpersonal Assn., Assn. Transpersonal Psychology, Acad. Religion and Psychical Research, Assn. Humanistic Psychology, Maine State Nurses Assn., Am. Nurses Assn., Va. State Nurses Assn. Office: 6324 Georgetown Pike McLean VA 22101

DUNEIER, DEBRA HOPE, gemologist; b. N.Y.C., Aug. 30, 1954; d. Jacob and Anita Arkow; student Queens Coll., 1976; grad. Gemological Inst. Am., 1980; m. Dana Brad Duneier, Sept. 2, 1971; children—Jamie Troy, Danielle Taylor. With Clyde Duneier Inc., N.Y.C., 1975—, v.p. loose stone div., 1980—; lectr., seminar leader in field. Mem. Am. Gem Soc., Women's Jewelry Assn., Assn. Women Gemologists, Am. Gem Trade Assn. Retail Jewelers Am. Address: 1212 Ave Americas New York NY 10036

DUNHAM, ANEVA JO, educator; b. Portsmouth, Va., Mar. 20, 1938; d. Joseph William and Rachel Lorraine (Kight) D.; B.S. in Edn. cum laude, S.E. Mo. State Coll., 1960; M.Ed. in Elem. Edn., St. Louis U., 1972; M.A. in Mgmt., Webster U., 1983. Tchr., Ritenour Consol. Sch. Dist., St. Louis, 1960—; Tri-Hi-Y coordinator YMCA, Overland, Mo., 1963-68; mem. nominating com. Ednl. Employees Credit Union, 1976-77, bldg. rep., 1975—. Bd. dirs. The Connection, 1986—. Coro Found. Women in Leadership tng. award, 1984. Mem. NEA, Women's Polit. Caucus. Kappa Delta Pi, Phi Alpha Theta. Democrat. Presbyterian. Home: 16 Coach Ct Saint Peters MO 63376 Office: 4301 Edmundson Rd Saint Louis MO 63134

DUNHAM, BARBARA BONONI, temporary service company executive; b. Mpls., Sept. 19, 1939; d. John Michael and Evelyn (Schwartz) Gleason; m. Charles Bononi, Mar. 21, 1959 (div.); m. Gordon Raymond Dunham, May 22, 1980; children—Michele Bononi Schuur, Michael John Bononi. Student Ill. State U. Owner, pres. Action Temps, Inc., Sacramento, Calif., 1977—, Action Secretarial Services, Sacramento, 1983—. Author: You're the Boss, 1983. Bd. dirs. ARC, 1984-87, Salvation Army, 1984-87, Point West Bus. Assn., 1984-87, Eskaton, 1983-86, Healds Bus. Coll., 1985-86, United Way, 1985-88, Vols. in Victim Assistance, 1985-86; fundraiser Am. Lung Assn., 1983, 84, 85, Sacramento Symphony, 1983. Recipient Outstanding Working Exceptional Achievement award The Woman's Advocate, 1982, First Place award Nat. Assn. Temporary Services, 1982, Grand Prize, Nat. Assn. Temporary Services, 1983. Mem. Internat. Temporary Services Assn. (dir. 1980-81, v.p. western region 1981-82), Internat. Assn. Profl. Women, (program chmn. 1984-85), Sacramento Met. C. of C. (com. mem. state Capitol trip and econ. devel. 1985, team capt. econ. devel. indsl. contact 1985), Sacramento C. of C. (mem. county suprs. bus. adv. com. 1985-86, bd. dirs. 1984—; Woman of Yr. award 1985), Citrus Heights C. of C. (sec., Disting. Businesswoman award 1982), Folsom C. of C., Roseville C. of C., Sacramento Women's Network. Clubs: Ambassadors (co-chmn. 1982-83); Soroptomist Internat. (com. mem. ways and means 1984-85, charter pres. 1983-84, Women Helping Women award 1984), Comstock. Avocations: golf; boating. Office: Action Temps Inc 1555 River Park Dr Suite 105 Sacramento CA 95815

DUNHAM, DURLINE, marketing executive, TV personality/producer; b. Dallas, Nov. 22, 1950; d. Harvey Lee and Pauline (Lawhon) D. B.S. summa cum laude, U. Tex.-Arlington, 1969-73; Spanish cert. Universidad Internacional de Cultura, Mex., 1971, dance cert. So. Meth. U., 1968; dance cert. Northwood Inst., Cedar Hill, Tex., 1968; cert. in fashion merchandising, 1983; cert. secondary edn. U. Tex.-Arlington, 1973. On-air personality, producer Sta. KFWT-TV, Ft. Worth, 1969-71, Sta. KXTX-TV, Dallas, 1977-78; mktg. dir./asst. mgr. Red Bird Mall, Dallas, 1981-83; instr./owner Am. Pageant Acad. Fine Arts, Dallas, 1983—; owner Miss Am. Sweetheart Cosmetics, Dallas, 1983—; feature writer Tribune Newspaper Group, Dallas, 1977—; mktg. dir. Am. Pageant System, Dallas, 1975—; advisor, local sponsor Miss Tex./Miss Am. Pageant, Ft. Worth, 1978—; part-time lectr. Northwood Inst., 1982—; mktg. cons. Northtown Mall, Dallas, 1983—, Forum 303, Arlington, Tex., 1983—; mktg. dir. Elvis Presley Mus., Honolulu, Orlando, Memphis, 1981—; producer/dir. The Sensational 60's, 1983, Miss American Sweetheart, 1976—, State Fair Tex., 1972. Author: Miss American Sweetheart, 1983. Spl. program dir. USO, Dallas, 1967-75, ARC, Dallas, 1967-75; spl. hostess for Gov. as Yellow Rose of Tex., 1973, for Mayor and City of Dallas, 1974-75. Recipient award Internat. Newspaper and Advt. Mktg. Execs., 1982. Mem. Women in Communications, Duncanville C. of C., Oak Cliff C. of C., Internat. Council Shopping Ctrs., Nat. Assn. Female Execs., Phi Beta Kappa, Alpha Chi, Sigma Delta Pi. Republican. Methodist. Home: 2734 Brandon St Dallas TX 75211 Office: Am Pageant System Inc 2742 Brandon St Dallas TX 75211

DUNHAM, FRANCES STEVENSON, federal mediator; b. N.Y.C., Aug. 20, 1937; d. Roosevelt K. and Georgette (Murphy) Stevenson; div.; 1 child, Darrell Miliane. B.A., CCNY, 1955; student U. Md., 1973. Organizer Am. Fedn. State, County & Mcpl. Workers, AFL-CIO, N.Y.C., 1960-65, internat. rep., Trenton, N.J., 1965-71, exec. dir., N.J., 1971-77; Fed. mediator Fed. Mediation and Conciliation Service, East Orange, N.J., 1977—. Trustee, ch. clk. Spiritual Ch., Hackensack, N.J., 1978—, editor jour., 1985—. Recipient Superior Performance award Fed. Mediation and Conciliation Service, 1984, Sustained Performance award, 1985; Tng. cert. Office Personnel Mgmt., Ocean City, Md., 1982. Democrat. Club: Universal Hagar's (pres. 1978-81) (Hackensack, N.J.). Avocations: plants, swimming, horseback riding. Home: 54 Morgan Pl East Brunswick NJ 08816 Office: Fed Mediation and Conciliation Service 20 Evergreen Pl East Orange NJ 07018

DUNHAM, PATRICIA ANN, educator; b. Jersey City, May 13, 1948; d. Joseph John and Edith Mae (Dayton) Garvey; m. David Willard Dunham Jr., July 21, 1973; children—Devon Joseph, Dorie Anne. Student, Notre Dame Coll., 1966-67; B.A., Jersey City State Coll., 1971; postgrad., 1973-75. Clk., typist Nat. Employment Exchange Inc., N.Y.C., 1967-71; tchr. Jersey City Bd. Edn., 1971—. Active in Com. Pub. Edn., Jersey City, 1983-84; treas. Parents Council Jersey City, 1983-85; sec., v.p. Parents Council Pub. Sch. 30, Jersey City, 1983-85, pres., 1985—; adv. com. Confraternity of Christian Doctrine, Our Lady Mercy Ch., Jersey City, 1983—. Mem. Nat. Edn. Assn., N.J. Edn. Assn., Jersey City Edn. Assn. (sch. dir., violence and vandalism com. 1980-81), Kappa Delta Pi. Democrat. Roman Catholic. Avocations: reading; needlecraft; ceramics; drawing; design; sewing. Home: 30 Linden Ave Jersey City NJ 07305

DUNHAM, SARA LYNNE, dental hygienist; b. Milw., June 4, 1948; d. Roy Henry and Helen Marie (Wagner) Dunham. Student E. Tenn. State U., 1967, U. Tenn.-Memphis, 1970; cert. in dental hygiene U. Tenn., 1970. Lic. dental hygienist, Ga., N.C. Pvt. practice dental hygiene, Atlanta, 1970-83; pres. Am. Dental Hygienists Assn. Found., Chgo., 1983-84, chmn. bd., 1984-85. Contbr. articles to profl. jours. Mem. Atlanta High Mus. Art, Atlanta Children's Guild. Named Outstanding Young Women of Am., 1982. Mem. Ga. Dental Hygienists Assn. (pres. 1973-74), Atlanta Dental Hygienists Assn. (pres. 1972-74), Am. Dental Hygienists Assn. (trustee 1977-80, 2d v.p. 1980-81, 1st v.p. 1981-82, pres.-elect 1982-83, pres. 1983-84, vice chmn. polit. action com. 1979-80), Nat. Assn. Female Execs., Sigma Phi Alpha. Republican. Methodist Office: Am Dental Hygienists Assn 444 N Michigan Ave Suite 3400 Chicago IL 60611

DUNIHUE, ANNE WUNDUKE, city official, steel company executive; b. Slovan, Pa., Sept. 22, 1924; d. George and Katherine (Yanchiak) Wunduke; Asso. Sci., Chaffey Coll., 1978; B.S., U. Redlands, 1979; m. George Van Sotraidis, Oct. 9, 1942; children—George Thomas, Steven Barry; m. 2d, Donald Wallace Dunihue, Nov. 5, 1952; 1 child, David Brian. With Kaiser Steel Corp., Fontana, Calif., 1951—, acctg. clk., 1968—; cons., lectr. C.S.W. Assocs. city councilwoman Fontana, 1976-80, mayor pro-tem, 1977-79, mem. Planning Commn., 1981—; chmn. bd. dirs. Omnitrans, 1979-80; chmn. Fontana Redevel. Agy., 1979-80; bd. dirs. San Bernardino County Transp. Commn.,

1977—, East Valley Transit Service Authority, 1976—, Steelworkers Oldtimers Found., 1965—, YWCA, 1977—. United Way, 1979—, Kaiser Cares Found., 1984—, Chino Basin Municipal Water Dist., 1985—; mem. Fontana adv. council Chaffey Coll., 1979—. Mem. Calif. Elected Women's Assn. for Edn. and Research, AAUW, United Steelworkers Am., Fontana C. of C., San Bernardino Asso. Govts. (dir.), So. Calif. Assn. Govts. (energy and environment com. 1977-80). Democrat. Baptist. Clubs: Fontana Bus. and Profl. and Women's (Woman of Yr. 1965, Woman of Achievement 1978), Zonta. Home: 9395 Mango Ave Fontana CA 92335 Office: PO Box 217 Fontana CA 92335

DUNIKOSKI, SARAH BEELS, vocal music educator; b. Oil City, Pa., Dec. 11, 1947; d. Kenneth Woodrow and Kathryn Elizabeth (McClure) Beels; m. Leonard Karol Dunikoski, Jr., June 24, 1972. B.Mus., Westminster Coll., 1969; M.Ed., Pa. State U., 1970. Tchr. vocal music Butler Area Sch. Dist., Pa., 1970-72, Montgomery County Sch. Dist., Rockville, Md., 1972-73, Rumson Bd. Edn., N.J., 1974—; vol. tchr. Rumson Community Edn., 1977-84. Chmn. Greater Red Bank (N.J.) Crop Hunger Walk, 1981-82, recruitment dir., 1983—; ordained deacon Presbyterian Ch. (U.S.A.), 1983; sec. bd. deacons Shrewsbury Presbyn. Ch., N.J., 1985—; pianist Butler Community Theater, 1970. Mem. Nat. Guild Piano Tchrs., NEA, N.J. Edn. Assn., Music Educators Nat. Conf., N.J. Music Educators, Mu Phi Epsilon, Kappa Delta Pi, Delta Zeta. Republican. Presbyterian. Avocations: sailing; horseback riding; tennis; gardening. Office: Rumson Bd Edn Forrest Ave Rumson NJ 07760

DUNKER, LAVONNE BERNIECE, technician nurse; b. Albert Lea, Minn., Apr. 16, 1931; d. Herman Albert and Stella Elizabeth (Larson) Luthe; m. Lowell Herman Dunker, June 21, 1949 (div. 1975); children—Katherine Boylan, Krystal Frink Steven, Julie Wilson. B.S. in Community Service, Bemidji State U., 1975. Program clk. ASCS, Wadena, Minn., 1965-67; bookkeeper Verndale Bank (Minn.), 1966-69; sch. health technician Wadena Pub. Schs., 1970-78; house dir. Kappa Kappa Gamma, U. Minn., Mpls., 1978—; technician Phys. Measurements, Inc., Mpls., 1983—; camp nurse Herzl Camp, Webster, Wis., Summers 1984, 85. Mem. Human Services Task Force, Mpls., 1980-81; govt. agy. monitor United Way Mpls., 1979-81; organizer, project leader 4-H, Wadena, 1960-76; sponsor, chaperone Alateen Teen Ctr., 1970-75. Lutheran. Republican. Home: 329 10th Ave SE Minneapolis MN 55414 Office: Kappa Kappa Gamma 329 10th Ave SE Minneapolis MN 55414

DUNLAP, EMILY TROYER, nurse; b. Tampa, Fla., Dec. 22, 1952; d. Carl Wayne and Gertrude Ardath (Futch) Troyer; m. Gary Cole Dunlap, July 30, 1977 (div. July 1980); m. 2d Gary Cole Dunlap, July 30, 1982. B.S. in Nursing with honors, U. Tex., 1975. R.N., Tex. Staff nurse St. Paul Hosp., Dallas, 1976-80; office nurse Dr. Robert Franklin, Obstetrics-Gynecology Assocs., Houston, 1980-82. Bd. dirs. Tex. Exes.; vol. various charities. Mem. U. Tex. Ex-Students Assn. (dir. Dallas 1983). Republican. Methodist. Home: 17126 Club Hill Dr Dallas TX 75248

DUNLAP, MARGIE CARROLL, retired auto dealer; b. Stokes County, N.C., Nov. 10, 1924; d. Abram Monroe and Betty Jane (Holland) Carroll; m. Wesley Taylor Dunlap, Jan. 25, 1944 (dec. 1970); children—Wesley Carroll, William Durwood. Cert. Draughns Bus. Coll., 1959. Asst. mgr. Western Auto Store, Walnut Cove, N.C., 1946-72, owner, mgr., 1972-83, ret., 1983. Commr. County of Stokes, Danbury, N.C., 1978-82; vice chmn. Bd. Commrs., Danbury, 1980-82; vice chmn. Stokes County Republican Com., 1972-76; registration commr. Stokes County Bd. Elections, 1983—; treas. Stokes County Mental Health Assn., 1984—. Baptist. Club: Hemlock Golf Assn. (treas.). Avocations: Golf; potter; gardening; sewing. Home: PO Box 222 Walnut Cove NC 27052

DUNLAVEY, MARY ANN, police captain; b. Keokuk, Iowa, Mar. 14, 1929; d. Ralph Anthony and Ruth Irene (Cramer) Wilkens; m. Richard Emile Dunlavey, Aug. 12, 1948; children—Michael R., Mark A., Cheryl A., James P. A.A. in Adminstrn. Criminal Justice, Ill. Central Coll., 1971; B.S. in Adminstrn. of Criminal Justice, Bradley U., 1973, M.A. in Counseling, 1975; M.A. in Adminstrn. of Criminal Justice, Sangamon State U., 1978; Cert., Delinquency Control Inst. U. So. Calif., 1980; Cert. Bus. Mgmt., Bradley U., 1979. Police officer Peoria Police Dept., Ill., 1964-69, police sgt., 1969-77, police lt., 1977-82, police capt., 1982—. Contbr. articles to profl. jours. Mem. Internat. Police Mgmt. Assn. (bd. dirs., founding mem.), Peoria Police Benevolent and Protective Assn. (local and state). Avocations: aerobics, gardening, crafts, biking, fishing. Home: 4904 Lionel Ct Mapleton IL 61547 Office: Peoria Police Dept 542 S W Adams St Peoria IL 61602

DUNN, BETTY, realtor; b. Montpelier, Idaho, Feb. 16, 1931; d. Mark Alvin and Lucille (Grunig) Dunn. B.S., Weber State Coll., Ogden, Utah, 1961; grad. in comml. sci., Steven Henegar Sch., Ogden, 1978. Cert. realtor, residential specialist. Mgr. dry goods F.W. Woolworth Corp., Ogden, 1949-54; prodn. mgt. specialist, supr. USAF, Hill AFB, Utah, 1957-80; realtor Wardley Corp. BH &G, Ogden, 1979—. Contbr. articles, poem to publs. Chmn. Tri-County Planning Bd., Weber County, 1981; chmn. Women's Council Realtors-Utah Realtors Polit. Action Com., Ogden, 1983; chmn. Polit. Action Com., Ogden, 1983-84, pub. relations com. chmn., 1982-83; leader Troubled Teenagers, Sunset, Utah, 1974-76; Cub Scout Leader, Den 2 Pack 239, Lake Bonneville, Ogden, 1981-83. Served to sgt. USAF, 1954-57. Recipient Value Engring. Award, U.S. Air Force dept. defense, Hill Air Force Base, 1979. Mem. Nat. Assn. Realtor (Nat. Pvt. Property award 1983), Women's Council Realtors, Grad. Real Estate Inst., Nat. Real Estate Marketing Inst., Ogden C. of C., Democrat. Mormon. Club: Internat. Toastmistress (1960-70) Home: 2906 W 2900 S Ogden UT 84401

DUNN, CHARLOTTE MCCRARY, clinic administrator; b. Hattiesburg, Miss., June 24, 1953; d. William M. and Myrtis Rae (Malone) McCrary; m. Thomas Michael Dunn, June 5, 1971 (div. 1985). Student U. So. Miss. Sch. of Profl. Acctg., 1986—. Computer operator Ross-King-Walker, Hattiesburg, 1971-74; acct. Red & White Supermarkets, Hattiesburg, 1974-77; bookkeeper Larry H. Day, M.D., Hattiesburg, 1977-80; clinic adminstr. The Orthopedic Clinic, Hattiesburg, 1980—; mem. adv. com. bus. dept. Pub. Schs. System, Hattiesburg, 1985—. Vol. Am. Cancer Soc., Heart Fund, March of Dimes. Mem. Am. Mgmt. Assn., Med. Group Mgmt. Assn., Hattiesburg Med. Mgmt. Group, So. Ctr. for Research and Devel., Hattiesburg Area C. of C. Republican. Baptist. Home: 2300 Lincoln Rd Apt 1 Hattiesburg MS 39401 Office: The Orthopedic Clinic PA 7 Medical Blvd Hattiesburg MS 39401

DUNN, DEBRA MICHELLE, marketing specialist; b. Rantoul, Ill., May 24, 1956; d. James Madison and Marilyn Louise (Miller) D. B.A., George Mason U., 1978; student Am. Coll. Paris, 1974-75. Staff aide Congressman W.H. Natcher, Washington, 1979; internat. travel specialist Carlson Mktg. Co., Dayton, Ohio, 1980-81; sales promotion supr. Stauffer Chem. Co., Westport, Conn., 1981-83; ops. mgr. Royal Am., Newton Centre, Mass., 1983; sales promotion mgr. Princess House/Colgate Palmolive, North Dighton, Mass., 1983—. Mem. Soc. Incentive Travel Execs., Meeting Planners Internat. Republican. Home: 3-5 Christopher Dr South Easton MA 02375 Office: Princess House Inc/Colgate Palmolive 455 Somerset St North Dighton MA 02764

DUNN, ERAINA BURKE, school district coordinator; b. Chgo., Oct. 4, 1945; d. Marion H. and Lolita D. (Ward) Burke; B.A., Wilberforce U., 1968; m. James Dunn, July 23, 1981; children—Kyle T., Jamison L. Programmer, analyst Blue Cross/Blue Shield, Chgo., 1968-74, membership cons. Blue Cross Assn., 1975; personnel, benefits specialist Kimberly-Clark Corp., Atlanta, 1976-78; community coordinator Sch. Dist. 147, Harvey, Ill., 1980—. Active community-based edn., tng. workshops, voter registration, mgmt. tng., crime prevention, adult literacy, effective parenting, 1971-84; coordinator Tchr. Corps. Project, Community Council, 1980—; vol. After sch. Tutorial Program, 1981—, United Family Found., 1981—, South Area Literacy Council, South Suburban Act-So, West Harvey Block Captains, PAC, Community Leaders Program, 1982-86, Minority Women's Devel. Project, Human Action Community Orgn., 1985-86. Recipient Outstanding Vol. Service award B.U.I.L.D., 1971, Outstanding Community Service award Dist. 147, 1981, Vol. After sch. Tutorial Program award, 1981, Bus. and Profl. Women's Seminar, 1985. Mem. Ill. Community Edn. Assn., Delta Sigma Theta. United Methodist. Home: 15221 Lincoln St Harvey IL 60426 Office: Sch Dist 147 Washington Sch 153d St and Lincoln Ave Harvey IL 60426

DUNN, JOHANNA ALEXANDRA READ, financial executive; b. N.Y.C., Mar. 7, 1946. B.A. summa cum laude, Barnard Coll., 1965; M.A. summa cum laude, Columbia U., 1967, Ph.D. magna cum laude, 1970; postgrad. The Sorbonne, U. Paris, 1969-70. With McKinsey & Co., Inc., N.Y.C., 1967; mng. editor European Bus., Paris, 1969-70; co-founder, chief bus. editor Tempo Economico, Lisbon, Portugal, 1970-74; chief fin. writer for Expresso Lisbon, 1970-74; fgn. correspondent Manchester Guardian, Portugal, 1973-74; communications cons. Citicorp, 1975-76, Norton Simon Inc., 1975-76, Council of Americas, 1975-76; communications specialist N.Y. Stock Exchange, Inc., 1976-78; exec. asst. to office of chmn. N.Y. Stock Exchange, 1978-79, asst. v.p. corp. planning, 1979-80; v.p. mktg. planning and support N.Y. Futures Exchange, 1980-81; asst. v.p. market ops. N.Y. Stock Exchange, 1981-83, asst. v.p. mktg. group, 1984—; cons. State Edn. Dept., State U. N.Y., 1975-81. Mem. Pres.'s Council Marymount Manhattan Coll., 1981—; mem. Cardinal's Com. of Laity for the 1980's, Archdiocese of N.Y. Woodrow Wilson vis. fellow, 1979-81. Mem. Fin. Women's Assn., Investment Assn. N.Y., Bond Club, Wall St. Planning Group (v.p.), Phi Beta Kappa. Democrat. Presbyterian. Author: Counterpoint: A Book of Poetry, 1966; contbg. author Business: Its Nature and Environment; contbr. numerous poems to lit. publs. Home: 785 Park Ave New York NY 10021 Office: NY Stock Exchange Inc 11 Wall St New York NY 10005

DUNN, LINDA SMITH, college administrator; b. Winchester, Va., Oct. 30, 1947; d. Roy Herbert and Lee Mae (Heishman) Smith; m. Keenan Ray Dunn, July 3, 1976. B.A. in Math. Edn., Shepherd Coll., 1968; M.S. in Math., W.Va. U., 1971, postgrad., 1974-80. Dir. spl. project W.Va. No. Coll., Wheeling, 1972-73, asst. to pres., 1973-76; dir. Title I, Shepherd Coll., Shepherdstown, W.Va., 1976-78, dir. continuing edn., 1978-82, asst. acad. dean, 1982-83, acting acad. dean, 1983-84, asst. to pres., 1984—; mem. Jefferson County Ednl. Council, Charles Town, W.Va., 1981-83. Mem. AAUW (corr. sec. 1979-81), W.Va. Continuing Edn. Assn. (sec. 1980), Delta Kappa Gamma. Democrat. Baptist.

DUNN, LORETTA LYNN, lawyer; b. Owensboro, Ky., Dec. 3, 1955; d. John Edwin and Arnetta Mae (Trunnell) D.; m. Herbert S. Lunenfeld, Oct. 18, 1985. B.A., U. Ky., 1976, J.D., 1979; LL.M., Georgetown U., 1983. Bar: Ky. 1979, D.C. 1984. Staff atty. U.S. Senate, Com. Commerce, Sci. and Transp., Washington, 1979—. Mem. D.C. Ky. Bar Assn., Phi Beta Kappa, Order of Coif.

DUNN, MARGARET MARY COYNE, journalist; b. Pittsfield, Mass., Sept. 9, 1909; d. Robert Joseph and Margaret Jane (O'Neill) Coyne; student Berkshire Bus. Coll., Pittsfield, Mass., 1928-29; m. John Raymond Dunn, May 29, 1933 (dec.); children—Joyce Dunn Higgins, John Raymond, Joel. Freelance contbr. articles to numerous newspapers, including Boston Post, Boston Globe, The Pilot, Beverly Times, Providence Jour., The Tablet, Montreal Herald and Weekly Star, 1937—, to mags. including Better Homes and Garden, Yankee, Conn. Circle, Modern Baby, Family Digest, others; lectr. in field. Mem. Nat. League Am. Pen Women (pres. Boston br. 1968-70, 74-76, rec. sec. 1970-72, membership chmn. 1972-74, nat. charter chmn. 1974-76, mature women's scholarship com. 1978—, Mass. State pres. 1978-80, nat. auditor 1978-80, nat. roster chmn. 1978-80, nat. orgn. and bylaws chmn. 1982-84 co-editor Fifty Year history Boston br., contbg. editor Pen Woman mag., asso. editor 1980—), Boston Authors Club (rec. sec. 1973, 1st v.p. 1980-82, pres. 1982—), Dickens Fellowship (council mem. 1972—), treas. 1977—), Boston Browning Soc. Club: Women's City (heritage com.). Author: (with Barbara B. Reese) Capture of the Johnson Family (hist. pageant for Charlestown, N.H.), 1954; editor Between Branches, 1974-80. Home: 19 Pilgrim Rd Wellesley MA 02181

DUNN, MARILYN CLAIRE, toy company executive; b. Teaneck, N.J., May 9, 1953; d. Bernard Joseph and Claire Margaret (Langenstein) Dunn. A. in Applied Sci., Bergen Community Coll., 1972. Exec. sec. Fer. Schmetz Needle Corp., Leonia, N.J., 1972-75, Walter Dental Supply, South Hackensack, N.J., 1975-78, Heyward-Robinson Co., N.Y.C., 1978-79, Jones Lang Wootton, N.Y.C., 1979-81; personnel adminstr. Gen. Mills Toy Group, N.Y.C., 1981—. Mem. parish council St. John's Roman Catholic Ch., Leonia, 1973. Mem. Nat. Assn. for Female Execs. Leonia Bowling League (sec. 1978). Home: 266 Broad Ave Apt E 1 Leonia NJ 07605 Office: General Mills Toy Group 41 Madison Ave New York NY 10010

DUNN, MARY FRANCENE, employment company supervisor; b. Texarkana, Ark., Oct. 20, 1944; d. Vincent John and Lois Elizabeth (Cigainero) Glorioso; m. Winford L. Dunn Jr., Mar. 30, 1963 (div. Feb. 1980); 1 child, Ina Margaret. A.S. in Bus., Texarkana Community Coll., 1969; B.B.A., East Tex. State U., 1974, M.B.A., 1977. Sr. sec. U. Tex.-Austin, 1963-65; job placement supr. Tex. Employment Commn., Texarkana, 1971—; alumni career counselor East Tex. State U., Texarkana, 1984—; owner, author Heart Hugs Greeting Card Co., Texarkana, 1984—. Author: Keep Texarkana Working, 1980; Keep the Valley Working, 1985. Editor: Borderline, 1985. Poll worker Democratic Party, 1979. Recipient Outstanding Service and Assistance award Am. Legion, 1984. Alumni Achievement award East Tex. State U., 1984-85. Mem. Tex. Alumni Assn., Texarkana C. of C., Four States Personnel Assn., Internat. Assn. Personnel in Employment Security, Hildago County Personnel Assn., Texarkana Jr. League. Roman Catholic. Avocations: writing; water sports; travel; golf; dancing. Home: PO Box 735 Texarkana TX 77504 Office: Texarkana State Employment Office PO Box 241 Texarkana TX 75501

DUNN, NANCY GAIL, public relations specialist; b. Boston, Apr. 20, 1954; d. Albert Howard and Jean (Shimp) D. Student Wesley Coll., 1972-73; B.A., U. Del., 1976. Dir. customer service N.M.I. Del. Dry Goods, Inc., New Castle, 1977-78, regional sales rep., Del., Pa., Va., Md., 1978-79; industry cons., Newark, Del., 1979-80; free-lance writer Wilmington News Jour., Newsday, L.I. Newspaper, 1975—; dir. pub. info. ARC, Patchogue, N.Y., 1980-82; adminstr. mktg. services NEC Telephones, Inc., Melville, N.Y., 1982-84; publs. mgr. Ricoh Corp., West Caldwell, N.J., 1984—. NEH grantee, 1976. Contbr. articles to profl. jours. Office: 5 Dedrick Pl West Caldwell NJ

DUNN, PAULINE GIBSON, retired music educator, minister of music; b. Miami, Fla., Aug. 1, 1916; d. Richard Alfred and Maggie (Grant) Gibson; m. Jarius Wilson Dunn, 1 child, Richard Paul. B.A. in Edn., Ala. State U., 1939; B.A. in Music, Fla. A&M U., 1944; M.A. in Music Edn., Columbia U., 1953; postgrad. Union Theol. Sem., 1959-60, U. Miami, 1968-69. Music tchr. Dunbar Elem. Sch., Frank C. Martin Elem. Sch. and J.R.E. Lee Elem. Sch., 1937-42, Holmes Elementary Sch., Orchard Villa Elem. Sch., Coconut Grove Elem. Sch., J.S. Johnson Elem. Sch., Edition Park Elem. Sch., 1942-54, Lake Stevens Elem. Sch., Rainbow Park Elem. Sch., Skyway Elem. Sch., Twin Lakes Elem. Sch., Amelia Earhart Elem. Sch., 1954-69, Bunche Park Elementary Sch., Miami, Fla., 1969-81; minister of music St. John Baptist Ch., Miami, 1931-66, Drake Meml. Bapt. Ch., Miami, 1966—. Mem. Ch. Women United, Urban League, Miami, 1985. Recipient Service award St. John Instnl. Bapt. Ch., 1950, 81, So. Singers, 1976, Metro-Dade County Model City Gov. Bd., 1976, Blanche Park Elementary Sch. PTA, 1980, 81, Drake Meml. Bapt. Ch., 1982, 84, 85, Drake Meml. Daycare Ctr., 1984, award Frank Crawford Martin Elem. Sch., 1970, Nat. Council Negro Women, Inc., 1980, 81, Nat. Assn. Negro Bus. and Profl. Women's Club, Inc., 1981, Tchr. of Yr. award Dade County Pub. Schs., 1981, Proclamation award City of Miami, 1981, Met. Dade County, 1981, Felix McCool Aremicanism award VFW, 1977. Mem. AAUW (chaplain), Music Educator's Nat. Assn., Fla. Elem. Music Educator's Assn., Dade County Music Educator's Assn., Phi Delta Kappa, Delta Sigma Theta (service award 1975, 79). Avocations: reading; travel; decorating; listening to music. Home: 1895 NW 57 Miami FL 33142 Office: Drake Meml Bapt Ch 5800 NW 2d Ave Miami FL 33127

DUNN, SISTER CATHERINE, college president. Pres. Clarke Coll., Dubuque. Office: Clarke Coll Office of Pres Dubuque IA 52001*

DUNN, THERESA MARIE, airlines executive; b. Balt., Sept. 4, 1956; d. Jonah Marshall and Elizabeth Theresa (Rice) D. B.S. magna cum laude, Mt. St. Mary's Coll., Emmitsburg, Md., 1978; M.B.A., Loyola Coll., Balt., 1982. Staff acct. Price Waterhouse, Balt., 1978-80; internal auditor Black & Decker, Towson, Md., 1980-81; customer service mgr. People Express Airlines, Newark, 1984—, inflight mgr., 1984-85, acctg. and mktg. cons., mem. task force to open new operational bases, 1985. Mem. Citizens for Washington Hill, Inc., Balt., 1983—. Mem. Am. Mktg. Assn., Southwest Travel Industry Assn., Fort Myers C. of C., Delta Mu Delta. Democrat. Roman Catholic. Avocations: travel; fine dining; theatre; physical fitness; reading. Home: 2224 Tyrone Rd Westminster MD 21157 Office: People Express Airlines Newark Internat Airport Newark NJ 07114

DUNNAVAN, CAROL CHAMBLIN, educator; b. Maysville, Ky, Feb. 5, 1954; d. Kenneth Harold and Anna Elizabeth (King) Chamblin; m. Jay Calvin Dunnavan, July 7, 1979. Student Cin. Bible Coll., 1972-74; B.A., Morehead State U., 1976, M.A., 1980, Rank I in Edn., 1985. Cert. elem. tchr., Ky. Tour guide Washington Hist. Soc., Ky., 1972-75; tchr. Washington Elem. Sch., Maysville, 1976-78, Mason County Elem. Sch., Maysville, 1978-80; tchr. Straub Elem. Sch., Maysville, 1980—; supervising tchr. for student tchr. tng. Morehead State U., 1980, 83-84; tchr. in film Emergency Preparedness, Ky. Dept. Edn., 1983; activities demonstrator on Edn. Notebook, TV Program, 1985. Active Germantown Christian Ch., Ky., 1975—, Maysville-Mason County PTA., 1976—; camp counselor Northward Christian Assembly, Falmouth, Ky., 1973. Named Outstanding Elem. Tchr. at Morehead State U. Sci. Fair, 1981, 84. Mem. NEA, Eastern Ky. Edn. Assn., Mason County Edn. Assn., AAUW, Kappa Delta Pi. Democrat. Club: Mason County Homemakers. Avocations: Interior decorating; floral arranging; needlework; reading. Home: Route 3 Box 610-A Maysville KY 41056 Office: Straub Elem Sch 387 Chenault Dr Maysville KY 41056

DUNNE, CINDY LOU, television producer; b. Sacramento, July 26, 1947; d. Elton H. and Betty L. (Bender) Rule; m. Peter A. Dunne (div. July 1975); 1 child, Patrick Elton. Student Los Angeles Valley Coll., 1965-67, U. Oreg., 1967-68. Prodn. asst. Laroche, McCaffrey, McCall Advt., N.Y.C., 1968-69, Sta. KRON-TV, San Francisco, 1969-70, Needham, Harper & Steers, Los Angeles, 1970-71; dir. program devel. Spelling/Goldberg Prodns., Los Angeles, 1974-77; v.p. program devel. Aaron Spelling Prodns., Los Angeles, 1977-81, Lorimar Prodns., Los Angeles, 1981-82, Warner Bros. TV, Burbank, Calif., 1982-85; ind. producer Warner Bros. TV, 1985—. Producer: Boy in the Plastic Bubble, 1976; Friends series, 1979. Recipient Excellence award Film Adv. Bd., 1979. Mem. Women in Film (dir. 1982-84), Acad. TV Arts and Scis., Writers Guild Am. W. Democrat. Episcopalian. Avocations: painting; sailing; scuba diving. Office: Warner Bros TV 4000 Warner Blvd Burbank CA 91522

DUNNING, DARLENE CHERYL, private investigator, consultant; b. Jersey City, June 8, 1947; d. Gilbert Franklin and Mildred Anna (D'Oddo) D.; children—James, Jason, Christian, Timothy. Cert. in self def., small arms and security Cobary Tng. Ctr. and Sionics, Powder Springs, Ga., 1981. Adminstr., Sionics, Inc., Powder Springs, 1979-82; owner, dir. Clemons & Dunning, N.Y.C., 1982—; cons. security. Named Countess, His Majesty King Hassan, King in exile Afghanistan, 1981, named maj. Royal Free Afghan Army, His Majesty King Hassan, 1981. Republican. Office: Clemons & Dunning 212 E 47th St 10th Floor New York NY 10017

DUNNING, ETTA MARIE EATMAN, lawyer; b. Birmingham, Ala., Jan. 15, 1949; d. Matthew Eatman and Roberta (Smith) Hampton; m. Jessie James Dunning, Mar. 15, 1975; children—Jessie James and Jason Jarrod (twins). B.A., Ala. A&M U., 1970; J.D. cum laude, Miles Coll., 1977. Bar: Ala. 1981. Dir. Alcoholism Ctr., Jefferson County Com. for Econ. Opportunity, Birmingham, 1970-72; probation officer Jefferson County, Birmingham, 1972-81; equal opportunity specialist EEOC, Birmingham, 1981—; sole practice law, Birmingham, 1981-84, ptnr. firm Barnes, Dunning, May and Miller, Birmingham, 1984—. Pres. Forestdale Community Devel. Assn., Birmingham, 1978-82; v.p. Coalition of 100 Black Women, Birmingham, 1984-85; adviser, asst. A.H. Parker High Sch. Band, 1978-82; mem. task force Mayor's Commn. on Status of Women, Birmingham, 1984—. Recipient Community Service award Forestdale Community Devel. Assn., 1982. Mem. ABA, Ala. Bar Assn., Nat. Bar Assn., Ala. Lawyers Assn. (v.p. 1983—), Delta Theta Phi, Delta Sigma Theta (exec. bd. 1983—, Acad. Achievement award Birmingham Alumnae Chpt. 1982). Baptist. Clubs: Ben Marcata, Order Eastern Star. Home: 1320 Echols Dr Birmingham AL 35214

DUNNING, KAREN ELLEN, electronics manufacturing company executive; b. Danville, Ill., Mar. 16, 1956; d. Thomas Wesley and Sarah Anne (Lewis) D. B.B.A. in Fin., Fla. Atlantic U., 1979, M.B.A., 1981. Researcher, Fla. Atlantic U., Boca Raton, Fla., 1979-81, cons., research assoc., 1981-85; research analyst asst. IBM, Boca Raton, 1985-86, Motorola, Inc., 1986—; freelance computer programmer and cons., Boca Raton, Fla., 1983—. Mem. Beta Gamma Sigma, Phi Kappa Phi. Republican. Avocations: golf; tennis; woodworking; mechanic; running. Home: 8176 A Thames Blvd Boca Raton FL 33433 Office: 8000 W Sunrise Blvd Fort Lauderdale FL 33322

DUNNING, LINDA SCHMIDT, medical education administrator, nurse; b. Farmville, Va., Jan. 29, 1952; d. Leroy Wheeler and Edith Elizabeth (Elliott) Schmidt; m. Frederick Graydon Dunning, Nov. 24, 1979; children—Meredith Lin, Allison Gray. Diploma with honors, Richmond Meml. Hosp. Sch. Nursing, 1973; postgrad. St. Joseph's Coll., North Wyndam, Maine, 1982-86. Cert. occupational health nurse, Conn. Nursing asst. Richmond Meml. Hosp., Va., 1971-73; staff nurse Philip Morris, U.S.A., Richmond, 1973-79, coordinator med. edn. programs, 1979-84, supr. med. edn. and supply, 1984—, chairperson developed health awareness and phys. fitness program, 1985. Recipient Service medal award ARC, 1985. Mem. Capital Area Assn. Occupational Health Nurses (pres. 1979-81), Va. Assn. Occupational Health Nurses. Republican. Baptist. Avocations: volleyball; biking; traveling; dancing. Home: 1219 Kingscross Rd Midlothian VA 23113 Office: Philip Morris USA 1600 Jefferson Davis Hwy PO Box 26603 Richmond VA 23261

DUNNING, TESSA FRANCES ELEANOR, real estate broker; b. Whitchurch, Shropshire, Eng., Jan. 11, 1943; came to U.S., 1967; d. Gerald Clough and Muriel Ellen (Higham) D. B.S. in Occupational Therapy, St. Andrews, Northampton, Eng., 1964; M.S. in Mgmt., MIT, 1977. Lic. real estate broker. Dir. occupational therapy Lindemann Mental Health Ctr., Boston, 1972-76; cons. Medicus Systems Corp., Bethesda, Md., 1977-80, Libra Tech., Rockville, Md., 1980-82; assoc. Joseph & Cohen, Washington, 1982-85; dir. leasing James Andrew, Badger Ltd., Washington, 1985—; dir. MIT Enterprise Forum, Washington, 1982-84. Dir. theatrical prodn. Pygmalion (G.B. Shaw), 1985. Trustee Brit. Embassy Players, Washington, 1985. Sloan fellow MIT, 1976-77. Fellow Roster of Sloan Fellows; mem. Comml. Real Estate Women, Mediaeval Pottery Research Group (hon.), Brit. Embassy Players. Democrat. Clubs: Capitol Toastmasters, MIT (Washington) (bd. dirs. 1982—). Office: James Andrew Badger Ltd 1625 K St NW Washington DC 20006

DUNPHY, PATRICIA M., lawyer; b. Ft. Benning, Ga., Oct. 11, 1949; d. John T. and Mary (Young) D. B.A., Douglass Coll., Rutgers U., 1971; J.D., N.Y. Law Sch., 1977. Bar: N.Y. 1978, N.J. 1978, U.S. Dist. Ct. (so. dist.) N.Y. 1978, U.S. Dist. Ct. (ea. dist.) N.Y. 1983. Atty., CBS Inc., N.Y.C., 1978-80, asst. gen. atty., 1980-82, litigation counsel, 1982-83, broadcast counsel, 1983—; panelist Practising Law Inst., N.Y.C., 1983. Mem. ABA (chmn. sect. patent, trademark and copyright law subcom. 1980), N.Y. Bar Assn., Copyright Soc. U.S.A., Internat. Radio and TV Soc., Nat. Acad. TV Art and Scis. Home: 527 E 72d St New York NY 10021 Office: CBS Inc 51 W 52d St New York NY 10019

DUNWIDDIE, CHARLOTTE, sculptor; b. Strasbourg, France, June 19, 1907; student Acad. Fine Arts, Berlin; pupil of Mariano Beullure, Alberto Lagos. Sculpture represented in Mus. of Brookgreen Gardens, S.C., Marine Corps Mus., Washington, Aquaduct Racetrack, N.Y.C., New Britain (Conn.) Mus. Am. Art, Madrid, Buenos Aires, Argentina, Lima, Peru, also others; also represented in pvt. collections. Recipient 15 gold medals, 30 other awards. Fellow Nat. Sculpture Soc. (pres. 1982—), Royal Soc. Arts (London); mem. NAD (academician), Allied Artists Am., Nat. Arts Club, Hudson Valley Art Assn., Pen and Brush (past pres.). Club: Cosmopolitan (N.Y.C.).

DUPEY, MICHELE MARY, advertising company executive; b. Bronx, N.Y., Feb. 26, 1953; d. William B. and Sandra Nancy (Raia) D.; m. Daniel Michael Gieser, July 14, 1980. B.A., Montclair State Coll., 1975; postgrad. NYU, 1981. Product analyst Internat. Playtex, Paramus, N.J., 1975-79; child care counsellor Bergen Residential Ctr., Rockleigh, N.J., 1979-80; asst. to editor Standard & Poor's Corp., N.Y.C., 1981-84; sec. Doyle Dane Berbach Advt. Co., N.Y.C., 1985—. Contbr. articles to profl. publs. Mem. NOW (pres. local chpt. 1982-83, 84-86, chmn. fin. com. N.J. orgn. 1984-85, chmn. fund raising com. 1984-85). Democrat. Roman Catholic. Home: 217 7th St Jersey City NJ 07302 Office: Doyle Dane Berbach Advt Co 437 Madison Ave New York NY 10022

DUPLAGA, TINA MARIE, sales representative; b. Wheeling, W.Va., June 28, 1956; d. Michael F. and Susan (Skinto) D. B.A., W.Va. U., 1978; M.B.A., U. Fla., 1983. Mgr., D & D Investments, Wheeling, 1978-79; field ops. supr. U.S. Census Bur., New Orleans, 1979-80, geog. technician supr., 1980-81; profl. sales rep., pharmacy mgmt. cons. DuPont Pharms., Wheeling, 1983—. Mem. allocations rev. panel Wheeling United Way, 1986; active Big Bros./Big Sisters, Friends of Wheeling, Oglebay Inst. Fine Arts Ctr. Mem. Profls. for Progress, Psi Chi, Mortar Bd., LWV (exec. com. 1986), Alpha Xi Delta (pres. 1975-76).

Republican. Roman Catholic. Avocations: tennis; jewelry making; golf; photography; travel. Home: 417 N 16th St Apt 12 Wheeling WV 26003 Office: DuPont Pharms BRML Laverly Mill Bldg Wilmington DE 19898

DUPLESSIS, GWENDOLYN MARIE, educator; b. New Orleans, Oct. 10, 1949; d. Charles Anthony Andrews and Joyce (Frances) Montana; m. Victor Louis Duplessis, Dec. 18, 1976; children—Duane, Candis. B.S., So. U., 1972. Phys. edn. tchr. Carver Sr. High Sch., New Orleans, 1973-74; spl edn. tchr. Lawless Sr. High Sch., New Orleans, 1976—, tennis coach, 1983—; br. mgr. Jewelry by Park Lane, Inc., 1985—. Mem. La. High Sch. Athletic Assn. Democrat. Roman Catholic. Avocations: traveling; tennis; dancing; reading; music. Home: 7601 Trapier Ave New Orleans LA 70127 Office: Lawless Sr High Sch 5300 Law St New Orleans LA 70117

DU PONT, ELISE RAVENEL WOOD, lawyer; b. N.Y.C., Dec. 27, 1935; d. Richard D. and Margaretta (Duane) Wood; B.A., Temple U., 1976; J.D., U. Pa., 1979; m. Pierre S. du Pont IV, May 4, 1957; children—Elise R., Pierre V, Benjamin, Eleuthere Irenee II. Bar: Pa. 1981. Real estate developer, Washington, 1973—; assoc. corporate law dept. Montgomery, McCracken, Walker and Rhoads, Phila., 1978-80; asst. adminstr. Bur. Pvt. Enterprise, AID, 1981-84; candidate for U.S. Ho. of Reps., 1984; leader U.S. Dept. Commerce State Trade Mission to People's Republic of China, 1980. Mem. Del. World Affairs Council, Del. Bd. Health, 1969-72; chmn. State Council on Public Health; founder, chmn. Women's Campaign Fund, Washington; bd. mgrs. Franklin Inst., Phila., 1976-81. Recipient Speiser award U. Pa. Law Sch., 1979. Republican. Home: Rockland Rd Rockland DE 19732

DUPONT, JOHANNA HARMANNA, accountant; b. Coevorden, Netherlands, May 6, 1912; came to U.S., 1956, naturalized, 1986; d. Hendrik Lucas and Margaretha (Ter Braake) van der Vecht; m. Johannes Martinus Caspers, Dec. 13, 1943 (div. Feb. 1953); 1 child, Margaretha E.H. Caspers Frank; m. Bernard J. DuPont, July 29, 1958. B.B.A., Fla. Internat. U., 1974. Bookkeeper, Rotterdam/Amsterdam Bank, 1930-34, 45-48, Dutch Heather Co., Arnhem, Netherlands, 1934-44, Keyes Co., Miami, Fla., 1957-63; gen. acct. Miller Assocs., Miami, 1963-84; pvt. practice acctg., Miami, 1984—. Republican. Presbyterian. Club: Coco Plum Woman's (chmn. lit./poetry 1985-86, treas. 1986—). Avocations: reading, walking, swimming, writing. Home: 7412 S W 105th Pl Miami FL 33173

DUPRE, CONSTANCE LOUISE, lawyer; b. N.Y.C., July 23, 1933; d. John David and Mary Edith (Pfautz) Pierson; m. Louis Dupre, Dec. 18, 1965 (div. Dec. 1974); 1 son, Christian. B.A., Dunbarton Coll., 1953; M.A., Georgetown U., 1960, J.D., 1966. Bar: D.C. 1967. Law clk. U.S. Ct. Appeals, D.C. cir., Washington, 1966-67; br. chief OEO, Washington, 1967-73; supervisory atty. EEOC, Washington, 1973-75, assoc. gen. counsel, 1975-82, legal counsel, 1982-85, program dir. region I, 1985—. Editor, Georgetown Law Jour., 1965-66. Recipient awards for superior and outstanding performance EEOC, 1976, 78, 80, 81, 82. Mem. Sr. Execs. Assn., D.C. Bar Assn., Bar Assn. D.C. Democrat. Roman Catholic. Office: Region I Programs Office Program Ops 2401 E St NW Washington DC 20507

DUPRE, JUDITH ANN NEIL, real estate agent, interior decorator; b. Houma, La., May 7, 1945; d. Herbert Joseph and Doris Mae (LeBouef) Neil; m. Michael Anthony Dupre, Jan. 7, 1962; children—Arienne Danielle, Travis Lance. B.A. in Psychology, Southeast Okla. State U., 1982. Fin. mgr. Gen. Fin., La., Colo., 1960-69; exec. sec. Progressive Bank & Trust Co., Houma, La., 1973-74; health coordinator Spring Cypress Recreation Ctr., 1974-75; actress, model David Payne Agy., Dallas, 1985—; real estate agt. J. Nordquist Realtors, Sugar Land, Tex., 1985—; mgr., buyer June Morris Boutique, Ardmore, Okla., 1978-79. Mem. Strake Jesuit-Mothers' Club, Houston, 1985-86, St. Agnes Acad. Women's Club, Houston, 1985-86, Ft. Bend Republican Women, Sugar Land, 1985-86; chmn. Texans War on Drugs, Sugar Land, 1985-86; bd. dirs. MUD (Dist. 6), Sugar Land, 1986—. Mem. Cath. Daughters of the Americas, Nat. Assn. Realtors, Tex. Assn. Realtors, Alpha Chi. Roman Catholic. Clubs: Sweetwater Ladies Golf Assn., Sweetwater Country (Sugar Land). Avocations: tennis; golf; fishing; boating; dancing. Home: 3711 Springhill Ln Sugar Land TX 77479

DUPREY, JANET MARIE, county official; b. Plattsburgh, N.Y., Nov. 27, 1945; d. Peter Joseph and Edna Mae Lacy; student Empire State Coll., 1979—; m. Elmer C. Duprey, Sept. 9, 1967; children—John, Michelle. Exec. sec. Eastman Kodak Co., Rochester, N.Y., 1965-66; legal sec. John L. Bell, Plattsburgh, 1966-68; legis. asst. to Sen. Ronald B. Stafford, Plattsburgh, 1968-70; co-owner Rustic Restaurant, Peru, 1967-85; mem. Clinton County Legislature, 1976-86, chmn., 1981-82; treas. Clinton County, 1986—; mem. Champlain Valley Physicians Hosp. Med. Ctr. Corp. Sec. bd. dirs. Apple Valley Sr. Housing Corp., Inc., 1977-83; mem. N.Y. State Dept. Social Services Statewide Adv. Council, 1979-81; Clinton County Social Services Adv. Council, 1976-86, Office Aging Adv. Council, Child Abuse Task Force. Mem. adv. bd. Clinton County Div. for Youth; bd. dirs. Hospice Care Services, Council Community Services; mem. SUNY-Plattsburgh Coll. Found. Mem. LWV, SUNY Plattsburgh Coll. Found., Clinton Community Coll. Found., N.Y. State Treas. Assn., Clinton County Hotel, Restaurant and Liquor Dealers Assn. (past pres.), Champlain Valley Bus. and Profl. Women's Club (Woman of Yr. award 1985), Delta Kappa Gamma (hon.). Republican. Roman Catholic. Club: Plattsburgh AFB Officers (hon.). Home: Telegraph St Peru NY 12972 Office: 137 Margaret St Plattsburgh NY 12901

DUPUIS, SHARON BULLOCK, lawyer; b. Lincoln, Nebr., May 3, 1944; d. Richard Brooks, and Betty June (Martin) Bullock; m. Daniel G. DuPuis. A.A., Riverside City Coll., 1968; B.S.L., Citrus Belt Law Sch., 1976, J.D., 1978. Bar: Calif. 1978, U.S. Dist. Ct. (cen. dist.) Calif. Customer service rep. Alumax, Riverside and Joliet, Ill., 1968-70; ptnr. DuPuis & DuPuis, Fontana, Calif., 1979-85; sole practice, Fontana, 1985—. Mem. Attys. for Criminal Justice Los Angeles, 1982—, Attys. for Animal Rights, Los Angeles, 1982—; mem. Democratic steering com. for Tom Bradley, San Bernardino, Calif., 1982. Mem. Inland Counties Women at Law (v.p.), Valley Trial Lawyers Assn. (pres.), ABA, Calif. State Bar, San Bernardino County Bar Assn., Trial Lawyers Am., DAR, Sigma Iota Delta. Democrat. Clubs: Fontana Bus. and Profl. Women's (Woman of Achievement 1982, v.p. 1985-86), Zonta. Office: DuPuis Law Offices 8414 Sierra Ave Fontana CA 92335

DURALL, MARTHA LOUISE, personnel executive; b. Fairmont, W. Va., Dec. 10, 1950; d. Charles Oliver and Dorothy (Morris) McIntire; m. James Raymond DuRall, Dec. 29, 1970; children—Christine Elizabeth. A.G.S., Ind. U.-Purdue U.-Indpls., 1985. Sec., Flint Osteo. Hosp., Mich., 1968-69; office mgr. pvt. physician, Mt. Morris, Mich., 1969-74; personnel sec. Westview Hosp., Indpls., 1974-76; employment coordinator Westview Hosp., Indpls., 1976-81, dir. personnel services, 1981—. Chmn. volunteer devel. com. Indpls. YWCA, 1983-84, pres. bd., 1984-85, nat. conv. del., 1985, bd. dirs., 1983-86, bd. dirs. Marion County Farm Bur. Credit Union, Indpls., 1976-78, Pvt. Industry Council, 1985-86, Pro-Health, 1985—; vice chmn. fund drive Indpls. Mus. Art, 1983. Mem. Am. Soc. Hosp. Personnel Adminstrn., Am. Soc. Personnel Adminstrn., Indpls. Soc. Hosp. Personnel Adminstrn., Ind. Soc. Personnel Adminstrs., Am. Osteo. Assn. (nat. del. aux.), Ind. Aux. Osteo. Physicians and Surgeons (state sec. 1982-83, v.p. 1983-84).

DURANT, SANDRA JACQUELINE, nurse; b. Milw., Apr. 1, 1954; d. Thomas Daryl and Edna Theresa (Balczerak) Smigelski; m. Lary Allan Durant, Aug. 6, 1977 (div. Sept. 1979); 1 child, Jocelyn Anne. Student U. Wis.-Milw., 1972-75, Tex. Christian U., 1975-77; B.S. in Nursing, Marquette U., 1981. Lic. R.N., Wis. Staff nurse St. Lukes Hosp., Milw., 1981-82, Trinity Meml. Hosp., Cudahy, Wis., 1982, Mt. Sinai Med. Ctr., Milw., 1982-85, St. Mary's Hosp., Milw., 1985—. Mem., past regional dir. Presdl. Classroom for Young Ams., Washington, 1972—; mem. 4th of July Commn., Milw., 1972—. Mem. Assn. Critical Care Nurses, Am. Nurses Assn., U.S. Homeopathic Assn., Marquette U. Women. Democrat. Roman Catholic. Club: Kappa Delta (Colo.). Home: 2415 S 10th St Milwaukee WI 52315

DURANTE, ANGELA, university official, writer-editor; b. Hackensack, N.J., Nov. 20, 1949; d. Louis Anthony and Adeline (Puntolillo) Durante. B.A. in Comml. Art, Jersey City State Coll., 1972; M.A. Communications, Fordham U., 1979. Cert. art tchr kindergarten-12, N.J. Tchr. scholastic journalism, art dir. student publs. Pope Piux XII High Sch., Passic, N.J., 1972-74, 78-79, St. Francis Xavier Sch., Kansas City, Mo., 1974-75 Neumann Prep. Sch., Wayne, N.J., 1975-78; reporter, editor, designer Key to the News, paper, Kansas City, 1974-75; dir. adult edn. Lyndhurst (N.J.) Pub. Schs., 1975-78; intern, researcher Sta. WCBS-TV, N.Y.C., 1978; corr. The Record, Hackensack, 1978-79; mgr. univ. relations Fairleigh Dickinson U., Rutherford, N.J., 1979-82; dir. news services U. Mo.-Columbia 1982-85; dir. pub. relations Fordham U., N.Y.C., 1985—; bd. judges Quill and Scroll Soc., U. Iowa, Iowa City; bd. advisors Sta. KBIA-FM, Columbia, 1983-85; pub. relations cons. RENEW program Roman Catholic Archdiocese. Newark, 1979-80, editor Renew program handbook, 1979; designer religious art Sacred Heart Ch., Lyndhurst, N.J., 1973-78, 79. Fellow Dow Jones Newspaper Fund, Mem. Soc. Profl. Journalists (v.p. mid-Mo. chpt. 1977-78), Council for Advancement and Support. Edn. (scholar 1982, exceptional achievement in editorial content award dist. VI 1983, Nat. Silver medal 1985), Women in Communications. Democrat.

DURBAHN, JANET SUE, newspaper editor; b. Anoka, Minn., Mar. 23, 1935; d. Cortes Frederick and Erma Rae (Jenks) Reed; m. Paul A. Durbahn, Aug. 21, 1954; children—Paula, William, Karen, Mark Student Stephens Coll., 1955. Reporter, Anoka Herald, 1961-64, Edina (Minn.) Courier, 1962-66; editor Stewartville (Minn.) Star, 1970—. Vice chmn. Stewartville Spl. Events Commn., 1976—; Mem. Olmsted County Democratic-Farmer-Labor Central Com., 1984—. Mem. Minn. Newspaper Assn. (1st place winner 1984), Press Women of Minn. (edn. dir.). Methodist. Club: Home Econs. Home: 203 6th Ave NW Stewartville MN 55976 Office: Stewartville Star PO Box 365 301 N Main St Stewartville MN 55976

DURBIN, HAZEL MARINDA, licensed practical nurse; b. Alton, Ill., Aug. 15, 1906; d. Reubin Samuel and Mary Charlottie (Sawyer) Spurling; m. Albert Michael Durbin, Oct. 8, 1924; children—Wilbur Lee, Shirley Jean, Herbert Dale, Betty Louise, Delmer Dean. Diploma, Chgo. Sch. Practical Nursing, 1946; grad. Decatur (Ill.) Sch. Practical Nursing, 1960. Lic. practical nurse, Ill. Insp., Illiopolis War Plant, 1943-45; practical nurse Decatur Macon County Hosp. (now Decatur Meml. Hosp.) 1947-79, pvt. duty nursing, 1979—; nurse St. Mary's Hosp., Decatur, 1956-79, med. nurse, 1965-79. Mem. Lic. Practical Nurse Assn. (active Local Div. 10, pres. 1982—, mem. state exec. bd., nat. del., 1983—), Am. Bus. Woman's Assn. (1st v.p. 1978-79). Home: 3365 Greenlake Dr Decatur IL 62521

DURBROW, BARBARA HELEN, management consultant; b. Washington Court House, Ohio, Mar. 29, 1936; d. Roy Lee and Esta Pearl (Sword) Mustain; attended U. Cinn., Central Mich. U., U. Ala.; m. Brian Durbrow; children—Robert E., William D. Sr. cons. B.R. Durbrow & Assos., Cin., 1969-72; v.p., sec., treas., dir. Barbrisons Mgmt. Systems, Inc., Cin., 1972—; v.p. Mgmt. Research and Devel., Inc. (merged with Barbrisons Mgmt. Systems, Inc.), Cin., 1975-80; v.p., dir. IE, Inc., 1980—; v.p. Durbrow Assocs. Properties, 1984—; co-developer ACCUTRAC Evaluation Systems. Mem. Republican Presdl. Task Force, U.S. Senatorial Club, U.S. Congl. Adv. Bd. Mem. Nat. Mgmt. Assn., Acad. Mgmt. Co-author: Modern Research on Accident Proneness; contbr. articles to profl. jours.; research on employee selection, honesty, substance abuse and accident predisposition. Office: 10451 Grand Oaks Suite 200 Cincinnati OH 45242 also 3040 Madison Rd Suite 203 Cincinnati OH 45209

DURCHHOLZ, PATRICIA, sociologist; b. Cin., Apr. 5, 1933; d. Robert Patrick and Helen (Lippert) White; m. Richard Francis Durchholz, Aug. 9, 1952 (dec. May 1982); children—Kim Benz, Leslie Chamberlain, Mark, Andrea Harpen, Theresa Hill, Anthony, Amy. B.A., U. Cin., 1973; Ph.D., Union Grad. Sch., Yellow Springs, Ohio, 1977. Ford Found. intern, U. Cin., 1973-74, asst. to pres., 1974-76; dir., adj. prof. U. Ky., Lexingon, 1977-79; cons. Cin. Family Health Care, Mason, Ohio, 1983—; v.p. RFD Enterprises, Mason, Ohio, 1984—; cons. Trillium Hills Coop., Clarksville, Ohio, 1985—; lectr. English, Clermont Coll., Batavia, Ohio, 1986—. Danforth fellow, 1975. Mem. Soc. Values in Higher Edn., Am. Sociol. Assn., U. Cin. Library Guild, Phi Beta Kappa. Democrat. Roman Catholic. Avocations: biking; running; gardening. Home: 9307 Greenhedge Ln Loveland OH 45140

DURDEN, ZELDA DENISE, quality engineer; b. Los Angeles, Dec. 28, 1959; d. Sylvester, Jr., and Lorene (Griffin) D. Grad. in Indsl. Engring. and Operation Research, U. Calif.-Berkeley, 1982. Contract engr. SOHIO Constrn., San Francisco, 1982-83; quality program specialist, STC Computer Systems Corp., Santa Clara, Calif., 1983-84, cert. instr. quality circle facilitator, 1983-84; adminstr. quality edn. systems Convergent Techs., Santa Clara, 1984—. Vol. San Francisco Bay council Girl Scouts U.S.A., 1981—. State of Calif. scholar, 1977. Mem. Am. Inst. Indsl. Engrs., Soc. Women Engrs., Am. Soc. for Quality Control, Nat. Assn. Female Execs. Democrat.

DURGOM, JANE ELLYN, lawyer; b. Sept. 1, 1948; d. John Albert and Rosemarie (Scordino) Durgom. B.S., Purdue U., 1971; J.D., Georgetown U., Washington, 1974. Asst. dist. atty. N.Y. County Dist. Atty.'s Office, N.Y.C., 1974-78; atty. Gen. Motors Corp., N.Y.C., 1978-81; gen. counsel Genway Corp., Chgo., 1981-83; asst. gen. counsel Nissan Motor Corp., Carson, Calif., 1983—, gen. counsel Nissan Motor Acceptance Corp., Carson, 1983—. Co-author Fed. Regulation of Consumer Credit, 1982. Recipient Personalities of Am. award, 1985). Mem. ABA, Women in Mgmt., Inc. (women of achievement award, 1982, outstanding young woman Am. award 1981), Kappa Alpha Theta (exec. v.p. Purdue U. 1970-71). Home: 736 Gould Ave Unit 14 Hermosa Beach CA 90254

DURHAM, BARBARA, state justice; b. 1942. B.S.B.A., Georgetown U.; law degree, Stanford U. Bar: Wash. 1968. Formerly judge Wash. Superior Ct., King County; then judge Wash. Ct. Appeals; assoc. justice Wash. Supreme Ct., 1985—. Office: Temple of Justice Olympia WA 98504*

DURHAM, CHRISTINE MEADERS, state supreme court justice; b. Los Angeles, Aug. 3, 1945; d. William Anderson and Louise (Christensen) Meaders; m. George H. Durham, Dec. 28, 1966; children—Jennifer, Meghan, Troy, Melinda, Isaac. A.B., Wellesley Coll., 1967; J.D., Duke U., 1971. Bar: N.C. 1971, Utah 1973, U.S. Ct. Appeals (10th cir.) 1973. Sole practice, Durham, N.C., 1971-73; ptnr. Johnson, Durham & Moxley, Salt Lake City, 1973-78; adj. prof. J. Reuben Clark Law Sch., Brigham Young U., Provo, 1973-78; judge Utah Dist. Ct., Salt Lake City, 1978-82; assoc. justice Utah Supreme Ct., Salt Lake City, 1982—; instr. Nat. Jud. Coll., Reno, Nev. Fellow Am. Bar Found.; mem. Am. Law Inst., Am. Judicature Soc. (bd. dirs.), Utah State Bar Assn., ABA (subcom. state-fed. ct. relations of jud. adminstrn. div.), Nat. Assn. Women Judges (pres.-elect). Office: Utah Supreme Ct 332 State Capitol Bldg Salt Lake City UT 84114

DURHAM, INEZ M., former parish official; b. Woodville, Miss., May 30, 1909; d. John Riley and Nancy Virginia (Hastings) McCearley; m. Louis Stanley Durham, Aug. 14, 1929 (dec. Feb. 1943); children—Louis Stanley, John Weldon; m. Frank A. Bailey, Feb. 5, 1977. Student pub. schs., Fayette, Miss. Clk. of ct. East Feliciana Parish, La., 1943-80, ret., 1980. Named Woman of Yr., Krewe of Adonis, New Orleans, 1962. Mem. La. Clks. of Ct. Assn. (past mem. bd. dirs.), Hist. Soc. East Feliciana Parish (charter), Jackson Assembly, East Feliciana Pilgrimage and Garden Club, Am. Legion Aux. Democrat. Methodist. Lodge: Order Ea. Star. Home: PO Box 903 Clinton LA 70722

DURHAM, LINDA GRAVES, art gallery owner; b. Phila., Nov. 19, 1942; d. Everett Harold and Lenore (Bailey) Graves; children—Donna Lynn, Everett Andrew; m. Peter H. Goodwin, June 1985. Student Ithaca Coll., 1960-62, Plymouth Coll., 1971-72, Mary Baldwin Coll., 1974-76. Playboy bunny Playboy Club, N.Y.C., 1962-65; producer/dir. Tiffany Melodrama Theatre, Cerrillos, N.Mex., 1966-69; founder, dir. N.Mex. Prisoners Aid Soc., Santa Fe, 1972-73; dir. research Fenn Galleries, Santa Fe, 1978-79; owner, pres. Linda Durham Gallery, Inc., Santa Fe, 1979—; producer host Artworks, Santa Fe, 1983; panelist N.Mex. Arts Commn.; lectr. in field; panelist Artnews World, Art Market Conf., Los Angeles, N.Y.C., 1983, 84. Contbr. articles to profl. jours. Bd. dirs. Ctr. for Contemporary Art, Santa Fe, 1984-85, Visual Arts Bd. Coll. of Santa Fe, 1985, Inst. Fine Arts, Santa Fe, 1984-85, Santa Fe Festival of Arts, 1980-82; chmn. Unicef Adv. Bd., N.Mex., 1983-85. Mem. Santa Fe Gallery Assn., C. of C., Better Bus. Bur., Nat. Assn. Female Execs., Santa Fe Council on Internat. Relations. Avocations: hiking; reading; travel; entertaining; writing. Office: Linda Durham Gallery Inc 400 Canyon Rd Santa Fe NM 87501

DURHAM, LINDA THEUNE, editor; b. Ft. Leavenworth, Kan., Nov. 11, 1951; d. Stanley William and Carol Ann (Feld) Theune; student U. Ga., 1969-70; B.A., West Ga. Coll., 1973; m. Michael Bryan Durham, Aug. 4, 1973. Sec. The Coca-Cola Co., Atlanta, 1973-75, research asst., 1975-76, research specialist, 1976-77, supr. editorial services, 1977-79, editor internal. publs., 1979-81, mgr. consumer info. center, 1981-83, mng. editor fin. communications, 1983-85, free lance writer, 1985—. Mem. Assn. to Revive Grant Park, 1980—. Nat. Merit scholar, 1969-73. Mem. Internat. Assn. Bus. Communicators. Roman Catholic. Home: 366 Oakland Ave Atlanta GA 30312 Office: 366 Oakland Ave Atlanta GA 30312

DURHAM, PEGGY J., freelance journalist; b. Boise City, Okla., Aug. 19, 1941; d. John M. and Mildred C. (Phillips) D.; 1 dau., Erin Christine Phillips Durham. B.A. in Journalism, U. Okla., 1963. Dir. public info. U. Tulsa, 1967-70; mgr. communications Honeywell Info. Systems, Oklahoma City, 1970-75; dir. public info. Okla. Bar Assn., Oklahoma City, 1975-77; chmn. bd., partner Metro Media Ltd. Advt. Agy., Oklahoma City, 1977-78; pres. The Word Place Advt. Agy., Oklahoma City, 1978-82; pres. Okla. Feminist Enterprises, Inc., Oklahoma City, 1977-80; freelance journalist. Bd. dirs. PASEO Drug Counseling Center, Oklahoma City, 1970-73; bd. dirs., co-founder Okla. Women's Center, 1973-74; mem. ERA coalition NOW, 1973-75. Named one of Okla.'s 10 movers and shakers in women's movement Okla. Monthly Mag., 1976. Mem. Internat. Assn. Bus. Communicators, Oklahoma City Press Club, ACLU, Okla. Press Assn. Democrat. Editor Okla. Halfway House newsletter Alternatives, 1973; founder, editor Sister Advocate newspaper, Okla.'s only feminist newspaper, 1975-80. Home and office: 1522 NW 30th Oklahoma City OK 73118

DURHAM-JONES, BONNIE DEE ROETMAN, lawyer; b. Ansted, W.Va., Oct. 5, 1935; d. Edward Terrink and Fern Catherine (McCleary) Roetman; m. Edward Allen Durham, Oct. 1, 1960 (div. 1976); 1 child, Mark Allen; m. 2d, Roger Rittenhouse Jones, Dec. 19, 1981. B.S., U. Nebr., 1972; J.D., Creighton U., 1976. Bar: U.S. Supreme Ct. 1983, U.S. Dist. Ct. (Nebr.) 1972, U.S. Dist. Ct. (N.C.) 1983. Asst. city prosecutor legal dept., prosecution div. City of Omaha, 1977-82; v.p., legal counsel Piedmont Record Classics, Winston-Salem, N.C., 1983—; sole practice, Winston-Salem, 1983-84; with Womble Carlyle Sanoridge & Rice, 1984—; research cons. Nat. Coll. State Judiciary, Reno, 1970-71, Met. Criminal Justice Commn., Omaha, 1971-73. Author: Court Systems Analysis 4th Judicial District Court System, 1972. Pres., Nebr. PTA, Omaha, 1969; chmn. library and reading services Nat. Congress Parents and Tchrs. State Nebr., Omaha City Council, 1972; chmn. legis. com. sch. unit Nat. Congress Parents and Tchrs. 1972, pres. 1972-73; bd. dirs. Halfway House Stop-Over Homes, Inc., 1972; cons. com. mem. Omaha Pub. Schs. Self-Study and Eval., 1972-73. Recipient Service award Nat. Cystic Fibrosis Research Found., Nebr. chpt., 1963. Mem. ABA, Am. Trial Lawyers Assn., N.C. Acad. Trial Lawyers, N.C. Women Attys. Assn. Nebr. State Bar Assn., N.C. State Bar Assn., Forsyth County Bar Assn, Forsyth County Women Attys. Assn., Forsyth County Def. Attys. Assn. (v.p.), Nebr. Personnel and Guidance Assn., AAUW Alpha Phi Sigma. Lutheran. Home: 7022 Brandemere Ln Winston-Salem NC 27106 Office: 5000 Wachovia Bldg Winston-Salem NC 27101

DURKEE, JEAN KELLNER, home economist; b. Chgo., Feb. 7, 1932; d. Herbert Ernest and Lucy (Stevens) Kellner; B.S. in Home Econs., U. Tex., Austin, 1953; m. Robert Rosswell Durkee, Jr., Oct. 3, 1953; children—Robert III, Mark, Todd. Dir., First Presbyn. Nursery Sch. and Kindergarten, Lafayette, La., 1954-56; dir. Grace Presbyn. Nursery Sch. and Kindergarten, Lafayette, 1965-67; pres. Tout de Suite, Inc., Lafayette, 1978—; tchr. microwave cooking. Pres., Lafayette Natural History Mus. Mem. Am. Home Econs. Assn., Home Economists in Bus., La. Home Econs. Assn. Internat. Microwave Power Inst., Internat. Assn. Cooking Profls. (cert.), P.E.O. (pres. chpt., 1961-62). Republican. Methodist. Clubs: Jr. League (pres. club 1959-60) (Lafayette); Chez Amis Women's (pres. 1957-58). Author, pub.: Tout de Suite à la Microwave, I, 1977, II, 1980; co-author Blades and Waves column, 1978-83; author: Voilà! Lafayette Centennial Cookbook, 1884-1984, 1983. Office: PO Box 30121 Lafayette LA 70503

DURKIN, DOROTHY ANGELA, university administrator; b. Glen Cove, N.Y., June 23, 1945; d. Frank Vincent and Rose Marie D.; B.A., SUNY, Stony Brook, 1968; M.A., N.Y. U., 1974; m. David Lawrence Hawthorne, July 13, 1975; 1 son, David Francis Hawthorne. Adminstrv. asst. State U. N.Y., Stony Brook, 1965-67; prodn. editor Holt, Rhinehart & Winston, Inc., 1967-69; editor Hill & Wang Pub., Inc., N.Y.C., 1969-70; asst. dir. public info. N.Y.U. Sch. Continuing Edn., N.Y.C., 1970-72, asst. dean pub. affairs and student services, 1972—; cons. N.Y.C. Center for Lifelong Learning, 1974. Recipient Andy Advt. award of merit, 1972, Direct Mktg. Leadership award, 1977, 80, Nat. U. Continuing Edn. Assn. awards, 1978, 81-86, Big Apple award N.Y. Radio Broadcasters, 1985. Mem. Am. Coll. Public Relations Assn. (nat. award 1973), Council for Advancement and Support of Edn. (nat. award 1981, 82, 83), Women in Communications (chmn. job info. N.Y.C. chpt. 1981-82), Nat. Univ. Continuing Edn. Assn. (cons. 1977-78, chmn. info. services div. 1980, mktg. task force 1986—), Pub. Relations Soc. Am. Direct Mail/Mktg. Assn. (Echo award 1983). Clubs: Scuba Diving, Community Sing. Producer TV series Continuum, WNYC, 1974; editor NSF student mag., 1961. Home: 200 Mercer St New York NY 10012 Office: NYU Sch Continuing Edn 126 Shimkin Hall New York NY 10003

DURLACH, MARGARET ROSANNA, automotive supplier; b. Enid, Okla., Oct. 13, 1951; d. James Gerald and Lorraine Freda (Loucks) Aust; m. Christopher Lee Durlach, Nov. 24, 1973. B.A. with honors, Potsdam State Coll., 1973; M.B.A. with honors, Cleve. State U., 1978. Caseworker, Fairfield County Welfare Dept., Lancaster, Ohio, 1974-76; research asst. Cleve. State U., 1976-78; mktg. analyst Valve div. TRW Inc., Cleve., 1979-82, supr. mktg. services, 1982—. Exec. advisor co.-sponsored Jr. Achievement, Euclid, Ohio, 1980-82. Mem. Am. Mktg. Assn. (sec. 1985-86, various coms. 1978—), Automotive Market Research Council (rep. 1981—), Cleve. State U. M.B.A. Alumni Soc. (dir., sec. 1983—). Club: Toastmasters (ednl. v.p. 1985—). Office: TRW Inc Valve Div 1455 E 185th St Cleveland OH 44110

DURON, YSABEL, newscaster; b. Salinas, Calif., Apr. 14, 1947; d. Eligio and Jessie (Salgado) D. B.A. in Journalism, San Jose State U., 1970. Writer, KNXT CBS, Los Angeles, 1970-71; reporter KPIX TV, San Francisco, 1971-72; newscaster, reporter KTVU TV, Oakland, Calif., 1972-79, WBZ TV, Boston, 1979-80; reporter KCST TV, San Diego, 1980-81; newscaster KICU TV, San Jose, 1981—. Chmn. San Jose Devel. Corp., 1986; 1st v.p. League of Friends, San Jose, 1985; editorial bd. Nat. Network of Hispanic Women, Palo Alto, 1985. Washington Journalism fellow, 1970; Nat. Cath. Conf. fellow, 1970; Columbia U./Ford Found. fellow, 1970; recipient Tchr. Advocate award Calif. Tchrs. Assn., 1973, John Swett award, 1982; award for best feature series "Trouble with Teachers", No. Calif. Radio/TV News Dirs. Assn., 1982. Mem. Nat. Assn. TV and Radio Artists (Emmy award 1974), Latinos in Communication. Avocations: interior design; fashion cons. Office: KICU TV 36 1585 Schallenberger Rd San Jose CA 95131

DURR, JANIS JOY, home entertainment corporation executive; b. Ann Arbor, Mich., Mar. 3, 1947; d. Elwood Harry and Genevieve Joy (Southworth) Ball; m. Richard Theodore Durr, Sept. 8, 1973 (div. Aug. 1980). B.A. in Psychology, Monmouth Coll., 1969. Computer saleswoman LAG Drug Co., Chgo., 1976-77; regional mgr. Sales Maids of Am., Westport, Conn., 1977-78; sales rep. MST, Inc., Skokie, Ill., 1979, Northrop Data Systems Corp., Rosemont, Ill., 1979-80; video specialist MCA, Inc., Rosemont, 1980-81, regional video dir., 1981—. Active Am. Film Inst., Mus. Sci. and Industry, 1982—. Ill. State scholar, 1965; Mellinger Found. fellow, 1966-69. Mem. NOW. Presbyterian. Office: MCA Inc 10700 W Higgins Rd Rosemont IL 60018

DURST, BARBARA, non-profit company executive; b. N.Y.C., Jan. 9, 1943; d. Marc and Beatrice (Grossfeld) Durst. B.A. in Polit. Sci., Hunter Coll., 1964; student Sarah Lawrence Summer Inst.-Paris, 1962; student NYU Grad. Sch. Pub. Adminstrn., 1965-66. English tchr. Bd. Edn., N.Y.C., 1964-66; community relations specialist Urban Renewal Agy., Tarrytown, N.Y., 1966-67; urban planner Hudson River Valley Community Tarrytown, 1967-69; urban renewal rep. N.Y. Div. Housing, N.Y.C., 1970; project dir. N.Y.C. Housing Preservation & Devel., 1970-79; exec. dir. NHS of Ft. Worth, Tex., 1979—. Bd. dirs. Dan Danciger Jewish Community Ctr., 1981—, Hebrew Day Sch., Ft. Worth, 1985—; council mem. Englewood Community Ctr. to present; chmn. Neighborhood Adv. Council, 1985-86. Recipient Cert. of Recognition for service to Poly. Neighborhood Adv. Council, City of Ft. Worth, 1986. Fellow Nat. Assn. Housing and Renewal Ofcls., Nat. Trust for Historic Preservation. Democrat. Jewish. Avocations: reading; traveling; needlework. Office: Neighborhood Housing Services of Fort Worth 3301 E Rosedale Fort Worth TX 76112

DURYEA, LOVEJOY REEVES, business executive; b. Bronxville, N.Y., May 7, 1944; d. Rosser and Elizabeth Lovejoy (Street) Reeves; B.A., St. John's Coll., 1967; m. William M. Duryea, Jr., Aug. 7, 1976; children—Robert Atwell, David Rosser McShane, Sr. copywriter Compton Advt. Co., N.Y.C., 1967-70; copywriter Avon Products Inc., N.Y.C., 1970-71, copychief, 1971-73, group-coordinator, 1973-74, mgr., 1974, creative mgr., 1975, project mgr., 1975-76, mgr. nat. rep. recruiting, 1976-80, cons., 1980—; dir. Alderney Design Ltd.; pres. Dorset Design; bd. dirs. St. John's Coll., 1983. dir. Boothsroy Stuart Ltd. Founder N.Y. chpt. Achievement Rewards Scientists Found. Inc., 1972, dir. at large, 1974-76, membership chmn., 1976-77, 1st v.p., 1978-79, chmn. exec. com., 1979-80; active Jr. League N.Y., 1968—; bd. visitors and govs. St. John's Coll., 1983. Recipient cert. of achievement Avon Products Inc., 1978. Clubs: Nat. Arts, Cold Spring Harbor Beach, Leash, Westminster Kennel, Jr. League. Home and Office: 173 E 80th St New York NY 10021

DUSAULT, DEBORAH SULLIVAN, government official; b. Boston, June 20, 1944; d. John Lawrence and Priscilla (Manning) Sullivan; m. Philip Ames DuSault, Sept. 30, 1967. B.A., George Washington U., 1966. Personnel mgmt. specialist HUD, Washington, 1966-72, personnel officer, 1972-75, supervisory personnel specialist, 1975-78, dep. dir. field div., 1978-79, dir. personnel systems and payroll div., 1979-83, dir. mgmt. services div. ADP, 1983-84, dir. project mgmt. staff, 1984—. Recipient Spl. Achievement award HUD, 1978. Mem. EDP Auditors Assn. Roman Catholic. Home: 826 25th St NW Washington DC 20037 Office: HUD 451 7th St SW Washington DC 20410

DUTCH, DORIS ANN, publications specialist; b. Washington, May 7, 1939; d. Norris W. and Elizabeth V. (Poe) D.; 1 dau., Doretha Annette Johnson. Student Washington pub. schs. Publications specialist Fed. Aviation Adminstrn., Dept. Transp., Washington, 1964—; dir. Small World Prodns., Inc., Washington, 1978—. Active Urban League, Washington, Mayor's Com. to Promote Washington (grantee 1983), Trinity Coll. Upward Bound Parent Adv. Com. (v.p., then pres. 1973-75). Democrat. Home: 3640 13th St NW Washington DC 20010 Office: Federal Aviation Administration 800 Independence Ave SW Washington DC 20591

DUTCHER, LISA DELAYNE, municipal operations analyst; b. Grand Rapids, Mich., Apr. 7, 1956; d. Bruce Irwin and Patricia Louise (Campbell) Dutcher. Student Grand Valley State U., 1975-76, Mich. State U., 1976-77, Davenport Coll., 1977, Internat. Acad. Merchandising and Design, 1978, Rock Valley Coll., 1979, 84—. Draftsman, surveyor Heritage Engring., Rockford, Ill., 1979; engr. technician II City Belvidere (Ill.), 1979-81; adminstrv. asst. City of Rockford, 1981-82, ops. analyst, 1982—. Rep. City of Rockford Emergency Services, 1981—; group leader quality circle Rockford (Ill.) Pub. Works, 1983—; mem. Rockford Interactions Teams, Rockford, 1983—. Mem. Nat. Assn. Female Execs., NOW, Am. Pub. Works Assn., Nat. Assn. Women in Construction, Internat. Assn. Quality Circles, DAR. Congregationalist. Lodge: KC. Home: 51 Johns Woods Dr Rockford IL 61103 Office: City of Rockford Pub Works 425 E State St Rockford IL 61104

DUTTON, LOIS ANN, consulting firm executive; b. Pensacola, Fla., Mar. 9, 1939; d. Cecil Ivor and Juanita (Locklear) D. B.S. in Nursing, U. N.C., 1965; M.P.H., 1966; Ph.D., U. Ala., 1984. R.N., Fla., Ala. Program dir. Alcoholism Services, Winter Haven, Fla., 1973-77; exec. dir. Tri-County Alcoholism Services, Inc., Winter Haven, 1975-80; asst. prof. U. Ala.-Birmingham, 1980-85; cons. Comprehensive Care Corp., Irvine, Calif., 1985-86; pres. Dutton Assocs., Inc, Tampa, Fla., 1985—; cons. Fla. Adv. Bd. for Profl. Alcoholism Edn. and Tng., Tallahassee, 1978-80; chairperson community health council U. Ala.-Birmingham, 1981-83. Mem. adv. task force Gov.'s Task Force for Devel. Alcoholism Program Standards, Tallahassee, 1977-80; adv. counsel Spouse Abuse Program, Lakeland, Fla., 1979-80; mem. edn. com. Am. Cancer Soc., Birmingham, 1981-85; instructional specialist ARC, Birmingham, 1984—; active Track Club, Tampa. Recipient Outstanding Faculty award U. Ala.-Birmingham sr. nursing students, 1983. Mem. Am. Nurses Assn., Am. Pub. Health Assn., Fla. Nurses Assn., Nat. Assn. Female Execs., Sigma Theta Tau, Kappa Delta Pi. Democrat. Roman Catholic. Avocations: running; painting; guitar.

DUTTON, PAULINE MAE, fine arts librarian; b. Detroit, July 15; d. Thoralf Andreas and Esther Ruth (Clyde) Tandberg; B.A. in Art, Calif. State U., Fullerton, 1967; M.S. in Library Sci., U. So. Calif., 1971; m. Richard Hawkins Dutton, June 21, 1969. Elem. tchr., Anaheim, Calif., 1967-68, Corona, Calif., 1968-69; fine arts librarian Pasadena (Calif.) Public Library, 1971-80; art cons., researcher, 1981—. Mem. Pasadena Librarians Assn. (sec. 1978, treas. 1979-80), Calif. Library Assn., Calif. Soc. Librarians, Art Librarians N.Am., Nat. Assn. Female Execs., Am. Film Inst., Am. Entrepreneurs Assn., Gilbert and Sullivan Soc., Alpha Sigma Phi. Club: Toastmistress (local pres. 1974).

DUVAL, CYNTHIA, museum curator; b. Port Talbot, South Wales, Oct. 6, 1932; came to U.S., 1972; d. Joseph and Esther (Goldberg) Armstrong; m. Marcel Duval, Aug. 26, 1973; 1 son, Jonathan Armstrong. Intermediate degree, Chelsea Sch. Art, London, 1953. Antiques buyer Harrod's, London, 1972-73; gen. appraiser Sotheby's, N.Y., 1973-77; lectr. Ringling Sch. Art, Sarasota, Fla., 1977-79; adminstr. Ringling program Tampa Ringling Mus. Art, Sarasota, 1979-80, sr. curator decorative arts, 1980—; advisor State Div. of Culture, 1985—; grants panelist for visual arts, Fla., 1985—; liaison to Gov.'s Mansion, Tallahassee. Author: History of Lighting and Lamps, 1972; Toys of Long Ago, 1972; The Life of a Gentleman, 1972; Love and Marriage, 1972. Author: (catalog) 500 Years of the Decorative Arts, 1984; Medieval and Renaissance Armor, 1984. Recipient Designers Image award Am. Assn. Interior Designers, 1983. Mem. Hist. House Assn., The Decorative Arts Trust, Appraisers Assn. Am. (fine and decorative arts appraiser 1977—), Am. Assn. Mus., Internat. Assn. Mus. (mem. internat. exhibitions exchange com.). Avocation: study of social history. Office: Ringling Mus Art 5401 Bayshore Rd Sarasota FL 33580

DUVALL, LORRAINE, recreation center owner; b. Hamilton, Ohio, Jan. 31, 1925; d. Saul and Martha Jane (Huff) Baker; m. Ray DuVall, June 12, 1951; children—Sharon DuVall Keese, Deborah D. Velchoff, Steve, Annette. B.A., U. Cin., 1951; M.A., Tex. A&I U., 1963; postgrad. Miami U., Oxford, Ohio, 1958, U. Toledo, 1959, U. Tex.-Austin, 1968. Elem. tchr. Larkmoor, Lorain, Ohio, 1956-60; tchr. math. Incarnate Word High Sch., Corpus Christi, 1964-70; owner, instr. Aerobic Fitness, Corpus Christi, 1973—; owner, coach Corpus Christi Marlin Swim Team, 1972—; mgr. Corpus Christi Country Club Pool, 1973—; pres., mgr. Club Estates Pool Chems., Corpus Christi, 1980—, Club Estates Recreation, Corpus Christi, 1977—. Vol. psychiat. ward Meml. Hosp., Corpus Christi, 1966-70; bd. dirs. vol. YWCA, Corpus Christi, 1970-77; water safety trainer ARC, Corpus Christi, 1975-82; CPR instr. Am. Heart Assn., Corpus Christi, 1980-84; vol. children's choir dir. St. John Methodist Ch., Corpus Christi, 1966-78, Asbury United Meth. Ch., 1980—. NSF grantee U. Tex.-Austin, 1968. Mem. Am. Swim Coaches Assn. Republican. Avocations: music; swimming; tennis; skiing; backpacking. Home: 6709 Pintail Dr Corpus Christi TX 78413 Office: 4902 Snowgoose St Corpus Christi TX 78413

DUVALL, PATRICIA ARLENE, educator; b. Pitts., June 27, 1950; d. William Richard and Willene Alberta (Goode) Addison; 1 child, Tiyonda Aikee. B.A. in Math., Carnegie-Mellon U., 1972; M.Ed., U. Pitts., 1981. Long distance telephone operator AT&T, Pitts., summers 1968-71; switchboard operator Union Nat. Bank, Pitts., summers 1972; math tchr. Allegheny Intermediate Unit, Pitts., summers, 1978-79; math skills program Chatham Coll., Pitts., 1983—; tchr. math Pitts. Bd. Pub. Edn., 1972—; tennis coach Allegheny High Sch., Pitts., 1979-81. Mem. U.S. Tennis Assn., Nat. Assn. Female Execs., Am. Alliance for Health, Phys. Edn., Recreation and Dance. Jehovah's Witness. Avocations: stamp collecting; tennis; reading; collecting comic book; home computers.

DUXBURY, SHEILA NOLAN, buyer; b. Waterbury, Conn., Jan. 9, 1958; d. John William and Theresa (Langey) N.; m. Hampton David Duxbury, Oct. 30, 1982. B.B.A., Bryant Coll., 1980. Mgmt. trainee Navy Exchange, Davisville, R.I., 1980-81, buyer, Patuxent River, Md., 1981-82; store mgr. Open Country, Warwick, R.I., 1982-83; asst. buyer Bradlees, Braintree, Mass., 1983-85, buyer, 1985—. Democrat. Roman Catholic. Avocations: swimming, crafts. Home: 24 Peabody Terr Apt 1004 Cambridge MA 02138 Office: Bradlees 1 Bradlee Circle Braintree MA 02184

DVORAK, NANCY GERALDINE, physician, artist; b. New Rochelle, N.Y., Feb. 24, 1943; d. Francis Vincent and Bertha (Emanogsky) D.; B.S. cum laude, Fordham U., 1966; M.A., Coll. New Rochelle, 1973; B.S., Columbia U. 1975; M.D. SUNY-Buffalo, 1979; resident in internal medicine Med. Coll. Ohio, 1979-82. Cert. art edn. Elem. and high sch. tchr. Sisters of Resurrection, Albany, N.Y., 1966-71, Holy Family Sch., New Rochelle, N.Y., 1971-72; internist Community Health Plan, Latham, N.Y., 1982-84; clinical instr. dept. medicine Albany Med. Coll. Union U., 182-84; clin. physician Sunmount Developmental Center, Tupper Lake, N.Y., 1983—; med. advisor dept. continuing care Community Health Plan, Latham, N.Y., 1983-84. Contbr. articles on clinical medicine to profl. jours. Oil, watercolor paintings represented in pvt. collections. Regents' scholar SUNY, 1961-65; SHIP scholar Nat. Art Edn. Assn., 1971. Democrat. Roman Catholic. Home: 2481 Troy Rd Schenectady NY 12309 Office: Sunmount Developmental Center Tupper Lake NY 12986

DVORAK-LEVY, SUSAN ELAINE, writer, editor; b. New London, Conn., Aug. 9, 1950; d. Francis Charles and Sophie Mary (Renkiewicz) Dvorak; m. Harold Charles Levy, Apr. 5, 1975. B.A. cum laude, Eastern Conn. State Coll., 1975. Staff reporter Norwich Bull. (Conn.), 1972-73; staff reporter, newscaster Willie Broadcasting Co., Willimantic, Conn., 1973-74; staff reporter, supr. Hartford Times, 1975-76; copy editor, writer Bur. Bus. Practice div. Prentice Hall Co., Waterford, Conn., 1976-78; editor Wallingford Post (Conn.), 1978-84; editor communications div., pub. affairs and govtl. relations. Conn. Mut. Life Ins. Co., Hartford, 1984—; adult edn. instr., Wallingford, 1983. Corporator Town of Wallingford, 1984—; bd. dirs., 2d v.p., com. chmn. Wallingford Boys and Girls Club, 1981-84, recipient Pub. Service award, 1981. Recipient Media award Conn. Edn. Assn., 1983, Disting. Service award Wallingford Edn. Assn., 1983. Mem. Greater New Haven C. of C. (mem. model leadership program 1983), Pub. Relations Soc. Am. Roman Catholic. Clubs: Zonta (chmn. status of women com. 1982-83), Toastmasters. Home: 392 Wallingford Rd RD Box 382 Durham CT 06422 Office: Communications Div Conn Mut Life Ins Co 140 Garden St Hartford CT 06154

DWIGHT, MARGARET LEOLA, historian, educator; b. Hattiesburg, Miss., Dec. 12, 1947; d. Benton and Lula M. (Hicks) D. B.S., U. So. Miss., 1970; M.A., So. Ill. U., 1973; Ph.D., U. Mo., 1978; postgrad. Northwestern U., 1978. High sch. history Hattiesburg pub. schs., 1969-70; teaching and research asst. So. Ill. U., Carbondale, 1970-72; instr. history Lincoln U., Jefferson City, Mo., 1973-74; teaching and research asst. U. Mo., Columbia, 1974-77; dir. Black Culture Ctr., asst. prof. U. Va., Charlottesville, 1977-80; prof. history Alcorn State U., Lorman, Miss., 1981—; cons. Charlottesville Pub. Sch. System, 1980, Hattiesburg Pub. Sch. System, 1984, NEH, Washington, 1979—, Nat. Negro Women Bus. and Profl. Club, Washington, 1979-80, Yorktown Bicentennial Commn. (Va.), 1981, Miss. Commn. Humanities, Jackson, 1981—, Va. Pub. Policy and Humanities Program, 1978-80. Author: (with G.A. Sewell) Miss. Black Historymakers, 1984; also articles on Negro history. Advisor, NAACP-Youth, Alcorn State U., 1981—. NEH fellow, Washington, 1979; CIC fellow Lilly Found., N.Y.C., 1983; internat. study grantee Dept. Edn., Washington, 1983; Lily Found. mini-grantee, 1982-83; Fulbright-Hays fellow, Cameroon, 1984. Mem. Assn. Study Afro-Am. Life and History, So. Hist. Assn., So. Conf. Afro-Am. Studies, Assn. Women Historians, NAACP, Phi Alpha Theta, Phi Delta Kappa. Democrat. Penecostal. Home: 1004 Spencer St Hattiesburg MS 39401 Office: Dept History Alcorn State U Lorman MS 39096

DWIRE, DOROTHY RICE, investment banker; b. Pitts.; d. Benjamin William and Rebecca (Zaks) Rice; children—Stephen Matthew, Neal Jay. Student pub. schs., Riga, Latvia, N.Y.C.. Speaker's bur. dir. Hugh Carey for Gov., N.Y.C., 1977; campaign mgr. John V. Lindsay for Senator, N.Y. State, 1978-79; sales person Murry Roth Real Estate Co., N.Y.C., 1982—; exec. v.p. Barsily Internat., N.Y.C., 1983—. Pres. bd. dirs. Concert Artists Guild, N.Y.C., 1983-85; bd. dirs. Westchester County Mental Health, Harrison, N.Y., 1958-64, Westchester O.R.T., Harrison, 1957-61; primary day coordinator Howard Samuels for Gov., N.Y.C., 1970. Home: 215 E 68 St New York NY 10022

DWORSKY, CLARA WEINER, merchandise brokerage executive, lawyer; b. N.Y.C., Apr. 28, 1918; d. Charles and Rebecca (Becker) Weiner; m. Bernard Ezra Dworsky, Jan. 2, 1944; 1 dau., Barbara G. Goodman. B.S., St. John's U., N.Y.C., 1937, LL.B., 1939, J.D., 1968. Bar: N.Y. 1939, U.S. Dist. Ct. (ea. dist.) N.Y. 1942. Law clk. Milton Ehreneich, N.Y.C., 1938-39; sole practice, N.Y.C., 1939-51; assoc. Bessie Farberman, N.Y.C., 1942; clk., sec. U.S. Armed Forces, Camp Carson, Colo., Camp Claiborne, La., 1944-45; abstractor, dir. Realty Title, Rockville, Md., 1954-55; v.p. Kelley & Dworsky Inc., Houston, 1960—; appeals agt. Gasoline Rationing Apls. Bd., N.Y.C., 1942; dir. Southlan Sales Assocs., Houston. Vol., ARC, N.Y.C.; vice chmn. War Bond pledge drive, Bklyn.; vol. Houston Legal Found., 1972-73; pres. Women's Aux. Washington Hebrew Acad., 1958-60, v.p. bd. trustees, 1959-60; co-founder, v.p. S. Tex. Hebrew Acad. (now Hebrew Acad.), Houston, 1970-75, hon. pres. women's div., 1973. Recipient Certificate award Treas. of U.S., 1943; Commendation Office of Chief Magistrate of City N.Y., 1948; Pietas medal St. Johns U., 1985. Mem. ABA, N.Y. State Bar Assn., Nat. Assn. Women Lawyers (chmn. organizer Juvenile Delinquency Clinic N.Y. 1948-51), St. Johns U. Alumni Assn. (coordinator Houston chpt. 1983-86, pres. 1986). Jewish. Clubs: Delphian Soc., Amit Women. Lodges: B'nai B'rith Women, Hadassah. Home: 9726 Cliffwood Dr Houston TX 77096

DWORSKY, DORIS GORDON, state researcher, jewelry company executive; b. Bklyn., Oct. 1, 1925; d. Julius Dewey Gordon and Florence (Levinson) Gordon Feldman; m. Milton Barnette Dworsky, Mar. 4, 1945 (dec. Sept. 1964); children—Myrna, Risa, Lee. Student NYU, 1942-45. Buyer Felix Lilienthal & Co., N.Y.C., 1942-44; owner, operator Dworsky's Juvenile Ctr., Raleigh, N.C., 1945-48, Esquire Jewelers, Raleigh, 1960-63; buyer, mgr. Parisian Shop, Raleigh, 1964-67; statis. aide N.C. Div. Social Services, Raleigh, 1967-78, statis. research asst., 1978—; owner, operator Myrilee Jewelry Co. Contbr. articles to profl. jours. Actress Raleigh Little Theatre, 1962-78, house mgr., 1964-68; pub. relations worker Democratic Gubernatorial Race, Raleigh, 1984; v.p. Bethmeyer Sisterhood, Raleigh, 1949-51; pres. N.C. Assn. Jewish Women, Raleigh, 1979-81; bd. dirs. N.C. Blumenthal Home for Aged, Clemmons, 1979—. Recipient Best Supporting Actress award Raleigh Little Theatre, 1962, Spl. Vol. award Gov. N.C., 1965, Tech. Service award Raleigh Little Theatre, 1967, cert. appreciation Women in State Govt., 1983, cert. appreciation N.C. Central U., 1984. Mem. N.C. Social Services Orgn., N.C. Group Behavioral Soc. Avocations: philanthropic and community activity; acting; singing. Office: NC Div Social Services 325 N Salisbury St Raleigh NC 27611

DWYER, CAROL JONES, lawyer; b. Ann Arbor, Mich., Aug. 9, 1953; d. Lawrence William Jones and Ruth (Reavley) Drummond; m. Robert Eugene Dwyer, Jan. 8, 1977. B.A., U. Mich., 1974, J.D., 1980. Bar: Mich. 1981. Press advanceperson for Vice Pres. Walter Mondale, 1980; assoc. firm Kohl, Secrest, Wardle, Lynch, Clark & Hampton, P.C., Detroit and Farmington Hills, Mich., 1981-85; v.p. Dem. Lawyers of Mich., 1984—. Mem. Ann Arbor City Council, 1973-77. Mem. Am. Trial Lawyers Assn., State Bar Mich., Women Lawyers Assn. Mich. (regional dir. 1983-85).

DWYER, DORIOT ANTHONY, flutist; d. William C. and Edith (Maurer) Anthony; B.Music, Eastman Sch. Music, 1943; hon. degrees Harvard U., 1982, Simmons Coll., 1982; 1 child, Arienne. Second flutist Nat. Symphony, Washington, 1943, Los Angeles Philharm., 1945-52; 1st flutist Boston Symphony Orch., 1952—; flutist numerous chamber groups including: Boston Symphony Chamber Players, Doriot Anthony Dwyer and Friends; appeared at numerous music festivals including: Camel Back Festival, Berkshire Festival at Tanglewood, Rocky Mountain Music Festival; former mem. faculty Pomona Coll., New Eng. Conservatory Music; adj. prof. flute Boston U.; mem. faculty Berkshire Music Festival. Mem. Nat. Council of Women, Audubon Soc. Home: 3 Cleveland Rd Brookline MA 02146 Office: care Boston Symphony Symphony Hall Boston MA 02115*

DWYER, ETHEL THERESA, psychologist; b. Manchester, N.H., July 30, 1931; d. Joseph George and Florence Theresa (Kittredge) Thibodeau; Mus.B., Boston U., 1953, Ed.M., 1962, cert. advanced grad. study, 1965, Ed.D., 1968; m. John Philip Dwyer, June 22, 1957. Tchr., Miss Jacques Pvt. Sch., Manchester, 1953-54; asst. dir. Girls Club, Manchester, 1954-57; tchr. Manchester Public Schs., 1957-65; instr. edn. Boston U. Sch. Edn., 1965-66; asst. prof. psychology New Eng. Coll., Henniker, N.H., 1965-67; assoc. prof. Mt. St. Mary Coll., Hooksett, N.H., 1968-70; staff psychologist N.H. Hosp., Concord, 1968-71; ind. practice child psychology, 1970—; mem. N.H. Bd. Examiners Psychologists, 1976-77, chmn., 1977-79, investigator, 1984; mem. peer rev. com. APA/CHAMPUS, 1977-78; profl. adv. bd. N. River Sch., 1978-80, chmn., 1977; mem. teen age pregnancy/mother adv. bd. Vis. Nurse Assn. Manchester, 1978—; research asst. Boston U. Center Exceptional Children, 1962-63; curriculum cons. Concord Public Schs., 1967-68; psychologist, cons. Easter Seal Rehab. Center, 1971-72. Instr. water safety and first aid ARC; active YWCA. Diplomate sch. psychology Am. Bd. Profl. Psychology; cert. psychologist, N.H.; lic. psychologist, Mass.; listed Nat. Register Health Service Providers in Psychology. Mem. Am. Psychol. Assn., NEA (state rep. elem. educators 1965-70), Am. Edn. Research Assn., Music Educators Nat. Conf., Eastern Psychol. Assn., New Eng. Psychol. Assn., Mass. Psychol. Assn., N.H. Dental Assn. Women's Aux., Hillsboro County Kennel Club (dir. 1980), Mu Phi Epsilon, Pi Lamda Theta. Republican. Roman Catholic. Home: 2071 N River Rd Manchester NH 03104 Office: 1480 Elm St Manchester NH 03101

DWYER, MARGARET RELLA, management consulting executive; b. Chgo., Feb. 22, 1937; d. Niles Michael and Margaret Estelle (Walsh) D. B.A., Mundelein Coll., Chgo., 1958; cert. Am. Inst. Baking, Chgo., 1969. Bakery technician W.E. Long Co., Chgo., 1958-69, asst. dir. prodn., 1969-74, dir., adminstr. mfg., 1974-83, dir. tech. services, 1984—. Contbr. articles to mags. Mem. Am. Bakers Assn. (chmn. regulatory and tech. affairs com. 1984—), Am. Soc. Bakery Engrs. (chmn. tech. terms com. 1985—), Inst. Food Technologists, Chgo. Bakery Prodn. Club, Bakers Courtesy Club, Am. Inst. Baking (sci. adv. bd.), Wheat Industry Council. Republican. Roman Catholic. Avocations: reading, skiing, boating, golf, watching football, gardening. Home: 535 No Dee Rd Park Ridge IL 60068 Office: WE Long Co IBC 309 W Washington St Chicago IL 60606

DWYER, MARIE RITA ROZELLE (MRS. JOHN D. DWYER), educator; b. N.Y.C., Sept. 4, 1915; d. Charles W. and Agnes (Coyle) Rozelle; student L'Assomption, Paris, 1932-33; B.A., Notre Dame Coll., 1936; M.A., Fordham U., 1938, also postgrad; postgrad. St. Louis U.; student Sorbonne, Paris, summers 1933-37, 52; m. John D. Dwyer, Sept. 8, 1942; children—John Duncan, Joseph Charles, James Gerard, Jerome Valentine. Tchr. French, Sch. of Edn., Fordham U., N.Y.C., 1938-42, Notre Dame Coll., N.Y.C., 1939-40, Coll. of St. Rose, Albany, N.Y., 1949-53, Washington U., St. Louis, 1959-60; faculty French dept. Webster Coll., 1966-74; dir. community services Internat. Students Program, St. Louis U., 1974-83, with internat. programs, 1984—; mem. faculty Meramec Community Coll., St. Louis, 1968-70. Active community fund drives, including Greater St. Louis Fund for Arts and Edn.; bd. dirs. St. Louis Christmas Carols Assn., 1962-64, Parish Council, 1966-67; adult adviser cultural program for young adults Archdiocesan Council Cath. Youth, 1961-67; mem. Archdiocesan Council Laity Charities; chmn. internat. friendship program Archdiocesan Council of Laity of St. Louis, 1984. Mem. Am. Assn. Tchrs. French (pres. St. Louis chpt. 1955-56), Mo. Acad. Sci. (life mem., editorial staff transactions 1969-72, chmn. linguistics sect. 1970-76, past mem. exec. bd.), Alliance Française (past sec. St. Louis), Société Française (past sec.), KC Aux. (past pres.), AAAS (rep. Mo. Acad. Sci. at conv. in Mexico City 1973), Notre Dame Coll. Alumnae Assn. (past pres.), Internat. Fedn. Cath. Alumnae (past pres. Albany), Jesuit Mothers Guild (pres. 1963-65), Cath. Women's League (pres. 1964-66), Archdiocesan Council Cath. Women (mem. coms. family life teen-age code, corr. sec. 1963-64, pres. 1964-66 South Central dist., adv. council 1968—), Nat. French Honor Soc., AAUP, MLA, Mo. MLA (pres. 1961-63), Central States Conf. on Teaching Fgn. Langs., Société International de la Linguistique, Linguistic Soc. Am., Fgn. Lang. Assn. Mo. (v.p. 1973, sec. 4-Coll. Consortium (Webster, Fontbonne, Maryville and Lindenwood) 1972-73), Centro Studie Scambi Internazionali (mem. internat. com.), Smithsonian Instn. Nat. Assos., Internat. Platform Assn., Pi Delta Phi, Alpha Sigma Nu. Club: St. Louis University Faculty Women's (pres. 1956-58, dir. 1959—, v.p. 1983-84). Extensive travel for ednl. and linguistic research. Home: 526 Oakwood Ave Webster Groves MO 63119 Office: Internat Programs St Louis U 220 N Grand Blvd Saint Louis MO 63103

DYCHTWALD, MADELYN KENT, film and video producer; b. Newark, Feb. 13, 1952; s. Stanley and Sally Susan (Gordet) Kent; m. James Gregory Asher, Dec. 1, 1974 (div. 1977); m. Kenneth Mark Dychtwald, Nov. 24, 1983. Student in media communications, U. Wis.-Madison, 1968-70; B.A., NYU, 1974. Actress, N.Y.C. and Los Angeles, 1974-83; dir. spl. projects Dychtwald & Assocs., Emeryville, Calif., 1983-86; dir. communications Age Wave, Inc., Emeryville, 1986—. Producer slide shows, video. Author, editor: New Images of Aging, forthcoming. Mem. Screen Actor's Guild, Am. Fedn. TV and Radio Actors, Am. Film Inst., Nat. Assn. Female Execs. Avocations: movies; reading; skiing; snorkeling; swimming. Home: 1023 Amito Ave Berkeley CA 94705 Office: Age Wave Inc 1900 Powell St #700 Emeryville CA 94608

DYE, ANNA MARIA JAWORSKI, English as a second language educator; b. Newark, Apr. 26, 1953; d. Zbigniew Stanislaw and Teresa Marianna (Pekacka) Jaworski; m. Dana Blair Dye, Dec. 30, 1978; children—Thomas Blair, Adam Blair. A.B., Rutgers U., 1975, M.Ed., 1978. Instr., curriculum developer English as a second lang. Piscataway Twp. Schs., N.J., 1976-77, mem. parents' adv. council, 1976-77; instr. coordinator English as a second lang. Houston Ind. Sch. Dist., 1978-80; instr. intensive English program U. Tex., Austin, 1985—. Mem. Tchrs. of English to Speakers of Other Langs., Phi Delta Kappa. Avocations: travel; learning languages; swimming; volleyball.

DYER, DOLORES, psychologist; b. Ft. Worth; d. William Leon and Frances Louise (Cargill) D.; B.A. with highest honors, N. Tex. State U., 1963; grad. (scholar) So. Meth. U. Grad. Sch., 1964-65; Ph.D. (fellow), Southwestern Med. Sch., U. Tex., Dallas, 1973; m. Mark Howard Perkins; children—Michael Dexter Allen, Benjamin Seth Dyer Perkins, Eden Dyer Perkins. Adminstr., Child and Adolescent Community Mental Health Center, Dallas, 1969-70; asst. to dir. Dallas County Mental Health and Mental Retardation Center, 1970-73, project dir. Dallas County Comprehensive Child Care Program, 1973; dir. Dallas Commn. on Children and Youth, 1974; pvt. practice psychology, Dallas, 1975—; former tchr. Adult Sch. Continuing Edn., So. Meth. U.; mem. clin. adv. bd., bd. dirs. Suicide Prevention Center of Dallas; trainer group tng. program Dallas Group Psychotherapy Soc. Mem. children and youth adv. com. Dallas Office of Human Devel., 1974-76; bd. dirs. Dallas County Mental Health Assn., Dallas Area Women's Polit. Caucus, 1982—; mem. steering com. Dallas Women's Issues Congress; mem. adv. bd. Women's Ctr. of Dallas; mem. Health and Human Services Commn., Dallas. Mem. Am. Psychol. Assn., Dallas Psychol. Assn., Tex. Psychol. Assn., Am., Southwest, Dallas group psychotherapy assns., Am., Dallas socs. clin. hypnosis, Women's Coalition Dallas. Democrat. Clubs: The 500 Inc. Home: 4031 Inwood Rd Dallas TX 75209 Office: 2505 Wycliff Dallas TX 75219

DYER, DORIS ANNE, nurse; b. Washington, Jan. 14, 1944; d. William Edward and Helen Gertrude (Smith) Swain; R.N., Sibley Nursing Sch., Washington, 1964; B.S., Am. U., 1966, M.Ed., 1969; m. Robert Francis Dyer, Jr., June 27, 1970; children—Robert Francis, William Edward, Anne-Marie Helen Sallie, Scott Robertson McGavin. Mem. staff emergency medicine dept. George Washington U. Hosp., 1960-69, emergency specialist protective services clinic, 1967-70, adminstr. asst. to dir. clinic, 1970-78. Cubscout leader Boy Scouts Am., 1979—. Trinity Coll. scholar, 1960; Lucy Webb Hayes scholar, 1964; recipient Martha Washington award Md. Soc. SAR, 1977; Washington medal, 1984; decorated comdr. Order of St. Lazarus; created dame Order of Sovereign Mil. Order. Mem. Am., D.C. nurses assns., Am. Acad. Ambulatory Nursing Adminstrs., Washington Med.-Surg. Soc. Aux. (pres.), Am. U. Grads. Assn., DAR, Washington Assembly. Clubs: Washington, Annapolis Yacht, Kenwood Golf and Country. Author: Say Ah, 1971; also articles. Address: 5608 Albia Rd Bethesda MD 20816

DYER, GERALDINE ANN, artist; b. Bklyn., Nov. 4, 1921; d. Edward and Chattie (Holmes) Bingham; m. Ralph Dyer, Oct. 1956. Student N.Y. Phoenix

Sch. Design, N.Y.C., 1946-48, Bklyn. Mus. Art Sch., 1959. Commd. with U.S. Coast Guard, 1941-79. Exhibited in one-woman shows Henry Hicks Gallery, N.Y.C., 1978-79, 81, Womanart Gallery, N.Y.C., 1980, Keane Mason Gallery, N.Y.C., 1981, Esta Robinson Gallery, N.Y.C., 1983, Brooklyn Heights Br. Library, Bklyn., 1986; represented in permanent collection Samuel Schulman Inst., Bklyn. Mem. Womeninterart Ctr., Drawing Ctr., Nat. Assn. Female Execs., also galleries, mus. Club: Officers (N.Y.C.). Avocation: writing poetry.

DYER, JANICE RAE MOSER, entertainment company executive; b. Lynwood, Calif., Sept. 14, 1946; d. Raymond Paul and Verena Clara (Wemhoff) Moser; B.S., U. So. Calif., 1968; m. John Lockwood Dyer, Dec. 15, 1973. In charge staff auditor Price Waterhouse & Co., Los Angeles, 1968-72; controller Mor-Win Products, Inc., Los Angeles, 1972-73, Monogram/Custom Craft, Culver City, Calif., 1973-76; chief fin. officer, corp. sec. Photo-Sonic's, Inc., Burbank, Calif., 1976-84, Instrumentation Mktg. Corp., Burbank, 1976-84, Photo Digitizing Systems, Inc., 1979-84; v.p., controller Embassy Home Entertainment, Century City, Calif., 1984—. C.P.A., Calif. Mem. Am. Inst. C.P.A.s, Am. Women's Soc. C.P.A.s, Calif. Soc. C.P.A.s, Am. Mgmt. Assn., Nat. Assn. Accts., U. So. Calif. Alumni Assn., Alpha Chi Omega, Beta Alpha Psi, Phi Chi Theta. Office: Embassy Home Entertainment 1901 Ave of the Stars Century City CA 90067

DYKE, NANCY BEARG, U.S. govt. ofcl; b. Mpls., Feb. 11, 1947; d. Richard W. and Hildegarde V. Bearg; B.A., Williamette U. 1969, M.P.A. Harvard U. 1978; m. Charles W. Dyke, June 22, 1980; 2 daus. With U.S. Dept. State, 1969; with NSC, 1969-70; mem. profl. staff com. on armed services U.S. Senate 1970-75; analyst Congressional Budget Office 1975-77; dir. policy analysis for N. East, Africa and South Asia, U.S. Dept. Def. 1978-79; dep. asst. sec. of air force 1980; asst. to v.p. for nat. security affairs The White House, Washington 1981-82; mem. Army Sci. Bd. Recipient Sec. Def. Meritorious Civilian Service medal 1979, Air Force Exceptional Civilian Service award 1980. Contbr. in field. Home: Office of Comdg Gen US Army Japan IX Corps San Francisco CA 96343

DYKEMAN, ALICE MARIE, public relations executive; b. Fremont, Nebr., May 18; d. Cecil V. and Dorothy Lillian (Sillik) Jansen; children—David Clair, Cinda Cecille. Student Nebr. Wesleyan U., 1949-50, So. Meth. U., 1960-69. Women's editor, feature writer Fremont Guide and Tribune, also Biloxi Daily Herald, Miss., 1950-55; adminstrv. asst. A. Harris & Co. (now part of Sanger-Harris), Dallas, 1957-60; account exec. Contact Corp., Dallas, 1960-61; pub. relations dir. Methodist Hosp. Dallas, 1961-72; regional pub. info. officer SBA, Dallas, 1972-74; founder, pres. Dykeman Assocs., Inc., pub. relations consultants, Dallas, 1974—; adj. prof. U. Dallas Grad. Sch. Mgmt., Irving, 1972-78; guest lectr. various colls. and univs.; speaker before numerous profl. and civic groups. Contbr. articles to bus., hosp. and ch. jours.; writer-producer slide-films, filmstrips and videotapes. Mem. fgn. visitors com. Dallas Council on World Affairs, 1962—; mem. Dallas Pub. Health Bd., 1972-74, Dallas-Urban Rehab. Standards Bd., 1981-83, Econ. Devel. Adv. Bd. City of Dallas, 1983-86; mem. pub. relations com. Dallas-Ft. Worth Fed. Exec. Bd., 1973; mem. Tex. Gov.'s Council on Small Bus., 1980-81. Mem. Pub. Relations Soc. Am. (accredited; mem. numerous nat. coms.; chairperson SW Dist. 1965-72; bd. dirs. N.Tex. chpt. 1966-72, chpt. pres. 1969), Nat. Assn. Women Bus. Owners, North Dallas C. of C., Dallas C. of C. Clubs: Press of Dallas (Headliner 1975, 76, 83, 85, bd. dirs. 1981-83), Rep. Men's, Premier. Avocations: swimming, dancing, yardwork. Office: Dykeman Assocs Inc 4205 Herschel St Dallas TX 75219

DYKEMAN, WILMA, author, educator; b. Asheville, N.C., May 20, 1920; d. Willard J. and Bonnie (Cole) Dykeman; B.S. in Speech, Northwestern U., 1940; Litt.D., Maryville Coll., 1974; L.H.D., Tenn. Wesleyan Coll., 1978; m. James R. Stokely Jr., Oct. 12, 1940; children—Dykeman Cole, James R. III. Lectr. English dept. U. Tenn., Knoxville, 1975—, adj. prof., 1985—; columnist Knoxville News-Sentinel, 1962—; historian State of Tenn., 1980—; author 14 books including: The French Broad: A Rivers of America Volume, 1955, The Tall Woman, 1962, Seeds of Southern Change, 1962, The Far Family, 1966, Return the Innocent Earth, 1973, others; co-author: Neither Black Nor White, 1957; Tennessee: A Bicentennial History, 1976; Explorations, a collection of essays, 1984; contbr. articles to nat. mags. Ency. Brit.; nat. lectr. in field; dir. Merchants & Planters Bank. Trustee Berea Coll., 1971—, Phelps Stokes Fund, 1981—, U. N.C.-Asheville, 1985—. Guggenheim fellow, 1956-57, NEH fellow, 1976-77; recipient Hillman award, 1967; N.C. Gold medal for Contbn. to Am. letters, 1985. Mem. PEN, Authors Guild, So. Hist. Assn., Phi Beta Kappa, Sigma Delta Chi. Home: 405 Clifton Heights Newport TN 37821

DYM, FRAN GLORIA, public relations consultant; b. N.Y.C.; d. Aaron and Goldie (Lustig) D.; m. Henry V. Goldstein, Feb. 13, 1958 (div. Dec. 1972); children—Janet, Jonathan. B.A., Hunter Coll., 1976; postgrad. NYU, 1976-78. Vice-pres. Kalmus Corp., N.Y.C., 1965-77, Keller Haver Advt., N.Y.C., 1978-79; sr. v.p. Daniel S. Roher, Inc., N.Y.C., 1979-83; pres. Dym/SR&A, Inc., N.Y.C., 1983—; cons. KLH R&D Corp., Canoga Park, Calif., 1979-82, Bang & Olufsen of Am., Mount Prospect, Ill., 1980, dbx, Inc., Newton, Mass., 1979—, Studer Revox of Am., Inc., Nashville, 1982—, Sparkomatic Corp., Milford, Pa., 1983—, Inter-Link Technology, Ltd., London, 1984—, Altec Lansing Consumer Products, Milford, 1986—, Finial Tech., Sunnyvale, Calif., 1986—, Lexicon Inc., Waltham, Mass., 1984—. Contbr. articles to profl. jours. Mem. Nat. Assn. Female Execs., Audio Engrng. Soc., Internat. Motor Press Assn., Am. Women's Econ. Devel. Corp., Roosevelt Island Residents Assn. Office: Dym/SR&A Inc 355 Lexington Ave New York NY 10017

DYME, ROCHELLE SECEMSKY, lawyer; b. Chgo., June 11, 1955; d. Morris and Emma (Kleiman) Secemsky; m. Bernard Samuel Dyme, Aug. 20, 1978; children—Jason Ross, Michael Scott. B.A. cum laude with distinction in English, U. Ill., 1976; J.D., Northwestern U., 1979. Bar: Ill. 1979; U.S. Dist. Ct. (no. dist.) Ill. 1979, also trial bar 1983. Ptnr. firm Rosenthal & Schanfield, Chgo., 1979—. Mem. Chgo. Bar Assn., Women's Bar Assn. Ill., Chgo. Council Lawyers, Lawyers Alliance for Nuclear Arms Control, Assn. Children of Holocaust Survivors, Phi Kappa Phi. Office: Rosenthal & Schanfield 55 E Monroe St Chicago IL 60603

DY-RAGOS, LYDIA SY, investment company executive; b. Manila, Apr. 17, 1946; came to U.S., 1969; d. Thomas Tan and Maxima Co (Uy) Syling; B.S. in Bus. Adminstrn., St. Scholastica Coll., 1968; m. Ramon R. Dy-Ragos, June 28, 1969; children—R. Leonard, Julian B., Phillip L., Mark J. Credit/collection Sy Ling Chong Sons, Manila, part-time 1965-68, controller, 1968-69; mktg. researcher Va. Nat. Bank, Charlottesville, 1969-70; bus. mgr., corp. sec. Ramon R. Dy-Ragos M.D., Inc., Kansas City, Mo., 1977—; mng. partner D.T.K. Investment Co., Kansas City, Mo., 1978—, H.D.H. Investment Co., 1980—. Charter mem. Nat. Bank in North Kansas City Women's Adv. Council, 1978; mem. North Kansas City Meml. Hosp. Aux., 1981—; 1st dist. dir. Mo. State Med. Assn. Aux., 1983-85; council mem. St. Therese Roman Cath. Ch., 1978-79, social chmn., 1978-79. Recipient Recognition cert. Bicentennial Ethnic Heritage Community Plan, 1976, Appreciation cert. St. Therese Ch., 1979. Mem. Filipino Assn. Greater Kansas City (social chmn. 1975, ways and means chmn. 1981, Appreciation award 1981), Clay County Med. Assn. Aux. (pres. 1982, county rep. to AMA Aux. 1981). Office: D T K Investment Co Northwoods Office Park 5700 N Broadway Kansas City MO 64118

DYSON, ANNE ELIZABETH, pediatrician, foundation executive; b. White Plains, N.Y., Nov. 30, 1947; d. Charles Henry and Margaret Helen (Macgregor) D.; m. Roger Harold Hull, July 4, 1980. A.A., Bennett Coll., Millbrook, N.Y., 1967; B.A., NYU, 1969; M.D., N.Y. Med. Coll., Valhalla, 1977. Diplomate Am. Bd. Pediatrics, Nat. Bd. Med. Examiners. Intern, St. Christopher's Hosp., Phila., 1977-78; guest investigator Rockefeller U., N.Y.C., 1978-79; resident in pediatrics N.Y. Hosp.-Cornell U. Med. Ctr., N.Y.C., 1979-80; fellow in pediatrics Upstate Med. Ctr., Syracuse, N.Y., 1980-81; asst. prof. clin. pediatrics U. Ill. Coll. Medicine, Rockford, 1982—; adj. asst. prof. pediatrics, clin. affiliate Cornell U. Med. Ctr., N.Y.C., 1983—; pres. Dyson Found., 1979—; chmn. exec. com., dir. Esterline Corp., Darien, Conn.; dir. Dyson-Kissner-Moran Corp., N.Y.C. Bd. dirs. Planned Parenthood N.Y.C., 1982; mem. corp. Dana-Farber Cancer Inst., Boston, 1980; mem. council Rockefeller U., N.Y.C., 1983; health adv. com. Head Start of Rock and Walworth Counties, Wis., 1982. Fellow Am. Acad. Pediatrics; mem. Wis. Med. Soc., Rock County Med. Soc. Democrat.

DYSON, LUCINDA STEDFELD, real estate developer; b. Burbank, Calif., Dec. 21, 1951; d. Rowland Reroy Stedfeld and Marilyn Ann (Mercier) Wetzler; m. John William Dyson, Jr., Nov. 6, 1982 (div. 1985). B.S.B.A. in Stats., Econs., Butler U., 1973. Lic. real estate broker, N.C., S.C., Va.; accredited personnel mgr.; cert. shopping ctr. mgr. Buyer trainee L.S. Ayres & Co., Indpls., 1973-74; property mgr., leasing mgr. Centennial Properties, Dallas, 1974; asst. to v.p., tech. specialist, community mgr. Paragon Group, Inc. Charlotte, N.C., 1974-79, dir. personnel, 1979-83, dir. comml. mgmt., 1982-84; project mgr. John Crosland & Assoc., Charlotte, 1984—; treas. Charlotte Apt. Assn., 1984-84. Mem. Bldg. Owners and Mgrs. Assn. (sec. 1984—), Internat. Council Shopping Ctrs., Charlotte C. of C. (econ. devel. com. 1985). Republican. Avocations: golf; boating. Home: 707 Rome Ct Charlotte NC 28209 Office: John Crosland-Erwin Assocs 125 Scaleybark Rd Charlotte NC 28209

DZAMAN, FERN LORETTA, publishing company executive; b. Decker, Man., Can., Apr. 25, 1932; came to U.S., 1968, resident, 1968; d. Alfred Ernest and Euretta Jane (Doupe) Lints; grad. Man. Tchrs. Coll., 1952; postgrad U. Man., 1953-54, U. Sask, 1958; m. Russell Dzaman, July 2, 1953; children—Randall, Julie, Lesa, Kenneth, Grant.; Tchr. schs. Winnipeg and Flin Flon, Man. and Estevan, Sask., Can., 1952-62; co-pub. Estevan Sun, 1962-68; exec. dir. public relations Spears Chiropractic Hosp., Denver, 1973-84; founder, pres. WWIC Internat. Pub. Co., Littleton, Colo., 1976—. Active PTA. Mem. Chiropractic Editors Guild, Assn. History of Chiropractic (founding). Clubs: Lions Women's Aux. Home: 3152 E Weaver Ave Littleton CO 80121 Office: PO Box 2615 Littleton CO 80161

DZIEDZIC, INGEBORG SVETLANA, ophthalmologist; b. Zagreb, Yugoslavia, June 6, 1952; came to U.S., 1970; d. Svetozar and Ivanka (Uhrl) Vlascic; m. John David Dziedzic, Feb. 9, 1974; children—John Jr., Stephan, Michael. Student Atlantic Coll. (Gt. Britain), 1968-70; B.S., Fordham U., 1974; M.D., Albert Einstein Sch. Medicine, Yeshiva U., 1979. Intern pediatrics Med. Coll. Pa., Phila., 1979-80; resident in ophthalmology Montefiore Hosp., N.Y.C., 1980-83; practice medicine specializing in ophthalmology, Yorktown Heights, N.Y., 1983-84, Pleasantville, N.Y., 1984—. Mem. Am. Acad. Ophthamology, Phi Beta Kappa. Roman Catholic. Office: 320 Manville Rd Pleasantville NY 10570

EADS, LINDA SUSAN, lawyer; b. Pitts., Nov. 24, 1949; d. James Thomas and Georgette (Camberis) E. B.A., Am. U., 1971; J.D., U. Tex., 1975. Bar: Tex. 1975, D.C. 1976. Atty., D.C. Superior Ct., Washington, 1975-77; trial atty. tax div. criminal sect. Dept. Justice, Washington, 1977-83, tax div. tax shelter unit, 1983—; mem. civil rules com. D.C. Superior Ct., 1977—. Named Outstanding Atty., Dept. Justice, 1981, recipient Spl. Commendation award tax div., 1983. Mem. Assn. Trial Lawyers Am., ABA, State Bar Tex., Bar Assn. D.C. Democrat. Home: 6443 Del Norte Dallas TX 75225

EADS, M. ADELA, state legislator; b. Mar. 2, 1920. Mem. Conn. Ho. of Reps., from 1976; now mem. Conn. Senate. Republican. Mem. Conn. Bd. Edn., 1972-76. Office: Conn Senate State Capitol Hartford CT 06106*

EAGLEN, AUDREY BERYL, librarian; b. Cleve., Oct. 22, 1930; d. Harold G. and Gertrude E. Eaglen. B.S., John Carroll U.; M.A., U. Chgo. Tchr. pub. schs., Cleve., 1950-63; lang. arts cons. Reardon-Baer Pub. Co., Cleve., 1963-67; research assoc. Ednl. Research Council Am., Cleve., 1967-70; acquisitions librarian Cuyahoga County Pub. Library, Cleve., 1970—; vis. asst. prof. Kent State U. (Ohio), 1982—. Author: Judy Blume: A Critical Study, 1984; author, editor: (text book series) Concepts and Inquiry Series, 1967-70; editor Top of the News, 1977-83; contbr. articles to profl. jours. Trustee, Cleve. Rape Crisis Ctr., 1976-78. Mem. ALA (councilor 1982-86) pres. Young Adult Services div. 1981-82). Office: Cuyahoga Public Library 4510 Memphis Ave Cleveland OH 44144

EARHART, EILEEN MAGIE, educator; b. Hamilton, Ohio, Oct. 21, 1928; d. Andrew J. and Martha (Waldorf) Magie; B.S., Miami U., Oxford, Ohio, 1950, H.H.D. (hon.), 1980; M.Ed. in Elem. Edn. and Adminstrn., Mich. State U., East Lansing, 1962, Ph.D. in Edn., 1969; m. Paul G. Earhart; children—Anthony G., Bruce P., Daniel T. Tchr. home econs. West Alexandria Schs., 1950-51; elementary tchr. Waterford Twp. Schs., Pontiac, Mich., 1958-65, reading specialist, 1965-67; chmn. family and child ecology dept. Mich. State U., 1974-83, prof., 1968-84; prof. head dept. home and family life Fla. State U., 1984—. Mem. adv. bd. Lansing Com. on Children's TV; bd. dirs. Women's Resource Center, Grand Rapids, Mich. Named a leader in home econs. Am. Home Econs. Assn., 1984. Mem. Soc. Research in Child Devel., AAUW, Nat. Assn. Edn. Young Children, Assn. Childhood Edn. Internat., Am. Home Econs. Assn., Am. Ednl. Research Assn., Internat. Fedn. for Home Econs., Internat. Reading Assn., Am. Vocat. Assn., Nat. Council Family Relations, Fla. Council on Family Relations (pres. 1986-87), Mich. Home Econs. Assn. (pres. 1980-82), Assn. Supervision and Curriculum Devel., Delta Kappa Gamma., Phi Kappa Phi, Omicron Nu (advisor 1984-87). Author: Building the Child's Learning Skills; Attention and Classification Training Curriculum; many others; assoc. editor Family Relations, 1980—; co-editor spl. issue The Family with Handicapped Members, 1984; mem. editorial bd. Home Econs. Research Jour., 1984-85; reviewer Home Econs. Research Jour., 1982—. Home: 3717 Galway Dr Tallahassee FL 32308 Office: Home and Family Life Dept 222 Sandels Bldg Coll Home Econs Fla State U Tallahassee FL 32306

EARLY, TERI (DENISE) WILSON, financial representative, educator; b. Jacksonville, Ill., Sept. 3, 1952; d. Arthur Amos and LaVada Inez (Norton) W.; m. Lorenzo E. Early, Dec. 28, 1984. 1 son, Bill Duane (dec.). B.S., No. Ill. U., 1973, M.S., 1974. Head Start tng. and tech. grad. asst. No. Ill. U., DeKalb, 1973-74; tchr. 2d grade North Chicago (Ill.) Dist. 64, 1974-75; Head Start site administr. Archdiocese Bd. Edn., Chgo., 1975-76; Head Start tchr. Denver Pub. Schs., 1976-77; tchr., dir. Met. State Coll., Denver, 1977; instr. Community Coll. Denver, 1980; toddler day-care dir. Denver Pub. Schs., 1977-80, tchr. 4th grade, 1980-81, kindergarten tchr., 1981-85; fin. rep. Equitable Fin. Services, 1985-86. Mem. Gov.'s Subcom. on Infants and Toddlers, State of Colo., 1979-80. Women's equity grantee Far West Labs, 1982. Mem. Nat. Assn. Edn. Young Children, Denver Classroom Tchrs. Assn., Black Educators United Den Co., Alpha Kappa Alpha, Pi Lamba Theta. Methodist. Home: 4477 Mentone #202 San Diego CA 92107 Office: Imperial Bank 701 B St Suite 855 San Diego CA 92101

EARMAN, VELMA PORTER, lighting fixture designer, consultant; b. New Orleans, July 31, 1910; d. Albert Arthur and Mabel (Long) Porter; m. John William Hulsey, Feb. 18, 1933 (dec. 1957); children—Carroll Joan, Gloria Faye; m. Clarence G. Earman, Jr., Sept. 23, 1963. Student So. Meth. U., 1928-30, Dallas Art Inst., 1930-31. Free-lance fashion designer, Dallas, 1930-33; tchr. art and Spanish lang., Dallas Pub. Schs., 1933-36; owner, contractor Hulsey Constrn. Co., Dallas, 1936-57; owner, designer A.A. Porter Lighting Co., Inc., Dallas, 1958—; cons. in field. Campaign worker Dallas Republican party. Christian Scientist. Avocation: gardening.

EARNEST, MARIAN, art museum administrator, historian, researcher; b. Lamesa, Tex., Mar. 7, 1954; d. J.R. and Kathryn (Oliver) E. B.A. in Art History, So. Meth. U., 1979; postgrad. Sotheby's (London), 1979-80, Hunter Coll., 1980-82, Salzburg Seminar (Austria), 1984. Asst. to coordinator membership vols. Met. Mus. Art, N.Y.C., 1981-84; McDermott intern for adminstrn. Dallas Mus. Art, 1984—; researcher. Mem. Am. Mus. Assn., Coll. Art Assn.

EARNSHAW, JOAN SALISBURY, government revenue agent; b. Billings, Mont., Jan. 16, 1943; d. Donovan Dee and Florence (Chandler) Salisbury; m. Joseph B. Earnshaw, Mar. 27, 1965; children—Deborah, Mary. Student Mont. State U., 1960-61, Brigham Young U., 1961-62, Ariz. State Coll. (now. No. Ariz. U.), spring 1963, spring 1964, U. Calif.-Berkeley, 1971—; student in bus. adminstrn. Thomas Edison State Coll., 1980—. Acctg. clk. Nat. Park Service, Yellowstone Nat. Park, 1960-67; clk. IRS, Phoenix, 1974-75, tax auditor, Phoenix, 1975-78; tax auditor, Farmington, N. Mex., 1978-84, revenue agt., 1984—, also site dir. Vol. Income Tax Assistance, Phoenix, 1977, Vol. Income Tax Assistance instr., Farmington, 1979—; various TV and radio appearances for IRS, 1979—; mem. speakers panel San Juan Coll., Farmington, 1980—, mem. adv. bd. dept. acctg., 1984—. Leader, fundraiser Campfire, Fontana, Calif., then Phoenix, 1971-78; fundraiser for schs., ch., 1973—; mem. Community Action Council, Phoenix, 1975-78. Recipient Wakan award Camp Fire, 1977, Performance award IRS, 1981, Spl. Act award IRS, 1982. Mem. Sodality of Our Lady Club. Democrat. Roman Catholic. Avocations: building underground home; herb gardening; sewing; historical research. Office: IRS 3539 E 39th Farmington NM 87401

EARP, BRENDA CAROL, med. technologist; b. Lafe, Ark., Aug. 25, 1946; d. A.G. Harrison and Clarice Beatrice (Harris) Earp; A.S., Mott Community Coll., 1966; A.B., U. Mich., 1969; cert. Hurley Med. Center Sch. Med. Technology, 1970. Lab. asst. Dr. F.W. Baske, Flint, Mich., 1966-68; substitute tchr. Flint Community Schs., 1969; med. technologist microchemistry lab. Hurley Med. Center, Flint, 1970—; lectr. in field. Vol. ARC. Named Hurley Med. Center Employee of Month, 1976, of Yr., 1977; Brenda Earp Day proclaimed by mayor of Flint, 1977. Mem. U. Mich. Alumni Assn., Hurley Med. Center Med. Technologist Orgn., Am. Soc. Clin. Pathologists. Democrat. Baptist. Contbr. articles to profl. jours. Home: 652 Vermilya Ave Flint MI 48507 Office: 1 Hurley Plaza Flint MI 48502

EASBEY, MARION MORIARTY, former telephone co. mgr.; b. New Bedford, Mass., Apr. 8, 1930; d. Walter Vincent and Marion Elizabeth (Rigby) Moriarty; B.S., U. R.I., 1947-51; student Bell Cor Tech. Edn. Center, 1973—. Service rep. N.E. Telephone & Northwestern Bell, Providence and St. Paul, 1952-58; office supr. Northwestern Bell, St. Paul, 1958-63, engrng. staff asst., 1963-64; engrng. technician, asso. engr. and engr. Northwestern Bell, St. Paul and N.E. Telephone, Providence, 1967-79, project mgr. N.E. Telephone, Framingham, Mass., 1979-86; engr. chief clk. Northwestern Bell, 1964-67. Practical politics instr. St. Paul C. of C., 1970; Lake Elmo Precinct chmn. and county conv. del., 1973; 1st lt., adj., fiscal officer, personnel officer CAP, 1953-69. Recipient cert. of Accomplishment, CAP, 1968, cert. of Merit, 1968. Mem. Common Cause (state network chmn. 1976-79), Assn. Mgmt. Women, Nat. Assn. Female Execs., AAUW, ACLU, NOW. Democrat Unitarian. Club: Appalachian Mountain. Home: 100 Girard Rd Cumberland RI 02864

EASLEY, BETTY, state legislator; b. Victoria, Tex., Aug. 5, 1929; d. Clifford Pennington and Inez (Cary) Chapman; student U. Tex., 1947-49; B.A. in Pub. Adminstrn., Eckerd Coll., 1984; m. Kenneth E. Easley, Nov. 11, 1966; children—Cary, Barbara, Katherine, Virginia, William (dec.). Med. illustrator Walter Reed Med. Center, Washington, 1952-55; owner B&K Acctg. System, Tampa, Fla., 1962-66; newspaper columnist, Clearwater, Fla., 1969-72; mem. Fla. Ho. of Reps., 1972-86, minority leader pro tempore, 1984-86, mem. subcom. on edn. appropriations com. fin. and taxation com. transp. com., rules com. Vice chmn. Fla. Human Relations Commn., 1974-75; women's chmn. United Cerebral Palsy of Fla., 1973-75; mem. Fla. State Adv. Com. on U.S. Commn. Civil Rights, 1972-74, Pinellas County Met. Criminal Justice Planning Unit, 1972-80; bd. dirs. Morton Plant Hosp., 1984—, Eckerd Coll., 1985—; mem. U.S. Intergovtl. Policy Adv. Com., 1984—, U.S. Comml. Motor Vehicle Safety Regulatory Rev. Panel, 1985—, U.S. Adv. Council on Edn. Stats., 1984-85; mem. Intergovtl. Adv. Council on Edn., 1986—; co-chmn. Fla. Reagan-Bush, 1984; del. Republican Nat. Conv., 1976, 84; chmn. Pinellas Legis. Del., 1978-79; mem. Dist. V Mental Health Bd., 1974-78; bd. dirs. Upper Pinellas Assn. for Retarded Citizens, 1984—; mem. Women's Living and Learning Program Adv. Council, Fla. State Panel Am. Council on Edn., Fed. Edn. Data Acquisition Council. Recipient legis. award, Property Appraiser's Assn. Fla., 1981, presdl. award, 1981; legis. awards Fla. Phosphate Council, 1982, Juvenile Welfare Bd., 1976, Commn. on Human Rights, 1977, Fla. Assn. Community Colls., 1977, 80, 83, 84; TIGER award, 1977, 79, 80, 81; Fla. Sch. Bd. Assn. award, 1979, 80, 81, 82, 84; Friend of Edn. award, Pinellas Classroom Tchrs. Assn., 1980, 82; Gavel of Authority award Fla. Assn. Sch. Adminstrs., 1981, 82, 84; Allen Morris award, 1981; named rep. of year Fla. Assn. Community Colls., 1979, 81, 82, 84; nominated Most Valuable Mem. of the House, St. Petersburg Times, 1979, 80; Legislator of Yr. award Nat. Rep. Legislators Assn., 1983; Legis. award for disting. service Fla. Vocat. Assn., 1983, 84; Rep. Leadership award, 1984; Outstanding Layman award Phi Delta Kappa, 1983; service award Fla. Assn. Broadcasters, 1985; PACE award Pinellas Emergency Mental Health Services, 1985. Mem. Bus. and Profl. Women's Club, Fla. Fedn. Rep. Women's Clubs, Nat. Order Women Legislators (pres. 1982-83), Nat. Conf. State Legislators (SFA vice chmn.), Nat. Rep. Legislators Assn. (treas.), Beta Sigma Phi, Phi Theta Kappa. Episcopalian. Clubs: Zonta, Suncoast Tiger Bay. Office: 12800 Indian Rocks Rd Largo FL 33544

EASLEY, ELEANOR LUCIE, social worker; b. Atmore, Ala., Feb. 14, 1950; d. Anselm Thedford and Sara Ella (Stewart) Easley; B.S., Judson Coll., 1971; M.R.E., So. Bapt. Theol. Sem., 1974; M.S.W., U. Louisville, Kent Sch. Social Work, 1975; doctoral student U. Ala. Asst. social worker Norton Psychiat. Clinic, Louisville, 1973-75; mem. faculty So. Bapt. Theol. Sem., Louisville, 1975-82, asst. prof. social work edn., 1976-82. Bd. dirs. Hospice of Louisville, Inc.; mem. adv. com. Can Surmount; mem. allocation com. Metro United Way. Recipient Kentuckiana Metroversity Instructional Devel. award, 1979. Mem. Nat. Assn. Social Workers, Acad. Cert. Social Workers, So. Bapt. Social Services Assn. Democrat. Baptist. Home: 1002 N White Ave Bay Minette AL 36502

EAST, DOROTHY GAIL, school counselor; b. Atlanta, Oct. 16, 1940; d. Robert Leon and Verna Dorothy (Bryce) Gordon; A.B., Emory U., 1962; M.Ed., Ga. State U., 1972; m. Donald Paul East, July 15, 1962. Tchr. English, then tchr. remedial reading Forest Park (Ga.) Jr. High Sch., 1962-69; tchr. English, Morrow (Ga.) Jr. High Sch., 1969-70, guidance counselor, 1970—, chmn. English dept., 1966-70. Mem. Am., Ga. sch. counselors assns., Am. Personnel and Guidance Assn., PTA. Episcopalian. Home: 166 Foster Dr McDonough GA 30253 Office: Morrow Jr High Sch Maddox Rd Morrow GA 30260

EASTERBROOK, HELEN LOUISE, bank officer; b. Cowles, Nebr., Feb. 2, 1917; d. Jesse M. and Lora Belle (Holland) Marsh; A.B., Hastings (Nebr.) Coll., 1938; M.S. in Edn., Kearney (Nebr.) State Coll., 1961; m. Carl W. Easterbrook, May 25, 1940; 1 dau., Leslie Eileen Easterbrook Holchak. Tchr. English, Nebr. high schs., 1939-58, Lab. Sch., U. No. Colo., Greeley, 1963-65; instr. English, Kearney State Coll., 1960-72; trust adminstrn. officer Platte Valley State Bank & Trust Co., Kearney, 1973-83. Mem. Nat. Assn. Bank Women (pres. Central Nebr. Group 1980-81), Am. Inst. Banking. Presbyterian. Home: 3117 10th Ave Kearney NE 68847

EASTERDAY, VICKIE VOELLER, advertising account executive; b. Columbus, Ohio, Feb. 15, 1952; d. Leon Henry and Laura Elizabeth (McCoy) Voeller; m. William Stephen Easterday, Sept. 7, 1974. B.A. in Communications, Ohio State U. Asst. mktg. officer Ohio Fed. Savs. and Loan, Columbus, 1974-78, personnel officer, 1978-80, mktg. officer, 1978-82; dir. mktg. Mid-Am. Fed., Columbus, 1982-85; account exec. JAM and Corbett Advt., Columbus, 1985—; instr. Inst. Fin. Edn., 1978—. Trustee Mid-Ohio Multiple Sclerosis Soc., Columbus, 1983-85, Days of Creative Arts Program for Kids, Columbus, 1985—. Mem. Am. Mktg. Assn., 1988 Columbus U.S.A. Assn. (bd. dirs. 1986—), Fin. Instns. Mktg. Assn., Columbus Advt. Fedn. (bd. dirs. 1984—, Outstanding Performance award 1985). Democrat. Home: 195 S Riverview St Dublin OH 43017 Office: JAM & Corbett Advt Co 40 S 3d St Columbus OH 43215

EASTERLY-SPENCER, BONNIE MARIETTA, lawyer; b. Jackson, Miss., Sept. 20, 1954; d. Clay Elliot and Mary (Anderson) Easterly; m. Gerald Roy Spencer, July 31, 1982. B.B.A. magna cum laude, Loyola U., New Orleans, 1976; M.B.A., 1980, J.D., 1980. Bar. Tex. 1980. Asst. atty. in contracts lease maintenance dept. Chevron USA Inc., New Orleans, 1978; mktg. asst. Gulf Coast Safety Co., Houston, 1980-82, sole practice Bonnie E. Spencer, Atty.-at-Law, Houston, 1982-86; corp./securities atty. Sonfield & Sonfield, 1986—. corp. atty., fin. cons.; dir. Spencer Engrs., Inc., Houston. Mem. Houston Rose Soc., Am. Rose Soc., Houston Grand Opera Assn., all Houston. Named Best Speaker Moot Ct. Competition, Loyola U. Sch. Law, New Orleans, 1977-78; recipient Delta Sigma Pi Outstanding Freshman award Loyola U., 1971-72. Mem. ABA, Tex. State Bar Assn., Houston Bar Assn., Houston Engrng. Sci. Soc. Aux., AIA Women's Aux. Republican. Roman Catholic. Home: 4000 Purdue Ave #115 Houston TX 77005 Office: 4041 Richmond Suite 300 Houston TX 77027

EASTLAND, MARY LOU, educator; b. McComb, Miss., July 3, 1939; d. James DeWitt and Mary Belle (Barnes) White; B.S.E., Delta State U., 1961; postgrad. U. So. Miss., 1978; m. Charles Lamar Eastland, Sr., Dec. 25, 1961; children—Charles Lamar, James Denson, Laura Lynette. Instr. phys. edn. and health El Paso (Tex.) Pub. Sch. System, 1961-62; accounts researcher, clk.-typist IRS, Jackson, Miss., 1963-65; co-owner, operator Bresler's 33 Flavors, Gulfport, Miss., 1974-76; instr. sci. Harrison County (Miss.) Sch. System, 1977-82; theater mgmt., 1982—. Active YWCA, Girl Scouts U.S., baseball and softball programs of Orange Grove Youth Assn., youth basketball program of Orange Grove C. of C. Home: 10 Edington Pl Gulfport MS 39503

EASTMAN, LINDA SUZANNE, consulting organization executive, corporate image consultant; b. Evanston, Ill., Sept. 21, 1946; d. Robert William and Ardath Louis (Stoddard) Ellis; m. Albert Henry Eastman, Nov. 20, 1971; 1 dau., Suzanne Elisabeth. Student No. Ill. U., 1965-66, U. Louisville, 1986—. Model, Jack Winter, Chgo., 1969-71, Saks Fifth Avenue, N.Y.C., 1969; stewardess Am. Airlines, Chgo. and N.Y.C., 1969-71; owner, operator Louisville Model Agy., 1973—; pres. The Profl. Woman Network, Prospect, Ky., 1981—; corp. image cons. Author: The Professional Woman; The Tean Image Guide, 1984. Mem. Nat. Assn. Female Execs., Am. Soc. Tng. and Devel., Am. Assn. Women Bus. Owners. Republican. Episcopalian. Club: Louisville Tennis. Lodge: Zonta. Avocations: tennis; water skiing. Home: 14107 Harbour Pl Prospect KY 40059 Office: The Profl Woman Network PO Box 333 Prospect KY 40059

EATON, EDNA DOROTHY, nursing administrator; b. Van Meter, Iowa, Mar. 21, 1938; d. Walter Clifford and Rosemarie Rose (Lienemann); m. Edward Eugene Eaton, July 1, 1962; children—David Clifford, Thomas Eugene. B.S.N., R.N., U. Iowa, 1961. Staff nurse Shenandoah Hosp., Iowa, 1961-62, 63-65, Hamburg Community Hosp., Iowa, 1965-73; surg. supr. Grape Community Hosp., Hamburg, 1973-79, dir. nursing, 1979—. Bd. govs. Iowa Bd. Nursing, 1984—. Named Booster of Yr., Booster Club Sidney, 1985. Republican. Lutheran. Home: Box 429 Sidney IA 51652 Office: Grape Community Hosp N Hwy 275 Hamburg IA 51640

EATON, JOANNE WALTON, lawyer, writer; b. Windsor, N.C., Nov. 17, 1936; d. John Odell and Lois (King) Walton; children—Richard E.P., John W.T., Edward V.H. Student Wake Forest Coll., 1961-62; B.A., W.Va., U., 1975, J.D., 1978. Bar: W. Va. 1978. Actress, W.Va., 1968-78; contbg. editor Victorian Poetry W.Va. U., Morgantown, 1970-75; assoc. Love, Wise, Robinson & Woodroe, Charleston, W.Va., 1978-82; adj. prof. U. Charleston, 1982—; prof. Hebei Tchrs. U., Shijiazhuang, Hebei Province, People's Republic China, 1983-84; lectr. Harvard Med. Sch., 1985—; lead articles editor W.Va. Law Rev., Morgantown, 1977-78; asst. editor Mountain State Press, Charleston, 1980-83. Bd. dirs. Women's Health Ctr., Charleston, 1980-81; bd. dirs. Legal Aid Soc., Charleston, 1980-81. Winner 1st prize Nathan Burke Competition ASCAP, W.Va., 1977; nominee for Best Supporting Actress W.Va. U., Morgantown, 1974. Mem. W.Va. State Bar Assn., ABA. Clubs: University (Wichita Falls, Tex.); Harvard (Boston). Contbr. articles to profl. jours. Home: 2100 Santa Fe #903 Wichita Falls TX 76309

EATON, LYNDA LOU, aircraft manufacturing company executive; b. Nevada, Mo., Aug. 31, 1946; d. Ira and Anna Mae (Welch) E.; B.S. in Chemistry, Central Mo. State U., Warrensburg, 1967; M.B.A., Pepperdine U., 1981; m. John C. Carlisle, Dec. 1980. Blood bank supr. St. Luke's Hosp., Kansas City, Mo., 1968-71; acting blood bank supr. Hoag Meml. Hosp., Newport Beach, Calif., 1971-72; blood bank supr. City of Hope Nat. Med. Center, Duarte, Calif., 1975-77; mgr. Immuno-Science, Inc., Los Angeles, 1977-82; materials mgr. Ortho Diagnostic Systems, Inc., Irvine, Calif., 1982-85; br. mgr. Douglas Aircraft Co., Long Beach, Calif., 1985—. Mem. Am. Soc. Clin. Pathology (med. technologist, specialist in blood banking), Am. Assn. Blood Banks, Am. Prodn. and Inventory Soc. Republican. Home: 8116 Pawtucket Dr Huntington Beach CA 92646 Office: Douglas Aircraft Co 3855 Lakewood Blvd Long Beach CA 90846

EATON, NANCY LINTON, library administrator; b. Berkeley, Calif., May 2, 1943; d. Don Thomas and Lena Ruth (McClellan) Linton; m. Edward Arthur Eaton III, June 19, 1965 (div. 1979). A.B., Stanford U., 1965; M.L.S., U. Tex., 1968, postgrad., 1968. Cataloger, head Machine Readable Cataloging unit, asst. to univ. librarian U. Tex., Austin, 1968-74; automation librarian SUNY-Stony Brook, 1974-76; head tech. services Atlanta Pub. Library, 1976-82; dir. libraries U. Vt., Burlington, 1982—; cons. in field, 1978—; evaluator Commn. on Instns. of Higher Edn., New Eng. Assn. Schs. and Colls., Winchester, Mass., 1985—. Author: (with others) Book Selection Policies in American Libraries, 1971. Editor Southwestern Library Assn. Newsletter, 1970-74. Contbr. articles to profl. jours. State of Calif. fellow, 1961-65; U. Tex. fellow, 1966-68, U.S. Office Edn. fellow, 1968. Mem. ALA, Library and Info. Tech. Assn. (pres. 1984—), Online Computerized Library Ctr. Users Council (exec. com. 1982), AAUW, Consortium of New Eng. State Univ. Libraries (chmn. 1984—). Democrat. Avocations: tennis; jogging; reading. Office: U Vt Libraries 113 Bailey/Howe Library Burlington VT 05405

EATON, PAULINE, artist; b. Neptune, N.J., Mar. 20, 1935; d. Paul A. and Florence Elizabeth (Rogers) Friedrich; m. Charles Adams Eaton, June 15, 1957; children—Gregory, Eric, Paul, Joy. B.A., Dickinson Coll., 1957; M.A., Northwestern U., 1958. Lic. instr., Calif. Instr., Mira Costa Coll., Oceanside, Calif., 1980-82, Idyllwild Sch. Music and Arts, Calif., 1983—; juror, demonstrator numerous art socs. Exhibited one-woman shows Nat. Arts Club, N.Y.C., 1977, Designs Recycled Gallery, Fullerton, Calif., 1978, 80, 84, San Diego Art Inst., 1980, Spectrum Gallery, San Diego, 1981, San Diego Jung Ctr., 1983, Marin Civic Ctr. Gallery, 1984; group shows include: Am. Watercolor Soc., 1975, 77, Butler Inst. Am. Art, Youngstown, Ohio, 1977, 78, 79, 81, NAD, 1978; represented in permanent collections including: Butler Inst. Am. Art, St. Mary's Coll., Md., Mercy Hosp., San Diego, Sharp Hosp., San Diego; work featured in books: Watercolor, The Creative Experience, 1978, Creative Seascape Painting, 1980, Painting the Spirit in Nature, 1984. Trustee San Diego Art Inst., 1977-78, San Diego Mus. Art, 1982-83. Mem. Nat. Watercolor Soc. (exhibited traveling shows 1978, 79, 83, 85), Rocky Mountain Watermedia Soc. (Golden award 1979, Mustard Seed award 1983), Nat. Soc. Painters in Acrylic and Casein (hon.), Watercolor West (Strathmore award 1979, Purchase award 1986), Marin Arts Guild (instr. 1984—), San Diego Watercolor Soc. (pres. 1976-77, workshop dir. 1977-80), Artists Equity (v.p. San Diego 1979-81), San Diego Artists Guild (pres. 1982-83), Western Fedn. Watercolor Socs. (chmn. 1983, 3d prize 1982, Grumbacher Gold medal 1983), West Coast Watercolor Soc. (exhbns. chmn. 1983—). Democrat. Presbyterian. Home: 10 Alta Mira Ave Kentfield CA 94904

EATON-BOWEN, CAROL LEAH, photographer, art educator, broker, communications consultant; b. Berkeley, Calif., Oct. 4, 1933; d. Gerald Esley Eaton and Marileah (Speas) Russ; m. Jerome Joseph Bowen, Nov. 17, 1966 (div. Jan. 1977); children—Westanna Leah, Brecon Nelle. B.A., U. Calif.-Berkeley, 1954; M.F.A., Pratt Inst., 1960. Asst. prof. art San Francisco State U., 1967-71, Calif. State U., Hayward, 1971-73, U. Calif., 1973-75; owner, mgr. Old Hill Ranch Vineyard, Glen Ellen, Calif., 1973-81; pres. Resources, Unlimited, Kamuela, Hawaii, 1980-85; asst. prof. U. Hawaii, Hilo, 1982-83; art broker Bowles/Hopkins Gallery, San Francisco, 1985-86. Mem. Soc. Photog. Educators, Nat. Assn. Female Execs. Clubs: Mensa, Intertel. Home: 48 Lucky Dr Greenbrae CA 94904

EBAUGH, ELIZABETH BROWN (MRS. FRANK WRIGHT EBAUGH), civic worker; b. Jacksonville, Tex.; d. John Lemuel and Jewel (Newton) Brown; B.A., U. Colo., 1925; M.A., Tchrs. Coll., Columbia U., 1927; m. Frank Wright Ebaugh, Feb. 22, 1930; 1 dau., Betty Jane Ebaugh McFarland. Kindergarten tchr., Port Arthur, Tex., 1927-30. Bd. dirs. Jacksonville Pub. Library, 1944-77, pres., 1944-46, hon. mem. bd., 1977—, curator, organizer Vanishing Texana Mus., 1965-79. Mem. Cherokee County Hist. Commn., 1964-82. Recipient Appreciation plaque Jacksonville Library, 1969. Mem. D.A.R. (charter; registrar 1965—), Chi Omega. Presbyterian (historian 1965-66). Home: 428 S Patton St Jacksonville TX 75766

EBEL, CAROLYN W., language educator, consultant; b. Rochester, N.Y., Nov. 1, 1936; d. Kent Dane and Emily A. (Masonic) Williams; m. William K. Ebel Jr., June 25, 1960 (div.); children—William III, Jennifer A., Bruce K. B.A. in French, Wells Coll., 1958; M.Ed. in TESOL, Temple U., 1973, Ed.D., 1978. Coordinator adult edn. English as 2d lang. Lancaster-Lebanon Intermediate Unit 13, Lancaster, Pa., 1969-72, dir. bilingual edn., 1972-80; acting exec. dir. Nat. Assn. Bilingual Edn., Washington, 1980-81; asst. prof. English as 2d. lang. Georgetown U., Washington, 1983-85; pres. BESL/EDR, Inc., Drumore, Pa., 1979-82; dir. pub. info. strategies bilingual edn. NEA, Washington, 1981-82; asst. dir. SPECTRA Sch. of Design, McLean, Va., 1982—. Contbr. articles, book revs. to profl. jours. Pres. Friends of Lancaster Pub. Library, 1961-62. Cited for Outstanding Service to Hispanic Community, Pa. State Hispanic Concerns Orgn., Harrisburg, 1976; recipient Award of Merit for Service to Hispanic Community of Lancaster, El Centro Hispano, 1978. Mem. Internat. Reading Assn., TESOL (founder Pa. affiliate, pres. 1976-77), Phi Delta Kappa. Clubs: Cliosophic Soc., Los Besol (pres. 1976-77) (Lancaster). Office: Spectra Sch Design Inc Box 1054 McLean VA 22210

EBEL, LYNN ELIZABETH, lawyer, educator; b. Ft. Riley, Kans., Sept. 1, 1956; d. William Edward and Lois Lorraine (Lasewicz) E. B.S., U. Kans., 1978, J.D., 1982. Bar: Kans. 1982. Assoc. firm Davis, Davis, McGuire & Thompson, Chartered, Leavenworth, Kans., 1979—; atty. land use planning, Johnson County, Kans., 1984—; prof. Park Coll., Parkville, Mo., 1982—, Johnson County Community Coll., 1984. Active Human Relations Commn., Leavenworth, 1982-83. Mem. ABA, Kans. Bar Assn., Leavenworth County Bar Assn., Johnson County Bar Assn., Am. Planning Assn., Johnson County Coalition Against Child Abuse, Am. Judicature Soc. Republican. Roman Catholic. Home: 6602 Halsey St Shawnee KS 66216 Office: Johnson County Legal Dept Courthouse Olathe KS 66061

EBELING, ELINOR RUTH, library administrator; b. Detroit, Aug. 23, 1932; d. Vergil McKinley and Edith Athlee (Graves) Hodges; B.A., Wayne State U., 1954; M.L.S., U. Mich., 1957; hon. fellow Western Mich. U., 1967-68. Circulation/reference librarian Fordson High Sch., Dearborn, Mich., 1954-61; supr. tech. services Henry Ford Community Coll., Dearborn, 1961-67; asst. profl. library sci. Ill. State U., Normal, 1968-69; dir. Brookdale Community Coll., Lincroft, N.J., 1969—. Mem. N.J. Edn. Assn., N.J. Library Assn., ALA, Delta Zeta, Pi Lambda Theta, Beta Phi Mu. Home: 228 Clubhouse Dr Middletown NJ 07748 Office: Brookdale Community Coll Newman Springs Rd Lincroft NJ 07738

EBERHART, MARY ANN PETESIE, wholesale company executive; b. Baton Rouge, Aug. 20, 1940; d. Wilford Malvern and Mary Gordon (Davidson) Eberhart. B.S., McNeese State U., 1963. With United Service Warehouse, Inc., Baton Rouge, 1963-82, v.p., 1974-82, sales mgr., 1979—; v.p. United Engine Service, Inc., Baton Rouge, 1980-83, pres., 1983—, gen. mgr., 1981—. Recipient Worlds Champion Cutting Horse award Womens Profl. Rodeo Assn., 1971. Mem. Automotive Wholesalers Assn. La. (credit com. chair, sec. fed. credit union), Women's Profl. Rodeo Assn. (v.p. 1978-83), McNeese State U. Alumni Assn., NOW, Baton Rouge C. of C., Delta Zeta. Democrat. Episcopalian. Club: Baton Rouge Country. Home: 4070 Stumberg Ln Baton Rouge LA 70816 Office: 11923 Cloverland Ave Baton Rouge LA 70809

EBERSOLE, GUYLEENE HARMON, accountant; b. Minden, La., Jan. 4, 1941; d. Guy Augustus and Anna Belle (Shinpoch) Harmon; children—Ross Harmon, Rachel, Jason. Student Kilgore Coll., 1959-60, 74, Houston Community Coll., 1976-77; B.A. in Acctg. summa cum laude, U. St. Thomas, 1979, M.B.A., 1983. C.P.A., Tex. Acct., Deloitte Haskins & Sells, Houston, 1980-82; controller Oilfield Pipe & Supply Co., Houston, 1982; prin. Guyleene Harmon Ebersole, C.P.A., Houston, 1982—; sec.-treas., dir. Sand Dollar, Inc.; lectr. U. St. Thomas, Houston, 1984. Treas., bd. dirs. Heights Area Polit. Action Com., Houston, 1983—; bd. dirs. North Main Redevel. Task Force, Houston, 1983; sec. Woodland Heights Civic Club, Houston, 1984. Heights coordinator Mayor Kathy Whitmire campaign, Houston, 1983; treas. Harris County Dem. Exec. Com., 1984—; mem. parks steering com. Harris County Precinct I, 1985—. Mem. Am. Inst. C.P.A.s, Tex. Soc. C.P.A.s (nat. fiscal issues com. 1983—, acctg. and auditing com. 1984—, primary key person 1983—; Houston chpt. mgmt. adv. services com. 1984, vice chair 1986, pub. affairs com. 1985—, vice chair 1986), AAUW, Am. Contract Bridge League (cert. dir.), Harris County Women's Polit. Caucus (treas. 1985—), Phi Theta Kappa. Democrat. Episcopalian. Home: 1741 Branard Houston TX 77098 Office: 5100 Westheimer Suite 256 Houston TX 77056

EBERT, GLADYS EILEEN MEYER, home economist, adult education specialist, counselor; b. Wellsburg, Iowa, Jan. 16, 1921; d. Eilert J. and Juliet O'Ressa (Thompson) Meyer; B.A., U. No. Iowa, 1942; M.S., Iowa State U., 1967, M.S., 1968, Ph.D., 1978; m. George Henry Ebert, Sept. 16, 1950; children—George Meyer, Ann Louise, Barbara Eileen. Tchr., McGregor (Iowa) High Sch., 1942-43, Sigourney (Iowa) High Sch., 1943-44, Wellsburg (Iowa) High Sch., 1944-46, Nevada (Iowa) High Sch., 1946-52, Freeborn (Minn.) High Sch., 1952-53, Westmarshall Community Sch., State Center, Iowa, 1962-65; research asst. home econs. home econs. Iowa State U., Ames, 1965-67, instr. home econs., 1967-78, asst. prof., 1979—, acting coordinator Office of Distance Learning Programs, summer 1980; vis. prof. S.D. State U., summer 1977; mem. Iowa Task Force on Needs of Incarcerated Mothers, 1981-82; participant profl. confs. Mem. Am. Home Econs. Assn., Iowa Home Econs. Assn., Am. Vocat. Edn. Research Assn., Am. Ednl. Research Assn., Adult Edn. Research Assn., Assn. Tchr. Edn., Nat. Assn. Tchr. Educators for Home Econs., AAUW, Phi Delta Kappa, Omicron Nu, Theta Theta Epsilon, Phi Delta Gamma, Alpha Chi Omega. Presbyterian (deacon, elder). Contbr. articles to profl. jours. Home: 2114 Greenbriar Circle Ames IA 50010 Office: Coll Home Econs Iowa State U Ames IA 50010

EBERT, REGAN DANIELLE, lawyer; b. Chgo., June 13, 1954; d. Carl Henry and Florence (Sonerin) Ebert; m. Daniel Lee Balzano, July 14, 1981; 1 son, Daniel Carl. B.S., U. Ill., 1976, M.S., 1977; J.D. with honors, John Marshall Law Sch., 1979. Bar: Ill. 1979, U.S. Dist. Ct. (no. dist.) Ill. 1979, U.S. Ct. Appeals (7th cir.) 1980, U.S. Dist. Ct. (no. dist.) Ill. 1983. Law clk. Ritsos & Ritsos, Chgo., 1978-79; assoc. Carl H. Ebert & Assocs., Chgo., 1979-80; appellate atty. City of Chgo., 1980; adj. prof. law John Marshall Law Sch., Chgo., 1980—; assoc. Roderick J. Bergin Law Offices, Chgo., 1980-84; assoc. Judge & Knight Ltd., Park Ridge, Ill., 1984—; prosecutor Village of Park Ridge, 1984—. Precinct capt. 41st ward Regular Dem. Orgn., Chgo., 1977—, legal advisor, 1979—, mem. Women's Club. Mem. Chgo. Bar Assn., Ill. Bar Assn., ABA, Ill. Trial Lawyer's Assn., Assn. Trial Lawyers Am., Delta Theta Phi. Office: Judge & Knight Ltd 422 N Northwest Hwy Park Ridge IL 60068

EBERT, TINA ANITA, nurse; b. Fremont, Ohio, Sept. 11, 1958; d. Lloyd Fuller and Doris Jean (Parlow) E. B.S. in Nursing, Bowling Green State U., 1980. Registered nurse, Ohio. Camp nurse Luth. Meml. Camp, Fulton, Ohio, summer 1980, program-health and safety mgr., 1983-85; staff nurse Meml. Hosp. of Sandusky County, Fremont, Ohio, 1980-83, Mt. Carmel Hosp., Columbus, Ohio, 1983-85, Traveling Nurse Corps, 1985—; CPR instr. Am. Heart Assn., 1983-85. Youth adviser St. John Lutheran Ch., Fremont, 1980-83. Mem. Am. Nurses Assn., Ohio Nurses Assn., Nat. Parks and Conservation Assn., World Wildlife Fund, Nature Conservancy, Appalachian Trail Conf., Bread for the World, Ohio Nuclear Weapons Freeze Campaign. Avocations: hiking; swimming; reading; sewing; running; skiing. Home: 1695 County Road 236 Clyde OH 43410

EBITZ, ELIZABETH KELLY, lawyer; b. LaPorte, Ind., June 9, 1950; d. Joseph Monahan and Ann Mary (Barrett) Kelly; m. David MacKinnon Ebitz, Jan. 23, 1971 (div. 1981). A.B., Smith Coll., 1972; J.D. cum laude, Boston U., 1975. Bar: Maine, Mass, U.S. Supreme Ct. Law clk. Boston Legal Assistance Project, 1973-75; law clk., assoc. Law Offices of John J. Thornton, Boston, 1974-76; ptnr. Ebitz & Zurn, Northampton, Mass., 1976-79; assoc. Gross, Minsky, Mogul & Singal, Bangor, Maine, 1979-80; sole practice, pres. firm, Bangor, 1980—. Pres. Greater Bangor Rape Crisis Bd., 1983-85; mem. various peace and hunger orgns., Bangor, 1981-86; mem., legal counsel Greater Bangor Area Shelter Bd., 1985-86. Named Young Career Woman of Hampshire County, Nat. Bus. and Profl. Women, Northampton, 1979. Mem. ABA, Assn. Trial Lawyers Am., Sigma Xi. Democrat. Roman Catholic. Home: 111 Maple St Bangor ME 04401 Office: 15 Columbia St PO Box 641 Bangor ME 04401

EBNER, MYRA RHUNA, market research company executive; b. Hohenwald, Tenn., Mar. 16, 1948; d. Edward and Bertie Lou (Coble) Churchwell; m. Bruce A. Ebner, Aug. 1, 1970; children—Kimberly D., William A. Student Columbia State Community Coll., 1966-68. Data Entry operator T. Jefferson Ins. Co., Nashville, 1968-69; data processing mgr. Coca-Cola Co., Nashville, 1969-76; field dir. Mktg. Research Counsel, Atlanta, 1977-83; pres., owner Peachtree Surveys, Ltd., Atlanta, 1983—. Arbitrator Better Bus. Bur., Atlanta, 1983. Mem. Mktg. Research Assn. (Southeast chpt. sec. 1981-82, pres. 1983-84), Am. Mktg. Assn., Nat. Assn. Female Execs. Home: 3823 Vineyard Ct Marietta GA 30062 Office: Peachtree Surveys Ltd 6095 Barfield Rd Suite 120 Atlanta GA 30328

ECHOLS, IVOR TATUM (MRS. SYLVESTER J. ECHOLS), educator, asst. dean; b. Oklahoma City, Dec. 28, 1919; d. Israel E. and Katie (Bingley) Tatum; A.B., U. Kans., 1942; postgrad. (A.R.C. scholar) U. Nebr., 1945-46; M.S. in Social Work (Nat. Urban League fellow, Porter R. Lee fellow), Columbia, 1952, postgrad. (NIMH fellow), U. So. Calif., 1961-62, D.S.W., 1968; m. Kenneth Johnston, Dec. 28, 1948 (div. June 1951); 1 dau., Kalu Helene; m. 2d, Sylvester J. Echols, June 13, 1954 (div. 1976); 1 son, Kim Arnett. Tchr. social studies high sch., Holdenville, Okla., 1942-43, Geary, Okla., 1943-45; caseworker A.R.C., Chgo., 1946-47; resident group worker, Dosoris House for Teen-Age Girls, Community Services Soc., N.Y.C., 1950-51; supr. group work Walnut Grove Center Neighborhood Clubs, Oklahoma City, 1948-51; program dir. Camp Lookout YWCA, Denver, 1951; dir. program services Presbyn. Neighborhood Services, Detroit, summer 1960, supr. group work Merrill-Palmer Inst., Detroit, 1951-70; asst. dir. Merrill-Palmer Camp, Dryden, Mich., 1951-59; prof. Sch. Social Work, U. Conn., West Hartford, 1970—, now also asst. dean; del. Inter-Univ. Consortium of Social Devel., Hong Kong, 1980; mem. conn. adv. com. U.S. Commn. Civil Rights. Mem. Ad Hoc Com. Citizens Concerned with Equal Ednl. Opportunity, Detroit, 1964—; cons. to N.E.A. Conf. Family Camping Washington, 1959, ednl. film Scott Paper Co., Phila., 1963, 64; summer study skills project Presbyn. Ch. Bd. Nat. Missions, Knoxville, Tenn., 1965—; sec. United Neighborhood Centers Am.; pres. Protestant Community Services, Detroit, 1969-70. Recipient Sojourner Truth award Detroit chpt. Nat. Assn. Negro Bus. and Profl. Women, 1969; Conn. Social Worker of Year, 1979. Mem. Nat. Assn. Colored Women's Clubs (participant White House Conf. on Children and Youth 1960), A.M.E. Ministers Wives, Acad. Certified Social Workers, Delta Sigma Theta. Mem. A.M.E. Ch. Home: 51 Chestnut Dr Windsor CT 06095 Office: U Conn 1800 Asylum Ave West Hartford CT 06007

ECHOLS, JERRI LYNN, insurance company executive; b. Brimingham, Ala., Oct. 31, 1953; d. Harry Clay and Osie Virginia (Johnson) Griffin; m. James Willard Echols, Mar. 24, 1972; 1 child, Diana Lynn. Student Samford U., Birmingham, 1983-87. Sec. Conn. Gen. Life Ins. Co., Birmingham, 1978-81, service rep., 1981-83, sales rep., 1983-85; sales rep. Life Ins. Co. N.Am., Birmingham, 1985—. Troop leader Cahaba council Girl Scouts U.S.A., 1979-85. Mem. Assn. Health Underwriters, Nat. Assn. Female Execs., Network Birmingham. Avocations: reading; camping; motorcycling; hiking. Office: Life Ins Co N AM 31 Inverness Ctr Pkwy Suite 340 Birmingham AL 35243

ECHOLS, LINDA KAYE, sales executive; b. Oklahoma City, May 16, 1946; d. Lowery Edwin and Zelma Farris (Shive) Echols. B.S., U. Okla., 1969. Lic. phys. therapist. Staff phys. therapist Tex. Inst. for Rehab./Research, Houston, 1969-71, J.T. Gilbert & Assocs., Jackson, Miss., 1971; dir. Okfuskee Meml. Hosp., Okemah, Okla., 1971-73; staff phys. therapist Diagnostic Hosp., Houston, 1973-74; sr. phys. therapist St. Anthony Rehab., Houston, 1974-78; asst. dir. Plaza del Oro Rehab., Houston, 1978; cons. Harris County Dept. Edn., Houston, 1978-79, program asst., 1979-81, asst. coordinator, 1981-84; regional sales rep. Mettler Electronics, Anaheim, Calif., 1984—. Mem. Pediatric Spl. Interest, City of Houston, 1980-83, chmn. Recipient Civitan Citizenship award, 1964. Mem. Am. Phys. Therapy Assn., Tex. Phys. Therapy Assn., Southeastern Dist. Phys. Therapy Assn., Nat. Assn. Female Execs., Council for Exceptional Children. Republican. Home: 4227 San Felipe 34 Houston TX 77027 Office: Mettler Electronics 1333 S Claudina St Anaheim CA 92805

ECK, ANDREA LOUISE, advertising and marketing executive; b. Easton, Pa., Oct. 31, 1962; d. Charles Anthony Bottiglieri and Almeda Louise (Eck) Migliazza. Student Northampton County Area Community Coll., Boston Ctr. for Edn., Weist Barron Acting. Asst. mgr., salesperson Sigals Country Corner Shoe Dept., Easton, Pa., 1980; telemarketing rep. Simmons Communications, Easton, 1981; customer service rep. Christmas Club Corp., Easton, 1980-81, mgr., 1982-83, account exec., Framingham, Mass., 1984-86; self-employed advt. sales and mktg. exec., Phila., 1986—; telemktg. rep. Phila. Drama Guild, 1986—. Sponsor Christian Children's Fund, Richmond, Va., 1984, 85, 86. Recipient Disting. Achievement award Christmas Club Corp., 1985. Mem. Nat. Assn. Female Execs. Lutheran. Avocations: acting; dancing; travel; nautilus; sports. Home: 1000-12 South St Apt B Philadelphia PA 19147

ECK, DOROTHY FRITZ, state senator; b. Sequim, Wash., Jan. 23, 1924; d. Ira Edward and Ida (Hokanson) Fritz; B.S. in Secondary Edn., Mont. State U., 1961, M.S. in Applied Sci., 1966; m. Hugo Eck, Dec. 16, 1942; children—Lauvrence, Diana. Co-mgr. archtl. and property mgmt. bus., 1955—; conf. coordinator Am. Agrl. Econs. Assn., 1967-68; state-local coordinator Office of Gov. Mont., Helena, 1972-77; mem. Mont. State Senate, 1981—; mem. Mont. Environ. Quality Council, 1981—. Bd. dirs. Methodist Youth Fellowship, 1960-64, Mont. Council for Effective Legislature, 1977-78, Rocky Mountain Environ. Council, 1982—; del., Western v.p. Mont. Constl. Conv., 1971-72; chmn. Gov.'s Task Force on Citizen Participation, 1976-77; mem. adv. com. No. Rockies Resource and Tng. Center (now No. Lights Inst.), 1979-81. Recipient Outstanding Alumna award Mont. State U., 1981. Mem. LWV (state pres. 1967-70), Common Cause, Nat. Women's Polit. Caucus. Democrat. Office: Mont Senate Helena MT 59620*

ECKARDT, GLADYS EVANGELINE (MRS. KARL PAUL KONRAD ECKARDT), librarian; b. Hartland, N.Y., Sept. 7, 1912; d. Isaac John and Flora Caroline (Hofmeister) Beach; student U. Buffalo, 1930-32; B.A., U. Rochester, 1934; M.L.S., Rutgers State U., 1958; m. Karl Paul Konrad Eckardt, Oct. 19, 1940; 1 dau., Susan (Mrs. Edward Misiewicz). Dir. Wood-Ridge (N.J.) Pub. Library, 1956-59, Rutherford (N.J.) Pub. Library, 1959—. Trustee Wood-Ridge Pub. Library, 1954-56. Mem. Am., N.J. (sec. 1964-65, chmn. N.J. insts. 1968), Bergen-Passaic (pres. 1964-66), N.Y. library assn., Pub. Relations Council, Bergen County Small Libraries (v.p. 1963), Rutgers Alumni Assn. Club: Rutherford Women's College. Office: Rutherford Pub Library Park Ave Rutherford NJ 07070

ECKENDORF, LYNN ELLEN, data systems analyst; b. Cleve., Aug. 11, 1953; d. Stephen Albert and Ruth Marie (Shenk) Brado; m. John David Eckendorf, Oct. 1, 1977; 1 child, Peter Stonestreet. B.S., Miami U., Oxford, Ohio, 1974; M.B.A., Baldwin-Wallace Coll., 1980. Adminstrv. asst. Hilti, Inc., Cleve., 1975-79; user liaison Progressive Ins. Co., Mayfield Village, Ohio, 1979; sr. data systems specialist Ernst & Whinney, Cleve., 1979-83, mgr. data systems 1983—. Co-chmn. residential/community bus. campaign United Way, Cleve., 1983, vice chmn. 1981, 82; mem. house com. Cleve. Civic House, 1981; mem. women's com. Cleve. Orch. Mem. Data Processing Mgmt. Assn., Assn. for Computing Machinery (chmn. publs. 1981-82), Northcoast Exec. Women's Network, Nat. Assn. Female Execs. Republican. Roman Catholic. Club: Women's City (co-chmn. Exec. Women's Network 1983-85, trustee 1984—, fin. com. 1984-85). Office: 2000 National City Ctr Cleveland OH 44114

ECKERLY, JEAN RUTH, physician; b. Chgo., June 25, 1937; d. Wilbur Joseph and Carrie Minnie (Wendorf) E. B.S., U. Chgo., 1958, M.D., 1962. Diplomate Am. Bd. Internal Medicine. Intern, Mpls. Gen. Hosp., 1962-63; resident Hennepin County Med. Ctr., 1963-66, dir. outpatient dept., 1965-69; practice medicine specializing in internal medicine, Mpls., 1977—; dir. medicine Pilot City Health Ctr., Mpls., 1969-73, Hennepin County Methadone, Mpls., 1974-81, Chrysalis, Mpls., 1980-81; pres. Preventive Med. Assocs., Mpls., 1982—; asst. prof. medicine U. Minn., Mpls., 1969-73. Mem. Am. Soc. Internal Medicine, Am. Acad. Med. Prevention, Am. Med. Women's Assn., Am. Holistic Med. Assn., Am. Assn. Physicians for Human Rights. Democratic Farm Labor. Office: Preventive Med Assocs 5851 Duluth St Minneapolis MN 55422

ECKERT, SUSAN MARIE, publisher, editor; b. Rochester, N.Y., May 17, 1950; d. Louis Joseph and Pearl Clara (Stiles) Eckert. B.A. in English, Houghton Coll., 1972; postgrad. in English, U. Rochester, 1979-85. Editor, Wolfe Publs., Pittsford, N.Y., 1973-75; promotion dir. Sta. WXXI-TV-FM, Rochester, 1975-76; freelance writer, Rochester, 1976-79; corp. info. editor Rochester Telephone Corp., 1979-84; newsletter pub. The Bookery, Rochester, 1984—; cons. Xerox Corp., 1982—; adj. faculty St. John Fisher Coll., Rochester, 1984-86; publicist Greece Performing Arts Soc. Summer Theatre, Greece, N.Y., 1976—. Contbr. articles to mags. Editor press kit United Way Greater Rochester, 1982. N.Y. State Regents scholar Houghton Coll., 1968-72,

Houghton Coll. scholar, 1968-69. Mem. Women in Communications (chpt. v.p. programs 1982-83, pres. 1984-85), Internat. Assn. Bus. Communicators (jr. del. 1982—). Lutheran. Office: Bookery Newsletter for Booklovers PO Box 40247 Rochester NY 14604

ECKHOFF, ROSALEE, nurse; b. Falls City, Nebr., Apr. 24, 1930; d. George and Blanche (Montague) Rieger; R.N., Nebr. Meth. Sch. Nursing, 1951; m. Robert Dale Eckhoff, Feb. 21, 1954; children—Dixie Dee, Monte Ray. Dir. nursing Sutherland (Nebr.) Hosp., 1952-55; head nurse med. ward Hastings (Nebr.) Regional Center, 1957-61; night supr. Good Samaritan Village, Hastings, 1962; charge nurse pediatrics Mary Lanning Hosp., Hastings, 1962-65; night supr. Broken Bow (Nebr.) Hosp., 1965-66; dir. nursing Bethel Nursing Home, Ainsworth, Nebr., 1966-67, adminstr., 1967-69; part-time staff nurse Ainsworth Hosp., 1969-70; nursing home counselor Norfolk (Nebr.) Regional Center, 1970-72; night supr. Albion (Nebr.) Boone County Hosp., 1970-75; adminstrv. dir. Mideast Nebr., Albion and Columbus Mental Health Clinic, 1975-76; dir. nursing Phelps Meml. Health Center, Holdrege, Nebr., 1976—. Mem. Nebr. Soc. Nursing Service Adminstrs. (sec.-treas.), Nebr. Mental Health Assn., Luth. Ch. Women, Dist. 4 Hosp. Assn. (dir. nurses), Am. Orgn. Nurse Execs., Nebr. Orgn. Nurse Execs. Home: 1015 West Ave Holdrege NE 68949 Office: 1220 Miller St Holdrege NE 68949

ECKLEY, ALICIA KATHRYN, writer, editor, public relations specialist; b. Columbus, Ohio, Mar. 31, 1959; d. Richard McCoy and Helen Louise (Martin) E. B.A. in Journalism, Ohio State U., 1981. Freelance mktg. research Lexikos Pub., San Francisco, 1982; editorial asst. Diagnostic Imaging Mag., Miller Freeman Publs., San Francisco, 1982-83, asst. editor, 1983-84; pub. affairs mgr. Squibb Corp., Princeton, N.J., 1984—. Mem. Women in Communications, Inc. Office: PO Box 4000 Princeton NJ 08543

ECKLEY, GRACE ESTER, English language educator; b. Alliance, Ohio, Nov. 30, 1932; d. Clyde L. and Wilma Agnes (Hahn) Williamson; B.A., Mount Union Coll., 1955; M.A., Case Western Res. U., 1964; Ph.D., Kent State U., 1970; m. Wilton Eckley, Sept. 12, 1954; children—Douglas, Stephen, Timothy. Instr. English, Simpson Coll., Indianola, Iowa, 1965-68; prof. dept. English, Drake U., Des Moines, 1968—NEH fellow, 1984-85. Mem. AAUW. Author: Benedict Kiely, 1972; Edna O'Brien, 1974; (with Michael Begnal) Narrator and Character in Finnegans Wake, 1974; Finley Peter Dunne, 1981; Children's Lore in Finnegans Wake, 1984; contbr. articles to profl. jours. Home: 14 S Holman Way Apt 2-D Golden CO 80401 Office: Drake U Des Moines IA 50311

ECKMAN, BERTHA ELIZABETH, educator; b. Berlin, Pa.; d. Frank and Augusta (Olson) Eckman; student Calif. Tchrs. Coll., 1929-31; B.S., U. Pitts., 1940, postgrad., 1950-61; in service tng. Ind. Tchrs. Coll., 1959-61. Tchr., Brothers Valley Twp. Sch., Berlin, Pa., 1931-33, Lincoln Twp., Somerset, Pa., 1934, Garrett, Pa., 1934-44, Maple Ridge Sch., 1944—; supervising tchr. California (Pa.) State Tchrs. Coll. Exec. sec. Somerset County Council Christian Edn., 1956—, editor yearbooks, 1958-82; youth counselor Somerset County Youth Camp, 1954—, tchr. young people's class; campaign chmn. ARC, Somerset, 1954-57; promotional sec. Somerset Council Sunday Sch. Convs., 1957—; mem. synodical affairs com. Fgn. Missions West Allegheny Conf. Central Pa.; campaign chmn. Allegheny Luth. Homes Aux., Johnstown, Pa.; pres. Garrett Parish Joint Council Luth. Ch. Am.; exec. sec. Garrett Parish Luth. Ch. Am.; pres. Somerset County aux. Allegheny Luth. Home for the Aged, Johnstown, Pa. Mem. NEA (del. to centennial conv. 1957, del. to classroom tchrs. conf.), Pa. Edn. Assn. (pres. Somerset County), United Ch. Women, Nat. Geog. Soc. Educators Beneficial Assn., Delta Kappa Gamma (chpt. pres., dir. work program), Internat. Platform Assn., Marquis Biog. Library Soc. Republican. Lutheran (program coordinator spl. spiritual programs 1936-82). Home: RD 3 Berlin PA 15530

ECKSTEIN, ETHEL GINSBERG, educator, consultant; b. Glen Cove, N.Y., Oct. 15, 1915; d. Philip and Bessie (Idelewitz) Zendle; m. Henry H. Ginsberg, May 11, 1944 (dec. Mar. 1965); children—Sheila, Nisan J.; m. Walter Eckstein, Apr. 14, 1973 (dec.). B.A. in French with honors, U. Ky., 1940; M.S. in Edn., Hofstra U., 1956; postgrad. Iona Coll., summer 1961, Emory Coll., Besanoon, France, 1963. Tchr. French and English, Huntington High Sch., N.Y., 1942-44, tchr. 7th grade Jericho Elem. Sch., N.Y., 1953; instr. conversational French to adults, Glen Cove High Sch., 1952-55; tchr. remedial reading Deasy Sch., Glen Cove, summers 1951-61, 66; tchr. Landing Sch., Glen Cove, 1954-61; curriculum assoc. Middle Sch., Glen Cove, 1961-65; tchr. 3d grade Coles Sch., 1965-76; asst. prof. grad. level CCNY, 1964-66. Mem. Kappa Delta Pi. Republican. Jewish. Avocations: reading; golf; dancing; writing; poetry. Home: 13755 Flora Pl Delray Beach FL 33445

ECONOMIDES, ELAINE, lawyer; b. N.Y.C., Sept. 14, 1948; d. Basil and Anastasia (Pavlakis) E.; B.A. cum laude (Granite State Merit scholar, Elks Assn. scholar), U. N.H., 1970; postgrad. London Sch. Econs., 1970-71; J.D., Suffolk U., 1977. Civil rights specialist GSA, Boston, 1972-73; contract negotiator Transp. Systems Center, Cambridge, Mass., 1973-78, spl. asst. to dir., 1978-79; spl. asst. to dir. Materials Transp. Bur., Washington, 1979-80, exec. officer, 1980-82; atty.-adv. RSPA, Dept. Transp., Washington, 1982—; fed. women's program coordinator GSA, 1972-73, Transp. Systems Center, 1973-74; bd. dirs. Kendall Sq. Fed. Credit Union, 1979; admitted to Mass. bar, 1977, Fed. bar, 1978. Mem. Am. Bar Assn., ACLU, Mensa, Pi Sigma Alpha, Phi Kappa Phi, Pi Gamma Mu. Greek Orthodox. Office: US Dept Transp 400 7th St SW Washington DC 20590

EDDIE-CALLAGAIN, ANNETTE MARIE, lawyer; b. Lafayette, La., Feb. 11, 1953; d. Joseph Charles Eddie and Lorenza (Roman) Johnson; m. Glynn Mark Callagain, Aug. 9, 1975 (div. 1983); 1 son, Glynn Mark. B.S. So. U. A&M Coll., Baton Rouge, 1975, J.D., 1981. Bar: La. 1982; cert high sch. tchr. Tchr. Nebr. Coll. Bus., Omaha, 1977-78, Central High Sch., Omaha, 1975-77; atty. La. Dept. Justice, Baton Rouge, 1982-83; capt. U.S. Air Force, 1983—; asst. staff judge adv. U.S. Air Force, Victorville, Calif., 1983—. Counseling asst. Alcohol and Drug Rehab. Council of Elderly; domestic counselor Preventive Law Program; vol. leader Girl Scouts U.S.A., 1983-84 (all George AFB, Calif.). So. U. scholar, 1978-81. Mem. ABA, La. Bar Assn., High Desert Bar Assn. (v.p. mil. liason), Delta Sigma Theta, Pi Omega Pi, Phi Alpha Delta. Democrat. Roman Catholic. Office: USAF 831 CSG/JA Bldg 245 George AFB CA 92394

EDDINGS, ALICE FAYE, retail ofcl.; b. Sherman, Tex., July 30, 1939; d. Allen and Ethel Aline (Tumey) Tatum; student N. Tex. Bus. Coll., 1954, LaSalle Extension U.; children by previous marriage—Lori Driggers, Donald Driggers, David Driggers. Employed in various credit, accounting and mgmt. positions, Tex., Fla., Ala. and Germany, 1954-71; office, credit mgr. Pioneer Logging Machinery, Inc., Columbia, S.C., 1971-74; office mgr. Camden Lugoff Chrysler-Plymouth-Dodge, Inc., Lugoff, S.C., 1974-76; dep. clk. in bankruptcy ct., clks. office U.S. Dist. Ct., Columbia, S.C., 1976-77; credit mgr. Salem Carpets, Inc., Columbia, 1977-78, officer, credit mgr., 1978—. Founder, exec. dir. Friendly Faces, Columbia, 1977—; bd. dirs. Columbia YWCA, 1981-82. Mem. Nat. Assn. Credit Mgrs., Am. Soc. Profl. and Exec. Women, Am. Bus. Womens Assn., Nat. Assn. Female Execs., Columbia Credit Mgrs. Assn., NOW, Credit Women Internat. (chpt. pres. 1981-82), Columbia Area LWV (dir. 1978-82), Soc. Cert. Consumer Credit Execs. Republican. Roman Catholic. Office: Cogdill Carpets Inc PO Box 21306 Columbia SC 29221

EDDISON, ELIZABETH BOLE, entrepreneur, information specialist; b. Bronxville, N.Y., June 3, 1928; d. Hamilton Biggar and Elizabeth Owsley (Boyle) Bole; m. John Corbin Eddison, Feb. 10, 1951; children—Jonathan B., Elizabeth O., Martha C. A.B., Vassar Coll., 1948; M.S., Simmons Coll., 1973. Pres. bd. dirs. Lahore Am. Sch., Pakistan, 1959-61; chmn. evaluation com. Karachi Am. Sch., Pakistan, 1961-63; treas. bd. dirs. La Paz Coop. Sch., Bolivia, 1963-65; v.p. Assn. Am. Fgn. Service Women, coordinator social services Urban Service Corps, Washington Pub. Schs., 1965-69; sec. bd. dirs. Colegio Nueva Granada, Bogota, Colombia, 1969-71; chmn., treas. Warner-Eddison Assocs., Inc., Cambridge, Mass., 1973—, pres., 1981—; chmn., dir. bus. devel. Inmagic Inc., Cambridge, 1984—. Author: Database Design Workbook, 1986. Compiler: Words that Mean Business, 1981. Contbr. articles to profl. jours. Mem. adv. com. on internat. investment, tech. devel. U.S. Dept. State, 1980-83. Mem. Info. Industry Assn. (chmn. emeriti com. 1983—, co-chmn. publs. com. 1984—), Assoc. Info. Mgrs. (chmn. publs. com. 1984—, bd. dirs.), Spl. Libraries Assn. (chmn. program com./library mgmt. div. 1984-85), Am. Soc. Info. Scientists, Beta Phi Mu. Democrat. Office: Inmagic Inc 238 Broadway Cambridge MA 02139

EDDY, DARLENE MATHIS, English language educator, poet; b. Elkhart, Ind., Mar. 19, 1937; d. William Eugene and Fern (Paulmer) Mathis; B.A., Goshen Coll., 1959; M.A., Rutgers U., 1961, Ph.D., 1967; m. Spencer Livingston Eddy, Jr., May 23, 1964 (dec. May 1971). Instr., lectr. Douglass Coll. and Rutgers U., 1962-64, 66-67; asst. prof. English, Ball State U., Muncie, Ind., 1967-70, assoc. prof., 1971-75, prof., 1975—. Recipient numerous research, creative teaching and creative arts grants; Woodrow Wilson Nat. fellow, 1959-62; Rutgers U. Grad. Honors fellow, 1964-65. Mem. Nat. Council Tchrs. of English, MLA, AAUP, Shakespeare Assn., DAR. Author: The Worlds of King Lear, 1968; Leaf Threads, Wind Rhymes, 1985; Weathering, 1986; contbr. articles to Am. Lit., English Lang. Notes and others, poetry to Green River Rev., Calyx, Bitterroot, Pebble, Hiram Poetry Rev., Forum, Rendezvous, Barnwood Mag., others. Home: 1409 W Cardinal St Muncie IN 47303 Office: RB248 English Ball State Muncie IN 47303

EDDY, KATHLEEN SUE, trucking company executive; b. Grand Rapids, Mich., July 21, 1951; d. Francis Milo and LaVerne (Graham) Cook; m. Gilbert Sherman Eddy, Nov. 7, 1971 (div. Nov. 1978). Student pub. schs., Grand Rapids. Truck broker Brokers Distbg. Co., Inc., Grand Rapids, 1972-76, owner, operator, 1976-79; terminal mgr. Truckers Brokers Inc., Grand Rapids, 1979-82; pres., owner Amazon Ind. Transp. Inc., Grand Rapids, 1982—. Avocations: reading; gardening. Office: Amazon Ind Transp Inc 1020 Hall St SW Grand Rapids MI 49503

EDDY, LINDA JOAN, mortgage bank executive; b. South Weymouth, Mass., Dec. 20, 1949; d. LaRue Ernest and Ruth (Adams) Eddy. A.A., Palm Beach Jr. Coll., 1969; B.S.E., Fla. Atlantic U., 1971. Cert. tchr., Fla. Tchr. math. Lyman High Sch., Longwood, Fla., 1971-81; tng. dir. asst. v.p. Citizens Mortgage Corp., St. Petersburg, Fla., 1981-82, compliance officer, v.p. Loan Am. Fin. Corp., 1982-85, asst. to pres., 1985-86, sr. v.p. adminstrn., 1986—. Squadron comdr. CAP, Orlando, Fla., 1972-75, group dep. for cadets, 1976-77, group comdr., 1979-80, sector comdr., 1980-81, wing dep. for cadets, St. Petersburg, 1982—, recipient various awards, 1974, 76, 78, 81; creator, comdr. Encampment Cadet Command and Staff Sch., 1981—. Mem. Nat. Assn. Female Execs., Mortgage Brokers Assn. Office: Loan Am Fin Corp 8100 Oak Ln Miami Lakes FL 33016

EDDY, LINDA PEET, educational administrator, child development educator; b. Eaton Rapids, Mich., May 23, 1948; d. James Ray and Louisa (Kunkel) N.; m. Thomas Michael Peet, Oct. 6, 1969 (div.); m. Jon Randolph Eddy, June 7, 1980; 1 child, Gregory Peet. B.S., Mich. State U., 1970, M.A., 1974. Tchr. Morrice Pub. Sch., Mich., 1970-71; teaching asst. Mich. State U., East Lansing, Mich., 1971-72; dir. Haslett Child Devel. Ctr., Mich., 1975—; instr. Mich. State U., East Lansing, part-time 1979—, Lansing Community Coll., part-time 1976-81; cons. several schs. in area East Lansing, Grand Ledge, etc. on setting up before and after sch. programs, 1979—. Mem. Central Mich. Assn. for Edn. of Young Children (treas. 1977-80). Avocations: quilting; sewing; reading; travel; history. Office: Haslett Child Devel Ctr 5655 School St Haslett MI 48840

EDDY, SARA LEPPER, book publishing consultant; b. Topeka, Mar. 30, 1915; d. Harold Arthur and Ferne Haun (Williams) Lepper; m. Richard Carl DeLong, Sept. 29, 1940 (div. Jan. 1949); children—John Richard DeLong (dec.), Robert Gary DeLong, m. 2d, G. Russell Eddy, Apr. 25, 1964. B.F.A., U. Kans., 1937. Asst. instr. design U. Kans., Lawrence, 1937-38; chief draftsman Western Air Lines, Burbank, Calif., 1940-45; art dir. Bert Ray Studios, Chgo., 1949-64; design prodn. mgr. Syracuse U. Press (N.Y.), 1973-85. Designer: Landmarks of Rochester and Monroe County, 1975; The Catskill Witch, 1975; Wood Structure and Identification, 1977; Tomatoes were Cheaper, 1978. Recipient Certs. of award AAUP, 1975, 78, Printing Industries of Am., 1977. Life mem. Am. Inst. Graphic Arts, Kappa Kappa Gamma, Delta Phi Delta. Republican. Congregationalist. Home: Wind Rush Farm Manlius NY 13104

EDE, JOYCE KINLAW, counselor, marketing executive; b. Lumberton, N.C., Aug. 9, 1936; d. Neil Archibald and Myrtle Carolyn (Kinlaw) Kinlaw; m. William L. Schmid, Sept. 17, 1954 (dec. Nov. 1956); 1 dau., Cheryl Ann; m. Archie L. Phillips, Jr., Nov. 11, 1960 (div. July 1973); children—Archie L. III, Michael Bartley, John Wade; m. Kenneth Russell Ede, Dec. 27, 1984. Certs. Lake Sumter Community Coll., 1976, 77, 79, Volusia Community Coll., 1977, Ocala Jr. Coll., 1979, Univ. Central, Orlando, Fla., 1980, Triton Coll., 1981. Counselor, social worker Epilepsy Assn. Central Fla.-Lake County, 1973-76; social worker Lake Sumter Community Mental Health, Med. Social Services, Leesburg, Fla., 1976-79; counselor, social worker Epilepsy Assn. Central Fla.-Lake County, 1979-81; mktg. coordinator Friendship Village, Schaumburg, Ill., 1981-84; retirement counselor Health Care Assocs., Winter Haven, Fla., 1984-85; in mktg. Cambridge Park Manor, Wheaton, Ill., 1985—; pres. Lake County Services Council, Leesburg, 1978-79; del. central Fla. Nat. Conf. on Epilepsy, Washington, 1975; mem. State Conf. on Epilepsy, Tampa, Fla., 1977-81; dir. Lake County, Epilepsy Job Tng., Tavares, Fla., 1979-81; mem., advocate Lake/Sumter County Geriatric Program, 1979; chairperson Epilepsy Bd. Fla., Tavares, 1974-75. Contbr. articles on epilepsy to profl. jours. Mem. Lake County PTA, Leesburg, 1970-76; mem. Parents Adv. Council, Lake County, Leesburg, 1977-80; mem. Parents Council, Dixie Youth Baseball League, Fruitland Park, Fla., 1980. Recipient Certs. Epilepsy Assn. Central Fla., Orlando, 1980, Kiwanis Clubs, Leesburg and Mt. Dora, Fla., 1974, Rotary Clubs, Leesburg, Mt. Dora, Groveland, Fla., 1974, Lions Clubs, Leesburg, Mt. Dora, Tavares, 1974-75. Mem. Am. Bus. Women's Assn. (hosp. chairperson 1979-80), Concerned Women for Am., Nat. Assn. Female Execs. Avocations: reading; sports; art; music; cooking; crafts; visiting library; playing piano. Home: 680 Bluff St Apt 303 Carol Stream IL 60188

EDELEN, MARY BEATY, state legislator; b. Vermillion, S.D., Dec. 9, 1944; d. Donald William and Marjorie (Heckel) Beaty; m. Joseph Ruey Edelen, Jr., June 8, 1968; children—Audra Angelica, Anthony Callaghan, Jarrod Arthur. Student Cottey Coll., Nevada, Mo., 1963-64; B.A., U. S.D., 1967; M.A., Trinity U., 1971. Asst. med. librarian U. S.D., Vermillion, 1965-67; lectr. U. S.D., Vermillion, 1969-70, Yankton (S.D.) Coll., 1973-74; mem. S.D. Ho. of Reps., 1972-80, 82—. Vice chmn. Clay County Republican Party, Vermillion, S.D., 1982—; mem. exec. com. Southeastern Council of Govts.; mem. U. S.D. Community Edn. Adv. Council; mem. S.D. Safety Council's Restraint Coalition. Recipient Burgess Book award U. S.D., 1966; S.D. Safety Council award, 1984. Mem. Nat. Order Women Legislators (v.p. 1983-84, pres. 1985-86), Nat. Conf. State Legislators (com. children and youth 1983—), PEO, Zeta Phi Eta. Republican. Mem. United Ch. of Christ. Lodge: Order Eastern Star (worthy matron). Home: 311 Canby St Vermillion SD 57069

EDELMAN, DIANE LYNN, human resource consultant; b. Chgo., Aug. 11, 1956; d. Donald R. and Harriette P. (Duncan) E. B.S. in Math., Chgo. State U., 1977. Systems analyst Zurich Am., Chgo., 1978-80; account mgr. Cyborg Systems, Chgo., 1980-83; sr. systems analyst Marsh & McLennan, Chgo., 1983; mgmt. info. systems mgr. Saxon Paint, Chgo., 1983-85; account mgr., cons. ISI, Downers Grove, Ill., 1985-86; pres. Edelman & Assocs., Ltd., Hinsdale, Ill., 1986—. Mem. Young Profls. for Heart Assn., Nat. Assn. Female Execs., U.S. Polo Assn., Hinsdale C. of C., Kappa Delta Pi. Episcopalian. Club: Oak Brook Polo (Ill.). Avocations: polo, architectural art.

EDELMAN, JUDITH HOCHBERG, architect; b. Bklyn., Sept. 16, 1923; d. Abraham and Frances (Israel) Hochberg; m. Harold Edelman, Dec. 26, 1947; children—Marc, Joshua. Student, Conn. Coll., 1940-41, NYU, 1941-42; B.Arch., Columbia U., 1946. Designer, drafter Huson Jackson, N.Y.C., 1948-58; Schermerhorn traveling fellow, 1950; pvt. practice architecture, 1958-60; partner Edelman & Salzman, N.Y.C., 1960-79, Edelman Partnership (Architects), 1979—; adj. prof. Sch. Architecture, City U. N.Y., 1972-76; vis. lectr. urban renewal New Sch., 1968; vis. lectr. Washington U., St. Louis, 1974, U. Oreg., 1974, Mass. Inst. Tech., 1975, City U. N.Y. Grad. Program Environ. Psychology, 1975, Pa. State U., City U. N.Y. Grad. Program Environ. Psychology, 1977, Rensselaer Poly Inst., 1977, Columbia U., 1979; First Claire Watson Forrest Meml. lectr. U. Oreg., U. Calif.-Berkeley, U. So. Calif., 1982. Major archtl. works include: Restoration of St. Mark's Ch. in the Bowery, N.Y.C., 1970-82, Two Bridges Urban Renewal Area Housing, 1970-84, Jennings Hall Sr. Citizens Housing, Bklyn., 1980, Goddard Riverside Elderly Housing and Community Ctr., N.Y.C., 1983. Recipient Bard 1st honor award City Club N.Y., 1969, Bard award of merit, 1975, 82; Residential Design award A.I.A., 1969; award for design excellence HUD, 1970; Honor award N.Y. State Assn. Architects-AIA, 1975; 1st prize Nat. Trust Historic Preservation, 1975; Honor award Nat. Trust Historic Preservation, 1983; art. of merit Mcpl. Art Soc. N.Y., 1983; Pub. Service award Settlement Service award, 1983. Fellow AIA (dir. N.Y. chpt., chmn. commn. archtl. edn. 1971-73, chmn. nat. task force on women in architecture 1974-75, v.p. N.Y. chpt. 1975-77, chmn. ethics com. 1975-77); mem. Alliance of Women in Architecture (founding mem., mem. steering com. 1972-74), Architects for Social Responsibility (exec. com. 1982—), Columbia Archtl. Alumni Assn. (dir. 1968-71). Home: 13 Bank St New York NY 10014 Office: 434 6th Ave New York NY 10011

EDELSON, ZELDA SARAH TOLL, editor; b. Phila., Oct. 18, 1929; d. Louis David and Rose (Eisenstein) Toll; m. Marshall Edelson, Dec. 27, 1952; children—Jonathan Toll, Rebecca Jo, David Jan. B.A., U. Chgo., 1949, postgrad., 1949-52. Editor-writer Consol. Book Pubs., Chgo., 1953-56; social worker Balt. City Dept. Pub. Welfare, 1956-57; pub. relations writer Md. Dept. Employment Security, Balt., 1958-59; museum editor Yale Peabody Mus., New Haven, 1970-76, head publs., 1976—, editor mus.'s Discovery mag., 1983—; lectr. in sci. writing Yale U., 1983-84. Editor numerous publs. including: A Guide to the Age of Mammals, 1978. U. Chgo. scholar, 1947-51. Mem Council Biology Editors, Soc. Scholarly Publishing, Am. Assn. Museums (awards of distinction 1985, 86), New Eng. Conf. Museums. Office: Publications Office Yale Peabody Mus Natural History 170 Whitney Ave PO Box 6666 New Haven CT 06511

EDELSTEIN, PAULA CRAVEN, entertainment company executive; b. Houston, Oct. 10, 1950; d. Moritz Virano and Judith (Berwick) Craven; m. Ronald Steven Edelstein, Dec. 27, 1981. B.A., U. Ill.-Chgo., 1974; student U. Houston, 1969-71. Pres., Adesta Prodns., Los Angeles, 1983-85; exec. asst. to v.p. Walt Disney Prodns., Los Angeles, 1985; exec. asst. to pres. Motown Prodns., Los Angeles, 1985—. Author: Love Poems for Disappointed Mistresses, 1983. Mem. Women in Film, Hollywood Radio and TV Soc., Nat. Assn. for Female Execs., Am. Mgmt. Assn., Phi Theta Kappa. Democrat. Episcopalian. Avocation: horseback riding.

EDELSTEIN, ROSEMARIE HUBLOU, nurse, educator, consultant; b. Drake, N.D., Mar. 3, 1935; d. Francis Jerome and Myrtle Josephine (Merbach) Hublou; B.S. in Nursing, St. Teresa's Coll., 1956; M.A. in Edn., Holy Names Coll., 1977; Ed.D., U. San Francisco, 1982; cert. public health nurse U. Calif., Berkeley, 1972; postgrad. in Pub. Health, U. Ariz., 1985; m. Harry Georg Edelstein, June 22, 1957 (div.); children—Julie, Lori, Lynn, Toni Anne. Dir., clin. supr. San Francisco Sch. for Health Professions, 1971-74, Rancho Arroyo Sch. Vocat. Nursing, Sacramento, 1974-75; intensive care nurse Kaiser-Permanente Hosp., San Rafael, Calif., 1976-77; dir. inservice edn. Ross (Calif.) Hosp., 1977-78; assoc. dir. nursing edn. St. Francis Meml. Hosp., San Francisco, 1978—; clin. and home health cons. instr. CPR. Served to USAR. Mem. Calif. Nurses Assn., Am. Heart Assn., Sigma Theta Tau. Roman Catholic. Author: (with Jane F. Lee) Acupuncture Atlas, 1974; The Influence of Motivator and Hygiene Factors in Job Changes by Graduate Registered Nurses, 1977; Effects of Two Educational Methods Upon Retention of Knowledge in Pharmacology, 1981; contbr. articles to profl. jours. Office: PO Box 696 Ross CA 94957

EDENFIELD, VIRGINIA ANNE, lawyer; b. Augusta, Ga., Jan. 16, 1949; d. John Greenwood and Virginia (Jameson) Lyon. B.A., U. N.C., 1970; J.D., 1975. Bar: Va. 1975. Atty., Legal Aid Soc. Roanoke Valley, Va., 1975—. Contbg. writer, editor A Women And the Law-A Handbook for North Carolina, 1975. Bd. dirs. Planned Parenthood, 1982—, Mahala (shelter for abused women), 1975—, Free Clinic of Roanoke Valley, 1977-82, Acting Co. of Roanoke Valley, 1985—. Mem. ABA, Va. State Bar Assn. (mem. dist. ethics com.), Roanoke Bar Assn., Va. Women Attys. Assn. (bd. dirs. 1981-83, legis. com. 1984-85), Va. Trial Lawyers Assn., Am. Trial Lawyers Assn. ACLU, NOW, Phi Beta Kappa. Democrat. Home: Route 4 Box 480 Roanoke VA 24018 Office: Legal Aid Soc Roanoke Valley 312 Church Ave SW Roanoke VA 24016

EDERER-SCHWARTZ, JANE, dance therapist; b. N.Y.C., Dec. 1, 1939; d. Abel and Gertrude (Glass) Ederer; A.B., Queen's Coll., City U. N.Y., 1961; M.S.W., Columbia U., 1966, M.A., 1975. Movement therapist Day Hosp., St. Luke's Hosp., N.Y.C., 1975-79; program dir. Shellbank Jewish Center, Bklyn., 1978—; movement therapist Shaaray Tefila, N.Y.C., 1978—, Creative Arts Rehab. Center, N.Y.C., 1980—; faculty dept. dance N.Y.U., 1980—; pvt. practice, supr. dance therapy; founding bd. dirs. Laban Inst. Movement Studies, N.Y.C., 1977—. Grantee, NIMH, 1964-66; cert. movement analyst Laban Inst. Movement Studies; cert. social worker, N.Y. State. Mem. Nat. Assn. Social Workers, Am. Dance Therapy Assn. (chmn. edn. N.Y. State 1980—, chmn. N.Y. State 1985—), Acad. Registered Dance Therapist. Home: 544 E 86th St New York NY 10028 Office: 251 W 51st St New York NY

EDGAR, KATHRYN MARIE SNYDER, guidance counselor; b. Belle Fourche, S.D., Nov. 11, 1960; d. Gerald Dean Snyder and Alfreda Ann Kayras; m. John Frederick Edgar, Nov. 5, 1980; 1 child, John. A.A.S, Community Coll. Air Force, 1982; B.S., Black Hills State Coll., 1981; M.P.A., U. S.D., 1983; M.Ed., S.D. State U., 1985. Alcoholism counselor Intercept Program, Custer, S.D., 1984-85; guidance counselor Dept Air Force, Edwards AFB, Calif., 1985—; crisis counselor HelpLine, Edwards, Calif., 1985—. Served with USAF, 1978-84. Mem. Am. Assn. Counseling and Devel., NOW, Nat. Abortion Rights Action League, Com. for Peace and Social Justice, NAACP. Democrat. Avocations: sports; fundraising for community projects. Office: Education Service Office 6510 ABG/DPE Edwards AFB CA 93523

EDGERTON, ADELE PLEASANCE, lawyer; b. N.Y.C., May 17, 1949; d. Malcolm James and Adele (Pleasance) E.; m. Todd Rofuth, June 19, 1982. B.A., Yale U., 1971; J.D., Boston U., 1976; LL.M. in Taxation, NYU, 1981. Bar: N.Y. 1977, Mass. 1983, Pa. 1984. Assoc. Curtis, Mallet-Prevost, Colt & Mosle, N.Y.C., 1977-81, Fine & Ambrogne, Boston, 1981-83; asst. counsel Pa. Dept. Revenue, Harrisburg, 1983-84; assoc. Rhoads & Sinon, Harrisburg, 1984—. Mem. Pa. Bar Assn., Mass. Bar Assn., N.Y. State Bar Assn., ABA. Office: Rhoads & Sinon 410 N 3d St Harrisburg PA 17108

EDGERTON, MARY ALICE, networking executive; b. Atlanta, Tex., Dec. 9, 1920; d. Raymond William and Ada Lou (Blades) Riley; student Pasadena Community Playhouse, 1939-41; m. James E. Edgerton, Feb. 8, 1942; 1 dau., Sarah Jane. City clk. Hermosa Beach, Calif., 1967-71; election cons. Computer Election Systems, Berkeley, Calif., 1970-73, legis. agt., 1973-77, project dir., 1975-77; Calif. state mgr. News Election Service, Los Angeles, 1978; founder, dir. Creative Services Network, Pub. Network News, San Pedro, Calif., 1980—; writer, lectr. on networking, 1980—. Life mem. PTA; pres. Friends of Library, 1962-63; ministerial student Redondo Beach Ch. of Religious Sci. Named Hermosa Beach Woman of Yr., 1968; recipient Disting. Service award City of Hermosa Beach, 1971. Deomcrat. Pub., Creative Mind in Action, 1985. Home: 17327 E Boca Dr Fountain Hills AZ 85268

EDGMON, JOYCE ANN, cosmetics co. exec.; b. Tuttle, Okla., Sept. 6, 1939; d. Leroy A. and Sarah Alice (Mc Bride) Mc Clure; B.A. in Bus., Okla. U., 1957; student Okla. Real Estate Coll., 1975-76; children—Ricky Joe, Vicki Diane. Owner, operator beauty shop Blanchard, Okla., 1968-70; spl. agt. Gt. So. Life, Oklahoma City, 1971-75; sales agt. Employers of Wausau, Oklahoma City, 1976-78; field rep. Redken Labs., Inc., Oklahoma City, 1978, dist. mgr., St. Louis, 1978—; hon. dep. ins. commr. State Okla., 1973-74. Pres. PTA, Blanchard Sch. System, 1970-78; state v.p. Okla. Dairy Assn., 1968-72; v.p., sec. Blanchard Rodeo Assn. Mem. Am. Bus. Women's Assn., Beta Sigma Phi. Republican. Baptist. Office: 6625 Variel Ave Canoga Park CA 91303

EDIN, KAREN GREEN, corporate management company executive; b. Chgo., Dec. 30, 1959; d. Daniel L. and Wanda (Golik) Green; m. Ronald C. Edin, June 7, 1980. Student Elgin Community Coll., 1978. Mgr. Corporate Mgmt. Co., Slidell, La., 1979-83, v.p., 1984-85, pres., 1986—. Author: Surplus Digest, 1979. Mem. Nat. Assn. Female Execs. Avocations: tennis; painting; scuba diving; golf. Home: 100 Royal Dr Slidell LA 70460 Office: Corporate Mgmt Co Slidell Tower Suite 400 Slidell LA 70458

EDMISTEN, JANE MORETZ, lawyer; b. Boone, N.C., Oct. 25, 1938; d. Ralph D. and Lola (Thompson) Moretz; B.A. with honors, U.N.C., 1960, M.A. with honors, 1962; J.D. with honors, George Washington U., 1967; 1 dau., Martha. Research analyst Georgetown U., 1962-63, Herner & Co., Washington, 1964; mil. assistance analyst USAF, Washington, 1964-66; chief, legis. reference sect. NASA, 1966-69; admitted to N.C. bar, 1967, D.C. bar, 1967, U.S. Supreme Ct. bar, 1972; faculty N.C. Central Law Sch., Durham, 1975-76;

individual practice law, 1975-76; trial atty. tax div., appellate sect. U.S. Dept. Justice, Washington, 1970-74, 76-77; asst. gen. counsel HUD, 1977-79; dep. gen. counsel Merit Systems Protection Bd., 1979-81; mem. firm Moore & Foster, Washington, 1981-82; ptnr. Prokop & Edmisten, Washington, 1983-85; adj. faculty Am. U. Sch. Law, Washington, Nat. Law Ctr., George Washington U. Recipient Outstanding Adj. Faculty award Am. U., 1984. Mem. Am. Bar Assn., D.C. Bar Assn., Fed. Bar Assn. (Tom C. Clark award 1980), Kappa Beta Pi, Phi Delta Delta. Contbg. author BNA Portfolio. Office: 4801 Massachusetts Ave NW Suite 400 Washington DC 20016

EDMOND, PATRICIA DUFFUS, mortgage banker; b. Nacozari, Senora, Mexico, Mar. 23, 1928 (parents Am. citizens); d. John Trent and Glynton (Small) Duffus; student U. Tex., El Paso, 1946-47; m. Robert D. Edmond, Jan. 31, 1963; children—Patricia, Michael, Trent. Clk. typist Mortgage Investment Co., El Paso, 1965-70, br. mgr., 1970-78, sr. v.p., chief underwriter, 1978—. Mem. women's aux. U. Tex., El Paso. Mem. El Paso Bd. Realtors (women's council), Nat. Assn. Home Builders (past dir.), Women's Aux., Am. Bus. Women's Assn. Republican. Episcopalian. Club: Ladies Shrine. Home: 94 Sutton Pl El Paso TX 79912 Office: 5801 Trowbridge El Paso TX 79925

EDMONDS, ANNE CAREY, librarian; b. Penang, Malaysia, Dec. 19, 1924; d. William John and Nell (Carey) E. Student, U. Reading, Eng., 1942-44; B.A., Barnard Coll., 1948; M.S. in L.S, Columbia U., 1950; M.A., Johns Hopkins U., 1959; postgrad., Western Res. U., 1960-61. With War Damage Commn., London, Eng., 1944-46; children's asst. Enoch Pratt Free Library, Balt., 1948-49; reference librarian Sch. Bus. Adminstrn., CCNY, 1950-51; reference librarian, then asst. librarian readers' services Goucher Coll., Balt., 1951-60; exchange reference librarian European services library BBC, London, 1955; instr. Sch. L.S., Syracuse U., summer 1960; librarian Douglass Coll., Rutgers U., New Brunswick, N.J., 1961-64, instr., summer 1962, fall 1963; librarian Mt. Holyoke Coll., 1964—; vis. librarian U. North, Turfloop, South Africa, 1976-77; mem. library vis. com. Wheaton Coll., Norton, Mass., 1978—; Mem. South Hadley (Mass.) Bicentennial Com., 1975-76; mem. accreditation teams Middle States Assn. Colls. and Secondary Schs., 1963—; bd. dirs. U.S. Book Exchange, 1973-76, 80-83; exec. com. New Eng. Library Info. Network, 1974-76, 79-85, chmn., 1982-84; mem. Adv. Commn. Historic Deerfield, 1975-81. Mem. ALA, Am. Hist. Assn., Assn. Coll. Research Libraries (pres. 1970-71, chmn. constn. and bylaws com. New Eng. chpt. 1975-76, pres. New Eng. chpt. 1983-84), AAUP, AAUW. Home: 79 Cold Hill Granby MA 01033

EDMONDS, SLIVY, insurance company executive; b. Norfolk, Va., July 19, 1947; d. Carlton Lee Perkins and Doris Elaine (Edmonds) Dukes. B.A. in Bus. Mgmt., Marymount Manhattan Coll., N.Y.C., 1977; M.B.A. in Fin., Wharton Sch. U. Pa., Phila., 1979. Flight attendant TWA, N.Y.C., 1970-72, analyst, sr. analyst, 1972-77; sr. analyst Bristol-Meyers Co., N.Y.C., 1979-81; sr. investment mgr., v.p. Equitable Life Assurance Soc., N.Y.C., 1981—; pvt. practice personal fin. planning, N.Y.C., 1980-83; tutor N.Y.C. Bd. Edn., 1982. Named 1 of 10 Outstanding Young Working Women, Glamour mag., 1984. Mem. Wharton Bus. Sch. Club N.Y. (treas. 1981-84). Democrat. Office: The Equitable Life Assurance Soc 1285 Ave of Americas New York NY 10019

EDMONDS-GOZA, SHIRLEY EILEEN, lawyer; b. Garnett, Kans., Apr. 12, 1957; d. Thomas Franklin and Ida Mae Sarah (Moon) Edmonds; m. Kirk John Goza, Sept. 11, 1982. B.A., Pittsburg State U. (Kans.), 1979; J.D., U. Kans., 1982. Bar: Mo. 1982. Assoc. Spencer, Fane, Britt & Browne, Kansas City, Mo., 1982—. Tchr. Jr. Achievement, Kansas City, 1982—; mem. Downtown Republicans, Kansas City, 1982—. Recipient Am. Jurisprudence award, 1980; Bus. and Profl. Women scholar, 1977. Mem. ABA, Kans. City Bar Assn. (chmn. publicity 1982-85), Lawyers Assn. (dir. young lawyers sect. 1984—), Phi Alpha Delta (chairperson membership), Kappa Delta Pi (scholar 1977), Phi Kappa Phi, Omicron Delta Kappa, Lambda Sigma. Roman Catholic. Home: 8698 W 101st St Overland Park KS 66212 Office: Spencer Fane Britt & Browne 106 W 14th St Suite 1000 Kansas City MO 64105

EDMONDSON, CAROLYN CRAFT, radio station executive; b. Charlotte, N.C., Aug. 14, 1950; d. Denzel Ray and Alice Elizabeth (Lockwood) Craft; m. Rigdon Osmond Dees, III, Dec. 1, 1973 (div. 1977); m. James Kenneth Edmondson, Jr., Mar. 15, 1980. B.A., U. N.C., 1972. Copywriter Sta. WPIF, Durham Life, Raleigh, N.C., 1972-73; media buyer Luckie and Forney Advt., Birmingham, Ala., 1973-74; account exec., regional mgr. Sta. WEZI, Internat. Harte Hanks Communications, Memphis, 1974-79; gen. sales mgr. Sta. WRVR, Viacom, Memphis, 1979-85; owner Craft Communications Inc., 1985—; chmn. and host TV Cable Mktg. Program, Sales and Mktg., Memphis, 1984—. Sta. WCHL scholar, 1968. Mem. Sales and Mktg. (bd. dirs.), Advt. Fedn. (v.p., bd. dirs., Pyramid award 1984), Uniport Assn. Episcopalian. Home: 7544 Apple Valley Rd Germantown TN 38138 Office: Sta WRVR-AM-FM Radio 5904 Ridgeway St Memphis TN 38119

EDMONDSON, HAZEL MARIE, plumbing and heating supply company executive; b. Mercer County, Ky., June 24, 1929; d. Harlan and Jennie (Chapman) Parker; m. Henry Nathan Edmondson, May 27, 1950; 1 child, Nathan Alan. Grad. high sch., Harrodsburg, Ky. Pres., bookkeeper, office mgr. Edmondson Plumbing and Heating Supply, Inc., Lawrenceburg, Ky., 1975—. Democrat. Methodist. Avocations: china painting; ceramics. Home: 103 Elm St Lawrenceburg KY 40342 Office: Edmondson Plumbing and Heating Inc PO Box 118 Lawrenceburg KY 40342

EDMONDSON, JEANNETTE B., sec. state Okla.; b. Muskogee, Okla., June 6, 1925; d. A. Chapman and Georgia (Shutt) Bartleson; B.A., U. Okla., 1946; m. J. Howard Edmondson, May 15, 1946 (dec.); children—James H. (dec.), Jeanne E. Watkins, Patricia E. Zimmer. Sec. of state State of Okla., Oklahoma City, 1979—. Pres. Okla. affiliate Am. Heart Assn., 1985-86. Mem. Nat. Assn. Secs. of State (pres.). Democrat. Methodist. Office: Office of Sec of State 101 State Capitol Oklahoma City OK 73105

EDMONDSON, LYNN ELLEN, physical therapist facility executive; b. Lodi, Calif., June 11, 1952; d. Leonard and Mildred Irene (Thompson) Preszler; divorced; 1 child, Matthew Armstrong. B.S. in Phys. Therapy, Long Beach State U., 1976. Lic. phys. therapist, Ohio, W.Va., Calif. Staff phys. therapist Dominques Valley Hosp., Compton, Calif., 1976-77; dir. phys. therapy Los Altos Hosp., Long Beach, Calif., 1977-79, Cerritos Gardens Hosp., Hawaiian Gardens, Calif., 1979-80, East Liverpool City Hosp., Ohio, 1980-85; contracted phys. therapist Ohio Valley Home Health Ctr., East Liverpool, 1980-85; pres. Edmondson Phys. Therapy, Inc., Youngstown, Ohio, 1985—; cons. arthritis patient edn. Ohio State Dept. Health, Columbus, 1985—; tchr., lectr. Compton Community Coll., Calif., 1977-78. Mem. com. patient care Cleve. Arthritis Found., 1984—; bd. dirs. Youngstown Arthritis found., 1984—. Ohio Dept. Health grantee, 1983-85. Mem. Am. Phys. Therapy Assn., Allied Health Profls. Arthritis Found., Bus. Profl. Women's Club (treas.). Democrat. Avocations: arts and crafts; reading; golf; bowling; skiing. Office: Edmondson Phys Therapy Inc 1745 Belmont Ave Youngstown OH 44504

EDMUNDS, FRANCES RAVENEL, historical foundation executive; b. Charleston, S.C., Dec. 11, 1916; d. Augustine T. and Harriott (Buist) Smythe; grad. Coll. of Charleston, 1937, hon. degree, 1972; m. S. Henry Edmunds, Dec. 23, 1943; children—Harriott, Eliza, Langdon. With Hist. Charleston Found., 1947—, dir. Ann. Festival of Houses, 1948, dir. Nathaniel Russell House Mus. and Edmondston-Alston House Mus., 1956, dir. Ansonborough Rehab. Project, 1958-77, exec. dir. found., 1947—; dir. Historic Charleston Reprodns. program; chmn. Drayton Hall Council; bd. dirs. Spoleto Festival USA, Thomas Jefferson Meml. Found.; radio and TV appearances; speaker on preservation. Recipient Historic Savannah Preservation award; Charleston Realtor Appreciation award; citation Preservation Soc. Charleston; Conservation Service award U.S. Dept. Interior; U.S. Dept. Interior Conservation award, others. Mem. Nat. Trust Historic Preservation (citation 1968, Louise duPont Crowninshield award 1971), Am. Assn. State and local History, Am. Mus. Assn. Home: 10 Bedon's Alley Charleston SC 29401

EDSALL, DEBORAH CHRISTINE (ROSE), landscape architect, consultant; b. Rochester, N.Y., Aug. 12, 1942; d. Earl Arlington and Mildred Carol (Schoenheit) Rose; m. John Frederick Edsall, June 21, 1964; 1 child, Scott Christopher. B.S. in Biol. Sci., Mich. State U., 1964; B. Land Architecture, Ohio State U., 1970. Registered landscape architect, Ky., Ohio. Land architect Ohio State U., Columbus, 1968, Ohio Dept. Hwys., Columbus, 1968; planning technician Parkins, Rogers & Assocs., Detroit and Columbus, 1969; landscape architect technician Schooley Cornelius Assoc., Columbus, 1972-73; landscape architect Edsall & Assocs., Columbus, 1973—; people to people landscape architect, planner del. People's Republic of China, 1981; vis. lectr. Mich. State U. Author: (with others) Brooklyn Botanical Gardens: Plants and Gardens, 1967. Mem. Ohio Arts Council, Columbus, 1984—, chmn. art in pub. places panel, 1984; mem. Columbus Devel. Commn., 1985—. Recipient numerous awards Illuminating Engring. Soc. N.Am., Kingsdale Shopping Ctr., Ohio chpt. Am. Soc. Landscape Architects, 1978; Franklin Commons, 1979; Goodale Park Playground, Fifth Ave. Elementary Sch., 1984, Parsons Ave. Urban Design Action Plan, 1984, exterior recognition award One Crosswoods Ctr., 1985, others; landscape design winner Women in Design Internat. cert. of honor 1983. Mem. Urban Land Inst., Soc. Environ. Graphic Designers, Constrn. Specifications Inst., Am. Soc. Landscape Architects (Ohio chpt. and Buckeye sect., Columbus C. of C. (local legis. affairs com. 1981-86, taxation subcommittee 1983). Republican. Avocations: music; reading; family activities. Home and Office: Edsall & Associates 754 Neil Ave Columbus OH 43215

EDWARDS, AUDREY MARIE, editor, writer; b. Tacoma, Apr. 21, 1947; d. Cyril Alfred and Bertie Marie (Edwards) E. B.A., U. Wash., 1969; M.A., Columbia U., 1974. News editor Community News Service, N.Y.C., 1974-75; promotion news editor Fairchild Publs., N.Y.C., 1975-77; assoc. editor Black Enterprise, N.Y.C., 1977-78; sr. editor Family Circle mag., N.Y.C., 1978-81; editor Essence mag., N.Y.C., 1981—; instr. NYU, N.Y.C., 1983-84; lectr. New Sch. for Social Research, N.Y.C., 1984. Author children's books: Muhammad Ali: The Peoples' Champ, 1977; The Picture Life of Stevie Wonder, 1977. Mem. Am. Soc. Mag. Editors, Nat. Assn. Black Journalists (regional dir. 1981-83). Home: 45 Plaza St New York NY 11217 Office: Essence Communications 1500 Broadway New York NY 10036

EDWARDS, CARLA LEE CARLIN, recreation and theme park management consultant; b. Oakland, Calif., Apr. 12, 1945; d. Clay Thomas and Eileen (Laughlin) Birdsall; m. Robert Joseph Edwards, Aug. 29, 1964 (div. 1979); children—Kent Joseph, Kelly Marie. Student San Joaquin Delta Coll., 1964-68. Announcer, K-Joy Radio Sta., Stockton, Calif., 1962-63; telephone operator San Joaquin Telephone Co. Manteca, Calif., 1963-65; co-owner Creative Touch, Manteca, 1967-70; chief communications div. Defence Depot Tracy (Calif.), 1965-81; owner Carla Edwards Rental Properties, Manteca, 1979—; co-owner Gemini Investments, Stockton, Calif., 1982—; owner Carla Edwards & Assocs., Manteca, 1979-81; mgr. advt. Oakwood Lake, Inc., Manteca, 1981-82, gen. mgr., 1982-8613 ; bd. dirs. Stockton Conv. and Visitors Bur., Manteca, 1982-83. South county dir. United Cerebral Palsey, Stockton, 1981; dir. publicity Manteca Pumpkin Festival, Manteca, 1979-83; promotions dir. Muscular Distrophy, Manteca, 1982. Served with USCGR, 1973-75. Mem. San Joaquin Rental Property Owners Assn., Pacific Athletic Found., Womens Network, Delta C. of C. (dir.), Manteca C. of C., Stockton C. of C., Am. Back Soc. Republican. Roman Catholic. Clubs: Marina West Yacht, Stockton Women's Profl., Pacific Athletic Found. (Stockton). Home: 755 14th Ave Apt 515 Santa Cruz CA 95062 also Village West Marina C-Dock Berth 43 6465 Embarcadero Stockton CA Office: Oakwood Lake Inc 874 E Woodward Manteca CA 95336

EDWARDS, CORDELIA MAE (CORDELIA MCFARLAND), writer; b. Runnels County, Tex., Feb. 11, 1917; d. Wilburn Jones and Cynthia Cordelia (Dowdy) McFarland; student So. Meth. U., 1935-39, Okla. State U., 1951-52, Bapt. Coll., 1975-77; m. Carl S. Edwards, Dec. 16, 1939; children—Gregg Stanley, Cholly Clayton, Carolyn Diane, Jean (dec.). Sec., So., Meth. U., Dallas, 1937-38; sec., contbr. stories Oak Cliff Tribune, Dallas, 1953-56; contbr. Dallas Library Anthology Dallas Families, 1979-80, 81-82; mktg. researcher, pollster T.O.P.S., Dallas; mktg. researcher, pollster Bauman Research and Elrick and Lavidge, 1980—. contbr. Historic Dallas Jour., Historic Preservation League, Dallas, 1982. Chmn. resource com. LWV, 1963-65. Mem. Women's Equity Action League, Women's S.W. Fed. Credit Union, Nat. Historic Preservation Assn.; Daus. Republic Tex. Methodist. Clubs: Spa and Racquet (pres.); Old Oak Cliff Conservation League. Author: Happiness is Struggle, 19 . Office: 1707 Rio Vista Dr Dallas TX

EDWARDS, DORIS STECK, nursing educator; b. Montgomery County, Ohio, Dec. 27, 1944; d. Russell Luther and Elsie Elizabeth (Schumaker) Steck; m. Neil Kenneth Edwards, Sept. 17, 1966; children—Jeffrey Kenneth, Steven Donald. Diploma, Miami Valley Hosp. Sch. Nursing, 1965; B.S.N. summa cum laude, U. Cin., 1976, Ed.D., 1984; M.S., Wright State U., 1980. R.N., Ohio. Head nurse Dayton State Hosp. (Ohio), 1965-66; clinic nurse Hamilton County Ct., Cin., 1967-68; nursing instr. Jewish Hosp. Sch. Nursing, Cin., 1976-80; nursing instr. U. Cin., 1980-82, asst. prof. nursing, 1982-86, assoc. prof., 1986—, sophomore dept. chmn., 1983—, exec. com. Women's Studies Faculty, 1983-85. Mem. Southwestern Ohio Nurses Assn. (dir. 1979-82, pres. 1982—, legis liaison 1982-83), Ohio Nurses Assn. (bd. dirs. 1983—, Mary/Hamer Greenwood award), Assembly of Nurse Educators (chmn.), Am. Nurses Assn. (council nurse researchers), Assn. Women Faculty U. Cin. (bd. dirs.), Sigma Theta Tau (3d v.p.), Kappa Delta Pi, Phi Delta Kappa. Lutheran. Home: 7711 Shadow Hill Way Cincinnati OH 45242 Office: College of Nursing and Health U Cin ML 38 3110 Vine St Cincinnati OH 45221

EDWARDS, EDNA JANE, broadcasting company executive; b. Kenton, Ohio, Oct. 9, 1934; d. Leroy Alfred and Stella Josephine (Long) Wilcox; m. Phil Milton Edwards, Aug. 25, 1954. Student Marion Coll., 1952-54. Sec. YWCA, Lima, Ohio, 1954-55; asst. librarian Ohio Wesleyan U., Delaware, 1955-59, Kans. Wesleyan U., Salina, 1959-61; med. sec. various hosps., Ohio, Kans., 1961-64; exec. sec. Blue Ridge Broadcasting, Black Mountain, N.C., 1969-73, gen. mgr., 1973—. Producer, host radio programs Know Your Neighbor, 1974—, Skip A Beat, 1978—, Morning Manna, 1980—. Mem. Christian Bus. and Profl. Women (chmn. 1978-80), Nat. Religious Broadcasters (bd. dirs. 1974—, sec. 1985—, treas. S.E. chpt. 1984—), Christian Writers Conf. (sec. and asst. registrar 1979—), Black Mountain C. of C. Republican. Mem. Christian-Missionary Alliance. Avocations: reading; theatre; sewing; cooking. Office: Blue Ridge Broadcasting Corp Hwy 70 PO Box 158 Black Mountain NC 28711

EDWARDS, ELEANOR MATTIASICH, singer, voice teacher; b. Mt. Vernon, N.Y., May 14, 1938; d. Anton Casimir and Eleanor (Gallessich) Mattiasich; m. Peter L. Edwards, Sept. 4, 1960; 1 child, Jonathan Anthony. Mus.B., Oberlin Coll., 1960; Mus.M., New Eng. Conservatory, Boston, 1963; Sommer Akademie cert. Das Mozarteum, Salzburg, Austria, 1959. Soprano soloist Temple Israel, Brookline, Mass., 1964-76, Trinity Ch., Boston, 1966-80, Boston Pops Orch., 1965, 74; presented by Concert Artists Guild in recital Town Hall, N.Y.C., 1967; voice tchr. pvt. studio, 1972—, South Shore Conservatory, Hingham, Mass., 1978—; soprano soloist with maj. choral orgns. in Boston area; soloist numerous chs., temples; recitalist Isabella Stewart Gardner Mus., other New Eng. locations; soloist European Choral Symposium, Salzburg and Linz, Austria, 1980. Co-chmn. communications com. Derby Parent's Assn., Hingham, 1984-85; choir mem. Old South Union Ch. (Congregational), South Weymouth, Mass., 1980—. Mem. Pi Kappa Lambda. Recipient 2d place award Met. Opera Auditions, Boston, 1966. Democrat. Avocations: needlework; old house restoration. Address: 779 Main St South Weymouth MA 02190

EDWARDS, EVA K., field underwriter; b. Pontllanfraith, S. Wales, U.K., Sept. 18, 1942; came to U.S. 1963, naturalized 1967; d. Sydney James and Kathleen (Jones) Edwards; 1 child, Scott Jason. Basic Tng. Degree, U. Ill., 1972; A.Criminal Justice, Prairie State Coll., 1974. Field underwriter N.Y. Life Ins., Oak Brook, Ill., 1977-79, sales mgr., 1979-85, field underwriter, 1985—; juvenile officer Glenwood Police Dept., Ill., 1965-69; police officer Olympia Fields Police Dept., Ill., 1969-77. Contbr. articles to profl. jours. Named Boss of Year, Profl. Bus. Women's Assn., 1985; Rookie of Year, N.Y. Life Ins. Co., 1978; Counselor of Year, Rich Central High Sch., 1975. Avocations: singing. Office: Edwards Financial Group PO Box 5241 Oak Brook IL 60522-5241

EDWARDS, GAIL WARREN, polygraph examiner, security consultant; b. Wilson, N.C., Sept. 21, 1947; d. Oscar Aaron and Bettie (Pridgen) Warren; m. Johnnie Warren Edwards, Jr., Feb. 18, 1967; 1 child, Phillip Dean. Diploma practical nurse edn. Nash Tech. Inst., 1972, A.S., 1978; diploma Acad. Polygraph Sci. and Methodology, Charlotte, 1984-85. R.N.; lic. polygraph examiner. House supr. Community Hosp., Rocky Mount, N.C., part time 1979-81; staff nurse Nash Gen. Hosp., Rocky Mount, part time 1979-82; office nurse, mgr. Dr. H.E. Hendriks, Jr., Rocky Mount, 1979-84; polygraph examiner Edwards Polygraph Services, Rocky Mount, 1984—. Mem. N.C. Polygraph Assn., Am. Polygraph Assn. (asso.), Am. Soc. Plastic and Reconstructive Surg. Nurses, (co-pres. 1982-84), Am. Bus. Women's Assn., Rocky Mount C. of C. Nat. Assn. Women Polygraphists, Nat. Assn. Female Execs., Republican. Home: 605 S Tillery St Rocky Mount NC 27801 Office: Edwards Polygraph Services 225 Station Square Mall Rocky Mount NC 27801

EDWARDS, GLORIA BANKS, management consultant, educator; b. Yonkers, N.Y., Sept. 18, 1932; d. Richard Henry and Pinkie (Moore) Banks; m. Esmond Herbert Edwards, Aug. 7, 1954 (div. May 1961). B.S., Tchrs. Coll. Columbia U., 1961, M.A., M.Ed., 1977, Ed.D., 1985. Nat. cert. counselor. Research assoc. Met. Applied Research Ctr., N.Y.C., 1969-70; spl. projects coordinator N.Y. Urban Coalition, N.Y.C., 1970-77; field faculty advisor Vt. Coll., 1983—; adj. asst. prof. Herbert H. Lehman Coll., Bronx, N.Y., 1981-84; sr. assoc. Arawak Consulting Corp., N.Y.C., 1984—. Contbr. articles to profl. jours. Mem. Lincoln Ave. Assn. Democrat. Baptist. Club: L'54 (N.Y.C.). Avocations: sculptoring; sketching. Office: Arawak Consulting Corp 210 E 86th St New York NY 10028

EDWARDS, HELEN JEX, lawyer; b. San Francisco, Nov. 17, 1938; d. Cooper Lee and Bettie Marian (Hayes) Jex; m. E. Daniel Edwards, Feb. 4, 1960 (div. 1972); children—Marian Kaye, Steven Daniel. J.D., U. Utah-Salt Lake City, 1978. Bar: Utah 1978, U.S. Dist. Ct. Utah 1978. Legal sec., various firms and locations, 1956-70; placement dir. Law Sch. U. Utah, Salt Lake City, 1970-75; law clk. Utah Sup. Ct., Salt Lake City, 1976-78; atty., 1978-79; corp. atty. Utah Power & Light Co., Salt Lake City, 1979—; instr. Paralegal Program, Salt Lake City, 1980-81, Community Edn., Salt Lake City, 1980; speaker in field. Merlin J. Norton Found. scholar, 1975-78. Mem. ABA, Fed. Bar Assn., Utah State Bar Assn., Salt Lake County Bar Assn., Women Lawyers Utah. Democrat. Office: Utah Power & Light Co PO Box 899 Salt Lake City UT 84110

EDWARDS, JANE ELIZABETH, state administrator; b. Chgo., Oct. 9, 1942; d. Walter William and Helen Lacy (Rummons) Schaible; m. Harvey Jay Edwards, Dec. 31, 1968; children—Amy, Lucy, Julie. B.A. in English, U. Alaska, 1964; J.D., U. Oreg., 1970. Bar: Oreg. Assoc., Keith Burns, Atty., Portland, Oreg., 1971-74; ptnr. Edwards & Edwards, Portland, 1974-75; equal employment coordinator State of Oreg., Salem, 1975-78, budget analyst, 1978-84, corp. commr., 1984—. Contbr. articles to profl. jours. Treas., Salem Aquatic Club, 1983-85. Mem. Oreg. State Bar Assn., Marion County Bar Assn., Mary Leonard Law Soc. Democrat. Home: 1925 Margarett NW Salem OR 97304 Office: Corp Div 158 12th NE Salem OR 97310

EDWARDS, JANNETTE ETTA MARIE, image consultant, personal shopper; b. Ventura, Calif., Jan. 3, 1940; d. William Frank and Janet Elva (Everett) Davis; m. Gary Lynn Lodmell, Aug. 15, 1964 (div. 1973); children—Douglass Scott, Benjamin Reid; m. Melvin P. Edwards, June 20, 1980. B.S., Grand Canyon Coll., 1961; postgrad. Lang. Sch., Geneva, Switzerland, 1965; M.Guidance Counseling, Ariz. State U., 1967. Cert. profl. counselor. Fin. assoc. H.J. Tessier Assocs., Phoenix, 1968-73; dir. of sales Barbizon Sch. Modeling, San Francisco, 1973-74; pres. Metamorphosis, Ltd., Laguna Beach, Calif., 1974-80, Huntsville, Ala., 1984—; dir. advt. Bellevue News, Omaha, 1980-83. Contbr. articles to newspapers and mag. Election team campaigns Huntsville, 1984, 86. Named Women of Accomplishment, Orange Coast Mag., 1978; featured exec. Executive Mag., 1979; featured Los Angeles Times, 1978. Mem. Sales and Mktg. Execs. Ala., Assn. for Humanistic Psychology, Huntsville C. of C. (small bus. com. 1984—), Entrepreneurs of Ala. (charter), Assn. Fashion and Image Cons. (del.), Women's Network of Huntsville (v.p. membership 1986), Am. Bus. Women, Nat. Assn. Female Execs. Democrat. Unitarian Universalist. Clubs: Toastmasters (v.p. Huntsville 1984-86), Heritage. Home: 2210 Lytle St Huntsville AL 35801 Office: Metamorphosis Ltd 2603 Artie St Suite 16405 Huntsville AL 35801

EDWARDS, JULIA WARNER, association executive; b. Houston; d. Frederick Ralph and Diana (Adolph) Warner; m. William F. Edwards, May 2, 1953 (div.); children—William Steven, John David, Victoria Ann Edwards Baumer. B.A., Occidental Coll. Editorial asst. Security World, Los Angeles, 1965-66; tech. writer Auto Club of So. Calif., Los Angeles, 1967-72, communications analyst, 1972-80, supr. personnel communications, 1980—, founder Auto Club Employee Fed. Credit Union, Los Angeles, 1975, pres., 1978-79, bd. dirs., 1976-79. Contbr. articles to Auto Club News. Bd. dirs. Vols. of Am. Maud Booth Family Ctr., North Hollywood, Calif., 1970-77, pres., 1976-77; deacon 1st Presbyn. Ch., North Hollywood, 1974-77, elder, 1978—. Mem. Internat. Assn. Bus. Communicators (conf. planner Los Angeles chpt. 1983, competition judge, 1984-85, various awards for publs.). Avocations: art, theater, watercolor painting, backpacking, cooking. Office: Auto Club of So Calif 2601 S Figueroa St Los Angeles CA 90007

EDWARDS, KATHRYN INEZ, instructional media consultant; b. Los Angeles, Aug. 26, 1947; d. Lloyd and Geraldine E. (Smith) Price; m. Gregor Quentin Edwards, June 7, 1969; 1 child, Bryan. B.A. in English, Calif. State U.-Los Angeles, 1969, supervision credential, 1974, adminstrn. credential, 1975; M.Edn. Curriculum, UCLA, 1971; Ph.D., Claremont Grad. Sch., 1979. Tchr., Los Angles Pub. Schs., 1969-78, adv. specially funded programs, 1978-80, libraries and learning-resource program, 1980-81, instructional specialist, 1981-84; cons. instructional media Los Angeles County Office of Edn., Downey, Calif., 1984—; cons. Walt Disney Prodns., Alfred Higgins Prodns., others. Author guides and curriclum kits. Mabel Wilson Richards scholar, 1968; Calif. Congress Parents and Tchrs. scholar, 1968; UCLA fellow, 1968; others. Mem. Nat. Assn. Minority Polit. Women, Alpha Kappa Alpha, Los Angeles Reading Assn. (v.p.), Calif. Assn. Tchrs. of English (conf. del. 1982), Assn. Supervision and Curriculum Devel., Calif. Media and Library Educators Assn., Nat. Assn. Women in Media. Democrat. Roman Catholic. Avocations: reading; gardening; sewing. Home: 6005 Wooster Ave Los Angeles CA 90056 Office: 9300 E Imperial Hwy Downey CA 90242

EDWARDS, LAURIE ELLEN, home-based services company executive, educator; b. San Diego, June 3, 1951; d. Donald Morgan and Doral (Erickson) Hurd; m. William E. Edwards, Dec. 5, 1981. Student Calif. Poly. State U., 1977; B.A., Nat. U., San Diego, 1978; postgrad. U. Calif.-San Diego, 1982-84; M.S., Chapman Coll., 1986. Founder, owner La Jolla Village Secretarial Services, Calif., 1981-82; founder, owner Am. Med. Claims, La Jolla, 1981-86; pres., originator At Your Home Services, San Diego, 1984—; cons. LaJolla Light Printers, 1985—; instr. bus. Palomar Coll., Mira Costa Coll., San Diego Community Colls., 1981—; lectr. in field. Columnist, University City Gazette, 1982. Mem. La Jolla Town Council, 1981-84; assoc. Indsl. Recreational Council, San Diego, 1983-85. Mem. Nat. Assn. Female Execs., Calif. Bus. Edn. Assn., ASTD, Nat. U. Alumni Assn. Republican. Avocations: photography; travel; exercising; family life. Home and Office: 1512 Laurel Rd Oceanside CA 92054

EDWARDS, MARIE BABARE, psychologist; b. Tacoma; d. Nick and Mary (Mardesich) Babare; B.A., Stanford, 1948, M.A., 1949; m. Tilden Hampton Edwards (div.); 1 son, Tilden Hampton Edwards III. Counselor guidance center U. So. Calif., Los Angeles, 1950-52; project coordinator So. Calif. Soc. Mental Hygiene, 1952-54; pub. speaker Welfare Fedn. Los Angeles, 1953-57; field rep. Los Angeles County Assn. Mental Health, 1957-58; intern psychologist UCLA, 1958-60; pvt. practice, human relations tng., counselor tng. Mem. Calif., Am., Western, Los Angeles psychol. assns., AAAS, Nat. Acad. Religion and Mental Health, Soc. Advancement Mgmt., So. Calif. Soc. Clin. Hypnosis, Internat. Platform Assn. Author: (with Eleanor Hoover) The Challenge of Being Single, 1974, paperback edit., 1975. Office: 6100 Buckingham Pkwy Culver City CA 90230

EDWARDS, MILDRED HOPKINS, county administrator; b. Daytona Beach, Fla., Mar. 24, 1943; d. Andrew Hopkins and Eula (Prince) Hayes; m. Roland Bernard, Sr., July 9, 1963 (dec. 1977); children—Shannel, Roland, Albert III, Mario T. Student Daytona Beach Community Coll., 1972-74; B.S., Bethune-Cookman Coll., 1977. Adminstrv. aide I, Volusia County Govt., Daytona Beach, 1978-79; field ops. asst. Dept. Commerce and Census, Daytona Beach, 1980; utilities clk. Bethune-Cookman Coll., Daytona Beach, 1980-81, asst. research devel., 1981; interim exec. dir. Volusia County Community Action Agy., Daytona Beach, 1981-82, exec. dir., 1982—; staff acct. I, Volusia County Govt., DeLand, Fla., 1977-78; cashier Atlanta Life Ins. Co., Daytona Beach, 1969-72. Mem. NAACP, 1984, Community Forum, Daytona Beach, 1983. Recipient Richard V. Moore Service award Westside Bus. and Profls. Assn., 1983. Mem. Fla. Assn. Community Action Agys., Alpha Kappa Alpha. Democrat. Methodist. Home: 135 S Keech St Daytona Beach FL 32014 Office: Volusia County Community Action Agy 512 S Keech PO Box 2116 Daytona Beach FL 32015

EDWARDS, REGINA BELLE, employment and research firm executive; b. Pensacola, Fla., May 11, 1938; d. Renty Benjamin Franklin and Esther Pearl (Wilson) Franklin Smith; m. Hartwell Ervin Edwards, May 21, 1956 (div. June 1969); children—Calvin, Tina, Ethelyne, Pamela, Mitzi. A.A. in Computer Sci., Southwestern State Coll., Altus, Okla., 1969; B.B.A., Central State U., Edmond, Okla., 1973. Lic. ins. mgr. Account technician Liberty Nat. Bank, Oklahoma City, 1969-71; ins. sales mgr. Universal Life Ins. Co., Oklahoma City, 1971-73; job developer Urban League, Oklahoma City, 1974-76; human resource specialist city of Oklahoma City, 1976-81, personnel technician, 1981-83, on-the-job tng. coordinator, 1983-85; chief exec. officer, pres. Personnel Network, Inc., Oklahoma City, 1985—; mktg. research specialist Burke Research, Cin., part-time 1973-79; research enumerator Dept. Agr., Oklahoma City, part-time 1980-84. Writer PTA handbook, 1967, employment manuals, 1980, 82. Active ARC, Altus, Okla., 1966-68, Cub Scouts, Altus, 1967-68, Okla. Women's Polit. Caucus, 1977-79, Urban League, Oklahoma City, 1973-76. Recipient Nat. Betty Crocker Homemaking award, 1956; Regional Ins. Sales award Universal Life Ins., Memphis, 1972; Humanitarian Services award DAV, 1980; Community Service award Regents Higher Edn., Oklahoma City, 1982. Mem. Am. Bus. Women's Assn., Exec. Females, PTA (local pres. 1966-67, Honor cert. 1967), Delta Sigma Theta. Democrat. Avocations: piano, sewing, golf, travel, French and German languages. Home: 27 NE 65th St Oklahoma City OK 73105 Office: Personnel Network Inc 4501 Classen Blvd Suite 107 Oklahoma City OK 73118

EDWARDS, RUTH BAX, nurse, educator; b. Waynesville, Mo., Feb. 13, 1947; d. Martin Bernard and Gertrude Cecelia (Luebbert) Bax; m. William Lane Edwards, Oct. 27, 1973 (div. Dec. 1978). B.S. in Nursing, U. Mo., 1969; M.S. in Nursing, U. Tex., 1973; Ed.D. in Curriculum and Instrn., U. Kans., 1984. Staff nurse U. Mo. Med. Ctr., Columbia, 1969-70; instr. nursing U. Mo., 1970-71; staff nurse St. Luke's Hosp., Kansas City, Mo., 1971-72; assoc. prof. nursing William Jewell Coll., Liberty, Mo., 1973-86, prof., 1986—; staff nurse Bapt. Med. Ctr., Kansas City, Mo., 1975—. Author: (with others) Medical Terminology, computer program, 1981. Mem. Am. Nurses Assn., Am. Assn. Critical Care Nurses (cert.), Sigma Theta Tau. Republican. Roman Catholic. Home: 8801 W 102d St Apt 4 Overland Park KS 66212 Office: William Jewell Coll Liberty MO 64068

EDWARDS, RUTH ELLEN CHARLES, social worker; b. Boston, May 24, 1945; d. Jacob and Anne (Rosenfelt) Charles; A.B., Boston U., 1967; A.M. (VA grantee), U. Chgo., 1969; m. William H. Edwards, Dec. 22, 1973; 1 child, Jacob. Faculty, Morraine Valley Community Coll., Palos Hills, Ill., 1972-73; clin. social work adminstr. Pilsen-Little Village Mental Health Center, Chgo., 1969-76; adminstr. admissions Tinley Park (Ill.) Mental Health Center, 1976-78; aftercare program coordinator Beverly-Morgan Park Mental Health Center, Chgo., 1978-84; partner, Chgo. Women's Therapy Collective, 1976—. Mem. Nat. Assn. Social Workers, Council on Women's Programs, Acad. Cert. Social Workers, State Street Bus. and Profl. Women's Club. Home: 10106 S Prospect Ave Chicago IL 60643 Office: Chgo Women's Therapy Collective Suite 1934 55 E Washington St Chicago IL 60602

EDWARDS, RUTH MARIE, nursing adminstrator; b. Oklahoma City, May 20, 1957; d. John Edward and Elizabeth Irene (Shiplet) E. B.S. in Nursing, U. Okla., 1980. Night supr. Stroud Mcpl. Hosp., Stroud, Okla., 1980-81, dir. nursing, 1981-84; clin. nurse mgr. St. Mary Hosp., Langhorne, Pa., 1984—. Bd. advisors Lincoln County Home Health Care, Chandler, Okla., 1981-83; camp nurse Falls Creek Bapt. Assembly, Davis, Okla., 1981, 82, Chandler council Girl Scouts Am., 1981. Mem. Nat. League Nursing, Nat. Soc. Nursing Service Administrs. Democrat. Bapt. Avocations; training and teaching horses; skiing. Home: 130 S State St Apt C Newtown PA 18940 Office: St Mary Hosp Langhorne-Newtown Rd Langhorne PA 19047

EDWARDS, VIVIAN WIGGS, personnel official; b. Rhome, Miss., Oct. 17, 1941; d. Thurman Allen Wiggs and Mattie (Richey) Burchfield; m. Lester Bussell, June 14, 1959 (div. May 1967); children—Dennis, Allen, Roger, Terry; m. 2d Gregory Kent Edwards, Feb. 14, 1976; 1 son, Ryan. A.S., Sierra Coll., Rocklin, Calif., 1972; student North Tex. State U., 1976—. Tchrs. asst. Sierra Coll., 1969-72; acctg. clk. Internat. Meat Co., El Paso, Tex., 1975-76; acctg. clk. Poco Graphite, Decatur, Tex., 1976-78; personnel dir. 1st Tex. Med., Inc., Lewisville, Tex., 1978—. Mem. Pvt. Industry Council, co chmn., 1982, trustee Fairhaven Retirement Ctr., 1983—; mem. Denton Citizens Traffic Safety Commn. Served with U.S. Army, 1973-75. Mem. Denton Personnel Assn. (treas. 1982-84), Dallas Personnel Assn., Med. Group Mgmt. Assn., Bus. and Profl. Women's Club (pres. 1982), North Tex. Assn. Med. Adminstrs., Med. Adminstrs. Tex., Denton C. of C. Home: 1300 Dallas Dr Apt 1214 Denton TX 76205

EDWIN, ELIZABETH HOPE, assistant editor Paso del Norte magazine; b. Colorado City, Tex., Aug. 26, 1959; d. John Reed and Fanelle (Boney) E. B.A., Tex. Tech. U., 1981. Editor, La Ventana, Tex. Tech. U., 1978-80; mktg. rep. pub. relations Stewart Title Co., El Paso, Tex., 1982, freelance prodn., 1981-83; prodn. asst. Paso del Norte mag., El Paso, 1983, asst. editor, 1984—; bookkeeper Southwest Veterinary Hosp., El Paso, 1976-81, Vista del Sol Veterinary Hosp., El Paso, 1977—; prodn. asst. Miss Tex. USA Pageant, 1979, 83, Miss California USA Pageant, 1979, 83. Mem., El Paso Rehab. Aux., 1982—. Named Maid of Cotton, Faben's Cotton Festival, 1979, Sun Princess El Paso Sun Bowl Assn., 1978. Mem. Women in Communications Inc., Pub. Relations Soc. Am., Sigma Delta Chi, Pi Beta Phi (yearbook chmn. 1983-84). Club: El Paso Woman's. Home: 8700 Parkland Dr El Paso TX 79925 Office: 300 E Santonio St Paso del Norte Suite 415 El Paso TX 79925

EFFINGER, KATHARINA VIOLA, hosp. exec.; b. Milw., June 15, 1941; d. Charles William and Eleanora (Hauer) E.; student Ft. Wayne (Ind.) Luth. Sch. Nursing, 1959-61; B.A. in Behavior Scis., Nat. Coll. Edn., Evanston, Ill., 1981. Reservation supr. Braniff Internat., 1961-69; sales rep. United Gasket Corp., 1969-70; admitting mgr. MacNeal Meml. Hosp., Berwyn, Ill., 1970-73; bus. office mgr. Lake Forest (Ill.) Hosp., 1974-77; asst. v.p. fin. Victory Meml. Hosp., Waukegan, Ill., 1978—; adv. bd. Lake County Vocat. Center. Mem. Hosp. Fin. Mgmt. Assn., Nat. Assn. Patient Accounts Mgrs. Office: 1324 N Sheridan Rd Waukegan IL 60085

EGAN, SISTER EILEEN MARY, college president, English educator; b. Boston, Jan. 11, 1925; d. Eugene O. and Mary B. (Condon) E. B.A., Spalding Coll., 1956; M.A., Catholic U. Am., 1963, Ph.D., 1966; postgrad. (Inst. Internat. Edn. fellow) Oxford U. (Eng.), 1963; postgrad. Smith Coll., 1967-68; J.D., U. Louisville, 1981. Bar: Ky. 1981. Tchr., adminstr. secondary schs., 1956-63; tchr. dept. English Catholic U. Am., 1963-66; chmn. dept. English Spalding Coll., 1966-67, v.p., 1968-69, pres., 1969—; adminstrn. intern Smith Coll., 1967-68; bd. dirs. Kentuckiana Metroversity, 1972—, exec. com., 1977—, chmn. 1982-83; dir. Fed. Res. Bank of St. Louis. Bd. dirs. Louisville Central Area, Inc., 1979, 80—; bd. dirs. Met. United Way, 1976-80; mem. exec. bd. Old Ky. Home council Boy Scouts Am., 1976—; bd. dirs. Internat. Ctr. U. Louisville, 1980—; mem. community audit com. Jefferson County Bd. Edn., 1980-83; trustee Jewish Hosp. Assn., 1982—; mem. Ky. Country Day Sch. Bd., mem. nominating com., 1982-83, mem. long-range planning com., 1983—. Recipient Equality award Louisville Urban League, 1978; Blanche B. Ottenheimer award Louisville Jewish Community Ctr., 1978; Brotherhood award NCCJ, 1979; award Phi Delta Kappa, 1979. Mem. Am. Assn. Higher Edn., AAUW, English Speaking Union, ABA, Ky. Bar Assn., Louisville Area C. of C. (dir. 1981—), Am. Council on Edn., Council Ind. Ky. Colls. and Univs., So. Assn. Colls. and Schs., Council of Ind. Colls. (dir. 1980—), Nat. Assn. Ind. Colls. and Univs. Office: Spalding Univ 851 S 4th St Louisville KY 40203

EGAN, LINDA LEE, nurse; b. Daretown, N.J., Mar. 25, 1947; d. John Joseph and Mary Elizabeth (Woodruff) Egan; A.S. in Nursing, Cumberland County Coll., 1972; B.S.N., Stockton State Coll., 1978. Cottage attendant Vineland (N.J.) State Sch., 1965-69, cottage supr., 1969-72, staff nurse, 1972-74, head nurse intensive care, 1974-75; staff nurse intensive care Cooper Med. Center, Camden, N.J., 1975-77, inservice clinician, 1977-78; dir. nursing Vineland (N.J.) State Sch. Hosp., 1978-79, instr. nursing inservice, 1979-82; rehab. specialist Staff Builders, San Diego, 1982-83; self-employed rehab. specialist, 1983-86; nursing care cons. (part-time) Am. Inst. for Mental Studies, 1980. Respiratory/circulatory emergency instr./multimedia first aide instr. ARC, Vineland, 1975-81; staff nurse Hemet Valley Hosp., Calif., 1986—. Recipient Instl. award N.J. Assn. for Retarded Children, 1969. Mem. Profl. Traveling Nurses Assn., S.Jersey Inservice Exchange, Am. Nurses Assn., N.J. Nurses Assn., Calif. Nurses Assn., Am. Assn. Critical Care Nurses, Am. Nurses Found., Century Club. Roman Catholic.

EGAN, SHIRLEY ANNE, nursing educator; b. Haverhill, Mass.; d. Rush B. and Beatrice (Bengle) Willard; diploma St. Joseph's Hosp. Sch. Nursing, Nashua, N.H., 1945; B.S. in Nursing Edn., Boston U., 1949, M.S., 1956. Instr. sci. Sturdy Meml. Hosp. Sch. Nursing, Attleboro, Mass., 1949-51; instr. sci. Peter Bent Brigham Sch. Nursing, Boston, 1951-53, ednl. dir., 1953-55, assoc. dir. Sch. Nursing, 1955-59; nurse edn. adviser AID (formerly ICA), Karachi, Pakistan, 1959-67; prin. Coll. Nursing, Karachi, 1959-67; dir. Vis. Nurse Service, Nashua, 1967-70; exec. dir. Lowell (Mass.) Vis. Nurse Assn., 1970-71; cons. nursing edn. Pan Am. Health Orgn./WHO to faculty of medicine U. W.I., Jamaica, 1971-72; med.-surg. coordinator Peter Bent Brigham Sch. Nursing, Boston, 1971-73, asso. dir., 1973-79, dir., 1979-85; cons. North Country Hosp., Newport, Vt., 1985—; cons. nursing edn. Pakistan Ministry of Health, Labour and Social Welfare, 1959-67; adviser to editor Pakistan Nursing and Health Rev., 1959-67; mem. exec. bd. Nat. Health Edn. Com., Pakistan. Mem. Nashua Service League, 1970-81, pres., 1973-75; bd. dirs. Nashua Child Care Center, 1968-71; bd. dirs. Matthew Thornton Health Center, Nashua, 1971-81, sec. bd. dirs., 1971-75. Served as 1st lt. Army Nurse Corps, 1945-47. Mem. Nat. League Nursing, Diploma Nurses Assn. (treas. 1981—), Trained Nurses Assn. Pakistan, St. Joseph's Sch. Nursing Alumnae Assn., Boston U. Alumnae Assn., Brit. Soc. Health Edn., Sigma Theta Tau. Contbr. articles to profl. publs. Home: Star Route Darling Hill Lyndonville VT 05851

EGENDORF, NORMA LUCY, advertising agency executive; b. Phila., Oct. 7, 1928; d. Louis R. and Alice Joan (Petrarch) Testardi; m. Irwin A. Egendorf, Feb. 10, 1961 (div. Dec. 1980). Student Charles Morris Price Sch. Advt. and Journalism, 1946-48, Temple U., 1950-52. Advt. asst. Internat. Resistance Co., Phila., 1952-54; advt.-sales promotion mgr. Internat. Resistance Co., Phila., 1954-61; account exec. Mel Richman, Inc., Bala Cynwyd, Pa., 1961-68, v.p., account supr., 1968-72; pres. The Advt. People, Inc., Bala Cynwyd, 1972-84, De Marco Brown Egendorf, Bala Cynwyd, 1984—; lectr. in field. Contbr. articles to profl. jours. Bd. dirs. Muscular Dystrophy Assn. Southeastern Pa., 1960-72, 80-85, pres., 1972-74, 76-80; bd. govs. Main Line YMCA, Ardmore, Pa., 1975-79; bd. dirs. Com. of 70, Phila., 1978-82, 84-85, vice chmn., 1982-84; mem. sch. com. Charles Morris Price Sch., 1980-82, trustee, 1980-85, chmn., 1982-84; mem. publicity com. Am. Swedish Hist. Mus. Recipient Gold Mail Box award Nat. Direct Mktg. Assn., 1968; Silver Medal award Am. Advt. Fedn., 1980; award of merit Artists Guild Delaware Valley, 1981; Disting. Alumna award Charles Morris Price Sch. Advt. and Journalism, Phila., 1982. Mem. Mktg. Communications Execs. Internat. (bd. dirs. 1982-85), Direct Mktg. Assn., Phila. Club Advt. Women. Democrat. Clubs: Germantown Cricket, Poor Richard (pres. 1984-86) (Phila.) (bd. dirs. 1980-85). Avocations: tennis; art; sculpture; theatre. Office: De Marco Brown Egendorf 201 N Presidential Blvd Bala Cynwyd PA 19004

EGET, SUSAN MARIE, association executive; b. Chgo.; d. Peter Paul and Belle Mae (Enyart) E. B.A. in Polit. Sci., Northeastern Ill. U., 1978. Adminstrv. asst., profl. chpt. services, Am. Mktg. Assn., Chgo., 1978-80, dir. profl. chpt. services, 1980—, mem. steering com. Your Opinion Counts, 1985—. Mem. Chgo. Council Fgn. Relations, 1979—. Mem. Am. Soc. Assn. Execs. (Mgmt. Achievement award 1985), Pi Sigma Alpha (Theta Lambda chpt. sec.-treas. 1977-78). Republican. Roman Catholic. Avocations: photography; foreign travel; international affairs. Office: Am Mktg Assn 250 S Wacker Dr Chicago IL 60606

EGGERT, LUCILLE D., service company executive; b. Chgo.; d. Louis B. and Betty M. Duckmann; B.S., Northwestern U.; m. Warren C. Eggert; children—Kenneth, Jeffrey, Gerald. Exec., Capital Bus. Service, Chgo., 1958-63; co-founder, co-owner, exec. Cert. Bus. Service, San Francisco, 1963—; exec. dir. Cert. Career Adv. Service div. CBS Inc., San Francisco, 1977—. Mem. adv. bd., work readiness instr. Regional Occupational Program, 1975-80; chmn. bus. adv. bd. Goodwill Industries, San Francisco, 1985—; pres. bd. dirs. Christian Sci. Ch., 1975-78; arbitrator Better Bus. Bur. Mem. Am. Soc. Tng. and Devel., Bus. and Profl. Women (pres. 1972), Profl. Secs. Internat., Exec. Women Internat., Bay Area Exec. Women's Forum, San Francisco C. of C., Delta Zeta. Clubs: Commonwealth of Calif., Soroptimists. Office: 111 New Montgomery St Suite 700 San Francisco CA 94105

EGGLESTON, SYLVIA JOHNSON, university administrator; b. Balt., Oct. 24, 1940; d. Ralph Ignatius and Hazel Elizabeth (Ring) Johnson; m. Joseph Carr Eggleston, June 16, 1962; children—Elizabeth Ridley, Anne Fleming, Elaine Price. B.A., Goucher Coll., 1962; M. Adminstrv. Sci., Johns Hopkins U., 1981. Research asst. children's psychiat. ctr. Johns Hopkins Hosp., Balt., 1962-63; case worker San Bernardino County Welfare Dept. (Calif.), 1963-65; ednl. psychologist Balt. City Pub. Schs., 1965-68; dir. Goucher II, Goucher Coll., Towson, Md., 1979-82, dir. Goucher Ctr. for Ednl. Resources, 1982-84; dir. devel. for medicine U. Md., Balt., 1984-85; dir. devel. Johns Hopkins U. Sch. Hygiene and Pub. Health, 1985—; cons. pub. affairs Wills & Assocs., Inc., Balt., 1981—; lectr. dept. bus. mgr. and econs. Goucher Coll., 1981-83. Vice pres. bd. trustees Bryn Mawr Sch., Balt., 1981-84; mem. Balt. City Commn. for Women, 1979-82; chmn. Citizens in Volunteerism in City Schs., Balt., 1975-78. Mem. Am. Mktg. Assn. Democrat. Episcopalian. Club: Jr. League Balt. (pres. 1977-79). Home: 705 Stoneleigh Rd Baltimore MD 21212 Office: Johns Hopkins U Sch Hygiene & Pub Health 615 N Wolfe St Baltimore MD 21205

EGLAND, SANDRA LEE, manufacturing company executive; b. Milw., June 12, 1948; d. Elmer William and Evelyn Helen (Salmon) Fricker; m. Kenneth Dean Egland, Aug. 7, 1971. B.S., Bradley U., 1970; M.A., Marquette U., 1973. Teaching asst. Marquette U., Milw., 1970-72; instr. Waukesha Tech. Inst., Wis., 1972-77; compensation analyst Allen Bradley Co., Milw., 1978-79, human resource planning specialist, 1979-81, mgr. personnel research and devel., 1981-83, corp. mgr. staffing and devel., 1983—. Adv. bd. Boston Store, Milw., 1982—; mem. Employee Polit. Action Com., Milw., 1982—. Ill. State scholar, 1966-68; Bradley U. scholar, 1966-68. Mem. Am. Soc. Personnel Adminstrs., Midwest Human Resources Planning Assn., Mortar Bd. (sec. 1969-70), Pi Gamma Mu, Alpha Kappa Delta. Home: W246 S6855 Maple Hill Dr Waukesha WI 53186 Office: Allen Bradley Co 1201 S 2d St Milwaukee WI 53204

EGRESITS, MONICA MARIA, lawyer; Kophaza, Sopron, Hungary, July 27, 1953; came to U.S. 1956; d. Lawrence and Maria (Wild) E.; m. Joseph William O'Neill, Jr., June 6, 1981. A.A., Harrisburg (Pa.) Area Community Coll., 1973; B.A. magna cum laude, Roger Williams Coll., Bristol, R.I., 1975; J.D., Temple U., 1979. Bar: N.Y. 1980. Exam. atty. N.Y.C. Dept. Investigation, 1979-80; dir. check fraud unit, 1980-82; asst. dist. atty. econ. crimes and arson bur. Kings County, Dist. Atty. Office, Bklyn., 1982—. Lector, Sacred Heart Roman Catholic Ch., Bklyn., 1983—. Mem. ABA, N.Y. State Bar Assn., N.Y. County Lawyers Assn., Phi Alpha Delta. Office: Kings County Dist Atty 210 Joralemon St Brooklyn NY 11201

EGRY, ANNE MARIE, business educator; b. Blawnox, Pa., Apr. 10, 1938; d. Julius R. and Anna (Dolhi) E. B.S., U. Pitts., 1968, M.Ed., 1970, Ed.D., 1976. Sec., Blaw-Knox Co., Blawnox, Pa., 1956-68; bus. tcr. New Kensington Comml. Sch., Pa., 1968-69, Gateway High Sch., Monroeville, Pa., 1969-70; bus. tcr., curriculum specialist Pits. Public Schs., 1970—. Tchr.'s aide Pitts. Civic Garden Ctr., 1985. Mem. Eastern Bus. Edn. Assn. (advt. chmn. 1979), Nat. Secs. Assn., Nat. Bus. Edn. Assn., Tri State Bus. Edn. Assn. (exhbns. chmn. 1974-84), Pa. Bus. Edn. Assn., Am. Edn. Research Assn., Internat. Word Processing Assn. (nat. task force on work processing 1979—; bd. dirs. 1980), Delta Pi Epsilon. Grantee Pa. State Dept. Edn., 1982, Allegheny Conf. Community Devel., 1983, 85. Democrat. Roman Catholic. Home: 108 Mattier Dr Pittsburgh PA 15238 Office: Brashear High Sch 590 Crane Ave Pittsburgh PA 15216

EHLERS, ELEANOR MAY COLLIER (MRS. FREDERICK BURTON EHLERS), civic worker; b. Klamath Falls, Oreg., Apr. 23, 1920; d. Alfred Douglas and Ethel (Foster) Collier; B.A., U. Oreg., 1941; secondary tchrs. credentials Stanford, 1942; m. Frederick Burton Ehlers, June 26, 1943; children—Frederick Douglas, Charles Collier. Tchr., Salinas Union High Sch., 1942-43; piano tchr. pvt. lessons, Klamath Falls, 1958—. Mem. Child Guidance Adv. Council, 1956-60; mem. adv. com. Boys and Girls Aid Soc., 1965—; mem. Gov.'s Adv. Com. Arts and Humanities, 1966-67; bd. mem. Friends of Mus. U. Oreg., 1966-69, Arts in Oreg., 1966-68, Klamath County Colls. for Oreg.'s Future, 1968—; chpt. pres. Am. Field Service, 1962-63; mem. Gov.'s Com. Governance of Community Colls., 1967; bd. dirs. Favell Mus. Western Art and Artifacts, 1971—, Community Concert Assn., 1950—, pres., 1966-74; established Women's Guild at Presbyn. Intercommunity Hosp., 1965, trustee hosp. sec. bd. trustees, 1962-65, 76—, mem. bldg. com. 1962-67, mem. planning com., chmn. edn. and research com. hosp. bd., 1967—. Named Woman of Month, Klamath Herald News, 1965; named grant to Oreg. Endowed Fellowship Fund, AAUW, 1971; recipient greatest Service award Oreg. Tech. Inst., 1970-71, Internat. Woman of Achievement award Quota Club, 1981, U. Oreg. Pioneer award, 1981. Mem. AAUW (local pres. 1955-56), Oreg. Music Tchrs. Assn. (pres. Klamath Basin dist. 1979—), P.E.O. (Oreg. dir. 1968-75, state pres. 1974-75, trustee internat. Continuing Edn. Fund 1977-83, chmn. 1981-83), Pi Beta Phi, Mu Phi Epsilon, Pi Lambda Theta. Presbyterian. Address: 1338 Pacific Terr Klamath Falls OR 97601

EHRENBERG, DARLENE BREGMAN, psychoanalyst; b. N.Y.C., Aug. 15, 1942; d. Samuel and Pauline (Gellman) Bregman; B.A. magna cum laude, CCNY, 1963; M.S. (Harrison fellow), Yale U., 1965; Ph.D. (NIMH tng. fellow), N.Y. U., 1970; cert. William Alanson White Inst. Psychiatry, Psychoanalysis and Psychology, 1973; m. Bernard Ehrenberg, Nov. 26, 1970; children—Jonathan, Erica. Pvt. practice psychoanalysis and psychotherapy, N.Y.C., 1969—; supervising analyst and supr. psychotherapy William Alanson White Inst. Psychiatry, Psychoanalysis and Psychology, N.Y.C., 1977—; supr. Inst. Contemporary Psychotherapy, 1974—; clin. instr. psychiatry Albert Einstein Coll. Medicine, 1968-69; conf. presenter. Carnegie Teaching fellow CCNY, 1964. Mem. Am. Psychol. Assn., William Alanson White Psychoanalytic Soc., Phi Beta Kappa. Asst. editor: Contemporary Psychoanalysis, 1979—, editorial bd., 1975-79; contbr. articles to profl. jours. Home and Office: 11 E 68th St New York NY 10021

EHRENKRANZ, SHIRLEY MALAKOFF, university dean, social work educator; b. N.Y.C., Nov. 9, 1920; d. Isidore and Diana Frances (Lewis) Malakoff; A.B., Hunter Coll., 1939; M.A., Bryn Mawr Coll., 1943; M.S.W., U. Pa., 1945; D.S.W., Columbia U., 1967; m. Gilbert Ehrenkranz, Mar. 29, 1946 (dec.); children—Jean, Joel, Pamela; m. 2d, Fred Kasoff, July 11, 1982. Case worker Jewish Welfare Soc., Phila., 1943-44; case supr. S.I. Social Service, N.Y., 1945-48; case supr. United Family & Children's Service, Plainfield, N.J. 1949-53; field instr. Rutgers U., 1960-62; research asst. Columbia U., 1964-65; asst. prof. social work NYU, 1966-68, assoc. prof., 1968-73, prof., 1973—, assoc. dean Sch. Social Work, 1969-76, acting dean, 1976-77, dean, 1977—. NIMH grantee, 1963-64, 65; recipient Disting. Alumna award U. Pa., 1979. Mem. N.Y. State Assn. Deans (v.p. 1979-80, pres. 1980-81), Nat. Assn. Social Workers, Acad. Cert. Social Workers. Contbr. book revs. and articles in field of social work to profl. jours. Office: NY Sch Social Work 3 Washington Sq N New York NY 10003

EHRENREICH, BARBARA, author; b. Butte, Mont., Aug. 26, 1941; d. Ben Howes and Isabelle (Oxley) Alexander; m. John H. Ehrenreich, Aug. 6, 1966; children—Rosa, Benjamin; m. Gary Stevenson, 1983; B.A., Reed Coll., 1963; Ph.D., Rockefeller U., 1968. Editor Health Policy Adv. Ctr., N.Y.C., 1969-70; asst. prof. SUNY-Old Westbury, 1971-74; freelance writer, lectr.; vis. fellow N.Y. Inst. Humanities, N.Y.C., 1980-; editor Seven Days mag., N.Y.C., 1974—; contbg. editor Ms. mag., 1981—. Author: For Her Own Good: 150 Years of the Experts' Advice to Women, 1978, (with Deirdre English) The American Health Empire, 1970, (with John Ehrenreich) Long March, Short Spring, 1969, The American Health Empire, 1970; (with D. English) Witches, Midwives and Nurses: A History of Women Healers, 1972, Complaints and Disorders: The Sexual Politics of Sickness, 1973, For Her Own Good, 1978, The Hearts of Men: American Dreams and the Flight from Commitment, 1983. Recipient award Nat. Mag., 1980; Ford Found. award, 1981; fellow Inst. Policy Studies, 1982—. Mem. PEN, Soc. Study of Social Problems, Health Right. Home: 9 Devine Ave Syosset NY 11791 Office: 19 Univ Pl New York NY 10003

EHRENWERTH, CHARLENE REIDBORD, lawyer, law educator; b. Pitts., Sept. 8, 1949; d. Julius Martin and Patricia B. (Postar) Reidbord; m. David H. Ehrenwerth, July 8, 1973; children—Justin Reid, Lindsey Royce. B.A., Barnard Coll. Columbia U., 1971; J.D., Duquesne U., 1974. Bar: Pa. 1974, U.S. Dist. Ct. (we. dist.) Pa. 1974, U.S. Ct. Appeals (3d cir.) 1977. Asst. dist. atty. Allegheny County, Pa., 1974-76; instr. Carlow Coll., 1977; asst. atty. gen. State of Pa., Pitts., 1976-79; asst. chief counsel Dept. Labor and Industry, Pitts., 1979—, adj. prof. U. Pitts., 1982—. Bd. dirs., vice chmn. Mt. Lebanon Zoning Appeal Bd., Pitts., 1983; area rep. Barnard Coll Columbia U., 1972; social action chmn. Women's League of Conservative Judaism, 1982—. ABA, Pa. Bar Assn., Mem. Allegheny County Bar Assn. (mem. indigent divorce panel 1983—), Assn. Trial Lawyers Am. Republican. Jewish. Clubs: 57 Club (asst. chmn.). Home; 761 Pin Oak Rd Pittsburgh PA 15243

EHRESMANN, KATHLEEN JANE, oil company executive; b. Bklyn., Aug. 6, 1954; d. Frank James and Lydia Catherine (Surdi) E.; m. John J. Janczewski, May 20, 1979 (div. Aug. 1985). B.B.A. with high honors, Pace U., 1983, M.B.A., 1985. Asst. to v.p. exploration Nepco Exploration, N.Y.C., 1975-79; asst. to pres. Ogle Petroleum Inc., N.Y.C., 1980-81; v.p. Interocean Oil & Land Co., N.Y.C., 1981—, also dir.; assoc. Gillis, Haldi & Clark, N.Y.C., 1982—; dir. Interocean Oil Co. of Del., N.Y.C.; adviser Acquisition Capital Ptnrs., N.Y.C., 1983—. Designer leaded stained glass. Pres. Monitor East Assn., Bklyn., 1982-84. Republican. Roman Catholic. Home: 185 Monitor St Brooklyn NY 11222 Office: Interocean Oil & Land Co 680 Fifth Ave New York NY 11222

EHRLICH, GERALDINE ELIZABETH, food service management consultant; b. Phila., Nov. 28, 1939; d. Joseph Vincent and Agnes Barbara (Campbell) McKenna; m. S. Paul Ehrlich, Jr., June 20, 1959; children—Susan Patricia, Paula Jeanne, Jill Marie. B.S., Drexel Inst. Tech., 1957—. Supervisory dietitian ARA Service Co., Phila. and San Francisco, 1959-65; dietary mgmt. cons. HEW, Washington, 1967-68; nutrition cons., hypertension research team U. Calif. Micronesia, 1970; regional sales dir. Marriott Corp., Bethesda, Md., 1976-78; dir. sales and profl. services Coll. and Health Care div. Macke Co., Cheverly, Md., 1978, gen. mgr., 1978-79; v.p. ops., div., 1979-80, rpes. Health Care div., 1980-81; regional v.p. Custom Mgmt. Corp., Alexandria, Va., 1981-83, v.p. mktg., 1983—; dir. Ed M. Bartikowsky Inc., Kingston, Pa., 1983—, Custom Mgmt. Corp., Kingston, Pa., Tennis Patrons, Washington. Mem. Health Systems Agy. No. Va., 1976-77; chmn. Health Care Adv. Bd. Fairfax County Va., 1973-77; vice chmn. Fairfax County Community Action Com., 1973-77; treas. Fairfax County Democratic Com., 1969-73; trustee Fairfax Hosp., 1973-77. Mem. Internat. Women's Assn., Am. Mgmt. Assn., Nat. Assn. Female Execs., Rountable for Women in Food Service, Soc. Mktg. Profls. Club: Interntional (Washington). Avocations: reading. Home: 6512 Lakeview Dr Falls Church VA 22041 Office: Custom Management Corp 700 N Fairfax St Suite 500 Alexandria VA 22314

EHRLICH, LESLIE SHARON, telecommunications executive; b. Bklyn., N.Y., July 30, 1952; d. Abraham and Evelyn (Kuznetz) Ehrlich; m. Lee Marc Kaswiner, Aug. 11, 1979; 1 child, Adam Jason. B.A., New Coll. at Hofstra, 1973; Cert. Paralegal, Adelphia U., 1974; M.A., Montclair State U., 1977; J.D., Pace U. Sch. of Law, 1981. Bar: N.Y. 1981, N.J. 1981. Paralegal AT&T, N.Y.C., 1977-81; mgr. state regulations N.Y. Telephone, 1981-82; atty. Bell Communications Research, 1983-84; mgr. contracts AT&T, Morristown, N.J., 1984—; adj. prof. Seton Hall U., Newark, 1983-84, Am. Paralegal Inst., South Orange, N.J., 1982-83. Chmn. state regulations Nat. Council of Jewish Women, N.J., 1981-82; chmn. edn. Suburban Jewish Ctr., Florham Park, N.J., 1984—. Recipient Gold Key award Pace U., White Plains, N.Y., 1979. Mem. ABA (young lawyers corp. council sec. 1984—, antitrust commn. student liaison 1979-80, Silver Key award 1979), N.Y. Bar Assn., N.J. Bar Assn. Avocations: tennis; horseback riding; water sports; arts; travelling. Office: AT&T 1 Speedwell Ave Morristown NJ 07960

EHRMAN, MADELINE ELIZABETH, government administrator; b. N.Y.C., July 4, 1942; d. Donald McKinley and Marie Madeleine (Brandeis) Ehrman. B.A. summa cum laude Brown U., 1964, M.A., 1965; M.Phil., Yale U., 1967. Sci. linguist U.S. Dept. State, Washington, 1969-73, regional lang. supr. U.S. Embassy, Bangkok, Thailand, 1973-75, lang. tng. supr. U.S. Dept. State, Washington, 1975-84, curriculum and tng. specialist, 1984-85, acting chmn. dept. Asian and African Langs., 1985, chmn. dept. Asian and African Langs., 1986—. Author: The Meanings of the Modals in Present Day American English, 1966; Contemporary Cambodian, 1975; Indonesian Fast Course, 1982; Communicative Japanese Materials, 1984. Mem., ESOL/HILT Citizen's Adv. Council, Arlington County, Va., 1985—, ESOL/HILT Coordinating Com., 1985—. Woodrow Wilson Found. fellow, 1964; NSF fellow, 1964-69; recipient Meritorious Honor award U.S. Dept. State, 1983. Mem. Tchrs. of English to Speakers of Other Langs., Computer Assisted Lang. Instruction Consortium, Am. Assn. Asian Studies, Assn. Devel. Computer Instruction Systems, Phi

Beta Kappa. Avocations: reading; bicycling; gardening. Office: Fgn Service Inst 1400 Key Blvd Arlington VA 22209

EHRMANN, SUSANNA, foreign language educator; b. Detroit, Oct. 17, 1944; d. Frederick Michael and Stephanie (Fiala) Ehrmann. Student Universite Laval, summer, 1965; B.A., Antioch Coll., 1966; M.A.T., U. Chgo., 1968. Cert. tchr., Ill., Tex., Mass. Tchr. fgn. lang. U. Chgo. Lab. Schs., 1967-74, Maimonides Sch., Brookline, Mass., 1975-76, North Shore Country Day Sch., Winnetka, Ill., 1977-78, Copenhagen Internat. Jr. Sch., 1978-79, Houston Community Coll., 1979-81, 84, Kinkaid Sch., Houston, 1980-82, Alief Ind. Sch. Dist., Houston, 1982-85; mem. North Central evaluating team, Chgo., Rockford, 1971; mem. M.A.T. coordinating com. on Romance langs., U. Chgo., 1971-74. Creator German Grammar Game, 1982. Reader for the blind, Chgo., 1972-74. NDEA fellow, 1966-68; Goethe Inst. grantee, summer, 1983. Mem. Am. Assn. Tchrs. of French, Am. Assn. Tchrs. of German. Jewish. Home: 6158 Cedar Creek Dr Houston TX 77057

EHWA, MARY L., tobacco company executive; b. Kansas City, Mo., Aug. 27, 1945; d. James A. and Ora Lee (Elam) Baruxis; m. Carl Robert Ehwa, Jr., June 16, 1967 (div. Apr. 1985). B.J., U. Mo., 1967. Asst. editor NCAA, 1968-71; editor corp. publs. Yellow Freight System, Inc., Overland Park, Kans., 1971-77; ptnr. McClelland Tobacco Co., Kansas City, Mo., 1977-84, pres., 1984—. Recipient awards Am. Trucking Assn., 1973-77, Pipe Collectors Internat., 1985. Office: McClelland Tobacco Co PO Box 7005 Country Club Station Kansas City MO 64113

EIBEN, MARY FRANCES, photographer, editor; b. Dayton, Ohio, Feb. 2, 1958; d. Frank Joseph and Dorothy Helen (Boyle) E. B.S. in Communications, Ohio U., 1982, cert. women's studies, 1982; postgrad. Bowling Green State U., 1984-85. Television news photographer Sta. WCPO-TV (CBS), Cin., 1982-83, Sta. WDHO-TV (ABC), Toledo, 1983-85; television grad. teaching asst. Bowling Green State U., Ohio, 1984-85; film prodn. asst. Woody Allen Fall Project, N.Y.C., 1985—. Avocation: bodybuilding. Home: 240 E 2d St 1C New York NY 10009

EICHEL, GLORIA LILLIAN, guidance counselor; b. Bklyn.; d. Meyer and Anna Rita (Housman) Jacobs; B.A., Hunter Coll., 1936; M.S. in Guidance, Bklyn. Coll., 1969; m. Arthur Eichel, Sept. 9, 1936 (dec. Aug. 1969); children—Alan Charles, Diane Sara, Martin Alexander. Caseworker home relief div. Dept. Welfare, Bklyn., 1938-42; tchr. Bklyn. Bd. Edn., 1950-65, guidance counselor, 1965-80; Supporting Services-Careers cons. Bur. Edn. and Vocat. Guidance N.Y.C., 1981-85; condr. workshops on careers at profl. convs. Active Boy Scouts Am., 1950-81. Recipient plaque for services to parents and students Parents Assn. Public Sch. 181, Bklyn., 1979; Counselor of Yr. award Community Sch. Bd. 17, Bklyn., 1980; plaque for outstanding dedication and commitment to counseling profession N.Y. State Counseling Assn., 1985. Mem. Bklyn. Coll. Guidance Assn. (pres. 1976-79), N.Y.C. Personnel and Guidance Assn. (sec. 1976-79), Nat. Vocat. Guidance Assn. (nat. chair career poetry contest 1979—, rep. nat. conv. 1979, 80, 81), N.Y. State Vocat. Guidance Assn. (pres. 1982—), N.Y. State Personnel and Guidance Assn. (chairperson membership 1980-81, chmn. ret. counselors 1982—), Nat. Career Devel. Assn. (chmn. spl. events and meals for nat. conv. 1985), AAUW (chairperson chpt. edn.). Contbr. articles to N.Y. State Sch. Counselors Newsletters, poems to anthologies; columnist Ret. Counselors Network, 1978-81. Home: 1410 Ave L Brooklyn NY 11230

EICHER, JOANNE BUBOLZ, design educator; b. Lansing, Mich., Sept. 18, 1930; d. George C. and Stella L. (Mangold) Bubolz; m. Carl K. Eicher, June 8, 1952 (div. Dec. 1974); children—Cynthia, Carolyn, Diana. B.A., Mich. State U., 1952, M.A., 1956, Ph.D., 1959. Instr., asst. prof. dept. social sci. Boston U., 1957-61; asst. prof. dept. human environment and design Coll. Human Ecology, Mich. State U., 1961-69, asso. prof., 1969-72, prof., 1972-77; prof. U. Minn., 1977—, head dept. textiles and clothing, 1977-83, head dept. design, housing and apparel, 1983—; dir. Goldstein Gallery, 1983—; research assoc. Econ. Devel. Inst., U. Nigeria, 1963-66; cons. Time-Life, Inc., Howard U., Prentice Hall, Inc. Author: (with Mary Ellen Roach) Dress, Adornment and the Social Order, 1965, The Visible Self: Perspectives on Dress, 1973; African Dress: A Select and Annotated Bibliography of Subsaharan Countries, Vol. I, 1970; Nigerian Handcrafted Textiles, 1976; (with Erekosima and Thieme) Pelete Bite: Kalabari Cut-Thread Cloth, 1982; (with Pokornowski, Thieme and Harris) African Dress Bibliography, Vol. II, 1985. Contbr. articles to profl. jours. Research grantee Internat. Programs, Mich. State U., 1963-64, African Studies Center, 1965-66, 4-H Programs grantee Ethnic Heritage Program, 1974, research grantee Midwest U. Consortium for Internat. Affairs, 1968, 81; Ford Found. individual grantee, 1973; resident scholar Rockefeller Found. Study and Conf. Center, Bellagio, Italy, 1973; research grantee Buguma Internat. Affairs Soc., 1982, 84. Mem. Costume Soc. Am., Walker Art Ctr., Textile Mus., Mpls. Inst. Art, Am. Home Econs. Assn., Am. Sociol. Assn., Assn. Coll. Profs. Textiles and Clothing, Costume Soc. (London, Eng.), Nigerian Nat. Mus. Soc., African Studies Assn., Gamma Sigma Delta, Phi Kappa Phi, Alpha Kappa Delta, Tau Sigma, Alpha Gamma Delta. Democrat. Lutheran. Home: 2179 Folwell St Saint Paul MN 55108

EICHOR, JANICE MUSIC, communications executive; b. Des Moines, Oct. 28, 1941; d. John George and Mignon Emma (Eaton) Music Pauelka; m. John F. Eichor, Dec. 26, 1965; 1 dau., Kristin Mignon. B.F.A., Drake U., 1963; A.A., Stephens Coll., 1961; postgrad. Drake U., 1963-64. Communications cons. South Central Bell, Baton Rouge, La., 1979-80, Southwestern Bell, Houston, 1980-82, AT&T Info. Systems, Houston, 1982-83; account exec. AT&T Communications, Houston, 1983—. Actor, singer, dir., stage mgr. Des Moines Community Playhouse, Drake U., Drama Workshop, Pasadena Playhouse, Red Barn Summer Theatre, Dallas Reperatory Theatre, Richardson Civic Theatre, Garland Civic Theatre, Baton Rouge Little Theatre, Okoboji Summer Theatre, Stephens Coll. Named Outstanding Cons., AT&T Info. Systems, Houston, 1983. Mem. Nat. Assn. Female Execs. Democrat. Home: 16603 Dounreay Houston TX 77084 Office: AT&T Communications 333 Clay St Suite 7700 Houston TX 77002

EICK, NANCY TERESA, financial manager, cost analyst; b. Plainfield, N.J., Feb. 23, 1954; d. Henry Lawrence and Mary Virginia (Meaney) E. B.S., LeMoyne Coll., 1976; M.B.A., George Washington U., 1983. Acctg. analyst W.R. Grace & Co., Somerville, N.J., 1976-77; acctg. asst. Am. Export Group Internat. Services, Inc., Washington, 1978, accounts payable supr., 1978-79, mgmt. acct., 1980-82, mgr. acctg. ops., 1982-85; fin. analyst GTE Govt. Systems Corp., Vienna, Va., 1985—. Vol. Crisis Assistance Info. and Referral Hotline, Alexandria, Va., 1984—; mem. Mental Health Assn., Alexandria, 1984—. Mem. Nat. Assn. Female Execs. Roman Catholic. Club: Maureen Malcolm Irish Dancers. Avocations: jogging; photography; travel. Home: 6490 King Louis Dr 202 Alexandria VA 22312 Office: GTE Government Systems Corp 8330 Old Courthouse Rd Vienna VA 22180

EICK, SHIRLEY A., management information systems executive; b. Trenton, July 3, 1935; d. Benjamin Louis and Ethel Mae (Levering) Hartman; m. Jacob Eick; children—Linda Rae, Wayne, David. A.A.S. summa cum laude, Burlington Coll., Pemberton, N.J., 1982; postgrad. Thomas Edison Coll., Trenton, 1982—. Cert. systems profl. Asst. credit mgr. F.W. Donnelly, Trenton, 1952-53; gen. acctg. Goodall Rubber Co., Trenton, 1953-66, programmer, 1966-68, systems analyst, 1968-72, data processing mgr., 1972-81, asst. v.p. mgmt. info. systems, 1981-85; computer cons. AGS Computers Inc., N.Y.C., 1985—. Mem. Data Processing Mgmt. Assn., Met. N.Y. Honeywell Users (pres. 1982-84), N.Am. Honeywell Users (nat. dir. 1983-84, nat. treas. 1984-86, pres. 1986—), Lutheran Women's Assn. (v.p. Morrisville, Pa. 1967-69), Goodall Bowling League (v.p. 1980-81), Phi Theta Kappa. Home: 1660 Hunters Ct Yardley PA 19067 Office: AGS Computers 111 Broadway New York NY 10016

EICKMAN, JENNIFER LYNN, conference center manager, writer, artist; b. Urbana, Ill., Nov. 7, 1946; d. Marvin A. and Emma L. (Hartrick) Smith; B.F.A., U. Ill., 1967, postgrad. in Art History, 1967-70; m. Gary Edwin Eickman, June 9, 1968. Tchr., Univ. High Sch., Urbana, 1968, Champaign (Ill.) Public Schs., 1969-70; mem. faculty U. Ill., 1968-77, Richland Coll., Decatur, Ill., 1975-77; asst. to dir. of extension in visual arts U. Ill., 1969-70, asst. dir. Allerton House Conf. Center, 1974—; dir. Allerton Art Inst., 1985—; guest lectr., tchr. art workshops. Mem. Pacific Tropical Bot. Gardens, Defenders of Wildlife, Nat. Trust Hist. Preservation, Internat. Platform Assn., Kappa Alpha Theta. Staff writer Champaign-Urbana mag.; author articles on art history, music, edn. and natural history. Home: Gate House Allerton Park Monticello IL 61856 Office: Allerton House Allerton Park Monticello IL 61856

EIDE, MARLENE, county government official, law firm executive; b. Great Falls, Mont., Mar. 4, 1932; d. Howard A. and Maud (Ray) Lund; m. Donald H. Eide, Apr. 2, 1952; children—David, Don Allen, Kjersti, Jennifer. Student, U. N.D., 1949-50. Coordinator, editor, writer Williams County Hist. Soc., Williston, N.D., 1974-77; legal asst. Bjella Neff Rathert Wahl & Eiken, Williston, 1977—; mem. Fort Buford-Fort Union Council, Williston, 1977—; commr. Williams County, Williston, 1981—; mem. N.D. State Banking Bd., Bismark, 1986—. Author, editor: Wonder of Williams, 1976; also articles. Clk.-treas. Williston Twp., 1975-80; active Northwest Human Resources, 1982—. Named Outstanding Woman, Williston Jaycettes, 1976; recipient Appreciation cert. for service on bd. Williston Community Library, 1985. Mem. N.D. Press Women, Assn. Oil and Gas Producing Counties (v.p. 1981—), N.D. County Commrs. Assn. (exec. com. 1982, treas. 1982—). Democrat. Lutheran. Lodges: Eastern Star (worthy matron 1962-63), Rainbow Girls (mother advisor 1961-63). Home: Route 1 Box 56-E Williston ND 58801 Office: Williams County Courthouse PO Box 1246 201 E Broadway Williston ND 58801

EIESLAND, KRISTINE LYN, law enforcement officer; b. Eureka, Calif., Sept. 14, 1951; d. Richard Delbert and Carolyn Joan (Atsatt) Dimick; m. Vern Lee Eiesland, Sept. 16, 1972; 1 child, Benjamin John. B.S., Eastern Oreg. State U., 1973; M.S. U. Portland, 1977; cert. Bd. on Police Standards and Tng., 1978, FBI Nat. Acad., 1983. Probation officer State Oreg., Portland, 1972; dispatcher City Beaverton, Oreg., 1973-75, crime prevention officer, 1978-80, police officer, 1975-81, sgt., 1981—; dir. Beaverton Police Cadets and Reserves Program, 1983—. Founder Police Chaplain Program, 1980-82, Sex Crimes Assistance Team, 1980. Named Police Officer of Yr. Optimist Club, 1980; recipient Woman of Achievement award LLoyd Mushaw Ctr., 1983. Mem. Oreg. Police Officers Assn. (top woman shooter 1976), FBI Nat. Acad. Assn. (master shooter 1983), Beaverton Police Athletic Assn. (pres. 1979-81), Oreg. Assn. Women Police (co-founder), Internat. Assn. Women Police, Internat. Law Enforcement Stress Assn. Republican. Office: City Beaverton 4950 SW Hall Blvd Beaverton OR 97005

EIGEN, JUDITH ANN, designer, crafts developer, importer, consultant; b. N.Y.C., Oct. 11, 1938; d. Morris and Beatrice (Bronfman) E.; m. Morris Sarna, May 1, 1983. B.A., U. Mich., 1961. Social worker Riverdale Children's Assn., N.Y.C., 1960-62; interior designer, owner Designs by Judith Ann, N.Y.C., 1962-69, also importer of crafts; developer of crafts Disney World, J.C. Penny, self, N.Y.C., 1969-80; importer, designer, owner Judith Ann Creations, N.Y.C., 1980—; cons. in field. Designer stage and costume show Casino-Estorial, 1984 (1st prize); costumes show Maderia, Portugal, 1983. Cons., Indian Women's Bur., New Delhi, 1980—. Mem. Women's Bur., Sundar Nagar Assn., Threshold. Jewish. Avocations: skiing, traveling, art. Home: 6 West 77 St New York NY 10024 Office: Judith Ann Creations 530 7th Ave New York NY 10018

EILAND, DEANIE IVA, sales representative, counselor, writer, poet; b. Bryson City, N.C., May 25, 1938; d. James Noel and Ellen (Waldroup) Cochran; m. Royce L. Eiland, Dec. 31, 1955 (dec. Apr. 1963); children—Janice, Lynne, Sue. B.S., Bryce Bus. Coll., High Point, N.C., 1966; B.S. in Radio Tech. and Photog. Sci., Career Tng. Inst., Atlanta, 1972. Tchr. Electronic Computer Programming Inst., Atlanta, 1968-72; salesperson E.R.A. Realty, Atlanta, 1973-78; sales rep. Pitney Bowes, Atlanta, 1979-82, Dallas, 1984—; active counselor, youth orgn., Dallas. Author: Dawn Awaken, 1968; (poetry) End of the Road, 1983; Best of Sunshine, 1984. Pres. Republican fund raising group, Atlanta, 1980. Recipient 84 sales awards, 1979-86. Jewish. Avocations: flying; golfing; swimming; tennis. Home: PO Box 515801 Dallas TX 75251

EILER, MARY KATHERINE, nurse; b. Atlantic City, N.J., Jan. 15, 1957; d. William and Margaret (Speir) E. B.S. in Nursing, Duquesne U., 1979. Registered nurse, Pa. Nurse ICU, Mercy Hosp., Pitts., 1979, nurse neurosurg. unit, 1979; nurse Med.-Surg. Nursing unit Divine Providence Hosp., Pitts., 1979-81; nurse delivery room St. Clair Hosp., Pitts., 1981, nurse cardiac step down/med. surg. unit, 1981—, mem. policy and procedure com., 1984-85; nurse recruiter Divine Providence Hosp., Pitts., 1980-81. Choir mem. Duquesne U. Chapel Choir, Pitts., 1979. Democrat. Roman Catholic. Club: Catholic Alumnae (Pitts.). Avocations: traveling; golf; cross country skiing; theater; symphony. Home: 1290 Highfield Ct Apt 5 Bethel Park PA 15102 Office: St Clair Hosp 1000 Bower Hill Rd Pittsburgh PA 15228

EINIGER, CAROL BLUM, investment banker; b. Phila., Nov. 30, 1949; d. Bernard Michael and Bella (Karff) Blum; m. Roger William Einiger, Dec. 21, 1969; 1 child. B.A., U. Pa., 1970; M.B.A., Columbia U., 1973. With Conde Nast Publs., N.Y.C., 1970-71, Goldman, Sachs & Co., N.Y.C., 1971-72; with First Boston Corp., N.Y.C., 1973—, mng. dir., 1982—, head short-term fin. dept., 1983—, head capital markets dept., 1985—. Honoree Women in Corp. Leadership, Catalyst, 1984; named to Acad. of Women Achievers, YWCA, 1983. Office: First Boston Corp 55 E 52 St New York NY 10055

EINODER, CAMILLE ELIZABETH, educator; b. Chgo., June 15, 1937; d. Isadore and Elizabeth T. (Czerwinski) Popowski; student Fox Bus. Coll., 1954; B.Ed. in Biology, Chgo. Tchrs. Coll., 1964; M.A. in Analytical Chemistry, Gov.'s State U., 1977; M.A. in Edn. Adminstrn. and Supervision, Roosevelt U., 1986; m. Joseph X. Einoder, Aug. 5, 1978; children—Carl Frank, Mark Frank, Vivian Einoder, Joe Einoder, Tim Einoder, Sheila Einoder, Jude Einoder. Secretarial positions, Chgo., 1955-64; tchr. biology Chgo. Bd. Edn., 1964, tchr., biology-agr. 1975-81, tchr. chemistry, 1981—; human relations coordinator Morgan Park High Sch., 1980—; career devel. cons. for agr. related curriculum. Bds. dirs. Community Council, 1970—, Neighborhood Council, 1974; rep. Chgo. Tchrs. Union, 1969. Sculptor bronze unicorn, 1971; contributed quilt sect. to Judy Chicago's Dinner Party, 1982; author research paper. Home: 10637 S Claremont St Chicago IL 60643 Office: 1744 W Pryor St Chicago IL 60643

EISEL, MARIE TERESA, graphic arts director; b. Bronx, N.Y., June 5, 1946; d. Franz and Lina Eisel. B.S. in Earth and Space Scis., SUNY-Stony Brook. Lab. technician Marine Scis. Research Ctr. SUNY-Stony Brook, 1969-75, draftsman, 1977-79, dir. graphic arts dept., 1979—. Author: A Shoreline Survey of Great Peconic, Little Peconic, Gardiners and Neapeague Bays, 1977; illustrator: (J. Levington) Marine Ecology, 1981, (I.W. Duedall) Wastes in the Ocean, 1983. Office: Marine Scis Research Ctr SUNY Stony Brook NY 11790

EISELE, KARIN, educational foundation executive; b. N.Y.C., Aug. 23, 1938; d. Arthur and Florence (Nylen) Friedenheit; m. Paul Michael Eisele, June 9, 1952; children—Lauren Russell, Gretchen Ann, Rebecca Nylen. B.A., Smith Coll., 1959; student Ecole de Louvres, Ecole de Sciences Politiques, Paris, 1957-58. Dir. selection and placement Am. Field Service Internat. Exchange, 1959-75, dir. devel., 1975-79; v.p. external affairs Project ORBIS, N.Y.C., 1979-82; exec. dir. Eastern Center Coro Found., N.Y.C., 1983—; Union Settlement exec. com., bd. dirs.; cons. state-based program NEH. Bd. dirs. Home Health Care Exec. Com., Lenox Sch., 1974-79; mem. Goat Hill Neighborhood Assn.; assoc. Environ. Def. Fund. Mem. Nat. Soc. Fundraising Execs., Fin. Women's Assn. N.Y., Publicity Club N.Y., Nat. Assn. Fgn. Student Advisers, East Coast Coll. Placement Officers, Women and Founds. Corp. Philanthropy. Clubs: Smith Coll., Cosmopolitan, Point-o'Woods. Home: 135 E 95th St New York NY 10128 Office: 20 W 40th St New York NY 10018

EISELE, MARY MARIAM, clinical psychologist; b. Chgo., Oct. 3, 1939; d. Charles Wesley and Blanche Mae (Kennell) Eisele; B.A., Radcliffe Coll., 1962; M.A. (NIMH fellow), U. Ariz., 1970, Ph.D. in Psychology, 1973; 1 son, John Miller Adam. High sch. tchr. Valley Sch. Girls, Tucson, 1963-66; clin. psychologist student counseling service U. Ariz., 1972-76, asst. dir., 1976-85, assoc. dir., 1985—, acting dir., 1980, dir. univ.-wide honors program, 1980-85, lectr. psychology, 1974-76. Co-founder Tucson Gilbert and Sullivan Theatre, 1966, bd. dirs., 1966-71; alumni interviewer Harvard-Radcliffe Admissions Office, 1976—; adminstrv. bd. St. Francis in the Foothills Meth. Ch., 1978-81; mem. Ariz. Opera Co. Cert. psychologist, Ariz.; cert. Nat. Register Health Service Providers in Psychology; recipient Faculty Achievement award U. Ariz. Alumni Assn., 1983. Mem. Am. Psychol. Assn., Ariz. Psychol. Assn., So. Ariz. Psychol. Assn., Internat. Transactional Analysis Assn., Ariz. Group Psychotherapy Soc., Nat. Collegiate Honors Council, Catalyst Network Nat. Women's Info. Democrat. Episcopalian. Office: Student Counseling Service Old Main U Ariz Tucson AZ 85721

EISELE, PATRICIA O'LEARY, shopping center mgr.; b. Kansas City, Mo., Aug. 31, 1935; d. George Sexton and Dorothy Madeline (Stubbs) O'Leary; student Sarachon Hooley Bus. Sch., 1954-55, Rockhurst Coll., 1982-83; cert. Internat. Council Shopping Centers Mktg. Inst., 1978; m. John G. Eisele, July 16, 1955; children—Kathleen, Janice, Melissa, Patricia, John. Mktg. dir. Ward Pkwy. Center, Kansas City, Mo., 1974-79, mgr., 1979-80; mktg. counselor John Knox Village, Lee's Summit, Mo., 1981-83; gen. mgr. Leavenworth Plaza Shopping Ctr., 1983—; bd. dirs. local merchant's assn., 1977-80. Bd. dirs. Arthritis Found., Kansas City, Mo., 1980-82; bd. dirs., sec. Mid-Winter Art Fair Assn., Kansas City, 1980-82. Recipient award Heart Assn., 1979, 80, Easter Seal Soc., 1979, Muscular Dystrophy Assn., 1978, Ararat Shrine, 1980, Boy Scouts Am., 1979, 80. Mem. Am. Bus. Women's Assn., Women's C. of C., Chi Omega. Clubs: Altar Soc., Catholic Women's. Home: 2803 W 73d Terr Prairie Village KS 66208 Office: 3400 S 4th Trafficway Leavenworth KS 66048

EISENBERG, RUTH F., literature and communications educator, consultant; b. N.Y.C., Jan. 20, 1927; d. Samuel I. and Ida (Hollander) Berman; m. Arthur Eisenberg, Nov. 9, 1947 (div. Dec. 1963); children—Jay M., Stephen J. B.A., NYU, 1946; M.A., U. Wis., 1947. Asst. prof. Westchester Community Coll., Valhalla, N.Y., 1954-67; prof. lit. and communications Pace U., Pleasantville, N.Y., 1967—; cons. to industry. Editor: (with Carol Swidorski) Reading for Recognition, 1969; Not Quite Twenty, 1970; contbr. poetry to periodicals and mags. including I Must Explain (All Nations Poetry award 1981). Bd. dirs. Planned Parenthood of Westchester, 1981-83. Recipient Disting. Teaching award Pace U., 1973, 3d place award for poem Pteranodon Mag., 1983. Mem. Poetry Soc. Am., Speech Communication Assn., Nat. Council Tchrs. English, Women in Communications (chmn. Westchester 1980-82, Founders award 1982), Internat. Platform Assn. Democrat. Jewish. Home: 90 Bryant Ave White Plains NY 10605 Office: Pace University Bedford Rd Pleasantville NY 10570

EISENBERG, SONJA MIRIAM, artist; b. Berlin, June 10, 1926; came to U.S., 1938, naturalized, 1947; d. Adolf and Meta Cecilie (Bettauer) Weinberger; student Queens Coll., 1943-46, Middlebury Coll., 1945; N.Y.U., 1952-54; B.A., N.Y.U., 1954; postgrad. Nat. Acad. Sch. Fine Arts, 1961; m. Jack Eisenberg, Mar. 31, 1946; children—Ralph, Lynn, Lauren. One-woman shows: Bodley Gallery, N.Y.C., 1970, 73, 75, 80, Galerie Art du Monde, Paris, 1973, Buyways Gallery, Sarasota, Fla., 1973, 74, 75, 78, Galerie de Sfinx, Amsterdam, Netherlands, 1974, Huntsville (Ala.) Mus. Art, 1974, Anglo-Am. Art Mus., Baton Rouge, 1974, Comara Gallery, Los Angeles, 1974, Palm Spring (Calif.) Desert Mus., 1975, Fordham U., N.Y.C., 1976, Omega Inst., New Lebanon, N.Y., 1979, Am. Mus., Hayden Planetarium, N.Y.C., 1980, Avila Graphics, Ltd., 1981, YWCA, N.Y.C., 1981, Cathedral of St. John the Divine, N.Y.C., 1983, 85; group shows include: Mus. Fine Arts, St. Petersburg, Fla., 1973, Am. Watercolor Soc., 107th, 108th Exhbn., 1974, 75, Galerie Frederic Gollong, St. Paul de Vence, France, 1978, Betty Parson's Gallery, N.Y.C., 1981; represented in permanent collections: Archives Am. Art, Smithsonian Instn., Jewish Mus., N.Y.C., Fordham U. Mus., N.Y.C., Palm Springs Desert Mus., Omega Inst., Cathedral St. John the Divine; apptd. artist-in-residence Cathedral of St. John the Divine, N.Y.C., 1983; designer WFUNA cachet for UN Water Power Conf., 1977, UN Internat. Yr. of Disabled Persons, 1981. Recipient gold medal for artistic merit Internat. Parliament for Safety and Peace, 1983. Mem. Accademia Italia delle Arti e del Lavoro (Gold medal 1981). medal 1981. Home and Office: 1020 Park Ave New York NY 10028

EISENBERG, VICKI LEE, advertising agency executive, literary agency executive; b. Kansas City, Mo., Sept. 25, 1948; d. Boris David Kleiman and Helen (Kaminsky) Kleiman Bold; m. Arthur Eisenberg, Aug. 31, 1969 (div. May 1977); children—Arlo David, Josie Brook. Student U. Mo., 1966; B.S. in Polit. Sci., U. Tex., 1970; postgrad. North Tex. State U., 1971. Program dir. Park North YWCA, Dallas, 1971-73; media buyer Midway Agy., Dallas, 1977-80; media dir. Allday & Assoc., Dallas, 1980-81; pres., owner Ad Motion, Inc., Dallas, 1981—, Vicki Eisenberg Agy, Dallas, 1985—. Agt. (book) Evidence of Love, 1984 (Carr P. Collins nominee 1985, Ed. Allan Poe award 1985). Democrat. Jewish. Office: Vicki Eisenberg Agy Inc 5207 McKinney Dallas TX 75205

EISENDRATH, KATHLEEN GILLMAN, physical therapist; b. Milw., Sept. 19, 1948; d. Abraham S. and Jennie (Shovers) G.; m. David Howard Eisendrath, Feb. 20, 1977; children—Richelle, Sari. B.S., U. Pa., 1970. Cert. physical therapist. Sr. physical therapist Rehab. Inst. Chgo., 1972-74; asst. dir. phys. therapy U. Chgo. Hosp., 1974-77; chief phys. therapist Downstate Med. Hosp., Bklyn., 1977-78; phys. therapist, Croton-on-Hudson, N.Y., 1978—. Pres. Hadassah, Croton, 1981-83. Mem. Am. Phys. Therapy Assn. Jewish. Avocations: knitting; skiing. Office: 5 Patricia Ave Briarcliff Manor NY 10510

EISENKRAMER, JOAN HESSEL, marketing and public relations firm executive; b. St. Louis, Oct. 2, 1947; d. Meyer and Mildred R. (Margulis) Hessel; m. Larry Jay Eisenkramer, May 16, 1980; 1 child, Eric. B.A., Washington U., St. Louis, 1969; M.A., Case Western Res. U., 1972. Founder, dir. Early Childhood Enrichment Ctr., Cleve., 1971-74; founder Design 3, St. Louis, 1975-79; account exec. Eisenkramer Assocs., Inc., St. Louis, 1979-80, exec. v.p., 1980-82, pres., 1982—. Com. mem., fundraiser United Way Greater St. Louis, March of Dimes, St. Louis, Jewish Hosp., St. Louis, Washington U. Med. Sch., Human Growth Found., St. Louis; com. mem. NCCJ, St. Louis; bd. dirs. Kammergild Orch., Scholarshop, Am. Cancer Soc., St. Louis; mem. adv. com. English Lang. sch., St. Louis. Recipient Show Merit award N.Y. Art Dirs., 1984, Flair awards Adv. Fedn. St. Louis, 1983, 84, 85. Mem. Women in Communications, St. Louis Women's Commerce Assn., Ladies Lit. League. Club: Press of St. Louis. Avocations: swimming; Nautilus; dancing; reading; art. Office: Eisenkramer Assocs Inc 300 Hunter Ave Suite 100 Saint Louis MO 63124

EISENMAN, TRUDY FOX, dermatologist; b. Chgo., Oct. 14, 1940; d. Nathan Henry and Bernice (Greenberg) Fox; student U. Ill. at Navy Pier, Chgo., 1958-60; M.D., U. Ill., 1964; m. Theodore S. Eisenman, Aug. 19, 1962; children—Lawrence, Robert. Rotating intern Milw. County Gen. Hosp., 1964-65, med. resident, 1965-66; resident in dermatology Northwestern U. Med. Sch., Chgo., 1970-73, instr., 1973—; practice medicine specializing in dermatology, Chgo., 1973—; attending dermatologist Louis A. Weiss Meml. Hosp., Chgo., 1973—. Diplomate Am. Bd. Dermatology. Fellow Am. Acad. Dermatology; mem. Chgo. Dermatol. Soc., Soc. for Investigative Dermatology, Am. Med. Women's Assn., AMA, Chgo. Med. Soc., Alpha Omega Alpha. Home: 2526 Thornwood Ave Wilmette IL 60091 Office: 4640 N Marine Dr Chicago IL 60640

EISENSTADT, KAREN MARCIA, banker; b. Bklyn., Apr. 9, 1948; d. Nathan M. and Anne (Krugman) E.; m. Cary Reich, 1985. B.A. cum laude, Bklyn. Coll., 1968; M.Regional Planning (NDEA fellow 1968-70), U. N.C., Chapel Hill, 1971. Mem. research staff Rand Corp., Santa Monica, Calif., 1970-72; with N.Y.C. Office Mgmt. and Budget, 1972-79, dep. asst. budget dir. for fin., 1977-79; asst. v.p. public fin. dept. Morgan Guaranty Trust Co., N.Y.C., 1979-82, v.p., 1982—; mem. adj. faculty New Sch., 1974, Columbia U., 1976; dir. Critical Options Mgmt. Corp. Mem. N.Y.C. Rent Guidelines Bd., 1981—; bd. dirs. Citizens Housing and Planning Council, 1982. Mem. Phi Beta Kappa. Office: 23 Wall St New York NY 10015

EISENSTADT, MERRIE MADWAY, journalist; b. Phila., Apr. 25, 1957; d. Ralph K. and Bette Melba (Davis) Madway; B.J., U. Mo., Columbia, 1978; Isaac M. Wise program cert. Gratz Hebrew Coll., Phila., 1975; m. David Michael Eisenstadt, Nov. 19, 1978; children—Rebecca Karen, Rachel Leah. Reporter, Sentinel Newspapers, Montgomery and Prince George's counties, Md., 1979-80, Balt. Jewish Times, 1980-83. Theme Exhbn. chmn. Balt. Jewish Am. Festival, 1981. Recipient Smolar award for excellence in N.Am. Jewish journalism, 1981. Mem. Sigma Delta Chi, Alpha Epsilon Phi (scholarship award 1976), Phi Eta Sigma, Kappa Epsilon Alpha, Omicron Delta Kappa, Kappa Tau Alpha. Jewish.

EISENSTADT, PAULINE DOREEN BAUMAN, investment company executive, state legislator; b. N.Y.C., Dec. 31, 1938; d. Morris and Anne (Lautenberg) Bauman; B.A., U. Fla., 1960; M.S. (NSF grantee), U. Ariz., 1965; postgrad. U. N.Mex.; m. Melvin M. Eisenstadt, Nov. 20, 1960; children—Todd Alan, Keith Mark. Tchr., Ariz., 1961-65, P.R., 1972-73; adminstrv. asst. Inst. Social Research U. N.Mex., 1973-74; founder, 1st exec. dir. Energy Consumers N.Mex., 1977-81; dir., host TV program Consumer Viewpoint, 1980-82; chmn. consumer affairs adv. com. Dept. Energy, 1979-80; v.p. tech. bd. Nat. Center Appropiate Tech., 1980—; pres. Eisenstadt Enterprises, investments, 1983—; mem. N.Mex. Legislature, 1985—. Vice chmn. Sandoval County (N.Mex.)

Democratic Party, 1981—; mem. N.Mex. Dem. State Central Com., 1981—; N.Mex. del. Dem. Nat. Platform Com., 1984, Dem. Nat. Conv., 1984; pres. Sandoval County Dem. Women's Assn., 1979-81; vice chmn. N.Mex. Dem. Platform Com., 1984—; mem. Sandoval County Redistricting Task Force, 1983-84; bd. dirs. Mediation Ctr., 1983-84; mem. Rio Rancho Ednl. Study Com., 1984—. Mem. NEA, LWV, NOW. Author: Corrales, Portrait of a Changing Village, 1980. Address: PO Box 658 Corrales NM 87048

EISENSTOCK, BARBARA ANN, communication educator; b. Hartford, Conn., Nov. 9, 1950; d. Milford Michael and Rose Lillian (Barrabee) Goldman; m. Alan Stuart Eisenstock, Aug. 31, 1969. B.A. with highest honors U. Mich., 1972, M.A., 1973; M.A., U. So. Calif., 1978, Ph.D., 1979. Editor, Sage Publs., Beverly Hills, Calif., 1974—; project dir. Center for Communications Policy Research, Los Angeles, 1975-78; sr. research assoc. Applied Communications Networks, Santa Monica, Calif., 1979-83; vis. asst. prof. UCLA, 1982; adj. faculty Antioch U., Venice, Calif., 1982—; research cons. McCorkle Research Services, Los Angeles, 1984—; adj. faculty Calif. State U.-Northridge, 1980—; instr. Calif. Instn. for Women, Frontera, 1982—; pres. M.E. Prodns., Los Angeles, 1977—; cons. Cox Cable, Santa Barbara, Calif., 1984, Pub. Broadcasting, Los Angeles, 1978-82. Mem. Broadcast Edn. Assn., Internat. Communications Assn., Speech Communication Assn., Women in Communications (bd. dirs. 1974-75, 79-81), Kappa Tau Alpha. Office: Calif State U Northridge CA 91330

EISENZIMMER, BETTY WENNER, insurance agent executive; b. Twisp, Wash., July 25, 1939; d. Bren William and Julia Emogene (Salmon) Wenner; m. Erwin LeRoy Cook, June 19, 1955 (div. 1960); 1 son, Richard Jeffrey; m. 2d, Jerome Anthony Eisenzimmer, Feb. 18, 1966. Cert. in gen. ins. Ins. Inst. Am., 1981. Clk. typist MR Ins., Seattle, 1957-59; records clk. Assigned Risk Plan, Seattle, 1959-61; acct. asst. Robinson Jenner, Inc., Seattle, 1961-66; sec., acct. asst. Falkenberg & Co., Seattle, 1966-75, adminstrv. asst., 1975-77; ins. agt., corp. officer Service Ins. Inc., Seattle, 1975—; mem. adv. bd. Sch. Ins., Wash. State U. Coll. Bus., 1981—. Asst. editor Today's Ins. Woman, 1980-81. Exec. bd. Wash. chpt. Cystic Fibrosis Found., 1978-84, pres., 1983-85. Mem. long range planning com. Cedar Cross United Meth. Ch., 1986—. Named Vol. of Yr., Wash. chpt. Cystic Fibrosis Found., 1980. Fellow Acad. of Producer Ins. Studies; mem. Seattle Assn. Life Underwriters, Nat. Assn. Life Underwriters (women life underwriters conf.), Network of Exec. Women, Nat. Assn. Female Execs., Mem. Seattle C. of C., Ins. Women Puget Sound (pres. 1970-72, Industry award 1984), Ins. Women's Assn. Seattle (Ins. Woman of Yr. 1978, 81), Ins. Women of Lower Yakima Valley, Nat. Assn. Ins. Women (nat. sec. 1976-77, regional dir. 1981-82 mem. exec. bd.), Ind. Ins. Agts. and Brokers Wash. (edn. com. 1982-83), Ind. Ins. Agts. and Brokers King County (chmn. bylaws 1984—), Profl. Ins. Agts. Washington (edn. com. 1982—, chmn. 1983—), Washington Ins. Council (mem. speakers bur. 1980—), Women's Bus. Exchange, Women's Profl. and Managerial Network (chmn. 1983-86), Toastmasters Internat. (pres. club 1986—). Office: Service Ins Inc 332 Securities Bldg Seattle WA 98101

EISLER, SUSAN KRAWETZ, advertising agency executive; b. N.Y.C., Aug. 18, 1946; d. Aaron and Bertha (Platt) Krawetz; m. Howard Irwin Eisler, June 8, 1980; 1 stepchild, Robin Joy. B.A., U. Pitts., 1967; M.A., New Sch. for Social Research, 1971. Analyst, Marplan, Inc., N.Y.C., 1968-69; project dir. Market Facts, Inc., N.Y.C., 1969-70; assoc. research mgr. Gen. Foods, Inc., White Plains, N.Y., 1970-75, product mgr., 1975-80; research dir. Elizabeth Arden, N.Y.C., 1980-81; v.p., assoc. research dir. SSC&B: Lintas Worldwide, N.Y.C., 1981—. Mem. Am. Mktg. Assn., Advt. Women N.Y. Office: SSC&B Lintas Worldwide 1 Dag Hammarskjold Plaza New York NY 10017

EISNER, SISTER JANET, educational administrator, nun; b. Boston, Oct. 10, 1940; d. Eldon and Ada (Martin) Eisner; A.B., Emmanuel Coll., 1963; M.A., Boston Coll., 1969; Ph.D., U. Mich., 1975. Joined Sisters of Notre Dame de Namur, Roman Catholic Ch., 1958; dir. admissions Emmanuel Coll., Boston, 1967-71, dir. Emmanuel Coll. and City of Boston Pairings, 1976-78, chmn. English Dept., 1977-78, acting pres., 1978-79, pres., 1979—; Trustee Trinity Coll.; dir. Regional Com. Colls.; mem. Mass. Bd. Regents, Ford fellow, 1971-73; Rockham Prize fellow, 1973-75. Mem. Assn. of Governing Bds. (pres.'s adv. council), Am. Council on Edn., Women's Coll. Coalition, Assn. of Cath. Colls. and Univs., New Eng. Enrollment Planning Council. Office: Emmanuel College 400 The Fenway Boston MA 02115

EISNER, SUSAN PAMELA, communications executive, consultant; b. N.Y.C., Apr. 19, 1950; d. Nathaniel Julius and Frances Rochelle (Linick) E. Student Smith Coll., 1968-69; B.A., Wellesley Coll., 1971; M.P.A., Kennedy Sch. Govt., Harvard U., 1974. Staff intern to Senator Javits, U.S. Senate, Washington, 1970; mem. staff HEW, Washington, 1971; asst. to dir. communications Democratic Nat. Com., Washington, 1972; nat. coordinator press ops. McGovern Presdl. Campaign, Washington, 1972; dir. communications Dem. Nat. Com. Telethons II and III, Washington, N.Y.C. and Los Angeles, 1973-74; creative dir. Ways and Means, Inc., Louisville, 1974; producer/writer WNET-Thirteen, N.Y.C., 1975-81, dir. acquisitions, scheduling and spls., 1981, dir. broadcasting, 1981-83, spl. adviser to sr. v.p., 1983; pres. Susan Eisner Assocs., 1983-85; dir. communications March of Dimes Birth Defects Found., 1985—, folk singer, Boston, 1969-71; spl. cons. to exec. dir. Nat. Urban League, 1969-71; tutor MIT, 1972. Dir. broadcasting various programs, mini-series, including Cinema Thirteen, Classics Showcase, Star Movie, Viewer's Choice, Gala of Stars, Astaire, Hepburn, Years of Darkness, The Am. Worker, Black History, Celebrate Dance, Chanukah/Christmas, Disarmament, Remember the Holocaust, A Salute to Britain. Exec. producer and producer various spots, reports, segments including: Listening To You (Nat. Assn. Ednl. Broadcasters Graphics and Design award), 1978; Masterpiece Theatre Quotes Montage (Nat. assn. Ednl. Broadcasters Graphics and Design award), 1978; Haven't Stopped Dancin' Yet (Nat. Assn. Ednl. Broadcasters Graphics and Design award), 1979; Window on the World (Nat. Assn. Ednl. Broadcasters Graphics and Design award), 1979; Everything Beautiful At the Ballet (Nat. Assn. Ednl. Broadcasters Graphics and Design award 1979); Making Poldark--Location (Nat. Assn. Ednl. Broadcasters Graphics and Design award), 1979; Work in Progress, Dance in America (Nat. Assn. Ednl. Broadcasters Graphics and Design award), 1979; Cavett Conversation with Baryshnikov-Gregory, Claudius, Poldark, Duchess of Duke Street, Upstairs-Downstairs Farewells, Masterpiece Theatre's Tenth Anniversary Party, On location: Dance in America, Summercast Live, Starfest Finale, Thirteen: The First Twenty Years. Writer contemporary folksongs, 1969-71. Author speeches, press, and promotional materials; research on various topics. Recipient award for citizenship Am. Legion, 1965, Mayor's award for Young Citizenship, Mayor New Rochelle (N.Y.), 1965; named to Outstanding Young Women Am., U.S. Jaycees, 1981; Durant scholar, 1971; Harvard U. Kennedy Sch. adminstrn. fellow, 1971-74.

EITNIER, CYNTHIA KAY, nurse; b. Lancaster, Pa., June 16, 1953; d. C. Quentin and Nancy Lee (Fisher) Martin. Lic. Practical Nurse, Willow State Vocat.-Tech. Coll., 1972; Assoc. Nursing, Harrisburg Area Community Coll., 1981; B.S. in Nursing, Millersville U., 1984; postgrad. U. Ariz., 1985—. Lic practical nurse Conestoga View, Lancaster, 1973-77, Polyclinic Med. Ctr., Harrisburg, Pa., 1977-81; R.N., 1981-85; R.N., St. Joseph Hosp., Tucson, 1985—, mem. code team, pulmonary rehab. teams, 1985—. Mem. Nat. Assn. Female Execs., Pa. Nurses Assn. Democrat. Avocations: computers; swimming; hiking. Home: Apt 1205 4601 E Skyline Dr Tucson AZ 85718

EKBERG-WILENSKY, CHRISTINE LEE, financial consultant; b. Coronado, Calif., Aug. 11, 1957; d. Gerald Von Ekberg and Kathleen Marie (Horrell) Ekberg Culver; m. Terrance Allan Wilensky, Oct. 31, 1985. B.S. in Bus. Adminstrn., Rockhurst Coll., 1979. Cost acct. Solar Turbines, San Diego, 1980-81; fin. analyst Marion Labs., Kansas City, Mo., 1981-83; ind. mgmt. cons., Villanova, Pa., 1983-85; fin. cons. Merrill Lynch, Kansas City, Mo., 1985—. Vol. worker United Way, Kansas City, Mo., 1985, Spl. Olympics, Villanova, Pa., 1984-85. Mem. Nat. Assn. Female Execs., Rockhurst Alumni Assn. Office: Merrill Lynch 801 W 47th St 5th Floor Kansas City MO 64112

EKEMA, EMMA YOTI, pharmacist; b. Bimbia, Cameroon, May 24, 1947; came to U.S., 1976; d. Samuel Ikoli and Susan Eposi (Bwindi) Ekema. U. London gen. cert. of edn. advanced level Coll. Arts, Sci. & Tech., Bambili, Cameroon, 1968; student Northwestern Okla. State U., 1976-78; B.Sc. in Pharmacy, Southwestern Okla. State U., 1981. Registered pharmacist. Lab. technician Nat. Research Inst., Ekona, Cameroon, 1974-76; math. tchr. Saker Baptist Sch., Victoria, Cameroon, 1973-74; pharmacist, asst. mgr. Revco DS Inc., Dallas, 1981—. Vol. worker Hospice Program, Dallas, 1983—. Mem. Southwestern Pharm. Assn., Am. Pharm. Assn., AAUW, Nat. Assn. Female Execs. Baptist. Home: 417 West Hayes Norman OK 73069 Office: 3435 Webb Chapel #332 Dallas TX 75220

EKLUND-EASLEY, MOLLY SUE, lawyer; b. Benton Harbor, Mich., Aug. 17, 1953; d. Robert Gordon and Arlene Ann (Weinlander) Eklund; m. Herman Easley Jr., July 18, 1981; 1 dau., Rachel Nicole. B.A., Grand Valley State Coll., 1975; J.D., U. Detroit, 1979. Bar: Mich. 1979. Assoc. firm Stalburg Fischer & Weberman, P.C., Detroit, 1979—. Mem. ABA, Women Lawyers Assn. Mich., State Bar Mich., Assn. Trial Lawyers Am., Mich. Trial Lawyers Assn. Lutheran. Office: Stalburg Fischer & Weberman PC 139 Cadillac Sq Detroit MI 48226

EKSTROM, RUTH BURT (MRS. LINCOLN EKSTROM), psychologist; b. Bennington, Vt., July 2, 1931; d. Ralph Amos and Bertha Paisley (Lambert) Burt; A.B., Brown U., 1953; M.Ed., Boston U., 1956; Ed.D., Rutgers U., 1967; m. Lincoln Ekstrom, Nov. 9, 1957. Tchr. pub. schs., Beverly, Mass., 1953-57; research asst. Ednl. Testing Service, 1957-64, profl. assoc., 1964-66, dir. documentation services, 1966-68, research scientist, 1968-80, sr. research scientist, 1980—; vis. lectr. Grad. Sch. Edn., Rutgers U., 1958-60. Trustee, Brown U., 1972-77, Fellow, 1977—, sec. corp., 1982—. Fellow Am. Psychol. Assn., AAAS; mem. Am. Assn. Higher Edn., Am. Ednl. Research Assn., Am. Assn. Counseling and Devel., Nat. Council for Measurement in Edn., Pi Lambda Theta. Co-editor: Kit of Factor Referenced Cognitive Tests, 1963, 76; editor: Measurement, Technology, and Individuality in Education, 1983; contbr. articles to profl. publs. Home: 78 Westerly Rd Princeton NJ 08540 Office: Educational Testing Service Princeton NJ 08541

ELAM, PAMELA LYNN, historian; b. Ashland, Ky., Apr. 28, 1950; d. James Harve, Jr. and Mildred (Hayes) E.; B.A. in Polit. Sci., U. Ky., 1972, J.D., 1975; M.A. in Women's History, Sarah Lawrence Coll., 1980. Staff asst. Ky. Commn. on Women, Frankfort, 1973-74; asst. Mcpl. Statute Revision, Ky. Gen. Assembly, Lexington, 1975; exec. dir. Ky. Civil Liberties Union, Louisville, 1976-77; teaching asst. Sarah Lawrence Coll., Bronxville, N.Y., 1979; legis. aide N.Y.C. Council, 1980—. Exec. com. Congressional Union Inc., 1980-84; organizer Nat. Women's History Week activities, 1979—; lobbyist, lectr. women's issues, 1971—; del. Nat. Internat. Women's Yr. Conf., 1977; exec. com., program chmn. Ky. Internat. Women's Yr. Com., 1977; chmn. Ky. Women's Agenda Coalition, 1976-78; coordinator Women's Center of Lexington, Inc., 1974; chmn. Internat. Woman's Year Com. Lexington-Fayette County, 1975; mem. state policy council Ky. Women's Polit. Caucus, 1971-78; chairwoman U. Ky. Council on Women's Concerns, 1973; alt. del. Democratic Nat. Conv., 1972. Recipient award, Ky. Women's Agenda Coalition, 1978. Mem. Orgn. Am. Historians, Am. Hist. Assn., Nat. Women's Studies Assn., Nat. Women's Polit. Caucus, NOW. Author: How Long Must Women Wait for Liberty?: Perceptions of the Militant Woman Suffrage Movement in the United States, 1916-1920, 1980. Home: 214 W 82d St New York NY 10024 Office: City Council City Hall New York NY 10007

ELBERT, JOANNA, real estate executive; b. Chgo.; d. Joseph and Mary (Alesia) Germano; m. Phillip Myron Elbert (div. 1977); children—Kimberly, Scott, Keith, Lynn, Phillip. B.S. in Journalism, U. Ill., 1951. Personnel mgr. Adminstrv. Offices Jewel-Osco Co., Inc., Melrose Park, Ill., 1962-67; personnel adminstr. Anocut Engring. Co., Chgo., 1967-69; pres. Joanna Elbert, Inc., real estate sales, Houston, 1978—. Contbr. poetry to various quars. and anthologies including Indigo, Poetry Today, Invictus, Am. Poet, N.Am. Mentor, Driftwood East, Mem. Million Dollar Club. Republican. Roman Catholic. Home: 201 Vanderpool Houston TX 77024 Office: Joanna Elbert Inc 3300 Chimney Rock Houston TX 77056

ELBIN-SCHELL, CAROL GERTRUDE, television promotion manager; b. Morgantown, W.Va., Sept. 30, 1937; d. Harry C. and Gertrude I. (Simms) Elbin. B.F.A., Cin. Coll.-Conservatory, 1959; student Foley Modeling Sch., 1961; postgrad. Tidewater Community Coll., 1976-77. Promotion mgr. Sta. WAVY-TV, Norfolk, Va., 1975-76; promotion pub. service mgr. Sta. WNYS-TV (now WIXT), Syracuse, N.Y., 1962-71; asst. promotion dept. Sta. KRCA (now KNBC-TV), Hollywood, Calif., 1959; asst. promotion-pub. service mgr. Sta. WCPO-TV, Cin., 1956-59, 60-61; promotion pub. service mgr. Sta. KUSK-TV, Prescott, Ariz., 1982-83; promotion mgr. Sta. KMIR-TV, Palm Springs, 1983; freelance writer, Prescott, 1983—. Campaign coordinator Senator John W. Warner of Va., 1977-78; campaign worker Senator Barry Goldwater of Ariz., 1980. Author: Great Hospital Connection, 1976; Self Signs, 1976. Recipient Gabriel award Office of Catholic Dioceses, Washington, 1971. Mem. Women in Communications, Am. Women in Radio and TV, Broadcast Promotion Assn., Am. Film Inst., Delta Omicron. Republican. Methodist. Home: Prescott AZ 86301

ELDER, BEVERLY GLORIA, real estate company executive, mortgage broker; b. Montreal, Que., Can., July 1, 1917; came to U.S., 1921; d. J.A. Emile and Theresa Bernadette (Carroll) De Celles; m. Willard F. Elder, June 12, 1943 (dec. 1944). Student U. Tampa, 1955. Lic. realtor and mortgage broker, Fla. Salesman Powell Real Estate Co., St. Petersburg, Fla., 1946-47; broker, ptnr. Elder & Powell Real Estate Inc., St. Petersburg, 1947—, mortgage broker, 1950—, v.p., 1954-59, pres., 1959—; dir. Rutland Bank, St. Petersburg. Mem. com. Goals for St. Petersburg, 1973; mem. com. Community Improvement Project, St. Petersburg, 1974, 75; mem. Bd. of Adjustment, St. Petersburg, 1984—; Recipient Stephen McCready award N.Y. Times Advt., 1966. Mem. Mortgage Brokers Assn. (pres. 1968-69, bd. dirs., 1968-75), St. Petersburg Bd. Realtors (sec. 1976-77, bd. dirs.), Fla. Assn. Bd. Realtors (bd. dirs.), St. Petersburg C. of C. (bd. govs. 1971-73), St. Petersburg and Pinellas County C. of C., 1971, 72), Mortgage Brokers Assn. (pres. 1968-69, Achievement award 1968), Nat. Assn. Realtors. Republican. Roman Catholic. Clubs: Bath (North Redington Beach, Fla.); St. Petersburg Yacht. Avocation: golf. Office: C-21 Elder & Powell Inc 1935 Central Ave Saint Petersburg FL 33713

ELDER, JEAN KATHERINE, government official; b. Virginia, Minn., May 30, 1941; d. Clarence Adrian and Katherine C. (Miltich) Samuelson; B.S., U. Mich., 1963, A.M., 1966, Ph.D., 1969; L.H.D. (hon.), Elkins Coll., 1985. Tchr. 5th grade Ypsilanti (Mich.) pub. schs., 1963-64; tchr. educable mentally retarded Quantico (Va.) Marine Corps Dependent Sch., 1964-65; dir. remedial reading program Iron Mountain (Mich.) pub. schs., 1966; asst. prof. spl. edn. Ind. U., Bloomington, 1969-71; dir. delinquency modification through edn. project Marquette (Mich.)-Alger Intermediate Sch. Dist.-Marquette County Probate Ct., 1971-72; asst. prof. edn. No. Mich. U., Marquette, 1972-76, asso. prof., 1977-78, coordinator Title IX, 1975-76; project dir., assoc. scientist Specialist Office Three, Wis. Research and Devel. Center Cognitive Learning, U. Wis., Madison, 1976-77; assoc. prof. med. edn. Coll. Human Medicine, Mich. State U., 1978-81; commr. Adminstrn. on Developmental Disabilities, HHS, Washington, 1981-86, acting asst. sec. Office of Human Devel., 1986—; cons. in field. Bd. dirs. Rehab. Internat., U.S.A.; mem. Pres.'s Com. on Mental Retardation, 1976—. U.S. Office Edn. fellow, 1966-69. Fellow Am. Assn. Mental Deficiency; mem. Assns. Retarded Citizens, Internat. Assn. for Sci. Study Mental Deficiency (mem. council), Council Exceptional Children, Pi Lambda Theta, Phi Delta Kappa, Delta Kappa Gamma. Lutheran. Club: Zonta. Author: (with others) Planning Individualized Education Program in Special Education, 1977; Pathways to Employment for Adults with Developmental Disabilities, 1985. Contbr. articles to profl. jours. Home: 7375 Hallcrest Dr McLean VA 22102 Office: 200 Independence Ave SW Washington DC 20201

ELDER, JEAN LOUISE, school system business manager; b. Mattoon, Ill., Dec. 20, 1955; d. Paul Leroy and Maria (Brandlhofer) Smith; m. Chris Alan Pfeiffer, June 1, 1974 (div. Nov. 1979); 1 child, Lisa Marie; m. Bradley Ray Elder, Sept. 4, 1982. B.S. in Bus., Eastern Ill. U., 1977, M.B.A., 1980. Office mgr. ED Buxton & Assocs., Charleston, Ill., 1974-77; personnel mgr. Unibuilt Structures, Charleston, 1977-80; bus. mgr. Eastern Ill Area Spl. Edn., Mattoon, 1980—. Ill. Assn. Sch. Bus. Ofcls. (scholarship 1984, com. mem. 1984—), Assn. Sch. Bus. Ofcls., Ill. Adminstrs. Spl. Edn. Republican. Baptist. Avocations: sewing; jogging; swimming; racquetball; tennis.

ELDER, ROBERTA ANNE, transportation executive, educator; b. Dublin, Ireland, Aug. 8, 1942; came to U.S., 1966, naturalized, 1971; d. Philip Nicholas and Margaret-Mary (McElligott) Feanny; m. Ian Frederick Elder, Jan. 7, 1961; children—James Rudolf, Julie Anne, Anita Margaret. A.A., Broward Community Coll., 1978; B.A., Fla. Atlantic U., 1980, M.A., 1982; student Nova Law Sch., 1982-83. Pres. Elder and Co., Inc., Ft. Lauderdale, Fla., 1976-82, REMM, Inc., Ft. Lauderdale, 1985—; lectr. polit. sci. Broward Community Coll., Ft. Lauderdale, 1982-85; v.p. sales Road Runner Transport, Ft. Lauderdale, 1984-85; dir. Accredited Trading, Ft. Lauderdale; lectr. Palm Beach Adult Edn., Fla., 1982-83; cons. Grace Group, Kingston, Jamaica, 1983—, Caribbean Basin Initiative, Council on Foreign Relations, Ft. Lauderdale, Washington, 1982-83. Campaign aide Clay Shaw for Congress, Ft. Lauderdale, 1984; staff intern Congl. Dist. 15, Ft. Lauderdale, 1983. Mem. AAUW, Women in Transp. (pres. 1985—), Eastern States Women's Traffic Conf., Am. Polit. Sci. Assn., Nat. Assn. Female Execs., Jade Beach Democratic Club, Port Everglades Assn., Delta Nu Alpha, Phi Kappa Phi, Phi Theta Kappa, Phi Alpha Theta. Roman Catholic. Avocations: boating, reading, golf. Home: 2013 SE 17th Ct Pompano Beach FL 33062 Office: BIGT Trucking Inc PO Box 350582 950 Eller Dr Ft Lauderdale FL 33335

ELDER-JUCKER, PATRICIA LOUISA, psychologist; b. Trinidad, W.I., Dec. 10, 1945; d. Jacob Delworth and Nevada Lenora Elder; B.A., Temple U., 1972, M.Ed., 1974, Ph.D., 1979; m. Walter Jucker, May 27, 1978. Staff psychologist Northwestern Inst. of Psychiatry, Phila., 1978-80, adj. profl. staff mem., 1980—; clin. psychologist ACORN, Phila., 1980—; cons. Pastoral Care Program, Phila., 1980—; pvt. practice psychology, Phila., 1980—; clin. dir. The Bridge, Phila., 1981-83; cons., assoc. Rutman-Miller Assocs., 1982-84. Participant Winner project, Community Coll. Phila., 1982; bd. dirs. Family Service Assn. Bucks County. Mem. Am. Personnel and Guidance Assn., Am. Psychol. Assn., Delaware Valley Assn. Black Psychologists (pres. 1984-85), Assn. Black Psychologists, Pa. Psychol. Assn., Phila. Soc. Clin. Psychologists. Office: 10890 Bustleton Ave Suite 207 Philadelphia PA 19116

ELDREDGE, EDDA ROGERS, securities transfer company executive; b. Deseret, Utah, Feb. 15, 1915; d. James Noah and Alice (Critchley) Rogers; student Henager Bus. Coll., 1930-31, U. Utah, 1932-35; m. Frank Aubrey Eldredge, Sept. 5, 1936; children—Frank A., Noah R., Alice Lou, Julie, Joseph U. With Gen. Petroleum Corp., 1945-55; mgr. land dept. Utah So. Oil Co., 1955-62, asst. sec., 1956-62; pres., dir. Edda R. Eldredge & Co., Inc., Salt Lake City, 1967—; pres., dir. Bonneville Petroleum Corp., 1974—. Republican. Mormon. Office: 315 Newhouse Bldg 10 Exchange Pl Salt Lake City UT 84111

ELDRIDGE, BETH ANN, broadcasting executive; b. Dallas, Aug. 20, 1949; d. Zellner Edward and Evelyn Virginia (Wortsman) Eldridge; B.Jour., U. Tex., 1971; postgrad. U. Houston, 1982—. Lic. broadcaster FCC. Pres., owner Traffic Central Inc., Houston, 1977-80; news editor, producer Sta. KTRH, Houston, 1980-81; news dir. Sta. KRBE, Houston, 1981-83; exec. dir. Taping for Blind, Houston, 1982—; lectr. U. Houston, 1982—. Recipient Best News Broadcast award, AP, Dallas, 1972. Mem. Futurist Soc., Assn. Radio Reading Services. Home: 7730 Romney St Houston TX 77036

ELDRIDGE, MARIE DELANEY, statistician, education researcher; b. Balt., June 1, 1926; d. James Howard and Mathilda (Belz) Delaney; A.B. in Math., Coll. Notre Dame Md., 1948; Sc.M. in Biostatistics, Johns Hopkins U., 1953; m. Paul Eldridge, Apr. 3, 1961; children—Julia Delaney, Dan Pattengill. Statistician, indsl. quality control Revere Copper and Brass, Balt., 1948-49; statistician Ralph Parsons & Co., Frederick, Md., 1953-54, U.S. Govt., 1954-60; instr. U. Balt., 1958-60; supr. statistician HEW, Washington, 1960-65; with Office Stats. Programs and Standards, U.S. Postal Service, Washington, 1965-72, dep. dir., 1968-70, dir., 1970-72; dir. math. analysis div. Nat. Hwy. Traffic Safety Adminstrn., Dept. Transp., 1972-73, dir. office stats. and analysis, 1973-75; adminstr. Nat. Center Edn. Stats., Dept. Edn., Washington, 1976-84; dir. ctr. for ednl. studies Research Triangle Inst., Research Triangle Park, N.C., 1984—; mem. Edn. Commn. of States, 1976-84; mem. tech. adv. com. Calif. Assessment Program, 1978—; mem. nat. accident sample adv. com. Dept. Transp.; professorial lectr. George Washington U., 1981-84; adj. faculty Fed. Exec. Inst., 1982—. Recipient Superior Accomplishment award U.S. Postal Service, 1970; Outstanding Performance award Dept. Transp., 1975; cert. recognition HEW, 1976, 80; Presdl. Rank award, 1981. Fellow Am. Statis. Assn. (exec. council 1975-79, co-chmn. subcom. tng. statisticians for govt. 1979-81, com. fellows 1978-80); mem. Am. Edn. Research Assn., Internat. Assn. Survey Statisticians, Fed. Exec. Inst. (dir. 1982-85), Washington Statis. Soc. (pres. 1976-77), Phi Delta Kappa. Democrat. Episcopalian. Office: PO Box 12194 Research Triangle Park NC 27709

ELDRIDGE, RITA HAZEL, mathematics educator, institute administrator; b. Trenton, N.J., Feb. 4, 1933; d. James Clarence and Jessie Edna (McCully) Nearing; m. Pasquale C. DaLoisio, Aug. 21, 1953 (div. Nov. 1974); children—Pat James, Gregory Arthur; m. 2d, David Rogers Eldridge, Aug. 8, 1975. B.S., Trenton State Coll., 1953; M.Ed., Beaver Coll., Glenside, Pa., 1980. Cert. tchr., supr. math., N.J., Pa. Tchr., Upper Freehold Twp. Sch., Allentown, N.J., 1953-54, Hamilton Twp. Schs., Trenton, 1957-60, N. Burlington Regional Sch., Columbus, N.J., 1964-65; tchr. math. Pennsbury Schs., Fallsington, Pa., 1968—; adj. prof. Mercer County Coll., East Windsor, N.J., 1983—; pres. Inservice Computer Inst., Trenton, N.J., 1982—. Dreyfus Found. grantee, 1969-70. Mem. Pa. State Edn. Assn., Pennsbury Edn. Assn., NEA, Nat. Council Tchrs. Math., Pa. Council Tchrs. Math. Unitarian-Universalist. Club: Ewing Apple Users (pres., founder) (Trenton). Home: 828 River Rd West Trenton NJ 08628

ELGIN, SARAH CARLISLE ROBERTS, biology researcher and educator; b. Washington, July 16, 1945; d. Carlisle Bishop and Lorene (West) Roberts; m. Robert Lawrence Elgin, June 9, 1967; children—Benjamin Carlisle, Thomas James. B.A. in Chemistry, Pomona Coll., 1967; Ph.D. in Biochemistry, Calif. Inst. Tech., 1971. Research fellow Calif. Inst. Tech., Pasadena, 1971-73; asst. prof. biochemistry and molecular biology Harvard U., Cambridge, Mass., 1973-77, assoc. prof., 1977-81; assoc. prof. biology Washington U., St. Louis, 1981-84, prof., 1984—. Mem. editorial bd. Jour. Cell Biology, N.Y.C., 1980-82; exec. editor Nucleic Acids Research, 1983—; editorial bd. Jour. Biol. Chemistry, 1985—; contbr. papers in field. Research grantee NIH, 1981, 83. Mem. Am. Chem. Soc., Am. Soc. Biol. Chemists (program com. 1984), Am. Soc. Cell Biology (council 1983-86), Genetics Soc. Am., AAAS. Office: Washington U Biology Dept Box 1137 Saint Louis MO 63130

ELGIN, SUSAN CAROL, lawyer; b. Hagerstown, Md., Sept. 22, 1954; d. Harold Lester and Mary Susan (Rinehart) E. B.A. cum laude, Franklin and Marshall Coll., 1976; J.D., George Washington U., 1979. Bar: Md. 1979, U.S. Dist. Ct. Md. 1982. Ptnr. Berkson & Berryman, Williamsport, Md., 1979-80, France & Metzner, Hagerstown, Md., 1980-81, Snyder & Elgin, P.A., Hagerstown, 1982—; dir., legal counsel Citizens Assisting and Sheltering the Abused, Hagerstown, 1982—; dir., legal advisor Big Bros., Hagerstown, 1982—; advising legal counsel Parents Without Ptnrs., Hagerstown, 1983—. Legal counsel, regional chmn. Md. Fedn. Republican Women, 1981—; mem. Rep. Central Com. Washington County, Md., 1982—; pres. Advocates for Women in Politics, Washington County. Named Young Careerist, Bus. and Profl. Women, Hagerstown, 1982. Mem. Assn. Trial Lawyers Am., Md. Trial Lawyers Assn. (gov. 1983—), ABA, Md. Bar Assn., Washington County Bar Assn. (dir. 1982—, chmn. continuing legal edn. com.). Lutheran. Clubs: Torch, Republican. Office: Snyder & Elgin PA 28 Jonathan St Hagerstown MD 21740

ELGIN, TAMMY J., journalist, youth director; b. Indiana, Pa., July 24, 1960; d. Thomas Gerald and Barbara Ann (Jacob) E. B.S. in Journalism, Indiana U. of Pa., 1985. Research asst. Sta. KDKA-TV, Pitts., 1980-81; prodn. asst. Washington Hosp., Pa., 1981; reporter Nor'wester Group of Publs., Grand Cayman, B.W.I., 1983-85; account exec. Sta. WNQQ, Pa., 1985—; part-time youth dir., Grand Cayman, 1983-85. Mem. Graystone Ch. Choir, Indiana. Mem. Women in Communications, Inc., Sigma Delta Chi. Republican. Presbyterian. Club: Indiana Garden. Home: 21 N 10th St Indiana PA 15701 Office: WNQQ Inc Blairsville PA 15717

ELGUIN-BÖDY, GITA, psychologist; b. Santiago, Chile; came to U.S., 1968; d. Serafín and Regina (Urízar) Elguin; B.S. summa cum laude, in Biology, U. Chile, Santiago, Psy.D., 1964; Ph.D. in Counseling Psychology (Chancellor's fellow, NIMH fellow), U. Calif., Berkeley, 1976; m. Bart Bödy, Oct. 23, 1971. Clin. psychologist Barros Luco-Trudeau Gen. Hosp., Santiago, 1964-65; co-founder, co-dir. Lab. for Parapsychol. Research, Psychiat. Clinic, U. Chile, Santiago, 1965-68; research fellow Found. Research on Nature of Man, Durham, N.C., 1968; researcher psychol. correlates of EEG-Alpha waves U. Calif., Berkeley, 1972-76; originator holistic method of psychotherapy Psychotherapy for a Crowd of One, 1978; co-founder, clin. dir. Holistic Health Assos., Oakland, Calif., 1979—; lectr. holistic health Piedmont (Calif.) Adult Sch., 1979-80; hostess Holistic Perspective, Sta. KALW-FM, Nat. Public Radio, 1980. Lic. psychologist, Chile, Calif. Mem. Am. Psychol. Assn., Calif. Psychol. Assn., Alameda County Psychol. Assn., Assn. Advancement Psychology, Assn. for Holistic Health, AAAS, Montclair Health Profls. Assn. (co-founder, pres. 1983-85), Sierra Club, U. Calif. Alumni Assn. Contbr. articles in clin. psychology and holistic health to profl. jours. and local periodicals. Presenter Whole Life Expo, 1986. Office: Montclair Profl Bldg 2080 Mountain Blvd Suite 203 Oakland CA 94611

ELIAS, ARLENE, sanitation service company executive; b. Perth Amboy, N.J., Mar. 9, 1932; d. Edward and Ann (Christensen) Ostergaard; m. Bernard W. Thompson, May 2, 1953 (div. 1969); children—Dawn Marie Lozak, William Jesse, Tami Ann Maxwell; m. Albert Elias, Mar. 21, 1970 (dec. 1981). Vice-pres., founder Madison Septic, Matawan, N.J., 1957-69, Central Jersey Septic, Matawan, 1970-80, Johnny on the Spot, Matawan, 1971-80; pres. Central Jersey Septic, Parlin, N.J., 1980—, Johnny on the Spot, Parlin, 1980—. Mem. N.J. Portable Sanitation Assn., Internat. Portable Sanitation Assn. Home: 10 Cambridge Ln Somerset NJ 08873 Office: Johnny on the Spot 3143 Bordentown Ave Parlin NJ 08859

ELIAS, SANDRA CHIAVARAS, educator; b. Clinton, Mass., Apr. 8, 1949; B.S. in Spl. Edn., Fitchburg (Mass.) State Coll., 1970, M.Ed. in Reading, 1976; postgrad. (fellow) Clark U., 1981-83; married; 1 child. Tchr. spl. class Webster (Mass.) Schs., 1970-73, asst. coordinator program materials, resource room, 1974, tchr./coordinator primary spl. needs program, 1975—, tchr. jr. high English, 1978-79, reading tchr. jr. high, 1979-80 adminstrv. asst. intern Shepherd Hill Regional Sch., Dudley, Mass., 1980-81; dir., owner Teddy Bear Day Care Ctr., Dudley, Mass., 1983-85; developmental specialist Ft. Devens Post Learning Ctr., Shirley, Mass., 1985-86; resource room tchr. Murdock High Sch., Winchendon, Mass., 1986—. Mem. Nat. Council Tchrs. English. Club: Webster Emblem (pres. 1984-85). Cert. in elem. and spl. edn., reading, reading supervision, learning disabilities, Mass. Home: Bemis Rd Fitchburg MA 01420

ELIOT, JUDI, personnel consulting company executive; b. Phila., Apr. 9, 1946; d. Harry and Bernice (Page) Katz. Student Temple U., Media buyer, adminstrv. asst., copywriter Elkman Advt. Co., Bala Cynwyd, Pa., 1967-70; mgr., cons. C.W. Harvey Personnel, Phila., 1971-75; pres. Judi Eliot, Inc., Phila., 1976—, also cons.; leader seminars in field. Author articles. Bd. dirs. Am. Cancer Soc., Phila., 1980-83, mem. spl. events steering com., 1983—, corp. sponsor Triathlon, 1985; fundraiser Sunshine Found., Phila., 1984—; mem. Orgn. for Rehab. Through Tng., Phila., 1970—. Recipient Outstanding Service award Am. Cancer Soc., 1981, 82. Mem. Internat. Assn. for Personnel Women (bd. dirs. Phila. affiliate, dir. communications 1983, v.p. 1984-85, pres. 1985-86), Exec. Women Internat. Democrat. Jewish. Avocations: neurolinguistics; communication theory; psychology; creative writing; travel. Office: Judi Eliot Inc Suite 3 Penn Center Plaza Suite 2005 Philadelphia PA 19102

ELIOT, LUCY CARTER, painter; b. N.Y.C., May 8, 1913; d. Ellsworth, Jr., and Lucy Carter (Byrd) E.; B.A., Vassar Coll., 1935; student Art Students League, N.Y.C., 1935-40. One-woman shows include: Cazenovia Coll., 1941, 42, Rochester Meml. Art Gallery, 1946, Syracuse (N.Y.) Mus. Fine Arts, 1947, Wells Coll., 1953, Ft. Schuyler Club, Utica, N.Y., 1971; works exhibited many nat. and regional exhbns., including Silvermine Guild; represented in permanent collections Munson-Williams-Proctor Inst., Utica, Rochester Meml. Art Gallery, also pvt. collections. Recipient 1st prize Rochester Meml. Art Gallery, 1946; prize for painting Silvermine Guild, 1957; 1st prize in painting, Cooperstown (N.Y.) Art Assn., 1978. Mem. N.Y. Soc. Women Artists (pres. 1973-75), Artists Tech. Research Inst. (dir. 1975-79), Audubon Artists (dir. oils 1983-85, awards chmn. 1987—). Episcopalian. Clubs: Cosmopolitan (N.Y.C.), Cazenovia (N.Y.). Home: 131 E 66th St New York NY 10021 also 70 Sullivan St Cazenovia NY 13035

ELIZONDO, PATRICIA IRENE, TV/film production executive; b. San Antonio, Jan. 11, 1955; d. Oscar Andres and Rosalinda (Elizondo) Elizondo. B.A. magna cum laude, Trinity U., 1978. Crew mem. Trinity TV Prodn. Unit, San Antonio, 1977-78; coordinator publicity and audio visual services Nat. Autonomous U. Mex., San Antonio, 1978-79; mem. prodn. crew KLRN-TV, San Antonio, 1978-79; asst. prodn. mgr. Rogers Cablesystems, San Antonio, 1979-85, spl. programs mgr., 1985—, mgr. pay per view ops. Producer/dir. Spanish TV series Plaza Mexico, 1982; producer, host series Cable Connections, 1984—. Recipient spl. photography award Hispanic Woman, 1980. Mem. Mortar Board (sec. 1977-78), Phi Beta Kappa. Roman Catholic. Home: 13259 Hunters View San Antonio TX 78230 Office: Rogers Cablesystems 403 Urban Loop San Antonio TX 78207

ELKHANIALY, HEKMAT ABDUL RAZEK, real estate company executive; b. Egypt, Dec. 17, 1935; came to U.S., 1961, naturalized, 1975; d. Abdul Razek Hussein and Nabiha Mursi (Kutb) E.; B. Commerce/Econs., Cairo U., 1959; Ph.D. in Sociology, U. Chgo., 1968; m. Chandra Kant Jha, Dec. 20, 1969; 1 dau., Lakshmi. Mem. faculty Roosevelt U., Chgo., 1968-75, assoc. prof. sociology, 1973-75; research assoc. Population Research Ctr., U. Chgo., 1977-80; demographic cons., Chgo., 1975—; v.p. PSM Realty, Inc.; sec., treas. PSM Internat. Mem. Population Assn. Am., Am. Sociol. Assn., Chgo. Council Fgn. Relations, City Club of Chgo. Contbr. articles to profl. jours. Home: 2800 N Lake Shore Dr Chicago IL 60657 Office: care PSM Realty Inc 444 E Ontario St Chicago IL 60611

ELKINS, EVANGELINE CANONIZADO, consumer coop. ofcl.; b. San Pedro, Calif., Aug. 28, 1932; d. Estanislao C. and Felicia (Stokes) Canonizado; student San Jose State Coll., 1952-53; grad. U. San Francisco, 1978; m. Robert Alexander Elkins, July 1, 1961; children—Nikki Isaacs, Stacey Vilas, Danni Vilas Plump. With Consumers Coop. of Berkeley (Calif.) Inc., 1958—, edn. asst. for community relations, 1964-73, supr. edn. dept., 1973-76, asst. to edn. dir., 1976-78, program coordinator edn. dept., 1980-81, personnel tng. coordinator, 1981—; events coordinator Internat. House, U. Calif., Berkeley, 1984; also guitar tchr. Mem. Community Adv. Com., Bonita House, Berkeley, 1974; mem. steering com. for cultural and ethnic affairs Guild of Oakland Mus., 1973-74; dir. various activities YMCA, YWCA, Oakland City Recreation Dept., 1959-73. Recipient Honor award U. Calif. Student Coop., 1965, other awards. Mem. Coop. Educators Network Calif. Democrat. Unitarian. Columnist Coop. News, 1964—. Home: 516 Santa Barbara Rd Berkeley CA 94707 Office: 2299 Piedmont Berkeley CA 94720

ELKINS, SUSAN LEE, lawyer; b. Elgin, Ill., Jan. 17, 1951; d. Robert L. and Zelma C. (Beggs) E.; m. Douglas L. Jameson, Jan. 12, 1985; children—Brian, Brandon. B.A., Aurora (Ill.) Coll., 1972; J.D., Ariz. State U., 1979. Bar: Ohio 1979, Ariz. 1982, Calif. 1982. Tchr., Batavia (Ill.) Jr. High Sch., 1972-74, Thunderbird High Sch., Glendale, Ariz., 1974-76; assoc. Kahn, Kleinman, Yanowitz & Arnson, Cleve., 1979-81; atty. Globe Am. Casualty Co., Pepper Pike, Ohio, 1981-82; assoc. Meyers, Greger & Pohlman, Phoenix, 1983; ptnr. Horne, Kaplan & Bistrow, P.C., 1983—. Recipient Am. Jurisprudence award, 1976, Corpus Juris award, 1979. Mem. Ariz. Bar Assn., Calif. Bar Assn., Maricopa County Bar Assn., ABA, Ariz. State U. Coll. Law Alumni Assn. (dir. 1984). Home: 1421 W Medlock Dr Phoenix AZ 85013 Office: Horne Kaplan & Bistrow PC 2480 Valley Bank Center Phoenix AZ 85073

ELLEN, ROBERTA DORIS, leasing company controller; b. Bklyn., May 24, 1944; d. Julius and Lillian (Zuckerman) Richer; m. Howard Ellen, Apr. 16, 1967; children—Steven, David. B.S., L.I. U., 1968. Internal auditor Brown Bros. Harriman, N.Y.C., 1966-68; staff acct. N.Y. Stock Exchange, N.Y.C., 1968-69; asst. to pres. Franklin G. Bishop Co., Rockville Centre, N.Y., 1980-82; controller Cons. Property Mgmt., Valley Stream, N.Y., 1982-85; controller A to Z Equipment Corp., div. Welsbach Corp., Westbury, N.Y., 1985—. First prize for stained glass Middlesex County Fair, 1981. Pres. Valley Stream Spl. Edn. PTA, 1981-83; v.p. Valley Stream Council, 1982. Mem. Nat. Assn. Female Execs. Avocation: Stained glass. Office: A to Z Equipment Corp 610 A Old Country Rd Westbury NY 11590

ELLENBERGER, DIANE MARIE, nurse; b. St. Louis, Oct. 5, 1946; d. Charles Ernst and Celeste Loraine (Neudecker) E.; R.N., Barnes Hosp., St. Louis, 1970; B.S. in Nursing St. Louis U., 1976; M.S., U. Colo., 1977. Staff nurse hosps., clin. nurse, St. Louis, 1973-76; nurse clinician, Sedalia, Mo., 1977-78; nurse clinician, educator Bothwell Hosp., Sedalia, 1977-78; clin. nurse specialist, coordinator perinatal outreach edn. Cardinal Glennon Meml. Hosp. Children, St. Louis, 1978-80; instr. McKendree Coll., Lebanon, Ill., 1980; asst. prof. Maryville Coll., St. Louis, 1982-85; nurse cons. Carr, Korein, Kunan, Schlichter Montroy and Brennan Attys. at Law, 1986—; owner, operator Diane Designs Needlepoint, St. Louis, 1981—. Served with Nurse Corps, USAF, 1970-72. Mem. Am. Nurses Assn., Nurses Assn. Am. Coll. Ob-Gyn, Nat. Perinatal Assn., Mo. Nurses Assn., Mo. Perinatal Assn. (v.p. 1980), Sigma Theta Tau. Mem. Divine Sci. Ch. Contbr. articles profl. jours. Office: 412 Missouri Ave East Saint Louis IL 62201

ELLERIN, SUSAN MORRIS, statistics educator, consultant, market researcher; b. Riverdale, Md., May 13, 1948; d. Albert A. and Pearl Q. E.; married, 1982; 1 child. B.A., U. Pa., 1971, M.S., 1972, Ph.D., 1976. Mem. faculty research methods and stats. Northeastern U., 1973-85, asst. prof., 1975-79, assoc. prof., 1979-85, assoc. dean arts and scis. for humanities and social scis., 1979-82; pres. STAT Resources, Boston, 1982—; cons. in field; specialist in application of statis. and psychometric techniques to understanding market and human issues. Mem. Am. Mktg. Assn., Am. Psychol. Assn. Office: 22 Borland St Brookline MA 02146

ELLINGHAUSEN, CATHERINE ANN, public relations consultant; b. Oklahoma City, June 18, 1955; d. John Richard and Mary Theressa (Myracle) Ellinghausen. B.F.A., So. Meth. U., 1976, M.L.A., 1982; postgrad. U. So. Calif., 1978. Pub. relations dir. USA Film Festival, Dallas, 1975-76; asst. to pub. Soc. Sect. mag., Dallas, 1976; news editor, reporter, producer sta. KVIL-FM, Dallas, 1976, 80; dir. pub. relations Hoyt R. Matise Co., Dallas, 1977-78; free-lance pub. relations, Oklahoma City, 1979-80, Dallas, 1980-83; dir. pub. edn. Northwood Inst., Dallas, 1983-84, now chmn. women's bd.; cons. on broadcasting/pub. relations Mayor's Office of Protocol, Dallas, 1983—. Contbr. articles to profl. jours. Pres. Singles of St. Michael Episcopal Ch., Dallas, 1981-83; bd. dirs. Dallas County Diabetes Assn., 1976-78; co-chmn. provisional transfers Jr. League, 1983-84; mktg. chmn. Vol. Connection, 1984-85. Recipient Outstanding Pub. Service award Am. Diabetes Assn., 1977. Mem. Soc. Profl. Journalists, Women in Communications (co-chmn. job placement Dallas 1983—), Dallas Theatre Ctr., Dallas Symphony Innovators, Zeta Tau Alpha, Pi Delta Phi. Republican. Clubs: Alliance Francaise, 500. Home: 2415 Connecticut Ln Dallas TX 75214

ELLIOT, GLADYS CRISLER, oboist; b. Macon, Ga., Sept. 5, 1929; d. George Edwin and Celeste (Rhyne) Crisler; B.Mus., N.Tex. State U., Denton, 1951; m. Willard Elliot, Sept. 3, 1951 (div. June 1976). Oboist, Dallas Symphony Orch., 1951-64; Contemporary Chamber Players, U. Chgo., 1964-81, WGN Staff Orch., 1966-69; prin. oboist Lyric Opera Chgo., 1964—, Chgo. Grant Park Summer Symphony, 1966—, Orch. of Ill., 1979—; instr. DePaul U. Sch. Music, Chgo. Mem. Internat. Double Reed Soc.

ELLIOTT, DOROTHY GALE, library administrator; b. Waltham, Mass., Mar. 6, 1948; d. Robert Straight and Grace Moore (Mills) Sanborn; m. W. Mitchell Elliott, Oct. 10, 1970. B.A., Wellesley Coll., 1970; M.A., U. Mo., 1977. Exec. sec. Council for Pub. Schs., Boston, 1970-72; asst. Jerry Litton for Congress, North Kansas City, Mo., 1972; exec. sec. Stephens Coll., Columbia, Mo., 1972-74; coordinator Univ. Without Walls, Stephens Coll., Columbia, Mo., 1975-76; pub. services librarian St. Joseph Pub. Library, Mo., 1977-78, dir., 1978—. Sec., Grand River Library Conf., 1982-84; bd. dirs. Mo. Libraries Film Coop., 1980-83; sec./treas. Mo. Libraries Network Bd., 1984-85; pres. N.W. Mo. Library Network Bd., 1983-85; pres. adv. council Sch. Library and Info. Sci., U. Mo., Columbia, 1985. Editor newsletter Jr. League St. Joseph, 1985-86. Bd. dirs. Mental Health Assn. St. Joseph, 1978-81; com. mem. United Way Greater St. Joseph, 1981—; bd. dirs. Interfaith Community Services, 1982-85; mem. steering com. Lifelong Learning, St. Joseph, 1983—; mem. St. Joseph Area Women's Career Network, 1983—, Downtown St. Joseph, Inc., 1983—. Wellesley scholar, 1969. Mem. ALA, Mo. Library Assn. (sec. 1983-84), Beta Phi Mu, St. Joseph Area C. of C. Democrat. Methodist. Clubs: Wellesley (Kansas City); Runcie (St. Joseph). Office: St Joseph Public Library 10th and Felix Sts St Joseph MO 64501

ELLIOTT, ELEANOR THOMAS, chem. co. exec.; b. N.Y.C., Apr. 26, 1926; d. James A. and Dorothy Q. (Read) Thomas; B.A., Barnard Coll., 1948; m. John Elliott, Jr., July 26, 1956. Staff writer Vogue Mag., N.Y.C., 1948, asso. editor, to 1952; asst. dir. research and speech writing div. N.Y. State Republican Com., 1952, 53-56; social sec. to Sec. of State and Mrs. John Foster Dulles, Washington, 1953-56; dir. Celanese Corp., N.Y.C., 1974—, C.I.T. Fin. Corp., 1978-81. Trustee, Barnard Coll., 1959—, chmn., 1973-76; chmn. bd. dirs. Found. for Child Devel., 1972-79; bd. govs. N.Y. Hosp., 1970—; bd. dirs. United Way of Greater N.Y., 1977—, Catalyst Inc., 1978—, Am. Women's Econ. Devel. Corp., 1978—, NOW Legal Def. and Edn. Fund, 1983—; trustee Woodrow Wilson Nat. Fellowship Found., 1983—, Edna McConnell Clark Found., 1984—. Recipient Columbia U. medal, 1977, Barnard Coll. medal, 1979; named Extraordinary Woman of Achievement, NCCJ, 1978. Mem. Nat. Assn. Women, Nat. Women's Polit. Caucus. Republican. Episcopalian. Club: Colony. Author: Glamour Magazine Party Book, 1966. Address: 1035 Fifth Ave New York NY 10028

ELLIOTT, ELIZABETH ANN, market researcher; b. Cin., Apr. 27, 1932; d. Howard E. Elliott and Kathryn E. (Forsman) Byers. B.A., Denison U., 1954. Interviewer market research dept. Procter & Gamble Co., Cin., 1954-55, field supr., 1955-58, chief field supr., 1958-60, personnel dir. and scheduler, 1960-77, tech. cons., 1977—; career adv. Denison U., 1980—; market research cons. Community Chest and other service agys., 1983—. Mem. Delta Gamma. Republican. Presbyterian. Avocations: photography; travel; antiques; gardening; music. Home: 1326 Deliquia Dr Cincinnati OH 45230 Office: 2 Procter & Gamble Plaza Cincinnati OH 45201

ELLIOTT, GLORIA J., management consultant; b. Canonsburg, Pa., Mar. 7, 1947; d. George and Victoria (Guzik) Hadanich. B.S., California U. of Pa., 1969; M.S., Shippensburg U., 1975; nat. cert. in rehab. counseling; cert. in adminstrn. U. Wis., 1977. Youth rehab. counselor Pa. Dept. Pub. Welfare, Waynesburg and Loysville, 1971-73; exec. dir. Counseling Services Ctr., Corry, Pa., 1975-78; CMHC unit dir. Mental Health Services, Roanoke, Va., 1978-80; prin., sr. cons. Elliott & Assocs., orgnl. and human resources devel. cons., Roanoke, 1981—; former mem. adj. faculty U. Va. Roanoke Extension, Va. Western Community Coll., Pa. State U.; mem. adj. faculty M.B.A. program Lynchburg Coll., U. Richmond, Roanoke Coll. Contbr. articles to profl. jours. Trainer Nat. Alliance of Bus., 1978; bd. dirs., mem. exec. com. Girl Scouts U.S.A., 1981-87, Mental Health Assn., Roanoke, 1981-85; bd. dirs., pres. Jr. Achievement, Roanoke, 1981—, pres., 1985; mem. Roanoke Centennial Com., 1982; mem. campaign cabinet United Way, 1985, 86. Recipient SBA award, Va., 1986. Mem. Am. Soc. Tng. and Devel. (dir. 1981-82, pres. 1983, chmn. 1984-85), Am. Soc. Personnel Adminstrs., Va. Mental Health Counselors Assn. (sec. 1979), Am. Soc. Profl. Cons., Am. Mgmt. Assn., Roanoke Profl. and Managerial Network, Nat. Assn. Female Execs., Women Bus. Owners of S.W. Va. (founder, pres.), Roanoke Valley C. of C. (chmn. small bus. council 1983, 86), Va. State C. of C. (mem. small bus. council). Address: Elliott and Assocs PO Box 12386 Roanoke VA 24025

ELLIOTT, INGER MCCABE (MRS. OSBORN ELLIOTT), designer, textile company executive, author; b. Oslo, Norway, Feb. 23, 1933; d. David and Lova (Katz) Abrahamsen; came to U.S., 1941, naturalized, 1946; B.A. in History with honors, Cornell U., 1954; postgrad. Harvard U., 1955; A.M. (Jean Birdsall fellow), Radcliffe Coll., 1957; m. Osborn Elliott, Oct. 20, 1973; children by previous marriage-Kari McCabe, Alexander McCabe, Molly McCabe. Editor, East European Student and Youth Service, N.Y.C., 1957-60; photographer Photo Researchers, U.S. and fgn. countries, 1960—; pres. China Seas, Inc., N.Y.C., 1972—; tchr. Newton (Mass.) Public Schs., 1955-56. Mem. adv. council Cornell U., 1985; mem. East Asia vis com. Harvard U., 1981—. Recipient award Resources Council, 1977-83, Roscoe award, 1978, 80, 82, 83, 84, Mem. Am. Soc. Mag. Photographers, Com. of 200, Am. Women's Econ. Devel. Corp. (bd. dirs. 1973-83), Nat. Home Fashion League, Am. Soc. Interior Designers (industry found.), Phi Beta Kappa. Author: Women Photographers, 1970; A Week in Amy's World, 1970; A Week in Henry's World, 1971; Batik: Fabled Cloth of Java, 1984; also portfolio in Infinity mag., 1969. Home: 10 Gracie Sq New York NY 10028 Office: China Seas Inc 21 E 4th St New York NY 10003

ELLIOTT, LEE ANN, psychologist; b. Tulsa, Jan. 22, 1923; d. John Lewis and Evelyn (Peters) Moore; m. Craig Judson Elliott (dec. Feb. 1971). B.S., Okla. State U., 1945; postgrad. UCLA, 1947-50. Part owner, Profl. Guidance Assocs., Sherman Oaks, Calif., 1961-66; mgr., dir., spokesperson Alpha Oxi Omega, North Hollywood, Calif., 1967-75, 78—; vis. nurse Vis. Nurses Assn., Hollywood, Calif., 1977-78, 1978—. Mem. Republican Presdl. Task Force, 1984—, U.S. Senatorial Club, 1984—. Fellow Nat. Assn. Female Execs., Smithsonian Instn. Avocations: Dress design; writing. Home: 5251 Strohm St North Hollywood CA 91601 Office: Alpha Oxi Omega 5149 Bakman St North Hollywood CA 91601

ELLIOTT, LINNÉA CONSTANCE, publisher; b. N.Y.C., Feb. 23, 1948; d. Samuel and Edith Anna (Peterson) Whyte, Jr.; m. Peter Thomas Elliott, Aug. 31, 1969. Ground hostess Japan Airlines, N.Y.C., 1967-68; asst. to mng. editor Southmayd Corp., Yonkers, N.Y., 1968; public relations model Seagrams Corp., N.Y.C., 1968; prodn. editor, mgr. jours., editorial dept. Pergamon Press, Elmsford, N.Y., 1968-74; assoc. pub. Appleton Century-Crofts div. Prentice-Hall, East Norwalk, Conn., 1974-84; dir. mktg. services HP Pub. Co., N.Y.C., 1986—; cons. in field. Mem. Healthcare Businesswomen's Assn., Pharm. Advt. Council, Assn. Ind. Clin. Pubs. (treas. 1981-83, pres.-elect 1984), Nat. Assn. Female Execs. Episcopalian. Mng. editor Jour. Family Practice, 1974-83, Jour. Nat. Med. Assn., 1975-79. Home: Colonial Hill RFD #1 Kisco NY 10549 Office: HP Publishing Co 10 Astor Place New York NY 10003

ELLIOTT, MARGARET HENDERSON, reading educator, clinical diagnostician, consultant; b. Pittsylvania County, Va., Oct. 28, 1942; d. David Lawson and Louise (Puryear) Henderson; m. Lauriston Kennerly Elliott, Nov. 15, 1963; children—Alice Marilyn, David Kennerly. Diploma Phillips Bus. Coll., Lynchburg, Va., 1961; student U. Va., 1970-71, postgrad. in edn., 1986—; student Stratford Coll., 1972; B.A. in Edn., Averett Coll., 1974; M.S. in Edn. summa cum laude, Longwood Coll., 1982. Cert. tchr., reading specialist, supr., Va. Stenographer, Va. chpt. Arthritis and Rheumatism Found., Lynchburg, 1962; sec., office mgr. Riverside Constrn. Co., South Boston, Va., 1963-68; pvt. piano tchr., Halifax, Va., 1968-71; adminstrv. tchr. Cluster Springs Acad. (Va.), 1971-74; resource tchr. Charlotte County Pub. Schs. Reading Ctr., 1974-76; reading specialist, diagnostician, resource tchr. Chase City Acad. (Va.), 1976-82, master tchr., cons., 1982-85; elem. supr. Mecklenburg County Edni. Found., Chase City, asst. adminstr. K-12, 1986—; cons. Mecklenburg Ednl. Found., 1982-83. Bd. dirs. Dan River Youth; Dan River Assn. Mission Action dir., 1979-81, Acteen dir., 1981-83. Recipient Community Service Program award Southside Community Coll., 1975, Superior Instrn. award State AAA. Mem. Averett Alumni Assn., Longwood Alumni Assn., Kappa Delta Pi. So. Baptist. Club: Lakewood Homemakers (Halifax). Home: Route 2 Box 522 Halifax VA 24558 Office: Route 3 Box 1050 St Chase City VA 23924

ELLIOTT, MARGARET MCKEAGUE, lawyer; b. Lansing, Mich., May 16, 1950; d. Herbert William McKeague and Phyllis (Forsyth) McKeague Jones; m. Theodore Roosevelt Elliott, June 5, 1982. B.A., U. Mich., 1972; J.D., U. Calif.-San Franciso, 1981. Bar: Calif. Paralegal, summer assoc. Cooley, Godward et al, San Francisco, 1972-79; summer assoc. Brobeck, Phleger et al, San Francisco, 1980; jud. extern U.S. Dist. Ct., San Francisco, 1981; assoc. Anderson, Zeigler, Disharoon & Gray, Santa Rosa, Calif., 1981—; asst. prof. Sonoma U., Rohnert Park, Calif., 1982-83; prof. Empire Law Sch., Santa Rosa, 1984. Bd. dirs. Goodwill Industries, Santa Rosa, 1983—; trustee Sonoma Land Trust, Santa Rosa, 1983—. James B. Angell scholar U. Mich., 1970-72; Thurston scholar U. Calif.-San Francisco, 1980-81. Mem. ABA, Calif. Bar Assn., Sonoma County Bar Assn., Redwood Empire Estate Planning Council. Clubs: Forum, Parkpoint (Santa Rosa). Office: Anderson Zeigler Disharoon Gray 50 Old Courthouse Sq Santa Rosa CA 95402

ELLIOTT, MYRTLE EVELYN KEENER, educator; b. Annawan, Ill., Apr. 11, 1898; d. John William and Mary (Baldwin) Keener; A.B., Cornell Coll., 1921; M.A., Columbia, 1926; postgrad. summers U. Iowa, 1928, Ohio State U., 1930, 31, U. Chgo., 1933, San Francisco State Coll., 1949, Fresno State Coll., 1958, 59, 60; m. Leo Louis Elliott, Aug. 10, 1935 (dec. 1948); children—Mary Ellen (Mrs. Jack Agan), Winona (Mrs. Herbert C. Sample), James, Joan. Tchr. pub. high schs., Panora, Iowa, 1921-23, Dewitt, Iowa, 1923-25; head English dept., dean girls, Kemmerer, Wyo., 1926-29; dean girls and English, Pendelton, Oreg., 1929-30; tchr., Ely, Nev., 1930-31; girls' adviser boarding schs. U.S. Indian Service, 1931-35; tchr. Latin and English, Cut Bank, Mont., 1944-46; tchr. older educable retarded children for Kern County Supt. Schs., Bakersfield, Calif., 1949-68; pvt. work with children with learning disabilities. Recipient Alumni Merit award Cornell Coll., 1977. Fellow Am. Assn. Mental Deficiency; mem. Council for Exceptional Children, Calif. Tchrs. Assn., Nat. (hon. life), Calif. (hon. life) congresses parents and tchrs., Catholic Daus. Am., Columbia Tchrs. Coll. Alumni Assn. (past local chmn.), Cornell Coll. Alumni Assn., AAUW, Internat. Reading Assn., Phi Beta Kappa. Home: 2709 4th St Bakersfield CA 93304

ELLIOTT, PATRICIA ANN, systems engineer; b. St. Louis, Mar. 30. 1951; d. Thomas and Emma Madge (Everette) E. B.S.E. In Math., Northeast Mo. State U., Kirksville, 1973. Tchr. math. Elk Grove Sch. Dist., Sacramento, Calif., 1973-74, Hazelwood Sch. Dist., St. Louis, 1974-75; engring. programmer Emerson Electric Co., St. Louis, 1975-77; software programmer Ralston Purina, St. Louis, 1977-81; system engr. Four Phase Systems Inc., St. Louis, 1981—. Mem. choir Antioch Bapt. Ch., St. Louis, also Sunday sch. tchr. Recipient cert. of recognition Antioch Bapt. Sunday Sch., 1980, 1981. Mem. Nat. Assn. Female Execs.

ELLIOTT, ROSALIE CONN (MRS. F. SCOTT ELLIOTT), educator, club woman; b. Kosciusko, Miss.; d. Jefferson P. and Ada (Russell) Conn.; B.S., George Peabody Coll. Tchrs., 1924; M.A., U. N.C., 1935; postgrad. U. Chgo., several summers; m. F. Scott Elliott, Dec. 22, 1933 (dec.); 1 son, F. Scott, Jr. Tchr. English, Columbia (S.C.) High Sch., 1924-26; tchr. head math. dept. Lee H. Edwards High Sch., Asheville, N.C., 1926-39; math. tchr. Durham (N.C.) High Sch., 1939-46; tchr. English and French, Whitmire (S.C.) High Sch., 1957-65. Past exec. bd., past sec. Newberry Civic League; active Crippled Children Soc.; sec. United Meth. Ch. Central, United Meth. Women. Mem. AAUW (chmn. local lit. div., past pres. Newberry br. 1958-60, 70-72, mass media chmn. state div. 1960-62), N.E.A., Newberry County Classroom Tchrs. (pres. 1959), Newberry Hist. Soc. (publicity chmn.), NEA (pres. math. div.), N.C. Edn. Assn., S.C. Fedn. Women's Clubs (div. chmn. 1951-72, dir. N. dist. 1952-55, chmn. library services 1968-72), Nat. League Am. Pen Women (chmn. Piedmont poetry div.), Am. Legion Aux. (local pres. 1948-50), Women's Soc. Christian Service (local pres. 1952-56; dist. pres. 1956-60), U.D.C. (twice chpt. pres., recorder crosses S.C. div.), D.A.R. (past regent Jasper, state motion picture chmn., past treas., S.C. arts com.), S.C. Soc. Poets, Delta Kappa Gamma (chpt. pres. 1970-72), Epsilon Sigma Omicron (past chpt. pres.). Methodist (circle leader, Sunday sch. tchr.). Club: Woman's (pres. 1948-50). Poems included in Nat. Poetry Anthology, 1958-81, S.C. Mag. Home: 718 Glenn St Newberry SC 29108

ELLIOTT, ROXANNE SNELLING, consultant to independent schools; b. Ft. Eustis, Va., Aug. 17, 1954; d. William Rodman and Anne Louise (Kurtz) Snelling; m. Vincent James Elliott, Oct. 1, 1983; 1 child, Brian William. B.A., Denison U., 1976; M.B.A., Syracuse U., 1978. Internat. loan officer First Pa. Bank, Phila., 1978-82; ins. assoc. Ind. Sch. Mgmt., Wilmington, Del, 1982-83, dir. mgmt. insts., 1983—, assoc. cons., exec. dir. consortium, 1984—, v.p., 1986—. Republican. Episcopalian. Office: Independent Sch Mgmt 1316 N Union St Wilmington DE 19806

ELLIOTT, SHIRLEY RAE, medical technologist; b. Binghamton, N.Y., Oct. 21, 1922; d. John Rook and Carrie Marie (Keeney) Reynolds; student Duke U., 1940-42; student U. Tex., 1942-43, Sch. Med. Tech. VA Med. Ctr., 1955-56; m. Floyd Strother Elliott, Nov. 13, 1943; children—Linda Rae, Teresa Marie, Rita Kay, Susan Irene, John Roger, Katherine Claire, Floyd Strother. Research technologist VA Med. Center, Nashville, 1956, med. technologist microbiology, chemistry, 1956-59, med. technologist, generalist, 1959-66, coagulation/parasitology, technologist, 1966-72, supr. med. technology, 1972—. Named Mother of the Yr., (Gallatin) Jaycettes, 1976, others. Mem. Nat. Geographic Soc., Cousteau Soc., Duke Alumni Assn., Met. Opera Guild, Am. Soc. Med. Technologists, Internat. Soc. Med. Technologists, Tenn. Soc. Microbiology, Am. Soc. Clin. Pathologists. Methodist. Clubs: Toastmasters, Nat. Commodore, Iron Dukes. Home: 1007 Bentley Cir Gallatin TN 37066 Office: 1310 24th Ave S Nashville TN 37203

ELLIOTT, SUSAN ALBERTA, lawyer, govt. ofcl.; b. Palm Springs, Calif., Mar. 28, 1948; d. William Henry and Ruth Elizabeth (Schureman) Elliott; B.A. magna cum laude, Harvard U., 1970; J.D., Boston U., 1974; m. Jean Pierre Swennen, Oct. 18, 1975; children—Tara, Kimberly. Admitted to D.C. bar, 1975, U.S. Supreme Ct. bar, 1978; asso. Jones, Day, Reavis & Pogue, Washington, 1974-76, Cadwallader, Wickersham & Taft, 1976-78; staff atty. div. advt. practices FTC, 1978-80, dep. asst., 1980-82, asst. dir., 1982—. Mem. Womens Legal Def. Fund, 1974—. Mem. D.C. Bar Assn. Methodist. Office: FTC 600 E St Suite 407 Washington DC 20580

ELLIS, ANGELA ELAINE, real estate development company executive; b. Oklahoma City, Okla., Feb. 14, 1958; d. Roger Sherman and Ilene Faye (Forrester) Bailey; m. Hal William Ellis, May, 1980 (div. Aug. 1982). B.S. in Acctg., Okla. State U.-Stillwater, 1979. C.P.A., Okla., Tex. Staff acct. Thomas F. Riley, Jr. C.P.A., Stillwater, 1979-80; staff acct. Call, Barrick, Ethridge, Webb & Co., Stillwater, 1980-81; asst. controller Rockie Smith Enterprises, Cushing, Okla., 1981-83; asst. controller The Talmadge Tinsley Co., Inc., Dallas, 1983—. Reading & Bates Offshore Drilling scholar, 1977, Okla. Gas & Electric scholar, 1976, Okla. State U. Regent's Disting. scholar, 1978. Mem. Okla. Soc. C.P.A.s, Tex. Soc. C.P.A.s, Real Estate Fin. Execs., Beta Alpha Psi, Alpha Kappa Psi. Republican. Baptist. Home: 5963B Mendocino Dr Dallas TX 75248 Office: The Talmadge Tinsley Co Inc 17000 Preston Rd Suite 400 Dallas TX 75248

ELLIS, CAROLYN TERRY, lawyer; b. N.Y.C., Apr. 20, 1949; d. Francis Martin and Sarah Baker (Ames) Ellis; m. H. Lake Wise, Feb. 27, 1982; children—Carolyn Campbell Wise, Burke Ames. B.A., U. Chgo., 1971; J.D., NYU, 1974. Bar: N.Y. 1975. Research analyst Dept. Justice, N.Y.C., 1973-74; assoc. Lord, Day & Lord, N.Y.C., 1974-84, ptnr., 1984—; instr. Bklyn. Law Sch., 1980-82. Mem. ABA, N.Y. State Bar Assn. Club: Heights Casino. Office: Lord Day & Lord 25 Broadway New York NY 10004

ELLIS, ELIZABETH GILL, librarian; b. Raleigh, N.C., Nov. 6; d. Samuel J. and Annie (Shepard) Gill; m. Edward V. Ellis, June 24, 1950; children—Ednetta, Bruce, Gary. A.B., B.S. in L.S., N.C. Central U., 1949, M.L.S., 1962; postgrad. Pa. State U., 1980—. Coordinator librarian Raleigh City Schs., 1951-53; serials accessioner Library of Congress, Washington, 1954; head Pa. Dept. Health Library, Harrisburg, 1956-58; head govt. pubs. State Library of Pa., Harrisburg, 1958-67; head undergrad. library Pa. State U., University Park, 1969-76, head library studies, 1976—; adj. prof. Drexel U., Phila., 1965-67, dir. workshops on govt. pubs., 1965-75; lectr. Tex. So. U., 1973; mem. state adv. council on sch. media Pa. Dept. Edn., Harrisburg, 1976-78. Contbr. articles to profl. jours. Bd. chmn. Library Service Vol. Assn. U. Minn. Hosp., Mpls., 1967-69. Mem. ALA (chmn. GODORT task force on edn. legis. 1975-78), Pa. Library Assn. (dir. 1965-66, 74-78), N.C. Library Assn. (sec.; Librarian of Yr. award 1950), Am. Assn. Higher Edn., AAUW, LWV, Delta Sigma Theta, Pi Lambda Theta. Democrat. Presbyterian. Office: Pa State Univ Pattee Library University Park PA 16802

ELLIS, ETHEL MAE, librarian; b. Lawrenceville, Va., Feb. 28, 1924; d. Charles Roman and Kate Delina (Travis) Vaughan; m. Albert Thomas Ellis, July 5, 1947 (dec. Aug. 1975); children—Willette, Albert Thomas, Mildred. B.S., Va. State U., 1944; B.S.L.S., Atlanta U., 1946; M.S., Howard U., 1980. Librarian, Christianburg (Va.) High Sch., 1944-45; asst. librarian Va. State U., Ettrick, 1946-47; librarian, cataloger D.C. Pub. Library, Washington, 1947-62; cataloger, head tech. service Moorland-Spingarn Research Ctr., Howard U., Washington, 1962—. Compiler: (with Porter) Journal of Negro Education Index 1932-1962, 1963; The American Negro, 1968; Opportunity, Cumulative Index, 1971. Mem. ALA, Potomac Tech. Processing Librarians, D.C. Library Assn., Assn. for Study Negro Life and History, Ch. Library Council, Alpha Kappa Alpha. Home: 512 Hillsboro Dr Silver Spring MD 20902 Office: Moorland-Spingarn Research Center Howard University Washington DC 20059

ELLIS, EVA LILLIAN, artist; b. Seattle, June 4, 1920; d. Carl Martin and Hilda (Persson) Johnson; B.A., U. Wash., 1941; M.A., U. Idaho, 1950; M.Painting (h.c.), U. delle Arti, 1983; m. Everett Lincoln Ellis, May 1, 1943; children—Karin, Kristy, Hildy, Erik. Assoc. dir. art Best & Co., Seattle, 1943; dir. Am. Art Week, Idaho, 1949-55; mem. faculty dept. art U. Idaho, 1946-48; dir., tchr. Children's Art Oreg., 1966-71; exhbns. include: Henry Gallery, U. Wash., 1941, Immanuel Gallery, N.Y.C., 1943-46, U. Mich., 1956-65, Detroit Inst. Art, 1959, Kresge Gallery, 1959-64, Portland Art Mus., 1967, Corvallis Art Center, Oreg., 1966, U. Idaho, 1946-56, U. Canterbury, N.Z., 1979, Boise Mus., 1949-55, CSA, 1972, 79, Survey of New Zealand Art, 1979, Shoreline Mus., Seattle, 1981, N.Z. Embassy, London, 1979, Karlshamn Art Soc., Sweden, 1979, Italian Acad. Art, 1982, Palos Verdes Art Ctr., calif., 1982, Aigantighe Gallery, N.Z., 1983; represented in permanent collections: U. Calif. Berkeley, U. Wash.; guest appearances on NBC-TV, N.Y.C. Counselor Cancer Soc., active Girl Scouts U.S.A. Recipient awards Acad. Art and Sci., 1958-66, Ann Arbor Women Painters, diploma with gold medal, Italian Acad. Art, 1980, hon. diploma fine art; World Culture prize, 1984; Internat. Peace award in Art, 1984; Internat. Art Promotion award, 1986, others. Mem. Mich. Acad. Art and Sci., Nat. League Am. Pen Women, Fine Arts Soc. Idaho, Canterbury Soc. Art New Zealand, Copely Soc. Fine Arts (Boston), Alpha Omicron Pi. (featured in nat. mag.). Clubs: Scandinavian (pres. 1977—), Faculty Wives (pres. 1979). Address: 2603 NW 98th St Seattle WA 98117

ELLIS, FRANCES LORENE ARNOLD, civic worker; b. Greenville, Tex., Jan. 8, 1913; d. Horace Robert and Fay (Hall) Arnold; m. Printis E. Ellis, Apr. 19, 1954 (dec. Feb. 1981). A.A., Wesley Jr. Coll., Greenville, 1932; B.A., East Tex. State U., 1933; B.S., Tex. Woman's U., 1937; postgrad. in journalism Iowa State U., 1951. Phys. edn. instr. Wesley Jr. Coll., Greenville, 1932-33; sec. Hunt County Agrl. Extension Service, Greenville, 1933-35; home demonstration agt. Red River, Cass and Lamar Counties (Tex.), 1937-47; home econs. editor Agrl. Extension Service, Tex. A&M U., College Station, 1947-53; asst. dir. nat. project in agrl. communications Mich. State U., East Lansing, 1954; sec. Am. Nat. Ins. Co., Paris, Tex., 1954—. Contbr. articles to Farmer Stockman, Prog. Farmer, Together mag., other publs. Chmn. Lamar County Adv. Bd. Health, 1971—; mem. Tex. Gov.'s Com. on Aging, 1970-79; chmn. adv. council and bd. Red River Valley Home Health Services, 1972—; sec. adv. bd. Paris Pub. Library, 1965—; mem. adv. council Area Agy. on Aging, Ark.-Tex. Council Govts., 1982—; mem. adv. council Tex. Dept. Aging, 1983—; chmn. litter, reclamation and recycling Nat. Council State Garden Clubs, 1982—; local unit reporter Am. Cancer Soc., 1972—; dist. archives and history chmn. United Methodist Ch., 1972-82; sec. ofcl. bd. 1st United Meth. Ch., Paris, 1983—, author, pub. history, 1985; pub. Early Families of Hunt County; v.p. Tex. Meth. Hist. Soc., 1986—; mem. mng. com. Tridens Prairie. Recipient Nat. Radio award Nat. Assn. Agrl. Coll. Editors, 1947; Disting. Alumna award Tex. Woman's U., 1970; honoree 5th Ann Wildflower Day awards luncheon Tex. Woman's U., 1984. Mem. Women in Journalism (Clarion award 1978), Am. Home Econs. Assn. (40 Yr. Membership award 1982), Paris Bus. and Profl. Women's Club (Women of Yr. 1968), Lamar County Home Econs. Assn., Mary Emma Bible Study Club, Tex. Garden Clubs (v.p., editor Lone Star Gardener 1971-73, chmn. bd. trustees 1979-82), Epsilon Sigma Phi, Delta Kappa Gamma. Home: 1003 S Main St Paris TX 75460

ELLIS, GLORIA BURROW, library director; b. Long Branch, N.J., Oct. 30, 1930; d. Robert and Mary Celia (Katz) Burrow; B.A., Rutgers U., 1951; tchr. cert. Wayne State U., 1967, M.S.L.S., 1972; m. Robert Lowell Ellis, Feb. 5, 1956; children—Wendy Lee, Jeffrey B., Richard C. Newspaper reporter, 1951-55; tchr. Hillel Day Sch., Farmington, Mich., 1968-71; librarian Walsh Coll. Accountancy and Bus. Adminstrn., Troy, Mich., 1973—, library dir., 1974—. chmn. Mich. region bd. dirs. B'nai B'rith Youth Orgn., 1981-83. Mem. ALA, Spl. Libraries Assn., Southeastern Mich. League Libraries (chmn. 1984—), Mich. Library Assn. Club: B'nai B'rith Women (chmn. Midwest region 1978-80, mem. nat. exec. bd. 1982-84). Home: 7123 Pebble Park Dr West Bloomfield MI 48033 Office: 3838 Livernois Troy MI 48084

ELLIS, GRACE CAROL, businesswoman; b. Fairview, Mo., Dec. 4, 1935; d. Leo Leslie and Grace (Allinder) Eurit; m. Leonard Eugene Ellis, Dec. 17, 1955; children—Susan Diane, Linda Jeanne, Leonard Eugene. Grad. Draughon's Bus. Sch., 1954. Real estate broker, Stillwater, Okla., 1970—; ptnr., mgr. Crestview Estates, Stillwater, 1971-85, Crestview Quick Shop and Laundry, 1971—. Republican. Baptist. Avocations: reading; gardening; traveling. Office: Crestview Quick Shop 2319 E 6th St Stillwater OK 74074

ELLIS, GWEN BOYD, personnel representative; b. Champaign, Ill., Apr. 2, 1952; d. Elijah L. and Debora (Hall) Boyd; div. 1980. B.S. in Pub. Sch. Music cum laude, Morris Brown Coll., 1972. Tchr. music East Atlanta High Sch., 1972; head payroll and receiving teller C&S Nat. Bank, Atlanta, 1972; customer service II, office mgr., 1972-76; flight attendant Delta Airlines, Houston, Dallas, Atlanta, 1976—, personnel rep., Atlanta, 1983—. Speaker career day Delta, Tex., Ga., 1976-83; tour guide Internat. Airport Summer Safe Camp, Atlanta, 1981-82, instr. music, 1981-82; actress nat. TV commls. Delta Airlines, Atlanta, 1983; asst. producer, host Video-Host Video-Pub. Access TV, Women of 80's, 1983. Team leader March of Dimes Walk, Atlanta, 1982-83; co-host Mayor's Christmas party for children of Atlanta, 1981-83; singer JEL Choraliers, Atlanta, 1981-83. Mem. Nat. Assn. Female Execs., Pub. Access Users Assn. Democrat. Methodist. Home: 1599 Rogers Ave SW Atlanta GA 30310 Office: Delta Airlines Hartsfield Atlanta Internat Airport Dept 961 Atlanta GA 30320

ELLIS, HELEN CHARD, writer, former health agency executive; b. East Orange, N.J., Oct. 16, 1914; d. Claude Franklin and Harriet Correll (Wallen) Chard; m. Harlan Reed Ellis, Dec. 23, 1937; children—Reed Ellis, Karen Anne Ellis Stonesifer. Student, Wooster Coll., 1931-33, U. Fla.-Gainesville, 1966-67; B.S., Simmons Coll., 1936. Part-time editorial work U. Fla.-Gainesville, 1957-70; exec. dir. Birth Defects Found., Gainesville, 1970-79; freelance writer, 1982—; instr. community edn. program Santa Fe Jr. Coll., 1984—. Compiler series of articles in Jour. of Teacher Edn., 1957-67; contbr. articles to mags. Mem., Fla. Gov.'s Alachua County Children's Commn., 1965-69, Alachua County Crime Victim Fund Rev. Com., 1979-83. Recipient March of Dimes Service award, 1982, 83, AAUW Service award, 1983, Fla. Fedn. Women's Clubs Service award, 1983. Mem. Nat. League Am. Pen Women (pres. Gainesville br. 1978-84, Fla. pres. 1986—), Women in Communications, Fla. Freelance Writer's Assn., AAUW (past pres.), Gainesville Fine Arts Assn. (1st v.p. 1980-82). Club: Gainesville Woman's (chmn. internat. affairs 1982-83). Home: 4041 NW 12th Ave Gainesville FL 32605

ELLIS, JANE FINCKE, marketing director; b. Newark, Aug. 27, 1956; d. Melvin R. and Estelle (Seiff) Fincke; m. Richard Lowes Ellis, Jr., June 2, 1985. B.A. in Philosophy cum laude, Yale U., 1978; M.B.A., Harvard U., 1982. Asst. treas. Chase Manhattan Bank, N.Y.C., 1978-80; corp. planner The Rockefeller Group, N.Y.C., 1982-84; dir. mktg. Rockefeller Ctr. Mgmt. Corp., 1984—. Pub. mag. Center. Treas. Yale Class of 1978, chair Quarter Century Fund. Mem. Nat. Assn. Female Execs., Yale U. Alumni Assn. Club: Harvard Business School, Harvard (N.Y.C.). Avocations: running; bicycling; piano. Home: 7 Midland Gardens 5M Bronxville NY 10708 Office: Rockefeller Ctr Mgmt Corp 1230 Ave of Americas New York NY 10020

ELLIS, JOANNNE HAMMONDS, computer executive; b. Rome, Ga., Aug. 15, 1946; d. James Randolph and Louise (Glass) Hammonds; B.S., A.B., Jacksonville (Ala.) U., 1968; M.G.A., Ga. State U., 1979, M.P.A., 1981; 1 dau., Stephanie Louise. With GSA, 1969—, computer systems analyst, 1979-80, now dir. mgmt. services. Named Profl. Employee of Year, 1979. Mem. Assn. Women in Computing, Federally Employed Women, Atlanta Assn. Fed. Execs., Beta Sigma Phi. Baptist. Home: 1143 Seabreeze Ln Gulf Breeze FL 32561 Office: Navy Regional Data Automation Center NAS Pensacola FL 32508

ELLIS, LAURA CAREY, art advisor, curatorial consultant; b. N.Y.C., Sept. 30, 1951; d. William and Paulette Marcelle (Vidal) Carey; m. Ralph Winston Ellis, Nov. 19, 1979; children—Phillip, Alexandra. Student U. St. Thomas, 1969-71, Roanoke Coll., 1971; B.F.A., U. Tex., 1975; postgrad. U. Grenoble, France, 1975-76. Pres. Carey Ellis Co., Houston, 1978—. Author and editor: American Works of the 19th and 20th Centuries, 1985; Tex. Am. Bank Art Catalogue. Mem. allocations rev. com. Cultural Arts Council of Houston, exhbn. com. Nave Mus., Victoria, Tex., Women's Bd. of Northwood Inst., Dallas. Mem. Assn. Profl. Art Advisors (1st Tex. mem.). Democrat. Roman Catholic. Home: 2045 Goldsmith St Houston TX 77030 Office: Carey Ellis Co 1414 Sul Ross Houston TX 77006

ELLIS, MARCIA MARY, utility consultant; b. Herkimer, N.Y., Sept. 23, 1951; d. Frederick E. and Elizabeth Louina (Leonard) E. Student SUNY-Oswego, 1969-73. Sr. records clk. Stone & Webster Engring. Corp., Oswego, N.Y., 1977-80, documentation coordinator, Oswego and Boston, 1980-81, mgmt. systems analyst, Boston, 1981-82, sr. systems analyst, Boston, 1982-83; utility cons. Mgmt. Analysis Co., San Diego, 1983—. Mem. Nuclear Info. and Records Mgmt. Assn., Assn. Records Mgrs. and Adminstrs. Democrat. Avocations: reading; writing. Office: Mgmt Analysis Co 12671 High Bluff Dr San Diego CA 92130

ELLIS, MARIQUIT PANOPIO (KIT), insurance executive; b. Batangas, Philippines, Oct. 2, 1946; came to U.S., 1972, naturalized, 1972; d. Felix Panopio and Aurora Yance; m. Keith E. Ellis, Feb. 14, 1972; 1 child, Duster S. Student Phila. Coll. Commerce, 1964. Lic. ins. agt., broker. Owner, mgr. The Flame, Stratton, Nebr., 1973-83; ins. agt. Druliner Ins. Agy., Benkelman, Nebr., 1979-84; mgr. Trenton Agy., Inc., Nebr., 1984—. Mem. Ind. Ins. Agts. Am., Ind. Ins. Agts. Nebr., Profl. Women Nebr. Roman Catholic. Club: Stratton Recreation (Nebr.). Lodge: Eagles Aux. Avocation: sewing.

ELLIS, MARY JO, county official; b. Scottsbluff, Nebr., Nov. 13, 1928; d. Roy Edward and Hazel Belle (Parmenter) Kronberg; m. Vinton Maurice Ellis, Aug. 3, 1949; children—Martin F., Mary Ellis Shaughnessy. Dep. register of deeds Scotts Bluff County, Gering, Nebr., 1946-52, register of deeds, 1963—; asst. mgr. Fed. Land Bank, Scottsbluff, 1955-62. Sec., treas. United Way, Scottsbluff, 1974-76; v.p., bd. dirs. Foster Grandparents Assn., Scottsbluff, 1980—. Mem. Nebr. Recorders and Clks. Assn. (pres. 1971-72), Nat. Assn. Recorders and Clks. Assn. (historian 1979—, Cert. merit 1967, 85), Panhandle County Ofcls. Assn. (pres. 1985), Scottsbluff Bus. and Profl. Women's Club (pres. 1974-75, Woman of Achievement award 1979), Scottsbluff C. of C. (chmn. women's div. 1958). Republican. Club: Twin-City Toastmistress (pres. 1968-69). Avocations: travel; flower gardening. Home: 3023 8th Ave Scottsbluff NE 69361 Office: Scotts Bluff County Adminstrv Bldg 10th St Gering NE 69341

ELLIS, MARY JUDITH, real estate broker; b. Stephenville, Nfld., Can., Mar. 1, 1955; came to U.S., 1960, naturalized, 1960; d. Ronald M. and Eileen (Benoit) E. Student, Western Coll., 1979, 83. Lic. real estate salesperson, real estate broker, Ariz. Accts. payable sr. clk. Ramada Inns, Phoenix, 1973-79; adminstrv. mgr. Century 21 Bliss Widger, Phoenix, 1979; co-owner, adminstrv. mgr. Century 21 Odyssey, Phoenix, 1980; real estate salesperson with various offices, Phoenix, 1981-83; co-owner, sec.-treas., adminstrv. mgr. broker Am. First Realty, Inc., Phoenix, 1983—, also dir. Vol., Ariz. Valley Big Sisters, Phoenix, 1982—, ARC, Phoenix, 1982-84. Recipient You Are Concerned award Ramada Inns, 1978; Cert. of Achievement, Century 21, 1979, 21 Club Mem. award, 1979. Mem. Ind. Real Estate Brokers Assn. Ariz. (steering com. 1983, sec. bd. dirs. 1984-86, referral and relocation com. 1984, editor newsletter 1986), Phoenix Bd. Realtors, Avocations: camping; hiking; swimming; reading; dancing. Office: Am First Realty Inc 2432 W Peoria Ave Suite 1045 Phoenix AZ 85029

ELLIS, MYRNA JOYCE, pipe and supply company executive; b. Camden, N.J., Nov. 12, 1942; d. LeRoy and Margaret Etta (Harris) Malloy; children—Dawn Danise, William Stuart. Adminstrv. asst. to pres. LaMonte Owens Assn., Phila., 1972-74; dist. sales mgr. Avon Products, Inc., Newark, Del., 1974-76; dir. sales Inntowner Motor Hotel, Phila., 1976-81; mgr. Showcase One, Camden, N.J., 1981-83; ptnr., owner Nova Pipe & Supply Co., Camden, 1984—. Democrat. Bahai. Avocation: ballet. Office: Nova Pipe and Supply Co 1408 Sayrs Ave Bldg #1 Camden NJ 08104

ELLIS, RANDI SUE, marketing company executive, marketing educator; b. Chgo., Sept. 10, 1948; d. Averon Harold and Phyllis Ruth (Weil) E. B.A. with honors, U. N.C., 1969, M.A., 1972; Ph.D., Rice U., 1985. Research psychologist U.S. Govt., Bethesda, Md., 1972-73; cons. psychometrician London Sch. Econs., Eng., 1973; mktg. researcher Interpublic Group of Cos., N.Y.C., Houston, 1974-77; mktg. mgr. Coca-Cola Foods, Houston, 1977-81; prof. mktg. North Harris County Coll., Houston, 1981—; pres. Ellis Pedersen Forbes, Houston, 1983—. Contbr. numerous articles to profl. jours. Mem. Am. Mktg. Assn., Acad. Mgmt., Am. Mgmt. Assn., Psi Chi, Phi Beta Kappa, Phi Mu. Office: Ellis Pedersen Forbes Inc 15710 Drummet Blvd Ste 285 Houston TX 77032

ELLIS, SANDRA ANN RUBICO, company executive; b. East Boston, Mass., June 22, 1940; d. Jerome Anthony and Amelia Catherine (Cecchino) Rubico; m. Harry B. Ellis, Jr., Aug. 28, 1982. With Harbridge House, Inc., Washington, 1970-85, office mgr., 1970-74, research cons., 1974-76, adminstrv. services mgr., 1976-85; corp. sec. Devel. Sci. Services, Inc., Boston, 1978-85; now pres. Sare Enterprises. Mem. Nat. Assn. Female Execs. Office: Harbridge House Inc 1301 Pennsylvania Ave NW Washington DC 20004

ELLIS, SHARON MARIE, retail company buyer, writer; b. Danville, Va.; d. Clarence Bernard and Tommie Rene (Young) Jones. B.S., Howard U., 1971. Claims reviewer Civil Service Commn., Washington, 1968-70; adminstr. Fed. City Coll., Washington, 1971; mgmt. trainee Sears Roebuck, N.Y.C., 1972, asst. buyer, 1973-76, buyer, N.Y.C., 1976-79, Chgo., 1979—. Contbr. articles to profl. mags. Vol. Northwestern Hosp., Chgo., 1983, CARE, Chgo., 1985, 4th Presbyterian Ch., Chgo., 1986. Mem. Best-Black Exec. Support Team. Democrat. Avocations: dancing; skiing; gourmet cooking; reading. Office: Sears Roebuck & Co Sears Tower Chicago IL 60684

ELLIS, SUSAN GOTTENBERG, psychologist; b. N.Y.C., Jan. 24, 1949; d. Sam and Sally (Hirschman) Gottenberg; B.S., Cornell U., 1970; M.A., Columbia U., 1971; M.A., Hofstra U., 1975, Ph.D., 1976; m. David Roy Ellis, July 23, 1972; children—Sharon Rachel, Dana Michelle. Instr. health edn. Nassau Community Coll., Garden City, N.Y., 1971-73; sch. psychologist public schs., Somerville, N.J., 1976-77; clin. psychologist Somerset County Community Mental Health Center, Somerville, 1976-77; sch. psychologist, Pinellas County, Fla., 1977-78; instr. St. Petersburg (Fla.) Jr. Coll., 1978; clin. psychologist, Largo, Fla., 1977—; cons. Fla. Dept. Health and Rehab. Services, Med. Center Hosp., Largo, Morton Plant Hosp., Clearwater, Fla., N.Y. State Regents scholar, 1966-71. Mem. Am. Psychol. Assn., Fla. Psychol. Assn., Pinellas Psychol. Assn. (treas. 1978, polit. action chmn. 1979), Kappa Delta Pi. Club: Cornell U. Suncoast (v.p. 1979-80). Home: 1904 Oakdale Ln North Clearwater FL 33546 Office: 3300 East Bay Drive Suite 100 Largo FL 33541

ELLISON, ALISON ARMSTRONG, nurse; b. West Point, N.Y., Nov. 27, 1948; d. Robert Hawkins and Sally (Miller) Armstrong; m. Ketron Hugh Ellison, Jan. 14, 1977; 1 child, Sara Lesley. B.S. in Nursing, U. Md., 1970; postgrad. U. Va., 1973, 75-76. R.N., N.C., Va., Fla., Ariz. Staff nurse Walter Reed Gen. Hosp., Washington, 1970-72, head nurse pediatrics, 1972-73; pediatric nurse practitioner Pitt County Health Dept., Greenville, N.C., 1974; clin. instr. East Carolina U., Greenville, 1974-75, Auburn U., Montgomery, Ala., 1982; child health cons. Dept. Human Resources, Greenville, 1976-77; maternal child health supr. Pitt Meml. Hosp., Greenville, 1977-78; head nurse pediatrics Yuma Regional Med. Ctr., Ariz., 1978-81; prof. nursing Ariz. Western Coll., Yuma, 1982; clin. dir. nursing Craven County Hosp., New Bern, N.C., 1983-84; pediatric nurse practitioner Craven County Health Dept., 1984—. Vol. Spl. Olympics, Greenville, 1974, 80. Served to capt. U.S. Army, 1966-73. Fellow Nat. Assn. Pediatric Nurse Practitioners; mem. Am. Nurses Assn., Sigma Theta Tau. Democrat. Methodist. Home: 1990 Hoods Creek Dr New Bern NC 28560 Office: Craven County Health Dept PO Box 1390 New Bern NC 28560

ELLISON, MARCIA MANSFIELD, spatial designer, photographer; b. Chgo., Jan. 24, 1946; d. Sheldon E. and Marcia E. (Segal) Berkson; A.A., Stephens Coll., Columbia, Mo., 1965; B.Ed., Nat. Coll. Edn., Evanston, Ill., 1967; M.A., Northwestern U., 1967; grad. Chgo. Real Estate Sch., 1973; m. Stuart H. Ellison, May 26, 1977; children—Robert, Jon, Adam. Tchr. schs. in Ill., 1967-75; saleswoman Ringer Realty, Highland Park, Ill., 1973; with Lord & Taylor, Northbrook, Ill., 1976-77; lic. practical nurse to doctor, Highland Park, 1977-78; model, actress, 1967-78; owner Pandy Enterprises, Ltd., Glencoe, Ill., 1978—, By Design, Glencoe; creator Pandy Poppins, Evanston Hosp. pediatric ward. Mem. exec. bd. Michael Reese Hosp., Chgo., 1979-84. Jewish. Address: 537 Greenleaf Ave Glencoe IL 60022

ELLMANN, SHEILA FRENKEL, investment company executive; b. Detroit, June 8, 1931; d. Joseph and Rose (Neback) Frenkel; B.A. in English, U. Mich., 1953; m. William M. Ellmann, Nov. 1, 1953; children—Douglas Stanley, Carol Elizabeth, Robert Lawrence. Dir. Advance Glove Mfg. Co., Detroit, 1954-78; v.p. Frome Investment Co., Detroit, 1980—. Mem. Nat. Trust Hist. Preservation, U. Mich. Alumni Assn. Home: 28000 Weymouth Dr Farmington Hills MI 48018

ELLNER, CAROLYN LIPTON, university dean, consultant; b. N.Y.C., Jan. 17, 1932; d. Robert Mitchell and Rose (Pearlman) Lipton; m. Richard Ellner, June 21, 1953; children—David Lipton, Alison Lipton. A.B. cum laude, Mt. Holyoke Coll., 1953; A.M., Columbia Tchrs. Coll., 1957; Ph.D. with distinction, UCLA, 1968. Tchr., prof., adminstr., N.Y. and Md., 1957-62; dir. tchr. edn. Claremont Grad. Sch. (Calif.) 1967-82; prof., dean sch. edn. Calif. State U., Northridge, 1982—. Co-author: Schoolmaking, 1977; Studies of College Teaching (Orange County Authors award 1984), 1983. Trustee Ctr. for Early Edn., Los Angeles, 1968-71, Oakwood Sch., Los Angeles, 1972-78, Mt. Holyoke Coll., South Hadley, Mass., 1979-84; commr. Economy and Efficiency Com., Los Angeles, 1974-82; bd. dirs. Found. for Effective Govt., Los Angeles, 1982, Calif. Coalition for Pub. Edn., 1985—. Ford Found. fellow, 1964-67; recipient Office of Edn. award U.S. Office of Edn., 1969-72; W. M. Keck Found. grantee, 1983. Mem. Am. Edn. Research Assn. (governing council), Assn. for Supervision and Curriculum Devel., Nat. Assn. for Study of Edn. Office: Sch of Edn Calif State U 18111 Nordhoff St Northridge CA 91330

ELLSWEIG, PHYLLIS LEAH, psychotherapist; b. Irvington, N.J., Apr. 19, 1927; d. Sumar and Jeanette (Geffner) Schwartz; B.S., East Stroudsburg U. (Pa.), 1947; Ed.M., Lehigh U., 1966, Ed.D., 1972; m. Martin Richard Ellsweig, Dec. 25, 1947; children—Bruce, Steven. Tchr., Stroud Union High Sch., 1963-66; guidance counselor East Stroudsburg Schs., 1966-68; asst. prof. edn. East Stroudsburg U. 1968; staff psychologist, outpatient supr. Mental Health Center Carbon, Monroe and Pike Counties, Stroudsburg, 1968-80; pvt. practice, 1969—; staff Pocono Hosp.; pub. speaker, cons. to schs., orgns. Mem. Am., Eastern, Pa. psychol. assns., Am. Acad. Psychotherapists, Am. Group Psychotherapy Assn., Am. Soc. Clin. Hypnosis, Internat. Soc. Hypnosis, NOW (profl. cons. 1973—), Internat. Assn. Group Psychotherapy. Club: Torch. Home: 58 S Green St East Stroudsburg PA 18301 Office: 322 Park Ave Stroudsburg PA 18360

ELLSWORTH, GRETCHEN GAYLE, museum administrator; b. Atlanta, Feb. 10, 1939; d. William Thomas and Margot (McCoy) Gayle; m. Robert W. Ellsworth, Dec. 21, 1971; children—Eric Matthew, Brian Paul, Andrew William. B.A. with honors, Swarthmore Coll., 1961; M.A., Stanford U., 1962. Grad. tchr. Stanford U., Calif., 1961-64, found. specialist, devel. office, 1964; staff legis. aide Congl. Office, 1965-68; fellowship specialist, higher edn. program officer Smithsonian Inst., Washington, 1968-78, dir. fellowships and grants, 1978-84, dep. dir. directorate of internat. activities, 1984—. Sec., treas. Nat. Conservation Adv. Council, Inc.; precinct capt., compaign worker, intermittently, 1954-68. Mem. Am. Hist. Assn. Orgn., Am. Historians. Office: Dep Dir Directorate Internat Activities Smithsonian Inst 1000 Jefferson Dr SW Washington DC 20560

ELLSWORTH, MYRNA RUTH, accountant; b. Port Arthur, Tex., May 13, 1948; d. Joseph Curry and Ada Ruth (Pate) Meyer; m. Alfred Wells Ellsworth, May 25, 1973; children—Gordon Wells, Carleton Curry. B.B.A., Lamar U., 1977. Mem. acctg. dept. Port Iron and Supply Co., Inc., Port Arthur, 1970-76; acct. Wathen Deshong & Co., C.P.A.s, Beaumont, Tex., 1977-79; prin. Myrna R. Ellsworth, C.P.A., Port Arthur, 1980-81; mgr. acctg. and data processing depts. Hayes Enterprises, Port Arthur, 1981-83; acct. Alan Hefty, C.P.A., Beaumont, Tex. C.P.A., Tex. Mem. Tex. Soc. C.P.A.s (pres. SE Tex. chpt.), Am. Inst. C.P.A.s, Am. Women's Soc. C.P.A.s, Lamar U. Ex-Students Assn., Port Arthur Bus. and Profl. Women's Club, Beaumont Spindletop Bus. and Profl. Woman's Club, Delta Sigma Pi. Home: 3175 Sandalwood Port Neches TX 77651 Office: 2192 Eastex Freeway Beaumont TX 77703

ELLSWORTH, WANDA THURMAN, county official, stenographer, typist; b. Harviell, Mo., Dec. 29, 1945; d. Roy Lee and Iva DeBoin (White) Wolverton; m. Harlon Roy Thurman, Jr., June 28, 1963 (div. Mar. 1979); 1 dau., Angela Dawn Thurman Hodge. Student Three Rivers Coll., Poplar Bluff, Mo. Credit mgr. Newberrys, Poplar Bluff, 1964-66; chief dep. clk. Cir. Ct., Poplar Bluff, 1966-78, cir. ct. clk., 1979—. Mem. Butler County Republican Women, Poplar Bluff, 1978, Butler County Central Com., Poplar Bluff. Recipient Gold award United Way, 1979; Service award U.S. Passport Agy., 1982. Mem. Bus. and Profl. Women, Nat. Fedn. Republican Women. Baptist. Club: Beta Sigma Phi (chpt. Woman of Yr. 1983, Valentine Queen, 1984; pres., v.p. chpt. 1985—). Avocations: fishing; camping; volley ball; walking; collecting rocks and crystal. Home: 619 N Main St Townhouse 3 Poplar Bluff MO 63901 Office: Circuit Clk Butler County Courthouse Poplar Bluff MO 63901

ELLZY, RENA CROSBY, business educator; b. Anderson, S.C., Mar. 2, 1941; d. Paul and Lorene Crosby; B.A., Clark Coll., Atlanta, 1964; M.Ed., S.C. State Coll., Orangeburg, 1972; Ed.D. in Bus. Edn., No. Ill. U., 1974; m. James A. Ellzy, Oct. 8, 1965; children—James, Kenneth Lyle. Sec. to head librarian Md. State Coll., Princess Anne, 1964-68; sec. to office mgr. Blayton's C.P.A. Office,

Atlanta, 1962-63; prof. bus. Tenn. State U., Nashville, 1974—; affiliate broker Estes-Taylor Co., Inc., 1984—. Bd. dirs. Nashville Urban League, 1986—; mem. Hosp. Hospitality House, Nashville. Mem. Nat. Bus. Edn. Assn., S.E. Bus. Edn. Assn., Tenn. Bus. Edn. Assn., Am. Vocat. Assn. (life), Nat. Assn. Realtors, Delta Pi Epsilon, Pi Omega Pi, Delta Mu Delta, Delta Sigma Theta. Lutheran. Clubs: Jack and Jill Am. Contbr. articles to profl. jours. Home: 6328 Chickering Circle Nashville TN 37215 Office: Tenn State U Charlotte Campus Nashville TN 37303 also 2000 Richard Jones Rd Nashville TN 37215

ELMER, KATHERINE, wholesale knitwear executive; b. Jacksonville, Fla.; d. Slocum and Esther (Boardman) Ball; m. Harold T. Elmer, Apr. 28, 1962; children—Layne Elizabeth, Todd Thomas, Trey Grant, Paige Ansley. B.S., Fla. State U. Owner, ptnr. Prodns. II, Atlanta, 1973-75, Prodns. III, Charlotte, N.C., 1977-80; pres., owner Norcross Knits Inc., Atlanta, 1980—, K&S Distbg. Inc., Atlanta, 1983—; owner Peachtree Embroidery, Atlanta, 1984—. Mem. Sales and Mktg. Execs. Democrat. Episcopalian. Office: K&S Distbg Inc 3259 Peachtree Corners Circle Norcross GA 30092

ELMER, MARY ELIZABETH, executive recruiter; consultant; b. Utica, N.Y., Dec. 23, 1954; d. Bernard Edward and Ruth Marion (York) E.; m. Peter Julian Baskin, July 28, 1984. B.A., Siena Coll., 1977. Mktg. rep. Hartford Ins., Albany, N.Y., 1977-80, Gt. Am., Syracuse, N.Y., 1981-82; v.p., sec. Personnel Assocs., Inc., Syracuse, 1982—. Mem. Nat. Assn. Female Execs. (network dir.), Am. Soc. Profl. and Exec. Women, Nat. Assn. Woman Bus. Owners (Greater Syracuse chpt.), Nat. Assn. Personnel Cons. (cert. personnel cons; regent 1986—), Ind. Personnel Cons. Central N.Y., Siena Alumni Assn., Nat. Mus. of Women in Arts (charter), Winterthur Guild. Republican. Roman Catholic. Avocations: reading; collecting antiques; refinishing furniture. Office: Personnel Assocs Inc 731 James St Suite 206 Syracuse NY 13203

ELMORE, DOLORES DALY, city official; b. Colonial Heights, Va., Mar. 9, 1930; d. Frank Benjamin and Lillian Essig (Watkins) Daly; m. Collin Eldred Elmore, Apr. 13, 1950; children—Collin Eldred Jr., Katherine Gail, Stephen Mark, Michael Lawrence. Grad., Inst. Mcpl. Clks., Old Dominion U. Cert. mcpl. clk. Office mgr. Wiley Ins. Agy., Petersburg, 1947-50; clk.-typist U.S. Navy Tng. Facilities, Jacksonville, Fla., 1951-53; payroll clk., sec. Petersburg-Hopewell Gas Co., Petersburg, 1954-56; sec. personnel dept. Brown and Williamson, Petersburg, 1956-57; city clk., clk. of council City of Colonial Heights, 1969—; sec.-treas. Indsl. Devel. Authority, Colonial Heights, 1976—. Sec. Colonial Heights Bapt. Ch., 1957-59. Mem. Internat. Mcpl. Clks. Assn., Va. Mcpl. Clks. Assn. (regional dir. 1983—), Advanced Acad. Mcpl. Clks. of Old Dominion U. Avocations: handcrafts; reading; gardening.

ELMORE, GAIL LARAYNE, data processing accessories manufacturing company executive; b. Oak Ridge, Jan. 16, 1947; d. George Arthur and Dorothea LaRayne (Haynes) Anderson; m. Marc Andrew Bartlett, Aug. 1970 (div. Dec. 1981); m. 2d, George Lee Elmore, Aug. 7, 1982. B.A. in Sociology, Muhlenberg Coll., 1969. From supr. to group dental expert John Hancock Ins. Co., Phila. and Boston, 1974-80; sales specialist Wright Line Inc., Denver, 1980-82, program mgr., Worcester, Mass., 1982-84, engring. systems mgr., 1984-86, comml. sales mgr., 1986—; rep. Bus. and Instl. Furniture Mfrs. Assn., Grand Rapids, Mich., 1982—. Advisor Computer Adv. Com., Grafton, Mass., 1983. Home: 13 Barbara Jean St Grafton MA 01519 Office: Wright Line Inc 135 Gold Star Blvd Worcester MA 01606

ELMORE, PATRICIA CONNER, city official; b. Anderson, Ind., Oct. 30, 1935; d. Kenneth Wilbur Conner and Vivian Louise (Wells) Conner Basey; m. Delzie Edward Elmore, Aug. 14, 1954; children—Rebecca Rea, Darrell, Sherri Reeves, Bryan, Lori. Student Central Bus. Coll., Indpls., 1954-55. Cert. mcpl. clk. Sec. Eli Lilly and Co., Indpls., 1953-63; billing dept. head City of Greenfield, Ind., 1963-65, clk.-treas., 1976—; clk. Circuit Ct. Hancock County, Ind., 1966-74, mgr. CETA, 1975. Past sec. Hancock County Republican Women, Greenfield; bd. dirs. Santa's Helpers, 1975; exec. com. for higher edn. Ball State U., 1985—; elder Greenfield Christian Ch. Named Rep. Woman of Yr. Hancock County, 1982; Outstanding Clk. of Circuit Ct. Ind. Clks., 1974; Outstanding Citizen United Way, 1982. Ind. League Mcpl. Clks. and Treas. (bd. dirs. dist. 4, chmn. state bd. accts. sch. instrn.). Lodge: Order Eastern Star. Avocations: flower arranging; knitting; boating; engraving; grandchildren. Home: 630 N Spring St Greenfield IN 46140 Office: City of Greenfield 110 S State St Greenfield IN 46140

ELMS, LOIS JANET, professional meeting coordinator; b. Hutchinson, Kans., June 27, 1936; d. J. Wilbert and Katherine (Schoenhoff) Estabrooks; m. Bruce R. Elms, Aug. 24, 1956 (div. June 1972); children—Laura Lanette Smith, Bruce Ronald, Jr. A.A. with honors, Hutchinson Jr. Coll., 1956; postgrad. U. Colo. Meeting planner Geol. Soc. Am., Boulder, Colo., 1969-77; pres., owner Western Experience, Ltd., Boulder, 1977—; guest lectr. Met. State Coll., 1975; exec. dir. Conv. and Visitors Bur., Boulder, 1975; mem. Denver Conv. and Visitors Bur., 1982—. Mem. Boulder Community Hosp. Aux., 1984-85. Mem. Meeting Consultants Club, Meeting Planners Internat. (various coms. 1972-82, inst. instr. 1979), Boulder C. of C. Republican. Episcopalian. Avocations: skiing, reading, gourmet cooking, traveling. Address: 2369 Carriage Circle Oceanside CA 92056

ELROD, MARGARET ANN, nurse, consultant; b. Fitzgerald, Ga., Dec. 13, 1919; d. Joseph Thomas and Della Ann (Booker) Hendricks; m. James William Elrod, Sept. 9, 1942 (div. 1967, dec.); children—Linda Sue, James Thomas (dec.), Robert Lee. Student Middle Ga. Coll., Cochran, 1936-37; R.N., Macon City Hosp., 1942. Pvt. duty nurse, Macon, Ga., 1942-49; dir. nurses Mitchell County Hosp., Camilla, Ga., 1953-57, Howard Hosp., Pelham, Ga., 1957-63, Rest Awhile Nursing Home, Moultrie, Ga., Jesup, Ga., 1963-67, Templeton Nursing Homes, Valdosta, Ga., 1967-78, Parkwood Devel. Ctr., Valdosta, 1978—. Mem. Ga. State Nurses Assn. (pres. 15th dist. 1970-71), Loundes County Mental Health Assn. (v.p. 1984-85), Loundes Assn. Retarded Citizens (bd. dirs. 1983-85, service award 1983). Democrat. Methodist. Clubs: United Spanish War Aux. (state pres. 1973-74); Pilot of Valdosta (pres. 1975-76, 77-78, 84-85). Avocation: fishing. Home: Route 8 Box 31 Lot 10 Valdosta GA 31602

EL SAFFAR, RUTH SNODGRASS, Spanish literature educator; b. N.Y.C., June 12, 1941; d. John Tabb and Ruth (Wheelwright) Snodgrass; B.A., Colo. Coll., 1962; Ph.D., Johns Hopkins U., 1966; m. Zuhair M. El Saffar, Apr. 11, 1965; children—Ali, Dena, Amir. Instr. Spanish, Johns Hopkins U., 1963-65; instr. English, Univ. Coll. Baghdad, 1966-67; asst. prof. Spanish, U. Md., Balt. County, 1967-68; asst. prof. U. Ill., Chgo. Circle, 1968-73, assoc. prof., 1973-78, prof., 1978-83, univ. research prof., 1983—; Nat. Endowment for Humanities summer seminar dir., 1979, 82. Woodrow Wilson fellow, 1962; Nat. Endowment for Humanities fellow, 1970-71; Guggenheim fellow, 1975-76; Am. Council Learned Socs. grantee, 1978; Newberry Library fellow, 1982. Mem. MLA (exec. council 1974-78, council on future of profession 1980-82), Am. Assn. Tchrs. Spanish and Portuguese, Midwest MLA, Cervantes Soc. Am. (exec. com. 1978—), Author: Novel to Romance: A Study of Cervantes' Novelas Ejemplares, 1974; Distance and Control in Don Quixote, 1975; Cervantes' Casamiento engañoso and Coloquio de los perros, 1976; Beyond Fiction, 1984; Critical Essays on Cervantes, 1986. Home: 7811 Greenfield River Forest IL 60305 Office: Dept Spanish U Ill Chicago IL 60680

ELSBREE, ROSA TREVINO, equal employment opportunity manager, consultant; b. Granger, Tex., Aug. 30, 1935; d. Pilar Flores and Guadalupe (Reyes) Trevino; m. David Peter Adaska, June 29, 1968 (div. Oct. 1978); children—David P., Jr., Christina G.; m. 2d, Truman Wayne Elsbree, Mar. 17, 1979. B.A. in Psychology, Golden State U., 1982, postgrad., 1982—. Farm worker, Granger, Tex., 1945-54; with U.S. Govt., 1959—, EEO mgr. Naval Ocean Systems, San Diego, 1979—, trainer/project mgr., 1979—; owner Elsbree & Elsbree, San Diego, 1983—, also pres. Author: Working Through The EEO Maze, 1982. Author tng. modules. Mem. Adv. council Padre Serra Ctr., San Diego, 1985—. Mem. Nat. Federally Employed Women, Inc. (spl. asst. cultural awareness 1985-86, v.p. tng. 1983-85, v.p. compliance 1981-83), Fed. Equal Employment Opportunity Council (pres. 1976-77), Nat. Assn. Female Execs. Republican. Roman Catholic. Avocations: bowling; gardening; camping; traveling. Home: 4216 Darwin Way San Diego CA 92154 Office: Naval Ocean Systems Ctr Code 002 San Diego CA 92154

ELSE, CAROLYN JOAN, library administrator; b. Mpls., Jan. 31, 1934; d. Elmer Oscar and Irma Carolyn (Seibert) Wahlberg; m. Floyd Warren Else, Feb. 11, 1962 (div.); children—Stephen Alexander, Catherine Elizabeth. B.A., Stanford U.; M.L.S., U. Wash. Librarian Queens Borough Pub. Library, N.Y.C., 1957-59, U.S. Army Spl. Service, France and Germany, 1959-62; info. librarian Bennett Martin Library, Lincoln, Nebr., 1962-63; br. librarian Pierce County Library, Tacoma, Wash., 1963-65, dir., 1965—. Bd. dirs. Campfire, Tacoma, 1984; bd. dirs. South Sound Women's Network, Tacoma, 1982-84. Mem. Wash. Library Assn. (v.p. 1969-71), Pacific Northwest Library Assn. (sec. 1969-71), ALA. Club: City of Tacoma. Office: Pierce County Library Dist 2356 Tacoma Ave S Tacoma WA 98402

ELSON, ELIZABETH, educator, cultural organizations executive; b. Radomisl, Kiev, Russia, Mar. 19, 1904; came to U.S., 1906, naturalized, 1913; d. Jacob and Rebecca (Brodsky) E.; m. Myer Cohen, Aug. 21, 1933; children—Arthur Elson, Judith Cohen Kretzmann. Ph.B., U. Chgo., 1924; M.F.A., Yale U., 1934. Instr., U. Chgo., summers 1927-28, Yale Drama Sch. Yale U., Newhaven, Conn., 1929-35; exec. dir. WPA-N. Calif. Theatre Producers, San Francisco, 1935-37; dir. cultural prod. NYA-State of Calif., San Francisco, 1938-42; dir. plays Plays for Living, N.Y.C., 1956-57; World Fedn. Mental Health rep. to UN, N.Y.C., 1960-85. Mem. U.S. del. Internat. Theatre Inst. World Conf., Dubrovnik, Yugoslavia, 1955, Budapest, Hungary, 1969. Recipient two Service awards World Fedn. Mental Health 1976, 79. Mem. Am. Nat. Theatre Assn., Phi Beta Kappa. Home and Office: 2 Peter Cooper Rd 13F New York NY 10010

ELSON, SUZANNE GOODMAN, retail executive; b. Memphis, Oct. 17, 1937; d. Charles F. and Isabel (Ehrlich) Goodman; m. Edward Elliott Elson, Aug. 24, 1957; children—Charles Myer, Louis Goodman, Harry II. Student Randolph-Macon Women's Coll., Lynchburg, Va.; B.A., Agnes Scott Coll., 1959. Vice pres. mktg. Elson's, Atlanta, 1977—. Ga. coordinator 51.3 Women's Com. for Carter campaign, 1975-77; sec. Nat. Council Jewish Women, N.Y.C., 1977-79; pres. Mental Health Assn. Ga., 1977-78; pres.-elect Nat. Mental Health Assn.; v.p., Nat. Mental Health Assn., 1980-82. Recipient Human Relations award Atlanta Jewish Com., 1975; Community Service award Channel 11, Atlanta, 1976. Named in 100 Shapers of Future article, Atlanta Mag. Mem. Am. Craft Council (trustee), High Mus. Art. (v.p. 1980-82), Am. Jewish Com. (bd. govs. women's issues com.). Home: 65 Valley Rd NW Atlanta GA 30305 Office: Elson's 4070 Shirley Dr SW Atlanta GA 30336

ELSTIEN, CYNTHIA FERRARA, b. Chgo., Mar. 31, 1948; d. Robert Joseph and Saretta (DeSalvo) F.; m. Morris Joseph Elstien, July 24, 1980. Student No. Ill. U., 1967-69, Ins. Sch. Chgo., 1976-77. Claims examiner Lynn Ins. Group or Universal Underwriters, Des Plaines, Ill., 1966-70; sec., v.p. mfg. Stenographic Machines, Skokie, Ill., 1970-71; v.p. employee relations Fred S. James & Co. of Ill., Chgo., 1971—. Campaign worker for candidate for state's atty. 1972. Mem. Soc. Personnel Adminstrs. (v.p. programs Chgo. 1982-83 treas. 1983—), Ins. Personnel Council (pres. Chgo. 1982). Roman Catholic. Club: East Bank (Chgo.). Home: 327 Hambletonian Dr Oak Brook IL 60521 Office: Fred S James & Co Ill 230 W Monroe St Chicago IL 60606

ELTGROTH, MARLENE BUMGARNER, author, educator; b. Yorkshire, Eng., Nov. 6, 1947; came to U.S., 1949, naturalized, 1965; d. Rowland and May (Whittaker) Skirrow; A.A., Coll. San Mateo, 1967; B.A., San Diego State Coll., 1970; M.A., San Jose State U., 1982; m. John Owen Bumgarner, June 17, 1967 (div. 1982); children—Doña Ana, John Rowland, Deborah Ruth; m. Robert John Eltgroth, Feb. 19, 1983. Tech. editor electronics firms, 1967-70; coordinator Peer Counseling Center, Las Cruces, N.Mex., 1970-72; tchr. elem. sch., 1974-76; owner, mgr. Morgan Hill Trading Post, natural food store, Morgan Hill, Calif., 1976-78; editor Natural Living Newsline, Morgan Hill, 1979-81; mgr. Natural Living Assocs., 1979—; dir. Morgan Hill Country Day Sch., 1980-82; instr. Gavilan Coll., 1979—, coordinator child devel. program, 1985—. Leader, founder La Leche League of Morgan Hill, 1977-85; supt. Sunday Sch., St. John's Episcopal Ch., 1982-84; coordinator Morgan Hill Community Garden, 1983-85. Mem. Soc. Children's Book Writers, Nat. Newspaper Food Writers and Editors Assn., AAUW, Calif. Press Women. Author: Book of Whole Grains, 1976; Organic Cooking for (not-so-organic) Mothers, 1980; columnist San Jose (Calif.) Mercury, 1977-80; contbr. People's Cookbook, 1977, Real Food Places, 1981; sr. tech. writer Boole and Babbage, Inc., 1982-83; contbg. editor Mothering mag., 1981—; new products editor Classroom Computer Learning, 1983-85; columnist Gilroy Dispatch, Calif., 1984—. Office: PO Box 1326 Morgan Hill CA 95037

ELVIDGE, VIVIAN PATRICIA, mus. dir.; b. Okanogan, Wash., Jan. 6, 1940; d. Floyd Kenneth and Martha Grace (Hinshaw) Byrd; A.B., Bellevue Community Coll., 1974; B.A. cum laude in Anthropology, U. Wash., 1977, M.A. cum laude in Anthropology, 1980; m. Robert Fred Elvidge, Dec. 26, 1962; 1 dau., Janice April. Vol. coordinator Marymoor Mus., Redmond, Wash., 1979, curator, 1978-80, dir., 1980—. Mem. Am. Assn. of Mus., Wash. Mus. Assn., Am. Assn. for State and Local History, Phi Beta Kappa. Methodist. Author: Redmond Historic Tour Guide, 1981; Report on Collections, Marymoor Mus.: Lace Collection, 1979, Indian Artifacts, 1978; Eastside Historic Resource Guide, 1982. Co-editor: Eastside Historic Color Book, 1985. Home: 17511 Avondale Rd Woodinville WA 98072 Office: PO Box 162 6046 W Lake Sammamish Pkwy Redmond WA 98073

ELWELL, ELLEN C., sales training and marketing promotions executive, instructional design and marketing promotions consultant; b. Jacksonville, Fla.; d. Merrill K. and Hermine (Chalfin) Cohen; B.A., U. Mich., 1967; M.A., N.Y.U., U. Ill., 1968; m. John Lee Elwell, Feb. 10, 1968; 1 dau., Melissa Mae. Advanced mktg. support rep. IBM, Oklahoma City, 1969-73, program planner/designer sales tng. programs, Dallas, 1973-79; owner, operator Elwell Assos., Inc., Dallas, 1979—; dir. Indsl. Catering Co., Indpls., A. Rose Prodns., St. Louis. Recipient Outstanding Contbn. award IBM, 1976, Notable Women of Tex. award. Mem. Am. Soc. Tng. and Devel., Am. Soc. Profl. Cons., Am. Mgmt. Assn. Club: 2001 (Dallas). Author numerous corp. tng. books, 1976—. Office: 7230 Briarmeadow St Dallas TX 75230

ELWELL, PATRICIA ANN, real estate broker; b. Newburgh, N.Y., May 17, 1940; d. John Clement and Ruth Culver (Ahrensdorf-Booth) King; m. Floyd Allen Elwell, Apr. 5, 1959 (div. 1972); children—Lori Ann, Floyd Allen Jr., Robert Jay. Student Mohave Community Coll., 1982-83, Kelley Sch. Real Estate, 1973, 79. Sales assoc. King Realty, Fort Mojave, Ariz., 1973-79, broker, 1979-85, broker, owner, 1985—. Bd. dirs. Fort Mojave Mesa Fire Dist., 1985-87. Mem. Nat. Assn. Female Execs., Nat. Fedn. Ind. Businessmen. Episcopalian. Club: Gold Prospectors Ariz. Avocations: gold prospecting; reading; health activities; needlework. Office: 5287 Hwy 95 Suite 5 PO Box 8549 Fort Mojave AZ 86427

ELWOOD-AKERS, VIRGINIA EDYTHE, university librarian; b. Los Angeles, Nov. 9, 1938; d. George Henry and Eileen Edythe (Kelterer) Elwood; m. Roy S. Akers, Apr. 12, 1980. B.A., UCLA, 1964; M.L.S., U. Oreg., 1972; M.A., Calif. State U.-Northridge, 1981. Editor, UCLA, 1970-71, writer, 1971-72; librarian Calif. State U., Northridge, 1972—, assoc. librarian, univ. archivist, 19—. Author: (bibliography) Media Image of Women, 1975, Women Correspondents, 1983. Mem. Soc. Calif. Archivists, Nat. Women Studies Assn., Calif. Women in Higher Edn. (chmn. 1981-82), Calif. State U. Librarians (chmn. 1984). Democrat. Episcopalian. Office: Calif State Univ-Northridge Library 18111 Nordhoff St Northridge CA 91344

ELWORTH, MARY L., land developer/broker; b. Omaha, Sept. 12, 1957; d. Herbert J. and Josephine A. (Polito) E. B.A., Northwestern U., 1978; M.B.A., U. Chgo., 1982. Systems engr. IBM, Omaha and Chgo., 1978-80, mktg. rep., Chgo., 1980-84; assoc. LaSalle Ptnrs. Inc., Chgo., 1984-85, sr. assoc., Boca Raton, Fla., 1985—. Mem. U. Chgo. Women's Bus. Group, U. Chgo. Alumni Assn., Northwestern U. Alumni Assn., Urban Land Inst., Nat. Assn. Indsl. and Office Parks, Comml. Real Estate Orgn., Jr. League Chgo./Palm Beaches, Phi Beta Kappa, Alpha Phi. Club: Palm Beach Polo and Country (West Palm Beach). Office: LaSalle Ptnrs 1900 Glades Rd Suite 441 Boca Raton FL 33431

ELY, MARICA MCCANN, interior designer; b. Pachuca, Mex., May 2, 1907 (parents Am. citizens); d. Warner and Mary Evans (Cook) McCann; m. Northcutt Ely, Dec. 2, 1931; children—Michael and Craig (twins), Parry Haines. B.A., U. Calif.-Berkeley, 1929; diploma Pratt Inst. of Art, N.Y.C., 1931. Free-lance interior designer, Washington and Redlands, Calif., 1931—; lectr. on flower arranging and fgn. travel, 1931—; prof. Sogetsu Ikebana Sch., Tokyo, 1972. Art editor (calendar) Nat. Capital Garden Club, 1957-58. Pres. Kenwood Garden Club, Md.; bd. dirs. Nat. Library Blind, Washington; v.p. bd. dirs. Washington Hearing and Speech Soc., 1969; co-founder Delta Gamma Found. Pre-Sch. Blind Children, Washington. Finalist Nat. Silver Bowl Competition, Jackson-Perkins Co., 1966; garden shown on nat. tour Am. Hort. Soc., 1985. Mem. Calif. Arboretum Found., Redlands Hort. and Improvement Soc. (bd. dirs. 1982—), Town and Country African Violet Soc., Hemerocallis Soc., Delta Gamma. Clubs: Redlands Country (Calif.); Washington, Chevy Chase (Washington); Berkeley Tennis (Calif.).

ELY, STEPHANIE, real estate publishing service executive; b. Edgartown, Mass., Oct. 25, 1955; d. RobertrNewell and Marianne (Bearer) E.; m. John Joseph Frisby, Apr. 28, 1981 (div. Jan. 1984). B.A., UCLA, 1976. Prodn. mgr. Volt Tech. Corp., Los Angeles, 1977-81; pres., chief exec. officer Real Estate Digest, Santa Monica, Calif., 1982—, also chmn. bd., 1982—; dir. Philip Norton, Inc., Los Angeles; cons. Los Angeles Bd. Realtors, 1983—. Vol. blood bank ARC, Santa Monica, Calif., 1980—; tournament dir. Santa Monica Recreation and Parks, 1984—; campaign dir. Republican Party, Los Angeles, 1976—. Mem. Nat. Assn. Female Execs., Westwide Realtors Assn., Women in Bus. Roman Catholic. Avocations: camping; softball; bowling; writing; surfing. Office: Real Estate Digest Inc 933 Pico Blvd Suite 2 Santa Monica CA 90405

EMAN, EVELYN, public relations executive; b. N.Y.C., Dec. 31, 1949; d. John and Gay (Simon) Eman; m. Larry Edward Delmar, Nov. 26, 1982. Student, NYU, 1975-76, Baruch Coll., 1981-82. Asst. mgr. Vanderbilt Athletic Club, N.Y.C., 1967-68; pub. relations mgr. DEC Enterprises, Inc., N.Y.C., 1968-73; exec. interviewer Dun & Bradstreet, Inc., N.Y.C., 1974; pub. relations rep. Parsons & Whittemore, Inc., N.Y.C., 1974-77; corp. mgr. pub. relations NEC America, Inc., Melville, N.Y., 1977-82; pres. Perception +, Colorado Springs, Colo., 1982—. Contbr. articles to mags. Media relations chmn. World Cycling Championships Communication Adv. Council, 1986. Recipient Merit cert. Publicity Club N.Y., 1976, 77. Mem. Colorado Springs C. of C., Colorado Springs Press Assn. (Gridiron award 1986), Internat. Assn. Bus. Communicators (v.p. programming So. Colo. 1984-85, pres. 1985-86; Gold Nugget award 1984, 85), The Promoters (bd. dirs. 1983-84, pres. 1984-85, chmn. 1985-86), Pub. Relations Soc. Am., Women's Exchange Network (editor newsletter 1983-84). Jewish. Office: Perception Plus 100 E St Vrain Suite 105 Colorado Springs CO 80903

EMANUEL, DIANE MARIE, labor relations executive; b. Mpls., Apr. 17, 1947; d. Clinton David and Muriel Ruth (Jensen) Gustafson; m. Bruce A. Bakke, June 29, 1967 (div.); 1 son, Brian Allen; m. David Harris Emanuel, Jan. 28, 1978; 1 son, Frederick Paul. Cert. profl. in human resource. Student U. Minn., 1973-77, North Tex. State U., 1978-79, 85; A.A., A.S., Tarrant County Jr. Coll., 1984. Personnel mgr. ITT Thermotech, Hopkins, Minn., 1967-77; mgr. employment and equal opportunity Fingerhut Corp., Minnetonka, Minn., 1977-78; personnel mgr. Automatic Data Processing, Dallas, 1978-79; compensation adminstr. Sky Chefs, Arlington, Tex., 1979-81, employee relations specialist, 1981-83, mgr. labor relations, 1983—; cons. Assoc. Clerical Specialist, Mpls., 1976-78. Editor: Fingerprints, 1977-78, ITT Thermotech News, 1970-77, ADP News, 1978-79. Dir. concessions Coppell Pee Wee Football Assn. (Tex.), 1983-85; den leader Coppell council Boy Scouts Am., 1982, asst. den leader Webelos, 1983; campaign chmn. City Council election campaign City of Coppell, 1983. Mem. Am. Soc. Personnel Adminstrn., Twin City Personnel Assn., Dallas Personnel Assn., Mid-Cities Personnel Assn., Nat. Assn. Female Execs. Home: 541 Rolling Hills Rd Coppell TX 75019 Office: Sky Chefs PO Box 61777 Dallas-Fort Worth Airport TX 75261

EMANUEL, GLORIA PAGE, social studies educator; b. Dallas, Apr. 5, 1947; d. Daniel and Leola (Green) Page; m. Lawrence Ray Emanuel, Oct. 2, 1971; children—Lawrence Ray, Jr., Kevin Lawrence. B.S., E. Tex. State U., 1970; student Paul Quinn Coll., 1966-67; M.Ed., Prairie View A & M U., 1975. Cert. tchr., profl. counselor, Tex. Tchr. social studies Waco High Sch., Tex., 1971-82, University Middle Sch., Waco, 1982—, chairperson social studies, 1985—. Mem. Central Tex. Minister Wives, Waco-Temple Dist., 1971—; mem. sr. choir Wayman Chapel A.M.E. Ch., Temple, Tex., 1983—, tchr. Sunday sch.; histotiographer Gloria Emanuel Unit, Temple, 1985—. Mem. Waco Classroom Tchrs. (faculty rep. 1973-74), Tex. State Tchrs. Assn., NEA, Nat. Assn. Female Execs. (cert. 1984), Sigma Gamma Rho. Lodge: Order of Eastern Star. Avocations: photography; reading; travel. Home: 2024 King Cole Dr Waco TX 76705

EMANUEL, HELENE RICH, lawyer, musician, educator; b. N.Y.C., Mar. 31, 1926; d. Irving Wolf and Annette (Moskowitz) Rich; B.A., U. Mich., 1947; J.D., Cardozo Schl. of Law, Yeshiva U., 1982; m. Paul Emanuel, 1950; children—Irene, Carol, Ruth. Chmn. bd. N.J. Fedn. Music Clubs, mem. legis. action com.; trustee Bergen Philharm.; adjudicator N.J. Fed. Festivals; French horn player U. Mich. Concert Band, 1945-47, Bklyn. Philharm., 1948; pvt. tchr. of piano, 1948—; jud. clk. to Hon. Morris Malech, Superior Ct., Bergen City, N.J.; tchr. folk dance Bklyn. youth groups, 1948-50; composer, dir. confirmation programs, North Bergen, N.J., 1954-59; choir dir. Temple Israel, Cliffside Park, N.J., 1954-57, Bergenfield (N.J.) Jewish Center, 1960-62. Chmn. Bklyn Jewish Music Festival, 1949; children's concerts Bergen County YMHA, 1977. Recipient award Music Edn. League, 1936; Founder's medal Theodore Roosevelt Soc., 1938; scholar Brandeis Camp Inst., 1949. Mem. Bergen County Bar Assn., N.J. Bar Assn., Vol. Lawyers Arts, Women Lawyers in Bergen, Bklyn. Music Tchrs. Guild, Profl. Music Tchrs. Assn., Interstate Music Tchrs. Assn. Co-author: Tercentenary History of Jews, 1954. Home: 468 Churchill Rd Teaneck NJ 07666 Office: 197 Main St Ridgefield Park NJ

EMBRY, CARLOTTA EVANS, Congressional aide; b. Muskogee, Okla., Mar. 28, 1952; d. Leonard DeVoda and Ella Lean (Martin) Evans; m. Robert Wayne Embry, Oct. 14, 1983; children—Humeta Jeru Embry, Shechinah Iman Embry, Taj Ransaan Sourie. Student Okla. U., 1970-71, 76-77. Receptionist, sec. Devel. Dist. Eastern Okla., Muskogee, 1971-73; with classified ads dept. Muskogee Daily Phoenix, 1973-74; traffic clk. Sta. KKUL, Tulsa, Okla., 1974-75; sec. Blue Cross/Blue Shield, Muskogee, 1975-76, City of Muskogee, 1977-78; congl. aide Congressman Mike Synar, Muskogee, 1979-86; state coordinator Nat. Black Women's Health Project, 1986—; v.p. Federally Employed Women, Muskogee, 1983. Bd. dirs. Eastern Okla. Hospice, Muskogee, 1985, Muskogee YMCA/YWCA, 1985; mem. Nat. Black Women's Health Project, Atlanta, 1986. Recipient cert. Nat. Black Women's Health Project, 1985, Alpha Lambda Zeta/Zeta Phi Beta, 1986. Mem. NAACP. Avocations: horseback riding; swimming; jogging; dancing.

EMBRY, ZORA ROMANS, newspaper publisher, shopping center owner; b. Flint Spring, Ky., Aug. 12, 1908; d. Richard D. and Ora (Haven) Romans; m. Carlos B. Embry, June 30, 1940 (dec.); 1 son, Carlos B. Student U. Ariz., 1948-49; B.S., Western Ky. U., 1963. Tchr., Central Park High Sch., McHenry, Ky., 1932-44; prin. Pleasant Ridge Elem. Sch. (Ky.), 1959-74; v.p. The Embry Newspapers, Beaver Dam, Ky., 1944-74; pub. Ohio County Messenger, Beaver Dam, 1974—; owner Embry Valley Shopping Center, Beaver Dam, 1974—; tchr. spl. handicapped children, 1958-59. Chmn. ARC, Beaver Dam, 1946-47; pres. Beaver Dam PTA, 1947-48; 2d v.p. Ky. PTA, 1948-50; v.p. 4th dist. Ky. PTA, 1950-52; youth dir. Beaver Dam Baptist Ch., 1981—; founder, advisor Zora Embry Home for Girls; vol. Western Pkwy. Nursing Home. Mem. Ky. Weekly Newspaper Assn., Alpha Delta Kappa (pres. Beaver Dam 1979-80). Republican. Clubs: Ky. Rep. Women's (state treas. 1955-56), Ky. Fedn. Women's Clubs (gov. 1st dist. 1953-55), 20th Century Woman's (pres. Beaver Dam 1957-59), Beaver Dam Woman's (pres. 1951-53), Order Eastern Star (worthy matron 1982—), White Shrine. Home: 211 N Main St Beaver Dam KY 42320 Office: Embry Newspapers Inc 220 N Main St Beaver Dam KY 42320

EMBURY, SHEILA BARBARA, Canadian provincial legislator, nurse; b. Calgary, Alta., Can., June 6, 1931; d. Herbert Leonard and Beatrice Mary (Taffler) Pease; R.N. diploma Calgary Gen. Hosp. Sch. Nursing, 1953; diploma in teaching and supervision U. Alta. Sch. Nursing, Edmonton, 1955, B.Sc. in Nursing, 1971; postgrad. in edn1. psychology U. Calgary, 1974-75; m. David Edward Embury, June 4, 1955; children—Barbara Lynn, James Edwin. Mem. faculty Calgary Gen. Hosp. Sch. Nursing, 1953-54, 55-56; gen. staff nurse med. ward Vancouver (B.C., Can.) Gen. Hosp., 1954; gen. staff nurse, emergency dept. Peace River (Alta.) Mcpl. Hosp., 1964-66; gen. staff nurse, med. ward Royal Alexandra Hosp., Edmonton, 1967; mem. nursing res. Foothills Hosp., Calgary, 1969-71; clin. instr. Sch. Nursing, U. Calgary, 1971-72, profl. assoc., 1972-73, asst. prof. nursing, 1973-74, asst. prof. Faculty Nursing, 1974-79, research assoc., 1980-81, adj. assoc. prof. nursing, 1982-85; mem. Legis. Assembly Alta., Edmonton, 1979—, chmn. health and social services, vice chmn. legis. com. Senate reform, 1983, party whip, 1983—; lectr. on politics and health issues. Pres., Calgary West Progressive Conservative Provincial Constituency Assn., 1977-78; bd. dirs. Alta. Housing Corp. Mem. Internat. Council Nurses, Can. Nurses' Assn., Alta. Assn. RNs (v.p. North Dist. 1966-67, mem. South Central Exec. 1970-71, 78-79), Can. Assn. Univ. Schs.

Nursing, Can. Nurses' Found. Home: Legislative Assembly of Alberta 1204 Varsity Estates Rd NW Calgary AB T3B 2X2 Canada

EMEK, SHARON HELENE, business consultant; b. Bklyn., Oct. 23, 1945; d. Hyman Sampson and Cynthia Gertrude (Roth) Rabinowitz; children—Aleeza Judith, Joshua Michael, Elana Yael. B.A., CCNY, 1967; M.A., Bklyn. Coll., 1970; Ed.D., Rutgers U., 1977. Dir. preliminary program for small coll. Bklyn. Coll., 1969-71, 73-74; dir. Am. Ctr. Reading Skills, Tel Aviv, 1972; asst. prof. Brookdale Community Coll., Lincroft, N.J., 1975-77, Rutgers U., New Brunswick, N.J., 1977-82; v.p. Radzik & Emek, Princeton, N.J., 1980—; speaker profl. meetings. Author (with Adam Radzik); Managing Employees the Easy Way, 1986; Dealing Successfully with Key Management Issues, 1986. Contbr. articles to profl. jours. Recipient Promising Research award Nat. Council Tchrs. of English, 1978. Mem. Am. Mgmt. Assn., Am. Soc. Profl. Cons. Avocations: writing; reading; jogging; tennis; travel. Office: Radzik & Emek PO Box 7185 Princeton NJ 08543

EMERING, SANDRA ANN, actuary; b. Chgo., Sept. 12, 1949; d. Adrian Douglas and Marie (Wojnowiak) Troutman; m. Edward John Emering, July 11, 1981; 1 son, Daniel T. B.S. in Math., U. Ill., 1970. Enrolled actuary. Mgr. CNA Ins. Co., Chgo., 1970-75; pension actuary Reed Ramsey, Inc., Oakbrook, Ill., 1975-77, Kemper Life Ins. Co., Long Grove, Ill., 1977-78; actuary Karel & Assocs., Northbrook, Ill., 1979-80; pres. Consulting Actuarial Group, Northfield, 1981—. Adviser Northfield Community Ch., 1982. Mem. Am. Acad. Actuaries, Am. Soc. Pension Actuaries, Women in Mgmt. Republican. Congregationalist. Clubs: Chgo. Actuarial, East Bank (Chgo.). Office: Cons Actuarial Group 778 Frontage Rd Northfield IL 60093

EMERSON, ALICE FREY, college president; b. Durham, N.C., Oct. 26, 1931; d. Alexander Hamilton and Alice (Hubbard) Frey; A.B., Vassar Coll., 1953; Ph.D., Bryn Mawr Coll., 1964; LL.D., Wheaton Coll., 1986; div.; children—Rebecca, Peter. Tchr., Newton (Mass.) High Sch., 1956-58; mem. faculty Bryn Mawr (Pa.) Coll., 1961-64; mem. faculty U. Pa., Phila., 1966-75, asst. prof. polit. sci., 1966-75, dean women, 1966-69, dean students, 1969-75; pres. Wheaton Coll., Norton, Mass., 1975—; dir. Bank of Boston Corp., Bank of Boston; trustee Penn Mut. Life Ins. Co., Pub./Pvt. Ventures; adv. bd. HERS Mid-Am., 1973—. Mem. com. on coll. athletics Am. Council on Edn., 1979—; trustee Vassar Coll., 1978-85, Sturdy Meml. Hosp., 1977—; mem. adv. bd. Com. for Nat. Security, 1982—. Mem. Assn. Am. Colls. (dir. 1984—), Council on Fgn. Relations, Am. Polit. Sci. Assn., AAUP, Americal Council Edn., Women's Coll. Coalition. Office: Office of Pres Wheaton Coll Norton MA 02766

EMERSON, ANDI, sales and advertising executive; b. N.Y.C.; d. Willard Ingham and Ethel (Mole) E.; student Barnard Coll.; m. George G. Fawcett, Jr. (div.); children—Ann Emerson II, George Gifford III, Christopher Babcock; m. 2d, Kenneth E. Weeks (div.); 1 dau., Electra Ingham. Exec. v.p., ptnr. Eugene Stevens, Inc., N.Y.C., 1956-60; pres., dir. Emerson Mktg. Agy., Inc., 1960—, Mail Order Operating Co. Ltd., London and N.Y.C., 1976—, Ingham Hall Ltd., 1977-79; chmn. bd., sec. Sonal World Mktg., Ltd., N.Y.C. and Delhi, India, 1983—; instr. NYU, 1960-65. Block chmn. fund raising ARC, Multiple Sclerosis, Nat. Found., Crippled Children, Found. for Blind, 1954-63; vol. worker Children's Ward, Meml. Hosp., 1964-66, Hosp. Spl. Surgery, 1967; mem. adv. com. African Students League, 1965-67; bd. dirs. Violet Oakley Meml. Found., Phila., 1964-81; del. White House Conf. on Small Bus., 1986. Mem. Direct Mktg. Assn., Mktg. Execs., Direct Mktg. Creative Guild (pres. 1974—), Mail Order Profls. Group, Soc. Profl. Writers, Direct Mkgt. Club of N.Y. (treas. 1960-61). Clubs: N.Y. Jr. League, Barnard (ex-moms squadron A). Home: 16 E 96th St New York NY 10128 Office: 44 E 29th St New York NY 10016

EMERSON, ANN PARKER, dietitian; b. Twin Lakes, Fla., Dec. 3, 1925; d. Charles Dendy and Gladys Agnes (Chalker) Parker; B.S., Fla. State U., 1947; M.S., U. Fla., 1968; m. Donald McGeachy Emerson, Sept. 22, 1950; children—Mary Ann, Donald McGeachy, Charles Parker, William John. Research dietitian U. Chgo., 1948-50; adminstrv. research dietitian U. Fla. Coll. Medicine, Gainesville, 1962-68, dir. dietetic edn., 1968-74, dir. dietetic internship program, 1968-75, dir. program in clin. and community dietetics, 1974-83; mem. Commn. on Dietetic Registration, 1974-77, Commn. on Accreditation, 1980-83. Pres., Gainesville chpt. Altrusa, Internat., 1977-78. VA Allied Health Manpower grantee, 1974-81; HEW Allied Health Manpower grantee, 1975-78, 78-81. Mem. Am., Fla. dietetic assns. Democrat. Roman Catholic. Club: Jr. League (Gainesville). Office: PO Box J-184 JHMHC Gainesville FL 32610

EMERSON, DOROTHY, home economist; b. Waltham, Mass.; d. Philip and M. Evelyn (Dewey) E.; grad. in home econs. Framingham State Tchrs. Coll.; summer study Dartmouth Coll., Columbia U., Amherst. Tchr., Boston Public Schs., Kimball Union Acad. Urban home demonstration agt., Portsmouth, N.H.; county club agt. Sussex County, Del.; prof., asso. state 4-H Club agt. Md. Extension Service, 1923-61, now extension prof. emeritus; now cons. citizenship-leadership div. Nat. 4-H Council, also lectr. on 4-H Club work. Mem. Pen Women, Delta Kappa Gamma (hon.), Epsilon Sigma Phi (Ruby award 1975) Phi Kappa Phi. Author: Scrapbook, 1966; also articles. Home: 3445 S Leisure World Blvd Silver Spring MD 20906 Office: 7100 Connecticut Ave Chevy Chase MD 20815

EMERSON, JUDI LOEWEN, social worker; b. Los Angeles, Aug. 11, 1946; d. Wallace and Esther (Hiebert) Loewen; m. Ted Ross Emerson, May 23, 1976; children—Travis, Ashley. M. Social Work, U. Kans., 1976; B.S. summa cum laude, McPherson Coll., 1974. Cert. social worker, 1978. Social worker Topeka State Hosp., Kans., 1974-76, Kans. Children's Service League, Wichita, 1976-78; supr. State of Kans., Wichita, 1978-80; cons., edn. specialist S. Central Mental Health Ctr., El Dorado, Kans., 1980-82; cons. Rainbow Day Care, Hutchinson, Kans., 1982-84; cons., edn. coordinator Horizons Mental Health Ctr., Hutchinson, Kans., 1985—. Treas., United Methodist Women, Nickerson, 1985; bd. dirs. Big Sisters, 1983, Arts Council, 1983. Mem. Acad. Cert. Social Workers. Clubs: Idona Women's (pres. 1985-86), Mother's (pres. 1982-83). Avocation: tennis. Home: Box 7 Nickerson KS 67561

EMERSON, SUZANNE MICHEL, marriage, family and child counselor; b. Marion, Ohio, Mar. 13, 1934; d. Paul Devere and Esther (Kent) Michel; student U. Dayton, 1952-53; B.S., Ohio State U., 1953-56; M.A., Loyola U., Los Angeles, 1974; Ph.D., U.S. Internat. U., San Diego, 1981; 1 son, Dane E.M. Little. Staff occupational therapist Ohio State U. Hosp., Columbus, 1956-60; sr. psychiat. therapist VA Hosp., Brentwood, Calif., 1960-61; coordinator adjunctive therapy and adult treatment program Westwood Hosp., Los Angeles, 1961-73; pvt. practice as therapist, also cons., Los Angeles, 1966-74; pvt. psychotherapist, La Jolla, Calif., 1975—; research coordinator U. Calif. Hosp., San Diego, 1975-77; instr. U. Calif., San Diego; cons. Calif. Assn. Mental Health, 1968-69; lectr. in field. HEW grantee, 1958-1962. Mem. So. Calif. Occupational Therapy Assn. (office chmn. 1968-69), Psi Chi, Kappa Alpha Theta. Democrat. Office: 6525 La Jolla Blvd La Jolla CA 92037

EMERY, IRIS REDFERN, public relations executive; b. Heidelburg, Fed. Republica of Germany, Nov. 11, 1947; d. Ira Cornelius and Miriam Beverly (Nelson) Redfern; m. Ronald Eugene Quale, Sept. 30, 1967 (div. 1978); 1 child, Christopher Redfern; m. John Ernest Emery, July 1, 1978. B.A., Columbia Coll., S.C., 1984. Cons. MRL Resources, Columbia, 1984-85, ptnr., 1986—. Mem. LWV, Columbia, 1985—; mem. chmn. 5 Points Civitan Club, Columbia, 1985—, sec.-treas., bd. dirs., 1986—; dir. Army Community Services Red Cross, Baumholder, Fed. Republic of Germany, 1967-68, vol., Ft. Jackson, S.C., 1978-80; mem. communications commn. St. Martin's Episcopal Ch. Mem. Parents without Ptnrs. (scholarship chmn. 1981-83), Nat. Assn. Female Execs., VFW Aux. Democrat. Episcopalian. Office: MRL Resources P O Box 4854 Columbia SC 29240

EMERY, JENNIFER ELIZABETH, inventor, designer, consultant; b. Akron, Ohio, Dec. 9, 1944; d. Sherman Webster and Elizabeth (Schneider) Horn; m. Thomas E. Emery, Feb. 17, 1964 (div. 1982); children—Christopher, Jacquelyn, Bethani. Student, U. Akron, 1962-65, Kent State U., 1965-66. Mgr. Prinz Design Group, Akron, 1964-74; ptnr., v.p. Bus. Interiors, Inc., Akron, Cleve., 1974-79; prin. AFC Interior Constrn. Co., Tallmadge, Ohio, 1980-82; pres. Emery & Assocs., Cleve., 1982—; bus. cons. The Airplane Companies, Cleve., 1979-85; spl. instr. Kent State U., Ohio, 1982-84; computer-graphic lectr. Design Decisions, Bedford, Ohio, 1982-84; cons. Am. Hosp. Corps., Chgo., 1984-85. Author: Survival As The Female Executive, 1986. Artist, monumental canvas, 1966. Creator prototype dealership for Steelcase, 1980. Mem. exec. com. Playhouse Found. Benefit Group, Cleve., 1984-85; designer exhbn. Gourmet Gala, Am. Soc. Interior Designers, Cleve., 1984; Jr. League Hope House, Bath, Ohio, 1985—; vol. ARC, Ohio Ballet, Cleve., 1983-85. Recipient Best Renovation in City award AIA, Highland Square, Ohio, 1980. Mem. Nat. Assn. Female Execs., Am. Soc. Interior Designers, Womens City Club of Cleve. (com. mem. 1984—), Inst. Bus. Designers, Akron City Club. Avocations: flying; power boating. Office: Emery and Assocs 23600 Mercantile St Beachwood OH 44122

EMERY, JILL HOUGHTON, federal government administrator. Former pres. Emery Corp., Geneso, N.Y.; dir. Women's Bus. Ownership Office, SBA, Washington, 1985—. Office: SBA 1441 L St NW Washington DC 20416*

EMERY, MARCIA ROSE, parapsychologist; b. Phila., Mar. 19, 1937; d. David Joshua and Naomi (Carner) Rose; B.A. in Psychology, Adelphi U., Garden City, N.Y., 1958; M.S. in Clin. Psychology, CCNY, 1960; M.A. in Social Psychology, New Sch. Social Research, 1964, Ph.D., 1968; m. Gordon M. Becker, 1970 (div.); m. 2d, James D. Emery, 1982; stepchildren—Stephen, Alicia, Jamie. Research asst. Office Instl. Research, Hunter Coll., N.Y.C., 1959-62, Community Service Soc., N.Y.C., 1962-65; lectr. psychology Hunter Coll., 1965-67; asso. prof. psychology, chmn. M.A. program in community psychology Fed. City Coll., Washington, 1968-74; ind. practice psychology and astrological counseling, Hollywood, Fla., 1981—; pres. Intuitive Mgmt. Cons. Corp.; adj. faculty Aquinas Coll., Grand Rapids; psychologist Renaissance Revitalization Center, Nassau, Bahamas, 1975; lectr., coordinator counseling Coll. Bahamas, 1976-80; condr. workshops in parapsychology throughout U.S. Author: Developing Your Intuition: A Beginner's Guide; Manage Intuitively to Improve Decision Making and Problem Solving. Grantee NIMH, 1972. Mem. Am. Psychol. Assn., Assn. Humanistic Psychology, Parapsychol. Assn., Spiritual Frontiers Fellowship, Am. Soc. Psychical Research, Am. Fedn. Astrology, Assn. Past Life Research and Therapy. Mem. Unity Ch. Address: 3512 McCoy SE Grand Rapids MI 49506

EMERY, NANCY BETH, lawyer; b. Shawnee, Okla., July 9, 1952; d. Paul Dodd Finefrock and Kathryn Jo (Saling) Hutchens; m. Lee Monroe Emery, May 18, 1974. B.A., U. Okla., 1974; J.D. Harvard U., 1977. Bar: Okla. 1977, D.C. 1981. Atty. advisor Office Gen. Counsel, U.S. Dept. Agri., Washington, 1977-79; legal adv. to Fed. Energy Regulatory Commr. Matthew Holden, Jr., Washington, 1979-81; assoc. firm Pierson, Ball & Dowd, and predecessor Sullivan & Beauregard, Washington, 1981-83; assoc. firm Paul Hastings, Janofsky & Walker, Washington, 1983—. Bd. dirs., sec. Park Place Condominium Assn., Inc., Washington, 1982—; page Continental Congress, DAR, 1978-82, chpt. del. Continental Congress, 1981, 84. Mem. ABA (adminstrv. and nat. resources law sect.), Fed. Energy Bar Assn., Soc. Profl. Journalists, Mortar Bd., Phi Beta Kappa. Democrat. Home: 31123 Hawthorne Dr NE Washington DC 20017 Office: Paul Hastings Janofsky & Walker 1050 Thomas Jefferson St NW Washington DC 20007

EMIG, LOIS IRENE MYERS, composer; b. Roseville, Ohio, Oct. 12, 1925; d. Earl Francis and Margaret Byrd (Weaver) Myers; B.S. with distinction, Ohio State U., 1946; postgrad. Ohio State U., Queens Coll.; m. Jack Wayne Emig, June 7, 1947; children—Sandra Jill, Keith Jack. Public sch. vocal and instrumental music tchr., Ohio and N.Y., 1946-65; pvt. tchr. piano and theory, 1954—; composer and librettist for adult and children's choirs; church organist; pub. works include 9 cantatas, 2 piano books, over 185 varied choral works. Mem. AAUW, ASCAP, Delta Omicron. Contbr. music to profl. jours. Home and Studio: 2149 N Hampton Circle Winter Park FL 32792

EMLER, DIXIE GWEN, nursing administrator; b. Logansport, Ind., May 21, 1939; d. Conn and Betty (Sixbey) Frey. B.S., Ind. U., 1961, M.S., 1962. Assoc. nursing service dir. Bethany Hosp., Kansas City, Kans., 1965-66; sect. chmn. Assoc. Degree Nursing Program, Purdue U., West Lafayette, Ind., 1966-74; v.p. Lafayette Home Hosp., Ind., 1974—; adj. prof. Purdue U., 1974—. Mem. hosp. licensing council Ind. Bd. Health, 1980—. Recipient Leadership Excellence award Sigma Theta Tau, 1984. Mem. Ind. Nurses Assn. (bd. dirs. 1980—, dist. VIII 2d v.p.), Am. Orgn. Nurse Execs., Inq. Soc. Nursing Service Adminstrs. Republican. Club: Altrusa. Avocations: outdoor activities; gardening; reading. Home: Rural Route 2 Box 111B Thorntown IN 46071 Office: 2400 South St Lafayette IN 47904

EMMERICH, JO ANN, broadcasting executive; b. St. Louis, Sept. 1; d. William K. and Leora M. (Wolff) E. B.A., Catholic U. Am., 1964, M.A., 1971. Drama specialist Dept. State, Europe and Middle East, 1965-66; exec. staff Olney Theatre (Md.), 1967-68; agt. TV dept. Internat. Famous Agy., N.Y.C., 1972-75; asst. producer As the World Turns, CBS, N.Y.C., 1975-76; mgr. daytime programming ABC, N.Y.C., 1976-77, dir. daytime programming, 1977-80, v.p. daytime programs East Coast, 1980-86, v.p. daytime programs, 1986—. Mem. Am. Film Inst., Nat. Acad. TV Arts and Scis. Office: ABC 1330 Ave of Americas New York NY 10019

EMMONS, CAROL ANN, mortgage banker; b. Jersey City; d. Max and Dorothy (Peters) Leuck; student El Camino Jr. Coll., Torrance, Calif., 1960-61, Dutchess Community Coll., 1974-75, D'Youville Coll., 1977-81, various courses SUNY, Buffalo, and Dale Carnegie; children—Linda, Conrad, Rodney. Mortgage adminstr., asst. br. mgr. Soc. for Savs., Hartford, Conn., 1965-75; asst. br. mgr. Reliance Equities, Inc., Poughkeepsie, N.Y., 1975-76, br. mgr., Buffalo, 1976-80, asst. v.p., 1980, pres., dir., Buffalo, 1981-83; sr. v.p. Comfed Mortgage Co., Lowell, Mass., 1983—; pres. Nat. Mortgage Banking Corp. Bus. adv. bd. High Sch. Students. Notary public. Mem. Mortgage Bankers Assn. Western N.Y. (pres. 1981), Conn. Mortgage Bankers Assn. (dir.), Greater Buffalo Bd. Realtors, Nat. Assn. Female Execs., Council Small Bus. Enterprises, Better Bus. Bur., Buffalo C. of C., Center for Women in Mgmt. of D'Youville Coll., Women for Downtown Buffalo. Office: One Corporate Dr Windsor Locks CT 06096

EMMONS, LINDA NYE, state legislator; b. Ridgewood, N.J., July 8, 1937; d. Drake and Helen N. Pinkney; A.A., Centenary Coll. Women, Hackettstown, N.J., 1957; B.A., Conn. Coll., 1972; m. Richard L. Emmons, Dec. 13, 1958; children—Mark Richard, Dwight Nye. Staff asst. AT&T Co., 1957-61; self-employed accountant, 1975—; mem. Conn. Ho. of Reps. from 101st Dist., 1977—, mem. com. on revenue, bonding and fin., 1977-81, 83—, house chmn., 1985—, mem. com. on appropriations, 1981-83, ranking mem., 1981-85, asst. minority leader for fiscal affairs; mem. Conn. Bond Commn. Mem. Madison (Conn.) Charter Commn., 1967-69, Madison Republican Town Com., 1970-77; chmn. Madison Bd. Fin., 1977-79; bd. dirs. E.C. Scranton Meml. Library, 1973—. Mem. Order Women Legislators, LWV (voters service chmn. 1968-69). Address: 111 Yankee Peddler Path Madison CT 06443

EMSHWILLER, CAROL FRIES, writer, educator; b. Ann Arbor, Mich., Apr. 12, 1921; d. Charles Carpenter and Agnes (Carswell) Fries; m. Edmund Alexander Emshwiller, Aug. 30, 1949; children—Eve, Susan, Peter. B.A. in Music, U. Mich., 1945; B.Design, U. Mich. Art Sch., 1949. Guest, Sarah Laurence Coll., Bronxville, N.Y., 1983; faculty Clarion Sci. Fiction Workshop, 1976-77; adj. asst. prof. continuing edn. NYU, N.Y.C., 1978—. Author: Joy in our Cause, 1974. Contbr. stories to lit. mags. and sci. fiction mags. Nat. Endowment for Arts grantee, 1980; Pub. Service grantee, N.Y. State, 1975; McDowell Colony fellow. Mem. PEN, Sci. Fiction Writers of Am. Address: 260 E 10th St Apt 10 New York NY 10009

ENDICOTT, MARGARET AILEEN, lawyer; b. Glazier, Tex., July 1, 1911; d. Harry LeRoy and Georgia Lois (Brizendine) E. LL.B., Oklahoma City U., 1958. Bar: Okla. 1958. Sec. to judge Okla. Dist. Ct., Oklahoma City, 1935-43; dep. ct. clk. U.S. Dist. Ct. (we. dist.) Okla., Oklahoma City, 1943-50; sec. to judge U.S. Dist. Ct. (we. dist.) Okla., 1950-60; civilian atty. U.S. Air Force, Tinker Air Force Base, Okla., 1960-76. Recipient award for meritorious civilian service U.S. Air Force, 1976. Mem. Okla. Bar Assn., ABA, Fed. Bar Assn., Inter-Am. Bar Assn., Iota Tau Tau. Democrat. Baptist. Home: 2529 NW 118th St Oklahoma City OK 73120 Office: PO Box 60287 Oklahoma City OK 73106

ENDSLEY, CAROLYN FRANCES, industrial nursing supervisor; b. Landess, Ind., Nov. 4, 1936; d. Francis Levi and Pauline Lucille (Foust) Franks; m. Rodger Malcolm Endsley, Apr. 15, 1972 (dec. 1979); 1 son, Rod Travis. R.N., Meth. Hosp.-Indpls., 1957; B.S. in Health Care Adminstrn., St. Joseph Coll., North Windham, Maine. R.N.; cert. spirometry technician, occupational health nurse, hearing conservationist. Charge nurse Marion Gen. Hosp., (Ind.), 1957-60, 67; sch. nurse Marion Coll., 1959-60; staff nurse Fisher Body, Inc., Marion, 1960-78, supr. med. dept., 1978—. Mem. Am. Occupational Health Nurses Assn., Mid Ind. Assn. Occupational Health Nurses (bd. dirs., v.p. 1979-83, pres. 1983-85), Ind. Assn. Occupational Health Nurses (com. chmn. 1983-86, bd. dirs. 1984-87, Nurse of Yr. award 1985), Ind. Acad. Occupational Nurses. Democrat. Club: Home Extension (treas. Fowlerton, Ind. 1978-80). Home: 4312 S Washington St Marion IN 46953 Office: Fisher Body Div GMC 2400 W 2d St Marion IN 46952

ENEGUESS, ANN CAVANAUGH, fund development administrator; b. Evanston, Ill., Sept. 27, 1924; d. Matthew Patrick and Mary Ethel (Kelleher) Cavanaugh; m. Daniel Francis Eneguess, July 29, 1950; children—David Michael (dec.), Katharine Ann, Daniel Francis, John Matthew. B.A., Regis Coll., Weston, Mass., 1946. Field dir. So. Nassau Girl Scout Council, Freeport, N.Y., 1946-49; exec. dir. Wellesley Girl Scout Council, Mass., 1949-51; reporter, feature writer Keene Evening Sentinel, N.H., 1957-64; owner, operator Deer Run Day Camp, Deer Run No. White Water, Peterborough, N.H., 1958-68, 70—; field exec. mem., edn. dir. Swift Water Girl Scout Council, Manchester, N.H., 1962-84, fund devel dir., 1984—. Pres., Monadnock Chorus & Orch., Peterborough, 1985 Recipient Thanks Badge Swift Water Girl Scout Council, 1954, St. Ann's award Diocese of Manchester, 1978; Named Career Girl of USA Internat. Friendship League, 1947, Named Outstanding Woman of Yr., Beta Sigma Phi, 1983-85. Mem. Assn. Girl Scout Exec. Staff (v.p. 1964-66, sec. 1978-80), AAUW (pres. 1965-67), Audubon Soc., Soc. Protection N.H. Forest. Republican. Roman Catholic. Club: Woman's. Avocations: skiing; chorus; community service. Home: Old Dublin Rd PO Box 179 Peterborough NH 03458 Office: Swift Water Girl Scout Council 325 Merrill St Manchester NH 03103

ENEVOLDSEN, BERNADINE LOUISE, home economist; b. Parkston, S.D., July 13, 1942; d. Henry Ferdinand and Augusta Katherine (Ruff) Blume; B.S., S.D. State U., 1964, M.S., 1986; m. Myron E. Enevoldsen, July 25, 1969; 1 dau., Victoria Katherine. Area extension home economist, Plankinton, S.D., 1964-67; extension home economist Brookings County (S.D.), 1967—; extension family fin. mgmt. specialist S.D. State U., Brookings, 1967-86. Mem. Bus. and Profl. Women Brookings (Outstanding Young Career Woman 1968), S.D. Home Econs. Assn. (named Outstanding Young Home Economist 1978), Am. Home Econs. Assn., S.D. Assn. Extension Home Economists (Disting. Service award 1978), Nat. Assn. Extension Home Economists, Brookings Area Geneal. Soc. Epsilon Sigma Phi. Lutheran. Office: SD State U Home Econs Nursing Bldg 243 Box 2275A Brookings SD 57007

ENFINGER, SHERON ANN, city clerk; b. Hartford, Ala., Mar. 13, 1944; d. Lunice E. and Willie E. (Skinner) Newsome; divorced; 1 child, Teresa Kay Enfinger Tripp. Student George C. Wallace Coll., 1962. Clk., typist I, City of Geneva, Ala., 1962-80, city clk., 1980—. Recipient Disting. Service award Ala. League Municipalities, 1983, Cert. Appreciation ARC. 1979. Mem. Geneva-Geneva County C. of C. (mem. beautification com. 1984—). Methodist. Avocations: reading, dancing. Home: Rt 1 Box 345 Hartford AL 36344 Office: City of Geneva PO Box 37 517 S Commerce St Geneva AL 36340

ENG, ANNE (CHING), broadcast account executive; b. N.Y.C., Aug. 9, 1950; d. Fuen and Suit Fong (Mark) Eng; m. George Chin, June 28, 1978; 1 child, Lauren. A.A.S., Manhattan Community Coll., 1970; student Baruch Coll., 1972. Sales asst. AVCO Radio Sales, N.Y.C., 1972; asst., jr. media buyer R.D.R. Timebuying Services, N.Y.C., 1972-74; TV media buyer, planner Ogilvy & Mather Advt., N.Y.C., 1974-78; broadcast account exec. H.R. Television, N.Y.C., 1978-79, RKO TV Reps., N.Y.C., 1979-80, Petry TV, N.Y.C., 1980—. Avocations: Plate collecting; exercise; skiing. Office: Petry Television 3 E 54th St New York NY 10022

ENG, JOYCE FRANCES, government official; b. East Orange, N.J., Aug. 16, 1946; d. Walter K. and Caroline C. (Young) E.; B.S. in Med. Tech., Fairleigh Dickinson U., 1969; M.S., C.W. Post Center of L.I. U., 1972; M.A. in Theology, Ecumenical Inst. Theology, St. Mary's Sem. and U., 1980. Med. tech. intern Sch. Med. Tech., Morristown (N.J.) Hosp., 1968-69, med. technologist, 1969-70; blood bank technologist Dover (N.J.) Gen. Hosp., 1971; med. technologist Glenridge Labs., Bklyn., part-time 1972; instr. dept. clin. pathology U. Md. Sch. Medicine, Balt., 1972-73, asst. prof. dept. med. tech., 1972-73; chief bacteriologist Howard County Gen. Hosp., Columbia, Md., 1973-74; instr. anatomy and physiology div. biology Catonsville (Md.) Community Coll., 1975; health care specialist Bur. Health Ins., Social Security Adminstrn., HEW, Balt., 1975-78, standards and cert. analyst Health Care Financing Adminstrn., Health Standards and Quality Bur., Dept. Health and Human Services, Balt., 1978-82, Bur. Eligibility, Reimbursement, and Coverage, 1982—. Recipient cert. of appreciation Health Care Financing Adminstrn., 1981; Spl. Achievement award Health Care Financing Adminstrn., 1980; USPHS Allied Health trainee, 1971-72; AAUW award, 1968-69. Mem. Am. Soc. Med. Tech. (ho. of dels. 1981, 82, 85), Md. Soc. Med. Tech. (chmn. civil service subcom. 1981-82, bd. dirs., Western Md. rep. 1984-85, 86-87), Am. Soc. Clin. Pathologists, Am. Soc. Microbiology, Nat. Registry Microbiologists, Assn. Mil. Surgeons U.S.

ENGEBRETSON, MARY EVONE, librarian; b. Albert Lea, Minn., Apr. 9, 1947; d. Merel Harlan and Darlyne Geneva (Johnson) E.; B.A., Luther Coll., 1969; M.A., U. Denver, 1971; M.B.A., Ariz. State U., 1977. Head, bookmobile dept. Whatcom County Library, Bellingham, Wash., 1971-75; market research analyst Helene Curtis, Inc., Chgo., 1977-78; assoc. librarian U. Fla., Gainesville, 1978-85; head reference U. South Ala. Library, Mobile, 1985—. Mem. ALA, Ala. Library Assn., Spl. Library Assn. Home: 1601 Hillcrest Rd Apt 42 Mobile AL 36609 Office: U South Ala Reference Dept Mobile AL 36688

ENGEL, GLORIA JILL, state court official; b. Onida, S.D., July 22, 1937; d. Newel and Eleanore Ruth (Kane) Bever; m. LeRoy Carl Engel (dec. 1981); children—Bernadette, Shawn, Stephen, Heather. Adminstrv. asst. to chief justice Supreme Ct. of S.D., Pierre, 1965-73, dep. clk. of ct., 1973-77, clk. of supreme ct., 1977—. Author: (study) Time Analysis of Appellate Stages: An Effective Method of Identifying Areas of Delay, 1983. Grad. fellow Inst. Ct. Mgmt., 1983. Mem. Nat. Conf. Appellate Ct. Clks. (sec. 1982-84, exec. bd. 1985-87), Am. Judicature Soc., Nat. Orgn. Bus. Profl. Women. Democrat. Roman Catholic. Avocations: reading; swimming; bridge. Home: 512 N Highland Ave Pierre SD 57501 Office: Supreme Ct of SD 500 E Capitol Ave Pierre SD 57501

ENGEL, IVY ANNE, radiologist, educator; b. N.Y.C., Sept. 16, 1950; d. Stanley Morton and Mildred (Cassel) E.; m. Mark Edward Jacobs, June 9, 1977. B.A., Queens Coll., Flushing, N.Y., 1973; M.D., N.Y. Med. Coll., Valhalla, 1977. Diplomate Am. Bd. Diagnostic Radiology. Intern Stamford Hosp. (Conn.), 1977-78; resident in diagnostic radiology N.Y. Hosp., N.Y.C., 1978-81, fellow in radiology, 1981-82, instr. diagnostic radiology, 1982-83, asst. prof., 1983-84; asst. prof. NYU Med. Ctr., N.Y.C., 1984-85; with L.I. Diagnostic Imaging, Stony Brook, N.Y., 1986—. Contbr. articles to profl. jours. Mem. Radiol. Soc. N.Am., Am. Coll. Radiology, Am. Roentgen Ray Soc., N.Y. Roentgen Ray Soc., Phi Beta Kappa. 11050Office: LI Diagnostic Imaging PC 2500-15 Nesconset Hwy Stony Brook NY

ENGEL, JULIE LISBETH, machining company executive; b. Rochester, N.Y., June 16, 1956; d. Paul Richard and Mildred Adele (Adams) Engel. A.A.S., Monroe Community Coll., 1976. Dispatcher Regional Transit Service, Rochester, N.Y., 1975-77, customer service rep., 1977-78; shipping clk., insp. Carl Wirth & Son, Inc., Rochester, 1978, office mgr., 1978-82, exec. v.p., 1982-83, pres., 1983—. Mem. Nat. Assn. Female Execs. Avocations: reading; music; boating; restoring classic cars. Office: Carl Wirth & Son Inc PO Box 17801 Rochester NY 14617

ENGEL, MARGORIE LOUISE, personnel firm executive, consultant; b. Balt., Nov. 12, 1943; d. William Herman and Margorie Claire (Gladmon) Engel; children—Sharon Elizabeth, Jennifer Claire. B.A., Western Md. Coll., 1965; M.A., Fairfield U., 1975; M.B.A., U. New Haven. Edn. program developer pub./pvt. schs., Va., Calif., N.Y., Conn., 1965-76; coordinator pub. relations Fairfield U., Conn., 1976-78; ptnr. Siebert Assocs., Fairfield, 1978-85; pres. Hamilton-Forbes, Norwalk, Conn., 1984—; dir. CLG Technologists. Editor: Wheels of Life, 1976; editorial bd. A Guide to Mergers and Acquisitions Publications, 1984. Rep. Conn. Women's Adv. Com., Hartford, 1985—; bd. dirs. Children's Mus., Fairfield, 1985—. Mem. Assn. Corporate Growth (v.p. 1983—), Investors' Strategy Inst. (v.p. bd. 1983—), Conn. Venture Group, Fairfield County Bus. Roundtable (pres. 1981-82, exec. bd. 1982—). Republican. Episcopalian. Club: Landmark (Stamford, Conn.). Avocations: sailing; wedding cake decorating; internat. travel. Home: 4029 Park Ave Fairfield CT 06430 Office: Hamilton-Forbes Assocs Ltd 50 Washington St Norwalk CT 06854

ENGELBERG, JANE LINDA, genetic counselor; b. N.Y.C., Apr. 5, 1941; d. Daniel and Vivian (Lipkind) Sanders; m. Alfred Benjamin Engelberg, Aug. 16, 1964. B.S. in Edn., CCNY, 1962; M.S. in Human Genetics and Genetic Counseling, Sarah Lawrence Coll., 1973. Diplomate Am. Coll. Med. Genetics. Elem. sch. tchr., N.Y.C., 1962-65; tchr. children with learning difficulties Fairland Elem. Sch., Silver Spring, Md., 1965-66; sci. tchr. Francis Scott Key Jr. High Sch., Silver Spring, 1966-69; genetic counselor-coordinator Beth Israel Med. Ctr., N.Y.C., 1973-77; genetic counseling assoc. Nat. Genetics Found., N.Y.C., 1977-78; genetic counselor-coordinator satellite genetic clinic program L.I. Jewish Med. Ctr., New Hyde Park, N.Y., 1979—; mem. Genetics Task Force, N.Y.C., 1979—; mem. genetic counseling adv. com. Prenatal Diagnosis Lab., N.Y.C., 1975—. Mem. community bd. Roosevelt-St. Luke's Med. Ctr., N.Y.C., 1983—. Mem. Am. Soc. Human Genetics, Nat. Soc. Genetic Counselors, N.Y. Acad. Scis. Jewish. Avocations: studying Spanish, travel, skiing, golf, attending cultural events. Home: 20 W 64th St New York NY 10023 Office: Long Island Jewish Med Ctr Schneider Children's Hosp New Hyde Park NY 11042

ENGELEITER, SUSAN SHANNON, state legislator; b. Mar. 18, 1952. B.S., U. Wis., 1974, J.D., 1981. Mem. Wis. Assembly, from 1974; mem. Wis. Senate, 1980—. Republican. Office: Wis Senate State Capitol Madison WI 53702*

ENGELHARDT, DIANE MARY, light and power company official; b. Postville, Iowa, Sept. 9, 1956; d. Rachel Kathleen (Connor) E. B.A. in Criminal Justice Adminstrn., Mount Mercy Coll., 1978. Security supr. Duane Arnold Energy Ctr., Iowa Electric Light & Power Co., Cedar Rapids, Iowa, 1978—; v.p. Hawkeye Services, Cedar Rapids, 1982—. Mem. Am. Mgmt. Assn., Midwest Nuclear Security Assn. Roman Catholic. Avocations: boating; arts and crafts. Home: 1067 Juniper Dr SW Cedar Rapids IA 52404

ENGELHARDT, SARA LAWRENCE, foundation executive; b. Phila., Aug. 23, 1943; d. Ruddick Carpenter and Barbara (Dole) Lawrence; B.A., Wellesley Coll., 1965; M.A., Tchrs. Coll., Columbia U., 1970; m. Dean Lee Engelhardt, June 20, 1970; children—Barbara Elizabeth, Margaret Ann. Staff asst. Carnegie Corp., N.Y.C., 1966-70, asst. sec., 1972-74, assoc. sec., 1974-75, sec., 1975—; free-lance editor and writer, Storrs, Conn., 1970-72. Mem. bd. overseers Wellesley Coll. Ctr. for Research on Women, 1979—; bd. dirs. Nat. Charities Info. Bur., 1983—; trustee Found. Ctr., 1984—. Home: 173 Riverside Dr New York NY 10024 Office: Carnegie Corp 437 Madison Ave New York NY 10022

ENGELKING, ELLEN MELINDA, pattern company executive, real estate broker; b. Columbus, Ind., May 12, 1942; d. Lowell Eugene and Marcella (Brane) E.; children—Melissa Claire Prohaska, John David Prohaska, Ellen Margaret Prohaska. Student Sullins Coll., 1961, Franklin Coll., 1982; B.Ed., Ind. U., 1983. Broker Engelking Realty, Columbus, Ind., 1980—; pres., chief exec. officer Engelking Patterns, Inc., Columbus, 1980—, also dir.; vice-chmn. dir. Engelking Properties, Columbus, 1980—; guest speaker Bus. Sch., Ind. U., Bloomington, 1985. Campaign chmn. Am. Heart Assn., Columbus, 1980-81; chmn. Mothers March of Dimes, Columbus, 1967; sec. Bartholomew County Republican Party, 1976-80; bd. dirs. Found. for Youth, 1975-79. Mem. Columbus C. of C. (lectr. 1980—), Am. Foundry Assn., Ind. C. of C., Ind. Mfg. Assn., Delta Delta Delta. Roman Catholic. Avocations: study and present adaptation of Shaker work ethic; remote controlled aircraft; literature; oil painting. Office: Engelking Patterns Inc PO Box 607 Columbus IN 47202-0607

ENGELSCHALL, JULIA ANN, technical communications executive, consultant; b. Encino, Calif., Sept. 27, 1956; d. James Joseph and Roberta Jean (Bauer) E. B.A., UCLA, 1978; postgrad. Calif. State U.-Northridge, 1982-83. Cert. tchr., Calif. Tchr. secondary sch., Las Virgenes Unified Sch. Dist., Westlake Village, Calif., 1978-79; sr. editor Xyzyx Info. Corp., Canoga Park, Calif., 1979-81; publs. analyst TRE Semiconductor, Woodland Hills, Calif., 1981-82; free-lance communications cons., Reseda, Calif., 1982-84; owner, mgr. CommuniClear, Van Nuys, Calif., 1984—. Author, co-author reports and manuals. Designer tng. programs. Contbr. articles to profl. jours. Communications cons. Miriam Ojeda, Republican candidate 26th Congl. Dist., 1984, corp. scholars program, Calif. State U., 1983, Chaverim, Los Angeles, 1984. Mem. Soc. for Tech. Communications, Nat. Assn. Women Bus. Owners, Nat. Assn. Female Execs., MENSA, Phi Beta Kappa. Clubs: Grad. Bus. Students Assn. (pres. 1983) (Northridge). Office: CommuniClear 15120 Vanowen St #29 Van Nuys CA 91405

ENGERRAND, DORIS DIESKOW, educator; b. Chgo., Aug. 7, 1925; d. William Jacob and Alma Willhelmina (Cords) D.; B.S. in Bus. Adminstrn., N. Ga. Coll., 1958, B.S. in Elementary Edn., 1959; M. Bus. Edn., Ga. State U., 1966, Ph.D., 1970; m. Gabriel H. Engerrand, Oct. 26, 1946; children—Steven, Kenneth, Jeannine. Tchr., dept. chmn. Lumpkin County High Sch., Dahlonega, Ga., 1960-63, 65-68; tchr., Gainesville, Ga., 1965; asst. prof. Troy (Ala.) State U., 1969-71; asst. prof. bus. Ga. Coll., Milledgeville, 1971-74, asso. prof., 1974-78, prof., 1978—, chmn. dept. bus. info. systems and communications, 1984—; cons. Named Outstanding Tchr. Lumpkin County Pub. Schs., 1963, 66; Outstanding Educator bus. faculty Ga. Coll., 1975, Exec. of Yr. award, 1983. Fellow Am. Bus. Communication Assn.; mem. Am. Bus. Communication Assn. (nat. dir.; v.p. S.E. 1978-80, 81-84), Soc. Tech. Communication, Acad. Mgmt., So. Mgmt. Assn., Nat., Ga. (Postsecondary Tchr. of Yr. award 10th dist. 1983, Postsecondary Tchr. of Yr. award 1984) bus. edn. assns., Am., Ga. (Educator of Yr. award 1984) vocat. assns., Profl. Secs. Internat., Office Systems Research Assn., Ninety-nines Internat. (chmn. N. Ga. chpt. 1975-76, named Pilot of Year N. Ga. chpt. 1973). Methodist. Contbr. articles on bus. edn. to profl. publs. Home: 1674 Pine Valley Rd Milledgeville GA 31061 Office: Ga Coll Milledgeville GA 31061

ENGHOLM, MARY KORSTAD MUELLER, art education consultant; author; b. Seattle, May 7, 1918; d. Martin and Mary Emily (Greene) Korstad; B.E., UCLA, 1940; M.Ed., St. Lawrence U., 1949; postgrad. Syracuse U., 1950-52; m. Walter Weigel, Dec. 22, 1949 (div. 1967); 1 child, Erica K. Weigel; m. 2d, Paul G. Mueller, Nov. 9, 1968 (dec. 1976); m. 3d, Glenn S. Engholm, Aug. 6, 1982. Tchr. art Riverside (Calif.) City Schs., 1944-46; art supr. Canton (N.Y.) Sch. Dist., 1946-48; asst. prof. art SUNY, Potsdam, 1948-58; art supr. Watertown (N.Y.) City Sch. Dist., 1962-67; cons., lectr. U. Nebr., Lincoln, summer 1966; art supr. Bakersfield (Calif.) City Sch. Dist., 1967-78; instr. art, continuing edn. Calif. State Coll., Bakersfield, 1971-74, 76, adj. instr., lectr., 1982-83; free-lance art cons., Bakersfield, 1978—. Trustee Kern County Arts Council, 1976-83, Bakersfield Sister City Com., 1978-83, H. Weil Child Guidance Clinic, 1980-83, Kern County Mus. Alliance, 1978-84; pres. Kern County chpt. Young Audiences of Am., 1978-83; pres. bd. dirs. H. Weill Meml. Child Guidance Clinic, 1981-83; community adv. Jr. League Bakersfield, 1980-83; v.p. Am. Scandinavians Assn. (Montery Bay chpt.), 1986—; bd. dirs. Lori Brock Jr. Mus., 1975-78, Monterey History and Art Assn., 1986—. Mem. Nat. Art Edn. Assn., Greater Bakersfield C. of C. (Woman of Yr. women's div. 1983), Calif. Art Edn. Assn. (trustee 1979-82), Kern County Art Edn. Assn., AAUW, Calif. Tchrs. Assn., Delta Kappa Gamma. Republican. Lutheran. Author: (with Thomas and Wells) Elementary Art, 1967; Murals: Creating an Environment, 1979; contbr. articles to profl. jours.

ENGLAND, LYNNE LIPTON, lawyer, speech pathologist, audiologist; b. Youngstown, Ohio, Apr. 11, 1949; d. Sanford Y. and Sally (Kentor) Lipton; m. Richard E. England, Mar. 5, 1977. B.A., U. Mich., 1970; M.A., Temple U., 1972; J.D., Tulane U., 1981. Bar: Fla. 1981. Cert. clin. competence in speech pathology and audiology. Speech pathologist Rockland Children's Hosp. (N.Y.), 1972-74, Jefferson Parish Sch., Gretna, La., 1977-81; audiologist Rehab. Inst. Chgo., 1974-76; assoc. Trenam, Simmons, Kemker, Scharf, Barkin, Frye & O'Neill, Tampa, Fla., 1981-84; asst. U.S. atty. for Middle Dist. Fla., Tampa, 1984—. Editor Fla. Bankruptcy Casenotes, 1983. Recipient clin. assistantship Temple U., 1972-74. Mem. Am. Speech and Hearing Assn., Fla. Bar Assn., ABA, Hillsborough County Bar Assn., Am. Congress Phys. Medicine and Rehab., Order of Coif. Jewish. Home: 3054 Wister Circle Valrico FL 33594 Office: US Atty's Office 500 Zach St Tampa FL 33602

ENGLAND, MARY JANE, public administration specialist, dean; b. Brighton, Mass., July 22, 1938; d. Thomas J. and Anna Elizabeth Fahey; A.B., Regis Coll., Weston, Mass., 1959; M.D., Boston U., 1965; m. Robert A. England, July 8, 1962; children—Alexandra, Kara, Thomas. Rotating intern Framingham (Mass.) Union Hosp., 1964-65; resident in psychiatry Boston U. Hosp., 1965-66, also teaching fellow Med. Sch.; resident in psychiatry, cons. adolescent med. clinic Mt. Zion Hosp., San Francisco, 1966-67; fellow child and adolescent psychiatry Boston U.-Boston City Hosp. Child Guidance Clinic, 1967-69; dir. child psychiatry St. Elizabeth's Hosp., Brighton, 1969-72; dir. clin. psychiatry Brighton-Allston Mental Health Clinic, 1972-74; with Mass. Dept. Mental Health, 1974-79, assoc. commnr., 1976-79; commr. Mass. Dept. Social Services, 1979-83; asst. dean, dir. M.P.A. Program, John F. Kennedy Sch. Govt., Harvard U., 1983—; chmn. manpower policy com. NIMH, 1977—. Pres. Action for Boston Community Devel., 1973-75; Bd. dirs. United Way Boston, 1980—, v.p., 1983—; bd. dirs. Mass. Children's Lobby, 1972-73; chmn. regional subpanel United Community Planning Corp., 1971-73; exec. bd. Mass. Com. Children and Youth, 1973-76; chmn. policy com., bd. dirs. Boston-Brookline Collaborative Center, 1971-75; pres. bd. dirs. Brighton-Allston Mental Health Assn., 1969-71; mem. Mass. Mental Health Center Area Bd., 1970-72; bd. dirs. The Partnership, 1982—. Mem. Am. Acad. Child Psychiatry, Am. Assn. Psychiat. Services to Children, Am. Orthopsychiat. Assn., Am. Psychiat. Assn. (cons. govt. relations com. 1985—), Am. Med. Women's Assn. (pres.-elect 1986—), Assn. Psychiat. Treatment Offenders, Am. Coll. Mental Health Adminstrs., Mass. Psychiat. Soc., New Eng. Council Child Psychiatry (co-chmn. legis. com. 1973-75, dir. 1975—). Office: John F Kennedy Sch Govt 79 Kennedy St Cambridge MA 02138

ENGLAND, PATSY COLLEEN, health care direct marketing executive; b. Coleman, Tex., Apr. 14, 1930; d. Joe Collin and Thelma (Boyd) Price; m. Al England, Aug. 17, 1947; children—Al'An England Kesler, Traci Kai. Student Tex. Tech U., 1946, Tech. Art Inst., 1946-47, Harvard U. Sch. Bus., 1951, N.Y. Sch. Mktg., 1952. Editorial asst. Coleman Democrat-Voice (Tex.), 1944-47; adv. editor Santa Anna News (Tex.), 1948-49; advt. account exec. Abilene Reporter News (Tex.), 1949-52; advt., promotion dir. Grissom's Dept. Stores, Abilene, 1952-61; promotion dir. River Oaks Shopping Centre, Abilene, 1961-62; advt., promotion dir. Colberts Dept. Stores, Amarillo, Tex., 1962-66; advt. cons. England's Studio, Dallas, 1967-68; pres., co-owner Wig Imports, Inc., Dallas, 1968-71; v.p. communications Aloe Vera Am. Cosmetics, Dallas, 1972; div. mgr. AVACARE, Inc., 1972—; pres., owner England Enterprises, Dallas, 1974—; regional dir. Direct Success, Inc., 1984—; cons., dir. Charm, Inc. (Charmay); guest instr. Hardin Simmons U., Abilene, 1953-60. Publicity telethon dir. West Tex. March of Dimes Campaign, Abilene, 1956-57; publicity chmn. Diamond Jubilee, City of Abilene, 1956; fund raising chmn. Tex. Soc. Crippled Children, West Tex. Rehab. Ctr., Abilene, 1955-60; dir. Miss Abilene preliminary pageant, 1952-59, West Tex. Fair Queen contest, 1956-58; judge State Miss Tex., 1954-55; nat. del., regional trainer Tejas council Girl Scouts U.S.A., 1964-80. Recipient First Place Float awards City of Abilene, 1955, 56, 57; honored for Nat. Formfit Ad of Yr., 1961, Nat. Formfit Campaign of Yr., 1961. Mem. Advt. Fedn. Am. (dist. dir. 1956-59, silver medal Advt. Fedn. Am.-Printers Ink 1962, first place awards regional Addy contest 1952-66, first place advt. award state contest, 1966), Nat. Assn. Female Execs., NOW, Dallas Advt. League, Beta Sigma Phi (Outstanding Mem. Abilene 1954, 56, Outstanding Mem. Amarillo 1963, Outstanding Mem. Dallas 1972, City-Wide Woman of Yr. 1956, 63, 72, council pres. 1956-58). Office: England Enterprises 9595 Highedge Dr Dallas TX 75238

ENGLAND, SUSAN LOUISE, lawyer; b. Pasedena, Calif., Dec. 20, 1936; d. Henry Joseph and Aletha Marie Schreiner; m. William England, Mar. 13, 1968 (div. Feb. 1978); children—Eleonor Aletha, Rebecca Sue. A.B., U. So. Calif., 1958, J.D., 1961. Bar: Calif. 1962, Wash. 1976. Assoc. Taylor, Heller and Sherman, Los Angeles, 1961-63, Law Office of Frank Heller, Los Angeles, 1963-64; sole practice, Los Angeles, 1964-66; assoc. atty. State Compensation Ins. Fund, South Pasedana and Santa Ana, Calif., 1966-70; judge Workers Compensation Appeals Bd., Santa Ana, 1970-74; pres. Law Offices of Susan L. England, P.C., San Diego, 1977—; instr. Ins. Edn. Assn., San Diego, 1978—; cons. in field. Univ. scholar U. So. Calif., 1954-58. Mem. Calif. Bar Assn. (com. mem. 1981-83, worker's comp specialization com.), Phi Alpha Delta. Republican. Presbyterian. Office: Law Offices of Susan L England 438 Camino del Rio S Suite B 118 San Diego CA 92108

ENGLAND, TERESA NOFFSINGER, lawyer; b. Wichita, Kans., Oct. 1, 1954; d. John William Noffsinger and Helen Marrie (Hughes) Story; m. Daniel Kirk England, Apr. 16, 1983. B.S. cum laude, Kans. State U., 1976; J.D. with honors, U. Denver, 1979. Bar: Colo. 1979. Asst. atty. gen. Colo. Dept. Law, Denver, 1979-80; assoc. counsel Mission Viejo Co., Denver, 1980-82; assoc. firm Davis, Graham & Stubbs, Denver, 1982-85; dir. sales adminstrn. Mission Viejo Bus. Properties, Denver, 1985—. Mem. ABA, Colo. Bar Assn. (conv. com. 1983-84), Denver Bar Assn. (young lawyers conv. com. 1983, 84). Republican. Lutheran. Office: 6 Inverness Ct E Englewood CO 80112

ENGLANDER, CELIA ANN, physician; b. Portsmouth, N.H., Mar. 4, 1944; d. Chester Elmer and Charlotte Winona (Miller) Williams; m. Joseph Morrell Dodge II, Sept. 18, 1964; children—Joseph Morrell III, Jeffers Rhouee; m. David Murray Englander, July 18, 1975; children—Chester Allen, Chip. B.A., Wellesley Coll., 1965; M.D., N.Y. Med. Coll., 1975. Pathology intern NYU Med. Ctr.-Bellevue Hosp., N.Y.C., 1975-76; med. intern U. So. Calif., 1978-79; med. resident Martin Luther King Jr. Gen. Hosp., Los Angeles, 1979-81; fellow hematology-oncology U. Calif.-Irvine, Orange, 1981-83; geriatrics fellow UCLA Sch. Medicine, 1983-85, Andrus Ctr. fellow, 1983—. Sarah Perry Wood med. fellowWellesley Coll., 1974; recipient David T. Spiro Pathology prize N.Y. Med. Coll., 1975. Mem. Am. Med. Women's Assn., Los Angeles County Med. Assn., DAR, Alpha Omega Alpha. Club: Wellesley. Office: 2200 Santa Monica Blvd Suite 112 Santa Monica CA 90404

ENGLANDER, PAULA TYO, lawyer; b. Syracuse, N.Y., Dec. 25, 1951; d. Howard James and Pauline (Henderson) Tyo; m. Ronald Englander, Jan. 24, 1971. B.A. magna cum laude, SUNY-Oswego, 1978; J.D. Syracuse U., 1981. Bar: Colo. 1982. Cons. Orthotic & Prosthetic Assocs., Inc., Syracuse, 1982; law clk. Kintzele & Collins, Denver, 1982; sole practice law specializing in bus. law and litigation, Denver, 1983—; assoc. coordinator export assistance program Fed. Bar Assn., 1983—; founding mem., dir. Orthopedic Techs., Inc., Syracuse, Aurora Orthopedics, Inc., Aurora, Colo. Mem. Onondaga County Environ. Mgmt. Council, Syracuse, 1982. Mem. ABA (data base computer com. 1984—), Colo. Bar Assn. (gen. and small practice sect. 1985—, internat. law com. 1985—), Colo. Women's Bar Assn. Denver Bar Assn., Alliance Profl. Women (founding mem.). Office: Paula Tyo Englander Atty at Law 1321 Delware St Denver CO 80204

ENGLE, JUNE LESTER, library-information management educator; b. Sandersville, Ga., Aug. 25, 1942; d. Charles DuBose and Frances Irene (Cheney) Lester; m. David Stuart Engle, Dec. 22, 1972; 1 child, Anna Elisabeth. B.A., Emory U., 1963, M.Librarianship, 1971; cert. in advanced librarianship Columbia U., 1982. Asst. prof., cataloger U. Tenn. Library, Knoxville, 1971-73; librarian div. library and info. mgmt. Emory U., Atlanta, 1973-81, asst. prof. div. library and info. mgmt., 1976-80, assoc. prof., 1980—. Mem. ALA, Assn. for Library and Info. Sci. Edn. (bd. dirs. 1985—), Ga. Library Assn., Phi Beta Kappa, Beta Phi Mu. Unitarian. Home: 128 Clarion Ave Decatur GA 30030 Office: Div Library and Info Mgmt Emory U Atlanta GA 30322

ENGLISH, BEA LOLA, beauty salon executive, interior decorator; b. Arley, Ala., May 21, 1924; d. Emanuel Robert and Leola (Phillips) Benson; m. Herbert Edwin English, Aug. 19, 1944; children—Patricia Ann, Pamela Gwen. B.A., Modesto Jr. Coll., Supr. women Patterson Frozen Foods, Patterson, Calif., 1948-70; owner interior, gift boutique Busy Bee, Patterson, Modesto, Calif., 1979-82; salon owner Honey Comb, Modesto, 1979-82, 84—. Bd. dirs. Del Puerto Hosp. Found., Patterson, 1980-85. Mem. Patterson C. of C., Wesley C. of C., Modeston C. of C., Stanislaus C. of C., Calif. Cosmetologist Assn. (mem. bd. 1984—). Democrat. Avocations: boating; golf; hiking; travel. Home: 1908 Laurel Oak Dr Modesto CA 95354 Office: Images 2404 E Orangeburg Modesto CA 95355

ENGLISH, DOROTHY LOUISE, med. technologist; b. Rosiclare, Ill., June 14, 1927; d. Walter Pierce and Nina Mae (Lynch) Coram; A.S., Paducah Jr. Coll., 1960; B.S. in Med. Tech., U. Tenn., 1961; m. Ardell English, June 24, 1943 (dec.); 1 dau., Carolyn Sue. Med. technologist Western Bapt. Hosp., Paducah, Ky., 1961-63; asst. chief technologist Med. Center Hosp., Punta Gorda, Fla., 1963-71; chief med. technologist, lab. mgr. St. Joseph Hosp., Port Charlotte, Fla., 1971—. Lic. lab. supr., Fla., cert. bioanalyst lab. dir. Mem. Am. Soc. Clin. Pathologists, Am. Soc. Med. Technologists, Am. Assn. Blood Banks (dir.), Fla. Assn. Blood Banks, Nat. Crediting Agy. Republican. Mem. Ch. of Christ. Home: 4151 Harbor Blvd Port Charlotte FL 33952 Office: 2500 NE Harbor Blvd Port Charlotte FL 33952

ENGLISH, RUTH HILL, artist, educator, art consultant; b. Andover, Mass., Feb. 7, 1904; d. Herbert Hudson and Ada Jane (Wells) Hill; grad. Abbot Acad., Andover; m. A. Evans Kephart, June 28, 1929; children—Susan K. (Mrs. Howard K. Simpson), Katharine K. (Mrs. Christopher R. Barnes); m. 2d, E. Schuyler English, July 4, 1959. Mem. faculty Hampton Inst., 1924-25, Bryn Mawr Art Center (later Main Line Center of Arts), 1945-65, Wayne Art Center, 1947-49; dir. Hedgeabout Studio, Wynnewood, Pa., 1965—; lectr. throughout East, 1960-70. Past mem. women's bd. Pa. Hosp.; mem. women's bd. Babies Hosp., 1934-39. Mem. Hist. Soc. Early Am. Decoration (pres. William Penn chpt. 1950-51), Pa. Craftsmans Guild (dir. 1952-54). Republican. Episcopalian. Clubs: Acorn, Skytop. Home: 47 E Wynnewood Rd Merion PA 19066 also Skytop PA 18357 Studio: 1124 Rose Glen Rd Gladwyne PA 19035

ENGLUND, GAGE BUSH, dancer, educator; b. Birmingham, Ala., Sept. 7, 1931; d. Morris Williams and Margaret Wallace (Gagé) Bush; student Sweet Briar Coll.; student (Ford Found. scholar) Sch. Am. Ballet, 1960; m. Richard Bernard Englund, Dec. 1, 1959; children—Alixandra, Rachel Rutherford. Founder, Birmingham Civic Ballet, 1952; mem. Robert Joffrey Ballet, N.Y.C., 1957-60, soloist, 1959-60; mem. Am. Ballet Theatre, N.Y.C., 1960-63, Huntington Dance Ensemble, L.I., N.Y., 1968-69; soloist Dance Repertory Co., 1969-72; tchr. ballet, assoc. chmn. Friends of Am. Ballet Theatre, N.Y.C., 1972—; mem. scholarship com. Am. Ballet Theatre Sch., N.Y.C., 1974—; dir. Ala. By-products Corp., 1971-77. Bd. dirs. Children's Hosp. Clinic, Birmingham, 1955-57, Spoleto Festival, U.S.A., 1980-83, Ala. State Ballet, 1967——, Birmingham Civic Ballet, 1952-67; trustee Ballet Theatre Found., 1974—, v.p., 1980-81; trustee Episcopal Sch. of N.Y., 1979-83, Chapin Sch., 1982—, Animal Med. Center, N.Y.C., 1982—, Cancer Research Inst., 1984—. Recipient Silver Bowl award Birmingham Festival of Arts, 1955; named Queen of Birmingham Festival of Arts, 1957. Mem. Am. Guild Mus. Artists, Colonial Dames Ala., Jr. League N.Y.C. Episcopalian. Club: Lakewood Country. Home: PO Box 469 Point Clear AL 36564 Office: 326 W 80th St New York NY 10024

ENGLUND, JANET LYNN, lawyer; b. St. Paul, Nov. 17, 1953; d. Curtis John and Priscilla Ruth (Widen) Englund. B.A., Trinity Coll., 1975; J.D., Hamline U., 1978. Bar: Minn. 1979, U.S. Dist. Ct. Minn. 1979. Admitting clk. Luth. Deaconess Hosp., Mpls., 1975-76; law clk. O'Connor & Hannan, Mpls., 1978-79; assoc. Kuduk & Walling, Mpls., 1979-80; fin. analyst, atty. Fed. Land Bank, St. Paul, 1980-81, fin. services coordinator, 1981-82; fin. planning analyst, mgr. IDS/Am. Express, Mpls., 1982-83, regional mgr. fin., 1983-84, mgr. analysis plans devel., 1984—; lectr. fin. planning, 1978—; sole practice law, Mpls., 1979—. Editor Hamline U. Law Rev. Contbr. articles to profl. jours. Vol., dist. coordinator United Way of Mpls., 1981-82, 71; musician local/regional chs., 1971—. Hamline U. Legal Research scholar, 1978. Mem. Christian Legal Soc., Cert. Fin. Planners, Internat. Assn. Fin. Planners, ABA, Ctr. for Law and Religious Freedom, Sigma Nu Phi. Republican. Baptist. Club: Christian Bus. Women's. Home: 5546 Donegal Dr Shoreview MN 55112 Office: IDS/Am Express IDS Tower Minneapolis MN 55402

ENGRAM, BEVERLY LEIGH, state legislator; b. Feb. 2. Mem. Ga. Senate. Democrat. Office: Ga Senate State Capitol Atlanta GA 30334*

ENIS, CAROL ANN, physical education educator; b. Lowell, Mass., Mar. 15, 1947; d. Martin and Alma Elizabeth (Bergsten) Enis; m. Dana Arnold Simpson, Jan. 2, 1983. B.S., Boston U., 1968, M.Ed., 1974. Tchr. phys. edn. Perkins Sch. for Blind, Watertown, Mass., 1967-71; motor specialist Corry Coll., Milton, Mass., summers, 1971-74; tchr. phys. edn. Dana Hall Sch., Wellesley, Mass., 1971—, chmn. phys. edn. dept., 1981—; motor specialist Curry Coll. Lab. Sch., Milton, Mass., 1971-74; co-owner Points North, Inc., Woodstock, N.H., 1974-79. Contbr. articles to profl. jours. Chmn. girls sports Eastern Athletic Assn. for Blind, 1968-69. Mem. Boston Bd. Women's Ofcls. (treas. 1972-74, co-chmn. softball 1974-78). Roman Catholic.

ENIX, AGNES LUCILLE, editorial consultant; b. Drummond, Okla., Jan. 17, 1933; d. James Robert and Alma Frances (Hodges) E. B.S., Okla. State U., 1955; M.S., Northwestern U., 1966. Writer Chgo. Tribune, 1966-67; editor Dallas Mag., 1968-75, Dallas Morning News, 1976-79, Vision Mag., Dallas, 1980-81; editorial cons., Dallas, 1981—. Recipient Katy award Dallas Press Club, 1975-81, Matrix award Women in Communications 1971, SW Journalism Forum award So. Meth. U. 1970, Creativity award Art Direction Mag. 1981, Anson Jones award Tex. Med. Assn. 1971. Mem. Tex. Pub. Assn., Southwestern Booksellers Assn., Southwest Film Video Archives., Buckner Terr. Homeowners Assn. Avocations: bicycling; travel; writing.

ENLOE, JOAN CATHERINE, weight loss counselor; b. Duluth, Minn., Dec. 11, 1931; d. Chester Charles and Mabel Elizabeth (Hyland) Drake; m. Richard Leonard Enloe, Aug. 20, 1950; children—Jeanne, Donald, David, Thomas. B.S. in Bus. Adminstrn., So. Oreg. State Coll., 1972. Owner, mgr. Rogue Office Services, Medford, Oreg., 1968-76; office mgr. Goldberg Furniture, Olympia, Wash., 1976-78; real estate sales rep. Severson Realestate, Medford, 1978; owner, mgr. Diet Center, Medford, 1979—. Pres. So. Oreg. Land Conservancy, Medford, 1982, 83, 84. Mem. AAUW (sec. 1986—), Bus. and Profl. Women (sec. Medford 1982-83). Republican. Club: Altrusa (v.p. Medford 1982-83). Avocations: custom dressmaking and tailoring; cross country skiing. Home: 2271 W Hillside Dr Central Point OR 97502

ENLOW, KAREN LESLEY, community development grants administrator; b. Columbus, Ohio, June 21, 1961; d. George William and Learntene (Branch) Enlow. Student U. Mo., 1979-83. Account rep. Columbia Missourian, 1982; pre-sch. asst. U. Mo.-Columbia Student-Parent Ctr., 1983; field rep. Community Devel. Block Grant Program, State of Mo., Jefferson City, 1983-84, civil rights officer, 1983-84. Sloan fellow, SUNY-Stony Brook, 1984-86. Mem. Women in Communications, Inc. Club: Women's Aglow (Jefferson City). Home: 1503 Chestnut St Jefferson City MO 65101 Office: W Averell Harriman Coll for Policy Analysis and Pub Mgmt SUNY Stony Brook NY 11794

ENNIS, REBECCA LEE, government/economics educator; b. N.Y.C., Mar. 23, 1953; d. Cairn Cross and Virginia (McNary) E. B.A., Stephen F. Austin State U., 1975; M.Ed., U. Houston, 1981. Tchr., chmn. social studies dept. Houston Ind. Sch. Dist.-Yates High Sch., 1976-85, Sharpstown High Sch., 1986—. Mem. Am. Fedn. Tchrs., Nat. Council Social Studies, Tex. Council Social Studies, Houston Council Social Studies. Republican. Presbyterian. Home: 12211 Fondren Apt 808 Houston TX 77035 Office: Houston Ind Sch Dist Sharpstown High Sch 7504 Bissonnet Houston TX 77074

ENOS, ANDREA WORONKA, librarian; b. Boston, Dec. 22, 1940; d. Andrew J. and Mary (Kolba) Woronka; m. Dan S. Enos, Sept. 8, 1969; children—Anastasia, Jennifer. A.A., Colby Jr. Coll., N.H., 1960; B.S., Plymouth State Coll., N.H., 1963; M.Ed., U. N.H., 1971; postgrad. CUNY. Educator, Alvivne High Sch., Hudson, N.H., 1963-70; supervising librarian Haverhill Pub. Schs., Mass., 1970—. Chmn. com. West El PTA, Andover, Mass. Mem. NEA, ALA, Mass. Tchrs. Assn., Mass. Sch. Librarians Assn., Haverhill Tchrs. Assn., Hospice Greater Lawrence. Congregationalist. Avocations: Folk artist; antique dealer. Office: Nettle Sch Library Boardman St Haverhill MA 01830

ENRIGHT, DOROTHY PATE, chemist; b. Blountsville, Ala., Jan. 19, 1922; d. Clarence Judson and Lillie Irene (Tidwell) Pate; m. Lee John Enright, Sept. 20, 1947 (dec.). B.S., U. Ala., 1943; M.S., Pa. State Coll., 1948. Research assoc. Pa. State U., University Park, 1945-52; chemist U.S. Naval Ordnance Lab., Silver Springs, Md., 1953-60; engr. Tex. Instruments, Inc., Dallas, 1960-63; chemist Dow Chem. Co., Indpls., 1964-65; instr. research Washington U. Sch. Medicine, St. Louis, 1965-66; research assoc. Milchem. Inc., Houston, 1967—. Patentee inhibition of swelling shales, 1974, drilling fluid additive, 1981, 82, copolymer for filtration control, 1981; contbr. articles to profl. jours. Recipient Meritorious Civilian Service award U.S. Navy, 1959. Mem. Soc. Petroleum Engrs., Keramos, Sigma Xi, Sigma Delta Epsilon, Iota Sigma Pi. Home: 5446 Jackwood St Houston TX 77096 Office: MilPark 7000 Hollister Rd Suite 30 Houston TX 77040

ENRIGHT, JANICE MARIE, med. clinic ofcl.; b. San Jose, Calif., Jan. 2, 1951; d. John George and Antoinette H. (Burgos) Lesch; student West Valley Jr. Coll., 1969-71; m. David Enright, Nov. 18, 1980. 1 son, Jason Aaron Baca. Emergency room clk. O'Connor Hosp., San Jose, 1967-73; auditing sec. Ernst

& Whinney, San Jose, 1974-76; exec. sec. San Jose Med. Clinic, 1976—. Vol. worker Muscular Dystrophy Telethon, San Jose, 1974-76, O'Connor Hosp., 1965-66, San Jose Bicentennial Celebration, No. Calif. chpt. Hosp. Fin. Mgmt. Assn., 1976-78; sec. Econ. Opportunity Commn., 1965-66. Notary public, Calif. Mem. Exec. Women Internat., Nat. Assn. Exec. Secs. Address: 17781 Cherokee Trail Los Gatos CA 95030

ENSOR, JOAN ELIZABETH, government official; b. Arlington, Va., Mar. 24, 1944; d. Leonard Joel and Doris Elizabeth (Hindman) E.; 1 child, Courtney Lynne. B.A., Westhampton Coll., 1966. Service rep. Va. Electric Power Co., Richmond and Fairfax, 1966-68; pub. health analyst Pub. Health Service, HHS, Arlington, 1968-73, program analyst Social Security, Balt. and Arlington, 1973-77, program analysis officer, 1977—. Recipient awards U.S. Govt., 1968—. Democrat. Avocations: sewing; writing; poetry. Home: 3013 Strathmeade St Falls Church VA 22042 Office: Dept Health and Human Services 3833 N Fairfax Dr Arlington VA 22203

ENTMAN, BARBARA SUE, broadcaster, writer, photographer; b. Glen Cove, N.Y., Sept. 24, 1954; d. Bernard Entman and Rose (Jacobson) Entman Pachter; B.A., U. Conn., 1976. Freelance writer/photographer, 1975—; announcer, publicity dir. Sta. WHUS-FM, Storrs, Conn., 1975-76; announcer, copywriter Sta. WKAJ-AM-FM, Saratoga Springs, N.Y., 1976-77; traffic coordinator Sta. WMHT-FM, Schenectady, 1977-79; ops. dir. Sta. WNIU-FM, DeKalb, Ill., 1980-82; ops. mgr. Sta. KUHF, Houston, 1982—; media cons. Ill. Heart Assn., DeKalb, 1982, Sojourner Women's Bookstore, DeKalb, 1980-81; exhibited fine arts in galleries and univs., 1970—; contbr. articles and poetry to mags. and newspapers. Newsletter editor Congregation Aytz Chayim, Houston, 1983-84; founder DeKalb Area Women's Network, 1981; bd. dirs., newsletter editor Art Resources Open to Women, 1977-79; mem. Chgo. Artists Coalition, 1981-82; mem. mems. adv. bd. Houston Women's Caucus for Arts, 1985—; del. Tex. Democratic Conv., 1984, 86. Mem. Houston Ctr. Photography, Art League of Houston, Cultural Arts Council Houston, NOW, ACLU.

EPHRON, NORA, author; b. N.Y.C., May 19, 1941; d. Henry and Phoebe (Wolkind) Ephron; B.A., Wellesley Coll., 1962; m. Carl Bernstein, Apr. 14, 1976 (div.); children—Jacob, Max. Reporter, N.Y. Post, 1963-68; freelance writer, 1968—; contbg. editor, columnist Esquire mag., 1972-73, sr. editor, columnist, 1974-78; contbg. editor N.Y. mag., 1973-74. Mem. Writers Guild Am., AFTRA, Authors Guild. Author: Wallflower at the Orgy, 1970; Crazy Salad, 1975; Scribble Scribble, 1978; Heartburn, 1983; author screenplay: Heatburn, 1986; co-author screenplay: Silkwood, 1983. Address: care Lynn Nesbit ICM 40 W 57th St New York NY 10019

EPP, MARY ELIZABETH, software engineer, consultant; b. Buffalo, Aug. 7, 1941; d. John Conrad and Gertrude Marie (Murphy) Winkelman; m. Harry Francis Epp, Aug. 31, 1963. B.A. in Math., D'Youville Coll., 1963; M.S. in Math., Xavier U., 1974, M.B.A. in Fin., 1981. Systems analyst Gen. Electric, Evendale, Ohio, 1965-71; techniques and ops. mgr. Palm Beach Co., Cin., 1972-73; hardware systems engr. Procter & Gamble, Cin., 1973-76; systems engr. CalComp Inc., Anaheim, Calif., 1980-84; software engr. SDRC Inc., Cin., 1984-86; sr. software engr. Burke Mktg. Services, Cin., 1986—; cons. Shelley & Sands, Zanesville, Ohio, 1983-85. Contbr. articles to profl. jours. Mem. Fairfield Charter Rev. Commn., 1981-83. Mem. AAUW (br. treas. 1975-79, state women's chair 1979-80, state treas. 1980-82), Nat. Assn. Female Execs. Republican. Roman Catholic. Clubs: Mercy Hosp. Aux. (treas. 1978-79), Musical Arts Club. Avocations: bridge; skiing; music; fishing; travel. Home: 4900 Pleasant Ave Fairfield OH 45014 Office: Burke Mktg Services 800 Broadway Cincinnati OH 45202

EPPERT, LORNA MAE, nursing home administrator, nurse; b. New Albin, Iowa, July 22, 1931; d. Frank Louis and Kathryn Marie (Moore) Hurley; m. Gerald Lee Eppert, Feb. 11, 1956; children—James, Steven, Mark, Lynn, Dale. B.S. in Nursing, U. Cin., 1971, M.S. in Nursing, 1974. Lic. nursing home adminstr., Ohio. Staff nurse Good Samaritan Hosp., Cin., 1957-64, evening supr., 1964-85, staff nurse, 1985—; instr. nursing U. Cin., 1974-78, asst. prof., 1978-81; vis. asst. prof. nursing Miami U., Hamilton, Ohio, 1985—. Served to 1st lt. USAF, 1953-56. Mem. Am. Coll. Health Care Adminstrs., Nat. League Nursing. Republican. Roman Catholic. Avocations: rafting, sewing, reading. Home: 6721 Schuster Ct Cincinnati OH 45239 Office: Miami U Hamilton Campus Hamilton OH 45011

EPPES, MAVIS, law firm records manager; b. Teague, Tex., Jan. 31, 1937; d. Rich and Ruth (Haynie) E. Student Sam Houston State U., 1955-58. Records mgr. Vinson & Elkins, Houston, 1959—; curriculum adv. com. records mgmt. N. Harris County Coll., 1983, 85. Recipient Records Mgmt. award The Office, 1982. Mem. Assn. Records Mgrs. and Adminstrs. (info. mgmt. achievement award Houston chpt. 1982, award of Achievement 1984, pres. 1986-86, internat. chmn. legal services industry action com. 1985-87), Soc. Descendants of Francis Epes I Va. Republican. Baptist. Home: 1310 Springrock Ln Houston TX 77055 Office: Vinson & Elkins 1001 Fannin 2968 First City Tower Houston TX 77002

EPPLEY, FRANCES FIELDEN, educator, author; b. Knoxville, Tenn., July 18, 1921; d. Chester Earl and Beulah Magnolia (Wells) Fielden; m. Gordon Talmage Cougle, July 25, 1942; children—Russell Gordon, Eppley, Carolyn Eppley Horseman; m. Fred Coan Eppley, Mar. 8, 1953; 1 child, Charlene Eppley Sellers. B.A. in English, Carson Newman Coll., 1942; M.A., Winthrop Coll., 1963. Tchr., East Corinth (Maine) Acad., 1942-43; tchr. pub. schs., Charlotte, N.C., 1950-53, 59-83, Greenville, S.C., 1954-56, Spartanburg, S.C., 1957-58; head start tchr., summers 1964-68. Mem. hist. com. N.C. Bapt. Conv., 1985-86. Alpha Delta Kappa grantee, 1970. Mem. NEA, N.C. Social Studies Conf., Writers Assn., Alpha Delta Kappa, Pi Kappa Delta, Alpha Psi Omega. Baptist. Author: First Baptist Church of Charlotte, North Carolina: Its Heritage, 1981; History of Flint Hill, 1983; The First Astrologer, 1983; Sammy's Song, 1984; No Show Dog, 1985; Sun Signs for Christians, 1985; (mus. drama): The Place To Be, 1982; (mus. show): Songs of The People, 1983; (song): Katie, 1985, (cantata) How Come, Jesus?

EPPS, BARBARA ANNE, city official; b. Englewood, N.J., July 17, 1941; d. Roy Sherman and Lillian Grace (McCloud) Watson; student U. Ill., Navy Pier, 1959, Roosevelt U., 1967, 85—. Adminstrv. asst., labs. applied scis., lab. astrophysics and space research U. Chgo., 1959-69, asst. compensation mgr., personnel office, 1969-76; salary adminstrn. specialist Montgomery Ward and Co., Chgo., 1976-79, corp. wage adminstrn. mgr., 1979-84; personnel analyst Chgo. Transit Authority, 1985—; asst. developer compensation plan Provident Hosp., 1970. Recipient HEW award, 1977. Mem. Coll. and Univ. Personnel Assn., Am. Soc. Profl. and Exec. Women, Delta Sigma Theta. Episcopalian. Home: 4800 S Chicago Beach Dr Apt 1111N Chicago IL 60615 Office: Mdse Mart Chicago IL 60654

EPPS, MAVIS CINDY, equal employment opportunity specialist; b. Washington, July 2, 1944; d. Maceo Livingston and Viola Ernestine (Livingston) Churchill; m. Julian Epps, Sr., Dec. 10, 1983; children—Rondella, Patricia, Alvin, Jr., Maceo. M.Ed., Antioch U. Inst. Open Edn., 1980. File clk. N.Y. Life Ins. Co., N.Y.C., 1962-63, jr. clk. and typist, 1963-65; sec./timekeeper Vulcan Basement & Waterproofing Co., Patterson, N.J., 1966; clk.-typist N.Y. State Div. Employment Security, New Rochelle, 1967, Mass. Div. Employment Security, Boston, 1969-70; officer mgr. Ecumenical Center, Boston, 1970-71; sec., adminstrv. asst. Roxbury Multi-Service Center, Boston, 1971-79, employment counselor, 1979-80; regional affirmative action dir. Dept. Mental Health, Boston, 1980-81; equal employment opportunity specialist Perini Corp., Framingham, Mass., 1981—; tchr. South End Adult Edn. Program, Boston, 1983—; cons. Girl Scout Council, Danvers, Mass., 1980, Dept. Mental Health, Lawrence, Mass., 1982. Recipient Merit award Mass. Bay United Way, 1975; Outstanding Staff award Roxbury Multi-Service Center, 1977. Mem. Am. Assn. Affirmative Action Profls., Martin Luther King Parent Bd. (chmn. 1978-79), St. John's Parent Bd. (pres. 1972-73). Home: 8 Shafter St Dorchester MA 02121 Office: Perini Corp 73 Mt Wayte Ave Framingham MA 01701

EPSTEIN, BARBARA, editor; b. Boston, Aug. 30, 1929; d. H.W. and Helen (Diamond) Zimmerman; children—Jacob, Helen. B.A., Radcliffe Coll., 1949. Co-editor N.Y. Rev. of Books, N.Y.C., 1963—. Office: New York Review 250 W 57th St New York NY 10019

EPSTEIN, BEE J., consultant, professional speaker; b. Tubingen, Germany, July 14, 1937; came to U.S., 1940, naturalized, 1945; d. Paul and Milly (Stern) Singer; student Reed Coll., 1954-57; B.A., U. Calif., Berkeley, 1958; M.A., Goddard Coll., 1976; Ph.D., Internat. Coll., 1982; m. Leonard Epstein, June 14, 1959 (div. 1982); children—Bettina, Nicole, Seth. Bus. instr. Monterey Peninsula Coll., 1975—; owner, mgr. Bee Epstein Assocs., Cons. to Mgmt., Carmel, Calif., 1977—; pres. Success Tours Inc., Carmel, 1981—; founder, prin. Monterey Profl. speakers, 1982; instr. Monterey Peninsula Coll., Golden Gate U., U. Calif., Santa Cruz, Am. Inst. Banking, Inst. Ednl. Leadership, Calif. State Fire Acad. Monterey Peninsula Coll., U. Calif.-Berkeley, Foothill Coll., U. Alaska. Author: The Working Woman's Stress First Aid Handbook; contbr. articles to newspapers and trade mags. Research grantee, 1976. Mem. Nat. Speakers' Assn., Am. Soc. Tng. and Devel., Nat. Assn. Female Execs., Peninsula Profl. Women's Network, Calif. Tchrs. Assn. Democrat. Jewish. Office: PO Box 221383 Carmel CA 93922

EPSTEIN, FRAN ANDRON, personnel administrator; b. Oceanside, N.Y., July 3, 1955; d. Arnold I. and Shirley Andron Wallace; B.S. with distinction, Cornell U., 1977; M.Ed., Harvard U., 1978; postgrad. U. San Francisco. Asst. dir. career planning Ithaca (N.Y.) Coll., 1978-79, dir. career planning, 1979-81; staff mem. Nat. Career Devel. Project, Walnut Creek, Calif., 1981; personnel mgr. REMAC Systems, San Jose, Calif., 1981-82; asst. dean students Mills Coll., Oakland, Calif., 1981-82; employee relations and tng. mgr. Bay View Fed. Savs., San Mateo, Calif., 1983-86; mgr. human resources Nimbus, Inc., 1986—. Mem. Nat. Vocat. Guidance Assn. (mem. com. on occupational status of women), Am. Soc. Tng. and Devel., Am. Psychol. Assn., Assn. Advancement Behavior Therapy, Am. Assn. Counseling and Devel., Bay Area Personnel Assn. Contbr. articles to profl. jours. Editor: Career Counseling and Placement, 1980-81. Home: 5025 Gerhardt Pl Fair Oaks CA 95628

EPSTEIN, HARRIET ANNE, promotion agency executive; b. Newark, Apr. 19, 1943; d. Louis and Shirley (Rabinowitz) Rosenblatt; m. Henry Michael Epstein, June 10, 1962; children—Sheryl Lynn, Robin Beth. Student Fairleigh Dickinson U., 1961-62. Pub. relations exec. Bamberger's, Paramus, N.J., Wayne, N.J. and Nanuet, N.Y., 1974-76; pres. SOAPS ALIVE!, Paramus, 1976—. Contbg. editor Soap Opera Digest, 1983-84. Fund raiser Juvenile Diabetes Found., Chgo., Phila., 1984-85, Am. Cancer Soc., N.J., 1985; organizer program U.S. Dept. Transp. on drinking and driving, Springfield, Mo., 1984, others. Mem. Nat. Acad. TV arts and Scis., Internat. Council Shopping Ctrs., Broadcasters Promotion Assn. Office: Soaps Alive 256 Beechwood Dr Suite 228 Paramus NJ 07652

EPSTEIN, HARRIET PIKE, state official; b. N.Y.C.; d. Samuel and Sonia (Kuchinok) Pike; m. Stanley H. Epstein; children—Lois N., Susan A. B.A. cum laude, NYU. Newspaper reporter Newsday, Garden City, N.Y., 1956-60; free-lance writer, 1961-69; pub. relations exec. Townsend Communications Inc., Syosset, N.Y., 1970-75; mng. editor L.I. Bus. Rev., Plainview, N.Y., 1975-80; v.p. Howard Rubenstein Assocs., N.Y.C., 1980-81; dir. communications N.Y. State Assembly Ways and Means Com., Albany, 1981—. Contbr. articles to various newspapers. Pres. Princeton Park Civic Assn., Jericho, N.Y., 1963-65. Mem. L.I. Women's Network (membership chmn. 1980-82), N.Y. Women in Communications, Phi Beta Kappa. Club: L.I. Press. Office: NY State Assembly Ways and Means Com Room 923 Legislative Office Bldg Albany NY 12248 Also: 303 E Park Ave Long Beach NY 11561

EPSTEIN, JUDITH ANN, lawyer; b. Los Angeles, Dec. 23, 1942; d. Gerald Elliot and Harriet (Hirsh) Rubens; m. Joseph Irving Epstein, Oct. 4, 1964; children—Mark Douglas, Laura Ann. A.B., U. Calif.-Berkeley, 1964; M.A., U. San Francisco, 1975, J.D., 1977. Bar: Calif. 1978, U.S. Supreme Ct. 1983. Social services worker Sutter County Welfare, Yuba City, Calif., 1964-66; dir. indsl. devel. Marysville C. of C. (Calif.), 1967-68; extern clk. Calif. Supreme Ct., San Francisco, 1977; assoc. firm Crosby, Heafey, Roach & May, Oakland, Calif., 1977-85; mem., v.p. dir., 1985—; dir. Sierra Pacific Steel, Hayward, Calif. Contbr. articles to legal publs. Bd. dirs. v.p. Oakland Ballet, 1980—; mem. Internat. Host Com., Oakland, 1980—. Mem. Law Rev., U. San Francisco, 1977. Mem. ABA, Queen's Bench. Democrat. Jewish. Club: Berkeley Tennis. Office: Crosby Heafey Roach & May 1999 Harrison St Oakland CA 94612

EPSTEIN, PHYLLIS GORIN, marketing research executive; b. Queens, N.Y., Mar. 6, 1940; d. Louis and Bella (Bialer) Gorin; m. Edward Epstein, June 28, 1958; children—Jeffrey Stuart, Sheryl Lynn, Brian David. B.S. in Elem. Edn., Hofstra U., 1959; M.S. in Remedial Reading, C.W. Post Coll., 1974. Cert. reading specialist, N.Y. Tchr., Island Trees Sch. Dist. (N.Y.), 1959-62; substitute tchr. Island Trees and Syosset Dists. (N.Y.), 1963-72; reading tutor, 1973; tchr. reading CETA, Port Washington, N.Y., 1974; field dir. Edward Epstein & Assocs., Syosset, 1974-76, exec. v.p., 1976—; vis. lectr. NYU Sch. Continuing Edn., N.Y.C., 1980, 81. Vice pres. PTA Council, Syosset, 1972; pres. Split Rock Elem. Sch. PTA, Syosset, 1971. Mem. Market Research Assn. (N.Y./Northeast chpt.; pres. 1982-83, bd. dirs. 1981—), Market Research Assn. (moderator, panelist, speaker various confs. 1979—, Appreciation of Services award 1979-83). Am. Mktg. Assn., Council Am. Survey Research Orgn. Democrat. Jewish. Home: 140 Split Rock Rd Syosset NY 11791 Office: Edward Epstein & Assocs Inc 420 Jericho Tpke Jericho NY 11753

EPSTEIN, SARAH GUNY, library media specialist; b. Providence; d. Maurice and May (Guny) Epstein; student R.I. Coll. Edn., 1943-45, U. Miami, Coral Gables, 1955; B.A., U. R.I., 1957; M.L.S., Pratt Inst., 1958. Asst. catalog dept. Providence Pub. Library, 1946-55; library media specialist George J. West Elem. Sch., Providence, 1958—. Mem. ALA, Am. Assn. Sch. Librarians, (state assembly del. 1974-75), New Eng. Ednl. Media Assn., R.I. Sch. Media Assn. (treas. 1963-65), R.I. Library Assn., Pratt Inst. Grad. Library Sch. Alumni Assn. Jewish. Home: 36 Lincoln Ave Providence RI 02906 Office: 145 Beaufort St Providence RI 02908

EPSTEIN, SELMA, pianist; b. Bklyn.; m. Joseph Epstein, 1950. Grad. Juilliard Acad. Debut as concert pianist Carnegie Hall, N.Y.C., 1942; pianist numerous concerts, recitals and symphonies; recorded numerous albums; composer piano pieces. Most recent recital: Donnel Library, N.Y.C., 1985 (UN Day Program); numerous lecture-recitals including univs. and profl. orgns. Lectr., U.S. Info. Service, Europe, Australia, Japan, Hong Kong, Okinawa, New Zealand, introducing music of U.S. 20th Century composers, women and black composers. First American to teach full time at an Australian Conservatory, Newcastle Conservatory, 1972-75. Founder of Group Piano Studios and author of 8 group teaching manuals. Co-founder Md. Women's Symphony; founder, bd. dirs. Chromattica USA Chamber Music Group of Balt. Mem. Am. Grainger Soc. (pres.), Internat. Congress Women in Music (bd. dirs. Mid-Atlantic region). Club: West Point Parents' (founder 1979). Address: Epstein House 2443 Pickwick Rd Dickeyville MD 21207

EPSTEIN, SUSAN DERMAN, public health administrator; b. N.Y.C., Apr. 9, 1948; d. Sidney C. and Sheila R. (Pollock) Derman; m. Matthew S. Epstein, May 9, 1971; children—Dale Judith, Andrew Jacob. B.A., Conn. Coll., 1970; M.Pub. Adminstrn., U. N.H., 1975. Adminstrv. asst. planning and budget N.Y.C. Health Services Adminstrn., 1970-71; sr. planner Mass. Dept. Youth Services, Boston, 1971-73; exec. dir. Newmarket Regional Health Ctr. (N.H.), 1975-76; asst. chief med. services N.H. Dept. Health and Welfare, Concord, 1976-77; program dir. United Health Systems Agy., Concord, 1977-81; dep. dir. pub. health services State of N.H., Concord, 1981—; cons. in field. Treas., sec. N.H. Civil Liberties Union, Concord, 1976-81; del. N.H. Democratic Conv., Manchester, 1978; chmn. med. care adv. com. N.H. Dept. Health and Welfare, 1979-81. Jewish. Club: West Concord Garden (treas. 1983-84). Office: State of NH Public Health Services Hazen Dr Concord NH 03301

EPSTEIN, SUZANNE PAULINE, computer marketing executive; b. Watsonville, Calif., Nov. 7, 1951; d. Lloyd Anthony and Myrtle Effie (Kliewer) Lettis; m. Dan Lester Masdeo, Feb. 22, 1975 (div. 1980); m. Allan Epstein, May 30, 1982; children—Aaron Justin, Aimee Mikhaile. B.A. in Indsl. Psychology, U. Calif.-Berkeley, 1972, M.B.A. in Mktg. Mgmt., 1981. Mgr. selling services Macy's Dept. Store, San Francisco, 1972-74; Saleswoman Better Homes Realty, Hayward, Calif., 1974-76; product mgr. Berkeley Bio-Engring., San Leandro, Calif., 1975-79; advt. mgr. Cooper-Med., Mountain View, Calif., 1979-81, mktg. mgr., 1981-83; dir. bus. devel. Cooper Lasersonics, Santa Clara, Calif., 1983-84; dir. mktg. and internat. sales Formaster, San Jose, Calif., 1984-85; cons. Bus. Devel. Assocs., Fremont, Calif., 1985—. U. Calif.-Berkeley Alumni scholar. Mem. Nat. Assn. Female Execs., Am. Mktg. Assn., U. Calif. Bus. Alumni Assn., Calif. Scholarship Fedn., Phi Beta Kappa. Democrat. Jewish.

ERB, DONNA ELAINE, lawyer; b. North Platte, Nebr., Sept. 26, 1955; d. Donald Leon and Bettymae (Miller) E. B.A., U. Nebr., 1977; J.D., U. Mich., 1980. Bar: Calif. 1980. Assoc. Weissburg & Aronson, Los Angeles, 1980-83; asst. v.p., corporate counsel Am. Med. Internat., Inc., Beverly Hills, Calif., 1983—. Mem. ABA, State of Calif. Bar Assn., Los Angeles County Bar Assn., Phi Beta Kappa. Office: Am Med Internat Inc 414 N Camden Dr Beverly Hills CA 90210

ERB, PHYLLIS, chemical engineer; b. Milw., Aug. 7, 1941; d. Ernest Wilhelm and Mary (Anderson) Erb; B.S. in Chem. Engring., U. Wis.-Madison, 1964. Research engr. DuPont Co., Wilmington, Del., 1964-70, advt. rep. for indsl. chem., synthetic films, x-ray testing products, 1970-73; tech. rep. x-ray products, N.Y.C., 1974-77; sales mgr. Celanese Corp., Charlotte, N.C., 1977-80; advt. mgr. Ga.-Pacific Corp., Atlanta, 1980-83, dir. communications chems., 1984—. Active campaigns for gov. Del. R. Peterson and P.S. DuPont; active Young Republicans N.C.; sec. Carriage Post Condominium, N.J., 1975, 76; controller Sir Johns Hill Condominium, N.C., 1977-80; bd. dirs. Chamber Music Soc., Charlotte, 1979. Mem. Internat. Assn. Bus. Communicators, Soc. Plastics Engrs., Atlanta Women's C. of C., Am. Chem. Soc., Formaldehyde Inst. (communications com.), Chem. Mfrs. Assn. (energy task force). Home: 4 Pointe Terr Atlanta GA 30339 Office: 133 Peachtree St Atlanta GA 30303

ERBACHER, KATHRYN ANNE, writer, editor; b. Kansas City, Mo., Dec. 11, 1947; d. Philip Joseph and Thelma Lillian (Hines) Erbacher; m. Howard John Pankratz, Jr., Aug. 20, 1981. B.S. in Edn., U. Kans., 1970; B.A. magna cum laude in Art, Metro State Coll., Denver, 1983. Reporter, Kansas City Star (Mo.), 1970-71; newswriter Washington U., St. Louis, 1972-76; copy editor Kansas City Star-Times (Mo.), 1976-79; editor Petro-Lewis Corp., Denver, 1979-82; assoc. Artours, Inc., Denver, 1983-84; assoc. editor arts and travel editor Denver Mag., 1984-86, arts columnist, 1986—; freelance writer, editor, 1986—. Creative dir. TV shorts for contemporary art collection Denver Art Mus., 1983. Recipient award for arts writing Denver Partnership, 1986. Mem. Women in Communications (jobs chmn. Denver 1981-82). Home: 142 Jackson Denver CO 80206

ERBE, YVONNE MARY, marketing specialist, educator; b. Wausau, Wis., Nov. 18, 1947; d. Rudolf Anthony and Lucille Virginia (Andrew) Karlen; m. Drake H. Erbe, June 26, 1971; children—Daniel, Heather. B.Mus.Edn., U. Wis., Madison, 1969; postgrad. U. Wis.-Milw. Lic. music educator, Wis. Music-vocal tchr. Bayport Jr. High Sch., Greenbay, Wis., 1969-70; tchr. bassoon, oboe U. Wis.-Greenbay, 1969-70; jr. high choral dir. Kenosha Unified Schs., Wis., 1970-76; univ. supr.-edn. U. Wis.-Parkside, Kenosha, 1976-78; mktg. specialist Metro Prodns., La Crosse, Wis., 1984-85. Mem. parent adv. com. No. Hills Sch., Onalaska Pub. Sch. System, Wis., 1981—, parent vol. coordinator Fauver Hill Sch., 1983-84; sec. exec. bd. Gt. River Festival of Arts, La Crosse, 1982-83, 1st v.p. exec. bd., chmn. adult choral workshop and performance, chmn. swing choir workshop, 1983-84, pres. bd. dirs., 1984-85; pres. La Crosse Area Newcomers Club, 1982-83; tchr. Confraternity of Christian Doctrine, 1981-82, pres., 1985—, bd. dirs. La Crosse Boy Choir, 1985—. Roman Catholic. Avocations: tennis; cross-country skiing; aerobic exercises; needlecrafts; gourmet cooking. Home: 520 16th Ave N Onalaska WI 54650

ERICH, DOROTHY BEATRICE, nurse; b. Chillicothe, Ohio, Oct. 4, 1915; d. Oliver Gustave and Daisy Mae (Orr) E.; R.N., Bethesda Hosp., 1941; B.Th., Olivet Nazarene Coll., 1953. Nurse, Ft. Hamilton Hosp., Hamilton, Ohio, 1953-55, Chillicothe Hosp., 1955-60; orthopedic nurse Mt. Logan Sanitorium, Chillicothe, 1960-70; nurse surgery Greenfield (Ohio) Hosp., 1970-73; nursing cons. Gospel Light Nursing Home, Kingston, Ohio, 1980-84; part-time preacher in youth work. Mem. Am. Nurses Assn. Mem. Nazarene Ch. Republican.

ERICHSEN-HUBBARD, ISABEL JANICE, educator; b. LaCrosse, Wis., June 18, 1935; d. Frank Peter August and Janice May (Grutzmacher) Erichsen; B.S. with honors, U. Wis., Madison, 1957, M.S., 1979, postgrad., 1980; m. Allan Paterson, Apr. 4, 1959; children—Janel Isabel, John Allan. Tchr., Kenosha (Wis.) Bd. Edn., 1957-60; tchr., supr. Madison (Wis.) Bd. Edn., 1968—; cooperating tchr. sr. program U. Wis. master tchr. seminars, 1978—; pvt. piano and vocal coach, 1950—; choir dir. St. Mary's Lutheran Ch., Kenosha, 1959-61. Program chair YWCA, 1961-65; chmn. UNICEF, 1960, Camp Nursery Sch., 1960; info. chmn. Am. Cancer Soc., Dane County, 1960-68; active Methodist Women's Soc., United Ch. Women, Madison Civic Assn., Opera Buffs, Wis. Exec. Mansion Guides, Wexford Homeowners Assn. Recipient Carol award Madison Jaycette Club, 1966, 3d grand prize Wis. State Jour. Cookbook, 1971. Mem. Am. Ednl. Research Assn., NEA, Wis. Edn. Assn., Madison Tchrs., Inc., Lafollette Area Lang. Arts Cadre, Madison Met. Sch. Dist. Human Relations Cadre, U. Wis. Alumni Assn. (life), Sigma Alpha Iota (Sword of Honor, past pres.), Chi Omega (alumni sec.), Phi Lambda Theta, Pi Kappa Delta. Methodist. Clubs: Cherokee Country, Jr. Golf (dir. 1974-75), Eastern Star. Author: Reading Techniques Using the Newspapers, Magazines, 1975; Spell It Again Sam, 1978; Hidden Curriculum, 1979; contbr. to Kenosha Kindergarten Teacher's Handbook, 1958. Home: 26 E Newhaven Circle Wexford Village Madison WI 53717-1051 Office: 2421 E Johnson St Madison WI 53704

ERICKSEN, ANNA MAE, nursing administrator; b. Moose Jaw, Sask., Can., Nov. 1, 1919; d. Eric Andrew and Evelyn (Kyle) E.; R.N., Deaconess Hosp., Spokane, Wash., 1943. Night charge nurse Deaconess Hosp., Spokane, 1943, pvt. duty nurse, 1946, staff nurse, 1947; head nurse emergency dept., outpatient dept., Spokane Poison Center, Deaconess Hosp., 1948-57, supr., 1957-70, asst. dir., 1970-73, assoc. dir. nursing service, 1973-78, adminstrv. asst. regional out research services, physician liaison, 1978, asst. to adminstr., dir. outreach program, coordinator continuing edn., 1978-82, dir. Spokane Poison Center, dir. physician liaison, 1979-82; dir. outreach program Physician Liaison and Reg. Poison Ctr. Deaconess Med. Ctr., 1982—; chmn. disaster com., mem. safety com.; advisor to Wash. State Assn. Nursing Students, 1956-60; bd. dirs. Regional Emergency Med. Services Council, 1975—, 1st v.p., 1978-79, chmn., 1979—; mem. N.E. Hosp. Disaster Com., Gov.'s ad hoc com. Emergency Med. Services, Emergency Med. Ambulance Pier Com., Emergency Med. and Ambulance Review Com., Review Com. for Tng. Emergency Med. and Paramed. Technicians; bd. dirs. Nat. Poison Center Network. Mem. Spokane Health Assn.; v.p. NE Heart Assn.; recruitment nurse for ARC in Inland Empire, 1960-68; bd. dirs. Spokane Area Safety Council, 1963-67, vice chmn., 1966-67; bd. govs. Home Safety Council Wash. State, 1966-69, v.p., 1969-70; bd. dirs. NE chpt. Wash. State Heart Assn., 1966—, v.p., 1974-75; polio fund com. Spokane County Med. Soc.; chmn. adv. bd. Rape Crisis Network 1978, 1980, 1982-84; program chmn. Spokane Youth Health Council; bd. dirs. Human Tng. Services Inst., Spokane, 1974-80, sec.-treas., 1976-77; mem. panels United Crusade; panel mem. campaign com. United Way, 1978-81; active Polio Program, 1962-69; adv. bd. Samaritan Ctr. of Inland Empire, 1981-85. Served to capt. Nurse Corps, U.S. Army, 1943-46. Named Spokane Woman of Achievement, Am. Bus. and Profl. Women, 1961, Theta Sigma Phi, 1968, Wash. State's Most Involved Nurse, 1970, Outstanding Lady of Year, Spokane, 1972; recipient Key award Inland Empire chpt. Safety Council, 1976, disting. citizen award Rotary Club of Spokane, 1982, 1st Ericksen award for emergency nursing, 1985; award of appreciation Am. Lupus Soc., 1985. Mem. Inland Empire (bd. 1956-60), Wash. State (bd. dirs. 1959-63, pres. 1960-64, chmn. careers com. 1970-72), Am. (del. 1960-62, 64), Emergency Dept. (founder Inland Empire chpt., pres. 1971, region X rep., 1970-77, asst. exec. dir. 1972, nat. pres. 1975-76, nat. bd. dirs. 1970-77) nurses assns., Spokane Greater Community Found., 1978—. Presbyterian. Clubs: Altrusa (pres. 1965-68), Epsilon Sigma Alpha (pres. Spokane chpt. 1960-62, treas. 1958-59, mem. state coms.). Home: 2311 W 16th Ave Apt 70 Spokane WA 99204 Office: Deaconess Med Ctr-Spokane W 800 Fifth Ave PO Box 248 Spokane WA 99210-0248

ERICKSON, CATHY ELIZABETH, cable company executive, ski instructor; b. Augusta, Ga., Oct. 9, 1958; d. Carl Max and Lou Ann (Holsing) Erickson. Student Allegheny Coll., 1976-78; B.A. in English Lit., Ohio U., Athens, 1980. Sales rep. Omnicom of Mich. Inc., Plymouth, 1981, sales mgr., Hamtramck, 1981-82; v.p., gen. mgr. Capital Cities Cable of Ind., Inc., Greenwood, 1982—; ski instr. Ski World, Inc., 1985—. Co-founder Com. on Peaceful Existence, Athens, Ohio, 1980; recruiter Informal, Capital Cities Affirmative Action Plan, 1982—. Mem. Cable TV Adminstrv. and Mktg., Nat. Cable TV Assn., Ill.-Ind. Cable TV Assn. (bd. mem. 1985-88), Greater Greenwood C. of C. (2d v.p., legis. and small bus. affairs 1983-86). Democrat. Presbyterian. Avocations: guitar; write music; singing; acting; traveling; entertaining. Office: Capital Cities Cable of Ind Inc 2520 Endress Pl Greenwood IN 46142

ERICKSON, CHARLOTTE HELEN, consultant, author; b. Los Angeles, May 3, 1930; d. Kurt William and Helen (Rall) Zimmer; m. Howard Lee Erickson, Nov. 23, 1951; children—Kenneth, Russel, Daniel. Student U. Ill., 1948-50. Pres. Erickson & Erickson Cons., Bensenville, Ill., 1985—; cons. Beatrice Foods, Chgo., Sunbeam, Oakbrook, Ill., Charmglow, Bristol, Wis.; advisor Fenton High Sch., Bensenville, 1985. Author: (cookbooks) The Freezer Cookbook, 1968, The Working Person's Cookbook, 1979, The Complete Barbeque, 1984. Mem. Midwest Soc. Profl. Cons. Lutheran. Home and Office: 4 N 324 Briar Ln Bensenville IL 60106

ERICKSON, DEBORAH LYNN OLDENBURG, nurse, educator; b. Benton Harbor, Mich., Dec. 2, 1954; d. Howard Elton and Joan Kay (Ackerman) O.; B.S. in Nursing, U. Mich., 1977; M.S. in Nursing, Vanderbilt U., 1980. Staff and charge nurse Meml. Hosp., St. Joseph, Mich., 1977-78; traveling collegiate sec. Alpha Delta Pi Sorority, Atlanta, 1978-79; part-time staff nurse Vanderbilt U. Hosp., Nashville, 1980, Greenview Hosp., Bowling Green, Ky., 1982-85; asst. prof. nursing Western Ky. U., Bowling Green, 1980-85, coordinator assoc. degree nursing program, 1984-85, mem. dept. nursing adv. com., 1984-85; staff nurse ICU/CCU, Pekin Mem. Hosp., Ill., 1985-86; instr. nursing Methodist Med. Ctr. Sch. Nursing, Peoria, Ill., 1986—. Mem. steering com. Coronary Club affiliate Am. Heart Assn., 1982. Recipient Dorothy Shaw Leadership award Alpha Delta Pi, 1977; U. Mich. Regents Alumni scholar, 1973; Sawyer Community Assn. scholar, 1974, 75, 76; Panhellenic Achievement Award scholar, 1976; Alpha Delta Pi 125th Anniversary scholar, 1979; Vanderbilt U. Sch. Nursing trainee, 1979-80. Mem. Am. Nurses Assn., Ky. Nurses Assn., Nat. League for Nursing, Am. Assn. Critical Care Nurses, Sigma Theta Tau (Bradley U. chpt. sec.), Alpha Delta Pi (pres. U. Mich. chpt. 1975-76). Home: 2 Lisa Ct Pekin IL 61554 Office: Meth Med Ctr Sch Nursing 221 NE Glen Oak Peoria IL 61636

ERICKSON, DENISE ANN GRIFFIN, lawyer, army officer; b. Boston, Apr. 19, 1952; d. Edward John and Margaret Ann (Ryan) Griffin; m. Robert Charles Erickson, Jr., Aug. 9, 1980; 1 son, Robert Charles III. B.A. in Polit. Sci., Boston U., 1974; J.D., New Eng. Sch. Law, Boston, 1978. Bar: Mass. 1979, U.S. Ct. Mil. Appeals 1980, U.S. Supreme Ct. 1983, U.S. Ct. Mil. Rev. 1983. Commd. 1st lt. U.S. Army, 1980, advanced through grades to capt., 1980; prosecutor Aschaffenburg, W.Ger., 1980-81, legal asst. officer, 1980-81, claims officer, 1980-81, def. counsel, 1981-82, sr. def. counsel, 1982-83, govt. appellate counsel, Falls Church, Va., 1983—. Nuclear surety officer, mem. child protection and placement services, mem. women's adv. com., Aschaffenburg, 1980-82. Recipient Community Service award Aschaffenburg Mil. Community, 1980. Mem. Mass. Bar Assn., Boston Bar Assn., Fed. Bar Assn., ABA, Assn. Trial Lawyers Am. Roman Catholic. Home: 7475 DeMille Ct Annandale VA 22003

ERICKSON, DOROTHY ANNE, construction company executive, construction management consultant; b. Portola, Calif., Dec. 17, 1932; d. Stanley N. and Virginia (Blair) Bailey; divorced; children—Elizabeth, Michael, Susan Blair. Student Sacramento City Coll., 1951. Sec. FHA, Sacramento, 1958-59, Edward R. Bacon, Oakland, Calif., 1961-69; office mgr. safety Homer J. Olsen, Inc., Union City, Calif., 1969-80; owner, operator D Enterprises, San Ramon, Calif., 1980—; exec. v.p. Nationwide Constrn. Cons., Inc., San Francisco, 1984—. Editor Constrn. Hi-Lights, 1981—. Contbr. articles to newspapers, 1981-85. Recipient cert. Met. Transit Authority, San Francisco, 1982. Mem. Women Constrn. Owners and Execs., U.S.A. (sr. v.p.), Nat. Assn. Women in Constrn. (Mem. of Yr. 1974), Associated Gen. Contractors (bd. dirs.), Am. Soc. Safety Engrs. (nat. sec. constrn. div. 1981-84). Democrat. Avocations: traveling; reading; entertaining; walking. Office: Nationwide Constrn Co Inc PO Box 265 San Ramon CA 94583

ERICKSON, GAIL, lawyer; b. Pasadena, Calif., Feb. 9, 1934; d. Alfred L. and Helen (Baker) E. B.A., Stanford U., 1955; J.D., Harvard Law Sch., 1958. Bar: N.Y., 1959. Lawyer W.R. Grace & Co., N.Y.C., 1958-84, v.p., assoc. gen. counsel, 1984—. Mem. ABA. Democrat. Club: Harvard (N.Y.C.). Office: WR Grace & Co 1114 Ave of Americas New York NY 10036

ERICKSON, JANE B., speech communications educator, consultant; b. Grosse Pointe, Mich., Apr. 7, 1945; d. Deverr and Nettie Marie (Ballard) Turrell; m. Mark Kevin Erickson, Aug. 14, 1976; 1 child, Kathryn DeVere. A.A., Highland Park Community Coll., 1965; B.S., Eastern Mich. U., 1967; M.Ed., Wayne State U., 1974. Tchr. English and drama Lake Shore Schs., St. Clair Shores, Mich., 1967-69, tchr. English and debate, 1969-73, coordinator, 1973—; pvt. ednl. cons., Utica, Mich., 1974—; puppeteer Mattel Toys, Sterling Heights, Mich., 1986. Vol. sr. citizens, St. Clair Shores, 1985-86. Recipient Forensic award Detroit Free Press, 1962-63; Key to City award St. Clair Shores, 1963. Mem. Nat. Indian Edn. Assn., Mich. Indian Community Edn. Assn. (sec.-treas.), Kappa Delta Pi, Pi Lambda Theta. Avocations: puppetry; music; reading; travel; quilting; brainstorming. Office: Lake Shore Schs 30401 Taylor Saint Clair Shores MI 48082

ERICKSON, JEANNE HOLLAND, pharmacist, business executive; b. Warroad, Minn., Nov. 17, 1921; d. Edward James and Henrietta (Berglund) Holland; m. Martin A. Erickson, June 21, 1941; children—Martin III, Kirk E., Marilyn J. Student Macalester Coll., 1939-40; B.S. in Pharmacy, U. Minn., 1946; postgrad. Cornell U., 1958. Registered pharmacist, Minn. Analyst Minn. Bd. Pharmacy, Mpls., 1943-46; pharmacist in charge Holland Pharmacy, Warroad, Minn., 1946-56, Heritage Pharmacy, Warroad, 1975—; staff pharmacist Olson Bros. Pharmacy, Edina, Minn., 1966-71; mgr. Rembrandt Pharmacy, Edina, 1971-75; mem. adv. com. Minn. Bd. Pharmacy, 1973; v.p. Warroad Heritage, Inc., retail sales-rental property, 1975—; pharmacy cons., mem. infection control com. Warroad Care Ctr., 1979—. Leader Girls Scouts U.S.A., Minn. and N.Y.; v.p. PTA, Wanaka, N.Y., 1962; dir. religious edn. Hamburg Schs. Release Time Edn., N.Y., 1963-66; crusade chmn. Erie County unit Am. Cancer Soc., Hamburg, 1965. Recipient Hall of Fame award Rembrandt Corp., Cert. of Appreciation Warroad Care Ctr., 1985. Mem. Am. Pharm. Assn., Nat. Assn. Retail Pharmacists, Am. Soc. Hosp. Pharmacists, Minn. Pharm. Assn. (del. 1972-74), Am. Legion Aux., U. Minn. Alumni. Lodge: Order of Eastern Star. Avocations: boating; swimming; music; flying. Office: Warroad Heritage Inc 321 E Lake St Warroad MN 56763

ERICKSON, MILDRED BRINKMEIER, emeritus university dean, counseling consultant; b. Hannibal, Mo., Sept. 8, 1913; d. Louis C. and Anna G. (Schmidt) Brinkmeier; A.A., Hannibal-LaGrange Coll., 1932; B.S., Northwestern U., 1934, M.A., 1937; Ph.D., Mich. State U., 1968; m. Clifford E. Erickson, June 10, 1937; children—W. Bruce, Marilyn Kay. Tchr., Central Jr. High Sch., Hannibal, 1934-35, Sycamore (Ill.) Community High Sch., 1935-37; asst. instr. Am. thought and lang. Mich. State U., East Lansing, 1963-65, instr., 1965-68, counselor U. Coll., 1965-68, asst. prof. Am. thought and lang., 1968-71, asso. prof., 1971-75, prof., 1975-81, counselor, 1968-75, asst. dean continuing edn., 1972-75, asst. dean lifelong edn. programs, 1975-81, asst. dean and prof. emeritus, 1981—, mem. univ. com. on aging, 1974—, univ. devel. fund com., 1979—; cons. various bus. firms, instns., 1972—; appeared as guest various radio and TV programs, 1970—. Mem. Tng. Plan Adv. Task Force, Mich. Dept. Civil Service, 1979, 84—; mem. citizens budget com. East Lansing Bd. Edn., 1984—; active Mich. Edn. Forum, 1981-83, Mich. Equal Ptnrs in Edn., 1982—, Mich. Arthritis Found., 1979-83, Mich. Health Adv. Council, 1981-83; mem. adv. bd. Lansing Sch. Health Project, 1977, 78; officer Band Parents, 1952-54; bd. dirs. YWCA, East Lansing, Mich., 1950-52, Lansing Women's Bur., 1978—; bd. dirs. Mildred B. Erickson Fellowship in Support of Lifelong Edn. for Women, 1974—, sec., 1974-78, mem. various coms., 1974—. Recipient Maharishi Community award, 1978, Citation of Excellence, Gov. Mich., 1978, Cert. of Recognition, YWCA, 1975; Woman of Yr. award Mich. Assn. Professions, 1980; Service to Lifelong Edn. award Mich. State U., 1980; named lifetime hon. mem. Adult and Continuing Edn. Assn. of Mich. Mem. Am. Personnel and Guidance Assn., Am. Coll. Personnel Assn., Adult Edn. Assn., Nat. Univ. Extension Assn., NEA, Soc. Study of Midwestern Lit., Mich. Women's Studies Assn., Acad. Affairs Adminstrs., Am. Assn. Higher Edn., LWV, Assn. Gen. and Liberal Studies, AAUW (state legis. com. 1981-83, state edn. com. 1983—), P.E.O., Phi Mu, Sigma Alpha Iota (patroness 1971—), Phi Delta Kappa, Pi Lambda Theta (chpt. pres. 1933-35), Sigma Alpha Iota, Phi Kappa Phi (chpt. pres. 1977). Club: Zonta Internat. (Outstanding Community Service award 1981). Author: (with Francoise Murray) The Adult Female Human Being, 1975, 77, 80; contbr. articles on counseling and ednl. research to profl. jours. Home: 511 Wildwood Dr East Lansing MI 48823 Office: 7 Kellogg Center Mich State Univ East Lansing MI 48824

ERICKSON, NANCY SALOME, lawyer; b. Orange, N.J., Sept. 26, 1945; d. George Hugh and Salome Celestia (Brennesholtz) E.; B.A., Vassar Coll., 1967; J.D. (editor-in-chief law rev. 1972-73), Bklyn. Law Sch., 1973; LL.M., Yale U., 1979; 1 dau., Laura. Admitted to N.Y. bar, 1974; assoc. atty. firm Botein, Hays, Sklar & Herzberg, N.Y.C., 1973-75; asst. prof., then assoc. prof. N.Y. Law Sch., 1975-80; vis. assoc. prof. law Cornell U. Law Sch., spring 1980; assoc. prof., then prof. law Ohio State U. Coll. Law, Columbus, 1980—; vis. prof. history NYU, summer 1984; Richard J. Hughes Disting. vis. prof. law Seton Hall Sch. of Law, Newark, 1986—. Mem. Soc. Study Women in Legal History (founder, coordinator 1980), Assn. Am. Law Schs. (newsletter editor sect. women in legal edn. 1978—), Am. Soc. Legal History, Orgn. Am. Historians, Soc. Am. Law Tchrs., Met. Women Law Tchrs. Assn. N.Y.C. (a founder). Author articles on sex discrimination, family law, constl. law. Address: 619 Carroll St Brooklyn NY 11215

ERICKSON, SHARON K., investment broker, tax specialist; b. Mpls., Nov. 14, 1938; d. Ivar Carl and Beatrice Josephine (Wiberg) Erickson; B.A. in Sociology and Psychology, Macalester Coll., St. Paul, 1961; postgrad. in bus. adminstrn., fin. U. Minn., N.Y.U.; div.; children—Kathleen Ann, Deborah Jean, Rebecca Joanne. Chief exec. officer Erickson Motor & Oil Co., Inc., Mpls., 1972—; pres., owner Kabobs, Inc., St. Paul and Edina, Minn., 1972-76; investment broker Prudential-Bache Securities, Mpls., 1977—; cons., seminar speaker in field. Founder Minn. chpt. Alliance Displaced Homemakers, also chmn., regional cons., 1974-77; nat. speaker, local officer, chmn. employment com. Mpls. chpt. NOW, 1972-76; founding mem., mem. steering com. Minn. Women's Polit. Caucus, 1971; Minn. rep. LWV, 1974-75; founder St. Croix Valley Human Rights Com., 1965; exec. com., treas. Epilepsy Found. of Minn., 1982-85; founder, pres. Horizon 100, 1981. Mem. Internat. Soc. Registered Reps., Am. Mgmt. Assn., Minn. Investment Brokers Assn., AMEX Club. Lutheran. Club: Greenway Athletic. Home: 9714 Brighton Ln Eden Prairie MN 55344 Office: 2020 IDS Tower Minneapolis MN 55402

ERICSON, RUTH ANN, psychiatrist; b. Assaria, Kans., May 15; d. William Albert and Anna Mathilda (Almquist) E.; student So. Meth. U., 1945-47; B.S., Bethany Coll.; M.D., U. Tex., 1951. Intern, Calif. Hosp., Los Angeles, 1951-52; resident in psychiatry U. Tex. Med. Br., Galveston, 1952-55; psychiatrist Child Guidance Clinic, Dallas, 1955-63; clin. instr. Southwestern Med. Sch., Dallas, 1955-72; practice medicine specializing in psychiatry, Dallas, 1955—; cons. Dallas Intertribal Council Clinic, 1974-81, Dallas Ind. Sch. Dist., U.S. Army, Welfare Dept., Tribal Concerns, alcoholism, Adv. Bd. Intertribal Council. Fellow Am. Geriatrics Assn.; mem. So., Tex., Dallas med. assns., Am. (life), Tex., North Tex. psychiat. assns., Am. Med. Women's Assn., Dallas Area Women Psychiatrists, Alumni Assn. U. Tex. (Med. Br.), Navy League (life), Air Force Assn., Tex. (life mem.), Dallas (life mem., pres. 1972-73, 82-84) archaeol. socs., C., South Tex. Archaeol. Soc., N. Mex. Archaeol. Soc., Paleopathology Soc., Alpha Omega Alpha, Delta Psi Omega, Alpha Psi Omega, Pi Gamma Mu, Lambda Sigma, Alpha Epsilon Iota. Lutheran. Home: 4007 Shady Hill Dr Dallas TX 75229 Office: 2915 LBJ Freeway Suite 135 Dallas TX 75234

ERINAKES, DOROTHY MAY EDEN, educator; b. Pawtucket, R.I., Dec. 18, 1919; d. Richard William and Isabelle May (Pilblad) Eden; m. Peter C.H. Erinakes, July 10, 1972; children—(by previous marriage) Richard Lucius Trayner, Patricia Florence Trayner Recchia, Dorothy Eden Trayner Newmann, William Wesgarth Trayner, Sarah-Anne Eliza Trayner. B.S., U. Conn., 1967, M.A., 1970, Ph.D., 1980. Tchr., Preston Sch. (Conn.), 1967-70; coordinator spl. edn. Town of Preston, 1969-70; tchr. Lisbon Central Sch., Conn., 1970-71; resource room tchr. Donald Kramer Sch., Willimantic, Conn., 1971-72, Nelson Aldrich Sch., Warwick, R.I., 1972—; resource dir. workshops Conn. Coll., Annhurst Coll. (Conn.), 1971. Active 4-H Clubs; mem. Nat. PTA. Named Miss New Eng., 1935, Miss R.I., 1937. Mem. Council Exceptional Children, Am. Assn. Mental Deficiency, Delta Kappa Gamma. Home: 311 Love Ln Warwick RI 02886

ERLAND, SHIRLEY, nurse; b. N.Y.C., Sept. 24, 1947; d. Endre and Sigrid (Hoiland) Erland; diploma Meth. Hosp. Sch. Nursing, 1968; B.S., Molloy Coll., 1981; postgrad. Adelphia U. Surg. nurse Meth. Hosp., Bklyn., 1968-70; staff nurse J. B. Thomas Hosp., Peabody, Mass., 1971-73; staff nurse Mercy Hosp., Rockville Centre, N.Y., 1973-75, critical care nurse, 1975-78, staff nurse CCU, 1978-86, asst. head nurse, 1986—. Mem. Am. Assn. Critical Care Nurses, Am. Heart Assn., N.Y. State Nurses Assn., Sierra Club, Sigma Theta Tau, Phi Sigma Tau. Club: Sons of Norway. Home: 2120 Wantagh Ave Wantagh NY 11793 Office: 1000 N Village Ave Rockville Centre NY 11579

ERNEST, DORA PAGE, educator; b. Stanton, Ala., July 23, 1926; s. George L. and Lillie Mae (Mull) Grover; m. Gerald R. Page, Apr. 20, 1946 (dec.); children—Sarah Bowles Page Schisel, Allen Page, Ann Page Gafford; m. 2d, Jimmy F. Ernest, July 31, 1959. B.A., Troy State U., 1958. Tchr., Brewton Elem. Sch., 1958-59, Parker Elem. Sch., Bay County, Fla., 1959-69, Northside Elem. Sch., Panama City, Fla., 1969—. Mem. Assn. Bay County Educators, Fla. Teaching Profession, Nat. Tchrs. Assn., NEA. Democrat. Baptist.

ERNOUF, ANITA BONILLA, educator; b. Santurce, P.R., Feb. 22, 1920; d. John and Dolores (Asencio) Bonilla; B.A., Hunter Coll., 1944; M.A., Columbia U., 1946, Ph.D., 1970; m. Edward Ernouf, Feb. 8, 1946 (div. 1985); children—Edward, Roderic. French, Spanish and Portuguese examiner U.S. Postal Service, N.Y.C., 1942-44; research asst., librarian Hispanic Inst. Columbia U., 1945-47; asst. prof. Spanish, Hollins Coll., Va., 1947-60; prof. Longwood Coll., Farmville, Va., 1960-85, prof. emeritus, 1985—, chmn. dept. fgn. langs., 1972-79. Mem. NEA, Longwood Edn. Assn. (v.p. 1981), AAUW (br. pres. 1980-81), Am. Assn. Tchrs. Spanish and Portuguese, Tchrs. French, Tchrs. German, Am. Council on Teaching Fgn. Langs. (pres.), Va. Fgn. Lang. Assn. (pres. 1972-73, pres. elect 1978, pres. 1979).

ERNST, KAREN M., public relations executive; b. Boston, June 23, 1954; d. Donald Charles and Catherine Patricia (Clancy) Ernst, Sr. B.A., Syracuse U., 1976. Pub. relations asst. New Eng. Sch. Law, Boston, 1976-79; staff asst. dedication com. Kennedy Library, Boston, 1979; mus. interpreter John F. Kennedy Library, Boston, 1979-80; campaign press aide Kennedy for Pres., Ind. and Calif., 1980; campaign mgr. Frances Shaine for Gov.'s Council, Manchester, N.H., 1980; pub. info. dir. Mass. Commerce Dept., Boston, 1980-83; corp. communications exec. Fidelity Group, Boston, 1983—. Founding mem., treas. Friends of Kennedy Library, Boston, 1980—; alt. del. Mass. Democratic Conv., Springfield, 1983; active Mass. Spl. Olympics, 1982. Mem. Women in Communications, Mass. Women's Polit. Caucus. Democrat. Roman Catholic. Home: 300 River Apt 7 Weymouth MA 02191 Office: Fidelity Group 82 Devonshire St Suite A4 Boston MA 02109

ERNST, KATHRYN FITZGERALD, management consulting firm executive, author; b. N.Y.C., Nov. 12, 1942; d. Joseph Michael and Helen Ann (Dougherty) Fitzgerald; m. John Lyman Ernst, Dec. 7, 1971 (div. Apr. 1977). B.A. in Econs., Wells Coll., Aurora, N.Y., 1963; postgrad N.Y. U., 1964. Portiolio analyst Donaldson, Lufkin & Jenrette, N.Y.C., 1966-68; asst. v.p. Prentice-Hall, Englewood Cliffs, N.J., 1968-74; v.p. Franklin Watts/Grolier, N.Y.C., 1975-77; mktg. mgr. ITT, N.Y.C., 1977-80: mng. dir. Warburg, Paribas Becker, N.Y.C., 1980-82; pres., owner Ernst Assocs., Inc., N.Y.C., 1982—; editorial adv. bd. com. Boardroom Reports, N.Y.C., 1982—. Author: The Complete Carbohydrate Counter for Eating Out, 1979, The Complete Calorie Counter for Eating Out, 1979; Danny and His Thumb, 1972, Mr. Tamerin's Trees, 1978 (Nat. Sci. Tcrh.s award 1979), Owl's New Cards, 1979 (ALA-Children's Choice award 1980), Charlie's Pets, 1980, Indians: The First Americans, 1981, ESP McGee & The Mysterious Magician, 1984. Recipient Outstanding Achievement award Fed. Govt., 1966, Pub. Achievement award Christopher Soc., 1973, Acad. Women Achievers YWCA, 1979. Mem. Direct Mktg. Assn. (Echo award 1985), Nat. Assn. Securities Dealers, Women's Econ. Roundtable. Club: Williams. Avocations: bridge, chess, golf, modern art, jazz. Office: Ernst Assocs Inc 59E 54th St Suite 64 New York NY 10022

ERNSTER, SISTER JACQUELYN, College president; b. Salem, S.D., Oct. 3, 1939; d. John Ernster and Eleanor (Bie) Ingalls. B.A., Mount Marty Coll., 1965; M.A., Ind. U., 1969; Ph.D., Ohio State U., 1976. Mem. faculty Mount Marty Coll., Yankton, S.D., 1970-76, v.p. acad. affairs, 1976-83, pres., 1983—; speaker S.D. Commn. on Humanities Pub. Issues Forum, 1980-82. Corp. bd. dirs. Sisters of Sacred Heart Convent, Yankton, 1976-82; trustee Madonna Profl. Care Ctr., Lincoln, Nebr., 1977-82. Mem. editorial bd. Yankton Press and Dakotan, 1984. Bush Found. fellow, 1982-83. Mem. Am. Council on Edn. (nat. identification program 1979, nat. com. on women in higher edn. 1984—), Council for Ind. Colls., S.D. Pvt. Coll. Found., Consortium for Mid-Am. (chmn. deans 1980-81), Delta Kappa Gamma (pres. 1980-82). Club: Interchange (bd. dirs. 1985) (Yankton). Office: Mount Marty Coll 1105 W 8th Yankton SD 57078

ERON, CAROL LEHMAN, author, editor; b. Bryn Mawr, Pa., Jan. 11, 1945; d. Richard Long and Ellen Elizabeth (Walters) Lehman; m. Lawrence Joseph Eron, Jan. 2, 1967; children—Ethan Thornton, Lucy Elizabeth, Amanda Emily. B.A., Douglass Coll., 1966. Asst., then assoc. editor Boston Mag., 1967-70; mng. editor The Phoenix, Boston, 1971-72; asst. editor Washington Post Book World, 1972-74; asst. prof. Boston U., 1974-75. Author: The Virus That Ate Cannibals, 1981. Contbr. articles to newspapers and jours. Mem. Nat. Book Critics Circle, Washington Ind. Writers. Avocations: sailing; gardening; travel. Home: Bethesda MD 20817 Office: Theron Raines 71 Park Ave Suite 4A New York NY 10016

ERRICKSON, BARBARA BAUER, electronic equipment company executive; b. Pitts., Apr. 5, 1944; d. Edward Ewing Bauer and Margaret J. McConnell; m. James Jay Burcham, June 30, 1966 (div. May 1972); children—James Jay II, Linda Lee; m. William Newell Errickson, Apr. 9, 1976; children—David Newell, Amy Beth. B.A., U. Ill., 1966; M.B.A., So. Meth. U., 1981. Programming trainee Allstate Ins. Co., Northbrook, Ill., 1973; program-mer, team leader Motorola, Inc., Chgo., 1974-78; supr. systems Tex. Instruments, Inc., Dallas, 1978-81, product line mgr. worldwide shipping systems, 1981-83, product line mgr. shipping, inventory systems, 1983-84, mgr. mktg. info. systems, 1985, mgr. benefit systems, 1986—; dir., billing/software developer Spring Park Home Owners, Garland-Richardson, Tex., 1983—, fin. chmn., 1986; active Dallas Women's Ctr., 1984—; United Way chmn. mktg. systems Tex. Instruments, 1985. Recipient Women in Leadership cert. YWCA Met. Chgo., 1977. Mem. Am. Mgmt. Assn., Am. Women in Computing, Community Assns. Inst., So. Meth. U. M.B.A. Soc., Beta Gamma Sigma. Republican. Presbyterian. Club: Spring Park Racqette. Avocations: sailing, horseback riding, reading, oil painting. Home: 6702 Lakeshore Dr Garland TX 75042 Office: Tex Instruments Inc PO Box 869305 6500 Chase Oaks Blvd Plano TX 75086

ERRINGTON, SUE ELLEN, community and political organizer; b. Warsaw, Ind., Feb. 15, 1942; d. John S. and Juanita Hope (Wolf) Frederich; m. Paul R. Errington, Dec. 21, 1966; children—Sara Beth, Amy Ellen. B.A., Ind. U., 1964; postgrad. Middlebury Coll., 1964, 1966; M.A., U. Mich., 1965; postgrad. Cath. U., Lima, Peru, 1969, Ball State U. 1977-78. Teaching fellow U. Mich., Ann Arbor, 1964-65; instr. Spanish, Bethany Coll., W.Va., 1965-68; instr. English, Cath. U., Lima, Peru, 1969; instr. Spanish, Ball State U., Muncie, Ind., 1970-72, 76-77, Anderson Coll., Ind., 1970; dir. communications ERA Countdown Campaign, NOW, Oklahoma City, 1981-82; dir. Ind. Now, Ind. Fedn. Dem. Women, Dem. Women in the Running project, 1982-83; field dir. McCarty for Gov. campaign, Ind., 1983-84; campaign mgr. Friends Phil Sharp, Ind. 2nd Congl. Dist., 1984; cons. L&B Broadcasting, Muncie, Ind., 1985—, Planned Parenthood of East Central Ind., 1985—. Vol. coordinator Delaware County, Ind. Senate candidates, 1978, 83, Birch Bayh U.S. Senate campaign, 1979-80, mem. steering com. Edward Kennedy presdl. primary campaign, 1980; mem. campaign com. Mary Alice Cherry for Mayor, 1983; vice precinct com., 1979-80; del. Dem. Nat. Conv., 1980, State Convention, 1980, 84; active Unitarian Universalist Ch. of Muncie, 1975—. Co-dir. grant Ind. Commn. for Humanities, 1975-76. Mem. Planned Parenthood of East Central Ind. (bd. dirs, chmn. pub. affairs com. 1976-82, Muncie adv. com. 1985—, co-chmn. spl. gift campaign 1985), Phi Beta Kappa, Phi Sigma Iota, Alpha Lambda Delta. Avocations: aerobics; reading; music. Home: 3200 Brook Dr Muncie IN 47204

ERVIN-CARR, CHARLESETTA YVONNE, educator; b. Seattle, June 10, 1946; d. Charles Woodrow and Christene Rosetta (Griffin) Ervin; B.A. in Speech and English, U. Wash., 1969, M.Ed., 1971; 1 son, David Anthony Carr. Tchr. Seattle Public Schs. Dist. 1, 1971—; instr. Seattle Central Community Coll., part-time, 1977—; instr. U. Wash., Seattle, 1979—; instr. North Seattle Community Coll., part-time, 1984—; tng. and employee devel. cons. City of Seattle, 1981—; owner, cons. Effective Communication Skills, Seattle, 1980—. Bd. dirs. Shades of Beauty, Seattle, 1979—. Mem. Am. Soc. Tng. and Devel., AAUW, Black Profl. Educators of Greater Puget Sound, Nat. Council Negro Women (Seattle sect.), Council on Black Am. Affairs, Women's Profl. and Managerial Network, Nat. Assn. Female Execs., Delta Kappa Gamma. Office: PO Box 18965 Seattle WA 98118

ERWIN SAUVÉ, JACQUELINE ANNMARY, management consultant; b. Toledo, Dec. 21, 1943; d. Elwood Jack and Marie Erwin; m. Daniel Sauvé. B.S. in Indsl. Relations and Humanities, U. Toledo, 1980; grad. Am. Bankers Assn. Sch. Bookkeeper, Toledo Automobile Club, 1965-69; compensation specialist Questor Corp., Toledo, 1976-79; personnel dir. People's Jewelry Co., Toledo, 1976-79; asst. dir. tng. Toledo Trust Co., 1979-81; owner, cons. Comprehensive Profl. Services, Toledo, 1981—; facilitator U. Toledo seminars. Bd. govs. Rescue/Crises Services. Mem. Internat. Assn. Personnel Women (nat. dir., past pres. Toledo chpt.), Am. Soc. Tng. and Devel., Am. Soc. Personnel Adminstrn., Am. Compensation Assn., Toledo Indsl. Recreation and Employee Services Council (exec. dir., past pres.), Toledo Personnel Mgmt. Assn. (dir.), Hotel and Motel Assn. (dir.), Profl. Network (exec. dir.). Republican. Lutheran. Contbr. articles to profl. jours. Office: 800 Washington Toledo OH 43624

ESAKI, AMY ITSUMI, lawyer; b. Hilo, Hawaii, Apr. 3, 1955; d. James Umetaro and Chiyoko (Mori) Ishii; m. Clement Teruo Esaki, July 21, 1979; children—Ryan Akira, Stephen James Kiyoshi. B.B.A., U. Hawaii, 1977; J.D., U. Oreg., 1980. Bar: Hawaii 1980. Law clk. to county council, Lihue, Hawaii, 1980-81; 3d dep. county atty. County of Kauai, Lihue, 1981-84; pvt. practice law, 1984—. Mem. ABA, Hawaii Bar Assn., Kauai Bar Assn. (sec. 1983—), Anahola Japanese Community Assn., Beta Alpha Psi, Beta Gamma Sigma, Phi Kappa Phi, Phi Delta Kappa. Democrat. Office: 1981 Hulali Loop Kapaa HI 96746

ESAU, KATHERINE, retired botanist, educator; b. Ekaterinoslav, Russia, Apr. 3, 1898; naturalized. Ph.D., U. Caif., 1931, LL.D. (hon.), 1966; D.Sc. (hon.), Mills Coll., 1962. Instr. botany, jr. botanist U. Calif.-Davis, 1931-37, asst. prof., asst. botanist, 1937-43, assoc. prof., assoc. botanist, 1943-49, prof., botanist, 1949-63; prof. botany U. Calif.-Santa Barbara, 1963-65, emeritus prof. botany, 1965—; Prather lectr. Harvard U., 1960. Guggenheim fellow, 1940. Fellow Am. Acad. Arts and Scis.; mem. Nat. Acad. Sci., AAAS, Swedish Royal Acad. Sci., Am. Philos. Soc., Bot. Soc. Am. (pres. 1951). Address: Dept Biol Sci U Calif Santa Barbara CA 93106*

ESCALANTE, MILLIE MARGARETTE, nursing educator; b. Long Beach, Calif., Jan. 24, 1939; d. George B. and Millie N. (Doyle) Williams; m. Frank R. Escalante, Sept. 28, 1966; children—Kathleen Ann and Christina Marie (twins). R.N., Loma Linda U., 1961, B.S. in Nursing, 1961, diploma in pub. health nursing, 1961; diploma teaching Santa Barbara U., 1975, Calif. Luth. Coll., 1975; B.M.S., Am. Nat. Inst., 1984. R.N., San Bernardino County Hosp. (Calif.), 1962; pub. health nurse Los Angeles City Health Dept., Hollywood/Glendale areas, 1962-65; sch. nurse Los Angeles City Sch. Dist., 1965-67; emergency room nurse Los Angeles City Central Receiving Hosp., summer, 1966; sch. nurse Conejo Valley Unified Sch. Dist., Thousand Oaks, Calif., 1967-68, instr. nursing, 1974-82; adminstrv. asst. supr. Los Robles Regional Med. Ctr., Thousand Oaks, 1968-74; instr. nursing Am. Nat. Inst. Agoura Hills, Calif., 1982—; instr. Am. Heart Assn., Thousand Oaks, 1977—, ARC, Ventura, Calif., 1981—. Mem. Booster Club, Thousand Oaks, 1983. Mem. Calif. Vocat. Nurse Educators, Republican. Home: 3139 Calle Quebracho Thousand Oaks CA 91360

ESCALERA, KAREN WEINER, public relations company executive; b. Phila., Dec. 7, 1944; d. George Joseph and Gladys (Lieberman) Weiner; m. Alfonso G. Escalera, Sept. 8, 1978; 1 child, Kent. B.A. cum laude, U. Pa., 1966. Assoc. editor United Bus. Publs., N.Y.C., 1967-68; account exec. Jacobson/Wallace/Westphal, N.Y.C., 1968-69; news and feature editor Hilton Internat. Hotels, N.Y.C., 1969-74, dir. pub. relations western hemisphere, N.Y.C., 1974-79; pres. Karen Weiner Escalera Assocs., N.Y.C., 1979—. Contbr. articles to profl. jours. Mem. Soc. Am. Travel Writers (treas. northeast chpt. 1982-84), Pub. Relations Soc. Am., Hotel Sales and Mktg. Assn., Caribbean Tourism Assn., Caribbean Hotel Assn. Avocations: cultural activities; travel. Office: Karen Weiner Escalera Assocs Inc 555 Madison Ave New York NY 10022

ESCALERA, LYDIA N., insurance company executive; b. San Juan, P.R., Jan. 25, 1936; d. Francisco Navarro and Esperanza Ayala; m. Angel L. Escalera,

Sept. 6, 1957; children—Teresita, Angel L., Alfredo L. B.B.A., U. P.R., 1958. Statistician, Govt. P.R., San Juan, 1958-64; with Blue Cross P.R., San Juan, 1964—, mgr., 1970-71, dir. human resources and indsl. relations, 1971—. Bd. dirs. Jesus de Nazareth Coll., Carolina, P.R., 1973—, PTA, Colegio La Piedad, 1977-80, Camp Bethania, Isla Verde, 1973—; counsellor Club Pro-Cancer Hosps., Rio Piedras. Mem. Am. Soc. Personnel Adminstrn. (program dir. 1981-82), Pub. Relations Mfrs. Assn., Kotten Assocs. P.R. (bd. dirs. 1980—), Execs. Assn. (pres.). Popular Democrat. Roman Catholic. Home: 178 5th St Villamar Isla Verde PR 00913 Office: Blue Cross PR GPO Box 6068-G San Juan PR 00936

ESCHUK, MARY ELIZABETH, educational administrator; b. Daytona Beach, Fla.; d. Lloyd James and Annie (Coleman) Appleby; B.A. in English, Cleve. State U., 1969, M.Ed., 1972, Ed.S., 1979; m. Steven Eschuk, Oct. 22, 1949; children—Holly, Lauren, Steven. Tchr. English public schs., Cleve., Parma, Ohio, 1969-74; dept. head English Normandy High Sch., Parma, 1972-74; asst. prin. Hillside Jr. High Sch., Parma, 1974-76; prin. Schaaf Jr. High Sch., Parma, 1976-82, Parma High Sch., 1982—. NEH grantee, 1981; named Outstanding Educator Ohio PTA, 1981. Mem. Nat. Assn. Secondary Sch. Adminstrs., Ohio Assn. Secondary Sch. Adminstrs. (dir.), Assn. Parma Adminstrs. Co-author, lyricist musical Chicken Little; author, lyricist musicals The Butterfly that Stamped, The Cat that Walked Alone. Home: 7195 Glencairn Dr Parma OH 44134 Office: 5983 W 54th St Parma OH 44129

ESCOBAR, HILDA LOPEZ, nurse practitioner, physician assistant; b. N.Y.C., Aug. 6, 1929; d. Eladio and Josephine (Justiniano) Lopez; A.A.S., Nassau Community Coll., 1967; B.S.N., C.W. Post U., 1975; Adult nurse practitioner, SUNY, Upstate Med. Ctr., Syracuse, 1978; m. John Louis Escobar, Sept. 10, 1949; children—Linda, Michael, Jean. Staff nurse, South Nassau Community Hosp., Oceanside, N.Y., 1967-68; staff nurse Nassau Hosp., Mineola, N.Y., 1968-78, head nurse hemodialysis unit, 1976-78; adult nurse practitioner Community Health Orgn., New Hyde Park, N.Y., 1978—. Certified hemodialysis nurse, 1978; adult health practicioner, 1978. Mem. Am. Assn. Nephrology Nurses and Technicians, Phi Theta Kappa, Sigma Theta Tau. Home: New Hyde Park

ESCRIBANO, ELVIRA AMELIA, consulting engineer company executive; b. Havana, Cuba, Feb. 25, 1945; came to U.S., 1954; d. Alfredo Manuel and Manuela (Lopez) Vizcaino; m. Julio Escribano, July 6, 1963; children—Elvira A., Vivian. Student Akron U. Exec. v.p. J. Escribano & Assocs. Cons. Engrs., Miami, Fla., 1972—. Bd. dirs. Young Patronesses of the Opera, Miami, 1977—; bd. dirs. Telemarathon League Against Cancer, 1975, Am. Heart Assn., Miami, 1979-83, Project Newborn U. Miami, 1979—, pres., organizer 1st Cuban Mus of Arts and Culture outside of a communist country, 1981. Recipient Bronze medal Am. Heart Assn., 1980, Floridana award Cuban Women's Club, Miami, 1981, Outstanding Service award Project Newborn, 1982, award Miami Ballet Soc., 1981. Mem. Latin Bus. & Profl. Women's Club (nominee for Woman of Yr. 1982). Republican. Roman Catholic. Clubs: Cuban Women's, Big 5 (Miami). Office: J Escribano & Assocs 2320 SW 57th Ave Miami FL 33155

ESH, DALIA REGINA, insurance educator, financial planner; b. Jerusalem, May 15, 1950; came to U.S., 1980, naturalized, 1983; d. Jedidya Mizrahi and Orah (Debby) Mizrahi Malka; m. David Esh, Dec. 18, 1948; children—Odelia, Roy. B.A., Bar Ilan U., Tel Aviv, 1972, Teaching Cert., 1976; postgrad. U. Mo.-St. Louis, 1981-82, Washington U., St. Louis, 1983-84. English tchr. Lady Davis Sch., Tel Aviv, 1973-80; Hebrew tchr. Epstein Acad., St. Louis, 1981-82; sales rep. Met. Ins. Co., St. Louis, 1982-85, mktg. specialist, instr., Tulsa, 1985—, originated universal life-term sales concept, 1985. Active Jewish Community Ctrs. Assn., St. Louis, 1984-85. Human resources mgmt. grantee Washington U., 1983; recipient Career Builders award Met. Ins. Co., 1982, Leader's Conf. award, 1984; named to Million Dollar Round Table, 1985. Mem. Nat. Assn. Life Underwriters, Internat. Assn. Fin. Planning, Nat. Assn. Female Execs. Jewish. Avocation: folk dancing. Office: Met Ins Co (CSS) 12902 E 51st St Tulsa OK 74121

ESKEW, SUE ELLEN, nurse anesthetist; b. Chgo., Nov. 13, 1947; d. Robert Edmund and Eleonore Marie (Adams) Michalak; m. Patrick Fredrick Eskew, Jan. 3, 1979; children—Rebekah Sue, Rachel Marie, Patrick III. Diploma in nursing cum laude Los Angeles County Hosp., 1968; diploma with honors Brooke Sch. Aerospace Medicine, 1969; diploma in nursing anesthesiology Charity Hosp. Sch. Anesthesia, 1973; B.A., Ottawa U., 1979. Cert. R.N. anesthetist, lic. pvt. pilot. Charge nurse Los Angeles County Gen. Hosp., 1968-70, St. Joseph Hosp., Burbank, Calif., 1971; staff anesthetist Meth. Hosp., New Orleans, 1973; anesthesia supr. and instr. Baylor Hosp., Dallas, 1973-79; free-lance nurse anesthetist, Dallas, 1979—; flight nurse Air N.G., Van Nuys, Calif., 1968-71, New Orleans, 1971-73; part-time staff anesthetist St. Paul Hosp., Dallas, 1973—. Mem. kick-off campaign Am. Heart Assn., Dallas, 1978; block coordinator Neighborhood Crime Watch, Dallas, 1983; den mother Cub Scouts Am., Dallas, 1980-81, sch. coordinator St. Elizabeth's Dallas, 1981. Served to 1st lt. Air N.G., 1968-73. Mem. Am. Assn. Nurse Anesthetists, Calif. Nurses Assn., Tex. Assn. Nurse Anesthetists (sec. 1974, v.p. 1975, pres. 1976). Republican. Roman Catholic. Home: 3040 Coombs Creek Dallas TX 75233

ESPENLAUB, SHARON KAY JURY, advertising agency executive; b. Bucyrus, Ohio, Apr. 9, 1946; d. Sheridan Windslow Jury and Mary Jane (Hilborn) Jury McCartney; m. Timothy J. Esenlaub, Mar. 16, 1968. Grad. high sch., Wynford, Ohio, 1964. Head dairy clk. Kroger Grocery Co., Marion, Ohio, 1966-72, asst. head cashier, Madisonville, Ky., 1972-77; ptnr. McKee Advt. Spltys., Birmingham, Ala., 1977-83; owner, operator Key To Spltys., Birmingham, 1983—. Mem. Birmingham Advt. Club, Birmingham C. of C., Sunbelt Advt. Splty. Assn. (treas.), Advt. Splty. Inst., Splty. Advt. Assn. Avocations: horses; knitting; stained glass; traveling. Office: Key To Spltys 4019 St John Way Birmingham AL 35215

ESPINAS, GLENDA ZAMUDIO, accountant; b. Daraga, Albay, Philippines, Oct. 7, 1939; came to U.S., 1974, naturalized, 1980; d. Beato Mayores and Purita Amaranto (Zamudio) E.; student in elem. edn. Albay Normal Coll., Legaspi City, Philippines, 1955-56; student in secretarial sci. U. of East, Manila, 1956-57, B.B.A. in Acctg., 1964; 1 dau., Glendalie Espinas Fabia. Personal sec. to project dir. UN Devel. Program, Laguna de Bay Feasibility Study, Manila, 1968-70; sec. Laguna Lake Devel. Authority, Pasig, Rizal, Philippines, 1970-71; sec. Internat. Rice Research Inst., Laguna, Philippines, 1971-74; acct. Kramer Assos., Inc., Washington, 1974-77, also dir. and sec. bd. dirs.; acct. Found. for Applied Research, Inc., 1974-77; acct. Washington Bd. Realtors, 1977-78, dir. fin., 1979-84; acct. Washington Realtors Polit. Action Com., Inc., 1978-84, Washington Home Ownership Council, 1979-84; pvt. practice acctg., 1984—. Vol. telethon, art shows, fund-raising drives Leukemia Soc. Am., Washington, 1979—. Recipient Most Outstanding Betan award Sigma Beta Lambda, 1964. Mem. Am. Soc. Women Accts. (editor D.C. chpt. Capitol Accounts 1979-80, sec. and dir. D.C. chpt. 1981-82, chmn. registration com. Nat. Spring Conf. 1982, v.p. and dir. D.C. chpt. 1982-83, pres. D.C. chpt. 1984-85), Inst. Mgmt. Acctg., Nat. Assn. Accts. (asso. dir. membership D.C. chpt. 1981-83), Internat. Platform Assn. Home: 1414 17th St NW Washington DC 20036

ESPINOZA, REBECCA ANN, municipal official, consultant; b. Pueblo, Colo., Oct. 30, 1952; d. Charles D. and Mary Orlinda (Ortega) E. B.S., U. So. Colo., 1974; M.P.A., North Tex. State U., Denton, 1985. Investigator for Dist. Atty., Pueblo, 1974; pvt. investigator Romar Security, Pueblo West, Colo., 1974-75; urban rehab. specialist City of Dallas, 1975-82, neighborhood rep., 1982-83, mgmt. asst., 1983-85; budget and fin. coordinator Dallas Mcpl. Ct. Judiciary, 1985—; personnel and orgn. cons., 1986—. Author: Guide to Basic Construction, 1983. Dir. Dallas County Rape Crisis Ctr., 1975-78, Central YWCA, 1982-84, Women's Coalition and Women's Issues Network, 1977-84 community chmn. rape edn., coordinator mktg. plan, 1987. Recipient cert. of appreciation City of Dallas, 1982, cert. of recognition, 1983, cert. of appreciation Goals for Dallas, 1985. Mem. Internat. City Mgmt. Assn. (assoc.), Am. Soc. Pub. Adminstrn., AAUW, Urban Mgrs. North Tex., Tex. City Mgrs. Assn., Dallas LWV, Dallas Area Women's Polit. Caucus, Am. Scholars of Phi Beta Kappa. Democrat. Home and Office: 3333 Blackburn St Apt 111 Dallas TX 75204

ESPOSITO, DEBORAH SOULE, photographic products company official; b. Ithaca, N.Y., Sept. 11, 1950; d. Lauren M. and Maureen E. (Casterline) Soule; m. Gerard F. Esposito, Nov. 29, 1975. B.A. in Chemistry, Wells Coll., 1972; postgrad. Rochester Inst. Tech., 1973-74, Carnegie-Mellon U., 1980. With Eastman Kodak Co., Rochester, N.Y., 1972—, ops. mgr., 1980-82, head dept. material inspection 1982-85, program mgr. delivery of corp. tng. programs; cons. and investor real estate. Fundraiser Wells Coll., 1972—. Mem. Nat. Assn. Female Execs., Strong Family Assn. Am. (dir. 1982-85), Bakers Bridge Hist. Soc., Jr. League Rochester (chmn. women's issues 1985-86), Landmark Soc. Western N.Y. Club: Wells (pres. 1974-76) (Rochester).

ESPOSITO, JANICE LYNN, computer programmer; b. New Haven, June 13, 1960; d. Harry Salavatore and Carol Lee (Brousseau) Edwards E. B.S. summa cum laude, in Computer Info. Systems and Math., Quinnipiac Coll., Conn., 1982. Acad. programmer Quinnipiac Coll., Hamden, Conn., 1982-85, CIS instr., 1983—, acad. lab. supr., 1985—; cons. in field. Fund raiser Quinnipiac Coll. Alumni Assn., 1982—. Mem. Nat. Assn. Female Execs., Data Processing Mgmt. Assn. (treas. 1980-81), Conn. Women Higher Edn., Delta Mu Delta. Republican. Roman Catholic. Avocations: camping; traveling. Office: Quinnipiac Coll Mount Carmel Ave Hamden CT 06518

ESPOSITO, MARLENE THERESA MARY, librarian; b. Phila., Oct. 4, 1941; d. Vincent James and Mary Theresa (Taritero) Esposito. B.S. in Edn., Chestnut Hill Coll., 1971; M.S. in L.S., Villanova U., 1981. Joined Sisters of St. Joseph, Roman Catholic Ch., 1959; cert. in edn., library sci., supervision, Pa. Tchr., Our Lady of Rosary Sch., Phila., 1961-67, St. Augustine Sch., Ocean City, N.J., 1967-70, Ascension of Our Lord Sch., Phila., 1970-76; prin. St. Vincent de Paul Sch., Phila., 1976-82; librarian Mt. St. Joseph Acad., Flourtown, Pa., 1982—. Mem. Cath. Library Assn., ALA, Pa. Sch. Library Assn., Pa. Library Assn., Pa. Citizens for Better Libraries, Nat. Cath. Edn. Assn. Democrat. Address: Mount St Joseph Acad Wissahickon and Stenton Aves Flourtown PA 19031

ESPOSITO, PATRICIA, assn. exec.; b. Bklyn., Nov. 28, 1944; d. Charles and Camille (D'Andrea) Butindaro; B.S., L.I. U., 1968; m. Ralph Esposito, July 9, 1966; children—Vincent, Matthew. Bus. edn. instr. N.Y.C. Bd. Edn., 1968-73; free-lance corp. tng. cons., Westchester and N.Y.C., 1973-78; asst. dir. DETO, Scarsdale, N.Y., 1978-80; exec. dir. Plumbing Industry Promotion Fund, Hartsdale, N.Y., 1980—, Westchester Mech. Contractors Assn., 1980—. Mem. Westchester County Pvt. Indsl. Council, 1981—; Westchester County Drought Emergency Task Force, 1981—; chmn. Yorktown Community Devel. Adv. Council, 1980—; co-chmn. Yorktown Youth Council, 1980—; dir. Youth Employment Service, 1974-75. Mem. Am. Soc. Assn. Execs., Nat. Assn. Female Execs., NOW. Home: 435 Yorkhill Rd Yorktown Heights NY 10598 Office: 250 E Hartsdale Ave Hartsdale NY 10530

ESQUELL, MARY LOUISE, insurance company executive; b. San Antonio, May 16, 1952; d. Lee William and Victoria Bernard (Hoffman) Wilson; m. Herschell A. Esquell, July 18, 1970; children—Timothy Andrew, Melissa Diane. Student Austin Bus. Sch., 1968-69. Cert. ins. counselor, Tex. Pres. Tex. Ins. Assocs., Inc., Austin, 1983—; ptnr. Assocs. Leasing and Fin. Services, Austin, 1985—. Mem. CPCU, Ins. Women of Austin (chmn. Austin State Hosp. 1978), Fedn. Ins. Women of Tex., Ind. Agts. Tex., Ind. Agts. of Austin, Profl. Ins. Agts. of Austin, Nat. Assn. Female Execs. Republican. Baptist. Avocations: handwork; sewing; painting; swimming; boating. Home: 5210 Maulding Pass Austin TX 78749 Office: Tex Ins Assocs Inc 4307 S 1st St Austin TX 78745

ESQUIBEL, GLADYS MONTOYA, rehabilitation counselor, consultant; b. Whealand, Wyo., Aug. 6, 1939; d. Mike G. and Celia R. (Romero) Montoya; m. Augustine Esquibel, Feb. 14, 1957; children—Russell, Milton, Gaynol Lee. Student Highlands U., 1959; B.A., U. N.Mex., 1962; Student Southwestern Ednl. Lab., Albuquerque. Social worker Cassia County Schs., Idaho, 1965; exec. dir. Idaho Citizens for Migrant Affairs, 1971; cons. Human Advancement, Boise, Idaho, 1975; paralegal Idaho Legal Services, 1980-84; rehab. counselor Idaho Vocat. Rehab., Burley, 1984—; cons. Minority Assistance Ctr., Boise. Pres. Idaho Citizens for Minority Affairs; chmn. vols. Cassia County Red Cross. Recipient Culture Awareness award, 1972, Hispanic Ministry award, 1983, named Outstanding Precinct Committeewoman. Roman Catholic. Home: 511 Elba Ave PO Box 835 Burley ID 83318

ESSEX, JUDY TOWNE, hospital administrator; b. Jersey City, June 7, 1954; d. John Franklin and Margaret Ida (Miller) Towne; m. Paul Denison Essex, Aug. 7, 1976; children—Kyle Towne, Ryan Denison. B.S., Davis and Elkins Coll., 1976; M.P.A., C.W. Post Ctr., L.I.U., 1981. Cert. tchr. health and phys. edn., N.Y. Natural resource planner Town of Denning, N.Y., 1978-80; substitute tchr. Tri Valley Central Sch., Grahamsville, N.Y., 1980-84; night mgr. New Age Health Farm, Neversink, N.Y., 1982-84; exec. dir. Liberty Community Coalition, N.Y., 1984-86; dir. grants and planning research Community Gen. Hosp. Harris, N.Y., 1986—; exec. bd. dirs. Sullivan Diagnostic Treatment Ctr., Harris, Sec., exec. bd. dirs. Sullivan County Cares Coalition, Liberty, 1985—; chmn. Liberty Internat. Festival and Exposition, Liberty, 1984-85. Mem. Nat. Assn. Female Execs., Sullivan County C. of C. (corr. sec., exec. bd. dirs. 1985—). Avocations: crocheting; skiing; cooking; candy making. Home: Route 1 PO Box 21 Neversink NY 12765 Office: Community Gen Hosp of Sullivan County PO Box 800 Harris NY 12742

ESSMAN, DENISE IRENE, marketing executive; b. Greenfield, Iowa, Mar. 31, 1948; d. Harold William and Eleanor Irene (Johnson) Bricker; m. Allen Kent Essman, June 1, 1968; children: Bradly Allen, Brady Kent, Barrett William. B.S., Iowa State U., 1973, postgrad., 1977-78; M.B.A., Drake U., 1980. Mktg. trainee The Bankers Life, Des Moines, 1975-76; v.p. mktg. Essman & Assocs., 1977—; instr. mktg. Iowa State U., Ames, 1978-79, 81-84; cons. Small Bus. Devel. Ctr., 1984—, instr. mktg. Drake U., Des Moines, 1984—. Com. mem. Des Moines Art Ctr., 1975—. Mem. AAUP, Am. Mktg. Assn. (dir. 1983—, v.p. midwestern region 1983—85, fin. com. 1985-86, mem. activities council 1985-86, chmn. chpt. excellence awards 1985-86), Iowa Mktg. Assn. (dir. 1982-85, treas. 1979-80, v.p. 1980-81, pres. 1981-82), Life Office Mgmt. Assn., Acad. Health Services Mktg. (contbns. and awards judge 1985-86), Nat. Assn. Female Execs. Alpha Mu Alpha (advisor). Democrat. Lutheran. Home: 3008 SW Thornton Ave Des Moines IA 50321

ESSMAN, PANSY ELLEN, manufacturing company executive; b. Anomoose, N.D., Dec. 11, 1918; d. Robert John and Anna (Spivack) Hurt; m. Lewis John Essman, Mar. 29, 1942 (dec. Nov. 1967); children—Caroline Thompson, Katheen Kelly. Aircraft mechanic helper Civil Service, Sacramento, 1940-45; electric assembler, welder Jennings Radio, San Jose, Calif., 1945-67; electronic parts insp. Watkins & Johnson, Palo Alto, Calif., 1967-72; pres., v.p., chmn. bd. Pansy Ellen Products, San Jose, Calif., 1969—. Author: Success Secrets, 1978; Pearls of Potentiality, 1979; subject of Six Figure Women, 1983; patentee infant bath aid. Recipient Oustanding Small Bus. Woman of Yr. award Internat. Council Small Bus. Mgmt. and Devel., 1976; Nat. Ind. Nursery Furniture Retailers Assn. award, 1976. Office: Pansy Ellen Products Inc 7025-A Amwiler Industrial Dr Atlanta GA 30360

ESTEP, M(ARGARET) FRANCES, consumer psychologist; b. Peru, Ind., Feb. 5, 1922; d. Arthur W. and Minnie (Coburn) E. B.S., Purdue U., 1945; M.A., Wayne U., 1948; postgrad. U. Mich., U. Detroit, Wayne U., 1948; Ph.D. (grad. asst.), Ohio State U., 1951. With advt. dept. Procter & Gamble Co., Cin., 1942, mfg. dept., Milan, Tenn., 1943-44; with mfg. dept. Joseph E. Seagram & Sons, Lawrenceburg, Ind., 1946; mem. research staff J.L. Hudson Co., Detroit, 1946-47; instr. and research assoc., mng. editor Indsl. Tng. Abstracts, Wayne U., Detroit, 1947-52; instr. Marygrove Coll., Detroit, 1949; psychologist, mgmt. cons. Roger Bellows & Assocs., Detroit, 1947-53; research psychologist Psychol. Research Service of Pitts., 1954; research and cons. psychologist Winkelman Bros., Detroit, 1955-56; pvt. practice psychology, Detroit, N.Y.C., 1954-57; pres. and consumer psychologist Estep and Assocs., Inc., N.Y.C., 1957—; lectr. psychology CUNY, Queens Coll., 1961-69, CUNY, Hunter Coll., 1970; lectr. Mercy Coll., Dobbs Ferry, N.Y., 1982. Lic. psychologist, N.Y. Contbr. articles to profl. jours.; Co-author textbooks on psychology. Office: 33 Gold St New York NY 10038

ESTER, MARY ELLEN, cosmetologist, cosmetician, esthetician; b. Carey, Ohio, Apr. 26, 1926; d. John Cleveland and Flora Effie Ellen (Snider) Leasure; lic. Cleve. Acad. Cosmetology, 1945; grad. Realtors Inst., U. Mich., 1975; cert. Newspaper Inst. Am., 1980; m. Henry Ester, Aug. 25, 1946; 1 dau., Barbara Rosanne Ester Christensen. Tchr. cosmetology Am. Beauty Sch., Cleve., 1969-70; owner, mgr. Fair Lady Beauty Salon, Fairview Park, Ohio, 1960-70; staff Martin, Ketchum & Martin Inc., Realtors, Livonia, Mich., 1972-76; esthetician, rep. Adrien Arpel Skin Care and Cosmetics, Directives Hair Design, Rocky River, Ohio, 1977—; tchr. adult edn., cons. adult classes Lakewood High Sch. Campaign mgr. local polit. elections, 1959, 63, 71. Mem. Women's Council of Realtors, Bus. and Profl. Women, Nat. Hairdressers and Cosmetologists Assn. Office: Directives Hair Design 20629 Center Ridge Rd Rocky River OH 44116

ESTERLINE, SHIRLEY JEANNE, lithograph company executive; b. Paulding, Ohio, June 6, 1936; d. George Gary and Catherine Genevieve (Durbin) Sontchi; m. Meredith Esterline, Apr. 1, 1956; children—Gordon Alan, Amy Jeanne. Cert. med. technologist, Elkhart U., Ind., 1956. Lab technician, Fort Wayne, Ind., 1956-57; sec. Zollner Corp., Fort Wayne, 1957-58, Magnavox Corp., Fort Wayne, 1958-61; sales coordinator Doty Lithograph Inc., Fort Wayne, 1975-77; sales mgr. Dot Line div. Dot Corp., Auburn, Ind., 1977—. Recipient Top Sales award Dot Corp., 1985. Mem. Specialty Advt. Assn. Internat. (suppliers com. 1983—, cert. advt. specialist 1985—, chmn. 100 club 1983—, facilitator tng. 1985—, CAS Alumni 1985—, mgmt. awards 1984, 85, 86). Methodist. Avocations: reading; gardening. Office: Dot Line 318 E Seventh St Auburn IN 46706

ESTES, CARROLL LYNN, sociologist, educator; b. Fort Worth, May 30, 1938; d. Joe Ewing and Carroll (Cox) E.; A.B., Stanford U., 1959; M.A., So. Meth. U., 1961; Ph.D., U. Calif.-San Diego, 1972; m. Philip R. Lee; 1 child, Duskie Lynn Gelfand. Research asst., asst. study dir. Brandeis U. Social Welfare Research Ctr., 1962-63, research assoc., 1964-65, project dir., 1965-67, vis. lectr. Florence Heller Grad. Sch., 1964-65; research dir. Simmons Coll., 1963-64; asst. prof. social work San Diego State Coll., 1967-72; asst. prof. in residence dept. psychiatry U. Calif.-San Francisco, 1972-75, assoc. prof. dept. social and behavioral scis., 1975-79, prof. 1979—, chair dept. social and behavioral scis., from 1981, coordinator human devel. tng. program, 1974-75, dir. Aging Health Policy Research Center, 1979-85. Mem. Calif. Commn. on Aging, 1974-77; cons. U.S. Senate Spl. Com. on Aging from 1976. Recipient Matrix award Theta Sigma Phi, 1964; award for contbns. to lives of older Californians, Calif. Commn. on Aging, 1977; NIMH spl. fellow for research, 1970-72. Mem. ACLU, Am. Sociol. Assn., Gerontol. Soc., Assn. Gerontology in Higher Edn. (pres. 1980-81), Western Gerontol. Soc. (pres. from 1982), Soc. Study Social Problems, Sociologists for Women in Soc., Alpha Kappa Delta, Pi Beta Phi. Democrat. Author: The Decision-Makers: The Power Structure of Dallas, 1963; co-author: Protective Services for Older People, 1972; U.S. Senate Special Committee on Aging Report, Paperwork and the Older Americans Act, 1978; The Aging Enterprise, 1979; co-author: Fiscal Austerity and Aging, 1983; Long Term Care of the Elderly, 1985, Political Economy Health and Aging, 1984; contbr. articles to profl. jours. Office: Dept Social and Behavioral Scis U Calif San Francisco CA 94143*

ESTES, ELEANOR, author; b. West Haven, Conn., May 9, 1906; d. Louis and Caroline (Gewecke) Rosenfeld; m. Rice Estes, Dec. 8, 1932; 1 child, Helena. Grad. (Caroline M. Hewins scholar 1931), Pratt Inst. Sch. Library Sci., 1932. Children's librarian Free Pub. Library, New Haven, 1924-31, N.Y. Pub. Library, 1932-40. Author: The Moffats, 1941; The Middle Moffat, 1942; The Sun and the Wind and Mr. Todd, 1943; Rufus M., 1943; The Hundred Dresses, 1944; The Echoing Green, 1947; The Sleeping Giant, 1948; Ginger Pye (winer Herald Tribune Spring Book Festival award), 1951; A Little Oven, 1955; Pinky Pye, 1958; The Witch Family, 1960; The Alley, 1964; Miranda the Great, 1967; The Lollipop Princess, 1967; The Tunnel of Hugsy Goode, 1972; Coat Hanger Christmas Tree, 1973; The Lost Umbrella of Kim Chu, 1978; The Moffat Museum, 1983. Recipient Newbery medal for disting. contbn. to Am. lit. for children, 1951; Outstanding Alumni award Pratt Inst., 1969. Mem. P.E.N. Episcopalian. Home: New Haven CT 06511

ESTES, LYNN ANGELIQUE ROE, university administrator; b. Gulfport, Miss., June 24, 1953; d. Charles Alva and Agnes (Gaddy) Roe Adams; m. James Neal Estes, Feb. 18, 1978; 1 dau., Leslie Renee. B.A., U. So. Miss., 1975, M.S., 1981. Admissions counselor U. So. Miss., Hattiesburg, 1976-78; exec. dir. Am. Cancer Soc., Gulfport, Miss., 1978-80; fin. aid-VA-admissions counselor U. So. Miss., Long Beach, 1980-84, dir. student services, 1984—; judge officers' wives scholarship program Keesler AFB, Biloxi, Miss., 1981—; instr. fin. aid workshops Gulf Coast area high schs. (Miss.), 1982—; instr. Miss. Assn. Student Fin. Aid Adminstrs. Workshop, Biloxi, 1982. Performer, Miss. Gulf Coast Opera Theater, 1973—; mem. spl. events com. Miss USA Pageant, Biloxi, 1981, 82; bd. dirs. Miss Gulfport Pageant, 1982; pres. Jaycee Women, Gulfport, 1983-84. Recipient Disting. Service award United Way, Harrison County, Miss., 1982; named to Top Ten Speakers in Nation, U.S. Jaycee Women, 1982, Outstanding Sparkette in Nation, 1983. Mem. Miss. Assn. Student Fin. Aid Adminstrs. (contbg. editor newsletter 1983-84), So. Assn. Student Fin. Aid Adminstrs., Miss. Assn. Collegiate Registrars and Admissions Officers, United Daus. of Confederacy, U. So. Miss. Alumni Assn. (sec. chpt. 1985-86), Omicron Delta Kappa (v.p. 1975-76), Phi Kappa Phi, Phi Alpha Theta, Pi Gamma Mu, Alpha Sigma Alpha (pres. U. So. Miss. chpt. 1975-76, Gulf Coast chpt. 1981-83). Baptist. Office: U So Miss Gulf Park Regional Campus Long Beach MS 39560

ESTES, MARGARET TURNER, university official, educator; b. Caldwell, Kans., July 1, 1924; d. William Jennings Bryant and Margaret Violet (Kern) Turner; B.A., U. Kans., 1965, M.A., 1967, Ph.D. in Sociology, 1972; m. John King Estes, Jan. 13, 1943; (dec.), children—John, Greg, David, Jennifer. Instr., U. Kans., 1965-68; asst. prof. sociology Millersville State U., Pa., 1968-70; asst. prof. anthropology/sociology Haskell Indian Coll., Lawrence, Kans., 1970-71, prof. sociology, chmn. dept. No. Ariz. U., Flagstaff, 1972-78; assoc. v.p. acad. affairs, prof. sociology Miss. State U., Starkville, 1978—. Mem. Gov. Ariz. Commn. Women, 1976, Gov. Ariz. Task Force Marriage and Family, 1976-78. Named Faculty Woman of Year, No. Ariz. U., 1973; Margaret Turner Estes scholarship established, 1978. Mem. Am. Assn. Higher Edn., N.Am. Assn. Summer Sessions, So. Sociol. Assn., AAAS (past dir.), Am. Sociol. Assn., Phi Kappa Phi, Phi Delta Kappa. Democrat. Congregationalist. Office: Drawer BQ Miss State U Mississippi State MS 39762

ESTEVE, MARIA DEL PILAR, petroleum company executive; b. Dallas, Sept. 7, 1954; d. Francisco Javier Esteve and Carmen Sommers Esteve Slaton; m. James Thomas Prokupek, June 20, 1977 (div. Nov. 1980); m. 2d, James Richard Iler, Nov. 20, 1982 (div. 1986). B.C.E., Ga. Inst. Tech., 1976; M.B.A., U. Houston, 1981. Project engr. Owens-Corning Fiberglas, Anderson, S.C., 1976-77; proposal project engr. Black Sivalls & Bryson, Houston, 1977-78; proposal mgr. CE Crest Engring., Houston, 1978, bus. devel. mgr., 1979-81; sr. sales engr. Black Sivalls & Bryson, Houston, 1981-83; div. contracts mgr. Sohio Petroleum Co., Houston, 1983—. Mem. Nat. Assn. Contract Mgrs. (membership com. 1982-84), Am. Petroleum Inst., Soc. Women Engrs. (chmn. Speaker's Bur. 1981-82 sec. Houston sect. 1984-85), Engrs. Council Houston (sect. rep. 1980-81). Republican. Roman Catholic. Office: Standard Oil Petroleum Co 5420 LBJ Freeway Suite 1200 Dallas TX 75240

ESTEY, AUDREE, exec., cons. ballet soc.; b. Winnipeg, Man., Can., Jan. 7, 1910; d. Robert and Anna (Harrington) Phipps; student Immaculate Heart Coll., 1927-29; m. L. Wendell Estey, Sept. 18, 1933; children—Lawrence Mitchell, Carol. Ballet tchr. Lawrenceville and Princeton, N.J., 1938-80, Perry Mansfield Camp, Steamboat Springs Colo., summers 1949-50; head dance dept. Les Chalets Francais, Deer Isle, Maine, 1951-73; founder non-profit Princeton (N.J.) Ballet Soc., 1954, dir., cons.; founder Princeton Regional Ballet Co., 1963; founder profl. co., Princeton Ballet, 1979. Apptd. by gov. N.J. State Commn. to Study Arts, 1968, trustee N.J. Sch. of the Arts, 1980. Recipient Rutgers U. award for contbn. to arts in N.J., 1982. Mem. N.E. Regional Ballet Assn. (pres., 1967-68, exec. v.p., 1968-71). Episcopalian. Choreographer over 20 ballets for children and young dancers including: Festival of the Gnomes, Pastels, Peter and the Wolf, Sleeping Beauty, Cinderella, Pied Piper, The Nutcracker (choreography for Act I currently used by Princeton Ballet), Chanson Innocente, Graduation Ball, Coppelia. Office: 262 Alexander St Princeton NJ 08540

ESTIN-KLEIN, LIBBYADA, advertising executive, medical writer; b. Newark, July 13, 1937; d. Barney and Florence B. (Tenkin) Straver; m. Harvey M. Klein, Sept. 9, 1984. Student Syracuse U., 1955-57; B.S., Columbia, 1960; R.N., Columbia-Presbyn. Med. Center, 1960; certificate N.Y. Sch. Interior Design, 1962. Med. research tech. writer, N.Y.C., 1960-62; pres. Libbyada Estin Interiors, N.Y.C., 1962-65; v.p. advt. and pub. relations Behrman/Estin Inc., N.Y.C., 1965-67; account exec., dir. pub. relations J.S. Fullerton, Inc., N.Y.C., 1967-68; med. writer L.W. Frohlich & Co., Intercon Internat. Inc., N.Y.C., 1968-69, Kallir Philips Ross Inc., N.Y.C., 1969-71; copy supr. William Douglas McAdams Inc., N.Y.C., 1971-75, Sudler & Hennessey Inc., N.Y.C., 1975-80; v.p., exec. adminstr./creative dir. Grey Med. Advt. Inc., N.Y.C., from 1980; founder, ptnr. Estin-Sandler, Communications Inc., N.Y.C., 1984; v.p. Barnum Communications Inc., N.Y.C., 1984-86; sr. v.p. ICE Communications, Inc.,

Rochester, N.Y., 1986—. Mem. Public Relations Soc. Am., Advt. Women N.Y., Am. Advt. Fedn., Am. Med. Writers Assn., Pharm. Advt. Club, Am. Nurses Assn., Allied Bd. Trade, Columbia-Presbyn. Hosp. Alumnae Assn., Syracuse U. Alumnae Assn., Sigma Theta Tau, Delta Phi Epsilon. Home: 289 Garnsey Rd Pittsford NY 14534 Office: 2290 East Ave Rochester NY 14610

ESTLER, ELIZABETH DOWNING, army officer; b. Ames, Iowa, Dec. 30, 1955; d. James Ray and Maria Tulia (Quiros) Downing. m. Gary Lee Estler, May 21, 1983. B.S., Nebr. Wesleyan U., 1975; postgrad. U. Okla. at Canal Zone, 1978-80. Commd. 2d lt. U.S. Army, 1977, advanced through grades to capt., 1981; chief All Source Intelligence Ctr., 1st Inf. Div., Ft. Riley, Kans., 1980-81, 2d brigade asst. sr. intelligence officer, phys. security crime prevention officer, 1981-82; chief Intelligence Collection Mgmt. and Dissemination Ctr., 513th M.I. Group, Ft. Monmouth, N.J., 1983-84; comdr. 174th M.I. Co., Ft. Monmouth, 1984-85; officer Intelligence Communications Security, U.S. Army Europe, Heidelberg, Fed. Republic Germany, 1985—; mem. working women's panel Glamour mag., 1982. Editor 201st Mil. Intelligence Bn. Newsletter, 1983-84. Mem. Junction City-Ft. Riley Ambassadors Program, 1981. Mem. Assn. U.S. Army, Nat. Mil. Intelligence Assn. Minerva Mil. Women Network, Nat. Assn. Female Execs., Mil. Network, Nat. Assn. Female Execs., Roman Catholic. Club: Heidelberg Internat. Ski. Office: PO Box 296 APO NY 09333

ESTRADA, NORMA RUTH, pyschologist; b. Oakland, Calif., Oct. 29, 1926; d. Fred and Evelyn (Costa) Cambra; student Calif. Coll. Arts and Crafts, 1946-47; B.A., Antioch Coll. West, 1975; Ph.D., Union Grad. Sch. West, 1978; m. Marce Estrada, Aug. 22, 1959; children—Jeffrey, Jamie. Adminstrv. asst. research and devel. Gladman Meml. Hosp., Oakland, 1966—, also exec. dir. The Gladman Center, 1975—; co-therapist in pvt. practice Hotel Claremont, Berkeley, Calif., 1972—; bd. dirs. Health Research Found., 1977—. Fellow Menninger Found.; mem. Am. Psychol. Assn., Biofeedback Soc. Am., Am. Assn. Biofeedback Clinicians, Biofeedback Soc. Calif. (dir. 1979-80), AAAS. Democrat. Roman Catholic. Contbg. author: Psychiatry and Mysticism (Stanley Dean, editor), 1975. Office: 2633 E 27th St Oakland CA 94601

ETCHESON, DENISE ELENE, architect; b. Iowa City, Iowa, May 17, 1950; d. Warren Wade and Marianne (Newgent) E.; m. Alejandro Sanchez, May 26, 1984. B.A. in Environ. Design, U. Washington, 1974, Cert. in Urban Design, 1977, M.Arch., 1977. Planner, designer Temel Muhendislik A.S., Istanbul, Turkey, 1974; project designer Astra Zarina Assocs., Seattle, 1973-74, 76-77; project designer, constrn. coordinator G.R. Bartholick Architect/Planner, Seattle, 1975, 78; project mgr. TRA Airport Cons., Seattle, 1978-84; pres. Portico Architects, Houston, 1985—; lectr. U. Wash., 1977. Mem. City of Seattle Pike Pl. Market Hist. Commn., 1975-82, vice chmn., 1977-79, chmn., 1979-81, mem. Landmarks Preservation Bd., 1976-77. Recipient U. Wash. Archtl. Found. award, 1975. Mem. Am. Planning Assn., Historic Seattle Preservation and Devel. Authority, Nat. Trust Historic Preservation, Internat. Council Monuments and Sites. Office: PO Box 60491 Houston TX 77205

ETCHISON, ANNIE LAURIE, librarian, artist; b. Cana, N.C., Dec. 5, 1908; d. John W. and Nana (Cain) E. A.B., Western Res. U., 1939, B.L.S., 1940. Librarian, Cleve. Pub. Library, 1941-42; chief librarian Langley AFB, Va., 1942-44; supervisory librarian U.S. Army, Hawaii, 1945; chief librarian Armed Forces Western Pacific, Philippines, Okinawa 1945-46; command librarian 2d Mil. Dist. U.S. Army, Europe, 1947-48, Hdqrs. U.S. Air Force, Alaska, 1950-52; librarian recruitment Dept. Army, Washington, 1952-54; librarian Dept. Navy, Washington, 1956; chief librarian Ft. Bragg, N.C., 1957-63; staff librarian Hdqrs., 3d U.S. Army, Atlanta, 1963-72; library dir. U.S. Army Europe, 1972-78; cons. automation of libraries and library design. Designed the first computer based library system for post libraries, U.S. Army. Recipient U.S. Army Meritorious Service medal, Armed Forces Achievement citation, 1978. Home: RFD 5 Box 58 Mocksville NC 27028

ETESS, SUSAN LYNN, educational adminstator; b. Syracuse, N.Y., Sept. 19, 1948; d. Abraham David and Elaine (Grossinger) Etess; B.A., Russell Sage Coll., 1970; M.A., Columbia U., 1977, postgrad.; m. Howard Lawrence Zimmerman, Dec. 17, 1979; children—Harron Etess, Andrew Etess. Tchr. social studies Dalton Sch., N.Y.C., 1971-72, coordinator for middle and lower sch. social studies, 1972-76, asst. dir. middle sch., 1975-76, dir., 1976—; project dir. Fischer-Landau Program for Gifted Children with Learning Disabilities, 1984—; adj. prof. dept. supervision and adminstrn. Bank Street Coll. Edn., 1986—. Mem. Nat. Assn. Elem. Prins., Nat. Middle Sch. Assn., Assn. Supervision and Curriculum Devel., Nat. Assn. Ind. Schs., Ind. Sch. Middle Sch. Dirs. Assn. (co-founder N.Y.C.). Home: 60 E 96th St New York NY 10028 Office: 108 E 89th St New York NY 10028

ETHAN, CAROL BAEHR, psychotherapist; b. N.Y.C., May 30, 1920; d. Irving and Sadie (Goldman) Baehr; trained Met. Inst. Psychoanalytic Studies, 1965-70; B.A. in Psychology with honors, N.Y. U., 1978; M.A. in Psychology, New Sch. Social Research, 1981; m. Sy Ethan, Mar. 18, 1955; children—Willa Capraro, Barbara, Ethan. Writer, Irvington (N.J.) Herald, 1946, Walt Framer Prodns., 1949-50; tchr. Queens Coll., 1956-57; consumer psychology researcher and cons., 1950-70; staff psychotherapist Fifth Ave. Center Counseling and Psychotherapy, 1965-70; pvt. practice psychotherapy, N.Y.C., 1967—; columnist Rhinebeck Gazette-Advertiser, 1981—. Democratic committeewoman for Queens County, 1960; vol. social rehab. program Queens County Mental Health Soc., 1965-66; fellow internat. council sex edn. and parenthood Am. U. Recipient Founders Day award N.Y. U. 1978. Fellow Am. Orthopsychiat. Assn.; mem. N.Y. State Assn. Practicing Psychotherapists (cert.), Am. Mental Health Counselors Assn., Divorce Mediation Council, Am. Psychol. Assn., Internat. Acad. Profl. Counseling and Psychotherapy (clin. mem.). Address: 235 W 76th St New York NY 10023

ETHERIDGE, BARBARA RUGA, lawyer; b. Columbia, Mo., Dec. 13, 1952; d. William Joseph and Irene Anne (de Uriarte) Ruga; m. W. Mark Etheridge, Aug. 4, 1973; children—Brian Mark, Erica Darai. B.A. cum laude, U. Mich., 1973, J.D. cum laude, 1977. Bar: Mich. 1977. Assoc., Varnum Riddering Wierengo & Christenson, Grand Rapids, Mich., 1977-82; assoc. gen. counsel Amway Corp., Ada, Mich., 1982—; adj. instr. Grand Valley State Colls., Allendale, Mich., 1982-83; mem. Atty. Grievance Co., Lansing, Mich., 1983-84. Adv. bd. Villa Maria, Grand Rapids, 1982-84. Mem. ABA, Mich. Bar Assn., Grand Rapids Bar Assn. (chmn. young lawyers sect. 1983-84), Fed. Bar Assn., Women Lawyers Assn. Mich. (dir. 1981-82). Roman Catholic. Home: 2009 Wolfboro Dr SE Kentwood MI 49508 Office: 7575 E Fulton Rd Ada MI 49355

ETHIER, PATRICIA KELLEHER, ins. co. exec.; b. Montague, Mass., June 28, 1951; d. Edward Patterson and Mary Elizabeth (Masterson) Kelleher; A.A., Greenfield Community Coll., 1971; student Am. Coll., 1979—; m. Gerard R. Ethier, Aug. 3, 1973. Titlist policy title Phoenix Mut. Life Ins. Co., Greenfield, Mass., 1971-76, supr. group major med. claims, 1976-78, asso. mgr. group claims, 1978-79, mgr. policy title, 1979-82, mgr. new products adminstrn., 1982-85, dir. ins. service systems, 1985—. Allocations chmn. Franklin County United Way, 1980-85, bd. dirs., 1980—; mem. adv. bd. Dept. Social Services, Franklin County, 1981—; bd. dirs. New England Learning Center Women in Transition, 1981—. Fellow Life Office Mgmt. Assn. Roman Catholic. Home: 205 Fairview West Greenfield MA 01301 Office: 101 Munson St Greenfield MA 01301

ETHRIDGE, LURA CLARK, lawyer; b. Greenville, Miss., Mar. 27, 1923; d. Hampton C. and Mossye (Ferguson) Clark; m. William N. Ethridge, III, Dec. 14, 1946 (dec. 1971); children—William N. IV, David F., Paul R., Ruby M., Thomas C. Student Cumberland Coll., 1940-42; B.A., Blue Mountain Coll., 1944; postgrad. U. Miss. Sch. Law, 1957; LL.B., Jackson Sch. Law, 1959. Bar: Miss. 1959. Exec. sec. Miss. State Bar, 1947-48; sole practice law, Jackson, Miss., 1959-64, 77-78; assoc. Brunini, Grantham, Grower & Hewes, 1964-77; social worker St. John's Regional Health Ctr., 1978-80; advocate Tribunal of Roman Catholic bishop Diocese of Springfield (Mo.)-Cape Girardeau, 1980-85. Chmn. Cancer Tea, Jackson, 1961; bd. dirs. Children's Home Soc., Jackson, Hough Home, Jackson, 1970-78. Mem. ABA, Miss. State Bar Assn., Miss. Oil and Gas Lawyers Assn. (v.p. 1970). Roman Catholic. Home: 665 W Roxbury Pkwy West Roxbury MA 02132

ETTINGER, SUSI STEINITZ, artist; b. Berlin, July 29, 1922; came to U.S., 1939, naturalized, 1944; d. Otto and Grethe Steinitz; B.F.A. cum laude, U. Louisville, 1943; m. Manford F. Ettinger, June 2, 1944; children—Linda, Daniel. Staff lectr. Met. Mus. Art, N.Y.C., 1944-45; staff instr., dir. children's classes Springfield (Mo.) Art Mus., 1960-66; instr. and lectr. art S.W. Mo. State U., Springfield, 1964-84, ret., 1984, also former area head found. art program; one-woman shows include: Ft. Smith (Ark.) Art Mus., 1968, Sch. of Ozarks, 1972, 86, Springfield Art Mus., 1976, S.W. Mo. State U., 1980; two-artist shows, Springfield, 1974, 84; exhibited group shows in Ark., Kans., Mo., Nebr., Tenn., 1966—; represented in permanent collections: Mo. Hist. Soc., Springfield Art Mus. Recipient Appreciation cert. Mo. Women in Arts, 1974. Home: 2020 Ventura Ave Springfield MO 65804

ETTUS, SANDRA HELENE, marketing research executive; b. Fort Benning, Ga., Aug. 21, 1943; d. Avery Aaron and Miriam (Bitensky) Waldman; m. Frank Ettus, Oct. 18, 1969; children—Samantha, Timothy. B.A., NYU, 1972, postgrad., 1975-76. Mktg. research trainee Alfred Politz Research, N.Y.C., 1965-66; mktg. research project supr. Decisions Ctr. Inc., N.Y.C., 1966-68; mktg. research sr. analyst D'Arcy Advt., N.Y.C., 1968-69; mktg. research cons., N.Y.C., 1969-76; pres. SE Surveys, Inc., N.Y.C., 1976—. Instr. workshop in Bus. Opportunities, Bedford Stuyvesant, Bklyn., 1967, coordinator, 1968; mem. Community Bd. 8, N.Y.C., 1980—, vice chmn., 1983-84. Mem. Am. Mktg. Assn., Mktg. Research Assn., NOW. Democrat. Jewish. Office: SE Surveys Inc 971 Madison Ave New York NY 10021

ETZEL, BARBARA COLEMAN, psychologist, educator; b. Pitts., Sept. 19, 1926; d. Walter T. and Ruth (Coleman) E.; A.A., Stephens Coll., 1946; B.S. in Psychology, Denison U., 1948; M.S., U. Miami (Fla.), 1950; Ph.D. in Exptl. Child Psychology, State U. Iowa, 1953. Staff psychologist Ohio State Bur. Juvenile Research, Columbus, 1953-54; asst. prof. psychology Fla. State U., Tallahassee, 1954-56; chief psychologist, child psychiatry U. Wash. Med. Sch., Seattle, 1956-61; asso. prof. psychology Western Wash. State U., Bellingham, 1961-65, dir. grad. program in psychology, 1963-65; spl. fellow sect. early learning and devel. NIMH, Bethesda, Md., 1965-66; asso. prof. dept. human devel. U. Kans., Lawrence, 1965-69, mem. grad. faculty, 1965—, prof. dept. human devel., 1969—, dir. Edna A. Hill Child Devel. Lab., 1965-72, dir. Kansas Center for Research in Early Childhood Edn., 1968-71, asso. dean Office of Research Adminstrn. and Grad. Sch., 1972-74, dir. John T. Stewart Children's Center, 1975-85; vis. prof. Universidad Central de Venezuela, Caracas, 1981-82; cons. Manchester Sch. Presch. Program, U. Mex., Mexico City, 1973-75, George Peabody Tchrs. Coll., 1978, St. Luke's Hosp., Kansas City, Mo., 1981-83, Anne Sullivan Sch. for Handicapped Children, Lima, Peru, 1982—. Bd. dirs. Community Children's Center, Inc., 1968-71; trustee Center for Research, Inc., U. Kans., 1975-78. Elected to U. Kans. Women's Hall of Fame, 1975; Japan Soc. for Promotion for Sci. fellow, 1981. Fellow Am. Psychol. Assn.; mem. Soc. for Research in Child Devel., Midwestern Psychol. Assn., Am. Ednl. Research Assn., AAAS, AAUP, Southwestern Soc. for Research in Human Devel., Assn. Behavior Analysis (pres.-elect 1986-87, pres. 1987-88), Sigma Xi, Psi Chi, Pi Lambda Theta. Author: (with J.M. LeBlanc and D.M. Baer) New Developments in Behavioral Research, 1977; contbr. numerous articles on learning and human devel. to profl. publs.; mem. editorial bd. Behavior Analyst, 1979-83, 84-87. Home: Woodsong at JB Ranch Rt 1 PO Box 82-E Oskaloosa KS 66066 Office: Dept of Human Development U Kans Lawrence KS 66045

ETZLER, LOIS RUTH, medical technologist; b. Lancaster, Ohio, Jan. 27, 1941; d. Edward Ferdinand and Ruth Faye (Cofman) Walter; B.S. in Med. Tech., Ohio State U., 1963; postgrad. Central Mich. U.; m. Alvin Lorenz Etzler, May 4, 1963; children—Paul, Janice. Med. technologist Ohio State U. Hosp., 1962-63; blood bank technologist OB Hunter Lab., Washington, 1963-65; blood bank supr. Jewish Hosp., Louisville, 1965-66; staff technologist Greater S.E. Community Hosp., Washington, 1969-72, tech. supr., instr. Med. Tech. Sch., 1972-75, edn. coordinator Med. Tech. Sch., 1975-77, quality control supr., edn. coordinator, 1977-81, computer coordinator, quality control supr., 1981-85; programmer analyst Greater S.E. Mgmt. Co., 1985—. Fin. sec. Chesapeake dist. Lutheran Women's Missionary League, 1978-82, pres. zone, 1976-78, v.p. zone, 1983-85, v.p. Chesapeake Dist., 1984—, chmn. Chesapeake dist. nominating com., 1984; pres. Women's Guild, 1st Luth. Ch., Sunderland, Md., 1984—; del. Nat. Capitol area Luth. High Sch. Assn., 1978—. Mem. Am. Soc. Clin. Pathologists, Echo. Home: 2211 Green Valley Dr Sunderland MD 20689 Office: Dept Pathology 1310 Southern Ave Washington DC 20032

EU, MARCH KONG FONG, state official; b. Oakdale, Calif., Mar. 29, 1927; d. Yuen and Shiu (Shee) Kong; student Salinas Jr. Coll.; B.S., U. Calif.-Berkeley; M.Ed., Mills Coll., 1951; Ed.D., Stanford U., 1956; postgrad. Columbia U., Calif. State Coll., Hayward; children by previous marriage—Matthew Kipling, Marchesa Suyin; m. Henry Eu, July 30, 1973; stepchildren—Henry, Adeline, Yvonne, Conroy, Alaric. Chmn. div. dental hygiene U. Calif. Med. Center, San Francisco, dental hygienist Oakland (Calif.) Pub. Schs.; supr. dental health edn. Alameda County (Calif.) Schs.; lectr. health edn. Mills Coll., Oakland; mem. Calif. Legislature, 1966-74, chmn. select com. on agr., foods and nutrition, 1973-74, mem. com. natural resources and conservation, com. commerce and pub. utilities, select com. med. malpractice; sec. state State of Calif., 1975—; chairperson Calif. State World Trade Commn. Spl. cons. Bur. Intergroup Relations Calif. Dept. Edn.; ednl., legis. cons. Sausalito (Calif.) Pub. Schs., Santa Clara County Office Edn., Jefferson Elem. Union Sch. Dist., Santa Clara High Sch. Dist., Santa Clara Elem. Sch. Dist., Live Oak Union High Sch. Dist. Mem. Alameda County Bd. Edn., 1956-66, pres., 1961-62, legis. adv., 1963; mem. budget panel Bay Area United Fund Crusade; mem. Oakland Econ. Devel. Council; mem. tourism devel. com. Calif. Econ. Devel. Commn., mem. citizens com. on housing Council Social Planning; mem. Calif. Interagy. Council Family Planning; edn. chmn., mem. council social planning, dir. Oakland Area Baymont Dist. Community Council; charter pres. hon. life mem. Howard Elementary Sch. PTA; charter pres. Chinese Young Ladies Soc., Oakland; mem., vice chmn. adv. com. Youth Study Centers and Ford Found. Interagy. Project, 1962-63; chmn. Alameda County Mothers' March, 1971-72. Mem. exec. com. Calif. Democratic Central Com., mem. central com., 1963-70; asst. sec., del. Dem. Nat. Conv., 1968; dir. 8th Congl. Dist. Dem. Council, 1963; v.p. Dems. of 8th Congl. Dist., 1963; dir. Key Women for Kennedy, 1963; women's vice chmn. No. Calif. Johnson for Pres., 1964. Bd. dirs. Oakland YMCA, 1965. Recipient ann. award for outstanding achievement Eastbay Intercultural Fellowship, 1959, Phoebe Apperson Hearst Distinguished Bay Area Women of Year award, Woman of Year award Calif. Retail Liquor Dealers Inst., 1969, Merit citation Calif. Assn. Adult Edn. Adminstrs., 1970, Art Edn. award. Mem. Am. (life, pres. 1956-57), No. Calif. (life) dental hygienists assns., Oakland LWV, AAUW (area rep. in edn. Oakland br.), Calif. Tchrs. Assn., Calif., Alameda County (pres. 1965) sch. bds. assns., So. Calif. Dental Assn. (hon.). Bus. and Profl. Women's Club, Delta Kappa Gamma. Office: 1230 J St Suite 605 Sacramento CA 95814

EUBANK, CHRISTINA, oil company executive; b. Temple, Tex., Jan. 17, 1944; d. G.R. and Catherine (Andrews) E. B.A., Baylor U., 1966, J.D., 1973. Bar: Tex. 1973. Atty. Champlin Petroleum Co., Ft. Worth, Tex., 1973-76, asst. gen. atty., 1976-78; staff atty., 1978-79; sr. staff atty., 1979-81; gen. atty., 1981-83; sr. gen. atty., 1983-84; asst. gen. counsel, 1984—. Contbr. Baylor Law Rev., 1973; mem. Presdl. task force Grace Commn. War on Waste, 1984. Recipient Am. Jurisprudence award, 1973; letter of commendation Pres. Reagan, 1982. Mem. ABA, Tex. Bar. Assn., Am. Corp. Counsel Assn. Greek Orthodox. Clubs: Shady Oaks Country, Woman's, Petroleum (Ft. Worth). Home: 1239 Roaring Springs Rd Fort Worth TX 76114 Office: Champlin Petroleum Co 801 Cherry St Fort Worth TX 76101

EUBANKS, FRANCES OLIVE DOWELL (MRS. ELI T. EUBANKS), oil company manager; b. Wellsford, Kans.; d. Frank E. and Eva (Thomas) Dowell; student U. Kans., 1945-46; B.S., Kans. State U., 1949, M.S., 1950; m. Eli T. Eubanks, Dec. 23, 1940. Teaching fellow dept. home mgmt. Kans. State Coll., Manhattan, 1949-50; instr. U. Louisville, 1950-51, U. Wash., Seattle, 1951-52; mgr. records dept. Adair Oil Co., Wichita, Kans., 1955-86. Sec. Young Democrats Club, U. Kans., 1945-46. Mem. Omicron Nu, Phi Kappa Phi. Home: Route 1 Viola KS 67149 Office: POB 2823 Wichita KS 67201

EUBANKS, GINGER GIDDENS, clerk of superior and magistrate courts; b. Eastman, Ga., Feb. 25, 1955; d. Lawton Wendell and Marie Elizabeth (McDuffie) Giddens; M. Larry Dale Eubanks, Aug. 13, 1977; children—Lauren Marie, Larry D. Jr. Student Ga. Southwestern Coll., 1973-75. Elected clk. Superior Court Schley County, Ellaville, Ga., 1980-84, 1985—; apptd. clerk, 1981—. Organist, pianist Ellaville Bapt. Ch., 1969—. Democrat. Club: Bapt. Young Women. Avocations: sewing; needlepoint. Home: PO Box 105 Ellaville GA 31806 Office: Clerk Superior Court Schley County Seat County Courthouse Ellaville GA 31806

EUBANKS, MARY WALTINE BANKS, educator; b. Esmont, Va., May 21, 1941; d. Walter Earl Banks and Madolia (Scott) Banks Chambers; m. Jack Junior Eubanks, July 3, 1982. B.S., Va. State Coll., 1964; M.Ed., U. Va. 1972. Tchr., Nelson County, Va., 1964-77, B.F. Yancey Elem. Sch., Esmont, Va., 1977—. Editor New Hope Ch. Yearbook, 1976. Pres. bd. dirs. Southside Health Ctr.; active Albermarle Democratic Com., Southside Albemarle NAACP, Albemarle County Parks and Recreation Commn.; lead soprano singing group Echoes. Recipient Recognition award Va. Edn. Jour., 1981. Mem. Va. Edn. Assn. (del.), NEA, Albemarle Edn. Assn. Baptist. Club: Greencroft Garden. Lodge: Household of Ruth. Home: Route 1 PO Box 51 Esmont VA 22937 Office: Route 1 Box 285 Esmont VA 22937

EUFEMIA-VECCHIO, MARIA THERESA, history educator, research-writer; b. N.Y.C., July 8, 1949; d. Joseph Anthony and Lorenza Augustina (Mattei) Eufemia; m. Russell Paul Vecchio, Nov. 20, 1983. B.A., Fordham U., 1970, M.A., 1972, Ph.D., 1976. Adj. asst. prof. history Fordham U., N.Y.C., Bronx, 1972—, tutor higher edn. opportunity program, 1983—; adj. assoc. prof. Pace U., N.Y.C., 1975—; adj. prof. Coll. Mt. St. Vincent, Riverdale, N.Y., 1975-79; lectr. Mercy Coll., Dobbs Ferry, N.Y., 1980; adj. asst. prof. N.Y. Inst. Tech., N.Y.C., 1983; asst. prof. A.A. degree program Wood Sch., N.Y.C., 1984—; asst. prof., coordinator Learning Ctr., Felician Coll., Lodi, N.J.; tchr. bridge program St. Michael's High Sch., N.Y., 1975-84. Author: (with Russell Paul Vecchio) Across the Rubicon: Speculations on the Philosophy of History, 1983; Fellow NDEA, Fordham U., 1972-73; Fordham U. assistantship, 1973. Mem. Am. Hist. Assn., Orgn. Am. Historians, Nat. Hist. Soc. Republican. Roman Catholic. Home: 280 C Grove St Lodi NJ 07644 Office: Felician Coll Learning Ctr 260 S Main St Lodi NJ 07644

EUSTER, JOANNE REED, librarian; b. Grants Pass, Oreg., Apr. 7, 1936; d. Robert Lewis and Mabel Louise (Jones) Reed; m. William T. Euster Jr., Apr. 2, 1955 (div.); children—Shron Lee, Carol Lynn, Lisa Joan; m. 2d, Stephen Lynn Gerhardt, May 14, 1977. Student Lewis and Clark Coll., 1953-56; B.A., Portland State Coll., 1965; M.L.S., U. Wash., 1968, M.B.A., 1977; Ph.D., U. Calif.-Berkeley, 1986. Asst. librarian Edmonds Community Coll., Lynnwood, Wash., 1968-73, dir. Library-Media Ctr., 1973-77; univ. librarian Loyola U., New Orleans, La., 1977-80; library dir. San Francisco State U., 1980—; library cons. Union Ejidal, La Peñita, Nayarit, Mex., 1973; library cons. Office Mgmt. Studies Assn. Research Libraries, Washington, 1979—. Mem. adv. bd. City Coll. San Francisco Library Tech. Program, 1984—. Mem. ALA, Assn. Coll. Research Libraries, Am. Assn. Higher Edn., Calif. Library Assn., Am. Soc. for Info. Sci. Democrat. Unitarian. Author: Changing Patterns of Internal Communication in Large Academic Libraries, 1981; contbr. articles to profl. jours.

EVALE, NANCY MCALAINE, nurse practitioner, educator; b. Phila., Sept. 1, 1944; d. Daniel Paul and Ann Catherine (Morris) McAlaine; m. John William Evale, Oct. 5, 1968; children—Amy Elizabeth, Colleen Margaret, Christina Anne. R.N., Chester County Sch. Nursing, 1965; B.Profl. Studies, SUNY-Saratoga Springs, 1982; adult nurse practitioner program SUNY-Syracuse, 1982. Staff and head nurse Upstate Med. Ctr., Syracuse, N.Y., 1965-68; office nurse, 1968-71; nurse educator, nurse practitioner Bd. Coop. Edn. Services, Oswego, N.Y., 1971—; nursing cons. utilization review St. Luke's Health Facility, 1978—; chmn., coordinator Continuing Health Edn. Com., 1978—; curriculum cons. N.Y. State Edn. Dept., 1980—; nursing dir. Quality Care Nursing Service, Oswego, 1984—; nurse practitioner Oswego County Opportunities, 1984—. Bd. dirs. Health Systems Agy., Subarea Council, 1980—; mem. internat. adv. bd. North Country Inst. Natural Philosophy. Mem. Nat. Ctr. Health Edn. (charter assoc.), Coalition Nurse Practitioners Inc., Community Planning Group for Nurses. Republican. Roman Catholic. Office: Quality Care 28 W Bridge St Oswego NY 13126

EVANKO, MELANIE LUCAS, trust company executive; b. Staten Island, N.Y., Apr. 17, 1954; d. Harold Warde and Billie Arwin (Clift) Lucas; m. Robert James Evanko, Oct. 15, 1983. B.B.A., U. Ga., 1976. C.P.A., Ga. Internal auditor Trust Co. Ga., Atlanta, 1976-79, ops. officer corp. planning, 1979-81, asst. v.p. corp. tax, 1981—. Co. coordinator United Way, Atlanta, 1982; team capt. High Mus. Art-Young Careers, Atlanta, 1980-83. Mem. Am. Inst. Banking, Am. Inst. C.P.A.s (edn. com.), Ga. Soc. C.P.A.s, Atlanta C. of C. (pres. com. 1982). Republican. Presbyterian. Office: Trust Co Ga 25 Park Pl NE Atlanta GA 30302

EVANS, ANGELA MARIA, public policy analyst; b. Buffalo, June 20, 1947; d. Guy Frank and Connie Nina (Latona) Giordano; m. Gary Lee Evans, Apr. 27, 1974; children—Kyle, Michael, Rachel. B.A. summa cum laude, Canisius Coll., 1969; M.A., U. Wis., 1971. Analyst in pub. policy Congl. Research Service, Library of Congress, Washington, 1971-76, specialist in edn. policy, 1978-84, supr. edn. specialists in pub. policy, 1985—. Mem. Blvd. Manor Civic Assn., Arlington, 1980—. Recipient Meritorious Service award Congl. Research Service, 1985. Mem. Women in Govt. Relations, Inc., Congl. Research Employees Assn. (bd. govs. 1983-85), Am. Ednl. Research Assn., AAUW. Avocations: painting water colors, crafts. Office: Congl Research Service 101 Independence Ave SE Washington DC 20540

EVANS, BARBARA JEAN, county official; b. Cheyenne, Wyo., Sept. 20, 1934; d. William Aaron Muir and Margaret Lee (Green) Muir Blotzke; m. Allan Edward Evans, Sept. 6, 1952; children—Larry Allan, Karyn Gayle, Richard David, Terry Wayne. County commr. Missoula County, Mont., 1978-84, 84—. Local govt. study commn. Missoula City/County, 1973-76; mem. police commn. City of Missoula, 1975-80; state pres. Mont. Citizens for Ct. Improvement, 1974-75; gov.'s appointee criminal justice standards and goals task force on cts., Mont., 1975; vice-chair law enforcement subcom. Nat. Assn. Counties, Washington, 1980—; del. NACO justice and pub. safety steering com. Mont. Assn. Counties, Helena, 1980—; active Child Abuse Protection Team, Missoula, 1982. Republican. Mormon. Avocations: soil and water gardening; sewing; reading; writing. Home: 2415 56th St Missoula MT 59803 Office: Missoula County Courthouse 200 W Broadway Missoula MT 59802

EVANS, BETTY BOLLBACK, audiologist, educator; b. Bklyn., May 28, 1927; d. Anthony J. and Elizabeth (Balzer) Bollback; m. C. Hans Evans, June 10, 1961. B.R.E., Nyack Coll., 1949; M.A., NYU, 1951; postgrad. Northwestern U., 1953, Columbia U., 1952-57. Audiologist Manhattan Eye, Ear, Nose and Throat Hosp., N.Y.C., 1949-54; tchr. Lexington Sch. for Deaf, N.Y.C., 1954-59; supervising Deaf, Phila., 1960-68; prin. Middle Sch., Pa. Sch. for Deaf, 1968-71; asst. prof. spl. edn. Pa. State U., University Park, 1962-71; specialist in deaf edn. Chester County Child Devel. Ctr., Coatesville, 1971-78; assoc. dean students King's Coll., Briarcliff Manor, N.Y., 1978—, instr. speech, 1978-79, dir. dept. continuing edn., 1980—, cons. study skills ctr., 1982—; cons. Nat. Com. Library Standards for Schs. for Deaf, N.Y., 1965-66; lectr. civic, religious and profl. groups. Active Chester County Health and Welfare Assn., 1962; social dir. Word of Life Summer Confs., N.Y., 1955-60; corp. mem. Lancaster Sch. of Bible, 1973; v.p. Living Word Radio Ministry Internat., 1974-77; summer seminar coordinator Camp of Woods, Speculator, N.Y., 1978—; hon. mem. program agy. United Presbyn. Ch. U.S.A., 1977—. Recipient Outstanding Service award Coatesville Area Council PTA. Mem. Coatesville Hosp. Aux., Alexander Graham Bell Assn. for Deaf, Conv. Am. Instrs. for Deaf, Presbyn. Women's Assn. (pres. 1976-77), Assn. Christians in Student Devel., Delta Kappa Gamma. Republican. Address: Kings Coll Briarcliff Manor NY 10510

EVANS, CAROLYN MARGARET, court administrator; b. Camden, N.J., Jan. 19, 1946; d. Philip Louis and Margaret Caroline (Henry) Iuliucci; B.A., Rutgers U., 1968; postgrad. LaSalle Coll., 1981—. Probation officer Camden (N.J.) County Probation Dept., 1968-70, sr. probation officer, dir. vols., 1970-74; dir. vol. services Adminstrv. Office of Cts., Trenton, N.J., 1974-81, asst. chief jud. edn., 1981-83, chief ct. reporting services, 1983—. Mem. Nat. Assn. for Female Execs., Am. Soc. for Tng. and Devel., Vols. in Cts. and Corrections Assn. of N.J. (pres. 1980-82), Nat. Assn. on Vols. in Criminal Justice (sec. 1977-79, adv. bd., chmn. com. on adult cts. and probation Nat. Guidelines Project 1980-82). Home: 3301 N Elberta Ln Marlton NJ 08053 Office: Justice Complex CN 037 Trenton NJ 08625

EVANS, CHARLENE TAYLOR, English educator; b. LaGrange, Tex., Mar. 3, 1948; d. John and Rachel (Hughes) Taylor; m. Travis Whitfield, Oct. 28, 1969 (div. Jan. 1978); m. 2d Larry Quincy Evans, Feb. 27, 1980; children—Larry Quincy II, Jon Alan. B.A., U. Tex., 1970; M.A., Atlanta U., 1977; postgrad. Rice U., 1981—. Instr., U. Houston Downtown, 1977-78; dir. edn.

Houston Urban League, 1979-80; instr. Houston Community Coll., 1976-77; instr. English, Tex. So. U., Houston, 1977—; cons. Practical Sci. Inst., Houston, 1979-80, Thurgood Marshall Sch. Law, Houston, 1981. Pub. relations coordinator Democratic candidate for Tex. Legislature, Houston, 1982. Bodkin scholar Atlanta U., 1974. Mem. YWCA. Baptist. Home: 3312 Binz St Houston TX 77004 Office: Tex Southern U 3201 Wheeler St Houston TX 77004

EVANS, CHARLOTTE MORTIMER, writer, communications consultant; b. Newton, N.J., Nov. 26, 1933; d. Karl Otto and Wilhelmina (Otterbach) Pfau; student Douglass Coll., 1952-54; B.S., R.N., Columbia U. Presbyn. Hosp., 1957, postgrad., 1957-59; postgrad. N.Y.U., 1959-60; M.P.A., Coll. of Notre Dame, 1979; m. John Atterbury Mortimer, Nov. 20, 1964; children—Meredith Elizabeth, Mandy Leigh; m. G. Robert Evans, Sept. 4, 1982. Spl. assignment nurse Columbia-Presbyn. Med. Center, N.Y.C., 1957-59; med. advt. copywriter Paul Klemtner & Co., N.Y.C., 1959-61, William Douglas McAdams Agy., N.Y.C., 1961-62; account exec. Arndt, Preston, Chapin, Lamb & Keen, N.Y.C., 1962-63; Rocky Mountain corr. Med. World News, Denver, 1963-64; owner Publicite, Denver; gen. mgr. Center Mktg. Assos., Palo Alto, Calif., 1964-66; freelance writer, pub. relations and mgmt. cons., Woodside, Calif., 1966-85; pres. Communications for Youth, 1979—. Mem. Palo Alto-Stanford Hosp. Aux., 1968-72; pub. relations assistance Peninsula Children's Center, Palo Alto, 1968-73, Triton Mus. Art, San Jose, Calif., 1966-70; chmn. citizens adv. com. San Mateo County Juvenile Social Services; health component Early Childhood Com., Woodside Elem. Sch. Dist.; mem. adv. com. South County Youth and Family Services Program; bd. dirs. N.J. Jr. C. of C./UNICEF/African Project, 1960-61; mem. San Mateo County Mental Health Adv. Bd., Friends of Woodside Library Bd, 1983-85; mem. Rep. Senatorial Inner Circle, 1982—. Home: PO Box 501 Wayne IL 60184 Office: Communications for Youth PO Box 462 Wayne IL 60184

EVANS, CONNIE ODESSA, small business consultant, office systems specialist; b. Des Moines, June 18, 1946; d. Elmer Edward and Violet Beatrice (Brooks) E.; 1 child, Nia Malika Azurée. B.A., Drake U., 1974, M.P.A., 1976, postgrad. Law Sch., 1976. Statis. clk. Exec. Office of Pres., Washington, 1964-69; adminstrv. analyst City of Des Moines, 1970-73; sr. planner employment, tng. and econ. devel. Central Iowa Regional Assn. Local Govt., Des Moines, 1977-81; founder, pres. Inst. Community Devel., Des Moines, 1980—; owner, mgr. Coe & Assocs., Denver, 1981—; owner, mgr. Internat. Computer & Mgmt. Cons. Services, 1981—; cons. Des Moines C. of C., 1980-82, Minority Bus. Assn., Des Moines, 1982; instr. Small Bus. Devel. and Computer Applications, Des Moines, 1982-84; mem. Nat. Assn. Counties, Conf. Mayors Task Force Econ. Devel. and Energy, Small Bus. and Econ. Devel., 1979-81. Co-chmn. overview adv. com. Black Leadership Council Des Moines; leader Mile-Hi chpt. Montebello council Girl Scouts U.S.A., Denver, 1982; del. Polk County Dem. Conv., 1984. Scholar Des Moines chpt. Nat. Assn. Profl. Colored Women, 1975-76. Mem. Am. Soc. Pub. Adminstrn., Nat. Assn. Female Execs., Pi Alpha Alpha. Baptist. Home: 1320 Laurel St Des Moines IA 50314

EVANS, DARDANELLA LISTER, nurse, writer, engineering company executive; b. Vernon, Tex., Jan. 26, 1921; d. Jack and Jenna Ferol (Bradley) Lister; grad. U. Okla. Sch. Nursing, 1943; grad. Nat. Landscape Inst., 1959; m. Kent E. Evans, May 21, 1946; children—Karen Louise Evans Ulehla, Sharon Jean Evans Wilson. With Okla. Pub. Co. and Sta. WKY, 1939-40; nurse U. Hosp. and Crippled Childrens' Hosp., Oklahoma City, 1940-43; vol. nurse Sch. Immunization Community Program, Dallas, 1958-69; key market editor for N.Y. publs. including Radio & TV Weekly, 1964-71, U.S. Tobacco Jour., 1964-71; v.p. Atlas Engring. Services, Inc., Atlanta, 1976—; free lance writer health and safety, 1939—. PTA room rep. Lakewood, Long and Woodrow Wilson high schs., Dallas, 1953-69; girl scout leader Lakewood Sch. council Girl Scouts U.S., 1956-63; Sunday sch. tchr. Skillman Ave. Ch. of Christ, 1962-65; mem. dir.'s com. U.S. Senatorial Bus. Adv. Bd., 1981. Served with U.S. Army Nurse Corp., 1943-46. Mem. Women in Communications, Am. Heart Assn., Nutrition Today Soc., Nat. Writers Club, Associated Bus. Writers Am., Smithsonian Nat. Assn., Am. Trauma Soc., Am. Name Soc., Ret. Officers Assn., Ret. Army Nurse Corps Assn., DeKalb North Art Alliance, Riverview Assn., Nat. Safety Council. Republican. Mem. Ch. of Christ. Club: Atlanta Athletic. Author: Nest Not in My Hair!, 1978; contbr. poetry to various lit. publs. Home: 4324 Ridgegate Dr Duluth GA 30136 Office: PO Box 81292 atlanta GA 30366

EVANS, HANNAH IMOGENE, psychologist; b. Richmond, Va., Nov. 6, 1945; d. Charles and Ruth (Powell) E.; B.A., U. Vt., 1967; M.S., Pa. State U., 1970, Ph.D., 1972; M.P.A., U. Colo., Denver, 1981; m. Robert F. McKenzie, July 12, 1975. Clin. psychology intern, psychol. cons. II, Denver Dept. Health and Hosps., 1972-77; adj. faculty U. Colo., Denver, summer 1978; resource counselor Regional Transp. Dist., 1978-79; pvt. practice psychotherapy, Denver, 1976—. Mem. community adv. bd. Sch. Profl. Psychology, U. Denver; mem. grievance com. Colo. Supreme Ct., 1982—; mem. transp. group Project Colo., 1982—; mem. Gov.'s Front Range Task Force, 1980-81; bd. dirs. Denver Sexual Assault Council, 1974-80; founding bd. Colo. Center Women and Work, 1979-81; mem. Women's Forum of Colo., 1979—, selection com., 1980-84; chmn. victim and law enforcement bd., 2d jud. dist., 1985—. USPHS fellow, 1968-70; named one of Faces of Colo., Colo. mag., 1976. Mem. Am. Psychol. Assn., Colo. Psychol. Assn., Colo. Women Psychologists, Rocky Mountain Road Runners. Club: Phiddipides Track. Contbr. articles to profl. jours. and popular mags. Office: 146 W 11th Ave Denver CO 80204

EVANS, HAZEL BAKER, real estate broker; b. Vanndale, Ark., Mar. 26, 1932; d. Charlie and Lillie Mae (Miller) Baker; m. Robert Liles Evans, May 2, 1952; children—Robert Baker, Jeffrey Lynn. Student Draughans Bus. Coll., Memphis, 1951. Grad., Realtors Inst. With Wynne Fed. Savs. & Loan (Ark.), 1956-58, Pima Savs. & Loan, Tucson, 1958-65; mortgage loan processer Catalina Savs. Bank, Tucson, 1965-69, 1st Fed. Bank, Ft. Smith, 1969-70; real estate broker Jimmie Taylor Co., Ft. Smith, 1971-74; pres., broker Hazel Evans Real Estate, Ft. Smith, 1974-82; broker Coldwell Banker, Fort Smith, 1982—. Adv. trustee Sparks Regional Med. Ctr., 1984—. Mem. Fort Smith Bd. Realtors (realtor of yr. 1982; pres. 1983), Ft. Smith C. of C. (bd. dirs. 1978), Assn. Bus. Women Am. (pres. 1974), Women's Council Realtors (woman of yr. 1982, pres. 1977), Nat. Assn. Realtors, Ark. Assn. Realtors (cert. residential specialist, sec. 1984, state edn l. com. 1983-84, dist. v.p.). Republican. Baptist. Home: 7100 S Q St Fort Smith AR 72913 Office: Coldwell Banker Fleming Realty 2910 Rogers Ave Fort Smith AR 72901

EVANS, HEATHER HELEN, investment banker, entrepreneur; b. N.Y.C., Oct. 18, 1958; d. Thomas William and Lois DeBaun (Logan) E.; m. Peter John Christus, July 16, 1983. B.A., Harvard U., 1980, M.B.A., 1983. Model, Ford Models, Inc., N.Y.C., 1975-79; fin. analyst Morgan Stanley Inc., N.Y.C., 1979-81; pres. Heather Evans Inc., N.Y.C., 1983-84; v.p. Bear, Stearns & Co., N.Y.C., 1985—; instr. econs. dept. Harvard U., Cambridge, Mass., 1982. Contbr. articles to mags. Recipient Bus. Achievement award SAVVY mag., 1984. Mem. Phi Beta Kappa. Club: Down Town Assn. Office: Bear Stearns & Co Inc 55 Water St New York NY 10003

EVANS, JANE, fashion industry executive; b. Hannibal, Mo., July 26, 1944; d. L. Terrell Evans and Katherine (Rosser) Evans Pierce; m. George sheer, June 17, 1970; 1 child, Jonathan. B.A., Vanderbilt U., 1965; student L'Universite d'Aix-Marseille, France, 1962. Pres. I. Miller, N.Y.C., 1970-73; v.p. internat. mktg. Genesco, N.Y.C., 1973-74; pres. Butterick/Vogue Patterns, N.Y.C., 1974-77; v.p. adminstrn. and corp. devel. Fingerhut, Mpls., 1977-79; exec. v.p. fashion Gen. Mills, Inc., N.Y.C., 1979-84; pres., chief exec. officer Monet Jewelers, N.Y.C., 1984—; dir. Equitable Life Assurance Soc., Philip Morris, N.Y.C., The Fashion Group, Catalyst, N.Y.C., Fashion Inst. Tech., N.Y.C. Recipient Women's Equity Action League award, 1982, Entrepreneurial Woman award Women Bus. Owners of N.Y., 1982; named one of All Time Ten Outstanding Working Women, Glamour Mag., 1984, Corp. Am's. Top Women Execs., Savvy Mag., 1983. Mem. Young Pres.'s Orgn., Com of 200, Fashion Group of N.Y., Women's Forum. Avocations: golf; tennis; gourmet cooking; piano. Office: Monet 16 E 34th St New York NY 10016

EVANS, JANE G., home economist; b. Olney, Md., June 15, 1951; d. Ulysses IV and Marion Margaret (Taylor) G.; 1 child, Benjamin Matthew. B.Sc. in Human Ecology, U. Md., 1973; M. Adminstrv. Sci., Johns Hopkins U., 1983; postgrad. in acctg. Montgomery Coll., 1983—. Tchr. home econs. Berlin (Md.) Middle Sch., 1973-75; youth program developer, Swaziland, 1975-76; vis. lectr. Md. Coop. Extension Service, 1977, 4-H and youth agt. Howard County, 1977-84; mem. faculty U. Md., 1977-84; asst. supt. 4-H foods dept. Md. State Fair, 1978-81; tchr. home econs. Jessup Correctional Inst. Women, 1972. Mem. Laytonsville Town Council, Md., 1985—. Mary Faulkner scholar, 1969; Md. Senatorial scholar, 1969; Johns Hopkins U. fellow in Orgnl. and Community Systems, 1980-81. Mem. Am. Home Econs. Assn., Md. Home Econs. Assn. (chmn. by-laws com. 1979, v.p. for programs 1980-82), Nat. Assn. 4-H Agts. (N.E. regional contact for public relations and info. com. 1981-82), Md. Assn. 4-H Agts. (chmn. nominating com. 1980-81), Md. Internat. 4-H Youth Exchange Assn., Md. 4-H All Stars, Mortar Board, Omicron Nu, Epsilon Sigma Phi. Author newsletters in field. Home: 21512 Montgomery Ave Laytonsville MD 20879

EVANS, JENNIE QUICK, real estate broker; b. Flintville, Tenn., Aug. 15, 1937; d. Richard L. and Rossie (King) Quick; m. Harvell Ray Evans, Aug. 22, 1958; children—Treva A. Richardson, Richard A., Ronald A. Student Middle Tenn. State U., 1955-58, Central Tex. Coll., 1980-81. Mgmt. analyst U.S. Army, Ft. Hood, Tex., 1969-72, computer specialist, 1972-80; real estate broker, owner Century 21 Preferred, Killeen and Copperas Cove, Tex., 1980—, pres., 1983—. Bd. dirs., profl. chairperson Copperas Cove United Way, 1980—; trustee Grace United Methodist Ch., Copperas Cove, 1984—. Mem. Ft. Hood Area Bd. Realtors (chairperson Multiple Listing Service com. 1985, numerous Producer awards 1980—, 6 Million Dollar Producer 1983), Am. Bus. Women's Assn. (v.p. Copperas Cove 1972-73, pres. 1973-74). Democrat. Avocation: reading. Home: 703 Judy Ln Copperas Cove TX 76522

EVANS, JO BURT, TV translator company executive, rancher; b. Kimble County, Tex., Dec. 18, 1928; d. John Fred and Sadie (Oliver) Burt; B.A., Mary Hardin-Baylor Coll., 1948; M.A., Trinity U., 1967; m. Charles Wayne Evans II, Apr. 17, 1949; children—Charles Wayne III, John Burt, Elizabeth Wisart. Owner, mgr. Sta. KMBL, Junction, Tex., 1959-61; real estate broker, Junction, 1965-74; staff economist, adv. on 21st Congl. Dist., polit. campaign Nelson Wolff, 1974-75; asst. mgr., bookkeeper family owned ranches and rent property, Junction, 1948—; gen. mgr. TV Translator Corp., Junction, 1968—, sec.-treas., 1980—. Treas., asst. to coordinator Citizens for Tex., 1972; historian Kimble Hist. Soc.; mem. Com. of Conservation Soc. to Save the Edwards Aquifer, San Antonio, 1973; homecoming chmn. Sesquicentennial Year, Junction; treas., asst. coordinator New Constitution, San Antonio, 1974. AAUW scholarship named in honor, 1973; named an outstanding Texan, Tex. Senate, 1973. Mem. Nat. Translator Assn., AAUW, Daus. Republic Tex., Tex. Sheriffs Assn., Internat. Platform Assn., Bus. and Profl. Women (pres. 1981-82). Democrat. Mem. Unity Ch. Home: PO Box 283 Junction TX 76849 Office: 618 Main St Junction TX 76849

EVANS, JUDY ANN, real estate broker, interior designer; b. Grand Rapids, Mich., June 28, 1936; d. Abner W. and Margaret J. (Whitford) Wilson; m. Douglas M. Carlson, Nov. 19, 1955 (div. 1969); children—Mark William, Gregory Scott, Jeffrey Martin; m. Roy Evan Evans, Jr., Dec. 30, 1972; children—Roy Evan, Victoria Leigh. B.A., U. Colo., 1958; B.S., Northwestern U., 1979; student Realtors Inst., 1974-79. Cert. residential specialist. Payroll clk. Oceana Hwy. Dept., Hart, Mich., 1969; designer Hart Builders Supply Co., 1969-72, Peterson Interiors, Arlington Heights, Ill., 1973; real estate broker Whitney Real Estate Co., Barrington, Ill., 1973-76, Realty World, Robert, 1976-78; assoc. broker Baird & Warner Inc., Barrington, 1978—, corp. specialist, Chgo., 1980—. Active Arden Shore Home for Boys, 1979—, Chgo. Art Inst. Mem. Nat. Assn. Realtors, Ill. Assn. Realtors (lifetime Two Millon Dollar Club), Barrington Bd. Realtors (Realtor of Yr. 1977), Am. Assn. Interior Designers, Nat. Assn. Female Execs., Alpha Phi Alumni. Republican. Club: Biltmore Country (Barrington). Contbr. articles to profl. jours. Home: 559 Eton Dr Barrington IL 60010 Office: Baird & Warner Inc 303 Northwest Hwy Barrington IL 60010

EVANS, LINDA, actress; b. Hartford, Conn., Nov. 18, 1942; m. John Derek (div.). Film debut Twilight of Honor, 1963; other films include Tom Horn, 1980, The Klansman, 1974, Avalanche Express, 1979; TV series: Dynasty, 1980—, The Big Valley, 1965-69; TV miniseries: Bare Essence, 1982, Gambler II, 1983. Author: Linda Evans Beauty and Exercise Book, 1983. Address: care Charter Mgmt 9000 Sunset Blvd Los Angeles CA 90069*

EVANS, LOIS LOGAN, investment banker, government official; b. Boston, Dec. 1, 1937; d. Harlan DeBaun and Barbara (Rollins) Logan; m. Thomas W. Evans, Dec. 22, 1956; children—Heather, Logan, Paige. Student Vassar Coll., 1954-55; B.A., Barnard Coll., 1957. Mem. U.S. del. to UN, N.Y.C., 1972-74; alt. chief del. UN Commn. on Status of Women, 1974; mem. bd. U.S. Commn. to UNESCO, 1974-78; pres. Acquisition Specialists, Inc., N.Y.C., 1977-81, 83—; asst. chief of protocol of U.S., Washington, 1981-83; mem. bd. Fed. Home Loan Bank N.Y., 1984—, chmn. bd., 1986—; dir. D.G. Beauty Systems, N.Y.C., Campbell Shea, Inc., N.Y.C. State co-chmn. Reagan-Bush Campaign, N.Y., 1984, state fin. co-chmn., 1983-84; mem. bd. Jr. League, Bklyn., 1968-72; vice chmn. devel. council Williams Coll., 1979-81. Republican. Episcopalian. Office: Acquisition Specialists Inc 142 E 35th St New York NY 10016

EVANS, LOUISE, psychologist; b. San Antonio; d. Henry Daniel and Adela (Pariser) E.; B.S., Northwestern U., 1949; M.S. in Psychology, Purdue U., 1952, Ph.D. in Clin. Psychology, 1955; m. Thomas Ross Gambrell, Feb. 23, 1960. Intern clin. psychology Menninger Found., Topeka (Kans.) State Hosp., 1952-53, USPHS-Menninger Found. fellow clin. child psychology, 1955-56; staff psychologist Kankakee (Ill.) State Hosp., 1954; head staff psychologist child guidance clinic Kings County Hosp., Bklyn., 1957-58; dir. psychology clinic, instr. med. psychology Washington U. Sch. Medicine, 1959; clin. research cons. Episcopal City Mission, St. Louis, 1959; pvt. practice clin. psychology, 1960—; psychol. cons. Fullerton (Calif.) Community Hosp., 1961-81; staff cons. clin. psychology Martin Luther Hosp., Anaheim, Calif., 1963-70; lectr. clin. psychology schs. and profl. groups, 1950—; participant psychol. symposiums, 1956—; guest speaker clin. psychology civic and community orgns., 1950—. Elected to Hall of Fame, Central High Sch., Ind., 1966; recipient Service award Yuma County Head Start Program, 1972; named Miss Heritage, Heritage Publs., 1965; lic. psychologist N.Y., Calif.; diplomate Clin. Psychology. Fellow Am. Psychol. Assn., Royal Soc. Health of England, Internat. Council of Psychologists (dir. 1977-79, sec. 1962-64, 73-76), AAAS, Am. Orthopsychiat. Assn., World Wide Acad. of Scholars of N.Z.; mem. AAUP, Los Angeles Soc. Clin. Psychologists (exec. bd. 1966-67), Calif. State Psychol. Assn., Los Angeles County Psychol. Assn., Orange County Psychol. Assn. (exec. bd. 1963-65, pres. 1964-65), Am. Public Health Assn., Rehab. Internat., Internat. Platform Assn., Am. Acad. Polit. and Social Scis., N.Y. Acad. Scis., Purdue U. Alumni Assn. (Citizenship award 1975), Am. Judicature Soc., Center for Study of Presidency, Alumni Assn. Menninger Sch. Psychiatry, Sigma Xi, Pi Sigma Pi. Contbr. articles on clin. psychology to profl. publs. Office: 905-907 W Wilshire Ave Fullerton CA 92632-1650

EVANS, LYNN S(USAN), financial planner; b. Scranton, Pa., Sept. 15, 1951; d. William P. and Shirley R. (Zenker) E.; B.A., Cedar Crest Coll., 1973. Field underwriter Mut. N.Y., Scranton, 1975-79; sales asso. Alden-Levine Assos., Allentown, Pa., 1979; fin. planner Profl. Econs., Inc., Bethlehem, Pa., 1979—; pres., fin. planner Assoc. Fin. Planners, Inc., Scranton, 1980—; fin. planner Robert J. Oberst, Sr. CFP & Assocs., Red Bank, N.J., 1984; ins. cons. Creative Planning, Scranton, 1980-84. Panelist, allocations com. United Way of Lackawanna County (Pa.), 1980-84; chairperson adv. com. Women's Resource Center, Inc., Scranton, 1981-84; pres. YWCA, Scranton. Mem. Inst. Cert. Fin. Planners (cert.; chmn. chpt.), Internat. Assn. Fin. Planners. Office: 723 S State St Clarks Summit PA 18411

EVANS, M. JANE, college president. Pres. Mount Vernon Coll., Washington. Office: Mount Vernon Coll 2100 Foxhall Rd NW Washington DC 20007*

EVANS, MARGARET A., civic worker; b. N.Y.C., Jan. 20, 1924; d. Bernard J. and Katherine (Walsh) Markey; B.A., Coll. Mt. St. Vincent, Mt. St. Vincent-on-Hudson, N.Y., 1944; evening student Columbia U.; m. John Cullen Evans, Jr., Nov. 24, 1951. Rep. N.Y. Telephone Co., 1944; personnel office Sak's 34th, N.Y.C., 1944-45, tng. supr., selling and non-selling depts., 1945-49, spl. assignment for store mgr. 1949-50; non-selling tng. supr. Gimbel Bros., 1950-51; rep. Gimbels and Sak's 34th at NCCJ Retail Group meeting, 1949-50. Instr. textile painting for ARC, Chelsea Navy Hosp., 1952-54, ARC vol., 1980—; bd. dirs. Marblehead Hosp. Aid Assn., 1954, pres., 1955-58; sec. Mass. Hosp. Assn. Council of Hosp. Auxiliaries, 1957-59, chmn. North Shore region, 1959-61, chmn.-elect, 1961-62, chmn., 1962-64; exofficio trustee Salem Hosp.; trustee Mary A. Alley Hosp., 1956-79, chmn., 1962-79; mem. Welcome Wagon of Fairfield/Easton (Conn.), 1979-83; chmn. Fairfield/Easton Theater Group, Fifth Wheel Club of Fairfield, 1983—. Mem. Alumnae Assn. Coll. Mt. Saint Vincent, Arrangers of Marblehead (chmn. garden therapy 1967-79). Clubs: Marblehead Women's Newcomers (pres. 1953). Home: 108 Cedarwoods Ln Fairfield CT 06430

EVANS, MARGARET MARY, client service executive; b. Annapolis, Md., Oct. 6, 1938; d. Frank Joseph and Margaret Mary (Ruzicka) Wanex; B.A., Newcomb Coll., 1960; student Sorbonne, 1958-59; m. Glen Evans, Jan 2, 1962; 1 dau., Lisa Glyn. Systems analyst IBM Corp., Balt., 1961-62; systems supr. U.S. Naval Acad., Annapolis, Md., 1963-67; mktg. dir. Fawcett Pubs., Inc., Greenwich, Conn., 1967-77; sales v.p. Neodata Services/A.C. Nielsen Co., N.Y.C., 1977-83, v.p., dir. client service, Boulder, Colo., 1983-85, N.Y.C., 1985—. Co-chmn. Parent's Assn., White Mt. Sch., Littleton, N.H., 1979-80; bd. dirs. White Mt. Sch., 1979-80. Recipient Spl. Service award, Fulfillment Mgmt. Assn., 1980. Mem. Fulfillment Mgmt. Assn. (program chmn. 1978-80, dir. 1980-84), Am. Mgmt. Assn., Data Processing Mgmt. Assn., Women's Direct Response Group. Democrat. Clubs: Sales Execs. of N.Y., Direct Mktg. Club N.Y. Home: 122 Cedar Heights Rd Stamford CT 06905 Office: 1290 Ave of Americas New York NY 10104

EVANS, MARY ELOISE, retired county official; b. Sandusky, Ohio, June 28, 1920; d. John A and Zura F. (Kahler) Von-Eitzen; m. Marvin Evans, Nov. 1, 1952; 1 child, Gary M. Bus. degree, Sandusky Bus. Coll., 1939. With sales and personnel depts. Apex Electric Mfg. Co., Sandusky, 1941-58; dep. sheriff Erie County, Ohio, 1958-70; clk. of cts. Erie County, 1970-81, commr., 1981-85, ret. 1985. Mem. Sandusky Bus. and Profl. Women, Ohio Bus. and Profl. Women, Nat. Bus. and Profl. Women. Republican. Methodist. Avocations: bowling, ceramics. Home: 3515 South Ave Sandusky OH 44870

EVANS, MARY JOHNSTON, corporation director; b. Shawnee, Okla., Feb. 28, 1930; d. Paul Xenophon and Helen Elizabeth (Alford) Johnston; student Wellesley Coll., 1947-48, U. Okla., 1949; m. James H. Evans, 1984; children by previous marriage—Marcia Lee Head, Paul Johnston Head, Eric Talbott Head. Mem. Citizens Adv. Com. on Transp. Quality, Washington, 1968-73, Urban Transp. Adv. Council, Washington, 1973; dir. Amtrak, 1974-80, vice chmn., 1975-79; dir. Household Internat., CertainTeed Corp., The Sun Co., Baxter Travenol Labs., Inc., Delta Air Lines; mem. adv. bd. Morgan Stanley, Inc. Pres., Jr. League Oklahoma City, 1968-69; trustee Nat. Council Crime and Delinquency, 1971-75, Presbyn. Med. Ctr., Oklahoma City, 1969-75, Mary Baldwin Coll., 1976-83, Scudder-AARP Trusts, Carnegie Hall, 1985—, Brick Presbyn. Ch.; bd. dirs. St. Anthony Hosp., Oklahoma City, 1973-75; bd. visitors U. Pitts. Grad. Sch. Bus., 1978-85. Recipient Law Day award-Liberty Bell award Okla. Bar Assn., 1971; named to Okla. Hall of Fame, 1978; Disting. Service citation U. Okla. Mem. Conference Board (sr.), Pi Beta Phi. Presbyterian (elder). Clubs: River, Colony, Maidstone (East Hampton). Address: 920 Fifth Ave New York NY 10021

EVANS, PAULA LORRAINE, businesswoman; b. Hot Springs, Ark., May 10, 1941; d. Paul Carter and Susie (Rixie) Wright; student Ark. schs.; m. William R. Evans, Feb. 10, 1973; children—Christopher C., Kelly Ann. Office mgr. Hot Springs Conv. Bur., 1970-71; bus. mgr. Therapy Services, Inc., 1971-73; partner The Crystal House, 1974-76; dir., bus. and fin. adminstr. Evco, Inc., Hot Springs, 1976—, also co-owner Paula's. Lic. nursing home adminstr., Ark. Mem. New Downtown Mchts. Assn. (treas.). Democrat. Roman Catholic. Club: Hot Springs Altrusa (pres.). Office: 308 Central Ave Hot Springs AR 71901

EVANS, PAULINE (DAVIDSON), physicist, educator; b. Bklyn., Mar. 24, 1922; d. John A. and Hannah (Brandt) Davidson; B.A., Hofstra Coll., 1942; postgrad. N.Y. U., 1943, 46-47, Cornell U., 1946, Syracuse U., 1947-50; m. Melbourne Griffith Evans, Sept. 6, 1950; children—Lynn Janet Evans Hannemann, Brian Griffith. Jr. physicist Signal Corps Ground Signal Service, Eatontown, N.J., 1942-43; physicist Kellex Corp. (Manhattan Project), N.Y.C., 1944; faculty dept. physics Queens Coll., N.Y.C., 1944-47; teaching asst. Syracuse U., 1947-50; instr. Wheaton Coll., Norton, Mass., 1952; physicist Nat. Bur. Standards, Washington, 1954-55; instr. physics U. Ala., 1955, U. N.Mex., 1955, 57-58; staff mem. Sandia Corp., Albuquerque, 1956-57; physicist Naval Nuclear Ordnance Evaluation Unit, Kirtland AFB, N.Mex., 1958-60; programmer Teaching Machines, Inc., Albuquerque, 1961; mem. faculty dept. physics Coll. St. Joseph on the Rio Grande (name changed to U. Albuquerque 1966), 1961—, assoc. prof., 1963—, chmn. dept., 1961—. Mem. Am. Phys. Soc., Am. Assn. Physics Tchrs., Fedn. Am. Scientists, AAUP, Sigma Pi Sigma, Sigma Delta Epsilon. Patentee in field. Home: 730 Loma Alta Ct NW Albuquerque NM 87105 Office: Dept Physics Univ of Albuquerque Albuquerque NM 87140

EVANS, ROSEMARY KING (MRS. HOWELL DEXTER EVANS), librarian, educator; b. Forsyth, Ga., Nov. 16, 1924; d. Wiley Gwin and Mary (Goggans) King; B.S., Tift Coll., 1957; librarian's certificate Woman's Coll. of Ga., 1963; M. Library Edn., U. Ga., 1972, postgrad. in library edn., 1975; m. Howell Dexter Evans, June 29, 1945; children—Joseph William, Curtis McKenney. Tchr. elementary sch., Forsyth, Ga., 1946-48, 54-62; librarian Mary Persons High Sch., Forsyth, 1962-73; catalog librarian Tift Coll., Forsyth, 1973-74, head librarian Stratford Acad., Macon, Ga., 1974-77; head librarian, assoc. prof. Gordon Jr. Coll., Barnesville, Ga., 1977—; chmn. regents' acad. com. libraries State Bd. Regents Univ. System of Ga.: Mem. Ga. State Bd. Certification of Librarians. Spiritual edn. chmn. PTA, 1960-61. Named Star Tchr., 1966. Mem. Nat., Ga., Monroe County (sec. 1959-60, v.p. 1961-62, pres. 1962-63) edn. assns., Ga. (dis. pres. 1965), ALA, Southeastern library assns., Ga. Library Assn. Methodist (chmn. local edn. bd. 1964-65, chmn. commn. on Christian vocation 1965—, exec. com., tchr. adult Bible class). Author: Backhome Cuisine, 1984. Office: Gordon Junior Coll Barnesville GA 30204

EVANS, RUTH TODD, internist; b. Washington, Sept. 2, 1945; d. Benjamin Johnson and Margaret Wayne (Williams) Todd; m. Edward B. Evans, Dec. 24, 1967; children—Elizabeth Todd, Andrew Todd, Susanne Williams. A.B., Goucher Coll., Balt., 1967; M.D., U. Rochester, N.Y., 1971. Diplomate Nat. Bd. Med. Examiners, Am. Bd. Internal Medicine. Intern, Univ. Hosps. of Cin., 1971-72; resident in internal medicine Univ. Hosps. of Cleve., 1972-74; pub. health officer Newport News Health Dept. (Va.), 1974-76; internist Hough Norwood Family Health Care Ctr., Cleve., 1976-78, chief adult medicine dept., 1977-78; practice medicine specializing in internal medicine, Elmira, N.Y., 1979-81, Oceanside, Calif., 1981—; med. adviser RSF Swimming Assn., 1983. Mem. Jr. League San Diego, 1983; mem. policy women's com. Beach and Country Guild, 1981—; mem. Country Friends, 1983; bd. dirs. Parent-Tchr. Orgn., 1983. Ford Found. fellow, 1965; U. Rochester fellow, 1967, 68; U. Buffalo fellow, 1966. Mem. ACP, Am. Soc. Internal Medicine, Calif. Med. Soc., San Diego Med. Soc. Republican. Presbyterian. Home: Box 2531 Rancho Santa Fe CA 92067 Office: 145 Thunder Dr Vista CA 92083

EVANS, SARAH FRANCES HINTON, nurse; b. Athens, Clark County, Ga., July 19, 1924; d. Charles Jackson and Bessie Marie (Hickman) Hinton; R.N., Macon Hosp. Sch. Nursing, 1945; B.S. in Nursing, Med. Coll. Ga., 1975; m. Omer Fountain, Oct. 9, 1948 (div. 1964); children—Anita Francine, Sarah Alice; m. John Duggan Evans, Feb. 14, 1969 (dec. Apr. 1971). Night supr. Ware County Hosp., Waycross, Ga., 1946-47; staff nurse nursery and obstetrics Mercy Hosp., Macon, Ga., 1947-48; staff nurse obstetrics Macon (Ga.) Hosp., 1952-54, 55-56, head nurse colored labor and delivery, 1956-64, obstet. staff nurse, 1964-65; head nurse newborn nursery Med. Center Central Ga., Macon, 1965-74, infection control nurse, 1974—; mem. Ga. Bd. Nursing, 1977-80. Mem. Am. Nurses Assn. (del. from Ga. 1976, 78), Assn. Practitioners in Infection Control (cert.), Ga. Heart Assn., Ga. Public Health Assn., Sixth Dist. Ga. Nurses Assn., Med. Center Central Ga. Alumnae, Med. Coll. Ga. Alumnae Assn. Baptist. Home: 6375 Houston Rd Macon GA 31206 Office: Med Center Central GA Box 6000 Macon GA 31208

EVANS, SHIRLEY A(NN), government official accountant; b. Minden, Nebr., Dec. 23, 1926; d. George V. and Kathryn F. (Bayer) Saltzgaber; m. George P.H. Evans, July 3, 1946; children—Renee Kathryn Evans Gregorio, Nancy Evans Whitestone. With Dept. Navy, Washington, 1944-69; dir. systems and acctg. div. Bur. Navy Personnel, Washington, 1969-74; spl. asst. to dir. Office Fin. and Acctg., HUD, Washington, 1974-80, dir. Office Fin. and Acctg., 1980—. Recipient numerous Outstanding Performance awards Dept. Navy and HUD, 1960—, Cash Mgmt. Savs. award U.S. Treasury, 1984. Mem. Assn. Govt. Accts. Home: 7200 Constantine Ave Springfield VA 22150 Office: HUD Office Fin and Acctg Bldg 451 7th St SW Washington DC 20410

EVANS, SUSAN A., lawyer; b. Washington, Aug. 31, 1954; d. Robert David and Clara Mae (Messick) Evans; m. Robert Stevens Greenlief, Dec. 26, 1980 (div. 1983); m. Ralph N. Boccarosse, May 27, 1986. B.A., U. Va., Charlottesville, 1976; J.D., U. Richmond, Va., 1979. Bar: Va. 1979, D.C. 1982. Law clk. 19th Jud. Cir. Va., Fairfax, 1979-80; ptnr. Siciliano, Ellis, Dyer & Boccarosse, Fairfax, 1980—. Mem. Va. State Bar Assn., Fairfax Bar Assn., No. Va. Def. Lawyers (v.p. 1986—). Baptist. Home: 2404 Ansdel Ct Reston VA 22091 Office: Siciliano Ellis Dyer & Boccarosse 10521 Judicial Dr Suite 300 Fairfax VA 22030

EVANS, VERA FRAZIER, food service executive, caterer; b. Dermott, Ark., Mar. 11, 1935; d. Leon W. and Alberta (Hall) Frazier; divorced, 1974; 1 dau., Kim Denise Azadiani. Cert. Loop Coll., Chgo., 1965, 1977; cert. Saga Mgmt. Sch., Kalamazoo, 1980. Food service worker Michael Reese Hosp., Chgo., 1953-56, food service supr., 1959-63, cost control analyst, 1963-64, food service mgr., 1964—. Co-chmn. Michael Reese Hosp. and Martin Luther King Scholarship Com., 1971, treas., 1974; bd. dirs. Michael L. Reese Hosp. Fed. Credit Union, 1979. Mem. Dietary Mgrs. Assn. (treas. 1976-78, pres.-elect 1985-86). Methodist. Avocations: collector African sculpture and pressed glass. Home: 9356 S King Dr Chicago IL 60619

EVANS, VICTORIA A., environmental company executive; b. Louisville, June 19, 1950; d. Frank William and Kathryn Cecilia (Finn) Evans; m. Douglas Alan Latimer, Feb. 14, 1982. Student Bowling Green U., 1968-71; B.S. in Natural Resources, U. Mich., 1972, M.S. in Natural Resources, 1976. Environ. planner Gilbert-Commonwealth Assocs., Jackson, Miss., 1974-76; environ. rev. officer Dept. Interior, Washington, 1976-78; bur. chief Wis. Pub. Service Commn., Madison, 1978-79; visibility program mgr. Nat. Park Service, Washington, 1979-82; environ. cons. Gaia Assocs., Sausalito, Calif., 1982—. Author numerous papers in field. Bd. dirs. Lucas Valley Home Owners Assn., San Rafael, 1984, v.p., 1985-86, pres., 1986; bd. dirs. Marin Citizens for Energy Planning, San Rafael, 1984, mem. environ. forum, Larkspur, Calif., 1984, Marin Conservation League, 1984. Recipient Spl. Achievement award Nat. Park Service, 1980. Mem. Women Energy Assn. (bd. dirs. 1984—), Air Pollution Control Assn., TE-5 Visibility Com., Golden Gate Energy Ctr. Democrat. Avocations: cross-country skiing, gardening, natural history. Home: 1268 Idylberry Rd San Rafael CA 94903 Office: Gaia Assocs Fort Cronkhite Bldg 1055 Sausalito CA 94965

EVANS, ZOE ANDES, microbiologist; b. Knoxville, Tenn., Mar 5, 1934; d. James Osborn and Esther Marie (Crawford) Andes; B.S., Coll. of William and Mary, 1955; M.S., U. Tenn., 1972; Ph.D. (NIH trainee), Med. Coll. Va., 1977; m. James Montgomery Evans, Sept. 26, 1956; children—Janet Marie, Karen Hungerford. Microbiologist, Bapt. Meml. Hosp., Memphis, 1956-58, 68-70; research asst. Vanderbilt U., Nashville, 1966-68; instr., asst. dir. clin. microbiology U. Va. Sch. Medicine, Charlottesville, 1972-75; asst. prof. U. Ala., Huntsville, 1977-81; asso. prof., chmn. dept. med. tech. U. Tex. Health Sci. Center, Dallas, 1981-83, assoc. prof., chmn. dept. med. lab. scis., 1983—; cons. microbiology, 1977—. Specialist in public health, med. lab. microbiology Am. Acad. Microbiology. Mem. AAAS, Am. Soc. for Microbiology, Southeastern Immunology Conf., Ala. Acad. Sci., Am. Soc. Clin. Pathologists, Reticuloendothelial Soc., Am. Soc. Med. Tech., Bus. and Profl. Women's Assn., Phi Kappa Phi, Sigma Xi. Presbyterian. Contbr. papers, abstracts in field to profl. lit. Office: Dept Med Lab Scis U Tex Health Sci Center Dallas TX 75235

EVANSON, JANE LOUISE, educator; b. San Francisco, July 20, 1944; d. Charles William and Margaret (Bull) Evanson; B.S., Calif. Poly. State U., 1965; M.Ed., U. Va., 1972; Ph.D., Fla. State U., 1974. Asso. dir. Adult Edn. Resource Center, Montclair (N.J.) State Coll., 1974-75; asst. prof., asso. prof. Worcester (Mass.) State Coll., 1975-79; assoc. prof. Alaska Pacific U., Anchorage, 1979-80, prof., from 1980, chmn. human resource devel., from 1983, dean of students 1980—; editorial cons. Contemporary Books, Inc., Chgo. Bd. dirs. Alaska Native Social and Recreation Center. Recipient Outstanding Service Award, Adult Edn. Assn. U.S.A., 1981. Mem. Internat. Reading Assn., Western Coll. Reading Assn., Phi Delta Kappa. Presbyterian. Club: Soroptomist Internat. (Cook Inlet, Anchorage). Author: From Pictures to Passages: Building Skills in Reading Comprehension, 1968; contbr. articles to profl. jours. Office: 319 Grant Hall Alaska Pacific U Dept Edn 4101 University Dr Anchorage AK 99508

EVENSTEIN, JOSEPHINE JIHRLL, apparel mfg. co. exec.; b. Chgo.; d. Louis Benjamin and Fannie (Gluckman) Evenstein; B.S., Ill. Inst. Tech., 1944. Credit mgr. Catalina, Inc., Los Angeles, 1946-52, Jerry Mann of Calif., Los Angeles, 1953-63; controller Hartog of Calif., Los Angeles, 1964-73; controller Lucie Ann, Beverly Hills, Calif., 1973—. Mem. Greater Los Angeles Zoo Assn., Brentwood-Westwood Symphony Assn., Concern Found. for Cancer Research, Los Angeles County Mus. Art and Natural History. Democrat. Jewish. Clubs: Hadassah (fin. sec. 1977-78), B'nai B'rith. Home: 350 S Fuller Ave Apt 7-E Los Angeles CA 90036 Office: 1 Lucie Ann Ln Beverly Hills CA 90210

EVERETEZE, JUANITA ANN, physician; b. Cambridge, Mass., Apr. 18, 1953; d. Enricius and Clorae Donnell (Hunt) Evereteze. B.A. in Biology, Boston U., 1975; M.D., SUNY-Buffalo, 1979; M.P.H., Columbia U., 1983. Intern Mt. Auburn Hosp., Cambridge, Mass., 1979-80; resident, sr. resident Harlem Hosp., N.Y.C., 1980-82; jr. attending physician dept. medicine, 1982—; fellow nephrology Cornell U., 1984—. Mem. Nat. Acad. Sci., AMA, ACP, Nat. Med. Assn., Coalition 100 Black Women. Office: Harlem Hosp 506 Lenox Ave New York NY 10037

EVERETT, NANCY LEE, advertising agency executive, custom furniture crafter executive; b. Richmond, Va., Nov. 13, 1940; d. Ernest Rexford and Clarice (Ryland) E.; m. James F. Dalby, Jan. 26, 1957 (div. Aug. 1979); children—James F. Jr., Ernest Fleet, Joseph Reynolds. B.A., U. N.C., 1958; M.F.A., U. Md., 1976. Pres. Mktg. Communication Inc., Arlington, Va., 1978—, Everett Ross Communications Inc., Christiansted, St. Croix, V.I., 1984—, Solid Wood Design, Falls Church, 1983—. One women shows: Rice U., Houston, 1960, Carnegie Hall, N.Y.C., 1973; group shows include: Houston Project for the Arts, 1960, Washington Project for the Arts, 1980. Mem. com. Superball Charity event Easter Seals, Washington, 1981, 82, 83. Recipient numerous 1st place art shows awards. Mem. Washington Performing Arts Soc. Republican. Episcopalian. Avocation: oil painting. Office: Mktg Communications Inc 1021 N Kentucky St Arlington VA 22205

EVERINGHAM, JOYCE DUBERT, library administrator; b. Hornell, N.Y., May 14, 1929; d. John Griniliffe and Genie Mae (Herda) Dubert; m. Neil Gilbert Everingham, Sept. 17, 1955; 1 child, N. Mark. B.A., SUNY-Albany, 1950; M.L.S., SUNY-Geneseo, 1957, postgrad., 1974. Librarian, East Pembroke Sch., N.Y., 1957-59, City Sch. Dist., Williamsport, Pa., 1959-62; coordinator libraries Westhill Schs., Syracuse, N.Y., 1963-69; dir. pilot project Sch. Library System Syracuse City Schs., 1979-82, supr. libraries, 1969-82; exec. dir. Western N.Y. Library Resources Council, Buffalo, 1983—; mem. N.Y. Hist. Documents Inventory State Com., 1984—. Mem. ALA, N.Y. Library Assn., Western N.Y. Hosp. Library Assn., Mid-Atlantic Records & Archives, Pub. Library Sect. N.Y. Library Assn., Western N.Y. Ry. Hist. Soc. Avocations: music, basketball, sports, camping, crafts. Office: Western New York Library Resources Council Lafayette Square Buffalo NY 14203

EVERSBERG, HELEN M., government lawyer. U.S. atty. western dist. Tex., San Antonio. Office: US Attys Office John H Wood Jr Fed Bldg 655 E Durango Blvd San Antonio TX 78206*

EVERSON, SUSAN TOFT, field services director; b. St. Louis, Nov. 22, 1944; d. Martin John and Edna Ann (Mortensen) Toft; B.S., U. Mo., 1966; M.A., Peabody Coll., 1974; postgrad. U. Wis., 1977-78; m. David E. Everson, Jr., June 11, 1966; 1 dau., Courtney Anne. Tchr., Webster Groves (Mo.) Schs., 1966-67; resident dir. U. Mich., Ann Arbor, 1968-69; dir. child devel. program, Cape Elizabeth, Maine, 1972-73; instr. U. Ga., 1974-77; program asso. Mid-Continent Regional Edn1. Lab., Kansas City, Mo., 1978-79, project dir., 1979—. Mem. Adult Basic Edn. Bd., Kansas City, Mo., 1981-82. Mem. Kansas City Citizen's Assn. (bd. govs.), Central Exchange, Assn. Supervision and Curriculum Devel., Am. Ednl. Research Assn., Nat. Assn. Exec. Women, Phi Delta Kappa. Democrat. Clubs: Sierra, Internat. Relations, Audubon Soc. Home: 831 Westover Rd Kansas City MO 64113 Office: 4709 Belleview Kansas City MO 64112

EVERT-LLOYD, CHRISTINE MARIE (CHRIS), professional tennis player; b. Ft. Lauderdale, Fla., Dec. 21, 1954; d. James and Colette Evert; ed. pvt. schs. Ft. Lauderdale; m. John Lloyd, Apr. 17, 1979. Amateur tennis player until Dec., 1972; now profl. player, mem. Women's Pro Tennis Tour; U.S. jr. champion, 1970-71; singles titlist U.S. Clay Ct. Championship, 1972, 73, 74, 75, 79, 80, U.S. Lawn Tennis Assn. tournament, 1973, South African Open, 1973, 84, Wimbledon, 1974, 76, 81, Italian Open, 1974, 75, 79, 80, 81, 82, French Open, 1974, 75, 79, 80, 83, 85, Canadian Open, 1974, 80, 84, 85, Family Circle Mag. Cup tournament, 1974, 75, 77, 78, U.S. Open, 1975, 76, 77, 78, 80, 82, Va. Slims Championship, 1975, 77; ITF world champion, 1978, 80, 81; numerous others. Mem. Wightmen Cup team, 1971, 72, 73, 75, 82, 84, 85, Bell Cup team, 1972, 73. Recipient Most Valuable Player trophy Wightman Cup Championship 1971; Lebair Sportsmanship trophy, 1971, named Female Athlete of Year AP, 1974, 75, 77, 80. Mem. U.S. Lawn Tennis Assn. (named top Women's Singles Player 1974), Nat. Honor Soc. Address: 1628 7th Pl NE Fort Lauderdale FL 33304*

EVERTON, MARTA VE, ophthalmologist; b. Luling, Tex., Nov. 12, 1926; d. T.W. and Nora E. (Eckols) O'Leavy; B.A., Hardin-Simmons U., 1945; M.A., Stanford U., 1947; M.D., Baylor U., 1955; postgrad. N.Y.U.-Bellevue Hosp., 1956-57; m. Robert K. Graham, Oct. 15, 1960; children—Marcia, Christie, Leslie Fox. Intern, Meth. Hosp., Houston, 1955-56; resident in ophthalmology Baylor Affiliated Hosps., Houston, 1957-59; clin. instr. ophthalmology Baylor U., 1959-60; asst. clin. prof. ophthalmology Loma Linda U., 1962-73; practice medicine specializing in ophthalmology, Houston, 1959-60, Pasadena, Calif., 1961-74, Escondido, Calif., 1974—. Mem. AMA, Am. Acad. Ophthalmology, Am. Med. Women's Assn., Alpha Omega Alpha. Home: 3024 Sycamore Ln Escondido CA 92025 Office: 810 E Ohio Ave Escondido CA 92025

EVERTS, DELORES JEAN, graphic services executive; b. Madison, Wis., May 13, 1943; d. William Robert and Agnes Anna (Schwartz) Bennett; m. Gordon Clifford Conley, Nov. 30, 1963 (div. 1965); 1 child, William Earl; m. R. Alain Everts, Aug. 31, 1974. Student U. Wis.-Madison, 1961-62, Madison Area Tech. Coll., 1972-74. Pres., chmn. bd. Madison Graphic Services, Inc., 1980—. Editor Etchings & Odysseys mag., 1983—. Served with USMC, 1962. Mem. World Fantasy Conv., MadCon (v.p. 1974-85, Weirdfield award 1985), MinnCon, Madison Area C. of C., Ind. Bus. Assn. of Wis. Avocations: books; science fiction; Dr. Who. Office: Madison Graphic Services Inc 120 E Wilson St Madison WI 53703

EWALD, ROBERTA GRANT, artist, playwright, composer; b. Mpls., Aug. 25, 1915; d. Oscar and Hanna Theolinda (Johannson) Grant; m. Henry C. Ewald, Sept. 7, 1946; 1 child, Grant Christian. Student U. Minn., Calif. Sch. Fine Arts, Coll. of San Mateo, Golden Gate Coll. Acct. various firms, San Francisco, 1946-64; owner, artist Travelers Art Gallery, South San Francisco, Calif., 1973—; owner, adminstr. Ewald Travel Service, South San Francisco and San Bruno, Calif., 1967—; cons. Capuchino Community Theater, 1984. Lead role and author musical: The Wanderers, 1978, co-producer revision, 1982. Illustrator, pub. (poetry): I'm All I Know, 1983; co-producer TV show, Pacifica, 1982; dir. children's choirs, music events, songwriter, singer, actress, musician (piano and guitar). Recipient Merit award Capuchino Community Theater, 1983, 84; numerous awards for paintings San Francisco and Calif. art exhibits; named Outstanding Mem. Pacifica Spindrift Players, 1980. Mem. Internat. Platform Assn., Pacifica Area Travel Assn., Am. Assn. Travel Agts., Internat. Assn. Travel Agts., Pacifica Arts and Heritage Assn., ArtRise, Citizens Against Waste, Pacifica Spindrift Players, Art Guild of Pacifica (past pres.), Playwrights Continuon, LWV, Beta Sigma Phi (pres. 1940-41). Republican. Presbyterian. Office: Travelers Art Gallery 345-9 Baden Ave South San Francisco CA 94080 also Ewald Travel Service 757 Kains Ave San Bruno CA 94066

EWELL, YVONNE AMARYLLIS, educational administrator; b. Frankston, Tex., Sept. 19, 1926; d. Valcris Olenthus and Marjorie (Morris) E. B.A., Prairie View A&M Coll., 1947; M.A., U. Colo., 1960; LL.D. (hon.), Bishop Coll., 1979. Elem. tchr. Ladonia (Tex.) Pub. Schs., 1947-54; elem./secondary tchr. Dallas Ind. Sch. Dist., 1954-61, elem. prin., 1961-64, elem. cons., 1964-68, dep. asst. supt., 1974-76, asst. supt., 1976, assoc. supt., 1976-82, spl. asst. to gen. supt., 1982-83, adminstr. Townview Magnet Ctr., 1983—; bd. dirs. KERA Pub. TV, 1978—; cons. Com. on Race, United Meth. Ch., N.Y.C., 1981-82, Bd. Edn. and Adminstrn., Chgo., 1983. Developer Model Program for Desegregation - East Oak Cliff, 1976, Citation by Fed. Judge, 1981. Bd. dirs. Park Bd., City of Dallas, 1983—; fin. chmn. Nat. Council Negro Women, Washington, 1980—; nat. bd. dirs. YWCA, 1973—, chmn. racial justice com., 1975-82; edn. chmn. Tex. Adv. Commn., U.S. Commn. on Civil Rights, Austin, 1980. Named Woman of Yr., Zeta Phi Beta, Dallas, 1964; recipient State Human Relations award Tex. State Tchrs. Assn., Austin, 1976; Meritorious Service award Phi Delta Kappa, 1979. Mem. Assn. for Supervision and Curriculum Devel., Am. Assn. Sch. Adminstrs. (adv. panel 1979-83), Dallas Sch. Adminstrs. Assn. (sec. 1968—), Delta Sigma Theta. Baptist. Clubs: Zonta, So. Dallas Bus. and Profl. Women (Dallas). Home: 4641 Kushla Ave Dallas TX 75216 Office: Dallas Ind Sch Dist 3700 Ross Ave Dallas TX 75204

EWEN, PAMELA BINNINGS, lawyer; b. Phila., Mar. 22, 1944; d. Walter James and Barbara (Perkins) Binnings; m. Jerome Francis Ayers, Aug. 22, 1965 (div. July 1974); 1 son, Scott Dylan; m. 2d, John Alexander Ewen, Dec. 13, 1974. B.A., Tulane U., 1977; J.D. cum laude, U. Houston, 1979. Bar: Tex. 1979, U.S. Dist. Ct. (so. dist.) Tex. 1981, U.S. Ct. Appeals (5th cir.) 1981. Law clk. firm Harris, Cook, Browning & Barker, Corpus Christi, Tex., 1977-79; assoc. firm Kleberg, Dyer, Redford & Weil, Corpus Christi, 1979-80; atty. law dept. Gulf Oil Corp., Houston, 1980-84; assoc. Baker & Botts, Houston, 1984—. La. Legis. scholar, New Orleans, 1976-77. Mem. ABA (forum com. on franchising 1983—), Am. Petroleum Inst. (spl. subcom. to gen. com. on law, com. on product liability 1982-85), Order of Barons. Office: 3000 One Shell Plaza Houston TX 77002

EWERSEN, MARY VIRGINIA, educator; b. Von Wert County, Ohio, June 7, 1922; B.S. in Elem. Edn., Bowling Green, Toledo and Ohio State U. State U., 1966, now postgrad.; m. Herbert Ewersen (dec.); 2 children. Remedial reading tchr. Port Clinton (Ohio) City Schs., 1966-70, reading tchr./coordinator, 1970—Cert., Ohio. Mem. NEA, Ohio, N.W. Ohio, Port Clinton edn. assns., Internat. Reading Assn., Sandusky Choral Soc., Kappa Delta Pi. Author activity card set: From Hyperactive to Happy-Active in Limited Spaces, 1979. Home: 1786 S Hickory Grove Rd Port Clinton OH 43452 Office: 431 Portage Dr Port Clinton OH 43452

EWERT, KARLA RUTH, telephone company official; b. Des Moines, Aug. 16, 1949; d. Lowell E. and Martha H. (Henry) Strahan; B.S. in Christian Edn. and Music, Grace Coll. Bible, Omaha, 1971; m. Stanley B. Ewert, June 19, 1971; 1 dau., Lisa Renae. With Northwestern Bell Telephone Co., Omaha, 1971-72, 73—, staff supr. ednl. relations, 1977-78, mgr. community relations, 1978—; speaker in field. Coordinator, Wintertainment Festival, 1981; bd. dirs. Omaha Summer Arts Festival, 1981, YWCA, 1983, 84, Leadership Omaha, 1982-83, Nebraskaland Found.; coordinator Sundae Sunday, Omaha Children's Museum Festival, 1982; mem. River City Roundup Com., 1982-84. Mem. Soc. Consumer Affairs Profls., Jr. League Omaha. Home: 2503 N 55th St Omaha NE 68104 Office: 100 S 19th St Room 1270 Dodge Omaha NE 68102

EWING, JUDITH COATS, architectural design executive, real estate broker, counselor; b. Beaumont, Tex., Apr. 30, 1941; d. James D. and Dru Elaine (Sheffield) Coats; m. Joe L. Ewing, Jan. 12, 1973. B.S., Lamar U., 1963; M.Ed., U. Houston, 1974; postgrad. Fielding Inst., 1982—. Lic. profl. counselor. Tchr., Nederland Ind. Sch. Dist. (Tex.), 1963-64, Silsbee Ind. Sch. Dist. (Tex.), 1964-69; dep. clk. Harris County Courthouse, Houston, 1970; tchr., ednl. diagnostician Aldine Ind. Sch. Dist. (Tex.), 1968-76; office mgr. Windermere Chase Corp., Houston, 1976, Ewing Design Group, Spicewood, Tex., 1977-78; realtor assoc. Century 21, Howard Itten Co., Austin, Tex., 1978-79; tchr. spl. edn. San Antonio Ind. Sch. Dist., 1979-80; coordinator spl. services, secondary counselor Cimarron Mcpl. Schs. (N.Mex.), 1980-81; sales/property mgr. Bailey-Mertz Venture, Angel Fire, N.Mex., 1981-82; elem. counselor Fort Bend Ind. Sch. Dist., Sugarland, Tex., 1982-83, coordinator Lakeview Career Fair, mem. com. for devel. 1st elem. summer sch. program, 1983; v.p. Ewing Design Group, Houston, 1983—; cons. to assist in updating and reevaluation of counselor edn. program Sam Houston State U., Huntsville, Tex., 1983. Tchr., vol. Silsbee Woman's Club Adult Basic Edn. Program, 1967; co-chmn., organizer program on communication and behavior control for parent and family life edn. PTA, Houston, 1975. Mem. Tex. Personnel and Guidance Assn., Tex. Sch. Counselors Assn., Tex. Mental Health Counselor Assn., Tex. Real Estate Commn., Fort Bend County Personnel and Guidance Assn. (sec. 1983), DAR, Am. Needlepoint Guild, Alpha Delta Kappa, Beta Sigma Phi. Methodist. Lodge: Order of Rainbow for Girls (life, worthy advisor 1958, Grand Cross of Color), Order Eastern Star. Office: Ewing Design Group 2400 Augusta St Suite 236 Houston TX 77057

EWING, MARY ARNOLD, lawyer; b. Shreveport, La., Feb. 21, 1948; d. George and Christine (Cocek) Hengy; B.A., U. Colo., 1972; J.D., U. Denver, 1975; m. Robert Craig Ewing, Aug. 30, 1981; 1 child, Kyle Ross. Bar: Colo. 1975, U.S. Supreme Ct. 1979; cert. trial specialist Nat. Bd. Trial Advocacy. Law clk. Johnson and Mahoney, P.C., Denver, 1972-75, asso., 1975-80; partner firm Branney, Hillyard, Ewing and Barnes, Englewood, Colo., 1980-85, Bucholtz, Bull & Ewing P.C., 1986—; asst. prof. law U. Denver Coll. Law, 1977-78, part-time prof., 1978—; judge continuing legal edn. Course in Trial Advocacy, 1979, 80; mem. faculty Nat. Inst. Trial Advocacy, 1984-86; guest lectr. local colls. and univs.; instr. nat. session Nat. Bd. Trial Advocacy, Boulder, Colo., 1984, 85, instr. regional session U. Denver Coll. Law, 1986. Chmn., Denver County Task Force, Health and Hosp., 1976-77; treas. 1st. Congressional Dist. Central Com., 1976-77; v.p. Young Republican League of Denver, 1975, pres., 1976; mem. govt. relations com. Jr. Symphony Guild, 1978—. Mem. ABA, Colo. Bar Assn. (ethics com.), Denver Bar Assn. (vice chmn. new lawyers assistance com. 1977), Colo. Women's Bar Assn., Internat. Platform Assn., Mountain States Combined Tng. Assn., Rocky Mountain Dressage Soc. (sec. High Plains chpt. 1979, 80), Am. Trial Lawyers Assn., Colo. Trial Lawyers Assn. (bd. govs., chmn. interprofl. com. 1980, dir. 1981—), Am. Arbitration Assn., U. Denver Coll. Law Alumni Council, Kappa Beta Pi (pres. 1977-78). Club: Toastmasters Internat. Home: 816 W Quarry Rd Littleton CO 80124 Office: 1666 S University Blvd Denver CO 80210

EWING, TERRY LYNN GARDNER, graphic arts co. exec.; b. Indpls., Aug. 18, 1950; d. William Clyde and Donna Louise (Lain) Gardner; student Ind. U., Indpls., 1971-76; m. Michael Paul Ewing, June 27, 1980; 1 dau., Lauren Noel. Graphic artist, typesetter, Indpls., 1968-70; corp. artist Am. Monitor Corp., Indpls., 1970-71, 73-74; adminstrv. asst. Campaign Communicators, Inc., Indpls., 1972; customer coordinator Universal Printing Co., Indpls., 1974; prodn. mgr. Plywood & Panel Mag., Indpls., 1974-75; prodn. mgr. Indytype, Inc., Indpls., 1975-79, v.p. prodn. div., 1979—, editor-in-chief Art Product News, bd. dirs. Indytype, Inc., exec. editorial bd. Art Product News Mag., Mimar Corp.; pvt. tutor, tchr. migrant children. Mem. Women in Communications, Ind. Bus. Communicators. Home: 4923 W 14th St Speedway IN 46224 Office: 4040 W 10th St Indianapolis IN 46222

EX, MIRIAM GOLUB, credit union executive; b. Chgo., Aug. 2, 1936; d. Arthur J. and Helen (Solomon) Golub; m. Jerome J. Ex, Apr. 3, 1955; children—Rachel B. Ex Connelly, Francine J., Barbara. B.Ed., Northeastern Coll., Chgo., 1966. Asst. mgr. Tempel Fed. Credit Union, Chgo., 1977-79; pres. Kraft Employees Credit Union, Glenview, Ill., 1979—. Home: 2815 W Chase St Chicago IL 60645 Office: Kraft Employees Credit Union Kraft Court Glenview IL 60025

EXUM, FRANCES BELL, foreign language educator; b. Birmingham, Ala., May 11, 1940; d. Frank Kinney and Frances Henrietta (Bell) E.; B.A. in Spanish cum laude, Fla. State U., 1962, M.A. in Spanish, 1963, Ph.D. in Spanish, 1970. Instr. Spanish, N.C. Wesleyan Coll., 1963-65, Greensboro Coll., 1965-67; asst. prof. Spanish, Winthrop Coll., 1970-73, assoc. prof., 1973-77, prof., 1977—. Mem. MLA, South Atlantic MLA (exec. v.p. 1986—, Spanish I chmn. 1985), Asociación Internacional de Hispanistas, Am. Assn. Tchrs. Spanish and Portuguese (pres. S.C. chpt. 1979-80), Cervantes Soc. Am., Soc. Spanish and Portuguese Hist. Studies, AAUP (pres. chpt. 1976-77), Renaissance Soc. Am., Phi Beta Kappa, Phi Kappa Phi (pres. chpt. 1984-85), Pi Beta Phi. Author: The Metamorphosis of Lope de Vega's King Pedro, 1974; contbr. articles and book revs. to profl. publs. Home: 3757 Harwick Place Charlotte NC 28211 Office: Dept Modern and Classical Langs Winthrop Coll Rock Hill SC 29733

EYRE, PAMELA CATHERINE, army officer; b. Chgo., Nov. 3, 1948; d. Francis Thomas and Jane (Burd) E.; m. Burke Owen Buntz, Jan. 10, 1986. B.A., Central State U. Okla., 1972; M.P.A., U. Okla., 1976. Commd. 2d lt. U.S. Army, 1973, advanced through grades to maj., 1986; test and evaluation officer Fort Gordon, Ga., 1982-85, research and devel. coordinator Pentagon, Washington, 1985—. Fellow Armed Forces Communications Electronics Assn. Avocation: foxhunting. Home: 5011 Larno Dr Alexandria VA 22310

EYSTER, CAROL IRENE, educational administrator; b. Massillon, Ohio, July 23, 1938; d. Robert Lee and Mildred Florence (Klick) E.; m. Irving Wallace, Oct. 18, 1969 (div. 1970). B.S., U. Ariz., 1961, M.S., 1968. Cert. elem. and secondary tchr., Calif. Sci. tchr. Glendale Unified Sch. Dist., Ariz., 1961-63; tchr., Valencia, Venezuela, 1963-67, Los Angeles Unified Sch. Dist., 1968-78; dir. San Pedro Sci. Ctr., 1978—; dir. San Pedro and 186th Sci. Ctr. Specializing in Sci. Edn., 1984—; judge Sci. Fair Com., Los Angeles, 1983-85; evaluator Textbook Evaluation Com., Los Angeles, 1984-85. Mem. Sierra Club, Nat. Audubon Soc., Desert Tortoise Preserve Com. Inc., Red Rock Canyon Interpretive Assn., Los Angeles Sci. Tchrs. Assn., Calif. Sci. Tchrs. Assn., Nat. Sci. Tchrs. Assn., Phi Kappa Phi, Delta Kappa Gamma. Avocations: collecting houses; travel; photography. Home: 623 1/2 S PCH Redondo Beach CA 90277 Office: San Pedro Sci Ctr 2201 Barrywood Ave San Pedro CA 90732

EYTAN, RACHEL, novelist, educator; b. Israel, May 4, 1932; came to U.S., 1967, naturalized, 1979; d. Yaacov Litai and Sara Zweig; B.A., Hakibutzim Tchrs. Coll., Israel, 1950; B.A., NYU, M.A., 1975, doctoral student, 1976-79; m. Jerry H. Fishman, Oct., 1967; children—Omry, Hamutal, Yonatan. Tchr., Israeli Kibbutz, Tel Aviv, 1950-53; novelist; books include: The Fifth Heaven, 1963; Shida Veshidot, 1973; The Fifth Heaven (in English), 1985; contbr. short stories and articles to Am. lit. mags.; editor, contbr. to Israeli and Am. lit. mags. and newspapers; prof. Israeli lit. Gratz Coll., Phila., 1967-68; prof. Israeli, Hebrew and Yiddish lit. Hofstra U., 1968—; lectr. Am., European and Israeli univs., TV and radio. Active Israeli-Arab Peace Movement, NOW, Women Ink Writers. Recipient Brenner prize for lit., Israel, 1966, Founders Day award N.Y.U., 1973. Mem. MLA, AAUP, Am. PEN Club, Israeli Pen Club, Israeli Writers Assn., Herzle Inst., Concerned Scientists. Home: 227 Central Park W New York NY 10024 Office: Hofstra U Hempstead NY 11550

EZELL, ANNETTE SCHRAM, nursing educator, university dean; b. West Frankfort, Ill., June 19, 1940; d. Woodrow C. and Rosa (Franich) Schram; student Evansville Coll., 1957, Protestant Deaconess Hosp. Sch. Nursing, 1957-59, Ind. U., 1959; B.S. in Nursing, U. Nev., 1962, M.S. in Physiology, 1967, postgrad., 1969; Ed.D., Brigham Young U., 1977; children—Michael L., Rona Maria. Staff nurse Washoe Med. Center, Reno, 1962; teaching asst. U. Nev., Reno, 1962-63, instr., 1963-64, 1965-67, asst. prof. nursing, 1967-71; curriculum specialist U. Nev. Med. Sch., 1971-72, project mgr. Fed. Grant Intercampus Nursing Edn. Project, 1969-71, assoc. prof. nursing, curriculum specialist rural nurse practitioner program, 1971-73, staff assoc. Mountain States Regional Med. Program, 1974-75; cons. Nev. Dept. Edn., 1975-77; asst. dean acad. affairs Coll. Nursing, U. Utah, Salt Lake City, 1977-80; acting Dean, 1981, dir., prof. doctoral program Nursing Edn. Adminstrn.; prof., dept. head for nursing, Coll. Human Development, Pa. State U., 1982-85; dean Coll. Profl. Studies, U. So. Colo., Pueblo, 1985—; cons. nursing edn., TV edn., research methology; adviser to various research, polit. and ednl. bds. Mem. Am. Nurses Assn., Am. Ednl. Research Assn., Am. Assn. Humanistic Psychiatry, AAAS, Am. Acad. Arts and Scis., AAUP, Western Ednl. Soc. for Telecommunications, Sigma Xi, Phi Kappa Phi, Delta Kappa Gamma. Home: 11 Sedum Ct Pueblo CO 81001 Office: Coll Profl Studies U So Colo Pueblo CO 81001

EZELL, DHE LEE, community development and human services agency executive; b. Perry, Ga., Feb. 24, 1944; d. John Thomas and Rosa Bell (Hill) E.; children—Hansi Jones, Stacey Jones, Theronn Dozier. Cert. Columbia U., 1979; B.A. in Profl. Studies and Human Services, Coll. for Human Services, N.Y.C., 1980; postgrad Baruch Coll., CUNY, 1982. Past bus. rep. N.Y. Telephone Co., N.Y.C.; then clk. U.S. Post Office, N.Y.C.; community organizer Morris Heights, Bronx, N.Y., 1978-80; exec. asst. Assn. Neighborhood and Housing Devel., 1980-81, acting exec. dir., N.Y.C., 1981-83; exec. dir. Bronx Heights Corp., 1985—; tech. adviser Quality Housing Mgmt. Co., Bronx, 1985—. Editor Moore News newsletter, 1976 (N.Y.C. Housing Authority Best Publ. award 1976); co-editor IRT Express trade newspaper, 1978, Speaking Out newspaper, 1978—. Vice pres. Moore Tenants Assn., Bronx, 1975-78, People Networking Unltd., Bronx, 1985—; pres. Moore

Houses Community Ctr., Bronx, 1975-76; chairperson Congl. Planning Council, Bronx, 1976. Served to pfc. U.S. Army, 1962-64. Recipient Service to Humanity award Morrisania Hosp., Bronx, 1968; fellow Baruch Coll., CUNY, N.Y.C., 1982. Mem. Nat. Assn. Female Execs. Democrat. Avocations: sewing; writing; reading; collecting social and political buttons. Home: 535 Jackson Ave Bronx NY 10455 Office: Bronx Heights Community Corp 99 Featherbed Ln Bronx NY 10452

EZELL, IDA HAMILTON (THOMPSON) GAYDEN, physical education educator and administrator; b. Nashville, Apr. 23, 1949; d. Hamilton Virgil and Ann (Dickinson) Gayden; B.S. in Phys. Edn. and Art Edn. (Delta Zeta scholar), U. Miami, Coral Gables, Fla., 1972; M.S. in Phys. Edn. and Spl. Edn., U. Tenn., 1975; m. John Calvin Ezell, June 5, 1972. Mgr. Crestwood Hills Recreation Center, Oak Ridge, 1973-74; tchr. phys. edn., spl. edn., public schs., Oak Ridge, 1974-77; mgr. Homeland Apts., Balt., 1978; mgr., coach L'Hirondelle Country Club, Balt., 1979; asst. prof., athletic dir. women's athletics, chmn. dept. phys. edn. Coll. Notre Dame, Balt., 1977—; mem. adv. com. YWCA Greater Balt. Aerobics, 1979-80; mem. Balt. Water Safety Com., 1980-82; aquatics dir. Teen Odyssey, 1982 Chmn. standards com., mem. exec. com. ARC. Recipient vol. recognizition awards ARC, 1976, 79; cert. tchr., Md., Tenn., Fla. Mem. NEA, AAHPER, Md. Assn. Intercollegiate Athletics for Women (sec. 1978-80), Nat. Volleyball Coaches Assn., Nat. Collegiate Women's Swimming Coaches Assn., Phi Delta Phi, Delta Psi Kappa. Democrat. Presbyterian. Home: PO Box 10153 Towson MD 21204 Office: 4701 N Charles St Baltimore MD 21210

EZOP, PHYLLIS P., marketing and planning executive; b. Chgo., Sept. 27, 1950; d. Frank Joseph and Helen (Rocen) Panno; m. Richard V. Ezop, July 4, 1970. B.S. in Math., U. Ill.-Chgo., 1971; M.B.A., U. Chgo., 1976. Statis. analyst 1st Fed. Savs. & Loan, Chgo., 1971-73; research analyst Allied Van Lines, Broadview, Ill., 1974-77, dir. mktg. support, 1981-82; planning analyst U.S. Gypsum Co., Chgo., 1978-79; product cons. Western Electric unit AT&T, Warrenville, 1979-81; prin. Ezop & Assocs., LaGrange Park, Ill., 1982—; Mem. U. Chgo. Women's Bus. Group (dir. 1982—, continuing edn. chmn. 1982—), Am. Mktg. Assn. Club: Hinsdale Toastmasters (ednl. v.p. 1984—). Home and Office: 321 N Catherine St LaGrange Park IL 60525

EZZARD, MARTHA MCELVEEN, state senator, lawyer; b. Atlanta, Nov. 8, 1938; d. George Davant and Gladys Caroline (Lewis) McElveen; A.B. in Journalism, U. Ga., 1960; M.A., U. Mo., 1968; J.D., U. Denver, 1982; m. John A. Ezzard, Dec. 27, 1960; children—Shelly Lynne, Lisa Annette, John A. With Atlanta Jour., 1959-60, Sta. WSB-TV, Atlanta, 1960; tchr. Littleton (Colo.) High Sch., 1961-62; with Sta. KOMU-TV, Columbia, Mo., 1965-68; gov.'s press aide, 1973-75; polit. columnist Rocky Mountain Jour., Denver, 1976-77; mem. Colo. Ho. of Reps. from 37th Dist., 1978-80, Colo. Senate from 20th Dist., 1980—; atty. Bader & Cox, Denver; dir. United Bank Littleton. Bd. dirs. Women's Forum. Named Outstanding Republican Legislator, 1980, 81. Mem. Colo. Press Women (Feature and Editorial Writing awards), Colo. Bar Assn., Denver Bar Assn., Women's Forum. Episcopalian. Clubs: Cherry Hills Country, Oxford. Office: Colo Senate State Capitol Denver CO 80203 also 1660 17th St Denver CO 80202

FAATZ, JEANNE RYAN, state legislator; b. Cumberland, Md., July 30, 1941; d. Charles Keith and Myrtle Elizabeth (McIntyre) Ryan; B.S., U. Ill., 1962; postgrad. (Gates fellow) Harvard U. Program Sr. Execs. in state and local Govt., 1984; M.A., U. Colo.-Denver, 1985. children—Kristin, Susan. Tchr., English and speech, Ill. and Colo., 1963-67; sec. to majority leader Colo. Senate, 1976-78; mem. Colo. Ho. Reps. from Dist. 1, 1978—, chmn. local govt. com., mem. judiciary com.; coll. instr. Metro State Coll., Regis Coll., 1985. Past pres. Harvey Park (Colo.) Homeowners Assn., Southwest Denver YWCA Adult Edn. Club; Southwest met. coordinator UN Children's Fund, 1969-74; mem. citizens adv. council Ft. Logan Mental Health Center; bd. mgrs. Southwest Denver YMCA; bd. dirs. Southwest Denver Community Health Services. Mem. Bear Creek Republican Women's Club. Home: 2903 S Quitman St Denver CO 80236 Office: State Capitol Denver CO 80203

FABBRI, ANNE R., art museum administrator; b. Norristown, Pa.; d. Remo and Anne Wilde (Butterworth) F.; A.B. cum laude, Radcliffe Coll.; M.A. in Art History, Bryn Mawr Coll., 1971; m. Joseph Henry Butera (div.); children—Virginia, Remo, Jay. Art lectr. Villanova U., Pa., 1971-73, Drexel U., Phila., 1974-76; art critic, art editor The Drummer, Phila., 1976-79; art critic The Bulletin, Phila., 1978-80; dir. Alfred O. Deshong Mus., Widener U., Chester, Pa., 1980-82, The Noyes Mus., Oceanville, N.J., 1982—; vis NEH fellow U. Calif.-Berkeley, 1979, Princeton U., 1980. Mem. Am. Assn. Museums, Artists Equity Assn., Coll. Art Assn., Internat. Assn. Art Critics. Home: One Independence Pl 305 6th St and Locust Walk Philadelphia PA 19106 Office: The Noyes Museum Lily Lake Rd Oceanville NJ 08231

FABER, EMMY-LOU EATON, nurse, educator; b. Utica, N.Y., May 19, 1930; d. Tom and Agnes (Barker) Eaton; student Paterson State Tchrs. Coll., 1947-49, Middle Tenn. State U., 1963; R.N., Oglethorpe U., 1970; M.Community Health, Emory U., 1977; m. Theodore Faber, Dec. 10, 1949; children—Christopher Jay, Theodore Tom, Timothy Andrew. Nurse, Emory U. Hosp., Atlanta, 1967-70; nurse recruiter Northside Hosp., Atlanta, 1970—, dir. edn. dept., 1971—; clin. asst. prof. Sch. Nursing, Ga. State U.; sch. cons. DeKalb County Bd. Edn. Mem. Am., Ga. nurses assns., Nat., Ga. leagues nursing, Am., Ga. (sec. 1982-83) socs. health manpower edn. and teaching, Ga. Heart Assn., Ga. Adult Edn. Assn., Am. Cancer Soc., Sigma Theta Tau. Episcopalian. Home: 14155 Hopewell Rd Alpharetta GA 30201 Office: 1000 Johnsons Ferry Rd Atlanta GA 30042

FABER, SANDRA MOORE, astronomer, educator; b. Boston, Dec. 28, 1944; d. Donald Edwin and Elizabeth Mackenzie (Borwick) Moore; B.A., Swarthmore Coll., 1966; Ph.D., Harvard U., 1972; m. Andrew L. Faber, June 9, 1967; children—Robin, Holly. Asst. prof., astromomer Lick Obs., U. Calif. Santa Cruz, 1972-77, assoc. prof., astronomer 1977-79, prof., astronomer 1979—; mem. NSF astronomy adv. panel; Phillips visitor Haverford Coll., 1982; vis. lectr. Inst. Astonomy, U. Hawaii, 1983. NSF fellow; Woodrow Wilson fellow; Alfred P. Sloan fellow. Mem. Am. Astron. Soc., Internat. Astron. Union, Phi Beta Kappa, Sigma Xi. Editorial bd. Ann. Revs. of Astronomy and Astrophysics, 1982—; assoc. editor Astrophys. Jour. Letters, 1982—. Contbr. articles to profl. jours. Office: Lick Obs U Calif Santa Cruz CA 95060

FABIAN, SHARON L., real estate executive, lawyer; b. South Bend, Ind., July 14, 1948; d. Stephen Louis and Lucille Paulina (Alfinito) Fabian. B.S., Northwestern U., 1976, J.D., 1979. Bar: Ill. 1979; real estate broker, Ill. Mgr. compensation and tng. Trailer Train, Chgo., 1971-77, cons., 1977-79; assoc. Sidley & Austin, Chgo., 1979-83; v.p. US Equities Realty, Chgo., 1984—; adv. com. Flexible Careers, Chgo., 1970s. Bd. dirs. Chase House Inc., Chgo., 1982-83. Mem. Northwestern Law Sch. Alumni Assn. (dir. 1981—), Comml. Real Estate Orgn., ABA (Young Lawyers Div. 1980—, liaison mem. Young Lawyers Com. Citizenship Edn. 1982-83, gen. practice sect. 1981—, Pub. Interest Practice Subcom. 1982-83, real property, probate and trust law sect. 1981—, litigation sect. 1980-81), Chgo. Bar Assn. (Young Lawyers sect. 1980—, exec. council 1982—, community action com. co-chmn. 1982-83, Law Week com. coordinator Downtown Law Fairs 1981-82, Assn. meetings com. 1982—, urban affairs com. 1982-84, future home com. 1984—, entertainment com 1980—, Community Orgn. Spl. Recognition award 1984, Broadcast Achievement award 1984, Maurice Weigle award), Ill. Bar Assn. (Young Lawyers sect. 1980—, real estate sect. council 1981—), Chgo. Area Broadcast Pub. Affairs Assn., Phi Alpha Delta. Office: US Equities Realty Inc 840 N Michigan Ave Chicago IL 60611

FABRAY, NANETTE, actress; b. San Diego, Oct. 27; d. Racul Bernard and Lillian (McGovern) Fabares; student Los Angeles City Coll.; D.H.L., (hon.), Gallaudet Coll., 1970; D.F.A. (hon.), Md. Coll., 1972; m. David Tebet, Oct. 26, 1947 (div. July 1951); m. 2d, Ranald MacDougall, 1957 (dec. Dec. 1973); 1 son, Jamie. Appeared as actress in Broadway shows Let's Face It, 1941, Meet the People, 1940, By Jupiter, 1943, Bloomer Girl, 1944, High Button Shoes, 1947, Arms and the Girls, 1950, Love Life, 1948, Make A Wish, 1951, Mr. President, 1962, Jackpot, No Hard Feelings, 1973, Applause, 1973-74, Plaza Suite, 1973-74, The Secret Affairs of Mildred Wild, 1977; co-star with Sid Caesar on Caesar's Hour, CBS-TV, 1954-56; star TV series Yes, Yes Nanette, 1961-62, spls. Happy Birthday & Goodby, 1974, George M!, 1970; motion pictures include Private Lives of Elizabeth and Essex, 1939, The Bandwagon, 1952, The Happy Ending, 1969, A Child is Born, 1940, Cockeyed Cowboys of Calico County, 1970, That's Entertainment, Part 2, 1976, Harper Valley PTA, 1978, Amy, 1981; toured in Upper Broadway, 1985; role TV One Day at a Time. Trustee Eugene O'Neill Meml. Found., Nat. Theatre of Deaf; past chmn. Pres.'s Nat. Adv. Com. on Edn. Deaf, bd. dirs. Pres.'s Com. on Employment Handicapped, House Ear Inst., Nat. Adv. Com. on Handicapped, Muses of Calif. Mus. Found. Recipient 2 Donaldson awards for High Button Shoes, 1947; Tony award for Love Life, 1949; Emmy award as best comedienne, 1955, 56, best supporting performer Caesar's Hour, 1955; Eleanor Roosevelt Humanitarian award, 1964; Human Relations award Anti-Defamation League, 1969; 1st ann. Cogswell award Gallaudet Coll., 1970; Pres.'s Disting. Service award, 1970; named Woman of yr., Radio and TV Editors, 1963, Jewish War Vets. Am., 1969. Office: care Writers and Artists 11726 San Vincente Blvd Suite 300 Los Angeles CA 90049

FABRIZIO, ANGELINA MARIA, educator, medical researcher, microbiologist; b. Montenero Valcocchiaro, Italy (parents Am. citizens); d. Amico Gaetano and Felicita Francesca (Danese) F.; B.S., Villa Maria Coll., Erie, Pa., 1944; M.S. (fellow 1944-45), U. Ky., 1947; Ph.D., U. Pa., 1952; cert. Hahnemann Med. Coll. and Hosp., Phila., 1955. Asst. bacteriology U. Ky., 1945-46, instr. Italian, 1946-47; research bacteriologist antibiotics U. Cin. Coll. Medicine, Cin. Gen. Hosp., 1947-48; research asso. exptl. cancer and tissue culture Presbyn. Hosp., Phila., 1951-65; research asso. exptl. cancer and tissue culture Jefferson Med. Coll., Phila., 1965-67, asst. prof. pathology, 1967—; mem. faculty Coll. Grad. Studies, 1971—; instr. U. Pa. Sch. Medicine, 1960; cons. VA Hosp., Coatesville, Pa., 1968—. Recipient Career award Villa Maria Coll. Alumnae, 1974; Nat. Tb Assn. fellow, 1948-51. Fellow AAAS; mem. Tissue Culture Assn., Am. Soc. Microbiology, N.Y. Acad. Sci., Am. Assn. Pathologists, Sigma Xi, Sigma Delta Epsilon (chpt. pres. 1959-60, nat. pres. 1973-74, dir. 1975-80, chpt. v.p. 1983-84, chpt. pres. 1984-85). Home: 2045 Spruce St Philadelphia PA 19103

FACTOR, ELLEN LEE, publishing company executive; b. Boston, Feb. 7, 1945; d. Martin and Natalie (Green) Weiner. Student Boston U. Sch. Edn., 1967-68; B.S. in Bus. Edn., U. Mich., 1969; postgrad. in edn. NYU, 1973-74; M.B.A. in Mktg., Fordham U., 1983. Circulation mgr. McGraw Hill Publs. Co., N.Y.C., 1973-76, mgr. distbn. research McGraw Hill Info. Systems Co., 1976-80, distbn. mgr., 1980-85, mgr. Market adminstrn., 1985—. Cons. Arts and Bus. Council, N.Y.C., 1979-80, 84. Office: McGraw Hill Info Systems Co 1221 Ave of Americas New York NY 10020

FADER, SHIRLEY SLOAN, writer; b. Paterson, N.J.; d. Samuel Louis and Miriam (Marcus) Sloan; B.S., M.S., U. Pa.; m. Seymour J. Fader; children—Susan Deborah, Steven Micah Kimchi. Writer, journalist, author, Paramus, N.J., 1956—; writer of People and You, Jobmanship columns Family Weekly, 1971-81, contbg. writer, 1977-81; columnist, writer How To Get More From Your Job column, contbg. editor Glamour mag., 1978-81; columnist, writer Start Here column Working Woman mag., 1980—, contbg. editor, 1982—; writer Women Getting Ahead column Ladies' Home Jour., 1981—; contbr. articles to numerous nat. mags.; coordinator ann. writers' seminar Bergen Community Coll., 1973-75. Mem. Authors Guild, Am. Soc. Journalists and Authors (nat. v.p. 1976-77, nat. exec. council 1976-78, 83-86), Nat. Press Club. Author: The Princess Who Grew Down, 1968; From Kitchen to Career, 1977; Jobmanship, 1978; Successfully Ever After: A Young Woman's Guide to Career Happiness, 1982. Address: 377 McKinley Blvd Paramus NJ 07652

FADOK, VALERIE ANNE, veterinarian; b. N.Y.C., Jan. 12, 1954; d. George T. and Evelyn M. (Stoutland) Fadok. B.S., Wash. State U., 1976, D.V.M., 1978. Diplomate Am. Coll. Vet. Dermatology. Intern in medicine and surgery West Los Angeles (Calif.) Vet. Med. Group, 1978-79; resident in dermatology U. Fla., Gainesville, 1979-81, asst. prof. dermatology, 1983—; asst. prof. dermatology U. Tenn., Knoxville, 1981-83; cons. in dermatology Stage Road Animal Hosp., Memphis, 1983-84; lectr. in field. Contbr. articles to profl. jours. Hon. bd. mem. Wildlife Way Sta., San Fernando, Calif., 1979-80. Named Small Animal Clinician of Yr., U. Tenn., 1982; Am. Acad. Vet. Dermatology grantee, 1980-82, 84. Mem. Am. Acad. Vet. Dermatology, Acad. Vet. Allergy (sec.), Am. Animal Hosp. Assn., AVMA, Am. Coll. Vet. Dermatology. Roman Catholic. Home: 2712 SW 34th St Apt 236 Gainesville FL 32608 Office: Dept Med Sci CVM PO Box J126 JHMHC Gainesville FL 32610

FADUM, NANCY FIELDS, lawyer; b. Bedford, Ind.; d. Albert J. and Alma (Braden) Fields; m. Ralph E. Fadum, July 19, 1939; 1 dau., Jane Fields. Student Oberlin Conservatory Music, 1936-37, Radcliffe Coll., 1937-40; J.D., Wake Forest U., 1954. Bar: N.C. 1954. Assoc. Fletcher & Dupree, Raleigh, N.C., 1954-57; sole practice, Raleigh, 1957-81; pres. Meml. Enterprises Inc., 1964—, Fields Enterprises Inc., 1978—. Bd. dirs. Salvation Army, Raleigh, 1957-60, YWCA, 1961-62, United Fund Raleigh, 1962-63; legal dir., counsel Raleigh Little Theatre, 1970-73; chmn. Four County Heart Assn., 1959-60; chmn. women's div. Raleigh C. of C., 1961-62. Mem. ABA, N.C. Bar Assn., Wake County Bar Assn. (exec com. 1957-58), N.C. State Bar, N.C. State Art Soc., N.C. State Symphony Soc., N.C. Hist. Soc., N.C. Natural History Soc. Club: Carolina Country. Home: 3056 Granville Dr Raleigh NC 27609 Office: Suite 148 505 Oberlin Rd Raleigh NC 27605

FAEGENBURG, BERNICE, artist; b. Phila.; d. Simon and Dora (Rudnick) Kaufman; B.S., Tyler Sch. Fine Arts, Temple U.; postgrad. Art Students League, Nat. Acad. Design; M.S. in Art Edn., C.W. Post Coll., 1972; m. David Faegenberg; children—Nancy, Glenn, Russell. Tchr. children's classes Phila. Art Mus.; tchr. art Phila. Public Schs., Westbury (N.Y.) Schs.; tchr. art to emotionally disturbed children Roslyn (N.Y.) Jr. High Sch., 1972, silk screen printing to adults Roslyn, 1975—, tchr. creative arts workshop, 1977—; exhibited numerous one-person shows including: C.W. Post Coll., 1972, Syosset Library, 1973, Locust Valley (N.Y.) Library, 1973, Shelter Rock Library, 1976, B.J. Spoke Gallery, N.Y.C., 1977, 80, 85, Viridian Gallery, 1978, 80, Country Art Gallery, Locust Valley, 1982, Concordia Coll., Bronxville, N.Y., 1984, Isis Gallery, Port Washington, N.Y., 1985, St. Peter's Ch., N.Y.C., 1986; exhibited numerous group shows including: Firehouse Gallery Nassau Community Coll., 1975, Long Beach Art Assn., 1976, Nat. Assn. Women Artists, 1976, 77, Locust Valley Art Show, 1976, 77, Huntington Township Art League, 1977, Nat. Soc. Painters in Casein & Acrylic, 1977, Avery Fisher Hall at Lincoln Center, 1978, Concordia Coll., 1979, Silvermine Guild of Artists, 1979, Gracie Sq. Art Show, 1979 Parrish Art Mus., 1981, City Gallery, N.Y.C., 1982, travelling graphics show, Egypt and Israel, 1981-82, Guild Hall, East Hampton, 1985, Sarah Lawrence Coll., Bronxville, 1985, Frostburg State Coll., Md., 1985; also represented in permanent collections. Pres. East Hills PTA, 1970; co-pres. L.I. Artists Alliance, 1975. Recipient award excellence Long Beach Art Assn., 1976; Henningsen Meml. prize, 1980. Mem. Internat. Assn. Art, Nat. Assn. Women Artists (Grumbacher award of merit 1978, chmn. program com. 1986). Treas., B.J. Spoke Gallery, Port Washington, N.Y., 1976—; membership chmn. Viridian Gallery, N.Y.C., 1977—, treas., 1981. Home and Studio: 31 Canterbury Ln Roslyn Heights NY 11577

FAGAN, ANN BUCKMASTER, financial planner; b. Stockton, Calif., Sept. 16, 1948; d. LaNeil Newton and Margaret Anglin (Woods) Buckmaster. Student Santa Rosa Coll., 1966-68; B.A., Calif. State U.-Sacramento, 1971, elem. teaching degree, 1972. Cert. fin. planner, registered investment advisor. Tchr., Dixon Unified Sch. Dist., Calif., 1972-79; faculty U. Calif.-Davis, 1976-78; ins. agt., Davis, 1979-80; fin. planner Ann B. Fagan & Assocs., Davis, 1980—. Chmn. Pvt. Industry Council, Yolo County, Calif., 1983—; trustee Dixon Unified Sch. Dist., 1981—, v.p., 1983—; bd. dirs. Econ. Devel. Corp., Davis, 1985—. Mem. Davis C. of C., Nat. Assn. Life Underwriters (Nat. Sales Achievement award, Nat. Quality award 1981), Million Dollar Round Table, Internat. Assn. Fin. Planners, Cert. Inst. Fin. Planners, Leading Life Ins. Producers No. Calif. Club: Soroptimist. Avocations: speaking to groups, cooking, yachting.

FAGAN, BETTY MAHON, financial executive; b. Jackson, Tenn., Apr. 25, 1932; d. Robert Perry and Claire (Rogers) Mahon; B.A. cum laude, Vanderbilt U., 1953; m. Arthur Lawrence Fagan, Jr., Dec. 27, 1962; children—Perry Lawrence, Mark Malone, Anthony Rogers. Jr. analyst Smith Barney & Co., N.Y.C., 1960-65; v.p., sr. analyst White, Weld & Co., Inc., N.Y.C., 1972-78, Merrill Lynch, N.Y.C., 1978-80, First Boston Corp., N.Y.C., 1980-82; portfolio strategist Ford Found., N.Y.C., 1982—. Trustee, chmn. fin. com. Greenfield Hill Congregational Ch.; bd. dirs., chmn. fin. com. YWCA of N.Y.; bd. dirs., mem. investment com. United Ch. Found. Mem. Fin. Women's Assn., Fin. Analysts Fedn., N.Y. Soc. Security Analysts. Club: Cosmopolitan (past gov., chmn. fin. com.) (N.Y.C.).

FAGIN, CLAIRE MINTZER, nursing school dean; b. N.Y.C., Nov. 25, 1926; d. Harry and Mae (Slatin) Mintzer; m. Samuel Fagin, Feb. 17, 1952; children—Joshua, Charles. B.S., Wagner Coll., 1948; M.A., Tchrs. Coll. Columbia, 1951; Ph.D., N.Y. U., 1964; D.Sc. (hon.), Lycoming Coll., 1983. Staff nurse Sea View Hosp., Staten I., N.Y., 1947, clin. instr., 1947-48, Bellevue Hosp., N.Y.C., 1948-50; psychiat. nurse cons. Nat. League for Nursing, N.Y.C., 1951-52; asst. chief psychiat. nursing service clin. center NIH, 1953-54, supr., 1955; research project coordinator Children's Hosp. Dept. Psychiatry, Washington, 1956; instr. psychiat.-mental health nursing N.Y. U., N.Y.C., 1956-58, asst. prof., 1964-67, dir. grad. programs in psychiat. mental health nursing, 1965-69, asso. prof., 1967-69; chmn. nursing dept., prof. Herbert H. Lehman Coll., CUNY, N.Y.C., 1969-77; dir. Health Professions Inst., Montefiore Hosp. and Med. Center, 1975-77; dean sch. of nursing, U. Pa., Phila., 1977—; mem. task force Joint Commn. Mental Health of Children, 1966-69; gov.'s com. on children N.Y. State, 1971-75; pres. Council on Deans of Nursing, Sr. Colls. and Univs. N.Y. State, 1974-76; cons. to many pub. and private univs. and health care agys.; cons. Pan Am. Health Nursing, Washington, 1972-74, WHO, Geneva, Switzerland, 1974—, NIMH, HEW, 1974-76, NIMH, 1979, 83; mem. expert adv. panel on nursing WHO, 1974—; mem.-at-large Nat. Bd. Med. Examiners, 1980—; Bd. dirs. Provident Mut. Ins. Co., 1977—, audit com., 1978—. Editorial bds.: Cancer Nursing: An International Jour. of Cancer Care, 1977—, Jour. of Pub. Health Policy, Am. Jour. Nursing; Chmn. editorial bd.: Jour. for Nursing Leadership, 1978-81; speaker profl. convs.; contbr. articles to profl. publs.; speaker radio and TV. Recipient achievement award Wagner Coll., 1956, Wagner Coll. Sch. Nursing, 1973, Tchrs. Coll., 1975, disting. alumna award N.Y. U., 1979, Founders award Sigma Theta Tau, 1981; NIMH fellow, 1950-51, 60-64. Mem. Inst. of Medicine, Nat. Acad. Scis. (governing council 1981-83), Am. Acad. Nursing (governing council 1976-78), Am. Orthopsychiat. Assn. (bd. dirs. 1972-75, exec. com. of bd. 1973-75), Am. Assn. Colls. Nursing (data bank task force). Office: Nursing Education Bldg Univ Pennsylvania Philadelphia PA 19104

FAHEY, PATRICIA ANN, civic worker; b. Cleve., Jan. 3, 1946; d. Maurice Arthur and Eleanor Johanna (Anderson) Myhrvold; m. John C. Weathers, Oct. 26, 1963 (div. 1977); children—Amy, John, Tricia; m. 2d Paul S. Fahey, Oct. 23, 1977 (dec. 1980). Patient rep. J.F. Kennedy Hosp., Lake Worth, Fla., 1970-77; med. sec. to physician, Brunswick, Ga., 1980-85; dir. quality assurance ABC Home Health, 1985—. Med. record cons. Hospice of the Golden Isle, 1982—; pres. Amity House, 1984—; mem. task force Chem. People, 1984—. Mem. Am. Med. Record Assn., Am. Bus. Womens Assn. (sec. 1984—). Republican. Lutheran. Home: 16A Woodland Circle Brunswick GA 31520 Office: ABC Home Health Services Inc PO Box 1056 Brunswick GA 31520

FAHLSTROM, DIANE LYNN, programmer/analyst; b. Chgo., Aug. 7, 1960; d. Richard John and Anna Mae (Petersen) F. A.A.S. in Bus. Adminstrn., Thornton Community Coll., 1980; B.S. in Computer Sci., North Central Coll., 1986. Programmer Harris Hub Co., Inc., Harvey, Ill., 1977-81; tech. assoc. AT&T Bell Labs., Naperville, Ill., 1981-86; programmer/analyst Authur Anderson & Co., Chgo., 1986—. Mem. Nat. Assn. Female Execs. Avocations: writing; journalism. Home: 3S 567 Lorraine Ave Warrenville IL 60555 Office: Arthur Anderson & Co 1 N Dearborn Chicago IL

FAHR, LINDA MEYERS, radiologist, educator; b. N.Y.C., Sept. 20, 1942; d. Paul Tabor and Jessie V. (Jones) Meyers; B.A., Barnard Coll., 1964; M.D., U. Iowa, 1968; m. James Dwight Watson, Mar. 29, 1980; children—John Pearson Fahr, Bruce Tabor Fahr. Resident in radiology U. Iowa, Iowa City, 1971-74; staff radiologist VA Hosp., Houston, 1974-77, chief dept. radiology, 1977-79; chief radiologist MacGregor Med. Clinic, Houston, from 1980; now asst. prof. radiology Loma Linda U., Calif.; clin. asst. prof. Baylor Coll. Medicine, Houston, 1974-79. Mem. Am. Assn. Women Radiologists (pres.-elect 1982, pres. 1983), Am. Coll. Radiology, Radiol. Soc. N.Am., Tex. Radiol. Soc., Houston Radiol. Soc. (treas. 1982, sec. 1983), Tex. Med. Assn., Harris County Med. Assn., Women's Profl. Assn. Office: Loma Linda U Med Ctr Loma Linda CA 92354

FAHR, MICHELE BLAKESLEE, automotive company executive; b. Kalamazoo, Sept. 27, 1959; d. Russell Harold Blakeslee and Mie (Yamada) Blakeslee Stevens; m. Jeffery Russell Fahr, June 23, 1984. B.S. in Packaging Engring., Mich. State U., 1982. Quality analyst Buck Motor div. Gen. Motors Corp., Flint, Mich., 1982-83, supr. quality control, 1983, specifications analyst, 1983-84; project engr. B-O-C Powertrain div. Gen. Motors Corp., Flint, 1984-85, sr. buyer, 1985—. Humphrey scholar, 1977-81. Democrat. Lutheran. Avocations: tennis; golf; swimming. Home: 4757 Parkridge Dr Waterford MI 48095 Office: Gen Motors Corp B-O-C Powertrain 902 E Hamilton St Bldg 84 Dept 78 Flint MI 48550

FAHRENKAMP, BETTYE, state legislator; b. Wilder, Tenn.; m. Gilbert H. Fahrenkamp, 1952 (dec.). B.S., U. Tenn., 1949; M.A., U. Alaska, 1962. Formerly sch. music tchr.; mem. Alaska Senate, 1978—. Served with WAC, 1944-46. Chmn. dist. Democratic com., 1968-72; nat. Dem. committeewoman, 1972-78. Office: Alaska Senate PO Box V Juneau AK 99811

FAIKS, JAN OGOZALEK, state legislator; b. Long Island, N.Y.; m. James Faiks (div. 1983); m. Dick Lyon. Formerly tchr. math. East High Sch., Anchorage; owner, operator Green Connection leasing, 1978-80; mem. Alaska Senate, 1982—; chmn. rules com., 1983; now chmn. fin. com. Republican. Office: Alaska Senate State Capitol Juneau AK 99811

FAILINGER, DIANNE MARIE, personnel executive; b. Frostburg, Md., Nov. 27, 1958; d. Kermit Belvin and Thelma Josephine F. B.S., Frostburg State Coll., 1980. Intern guidance counseling Braddock Jr. High, Cumberland, Md., 1980; field supr. Western Md. Consortium, Cumberland, 1980; residential services specialist Friends Aware, Cumberland, 1977-81; equal opportunity officer Allegany County Human Resources Devel. Commn., Inc., Cumberland, 1980-82, personnel officer, 1982-84; personnel adminstr. Precise Metals and Plastics, Inc., Cumberland, 1984—. Bd. dirs. Community Housing Resources, Cumberland, 1982-84; program advisor Coop. Extension Service, Cumberland, 1983—; human rights advisor Archway Sta., Cumberland, 1983—; chmn. pub. relations Gov.'s Youth Adv. Council, Balt., 1978-82; mem. Allegany County Children's Council, Cumberland, 1979-83; mem. ch. council St. Paul's Luth. Ch., Frostburg, 1984—; mem. Cumberland Choral Soc. Recipient Letter of Appreciation/Commendation, Gov. Md., 1982. Mem. NOW (treas. local chpt.), Delta Omicron, Psi Chi. Republican. Lutheran. Home: 216 Shaw St Apt 32 Frostburg MD 21532 Office: Precise Metals and Plastics Inc Day Rd RFD #4 Box 244B Cumberland MD 21502

FAIN, REBECCA ANN, nursing administrator; b. Rupert, W.Va., Jan. 8, 1951; d. Virgil W. and Helen Rose (Surbaugh) F. B.S. in Nursing, Tex. Woman's U., 1973; M.S. in Nursing, W.Va. U., 1985. R.N., W.Va., Tex., Fla. Staff nurse Winter Park Hosp., Fla., 1973-74; nurse clinician Fla. Hosp., Orlando, 1974-75; head nurse Charleston Area Med. Ctr.-Meml. Div., W.Va., 1975-83, OA dir., 1983—. Nurse pracitioner W.Va. Health Right Clinic, Charleston, 1982-85. Mem. Am. Nurses Assn., W.Va. Nurses Assn. (legis. and health planning com. 1984-85, 2d v.p.), Nat. Assn. Orthopedic Nurses, Nat. Assn. Quality Assurance Profls., Sigma Theta Tau. Episcopalian. Avocations: skiing; jogging. Home: 2106 Kanawha Blvd E Apt A604 Charleston WV 25311 Office: Charleston Area Med Ctr PO Box 1547 Charleston WV 25326

FAIR, PAMELA JEANNE, real estate broker; b. Lincoln, Nebr., June 28, 1949; d. Harold William and Mary Ann (Gregory) Ohlrich; m. John Edmund Fair, May 31, 1970 (div. Oct. 1973); 1 dau., Tiffanie Nicole. B.S., Okla. State U., 1971. Lic. real estate broker, Tex. Stenographer mktg. Texaco, Inc., Houston, 1971-78; regional ops. mgr. RRS, Inc., Houston, 1978-82; broker Real Property Mgmt., Inc., Houston, 1982-84; mgr. transferee services Southwest region Merrill Lynch, 1984—; substitute tchr. Houston Community Coll., 1982. Fellow Nat. Assn. Realtors; mem. Tex. Assn. Realtors, Houston Bd. Realtors (cert. comml. investment mem.). Republican. Episcopalian. Home: 10114 Enchanted Stone Houston TX 77070

FAIR, TAMERA L., engineer; b. Anderson, S.C., Jan. 5, 1960; d. Frank T. and Thelma B. (Belton) F. B.S. in Metallurgy and Materials Sci., Carnegie-Mellon U., 1981. Summer engr. E.I. duPont de Nemours, Inc., Belle, W.Va., 1979, summer metall. engr., New Cumberland, Pa., 1980, product engr., Camp Hill, Pa., 1981-85, research and devel. engr., 1985—; resident asst. Carnegie-Mellon U., Pitts., 1980-81. Co-patentee elec. jumper. Bd. dirs. Mus. Sci. Discovery, Harrisburg, Pa., 1985—, chmn. ednl. events, 1986—; assoc. mem. Talented Tenth. Mem. Soc. Women Engrs., Soc. Plastic Engrs., Carnegie Mellon Black

Alumni Assn. Democrat. Baptist. Club: Isshoniryu Karate (asst. instr. Lemoyne, Pa. 1985—). Office: EI duPont de Nemours & Co 30 Hunter Ln Camp Hill PA 17011

FAIRBANKS, MARY JOANNE, educational administrator; b. Massena, N.Y., Dec. 21, 1939; d. James William and Inez (Cappiello) Phillips; Assoc. in Bus. Adminstrn., Central City Bus. Inst., Syracuse, N.Y. 1959; A.S. in Accounting LaSalle Extension U., 1974; student in mgmt., Syracuse U., 1974—. Sec. elec. and computer engring. dept. Syracuse U., 1959-65, asst. to adminstrv. asst., 1965-72, publs. mgr. Assembly on U. Governance, 1970-72, coordinator computer confs., 1972-81, adminstr. short course Air Force intrasystem analysis program, 1974-78, supervisory asst. to chmn. dept. elec. and computer engring. and mgr. Air Force Post-Doctoral Program, Rome Air Devel. Center, 1972-78, adminstrv. asst. to chmn. dept. indsl. engring. and ops. research 1978-82, dir. Engring. Coop. Edn. program, 1982—; mgr. electromagnetic compatibility analysis techniques advancement program, 1978-82; coordinator workshops on computer architecture, 1977-79; ofcl. stenographer 1985 Project, USMC, 1963; mem. computer scoring team XIII Olympic Winter Games, Lake Placid, N.Y., 1980; Alpine ofcl. U.S. Ski Assn., 1980—. Pres. LWV Met. Syracuse, 1981-83, voters service dir. N.Y. State, 1983—, 2d v.p. N.Y. State, 1986. Mgr., editor publs. Onondaga County Bicentennial Quilt, 1976; editor 7 elec. engring. textbooks, 1960-78; author: The Road to the Voting Booth, 2 vols., 1986; co-author: Career Portfolio for Volunteers, 1980, Patterns of Government in Onondaga County, 1981. Mem. Am. Soc. Engring. Edn. (coop. edn. div.), Coop. Edn. Assn., Ohio Coop. Edn. Assn., N.Y. State Coop. and Experiential Edn. Assn., Middle Atlantic Placement Assn. Home: 140 Edgehill Rd Syracuse NY 13224 Office: 359 Link Hall Syracuse U Syracuse NY 13210

FAIRCHILD, CAROL MICHAEL, architect, engineer; b. Dallas, Oct. 13, 1953; s. Leo Anthony and Bettie Joe (Roden) F.; m. Walter Barry Davis, Nov. 24, 1984. B.Environ. Design, Tex. A&M U., 1976, M.Arch., 1979. Registered architect, Wash., Tex. ACLM engr. Boeing Aerospace, Seattle, 1977; site architect IBM Corp., Austin, Tex., 1977-82, software engr., 1982-84, test engr., testing engring. architect, 1984—, now mgr. facilities engring. and fast track design CADAM ops.; interior designer Daven, Austin, 1984—. Commr. Boy Scouts of Am., Austin, 1980—. Mem. Am. Soc. Interior Designers, ASCE, Inst. Indsl. Engrs., Soc. Women Engrs., Soc. Am. Magicians, Internat. Brotherhood of Magicians. Republican. Presbyterian. Avocations: flying; scuba diving; amatuer radio; geneology; skiing. Home: 401 Meadow Creek Dr Pflugerville TX 78660

FAIRCLOUGH, ELLEN LOUKS, Can. politician, mem. Privy Council; b. Hamilton, Ont., Can., Jan. 28, 1905; d. Norman Ellsworth and Nellie Bell (Louks) Cook; student schs. Hamilton, Ont.; LL.D., McMaster U., 1975; m. David Henry Gordon Fairclough, Jan. 28, 1931; 1 son, Howard Gordon. Founder, prin. acctg. practice, 1935-57; mem. Ho. of Commons Can., 1950-63, sec. of state, 1957-58, minister citizenship and immigration, 1958-62, mem. Privy Council, 1957—, postmaster gen., 1962-63; adv. mem. Can. del. to UN, 1950; del. to Conf. of Parliamentarians from NATO Countries, Paris, 1955; ambassador extraordinary to Argentina for presdl. inauguration, 1958; apptd. sec. Hamilton Trust & Savs. Corp., 1963-77 (amalgamated with Can. Permanent Trust); chmn. Hamilton Hydro Electric Commn. Past v.p. Young Conservatives Ont.; alderman Hamilton City Council, 1946-50, controller, 1950; bd. dirs. Can. Council Christians and Jews; patron Huguenot Soc., United Empire Loyalists' Assn., Hamilton br. Can.; hon. treas. and exec. dir. Chedoke-McMaster Hosps. Found., 1983—. Decorated officer Order of Can.; govt. bldg. named in her honor, 1982. Fellow Chartered Accts.; mem. Gen. Accts. Assn. Can. (life), United Empire Loyalist Assn. (dominion sec. 1935-40), Imperial Order Daus. of Empire (officer provincial and nat. chpts. 1935-48), Hamilton C. of C. Anglican. Club: Zonta Internat. (pres., Hamilton 1940-42, dist. gov. 1948-49, internat. treas. 1972-76). Office: Hamilton Hydro Electric Commn 55 John St N Hamilton ON L8N 3E4 Canada

FAIRLEY, WILMA K., ednl. adminstr.; b. Washington, Apr. 25, 1933; d. Elton F. and Edith King; B.A., D.C. Tchrs. Coll., 1956; M.A., Stanford U., 1970; children—Ricki F. Sharon R. Tchr. various sch. systems, 1960-69; lang. arts tchr.-specialist Montgomery County Public Schs., Rockville, Md., 1969-70, coordinator human relations tng., 1970-71, dir. human relations, 1971—, EEO officer, 1973—. Second v.p. Nat. Tots and Teens, 1972-73; bd. dirs. YWCA, 1974-75; mem. nat. bd. dirs. Girl Scouts U.S.A., 1974-75. Named Woman of Yr., Montgomery County chpt. NAACP, 1978. Mem. Am. Assn. Sch. Adminstrs., Nat. Assn. Elem. Prins., Nat. Alliance Black Sch. Educators, NAACP (life) NCCJ (bd. dirs. 1982—), Delta Sigma Theta, Phi Delta Kappa. Office: Dept Human Relations Montgomery County Public Schs 850 Hungerford Dr Rockville MD 20850

FAIRWELL, KAY LORRAINE, editor; b. Waukegan, Ill., Aug. 20, 1947; d. Edwin Henry and Doris Lorraine (Warren) Siemons; B.A. in Communications and Public Policy, U. Calif., Berkeley, 1969. Asst. to ops. officer Am. Savs. Assn., Oakland, Calif., 1971-72; sr. editor Lawrence Hall Sci., U. Calif., Berkeley, 1972—; editor sci. edn. publs., Berkeley, 1972—. Recipient Outstanding Service award U. Calif., Berkeley, 1979, 82. Mem. Nat. Assn. Female Execs., Am. Film Inst., Smithsonian Inst. Democrat. Editor The LHS Quar., 1983—. Office: Lawrence Hall Sci Univ Calif Berkeley CA 94720

FAISON, DELORES, government accountant; b. Atlanta, Aug. 28, 1945; d. Harry and Ella Maud (Hunter) Campbell; 1 child, Harold Ernest Campbell. Student CUNY, Helene Fuld Sch. Nursing, N.Y.C., U. Ariz.; grad. with high honors, Pima Coll., 1984. In various positions U.S. Govt., N.Y.C., 1965-74; health unit coordinator Polyclinic Med. Ctr., Harrisburg, Pa., 1978-81, St. Joseph's Hosp., Tucson, 1981-86; acctg. technician Agrl. Research Service, Dept. Agr., Tucson, 1984—; v.p. Tucson Employees Benefit Assn., 1984-85. Recipient Woman On The Move award YWCA, Tucson, 1985. Mem. Nat. Assn. Health Unit Coordinators, Nat. Assn. Female Execs., Federally Employed Women, Fed. Women's Program (alt. rep.), Phi Theta Kappa. Democrat. Baptist. Club: Federally Employed Women (com. chairperson 1985—) (Tucson). Avocations: reading; writing; singing; public speaking.

FAISON, FRANCES WATKINS, inn executive; b. Johnson County, N.C., July 20, 1935; d. Mallie Leon and Lola (Lamm) Watkins; m. Donald Taylor Faison, Dec. 15, 1956; children—Michele Lamm, Taylor Windham, Donald Winter. With real estate sales dept. Oglesby & Barclift, Virginia Beach, Va., 1973-74; dir. sales Omni Internat. Hotel, Norfolk, Va., 1974-83; gen. mgr. Park Central Hotel, Washington, 1983-84, State Plaza Hotel, Washington, 1984-85, Sheraton Airport Inn, Warwick, R.I., 1985—. Bd. dirs. Providence Conv. and Visitors Bur., 1985—. Mem. Tidewater Womens Network (founder 1982, pres. 1982-83), Nat. Assn. Female Execs. (Network dir. 1981-83), Sales and Mktg. Execs. (sec. 1983), Hotel Sales Mgmt. Assn., Hotel Assn. of Washington, Warwick C. of C. (tourism com. 1985). Home: 1482 Poinsettia Arch Virginia Beach Va 23456 Office: Sheraton Airport Inn 1850 Post Rd Warwick RI 02886

FAISON, LOIS PARKER, marketing executive; b. Chgo., Oct. 25, 1929; d. Ross I. and Lois B. (Harger) Parker; m. Edmund Winston J. Faison; children—Charles, Dorothy, Barbara. B.A., U. Hawaii, 1971, M.A., 1973. Pres., Lois Faison Research, Honolulu, 1968-73, East West Research Design, Kailua, Hawaii, 1973—, also dir.; editor Hawaii Advt. Agy. Directory, 1985, 86. Contbr. articles on mktg. to profl. jours; editor Mktg. Sci. Jour., Hawaii Advt. Agy. Dir., 1985-86. Mem. Am. Mktg. Assn., Small Bus. Assn., Pacific and Asia Affairs Council, Soc. Corp. Planners, Am. Acad. Advt., Women in Communications (bd. dirs.), Honolulu C. of C., Kailua C. of C. (bd. dirs.), Japan-Am. Soc. Club: Soroptimist (bd. dirs.). Office: 735 Bishop St Suite 235 Honolulu HI 96813

FAIT, LINDA, educational administrator; b. Tooele, Utah, Oct. 22, 1945; d. Joseph Vicevich and Lucille (Murray) Fait. B.S., Utah State U., 1967; M.Ed., Brigham Young U., 1971, Ed.S., 1980, Ed.D., 1982. Tchr. Granite Sch. Dist., Salt Lake City, 1967-83, asst. prin., 1983-84, prin., 1984—. Mem. Nat. Assn. Elem. Sch. Prins., Utah Assn. Elem. Sch. Prins., Granite Assn. Sch. Adminstrs., Granite Assn. Elem. Sch. Prins., Delta Kappa Gamma (pres. 1982-84), Delta Delta Delta. Mem. Ch. of Jesus Christ of Latter-day Saints. Office: Oakwood Elem Sch 5818 Highland Dr Salt Lake City UT 84121

FAJARDO, KATHARINE LYNN, computer consultant, former mining company executive, actress; b. Akron, Ohio, Mar. 19, 1951; d. Edwin Murray and Diane (Zabiegalski) H.; B.A., Johns Hopkins U., 1973; M.B.A., U. Calif.-Irvine, 1987. Dir. pub. affairs council Electronic Industries Assn., Washington, 1974-75; pension cons. Proskauer, Rose, Goetz & Mendelsohn, N.Y.C., 1976-77; sr. mktg. cons. The Equitable Life Assurance Soc., N.Y.C., 1977-79; dir. advt., assoc. dir. public affairs St. Joe Minerals Corp., N.Y.C., 1979-82, mgr. communications projects, 1982-83; computer cons., 1984—; actress, 1983—; leading roles include Goodbye Charlie, Picnic, Witness for the Prosecution. Recipient Nicholson award, 1980, 81; named Best Supporting Actress, Orange County, Calif., 1983. Mem. Am. Mgmt. Assn. Home: 1076 Miramar St Laguna Beach CA 92651

FAKO, WANDA LEE, sales and marketing executive; b. Chardon, Ohio, July 26, 1949; d. Thomas Edgar and Wanda Marie (Bard) Beattie; m. Gary Lee Fako, July 8, 1972 (div. Dec. 1985). B.S. in Nursing, Kent State U., 1972; M.S., Ohio State U., 1978. R.N., Ohio. Staff nurse Fairview Gen. Hosp., Cleve., 1972-73; instr. ob-gyn Fairview Gen. Hosp. Sch. Nursing, Cleve., 1973-77, asst. prodn. coordinator, 1977-78, patient edn. coordinator, 1978-79; sales rep. Critikon, Inc., Tampa, Fla., 1979-82, clin. research assoc., 1982-83, profl. relations adminstr., 1983-85; v.p. mktg. and sales Hyper Scan Dallas, Inc., Dallas, 1985—; cons. Beckton-Dickinson, Rutherford, N.J., 1977-79, Auto-Syringe, Hooksett, N.H., 1977-79, Ancer, Columbus, Ohio, 1979-82. Trustee Far West Center, North Olmstead, Ohio, 1978-82, 1st v.p. bd. trustees, 1980-82; mem. Rep. Assembly for Community Planning, Cuyahoga County, Ohio, 1980-82, Author (16mm films) Central Venous Pressure Part I, 1977, Central Venous Pressure Part II, 1977, Bathing Your Baby, 1977, Infant Nutrition Part I, 1977, Infant Nutrition Part II, 1977, Problem Oriented Nursing Part I, 1978, Problem Oriented Nursing Part II, 1978, The Teaching Learning Process, 1978, Writing Behavioral Objectives, 1978, The Evaluation Process, 1978; author, producer slide tape program Dinamap 1846 Inservice Program, 1983, Simplicity Plus Infusion Pump Inservice Program, 1984. Mem. Nurses Assn. Am. Coll. Obstetricians and Gynecologists, Nat. Assn. Female Execs., Ohio State U. Alumni Assn. Republican. Roman Catholic. Home: 12610 Jupiter Pl Apt 626 Dallas TX 75238 Office: Hyper Scan Dallas Inc 4809 Cole Ave Suite 330 Dallas TX 75205

FALASCO, AUDREY ROBINSON, management development consultant, educator, lecturer; b. Phila.; d. Ellwood Souder and Dorothy (Lohr) Robinson; m. Eugene C. Falasco; children—Colette, Ilise. B.S. in Acctg. and Mgmt., St. Joseph's U., Phila., also M.S. in Edn.; postgrad. in bus. Temple U. Pres. Balance Concepts, Mgmt. Cons. Co., Spring City, 1976—; adj. instr. Immaculata Coll., Pa., 1983—, Pa. State U., 1982—, Albright Coll., Reading, Pa., 1982—, Reading Area Community Coll., 1984—, Ursinus Coll.; pres., treas. Genesco, Inc., Spring City, Pa., 1981—. Contbr. articles to profl. jours. Designer performance evaluation instrument for service industry. Bd. dirs., vol. Rape Crisis Ctr., Norristown, Pa., 1974-82; mem. Pa. Trial Ct. Nominating Commn., 1978; mem. citizen rev. panel Pa. Dept. Pub. Welfare, Children and Youth Facilities, 1979; Chester County Republican precinct com. person, Pa. 1976-79; active Hanna Penn House, Rep. Women Pa., Phila., 1978—. Mem. Nat. Speakers Assn. (treas. 1981—), Nat. Assn. Accts., Am. Soc. Tng. and Devel., Internat. Mgmt. Council, Am. Soc. Personnel Adminstrn., NOW, AAUW. Avocations: organic gardening; bird watching; water colors; modern jazz.

FALCO, JOANN, fundraising consultant; b. N.Y.C., Aug. 9, 1952; d. Joseph J. and Mary J. Falco. B.A. summa cum laude in English, Barry Coll., 1974, M.A., 1976; postgrad. U. Miami. Asst. dir. Fla. Pub. Interest Research Group, U. Miami, Fla., 1976-79, adminstrv. aide to asst. v.p. devel., 1980-81; ind. devel. cons., Washington and Miami, 1981—.

FALCO, MARIA JOSEPHINE, political scientist, university official; b. Wildwood, N.J., July 7, 1932; d. John J. and Mafalda M. (Barbieri) Falco; A.B., Immaculata (Pa.) Coll., 1954; Fulbright scholar, U. Florence, Italy, 1954-55; M.A. in Polit. Philosophy, Fordham U., 1958; Ph.D., Bryn Mawr (Pa.) Coll., 1963; postdoctoral research fellow, Yale U., 1965-66; NSF grantee, U. Mich., summer 1968; postgrad. Carnegie-Mellon U., 1983. Instr., asst. prof. history and polit. sci. Immaculata Coll., Pa., 1957-63; asst. prof. polit. sci. Washington Coll., Chestertown, Md., 1963-64; research asst. to Genevieve Blatt, candidate for U.S. Senator from Pa., 1964-65; asst. prof., asso. prof. polit. sci. LeMoyne Coll., Syracuse, N.Y., 1966-73, chmn. polit. sci. dept., 1967-73; prof. polit. sci. Stockton State Coll., Pomona, N.J., 1973-76; chmn. social and behavioral scis. faculty U. Tulsa, 1976-79; dean Coll. Arts and Scis., Loyola U., New Orleans, 1979-85, prof. polit. sci., 1985-86; acad. v.p. DePauw U., Greencastle, Ind., 1986—; pres. Women's Caucus for Polit. Sci., 1976. Pres., Syracuse chpt. New Democratic Coalition, 1970-71; bd. dirs. Am. Council Acad. Deans, 1984-85. Named Outstanding Educator in U.S., 1975. Faculty fellow in state and local politics Nat. Center for Edn. in Politics, 1964. Mem. Am. Polit. Sci. Assn. (mem. Benjamin Evans Lippincott award com. 1976, chmn. sect. program com. 1975, mem. profl. ethics and acad. freedom com. 1977-80), Midwest Polit. Sci. Assn. (com. on status of women), S.W. Polit. Sci. Assn. (outstanding conv. paper award com.), Northeastern Polit. Sci. Assn., AAUP (v.p. LeMoyne chpt. 1971-72), Founds. Polit. Theory Group. Roman Catholic. Author: Truth and Meaning in Political Science: An Introduction to Political Inquiry, 1973; Through the Looking Glass: Epistemology and the Conduct of Political Inquiry, 1979; —Bigotry—!: Ethnic, Machine and Sexual Politics in a Senatorial Election, 1980; contbr. articles to profl. publs. Office: Office of Acad Vice Pres De Pauw U Greencastle IN 46135

FALCON, KAREN GAY, bedspread manufacturer; b. N.Y.C., Jan. 31, 1949; d. Joseph Albert Falcon and Olcay Kent. A.A., Pierce Coll., 1970; B.A., Calif. State U.-Los Angeles, 1972. Sales mgr. Animan Designs, Los Angeles, 1972-76; pres. Kare-Free, Los Angeles, 1976-79; founder, chief exec. officer Hollywood Nights, Inc., Los Angeles, 1979—; pres. Hollywood Nights of Jamaica Ltd., 1985—; cons. Laguna Mfg., 1980—; cons. European mktg. Magma Heimtex, Friesenheim, Fed. Republic Germany, 1985—; seminar speaker SBA, Los Angeles, 1982—. Sponsor Soc. for Prevention Cruelty to Animals, Los Angeles, since 1980—. Mem. Nat. Bath, Bed and Linen Assn., Waterbed Mfrs. Assn. (speaker 1977—, best trade show exhibit awards 1981, 83, 84, 85), Nichiren Shoshu Am. Democrat. Avocations: travel; music. Office: Hollywood Nights Inc 1930 E 15th St Los Angeles CA 90021

FALCONE, NOLA MADDOX, investment company executive; b. Augusta, Ga., July 8, 1939; s. Louis Vernon and Geneva Elizabeth (Fox) Maddox; m. Charles Anthony Falcone, Dec. 6, 1968; 1 child, Charles Maddox. B.A., Duke U., 1961; M.B.A., U. Pa., 1966. Chartered fin. analyst, 1980. Security analyst, portfolio mgr. pension and personal trust dept. Chase Manhattan Bank, N.Y.C., 1961-63, investment officer personal trust dept., 1966-70; protfolio mgr., registered rep. Lieber & Co., Harrison, N.Y., 1974-75, br. mgr., Arlington, Va., 1978-79, portfolio mgr., 1979-80, ptnr., 1981—, pres. The Evergreen Total Return Fund, Inc., 1985—; dir. Saxon Woods Asset Mgmt. Corp., Harrison, 1981—. Mem. fin. com. Jr. League, Scarsdale, N.Y., 1971-75; trustee 1st Baptist Ch. White Plains, 1973-74. Mem. Fin. Analysts Soc. Democrat. Avocations: reading; gardening; swimming. Office: Leiber & Co 550 Mamaroneck Ave Harrison NY 10528

FALK, ALMA MARTHA, former educator; b. Chgo., Apr. 18, 1910; d. Henry and Alma (Wolowski) Weihofen; cert. Chgo. Tchrs. Coll., 1932; B.A., George Washington U., 1937, M.A., 1957; postgrad. Howard U.; m. James E. Curry, Apr. 28, 1934 (dec. Aug. 1972); 1 dau., Aileen Curry-Cloonan; m. 2d, Byron A. Falk, Nov. 22, 1966 (dec. Mar. 1984). Tchr., Hull House, Chgo., 1930-32; social worker Ill. Relief Commn., 1932-35; tchr. elem. sch., Chgo., 1937-38, 46-47; office mgr. law firms in P.R. and Washington, 1948-53; elem. tchr. Jr. Village Sch., Washington, 1953-57; reading coordinator Washington Public Schs., 1957-72; instr. George Washington Reading Clinic, 1957-66; pres. Greater Washington Reading Council, 1966-67. Vol. asst. CD Milk Sta. Program, San Juan, P.R., 1942-46; instr. Urban Service Corps. of Vols., 1952-56; bd. dirs. Internat. Student House, Washington, 1980—. Recipient citation White House Conf. on Children, 1962. Mem. AAUW (chmn. edn. com. Washington br. 1959-61, dir. 1976-80, 84—), Nat. Mil. Wives, Internat. Reading Assn., Am. Fedn. Tchrs., Women's Internat. League for Peace and Freedom, Washington Tchrs. Union (rep. reading specialists 1968-70), Internat. Platform Assn., Ret. Tchrs. Assn., Am. Humanist Assn., UN Assn., Internat. Platform Assn., Phi Delta Gamma. Clubs: George Washington U. (charter), Army and Navy (Washington). Home: 922 24th St NW Washington DC 20037

FALK, BARBARA ANN, financial analyst b. Eugene, Oreg., Feb. 1, 1944; d. Everett Henry and Phyllis Ruth (Wetgen) F.; student So. Oreg. State Coll., 1962-63; A.S., Lane Community Coll., 1971. Accounts receivable bookkeeper Junction City Implement Co. (Oreg.), 1963-64, Eugene Farmers' Co-op, 1964-65; bookkeeper Chef Francisco, Inc., Eugene, 1978-79, sr. acct., 1979, acctg. supr., 1980-84, corp. fin. analyst, 1984—. Mem. acctg. adv. com. Lane Community Coll., 1982—, chmn., 1983—. Mem. Nat. Assn. Female Execs., Nat. Assn. Accts. (dir. chpt. 1971-79, pres. chpt. 1979-80, nat. dir. 1981-83, Pacific N.W. council prin. 1983-84, Eugene-Springfield chpt. Most Valuable Mem. 1979, 82), Eugene-Springfield Credit Assocs. (dir. 1978-82), Am. Mgmt. Soc. Republican. Baptist. Home: 140 Tatum Ln Eugene OR 97404 Office: 1500 Valley River Dr Eugene OR 97401

FALK, DIANE SENA, psychiatric social worker; b. Oak Park, Ill., Mar. 15, 1941; d. Philip and Leta Jessie (Edgecombe) Miller; B.A., U. Chgo., 1963, M.A., 1966; M.S.W., U. Pa., 1971; predoctoral fellow Rutgers U.-Princeton U. Program in Mental Health Policy Research, 1982-84; Ph.D., Rutgers U., 1985; m. Charles D. Falk, July 16, 1965 (div. Oct. 1980); 1 child, David Andrew. Social worker Del. Dept. Pub. Welfare, Wilmington, 1967-69; staff social worker Children's Psychiat. Center, Eatontown, N.J., 1971; dir. transitional services Raritan Bay Mental Health Center, Perth Amboy, N.J., 1972-80, dir. adult outpatient services, 1980—; field work instr. Sch. Social Work, Rutgers U., 1976—. Bd. dirs. ACLU Monmouth County, 1973-76. Mem. Nat. Assn. Social Workers (sec. to bd. dirs. N.J. chpt. 1978-80), Acad. Cert. Social Workers, Am. Orthopsychiat. Assn., Otto Rank Assn. Episcopalian. Contbr. articles to profl. jours. Home: 94 Conover Rd Marlboro NJ 07746 Office: 570 Lee St Perth Amboy NJ 08861

FALK, JULIA FERGUSON, state library commissioner; b. Shenandoah, Iowa, Jan. 27, 1928; d. William Paul and Lina (Coxedge) Ferguson; m. William Edward Falk, June 28, 1949; children—Mark Ferguson, Elizabeth Ann. B.A., U. Iowa, 1949. Mem. Iowa State Library Commn., Des Moines, 1979—. Mem. ALA, Iowa Library Assn., Phi Beta Kappa, AAUW. (past pres. Shenandoah chpt.). Republican. Episcopalian.

FALK, MIRI, urban planner; b. Tel Aviv, Israel, Dec. 11, 1947; came to U.S., 1975, naturalized, 1983; d. Nachman and Devora (Fineberg) Bar-Shalom; m. Yeshayahu Arie Falk, Apr. 10, 1975; children—Tomer Menachem, Idan Dor. B.S. in Civil Engring., Technion Inst., Israel, 1974; M.Urban Planning, NYU, 1981. Profl. engr., Israel. Engr., Urban Planning Dept., Tel Aviv, 1973-75; asst. traffic mgr. Govt. Israel, N.Y.C., 1976-81; fin., planning coordinator N.Y. Hill Park Corp., N.Y.C., 1982—. Served with Israeli Army, 1966-68. Mem. Israel Architects and Engrs., Nat. Assn. Female Execs., Am. Planning Assn. Avocations: painting, art, music.

FALKENBERG, MARY ANN THERESA, realtor; b. Chgo., Dec. 8, 1931; d. Joseph and Catherine (Bausch) Haselsteiner; student Barat Coll., 1953; m. Charles V. Falkenberg, Jr., Apr. 9, 1955; children—Catherine, Grace Ann, Susan Marie, Charles V., Robert, Thomas, Martin, Mary, Elizabeth, Joseph. Tchr. piano, 1946-73; organist St. Thomas of Villanova Ch., 1960—, choir dir., 1960—; sales staff Quinlan & Tyson, Realtors, Inc., Palatine, Ill., 1970-77; broker, mgr., co-owner Assos. Realty Corp., Palatine, 1978—. Named Palatine Woman of Yr., Surburban Press Found., 1962; cert. home protection cons. Mem. Women in Mgmt., Am. Mgmt. Assn., Ill. Assn. Realtors (life mem. two million dollar club), Nat. Assn. Realtors (accredited profl. residential appraiser, cert. real property appraiser), Nat. Assn. Female Execs., N.W. Suburban Bd. Realtors (edn. com. 1977-78, non-resident com. 1982, broker-lawyer com. 1986), MAP (bd. dirs. 1986), Women in Sales, Barat Coll. Alumni Assn. Club: Women's. Republican. Roman Catholic. Home: 517 Warwick St Palatine IL 60067 Office: 670 First Bank Dr Palatine IL 60067

FALKENBURG, SHARON ANN, health and ergonomic consultant, occupational therapist; b. Milw., Feb. 2, 1955; d. Donald Edward and Eunice Ester (Schneider) Greiten; m. Douglas Gilbert Falkenburg, May 7, 1983. B.S. in Occupational Therapy, Mount Mary Coll., 1978; M.S., Cardinal Stritch Coll., 1985. Registered occupational therapist. Occupational therapist Sage Nursing Home, Milw., 1978-79, Curative Rehab. Ctr., Milw., 1979-81; med. consultant Nat. Loss Control Service Corp., Milw., 1981-83, state supr., 1983-84, regional supr., Long Grove, Ill., 1984—, corp. health and ergonomic cons., 1984—. Mem. Wis. Occupational Therapy Assn., Am. Occupational Therapy Assn. Lutheran. Avocations: bicycle riding; racquetball; cross country skiing; snowmobile riding; fishing. Home: 707 Old Prospectors Trail Eagle WI 53119 Office: Nat Loss Control Service Corp Route 22 Kemper Dr K-3 Long Grove IL 60049

FALKSON, SUSAN DORY, lawyer; b. N.Y.C., Mar. 20, 1948; d. Leo and Mildred (Novick) Rashkin; m. Joseph L. Falkson, May 22, 1971. B.A. cum laude, NYU, 1968; M.S., U. Mich., 1969, J.D. magna cum laude, 1977. Bar: D.C. 1977. Systems analyst Ann Arbor Computer Corp. (Mich.), 1969-71, EPA, Washington, 1971-74; assoc. Shaw, Pittman, Potts & Trowbridge, Washington, 1977-81, Willkie, Farr & Gallagher, Washington, 1981-85; assoc. gen. counsel Electronic Data Systems Corp., 1985—. Mem. ABA, D.C. Bar Assn., Nat. Contracts Mgmt. Assn., Order of Coif, Phi Beta Kappa. Home: 907 B Seneca Rd Great Falls VA 22066 Office: Electronic Data Systems Corp 6430 Rockledge Dr Bethesda MD 20817

FALLER, SUSAN GROGAN, lawyer; b. Cin., Mar. 1, 1950; d. William M. and Jane (Eagen) Grogan; m. Kenneth R. Faller, June 8, 1973; children—Susan Elisabeth, Maura Christine. B.A., U. Cin., 1972; J.D., U. Mich., 1975. Bar: Ohio 1975, U.S. Dist. Ct. (so. dist.) Ohio 1975; U.S. Supreme Ct. 1982, U.S. Ct. Claims 1982, U.S. Ct. Appeals (6th cir.) 1982; U.S. Tax Ct. 1984. Assoc. firm Frost & Jacobs, Cin., 1975-82, ptnr., 1982—. Trustee, Newman Found., Cin., 1980—, v.p., 1982—; trustee Bd. Cath. Service S.W. Ohio, 1984—; bd. dirs. Summit Country Day Alumni Council, Cin., 1983-85. Assoc. editor, note editor Mich. Law Rev., 1974-75. Mem. ABA, Fed. Bar Assn., Ohio Bar Assn., Cin. Bar Assn., Greater Cin. Women Lawyers Assn., Lawyers Club Cin., Assn. Profl. Women, Nat. Assn. Female Execs., Libel Def. Resource Ctr., Miami Purchase Assn. for Hist. Preservation, U. Cin. Friends of Women's Studies, Alumni Assn. U. Cin., U. Mich. Alumni Assn., Mortar Bd., Phi Beta Kappa, Theta Phi Alpha. Roman Catholic. Clubs: Leland (Mich.) Yacht; College, Greater Cin. Bus. and Profl. Women, Clifton Meadows (Cin.). Office: Frost & Jacobs 2500 Central Trust Ctr 201 E 5th St Cincinnati OH 45202

FALLIS, MARY MARGARET GAYNOR, magazine publisher; b. Kansas City, Kans., Feb. 19, 1924; d. Philip Patrick and Ethel (Williams) Gaynor; m. Gordon Douglas Fallis, Oct. 8, 1950; children—Lynn, Nancy, Mark, Dean, Keith. Feature writer, photographer Weekly Highlights, Kansas City, Mo., 1946-47; reporter St. Joseph (Mo.) Gazette, 1947-51; freelance writer Tulsa Tribune, 1961-68; editor, pub. Tulsalite, Inc., Tulsa, 1967—; freelance writer; founder, pub. Spotlite. Trustee William Allen White Found., Lawrence, Kans., 1983—; past pres. PTA; mem. Tulsa Opera Guild, Tulsa Ballet Guild, Vol. Council Tulsa Philharm. Soc.; past state pres. Sooner chpt. Cystic Fibrosis Found.; hon. dir. March of Dimes, also chmn. Mother's March; dir. Theatre Tulsa, Tulsa Alliance Classical Theatre, Am. Theatre Co. Recipient citation Okla. Ho. of Reps., 1978, plaque of appreciation Okla. Osteo. Soc., 1975, plaque NCCJ, 1981. Mem. Women in Communications, Nat. Soc. Interior Designers (hon.), Am. Soc. Interior Designers (affiliate), Sigma Delta Chi, Beta Sigma Phi, Alpha Omicron Pi. Republican. Episcopalian. Clubs: Tulsa Press, Summit. Home: 3138 S 85th East Ave Tulsa OK 74145 Office: Tulsalite Inc 2164 E 61st St Tulsa OK 74136

FALLON, JANICE ANN, insurance company executive; b. Jersey City, N.J., Sept. 13, 1949; d. John Frederick and Regina Teresa (Russell) F.; divorced; children—Benjamin James, Michael Joseph. File clk., gen. clk. Chubb Group Ins. Cos., N.Y.C., 1967-70, policy typist, 1970-71, asst. underwriter, 1972-76, underwriter mandated bus., 1976-77, retro-dividend analyst, 1977-80, spl. risk underwriter, 1980—. Democrat. Roman Catholic. Home: 2600 Kennedy Blvd Jersey City NJ 07306 Office: 15 Mountain View Rd Warren NJ

FALLS, WALDTRAUT MARGRETE GOETZE, medical librarian; b. N.Y.C., June 28, 1941; d. Otto Paul and Anna Irma (Zander) Goetze; A.B., State U. N.Y. at Albany, 1963, M.A. (scholar), 1964; M.S., Columbia U., 1967; m. John Allen Falls, Jr.; children—John Francis, Michael Gregory. Asst. advt. librarian Curtis Pub. Co., N.Y.C., 1964-65; library asso. N.Y. U. Commerce Library, N.Y.C., 1965-67; librarian, instr. N.Y.C. Community Coll., Bklyn., 1967-69, 70, 73-75; med. librarian Victory Meml. Hosp., Bklyn., 1975—. Mem. ALA, Med. Library Assn., Bklyn., Queens and S.I. Health Scis. Librarians, N.Y. Library Club (life). Home: 328 78th St Brooklyn NY 11209 Office: Victory Meml Hosp 9036 7th Ave Brooklyn NY 11228

FAN, SUSIE WU, medical technologist; b. Taiwan, Republic of China, Oct. 24, 1938; came to U.S., 1963, naturalized, 1973; d. Fu-Tzu and Yan-Chu (Chang) Wu; m. Hsin-Ya Fan, Nov. 3, 1963; children—Calvin A., Carol E., Cathyn S. B.Ed., Taiwan Normal U., 1963; M. Pub. Health, UCLA., 1966; Cert. City of Hope Med. Technologist Tng. Sch., 1978. Cert. med. technologist, Calif. Teaching asst. UCLA Sch. Pub. Health, 1965-66, biochemist, 1966-69; microbiologist, biochemist GEOMET, Pomona, Calif., 1976-77; med. technologist City of Hope Med. Ctr., Duarte, Calif., 1978-83, chemist, 1978-80, microbiologist, 1980-83; med. technologist Kaiser Hosp., Fontana, Calif., 1983—. Mem. Am. Soc. Microbiology, Am. Soc. Clin. Pathologists, Nat. Certifing Agency. Republican. Methodist. Home: 615 Wellesley Dr Claremont CA 91711 Office: Kaiser Hosp 9961 Sierra Ave Fontana CA 92335

FANCETT, CARRIE SUSAN, psychologist, educator, consultant; b. Newberry, Mich., Jan. 5, 1958; d. William Henry and Ruby Evelyn (Skidmore) F. B.A. in Psychology, Lake Superior State Coll., 1978; student Whittier Coll., 1976-77; M.A. in Sch. Psychology, U. S.C., 1981; Ph.D. in Sch. Psychology, 1984. Cert. sch. psychologist, III, S.C. Research asst. U. S.C., Columbia, 1979-80, 81-83; instr., 1983; instr. Lake Superior State Coll., Sault Ste. Marie, Mich., 1981; sch. psychologist III Head Start Program, Columbia, 1983—; child psychotherapist Counseling and Readjustment Services, Columbia, 1985—; psychologist Children's Hosp., Columbia, 1983—; clin. asst. prof. U. S.C. Sch. Medicine, Columbia, 1984—; cons. Richland Meml. Hosp., Columbia, 1983, Divorce Mediation Project, Columbia, 1982, Life Satisfaction Grant, Columbia, 1979-81. Contbr. chpt. to book. Campaign aide Democratic party, U.S. Senate race, Sault Ste. Marie, Mich., 1978. Stephenson scholar, 1978; NIMH fellow, 1980-81. Mem. Am. Psychol. Assn., Nat. Perinatal Assn., S.C. Perinatal Assn., Nat. Assn. Female Execs. Democrat. Episcopalian. Club: Palmette Personal Computer (Columbia). Avocations: writing fiction; computers; reading; aerobics. Home: 105 Hillpine Rd Apt F3 Columbia SC 29210 Office: Div Neonatology Richland Meml Hosp Columbia SC 29210

FANCHER, EVELYN PITTS, librarian; b. Marion, Ala.; d. D.C. and Nell Lenora Pitts; B.S., Ala. State U., 1946; M.S.L.S., Atlanta U., 1961; Ed.S., George Peabody Coll., 1969, Ph.D., 1974; m. Charles B. Fancher, Dec. 20, 1947; children—Charles B., Mark Pitts, Adrienne Lenore. Tchr. biology, chemistry public schs., Marion, Ala., 1946-56; library tech. asst. A&M U., Huntsville, 1956; dir. media center Council High Sch., Huntsville, Ala., 1959-62; circulation, reference librarian, instr. Tenn. State U., Nashville, 1962-74, dir. univ. library, 1975—; cons. Tenn. State Library Adv. Bd. on Libraries, 1983-85. Bd. dirs. Tenn. Girl Scouts U.S.A., 1982-85. Mem. ALA, Southeastern Library Assn., Tenn. Library Assn., (pres. 1984-85), Mid State Library Assn., Nashville Library Club, AAUW, Phi Delta Kappa. Congregationalist. Home: 3948 Drakes Branch Rd Nashville TN 37218 Office: Brown-Daniel Library Tenn State Univ Nashville TN 37203

FANCHER, HELEN IRENE, former state legislator, rancher, lobbyist; b. Seattle, Mar. 1, 1931; d. Robert Warren and Mary Caroline (Foy) Walker; student U. Wash., 1948, Eastern Wash. U., 1949-50; m. John T. Fancher, Aug. 14, 1950; children—Scott, Donald, Nancy Connelly. Profl. musician, Seattle, Spokane, Wash., 1947; sec.-treas., dir. Pilot Wheel Ranch, Inc., Tonasket, Wash., Three Toed Feedlot, Inc., Quincy, Wash., 1971—; mem. Tri-County Law and Justice Commn., 1970, Okanogan County Planning Commn., 1974; mem. Wash. Ho. of Reps., 1976-82, asst. majority leader, 1981-82. Precinct committeeman Republican party; dir. Agr.-Forestry Leadership Found., 1982; pres. Okanogan County Cow Belles, 1972-73; v.p. Wash. State Cow Belles, 1975-76; mem. Wash. State Timber Tax Adv. Com. mem. Quincy City Planning Commn. and Bd. Appeals; mem. Quincy City Council, 1985—; mem. Grant County Clean Air Bd., 1985—. Named Hon. State Farmer, Future Farmers Am., 1982. Mem. Nat. Cow Belles and Cattlemen's Assn., Musicians Union, Am. Legis. Exchange Council, Quincy C. of C. (bd. dirs. 1984); Mu Phi Epsilon. Home: 216 M St SE Quincy WA 98848

FANCHER, VIVIAN KRAMER, author, guidance counselor; b. Phila., Sept. 23, 1931; d. Edward Julius and Rose (Marian) Kramer; m. Edwin Crawford Fancher, Nov. 7, 1969; children—Bruce, Emily. B.S. in Edn., Temple U., 1953; M.S. in Guidance and Counseling, CCNY, 1959. Tchr. N.Y.C. Bd. Edn., 1954-59, guidance counselor, 1959-70; freelance writer, N.Y.C., 1981—. Author: Greenwich Village Cookbook, 1969, also articles. Vol., Congressman William Green, N.Y., 1977, 78, 80. Republican. Club: Gipsy Trail. Avocations: reading; sewing; contests. Home: 40 5th Ave New York NY 10011

FANNING, ELEANOR, lawyer; b. Warren, Ohio, May 19, 1949; d. Arthur and Irene Lillian (Elefant) F. B.A., Syracuse U., 1968; J.D., Temple U., 1974. Bar: Pa. 1974. Law clk. Isaac S. Garb, Pres. Judge Bucks County, Doylestown, Pa., 1974-75; mental health rev. officer County of Bucks, Doylestown, 1975—; sole practice law, Trevose, Pa., 1980—. Bd. dirs. Blind Assn. Bucks County, Newtown; Big Sister, Phila., 1982-84. Recipient Sara A. Shulman award Temple U. Law Sch., 1974. Mem. ABA, Pa. Bar Assn., Bucks County Bar Assn. Democrat. Office: One Neshaminy Interplex Suite 205 Trevose PA 19047

FANNING, KATHERINE WOODRUFF, editor; b. Chgo., Oct. 18, 1927; d. Frederick William and Katherine Bower (Miller) Woodruff; m. Marshall Field, Jr., May 12, 1950 (div. 1963); children—Frederick Woodruff, Katherine Woodruff, Barbara Woodruff; m. Lawrence S. Fanning, 1966 (dec. 1971); m. Amos Mathews, Jan. 6, 1984. B.A., Smith Coll., 1949; LL.D. (hon.), Colby Coll., 1979; Litt. D. (hon.), Pine Manor Jr. Coll., 1984; L.H.D. (hon.), Northeastern U., 1984. With Anchorage Daily News, 1965—, editor, pub., 1972-83; editor The Christian Science Monitor, 1983—. Mem. Anchorage Urban Beautification Commn., 1968-71, Alaska Ednl. Broadcasting Commn., 1971-75; dir. Alaska Repertory Theater, 1975-81; pres. Greater Anchorage Community Chest, 1973-74. Recipient Elijah Parish Lovejoy award Colby Coll., 1979; Smith Coll. medal, 1980; Mo. medal of Honor U. Mo. Journalism award, 1980. Mem. Am. Soc. Newspaper Editors (dir., v.p. 1984), Sigma Delta Chi. Office: One Norway St Boston MA 02115

FANNING, KAY EILENE, retail cosmetics company executive; b. Springfield, Ohio, Sept. 4, 1942; d. Wilbur J. and Ethel Waddle; B.S., Wittenberg U., 1964; student U. Dayton, summer 1965, Bowling Green U., summer 1966; m. Robert H. Fanning, Feb. 1, 1964; children—Leann Kay, (Robert) Shane, Aaron Carter. Tchr., Shawnee High Sch., Springfield, Ohio, 1964-67; tchr. Clark Tech. Coll., 1967-70; beauty cons. Fashion Two Twenty Cosmetics, Springfield, 1969-70, assoc. dir., 1970-78, dir., 1978; pres. Mic-Kay, Inc., Springfield, 1979—; regional mgr. Cher-Beli Creations, Inc., Memphis, 1981-82, v.p., 1982-83; pres. Leana Internat., Inc., 1983—. Mem. Clark County Bd. Edn., 1974—, v.p., 1978, pres., 1979; mem. Springfield-Clark County Joint Vocat. Sch. Bd. Edn., 1979—, v.p., 1981-82, pres., 1982—; mem. Clark County Republican Women. Mem. Nat. Assn. Female Execs., Springfield Area C. of C., Alpha Delta Pi. Republican. Baptist. Address: 364 W Jackson Rd Springfield OH 45502

FAOUR, ANNA ROSE, writer, educator; b. Houston, Nov. 27, 1929; d. Jack and Alice (Emmett) Faour. B.S., U. Houston, 1952. Reporter, Houston Chronicle, 1952-53, 58-59; reporter women's dept. Houston Post, 1953-54; proof-reader McCann-Erickson, Houston, 1962-64; tchr. English, Cypress-Fairbanks Ind. Sch. Dist., Houston, 1965-79; reporter Brazosport Facts, Clute, Tex., 1981; tchr. English, Houston Ind. Sch. Dist., 1957-61, 64-65, 81-83; author, pub. TexAnna greeting cards, 1981—; freelance writer. Publicity writer Eisenhower campaign, Houston, 1956. Named Foremost Women in Communications, Foremost Am. Pub. Corp., 1970; pub. relations scholar U. Houston, 1950-52. Mem. Tex. Tchrs. Assn., San Jacinto Mus. History, Women in Communications, Theta Sigma Phi. Antiochian Orthodox Christian. Address: 16615 Torrington Ct Spring TX 77379

FARACE-EPLEY, DIANA MARIA, educator, human relations counselor; b. Bklyn., Jan. 2, 1948; d. Nicholas Vincent and Catherine (Mauro) F.; m. James Pascal Epley, Jr., July 29, 1973. A.A.S., Suffolk County Community Coll., 1968; B.A. in Psychology summa cum laude, St. Leo Coll., 1976; M.A. in Human Relations, Webster U., 1984. Figure cons. Barbara-Wayne Figure Salon, N.Y.C., 1970-71; evening mgr. Nu-Dimensions Figure Salon, N.Y.C., 1971-72; adminstrv. asst. to dir. sales/mktg. Hazletine Corp., Greenlawn, N.Y., 1972-73; faculty City Colls. of Chgo., Zaragoza, Spain, 1973-74, Stratford Women's Coll., Tampa, Fla., 1974; ops. mgr. Stanton & Assocs. Constrn., 1976-78; officer Richard's Auto Grooming, Inc., 1978-79; faculty Florence-Darlington TEC, Florence, S.C., 1979-81, St. Anne's Cath. Elem. Sch., 1982; tutor, tchr., counselor Darlington Acad. (S.C.), 1982; area dir. office occupations Preston Coll. Tech. and Bus. Careers, Columbia, S.C., 1983-84; owner, mental health counselor PMS Research and Peripheral Treatment Clinic, 1985; ednl. resource adviser Davis-Monthan AFB Learning Ctr., Cochise Coll., Sierra Vista, Ariz., 1986—. Exhibited paintings Sumter Gallery Art, 1983. Benefactor, St. LeBre Missionary for Indians in Utah, 1983-84, Christian Appalachian Project in Ky., 1984—; mem. Florence-Darlington Tech. Coll. Ednl. Found., 1981—. Mem. Secretarial Guild Am., S.C. Ednl. Tchrs. Assn., Sumter Artists Guild, Smithsonian Assocs. Roman Catholic.

FARAH, CYNTHIA WEBER, photographer, publisher; b. Long Island, N.Y., June 2, 1949; d. Andrew John and Aria Emma (Jelnikova) Weber; m. James Clifton Farah, Jan. 12, 1974; children—Elise, Alexa. B.A. in Communications, Stanford U., 1971. Prodn. staff Sta. KDBC-TV, El Paso, Tex., 1971-73; v.p. Sanders Co. Advt., El Paso, 1973-74, film critic El Paso Times, 1972-77; free lance photographer, El Paso, 1974—; pres. CM Pub., El Paso, 1981—. Photographer, co-author: Country Music: A Look at the Men Who've Made It, 1982. Bd. dirs. N. Mex. State U. Mus. Adv. Bd., Las Cruces, 1982—; dir., vice-chmn. Shelter for Battered Women, El Paso, 1982; active Jr. League, 1977—, C. of C. Leadership El Paso Program, 1983-84; mem. El Paso County Hist. Commn., 1984—, vice chmn., 1986; trustee El Paso Community Found., 1984—. Recipient Clara Barton Medallion ARC, 1979. Mem. Tex. Profl. Photographers Assn., Stanford U. Alumni Assn. Episcopalian. Office: CM Pub 330 Eubank El Paso TX 79902

FARAJ, BETH ANNE, pharmacist, pharmacy executive; b. Phila., Feb. 7, 1951; d. Sylvester Edmund and Marian Audrey (Walker) Kasnikowski; m. Ramzi Bahjat Faraj, June 10, 1984. B.S. in Pharmacy, Wayne State U., 1975. Registered pharmacist, Mich. Pharmacy intern Michaels Pharmacy, Detroit, 1972-75; pharmacist Dale Drugs, Union Lake, Mich., 1976-77; pharmacist, owner Franks Pharmacy, Detroit, 1978-82; staff pharmacist Lakeside Hosp., Detroit, 1981-82; pharmacist, mgr. King Pharmacy, Detroit, 1983-86; cons. adult foster-care homes. Active Washington Square Estates, Troy, Mich., 1984—. Mem. Mich. Pharmacist Assn., Oakland County Pharmacist Assn., Wayne State Alumni Assn., Rho Pi Phi. Republican. Roman Catholic. Club: Franklin Racquet (Southfield). Avocations: bowling; crocheting; gardening. Office: Banner Pharmacy 14424 Schaefer Detroit MI 48227

FARB, CAROLYN FREEDMAN, free-lance journalist, fundraiser; b. Houston, Feb. 8; d. Nathan and Ruth (Epstein) Freedman; m. Harold Farb, July 14, 1977 (div. May 1983); 1 son, J. Kenyon Shulman. B.S. in Mktg., U. Okla. Contbr. to Houston City mag., Interview mag., 212 mag. Organizer 1st pub. TV auction, 1970; mem. steering com. for benefit St. Joseph Hosp., 1971; entertainment chmn. Nina Vance Theatre, 1971-72; benefit chmn. Neiman-Marcus awards Contemporary Arts Mus., 1973; chmn. Super Sports Night auction Channel 8, Houston, 1973; invitation chmn. Silver Anniversary ball March of Dimes, 1973; program dir. Mus. Theatre Guild Houston, 1976; chmn. souvenir program Jack Benny Meml. Tennis Classic for Juvenile Diabetes, 1977; Chili cook-off celebrity judge for Cancer Assistance League, 1978; organizer Angels fun raising group for Soc. Performing Arts, 1979, benefit advisor, 1984, chmn. Soiree on Swanee fundraiser Houston Ballet, 1980; chmn. Renaissance Evening fundraiser Mus. Fine Arts, 1981; creater art piece Winged Pegasus for Blaffer Gallery Benefit, 1981; chmn. benefit for Tex. project Archives Am. Art, Washington, 1982; chmn. Million Dollar Evening fundraiser Stehlin Found., Houston, 1983; benefit participant for Scott and White Meml. Hosp., Temple, Tex., 1983; mem. fin. com. reelection campaign Whitmire for Mayor, Houston, 1983; fundraiser Senator Percy re-election campaign, Houston, 1984; River Oaks Mother's March Against Birth Defects, 1984, Cancer Fighters, 1984; chmn. hon. host com. 1st Stars of Tex. Gala for Ms. Found. for Women, 1984; mem. host com. 1st internat. Dallas Grand Prix, 1984; bd. dirs. Mus. Fine Arts, Houston, Houston Ballet Found., Soc. for Performing Arts, Houston, Houston Grand Opera, Stehlin Found. for Cancer Research; mem. internat. com. N.Y.C. Ballet. Recipient Women's Fund award Stehlin Found., 1983; named Queen Isabella for XIX Ann. Noche de Las Americas Ball., 1984. Republican. Home: 1721 River Oaks Blvd Houston TX 77019

FARBMAN, ROBIN ELISE, financial and management consultant; b. Detroit, Jan. 22, 1951; d. Aaron A. and Marie A. (Prager) F. B.A., Mich. State U., 1974; postgrad. Wayne State U., 1976, Pace U., 1983. Drama critic Lansing State Jour., Mich., 1974, asst. editor Gale Research Co., Detroit, 1974-77; copy chief Ballantine Books, Random House, N.Y.C., 1977-79; fin. mgr. and adminstr. Ark Mgmt. Corp., N.Y.C., 1980-83; owner, pres. Robin Farbman Acctg. Services, N.Y.C., 1981—. Mem. Nat. Assn. Female Execs. Democrat. Unitarian. Avocations: writing; piano. Address: 59 W 76th St New York NY 10023

FARBMAN, ROBIN LORI, lawyer; b. Bklyn., July 22, 1955; d. Irving and Sheila Falk; m. Robert Jeffrey Farbman, July 19, 1975. Student Drew U., 1973-75; B.A. in Polit. Sci., George Washington U., 1977; postgrad. Cath. U. Law Sch., 1977-78; J.D., Suffolk U., 1980. Bar: Fla. 1980, U.S. Dist. Ct. (so. dist.) Fla. 1981, U.S. Tax Ct. 1981, U.S. Ct. Appeals (11th cir.) 1981. With div. consumer protection Mass. Atty. Gen.'s Office, Boston, 1978; with legal bur. Mass. Dept. Revenue, Boston, 1979, estate tax bur., 1979, rulings and regulations bur., 1979-80; with Suffolk Vol. Prosecutors, Boston Mcpl. Ct., Boston, 1979-80; asst. state's atty. State Atty.'s Office, Circuit and County Ct., Miami, Fla., 1980-81; assoc. pvt. practice, Fort Lauderdale, Fla., 1981-83; sole practice, Coral Springs, Fla., 1983—. Named to Dean's List Drew U., 1973-75, George Washington U., 1975-77, Suffolk U. Law Sch., 1979-80. Mem. Phi Delta Phi. Office: 1881 University Dr Suite 203-A Coral Springs FL 33065

FARENTHOLD, FRANCES TARLTON, lawyer, former college president; b. Corpus Christi, Tex., Oct. 2, 1926; d. Benjamin Dudley and Catherine (Bluntzer) Tarlton; A.B., Vassar Coll., 1946; J.D., U. Tex., 1949; LL.D., Hood Coll., 1973, Boston U., 1973, Regis Coll., 1976, Lake Erie Coll., 1979, Elmira Coll., 1981, Coll. of Santa Fe, 1985; children—Dudley Tarlton, George Edward, Emilie, James Dougherty, Vincent Bluntzer (dec.). Bar: Tex. 1949. Mem. Tex. Ho. of Reps., 1968-72; dir. legal aide Nueces County, 1965-67; asst. prof. law Tex. So. U., Houston; pres. Wells Coll., Aurora, N.Y., 1976-80. Mem. Human Relations Com., Corpus Christi, 1963-68, Corpus Christi Citizen's Com. Community Improvement, 1966-68; mem. Tex. adv. com. to U.S. Commn. on Civil Rights, 1968-76; mem. nat. adv. council ACLU; mem. Orgn. for Preservation Unblemished Shoreline, 1964—; Democratic candidate for Gov. of Tex., 1972; del. Dem. Nat. Conv., 1972, 1st woman nominated to be candidate v.p. U.S., 1972; nat. co-chmn. Citizens to Elect McGovern-Shriver, 1972; chmn. Nat. Women's Polit. Caucus, 1973-75; trustee Vassar Coll., 1975-83; bd. dirs. Texans for a Bilateral Nuclear Weapons Freeze, 1983-84, Fund for Constl. Govt., Ctr. for Devel. Policy, 1983—, Mexican Am. Legal Def. and Ednl. Fund, 1980-83; chmn. Inst. for Policy Studies, 1984—. Recipient Lyndon B. Johnson Woman of Year award, 1973. Mem. State Bar Tex. Office: 1203 Central Bank Bldg 2100 Travis Houston TX 77002

FARESE, MAUREEN, trainer consultant; b. Saratoga Springs, N.Y., July 29, 1956; d. Frank Louis and Elizabeth Mary (DelVecchio) Buffardi; m. John Michael Farese, Sept. 1, 1979. B.A. in Sociology, State U. Coll., Potsdam, N.Y., 1978, B.A. in Psychology, 1978. Cert. family tchr./trainer. Family tchr./parent trainer Kolburne Sch., New Marlboro, Mass., 1981; Fla. Mental Health Inst., Tampa, 1982-83; trainer, cons., evaluator Fla. Mental Health Inst., Tampa, 1983-84, dir. tng. and cons., 1985, dir. pub. relations, 1984-86, dir. dissemination, 1984—; program cons. 6 Community Mental Health Ctrs., Fla., 1985-86; parent trainer/therapist Northside Mental Health Agy., Tampa, 1986—; mem. research team Hillsborough County Charter Rev. Bd., Tampa, 1986—; trainer Nat. Teaching Family Assn., Chgo., 1984. Singer album Sing Out, 1973; author song, words and music: Take Back the Night, 1984. Career service senator U. South Fla., Tampa, 1985; mem. Women's Awareness Week Com., U. South Fla., 1986; chief organizer Western Mass. Coalition for Reproductive Freedom, Great Barrington, 1980; lobbyist Women's Rights Day in Congress, Washington, 1980. U. South Fla. grad. asst., 1986. Mem. Women in Pub. Adminstrn., Tampa Women's Bus. and Profl. Orgn., NOW, LWV, Am. Soc. Tng. and Devel., Nat. Audubon Soc. Democrat. Roman Catholic. Club: Women's Music Collective. Avocations: running; backpacking; environmental issues; gardening; music. Home: 801 W 114th Ave Tampa FL 33612 Office: Public Adminstrn Dept SOC 107 U South Fla Tampa FL 33620

FARGO, DIANE MARIE, nurse; b. Oil City, Pa., Apr. 12, 1958; d. Albert Joseph and Arlene Anna (Frankenberger) Geary; m. Douglas Larry Fargo, July 24, 1982. Licensed practical nurse Venargo County Vocat. Tech. Sch., 1977; registered nurse, Clarion U. Pa., 1982; postgrad., Slippery Rock U. Pa., 1984—. Registered nurse, Pa. Licenced practical nurse Titusville Hosp., Titusville, Pa., 1978, Oil City Hosp., 1978-82; registered nurse Oil City Area Health Ctr., 1982—. Mem. Sandy Lake Women's Aglow Fellowship, Sandy Lake, Pa., 1984, Rosary Soc. Saint Joseph's Ch. Mem. Am. Diabetes Assn. (mem. adv. council). Democrat. Club: Oil City Boat.

FARIAS, MARIA ELENA, psychotherapist, social worker; b. Los Angeles, Apr. 27, 1953; d. Guillermo Tapia and Maria de la Luz (Martinez) Farias; B.A., Loyola-Marymount U., 1975; M.S.W., Calif. State U., 1977. Lic. clin. social worker, Calif. Adoptions supr. Dept. Adoptions, Los Angeles, 1978-85; program coordinator Plaza Community Ctr., East Los Angeles, 1985; asst. dir. Orthopaedic Hosp., Los Angeles, 1985-86; family therapist Century City Hosp., Calif., 1986—; cons. Zapanta Med. Group, Monterey Park, Calif.; psychotherapist in pvt. practice, Beverly Hills, Calif. Bd. dirs. In Jesus Si Se Puede, East Los Angeles, 1986. Mem. Nat. Assn. Social Woekrs, Comision Femenil, Spanish-Speaking Child Abuse Council, Los Angeles County Child Abuse Task Force, NOW, Nat. Assn. Female Execs. Democrat. Roman Catholic. Office: 292 S La Cienega Suite 213 Beverly Hills CA 90211

FARINHOLT, (MARY) KATHARINE WOLTZ (MRS. WILLIAM WORTHAM FARINHOLT), writer, educational consultant; b. Chapel Hill, N.C., Feb. 5, 1912; d. Albert Edgar and Daisy (Mackie) Woltz; B.A. with honors, Agnes Scott Coll., 1933; M.Ed., Emory U., 1964; m. Holcombe Tucker Green, Oct. 16, 1934; children—Caroline Tucker, Holcombe Tucker; m. 2d, William Wortham Farinholt, July 18, 1959; 1 stepson, Lewis Sharp. Tchr. English, Belmont (N.C.) High Sch., 1933-34; tchr. English, Westminster Schs., Atlanta, 1958-59, 64-74, prin. Girls' Jr. High Sch., 1964-74; now cons. Author: Alexander's Daughter, 1984. Pres. Atlanta council Girl Scouts U.S.A., 1953, bd. dirs., 1950-53; pres. Child Service Assn. Atlanta, 1956-58; mem. exec. bd. Atlanta Music Club, 1951-59; hon. bd dirs. Met. Atlanta Child Service and Family Counseling Center, 1975—; trustee Agnes Scott Coll., 1944-45, Appleton Ch. Home, Macon, Ga., 1962-65; patron High Mus. Art. Named One of 10 Leading Ladies of Atlanta, 1975; recipient Outstanding Alumna award Agnes Scott Coll., 1983; collection named in her honor Emory U.; Katharine Woltz Farinholt Scholarship established her honor Agnes Scott Coll., 1983. Mem. Nat. (jr. high sect. chmn. 1969-70, mem. exec. bd. 1969-70, editorial bd. jour. 1972-74, adv. com. 1975, treas. 1975-77, citation 1982), Ga. assns. women deans, adminstrs. and counselors, Ga. Assn. Middle Sch. Prins. (sec.), Mortar Bd. (nat. treas. 1945-47, fellowship chair 1950-52), Nat. Soc. Colonial Dames Am. (bd. mgrs. Ga. 1985-87), Atlanta Opera Guild, Friends of Decorative Arts, Atlanta Bot. Gardens, Atlanta Hist. Soc., Dixie Council Authors and Journalists, Village Writers Group, Agnes Scott Coll. Alumnae Assn. (pres. 1944-45, bd. dirs. 1983-85, citation 1975), AAUW, Phi Beta Kappa, Delta Kappa Gamma. Episcopalian (pres. women's group). Club: Wayside Garden, Piedmont Driving, Tuesday Bridge, Thursday Book. Address: 3462 Paces Pl NW Atlanta GA 30327

FARIS, BARBARA GOEDEKE, lawyer; b. Morristown, N.J., Nov. 7, 1952; d. Philip George and Martha Melvine (Maines) Goedeke; m. Thomas Carmon Faris, Nov. 21, 1981; 1 dau., Michele Elizabeth. B.A., Maryville Coll., 1974; J.D., U. Tenn., 1978. Bar: Tenn. 1980. Corp. staff atty., lease agt. United Am. Energy, Kingston, Tenn., 1978-81; ptnr. firm Faris & Faris, Winchester, Tenn., 1981—; dir. Mafis, Inc., Knoxville, 1981-83; assoc. atty. Legal Services, Tullahoma, Tenn., 1984—. Mem. ABA, Tenn. Bar Assn., Tenn. Trial Attys Assn., Tenn. Oil and Gas Assn. Jewish. Office: Faris & Faris Public Sq Winchester TN 37398

FARIS, JANICE MARIE, accountant; b. Oak Park, Ill., Jan. 12, 1947; d. Arthur James and Betty Alice (Packer) Blumthal; m. Paul Thompson Faris; children—Bradford Paul, Jana Lind, Todd Arthur. B.S., No. Ill. U., 1979. Staff acct. Nalco Chem. Co., Oak Brook, Ill., 1979-80, internal auditor, 1980-82; acct., franchise owner Comprehensive Acctg. Service, Wheaton, Ill., 1982—. Parent adv. council Wheaton No. High Sch., 1982-83. Mem. EDP Auditors Assn., Info. Systems Resources (ednl. adv. bd.), Wheaton C. of C. Republican. Roman Catholic. Home: 412 N Washington St Wheaton IL 60187 Office: Comprehensive Accounting Services 221 S Hale St Wheaton IL 60187

FARLEY, DOROTHY BIEBER, artist, civic worker, educator; b. St. Louis, May 27, 1927; d. Ralph Paul and Ida (Parker) Bieber; B.F.A. in Art Edn., U. Ill., 1949; m. Donald Gene Farley, June 16, 1951; children—Dale Ellen, Ronald Wesley. Secondary sch. art tchr., Ferguson, Mo., 1949-51; secondary art tchr. Normandy, Mo., 1955-57; art gallery dir. Craft Alliance, St. Louis, 1970-81; exhbn. juror, lectr., cons., 1977—; treas. Craft Alliance, 1967-68; pres. Craft Alliance, 1968; enamel artist, tchr., 1955—. Community chmn. March of Dimes, Creve Coeur, Mo., 1963; mem. adv. commn. University City Loop Spl. Bus. Dist., 1981; city clk., Crystal Lake Park, Mo., 1981—; bd. dirs. Holistic Health Ctr. of St. Louis, 1983—. Mem. Am. Crafts Council (sec. n. central region, 1973-80), World Crafts Council, Mo. City Clks. and Fin. Officers Assn., Friends of St. Louis Art Mus., St. Louis Symphony Soc., Mo. Bot. Garden Assocs. Home: 2332 Putter Ln St Louis MO 63131

FARLEY, JENNIE TIFFANY TOWLE, industrial and labor relations educator; b. Fanwood, N.J., Nov. 2, 1932; d. Howard Albert and Dorothy Jane (Van Wagner) Towle; m. Donald Thorn Farley, Jr., June 16, 1956; children—Claire Hamlin, Anne Tiffany, Peter Towle. B.A., Cornell U., 1954, M.S., 1969, Ph.D., 1970. Mem. editorial staff Mademoiselle and Seventeen Mags., N.Y.C., 1954-56; free-lance writer, Eng., Sweden, Peru, 1956-67; lectr., research assoc., adj. asst. prof. Cornell U., Ithaca, N.Y., 1970-72, dir. women's studies, 1972-76, asst. prof. Sch. Indsl. and Labor Relations, 1976-82, assoc. prof., 1982—, exec. bd. dirs. women's studies program, 1970—; dir. Profl. Skills Roster, Ithaca. Author: Affirmative Action and the Woman Worker, 1979; Academic Women and Employment Discriminations, 1982. Editor: Sex Discrimination in Higher Education, 1982; The Woman in Management, 1983; Women Workers in Fifteen Countries, 1985. Vice pres. bd. dirs. City Fedn. of Women's Orgns., Ithaca, 1984-85; bd. dirs. Seven Lakes Girl Scouts U.S.A. Council, Geneva, N.Y., 1980-84. Mem. Ithaca AAUW (pres. 1980-82). Club: Cornell Women's of Tompkins County. Home: 711 Triphammer Rd Ithaca NY 14850 Office: Sch Indsl and Labor Relations Cornell U Ithaca NY 14853

FARLEY, LINDA NELL, chemical company executive; b. Charleston, W.Va., Nov. 24, 1941; d. Frederick Paul and Frances Eloise (Hale) Farley. Student Eastern Mont. Coll. of Edn., 1959-60, W.Va. State Coll. Instr. gymnastics Lawrence Frankel Inst., Charleston, 1960-61; sec. Union Carbide Corp., Institute, W.Va., 1961-73, office services supr., 1973-81, mgmt. devel. assoc., 1981—, sr. office supr., public relations adminstr., non-exempt tng. adminstrn. Mem. Nat. Assn. Female Execs., Am. Soc. Tng. and Devel. Club: Altrusa (corr. sec. 1976-77) (Charleston). Home: 4 Sitting Bull Dr Saint Albans WV 25177 Office: PO Box 2831 Charleston WV 25330

FARLEY, MARIAN DIEDRE, librarian; b. Manhasset, N.Y., Mar. 1, 1955; d. John Joseph and Rita Sarah (Johnston) Farley. B.A., St. Bonaventure U., 1977; M.L.S., SUNY-Albany, 1978. Librarian-instr. Iona Coll., New Rochelle, N.Y., 1980-82; head circulation dept. U. Lowell (Mass.), 1982-83; library dir. Analytic Scis. Corp., Reading, Mass., 1983—. Mem. ALA, Spl. Libraries Assn., Route 128 Librarians, New Eng. On-Line Users Group. Democrat. Roman Catholic. Home: 28 Fifth Ave Lowell MA 01854 Office: Analytic Sciences Corp One Jacob Way Reading MA 01867

FARLEY, NORMA SUE, educator; b. Kansas City, Mo., Nov. 15, 1936; d. Leroy James and A. Ione (Thompson) Markwell; student Northwestern U., 1954-55; B.S. in Edn., U. Kans., 1958, M.A., 1968; m. James W. Farley, June 27, 1981; children—R. Michael Murphy, Kathleen A. Murphy, James Mark Murphy. Tchr. social sci. dept. Park Hill Sr. High Sch., Kansas City, Mo., 1963—. Twp. committeewoman Kickapoo Twp., treas. Platte County Dem. Women's Club, chmn. Platte County Central Com., del. Dem. nat. conv., 1980. Recipient award Young Democrats of Mo., 1981. Mem. NEA, Mo. Edn. Assn., Park Hill Edn. Assn., Mo. State Tchrs. Assn., Nat. Council Social Studies, Mo. Council Social Studies, Platte County Hist. Soc., Delta Kappa Gamma, Sigma Alpha Iota, Pi Lambda Theta, Alpha Delta Pi. Methodist. Pianist; solo performance with Kansas City Philharm. Orch., 1951. Home: 6514 Fairway Dr Kansas City MO 64152

FARLEY, URSULA PATRICIA, copywriter/consultant; b. Bklyn., July 31, 1942; d. Walter Howard and Ursula Michaela (Kirsten) F.; student Marywood Coll., 1960-61, Columbia U., 1961-64. Asst. bus. mgr. book div. The Conde Nast Publs., Inc., 1966-68; mgr. client services, sr. copywriter Response Scis. Corp., 1968-70; creative dir. Throckmorton/Satin Assos., Inc., N.Y.C., 1970-73; free-lance copywriter/cons. direct mktg., N.Y.C., 1973—. N.Y.

County com. mem. Republican party, 1967, 68; dist. capt. Village Rep. Club, 1967-68; mem. bd. elections, 1967-68. Recipient award Lynchburg (Va.) Advt. Club, 1975; award Am. Printers Council, 1975. Mem. Nat. Assn. Female Execs. (past dir.), Direct Mktg. Creative Guild (past dir.), Women's Direct Response Group. Author: Kenneth Beauty Consultation, 1974; The Advertising Trivia Book, 1978; Resume Preparation Guide, 1977; co-author: Powertalk, 1983.

FARLING, ALICE MARIE, educational administrator; b. Terre Haute, Ind., Dec. 16, 1945; m. Robert Finley Farling, Dec. 17, 1967 (div. 1973); 1 child, Christopher; m. David Wilson Hennage, June 23, 1985; children—Michael, Daniel. B.S., Ball State U., 1967; M.S., No. Ill. U., 1975. Cert. dir. spl. edn., gen. adminstr. Speech-lang. therapist Denver pub. schs., 1967-68, Duval County pub. schs., Jacksonville, Fla., 1968-70; speech-lang. and psycho-ednl. diagnostician Schaumburg Sch. Dist. 54, Ill., 1970-77, asst. prin., learning disability coordinator, 1977-78, spl. services cons., 1978-80, dir. placement and curriculum/spl. services, 1980—; due process hearing officer Ill. State Bd. Edn., Springfield, 1980-82; mem. field work faculty Ill. State U., Normal, part-time 1981-83; strategic long-range planning facilitator intern Harper Community Coll., Palatine, Ill., 1984-85; pres., founder, communication-image cons. Profl. Image Consultants, Farling & Assocs., Chgo., 1986—. Chmn. bd. dirs. Elk Grove-Schaumburg Twps. Mental Health Ctr., Ill., 1985—, Profl. Counseling Assocs. (formerly Ill. Human Services Found.), Itasca, 1985—; temp. area leader Children's Channel Television, Schaumburg and Hoffman Estates, Ill., spring 1982. Mem. Women in Mgmt., Council for Exceptional Children, Ill. Council for Adminstrs. Spl. Edn., Ill. Dirs. Pupil Personnel, Ill. Assn. Spl. Edn. Adminstrs., Tchrs. English as 2d Lang.-Bilingual Edn., Nat. Assn. for Female Execs., Delta Kappa Gamma. Avocations: tennis, sailing, acting, bicycling, photography. Home: 405 N Wabash Ave Apt 4009 Chicago IL 60611 Office: Schaumburg TWP Schs-Dist 54 524 E Schaumburg Rd Schaumburg IL 60194 also Profl Image Assocs Three First Nat Plaza Suite 1400 Chicago IL 60602

FARMANN, KATHLEEN ELIZABETH, retired law librarian; b. Addison, N.Y., Aug. 21, 1920; d. Michael Francis and Elizabeth Lee (McClintock) Godfrey; A.B., Trinity Coll., Washington, 1941; J.D., Cath. U., 1945; M.L.L., U. Wash., Seattle, 1957; m. Stanley L. Farmann, June 14, 1958. Admitted to D.C. bar, 1945; asso. firm Covington & Burling, 1945-53; asst. law librarian Ohio State U., 1957-61, asst. dir. research services, 1962-66; law librarian Hawaii Supreme Ct., 1961-62; law librarian U. Notre Dame, 1966-85, asst. to dean Law Sch., 1975-77. Exchange student Dept. of State, 1942. Mem. Bar Assn. D.C., Ohio Regional Assn. Law Libraries (past pres.), Am. Assn. Law Libraries. Democrat. Roman Catholic. Home: 19053 Summers Dr South Bend IN 46637

FARMER, ALLENE VALERIE, information specialist, government executive; b. Washington, Sept. 23, 1958; d. Thomas Jonathan and Allena V. (Joyner) F. Student, Richmond Coll., London, 1980; B.A., Clark Coll., 1980; grad. cert. U. Oxford, Eng., 1981; M.L.S., U. Md., 1986. Library asst. NUS Corp., Gaithersburg, Md., 1981-82; cataloger Library of Congress, Washington, 1982-84, copyright specialist, 1984-85; congl. fellow Ho. of Reps. Com. on D.C., Washington, 1985—; English tutor, writer Natural Motion, Washington, 1983-84; intern, archivist Howard U., Washington, 1985. Compiler; Single Mother's Resource Directory, 1984. Compiler, editor: Policy Research, 1985. Author booklet: D.C. Statehood Issue, 1986. Mem. U. Md. College Park Black Women's council, College Park, Md., 1984; vol. Congl. Black Caucus Found., Washington, 1985. Recipient Fgn. Study award Am. Inst. for Fgn. Study, 1981; Congl. Black Caucus fellow, 1985. Mem. Library of Congress Profls. Assn., ALA, Daniel A.P. Murray Afro-Am. Culture Assn. of Library of Congress, NAACP, Delta Sigma Theta (tutor 1986). Avocations: travel; writing; dance; drama; tennis. Home: 8504 Barron St Takoma Park MD 20912 Office: Congress of US Ho of Reps Com on DC 2135 Rayburn House Office Bldg Washington DC 20515

FARMER, CATHERINE ARMBRUSTER, public relations consultant; b. Omaha, Jan. 12, 1948; d. Joseph Francis and Helen Jane (Grommesch) Armbruster; m. Samuel Carter Farmer, IV, May 9, 1981; 1 child, Catherine Carter. Student St. Mary's of Notre Dame, 1966-69; B.A., U. Mo., 1971. News dir. Sta. KSOO, Sioux Falls, S.D., 1971-73; talk show producer, hostess Sta. WLYH-TV, Lancaster, Pa., 1973-74, Sta. WBNG-TV, Binghamton, N.Y., 1974-75; dir. pub. relations Pa. Dutch Visitors Bur., Lancaster, 1976-77; owner Cathy Farmer Pub. Relations, Lancaster, 1978—; instr. writing Pa. State U.-Middletown, 1978; guest lectr. Millersville State U., Lancaster, 1978-79. Office: Cathy Farmer Pub Relations 411 Chelsea Dr Lancaster PA 17601

FARMER, DOROTHA F., administrative associate; b. New Bloomfield, Mo., Nov. 8, 1942; d. James B. and Bertha E. (Vaughan) Gray; student U. Mo., 1971—; m. John C. Farmer, Sept. 2, 1961; stepchildren—John C. (dec.), Michael A. Clinic sec. Ellis Fischel State Cancer Hosp., Columbia, Mo., 1961-64; sec. to dir. Mo. Div. Employment Security, Columbia, 1965-66; departmental sec., dept. indsl. engring. U. Mo., Columbia, 1966-71, office mgr. bioengring./advanced automation program, 1974-78, adminstrv. asso., radiology computer research center, Mid-Am. Bone Diagnostic Center, 1978-83, adminstrv. assoc. radiol. scis., 1983—; cons. NIH, 1980-82. Mem. Bus. and Profl. Women, Mo. Farmers Assn., Women's Progressive Farmers Assn. Roman Catholic. Contbr. articles to profl. jours. Home: RR 1 Clark MO 65243 Office: U Mo 410 Lewis Hall Columbia MO 65211

FARMER, (EVELYN) JOAN, educator; b. Wartburg, Tenn., Dec. 3, 1939; d. Noble Jack and Lydia (Thomas) Freytag; children—Kimberly Denise, Scott DeWayne. B.S., Carson Newman Coll., Jefferson City, Tenn., 1963. Tchr., Morgan County Sch. Dist., Wartburg, 1959-63, Lakota Sch. Dist., West Chester, Ohio, 1963-69, LaPorte Sch. Dist. (Tex.), 1979—. Treas. Lakota Hist. Soc., West Chester, 1973-76. Mem. PTA, Internat. Reading Assn., Bay Area Reading Council. Democrat. Baptist. Clubs: Bay Area Singles (treas. 1980-83) (Houston). Home: 1211 El Dorado Blvd Houston TX 77062 Office: LaPorte Ind Sch Dist Bayshore Sch 301 E Fairmont Pkwy La Porte TX 77571

FARMER, JANENE ELIZABETH, artist, educator; b. Albuquerque, Oct. 16, 1946; d. Charles John Watt and Regina M. (Brown) Kruger; m. Michael Hugh Bolton, Apr. 1965 (div.); m. Frank Urban Farmer, May, 1972 (div.). B.A. in Art, San Diego State U., 1969. Owner, operator Iron Walrus Pottery, 1972-79; designer ceramic and fabric murals, Coronado, Calif., 1979-82; executed commns. for clients in U.S.A., Can., Japan and Mex.; pvt. tchr. pottery; mem. faculty U. Calif.-San Diego; substitute tchr. Calif. community colls.; designer fabric murals and bldg. interiors, Coronado, 1982-85, La Jolla, 1985—; tchr. Blessed Sacrament Sch., San Diego, 1984—. Mem. Coronado Arts and Humanities Council; resident artist U. San Diego. Recipient grant Calif. Arts Council, 1980-81; U. Calif.-San Diego grad. fellow dept. edn., 1984. Mem. Am. Soc. Interior Designers (affiliate). Roman Catholic.

FARMER, KATHRYN LYNETTE, information management executive; b. Inglewood, Calif., Dec. 25, 1952; d. Richard Leon and Rosalie Mae Sanford; m. Michael Edward Farmer, July 19, 1975. B.A., Calif. State U.-Dominguez Hills, 1975; M.A., Grace Grad. Sch. Theology, 1977. Owner, mgr. Mike & Kathy Data Service, Gardena, Calif., 1978—; exec. asst. Coomputerland South Bay, Lawndale, Calif., 1978-82; dir. MIS, Arrays, Inc., Los Angeles, 1982-85; chief fin. officer Computer Sch., Inc., Gardena, 1983—, also dir. Deaconess, Grace Brethren Ch., Long Beach, 1978-81; vol. Youth for Christ, 1986. Mem. Nat. Assn. Female Execs. Republican. Avocations: reading; needlework; computer; mind puzzles. Home: 529 W 149th St Gardena CA 90248 Office: Computer Sch 11222 La Cienega Blvd Suite 450 Inglewood CA 90304

FARMER, MARJORIE ELIZABETH, electrochemist; b. Detroit; d. Henry and Jessie (Lodewyck) F.; B.A., Mt. Holyoke Coll. Research electrochemist Pratt & Whitney div. United Techs. Corp., East Hartford, Conn., 1942-51; electrochemist Chem. Corp., Springfield, Mass., 1953; research electrochemist Convair div. Gen. Dynamics Corp., Pomona, Calif., 1953; electrochemist U.S. Navy Shipyard, Long Beach, Calif., 1954-55; mem. tech. staff Rockwell Internat. Corp., Anaheim, Calif., from 1957, lead instr. in advanced career tng. program for high sch. students in coordination with Regional Occupation Program, now ret.; cons. in field; lectr., chmn. tech. sessions. Registered profl. engr., Calif. Fellow Am. Soc. for Metals (officer), Inst. Metal Finishing (Gt. Britain); mem. Am. Electroplaters Soc. (certified electroplater-finisher), New Eng. Anti-Vivisection Soc. Humane Soc. U.S., Nat. Assn. Corrosion Engrs., Def. Preparedness Assn., Am. Horse Protection Assn., Animal Protection Inst. Am., Mercy League, Amnesty Internat. Club: Mt. Holyoke. Contbr. articles to profl. jours.

FARMER, MARTHA LOUISE, retired educator; b. Cin., d. William S. and Genevieve (Fye) Farmer; B.A., Wheaton Coll., 1935; postgrad. Wellesley Coll., 1936; M.A., Columbia U., 1937, Ed.D., 1956. Assoc. prof. Manhattanville Coll. Sacred Heart, 1936-43, 46-48; assoc. prof. dept. student life City Coll., CUNY, 1948-69, prof. dept. student personnel services, 1969-75, prof. emeritus, 1975—; vis. prof. Grad. Sch. Edn., N.Y. U., 1967-69; cons. student personnel services for adults in higher edn., 1975—. Mem. mgmt. com. Emma Ransom YWCA, N.Y.C., 1958, mem. resident com. 1956-58; mem. jr. high teens com. YWCA, Ridgewood, N.J., 1962-75; mem. N.J. com. U.S. Commn. on Civil Rights; trustee Hispanic Commn. on Alcoholism in N.J. Served as lt. USNR (W), 1943-46. Recipient Winifred Fisher award, 1974. Mem. Am. Coll. Personnel Assn. (program com. 1960-62, mem. com. I, 1963-65, chmn. Com. XIII 1965-67, mem. Com. IV 1968-72), Am. Personnel and Guidance Assn., Assn. U. Evening Colls. (coms. 1961-72), U.S. Assn. Evening Students (chmn. bd. trustees 1970-71, hon. life trustee 1975—), Evening Student Personnel Assn. (pres. 1962-63), Adult Student Personnel Assn. (chmn. bd. trustees 1968-71, hon. life trustee 1975—). Editor: Student Personnel Services For Adults in Higher Education, 1967; Counseling Services for Adults in Higher Education, 1971. Home: 348 Lake St Upper Saddle River NJ 07458

FARMER, MARY MARGARET WILSON, medical technologist; b. Asheville, N.C., July 5, 1933; d. Roeby Bryant and Flossie Aurora (Montieth) Wilson; B.S., Wake Forest Coll., 1954; B.S. in Med. Tech., Bowman Gray Sch. Med. Tech., 1954; m. Gary Clayton Farmer, Apr. 28, 1962; children—Mary Elizabeth, Melissa Margaret. Med. technologist Aston Park Hosp., Asheville, 1954-56, Occupational Health Services, Asheville, 1956-58; med. technologist, asst. lab. supr. Meml. Mission Hosp., Asheville, 1958-62; med. technologist, lab. dir. Joseph E. Seagram & Co., N.Y.C., 1962-65; dir. blood collections and phlebotomy Richmond (Va.) Met. Blood Bank, 1974-77; lab. mgr., med. technologist Thoms Rehab. Hosp., Asheville, 1980—; lab. dir. Thoms Rehab. Hosp.; sec./treas. Assos. for Human Devel., Asheville. Chmn. fund raising Biltmore PTA, Asheville, 1978-79, chmn. membership, 1979-80; v.p. Valley Springs PTA, Skyland, N.C., 1980-81, pres., 1981-82; mem. Roberson dist. Buncombe County (N.C.) Schs. Adv. Council, 1981-82; mem. outreach, youth and worship commns. All Souls Episc. Ch., co-dir. acolyte program; v.p. Women of Gen. Theol. Sem., 1963-64. Recipient Citizenship award United Daus. of Confederacy. Mem. Am. Soc. Med. Technologists, Am. Soc. Clin. Pathologists (med. technologist), AAUW, N.Am. Benefit Assn., Western N.C. Lab. Mgrs. Assn., Clin. Lab. Mgmt. Assn., Episcopal Church Women, Beta Sigma Phi (pres. Beta Tau chpt. 1961-62). Democrat. Clubs: Mahjong, Bridge. Home: 8 Busbee Rd Asheville NC 28803 Office: 1 Rotary Dr Asheville NC 28803

FARMER, SUSAN LAWSON, secretary of state Rhode Island; b. Boston, May 29, 1942; d. Ralph and Margaret (Tyng) Lawson; m. Malcolm Farmer, III, Mar. 6, 1968; children—Heidi Benson, Stephanie Lawson. Student Garland Jr. Coll., 1961, Brown U.-Extension div., Providence, 1961-62. Ct. appointed spl. advocate for abused children Family Ct. R.I., 1978-83; mem. Providence Home Rule Charter Commn., 1979-80; sec. of state R.I., 1982—; vice-chmn. Nat. Voter Edn. Project, Nat. Assn. Secs. State, 1983-84; mem. Nat. Voting Systems Standards Adv. Panel, 1984; mem. Electoral Coll., 1984; mem. steering com. Project Vote/R.I., 1984; mem. adv. panel and teaching faculty Internat. Ctr. Election Law and Adminstrn. Trustee, Wheeler Sch., Providence, 1971-77; co-chmn. statewide mcpl. campaign United Way, 1981; bd. dirs., past chmn. Challenge House, Inc., 1974-80; exec. com. R.I. Republican State Central Com., 1980-84; mem. policy council Nat. Women's Polit. Caucus, 1981-83; mem. Providence Mayor's Task Force on Child Abuse, 1976—, Providence Human Relations Commn., 1976-83; mem. corp. Providence Vis. Nurses Assn., 1978—, R.I. Hosp., 1978—; bd. dirs., past chmn. Marathon House, Inc., 1968—; v.p. Miriam Hosp. Found., 1978—; bd. dirs. Justice Resource Corp., 1982—; trustee Stoneleigh-Burnham Sch., 1983—, Women in Polit. and Govtl. Careers Program, U. R.I.; bd. dirs. Alzheimer's Disease and Related Disorders Assn., pres. bd. dirs., 1985-86; mem. Commn. to Study Election Process, 1985; bd. dirs. Tng. Through Placement, 1985; bd. dirs., Com. on Election Ofcls.; chmn. Gov.'s Com. on Ethics in Govt., 1985-86; mem. Council on Govt. Ethics Laws. Mem. LWV R.I., Save the Bay, Common Cause, Providence Preservation Soc., Nat. Women's Polit. Caucus. Named Woman of Yr., R.I. chpt. Nat. Women's Polit. Caucus, 1980, Bus. and Profl. Women, 1984. Mem. Nat. Assn. Secs. of State (vice chmn. nat. voter edn. project), East Greenwich Bus. and Profl. Women, Newport County Women's Network. Republican. Office: State House Room 217 RI 02903

FARNE-JUMAWAN, JEAN FORTALEZA, physician; b. Manila, Philippines, June 6, 1941; came to U.S., 1970, naturalized, 1978; d. Melchor F. and Aurora (Fortaleza) Farne; m. Jesus A. Jumawan, Aug. 14, 1976. A.A., U. Santo Tomas, Philippines, 1961; M.D., U. East Ramon Magsaysay Meml. Med. Ctr., 1967. Med. examiner Outpatient Clinic, Quezon City Pub. Health Ctr., Philippines, 1967 68; resident in pediatrics Chinese Gen. Hosp., Manila, 1968-70; intern Columbus Cuneo Med. Ctr., Chgo., 1970-71, resident in internal medicine, 1971-74; med. examiner USPHS Outpatient Service, 1974; med. examiner Cancer Prevention Ctr. Chgo., 1975-77; mem. med. staff dept. internal medicine Union Health Service, Chgo., 1975—, med. examiner Disability Evaluation under Social Service, 1977-78; pvt. practice specializing in internal medicine, Chgo., 1978—; assoc. staff internal medicine Swedish Covenant Hosp., Chgo.; mem. med. staff dept. internal medicine, Union Health Service, Chgo. Mem. AMA, Ill. Med. Soc., Chgo. Med. Soc., Philippine Med. Assn. Chgo. Roman Catholic. Home: 3008 Mary Kay Ln Glenview IL 60025 Office: 3432 W Lawrence Ave Chicago IL 60625

FARNHAM, MARY GLADE SIEMER, women's sportswear manufacturing executive; b. Ross, Calif., Nov. 1, 1924; d. Albert Henry and Mabel Meta (Jones) Siemer; children—Thomas Ross, Evan Neil, Gwen Marie, William Blair, Hugh Porter. Student Marin Jr. Coll., 1942-43, Goucher Coll., 1943-44; B.A., U. Calif.-Berkeley, 1947. Profl. athlete, Curry Co., Yosemite, Calif., 1945; advt. prodn. mgr. City of Paris/Hale's, San Francisco, 1947; advt. artist Lipman Wolfe, Portland, Oreg., 1947-48; advt. layout artist Meier & Frank, Portland, 1948; art dir. Olds & King, Portland, 1948-50; free lance comml. artist, Portland, 1950-56; pres. Marin County Devel. Co., San Anselmo, Calif., 1963-78; pres., designer Mary Farnham Designs, Inc., Portland, 1983—. Exhibited in numerous West Coast one woman and nat. group shows, 1960-83. Mem. pub. art selection panel II, Met. Arts Commn., Portland, 1982-83; bd. dirs. N.W. Artists Workshop, Portland, 1977-78; sec. Artist Membership, Portland Art Assn., 1973-74. Episcopalian. Club: Multnomah Athletic. Avocations: swimming; diving.

FARNSWORTH, SUSAN STEELE HIGGINS, writer; b. New Braunfels, Tex., Sept. 8, 1949; d. Walter Sayers and Marian Louise (Schumann) Higgins; B.J., U. Tex., Austin, 1971; m. Dan Collins Farnsworth, Jan. 26, 1974; 1 son, Christopher Sayers. Editor, The Greater Houston Tchrs. Jour., Media Am. Inc., 1973; tax editor/editorial supr. Peat, Marwick, Mitchell & Co., N.Y.C., 1974-77; copywriter Cannon Advt. Agy., N.Y.C., 1977; columnist The News Tribune, Woodbridge, N.J., 1977-79; writer Peat, Marwick, Mitchell & Co., N.Y.C., 1977-78, Alden & Assocs., N.Y.C., 1979-80; writer/communications cons. Peat, Marwick, Mitchell & Co., Dallas, 1979-82; dir. profl. services unit Hill and Knowlton, Inc., Dallas, 1982; owner Farnsworth & Assocs., Miami, Fla., 1977—; cons. Holland & Knight, Fla. and Washington, 1983-84, Harrison & Lerch, Phoenix, 1985—. Named Outstanding Advt. Student, U. Tex., Austin, 1970-71. John E. McGary scholar. Mem. Nat. Assn. Female Execs. Episcopalian. Contbr. articles to profl. jours. Address: 7630 E Carol Way Scottsdale AZ 85260

FARQUHAR, KAREN LEE, business forms company executive, consultant; b. Warwick, N.Y., May 27, 1958; d. Wesley Thomas and Margaret Anne (Storms) Kervatt; m. David W. Farquhar, July 17, 1982. Assoc. Sci., Roger Williams Coll., 1978, B.S. cum laude, 1980. Office mgr. Price-Rite Printing Co., Dover, N.J., summer 1975-76; cons. SBA, Bristol, R.I., 1978-80; account exec. P.M. Press Inc., Dallas, 1980—, sales trainer, 1984-85; v.p. KDF Bus. Forms Co., Irving, Tex., 1984—. Printer, Tex. Aux. Charity Auction Orgn., Dallas, 1985, Crescent Gala, Dallas, 1986. Recipient various awards Clampitt Paper Co., Dallas, 1982, P.M. Press Inc., 1983-85, Mead Paper Co., 1985. Mem. Printing Industry in Am., Internat. Assn. Bus. Communicators, Nat. Bus. Forms Assn. Republican. Baptist. Avocations: piano; aerobics. Home: 429 Dillard Ln Coppell TX 75019

FARR, BEVERLY AGNES, shoe manufacturing company official; b. Middleboro, Mass., Dec. 6, 1928; d. George Sampson and Bertha Josephine (Duffany) Barney; m. Stanley Thomas Farr, May 30, 1949; 1 child, Paul Thomas. A.A., Arlington Acad. Music, 1947. Prodn. clk. W.L. Douglas Shoe Co., Brockton, Mass., 1948-49; customer service rep. Commonwealth Shoe, Whitman, Mass., 1950-51; schedule and prodn. dept. Knapp Shoe Co., Brockton, 1951-53; asst. to office mgr. Givren Shoe Co., Rockland, Mass., 1953-54, Porter Shoe Co., Milford, Mass., 1954-57; purchasing mgr., leather buyer Foot-Joy, Inc., Brockton, 1957—. Com. mem. Conservation Commn., Halifax, Mass., 1979. Mem. Nat. Assn. Female Execs. Republican. Avocations: aerobics; silk flower arranging; flower gardening. Home: 27 Cedar Ln PO Box 493 Halifax MA 02338 Office: Foot-Joy Inc 144 Field St Brockton MA 02403

FARR, PATRICIA HUDAK, librarian; b. Youngstown, Ohio, Mar. 10, 1945; d. Frank Francis and Anna Frances (Tylka) Hudak; m. William Howard Farr, Aug. 28, 1971; 1 dau., Jennifer Anne. B.A., Youngstown State U., 1970; M.L.S., U. Md., 1980. Children's librarian Pub. Library Youngstown and Mahoning (Ohio), 1970-71; asst. Fla. State U. Library, Tallahassee, 1971-73; research asst. John Hopkins U. Sch. Hygiene and Pub. Health, Balt., 1974-76; asst. Mary Washington Coll. Library, Fredericksburg, Va., 1976-79; children's librarian Central Rappahannock Regional Library, Fredericksburg, 1980-84, young adult coordinator, 1984—. Revision editor HEW pub. Thesaurus of Health Education Terminology, 1976; compiler Health Edn. Monographs, 1974-76. Youngstown State U. scholar, 1963-64; R.V. Lowery Meml. scholar, 1979-80. Mem. ALA, Va. Library Assn. Democrat. Episcopalian. Club: Rappahannock Twirlers Square Dance. Home: Route 11 Box 1634 Fredericksburg VA 22405 Office: Central Rappahannock Regional Library 1201 Caroline St Fredericksburg VA 22401

FARRAR, ELAINE WILLARDSON, artist; b. Los Angeles, Feb. 27, 1929; d. Eldon and Gladys Elsie (Larsen) Willardson; B.A., Ariz. State U., 1967, M.A., 1969, now doctoral candidate; children—Steve, Mark, Gregory, Leslie Jean, Monty, Susan. Tchr., Camelback Desert Sch., Paradise Valley, Ariz., 1966-69; mem. faculty Yavapai Coll., Prescott, Ariz., 1970—, chmn. dept. art, 1973-78, instr. art in watercolor and oil and acrylic painting and intaglio, 1971—; one-man shows include: R.P. Moffat's, Scottsdale, Ariz., 1969, Art Center, Battle Creek, Mich., 1969, The Woodpeddler, Costa Mesa, Calif., 1979; group show Prescott (Ariz.) Fine Arts Assn., 1982, 84, 86, N.Y. Nat. Am. Watercolorists, 1982; works rep. local and state exhibits; supt. fine arts dept. County Fair; com. mem., hanging chmn. Scholastic Art Awards. Mem. Mountain Artists Guild (past pres.), Nat. League Am. Pen Women (Prescott br.), NEA, Ariz. Edn. Assn., Nat. Art Edn. Assn., Ariz. Coll. and Univ. Faculty Assn., AAUW, Verde Valley Art Assn., Kappa Delta Pi, Phi Delta Kappa. Republican. Mormon. Home: 635 Copper Basin Rd Prescott AZ 86301 Office: Yavapai College Art Dept 1100 E Sheldon Rd Prescott AZ 86301

FARRAR, MARGARET MARION, educator, former sch. ofcl.; b. Schriever, La., Feb. 8, 1911; d. Louis James and Lillian Gertrude (Smith) F.; B.A. cum laude, Dillard U., 1941; M.Ed., Boston U., 1953; Ph.D., Laurence U., 1975. Tchr. kindergarten New Orleans Public Schs., 1931-60; kindergarten tchr. D.C. Public Schs., 1960-67, reading specialist, 1967-71, reading cons., 1971-81. Mem. Nat. Council Tchrs. Math., Nat. Council Tchrs. English, Nat. Assn. Univ. Women, AAUW, Nat. Council Negro Women, D.C. Reading Council (pres.) Internat. Reading Assn., NEA, Pi Lambda Theta. Democrat. Home: 5162 34th St NW Washington DC 20008

FARRELL, EILEEN, college president; b. Mineola, N.Y., Aug. 10, 1924; d. John A. and Anne V. (Hayes) F. B.A., Seton Hill Coll., 1946. Dir. Jersey City Job Corps Ctr. for Women, 1967-74; dir. personnel adminstrn. Hofstra U., 1974-77; now pres. Seton Hill Coll., Greensburg, Pa. Mem. nat. bd. YWCA, from 1976—; mem. citizens adv. bd. Westmoreland Hosp. Community Health Ctr., 1977; mem. bd. Hudson County, N.J. Council Social Agys., 1971-74, Hudson County Ancillary Manpower Planning Bd., 1972-74; commr. Westmoreland County Drug and Alcohol Abuse Program, 1978. Office: Office of Pres Seton Hill Coll Greensburg PA 15601*

FARRELL, EILEEN MARIE, nurse, administrator; b. N.Y.C., Oct. 8, 1950; d. William James and Ann Marie (Hogan) F.; B.S. in Nursing, Columbia U., 1972, M.P.H., Sch. Pub. Health, 1986. Cert. emergency nurse. Staff nurse Vanderbilt Clinic, Columbia Presbyn. Med. Center, N.Y.C., 1972-74, sr. supr. evenings Emergency Services, Vanderbilt Clinic, 1974-77, sr. supr. days, 1978-80, adminstrv. nurse clinician emergency services, 1980-86, tng. coordinator computer systems, nursing, 1986—, nursing liaison ambulatory care, 1982; preceptor, cons. Edna McConnell Clark and Columbia U. Sch. Nursing, 1978—, preceptor ambulatory care Columbia U. Sch. Public Health, 1980-82; tchr. seminars in field. Mem. Emergency Dept. Nurses Assn., Nat. Assn. Female Execs., Columbia U. Presbyn. Hosp. Alumnae Assn. Office: 622 W 168th St New York NY 10032

FARRELL, JUNE MARTINICK, public relations executive; b. New Brunswick, N.J., June 30, 1940; d. Ivan and Mary (Tomkovich) M.; B.S. in Journalism, Ohio U., 1962; M.S. in Public Relations, Am. U., Washington, 1977; m. Duncan G. Farrell, July 31, 1971. Public relations asst. Corning Glass Works, N.Y.C., 1963-65; assoc. beauty editor Good Housekeeping mag., N.Y.C., 1966; public relations specialist Gt. Am. Ins. Co., N.Y.C., 1967-68; assoc. editor Eastern Airlines, N.Y.C., 1968-82, regional public relations mgr., Washington, 1976-82; public relations dir. Nat. Captioning Inst., Falls Church, Va., 1982-83; dir. media relations Marriott Corp., 1984—; adj. instr. Montgomery County Community Coll., also mem. hotel/tourism adv. bd., 1980—; staff cons. Office of Public Liaison, White House, 1981-82. Creator, condr. spl. career awareness program for inner city youth, Washington, 1979-80; mem. public relations com. Jr. Achievement, 1979; motivational counselor for youth Nat. Alliance of Businessmen, 1979; trustee Nat. Hosp. Orthopedics and Rehab., 1984- . Mem. Pub. Relations Soc. Am., Washington Women's Network, Travel Industry Assn. Am. (nat. conf. planning com.), Women in Communication, Phi Mu. Republican. Clubs: Zonta, Internat. Aviation. Home: 6630 Lybrook Ct Bethesda MD 20817 Office: Marriott Corp One Marriott Dr Bethesda MD 20817

FARRELL, MARY C., psychologist, consultant; b. Tucson, Dec. 10, 1940; d. Charles Henry and Mary Agness (Harrington) F.; div. B.A., U. Ariz., 1960, M.A., 1967; postgrad. in psychology Pepperdine U., 1973-75. Adolescent psychologist Alhambra Schs., San Gabriel, Calif., 1978—; pres. Peer Counseling Consultants, Long Beach, Calif., 1984—; psychotherapist in pvt. practice, Pasadena, Calif., 1980—. Mem. NOW, Calif. Peer Counseling Assn., Western Assn. Coll. Admissions Counselors. Avocations: skiing, running, travel, reading, theater.

FARRELL, PATRICIA ANN, psychologist; b. N.Y.C., Mar. 11, 1945; d. Joseph Alexander and Pauline (Loth) F.; B.A., Queens Coll., 1976; M.A., N.Y. U., 1978, postgrad., 1980—. Assoc. editor Pubs. Weekly Mag., N.Y.C., 1968-72; editor Bestsellers Mag., N.Y.C., 1972-73; assoc. editor King Features Syndicate, N.Y.C., 1973-78; staff psychologist, intake coordinator Mid-Bergen Community Mental Health Center, Paramus, N.J., 1978—; instr. Bergen Community Coll., Paramus, 1978-84; cons. Family Counseling Service of Ridgewood, N.J., 1984; clin. psychology intern Marlboro Psychiat. Hosp., N.J., 1984-85, staff psychologist, 1985—; appeared on radio shows Sta. WWDJ, Hackensack, N.J. Mem. Bergen County Task Force on Crimes Against Children, Bergen County Task Force on Alcoholism and Drunken Driving, 1984. Recipient Social Scis. award Queens Coll., 1976. Mem. Am. Psychol. Assn. (assoc.), N.J. Psychol. Assn. (assoc.), Assn. Women in Psychology, Am. Soc. Clin. Hypnosis (student affiliate), AAAS. Contbr. articles to Writer's Digest, Real World, newspapers. Office: Marlboro Psychiat Hosp Marlboro NJ 07746

FARRELL, SUZANNE, ballerina; b. Cin.; study ballet Cin. Conservatory Music with Marian LaCour; Ford Found. scholar Sch. Am. Ballet, 1960; hon. doctorate Georgetown U., 1984; m. Paul Mejia, Feb. 1969. With N.Y. City Ballet, 1961-69, 75—, became featured dancer, 1962, prin. dancer, 1965-69, roles include Arcade, Movements for Piano and Orchestra, Apollo, Bugaku, Meditation, Clarinade, Episodes, Stars and Stripes, Glinkaiana, Chaconne, Metastaseis and Pithoprakta, Western Symphony, Symphony in C, Concerto Barocco, A Midsummer Night's Dream, Agon, Ballet Imperial, Irish Fantasy, The Nutcracker, Don Quixote, La Sonnambula, Raymonda Variations, Mozartiana, Brahms-Schoenberg Quartet, Variations, Swan Lake, Jewels, Prodigal Son, Divertimento 15, Slaughter on 10th Ave., (film version) Midsummer Night' Dream; with Bejart Ballet of 20th Century, Brussels, Belgium, 1971-75; created role in Bach Sonate #5; other ballets include Beethoven's 9th Symphony, Messe pour le temps present, Bhakti, Erotica pas de deux, Marteau Sans Maitre, Ah, Vous Dirais Je, Maman?, Juliet in Romeo and Juliet; created The Young Girl in Rose in Nijinsky . . . Clown of God, 1971, Bolero, The Rite of Spring, Laura in I Trionfi, Eight by Adler, 1985 (Emmy award); created roles with Chgo. City Ballet, N.Y.C. Ballet in New Ravel Festival, Tzigane, In G Major. 1976, Hon. lectr. dance U. Cin.; mem. faculty Sch. Am. Ballet; artistic adv. Chgo. City Ballet. Recipient Spl. award of merit in creative and performing arts, U. Cin., 1965; Merit award Mademoiselle mag., 1965; Dance Mag. award, 1976; Creative Arts award in dance Brandeis U., 1980; award of honor for arts and culture N.Y.C., 1980; featured in Sta. WNET-TV Dance in Am., Balanchine, Parts I-IV. Address: care New York City Ballet Lincoln Center Plaza New York NY 10023

FARRELL-RATH, MAUREEN ANN, builder; b. Evergreen Park, Ill., Apr. 13, 1954; d. Jeremiah and Patricia (Lannon) Farrell; m. Ronald Raymond Rath, Nov. 2, 1974 (div.); 1 dau., Patricia L. B.A., St. Xavier Coll., Chgo., 1982; postgrad. Roosevelt U. Securities specialist Becker Paribas, Inc., Chgo., 1972-73; clk. Rath Family Farm, Waupaca, Wis., 1975-77; interviewer Nat. Opinion Research Ctr., Chgo., 1979-80; mgr. Franchise Concepts, Inc., Olympia Fields, Ill., 1980-81; prodn. operation coordinator White-Meyer Wood Products, Orland Park, Ill., 1981; corp. sec. Kala Hari Builders, Inc., Evergreen Park, Ill., 1981—. Mem. Catholic League for Religious Civil Rights, Milw., 1984. Mem. Am. Sociol. Assn., Am. Mktg. Assn., Notaries Assn. Ill., Chgo. Council on Fgn. Affairs.

FARRENKOPF, JOAN HELEN, restorationist/artist; b. Massillon, Ohio, Aug. 7, 1953; d. Robert and Elizabeth F. Student, London Coll. Printing, 1974; B.F.A., Syracuse U., 1975. Pres., Farrenkopf Designs, Syracuse, N.Y., 1976—; tchr. Everson Mus. Art, 1972, Marshall U., 1975, Cortland Arts Council, 1979. Restored old Victorian houses that became nat. hist. dist., 1979. One woman shows include Canton Cultural Ctr., 1974, Lowe Art Ctr., 1974, Syracuse U., 1974, Massillon Mus., 1973, Marshall U., 1979, Canton Art Inst., 1979, Everson Mus., 1979. Recipient Pat Earle award Preservation League of Central N.Y., 1981; scholar London Coll. Printing, 1974. Mem. Tully Hist. Soc. (trustee), Landmarks Soc. Central N.Y. (exec. bd.), Nat. Trust Historic Preservation, N.E. Hawley Devel. Assn. (bd. dirs.), Nat. and Profl. Women (N.Y. State Young Careerist 1982). Home and Office: 209 Green St Syracuse NY 13203

FARRINGTON, HELEN AGNES, utility company executive; b. Elmhurst, N.Y., Dec. 1, 1945; d. Joseph Christopher and Therese Marie (Breazzano) F. A.S., Interboro Inst., N.Y.C., 1965; A.A., Ohio State U., 1983, student, 1983—. Coordinator employee relations Am. Electric Power Co., N.Y.C., 1974-76; employee and labor relations adminstr. Ohio Power Co., Canton, 1977-78; personnel supr. Ohio Power Co., Newark, 1979—. Mem. adv. bd. Newark High Sch., 1980-82, Central Ohio Tech. Coll., 1981-82, Licking County Joint Vocat. Sch., 1981-82; mem. Presdl. Republican Task Force, 1983-84. Mem. Nat. Assn. Female Execs., Am. Soc. Profl. and Exec. Women, Roman Catholic. Club: U.S. Senatorial (Washington). Home: 1380 Londondale Pky Apt C-1 Newark OH 43055

FARRINGTON-HOPF, SUSAN KAY, plumbing and heating contractor; b. Seattle, Dec. 17, 1940; d. Donald Robert and Dorothy May (Graf) Little; m. Edwin Terry Farrington, Sept. 4, 1959 (div. Apr. 1972); children—Cathe T., Jacqueline M.; m. William Desmond Hopf, Nov. 20, 1983. B.A. cum laude, U.S. Internat. U., 1975, M.A., 1976. Program speaker AMR Internat., N.Y.C., 1977-82; pres. Dawson Plumbing & Heating Co., Seattle, 1979—; tng. cons. Fred Sherman, Inc., San Marcos, Calif., 1982—; cons. Pacific SW Airlines, San Diego, 1977, Dept. Labor Job Corps, Moses Lake, Wash., 1978. Developer assertive mgmt. workshop, 1976. Mem. Seattle Execs. Assn., Am. Soc. Tng. and Devel., Nat. Assn. Plumbing Heating Cooling Contractors. Avocations: skiing, sailing, gardening. Home: 16419 261st Ave SE Issaquah WA 98027 Office: Dawson Plumbing & Heating Co 1522 12th Ave Seattle WA 98122

FARROW, MARGARET ANN, village executive; b. Kenosha, Wis., Nov. 28, 1934; d. William Charles and Margaret Ann (Horan) Nemitz; m. John Harvey Farrow, Dec. 29, 1956; children—John, William, Peter, Paul, Mark. Student Rosary Coll., 1952-53; B.S. in Polit. Sci., Marquette U., 1956, postgrad., 1975-77. Tchr., Archiodese of Milw., 1956-57; salesperson Bonerz Realty, Brookfield, Wis., 1971-76; trustee Elm Grove Village, Wis., 1976-81, pres., 1981—. Chairperson FLOW community coalition working for equitable sewer rates, New Berlin, Wis., 1982—; mem. budget com. Milw. Archdiocese, 1979—, mem. salary adminstrn. com., 1983—. Recipient community service award Elm Grove Jr. Guild, 1986. Mem. Assn. Marquette Univ. Women (bd. dirs. 1980—, 1st v.p. 1984-85), League Wis. Municipalities, League Insurance Trust (bd. dirs.), League Suburban Municipalities. Republican. Roman Catholic. Clubs: Elm Grove Woman's, Elm Grove Hist. Soc. Home: 14905 Watertown Plank Rd Elm Grove WI 53122 Office: Village Hall 13600 Juneau Blvd Elm Grove WI 53122

FARROW, MIA VILLIERS, actress; b. Los Angeles, Feb. 9, 1945; d. John Villiers and Maureen Paula (O'Sullivan) Farrow; student pub., pvt. schs.; m. Andre Previn, Sept. 10, 1970 (div. Feb. 1979); children—Matthew Phineas and Sascha Villiers (twins), Lark Song, Fletcher Farrow, Summer Song, Gigi Soon Mi, Misha. Actress appearing in TV and films; debut The Importance of Being Earnest, N.Y.C. 1964; starred in TV series Peyton Place, 1964-66; films include Guns at Batasi, A Dandy in Aspic, Rosemary's Baby, Secret Ceremony, John and Mary, Blind Terror, Doctor Paupul, See No Evil, The Public Eye, Goodbye Raggedy Ann, The Great Gatsby, Full Circle, Peter Pan, The Wedding, Death on the Nile, Hurricane, A Midsummer Night's Sex Comedy, Zelig, 1983, Broadway Danny Rose, 1984, Purple Rose of Cairo, 1985, Hannah and Her Sisters, 1986; appeared in stage plays Mary Rose, The Three Sisters, The House of Bernarda Alba, Romantic Comedy; joined Royal Shakespeare Co., London, 1974, appeared in the Marrying of Ann Leete, A Midsummer Nights Dream, The Zykovs, Ivanov. Recipient best actress award French Acad., 1969, Golden Globe award, 1967, Rio de Janero Film Festival award, 1969, Italian Acad. Award, 1970. Address: care Lionel Larner Ltd 850 7th Ave New York NY 10019*

FARROW, SALLIE, lawyer; b. Plainfield, N.J., Dec. 31, 1942; d. James R. and Sallie (Mitchell) Rivera; m. Richard H. Staton, July 11, 1964 (div. Feb. 1977); 1 child, Richard H., Jr. B.A. with honors, U. Denver, 1974; J.D., U. Nebr., 1976. Bar: Nebr. 1977. Laborer Standard Plastic Products, Plainfield, N.J., 1960-64; sr. line clk. N.J. Bell Telephone Co., Elizabeth, 1964-68; underwriter Allstate Ins. Co., Murray Hill, N.J., 1969-72; legal asst. Colo. Dept. Edn., Denver, 1974, City of Atlanta, 1976; asst. gen. counsel, asst. sec. Mut. of Omaha and United of Omaha, 1977—; panelist U.S. Office of Edn., Washington, 1978; ace counselor SBA, Omaha, 1980—; series speaker Creighton U., Omaha, 1981, moot ct. judge, 1983—. Organizer/adviser Met. Sci. and Engring. Fair Inc., Omaha, 1982—; chairperson Boy Scouts Am., Omaha, 1982, cons. career awareness, 1983; bd. dirs., officer Girls Club of Omaha, 1985—. Mem. Nebr. Bar Assn., ABA, Nat. Bar Assn., Kappa Delta Pi, Beta Chi. Democrat. Office: Mut of Omaha Ins Co Mut of Omaha Plaza Omaha NE 68175

FARROW, VICKY ROSE, marketing research and data processing official; b. Port Arthur, Tex., Nov. 27, 1952; d. L.D. and Dorothy Marie (Carter) F. B.B.A., Stephen F. Austin State U., 1973; M.B.A., Lamar U., 1977. Lectr., Lamar U., Beaumont, Tex., 1977-80; sr. project mgr. Pine Co., Los Angeles, 1980—. Mem. Am. Mktg. Assn. (eval. chmn. 1983-84). Club: Pacific Palisades Tennis. Home: 11937 Sunset Blvd F Los Angeles CA 90049 Office: Pine Co 2112 Cotner Ave Los Angeles CA 90025

FARVER, LINDA LOUISE, educator; b. Balt., July 30, 1948; d. Roby Thomas and Ethel LaRue (Waddell) Farver. B.S., Frostburg State Coll., 1970; M.Ed., Middle Tenn. State U., 1973. Phys. edn. tchr. Carroll County Bd. Edn., South Carroll High Sch., Sykesville, Md., 1970-72; grad. asst. Middle Tenn. State U., Murfreesboro, 1972-74; instr. phys. edn. Salisbury State Coll., Md., 1974-76, Cent. Va. Community Coll., Lynchburg, 1976-77; asst. prof. phys. edn. Liberty U., Lynchburg, 1977—, head coach women's basketball, 1977-86. First aid instr. ARC, Lynchburg, 1977—. Named Outstanding Female Athlete, Frostburg State Coll. Women's Athletic Assn., 1970; Outstanding Phys. Edn. Major, Frostburg State Coll., 1970. Mem. AAHPERD, World Basketball Coaches Assn., Va. Assn. Intercollegiate Athletics for Women (pres. 1980-81). Office: Liberty U Box 20000 Lynchburg VA 24506

FARWELL, MARGARET JOHN, medical foundation/medical center executive; b. Chgo., Sept. 8, 1947; s. John Howland and Carol (Bowers) F. Student U. Exeter, Devon, Eng., summer 1968; B.A., Baker U., 1969; postgrad. U. Kans., summers 1974-76. Jr. account exec. Biddle Advt. Agy., Kansas City, Mo., 1970-72; coll. admission officer Baker U., Baldwin, Kans., 1972-74, Benedictine Coll., Atchison, Kans., 1974-76; asst. dir. devel. Rush-Presbyn.-St. Luke's Med. Ctr., Chgo., 1978-81; devel. assoc. Mus. Sci. and Industry, Chgo., 1981-83; exec. v.p./dir. fund devel. Columbus-Cuneo-Cabrini Med. Found./Med. Ctr., Chgo., 1984—; program speaker Chgo. Planned Giving Officers Roundtable, 1984, 86. Bd. dirs., sec. women's bd. Travelers and Immigrants Aid, Chgo., 1982—. Mem. Nat. Soc. Fundraising Execs. (membership com. Chgo. chpt. 1981-83, cert. com. 1982-83, co-chmn. nat. conf. com. 1985-86), Nat. Assn. Hosp. Devel. (regional conf. speaker Chgo. 1984), Nat. Catholic Devel. Conf., 1200 Club of Ill. (bd. dirs. 1983-85) (Chgo.). Republican. Episcopalian. Office: Columbus-Cuneo-Cabrini Med Found 676 N St Clair Suite 1900 Chicago IL 60611

FARWELL, SIGRID OLAFSON, consulting company executive; b. Ithaca, N.Y., June 4, 1933; d. Peter and Harriette (Smith) O.; B.A., Cornell U., 1955; tchr. cert. U. Colo., 1972, M.A., 1978; m. Theodore Austin Farwell, Jr., July 11, 1954; children—Karin, Peter, Eric Edward. Owner, tchr. Farwell Ballet Sch., Littleton, N.H., 1960-68; inservice coordinator nine sch. dists. Northwest Colo., 1974-75; head theatre dept. Platt Jr. High Sch., Boulder, Colo., 1976-79, Fairview High Sch., Boulder, 1979-80; pres. Sigrid Farwell & Assos., Inc., Boulder, 1980—, BDF Reflections, Inc., 1982-84. Founder Evergreen Jr. Theatre, 1970, Storybook Players, 1973; mem. Council Arts and Humanities, Steamboat Springs, 1973-75; vol. horseback riding and skiing programs Fitzsimmons Army Hosp. Amputee programs, 1970-73. Recipient Internat. Yr. of Child award for service and dedication, Family Acad. Internat. Children's Center, Stravanger, Norway and San Francisco, 1979. Mem. Colo. Drama and Speech Assn. (pres.), Am. Soc. Tng. and Devel., Nat. Assn. Female Execs., Nat. Speakers Assn. Pub. play The Child of Fear, 1978. Home and Office: 7363 Cortez Ln Boulder CO 80303

FARY, DEBRA FAYE, pharmacist; b. Richmond, Va., Mar. 25, 1957; d. William Otway and Mildred Leona (Sears) F. B.A. in Biology, U. Va., 1979; B.S. in Pharmacy, Med. Coll. of Va., 1982. Registered pharmacist. Health services Officer Nat. Cancer Inst., Silver Spring, Md., 1981; pharmacist Waynesboro Community Hosp., Va., 1982-85, Med. Coll. Va. Hosp., Richmond, 1985—, Peoples Drug Stores, Waynesboro, 1983-85, Kroger Pharmacy, Waynesboro, 1983-85. Vol. U. Va. Hosp., Charlottesville, 1975-76. Mem. Va. Soc. Hosp. Pharmacists, Nat. Assn. Female Execs., Am. Soc. Hosp. Pharmacists, Va. Pharm. Assn., Am. Pharm. Assn. (mem. com. 1980-81), Sigma Zeta, Rho Chi, Kappa Epsilon (sec. 1980-81). Methodist. Avocations: travel; skiing; bicycling; reading; aerobic cande. Office: Med Coll Va Hosps MCV Sta Box 42 Richmond VA 23298

FARYNIARZ, DEBORAH ANN, manufacturing development engineer; b. Sacramento, Nov. 11, 1962; d. Jay and Michele (Daley) Wilson. B.S. in Mech. Engring., U. Calif.-Davis, 1985. Phys. therapist (part-time) St. Francis Clinic, Rancho Cordova, Calif., 1980-82; project engr. Weyerhaeuser Paper Co., Valliant, Okla., summer 1983; prodn. engr. Hewlett Packard, Santa Clara, Calif., 1984, mfg. devel. engr., 1985—. Elks Found. scholar, 1980-81, Scottish Rite Found. scholar, 1980-85, Panhellenic Assn. scholar, 1980-81, U. Calif. Regents scholar, 1980-84. Mem. Female Execs., Phi Kappa Phi, Tau Beta Pi. Avocations: triathalons; skiing; travel; languages; poetry; music; dance. Home: 20800 Valley Green Dr 485 Cupertino CA 95014 Office: Hewlett Packard 5301 Stevens Creek Blvd Santa Clara CA 95051

FASANO, CLARA, sculptor; b. Castellaneta, Italy, Dec. 14, 1900; emigrated to U.S., 1907, naturalized, 1939; d. Pasquale and Julia (de Feudis) F.; m. Jean de Marco, July 8, 1936. Student, Cooper Union Art Inst., Art Students League, N.Y.C., 1917-21, Julien Academie and Colarossi Academie, Paris, 1924-26; scholar, Rome, Italy, 1922-24. Tchr. sculpture adult edn. Bd. Edn., N.Y., 1948-58; tchr. Manhattanville Coll. Exhibited at, Salon d'Automne, Paris, 1925; worked in own studio, exhibited in, Rome, 1926-32; exhibited in numerous shows, including, Worlds Fair, N.Y.C., 1939, Whitney Museum, NAD, Pa. Acad., Art Inst. Chgo., Met. Mus. Art, Am.-Brit. Center N.Y.C., Ferragil, Buckholz galleries; works represented in permanent collections at, Met. Mus. Art, N.Y.C., Manhattanville Coll. Sacred Heart, Purchase, N.Y., Norfolk Mus. Arts and Scis., Smithsonian Instn., Washington, Syracuse U., also pvt. collections, U.S., abroad; important works include series of twelve portraits in bronze, the last being of His Excellency Giuseppe Cataldi, pres. Corte dei Conti of Italy. Grantee, recipient citation Nat. Inst. Arts and Letters, 1952; recipient medal of Honor with citation Am. Artists Mag., Audubon Annual Exhbn., 1956, hon. mention Archtl. League N.Y., Gold Medals Exhbn., 1956, Daniel Chester French medal NAD, 1965, Peter Caesar Alberti award Italian Execs. Am. Inc., 1967, Dessie Greer award for sculpture NAD, 1968, 2d pl. sculpture competitions for entrance Supreme Ct. of Bklyn., for fountain sculpture for lobby 100 Church St. bldg., N.Y.C., sculpture commn. for relief Middleport (Ohio) Post Office U.S. Treasury Dept. competition for Apex Bldg. in Washington. Academician NAD.; Fellow Nat. Sculpture Soc. (hon. mention 1956); mem. Audubon Artists (M. Grumbacher prize 1954), Sculptors Guild, Nat. Assn. Women Artists (Anonymous prize 1945, Marcia Brady Tucker prize 1950, medal of Honor for sculpture 63d ann. exhbn. 1955). Subject of articles, works reproduced in Am. Artist mag., Nat. Sculpture Rev., also books Sculpture in Modern America, Contemporary American Scultpure, The Materials and Methods of Sculpture. Home: 03044 Cervaro-Prov Frosinone Italy Office: 1083 Fifth Ave New York NY 10028

FASCIA, DOMENICA MARY, med. technologist; b. Mechanicsville, N.Y.; d. Anthony and Assunta (Dinardo) F.; B.S., Calif. State U., Los Angeles, 1970, M.A., 1974. Chief med. technologist St. Mary's Hosp., Troy, N.Y., 1951-56, Santa Teresita Hosp., Duarte, Calif., 1956—. Registered sanitarian; profl. entomologist; hazard control mgr. Mem. Am. Soc. Clin. Pathologists, Am. Registry Profl. Etomologists, Internat. Soc. Clin. Lab. Tech., Calif. Assn. Med. Tech., Am. Soc. Microbiology, Am. Assn. Blood Banks, Assn. of Practitioners in Infection Control, Healthcare Safety Profls., Am. Philatelic Soc. Democrat. Roman Catholic. Clubs: Am. Contract Bridge League, Federated Women's Am. Address: 403 N Grand Ave Monrovia CA 91016

FASS, BARBARA, city official. Mayor, Stockton, Calif., 1985—. Address: Office of the Mayor 425 N El Dorado St Stockton CA 95202*

FASSLER, CRYSTAL G., broadcasting executive; b. Marion, Ohio, Mar. 15, 1942; d. Lloyd C. and Iola M. (Runkle) Mahaffey; student public schs., Prospect, Ohio; m. Donald D. Fassler, May 6, 1960; 1 child, Curtis A. Media buyer H. Swink Advt., Marion, 1968-73; media buyer and planner Tracey Locke Advt., Columbus, Ohio, 1973-74, Lord, Sullivan & Yoder Advt., Marion, 1974-82; youth conselor State of Ohio Employment Services, Marion, 1982-83; nat. mktg. cons. sta. WMRN-AM and FM, Marion, 1983-84, asst. gen. mgr., 1985-86, sta. mgr., 1986—. Home: 1846 Smeltzer Rd Marion OH 43302 Office: WMRN-AM and FM 1330 N Main St Marion OH 43302

FAST, JUDITH ELLEN STEPHENSON, nurse, educator; consultant, researcher; b. Welch, W.Va., May 8, 1942; d. Leslie James and Rosa Ellen (Mullens) Stephenson; children—Carrie Lisa, Randolph Leslie. A.A. in Nursing, St. Petersburg Jr. Coll., 1971; B.S. in Biology cum laude, U. Tampa, 1973; M.S. in Physiology, U. Houston, 1977; D.Ph. in Internat. Health, (traineeship), U. Tex. Sch. Pub. Health, Houston, 1987. R.N., Fla., La., Tex.; lic. practical nurse, Fla., W.Va.; cert. first aid and CPR instr.; cert juvenile probation officer. Staff nurse Wyoming Gen. Hosp., Mullens, W.Va., 1967-69, St. Anthony's Hosp., St. Petersburg, Fla., 1969-71, team leader, charge nurse telemetry CCU and Med. ICU, 1971-74; teaching fellow in biology U. Houston, 1974-77; staff and charge nurse M.D. Anderson Hosp., Houston, 1974-77, critical care program dir., instr., 1977-79, dir. oncology program, 1979-80, mgmt. analyst, 1980-84; nurse mgmt. info. systems analyst Harris County Hosp., Houston, 1984-85, mem., chmn., vice chmn. various coms.; nurse clinician Harris County Juvenile Probation Dept., Houston, 1985—. Creator, author 52 ednl. videotapes on critical care, 1978-79; creator, author hosp. patient classification and staffing systems; researcher in field; speaker profl. groups; author articles. Judge exhibits Houston Sci. Fair, 1983, 84; vol. Am. Cancer Soc. research survey, 1982. Recipient numerous awards. Mem. Am. Assn. Critical Care Nurses (nat. and Gulf Coast chpts.), Oncology Nursing Soc. (cons.), Am. Pub. Health Assn., Greater Houston Hosp. Mgmt. Systems Soc., Houston Consortium Nurses (charter), Assn. Women in Sci. (Houston, sec. 1983-84), Fedn. Houston Profl. Women (del., affiliate), Houston Area League for IBM Personal Computer Users, Alpha Chi. Office: Harris County Juvenile Probation Dept Burnett Bayland Home 6500 Chimney Rock Houston TX 77081

FAUBEL, NANCY CAROLINE, business executive; b. Rochester, N.Y., July 10, 1958; d. Robert S. and Elisabeth (Torrey) F. B.S. Alfred U., 1979; M.B.A., U. Rochester, 1983. Cert. flight instr., comml. pilot; lic. real estate agt.; notary pub. Engr. I, Babcock & Wilcox, Augusta, Ga., 1979-80, sales engr., Phila., 1980-82; v.p. Precision Equipment Services, Rochester, 1983—. Del., 19th Ward Community Assn., Rochester, 1986; capt. CAP, 1985—. Mem. Nat. Assn. Female Execs., Rochester Pilots Assn., Rochester Real Estate Bd. Republican. Avocations: flying; carpentry; art. Home: 69 Oak Hill View Rochester NY 14611 Office: 484 Brooks Ave Rochester NY 14619

FAULCONER, KAY ANNE, mgmt. cons., educator; b. Shelbyville, Ind., Aug. 19, 1945; d. Clark J. and Charlotte Keenan; B.A. in English, Calif. State U., Northridge, 1968; M.B.A., Pepperdine U., 1975, M.A. in Public Communications, 1976; m. James R. Faulconer; children—Kevin Lee, Melissa Lynne. Personnel mgr. Uni-Systems, Inc., Ventura, Calif., 1977; pres. Kay Faulconer & Assos., mgmt. cons., Oxnard, Calif., 1977—; instr. U. LaVerne, 1978—, Oxnard Coll., 1978-85; div. dir. Ventura Coll., 1985—. Founder, past pres., sec. Oxnard Friends of Library, 1975-81; bd. dirs., sec. Girls Club Oxnard, 1980—; bd. dirs Oxnard Boys Club, 1981. Recipient Clubwoman of Year award Oxnard Jr. Women's Club, 1975, Bus. Woman of Year award Oxnard Bus. and Profl. Women's Club, 1977, Young Career Woman award; Mark Hopkins award Oxnard Coll., 1981-82. Mem. Am. Soc. Tng. and Devel. (dir. Los Padres chpt.), Am. Soc. Profl. Cons., Ventura County Profl. Women's Network, Am. Assn. Women in Community and Jr. Colls. Home and Office: 601 Janetwood Oxnard CA 93030

FAULL, DONNA MAY, publishing company executive; b. Royalton, Ill., June 3, 1938; d. George L. and Mary R. (Volner) F. Student Lexington Christian Acad., 1957-60. Sec., Wheaton Van Lines, Indpls., 1956-57; adminstrv. asst. to sales mgr. Mallard Pencil Co., Georgetown, Ky., 1957-61; exec. sec. Country Cos., Bloomington, Ill., 1961-67; layout artist McKnight Pub. Co., Bloomington, 1967-69, prodn. editor, 1970-78; mng. editor McKnight Pub. Co. div. Macmillan, Inc., 1979-84; dir. art/design Bennett & McKnight div. Macmillan, Inc., 1984—. Chmn., Area Vocat. Ctr. Adv. Com., Bloomington, 1978-83, mem., 1983—; team mem. Ill Bd. Edn. Vocat. Edn. Dept., 1979-82; active Eastview Christian Ch., Bloomington. Recipient Sales Service award McKnight Pub. Co., 1980. Mem. Chgo. Women in Pub., Am. Vocat. Assn., Am. Home Econs. Assn., Women in Communications. Contbr. numerous articles and poems to popular mags., Christian jours. Office: Bennett & McKnight 809 W Detweiller Peoria IL 61615

FAUNCE, SARAH CUSHING, museum curator; b. Tulsa, Aug. 19, 1929. B.A., Wellesley Coll., M.A., Washington U.; postgrad. Columbia U. Curator art collections Columbia U., N.Y.C., 1965-69; exhibits cons. Jewish Mus., 1968-70; curator painting and sculpture Bklyn. Mus., 1969—; lectr. art theory and criticism Barnard Coll., N.Y.C., 1964. Contbr. articles to profl. jours. and exhbn. catalogs. Mem. Coll. Art Assn. Am., Victorian Soc., Am. Assn. Mus., Internat. Council Mus. Address: c/o Bklyn Mus Eastern Pkwy Brooklyn NY 11238

FAUR, YVONNE CONSTANCE, microbiologist; b. Romania, Sept. 11, 1916; came to U.S., 1963, naturalized, 1968; d. Alexander S. and Clara I. (Abra) Ardan; M.D., U. Bucharest, 1940; m. Aurel Sebastian Faur, Nov. 20, 1943. Chief microbiology lab. Cantacuzino State Inst., Bucharest, 1948-62; research scientist immunohematology dept. N.Y.U., 1963-66; cons. microbiologist Bur. Labs., N.Y. State Dept. Health, 1966-73, sr. research scientist, 1973—, lectr. microbiology, 1967—. Recipient Sci. Paper award Am. Public Health Assn., 1979. Fellow Am. Acad. Microbiology; mem. Am. Soc. Microbiology. Author manual, 60 papers in field. Patentee medium for pathogenic neisseria. Office: 455 1st Ave New York NY 10016

FAUSETT, PATRICIA LEE, electronics company executive; b. Washington, Feb. 8, 1944; d. Gerald LeRoy and Bernice Kennedy; B.S., Purdue U., 1965; M.B.A. Golden Gate U., 1983; m. Richard Orlin Fausett, Sept. 15, 1979; children—Stephen Johnson, Jr., Michael Lee Johnson. Tchr., Franklin Sch., Burlingame, Calif., Peter Hoy Sch., Lombard, Ill., 1966-71; acct. Hewlett Packard, Palo Alto, Calif., 1978-81, buyer, 1981-84, corp. materials contract mgr., 1984—. Treas., Almond Sch. PTA, Los Altos, Calif., 1978-79. Mem. AAUW, Alpha Chi Omega, Alpha Delta Kappa. Democrat. Roman Catholic. Home: Los Altos CA 94022 Office: 3000 Hanover St Palo Alto CA 94303

FAUSNIGHT, VESTA LE, utility company executive; b. Zanesville, Ohio, July 27, 1952; d. Ivan Joseph Fausnight and Norma Rae (Taylor) Roberts. Student Manchester Coll., Ind. Meter reader Puritan/Diversified, Fort Wayne, 1974-75; surveyor Turnbell Engring., Fort Wayne, 1975-76; insp. Puritan/Diversifed, 1976-79; constrn. supr. Hartman Constrn. Co., Fort Wayne, 1979-81; project technician City of Fort Wayne, 1981-82; new devel. mgr. Utility Ctr., Inc., Fort Wayne, 1982—. Active YWCA, Women's Bur. Mem. Nat. Assn. Female Execs., Home Builders Assn., Nat. Mus. of Women in Arts. Mem. Ch. of the Brethren. Avocations: collectin stamps and ships; play softball and golf; photography; travel. Office: Utility Ctr Inc 2200 W Cook Rd Fort Wayne IN 46818

FAUST, ANNE SONIA, lawyer; b. Honolulu, Aug. 27, 1936; d. Alfred and Geneva Dora (Barnett) F. B.A., U. Hawaii, 1960; cert. of completion Coro Found. Internship in Pub. Affairs, San Francisco, 1961; J.D., Harvard U., 1964. Bar: Hawaii, 1964. Dep. corp. counsel City and County of Honolulu, 1964-66; asst. researcher Legis. Reference Bur., Honolulu, 1966-69; assoc. counsel Legal Aid Soc., Honolulu, 1969-70; dep. atty. gen. State of Hawaii, Honolulu, 1970-72; atty., exec. officer Hawaii Pub. Employment Relations Bd., Honolulu, 1972-80; 1st dep. corp. counsel County of Maui, Wailuku, Hawaii, 1980-81; chief antitrust div. Dept. Atty. Gen., State of Hawaii, Honolulu, 1981-86, supr. regulatory and Hawaii Housing Authority divs., 1986—; ex officio mem. Gov.'s Commn. on Status of Women, Hawaii, 1971-72; mem. Hawaii Bd. Bar Examiners, 1975-79. Contbr. articles to publs. Recycling chmn. Sierra Club, Honolulu, 1978; mem. Outdoor Circle. Mem. ABA (membership chmn. Hawaii 1965), Phi Beta Kappa, Phi Kappa Phi. Mem. United Ch. of Christ. Club: Obedience Tng. Hawaii (treas. 1982—). Home: 47-415A Kapehe St Kaneohe HI 96744 Office: Regulatory Div Dept Atty Gen 4th Floor State Capitol Honolulu HI 96813

FAUST, MARGARET SILER, psychology educator; b. Tientsin, China, Feb. 22, 1926; came to U.S., 1928; d. Charles Arthur and Marion Louise (Pierce) Siler; m. William Langdon Faust, Aug. 26, 1950; children—Katherine, Ann, Marion. B.A., Pomona Coll., 1948; M.A., Stanford U., 1951, Ph.D., 1957. Lic. psychologist, Calif. From asst. prof. to prof. Scripps Coll., Claremont, Calif., 1960-70, prof. psychology, 1970—. Author: Somatic Development of Adolescent Girls, 1977; contbr. articles to profl. jours. Bur. for Edn. of Handicapped Postdoctoral fellow UCLA, 1980; Grant Found. grantee, 1970-72. Mem. Am. Psychol. Assn., Soc. for Research in Child Devel., Sigma Xi. Office: Psychology Dept Scripps Coll Claremont CA 91711

FAUST, NAOMI FLOWE, educator, poet; b. Salisbury, N.C.; d. Christopher Leroy and Ada Luella (Graham) Flowe; A.B., Bennett Coll.; M.A., U. Mich., 1945; Ph.D., N.Y. U., 1963; m. Roy Malcolm Faust, Aug. 16, 1948. Elem. tchr. Public Schs. Gaffney (S.C.); tchr. English, French, phys. edn. Atkins High Sch., Winston-Salem; instr. English, Bennett Coll. and So. U., Scotlandville, La., 1944-46; prof. English, Morgan State Coll., Balt., 1946-48; tchr. English, Greensboro (N.C.) Public Schs., 1948-51, N.Y.C. Public Schs., 1954-63; prof. edn. Queens Coll. of City U. N.Y., Flushing, 1964-82; lectr. in field; writer, lectr., poetry readings, 1982—. Named Tchr.-Author of 1979, Tchr.-Writer; cert. of Merit for poem Cooper Hill Writers Conf., 1970; Achievement award L.I. br. AAUW, 1985. Mem. AAUP, Nat. Council Tchrs. English, Nat. Women's Book Assn., World Poetry Soc. Intercontinental, N.Y. Poetry Forum, NAACP, United Negro Coll. Fund, Alpha Kappa Alpha, Alpha Kappa Mu, Alpha Epsilon. Author: Discipline and the Classroom Teacher, 1977; (poetry) Speaking in Verse, 1974; All Beautiful Things, 1983; contbr. poetry to jours. Home: 112-01 175th St Jamaica NY 11433

FAUSTO-STERLING, ANNE, educator; b. N.Y.C., July 30, 1944; d. Philip and Dorothy Ruth (Dannenberg) Sterling; B.A., U. Wis., 1965; Ph.D., Brown U., 1970; m. Nelson Fausto, Dec. 3, 1966. Asst. prof. Brown U., Providence, 1971-76, asso. prof. biology, 1976—; NSF grant reviewer devel. biology. Mellon fellow Wellesley Center for Research on Women, 1980-81; fellow Pembroke Center Research and Teaching on Women, 1982-83. Mem. AAAS, Soc. Developmental Biology, Genetics Soc. Am., Nat. Women's Studies Assn.,

Internat. Soc. Developmental Biology. Contbr. articles to publs. sci. and women's studies. Office: Box G Brown Univ Providence RI 02912

FAVANT, SUSAN ELIZABETH, retailing company staff member; b. Bronxville, N.Y., Jan. 16, 1951; d. Eugene Frederic and Jacqueline Marie (Terreson) F. Student Russell Sage Coll., 1969-70; A.A. cum laude, Green Mountain Coll., 1972; B.S., N.Y. U., 1973. Asst. buyer merchandise trainee B. Altman & Co., N.Y.C., 1973-74, sr. asst. buyer, 1974-76, sr. group mgr. ready to wear, St. David's Pa., 1976-82, asst. store mgr., Short Hills, N.J., 1982—. Vol., United Way of Bronxville, 1973, Planned Parenthood of Mt. Vernon, N.Y., 1973, Lawrence Hosp., Bronxville, 1974-75. Mem. Green Mountain Coll. Alumni Assn., Edn. Alumni Assn. N.Y. U., Omicron Nu. Republican. Club: 7 Arts Soc. (Bronxville treas. 1976). Home: 154 The Fellsway Murray Hill NJ 07974 Office: B Altman & Co The Mall at Short Hills Short Hills NJ 07078

FAVARO, MARY KAYE ASPERHEIM, physician, author; b. Edgerton, Wis., Sept. 30, 1934; d. Harold Wilbur and Genevieve Catherine (Hyland) Asperheim; B.S. in Pharmacy, U. Wis., 1956, M.D., 1969; M.S. in Pharmacy, St. Louis Coll. Pharmacy, 1965; m. Biagino Philip Favaro, May 31, 1969; children—Justin Peter, Gina Sue. Instr. pharmacology St. Louis U. and St. Mary's Hosp., St. Louis, 1959-63; intern Albany Med. Coll., 1969-70; resident in pediatrics Albany Med. Coll., 1970-71, Med. U. S.C., 1972-73; asst. prof. pediatrics Med. U. S.C., 1973—; practice medicine specializing in pediatrics and family practice, Charleston, S.C., 1974—; books include: Pharmacology: An Introductory Text, 1985; The Pharmacologic Basis of Patient Care, 1986. Mem. AMA, S.C. Med. Assn., Charleston County Med. Assn., Charleston County Pediatric Soc. Home: 1866 Capri Dr Charleston SC 29407 Office: 5390 Dorchester Rd Charleston Heights SC 29418

FAVREAU, SUSAN DEBRA, management consulting firm executive; b. Cleve., Dec. 15, 1955; d. Donald Francis and Helen Patricia (Rafferty) F. Cert., N.Y. State Police Acad., 1974; student Hudson Valley Community Coll., 1983-85, SUNY, 1984—, Cornell U., 1984. Communications specialist N.Y. State Police, Loudonville, 1974—; mgmt. cons., sec.-treas., dir. Don Favreau Assocs., Inc., Clifton Park, N.Y., 1983-86. Recipient Dirs. commendation N.Y. State Police Acad., 1977, commendation N.Y. State Police, 1978. Mem. Nat. Assn. Female Execs., N.Y. State Civil Service Assn., Assoc. Pub. Safety Communications Officers (planning commn. mem. Atlantic chpt. 1986), N.Y. State Troopers Police Benevolent Assn. (hon.), Nat. Bus. Women Am., Internat. Assn. Chiefs Police, Am. Horse Shows Assn. Avocations: equestrienne, target shooting, reading, sewing. Republican. Roman Catholic. Home: 20 Columbia Gardens Cohoes NY 12047

FAWELL, BEVERLY, state legislator; b. Sept. 17, 1930; children—Jeffrey, Steven, Judith, Scott. B.A., Elmhurst Coll. Precinct committeewoman, 1960—; former Ill. State rep.; mem. Ill. State Senate from Dist. 20. Active Republican Fedn. Women, LWV. Mem. Bus. and Profl. Women, NOW. Episcopalian. Office: State Capitol Bldg Springfield IL 62706*

FAY, DARCY HUNT, international management and organizational consultant, educator; b. Cleve.; d. Horace Byron Jr. and Bette (Berne) Fay. B.A. in Polit. Sci., Boston Coll., 1970; M. in Internat. Adminstrn., Sch. for Internat. Tng., Brattleboro, Vt., 1979; postgrad. Fielding Inst. Cert. in intercultural tng. Tchr. Internat. Sch. Tokyo (Japan), 1971-74, Am. Sch. of Barcelona (Spain), 1974-75; dir. African/Am. Educators program AAUW Ednl. Found., Washington, 1977-81; cons. Internat. Soc. for Intercultural Edn., Tng. and Research, Washington, 1982-84; cons. Delphi Research Assocs., Washington, 1984—, World Bank, Washington, 1984-85. Contbr. articles to profl. jours. Recipient Japanese Flower Arrangement award Sogetsu Sch., Tokyo, 1974. Mem. Asia Soc., Capital Press Women, Internat. Soc. Intercultural Edn., Tng. and Research (1984 conf. steering com., program com., chmn. conf. publs. com.), Nat. Assn. Female Execs., Am. Soc. Tng. and Devel., NOW, Soc. for Accelerative Learning and Teaching, Soc. for Internat. Devel./Women in Devel., Nat. Mus. Women in Arts (charter), OD Network. Home: 4545 Connecticut Ave NW #635 Washington DC 20008

FAY, JOANNE LORRAINE (BICKLEY), consumer products company executive; b. Phila., Aug. 11, 1955; d. Homer Edward and Loretta (Duncan) Bickley; m. Robert Earl Fay, Jr., June 18, 1977. B.S., Bloomsburg State Coll., 1976; M.A. in Adminstrn., Antioch U., Phila., 1983. Cert. secondary tchr., Pa. with McNeil Consumer Products Co. subs. Johnson & Johnson, Ft. Washington, Pa., 1978—, ter. mgr., 1978-79, customer service mgr., 1980-82, inventory control and distbn. planner, 1982-83, tng. and devel. mgr., 1984—, cons., team leader, facilitator and co-chmn. steering com. Quality Circle, 1980-84. Mem. Orgn. Devel. Network, Acad. Mgmt., Am. Mgmt. Assn., Phi Sigma Iota, Kappa Delta Pi. Home: 7 Pebble Ridge Rd Warmington PA 18976 Office: McNeil Consumer Products Camp Hill Rd Fort Warrington PA 19034

FAY, NANCY ELIZABETH, nurse; b. Fulton, N.Y., May 10, 1943; d. Harold and Jean (Junker) Sant; m. Ronald George Fay, July 30, 1966; step children—Rory Patrick, Ronald George Jr. R.N., Genesee Hosp., Rochester, N.Y., 1964. Cert. nurse practitioner; cert. physician's asst., N.Y. Head maternity nurse St. Luke's Hosp., Utica, N.Y., 1975-78, diabetes clinician, 1978-82, co-dir. diabetes out-patient clinic, 1980-82; nurse practitioner, physician's asst. Slocum Dickson Med. Group, Utica, 1982—. Recipient Extra Mile award St. Luke's Hosp., 1979, Outstanding Citizenship award Am. Legion, Utica, 1982; Diabetes research grantee Diabetes Project, Ctr. Disease Control Utica, 1980-82. Mem. Am. Diabetes Assn. (pres. Utica chpt. 1983—, Outstanding Vol. of Yr. 1978, bd. dirs. N.Y. State affiliate 1983—, profl. edn. chmn. 1983—), Am. Acad. Physician's Assts., Am. Assn. Diabetes Educators. Republican. Methodist. Avocations: doll collecting, dancing, poetry, bike riding. Home: Valley Rd Oriskany NY 13424 Office: Slocum Dickson Med Group 430 Court St Utica NY 13502

FAY, PAMELA GALLOWAY, university official; b. Tucson, Dec. 2, 1952; d. David Barnes and Nancy (Harrison) Galloway; m. Peter Bunster Fay, Dec. 19, 1944. B.A., in Journalism, U. Nev., 1974. Feature writer Reno Gazette Jour., 1974-79, lifestyle editor, 1979-81, reporter, 1981-84; dir. pub. info. U. Nev. System, Reno, 1984—. Recipient numerous writing awards Nev. Press Assn., 1977-78. Mem. Nev. Press Women (writing awards 1974-77). Episcopalian. Office: Chancellor's Office U Nev System 405 Marsh Ave Reno NV 89511

FAY, TONI GEORGETTE, public affairs administrator; b. N.Y.C., Apr. 25, 1947; d. George E. and Allie C. (Smith) F.; B.A., Duquesne U., Pitts., 1968; M.S.W. (NIMH fellow 1970-72), U. Pitts., 1972, M.Ed., 1973; cert. Yale U. Drug Dependence Inst., 1973. Caseworker, N.Y.C. Dept. Welfare, 1968-70; regional commr. Gov. Pa. Council Drugs and Alcohol, 1973-76; dir. social services Pitts. Black Action Against Drug Abuse, 1972-73; dir. planning and devel. Nat. Council Negro Women, 1977-79; exec. v.p. D. Parke Gibson Assos., 1979-82; mgr. community relations Time Inc., N.Y.C., 1982-83, dir. corp. community relations, 1983—. Bd. dirs. N.C.Y. Pvt. Pub. Council, N.Y. Coalition of 100 Black Women; treas., sec. Mary McLeod Bethune Mus. and Archives, Washington; mem. Bus. Urban Issues Council of Conf. Bd. Named Woman of Yr., Pitts. YWCA, 1975. Mem. Alpha Kappa Alpha. Office: Time Life Bldg Rockefeller Center New York NY 10020

FEAGLES, GAIL WINTER, lawyer; b. Warrenton, Mo., Dec. 11, 1951; d. Henry George and Evelyn May (Schulze) Winter; m. Prentiss Eric Feagles, Aug. 9, 1975; 1 child, Eric. A.B. in French, B.S. in Edn., U. Mo., 1972; J.D., Duke U., 1976. Bar: Va. 1976. Assoc., Hazel, Beckhorn & Hanes, Fairfax, Va., 1976-82, ptnr., 1983—. Bd. dirs. Wesley Housing Devel. Corp., Alexandria, Va., 1983—; chmn. Community Outreach Devel., 1984—; active Fairfax United Methodist Ch., 1978—. Mem. ABA, Fairfax County Bar Assn. (mem. library com. 1979-82, mem. com. 1979-81, sec. real estate sect. 1982-84, chmn., 1984-85, mem. fee arbitration com. 1983—), Phi Beta Kappa. Office: Hazel Beckhorn & Hanes PO Box 547 Fairfax VA 22030

FEATHERMAN, SANDRA, political science educator; b. Phila., Apr. 14, 1934; d. Albert N. and Rebe (Burd) Green; B.A., U. Pa., 1955, M.A., 1978, Ph.D., 1978; m. Bernard Featherman, Mar. 29, 1958; children—Andrew Charles, John James. Asst. prof. polit. sci., 1978-84, assoc. prof., 1984—, Chmn. grad. program, 1982-84, dir. MBA program, 1984-85, pres. faculty Senate, 1985-86; cons. U.S. Office Personnel Mgmt., 1979. Mem. Sch. Bd. Nominating Panel, Phila., 1979-81; pres. Alliance Quality Edn., 1976-78; bd. dirs. Citizens Com. Public Edn. in Phila., 1977—, pres., 1979-81; pres. Pa. Fedn. Community Coll. Trustees, 1974-75; trustee Community Coll. Phila., 1970—, vice chmn., 1978-84, chmn., 1984—; life trustee Samuel Fels Found.; bd. dirs. United Way S.E. Pa., 1977—, United Way Pa., 1981-84, Concerto Soloists of Phila., 1978-81; mem. commn. jud. selection and evaluation Phila. Bar Assn., 1979-81; nat. bd. dirs. Girls Clubs Am., 1971-74, pres., Phila., 1971-73; mem. Pa. Council on Arts, 1979—. Recipient Brooks Graves award Pa. Polit. Sci. Assn., 1982; Community Service award City of Phila., 1984; Annual Youth Services award Bnai Brith' Quaker City lodge, 1985. Mem. Am. Planning Assn., Am. Polit. Sci. Assn., Am. Soc. Public Administrn., Public Choice Soc., AAUW (dir. Phila. chpt. 1975-78, pres. 1984-86, Outstanding Women award 1986). Author: Jews, Black and Ethnics, 1979; also articles. Home: 2100 Spruce St Philadelphia PA 19103 Office: Temple U Broad and Montgomery Sts Philadelphia PA 19122

FECHTEL, ALICIA MARIE, insurance executive, lawyer; b. Dallas, Nov. 30, 1946; d. Joseph Charles and Hazel Louise (Rustin) F.; m. Richard George Pfeil, May 15, 1967 (div. May 1971); children—Lisa Ann, Alison Louise. B.A., Mercer U., Macon, Ga., 1973; J.D., So. Meth. U. 1976. Bar: Tex. 1977. Staff atty. Lone Star Life Ins. Co., Dallas, 1977-79, asst. gen. counsel, 1979-82, dir., 1983—; v.p., gen. counsel, sec. Kmart Ins. Services, Inc., Dallas, 1982—; dir. Tex. Life, Accident & Health Guaranty Fund, KM Ins. Co., Dallas, Lone Star Life Ins. Co.; mem. adv. coms. Nat. Assn. Ins. Commrs., 1983—. Founder Woman's Crisis Ctr., Macon, 1973; mem. Women Meeting Women, Dallas, 1981. Mem. ABA, Tex. Bar Assn., Women Lawyers Assn. Roman Catholic. Office: Kmart Insurance Group 4050 Alpha Rd Dallas TX 75244

FEDELE, MARTHA JOSA, management executive; b. Bacsalmas, Hungary, Jan. 13, 1947; came to U.S., 1976; d. Szilard and Roza (Papp) Josza; children—Martha Carolina, Daniel Gregory. B.S., Liceo Venezuela, Caracas, 1969; B.A., Newton Jr. Coll., Mass., 1967. Exec. asst. personnel mgmt. Banco Nacional de Descuento, Caracas, 1969-71; exec. asst. to pres. Constructora Ripa S.A., Caracas, 1971-76; pres. 8460 Pealty Corp., N.Y.C., 1978—; pres. Andrei Inc., N.Y.C., 1985—; mgr. USA 561 NL Labs., Eng., 1985—. Vol. Our Lady Queen of Martyrs Sch., Forest Hills, N.Y., 1984—. Avocations: music; handcrafts.

FEDOROFF, NINA VSEVOLOD, research scientist, consultant; b. Cleve., Apr. 9, 1942; d. Vsevolod N. and Olga S. (Snegireff) Stacy; m. T. Patrick Gaganidze, June 18, 1966 (div. 1978); children—Natasha, Kyr. B.S., Syracuse U., 1966; Ph.D., Rockefeller U., 1972. Asst. Mgr. translation bur. Biol. Abstracts, Phila., 1962-63; flutist Syracuse Symphony Orch., N.Y., 1964-66; acting asst. prof. U. Calif., Los Angeles, 1972-74; postdoctoral fellow UCLA and Carnegie Instn. Washington, Los Angeles and Balt., 1974-78; staff scientist Carnegie Instn. of Washington, Balt., 1978—; mem. devel. biology panel NSF, Washington, 1979-80, sci. adv. panel Office of Tech. Assessment, Congress, Washington, 1979-80, recombinant DNA adv. com. NIH, Bethesda, Md., 1980-84; mem. commn. on life scis. NRC, Nat. Acad. Sci., Washington, 1984—. Contbr. articles to profl. jours., chpts. to books. Editor Gene, 1981-84; editor, bd. of rev. editors Sci., 1985—. Grantee NSF and U.S. Dept. Agr., 1979-84, NIH, 1984—. Mem. AAAS, Phi Beta Kappa (vis. scholar 1984-85), Sigma Xi. Avocations: chamber music; hiking; skiing. Office: Carnegie Inst of Washington Dept Embryology 115 W University Pkwy Baltimore MD 21210

FEELEY, KATHLEEN, college president; b. Balt., Jan. 7, 1929; d. Jerome Laurence and Theresa (Tasker) F. B.A. in English, Coll. Notre Dame of Md.; M.A. in English, Villanova U.; Ph.D. in English, Rutgers U.; student Claremont U. Ctr. Inst. for Study of Change. Joined School Sisters of Notre Dame, Roman Cath. Ch. Am. Council on Edn. intern in acad. adminstrn. to 1971; pres. Coll. Notre Dame of Md., Balt., 1971—, asst. prof. to prof. English; dir. Union Trust Bancorp, Balt. Gas and Electric Co., Comml. Credit, Inc.; trustee St. Vincent Coll., Latrobe, Pa., Marian House; lectured at St. John Coll., Santa Fe, Ga. State Coll., Longwood Coll., Wheaton Coll., Fairfield U.; lectr. colls., univs., Japan, 1981. Author: Flannery O'Connor: Voice of the Peacock; contbr. articles to profl. jours. Named Woman of Yr., Jewish Nat. Fund Women's Aux., 1975, Good Will Ambassador in Israel, Am. Israel Soc., 1976; recipient Woman of Yr. award Md. Colonial Soc., 1976, J. Jefferson Miller award Greater Balt. Com., 1979, Andrew White medal Loyola Coll., Balt., 1981. Mem. Balt. Council on Fgn. Affairs (bd. dirs.), Assn. Cath. Colls. and Univs. (trustee). Address: Coll Notre Dame of Md 4701 N Charles St Baltimore MD 21210

FEENEY, ANDREA CHARLTON, lawyer; b. San Francisco, June 8, 1955; d. Francis Joseph and Phyllis Dorothy (Mutch) Charlton; m. Thomas Joseph Feeney, Sept. 10, 1983; 1 child, Joseph Edward; B.A. English, Stanford U., 1977; J.D., U. Pacific, Mc George Sch. Law, 1980. Bar: Calif. 1980. Environ. policy analyst Nat. Commn. on Air Quality, Washington, 1980-81; Pacific Gas & Elec. Co., San Franciso, 1981, legis. rep., adminstr. legis. services, 1982, adminstr. state issues, 1983, adminstr. fed. issues, 1985—. Bd. dirs. Monterey Heights Homes Assn., 1985—. Recipient writing and speech awards U. Pacific McGeorge Sch. Law, 1979; mem. Internat. Law Moot Ct. Honors Bd., 1979-80; recipient regional award Jessup Internat. Law Moot Ct., 1979. Mem. ABA, State Bar Calif., Fed. Energy Bar Assn. Democrat, Roman Catholic. Clubs: Commonwealth, Metropolitan, Spinsters of San Francisco (charity chmn. 1981-82, mem. adv. bd. 1982-83). Office: Pacific Gas & Elec Co 77 Beale St San Francisco CA 94106

FEHL, PATRICIA KATHERINE, educator; b. Cin., May 29, 1927; d. Norman and Gertrude (Morris) F.; A.B. cum laude, DePauw U., 1949; M.S., Ind. U., 1955, Ed.D., 1966. Tchr., Crawfordsville Schs., Ind., 1950-52; critic tchr., lab. sch., coll. methods instr. Ind. U., Bloomington, 1952-62; assoc. prof. health, phys. edn. and recreation U. Cin., 1962-73; prof., chmn. dept. gen. program Sch. Phys. Edn., W.Va. U., Morgantown, 1973—. Kennedy Found. grantee, 1966. Fellow Am. Sch. Health Assn.; mem. Am. Alliance for Health, Phys. Edn., Recreation and Dance (honor award 1986, v.p. recreation 1973-75), Midwest Dist. AAHPERD (historian, 1974-78, pres. 1978-80, Pres.'s award, 1976, Honor award 1983), Ohio Assn. Health, Phys. Edn. and Recreation (v.p., chmn. div. girls and women's sports 1970-72, meritorious award 1973), W.Va. Assn. Health, Phys. Edn. and Recreation (v.p. recreation 1975; Honor award 1978), W.Va. Recreation and Parks Assn. (bd. dirs. 1978-81, treas. 1983, pres. 1982-84; profl. cert. 1980), Ohio Parks and Recreation Assn. (pres. 1972; Meritorious award 1974), Midwest Assn. Phys. Edn. for Coll. Women (governing bd.), Nat. Recreation and Park Assn., Phi Delta Kappa, Pi Lambda Theta, Delta Kappa Gamma. Contbr. articles to jours.; contbr. to Ohio Secondary Girls Phys. Edn. Curriculum Guide. Address: 1336 Cherry Ln Morgantown WV 26505

FEHRENBACH, ALICE R. O'SULLIVAN, psychologist; b. Denver, Nov. 14, 1910; d. John Alexander and Gertrude (Gaffney) McTammany; A.B., Barnard Coll., 1931; M.A., U. Denver, 1944, Ph.D., 1955; m. Frank O'Sullivan, July 6, 1940 (dec. Feb. 1941); m. 2d, Carl E. Fehrenbach, June 8, 1953 (dec. 1961). Tchr., Denver public schs., 1935-47, psychologist, 1948-68; pvt. practice psychology, Denver, 1948—; prof. psychology Regis Coll., 1968-76, prof. emeritus, 1976—, faculty lectr., 1972, acting dir. counseling service, 1971-73, dir. counseling services, 1974-76; staff Mt. Airy Psychiat. Center, 1976—; vis. lectr. U. Nev., Stanford U.; guest appearances radio, TV series, Denver; mem. interregional bd. Am. Bd. Profl. Psychology, 1978-83; mem. Colo. Bd. Psychologist Examiners. Bd. dirs. Camp Fire Girls, 1949-55. Recipient Alumnae Recognition award Barnard Coll., 1975; Dir.'s award Regis Coll., 1975; Outstanding Social Action award Colo. Mental Health Assn., 1975; Disting. Service award Am. Bd. Profl. Psychologists, 1983, 86. Diplomate in sch. psychology Am. Bd. Profl. Psychologists. Fellow Am. Psychol. Assn. (campus peer rev. bd. 1985—); mem. Colo. Psychol. Assn. (dir.; pres. 1973-74; Disting. Service award 1969, Disting. Past Pres. award 1984), Rocky Mountain Psychol. Assn. (exec. bd., Disting. Service award 1982), English-Speaking Union, Assn. Specialized Services (pres. 1953-54), Denver Mental Health Assn. (profl. adv. bd.), Columbia U. Women's Club Colo. (founder 1948, pres. 1948-50), Denver Women's Press Club, Women's Forum Colo., Delta Kappa Gamma. Author personality test; contbr. articles to profl. jours. Office: 3232 S Josephine St Denver CO 80210

FEIGEN, BRENDA, lawyer; b. Chgo., July 7, 1944; d. Arthur Paul Feigen and Shirley (Bierman) Feigen Kadison; B.A. cum laude in Math., Vassar Coll., 1966; J.D., Harvard U., 1969; m. Marc S. Fasteau, Dec. 21, 1968; 1 dau., Alexis Feigen-Fasteau. Admitted to Mass. bar, 1970, N.Y. bar, 1971; chief analyst Boston Redevel. Authority, 1969; assoc. firm Rosenman, Colin, Kaye, Petschek, Freund & Emil, N.Y.C., 1970; coordinating dir. Women's Action Alliance, N.Y.C., 1970-72; dir. nat. women's rights project ACLU, N.Y.C., 1972-74; partner firm Fasteau and Feigen, N.Y.C., 1974-80; asso. firm Hess, Segall, Guterman, Pelz & Steiner, N.Y.C., 1980-81; lawyer, motion picture agt. William Morris Agy., N.Y.C., 1982—; adj. instr. law Coll. of New Rochelle, 1976. Hon. pres.'s fellow Columbia U., 1977-78, also mem. program social sci. research on sex roles and social change; participant Exec. Seminar, Aspen Inst., 1979. Adv. bd. Working Women United; bd. dirs. Film Forum; candidate for N.Y. State Senate, 1978. Mem. NOW (nat. legis. v.p. 1970-71), N.Y. Women in Film (adv. com.), Women's Action Alliance (co-founder, dir.), Nat. Women's Polit. Caucus (nat. adv. com.). Democrat. Contbr. articles to mags., chpt. to book. Address: 944 Park Ave New York NY 10028

FEIGIN, BARBARA SOMMER, advertising agency executive; b. Berlin, Nov. 16, 1937; came to U.S., 1940, naturalized, 1949; d. Eric Daniel and Charlotte Martha (Demmer) S.; B.A., Whitman Coll., Walla Walla, Wash., 1959; cert. bus. adminstrn. Harvard U.-Radcliffe Coll., 1960; m. James Feigin, Sept. 17, 1961; children—Michael, Peter, Daniel. Mktg. research asst. Richardson-Vick Co., 1960-61; market research analyst SCM Corp., 1961-62; group research supr. Benton & Bowles, Inc., 1962-68; assoc. research dir. Marplan Research Co., 1968-69; exec. v.p. research and mktg. services Grey Advt., N.Y.C., 1969—, also mem. agency policy council. Vice chmn. bd. overseers Whitman Coll.; mem. bd. advisors M.Mktg. program U. Ga. Mem. Advt. Research Found., Am. Mktg. Assn. (2d v.p. chpt.), Am. Assn. Advt. Agys. (research com.), Copy Research Council, Agy. Research Dirs. Council. Contbr. articles to profl. jours. Office: 777 3d Ave New York NY 10017

FEIGON, JUDITH TOVA, physician, medical educator; b. Galveston, Tex., Dec. 2, 1947; d. Louis and Ethel (Goldberg) Feigon; m. Nathan C. Goldman. A.B., Barnard Coll., Columbia U., 1970; postgrad. in sci., Rice U. and U. Houston, 1970-71; M.D., U. Tex.-San Antonio, 1976. Diplomate Am. Bd. Ophthalmology. Intern, Mt. Auburn Hosp., Cambridge, Mass. Intern and clin. teaching fellow, Harvard U. Med. Sch., 1976-77; resident in ophthalmology, Baylor Coll. Medicine, Houston, 1977-80, fellow in retina, 1980-82, clin. instr., 1982—; asst. prof. ophthalmology U. Tex. Med. Br., Galveston, 1982-85, clin. asst. prof., 1985—; practice medicine specializing in ophthalmology, vitreoretinal diseases and surgery, Houston, 1983—; physician advisor to Houston br. Tex. Soc. to Prevent Blindness; mem. staff Methodist, St. Lukes/Tex. Children's, John Sealy, Rosewood hosps. Mem. Am. Acad. Ophthalmology, Tex. Med. Assn., Harris County Med. Soc., Barnard Club of Houston, U. Tex.-San Antonio Alumni Assn., Harvard Med. Sch. Associate Alumni, Vitreous Soc., AMA. Contbr. article to profl. publs. Office: 6410 Fannin Suite 404 Houston TX 77030

FEIK, LUCILE ANN, marketing educator; b. Chgo., May 6, 1938; d. George Raymond and Lucile Marie (Barrett) Jautz. B.A., Mundelein Coll., 1960; M.A., Georgetown U., 1965; M.B.A., Am. U., 1979. Econ. intelligence officer CIA, Washington, 1965-67; advt. copywriter Hecht's, Washington, 1968-69; sales promotion writer U.S. News & World Report, Washington, 1969-71; freelance writer, Washington, 1971-74; dir. publs. and promotion, assn. div. U.S. C. of C., Washington, 1974-77; co-founder Reston Mailing Service (Va.), 1977-79; instr. George Mason U., Fairfax, Va., 1979-81, LaSalle Coll., Phila., 1981-82; asst. prof. bus. adminstrn. St. Norbert Coll., DePere, Wis., 1982—. Contbr. articles to various publs. Founder Lucile Barrett Jautz award Mundelein Coll., Chgo., 1983; mem. adv. bd. People for Positive Involvement in South Africa. Recipient award Newsletter Clearinghouse, 1976, merit award Am. Soc. Assn. Execs., 1977; Mary Vogel Strasburg scholar Washington Fashion Group, 1977. Mem. Am. Mktg. Assn., Assn. on Third World Affairs, World Future Soc. Democrat. Roman Catholic. Office: St Norbert Coll DePere WI 54115

FEIL, NAOMI WEIL, script writer, gerontologist; b. Munich, Germany, July 22, 1932; came to U.S., 1937, naturalized, 1944; d. Julius and Helen (Kahn) Weil; student Oberlin Coll., 1950-51, Western Res. U., 1950-51, Columbia U., 1951-54; B.S. cum laude, Columbia U., 1954, M.S.W., 1956; m. Edward Feil, Dec. 29, 1963; children by previous marriage—Victoria, Beth; children—Edward G., Kenneth J. Dir. group work William Hodson Center, 1960-62, Bird S. Coler Hosp., Welfare Island, N.Y., 1962-63, Montefiore Home for Aged, 1963-80; script writer, actress documentary films Edward Feil Prodns., 1963—; cons. Case Western Res. U., also adj. field instr.; workshop leader; group worker, cons. Amasa Stone; author: Validation: The Feil Method, 1982; Resolution: The Final Life Task, 1985; writer books on gerontology, documentary films; films awarded internat. awards include: Where Life Still Means Living, 1965; The Inner World of Aphasia, 1967; Looking for Yesterday: 100 Years to Live, 1981; contbr. articles to Gerontology, Humanistic Jour., Pilgrimmage. Recipient award for human relations in pub. service, Cleve., 1974, Cine award for documentary films, 1965, 68, 82. Mem. Nat. Assn. Social Workers, Transpersonal Psychology Assn., Humanistic Psychology Assn., Univ. Film Assn., Gerontology Assn. Democrat. Jewish. Home: 21987 Byron Rd Cleveland OH 44122 Office: 4614 Prospect Ave Cleveland OH 44103

FEILD, RACHEL NANNEY, printing company executive; b. Spindale, N.C., Nov. 11, 1927; d. Roy and Cora Lillian (Beam) Nanney; B.S., Queens Coll., Charlotte, N.C., 1947; m. George Feild, Jr., May 26, 1951 (div. 1957); children—John Anthony, Kathryn Elizabeth. With Aerospace Industries Assn. Am., Inc., Washington, 1956-69, com. exec. procurement and finance, 1961-69; part-owner, sec.-treas. Taylor Printing Co., Inc., Hyattsville, Md., 1969—. Mem. Nat. Assn. Female Execs., Am. Soc. Profl. and Exec. Women. Episcopalian. Office: 5206 46th Ave Hyattsville MD 20772

FEIN, LEAH GOLD (MRS. ALFRED G. FEIN), psychologist; b. Minsk, Russia; d. Jacob Lyon and Sarah Freda (Meltzer) Gold; B.S., Albertus Magnus Coll., 1939; M.A., Yale U., 1942, Ph.D. (Marion Talbot fellow), 1944; m. Alfred Gustave Fein, June 10, 1944; 1 son, Ira Hirsh. Health educator New Haven Schs., 1930-43; instr. psychology Carleton Coll., 1944-45; research asso. Conn. Interracial Commn., 1946; chief psychologist Seattle Psychiat. Clinic, 1947-48; prof. U. Bridgeport, 1946-47, 52-58; ind. clin. practice, specializing in clin., child consultation, Seattle, 1948-52, Stamford, Conn., 1952-64, N.Y.C., 1967-81, West Palm Beach, Fla., 1982—; clin. cons. Conn. Commn. on Alcoholism Clinic, 1952-64; research asso. Soc. for Investigation Human Ecology; therapist Norwalk Psychiat. Clinic, 1952-64; cons. Child Edn. Found., 1953-56; dir. research Sch. Nursing Norwalk Hosp., 1961-64; dir. clin. services cerebral palsy and mental retardation, Waterbury, Conn., 1964-65; assoc. prof. Quinnipiac Coll., Hamden, Conn., 1965-66; cons., instr., med. staff N.Y. Hosp.-Cornell Med. Center, White Plains, 1966-67; dir. psychology Psychiat. Treatment Center, N.Y., 1967-68; research asso. Roosevelt Hosp. Child Psychiatry, 1968-69; supr., cons. research psychologist Bur. Child Guidance, N.Y.C. Board Edn., 1969-72; faculty Greenwich Inst. Psychoanalytic Studies, 1971-79; sr. research scientist Postgrad. Center for Mental Health, N.Y.C., 1980-82; mem. program com. Internat. Congress Social Psychiatry, 1974; research cons. N.Y.C. Mayor's Vol. Action Com., Human Resources Adminstrn., N.Y.C. Study of Delinquency and Study Abused and Neglected Children; cons., inservice trainer Center Group Counseling, Boca Raton, Fla., 1982-84; manuscript reviewer Perceptual Motor Skills. Diplomate clin. psychology Am. Bd. Profl. Psychology. Fellow Soc. Personality Assessment, Am. Psychol. Assn. (council of reps. div. 42, 1983-86), Am. Acad. Psychotherapists, Internat. Council Psychologists (v.p. 1961-62, 71-73, pres. 1973-75), Am. Orthopsychiat. Assn., N.Y. Acad. Sci.; mem. Nat. Assn. Gifted (v.p. 1961-62), Internat. Council Women Psychologists (chmn. profl. relations among psychologists), Psychologists in Pvt. Practice (treas. 1972-78), Am. Psychol. Assn. (sec. div. psychotherapy 1966-69; council of reps.), N.Y. State Psychol. Assn., Fla. Psychol Assn., Am. Assn. Group Psychotherapy and Psychodrama (council 1973-75), World Fedn. Mental Health, Nat. Council Jewish Women, Hadassah. Club: Yale (N.Y.C.). Author: The Three Dimensional Personality Test—Reliability, Validity and Clinical Implications, 1960; The Changing School Scene: Challenge to Psychology, 1974; editor Jour. Internat. Understanding, vol. 9-10, 1974; Jour. Psychology Div. Am. Friends Hebrew U.; guest editor Jour. Clin. Child Psychology, 1975; cons. editor Jour. Psychotherapy in Pvt. Practice; others; contbr. Jour. Clin. Psychology, other profl. jours. Address: 213 29th St West Palm Beach FL 33407

FEIN, LINDA ANN, nurse anesthetist, critical care nurse consultant; b. Cin., Dec. 10, 1949; d. Joseph and Elizabeth P. (Kannady) Stofle; m. Thomas Paul Fein, Dec. 11, 1971. Nursing diploma, Miami Valley Hosp. Sch. Nursing, Dayton, Ohio, 1971, Wright State U., Dayton, 1969; postgrad. U. Cin. Med. Ctr., 1978. Nursing asst. Miami Valley Hosp., Dayton, 1969-71; staff nurse operating room Cin. Children's Hosp. and Med. Ctr., 1971, 73, Peninsula Hosp., Burlingame, Calif., 1972-73; staff nurse operating room and emergency room Doctors Hosp., San Diego, 1972; staff nurse emergency room Ohio State U. Hosps., Columbus, 1973-75, head nurse operating room, 1975-76; staff nurse anesthetist Bethesda Hosps., Cin., 1978—; childbirth educator psychoprophylactic method, 1975—; critical care nursing cons. Med. Communicators & Assocs., Salt Lake City, 1985—; co-owner Exec. Shops, Cin., 1982-85; speaker in field. Mem. search com. Cin. Gen. Hosp. Sch. of Anesthesia for Nurses, 1981-82. Recipient Recognition of Profl. Excellence, First Nurse Anesthesia Faculty Assocs., 1982. Mem. Miami Valley Hosp. Sch. of Nursing Alumni Assn., Cin. Gen. Hosp. Sch. Anesthesia for Nurses Alumni Assn., Nurse Anesthetists of Greater Cin., Ohio Assn. Nurse Anesthetists, Am. Assn. Nurse Anesthetists, Am. Assn. Operating Room Nurses, Am. Assn. Critical Care Nurses, Nat. Assn. Female Execs., Altrusa Internat. (officer 1985—). Republican. Methodist. Lodge: Eastern Star. Avocations: antiques; gourmet cooking; African violets; roses; swimming; skiing; writing. Home: 1557 Oak Knoll Dr Cincinnati OH 45224 Office: Med Communicators and Assocs 3760 S Highland Dr Suite 252 Salt Lake City UT 84106

FEIN, SYLVIA, author, painter; b. Milw., Nov. 20, 1919; d. Alfred E. and Elizabeth (Routt) F.; B.S., U. Wis., Madison, 1942; M.A., U. Calif., Berkeley, 1951; m. William K. Scheuber, May 30, 1942; 1 dau., Heidi. One-woman exhbns. include: U. Wis. Meml. Union Gallery, 1942, Milw. Art Inst., 1942, Perls Galleries, N.Y.C., 1946, Feingarten Galleries, San Francisco, 1957, 59, Carmel, Calif., 1959, N.Y.C., 1961, Sagittarius Gallery, N.Y.C., 1958, St. Mary's Coll., Moraga, Calif., 1960, Kunstkabinett, Frankfurt, W.Ger., 1960, Mills Coll. Art Gallery, Oakland, Calif., 1962, Ruthermore Galleries, Oakland, 1962, Maxwell Galleries, San Francisco, 1963, Nicole of Berkeley (Calif.), 1965, Bresler Galleries, Milw., 1966, Oshkosh (Wis.) Pub. Mus., 1967; numerous group exhbns., 1941—, latest being 5th Winter invitational Calif. Palace Legion of Honor, 1964, Art of Landscape, San Francisco Art Inst. travelling exhibit, 1964-65, Three Painters, St. Mary's Coll., 1964, Magic and Fantastic Art, Walnut Creek (Calif.) Library, 1968; author: Heidi's Horse, 1976; owner, pub. Exelrod Press, 1975—; chmn. Archtl. Rev. Comm., Pleasant Hill, Calif., 1975. Recipient Elizabeth Water's Purchase prize U. Wis.; John Steuart Curry award 1942; Joseph E. Davies Purchase award Wis. Salon Art; Wis. Union Purchase prize. Home: 341 Strand Ave Pleasant Hill CA 94523 Office: PO Box 2303 Pleasant Hill CA 94523

FEINBERG, BARBARA, interior designer; b. N.Y.C., Oct. 23, 1941; d. Alexander and Eunice (Michael) Youngerman; m. Ira David Feinberg, Aug. 1964 (div. 1968). B.F.A., Boston U., 1963. Jr. designer Hans Krieks Assocs., Boston, 1963-66; prin. Barbara Feinberg Design, Boston, 1966-71, Miami, 1971-74; designer Designs for Interiors & Unigram, Inc., N.Y.C., 1974-77; pvt. practice interior designing, N.Y.C., 1977-79; owner Feinberg Orsini Assocs., N.Y.C., 1979-85, Feinberg Assocs., 1985—. Office: 30 E 23d St New York NY 10010

FEINBERG, SANDRA LEE, library administrator; b. Saginaw, Mich., July 31, 1946; d. Frank and Elisabeth Ann (Ackerman) Langeneker; m. Richard Philip Feinberg, June 12, 1969; children—Jacob, Theodore. B.A., Western Mich. U., 1968; A.M.L.S., U. Mich., 1971. Lic. pub. librarian, N.Y. Tchr., spl. edn. Romulus Community Schs., Mich., 1968-70; asst. dir. children's services Middle Country Pub. Library, Centereach, N.Y., 1971—. Steering com. Suffolk Coalition for Parents & Children, Suffolk County, N.Y., 1981—; bd. dirs. Child Care Council of Suffolk Inc., Huntington, 1986; com. mem., interviewer Child Watch Project of Children's Def. Fund, SUNY-Stony Brook, 1982; com. on pre-sch. activities handbook Youth Services, N.Y. Library Assn., N.Y.C., summer 1985; coordinator Early Childhood Resource Ctr. Program, N.Y. Pub. Library, N.Y.C., 1985. Author: Menu for Mealtimes, Family Resource Book. Mem. Children's Librarian Assn. (exec. bd. 1971-80, pres. Suffolk County 1976-78), Librarians Alliance for Parents and Children (coordinator 1982—). Avocations: jogging, reading. Home: 87 Quaker Path Stony Brook NY 11790 Office: Middle Country Pub Library 101 Eastwood Blvd Centereach NY 11720

FEINER, ARLENE MARIE, librarian, researcher, consultant; b. Spring Green, Wis., Mar. 23, 1937; d. Herman Joseph and Cecelia Margaret (Meixelsperger) F. B.A. in History, Alverno Coll., 1959; M.A. in Library Sci., Rosary Coll., 1971; M.A. in Community and Organizational Devel., Loyola U., Chgo., 1985. Gen. office worker USIA, Washington, 1959-60; adminstrv. sec. Nat. Council Cath. Women, Washington, 1960-62; asst. librarian Munich campus, U. Md., Fed. Republic Germany, 1962-64; preliminary cataloger, 1st editor MARC Pilot Project, Library of Congress, Washington, 1965-67, head librarian Acad. of the Holy Cross, Kensington, Md., 1967-70, Jesuit Sch. of Theology Library, Chgo., 1971-79, coordinator serial activities; women's studies bibliographer, Loyola U., Chgo., 1979—. Editor: (bibliography) Current Serials, 1980—. Compiler: (bibliography) Guide to Women's Studies Sources, 1985. Contbr. articles to profl. jours. Bd. dirs. Women's World Ctr., Chgo., 1985—. Assn. of Theol. Schs. in U.S. and Can. grantee, 1976. Mem. Chgo. Acad. Librarians Council (serials com.), Chgo. Area Women's Studies Assn., ALA, Loyola U. Women's Studies Com. Roman Catholic. Avocations: poetry; hiking; music. Home: 336 W Wellington Ave Apt 2102 Chicago IL 60657

FEINGOLD, NANCY JO, mortgage company executive; b. South Bend, Ind., Jan. 6, 1946; Jordan Herbert and Bette (Medow) Kapson; 1 dau., Denise Rae. B.A. in Sociology, U. Ariz., 1964. With Colonial Mortgage, South Bend, Ind., 1971-74, Tchrs. Credit Union, South Bend, 1974-77; processor and closer Hinton Mortgage, Dallas, 1982-83; loan officer Criterion Fin., Dallas, 1983-84; sr. loan officer Sunbelt Mortgage Div., Dallas, 1984—; devel. coordinator Women's Council Dallas, 1984—. Drama instr. Jewish Community Ctr., Dallas, 1977-81, fund coordinator, 1977-81; advisor B'nai B'rith Youth Orgn., Dallas, 1977-81. Mem. Dallas Bd. Realtors (conf. and bd. coordinator), Nat. Assn. Female Execs., Assn. Profl. Mortgage Women (fiscal coordinator). Office: Sunbelt Mortgage Div 4901 LBJ Freeway Suite 104 Dallas TX 75234

FEINN, BARBARA ANN, economist; b. Waterbury, Conn., Feb. 16, 1925; d. David Harris and Dora (Brandvein) F. A.B. magna cum laude, Smith Coll., 1946; M.A. (univ. scholar), Yale U., 1947, Ph.D. (univ. fellow), 1952; cert. Oxford (Eng.) U., 1949. Research economist First Nat. City Bank, N.Y.C., 1953-54; assoc. economist Office Messrs. Rockefeller, N.Y.C., 1954-61; asst. to dir. N.Y. State Office for Regional Devel., N.Y.C., 1961-62; cons. economist Nelson A. Rockefeller, N.Y.C., 1963-64; pvt. cons., 1965-68; sr. council economist N.Y. State Council Econ. Advisers, N.Y.C., 1969-72; chief economist Office S.C. Gov., Columbia, 1972—, mem. bd. econ. advisors, 1976—, sec. bd. econ. advisors, 1986—; adj. prof. bus. adminstrn. U. S.C., Columbia, 1972-74. Ofcl. participant White House Conf. on Balanced Nat. Growth and Econ. Devel., 1978; del. meetings on nat. balanced growth Nat. Govs. Assn., Leesburg, Va., 1977; mem. S.C. Gov.'s Task Force on the Economy, 1980—; mem. productivity measurement com. S.C. Council on Productivity, 1981—. Dir. Smith Coll. Alumnae Fund Program, N.Y.C., 1965-66, mem. spl. gifts com., 1971; del. assembly Assn. Yale Alumni, 1983-86. Mem. Am. Econ. Assn., Nat. Assn. Bus. Econs., Soc. Govt. Economists, Downtown Economists Luncheon Group, Western Econ. Assn., N.Y. Assn. Bus. Economists, Atlanta Econ. Club, Phi Beta Kappa. Clubs: Yale (N.Y.C.); Summit, Wildewood (Columbia, S.C.); Sea Pines (Hilton Head Island, S.C.). Contbr. articles to profl. jours. Home: 50 Mallet Hill Ct Columbia SC 29223 Office: Gov's Office Columbia SC 29201

FEINSTEIN, DIANNE, mayor San Francisco; b. San Francisco, June 22, 1933; d. Leon and Betty (Rosenburg) Goldman; B.S., Stanford U., 1955; D.Public Adminstrn. (hon.), U. Manila, 1981; H.H.D. (hon.), Philippine Women's U., 1981; m. Bertram Feinstein, Nov. 11, 1962; 1 dau., Katherine Anne; m. 2d, Richard Blum, Jan. 20, 1980. Intern public affairs Coro Found., San Francisco, 1955-56; asst. to Calif. Indsl. Welfare Commn., Los Angeles, also San Francisco, 1956-57; vice-chmn. Calif. Women's Bd. Terms and Parole, Los Angeles, also San Francisco, 1962-66; chmn. San Francisco City and County Adv. Com. for Adult Detention, also mem. Mayor's Com. on Crime, 1968-69; mem. Bd. Suprs. City and County of San Francisco, 1970-73, 74-77, 78, pres. bd., 1970-71, 74-75, 78; mayor of San Francisco, 1978—; mem. exec. com., del. gen. assembly Assn. Bay Area Govts., 1970-74, 76-78, chmn. Environ. Mgmt. Task Force, 1976-78; bd. govs. Bay Area Council, 1972-73; mem. Bay Conservation and Devel. Commn., 1973-78. Chmn. bd. regents Lone Mountain Coll., 1972-75. Recipient Women Achievement award Bus. and Profl. Women's Clubs San Francisco, 1970, Distinguished Woman award San Francisco Examiner, 1970; CORO award, 1979; SCOPUS award, 1981. Mem. Multi-Culture Inst. (dir.), Calif. Tomorrow, Bay Area Urban League, Planning and Conservation League, Friends of Earth, Chinese Culture Found., Sierra Club. Clubs: Propeller, Commonwealth. Office: City Hall San Francisco CA 94102

FEINSTEIN, RENE ELLEN, lawyer; b. Chattanooga, July 26, 1948; d. Leo and Constance (Blum) F. B.A., Lake Forest Coll. (Ill.), 1970; J.D., Golden Gate U., San Francisco, 1977, LL.M. in Taxation, 1981. Bar: Nev. 1978, Calif. 1978. Staff atty., Sup. Ct. Nev., Carson City, 1978-79; assoc. Lawrence J. Semenza, Reno, 1979-80, Stephen R. Harris, Ltd., Reno, 1981; ptnr. Chubb & Feinstein, Reno, 1982—. Mem. State Bar Nev., No. Nev. Women Lawyers Assn. (treas. 1979-80, pres. 1984), Washoe County Bar Assn. Office: Chubb & Feinstein 527 Lander St Reno NV 89509

FEINSTEIN, SHIRLEY, banker; b. N.Y.C., Nov. 23, 1929; d. Jacob and Yetta Klukolskey; m. Edward Feinstein, July 12, 1963; children—Eric, Deborah, Mark, Brian. Student pub. schs., Woodbridge, N.Y. Pres. Bird Rd. Comml. Sites, Miami, Fla., 1954—, Fla. Land Developers, Inc., Miami, 1960—; with Heritage Corp., S. Fla., Miami, 1963—, sec.-treas., 1965—; sec.-treas. Inter-Am. Title Corp., Miami, 1963—, Heritage Mortgage Corp., Miami, 1971—. Mem. Jewish Family and Children's Service, Miami, Fla. Mem. Am. Mortgage Bankers Assn., Fla. Mortgage Bankers Assn., Greater Miami Mortgage Bankers Assn. Democrat. Lodge: Hadassah. Home: 120 S Prospect Dr Coral Gables FL 33133 Office: 1318 NW 7th St Miami FL 33125

FEIR, DOROTHY JEAN, entomologist; b. St. Louis, Jan. 29, 1929; d. Alex R. and Lillian (Smith) F.; B.S., U. Mich., 1950; M.S., U. Wyo., 1956; Ph.D., U. Wis., 1960. Instr. biology U. Buffalo, 1960-61; mem. faculty St. Louis U., 1961—, prof. biology, 1967—; mem. tropical medicine and parasitology study sect. NIH, 1980-84. Mem. Emtomol. Soc. Am., AAAS, Am. Physiol. Soc., N.Y. Acad. Sci., Mo. Acad. Sci., Sigma Xi. Editor Environ. Entomology, 1977-84. Office: Biology Dept St Louis U Saint Louis MO 63103

FEIST-FITE, BERNADETTE, health, food and travel consultant; b. Linton, N.D., Sept. 28, 1945; d. John K. and Cecilia (Nagel) F.; B.S. in Dietetics, U. N.D., Grand Forks, 1967; M.S. in Edn., Troy (Ala.) State U., 1973; Ed.D. U. So. Calif.; m. William H. Fite. Commd. officer USAF, 1965, advanced through grades to maj., ret., 1985; prof. health and fitness Nat. Def. U., Ft. McNair, Washington; speaker, lectr.; instr. USAF dietetic internship. Mgr. coffee house Unitarian Ch., 1972-74; mem. Alexandria Little Theatre, 1977-78. Decorated Air Force Commendation medal, Dept. Def. Meritorious Service medal. Mem. Soc. Internat. Edn., Tng. and Research, Am. Dietetic Assn., Internat. Food Service Execs. Assn., VFW, Assn. Mil. Surgeons U.S., Exec. Female, Air Force Assn., Soc. Nutrition Edn., Dietitians in Bus. and Industry, Sports and Cardiovascular Nutritionists, Am. Soc. Profl. and Exec. Women. Roman Catholic. Clubs: Woodlawn Country, Andrews Officers. Home: 2-303 Montebello 5902 Mount Eagle Dr Alexandria VA 22303 Office: NDU-EDO-Health Fitness Fort McNair DC 20319

FEIT, EVELYN BARBARA, security analyst; b. N.Y.C., Oct. 6, 1932; d. Henry and Cecilia (Klapper) Weinrich; m. Theodore Feit, Oct. 24, 1954; children—Helen, Sheila, Norman. A.B., Barnard Coll., 1953. Chartered fin. analyst. Bond analyst Dun & Bradstreet, N.Y.C., 1953-54, statistician Brookings Instn., Washington, 1954-55; statistician, editor Wiesenberger Fin. Services, N.Y.C., 1972-73; pension fund performance analyst Wertheim & Co., N.Y.C., 1973-76; security analyst, v.p. Kidder, Peabody & Co., N.Y.C., 1976—. Contbr. articles to profl. jours. Pres., PTA, Hunter Coll. High Sch., N.Y.C., 1971. Mem. Investment Tech. Assn., Fin. Women's Assn., N.Y. Soc. Security Analysts. Jewish. Office: Kidder Peabody & Co Inc 10 Hanover Sq New York NY 10005

FELCHLIN, MARY KATHLEEN CONROY, financial executive; b. Cleve., Feb. 16, 1951; d. Ernest J. and Margaret Jane Conroy; B.A., U. Calif., Berkeley, 1973; M.B.A., U. So. Calif., 1977. Adminstrv. asst. Mason McDuffie Investment Co., Berkeley, 1974-75; mortage mktg. staff Gibraltar Savs. & Loan, Beverly Hills, summer 1976; account officer Wells Fargo Bank, Los Angeles, 1977-79; sr. account officer Citicorp Real Estate, Inc., Los Angeles, 1979-80, asst. v.p., 1981-82, v.p., 1982—; v.p. Citicorp Real Estate Capital, 1985—. Wittenberg fellow, 1975-76; Commerce Assos. fellow, 1976-77. Mem. Am. Mgmt. Assn. Home: 8960 Wonderland Ave Los Angeles CA 90046 Office: 444 S Flower St Los Angeles CA 90071

FELD, ILA LOU, advertising executive; b. N.Y.C., July 29, 1933; d. Philip and Audrey Joy (Nicthauser) F.; m. Geoffrey Leland Clarkson, Oct. 6, 1983. B.S. in TV Prodn., Syracuse U., 1974; M.B.A., CCNY, 1977. Media planner Ted Bates Worldwide, N.Y.C., 1974-75, account exec., 1975-79, v.p., account supr., 1980-83, mgmt. rep., 1983-84, sr. v.p., mgmt. rep., 1984—. Jewish. Office: Ted Bates Worldwide 1515 Broadway New York NY 10036

FELDER, ALYCE SCHERZER, former guidance counselor; b. N.Y.C., Sept. 17, 1917; d. Louis and Gussie Moskowitz; m. Michael Scherzer, 1939 (dec.); children—Larry, Judith, Donald; m. Karl Felder, Nov., 1977. B.B.A., St. John's U., 1938; M.S. in Edn., Hofstra U., 1960; student Spl. Edn., Adelphi U., 1975-76; student Herzlia Acad., 1933-56. Tchr. bus. subjects, Plainview (N.Y.) High Sch., 1957-62; guidance counselor Burr Jr. High Sch., Commack, N.Y., 1962-84; peer counselor No. County Interfaith Crisis Ctr., Escondido, Calif.; tchr. Hebrew Sch., 1964-74. Fund raising chmn. North Shore Hosp., Manhasset, N.Y.; founding mem., pres. Sisterhood Temple Sinai, Roslyn, trustee Temple Sinai. Mem. Sigma Tau Delta (sec.), Delta Mu Delta. Club: Hadassah. Home: 12142 Iron View Row San Diego CA 92128

FELDHAMER, THELMA LEE, architect; b. Bklyn., May 10, 1925; d. Frank and Anna Pearl (Shapiro) Sitzer; student Cooper Union, 1942-46, B.Arch. (hon.); student Bklyn. Coll., 1942; m. Carl Feldhamer, Aug. 27, 1950; children—Randi Judith Feldhamer Wathen, Mark David. Archtl. draftsman-designer Caleb Hornbostel, N.Y.C., 1946-47, John F. Milan, Denver, 1963-65, Lultcho Boduroff, Denver, 1965-66, Gerri Von Frellick, Denver, 1966-68; assoc. architect Joseph E. MacMillan, Denver, 1968-81; owner, pres. Feldhamer & Assocs., P.C., Inc., Denver, 1980—; mem. Colo. state tech. com. drafting. Democratic precinct committeewoman Dist. 13, 1977-78; capt., personnel officer Colo. wing CAP. Colo. Mem. AIA, Women in Architecture (co-founder), Bus. and Profl. Women's Club Denver (pres. 1974-76). Democrat. Clubs: Altrusa, Hadassah, Pres.'s Council of Denver. Lodge: Daus. of Nile. Prin. works include Pine Haven Nursing Home, Morrison, Colo., Harris Gardens I and II office bldgs., Denver, Linden Lea House Devel., Denver, The Reserve, Green Oaks, Cherry Hills. Office: Feldhamer & Assocs PC 205 La Plada Center 3650 S Yosemite St Denver CO 80237

FELDKAMP, BONNIE BETH, educational and social service organization consultant; b. Detroit, June 15, 1936; d. Lawrence Carlos and Agnes Carolyn (Broese) Speck; m. Ralph Elmer Feldkamp, June 22, 1957; children—Beth Feldkamp Kumfer, Beverly, Carole, Gretchen, John. A.A. in Liberal Arts, Concordia Jr. Coll., Ft. Wayne, Ind., 1955; student Concordia Coll., River Forest, Ill., 1955-57, St. Francis Coll., Ft. Wayne, 1975-77. Elem. tchr. Lutheran schs., Ft. Wayne, 1955-59; mgr., salesperson Tupperware, Ft. Wayne, 1962-67; tchr., dir. Ft. Wayne pre-sch. programs, 1969-77; pres., dir. Hope Alive, Inc., Ft. Wayne, 1979-82, editor newsletter, 1979-84, exec. dir., 1982-84; cons. in field, 1984-85; patient services dir. Allen County Cancer Soc., Ft. Wayne, 1985—. Mem. Women in Communications (chpt. chairperson spl. projects 1981—), Luth. Women's Missionary League (chairperson Christian growth 1964-66), Christian Women's Club (chairperson membership 1969-76) Ft. Wayne). Home: 3104 Alexander St Fort Wayne IN 46806 Office: 2925 E State St Fort Wayne IN 46805

FELDMAN, DONNA, account executive; b. Chgo., Nov. 15, 1945; d. Nathan and June (Somers) Feldman; m. Paul Ruch. B.S., So. Ill. U., 1966; M.S., Murray State U., 1968. Spl. promotions mgr. 1st Nat. Bank Chgo., 1966-67; asst. prof., dir. forensics Luzerne County Community Coll., Nanticoke, Pa., 1968-75; account exec. Merrill Lynch, Pierce, Fenner & Smith, Chgo., 1975-77; transp. supr. Johnson & Johnson Baby Products, Park Forest, Ill., 1977-78; account exec. Christmas Club a Corp., Easton, Pa., 1979—; v.p. Ruch and Feldman Inc., corp. meeting planners. Recipient Nat. Sales award Christmas Club a Corp., 1980. Mem. Network Women Execs., Nat. Network Women in Sales (career devel. chmn.), Nat. Assn. Female Execs., Inst. Gen. Semantics, Internat. Soc. Gen. Semantics, Speech Communications Assn. Home: 668 Mallard Ln Deerfield IL 60015

FELDMAN, JUDITH ELLEN, banker; b. N.Y.C., Apr. 7, 1945; d. Carl Benjamin and Florence Siskind; B.A., Vassar Coll., 1966; M.S., Stevens Inst. Tech., 1969; m. Melvyn J. Feldman, Aug. 18, 1968; 1 son, Jonathan. Mem. tech. staff Bell Telephone Labs., Holmdel, N.J., 1966-69; with Morgan Guaranty Trust Co. N.Y., N.Y.C., 1969-84, , v.p. fin. analysis; v.p., head securities industry div. First Nat. Bank Chgo., 1984—. Pres. 353 W. 29th St. Housing Corp., 1982-84; mem. nat. devel. council Stevens Inst. Tech. Office: 153 W 51st St 8th Floor New York NY 10019

FELDMAN, MARCIA SUE, communications executive; b. N.Y.C., Dec. 1, 1940; d. Alexander Sigmund and Sylvia (Straus) Smith; m. Mark Burton Feldman, Nov. 23, 1963; children—Ilana Kay, Rachel Leigh. B.A., Harpur Coll., SUNY-Binghamton, 1961. Staff writer Textile Workers Union, N.Y.C., 1961-64; editor Where Mag., Washington, 1965-71; contbg. editor Washingtonian, Washington, 1974-78; writer, producer Eli Prodns., Washington, 1976-80; dir. pub. affairs PATCO, Washington, 1980-81; dir. communications U.S. Holocaust Mem. Council, Washington, 1982—; consumer reporter Sta.-WJLA-TV, Washington, 1976-77; cons. Older Women's League, Oakland, Calif., 1982, People for Am. Way, Washington, 1982. Mem. Washington Ind. Writers (bd. dirs. 1976-77, treas. 1977-78), Nat. Assn. Gov. Communicators (Gold Screen award 1983, Blue Pencil award 1984), Internat. Assn. Bus. Communicators, AFTRA. Democrat. Jewish. Avocation: sculpting. Office: US Holocaust Meml Council 2000 L St NW Washington DC 20036

FELDMAN, MIRIAM ELLIN, nursing home administrator, nurse; b. N.Y.C., Dec. 12, 1924; d. Charles and Ida (Novick) Ellin; m. Herbert Feldman, Mar. 23, 1958; children—Leslie Ellin, Peter Hilton, Madeleine Elyse. R.N., N.Y. State U., 1965; A.A.S., Queens Coll., 1965; B.S., SUNY, 1974. Asst. adminstr. Five Towns Nursing Home, Woodmere, N.Y., 1963-65; cons. nursing service, N.Y., 1967-73; adminstr., developer Cerebral Palsy Domiciliary Care Program, N.Y., 1973-79; adminstr. Woodmere Health Care Ctr., N.Y., 1979—. Producer ednl. video tapes Patient Abuse Series, 1979-81. Recipient Outstanding Service award United Cerebral Palsy Assn., 1981. Fellow Am. Coll. Health Care Adminstrs.; mem. Am. Nursing Assn., Assn. for Help of Retarded Children. Club: Hadassah. Office: 39 Burton Ave Woodmere NY 11598

FELDMAN, SHERYL SANDRA (DEDE), journalist; b. Dallas, Feb. 24, 1947; d. Samuel Feldman and Pauline (Schaffer) DeNur. B.A. in Social Work, U. Wis., 1968; postgrad. U. Tex.-Austin, 1972-73. Cert. tchr., Tex. News reporter Sta. KLRN-TV, Austin, 1973-74, Sta. KTRK-TV, Houston, 1974-75; news anchor Radio Sta. KIKK, Houston, 1975; news reporter/anchor Radio Sta. KTRH, Houston, 1975-80; news reporter Sta. KPRC-TV, Houston, 1980-83; freelance Journalist, Houston, 1984—; co-host/producer spl. program Sta. KHTV, Houston, 1977. Co-recipient Best Newscast merit award Tex. A.P., 1983, Outstanding News Reporting award Friendswood Civic Assn., Houston, 1979; Outstanding News Reporting award Breakthrough Mag., 1979. Mem. Am. Film Inst., Motion Picture Council of Houston. Jewish. Home: 2414 Inwood Dr Houston TX 77019

FELDMAN, SUSAN LOIS, printing sales executive; b. N.Y.C., Sept. 13, 1952; d. Murray and Myra (Meyer) Feldman. B.A. in French magna cum laude, U. Miami, 1973. Sr. sales exec. Information Systems Group Xerox Corp., Tarrytown, N.Y., 1973-77; sales exec. R.R. Donnelley & Sons Co., N.Y.C., 1977-80; account exec. Communicolor div. of Standard Register Co., N.Y.C., 1980—. Recipient Xerox Nat. Sales award, 1974; Xerox Par Club, 1975; Standard Register 100 Plus Club, 1983, 84. Mem. Women's Direct Response Group, Phi Kappa Phi (hon.). Advocations: tennis; jogging; ice Skating; reading. Home: 44 N Broaadway Apt 2KS White Plains NY 10603 Office: Communicolor 201 E 42nd St Suite 3010 New York NY 10017

FELDON, JOAN SORGE, marketing researcher; b. Evanston, Ill., July 18, 1932; d. Clarence Christopher and Jane (Back) Sorge; m. Richard A. Feldon, June 11, 1954; children—Jill Allison, Richard Alden, Reed Andrew. B.S., Northwestern U., 1954. Mktg. asst., project dir. Action Data, Inc., Cin., 1976-77, project dir. client services, 1977-80, v.p., 1980-82; pres. The Answer Group, Cin., 1982—. Vice-pres. Terrace Park Community Theatre, 1959—; mem. Cin. Music Theatre, 1960—; actor Playhouse in the Park, Cin., Edgecliff Theatre, Cin.; pres. Playhouse Prompters, Cin. Mem. Actors Equity, Am. Mktg. Assn. (sec. 1982-83, hospitality chmn. 1981-82). Republican. Episcopalian. Clubs: Internat. of Frankfort (Ger.) (bd. dirs.); Terrace Park Country (Ohio). Avocations: tennis; golf; community theatre. Home: 7280 Drake Rd Cincinnati OH 45243 Office: The Answer Group 11161 Kenwood Rd Cincinnati OH 45242

FELICIANO, GLORIA, human resources executive; b. N.Y.C., July 10, 1946; d. Armando and Carmen (Lespier) F. B.B.A., Bernard Baruch Coll., 1982. Legal sec. to adminstrv. asst. in personnel Richardson-Vicks, Westport, Conn., 1967-75; mgr. adminstrv. services Internat. Basic Economy Corp., N.Y.C., 1975-79; personnel dir. Toyomenka (America) Inc., N.Y.C., 1979-84; personnel dir. PolyGram Records, Inc., N.Y.C., 1985—. Mem. Am. Soc. Personnel Adminstrn., Am. Mgmt. Assn. Republican. Roman Catholic.

FELIX-RETZKE, JO ANN, association executive, consultant; b. Denver, Sept. 19, 1946; d. Marvin Carl and Lilliam May (Theisen) Jorgensen; m. Richard M. Felix, Jan. 29, 1966 (div. Sept. 1972); children—Tina Jo, Maria Ann, Trisha; m. 2d George R. Retzke, Mar. 12, 1982. Student in bus. Barnes Coll., Denver, 1962-64. Lic. real estate salesperson, Ill. Underwriter Equity Gen. Agts., Los Angeles, 1972-76; asst. v.p. Alexander & Alexander, Mpls., 1976-80; staff dir. ABA, Chgo., 1981—; cons. malpractice and mgmt.; instr. Ill. Inst. Tech. Kent Sch. Law, Chgo., 1983. Author: A Lawyer's Guide to Legal Malpractice Insurance 1982; (with D. N. Stern) A Practical Guide to Preventing Legal Malpractice, 1983; contbr. articles on legal malpractice to profl. jours. Mem. Nat. Assn. Realtors, Lake County Bd. Realtors, Ill. Assn. Realtors, Nat. Assn. Female Execs. Democrat. Roman Catholic. Home: 21384 W Lakeview Pkwy Countryside Lake Mundelein IL 60060 Office: ABA 750 N Lake Shore Dr Chicago IL 60611

FELLENBAUM, DEBRA ANN, journalist; b. Bridgeton, N.J., Feb. 19, 1957; d. Raymond Thomas Fellenbaum and Ellen Elizabeth (Fuller) Fellenbaum Rodgers. B.S., Clarion State Coll., 1979. Tchr., coach Harford County Bd. Edn., Bel Air, Md., 1979-81; office mgr., bookkeeper Ray's Flight Service, Picayune, Miss., 1981-82; community editor Picayune Item, 1982—. Publicity dir. Heart Fund, Picayune, 1984; bd. dirs. Picayune On Stage, 1984—. Recipient Outstanding Service award Picayune Jaycees, 1984, Miss. Jaycee Women Outstanding New Local Pres., 1985, U.S. Jaycees Outstanding New Local Pres., 1985, other Jaycee honors. Mem. Bus. and Profl. Women's Club, U.S. Jaycees Pres.'s Club. Republican. Home: 608 2d St Picayune MS 39466 Office: Picayune Item 214 Curran Ave Picayune MS 39466

FELLENSTEIN, CORA ELLEN MULLIKIN, credit union executive; b. Edwardsville, Ill., June 2, 1930; d. Russell K. and Elberta Mable (Rheude) M.; m. Charles Frederick Fellenstein, Feb. 24, 1951; children—Keith David, Kimberly Diane. Student Community Coll., 1980-83. Teller, loan officer, officer mgr. Credit Union of Johnson County, Mission, Kans., 1976-84, 1st v.p., supr. lending, collections and Mastercard depts., 1984—. Author: Moore Family History, 1987. Precinct committeewoman Johnson County Republicans, Olathe, Kans., 1976—. Mem. Internat. Consumer Credit Assn., Kans. Consumer Credit Assn., Credit Women Internat. (dir. 1983—), Assn. Bus. and Profl. Women, DAR (treas. 1976-86), Daus. Am. Colonists (treas. 1976-86), Beta Sigma Phi. Republican. Mem. Christian Ch. Club: Friends of Historic Mahaffie Farmstead (Olathe), Seroptimist. Avocations: genealogy; philately; numismatics. Home: 2000 Arrowhead Dr Olathe KS 66062 Office: Credit Union Johnson County 6025 Lamar St Mission KS 66202

FELLER, SHERYL JANET, management consultant; b. Winnipeg, Man., Can., Dec. 13, 1950; d. George Arthur and Olga (Andersen) Nichols; m. Barry Feller, June 22, 1974; children—Jamie George, Lindsay Janet. Diploma dental hygiene U. Man., 1970, B.A., 1974, M.B.A., 1981. Demonstrator, Sch. Dental Hygiene U. Man., Winnipeg, 1971-73, lectr., 1973-75, asst. prof., 1975-78, acting dir., 1976-78, asst. prof. Faculty Dentistry, 1981; pres., owner SJB Mgmt. Cons., Stonewall, Man., 1982—; dental hygiene clin. practice, Winnipeg, 1970-81. Bd. dirs. Stonewall Children's Ctr., 1982-85. Vol. Centre Winnipeg, 1983-86. Isbister scholar Govt. Man., 1968. Mem. Can. Dental Hygienists Assn. (chmn. long-range planning com. 1983—), Man. Dental Hygienists Assn, Mgmt. Cons. Assn. Man., Inst. Cert. Mgmt. Cons. of Man. (exec. council 1985—), Man. Soc. Tng. and Devel., Winnipeg Women's Network, U. Man. Alumni Assn. (bd. dirs. 1984—). Home: 17 Oak Park Dr Stonewall MB R0C 2Z0 Canada Office: SJB Mgmt Cons Box 1052 Stonewall MB R0C 2Z0 Canada

FELLERS, RHONDA G., lawyer; b. Gainesville, Tex., July 20, 1955; d. James Norman and Gaytha Ann (Sanders) Fellers; m. Bruce Curtis Hinton, Oct. 15, 1981 (div. 1985). B.A., U. Tex.-Austin, 1977, J.D., 1980; LL.M. in Taxation, U. Denver, 1985. Bar: Tex. 1981, Colo. 1981, U.S. Dist. Ct. (no. dist.) Tex. 1982, U.S. Dist. Ct. Colo. 1985, U.S. Tax Ct. 1985, U.S. Dist. Ct. (we. dist.) Tex. 1986, U.S. Ct. Appeals (5th cir.) 1986. Assoc. Walters & Assocs. P.C., Lubbock, Tex., 1981-83; gen. counsel, sr. v.p. Security Nat. Bank, Lubbock, Tex., 1983; atty., sole practice law Rhonda G. Fellers, Atty.-at-Law, Lubbock Tex., 1983—; assoc. Melvin Coffee and Assocs, P.C., Denver, 1984-85. Mem. State Bar Tex., Lubbock County Bar Assn., Colo. Bar Assn., ABA.

FELLIN, OCTAVIA ANTOINETTE, librarian; b. Santa Monica, Calif.; d. Otto P. and Librada (Montoya) F.; student U. N.Mex., 1937-39; B.A., U. Denver, 1941; B.L.S., Rosary Coll., 1942. Asst. librarian, instr. library sci. St. Mary-of-Woods Coll., Terre Haute, Ind., 1942-44; librarian U.S. Army, Burns Gen. Hosp., Santa Fe, 1944-46; post librarian Camp McQuaide, Calif., 1947; librarian Gallup (N.Mex.) Pub. Library, 1947—; free-lance writer mags., newspapers, 1950—; dir. Nat. Library Week N.Mex., 1959. Vice pres., publicity dir. Gallup Community Concerts Assn., 1957-72, 75—; organizer Gt. Decision Discussion groups, 1963—; mem. Gallup St. Naming Com., 1958-59, Aging Com., 1964-68; chmn. Gallup Mus. Indian Arts and Crafts, 1964-78; mem. publicity com. Gallup Inter-Tribal Indian Ceremonial Assn. 1966-68; mem. N.Mex. Gov.'s Com. 100 on Aging, 1967-70; chmn. Sr. Citizens Adv. Com., 1970-72; del. N.Mex. Am. Revolution Bicentennial Commn., 1972; mem. N.Mex. Library Adv. Council, 1971-75; mem. nat. adv. council U.S. Cath. Bishops' Adv. Council, 1970-75; organizing chmn. McKinley County Hosp. Aux., 1968, editor newsletter, 1972-75, pres., 1983; chmn. Trick or Treat for UNICEF, 1971-79; corr. sec. Latin Am. Mission program, 1973-75; pledge chmn. Rancho del Nino San Huberto Home Children, Empalme, Mexico, 1973-76; mem. bicentennial steering com. Diocese of Gallup, also chmn. hist. com., 1975-76, corr. sec. liturgical commn., 1978-85; bd. dirs. Gallup Area Arts Council, 1974-78, 85—; mem. speakers bur. commn., 1978—; Bicentennial Com., 1976; mem. N.Mex. Humanities Council, 1979; publicity chmn. Gallup Opera Guild, 1977-79; pres. library div. N.Mex. Mcpl. League, 1979; mem. Cathedral Parish Council, 1980-83. Recipient Dorothy Canfield Fisher $1,000 Library award, 1961; Outstanding Community Service awards for mus. service Gallup C. of C., also Outstanding Community Service plaque, 1969, Outstanding Citizen award, 1973, Papal medal Benemerentl, 1977, Celebrate Literacy award Internat. Reading Assn., 1983-84; chmn. Harrison House Artists Coop., 1985—; co-chmn. scholarship com. Rehoboth McKinley County Christian Hosp., 1984—. Mem. ALA, N.Mex. Library Assn. (v.p., sec., chmn. hist. materials com. 1964-66, salary and tenure com., nat. coordinator N.Mex. legis. com., com. on pub. library standards 1965—, chmn. com. to extend library services 1969-72, chmn. local and regional hist. roundtable 1980; Librarian of Year award 1975), AAUW (v.p., co-organizer Gallup br., pub. relations dir. 1967-75, nominating com. 1968, br. chmn. com. on women, fellowship and scholarship chmn. 1973-78), Internat. Reading Assn., Plateau Scis. Soc., N.Mex. Folklore Soc. (v.p. 1964-65, pres. 1965-66), N.Mex. Hist. Soc. (dir.), Gallup Film Soc. (co-organizer, v.p. 1950-58), LWV (v.p. 1953-56), Gallup C. of C. (organizing chmn. women's div. 1972), NAACP, Audubon Soc., Alpha Delta Kappa (hon.). Roman Catholic (Cathedral Guild, Confrat. Christian Doctrine Bd. 1962-64, sec.-treas. diocese Gallup pastoral council 1972-74, Cursillo movement). Author booklet. Home: 513 E Mesa Ave Gallup NM 87301 Office: 115 W Hill St Gallup NM 87301

FELTON, ANN SHIREY, educator; b. Balt., Sept. 14, 1941; d. Herbert and Lucinda (Bright) Gardner; m. Maceo N. Felton, June 10, 1967; children—Joy T., Travis A. A.B., Morgan State Coll., 1963; M.S.W., Howard U., 1968. Social worker Onondaga County Health Dept., Syracuse, N.Y., 1968-70; acad. and vocat. advisor, social work supr. Coop. Coll. Ctr., SUNY, 1970-72; assoc. prof. human services dept. Onondaga Community Coll., 1975—. Contbr. articles to profl. jours. Vice pres. Benjamin Banneker Democratic Club, 1980—; bd. dirs. Consortium for Children's Services. Mem. NAACP, N.Y. Assn. Human Services, Assn. Black Social Workers, Assn. Black Women in Higher Edn., Alpha Kappa Alpha, others. Episcopalian. Office: Onondaga Community Coll Syracuse NY 13215

FELTON, BARBARA JANE, personnel executive; b. Dayton, Ohio, Nov. 11, 1954; d. Myron Heber and Helen Jean (Foster) Felton. B.A. in Sociology, Hanover Coll., 1977; M.S. Personnel and Counseling, Miami U. Ohio, 1979. Personnel mgr. Henny Penny Corp., Eaton, Ohio, 1979—. Mem. Preble County Personnel Assn. (pres.), Am. Soc. Personnel Adminstrn., Internat. Assn. Quality Circles. Republican. Methodist. Home: 180 S 45th St Richmond IN 47374

FELTON, JUDITH R., psychoanalyst, social worker; b. Phila., Aug. 21, 1942; d. Martin and Laura (Goldman) Kirshenbaum; A.B. in Govt., Wheaton (Mass.) Coll., 1963; M.S.W., Rutgers U., 1966, Ph.D., Rutgers U. Grad. Sch. Arts and Scis., 1983; grad. N.Y. Center for Psychoanalytic Tng., 1978; m. Stephen Felton, Feb. 8, 1966; 1 dau., Jane Jennifer. Clin. social worker VA, Newark, 1967; psychotherapist Santa Barbara (Calif.) Mental Health Services, 1967-69; supr. Santa Barbara Counselling Center, 1967-69; pvt. practice psychoanalysis, 1969—; psychoanalyst, therapist Fifth Ave. Center for Psychotherapy, N.Y.C., 1969-72; instr. Marymount Manhattan Coll., 1971; psychotherapy supr. clin. faculty, dept. psychiatry Rutgers U. Med. Sch., New Brunswick, N.J., 1972-75, teaching asst. Grad. Sch. Social Work, 1974-76; vis. lectr. Bryn Mawr Coll. Sch. Social Work and Social Research, 1980; mem. faculty N.Y. Center for Psychoanalytic Tng., 1980—, N.J. Inst. Psychoanalysis and Psychotherapy, 1982—. Bd. dirs. N.Y. Ctr. for Psychoanalytic Tng. and Inst. for Psychoanalysis and Psychotherapy N.J., 1986—. NIMH fellow, 1965; diplomate Am. Bd. Psychotherapy. Fellow N.J. Soc. for Clin. Social Work; mem. Nat. Assn. Social Workers, Conf. Psychoanalytic Psychotherapists, Nat. Assn. for Advancement Psychoanalysis, Groves Conf. on Family, Acad. Cert. Social Workers, Soc. for Psychoanalytic Tng. (bd. dirs. 1983—, dir. social sci. program 1983—), N.J. Inst. Psychoanalysis and Psychotherapy, AAUP, Am. Psychol. Assn. Mem. editorial bd. jour. Current Issues in Psychoanalytic Practice, 1983—; contbr. articles to profl. jours. Home and office: 159 Valley Rd Princeton NJ 08540

FELTON-COLLINS, VICTORIA C., financial psychologist; b. Quincy, Mass., Nov. 2, 1942; d. Stanley Winchester and Ellen Victoria (Peterson) Call; m. Robert W. Felton, June 30, 1962; children—Kimberly Felton, Todd Felton; m. David Paul Collins, Nov. 16, 1985; children—Jennifer, David, Nicole. B.A. with honors, San Diego State U., 1964; M.A., St. Mary's Coll., Calif., 1976; Ph.D., U. Calif.-Berkeley, 1981; C.F.P., Coll. Fin. Planning, Denver, 1986. Lectr. St. Mary's Coll., Moraga, Calif., 1977-82; ptnr. Capital Options, Lafayette, Calif., 1982-83. FM Assocs., Lafayette, 1983—, AIS Fin. Services, Oakland, Calif., 1986—. Co-author: Piagetion Theory, 1976; Problem Solving, 1978; (newspaper column) Monclarion Newspaper, 1984; contbr. articles to profl. jours. Bd. regents John F. Kennedy U., Orinda, Calif., 1984—, exec. com., 1986. Mem. Internat. Assn. Fin. Planners (pub. relations chair 1984, v.p. membership 1985—), Inst. Cert. Fin. Planners, AAUW (v.p. programs 1982-83, pres. 1983-84, Disting. Woman 1976, fellow 1981), Nat. Speakers Assn., Nat. Assn. Female Execs. Republican. Presbyterian. Avocations: skiing; travelling. Home: 634 Glorietta Blvd Lafayette CA 94549 Office: AIS Fin Services 300 Lakeside Dr Suite 1300 Oakland CA 94612

FEMAT, JUDITH ESTHER, wholesale distributor; b. Mission, Tex., Aug. 12, 1927; d. Tiburcio and Francisca (Perez) F. Student in Bus., McAllen Coll., 1948. Ptnr. Femat T & Co., Mission, Tex., 1950—. Bd. dirs. Mission Citrius Fiesta; pres. Las Damas Catolicas, Mission; dir. adult probation bd. Restitution Ctr., Edinburg, Tex.; mem. Mission Sesquicentennial, 1986; mem. senate Our Lady Guadalupe Cath. Ch. Mem. Mission C. of C. (bd. dirs.). Democrat. Avocation: bowling. Home: PO Box 1004 Mission TX 78572 Office: T Femat & Co 114 E Leo Najo St Mission TX 78572

FEND, EILEEN, personnel service owner; b. Salt Lake City, Oct. 29, 1927; d. Mark and Louise (Irvine) Warburton; m. Jack Hartman, Oct. 28, 1958 (dec. 1968); children—Pamela Greene, Teri Gervais, Mark Hartman; m. Helmut Fend, June 21, 1975. Student, Utah State U., 1945-49, U. So. Calif., 1985. Purchasing agt. Futurecraft Corp., City of Industry, Calif., 1959-64; dir. Vivian Woodard, Panorama City, Calif., 1964-75; pres., owner On Call Personnel, Manhattan Beach, Calif., 1977—; chmn. bd. dirs. Hour Gang Personnel, Orange County, Calif., 1982—; cons. and lectr. in field. Coordinator, Duologue Vendor Com.; mem. roundtable Calif. State U., Dominguez Hills South Bay Bus. Roundtable; scholarship bd. Bank of Am., Redondo Beach, El Segundo Rotary Club. Mem. Internat. Assn. Personnel Women (hostess nat. mid-winter bd. meetings), Personnel and Indsl. Relations Assn., Bus. Mgmt. Assn., Women in Mgmt., C. of C. (Calif.), Nat. Assn. Women Bus. Owners (pub. affairs com.), Calif. Assn. Personnel Consultants (temprary services sect.), South Bay Mktg. Network. Club: Leads. Avocations: skiing. Office: On Call Personnel 505 N Sepulveda Manhattan Beach CA 90277

FENG, LILLIAN WAN-MING LEI, nurse, nursing home adminstr.; b. Canton, China, May 5, 1923; came to U.S., 1968, naturalized, 1973; d. Chin Chang and Sui Ching (Chen) Lei; R.N., Turner Sch. Nursing, Canton, China, 1946; B.S. in Health Care Adminstrn., Central Mich. U., 1976, M.A., 1979; m. Ping Tien Feng, June 3, 1950; children—Paul, Lucy, May, Howard. Asst. head nurse, nursing instr. Turner Nursing Sch. of Hacket Hosp., Canton, China, 1946-47; head nurse, instr. Hoihow (China) Am. Presbyn. Hosp. and Nursing Sch., 1947-50; instr. Tb nursing, head nurse Taiwan Tb Control Center, 1950-56, supr., 1956-66; clin. head nurse U.S. Naval Med. Research Unit No. 2, Taiwan, China, 1966-67; asst. adminstr. Palolo Chinese Care Home, Honolulu, 1968—. U.S.A. Internat. Corp. Adminstrn. grantee, 1958. Mem. Hawaii Nurses Assn., Am. Nurses Assn., Nat. League for Nursing, Hawaii Pacific Gerontol. Soc., Am. Gerontol. Soc., Acupuncture Sci. Research Found. Hawaii, Am. Health Care Assn., Central Mich. U. Alumni Assn., Hawaii Long Term Care Assn. Address: 2459 10th Ave Honolulu HI 96816

FENGLER, SARAH VAN CORTLANDT (BANKS), educational administrator, consultant; b. Balt., May 10, 1942; d. William Bradford and Sarah Parker (Koppelman) Banks; m. Richard Neel Sutton, July 27, 1963 (div. Nov. 1979); children—Richard Banks Sutton, William Banks Sutton; m. Alf Jurgen Fengler, Aug. 20, 1980. B.A., Wellesley Coll., 1964; M.A., Bryn Mawr Coll., 1966. Systems engr. IBM, Detroit, 1966-69, mktg. rep., Kansas City, Mo., 1969-70; ednl. cons., pres. ICA, Woodbury, Conn., 1979-82; computer coordinator Westover Sch., Middlebury, Conn., 1980-83, dir. devel., 1983—; cons. John Brown Ltd., Peterborough, N.H., 1985—. Mem. Mayor's Commn. on Status of Women, Wichita Falls, Tex., 1976-79; mem. Commn. on Info. Systems, Wichita Falls, 1978-79; treas. Jr. League of Wichita Falls, 1978-79; chmn. pub. relations Com. for Rebldg. Wichita Falls, 1979. Mem. Council for Advancement and Support of Edn. Republican. Episcopalian. Avocations: piano; singing; racquetball; tennis; skiing. Home: 80 Park Rd Woodbury CT 06798 Office: Westover Sch Whittemore Rd Middlebury CT 06762

FENNELL, SISTER MARYLOUISE, college president. Pres. Carlow Coll., Pitts. Office: Carlow Coll 3333 Fifth Ave Pittsburgh PA 15213*

FENNELL, TERRESA ANN, counselor, consultant; b. Norfolk, Va., Feb. 18, 1955; d. Robert Wallace and Patricia Louise (Riley) F.; m. Duncan Marshall, Nov. 11, 1978 (div.). B.A. in Spanish, Erskine Coll., 1976; M.A. in Counseling Psychology, U. Pacific, 1982. Registered marriage, family, child counselor intern, Calif. Counselor Valley Community Counseling Services, Stockton, Calif., 1981—; exec. dir. Parents Anonymous Ala., Inc., 1985—. Active San Joaquin County Sexual Abuse Treatment Providers. Mem. Assn. Measurement and Evaluation in Guidance, Am. Mental Health Counselors Assn., Am. Personnel and Guidance Assn., Nat. Vocat. Guidance Assn., Assn. Religious and Value Issues in Counseling, Assn. Specialists in Group Work. Democrat. Presbyterian. Home: 904 Isabel Ave Anniston AL 36201 Office: PO Box 2638 Anniston AL 36202

FENNELL, VALERIE INA, anthropologist, educator; b. Horry County, S.C., June 12, 1942; d. Ina Mozelle (Causey). B.A., U. N.C.-Greensboro, 1967; Ph.D., U. N.C.-Chapel Hill, 1974. Instr. anthropology Appalachian State U., Boone, N.C., 1971-72; asst. prof. Ga. State U., Atlanta, 1974-78, assoc. prof., 1979—. Contbr. chapt. to Dimensions: Aging, Culture and Health, 1981. Bd. dirs. Atlanta Ctr. for Feminist Studies, 1984-85. Fellow Am. Anthrop. Assn.; mem. So. Anthrop. Soc. (sec.-treas. 1975-79), Assn. for Anthropology and Gerontology, NOW, Gray Panthers. Democrat. Mem. Universalist Unitarian. Avocations: gardening; animal watching; music; mime; drama. Office: Ga State U Dept Anthropology University Plaza Atlanta GA 30303

FENNELL ROBBINS, SALLY, free-lance writer, promotional consultant; b. Greensburg, Pa., Feb. 17, 1950; d. Clifford Seanor and Charlotte Louise (Hoffman) Fennell; B.S. in Journalism, Ohio U., 1972 cum laude; M.A. in Journalism, magna cum laude, Marshall U., 1974; cert. in writing for TV Ctr. Media Arts, 1986. Intern, reporter Tribune-Rev., Greensburg, Pa., 1972; prodn. asst. Harper's Bazaar, N.Y.C., 1972; reporter UPI, Birmingham, Ala., 1972-73; reporter, dept. editor HFD-Retailing Home Furnishings, Fairchild Pubs., N.Y.C., 1975-77; account exec. supr., client service mgr., v.p. Burson-Marsteller, N.Y.C., 1977-83; group mgr., v.p. pub. relations div. Ketchum Communications, 1983-84; grad. teaching asst. Sch. Journalism/Reporting, Marshall U., Huntington, W.Va., 1973-74. Recipient Lasher award Ohio U. Sch. Journalism, 1972. Mem. Soc. Profl. Journalists/Sigma Delta Chi, Am. Mgmt. Assn., Assn. Edn. in Journalism and Mass Communication, Pub. Relations Soc. Am. Home and Office: 237 East 20th St New York NY 10003

FENSTERMACHER, ANNE S., consumer relations executive; b. Rochester, N.Y., Oct. 22, 1942; d. Walter Alfred and Dorothy (Shaw) F. B.S., U. Wis., 1964; M.S., Cornell U., 1972; M.B.A., U. Rochester, 1983. Home service rep. Rochester Gas and Electric Corp. (N.Y.), 1966-70, staff asst. consumer affairs, 1972-79, dir. consumer affairs, 1979-81, mgr. consumer relations, 1981—; bd. dirs. Better Bus. Bur., Rochester, 1976—; consumer affairs com. Edison Electric Inst., Washington, 1975—. Pub. affairs chmn., bd. dirs. Jr. League Rochester, 1979-80. Office: Rochester Gas and Electric Corp 89 East Ave Rochester NY 14649

FENSTERSTOCK, JOYCE NARINS, investment banker; b. N.Y.C., Dec. 30, 1948; d. Charles S. and Frances D. (Kross) Narins; m. Blair C. Fensterstock, Sept. 16, 1979; children—Michael Bayard, Evan Steele. B.A., Wellesley Coll., 1970; M.B.A., Harvard U., 1973. Assoc. Goldman, Sachs & Co., N.Y.C., 1973-74, 75-78, Warburg Paribas Becker, Chgo., 1974-75; v.p. Paine Webber Inc., N.Y.C., 1978-83, sr. v.p., 1983—, exec. asst. to chmn., 1985—. Mem. Fin. Womens Assn. Club: Harvard (N.Y.C.). Office: Paine Webber Group Inc 1285 Ave of Americas New York NY 10019

FENWICK, MILLICENT HAMMOND, ambassador, former congresswoman; b. N.Y.C., Feb. 25, 1910; d. Ogden Haggerty and Mary Picton (Stevens) Hammond; student Foxcroft Sch., Columbia Extension Sch., New Sch. for Social Research; L.L.D. (hon.) Princeton U.; div.; children—Mary Fenwick Reckford, Hugh. Assoc. editor Conde Nast Publs., N.Y., 1938-52; mem. N.J. Gen. Assembly, 1970-73; dir. div. consumer affairs N.J. Dept. Law and Pub. Safety, 1973-74; mem. 94th-97th Congresses from 5th N.J. Dist.; U.S. del. UN FAO, 1983—. Vice chmn. N.J. adv. com. to U.S. Commn. on Civil Rights, 1958-72. Mem. Bd. Edn., Bernardsville, N.J., 1938-41; mem. Borough Council, 1958-64. Republican. Author: Vogue's Book of Etiquette, 1948; Speaking Up, 1982. Office: US Mission to United Nations for Food and Agrl Am Embassy Rome APO NY 09794-0007

FERDMAN, JOANNE, computer room supplies and furniture company executive; b. N.Y.C., Sept. 19, 1928; d. John and Ella (Gotterer) Deneau; m. Saul Ferdman, Sept. 19, 1948; children—Deborah, Susan, Sandra, Richard. B.A. in Psychology, Queens Coll., 1948, postgrad., 1971-74. Ter. mgr. Royal Bus. Machines, West Hempstead, N.Y., 1978-79; owner Bus. Accessories, Bethpage, N.Y., 1980—. Mem. Assn. Commerce and Industry, Ctr. for Bus. and Profl. Women. Home: 116 Whitewood Dr Massapequa Park NY 11762 Office: Business Accessories 4020 Hempstead Turnpike Bethpage NY 11714

FERDON, NONA STINSON, clinical psychologist, educator; b. Homerville, Ga., Jan. 19, 1938; d. Haskell and Ilda Marie (Stinson) F.; B.A., U. Ga., 1958; D.O., U. Innsbruck (Austria), 1950; postgrad. U. Calif.-Berkeley, 1964-65; Ph.D., U. Hawaii, Honolulu, 1971; m. Sheldon A. Davis, June 7, 1980; children—Steven, Sharon. Fgn. student guidance specialist Fulbright orientation, Honolulu, 1961-63; successively research asst. ednl. psychology, asst. dir. New Coll., asst. dir. Man in Soc. Program, instr. U. Hawaii, Honolulu, 1964-71; lectr. in psychology Clark U., 1971-72; asst. prof. U. Mass., 1972-73, Northeastern U., 1973-74; corp. psychologist Digital Equipment Corp., Maynard, Mass., 1973-81; founder, dir. Boston Psychol. Center for Women, 1974-82; prof. psychology Webster U., Geneva, 1982—; cons. multinat. industry. Bd. dirs. Samaritans of Boston. NIMH grantee, 1967-69; Univ. Research Council grantee, 1968-69. Mem. Am. Psychol. Assn., Mass. Psychol. Assn., Soc. Psychol. Study of Social Issues, Assn. Women in Psychology, Internat. Council Psychologists, Internat. Acad. Profl. Counseling and Psychotherapy, Psi Chi. Author: The Psychological Origins of a Public Life, in progress; contbr. articles to profl. jours. Home: 31 Rue Vautier Carouge 1229 Switzerland

FERENCE, PATRICIA SUSAN, nurse; b. N.Y.C., Nov. 19, 1950; d. Edward Joseph Ference and Ann Carol (Fox) Gray; R.N., Misericordia Hosp. Sch. Nursing, Bronx, N.Y., 1974. Nurse, Montefiore Hosp., Bronx, 1974-77, N. Shore Univ. Hosp., Manhasset, N.Y., 1977—. Mem. N.Y. State, Am. nurses' assns. Home and Office: 219-46 93d Ave Queens Village NY 11428

FERENS, MARCELLA (MRS. JOSEPH J. FERENS), educator, business woman; b. Pitts.; d. Ignatius and Marcella (Buzas) Slevinskas; student Greensburg Bus. Coll., 1934-35, Maison Frederic Cosmetology, 1936, Kree Inst. Electrolysis, N.Y., 1952; B.S., U. Pitts., 1957; postgrad. Mid-Western U., 1962; M.Ed., Duquesne U., 1964; m. Joseph J. Ferens, Nov. 27, 1937; children—Joseph Ferens, James. Cosmetologist and electrologist, Manor and Darragh, Pa., 1937—; research in hair regrowth, Darragh, 1954—; tchr. cosmetology Uniontown (Pa.) Vocat. High, 1954-55; tchr. algebra, reading and drama dir. Harold Jr. High Sch., Greensburg, Pa., 1958—; pres. Marcella Ferens Inc.; treas. Schumacher Labs. Inc., Darragh. Insp., Chem. Corps, Dept. Army, N.Y., 1951. Mem. Nat. Council Tchrs. Math., Nat., Pa. edn. assns. Patentee in field. Home: Box 84 Daragh PA 15625

FERGUS, PATRICIA MARGUERITA, educator emeritus, writer, editor; b. Mpls., Oct. 26, 1918; d. Golden Maughan and Mary Adella (Smith) F.; B.S., U. Minn., 1939, M.A., 1941, Ph.D., 1960. Various personnel and editing positions with U.S. Govt., 1943-59; mem. faculty U. Minn., 1964-79, asst. prof. English, 1972-79, coordinator writing program conf. on writing, 1975, dir. writing centre, 1975-77; prof. English and writing, dir. writing ctr., assoc. dean Coll., Mt. St. Mary's Coll., Emmitsburg, Md., 1979-81; dir. writing seminars Mack Truck, Inc., Hagerstown, Md., 1979-81; writer, 1964—; editorial asst. to pres. Met. State U., St. Paul, 1984-85; cons. in field; dir. 510 Groveland Assocs.; bus. mgr. Eitel Hosp. Gift Shop; mem. St. Olaf Ch. Choir, St. Olaf Parish Adv. Bd. Recipient Outstanding Contbn. award U. Minn. Twin Cities Student Assembly, 1975; Horace T. Morse-Amoco Found. award, 1976; Ednl. Devel. grantee U. Minn., 1975-76; Mt. St. Mary's Coll. grantee, 1980; 3d prize vocal-choral category Nat. Music Composition Contest, Nat. League Am. Pen Women, 1986. Mem. Internat. Biog. Centre Assn., Am. Biog. Research Assn., AAUW, Nat. (regional judge writing awards program 1974, 76-77, state coordinator 1977-79) Minn. (chmn. career and job opportunities com., mem. spl. com. on tchr. licensure, sec. legis. com.) councils tchrs. English, Nat. League Am. Pen Women (pres. Minn. br.), Internat. Acad. Poets, Mpls. Poetry Soc. (pres.; 1st prize Haiku contest 1984, 3d prize poetry contest 1986), League Minn. Poets, Midwest Fedn. Chaparral Poets, AAUP, Pi Lambda Theta (v.p. Epsilon chpt.). Roman Catholic. Author: Spelling Improvement, 4th edit., 1983; contbr. to Minn. English Jour., Downtown Cath. Voice, Mpls., Mountaineer Briefing; contbr. poems Minn. English Jour., Mpls. Muse, The Moccasin, Heartsong and Northstar Gold. Home and Office: 510 Groveland Ave Minneapolis MN 55403

FERGUSON, BARBARA ELIZABETH, manufacturing company executive; b. Memphis, July 6, 1942; d. Robert Alexander and Mary Ovaleen (Spencer) Ferguson. M.B.A., Pepperdine U., 1973; postgrad. Claremont U., 1983—. Mfg. foreman Burroughs Corp., Westlake, Calif., 1967-73; materials mgr. Bennett Corp., Los Angeles, 1974-79; plant mgr. Rainbird Corp., Glendora, Calif., 1979-81; v.p., gen. mgr. Myers Electric Products Inc., Montebello, Calif., 1981—. Lt. col. CAP, 1979—. Named Outstanding officer Calif. State CAP, 1975. Mem. Nat. Elec. Mfrs. Assn., Nat. Assn. Exec. Women. Republican. Office: Myers Electric Products Inc 1130 S Vail Ave Montebello CA 90640

FERGUSON, CHARLOTTE BRAINARD, wholesale lumber executive; b. Chicopee, Mass., June 18, 1929; d. Charles Duncan and Gladys (Hamilton) Brainard; B.A., Ohio Wesleyan U., 1950; M.Ed., Boston U., 1956; m. Albert D. Wood, 1957 (div. 1972); children—Jeffrey D., Maribeth L., Jennifer H.; m. Robert Bruce Ferguson, Dec. 28, 1973 (dec. 1983). Traffic mgr. sta. WHDH, Boston, 1951-52; sec. Harold Cabot Advt. Agy., Boston, 1953; copywriter Gabriel Stern Advt. Agy., Boston, 1954-55; tchr. Weston (Mass.) Elem. Sch., 1956-57; dir. Village Sch., Boxford, Mass., 1967-72; tchr. Tuftonboro (N.H.) Central Sch., Gov. Wentworth Regional Sch. Dist., 1973-80; v.p. Wood Dimensions Inc., Tuftonboro, 1980-83, pres., 1983—. Friend Tuftonboro Library; mem. Huggins Hosp. Fair Com., 1984, West Point Fund Com. U.S. Mil. Acad. Mem. Pi Lambda Theta, Alpha Delta Pi, Alpha Epsilon Rho. Republican. Congregationalist. Club: Lakes Region Women's Republican (v.p. 1985-86). Address: RFD 1 Box 144 Tuftonboro Corner Ossipee NH 03864

FERGUSON, ELIZABETH ADELE, dance educator, choreographer; b. Dallas, June 10, 1928; d. Fred Dillahunty and Nel Jennings (Ryan) Stewart; B.B.A., North Tex. State U., 1949; M.F.A. in Dance, Southern Meth. U., 1967; m. Joe Durwood, Mar. 31, 1950; children—Susan Adele, Joann Elizabeth. With So. Meth. U., Meadows Sch. of Arts, Dallas, 1968—, dir. Dance Preparatory, 1969-78, asst. prof., 1972, assoc. prof., 1979, acting dir. Grad. Dance Program, 1979-81, dir. Grad. Dance Program, 1981, interim chmn. dance div., 1982-84, assoc. chmn. dance, 1984—; lectr.; choreographer Dallas Jr. League Ball Shows, 1971—. Bd. dirs. Faculty Women's Research Group, 1982, Dallas Dance Council, 1980—; mem. Arts Magnet Adv. Bd.; mem. dance cert. com. Commn. Standards for Dance Edn., Tex. Edn. Agy., 1982. Recipient Outstanding Prof. award So. Meth. U., 1977. Mem. Nat. Assn. Schs. Dance, Council Dance Adminstrs., AAUP, Am. Dance Guild, Dance History Scholars, Congress on Research in Dance, Dallas Dance Council. Episcopalian. Club: Southern Methodist University Faculty (dir.). Home: 11628 Colmar St Dallas TX 75218 Office: Meadows Sch Arts Dance Div Dallas TX 75275

FERGUSON, ELIZABETH RANDALL, accounting, tax service company executive; b. Montevallo, Ala., Mar. 8, 1939; d. Jess Whitlock and Louise Elizabeth (Reynolds) Mills.; m. Russell Lee Withers, Dec. 16, 1967 (div. 1974); children—Roanne, Tyrrell; m. 2d, Marvin D. Ferguson, Nov. 16, 1975; children—Kim, Kris, Kacy. Student Valley Coll., San Bernardino, Calif., 1963-68. Office worker Garner, Tee, Tracadas & Troy, San Bernardino, 1963-67; asst. bookkeeper Hansen Plumbing Co., San Bernardino, 1967-68; adminstrv. asst. Operative Plasterers' Union, Riverside, Calif., 1968-74; acct., property mgr. Seaside Mgmt. Corp., Encinitas, Calif., and office mgr. Bob Landers Comml. Announcer, La Costa, Calif., 1974-78; owner, pres. Mother Lode Bookkeeping Inc., Encinitas, 1980—; fin. adv. Desert Mag., 1981—, Seacoast Mag., 1981—, Encinitas; editor Women in Constrn., (nat. 2nd place award), 1965. Mcht. Monitor, 1983. Bd. dirs., v.p. Community Festival Guild, Encinitas, 1979-83; treas. Community Resource Ctr., Encinitas 1982-83. Named Citizen of Yr., Leucadia-Encintas Town Council, 1983; recipient Lizzie award, Community Festival Guild Inc., 1982. Mem. Nat. Soc. Pub. Accts., Downtown Mchts. Assn. (communications chmn.), Encinitas C. of C. (dir. 1983). Democrat. Mem. Sci. Mind. Office: Mother Lode Bookkeeping Inc 788 2d St Encinitas CA 92024

FERGUSON, ELIZABETH SHANLEY, publisher; b. St. Louis, June 11, 1925; d. Connor Bernard and Marie (Maull) Shanley; m. Thomas Bruce Ferguson, Jan. 31, 1948; children—Linda Ferguson Benoist, Thomas Bruce Jr., Scott Shanley. A.B., Duke U., 1947. Pub., St. Louis Mag. Bd. dirs. Goodwill Industry, St. Louis, 1983—, Centerre Bank, 1984—. Mem. Vis. Nurse Assn. (bd. dirs. 1983—), City Regional Mag. Assn. (bd. dirs. 1978-81). Republican. Episcopalian. Avocations: tennis; golf. Home: 14 Hacienda Saint Louis MO 63124 Office: Saint Louis Mag 7110 Oakland St Saint Louis MO 63117

FERGUSON, JENNY LAURA, fitness company executive, retailer, real estate broker; b. Dallas, June 25, 1948; d. Hugh William Ferguson and Ruth Virginia (Perdue) Drewery. B.A., U. Tex., 1970. Sales rep., mgr. Adair Realty, Atlanta, 1970-72; broker Donald Kerr & Assocs., Dallas, 1972-74; pres. J.F. Dancewear, Inc., Dallas, 1983—, also pres. JFE, Inc., Dallas, 1979—; dir. Equitable Bank, Dallas. Bd. dirs. Susan G. Komen Found., 1983-84; assoc. Dallas Mus. Art, 1982-84. Mem. Jr. League Dallas, Phi Beta Kappa. Republican. Presbyterian. Home: 4102 1/2 Lovers Ln Dallas TX 75225 Office: Jenny Ferguson Exercise Inc 4616 Travis St Dallas TX 75205

FERGUSON, JOLENE EVA, psychologist, educator; b. Lawton, Okla., Dec. 15, 1950; d. Cleetis Wilson and Violet Normadeen (Hughey) Howell; m. Stephen Edward Ferguson, July 16, 1970 (div. Dec. 1981); 1 child, Amber Nicole, B.S., Cameron U., 1973; M.Ed., U. Okla., 1980. Cert. tchr., Okla. Tchr. bus. Apache High Sch., Okla., 1973-81; dir. pre-sch. camp YMCA, Lawton, 1974; psychologist Taliaferro Mental Health Ctr., Lawton, 1981-85, Okla. Youth Ctr., Norman, 1985-86, team leader, psychologist, 1986—; bd. dirs. Fairhaven Girls Home, Lawton, 1983, 84, pres., 1985, cons., 1986; mem. description com. Okla. State Dept. Edn., 1975, other coms., 1978-80; speaker in field; pres. Apache Edn. Assn., 1979-80, chief negotiator, 1979. Co-author, editor: Mommy, What Should I Do? 1984. Sexual abuse speaker Youth Advocacy Council, Lawton, Walters, Apache, Okla., 1983-84. Mem. Am. Bus. Women's Assn. (chmn. com. 1985), Youth Advocacy Council (sec. 1983-84), Nat. Assn. Female Execs., Okla. Masters Psychol. Assn., Okla. Pub. Employees Assn., NOW (pres. S.W. Okla. chpt. 1983-84). Democrat. Avocations: snow skiing; tennis; ballet; stained glass. Home: 1915 Oakhurst Norman OK 73071 Office: Okla Youth Ctr 1120 E Main PO Box 1008 Norman OK 73070

FERGUSON, SANDRA MAREA, educational consultant; b. N.Y.C., Dec. 18, 1946; d. Edward Augustus and Oletha Gertrude (Higgs) F. B.S.Ed., St. John's U., 1968; M.S. Ed., Fordham U., 1977. Primary tchr. Bd. Edn. N.Y.C., 1967-69; adult educator Manpower Inc., N.Y.C., 1969-70; reading instr. Youth Devel., Inc., N.Y.C., 1970-71; ednl. cons. Scott Foresman & Co., Oakland, N.J., 1971—. Mem. Internat. Reading Assn., Nat. Council Tchrs. English, N.Y. State Reading Assn., Nat. Geog. Soc., Delta Sigma Theta. Democrat. Roman Catholic. Clubs: N.Y. Bot. Gardens, Camera. Home: 700 Columbus Ave New York NY 10025 Office: Scott Foresman & Co 99 Bauer Dr Oakland NJ 07436

FERGUSON, SHANNON, accountant; b. Chattanooga, Tenn., June 26, 1945; d. William Fleming and Grace Gwendolyn (Marshall) Cargo; student Mount San Antonio Coll., 1963-64; student UCLA, 1966; m. William Clark Ferguson III, Dec. 30, 1967; children—William Jeffrey, Jill. Jr. acct. United Geophys. Corp., Pasadena, Calif., 1964-67; controller, chief fin. officer, corp. sec. Presto-Tek Corp., Los Angeles, 1979-81; corp. sec., chief fin. officer Accessory Supply, Arcadia, Calif., 1981—, also dir. Asst. treas. Holiday Homes Tour, 1981, safety chmn., 1980; chmn. 20th Anniversary Ball Meth. Hosp., 1977; bd. dirs. Arcadia Tournament of Roses, 1985—; mem. U.S. Bus. Adv. Bd., Washington, Republican Presdl. Task Force, Arcadia aux. Meth. Hosp.; sustaining mem. Rep. Nat. Com., Calif. Rep. Com. Mem. Internat. Div. Credit Mgrs., Exec. Female, Office Automation Mgmt. Adv. Bd., Credit Mgrs. So. Calif., Arcadia Bus. Assn., Arcadia C. of C. Republican. Home: 1230 Oakglen Ave Arcadia CA 91006

FERGUSON, SYBIL RAE, franchise business executive; b. Barnwell, Alta, Can., Feb. 7, 1934; came to U.S., 1938, naturalized, 1975, d. Alva John and Xarissa (Merkley) Clarke; student public schs.; m. Roger N. Ferguson, July 10, 1952; children—Debra Kay, Michael David, Wade Clarke, Lois Christine, Julie Xarissa. Founder, owner Diet Center, Inc., Rexburg, Idaho, 1970—; dir. Dietology Sch., Diet Center Inn, Ferguson's Pharm. Labs., Diet Center Shipping and Receiving Co., Diet Center Print Shop, Audio-Visual Studio, Sybils Inc., Ferguson and Assocs. Charter mem. women's aux. Madison Meml. Hosp.; adv. bd. dept. of bus. Ricks Coll.; mem. nat. adv. council Sch. Mgmt., Brigham Young U.; bd. dirs. Community Health Services Div., Boise State U.; mem. U.S. Congl. Adv. Bd.; active Mormon Relief Soc. Recipient Bus. Leader of Yr. award Ricks Coll., 1980. Mem. Rexburg C. of C. (program dir. 1976). Clubs: Rexburg Civic, Soroptimists (v.p. Rexburg 1975, award 1979). Author: The Diet Center Program: Lose Weight Fast and Keep it Off Forever, 1983; The New Diet Center Cook Book. Office: Diet Center Inc 220 W 2nd St S Rexburg ID 83440

FERGUSON, VIRGINIA WELPTON, computer accounting executive; b. Los Angeles, Aug. 29, 1943; d. Sherman Seymour and Dorothy Virginia (Felber) Welpton.; m. William Dean Ferguson, Jr., June 22, 1968; children—Amanda Jane, Melissa Deanne. B.A. in Dramatic Arts, Calif. State U.-Fresno, 1966; M.B.A. in Mktg., U. Calif.-Berkeley, 1968. Media researcher Campbell-Ewald Agy., Detroit, 1968-69; media buyer N.W. Ayer Agy., Phila., 1969-72; owner, mgr. V. Ferguson Acctg. Co., Sherborn, Mass., 1980-82; owner, mgr. Compacct Co., Macon, Ga., 1982-85. Vice pres. Macon Symphony Guild; fin. dir. Friends of Macon Library; vol. Walters Art Gallery; mem. Zoomerang com. Balt. Zoo, 1985-86; bd. dirs. Macon Mus. of Arts and Scis. Guild. Mem. Macon Heritage Found. Episcopalian. Club: Middle Ga. Computer (treas. 1983-84). Home and Office: 306 Lochview Terr Timonium MD 21093

FERGUSON, WILDA MARIE, state commissioner; b. Durham, A.C., Apr. 14, 1944; d. Elvin Henderson and Rebecca Helen (Davis) F. B.A., Meredith Coll., 1966; M.S.W., Va. Commonwealth U., 1973; M.P.A., Nova U., 1975. Child welfare worker Dept. Welfare, Lynchburg, Va., 1968-70; licensing specialist Dept. Welfare, Richmond, Va., 1970-71; child welfare supr. Richmond Social Services, 1973-74; dir. clin. services United Meth. Children's Home, Richmond, 1975; sr. social worker D.C. Gen. Hosp., Washington, 1976; dir. Dept. Social Services, Manassas Park, Va., 1976-77; city mgr. City of Manassas Park (Va.), 1977-79; commr. Va. Dept. Aging, Richmond, 1979—; mem. spl. faculty for continuing edn. Sch. Social Work, Va. Commonwealth U., Richmond, 1974-75; bd. dirs. No. Va. Planning Dist. Commn., Falls Church, 1978-79, Gov.'s Employment and Tng. Council, Richmond, 1979-81; adj. faculty No. Va. Community Coll., Annandale, 1980; mem. Va. Long-Term Care Council, Richmond, 1982—. Organist, chmn. com. on health and welfare ministeries Westover Hills United Methodist Ch., Richmond, Va., 1979—; mem. bd. ch. and soc. Va. Meth. Conf., 1984—; vice chmn. adv. bd. Va. Ctr. on Aging, 1980-85; mem. adv. bd. Va. Commonwealth U. Sch. Social Work, 1973—. Mem. Nat. Assn. State Units on Aging (bd. mem. 1983-85), Nat. Assn. Social Workers (bd. mem. Va. chpt. 1981-85), Am. Soc. Pub. Adminstrn., Va. Commonwealth U. Sch. Social Work Alumni Assn. (pres. 1973-76), So. Gerontol. Soc. (bd. dirs. 1981-84). Methodist. Office: Dept Aging 101 N 14th St 18th Richmond VA 23219

FERGUSON-SAKSENA, L. DIANE, nurse; b. Montague, P.E.I., Can., Apr. 6, 1949; came to U.S., 1956; d. Ellsworth and Audrey Mary (O'Brien) Ferguson; m. Sanjeev Saksena, Dec. 10, 1983. R.N., Mountainside Hosp., Montclair, N.J., 1971. Asst. head nurse intensive care Newark Beth Israel Med. Ctr., 1972-74, head nurse surgery, 1974-78, adminstrv. coordinator cardiac surgery and cardiac electrophysiology, 1978—. Contbr. papers in field to med. jours. Mem. Am. Heart Assn., Nat. Assn. Female Execs. Office: Newark Beth Israel Med Ctr 201 Lyons Ave Newark NJ 07112

FERN, KATHERINE MILLIKEN, garment manufacturing company executive, financial executive, consultant; b. Lafayette, Ind., Apr. 6, 1948; d. Arthur Thomas and Mary June (Thurnau) Weaver; m. Joseph Jacob Fern, June 5, 1982. B.A., UCLA, 1971. Controller Mort Ross Enterprises and Carol Ann of Calif., Los Angeles, 1973-82; cons., 1982-84; chief fin. officer Topson Downs Calif., Inc., Los Angeles, 1984—. Contbr. articles to profl. jours. Chmn. physician's com. United Way, 1979. Recipient award of merit United Cerebral Palsy, 1980. Mem. U.S. Ski Writers Assn., So. Calif. Ski Writers. Club: Single Ski (treas. 1981, Snow Queen 1981) (Los Angeles). Avocations: photography; amateur ski racing; skiing; sailing. Office: Topson Downs Calif Inc 830 E 14th Pl Los Angeles CA 90021

FERN, RUTH KANE (MRS. WALLACE EDWARD FERN), educator; b. Somerville, N.J., May 12, 1919; d. James Aloysius and Marguerite Anne (Carberry) Kane; B.S., Trenton State Coll., 1941; M.A., N.Y.U., 1944; M.A. in Adminstrn., Montclair State Coll., 1953; postgrad. Columbia U., 1957-69, New Coll., Oxford, Bedford Coll., U. London; m. Wallace Edward Fern, Sept. 3, 1960. Tchr. sr. English Flemington (N.J.) High Sch., 1941-44; dept. chmn., tchr. sr. English, Passaic Valley High Sch., Little Falls, 1944-51; instr. Newark State Coll., 1951-55, asst. prof., 1955-57, dir. pub. relations, 1952-57; asso. prof. English, edn., William Paterson Coll. of N.J., Wayne, 1958—. Cons., English Lang. Arts, Pequannock (N.J.) Pub. Schs., spring 1966, secondary sch. reading Pompton Lakes Pub. Schs., winter 1972. Vice-pres. Essex County (N.J.) Council State Employees, 1956-57; trustee, sec. bd. Passaic County Hist. Soc. Flemington (N.J.) Bd. Edn. grantee, 1942-43. Mem. NEA (life mem.), N.J. Edn. Assn. N.J. Assn. Tchrs. English (exec. bd. 1963—), Nat. Council Tchrs. English, Nat. Assn. Tchr. Educators, N.J. Hist. Soc., Delta Kappa Gamma (chpt. pres. 1970-72), Kappa Delta Pi, Pi Lambda Theta (adviser coll. chpt.). Contbr. articles to profl. publs. Home: 62 Alpine Dr Wayne NJ 07470 Office: 300 Pompton Rd Wayne NJ 07470

FERNANDES, CYNTHIA ANN, state official; b. New Bedford, Mass., Mar. 15, 1959; d. Gilbert and Sally (Nobrega) F. B.S., Northeastern U., 1982; postgrad., Suffolk U., 1986. Campaign hdqrs. mgr. Senator MacLean, New Bedford, 1980; substitute tchr. City New Bedford, 1981-82; dir. victim witness assistance program Dist. Atty. Ronald Pina, New Bedford, 1982—; vis. prof. colls., high schs., Bristol County, 1982—. Instr. Southeastern Mass. chpt. Cardiopulmonary Resuscitation, Brockton, 1976—; active New Bedford Democratic Ward Com., 1985—. Mem. Mass. Victim-Witness Dir. Assn., Jaycees, St. Mary's Women's Guild (corr. sec. 1982-84). Roman Catholic. Avocations: needlecrafts; walking; theater; reading. Home: 775 Rockdale Ave New Bedford MA 02740

FERNANDES, KAREN MARIE, nurse; b. Newburyport, Mass., July 12, 1949; d. Lionel Alfred and Mary Louise (Provencher) Chouinard; m. Michael Fernandes, Feb. 8, 1970; 1 child, Kevin Michael. Diploma in Nursing, New Eng. Bapt. Hosp., 1970. Lic. R.N., R.I., Mass., N.H., Okla. Night charge nurse Miriam Hosp., Providence, 1971-73; evening supr. Ridgewood Ct. Nursing Home, Attleboro, Mass., 1973; night supr. Exeter Hosp., N.H., 1976-81; clin. coordinator, chmn. nursing exec. council Broken Arrow Med. Ctr., Okla., 1981—; advisor Tulsa Jr. Coll., 1981—; advisor Tulsa organ donor com., ARC, 1985. Eucharistic minister Ch. of St. Benedict, Broken Arrow, 1981—; bd. dirs. N.H. Multiple Sclerosis Soc., Manchester, 1978-81. Recipient Outstanding Young Women Am. award, 1978, 81. Mem. Okla. Assn. Nurse Recruiters (sec. 1985—), Okla. Soc. Nursing Adminstrs., Tulsa Dirs. Nursing Service, N.H. Jaycees (first lady). Republican. Roman Catholic. Avocations: tennis; ceramics; sewing; plants. Home: 124 W Inglewood St Broken Arrow OK 74011 Office: Broken Arrow Med Ctr 3000 S Elm Pl Broken Arrow OK 74012

FERNANDEZ, LINDA FLAWN, entrepreneur, social worker; b. Tampa, Fla., Sept. 14, 1943; d. Frank and Rose (D'Amico) F.; 1 child, Marci. B.S., U. South Fla., 1965; M.S., U. Nev., 1976. Social worker Hillsborough County, Tampa, Fla., 1965-67; parole officer adult div. Fla. Parole Commn., Tampa, 1967-69; dir. social services Sunrise Hosp., Las Vegas, Nev., 1969-78; ind. real estate investor, Fla. and Nev., 1965—; pres. Las Vegas Color Separations, Inc., 1978—, Las Vegas Typesetting, Inc., 1983—; LMR Enterprises, Inc., Las Vegas, 1984—; sec.-treas. Sierra Color Graphics, Inc., Las Vegas, 1983—, Royal Playing Card Co., Inc., 1985—. Bernal's Internat. Imports and Wholesalers, Inc., 1985—; fin. cons. Hands Ink, Inc., Las Vegas, 1984—; dir. LV-The Mag. of Las Vegas, 1985—. Founder, organizer Human Relations, pet mascots for elderly; team ofcl. girls' softball, 1985; cons., adv. St. Joseph's Sch., Las Vegas, 1984—. Recipient numerous awards Ad Club Fedn. Mem. Las Vegas C. of C. (congl. com.), Women's Las Vegas C. of C., Ad Club Fedn., Citizens for Pvt. Enterprise, U.S. C. of C. Club: St. Joseph's Sch. Parents (athletic com. 1985-86) (Las Vegas). Avocations: tennis; water skiing. Office: 3351 S Highland Dr Suite 210 Las Vegas NV 89109

FERNANDEZ, NOEMI, business executive; b. Santurce P.R., Dec. 9, 1947; d. Julio and Rosa Maria (Dominguez) F.; children—Noemi, Richard, Rosemary Cabrera. Grad., Dickinson High Sch., Jersey City, 1966. Mgr., Fernandez Furniture Co., Inc., Jersey City, 1969-80, pres., 1980—; pres. Pleasure Limousine Service, Inc., Nutley, N.J., 1985—; cons. acctg. Republican. Avocations: reading; horseback riding; tennis.

FERNANDEZ, PRISCILLA, librarian; b. Pitts., Sept. 26, 1939; d. Robert Duff and Elizabeth P. (Watkins) McMillen; m. Ferdinand F. Fernandez, Jan. 31, 1959; children—Laura P., Jonathan F. B.A., UCLA, 1961; M.S.L.S., Calif. State U.-Fullerton, 1972; M.A., Claremont, Grad. Sch., 1978. Librarian, Chaffey Coll., Alta Loma, Calif., 1972—. Mem. AAUW, Chaffey Republican Women, Law Wives San Bernardino, Assistance League Pomona Valley, Calif. Library Assn., ALA. Lutheran. Office: Chaffey Coll 5885 Haven Ave Alta Loma CA 91701

FERNANDO, DUSHANTÉ ANTOINETTE, fashion designer; b. Colombo, Ceylon, Sri Lanka, May 6, 1952; came to U.S. 1973, naturalized 1977; d. Charles Vernon and Jeanette Lena (Dissanayake) Fernando. B.F.A., St. Martins Sch. Art, 1973. Asst. designer Bill Blass Ltd., N.Y.C., 1974-78; designer Kasper div. Leslie Fay, N.Y.C., 1978-79, Albert Nipon, N.Y.C., 1979-80, Gare Coat & Suit, 1980; owner, designer Dushanté Antoinette Ltd., N.Y.C., 1981—; illustrator N.Y. Times, Henri Bendel, 1974-75; handbag designer Pierre Cardin N.Y., 1978-79; shoe designer Raybuck Shoes, N.Y.C., 1975; designer underwear Bill Blass Flexknit, 1975. Mem. Nat. Assn. Female Execs. Avocations: Seido karate.

FERNSTROM, DOROTHY BOND, psychology educator; b. Dedham, Mass., Sept. 2; d. William Holden and Delia Henrietta (Hansen) Bond; m. Karl Dickson Fernstrom, May 1945 (dec. 1959); children—John Dickson, Henning II. A.B., Adelphi U., 1953; M.A., U. Houston, 1965; Ph.D., Nova U., 1976. Real estate salesman George Jarvis Co., Houston, 1955-58; counselor Houston Pub. Schs., 1958-67; asst. prof. edn., dean women C.W. Post Coll., Greenvale, LI., N.Y., 1967-71; prof. psychology Okaloosa-Walton Jr. Coll., Niceville, Fla., 1971—. Bd. dirs. Okaloosa Community Concert, Niceville, 1973—, chmn. publicity, 1981-85; chmn. publicity Okaloosa Symphony League, Ft. Walton Beach, Fla., 1983-84; precinct chmn. Republican Party, Okaloosa County, Fla., 1972—; sec. Mattie M. Kelly Ctr. for Arts, 1981-84, pres., 1984-85. Served to maj. USMCR, 1943-46. Mem. AAUW (chmn. advocacy 1981-85), LWV (bd. dirs.), Mental Health Assn. (bd. dirs.), Phi Delta Kappa, Delta Kappa Gamma. Episcopalian. Club: Ft. Walton Yacht. Avocations: tennis; foreign travel; swimming; reading; music. Home: 928 Bay Shore Dr PO Box 95 Niceville FL 32578 Office: Okaloosa-Walton Jr Coll College Blvd Niceville FL 32578

FERNSTROM, MEREDITH MITCHUM, financial services company executive; b. Rutherfordton, N.C., July 26, 1946; d. Lee Wallace and Ellie (Saine) Mitchum; m. John Richard Fernstrom, Jr., Dec. 28, 1968. B.S., U. N.C.-Greensboro, 1968; M.S., U. Md., 1972. Tchr. home econs. Prince George County Schs. (Md.), 1968-72; assoc. dir. market research H.J. Kaufman Advt., Washington, 1972-74; dir. consumer edn. D.C. Office Consumer Affairs, Washington, 1974-76; dir. consumer affairs U.S. Dept. Commerce, Washington, 1976-80; v.p. consumer affairs Am. Express Co., N.Y.C., 1980-82, sr. v.p. pub. responsibility, 1982—; mem. FRS Cons. Adv. Council, Washington, 1982-85; bd. dirs. Nat. Consumers League, Washington, 1982—, N.Y. Met. Better Bus. Bur., N.Y.C., 1983—, Internat. Credit Assn. Editor: (brochures) Consumer Card Series, 1981— (Pub. Relations Soc. Pub. Service award 1983); mem. policy bd. Jour. Retail Banking; contbr. articles to profl. jours. Mem. Va. Citizens Consumer Council, 1980—. Recipient Consumer Edn. award Nat. Consumer Credit Fedn., 1981; Matrix award for pub. relations N.Y. Women in Communications, 1986; Disting. Women's award Northwood Inst., 1985. Mem. Soc. Consumer Affairs Profls. (sec. 1981, v.p. 1982, 1st v.p. 1983, pres.-elect 1985), Advt. Women of N.Y., Fin. Women's Assn., Electronic Funds Transfer Assn. (consumer affairs com. 1985—), Women's Econ. Roundtable. U.S. C. of C. Office: Am Express Co 200 Vesey St New York NY 10285

FERRAR, JOYCE PATRICIA, child advocate, parent aide coordinator; b. Cleve., July 11, 1940; d. Michael L. and Theresa Raye (Potoker) Sabrack; m. Robert L. Ferrar, July 11, 1959; children—Robert Brian, John Paul, Jason Channing, Corey Wayne. Student Ohio U., 1958, Kent State U., 1962, U. Oreg., 1966, Allegheny Coll., 1969, Am. U. in Cairo (Egypt), 1974. Dir., Adoption Listing Service Ohio, 1972-73; instr. Am. U. in Cairo, 1974-75; chairperson N.Am. Adoption Week, U.S. and Can., 1977, 78; attendance officer Cuyahoga County Schs., Cleve., 1975-80; assoc. editor Dayton (Ohio) Mag., 1980-82; realtor Realty World, King Assocs., Dayton, 1983-85; cons. childrens placement services Ohio Dept. Pub. Welfare, 1984—, mem. social services adv. com., 1984; former admissions/pub. relations/mktg. coordinator Unicare Corp.; parent aide coordinator suspected abuse and neglect program Family Service Assn., 1986—. Contbr. articles on adoption to newspapers. Chmn. edn. com. NAACP, Meadville, Pa., 1969-71; v.p. Cleve. chpt. Council on Adoptable Children, 1975-80; regional rep. N.Am. Council on Adoptable Children, 1976-80; bd. dirs., sec. exec. council Spaulding for Children, Cleve., 1976-80; mem. Ohio Legal Rights Adv. Com., Columbus, 1981—; chmn. Ohio Citizens Coalition for Permanence for Children, 1982-85; mem. task force Ohio Com. for Child Welfare Services, 1983—; mem. Montgomery County Citizens Rev. Bd., 1983—. Named Humanitarian of Yr., N.Am. Council on Adoptable Children, 1977; recipient spl. commendation Cuyahoga County Bd. Edn., 1980; One of Top Ten Women award Dayton Newspapers Corp., 1985. Mem. Women in Communications. Democrat. Roman Catholic. Home: 3700 Pobst Dr Kettering OH 45420

FERRARA, RUTH REIORDAN, association executive; b. Ducktown, Tenn., Nov. 8, 1924; d. Robert Harrison and Lillian (Fralix) Reiordan; student public schs.; grad. Jones Bus. Coll.; m. Joseph James Ferrara, Oct. 10, 1946; children—James Michael, John Richard. Machinist, Jacksonville (Fla.) Naval Air Sta., 1942-44; with Greyhound Bus Co., Jacksonville, 1944-45; head cashier womens apparel Mangels Ladies Wear, Jacksonville, 1945-46; owner, operator restaurant, Jacksonville, 1946-47, Copperhill, Tenn., 1946-48; bookkeeper Henley & Beckwith, Inc., Jacksonville, 1949-50; mem. purchasing dept. Am. Hardware Corp., New Britain, Conn., 1948-49; sec.-mgr. Greater Jacksonville Fair Assn., 1966-69, dir., 1959-69, exec. sec., 1965-70; pres. Fla. Fedn. Fairs and Livestock Shows, 1969-70, also dir. public relations; exec. sec. Fla. Fedn. Fairs, 1970-85, S.C. State Fair, Greenville, 1972-77; exec. sec., mgr. North Fla. Fair, Tallahassee, 1977—. Mem. Fla. Council for Aged, 1966-70; mem. aging com. Community Planning Council, 1966-70. Bd. dirs. Jacksonville Fair, 1959-68, State and Provincial Assn. Fairs, 1976—; sec. Venetia Boys Club, 1958-62; bd. advisers Cathedral Towers, 1966-70. Democrat. Methodist. Clubs: Jacksonville Garden (dir. 1960-68), Order Eastern Star, Venetia Manor Garden Circle (pres. 1960-62). Home: 2795 Blair Stone Ct Tallahassee FL 32301 Office: 441 Paul Russell Rd Tallahassee FL 32301

FERRARO, GERALDINE ANNE, former congresswoman and candidate for Vice President of U.S.; b. Newburgh, N.Y., Aug. 26, 1935; d. Dominick and Antonetta L. (Corrieri) Ferraro; A.B., Marymount Coll., 1956; J.D., Fordham U., 1960; postgrad. NYU Law Sch., 1978; m. John A. Zaccaro, 1960; children—Donna Zaccaro, John Zaccaro, Laura Zaccaro. Tchr. pub. schs., N.Y.C., 1956-60; admitted to N.Y. bar, 1961, U.S. Ct. Appeals bar for 2d Circuit, 1975, U.S. Supreme Ct. bar, 1978; individual practice law, N.Y.C., 1961-74; asst. dist. atty. Queens County (N.Y.), 1974-78; mem. U.S. Ho. of Reps. from 9th dist. N.Y. State; candidate for Vice Pres. of U.S., 1984. Mem. Hunt Commn. on Presdl. Nominations, 1981-82; chmn. platform com. Democratic Nat. Conv., 1984. Roman Catholic. Office: 108-18 Queens Blvd Forest Hills NY 11375

FERRARO, MARGUERITE MARY, educator; b. Hartford, Conn., May 25, 1942; d. Thomas Wilson and Marguerite Rosalia (Roe) Henebry; B.S. in Edn., SUNY at Potsdam, 1964; M.S. in Edn., CUNY, 1966, 1 dau., Sarah Teresa. Tchr., Deer Park (N.Y. Public Schs., 1964-65; tchr. Yonkers (N.Y.) Public Schs., 1966—, tchr. math. lab., 1980-82. Mem. legis. adv. coms. for N.Y. State Senator Frank Padavan, N.Y. State Assemblyman Doug Prescott; mem. Action for Child Transp. Safety; mem. St. Joseph Lakota Devel. Council, St. Joseph's Indian Sch. Recipient Jenkins Meml. award Congress of Parents and Tchrs., 1975. Mem. Am. Fedn. Tchrs., N.Y. State United Tchrs., Yonkers Fedn. Tchrs., N.Y. State Reading Council, Yonkers Reading Council, Nat. Council Tchrs. Math., Assn. Supervision and Curriculum Devel., Assn. Children and Adults with Learning Disabilities, N.Y. Assn. Children with Learning Disabilities, AAUW, N.Y. Assn. Brain Injured Children, Orton Soc. Roman Catholic. Office: Mark Twain Sch Woodlawn and Wakefield Aves Yonkers NY 10704

FERRARO-KENNEDY, MARIAROSA DEL VALLE, communications company executive; b. Tucaman, Argentina, Apr. 10, 1953; came to U.S. 1960; d. Francesco and Nelda (Marigliano) Ferraro. B.A., St. Mary's Coll., 1969—. Export mgr. Bishop Graphics, Westlake Village, Calif., 1977-80; tech. writer EECO, Inc., Santa Ana, Calif., 1980-82; inventory control Up-Right Scaffolds, Berkeley, Calif., 1981-82; office mgr. Encom Systems, Concord, Calif., 1982-84, gen. mgr., 1984-86; br. adminstr. Gen. Telcom, Santa Clara, Calif., 1986—; writer/cons. Landscape Architects, Walnut Creek, Calif., 1983. Editor EECO News, 1981. Mem. Women in Telecommunications, Nat. Assn. Female Execs. Club: Pre-Med Club. Avocations: gardening, creative writing; home computers; piano; reading; gourmet cooking. Home: 7070 Bucktown Ln Vacaville CA 94688 Office: Gen Telcom Inc 416 Aldo Ave Santa Clara CA 95050

FERREIRA, AUDREY LEE BLISS, community worker; b. Palo Alto, Calif., Apr. 4, 1931; d. Paul Randolph and Lucile (Hartman) Bliss; student Humboldt State Coll., Arcata, Calif., 1948-49, Willamette U., Salem, Oreg., 1949-52; m. John Gordon Selby, Feb. 10, 1952; children—Clinton, Katherine, Janet, Barbara; m. Charles E. Ferreira, Dec. 27, 1982. Chmn., Young Audiences of Bay Area, 1974-75; del. Young Audiences Council Calif., 1974-75; chmn. vol. program Oakland (Calif.) pub. schs., 1975-76, vol. music performances, 1969-80; pres. Montclair PTA, 1969-71, dir. 28th Dist., 1973-75, v.p. 28th Dist., 1975-76, pres. 28th Dist., 1976-78; v.p. Oakland Unit Ch. Women United, 1975; news editor Oakland Girl Scout Assn., 1968-70, area chmn., leader, 1966-74; city sect. chmn. Am. Cancer Soc., 1970-75; bd. dirs. Vol. Bur. Alameda County, 1974-78; mem; commn. discipline, attendence and sch. safety Oakland pub. schs., 1974-78; deacon Presbyn. Ch., 1977—; mem. Republican State Central Com. Calif., 1973-74; bd. dirs. Marcus A. Foster Ednl. Inst., 1978-81; bd. mgrs. Calif. Congress Parents and Tchrs., 1978-81; legis. adv. Calif. PTA, 1979-81; mem. com. credentials Calif. Commn. on Tchr. Credentialing, 1979-84; pres. Georgetown Divide Health Care Aux., 1983-85; v.p. Georgetown Divide Rep. Women Federated, 1986; co-dir. ARC Disaster Services, Georgetown Divide, 1985—. Recipient Marcus Foster grant for elementary sch. museum, 1971, Order Golden Sword, Am. Cancer Soc., 1974, 75; named hon. life mem. Calif. PTA, recipient Continuing Service award, 1976. Mem. United Presbyn. Women, Nat. Fedn. Rep. Women, Am. Needlepoint Guild, P.E.O., Embroiderers Guild Am. (nat. standards council), Pi Beta Phi, Theta Alpha Phi. Address: PO Box 573 Garden Valley CA 95633

FERREIRA, JO ANN JEANETTE CHANOUX, management information systems executive; b. Melrose Park, Ill., Dec. 3, 1943; d. John W. and June B. Chanoux; B.S., Purdue U., 1965, M.S. (NSF fellow), 1969; m. G. Dodge Ferreira, Apr. 21, 1979. With systems devel. research IBM, San Jose, Calif., 1965-67; asst. dir. mgmt. info. systems edn. Union Carbide Corp., N.Y.C., 1969; mgmt. cons. Touche Ross & Co., N.Y.C., 1970-72, Peat Marwick Mitchell, N.Y.C., 1974-75; dir. corp. devel. strategy cons. A.T. Kearney-Mgmt. Cons., Chgo., 1975-83; dir. Computer Devel. Ctr., United Airlines, 1983—; lectr. Purdue U., 1969, 73-74; guest lectr. Northwestern U., 1981. Mem. Assn. for Corp. Growth (mergers and acquisitions profls.), Inst. Mgmt. Cons. (cert. mgmt. cons.), Am. Arbitration Assn., Phi Kappa Phi. Contbr. articles to profl. publs.; speaker various groups. Home: Rural Route 2 Box 110 Barrington Hills IL 60010 Office: 222 S Riverside Plaza Chicago IL 60606

FERRELL, ANNA BELLE, retail/wholesale company executive; b. Piggott, Ark., Mar. 15, 1927; d. Thomas J. and Nora (Griffin) Johnson; m. William A. Harder, Sept. 20, 1949 (dec. Nov. 1967); m. James R. Ferrell, Feb. 23, 1969; 1 dau., Nora. Corr. student U. Mo.-Columbia 1949-52; student Memphis State U., 1983. Credit mgr. Sears Roebuck & Co., Caruthersville, Mo., 1953-59; bookkeeper Bain Motor Co., Hayti, Mo., 1959-62; purchasing asst. E.L. Bruce Hardwoods, Memphis, 1963-69; v.p., office mgr. Choctaw Scale & Electronics Co., Memphis, 1969—. Vol. investigator Mo. Dept. Human Services, 1947-62; foster mother Boys Town, 1977-82. Mem. Nat. Scalemen's Assn. (sec. 1969-83), Nat. Fedn. Small Bus. Republican. Methodist. Lodge: Rebekah (state pres.). Office: Choctaw Scale and Electronics Inc 1805 Bartlett Rd Memphis TN 38134

FERRELL, RUTH MORRIS (MRS. FRANK M. FERRELL), lawyer; b. Portsmouth, Va., Apr. 29, 1928; d. Francis Hubert and Ruth (Whitehead)

Morris; B.A., Agnes Scott Coll., 1949; M.A., Emory U., 1952; J.D., U. Pa., 1960; m. Frank M. Ferrell, Apr. 7, 1958. Bar: Del. 1960, U.S. Supreme Ct. Practiced in Wilmington, Del., 1960—; law clk. judges Del. State Cts., 1961-62; dep. atty. gen. Del., 1963-70; head civil div. Del. Atty. Gen's Office, 1967-70; state solicitor of Del., 1969-70; asst. regional atty. Phila. Regional Litigation Center, U.S. EEO Commn., 1973; mem. Gov.'s Commn. on Status Women, 1963-68; mem. European adv. council U.S. Dept. State, 1971-72. Pres., Women's Republican Club Wilmington, 1965-67. Recipient award for outstanding pub. service Rep. Nat. Com. N.E. Regional Women's Conf., 1967. Mem. ABA (mem. council local govt. sect.), Del. Bar Assn., Fed. Bar Assn., Assn. Trial Lawyers Am., Supreme Ct. Hist. Soc., Christina Bus. and Profl. Women's Club (pres.), Mortar Bd., Phi Beta Kappa. Presbyterian. Contbr. articles to profl. publs. Home: 17 Cragmere Rd Wilmington DE 19809 Office: 912 Market Tower Bldg 901 Market St Wilmington DE 19801

FERRI, KAREN LYNN, lawyer, retail food company executive; b. McKeesport, Pa., Aug. 15, 1956; d. Edward James and Carole Elizabeth (Petterson) Ferri. B.A., Duquesne U., 1977, J.D., 1981. Bar: Pa. 1981, U.S. Dist. Ct. (we. dist.) Pa. 1981., U.S. Supreme Ct. 1986. Law clk. Weiler & Dolfi, Pitts., 1980-81, assoc., 1981-84; assoc. Stokes, Lurie & Cole, Pitts., 1984—; weekend mgr. Ferri Land Co., Inc., Murraysville, Pa., 1977—; atty. Ferri Enterprises, 1981—. Recipient Sr. Leaders award Duquesne U., 1977, Am. Jurisprudence award Joint Pubs. Total Client-Service Library Pitts., 1978-79. Mem. Allegheny County Bar Assn. (vol. indigent divorce program, high sch. edn. program), Pa. Bar Assn. (family law sect.), Westmoreland County Bar Assn., ABA. Republican. Roman Catholic. Clubs: AMAA Investment, Young Republicans, Variety (Pitts.) Home: Chatham Tower Unit 3C Chatham Ctr Pittsburgh PA 15219 Office: Stokes Lurie & Cole 2100 Law and Fin Bldg Pittsburgh PA 15219

FERRIGNO, HELEN FRANCES, librarian, musician, educator; b. Trenton, N.J., Aug. 25, 1937; d. Joseph John and Frances (Leniart) Klidzia; m. Maurice Ferrigno, Oct. 3, 1964; children—Lisa, Nina. Student Hartt Coll. Music, Hartford, Conn., 1962-64; B.A., Rivier Coll., Nashua, N.H., 1977-80; M.L.S., Simmons Coll., 1982. Pvt. music tchr., Conn. and N.H., 1965—; free-lance flutist and piccolist, 1974—; co-owner/mgr. Ancus Books, Nashua, 1974—; cataloger/info. cons. Digital Equipment Corp., Merrimack, N.H., 1984—; librarian Daniel Webster Coll., Nashua, 1982-84, chmn. lecture series, 1982-83; flutist Nashua Symphony Orch., 1975-77. Mem. parents adv. bd. New Eng. Conservatory Prep. Sch., Boston, 1981-82; vol. Am. Heart Assn. Mem. ALA, Assn. Coll. and Research Libraries, Library and Info. Tech. Assn., New Eng. Library Assn., Beta Phi Mu. Roman Catholic. Home: 76 Manchester St Nashua NH 03060

FERRIS, ANITA MARIE, video production professional; b. Akron, Ohio, Dec. 1, 1955; d. Robert John and Juliette (Brabhan) F. B.S., Ithaca Coll., 1978. Media coordinator Akron City Hosp., 1978-82; mgr. product communications Sony Corp. Am., Park Ridge, N.J., 1982-83; writer, producer Am. Greetings Corp., Cleve., 1983—. Contbr. articles to profl. mags. Mem. Internat. TV Assn. (internat. officer 1983-84), Women in Communications, Assn. for Multi-Image, Phi Kappa Phi. Republican. Eastern Orthodox. Home: 2160 Thurmont Rd 5 Akron OH 44313 Office: Am Greetings Corp 10500 American Rd Cleveland OH 44144

FERRIS, EILEEN GUNTER, lawyer; b. Los Angeles, Oct. 4, 1944; d. John Exum and Pauline (Smith) Gunter; m. Michael A. Ferris, Oct. 28, 1972. B.A., Calif. State U., 1967; M.S., U. Hartford, 1976; J.D., U. Conn., West Hartford, 1980. Bar: Conn. 1980. Claims rep. Social Security Adminstrn., Van Nuys, Calif., 1967-70; productivity systems analyst Aetna Life & Casualty, Los Angeles and Hartford, Conn., 1971-72; pension paralegal Reid & Riege, P.C., Hartford, Conn., 1972-74; pension cons. Phoenix Mut., Hartford, 1975-76; asst. supt. pension trust sales Mass. Mut., Springfield, Mass., 1976-79; mem. firm Williams & Brooke, P.C., Hartford, Conn., 1980—. Illustrator: Student Survival Guide, 1979. Mem. Hartford County Bar Assn., Conn. Bar Assn., ABA, Hartford Assn. Women Attys. Club Hartford Women's Network. Home: 148 Hunters Ln Newington CT 06111 Office: Williams & Brooke PC One Financial Plaza Hartford CT 06103

FERRIS, EVELYN SCOTT, lawyer; b. Detroit; d. Ross Ansel and Irene Mabel (Bowser) Nafus; m. Roy Shorey Ferris, May 21, 1969; (div.); children—Judith Ilene, Roy Sidney, Lorene Marjorie. J.D., Willamette U., 1961. Bar: Oreg. 1962. Law clk. Oreg. Tax Ct., Salem, 1961-62; dep. dist. atty. Marion County, Salem, 1962-65; judge Mcpl. Ct., Stayton, Oreg., 1965-76; ptnr. Brand, Lee, Ferris & Embick, Salem, 1965-82; chmn. Oreg. Workers' Compensation Bd., Salem, 1982—. Bd. dirs. Marion County Civil Service Commn., Salem, 1970-75, Salem City Club, 1972-75, Friends of Deepwood, Salem, 1979-82; commr. Polk County Hist. Commn., Dallas, Oreg., 1976-80; mem. Oreg. Gov.'s Task Force on Liability. Recipient Outstanding Restoration of Comml. Property award Marion County Hist. Soc., 1982. Mem. Oreg. State Bar Assn., Mary Leonard Law Soc., Phi Delta Delta. Republican. Episcopalian. Clubs: Altrusa (Salem) (dir. 1981-84); Capitol (Salem) (pres. 1977-79). Office: Oregon Workers Compensation Bd 480 Church St SE Salem OR 97310

FERRIS, MARY CHRISTINE, physician; b. Detroit, Oct. 18, 1953; d. Tony and Audrey (Zardis) F. B.A., U. Mich., 1975; D.O., Coll. of Osteo. Medicine and Surgery, Des Moines, Iowa, 1980. Diplomate Nat. Bd. Examiners. Practice medicine specializing in family medicine, Madison Hts., Mich., 1981-84, Sterling Hts., Mich., 1984—; staff Oakland Gen. Hosp., Madison Hts., 1981—. Mem. Am. Osteo. Assn., Mich. Assn. Osteo. Physicians and Surgeons, Macomb County Osteo. Soc. Greek Orthodox. Avocations: drawing; painting; running. Office: 4845 E 14 Mile Rd Sterling Heights MI 48077

FERRITER, SANDRA MCPHERSON, retail management educator, administrator; b. San Diego, Oct. 17, 1949; d. Howard Raymond and Lois Arlean (Mounts) McP.; m. John Michael Ferriter, May 31, 1970; children—Timothy Brandon, Erin Kathleen. B.S. in Home Econs., Fashion Merchandising, U. Mass., 1971; M.Adminstrv. Sci., Mgmt. Option, Johns Hopkins U., 1979. Floor supr. Steiger's Dept. Store, Springfield, Mass., 1970; asst. dept. mgr. Montgomery Wards, Bel Air, Md., 1971-72; tng. store mgr. Foxmoor Casuals, Balt., 1972-74; part-time faculty Harford Community Coll., Bel Air, 1975-81, full-time, 1981—, asst. prof. retail mgmt., 1983—, coordinator retail mgmt. program, 1984—, mem. Acad. Standards com., 1983—, chairperson, 1985-86, chairperson Affirmative Action com., 1982-83, mem. Coop. Edn. Adv. com., 1983—. Mem. exec. bd. William S. James Elem. Sch., Abingdon, Md., 1984—, Parent Adv. com., 1983—. Mem. AAUW (hospitality chairperson 1985—), Harford County C. of C. (bd. dirs. 1985—). Roman Catholic. Avocations: needlework, swimming. Office: Harford Community Coll Bel Air Hall Thomas Run Rd Bel Air MD 21014

FERRO, CECILIA CICCIU, real estate broker; b. Reggio Calabria, Italy, Sept. 6, 1951; came to U.S., 1952, naturalized, 1952; d. Fortunato and Eugenia (Minnitti) Cicciu; m. Guiseppe Ferro, Apr. 30, 1972; children—Maria Loretta, Eugenia Giovanna, Francesco Giuseppe. Grad., Data Processing Inst., N.Y.C., 1968, Berkeley Secretarial Sch., N.Y.C., 1970, Empire Sch. Real Estate, Yonkers, N.Y., 1984. Legal sec. various law firms, N.Y.C., 1969-74, Frank Giordano, Bronx, N.Y., 1976-84; asst. project dir. Belmont Local Devel. Corp., Bronx, 1983—; broker Cosmopolitan Realty, Bronx, 1985—. Chmn. Belmont Community Day Care Ctr., Bronx, 1983; sec. Fordham Save Our Neighborhood Local Devel., Bronx, 1985; v.p. Van Nest Housing Devel. Fund, Bronx, 1985. Home: 22 Croydon Rd Yonkers NY 10710 Office: Belmont-Arthur Ave Local Devel Corp 2322 Arthur Ave Bronx NY 10458

FERRO-NYALKA, RUTH RUDYS, librarian; b. Chgo., June 2, 1930; d. Joseph F. and Anna (Serbenta) Rudys; B.A., U. Chgo., 1950; M.A. in Library Sci., Rosary Coll., 1972; children—Keith A. Krisciunas, Kevin L. Krisciunas, Kenneth M. Krisciunas; stepchildren—Anita L. Abbate, Vincent A. Abbate; m. Frank Ferro-Nyalka; stepchildren—Eleanor, Christine, Sylvia, André, Annette Ferro-Nyalka. Tchr. elem. sch. Westmont, Ill., 1961-63; librarian Dist. 105 public schs., La Grange, Ill., 1972—, tchr. program for gifted children, 1979-81, 82-85, coordinator gifted program, 1981-82. Mem. ALA, Ill. Library Assn., NEA, Ill. Edn. Assn., Dist. 105 Tchrs. Assn. (pres. 1983-85), AAUW. Roman Catholic. Home: 5800 Doe Circle Westmont IL 60559 Office: 1001 Spring Ave La Grange IL 60525

FERRY, DEEDRA HUNTER, counselor, baby care products executive; b. Santa Monica, Calif., May 17, 1947; d. Robert Charles and Anita (Boyer) Dukoff; m. Richard Paul Ferry, Aug. 29, 1981; children—Robert Paul, Brandon Charles, Kristina Charlene. B.A., Fla. Internat. U., 1981; M.S., St. Thomas of Villanova U., 1984. Lectr., Weight Watchers, Inc., Miami, Fla., 1971-74; counselor in pvt. practice, Coral Gables, Fla., 1977—; owner Robbie Ray All Natural Baby Care Products, Coral Gables, 1981—; moderator radio show Facts About the Issues, 1976-81. Head pub. relations Miami LWV, 1975-82; bd. dirs. Commn. on Status of Women, Miami, 1981, YWCA, 1981. Republican. Home: 4665 SW 64th Ave Miami FL 33155 Office: 300 Aragon Ave Coral Gables FL 33134

FERRY, DIANE LOUISE, educator; b. Ligonier, Pa. Apr. 24, 1947; d. William Glenn and Marjorie (Houpt) F.; B.A., Gettysburg Coll., 1969; M.B.A., Shippensburg State Coll., 1974; Ph.D., U. Pa., 1978; m. David C. White, Nov. 25, 1983; 1 child, William Austin David White. Computer systems analyst Dept. Army, Chambersburg, Pa., 1970-74; research assoc. U. Pa., Phila., 1975-78; instr. Temple U., Phila., 1977-78; assoc. prof. bus. adminstrn. U. Del., Newark, 1979—; cons. Kappa Systems, Inc., Rosslyn, Va., 1981-83, Urban Inst., Washington, 1980—. Mem. Nat. Acad. Mgmt., Am. Mgmt. Assn., Assn. Computing Machinery, Am. Psychol. Assn., Phi Beta Kappa. Author: (with A.H. VandeVen) Measuring and Assessing Organizations, 1980. Address: Dept Bus Adminstrn Univ Del Newark DE 19716

FERRY, ROBERTA JOANNE, medical office manager; b. Chgo., Oct. 3, 1961; d. Dale Alfred and Karen Jean (Chute) Schneider; m. James Eugene Ferry, June 26, 1982. Student pub. schs., Huntington Beach, Calif. With Sears Roebuck & Co., Westminster, Calif., 1977-78, Nordstrom, Costa Mesa, Calif., 1978; sec. Warner Village Lab., Fountain Valley, Calif., 1978-80; office mgr. Orange Coast Urology, Huntington Beach, Calif., 1980—; mgr. NPSS, Los Angeles, 1984—. Vol., Spl. Olympics, Los Angeles, 1976-78; mem. council Luth. Ch. Resurrection, Huntington Beach, 1985—, cons., tchr., 1984—. Mem. Nat. Assn. Female execs. Democrat. Avocations: skiing; aerobics; camping; needlework. Office: Orange Coast Urology 18700 Main St #203 Huntington Beach CA 92648

FESLER, ELIZABETH, educator, psychologist; b. Youngstown, Ohio, Nov. 5, 1930; d. Raymond and Mary (Theodore) Cosetti; B.S., Kent State U., 1952, M.S., 1961, Ph.D., 1974; m. July 8, 1953; children—Kim. Tchr., Buchtel High Sch., Perkins Jr. High Sch., 1952-62; counselor, Akron, Ohio, 1962-70; psychologist Akron Public Schs., 1970-76, coordinator spl. needs, 1976-78, dir. spl. edn., 1978-80, prin. Goodrich Jr. High Sch., 1978-80, dir. spl. edn., 1980—. Pres., Support Inc., suicide prevention; bd. dirs., chmn. edn. div. Planned Parenthood Assn.; v.p. bd. dirs. Mental Health Assn.; mem. women's aux. bd. Summit County Juvenile Ct.; mem. Children's Transitionals Services Bd. Kent State U. scholar; community advisor Jr. League. Mem. Am. Assn. Psychologists, Ohio Assn. Psychologists, Akron Assn. Psychologists, Am. Assn. Secondary Sch. Prins., Ohio Assn. Secondary Sch. Prins., Akron Assn. Secondary Sch. Prins., Nat. Assn. Sch. Psychologists, Alpha Xi Delta. Home: 65 N Wheaton Rd Akron OH 44313 Office: 65 Steiner Ave Akron OH 44301

FESS, MARILYNN ELAINE (MRS. STEPHEN W. FESS), occupational therapist; b. Casper, Wyo., June 20, 1944; d. Frederick Eugene and Norma Pence (Jarrett) Ewing; B.S., Ind. U., 1967, M.S., 1977; m. Stephen W. Fess, Nov. 26, 1966. Staff occupational therapist Marion County Gen. Hosp., Indpls., 1966-70; supr. phys. dysfunction unit, 1970-72; supr. adult occupational therapy Ind. U. Med. Center, Indpls., 1972-74, instr. occupational therapy curriculum, 1974-76; hand therapist Strickland & Steichen, M.D.'s, Inc., 1974-79; designer, developer, dir. hand therapy Hand Rehab. Center Ind., 1976-79; cons. hand rehab. and hand research, 1979—; cons. to hand surgeons various hosps. and nursing homes. Mem. exec. bd. Ind. Cerebral Vascular Accident Com., 1973-76. Fellow Am. Occupational Therapy Assn. (sec. orgn. affiliate pres.'s 1976-78); mem. Am. Soc. Hand Therapists (founding, mem. at large exec. bd. 1978-79, sec. 1980-82), Ind. Occupational Therapy Assn. (sec. 1969-71, v.p. 1972-73, pres. 1974-76, hand therapy liaison to exec. bd. 1978—). Author: (with others) Hand Splinting Principles and Methods, 1980; also articles; mem. editorial rev. bd. Occupational Therapy Jour. Research, 1983-84, Am. Jour. Occupational Therapy, 1985-87. Patentee externally powered hand orthosis. Office: 635 Eagle Creek Ct Zionsville IN 46077

FESTE, ANNE MARIA, fashion designer, apparel manufacturing company executive; b. Tacoma, July 27, 1957; d. Jon and Florence Irene (Erickson) F. Student U. Puget Sound, 1975-77; B.F.A. in Apparel Design, R.I. Sch. Design, Providence, 1980. Asst. designer Kay Unger-St. Gillians, N.Y.C., 1979, Stephen Burrows, N.Y.C., 1980; designer Connie Banko, Miami, Fla., 1980-81, Helga Howie, San Francisco, 1981-83; owner, designer Feste Exclusive, San Francisco, 1983—; cons. Cool-Offs, Sausalito, Calif., 1985—, Lillian Tom, San Francisco, 1985—. Designer fashions Big Beautiful Woman mag., 1984, 85. Recipient Apparel Design award Singer Sewing Machine Co., Tacoma, 1973, Cranston Printworks, R.I., 1978; cert. of appreciation Miami-Dade Community Coll., 1982. Mem. R.I. Sch. Design Alumni Assn., U. Puget Sound Alumni Assn., San Francisco Fashion Industries. Avocations: running, skiing, travel, horse-back riding. Home: 1550 17th Ave San Francisco CA 94122 Office: Feste Exclusive PO Box 210143 San Francisco CA 94121

FETHEROLF, MIRIAM MARKHAM (MRS. RICHMOND D. FETHEROLF), retired newspaper editor; b. Baldwin, Kans., Sept. 28, 1901; d. William Colfax and Carrie (Hoover) Markham; music supr. certificate Baker U., 1922; A.B., Bucknell U., 1923; m. Richmond D. Fetherolf, June 24, 1927 (dec. Oct. 1954); 1 son, Donald Markham. Supr. music Mt. Holly (N.J.) Pub. Schs., 1923-31; food editor Van Nuys (Calif.) News, 1954-76, Los Angeles Suburban Newspapers, 1957-65. Vice pres. Van Nuys Pub. Co., 1956-58, treas., 1958-76. Chmn. mothers group Home and Sch., 1945-46, 49-50, chmn. of chairmen, 1947-48. Bd. dirs. ARC, Swarthmore, 1950-52. Recipient Disting. Service award Baker U., 1976. Mem. Nat. Fedn. Press Women (affiliate), P.E.O., Delta Delta Delta (pres. West Phila. 1947-50). Republican. Presbyn. Club: Old Treasurers (pres. 1965-67) (Van Nuys). Home: 17225 Gault St Van Nuys CA 91406

FETRIDGE, BONNIE-JEAN CLARK (MRS. WILLIAM HARRISON FETRIDGE), civic worker; b. Chgo., Feb. 3, 1915; d. Sheldon and Bonnie (Carrington) Clark; student Girls Latin Sch., Chgo., The Masters Sch., Dobbs Ferry, N.Y., Finch Coll., N.Y.C.; m. William Harrison Fetridge, June 27, 1941; children—Blakely (Mrs. Harvey H. Bundy III), Clark Worthington. Bd. dirs. region VII com. Girl Scouts U.S.A., 1939-43, mem. nat. program com., 1966-69, mem. nat. adv. council, 1972-85, mem. internat. commr.'s adv. panel, 1973-76, mem. Nat. Juliette Low Birthplace Com., 1966-69, region IV selections com., 1968-70; bd. dirs. Girl Scouts Chgo., 1936-51, 59-69, sec., 1936-38, v.p., 1946-49, 61-65, chmn. Juliette Low world friendship com., 1959-67, 71-72; mem. Friends of Our Cabana Com. World Assn. Girl Guides and Girl Scouts, London, Eng., 1969—, vice chmn., 1982-86; founder mem., pres. Olave Baden-Powell Soc. of World Assn. Girl Guides and Girl Scouts, 1984—; asst. sec. Dartnell Corp., bus. pubs., Chgo., 1981—; bd. dirs. Jr. League of Chgo., 1937-40, Vis. Nurse Assn. of Chgo., 1951-58, 61-63, asst. treas., 1962-63; women's bd. dirs. Children's Meml. Hosp., 1946-50. Staff aide, ARC and Motor Corps, World War II. Vice pres. Latin Sch. Parents Council, 1952-54; bd. dirs. Latin Sch. Alumni Assn. 1964-69, Fidelitas Soc., 1979; women's bd. U.S.O., 1965-75, treas., 1969-71, v.p., 1971-73; women's service bd. Chgo. Area council Boy Scouts Am., 1964-70, mem.-at-large Nat. council, 1973-76, mem. nat. Exploring com., 1973-76; governing mem. Anti-Cruelty Soc. of Chgo.; assoc. Nat. Archives. Recipient Citation of Merit for community contbns. in field of human relations Sta. WAIT, Chgo., 1971; Baden-Powell fellow World Scout Found., Geneva, 1983. Mem. Nat. Soc. Colonial Dames Am. (Ill. bd. mgrs. 1962-65, 69-76, 78-82, v.p. 1970-72, corr. sec. 1978-80, 1st v.p. 1980-82, state chmn. geneal. info. services com. 1972-76, hist. activities com. 1979-83, mus. house com. 1980-83, house gov. 1981-82), Youth for Understanding (couriers bicentennial project), English-Speaking Union, Chgo. Dobbs Alumnae Assn. (past pres.), Nat. Soc. DAR, Chgo. Geneal. Soc., Conn. Soc. Genealogists, New Eng. Historic Geneal. Soc., N.Y. Geneal. and Biog. Soc., Newberry Library Assos., Chgo. Hist. Soc. Guild. Republican. Episcopalian. Clubs: Casino, Saddle and Cycle, Woman's Athletic. Home: 2430 Lakeview Ave Chicago IL 60614

FETSKE, RUTH BETTY, advertising agency executive; b. Rahway, N.J., Sept. 24, 1922; d. Plato Settle and Mitzie (Mihalovics) Bumgarner; student public and pvt. schs., Rahway, N.J., N.Y.C.; m. William A. Fetske, Jan. 29, 1944. Editorial asst. Woman's Home Companion mag., N.Y.C., 1941-44; photog. stylist Anton Bruehl Studios, N.Y.C., 1944-45; fashion copywriter West-Marquis Advt. Agy., Los Angeles, 1945-46; copywriter Lerner Shops, N.Y.C., 1946-47; copywriter, account exec. Dorland Internat. Advt. Agy., N.Y.C., 1947-48; advt. mgr. Marcus Breier Sons, Inc., men's outerwear, N.Y.C., 1951-53; account exec. Lester Harrison Advt. Agy., N.Y.C., 1953-60, Mervin & Jesse Levine Advt. Agy., N.Y.C., 1960-68; pres., owner Ruth B. Fetske Assos., Inc., N.Y.C. and Conn., 1969-85. Mem. Fashion Group, Inc., Nat. Assn. Female Execs. Contbg. writer/photographer to profl. pubis. Office: PO Box 248 Cobalt CT 06414

FETSKO, NADINE ELIZABETH, accountant, helicopter pilot, aviation co. exec.; b. Phila., June 23, 1951; d. John J. and Nadine M. (Dopirak) F.; B.S. in Acctg. Widener U., 1977; student geology, Temple U., 1969-72. Helicopter pilot, reporter Shadow Traffic Network, Inc., 1979-81; v.p. fin. Fetsko Aviation Sales & Transp., Inc., 1979—; acct. Franklin Mint Corp., 1972-82; pilot Omniflight Airways/Pan Am. Shuttle, 1982-83, Caesars Atlantic City, 1983—; pub. speaker women's groups. Mem. Whirlygirls, Inc. (treas 1977-78), Nat. Assn. Female Execs., Delaware County Aviation Assn. (sec. 1977). Home: RD 2 Baker Rd Cochranville PA 19330 Office: New London Airport Box 91 New London PA 19360

FETTE, MARY PATRICIA, nurse; b. Waseca, Minn., Apr. 1, 1956; d. William Carl and Phyllis Barbara (Lynch) Poehler; m. Jeffrey Lynn Fette, Sept. 16, 1978. Assoc. in Nursing, Austin (Minn.) Community Coll., 1978. R.N., Minn.; cert. med.-surg. nurse, emergency nurse, Staff nurse Lakeshore Nursing Home, Waseca, 1974-75, nursing supr., 1975-77; head nurse Meml. Hosp., Waseca, 1977—; transport nurse Neste Ambulance, 1983—. Vol. ARC, 1978—. Mem. Am. Nurses Assn., Minn. Nurses Assn., Critical Care Nursing Assn., Emergency Nurses Assn. Roman Catholic. Home: 409 14th Ave NW Waseca MN 56093 Office: Memorial Hospital 100 5th Ave NW Weseca MN 56093

FETTER, CAROLYN MARIE, pharmaceutical company executive; b. Bklyn., Jan. 13, 1952; d. Edward H. and Teresa A. (Maloney) F.; m. N. Jay Diener, Sept. 16, 1978. B.A., St. John's U., 1973; M.B.A., Rutgers U., 1985. Owner, Family & Friends Rec. Co., Bklyn., 1974-76; media planner Benton & Bowles Advt., N.Y.C., 1976-77; product mgr. Block Drug Co., Jersey City, 1977-81; sr. product mgr. Sterling Drug Co., N.Y.C., 1981-82; dir. acquisitions and new product devel. Johnson & Johnson Co., New Brunswick, N.J., 1982—. Mem. Nat. Assn. Female Execs. Avocation: microcomputers. Office: Johnson & Johnson Co JH-315 501 George St New Brunswick NJ 08903

FETTERHOFF, BARBARA GILLAM, office administrator; b. Bryn Mawr, Pa., Mar. 17, 1929; d. Neal F. and Helen (Olson) Gillam; m. Ira L. Fetterhoff, May 28, 1955; children—Hans, Heidi. B.A., U. Del., 1951. Med. Sec. Smith Kline, Phila., 1951-55, Johns Hopkins U., Balt., 1955-56, Springfield St. Hosp., Sykesville, Md., 1957-59, Dr. John T. King, Balt., 1963-78; office mgr., med. sec. Ira L. Fetterhoff, M.D., Hagerstown, Md., 1980—. Compiler Outstanding Women of Washington County, Md., 1979, 84; editor, project dir. Reaching the Public: Publicity Guide for Community Groups in Tri-State Area, 1983. Local/state officer LWV, 1981—; mem. Md. Gov.'s Adv. Com. on Reapportionment and Redistricting, 1981; Md. Adminstrv. Bd. Election Laws, 1983—. Recipient citation for work on title IX, Gov. Md., 1984. Mem. AAUW (br. pres. 1975, 83, v.p. state membership 1980-82, assn. nominating com. 1981-83, v.p. state program 1985—, meritorious award 1984), Alpha Iota, Phi Kappa Phi. Republican. Episcopalian. Office: 1610 Oak Hill Ave Hagertown MD 21740-2929

FETTERMAN, CAROLE L., publicity/public relations coordinator, producer, writer; b. Buffalo, Jan. 7, 1953; d. Harry William Fetterman and Jean Audrey (Solters) Dailey. Cert. Pub. Relations and Advt., SUNY-Buffalo, 1981, A.A., 1982; B.A., State Univ. Coll.-Buffalo, 1983. Producer Sta. WGR-TV, Buffalo, 1981-83, assignment editor/writer, 1981-82, news writer, researcher Sta. WGR, 1982; comml. continuity coordinator Sta. WGRZ-TV, Buffalo, 1983-85; pub. affairs producer: Open Rap, Inquiry, 1981-83; broadcast publicity coordinator Curtains Up, 1985. Publicity coordinator Friends of Philharm. MUNY Tennis Tournament, 1985. Nat. Acad. TV Arts and Scis. Republican. Roman Catholic. Home: 78 Fairfield Ave Lancaster NY 14086

FETTERMAN, NELMA IRENE, home economist; b. Starbuck, Man., Can., Feb. 21, 1938; d. Laude and Hesper Orpha (Olsen) F.; B.Ed., U. Alta., 1965; M.A., Mich. State U., 1968; Ph.D., Ohio State U., 1977. Elem. sch. tchr., Domain, Man., Can., 1958-60; jr. high sch. English tchr., Lethbridge, Alta., Can., 1960-62; high sch. tchr., Nanton, Alta., 1965-66; jr. high sch. home econs. tchr., Edmonton, Alta., 1966-67; assoc. prof. home econs. U. Alta., Edmonton, 1968—. Contbr. articles to profl. jours. Mary A. Clarke scholar, 1974-75; Marion K. Piper internat. fellow, 1975-76. Mem. Am. Home Econs. Assn., Assn. Coll. Profs. Textiles and Clothing, Am. Soc. Info. Sci., Can. Home Econs. Assn., Alta. Home Econs. Assn. Mem. United Ch. Can. Home: 247 Surrey Gardens Edmonton AB T5T 1Z3 Canada Office: 223B Home Econs Bldg U Alta Edmonton AB T6G 2M8 Canada

FETTERS, JOAN FRANCES, child care center administrator, educator; b. South Sioux City, Nebr., Apr. 4, 1939; d. Elmer David and Rose Viola (Leuenhagen) Owen; m. Harold Lee Fetters, June 9, 1958; children—Ricky Lee, Troy Dow, Mark Owen. B.A., U. No. Colo., 1960; postgrad. Mesa Coll., 1975. Tchr. pub. schs., Los Angeles, Oakland and Woodland, Calif., 1960-67, Ft. Collins, Colo., 1967-70, Crow Indian Reservation, Pryor, Mont., 1971-72; owner, mgr. Children's Workshops, Ft. Collins, 1983—, Learning Tree Children's Ctrs., Grand Junction, Colo., 1975—. Mem. Mesa County Dirs. Orgn. (pres. 1978-79), Larimer County Assn. for Edn. of Young Children, Nat. Assn. for Edn. of Young Children. Avocations: piano; reading; biking. Home: 3206 Norwood Ct Fort Collins CO 80525 Office: Children's Workshops 635 S Grant Fort Collins CO 80521

FETTWEIS, YVONNE CACHÉ, archivist; b. Los Angeles, Nov. 28, 1935; d. Boyd Eugene and Georgette Louisa (Tilmann) Adams; m. Rolland Phillip Fettweis, July 22, 1967; children—Maurice C.B. II, Michele-Yvonne; m. Maurice Lee Caché, Jan. 8, 1955 (div. 1962). B.A., Wagner Coll., 1954; postgrad Am. U., 1973, Bentley Coll., 1981. Legal sec., asst. Judge, Davis & Stern, and Orfinger & Tindall, Daytona Beach, Fla., 1961-66; head recording sect., bd. dirs. First Ch. Christ, Scientist, Boston, 1969-71, research assoc., 1971-72, adminstrv. archivist, 1972-78, sr. assoc. archivist, 1979-84, records adminstr., 1984—. Exec. sec. Volusia County Goldwater campaign, Daytona Beach, 1964. Mem. Soc. Am. Archivists, Am. Mgmt. Assn., New Eng. Archivists, Assn. Records Mgrs. and Adminstrs. (bd. dirs. 1983—), Assn. Col. and Research Librarians, Bay State Hist. League. Republican. Christian Scientist. Lodges: Order Eastern Star, Order Rainbow (bd. dirs. 1972-77). Home: 42 Edgell Dr Framingham MA 01701 Office: 1st Ch Christ Scientist Christian Sci Center Boston MA 02115

FETZER, PATRICIA NASSIF, lawyer, educator; b. Cedar Rapids, Iowa, June 7, 1949; d. M. Morey and Barbara (Lindsey) Nassif; B.A. in history with honors, U. Iowa, 1971, J.D., 1974; m. William E. Fetzer, Aug. 29, 1970. Admitted to Iowa bar, 1974; assoc. atty. Simmons, Perrine, Albright & Ellwood, Cedar Rapids, 1974-78; sole practice, Cedar Rapids 1978-80; Bigelow teaching fellow, lectr. law U. Chgo. Law Sch., 1980-81; vis. assoc. prof. Coll. Law, U. Iowa, 1981-84, clin. assoc. prof., 1984-85, clin. prof., 1985—; vis. prof. U. Fla. Coll. Law, 1985. Mem. Iowa Bar Assn., Order of Coif, Phi Beta Kappa. Christian Scientist. Editor notes and comments The Iowa Law Rev. 1973-74; contbr. articles to profl. jours. Office: University of Iowa College of Law Iowa City IA 52242

FEUER, BARBARA APRIL, union executive; b. N.Y.C., Apr. 19, 1949; d. George Phillip and Norma June (Wolin) F. B.A., Am. U., 1971; cert. de la

Langue Francaise, Sorbonne, Paris, 1970; M.S. with honors, U. LaVerne, 1979, doctoral candidate, Columbia U. Tchr. French, Pub. Schs., Washington, 1973-75; program coordinator YMCA Human Devel. Ctr., San Diego, 1976-80; tng. specialist Assn. Flight Attendants, Washington, 1980-82, dir., 1982—; instr. U. Md., 1985—; instr. ESL, positive parenting San Diego Community Colls., 1976-79; psychol. asst. San Diego Family Inst., 1978-80. Contbr. articles to profl. publs. Mem. Task Force on Women and Alcoholism, Washington, 1981-83, N. Am. Commn. on Women, 1983-84; cons. human resource devel. Named one of Outstanding Young Women Am., 1983. Mem. Assn. Labor Mgmt. Adminstrs. and Cons. on Alcoholism (chpt. v.p. 1981- 82, chpt. pres. 1982-83, bd. dirs.), Am. Soc. Tng. and Devel., Soc. for Study of Traumatic Stress. Office: Assn Flight Attendants 1625 Massachusetts Ave NW Washington DC 20036

FEUERHELM, JILL ANN, media specialist, educational software designer; b. Pasadena, Calif., May 7, 1948; d. Robert Warren and Jane Mary (Bode) Feuerhelm; m. Thomas Glenn Layton, May 23, 1980. A.A., Pasadena City Coll., 1968; B.S. in Edn., No. Ariz. U., 1971. Cert. tchr., Ariz. Tchr. Tolleson Sch. Dist., Ariz., 1973-75; Title I coordinator Kilbuck Sch., Kuskokwim Sch. Dist., Bethel, Alaska, 1975-79; microcomputer specialist, children's librarian Eugene Pub. Library, Oreg., 1983-85; software designer The 22d Ave Wordshop, Eugene, 1982-85, prodn. mgr., 1983-85; pres. TJ, Inc., 1985—. Designer computer software The Hinky Pinky Game, 1983. Mem. ALA, Pacific Northwest Library Assn., Oreg. Ednl. Media Assn., Internat. Council for Computers in Edn., Northwest Council for Computers in Edn. Office: 1430 Willamette Suite 236 Eugene OR 97401

FEYTEN, CARINE MARIE, foreign language educator, translator, researcher; b. Mechelen, Belgium, Mar. 14, 1958; came to U.S., 1983; d. Edgard and Viviane (Limbourg) F. B.A. in Germanic Philology, Cath. U. Louvain, 1980, M.A. in Germanic Philology, 1981; cert. in edn. Univ. Ibero-Americana (Mex.), 1981; postgrad. U. South Fla., 1983—. Translator Industry and Minister of European Affairs, Brussels, 1976—; tchr.'s asst. high sch., Tournai, Belgium, 1979; lectr., asst. Faculte Universitaires Saint Louis, Brussels, 1978-80; lang. teaching cons., educator Inlingua Internat. Sch. Langs., Brussels, 1981-83; grad. research asst. U. South Fla., Tampa, 1983-86, adj. prof., 1986—, fgn. lang. supervising prof., 1986; French tutor, 1984—. Recipient Study Scholarship award for Venezuela, 1980; Research Scholarship award for Spain, 1980; Outstanding Student award Cath. U. of Louvain, 1981. Mem. Linguistic Soc. Am., Am. Council Teaching Fgn. Langs., Fla. Fgn. Lang. Assn., Nat. Assn. Female Execs., Phi Kappa Phi. Roman Catholic. Avocations: classical guitar; gymnastics; travel; languages; gourmet cooking. Home: 752 S Shore Dr Land O'Lakes FL 33539 Office: U South Fla Edu 316K 4202 Fowler Ave Tampa FL 33620

FIALA, JOANNE CHRISTINE, personnel executive; b. N.Y.C., June 23, 1946; d. Armando and Anne (Cavaliere) Siconolfi; m. Anthony John Fiala, May 27, 1971 (div. 1981); 1 child, Christine. B.S., Ohio State U., 1968. Asst. buyer Bloomingdales, N.Y.C., 1968-71; account exec. Covertemp, White Plains, N.Y., 1971-76; pres., owner Vantage Careers, White Plains, 1976-83; pres., owner Westfield/Westemp, White Plains, 1983—. Mem. Assn. Personnel Cons., Adminstrv. Mgmt. Soc., County C. of C. Republican. Avocations: skiing; jogging; tennis. Home: Weavers Hill 7-B Greenwich CT 06830 Office: Westfield Personnel 1 N Broad Way White Plains NY 10601

FIALKO, JOAN VALERIE, company executive; b. Winnipeg, Man., Can., Feb. 14, 1946; came to U.S., 1951; d. Harry William and Una Pearl (Lewis) Tyler; m. Thomas Murphy Pollitt, Sept. 4, 1965 (div.); m. John Thomas Fialko, Apr. 23, 1971. (div.). B.A. in Bus. Adminstrn., Pepperdine U., 1977; M.B.A., U. Phoenix, 1983. Sec. Rockwell Internat., Downey, Calif., 1965-72, statis. analyst, 1972-74, fin. analyst, 1974-81, cost analyst, 1981-84, supr. material performance reporting, 1984—. Recipient Sustained Superior Performance award Rockwell Internat., 1971, Astronauts/Customer award, 1971. Mem. Nat. Mgmt. Assn. Episcopalian. Home: 4126 Hackett Ave Lakewood CA 90713 Office: Rockwell Internat 12241 Lakewood Blvd Downey CA 90241

FIASCO, CAROLYN LEE, counselor; b. Wayne, Mich., Oct. 16, 1944; d. Manuel Maurice and Virginia Lee (Tapp) Graddy; B.S., Murray (Ky.) State U., 1966; M.A. in Communications, Purdue U., 1969, Ed.S. in Counseling and Personnel, 1971; m. John Mirrell Fiasco, May 1, 1981; 1 child, John Christopher. Family living editor, agrl. info. dept. Purdue U., 1969-72; tech. assoc. Center Vocat. and Tech. Edn., Ohio State U., Columbus, 1972, residence complex dir., 1972-74; dir. residence life Capital U., Columbus, 1975-78; counselor, faculty mem. Manatee Community Coll., Bradenton, Fla., 1978—, also mem. exec. bd.; workshop dir., cons. in field. Mem. Circle 12, Palma Sola Presbyterian Ch., Bradenton, 1982-83. Assoc. editor Fla. Speech Communication Jour. Contbr. articles tok profl. jours. Mem. Am. Personnel and Guidance Assn., Am. Coll. Personnel Assn., Nat. Assn. Student Personnel Adminstrs., Nat. Assn. Women Deans, Adminstrs. and Counselors, Speech Communication Assn., Fla. Community Coll. Press Assn. (pres.), Fla. Community Coll. Activities Assn. (exec. com.), Alphecca, Alpha Omicron Pi, Chi Delta Phi, Lambda Iota Tau. Home: 6521 Wood Pond Dr Bradenton FL 34202 Office: 5840 26th St W Bradenton FL 33507

FICKES, MARITA CLARK, accountant; b. Chappell, Nebr., Mar. 22, 1946; d. Irven Frank and Birdie Mae (Williams) Clark; m. Allen Horton Zimmer, June 11, 1966 (div. Nov. 1973); m. Mark Blaine Fickes, Jr., June 8, 1974; children—Matthew Clark, Morriah Lynn. B.S., U. Nebr., 1969, postgrad., 1977-78. C.P.A., Nebr. Tchr., Neligh pub. schs., Nebr., 1969-71, Elgin pub. schs., Nebr., 1971-72; salesperson Sears Roebuck Co./Gold Key Realty, Lincoln, 1972-74; mgmt. trainee Gen. Electric Co., Hendersonville, N.C., 1978-79; staff acct. Fred A. Lockwood & Co., C.P.A.s, Gering, Nebr., 1979-81; prin. M.C. Fickes, C.P.A., Chappell, 1981—. Bd. dirs. Chappell Area Med. Services, 1981—, Sidney Meml. Hosp., Nebr., 1985—; mem. Rural Health Manpower Commn., Nebr., 1984—. Mem. Am. Inst. C.P.A.s, Nebr. Soc. C.P.A.s, Am. Morgan Horse Assn., Phi Upsilon Omicron, Omicron Nu. Avocations: gardening; equitation; music. Home: 1302 6th St Chappell NE 69129 Office: MC Fickes CPA 641 2d St Chappell NE 69129

FIDDLE, LINDA WALDER, former public relations account executive, writer; b. Newark, Mar. 15, 1959; d. Justin P. and Ellen (Berkeley) W. A.B., Vassar Coll., 1981; now student Benjamin N. Cardozo Sch. Law. Intern, Drawing Ctr. Art Gallery, N.Y.C., 1981; asst. dir. pub. relations Lord & Taylor, N.Y.C., 1981-83; account exec. John R. Walsh Assocs., N.Y.C., 1983-85; advt. coordinator Norman, Craig Kummel Inc., N.Y.C., 1978. Contbr. articles to publs. Mem. Publicity Club of N.Y.

FIEDLER, BOBBI, congresswoman; b. Santa Monica, Calif., Apr. 22, 1937; student Santa Monica City Coll., Santa Monica Tech. Sch.; LL.D. (hon.), West Coast Coll. Law, 1979; children—Lisa, Randy. Owner, mgr. pharmacies; mem. Los Angeles Bd. Edn., 1977; co-founder BUSTOP antibusing orgn.; mem. 97th-99th Congresses from 21st Dist. Calif. Bd. dirs. Com. Investigating Valley Ind. City/County; mem. Los Angeles Bd. Edn., 1977; bd. sponsors B'nai B'rith Youth Orgn. Named Outstanding Freshman, 97th Congress. Mem. Bus. and Profl. Women's Assn. Republican. Office: 1607 Longworth House Office Bldg Washington DC 20515

FIEDOR, GENEVIEVE EILEEN, nurse; b. Big Goose Creek, Wyo., Nov. 22, 1919; d. John and Magdaline (Sefczyk) Kopchia; R.N., Providence Sch. Nursing, Detroit, 1944; B.A. with distinction, U. Redlands, 1976, M.A., 1979; m. Adolph J. Fiedor, Aug. 25, 1944; children—Jeanette M., Alan J., Diane L., John C. Nurse, Providence Hosp., Detroit, 1944, St. Mary's Hosp., San Francisco, 1944-46; office nurse Dr. Clyde Kennedy, San Diego, 1946-54; with Stanford U. Hosp., 1965—, adminstrv. clin. nursing supr., 1968—. Active, Girl Scouts U.S.A., 1956-67, Boy Scouts Am., 1959-61, Palo Alto PTA, 1956-77, Palo Alto Little League, 1959-63, 68-71, ARC, 1981-84. Mem. Am. Assn. Critical Care Nurses, Calif. Soc. Nursing Service Adminstrs., Providence Hosp. Nurses Assn. Republican. Roman Catholic. Contbr. in field. Home: 16 Tulip Ln Palo Alto CA 94303 Office: Nursing Service Stanford U Hosp Stanford CA 94305

FIELD, BARBARA ANN, telecommunications company executive; b. Clayton, N. Mex., d. Marion Malcolm and Katherine Florence (Scott) Watkins; m. Brayton Allen Field, Dec. 5, 1954; children—Steven, Barbara, Catherine, Gerald. Mem. personnel staff Royal Jet Aircraft, Alhambra, Calif., 1957-59, United Testing Labs., Alhambra, 1959-62; cons. Telephone Analysis Co. and predecessor firms, Los Angeles, Chgo., Oak Park and Forest Park, Ill., 1962—. Mem. Internat. Orgn. Women Telecommunications Cons., Frank Lloyd Wright Found. (vol. 1982—). Republican. Avocation: reading. Home: 177 N Grove Ave Oak Park IL 60301 Office: Telephone Analysis Co 1001 S Harlem Ave Forest Park IL 60130

FIELD, CHARLOTTE, retired association executive; b. Seattle, June 9, 1915; d. Charles Henry and Evelyn Maude (Westcott) F.; B.A., U. Wash., 1936. Fashion coordinator Bon Marche Dept. Store, Seattle, 1940-41, display coordinator, 1941-44, asst. merchandising mgr., 1944-45, asst. rep., N.Y.C., 1945-46; asst. dir. publicity Lord & Taylor Dept. Store, N.Y.C., 1946-47; merchandising coordinator, design cons., asst. to pres. Gump's Dept. Store, San Francisco, 1949-50; account exec. Abbott Kimball Agy., San Francisco, 1951-54; dir. nat. food publicity Wash. State Apple Commn., Seattle, 1957-75. Mem. Fashion Group, Am. Women in Radio and TV (pres. Evergreen chpt. 1966-67), Nat. Edn. Found. (rep. Am. Women in Radio and TV 1967-68), Elec. Women's Round Table. Club: Wash. Athletic. Home: 110-100 SE #29 Bellevue WA 98004

FIELD, ELIZABETH ASHLOCK, preservationist; b. Little Rock, Nov. 27, 1915; d. Jesse Vernon and Felecia Irene (Bruner) Ashlock; grad. Little Rock Jr. Coll., 1934; student Washington U., St. Louis, 1934-35, U. Ark., 1962-63; m. Henry Lamar Field, Sept. 8, 1938 (dec. Nov. 1960); 1 dau., Elizabeth Field Wassell. Dir. historic house mus. Angelo Marre House, 1965-71; dir. Ark. Commemorative Commn., Little Rock, 1972-74. Mem. Nat. Trust for Historic Preservation, Fla. Trust for Historic Preservation, Decorative Arts Trust, Folk Art Ctr. of the Americas, Lowe Art Mus., Am. Clan Gregor Soc., Dade Heritage Trust (trustee 1975-76), Vizcayans, Hist. Soc. So. Fla. (sec. 1980-81), Quapaw Quarter Assn. (pres. 1972-74), Phi Theta Kappa. Episcopalian. Home: 5520 Maggiore Coral Gables FL 33146

FIELD, JANE SEABORG, public relations executive; b. Evanston, Ill., Feb. 12, 1939; d. Ernest Bernard and Janet Louise (Hand) Seaborg; m. Leslie Edward Field, Oct. 28, 1962 (div. 1972); children—Alexander Huston, Daniel Adams. Student Beloit Coll., 1957, 58. Adminstrv. assoc. G.D. Searle & Co., Skokie, Ill., 1974-78; pub. info. and mktg. rep. Michael Reese Hosp. Health Plan, Chgo., 1978-80; mgr. pub. relations PruCare of Ill., Des Plaines, 1980-83; dir. pub. relations and advt. Prudential Health Care Plan, Inc., Roseland, N.J., 1984-85; dir. pub. affairs MacNeal Hosp., Berwyn, Ill., 1985—; communications cons. Old Orchard Country Club Theatre, Mt. Prospect, Ill., 1983-85. Contbg. writer Your Pony mag., 1955-57. Bd. dirs. Evanston Twp. Republican Orgn., Evanston, 1976-77; v.p. Women's Rep. Club, 10th Congl. Dist. Northeastern Ill., 1974-76; bd. dirs. Winnetka Community Theatre, 1978-80; mem. jr. bd. Hadley Sch. for Blind, Winnetka, Ill., 1964-69. Mem. Pub. Relations Soc. Am. (cert.), Women in Communications (v.p. 1981-82 North Shore Chgo. chpt.), Publicity Club N.Y., Publicity Club Chgo. (membership com. 1982-84), Republican. Episcopalian. Clubs: N.W. Press (edn. com. 1979-82); CHEC XXII, Cursillo. Home: 2430 Lawndale Ave Evanston IL 60201 Office: MacNeal Hosp 3249 S Oak Park Ave Berwyn IL 60402

FIELD, JEANNE ANNE, bank officer; b. Texarkana, Ark., Apr. 2, 1956; d. Buster Stanton and Lela Mae (Cunningham) F. B.A., Tex. Tech U., 1979; M.B.A., East Tex. State U.; postgrad. in banking Am. Inst. Banking, Texarkana, Tex. Regional editor Texarkana Gazette (Tex.), 1979-80; pub. info. officer Ark.-Tex. Council Govts., Texarkana, Ark., 1980-81; mktg. rep. Texarkana Nat. Bank (Tex.), 1981-83; mktg. dir., officer Oaklawn Bank, Texarkana, Tex., 1983—; pub. speaker, career counselor, local high schs., 1982—. Vol. various local charitable orgns., Texarkana, Tex. and Ark., 1979—; mem. choir First United Methodist Ch., Texarkana, Ark. Mem. Nat. Assn. Bank Women, Bank Mktg. Assn., Tex. Bankers Assn., Am. Bankers Assn., Tex. Tech Ex-Students Assn. (chmn. publicity 1980—), Texarkana C. of C. (women's involvement com. 1982—), Alpha Chi Omega Alumni, Sigma Delta Chi. Democrat. Club: Toastmasters (charter; treas. 1984—). Home: 409 Blanton St Texarkana TX 75501 Office: Oaklawn Bank 3000 New Boston Rd Texarkana TX 75501

FIELD, JUDITH JUDY, librarian; b. Bucyrus, Ohio, Sept. 30, 1939; d. William Harrison and Eva Gertrude (Miller) Judy; m. Nathaniel Lamson Field III, Jan. 25, 1959. B.B.A., U. Mich., 1961, M.L.S., 1963, M.B.A., 1969. Library mgr. Western Electric Bell Telephone Labs., Indpls., 1962-65; asst. librarian Natural Sci. Library, Ann Arbor, Mich., 1965-66; assoc. librarian Sch. Bus. Adminstrn., Ann Arbor, 1966-69; library mgr. Inst. Internat. Commerce, Ann Arbor, 1969-71, research assoc., 1971-72; head gen. references Flint Pub. Library, Mich., 1972—; pres. Mich. Interorgn. Council on Continuing Library Edn., Lansing, Mich., 1983—; bd. dirs. Continuing Library Edn. Network and Exchange, Washington, 1979-81. Editor: International Finance Bibliography, 1971; Apprentice and Training Program, 1972; Beginning Positions and Training Program, 1973. Mem. LWV, Friends of Detroit Pub. Library, Spl. Libraries Assn. (dep. conf. chmn. 1983—, chmn. library mgmt. div., 1983-84, pres. Mich. chpt. 1981-82), ALA, Am. Soc. Info. Scis., Am. Inst. Parliamentarians. Republican. Avocations: archaeology; backgammon; archery. Home: 20500 Clement Northville MI 48167 Office: Flint Pub Library 1026 E Kearsley Flint MI 48502

FIELD, JULIA ALLEN, futurist, conceptual planner, association executive; b. Boston, Jan. 5, 1937; d. Howard Locke and Julia Wright (Field) Allen. B.A. cum laude, Harvard U. 1960, postgrad. Grad Sch. Deign, 1964-65; postgrad. Pius XII Grad. Sch., Florence, Italy, 1961; postgrad. Walden U. Inst. for Advanced Studies, 1982—. Cons. to archtl. and environ. firms, 1964-69; cons. Forestry Dept. of Simla (India), 1968-69; founder, v.p. Black Grove, Inc., Miami, Fla., 1970-80; founder, pres. Amazona 2000, Bogotá, Colombia, 1971—; leader Task Force Amazona 2000, DAINCO, 1977-78; pres. Acad. Arts and Scis. of the Ams., Miami, Fla., 1979—; mem. presdl. adv. com. on tech. devel. Group of Yr. 2000, Colombia, 1971-74; mem. men and biosphere com. UNESCO, Colombia, 1972-78; mem. task force on colonization Report to Pres. Colombia, 1972; cons. So. Unified Command, Republic of Colombia 1981—; hon. nat. insp. resources and environment Republic of Colombia, 1982—; bd. visitors Duke U. Primate Ctr., 1979—; prin. speaker various seminars, congresses. Mem. City of Miami Bicentennial Com., 1975-76; coordinator Community of Man Task Force, Miami, 1975-76; mem. Blueprint for Miami 2000, 1982—. Recipient Rachel Carson award, 1967. Author: Amazona 2000, 1978; The Zoo is Dead: Let us Plan a New Place for a Living City, 1968; Amazonia as a World Model, 1972; editor: Game and Wildlife Preserves in the USSR, 1965; Man and Nature, 1965; illustrator: Bodymarkings in Southwestern Asia, 1960; Essays on American Culture, 1961; filmmaker: Man Against Nature, 1966; organized archtl. graffiti poster exhbn.: The Writing on the Wall, 1968. Fellow Royal Geog. Soc. (London); mem. World Future Soc., Internat. Assn. Hydrogen Energy, UN Assn. U.S., Planetary Citizens, Am. Farmland Trust, ACLU, Sociedad Colombiana de Ecología. Office: 3551 Main Hwy Miami FL 33133

FIELD, KAREN ANN, real estate broker; b. New Haven, Conn., Jan. 27, 1936; d. Abraham Terry and Ida (Smith) Rogovin; m. Barry S. Crown, June 29, 1954 (div. 1969); children—Laurie Jayne, Donna Lynn, Bruce Alan, Bradley David; m. 2d Michael Lehmann Field, Aug. 10, 1969 (div. 1977). Student Vassar Coll., 1953-54, Harrington Inst. Interior Design, 1973-74. Owner Karen Field Interiors, Chgo., 1970—, Karen Field & Assocs., Chgo., 1980-81; pres., ptnr. Field Pels & Assocs., Chgo., 1981-86. Mem. women's council Camp Henry Horner, Chgo., 1960; bd. dirs., treas. Winnetka Pub. Sch. Nursery (Ill.), 1961-63; mem. exec. com. woman's bd. U. Chgo. Cancer Research Found., 1965-66, pres. jr. aux., 1960-66; bd. dirs., sec. United Charities, Chgo., 1966-68, Victory Gardens Theatre, Chgo., 1979; co-founder, pres. Re-Entry Ctr., Wilmette, Ill., 1978-80; mem. br. Parental Stress Services, Chgo., 1981—. Recipient Servian award Jr. Aux. of U. Chgo. Cancer Research Found., 1966, Margarite Wolf award Women's Bd., U. Chgo. Cancer Research Found., 1967. Mem. Chgo. Real Estate Bd., Chgo. Council Fgn. Relations, English Speaking Union (jr. bd. 1958-59). Office: La Thomas & Co 15 E Superior Chicago IL 60611

FIELD, MARIA NOLTE, art administrator; b. New Ulm, Minn., Apr. 7, 1941; d. Edwin Adolph and Emma Clara Helen (Loeslin) Nolte; m. Teddy Duane Fuller, Feb. 22, 1959 (div. 1979); children—Jody, Kathy, Beth; m. Max Wayne Field, May 8, 1982. With H&W Motor Parts/Ostensons, Inc., Windom, Minn., 1969-77; head payroll dept. Nat. Office Benson Optical, Edina, Minn., 1978; art dir. Rembrandt Enterprises, Inc., Edina, 1980—; owner, pres. The Associates, St. Louis Park, Minn., 1984—; cons. Capitol Travel Inc., St. Paul, 1984—; dir. Oak Park Heights State Bank, Stillwater, Minn. Co-author: Entrepreneurship. Bd. dirs., sec. Midwest Assn. Comatose Care, Mpls., 1984—; bd. dirs. Cottonwood County Aid to Retarded Citizens, Windom, 1968-72, Kidney Found. Upper Midwest, Minn., 1970-77. Recipient Outstanding Service award Assn. Retarded Citizens, 1968-72, Kidney Found. Upper Midwest, 1972-76; Disting. Service award Windom Jaycees, 1975, Key Woman award Minn. Mrs. Jaycees, 1976; named One of 10 Outstanding Young Minnesotans, Minn. Jaycees, 1976. Mem. Key Woman Club, Minn. Women's Network, Nat. Assn. Female Execs. Republican. Unitarian. Avocations: sewing; flower gardening; interior decorating; walking; bicycling. Home: 3420 Heritage Dr Edina MN 55435 Office: Rembrandt Enterprises Inc 3434 Heritage Dr Edina MN 55435

FIELD, MARTHA AMANDA, law educator; b. Boston, Aug. 20, 1943; d. Donald T. and Adelaide (Anderson) F.; children—Maria Adelaide, Gabriel Hartry, Lucas Anthony. B.A., Harvard U., 1965; J.D., U. Chgo., 1968. Bar: D.C. 1969. Law clk. to Justice Abe Fortas, U.S. Supreme Ct., 1968-69; prof. law U. Pa., 1969-78, Harvard U., Cambridge, Mass., 1978—. Office: Harvard University Law Sch Langdell Hall #255 Cambridge MA 02138

FIELD, REBECCA ANN, psychologist, educator; b. Denver, Dec. 18, 1934; d. Herbert P. White and Marjorie (Sharp) F.; m. Kenneth Gordon, Sept. 5, 1959; children—David B., Robert W. B.A., No. Colo. State U., 1957; M.A., Calif. Inst. Integral Studies, 1977, Ph.D., 1981. Camp counselor Girl Scouts U.S.A., Colorado Springs, Colo., 1955, Flint, Mich., 1956; tchr. Anchorage Pub. Schs., 1957-58, Markham (Ill.) Pub. Schs., 1959-65; sr. citizens coordinator West Valley Coll., Saratoga, Calif., 1977-78; psychol. counselor, Los Gatos, Calif., 1981-85; cons., lectr. in field. Chmn. bd. CONTACT of Santa Clara County; active Speakers Bur., Lupus Found., Child Advocacy Council. Recipient 1st prize Sri Aurobindo Centennial Essay Contest, 1973; Kern Found. grantee, 1979-81. Mem. Assn. Transpersonal Psychology, Am. Futurist Assn., Am. Soc. Tng. and Devel., San Jose C. of C., Alpha Psi Omega. Clubs: Toastmasters (pres., area gov. of yr. award), Rebekah. Contbr. articles to profl. jours. Address: 105 Vista del Campo Los Gatos CA 95030

FIELD, SALLY, actress; b. Pasadena, Calif., 1946; student Actor's Studio, 1973-75; m. Allan Greisman, 1984; children—Peter, Eli, Maggie O'Mahoney. Starred in TV series: Gidget, 1965, The Flying Nun, 1967-69, The Girl With Something Extra, 1973; theatrical film debut in The Way West, 1967; other films include: Stay Hungry, 1976, Heroes, 1977, Smokey and the Bandit, 1977, Hooper, 1978, The End, 1978, Norma Rae, 1979 (Cannes Film Festival Best Actress award 1979, Acad. award 1980), Beyond the Poseidon Adventure, 1979, Smokey and the Bandit II, 1980, Back Roads, 1981, Absence of Malice, 1981, Kiss Me Goodbye, 1982, Places in the Heart (Acad. award best actress), 1984, Murphy's Romance, 1985; TV movies include: Maybe I'll Come Home In the Spring, 1971, Marriage: Year One, 1971, Home for the Holidays, 1972, Bridges, 1976, Sybil, 1976 (Emmy award 1977). Office: care Stan Kamen William Morris Agy 151 El Camino Beverly Hills CA 90212*

FIELD, SUSAN INGEBORG, business consultant; b. Providence, R.I., Nov. 20, 1953; d. Robert Eugene and Ellen Louise (Lewis) F.; B.S. in Biology, B.A. in Sociology, Providence Coll., 1976; M.B.A., 1980. Research biologist R.I. Hosp., Providence, 1977-83, adminstrv. intern, 1978-81; spl. lectr. Community Coll. R.I., 1979-81, 83; bus. cons. Field Mgmt. Group, 1983—; dir. Nutri Sea Foods, Inc. Rep. U.S. Congressional Adv. Bd., 1982—; researcher/canvasser People Acting Through Community Effort, 1970, 73; social worker Catholic Inner City Center, 1968-69. Serving as 2d lt. Army N.G., 1981—. Mem. Assn. M.B.A. Execs., Nat. Assn. Female Execs., Am. Hosp. Assn., AAUW. Club: Toastmasters. Home: 114 Veazie St Providence RI 02908 Office: 250 Admiral St Providence RI 02908

FIELDER, DEBORAH ANN, accountant; b. Fort Worth, Aug. 16, 1956; d. James Bartholomew and Ann Ruth (Rattner) Huba. B.S., Rollins Coll., 1977. Bookkeeper, Louis Arno, Acct., Satellite Beach, Fla., 1978-79; acct. TWA Services, Kennedy Space Ctr., Fla., 1979-81; bookkeeper Air & Sea Travel, Indialantic, Fla., 1981-83; acct. Premier Cruise Lines, Cape Canaveral, Fla., 1983—. Nat. Merit Scholar, 1972. Mem. Am. Bus. Womens Assn. Avocations: Horseback riding; reading. Home: 1315 N Fiske Blvd Cocoa FL 32922 Office: Premier Cruise Lines 101 George King Blvd Cape Canaveral FL 32920

FIELDING, PEGGY LOU MOSS, publishing company executive; b. Davenport, Okla., Oct. 28, 1928; d. John Richard and Hazel (Matlock) Moss; B.S., Central State U., 1949, M.A., U. Santo Tomás, 1971. Tchr. various U.S. govt. overseas schs., Japan, Cuba and Philippines, 1955-71; owner Partners in Pub., Tulsa, 1975—; instr. writing Tulsa Jr. Coll., 1976—. Mem. Okla. Writers Fedn., NE Okla. Romance Writers, Tulsa Night Writers Club, Small Pubs. Alliance, Romance Writers Am. Democrat. Baptist. Office: 1419 W 1st St Tulsa OK 74127

FIELDS, ANJALI VARMA, electronic warfare engineer; b. Chhindwara, M.P., India, Aug. 15, 1948; came to U.S., 1972; d. Vijay Bahadur and Radhey Kumari (Khare) Varma; m. Douglas Edward Fields, Jan. 6, 1980. B.E., U. Jabalpur, 1971; M.S., U. Utah, 1975, Ph.D., 1981. Research assoc. U. Mich., Ann Arbor, 1979; staff research engr. Kaiser Aluminum & Chem. Co., Pleasanton, Calif., 1980-82; co founder Livermore Assocs., Calif., 1982-83; sr. adv. engr. Shugart Corp., Sunnyvale, Calif., 1983-84; staff scientist Tracor MBA, San Ramon, Calif., 1984—. Coauthor: Pulverized Coal Combustion, 1979. Vice pres. Bhopal Cynate Disaster Relief Fund, San Leandro, Calif., 1984—. Mem. Am. Def. Preparedness Assn., Am. Assn. Old Crows, Nat. Assn. Female Execs. Republican. Hindu. Club: Toastmasters. Avocations: skiing; writing. Home: 31 Pulido Ct Danville CA 94536 Office: Tracor MBA Bollinger Canyon Rd San Ramon CA 94583

FIELDS, DAISY BRESLEY, human resource development consultant; b. Bklyn.; student Hunter Coll., 1932-35, Am. U., 1949-53; m. Victor Fields, Aug. 2, 1936; 1 dau., Barbara Fields Ochsman. Personnel officer USAF Base, Norfolk, Va., 1942-45; asst. personnel officer Dept. Agr., Phila., 1945-47; asst. dir. personnel Smithsonian Instn., Washington, 1954-60; chief spl. programs NASA, Washington, 1960-67; spl. asst. Fed. Women's Program, VA, Washington, 1967-70; sr. program asso. Nat. Civil Service League, 1971-72; cons. Equal Employment Opportunity/Affirmative Action, 1972-75, 78—; exec. dir. Federally Employed Women, Washington, 1975-77; pres. Fields Assocs., Silver Spring, Md., 1978—; exec. dir. The Women's Inst., Am. U.; instr. Mt. Vernon Coll., 1979-80, Am. U., 1982. Chmn., Montgomery County (Md.) Personnel Bd., 1972-78; chmn. legis. com. Comm. for Women in Public Adminstrn., 1976-79; commr. Md. Commn. for Women, 1973-77; commr. Montgomery County Commn. for Women, 1979-82; chmn. Clearinghouse on Women's Issues; v.p. Women's Inst./Am. U. Recipient award Federally Employed Women, 1974, 78, UN Assn. U.S.A., 1980. Mem. Am. Soc. Tng. and Devel., Am. Soc. Public Adminstrn., Internat. Assn. Personnel Women, Internat. Personnel Mgmt. Assn., Nat. Council Career Women, Women's Equity Action League (pres. Md. 1972-74; award 1978), Federally Employed Women (pres. 1969-71), Nat. Press Club, Am. News Women's Club, Capital Press Women, Fedn. Orgns. Profl. Women (exec. council 1976-77, 80-82), Nat. Assn. Women Bus. Owners. Author: A Woman's Guide to Moving Up in Business and Government, 1983; contbr. articles to profl. jours.; editor-at-large IAPW Jour., 1972-76; editor FEW News and Views, 1972-77, Washington Ind. Writers. Home and Office: 13905 N Gate Dr Silver Spring MD 20906

FIELDS, EVA LOU, business executive; b. Cordele, Ga., Sept. 7, 1927; d. Tommy and Bertha Pearl (Musselwhite) Chandler; student public schs., Jacksonville, Fla.; m. Richard L. Fields, June 29, 1972; children—Ross D Bruner, Jay C. Bruner. Partner, Bruner Constrn. Co., Madison, Wis., 1954-66; asst. to dir. tng. Blue Cross Blue Shield, Dallas, 1967-70; ter. mgr. Southern Ill., Hollister Inc., Chgo., 1971-74, sales edn. mgr., 1974-80; dir. sales devel.

Sween Corp., Lake Crystal, Minn., 1981-83; pres. ELF Assocs. Ltd., 1984—. Mem. Nat. Soc. Sales Tng. Execs., Am. Soc. Tng. and Devel. (past mem. exec. com. sales tng. div.), Nat. Speakers Assn., Internat. Listening Assn. Presbyterian. Home: 30 Hilltop Ln Mankato MN 56001 Office: PO Box 3485 Mankato MN 56002

FIELDS, FREDRICA HASTINGS, designer, craftsman; b. Phila., Jan. 10, 1912; d. Theodore Mitchell and Carolyn Corlies (Baily) Hastings; student Wellesley Coll., 1930-32, Art Students League, 1933; m. Kenneth E. Fields, July 10, 1934; children—David Edward (dec.), Luellen, Stephen Francis. Designer craftsman in stained glass, 1948—; exhibited in one man show Artists Mart, Washington, 1955, First Presbyn. Ch., Stamford, Conn., 1976, Concordia Coll., Bronxville, N.Y., 1982, Greenwich (Conn.) YWCA, 1982; exhibited in group shows Nat. Soc. Arts and Letters, Washington, 1951, Smithsonian Instn., 1951, 53, 54, 57, 58, Corcoran Gallery Art, 1955, 56, Nat. Conf. on Religious Architecture, N.Y.C., 1967, Washington, 1970, Greenwich (Conn.) Art Soc. Ann. Exhbns., 1968-78, Stamford (Conn.) Art Soc., 1972, Danbury (Conn.) Public Library, 1974, Stained Glass Internat., N.Y.C., 1982; represented in permanent installations at Washington Cathedral, Marie Cole Auditorium, Greenwich Library, YWCA, Greenwich, Assn. for Research and Enlightenment Meditation/Prayer Center, Virginia Beach, Va., Conn. Hospice Inc., Branford, Concordia Coll., Bronxville, N.Y., many pvt. collections; tchr. classes in stained glass, Washington, 1950, YWCA, Greenwich, 1966, at studio, 1968-71. Recipient awards in stained glass Corcoran Gallery Art, 1955, 56, B.F. Drakenfeld award 6th Internat. Exhbn. of Ceramic Arts, Nat. Collections Fine Arts, Smithsonian Instn., 1957. Mem. Stained Glass Assn. Am., Greenwich Art Soc. Address: 561 Lake Ave Greenwich CT 06830

FIELDS, JANE KOLBER, hospital administrator; b. Buffalo, Apr. 9, 1952; d. Joseph Charles and Irene Mary (Kencik) Kolber; m. Lyle A. Fields, May 1, 1977; children—Jake, Casey. B.S. in Nursing, U. Rochester, 1974; M.S., Boston U., 1976. Community health nurse Monroe County Dept. Health, Rochester, N.Y., 1974-75; home care coordinator Montefiore Hosp., Bronx, N.Y., 1976-78; home care adminstr. Nyack Hosp., N.Y., 1978-85, v.p. community health services, 1985—. Sec. bd. dirs. Am. Cancer Soc., Rockland County unit, Nyack, 1983-85. Mem. Nat. Assn. Home Care, Home Care Assn. N.Y. State (bd. dirs. 1985—), N.Y. State Pub. Health Assn., Sigma Theta Tau. Democrat. Roman Catholic. Avocations: tennis; skiing. Home: 32 Edgewood Rd Hartsdale NY 10530 Office: Nyack Hosp North Midland Ave Nyack NY 10960

FIELDS, JOAN R., chemical company executive; b. N.Y.C., Jan. 18, 1930; d. Albert and Etta (Levy) Ross; B.S., Adelphi U., 1951; cert. early childhood edn. Ann Reno Inst., 1951; children—Larry M., Paul B. Tchr., Woodward Sch., Bklyn., 1951-52, Syosset Sch. Dist., 1959-65; corp. sec. Albatross Chem. Co., Long Island City, N.Y., 1966-69, pres., chmn. bd., 1969—; chmn. bd., pres. Etro Realty Corp., 1969—, Apparel Innovations Inc., 1978—; pres. J.R.F. Properties Inc., 1980—. Mem. young profl. com. United Jewish Appeal; mem. Sutton Pl. Synagogue. Mem. N.Y. Assn. Women Bus. Owners, Internat. Platform Assn., Queens C. of C. (city affairs com.), Phi Sigma Sigma. Clubs: B'nai B'rith, Atrium. Home: 303 E 57th St New York NY 10022 Office: 36-55 36th St Long Island City 11106

FIELDS, KAREN KAY, management executive; b. Columbus, Ohio, Sept. 8, 1942; d. James Wilson and Leuara Jane (Fout) F.; cert. med. tech. Brown's Sch., Columbus, 1964; R.N., Los Angeles City Coll., 1974; B.S. in Nursing, Calif. State U.-Los Angeles, 1977, M.S. candidate, 1983. Med. technologist Ohio State U. Hosps., Columbus, 1965-67; med. instr., cons. Career Acad., Columbus and Los Angeles, 1967-71; nurse, nurse recruiter Cedars Sinai Med. Center, Los Angeles, 1974-79; asst. dir. nursing, nurse recruiter Los Angeles New Hosp., 1979-80; dir. nursing services Nursing Services Internat. (now NSI Services, Inc.), Los Angeles, 1980-83, adminstr. nursing services, 1983, v.p. ops., 1984—. Mem. Nat. Assn. Female Execs., AAUW. Office: 8383 Wilshire Blvd Suite 810 Beverly Hills CA 90211

FIELDS, MARTHA JACOBS, state official, educational adminstrator; b. Greensboro, Ala., Jan. 26, 1940; d. Homer Lee and Lois (Newell) Jacobs; m. John Pope Fields, July 12, 1980; 1 child, Leigh Bolt. B.S., Troy U.; M.Ed., Auburn U., also postgrad. Counselor, psychologist Henry County Pub. Schs., Hendland, Ala., 1970-71, local dir. spl. edn., Abbeville, Ala., 1971-72; local dir. spl. edn. Montgomery County Pub. Schs., Montgomery, Ala., 1972-76; staff specialist Md. Dept. Edn., Balt., 1976-77, dir. div. spl. edn., 1977-79, asst. state supt., 1979—; instr. Auburn U., Montgomery, 1973-76; mem. Md. Gov.'s Adv. Com. Coordinating Services to Handicapped, 1979—; chmn., mem. State Coordinating Com. for Services to Handicapped, Balt., 1979—; mem. Gov.'s Task Force on Spl. Edn. Funding. Named Educator of Yr., Girl Scouts Central Md., 1981; Woman Mgr. of Yr., State of Md., 1983. Mem. Council for Exceptional Children, Nat. Assn. State Dirs. Spl. Edn. (pres.-elect 1983-84, pres. 1984-85), Council Adminstrs. Spl. Edn. (legis. chair 1982-84). Democrat. Baptist. Office: Md Dept Edn 200 W Baltimore St Baltimore MD 21201

FIELDS, RONA MARCIA, psychologist; b. Chgo., Oct. 27, 1934; d. William Samuel and Kate Darcy (Goldman) Katz; B.A., Lake Forest Coll., 1953; M.S., U. Ill., 1955; M.A., Loyola U., Chgo., 1964; Ph.D., U. So. Calif., 1970; m. Armond Fields, June 9, 1953 (div. 1967); children—Louis Marc, Sean Steven, Cathy Nikema, Miriam Star. Community psychologist Chgo. Bd. Health, 1963-64; psychologist NDEA program Monrovia (Calif.) Guidance Center, 1964-67; asst. prof. psychology Pasadena (Calif.) City Coll., 1966-69; prof. human devel. Calif. State U., Los Angeles, 1967-72, Pacific Oaks Coll., Pasadena, 1969-71; vis. prof. edn. Calif. State U., Northridge, 1971-72; asso. prof. sociology Clark U., Worcester, Mass., 1972-76; founding mem. Sozialwissenschaftliches Institut fur Katastrophen und Umfallforschung, Kiel, W.Ger.; asso. Transnat. Family Research Inst., Bethesda, Md.; pres. Assos. in Community Health and Devel. Co-chmn. campaign Betty McCann for Va. State Legislature, 1979; sec. Alexandria (Va.) Mayor's Com. for Handicapped, 1980-82; bd. dirs. Nat. Capitol YMCA, 1982-85; v.p. Alexandria YMCA, 1982-84, pres., 1984—. Recipient Phila. Mayor's award for Outstanding Service in Human Rights, 1978. Mem. Am. Psychol. Assn. (task force status of women 1970-73, bd. social and ethical responsibility 1971-73), Am. Sociol. Assn., Internat. Studies Assn., Sociologists for Women in Soc., Soc. Psychol. Study of Social Issues, Gaelic League (exec. com. 1985-86), Irish Am. Cultural Inst., Psychologists for Social Action (nat. coordinator 1969-72), So. Calif. Peace Action Council (leadership collective 1969-72), Assn. Women in Psychology. Author: Society on the Run, 1973; The Armed Forces Movement and the Portuguese Revolution, 1978; Society Under Siege, 1976; Northern Ireland, 1979; The Future of Women, 1985; contbr. articles to profl. jours., chpts. to books. Home and Office: 222 E Del Ray Ave Alexandria VA 22301

FIELDS, SYLVIA KLEIMAN, medical publisher, nurse educator, consultant; b. N.Y.C., Jan. 20, 1934; d. Irving and Frieda (Berkowitz) Kleiman; children—Melissa Ellen, Andrew Gregory, Elizabeth Carrie. B.S., Adelphi U., 1954; M.A., Columbia U., 1960, M.Ed., 1975, Ed.D., 1977. R.N., N.Y., Ga. Instr., Mass. Gen. Hosp., Boston, 1955-57, Luth Med. Ctr., Bklyn., 1957-60, Queens Coll., N.Y.C., 1961-63; Title II nurse trainee Columbia U., 1959-60, 68-69; assoc. prof. SUNY-Farmingdale, 1963-72; assoc. prof. nursing SUNY-Stony Brook, 1972-78; dir. nursing program Emory U., Atlanta, 1978-82, lectr./cons., 1982—; sr. med. editor F.A. Davis Co., Phila., 1982—. Author: Guide to Patient Evaluation, 4th edit. 1982; editor: Adult Health, 1984; Child Health, 1984; Woman's Health, 1984; Psych Mental Health, 1984; contbr. articles to profl. jours. Chmn., Nassau Com. for Abortion Law Repeal, 1970; bd. dirs. Women's Health Alliance Phila., Fedn. Jewish Agys. Phila. Recipient award for meritorious service Planned Parenthood for Nassau County, 1971. Mem. Am. Nurses Assn., Bus. and Profl. Women (bd. dirs.), Phila. Book Clinic, Sigma Theta Tau, Kappa Delta Pi. Jewish. Home: 903 Latimer St Philadelphia PA 19107 Office: FA Davis Co 1915 Arch St Philadelphia PA 19103

FIELEKE, CATHARINE NICHOLSON (MRS. LESSLY C.A. FIELEKE), author, reader, lecturer, columnist; b. Ash Grove, Mo., Sept. 27, 1909; d. John Warren and Mattie (Duncan) Nicholson; student Drury Coll., Olivet Coll., U. Chgo.; m. Lessly C.A. Fieleke, Dec. 24, 1929; children—Norman, Sharon Fieleke Cohly, Cathy Fieleke Butterfield, Lessly, Laurel Fieleke Shoshani, Curtis, Teresa Fieleke Brooks. Pres., Fieleke Implement Co., 1965-67. Recipient awards Woman's Club, Am. Pen Women, others. Mem. World Soc. Poets Intercontinental, Pen Women (pres. Chgo. br. 1974-76, chmn. Nat. Mid-Adminstrn. Congress 1977), Nat. Writers Club, Internat. Platform Assn., Internat., Ill. (v.p.) poetry socs., Am. Acad. Poets, Internat. Biog. Assn., Friends Am. Writers, Children's Reading Round Table, Chgo. Poets and Patrons, Poets Club of Chgo., Kankakee Area Writers Group. Baptist. Club: Women's. Author: (poetry) Run-off from Northern Springs; Summer Solstices; Aspects of Autumn; The White Fields of Winter; author, prodn. asst. American Poetry Series, 1965; scripts for ednl. tapes Imperial Internat. Learning, Kankakee, Ill.; lectures and poetry editor Pen Woman mag.; contbr. articles and poems to newspapers and mags., column to area newspapers, ch. and community scripts. Home: 312 Ohio St Momence IL 60954

FIELO, MURIEL BRYANT, space engineer, interior designer; b. Bklyn., Dec. 11, 1921; d. Harry and Minnie (Dick) Bryant; student CCNY, evenings 1938-41, Rutgers U., evenings 1965-69; cert. N.Y. Sch. Interior Design, 1970; m. Julius Fielo, June 17; 1 son, Michael Kenneth. Gen. mgr. Fidelity Discount Corp., Irvington, N.J., adv. supr. Lincoln Loan Cos., Essex County, N.J., 1941-49; interior designer Alex Fielo Interior Decorators, Newark, part-time 1942-49, prin., 1949-69, owner, 1969—; designer, cons. space engr. Design Studios, East Orange, N.J., 1969—. Essex County freeholder clk. Bd. Freeholders, part-time 1972-76; commr. East Orange Bus. Devel. Authority, 1977—; mem. U.S. adv. council SBA-Region II, 1980-81; active LWV, 1950-55; organizer, 1st pres. South Orange chpt. Women's Am. ORT, 1952-54, mem. nat. speakers bur., 1952-65, parliamentarian No. N.J. council, 1955-65; pres. Amity chpt. B'nai B'rith, Newark, 1946-48, v.p. No. N.J. council, 1948-49, various nat. and state positions, 1948-80; mem. nat. com. on sect. fund raising Nat. Council Jewish Women, 1979-81, nat. tour. chmn., 1979-81; trustee community services council Oranges and Maplewood, United Way of Essex and West Hudson, 1981-83; bd. dirs. East Orange Central Ave. Mall Assn., 1979-83, chmn. new voter registration drive East Orange 2d Ward, 1955—, entire city, 1969; pres. East Orange Democratic Club, 1957-58, campaign coordinator for Dem. mayoral candidate, 1969, calendar coordinator Essex County Dem. party, 1970-76; mem. N.J. Bipartisan Coalition for Women's Appts., 1981—. Named Outstanding Entrepreneur of 1984, N.J. Gov., Outstanding Orgn. Pres., Kean Coll. Profl. Women's Assn., 1985, Wonder Woman of 1986, Bus. Jour. of N.J.; also recipient various awards for civic service. Mem. Internat. Soc. Interior Designers (dir. 1981-85), Nat. Home Fashions League (N.J. membership chmn. N.Y. chpt. 1981-82), Interior Design Soc., N.J. Assn. Women Bus. Owners (state bd. 1979-82), Women Entrepreneurs N.J. (pres. 1981-85), N.J. Home Furnishings Assn. (dir. 1981-84), Constrn. Specifications Inst., Guild Designer Woodworkers, Women Bus. Ownership Ednl. Coalition (N.J. State pres. 1985—, mem. steering com. interior designers for licensing in N.Y. 1985—), East Orange C. of C. (dir. 1977—, v.p. 1981-85), Bus. and Profl. Women's Club of Oranges (dir. 1958-66). Jewish. Mem. adv. panel Interior Design Mag., 1977—. Office: Mudge Interior Design and Gift Studio 185 S Clinton St East Orange NJ 07018

FIELSTRA, HELEN ADAMS, educator; b. Elkhorn, W.Va., Feb. 26, 1921; d. Fred Russell and Clara Sue (Williams) Adams; A.B., UCLA, 1950; M.A., Stanford U., 1954, Ed.D., 1967; m. Edmond T. Dooley, Jr., Nov. 15, 1941 (div. 1948); 1 dau., Dereth Dooley Pendleton; m. 2d, Clarence Fielstra, Jan. 1, 1956. Tchr., Santa Monica (Calif.) Unified Sch. Dist., 1947-50; elem. coordinator San Diego County Schs., 1950-52; lectr. edn. Stanford U., 1953-54, UCLA, 1957-58; gen. elem. supr. Burbank (Calif.) Unified Sch. Dist., 1954-56, Beverly Hills (Calif.) Unified Sch. Dist., 1959-61; asst. prof., assoc. prof., prof. edn. Calif. State U., Northridge, 1961—; tng. coordinator Office Econ. Opportunity Tng. and Devel. Center for So. Calif., 1965-66; cons., speaker curriculum devel. and instructional supervision, 1952—; prin. investigator prospective tchr. grad. fellowship project U.S. Office Edn., 1968-70; dir., prin. investigator NSF Interdisciplinary Social Sci. Projects, 1972-82; participant Nat. Forum on Excellence in Edn., 1983; sec.-treas. Hadco, Inc., Los Angeles, Fielstra Publs., Inc., Pacific Palisades. Recipient Disting. Teaching award Calif. State Univ. and Colls., 1969, Associated Students' cert. of service Calif. State U., Northridge, 1970. Mem. Am. Ednl. Research Assn., Nat. Soc. for Study Edn., Nat. Council Social Studies (publs. bd.), NEA (life), Assn. Supervision and Curriculum Devel., Calif. Assn. Supervision and Curriculum Devel. (chmn. com. supervision in structure public edn.), AAUP, Calif. Higher Edn. Assn. (dir. 1970-75, pres. 1973-74), Calif. Coll. and Univ. Faculty Assn. (pres. Calif. State U., Northridge chpt. 1969-70, state v.p. 1970-71, state pres. 1972-73), Am. Film Inst., Stanford U. Alumni Assn. (life); Delta Kappa Gamma (life; chpt. pres. 1960-62). Democrat. Clubs: Stanford, Town Hall Calif. (Los Angeles); Palisadian Woman's. Author: (with L.G. Thomas, A. Coladarci, Lucien Kinney) Perspective on Teaching, 1961; (with Clarence Fielstra) Africa-With Focus on Nigeria, 1963; author numerous curriculum guides, 6 ednl. films; editorial bd. Calif. Jour. Instructional Improvement, 1967-70; editor Reading Monograph, 1970; Social Studies in the Elementary School, 1972. Home: 14177 Sunset Blvd Pacific Palisades CA 90272 Office: Calif State U Northridge CA 91330

FIENBERG, LINDA DORIS, lawyer; b. Albany, N.Y., July 7, 1942; d. Chester Leonard F. and Marcia Doris Kartzman; B.A. with distinction, Cornell U., 1964; M.A.T. with honors, Wesleyan U., 1966; J.D., Georgetown U., 1973; m. Jeffrey D. Bauman, Mar. 2, 1980; children—Amy Bauman, Lane Blumenfeld, Jessica Bauman, Shawn Blumenfeld. Bar: D.C. 1973. Instr., Huntingdon Coll., Montgomery, Ala., 1966-67; research analyst U.S. EEO Commn., 1967-68, U.S. Civil Rights Commn., 1968-70; assoc. Arnold & Porter, Washington, 1973-78; spl. counsel. SEC, 1979-80, asst. gen. counsel, 1980-82, assoc. gen. counsel, 1982—. Mem. Am. Bar Assn., Women's Legal Defense Fund, Phi Beta Kappa. Office: 450 5th St NW Washington DC 20549

FIGUEROA, LINDA ROSA, lawyer; b. Bklyn., June 14, 1957; d. Arcadio and Doris Esther (Vega) Figueroa. B.A. in Econs., Harpur Coll., 1977; J.D., Cornell U., 1980. Bar: D.C. 1980. Atty., FCC, Washington, 1980—. Mem. ABA, Fed. Bar Assn., Hispanic Bar Assn., Omicron Delta Epsilon, Phi Delta Phi. Roman Catholic. Office: FCC 2025 M St NW Washington DC 20554

FIGURELLI, JENNIFER CONSTANCE, psychologist; b. Jersey City, May 11, 1945; d. Francesco Antonio and Jean (Bigler) F.; B.S., St. Lawrence U., 1966; M.A., U. S.C., 1970; Ph.D., Fordham U., 1977; postgrad. U. Calgary, Jersey City State Coll. Research psychologist Alta. (Can.) Mental Hosp., Ponoka, 1967; psychol. research asst. U. Calgary (Alta.), 1968-69; psychologist Columbia (S.C.) Public Schs., 1969-70; psychologist Jersey City Public Schs., 1970-82, dir. bur. spl. services, 1982—; asst. prof. psychology St. Peter's Coll., Jersey City, 1970—. Mem. S.C. State Com. on Legalization Abortion, 1970. Mem. NEA, N.J., Jersey City edn. assns., Nat. Assn. Sch. Psychologists (chmn. ad hoc com. 1972-73), Am., N.J., Inter-Am., Southeastern psychol. assns., Internat. Assn. Applied Psychology, N.J. Assn. Sch. Psychologists, Soc. Research in Child Devel., Am. Ednl. Research Assn. Editorial bd. Sch. Psychology Digest. Home: 88 Highland Ave Jersey City NJ 07306 Office: 241 Erie St Jersey City NJ 07306

FIKE, PATRICIA RUTH, health care institution administrator; b. Boston; Aug. 31, 1950; d. John William and Eleanor (Squires) F. Grad. Bridgeport Hosp Sch. Radiol. Tech., Conn., 1966; B.S. in Hosp. Adminstrn., Fla. Internat. U., 1979; M.H.A., St. Thomas Coll., Miami, 1984. Registered radiol. technologist, Fla. Asst. chief technologist, radio-therapist Park City Hosp, Bridgeport, Conn., 1966-68; asst. chief radiol. technologist Doctors' Hosp., Coral Gables, Fla., 1968-79; adminstrv. dir. Victoria Hosp., Miami, 1979—; adminstrv. cons. St. Vincent's Home Unwed Mothers, Miami, 1976-81. Mem. Am. Hosp. Radiology Adminstrs. (Quality Assurance award 1982), Am. Bus. and Profl. Women. Republican. Episcopalian. Avocations: gourmet cooking; sailing; astronomy. Office: Victoria Hosp 955 NW 3d St Miami FL 33134

FILER, ELIZABETH ANN, psychotherapist; b. N.Y.C., Oct. 16, 1923; d. Edwin and Edith Louise (Levy) Filer. B.S., Columbia U., 1944, M.A., 1945, M.S., 1954. Asst. tchr. to asst. dir. Mallay Nursery Sch., Bklyn., 1943-52; tchr., guidance staff N.Y. Sch. for Nursery Years, 1954-60; liaison social worker The Reece Sch., N.Y.C., 1954-60; cons. to schs. in N.Y.C., 1960-71; ednl. cons./therapist Ednl. Inst. for Learning and Research, N.Y.C., 1961-65; clin. social worker, psychotherapist in pvt. practice, N.Y.C., 1971—; cons. in field. Bd. dirs. Recreation Room and Settlement, N.Y.C., 1962-73. Recipient Founders Day award and Bicentennial medal Columbia U., 1954. Mem. Nat. Assn. Social Workers, N.Y. State Soc. Clin. Social Work Psychotherapists, Nat. Registry of Health Care Providers in Clin. Social Work, Soc. for Psychoanalytic Psychotherapy, World Fedn. for Mental Health. Avocations: swimming; sports; opera; reading; needlepoint; travel. Home: 240 E 79th St New York NY 10021

FILIPP, CAROLYN FRANCINE, music educator, insurance agent; b. Houston, Oct. 11, 1950; d. Emil Frank and Augustina Joyce (Klozik) Filipp. B.Music, U. Houston, 1973; M.Ed., Stephen F. Austin State U., 1977; postgrad. Houston Baptist U., 1979-80. Band dir. Ft. Bend Ind. Sch. Dist., Stafford, Tex., 1973-74, choral dir., 1974-76, choral dir., Missouri City, Tex., 1976-77; choral dir. Houston Ind. Sch. Dist., 1977—, band dir., 1985-86; pianist Houston Brethren Ch., 1964-73, choral dir., 1968-70; clarinetist, saxophonist, vocalist Space-City Dutchmen Orch., 1965-75; pvt. tchr. clarinet, saxophone and piano, Houston; ins. agt. Western Frat. Life Assn., Cedar Rapids, Iowa, 1977—, Farmers' Mut. Protective Assn. Tex., Temple, 1978—. Mem. Congress Houston Tchrs. (rec. sec. 1980-82, exec. v.p. 1982-84), Houston Music Educators Assn., Tex. Music Educators Assn., Houston Symphony Chorale, Am. Choral Dirs. Assn., Alpha Delta Kappa, Tau Beta Sigma, Gamma Sigma Sigma (chpt. sec.-treas. 1971-73). Clubs: Coll. Women's, Houston Liederkranz. Lodges: Western Fraternal Life Assn. (local sec. 1977-81, state liaison officer 1985-86), Slavonic Benevolent Order Tex., Farmers Mut. Protective Assn. Tex., Sons of Hermann, Sokol Houston. Home: 2515 Lazybrook Dr Houston TX 77008

FILKO, REGINA LIBY, realtor; b. Michalovce, Czechoslovakia, Apr. 28, 1936; came to U.S., 1947, naturalized, 1953; d. John and Mary (Evans) Voynik; m. Joseph Filko, Sept. 27, 1951; children—Alan Joseph, Nadine Elizabeth. Cosmetologist Maison Felix Beauty Coll., 1951. Hair stylist Kaufman and May Salon, Pitts., 1951-58; real estate investor, Pitts., 1951-68; investor Amway Products, Miami, 1958-79; realtor assoc. Riteway Inc., North Miami, 1975—. Miss Silver Skate, Ice Capades, Pitts., 1950; recipient numerous sales awards Riteway Realtors, 1975-83. Mem. Miami Beach Condominium Assn. (dir. 1980-83), Miami Bd. Realtors, Women's Council Realtors, Miami Real Estate Exchangers. Democrat. Roman Catholic. Clubs: Jockey; Racquet (Bay Harbor Village). Office: Riteway Inc 1055 NE 125th St North Miami FL 33161

FILZEN, CHRISTINE MARIE, photographer; b. New Ulm, Minn., Mar. 8, 1955; d. Joseph P. and Eleanor R. (Janni) F. A.S., St. Cloud State U., 1978, B.A., 1979. Photo asst. St. Cloud (Minn.) State U., 1976-79; photo processor Brown Photo Co., Mpls., 1978-79; photo tech. Sta. KSTP-TV, Mpls., 1979-81; sr. photographer U. Minn.-Mpls., 1981-84; color insp. Brown Photo Co., Mpls., 1984-85; mdse. technician Donaldsons Photo Studio, 1985—; freelance photographer, reporter, 1975-79; judge Minn. Edn. Assn. Sch. Bell Awards, 1977; producer sports video tapes, 1982-84; judge Southwestern Minn. Regional Sci. Fair, 1985-86. Active Youth Minn.; mem. Assn. Retarded Citizens, v.p., 1971-73. Mem. Sigma Delta Chi (v.p. 1977-78), Minn. Press Club, Women in Communications, Nat. Press Photographers Assn., Communicators Plus. Democrat. Roman Catholic. Office: Mdse Info Office Donaldsons 600 On the Mall Minneapolis MN 55402

FINBERG, BARBARA DENNING, foundation executive; b. Pueblo, Colo., Feb. 26, 1929; d. Rufus Raymond and Velma Aileen (Hopper) Denning; B.A., Stanford U., 1949; M.A., American U. of Beirut (Lebanon), 1951; m. Alan R. Finberg, June 21, 1953. Intern, U.S. Dept. State, Washington, 1949-50, fgn. affairs officer Tech. Coop. Adminstrn., 1952-53; program specialist, area chief, Inst. of Internat. Edn., N.Y.C., 1953-59; editorial asso., program officer, 1959-80, v.p. program Carnegie Corp. of N.Y., N.Y.C., 1980—; trustee N.Y. Found., 1979—, vice chmn. bd., 1983-85, chmn., 1985—. Trustee Stanford U., 1976-86, v.p. bd., 1980-85; mem. N.C. Central U. Sch. Library Sci. adv. council, 1973—; mem. adv. council Mailman Found., 1984—; chmn. vis. com. Stanford U. Library, 1985—; mem. accreditation com. Assn. Am. Law Schs., 1986—. Mem. Am. Ednl. Research Assn., Soc. for Research in Child Devel., Council Fgn. Relations. Democrat. Club: Cosmopolitan. Home: 165 E 72nd St New York NY 100212 Office: Carnegie Corp NY 437 Madison Ave New York NY 10021

FINCH, LINDA MARTIN, architect; b. Phila., Apr. 30, 1948; d. Thomas Vernon and Roma Northcutt (Morgan) F.; B.Arch. with honors, U. Fla., 1971. Registered architect, Fla., Tex.; cert. Nat. Council Archtl. Registration Bds. Project architect Oscar Vagi & Assos., Ft. Lauderdale, Fla., 1978-79; prin. Linda Finch, Architect, Ft. Lauderdale, 1978-81; dir. design Michael A. Shiff & Assos., Ft. Lauderdale, 1980—; works include: Margate Mcpl. Complex, Lauderhill Mcpl. Complex, rural housing rehab. No. Fla. county, Lauderdale Lakes Recreation Ctr., Ft. Lauderdale Country Club, Markham Park Phase I, Markham Park Native Animal Habitat, Royal Palm Park, Mission Lake, Wolf Park, Fire Station Park, Lighthouse Point Mcpl. Complex, Coral Springs Library, Lauderhill Library, Lauderdale Lakes Library, Oakland Park Community Ctr., Lauderhill Community Ctr., North Lauderdale Community Ctr., 30-story mixed use bldg., Ft. Lauderdale, numerous others; gov.'s appointee to Fla. Bd. Architecture. Advisor Greater Victoria Park Civic Assn.; mem. Nat. Sex Equity Demonstration Project, Broward County Bd. Zoning and Code Enforcement, Rural Housing Rehab. Adv. Project, Hist. Preservation Bd. for Broward County, Greater Victoria Park Civic Assn. Recipient design award for hdqrs. bldg. Internat. Union Operating Engrs., 1981, design award for Coral Springs br. Broward County Library, 1983, for Lauderhill Mcpl. Complex, 1984, for Royal Palm Park, Oakland Park, 1985. Mem. AIA (treas., v.p., pres. Broward County chpt.; mem. Women's task group liaison) Assn. Women in Architecture, Union Internationale des Femmes Architects, Nat. Assn. Female Execs. Democrat. Research on modern European architecture. Office: 2701 W Oakland Park Blvd Suite 300 Oakland Park FL 33311

FINCH, PEGGY ANNE, company executive, editor; b. Evergreen Park, Ill., Nov. 22, 1952; d. William Mathias and Ada Margaret (Ferguson) Schroeder; m. Nathan Francis Finch, Nov. 20, 1982. Student Miami-Dade Coll., 1975-77. New accounts rep., sec. Comml. Bank, Miami, 1970-74; office mgr., adminstrv. asst. Conv. Contractors, Miami, 1974-80; office mgr., bookkeeper R. E. Alexander Ltd., Chgo., 1980-81; officer mgr., exec. sec. R. G. Ibbotson Assocs., Inc., Chgo., 1981-83, mktg. div. mgr., editor, 1983-84; mktg. support rep. J F M Bus. Systems, Inc., computer hardware and software vendor, Chgo., 1984-86, mgr. mktg. and customer support, 1986—. Pres., founder South Suburban br. Am. Diabetes Assn., Flossmoor, Ill., 1982-83, chmn. Bike-A-Thon, Homewood, Ill., 1983; mem. pub. edn. com. Am. Diabetes Assn., No. Ill. affiliate, Chgo., 1983, mem. speakers bur. com., 1982—. Mem. Nat. Assn. Female Execs. Home: 1700 Forest Cove Dr Mount Pospect IL 60056 Office: J F M Business Systems Inc Merchandise Mart Suite 144 Chicago IL 60654

FINCH, SALLY JO, educator; b. Galesburg, Ill., July 7, 1943; d. E.A. and Alice L. (Hartman) Pople; B.S., Ill. State U., 1965; m. Robert E. Finch, June 12, 1966 (dec. Aug. 14, 1983); 1 son, Mark Paul. Tchr., Springfield (Ill.) Public Schs., 1965-66; tchr. Knoxville (Ill.) Sch. Dist., 1966-71, title I reading tchr., 1977—; tchr. Knox-Warren Spl. Edn. Co-op., Galesburg, 1971-74; office mgr. Dr. Donald L. Grieme, Galesburg, 1974-77; part-time prof. edn. Monmouth (Ill.) Coll., 1970-82, Carl Sandburg Jr. Coll., Galesburg, 1981-83; dir. multiple handicapped summer camp, 1986—. Treas., John Ericsson Republican League of Knox County, 1981-83; Henderson Twp. precinct committeewoman, 1980—; bd. dirs. Luth. Social Services. Mem. Ill. Reading Council, Knox County Home Extension, DAR, Republican Women, Beta Sigma Phi. Methodist. Clubs: Carl Sandburg Coll. Booster (bd. dirs.), Pilot Service. Lodge: Vasa. Home: 560 Kenwick Dr Galesburg IL 61401 Office: Knoxville Sch Dist Mill St Knoxville IL 61448

FINCH, SHERRIE TWEEDIE, sales representative; b. Cedar Rapids, Iowa, Sept. 23, 1953; d. Robert Louis and Inez Marie (Groote) Tweedie; m. Gordon Irwin Finch, May 28, 1977. B.A., Coe Coll., 1975. Buyer Zale Corp., Dallas, 1976-82; sales rep. S.W. region Girl Scouts U.S.A., N.Y.C., 1982—. Div. chmn. for Zale Corp., United Way Campaign, 1980-81; host Dallas Fgn. Visitor Com., 1978-80; vol. Am. Lung Assn., City of Dallas Bond Election; bd. dirs., vol. Operation Kindness; parliamentarian Republican Women's Caucus. Mem. Assn. Girl Scout Execs., AAUW, Nat. Assn. Female Execs., Bus. and Profl. Women's Clubs (pres. 1980-81, found. chmn. 1983-84), Alpha Xi Delta. Home: 11207 Park Central Pl Dallas TX 75230 Office: Girl Scouts USA 830 3d Ave New York NY 10022

FINCHER, MARGARET ANN, educator; b. Harrodsburg, Ky., June 2, 1934; d. Henry Alexander and Minnie Bee (White) Cathey; B.S. in Bus. Edn., Auburn U., 1955; M.Ed., U. New Orleans, 1978; m. Willie John Fincher, Jr., Apr. 1, 1955; children—John Richard, Joseph Michael, Judy Darlene, James Andrew. Bookkeeper, Markle's Drug Store, Auburn, Ala., 1952-54; asst. to dir. Auburn U. Library, 1955; elem. tchr., Birmingham, Ala., 1958-64; bus. edn. tchr. Abramson High Sch., New Orleans, 1964—; owner, mgr. craft shop Fanci Krafts, New Orleans, 1977-78; asst. supr. Shaklee Corp., 1979—. Supr. adult Bible tng. dept. Word of Faith Temple, 1982, cons. library devel., 1982, tchr., 1975-80, deaconess, 1983—; bd. dirs. Lamb Day Care Center, 1979-81; sustaining mem. Meth. Hosp. Aux., 1967—; adv./sponsor Christian Life on Campus Club. Recipient Am. Legion citation of appreciation, 1981; Future

Bus. Leaders Am., award of Appreciation, 1976. Mem. Donna Villa Improvement Assn., Metro. Ednl. Media Orgn., Ch. and Synagogue Library Assn., So. Bus. Edn. Assn., Nat. Bus. Edn. Assn., La. Assn. Bus. Edn., La. Vocat. Assn., United Tchrs. New Orleans, Policemen's Assn. New Orleans (hon.), Phi Delta Kappa. Democrat. Christian Ch. Office: 5553 Read Blvd New Orleans LA 70127

FINCKEN, MARY, accountant; b. Westwood, N.J., Aug. 30, 1962; d. Joseph and Anna Marie (Samsel) F. B.S. in Bus. and Adminstrn., Ramapo Coll. N.J., 1984. C.P.A., N.J. Asst. to mgr. of direct response mktg. plans dept. IBM, Montvale, N.J., 1984; jr. acct. N. L. Fish & Co., C.P.A.s, Englewood Cliffs, N.J., 1984-85; staff acct. Tribune Cable Communications, Inc., Mahwah, N.J., 1985-86; sr. staff acct. Minolta Corp., 1986—; vol. income tax asst. IRS, Mahwah, 1983, 84. Fellow N.J. Soc. C.P.A.s; mem. Nat. Assn. Female Execs., Ramapo Coll. Alumni Assn. Home: 56 W End Ave Westwood NJ 07675 Office: Minolta Corp 150 Hilltop Rd Ramsey NJ 07446

FINDLAY, HOLLY ROXANN, retail company executive; b. Bath, Maine, July 22, 1949; d. Hollis Lenard and Gerttrude (Carr) Leeman; m. Joseph Raffa, June 19, 1978 (div. June 1979); m. 2d, Albert E. Findlay, June 17, 1981; 1 son, Jason P. Adminstrv. asst. Bradford-Compo. Lowell, Mass., 1969-72, mgr. credit dept., 1972-73; inventory supr. Hirshberg Co., Andover, Mass., 1973; asst. mgr. Spencer Gifts, Atlantic City, 1977, mgr., 1978-80, ops. adminstr., 1980-81, sales promotion dir., 1981—. Mem. Nat. Retail Mchts. Assn., Am. Mgmt. Assn. Democrat. Baptist. Club: Bus. Womens Assn. (Ventnor, N.J.). Office: Spencer Gifts Inc 1050 Blackhorse Pike Atlantic City NJ 08232

FINDLAY, MARGERY WALDO, librarian; b. Boston, Feb. 28, 1935; d. Allen Worcester and Cherrie Katherine (Malcomson) Waldo; m. William Francis Findlay, Sept. 11, 1955; children—Wendy, Eric, Steven, Heidi. B.A., Stanford U., 1957; M.L.S., San Jose State U., 1977; postgrad. Calif. State U.-Sacramento, 1970-74. Librarian Rio Linda Union Sch. Dist. (Calif.), 1972-79, dist. librarian, 1979—; instr. Calif. State U., Sacramento, 1979; reference librarian Cosumnes River Coll., Sacramento, summer 1981. Bd. dirs. Sacramento Lit. Symposium, 1980—. Mem. Calif. Library Media Educators Assn. (treas. no. sect. 1982-86, regional rep. 1981-82), Calif. Reading Assn., Sacramento Area Library Orgn., Phi Beta Kappa, Beta Phi Mu. Republican. Club: Stanford. Home: 8510 Walden Woods Way Loomis CA 95650 Office: Library Services Rio Linda Union Sch Dist 6450 20th St Rio Linda CA 95673

FINDLEY, MARY BAKER, violinist; b. Norfolk, Va., May 9, 1943; d. Henry Givens and Virginia Marie (Bredenfoerder) Baker; B.Mus. (Outstanding Sr. Woman in Music), U. Cin., 1965, M.Mus., 1966, D.M.A., 1974; student Staatlich Hochschule Musik, Frankfurt/Main, W. Ger., 1966-68; m. David Francis Findley, Mar. 3, 1966. Pvt. studio, Cin., 1972-75, Tulsa, 1976-80; adj. asst. prof. violin Oral Roberts U., Tulsa, 1976-80; Arts Council Okla. artist-in-residence, 1977-81; concertmaster, soloist, founding mem., bd. dirs. Tulsa Little Symphony Orch., 1978-80; founder Tulsa Chamber Music Festival, 1980; founding mem. Washington Music Ensemble, 1981—; concert soloist and recitalist; pvt. studio tchr., Washington, 1981—; instr. violin George Washington U. and Selma M. Levine Sch. Music (both Washington), 1981—; founder All-Okla. String Symposium, 1977, Summer Serenades, 1986; concert master, bd. dirs. Amadeus Chamber Orch., 1984—. Mem. Am. String Tchrs. Assn., Music Educators Nat. Conf., Nat. Sch. Orch. Assn., Music Tchrs. Nat. Assn., Mortar Board, Suzuki Assn. Ams., Coll. Music Soc., Sigma Alpha Iota (Performance award 1972). Office: Music Dept George Washington U Washington DC 20052

FINDLEY, SUZANNE BAKER, park and recreation superintendent; b. Wabash, Ind., Jan. 8, 1951; d. Robert S. and Marthetta J. (Jackson) Baker; m. D. Kevin Findley, Apr. 22, 1972; children—Callaway, Alison. A.S., Vincennes U. Athletic dir. Columbus Girls Club, Ind., 1971-72; exec. dir. Shelbyville Girls Club, Ind., 1973; cons. Model Cities Girls Club, Indpls., 1975; recreation dir. Franklin Parks and Recreation Dept., Ind., 1977-81, supt., 1981—. Chmn. Franklin Heritage Festival, 1985; mem. Franklin Revitalization Com., 1984-85. Mem. Nat. Recreation and Park Assn., Ind. Parks and Recreation Assn. (bd. dirs. 1983 , exec. bd. 1985, community sect. chmn.-elect 1985, pres.-elect 1986—), Avocations: outdoor sports, antique collecting. Office: Franklin Parks and Recreations Dept 101 N Hurricane St Franklin IN 46131

FINE, FAY BLAIR, social worker; b. Dvinsk, Latvia, Feb. 10, 1920; d. Morris L. and Pauline (Kleinstine) Blair; m. Julius L. Fine, Nov. 18, 1945; children—Sandra Fine Thurm, Jeffrey. Community relations assoc. Jewish Community Fedn., Cleve., 1964-73; asst. prof., asst. dir. continuing edn. Case Western Res. U., Cleve., 1974-77; adminstr. staff devel. dept. Summit County Children's Services Bd., Akron, Ohio, 1978—; cons. children's agys.; adj. instr. Northeast Ohio Univ. Coll. Medicine; adj. prof. Sch. Applied Social Scis., Case Western Res. U. Pres. alumni bd. Sch. Applied Social Scis., Case Western Res. U.; mem. Ohio Gov.'s Com. Sexual Abuse Tng., 1985—. Scholar Tulane U. Mem. Nat. Assn. Social Workers, Ohio Assn. Child Care Worker Tng., Council on Continuing Edn. Unit, Acad. Cert. Social Workers, Pentelicus. Democrat. Jewish. Office: Summit County Children's Services Bd 264 S Arlington St Akron OH 44306

FINE, JO RENÉE, audio-visual prodn. co. exec.; b. Norfolk, Va., June 19, 1943; d. Ruby Arthur and Tillie Fern (Goldman) F.; B.A., Smith Coll., 1965; M.A., N.Y.U., 1968, Ph.D., 1973; m. Edward Trieber, Apr. 12, 1981; 1 child, Jessica Fine Trieber. Probation officer N.Y.C. Office Probation, 1966; research asst. N.Y.U., N.Y.C., 1966-68, asso. research scientist Inst. Developmental Studies, 1968-73, research scientist, 1973-77, adj. asst. prof. dept. ednl. psychology, 1973-76; program analyst N.Y. State Dept. Mental Hygiene, N.Y.C., 1977-78; pvt. practice psychotherapy, N.Y.C., 1978-81; pres. CVM Prodns., Inc., N.Y.C., 1978—; cons. to bds. edn., N.Y.C., also greater met. area, 1973—. Mem. Am. Psychol. Assn., Pharm. Advt. Council, Nat. Assn. Women Bus. Owners, Am. Jewish Com., Am. Women in Radio and TV. Co-author: The Synagogues of New York's Lower East Side, 1978. Home: 55 W 16th St New York NY 10011 Office: 13 E 16th St New York NY 10003

FINE, JOAN, sculptor; b. N.Y.C., Mar. 5, 1942; d. Benajmin L. and Phyllis (Fried) Greene; m. Daniel H. Fine, June 30, 1963; children—Rebecca, Jocelyn, Benjamin, Jonathan. B.A., Queens Coll., 1963; Sculpture Certificate, St. Martins Sch., London, 1980; M.F.A., Columbia U., 1983; postgrad. U. Pitts., Sch. Fine Arts, 1969-70; studied with Toshio Odate, Bklyn. Mus., 1966-67. Blackburn, Padovano, Niizuma, Columbia, 1972-77; Tony Caro, David Annesley, Philip King, St. Martin's Sch. Art, London, 1979-80, Camberwell Sch. Arts, London, 1979-80. Author: I Carve Stone, 1979. One-woman shows: Fifth Street Gallery, N.Y.C., 1978, 14 Sculptors Gallery, N.Y.C., 1979, Nat. Art Ctr., N.Y., 1979, Leonia Pub. Library, 1980, Bergen Community Mus., 1982, 14 Sculptors Gallery, N.Y.C., 1983, 85; group shows include: Audubon, NAD, N.Y.C., 1978, Nexus Gallery, Phila., 1978, Hurlbutt Gallery, Greenwich, Conn., 1979, Mari Galleries, Ltd., Mamaroneck, N.Y., 1979, Lever House, N.Y.C., 1979, Third Floor Gallery, Atlanta, 1979, American Standard, N.Y., 1980, Elaine Benson Gallery, N.Y., 1980, Sculpture Ctr., N.Y., 1980, N.J. Inst. Tech., 1981, Canton Art Inst., Ohio, 1981, Traveling Exhibition, Israel, Nat. Assn. Women Artists, 1981, N.Y. Botanical Garden, 1981, Lever House, 1981, 14 Sculptors Gallery, 1982, Exhbn. Space, N.Y.C., 1983, Summit Art Ctr., 1985, The Doll Show at C.W. Post Coll., 1985; tchr. workshops Met. Mus. Art, N.Y.C., 1981; Sculpture Assocs., N.Y.C., 1981. Fellow in sculpture N.J. State Arts Council, 1984-85. Mem. Sculptors Guild (exec. bd. 1982-84), Women's Caucus for Art. Address: 164 Mercer St New York NY 10012

FINE, VIVIAN, composer; b. Chgo., Sept. 28, 1913; d. David and Rose (Finder) F.; privately ed.; m. Benjamin Karp, Apr. 5, 1935; children—Margaret, Nina. Faculty, N.Y. U., 1945-48, Julliard Sch. Music, 1948, State U. N.Y. at Potsdam, 1951, Conn. Coll. Sch. Dance, 1963; music dir. B. deRothschild Found., 1954-60; faculty music div. Bennington (Vt.) Coll., 1964—. Recipient award Am. Acad. and Inst. Arts and Letters, 1979; Rockefeller Found. grantee, 1964; Ford Found. grantee, 1969; Nat. Endowment of Arts grantee, 1974; Woolley Fund grantee, 1973; Martha Baird Rockefeller Fund for Music grantee, 1981; Guggenheim fellow, 1980; Kousevitsky Found. grantee, 1984. Mem. ASCAP, Inst. of Am. Acad./Inst. Arts and Letters Composer: Race of Life, 1937, Suite for Piano, 1940, Four Elizabethan Songs, 1943, The Great Wall of China, 1947, A Guide to the Life Expectancy of a Rose, 1956, String Quartet, 1957, Concertante for Pieno and Orch., 1944, Sonata for Violin and Piano, 1952, Alcestis, 1960, Sinfonia and Fugato for Piano, 1963, Quintet for Trumpet, Harp and String Trio, 1967, Panean for Brass Emsemble and Female Chorus, 1969, Two Neruda Poems, 1971, Concerto for Piano, Strings and Percussion, 1972, Teisho, 1975, The Women in the Garden, 1977, Romantic Ode, 1976, Brass Quartet, 1977, Momenti, 1978, Missa Brevis, 1972, Sonnets for Baritone and Orch., 1976, Drama for Orch., 1982; commd. by Elizabeth Sprague Coolidge Found., San Francisco Symphony. Office: Bennington Coll Bennington VT 05201*

FINELLI, SUSAN CATHERINE, legal administrator; b. N.Y.C., Oct. 30, 1950; d. Alfons B. and Celia I. (Barberio) Paske; m. John J. Finelli, Apr. 7, 1973. B.A., NYU, 1978. Legal sec. Lord Day & Lord, N.Y.C., 1969-73, Miller & Summit, N.Y.C., 1973-78; paralegal Rogers Hoge & Hills, N.Y.C., 1978-81; legal adminstrn. Katz, Robinson Brog & Seymour, P.C., N.Y.C., 1981-83; dir. fin. and adminstrn. Kay Collyer & Boose, N.Y.C., 1984—; pres. Assn. Legal Adminstrs., N.Y.C., Hammarskjold Cons., Inc. Mem. Assn. Legal Adminstrs. (sec. exec. com. 1984—), N.Y. State Bar Assn. (com. law office econs. and mgmt.), Legal Adminstrs. Workshop, Nat. Female Exec. Assn., Internat. Platform Assn. Democrat. Roman Catholic. Club: N.Y. Health and Racquet. Contbr. articles to law jour. Office: Kay Collyer & Boose One Dag Hammarskjold Pl New York NY 10017

FINESMITH, BARBARA KADEN, lawyer, educator; b. N.Y.C., Feb. 5, 1937; d. Harry and Rose (Cohen) Kaden; m. Stephen H. Finesmith, Aug. 28, 1955; (div. 1977); children—Terri L. Horwich, Robin Sarah. B.A., Mankato (Minn.) State U., 1969; M.A. Governors State U., Park Forest South, Ill., 1972; J.D., U. Wis., 1983. Bar: Ill. 1983, Wis. 1983, U.S. Dist. Ct. (we. dist.) Wis. 1983, U.S. Dist. Ct. (no. dist.) Ill. 1984. Coordinator geriatrics program Rock County (Wis.) Health Care Ctr., Janesville, 1972-74; asst. prof. psychology Milton (Wis.) Coll., part-time 1973-75; spl. asst. Lt. Gov's Nursing Home Ombudsman Program, Madison, Wis., 1974-76; dir. client adv. program Wis. Dept. Health and Social Services, Madison, 1976-83, chmn. health and social services com., 1976-81; instr. law Ill Inst. Tech. Chgo.-Kent Coll. Law, 1983-85; assoc. Frankel and McKay, Ltd., 1985-86; asst. corp. counsel City of Chgo., 1986—; pres. Cons. Community Inc., Madison, 1980-82, bd. dirs., 1980-84; program chmn. Nat. Assn. State Mental Health Program Dirs., Washington, 1980, mem. adv. and patient rights com., 1978-83; cons. NIMH, Washington, 1979-81; mem. adv. bd. Nat. Paralegal Inst., Mental Health Adv. Tng., Washington, 1978-81. Editorial bd. Adv. Now jour., 1979-81; contbr. articles to publs., editor manual, pamphlet. Trustee United Madison, 1978-79; mem. Ctr. Pub. Representation, Madison, 1976-83, Wis. Women in State Employment, Madison, 1979-80. NIMH grantee, 1981-82. Mem. Chgo. Bar Assn. (young lawyers sect.), Ill. Bar Assn., Wis. Bar Assn. (service award 1976), ABA (young lawyers sect.), Assn. for Advancement Behavior Therapy (chmn. ethical and legal issues com. 1978-79). Democrat. Jewish. Home: 70 W Burton Pl Apt 608 Chicago IL 60610 Office: City of Chicago Corp Counsel 180 N LaSalle St Chicago IL 60602

FINETHY, BENNIE KILLINGSWORTH RIDGEWAY, nursing educator, nursing service administrator, health and special education adviser; b. Greenwood, S.C., Jan. 5, 1945; d. Benjamin Franklin and Grace Lamar (Killingsworth) Ridgeway; m. Robert William Finethy, June 8, 1968 (div. Nov. 1983); 1 dau., Cynthia Lynn. A.A. Lees-McRae Coll., 1965; Assoc. in Nursing, Lander Coll., 1967, B.S., 1982. R.N., S.C. staff nurse Roper Hosp., Charleston, S.C., 1967-68; supr. night nursing Bailey Meml. Hosp., Clinton, S.C., 1972-73, dir. nursing service, 1973-76, instr. coronary care, 1974-76; profl. standards rev. coordinator S.C. Med. Care Found., Cola, 1976-77; sch. dist. nurse, social worker S.C. Pub. Sch. Dist. 52, Ninety Six, S.C., 1977-82, instr. sex edn., 1978-81, instr. social work, spl. edn., 1977-82; instr. nursing Piedmont Tech. Coll., Greenwood, 1982-84; adminstrv. asst. Laurens County Health Care System, 1984—; mem. Lic. Practical Nurse Adv. Council 7 County Service Area, Greenwood, 1982—. Vol. Cerebral Palsy Found., Greenwood, 1982; mem. Ninety-Six Band Booster Club, 1983, Lower Lake Greenwood Fire Dept., Ninety-Six, S.C. Archeol. Soc., Columbia, 1981. Mem. Am. Nurses Assn., S.C. Soc. Nursing Service Adminstrs., Three Rivers Health System Agy., S.C. Tech. Edn. Assn., Profl. Standards Rev. Orgn., Nat. Assn. Quality Assurance Profls., DAR. Democrat. Methodist. Author instrn. packets; contbr. books in archeol. field. Home: Route 3 Lake Greenwood Ninety Six SC 29666

FINIZZI, MARGUERITE H(ELENE), educator; b. Allentown, Pa., Nov. 16, 1934; d. John Michael and Margaret Mary (Havrilla) Martin; B.S. in Secondary Edn., Kutztown State Coll., 1956; M.A. in English, Lehigh U., 1973; m. Joseph Anthony Finizzi, Nov. 19, 1954. Tchr. English, Harrison-Morton Jr. High Sch., Allentown, 1956-64, Louis E. Dieruff High Sch., Allentown, 1964-76, Allen High Sch., Allentown, 1976—, also adviser various groups; instr. to develop. drug edn. competency for tchrs.; mem. in-service council Allentown Sch. Dist., 1973—; discussion leader for jr. classes Jewish Day Sch., 1969-71; judge numerous acad. contests; lectr., speaker in field; seminar discussion leader Council of Youth, 1980. Pres. Lehigh County (Pa.) Coordinating Council, 1967-71; mem. steering com. Allentown Sch. Dist., 1984. Recipient Meritorious award Kutztown State Coll., 1956; Newspaper Fund fellow, 1981; Commonwealth Partnerships fellow for lit. Inst. Secondary Tchrs., 1985. Mem. Nat. Council Tchrs. English (co-chmn. conf. 1985), Pa. Council Tchrs. English, NEA, Pa. State Edn. Assn. (editor eastern region constn.), Allentown Edn. Assn. (social chairperson 1964-79, exec. sec. 1964-69), AAUW, Allentown Women Tchrs. Club (editor constn. and by-laws, welfare chmn. 1986), Lehigh U. Alumni, Kutztown U. Alumni (pres. Lehigh County 1969-72), Columbia Scholastic Press Assn. assn. adviser Reflector Sci. newsletter, 1979-80. Home: 3025 Pearl Ave Allentown PA 18103

FINK, LOIS MARIE, art historian; b. Michigan City, Ind., Dec. 30, 1927; d. George Edward and Marie Helen (Hensz) F. B.A., Capital U., 1951; M.A., U. Chgo., 1955, Ph.D., 1970; H.H.D. (hon.), Capital U., 1982. Instr. Lenoir Rhyne Coll., Hickory, N.C., 1955-56, Midland Coll., Fremont, Nebr., 1956-58; asst. prof. Roosevelt U., Chgo., 1958-70; curator Nat. Mus. of Am. Art, Smithsonian Instn., Washington, 1970—; adv. com. Washington area Archives Am. Art, 1979—. Co-author: Academy: The Academic Tradition in American Art, 1975; author: Elizabeth Nourse: A Salon Career, 1983; contbr. articles to profl. jours. Mem. Coll. Art Assn., Am. Studies Assn. Office: Nat Mus of Am Art Smithsonian Instn Washington DC 20560

FINK, RUTH GARVEY, company executive; b. Colby, Kans., Apr. 26, 1917; d. Ray Hugh and Olive (White) Garvey; student U. Wichita, 1934-37, U. Kans., 1940-41; B.A., U. Ill., 1938; H.H.D. (hon.), Washburn U., 1981; m. Richard L. Cochener, Feb. 17, 1942 (dec. 1954); children—Bruce G., Diana Cochener Broze, Caroline Cochener Bolene; m. 2d, H. Bernard Fink, Mar. 30, 1955. Vice pres., dir. C-G-F Grain Co., Inc., 1957-84; pres., dir. CGF Industries, Inc., 1972—; dir. Garvey, Inc., Stauffer Communications, Inc. Trustee, Garvey Found., Garvey Family Found.; pres. Fink Found., 1962—; bd. dirs. Topeka YWCA, ARC; trustee Washburn Coll., 1960—, Alumni award, 1968; chmn. Bible com. Washburn Coll. Bible, 1977—; Kans. regent Gunston Hall, Lorton, Va., 1966-79; trustee Shawnee Country Day Sch., 1982-84. Mem. Nat. Soc. Colonial Dames of Kans. (Roll of Honor 1980), Delta Gamma (Cable award 1965, Shield award 1970), PEO. Republican. Congregationalist. Office: 800 Bank IV Tower Topeka KS 66603

FINK, VALERIE ANN, home economics educator; b. Chgo., Feb. 13, 1954; d. Joseph Michael and Elsie (Daghi) Fink. B.A., Rosary Coll., 1976; M.S., No. Ill. U., 1983. Sales, gen. office Jamie Lynn Bridals, Chgo., 1976-77, Galzier Corp., Chgo., 1977-78; with Stone & Adler Advt., Chgo., 1978-79; substitute tchr. various high schs., Cook County, Ill., 1979; retail salesperson I. Magnin, Oak Brook, Ill., part-time, 1985-86; tchr., dept. chmn. Westchester Dist. 92 1/2, Ill., 1980—. Author cognitive skills test: Home Economics Basic Skills Indicator, 1982. Docent, Chgo. Archtl. Found., 1981—. Mem. Westchester Edn. Assn. (treas.), Am. Home Econs. Assn., Ill. Home Econs. Assn., Omicron Nu. Roman Catholic. Avocations: travel; sewing; cooking; local theater guild prodns. Office: Westchester Middle Sch 1620 Norfolk Westchester IL 60153

FINKEL, JEAN WILLA, personnel service executive; b. Washington, Nov. 11, 1959; d. E. Jay and Harriet L. (Schwartz) F. B.A. in Comparative Lit., Brandeis U., 1981. Personnel asst. Grover Cronin Inc., Waltham, Mass., 1981-82; personnel cons. Daniel Roberts Inc., Boston, 1982-84, asst. mgr., 1984-85, sales mgr., Menlo Park, Calif., 1985—. Mem. No. Calif. Human Resources Council, Resource Ctr. for Women, AAUW, Nat. Assn. Female Execs., Nat. Assn. Personnel Cons., Calif. Assn. Personnel Cons. Democrat. Avocations: tennis; running; music. Home: 1817 Parkwood Dr San Mateo CA 94403 Office: Daniel Roberts Inc 3000 Sand Hill Rd 1-110 Menlo Park CA 94025

FINKELSTEIN, ANITA JO, lawyer; b. Cleve., Jan. 2, 1957; d. Denis Edmund and Helen (Graber) Fabian; m. Ben Finkelstein, Mar. 20, 1983. B.A. in Bus. Adminstrn. and Econs., Wittenberg U., 1979; J.D., Yale U., 1982. Bar: D.C. 1982; C.P.A., Ill. Assoc. firm Shaw, Pittman, Potts & Trowbridge, Washington, 1982—. Mem. ABA, D.C. Bar Assn. Jewish. Office: Shaw Pittman Potts & Trowbridge 1800 M St NW Washington DC 20036

FINKELSTEIN, DOLLY ANN, nurse educator; b. Slaton, Tex., Jan. 7, 1930; d. James William and Ruby Estelle (Bramlett) Payton; m. George Hugh Frank, Mar. 15, 1952 (div. 1975); children—Beth, Judith, Deborah, David, Daniel; m. Edward S. Finkelstein, June 10, 1982. B.S.Nursing, Coll. St. Teresa, Winona, Minn., 1951; M.Nursing, Hunter Coll., 1980. Head nurse Parkway Hosp., Forest Hills, N.Y., 1972-73; tchr. N.Y.C. Bd. Edn., 1973—. Mem. Sigma Theta Tau. Home: 63-42 Bourton St Rego Park NY 11374 Office: Julia Richman High Sch 317 E 67th St New York NY 10017

FINLEY, MYNELLE SPIERS, educator; b. New Caney, Tex., June 20, 1928; d. Clarence H. and Vera Lee (Gassett) Spiers; children—Jan, Tom S. B.A., Sam Houston State U., 1960, M.Ed., 1970; postgrad. U. London, 1974, Lamar U., 1980, Tex. Woman's U., 1982. Classroom tchr. Liberty Ind. Sch. Dist. (Tex.), 1955-60, music tchr., 1961-64, classroom and music tchr., jr. high, 1965-67; librarian Hardin Ind. Sch. Dist., Tex., 1967-71, Liberty Ind. Sch. Dist., 1971-77, East Chambers Ind. Sch. Dist., Winnie, Tex., 1977-82, Dallas Ind. Sch. Dist., 1982—; sponsor library club Liberty High Sch., 1972-77; chmn. media services com. So. Assn. Evaluation, Liberty, 1973-74; lectr. in field. Writer, artist, producer, stage prodns., verse plays, 1955-60; composer, artist, producer plays, 1961-67; art editor, artist posters, cartoons, illustrations, 1941-84. Active various charitable orgns.; precinct sec. Republican Party, Liberty, 1960; officer PTA, Liberty, 1962. Inst. Librarianship grantee, 1969-70. Mem. Tex. Library Assn. (chmn. young adult div. 1980), Tex. South Tchrs. Assn. (state del., v.p. 1978-79), Tex. Assn. Sch. Librarians, Dallas Assn. Sch. Librarians, Tex. Classroom Tchrs. Assn., Classroom Tchrs. Dallas, NEA, ALA, Am. Assn. Sch. Librarians, Teen Age Library Assn. (state sponsor 1975-77). Republican. Presbyterian. Clubs: Lions Club Sweetheart, Jr. Trivium (v.p. 1960), Couples Bridge. Office: Dallas Ind Sch Dist 3700 Ross Ave Dallas TX 75204

FINLEY, SUSIE Q., solar energy industry executive; b. Kewanee, Ill., Mar. 3, 1950; d. Melvin Dale and Annamae (Kubelius) Quanstrom; m. Dana J. Finley, July 12, 1980; 1 dau., Tiffany Nicole. B.S. in Edn., N.Tex. State U., 1972; cert. in bus. and legal secretarial, Draughan's Bus. Coll., Albuquerque, 1973, pub. relations, N.Mex. Jr. Coll., Hobbs, 1985, English Lit., U. N.Mex., 1975. Owner, dealer Solar Age Industries, Hobbs, N.Mex., 1982—, v.p. advt. and pub. relations, Albuquerque, 1986—; lobbyist N.Mex. Solar Energy Inst., 1985-86. Recipient sales awards, Solar Age Industries, Inc. Mem. Nat. Assn. Female Execs., N.Mex. Solar Energy Inst. Republican. Christian. Avocations: camping, reading, travel, ante-bellum southern history. Home: 12305 Loyola St NE Albuquerque NM 87112 Office: Solar Age Industries Inc Suite 457W 6400 Uptown Blvd Albuquerque NM 87110

FINLEY, TARA ANA, fine arts appraiser and auctioneer; b. Portland, Oreg., July 23, 1948; d. A. Craig and Charlotte (Welsh) F.; B.A. in Art History, Finch Coll., N.Y.C., 1973. Cataloguer and appraiser antiquities and ethnographic arts, dir. customer service and bids and reserves dept. Sotheby Parke Bernet, N.Y.C., 1973-78; v.p., auctioneer, cataloguer, appraiser, gallery dir. Phillips Auctioneers, N.Y.C., 1978-81; auctioneer, lead soldier and military miniature, antiquities and ethnographic art specialist Christie's, Manson and Woods, N.Y.C., 1981—. Mem. Appraisers Assn. Am., Model Figure Collector's Assn., N.Y. Jr. League. Republican. Episcopalian. Club: St. Bartholomew Community. Home: 110 E 87th St New York NY 10028

FINN, BARBARA JUNE, nurse, educator; b. Evansville, Ind., Dec. 18, 1938; d. Roscoe F. and Doris J. (Lehmann) Norris; diploma Protestant Deaconess Hosp. Sch. Nursing, 1959; student U. Evansville, 1956-57, St. Petersburg Jr. Coll., 1968, U. South Fla., 1976-78; 1 dau., Melissa Ann. Nurse physician's office, Clearwater, Fla., 1959-63; gen. med. nurse Morton F. Plant Hosp., Clearwater, 1963-66, nurse physician's office, Clearwater, 1966-68; head nurse emergency dept. Clearwater Community Hosp., 1968-72; adminstrv. coordinator to emergency physicians, Clearwater, 1972-76; chairperson emergency med. tech. program St. Petersburg (Fla.) Jr. Coll., 1976—; cons. to Fla. Dept. Edn., 1980-81, Tampa Bay Med. Center (Fla.), 1974-75; chmn. edn. com. Tampa Bay Regional Health Planning Council, 1979-80. Mem. Pinellas County Emergency Med. Services Adv. Council, vice-chmn., 1979-80, chmn. edn. and tng. com., 1981-82, chmn. subcom. C.P.R., 1982; mem. adv. council Fla. Gulf Health Systems Agy., 1981-82; instr.-trainer Am. Heart Assn., 1978—; sec. bd. dirs. Pinellas County Tchrs. Credit Union, 1984—; mem. Clearwater Community Chorus. Mem. Fla. Nurses Assn. (dir. 1968-70, v.p. 1968-69), Nat. Assn. Emergency Med. Technicians and Paramedics, Fla. Emergency Med. Technician Assn., Emergency Med. Service Educators Fla. (rec. sec. 1982-83). Democrat. Presbyterian. Home: 1316 S Evergreen Dr Clearwater FL 33516 Office: PO Box 13489 St Petersburg FL 33733

FINN, CHARLOTTE KAYE, interior designer; b. N.Y.C., May 11; d. Edward and Florence (Karp) Kaye; B.A. cum laude, Hunter Coll.; m. Allen Charles Finn, June 25, 1950; children—Andrew, Richard, Gregg. Apprentice designer J.H. Harvey, 1958-64; pvt. practice interior design, White Plains, N.Y., 1964, inc., Charlotte Finn, Inc., 1969—; design cons. R.H. Macy's, 1977-78; product designer H.J. Stotter, George Kovacs, Grindley-of-Stoke, Sigma Marketing, Smith & Weigler. Active Westchester Reformed Synagogue, Guild for Jewish Blind, LWV, United Jewish Appeal, Anti Defamation League, NOW. Recipient S.H. Hexter award, Burlington House award; cert. Braille transcriber, Library of Congress. Mem. Am. Soc. Interior Designers (speaker, panel mem.), Nat Home Furnishings League, Phi Beta Kappa. Work featured in publs. including House Beautiful, Interior Design, Residential Interiors, N.Y. Times, Palm Beach Life, Palm Beach Daily News, Home Furnishing Daily The Designer, Home Environment, Sensuous Interiors. Home: 12 Oxford Rd White Plains NY 10605 Office: 12 Oxford Rd White Plains NY 10605 also: 251 Royal Palm Way Palm Beech FL 33480

FINN, ELIZABETH PATRICIA, nurse; b. Boston, Feb. 18, 1930; d. Robert Michael and Mary Agnes (Hurley) F. B.S. in Nursing, Spalding U., 1955; M.S. in Nursing, Cath. U. Am., Washington, 1971. Joined Sisters of Charity, Roman Cath. Ch., 1948, served in various nursing positions until 1966; operating room supr. St. Vincent's Infirmary, Little Rock, 1956-58; emergency room supr., dir. nursing service, radiation therapist St. Joseph's Infirmary, Louisville, 1958-66; commd. U.S. Nurse Corps, Army, 1966, advanced through grades to col., 1984; head nurse CCU, 93d Evacuation Hosp., Vietnam, 1967-68; cardiovascular clin. nurse specialist Walter Reed, Tripler, William Beaumont Hosps., 1968-78; ambulatory care cons. U.S. Army, San Antonio, 1978-82; chief clin. nursing service Walter Reed Army Hosp., Washington, 1982-85; nursing cons. to Surgeon Gen. Pentagon, Washington, 1985—; ambulatory care cons. Health Service Command, Fort Sam Houston, 1978-82; med./surg. nursing cons. U.S. Army, Washington, 1982—. Decorated Bronze Star, Army Commendation medal with oak leaf cluster, Meritorious Service medal with 3 oak leaf clusters; Named Mana O'Lana Nurse of Hope, Hawaii div. Am. Cancer Soc., 1977. Mem. Am. Nurses Assn., Nat. League Nursing, Kennedy Inst. Bioethics, Hastings Inst. Bioethics, Sigma Theta Tau. Roman Catholic. Avocations: running; cooking; literature. Office: Walter Reed Army Med Center Washington DC

FINN, SUSAN KUDLA, foundation executive; b. Chicopee, Mass., Nov. 8, 1952; d. Robert F. and Phyllis T. (Swol) Kudla; student Springfield Coll., 1970-71; A.B., Georgetown U., 1974; M.A., George Washington U., 1978; m. Peter C. Finn, May 31, 1975; children—Daniel Patrick, Robert Peter. Intern, Office of Congresswoman Margaret Heckler, 1971-72; correctional intern U.S. Dept. Justice, 1973; intern, editor U.S. Dept. Justice, 1972-74; fed. public affairs R.J. Reynolds Industries, Winston-Salem, N.C., 1974-77; account exec. Smith, Bucklin & Assos., 1978—; exec. dir. Am. Women in Radio and TV Edn. Found.; dir. regulatory affairs Pet Food Inst., Washington, 1978—. Recipient Spl. Performance award U.S. Dept. Justice, 1973. Mem. Women in Govt. Relations, Inc. (past pres.). Roman Catholic. Home: 2601 Valley Dr Alexandria VA 22302 Office: 1101 Connecticut Ave Suite 700 Washington DC 20036

FINN-BUNALES, FRANCES CONCETTA, nurse; b. Bethesda, Md., Oct. 15, 1952; d. James Philip and Louise (Cranford) F.; m. Roy H. Bunales, Nov. 22, 1985. B.S. in Nursing, U.N.C.-Greensboro, 1974. Registered nurse, Md.,

D.C. Staff nurse Greater Southeast Community Hosp., Washington, 1974-78; staff nurse So. Md. Hosp. Ctr., Clinton, 1978-83, head nurse, 1983—. Named Outstanding Nurse, So. Md. Hosp. Ctr., 1980. Democrat. Roman Catholic. Avocations: auto racing; reading; bowling. Home: 2001 Arona Rd Fort Washington MD 20744

FINNEGAN, LANNETTA KAYE, financial analyst; b. Havre de Grace, Md., Feb. 26, 1956; d. Wilbur Jesse and Joan Belle (Martin) Hildebrand. B.A., U. Md.-Balt., 1976; M.City and Regional Planning, Cath. U. Am., 1981. Cons., Peat Marwick Mitchell, Washington, 1974-81; transp. analyst Mass Transit Adminstrn., Balt., 1981-83, spl. asst. to dir. fin., 1983-85, mgr. fin. analysis, 1985—. Mem. Smithsonian Resident Assoc. Program, 1977—; lector, eucharistic minister St. Joseph's Catholic Ch., Odenton, Md., 1979-83. Mem. Am. Mgmt. Assn., Am. Planning Assn., Am. Inst. Cert. Planners, Women's Transp. Seminar (pres. 1983-84; award 1984), U. Md. Alumni Assn. Home: 301 Warren Ave Apt 409 Baltimore MD 21230 Office: Mass Transit Adminstrn 300 W Lexington St Baltimore MD 21201

FINNERAN, SUSAN ROGERS, lawyer; b. Lynn, Mass., Oct. 12, 1947; d. Robert Edward and Alice Helen (Rogers) F. B.A., U. Mass., 1969; J.D., U. Notre Dame, 1977. Bar: N.Y. 1978, Mass. 1980. Tchr., Hamilton-Wenham Sch., Hamilton, Mass., 1973-74; assoc. Shearman & Sterling, N.Y.C., 1977-80, 81-82, Bingham, Dana & Gould, Boston, 1980-81, 82-84; sole practice, Boston, 1984—; atty. Voluntary Lawyers Project, Mass., 1983—; dir. Pub. Space Collaborative, N.Y.C., 1980—; mem. faculty New Eng. Sch. Law. Author articles in field. Mem. Merrimack Valley Council for Nuclear Freeze, 1983—, Lawyers Alliance for Nuclear Freeze, 1983—. Mem. ABA, Mass. Bar Assn., Boston Bar Assn., Newburyport Hist. Soc. Democrat. Roman Catholic. Home: 37 Prospect St Newburyport MA 01950 Office: 154 Stuart St Boston MA 02116

FINNEY, JOAN MARIE MCINROY, state official; b. Topeka, Feb. 12, 1925; d. Leonard L. and Mary M. (Sands) McInroy; B.A., Washburn U., 1974; m. Spencer W. Finney, Jr., July 24, 1957; children—Sally, Dick, Mary. Asst., Washington and Topeka offices U.S. Senator Frank Carlson, 1953-69; commr. elections Shawnee County, Kans., 1970-72; adminstrv. asst. to mayor of Topeka, 1973-74; treas. State of Kans., Topeka, 1974—; mem. exec. bd. Council State Govts. Bd. dirs. Kans. Community Service Orgn., YWCA. Mem. Nat. Assn. State Treasurers, Nat. Assn. Unclaimed Property Assn. (v.p.), Nat. Assn. State Auditors, Comptrollers and Treasurers (pres. elect), Am. Legion Aux., Helping Hands Humane Soc., Reinsch Rose Garden Soc., A. Philip Randolph Inst. (hon.), LWV (bd. dirs.), Kans. Young Democrats (hon. life), Kans. Fedn. Women's Dem. Clubs, Jeffersonian Club, St. Francis Hosp. and Med. Ctr. Aux., Santa Fe Ry. Ret. Employees' Club, Mended Hearts Inc., Hayden High Sch. Alumni Assn. (bd. dirs.), Washburn Alumni Assn., Sigma Alpha Iota. Democrat. Roman Catholic. Home: 4519 SW 33d Terr Topeka KS 66614 Office: Office of State Treasurer 700 Harrison St Topeka KS 66612

FINNEY, MARIAN ROUSE, health educator, immunohematologist; b. Washington, July 7, 1939; d. John Henry and Fannie Hope (Thompson) Rouse; m. Robert Finney, June 13, 1959; children—Robyne, Jananne. B.S. in Chemistry, Morgan State U., 1960; Cert. Immunohematology and Blood Banking, Philip Levine Labs., Ortho Research Found., 1969; M.T., U. Md., 1972; M.Ed. in Health Sci., Towson State U., 1976. Chief of labs. Med. Ctr., Balt., 1967-74; immunohematologist Francis Scott Key, Balt., 1960-67; health educator Sch. System, Balt., 1975-80; dept. head health edn. City Pub. Schs., Balt., 1981-85; project dir. coalition of Essential Schs., Balt., 1985—. Contbr. articles to profl. jours. Author curriculum gudes various ares med. tech., 1975-84. Bd. dirs. Health Edn. Adv. Bd., Balt., 1983—; assoc. mem. Balt. Council Pregnancy and Prevention, Balt., 1982-84; advisor Health Club, Balt., 1978—; cons. Health Material Selection Com., Balt., 1977—. Named Outstanding Woman of Baltimore County, AAUW, 1976; awards for outstanding service Kidney Found., 1982-84, Office of Health, Balt. Pub. Schs., 1985, others. Mem. Am. Assn. Blood Banks, Am. Sch. Health Assn., Am. Soc. Clin. Pathologists, Am. Heart Assn., Nat. Assn. Negro Bus. and Profl. Women, Morgan State U. Alumni Assn., Nat. Council Negro Women, Delta Sigma Theta, Eta Sigma Gamma. Democrat. Ch. of Christ. Clubs: Child Study Assn. (pres. 1972-75), Daisy Inc. Avocations: writing; reading; interior design. Home: 2813 Alrene Circle Baltimore MD 21207 Office: Walbrook Senior High Sch 2000 Edgewood St Baltimore MD 21216

FIOCK, SHARI LEE, design entrepreneur, researcher; b. Weed, Calif., Oct. 25, 1941; d. Webster Bruce and Olevia May (Pruett) F.; m. June 6, 1966 (div. 1974); children—Webster Clinton Pfingsten, Sterling Curtis. Cert. Art Instrn. Sch., Mpls., 1964; pvt. student, Lic. health, life and disability, Calif. Copywriter Darron Assocs., Eugene, Oreg., 1964-66; staff artist Oreg. Holidays, Springfield, 1966-69, part-time 1971; co-owner, designer Artre Enterprises, Eugene, 1969-74; design entrepreneur Shari & Assocs., Yreka, Calif., 1978—; devel. sec., chief fin. officer Cascade World Four Season Resort, Siskiyou County, Calif., 1980—; cons., pres. Reunions, Family, Yreka, 1984—. Designer 5 ton chain saw sculpture, Oreg. Beaver, 1967; illustrator: Holiday Fun Book, 1978. Creator Klamath Nat. Forest Interpretive Mus., 1979—. Author, illustrator Calling All Descendants, 1986. Residential capt. United Way, Eugene, 1972; researcher Beaver Ofcl. State Animal, Eugene, 1965-71; counselor Boy Scouts, 1983—. Mem. Western Interpreters Assn., Boston Computer Soc., Nat. Mus. of Women in the Arts, Nat. Assn. Female Execs., Nat. Writers Club. Avocations: family activities; outdoor recreation; travel; theater; music. Home and Office: 406 Walter's Ln Yreka CA 96097

FIONDELLA, JUNE LEA BELL, public utility executive; b. Meriden, Conn., May 24, 1941; d. Joseph Doran and Mildred (Hourigan) Bell; m. Louis Andrew Fiondella, Sept. 2, 1963; children—Kim Lisa, Tracy Lea. B.S. in Bus. Mgmt. cum laude, Post Coll., 1983. With Northeast Utilities, Hartford, Conn., 1959—, mgr. communications services, 1976-80, mgr. communications and adv. services, 1980-83, mgr. communications services and spl. projects, 1983—; chmn. Electric Council N.E. Pub. Info. Com., 1982. Recipient Pres.'s Circle of Distinction for acad. excellence, Post Coll., 1982. Mem. Women in Communications, Pub. Relations Soc. Am., Internat. Assn. Bus. Communicators, Nuclear Energy Women, Pub. Utilities Communicators Assn. (1st v.p. 1985, pres. 1986, regional chmn. New Eng. 1983, Maple Leaf award 1984), Advt. Club Greater Hartford, Conn. Assn. Bus. Communicators, Hartford Woman's Network, Nat. Assn. Female Execs. Democrat. Roman Catholic. Home: 1414 Meriden Ave Southington CT 06489 Office: Northeast Utilities Box 270 Hartford CT 06141

FIORATTI, HELEN COSTANTINO, designer, antique dealer; b. N.Y.C., Mar. 16, 1931; d. Arturo and Ruth (Teschner) Costantino; B.S., Parsons Sch. Design; m. Nereo Fioratti, Nov. 19, 1963; 1 dau., Arianna. Jewelry, furniture designer; v.p. L'Antiquaire, Inc., N.Y.C. Republican. Club: Tennis (Florence, Italy). Author: How to Know French Antiques. Home: 555 Park Ave New York NY 10021 Office: 36 E 73d St New York NY 10021

FIORAVANTI, NANCY ELEANOR, banker; b. Gloucester, Mass., Apr. 10, 1935; d. Richard Joseph and Evelyn Grace (Souza) Fioravanti; grad. high sch. Various positions and depts. Bank of New Eng.-North Shore (formerly Cape Ann Bank and Trust Co., successor to Gloucester Safe Deposit & Trust Co.), Gloucester, 1953—, with trust dept., 1959—, asst. trust officer, 1970-84, trust officer, 1984—. Treas. art adv. com. Gloucester Lyceum and Sawyer Free Library. Mem. Nat. Assn. Bank Women, Bus. and Profl. Women's Club. Home: PO Box 1638 Gloucester MA 01930 Office: 154 Main St Gloucester MA 01930

FIORE, JOAN DE WOLF, civic leader; b. Detroit, July 15, 1924; d. Richard Perrien and Rachel Elizabeth De Wolf; m. Pasquale Peter Fiore, Nov. 25, 1949; children—Richard, Jill. Grad. Kingswood Girls Sch., Cranbrook, Mich.; student UCLA. Vice pres. Fitness with Finesse, Inc., Houston; regent, Princeton chpt. DAR, 1974-77, Seimes microfilm chmn., Washington, 1977—; state regent N.J., Nat. Soc. Magna Charta Dames; mem. Assn. of Descs. of Knights of the Garter, Gen. Soc. Mayflower Descs., Elder William Brewster Soc., First Colony of Mayflower Descs., Plantagenet Kings of Eng. Soc., Sovereign Colonial Soc. Americans of Royal Descent, Richard 3d Soc., Nat. Soc. Colonial Dames of XVII Century, Japan Soc. Vol. chmn. Med. Ctr., Princeton, N.J., 1960-77; mem. Met. Mus. Art, N.Y.C., Natural History Mus., N.Y.C., Nat. Trust Historic Preservation. Republican. Quaker. Home: 18 Sturgis Rd Kendall Park NJ 08824

FIORE, MARY, magazine editor. Former editor Photoplay mag.; mng. editor Good Housekeeping mag. Office: Good Housekeeping Hearst Corp 959 Eighth Ave New York NY 10019*

FIORELLA, BEVERLY JEAN, medical laboratory scientist; b. Owensboro, Ky., Oct. 29, 1930; d. Gabriel and Agnes Loretta (Kurz) F.; B.S., Webster Coll./St. Louis U., 1952; M.A., Central Mich. U., 1976. Chief microbiology and blood bank St. Mary's Hosp., Kansas City, Mo., 1956-67; instr., asst. prof. med. lab. scis. dept. Coll. Assoc. Health Professions, U. Ill., Chgo., 1967-74, assoc. prof., 1974-80, prof., 1980—, assoc. head dept. med. lab. scis., 1977—, grad. program coordinator, 1977-81; mem. adv. panel on health ins. Subcom. Health of Com. on Ways and Means, Ho. of Reps., 1975-80; cons. lab. improvement sect. immunohematology divs. labs. Dept. Public Health State of Ill., 1975—. Named Med. Technologist of Yr., Mo. Soc. Med. Technologists, 1967. Mem. Am. Soc. Med. Tech. (pres. 1976-77), Am. Assn. Blood Banks, Ill. Med. Technologists Assn. (named Ill. Med. Technologist of Yr. 1976), Chgo. Soc. Med. Technologists (treas., dir. 1969-70), Chicagoland Blood Bank Soc. (v.p. 1975-76), Acad. Clin. Lab. Physicians and Scientists, Am. Soc. Allied Health Professions, Internat. Soc. Blood Transfusion, Alpha Mu Tau. Mem. bd. editors Med. Tech.- A Series, 1970-74. Office: Dept Med Lab Scis Coll Assoc Health Professions U Ill at Chgo 808 S Wood St Suite 690 CME Chicago IL 60616

FIORENTINO, NANCY L., state alcoholism agency administrator, social work educator; b. Rochester, N.Y., July 6, 1947; d. Lawrence John and Jean Isabell (Bailey) Ferry; m. Clement Joseph Fiorentino, Jan. 30, 1971; children—Joseph Andrew, Todd Jeffrey. B.A., SUNY-Fredonia, 1969; M.S.W., Rutgers U., 1974, postgrad., 1985. Caseworker Div. Children's Services, Mayville, N.Y., 1969-70; psychiat. social worker State Psychiat. Hosp., Rochester, N.Y., 1970-71; social worker State Sch. for Retarded, Apple Creek, Ohio, 1971-72; program specialist Alcoholism Control Program, Trenton, N.J., 1972-77; chief treatment, tng. and edn. N.J. State Div. Alcoholism, Trenton, 1977—; coadj. faculty dept. sociology Upsala Coll., East Orange, N.J., 1975-78, Rutgers U. Grad. Sch. Social Work, New Brunswick, N.J., 1978-84, Rider Coll., Lawrenceville, N.J., 1981. Trustee Unitarian Soc. New Brunswick, 1982-84, mem. nominating com., 1984-85. Mem. Nat. Assn. Social Workers (nominating com. 1985-86, chmn. alcoholism com. 1979—). Democrat. Unitarian Universalist. Club: Book, Sierra (Somerset, N.J.). Avocations: reading; swimming; poetry writing. Home: 71 Drake Rd Somerset NJ 08873 Office: NJ State Dept Health Div Alcoholism 129 E Hanover St Trenton NJ 08608

FIORI, PAMELA ANNE, editor; b. Newark, Feb. 26, 1944; d. Edward and Rita Marie (Rascati) F.; m. Colton Givner. B.A. cum laude, Jersey City State Coll., 1966. Tchr. English Gov. Livingston High Sch., Berkeley Heights, N.J., 1966-67; assoc. editor Holiday Mag., N.Y.C., 1968-71, Travel and Leisure Mag., 1971-74, sr. editor, 1974-75, editor-in-chief, 1975-80; editor-in-chief, exec. v.p. Am. Express Pub. Corp. (Travel and Leisure/Food and Wine), 1980—. Contbr. articles to periodicals; columnist; Window Seat, 1976—. Named an Outstanding Young Woman of Am., 1976. Mem. Am. Soc. Mag. Editors (exec. com.), N.Y. Travel Writers. Home: 345 E 57th St New York NY 10022 Office: 1120 Ave of Americas New York NY 10036

FIPPINGER, GRACE J., telecommunications executive; b. N.Y.C., Nov. 24, 1927; d. Fred Herman and Johanna Rose (Tesio) F.; B.A., St. Lawrence U., Canton, N.Y., 1948; LL.D. (hon.), Marymount Manhattan Coll., 1980; D.C.S. (hon.), Molloy Coll., 1982. With N.Y. Telephone Co., N.Y.C., 1948—, div. mgr., Nassau, 1966-71, gen. comml. mgr., Queens, 1971-74, Bklyn., 1973-74, v.p., sec.-treas., 1974-84; v.p., sec.-treas. NYNEX Corp., N.Y.C., 1984—; dir. Conn. Mut. Life Ins. Co., Pfizer, Inc., Gulf & Western Industries, Inc., L.I. Trust; mem. adv. bd. Manhattan East, Mfrs. Hanover Trust Co. Hon. bd. dirs. L.I. div. Am. Cancer Soc.; bd. dirs. Greater N.Y. Fund; trustee Citizens Budget Commn. Recipient John Peter Zenger award Nassau County Press Assn., 1975; named Woman of Year, Bus. and Profl. Women Nassau County, 1969, Woman of Achievement, Flatbush Bus. and Profl. Women's Assn., 1974; Outstanding Bus. Woman award Marymount Manhattan Coll., 1978; award for achievement and excellence Cath. Med. Ctr., 1983. Mem. Am. Soc. Corp. Secs., Fin. Execs. Inst., N.Y. C. of C. and Industry, Ladies Profl. Golf Assn. (hon.). Clubs: St. Lawrence of L.I.; Soroptimist, Columbus, Board Room. Office: NYNEX Corp 335 Madison Ave New York NY 10017

FIREBAUGH, EMILY ROULETTE, newspaper editor-publisher; b. Cape Girardeau, Mo., Sept. 8, 1941; d. Leon Roulette and Mary Jane (Benjamin) Brennecke; B.S. in Secondary Edn., Southeast Mo. State Coll., Cape Girardeau, 1963; Married; children—Kathryn Ryan, Art supr. Sikeston (Mo.) High Sch., 1963-66; elem. art supr. Fredericktown (Mo.) R-1 Sch. System, 1966-69; advt. mgr. Democrat-News, Fredericktown, 1968-79, editor-pub., 1979—; editor-pub. Press-Advertiser, Farmington, Mo., 1983—; pres. Mineral Area Pubs., Inc. Del., Mo. Democratic Conv., 1980, 84. Mem. Nat. Newspaper Assn., U.S. C. of C., Mo. Press Assn. (sec. 1982—, pres. 1984—), Mo. Dem. Editors Assn. (2d v.p. 1982—, pres. 1984—), Southeast Mo. Press Assn. (dir. 1981-82, pres. 1984—), Fredericktown C. of C. (dir. 1981-82), Mo. C. of C., Fredericktown Retail Mchts. Assn., Ironton Retailers Assn., Farmington C. of C. Roman Catholic. Clubs: Friday, Federated Women's. Office: 148 E Main St Fredericktown MO 63645

FIREBAUGH, FRANCILLE MALOCH, university official; b. El Dorado, Ark., July 15, 1933; d. Delton Verdis and Dorothy Lucille (Measeles) Maloch; B.S., U. Ark., 1955; M.S., U. Tenn., 1956; Ph.D., Cornell U., 1962; m. John David Firebaugh, Dec. 28, 1970. Instr., U. Tex., Austin, 1956-58; asst. prof. home econs. Ohio State U., Columbus, 1962-65, assoc. prof., 1965-69, prof., 1969—, dir. Sch. Home Econs., 1973-82, acting v.p. agrl. adminstrn., exec. dean of agr., home econs., natural resources, 1982-83, assoc. provost Office Acad. Affairs, 1983-84, vice provost for internat. affairs, 1984—. Mem. joint com. on agrl. research and devel. Bd. Internat. Food and Agr., 1982—; moderator First Baptist Ch., 1981-83. Mem. Nat. Council Family Relations, AAAS, Am. Home Econs. Assn., Ohio Home Econs. Assn., Sigma Xi, Sigma Delta Epsilon, Omicron Nu, Phi Upsilon Omicron, Gamma Sigma Delta, Phi Kappa Phi, Epsilon Sigma Phi. Clubs: Torch, Columbus Met. Author: Home Management: Context and Concepts, 1975; Family Resource Management, 1981. Office: Ohio State U 190 N Oval Mall Columbus OH 43210

FIRESTONE, (REBECCA) DARLENE, relocation executive; b. Norman, Okla., Nov. 4, 1946; d. Jesse Gerald and Dorothy Charlene F.; student Mt. San Antonio Coll., 1964-66; B.A., Pasadena Coll., 1969; postgrad. Iona Coll., 1979—. With Merrill Lynch Relocation Mgmt., White Plains, N.Y., 1970-85, successively receptionist, sec., admistv. asst., research analyst, Los Angeles, 1970-74, successively homefinding cons., mgr. homefinding ops., asst. v.p., v.p. homefinding and property mgmt. services, v.p. corp. services, N.Y.C., 1974-81, v.p. homesale ops., 1982-85; pres. Group 4 Assocs., Inc., Irvine, Calif., 1985—; cons. relocation Fed. Res.; Bank of N.Y. Bd. dirs. Homeowners Assn., 1979-81; pres. Newport Chamber Orch., 1984-85. Mem. Nat. Assn. Female Execs., Indsl. League Orange County. Republican. Contbr. articles to profl. jours., newspapers. Office: 4600 Barranca Irvine CA 92714

FIRETTO, MARCIA KUKLINSKI, association executive; b. New Britain, Conn., July 27, 1950; d. Edward Stanley and Wanda (Mieczkowski) Kuklinski; m. Dennis A. Firetto, May 25, 1973; children—Maegan, Brendan. Student Northwestern Community Coll., Winsted, Conn., 1968-69. Turst investment supr. New Britain Bank and Trust Co., Conn., 1969-75; asst. to adminstrv. mgr. Meriden-Wallingford Soc. for Handicapped, Conn., 1984—. Rec. sec. Jr. Woman's Club., Plainville, Conn., 1978-80, pres. Southington, Conn., 1981-83 (hon. membership 1985). dist. rep. Conn. Jr. Woman, Inc., 1984-86. Democrat. Roman Catholic. Home: 64 Belleview Ave Southington CT 06489 Office: Meriden Wallingford Soc for the Handicapped Inc 224-226 Cook Ave Meriden CT 06450

FIRGER, BETSY HEILPERN, lawyer; b. Hartford, Conn. B.S., Jackson Coll., Tufts U., 1970; J.D., U. Conn., 1975; student London Sch. Econs., 1969, Boston Coll. Sch. Law, 1972-73. Bar: Conn. 1975. Assoc., Day, Berry & Howard, Hartford, Conn., 1975-80; real estate investment counsel, head equity acquisition unit Aetna Life & Casualty, Hartford, Conn., 1980—. Mem. ABA. Office: Aetna Life & Casualty City Pl Hartford CT 06156

FIRTH, GAIL PATRICIA, business forms company executive; b. Marlboro, Mass., Apr. 30, 1953; d. Joseph Daniel and Barbara Ann (Karras) Souza; m. Robert Glenn Firth, Aug. 28, 1975; children—James Robert, Kelli Karras. B.B.A. cum laude, U. Mass., 1975; postgrad. Clark U., 1984—. Fin. analyst Investors Diversified Services, Worcester, Mass., 1976-78; market research analyst New Eng. Bus. Service, Groton, Mass., 1978-80, asst. project mgr., 1980-83, computer forms product mgr., 1983—. Mem. product mgrs. council U. Mass. Mem. Am. Mktg. Assn., Am. Soc. Profl. and Exec. Women. Home: 689 Flat Hill Rd Lunenburg MA 01462 Office: New Eng Bus Service 500 Main St Groton MA 01450

FIRTH, LETITIA CORINNA, communications trainer, consultant; b. Glen Cove, N.Y., Nov. 7, 1954; d. Lewis Gerald and Harriette (Campbell) F. B.S., Georgetown U., 1977. Lectr., Sao Paolo, Brazil, 1975-76; speech writer Am. Petroleum Inst., Washington, 1976-77; trainer Youth Understanding, Washington, 1978; communications trainer Burson Marsteller, N.Y.C., 1978—. Active LWV, UN Assn., Council Religion and Internat. Affairs. Mem. Women in Communications, Inc. Democrat. Episcopalian. Home: 505 West End Ave New York NY 10024 Office: Burson Marsteller 866 3d Ave New York NY 10022

FISCHBACH, MARILYN, company executive; b. Pueblo, Colo., Dec. 17, 1947; d. Hyman S. and Emma A. (Cortellini) F. B.A., Colo. Coll., 1970; M.Ed., U. Ill., 1971. Assoc. dean U. Calif.-Irvine, 1974-75; cons. Creative Design Assocs., Minot, N.D., 1975-77; dir. continuing learning ctr. Boys Town Ctr., Omaha, 1977-81; tng. dir. Lozier Corp., Omaha, 1981—. Co-author: Self-Help Group for Abused Adolescents, 1981. Advisor edn. com. Am. Cancer Soc., Omaha, 1983-84. Mem. Am. Soc. Tng. and Devel. (v.p., info officer, dir. 1978—; pres. Nebr. chpt. 1984-85, outstanding mem. award 1983). Democrat. Roman Catholic. Home: 1110 S 51st St Omaha NE 68110 Office: Lozier Corp 4401 N 21st St Omaha NE 68110

FISCHER, ASMA QURESHI, pediatric neurologist; b. Pakistan, Apr. 8, 1950; came to U.S., 1975; d. Muhammad Siddique and Mahmudah Qureshi; M.B., B.S., U. Karachi, 1973; m. Paul Mehdi Fischer, Dec. 30, 1977. Resident in pediatrics Waterbury (Conn.) Regional Hosp.-U. Conn., 1975-77, Brookdale Hosp. Med. Center, Bklyn., 1977-78; fellow in pediatric neurology Bowman-Gray Med. Sch., Winston-Salem, N.C., 1978-81; instr. pediatric neurology U. Nebr.-Creighton U. med. schs., Omaha, from 1981; now faculty dept. neurology Med. Coll. Ga., Augusta. cons. in field. Mem. Am. Acad. Neurology, Child Neurology Soc., Assn. Pakistan Physicians, Internat. Assn. Child Neurology, Nat. Assn. Female Execs. Muslim. Author papers in field. Office: Dept Neurology Med Coll Ga Augusta GA 30907

FISCHER, DALE SUSAN, lawyer; b. East Orange, N.J., Oct. 17, 1951; d. Edward L. and Audrey (Tenner) F. B.A. magna cum laude, U. So. Fla., 1977; J.D., Harvard U., 1980; student Dickinson Coll., 1969-70. Bar: Calif. 1980. Ptnr. law firm Kindel & Anderson, Los Angeles, 1980—; lawyer in classroom Constl. Rights Found., 1981—. Mem. ABA, Los Angeles County Bar, Beverly Hills Bar Assn. (vice chmn. atty.-client relations com.). Home: 3695 Hampton Rd Pasadena CA 91107 Office: Kindel and Anderson 555 S Flower St Los Angeles CA 90071

FISCHER, DOROTHY ELLEN, financial analyst; b. Kansas City, Kans., Dec. 26, 1956; d. Robbins Warren and J. Noreen (Greenawalt) F. B.A. cum laude, Lawrence U., 1977; M.B.A., U. Mich., 1979. Asst. to pres. Soypro Internat., Cedar Falls, Iowa, 1975; asst. export mgr. Internat. Bus. Assocs., 1976-77; bus. analyst intern Owens-Ill., Toledo, 1978; bus. analyst Frito-Lay, Inc., Dallas, 1979-81; fin. analyst Carborundum Co. div. SOHIO, Dallas, 1981—. Mem. Assn. Women Execs. (v.p. 1984—), PEO, Omicron Delta Epsilon, Pi Beta Phi. Republican. Mem. Christian Ch. Home: 400 Sandy Knoll Coppell TX 75019 Office: Proppants Div Carborundum Co 130 E Carpenter Freeway Suite 250 Irving TX 75026

FISCHER, LINDA DEMOSS, charter boat company executive; b. Saginaw, Mich., Jan. 8, 1951; d. Duane LaGene and Esther Ella (Rine) DeMoss; m. Jerry Lewis Bowles, Nov. 17, 1967 (div. 1969); 1 dau., Christie Janean; m. 2d, Ronald Louis Fischer, July 4, 1981; 1 son, Ryan Louis. Student pub. schs., Satellite Beach, Fla. Bookkeeper Patrick AFB (Fla.) Officers Club, 1966-70; sec. Virginia Constrn. Co., Cocoa Beach, Fla., 1973-74; hostess, waitress Bernard's Surf, Cocoa Beach, 1974-79; cocktail waitress, waitress Pelican Point Inn, Cocoa Beach, 1979-81; owner, mgr. Fischer's Harbor Sea Foods, Port Canaveral, Fla., 1982—; owner, mgr. Canaveral Charter Boats, Inc., Port Canaveral, 1981—; broadcaster, author radio program Angler's Angle, Sta. WEZY, 1983-86. Mem. Port Canaveral Tenants Assn., Southeastern Fisheries Assn., Organized Fisherman of Fla., Cocoa Beach C. of C., Astron. Soc. Pacific, Am. Soc. Notaries, Internat. Fund for Animal Welfare, Greenpeace, Humane Soc. U.S. Democrat. Baptist. Home: 2570 Newfound Harbor Dr Merritt Island FL 32952 Office: Canaveral Charter Boats Inc PO Box 962 Cape Canaveral FL 32920

FISCHER, MARGARET ELEANOR, psychologist, educator; b. Newark; d. John T. and Mary (Worden) F.; B.S. cum laude in Psychology, Seton Hall U., 1958; postgrad. U. Paris, 1958, Carl G. Jung Inst., Switzerland, 1958-59, NYU, 1959-60, U. Md., 1960-63; M.A. magna cum laude in Ednl. Psychology, San Diego State U., 1966; postgrad. (NDEA grantee), U. Alaska, 1965; Ph.D. cum laude in Psychology, U. Wash., 1970. Lic. pilot, comml. helicopter, fixed wing. Resident counselor Children's Center, N.Y.C., 1959-60; tchr. Am. Dependents' Schs., Okinawa, Germany, Turkey, France, 1960-64; tchr. English as fgn. lang. Jean Giraudoux Lycée, Chateauroux, France, 1963-64; tchr. English and French, Sweetwater Sch. Dist., Chula Vista, Calif., 1964-66; asst. to editor Rev. of Ednl. Research Jour., Seattle, 1967-68; psychologist vocat. rehab. program Edmonds Sch. Dist., Lynnwood, Wash., 1968-70, Charles Denny Youth Center, Everett, Wash., 1969-71; instr. psychology Seattle Community Coll., 1971; asst. prof. dept. social scis., humanities and edn. Purdue U., Lafayette, Ind., 1971-72; lang. evaluation specialist Def. Lang. Inst., Monterey, Calif., 1972; research psychologist U. Calif., San Francisco, 1972; asst. prof. psychology U. Calif., Santa Cruz, 1973, Mass. State Colls., 1973-76; pvt. practice psychology, Mass., 1976-78; psychologist N.Y. State Dept. Mental Hygiene, 1978, Alaska div. mental health Harborview Devel. Center, Valdez, 1978-79; psychologist Alaska Psychiat. Inst., Anchorage, 1979—; mem. Alaska State Bd. Psychologists and Psychol. Assocs. Examiners, 1986—. Recipient internat. travel award Purdue U., 1972, scholarly support award Mass. State Coll., 1974, 75, 76; lic. psychologist, Alaska. Mem. Am. Psychol. Assn., Internat. Council Psychologists (area chmn. Alaska 1979-80), Interam. Soc. Psychologists, DAR, Mensa. Contbr. articles to psychol. jours. Home: 7935 Hillside Dr Anchorage AK 99516 Office: Alaska Psychiat Inst 2900 Providence Dr Anchorage AK 99508

FISCHER, ZOE ANN, property marketing and sales company executive, real estate consultant; b. Los Angeles, Aug. 26, 1937; d. George and Marguerite (Carrasco) Routsos; m. Douglas Clare Fischer, Aug. 6, 1960 (div. 1970); children—Brent Sean Cecil, Tahlia Georgienne Marguerite Bianca. B.F.A. in Design, UCLA, 1964. Pres. Zoe Antiques, Beverly Hills, Calif., 1973-77; v.p. Harleigh Sandler Real Estate Corp. (now Merrill Lynch), 1980-81; Coast to Coast Real Estate & Land Devel. Corp., Century City, Calif., 1981-83; pres. New Market Devel., Inc., Beverly Hills, 1983—; dir. mktg. Mirabella, Los Angeles, 1983, Autumn Pointe, Los Angeles, 1983-84, Desert Hills, Antelope Valley, Calif., 1984-85; cons. Lowe Corp., Los Angeles, 1985. Designer album cover for Clare Fischer Orch. (Grammy award nomination 1962). Soprano Roger Wagner Choir, UCLA, 1963-64. Mem. UCLA Alumni Assn. Democrat. Roman Catholic. Avocations: skiing; jewelry design hand wrought in gold and sterling silver; commercial and residential interior design; fine art and antique collecting. Home: 446 S Crescent Dr Beverly Hills CA 90212

FISCHLER, BARBARA BRAND, librarian, educator, administrator; b. Pitts., May 24, 1930; d. Carl Frederick and Emma Georgia (Piltz) Brand; m. Edward McGough, Aug. 15, 1953 (div. Dec. 1957); m. Drake Anthony Fischler, June 3, 1961; 1 child, Owen Wesley. A.B. cum laude, Wilson Coll., 1952; M.M. with distinction, Ind. U., 1954, A.M.L.S., 1964. Asst. reference librarian Ind. U., Bloomington, 1958-61, asst. librarian undergrad. library, 1961-63, acting librarian undergrad. library, 1963; circulation librarian Ind. U.-Purdue U. at Indpls., 1970-76, pub. services librarian Univ. Library-Sci., Engring. and Tech. Unit, 1976-81, acting dir. univ. libraries, 1981-82, dir. univ. libraries, 1982—; vis. and assoc. prof. (part-time) Sch. of Library and Info. Sci. Ind. U., Bloomington, 1972—, counselor, coordinator, Indpls., 1974-82; cons. in field. Contbr. articles to profl. jours., revs. to jours. Fund raiser Am. Cancer Soc., Indpls., 1975, Am. Heart Assn., Indpls., 1985, Indpls. Mus. of Art, 1971; mem. core com. and program chairperson Ind. Gov.'s Conf. on Libraries and Info. Services, Indpls., 1976-78; vol. tchr. St. Thomas Aquinas Sch., Indpls., 1974-75; bd. dirs., treas. Hist. Amusement Found., Inc., Indpls., 1984—; bd.

advisors N.Am. Wildlife Park Found., Battle Ground, Inc., 1985—. Recipient Outstanding Service award Central Ind. Library Services Authority, 1979. Mem. ALA, Ind. Library Assn. (chmn. coll. and univ. div. 1977-78; chmn. library edn. div. 1981-82, treas. 1984-85), German Shepherd Dog Club of Central Ind. (sec. 1973-74, pres. 1978-79), Central Ind. Kennel Club (bd. dirs. 1985-86), Wabash Valley German Shepherd Dog Club (sec. 1980-81, 83-84, pres. 1982-83), Beta Phi Mu, Pi Kappa Lambda. Republican. Presbyterian. Avocations: breeding and exhibiting German Shepherd dogs; ethology. Home: 4232 Central Ave Indianapolis IN 46205 Office: Univ Libraries-Ind U-Purdue U at Indpls 815 W Michigan St Indianapolis IN 46202

FISCHLER, PAMELA FRAN, advertising executive; b. Bklyn., Sept. 25, 1951; d. Martin Lee and Gilda Augusta (Gerber) Greenfield; student Stephens Coll., 1969-71; B.A., Hofstra U., 1973; m. Burton Fischler, July 3, 1973. New account exec. Unique Security Agy., Great Neck, N.Y., 1973-75; career counsellor, account exec. Dartmouth Consultants, recruiting agy. personnel, N.Y.C., 1975; account liaison MGA Inc. advt., Great Neck, 1975-76, v.p. public relations and media, 1977-80, exec. v.p., 1980—. Home: 1495 Cleveland Ave East Meadow NY 11554 Office: MGA Plaza 28 Urban Ave Westbury NY 11590

FISCHLER, SHIRLEY BALTER, lawyer; b. Bklyn., Oct. 9, 1926; d. David and Rose (Shapiro) Balter; m. Abraham Saul Fischler, Apr. 9, 1949; children—Bruce Evan, Michael Alan, Lori Faye. B.A., Bklyn. Coll., 1947, M.A., 1951; J.D., Nova U., Ft. Lauderdale, Fla., 1977. Tchr., N.Y.C. Bd. Edn., 1948-50, Richmond (Calif.) Pub. Schs., 1965-66; assoc. firm Panza & Maurer, Ft. Lauderdale, 1977—; pro bono atty. Broward Lawyers Care, 1982-86. Bd. govs. Nova. U. Law Ctr., 1982—; mem. Commn. on Status of Women, Broward County, Fla., 1982—, vice chair, 1983-84. Mem. ABA, Fla. Bar Assn., Broward County Bar Assn., Fla. Assn. Women Lawyers. Home: 5000 Taylor St Hollywood FL 33021 Office: Panza & Maurer 3081 E Commercial Blvd Fort Lauderdale FL 33308

FISCHMAN, MYRNA LEAH, accountant, educator; b. N.Y.C., d. Isidore and Sally (Goldstein) F. B.S., CUNY, 1960, M.S., 1964; Ph.D., NYU, 1976. Asst. to controller Sam Goody, Inc., N.Y.C.; tchr. acctg. Central Comml. High Sch., N.Y.C., 1960-63, William Cullen Bryant High Sch., Queens, N.Y., 1963-66, vocat. adviser, 1963-66; instr. acctg. Borough of Manhattan Community Coll., N.Y.C., 1966-69; pvt. practice acct., N.Y.C., 1960—; chief acct. investigator rackets, Office Queens Dist. Atty., 1969-70, community relations coordinator, 1970-71; adj. prof. L.I. U., 1970-79, prof. acctg. taxation and law, 1979—, coordinator Capstone Games M.B.A. Grad. Program, 1982; dir. Sch. Profl. Acctg., L.I. U., Bklyn., 1984—; research cons. pre-tech. program Bd. Edn., City N.Y.; acct.-adviser Inst. for Advancement Criminal Justice; acct.-cons. Coalition Devel. Corp., Interracial Council for Bus. Opportunities; treas. Breakfree Inc., Lower East Side Prep. Sch.; mem. edn. task force Am. Jewish Com., 1972—; mem. supevisory com. Fed. Credit Union 1532, N.Y.C., 1983; chmn. Health Ins. Plan Astoria Consumer Council, N.Y., 1980—; speaker various profl. orgns. Mem. steering com., youth div. N.Y. Democratic County Com., 1967-68, del. to Nat. Conv., Young Dems. Am., 1967; mem. Chanceller Com. Against Discrimination in Edn., 1976—; mem. legis. adv. bd. N.Y. State Assemblyman Denis Butler, 1979—; mem. Jewish Guild for Blind, Jewish Brailler Inst., Friends Am. Ballet Theatre, Friends Met. Mus. Art, Community Welfare Com., Emanu-El League Congregation Emanu-El, N.Y., (chmn. community services com., 1967-68; elected chmn. Astoria H.I.P. Med. Group Consumer Council, 1980, 81, 82. Recipient award for meritorious service Community Service Soc., 1969. Mem. Am. Acctg. Assn., Nat. Bus. Edn. Assn., Eastern Bus. Edn. Assn. (co-chmn. annual meeting 1967), Nat. Bus. Tchrs. Assn., Eastern Bus. Tchrs. Assn. (chmn. annual meeting 1968), Internat. Soc. Bus. Edn., Grad. Students Orgn. NYU (treas. 1972-73, v.p. 1973-74), NEA, AAUP, Doctorate Assn. N.Y. Educators (v.p. 1975—), Am. Assn. Jr. Colls., Young Alumni Assn. City Coll. (council), Delta Pi Epsilon (treas. 1976). Jewish. Democrat. Club: Women's City (N.Y.C.). Developer new bus. machine course and curriculum Borough Manhattan Bus. Community Coll. Home: PO Box 6241 Astoria NY 11106 Office: Zeckendorf Campus Long Island U Brooklyn NY 11201

FISH, KATHLEEN ANN, association executive; b. Milw., Apr. 6, 1943; d. Ralph Eugene and Aurelia Mary (Armbruster) F.; student U. Wis., 1961-62; grad. Inst. Orgn. Mgmt., U. Del., 1983; m. Michael Kessenich, May 3, 1974 (div. 1984). Office mgr. Karan, Roth, Frank & Co., C.P.A.'s, Milw., 1963-73; treas. Maggie's Travel Shoppe, Milw., 1971-74, also dir.; with customer relations dept. Italian Line Cruises, N.Y.C., 1978-79; communications mgr. U.S. C. of C., N.Y.C., 1979-81, pub. affairs mgr., 1981-84, regional pub. affairs mgr., 1984—. Mem. Pub. Relations Soc. Am., Women in Communications Inc., Govt. Affairs Profls., N.Y. Soc. Assn. Execs. Republican. Congregationalist. Home: 20 Waterside Plaza 10 H New York NY 10010 Office: 711 3d Ave New York NY 10017

FISH, LILIAN MANN, lawyer; b. Methuen, Mass., Sept. 6, 1901; d. Samuel Eleazer and Ella Agnes (Hobbs) Mann; m. Charles Melvin Fish, Dec. 25, 1923 (div. 1933). Student U. So. Calif., 1930's-40's; J.D. magna cum laude, Southwestern U., 1932. Bar: Calif. 1932, U.S. Dist. Ct. (so. dist.) Calif. 1932, U.S. Ct. Appeals (9th cir.) 1934, U.S. Supreme Ct. 1936. Sec. Lloyd S. Nix, Atty., San Pedro, Calif., 1926-29, Los Angeles, 1931-32; sec. Office of City Prosecutor (Lloyd S. Nix), Los Angeles, 1929-30, Victor R. Hansen, atty., Los Angeles, 1930-31; assoc. Lloyd S. Nix, Los Angeles, 1932-44, Price, Postel & Parma, Santa Barbara, Calif., 1949-71; sole practice, Los Angeles, 1944—, Santa Barbara, 1971—; editor Ancestors West quar., 1979—. Vice pres. Los Angeles County Young Republicans, 1939-40; bd. dirs. Santa Barbara Trust Hist. Preservation, pres., 1975, also sec.; bd. dirs. Santa Barbara County Geneal. Soc., 1978—, also editor, hon. life mem.; bd. dirs. Santa Barbara Hist. Soc., 1971-76, chmn. library com., 1978-83; pres. Santa Barbara Bus. and Profl. Women, 1955-56, Nat. Bus. and Profl. Women, Los Angeles, 1945-46; registrar Mission Canyon chpt. DAR, Santa Barbara, 1965-80, 85— (Roll of Honor cert. 1978). Recipient Cert. of Recognition for service Calif. Senate, 1980; Cert. of Service, Bicentennial Com., City of Santa Barbara, 1975-77; named Woman of Yr., Mar Vista Bus. and Profl. Women's Assn., 1979. Mem. ABA, Santa Barbara County Bar Assn. (del. state bar convs. 1950s), Women Lawyers Club Los Angeles (pres. 1940-41), Soc. Genealogists (London), Phi Delta Delta. Republican. Mem. United Ch. of Christ. Home: 2546 Murrell Rd Santa Barbara CA 93109 Office: 225 E Carrillo St Suite 202 Santa Barbara CA 93101-2185

FISH, RUBY MAE BERTRAM (MRS. FREDERICK GOODRICH FISH), civic worker; b. Sheridan, Wyo., July 24, 1918; d. Ryan Lawrence and Ruby (Beckwith) Bertram; R.N., St. Luke's Hosp., 1936; postgrad. Washington U., St. Louis, 1941; m. Frederick Goodrich Fish, Apr. 12, 1942; children—Bertram Frederick, Lisbeth Ann Fish Kalstein. Staff nurse Huntington Meml. Hosp., Pasadena, Calif., 1941-42; dr.'s office nurse, Denver, 1943-44; travel cons. Buckingham Travel Agy., Aurora, Colo., 1976—. Bd. dirs. Jefferson County Easter Seal Soc., 1949—, pres., 1952-53, 56-57, 66-67; pres. Colo. Easter Seal Soc., 1960-61; bd. dirs. Nat. Easter Seal Soc., 1968-69, sec. ho. of dels., 1976-77; bd. dirs. Assistance League Denver, 1968-70, 75-76, People to People for Handicapped; mem. Pres.'s Com. on Employing Handicapped, 1976—; active Rehab. Internat. of U.S.A., 1972—, Rehab. Internat., 1960—; v.p. Denver chpt. Freedom Found. at Valley Forge. Mem. Dau. of Nile-El Mejedel. Home: 4646 Bow Mar Dr Littleton CO 80123 Office: 1387 Joliet St Aurora CO 80012

FISH, SALLY R., marketing consultant; b. Albuquerque, Dec. 3, 1936; d. Jackson Cooper and Virginia (Weldey) Fish; B.A. with distinction in journalism, San Diego State U., 1961, postgrad., 1977—; M.B.A. with honors in mktg., Nat. U., San Diego, 1980. Airline hostess various airlines, Los Angeles, 1955-59; data processor Douglas Aircrft El Segundo, Calif., 1957-58; statistician aide San Diego State U., 1958; editor, writer Splty. Mags., San Diego, 1959-62; public relations writer, coordinator Melvin Agy., Las Vegas, Nev., also Phillips-Ramsey Agy., San Diego, 1962-63; coordinator, adminstr., tchr. Lakeside (Calif.) Sch. Dist., 1965-77, 78-80; cons. sales Joan Bodin Fashions UTA, Los Angeles, Tanners Indian Arts, La Jolla, Calif., 1970-80; cons. mktg. Grossmont Coll. and Dist., 1978; partner, cons. PR Assocs. Agy., San Diego, 1977-78; market adminstr. Pacific Telephone, Orange, Calif., 1981-82, AT&T Long Lines, Santa Clara, Calif., 1982-83; project coordinator Western region mktg. ATTIX, AT&T Communications, San Francisco, 1983—, acct. exec., industry cons. internat. airlines 1985-86; nat. account exec. Greyhound Corp., 1986—; cons. in field. Project coordinator Democratic Nat. Conv., 1984. Recipient Outstanding Cert. for Service and Achievement in Journalism, San Diego State U., 1961; Eagle awards for outstanding contbns. AT&T-C, 1984, 85; award for profl. performance AT&T, 1983. Edith R. Allen Meml. scholar, 1959-60. Mem. AAUW, Career Women's Assn., Women in Sales, Sigma Delta Chi. Contbr. articles to profl. jours. Office: 3101 N Central Ave Phoenix AZ 85012

FISHER, AGNES, beauty products company manager; b. Richmond, Ind., Nov. 17, 1943; d. George Washington and Ruth (Craig) Barker; m. Melvin K. Fisher, Oct. 20, 1961; children—Lisa Fisher Eldridge, Linda. Sec., office mgr. Rice's Monuments, Richmond, 1973-76; sales rep. Avon Products, Inc., Cin., 1977-79, dist. sales mgr., 1979—, leadership trainer, 1981, div. panel mem., 1985-86. Recipient Circle of Excellence award Avon Products, Inc., 1981, Activity Leadership award, 1985. Mem. Nat. Assn. Female Execs. Republican. Club: Nettle Creek Steppers (v.p. 1973, pres. 1974, treas. 1976, 80, sec. 1981) (Hagerstown, Ind.). Avocations: reading; camping. Home: RR 1 Box 295 Cambridge City IN 47327 Office: Avon Products Inc 175 Progress Pl Cincinnati OH 45214

FISHER, ALICE JANET, librarian; b. Trenton, Sept. 18, 1925; d. Joseph and Nessia (Kantor) Rosenfeld; m. Arthur David Fisher, Jan. 26, 1947; children—Mark Andrew, Linda Diane, Amy Susan. Litt.B., Douglass Coll., 1946; M.S.L.S., U. So. Calif., 1975. News reporter Trenton Times Newspapers, 1945-47; pub. relations writer Pan Am. Airways, Seattle, 1947-48; art librarian CBS-TV Network Art Library, Los Angeles, 1975-76; free-lance researcher/editor, 1975—; reference librarian Beverly Hills (Calif.) Pub. Library, 1976-77, Santa Monica (Calif.) Pub. Library, 1977—, vol. coordinator, 1980—. Author, editor newsletter, Study Peace, 1982-83, LNAC Almanac, 1984—; author book revs.; contbr. articles to jours.; author, compiler: Health Care in the 70's, 1974. Vice pres. Librarians for Nuclear Arms Control, Pasadena, 1984—; mem. Women's Internat. League for Peace and Freedom, Los Angeles, Recipient Beta Phi Mu annual award, 1975. Mem. ALA, Calif. Library Assn., Calif. Soc. Librarians, Beta Phi Mu (ann. award 1975, dir. 1980-83), Phi Kappa Phi. Democrat. Club: Thursday Night Group. Home: 100 Larkin Pl Santa Monica CA 90402 Office: Santa Monica Pub Library 1343 6th St Santa Monica CA 90401

FISHER, ALICIA RAE, government exeutive; b. Orlando, Fla., Jan. 14, 1944; d. John Raymond and Agatha Rita (Winn) Garland; m. Thomas Frederick Fisher, Mar. 27, 1967; children—Meredith Marie, John Carroll, Amanda Rae. Staff asst. Senator Claiborne Pell, Washington, 1963-67; mgr. directory system Smithsonian Instn., Washington, 1967-72, asst. supt. Pub. Records U.S. Senate, Washington, 1972-76, supt., 1976—. Recipient Eagle of the Cross award Cath. Youth Orgn., 1962. Mem. NOW. Roman Catholic. Office: US Senate Office of Pub Records 2d St and C St NE Washington DC 20510

FISHER, ANN, business executive, lawyer; b. N.Y.C., Apr. 5, 1939; d. William Parker and Dorothy Howe (Douglas) Fisher; m. William J. Danaher, Feb. 22, 1958 (div. 1963); children—Dorothy Lynn Danaher, Jo Ann Danaher Chitty. M.B.A., U. Miami, 1976, J.D., 1981. Bar: Fla. 1981. Sales promotion mgr. Aristar Mgmt. Corp., Miami, 1965-71, dir. instl. sales Terner's of Miami Corp., Miami, 1971-80; assoc. Jorden, Melrose et al, Miami, 1981-83; co-owner Now Courier, Inc., Hialeah, Fla., 1983-85, Cannon & Fisher, gen. contractor, 1984-86; owner Corp. Records, Inc., 1986—. Mem. Nat. Assn. Women Bus. Owners (com. chmn. Dade County chpt. 1984, sec.), Fla. Bar Assn., Fla. Assn. Women Lawyers, Beta Gamma Sigma. Republican. Home: 1514 Zuleta Ave Coral Gables FL 33146

FISHER, ANNA LEE, physician, astronaut; b. Albany, N.Y., Aug. 24, 1949; m. William Frederick Fisher; 1 child, Kristin Anne. B.S. in Chemistry, UCLA, 1971, M.D., 1976. Physician, 1976-78; astronaut NASA, Johnson Space Ctr., 1978—, mission specialist STS, 51-A, 1984. Office: NASA Johnson Space Ctr Astronaut Office Houston TX 77038*

FISHER, BARBARA ALDEN MOLNAR, writer, editor; b. Hamilton, Ohio, May 30, 1942; d. George William and Marion Shepard (Drew) Molnar; m. Thomas Graham Fisher, June 2, 1963; children—Anne Corwin, Thomas Molnar. B.A., Ind. U., 1964, M.A., 1968. Library dir. Rensselaer Pub. Library (Ind.), 1965-68; tchr. pvt. sch., Remington, Ind., 1969-70; reporter Rensselaer Republican, 1972-74; owner, mgr. Barbara's Plants, Remington, 1975-76; freelance writer, Remington, 1979—; mng. dir. Jasper County Council on Aging, 1979-81; editor Remington Press, 1981-83; advt. dir., contbg. editor Lafayette Bus. Digest, 1984; owner Words Work, 1985—; dir. advt., asst. editor The Purdue Alumnus, 1985—. Contbr. numerous articles to newspapers and mags. Bd. advisors Planned Parenthood of Jasper County, Rensselaer, 1974-78; mem. Jasper County Welfare Bd., Jasper County Mental Health Assn., 1968-78; sec. Remington Park Bd., 1981-86. Recipient Vanguard award Greater Lafayette Women in Communication, 1984. Mem. Am. Bus. Women's Assn.Democrat. Presbyterian. Club: Remington Reading. Home and office: 227 Brown St PO Box 155 Remington IN 47977

FISHER, BARBARA LOUISE, businesswoman, interior designer; b. Kansas City, Mo., June 14, 1951; d. Robert Burton and Susan Elizabeth (Patten) F. B.F.A., Drake U., 1973. Tchr. art Barrington Pub. Schs., Ill., 1973-80; owner, operator The Great Frame Up, Charlotte, N.C., 1980—; pres. Interiors By Barbara, Charlotte, 1980—; ptnr. Princeton Properties, Charlotte, 1984—. Recipient Mirm award Nat. Home Builders Assn., 1984. Office: The Great Frame Up 6445 Albemarle Rd Charlotte NC 28212

FISHER, CARRIE FRANCES, actress; b. Oct. 21, 1956; d. Eddie Fisher and Debbie Reynolds; m. Paul Simon, Aug., 1983; ed. high sch., Beverly Hills, Calif. Mem. chorus in Broadway musical Irene, 1972; appeared motion pictures Shampoo, 1975, Star Wars, 1977, Mr. Mike's Mondo Video, 1979, The Blues Brothers, 1980, The Empire Strikes Back, 1980, Under the Rainbow, 1981, Return of the Jedi, 1983, TV movie Come Back, Little Sheba, 1977, Leave Yesterday Behind, 1978, Garbo Talks, 1984, Hannah and Her Sisters, 1986. Office: care Creative Artists Agy 1888 Century Park E Suite 1400 Los Angeles CA 90069*

FISHER, CONSUELO C. (CONNIE), communications executive, writer, editor; b. Oakland, Calif., Dec. 30, 1933; d. George Thomas and Laura (Koski) Carmona; m. Russell Craig Fisher, June 4, 1967; children—Laura Elizabeth, Landrum Bilyeu, Belinda Marie, Nadine Gerry. Student, Sch. Journalism, Mexico City Coll., 1952-55. Reporter-columnist El Excelsior & The News, Mexico City. 1949-54; travel agt. Redwood Travel Advisors & GTS Travel, San Rafael, Calif., 1962-72; dir. community relations Vitam Ctr. Inc, Norwalk, Conn., 1973-75; owner, dir. Connie Fisher Communications, Wilton, Conn., 1975-78; writer The Hour, Norwalk, 1978-80; pub. affairs coordinator Continental Telephone of Tex., Dallas, 1980-83; mgr. mktg. communications publs. No. Telecom Inc., Richardson, Tex., 1983—; press liason Conn. senatorial candidate, Wilton, 1974; pub. relations dir., v.p. Wilton Playshop, 1974-80. Contbr. articles to profl. jours. Parish directory editor, eucharistic minister All Saints Cath. Ch., Dallas, 1983-84. Mem. Am. Sch. Alumni Assn. (Bronze Quill award 1982, 83) (Mexico City), Internat. Assn. Bus. Communicators (coordinator cons. service 1982-83, mem. recognition com. 1983-84, Coty award 1984-85). Home: 6533 Clearhaven Circle Dallas TX 75248 Office: Northern Telecom Inc 2100 Lakeside Blvd Richardson TX 75081

FISHER, CYNTHIA KRAUSE, TV station administrator; b. Pitts., June 15, 1955; d. Glenn Herbert and Dorothy Louise (Poppleton) Krause; m. Richard Alan Fisher, July 5, 1985. B.A. magna cum laude, Bethany Coll., 1977. Service mgr. Marriott Corp., Washington, 1977-79; editor, abstractor Capital Services, Inc., Washington, 1979-80; publicity mgr. HERCO, Inc., Hershey, Pa., 1980-82; promotion mgr. Sta. WHA-TV and Radio, Madison, Wis., 1982-84; dir. TV promotion Sta. WBGU-TV, Bowling Green, Ohio, 1985—; freelance promotion/advt. cons., Napoleon, Ohio, 1985—. Contbr. articles to profl. jours. Mem. Lima Advt. Assn., Broadcast Promotion & Mktg. Execs., Gamma Sigma Kappa, Lambda Iota Tau. Avocations: running; swimming; tennis; equestrian sports. Office: WBGU-TV Bowling Green State U Troup Ave Bowling Green OH 43403

FISHER, ELIZABETH ANN, owner travel agency; b. Ann Arbor, Mich., Aug. 28, 1945; d. Robert Francis and Mary Angeline (Marchese) F. B.A., Reed Coll., 1967. Owner, mgr. Pace Travel, San Francisco, 1982—. Avocations: rough-water swimming; Italian cars. Office: Pace Travel 870 Market St Room 1012 San Francisco CA 94102

FISHER, FLORENCE ANNA, assn. exec., author, lectr.; b. Bklyn., May 28, 1928; d. Frederick I. and Florence (Goldstein) Fisher; student pub. schs., Phila.; m. Stanley Eigenfeld, Dec. 20, 1953; 1 son, Glenn Mark Love. Founder, pres. The Alma Soc., Inc. (Adoptees' Liberty Movement Assn.), N.Y.C., 1971—; mem. Mabon Policy Advisory Council Odyssey Inst., Inc., N.Y.C., 1977-78; author: (autobiography) The Search for Anna Fisher, 1973. Office: PO Box 154 Washington Bridge Station New York NY 10033

FISHER, JOANNE LOUISE, lawyer; b. Detroit, Dec. 13, 1949; d. Charles Eugene and Helen Ruth (Bluhm) F.; B.A., Oberlin Coll., 1972; J.D., Wayne State U., 1975. Bar: Mich. 1975. Mem. firm Leonard C. Jaques, Detroit, 1976-78; asst. cashier, legal counsel Bank of Commonwealth, Detroit, 1978-79, asst. v.p., legal counsel, 1979-80; legal officer Mich. Nat. Bank Detroit, Clawson, 1980-83; staff counsel Mich. Nat. Corp., Clawson, 1983-86; assoc. Shermeta and Chimko, P.C., Rochester, Mich., 1986—. Mem. Women Lawyers Assn. Mich. (corr. sec. 1981-82, treas. 1982-83), ABA, State Bar Mich., Detroit Bar Assn. Lutheran. Office: 1812 Rochester Rd PO Box 644 Rochester MI 48063

FISHER, KATHRYN MARIE, aerospace facilities planner; b. Helena, Mont., Jan. 21, 1958; d. William Joseph and Joyce Elizabeth (Dewey) Hrouda; m. John Dennis Fisher, Aug. 27, 1983. B.S. in Bus. Adminstrn., U. No. Colo., 1980. Assoc. engr. Martin Marietta Aerospace, Denver, 1980-81, layout specialist, 1981-83, sr. layout specialist, 1983, acting chief facilities layout, 1983, chief facilities planning, 1983—. Democrat. Methodist. Home: 6969 S Sheridan Blvd Littleton CO 80123 Office: Martin Marietta Denver Aerospace PO Box 179 Denver CO 80201

FISHER, LETITIA CATHERINE, marketing educator, educational consultant; b. Mineola, N.Y., Apr. 25, 1932; d. Thomas Joseph and Letitia Catherine (Hanley) F. B.S., U. New Haven, 1966; M.S., U. Bridgeport, 1968, cert. in advanced studies, 1974; M.P.A., NYU, 1982. Cert. distributive edn. tchr./coordinator, N.Y., Conn.; cert. intermediate adminstr., supr., Conn. Distributive edn. coordinator West Haven High Sch. (Conn.), 1967-69; asst. mgr. employee benefits R.H. Macy & Co., N.Y.C., 1969-73; merchandising specialist Bloomingdale's, New Rochelle, N.Y., 1973-74; job placement/mktg. instr. Bd. Coop. Ednl. Services, North Westchester Tech. Ctr., Yorktown Heights, N.Y., 1974-76; assoc. prof., chmn. bus. dept. Elizabeth Seton Coll., Yonkers, N.Y., 1976-83; asst. prof., curriculum chmn. retail bus. mgmt. SUNY at Westchester Community Coll., Valhalla, 1983—; reviewer texts, simulations McGraw-Hill Book Co., N.Y.C., 1979, 83; reviewer computer simulations Prentice-Hall, Inc., Englewood Cliffs., N.J., 1983. Vol. Am. Cancer Soc., N.Y.C., 1955-64; campus rep. United Way of Westchester, Yonkers, N.Y., 1978-79. Recipient scholastic award J. C. Penney & Co., 1956, citation Am. Cancer Soc., 1957, Citizens Adv. Transp. award City of Yorktown (N.Y.), 1976, Service to Youth award Kinney Corp., 1982; grantee Sears Found., 1968-69. Mem. Assn. Mktg. Educators (v.p. 1982-83, pres. 1983-85), Distributive Edn. Clubs Am. (cert. appreciation 1979, recognition service 1983, county-state adviser 1983), Mktg. and Distributive Edn. Assn. (life), Am. Mktg. Assn. Home: 126 Church St Apt 5-C New Rochelle NY 10805 Office: SUNY at Westchester Community Coll 75 Grasslands Rd Valhalla NY 10595

FISHER, LYNN ELLEN, program coordinator, wildlife ecologist; b. Phila., Jan. 21, 1953; d. David and Marcia Ann (Jaspan) F. Student Durham U., Eng., 1971-72; B.A. in Biology cum laude, Hiram Coll., Ohio, 1974; M.S. in Wildlife Ecology, Mich. State U., 1977. Research asst. Mich. State U., East Lansing, 1975-77; student asst., Pub. Service Commn., Lansing, Mich., 1977; project coordinator S&R Environ. Cons., Jenison, Mich., 1978; wildlife ecologist U.S. Bur. Reclamation, Denver, 1978-81; pvt. practice ecologist cons., Pinecliffe, Colo., 1981-84; program coordinator U.S. Fish & Wildlife Service, Anchorage, 1984—, cons. in field. Author: (with others) A Survey of Wintering Bald Eagles & Their Habitat in the Lower Missouri Region, 1981; Contbr. articles to profl publs. Mem. Audubon Soc., Nature Conservancy, Wildlife Soc., Nat. Wildlife Fed. (cert. Wildlife Biologist), Phi Beta Kappa, Alpha Soc. Avocations: skiing; sailing; hiking; bicycling; swimming. Home: 13540 Tahoe Circle Anchorage AK 99516 Office: U S Fish and Wildlife Service 1011 E Tudor Rd Anchorage AK 99502

FISHER, MARJORIE, investment management company executive; b. Barcelona, Spain, Nov. 10, 1920; d. George H.B. and Marjorie A. (Wheeler) F. (parents Am. citizens); B.A., Mt. Holyoke Coll., 1942. Mem. editorial staff Dun's Rev., N.Y.C., 1943-45; asst. field dir. ARC, Philippines and Japan, 1945-47; with Babson's Reports, Wellesley Hills, Mass., 1948-50; security analyst Capital Research & Mgmt. Co., Los Angeles, 1951-58, v.p., 1958—; exec. v.p. Am. Mut. Fund, Inc., Los Angeles, 1968-80; pres., 1980—, dir., 1968—. Trustee, Fellowships Endowment Fund, AAUW, 1965-75, Mt. Holyoke Coll., 1962-67. Mem. Fin. Analysts Fedn. (chartered fin. analyst, chmn. admissions com. 1963-64, regent Fin. Analysts Seminar 1969-72, bd. govs. 1970-72), Los Angeles Soc. Fin. Analyst (pres. 1961-62). Republican. Club: Mt. Holyoke of So. Calif. Home: 21 Maygreen Ct Glendale CA 91206 Office: Am Mut Fund Inc 51st Floor 333 S Hope St Los Angeles CA 90071

FISHER, (MARY) JEWEL TANNER, former construction company executive; b. Port Lavaca, Tex., Oct. 31, 1918; d. Thomas M. and Minnie Frances (Dunks) Tanner; grad. Tex. Lutheran Coll., 1937; m. King Fisher, Aug. 13, 1937; children—Ann Fisher Boyd, Linda Fisher LaQuay. Sec. treas. King Fisher Marine Service, Inc., Port Lavaca, 1959-82; dir., cons. King Fisher Marine Service; artist. Trustee Champ Traylor Hosp., 1976-81, Golden Crescent Council Govts., 1980-81. Lic. pvt. pilot. Mem. DAR (regent Guadalupe Victoria chpt. 1986—), 99's, Internat. Orgn. Women Pilots. Home: Box 183 Port Lavaca TX 77979 Office: Box 108 Port Lavaca TX 77979

FISHER, MILDRED LUCILLE, retired nurse; b. Briggs, Tex., Feb. 12, 1919; d. Hubert W. and Zula (Stewart) Hall; m. Gordon Williams, Sept. 26, 1936 (div. 1979); children—Barbara, Marilyn Williams Stone. Student, Tex. Woman's U., U. Houston. Lic. R.N., Tex. Pvt. office nurse Dr. Alan Lambert, Houston, 1955-56, 57-60, Dr. Victor Zima, Houston, 1956-57; nurse Galena Park Schs. (Tex.), 1960-73, Sam Houston Hosp., Houston, 1973-77, Gen. Post Office, Houston, 1978-79, Leander Schs. (Tex.), 1979-85. Campaign worker Senator Lloyd Doggett, Austin, Tex., 1981-83. Democrat. Methodist. Home: 1617 Cimarron 12F Portland TX 78374

FISHER, MIRIAM LUCILE (BLALOCK), child development center administrator, church music administrator; b. Griffin, Ga., Jan. 12, 1948; d. Thomas Hubert and Hessie Miriam (Lusier) Blalock; m. John Lee Fisher, June 19, 1976 (div. June 1978); 1 child, TaMiria Johnessa. B.A. in Psychology, Spelman Coll., 1970; M.Ed. in Spl. Edn., Speech, and Lang. Pathology, Ala. A&M U., 1984. Field dir. Girl Scouts No. Ala., Huntsville, 1972-74; counseling dir. Huntsville Sickle Cell Ctr., 1974-75, asst. dir., health educator, 1975-77; counselor, recruiter No. Ala. Ednl. Opportunity Ctr., Huntsville, 1978-81; counselor health careers opportunity program Ala. A&M U., Normal, 1981-84, also host Montage TV show, 1980; dir. First Missionary Baptist Ch. Child Devel. Ctr., Huntsville, 1985—; dir. inspirational choir First Missionary Bapt. Ch., Huntsville, 1981-85, assisting dir. mass and intermediate choirs, 1981—, asst. minister of music, 1986—. Composer song: My Heavenly Father, 1985. Mem. cast world premiere Treemonisha, dept. music Morehouse Coll., Atlanta, 1972. Recipient Superior Performance award Health Opportunities Program, Ala. A&M U., 1983, 84, Dedicated Services award First Missionary Bapt. Ch. Inspirational Choir, 1983, 84; named to Outstanding Young Women Am., U.S. Jaycees, 1975, 78; extensive tng. program grad. fellow Ala. A&M U., 1983-84. Mem. Delta Sigma Theta (Huntsville Alumnae chpt.) (sec. 1973-75, pres. 1975-78, Outstanding Service award 1978, 84). Democrat. Avocations: singing; public speaking; drawing; writing. Home: 6000-A Lincoya Dr Huntsville AL 35810 Office: First Missionary Bapt Ch Child Devel Ctr 3509 Blue Spring Rd Huntsville AL 35810

FISHER, NANCY, TV writer, producer; b. N.Y.C., Oct. 21, 1941; d. Seymour and Tema F.; m. Peter David Wild, Aug. 25, 1973; children—Sarah Olivia Fisher. B.A., Barnard Coll., 1962. Prodn. supr. CBS, N.Y.C., 1964-66; owner, mgr. Serendipity Talent Agy., N.Y.C., 1966-68; writer, producer Grey Advt., N.Y.C., 1968-70; creative group head Benton & Bowles Advt., London,

1970-74, McCann Erickson Advt., N.Y.C., 1974-75; creative dir. Norman, Craig & Kummel Advt., N.Y.C., 1975-78; pres. Nancy Fisher Inc., Weston, Conn., 1978-81; pres. Creative Programming, Inc., N.Y.C., 1981—. Creator, writer, producer TV series Womanwatch, 1982—, Celebrity Chefs, 1983—. Recipient 3 broadcast awards Network Documentary Series, 1982-843. Mem. Am. Women in Radio and TV. Club: Wings (N.Y.C.) Office: Creative Programming 30 E 60th St New York NY 10022

FISHER, PAMELA STOWE, lawyer; b. Bryn Mawr, Pa., July 28, 1944; d. Putnam Thomas and Thelma (Black) Stowe; m. William Freeman Holmes, Nov. 15, 1963 (div. Mar. 1979); children—William Taylor, Matthew Franklin, Andrew Stowe; m. Thomas Fisher III, June 16, 1979. Student Bennington Coll., 1962-64; B.A. summa cum laude, U. Pa., 1973; J.D., Villanova U., 1976. Bar: Pa. 1976, U.S. Dist. Ct. (ea. dist.) Pa. 1976, U.S. Ct. Appeals (3d cir.) 1976. Assoc., Rawle & Henderson, Phila., 1976-78; staff atty. Montgomery County Legal Aid, Norristown, Pa., 1978-83; assoc. Sager and Sager, Pottstown, Pa., 1983—. Mem. ABA, Pa. Bar Assn. (family law sect.), Montgomery County Bar Assn. Home: 108 Bleddyn Rd Ardmore PA 19003 Office: Sager and Sager 45 High St Pottstown PA 19464

FISHER, PAULA SENIOR, mental health executive; b. N.Y.C., Feb. 27, 1947; d. Frederick Bernard Senior and Glenna (Senior) Emanuel. B.A., Howard U., 1968, M.A., 1970; M.H.S., Johns Hopkins U., 1981. Counselor Prince Georges Community Coll., Largo, Md., 1970-73; spl. asst. to adminstr. Mental Health Services Adminstrn., Washington, 1973-83, acting adminstrv. officer, 1975-76, spl. asst. for program ops., 1983—. Active Camp Springs Civic Assn., 1986, Statewide Coalition Fair Econ. Policy, 1986. Recipient Sustained Superior Performance award Dept. Human Services, cert. of commendation, 1984; Youth Motivation Task Force commendation, 1984. Mem. Am. Pub. Health Assn., Am. Bus. Women's Assn., Nat. Assn. Female Execs., Johns Hopkins Alumni Assn., Howard U. Alumni Assn. Democrat. Roman Catholic. Avocations: tennis; horseback riding; reading. Office: Mental Health Services Adminstrn 1875 Connecticut Ave NW Room 823 Washington DC 20009

FISHER, PEG JEAN, marketing and training consultant; b. Kenosha, Wis., Oct. 15, 1940; d. Edwin and Lucille (Grimm) Reuter; B.S., U. Wis., Milw., 1964, M.S., 1969. Curriculum officer Nat. Assn. Housing and Redevel. Ofcls., Washington, 1971-72; dir. tng. and mgmt. devel. N. Am. ops. Manpower Temporary Services, Milw., 1973-76; cons., trainer Manpower Temporary Services, Milw. also Universal Tng. Systems Co., Northbrook, Ill., 1976-77; gen. mgr. Universal Tng. Systems, 1977-80; pres. Peg Fisher & Assos., Racine, Wis., 1980—; internat. mktg. cons. CREACTIVE, internat. cons. and mktg. firm, Belgium, 1981—; profl. assoc., mem. adv. bd. communication program U. Wis., Parkside, 1982—. Sec., Preservation-Racine Inc., 1981-82; chmn. Starving Artists Outdoor Art Fair, Racine Art Guild, 1981. Mem Wis. Women Execs., Inst. Mgmt. Consultants. Author: Successful Telemarketing, 1985; Telemarketing Excellence, 1985. Contbg. editor Supply House Times, Elec. Distbr., Indsl. Distbn., Modern Distbn. Mgmt., Telemktg. mags., others; mem. bd. editorial advisers Teleprofl. mag. Home: 1201 S Wisconsin Ave Racine WI 53403

FISHER, SHEILA ABUGOV, clinical psychologist; b. Cornwall, Ont., Can., July 20, 1932; d. Philip and Ada (Cohen) Abugov; B.A. magna cum laude, Case Western Res. U., 1970, M.A., 1971, Ph.D., 1972; m. Jack B. Fisher, June 3, 1952; children—Jeffry A., Barbara L., Pamela S. Lic. psychologist, Ohio, Fla. Cons. drug outreach tng. program Cath. Community League, Canton, Ohio, 1970-71; cons., trainer Suicide and Crisis Help Service of Stark County (Ohio), 1969-75; psychologist Cath. Community League, Canton, 1970-72; psychologist Psychol. Services, Canton, 1972-73; pvt. practice psychology, Canton, 1973—; bd. dirs. Acad. Research in Ednl. Devel., Wright State Sch. Profl. Psychology, 1977-80; cons. befriender tng. program Massilon State Hosp., 1973. Pres., founder Suicide and Crisis Help Service Stark County, 1969-74; bd. mem. Mental Health Assn. Stark County, 1969-75; pres. Human Effectiveness Cons., Inc., 1979-80. Recipient Virda Laura Stewart award Case Western Res. U., 1970; named Vol. of Year, Mental Health Assn., 1970. Mem. Am. Psychol. Assn., Am. Assn. Marriage and Family Therapists (clin. mem. 1972—), Ohio Psychol. Assn. (dir. 1972-76), Soc. Clin. and Exptl. Hypnosis, Fla. Psychol. Assn., Delta Kappa Gamma (hon.). Author: Suicide and Crisis Intervention: A Guide to Services, 1974; Productive Power of Stress Seminars, 1975. Office: 2121 Fulton Rd Canton OH 44709

FISHER, SUSAN GROSSMAN, banker; b. N.Y.C., July 27, 1946; d. Bernard and Leah Irene (Gordon) Grossman; B.A. in Math., U. Wis., 1967; M.A., Columbia U., 1968, M.B.A., 1976; m. Yale L. Fisher, June 17, 1968; children—Douglas Carl, Robin Leah. Asst. trust officer Mfrs. Hanover Trust Co., N.Y.C., 1971-73, asst. v.p., 1973-76, v.p. trust div., 1977-79; v.p. Wells, Rich, Greene, Inc., N.Y.C., 1979-80; v.p., dir. mktg. met. div. Chem. Bank, N.Y.C., 1980-82, v.p., dist. head worldwide pvt. banking div., 1982-83; sr. v.p. Marine Midland Bank, N.Y.C., 1983-85; sr. v.p. Mfrs. & Traders Trust Co., 1985—; dir. Veeco Instruments, Inc.; mem. leadership devel. group for execs. Brandeis U., 1974—. Bd. dirs. Emanuel Midtown YM-YWHA, YWCA of City of N.Y., 1979-82, Manhattan Community Bd. #5, 1981—, Dance Notation Bur., United Neighborhood Houses N.Y., Women's Forum; mem. women's bd. Jewish Guild for Blind; mem. Nat. Choral Council, 1981—. Mem. Inst. Quantitative Research in Fin. (dir. 1975-79), N.Y. State Bankers Assn. (com. communications policy 1981—), Fin. Women's Assn. (dir., chmn. corp. bd. com.; pres. 1980-81), Women's Forum, Investment Tech. Symposium (dir. 1974-78), Council Mcpl. Performance (dir.), Communications Industry Council (steering com.), Columbia Grad. Sch. Bus. Alumni Assn. (dir. 1981—), Beta Gamma Sigma. Club: Econ. (N.Y.C.). Office: Mfrs & Traders Trust Co 654 Madison Ave New York NY 10021

FISHER-DICKENS, JOANN YVONNE, naval petty officer; b. Washington, Mar. 8, 1947; d. Warren G.H. and Irene (Warren) Fisher; m. Robert Lawrence Dickens, Jan. 19, 1976 (div. 1978); children—Phyllis Ann Fisher, Ericka Lynn Fisher, Donald Steven Fisher. Student Merrit Jr. Coll., Oakland, Calif., 1970, Laney Jr. Coll., Oakland, 1970-71, J.F.K. U., Orinda, Calif., 1980-84. Enlisted U.S. Navy Res., 1976, active duty, 1978—, petty officer 1st class, 1982; with adminstrv. dept. Navy Recruiting Exhibit Ctr., Washington, 1985—. Democrat. Methodist. Home: 249 Burwell St Bolling AFB Washington DC 20332 Office: Navy Recruiting Exhibit Ctr Washington Navy Yard Washington DC 20374

FISHMAN, BARBARA J., psychiatric nurse; b. Goodland, Kans., Jan. 19, 1952; d. Thomas Harold and Geraldine Louise (Gottberg) Linneberger; m. Stephen A. Fishman, Oct. 13, 1974. B.S. in Nursing, U. Kans., 1974, M.N. in Nursing, 1978. Staff nurse Psychiat. Units, Kansas City Area, 1974-76; teaching asst. U. Kans., Kansas City, 1976-77; psychiat. nurse cons. VA Med. Ctr., Topeka, 1981-82; cons. Ctr. Health Promotion, Research Med. Ctr., Kansas City, Mo., 1981-82; from instr. to asst. prof. U. Kans. Sch. Nursing, Kansas City, 1977-82, adj. asst. prof., 1983—; psychiat. clin. nurse specialist Vis. Nurse Assn. Greater Kansas City, Mo., 1982—; cons., lectr. Contbr. chpt. Psychiat. Nursing. Bd. dirs. Human Rescue Inc., Kansas City Area, 1979-83; vol. Leukemia Soc., Kansas City Area, 1979-83. Mem. Am. Nurse's Assn., Kansas State Nurse's Assn., U. Kans. Nursing Alumni Assn. (pres. 1982-84), Sigma Theta Tau (v.p. 1978-80). Office: Vis Nurse Assn Greater Kansas City 527 W 39th St Kansas City MO 64111

FISHMAN, HELENE BETH, social worker; b. Portchester, N.Y., Oct. 23, 1937; d. Henry William and Hortense (Baumblatt) Sandground; B.A., Mt. Holyoke Coll., 1959; M.S. in Social Work, Columbia U., 1961; m. Bernard Fishman, Feb. 14, 1959; children—Kara Jo, Charles Lee. Psychiat. social worker Children's Village, Dobbs Ferry, N.Y., 1961, 1965-66; asst. dir. Afro-Am. Cultural Found., White Plains, N.Y., 1968-78; mental health technician tchr., White Plains, 1970-71; cons. social worker, Hartsdale, N.Y., 1978—; cons. edn./research Oceanic Soc., Stamford, Conn., 1985-86. Chmn. cottage program Greenburgh Dist. 7; active PTA. Mem. Assn. for Children with Learning Disabilities (chmn. dist. 7). Jewish. Home: 6 Old Farm Ln Hartsdale NY 10530

FISHMAN, LOIS JUDY, financial planner; b. N.Y.C., Apr. 22, 1948; d. Benjamin and Mildred Ellen (Goldberg) Schnapp; children—Susan Rachel, David Alan. B.A., Bklyn. Coll., 1969; M.S., L.I. U., 1974; C.F.P., Coll. for Fin. Planning, 1985. Cert. fin. planner; registered investment advisor; registered rep. Tchr., N.Y.C. Bd. Edn., 1969-74; propr., and tax preparer Suburban Tax Service, Gaithersburg, Md., 1976; life underwriter Mut. of N.Y., Rockville, Md., 1981-83; fin. planner CFPA, Gaithersburg, 1983—; columnist Recreation Register, Gaithersburg, 1983-85. Recipient Silver award WLUC, 1984-85. Mem. Internat. Assn. Fin. Planners, Nat. Assn. Life Underwriters, Inst. Cert. Fin. Planners, Women Life Underwriters Conf. Greater Washington (pres. 1985-86), Rockville C. of C. (membership com. 1984), Rockville Woman Bus. Owners. Republican. Avocations: reading; travel; art. Home: 16605 Bethayres Rd Rockville MD 20855 Office: CFPA 8939 Shady Grove Ct Gaithersburg MD 20877

FISHMAN, MADELINE DOTTI, management consulting company executive, educator, consultant; b. Chgo., Oct. 7, 1942; d. Martin and Anne (Sweet) Binder; m. Norton Lee Fishman, Apr. 7, 1963; children—Mark Nathan, Marla Susan. B.Ed., Nat. Coll. Edn., 1964, M.S., 1972. Tchr., Rochester Schs. (Minn.), 1963-64, Orange County Schs., Orlando, Fla., 1967-68; reading cons. Palatine Schs. (Ill.), 1972-73; instr. Parent Effective Tng., Wilmette, Ill., 1974-76, tchr. effective tng., 1974-76; pres. Profls. Diversified, Wilmette, Ill. 1976—; mgmt. cons. World Wide Diamonds Assn., Schaumburg, Ill., 1979—, Artistic Color, Dallas, 1983—; Pearl direct distbr. Amway Corp., Ada, Mich., 1976—; tchr. reading, Waukegan, Ill., 1986. Author: Organic Gardening, 1975. Leader, Camp Fire Girls, Evanston, Ill., 1963, 75. Recipient Ednl. Scholarship, Nat. Coll. Edn., 1971. Mem. Kappa Delta Pi. Republican. Jewish.

FISK, JEAN A., child devel. clinic adminstr.; b. Aberdeen, S.D., June 11, 1946; d. Darwin A. and Ardith (Severance) F.; B.S., U. Wis., Oshkosh, 1972; M.S.Ed., U. Wis., Whitewater, 1974; postgrad. Nat. Coll. Edn., Evanston, Ill., 1975, No. Colo. U., 1979. Supr., N.W. Spl. Edn. Dist., Freeport, Ill., 1972-73; cons. Racine County Spl. Edn., Union Grove, Wis., 1973-74; instr. Nat. Coll. Edn., 1974-77; founder, exec. dir. Chgo. Clinic for Child Devel., 1976—; in-service dir., cons. to schs. Recipient Title VI-D fellowship award, 1972. Mem. Assn. for Children with Learning Disabilities, Exec. Female Assn., Hyde Park Businessmen's Assn., Council for Exceptional Children. Christian. Club: Zonta. Author: EmH-SLD????, 1972; Handbook for Parents of Children with Learning Disabilities, 1973; Nonsense Syllables as an Aide to Teaching Reading, 1973. Office: 1525 E 53d St Chicago IL 60615

FITCH, MARY KILLEEN, insurance company administrator; b. Carroll, Iowa, July 15, 1949; d. Michael Francis and Mildred (Pauley) Killeen; m. David Paul Fitch, July 3, 1971. B.S., Iowa State U., 1971, M.S., 1975; postgrad. U. Minn., 1982—. Personnel adminstr. Control Data Corp., Roseville, Minn., 1976-77; sr. compensation analyst/employee relations rep. Honeywell, Inc., Mpls., 1977-80; human resource mgr./compensation and benefits mgr. No. Telecom, Inc., Minnetonka, Minn., 1980-82; adj. instr., teaching asst. Lakewood Community Coll./U. Minn., Mpls., 1982-84; compensation cons. Gen. Mills, Wayzata, Minn., 1984-85; mgr. compensation Northwestern Nat. Life Ins., Mpls., 1985—; cons. exec. compensation Honeywell Inc., Mpls., 1984; cons. human resources Les Kraus & Assocs., Edina, Minn., 1984; pres. Personnel Mgmt. Services of Twin Cities, St. Paul, 1983—. Author: (with Paul Muchinsky) Organization Behavior and Human Performance, 1975; (with John Fossum) Personnel Psychology, 1985. Bd. dirs. Kathadin, United Way Agy., Mpls., 1985—; curriculum com. U. Minn., 1983-84. George Catt Iowa State U. scholar, 1970. Mem. Am. Soc. Personnel Adminstrn., Twin Cities Personnel Assn. (program chmn. 1978-81), Indsl. Relations Research Assn., AAUW, Am. Psychol. Assn., Acad. Mgmt., Am. Compensation Assn., Psi Chi, Phi Kappa Phi. Avocations: dressage; karate. Home: 1188 90th St E Inver Grove Heights MN 55075

FITCH, NANCY E. HARVEY, civic worker, former municipal official; b. Spartanburg, S.C., Nov. 7; d. David and Alsia Penola (Edwards) Zeigler; m. Robert Franklin Fitch, Sept. 19, 1946; children—Nancy Elizabeth, Robert Franklin, Kevin David. Student CCNY, 1943-46. Lic. real estate saleswoman, N.Y. Staff mem. Westchester Library System, Mt. Vernon, N.Y., 1965-67; dep. city clk. City of Mt. Vernon, 1968-79, city clk., 1980-82; vol. service and recruitment cons. Urban League of Westchester County, White Plains, N.Y., 1982—. Pres. Urban League Guild of Westchester County, White Plains, 1963-75, bd. dirs., 1967—; committeewoman 9th Dist. of Mt. Vernon, 1968—; bd. dirs. Mt. Vernon Day Care Ctr., 1970—; trustee Afro-Am. Cultural Found., White Plains, 1973-81; v.p. Mt. Vernon Republich Club, 1973-83; founder, past pres. Westchester, Rockland and Putnam Counties Conf. of Black Republicans, 1973-76; bd. dirs. United Way of Westchester County, 1980-83; mem. Nat. Women's Polit. Caucus, 1982—. Recipient Legislative Resolution for Outstanding Work in Mt. Vernon Community, State of N.Y., 1981; named Outstanding Woman of Yr., NAACP Nat. Women's Conf., 1981. Episcopalian. Clubs: Women's Service League Mt Vernon (pres. 1974—), Key Women of Am. (Mt. Venon).

FITCH, RACHEL, nurse; b. Deering, Mo., July 27, 1933; d. Allen Edward and Rosie Leola (Jones) Farr; R.N., St. Vincent Hosp., 1954; student Little Rock U., 1965-67; B.S., St. Louis U., 1974, M.S., 1976, Ph.D., 1983; m. Coy Dean Fitch, Mar. 31, 1956; children—Julia Anne, Jaquelyn Kay. Psychiat. staff nurse VA Ft. Root Hosp., North Little Rock, Ark., 1954-57; surg.-med. staff nurse St. Vincent Infirmary, Little Rock, 1957-65; acute care nurse Georgetown U. Hosp., Washington, 1968-69; public health nurse to adminstr. South office Vis. Nurse Assn. Greater St. Louis, 1970-73; cons. in edn. St. Louis City Health Dept., 1977-80; research specialist Sen. John C. Danforth, St. Louis, 1980; owner RFF Assocs., 1983—; project dir. study of infant mortality in city of St. Louis, 1978. Vol. cert. instr. CPR, mem. community health edn. com. Am. Heart Assn., 1977—; bd. dir. League of Women Voters of Mo., 1984—, editor newspaper, 1984—. Mem. Am. Nurses Assn., Mo. Nurses Assn. (Nurse of Yr. 3d Dist. 1980), Am. Public Health Assn., Acad. Polit. Sci., AAAS, Sigma Theta Tau.

FITCH, SUE ANN, lawyer; b. Garrett, Ind., Feb. 13, 1952; d. Kenneth Duane Fitch and Wilma Loyola (Smith) Sites; m. Gary Duane Shaver, Dec. 15, 1973; (div. Sept. 1977). B.A. cum laude, Colo. State U., 1975; J.D., U. Denver, 1980. Bar: Colo. 1981, U.S. Dist. Ct. Colo. 1981, U.S. Ct. Appeals (10th cir.) 1981; cert. tchr. secondary English edn., Colo. Tchr., Arvada (Colo.) Jr. High Sch., 1976-78; dep. state pub. defender State of Colo., Golden, 1981—. Mem. Colo. Bar Assn., Denver Bar Assn., Colo. Trial Lawyers Assn., Assn. Trial Lawyers Am., ABA, Colo. Criminal Def. Bar Assn. Office: Public Defender Office 815 16th St Golden CO 80401

FITE, BARBARA ALICE, home economist, educator; b. Weaver, Ala.; d. Howard Wester and Edith (Williamson) F.; B.S., Ala. Coll., 1955; M.A., U. Ala., 1966, Ed.D., 1973. Home econs. tchr. West Point (Ala.) High Sch., 1955-56; extension home demonstration agt. Ala. Extension Service, Birmingham, 1956-66; specialist in human devel. Ala. Extension Service, Auburn U., 1966-74; assoc. prof. and staff devel. specialist Va. Poly. Inst. and State U., Blacksburg, 1974-79, interim dir. family resources, 1979-81, dir. family resources, 1981—, assoc. dean Coll. Human Resources, 1982—; adv. Va. Assn. Extension Home Economists, 1979—. Mem. Ala. State Adv. Com. Children and Youth; Ala. planning com. sec. White House Conf. Children and Youth; del. White House Conf. on Children, 1970, White House Conf. on Youth, 1971. Mem. AAUW, AAUP, Ala. Coll. Home Econs. Alumni Adv. Council, Am. Soc. Tng. and Devel., Am., Ala. (liaison to nat. assn. family planning com. 1973, v.p. 1974) home econs. assns., Ala. Coll., U. Ala. alumni assns., Va. Adult Edn. Assn., Internat. Fedn. Home Econs., Kappa Delta Pi, Delta Kappa Gamma (1st v.p. chpt. 1978-80, pres. 1980—), Phi Delta Kappa, Epsilon Sigma Phi. Home: PO Box 745 Blacksburg VA 24060

FITE, DIANA LYNN, physician; b. Amarillo, Tex., Apr. 10, 1953; d. John Victor and Sylvia Mae (Hancock) Ellis; m. Ronald Patrick Patton, Dec. 15, 1977; children—Tracy Patton, Anna Patton, Arthur Patton, Elizabeth Patton. B.S., West Tex. State U., 1975; M.D., U. Tex., 1978. Intern, Hermann Hosp., Houston, 1978-79, resident, 1979; dir. gynecology clinic U. Houston, 1980-81; emergency physician Sam Houston Hosp., Houston, 1979-83; emergency room physician Spring Branch Hosp., Houston, 1983—; owner Gyncare-Pedicare: A Clinic for Women and Children, Houston, 1981—, Audio Prophiles, Inc., Houston, 1983—; dir. Cyfair Vol. Fire Dept., Houston, 1984—; med. dir. Village Fire Dept., Houston, 1985—, Jersey Village Fire Dept., 1985—. Mem. Am. Coll. Emergency Physicians, Harris County Med. Soc., Tex. Med. Assn., Nat. Assn. EMS Physician Dirs., Western Br. Med. Soc. (sec.-treas.). Republican. Episcopalian. Office: Gyncare 4536 Hwy 6 N Houston TX 77084

FITTERER, BARBARA TROMBLEY, clergywoman; m. John A. Fitterer, Dec. 23, 1977. A.B. in English, magna cum laude, U. Rochester, 1966, M.A. in English Lit., 1967; M.Div. magna cum laude, Wesley Theol. Sem., 1979; postgrad. Princeton Theol. Sem., 1983-84. Ordained deacon Episcopal Ch., 1979, ordained priest, 1979. Tchr. English, Pittsford High Sch., N.Y., 1967-68; instr. English, U. Rochester, N.Y., 1967-68; editor, nat. cons. Houghton Mifflin Pub. Co., 1968-75, mgr. Washington office, 1976-79; Presdl. fellow Pres.'s Exec. Exchange Program, Washington, 1975-76; interim curate Parish of St. John the Evangelist, Hingham, Mass., 1979-80; co-dir. The Dream of Calif. for Episcopal Diocese Calif., 1980-83; assoc. rector St. Stephen's Episcopal Ch., Belvedere, Calif., 1983-84, St. John's Episcopal Ch., Ross, Calif., 1984—; dir. ecumenical and young adults ministry First Baptist Ch. Washington, 1976-78; liturgist U.S. Naval Chapel, Washington, 1977-79; clin. pastoral edn. assoc. Sibley Hosp., Washington, 1978; seminarian asst. St. Columba's Episcopal Ch., Washington, 1978-79; offered opening prayers U.S. Ho. of Reps. and U.S. Senate, 1982, 83, 85. Mem. trustees council U. Rochester, 1975-85. Served with Chaplain's Res. Corps, USN, 1978-80. Named to Outstanding Young Women Am., U.S. Jaycees, 1976; Reading fellow Coll. Preachers, Washington, 1983. Hon. mem. Am. Bus. Women's Assn. Office: St. John's Episcopal Ch 14 Lagunitas Rd PO Box 217 Ross CA 94957 Mailing Address: Box 534 Ross CA 94957

FITZER, MARY M(OLINA), compensation planning professional; b. N.Y.C., July 21, 1947; d. Carlos F. Molina and Isabel F. Huth; m. Joseph P. Fitzer, June 27, 1978; 1 stepson, Paul. B.A. magna cum laude, St. John's U., 1969, M.A., 1971. Tchr., Holy Trinity High Sch., Hicksville, N.Y., 1971; asst. to dean St. John's U., S.I., N.Y., 1972-75, asst. personnel dir., Jamaica, N.Y., 1975-77; compensation mgr. Research Inst. Am., N.Y.C., 1977-83; mgr. human resource cons. Peat, Marwick, Mitchell & Co., N.Y.C., 1984-85; asst. v.p. compensation planning Chem. Bank, N.Y.C., 1986—; manuscript reviewer Am. Soc. Personnel Adminstrn., Alexandria, Va., 1982—. Author reports in field. Mem. Am. Compensation Assn. (cert. compensation profl.), Adminstrv. Mgmt. Soc., Nat. Assn. Female Execs., Alumni Assn. St. John's U. (President's Soc.; exec. com. 1983). Office: Chem Bank 380 Madison Ave New York NY 10017

FITZGERALD, DONNA SUE, data systems executive, real estate broker; b. Meriden, Conn., Mar. 1, 1947; d. Anthony and Doris Marie (Hoffman) Bovini (Bolovinos); m. Bruce Paul Fitzgerald (div. Dec. 1984); children—Kirsten Ruth, Lee Wayne. Student Quinnipiac Jr. Coll., Hamden, Conn., 1965, So. Conn. State Coll., 1965-1967. Acct., Tenneco Oil Co., Atlanta, 1970-73; br. acct. Jaguar Research Corp., Atlanta, 1973; controller Jeryl's, Inc., Altnata, 1974-80, Broadwalk at Park Place, Atlanta, 1981, Nat. Semicondr., Datachecker/DTS, Norcross, Ga., 1981-84; adminstrv. mgr. Century Data Systems, Norcross, 1984—; prin. Donna Fitzgerald Realty. Founding editor Mag. Sch. Odds 'n Ends, 1964-65. Mem. Nat. Assn. Credit Mgrs. Roman Catholic. Club: Cherokee Appaloosa Horse (treas. 1979-81). Avocations: raising horses; needlework; writing prose; grapite sketching. Home: 201 Denna Dr Alpharetta GA 30201

FITZGERALD, EDITH JACKSON, real estate and farming executive; b. Lumberton, N.C., May 6, 1932; d. Corbett and Blanche (Wilkins) Jackson; m. James Thomas Fitzgerald, June 24, 1972; children—S. Dianne Martin, Candi Swinson, Angela Fitzgerald Hanno. Student in Econs., N.C. State U., 1973, postgrad., 1979. Adminstr., N.C. Cancer Inst., Lumberton, 1960-70; instr. Army Edn. Ctr., Fort Bragg, N.C., 1970-78; pres. Shamrock Farms, Hope Mills, N.C., 1985—, Shamrock Isle Estate, Ltd., Raeford, N.C., 1985—, also founder. Bd. dirs. Fayetteville Tech. Bus. Club, N.C., Fayetteville Tech. Inst. Democrat. Baptist. Avocations: reading; outdoor sports. Office: Shamrock Isle Estate LTD Route 2 Box 177 Raeford NC 28376

FITZGERALD, ELLA, singer; b. Newport News, Va., Apr. 25, 1918; m. Ray Brown (div. 1953); 1 son, Ray. Began singing with Chick Webb Orch., 1934-39; tours throughout U.S., Japan, Europe with Jazz at the Philharm. troupe, 1948-57; rec. artist for Decca, 1936-55, Verve, from 1956, now Pablo Records; appeared in motion picture Pete Kelly's Blues, 1955; nightclub appearances include Sahara Hotel, Caesar's Palace (both Las Vegas), Fairmont Hotel, San Francisco, Ronnie Scott's Club, London; appeared on TV in spls. with Frank Sinatra, also on Screen Gems hours with Duke Ellington, All Star Swing Festival, 1972; concert with Boston Pops, 1972, later with more than 40 Symphony orchs. throughout U.S. Recipient numerous popularity awards from Down Beat mag., Metronome mag., Musicians Poll. JAY Award Poll; 11 Grammy awards, Am. Music award, 1978; named number 1 female singer 16th Internat. Jazz Critics Poll, 1968; Kennedy Center honor, 1979; Grammy award as best female jazz vocalist, 1981-84. Records include: At Duke's Place, 1966; Best, 1967; Clap Hands, 1961; Cote d' Azur (with Ellington), 1967; Ella; Ella Fitzgerald; In Hamburg, 1965; Mack the Knife. Ella in Berlin, 1960; Sunshine of Your Love; Things Ain't What They Used to Be; Tribute to Porter, 1965; Whisper Not, 1966; Watch What Happens, 1972; Take Love Easy, 1975; Ella in London, 1975; Montreux Ella. Address: care Pablo Records 451 N Canon Dr Beverly Hills CA 90210

FITZGERALD, JANET ANNE, college president; b. Woodside, N.Y., Sept. 4, 1935; d. Robert William and Lillian (Shannon) F.; B.A. in Math. magna cum laude, St. John's U., 1965, M.A. in Philosophy of Sci., 1967, Ph.D. in Philosophy, 1971, LL.D. (hon.), 1982. Joined Sisters of St. Dominic, Roman Catholic Ch., 1953; elem. tchr. St. Ignatius Sch., 1955-56, St. Thomas Apostle Sch., 1956-65; math. tchr. Bishop McDonnell High Sch., 1965-69; prof. philosophy Molloy Coll., Rockville Centre, N.Y., 1969—, pres., 1972—; chmn. L.I. Regional Adv. Council on Higher Edn.; trustee Commn. Ind. Colls. and Univs.; mem. instl. rev. bd. St. John's U., Jamaica, N.Y.; bd. advisors Sem. Immaculate Conception, 1975-80; Cath. del. Nat. Congress Church-Related Colls. and Univs., 1979. Trustee, Cath. Charities, Diocese of Rockville Centre, 1979-82. Named Educator of Year, Assn. Tchrs. N.Y., 1980; cited Achiever in Edn., Bus. and Profl. Women, L.I. Center of Poly. Inst. N.Y., 1977; cited Fall Gal (lifetime governship) L.I. Sky Club, 1980. Mem. Assn. Am. Colls., Assn. Colls. and Univs. State of N.Y., Assn. Governing Bds. Univs. and Colls., Council Ind. Colls., Small Coll. Consortium, Nat. Assn. Ind. Colls. and Univs., Fellowship Cath. Scholars (trustee 1977, v.p. 1977-80). Author: Alfred North Whitehead's Early Philosophy of Space and Time, 1979; contbr. article to L.I. Bus. Rev. Home and Office: Molloy Coll 1000 Hempstead Ave Rockville Centre NY 11570

FITZGERALD, JOY BEVERLY, business executive, lawyer; b. Zearing, Iowa, Apr. 22, 1917; d. Seymour Robert and Jennie Blanche (Stevens) Hix; m. Craig William Fitzgerald, June 17, 1963. B.A., Morningside Coll., Sioux City, 1938; J.D., Drake U., 1941. Bar: Iowa 1941. Atty. Hers, Nevada, Iowa, 1941-44; spl. agent U.S. Dept. Agr., Chgo., 1944-49; interviewer Iowa Employment Security Commn., Amex, 1950-54, mgr., 1954-58; exec. sec. Iowa State Reciprocity Bd., Des Moines, 1958-71; pres. Joy B. Fitzgerald, Inc., Altoona, Iowa, 1971—; pres. Joy B. Fitzgerald Resident Agts., Inc., Altoona, 1983—; broadcaster Sta. WMAQ, Chgo., 1975—. Mem. motor carrier adv. com. U.S. Dept. Transp., 1982—. Name Iowa Lawyer Advocate of Yr. SBA, 1983. Mem. ABA, Ind. Trucker's Assn. (sec. Iowa div. 1975, nat. sec. 1972—). Democrat. Author: Overdrive Magazine, 1971—. Home: Rural Route Collins Iowa 50055

FITZGERALD, JOYCE LUCILLE, biologist, coal co. official, environmental consultant, outdoor writer; b. Coshocton, Ohio, Mar. 9, 1947; d. Earl Lester and Doris Lucille (Lapp) F.; B.S. in Edn. and Biol. Scis., Ohio U., 1970, postgrad., 1971; postgrad. Ohio State U., 1972. Instr. biol. sci. Zanesville (Ohio) Public Schs., 1970-72; adminstrv. asst. Ohio Dept. Natural Resources, Columbus, 1972-73; adminstrv. dir. Boys, Inc., Columbus, 1973-74; biologist Skelly & Loy, Cons. Engrs., Harrisburg, Pa., 1975-76; adminstrv. chief Ohio EPA, Columbus, 1976-78; mgr. environ. affairs Ind. div. Peabody Coal Co., Evansville, 1978-85, mgr. office pub. affairs, 1985-86, corp. mgr. environ. affairs post mined lands, Henderson, Ky., 1986—; environ. assoc. Zimmer Water Systems, Evansville, 1986—. Named Ohio Wildlife Conservationist of Yr., 1977; cert. wastewater operator, Ind.; cert. biologist U.S. Fish and Wildlife Service; lic. pvt. pilot FAA. Mem. Ind. Wildlife Soc., Women in Mining (nat. pres.), Nat. Wildlife Fedn., Ind. Coal Inst., Ind. Sportsman Alliance. Office: Peabody Coal Co 1951 Barret Ct Henderson KY 42420

FITZGERALD, JUNE GILL, trade association executive; b. Coconut Grove, Fla., Oct. 16, 1925; d. Alan Lawson and Chadsey Rebecca (Edwards) Gill; m. Frank S. Fitzgerald, June 29, 1950; children—April Ann Fitzgerald Pena Marsden, Kathryn Ruth Fitzgerald Pachuta. Student U. Miami, 1947. Meetings mgr. Archtl. Aluminum Mfrs. Assn., 1966-74; exec. asst. Pan Am. World Airways, Miami, Fla., 1942-57; exec. sec. Noise Control Products and Material Assn., Chgo., 1976-82; pres. Fitzgerald Corp., Chgo., 1971—. Mem. Am. Soc. Assn. Execs., Chgo. Soc. Assn. Execs., Inst. Assn. Mgmt. Cos., Garage Door Council (exec. sec. 1982—), Nat. Assn. Garage Door Mfrs. (exec. sec. 1974—), Screen Mfrs. Assn. (exec. sec. 1974—), Broadcast Advt. Club (exec. dir. and sec. 1974—), Am. Assn. Ret. Persons, Nat. Assn. for Female Execs. Home: 3950 Lake Shore Dr Apt 502A Chicago IL 60613 Address: 1140 NW 199th St North Miami Beach FL 33169 Office: Fitzgerald Corp 655 Irving Park Rd Chicago IL 60613

FITZGERALD, LAURINE ELISABETH, educator, university dean; b. New London, Wis., Aug. 24, 1930; d. Thomas F. and Laurine (Branchflower) F.; B.S., Northwestern U., 1952, M.A., 1953; Ph.D., Mich. State U., 1959. Instr. English, dir. devel. reading lab., head resident-dir. Wis. State Coll., Whitewater, 1953-55; area dir. residence and counseling Ind. U., 1955-57; teaching grad. asst. guidance and counseling, then instr., counselor Mich. State U., East Lansing, 1957-59; asst. prof. psychology and edn., asso. dean students U. Denver, 1959-62; asst. prof. counseling psychology, staff counselor for Carnegie Found. project U. Minn., 1962-63; asst. dean, asst. prof. Mich. State U., 1963-70, asso. dean students, prof. adminstrn. and higher edn., dir. div. edn. and research, 1970-74; dean Grad. Sch., prof. counselor edn., dir. NE Wis. Coop. Regional Grad. Center, U. Wis., Oshkosh, 1974-85; dean, dir., prof. ednl. policy and leadership Ohio State U.-Mansfield Campus, 1985—; vis. lectr. U. Okla., Norman, 1961; vis. prof. Oreg. State U., 1977; cons. in field. Recipient Higher Edn. award Rocky Mountain council Girl Scouts, 1961; Evelyn Hosmer award U. Denver, 1962; fellow Elin Wagner Found., 1963-64. Mem. Am., Mich. psychol. assns., Am. Personnel and Guidance Assn., Am. Coll. Personnel Assn. (sec. 1965-67, exec. bd. 1968-70, chmn. women's task force 1970-71, editor jour. 1976-82), Assn. Counselor Edn. and Supervision, Am. Assn. Higher Edn., Nat. Assn. Women Deans, Adminstrs. and Counselors (pres. 1980-81), AAUP (chpt. treas. 1955-56), NEA, Mich. Assn. Women Deans, Adminstrs. and Counselors (pres. 1967-69), Mich., Wis. coll. personnel assns., Midwest Assn. Grad. Schs. (pres. 1980-81), Intercollegiate Assn. Women Students (editorial bd., nat. adviser), AAUW, Women's Equity Action League (past pres. Mich.; nat. sec.-treas. legal and edn. def. fund), Bus. and Profl. Women's Club (Lena Lake Forrest fellow 1966-67; named Most Disting. Woman in Edn., Mich. 1973, Harriet Meyer award 1977, pres. Oshkosh 1980-81), Mortar Bd., Beta Beta Beta, Psi Chi, Alpha Lambda Delta, Delta Kappa Gamma. Clubs: Altrusa, Zonta Internat. (pres. Lansing; chmn. internat. status of women). Author numerous articles in field; co-author monograms, texts. Home: 1430 Royal Oak Dr Mansfield OH 44906 Office: Ohio State U 1680 University Dr Mansfield OH 44906

FITZGERALD, LINDA, restaurateur; b. Kingston, N.Y., July 28, 1946; d. Henry J. and Anne C. (Doyle) F. Mem. staff Pagosa Lodge, Pagosa Springs, Colo., 1978-80; owner, chef Eagle & Owl Restaurant, Pagosa Springs, 1980—. Avocations: cooking, horseback riding, reading, metaphysical sciences. Home: PO Box 937 Pagosa Springs CO 81147

FITZGERALD, MARCIA ANN, management consultant; b. Pueblo, Colo., Apr. 14, 1932; d. Robert Russell and Beulah Elizabeth (Coe) Atchison; B.A., Regis Coll., 82; m. William R. John, Feb. 7, 1949 (dec.); m. 2d, Robert Russell Fitzgerald, June 1, 1974; children—Linda Lee John, Laura Lynn John Egan, Lisa C. John York, Daniel R. John. Indsl. relations rep. Sun Oil Co., Denver, 1968-73; personnel dir. Sturgeon Electric Co., Denver, 1974-75; adminstrv. mgr. Nat. Controls Inc., Denver, 1975-79; asst. v.p. human resources Central Bank Denver, 1980-85; prin., chief exec. officer Fitzgerald & Assocs., 1985—. Mem. Denver C. of C., Colo. Soc. Personnel Adminstrs., Am. Mgmt. Assn., Am. Soc. Personnel Adminstrs., Nat. Assn. Bank Women. Republican. Home: 7141 S Vine Circle W Littleton CO 80122 Office: PO Box 2208 Littleton CO 80161

FITZGERALD, PATRICIA ANN, motivational and management consultant; b. Dallas, Sept. 16, 1937; d. Thomas O'Neil and Minerva Hannah (Gililland) Anderson; student Sawyer Bus. Coll., 1955, Phoenix City Coll., 1960-66, Brigham Young U., Hawaii, 1979, U. Calif.-Irvine, 1979, UCLA, 1979-80; m. Gerald William Fitzgerald, Mar. 6, 1976; children by previous marriage—Vicki Lee Jones Duncan, Gregg Ronald Jones, Randall Thomas Jones, Lori Lynn Jones Newman. Service rep. So. Calif. Gas Co., 1956-60, Ariz. Public Service, 1961; sales rep. Shaw Walker Co., 1967-68; sales mgr. Selective Office Service, 1968-69; communications cons., mktg. mgr. Pacific Telephone Co., Orange, Calif., 1970-80; pres. Fitzgerald & Assocs., Anaheim Hills, Calif. and Denver, 1979—; cons. in field. Recipient awards of appreciation Personnel and Indsl. Relations Assn., Brooks Coll., Pacific Telephone. Mem. Am. Soc. Tng. and Devel. (appreciation award), Am. Mktg. Assn., Women in Mgmt. (appreciation award), Internat. Platform Assn., Nat. Speakers Assn., Relief Soc. Republican. Mormon. Contbr. articles to bus. mags. and newspapers, Long Beach and Los Angeles; various appearances ednl. TV, Orange County. Home and Office: 6241 S Pennsylvania St Littleton CO 80121

FITZGERALD, RITA LOUISE, author; b. Boston, Feb. 8, 1925; d. Joseph Patrick and Agnes (Coyne) Howley; grad. Boston Tchrs. Coll., 1947; postgrad. U. Calif., Berkeley, 1971-74, Hayward State U., 1974, U. Calif., Santa Clara, 1972, St. Mary's of Notre Dame, Belmont, Calif., 1975, San Jose State U., 1967-68; m. John Gerald Fitzgerald, Aug. 9, 1947 (dec.); children—John Joseph, Robert Vincent. Tchr., Boston Public Schs., 1947-56, Richmond (Calif.) Unified Sch. Dist., 1956-76, ret., 1976; West Coast rep. Louise Downey McNamara and Assos., Quincy, Mass., 1979—; asso. author edn. div. World Almanac, Cleve., 1980—; tutor; ednl. cons., scholarship advisor, public speaker, reading asso. Marlborough Sch., London, 1975-76. Active Mt. Diablo Hosp. Vols. Assn., Mt. Diablo Hosp. Found. Assn., Roundtree Homeowners Assn., Concord High Sch. Boosters Club. Served with USN, 1945-46. Cert. in hosp. ministry tng.; reading specialist and elem. edn. lifetime teaching credentials, Mass., Calif. Life mem. NEA, Calif. Tchrs. Assn.; mem. Fairmede Tchrs. Assn., Boston Tchrs. Coll. Alumnae Assn., U. Calif. Alumnae Assn., AAUW, Internat. Assn. Childhood Edn., Internat. Platform Assn. Democrat. Roman Catholic. Author: Amanda Panda, 1981 (ednl. program); author 9 books on phonics, numbers, vocabulary, art. Home and Office: 1722 D Sapling Ct Concord CA 94520

FITZGERALD, SARA JEAN, journalist; b. Flint, Mich., Aug. 22, 1951; d. Glen Ray and Mary Louise (Ellis) F.; B.A., U. Mich., 1973; m. Walter W. Wurfel, Aug. 30, 1975; 1 son, Stephen Fitzgerald. Reporter, copy editor St. Petersburg Times, 1973-75; asso. editor Nat. Jour. mag., Washington, 1975-79; CompuServe editor, asst. city editor, editor fed. report page Washington Post, 1979—, assoc. editor nat. weekly edition. Recipient Mark of Excellence award Sigma Delta Chi, 1973. Mem. Women in Communications, Inc., Phi Beta Kappa. Office: 1150 15th St NW Washington DC 20071

FITZ-HUGH, SUSAN HARRISON, state official; b. Charlottesville, Va., Dec. 21, 1943; d. William Wright and Janet (Phillips) Harrison; m. Glassell Slaughter Fitz-Hugh Jr., May 11, 1963; children—Glassell Slaughter, III, Meredith Harrison. Student, Salem Coll., 1961-63. Kindergarten tchr., Martinsville, Va., 1969-74; clk. Va. Senate Privileges and Election Com. and Rules Com., 1978-82; exec. sec. Va. Bd. Elections, Richmond, 1983—. Mem. Internat. Assn. Clks., Recorders, Election Ofcls. and Treasurers, Nat. Assn. Secs. of State (assoc.). Office: State Bd Elections 101 9th St Office Bldg Richmond VA 23219

FITZPATRICK, DONNA R., government official; b. Washington, May 9, 1948; B.A., Am. U., 1972; J.D., George Washington U., 1980. Legal asst. O'Connor & Hannan, 1976-80, assoc., 1980-83; sole practice, also cons. to Dept. Energy, 1983-84; prin. dep. asst. sec. for conservation and renewable energy Dept. Energy, Washington, 1984-85, asst. sec., 1985—. Office: Dept of Energy 1000 Independence Ave SW Washington DC 20585*

FITZPATRICK, JANE MARIE, mail order company executive; b. Los Angeles, June 11, 1940; d. Thomas Harold and Marie (Maxcy) F.; B.S.B.A., Calif. State Poly. Coll., 1962. Buyer, Venberg's, Glendora, Calif., 1955-59; asst. buyer costume jewelry Broadway Stores, Los Angeles, 1962-69; buyer accessories Desmonds, Los Angeles, 1969; buyer costume jewelry and handbags Weinstock Stores, Sacramento, 1969-73; divisional group mdse. mgr., br. store Donaldsons, Mpls., 1974; buyer jewelry H. C. Prange's, Green Bay, Wis., 1974-77; exec. v.p. Jhirmack of N.E. Wis., Green Bay, 1979; owner Jane Elff Enterprises, Green Bay, 1982—; creator TV program Self-Help for the Unemployed, 1983; mgmt. cons. B&B Clothing, Milw., 1983-85; artist in watercolor and acrylic painting. Bd. dirs. Family Life and Growth Center; pres. bd. dirs. 218 Club, Inc., 1983-84. Creator board game Ricochet, 1978; author: Pop-Cubes Plus, 1980.

FITZPATRICK, MARY BLANCHE, economist, educator; b. Medford, Mass.; d. Joseph Leo and Elizabeth Dorothy (Bresnahan) F.; A.B. summa cum laude, Tufts U.; A.M., Stanford U.; Ph.D., Harvard U., 1966. Labor relations analyst Raytheon, Boston, 1949; price economist U.S. Dept. Labor, Boston, 1949-53; dir. sales analysis Polaroid, Cambridge, Mass., 1953-58; mem. faculty dept. econs. Lesley Coll., 1958-64; asst. prof. Calif. State U., Fullerton, 1964-65; asst. prof. econs. Boston U., 1965-66, assoc. prof, 1966-71, prof., 1971—; chmn. econ. Goucher Coll., 1980-82; lecturer Harvard U. Extension, 1971-77; mem. faculty adv. com. Md. Bd. Higher Edn., 1981-82; cons. in field. Mem. Mass. Gov.'s Commn. on Status of Women, 1971-74; mem. Mass. Bd. Higher Edn., 1975-76; trustee U. Lowell, 1975-78. Mem. Am. Econ. Assn., Eastern Econ. Assn., Indsl. Relations and Research Assn., Chesapeake Assn. Econ. Educators, Phi Beta Kappa. Author: Women's Inferior Education: An Economic Analysis, 1976. Office: 270 Bay State Rd Boston MA 02215

FITZPATRICK, MARY THERESE, psychologist, educator; b. Bklyn.; d. John and Elizabeth Fitzpatrick; Ph.D., Fordham U., 1966. Tchr., counselor high sch. Diocese of Bklyn., 1957-59; jr. high counselor, tchr. Diocese of N.Y., 1961-64; prof. Molloy Coll., Rockville Centre, N.Y., also chmn. dept.; cons. in field. Recipient Disting. Service medal Molloy Coll. Mem. Am. Psychol. Assn., Eastern Psychol. Assn., Internat. Transactional Analysis Assn., Fordham Counseling Assn., Assn. Advancement Higher Edn., Nassau County Psychol. Assn. Author: Getting to Know Me, 1967; Understanding Death, 1976. Office: Molloy Coll Rockville Centre NY 11570

FITZPATRICK, MYRTIE CONSTANCE JACKSON, educational administrator; b. Tyler, Tex., Nov. 28, 1934; d. Flemmie Alorronza and Lillie Jane (Burnley) Jackson; m. David Oakley Fitzpatrick, May 25, 1958; children—Sabrina Rochelle Fitzpatrick Jackson, Deenean Yolanda. B.S., Tex. Coll., 1954; reading specialist cert. Calif. State U.-San Jose, 1959; M.S., Calif. State U.-Hayward, 1974; postgrad. Laurence U., Santa Barbara, Calif. Operator/supr. Pacific Telephone-AT&T, Redwood City, Calif., 1959-62; tchr. Ravenswood Sch. Dist., Palo Alto, Calif., 1962-69, resource tchr., 1969-70, follow-through dir. U.S. Office of Edn., 1970-81, prin., 1981—; dir. My-Dae Creations, Menlo Park, Calif. Mem. Menlo Park Bicentennial Com., 1976, City Council Election Com., 1968, Homeowners Improvement Assn., Menlo Park. Recipient profl. awards. Mem. Calif. Tchrs. Assn., Ravenswood Tchrs. Assn. (sec.), Assn. Calif. Sch. Adminstrs., NEA, AAUW, Alpha Kappa Alpha, Beta Kappa Chi. Democrat. Mem. Ch. of Christ. Home: 1307 Windermere Ave Menlo Park CA 94025

FITZPATRICK, NANCY HECHT, corporation executive; b. East Orange, N.J., Dec. 29, 1942; d. Ira Youngwood and Bettie Jane (Van Cleave) Hecht; student Upsala Coll., 1960-62, New Sch. Social Research, 1962-64; m. Alan Rush Fitzpatrick, Dec. 15, 1973. Copy trainee Am. Home mag., N.Y.C., 1962-64, asst. copy editor, 1964-68; v.p. Creative Communications Assos., Newark, 1968-70; sr. editor Family Circle mag., N.Y.C., 1970-77, corp. sec., v.p. mktg. Alternative Telecommunications Corp., N.Y.C., 1977—. Mem. N.Y. Women in Communications (screening com. Matrix Awards 1977), NOW, Nat. Abortion Rights Action League, Empire Women in Telecommunications (pres.), LWV, Nat. Fedn. Bus. and Profl. Women's Clubs, Eastern Bedford Environ. Assn. (treas.). Editor various publs. Office: 80 8th Ave New York NY 10011

FITZPATRICK, SANDRA MARLENE, lawyer; b. East St. Louis, Ill., Jan. 21, 1940; d. Clottis F. and Louise (Campbell) Gray; m. Lorenzo Fitzpatrick, May 5, 1960; children—Andre Renard, Eric D'Wayne. B.A., U. Tex., 1973, J.D., 1976. Bar: Tex. 1977, U.S. Dist. Ct. (we. dist.) Tex. 1980, U.S. Ct. Appeals (5th and 11th cirs.) 1981, U.S. Supreme Ct. 1982. Appeals referee Tex. Employment Commn., Austin, 1976-78; hearings examiner Tex. Water Commn., Austin, 1978-83; sole practice, Austin, 1983—; mcpl. ct. relief judge City of Austin, 1980-82; pro bono Austin Lawyers Care, 1982—. Bd. dirs. Ctr. Battered Women, Lawyers Referral Service. Mem. Austin Black Lawyers (rec. sec.), Tex. State Bar (environ. sect.), Travis County Women Lawyers, Travis County Bar Assn., NAACP (appreciation award 1980), Tex. Coalition Black Democrats, Black Austin Dems., Nat. Polit. Congress Black Women. Baptist. Home: 7516 Downridge Dr Austin TX 78731 Office: 314 Highland Mall Blvd Suite 407 Austin TX 78752

FITZSIMMONS, KATHLEEN MARION, consumer affairs executive; b. Bklyn., June 13; d. James W. and Helena A. (Ritter) F.; B.S., U. Dayton, 1968; M.S., Purdue U., 1971. Supr., Practical Evaluations Lab., Colgate-Palmolive, Piscataway, N.J., 1971-73, supr. consumer relations, N.Y.C., 1973-77, mgr consumer affairs, 1978-85; dir. consumer affairs Richardson-Vicks, Inc., Wilton, Conn., 1985—. Vol. Bellevue Hosp., N.Y. Hosp., vol. arbitrator N.Y. Better Bus. Bur., 1984—. Recipient Silver Trivet award Stokely Van Camp, 1968, TWIN Tribute to Women in Industry, YWCA, 1981. Mem. Soap and Detergent Assn. (chmn. consumer affairs com. 1981-83), Home Economists in Bus. (chmn. N.Y.C. 1980-81), Soc. Consumer Affairs Profls., Am. Home Econs. Assn. Office: Ten Westport Rd Wilton CT 06897

FITZSIMON, JEAN KATHLEEN, lawyer; b. Evanston, Ill., Jan. 23, 1951; d. Robert Theodore and Kathleen Theresa (Daley) FitzSimon. B.A., St. John's Coll., Annapolis, Md., 1973; J.D., U. Notre Dame, 1976. Bar: Ill. 1976, D.C. 1983. Staff atty. U.S. Dept. Justice, Washington, 1976-80, unit chief, 1980-81, dep. dir., 1981-82, asst. U.S. trustee, Chgo., 1982-83, sr. atty.-advisor, Washington, 1983—; dir. Am. Bankruptcy Inst. Mem. ABA, Dist. Bar Assn., St. John's Coll. Alumni Assn. (v.p. 1982—). Office: Office of Legal Policy US Dept Justice Washington DC 20530

FITZSIMONS, ELEANOR, public relations counsel; b. N.Y.C.; d. Ludwig and Helene (Wolf) Brandt. Exec. v.p. Weintraub & FitzSimons, Inc., N.Y.C., 1961—, Photo Communications Co. Inc., N.Y.C., 1961—. Trustee Citizens Budget Commn., N.Y.C. Recipient citation for meritorious service Pres.'s Com. on Employment of Handicapped; Disting. Service award Fgn. Press Assn. Mem. Advt. Women N.Y. (bd. dirs., Pres.'s award) Fgn. Press Assn., Pub. Relations Soc. Am. (Counselors Acad.), Internat. Radio and TV Soc., Radio-TV News Dirs. Assn., Women's Econ. Round Table. Clubs: NYU, Atrium. Home: 254 E 68th St New York NY 10021 Office: 292 Madison Ave New York NY 10017

FITZSIMONS, SHARON RUSSELL, logistics executive; b. Toronto, Ont., Can., June 25, 1945; d. Leslie Alfred and Winifred Marjorie (Williston) Russell; B.A., U. So. Calif., 1968; M.A., Calif. State U., 1971; M.S. in Bus. Adminstrn., U. Calif.-Irvine, 1978; m. John Henry FitzSimons, Jan. 4, 1969; children—Luke Edward, Michael Russell. Mgr. research William Pereira Assoc., Newport Beach, Calif., 1970-71; asst. mgr. interior design Concept Environment Inc. subs. Ford Motor Co., Orange County, Calif., 1971-72; v.p. Urban Interface Group, Orange County, 1972-74; cons., 1975-76; mgr. strategic planning Mission Viejo Co., Orange County, Calif., 1976-80; mgr. fin. Philip Morris Internat., N.Y.C., 1980—, asst. treas., 1982—; logistics exec. Philip Morris Ltd., Melbourne, Australia, 1984—. Office: c/o Philip Morris Internat 120 Park Ave New York NY 10017*

FIVEHOUSE, BERNADETTE, office services supervisor; b. Paterson, N.J., Dec. 29, 1961; d. George W. and Dolores M. (Guarino) Cattiny; m. Harry David Fivehouse, June 11, 1983. B.A., Upsala Coll., 1983. Purchasing agt. Boorum & Pease Co., Elizabeth, N.J., 1982-83, office services supr., 1983—. Mem. Assn. Info. System Profls., Nat. Assn. Female Execs. Roman Catholic. Avocation: gourmet cooking. Home: 269 Ramapo St Pompton Lakes NJ 07442 Office: Boorum & Pease Co 801 Newark Ave Elizabeth NJ 07208

FIX, DOROTHY KAREN, banker; b. Streeter, N.D., Aug. 6, 1943; d. Andrew and Leah Pauline (Schauer) Meisch; m. Burnel Duane Fix, Feb. 8, 1964; children—Denette, Denise, Andrea. Corr. student Inst. Fin. Edn., Chgo., 1975—. Teller, bookkeeper Garrison State Bank, N.D., 1960-65; clk. USDA, Garrison, 1965-73; med. records sec. Garrison Clinic PC, N.D., 1974-75; customer service rep. Midwest Fed. Bank, Garrison, 1975-79, br. mgr., 1979—. Mem. Am. Legion Aux., Garrison Indsl. Devel. Com. Republican. Congregationalist. Clubs: Garrison Civic, Garrison Country. Avocations: reading; golfing; fishing; hunting. Home: RR Box 33 Garrison ND 58540 Office: Midwest Fed Savs Bank 68 N Main St Garrison ND 58540

FLACK, DORA DUTSON, writer, performing artist, lecturer; b. Kimberly, Idaho, July 9, 1919; d. Alonzo Edmund and Iona (James) Dutson; student Brigham Young U., U. Utah, Utah State U.; m. A. LeGrand Flack, Jan. 7, 1946; children—Marc Douglas, Lane LeGrand, Kent Dutson, Marlane, Karen, Marie. Exec. sec. Utah State Nat. Bank, Salt Lake City, 1938-46; author: (with Vernice G. Rosenvall and Mabel H. Miller) Wheat for Man...Why and How, 1952; England's First Mormon Convert, 1957; (with Louise Nielson) Dutson Family History, 1957; What About Christmas?, 1971; Fun with Fruit Preservation, 1972; (with others) The Joy of Being a Woman, 1972; (with Lula P. Betenson) Butch Cassidy, My Brother, 1975; Dry and Save, 1976 (U.S. Info. Service selection for Internat. Book Fair, Cairo, 1978); (with Janice T. Dixon) Preserving Your Past, 1977; Christmas Magic, 1977; Testimony in Bronze, 1980; (with Karla C. Erikson) Gifts Only You Can Give, 1984; Bread Baking Made Easy, 1984; (with others) Flood Fighters, 1984; contbr. numerous articles, stories to hist., religious and homemaking mags.; performing artist western U.S.; TV and radio appearances; mem. lit. panel Utah Arts Council, 1979-81; mem. faculty Brigham Young U. Edn. Week, 1976-83; mem. faculty World Conf. on Records, Salt Lake City, 1980. Mem. Utah Gov.'s Com. on Employment Handicapped, 1975-81. Recipient numerous state and nat. writing awards, including Utah State Inst. Fine Arts, 1969, 73-75, 77, 80, 84. Mem. League Utah Writers (Writer of Yr. award 1982), Nat. League Am. Pen Women (award), Daus. Utah Pioneers. Republican. Mormon. Club: Soroptimists. Home and Office: 448 E 775 N Bountiful UT 84010

FLACK, ROBERTA, singer; b. Feb. 10, 1939; d. Laron and Irene Flack; B.A. in Music Edn., 1958; m. Stephen Novosel, 1966 (div. 1972). Tchr. music and English lit. pub. schs., Farmville, N.C. and Washington, 1959-67; rec. artist Atlantic Records, 1968—; star ABC TV spl. The First Time Ever, 1973. Recipient Gold Record for The First Time Ever I Saw Your Face, 1972, Grammy award for song and record of year, 1972; winner Downbeat's reader poll as best female vocalist, 1971-73; Grammy award best popular female vocal for Killing Me Softly with His Song, 1973. City of Washington celebrated Roberta Flack Human Kindness Day, 1972. Mem. Sigma Delta Chi. Composer: (with Jesse Jackson and Joel Dorn) Go Up, Moses. Address: Magic Lady Inc 1 W 72d St New York NY 10023

FLADELAND, BETTY, historian, educator; b. Grygla, Minn., Jan. 18, 1919; d. Arne O. and Bertha (Nygaard) F.; B.S., Duluth State Coll., 1940; M.A., U. Minn., 1944; Ph.D. (Rackham fellow), U. Mich., 1952. Mem. faculty Wells Coll., Aurora, N.Y., 1952-55, Central Mich. U., 1956-59, Central Mo. State Coll., 1959-62; mem. faculty So. Ill. U., Carbondale, 1962—, prof. history, 1968—, disting. prof., 1985—; vis. prof. U. Ill., summer 1966. Recipient Anisfield-Wolf award in race relations, 1972; grantee Am. Philos. Soc., 1963, 75, Lilly Found., 1962. Mem. Am. Hist. Assn., So. Hist. Assn. Orgn. Am. Historians (chmn. nominating com. 1973, exec. bd. 1976-78), Assn. Study Afro-Am. Life and History, Norwegian-Am. Hist. Soc., Soc. Historians Early Am. Republic (adv. bd., bd. editors, pres. 1984-85), ACLU, Phi Beta Kappa, Phi Kappa Phi. Author: James Gillespie Birney: Slaveholder to Abolitionist, 1955; Men and Brothers: Anglo-American Antislavery Cooperation, 1972; Abolitionists and Working-Class Problems in the Age of Industralization, 1984; also articles. Home: Route 2 Carbondale IL 62901 Office: Dept of History Southern Illinois University Carbondale IL 62901

FLADMARK, SHEILA GWEN, business executive; b. Colorado Springs, Oct. 9, 1957; d. Lorentz Walter and Edith (Hunter) F. B.A.S., U. Fla., 1978. Engr., McDonnell Douglas Aircraft, Long Beach, Calif., 1978-80; sales rep. Evans & Sutherland, Irvine, Calif., 1980-82, Apollo Computer Co., Schaumburg, Ill., 1982-83; mgr. software integration Orcatech, Schaumburg, 1983-84; account mgr. Mentor Graphics, Schaumburg, 1984-85; sr. account mgr. Ridge Computer, Schaumburg, 1985-86; pres., cons. SMI, Inc., Chgo., 1986; pres. Concepts in Achievement, Melbourne, Fla., 1986—. Mem. Nat. Assn. Female Execs. Lutheran. Avocations: scuba diving; dancing; piano; travel; racquetball. Home: 909 Bluewater Dr Indian Harbour Beach FL 32937 Office: Concepts in Achievement The 1900 Bldg 1900 S Harbor City Blvd Melbourne FL 32901

FLAHAVEN, MARY JEANETTE, elementary educator; b. Canton, Ill., Dec. 19, 1918; d. Glen Wilbur Zeilman and Verna M. (Purman) St. John; m. John Eldon Flahaven, July 9, 1949; children—John Eldon, Jr. (dec.), James Douglas. B.A. in Edn., Ill. State Normal U., 1941. Cert. secondary and elem. tchr., Ill., Tchr. home econs. and biol. sci. Easton High Sch., Ill., 1941-43; tchr. home econs. Oswego High Sch., Ill., 1943-44, Wenona High Sch., Ill., 1944-46, Long Point Community High Sch., Ill. 1946-51; elem. tchr. Streator Elem. Dist., Ill., 1960-80, retired, 1980. Mem. DAR (regent Streator chpt. 1980-85, state chmn. biennial procs. sales Ill. chpt. 1983-85, state chmn. geneal. records 1985—), NEA (life), Ill. Ret. Tchrs. Assn. (life), LaSalle County Ret. Tchrs. Assn (parliamentarian), Bus. and Profl. Women Streator, Colonial Daus. of 17th Century. Roman Catholic. Avocations: sewing; needlepoint; embroidery; tole painting; reading; travel. Home: 57 Sunset Dr Streator IL 61364

FLAHERTY, GERLINDE M. (LYNN), electronic information systems company official; b. Stuttgart, Fed. Republic Germany, Feb. 19, 1942; came to U.S., 1959; d. Wilhelm and Frida (Lorenz) Klenk; m. Gerard Eugene Flaherty, June 9, 1962; children—Curt P., Wayne T. Ed., Germany. With Honeywell Corp., 1959—, word processing coordinator, Ft. Washington, Pa., 1977-83, sr. systems rep. Honeywell Info. Systems, Bala Cynwyd, Pa., 1983—. Mem. Assn. Info. Systems Profls. (pres. Ft. Washington chpt. 1982-86), Am. Bus. Women's Assn. (v.p. membership 1984; Woman of Yr. 1983). Home: 1194 Emma Ln Warminster PA 18974 Office: Honeywell Info Systems 121 Presidential Blvd Bala Cynwyd PA 19004

FLAHERTY, MARIE GLORIA, comparative literature educator; b. Kearny, N.J., May 30, 1938. B.A., Rutgers U., 1959; M.A., Johns Hopkins U., 1960, Ph.D., 1965. Asst. prof. German, Northwestern U., 1964-71; assoc. prof. German and chmn. dept. Bryn Mawr Coll., 1971-84; prof. Humanities Inst., U. Ill.-Chgo.; mem. faculty Aston Magna Acad. Mem. Am. Soc. 18th Century Studies, Am. Lessing Soc., Renaissance Soc. Am., Am. Musicol. Soc., MLA. Contbr. articles to profl. jours. Address: Humanities Inst U Ill Box 4348 MC189 Chicago IL 60680

FLAKE, LYNDA KERBY, video store chain executive; b. Safford, Ariz., July 9, 1948; d. Rex Marvin and Ruth (Norton) Kerby; m. Keith Madison Flake, July 28, 1967; children—Troy, Shana, Jennifer, Rachel, Rex, Justin, Kelyn, Jordan. Grad. Mesa High Sch., 1966. Vice pres. Nootka Sailmaker, Ltd., Tacoma, Wash., 1976-81; owner Rent a Flik, Snowflake, Ariz., 1983—. Designer solar adobe home. Mem. Liberty Belles (singing group), Snowflake, 1980-85; organizer Young Artists Festival, Snowflake, 1982; pres. Parent Tchr. Orgn., Snowflake, 1983. Mem. Video Software Dealers Assn. Republican. Mormon. Avocations: piano; singing; skiing; sewing. Home: PO Box 296 Snowflake AZ 85937 Office: Rent a Flik 123 N Main St Snowflake AZ 85937

FLAMMANG, DONNA MAE, machine tool corporation officer, lawyer; b. Cleve., Jan. 15, 1951; d. John Joseph and Irene Lillian (Buzash) Ungvary; m. John Frank Flammang, Jr., May 13, 1979; 1 son, Christopher James. B.A., Albion Coll., 1971; J.D., Cleve. State U., 1975. Bar: Ohio 1975. C.P.A., Ohio. Acct., N.L. Industries, Cleve., 1971-74; asst. mgr. corp acctg. ACME-Cleve. Corp., Cleve., 1974-76, mgr. acctg., 1976—, asst. to v.p. fin., 1979-81, asst. corp. counsel, asst. sec., 1981-83, corp. counsel, asst. sec., 1983—. Trustee, ABC Day Care Ctr., Bainbridge, Ohio, 1980-81. Mem. ABA, Ohio Bar Assn., Cuyahoga County Bar Assn., Phi Alpha Delta. Republican. Office: ACME-Cleveland Corp 30195 Chagrin Blvd Cleveland OH 44124

FLANAGAN, DEBORAH MARY, lawyer; b. Hackensack, N.J., Sept. 17, 1956; d. Joseph Francis and Mary Agnes (Fitzsimmons) F.; m. Glen H. Koch, Aug. 27, 1983. B.A. summa cum laude, Fordham U., 1978, J.D., 1981; postgrad. Sch. Law NYU, 1982—. Bar: N.Y. Law clk. Breslin, Herten & LePore Esqs., Hackensack, N.J., 1979-80, Schweiger, Novod & Meier Esqs., N.Y.C., 1980-81; tax atty. McGraw-Hill, Inc., N.Y.C., 1981—; sec., v.p. Internat. Archtl. Found., Inc., N.Y.C., 1982—; v.p. MHFSCO, Ltd. Contbr. articles to history and social sci. publs. Mem. ABA, N.Y. State Bar Assn., N.Y. County Lawyers Assn., Assn. Bar City of N.Y., Fordham Law Alumni Assn. Home: 114 Harrison Ave Hasbrouck Heights NJ 07604 Office: McGraw-Hill Inc 1221 Ave of Americas New York NY 10021

FLANIGAN, PEGGY TUCKER, writer; b. Concord, N.C., Feb. 7, 1935; d. Paul and Vassie Alma (Love) T.; m. Michael John Flanigan, May 24, 1958 (div. 1982); children—Patrick, Erin. B.A., U. N.C., 1957; postgrad. Northwestern U., 1980—. Writer CIA, Washington, 1957-61; free lance writer, 1961-73; editor U.S. Army Recruiting Command, Fort Sheridan, Ill., 1973-79, writer, mgr. mag. and book programs book program Hdqrs., 1984—; newspaper editor, 1979-84. Contbr. articles to profl. jours. Recipient award for excellence in journalism U.S. Army, 1983. Mem. Nat. Assn. Female Execs., Chgo.

Council Fgn. Relations, Highland Park Hist. Soc. Club: Chgo. Press. Republican. Presbyterian.

FLANNIGAN, GAIL ELIZABETH, hotel marketing and tourism executive, consultant; b. Staten Island, N.Y., Dec. 15, 1946; d. Charles Joseph and Winifred Mae (Kinder) F.; m. Terence William Rufer, Sept. 18, 1982. B.A., Georgian Ct. Coll., 1968; postgrad. U. Maine, 1968, Fairleigh Dickinson U., 1970-73; diploma Sch. Hotel Mgmt. NYU, 1977. Tchr. John F. Kennedy Meml. High Sch., Iselin, N.J., 1968-69, Saddle River Country Day Sch., N.J., 1968-73; research asst. to author Gay Talese, N.Y.C., 1973-77; account exec. Hyatt Hotels, N.Y.C., 1977-79; mktg. rep. Monaco Tourist Office, N.Y.C., 1979-80; dir. sales and mktg. Gulf and Western Hotels, N.Y.C., 1980-85; pres. Gail Flannigan Assocs., N.Y.C., 1985—; pres. nat. meeting planners orgn. TWR Inc., N.Y.C., 1985—. Author poetry in mags. Community lectr., high sch. speaker on alcoholism, N.Y.C., 1980—. French govt. grantee, U. Maine, 1968. Mem. Nat. Assn. Female Execs. (networking program 1981-82), Meeting Planners Internat., Soc. Incentive Travel Execs., N.Y. Soc. Assn. Execs., Phi Sigma Epsilon. Republican. Roman Catholic. Avocations: Writing; skiing; running. Office: Gail Flannigan Assocs 260 Madison Ave New York NY 10016

FLECHNER, ROBERTA FAY, graphic designer; b. N.Y.C., June 7, 1949; d. Abraham Julius and Evelyn (Medwin) F. B.A., CCNY, 1970; M.A., NYU, 1972; cert. Printing Industries Met. N.Y., N.Y.C., 1974, 75, 79. Researcher, asst. editor Arno Press, N.Y.C., 1970-73; free-lance editor Random House, N.Y.C., 1973-74, graphic designer/compositor coll. dept., 1984—; graphic designer Core Communications in Health, N.Y.C., 1974-76; prodn. mgr. Heights-Inwood News, N.Y.C., 1976-77; art dir., graphic designer Jour. Advt. Research, N.Y.C., 1976-81; prin., graphic designer/compositor Roberta Flechner Graphics, N.Y.C., 1976—; graphic designer/compositor W. W. Norton & Co., Inc., 1977—; mech. artist Fawcett, N.Y.C., 1979-80; graphic designer Avon Internat., N.Y.C., 1982; art dir., compositor, layout artist Source: Notes in the History of Art, N.Y.C., 1982—; graphic designer John Wiley & Sons, Inc., N.Y.C., 1985. Designer stationery, 1979 (Art Direction mag., Creativity-cert. distinction 1979). Art dir. enviroNews, N.Y. State Atty. Gen.'s Environ. Protection Bur., N.Y.C., 1977-78. Mem. Graphic Artists Guild, NOW, Women's Nat. Book Assn. (cons.), Nat. Assn. Female Execs., Women's Caucus for Art, Am. Inst. Graphic Arts, CCNY Alumni, NYU Alumni. Office: 106-15 Queens Blvd Forest Hills NY 11375

FLEEMAN, MARY GRACE, lawyer, librarian; b. Morgantown, W.Va., Aug. 24, 1947; d. George Ellis and Mary Jane (Stackpole) Moore; m. Keith Patrick Fleeman, Oct. 25, 1980. B.S., Allegheny Coll., 1969; M.S. in L.S., U. N.C., 1971; M.S.M., Frostburg State Coll., 1979; J.D. with highest honors, George Washington U., 1985. Library fellow U. N.C., Chapel Hill, 1970-71; asst. exchange and gift librarian U.S. Geol. Survey, Reston, Va., 1971-73, serials cataloger, 1973-74; cataloger Frostburg State Coll. (Md.), 1974-79; serials cataloger U. Okla., Norman, 1979-80; head cataloger George Washington U. Law Library, Washington, 1980-85; atty. Arnold & Porter, Washington, 1985—. Mem. ABA, Bar Assn. D.C., ALA, Am. Assn. Law Libraries, Law Librarians Soc. of Washington, AAUW, Order of Coif, Beta Phi Mu, Alpha Xi Delta. Methodist. Home: 4923 McCall St Rockville MD 20853 Office: Arnold & Porter 1200 New Hamphire Ave NW Washington DC 20036

FLEISCHHACKER, SUSAN ELLEN KATHRYN ANNE, marketing executive, computer systems designer; b. Iowa City, June 7, 1952; d. Rudolph Joseph Fleischhacker and Margaret Ellen (Gardner) Gardner. A.L.B. cum laude, Harvard U., 1985. Systems engr. Electronic Data Systems, Dallas, 1975-77; systems analyst Textron, Tehran, Iran, 1977-79; sr. systems analyst Am. Can Co., Greenwich, Conn., 1979-81; cash mgmt. Chem. Bank, N.Y.C., 1981-83; ops. mgr. Gartner Group, Mecinite, Stamford, Conn., 1983; sr. v.p. mktg., CD Pub. Co., Mecinite, N.Y.C., 1984—. Bd. dirs. Urban League of Southwestern Fairfield County, Stamford, 1983—; pres. Urban League Guild, 1984; founder Greenwich Exec. Roundtable, 1980, pres., 1980-82. Republican. Roman Catholic.

FLEISCHMAN, BARBARA GREENBERG, public relations consultant; b. Detroit, Mar. 20, 1924; d. Samuel J. and Theresa (Keil) Greenberg; B.A., U. Mich., 1944; m. Lawrence A. Fleischman, Dec. 18, 1948; children—Rebecca, Arthur, Martha. Tchr., Detroit Public Schs., 1944-45, psychoanalyst's sec., Detroit, 1947-49; sec. Greenberg Ins. Agy., Detroit, 1947-49; customer/public relations cons. Kennedy Galleries, N.Y.C., 1976—. Bd. dirs. Detroit Artists Market, 1958-66; mem. women's com. Detroit Inst. Arts, 1957-66, founder, pres. vol. com., 1961-66; bd. dirs. Friends of Channel 13, 1968-80, pres., N.Y.C., 1975-79, chmn. auction, 1975, trustee, 1975-84; pres. Friends of N.Y. Pub. Library, 1979—, trustee, 1980—; governing bd. Off the Record Luncheons, Fgn. Policy Assn., 1978-85; asso. producer Channel 13 Auction, 1978-80. Club: Cosmopolitan. Office: care Kennedy Galleries Inc 40 W 57th St New York NY 10019

FLEISCHMAN, JOAN WALDEN, social worker; b. Boston, Nov. 11, 1931; d. Daniel and Gertrude (Perry) Walden; m. Edward Hirsh Fleischman, Dec. 27, 1953; children—Charles M., Janet S. B.A., Wellesley Coll., 1953; M.Ed., Boston U., 1957; M.S.W., Fordham U., 1980. Cert. social worker, N.Y., N.J. Tchr., Natick, Mass., Mt. Vernon, N.Y., 1955-58; social worker Family Life Ctr. of Hackensack Med. Ctr., N.J., 1980—. Mem. Nat. Assn. Social Workers, Acad. Cert. Social Workers. Jewish. Home: 10 Glen Blvd Glen Rock NJ 07452 Office: Family Life Ctr of Hackensack Med Ctr 214 State St Hackensack NJ 07601

FLEISHMAN, MARTHA STONE, interior designer; b. Peace Dale, R.I., Sept. 16, 1946; d. Leslie Roland and Margaret Rodman (Thackeray) Stone; B.F.A., R.I. Sch. Design, 1968; m. Jay Fleishman, June 27, 1981; 2 children. Designer, William D. Warner AIA, Providence, 1967-68; interior designer Richard Sharpe AIA, Norwitchtown, Conn., 1968; interior designer Space Design Group, N.Y.C., 1969-73; dir. interior design Carson, Lundin & Shaw, N.Y.C., 1973-75; interior designer Duffy, Inc., N.Y.C., 1976-77; dir. design Chemical Bank, N.Y.C., 1977-83; owner design studio, 1983-85; dir. design Citibank, N.Y.C., 1985—; mem. adj. faculty R.I. Sch. Design, 1978. Mem. Am. Soc. Interior Designers, Inst. Facility Mgrs. Assn., AIA (assoc.). Interior designer Dime Savs. Bank, Franklin Savs. Bank, 1975, Chem. Bank World Hdqrs., 1981. Home: 127 E 94th St New York NY 10028

FLEISHMAN, WENDY RUTH, lawyer; b. Phila., Dec. 28, 1954; d. Harry and Sylvia (Laub) F. B.A., Sarah Lawrence Coll., 1974; J.D., Temple U., 1977. Bar: Pa. 1977. Asst. dist. atty. City of Phila., 1977-84; assoc. Ballard, Spahr, Andrews & Ingersoll, Phila., 1984—. Bd. dirs. Women Organized Against Rape, Women's Way (both Phila.). Mem. Assn. Trial Lawyers Am., Pa. Trial Atty. Assn., ABA, Pa. Bar Assn., Phila. Bar Assn. Democrat. Jewish. Office: Ballard Spahr Andrews & Ingersoll 30 S 17th St 20th Fl Philadelphia PA 19103

FLEMING, ALICE CAREW MULCAHEY (MRS. THOMAS J. FLEMING), author; b. New Haven, Dec. 21, 1928; d. Albert Leo and Agnes (Foley) Mulcahey; A.B., Trinity Coll., 1950; M.A., Columbia, 1951; m. Thomas J. Fleming, Jan. 19, 1951; children—Alice, Thomas, David, Richard. Trustee Trinity Coll., Washington; bd. dirs. N.Y. chpt. Medic Alert Found. Internat., United Hosp. Fund of N.Y., St. Vincent's Fund of N.Y. Recipient Nat. Media award Family Service Assn. Am., 1973; Alumnae Achievement award Trinity Coll., 1979. Mem. PEN, Authors Guild. Author: The Key to New York, 1960; Wheels, 1960; A Son of Liberty, 1961; Doctors in Petticoats, 1964; Great Women Teachers, 1965; The Senator from Maine: Margaret Chase Smith, 1969; Alice Freeman Palmer: Pioneer College President, 1970; Reporters At War, 1970; General's Lady, 1971; Highways into History, 1971; Pioneers in Print, 1971; Ida Tarbell, The First of the Muckrakers, 1971; Nine Months, 1972; Psychiatry, What's it All About?, 1972; The Moviemakers, 1973; Trials that Made Headlines, 1974; Contraception, Abortion, Pregnancy, 1974; New on the Beat, 1975; Alcohol: The Delightful Poison, 1975; Something for Nothing, 1978, The Mysteries of ESP, 1980; What to Say When You Don't Know What to Say, 1982; Welcome to Grossville, 1985. Editor: Hosannah the Home Run!, 1972; America Is Not All Traffic Lights, 1976; Welcome to Grossville, 1985. Contbr. articles to mags. Address: 315 E 72d St New York NY 10021

FLEMING, ALICE MAY, psychiatrist; b. Boston; d. Michael J. and Julia M. (Penney) F.; B.A., Radcliffe Coll., 1933; Ed.M., Harvard U., 1938; M.D., Boston U. Sch. Medicine, 1950. Intern, St. Vincent Hosp., N.Y.C., 1950-51; resident Boston State Hosp., 1951-52, Univ. Hosp., 1952-53, Putnam Children's Center, 1953-55, Judge Baker Guidance Center, 1955—; pvt. practice, dir. Boston unit Judge Baker Pilot Tng. Program in Delinquency, 1956-61; dir. Cape Cod Child Guidance Clinic, Barnstable, Mass., 1954-65; dir. Boston Juvenile Ct. Clinic, 1965-81; mem. staff Children's Hosp. Med. Center and Judge Baker Guidance Center, Boston, 1955-81; mem. faculty Harvard Med. Sch., Boston, 1955—, vis. lectr. psychiatry, 1981—; pvt. practice specializing in child psychiatry, Boston, 1953—; cons. psychiatrist May Sch. for Autistic Children, Chatham, Mass., 1957-78, Kennebec Mental Health Clinic, 1964-77; mem. corp. Boston Children's Services, 1981—; mem. staff Children's Hosp. and Med. Center. Served to lt. (j.g.) USNR, 1943-46. Recipient Marsalin award, 1966; Judge John F. Perkins award Boston Juvenile Ct., 1982; Harvard Chair award, 1984. Mem. AMA, New Eng. Council Child Psychiatry, Am. Psychiat. Assn. Home: Box 353 East Wareham MA 02538 Office: 295 Longwood Ave Boston MA 02115

FLEMING, (BEVERLY) JEANNE, psychologist; b. Chattanooga, Apr. 3, 1949; d. Delbert and Gladys Marie (Hicks) Swanson; B.S., U. Fla., 1971; M.S. in Marriage and Family Counseling, Loma Linda (Calif.) U., 1975; Ph.D., U.S. Internat. U., San Diego, 1979; m. John Richard Fleming, Sept. 6, 1973; 1 son, Jason. Ind. practice marriage-family counseling, Calif., 1975-78; custody investigator Cowlitz County (Wash.) Family Ct., 1979-81; psychology resident Dean V. Harris & Assocs., Vancouver and Longview, Wash., 1981-82; pvt. practice psychology, Vancouver, 1982-84, Longview, Wash., 1983—; mem. family life com. Oreg. conf. Seventh-day Adventists; bd. dirs. Children's Home Soc. Wash.; cons. in field. Mem. Am. Psychol. Assn., Am. Assn. Marriage and Family Therapists, Western Psychol. Assn., Wash. Psychol. Assn. (exec. bd. 1981-83), S.W. Wash. Assn. Psychologist (sec.-treas. 1981-82). Author articles in field. Office: 900 Fir St Suite 2N Longview WA 98632

FLEMING, BONNIE MARGARET, casino-hotel company executive; b. Morristown, N.J., Mar. 27, 1955; d. Douglas Haig and Mildred Lillian (Lachenauer) F. B.A., Stockton State Coll., Pomona, N.J., 1977; student Susquehanna U., Selinsgrove, Pa., 1973-75. Exec. trainee, Montgomery Ward's, Johnson City, N.Y., 1977-79; systems analyst Reese Pally-Zipp Ltd., Atlantic City, 1979-80; retail shop mgr. Holiday Inn Harrahs Casino, Atlantic City, 1980; asst. dir. purchasing Ramada Tropicana Casino, Atlantic City, 1980-82; dir. purchasing Del Webb Claridge Casino, Atlantic City, 1982—. Vice chairperson N.J.-Pa.-Del. Regional Minority Council, Phila., 1985—. Mem. Atlantic City Purchasing Assn. (pres. 1986—), Nat. Assn. Female Execs. Republican. Episcopalian. Home: 112 Roosevelt Ave Northfield NJ 08225 Office: Claridge Casino Hotel Indiana Ave Atlantic City NJ 08401

FLEMING, CYNTHIA ANN, alcoholism therapist; b. Balt., Feb. 29, 1960; d. Charles Hall and Rebecca Ann (Hamilton) Fleming. B.A. in Social Work, Colo. State U., 1982; student Tex. Woman's U., 1981. Cert. alcohol and drug abuse counselor. Substance Abuse counselor Sheriff's Office, Eagle, Colo., 1985—; youth counselor Garfield Youth Services, Glenwood Springs, Colo., 1982-83; detox counselor Mountain Rivers Addictions Rehab., Glenwood Springs, 1983-84, DUI group counselor, 1983-84, halfway house coordinator, 1984-85. Bd. dirs. Senior Home, Glenwood Springs, 1985—. Mem. Nat. Assn. Female Execs. Democrat. Presbyterian. Office: Eagle County Sheriff's Office PO Box 359 Eagle CO 81631

FLEMING, JACQUELINE ANTOINETTE, educator; b. Balt., May 12; d. Ollie Edward and Sarah Lorette (Watson) F. B.A., U. Md., 1964; M.Ed., Coppin State Coll., 1970, postgrad., 1971. Advanced profl. tchr.'s cert., Md. Tchr., Balt. Mem. Fedn. Republican Women, 1977—; mem. Theodore R. McKeldin Rep. Women Civic Club, 1977—, rep., 1977, 79; vol. Provident Hosp., 1976; mem. nominating com. Central Md. council Girl Scouts U.S.A., 1976-68, mem. stretching out com., 1977; bd. dirs., chmn. scholarship com. Morgan Christian Ctr., Morgan State U., 1977-80; mem. Nat. Urban League, 1969—, YWCA, 1964—, NAACP, 1964—; chmn. exptl. studies Herbert M. Frisby Hist. Soc., 1972-74; chmn. Bapt. Trustee Bd., 1982—; mem. Statue of Liberty-Ellis Island Found. Register, 1984—. Recipient Cert. of Appreciation, Provident Hosp., 1974, Outstanding Service award and pin, 1976; presdl. citation Herbert M. Frisby Hist. Soc., 1971, cert. for outstanding contbn. Morgan State U., 1983, Appreciation award St. John's Bapt. Ch., 1985. Mem. AAUW, Nat. Assn. Negro and Profl. Women (life, exec. com. 1969—, publicity chmn. 1969-71), Lambda Kappa Mu (chmn. edn. and scholarship com. 1971—, chmn. Lambda Kappa Mu Week 1972, award 1971). Baptist. Avocations: reading; travelling; music; drawing and painting; sewing. Home: 3660 Forest Garden Ave Baltimore MD 21207

FLEMING, KATHLEEN ADAIR, chemist; b. Glendale, Calif., Apr. 7, 1944; d. Charles MacGregor and Kathleen Adair (Sanders) Brown; m. Thomas Michael Fleming, Jan. 28, 1984; 1 dau., Iolana Adair Carver. B.A., Coll. Notre Dame, Belmont, Calif., 1977; postgrad. U. Calif.-Davis, 1977-79. Chemist, Hunt Products Co., Dallas, 1979—; beauty cons. Mary Kay Cosmetics, Dallas, 1982—. Mem. Soc. Cosmetic Chemists. Republican. Presbyterian. Home: 1944 Oak Bluff Dr Carrollton TX 75007 Office: Hunt Products Co 8321 Carpenter Freeway Dallas TX 75247

FLEMING, LINDA GAIL, business executive; b. State Center, Iowa, Mar. 20, 1943; d. Roy Marcus and Eleanor Elizabeth (Easton) Norman; m. Hugh Norman Fleming, June 1, 1962 (div. 1985); children—Victoria Jo, Hugh Bryan. Student schs. Kalispell, Mont. Dir. Central Ohio Soccer Assn., Columbus, 1979-81; gen. mgr. Columbus Lodging Inc., 1981—. Precinct com. chmn. Republican Party, Mountlake Terrace, Wash., 1968-69. Recipient Vol. award Ohio Spl. Olympics, 1985; Gold medal Arthur Murray Dance Studio, Detroit, 1985. Mem. Nat. Assn. Female Execs. Club: Central Ohio Rally. Avocations: dancing; driving road rallies; collecting miniatures; bowling. Office: Columbus Lodging Inc 14 E Gay St Columbus OH 43215

FLEMING, MARGARET GRACE, association executive; b. N.Y.C., May 24, 1936; d. Maurice and Anna (Christopher) Walsh; m. Cornelius J. Fleming, June 22, 1957. Cert. women's program Am. Inst. Banking, 1963, comml. banking cert., 1965. Exec. asst. Mfrs. Hanover Trust, N.Y.C., 1954-67; bus. devel. officer Franklin Nat. Bank, N.Y.C., 1967-75; asst. v.p. First Women's Bank, N.Y.C., 1975-77; bus. mgr. Accreditation Bd. Engring. and Tech., N.Y.C., 1978-85; controller Sholom & Zuckerbrot Realty Corp., Long Island City, N.Y., 1985; exec. dir. Eastern Assn. Equipment Lessors, Inc., Hicksville, N.Y., 1985—; meeting planner, 1955—. Editor newsletters and ann. reports. Recipient awards Franklin Nat. Bank, 1971, 72. Mem. Nat. Assn. Female Execs., Am. Soc. Assn. Execs., Carle Place Civic Assn. Republican. Roman Catholic. Avocations: fencing; reading; collecting elephants. Office: Eastern Assn Equipment Lessors 479 S Broadway Hicksville NY 11801

FLEMING, MARIAN VERONICA, lawyer; b. Washington, May 11, 1954; d. Raymond Francis and Marguerite Mary (Frost) F.; m. R. Stephen S. Amato, Jan. 8, 1983. B.A., U. Md.-College Park, 1975; J.D., U. Md.-Balt., 1979. Bar: Md., Hawaii. Assoc. Seidenman & Dugan, P.A., Balt., 1978-80; ptnr. Robinette, Dugan, Seiden & Fleming, P.A., Balt., 1980-85; of counsel Robinette, Dugan, Seiden & Jakubowski, P.A., Balt., 1985—, W.Va. U. Sch. Medicine, 1985—. Mem. Assn. Trial Lawyers Am. (grad. Nat. Coll. and Advanced Coll. Advocacy) 1981, 82, mem. coms.), Md. State Bar Assn. (coms.), Md. Trial Lawyers Assn., Am. Judicature Soc., ABA. Democrat. Home: 161 Scenery Dr Morgantown WV 26505 Office: Robinette Dugan Seiden & Fleming PA 801 St Paul St Baltimore MD 21202

FLEMING, RHONDA, actress; b. Calif., Aug. 10, 1925; d. Harold Louis and Effie Graham; m. Ted Mann. Appeared in Broadway plays The Women, 1973, Kismet, 1976; films include: The Spiral Staircase, 1945, A Connecticut Yankee in King Arthur's Court, 1949, Gunfight at OK Corral, 1956, Home Before Dark, 1956, others; guest appearances TV series McMillan and Wife, Police Woman, Love Boat, Doctors' Private Lives, TV movie The Last Hours Before Morning, Bob Hope's Road to Hollywood, Legends of the Screen; performed in stage musical Tropicana Hotel, concert Hollywood Bowl. Mem. Cerebral Palsy/Spastic Children's Found., Child-Help, U.S.A., ARCS scholarship program; assoc. Pepperdine U., Freedoms Found. at Valley Forge, Los Angeles Philanthropic Assn., Found. for the Blind; pres. Screen Smart Set. Recipient Woman of Yr. award City of Hope; Bronze award Motion Picture Council; Silver Angel award Religion in Media; Humanitarian award Desert Charities, Founder's award Child-Help, U.S.A.; Women of the World award Child-Help, U.S.A.; award NCCJ; Outstanding Career Achievement award Hollywood Internat. Orgn.; Gold Angel award Religion in Media; Eve award Mannequins of the Assistance League of So. Calif.

FLEMING, SIDNEY HOWELL, psychiatrist, educator; b. Lubbock, Tex., May 22, 1938; d. McKinley and Wilna Adrian (Simer) Howell; B.A., Agnes Scott Coll., Decatur, Ga., 1959; M.D., Emory U., 1964; m. J.D. Fleming, Jr., June 28, 1960; 1 dau., Julie Adrianne. Intern, Emory U./Va. Hosp., Atlanta, 1964-65, resident in psychiatry, 1965-68; mem. faculty Emory U. Med. Sch., 1968—, assoc. prof. psychiatry, 1979—, chmn. Pres.'s Commn. on Status of Women, 1984-85. Grantee NIMH, 1969-71; diplomate Am. Bd. Psychiatry and Neurology. Mem. Am. Psychiat. Assn. (editorial bd. on curriculum on psychiatry of women and men 1979-81, com. on women 1985), AMA, Assn. Acad. Psychiatrists, Ga. Psychiat. Assn., Med. Assn. Ga. Republican. Club: Druid Hills. Address: 2238 Hill Park Ct Decatur GA 30033

FLESCHNER, MARCIA HARRIET, marketing executive, personnel consultant; b. Bklyn., Mar. 31, 1947; d. Max and Bettina (Koerner) F.; m. Arthur Mace Teicher, Nov. 23, 1974; 1 son, Craig Morgan. B.A., CUNY, 1967. Sr. vice pres. market research, placement dir. Smith's 5th Ave Agy., Inc., N.Y.C., 1965—. Mem. Am. Mktg. Assn. (dir. N.Y.C. chpt. 1973—, cert. 1975, 82), Nat. Assn. Personnel Cons., Advt. Women N.Y., Assn. Personnel Cons. N.Y. (dir. 1979-80). Club: Castaways Yacht (New Rochelle, N.Y.). Office: Smith's 5th Ave Agy Inc 17 E 45th St New York NY 10017

FLESHMAN, LINDA EILENE SCALF, training official; b. Oklahoma City, Sept. 17, 1950; d. James Truman and Dortcha Virginia (Stiles) Scalf; children—Leatha Michele, Misty Dawn. A.A., Tarrant County Jr. Coll., 1977; B.A., North Tex. State U., 1979. Copywriter, Advt., Graphics & Mktg., Ft. Worth, 1978-80; editor Ft. Worth mag. Ft. Worth C. of C., 1980-81; mktg. prodn. coordinator City of Fort Worth, 1981-83; dir. pub. relations Circle T council Girl Scouts U.S.A., Ft. Worth, 1983-85; mgr. corp. tng. Am. Airlines Direct Mktg., 1984—. Mem. Internat. Bus. Communicators, Am. Women in Radio and TV, Women in Communication. Democrat. Roman Catholic. Home: PO Box 14807 Fort Worth TX 76117 Office: American Airlines Dallas/Fort Worth Airport TX

FLESNER, MARCIA KAY, nursing administrator; b. Macomb, Ill., May 21, 1950; d. Virgil Leroy and Marilyn Lucille (Schuster) F. Diploma in Nursing, Blessing Hosp., Quincy, Ill., 1971; B.A. in Health Scis., Quincy Coll., 1977; M. in Health Care Adminstrn., U. Miss., 1978. Cert. in nursing adminstrn. Staff nurse emergency room, spl. care area, Blessing Hosp., Quincy, 1971-74, head nurse emergency room, 1974-76, house supr., 1976-77, adminstrv. dir., 1979—; asst. dir. Oxford-Lafayette Hosp., Oxford, Miss., 1978-79. Vice pres. Family Planning Agy., Quincy, 1983—. Mem. Ill. Nurses Assn., Ill. Soc. Nursing Adminstrs. Democrat. Lutheran. Home: 2210 Washington Quincy IL 62301 Office: Blessing Hosp 1005 Broadway Quincy IL 62301

FLETCHER, ANNA LOU, investment banker; b Kansas City, Mo., Oct. 4 1944; d. George Richard and Mary Louise (Williams) Rodelander; B.A., U. Kans., 1965; M.S., Iowa State U., 1973; M.A., U. Md., 1977; children—Ethan H. Haggard, Frederick C. Haggard. Dir., Office Strategic Res. and Internat. Ops., Fed. Energy Adminstrn., Washington, 1974-77; sr. asso. energy div., Booz-Allen & Hamilton, Bethesda, Md., 1977-80; dir. bus. devel. alt. energy group EG & G, Inc., Wellesley, Mass., 1980-83; v.p. Kidder Peabody & Co., Inc., N.Y.C., 1983—. Recipient Superior Service award Fed. Energy Adminstrn., 1976. Mem. Internat. Assn. Energy Economists, Am. Econ. Assn., Nat. Assn. Bus. Economists, Kappa Kappa Gamma, Sigma Delta Pi, Phi Kappa Phi. Office: 10 Hanover Sq New York NY 10005

FLETCHER, BETTY BINNS, judge; b. Tacoma, Mar. 29, 1923; d. John Howard and Caroline (Hammond) Binns; B.A., Stanford U., 1943; LL.B., U. Wash., 1956; m. Robert L. Fletcher, June 13, 1942; children—Susan Fletcher French, William Alan, Katherine, Paul Robert. Admitted to Wash. bar, 1956, U.S. Sup. Ct., 1972; ptnr. Preston, Thorgrimson, Ellis, Holman & Fletcher, Seattle, 1963-79; judge U.S. Cir. Ct. Appeals 9th Circuit Wash.; 1979—; chmn. judges adv. com. to Com. on Ethics and Profl. Responsibility, 1981-83. Mem. adv. bd. Children's Home Soc. Wash.; trustee Seattle Symphony; bd. visitors Stanford U. Law Sch., 1981-83; mem. State Selection Com. for Rhodes Scholars, 1980—. Named Woman of Year, Quota Club, 1971. Mem. Am. Bar Assn. (cons. commn. on evaluation profl. standards), Nat. Conf. Bar Pres., Am. Bar Found., Am. Judicature Soc. (dir.). Office: 1010 5th Ave Seattle WA 98104

FLETCHER, CATHY ANN, auditor; b. Barnesville, Ga., Aug. 23, 1949; d. John James and Dorothy Lee (Banks) Fletcher; 1 child, Lisa Faye. Student, Ohio State U., 1969-70; A.S., Mass. Bay Community Coll., 1982; A.S., Northeastern U., Boston, 1984; B.S., Northeastern U., 1984. Mail clk. Fed. Reserve Bank, Boston, 1971-72; office mgr. Breckenridge Sportswear, Boston, 1973-74; asst. dir. Whittier Street Health Ctr., Boston, 1974-81; sec. to dir. Northeastern U., Boston, 1981-84; auditor Def. Contract Audit Agy., Burlington, Mass., 1984—; sec., bd. dirs. Boston Tenant Policy Council, 1977-79. Author: Softball Team Book, 1975. Vice pres., bd. dirs. Bromley Health Tenant Mgmt. Corp., Jamaica Plain, Mass., 1976—; mem. fund-raising com. Com. to Elect Jessie Jackson Pres., Boston, 1984. Mem. AAUW, Nat. Assn. Female Execs. Nat. Tenants Orgn., NAACP, Sigma Epsilon Rho. Club: Hawkettes Social (pres. 1971-80). Lodge: Elks. Avocations: reading, swimming, cooking, walking. Office: Def Contract Audit Agy 2 Wayside Rd Burlington MA 01803

FLETCHER, JULIANNE, publisher, editor; b. Chgo., Apr. 11, 1946; d. John Stephen and Alice (Jones) Palman; m. Robert Bruce Fletcher, Jr., Nov. 27, 1965; children—Susan Elizabeth, Stephanie Allison. Student Ball State U., 1963-65. Reporter, photographer Starke County Democrat, Knox, Ind., 1961-63; photographer The Anderson Herald (Ind.), 1969; owner, mgr. First Fruits Fabric Design, Alexandria, Ind., 1970-80; mng. editor The News, Alexadria, Ind., 1981-83; editor, publisher The Alexandrian, 1983—. Mem. com. Central Alexandria Revitalization Effort Project, 1982—. Worker, Monroe Twp. Republican Precinct Com., 1967—; pres. Monroe Twp. Republican Women, 1972-73. Vice pres. Aid Assn. Lutherans, 1981—, Alexandria Sesquicentennial Celebration, 1986. Recipient Disting. Community Service and Editorial Writing awards Hoosier State Press Assn., 1985; Woman of Yr., Alexandria Bus. and Profl. Women, 1985. Mem. Alexandria C. of C. (dir., pres. 1986). Office: The Alexandrian Inc 206 W Washington St PO Box 26 Alexandria IN 46001

FLETCHER, LOUISE, actress; b. Birmingham, Ala., 1936; d. Robert Capers F.; B.A., U. N.C.; student acting Jeff Corey. TV appearances include: Playhouse 90, Perry Mason, Bat Masterson, Maverick; films include: Thieves Like Us, 1974, Russian Roulette, 1975, One Flew Over the Cuckoo's Nest (Acad. award Best Actress), 1975, Exorcist II: The Heretic, 1977, The Cheap Detective, 1977, The Magician of Lublin, 1978, The Lady in Red, 1979, Natural Enemies, 1979, Lucky Star 1980, Strange Behavior, 1981, Strange Invaders, 1982, Brainstorm, 1982, Firestarter, 1984, Invaders from Mars, 1986, also TV films. Office: care William Morris Agy 151 El Camino Beverly Hills CA 90212

FLETCHER, MARJORIE AMOS, librarian; b. Easton, Pa., July 10, 1923; d. Alexander Robert and Margaret Ashton (Arnold) Amos; A.B., Bryn Mawr Coll., 1946; m. Charles Mann Fletcher, May 14, 1949; children—Robert Amos, Elizabeth Ashton, Anne Kennard. Asst. to dir. research, then research asst. to pres. Pa. Mut. Life Ins. Co., 1946-49; officer A.R. Amos Co., Phila., 1949-66; part-time tchr., 1965-68; librarian Am. Coll., Bryn Mawr, Pa., 1968-77, archivist, 1973—, dir. oral history collection, 1975—, lectr. on archives, 1975—, asst. prof. edn., 1973—, dir. archives and oral history, 1977—. Recipient awards Phila. Flower Show, 1965—. Mem. Spl. Libraries Assn. (pres. Phila. 1977-78), Soc. Am. Archivists (chairperson oral history sect. 1981—), Oral History Assn., Hist. Soc. Pa., U.S. Pony Club, D.A.R., Nat. Soc. Colonial Dames in Commonwealth of Pa. Republican. Presbyterian. Clubs: Phila. Skating; Bridlewild Pony (sponsor), Bridlewild Trails (Gladwyne). Author articles in field. Home: 1135 Norsam Rd Gladwyne PA 19035 Office: American Coll Bryn Mawr PA 19010

FLETCHER, MARVELLA KAY, city official; b. Anderson, Ind., Aug. 28, 1946; d. Paul Jacob and Ella Marie (Beeman) Clawson; m. Thomas Paul Fletcher, Sept. 17, 1966; children—Annmarie, Thomas Paul II. Student Ball State U., 1964-65. Cert. mcpl. clk. Communications officer Darke County Sheriff, Greenville, Ohio, 1974-79; clk. of council City of Greenville, Ohio, 1980—, city auditor, 1980—; dir. Greenville Indsl. Park, Greenville Community Improvement Corp. Named Citizen of Yr., Greenville K.C., 1984. Mem. Darke County Republican Women, Greenville Bus. and Profl. Women (legis. chmn. 1982-83, 2d v.p. 1983-84, pres. 1984—; Woman of Yr. 1986), Municipal Fin. Officers Assn. Ohio (bd. dirs. 1985—, fin. com.), Lambda Chi Omega (past pres. Gamma Epsilon chpt.). Avocations: reading; crossword puzzles. Office: City of Greenville Room 202 Mcpl Bldg Greenville OH 45331

FLETCHER, MARY LEE, business executive; b. Farnborough, Eng.; d. Dugald Angus and Mary Lee (Thurman) F.; B.A., Pembroke Coll., 1951. Ops. officer CIA, Washington, 1951-53; exec. trainee Gimbles, N.Y.C., 1954; copywriter Benton & Bowles, Inc., N.Y.C., 1955-63; creative dir. Alberto-Culver Co., Melrose Park, Ill., 1964-66; v.p. advt. and publicity Christian Dior Perfumes, N.Y.C., 1967-71; v.p. Christian Dior-N.Y., N.Y.C., 1972-78, exec. v.p., dir., 1978-85; exec. dir. licensing Fletcher & Co., N.Y.C., 1985—. Home: 12 Beekman Pl New York NY 10022 Office: Fletcher & Co Inc 1 Rockefeller Plaza New York NY 10020

FLETCHER, RAMONA NEAL, textile company supervisor; b. Danville, Va., Aug. 12, 1943; d. J. Edward and Mattie Sue (Guill) Neal; student Danville Community Coll., 1980—; m. Floyd Fletcher, Jr., Sept. 27, 1980; 1 stepson, James Christopher; 1 dau., Deborah. Office cashier G.C. Murphy Co., 1964-70; sec. to supt. yarn dyeing Dan River, Inc., Danville, 1970-80, dyeing supr., 1980—. Chmn. safety com. and waste com. March of Dimes, 1975-80; active Spl. Olympics, 1978. Named ambassador City of Danville, 1982-83. Mem. Am. Bus. Women's Assn., Tobacco Textile Mus., Internat. Platform Assn., Am. Film Inst., Beta Sigma Phi. Republican. Baptist. Home: 130 D2 Navajo Ct Danville VA 24540 Office: Dan River Inc W Main St Danville VA 24541

FLETCHER, ROSE MARIE, mortgage banker, consultant; b. Oakland, Calif., Dec. 8, 1940; d. Martin George Maher and Gertrude Elizabeth (Noe) Maher McCarthy; m. Jamie Franklin Fletcher, Aug. 1, 1960; children—Roberta JoAnne, Rebecca Louise, Jamie Suzanne. Student San Jose State U., 1958-60, West Valley Coll., 1972-76. Lic. real estate broker, Calif. Formerly br. mgr. Sutro Mortgage Co., San Jose, Calif., 3 yrs.; sr. v.p. Unified Mortgage Co., Cupertino, Calif., 1981-85; owner, pres., cons. Processing Place, San Jose, 1985—; dir. ops. Mortgage Loans Am., Campbell, Calif., 1986—; cons., lectr., trainer in lending field. Mem. Calif. Assn. Residential Lenders (1st v.p. 1985, pres. 1986), Assn. Profl. Mortgage Women (regional gov. 1980-81, Woman of Yr. 1979). Democrat. Roman Catholic. Avocations: water skiing; swimming; dancing. Home: 3704 Heppner Ln San Jose CA 95136 Office: Mortgage Loans Am 62 San Thomas Aquino Rd Campbell CA 95008

FLETCHER, WENDY SCOTT, educator; b. White Plains, N.Y., Dec. 13, 1945; d. Cyril Scott and Olga Noreen (Brigg) F.; m. Richard Morse Low, Mar. 13, 1982; 1 dau., Heather Morse. B.A., U. South Fla., 1968; postgrad. UCLA, 1972-74. Tutor autistic children Child Guidance Center, Tampa, Fla., 1968-69; art tchr. Summer Gifted Program, U. South Fla., Tampa, 1968; tchr. Hillsborough County, Fla., 1968-69, Sydney (Australia) Ch. of Eng. Girls Grammar Sch., 1970; tchr. remedial reading Garvey Jr. High Sch., Rosemead, Calif., 1971-72; Title I math specialist Garvey Sch. Dist., Rosemead, Calif., 1972-75; tchr. Lexington (Mass.) Pub. Schs., 1976—. Club: New Eng. Aquarium Dive. Author and illustrator: My Ancestors Are From Australia and Canada, 1975. Home: 5A Fulling Mill Ln Hingham MA 02043

FLICK, SONDRA CAROLINE, animal health products company executive; b. Cin., Jan. 27, 1947; d. Elmer and Evelyn June (Bauer) F. B.S. cum laude, Ohio State U., 1969; M.B.A., Pepperdine U., 1980. Research analyst, Shell Chem. Co., Princeton, N.J., 1969-70, technologist, San Ramon, Calif., 1974-77; biologist Shell Devel. Co., Modesto, Calif., 1970-74; technologist Shell Oil Co., Houston, 1977-79; mgr. regulatory affairs Diamond Shamrock, Cleve., 1979-83; mgr. FDA regulatory affairs SDS Biotech Corp., Painesville, Ohio, 1983-86; mgr. FDA regulatory affairs Fermenta Animal Health Co., Painesville, 1986—; chairperson task force Animal Health Inst., Alexandria, Va., 1980—, chairperson regulatory com., 1985-86. Scholar Ohio State U., 1965-69; recipient Cert. of Merit YWCA, 1985. Mem. Nat. Assn. Female Execs., Regulatory Affairs Profl. Soc. Republican. Avocations: breeding and racing thoroughbred horses; reading; tennis; bowling; water sports. Office: Fermenta Animal Health Co 7528 Auburn Rd Painesville OH 44077

FLIEGELMAN, AVRA LEAH, editor; b. Hartford, Conn., Mar. 5; d. Irving and Rose (Bason) F.; student public schs. With publicity dept. Columbia Pictures Corp., N.Y.C., 1949; with Asso. Artists Prodns., and successor UA-TV, N.Y.C., 1955-58; with Broadcast Info. Bur. Inc., N.Y.C., 1958—, editor-in-chief, 1969—, exec. v.p., 1979—. Mem. Am. Women in Radio and TV. Democrat. Jewish. Home: 174 Dix Hills Rd Huntington Station NY 11746 Office: 100 Lafayette Dr Syosset NY 11791

FLINCHBAUGH, PATRICE LYNNE, journalist; b. York, Pa., Aug. 1, 1957; d. Glenn Dale and Patricia Ann (Frey) Flinchbaugh. B.A. in Polit. Sci., Dickinson Coll., 1978; M.A. in Journalism, U. Mich., 1980. Intern, Modern Media Inst., St. Petersburg, Fla., 1979, Capitol Hill, Washington, 1976; graphics asst. Pa. Bar Assn., Harrisburg, Pa., 1978; teaching asst. U. Mich., Ann Arbor, 1980; reporter York Daily Record, Pa., 1980-81; polit. editorTampa Tribune, Fla., 1981—. Researcher, trade jour. Columbia Journalism Rev., 1979; editor-in-chief internat. grad. sch. mag. Mich. Journalism, 1980. Club: Tampa Bay Press (program com. and charter mem.). Address: Tampa Tribune 202 Parker St Tampa FL 33606

FLINK, JANE DUNCAN, public relations exective; b. Atlanta, Feb. 17, 1929; d. James Archibald and Frances (Watkins) Duncan; student Carleton Coll., 1948-49, U. Mo., 1967, Columbia (Mo.) Coll., 1974-75; m. Richard Albert Flink, Nov. 20, 1954; children—Jennifer, Elizabeth, Caroline, Charles Albert, James Duncan. Reporter, Tri-Town News, Greendale, Wis., 1958-61; reporter, photographer, feature writer, editor Central Mo. Rural and Farm Life Mag., Centralia (Mo.) Fireside Guard, 1973-78; briefly editor Bus. Briefs, MFA Oil Co., Columbia, Mo., 1977; editor Lifestyles, Kingdom Daily News, Fulton, Mo., 1978-82; asst. editor Centralia Fireside Guard, 1982-83, Mo. Ruralist, Columbia, 1983-85; dir. external relations Winston Churchill Meml. and Library, Westminster Coll., Fulton, Mo., 1985—. Republican committeewoman Ward I, Centralia, 1972, 74, 76; mem. exec. bd. Friends of Churchill Meml., Fulton; mem. Boone County Commn. on Child Abuse, 1978-81. Recipient numerous editorial awards. Mem. Nat. Fedn. Press Women (nat. achievement award 1982), Mo. Press Women (dist. v.p. 1978-79, v.p. 1985—; chmn. honors, awards 1979-81), Mo. Press Assn., PEO, Sigma Delta Chi, Centralia C. of C. (dir. 1983—), Centralia Hist. Soc. Clubs: Centralia Country. Home: The Clearing Route 4 Centralia MO 65240 Office: Winston Churchill Meml and Library Westminster Coll Fulton MO 65251

FLINN, ROBERTA JEANNE, computer company executive; b. Twin Falls, Idaho, Dec. 19, 1947; d. Richard H. and Ruth (Johnson) F. Student Colo. State U., 1966-67. Ptnr., Aqua-Star Pools & Spas, Boise, Idaho, from 1978—, mng. ptnr., 1981-83; ops. mgr. Polly Pools, Inc., Canby, Oreg., 1983-84, br. mgr. Polly Pools, Inc., A-One Distributing, 1984-85; sales mgr. Out Front Home/Sch. Computers, Portland, 1985—. Mem. Nat. Assn. Female Execs., Nat. Appaloosa Horse Club. Republican. Mem. Christian Ch. Home: 24687 S Central Point Rd Canby OR 97013 Office: 8122 SW Beaverton Hilldale Hwy Portland OR 97225

FLINNER, LIISAMAIJA CARMELA, insurance executive; b. London, Nov. 21, 1955 (parents Am. citizens); d. James Clark and Eila Mirjam (Kamppi) Flinner. Student Oxford U., 1976, 77; A.B. cum laude, Lake Erie Coll., 1977; postgrad. Western New Eng. Coll., 1977-78, Internat. Found. Employee Benefit Plans, Wharton Coll. Cert. employee benefit specialist. Group pension cons. Mass. Mut. Life Ins. Co., Springfield, 1977—; pension cons. Monarch Life Ins. Co., 1982—; group pension cons. in field. Recipient numerous scholarships and grants. Mem. Hampden County Assn. Ins. Women (edn. chmn. 1979-80, sec. 1980-81), Nat. Assn. Ins. Women, Nat. Assn. Female Execs., Internat. Platform Assn., Bus. and Profl. Womens Club, Mensa, Nature Conservancy, Jacques Cousteau Soc., World Wildlife Fund, Mortar Bd., Alpha Lambda Delta. Clubs: Indian Orchard Women's (pres. 1982—), Finnish Women's (membership chmn. 1983—). Home: 30 Wing St Indian Orchard MA 01151 Office: 1250 State St Springfield MA 01103

FLINT, JANET ALTIC, gallery executive; b. Louisville, Aug. 24, 1935; d. Luther Albert and Betty Drusilla (Devine) Altic; m. Roland H. Flint, June, 1962 (div.); children—Elizabeth, Pamela. B.S., U. Louisville, 1957; M.A., U. Minn.-Mpls., 1969. Asst. curator Mpls. Inst. Arts, 1959-66; curator graphic arts Nat. Mus. of Am. Art Smithsonian Instn., Washington, 1970-84; dir. dept. Am. prints Hirschl and Adler Galleries, Inc., N.Y.C., 1985—. Author exhbn. catalogues. Office: 21 East 70th St New York NY 10021

FLINTON, JENNIFER STRAIGHT, health care executive; b. Medford, Mass., Nov. 19, 1945; d. Edgar William and Doris Saunders (Holt) F. B.A., Harvard U., 1967, M.B.A., 1972. Editorial asst. Addison-Wesley Publications, Reading, Mass., 1967-69; asst. fund dir. Radcliffe Coll., Cambridge, 1969-70; with Am. Med. Internat., Los Angeles, 1973—, sr. v.p. mktg. and communications, 1983—, mem. mgmt. com., 1985—. Clubs: Regency, Riviera Tennis (Los Angeles); Calif. Yacht (Marina del Rey). Office: Am Med Internat 414 N Camden Dr Beverly Hills CA 90210

FLINT-SHAW, LYNN MARIE, speech-language pathologist; b. New Orleans, Aug. 31, 1954; d. Eddie Nicholas and Lena Mary (Hernandez) Flint; m. Rufus Shaw, Jr., Oct. 1, 1983. B.S. with honors, Xavier U., 1975; M.c.D. in Communication Disorders, La. State U. Med. Ctr., 1977. Speech-lang. pathologist Callier Ctr., U. Tex.-Dallas, 1977-79; speech-lang. pathologist, cons., Dallas, 1979-85; cons. Head Start Program, Dallas, 1979-85. Bd. dirs. Women of Arts, Dallas, 1982, Dallas Ballet, 1983-84; v.p. United Cerebral Palsy, Dallas, 1981—; bd. dirs. ASHA Minority Ethnic Com., Washington, 1983—, chmn. com., 1986—; cons. speech pathologist Plano Gen. Hosp. (Tex.), 1981, 82, 83. Recipient Cert. of Appreciation Head Start Program, Dallas, 1981; award Ctr. Inner City Studies, Ill., 1981. Mem. Am. Speech-Lang.-Hearing Assn., Nat. Black Assn. Speech, Lang. and Hearing (recruitment chair 1980—), Tex. Speech and Hearing Assn., Dallas Assn. Speech Pathologists and Audiologists. Roman Catholic. Home: 6616 Braddock Pl Dallas TX 75232 Office: 7557 Rambler Rd Suite 750 Dallas TX 75231

FLIPPO, CAROLE MCKEE, title company executive; b. Ft. Worth, Jan. 3, 1947; d. John Charles and Gwendolyn (Wilshire) McKee; m. Kenneth Wayne Flippo, Sr., Apr. 30, 1966; children—Kristie, Kenneth Wayne, Korie. Student Baylor U., 1964-66, U. Tex.-Arlington, 1983, Massey Coll., Dallas, 1983. Bookkeeper, Harris Hosp., Ft. Worth, 1966-68; acct. Chamblis & Chamblis, Houston, 1968-69, DuBose & Assocs., Ft. Worth, 1969-72; comptroller J.B. Kirshenbaum, Dallas, 1972-74; escrow mgr., v.p. Stewart Title Co., Ft. Worth, 1975-79; v.p. Hexter Fair Title Co., Dallas, 1979—; lectr. Tarrant County Jr. Coll., 1976-79; tutor math. for brokers exam., 1976-79. Author: Everything You Always Wanted to Know About Closing, 1978. Mem. Diamond Loch Homeowners Assn., St. Michael's Women's Assn. Mem. Nat. Assn. Female Execs. Republican. Episcopalian. Office: Hexter Fair Title Co 1307 Pacific St Dallas TX 75202

FLISS, MELINDA PATRICIA, human resource consultant; b. Durham, N.C., July 1, 1936; d. John Terrance and Lillie M. (Johnson) Wood; m. Daniel Joseph Fliss, Apr. 19, 1958; children—David, Michael, Diana. B.A. in Human Growth and Orgn. Communication, Northeastern Ill. U., Chgo., 1983; postgrad. in human orgn. and devel. Fielding Inst., Calif., 1983—. Pres., Focus Unltd., Inc., Northbrook, Ill., 1982—; mem. adv. bd., coordinating council for mental health, substance abuse and devel. disabilities Lake County Bd. Health, Waukegan, Ill., 1982—; chmn. Substance Abuse Adv. Com. AB/C Council, 1983—, vice chmn. Mental Health Adv. Com., 1982—, mem. Grant Rev. Com., 1983—; mem. program com. Community Adv. Bd. Program on Women, Northwestern U., Evanston, Ill., 1983—; founder Nat. Forum for Women, Woodstock, Ill., 1983—; mem. Funding Task Force, Planning Com. AB/C Council, 1983—; chmn. Spl. Study on DUI Problem and Alcoholism Services, Lake County, 1983. Mem. Assn. Labor/Mgmt. Adminstrs. Cons. on Alcoholism, Ill. Alcoholism and Drug Dependence Assn. Unitarian. Clubs: Tennaqua, Deerfield Woman's (Deerfield). Office: Focus Unltd Inc One Northbrook Pl 5 Revere Dr Suite 200 Northbrook IL 60062

FLOCKE, JENELLE LOUISE, congressional fellow, administrative assistant; b. Bellville, Tex., July 3, 1949; d. Calvin Joe and Rose Amy (Grubb) Mikeska; m. Robert Alfred Flocke, Oct. 5, 1968; 1 child, Catherine Rose. Student Blinn Coll., George Mason U. Battalion sec. 1st Battalion, 68th Armored Div., Baumholder, Fed. Republic Germany, 1978-79; Staff sec., stenographer Soldiers Mag., Alexandria, Va., 1980-81; sec., stenographer warrant officer div. U.S. Army, Alexandria, 1981-83, office personnel mgmt. dir., Alexandria, 1983, sec., adminstrv. asst. OASA (M&RA) Dept. Army, Pentagon, Washington, 1984-85; congl. fellow Congl. Caucus, Women's Issues, Washington, 1985—; pub. relations and program dir. Sec. Army Fed. Women's Program, Pentagon, 1984—. Editor Timbers' Tattler (community newsletter), Springfield, Va., 1983-85, Women in Def., Inc. (nat. newsletter). Instr. CPR, Alexandria, 1982-86; troop leader Girl Scouts U.S.A. Troop 1685, Springfield, 1980-84, Troop 00553, Baumholder, 1977-78. Recipient Outstanding Performance awards Dept. Army, 1979-85, Spl. Service award Combined Fed. Campaign, 1985. Mem. Nat. Assn. Female Execs., Federally Employed Women, Women in Def., Phi Beta Lambda (state sec. 1967-68). Lutheran. Club: Konza Klub (Brenham, Tex.). Avocations: horseback riding, reading, camping, dancing, cooking. Home: 8812 Winding Hollow Way Springfield VA 22152 Office: Congl Caucus for Women's Issues 2471 Rayburn House Office Bldg Washington DC 20515

FLOERSHEIM, MARY THERESA, stained glass artisan, business consultant; b. Clovis, N.Mex., Dec. 17, 1949; d. Edgar Jake and Norma Laverne (Harmon) F.; m. Max L. Reininger, Mar. 20, 1970 (div. Jan. 1975). A. in Bus. Data Processing, N.Mex. State U., 1970. Bookkeeper Johnson Trailer Sales, Spokane, Wash., 1973-74; sr. acctg. clk. Pub. Service Co., Albuquerque, 1974-76, methods analyst, 1976-79, ops. analyst, 1979-81, applications analyst, 1981-83; free-lance stained glass artisan, Albuquerque, 1983—. Bd. dirs. Shelter for Victims of Domestic Violence, Albuquerque, 1980; mem. Right to Choice, Albuquerque, 1983—, Animal Humane Assn., Albuquerque, 1983. Mem. Assn. for Female Execs., Assn. for Research and Enlightenment. Avocations: metaphysical studies; camping; crossword and jigsaw puzzles.

FLOOD, DIANE LUCY, marketing specialist; b. Plainfield, N.J., June 13, 1937; d. William Edward and Lucy (Dycker) Flood. B.A., Vassar Coll., 1959; postgrad. Fontainebleau Sch. Fine Arts (France), 1961. Advt. prodn. aide indsl. chem. div. Am. Cyanamid Co., Wayne, N.J., 1959-62, prodn. supr., 1962-64, creative coordinator organic chems. div. advt., 1964-66, design art and copy mgr., 1966-70, advt. rep., 1970-72, advt. rep. paper, process chems. and resins, indsl. chem. div., 1972-77, advt. coordinator water treating, mining, paper and enhanced oil recovery chems., 1977-83, mgr. mktg. communications indsl. products div., 1983—, mgr. venture chemicals div., 1986—; pres., dir. 103 Gedney St. Owners Co-op, 1985-86. Mem. Vassar Coll. Alumnae Assn. Mem. Consistory of Reformed Ch. Club: Vassar of N.Y.C. Home: 103 Gedney St 3C Nyack NY 10960 Office: Am Cyanamid Co Chems Group Wayne NJ 07470

FLOOD, FREDA PHOEBE, TV exec., astrologer cons.; b. Bklyn.; d. Joseph and Rose (Bauman) Roberts; A.A. cum laude, Morris County Coll., 1973; B.A. magna cum laude, William Paterson Coll., 1976; m. Jim Flood, May 29, 1963. Asst. to pres. Spanish Internat. Network, N.Y.C., 1962; ops. mgr. Channel 41, Secaucus, N.J., 1976—; pres. Astro Greetings, Inc., 1982—; astrological cons. World Fragrances Ltd.; astrologer cons., lectr., 1962—; astrology tchr. Adult div. N.J. Bd. Edn., 1970—; Mem. Am. Women in Radio-TV, Nat. Soc. Geocosmic Research (pres. N.J. div. 1974), Nat. Assn. Female Execs., Astrol. Assn. Am., Psi Chi. Columnist, Lincoln Herald, Lincoln Park, N.J., 1974—. Address: 15 Pine Brook Rd Lincoln Park NJ 07035

FLORA, JOANNE M., communications executive; b. Newark, Jan. 6, 1949; d. Angelo R. and Mary A. (Norton) Flora; B.A. in Communication Arts, Fordham U., 1970. Asst. to dir. advt. and pub. relations subsidiary Continental Ins. Cos., N.Y.C., 1970-71, pub. relations asst. parent co. N.Y.C., 1971, asso. editor publs. div., 1971-73, editor, 1973-74, mgr., 1974-76; fin. editor Morgan Stanley & Co., Inc., N.Y.C., 1976-79; communications officer human resources div. Chem. Bank, N.Y.C., 1979-80, communications mgr. div., 1980-84; v.p. corp. communication Morgan Guaranty Trust Co. N.Y., N.Y.C., 1984—. Mem. Internat. Assn. Bus. Communicators, Women in Communications, NOW. Home: 2600 Kennedy Blvd Jersey City NJ 07306 Office: Morgan Guaranty Trust Co NY 20 Pine St New York 10015

FLORA, PATRICIA LEE, marketing executive; b. Litchfield, Ill., Sept. 18, 1934; d. Fred L. and Ruby O. (Martin) Dively; student public schs., Litchfield; m. Anthony G. Flora, June 21, 1979; children—Michael Meyer, Kim DuPont, Todd Meyer, Shanna Meyer. Exec. sec. Internat. Paper Co., Litchfield, 1958-68, adminstr. asst. in research and devel., 1968-74; personnel mgr. Hecon Corp., Eatontown, N.J., 1974-83, mgr. mktg. services, 1983—, nat. sales mgr. bus. products div., 1983—; owner Phlora Line Cosmetic Co., Flora Enterprizes, mgmt. personnel cons. co. ; cons. flexible work hours, total woman, indsl. methods and procedures. Mem. Nat. Assn. Female Execs. Lutheran. Developer Phlawless Facial Cream. Home: RD 4 125 A Jackson Mills Rd Freehold NJ 07728 Office: 15 Meridian Rd Eatontown NJ 07724

FLORCZYK-MATT, SANDRA, personnel executive; b. Syracuse, N.Y., Oct. 29, 1955; d. Alexander Stephen and Josephine (Iorio) Florczyk; m. Louis C. Matt, Jr., Nov. 1, 1980. B.A., Syracuse U., 1977; M.B.A., Nova U., 1984. Personnel dir. Venetian Bay Constructors, Inc., Naples, Fla., 1981—. Co-editor Community Link, 1976. Mem. Nat. Assn. Female Execs. Republican. Roman Catholic. Avocations: art; tennis; traveling; golf. Home: PO Box 707 Mango FL 33550 Office: Claims Center PO Box 2928 Lakeland FL 33803

FLORES, DEBRA MOSLEY, educational administrator; b. Bakersfield, Calif., June 1, 1956; d. Orval C. and Bobbie Jean (Laxson) Mosley; m. Joseph Wayne Flores, Aug. 27, 1976; 1 child, Israel Joseph. Cert. early childhood edn., Riverside City Coll.; student Calif. State U., San Bernardino, 1979; cert. supr. Accelerated Christian Sch., Lewisville, Tex., 1980. Instructional asst. Head Start Pre School, Moreno Valley, Calif., 1975-77; tchr. Sunnyside Pre Sch., Moreno Valley, Calif., 1979; tchr. Kings Chapel Acad., Moreno Valley, 1980-83, adminstr., 1983—; dir., founder Rainbow Ranch Pre Sch., Moreno Valley, 1983, Rainbow Ranch Child Care Ctr. II, 1985. Recipient Cert. of Merit, Moreno Valley Unifed Sch. Dist., 1974. Mem. Accelerated Christian Edn., Pre-Schs. Assn., Moreno Valley C. of C. Avocations: study ancient history; reading; swimming; animal husbandry. Office: Kings Chapel Christian Ctr 15795 Perris Blvd Moreno Valley CA 92388

FLORES, ROBIN ANN, social worker, administrator; b. Allentown, Pa., Oct. 6, 1949; d. Norman Henry and Ann May (Huff) Flores. B.S. in Edn., Kutztown U., 1971; M.S. in Adminstrn., U. Scranton, 1983. Caseworker gerontology Lehigh County Area Agy. for Aging, Allentown, Pa., 1973-75, info. referral outreach coordinator, 1975-78, supr. community services, 1979—; lectr. on aging process, Lehigh County, Pa., 1978—; utilization community resources, Lehigh County, 1978—. Mem. adv. bd. Community Action Com. of Lehigh Valley, 1979-82; Pa. del. White House Conf. on Aging, Hershey, Pa., 1981; bd. dirs. Vis. Nurse Assn. of Lehigh County, 1982—, Women Inc., 1983—; adv. bd. Homecare, Inc., 1982—, Geriatric Edn. Modules, Allentown Osteo. Hosp., 1979; mem. profl. adv. com. Lehigh Valley Hospice, 1984—; mem. utilization and rev. bd. Vis. Nurse Assn., 1979—; consumer rep. Pa. Power and Light Co., Lehigh County, Pa., 1978—; co-chmn. Human Services Tng. Coop., 1975-81. Mem. Allentown Art Mus., Old Allentown Preservation Assn. Home: 237 N Lumber St Allentown PA 18102 Office: Lehigh County Area Agy on Aging 523 Hamilton St Allentown PA 18101

FLORESCUE, JUNE AVA, lawyer; b. Rochester, N.Y., Aug. 28, 1954; d. Harold Milton and Gertrude (Lapides) F. B.A., U. Ariz., 1976; J.D. cum laude, Tulane U., 1980. Bar: Ariz. 1980, U.S. Dist. Ct. Ariz. 1980. Atty.-advisor Fed. Labor Relations Authority, Washington, 1981-82; assoc. Jekel & Howard, Scottsdale, Ariz., 1982; atty. Ariz., Am. Fedn. State, County & Mcpl. Employees, Phoenix, 1982-84; asst. atty. gen. civil rights div. Ariz. Atty. Gen.'s Office, Phoenix, 1984—. Mem. Ariz. Bar Assn. (labor sect. 1983—), ABA (labor relations sect. 1981—), Assn. Trial Lawyers Am. Home: 6560 N 17th Ave #229 Phoenix AZ 85015 Office: Atty Gen's Office Civil Rights Div 1275 W Washington St Phoenix AZ 85007

FLORESTANO, PATRICIA SHERER, university official; b. Washington, Mar. 15, 1936; d. Wilbur L. and Virginia M. (Moriconi) F.; B.A. in Am. Civilization, U. Md., 1958, M.A. in Govt. and Politics, 1970, Ph.D. in Pub. Adminstrn. and Am. Govt., 1974; m. Thomas Florestano, Nov. 29, 1959; children—Leslie C., Thomas. Research staff State Legis. Commn. on Intergovt. Coop., 1972-75, State Gov.'s Commn. on Functions of Govt., 1973-75; staff asst. to pres. Md. Senate, 1975-78; asst. prof. Inst. Urban Studies, U. Md., College Park, 1974-79, dir. Inst. Govtl. Service, 1979-85; v.p. govtl. relations U. Md.-Adelphi, 1985—; cons. ednl. evaluation, mgmt. and survey research. Lector St. Elizabeth Ann Seton Ch., 1970—; vice chmn. Anne Arundel County (Md.) Commn. on Women, 1975; mem. Anne Arundel County Schs. Adv. Forum, 1975-76, chmn. nominations com., 1976-78. Recipient Outstanding Teaching award Students Assn. of U. Md., 1979. Mem. Am. Soc. Pub. Adminstrn. (pres. 1983-84, conf. fellow), Am. Polit. Sci. Assn., So. Polit. Sci. Assn., Urban Affairs Assn. (past chmn. governing bd.), So. Consortium Univ., Pub. Service Orgns. (former editor). Democrat. Roman Catholic. Author: (with other) The States and Metropolitan Areas, 1981; Attitudes of Special Interest Groups and the Public on Chesapeake Bay Areas, 1980; also articles. Home: 1516 Farlow Ave Crofton Ave Crofton MD 21114 Office: Central Adminstrn U Md 3300 Metzerott Rd Adelphi MD 20783

FLORIAN, MARIANNA BOLOGNESI, civic leader; b. Chgo.; d. Giulio and Rose (Garibaldi) Bolognesi, B.A. cum laude, Barat Coll., 1940; postgrad. Moser Bus. Sch., 1941-42; m. Paul A. Florian III, June 4, 1949; children—Paul, Marina, Peter, Mark. Asst. credit mgr. Stella Cheese Co., Chgo., 1942-45; With ARC ETO Clubmobile Unit, 1945-47; mgr. Passavant Hosp. Gift Shop, 1947-49; pres., Jr. League Chgo., Inc., 1957-59; pres. woman's bd. Passavant Hosp., 1966-68; bd. dirs. Northwestern Meml. Hosp., 1974-81, mem. exec. com., 1974-79; pres. Women's Assn., Chgo. Symphony Orch., 1974-77; v.p. Guild Chgo. Hist. Soc., 1977-81, chmn., 1981-84, mem. exec. com. Orchestral Assn., 1978—, v.p., 1978-83, vice chmn., 1983—; mem. women's bd. Northwestern U. Recipient Citizen Fellowship, Inst. Medicine Chgo., 1975. Clubs: Friday (pres. 1972-74), Contemporary; Winnetka Garden.

FLOURNOY, MARY FRANCES, educator; b. Snyder, Ark., Feb. 6, 1921; d. George Robert and Emma Harrell F.; B.A., Northwestern State Coll. La., 1942; M.A., George Peabody Coll., 1946; Ph.D., U. Iowa, 1953. Asst. prof. U. Ariz., 1953-55; asst. prof. U. Tex., Austin, 1955-59, asso. prof., 1959-69, prof. dept. curriculum and instrn., 1969—, in-service tchr. workshops on teaching elem. math.; vis. prof. U. Md., summer 1966. U. Tex. Univ. Research grantee, 1969-70. Mem. Nat. Council Tchrs. Math., Tex. Council Tchrs. Math., Am. Ednl. Research Assn., Pi Lambda Theta, Delta Kappa Gamma, Phi Kappa Phi. Contbr. articles to profl. jours. Author: Elementary School Mathematics, 1966; Mathematics Textbook Series, Kindergarten to Grade 8, 1966, 74, 78, 81, 85. Office: Edn Bldg 406 Dept Curriculum and Instrn U Tex Austin TX 78712

FLOWERS, JACQUELINE BROADBENT, nurse, flutist; b. Kingston, Pa., Mar. 13, 1939; d. Clyde E. and Mary (Kalina) Broadbent; R.N., McKeesport (Pa.) Hosp., 1960; A.A., Santa Rosa Jr. Coll., 1973; B.A., St. Marys Coll., 1978; M.A. in Counseling, Sonoma State U., 1981; Ph.D. in Nursing Adminstrn. and Gerontology, Columbia Pacific U., 1981, M.A. in Music, 1982; m. James Flowers, Jan. 14, 1971; children—Terry, Amy; stepchildren—James, Jeffrey. Staff nurse McKeesport Hosp., 1960-62; office nurse and dr.'s office mgr., Garden Grove, Calif., 1962-71; staff nurse Warrack Hosp., Santa Rosa, Calif., 1971-73; R.N. team leader Palm Drive Hosp., Sebastopol, Calif., 1973-77; dir. nursing Manzanita Convalescent Hosp., Cloverdale, Calif., 1977-79; dir. nursing Driftwood Convalescent Hosp., Santa Rosa, 1979-82; nurse educator Garland County Community Coll., Hot Springs, Ark., 1982-86, music educator, 1982-86; co-owner West Wind Music, 1982-85; nursing cons., 1986—; nurse adminstr. Area Agy. on Aging S.W. Ark., Hot Springs, 1986—; flutist Baroque Sinfonia of Santa Rosa, 1971-82, Santa Rosa Baroque Ensemble, 1971-82; participant Bath Sch. Baroque Music, 1979; pvt. instr. modern and baroque flute; harpsichordist; flute soloist Los Angeles Doctors Symphony, Middle East tour, 1970. Elder, Knox Presbyterian Ch., Santa Rosa; founder, trustee Baroque Sinfonia of Santa Rosa, 1971-82; personnel mgr. Long Beach and Orange County Doctors' Symphony, 1968-71. Mem. Am., Calif. nurses assns., Nat. Flute Assn., Calif. Music Tchrs. Assn. Republican. Past prin. flutist, Bell Flower Symphony, Calif., Long Beach and Orange County Doctors Symphony, Vallejo Symphony, Napa (Calif.) Symphony; past mem. Santa Rosa Symphony; decorator harpsichords in hist. patterns. Home: 108 Leslie Dr Hot Springs AR 71913

FLOWERS, JUANZETTA SHEW, nursing educator; b. Gadsden, Ala., Aug. 8, 1941; d. Shelly Jerome and Pluma Lee (Odom) Shew; m. Charles Ely Flowers, Jr., Sept. 25, 1972. B.S.N., U. Ala., 1966; M.A., U. Ala.-Birmingham,

1978, M.S.N., 1983, D.S.N., 1985. Pub. health nurse, Birmingham, Ala., 1966-68; sch. nurse, New Ulm, Germany, 1970; head nurse, cons., instr. U. Ala. Sch. Medicine-Birmingham, 1974-78, assoc. prof. dept. ob-gyn, 1978—, asst. prof. Sch. Nursing, 1985—. Pres., Birmingham Humane Soc., 1975-77. Mem. NOW, AAUW, Am. Nurses Assn., Soc. Sci. Study Sex, Nurses Assn. of Am. Coll. Obstetricians and Gynecologists (chmn. Ala. sect. 1977-81), Nat. League Nursing, Am. Assn. Sex Educators, Counselors and Therapists, Sigma Theta Tau, Phi Kappa Phi. Methodist. Home: 3757 Rockhill Rd Birmingham AL 35223 Office: U Ala Birmingham Sch Nursing Grad Programs University Station Birmingham AL 35294

FLOWERS, KATHRYN, writer; b. Cass City, Mich., Sept. 23, 1939; d. John Claud Lakin Zemke and Madeline Mary Zemke Beaudry; B.A., Mich. State U., 1961; M.A., San Francisco State U., 1972; divorced; children—John Lakin, David Brandon. News editor, editorial writer Sta. KCBS, San Francisco, 1972-77; anchor reporter, dir. ops. AMI Radio News Bur., San Francisco, 1977-80; contbg. editor Nat. Opinion Mag., San Rafael, Calif., 1978. Mem. Tiburon Parks Commn., Calif., 1977-82, chmn., 1978; mem. Joint Belvedere Tiburon Commn., 1978-79, Tiburon Downtown Com., 1981; commr., founder, dir. San Anslemo Youth Soccer Assn., 1973. Mem. Nat. Assn. Press Women, AFTRA, Calif. Press Women, World Affairs Council, Sierra Club, Marin Arts Council, Alpha Epsilon Rho, Gamma Alpha Chi. Clubs: Marin Cyclists, Mt. Tam Racquet. Address: PO Box 682 Tiburon CA 94920

FLOWERS, MARIAN WILLIAMS, educator; b. Houston, Dec. 5, 1933; d. Isaac Leon and Clara Louise (Petrie) Williams; m. Roosevelt Flowers, Dec. 27, 1969. B.S. in Phys. Edn. and Health, Tex. So. U., 1955, M.S. in Phys. Edn. and Health, 1959. Tchr. high sch., Houston, 1955-70; tchr. Crenshaw High Sch., Los Angeles, 1970—. Recreational dir. summer program City Parks and Recreation, Houston, 1955-65; docent March of Dimes, Los Angeles, 1982. Recipient plaque Girls Athletic Assn., 1979; Crenshaw-Dorsey Community Salute award Push for Excellence, 1977; named Outstanding Basketball and Softball Coach, Girls' Athletic Assn., 1975, 76, 78, Coach of Yr. for championship team Los Angeles Unified Sch. Dist., 1985. Mem. NAACP, Alpha Kappa Alpha (chmn. com.). Office: Crenshaw High Sch 5010 11th Ave Los Angeles CA 90043

FLOWERS, MAXINE ROGERS, psychiat. social worker; b. South Pittsburg, Tenn., Jan. 7, 1935; d. Omer Leighton and Mamie Gertrude (Parker) Rogers; A.B., Birmingham So. Coll., 1956; M.S., Columbia U., 1964; postgrad. Menninger Found., 1965; m. John Baxton Flowers, III, Oct. 4, 1969; 1 son, Bryan. Child welfare worker Dept. Public Welfare, Nashville, 1956-59; caseworker Children's Home Soc., Miami, Fla., 1959-63; caseworker Menninger Found. Children's Service, 1965-69; supr. adult services Pitt County Mental Health Center, 1969-71; staff social worker div. child psychiatry Duke U. Med. Center, Durham, N.C., 1971-76, chief social worker div. child psychiatry 1976—; cons. day care centers; bd. dirs. Durham Nurses Assn., Family Counseling Services Durham; mem. profl. adv. com. Mental Health Assn. Trustee, Hist. Preservation Soc. Durham; mem. Assn. Preservation of Eno Valley, Mus. Life and Sci. Mem. Acad. Cert. Social Workers, Nat. Assn. Social Workers, N.C. Soc. Clin. Social Work (ethics chmn.), N.C. Soc. Colonial Dames Am. (chmn. hist. activities com., mem. Durham-Orange com.). Democrat. Methodist. Home: 128 Pinecrest Rd Durham NC 27705 Office: Duke U Medical Center Trent and Elba Sts Durham NC 27705

FLOWERS, VIRGINIA ANNE, university system administrator; b. Dothan, Ala.; d. Kyrie Neal and Annie Laurie (Stewart) F.; B.A., Fla. State U., 1949; M.Ed., Auburn U., 1958; Ed.D., Duke U., 1963. Elem. tchr. Minnie T. Heard Sch., Dothan, Ala., 1949-52; secondary tchr. Dalton (Ga.) High Sch., 1952-55, personnel dir., asst. prin., 1955-61; instr. U.S. history U. Ga. Extension, Dalton, 1960-61; part-time instr. Duke U., Durham, N.C., 1961-62, vis. prof., summers 1966, 67, 69, 70, asst. provost, assoc. dean Trinity Coll. Arts and Scis. Duke, 1972—, acting vice provost, acting dean, 1973-74, chmn. dept. edn., asst. provost ednl. program devel., Duke, 1974-80; assoc. prof. edn. Columbia (S.C.) Coll., 1962-66, prof. edn., 1966-68, head dept. edn., 1966-68, assoc. dean, 1969-71, dean, 1971-72; prof. elem. edn. Va. Commonwealth U., Richmond, Va., 1968-69, assoc. dean Columbia Coll., 1969-71, dean, 1971-72; dean Sch. Edn., Ga. So. Coll., Statesboro, 1980-85, asst. vice chancellor acad. affairs, 1985—; mem. Commn. on Colls., So. Assn. Colls. and Schs., 1979—, Ga. Profl. Standards Commn. Mem. Nat. Merit Pay Task Force. Mem. NEA, Nat. Orgn. Legal Problems in Edn., Am. Ednl. Research Assn., Assn. Study of Higher Edn., Am. Assn. Colls. Tchr. Edn. (dir. 1979—, pres. 1983-84), AAUP, Am. Assn. Higher Edn., Kappa Delta Epsilon, Kappa Delta Pi, Delta Kappa Gamma, Phi Delta Kappa, Alpha Kappa Gamma. Research and publs. in field. Home: 619 N Superior Ave Decatur GA 30033

FLOYD, ANDRE' LAVERNE, family service association executive; b. Chgo., Nov. 24, 1929; d. Daniel Joseph and Opal Ruth (Pearson) Johnston; 1 son, David Richard. B.Nursing Edn., Fla. State U., 1956, M.S.W., 1959. Lic. clin. social worker, Fla. Sr. caseworker Family Service, Tampa, Fla., 1963-66; psychiat. social worker Fla. Alcoholic Rehab., Tampa, 1966-67; pvt. practice marriage/family therapy, Tampa, 1967-71; dir. psychiat. unit Athens Gen. Hosp. (Ga.), 1972-74; asst. prof. social work Fla. State U., Tallahassee, 1974-76; exec. dir. Family Service Assn., Tampa, 1976—; adj. prof. U. South Fla., Tampa, 1978—; pres. Fla. Council Family Service Agys., 1981-82; cons. in field. Vol. in stage set constrn. Playmakers Tampa, 1981-83. Mem. Nat. Assn. Social Workers (area coordinator voter registration), Women's Caucus Family Service Am. (S.E. region rep. 1981-83, chairperson nat. nominating com. 1983). Club: Zonta (sec. 1977-80 Tampa). Home: 706 E Hanlon St Tampa FL 33604 Office: Family Service Assn Greater Tampa 205 W Brorein St Tampa FL 33606

FLOYD, ANGELEITA STEVENS, flutist; b. Concord, N.C., Aug. 6, 1952; d. William Russel and Elizabeth (Hopkins) F.; B.Mus., Stetson U., 1974; M.Mus., Fla. State U., 1979, M.Mus. Edn., 1981, D.Mus., 1986. Music tchr., Rockhill, S.C., Charlotte and Concord, N.C., 1974-77; appearances with Charlotte Opera Assn., Charlotte Summer Pops Orch., Ice Capades, Oratorio Singers; concert tours as soloist and with chamber groups in S.E., 1977-82; mem. faculty Valdosta (Ga.) State Coll., 1977-84; grad. asst. Fla. State U., Tallahassee, 1980-82; prin. flute Naples/Marco Philharm. Orch., 1984-85; vis. instr. U. Idaho, Moscow, 1984-85; asst. prof. Flute U. Wis.-Eau Claire, 1985—, also dir. flute choir; asst. prof. flute U. No. Iowa, Cedar Falls, 1986—. Mem. NOW, Nat. Flute Assn., Charlotte Flute Assn., Music Educators Nat. Conf. Presbyterian. Home and Office: 307 Niagara St Eau Claire WI 54703

FLOYD, ANN DALEY, television executive; b. Bogalusa, La., May 30, 1941; d. Walter E. and Margie (Carroll) Gibbons; m. Graham A. Floyd, Feb. 26, 1983; children—Walter M. West, Terry West, Lori Anne West; m. J. Willard Daley, Oct. 24, 1969 (dec. Aug. 1981). Student U. So. Miss. Vice-pres. programming WDAM-TV, Hattiesburg, Miss., 1969—. Chmn. Forrest County Easter Seals, Hattiesburg; former com. mem. Forrest/Lamar United Way, Miss. Heart Assn. Mem. Broadcasting Promotion Assn., Kappa Delta Pi. Methodist. Home: 108 W Hills Dr Hattiesburg MS 39401 Office: WDAM-TV Hwy 11 N PO Box 1978 Hattiesburg MS 39401

FLOYD, BILLIE JEAN, state legislator, educator; b. Ada, Okla., Dec. 24, 1929; m. Ben C. Floyd; 2 daus. Asst. prof. East Central U.; mem. Okla. Senate from Dist. 13, 1985—. Active Federated Democratic Women's Club. Mem. AAHPER, Bus. and Profl. Women. Mem. Christian Ch. Office: Okla State Capitol Bldg Oklahoma City OK 73105*

FLOYD, BRENDA CAROL, optometrist; b. Sacremento, Jan. 8, 1955; d. Louis Carrell and Catherine Louise (Hawkins) Floyd. A.A. summa cum laude, Gaston Coll., 1975; B.S. in Chemistry summa cum laude, U. N.C.-Charlotte, 1977; B.S. in Physiol. Optics cum laude, U. Ala.-Birmingham, 1979, O.D. cum laude, 1981. Research asst. U. Ala., Birmingham, 1977-79, researcher, 1980-81; clinician Diabetes Hosp., Birmingham, 1980-81; optometrist Optical Clinic, Dallas, 1981-85; pvt. practice, 1985—. Author: Lab. Manual for Ocular Anatomy, 1978. Mem. Tex. Assn. Optometrists, Am. Optometric Found., Women in Optometry, Gamma Beta Phi. Republican. Baptist. Home: 3745 Casa Del Sol Dallas TX 75228 Office: 724 M Main St Suite 200 Lewisville TX 75067

FLOYD, CATHERINE J., city official; b. Corinth, Miss., July 3, 1920; d. Jesse Harris and Mary Elizabeth (Gray) Jones; m. William Thomas Floyd, June 20, 1942; children—Gloria A. Craig, William Thomas Floyd, III, James Milton (dec.), Catherine Jennifer Holder, Pamala Anchondo, Nancy Elizabeth. Student La. Tech. Coll., Ruston, 1937-41. Sec. City of League City, Tex., 1960-77, fin. dir., 1977—. Mem. Govt. Fin. Officers Assn. Club: League City Lioness (treas.). Home: 2935 Calder M-11 PO Box 489 League City TX 77573 Office: City Hall W Walker St League City TX 77573

FLOYD, JANE BIGGERSTAFF, nurse, educator; b. Rutherfordton, N.C., Feb. 15, 1943; d. James Garland and Katie (Earley) Biggerstaff; B.S. in Nursing, Lenoir Rhyne Coll., Hickory, N.C., 1965; M.Nursing (HEW grantee), Emory U., Atlanta, 1967; m. John G. Floyd, June 18, 1967; children—Kelly Jane, John Robert II. Instr., Lenoir Rhyne Coll., Hickory, N.C., 1966, 67-71, Druid City Hosp., Tuscaloosa, Ala., 1972-75; asst. prof. Samford U., Birmingham, 1977-79; asst. prof. U. South Fla., Tampa, 1980—; cons. Sch. Bd. Hillsborough County (Fla.), Women's Hosp. Mem. adv. bd. Crippled Children's Assn.; chmn. public edn. Am. Heart Assn.; active Girl Scouts U.S.A.; chmn. bd. Wee World Day Sch.; bd. cons. Childbirth Edn. Assn. Mem. Am. Nurses Assn., Nurses Assn. Am. Coll. Obstetricians and Gynecologists, Sigma Theta Tau, Zeta Tau Alpha. Baptist. Clubs: U. South Fla. Women's. Home: 5741 Whiteway Dr Tannahill Circle SE Huntsville AL 35802 Office: U South Fla Med Center Coll Nursing Box 22 12901 N 30th St Tampa FL 33612

FLOYD, PATSY MARIE, government official; b. Big Sandy, Tex., Dec. 16, 1953; B.A. in Polit. Sci., Tex. Woman's U., 1975, M.A. in Bus. and Govt., 1981. Office systems staff IBM, Milw., 1978; sch. cons. Wis. Bell Telephone Co., Milw., 1978-79; asst. unit mgr. Baylor Med. Ctr., Dallas, 1979; spl. asst. to dep. asst. sec. vets. employment Dept. Labor; ind. monitoring specialist N. Tex. Edn. Tng. Coop., Sanger, 1980-81; presdl. mgmt. intern Dept. Navy, Washington, 1981-83, Office Personnel Mgmt., Washington, 1981-82, Senate Com. Vets. Affairs, 1982; program analyst Naval Air Systems Command, Dept. Navy, Washington, 1983—. Pres. Coll. Republicans, Denton, Tex., 1980-81; mem. Fed. Summer Intern Bd., Washington, 1980. Served as lt. U.S. Army, 1976-78; capt. USAR. Recipient Law Day award Gregg County Bar Assn. (Tex.), 1972; Outstanding Young Am. award Nat. Bd. Advt., 1980, 82, 83; Presdl. Mgmt. Intern award, 1981-83; Rotary Internat. scholar, 1972. Mem. Nat. Assn. Female Execs., Res. Officers Assn. (life), Am. Soc. Pub. Adminstrn., Presdl. Mgmt. Intern Alumni Group, Profl. Bus. Women's Club. Republican. Baptist. Home: 3900 16th St NW Apt 510 Washington DC 20011

FLOYD-TENIYA, KATHLEEN A., business services executive; b. Berwyn, Ill., June 23, 1953; d. David James and Phyllis L. (Lyons) Floyd; m. Robert Don Teniya, June 20, 1982; one child: James David. Cert. credit and fin. analyst, lic. realtor, Ill. Indsl. specialist Technicon Instrument Corp., Elmhurst, Ill., 1971-74, service contract adminstr., 1974-76; asst. to pres. Ebend, Inc., Addison, Ill., 1976-77; credit rep. mgr. Memorex Corp., Lombard, Ill., 1977-79; nat. sales rep. Midcontinent Adjustment Co., Glenview, Ill., 1979-83, asst. v.p. sales, 1983-86; pres., chief exec. officer, Inteletek Inc., Itasca, Ill., 1986—. Newspaper editor, publicity chmn. Dupage County chpt. Young Ams. for Freedom, 1969-70, pres., 1970-71; mem. Teenage Republican Orgn., 1968-71. Mem. Nat. Assn. Female Execs. Lutheran. Clubs: Lombard Women's Rep., Ill. Fedn. Rep. Women. Home: 263 Evergreen Ln Bloomingdale IL 60108 Office: Inteletek Inc PO Box 0163 Itasca IL 60143-0163

FLUCKIGER, ADRIENNE NORTHAM, librarian; b. Branford, Conn., Aug. 28, 1926; d. Robert Hazen and Alice May (Hill) Northam; m. James R. Fluckiger, Nov. 4, 1949 (dec.); children—John, James, Anne, Elizabeth. B.A., Middlebury Coll., 1947; M.L.S., Palmer Grad. Library Sch., 1967. Social worker Conn. Dept. Child Welfare, New Haven, 1947-49; librarian Seaford Pub. Library, N.Y., 1963-68; head children's services Syosset Pub. Library, (N.Y.), 1968—; adj. prof. Palmer Sch. Library and Info. Sci., L.I.U., 1984, 86. Mem. Palmer Library Sch. Alumni (pres. 1982-84), ALA (Newbery-Caldecott com. 1978-79), N.Y. Library Assn., Nassau County Library Assn. (pres. 1981). Democrat. Unitarian. Home: 3964 Marilyn Dr Seaford NY 11783 Office: Syosset Pub Library 225 S Oyster Bay Rd Syosset NY 11791

FLUELLEN, SHIRLEY ANN, optics researcher; b. Macon, Ga., Nov. 17, 1952; d. Alexander Hamilton and Mamie L. (Stanley) F. B.S., Fort Valley State Coll., Ga., 1973; postgrad. U. Mich. Dental Sch., 1973-74; O.D., Ind. U., 1979; specialist cert. Manila Central U., 1981. Cert. optometrist. Optometrist, Manila and Va., 1979—; optics research specialist Naval Space Surveillance System, Dahlgren, Va., 1982—. Chair polit. action group for Va., NAACP, 1985; organizer, pres. Fredericksburg Area Pan-Hellenic Council 1984—; mem. Nat. Council Negro Women, 1984—. Am. Fund Minority Dental Edn. scholar, 1972-74; Ga. Bd. Regents Scholar, 1969-72. Mem. Nat. Optometric Assn. (chair regional membership com.; Student Service award 1977), Beta Kappa Chi, Alpha Kappa Mu (chpt. v.p. 1972-73), Alpha Kappa Alpha, Ruby Bell Missionary Soc. Mem. Christian Methodist Episcopal Ch. Lodges: Order of Eastern Star, Daus. of Elks. Avocations: reading; travel; sewing; jogging. Office: Naval Space Surveillance System Dahlgren VA 22448

FLUELLEN, VIRGINIA LORRAINE, nurse; b. Gilmor, Tex., Mar. 13, 1938; d. Olie and Iwana (Owens) F. Student Tex. Coll., Tyler, South Tex. Coll., Houston; Assoc. in Nursing, Alvin Sch. Nursing (Tex.), 1972. R.N., Tex. Staff nurse Herman Hosp., Houston, 1972-73, asst. head nurse, 1973—. Recipient Tina award Found. for Children, 1979. Mem. Tex. Perinatal Assn. Democrat. Baptist. Club: Las Vegas Social & Charity (Houston). Office: Hermann Hosp 1203 Ross Sterling Ave Houston TX 77037

FLUKE, LYLA SCHRAM, publisher, educator; b. Maddock, N.D.; d. Olaf John and Anne Marie (Rodberg) Schram; B.S. in Zoology and Physiology, U. Wash., Seattle, 1934, teaching diploma, 1935; m. John M. Fluke, June 5, 1937; children—Virginia Fluke Gabelein, John M., David Lynd. High sch. tchr., 1935-37; tutor Seattle schs., 1974-75; pub. Portage quar. mag. Hist. Soc. Seattle-King County, 1980—. Founder, N.W. chpt. Myasthenia Gravis Found., 1953, pres., 1953-55; obtained N.W. artifacts for destroyer tender Puget Sound, 1966; mem. Seattle Mayor's Com. for Seattle Beautiful, 1968-69; sponsor Seattle World's Fair, 1962, Seattle Symphony, Seattle Youth Symphony, 1983—; charter mem. Seattle Youth Symphony Aux., 1974; bd. dirs. Cascade Symphony, 1983—, Salvation Army, 1985-87; benefactor U. Wash., 1983—, Stanford U., 1984—. Fellow Seattle Pacific U., 1972—. Mem. Nat. Assn. Parliamentarians (charter mem., pres. N.W. unit 1961), Wash. Parliamentarians Assn. (charter), IEEE Aux. (chpt. charter mem., pres. 1970-72), Seattle C. of C. (women's div.), Seattle Symphony Women's Assn. (life mem.; pres. 1985-86), Hist. Soc. Seattle and King County (exec. com. 1975-78), Women's Mus. League (pres. 1975-78), Moritz Thomsen Guild of Hist. Soc. (pres. 1978-80, 84-87), Northwest Horticulture Soc., Nat. Trust Historic Preservation, Wash. State Hist. Soc., Seattle Orthopedic Guild. Republican. Lutheran. Clubs: Women's U., Rainier, Seattle Golf, U. Wash. Presidents, Sterling Circle of Stanford U. Author articles on history. Address: 1206 NW Culbertson Dr Seattle WA 98177

FLUKER, BRENDA ANN, lawyer; b. Demopolis, Ala., Mar. 3, 1952; d. Clinton and Pandora Eva (Essex) F.; 1 child, Brandy Fluker Oakley. B.S., Ala. A&M U., 1972; J.D., Tulane U., 1978. Bar: Mass. 1979, U.S. Supreme Ct. 1984. Group ins. underwriter Liberty Life Assurance Co., Boston, 1972-74; statis. filing analyst Liberty Mut. Ins. Co., Boston, 1974-75, assoc. counsel in charge of mktg. and underwriting support group, 1979—; part-time office mgr. and underwriter Fulton & Johnson Ins. Agy., New Orleans, 1975-78; mem. workers compensation self-insurers study com. Nat. Assn. Ins. Commrs., 1982-83; vis. prof. Nat. Urban League Black Exec. Exchange Program, N.Y.C., 1980—; of counsel Rosa Parks Day Care Ctr., Boston, 1980—. Mem. adv. council Roxbury (Mass.) Community Sch., 1979-81; loaned exec. United Way of Massachusetts Bay, Boston, 1979; vol. Boston pub. schs., 1983-85. Recipient Black Achievers award Boston YMCA, 1981, mem. Alumni Assn., 1984—. Mem. ABA, Nat. Bar Assn. (gov., regional dir. 1982-83, vice chmn. instl./corp. sect. 1982-83, editor regional newsletter 1982-83), Mass. Bar Assn. (co-chmn. Barristers Ball com. 1985-86), Mass. Black Lawyers Assn. (sec., exec. com. 1982-86, chmn. interorgnl. activities com. 1981-83), Mass. Black Women Attys. (exec. com. 1981-83), Nat. Assn. Ins. Commrs. (adv. com. on comml. premium payment plans 1985-86). Democrat. Baptist. Home: 42 Gladeside Ave Mattapan MA 02126 Office: Liberty Mut Ins Co 175 Berkeley St Boston MA 02117

FLY, CELIA PATTERSON, research company executive; b. Direct, Tex., Aug. 15, 1928; d. Martin and Laura (Hollingshead) Patterson; B.S., Tex. Tech. U., 1951; m. A.B. Fly, July 6, 1947; children—Charles Bruce, Gerald Wayne. Adminstrv. dietitian St. Anthony's Hosp., Amarillo, Tex., 1955-57, Calif. Hosp., Los Angeles, 1967-68; office mgr. Hydro-Jet Service, Inc., Hydro-Torq Pump Co., Amarillo, 1959—; also dir.; dir., sec. treas. Marine Metals Inc., Fly Enterprises, Inc., Aero-Span, Inc., Amarillo; controller Aero-Span Research Ltd., Hi-Plains Minerals Ltd., Amarillo, 1980—; sec., treas., office mgr. Tuff-N-Lite Inc., 1980—. Mem. Aircraft Owners and Pilots Assn., The Ninety-Nines. Republican. Inventor vapor suppression solar collector film system. Home: 136 Bayrock Circle PO Box 30400 Amarillo TX 79120 Office: 500 W Farmers Ave Box 30400 Amarillo TX 79120

FLY, MARY, lawyer; b. Houston, Mar. 13, 1937; d. William Madden and Mary Beth (Deans) F. B.S. cum laude, U. Mo.-St. Louis, 1968, M.Ed., 1970; J.D., U. Tex., 1977. Bar: Tex. 1978, U.S. Dist. Ct. (ea. dist.) Tex. 1979. Tchr., St. John and James Sch., Ferguson, Mo., 1966-68, Hazelwood Jr. High Sch., Florissant, Mo., 1968-69; teaching asst. U. Mo.-St. Louis, 1969-70; tchr. Dept. Def. Overseas Dependent Sch., Japan, Okinawa, Philippines, 1970-75; staff atty. East Tex. Legal Services, Beaumont, 1978-81; sole practice, Beaumont, 1981—. Staff mem. Am. Jour. Criminal Law, 1977. Bd. dirs. Family Violence Ctr., Inc., Beaumont, 1978-80; rec. sec. Beaumont Interfaith Choral Soc., 1982-84, pres., 1984-85; S.E. Tex. Chorale, Beaumont Civic Opera. Mem. ABA, State Bar Tex., Jefferson County Bar Assn. Democrat. Episcopalian. Office: 2349 North St Beaumont TX 77702

FLYNN, ELIZABETH ANNE, advertising and public relations company executive; b. Washington, Aug. 21, 1951; d. John William and Elizabeth Goodwin (Mahoney) F. A.A., Montgomery Coll., Rockville, Md., 1972; B.S. in Journalism, U. Md., 1976; postgrad. San Diego State U., 1976. Writer, researcher, Sea World, Inc., San Diego, 1977-79; sr. writer Lane & Huff Advt., San Diego, 1979-80; account exec. Kaufman, Lansky, Baker Advt., San Diego, 1980-82; mng. dir. Excelsior Enterprises, Beverly Hills, Calif., 1983-84; sr. account exec. Berkhemer & Kline, Inc., Los Angeles, 1985; pres. Flynn Advt. & Pub. Relations, Los Angeles, 1985—; cons. Coca-Cola Bottling Co. Los Angeles, 1982-84. Bd. dirs. Friends of Reconstructive Surgery, Beverly Hills, 1983—. Recipient Cert. of Distinction, Art Direction Mag., 1982. Mem. Nat. Assn. Female Execs., Beverly Hills C. of C., Republican. Roman Catholic. Avocations: screenwriting; short stories; painting; horseback riding. Office: Flynn Advt & Pub Relations 1440 Reeves St Suite 104 Los Angeles CA 90035

FLYNN, JANE MIRIAM, librarian; b. Phila., June 20, 1957; d. Charles L. and Sarah E. (MacDonald) F. B.A. in Spanish, Georgian Ct. Coll., 1979; M.L.S., Rutgers U., 1981; cert. youth ministry program Seton Hall U., 1983. Library assoc. Prudential Property and Casualty Ins. Co., Holmdel, N.J., 1981-82, librarian, 1982—; bus. mgr. N.J. Libraries Jour., 1982—. Active youth ministry St. Justin's Roman Cath. Ch., 1983—. Recipient Donald S. MacNaughton award for community service Prudential Ins. Co., 1984. Mem. Spl. Libraries Assn., ALA, N.J. Library Assn. Democrat. Home: 1956 Ship Ct Toms River NJ 08753 Office: Prudential Property and Casualty Insurance Co 23 Main St Holmdel NJ 07733

FLYNN, JUDITH ANNE, public relations executive; b. Hartford, Conn.; d. Jere J. and Helen P. (Kelly) F. B.A., U. Pa., 1959; M.A., Trinity Coll., Hartford, 1963. Pub. health edn. cons. Conn. Dept. Health, Hartford, 1962-64; assoc. editor Macmillan Co., N.Y.C., 1964-66; staff publicist Pub. Relations Soc. Am., N.Y.C., 1966-68; asst. v.p. pub. relations Bankers Trust Co., N.Y.C., 1968-75, asst. v.p., pub. relations Marine Midland Bank, N.Y.C., 1978-80; nat. dir. pub. relations Arthur Young & Co., N.Y.C., 1980-83; owner, dir. Flynn Communications Group, N.Y.C., 1983—. Bd. dirs. Brownstone Revival Commn., N.Y.C., 1984. Mem. New Eng. Soc. (N.Y.C.), Pub. Relations Soc. Am., Am. Women Entrepreneurs Nat. Assn. Female Execs. Club: Princeton (N.Y.C.). Home and office: 153 E 57th St New York NY 10022

FLYNN, JUDITH C. S., business exec.; b. Wichita Falls, Tex., Nov. 27, 1945; d. W.H. and Teena H. Chittum; B.A., Grove City (Pa.) Coll., 1966; M.A. in Teaching (teaching fellow 1967), Brown U., 1967; m. Harold F. Flynn, Jr.; children—Harold F., III, Peter Craig, Alison J. Tchr., Franklin (N.H.) High Sch., 1967-68; internat. advt. coordinator Franklin Mint, Franklin Center, Pa., 1969-72; fin. mgr. Fire Service Agy., Annapolis, Md., 1972-74; asst. to comptroller Alcoa Marine Corp., Washington, 1974-76; v.p. fin., dir. Martel Labs., Inc., Balt., 1977-80, exec. v.p., 1982—; pres., dir. Martel Lab. Services, St. Petersburg, Fla., 1982—; dir. Leartek Corp., 1977—, Chgo. Aerial Survey, Inc., 1982—. Mem. Engring. Soc. Balt., Nat. Assn. Female Execs., Internat. Oceanographic Found., Nat. Assn. Women Bus. Owners, Com. of 200, Assn. Women Govt. Contractors. Republican. Episcopalian. Office: 7100 30th Ave N Saint Petersburg FL 33710

FLYNN, KATHLEEN DOROTHY, architect; b. Washington, June 21, 1948; d. Charles Lenean and Winifred Judith (Carocari) F.; A.B., Manhattanville Coll., 1970; student So. Conn. State Coll., 1973-74; M.A., St. John's Coll., Santa Fe, N.Mex., 1979; M.Arch., U. Wash., 1984. Art tchr. Found. Sch., Orange, Conn., 1970-72; art tchr. Milford Pub. Sch., Conn., 1974-78; housing intern Office of Housing Devel., Dept. Community Devel., City of Seattle, 1980; intern architect Olson/Walker Architects, Seattle, 1981-82, Bassetti, Norton, Metler, Rekevics, Architects, P.C., Seattle, 1984—. NEA grantee, 1981.

FLYNN, MARIE COSGROVE, investment management company executive; b. Honolulu, Jan. 1, 1945; d. John Aloysius and Emeline Frances (Cael) Cosgrove; B.A., Trinity Coll., 1966; student U. Fribourg (Switzerland), 1964-65; m. John Thomas Flynn, Jr., June 3, 1968; children—Jamie Marie, Jacqueline Elizabeth. Mgmt. trainee, analyst U.S. Govt., Washington, 1967-70; coordinator nat. reading council F.X. Doherty Assos., N.Y.C., 1970-71; security analyst Corinthian Capital Co., N.Y.C., 1971-73; portfolio mgr. Clark Mgmt. Co., Inc., N.Y.C., 1973-78; v.p., sr. portfolio mgr. Lexington Mgmt. Corp., Saddle Brook, N.J., 1978—. Mem. Fin. Analysts Fedn., Inst. Chartered Fin. Analysts, Fin. Women's Assn., N.Y. Soc. Security Analysts, Bus. and Profl. Women's Club, Profl. Women's Network. Home: 70 Evergreen Dr Berkeley Heights NJ 07922 Office: Park 80 West Plaza Two PO Box 1515 Saddle Brook NJ 07662

FLYNN, MARYELLEN, advertising agency executive; b. Boston, Aug. 22; d. Cornelius and Helen G. Flynn; student Fordham U., 1957-60, Am. Acad. Dramatic Arts, 1960-62. Creative supr. Young & Rubicam, N.Y.C., 1970-73; creative dir. Revlon Inc., N.Y.C., 1973-75; founding partner, v.p., creative dir. Renning, Kuryla, Lieberman, Flynn Inc., N.Y.C., 1975-78; v.p., creative dir. Grey Advt., N.Y.C., 1979-84; pres. Mag Mell Enterprises, N.Y.C., 1985—; creative dir. Grey Entertainment & Media, 1986—. Founder, producing dir. Gryphon Theatricals, Inc., 1979; producer off-Broadway play A Coupla White Chicks Sitting Around Talking, 1980. Recipient Clio award, 1969, 74, 83, Andy award, 1965, 83, IBA award, 1963, Venice Grand Prix award, 1962. Mem. Nat. Assn. TV Arts and Scis., Actors Equity. Office: 875 Third Ave New York NY 10022

FLYNN, SHARON ANN, marketing executive, educator; b. Kings Park, N.Y., Apr. 14, 1955; d. John Joseph and Mary Rose (Dwyer) F. Nursing Sci. Degree, Suffolk County Community Coll., 1976; R.N., N.Y. State Psychiat. Sch. Nursing, 1977. Psychiat. therapist Kings Park Psychiat. Ctr., N.Y., 1971-77, psychiat. registered nurse, 1977-79; acute hemodialysis nurse Boca Raton Community Hosp., Fla., 1981-83; home infusion therapy educator Am. Hosp. Supply Corp., S.E. Fla., 1983-84, mktg./territory mgr., 1984-85; mktg. specialist Home Infusion Therapy Hosp. Corp. Am., Ft. Lauderdale, Fla., 1985—; cons. advisor HomeCare Palm Beaches, Inc., Lake Worth, Fla., 1984—; instr. continuous ambulatory peritoneal dialysis Boca Raton Community Hosp., 1982, instr. diabetic edn., 1981. Mem. Nat. Assn. Female Execs., Discharge Planners Assn., Assn. Profl. Saleswomen, Am. Legion Aux. Republican. Roman Catholic. Avocations: scuba diving; tennis. Office: Hosp Corp Am/Transmed 3351 NW 55th St Fort Lauderdale FL 33309

FLYNN, SUZANNE KENNEDY, writer-producer, beauty, health and fashion workshop executive; b. N.Y.C., Jan. 9, 1937; d. Patrick Joseph and Anna (Sullivan) Kennedy; m. Arthur E.P. Flynn, Mar. 25, 1961 (div. July 1967);

children—Kerry Kennedy, Tracy Kennedy. Student pub. schs., N.Y.C. Sr. beauty and health editor Seventeen mag., N.Y.C., 1966-69, 73-76, Harper's Bazaar, N.Y.C., 1971-73; assoc. editor Town and Country mag., 1969-71; founder, pres., chief exec. officer Buzzwords, Ink, Nantucket, Mass., 1976—; sr. cons. Revlon, Inc., 1976—, Clock Models, 1980—, Estee Lauder, Inc., 1985—; creative dir. Yardley of London, 1969-71; assoc. creative dir. Parker Advt., Calif., 1976-77; copy voice for Princess Marcella Borghese, Revlon, Pierre Balmain perfume. Columnist Trends, N.Y. Post; writer/producer The Contemporary Woman, 1st TV nat. women's mag., ABC; co-author: Seventeen Book of Beauty and Fashion, 1969; author: How To Save Your Hair...A Man's Guide, 1985; contbg. editor: Scavullo on Beauty, 1972, Revlon—The Art of Beauty, 1984. Recipient Excellence in Writing award Fragrance Found., 1967, 69, 71, 78; Fashion Video award, In Fashion, 1986. Republican. Club: Nantucket Yacht. Avocations: flying; pre-Revolutionary Russia. Office: Buzzwords Ink 12 E 86 St New York NY 10028

FOBES, JACQUELINE THERESA MITCHELL, psychologist, educator, research consultant; b. Calgary, Alta., Can., June 5, 1946; came to U.S., 1966; d. Jack and Marie Jane (Powell) Mitchell; m. James Lewis Fobes, Feb. 28, 1970. A.A., Pasadena City Coll., 1969; B.A., M.Ed., U. Ariz., 1973, 74; postgrad. U. Wis.-Madison, 1975, Ph.D. candidate Claremont Grad. Sch., Calif., 1978-86. Lic. ednl. psychologist, Calif.; lic. marriage, family and child therapist, Calif. Edn. psychologist Los Angeles Unified Schs., Calif., 1976-82; Fobes Assocs., Pacific Grove, Calif., 1978—, Monterey Unified Schs., Calif., 1982-86, Pajaro Valley Schs., Watsonville, Calif., 1984-85; devel. cons. Monterey County Office Edn., Salinas, Calif., 1983—. Author: A Papapo Boy and His Friends, 1979. Editor Ostomy Quar., 1985. Project dir. Salinas Reduction Minority Isolation Study, Calif., 1985; sr. sci. Mainstreaming Spl. Edn. Students Study, 1981; initiator, leader Sexual Assault Victims Group, Rape Crisis Ctr., Monterey; program initiator, cons. The Writing and Thinking Workshops for Children, Monterey, 1983-86, Monterey Writing Conf., summer 1985; bd. dirs. Found. to Support Monterey Unified Schs., 1985-88; cons. Agnese N. Lindley Found., Tucson, 1984—. Mem. AAUW (bd. dirs. 1984-86, program initiator, chmn. workshop series spring 1985), Monterey Bay Women's Sch. Psychol. Assn., Ostomy Soc. Roman Catholic. Avocations: writing; gourmet cooking; walking; gardening; restoration of antique furniture. Home: 3067 Larkin Rd Pebble Beach CA 93953 Office: Fobes Assocs 302-667 Lighthouse Ave Pacific Grove CA 93950

FOCH, NINA, actress, educator; b. Leyden, Netherlands, Apr. 20, 1924; d. Dirk and Consuelo (Flowerton) F.; came to U.S., 1928; grad. Lincoln Sch., N.Y.C., 1939; m. James Lipton, June 6, 1954; m. 2d, Dennis R. Brite, Nov. 27, 1959; 1 son, Schuyler Dirk; m. 3d, Michael Dewell, Oct. 31, 1967. Appeared in motion pictures: Nine Girls, 1944, Return of the Vampire, 1944, She's A Sweetheart, 1944, Shadows in the Night, 1944, Cry of the Werewolf, 1944, Escape in the Fog, 1945, A Song to Remember, 1945, My Name is Julia Ross, 1945, I Love A Mystery, 1945, Johnny O'Clock, 1947, The Guilt of Janet Ames, 1947, The Dark Past, 1948, The Undercover Man, 1949, Johnny Allegro, 1949, An American in Paris, 1951, Scaramouche, 1952, Young Man with Ideas, 1952, Sombrero, 1953, Fast Company, 1953, Executive Suite, 1954 (Acad. award nominee for supporting performance 1954), Four Guns to the Border, 1954, You're Never Too Young, 1955, Illegal, 1955, The Ten Commandments, 1956, Three Brave Men, 1957, Cash McCall, 1959, Spartacus, 1960, Such Good Friends, 1971, Salty, 1973, Mahogany, 1976, Jennifer, 1978; Broadway plays include: John Loves Mary, 1947, Twelfth Night, 1949, A Phoenix Too Frequent, 1950, King Lear, 1950, Second String, 1960; appeared with Am. Shakespeare Festival in Taming of the Shrew and Measure for Measure, 1956; appeared with San Francisco Ballet and Opera in The Seven Deadly Sins, 1966, also many regional theatre productions, including Seattle Repertory Theatre in All Over, 1972, The Seagull, 1973; actress TV, 1947—, including Playhouse 90, Studio One, Pulitzer Playhouse, Playwrights 56, Producers Show Case, Naked City, Kraft Suspense Theatre, Route 66, Arrest and Trial, Burke's Law, The Trailmaster, Dr. Kildare, The Outer Limits, The Steve Allen Show, Gunsmoke, McCloud, Mod Squad, I Spy, Columbo, Barnaby Jones, Hawaii Five-O, The Name of the Game, The Wonderful World of Disney, Lou Grant, also many other series, network spls. and films for TV; starring in series Shadowchasers, ABC-TV, 1985—; TV panelist and guest on numerous shows, including The Tonight Show, Dick Cavett Show, Merv Griffin Show, Mike Douglas Show, Dinah Shore Show; TV moderator Let's Take Sides, 1957-59; asso. dir. film The Diary of Anne Frank, 1959; dir. nat. tour and Broadway production Tonight at 8:30, 1966-67; asso. producer re-opening Ford's Theatre, Washington, 1968; adj. prof. U. So. Calif., 1966-68; artist-in-residence U. N.C., 1966, Ohio State U., 1967, Calif. Tech. Inst., 1969-70; mem. sr. faculty Am. Film Inst., 1973-77; founder, tchr. Nina Foch Studio, Hollywood, Calif., 1973—; adj. prof. U. So. Calif., 1978-80; a founder, actress Los Angeles Theatre Group, 1960-65; bd. dirs. Nat. Repertory Theatre, 1967-75. Hon. chmn. Los Angeles chpt. Am. Cancer Soc., 1970. Recipient Film Daily award, 1949. Mem. Acad. Motion Picture Arts and Scis. (co-chmn. exec. com. for fgn. film award 1973—), Hollywood Acad. TV Arts and Scis. (gov. 1976-77). Address: PO Box 1884 Beverly Hills CA 90213

FOCHLER, MARCIA LORRAINE, educator; b. Pasadena, Calif., Sept. 18, 1931; d. Raymond King and Olive Cecelia (McFarlane) Chamness; m. William Stanley Fochler, Mar. 26, 1954; children—Russell William, Teresa Lorraine, Patricia Lorene. A.A., Glendale Coll., 1951; B.A., Occidental Coll., 1953; M.A., Calif. State U.-Hayward, 1976. Cert. early childhood, elem., community coll., adult edn. tchr., Calif. Elem. tchr., Glendale Sch. (Calif.), 1953-54; master tchr. U. Nev., Reno, 1954-56; parent educator Grossmont Adult Sch., La Mesa, Calif., 1970-72; instr. child devel. San Diego Community Coll., 1972-73; vice prin. Acalanes High Sch., Lafayette, Calif., 1977-78; dir. Somerset Hills Adult Sch., Bernardsville, N.J., 1978-79; parent edn. coordinator Acalanes Adult Ctr., Walnut Creek, Calif., 1973-77, program coordinator, 1979—; exec. dir. Calif. Council for Adult Edn., 1985. Commr., City of Lafayette, 1981-82; intern Coro Found., Oakland, 1983; task force mem. Calif. Community Colls., Sacramento, 1982-83; bd. dirs. Bay Area Children's Mus., 1985. Recipient Recognition award Glendale Coll., 1951; PTA award, Los Angeles, 1953; citation City of Lafayette, 1983; program of excellence cert. Contra Costa County Schs, 1984. Mem. Calif. Congress Parents and Tchrs. (mem. 9th dist. bd. 1972-73), AAUW (mem. br. bd. 1981-82, edn. rep. Lafayette 1982, families and work chmn. 1984-86, developer Kid-Phone; Disting. Woman of Yr. 1986), Assn. Calif. Sch. Adminstrs., Calif. Assn. for Edn. Young Children (state pres. 1983-85), Nat. Assn. for Edn. Young Children (nat. conf. coordinator 1980), East Bay Assn. for Edn. Young Children (Outstanding Service award 1985), Republican. Office: Acalanes Adult Center 1963 Tice Valley Blvd Walnut Creek CA 94595

FODOR, MAGDA MARIA, civil engineer; b. Hungary, Sept. 21, 1942; d. Jeno and Edith Gotz; 1 child, Thomas. Ed. Europe. Civil squad leader Am. Cyanamid Co., Wayne, N.J., 1974-76; sr. engr. Merck & Co., Rahway, N.J., 1976-77; project engr. Exxon Research and Engring., Florham Park, N.J., 1977-79; mem. tech. staff TRW Inc., Redondo Beach, Calif., 1980-81; project engr. research and devel. Todd Pacific Shipyards Corp., San Pedro, Calif., 1981-83; aerospace engr. U.S. Air Force, Los Angeles, 1983-85; supervisory gen. engr. U.S. Navy, Long Beach, Calif., U.S. Air Force, Los Angeles, 1985—. Mem. Am. Soc. Naval Engrs. Office: 6592 ABG/DPCS PO Box 92960 Worldway Postal Ctr Los Angeles CA 90009-2960

FODOR, MARIANA DUARTE, army officer, nurse, educator; b. N.Y.C., Mar. 8, 1938; d. Rodulfo Sindulfo and Orosia (Perez) Diaz; Joseph E. Fodor, Sept. 1, 1972. R.N. diploma, NYU-Bellevue Hosp., 1958; B.A., Hunter Coll., 1972; M.Ed., NYU, 1975. Commd. 1st lt. Nurse Corps, U.S. Army, 1967, advanced through ranks to lt. col., 1983; nursing supr. Hosp. Spl. Surgery, N.Y.C., 1967-68; active duty, Yokohama, Japan, 1968-69; tchr., nurse Dept. Def. Schs.-Pacific, Japan, 1969-72; tchr. practical nursing New Rochelle High Sch. N.Y.C., 1972-74; bio-med. coordinator Lehman High Sch., N.Y. Bd. Edn., N.Y.C., 1974-81; pub. affairs officer 8th Med. Brigade, 1977-80; asst. chief nurse, tng. officer 344th Gen. Hosp., Ft. Totten, N.Y., 1981-85; bd. govs. 77th Army Res. Command, N.Y.C., 1982-85. Writer health edn. and family life curriculum Dept. Def. Schs., Pacific area, Japan, 1971. Recipient Meritorious Service medal Dept. Army, Washington, 1982, Achievement medal, 1983, Commendation medal, 1979; Community Service award Staten Island Hosp., N.Y.C., 1979; Tchr. of Yr. award Outstanding Secondary Educators Am., 1975; 1st woman mil. marshall Vets. Meml. Day Parade, N.Y.C., 1984. Mem. Res. Officers Assn. life; (adv. council), Assn. Mil. Surgeons U.S. (exec. council). Home: 230 Riverside Dr New York NY 10025

FOERSTEL, LENORA, art and anthropology educator; b. Phila., May 22, 1932; d. Carl Shargo and Olga Shargo Goldstein; m. Herbert Neil Foerstel, Sept. 5, 1961; children—Jonathon, Helen, Karen. B., Tyler Sch. Fine Arts, 1953; M.F.A., Temple U., 1959. Prof. art history Towson U., Md., 1959-60; prof. art and anthopology Md. Inst. Coll. of Art, Balt., 1960—; field asst. Dr. Margaret Mead, Papua New Guinea, 1953-54, field work, 1978; asst. Dr. M. Mead, Columbia U., N.Y.C., 1954-55. Producer, dir., writer Paola Soleri, 1968; producer Frederick Douglass, 1973, writer, cons. Anthopology on Trial, 1983. Instr. visual arts program for prisoners, 1982—. Ruth Benedict awardee, 1971; grantee Union of Ind. Colls., 1972, Nat. Endowment for Arts, 1973. Fellow Nat. Art Edn., Internat. Art Edn. Concerns; mem. Internat. Women's Research Agy. (sec. 1982—), People for Peace (pres. 1980—). Democrat. Club: Sounds Inc. (cons. 1985). Home: 5110 W Penfield Rd Columbia MD 21045 Office: Md Inst Coll of Art 1300 Mt Royal Ave Baltimore MD 21217

FOGARTY, JUDE CATHERINE, technical sales representative, medical technologist; b. Chgo., Oct. 8, 1948; d. Paul Francis and Esther Mae (Smith) Winkler; m. Michael Joseph Fogarty, Mar. 24, 1972. B.S. in Biology, U. Wis.-Whitewater, 1970; cert. in med. tech., Rush Presbyterian St. Luke's Hosp., 1971. Owner, operator Midwest Vet. Med. Lab., Willow Springs, Ill., 1974-81; lab. mgr. Damon Corp., Needham Heights, Mass., 1981-83; tech. sales rep. Am. Sci. Products, McGaw Park, Ill., 1983—; cons. Am. Midwest, Des Plaines, Ill., 1983; bd. advs. Morraine Valley Jr. Coll., Palos Hills, Ill., 1972-74. Sec. Oak Valley Homeowners Assn., Lockport, Ill., 1983—. Named Tech. Sales Rep. of Yr., Am. Sci. Products, 1983, 84. Mem. Am. Soc. Clin. Pathologists (assoc.), AAUW (v.p. 1980-81). Roman Catholic. Avocations: traveling; snow skiing; sailing. Home: 16026 Oak Valley Trail Lockport IL 60441 Office: Am Sci Products 1210 Waukegan Rd McGaw Park IL 60085

FOGEL, ADELAIDE FORST, lawyer; b. N.Y.C., July 26, 1915; d. Leon and Antoinette (Hahn) Forst; B.A., Washington Sq. Coll., 1936; LL.B., NYU, 1939; m. David Fogel, June 2, 1940; children—Ann Fogel Vivell, Susan Lee Fogel Lloyd. Admitted to N.Y. State bar; individual practice law, N.Y.C. Patron N.Y. Philharm.; trustee Temple Israel, N.Y.C., past pres. Sisterhood. Mem. Met. Mus. Art, Mus. Natural History, NYU Law Alumni Assn. Jewish. Address: New York NY 10021

FOGEL, MARJORIE, public relations executive; b. Port Chester, N.Y., Dec. 14, 1931; d. Maurice and Betty Schneider; student Pembroke Coll. of Brown U., 1949-50, N.Y.U., 1951-52, 78; m. Harold V. Fogel, June 12, 1954; children—Jonathan, Glenn. Prodn. asst., then prodn. mgr., copywriter, editor Jack Danowitz Advt., Inc., N.Y.C., 1951-56; community/public relations coordinator Planned Communities, Inc., Rye, N.Y., Washington, 1975-76; free-lance public relations, 1977; exec. dir. Energy Resources Devel. Inst., also exec. dir. Apt. Owners Adv. Council, White Plains, N.Y., 1978-79; founder, prin. Marje Fogel Communications, Rye Brook, N.Y., 1980—; founder, pres. Marjac Enterprises, producer Condo Showcase. Vol. ARC, 1955-59, United Hosp., 1968-77; mem. Westchester County Democratic Com., 1972-81; mem. exec. com. Port Chester-Town of Rye Voter Registration Dr., 1972-76; coordinator fund-raising, community relations Mental Health Assn. Westchester County, 1975; mem. steering com. Port Chester-Town of Rye Bicentennial, 1975-76; bd. dirs. Port Chester-Town of Rye Community Action Program, 1976-77; publicity coordinator Dem. candidates, 1975-77; mem. Rye Town Planning Bd., 1980-82, Village of Rye Brook Planning Bd., 1982-86. Recipient ARC service award; United Hosp. service award; Westchester Mental Health Vol. Service award. Mem. Advt. Club. Westchester, Am. Advt. Fedn. Club: Hampshire Country (Mamaroneck, N.Y.). Address: 201 Country Ridge Dr Rye Brook NY 10573

FOGGY, EARLIE BEATRICE KNOCKUM, educator; b. Cuthbert, Ga., Apr. 15, 1923; d. John and Mattie (Knockum) Pitman; m. William Foggy, July 16, 1946; B.S., Ga. State Coll., 1941; M.Ed., U. Ill., 1957; D. Christian Edn. (hon.), Ill. Bapt. Inst., 1975. Cert. adminstr., Ill. Tchr. East St. Louis, 1943-66, media supr., 1966-74, dir. project Continued Edn. for Pregnant Teens, 1974-81; spl. tchr. Venice Sch. Dist., Ill., 1981—. Active Bell Social Club, East St. Louis, Ill., 1980, The Ctr., 1981, Venus Temple, 1981, YWCA, Belleville, Ill., 1982, Democratic Women, East St. Louis, 1983. Recipient Civic award City of East St. Louis, 1981. Mem. Assn. Edn. and Communication Tech. (award 1970), Ill. Audio Visual Assn. (award 1973), Ill. Ret. Tchrs. Assn. (life), Ill. Alumni Assn. (life), Sigma Gamma Rho. Baptist. Lodge: Philo (affiliates coordinator). Avocations: writing; collecting records; travel; entertaining; youth work. Home: 1840 Saint Louis Ave East Saint Louis IL 62205 Office: East St Louis Pub Library 405 N 9th St East Saint Louis IL 62201

FOGLESONG, SUSAN LYN, insurance agent; b. Southwest City, Mo., July 7, 1948; d. Joseph August and Violet Aline (Wilfong) Minges; m. Marion David Foglesong, June 17, 1972 (div. Nov. 1974); 1 child, Violet Susanna Beasley. Med. Asst., Kansas City Bus. Coll., 1971. Med. asst., Midwest Orthopedic Group, Kansas City, Mo., 1971-72; med. transcriber Lakeside Osteopathic Hosp., Kansas City, Mo., 1974-76; new bus. coordinator ESCO Life Cons., Kansas City, Mo., 1977-82; adminstrv. asst. group rep. Bankers Life & Casualty Co., Kansas City, Mo., 1982-84; services coordinator Assn. Services Internat., Overland Park, Kans., 1985; sales service asst. U.S. Life Ins., Overland Park, Kans., 1985—. Columnist, Cub Communicator, 1984—. Regional coordinator, state rep. Concerned United Birthparents, 1984—, state rep., legis. reporter, 1980—; editor, legis. dir., liaison coordinator Kansas City Adult Adoptees, 1982—; legis. dir. Am. Adoption Congress Region VI, 1983—. Mem. Kansas City Life Underwriters, Life Ins. Co. Office Mgmt., Nat. Assn. Female Execs. Republican. Mem. Unity Church. Avocations: quilting; gardening; sewing; crafts; writing children's stories. Home: 7000 Jackson St Kansas City MO 64132 Office: US Life Ins Co 6400 Glenwood Suite 316 Overland Park KS 66202

FOKAKIS, CYNTHIA, court official; b. Mpls., Sept. 25, 1922; d. Andrew Theodore and Angeline (Kampile) Cappas; m. Emmanuel Arthur Fokakis, Sept. 5, 1943 (dec. 1983); 1 child, Irene. Grad. programs Inst. for Ct. Mgmt., 1976-83. Bookkeeper Cameron Ins. Agy., Mpls., 1941-43; bookkeeper, cashier restaurant, Madison, Wis., 1947-57; account clk. Clk. of Circuit Ct., Madison, 1957-59, judge's clk., 1960-75; clk. of ct. Dane County, Madison, 1976—; mem. Gov.'s Commn. on Fees, Fines and Forfeiture, 1980-81; mem. Wis. Com. for Rev. of Initiatives in Child Support, 1984—; mem. Jud. Council Jury Communication, State of Wis., 1982—. Mem. Clk. of Circuit Ct. Assn. (chairperson legislation 1983-85), Assn. County Officers (legis. chairperson 1985), LWV, Women's Polit. Caucus, Nat. Assn. Trial Ct. Adminstrs., Child Support Data System, Am. Judicature Soc. Democrat. Greek Orthodox. Avocations: reading, knitting, sewing. Home: 4417 Rolla Ln Madison WI 53711 Office: Clk of Circuit Ct City-County Bldg Madison WI 53709

FOKINE, IRINE, ballet educator; b. Vologda, Russia, Sept. 20, 1922; came to U.S., 1938, naturalized, 1943; d. Alexander and Alexandra (Federova) F.; m. Don Decker (div.); Nina Decker Marlow, Jon, Donna, Michael. Owner, tchr. Irine Fokine Sch. Ballet, Ridgewood, N.J., 1950—. Dir., choreographer Irine Fokine Ballet Co. Children's Theater, 1971-76, Pavlova Celebration, Ridgewood, 1982, Coppelia, Hamburg, Germany, 1983, The Nutcracker, Paramus, N.J., past 28 yrs; choreographer (ballets) Red Riding Hood, Peter and the Wolf, Nutcracker, Coppelia, Romeo and Juliet, Symphonie Fantastique, Christmas Carol, Sleeping Beauty, others. Active Kasschau Meml. Shell, Ridgewood, Ridgewood Nursing Home, Sr. Citizen Homes, Libraries, Handicapped Children. Recipient Commendation cert. Bergen County Bd. Chosen Freeholders, 1985, proclamation of Irine Fokine Day, Ridgewood, Mar. 22, 1985. Avocations: swimming; gardening. Office: Irine Fokine Sch Ballet 33 Chestnut St Ridgewood NJ 07450

FOLEY, ANNA BERNICE WILLIAMS (MRS. WARREN MASSEY FOLEY), author; b. Wigginsville, Ohio, Nov. 20, 1902; d. Karl Howland and Bertye (Young) Williams; B.A., U. Cin., 1924; postgrad. Nanking (China) Lang. Coll., 1926, Columbia U., 1931; grad. cert. Jesus Coll., Oxford (Eng.) U., 1969; m. Warren Massey Foley, Feb. 25, 1924; children—Williams Massey, Karlanne Foley Hauer. Commentator, Sta. WKRC, Cin., 1934, Sta. WSAI, Cin., 1938, Sta. WCPO-TV, Cin., 1939-44; spl. events coordinator Mabley & Carew Dept. Store, Cin., 1951-66; fashion model McCall Patterns and Singer Sewing Machines for Cultural Exchange for U.S. State Dept. and Russia, Moscow, 1957; dir. Martha Kinney Cooper Ohioana Library Assn., Columbus, Ohio, 1966-77, also editor Quar. mag., Yearbook, 1966-77; lectr. creative writing; lectr. U. Cin. Evening Coll., 1941-44; book reviewer Sunday Columbus Dispatch, 1967-77, Asia Mail, 1976-77. Bd. dirs. Ohio Poetry Day, 1968-77. Recipient Valley Forge Honor certificate Freedoms Found., 1976, certificate Columbus Art League, 1976; named hon. citizen of Paris, 1951; named to Ohio Women's Hall of Fame, 1982. Mem. English Speaking Union (br. pres. 1966-69), Ohio Arts Council (lit. panel 1966-70), Ohio Press Women, Women in Communication (pres. Columbus 1973), World Assn. Women Journalists and Writers, Nat. League Am. Pen Women, MacDowell Soc., Overseas Press Club, DAR, Sigma Delta Chi, Kappa Kappa Gamma (Woman of Achievement 1974). Author: (juvenile) Star Stories, 1970; Spaceships of the Ancients, 1978; Korean Legends, 1979; A Walk Among Clouds, 1980; Why the Cock Crows Three Times, 1980; The Gazelle and the Hunter, 1980; also weekly newspaper column. Home: 10224 Linden Ln Overland Park KS 66207

FOLEY, DONNA BRESLAWSKI, manufacturing engineer; b. Brockport, N.Y., Dec. 2, 1958; d. Daniel and Nancy Lee Breslawski; m. Kirk Andrew Foley, June 2, 1984. A.A.S. in Drafting and Design, SUNY at Morrisville, 1979; B.Tech. in Mech. Design Tech., SUNY at Utica, 1981. Asst. engr. Utica Screw Products, Inc. (N.Y.), 1980-81, engr., 1981-82; mfg. engr., mgr. quality control O.P. Held, Inc., Utica, 1982—. Mem. Nat. Screw Machine Products Assn., Soc. Mfg. Engrs. Home: 744 Herkimer Rd Utica NY 13502 Office: 1303 Rutger St Utica NY 13504

FOLEY, HELEN ANN, state legislator; b. Las Vegas, Nev., Oct. 20, 1953; student U. Nev., Reno, 1971-73; B.A. in Polit. Sci., U. Nev., Las Vegas, postgrad., 1982—. Mem. staff U.S. Senate Com. on Rules and Adminstrn., Washington, 1975-76; aide to Senator Howard W. Cannon, Washington, 1974-75, Congressman James Santini, Las Vegas, 1976-78; dir. devel. Opportunity Village for Retarded Citizens, Las Vegas, 1978-81; mem. Nev. Assembly, 1981-82; mem. Nev. Senate, 1983—. Bd. dirs. Aid to Adoption of Spl. Kids; past v.p. Nev. Young Democrats; mem. Clark County Dem. Central Com. Roman Catholic. Club: Jr. League. Office: Nev Senate State Capitol Carson City NV 89710

FOLEY, KATHLEEN A., advertising agency executive; b. Fresh Meadows, N.Y., Oct. 15, 1952; d. Thomas and Audrey Foley; grad. Marymount Coll., 1974; student Inst. European Studies, Vienna, Austria, 1973-74; grad. Mgmt. Program, Smith Coll., 1985. With Ogilvy & Mather, Inc., N.Y.C., 1974—, account exec., 1981-82, account supr., 1982—, v.p., 1983—. Class rep. Marymount Coll. Alumnae Assn., 1974—. Roman Catholic. Clubs: N.Y. Health and Racquet (N.Y.C.). Office: 2 E 48th St New York NY 10017

FOLEY, MARY MIX, architectural writer, editor; b. Muncie, Ind., Oct. 14, 1918; d. Charles Melvin and Margaret Louisa (Tracy) Mix; m. Justin John Foley, June 4, 1949; 1 son, Stephen Prescott. B.A., Syracuse U., 1940; postgrad. Columbia U., 1944-45. Asst. editor McCall's Mag., N.Y.C., 1940-43; assoc. editor Archtl. Forum, N.Y.C., 1943-49; exec. staff mem. pub. relations AIA, Washington, 1949-54; author: The American House, 1980; (with Albert Christ-Janer) Modern Church Architecture, 1969; (with others) Housing Choices and Housing Constraints, 1960, Building, U.S.A., 1955; contbr. articles to newspapers and mags.; author brochures. Mem. Soc. Archtl. Historians, Nat. Trust for Historic Preservation.

FOLIART-HARDIN, MARY-ELLEN, lawyer, dental service executive; b. Pitts., Sept. 16, 1948; d. Robert Layton and Eileen (McVay) Foliart; m. Dennis Ralph Hardin, Oct. 29, 1977; children—Robb Dennis, Brooke Ellen. B.A., Calif. State U., 1972; J.D., U. San Fernando Valley Coll. of Law, 1977. Bar: Calif. 1977. Atty. Law Office Melvin Belli, San Francisco, 1977-79; pres. Community Dental Service, Torrance, Calif., 1979—, M.E. Foliart Atty. at Law, Torrance, 1979—; dir. United Health Care Service, Los Angeles, 1983—. Mem. Calif. Bar Assn., Women Lawyers Assn., ABA, Los Angeles Bar Assn. Republican. Club: Palos Verdes Jr. Woman's Association. Office: Community Dental Services Inc 2235 Sepulveda Blvd Torrance CA 90501

FOLK, SHARON LYNN, printing company executive; b. Bellefontaine, Ohio, June 13, 1945; d. Emerson D. and Berdena Isabelle (Brown) F. A.A., Sacred Heart Coll., 1965; D.H.L., 1985; A.B., Belmont Abbey Coll., 1968. Exec. v.p. Nat. Bus. Forms, Inc., Greeneville, Tenn., 1968-73, pres., chmn. bd., 1973—; sec.-treas. Nat. Forms Co., Inc., Gastonia, N.C., 1969-73, chmn., pres., dir., 1973-79; dir. Andrew Johnson Bank, Greenville, chmn. long-range planning com., 1986—; mem.-at-large Forms Mfrs. Credit Interchange, 1975—. Mem. Presdl. steering com. Senator Howard Baker, 1979-80; mem. Republican Presdl. task force 1981—; life mem. Rep. Nat. Com., 1981—; charter mem. Com. 200 1981—, vice-chmn. S.E. region, 1983—, v.p., bd. dirs., Chgo., 1985-86; bd. dirs. Greeneville YMCA, 1977-80, mem. fin. com., 1977-78; bd. dirs. Greeneville United Way, 87, Tenn. Bus. Roundtable, Nashville, 1986—; oblate Order of St. Benedict, Our Lady Help of Christians Abbey, Belmont, N.C., 1967—; mem. parish council Notre Dame Catholic Ch., Greeneville, 1974-75, chmn. parish council, 1985-86; bd. adv. Belmont Abbey Coll., NC, 1984, trustee, 1986—; trustee Sacred Heart Coll., 1985—. Served to 2nd lt. USAF, Civil Air Patrol Aux., 1984—. Mem. Internat. Bus. Forms Industry Assn. (dir. 1982-84, chmn. employee relations com. 1978-83), mem.-at-large. Nat. Bus. Forms Assn., Am. Mgmt. Assn., U.S. Tennis Assn. (life) Airplane Owners and Pilots Assn. Ninety-Nines, Inc., 1980—. Home: 1131 Hixon Ave Greeneville TN 37743 Office: PO Box 1750 Greeneville TN 37744

FOLK, VALERIE, organizational consultant; b. Stoneham, Mass., Aug. 9, 1949; d. George J. and Theresa Sara (Moylan) F. B.S. summa cum laude, Northeastern U., 1978; M.Ed., U. Mass.-Amherst, 1984. Operator, New Eng. Telephone Co., Malden, Mass., 1971-72, clerical asst., Burlington, Mass., 1972-76, service adviser, Waltham, Mass., 1976-77, course developer, generic tng., Marlboro, Mass., 1977-81, tng. mgr. info. systems, Boston, 1981-84, orgnl. cons., Boston, 1984—. Mem. Sigma Epsilon Rho. Office: New Eng Telephone 99 High St Room 509 Boston MA 02110

FOLKINS, DOROTHEA MADISON, personnel agency executive, consultant; b. Springfield, Mass., Aug. 10, 1928; d. William Albert and Mae Bernardine (Boardway) Madison; m. Wallace Odber Folkins, Jan. 21, 1950; children—William Anthony, Jeffrey George. Student in acctg. Am. Internat. Coll., Springfield, Mass., 1945, student in math., 1973. Acct. for real estate firm, Longmeadow, Mass., 1963-75; field rep. March of Dimes, Springfield, 1975-76; personnel cons. Barker Personnel Service, Springfield, 1976-81, owner, personnel cons., 1981—; resume adviser; small bus. acct. Past treas. and exec. sec. Community Scholarship Clearing House, Springfield; past ofcl. Western Mass. Basketball Ofcls. Assn.; mem. by-law com., vice chmn. elem. sch. bldg. com., sec. town facilities study com., vice chmn. elem. sch. study com. Town of Longmeadow; co-chmn. games com. Longmeadow Bicentennial Com.; first pres., co-chmn. snack bar Longmeadow Baseball Assn. Aux.; chmn. Heart Sunday, Longmeadow, March of Dimes Mother's March, Longmeadow; various chairmanships Longmeadow Maternal Assn.; coffee shop chmn. Wesson Women's Hosp. Aux., Springfield; corporator Bay State Med. Ctr. Aux., Springfield; past pres., bd. dirs., sec., ways and means chmn., nominating chmn. St. Mary's Guild, Longmeadow. Recipient Life Membership award as founder Basketball Hall of Fame, Springfield, 1974. Mem. Nat. Personnel Assocs., Mass. Bus. Assn., Nat. Assn. Female Execs. Republican. Roman Catholic. Avocations: bridge; reading; antique glass collecting; sports. Home: 128 S Park Ave Longmeadow MA 01106 Office: Barker Personnel Service 333 Bridge St Springfield MA 01103

FOLLANSBEE, DOROTHY L. (DOROTHY L. LELAND), publisher; b. St. Louis, Mar. 24, 1911; d. Robert Leathan and Minnie Cowden (Yowell) Lund; grad. Sarah Lawrence Coll., 1931; m. Austin Porter Leland, Apr. 24, 1935 (dec. 1975); children—Mary Talbot Leland MacCarthy, Austin Porter Jr. (dec.), Irene Austin Leland Barzantny; m. 2d, Robert Kerr Follansbee, Oct. 20, 1979. Pres., Station List Publ. Co., St. Louis, 1975—; dir. Downtown St. Louis Inc. Hon. chmn. Old Post Office Landmark Com., 1975—; bd. dirs. Services Bur. St. Louis, 1943, pres., 1951; bd. dirs. Robert E. Lee Meml. Assn.; bd. dirs. Stratford Hall, Va., 1953—, pres., 1967-70, treas., 1970—; mem. St. Louis County Parks and Recreation Dept., 1969; bd. dirs. Historic Bldgs. Commn. St. Louis County, 1959-85, Mo. Hist. Soc., 1960-77, Mo. Mansion Preservation Com., 1975-80, Chatillon DeMenil House, 1977-79. Recipient Landmarks award Landmarks Assn. St. Louis, 1974; Pub. Service award GSA, 1978;

Crownenshield award Nat. Trust for Hist Preservation, 1979. Mem. Colonial Dames Am., Daus. of Cin., Episcopalian. Clubs: St. Louis Country, Fox Chapel Golf, Princeton of N.Y., St. Louis Jr. League. Home: 35 Pointer Ln St Louis MO 63124 also 1001 River Oaks Dr Pittsburgh PA 15215 Office: 1221 Locust St Saint Louis MO 63101

FOLLANSBEE, NANCY DAMON, investment management executive; b. Rochester, N.Y., Dec. 1, 1958; d. Winthrop Damon and Carolyn (Allen) Follansbee. B.A., William Smith Coll., 1980. Corp. sec., mgr. mktg. services Grace Capital Inc., N.Y.C., 1980—; corp. sec. Dirs. Capital Inc., N.Y.C., 1982—, Dirs. Mgmt. Corp., N.Y.C., 1983—; guest lectr. Am. Mgmt. Assn., N.Y.C., 1983. Tutor Vol. Services for Children, N.Y.C., 1982—; corr. Prison Action Group, Rochester, 1980. Mem. No-Load Mut. Fund Assn. Republican. Presbyterian. Home: 3 Nordling Ln Madison NJ 07940 Office: Grace Capital Inc 30 Broad St New York NY 10004

FOLLETT, JANE LOUISE, nurse, clinical nurse manager; b. Holyoke, Mass., July 12, 1958; d. Warren Osborne and Mary Jane (Salamon) F. B.S. in Nursing, Fitchburg State Coll., Mass., 1980. R.N. Staff nurse Baystate Med. Ctr., Springfield, Mass., 1980-83, clin. nurse mgr., 1983—, quality assurance, unit ops., 1984—, documentation task force mem., 1985—. Music com. Granby Congl. Ch., sec. 1982—. Recipient Donald F. Graham Meml. award S. Hadley High Sch., 1980. Mem. Sigma Theta Tau, Epsilon Beta. Club: Callboard Dance Theatre. Avocations: music; sing in musicals; cake decorating; calligraphy; arts and crafts. Home: 359 Hampden St Chicopee MA 01013 Office: Baystate Med Ctr Chestnut St Springfield MA 01107

FOLLETT, MARY VIERLING, artist, art conservator, appraiser; b. Chgo., Feb. 9, 1917; d. Arthur Garfield and Grace May (Cummings) Vierling; student U. Southern Calif., 1932-34, grad. Acad. Profl. Art Conservators, 1975, Masters, 1978; m. Garth Benepe Follett, Feb. 16, 1945; 1 dau., Dawn Goshorn; 3 stepchildren. Exhibited in group shows Palette and Chisel Acad. Fine Arts, 1975, 76, 77, 78, Municipal Art League, 1972-78, others; represented in permanent collection Fla., Calif., Italy, others; owner, operator Paintin' Place, gallery, Oak Park, Ill., 1973—; dir. Palette and Chisel Acad. Fine Arts, Chgo., 1975-76. Vice pres. Oak Park LWV, 1952-54, welfare chmn., 1956-58; treas. Oak Park Council Internat. Affairs, 1962-74. Recipient Gold medal Palette and Chisel Acad. Fine Arts, 1976-77, 1st award Civics and Art Found. Union League Chgo., 1977. Mem. Oak Park River Forest Art League (v.p., dir. 1981-82), Pen Women Am., Municipal Art League Chgo., Art Inst. Assos. Oak Park and River Forest (women's bd. 1967—), Oak Park River Forest Hist. Soc. Club: 19th Century Women's. Home: 1440 Park Ave River Forest IL 60305 Office: 820 North Blvd Oak Park IL 60301

FOLLETTE, LISA JOY, accountant; b. Washington, Dec. 7, 1961; d. Lysle Shirland and Denyce LaVerne (Hunt) F. B.S. in Acctg., Oakwood Coll., 1983; student Columbia Union Coll., 1980-81. Clk. typist FDA, Silver Spring, Md., 1980-83; acctg. clk. Oakwood Coll., Huntsville, Ala., 1982-83; asst. acct. Control Data Corp., Mpls., 1983-85, assoc. acct., 1985-86, acct., 1986—. Asst. treas. Glendale Seventh-day Adventist Ch., Mpls., 1983-86, DuPont Park Seventh-Day Adventist Ch., Washington, 1986—. Mem. Nat. Assn. Female Execs., Nat. Assn. Black Accts. Democrat. Avocations: piano, singing, bowling, golf. Home: 1603 Crestline Rd Silver Spring MD 20904 Office: Control Data Corp 1800 N Beauregard St Alexandria VA 22311

FOLSOM, RODDELLE BRANTLEY, librarian; b. Washington County, Ga., Mar. 8, 1925; d. Roger Tennyson and Evona (Smith) Brantley; student South Ga. Coll., 1941-42, 43-44; B.S. in Edn., U. Ga., 1955; M.L.S., Fla. State U., 1973; m. Elton Brown Folsom, May 30, 1946; 1 dau., Kathryn Yvonne. Tchr. elem. and high schs., Ga., 1944-51; extension librarian S. Ga. Regional Library, Valdosta, 1952-71, acting dir., 1971-73, dir., 1973—. Bd. dirs. Valdosta Girl's Club, 1977-79, sec., 1978-79; bd. dirs., adult edn. dir. Valdosta Tech. Sch., 1982-83. Mem. AAUW (editor newsletter 1975), Southeastern Library Assn., Ga. Library Assn., Lowndes Adult Edn. Assn. (pres. 1977-78), Valdosta and Lowndes County Library Assn. (pres. 1981-82), S. Ga. Associated Libraries, Tri-State Library Assn. Democrat. Baptist. Clubs: Wymoduasis (1st v.p. 1982-84, pres. 1984—), Quota (1st v.p. 1978-79, pres. 1979-80, governing bd. women's bldg. 1984—). Home: 1110 Dellwood Dr Valdosta GA 31602 Office: 300 Woodrow Wilson Dr Valdosta GA 31602

FOLSOM, WYNELLE STOUGH, wood products manufacturing executive; b. Bankston, Ala., July 19, 1924; d. Richard Carey and Ora Beatrice (Fowler) Stough; m. Eugene Bragg Folsom, Sept. 3, 1944; children—Don Wayne, Dana L. Student U. Ala., 1962-63, Draughan Bus. Coll., Montgomery, Ala., 1941-42, Alexander State Coll., Alexander City, Ala., 1967-68, Chilton Vocat. & Tech. Sch., Clanton, Ala., 1969-70. Sec., Ala. Power Co., Birmingham, 1942-44; med. librarian Santa Rosa Hosp., San Antonio, 1944-46; payroll clk. Dow Chem. Co., Freeport, Tex., 1946-48; with audit dept. Sears, Roebuck & Co., Selma, Ala., 1956-66; sec.-treas. Oakline Chair Co., Inc., Selma, 1967-83, pres., 1983—. Chmn. publicity Cahaba Regional Library, Clanton, Ala., 1979; mem. Selma-Dallas County Historic Preservation Soc., 1982-85. Mem. Selma C. of C., Bus. and Profl. Women's Club. Republican. Mem. Ch. of Christ. Clubs: Hemorcallis Garden (pres. 1979), Woman's Study (chmn. publicity 1967-79). Avocations: needlework; fishing; reading; painting; gardening. Home: 200 Chris Circle Selma AL 36701 Office: Oakline Chair Co Inc 5017 Water Ave PO Box 871 Selma AL 36701

FONDA, JANE, actress; b. N.Y.C., Dec. 21, 1937; d. Henry and Frances (Seymour) Fonda; student Vassar Coll., 2 years Art Students League, N.Y.C.; pupil acting with Lee Strasberg; m. Roger Vadim, 1966 (div.); 1 child, Vanessa; m. Tom Hayden, Jan. 20, 1973; 1 child, Troy. Appeared with father in summer stocks in The Country Girl, Omaha; actress on Broadway stage in There Was A Little Girl, 1960, The Fun Couple, 1962; in Actor's Studio prodn. Strange Interlude, 1963; appeared in films including: Tall Story, 1960, A Walk on the Wild Side, 1962, Period of Adjustment, 1962, Sunday In New York, 1963, In the Cool of the Day, 1963, The Love Cage, 1963, La Ronde, 1964, Barbarella, They Shoot Horses, Don't They?, 1969, Klute (Acad. award best actress), 1971, Steelyard Blues, 1973, A Doll's House, 1973, The Blue Bird, 1976, Fun With Dick and Jane, 1977, Julia, 1977, Coming Home, 1978 (Acad. award best actress), Comes A Horseman, 1978, California Suite, 1978, The China Syndrome, 1979, The Electric Horseman, 1979, Nine to Five, 1980, Rollover, 1981, On Golden Pond, 1982, The Dollmaker, 1984 (Emmy award best actress), Agnes of God, 1985; The Morning After, 1986. Star, Jane Fonda's Workout Video, others. Author: Jane Fonda's Workout Book, 1981; Jane Fonda's New Workout and Weight-Loss program, 1986; (with Mignon McCarthy) Women Coming of Age, 1984. Recipient Golden Globe award, 1978; N.Y. Film Critics award, 1969, 71; named #1 heroine of young Americans, U.S. News & World Report, 1985; 4th Most Admired Woman in Am., Roper Poll, Ladies Home Jour., 1985. Address: Fonda Films PO Box 491355 Los Angeles CA 90049*

FONDA, SUZANNE WEMYSS, computer manufacturing executive; b. Boston, Dec. 15, 1960; d. John Charles and Barbara (Wemyss) Fonda; m. Mark J. Fitzpatrick, Apr. 11, 1981 (div. 1982). Cert., Katherine Gibbs Sch., 1980. Clk. Town Clks. Office, Weston, Mass., 1978-79; buyer, inventory control The Stichery, Wellesley, Mass., 1979-80; inventory controller Merco Packaging, Canton, Mass., 1980-81; office mgr. Hiller Equip. Co., Okla. City, 1981-82, Welco Petroleum Co., Okla. City, 1982-83; co. coordinator U.S. Pixel Corp., Framingham, Mass., 1984—. Mem. Tng. for Intervention Procedures by Servers of Alcohol, Nat. Assn. Female Execs. Mem. United Meth. Ch. Clubs: Nautlas Fitness (Okla. City), Futura Health (Framingham). Avocations: skiing, water skiing, tennis, weight lifting, jazz dance. Office: U S Pixel Corp 59 Fountain St Framingham MA 01701

FONDILLER, SHIRLEY HOPE ALPERIN, nurse, journalist, educator; b. Holyoke, Mass.; d. Samuel and Rose (Sobiloff) Alperin; grad. Beth Israel Hosp. Sch. Nursing, Boston; B.S., Tchrs. Coll. Columbia U., 1962, M.A., 1963, M.Ed., 1971, Ed.D., 1979; m. Harvey V. Fondiller, Dec. 27, 1957; 1 son, David Stewart. Staff asst. Am. Nurses Assn., N.Y.C., 1963-64, dir. ednl. adminstrs., cons. and tchrs. sect., 1964-66, coordinator Am. Nurses Assn.-Nat. League for Nursing careers program, 1967-70; coordinator clin. sessions Am. Nurses Assn., 1971-72, editor Am. Nurse, Kansas City, Mo., 1975-79; asso. prof., asst. to dean for spl. projects Rush-Presbyn.-St. Luke's Med. Center, Chgo., 1979—. Mem. Kappa Delta Pi, Sigma Theta Tau. Writer, columnist Nursing World, 1955-60; film reviewer Am. Jour. Nursing, 1963-64, Film News, 1963-66; writer, dir. The Open Door, radio documentary, 1960; contbg. editor Am. Jour. Nursing, 1971-75; author books and articles on nursing, health care, edn. Home: 1550 N Lake Shore Dr Chicago IL 60610

FONES, BEATRICE DE HART WILLIAMS, government official; b. Swain County, N.C., Aug. 5, 1936; d. Arthur A. and Lexie I. (McMahan) DeH.; B.S.B.A., U. N.C., Chapel Hill, 1958; m. Ronald G. Williams, June 27, 1959; children—Roger David, Tina Marie; m. Robert W. Fones, Aug. 3, 1973. Staff auditor Hoffmann and Rink, C.P.A.s, summer 1957; traffic clk. DeHart Motor Lines, Inc., Hickory, N.C., 1958-59, personnel and safety dir., 1959-60; auditor Library of Congress, Washington, 1962-63, 68-70; owner, operator Hickory Custom Finishing Co. (N.C.), 1963-65; customer service rep. Nat. Cash Register Co., Hickory, 1965-66, Greensboro, N.C., 1966-67; cost acct. Western Electric Co., Greensboro, 1967; auditor D.C. Govt. Office Mcpl. Audit, 1970-73; sr. auditor Capital region Naval Audit Service, Washington, 1973-80, fed. women's program mgr., 1977-80; auditor office audit EEOC, Washington, 1980—; mem. Handicapped Employees Adv. Commn.; chairwoman supervisory com. D.C. Govt. Employee Credit Union; auditor Library of Congress Credit Union. Recipient Unit Meritorious award Sec. Navy, 1977, letter of appreciation Comptroller Gen. Navy, 1979, Audit of Quarter award Navy Audit, 1979, 80. Mem. Assn. Govt. Accts. (chpt. exec. com. 1971-73, 2d pl. in research competition 1972, cert. appreciation chpt. 1972, 73), Am. Soc. Mil. Comptrollers, Federally Employed Women (fin. chmn.), Nat. Assn. Female Execs., U. N.C. Alumni Assn. (life). Developed programmed text on appropriation acctg. for Navy Audit trainees. Home: 3423 Holly Rd Annandale VA 22003 Office: 2401 E St NW Washington DC

FONTAINE, BARBARA ALICE, lawyer, educator; b. Woonsocket, R.I., Dec. 8, 1935; d. John Nelson and Alice Claire (Hackett) Fontaine. A.B. in Chemistry, Brown U., 1959; M.A. L.S. in Physics, Wesleyan U., 1970; J.D., Pace U., 1981. Bar: 1982, Fed. 1983. Tchr. chemistry and physics Lincoln Sch., Providence, 1960-62; vol. U.S. Peace Corps, Ethiopia, 1962-64; tchr. chemistry and physics, head dept. Bellingham High Sch., (Mass.), 1964-69; tchr. chemistry and physics Ardsley High Sch. (N.Y.), 1969-81; lectr. math. Community Coll. of R.I., Lincoln, 1983-84; sole practice law, Wakefield, R.I., 1982—. Mem. Conservation Law Found., Providence, 1982-85; cons., spl. asst. atty. gen. R.I., 1985—; v.p. Cath. Alumni Club, N.Y.C., 1977-79; rep. Ardsley Tchrs.' Union, 1974-77; mem. Project Persona, Providence, 1982—; sec. Snug Harbor-East Matunuck Civic Assn., 1983—; bd. dirs. South County Community Action, 1983—, Heritage Playhouse, 1984-85; NSF fellow, 1966-68; recipient cert. of honor Westinghouse Ednl. Found., 1974, 78; Tchr. award Sci. Tchrs. of N.Y. State, 1973. Mem. R.I. Bar Assn., R.I. Trial Lawyers Assn., R.I. Law Inst., Lawyers in Mensa, Mensa (pres. R.I. chpt. 1982-84), Audubon Soc. Democrat. Roman Catholic. Club: R.I. Civic Chorale. Home: 70 Succotash Rd Wakefield RI 02879 Office: 72 Pine St Providence RI 02903

FONTAINE, SUE (JEANE), public relations practitioner; b. Rolfe, Iowa, June 28, 1928; d. Vernette M. and Dorothy (Messinger) Gaskins; B.A. in Journalism, U. Iowa, 1947; M.A. in L.S., U. Mo., 1977; m. Henry A. Fontaine, Jr., July 1, 1948 (div. 1970); children—Eva Joel, Jeffrey David. Radio and TV dir. Swigart Advt., Inc., New Orleans, 1948-54, 1962-65; producer Sta. WDSU-TV, New Orleans, 1954-60; dir. public relations La. State Library, Baton Rouge, 1960-62; Tulsa City-County Library, 1965-67, 70-76; spl. projects asst. U. Mo. Sch. Library/Info. Sci., Columbia, 1976-77; public info. officer Wash. State Library, Olympia, 1977-81; asso. mgr. public relations N.Y. Public Library, N.Y.C., 1981—; audio-visual, public relations cons. to various libraries and comml. clients, 1960—. Recipient 5 John Cotton Dana Public Relations award, 1965-75. Mem. Public Relations Soc., ALA (sect. and com. chmn., chmn. bd.), Women in Communications (chpt. pres.), N.Y. Library Assn., Alpha Xi Delta, Episcopalian. Editor: (with Susan Phelps) Communications for the Humanities, 1975; Public Relations: Tick/Click, 1975; Best of Library Literature, 1981; contbr. articles to profl. jours. Office: New York Public Library Fifth Ave at 42nd St New York NY 10018

FONTANA, BARBARA JEAN, legislative analyst, nutritionist; b. Chgo., Sept. 9, 1946; d. Robert Alfred and Virginia (Hartmann) Lubker; children—Brent, Ryan. B.S., Cornell U., 1968; M.A., San Francisco State U., 1974; Ph.D., U. Md.-College Park, 1983. Dietitian, Yale U., 1968-71; food service tng. Fremont Schs. (Calif.), 1973-77; research nutritionist Georgetown U., 1977-78; nutrition edn. chief food programs U.S. Dept. Agr., Washington, 1978-80, nutritionist Extension Service, 1980-81, exec. sec. Nat. Agrl. Research and Extension Users Adv. Bd., 1981-84; staff dir. agr. Nat. Govs. Assn., 1984—; lectr., advisor San Francisco State U., 1976-77. Office: Nat Govs Assn Hall of the States 444 N Capitol St Washington DC 20001

FONTENOT, JUDY DAVIS, entrepreneur; b. Bradenton, Fla., May 4, 1945; d. Glen Randolph and Louise (Duffey) D.; m. J. Roger Fontenot; children—Kristina Louise, Virginia Dianne, Georgia Glen. B.A., Brenau Coll., 1967. Owner Norrell Temporary Service, Orlando, Fla., 1973—. Dalindy Personnel, Orlando, 1980—; exec. v.p. Currier Davis Pub., Orlando, 1984—. Mem. Sales and Mktg. Execs. (v.p.), Fla. Exec. Women, Exec. Women Internat. Republican. Baptist. Clubs: Citrus (dir.), Horizon (chmn. bd.). Office: Norrell Services 2445 Lee Rd Winter Park FL 32789

FONTENOT, MARGARET MILNER, nurse, office manager; b. Eunice, La., Nov. 7, 1951; d. Garnett Alvin and Audrey (Clayton) Milner; m. Paul Roy Fontenot, Aug. 8, 1970; children—Kathryn, Donna, Jason, Kelly. Staff nurse Ville Platte Gen. Hosp., La., 1976-79; physician's asst., office mgr. Dr. Pedro Mora's Office, Ville Platte, 1981—. Mem. 1st Gov.'s Conf. on Women, Baton Rouge, 1976, pres., organizer Friends of the Library, Ville Platte. Mem. Am. Bus. Women's Assn. (chmn. membership com.), Beta Sigma Phi. Republican. Roman Catholic. Club: Magnolia Garden of Ville Platte. Avocations: reading; music; needlework; antique restoration. Home: Route 1 Box 704 Ville Platte LA 70586 Office: PO Box 299 1009 W Lincoln Rd Ville Platte LA 70586

FONTS, PATRICIA DIANNE, educator; b. Chgo.; d. Alfred Allen Crisler and Ida Lee (Brown) Crisler Thorpe; m. Brigido Castillo Fonts, III, June 24, 1973 (div.); 1 child, Brigido Castillo IV. B.S. in Edn., Chgo. State U., 1975; postgrad. Roosevelt U. Tchr. pub. schs., Chgo., 1975-80, Archdiocese of Chgo., 1985—; tng. specialist Mayor's Office of Employment Tng., 1980-84. Mem. Nat. Cath. Edn. Assn., NEA, Nat. Assn. Female Execs., Nat. Bus. Edn. Assn. Exec. Females, Alpha Kappa Alpha. Avocations: horticulture, cooking, music.

FOO, ANNABELLA SAI-YAN, pharmacy director; b. Taiwan, Mar. 23, 1956; came to U.S., 1974; d. Chan Yim and Tang Fong (Lai) Fu. Student Miss. U. for Women, 1974-76; B.S. in Pharmacy, SUNY-Buffalo, 1979; postgrad. in Fine Arts and Liberal Arts, U. Tex.-Arlington, 1980, in Mgmt., Am. Mgmt. Assn., 1982. Lic. pharmacist, Tex., Nev., Calif. Pharmacy intern Buffalo Gen. Hosp., 1978-79, Hurst-Euless-Bedford Hosp., Bedford, Tex., 1979; pharmacist John Peter Smith Hosp., Fort Worth, 1979-82, pharmacist supr., 1982-83, pharmacy dir., 1983—. Scholar, Miss. U. for Women, 1974-76; tuition waiver SUNY, Buffalo, 1977-79; recipient award for painting, Arlington Community Ctr., 1980. Mem. Am. Soc. Hosp. Pharmacists, Tex. Soc. Hosp. Pharmacists, N.Central Tex. Soc. Hosp. Pharmacists, Nat. Assn. Female Execs., Rho Chi. Avocations: Fine arts; theater; reading; travel. Home: 7509 Acapulco Rd Fort Worth TX 76112 Office: John Peter Smith Hospital 1500 S Main St Fort Worth TX 76104

FOOR, SHIRLEY JEAN, newspaper editor; b. Northville, Mich., Mar. 1, 1938; d. Royal Clarence and Dorothe Sara (Kent) Snow; m. Benjamin Charles Foor, Aug. 24, 1956 (div. Sept. 1981); children—Laurie Foor Meyer, Sharon, Timothy, Daniel, Jonathan. Student Black Hawk Coll., Moline, Ill., 1971-76, Manatee Jr. Coll., Bradenton, Fla., 1978-79, U. South Fla., Tampa, 1984—. Feature writer The Daily Dispatch, Moline, Ill., 1971-72, reporter, 1972-73, asst. state editor, 1973-76; asst. city editor The Bradenton (Fla.) Herald, 1976-77, city editor, 1977-80, mng. editor, 1980-85; editor, The Islander, Anna Maria, Fla. Bd. dirs. pres. Manatee County Girls Club, Inc., Bradenton, 1980-85; mem. Manatee County LWV, Bradenton, 1981; organizer, mem. Manatee County Women's Network, Bradenton, 1980—; bd. dirs. Manatee Artificial Kidney and Disease Prevention Ctr., Bradenton, 1981-82. Named Chpt. Woman of Yr., Am. Bus. Women's Assn., 1978. Mem. Nat. Fedn. Press Women (merit award, editorial writing 1984), Fla. Press Women (merit award, editorial writing 1984), Fla. Soc. Newspaper Editors, Am. Bus. Women's Assn. (charter pres. 1977-78). Democrat. Roman Catholic. Office: The Islander 314 Pine Ave Anna Maria FL 33501

FOOS, AVIS MAUREEN, lawyer; b. Portland, Oreg., Oct. 8, 1954; d. John David and Carolyn May (Faulkner) F. B.A. magna cum laude, in Human Services, Western Wash. State U., 1976; J.D. cum laude, U. Puget Sound, 1982. Bar: Calif. 1982, U.S. Dist. Ct. (no. dist.) Calif. 1982, U.S. Dist. Ct. (cen. dist.) Calif. 1983. Assoc. firm Cordova, Quinlan & Ruzicka, Newport Beach, Calif. Assoc. editor U. Puget Sound Law Rev., 1980-82; contbr. articles to legal jours. Mem. ABA, Calif. Bar Assn., Los Angeles County Bar Assn., White's Inn Soc. Home: 177 Riverside Ave Newport Beach CA 92663 Office: Cordova Quinlan & Ruzicka 359 San Miguel Ave Newport Beach CA 92660

FOOTE, RUTH ANNETTE, title company executive, land developer; b. Riverside, Calif., Nov. 2, 1925; d. Edgar Wallace and Murrel (Sibrell) Thomas; m. Harold Dale Borregard, July 15, 1945 (div.); children—Linda Gail, Valerie Louise, Jennifer; m. Robert Earl Foote, June 24, 1951; children—Robin David, James Wayne. Student pub. schs., San Bernardino, Calif. Comml. closer M.P. Crum Co., Dallas, 1964-67, Trammel Crow Co., Dallas, 1967-69; developer Hidden Valley Airpark, Denton, Tex., 1969-70, exec. sec., 1969-73; escrow officer, mgr. Southwest Land Title, Denton, 1970-75; exec. v.p. Lawyers Title Co, Denton, 1975-80, Attorneys Title Co., Dallas, 1980—; exec. sec., developer Whitehawk Valley, Denton, 1977—; developer Rainbow Valley Property Owners Assn., Denton, 1979—. Author: And the Truth Shall Set You Free, 1980. Mem. Women's Forum Dallas. Republican. Mormon. Pioneered (with Robert Foote) earth sheltered home communities which provide their own electricity, fuel and water. Home: 11700 Audelia St #813 Dallas TX 75243 Office: Attorney Title Co 9500 Forest Ln Suite 428 Dallas TX 75243

FORAKER-THOMPSON, JANE, criminal justice educator, researcher; b. Alhambra, Calif., Oct. 23, 1937; d. Field and Margaret Hall (Foraker) Thompson; m. Laurence E. Lynn, Jr., Aug. 24, 1958 (div. 1972); children—Stephen Louis, Daniel Laurence, Diana Jane, Julia Susanne; m. Edwin Watson Stockly, July 22, 1979. B.A., U. Calif.-Berkeley, 1959, M.A., 1965; postgrad. U. Leiden, Netherlands, summer 1973; Ph.D., Stanford U., 1985. Criminal justice specialist Bernalillo County, Albuquerque, 1974-75; chief planner N.Mex. State Police, Santa Fe, 1975-78; project mgr. restitution project N.Mex. Criminal Justice Dept., Santa Fe, 1978-80; pres. Analysis, Innovation, Devel., Inc., Santa Fe, 1980-81; prof. Boise State U., 1981—; cons. in field. Contbr. articles to profl. jours. Pres., chmn. bd. Alternatives Inc., Albuquerque, 1974-75, N.Mex. Assn. Women in Criminal Justice, 1980-81; exec. com. N.Mex. Council Community Mental Health Services, 1979-80; pres. N.Mex. Task Force on Victims of Sex Crimes, 1978-80; state chair Gov.'s Task Force on Family Policy, N.Mex., 1979-80; pres. Citizens for Prison Change, Inc., N.Mex., 1980-81; active Ada County Citizens for Peace, Idaho, 1983—; leader Northwest Regional New Call to Peacemaking Conf., 1983; bd. dirs., Friends Outside, 1983-85, peace and justice com. Episcopal Diocese Idaho, 1983—. Recipient Women of Yr. award Santa Fe Bus. and Profl. Women, 1980. Mem. Western Assn. Sociology and Anthropology (pres. 1986-87), Am. Soc. Pub. Adminstrn., ABA (criminal justice sect., jails incapacitation and prison com., 1982-83, juvenile justice com. 1983-85), Nat. Orgn. Victim Assistance, Internat. Soc. Law Enforcement and Criminal Justice Instrs., Acad. Criminal Justice Scis., Am. Soc. Criminology. Democrat. Quaker. Office: Boise State U Criminal Justice Dept 1910 University Dr Boise ID 83725

FORAN, KATHRYN ALICIA, social worker; b. Somerville, N.J., Oct. 1, 1943; d. Samuel and Anne (Boriek) Danzig; student Wilmington Coll., 1961-64; B.A., Central State Coll., 1966; postgrad. Okla. State U., 1966-67; M.S.W., U. Okla., 1973; m. William Gates Fink, Apr. 2, 1964 (div. 1974); m. 2d Arthur Francis Foran, III, Feb. 10, 1984. Social worker div. social services Okla. Dept. Human Services, Oklahoma City, 1967-72, social services supr., 1973-74, acting county adminstr., 1974-76, staff asst. for program devel., 1976-77; cons. div. youth and family services N.J. Dept. Human Services, Trenton, 1977, supervising systems analyst and adminstrv. analyst, 1977-79; asst. dir. Region III Adoption Resource Center, Phila., 1979-80; refugee resettlement specialist Office of Refugee Resettlement, U.S. Dept. Health and Human Services, Washington, 1980-81; project dir. Center for Social Policy and Community Devel., Sch. Social Adminstrn. Temple U., Phila., 1981-83; dir. welfare Gloucester County Welfare Bd., Woodbury, N.J., 1983-85; acting exec. dir. Community Services Planning Council Southeastern Pa., Phila., 1985-86, exec. dir., 1986—. Bd. dirs. Phila. Corp. for Aging; mem. adv. com. Phila. Mayor's Office Community Services; mem. rev. com. Gloucester County Human Services Adv. Com. Mem. Zool. Soc. Phila., Assn. Info. and Referral Systems. Nat. Assn. Social Workers, Am. Public Welfare Assn. Office: 7 Benjamin Franklin Pkwy Philadelphia PA

FORBES, CYNTHIA ANN, chemical company executive, marketing educator; b. Richmond, Calif., Dec. 27, 1951; d. James Martin and Mary Jane (Clafferty) Forbes; m. Larry Charles Osofsky, Mar. 20, 1970 (div. 1980); 1 child, Anna. B.A., U. Calif., 1977; M.S., Golden Gate U., 1981. Research asst. U. Calif., Berkeley, 1975-77, Chevron Research, Richmond, 1977-79; specialist dealer affairs Chevron USA, San Francisco, 1979-80, sales rep., San Fafael, Calif., 1981-84, adminstrv. supr., San Ramon, Calif.; 1984-85, advt. mgr. Chevron Chem. Co., San Francisco, 1986—; assoc. prof. Golden Gate U., San Francisco, 1981—. Mem. Contra Costra Women's Network, Nat. Agrimarketers Assn. Democrat. Jewish. Avocations: mountaineering, bicycling. Home: 139 Meadow View Rd Orinda CA 94563 Office: Chevron Chem Co 575 Market St San Francisco CA 94105

FORBES, HARRIETTE OLIVER, artist; b. Atlanta, May 24, 1907; d. James Connor and Harriet (Montgomery) Oliver; m. Philip Ibbotson Forbes, Oct. 21, 1933 (dec. 1973). Student Newcomb Coll. Art Tulane U., 1927-28. Artist-in-residence St. Luke's Ch., Atlanta, 1981—; mem. Art Workers Coalition, Atlanta, 1980-84, Nexus Ctr. Contemporary Art, Atlanta, 1983—. Mem. Nat. Assn. Women Artists (com. fgn. exhibits 1979, S.E. regional com. for exhibits 1984—). Home: 2292B Lindmont Circle NE Atlanta GA 30324

FORBES, JULIA LYNN, nurse; b. Austin, Tex., July 22, 1952; d. Herman Hayes and Connie Mae (Loney) Forbes. Student U. Tex., 1970-73; diploma Austin Community Coll., 1974; cert. paramedic City of Austin, 1976; A.S., San Jacinto Coll., 1982. R.N., Tex. Staff nurse Brackenridge Hosp., Austin, Tex., 1974-76; paramedic, asst. tng. coordinator City of Austin Emergency Med. Services, 1976-79, field evaluator, 1979-80; staff nurse Pasadena Gen. Hosp., Tex., 1980-81, Meml. Southeast Hosp., Houston, 1981-83; tng. coordinator Ft. Bend Co. Emergency Med. Service, Richmond, Tex., 1983-86; nurse in family medicine East Fort Bend Med. Ctr., Stafford, Tex., 1986—; instr. CPR and trainer Am. Heart Assn., Austin and Houston, 1977-80, 83-84; emergency med. service course coordinator Tex. Dept. Health, Austin and Richmond, 1977-80, 83-84; instr. CPR, ARC, Richmond, 1983-86; editor: Protocols and Standing Orders, 1983; developer continuing edn. programs. Troop leader Girl Scouts U.S.A., Austin, 1969-71, cons., 1968-75; instr. community CPR programs, Austin, 1977-80. Named Vol of Yr. Travis County, 1968. Good Samaritan Found. scholar, 1980-82. Mem. Tex. Assn. Emergency Med. Technicians, Emergency Dept. Nurses Assn. Democrat. Methodist. Club: Alief Belly Dance Group (Houston). Office: East Fort Bend Med Ctr 2503 B South Main Stafford TX 77477

FORBES, MAGGIE LOUISE, dietitian; b. Jackson, Miss., July 24, 1940; d. William Aaron and Juanita Louise (McGee) F.; B.S. in Foods, Nutrition and Instl. Mgmt., Wayne State U., 1962. Staff dietitian Fordham Hosp., City of N.Y. Hosp., 1964-66, head dietitian, 1966; asst. chief dietitian, V.I. Govt.-Charles Harwood Meml. Hosp., St. Croix, 1966-68; therapeutic dietitian Annapolis Hosp., Wayne, Mich., 1969-71, adminstrv. dietitian, 1971-75, dir. dietetics, 1975—; cons., preceptor for dietetic asst. and dietetic technician programs at various colls.; cons. comml. foods program Milton Middle Sch. Mem. Am. Dietetic Assn., Am. Soc. Hosp. Food Service Adminstrs., Mich. Dietetic Assn. Roman Catholic. Office: 33155 Annapolis Rd Wayne MI 48184

FORD, AGNES, insurance underwriter; b. Bklyn., Jan. 16, 1948; d. Edward and Anna (Anger) F.; 1 child, James. B.A., Bklyn. Coll., 1971. Cert. in ocean marine ins. Tchr., N.Y.C. Bd. Edn., 1971-72; asst. yacht underwriter Home Ins. Co., N.Y.C., 1972-75; offshore drilling rig underwriter Am. Marine Slip, N.Y.C., 1975-78; reinsurance underwriter Am. Internat. Underwriters, N.Y.C., 1978—. Chairperson Cub Scout pack Greater N.Y. council Boy Scouts Am., Bklyn., 1977-81, mem. com., 1981-84. Mem. Bklyn. Coll. Alumni Assn., Coll. Ins. Alumni Assn., Am. Marine Ins. Forum. Democrat. Roman Catholic. Avocations: dancing; camping; reading. Home: 2418 E 22d St Brooklyn NY 11235 Office: Am Internat Underwriters 70 Pine St New York NY 10270

FORD, ANN SUTER, health care consultant, educator, nurse; b. Mineola, N.Y., Oct. 31, 1943; d. Robert M. and Jennette (Van Derzee) Suter; m. W. Scott Ford, 1964; children—Tracey, Karin. R.N., White Plains Hosp. Sch. Nursing (N.Y.), 1964; B.S.N. with high distinction, U. Ky., 1967; M.S. in Health Planning, Fla. State U., 1971, Ph.D., 1975. Nurse, U. Ky. Med. Ctr., 1964-65, Tallahassee Meml. Hosp., 1968-69; guest lectr. health planning dept. urban and regional planning Fla. State U., Tallahassee, 1973-76, health planner and research assoc., 1974-76, vis. asst. prof., 1976-77, asst. prof. and dir. health planning splty., 1977-83, assoc. prof., 1982-83; health care analyst and policy cons., 1983—; mem. exec. com. human services and social planning tech. dept. Am. Inst. Planners, 1977-78. Author: The Physician's Assistant: A National and Local Analysis, 1975; contbr. numerous articles on health edn. and health planning to profl. jours.; contbr. chpts. to books; author research reports. USPHS grantee, 1965-67; HEW grantee, 1978; Univ. fellow Fla. State U., 1971-72; recipient Am. Inst. Planners' Student award, 1975. Mem. Am. Planning Assn. (charter mem. human services and social planning tech. dept. 1976—, chmn. health planning session Oct. 1978, 79, health policy liaison 1979-83, author assn. health policy statement), Am. Health Planning Assn., Phi Kappa Phi. Address: 2602 Cline St Tallahassee FL 32312

FORD, CYNTHIA, lawyer; b. San Francisco, Sept. 29, 1954; d. James Alexander Ford and June Josephine (Collins) Brack; m. Laurence Turner Paddock, Jr., May 28, 1977. A.B., Dartmouth Coll., 1975; J.D., Cornell U., 1978. Bar: Wash. Assoc., Crowley, Haughey, Hanson, Toole & Dietrich, Billings, Mont., 1978-83, Davis, Wright, Todd, Riese & Jones, Seattle, 1983—; vol. atty. King County Guardian ad Litem Program, Seattle, 1983—; v.p. women's law sect. Mont. Bar Assn., 1982. Bd. dirs. Seattle Rape Relief, 1983-84; adv. com. Bainbridge Trail System, 1984; docent Woodland Park Zoo, 1984; dir., counselor Billings Rape Task Force, 1979-82. Mem. ABA, Mont. Bar Assn., Washington/King County Bar Assn. Home: 7758 W Port Madison Rd Bainbridge Island WA 98110 Office: Davis Wright Todd Riese & Jones 4200 Seattle 1st National Bank Bldg Seattle WA 98104

FORD, DELORES CONLEY, learning resources specialist; b. Galveston, Tex., Aug. 17, 1949; d. James and Bertha Mae (Mallard) Conley; m. Roy Lee Ford, Aug. 14, 1971; children—Roy Princeton, Roy Shawn. B.S. in Elem. Edn., No. Tex. State U., 1970; M.S., U. Houston, 1981. Cert. tchr. elem. edn., learning resource specialist, Tex. Tchr., Port Arthur Ind. Sch. Dist. (Tex.), 1971, Houston Ind. Sch. Dist., 1971-77; tchr., North Forest Ind. Sch. Dist., Houston, 1977-78, librarian LaMarque Ind. Sch. Dist. (Tex.), 1978-79, tchr., 1979-80; computer coordinator Lakewood Elem. Sch., Houston, 1981—; presenter-story-telling Internat. Reading Assn. Conv., San Antonio, Jan., 1981; presenter other confs. Instr. C. H. Mason Bible Coll., Houston, 1983-84; PAFLE chmn. PTA, Houston, 1982-84. Mem. Tex. Library Assn., Greater Houston Are Reading Council, Tex. Assn. Ednl. Tech., Delta Sigma Theta. Democrat. Mem. Pentecostal Ch. Home: 8442 Bigwood St Houston TX 77078 Office: North Forest Ind Sch Dist Lakewood Elem Sch 8800 Grandriver Dr Houston TX 77078

FORD, E. DIANE, artist; b. Ruston, La., Mar. 28, 1934; d. Amos Weeks and Elizabeth M. (Clark) F.; B.A., La. Tech. U., 1956; M.A., Tex. Women's U., 1961; Ed.D., North Tex. State U., 1967; m. Robert William Gruebel, July 22, 1978. Tchr., Dallas schs., 1956-65; mem. faculty Stephen F. Austin State U., Nacogdoches, Tex., 1965—, asso. prof. art, 1972—. Mem. Nat. Art Edn. Assn., Handweavers Guild Am., Tex. Art Edn. Assn., Contemporary Handweavers Tex., Daus. Republic Tex., Colonial Dames 17th Century, Phi Delta Kappa. Home: 2408 Pinecrest Dr Nacogdoches TX 75961 Office: Stephen F Austin State U Box 13001 Nacogdoches TX 75962

FORD, ELIZABETH BLOOMER (BETTY FORD), wife of former Pres. U.S.; b. Chgo., Apr. 8, 1918; d. William Stephenson and Hortence (Neahr) Bloomer; student Bennington Sch. Dance, 1936-38; LL.D. (hon.), U. Mich., 1976; m. William Warren, 1942 (div. 1947); m. 2d, Gerald R. Ford (38th Pres. U.S.), Oct. 15, 1948; children—Michael Gerald, John Gardner, Steven Meigs, Susan Elizabeth. Dancer, Martha Graham Concert Group, N.Y.C., 1939-41; model John Powers Agy., N.Y.C., 1939-41; fashion dir. Herpolsheimer's Dept. Store, Grand Rapids, Mich., 1943-48; dance instr., Grand Rapids, 1932-1948. Chmn., Heart Sunday, Washington Heart Assn., 1974; pres. Red Cross Senate Wives Club; patron Salvation Army Aux. Ann. Fashion Show Luncheon; active benefits Hosp. for Sick Children, Washington; hon. chmn. crusade Am. Cancer Soc., 1975; trustee Eisenhower Med. Center; bd. dirs. Betty Ford Center; trustee Martha Graham Center Contemporary Dance; mem. Nat. Commn. Observance Internat. Women's Yr., 1977. Named Woman of Yr., Ladies Home Jour. Episcopalian (Sunday sch. tchr. 1961-64). Author: (autobiography) The Times of My Life, 1979.

FORD, EMMA MAE, educational administrator; b. Columbia, S.C., Mar. 25, 1954; d. Issac and Emma (Brown) Mundy; m. Willie Joseph Ford, June 12, 1982. A.A., Wayne County Community Coll., 1973; B.B.A., U. Detroit, 1980; M.A., Central Mich. U., 1982. Credit rep. Beneficial Fin. Co., Detroit, 1972-73; engring. asst. Mich. Bell Telephone Co., Livonia, 1973-75; acad. coordinator Wayne County Community Coll., Detroit, 1976—, part-time bus. faculty, 1980—; mgmt. cons. Ford's Cons. Firm, Southfield, Mich., 1982—. Editor: State Ch. Newspaper Mich. Triumphant Star, 1981. Mem. Female Execs. Inc., Am. Bus. Women's Assn., Booker T. Washington Bus. Assn. Democrat. Home: 20775 Greenview Rd Southfield MI 48075 Office: Wayne County Community Coll 801 W Fort St Detroit MI 48226

FORD, ERMA ALICE, retired educator, utility company executive; b. Stamford, Nebr., July 27, 1916; d. Henry and Alice Moss (Arnold) Busch; m. John Patterson Ford, Aug. 19, 1951; children—John Patterson III, Erma Kathleen. B.S. in Edn., Nebr. State Coll., 1938; postgrad. UCLA. Cert. secondary tchr., Nebr.; cert. secondary tchr., Calif. Bus. tchr. Clay Ctr. High Sch., Nebr., 1938-41, Paxton High Sch., Nebr., 1941-43, Deuel County High Sch., Chappell, Nebr., 1943-44, Scottsbluff High Sch., Nebr., 1946-49, Oxnard Union High Sch., Calif., 1949-53; secondary substitute Los Angeles Sch. System, 1960-66; pres., sec. A & B Electric Co., Inc., Oxnard, 1970—; mem. consumer adv. task force Gen. Telephone, Santa Monica, Calif., 1984—. Served with USN, 1944-46. Mem. Oxnard Bus. Profl. Women Assn. (pres. 1983-85), Coast Dist. Bus. Profl. Women Assn. (social service, civic edn. com. 1985—), Delta Kappa Gamma. Democrat. Mem. Christian Ch. Club: Navy Women (treas. 1981) (Ventura County, Calif.). Avocations: Crafts; needlework. Home: 392 Harvard St Oxnard CA 93030 Office: A & B Electric Co Inc 2965 Ventura Blvd Oxnard CA 93030

FORD, KATHLEEN, artist, designer, writer; b. San Francisco, Mar. 3, 1932; d. Edward Francis and Mary Catherine (Donnelly) Dowd; student San Francisco Coll. for Women. 1950-53; B.A. in Design, Salinger Sch. Design, San Francisco, 1954. Head designer swimwear Gantner of Calif., San Francisco, 1954-55; asst. designer Jantzen, Inc., Seattle, 1955-56; owner, mgr. Kathleen Dowd Boutique, Sausalito, Calif., 1956-62; designer Constructions For Sound and Video, objects for manufacture, 1976—; author: The Three-Cornered House, 1968; The End (film); Last And 1/2 (film); author, designer American Point 50 (film); author screenplays The Rocker and Sweetheart, Key Grip, Kicked Out!, Bel Air Bump!; authored kits for making miniature prodns.; dir. The Loyola Internat. Art Consortium. Mem. Contemporary Authors, Writers Guild of Am. Home: 425 Castenada Ave San Francisco CA 94116

FORD, LEE ELLEN, lawyer; b. Auburn, Ind., June 16, 1917; d. Arthur Whitten and Geneva Myrtle (Muhn) F. B.S., Wittenberg U., Springfield, Ohio, 1947; M.S. in Cytogenetics, U. Minn., 1949; Ph.D. in Cytogenetics, Iowa State Coll.-Ames, 1952; J.D., U. Notre Dame, 1972. Bar: Ind. 1972. Assoc. prof. Gustavus Adolphus Coll., St. Peter, Minn., 1950-51; assoc. prof. and prof. biology and cytogentics various colls., 1952-69; sci. researcher Inst. Research Mental Retardation, Seattle, 1965-66; prof. biology, head dept. Carson Coll., Carson City, Nev., 1966-67; sole practice law, Auburn Ind., 1972—; aide to gov. Ind., 1972-75; cons. in field. Contbr. articles in fields of sci., dog breeding and tng. to profl. jours; author/editor: Womens Legal Handbook Encyclopedia, over 100 vols., 1972—, Animal Welfare Encyclopedia, over 100 vols., 1972—. Mem., officer City Park Bd., Butler, Ind., 1973-76, City Econ. Devel. Com., Butler, 1973-76, City Planning Commn., Butler, 1973-76; bd. dirs. Assn. Migrant Opportunity Services; Indpls., 1975-80, Farm Workers Involved in Community Services, Indpls., 1980-82; bd. dirs. Social Services Bd. of Ind. Ky. Synod of Lutheran Ch. Am., 1981—; bd. dirs. Lutheran Social Services, Ft. Wayne, Ind., 1983—; mem., officer Sheriff Merit Bd., Auburn, Ind., 1983—; mem. U.S. Pres.'s Nat. Inst. Drug Adminstrn. Bd. Mem. ABA, Ind. Bar Assn., DeKalb County Bar Assn., Nat. Assn. Women Lawyers, AAUW. Republican.

FORD, LORETTA C., nurse, educator, univ. dean; b. N.Y.C., Dec. 28, 1920; d. Joseph F. and Nellie A. (Williams) Pfingstel; R.N., Middlesex Gen. Hosp., New Brunswick, N.J., 1941; B.S. in Nursing, U. Colo., 1949, M.S., 1951, Ed.D., 1961; D.Sc. (hon.), Ohio State Med Coll.; m. William J. Ford, May 2, 1947; 1 dau., Valerie. Staff nurse New Brunswick Vis. Nurse Service, 1941-42; supr., dir. Boulder County (Colo.) Health Dept., 1947-58; asst. prof., then prof. U. Colo. Sch. Nursing, 1960-72; dean Sch. Nursing, dir. nursing, prof. U. Rochester (N.Y.), 1972—; vis. prof. U. Fla., summer 1968, U. Wash., Seattle, 1974; mem. educators adv. panel GAO; dir. Security Trust Co., Rochester, Rochester Telephone Co. Bd. dirs. Threshold Alte. Youth Services, Easter Seal Soc. Served with Nurse Corps, USAAF, 1942-46. Named Colo. Nurse of Year; recipient N.Y. State Gov.'s award for women in sci., medicine and nursing. Fellow Am. Acad. Nursing; mem. Nat. League Nursing (fellowship, Linda Richards award), Am. Coll. Health Assn. (Boynton award), Am. Nurses Assn., Am. Public Health Assn., Inst. Medicine. Author articles in field, chpts. in books. Office: 601 Elmwood Ave Rochester NY 14618*

FORD, LUCILLE GARBER, college administrator; b. Ashland, Ohio, Dec. 31, 1921; d. Ora Myers and Edna Lucille (Armstrong) Garber; A.A., Stephens Coll., 1942; B.S. in Commerce, Northwestern U., 1944, M.B.A., 1945; Ph.D., Case Western Res. U., 1967; m. Laurence Welsey Ford, Sept. 1, 1946; children—Karen Elizabeth, JoAnn Christine. Asst. sec. corp., personnel dir. A.L. Garber Co., Ashland, 1947-67; chmn. econs. dept., prof. econs. Ashland Coll., 1970, dir. Gill Center for Bus. and Econs. Edn., 1974-86, dean spl. program, 1977-79, dean, 1979-80, v.p., dean Sch. Bus., 1980-86, v.p. acad. affairs, 1986—; dir. Ohio Edison, Nat. City Bank, Nat. City Corp., Shelby Mut. Ins. Co., A. Schulman Co.; instr. Allegheny Coll., Meadville, Pa., U. Ala. Past chmn. ARC Mobile, pres. Tb Assn., 1950's; bd. curators Stephens Coll., 1976-80; candidate for lt. gov. State of Ohio, 1978; elder Presbyn. Ch., 1960—; mem. nat. Presbyn. Found. Bd., 1981—. Recipient Disting. Alumni award Stephens Coll., NSF grantee; Martha Holden Jennings Found grantee. Mem. Am. Arbitration Assn. (nat. labor panel), Am. Econs. Assn., Indsl. Relations Research Assn., Nat. Platform Assn., Am. Acad. Sci., Ohio Assn. Economists and Polit. Scientists, Social Econs. Assn., AAUW. Club: Altrusa (hon.). Author: University Economics for Education Majors, 1979; Economics: Learning and Instruction, 1981; lectr. in field. Office: Gill Center Ashland Coll Ashland OH 44805

FORD, MARGARET GIBSON, lawyer; b. New Orleans, May 19, 1947; d. Johnie and Minnie Ree (McCarter) Gibson; m. Richard Henry South, Nov. 4, 1967 (div. 1981); m. 2d, Will Ford, Oct. 31, 1981; children—Richard Henry, James Christopher. B.A., So. U., 1972, J.D., 1983. Bar: La. 1983, U.S. Dist. Ct. La. 1983. Records analyst La. Family Planning, New Orleans, 1968-74; computer operator Fed. Res. Bank, New Orleans, 1973-74; substitute tchr. Orleans Parish Pub. Schs., New Orleans, 1975-77; claims investigator Blue Cross Ins., New Orleans, 1977-80; librarian asst. So. U., Baton Rouge, 1981-83; atty., New Orleans, 1983—; registered agt. Jackquelyn and Assocs., New Orleans, 1983—. Mem. Louis A. Martinet Soc., New Orleans, 1984. Scholar Council on Legal Edn. Opportunity, Washington, 1980-83. Mem. La. Bar Assn., ABA, Am. Judicature Soc. Democrat. Baptist. Home: 1429 Music St New Orleans LA 70117 also 3838 Saint Bernard Ave New Orleans LA 70122

FORD, MAUREEN MORRISSEY, civic worker; b. St. Joseph, Mo., July 1, 1936; d. Albert Joseph and Rosemary Kathryne (FitzSimons) Morrissey; student U. N.Mex., 1953-54, U. Bridgeport (Conn.), 1966-68; B.S., Fairfield U., 1986; m. James Henry Lee Ford, Jr., Feb. 12, 1954; children—Kathryne Elizabeth, Maryellen, James Henry Lee III, William Charles, Maureen Lee. Charity and sch. vol., 1959—; fundraiser for community causes, mus., agys., 1964—; active presdl. campaign Barry Goldwater, 1963-64, congressional campaign Senator Lowell Weiker, 1968; pre-sch. tchr. Nature Center Environ. Activities, 1966-68, trustee, v.p. bd. dirs., 1960-75, v.p. Women's League, 1966-70; mem. exec. com. Republican Women's Club, Westport, 1967-68; leader, trainer Troops on Fgn. Soil br. Girl Scouts USA, Caracas, Venezuela, 1971-72; founding trustee, treas. Kara Mus., Norwalk, Conn.; mem. adv. council Fairfield County (Conn.) for spl. edn. Staples High Sch.; bd. dirs. CLASP; mem. exec. com. Group Home Search; cons., facilitator life planning workshops Merideth Assos., Westport; mem. 1st selectmen's com. on recycling, 1974-75; bd. dirs. PTA, 1976-79; mem. YWCA of Bridgeport Com. of 100 and Task Force; v.p. bd. dirs. YWCA, 1980-87, pres., 1984-85; v.p. Conf. Women's Orgns., Bridgeport; founding mem. Concerned Women Colleagues of Bridgeport; pres. Jr. League Eastern Fairfield County, Inc., 1977-78; v.p., sec. J.H.L.F. Inc., Westport. Mem. Assn. Jr. League Am., Westport Tennis Assn. Roman Catholic. Home: 299 Sturges Hwy Westport CT 06880

FORD, PATRICIA, interior designer; b. Warsaw, N.Y., Feb. 17, 1947; d. Homer James and Ellen Louise (Dixon) F.; B.A. in Fine Arts, UCLA, 1969, M.A. in Fine Arts, 1971. Designer, Herb Rosenthal & Assos., Los Angeles, 1973; sr. designer Charles Kratka Planning and Design, Los Angeles, 1973-75; partner The Ford Wilson Partnership, Los Angeles, 1975-78; pres. Ford Design Group Inc., Los Angeles, 1978-82; dir. interior design Bobrow Thomas & Assocs., architects, Los Angeles, 1982-84; ptnr. Kaneko Ford Design, Los Angeles, 1985—; cons. to Los Angeles Olympic Organizing Com., 1984—. Mem citizens adv. council Los Angeles Olympics of 1984, 1980—; mem. Los Angeles Hdqrs. City Assn. 1980—. Mem. Assn. Women in Architeture (v.p.), Am. Soc. Interior Designers, AIA. Episcopalian. Contbr. articles to profl. jours. Office: 2200 Michigan Ave Santa Monica CA 90404

FORD, RUTH, financial printing executive, real estate broker; b. Westchester, Pa., July 24, 1951; d. Merton Eugene and Angela Anna (DiRuscio) F. Co-founder Century 21/Michael Shinn, Denver, 1973-78; mgr. Internat. Mgmt., Denver, 1979-82; owner Sand Dollar Investments, Denver, 1982-84; v.p. Merrill Denver, 1984—. Mem. devel. com. Eleanor Roosevelt Inst. for Cancer Research, Denver, 1985, guild com. Children's Diabetes Found., Denver, 1985; trustee Leukemia Soc., Denver, 1985—. Mem. Venture Capital Assn. of Colo., Rockies Club. Republican. Avocations: reading; scuba diving; skiing; tennis; swimming. Office: Merrill Denver 1660 17th St Suite 450 Denver CO 80202

FORD, SANDRA LEE, lawyer; b. Edgewood, Md., Jan. 12, 1944; d. William V. and Lydia (Schmitz) Ford; (div.); children—Robert L., Traci L. B.S., Sacramento State U., 1965; J.D., J.F. Kennedy U., 1986. Fingerprint agt. Dept. Justice, Sacramento, 1965-70; legal officer Calif. Beer Wholesalers Assn., Sacramento, 1975-80; with sales dept. Joseph Schlitz Brewing Co., San Francisco, 1980-82; nat. account mgr. Pabst Brewing, San Rafael, Calif., 1982-83; mktg. dir. Bracco Distbn. Co., San Francisco, 1983-84; with Office Dist. Atty., Martinez, Calif., 1986—. Mem. Nat. Assn. Female Execs. Republican. Roman Catholic. Office: Office Dist Atty 725 Court St Martinez CA 94553

FORD, SARAH JO, corporate executive, consultant; b. Oklahoma City, Apr. 16, 1956; d. Russell James and Mary Carolyn (Jones) F. Student William Woods Coll., Fulton, Mo., 1974-75, Duke U., 1975; B.A. in Am. Studies and Communication Arts with honors, Austin Coll., Sherman, Tex., 1979. Intern, Sta. KAUZ-TV, Wichita Falls, Tex., spring 1979; caseworker for tornado victims Tex. Dept. Human Resources, Wichita Falls, 1979; sec. Russell J. Ford, Inc., Wichita Falls, 1980; MPACT bank rep. Affiliated Computer Systems, Dallas, 1981-82; activities dir. Monticello West Retirement Ctr., Dallas, 1982-83; in-facilities program dir. Artreach, Inc., Dallas, 1983—; speaker; cons. Activities Dir. Assn., 1983-84; editor Monticello West Harbinger monthly newspaper, 1982-83. Exec. mem. 500, Inc., 1982-84; mem. Dallas Jr. League, cons. on handling the handicapped, 1984; mem. Dallas Area Young Republicans, Dallas Mus. Art; vol. Family Place of Dallas, 1984; founding assoc. Plaza Theatre, Inc., 1983-84; mem. benefit com. Shakespeare Festival; mem. Dallas Welcoming Com. Named Outstanding Activity Dir., Therapeutic Recreational Dirs. Dallas, 1983. Mem. Nat. Assn. Female Execs., Activities Dirs. Assn. Greater Dallas, P.E.O. (pres. Dallas 1982-84). Mem. Christian Ch. (Disciples of Christ). Clubs: Slipper, Dallas Cotillion. Home: 5349 Amesbury St 1001 Dallas TX 75206 Office: Artreach Inc PO Box 191266 Dallas TX 75219

FORD, VICTORIA, public relations executive; b. Carroll, Iowa, Nov. 1, 1946; d. Victor Sargent and Gertrude Francis (Headlee) Ford; m. John K. Frans, July 4, 1965 (div. Aug. 1975); m. David William Keller, May 2, 1981 (div. Nov. 1985). A.A., Iowa Lakes Community Coll., 1973; B.A. summa cum laude, Buena Vista Coll., 1974; postgrad. journalism, U. Nev., 1981—. Social work student Iowa Dept. Social Services, Spencer, 1973, juvenile parole officer, 1974-78; staff reporter Feather Pub. Co., Quincy, Calif., 1978-80; tng. counselor CETA, Quincy, 1980; pub. info. officer U. Nev.-Reno, 1982-84; pub. relations asst. Brodeur-Martin Co., Reno, 1984—. Contbr. articles on pub. relations to profl. jours. Adv. bd. Reno Philharm., Reno-Sparks Conv. and Visitors Authority. Named Outstanding Editor, U. Nev.-Reno Journalism Dept., 1982; Reno Newspapers scholar, 1983. Mem. Pub. Relations Soc. Am. (charter v.p. Sierra Nev. chpt.), Reno Women in Advt., NOW, ALA, Sigma Delta Chi. Democrat.

FORDE, CYNTHIA ANNETTE, special event coordinator, art consultant; b. Northwood, Iowa, July 16, 1939; d. Ervin G. and Rose Arlene (Miller) Vold; m. Stanley Roger Forde, July 16, 1955; children—Roxanne, Julie, Scott, Jon Paul. A.A. in Interior Design, Chgo. Sch. Interior Design, 1978; A.A., Iowa Western Community Coll., Council Bluffs, 1980; B.S., SUNY-Albany, 1982; B.F.A., U. Houston, 1983, postgrad., 1983—. Office mgr. Elk Horn Constrn. (Iowa), 1973-77; v.p. Stan Forde and Sons, Elk Horn, 1977-79; comml. artist Portraits by Cynthia, Elk Horn, 1965-80; corp. arts adviser Arena Art Gallery, Houston, 1981-82; spl. event coordinator United Exposition, Houston, 1982—; co-chmn. conv. Assoc. Gen. Contractors, Des Moines, 1977-79; founder, chmn. Tivoli Fest Art Exhibit, Elk Horn, 1980-81. Founder, pres. Elk Horn-Kimballton Community Arts Council, 1977-81; founder, bd. dirs. Hans Christian Andersen Theater, Elk Horn, 1977-81; mgr. ARC Swim Program, 1975-77; v.p. Achievements Rewards Coll. Scientists, 1984—. Named Mrs. Iowa Am., Mrs. Am. Pageant, Las Vegas, 1980. Mem. Iowa Amateur Artists (1st place award 1980), Cultural Arts Council Houston, Tex. Soc. Assn. Execs., Meeting Planners Internat., Nat. Soc. Assn. Execs., Golden Key Soc. Republican. Lutheran. Office: United Exposition Service Co 1293 N Post Oak Houston TX 77055

FORD ELLIOTT, CATHERINE VIRGINIA, lawyer, court administrator; b. Pitts., June 8, 1949; d. John Michael and Loretto Ann (O'Toole) Ford; m. Frederick B. Elliott, III, Oct. 31, 1981. B.A., U. Pitts., 1971; M.S., Duquesne U., 1973, J.D., 1978. Bar: Pa. 1978, U.S. Dist. Ct. (we. dist.) Pa. 1978, U.S. Supreme Ct. 1982. Reading specialist Pitts. Pub. Schs., 1971-78; appellate law clk. Superior Ct. Pa., Pitts., 1978-80, adminstrv. asst., 1980-82, chief staff atty., 1982—. Mem. ABA (chmn. publ. com. 1983—), Pa. Bar Assn., Allegheny County Bar Assn. Roman Catholic. Office: Superior Ct Pa Central Legal Staff 2701 Grant Bldg Pittsburgh PA 15219

FORDHAM, DEBORAH MOTLEY, marine electronics manufacturing company executive; b. Port St. Joe, Fla., Nov. 19, 1949; d. Carl Jessie Motley and Jamie (Barton) Martin; m. Wendell Allen Fordham, Feb. 11, 1973 (div. 1982). Student, Sparks State Tech. U., 1968, Troy State U., 1984, Judson Coll., 1985. Exec. sec. Great No. Paper Co., Cedar Springs, Ga., 1968-73; employee ins. coordinator Cooper Group, Apex, N.C., 1973-75; dir. admissions Johnston Meml. Hosp., Smithfield, N.C., 1976-80; office mgr. Edwin Hartman, M.D., Smithfield, 1980-82; personnel mgr. Techsonic Industries, Eufaula, Ala., 1982—; speaker, cons. in field. Asst. editor newspaper Techsonic Tribune, 1984—. Producer videotape Techsonic Memories, 1985. Industry coordinator United Way of Barbour County, Eufaula, 1983-85; coordinator blood drive div. ARC, Techsonic Industries, 1983—; rep. Eufaula High-Tech. Com., 1985; mem. Techsonic Exec. Com., 1984—. Recipient Outstanding Service award United Way, 1985. Mem. Am. Soc. Personnel Adminstrn., Columbus Area Personnel Assn., Nat. Assn. Female Execs., Eufaula Area Indsl. Relations Assn. (chmn. 1986). Republican. Methodist. Avocations: collecting Indian artifacts; reading; swimming; water sports. Home: Route 1 Box 334 Clayton AL 36016 Office: Techsonic Industries Inc 1 Humminbird Ln Eufaula AL 36027

FORD-WALKER, CONNIE JEAN, nurse; b. Frankfort, Ky., Nov. 2, 1948; d. Artist Edwin and Cornellia Isola (Riddle) Ford; m. William Benjamin Walker Jr. Dec. 27, 1970 (div. 1985). Assoc. in Nursing, St. Petersburg Jr. Coll., 1967; B.S. in Nursing, U. So. Fla., 1981; postgrad. Nova U., 1984—. R.N., Fla. Staff nurse Palms of Pasadena Hosp., St. Petersburg, Fla., 1976-78, clin. instr. edn., 1981-82, dir. surg. nursing, 1982-83, project coordinator internat. nursing course, 1983-84, dir. nursing resources, 1984-85; asst. dir. operating room Meml. Hosp., Sarasota, Fla., 1985—; instr. basic operating room nursing State Vocat. Coll., St. Petersburg, 1979-82. Mem. Assn. Operating Room Nursing (bd. dirs., chmn. nat. cert. bd. 1982-83), Am. Nurses Assn. (bd. dirs.), Nat. League for Nurses, Beta Sigma Phi. Republican. Mem. Christian Ch. (Disciples of Christ). Club: St. Petersburg Yacht. Avocations: sailing; cooking; reading; piano. Home: 1545 49th St N Saint Petersburg FL 33710

FORDYCE, DORIS ELLEN, educator; b. Wheeling, W.Va., Dec. 28, 1947; d. Clifford Alger and Helen Camilla (Campbell) Kemp; m. James Richard Fordyce, Aug. 22, 1970; children—Suzanne, Bradley, Sarah. B.S., Ohio State U., 1970. Cert. elem. tchr., Ohio. Elem. tchr. Cambridge City Schs., Ohio, 1970—; mem. reading com., advisor on minimum competency requirements. Officer Pike Home and Sch., Cambridge, 1984-85; advisor 4-H Club, Cambridge, 1972-74. Martha Jennings scholar, 1985-86. Mem. NEA, Ohio Edn. Assn., Eastern Ohio Tchr. Assn., Cambridge Edn. Assn. Presbyterian. Lodge: Rotary Anns (sec. 1982-83). Avocations: sewing; baking; yeast breads; walking. Home: 61566 Ridge Ave Cambridge OH 43725 Office: Washington Elem Sch 916 Foster Ave Cambridge OH 43725

FORE, NITA LORAINE LLOYD, hotel exec.; b. St. Louis, Oct. 4, 1930; d. Harold Troester and Helen Elsie (Kohr) Bouligny; student public schs., University, City, Mo.; m. Jay Lloyd, Jr., Nov. 27, 1947; children—Sunny Lee Lloyd Cloud, Pamela Jayne Lloyd Deal, Laura L. Lloyd Riegler; m. Joseph M. Fore, June 26, 1982. Adminstrv. asst. to exec. v.p. Dairy Queen Nat. Devel. Co., St. Louis, 1959-67; sales mgr. Hilton Inn of St. Louis, 1967-68, dir. sales, 1968-73; dir. sales, corp. accounts Hilton Hotels Corp., St. Louis, 1973-75, dir. sales corp. accounts So. region, 1975—; lectr. in field. Cert. hotel sales exec. Mem. Hotel Sales Mgmt. Assn. (internat. pres. 1980-82), Sales and Mktg. Execs., Meeting Planners Internat. (charter mem. Ga. chpt.), Women's C. of C. of Atlanta. Republican. Lutheran. Club: Zonta. Author: Women's Opportunity in Hotel Sales, 1978; Three Faces of Eve...And How She Travels, 1979. Home: 4684 Shallowford Rd Roswell GA 30075 Office: 2070 S Park Pl Suite 200 Atlanta GA 30339

FOREHAND, JENNIE MEADOR, state legislator; b. Nashville, Dec. 17, 1935; d. James T. and Estelle (Woodall) Meador; student Woman's Coll. of U. N.C., Greensboro, 1954-56; B.S. in Indsl. Relations, U. N.C., Chapel Hill, 1958; m. William E. Forehand, Jr., July 19, 1958; children—Mary Virginia, John Bentley. Reporter, Charlotte (N.C.) News, 1954-56; probation counselor Juvenile Ct., Charlotte, 1958; tchr. Anne Arundel County (Md.), 1958-60; statis. analyst NIH, Bethesda, Md., 1961-62; edn. research project evaluator Montgomery County (Md.) Bd. Edn., 1973-74; interior designer, owner Antiques and Interiors, Rockville, Md., 1971—; mem. Md. Ho. of Dels., 1978—; mem. appropriations com., joint capital budget com., health and environ. subcom.; adv. bd. First Women's Bank of Md. Planning bd. Montgomery County Health Systems Agy., chmn. edn. and community involvement; past chmn. Rockville Civic Improvement Adv. Commn.; consumer rep. Rockville Econ. Devel. Council; mem. Montgomery County Bd. of Edn. Med. Adv. Com.; mem. Md. Community Mental Health Adv. Bd.; pres. local civic assn.; bd. dirs. Mid-Md. Lung Assn., Montgomery County Hist. Soc.; bd. dirs. local sch. PTA; adv. bd. Mont. Hospice Soc., mem. Peerless Rockville Hist. Preservation, Ltd., Questers. Mem. Women's Caucus of Md. Gen. Assembly, AAUW, Nat. Order Women Legislators, Md. Assn. Elected Women, Women's Polit. Caucus. Democrat. Methodist. Office: 224B House Office Bldg State House Annapolis MD 21401

FOREMAN, CAROL LEE TUCKER, business executive; b. Little Rock, May 3, 1938; d. James Guy and Willie Maude (White) Tucker; A.A., William Woods Coll., Fulton, Mo., 1958; A.B., Washington U., St. Louis, 1960; postgrad. Am. U.; LL.D. (hon.), William Woods Coll., Fulton, Mo., 1976; m. Jay Howell Foreman, June 13, 1964; children—Guy Tucker, Rachel Marian. Research asst.

Com. on Govt. Ops., U.S. Senate, 1961; assoc. Fed. Counsel Assocs., 1961-63; instr. Am. govt. William Woods Coll., Fulton, 1963-64; exec. asst. to Rep. James Roosevelt, 1964; dir. research and publs. Democratic Nat. Com., 1965-66; Congressional liaison aide HUD, 1967-69; chief info. liaison Center for Family Planning Program Devel., Planned Parenthood-World Population, 1969-71; dir. policy coordination Commn. on Population and Am. Future, 1971-72; exec. dir. Citizens Com. on Population and Am. Future, 1972-73, Paul Douglas Consumer Research Center, 1973-77, Consumer Fedn. Am., 1973-77; asst. sec. food and consumer services Dept. Agr., Washington, 1977-81; pres. Foreman & Co., 1981—; exec. dir. Ctr. for Women Policy Studies, 1983—; mem. Interdeptl. Task Force on Women; mem. D.C. Commn. on Status Women, 1973-74; dir. Consumer's Union, 1982—, Food Research and Action Ctr., 1983—; dir. Commodity Credit Corp., 1977-81, Nat. Consumer Coop. Bank, 1979-81; vice-chmn. Center Nat. Policy, Center Population Options. Recipient Disting. Alumni award Washington U., 1979. Mem. Women's Equity Action League (past pres. local chpt.), Woman's Nat. Dem. Club, Pi Beta Phi. Presbyterian. Home: 5408 Trent St Chevy Chase MD 20015 Office: 1826 Jefferson Pl NW Suite 201 Washington DC 20036

FOREMAN, CAROLYN DENISE, business executive; b. East Chicago, Ind., Dec. 8, 1956; d. Carl Ray and Marilyn (Moldroski) F. B.S. in Bus. Adminstrn., Ball State U., 1980. Account rep. Burroughs Corp., Dallas, 1981-83; dist. mgr. SEI Corp., Oak Brook, Ill., 1983—. Mem. Golden Key. Methodist. Home: 17 W 706 Butterfield Rd Apt 105 Oak Brook Terrace IL 60181 Office: SEI Corp 2215 York Rd Suite 416 Oak Brook IL 60521

FOREMAN, JOYCE BLACKNALL, office products company executive; b. Thelma, Tex., July 6, 1948; d. Roy and Betty (Lockhart) Blacknall; m. Don Ellington Foreman (div.). A.A., El Centro Coll., Dallas, 1974; Student U. Tex.-Dallas, 1975-78. Purchasing agt. constrn. div. Zale Corp., Dallas, 1969-75; with U. Tex. Health Sci. Ctr., Dallas, 1976-78; purchasing coordinator Central and South West Services, Inc., Dallas, 1978-81; pres. Foreman Office Products, Inc., Dallas, 1981—. Mem. Entrepreneurial Devel. Com., 1982-84; bd. mgrs. Park South YMCA, 1983-84; mem. host com. Dallas Rep. Conv., 1984. Mem. Dallas Regional Minority Purchasing Council, Nat. Assn. Female Execs., Nat. Office Products Assn., Ft. Worth Regional Minority Purchasing Council, Dallas C. of C., Black C. of C. Methodist. Club: Sunday Network of Women. Office: Foreman Office Products Inc 1507 Main St Dallas TX 75201

FOREMAN, MOLLY ANN, marketing and communications firm executive; b. Detroit, Nov. 7, 1923; d. Abram and Sarah (Weinstein) Winokur; m. Milton N. Zimmerman, Sept. 15, 1946 (dec.); 1 dau., Amy Jo; m. 2d John Born Foreman, Aug. 3, 1972. B.B.A., U. Mich., 1944. Advt. and pub. relations dir. Zuieback's, Detroit, 1955-61; pres. Zimmerman & Assocs., Chgo., 1961-75; v.p. M.B. Simpson, Inc., Cin., 1975-80, Birkenes & Foreman, Boca Raton, Fla., 1980-83; pres. Foreman & Assocs., Boca Raton, 1983—. Vice pres. Boca Raton Symphony, 1983—; v.p. bd. govs. Philharm. Orch. of Fla., 1985; chmn. connoisseur gifts Pub. TV, Cin., 1978-79; bd. dirs., chmn. mktg. services com. Palm Beach Council for Arts, 1985; membership chmn. Ritter Art Gallery, Boca Raton, 1984; mem. devel. com. Boca Raton Mus. Art, 1985. Mem. Fashion Group, Am. Mktg. Assn., Advt. Club Ft. Lauderdale, Pub. Relations Soc. Am., Fla. Pub. Relations Soc., Boca Raton C. of C., C. of C. of the Palm Beaches, Exec. Women of the Palm Beaches (pub. relations liaison).

FOREMAN, YVONNE CLARICE, county official; b. Central City, S.D., Nov. 24, 1925; d. Charles C. and Jessie Mae (Pouriea) Martin; m. Robert J. Foreman, June 22, 1945; children—Richard R., Kristine Lynn. Grad. high sch., Deadwood, S.D., Operator service sta. Standard Oil, Portland, Oreg., 1943-44; catalogue order mgr. Montgomery Wards, Deadwood, 1948-59; dep. auditor Lawrence County, Deadwood, 1959-61, dep. treas., 1961-68, register of deeds, 1969—. Pres. Deadwood Pub. Sch. PTA, 1958, Twin City Republican Assn., Deadwood, 1979-80; mem. pastor-parish com. United Meth. Ch., Deadwood, 1982—, mem. fin. com. 1976-79. Mem. S.D. Assn. County Ofcls. (nominating com. 1976, exec. bd. 1970-75, legis. com. 1985), Nat. Assn. County Ofcls., Beta Sigma Phi. Clubs: Black Hills (bd. mem. 1985—), Hist. Soc. Lodge: Eastern Star (past matron 1956). Avocations: sewing; fishing; camping; flowers. Home: PO Box 165 Deadwood SD 57732 Office: PO Box 565 Deadwood SD 57732

FOREST, DORIS E., magazine publisher. Pub. Fgn. Affairs Mag., N.Y.C., 1977—. Address: Care Fgn Affairs Mag Council on Fgn Relations Inc 58 East 68th St New York NY 10021*

FOREST, SUZANNE ELISABETH, psychologist, lawyer; b. Magog, Que., Can., Aug. 5, 1948; d. Yves Lionel and Elizabeth Margaret (St. Martin) F.; B.A., U. Sherbrooke, 1968, B.Ps., 1970; M.Ps., U. Montreal, 1972, D.Psy., 1977; B.C.L., McGill U., 1981. Counseling psychologist U. Montreal, 1973-74; child and family therapist Marie-Enfant Hosp., Montreal, 1974-75; expert psychologist family div. Superior Ct. Montreal, 1976-81; ind. practice psychotherapy, part-time 1976-81; atty. firm Robinson Sheppard Borenstein Shapiro, Montreal, 1982-85; legal counsel Que. Order Psychologists, 1985—. Mem. Que. Bar, Can. Bar Assn., Am. Psychology-Law Soc. Address: 3475 Mountain St Apt 910 Montreal PQ H3G 2A4 Canada

FORESTER, JEAN MARTHA BROUILLETTE (MRS. JAMES LAWRENCE FORESTER), librarian; b. Port Barre, La., Sept. 7, 1934; d. Joseph Walter and Thelma (Brown) Brouillette; B.S., La. State U., 1955; M.A. (Carnegie fellow), George Peabody Coll. Tchrs., 1956; m. James Lawrence Forester, June 2, 1957; children—Jean Martha, James Lawrence. Librarian, Howell Elem. Sch., Springhill, La., 1956-58; asst. post librarian Fort Chaffee, Ark., 1958; command librarian Orleans Area Command, U.S. Army, Orleans, France, 1958-59; acquisitions librarian Northwestern State U., Natchitoches, La., 1960; serials librarian La. State U., New Orleans, 1960-66; mem. faculty La. State U., Eunice, 1966—, asst. librarian, 1972-85, assoc. librarian, asst. prof., 1972-85, assoc. librarian, 1985—. Active Eunice Assn. Retarded Children. Mem. La. Library Assn. (sect. sec. 1971-72, coordinator serials interest group 1984-85), UDC, Delta Kappa Gamma (chpt. parliamentarian 1972-74, rec. sec. 1984-86), Alpha Beta Alpha, Phi Gamma Mu, Phi Mu. Democrat. Baptist. Club: Order Eastern Star. Contbr. articles to profl. jours. Home: 1351 Gregg Ave Eunice LA 70535

FORGIONE, STEPHANIE JULIA, real estate management executive; b. Jamaica, N.Y., Dec. 11, 1942; d. Louis and Julia (Zawoluk) Majore; m. Joseph Edward Cox, Sept. 7, 1963 (div. Dec. 1975); 1 child, Debra Ann; m. Louis Victor Forgione, Dec. 28, 1980; stepchildren—Cheryl, Jay, JoAnn, Anthony. Student Jamaica Vocat. Sch. Sales recorder Rueben H. Donnelley, N.Y.C., 1960-62; sec. Durkee Famous Foods, Jamaica, N.Y., 1962-64; adminstrv. asst. Am. Home Products, N.Y.C., 1964-67; bookkeeper W.T. Grant Co., Riverhead, N.Y., 1967-69; sec. Scheinberg, Wolfet al, Riverhead, 1969-70; bookkeeper Hall Huntley, Middle Island, N.Y., 1970-73; asst. v.p. Bayport Assocs. (D.B.G. Mgmt. Corp.), N.Y.C., 1973—. Democrat. Roman Catholic. Avocations: boating; bowling; antiques. Home: 601 Terrace Rd Bayport NY 11705 Office: DBG Mgmt Corp 850 3d Ave New York NY 10022

FORIS-MILLER, CAROLYN M., histotechnologist; b. N.Y.C., Mar. 13, 1937; d. John Stephen and Caroline Bernice (Banoff) Foris; M. Herbert J. Miller. A.A., Thomas A. Edison Coll., 1979. Technician dept. Hosps. of City of NY., 1959-68; instr. histology Allen Sch. for Med. Tech.; supr. histology Wycoff Heights Hosp., 1968-70; mgr. tissue pathology lab. Metpath, Inc., Teterboro N.J., 1970-84; coordinator anatomic pathology services Woodhull Med. and Mental Health Ctr., Bklyn., 1985-86. Coordinator legis. adv. bd. dirs. for chmn. health for N.Y. State, 1974-75; moderator of community discussion sessions on drug abuse, 1973; bd. govs. Mid Queens Regular Democratic Orgn., 1965-75, sec., v.p., also campaign coordinator for candidates of this orgn., editor newsletter. Recipient certs. Merit and Appreciation, N.Y. State Assemblymen. Mem. Nat. Soc. for Histotech. (charter mem. pub. relations com.), N.Y. Soc. for Histotech. (charter mem., co-editor newsletter 1975-76, editor 1984-85, chmn. membership com.), N.J. Soc. for Histotech. (charter mem.), Am. Soc. Clin. Pathology (assoc. and affiliate member). Roman Catholic.

FORKAN, PATRICIA ANN, association executive; b. N.Y.C., June 13, 1944; d. Robert James and Elaine May (Van Horn) F.; B.A. in Polit. Sci., Pa. State U., 1966; postgrad. Am. U., 1968-69; m. Robert Eugene Eisenbud, Apr. 16, 1977. Manpower analyst Dept. Labor, Washington, 1967-69; nat. coordinator Fund for Animals, N.Y.C., 1970-76; v.p. program and communications Humane Soc. of U.S., Washington, 1976—; mem. U.S. del. Internat. Whaling Commn., 1978, Re-negotiation of Conv. for Regulation of Whaling, 1978, U.S. del. North Pacific Fur Seal Commn., 1985; mem. U.S. Public Adv. Com. to Law of the Sea, 1978-83; bd. dirs. Council for Ocean Law; advisor weekly TV show Pet Action Line; advisor Animal Polit. Action Com. Contbr. articles to environ. and animal welfare publs. Co-host weekly radio show. Office: Humane Soc of US 2100 L St Washington DC 20037

FORMAN, FLORENCE, publishing company executive; b. Bklyn., Nov. 11, 1941; d. Solomon and Rose (Cohen) Grossman; m. Robert Jay Forman, June 12, 1960 (div. 1979); children—Jill Allison, Eric Steven. A.A., Glendale Community Coll., 1967; B.S., Adelphi U., 1984. Sales mgr. Pennysaver Corp., Rockville Centre, N.Y., 1968-78, TV Informer, Lawrence, N.Y., 1978-79; advt. dir., assoc. pub. Gralla Publs., N.Y.C., 1979—. Mem. Nat. Assn. Plastic Fabricators, Nat. Kitchen Cabinet Assn., Delta Tau Alpha. Republican. Jewish. Club: Hempstead Bay (Sailing Island Park, N.Y.). Office: Gralla Publs 1515 Broadway New York NY 10036

FORMAN, JEANNE LEACH, piano teacher; b. Los Angeles, Mar. 3, 1916; d. Rowland E. and Charlotte F. (Van Wickle) Leach; student U. Redlands, 1934-36, UCLA, 1937; m. Edward S. Forman, July 28, 1945; children—Bonnie Jeanne (Mrs. James Field Ottinger), Karen Lynn (Mrs. Patrick Maginnis), Wendy K. Forman (Mrs. Michael Bolduc). Pvt. tchr. piano, Pasadena, Calif., 1945-52, Tucson, 1952-58, Sunnyvale, Calif., 1958-75, Santa Barbara, Calif., 1976—; owner, dir. Jeanne Forman Studios, Sunnyvale; owner/dir. Jeanne Forman Enterprises (Music to Write By), 1982—; owner J. Forman Advt. Agy.; propr. Jeanne Forman Advt. and Enterprises; writer Los Angeles Times, 1978-80; columnist The Galeria Santa Barbara News Press, 1978—; publicity writer Music Tchrs. Assn.; tchr. of blind Santa Clara County Assistance League; lectr. on blind techniques; freelance writer; gen. edn. staff Brooks Inst. Photography, Santa Barbara guest appearances There is a Way, Sta. KHJ-TV, Los Angeles. Active Santa Clara Assistance League. Mem. Calif. Assn. Profl. Music Tchrs., Music Tchrs. Nat. Assn., Compositions performed by U. Calif., Santa Barbara, 1971. Author: Security, 1984; Secret of the Pig, 1984. Home: 1119 Alameda Padre Serra Santa Barbara CA 93105

FORNACIARI, SHARON LEE, personnel consulting/placement firm owner; b. Framingham, Mass., Dec. 3, 1954; d. Augustine Alfred and Mary (Megliola) F. Student Providence Coll., 1972-74, Emerson Coll., 1984—. Sales rep. Mutual of Omaha, Waltham, Mass., 1974-75; office mgr. sales Quest Personnel, Natick, Mass., 1975-78; pres., owner Opportunities Unltd. of N.E. Inc., Framingham, Mass., 1978—; cons. Strehlke Co., Framingham, 1983—. Bd. dirs. YWCA, Boston/Natick, 1981-84, steering com., 1982-84. Mem. Nat. Assn. Personnel Cons., Route 128 Bus. Roundtable, Women in Outside Sales, Wellesley Area C. of C., South Middlesex Area C. of C. Avocations: aerobics; acting; drama; creative writing; sailing. Home: Boston MA 02110 Office: Opportunities Unltd of NE Inc 160 Speen St Framingham MA 01701

FORNELL, MARTHA STEINMETZ, educator, artist; b. Galveston, Tex., Dec. 19, 1920; d. Joseph Duncan and Martha Lillian (McRee) Steinmetz; m. Earl Wesley Fornell, Sept. 20, 1947 (dec. Mar. 1969). B.Mus. cum laude, U. Tex., 1943; postgrad. U. Houston, 1953-56, Lamar U., 1957-60. Music cons., fgn. program editor Voice of America, USIA, N.Y.C., 1944-46; advt. cons. fed. agys., San Antonio, 1946-47; tchr. music secondary schs., Houston, 1953-56; tchr. art Beaumont (Tex.) Ind. Sch. Dist., 1956-79; collages exhibited Galerie Paula Insel, N.Y.C., 1974-84, Ponce, P.R., 1976-79, 82, 84. Recipient Circuit awards Tex. Fine Arts Assn., 1962-64, Invitational awards, 1964-65. Mem. Mu Phi Epsilon. Contbr. articles to Am.-German Rev. Address: 2303 Evalon Ave Beaumont TX 77702

FORNERIS, JEANNE M., lawyer; b. Duluth, Minn., May 23, 1953; d. John Domenic and Elva Lorraine (McDonald) F.; m. Michael Scott Margulies, Feb. 6, 1982. A.B., Macalester Coll., 1975; J.D., U. Minn., 1978. Bar: Minn. 1978. Assoc. firm Halverson, Watters, Bye, Downs & Maki, Ltd., Duluth, Minn., 1978-81, firm Briggs & Morgan, P.A., Mpls. and St. Paul, 1981-83; ptnr. firm Hart & Bruner, P.A., Mpls., 1983-86; assoc. gen. counsel M.A. Mortenson Co., 1986—; instr. women's studies dept. U. Minn., Mpls., 1977-79. Author profl. edn. seminars, 1981—; author, editor articles. Bd. dirs. Good Will Industries Vocat. Enterprises, Inc., 1979-81; chmn. bd. trustees Duluth Bar Library, 1981; mem. United Way Family and Individual Services Task Force, Duluth, 1981. Nat. Merit Assn. scholar, 1971. Mem. ABA, Minn. State Bar Assn., Hennepin County Bar Assn., Minn. Women Lawyers (bd. dirs.). Democrat. Roman Catholic. Office: MA Mortenson Co 700 Meadow Ln N Minneapolis MN 55440

FORNES, MARIA IRENE, playwright; b. Havana, Cuba, May 14, 1930; came to U.S., 1945, naturalized, 1951; d. Carlos Luis and Carmen Hismenia (Collado) F.; Ed., Havana pub. schs. Pres., N.Y. Theatre Strategy, 1973-80. Author: plays Tango Palace, 1963, The Successful Life of 3, 1965, Promenade, 1965-69; The Office, 1966, A Vietnamese Wedding, 1967, The Annunciation, 1967, Dr. Kheal, 1968, The Red Burning Light, 1968, Molly's Dream, 1968, The Curse of the Langston House, 1972, Aurora, 1974, Cap-a-Pie, 1975, Lolita in the Garden, 1977, Fefu and Her Friends, 1977, Eyes on the Harem, 1979, In Service, 1978, Eyes on the Harem, 1979, Evelyn Brown (A Diary), 1980, Life is Dream, 1981, A Visit, 1981, The Danube, 1982, Mud, 1983, Sarita, 1984, The Conduct of Life, 1985, Lovers and Keepers, 1986. Grantee, John Hay Whitney Found., 1961, Centro Mexicano de Escritores, 1962; CADR-U. Minn., 1965, Cintas Found., 1967, Creative Artists Pub. Service Program, 1972, 75; Yale-ABC fellow, 1967; Yale-Levine Found. fellow, 1968; Rockefeller Found. fellow, 1971; Guggenheim fellow, 1972; Nat. Endowment Arts fellow, 1974, 85; Am. Acad. and Inst. Arts and Letters grantee, 1985; recipient Obie award, 1965, 77, 79, 82. Address: 1 Sheridan Sq New York NY 10014

FORNEY, VIRGINIA SUE, educational counselor; b. Little Rock, Sept. 15, 1925; d. Robert Millard and Susan Amanda (Ward) Tate; m. J.D. Mullen, Jr., Oct. 13, 1945 (div. 1966); children—Michael Dunn, Patricia Sue; m. Bill E. Forney, Apr. 29, 1967. Student Tex. State Coll. for Women, 1943-46; B.F.A., U. Okla., 1948; postgrad. Benedictine Heights Coll., Tulsa, 1957-58; M.Teaching Arts, Tulsa U., 1969; postgrad. Okla. State U., intermittently, 1969—. Cert. secondary tchr., sch. counselor, vis. sch. counselor, Okla. With Sta. WNAD, U. Okla., 1947-49; tchr. lang. arts Tulsa Bd. Edn., 1959-73; women's counselor Tulsa YWCA, 1980; vis. sch. counselor Tulsa County Supt. of Schs. Office, 1980—. Mem. budget com. United Way Greater Tulsa, 1980—, edn. com. Planned Parenthood Greater Tulsa, 1980—; mem. Tulsa County adv. council Okla. State U., 1983—; chairperson Tulsa Coalition for Parenting Edn., 1983-84; chairperson problems of youth study Tulsa Met. C. of C., 1984-85; mem. gen. bd. March of Dimes Greater Tulsa, 1985. Mem. Am. Assn. for Counseling and Devel., Internat. Assn. Pupil Personnel Workers (state bd. dirs. 1982—), Okla. Assn. Family Resource Programs (regional v.p. 1982—), LWV Okla. (chairperson juvenile justice study 1976-77). Democrat. Unitarian. Avocation: piano.

FORONDA, ELENA ISABEL, educator; b. N.Y.C., Jan. 15, 1947; d. Severino Deliso and LaVerne (Ibanez) F.; B.S. in Music, Hunter Coll., City U. N.Y., 1969, M.A. in Music Edn., 1971. Tchr. vocal music N.Y.C. Public Sch. System, 1970—; asst. dir. tchr. placement Hunter Coll., City U. N.Y., summers 1971-72. Sponsor children in Philippines and El Salvador, World Vision Internat.; del. Asian Am. Women's Caucus, 1977. Dist. winner Nat. Piano Playing Auditions, 1965; recipient N.Y. State permanent cert. Dept. Edn., 1971. Mem. Music Educators Nat. Conf., N.Y. State Sch. Music Assn., Amateur Chamber Players (Vienna, Va.), Internat. Platform Assn. Democrat. Episcopalian. Mem. choirs Hunter Coll., 1968-69, 71.

FORREST, DIANE, consulting firm executive; b. Bayonne, N.J., Oct. 22, 1946; d. Max D. and Selma (Winter) Forrest; m. Nicholas John LaHowchic, Sept. 11, 1981. B.A., Boston U., 1968; M.B.A., Pace U., 1982. Cert. prodn. and inventory mgmt. Programmer trainee Prudential Life Ins. Co., Newark, 1968-69; programmer analyst Computer Usage Corp., N.Y.C., 1970-71; systems analyst Plymouth Computers, Inc., N.Y.C., 1972-73; distbn. project leader T.J. Lipton Inc., Englewood Cliffs, N.J., 1973-74, fin. project leader, 1975-76, mktg. project mgr., 1977-78; project mgr. mfg. Nabisco Brands, Inc., N.Y.C., 1978-80, corp. mgr. mfg. systems, 1981-82; mgr. mfg. cons. Peat Marwick Mitchell & Co., N.Y.C., 1982-83, sr. mgr. mfg. practice, 1984-85, sr. mgr. in charge Stamford/White Plains, 1986—, editor newsletter, 1983-86. Contbr. articles to profl. jours. Mem. Am. Prodn. and Inventory Control Soc., Data Processing Mgmt. Assn., ASME, Robotics Assn., Nat. Assn. Female Execs., Assn. Women Bus. Owners. Office: Peat Marwick Mitchell & Co 3001 Summer St Stamford CT 06905

FORREST, GAIL, computer company executive; b. McAllen, Tex., Apr. 18, 1955; d. Richard Baker Forrest and Diane Mattison. B.A., U. So. Calif., 1977; postgrad. George Washington U., 1978-82, U. Md., 1983-86. Editorial asst. ABA, Washington, 1977-78; personnel asst. Sperry Computer Systems, McLean, Va., 1978-80, personnel rep., 1981-82, mgr. compensation and adminstrn., 1983—; cons. in field. Mem. Internat. Assn. Personnel Women (newsletter editor), Am. Soc. Personnel Adminstrn., Equal Employment Ofcls. Forum, PEO Nat. Women's Orgn., Wash. Tech. Personnel Forum. Republican. Methodist. Club: U. So. Calif. Alumni Club. Home: 521 N Armistead St Alexandria VA 22312 Office: Sperry Corp 8008 Westpark Dr McLean VA 22102

FORREST, VIRGINIA OGDEN RANSON (MRS. WILBUR STUDLEY FORREST), civic leader; b. Balt., June 24, 1896; d. Henry Warfield and Nannie Deaver (Cooper) Ranson; ed. Calvert Sch., Arundell Sch.; m. Frederick Beasley Williamson, Jr., July 5, 1917 (dec. July 1957); children—Virginia Williamson Hutton, Beverley Williamson Magill, Frederick Beasley III; m. 2d, Wilbur Studley Forrest, Apr. 20, 1960 (dec. 1977). Dir., Goodall Rubber Co., hon. dir., 1973—. Pres. Jr. League, Elizabeth, N.J., 1924-26, hon. mem., 1944; mem. hostess com. Franklin Inst., Phila., 1941; mem. N.J. Recreation Soc., Elizabeth, 1934-35, rep. N.J. to nat. conv., Chgo., 1935; chmn. New Hope (Pa.) chpt. ARC, 1939-43, head flood disaster chpt., 1955, chmn. home service, 1943-45; hon. v.p. New Hope Art Assos., 1940; mem. adv. com. Jonathan Dickinson State Park, Martin County, Fla., 1970—; organizer adviser Bucks County Conservation Alliance; mem. New Hope Centennial Com., 1976; bd. dirs. Martin County Conservation Alliance, 1966-74, Honey Hollow Watershed Assn., 1969—, Soc. Prevention Cruelty to Children Family Welfare Bd., Elizabeth, 1928, YWCA, Elizabeth, 1928, Abington (Pa.) Meml. Hosp. Women's Bd., 1941, Vis. Nurse Assn., New Hope, 1941-49; bd. dirs., 2d v.p. Garden Club, Stuart, Fla., 1951-60; trustee Egnolf Day Nursery, Elizabeth, 1923-36, New Hope, Martin County Public Library, Stuart, 1958-61; bd. dirs. Holmquist Sch. for Girls, Free Public Library Elizabeth, 1926-39, sec., 1927-36; bd. dirs. Keep Fla. Beautiful Com.; mem. founder's bd. Transylvania U., Lexington, Ky., 1979—. Recipient award Fla. Fedn. Garden Clubs, 1961; Gov.'s gold medal conservation award (1st woman recipient), 1959; Gov. Kirk's Conservation award, 1970; Conservation Heritage award U.S. Dept. Interior, 1979; Virginia Forrest Day observed by Martin County (Fla.) Audubon Soc., 1976; Virginia Forrest Beach dedicated, Hutchinson Island, Fla., 1976; Allan D. Cruickshank award Fla. Audubon Soc., 1981; Community Service award Commonwealth of Pa.; Delaware Canal Sesquicentennial award Pa. Dept. Environ. Resources, 1982. Mem. Fla. (recipient award 1960, chmn. Bald Eagle project 1959—, mem. wildlife com. 1959—, v.p. 1962-69, hon. v.p. 1970—), Martin County (dir. 1957—, chmn. exec. com. 1973-74), Bucks County (dir., adviser, citation for conservation 1972) Audubon socs., New Hope Hist. Soc. (dir. 1959-60, 67—, v.p. 1977-80), Fla. Fedn. Garden Clubs (hon. life), Colonial Dames N.J., Woman Fly Fishers Am. Clubs: Mt. Vernon (Balt.); Hartwood (Monticello, N.Y.); Martin County Anglers (dir. 1966—). Home: Pennswood Village D105 Newtown PA 18970

FORRESTER, ELAINE MARIE, nurse; b. Chester, Pa., Nov. 6, 1946; d. Richard Ernest and Helen Marie (Burns) F.; R.N. diploma Chester County (Pa.) Hosp. Sch. Nursing, 1968; B.S. in Nursing, U. Pa., 1973, M.S. in Nursing, 1976. Staff nurse Crozer-Chester Med. Center, Chester, 1968-73, night nursing supr., 1976-77, evening nursing supr., 1977-78, nurse coordinator, med.-surg., 1978-83, night nursing supr., 1983—. Mem. Republican Nat. Com. Recipient alumnae award for nursing ability Chester County Hosp., 1968, also Esther Eves Meml. award, 1968. Mem. Nat. League Nursing, Phila. Mus. Art, Phila. Zool. Gardens, Smithsonian Assos., Sigma Theta Tau. Baptist. Home: 112 Spring St Media PA 19063 Office: Crozer-Chester Med Center 15th and Upland Ave Chester PA 19013

FORRESTER, VICTORIA WADSWORTH, librarian, author-illustrator; b. Pasadena, Calif., Mar. 18, 1940; d. Victor and Leslie (Wadsworth) Parkin; m. Alan Harry Forrester, June 14, 1960; 1 son, Chad. B.A., UCLA, 1961, M.L.S., 1963, M.A., 1970. Reference librarian Santa Monica (Calif.) Library, 1963-66, children's librarian, 1969-71; head librarian St. Mark's Sch., San Rafael, Calif., 1980—; author-illustrator: Bears and Theirs, 1982; Oddward, 1982; The Touch Said Hello, 1982; The Magnificent Moo, 1983; Words to Keep Against the Night, 1983; author: The Candlemaker and other Tales, 1984. Mem. ALA, Soc. Children's Book Writers. Home: One Owlswood Dr Larkspur CA 94939

FORSMAN, SHIRLEY JEAN, nurse; b. Phila., Feb. 6, 1930; d. Hartley F. and Ellen T. (Carroll) Ness; A.A. in Nursing, Sacramento City Coll., 1966; B.S.N., Sacramento State Coll., 1971; M.A., Calif. State U., 1973; m. Willard John Forsman, June 18, 1949 (dec.); children—Daniel (dec.), John, Katie, Nancy. Staff nurse Kaiser Permanente Hosp., Sacramento, 1963-66; supervising head nurse psychiatry Eskaton Am. River Hosp., Carmichael, Calif., 1966-70, hosp. supr., 1970-71; dir. nursing edn. Golden Key Coll., Sacramento, 1971-74; dir. nursing services Douglas County Hosp., Alexandria, Minn., 1974-75; dir. public health Kandiyohi County Community Health Dept., Willmar, Minn., 1975-77; dir. nursing services Rice Meml. Hosp., Willmar, 1977-79; master staffing coordinator Roseville (Calif.) Community Hosp., 1979-80; instr. Am. River Coll., Sacramento, 1980-81; patient care coordinator Golden Valley Health Ctr. (Minn.), 1983—; dir. Beltrami County Pub. Nursing Service, Minn., 1985—; cons. Central Minn. Area Health Edn. Consortium, 1975—; mem. adv. com. to Lic. Practice Nurse Program, Minn.-Dakotas, 1974—; mem. Child Abuse Team, U. Minn. Continuing Edn. for R.N.s, 1978—; faculty/lectr. various schs., colls., instns., 1968—. HEW grantee, 1971. Mem. Am. Nurses Assn., Minn. Nurses Assn., Nat. Council Nursing Service Facilitators, Minn. State Council Nursing Service Adminstrs., Minn. Hosp. Assn. Area Nursing Service Adminstrs., Minn. Pub. Health Assn., Minn. Pub. Health Nursing Dirs. Assn., Minn. NW Dirs. Group, AAUW, Am. Legion Aux. Clubs: Bus. and Profl. Women, Eagles Aux. Home: 1515 Calihan Ave NE Bemidji MN 56601

FORSTER, JO ANN, harness racing, school executive, nurse; b. St. Bernard, Ohio, Feb. 27, 1929; d. Joe Homer and Dorothy (Roberts) Dahn; m. Eugene Forster, June 14, 1949 (div. 1971); children—Ellen, Janet Dahn (dec.); m. 2d, Lou Miller, Dec. 27, 1976. Diploma Met. Hosp. Sch. Nursing, N.Y.C., 1950; postgrad. in nursing edn. Hunter Coll., 1950-51, 54. Head nurse neurology service Met. Hosp., 1950-51, head nurse pediatrics service 1951-52, ward instr. pediatrics, 1952-53; co-founder, dir. Internat. Sch. Harness Racing, Westbury, N.Y., 1974—. Author curriculum Harness Horsemanship, 1981. Pres. LWV, Bronx, N.Y., 1957-60; mem. exec. com. Bronx Reform Democratic Com., 1960. Mem. U.S. Trotting Assn. (groom, owner 1966—, trainer 1974—), N.Y. Standardbred Owners Assn., N.J. Standardbred Owners and Breeders Assn., N.Y. Breeders Assn. Office: Internat Sch Harness Racing PO Box 978 Roosevelt Raceway Westbury NY 11590

FORSYTH, SUZANNE MARY, association administrator; b. Bklyn., Jan. 7, 1943; d. Douglas and Gloria (Morrison) F.; 1 adopted dau., Maura Patricia. B.S. in Indsl. Psychology, CCNY, 1963; postgrad. NYU, 1964-65. Cert. personnel exec. Personnel Accreditation Inst. Personnel officer Gen. Reins. Corp., Greenwich, Conn., 1964-67; mgr. employment Georgetown U., Washington, 1967-70, assoc. dean students, 1970-73; dir. human resources Am. Council on Edn., Washington, 1973—; guest lectr. U. Md., Am. U., Bowie State Coll., 1981-82; lectr. in field. Sec. bd. trustees Washington Internat. Coll., 1976-81; chmn. assn. div. United Way, Washington, 1977-78. Mem. Am. Soc. Personnel Adminstrn., AAUW (div. dir.), Washington Personnel Assn. (pres. 1981-82), Conf. Instnl. Adminstrs. (chmn. 1976-77). Roman Catholic. Home: 5306 MacArthur Blvd NW Washington DC 20016 Office: Am Council on Edn 1 Dupont Cir NW Washington DC 20036

FORSYTHE, MARY MACCORNACK, state legislator; b. Whitehall, Wis., May 23, 1920; d. Robert Lee and Gladys Fry MacCornack; B.Mus., St. Olaf Coll., 1942; m. Robert A. Forsythe, July 18, 1942; children—Robert A., Polly Forsythe Johnson, Jean Forsythe Peterson, Ann Forsythe Smith, Joan. Tchr., Viroqua, Wis., 1942-43, Whitehall, Wis., 1944-46; mem. Minn. Ho. of Reps., St. Paul, 1972—, chmn. appropriations com., 1985—. Mem. Guthrie Theater Found., 1973-80; mem. Minn. Commn. on Econ. Status of Women, 1976-79, Minn. News Council, 1979—; trustee Fairview Riverside Hosp.; mem. exec. com. Seat Belt Coalition, Gov.'s Residence Adv. Task Force, Fairview Corp. Bd.; mem. Gov.'s Adv. Task Force on Women and Corrections. Recipient Disting. Alumna award St. Olaf Coll., 1974; Dr. I. Michael Kuhn award Nat. Hemophilia Found., 1978; Outstanding Woman of Edina Bicentennial award, 1978; Community Service award Edina Optimists, 1982. Mem. Nat. Conf. State Legislators (vice chmn. human resources com. 1977-78). Republican. Lutheran.

Home: 5308 Brookview Ave Edina MN 55424 Office: State Office Bldg Saint Paul MN 55155

FORTI, CORINNE ANN, business executive; b. N.Y.C., July 26, 1941; d. Wilbur Walter and Sylvia Joan (Charap) Bastian; B.A., Hunter Coll., 1963; m. Joseph Donald Forti, Aug. 18, 1962 (dec.); 1 dau., Raina. Adminstrv. asst. Ednl. Broadcasting Corp., 1963-65; adminstrv. asst. W.R. Grace & Co., N.Y.C., 1965-67, public relations rep., 1967-70, mgr. info. services, 1970-79, dir. info. services, 1980—; lectr. photography and graphics Am. Mgmt. Assn. Bd. dirs. YM/YWCA Day Care Inc. Named to Acad. Women Achievers, YWCA, 1979; recipient citation award in communications Nat. Council of Women, 1979. Mem. Am. Women in Radio and TV, Women Execs. in Public Relations, Chem. Mfrs. Assn., Republican. Roman Catholic. Home: 10 E 85th St New York NY 10028 Office: 1114 Ave of Americas New York NY 10036

FORTNEY, ANNE PRICE, lawyer; b. Miami Beach, Fla., June 9, 1944; d. Camden Page and Margery (Shaut) F.; m. Richard A. Riddell, May 10, 1986. B.A., Mary Washington Coll., 1966; J.D., Georgetown U., 1969; postgrad. Harvard U. J.F. Kennedy Sch. Govt., 1985. Bar: D.C. 1969. Assoc. Cleary, Gottlieb, Steen & Hamilton, Washington, 1969-71; atty. FTC, Washington, 1971-76, adv. to commr., 1972-73; atty. Bur. Consumer Protection, 1972-76; atty. Washington Legal Office, J.C. Penney Co., Inc., 1976-82; assoc. dir. (credit practices) Bur. Consumer Protection, FTC, Washington, 1982—. Bd. dirs. Mary Washington Coll. Found., 1985—, mem. coll. alumni bd. dirs., 1980-82, mem. regional scholarship com., 1974-78, chmn., 1974-76, 1st v.p. alumni bd. dirs., 1972-74. Recipient Sr. Exec. Service award, 1983. Mem. ABA (chmn. consumer communications subcom. com. consumer fin. services), D.C. Bar Assn., Women's Bar Assn. D.C. Home: 1401 44th St NW Washington DC 20007 Office: Bur Consumer Protection FTC Washington DC 20580

FORTUNATA, JACQUELINE, computer software educator; b. Cleve., Nov. 18, 1945; d. Avery John Bunn and Fortunata (Dottore) B.; m. David Samuel Kinderlehrer, Aug. 2, 1968 (div. 1978). B.A. in Math. and Philosophy, Mills Coll., 1967; Ph.D., U. Minn., 1974. Assoc. engr. Lockheed Missiles & Space, Sunnyvale, Calif., 1967; statistician Dept. Pub. Welfare, St. Paul, 1968-69; teaching asst. U. Minn., Mpls., 1969-74; asst. prof. Coll. St. Catherine, St. Paul, 1974-78; edn. analyst Control Data Corp., Mpls., 1978-82; tech. instr. Floating Point Systems, Portland, Oreg., 1982—; cons. Am. Philos. Soc., 1978-81, Feminist Press, N.Y.C., 1977-78; bd. dirs. Oreg. Partnership in Edn., Corvallis, 1985—. Author computer-based edn. courses, chpts. in books. Editor Philos. Abstracts, Champaign, Ill., 1976-78. Vol. computer studies educator Boy Scouts Am., 1985; producer Women's Energy Prodn. Co., Portland, 1980-82; resident philosopher Muse: Women's Art Collective, Mpls., 1979-80. Scholar, Mills Coll., 1963-67, Calif. State scholar, 1963-67. Mem. Assn. for Devel. Interactive Instructional systems, Nat. Assn. Female Execs., Oreg. Mycology Soc. Democrat. Roman Catholic. Avocations: mycology, dancing, reading, graphology. Home: 6485 SW Murray Blvd Beaverton OR 97005 Office: Floating Point Systems Inc 3601 SW Murray Blvd Beaverton OR 97005

FORWARD, DOROTHY ELIZABETH, probate legal assistant; b. Medford, Mass., Oct. 12, 1919; d. Roy Clifford and Julia (Lane) Hurd; student UCLA, 1964; m. Winston W. Forward, Sept. 29, 1942. Sec. nat. dir. fund raising ARC, Washington, 1943-46; legal sec. William W. Waters, Esq., Los Angeles, 1953-56; office mgr. Winston W. Forward, Ins. Adjuster, Arcadia, Calif., 1956-64; legal asst. John M. Podlech, Esq., Pasadena, 1964-79; dir. Calif. Probate Insts., Arcadia, 1970—; ind. probate legal asst., 1979—; condr. workshops in probate procedures, 1969—. Recipient ARC Meritorious Service award, 1945; named Legal Sec. of Yr., Pasadena Legal Secs. Assn., 1974, 75, 77; Freedom Through Edn. award, Pasadena Legal Secs. Assn., 1975. Mem. Nat. Assn. Legal Secs., Legal Secs. Inc., Calif. Legal Secs. Assn. (parliamentarian 1982-84), Pasadena Legal Secs. Assn. (pres. 1976-78), Los Angeles County Forum of Legal Secs. (chmn. 1978-80), Nat. Assn. Legal Assts. (charter). Contbg. author: Calif. Legal Secretary's Handbook, 1984, 85. Office: PO Box 311 Arcadia CA 91006

FOSGATE, HEATHER LYNN, media specialist, librarian, educator, consultant; b. Watertown, Wis., Sept. 8, 1951; d. Olin Tracy and Grace Jean (Alverstrom) F. B.S. in Edn., U. Ga., 1974, postgrad., 1974-76; M.Ed., N. Ga. Coll., 1976. Cert. tchr. art edn., gifted edn., library edn., library media. Stewardess, United Airlines, Newark, 1972-74; middle sch. art tchr. Wilkes County Bd. Edn., Washington, Ga., 1974-76; elem. sch. tchr. Clarke County Bd. Edn., Athens, Ga., 1976-80, tchr. gifted edn. Habersham County Bd. Edn., Clarkesville, Ga., 1980-81; art tchr. Lumpkin County Bd. Edn., Dahlonega, Ga., 1981-85, community edn. coordinator, 1983-85, coordinator, artist in edn., 1984-85; media specialist Jackson County Bd. Edn., Jefferson, Ga., 1985, Atlanta Archdiocese, Athens, 1985—; coordinator student interns N. Ga. Coll., Dahlonega, 1982-85, instr. continuing edn., 1983-85, instr. Art Field Day, 1983-84; instr. Ga. State Dept. Edn., Atlanta, 1984; honors program U. Ga. steering com., 1983-85. Judge, coordinator Ga. Council of Arts, 1983-85; judge Ga. State Beauty Contests, 1980-85; mem., hostess Am. Cancer Soc., Athens, 1976-80. Finalist Ga. Tchr. in Space, 1985. Mem. NEA, Ga. Seen. Educators, Ga. Art Edn. Assn. (exec. bd. 1983-85), Ga. Library Dept., Ga. Assn. Community Edn., Nat. Assn. Female Execs., Kappa Delta (alumni fin. advisor), Beta Sigma Phi. Republican. Methodist. Avocations: drawing, travel, reading. Home: 230 Valleybrook Dr Athens GA 30606 Office: St Joseph School Atlanta Archdiocese 134 Prince Ave Athens GA 30606

FOSHAY, MAXINE VALENTINE SHOTTLAND, public relations firm executive; b. N.Y.C., Feb. 14, 1921; d. Maximillian Stanford and Violet Gertrude (Turner) Shottland; m. Robert Lethbridge Foshay, Mar. 16, 1956. B.A., Royal Acad. Dramatic Arts, London, 1943. Field rep. N.Y.C. div. Am. Cancer Soc., 1967-68; dir. fundraising and pub. relations Preventive Medicine Inst., Strang Clinic, 1969-71; dir. fundraising and pub. relations Fedn. Handicapped, N.Y.C., 1971-72; exec. dir. Irvington House, 1972-73; chmn. group affiliates Meml. Sloan Kettering, 1960-66; prin. Maxine V. Foshay & Assocs., N.Y.C. Vol. Meml. Sloan Kettering Cancer Ctr., N.Y.C., 1956-77; v.p. Meml. Sloan Kettering Soc., 1966-67; dir. vols. Children's Asthmatic Found. N.Y.; bd. dirs. Elder Craftsmen, N.Y.C. Mem. Nat. Soc. Fund Raisers (bd. dirs., v.p. N.Y. chpt. 1971-78), Daus. Brit. Empire in State N.Y. (pres.).

FOSLER, GAIL D., economist, government official; b. Los Angeles Dec. 7, 1947; d. Richard E. and Helen Elizabeth (O'Gorman) Deschner. A.B. in Econs. U. So. Calif., 1969; M.B.A. in Fin., NYU, 1972. Research analyst Chgo. Dept. Human Resources, 1970-72; research assoc. I.C.F., Inc., 1972-74; asst. v.p., economist Manufacturers Hanover, 1974-78; chief economist Senate Budget Com., Washington, 1981—. Address: Senate Budget Com SD-621 Washington DC 20510

FOSNIGHT, JOAN LADELLA, insurance company executive; b. Ft. Wayne, Ind., Mar. 17, 1938; d. Paul Stoner and Lorene (King) Moore; m. Wallace Jay Fosnight, Aug. 30, 1958; children—Wendy Jo, Jonell Marie. B.S. in Edn., Ind. U., 1963. Work mgmt. cons. Lincoln Nat. Life Ins. Co., Ft. Wayne, 1979-81; mgr. productivity mgmt. Time Ins. Co., Milw., 1981—. Vice pres. Channel 39 Pub. TV, Ft. Wayne, 1978-82; chmn. Adopt-A-Patient program Mental Health Assn., Ft. Wayne, 1978-82; pres. aux. Ft. Wayne Children's Zoo, 1979-80; pres. Civics, Inc., Ft. Wayne, 1980-81. Mem. Life Office Mgmt. Assn. (mem. nat. productivity com.), AAUW, Bus. and Profl. Women's Assn., LWV. Lutheran. Home: 15000 Westover Rd Elm Grove WI 53122 Office: 515 W Wells St Milwaukee WI 53201

FOSTER, BARBARA ANN, lawyer; b. Newberry, Mich., July 12, 1953; d. James Charles and Margaret Ann (Brennan) Foster; m. William Anthony Thielen, Aug. 5, 1978. B.A., Alma Coll., 1975; J.D., U. Ky., 1977; LL.M. in Taxation, Georgetown U., 1982. Bar: Ky. 1978. Tax atty. Office Chief Counsel, IRS, Washington, 1978-82; asst. prof. law U. Ky. Coll. Law, Lexington, 1982-84; assoc. Wyatt, Tarrant & Combs, Lexington, 1984—. Editor Ky. Law Jour., 1977. Mem. ABA, Ky. Bar Assn., Order Coif, Phi Delta Phi.

FOSTER, BETTY LOUISE, educator; b. Lincoln, Nebr., Nov. 12, 1943; d. Burt Willis and Elizabeth Julia Hunt; B.S. in Elem. Edn., U. Nebr., 1965, postgrad. in Elem. Edn. Reading; postgrad. in Elem. Edn. and Reading, Kearney State Coll., endorsement in teaching reading; m. Gary A. Foster; children—Ann Louise, Geofrey Algot; 1 foster son, Matt Urbaver. Tchr. reading departmentalized grades 5-6 South Sioux City (Nebr.) Schs., 1967-69, supplemental reading tchr. Title I, 1970-71; supplemental reading tchr. Title I Grand Island (Nebr.) Schs., 1971—. Organizer, tchr. Head Start in South Sioux City Community Center and Chs., 1968-69; active Girl Scouts U.S.A., 1970—; v.p. Neighborhood Taskforce, Inc., 1980-82; pres. S. Locust/Barr Neighborhood Assn., 1980-81; mem. Mayor's Taskforce for Tornado Recovery, 1980-81; v.p. YWCA Grand Island, 1983; organizer Grand Island Women's Network, 1984; coach elem. level Olympics of the Mind, 1986. Mem. Nat., Nebr., Grand Island edn. assns., Internat. (sec. Central Council 1974—), Nebr., State reading assns., PTA of Children with Learning Disabilities, AAUW (pres. Grand Island br., br. pres. 1979-80, state v.p. 1981-82, state topic chmn. 1980-81), Nebr. Coalition of Women, LWV, Grand Island Art Club (pres. 1985-86), Alpha Delta Kappa. Developed self correcting games. Certified in elementary edn., kindergarten-6th grade, Nebr., Iowa; specialist in diagnosis and remediation of reading problems with learning disabilities problems, gifted children; cert. foster home, Nebr. Home: 1311 S Lincoln St Grand Island NE 68801 Office: 1314 W 7th St Grand Island NE 68801

FOSTER, CAROLINE ROBINSON, personnel director; b. Mobile, Ala., Oct. 2, 1937; s. Lucius Waite and Vassar Austill (Bowling) Robinson; m. Edward Eugene Foster, May 23, 1964; children—Robin Caroline, Edward Eugene. Student, Troy State U., 1956-57; B.S. in Bus. Adminstrn., U. S. Ala., 1983. Sec., Pacific Fin. Corp., Yuma, Ariz., 1957-58; sec. Univ. Hosp., Mobile, 1962-64; sec. to dir., asst. dir. social service, 1966-68; asst. to pres., dir. personnal Goodwill Industries, Inc., Mobile, 1968-79; exec. asst. Mobile County Commr. Jeff Mims, Mobile County Commn., 1979; regional recruitor ARC Blood Service, Ga., Fla. and Ala., 1979; regional personnel mgr. Retail Consumer Services, Inc./Citicorp., 1980; job developer U. South Ala. Work Search Project, 1980—; exec. sec., asst. to minister Chicksasw United Methodist Ch., 1983—; chmn. program com. Personnel and Indsl. Relations Conf., Ala. Continuing Edn., 1977, conf. chmn., 1978; speaker in field. Mem. exec. com. Mobile County Republicans; regional rep. ARC, 1979; area rep. Am. Intercultrual Student Exchange; team leader bus. div. United Fund, 1981; area rep. Am. Scandinavian Student Exchange Program, 1980-81. Mem. Internat. Mgmt. Council (del. to USSR, Council-YMCA mgr. exchange program, named Key Person 1977), Am. Soc. Personnel Adminstrs. (dist. dir. 1979-80, mem. leadership tng. com. 1979-80, mem. coll. relations com. 1981—, mem. vocat. edn. com. 1983-84), Women in Mgmt., Mobile Personnel Assn. (bd. dirs. 1972-74, sec.-treas. 1975-76, v.p. 1976-77, pres. 1977-78). Baptist. Club: Gayfers Career Women. Home: 5778 Honor St Mobile AL 36608

FOSTER, CATHERINE RIERSON, metal components manufacturing company executive; b. Balt., Mar. 14, 1935; d. William Harman and Ella Fredericka (Magsamen) Rierson; m. Morgan Lawrence Foster, Nov. 17, 1957; children—Diana Kay, Susan Ann, Morgan Lawrence, Heather Lynne. Student Balt. City Coll., 1955, Johns Hopkins U., 1956-57, Glendale Coll., 1962-63. Sec., Martin Co., Balt., 1956-57, adminstrv. sec., 1957-58; v.p., corp. sec. Fostermation, Inc., Meadville, Pa., 1971—, also dir.; mem. adv. com. Vocat./Tech. Sch., Meadville, 1982-86. Pres. La Crescents, La Crescenta, Calif., 1962; active City Hosp. Aux., Meadville, 1969—; active Republican Women's Workshop, Glendale, Calif., 1966-68, Com. to Elect Ronald Reagan, Glendale, 1967. Lutheran. Lodge: Order Eastern Star. Avocations: genealogy; European history; bridge. Home: 1121 Lakemont Dr Meadville PA 16335 Office: Fostermation Inc 200 Valleyview Dr Meadville PA 16335

FOSTER, CORDELIA ANNETTE, engineer; b. Detroit, Apr. 28, 1950; d. Odell and Anna Mae (Henry) F. B.A. in Math., Grambling State U., 1972. Advt. records clk. Pacific Telephone, San Francisco, 1972-73; computer programmer Standard Oil Calif., San Francisco and Houston, 1973-77; programmer Lockheed Electronics, Houston, 1977-79; engr. NASA, U.S. Govt., Houston, 1979—. Mem. Grambling U. Alumni Assn., Delta Sigma Theta. Democrat. Home: 7908 Grove Ridge Houston TX 77061 Office: FS45 Johnson Space Center Houston TX 77058

FOSTER, DONNA KAYREN, counselor, sales leader; b. Cin., July 2, 1948; d. Charles and Mary Lou (Johnson) Warren; m. James Earl Foster, Jr., Jan. 11, 1964 (div.); children—James E., III, Antonio Dwayne, Denarius Milton; m. James Earl Foster, Jr., July 23, 1983. A.A., U. Cin., 1984, B.S., 1985. Insp. Heechst Phram, Cin., 1967-72; clk. Cin. Metro. Housing, Cin., 1972-80; counselor Juvenile Justice System, Cin., 1972—; sales leader A.L. Williams, Cin., 1985—. Contbr. articles to profl. jours. Tng. in child care, Hillcrest Sch., Cin., 1982, alcohol edn. tng., 1984; coordinator youth counseling, Cin., 1984—; child care worker, Ohio Assn. Child Care Workers, 1983—; motivator, Motivational Program, Cin., 1982—. Recipient Alcohol Edn. award, Hillcrest Sch., 1984; Am. Red Cross award, Riverfront Stadium, 1984. Mem. Mu Omega Beta (treas. 1982-83), U. Cin. Alumni Assn. Avocations: skating; reading; physical exercise.

FOSTER, F. BLANCHE, writer; b. Centerville, Tenn., Jan. 6, 1919; d. L. George and F. Blanche F.; B.S., Tenn. State U., 1940; B.L.S., Atlanta U., 1947; A.M.L.S., U. Mich., 1953. Librarian, Sam Houston Coll., 1947-50; librarian, lectr. Detroit Public Schs., 1951-70; lectr. U. Ibadan (Nigeria), 1971-73; librarian South Vigo High Sch., Terre Haute, Ind., 1974-81; author books, most recent being: Dahomey, 1971, West Indies, 1976, East Central Africa, 1981. Active NAACP, YWCA, African-Am. Mus., Detroit, Your Heritage House, Detroit. Named Outstanding Woman Ind., Ind. Black Caucus, 1975; recipient Outstanding Community Achievement award Alpha Kappa Alpha, 1976. Mem. ALA, Vigo County Ret. Tchrs. Assn., People to People, ACLU, Alpha Kappa Alpha. Home: 2239 Spruce Terre Haute IN 47807

FOSTER, FLORENCE PEREY, educational administrator; b. Hollis, N.Y., Jan. 26, 1924; d. John Francis and Florence Louise (Spilbor) Perey; B.S. in Foods and Nutrition, Beaver Coll., 1946; M.A. in Early Childhood Edn., Kean Coll. N.J., 1964; postgrad. Bank Street Coll. Edn., 1965, Rider Coll., 1968, Glassboro State Coll., 1972, Trenton State Coll., 1979; m. Gerald R. Foster, July 27, 1943; 1 son, Brian Gerald. Social worker Dept. Public Welfare, Long Island, N.Y., 1947-48; nutritionist Beechnut Co., N.Y.C., 1948-49; head tchr. Wesley Hall, Westfield, N.J., 1958-62; dir. Bound Brook (N.J.) Coop., 1962-63; head tchr. Pickwick Nursery East Orange, N.J., 1963-64; edn. dir. Child Service Assn., Newark, 1964-66; asst. in early childhood N.J. State Dept. Edn., Trenton, 1966-68, coordinator fed. early children programs, 1968-69, dir. early childhood and state follow through coordinator, 1969-70, dir. early childhood edn., 1971-72; asso. dir. Follow Through and Head Start Bank Street Coll. Edn., N.Y.C., 1970-71; dir. Bainbridge Nursery Sch. and Crosswicks (N.J.) Country Day Sch., 1972-73; N.J. head start regional tng. officer Region 2 Office Child Devel., HEW, Rider Coll., Lawrence, N.J., 1973-75; exec. dir. Egenolf Day Nursery Assn., Elizabeth, N.J., 1975-77; N.J. Head Start Regional tng. officer, Region 2 Adminstrn. for Children, Youth and Families, Dept. Health and Human Services, Rutgers U., New Brunswick, N.J., 1977-78; dir. child devel. assoc., head start supplementary tng. program dept. elem. early childhood and reading Trenton State Coll., 1978—. NDEA fellow for Early Childhood Adminstrs., 1965. Mem. Nat. Assn. Edn. Young Children, Organization Mondiali pour l'Education Prescolaire, N.J. Assn. Edn. Young Children (edn. and research chmn. 1962-84, chpt. pres. 1968-70), Assn. Childhood Edn. Internat. Congregationalist. Editor Young World, 1962-84; contbr. articles to profl. jours. Home: 810 Harding St Westfield NJ 07090 Office: Trenton State Coll Dept Elem Early Childhood and Reading Hillwood Lakes CN 550 Trenton NJ 08625

FOSTER, IRENE LORETTO, writer; b Lewistown, Mont., Dec. 18, 1924; d. James Nelson and Mary Ellen (Foley) Bailey; m. Vincent E. Foster, June 30, 1948 (div. June 1970); children—Vincent, Steven, Kevin, Margaret, Jeffrey; m. 2d, Bernard A. Carmin, Sept. 21, 1977. B.A., Gt. Falls Coll., 1946. Free lance writer, Seattle, 1957-68, 83—; writer Reverman Advt. Agy., Seattle, 1968-74, Evans Pacific Advt. Agy., Seattle, 1974-77, Stimpson Assocs., advt., Seattle, 1978-83. Contbr. articles and short stories to mags. including Good Housekeeping, Redbook, The Writer, Am. Girl. Mem. Seattle Free Lance (v.p. 1966-67, pres. 1967-68), Pacific N.W. Writers Conf. Roman Catholic.

FOSTER, MARGERY SOMERS, educator; b. Boston, Mar. 27, 1914; d. L. Brent and Grace (Butler) F.; B.A., Wellesley Coll., 1934; Ph.D., Radcliffe Coll., 1958; Litt.D., Russell Sage Coll., 1968. Asst. to actuary New Eng. Mut. Life Ins. Co., 1934-43; dep. comptroller and dir. devel. Wellesley Coll., 1946-54; lectr. econs. Harvard U. Sch. Bus. Adminstrn., 1956-58; lectr. econs., sec. coll. Mt. Holyoke Coll., 1958-64; prof. econs., dean coll. Hollins Coll., 1964-67; prof. econs., dean coll. Douglass Coll. of Rutgers U., 1967-75. Univ. prof. econs. Rutgers, 1975-80, prof. emeritus, 1980—; past dir. Prudential Ins. Co. Am. Mem. commn. on tests Coll. Entrance Exam. Bd., 1966-70, trustee, 1969-72; mem. commn. on instl. affairs Assn. Am. Colls., 1971-74; mem. Harvard U. overseer's vis. com. for Warren Center in Am. History, 1973-79; trustee Middle States Assn. Colls. and Schs., 1973-79. Served to lt. Women's Res., USNR, 1943-46. Mem. Am. Econ. Assn., Econ. History Assn., Econ. History Soc. Clubs: Appalachian Mountain, Cosmopolitan. Author: Out of Smalle Beginnings, An Economic History of Harvard College in the Puritan Period, 1962. Spl. research on Am. colonial econ. history, history of edn., pub. fin. Address: Box 60 Francestown NH 03043

FOSTER, MARTHA TYAHLA, educational administrator; b. Coaldale, Pa., Apr. 22, 1955; d. Stephen and Frances (Solomon) Tyahla; m. David Marion Foster, Jan. 3, 1981. B.A., U. Va., 1977, M.Ed., 1981, Ed.S., 1981. Legis. asst. U.S. Ho. of Reps., Washington, 1977-79; asst. dean summer session U. Va., Charlottesville, 1981; program cons. campus activities U. Houston, 1981; coordinator student affairs Capitol Inst. Tech., Kensington, Md., 1982-83, asst. dean students, Laurel, Md., 1983-84, assoc. dean students, 1984-86, dean students, 1986—. Named Woman of Yr., Bus. and Profl. Women's Club, Vienna, Va., 1986. Mem. Am. Coll. Personnel Assn., Am. Assn. Counseling and Devel., Am. Soc. Tng. and Devel. (met. D.C. chpt.), Va. Counselors Assn. Methodist. Lodge: Order of Eastern Star. Office: Capitol Inst Tech 11301 Springfield Rd Laurel MD 20708

FOSTER, MARY FRAZER (LECRON), anthropologist; b. Des Moines, Feb. 1, 1914; d. James and Helen (Cowles) LeCron; B.A., Northwestern U., 1936; Ph.D., U. Calif., Berkeley, 1965; m. George McClelland Foster, Jan. 6, 1938; children—Jeremy, Melissa Foster Bowerman. Research asso. dept. anthropology U. Calif., Berkeley, 1955-57, 75—; lectr. in anthropology Calif. State U., Hayward, 1966-75; mem. faculty Fromm Inst. Lifelong Learning, U. San Francisco, 1980. Fellow Am. Anthrop. Assn.; mem. Linguistic Soc. Am., Internat. Linguistic Assn., Southwestern Anthrop. Assn., AAAS, Soc. Woman Geographers. Democrat. Author: (with George M. Foster) Sierra Popoluca Speech, 1948; The Tarascan Language, 1969; editor: (with Stanley H. Brandes) Symbol As Sense: New Approaches to the Analysis of Meaning, 1980; (with Robert A. Rubinstein) Peace and War: Cross-cultural Perspectives, 1986. Home: 790 San Luis Rd Berkeley CA 94707

FOSTER, NICOLE WILLIAMS, financial executive; b. Langley Field, Va., July 23, 1944; d. Andrew Watts and Jacqueline Suzanne (Nicklin) Williams. A.A., Pensacola Jr. Coll., 1963; student U. Geneva (Switzerland), 1966; Licence es Sci. Polit., Grad. Inst. Internat. Affairs, Geneva, 1968; M.B.A., U. Chgo., 1970. Fin. cons. Perkins & Will, Chgo., 1973-75; asst. treas. Pullman, Inc., Chgo., 1975-79; treas. Trailmobile div., 1979-81, pres. Trailmobile Fin. Co., Chgo., 1980-81; treas. Swift Ind. Corp., Chgo., 1981-83, v.p., treas., 1983—. Author: Management of Hospital Employee Productivity, 1972. Bd. dirs. Ill. Devel. Fin. Authority, Chgo., 1977-83, Met. Housing and Planning Council, Chgo., 1977-83, Youth Guidance, Chgo., 1980-83. Club: Economic (Chgo.). Office: Swift Independent Corp 115 W Jackson Blvd Chicago IL 60604

FOSTER, PEARL DELPHINE, physician, educator; b. N.Y.C., Oct. 23, 1922; d. Isabel A. Courtney; m. Charles C. Hunt, June 25, 1950; children—Joanne Y., Patrice M. B.S., Queens Coll., 1943; M.D., Howard U., 1948; M.P.A., C.W. Post Coll., 1980. Intern, Harlem Hosp., N.Y.C., 1948-49, resident, 1950-53; resident Freedmen's Hosp., Washington, 1949-50; tchr. internal medicine Harlem Hosp. Sch. Nursing, 1955-65; practice medicine specializing in internal medicine, St. Albans, N.Y., 1953—; assoc. in clin. medicine Columbia U., 1970; chmn. utilization rev., mem. med. bd. Harlem Hosp.; mem. exec. com. Hillcrest Gen. Hosp., Flushing, N.Y. Recipient citation Harlem Hosp., 1958; Community Service award Nat. Urban Coalition, 1970-73. Mem. Am. Coll. Quality Assurance and Utilization Rev. Physicians, AMA (recipient Physicians Recognition award), N.Y. Heart Assn., Am. Geriatric Soc., Am. Pub. Health Assn., N.Y. State Pub. Health Assn., N.Y. Acad. Sci., N.Y. State Soc. Internal Medicine, Kappa Pi, Pi Alpha Alpha. Roman Catholic. Clubs: Carats, Coalition of 100 Black Women. Office: 200 15 Linden Blvd Saint Albans NY 11412

FOSTER, ROYCE PORTER, general contracting company executive; b. Wilkes County, Dec. 12, 1928; d. Lee Roy and Vassie Beatrice (Byrd) Porter; m. Roy George Foster, June 20, 1953; children—Karen Elizabeth, Melanie Ann, John Andrew. Student Draughon's Bus. Coll., 1945-46. Cert. ceramics tchr. Clk. typist Coble Dairies, Wilkesboro, N.C., 1946-47; bookkeeper Lineberry Foundry, North Wilkesboro, N.C., 1947-53; bookkeeper Nat. Meml. Park, Falls Church, Va., 1953; bookkeeper T.A. Talley & Son, Richmond, Va., 1955-56; bookkeeper Q.M. Tomlinson, Inc., Roanoke, Va., 1965-82, exec. v.p., 1982—. Mem. adv. bd. Va. Western Community Coll., Roanoke, 1980-81. Mem. Nat. Assn. Women in Constrn. (pres. 1979-81). Democrat. Presbyterian. Office: QM Tomlinson Inc 601 First Fed Bldg Roanoke VA 24011

FOSTER, RUTH IRENE, educator; b. Adair County, Iowa, Mar. 6, 1916; d. Clyde Manson and Rachel Virginia (Martin) Archer; B.S., Drake U., 1954, M.S., 1962; postgrad. U. Iowa, 1969, U. So. Calif., 1970; m. David R. Foster, June 30, 1938. Tchr. rural sch. Adair County (Iowa), 1934-38, Polk County Schs. (Iowa), 1942-54; tchr. Des Moines Pub. Schs., 1954-85, mem. adv. council staff devel., 1978; supr. elem. student tchrs. Coll. Edn., Iowa State U., 1986—. Mem. Cadre-Tchrs., Central Dist. Iowa State Edn., 1971-72; mem. teaching triad Classroom Tchr. Conf., U. Okla., summer 1969; mem. edn. and cert. com. Iowa Dept. Public Instrn., 1970-75; mem. Nat. Council Accreditation of Tchr. Tng. Edn., 1980—; mem. Iowa Profl. Teaching Practices Commn., 1971-76; mem. teaching staff, models of teaching Nat. Tchr. Corps Inst., U. Richmond (Va.), summer 1975; regional coordinator Nat. Survey for Preservice Preparation Tchrs., Nat. Center for Ednl. Stats., Stanford U., 1975-76; mem. vis. team Nat. Council for Accreditation Tchr. Edn., 1970—; mem. Project Profile taskforce Coll. Edn. Iowa State U., 1982—, mem. adv. com., 1984-86; mem. adv. com. div. edn. Grandview Coll., Des Moines, 1985—. Republican precinct committeewoman, 1967-69. Recipient Living Meml. scholarship, Delta Kappa Gamma, 1970; Charles Martin State Edn. award, 1981-82; Ruth Foster award for outstanding service to teaching profession named in her honor, 1985. Mem. Women's C. of C. (profl.), NEA (del. constl. conv. 1971-72), Des Moines Edn. Assn. (parliamentarian 1972-74), Am. Bus. Women Club, Iowa Edn. Assn. (dist. pres. 1966-68, rep. World Conf. Orgns. Teaching Profession 1972, mem. instrnl. profl. devel. council 1972-74, 77—), Iowa Instrnl. Profl. Devel., Nat. (sec. 1967-69), Iowa (pres. 1970-72) assns. classroom tchrs., Des Moines Edn. Assn. (1st v.p. 1966-68, chmn. instrnl. profl. devel. com. 1978-85), AAUW, Phi Delta Kappa, Kappa Kappa Iota (v.p. state chpt. 1974-75, pres. state central council presidents 1975-76, state pres. 1976-77, nat. exec. com., chmn. nat. conv. 1978, post III nat. exec. com. 1979-81), Delta Kappa Gamma Epsilon. Republican. Mem. Christian Ch. Mem. Order Eastern Star, Daus. of Nile. Home: 1004 McKinley Des Moines IA 50315

FOSTER, SALLY MARIE, legal consultant; b. Washington, Apr. 21, 1954; d. Eric Foster and Vera (Prevette) Foster Rollo. B.A., U. Md., 1976; J.D., Wake Forest U., 1980. Law intern Office Chief Counsel, FAA, Washington, 1980-81; contracts adminstr. Brit. Aerospace, Inc., Herndon, Va., 1981-83; contracts specialist JWK Internat. Corp., Arlington, Va., 1983; staff legal cons. systems internat. div. Computer Scis. Corp., Fairfax, Va., 1983—; sr. mem. CAP, Maxwell AFB, Ala., 1979—. Recipient First Honors, Dorothy Shaw Leadership award Alpha Delta Pi, 1976. Mem. Lawyer-Pilots Bar Assn., Nat. Contracts Mgmt. Assn., Nat. Assn. Female Execs., Phi Alpha Delta, Phi Alpha Theta. Democrat. Methodist. Lodge: Women of Moose. Home: 7203 Sewell Ave Falls Church VA 22046 Office: Computer Scis Corp 11150 Main St Fairfax VA 22030

FOSTER, SARA ANN, social work educator; b. Greencastle, Ind., Feb. 19, 1927; d. Harold and Anne May (Kemp) Zink; student DePauw U., 1944-47; B.A., U. N.Mex., 1948; M.A., Ohio State U., 1952; postgrad. U. Wis., 1972-74; 1 dau., Anne Claire Foster. Psychiat. social worker Div. Mental Hygiene, State of Ohio, 1952-53; research analyst High Commn. for Germany, Frankfort, 1950-51; social work researcher Westside Day Nursery, Northside Day Nursery, Columbus, 1954-55; caseworker, supr. Children's Services County of Franklin, Columbus, 1956-62; instr. dept. sociology Ohio Wesleyan U., 1963-69; asst. prof. social work Ohio State U., 1963—. NIMH grantee, 1972-74. Mem. Ohio Women Inc., Council on Social Work Edn. (ho. of dels. 1976-79, 81—), Nat. Assn. Social Workers (state bd. dirs. 1976-77), Acad. Cert. Social Workers, Ohio Coll. Assn. Social Service Educators, AAUP. Democrat. Methodist. Home: 5812 Olentangy Blvd Worthington OH 43085 Office: 1947 N College Rd Ohio State U Columbus OH 43210

FOSTER, TAMMY LEE, nurse, administrator; b. Richmond, Va., Sept. 25, 1958; d. Lee Roy and Rosalie Marion (Pritchett) F.; m. Edward Douglas Tyndall, Jr., Oct. 12, 1985. Diploma in Nursing, St. Luke's Sch. Nursing, 1979. R.N., Va. Salesperson Memco, Richmond, 1975-79; nurse St. Luke's Hosp.,

Richmond, 1979—, asst. head nurse, 1984—, staff blood pressure clinic St. Luke's Hosp., 1984—. Republican. Presbyterian. Avocation: bowling. Office: Humana St Lukes 7700 Parham Rd Richmond VA 23229

FOSTER, VELTA ALLENE, educational administrator; b. Pomona, Calif, June 9, 1935; d. Raymond A. and Velta Lucille (Jones) F. B.A., U. Redlands, 1957; M.A., Azusa Pacific U., 1971; postgrad. Ariz. State U. Tchr., Covina Sch. Dist., Calif., 1957-61, Rowland Sch. Dist., Rowland Heights, Calif., 1961-71; founder, adminstr. Northwest Christian Acad., Glendale, Ariz., 1971—. Mem. Assn. Christian Schs. Internat., Oral Roberts U. Ednl. Fellowship, Nat. Assn. Christian Educators, Bus. and Profl. Women. Republican. Mem. Full Gospel Ch. Avocations: quilting; gardening; camping; photography. Office: Northwest Christian Acad 14240 N 43d Ave Glendale AZ 85306

FOSTER-NOBEL, CAROL ANN, physician; b. Torrance, Calif., July 5, 1955; d. Duane Ray and Loretta Margaret (Hill) F. B.A. in Biology, Point Loma Coll., 1977; M.D., U. Calif.-San Diego, 1981. Resident in gen. surgery U. Calif.-San Diego Med. Ctr., 1981-82, resident in head and neck surgery, 1982-83; staff physician emergency medicine Rees Stealy Med. Group, San Diego, 1983-84; adj. prof. Point Loma Coll. Sch. Nursing, 1985—. Mackenzie Found. scholar, 1978-80; Country Friends of U. Calif.-San Diego, scholar, 1978-79; Ruth B. White Meml. Fund scholar, 1979-80. Mem. AMA, Calif. Med. Assn., Calif. House Officer Med. Soc., Phi Delta Lambda. Home: PO Box 3166 Rancho Santa Fe CA 92067 Office: 3023 Bunker Hill Suite 103A San Diego CA 92109

FOTINOS, KATHERINE, educator; b. San Francisco, Apr. 12, 1926; d. Christ Anastasios and Ageliki George (Pilarinos) F. B.A., San Francisco State Coll., 1948; M.A., Stanford U., 1955. Life diploma tchr. Calif. Tchr. Excelsior Sch., San Francisco, 1948-53, Ridgepoint III, San Francisco, 1953-54, Jedediah Smith Sch., San Francisco, 1954-55; head tchr. Washington Irving Sch., San Francisco, 1955-60, Jean Parker Sch., San Francisco, 1960—; curriculum designer 1951—; tchr. trainer for U. San Francisco, U. Calif., Berkley, Stanford U. and San Francisco State U. Co-author: Curriculum Guide for Language Arts, Curriculum Guide for Music, Curriculum Guide for Social Studies and Science (all for grades K-6 in San Francisco Unified Sch. Dist.). Designer Deaf Scrabball, 1981; artwork displayed deYoung Mus. Vol. Assn. for Deaf and Blind, 1980—; docent Calif. Hist. Soc., Sonoma; festival decoration chmn. Greek Orthodox Ch., Solono County 1982; vol. Sonoma Republican Com., 1982; chmn. Sonoma County for Senatorial Cand. GOP. Recipient commendations Pres. U.S., Gov. Calif., state senators, others. Mem. Sonoma Valley Rep. Women (charter), Nat. Fedn. Rep. Women (fedn. regent) Calif. PTA (hon. life), Calif. Tchrs. Assn., Stanford Edn. Club (sec. 1972-74), Alpha Delta Kappa (life; pres. 1962-64). Lodge: Daus. Penelope (v.p. 1974-76). Home: 150 El Portola Dr Sonoma CA 95476

FOTO, MARY ELIZABETH SMITH (MRS. STEPHEN ANTHONY FOTO), health cons.; b. Iowa Falls, Iowa, Sept. 1, 1941; d. Roy D. and Margaret Grace (Binnie) Smith; B.S., U. So. Calif., 1966; m. Stephen Anthony Foto, Aug. 29, 1964; 1 dau., Alison Marie. Clin. affiliate U. So. Calif.-Los Angeles County Med. Center, Rancho Los Amigos, Brentwood VA Hosp., 1966-67; staff therapist Crippled Children's Services Los Angeles County, 1967-68; staff therapist Coll. Vista Convalescent Hosp.; pvt. practice as occupational therapist, Eagle Rock, Calif., 1968-70; head therapist Glen Wheeler Assos., San Gabriel, Calif., 1970-73; cons. Hillhaven Convalescent Hosp., Inc., Tacoma, 1972-74; occupational therapy cons. Blue Cross So. Calif., Los Angeles, 1972—; tchr. restorative services sect. Western Center Continuing Edn. in Adminstrn. of Health Core Facilities, UCLA, 1971-74; lectr. Loma Linda U. Allied Health Sch., 1973, instr., 1978-81, asso. prof., 1981—; preclin. instr. U. So. Calif. Sch. Occupational Therapy, 1973, 74; tchr. restorative services Calif. Nursing Home Assn., 1973; lectr. Acad. Speech Pathology, 1974. Cons. Health Programs Evaluation Services, Inc., Los Angeles, 1973—, Westchester Phys. Therapy, Bakersfield, Calif., 1972-74. Mem. Parent involvement Com. All Saints Day Care Center, 1971-74, bd. dirs., 1978—. Mem. Am. (spl. adviser on pvt. practice-nat. legislative com. 1973, commn. on practice 1977—), So. Calif. (legislative chmn. 1972) occupational therapy assns., Alpha Chi Omega. Republican. Episcopalian. Home: 445 Pilgrim Pl San Marino CA 91108 Office: PO Box 70000 Van Nuys CA 91470

FOUCH, STEPHANIE SAUNDERS, advertising agency executive, consultant; b. Yonkers, N.Y., Apr. 22, 1947; d. Stephan L. and Rosetta J. (Arvonio) Saunders; B.A., Vassar Coll., 1968; m. Gregory G. Fouch, Mar. 6, 1976; 1 dau., Charlotte Michaux. Asst. account exec. Chirurg & Cairns, Inc., N.Y.C., 1968-70; account exec. Benton & Bowles, Inc., N.Y.C., 1971-75; pub. cons., N.Y.C. and Washington, 1975-77; v.p. Weitzman, Dym & Assos., Inc., Washington, 1978-82; v.p., client services dir. Abramson Assos., Washington, 1982-83; advt. cons., 1984—; speaker, adv. in field. Bd. dirs. Henry St. Settlement, N.Y.C., 1971-73. Recipient Merit award United Fund Greater N.Y., 1972. Mem. Am. Advt. Fedn., Washington Media Mgmt. Network, Advt. Club Washington. Clubs: Bethesda Country, Vassar (dir. N.Y.C. 1972-74).

FOULKES, DENISE DUBOSE, manufacturing company executive; b. N.Y.C., July 18, 1958; d. Vincent Gulf and Sadie Elizabeth (DuBose) Foulkes. B.S., Fordham U., 1980; M. Mgmt., Northwestern U., 1982. Market research intern Colgate-Palmolive Co., N.Y.C., summer 1979; mktg. mgmt. intern Johnson & Johnson, New Brunswick N.J., summers 1980, 81; asst. product mgr. S.C. Johnson & Son, Inc., Racine, Wis., 1982-84, assoc. product mgr., 1984—. Chairperson, First Thursday's Group, Racine, 1983—; counselor Catholic Charities, N.Y.C., 1975-76. Johnson & Johnson scholar, 1980-82. Mem. Am. Mktg. Assn. Democrat. Roman Catholic. Home: East Park Towers 111-11th St 3CS Racine WI 53403 Office: SC Johnson & Son Inc 1525 Howe St Racine WI 53403

FOULKES, MARTHA LEE ELLIOTT, real estate developer; b. Terre Haute, Ind., Oct. 4, 1925; d. Ross Edward and Norma Maybelle (Reichert) Elliott; student Ind. State U., Terre Haute, 1943-45; m. George Arthur Foulkes, Mar. 21, 1948 (dec. May 1977); children—Merrilee, Kathleen, Elizabeth, Jennifer, Arthur. Messenger, bookkeeper Ind. State Bank, Terre Haute, 1943-45; exec. sec. Mchts. Nat. Bank, Terre Haute, 1945-48; sec.-treas. Sta. WAAC, Terre Haute, 1963-77, pres., 1977-83; cons., speaker in field. Bd. dirs. Jr. Achievement Wabash Valley, Wabash Valley chpt. ARC, Terre Haute Area Clean Community; pres. Inactive League Terre Haute, 1975-76. Mem. Terre Haute Area C. of C., Terre Haute Downtown Bus. Council, Kappa Kappa Kappa, Delta Gamma (alumnae pres. 1965-66). Republican. Christian Scientist. Club: Terre Haute Country. Home: 80 Allendale Terre Haute IN 47802 Office: 601 Ohio St Terre Haute IN 47808

FOURCARD, INEZ GAREY, found. exec.; b. Bklyn., Sept. 26, 1930; d. George W. and Frances E. (MacDonald) Garey; student Pratt Inst., 1946-48; B.F.A., McNeese State U., 1963; m. Waldren Arthur Fourcard, Aug. 7, 1948; children—Chrystal Frances, Sharon Lynn, Waldren Arthur, Andrea Renee, David Marquard, Anita Lynn. Exhibited in numerous one man shows throughout U.S., also in Eng., France and Spain; mem. gifted and talented sect. of Spl. Edn. State of La., 1971-73; mem. adv. council Child Centered/Parent Tutored Kindergarden Program, 1974—; mem. La. Task Force for Community Edn., 1974-75; v.p. La. Assn. for Sickle Cell Anemia, 1974—, named best statewide vol.; mem. Calcasieu Parish Bicentennial Com., 1974—; exec. dir. Southwestern Sickle Cell Anemia Found., Lake Charles, La., 1973—. Named Hon. Citizen of Fort Worth, 1977; recipient Award of Merit, Human Relations Council of Lake Charles Deanery, award for services to sickle cell disease Sigma Gamma Rho, award for community service Phi Beta Sigma. Democrat. Roman Catholic. Important works include The Widow in pvt. collection Bertrand Russell Peace Found., London. Home: 1414 St John St Lake Charles LA 70601 Office: PO Box 3254 118 Enterprise Blvd Lake Charles LA 70601

FOURROUX, MARGARITA, insurance company manager; b. LaFeria, Tex., Dec. 18, 1950; d. Isidro and Elida (Trevino) Garcia; m. Melvin R. Fourroux, June 5, 1978; children—Josie, Matthew. Assoc. in Bus., Bellville Area Coll., Ill., 1986. Adminstrv. asst. Alpha Enterprises, Honolulu, 1978-81; purchasing agt. Poly Disc Systems, Torrance, Calif., 1981-83; purchasing mgr. Indicator Controls, Gardena, Calif., 1984-85; corp. office service mgr. Hickey Mitchell Ins., St. Louis, 1985—. Mem. Am. Purchasing Soc., Nat. Assn. Female Execs. Roman Catholic. Avocations: oil painting; reading; drawing. Office: Hickey Mitchell Ins 4242 Lindell Blvd Saint Louis MO 63108

FOUSHEE, OLA MAIE SUTTENFIELD, painter, author, lectr.; b. Avalon, N.C.; d. Emmett R. and Callie Jane (Keaton) Suttenfield; student U. N.C., intermittently 1953-57, pvt. tchrs.; m. John McIver Foushee, Sept. 5, 1931; children—John McIver, June Keaton. Tchr. arts and crafts Army Convalescent Hosp., 1945, U. N.C., 1946; tchr. art Allied Arts, Durham, N.C., 1955-56; now v.p., adv. mgr. Foushee Realty and Ins. Co., Chapel Hill, N.C.; one-woman shows in N.C., S.C.; exhibited in group shows, N.C., S.C., Pa., Va., also Rowan Art Gallery, Salisbury, N.C., Center Gallery, Carrboro, N.C., 1981, Meredith Coll., Raleigh, N.C., 1981, Atlantic Christian Coll., 1982, Salem Coll., 1982, Appalachian U., 1982, also others; paintings in numerous pvt. collections, also Wachovia Bank; lectr. on art; mem. art juries. Recipient citation N.C. State Art Soc., 1962. Founding mem. Durham Art Guild; Chapel Hill Jr. Service League; founder Chapel Hill Sch. Art Guild, co-founder Asso. Artists of N.C.; mem. State Art Soc. N.C. (life), Nat. Trust for Hist. Preservation, Phi Mu. Author: Art in North Carolina: Episodes and Developments 1585-1970, 1972; History of the Suttenfield Family, 1974; Avalon: A North Carolina Town of Joy and Tragedy, 1977; art columnist Greensboro Daily News, Durham Morning Herald, Rocky Mount Evening Telegram, High Point Enterprise, Charlotte Observer, Wilmington Star and others, 1958-63, Chapel Hill Weekly, 1963—; also TV series on N.C. Artists, 1975; TV Spl. on Outdoor Sculpture and Murals in N.C., 1978, 79. Home: Chapel Hill NC 27514

FOUST, JO ROBERSON, county ofcl.; b. Almance County, N.C., Sept. 25, 1937; d. Robert E. and Emma L. (Holt) Roberson; grad. Burlington (N.C.) Bus. Coll., 1960; student Inst. Govt., U. N.C., Chapel Hill, 1960-62; m. Robert A. Foust, Apr. 15, 1979; 1 son by previous marriage—Dale. Dep. register of deeds Alamance County Govt., Graham, N.C., 1958-71, adminstrv. asst. to county mgr., 1971-73, personnel dir., 1973—; v.p. Holt Constrn. Co., Graham, N.C.; dir. Nu-Med Ins. Co.; EEOC officer. Bd. dirs. United Way, Am. Heart Assn.; adv. council Employment Security Commn. Mem. Am. Soc. Personnel Adminstrs., Am. Soc. Public Administrs., Alamance County Personnel Assn., N.C. Heart Assn., Nat. Assn. County Ofcls. Democrat. Methodist. Club: Moose. Home: 520 Ward St Graham NC 27253 Office: 124 W Elm St Graham NC 27253

FOUST, SARAH (SALLY), county official; b. Sherman, Mich., Apr. 28, 1930; d. Stanley Whitmore and Mary Isabel (Munn) Teed; m. Donald Judson Foust, Sept. 9, 1950; children—Doris Jean Foust Lloyd, Dawn Janette Foust Bolock. Student Central Mich. U., 1947-50; B.S., Western Mich. U., 1968. Cert. secondary tchr., Mich. Elem. tchr. Edwardsburg Pub. Schs., Mich., 1963-68; register of deeds Cass County, Cassopolis, Mich., 1969—. Exec. mem. Cass County Republican Party, Mich., 1969—; officer, dir. Cass County Rep. Women's Club, Mich., 1969—; ruling elder Edwardsburg Presbyterian Ch., Mich., 1984-86, deacon, 1975-77. Mem. Mich. Assn. Registers of Deeds (pres. 1982-83, v.p. 1980-82, sec. 1977-79, dir. 1984—, Plaque award 1983), United County Officers Assn. of Mich. (del. 1971—), Bus. and Profl. Women's Club. Avocations: gardening; reading. Home: 68066 Elsie Ln PO Box 299 Edwardsburg MI 49112

FOWKE, EDITH MARGARET FULTON, author, educator; b. Lumsden, Sask., Can., Apr. 30, 1913; d. William Marshall and Margaret (Fyffe) Fulton; student Regina Coll., 1929-31; B.A. with high honours in English and History, U. Sask., 1933, M.A. in English, 1938; LL.D. (hon.), Brock U., 1974, U. Regina, 1986; D.Litt., Trent U., 1975, York U., 1982; m. Franklin George Fowke, Oct. 1, 1938. Editor, Western Tchr., Saskatoon, Sask., 1937-45; assoc. editor Mag. Digest, Toronto, Ont., Can., 1945-50; asso. prof. English dept. York U., Downsview, Ont., 1971-77, prof., 1977-84, emeritus, 1984—. Decorated Order of Can. Fellow Royal Soc. Can., Am. Folklore Soc.; mem. English Folk Dance and Song Soc., Assn. Canadian Univ. Tchrs. English, Folklore Studies Assn. Can., Canadian Folk Music Soc., Writers Union Can., Mensa. Author, editor; Folk Songs of Canada, 1954; Folk Songs of Quebec, 1957; Songs of Work and Freedom, 1960; Canada's Story in Song, 1960; Traditional Singers and Songs from Ontario, 1965; More Folk Songs of Canada, 1967; Lumbering Songs from the Northern Woods, 1970; Sally Go Round the Sun, 1969; Penguin Book of Canadian Folk Songs, 1974; Folklore of Canada, 1976; Ring Around the Moon, 1977; Folktales of French Canada, 1979; A Bibliography of Canadian Folklore in English, 1981; Sea Songs and Ballads from 19th Century Nova Scotia, 1982 Songs and Sayings of an Ulster Childhood (Alice Kane), 1983; Singing Our Heritage, 1984; Explorations in Canadian Folklore, 1985; Tales Told in Canada, 1986; editor Canadian Folk Music Jour., 1973—. Office: Winters College York U 4700 Keele St Downsview ON M3J IP3 Canada

FOWLER, BARBARA MASSEY WOODWARD, nursing administrator; b. Newport News, Va., Feb. 28, 1944; d. Horace Talmadge and Myrtle Virginia (Bland) Massey; R.N., Riverside Hosp. Sch. Nursing, Newport News, 1965; m. Robert Toy Fowler, Apr. 2, 1977; children—Richard Mark Woodward, Karen Jill Woodward; stepchildren—Robert Toy and Tamara Lynn Fowler. Coronary care nurse Riverside Hosp., Newport News, 1965-69; office nurse, Newport News, 1969-71; pediatric nurse Riverside Hosp., 1972-73, nurse adminstr., nursing leadership instr., 1973-74; exec. dir. Peninsula Planned Parenthood, Hampton, Va., 1974-78; co-owner, mgr. Footsteps Shoe Store, Hayes, Va. and Grafton, Va., 1978—; dir. nursing Saluda Home (Va.), 1982-84; instr. geriatric nurses aides Raphahannock Community Coll. Sec., Hayes Stores Tenants Assn.; mem. Heritage Tenants Assn.; bd. dirs. Peninsula Planned Parenthood, 1979-80, mem. expansion and merger com., budget com., 1980; cons. dir. Planned Parenthood Greater Tidewater, 1980; exec. com. S.E. region Planned Parenthood, 1980-81. Cert. rape crisis counselor, problem pregnancy counselor, sex edn. instr. Mem. Nat. League Nursing. Episcopalian. Home: PO Box 273 Gloucester VA 23061 Office: Saluda Home Route 17 Box 33 Saluda VA

FOWLER, BETTY JANMAE, dance company director, editor; b. Chgo., May 23, 1925; d. Harry and Mary (Jacques) Markin; student Art Inst., Chgo., 1937-39, Stratton Bus. Coll., Chgo., 1942-43, Columbia U., 1945-47; B.A., Eastern Wash. U., 1984; 1 dau., Sherry Mareth Connors. Mem. public relations dept. Girl Scouts U.S.A., N.Y.C., 1961-63; adminstrv. asst. to editor-in-chief Scholastic Mags., N.Y.C., 1963-68; adminstrv. dir. Leonard Fowler Dancers, Fowler Sch. Classical Ballet, Inc., N.Y.C., 1959-78, tchr. ballet, 1959-61; editor Bulletin, Kiwanis weekly publ., Spokane, Wash., 1978-82, also adminstrv. sec. Kiwanis Club; instr. Spokane Falls Community Coll., 1978. Cert. metabolic technician Internat. Health Inst. Address: W 5615 Lyons Ct Spokane WA 99208

FOWLER, CINDA PFENNIG, convention service company executive; b. Indpls., Sept. 25, 1942; d. John Richard and Ila Wayne (Reynolds) Pfennig; m. William Clifford Fowler, Dec. 21, 1965; children—Julia Irene, Mallory Leigh. B.S. in Edn., Ind. U., 1964. Tchr., Washington Twp., Indpls., 1964-66; owner, operator Presenting Atlanta, Inc., Ga., 1973—. Mem. Atlanta Jr. League, 1974—; mem., fund raiser Salvation Army, Atlanta; party arranger Am. Cancer Soc., Atlanta. Mem. Hotel Sales Mktg. Assn., Atlanta Conv. and Visitors Bur. (treas. 1980—), Meeting Planners Internat., Am. Soc. Assn. Execs., Profl. Conv. Mgrs. Assn. Republican. Methodist. Avocation: travel. Office: Presenting Atlanta Inc 110 E Andrews Dr NW Atlanta GA 30305

FOWLER, DORA CAMACHO, corporation executive; b. Cali, Valle, Colombia, Mar. 19, 1934; came to U.S., 1951; d. Jorge Enrique and Aminta (Rincon) Camacho; m. George Barton Fowler, May 30, 1960; children—David Mark, DeeAnn Michelle, Dwight Matthew. B.A. with honors, Nat. Coll. Edn. Linguist UN Gen. Assembly, N.Y.C., 1955; headmistress Montessori Children's House, West Des Moines, Iowa, 1968-71; dir. Children's Ctr., Schaumburg, Ill., 1972-74; exec. dir. Elk Grove Twp. Community Day Care Ctr., Elk Grove Village, Ill., 1974—; pres. Am. Assn. Exec. and Profl. Women, Palatine, Ill., 1983-85, Assocs. in Human Devel., 1985—; gov. Benedictine Coll., Atchison, Kans., 1974—; mem. adv. bd. on day care Nat. Coll. Edn., Evanston, Ill., 1982—. Author: The Complete Book of Home Day Care, 1983; A Guide to Effective Administration in Day Care, 1983; editor The Tng. Ctr. nat. newsletter, 1981. Contbr. articles to mags. Del., White House Conf. on Families, Chgo., Washington, 1980, Ill. Conf. on Children's Priorities for the 80's, Chgo., 1982; bd. dir. Elk Grove-Harper Coll. Lifelong Learning Program; mem. adv. bd. on day care State of Ill.; mem. State of Ill. Needs and Funding Subcommittee. Mem. Nat. Assn. Edn. Young Children, Chgo. Assn. Edn. Young Children (exec. bd., sec. 1978-79), Day Care Action Council, N.W. Suburban Council Community Services (v.p. 1980-81), Ill. Montessori Soc., Assn. Montessori Internat. Sigma Alpha Iota (pres. 1969-70). Roman Catholic. Club: Altrusa (Arlington Heights, Ill.). Office: Assocs in Human Devel Inc One E NW Hwy Suite 212 Palatine IL 60067

FOWLER, ELAINE DANIELSON, teacher educator; b. Concordia, Kans., Oct. 25, 1938; d. Clarence Frederick and Blanche Vendla (Magnus) Danielson; B.S., Kans. State U., 1960; M.S., U. Kans., 1964; Ph.D., U. Tex., Austin, 1969; m. Donald Fowler, Aug. 25, 1968; children—James, Thomas. Tchr. pub. schs., Topeka, 1960-63, Center Sch. Dist., Kansas City, Mo., 1964-66; teaching asst. U. Tex., Austin, 1966-69, asst. prof., 1969-75, assoc. prof. 1975—; cons. Pullman-Kellogg Project, Algeria, Africa, 1978. Vice pres. Austin Assn. Retarded Citizens, 1980-82. Mem. Nat. Council Tchrs. English, Internat. Reading Assn., Delta Kappa Gamma, Phi Kappa Phi, Phi Delta Kappa, Phi Lambda Theta. Methodist. Author: Banner English Series, 1981; contbr. articles to profl. jours. Home: 4801 Crestway Dr Austin TX 78731 Office: EDB 406 U Tex Austin TX 78712

FOWLER, ELIZABETH MILTON, real estate executive; b. Watertown, Fla., Jan. 11, 1919; d. Arthur Wellington and Mattie Jean (Hodges) Milton; student Bowling Green Bus. U., 1938-39; m. Albert L. Fowler, Jr., Aug. 6, 1948; children—Patricia Dawn Cecilia, Richard Gordon Sean. Sec. to dir. Workmen's Compensation Div., Fla. Indsl. Commn., Tallahassee, 1940-41; sec. to supt. div. Gibbs Ship Yard Repair, 1942-44; sec. to elec. engrs. Reynolds, Smith & Hills, Architects and Engrs., 1946-49; sec. to pres. Aichel Steel Corp., Jacksonville, Fla., 1949-50; adminstr. office mgr. for prin., vice-prin. Am. Dependent Sch., Moron Air Base, Spain, 1961-63; owner, mgr. Elizabeth Properties, Jacksonville, 1956—. Chmn. ways and means com. Chattanooga High Sch. PTA, 1956-57; asst. den mother Cub Scout Troop, 1970; block worker Gov. Reagan's Presdl. Campaign. Recipient Spl. Appreciation award Eglin AFB, Fla., 1969; Cert. of Recognition, Nat. Rep. Congl. Com. Mem. Nat. Assn. Female Execs., Am. Security Council (nat. adv. bd.), Dade County Crimewatch Orgn. Republican. Home and Office: 20101 SW 92d Ave Miami FL 33189

FOWLER, FRANCES JULIA, health care management consulting firm executive, consultant; b. Worcester, Mass., June 15, 1945; d. Frank and Regina (Banach) Kulig; m. Joseph E. Fowler, July 6, 1967. B.S., Ga. State U., 1974; M.S., Emory U., 1975. Various healthcare mgmt. positions, 1965-75; program coordinator Internat. Nursing Services Assn., Atlanta, 1975-76; cons. healthcare, Louisville, 1976-77; staff cons. Kurt Salmon Assocs., Atlanta, 1977-82, prin., 1982-84; pres. Fowler Healthcare Affiliates, Atlanta, 1984—. Mem. Internat. Health, Am. Assn. Healthcare Cons. (mktg. com. 1984—), Internat. Nursing Services Assn. (local devel. com. 1985—), Hosp. Soc. for Planning/Mktg. Home: 1115 Mitsy Hollow Dr Marietta GA 30067 Office: Fowler Healthcare Affiliates 1640-21 Powers Ferry Rd Atlanta GA 30067

FOWLER, HARRIET WHITTEMORE, art museum curator; b. Geneva, N.Y., Apr. 6, 1946. B.A., Cornell U., 1977, Ph.D., 1981; student Smith Coll., 1964-67. Interim dir. U. Ky. Art Mus., Lexington, 1982, curator, 1981—. Author (exhbn. catalogue) New Deal Art; WPA Works at the Univ. of Ky., 1985. Mem. Hist. Properties Adv. Commn. of Ky., 1985-87. Recipient Frances Sampson Fine Arts prize Cornell U., 1977. Mem. Am. Assn. Mus. Curators Com., Phi Kappa Phi. Home: 110 Broadway Versailles KY 40383 Office: Univ Ky Art Mus Rose and Euclid Sts Lexington KY 40506

FOWLER, LINDA MCKEEVER, hospital administrator, management educator; b. Greensburg, Pa., Aug. 7, 1948; d. Clay and Florence Elizabeth (Smith) McK.; m. Timothy L. Fowler, Sept. 13, 1969 (div. July 1985). Nursing diploma, Presbyterian U. Hosp., Pitts., 1969; B.S. in Nursing, U. Pitts., 1976, M.Nursing Adminstrn., 1980; D.Pub. Adminstrn., Nova U., 1985. Supr., head nurse Presbyn. Univ. Hosp., Pitts., 1969-76; mem. faculty Western Pa. Hosp. Sch. Nursing, Pitts., 1976-79; acute care coordinator Mercy Hosp., Miami, 1980-81; asst. adminstr. nursing North Shore Med. Ctr., Miami, 1981-84, v.p. patient care, 1984—; mem. adj. faculty Barry U., Miami, 1984—, Broward Community Coll., Ft. Lauderdale, 1984—, Nova U., 1986—; cons. Strategic Health Devel. Inc., Miami Shores, Fla., 1986—. Dept. HEW trainee, 1976, 79-80. Mem. Am. Orgn. Nurse Execs., Fla. Orgn. Nurse Execs., South Fla. Nurse Adminstrs. Assn. (sec. 1983-84, bd. dirs. 1984-86), U. Pitts. Alumni Assn., Presbyn. U. Alumni Assn., Nat. Assn. Female Execs., Sigma Theta Tau. Lutheran. Club: Ft. Lauderdale Dog (bd. dirs. 1981-82, 83-85, v.p. 1982-83). Home: 1040 SW 110th Terr Davie FL 33324

FOWLER, LORI S., financial consultant; b. Rutland, Vt., July 23, 1959; d. John Edward and Jean Avis (Petty) F. B.S., Castleton State Coll., 1981; postgrad. Lesley Coll., 1986—. Payroll clk. Castleton State Coll., Vt., 1979-81; fin. analyst Digital Equipment Corp., Maynard, Mass., 1981-83, sr. fin. analyst, 1983-85, fin. cons., 1985—. Vol., Vol. Income Tax Assistance, Castleton, 1980, coordinator, 1981. Mem. Nat. Assn. Female Execs. Home: 7 Holly St Watertown MA 02172 Office: Digital Equipment Corp 146 Main St Maynard MA 01754

FOWLER, NANCY CROWLEY, government economist; b. Newton, Mass., Aug. 8, 1922; d. Ralph Elmer and Margaret Bright (Tinkham) Crowley; m. Gordon Robert Fowler, Sept. 11, 1949; children—Gordon R., Nancy P., Betty Kainani, Diane Kuulei. A.B. cum laude, Radcliffe Coll., 1943; Grad. Cert., Harvard-Radcliffe Mgmt. Tng. Program, 1946; postgrad. U. Hawaii, 1971-76. Econ. research analyst Dept. Planning & Econ. Devel., Honolulu, 1963-69; assoc. chief research Regional Med. Program, Honolulu, 1969-70; economist V and VI, Dept. Planning and Econ. Devel., Honolulu, 1970-78, chief policy analysis br., 1978-85, tech. info. services officer, 1985—; staff rep. State Energy Functional Plan Adv. Com., Honolulu, 1983—, Hawaii Integrated Energy Assessment, 1978-81. Contbr. articles to profl. jours. Com. mem. Kailua Com. to Re-elect Mayor Eileen Anderson, 1984. Recipient Employee of Yr. award Dept. Planning and Econ. Devel., Honolulu, 1977, others. Mem. Hawaii Econs. Assn. (various offices). Democrat. Clubs: Radcliffe of Hawaii, Propeller of Honolulu (v.p.). Avocations: gardening; surfing. Home: 749 Mokapu Blvd Kailua HI 96734 Office: Dept Planning and Econ Devel 250 S King St Honolulu HI 96813

FOWLER, NANCY VIRGINIA, county official; b. Rosemont, W.Va., May 10, 1940; d. Wilson D. and Roxie C. (St. Clair) F. Office mgr. Taylor County W.Va. U. Extension Service, Grafton, 1958-74; county clk. Taylor County, Grafton, 1975—. Mem. W. Va. County and Circuit Clks. Assn. (sec. 1983—). Republican. Home: 109 Graham St Grafton WV 26354 Office: Taylor County Clks Office Courthouse Main St Grafton WV 26354

FOWLKES, MARTHA RICHMOND, sociology educator, researcher, consultant; b. Boston, May 6, 1940; d. David and Mary (Warren) Richmond; children—Lisa Bladen, Anne Bladen, Abigail Fowlkes, Margaret Fowlkes. A.B. magna cum laude, Smith Coll., 1961; M.A., London Sch. Econs. and Polit. Sci., 1965; Ph.D. with distinction, U. Mass.-Amherst, 1977. Med. sociologist Regional Med. Program, Memphis, 1970; researcher evaluator Northampton State Hosp., Mass., 1970-71; assoc. dean student affairs, 1978-80; dir. alumnae research Smith Coll., Northampton, 1980—, assoc. prof. pub. policy, 1980—; cons. in field. Author: Behind Every Successful Man: Wives of Medicine and Academe, 1980; also monographs and articles. Trustee Northampton State Hosp., 1975-78. Recipient Woodrow Wilson fellow, 1975-76; Nat. Research Service award NIMH, 1975-76. Mem. Am. Sociol. Assn., Eastern Sociol. Assn., Phi Beta Kappa. Democrat. Avocations: gardening; camping. Office: Smith Coll Jahnige Research Ctr Northampton MA 01063

FOX, CONNIE PATRICIA, writer; b. Chgo., Feb. 12, 1932; d. Hugh Bernard and Helen Marie (Mangan) F.; m. Lucio Ungaro de Zavallos, June 5, 1957 (div. 1970); children—Hugh, Cecilia, Marcella; m. Nono Woodyne Grimes, Oct. 3, 1970; children—Margaret, Alexandra, Christopher. B.S., Loyola U., Chgo., 1954, M.A., 1955; Ph.D., U. Ill., 1958. Author: (poetry) Blood Cocoon, 1980; The Dream of the Black Topaze Chamber, 1984; Babishka, 1985; Schreckliche Engel, 1985; Oma, 1985; Nachthymnen, 1986. Contbr. poetry and fiction to Telephone, Invisible City, Thirteenth Moon, Mockersatz, Big Scream, others. Spl. issue of Corona mag. devoted to Connie Fox, 1985. Mem. Com. Small Mag. Editors and Publishers. Home: 526 Forest St East Lansing MI 48823

FOX, DANIELLE DALEY, floral designer; b. Newark, Nov. 17, 1949; d. Daniel Daley and Clara (Reheis) Fox; student Centenary Coll. for Women, 1967-68; B.A., Finch Coll., 1973. Sec., Flavia's Creations, Summit, N.J., 1973-76, floral designer, 1976-79; freelance designer, 1979—. Mem. Jaguar Club Am., Finch Alumni Assn. Author: Extension - An Anthology of Modern Poetry, 1968. Home: 18 Cromwell Pkwy Summit NJ 07901

FOX, DEL FRANKLIN, counselor; b. Hartford, Conn., Oct. 11, 1923; d. Marcus Irving and Lee (Olshan) Franklin; B.A., N.Y. U., 1944; M.A., U. South Fla., 1968; m. Mark Edward Fox, Jan. 14, 1951; children—Andrew Eric, Steven Alan. Copywriter, WSRR, Stamford, Conn., 1945-48; pub. relations staff Sidney Ascher & Assos., 1949-51; feature writer Fla. Times Union, Jacksonville, 1952-59; feature writer Sarasota (Fla.) Mag., 1960-68; adult guidance counselor Sarasota County Vocat. Tech. Center, 1968—; weekly broadcast WSPB, 1969—. Mem. Sarasota Manatee Bi-County Commn. on Status of Women, 1975—; mem. Gov.'s Commn. on Status of Women, 1978—; bd. dirs. Women's Center of Sarasota, 1979—; mem. steering com. Fla. Women's Network, 1980—. Mem. Am. Personnel and Guidance Assn., Nat. Assn. Commns. for Women (dir. 1982—), Am. Vocat. Assn., Nat. League Am. Pen Women, Delta Kappa Gamma. Club: University. Home: 4634 Higel Ave Sarasota FL 33581 Office: 4748 Beneva Rd Sarasota FL 33581

FOX, ELLEN RANDI, business executive; b. Cheyenne, Wyo., Nov. 24, 1949; d. Abraham Harvey and Edith (Wolinsky) Fox; student public schs., Cheyenne. Microfilmer, City and County of Denver, 1969-70; asst. buyer Randall's Formalwear, Denver, 1970-72; owner, mgr. Firebird Motel, Cheyenne, 1972-83, Grandma Brindel's Waterbeds & Things, Cheyenne, 1979-83, Craft Collection, 1981-83; sec., treas. Fox Enterprises, Inc.; partner Lam-I-Dent Co. Active NOW, Wyo.; coordinator Multnomah County Low Cost Spay/Neuter Program, 1984—. Named Retailer of Yr., Am. Merchandising Enterprises Distributors, 1979. Mem. Bus. and Profl. Women. Jewish. Led demonstration against local newspapers for not inviting women on Treagle Train, 1979. Home: 3101 SE 11th St Portland OR 97202 Office: 2315 SE 38th St Portland OR 97214

FOX, HARRIET MINCHIN, educational administrator; b. Greenwich, Conn., Aug. 17, 1925; d. Henry Caleb and Hildegard Victoria (Larson) Minchin; m. Raymond Graham Fox, Apr. 17, 1948; children—Susan C., Christine A., Ellen B., Laura G., John G., II. B.A., Smith Coll., 1947. Analyst Moody's, N.Y.C., 1947-48, A.C. Nielson Co., N.Y.C., 1948; owner, mgr. Rockingham Farm, Warrenton, Va., 1961-75; pres. Learning Tech. Inst., Warrenton, 1975—, also dir.; dir. Inst. Delivery Machine Corp. Trustee Fauquier Ednl. Found., Warrenton, 1965-68; bd. dirs. Fauguier/Loudoun County Day Care, 1972-77; founder, life mem. Meadow Outdoors Found., 1983—, Nat. Mus. Women in Arts, 1984—. Sr. mem. Soc. Applied Learning Tech. Anglican. Clubs: Columbia Country (Chevy Chase, Md.); Moorings (Vero Beach, Fla.); Chestnut Forks (Warrenton). Home: Reynwood PO Box 376 Warrenton VA 22186 Office: Learning Tech Inst 50 Culpeper St Warrenton VA 22186

FOX, HARRIETT INA, leasing company executive; b. Brookline, Mass., Jan. 27, 1950; d. Louis and Irene Sylvia (Andelman) F. B.S. in Math., Simmons Coll., 1972; M.S. in Mgmt., MIT, 1975. Sr. cons. Touche Ross & Co., Boston, 1975-79; mgr. fin. planning staff Ryder Truck Rental, Inc., Miami, Fla., 1979-81, mgr. corp. planning, 1981-82, dir. contracts, 1982-85, dir. vehicle adminstrn., 1985—; dir. Ryder Credit Union, 1983—. Editor Sloan Mgmt. Rev., 1973-75. Founding mem. Miami Forum, 1979, treas., 1981-83, v.p. membership, 1983-84, pres., 1984—; dir. YMCA, Cambridge, 1978; pres. Grove Terr. Condominium Assn., Miami, 1980-83. Republican. Jewish. Office: Ryder Truck Rental Inc 3600 NW 82d Ave Miami FL 33166

FOX, JANE CAROLINE, automobile dealer; b. Auburn, N.Y., Dec. 14, 1945; d. Leo Norman and Elizabeth (Curtin) Fox. B.A., Nazareth Coll., 1968. Asst. buyer Sibley, Lindsay & Curr, Rochester, N.Y., 1968-70; buyer Fox Auto Sales, Weedsport, N.Y., 1970-76; pres. Fox Chevrolet, Inc., Auburn, 1976—, Fox Chrysler-Plymouth Dodge, Inc., Auburn, 1981—; cons. Fox Oldsmobile-Cadillac-Subaru, Auburn, 1980—, Sharon Chevrolet, Phoenix, N.Y., 1980—. Chmn. Dealer's Election Action Com., Washington, 1984-85. Mem. Nat. Automobile Dealer's Assn. (Chevrolet IV, chmn. 1984-85, lectr. 1978-84), N.Y. Auto Dealer's Assn. (bd. dirs. 1983-85), Syracuse Auto Dealer's Assn., Chevrolet Dealer Council (rep. 1984). Democrat. Roman Catholic. Avocations: skiing; travel; cooking. Home: 82 Greatwood Circle Fairport NY 14450 Office: Fox Chevrolet Inc 366 Genesee St Auburn NY 13021

FOX, JANICE THÉRÈSE JUDGE, manufacturing company executive; b. Peabody, Mass., Nov. 11, 1935; d. Bernard W. and Catherine M. (Romanowicz) Judge; m. Charles James Fox, Feb. 6, 1960; children—Mary Thérèsa, Charles James, Paul Judge. B.S., Boston Coll., 1958; R.N., Laboure Sch. Nursing, Dorchester, Mass., 1956. Sch. nurse, Boston, 1959-61; pres. Friend Box Co., Danvers, Mass., 1979—. Sec., New Eng. Bapt. Hosp. League, Boston, 1969-75; trustee Cath. Charitable Bur., Boston, 1984—, Fides com. Boston Coll., 1983—, Ireland Fund. Mem. Nat. Paper Box Assn., Nat. Assn. Female Execs. Republican. Roman Catholic. Clubs: Charles River Country (pres. 1982-84) (Newton, Mass.), Ace of Clubs. Avocations: fundraising for charities; piano; reading; history; gourmet cooking; interior design. Home: 5 Ruel Dr Dover MA 02030 Office: Friend Box Co 90 High St Danvers MA 01923

FOX, JOAN PHYLLIS, environmental engineer; b. Rockledge, Fla., July 16, 1945; d. John A. and Nonie L. (Knutson) Fox. B.S. with high honors in Physics, U. Fla., 1971; Ph.D. in San. Engring., U. Calif.-Berkeley, 1980. Engr., Bechtel, Inc., San Francisco, 1971-76; dir. and prin. investigator Lawrence Berkeley Lab., 1977-81; prin. engr., pres. Fox Cons., Berkeley, 1981—; guest lectr. dept. conservation and resource studies U. Calif.-Berkeley, 1980-84. EPA grantee, 1978-81; Dept. of Energy grantee, 1976-81. Mem. Am. Geo-phys. Union, Nat. Resources Def. Council, Am. Chem. Soc., ASTM, Water Pollution Control Fedn., Nat. Acad. Scis. (mem. subcom. on QA/QC of com. irrigation-induced water quality problems 1986—), AAAS, Audubon Soc., Phi Beta Kappa, Sigma Pi Sigma. Contbr. articles on oil shale, hazardous waste, and water quality control to profl. publs. Office: 1988 California St Berkeley CA 94703

FOX, JUDITH ELLEN, personnel executive; b. N.Y.C., Aug. 2, 1941; d. Murray A. and Harriette Schneider; student Pa. State U., 1959-60; m. Jerry Fox, Aug. 16, 1964; children—Brian Spencer, Jennifer Leslie. Asst. personnel dir. Miles Shoe Co., N.Y.C., 1961-63; freelance writer, photographer Coronet, The Progressive, U.S. Catholic, numerous local and state periodicals, 1962-77; asst. personnel dir. Wallachs, Inc., N.Y.C., 1963-64; co-owner, photographer J. Fox Photographers, Stony Brook, N.Y., 1968-72; mgr. Forbes Temporaries, Richmond, Va., 1975-78; pres. Fox-Huber Cos., 1978—; pres., founding partner Fox Huber Temporaries, Inc., Richmond, 1978—; pres. Rosemary Scott Temporaries, N.Y.C., 1983—, Fox-Huber Permanent Placements, Inc., Richmond, 1985—; mem. adv. bd. Womensbank, 1981-83; chmn. customer adv. bd. Va. Electric and Power Co., 1981—; personnel cons. pvt. industry and state govt., 1980—. Dist. chmn. Va. gubernatorial campaign, 1977; charter mem. Businesses Who Care, 1982; bd. dirs. Multiple Sclerosis Soc., Central Va. chpt., 1979-80, Met. YMCA, 1982—, Pvt. Industry Council, 1983—; bd. dirs. Sci. Mus. Va., 1985—; vice-chmn. Richmond area U.S. Olympic Com., 1983; mem. exec. bd. Gov.'s Adv. Com. on Small Bus., 1982—; mem. fundraising com. Hampton Inst., Mem. Nat. Assn. Temporary Services, Va. State C. of C. (small bus. com. 1983-84), Richmond C. of C. (chmn. small bus. council 1982-84, dir. 1983—, legis. affairs com., exec. bd. 1984—), Nat. Assn. Female Execs., Nat. Assn. Women Bus. Owners Richmond Assn. Women Bus. Owners (exec. bd. 1982—), Va. Assn. Temporary Services (v.p. 1981—) Office: 5006 Monument Ave Richmond VA 23230 also 515 Madison Ave New York NY 10022

FOX, KAREN FRANCES ANNE, marketing educator; b. San Francisco, Apr. 30, 1944; d. Karl August and Sylvia Olive (Cate) F. A.B., Stanford U., 1964, Ph.D., 1973; M.A.T., Harvard U., 1966; M.Mgmt., Northwestern U., 1980. Tchr. history Ames Sr. High Sch., Iowa, 1966-67; asst. prof. social sci. San Jose State U., Calif., 1969-71; assoc. research scientist Am. Insts. Research, Palo Alto, Calif., 1971-72; asst. prof. edn. Tchrs. Coll. Columbia U., N.Y.C., 1973-75, Northwestern U. Evanston, Ill., 1975-80; asst. prof. mktg. Santa Clara U., Calif., 1980—, dir. grad. edn. Leavey Sch. Bus. and Adminstrn., 1980-84; pres. Foxmark, Inc., 1985—. Co-author: Strategic Marketing for Educational Institutions, 1985. Contbr. articles to profl. jours. Mem. Am. Mktg. Assn., Assn. Consumer Research. Home: 640 Giralda Dr Los Altos CA 94022 Office: Mktg Dept Leavey Sch Bus and Adminstrn Santa Clara U Santa Clara CA 95053

FOX, KELLY DIANE, assistant buyer; b. Brockton, Mass., Sept. 9, 1959; d. James H. and Betty Jane (Calloway) F.; m. Alan David Goldberg, July 6, 1985. B.A., Allegheny Coll., 1980; postgrad. in Bus. Adminstrn., Suffolk U., 1983-84; student Temple U., London, 1978, Syracuse U., London, 1979. Asst. mgr. Casual Male, Braintree, Mass., 1980, Hit or Miss, Braintree, 1981-82; merchandiser Foxmoor, West Bridgewater, Mass., 1982; distbr. Hill's Dept. Stores, Canton, Mass., 1982-85; asst. buyer BJ's Wholesale Club, Natick, Mass., 1985—; cheerleading coach Avon High Sch., Mass., 1982-83. Mem. Nat. Assn. Female Execs. Methodist. Avocations: dance; exercise; cooking; art galleries.

FOX, LYNN (ELLEN) HUSSEY, teacher educator; b. Balt., Jan. 5, 1944; d. Harry and Gertrude (Leighs) F.; B.S. with honors, U. Fla., 1965, M.Ed., 1968; M.A. in Psychology, Johns Hopkins U., 1973, Ph.D., 1974; m. Harrison William Fox, Jr., Sept. 2, 1967; children—Harrison William III, Thomas Randolph and Leigh Lynn (twins). Tchr. math. Orange County Public Schs., Orlando, Fla., 1965-67; edn. specialist U.S. Office of Edn., 1969-71; research asst. dept. psychology Johns Hopkins U., Balt., 1972-73, asso. project dir. study of mathematically precocious youth, 1971-74, instr. evening div., 1974-75, asst. prof. edn. Evening Coll., 1975-78, assoc. prof., 1978-81, prof., 1981-85; cons. Harrison Group, 1985—; instr. Towson State U., Balt., 1974; cons. to Ford Found., 1979-80, Coll. Bd., 1982-85; reviewer jours. in psychology and child devel., 1977—. Mem. adv. com. gifted and talented programs and services Balt. City Schs., 1977—; mem. Balt. Mayors Vol. Cadre on Edn., 1976-77. Nat. Inst. Edn. grantee, 1977-81; Md. Dept. Edn. grantee 1977-78; Spencer Found. grantee, 1974-77, 79-82. Mem. Nat. Assn. for Gifted Children (exec. bd. 1977—), Council for Exceptional Children Am. Ednl. Research Assn. (program com. 1975-76), Am. Psychol. Assn., AAAS, Sigma Xi, Phi Delta Kappa. Democrat. Methodist. Author: The Problem of Women and Mathematics, 1981; Contbr. numerous articles to ednl. jours.; co-editor; Mathematical Talent, 1974, Women and the Mathematical Mystique, 1980, Learning Disabled/Gifted Children, 1983. Home: 217 41st Ave NE Saint Petersburg FL 33703 Office: The Harrison Group Koger Bldg-Koger Ct 9721 Executive Dr Saint Petersburg FL 33702

FOX, MARGARET BLACK, educator; b. Charlottesville, Va., Jan. 14, 1921; d. Daniel Nicholas and Sarah Eliza (Dollens) Black; m. Harold Heath Fox, Sept. 18, 1948; 1 son, Harold Heath. B.S., James Madison U., 1942; postgrad., 1977-79; postgrad. U. Va., 1966-67, Tchr. 1st grade, Dumfries, Prince William County, Va., 1942-45; tchr. 1st, 2d, 3d grade, Waynesboro (Va.) Pub. Schs., 1945-54, tchr. 2d grade, 1959-82. Historian, Westminster Presbyn. Ch., 1980-85, chmn. to research and compile Westminster Presbyn. Ch. History, 1980-85. Named life mem. Hist. Found. Presbyn. and Reformed Chs., Inc., Montreat, N.C., 1983; named One of Top 20 Tchrs. in Nation, Northwestern U., 1951. Mem. NEA, Va. Edn. Assn., Waynesboro Edn. Assn. (v.p. 1946-47), Alpha Delta Kappa (historian 1982-84), DAR (Col. James Patton chpt.), Augusta County Hist. Soc., Am. Assn. Retired Persons, Black Family Research Orgn. Presbyterian. Home: 1927 W Main St Waynesboro VA 22980

FOX, MURIEL CORINNE, public relations executive; b. Newark, Feb. 3, 1928; d. Morris and Anne L. (Rubinstein) F.; student Rollins Coll., 1944-46; B.A. summa cum laude, Barnard Coll., 1948; m. Shepard G. Aronson, July 1, 1955; children—Eric A., Lisa S. Reporter, UP, 1946-48; art critic and bridal editor Miami (Fla.) News, 1946; advt. copywriter Sears, Roebuck & Co., 1948-49; polit. speechwriter, publicist, 1949-50; with Carl Byoir & Assos., N.Y.C., 1950—, TV-radio writer, 1950-52, dir. TV-radio dept., 1952-57, v.p., 1957-74, group v.p., sr. cons., exec. com., 1974-76, exec. v.p., 1977—; pres. By/Media, Inc., 1978-80; dir. Harleysville Ins. Co., Rorer Group, 1979—. Co-chmn. Vice Presdl. Task Force on Women, 1968; bd. dirs. Women's Forum, 1974-78, pres., 1976-78; nat. adv. com. Nat. Women's Polit. Caucus; nat. adv. bd. Ethnic Woman; bd. dirs. N.Y. Diabetes Assn., 1956-66, Holy Land Conservation Fund, United Way of Tri State, Internat. Rescue Com., 1977—, Am. Arbitration Assn., 1982—; founder NOW, v.p., 1967-70, chmn. bd., 1971-73, chmn. nat. adv. com., 1973-74; bd. dirs. Legal Def. and Edn. Fund, 1974—, v.p., 1977, 78, pres., 1978-81, chmn. 1981—; mem. adv. council Democrats of the Senate, N.Y. State, 1979—; mem. mktg. and communications com. Pres.'s Adv. Council on Pvt. Sector Initiative, 1983—. Winner ADA Bus. Leader of Yr. award, 1979, Women in Communications Matrix award, 1975; recipient Eleanor Roosevelt Leadership award, 1985; Barnard Coll. Disting. Alumna award, 1985; named to 100 Top Corp. Women, Bus. Week, top-rated P.R. Woman, 1974. Mem. Am. Women in Radio and TV (dir. 1959-61, chmn. nat. publicity com. 1955-57, chmn. nat. pub. relations com. 1957-59; Achievement award 1983), Am. Arbitration Assn., Fin. Women's Assn. Office: Carl Byoir & Associates Inc 380 Madison Ave New York NY 10017

FOX, NANCY JAMES, company administrator; b. St. James, Minn., May 20, 1950; d. Latimer B. and Amy Pearl (Halverson) James; m. Jeffrey Michael Fox, Nov. 30, 1974; 1 child, Joshua James. B.A., Macalester Coll., 1972; postgrad. Hochschule fuer Musik, Frankfurt, West Ger., Wolfgang Goethe U., Frankfurt, Shenandoah Coll. Tchr. Jugendmusikschule, Frankfurt, 1971-74; paralegal Kuykendall, Costello & Hanes, Winchester, Va., 1976-77; sec. VDO Instruments, Inc., Winchester, 1978-79, credit mgr., 1979-81, br. mgr., 1982-85, regional sales mgr., 1985—. Recipient Janet Wallace Music award Macalester Coll., 1970. Mem. Nat. Assn. Female Execs., Am. Assn. Individual Investors. Office: VDO Instrument Inc PO Box 2897 Winchester VA 22601

FOX, PAULA (MRS. MARTIN GREENBERG), author; b. N.Y.C., Apr. 22, 1923; d. Paul Hervey and Elsie (de Sola) F.; m. Richard Sigerson (div. 1954); children—Adam, Gabriel; m. Martin Greenberg, June 9, 1962. Student, Columbia U. Condr. writing Seminars U. Pa. Author children's books, including How Many Miles to Babylon, 1966, Maurice's Room, 1966, A Likely Place, 1967, Portrait of Ivan, 1968, The King's Falcon, 1969, Blowfish Live in the Sea, 1970, Poor George, 1967; Desperate Characters, 1970, The Western Coast, 1972, Good Ethan, 1973, The Slave Dancer, 1974 (John Newbery medal), The Widow's Children, 1976, The Little Swineherd and Other Tales, 1978, A Place Apart, 1983 (Am. Book award), One-Eyed Cat, 1984. Guggenheim fellow, 1972; recipient Arts and Letters award Nat. Inst. Arts and Letters, 1972, Hans Christian Andersen medal, 1978; Creative Arts award Brandeis U., 1984. Mem. P.E.N., Authors League. Office: care Bradbury Press 2 Overhill Rd Scarsdale NY 10583

FOX, RENÉE CLAIRE, sociologist, educator; b. N.Y.C., Feb. 15, 1928; d. Paul Fred and Henrietta (Gold) F.; A.B. summa cum laude, Smith Coll., 1949, L.H.D., 1975; Ph.D., Harvard U., 1954; M.A. (hon.), U. Pa., 1971; Sc.D. (hon.), Med. Coll. Pa., 1974, St. Joseph's Coll., Phila., 1978; D. honoris causa, Katholieke U., Belgium, 1978. Research asst. Bur. Applied Social Research, Columbia U., 1953-55, research assoc., 1955-58; lectr. dept. sociology Barnard Coll., 1955-58, asst. prof., 1958-64, assoc. prof., 1964-66; lectr. sociology Harvard U., 1967-69, research fellow Center Internat. Affairs, 1967-68, research assoc. program tech. and society, 1968-71; prof. sociology, psychiatry and medicine U. Pa., Phila., 1969—, Annenberg prof. social scis., 1978—, chmn. dept. sociology, 1972-78. Sci. adviser Centre de Recherches Sociologiques, Kinshasa, Congo, 1963-67; vis. prof. sociology U. Officielle du Congo, Lubumbashi, 1965; vis. prof. Sir George Williams U., Montreal, Que., Can., summer 1968; Phi Beta Kappa vis. scholar, 1973-75; dir. humanities seminar med. practitioners NEH, 1975-76; maitre de cours U. Liege (Belgium), 1976-77; vis. prof. Katholieke U., Leuven, Belgium, 1976-77; Wm. Allen Neilson prof. Smith Coll., Mass., 1980; mem. bd. clin. scholars program Robert Wood Johnson Found., 1974-80; mem. Pres.'s Commn. on Study of Ethical Problems in Medicine, Biomed. and Behavioral Research, 1979-81; dir. human qualities of medicine program James Picker Found., 1980-83. 1980-83; pub. mem. Am. Bd. Med. Specialties, 1984—. dirs. medicine in Pub. Interest, 1979—; mem. tech. bd. Milbank Meml. Fund, 1979-85; mem. overseers com. to visit univ. health services Harvard Coll., 1979—; trustee Russell Sage Found., 1981—. Recipient E. Harris Harbison Gifted Teaching award Danforth Found., 1970; Radcliffe Grad. Soc. medal, 1977; Guggenheim fellow, 1962; China Assn. Sci. and Tech. and U.S. Nat. Acad. Scis. exchange scholar Peoples Republic of China, 1985. Fellow African Studies Assn., AAAS (dir. 1977-80; chmn.-elect sect. 1985-86). Am. Sociol. Assn. (rep. to Social Sci. Research Council 1970-73, v.p. 1980-81, Leo G. Reeder award for disting. scholarship in med. sociology), Am. Acad. Arts and Scis., Inst. Medicine (Nat. Acad. Scis.) (council 1979-82), Inst. Soc., Ethics and Life Scis. (founder, gov.); mem. AAUP, AAUW, Assn. Am. Med. Colls., Social Sci. Research Council (v.p., dir.), Eastern Sociol. Soc. (v.p. 1973-74, pres. 1976-77), N.Y. Acad. Scis., Soc. Sci. Study Religion, Inst. Intercultural Studies (asst. sec. 1969-78, sec. 1978-81), Phi Beta Kappa Assocs. Phi Beta Kappa (mem. senate united chpts. 1982—). Author: Experiment Perilous, 1959; (with Willy DeCraemer) The Emerging Physician, 1968; (with Judith P. Swazey) The Courage to Fall, 1974, rev. edit., 1978; Essays in Medical Sociology, 1979; assoc. editor Am. Sociol. Rev., 1963-66, Social Sci. and Medicine; editorial com. Ann. Rev. Sociology, 1975-79; editorial adv. bd. Ency. Bioethics, Jour. Medicine and Philosophy, Men and Medicine, Tech. in Soc., Science, 1982—. Editorial bd. Bibliography of Bioethics, 1979—, Culture, Medicine and Psychiatry, 1980—, Jour. of AMA, 1981—, Sci., 1985, Jour. Health and Social Behavior, 1985—. Contbr. articles to profl. jours. Home: 135 S 19 St Philadelphia PA 19103

FOX, ROBERTA FULTON, lawyer, state legislator; b. Phila., Nov. 25, 1943; d. Robert Fulton and Irmgard F.; B.A., U. Fla., 1964, J.D., 1967; m. Mike Gold; 1 stepdau., Shari Anna Gold. Admitted to Fla. bar, 1968; mem. Govt. Research Council, Miami-Dade C. of C., 1964-65; staff Goldin & Jones, Gainesville, Fla., 1968; atty. Migrant Legal Services, Miami, 1968-69, Legal Services Greater Miami, 1970-72; pvt. practice law, Coral Gables, Fla., 1972-80; partner firm Gold & Fox, P.A., from 1972; mem. Fla. Ho. Reps., 1976-82; mem. Fla. Senate, 1982—; mem. Gov.'s Commn. on Marriage and the Family Unit, 1974-76; chairperson Dade County Women's Polit. Caucus, 1971-74; counsel NOW, Women's Action Center, Inc.; chairperson sex-biased discrimination com. of minority affairs com. Democratic Issues Conv., 1976-78. Mem. affirmative action agy. adv. bd., treas. Transition, Inc.; mem. council, bd. dirs. Planned Parenthood of S. Fla.; bd. dirs. NOW Legal Def. and Edn. Fund.; hon. bd. dirs. Girls Clubs Greater Miami. Recipient Outstanding State Legislator award, 1979; Gov.'s award for Art, 1980. Mem. Bus. and Profl. Women, Fla. Women Lawyers Assn., Fla. Bar Assn., Voters Inc., Coral Gables C. of C., Nat. Women's Polit. Caucus, Fla. Women's Polit. Caucus, Dade County Women's Polit. Caucus, LWV, AAUW, Citizens League, Inc., ACLU, Panel of Am. Women, Common Cause, U. Fla. Law Center Assn., Zero Population Growth. Office: 7700 N Kendall Dr Suite 612 Miami FL 33156*

FOX, RONDA DIANE, lawyer; b. Port Angeles, Wash., Dec. 9, 1939; d. Curtis Brittain Barnard and Clio (Appleton) Barnard VanValkenburg; m. Milton M. Fox, Dec. 6, 1956 (dec. May 1979); children—Curtis Lewis, Eric Jay, Maureen Clio. B.A., U. Wash., 1956; J.D., St. John's U., 1980. Bar: N.Y. 1981. Assoc., Leffler & Samuel P.C., N.Y.C., 1983—. Mem. ABA, N.Y. County Lawyers Assn. Home: 180 East End Ave Apt 7H New York NY 10128 Office: Leffler & Samuel PC 360 Lexington Ave New York NY 10017

FOX, RUTH INABU, health planner, economist; b. Salt Lake City, Oct. 4, 1918; d. Masataro and Mitsuye (Kushigami) Inabu Kushiue; m. Jack Jay Fox, June 13, 1939; children—Dolores Fox Emspak, John Reed. B.A., U. Colo., 1940, M.A., 1946. Research assoc. U. Colo., Boulder, 1946-49; dir. Office Devel. Evaluation and Research, Westchester County, White Plains, N.Y., 1967-69; dir. div. health plannng and research Westchester County, 1969-74, asst. commr. health planning and program devel., 1974-79, program dir. regional emergency med. services system, 1974-79; emergency med. services cons Westchester County, Valhalla, N.Y., 1979—; asst. prof. community and preventive medicine N.Y. Med. Coll., Valhalla, 1970—. Del., adv. com to county execs. Stop Drinking and Driving Program, 1981—; v.p. Women of Westchester, 1980—; bd. dirs. Cage Teen Ctr., 1962—, Westchester County Mental Health Assn., 1968-83; pres. White Plains Council Community Services, 1979-84; Dist. leader Democratic Party White Plains, 1960-64; v.p. Nat. Womens Polit. Caucus, Westchester, 1982-84; voter service chmn. LWV, White Plains, 1956-58. Recipient Disting. Service award Commn. Human Rights White Plains, 1984. Fellow Inst. Trauma and Emergency Care; mem. Am. Pub. Health Assn., Westchester County Assos., Hudson Valley Regional Emergency Med. Services Council (del.), Westchester County Emergency Med. Services Council, Older Womens League, Gray Panthers, Advocacy League for Mentally Ill., N.Y. State Communities Aid Assn. Avocations: reading; travel. Home: 424 S Lexington Ave White Plains NY 10606 Office: NY Med Coll and Westchester County Med Ctr Valhalla NY 10595

FOX, SUSAN EVA, marketing executive; b. N.Y.C., Apr. 8, 1956; d. William and Barbara (Weil) Fox. B.B.A., George Washington U., 1978. Teaching asst. George Washington U., 1977-78; human resource assoc. Am. Can Co., Greenwich, Conn., 1978-79; project coordinator bus. resources Am. Can Internat., Greenwich, 1979-82; dir. mktg. ops. U.S. San. de Mex., Mexico City, 1982-83; sr. account mgr. Mass Mktg. Systems Internat. subs. Am. Can, N.Y.C., 1983-84; asst. v.p. Citibank U.S.A., Citicorp Credit Services Inc., N.Y.C., 1984—. Vol. Ford Presdl. Com., Washington, 1978, Nixon Presdl. Com., N.Y.C., 1974; bd. dirs. women's div. Jewish Guild for Blind, N.Y.C., 1982—, Am. Jewish Com., 1983—. Recipient Excellence in internat. bus. award George Washington U., 1978. Mem. Direct Mail Assn., Nat. Assn. Female Execs., N.Y. Jr. League. Club: Quaker Ridge Golf. Office: Citibank USA Citicorp Credit Services 575 Lexington Ave New York NY 10043

FOX, VIRGINIA GAINES, public broadcasting executive; b. Campbellsville, Ky., Apr. 30, 1939; d. Harold Durrett and Kathryn (Arnold) Gaines; m. Victor Fox, Dec. 27, 1963. B.A. in Edn., Morehead State U., 1961; M.S.L.S., U. Ky., 1969. Cert. tchr., librarian, Ky. Tchr. Franklin County Schs., Frankfort, Ky., 1961-62, Mason County Schs., Maysville, Ky., 1962-63, Whiteland Elem. Sch., Ind., 1963-64; tchr., librarian Fayette County Schs., Lexington, Ky., 1964-68; utilization specialist Ky. Ednl. TV, Lexington, 1968-69, asst. dir. edn. for evaluation, 1969-70, exec. asst. to exec. dir., 1970-71, dir. edn., 1971-74, dir. edn. and programming, 1974-75, dep. exec. dir., 1974-80; pres., chief exec. officer So. Ednl. Communications Assn., Columbia, S.C., 1980—; mem. nat. adv. com. Children's TV Workshop, N.Y.C., 1979—, informal sci. edn. panel NSF, Washington, 1986—; dir. Editorial Integrity Project, Columbia, 1984—. Exec. producer TV programs: Just One Day, 1979 (Eudora Welty award 1980), Vectoria, 1978 (Corp. for Pub. Broadcasting award 1979), GED. Named Woman of Yr. in Edn., Lexington Bus. and Profl. Women's Club, 1971-72. Mem. Am. Soc. Assn. Execs., Nat. Assn. Ednl. Broadcasters, ALA, Assn. for Ednl. Communications and Tech. (Edgar Dale award region V 1975), Wildlife Action. Episcopalian. Avocations: reading; golf; piano; running. Home: PO Box 5416 Columbia SC 29250 Office: Southern Ednl Communications PO Box 5008 Columbia SC 29250

FOXMAN, LORETTA DOROTHY, outplacement consultant; b. Los Angeles, Sept. 4, 1939; d. Frederick and Helen (Goldberg) F.; m. Walter L. Polsky, Aug. 9, 1964; children—Michael William, Susan Jennifer. B.A., Calif. State U.-Los Angeles, 1963; M.A., Columbia U., 1964. Tchr., Culver City Unified Sch. Dist. (Calif.), 1964-68; asst. dir. St. Christopher Acad., Westfield, N.J., 1971-75; curriculum cons. Middlesex Community Coll. Daycare Ctr., Edison, N.J., 1973, Lakeview Montessori Acad., Summit, N.J., 1975; instr. Northwestern U., Evanston, Ill., 1982—; prin. Jack Dill Assocs., Chgo., 1976-81; exec. v.p. CAMBRIDGE Human Resource Group, Inc., Chgo., 1981—. Chmn. various coms. LWV, Cranford, N.J. and Glencoe, Ill., 1971—; mem. Ad Hoc Rent Control Com., 1973; chmn. adv. bd. Northwestern U. Program on Women, 1982—. Author: Resumes That Work: How to Sell Yourself on Paper, 1984; contbg. editor Personnel Jour.; contbr. several articles to profl. jours. Mem. AAUW, Am. Soc. Personnel Adminstrn., Women in Mgmt., Human Resource Mgmt. Assn. Chgo. Club: Executives (Chgo.). Office: Cambridge Human Resource Group Inc 1500 Skokie Blvd Suite 5 Northbrook IL 60062

FOXX-GREEN, JANINA, municipal housing administrator; b. Charlotte, N.C., Sept. 14, 1953; d. Percy Washington and Sarah Catherine (Grier) Foxx; m. Janois Young, Dec. 21, 1974 (div. June 1980); m. Jerome Clay Green, Aug. 24, 1985. Student in acctg. Central Piedmont Community Coll., 1971-75; student in bus. mgmt. Pfeiffer Coll., 1985—. Order clk. Brodt Music, Charlotte, N.C., 1972; adminstrv. asst. Sch. Workers Fed. Credit Union, Charlotte, 1972-79; collection mgr. Barclay's Am., Charlotte, 1979-81; office mgr., loan officer Neighborhood Housing Services of Charlotte, 1981—; auditing cons. Neighborhood Reinvestment, Washington, 1984—. Democrat. Presbyterian. Avocations: tennis; backgammon; travel; singing. Home: 1117 Mount Kisco Dr Charlotte NC 28213 Office: Neighborhood Housing Services Charlotte 225 E Kingston Ave Charlotte NC 28204

FOY, JOAN MARIE, new home sales person; b. Medford, Mass., Apr. 12, 1930; d. David Leonard and Catherine (McKenzie) Fitzgerald; m. Edward James Foy, Jan. 15, 1955; children—Barbara Foy Walker, Edward James, Jr. B.A. in English Lit., Regis Coll., 1951; postgrad. N.Y. Inst. Fin., 1957-58. Cert. Nat. Assn. Security Dealers. Registered rep. N.Y. Stock Exchange, Washington, D.C., 1957-59, Boston Stock Exchange, 1967-69; mgr. Pres.'s Health and Racquet Ball Club, Dallas, 1977-84; sales Gen. Homes Corp., Dallas, 1984—. Actress Dallas Repertory Theatre, 1969-78 (Actress of Excellence award, 1976-77). Counselor, Suicide Prevention Dallas, 1969-72. Served to lt. (j.g.) USN, 1951-54. Recipient 1st pl. award Triathalon Women Over 45 Health and Tennis Corp., 1983. Democrat. Home: 3442 Whirlaway Dr Dallas TX 75229 Office: Gen Homes 15301 Dallas Pkwy Suite 1020 Dallas TX 75248

FOYTECK, KAREN EDNA, office services executive; b. Detroit, July 17, 1941; d. Edward W. and Evelyn E. (Gault) Webb; m. Douglas L. Foyteck, Aug.

26, 1961; children—Mark D., Michael D., Matthew W. B.A., Wayne State U., 1965. Tchr. English Birmingham Pub. Schs., Mich., 1965-66, Clarkston Community Schs., Mich., 1975-79; ptnr. The Drop'd Stitch, Clarkston, 1980-83; chief exec. officer, bus. mgr. North Oakland Office Services, Clarkston, 1983—. Active Clarkston Community Women's Club. Republican. Office: North Oakland Office Service PO Box 246 Clarkston MI 48016

FRACKMAN, NOEL, art critic; b. N.Y.C., May 27, 1930; d. Walter D. and Celeste (Barman) Stern; student (Sarah Williston scholar, 1950), Mt. Holyoke Coll., 1948-50; B.A., Sarah Lawrence Coll., 1952, M.A., 1953; postgrad. in art history Columbia U., 1964-67; M.A., Inst. Fine Arts, N.Y.U., 1976, now doctoral candidate; m. Richard B. Frackman, July 2, 1950; 1 dau., Noel Dru Frackman Pyne. Art critic Scarsdale (N.Y.) Inquirer, 1962-67; mus. lectr. Aldrich Mus. Contemporary Art, Ridgefield, Conn., 1967-75; lectr. Gallery Passport, Ltd., N.Y.C., 1968—; with Arts Mag., N.Y.C., 1968—, contbg. editor 1977—; curator of edn. Storm King Art Center, Mountainville, N.Y., 1973-75. Mem. Internat. Assn. Art Critics, Coll. Art Assn. Contbr. articles in field to various mags. Home: 3 Hadden Rd Scarsdale NY 10583

FRADKIN, MINDY SUE, fashion stylist; b. Balt., June 3, 1955; d. Robert Bernard Fradkin and Dorothy (Wolfe) Hight. Student Art Ctr., Los Angeles, 1979-81; A.A., Fashion Inst. Design and Mdse., Los Angeles, 1983. Freelance asst. stylist, Los Angeles, 1982-83, N.Y.C., 1983-84; stylist, prodn. coordinator Cailor Resnick Studio, N.Y.C., 1984; freelance fashion stylist, N.Y.C., 1985—. Mem. Assn. Stylists and Coordinators (sec. 1984-85), Stylists and Allied Services (bd. dirs. 1985-86). Democrat. Jewish. Avocations: reading; travel; music; movies; theater; swimming. Home: 236 E 80th St #19 New York NY 10021

FRAHM, SUE ADELE, university administrator; b. Beatrice, Nebr., Jan. 16, 1941; d. Berwin Richard and Kathryn Mary (Burroughs) Shaffer; m. Larry Dean Frahm, Aug. 17, 1963; children—Jeffrey Michael, Kristi Anne. B.A., Nebr. Wesleyan U., 1962; M.S., U. Nebr.-Lincoln, 1978. Instr., Southeast Community Coll., Lincoln, 1972-77, project asst. Ctr. on Aging, 1977-78, aging coordinator, 1978-79, asst. coordinator adult edn., 1979-80; dir. alumni Nebr. Wesleyan U., Lincoln, 1981—; trainer Minn. Couples Communication Program, Mpls., 1977-82. Pres., 1st v.p. YWCA, Lincoln, 1978-85; bd. dirs. Lincoln council Camp Fire, 1975-78, Lincoln Ctr. for Srs., 1970-76; co-pres. Community Adv. Council, Lincoln, 1985-86. Mem. Adult Continuing Edn. of Nebr., Omicron Nu. Avocations: jogging, reading, backpacking. Home: 8033 Sanborn Dr Lincoln NE 68505 Office: Nebr Wesleyan U 50th and Saint Paul Sts Lincoln NE 68504

FRAICHE, DONNA DIMARTINO, lawyer; b. New Orleans, Dec. 8, 1951; d. Anthony and Rose Mary (Batchelona) DiMartino; student St. Mary's Dominican Coll., New Orleans, 1971, La. State U., 1972; J.D., Loyola U., New Orleans, 1975; m. John F. Fraiche, Dec. 27, 1974; 1 son, Geoffrey Michael. Admitted to La. bar, 1975, U.S. Ct. Claims bar, 1979, U.S. Tax Ct. bar, 1977, U.S. Supreme Ct. bar, 1979, since practiced in New Orleans, Baton Rouge; law clk., assoc. Martzell & Montero, 1972-76; assoc. McCollister, McCleary, Fazio, Mixon, Holliday and Jones, 1976-78; individual practice law, 1978-80; pres. Donna D. Fraiche, P.C., 1980-84, Wyllie, Fraiche & Sullivan, 1984—; ptnr. Broadhurst Brook Mangham & Hardy. Mem. pres.'s adv. com. to bd. Our Lady of Holy Cross Coll., New Orleans, 1979; pres. La. State Arts Council, 1984—; mem. jr. women's com., Opus '81 com. New Orleans Symphony, chmn. Opus Ball, 1982, 83; bd. dirs. New Orleans chpt. Young Audiences; bd. dirs. Louise Davis Devel. Ctr. Recipient cert. of merit Loyola U. Sch. Law, 1975. Mem. ABA (mem. forum com. on health law, co-chmn. New Orleans forum com. on health law), Nat. Health Lawyers Assn. (dir. 1982-85, exec. dir., sec. 1984—), Am. Soc. Hosp. Attys., Am. Coll. Legal Medicine (asso.), La. Soc. Hosp. Attys. (founder, dir.), Am. Hosp. Assn., Acad. Hosp. Attys., Mortar Bd., Phi Delta Phi. Past editor in chief Delta mag. La. State U. Democrat. Roman Catholic. Home: 3924 Saint Charles Ave New Orleans LA 70115 Office: 400 Poydras St Suite 2600 New Orleans LA 70130

FRAIMAN, GENEVIEVE LAM, lawyer; b. Honolulu, May 18, 1928. B.A., Wellesley Coll., 1949; LL.B., Columbia Law Sch., 1952. Bar: N.Y. 1952. Ptnr. Lord, Day & Lord, N.Y.C. Mem. ABA, N.Y. State Bar Assn. Address: Lord Day and Lord 25 Broadway New York NY 10004

FRALEY, RUTH ANN, librarian; b. Peekskill, N.Y., Oct. 16, 1942; d. Joseph Edward and Cora Marie (McEachern) Salerno; B.A., SUNY-Albany, 1964, M.S. in L.S., 1966; M.B.A., Union Coll. Schenectady, 1981; m. James M. Fraley, Sept. 26, 1964; children—Christine, Melissa, Heather. Library media specialist Schenectady Public Schs., part-time 1966-72; reference librarian, then head tech. services Library Resources Center, Schenectady County Community Coll., 1972-79, chmn. adv. com., 1981—; head Hawley Library, SUNY, Albany, 1979-81, head Grad. Library Public Affairs and Policy, 1981-86; chief librarian WYS Unified Ct. System, 1986—. Recipient Chancellor's award for excellence in librarianship SUNY, 1979. Mem. ALA (chmn. publ. award jury resources and tech. services div. 1982—, chmn. circulation stats. com. library adminstrn. mgmt. div. 1982—, chmn. stats. sect.), Am. Soc. Info. Scis., N.Y. Library Assn. (past pres. resources and tech. services sect., pres. 1986), Hudson-Mohawk Library Assn., Albany Women's Forum. Roman Catholic. Author, editor in field. Home: 29 Roslyn Dr Ballston Lake NY 12019 Office: Office of Ct Adminstrn Agy Bldg 4 10th Floor Empire State Plaza Albany NY 12223

FRAME, ANNE PARSONS (TOOTELL-BRADY), civic worker; b. Berkeley, Calif., Jan. 3, 1904; d. Reginald H. and Maude (Bemis) Parsons; B.A., Mills Coll., 1924; postgrad. Columbia U., 1924-25; m. Frederic D. Tootell, Apr. 3, 1926 (div. July 1935); children—Geoffrey Howland, Natalie Anne Tootell Oliver; m. 2d, Jasper Ewing Brady, (dec. Dec. 1944), 1 son, Hugh Parsons; m. 3d, Howard Andres Frame, Mar. 29, 1948. Dir. Parsons, Hart & Co., Parsons Investment Co., Hillcrest Orchard Corp. Mem. Park and Recreation Commn., Town of Atherton, 1972-82, vice chmn. 1972-74; bd. dirs. Wash. State Bataan Relief Soc., chmn., 1943-46; bd. dirs. Children's Health Council, Palo Alto, Calif., 1953-58, 59-76, pres., 1954-58; bd. dirs. Nat. Recreation Assn., 1949-66; bd. dirs. Nat. Recreation and Park Assn. (award 1974), 1966-73, sr. aux. to Stanford (Calif.) Convalescent Home, 1958-62, v.p., 1964-65; bd. dirs. Children's Hosp., Stanford, 1967-81; mem. bd. mgmt. Palo Alto br. ARC, 1955-61, chmn. home service com., 1950-55; mem. bd. govs. San Francisco Symphony Assn., 1963-79; trustee Children's Orthopedic Hosp. and Med. Center, Seattle, 1942-48, Mills Coll., 1952-62, chmn. student life com., 1953-58. Mem. Chgo., Seattle, Calif., San Mateo County hist. socs., Nat. Soc. of Colonial Dames, Mus. Soc. of San Francisco , Nat. Trust for Hist. Preservation. Republican. Episcopalian. Clubs: Seattle Tennis, Sunset Club of Seattle; Francisca Club of San Francisco, Woodside-Atherton Garden. Home: 587 Fletcher Dr Atherton CA 94025 Office: Parsons Hart & Co 1218 3d Ave Seattle WA 98101

FRAME, JEAN GROETZ, educator, consultant; b. Medina, Ohio, July 18, 1951; d. Edward Joseph and Gwendolyn Mae (Lindley) G.; m. Carl Ralph Frame, Dec. 10, 1983. B.S., U. Akron, 1973, postgrad., 1973-83. Elem. tchr. Medina City Schs., Ohio, 1973—; cons. staff devel. team Medina Schs., 1982—; staff cons. Medina Drug Prevention Program, 1982—; dir. summer sch. age program Nurtury Presch., Medina, 1980-81. Composer of musical scores, 1972, 73. Jennings Found. scholar Kent State U., 1984-85. Mem. AAUW, Medina City Tchrs. Assn. (bldg. rep.) Medina City Staff Devel. Team, Kappa Delta Pi. Avocations: biking, travel, teaching piano, reading, gardening. Home: 955 Brookpoint Dr Medina OH 44256 Office: Sidney Fenn Elem Sch 320 N Spring Grove Medina OH 44256

FRANCA, CELIA, director, choreographer, dancer, narrator; b. London, Eng., June 25, 1921; m. James Morton, Dec. 7, 1960. Student, Guildhall Sch. Music, Royal Acad. Dancing; LL.D., U. Windsor, 1959, Mt. Allison U., 1966, U. Toronto, 1974, Dalhousie U., 1976, York U., 1976, Trent U., Peterborough, Ont., Can., 1977; D.C.L., Bishop's U., 1967; D.Litt., Guelph U., 1976. Mem. jury 5th Internat. Ballet Competition, Varna, Bulgaria, 1970, 2d Internat. Ballet Competition, Moscow, 1973. Debut: corps de ballet in Tudor, Mercury Theatre, London, 1936; soloist, Ballet Rambert, London, 1936-38; leading dramatic dancer, Ballet Rambert, 1938-39; guest artist, Ballet Rambert, 1950; dancer, Ballet des Trois Arts, London, 1939, Arts Theatre Ballet, London, 1940, Internat. Ballet, London, 1941; leading dramatic dancer, Sadler's Wells Ballet, 1941-46; guest artist, choreographer, Sadler's Wells Theatre Ballet, London, 1946-47; dancer, tchr., Ballets Jooss, Eng., 1947; ballet mistress, leading dancer, Met. Ballet, London, 1947-49; dancer, Ballet Workshop, London, 1949-51; founder, artistic dir., Nat. Ballet Can., Toronto, 1951-74; a prin. dancer, Nat. Ballet Can., 1951-59; co-founder, Nat. Ballet Sch., Toronto, 1959—; prin. roles include Black Queen in Swan Lake; title roles in Lady from the Sea; choreographer ballets including: Midas, London, 1939, Cancion, London, 1942, Khadra, London, 1946, Dance of Salome, The Eve of St. Agnes, BBC-TV, 1950, Afternoon of a Faun, Toronto, 1952, Le Pommier, Toronto, 1952, Casse-Noisette, 1955, Princess Aurora, 1960, The Nutcracker, 1964, Cinderella, 1968, numerous others for CBC, Can. Opera Co.; author: The National Ballet of Canada: A Celebration, 1978. Bd. dirs. Can. Council, York U., Theatre Ballet of Can.; mem. adv. bd. Quinte Sch. Dance, Belleville; bd. dirs. Pre-Profl. Program of Sch. Dance, Ottawa. Decorated Order of Can.; recipient Key to City of Washington, 1955; Woman of Year award B'nai B'rith, 1958; award for outstanding contbn. to arts Toronto Telegram, 1965; Centennial medal, 1967; Hadassah award of merit, 1967; Molson award, 1974; award Internat. Soc. Performing Arts Adminstrs., 1979; honored as a founder of Can.'s maj. ballet cos. at Alta. Ballet Co.'s 15th Anniversary, 1981; Can. Dance award, 1984; Can. Council sr. grantee, 1975. Office: 250 Clemow Ave Ottawa ON K1S 2B6 Canada

FRANCHIK, CAROL ANN, administrative executive; b. Chgo., Jan. 5, 1939; d. Florian J. and Mildred E. (Backofen) Ostrowski; student Morton Coll., 1964; m. Bill D. Franchik, Jan. 19, 1957; 1 son, Mark William. Legal sec. Hajek & Hucek, Cicero, Ill., 1956-58, Kirkland & Ellis, Chgo., 1958-59, 63-67; exec. sec. DeSoto Chem. Coatings, Chgo., 1961-63; adminstrv. mgr. Wildman, Harrold, Allen & Dixon, Chgo., 1967-79; v.p., controller Duff & Phelps, Inc., Chgo., 1979-83; adminstrv. mgr. Siegan, Barbakoff, Gomberg, Gordon & Elden, Ltd., Chgo., 1984—; pres. Law Officers Mgrs. Assn., Chgo., 1976. Mem. adv. bd. Prairie State Coll., 1978-79; exec. bd. Fullersburg Homeowners Assn., 1980-81. Mem. Assn. Legal Adminstrs. Nat. Fedn. Bus. and Profl. Women's Clubs, Inc. Home: 505 N Lake Shore Dr Chicago IL 60611 Office: 20 N Clark St Chicago IL 60602

FRANCHINI, ROXANNE, banker; b. N.Y.C., Mar. 20, 1951; d. Tullio and Jean (Brady) F.; ed. Emerson Coll., Ricker Coll., New Sch. Social Research. With Princess Marcella Borghese div. Revlon, N.Y.C., 1972-73; stewardess TWA Airlines, 1973-74; asst. to pres. N.Y. Shipping Assn., N.Y.C., 1974-79; benefits mgr. Kidde, Inc., 1979-83; 2d v.p. pension trust fin. services Chase Manhattan Bank, N.A., N.Y.C., 1983-85, v.p. mgr. global securities, 1985—; coordinator community fund raising campaigns. Mem. Nat. Assn. Female Execs., Am. Mgmt. Assn., AAUW, Internat. Founds. Employee Benefits, Internat. Ops. Assn., S.W. Pension Conf., Nat. Investment Co. Service Assn. Office: 1211 Ave of the Americas New York NY

FRANCIS, FADRA SUE, collection and repossession co. exec.; b. Winnsboro, Tex., Dec. 12, 1926; Henry Sylvester and Sally Mae (Boone) Brown; grad. Fed. Inst. Bus. Sch., Tyler, Tex., 1946; m. Robert H. Francis, Jan. 28, 1949 (dec.); children—Bobbie Sue, Debbie Lou. Sec., M. Oliver Rose Farm, Tyler, 1946-47, Reilly Oil Co., Tyler, 1947-48; office mgr. Caruthers Jewelry Store and Sch. Horology, Tyler, 1948-51; co-owner R. H. Francis Co., Tyler, 1951-54, owner, San Antonio, 1954—. Leader, San Antonio council Girl Scouts U.S.A. Mem. Allied Fin. Adjusters Conf., Nat. Fin. Adjusters (dir. 1983-84, 3d v.p. 1984-85, 2d v.p. 1985-86), Am. Recovery Assn., Nat. Fedn. Ind. Bus., Greater San Antonio C. of C. Baptist. Clubs: Sunridge, Daus. of Nile. Home: 1263 Bandera Rd San Antonio TX 78228 Office: 1263 Bandera Rd Sn Antonio TX 78228

FRANCIS, MARILYN MAE, editor, writer; b. Lakewood, N.J., May 28, 1935; d. Paul and Susanna (Komada) Milow; m. Ernest Charles Francis, Aug. 13, 1974. A.B., Hunter Coll., 1957. Asst. women's editor N.Y. World-Telegram & Sun, N.Y.C., 1957-66; account exec. Saul Krieg Assocs., N.Y.C., 1966-67; press and media contact Nat. Bd. YWCA, N.Y.C., 1967-73, editor writer, 1976-85; writer/advt. Del. County Times, 1986—; head publicity YWCA, London, Eng., 1973-74; fashion writer Soap Opera Digest, N.Y.C., 1975-76. Contbr. numerous articles to popular mags. Trustee Bovine Pub. Library. Mem. Newswomen's Club N.Y., Daus. Brit. Empire, Nat. Assn. Female Execs., Inc., Bovina Hist. Soc. Home: PO Box 27 Bovina Center NY 13740 Office: Delaware County Times 4 Ct St Delhi NY 13753

FRANCIS, REBECCA JANE, educator; b. Shreveport, La., Feb. 6, 1934; d. John Thomas and Mell (Smith) Gray; m. Albert Nolan Francis, Jr., Nov. 13, 1954; children—Robert Nolan, John Mark. B.S., Centenary Coll., 1955; M.Edn., Sam Houston State U., 1979. Cert. reading specialist. Tchr. Alaska On-Base Schs., Anchorage, 1955-56, Corpus Christi Ind. Sch. Dist. (Tex.), 1957-59; tchr. Houston Ind. Sch. Dist., 1970-76, reading specialist, 1977-79; reading specialist, tchr. Klein Ind. Sch. Dist., Spring, Tex., 1979—. Mem. NEA, Klein Edn. Assn., Tex. State Tchrs. Assn., Greater Houston Area Reading Council, No. Harris County Tchrs. English. Republican. Methodist. Home: 1423 Big Horn St Houston TX 77090 Office: Strack Intermediate Sch 18027 Kuykendahl St Spring TX 77373

FRANCIS, RUBY LEE, educator, media specialist; b. Paris, Tex., Nov. 5, 1922; d. Charles J. and Roberta (Allen) Chambliss; m. Homer Albert Francis, June 10, 1939 (dec. 1972); 1 dau., Nelda Francis Gossett. A.A., Paris Jr. Coll., 1960; B.S., East Tex. U., 1962, M.L.S., 1968. Elem. tchr. Nathaniel Hawthorne Sch., Dallas, 1962-83, media specialist, 1983—. Named Tchr. of Yr., Dallas Ind. Sch. Dist., 1978-81. Mem. Dallas Classrooms Tchrs. Assn., Tex. State Tchrs. Assn. (rep. 1965-88, 68), Nat. Tchrs. Assn., Nat. Assn. Bus. and Profl. Women. Democrat. Mem. Ch. of Christ. Home: 19232 LBJ Freeway Apt 2814 Mesquite TX 75150 Office: Nathaniel Hawthorne Sch 7800 Unphress St Dallas TX 75217

FRANCIS, THERESA P., medical record administrator, nursing home administrator; b. Thodupuzha, India, Mar. 20, 1938; came to U.S., 1976; naturalized, 1984; d. Frenchu (Francis) Aleykutty Nallanirappel; m. Francis Palayan Vargheese, May 10, 1970 (div. Sept. 1979); 1 child, Bobby Francis; m. Jacob Mathew Potheekattu, Jan. 7, 1980; Diploma nursing Cama and Albless Hosp., 1967, diploma midwifery, 1968; B.S. in Health Adminstrn., St. Joseph's Coll., Bklyn., 1986. Staff nurse Breach Candy Hosp. and Nursing Home, Bombay, India, 1968-76; dir. Panvel Mcpl. Hosp., Bombay, 1975-76; nurse's aide, lic. practical nurse Meth. Med. Ctr., Des Moines, 1976-78; staff nurse Ahn-Wyckoff Heights Hosp., Bklyn., 1978-81; supr. Willoughby Nursing Home, River Manor, Parkshore Manor, 1981-84; med. record adminstr. State Univ. Hosp., Bklyn., 1984—; sales mgr. Forever Living Prodocts, 1985—; real estate broker, 1986—. Author: (plays) This is Amerika, 1983; Slaughtered Sheeps; 1982; Barbed Wire, 1983. Mem. Indian Nat. Congress, Bombay, 1964-70, Kerala, 1953-59. Recipient awards Bombay Nursing State Bd., 1965, 67. Mem. N.Y. Assn. Quality Assurance Profls., Nat Assn. Female Execs., United Univ. Profls., Am. Nursing Assn., Kerala Samagam of Greater New York (sec. 1983-84). Roman Catholic. Lodge: Lionesses (Bklyn.). Avocations: reading; writing; cooking; dancing; teaching; yoga. Home: 262 Saint Nicholas Ave Brooklyn NY 11237

FRANCIS-VOGELSANG, CHAREE, business executive; b. Akron, Ohio, Aug. 22, 1946; d. William John and Mary Martha (Kemp) Francis; student Ohio Paralegal Inst., 1975-76; A.A., U. Akron, 1979, B.S.B.A., 1982. With gen. office and legal dept. Diebold, Inc., Canton, Ohio, 1964-72, asst. sec., 1972-78, sec., 1978-83, v.p., sec., 1983—. Mem. Am. Soc. Corp. Secs., Nat. Assn. Legal Assts. Republican. Presbyn. Home: 432 31st St NW Canton OH 44709 Office: 818 Mulberry Rd SE Canton OH 44711

FRANCK, ARDATH AMOND, educator, school psychologist; b. Wehrum, Pa., May 5, 1925; d. Arthur and Helen Lucille (Sharp) Amond; m. Frederick M. Franck, Mar. 18, 1945; children—Sheldon, Candace. B.S. in Edn., Kent State U., 1946, M.A., 1947; Ph.D., Western Res. U., 1956. Cert. high sch. tchr., elem. supr., sch. psychologist, speech and hearing therapist. Instr., Western Res. U., Cleve., summer 1953, U. Akron, 1947-50; sch. psychologist Summit County Schs., Ohio, 1950-60; cons. psychologist Wadsworth Pub. Schs., Ohio, 1946—; dir. Akron Speech & Reading Ctr., Ohio, 1950—; cons. dir. The Hobbitts, Richfield, Ohio, 1967-85. Author: Your Child Learns, 1976. Bd. dirs., pres. Twirling Unltd., 1982—. Mem. Am. Speech and Hearing Assn., Internat. Reading Assn., Ohio Psychol. Assn. Club: Soroptimist (Akron). Home: 631 Ghent Akron OH 44313 Office: Akron Speech & Reading Assn 700 Ghent Rd Akron OH 44313

FRANCK, IRENE MARY, author; b. Albany, N.Y., Mar. 14, 1941; d. Otto Charles and Pauline (Zuk) Franck; m. David M. Brownstone, Jan. 20, 1969; m. Lawrence E. Samuels, June 1961 (div. Mar. 1964). B.A., SUNY-Binghamton, 1962. Tchr. English, Susquehanna Valley Central Sch., Conklin, N.Y., 1962-63; writer Switchmen's Union N.Am., Conklin, 1962-67; office mgr. L.W. Hayes Real Estate & Ins., Binghamton, 1963-65, also folksinger, The Gate; chief operator N.Y. Telephone Co., Albany, 1966-67; tchr. English, Jefferson (N.Y.) Central Sch., 1967-68, Robert Louis Stevenson Sch., N.Y.C., 1968-70; editor John Wiley & Sons, N.Y.C., 1970-79; prin. The Hudson Group, Inc., Pleasantville, N.Y., 1979—, pres., 1980-82; sec. treas. Temeraire Enterprises, Chappaqua, N.Y., 1980—. Author: Island of Hope, Island of Tears: The Great Migration Through Ellis Island to America, 1979; The VNR Dictionary of Business and Finance, 1980; The VNR Real Estate Dictionary, 1981; The VNR Investor's Dictionary, 1981; The Dictionary of Publishing, 1982; The Sales Professional's Advisor, 1983; The Manager's Advisor, 1983; The Encyclopedia of Work: The Evolution of Careers, Occupations, and Trades from Their Origins to the Present, 1984; To The Ends of the Earth: The Great Travel and Trade Routes of Human History, 1984; editor Film Rev. Digest quar., 1975-77. Mem. Authors Guild, Orgn. Am. Historians, Oral History Assn., Am. Hist. Assn. Office: The Hudson Group Inc 74 Memorial Plaza Pleasantville NY 10570

FRANCK, JANE P., library administrator; b. Akron, Ohio, Jan. 11; d. Francis O. and Irene A. (Neumann) Paul; m. Wolf Franck, Sept. 4, 1953 (dec. 1966); children—Irene Cecily, Julie Louise. B.A. cum laude, Hofstra U.; B.S. in Library Service, Columbia U., M.A. with honors; postgrad. CCNY, 1968-74. Music librarian Columbia U., N.Y.C., 1943-49; adj. lectr. Pratt Inst. Library Sch., Bklyn., 1963-68; archivist and spl. coll. librarian CCNY, 1960-68; librarian and adminstrv. officer Ford Found., N.Y.C., 1968-77; dir. Tchr.'s Coll. Library, N.Y.C., 1977—; women's coordinating com. Ford Found., 1976-77; founder, chmn. Consortium Found. Libraries, 1970-74; chmn. adv. com. on post masters program for library dept. Queens Coll., 1975—; mem. adv. bd. St. John's U.; chmn. small libraries rountable, N.Y. Met. Reference and Research Library Agy. 1974-75, mem. adminstrv. services com., 1973-77; cons. libraries in U.S., Iran, Italy, Pakistan, Spain; organized seminars on exhbn. catalogs, reference standards, reference measurement. Contbr. articles to profl. jours. Active consumer, conservation and civil rights groups. William Mason scholar, 1947-48. Mem. Am. Musicological Soc., ALA, Internat. Fedn. Library Assns., Music Library Assn., Soc. Am. Archivists, LWV. Democrat. Mem. United Ch. of Christ. Office: Tchrs Coll Columbia U 525 W 120th St New York NY 10027

FRANCKE, GLORIA NIEMEYER, pharmacist, editor, publisher; b. Dillsboro, Ind., Apr. 28, 1922; d. Albert B. and Fannie K. (Libbert) Niemeyer; m. Donald Eugene Francke, Apr. 15, 1956. B.S. in Pharmacy, Purdue U., 1942; Pharm.D., U. Cin., 1971; postgrad. U. Mich., 1945. Pharmacist, Dillsboro Drug Store, 1943-44; instr. Sch. Pharmacy, Purdue U., Lafayette, Ind., 1943; asst. to chief pharmacist U. Mich. Hosp., Ann Arbor, 1944-46; assoc. editor Am. Jour. Hosp. Pharmacy, Washington, 1944-64; asst. dir. Div. Hosp. Pharmacy of Am. Pharm. Assn., Washington, 1946-56; exec. sec. Am. Soc. Hosp. Pharmacists, Ann Arbor, 1949-60; acting dir. dept. communications, Washington, 1963-64; drug lit. specialist Nat. Library Medicine, Bethesda, Md., 1965-67; clin. pharmacy teaching coordinator VA Hosp., Cin., 1967-71; asst. clin. prof. clin. pharmacy Coll. Pharmacy, U. Cin., 1967-71; chief program evaluation br. Alcohol and Drug Dependence Service, VA, Central Office, Washington, 1971-75; dir. Pharmacy Intelligence Ctr., Am. Pharm. Assn., Washington, 1975-85; mem. Roche Hosp. Pharmacy Adv. Bd., 1971-74; judge for ann. Lunsford Richardson Pharmacy awards, 1963, 64; mem. com. standards for drug abuse treatment and rehab. programs Joint Commn. Accreditation of Hosps., 1974-75. Author: (with D. E. Francke, C. J. Latiolais and N.F. H. Ho) Mirror to Hospital Pharmacy, 1964. Contbr. articles on hosp. pharmacy and clin. pharmacy to profl. jours. Recipient H.A.K. Whitney award Mich. Soc. Hosp. Pharmacists, 1953, Disting. Alumnus award Purdue U. Sch. of Pharmacy, 1985; also various commendations. Mem. Am. Pub. Health Assn., Internat. Pharm. Fedn., Am. Inst. History of Pharmacy (exec. sec. 1968-78), Tex. Soc. Hosp. Pharmacists (hon.), Am. Pharm. Assn. (hon. chmn. 1986), Am. Soc. Hosp. Pharmacists, Drug Info. Assn., Kappa Epsilon, Rho Chi. Presbyterian. Home and Office: 3900 Cathedral Ave NW #403-A Washington DC 20016

FRANK, DONNA JEAN PRANKA, government auditor; b. Waterbury, Conn., Sept. 19, 1952; m. Charles and Jean (Turner) Pranka; m. Ralph Joseph Frank, Jr., Apr. 15, 1978. B.S., U. Conn., 1974. Medicaid auditor State of Conn., Hartford, 1977-84, hosp. auditor, 1984, supr. hosp. audits, 1984—. Treas. Alsop A, Storrs, Conn., 1974; mem. Nat. Arbor Day Found., Nebraska City, Nebr., 1985. Mem. Am. Fed. Tchrs., Conn. Soc. Govtl. Accts. (sec. 1983-84, asst. sec. 1984-85, v.p. 1985—), United Council on Welfare Fraud. Avocation: amateur radio operator. Home: 31 Duane Ln Burlington CT 06013 Office: Dept Income Maintenance 110 Bartholomew Ave Hartford CT 06106

FRANK, EDITH SINAIKO, civic worker; b. Madison, Wis., July 16, 1902; d. Isaac and Sarah (Goldberg) Sinaiko; B.A., U. Wis., 1924, postgrad., 1963-66; grad. Wheeler Sch. Music, 1922, Cosmopolitan Sch. Music, 1926-42; m. David S. Frank, June 24, 1924 (dec. 1962); 1 dau., Suzanne Frank Freund. Pres., Toledo Friends of Library, 1949; pres. N.W. Ohio Fedn. Music Clubs, 1950; bd. dirs. Madison Friends of Library, 1973; mem. bd. Toledo Symphony Orch., 1951; mem. women's com. Chgo. Symphony, 1951; mem. bd. Met. Housing and Planning Council Chgo.; pres. women's council City Renewal, Chgo.; mem. bd. Madison Civic Center Commn., 1973-82; mem. bd. Found. for Arts, 1974—; bd. curators Aux. State Hist. Soc. Wis., 1976, pres. aux., 1974-76; mem. bd. Madison Found., 1976—. Recipient Service award Municipal Defense Council, Charleston, W.Va., 1945, Outstanding Citizen award Toledo Newspaper Guild, 1951, Page I Citizenship award Madison Newspaper Guild, 1976, award Rotary Club, 1976. Mem. Women in Communications (pres. Madison chpt. 1966), Madison Press Club (sec. 1969-70), Wis. Acad. Scis., Arts and Letters, LWV (past state bd. dirs., past pres. Toledo), Theta Sigma Phi. Clubs: Arts (Chgo.); University (Madison, Wis.). Home: 1515 Vilas Ave Madison WI 53711

FRANK, ELLEN, lawyer; b. Bklyn., Nov. 24, 1957; d. Leon and Gladys (Reznik) Frank. B.S., Bklyn. Coll., 1979; J.D., Boston Coll., 1982. Bar: N.Y. 1983, Mass. 1983. Fiscal analyst HUD, N.Y.C., summer, 1979; assoc. F. Strafaci, Bklyn., 1982-83; assoc. firm F. Lee Bailey and Aaron J. Broder, N.Y.C., 1984; sole practice law, N.Y.C., 1984—; tchr., coach mock trial team High Sch. Graphic Communication Arts, N.Y.C., 1985-86. Moderator Conf. on Legal Rights of Battered Women, N.Y.C., 1983; sec. 61st Civilian Patrol, Bklyn., 1979; mem. King's Hwy. Devel. Corp., Bklyn., 1982—. Recipient Alumni Assn. award Boston Coll., 1980. Mem. ABA, N.Y. Women's Bar Assn. (matrimonial law, internat. law coms.), N.Y. State Trial Lawyers Assn., New York County Lawyers Assn. (law, youth and citizenship com.), Phi Alpha Delta (publicity dir. Boston 1981-82). Democrat.

FRANK, HILDA RHEA KAPLAN, dancer; b. Houston, Dec. 30, 1939; d. Sam and Bertha (Grevsky) Kaplan; m. Robert Stuart Frank, Feb. 28, 1960; children—Karen Denise Frank Hurwitz, Daniel Steven, Nancy Alyson. Student Newcomb, Coll., New Orleans, 1957-59, U. Houston, 1959-60, Butler U., 1960. Dance tchr. Joy Alexander Sch. Dance, Houston, 1955-57, Jane Browning Sch. Dance, Houston, 1965-69, Rudy Jenkins, Sch. Ballet, Houston, 1968-69, Xperience Gymnastic Team, Houston, 1972-75; dance tchr. Jewish Community Ctr., Houston, 1975-80, dance com. chmn., 1978—; dance panelist Cultural Arts Council Houston, 1980-85; sec.-treas. Discovery Dance Group, Houston, 1981-84, pres., 1984-85; trustee Houston Dance Coalition, 1985-87. Choreographer: To Live Another Summer, 1980; Jewish Fairy Tale, 1974; My Son, The President, 1981; dir., choreographer Emanu El Israeli Dancers, Houston, 1973—. Recipient scholarship Jacob's Pillow Dance Festival, Lee, Mass., 1959; named Vol. of Yr., Jewish Community Ctr., Houston, 1985. Mem. Houston Dance Coalition (trustee 1985—), Cultural Arts Council Houston. Jewish. Clubs: Hadassah, Sisterhood of Emanu El (Houston) (Israeli dance dir. 1973—). Home: 1 Woods Edge Ln Houston TX 77024

FRANK, MAXINE SALVAGE, lawyer; b. Springfield, Mass., Sept. 23, 1930; d. Gasper and Gweyn (Slavin) Salvage; m. Lester Frank, June 15, 1950; children—Andrew, Barbara, Donald, Daniel. Student U. Vt., 1947-50; B.A., Am. Internat. Coll., Springfield, Mass., 1963; J.D., Western New Eng. Sch. Law, Springfield, 1976. Bar: Mass. 1976. Assoc., Skoler, Abbott & Hayes, Springfield, 1976-78, Skvirsky, Price, Weissman & Frank, Springfield, 1978-85; prin. Maxine Salvage Frank, 1985—; legal advisor No. Ednl. Soc., 1981—. Bd. dirs. Jewish Family Service, Springfield YWCA, Neurofibromatosis Assn., Inc.; corporator Jewish Nursing Home for Aged, Bay State Med. Ctr., Children's Study Home. Mem. Mass. Bar Assn., Hampden County Bar Assn., ABA, Am. Acad. Trial Attys., Mass. Acad. Trial Attys., Mass. Bar Assn. Jewish. Club:

Field (Longmeadow). Home: 113 Farmington Aae Longmeadow MA 01106 Office: 101 State St Springfield MA 01103

FRANK, PATRICIA ANNE, state senator; b. Cleve., Nov. 12, 1929; d. Paul Conrad and Mildred Patricia (Roane) Collier; m. Richard H. Frank; children—Stacy, Hillary, Courtney. B.B.A. in Fin. and Taxation, U. Fla., 1951; postgrad. Georgetown U. Sch. Law, 1951-52. Bus. economist anti-trust div. Dept. Justice, Washington, 1951-53; mem. staff Congressman John R. Foley, Washington, 1959-60; mem. Fla. Ho. of Reps., 1976-78; spl. U.S. ambassador to independence celebration of St. Vincent's Island, 1979; mem. Fla. State Senate, 1978—, chmn. econ., community and consumer affairs, govtl. ops., civil judiciary, fin., taxation and claims com., joint com. on info. tech. resources, chmn. edn. com., 1980-82. Vice chmn. assessment policy com. Nat. Assessment Ednl. Progress, 1983-86, Hillsboro County Juvenile Delinquency Task Force, 1984-85, Joint Exec. and Legis. Task Force for Tchr. Quality Improvement, 1982, Fla. Juvenile Justice and Delinquency Prevention Task Force, 1982-85, So. Regional Edn. Bd., 1979-82, 82-86; chmn. Hillsboro County Legis. Delegation, 1982-83; mem. Sch. Bd. of Hillsborough County, 1972-76, chmn., 1975-76. Recipient Outstanding spl. Service as Fla. State Senator award Fla. Fedn. Bus. and Profl. Women's Clubs, Inc., 1983; Human Rights award Office of Community Relations, City of Tampa, 1983; Women of Yr. award Zonta Club, Tampa, 1984; named Prominent Personality, Fla. League of Cities, 1985, Citizen of Yr., Tampa Bay unit Nat. Assn. Social workers; numerous other awards from municipalities, orgns. and civic groups. Office: 312 Senate Office Bldg Tallahassee FL 32301

FRANK, PAULA FELDMAN, business executive; b. Tulsa; d. Maurice M. and Sarah (Bergman) Feldman; B.S., Northwestern U., 1954; m. Gordon D. Frank, Dec. 15, 1955; children—Cynthia Jan, Margaret Jill. Directed, wrote and appeared in TV films for Nat. Safety Council, Chgo., 1954-55; appeared in TV commls., 1955-56; asst. prodn. mgr. Kling Films, Chgo., 1956; now pres. Gaston Ave. Optical Inc., Dallas. Social chmn. Baylor Hosp. Vol. Corp., Dallas, 1962—; asst. dir. Des Plaines (Ill.) Theater Guild, 1956-57, Pearl Chappell Playhouse, Dallas, 1962-63, Dallas Theater Center, 1964. Mem. Hockaday Alumni Assn., Idle Wives Book Rev. Club (treas.), Tau Gamma Epsilon, Phi Beta, Sigma Delta Tau. Home: 7123 Currin Dr Dallas TX 75230

FRANK, ROBYN CLAIRE, librarian; b. Washington, July 28, 1945; d. Vincent Leonard and Ann Elizabeth (Richards) Gingerich; m. Luther Kyle Baugham, Dec. 16, 1966 (div. 1970); m. 2d, Stephen Earl Frank, Mar. 22, 1975; children—Evelyn, Ingrid. B.S., U. Md., 1967; M.L.S., 1972. Research asst. Research Info. Ctr., Pub. Schs. D.C., 1967-69; asst. project dir. U.S. Office Edn., Ednl. Reference Ctr., Am. Soc. Info. Sci., Washington, 1971-73; tech. info. specialist Food and Nutrition Ctr., U.S. Dept. Agr., Beltsville, Md., 1978-78, dir., acting dep. adminstr. food and nutrition info., 1978-83, chief food, nutrition and human ecology Nat. Agrl. Library, 1983—, mem. young exec. com., 1976. Editor: Directory of Food and Nutrition Information Services and Resources, 1984. Recipient John Cotton Dana Library Pub. Relations award, 1986. Mem. Am. Soc. Info. Sci. (chmn. info. services to edn. 1979-80), Spl. Libraries Assn. (sec. food agr. and nutrition div. 1984-85, chair-elect food, agr. and nutrition div. 1986-87), Soc. Nutrition Edn., Assocs. of Nat. Agrl. Library, Alpha Chi Omega. Lutheran. Lodge: Vasa Order. Office: Food and Nutrition Info Ctr Room 304 Nat Agrl Library Beltsville MD 20705

FRANK, RUBY MERINDA, employment agency executive; b. McClusky, N.D., June 28, 1920; d. John J. and Olise (Stromme) Hanson; student in bus. adminstrn., coll., Mankato, Minn., also Aurora (Ill.) Coll.; m. Robert G. Frank, Jan. 14, 1944 (dec. 1973); children—Gary Frank, Craig. Exec. sec., office mgr. Nat. Container Corp., Chgo., 1943-50; owner, operator Frank's Office & Employment Service, St. Charles, Ill., 1957—; pres. Frank's Employment, Inc.; dir. St. Charles Savings & Loan Assn.; bd. govs. Baker Hotel. Vice chmn. bd. trustees Delnor Hosp., St. Charles, 1959-84, chmn. bd., 1985-86, also life mem. women's aux.; vice chairwoman Kane County (Ill.) Republican Com., 1968-77; pres. Women's Rep. Club, 1969-77; vice chmn. Delnor Community Health System; mem. St. Charles bd. dirs. Am. Cancer Soc.; bd. dirs. Aurora Found., Ill.; mem. adv. bd. Aurora U.; adv. council Dellora A. Norris Cultural Arts Center. Named Fox Valley Exec. of Yr., 1982, Fox Valley Woman of Achievement, Women in Mgmt., 1984, recipient Charlemagne award for outstanding service to St. Charles Community, 1982. Mem. St. Charles C. of C. (pres., dir. 1976—), Kane-DuPage Personnel Assn. (v.p. 1971—), Nat., Ill. employment assns., Ill. Assn. Personnel Cons. (trustee). Lutheran. Clubs: St. Charles Country; Execs. of Chgo. Contbr. weekly broadcast Sta. WGSB, 1965-80, weekly interviews WFXW, 1984—. Home: 534 Longmeadow Circle Saint Charles IL 60174 Office: Arcada Theater Bldg 12 S 1st Ave Saint Charles IL 60174

FRANK, SANDRA KAYE, mathematics educator; b. Springfield Twp., Mich., June 11, 1941; d. Virgil Euleas and Dorothy Arliene (Wells) Noble; m. Joseph Frederic Frank, Aug. 1, 1970; 1 child, Joseph Lindbergh. B.A., Central Mich. U., 1963; M.A., U. Mont., 1967. Tchr. math. Dearborn Pub. Sch., Mich., 1963—, Edsel Ford High Sch., 1978—. Mem. Nat. Council Tchrs. Math., Mich. Council Tchrs. Math., Mich. Assn. Computer Users and Learners, Internat. Platform Assn. Clubs: Mich. Flyers, Ninety-Nines. Home: 21222 Audette St Dearborn MI 48124

FRANK, SARAH RUTH, market and management consultant; b. Detroit, Mar. 3, 1939; d. Albert J. and Roselee A. (Madanes) Lippitt; m. Stewart D. Frank, June 12, 1965; children—Aaron Charles, Ethan Howard, Ivan Joseph. Student, U. Miami, 1956-58, Great Lakes Coll., 1958; cert. med. tech. Mich. Luth. Coll., 1959. Head med. technologist Bridgeton County Hosp., N.J., 1961-63; office, lab. mgr., assoc. H.L. Dorfmann, M.D., N.Y.C., 1963-65; office mgr., med. technologist Cantor Clinic, Huntington Woods, Mich., 1965-67; asst. mgr., book reviewer 1st Edition Book Store, West Bloomfield, Mich., 1977-78; owner, mktg. cons. A. Vitality, Birmingham, Mich., 1978—; exec. v.p., v.p. mktg. Lahaina Macadamia Nut & Coffee Co. Ltd., Hawaii, also Birmingham, 1984-85; cons. in field; writer, designer Get It: Write, West Bloomfield, 1985—. Author, editor, pub. newsletter Franklin Speaking, 1978—. Author, editor LMN&C Newsletter, 1985. Exec. v.p. fundraising Fairview chpt. Women's Am. ORT, Southfield, Mich., 1969-71, v.p. edn. edn. com. Mich. region, 1981-83, midwest rep., 1973; v.p., treas. Bloomfield Welcome Wagon, 1979-80. Mem. Nat. Assn. Female Execs., Delta Phi Epsilon Alumni (exec. v.p. 1965-67). Jewish. Club: Franklin Knolls Women's (exec. v.p. 1977-79) (Farmington). Avocations: skiing; horseback riding; swimming; writing; reading. Home: 502 Westbourne Dr Birmingham MI 48010 Office: A Vitality 502 Westbourne Dr Birmingham MI 48010

FRANKE, BONNY SMITH, college administrator; b. Ala., July 24, 1934; d. Nathan T. Smith; m. J. Paul Franke, Dec. 16, 1954 (div. 1972); children—Carole Franke DeMuth, Kim Franke Lepley, Paula. A.B., Birmingham-So. Coll., 1960; M.A., Austin Coll., 1968; Ph.D., U. Ala., 1976. Advt. coordinator Tenn. mag., Nashville, 1962-64; account exec. Powell Advt. Agy., Sherman, Tex., 1964-66; dir. counseling Jefferson State Jr. Coll., Birmingham, Ala., 1969-72, dir. fed. relations, 1971-73; dir. devl. S.C. State Bd. Tech. and Comprehensive Edn., Columbia, 1973-77; dir. resource devel. Dallas County Community Coll. Dist., Dallas, 1977—; field reader/cons. U.S. Dept. Edn., 1971-75, 78—; cons. colls. and univs., 1971—; painter. Trustee, Columbia (Md.) Visual Arts Coll., 1981-83, Highland Park United Methodist Ch., Dallas, 1981-83; mem. Dallas County Manpower Planning Council, 1979-83; vice-chair Mayor's Com. on Employment of Handicapped, 1982-84; Republican precinct chairperson, 1982. Kellogg fellow, 1974; Am. Assn. Community and Jr. Colls. grantee, 1971. Mem. Nat. Council Resource Devel. (regional coordinator 1971-77; founding), Delta Kappa Gamma. Republican. Home: 2525 Turtle Creek Blvd Dallas TX 75219 Office: 701 Elm St Dallas TX 75219

FRANKEL, DEXTRA LORENE, artist, educator; b. Los Angeles, Nov. 28, 1924; d. Melville and Lorene Leota (Radcliffe) Coakley; student John Muir Jr. Coll., Pasadena, Calif., 1950-52, Valley Jr. Coll., Van Nuys, Calif., 1955-56, Long Beach State Coll., 1957-60; cert. mus. mgmt., U. Calif., Berkeley, 1979; div.; 1 son, Kenneth. Exhibiting artist, 1956-70; organizer 24 major exhbns. mus. or galleries, also designer 13 exhbns. in Pasadena, Los Angeles, Laguna Beach, Long Beach, Calif., Honolulu, Phoenix, Albuquerque, and Tokyo; public lectr., 1957—; recipient archtl. commns. in metal sculpture, 1960-67; instr. art Calif. State U., Fullerton, 1965-67; dir. art gallery, prof. art Calif. State U., Fullerton, 1967—; partner Lax Design Studio 1976—; art exhbn. juror, 1958—; U.S. del. World Crafts Conf., Mex., 1976; mem. cultural and fine arts adv. com. Olympic Games, 1981-84; bd. dirs. Fine Arts Commn., Images and Issues mag., 1981-84; condr. exhbn. design workshops. Recipient design award for Print Casebooks, the Best in Exhn. Design, 1977, 79; design award For the Record: The West Coast Show, Western Art Dirs. Club, 1979; Silver Medallion award YWCA, 1981, design award The 1981 Chicago STA/100 Society of Typog. Arts, Union Bank History Mus., 1981; Nat. Endowment for Arts mus. profl. grantee, 1978; 13 individual and found. grants for spl. exhbns., 1970-81, 8 Nat. Endowment for Arts grants for spl. exhbns., 1975-83. Mem. Am. Assn. Mus., Am. Inst. Graphic Arts, Am. Craft Council (trustee 1975-78), Art Mus. Assn. (trustee 1978-81). Office: Calif State University 800 N State College Blvd Fullerton CA 92634

FRANKEL, LINDA DAIGNAULT, economic development council administrator; b. Springfield, Mass., Aug. 12, 1945; d. Alfred Philip and Jeane (Lacine) Daignault; m. James Melton Howell, Sept. 24, 1983. B.A., Wellesley Coll., 1967; M.A.T., Brown U., 1969. Sr. copy editor Wall St. Transcript, N.Y.C., 1970-74; dir. econ. devel. program New Eng. Regional Commn., Boston, 1974-75; spl. asst. to sr. v.p., fin. U. Mass., Boston, 1975-76; pres. Council for Econ. Action, Inc., Boston, 1976—, dir., 1980—; cons. urban affairs Bank of Boston, 1978—. Fundraiser, French Library, Boston, 1981; bd. dirs. New Eng. Congl. Inst., Washington, 1980—. Mem. Council Urban Econ. Devel., Wellesley Coll. Alumni Assn. Episcopalian. Home: 73 Beacon St Boston MA 02108 Office: Council Econ Action Inc 17th Floor 100 Federal St Boston MA 02110

FRANKEL, MARILYN LAUDAN, publishing company executive; b. Houston, Apr. 30, 1952; d. James A. Laudan and Florence (Shannon) Wrigley; m. Arthur J. Frankel, Sept. 17, 1976; 2 daus., Shannon Rebecca, Rachel Elise. B.S.W., U. Kans., 1973, M.S.W., 1974; postgrad. Gestalt Inst. Cleve., 1976. Lic. clin. social worker, Ky., 1976. Psychiat. social worker, River Region Mental Health Ctr., Louisville, 1974-76; instr. U. Louisville, Spalding Coll., 1975-76; psychotherapist Gestalt Growth Inst., Louisville, 1976-80; pres. Little People's Workshop, Ltd., publishing, Louisville, 1977—; cons., seminar, workshop leader, 1974—. Mem. Nat. Assn. Edn. Young Children, Bus. and Profl. Women Louisville, Nat. Council Social Work. Democrat. Author, editor: Pre-Sch. Master Plan, 1982; Just for Twos, 1983; Discovery Days, 1984.

FRANKEL, MARY ANN (KATE), librarian, teacher; b. San Francisco, Feb. 24, 1926; d. Samuel Joseph Spear and Julie Bernice (Calio) Le Pla; m. Benjamin Adam Frankel, June 14, 1950; children—Daniel Adam, Rachel Lynn. B.A., U. Calif.-Berkeley, 1949, cert. in teaching, 1951, M.L.S., 1965. Librarian, San Leandro Pub. Sch., Calif., 1965, Richmond Schs., Calif., 1965-67; librarian Berkeley Schs., Calif., 1967-78, teacher English, 1978-82, field librarian, 1982—. Chmn. PTA Council Study Elem. Libraries, Berkeley, 1964-65. Mem. East Bay Reading Assn., ALA, LWV (co-chmn. nat. security study 1984-85), San Francisco Recorder Soc. Avocations: early music; participant in recorder groups. Home: 1 Rochdale Way Berkeley CA 94708 Office: Berkeley Unified Sch Dist 1835 Allston Way Berkeley CA 94704

FRANKENTHALER, HELEN, painter; b. N.Y.C., Dec. 12, 1928; d. Alfred and Martha (Lowenstein) F.; B.A., Bennington Coll., 1949; L.H.D., Skidmore Coll., 1969; D.F.A., Smith Coll., 1973, Moore Coll. Art, 1974, Bard Coll., 1976, Radcliffe Coll., 1978, Amherst Coll., 1979, N.Y.U., 1979, Phila. Coll. Art, 1980, Williams Coll., 1980, Harvard U., 1980, Yale U., 1981, Brandus U., 1982, U. Hartford, 1983, Syracuse U., 1985; m. Robert Motherwell, Apr. 6, 1958 (div. 1971). One woman shows include: Tibor de Nagy Gallery, N.Y.C., 1951-58, Andre Emmerich Gallery, N.Y.C., 1959, 61, 63, 65, 66, 68, 69, 71-73, 75-77, 78, 79, 81, 82, 83, 84, Jewish Mus., N.Y.C., 1960, Everett Ellin Gallery, Los Angeles, 1961, Galerie Lawrence, Paris, 1961-63, Bennington Coll., 1962, 78, Galleria dell'Ariete, Milan, 1962, Kasmin Gallery, London, 1964, David Mirvish Gallery, Toronto, 1965-71, 73, 75, Gertrude Kasle Gallery, Detroit, 1967, 71, Nicholas Wilder Gallery, Los Angeles, 1967, Andre Emmerich Gallery, Zurich, 1974, Swarthmore (Pa.) Coll., 1974, Solomon R. Guggenheim Mus., N.Y.C., 1975, Corcoran Gallery Art, Washington, 1975, Seattle Art Mus., 1975, Mus. Fine Arts, Houston, 1975, Ace Gallery, Vancouver, B.C., Can., 1975, 1983, Rosa Esman Gallery, N.Y.C., 1975, 83, 3d Internat. Contemporary Art Fair, Paris, 1976, Gimpel-Hanover and Andre Emmerich Gallery, Zurich, 1980; retrospective Whitney Mus. Am. Art, 1979, Whitechapel Gallery, London, 1969, Kongresshalle, Berlin, Kunstverein, Hanover, 1969, Heath Gallery, Atlanta, 1971, Galerie Godard Lefort, Montreal, 1971, Fendrick Gallery, Washington, 1972, 74, 79, 80, Carl Solway, Cin., 1972, John Berggruen Gallery, San Francisco, 1972, 76, 79, 82, 86, Portland (Oreg.) Art Mus., 1972, Waddington Galleries II, London, 1973, 74, Janie C. Lee Gallery, Dallas, 1973, Houston, 1975, 76, 78, 80, 82, Met. Mus. Art, N.Y.C., 1973, Cologne Art Fair, 1974, Gallery Diane Gilson, Seattle, 1976, Greenberg Gallery, St. Louis, 1977, Galerie Wentzel, Hamburg, Ger., 1977, Jacksonville (Fla.) Art Mus., 1977-78, Ft. Lauderdale (Fla.) Mus. Arts, 1978, Loch Haven Art Center, Orlando, Fla., 1978, Internat. Communications Agy. Exhbn., N.Y.C., 1978 (travelled to Japan, Taiwan, Phillipines, Singapore, Australia, Mex., Venezuela, Colombia, Brazil 1978-79), Knoedler Gallery, London, 1978, 81, 83, 85, Atkins Mus. Fine Art, William Rockhill Nelson Gallery Art, Kansas City, Mo., 1978, Saginaw (Mich.) Art Mus., 1980, U. Mich. Art Mus., Ann Arbor, 1980, Grand Rapids (Mich.) Art Mus., 1980, Kalamazoo (Mich.) Inst. Arts, 1980, Sterling and Francine Clark Art Inst., Williamstown, Mass., 1980 (travelled to Phillips Collection, Washington, 1980, Birmingham (Ala.) Mus. Art, 1981, Toledo Mus. Art, 1981, Palm Springs (Calif.) Desert Mus., 1981, Santa Barbara (Calif.) Mus. Art, 1981, Mus. Fine Arts, Boston, 1981), Galerie Ulysses, Vienna, 1980, Rose Art Mus., Brandeis U., 1981, Thomas Segal Gallery, Boston, 1981; exhibited in group shows including: Whitney Mus., 1958, 71, 77, 78, 79, 81, 82, 83, Carnegie Internat., Pitts., 1955, 58, 61, 64, Columbus Gallery Fine Arts, 1960, Guggenheim Mus., 1961, 76, 77, Seattle World's Fair, 1962, Art Inst. Chgo., 1963, 69, 72, 76, San Francisco Mus. Art, 1963, 68, Krannert Mus., U. Ill., 1959, 63, 65, 67, Washington Gallery Modern Art, 1963, Pa. Acad. Fine Arts, 1963, 68, 76, N.Y. World's Fair, 1964, Am. Fedn. Arts Circulating Exhbn., 1964, U. Austin Art Mus., 1964, Rose Art Mus. Circulating Exhbn., 1964, Detroit Inst. Arts, 1965, 67, U. Mich. Mus. Art, 1965, Md. Inst., 1966, Norfolk Mus. Arts and Scis., 1966, Venice Biennale, 1966, Smithsonian Instn., 1966, 78, 80, Expo '67, Montreal, 1967, Washington Gallery Modern Art, 1967, Ga. Mus. Art, Athens, 1967, U. Okla. Mus. Art, Norman, 1968, Philbrook Art Center, Tulsa, 1968, Cin. Mus., 1968, U. Calif., San Diego, 1968, Mus. Modern Art, N.Y.C., 1969-75, 80, Met. Mus., N.Y.C., 1969-70, 76, 79, Va. Mus., Richmond, 1970, 74, Balt. Mus. Art, 1970, 76, Boston U., 1970, Boston Mus. Fine Arts, 1972, Des Moines Art Center, 1973, Mus. Fine Arts, Houston, 1974, Smith Coll. Mus. Art, Northampton, Mass., 1974, El Instituto de Cultura Puertorriquena, San Juan, 1974, Basil Art Fair, Basel, Switzerland, 1974, 76, 78, Finch Coll. Mus. Art, N.Y.C., 1974, S.I. Mus., 1975, Denver Art Mus., 1975, 76, Visual Arts Mus., N.Y.C., 1975, 76, Mus. Modern Art, Belgrade, Yugoslavia, 1976, Galleria d'Arts Moderna, Rome, 1976, Am. Art since 1945 from the collection of Mus. Modern Art, Worcester (Mass.) Art Mus., 1976, Toledo Art Mus., 1976, Denver Art Mus., 1976, Fine Arts Gallery San Diego, 1976, Dallas Mus. Fine Arts, 1976, Joslyn Art Mus., Omaha, Greenville (S.C.) County Mus., 1977, Va. Mus. Fine Arts, Richmond, 1977, Bronx Mus. Arts, 1977, Everson Mus. Art, Syracuse, 1976, Chrysler Mus. Norfolk, Art Ins. Chgo., 1976, Seibu Mus., Tokyo, 1977, 78, Orangerie of Charlottenburg Palace, West Berlin, W.Ger., 1977, Tacoma Art Mus., 1977, Mus. Art Wash. State U., Pullman, 1977, Cheney Dowles Meml. State Mus., Spokane, Wash., 1977, Detroit Inst. Arts, 1977, San Francisco Mus. Modern Art, 1977, Cooper-Hewitt Mus., 1977, Fogg Art Mus., Cambridge, Mass., 1978, Cranbrook Acad. Art Mus., Bloomfield Hills, Mich., 1978, Newport Harbor Art Mus., Newport, R.I., 1979, Oakland Mus., Cin., 1979, Mus. S.Tex., Corpus Christi, 1979, Krannert Art Mus., Champaign, Ill., 1979-80, Art Gallery Ont., Toronto, 1979, Sierra Nev. Mus., Reno, 1979, Corcoran Gallery Art, Washington, 1979, 81; represented in permanent collections: Met. Mus. Art, Bklyn. Mus., Solomon R. Guggenheim Mus., N.Y.U., Mus. Modern Art, Whitney Mus. (all N.Y.C.), Albright-Knox Art Gallery, Buffalo, Milw. Art Inst., Wadsworth Atheneum, Hartford, Newark Mus., Yale U. Art Gallery, U. Nebr. Art Gallery, Carnegie Inst., Pitts., Detroit Inst. Art, Balt., Mus. Art, Univ. Mus., Berkeley, Calif., Bennington (Vt.) Coll., Art Inst. Chgo., Cin. Art Mus., Cleve. Mus. Art, Honolulu Acad. Arts, Contemporary Arts Assn., Houston, Pasadena Art Mus., City Art Mus., St. Louis, Mus. Art, R.I. Sch. Design, Providence, San Francisco Mus. Art, Everson Mus., Syracuse, N.Y., Smithsonian Instn., Walker Art Inst., Mpls., Washington Gallery Modern Art, Nat. Gallery Victoria, Melbourne, Australia, Australian Nat. Gallery, Canberra, Victoria and Albert Mus., London, Tokyo Mus., Ulster Mus., Belfast, No. Ireland, Elvenhjem Art Center, U. Wis., Newark Mus., Phila. Mus. Art, Phoenix Art Mus., Corcoran Gallery Art, Washington, Boston Mus. Fine Arts, Springfield (Mass.) Mus. Fine Arts, Witte Mus., San Antonio, Abbott Hall Art Gallery, Kendal, Eng., Mus. Contemporary Art, Nagaoka, Japan, numerous others; lectures/seminars Yale U., 1966, 67, 70, 78, Hunter Coll., 1970, Princeton U., 1971, Cooper Union, N.Y.C., 1972, Skidmore Coll., 1973, Swarthmore Coll., 1974, Drew U., 1975, Harvard U., 1976, Radcliffe Coll., 1976, also N.Y.U., U. Pa., Sch. Visual Arts Goucher Coll., Washington U., Yale Grad. Sch., Detroit Inst. Arts, 1977, Bard Coll., Annandale-on-Hudson, N.Y., 1977, U. Ariz., Tucson, 1978, Davenport Coll., 1978, others. U.S. rep. Venice Biennale, 1966. Trustee Bennington Coll., 1967-82. Fellow Calhoun Coll., Yale U., 1968. Recipient 1st prize for painting Paris Biennale, 1959; Gold medal Pa. Acad. Fine Arts, 1968; Spirit of Achievement award Albert Einstein Coll. Medicine, 1970; Gold medal Commune of Catania, III, Biennale della Grafica d'Arte, Florence, Italy, 1972; Garrett award 70th Am. Exhbn., Art Inst. Chgo., 1972; Creative Arts awards Nat. Women's div. Am. Jewish Congress, 1974; Art and Humanities award Yale Women's Forum, 1976; An Extraordinary Woman of Achievement award 50th Anniversary NCCJ, 1978; Outstanding Achievement award Bennington Coll. Alumni, 1979, Mayor's Award of Honor for Art and Culture NYC, 1986. Mem. Nat. Inst. Arts and Letters, Am. Acad. & Instit. Arts and Letters, NEA Council on the Arts. Address: 173 E 94th St New York NY 10128

FRANKL, JEANNE SILVER, association executive; A.B. in Lit. summa cum laude, Brown U., 1952; LL.B., Yale U., 1955; m. Kenneth R. Frankl; 1 dau., Kathryn. Admitted to Conn. bar, 1955, N.Y. bar, 1956; law sec. to Hon. Edmund L. Palmieri, 1955-56; atty. Port of N.Y. Authority, 1956-60; assoc. firm Rosenman Colin Kaye Petschek Freund & Emil, N.Y.C., 1960-67; chief of program planning, office of edn. liaison, City Human Resources Adminstrn., 1967-69; spl. asst. to dep. adminstr. N.Y.C. Human Resources Adminstrn., 1969-70; asst. dir. Community Sch. System Project, N.Y. Lawyers Com. for Civil Rights under Law, 1970, dir., 1970-73; counsel and law project dir. Public Edn. Assn., N.Y.C., 1973-80, exec. dir., 1980—; lectr. Rutgers U. Law Sch. Edn. Law Seminar, 1972-73. Bd. dirs. Citizens Union City of N.Y., 1974—, local candidates com., 1971—, various coms. Mem. Assn. of Bar City of N.Y. (spl. com. on edn. and law), Phi Beta Kappa. Home: 45 Christopher St New York NY 10014 Office: 39 W 32d St New York NY 10001

FRANKLIN, BARBARA HACKMAN, educator, corporate director and consultant; b. Lancaster, Pa., Mar. 19, 1940; d. Arthur A. and Mayme M. (Haller) Hackman; B.A. with distinction, Pa. State U., 1962; M.B.A., Harvard U., 1964; D.Sc. (hon.), Bryant Coll., 1973. Mgr. environ. analysis Singer Co., N.Y.C., 1964-68; asst. v.p. Citibank, N.Y.C., 1969-71; mem. White House staff, Washington, 1971-73; vice chmn. U.S. Consumer Product Safety Commn., Washington, 1973-79; sr. fellow, dir. govt. and bus. program Wharton Sch., U. Pa., Phila., 1979—; adviser to comptroller gen. U.S.; dir. Aetna Life and Casualty Co., Dow Chem. Co., Westinghouse Electric Corp., Black & Decker Corp., Automatic Data Processing, Inc. Trustee, Pa. State U.; mem. Pres.'s Adv. Com. Trade Negotiations; bd. visitors Def. Systems Mgmt. Coll. Recipient Disting. Alumni award Pa. State U., 1972, Catalyst Award for Corp. Leadership, 1981, Excellence in Mgmt. award Simmons Coll., 1981, ann. award Am. Assn. Poison Control Centers, 1979, cert. appreciation, Am. Acad. Pediatrics, 1978. Mem. Am. Inst. C.P.A.s (bd. dirs.), Women's Forum Washington. Club: F Street (Washington). Contbr. articles to pubs. Office: 1320 19th St NW Washington DC 20036 also 107 Vance Hall CS Wharton Sch Univ Pa Philadelphia PA 19104

FRANKLIN, BEVERLY JEAN, artist; b. Los Angeles, Dec. 2, 1922; d. Harvey Franklin and Marian Ida (Cox) Keyse; student Baylor U., Waco, Tex., 1958-59; m. Charles Francis Franklin, Oct. 27, 1946; children—Christine Marie Franklin Carlin, Peter Charles, Kathleen Anne Franklin Watton. One-woman shows include La Jolla (Calif.) Art Assn., 1975, 76, Knowles Gallery, La Jolla, 1978, 80, 82, 84, 86. Mem. La Jolla Art Assn. (dir. 1973-76), San Diego Watercolor Soc. (dir. 1976-77), Nat. League Am. Pen Women (pres. La Jolla br. 1985-87), Los Angeles Art Assn. Address: 7205 Via Capri La Jolla CA 92037

FRANKLIN, BONNIE JOAN, designer, manufacturer, consultant; b. Woodland, Calif., June 2, 1949; d. William Lewis and Nora Adeline (Jensen) Holland; m. Michael Marion Franklin, Feb. 24, 1968; children—Dawn Marie, Christie Ann. Student U. Calif.-Davis, U. Calif.-Berkeley, Solano Jr. Coll., Calif. State Coll.-Sonoma, Mendocino Coll. Self employed doll mfr., Benicia, Calif., 1972-74; tchrs. aide Kelseyville Unified Sch. Dist., Calif., 1975-77, Fairfield-Suisun Unified Sch. Dist., Fairfield, Calif., 1978-80, sensory motor program coordinator, 1980-81, cons., lectr., 1981; designer, owner Bonnie Franklin Originals, Fairfield, Calif., 1981—; graphic artist Sch. Dist., Kelseyville and Fairfield, 1975-81; playground designer, 1976, cons. in field. Author/owner copyright Bear Facts series, 1983; artist miniatures, Nutshell News, 1983, 1986; author, artist Rocky Mountain Miniature Jour., 1984; exhibitor various orgns. Recipient First award shadow box Lake County Fair Assn., 1975. Mem. Bear Facts Collectors Club, Nat. Assn. Miniature Enthusiasts. Republican. Lutheran. Avocations: reading; writing; sketching; sculpting; piano. Home: 2245 Currier Pl Fairfield CA 94533

FRANKLIN, ELAINE A., communications specialist; b. N.Y.C., June 25, 1945; d. Abraham and Josephine (Epstein) Auerbach; B.A., Douglass Coll., 1967; M.B.A., Pace U., 1981; m. David Franklin, Aug. 28, 1966; children—Alisa, Daniel. Reporter Patterson (N.J.) Evening News, 1966; assoc. editor Reader's Digest, Pleasantville, N.Y., 1967-80; mgr. corp. publs. PepsiCo, Purchase, N.Y., 1980—. Bd. dirs. Westchester/Putnam council Girl Scouts U.S.; mem. communications curriculum adv. council Westchester Community Coll.; mem. Putnam Communications Com. Mem. Women in Communications, Internat. Assn. Bus. Communicators, Ossining Septa (pres.), Delta Mu Delta. Home: 65 Ganung Dr Ossining NY 10562 Office: Anderson Hill Rd Purchase NY 10577

FRANKLIN, JAN F., telephone company manager; b. Richmond, Calif., Feb. 3, 1945; d. Godfrey M. and Catharine D. (McElroy) Bishop; m. Marlin R. Franklin, Apr. 6, 1968. Student Oakland City Coll., 1963-65, Sacramento State U., 1965, Contra Costa Coll., 1965-67, 69, U. Hawaii, 1970. Order writer Pacific Telephone, Oakland, Calif., 1963-65, service rep., Oakland and Sacramento, 1965, bus. office supr., Richmond, Calif., 1965-71, bus. office mgr., Pittsburg, Calif., 1971-74, traffic mgr., personnel mgr., San Francisco, 1974-78; dist. mgr. Pacific Bell, San Ramon, Calif., 19—. Judge Bank of Am. Achievement awards, Oakland, 1975-78; mem. Richmond Police Task Force, 1971, Richmond Community Devel. Commn., 1975; liaison mem. Richmond/Shimada Friendship Commn., 1976. Mem. Richmond Bus. and Profl. Women (pres. 1970, 72, 78), Am. Mgmt. Assn., Am. Soc. Tng. and Devel., Nat. Assn. Female Execs. Republican. Lutheran. Club: PEO. Avocations: reading; public speaking; career counseling. Home: 5733 Amend Rd Richmond CA 94803

FRANKLIN, JOYCE, radio station manager; b. Meridian, Miss., July 8, 1954; d. Lancaster and Eunice (Davis) Greer; m. Lawrence Edward Franklin, May 27, 1977; children—LaToya, Jason, Donna. A. in Edn., East Miss. Jr. Coll., 1973; B.Ed., Miss. State U., 1976. Office asst. Miss. State Fin. Aid, Starksville, 1974-75; tchr. West Kemper High Sch., DeKalb, Miss., 1977; receptionist Sta. WDAL, Meridian, 1978-80; traffic mgr. Sta. WJDQ, Meridian, 1980—; cons. Sta. WYAM, Meridian, 1985. Dir. youth choir Unity Springs Ch., DeKalb, Miss., 1976, sec. Sunday Sch., 1976; jury commr. Lauderdale County Bd. Suprs., Meridian, Miss., 1980—. Mem. Phi Theta Kappa. Democrat. Avocations: sewing; reading; singing. Home: 1600 28th Ave Meridian MS 39301 Office: WJDQ Radio PO Box 5314 Hwy 45 S Meridian MS 39302

FRANKLIN, LORETTA WOODS, pipeline company executive; b. Clay County, Ky., Mar. 14, 1927; d. Robert and Ethel (Asher) Woods; m. Denver L. Franklin, May 6, 1956; children—John A., Darlene L. Vice pres. Delta Mech., Fairfield, Ohio, 1961—, pres., 1977—, chmn. bd., 1985—; v.p. Mo. Pipeline, Fairfield, 1965-77, pres., 1977-85, chmn. bd., 1985—. Mem. Am. Sub-Contractors Assn., Women in Constrn., Mech. Contractors Assn., Am. Arbitration Assn., Women Owned Bus. Assn., Ohio Women Entrepreneurs, Hamilton C. of C., Fairfield C. of C. Baptist. Avocations: golf; fishing.

FRANKLIN, LYNDA LONG, public relations agency executive; b. Macon, Ga., July 13, 1947; d. Hollis Alton and Lucile (Busbee) Long; B.S., U. South Fla., Tampa, 1969; m. Raymond Wesley Franklin, Feb. 10, 1979; 1 son, Jason Scott Foures. Tchr. English, drama and speech Leto High Sch., Tampa, 1976-78; chief copywriter Sta. WCTV, Tallahassee, 1978-80; account exec. First Mktg. Corp., Ft. Lauderdale, Fla., 1980-81; v.p. Azen & Assocs., Ft. Lauderdale, 1981-84; owner, pres. The Franklin Agy., 1984—. Participant Leadership Broward, 1983-84, v.p. communications alumni, 1984, vice chmn., 1986—. Recipient local Addy award, Tallahassee, 1979. Mem. Fla. Bank Mktg. Assn. (past editor newsletter), Women's Exec. Club Ft. Lauderdale (past pres.),

Council of Pres. (founding dir.). Office: 808 E Las Olas Blvd Suite 103 Fort Lauderdale FL 33301

FRANKLIN, MARGARET LAVONA BARNUM, civic worker; b. Caldwell, Kans., June 19, 1905; d. LeGrand Husted and Elva (Biddinger) Barnum; student U. No. Iowa, 1923-25, U. Iowa, 1937-38; B.A., Washburn U., 1952; m. C. Benjamin Franklin, Jan. 20, 1940 (dec. July 1983); children—Margaret Lee (Mrs. Michael John Felso), Benjamin Barnum. Tchr. pub. schs., Union, Iowa, 1925-27, Kearney, Nebr., 1927-28, Marshalltown, Iowa, 1928-40; advance rep. Chautauqua, summers 1926-30. Bd. dirs. state chpt. Nat. Multiple Sclerosis Soc., 1963-66; bd. dirs. Topeka Pub. Library, treas., 1962-65, chmn., 1965-67, sec., 1969-70, bd. rep. to N.E. Kans. Library System, 1968-71, awards for service, 1977, 80; mem. Mayor's Citizens Adv. Com., 1965-69; mem. Topeka Com. for Rescue Italian Art, 1966-67; bd. dirs. Friends of Library, 1960-79, Friends of Topeka Pub. Library Found., 1984—. Recipient Waldo B. Heywood award for cultural contbn. to Topeka, 1967; named Outstanding Mother of Kans., Alpha Delta Pi, 1971. Mem. Shawnee County Hist. Soc. (dir. 1963-75, sec. 1964-66), D.A.R. (state chmn. mus. 1968-71), AAUW, Topeka Art Guild, Topeka Civic Symphony (dir. 1952-57, service honor citation 1960), Doll Collectors Am., Stevengraph Collectors Assn., Marshalltown Community Theatre (pres. 1938-40), Topeka Geneal. Soc., Topeka Stamp Club, Nonoso, P.E.O. (chpt. pres. 1956-57, pres. coop. bd. 1964-65, chpt. honoree 1969), Alpha Beta Gamma. Republican. Mem. Christian Ch. Clubs: Western Sorosis (pres. 1960-61), Minerva (2d v.p. 1984-85), Woman's (1st v.p. 1952-54). Home: 4808 W Hills Dr Topeka KS 66606

FRANKSON-KENDRICK, SARAH JANE, publishing executive, publisher; b. Bradford, Pa., Sept. 24, 1949; d. Sophronus Ahimus and Elizabeth Jane (Sears) McCutcheon; m. James Michael Kendrick, Jr., May 22, 1982. Customer service rep. Laros Printing/Osceola Graphics, Bethlehem, Pa., 1972-73; assoc. editor Babcox Publs., Akron, Ohio, 1973-74; assoc. editor Bill Communications, Akron, 1974-75, sr. editor, 1975-77, editor-in chief, 1977-81; assoc. pub. Chilton Co./ABC Pub., Chgo., 1981-83, pub., 1983—. Recipient Automotive Replacement Edn. award Northwood Inst., 1983; award for young leadership and excellence Automotive Hall of Fame, 1984. Mem. Automotive Parts and Accessories Assn., Internat. Assn. Bus. Communicators, Am. Mgmt. Assn., Women in Communications. Republican. Club: Knollwood Country (Lake Forest, Ill.). Office: Chilton Co/ABC Publishing 100 S Wacker Dr Chicago IL 60606

FRANN, MARY, actress; b. St. Louis, Feb. 27. Studies at Northwestern U., Evanston, Ill. Formerly staff mem. KSDK-TV, St. Louis, later with ABC, Chgo.; various appearances Chgo. theaters; in Story Theatre, Los Angeles, N.Y.C., other theatre appearances Los Angeles; TV series: Newhart, 1982—, My Friend Tony, 1969, Days of Our Lives, Return to Peyton Place, King's Crossing, 1982; motion pictures for TV: Portrait of an Escort, Gidget's Summer Reunion. Address: care William Morris Agency 151 El Camino Beverly Hills CA 90212

FRANSEIN, DORIS LEWIS, judge; b. Germany, June 8, 1954; came to U.S., 1955, naturalized, 1955; d. Robert Richard and Anna (Iltchenko) Lewis; m. Steven Alan Foglesong, Jan. 9, 1976 (div. Apr. 11, 1980). B.A. cum laude in Psychology, Drury Coll., 1976; J.D., U. Tulsa, 1981. Bar: Okla. 1981, U.S. Dist. Ct. (no. dist.) Okla. 1981. With U.S. Med. Center for Fed. Prisoners, Springfield, Mo., 1975-76; probation clk. U.S. Probation and Parole Bd., Tulsa, 1976-78; dir. On The Bricks, Inc., Tulsa, 1979-81; asst. dist. atty. Tulsa County Dist. Atty.'s Office, 1981-84; sole practice, Tulsa, 1984; mcpl. judge City of Tulsa, 1984—, presiding judge, 1985—. Recipient Am. Jurisprudence award U. Tulsa, 1978. Mem. ABA, Okla. Bar Assn., Tulsa County Bar Assn., Assn. Trial Lawyers Am., Nat. Assn. Women Judges, Am. Judicature Soc., Okla. Trial Lawyers Assn., Mortar Board, Alpha Lambda Delta, Delta Delta Delta (scholarship chmn. 1971).

FRANSISCO, DEBORAH L., pharmacist; b. Detroit, Mar. 15, 1956; d. Theodore Joseph and Phyllis Irene (VanZant) F.; m. Gerald John Norris, Aug. 21, 1976 (div. May 1981). B.S. in Pharmacy, Ferris State Coll., 1978. Pharmacist, asst. mgr. Cunningham Drug Stores, 6 stores in met. Detroit area, 1978-81; cons. Specialized Pharmacy Services, Livonia, Mich., 1981-83; ptnr. Village Pharmacies, Harrison and Beaverton, Mich., 1983—. Mem. Central Mich. Pharmacists Assn. (sec. 1983-85), Nat. Assn. Retail Druggists. Republican. Avocations: cross country skiing, sailing. Home: 821 Westlawn St #12 Harrison MI 48625 Office: Village Pharmacy 158 N 1st St Harrison MI 48625

FRANTZ, MARY ALISON, archaeologist, photographer; b. Duluth, Minn., Sept. 27, 1903; d. Alfred J. and Mary Katherine (Gibson) F. B.A., Smith Coll., 1924; postgrad. Am. Acad. Rome, 1924-25, Am. Sch. Class. Studies, Athens, Greece, 1929-30; Ph.D., Columbia U., 1937; postgrad. (fellow) Dumbarton Oaks Research Library, Washington, 1941. Reader, Index of Christian Art, Princeton U., 1927-29; mem. staff Agora Excavations, Am. Sch. Classical Studies, Athens, 1933-40, 49-66, research fellow, 1967—; mem. Inst. Advanced Study, Princeton, N.J., 1976-77; polit. analyst OSS, Washington, 1942-45; cultural attache U.S. Embassy, Athens, 1947-49. Decorated Order of Benevolence (Greece), 1956. Mem. Am. Philos. Soc., Archaeol. Inst. Am., Medieaval Acad. Am., German Archaeol. Inst. Author: The Church of the Holy Apostles, 1971; (with others) Olympia, 1967; (with Martin Robertson) The Parthenon Frieze, 1975; assoc. editor Allied Mission to Observe the Greek Elections, 1946; contbr. photographs to archaeol. books, jours., articles to profl. jours. Address: 27 Haslet Ave Princeton NY 08540

FRANZ, LYDIA MILLICENT TRUC, real estate executive; b. Chgo., Jan. 11, 1924; d. Walter and Lydia (Kralovec) Truc; Mus.B., Ill. Wesleyan U., 1944; Mus.M., Northwestern U., 1949; m. Robert Franz, Aug. 27, 1952 (dec. Aug. 1983). Tchr. music pub. schs., Muskegon, Mich., 1947-48; marketing research analyst Grant Advt. Agy., Chgo., 1949; asst. to dir. mktg. research Buchen Co., 1949-52; asst. dir. mktg. research Sherman Marquette Advt. Co., Chgo., 1952; asst. to pres., dir. media and research Andover Advt. Agy., 1952-55; salesman Boehmer & Hedlund, realty, Barrington, Ill., 1960-63; pres. Country Squire Real Estate, Inc., Barrington, 1963-74, Century 21-Country Squire, Inc., 1974—; dir. Clyde Fed. Savs. & Loan Assn., North Riverside, Ill. Mem. real estate adv. com. William Rainey Harper Coll., Palatine, Ill., 1971—; mem. adv. com. Office Real Estate Research, U. Ill.,j Champa;ign-Urbana. Served with WAC, 1944-46. Mem. Women in Real Estate (pres. 1966-67), Barrington Bd. Realtors (pres. 1968-69), Ill. Assn. Real Estate Bds. (dir. 1981—, gov. Realtor's Inst. of Ill. 1972-78, pres. 1984), Nat. Assn. Realtors (dir. 1982—), Realtors Nat. Mktg. Inst. (bd. govs. 1978-82), Barrington C. of C. (pres. 1974, Merit award 1985), Am. Cryptogram Soc., Am. Contract Bridge League, Mensa, Barrington Bus. and Profl. Women's Club, Sigma Alpha Iota. Republican. Home: 408 E Hillside Ave Barrington IL 60010 Office: 209 Park Ave Barrington IL 60010

FRANZEN-HUNTER, MARCIA LEE, marketing executive; b. Chgo., Sept. 12, 1954; d. Donald Fred August and Ruth Helen (Johnson) Franzen; m. Steven R. Hunter, Dec. 18, 1982. B.S., Purdue U., 1975; M.B.A., Roosevelt U., 1979. Asst. product mgr. Wyler Foods, Northbrook, Ill., 1976-79; product mgr. Nat. Oats Co., Cedar Rapids, Iowa, 1979-81; asst. product mgr. Ore-Ida Foods, Boise, Idaho, 1981-82; mktg. instr. U. Iowa, Iowa City, 1983; industry mktg. mgr. Norand, Cedar Rapids, 1983-84; pres. Focus Mktg. Cons., Cedar Rapids, 1982—; mgr. Macy's of Calif., 1984—. Active Jr. Women's Club, Cedar Rapids, 1983, Profl. Women's Network, Cedar Rapids, 1982—; caller chmn. Christian Bus. Women, Cedar Rapids, 1979—. Mem. Am. Mktg. Assn., Inst. Food Technologists. Republican. Presbyterian. Home: 184 Tennyson Ave Palo Alto CA 94301 Office: Macy's Stanford CA 94303

FRANZHEIM-DROR, BARBARA, historic restoration company executive, fine arts consultant; b. Newark, Feb. 7, 1939; m. Kenneth Franzheim, II, Apr. 15, 1966 (div. 1973); children—Pamela Franzheim Tower, Sabrina, Melita; m. 2d, Daniel Dror, Sept. 27, 1974 (div. 1985); 1 son, Daniel. B.A., Montclair Coll., 1962; postgrad., NYU, 1962, Fordham U., 1965-66; M.E., Seton Hall U., 1964. Tchr. English, N.J., 1962-64; with editorial dept. McGraw-Hill, N.Y.C., 1965; with Batten Barton Durstine & Osborn, N.Y.C., 1965; various positions fashion industry, N.Y.C., 1965-66; with U.S. Fgn. Service, South Pacific, N.Z., Tonga, Fiji, Samoa, 1969-72; owner Hist. Restoration Co., Tex. and N.Y.C., 1976—; chief exec. officer Three Sources Corp., Houston, 1976—. Restorations include: Inness Hall, Lexington, Ky., 1975, Gardenside, Southhampton, 1979, La Favorita, Palm Beach, Fla., 1984, 635 Park Ave, N.Y.C., 1985. Bd. dirs. Tex. children's Hosp., Houston, 1967-68, Tex. Mental Health Assn., Houston, 1968-69, Contemporary Arts Mus., Houston, 1976-80, Houston Symphony, 1981-82, Houston Grand Opera, 1975-85. Republican. Roman Catholic. Clubs: Houston, Houstonian, University (Houston). Home: 160 Wells Rd Palm Beach FL also La Fleur Artists Village Southampton NY 11968 Office: Historic Restoration Co 502 Park Ave New York NY 10021

FRASER, ANN, association executive; b. Waterbury, Conn., May 23, 1931; d. Joseph and Rose (Romano) Daniele; 1 dau. by previous marriage, Ann Denise. Student Post Jr. Coll., 1967, U. Conn., 1968, Mattatuck Community Coll., 1970, 71, Inst. Orgn. Mgmt. U. Del., 1980, 81, 83, 84, San Jose State U., 1982. Buyer electronic components Benrus Watch Co., Waterbury, 1963-66; systems programmer Friden Inc., Waterbury, 1966-70; claims auditor, reviewer Conn. Gen. Life Ins. Co., Bloomfield, 1970-71; customer service rep. Risdon Mfg. Co., Thomaston, Conn., 1971-73; mktg. support rep. James R. Buchanan & Assocs., Plantsville, Conn., 1973-75; mgr. computer services Gen. Tours Inc., N.Y.C., 1976-78; membership records mgr. Am. Hotel and Motel Assn., N.Y.C., 1979—. Home: 300 W 55th St New York NY 10019

FRASER, HELEN MARIAN, museum curator; b. Milw., Apr. 5, 1928; d. Anthony and Mary Lunkiewicz; B.A., U. Wis., 1952, M.A. with honors, 1953; m. David Fraser, Aug. 29, 1953; children—Stephen, Suzette, Christine, Richard, James. With Naperville (Ill.) Park Dist., 1975-78; curator Caroline-Martin Mitchell Mus., Naperville, 1975—; assoc. dir. hist. complex Naperville Heritage Soc.-City of Naperville, 1978—; assoc. dir. Naper Settlement; pres. Edwardian House Inc. lectr., cons. in field. Author: Footsteps Through Old Naperville; contbg. author: DuPage Roots: A History of DuPage County. Mem. Am. Assn. State and Local History, Victorian Soc. in Am., Am. Mus. Assn., AAUW, Questors. One-woman art show, Milw., 1970. Home: 1244 Arthur Rd Naperville IL 60540 Office: 201 W Porter Naperville IL 60540

FRASER, LEILA, banker; b. Chgo., May 26, 1942; d. Paul and Emily (Dzierzyck) Hucko; A.B. with high distinction in Polit. Sci., U. Ill., 1964, M.A., 1966, Ph.D., 1971; 1 child, Alec. Teaching asst. Carleton U., Ottawa, Ont., Can., 1967-68; lectr. polit. sci. U. Ky., Lexington, 1970, asst. dir., then acting dir. Office Internat. Programs, 1970-72; staff asso., then asst. to vice chancellor U. Wis., Milw., 1972-76, asst. vice chancellor, 1976-77, asst. to chancellor, 1977; chief adminstr. to mayor City of Milw., 1977-82; sr. v.p. mktg. Marine Corp., Milw., 1982—. Mem. adv. com. on women and minorities Office Wis. Commr. Securities, 1976-80; mem. Gov.'s Commn. Wis. Strategic Devel., 1983-85; bd. dirs. Milw. Exposition, Conv. Center and Arena, 1978-82, Milw. Symphony Orch., 1979—, World Festivals Inc., 1982—, Milw. Urban League, 1984—; mem. corp. bd. Milw. Sch. Engring., 1983—; bd. dirs., past pres. Milw. Council Alcoholism, 1979-84; mem. planning and allocation council United Way Greater Milw., 1978-84, mem. campaign cabinet, 1986; bd. dirs. Planned Parenthood Wis., 1984—; mem. adv. council Robert M. LaFollette Inst. Pub. Affairs U. Wis.-Madison, 1984—; bd. dirs. Forward Wis., 1985—; U. Wis.-Milw. Found., 1986—; mem. Am. Council on Edn. Nat. Commn. on Higher Edn. Issues, 1981—; U.S. rep. 20th Gen. Conf. of UNESCO, Paris, 1978. Recipient Outstanding Achievement award 4th Dist. Wis. Fedn. Women's Clubs, 1978, YWCA, 1986; fellow Am. Council Edn., 1976-77. Mem. Am. Polit. Sci. Assn., Am. Bankers Assn. (ednl. policy and devel. council 1983—), Assn. Bank Holding Cos. (govt. relations com. 1983—), Bank Mktg. Assn., Phi Beta Kappa, Phi Delta Kappa. Author articles in field. Office: Marine Corp 111 E Wisconsin Ave Milwaukee WI 53202

FRASER, MADA MARGARET, cosmetic company executive; b. Monett, Mo., Jan. 2, 1931; d. Fred Wilber and Margaret Opal (Mullins) Gilbert; m. David William Fraser, Sept. 17, 1949; children—Terri Lynn, Loralee Wanda, Shirley Kay. Student pub. schs., Eagle Rock, Calif. Head instr. Joseph's Figure Studio, Pasadena, Calif., 1952-56, Vic Tanny Gym, LaCrescenta, Calif., 1956-60; regional mgr. Preview Products Inc., Van Nuys, Calif., 1969-70, Western tng. dir., 1970-72; dir. mktg. Jack LaLanne European Health Spas So. Calif., Los Angeles, 1972-76; founder, pres. Spa Formula Cosmetics, Inc., Hollywood, Calif., 1976—; cons. Neolife Corp., Pasadena, 1975, Jack LaLanne European Health Spas, Downey, Calif., 1976-80; speaker. Mem. Bus. and Profl. Women's Club. Home: 855 Moorside Dr Glendale CA 91207 Office: Spa Formula Cosmetics 2449 Hyperion Ave Hollywood CA 90027

FRATES, MRS. CLIFFORD LEROY, civic worker; b. Moweaqua, Ill., Jan 15, 1908; d. William James and Gertrude (Gunderson) Rodman; student Pine Manor Jr. Coll., 1924; B.A., U. Okla., 1929; m. Clifford L. Frates, Nov. 15, 1935; children—Rodman A., Kent F. Mem. bd. ARC, Oklahoma City; dir. Community Fund Bd.; trustee Jane Brooks Sch. Deaf, Okla. Art Center, Okla. Coll. for Women; chmn. adv. bd. Mercy Hosp., now also trustee; bd. dirs. Okla. State Library, League for Blind, dir. Jr. Leagues of Am.; mem. bd. Okla. Heritage Assn., Allied Arts of Oklahoma City, Oklahoma City Symphony, YWCA, Blood Inst., Better Bus. Bur.; mem. Children's Rehab. and Edn. Bd.; drive chmn. Central Vol. Bur.; chmn. women's div. United Fund; chmn. Art Center drive; chmn. Oklahoma City Savs. Bond Com.; chmn. Episcopal Women's Conf. Okla.; div. chmn. for Christian social relations; mem. Episcopal Bishop and Council; mem. vestry All Souls Ch. chmn. Re-act campaign for Oklahoma City Vol. Action Center, 1971. Named to Okla. Hall of Fame, 1969; recipient award NCCJ; By-Liners award Women in Communication, 1979; Okla. Gov.'s Arts award, 1985. Mem. Oklahoma City Art Assn., Oklahoma City C. of C. (dir.), Phi Beta Kappa (pres. Oklahoma City alumnae 1964-66, alumna award 1978), Kappa Alpha Theta, Mortar Bd. Republican. Home: 2607 Warwick Dr Oklahoma City OK 73116

FRAULINI, KAY ETTA, nurse, researcher, consultant; b. Benton, Ill., June 1, 1946; d. Leno and Leona Pearl (Upchurch) F. B.S.N., U. Ill., 1968; M.S.N., Loyola U., Chgo., 1981. Staff nurse U. Ill., Chgo., 1968-70, Wadsworth VA Hosp., Los Angeles, 1970-72; clin. nurse II UCLA Med. Ctr., Los Angeles, 1972-74; head nurse Grant Hosp. Chgo., 1974-79; practitioner, tchr., instr. Rush-Presbyn.-St. Lukes Rush U. Coll. Nursing, Chgo., 1981-84; now coordinator clin. research dept. anesthesiology Rush-Presbyn.-St. Luke's Med. Ctr.; lectr., cons., Chgo., 1984—; mem. cons. faculty Med. Media Assocs., East Hanover, N.J., 1984—; acad. leader Springhouse Corp. Nursing 84, Internat. Journey, 1984. Author, editor: After Anesthesia, 1986. Contbr. articles to profl. jours. Chmn. research com. Chgo. Lung Assn., 1981-83; vol. Al Ronan Reelect Campaign, Chgo., 1979. Link Belt Co. scholar U. Ill. Found., Champaign, Ill., 1966-68. Mem. Internat. Anesthesia Research Soc. (assoc.), Am. Nurses Assn., Am. Soc. Post Anesthesia Nurses, Ill. Soc. Recovery Room Nurses (pres. 1978-79), Sigma Theta Tau (treas. 1983, research award 1984). Clubs: Columbia Yacht, Lake Shore Ski (Chgo.). Avocations: photography; sailing; fashion retailing; travel. Home: 555 W Cornelia St Apt 1907 Chicago IL 60657 Office: Rush-Presbyn St Lukes Med Ctr 1753 W Congress Pkwy Chicago IL 60612

FRAZEE, PAMELA WALKER, marketing executive; b. New Brighton, Pa., July 8, 1947; d. Ralph Wayne and Pearl Armour W.; B.S., Edinboro State Coll., 1969; M.Ed., Memphis State U., 1975; postgrad. San Antonio Coll., 1977, U. Mex., 1977, U. Tex., Austin, 1978-80, Trinity U., 1979; children—Tasha Jane, Nikki Mila. Tchr., Erie (Pa.) City Schs., 1969, Norton (Ohio) City Schs., 1969-73, Trenors Day Sch., Memphis, 1973-74; project dir. Stanford Research Inst., Menlo Park, Calif., 1978; ednl. cons. Learning About Learning, San Antonio, 1978-80; mktg. dir. Colonial Life & Accident, San Antonio, 1980-83; v.p. mktg. Infotech Systems, Inc., 1983—. Mem. NOW, Nat. Art Edn. Assn., Nat. Assn. Profl. Saleswomen, Nat. Assn. Exec. Females, Ind. Automotive Service Assn., Phi Kappa Phi. Home: 14203 Ridgemeadow St San Antonio TX 78233

FRAZER, WENDY, nurse, physician's assistant; b. Steubenville, Ohio, June 3, 1943; d. Richard William and Mary Elizabeth (Sliday) F. R.N., Beaver Valley Gen. Hosp., New Brighton, Pa., 1964; A.A.S., Cuyahoga Community Coll., 1983. R.N., Ohio, Pa. Pediatrics nurse Cleve. Clinic Found., 1964-68; asst. head nurse Cardiovascular Lab., 1965-73; cardiac-vascular surg. nurse clinician Cleve. Clinic Found., 1978-86, thoracic surgery clinician, 1986—; admissions officer Lakewood Hosp., 1984-85; clin. preceptor Surg. Assistance Program, Cuyahoga Community Coll. Assoc. founder, counselor Inst. Creative Living, 1976-80. Mem. Nat. Acad. Physician Assts., Nat. Assn. Cardiovascular Physician Assts., Ohio Assn. Physician Assts., Cleve. Zool. Soc., Cleve. Mus. Art, Holden Arboretum, Nat. Geog. Soc., Smithsonian Soc. Republican. Baptist. Office: Cleveland Clinic Foundation 9500 Euclid St Cleveland OH 44106

FRAZIER, ADA VIRGINIA, training technician, truck leasing company executive; b. Pueblo, Colo., Mar. 13, 1935; d. John Rogers and Ada Fiana (Kachel) Blanc; m. Jimmie Gordon Frazier, Apr. 3, 1954; children—Jimmy Ray, John Timothy, Cynthia Rene, Francesca Lucille. B.A., U. So. Colo., 1972; M.A., U. No. Colo., 1985; postgrad. Chapman Coll., 1980, Brigham Young U., 1984, U. Tex., 1984. Tng. technician Dept. Army, Dept. Def., Ft. Carson, Colo., 1976—; sec.-treas. Frazier Truck Leasing, Inc., Pueblo, Colo., 1984—. Active Pueblo PTA, 1962-83, 4-H Club, Pueblo, 1966-81; mem. Ch. Bd. Edn., Pueblo, 1981-83; speech judge Colo. High Sch. Activities, Pueblo, 1980-86. Mem. Fed. Women's Program Com. (chair 1981-82), Mountain Plains Adult Edn., Federally Employed Women, AFL-CIO, Am. Fedn. Govt. Employees, Mountain Plains Adult Assn. Republican. Baptist. Avocations: bowling, cycling, reading, writing oral history. Home: 31281 Acoma Rd Pueblo CO 81006 Office: DOD Dept Army Army Edn Ctr Bldg 2217 Fort Carson CO 80913

FRAZIER, ELLEN ELIZABETH, accountant, consultant; b. Cambridge, Mass., Jan. 28, 1950; d. William Raymond, and Helen Rhoda (Brooks) Frazier. Student So. Meth. U., 1967-69; B.B.A., U. Houston, 1972; M.B.A., Houston Bapt. U., 1984. Acctg. mgr. Baker Internat. Co., Houston, 1979-81; acct., cons. NL Industries, Houston, 1981—. Vol. Gary Hart's Presdl. Campaign, Houston, 1983—; mem. speakers' bur. United Way Campaign, 1984. Mem. So. Meth. U. Alumni Assn., Houston Bapt. U. Alumni Assn., Assn. for Women in Computing. Democrat. Methodist. Club: Native Houstonian (charter mem.) Home: 1511 Burning Tree Road Kingwood TX 77339 Office: NL Industries/Corp MIS 3000 North Belt PO Box 60077 Houston TX 77206

FRAZIER, GENEVIEVE LAVERNE, lawyer; b. Warren, Ohio, Sept. 2, 1953; d. George Donald and Gladys Emma (Cooper) F. A.A., Dalton (Ga.) Jr. Coll., 1972; B.S. magna cum laude, U. Ga., 1974; J.D., Emory U., 1980. Bar: Ga. 1981. Ty. sales mgr. Wyeth Labs., Chattanooga, 1974-78; law clk. Dekalb Jud. Circuit, Atlanta, 1980-81; asst. dist. atty. Gwinnett Jud. Circuit, Ga., 1981-83; assoc. Chambers, Mabry, Mc Clelland & Brooks, Atlanta, 1984—; tchr. Gwinnett County and Mcpl. Police Depts., 1981-84, Gwinnett County Pub. Schs., 1981-84. Com. chmn. Gwinnett County LWV, 1982-83, treas., 1984; state v.p. Young Republicans, 1977-78; mem. Nat. Audubon Soc., 1982-84. P.W. Fattig Entomology scholar, 1973; Emory Acad. scholar, 1979; Dalton Jr. Coll. acad. scholar, 1971. Mem. Ga. Bar Assn., ABA, Atlanta Bar Assn., Gwinnett County Bar Assn., Phi Kappa Phi, Gamma Sigma Delta. Methodist. Club: Bus. and Profl. Women's of Gwinnett County (dir., Young Careerist). Home: 115 Michigan Ave Decatur GA 30030 Office: Chambers Mabry Mc Clelland & Brooks 2200 Century Center Pkwy 825 Atlanta GA 30345

FRAZIER, RAMONA ENID YANCEY, personnel executive; b. Boston, June 27, 1941; d. Raymond Ernest and Gladys Enid (Springer) Yancey; 1 child, Pamela Rae. B.A., Pace U., 1985; student Howard U., 1959-60, Simmons Coll., 1961-62. Employment mgr. Brown Bros. Harriman, N.Y.C., 1969-73; personnel officer, asst. v.p. Anchor Savs. Bank, N.Y.C., 1973-74, 77-79; personnel officer Boston U., 1974-77; EEO mgr. Raytheon Co., Lexington, Mass., 1977; dir. EEO, GAF Corp., N.Y.C., 1979-82; dir. personnel F.W. Woolworth Co., N.Y.C., 1982—; lectr. in field. Mem. Friends of Commn. on Status Women, N.Y.C.; bd. dirs. Bklyn. YWCA. Named to Black Achievers in Industry, Harlem YMCA, 1973, 78. Mem. Edges Group (pres.), others. Avocations: walking; reading; bridge; music collecting. Office: F W Woolworth Co 233 Broadway New York NY 10279

FREDE, MARTHA CHAMBERS, clin. psychologist; b. Marvell, Ark., June 18, 1926; d. Landon Benjamin and Marie (Quinelly) Chambers; B.A. cum laude, U. Tex., Austin, 1945; Ph.D., U. Houston, 1970; m. Ralph Edward Frede, Dec. 25, 1946; children—Phyllis, Bethann Frede Walmus, Gretchen (dec.), Ellen, Sarah Jane Frede Jenkins. Diagnostic bacteriologist Tex. Health Dept., Austin, 1945-48; pre-sch. tchr. St. Francis Episcopal Day Sch., Houston, 1961-65; center program coordinator Parent-Child Devel. Center, U. Houston, 1970-72, psychologist Counseling Center, 1972-75; pvt. practice clin. psychology, Houston, 1974—; tchr. Houston Community Coll., 1973-74; cons. to community groups and agys. Bd. dirs. Can-Do-It, 1982—. Mem. Am. Psychol. Assn., Am. Assn. Sex Educators, Counselors, and Therapists (cert. sex therapist), Tex. Psychol. Assn., Houston Psychol. Assn. (sec.-treas. 1974-75), Houston Behavior Therapy Assn., Family Mediation Network Houston (treas. 1985-86), Assn. for Advancement of Behavior Therapy, Houston Behavior Assn. (pres. 1976-77), Houston Zool. Soc., Houston Ballet Guild, Phi Kappa Phi. Episcopalian. Home: 849 Hickorywood St Houston TX 77024 Office: 2650 Fountainview Suite 210 Houston TX 77057

FREDERICK, ARLENE MAE WILLGING, nurse, educator; b. Passaic, N.J., Oct. 29, 1942; s. Arthur William and Mae Frances (Randazzo) Willging; m. Robert Arthur Frederick, June 19, 1965; children—Robert Arthur, Elyse, Dawn, Kristen. B.S.N., Georgetown U., 1964; M.S.N., U. Tex.-San Antonio, 1973; Ed.D., U. S.C., 1980. Project dir. S.C. Nurses Assn., Columbia, 1974-76; instr. Incarnate Word Coll., San Antonio, 1973-74; instr. Columbia Assn. Prepared Childbirth, 1974—; instr. Midlands Tech. Coll., Columbia, 1981-83; pres. Profl. Health Edn. Cons., Columbia, 1980—; nurse clinician Richland Meml. Hosp., Columbia, 1983-85; nursing edn. dir. William S. Hall Psychiat. Inst., Columbia, 1986—. Author: (with others) Are You Ready? A Guide for Prepared Childbirth, 1976, 2d edit., 1983, Expanding Horizons in Childbirth Education, 1985. Chmn. edn. com. S.C. Bd. Examiners Nursing Home Adminstrs., 1981-87; mem. S.C. Maternal Child Health Adv. Com., 1983—, chair, 1985—. Served to 1st lt. AUS, 1962-66. Mem. S.C. Nurses Assn. (chmn. council on edn., 1980-84), Central Midland Dist. Nurses Assn. (pres. 1985-87), Am. Nurses Assn., Am. Soc. Psychoprophlaxis Obstetrics (edn. cons. 1974—), Nurses Assn. of Am. Coll. Ob-Gyn., Sigma Theta Tau. Office: Profl Health Edn Cons PO Box 210372 Columbia SC 29221

FREDERICK, AUDREY ANN, real estate and interval ownership sales exec.; b. Nanticoke, Pa., Oct. 5, 1932; d. Irene Mary Drake; student SUNY, 1963-65; grad. in bus. adminstrn. Lowell Sch. Bus., 1968; m. Richard A. Frederick, Dec. 9, 1974; children—Christopher, Joseph, Douglas, Jan Marie, Victoria, Richard. Research and devel. technician Gen. Electric Corp., Johnson City, N.Y., 1951-64; research and devel. staff asst. IBM, Owego, N.Y., 1965-68; office mgr. Sta. WLOD, Pompano Beach, Fla., 1968-71; gen. mgr. Sta. WSBR, Boca Raton, Fla., 1971-73; asst. to pres. Tennis Championship Inc., Ft. Lauderdale, Fla., 1973-76; bus. mgr. U. Sarasota, 1977-79; pres. Orlando Internat. Investors (Fla.), 1979-83; assoc. Centre Plaza Realty, Orlando, 1983-85, Nat. Devel. Communities, Parkland, Fla., 1985—. Mem. Nat. Assn. Female Execs. Republican. Home: 1466 NE 57th Ct Fort Lauderdale FL 33334

FREDERICK, NANCY, government official; b. Lakewood, Ohio, Aug. 23, 1932; d. Howard Peter and Marian Bissell (Slater) F.; B.A., U. Colo., 1955; postgrad., George Washington U., 1962-63, U.S. Dept. Agr., 1964-65, Fgn. Service Inst., 1968; m. Francis Liell Wenger. Reporter/photographer, city editor Robinson (Ill.) Daily News, 1956-61; area reporter UPI, 1956-61; spl. asst. to Congressman Peter Mack, Washington, 1961-62; with AID, 1962—, info. officer/photographer, 1962-65, editor Front Lines, 1966-68, program analyst devel. planning offices Latin Am. and Africa Burs., 1968-69, asst. desk officer Nigeria Relief and Rehab., 5 Central African countries, also Sahelian Drought Emergency Unit, 1969-74, human resources devel. officer Central/West African Affairs, 1972-74, planning asst. to coordinator Women in Devel. AID, 1974-77, program analyst to dep. dir. Am. Schs. and Hosps. Abroad, 1978—; mem. AID Women's Adv. Com., 1973-75; AID adviser, U.S., del. UN World Conf. Internat. Women's Yr., Mexico City, 1975; U.S. del. UN Conf. Status of Women, Geneva, Switzerland, OAS Inter. Am. Conf. for Women, 1976; asst. founding spl. offices for women devel. activities, Peace Corps, WHO, FAO, World Bank; agy. speaker, panelist various confs., 1975-77. Trustee Chesapeake Environ. Protection Assn., editor Chesapeake Environ. Protection Assn. Quar., 1979—. Recipient five awards Fed. Editors Assn., 1966-69, various awards and citations AID, cert. Nat. Council of Negro Women, 1975. Author, co-author plans and papers in field. Home: Route 1 Box 170 West River MD 20778 Office: FVA/ASHA AID Washington DC 20523

FREDERICK, PAULINE, broadcast news analyst; b. Gallitzin, Pa.; d. Matthew Phillip and Susan (Stanley) F.; A.B., Am. U., Washington, also A.M.; numerous hon. degrees; m. Charles Robbins. State Dept. corr. U.S. Daily; radio editorial asst. H.R. Baukhage, Blue Network and ABC; free-lance Western Newspaper Union, N.Am. Newspaper Alliance, also news commentator ABC, 1946-53; news corr. NBC, 1953-74, also UN corr. ABC, NBC; radio anchor Dem. and Rep. Convs., NBC, 1956; internat. affairs analyst Nat. Public Radio; moderator 2d debate Pres. Ford-Gov. Carter, Oct. 6, 1976. Trustee Am. U., Save the Children, UN Assn. U.S.A. Recipient Headliner award Theta Sigma Phi, Alfred I duPont award, George Foster Peabody award for contbn. to internat. understanding, Golden Mike award for outstanding woman in radio-TV, McCall's; Paul White award for contbn. to broadcast journalism Radio and TV News Dirs. Assn.; voted radio's woman of yr. Radio-TV Daily poll; U. Mo. Sch. Journalism medal; spl. citation for UN coverage Nat. Fedn. Women's Clubs, East-West Center award; Journalism Achievment award U. So. Calif.; 1st Pa. Journalism Achievment award; Carr Van Anda award Ohio U. Sch. Journalism; named to N.Y. Profl. Journalists Soc. Hall of Fame. Fellow Soc. Profl. Journalists; mem. UN Corrs. Assn. (pres.), Assn. Radio and TV Analysts, Council on Fgn. Relations.

FREDERICK, SUSAN ANNE, publishing company executive, consultant, educator; b. Southington, Conn., Mar. 26, 1948; d. Kenneth Hall and Isabel (McKenna) Spaulding; m. Roger Henry Frederick, Oct. 10, 1970; 1 child, Stephen Andrew. B.S.E. cum laude, Westfield State Coll., 1970. Tchr., Russell Elem. Sch., Mass., 1970-71; exec. asst. Chase Farms, Inc., Newport, R.I., 1972-73; tchr., curriculum dir. Southside Acad., Portsmouth, Va., 1973-74; tchr. St. Lucy's Sch., Newark, 1979-82; purchasing reports mgr. Gordon Publs., Randolph, N.J., 1982, dir. list rentals, 1983—; instr. Coll. Morris County, Randolph, N.J., 1984-86; cons. NJS List Services, Green Village, N.J., 1985-86. Active Essex council Boy Scouts Am., 1982-86; mem. parish council St. Paul the Apostle Ch., Irvington, N.J., 1983-85. Mem. Direct Mktg. Assn. (Leaders Forum), Women's Direct Response Group (N.J. chpt.) (v.p. 1984-86, bd. dirs. 1985-86), Women's Direct Response Group (N.Y. chpt.), Nat. Assn. Female Execs. Republican. Roman Catholic. Avocations: photography; crafts; reading. Home: 216 Nesbit Terr Irvington NJ 07111 Office: Gordon Publs 13 Emery Ave Randolph NJ 07869

FREDERICK, VIRGINIA FIESTER, state legislator; b. Rock Island, Ill., Dec. 24, 1916; d. John Henry and Myrtle (Montgomery) Heise; B.A., U. Iowa, 1938; postgrad. Lake Forest Coll., 1942-43; m. C. Donnan Fiester (dec. 1975); children—Sheryl Fiester Ross, Alan R., James D.; m. 2d Kenneth Jacob Frederick, 1978. Free-lance fashion designer, Lake Forest, Ill., 1952-78; pres. Mid Am. China Exchange, Kenilworth, Ill., 1978-81; mem. Ill. Ho. of Reps., Springfield, 1979—. Alderman, first ward Lake Forest, 1974-78; del. World Food Conf., Rome, 1974. mem. Ill. Commn. on Status of Women subcom. pensions and employment, 1976-79; co-chmn. Conf. Women Legislators, 1982-85. Named Chgo. Area Woman of Achievement, Internat. Orgn. Women Execs., 1978. Recipient Lottie Holman O'Neal award, 1980, Jane Addams award, 1982. Mem. LWV (local pres. 1958-60, state dir. 1969-75, mem. nat. com. 1975-76), AAUW (local pres. 1968-70, state pres. 1975-77, state dir. 1963-69, mem. nat. commns. 1967-69), UN Assn. (dir.), Chgo. Assn. Commerce and Industry (dir.). Methodist. Address: 1540 Greenleaf Ave Lake Forest IL 60045

FREDERICK-MAIRS, T(HYRA) JULIE, alcohol agency official; b. Islip, N.Y., Jan. 4, 1941; d. Manuel and Thyra C. (Thorsen) Cajiao; B.A., Adelphi U., 1961; M.S.W., U. So. Calif., 1972. Social worker Los Angeles County Dept. Social Services, 1966-67, social work supr., 1967-70; planning cons. Los Angeles County Dept. Social Services and Los Angeles County Chief Adminstr.'s Office, 1972-76; dep. to supr. 4th Dist., Los Angeles County, 1976-80; asst. dir. Los Angeles County Office Alcohol Abuse and Alcoholism, 1980—. Mem. or past mem. Los Angeles Child Sexual Abuse Project, Commn. for Sex Equity, Los Angeles Unified Sch. Dist., Harbor Police Community Adv. Council, Los Angeles; mem. San Pedro and Peninsula Family Stress Task Force, Los Angeles; mem. ops. com. Interagy. Council on Child Abuse and Neglect; bd. dirs. Marshall High Sch. PTA, Los Angeles; adv. com. UCLA Alcohol Research Center; mem. Westside Child Trauma Council. Mem. Los Amigos de la Humanidad, Women in Health Adminstrn., Alpha Epsilon Delta, Beta Beta Beta. Clubs: Bus. and Profl. Women's, Soroptimists (pres. Los Angeles 1986-87), Catholic Maritime (dir.). Author: (with others) Youth Program Planning, 1975. Office: 849 S Broadway, Los Angeles, CA 90014

FREDMAN-(ZITLIN), SUSAN MIRIAM, interior designer; b. Chgo., Nov. 14, 1950; d. David Wolfe Fredman and Selma (Lobelson) Florio; m. Martin Zitlin, Jan. 28, 1984; 1 dau., Amanda Beth. B.S., Ill. State U., 1973. Display asst. Lane Bryant, Chgo., 1972-73, Lyttons, Chgo., 1973; asst. head visual merchandising Goldblatt's, Chgo., 1973-76; designer Advance Design Assocs., Chgo., 1976; prin. Susan Fredman & Assocs., Chgo., 1976—, Interior Accents, Ltd., 1985— dir. Seven-Thirty Network, 1980-85. Mem. steering com. women in professions and trades Jewish United Fund, 1984-85; mem. Hunger Project, Chgo., 1983; vol. Children's Meml. Hosp., Chgo., 1983; exec. com. audience devel. bd. Victory Gardens Theatre. Mem. Internat. Soc. Interior Designers (profl. mem., bd. dirs. 1984-85).

FREE, ANN COTTRELL, writer; b. Richmond, Va.; d. Emmett Drewry and Emily (Blake) Cottrell; grad. Collegiate Sch. for Girls, Richmond, 1934; A.B., Barnard Coll., Columbia, 1938; m. James Stillman Free, Feb. 24, 1950; 1 dau., Elissa. Reporter Richmond Times Dispatch, 1938-40; Washington corr., Newsweek, 1940-41, Chgo. Sun, 1941-43, N.Y. Herald Tribune, 1943-46; pub. information dir., spl. corr. UNRRA China Mission, Shanghai, 1946-47; corr. Middle and Nr. East and Europe, 1947-48; writer-photographer Marshall Plan, Washington and Western Europe, 1949-50; contbr. newspapers and mags., including Washington Post, N. Am. Newspaper Alliance, Women's News Service; Washington editor EnviroSouth Quar., 1977-82; contbg. editor Between the Species, 1986. Founding mem. Friends Nat. Zoo; chmn. Eleanor Roosevelt Award Commn., 1965; mem. adv. com. Council Livestock Protection; cons. expert Rachel Carson Council. Bd. dirs. Albert Schweitzer Fellowship, Soc. Study Ethics and Animals, 1980-82. Recipient Dodd Mead-Boys' Life Writing award, 1963, Albert Schweitzer medal, Animal Welfare Inst., 1963, Jr. Book award certificate Boys Clubs of Am., 1964; Humanitarian of Yr. awards Washington Animal Rescue League, 1971, Montgomery County Humane Soc., 1971, Washington Humane Soc., 1983, News Writing award Dog Writers Assn. Am., 1975, 78; recognition Dept. Interior, 1969. Mem. Soc. Woman Geographers. Clubs: Nat. Press, Am. News Women's. Author: Forever the Wild Mare, 1963; Animals, Nature and Albert Schweitzer, 1982; No Room, Save In the Heart, 1986. Home: 4700 Jamestown Rd Bethesda MD 20816

FREED, ANN SYBL, television producer; b. Wilmington, N.C., Sept. 16, 1945; d. Jack and Dorothy Jane (Duffy) Capling. A.S., Monroe Community Coll., 1965; B.S., U. Rochester, 1967; B.A., U. South Fla., 1981. Community activist social service orgns. in Colo. and N.Y., 1967-75; enlisted U.S. Army, 1975, advanced through grades to capt., 1986; instr. Signal Sch., Ft. Gordon, Ga., 1975-78, asst. broadcast supr. USAR, Tampa, 1978-81, radio/TV officer, 1981—; dir. media ctr. Fla. Mental Health Inst., Tampa, 1979-85; TV specialist ISFA Corp., Tampa, 1985—. Bd. dirs. Genesee Hosp., Rochester, N.Y., 1969; pres. Pub. Access Coalition Tampa, 1982-83. N.Y. State Merit scholar, 1965; Univ. fellow U. Rochester, 1967. Mem. Internat. TV Assn. (chpt. pres. 1982-84, recipient Pres.'s Cup 1982), Am. Soc. Tng. and Devel., Nat. Fedn. Local Cable Programmers. Democrat. Unitarian. Home: 1709 E Powhattan Ave Tampa FL 33610 Office: Investment Services for Am 5404 Cypress Center Tampa FL 33609

FREED, BARBARA BORAM, business administrator; b. Troy, Ohio, Mar. 7, 1943; d. William Jacob and Mabel Catherine (Mapes) Boram; m. Frederick David Freed, Sept. 1, 1972; children—Aaron S., Leah A. Grad. Glamour Sch. Modeling, Dayton, Ohio 1972. Lic. real estate agt. Legal sec. various law firms, Ohio, 1960-74, Freed, DeWeese and Virzi, Piqua, Ohio, 1974-85; corp. adminstr. A C D Corp., Dayton, Ohio, 1985—; mem. adv. bd. Upper Valley Joint Vocat. Sch., Piqua, 1976—, adult edn., 1980—, lectr., 1976—; mem. adv. bd. secretarial/office adminstrn. dept. Edison State Coll., Piqua, 1980—, participant Career Day, 1984—. Vice pres. bd. dirs. Miami County Family Abuse, Troy, 1975—; vol. Piqua Meml. Hosp. 1975-76, 1985, Dettmer Hosp., Troy, 1978-79; bd. dirs., legis. chmn. Piqua Meml. Med. Ctr. Aux.; pres. Temple Anshe Emeth, Piqua, 1981—; bd. dirs. Union Am. Hebrew Congregations, 1982—; mem. regional adv. bd. Anti-Defamation League of B'nai B'rith, Ohio, Ind., Ky.; lectr. on Women in Politics; Dem. precinct committeeman, Ward 5D, Piqua, 1984—; mem. central com. Miami County (Ohio) Dems., 1984—; active campaign worker numerous candidates. Mem. B'nai B'rith Women, Dayton Legal Secs. Assn., Ohio Assn. Legal Secs., Nat. Assn. Legal Secs., Miami County Legal Secs. Assn. (charter pres. 1972-74), Ohio PTA, Nat. Planned Parenthood Assn., Miami County Mental Health Assn., Tri-County NAACP. Club: Four Seasons Garden (pres. 1978-79). Avocations: gardening; nature walks; cooking; music; reading; style show modeling. Home: 303 Ron Aire Dr Piqua OH 45356 Office: A C D Corp 1336 Stanley Ave Dayton OH 45404

FREED, CATHERINE CAROL MOORE (MRS. DEBOW FREED), educator; b. Omaha, Dec. 27, 1925; d. Prentice Lauri and Henryetta (Baker) Moore; B.A., B.F.A., U. Tex., 1948; M.A., U. Kans., 1961; m. DeBow Freed, Sept. 10, 1949; 1 son, DeBow II. Mem. faculty St. Mary's Coll., Xavier, Kans., 1958-59, U. Kans., Lawrence, 1959-61, U. N.Mex., Albuquerque, 1961-65, Huntingdon Coll., Montgomery, Ala., 1965-67; lectr. in English, Ladycliff Coll., Highland Falls, N.Y., 1967-69. Adviser, Albuquerque Sch. System on Gifted Child Edn., 1962-64; writer, producer film on purposes and objectives of PTA, 1964; pres. Alliance Community Concert Assn., 1970-74; Alliance area chmn. Blossom women's com. Cleve. Symphony Orch., 1971-74; elder United Presbyn. Ch., U.S.A., 1976; commr. 189th Gen. Assembly, moderator Presbytery of Gt. Rivers, 1979; 1st v.p. Ada-Liberty United Way, 1981-83, pres., 1984; pres. Ada-Lima chpt. Liturgical Art Guild Ohio, 1980-84; lay speaker United Methodist Ch., 1983. Mem. Speech Assn. Am., Nat. Council Tchrs. English, Daus. of U.S. Army (pres. chpt. Ft. Benning, Ga. 1954-55), Internat. Platform Assn., PEO, DAR, Mortar Bd., Phi Beta Kappa, Delta Sigma Rho, Pi Kappa Delta, Kappa Phi, Alpha Psi Omega, Alpha Delta Pi. Home: 115 W Lima Ave Ada OH 45810 Office: Office of Pres Ohio No U Ada OH 45810

FREED, HERMINE, artist, educator; b. N.Y.C., May 29, 1940; d. Israel and Eleanor Herma (Schaap) Gerberg; m. Ned Benhaim, 1961 (div. 1965); m. James Ingo Freed, May 28, 1967; 1 child, Dara Michaella. Curator art rental Inst. Contemporary Art, Boston, 1963-65; instr. NYU Sch. Continuing Edn., N.Y.C., 1966-73; asst. curator NYU Art Collection, N.Y.C., 1965-67; asst. prof. Sch. of Art Inst. Chgo., 1977; instr. Sch. Visual Arts, N.Y.C., 1973—. One-woman shows include De Saisset Art Mus., U. Santa Clara, Calif., Herbert Johnson Mus., Cornell U., Ithaca, N.Y., Ileana Sonnabend Gallery, N.Y.C., 1975, Everson Mus., Syracuse, N.Y., 1978, Columbia U. Coll. Architecture, 1979, Stefanotti Gallery, N.Y.C., 1980, Leo Castelli Gallery, N.Y.C., 1981; exhibited in group shows at Leo Castelli Gallery, N.Y.C., 1973, 74, 78, Corcoran Gallery, Washington, 1975, 81, Whitney Mus., N.Y.C., 1975, 78, Art Gallery Ont., 1978, H. Johnson Mus., Cornell U., Ithaca, N.Y., 1978, Pratt Manhattan Ctr., 1979, Mus. Modern Art travelling exhbn., 1980, 81, Aspen Ctr. for Visual Arts, 1980, Mus. Folkwang, Essen, Germany, Am. Cultural Ctr. Exhbn., Paris, Weatherspoon Gallery, U. N.C., 1980, Stefanotti Gallery, N.Y.C., 1981, 82, S. Ohio Mus., 1981, Aldrich Mus., Ridgefield, Conn., 1982, Palais de Beaux Arts, Charleroi, Belgium, 1983, Taghinia-Milani Gallery, N.Y.C., 1983, Artists Space, N.Y.C., 1985, Am. Film Inst., 1985, Bernice Steinbaum Gallery, 1985, Gallery Camino Real, Boca Raton, Fla., 1986; represented in permanent collections Govt. Austria, Hartwick Coll., Oneonta, N.Y., Otis Art Inst., La., U. Mass., Amherst, Guild Hall, East Hampton, N.Y., Calif. Inst. Arts, Valencia, Va. Commonwealth U., De Saisset Art Mus., Santa Clara, Calif., U. N.C., Berlin Film Festival, Smith Coll., Northampton, Mass., Sch. of Chgo. Art Inst., Anthology Film Archives, N.Y., Donnell Library, N.Y., Grossmont Coll., El Cajun, Calif., U. Ga., Teheran Mus. Contemporary Art, Denver Art Mus., Queens U., Kingston, Can., Nat. Gallery Victoria, Melbourne, Australia, U. Ill., Chgo., Hamburger Kunsthaller, Hamburg, Germany, New Castle on Tyen Poly. Inst., Erg., Inter Communications Agy., Washington, Stedlijk Mus., Amsterdam, Epiphany br. N.Y. Pub. Library, N.Y.C.; also pvt. collections. Contbr. articles to profl. jours. Artists fellow Nat. Endowment on Arts, 1974, Creative Artists Pub. Service Program, N.Y. State, 1978, Rockefeller Found., 1978; artist-in-residence N.Y. State Council on Arts, WNET-TV Lab., 1974; grantee N.Y. State Council on Arts, Air Gallery Project, N.Y.C., 1972. Home: 60 Gramercy Park N New York NY 10010 Office: 40 Crosby St New York NY 10003

FREED, MARILYNNE MAUD, mfg. co. exec.; b. Youngstown, Ohio, Sept. 18, 1949; d. Warren P. and Phyllis I. (Avery) Freed; B.S., Case-Western Res. U., 1971; m. William E. Pastor, Jr., May 20, 1978; children—William A. Freed-Pastor, Daniel E. Freed-Pastor. Acctg. mgr. Sta. WFMJ-TV, Youngstown, Ohio, 1971-72; acctg. supr., Sta. WFLD-TV, Kaiser Industries, Chgo., 1973-74, chief acct., 1974-75; v.p., treas. Mahoning Culvert Co. Div. Youngstown Steel & Alloy Corp., Canfield, Ohio, 1975-82; pres. Life-Time Truck Products, Inc., Youngstown, Ohio, 1982—; v.p. Valley Truck & Trailer, Youngstown, 1979—. Chmn., Pvt. Industry Council of Mahoning County, 1981-84; mem. small bus. mgmt. adv. bd. Mahoning County Joint Vocat. Sch., 1980—, bd. dirs. Family Bus. Assn. Northeastern Ohio, 1978-80; mem. adminstrv. bd., choir dir. Ohltown United Methodist Ch. Mem. Youngstown Area C. of C., Audubon Soc. Republican. Office: 4300 Simon Rd Youngstown OH 44512 also Life-Time Truck Products Inc PO Box 3346 Youngstown OH 44512

FREEDLANDER, EVE SYLVIA, mortgage banker, real estate financier; b. Richmond, Va., Aug. 11, 1926; d. Max and Rebecca (Steinberg) Andelman; m. Ruben Freedlander, Aug. 31, 1941; children—Gwen Gertz, Eric, Benjamin, Melissa Landau. Lic. realtor, Va. Co-owner grocery store, Richmond, 1948-57; bookkeeper, receptionist 1958-60; bridal cons. 1960-63; pres. Town House Realty, Richmond, 1964-74 (name changed to Freedlander Realtors Inc. 1974-79; sr. exec. v.p., sec. So. Indsl. Loan Corp. (name changed to Freedlander Loan and Thrift Assn.), 1979—; pres. Freedlander Inc., 1964—; sr. exec. v.p. Freedlander Inc., The Mortgage People, 1979—. Vice pres. Rudlin Torah Acad., 1984—; mem. adv. bd. Med. Coll. Va. Hosp. Bd. Aux., 1984—; chmn. bd. dirs. Beth Shalom Home Va., 1983-84; bd. dirs. Richmond Hebrew Day Sch., Richmond Jewish Community Ctr., Beth Shalom Homes for Aged of Central Va. Recipient Service award Richmond Hebrew Day Sch., 1978, President's award Beth Shalom Home Va., 1982. Mem. Real Estate Women's Assn. Va. (pres. 1966), Richmond Realtors Assn. (v.p. women's div.), Mortgage Banker's Assn. Jewish. Club: Hadassah. Lodge: B'nai B'rith Woman. Avocations: Walking; dancing; travel; reading. Home: 300 Berwickshire Dr Richmond VA 23229

FREEDMAN, ANNE BELLER, public speaking and marketing consultant; b. Gardner, Mass., June 22, 1949; d. Gabriel Philip and Natalie Engler (Beller) Freedman Lyons; m. Edward A. Fischer, May 20, 1979; 1 child, Lynne Heather. B.S.J., U. Fla., 1971. Staff writer Coral Gables Times, Miami, 1972-73; reporter Miami News, 1973-74; assoc. editor Miami Phoenix, 1974-75; freelance writer, Miami, 1975-80; corr. Advt. Age, Miami, 1977-81; pres. Exec. S.O.S., Inc., Miami, 1980—. Contbr. articles to profl. jours. Bd. dirs. Miami/Bogota-Calé Sister Cities Program, 1983-85. Mem. South Miami/Kendall C. of C. (editor monthly newsletter 1980-83, dir., 1982-85, Presdl. award 1983), Nat. Assn. Women Bus. Owners (chmn. public relations 1981), Coral Gables C. of C., Kendall Bus. and Profl. Assn. Clubs: Toastmasters (pres. 1984), Kendall Bus. and Profl. Women, Zonta. Home: 6721 SW 113th Pl Miami FL 33173 Office: 10850 SW 113th Pl Suite 117 Miami FL 33176

FREEDMAN, AUDREY WILLOCK, labor economist; b. Cleve., Nov. 25, 1929; d. Sylvester Rhodes and Hilda Louise (Reiber) Willock; m. Monroe H. Freedman, Sept. 24, 1950; children—Alice, Sarah, Caleb, Judah. B.A. in Econs., Wellesley Coll., 1951. Labor economist Communications Workers Am., AFL-CIO, Washington, 1958-60; economist Bur. Labor Stats., Washington, 1961-67, Manpower Adminstrn., 1967-71; mem. policy staff Cost of Living Council, liaison U.S. Pay Bd., Washington, 1971-72; sr. cons. Orgn. Resources Counselors, N.Y.C., 1973-75; sr. research assoc. Conf. Bd., N.Y.C., 1976-85, exec. dir. Human Resources Program group, 1985—; mem. bus. research adv. council, price and indsl. relations subcoms. U.S. Bur. Labor Stats.; mem. econs. bd. U.S. Dept. Agr. Grad. Sch., 1972-75; mem. adv. bd. Columbia U. Bus. Sch., Syracuse U. Author: Security Bargains Reconsidered, 1978; Managing Labor Relations, 1979; Industry Response to Health Risk, 1981; The New Look in Wage Policy and Employee Relations, 1985; contbr. articles to profl. jours. Recipient Disting. Service award U.S. Dept. Labor, 1967, Presdl. citation, 1972. Mem. Am. Fedn. Govt. Employees (v.p. local chpt. 1965-68, chmn. civil rights com. 1964-69), Am. Econ. Assn., Indsl. Relations Research Assn., Am. Statis. Assn. Jewish. Office: Conf Bd 845 3d Ave New York NY 10022

FREEDMAN, BARBARA TWEEDLE, personnel and administration manager; b. Chgo., Feb. 9, 1948; d. Charles Earl and Barbara Maude (Bryant) Tweedle; m. Barry Leonard Freedman, June 30, 1985. Student Northfield Mt. Hermon Sch., 1963-66, U. Tampa, 1966-68. Service mgr. Saks Fifth Ave., Boston, 1971-72; supr. Filene's Boston, 1972-73; adminstrv. asst. Milliken & Co., N.Y.C., 1973-77, employment supr., 1975-77, personnel mgr., 1977-80; mgr. personnel and adminstrn. Hoechst Fibers Industries, N.Y.C., 1980—. Mem. Am. Soc. Personnel Adminstrn., Northfield Mt. Hermon Alumni Assn. (v.p. 1983-85), Republican. Episcopalian. Clubs: N.Y. Jr. League, Northfield Mt. Hermon-N.Y. (v.p. 1981-83, pres. 1985—). Home: 60 Gramercy Park Apt 5G New York NY 10010 Office: Hoechst Fibers Industries 1515 Broadway New York NY 10036

FREEDMAN, BARBARA WIDMAN, lawyer; b. Phila., Sept. 1, 1947; d. Robert and Lillian (Kartoz) Widman; m. Allan Perry Freedman, Dec. 22, 1968; children—Avraham, Reena, Noam. B.A. cum laude, Temple U., 1969, J.D. cum laude, 1977. Bar: Pa. 1977, D.C. 1980. Law clk. U.S. Dist. Ct. for Eastern Dist. Pa., Phila., 1977-78; tax atty. Dechert Price & Rhoads, Phila., 1978-82; tax atty. Rawle & Henderson, Phila., 1983—, ptnr., 1986—; adj. prof. Sch. Law, Temple U., Phila., 1981—. Editor Temple Law Quar., 1975-76; lectr.; contbr. articles to profl. jours. Barenkopf scholar, 1976-77. Mem. ABA, Phila. Bar Assn. (fed. tax com. 1983—, exec. council of tax sect. 1985—), Phila. Tax Supper Group (pres. 1986—), Templ Tax Forum (planning com. 1985—), Phila. Citywide Pension Lawyers Group. Office: Rawle & Henderson 211 S Broad St Philadelphia PA 19107

FREEDMAN, BETSY, fundraising consultant; b. Springfield, Mass., Aug. 16, 1942; d. Herman and Marcia (Glickman) F.; m. Seymour Golfond, Oct. 10, 1980; m. Neil Solomon, June 27, 1967 (div. May 1977); children—Leslie, Amy. A.S., Endicott Coll., 1962. Cons., Tamblyn & Brown, N.Y.C., 1962-67; exec. dir. East Mid Manhattan C. of C., N.Y.C., 1974-78; exec. v.p. Lawson Assocs., N.Y.C., 1978—. Cons., Orr Shalom Village, Jerusalem, 1980—, bd. dirs., 1982-83. Pres., Nat. Council Jewish Women, Monmouth County, N.J., 1972-73, recipient Outstanding Community work award, 1970. Mem. Nat. Soc. Fund Raising Execs. Republican. Jewish. Home: 80 East End Ave New York NY 10028 Office: Douglas M Lawson Assocs 39 E 51st St New York NY 10022

FREEDMAN, ELIZABETH IDA, lawyer; b. Albany, N.Y., Jan. 16, 1958; d. Alan Robert and Gloria (Silverstein) Freedman. B.A., SUNY-Albany, 1979; J.D., SUNY-Buffalo, 1982. Bar: N.Y. 1983, D.C. 1984. Bd. dirs. Buffalo Pub. Interest Law Program, Inc., 1981-82; research law clk. U.S. Ct. Appeals (2d cir.), N.Y.C., 1982-83; assoc. firm Finley, Kumble, Wagner, Heine, Underberg, Manley, Myerson & Casey, N.Y.C., 1983-85; asst. corp. counsel Office of Corp. Counsel N.Y.C. Law Dept., 1985—. Sea Grant Law fellow, 1981. Mem. ABA, N.Y. State Bar Assn., Assn. of Bar of City of N.Y. Office: NYC Law Dept Office Corp Counsel 100 Church St New York NY 10007

FREEDMAN, ESTELLE BRENDA, historian, educator; b. Harrisburg, Pa., July 2, 1947; d. Theodore Henry and Martha Harriet (Pincus) F. B.A. in History, Barnard Coll., 1969; M.A. in History, Columbia U., 1972, Ph.D. in History, 1976. Instr. Princeton U. (N.J.), 1974-76; asst. prof. Stanford U., Calif., 1976-83, assoc. prof. history, 1983—; assoc. editor: Signs: Jour. of Women in Culture and Society, 1980-85; mem. Coordinating Com. on Women in Hist. Profession. Author: Their Sisters' Keepers, 1981 (Hamilton manuscript prize 1978); assoc. editor: Victorian Women, 1981 (Sierra prize 1982); editor The Lesbian Issue, 1985; contbr. articles to publs. Hon. dissertation fellow Woodrow Wilson Found., 1974-75; ind. study fellow NEH, 1982-83; AAUW Founders fellow, 1985-86; Stanford Humanities Ctr. fellow, 1985-86; recipient Dean's award for Disting. Teaching, Stanford U., 1978, Dinkelspiel award for outstanding service to undergrad. edn., 1981. Mem. Orgn. Am. Historians, Am. Hist. Assn., Nat. Women's Studies Assn. Jewish. Office: Dept History Stanford U Stanford CA 94305

FREEDMAN, PHYLLIS B., civic worker; b. N.Y.C., Jan. 10, 1928; d. Irving and Pauline D. (Janowitz) Blonder; m. Jack I. Freedman, Jan. 19, 1947; children—Douglas S. Freedman, Robyn Freedman Spizman. Ed. Syracuse U. Pres., Brandeis U. Nat. Women's Commn., Atlanta, 1958-60, nat. v.p., 1970-73; sec. Atlanta Jewish Community Ctr., Atlanta, 1960-62; sec., asst. treas. Atlanta Jewish Fedn., 1970-75, pres. yr. round women's div., 1960-62; mem. nat. bd. Women's div. United Jewish Appeal, N.Y.C., 1960-62, 81-82, nat. chair Women's div. Council of Jewish Fedn., N.Y.C., 1981-83; co-chair Israel Expo, Atlanta Jewish Com. Ctr., 1985; bd. dirs. Council Jewish Fedns., 1981-85. Recipient Pres.'s Council award Brandeis U., 1976; Disting. Service award B'nai B'rith, 1983. Democrat. Jewish. Home: 1470 Wesley Pkwy NW Atlanta GA 30327

FREELAND, FRANCES JEANNETTE, alcoholism treatment center exec.; b. Danville, Ill., Apr. 11, 1938; d. John Terrence and Marie Amber (Iliff) F.; B.S. in Nursing, Coll. Mt. St. Joseph, Cin., 1960; M.S. in Extension Edn., Purdue U., Indpls., 1978, postgrad. in health adminstrn. Staff nurse in premature and critical care nursery Good Samaritan Hosp., Cin., 1960-61; joined Carmelite order, Roman Catholic Ch., 1961, with Carmelite Contemplative Community, Indpls., 1961-71; staff nurse VA Hosp., Indpsl., 1971-72; med./surg. staff nurse St. Francis Hosp., Beech Grove, Ind., 1972-74; dir. alcoholism detoxification unit Salvation Army, Indpls., 1974-79, program dir. Salvation Army Adult Rehab. Center, 1979—; tchr. alcoholism therapy; mem. Ind. Substance Abuse Task Force; v.p. Ind. Free Standing Addiction Agys. Coalition. Bd. dirs., mem. exec. bd. First Step Inc., half-way house for women, Indpls. Recipient award of appreciation Koala Center, Lebanon, Ind., 1978. Mem. Ind. Nurses Soc. on Alcoholism, Nat. Nurses Soc. on Alcoholism (planning com. 1982 Forum). Democrat. Home: 2335 Coyner Ave Indianapolis IN 46218 Office: 130 W Louisiana St Indianapolis IN 46218

FREEMAN, ANNE HOBSON, writer, English educator; b. Richmond, Va., Mar. 19, 1934; d. Joseph Reid Anderson and Mary Douthat (Marshall) Hobson; m. George Clemon Freeman, Jr., Dec. 6, 1958; children—Anne Colston, George Clemon, Joseph Reid Anderson. A.B., Bryn Mawr Coll., 1956; postgrad. London U., 1956-57; M.A., U. Va., 1973. Fiction writer, 1956—; reporter Internat. News Service, Eastern Europe, 1957; editor Va. Mus. Fine Arts, Richmond, 1959-63; lectr. English, U. Va., Charlottesville, 1973—; chmn. adv. com. Bryn Mawr Bull., Pa., 1978-81; firm historian Hunton & Williams, Richmond, 1984—. Contbr. stories to various mags., anthologies, lit. jours. Mem. Richmond Area Democratic Woman's Club, 1968—; bd. dirs. Va. Hist. Soc., Poe Found., Richmond, Nat. Council Friends of Kennedy Ctr., Washington, Mus. of Confederacy, Richmond. Fulbright scholar, 1956-57; Va. Ctr. for Creative Arts fellow, 1981-83, 85. Episcopalian. Clubs: Va. Writers (program com. 1983—), Country of Va., Woman's (Richmond). Home: 10 Paxton Rd Richmond VA 23226 Office: Dept English U Va Wilson Hall Charlottesville VA 22903

FREEMAN, ANTOINETTE ROSEFELDT, lawyer; b. Atlantic City, Oct. 7, 1937; d. Bernard Paul and Fannie (Levin) Rosefeldt; m. Alan Richard Freeman, June 22, 1958 (div. Apr. 1979); children—Barry David, Robin Lisa. B.A., Rutgers U., 1972; J.D., Ind. U., 1975; LL.M., Temple U., 1979. Bar: Pa. 1975, U.S. Dist. Ct. (ea. dist.) Pa. 1976, U.S. Ct. Appeals (3d cir.) 1982. Substitute tchr. Washington Twp. Sch. Dist., Indpls., 1972; dep. prosecutor intern Marion County Prosecutor, Indpls., 1974-75; asst. dist. atty. City of Phila., 1975-76; mgr. EEO, Wyeth Labs., Radnor, Pa., 1976-80, SmithKline & French Labs., Phila., 1980-82; atty. SmithKline Beckman Corp., Phila., 1982—; arbitrator Am. Arbitration Assn., 1976—. Counsel Regional Interests Developing Efficient Transp., 1983—; adv. bd. Family Service Phila., 1980-81, Greater Phila. C. of C., 1983; pres. Croskey Ct. Condominium Assn., 1983—; bd. dirs. Logan Sq. Neighborhood Assn., 1983—, pres., 1985—; v.p., sec. Friends of Logan Sq. Found.; chairperson Ctr. City Coalition for Quality of Life. Mem. ABA, Pa. Bar Assn., Phila. Bar Assn., Merit Employers Council (1st v.p. 1978-79), Phila. Women's Network, Phila. Lawyers Club, Phila. Vol. Lawyers for Arts. Democrat. Jewish. Office: SmithKline Beckman Corp One Franklin Plaza Philadelphia PA 19101

FREEMAN, BERNICE, retired educator; b. LaGrange, Ga., Aug. 8, 1909; d. Thomas Norman and Everette (Jenkins) F.; A.B., Tift Coll., 1930; M.A. in English, U. N.C., 1932; Ed.D. in English, Columbia U., 1952. Tchr. math. pub. schs., Dublin, Ga., 1930-31; tchr. social studies pub. schs., La Grange, Ga., 1932-42; tchr. social studies and English, Peabody Demonstration Sch., Ga. State Coll. Women, 1942-48, prin., tchr., 1948-51; dir. curriculum Troup County Schs., La Grange, 1951-67; asso. prof. edn. West Ga. Coll., Carrollton, 1967-69, prof. edn., 1969-74, coordinator secondary edn., 1969-73, chmn. dept. secondary edn., 1973-74; del. Washington Conf. Academically Talented, 1958, White House Conf. Children and Youth, 1960; chmn. English curriculum guide com. Ga. Pub. Schs., 1960-64, mem. steering com., English curriculum guide com., 1965-68; pres. Ga. Dept. Instructional Supervision, 1961-62, co-dir. English Study in Ga., 1951-52. Bd. dirs. Troup-Harris-Coweta Regional Library, 1954-67. Mem. LWV (pres. Carrollton br. 1970-72), AAUW (pres. Ga. div. 1957-59), Ga., Nat. councils tchrs. English, Ga. Writers Assn., Ga. Acad. Social Scis., World Edn. Fellowship (bd. dirs. U.S. sect. 1976-77), DAR (regent LaGrange br. 1977-79), Pi Lambda Theta, Kappa Delta Pi, Pi Gamma Mu, Delta Kappa Gamma. Preparation ednl. materials (with Lydia A. Thomas) The Reader's Digest, NEA (exec. com. dept. rural education 1965-69), Reading Skill Builder, Grade 5, Part 3, 1960, (with Bernice Cooper) Grade 1, Part 1, 1963. Home: 305 Park Ave LaGrange GA 30240

FREEMAN, CONSTANCE ANN, psychotherapist; b. N.Y.C., Oct. 18, 1946; d. Julius and Sylvia Hannah (Diamond) F. B.A., Hunter Coll., 1968; M.A., NYU, 1972, Ph.D., 1983. Tchr., N.Y.C. Bd. Edn., 1968-77; guidance counselor Ramsey High Sch. (N.J.), 1977-78, Hastings High Sch. (N.Y.), 1978-79; psychologist N.Y. State Office Mental Health, 1979-81, treatment team leader, 1981—; psychotherapist, Little Neck and Scarsdale, N.Y., 1980—; instr. White Plains Adult Edn. Program. Cert. sch. psychologist, N.J., guidance counselor, tchr. K-12, N.Y. Mem. Am. Psychol. Assn., MENSA. Home: 60 Morrow Ave Scarsdale NY 10583 Office: 45-13 Little Neck Pkwy Little Neck NY 11362

FREEMAN, EVELYN G., government official; b. Dayton, Tenn., Oct. 2, 1934; d. Charles Lee and Beulah Elizabeth (Swafford) Gentry; B.S., Tenn. Tech. U., 1968; postgrad. U. Tenn., 1970-72; Middle Tenn. State U., 1969-75; m. James R. Freeman, May 19, 1984; children by previous marriage—Thomas Lee Henderson (dec.), Yvonne Elizabeth Ownby. Legal sec. U.S. Atty. for Eastern Dist. Tenn., Dept. Justice, Chattanooga, 1963-66; with TVA, 1966-69, staff records officer, micrographics specialist, Chattanooga, 1975-83, mgr. micrographics dept. Dept. HUD, 1984-85, U.S. Dept. Commerce, 1985—; mktg. and mgmt. dept. head Walker County Tech. Sch., Lafayette, Ga., 1969-70; office occupations instr. State Area Vo-Tech. Sch., Chattanooga, 1970-72; instr. Edmondson Coll., Chattanooga, 1972-74; workshop instr. Chattanooga Area Literacy Movement Tchrs., 1978-83; notary pub., State of Tenn., 1962-83. Sec., Fed. Employed Women, 1976; vol. First Offender program, Chattanooga, 1972-74. Mem. Assn. of Records Mgrs. and Adminstrs. (chpt. pres. 1979-80, program chmn. 1980-81), Nat. Micrographics Assn. (pres. Tenn. Valley chpt. 1982-83), Chattanooga Paralegal Assn., Chattanooga Engrs. Club (pub. dir. for regional sci. and engring. fair 1976-79), Freedoms Found. Am., Assn. Info. and Image Mgmt., Assn. Records Mgmt. (Greater Washington chpt.), Fed. Govt. Micrographics Council. Democrat. Baptist. Clubs: Atlanta Skylarks Flying, Daisy Jr. Women's (pres. 1959-60). Home: 6471 Gildar St Alexandria VA 22310 Office: 2221 Jeff Davis Hwy Arlington VA 22202

FREEMAN, FLORENCE ELEANOR, lawyer; b. Cambridge, Mass., Feb. 25, 1921; s. Elbern and Olive Blanche (Rice) F.; A.B., Wellesley Coll., 1942; J.D., U. Pa., 1945. Bar: Del. 1947, U.S. Dist. Ct. Del. 1948, U.S. Ct. Appeals (3d cir.) 1950, Mass. 1954, U.S. Dist. Ct. Mass. 1960. Assoc., Lynch & Hermann, Wilmington, Del., 1946-53; sole practice, Weston, Mass., 1954-69; ptnr. Freeman & Conceison, Weston, 1970-83, Freeman & White, Weston, 1984—; town counsel Town of Weston, 1968—. Author: (play) Portrait of a Prince, 1965. Pres. Weston LWV, 1960-62, Weston Drama Workshop, 1963-71; mem. bd. selectmen Town of Weston, 1964-68; sec., trustee So. New Eng. Conf. United Meth. Ch., Boston, 1971-74, chancellor, 1976-85; bd. visitors Boston U. Sch. Theology, 1978-86; mem. council fin. and adminstrn. United Meth. Ch., Chgo., 1980—, alt. jud. council, 1980—, chmn. legal responsibilities com. 1984—; dir. Anna Howard Shaw. Mem. ABA, Am. Judicature Soc., Mass. Bar Assn. Republican. Club: Footlight (Boston) (pres. 1962-64); Wellesley Coll. Office: Freeman & White 483 Boston Post Rd Weston MA 02193

FREEMAN, GLORIA MARIE (EDWARDS), entrepreneur, former college official; b. Stanaford, W.Va., Feb. 15, 1939; d. Charles Abron and Helen Marie (Holliday) Edwards; B.S., Va. Union U., 1959; M.A. with highest honors, U. D.C., 1972; Ed.D., Va. Poly. Inst. and State U., 1983; children—Monica Marie, Cletis Anrique. Sec./stenographer to HEW, Washington, 1960-61, to surgeon-gen. USAF, Ramstein AFB, W. Ger., 1961-62; adminstrv. asst. to supt. schs. Dependents Edn., Kaiserslautern, W. Ger., also to Council of Govt., Washington, 1963-64; mgmt. asst. NASA, Washington, 1965; tchr. Chamberlain Vocat. High Sch., Washington, 1964-68; assoc. registrar U. D.C., Washington, 1968-75; registrar Essex County Coll., Newark, 1975-82, Passaic County Coll., 1982-84; self-employed, 1984—; cons. in field, lectr. Edn. com. D.C. Poor People's Campaign, 1968-69; del. Status Black Women's Nat. Conf., 1974; sec. Century Assn. Ednl. Excellence, Newark, 1976-78; recruitment dir. Miss Black Am. Essex County, 1978-80; adviser Montana Terr. Adult Edn. Center, Washington, den mother Boy Scouts Am.; pres. scholarship com. Bethel Baptist Ch.; bd. dirs. Bapt. Tng. Union-Youth. Mem. N.J. Registrars Assn. (sec.-treas. 1975—), Am. Assn. Registrars and Admissions Officers, Orgn. Women for Legal Awareness, Nat. Council Negro Women, Nat. Assn. Women Deans and Counselors, Nat. Assn. Black Adult Educators, Am. Ednl. Research Assn., other orgns. Baptist. Home and Office: 319 Self Pl South Orange NJ 07079

FREEMAN, JOYCE MARY, fast food company executive; b. Arlington, S.D., Dec. 5, 1932; d. Milo Andrew and Orpha Laurinda (Austad) Peterson; m. Meredith N. Freeman, Oct. 23, 1971; stepchildren—James Michael, Judith Ann; children—Mary Ann, Connie Jane, Keith Milo, Dawn Joy. Student N.W. Coll. Commerce, 1951, Dakota State Coll., 1969-71; B.S. summa cum laude, Black Hills State Coll., 1977; postgrad. W.Va., Coll., 1977—. Data processor, payroll, mail and supply clk., sec. Buckingham Transp. Co., Rapid City, S.D., 1951-53; night supr. at nursing home, Arlington, S.D., 1966-67; supr., Dakota State Coll. Alumni Assn. and coordinator Karl E. Mundt Library, Dakota State Coll., Madison, S.D., 1967-71; mgr. fed. program budget Temple U., Phila., 1971; substitute tchr. Mercer County Pub. Schs. (W.Va.), 1977-81; owner, mgr. Taco Hut, Princeton, W.Va., 1978—, Marion, Va., 1980-83, Wytheville, Va., 1981—, Wardrobes Unltd. Princeton, W.Va., 1982—. Mem. AAUW, Nat. Fedn. Ind. Bus., Princeton C. of C., Kappa Delta Pi. Methodist. Home and Office: PO Box 609 Athens WV 24712

FREEMAN, LEAH IDA, automotive company executive; b. Poland, May 12, 1911; came to U.S., 1921; d. Isaac and Norman (Warshawsky) Ziet; widowed; children—Robert, Naomi Bussel. J.D., Porta Law, Boston. Pres., owner N.E. Automotive Wholesalers, Inc., Belleville, N.J. Office: Northeast Automotive Wholesalers Inc 320 Washington Ave Belleville NJ 07109

FREEMAN, PATRICIA ELIZABETH, library and education specialist; b. El Dorado, Ark., Nov. 30, 1924; d. Herbert A. and M. Elizabeth (Pryor) Harper; m. Jack Freeman, June 15, 1949; 3 children. B.A., Centenary Coll., 1943; postgrad. Fine Arts Ctr., 1942-46, Art Students League, 1944-45; B.S.L.S., La. State U., 1946; postgrad. Calif. State U., 1959-61, U. N.Mex., 1964-74; Ed.S., Peabody Coll., Vanderbilt U., 1975. Librarian, U. Calif.-Berkeley, 1946-47, U.S. Air Force, Barksdale AFB, 1948-49, Albuquerque Pub. Schs., 1964-67; ind. sch. library media ctr. cons., 1967—. Painter lithographer; one-person show La. State Exhibit Bldg., 1948; author: Pathfinder: An Operational Guide for the School Librarian, 1975; compiler, editor: Elizabeth Pryor Harper's Twenty-One Southern Families, 1985. Mem. task force Goals for Dallas-Environ., 1977-82; pres. Friends of Sch. Libraries, Dallas, 1979-83. Honoree AAUW Ednl. Found., 1979; vol. award for outstanding service Dallas Ind. Sch. Dist., 1978; AAUW Pub. Service grantee 1980. Mem. ALA, AAUW (dir. Dallas 1976-82, Albuquerque 1983—), LWV (sec. Dallas 1982-83, editor Albuquerque 1984—), Nat. Trust Historic Preservation, Friends of Albuquerque Pub. Library, N.Mex. Symphony Guild, Alpha Xi Delta. Home: 3016 Santa Clara SE Albuquerque NM 87106

FREEMAN, SARA CELESTE, banker; b. Tulsa, Mar. 24, 1948; d. Walter F. and Helen (Smith) F.; B.A., St. Louis U., 1970, M.A., 1974. Teller, Webster Groves Trust Co., St. Louis, 1970-73; grad. asst. St. Louis U., summer 1973, adminstrv. asst. Mental Health Inst., 1973-74; with Bank of Okla., N.A., Tulsa, 1974-82, asst. v.p., 1978-82, v.p., mgr. secured lending adminstrn. dept., 1979-82; v.p., mgr. credit and collateral ops. RepublicBank 1st Nat. Midland (Tex.), 1982-83, div. mgr. credit adminstrn., 1983—; part-time instr. Tulsa Jr. Coll.; instr. banking courses, 1985, 86; guest speaker. Mem. Nat. Assn. Bank Women, Phi Alpha Theta. Author manuals. Office: PO Box 1599 Midland TX 79702

FREEMAN, SHANNON DEAN, banker, lawyer; b. Little Rock, Dec. 21, 1951; d. Eddie Lee and Willie Mae (Shaw) F. B.A. in Polit. Sci. cum laude, Johnson C. Smith U., 1973; J.D., U. Dayton, 1980. Bar: Ohio. Corp. trust adminstr. First Union Nat. Bank, Charlotte, N.C., 1975-80; utility staff atty. Duke Power Co., Charlotte, 1980-82; corp. trust adminstrn. asst. v.p. 1st Nat. Bank of Boston, 1982-84; asst. v.p., trust officer NCNB Nat. Bank N.C., Charlotte, 1984—. Vol. schs., Boston; vol., mgr. Community Tax Aid of Boston. Recipient awards Walter H. Rice Intramural Moot Ct. Competition, 1978, 79, Tri-State Moot Ct., 1979, 80. Mem. ABA, Ohio State Bar, Phi Delta Phi, Sigma Rho Sigma, Alpha Kappa Mu, Delta Sigma Theta (v.p. 1972-73). Office: NCNB National Bank NC One NCNB Plaza Corporate Service Services T10-3 Charlotte NC 28255

FREEMANZON, JUNE, aviation executive; b. Worcester, Mass., Jan. 4, 1933; d. Andrew and Mildred (Mitchell) F. Grad. Fisher Jr. Coll. Sec., Boston U., 1953-56; supr. Alitalia Airlines, N.Y.C., 1956-82; pres. Associated Products of Am., Inc. N.Y.C., 1982—. Founder, N.Y. Pops, 1983—, South St. Seaport Mus., 1967—. Mem. Sales Exec. Club of N.Y., Wings Club. Club: Atrium (N.Y.C.). Avocations: yachting; travel; cooking; horticulture. Office: Associated Products of Am Inc 175 Fifth Ave New York NY 10010

FREGOSI, MARY HELEN, headmaster; b. Proctor, Vt., July 27, 1944; d. Gino Joseph and Vera (Ravellini) F. B.S., U. Vt., 1966, M.A., 1969; postgrad. Universita di Firenze, Italy, 1966-67; M.A., Castleton State Coll., 1978, C.A.G.S., 1984. Tchr., Proctor Jr.-Sr. High Sch., 1969; tchr. Rutland High Sch., Vt., 1969-74, assoc. prin., 1974-80, prin., 1982-83, headmaster, 1983—, curriculum supr., 1980-82; mem. adj. faculty Castleton State Coll., 1981—. Chmn. Proctor Sch. Bd., 1970-74. Fulbright scholar, 1966-67. Mem. Nat. Assn. Secondary Sch. Prins., Assn. Curriculum and Supervision Devel., Vt. Headmasters Assn., New Eng. Assn. Secondary Schs., Kappa Delta Pi, Phi Beta Kappa. Democrat. Roman Catholic. Avocations: golf; reading; swimming. Office: Rutland High Sch Library Ave Rutland VT 05701

FREHNER, ELLEN, association executive; b. Plano, Idaho; children—Dalby, Craig, Lezle Ann, Linden. Cert. chamber exec. Sec., State Dept. Public Assistance, Rexburg, Idaho, 1953; exec. sec. Beneficial Life Inst. Co., Idaho Falls, Idaho, 1954; sec. dept. entomology Ednl. Field Service Placement Bur., U. Idaho, 1954-56; sec. to prin. Basic High Sch., Henderson, Nev., 1956; with telephone ops. dept. Henderson (Nev.) Telephone Co., 1957; publicity asst. Tropicana Hotel, Las Vegas, 1957-58; exec. dir. Henderson C. of C., 1958-72; exec. v.p. North Las Vegas (Nev.) C. of C., 1972—. State commr. EPA, 1973-76; bd. dirs., sec.-treas. So. Nev. Mus.; mem. Gov.'s Com. Fed. Landlaws Bd., 1971; sec. Nev. Indsl. Adv. Council, 1972; mem. State Energy Com., 1978-80; adv. bd. Regina Hall, Inc.; mem. North Las Vegas Planning Commn. Mem. Am. Bus. Woman's Assn., Am. C. of C. Execs. Assn., Nev. State C. of C. (dir.), Mountain States Assn. (pres.). Club: Toastmistress. Home: 1728 Arrowhead North Las Vegas NV 89030 Office: North Las Vegas Chamber of Commerce 1023 E Lake Mead Blvd North Las Vegas NV 89030

FREIDIN, ELLEN CATSMAN, lawyer; b. Miami, Fla., Aug. 24, 1946; d. David Philip and Elinor (Roth) Catsman. B.A., Am. U., 1968; J.D. cum laude, U. Miami, 1978. Dept. mgr. Saks Fifth Ave., Surfside, Fla., 1969-70; asst. buyer Jordan Marsh, Miami, Fla., 1970-71; adminstrv. aide State Senator Richard Pettigrew, 1972-73; campaign mgr. Pettigrew for Senate, Fla., 1973-74; assoc. Floyd, Pearson, Stewart, Richman, Greer & Weil, Miami, 1978-83; sole practice, Miami, 1983-86; of counsel Akerman, Senterfitt & Eidson, 1986—; instr. U. Miami Law Sch., Coral Gables, Fla., 1983-84, adj. prof. media law, 1984—; cir. rep. Fedn. Women Lawyers Jud. Screening Panel, Washington, 1979—; Author articles in law revs. Mem. Overall Econ. Devel. Program Com., Dade County (Fla.), 1979—; mem. Jud. Nominating Commn., Dade County, 1983-86. Mem. Fla. Bar Assn., ABA, Nat. Assn. Women Lawyers, Assn. Trial Lawyers Am., Acad. Fla. Trial Lawyers, Dade County Bar Assn. (bd. dirs. 1983-86) Dade County Trial Lawyers Assn. (bd. dirs., trustee 1980—). Office: 801 Brickell Ave 24th Floor Miami FL 33131

FREIER, SUSAN MARCIE, music educator, violinist; b. Bklyn., Dec. 13, 1953; d. George David and Ruth (Hollenberg) F.; m. Benjamin A. Miller, May 24, 1981; 1 child, Sarah. B.S., Stanford U., 1975, B.A., 1975; M.A., 1976; Mus.M., Eastman Sch. Music, 1980. Asst. prof. violin Ind. U., South Bend, 1980—; in residence Garth Newel Music Camp, summer 1985, Downeast Music Camp, Maine, summers 1984, 85, Grand Teton Music Festival, Wyo., summers 1980-84; vis. resident mem. string quartet Tex. Christian U., Ft. Worth, 1985—; mem. Chester String Quartet, 1978—; coach, South Bend Youth Symphony, 1980—. Winner top awards in quartet competitions, Munich, Germany, Portsmouth, Eng., Chgo. Mem. Chamber Music Soc. Am. Avocations: hiking; jogging. Office: Ind U Dept Music 1700 Mishawaka St South Bend IN 46634

FREILICHER, JANE, artist; b. N.Y.C., Nov. 29, 1924; B.A., Bklyn. Coll.; M.A., Columbia U.; studied Hans Hofmann Sch.; studied art history with Meyer Schapiro. One-woman shows include: Tibor de Nagy Gallery, N.Y.C., 14 exhbns., 1952—, Fischbach Gallery, N.Y.C., 1975, 77, 79, 80, 83, 84, Utah Mus. Fine Arts, 1979, Lafayette Coll., 1981, Coll. of the Mainland, 1982; group shows include: Whitney Mus. Am. Art Ann., 1955—, Vassar Coll., 1968, Dept. Interior Traveling Show, 1976, Denver Mus. Art, 1979, Met. Mus. Art, N.Y.C., 1979; vis. critic and lectr. U. Pa. Grad. Sch. Fine Arts, Skowhegan Sch. Art, Carnegie-Mellon Inst., Sch. of Mus. Fine Arts, Boston, Coll. Creative Studies, U. Calif., Santa Barbara. Recipient Hallmark Internat. Art award, 1960; AAUW award, 1974; Nat. Endowment for Arts grantee, 1976. Mem. NAD. Illustrator: Turandot and Other Poems, 1953; Paris Review (portfolio of drawings), 1965; subject of articles and revs.

FREIRE DE RODRIGUEZ, LINDA, company executive; b. N.Y.C., Apr. 23, 1946; d. Ramon and Luz (Montalvo) Freire; m. Rafael A. Rodriguez Mehrhof, June 5, 1971; 1 son, Eduardo Andres Rodriguez Freire. B.B.A., World U., Hato Rey, P.R., 1982, J.D., Interam. U., Santurce, P.R., 1984. Sec., Island Fin. Corp., Rio Piedras, P.R., 1965-67; statis. clerk Parke-Davis & Co., Carolina, P.R., 1967-70; purchasing asst. SK&F Co., Carolina, 1970-76, purchasing supr., 1976-77, personnel tech., 1977-79, administrator, 1979—. Editor: La Capsula (best cos. newspaper 1983), 1977. Active Vocat. and Rehab. Orgn. Com., Caguas, P.R., 1983. Mem. Am. Soc. Personnel Adminstrs., Assn. Labor Relations Practitioners, P.R. Mfrs. Assn. (indls. relations com.), P.R. Indsl. Editors Assn. (pres. 1980-81, v.p. 1978-80). Home: Cond Norte Plaza Apt 304 219 Rosario St Santurce PR 00912 Office: SK&F Co PO Box 745 Cidra PR 00639

FREITAS, ANTOINETTE JUNI, insurance company executive; b. Kansas City, Mo., Feb. 14, 1944; d. Anthony P. and Mariam L. Freitas; B.A., Calif. State U.-Long Beach, 1966; M.A., U. So. Calif., 1974; m. Stephen R. Krajcar, July 4, 1980. C.L.U., chartered life underwriter. Counselor, U. So. Calif., 1967-70, assoc. dir. fin. aid, 1970-75; sales agt. Equitable Life Assurance Co., 1975-79, dist. mgr., San Francisco, 1979-84; pres. Group Mktg. Services, Inc., field dir. Northwestern Mut. Life, San Francisco, 1984-86; pres. Freitas-Krajcar and Assocs., 1986—; mktg. mgr. Home Life, H.L. Fin. Group, San Jose, Calif., 1986—; registered rep. W.S. Griffith Co., securities. Recipient various sales and mgmt. awards; mem. Million Dollar Round Table. Mem. Nat. Assn. Life Underwriters, AAUW, U. So. Calif. Alumni Assn., Women Life Underwriters Conf. Republican. Episcopalian. Author: A Study in Changing Youth Values, 1974. Office: HL Financial Group N 1st St Plaza Suite 360 San Jose CA 95131

FREITAS, SUSAN CHESNEY, management trainer; b. N.Y.C., Aug. 12, 1943; d. Morton and Tillie (Talmadge) Chesney; m. Donald Lewis Freitas, Sept. 17, 1967 (div. May 1976); m. Robert Martin Rosenblatt, Apr. 9, 1980. A.B., U. Calif.-Berkeley, 1967. Placement interviewer U. Calif., Berkeley, 1972-74, program coordinator, 1974-79; personnel adminstr. Hewlett-Packard Co., Santa Rosa, Calif., 1982-84; pres. Mgmt. Resources, Santa Rosa, 1984—; cons. Kensington Electronics Group, Healdsburg, Calif., 1984-85, Behavioral Medicine Assocs., Santa Rosa, 1985—. Bd. dirs. Sonoma County Respite Services, Santa Rosa, 1985-86; bd. dirs., sec. Sonoma County Forum, 1986. Mem. Nat. Assn. Female Execs. Avocations: Asian cooking; gardening; music. Office: Mgmt Resources 2125 Hyland Ct Santa Rosa CA 95404

FREITAS, SUSAN ELAINE, training workshop company executive; b. Mexia, Tex., Apr. 28, 1946; d. Deward Forest and Charlene (Fetty) LeFevre; m. Michael Woodford Freitas, Apr. 29, 1967 (div.); children—Shannon Marie, Mika Michelle, Lindsay Lea. Student Navaro Jr. Coll., 1964-65. Legal sec. Alexander Firm, Dallas, 1965-68; self employed builder, bldg. sales rep., Dallas, 1976-81; tng. sales rep. Discovery Workshops, Dallas, 1982; owner, pres. TIPS, Dallas, 1982—. Mem. Home Builders of Carrollton (sec. 1981-82), Nat. Assn. Female Execs., Am. Soc. Tng. and Devel., Assn. Women Entrepreneurs of Dallas (scholarship chmn.). Republican. Methodist. Address: 13806 Wooded Creek Dallas TX 75234

FREIWALD, JOYCE GROSS, congressional staff, energy specialist; b. Fulton, Mo., June 22, 1944; d. Fred Alfred and Susan (Kist) Gross; B.S. in Math. (scholar), U. N.Mex., 1966; postgrad. in math. and physics, 1967-68, M.Arch. (scholar), 1976; m. David Allen Freiwald, Apr. 3, 1976; children—Wesley, Todd, Christopher. Mathematician, Air Force Weapons Lab., Albuquerque, 1963-65, Sandia Nat. Lab., Albuquerque, 1966-69; owner, mgr. Costello Cons. Co., Albuquerque, 1970-72; scientist Sci. Applications, Inc., Albuquerque, 1973-75; pres. Phoenix Forth, Inc., Albuquerque, 1975-76; mem. staff Los Alamos Nat. Lab., 1976-81; Republican staff dir. U.S. Ho. Reps. Com. on Sci. and Tech., Washington, 1981—. Candidate for Albuquerque City Commn., 1970, N.Mex. Senate, 1971; chairwoman N.Mex. Equal Rights Legis. Com., 1972, Citizen's Coalition for Land Use Planning, 1975; former mem. various state and county bds. and commns. Mem. Assn. Women in Sci., N.Mex. Women in Sci., Am. Nuclear Soc., Am. Astron. Soc., Women in Aerospace, AAUW, AAAS, Nat. Assn. Female Execs., Phi Kappa Phi, Kappa Mu Epsilon, Alpha Delta Pi. Republican. Contbr. numerous articles on energy, environ. and tech. issues to profl. jours. Home: 10401 LLoyd Rd Potomac MD 20854 Office: 2320 Rayburn House Office Bldg Washington DC 20515

FRELICH, PHYLLIS, actress; b. Devils Lake, N.D., Feb. 29, 1944; d. Phillip and Esther (Dockter) F.; m. Robert Steinberg, May 17, 1968; children—Reuben, Joshua. B.S. in Library Sci., Gallaudet Coll., 1967. Acting tchr. Nat. Theater of the Deaf, Waterford, Conn., 1977-79, 83, R.I. Sch. for Deaf, Providence, 1977-78, U. R.I., North Kingston, 1978; appeared in numerous stage plays, 1965—; latest being Woyzeck, all with Nat. Theatre of the Deaf, 1979, Songs from Milkwood, Broadway, Children of a Lesser God, Broadway, 1980; theater appearances in "The Hands of Its Enemy", Los Angeles, 1984 (Los Angeles Dramalogue award 1985), "The Debutante Ball", Costa Mesa, Calif., 1985; dir. Gin Game, N.Y. Deaf Theatre. Recipient Humanitarian award Gallaudet Coll., 1980; Rough Rider award State of N.D., 1981; California's Year of Handicapped award, 1980; Critic's Circle award, 1980; Tony award, 1980. Mem. Screen Actors Guild, Actors Equity Assn., Nat. Assn. Deaf. Office: care Bret Adams Ltd 448 W 44th St New York NY 10036

FRELS, LOIS MARIAN PARNELL (MRS. CALVIN EDWIN FRELS), educator; b. Geneseo, Ill., Nov. 20, 1929; d. Floyd Vinton and Mary Jane (Davis) Parnell; R.N., Moline (Ill.) Pub. Hosp., 1950; student pub. Health U. Minn., Loyola U., Chgo., 1951-54; B.N.S., Augustana Coll., Rock Island, Ill., 1959; M.A., U. Iowa, 1964; diploma for testing, Marianne Frostic Center Ednl. Therapy, Los Angeles, 1969; Ph.D., U. Minn., 1977; m. Calvin Edwin Frels, Oct. 28, 1950; children—Mark Edwin, Arlan James. Sch. nurse East Moline Elementary Schs., 1951-54; pub. health work East Moline Vis. Nurses Assn., 1955-57; sch. nurse, project dir., nurse cons. United Twp. High Sch., East Moline, 1957-67; instr. psychology Blackhawk Jr. Coll., Moline, part time 1966-68; tchr., dir. gifted program Silvis (Ill.) Elementary Schs., 1968; counselor Pleasant Valley (Ia.) High Sch., 1969-70; asst. prof. Marycrest Coll., Davenport, Iowa, 1970-73; chmn. nursing div. Iowa Wesleyan Coll., Mt. Pleasant, 1973-76; dir. div. nursing Bradley U., Peoria, Ill., 1976—. Sec., East Moline Community Resource Council, 1965-67; mem. Riverdale Unit 100 Bd. Edn., Port Byron, Ill., 1964-67, 68-73; chmn. Rock Island County Fact Finding Com. White House Conf. Children and Youth, 1970; organizer Little White House Conf. Children and Youth, Rock Island County, 1969; del. Nat. White House Conf. on Children and Youth, 1970; 2d v.p. Rock Island Country Welfare Council, 1968-70. Bd. dirs. Opportunity Mentally Handicapped. Ill. Dept. Pub. Recipient Mergen award Bradley U. Instrn. grantee Western Ill. U., 1968; Nurse traineeship grantee, 1973. Fellow Am. Sch. Health Assn. (chmn. sch. nurse study com. 1973-77, disting. service award 1978; chmn. sch. nurse subcom. 1984-86), mem. Nat. League Nursing, Iowa Citizens League for Nursing (pres. 1975-77), Am., Ill. nurses assns., Am. Edn. Research Assn., Am., Ill. public health assns., Ill. Sch. Health Assn. (chmn. legis. resolutions com. 1986), Nat. League Nursing (sec. Midland regional assembly 1979—), Ill. League Nursing (pres. 1983-84), Royal Soc. Health (London, Eng.), Am. Assn. Colls. Nursing, Phi Kappa Phi, Sigma Theta Tau, Pi Lambda Theta. Editorial bd. Jour. Sch. Health. Home: 25329 1st Ave N Hillsdale IL 61257

FREMONT-SMITH, MARION R., lawyer; b. Boston, Oct. 29, 1926; d. Max and Frances (Davis) Ritvo; m. Joseph Miller, Sept. 12, 1948 (div.); children—Beth Miller Hanson, Keith Lane, E. Bradley; m. 2d, Paul Fremont-Smith, July 6, 1961. B.A. with high honors, Wellesley Coll., 1948; J.D. cum laude, Boston U., 1951. Bar: Mass. 1951, U.S. Supreme Ct. 1979. Instr. dept. polit. sci. Wellesley (Mass.) Coll., 1958-59; asst. atty. gen., dir. div. pub. charities Commonwealth of Mass., Boston, 1961-62; project dir. Russell Sage Found., N.Y.C., 1963-65; assoc. firm Choate, Hall & Stewart, Boston, 1964-71, ptnr., 1971—, now head of estate planning dept.; mem. Boston Tax Forum, Ind. Sector Govt. Relations Com., Washington, Gov.'s Adv. Task Force on Dept. of Revenue, Boston; mem. adv. com. on trusts U.S. Dept. State; bd. dirs. Fed. Tax Inst. New Eng., Boston, Ind. Factor. Author: Foundations and Government, 1965; Philanthropy and the Business Corporation, 1972. Trustee The Found. Ctr., N.Y.C., 1970-76, Greater Boston Fund for Internat. Affairs, 1972—, Carnegie Endowment for Internat. Peace, 1972—; overseer Mus. Sci., Boston, 1971—, Mus. Fine Arts, Boston, 1983—; bd. dirs. Council on Founds., Washington, 1971-76, Forsyth Dental Ctr., Boston, 1978—. Fellow Am. Bar Found., Am. Coll. Probate Counsel, Am. Coll. Tax Counsel, Am. Law Inst.; mem. ABA (sect. taxation, com. on founds., sect. on real property, probate and trust law, com. on charities, vice chmn. sect. on taxation, com. on exempt orgns.), Boston Bar Assn. Office: Choate Hall & Stewart 53 State St Boston MA 02109

FRENCH, BECKY RUSSELL, lawyer, educator; b. Charleston, Mo., Dec. 4, 1953; d. William C. and Billie (Summers) Russell; m. Robert R. French, Mar. 18, 1971 (div. 1978); m. 2d, William Dennis Harazin, Mar. 13, 1981. B.S. in Bus. Adminstrn. Southeast Mo. State U., 1976; J.D., So. Ill. U., 1978; grad. Govt. Exec. Inst., U. N.C., 1982. Bar: Ill. 1979, N.C. 1982. Instr. Sch. Fin., So. Ill. U., 1978; legal asst. Sato & Tsuda, Tokyo, summer 1978; hearing officer State of N.C., Raleigh, 1979-80, dir. office adminstrv. hearings, 1980-84; adj. bus. law instr. N.C. State U., Raleigh, 1983—, contracts, patents officer, 1984-85, dir. Office of Tech. Adminstrn., 1985—, instr., 1982—, asst. univ. counsel, 1986—; instr. So. Ill. U., 1977-78. Bd. dirs. Down-Town Housing Improvement Corp., Raleigh, 1983—. Mem. ABA, N.C. Bar Assn., Am. Judicature Soc., Ill. Bar Assn. Methodist. Club: Hist. Oakwood Assn. (Raleigh).

FRENCH, BRENDA CAROLYN, computer company executive; b. Newburyport, Mass., May 16, 1940; d. Arthur Charles and Emily Lancey (Reid) Browne; m. Richard Enright French, Feb. 17, 1968; 1 son, Richard Enright. B.A. cum laude, U.N.H., 1961; M.A., Simmons Coll., 1977. With Digital Equipment Corp., Maynard, Mass., 1977—, material mgr., 1979-80, strategic planning mgr., 1980—. Adviser urban renewal project Hist. Commn., Newburyport, 1973-75; mgr. continuing edn. Newburyport YMCA, 1964-75. Mem. Simmons Alumni Assn. Unitarian. Office: Digital Equipment Corp Digital Dr Westminster MA 01473

FRENCH, CYNTHIA WALKER, medical center administrator; b. Moultrie, Ga., Jan. 6, 1960; d. Gilbert O'Neal and Corinne Maria (Covington) Walker; m. Nathaniel French, July 25, 1981; children—Shelia Michelle, Nathaniel. B.S. in Nursing, Valdosta State Coll., 1981. Staff nurse Colquitt Regional Med. Ctr., Moultrie, 1980-81, Columbus Med. Ctr., Ga., 1981-82; office nurse Dr. Newborn's Office, Moultrie, 1982-83; charge nurse Colquitt Regional Med. Ctr., Moultrie, 1982-85, asst. clin. dir., 1986—; inservice dir. Moultrie Rest a While, 1984-86. Mem. Ga. Assn. Nurses, Nat. Assn. Women Execs., Alpha Kappa Alpha. Democrat. Methodist. Avocations: piano, crafts, cooking.

FRENCH, ELIZABETH CHAMBERLAIN, harpsichordist, ednl. adminstr.; b. Altoona, Pa., Aug. 16, 1929; d. Alton Francis and Margaret (Griffith) Chamberlain; B.Mus. in Edn. with honors, Wheaton Coll., 1951; M.Mus., Coll. Conservatory of Music, U. Cin., 1963; postgrad. Peabody Conservatory of Music, 1967-70; Dr.Mus.Arts, Boston U., 1975; postgrad. U. Ariz., 1978; children—Eugene Thurman Vest, Jonathan Mark Vest, Harry Allan Vest, Michael Robert Vest. Dir. music Westminster Presbyn. Ch., Bluefield, W.Va., 1951-53, Bland St. Meth. Ch., Bluefield, 1959-70; instr. music Concord Coll., Athens, W.Va., 1964-66, asst. prof., 1966-70; mus. dir. Barter Theater, Abingdon, Va., 1968; dir. music Episcopal Ch. of St. Matthew, Tucson, 1973-76; organist Trinity Presbyn. Ch., Tucson, 1976-78; sr. staff asso. for acad. affairs Ala. Commn. on Higher Edn., Montgomery, 1978-82, asst. dir., 1982—; profl. appearances as harpsichord and organ recitalist in Ohio, Ky., W.Va., S.C., Mass., Ariz., Ala., 1951—; harpsichordist with chamber ensemble, Birmingham Musica Antiqua, 1980-83; dir. music Temple Beth Or, Montgomery, 1980—. Mem. Episcopal Diocesan Music Commn., State of Ariz., 1973-78; mem. Gov.'s Study Commn. on Library Coop., State of Ala., 1979-81; bd. dirs. Friends of Temple of Music and Art, Tucson, 1975-78; mem. exec. bd. Pres.'s Council of Montgomery, 1981-83; Montgomery bd. dirs. Ala. Symphony, 1980-81; mem. Ala. Pub. Library Service Adv. Council, 1981-84, chmn., 1982; mem. Ala. Hist. Records Adv. Bd. Task Force, 1984-85; chmn. State Higher Edn. Officers Nat. Planning Com., 1984; bd. dirs. Arrowhead Townhouse Owners Assn., 1979-80, 84-85, pres., 1984-85; mem. Montgomery Bus. Com.

for the Arts, 1983—. Mem. AAUW, Coll. Music Soc., Am. Musico. Soc., Am. Assn. Higher Edn., Assn. Study Higher Edn., Am. Guild Organists (Ala. state chmn. 1981—, regional chmn. ednl. concerns 1985—), Southeastern Hist. Keyboard Soc. (exec. bd. 1982-85), Phi Kappa Phi. Club: Capital City. Contbr. articles to profl. jours. Home: 37 Tecumseh Dr Montgomery AL 36117 Office: Suite 221 One Court Sq Montgomery AL 36104

FRENCH, GEORGINE LOUISE, guidance counselor; b. Lancaster, Pa., May 15, 1934; d. Richard Franklin and Elizabeth Georgine (Driesbach) Beacham; B.A., Calif. State U., San Bernardino, 1967; M.S., No. Ill. U., 1973; D.D., Am. Ministerial Assn., 1978; m. Barrie J. French, Feb. 4, 1956; children—Joel B., John D., James D., Jeffrey D. Personnel counselor Sages Dept. Store, San Bernardino, 1965-66; asst. bookkeeper Bank Calif., San Bernardino, 1964-65; tchr. Livermore (Calif.) Sch. Dist., 1968-69; guidance counselor Bur. Indian Affairs, Tuba City, Ariz., 1974-80, Sherman Indian High Sch., Riverside, Calif., 1980-82, Ft. Douglas Edn. Ctr., U.S. Army, Salt. Lake City, 1982—; extension tchr. Navajo Community Coll., Yavapai Jr. Coll.; personnel counselor USNR; ordained to ministry Am. Ministerial Assn., 1979. Served with USAF, 1954-56. Recipient Sustained Superior Performance certs. U.S. Army, 1983, 84, 85. Cert. guidance counselor, secondary tchr. Mem. Am. Assn. Counseling and Devel. Home: PO Box 8734 Salt Lake City UT 84108 Office: Army Edn Ctr Fort Douglas UT 84113

FRENCH, JEANA TURNER, health and social services agency executive; b. Tallahassee, Fla., Feb. 22, 1947; d. Cleveland Adelbert and Myra Alice (Hartsfield) Turner; B.S., Fla. State U., 1967, M.S., 1970, Ph.D., 1972; m. John H. French, Jr., Dec. 27, 1966. Tchr. 2d grade Leon County Sch. System, Tallahassee, 1967-69, tchr. Head Start program, 1968; instr. early childhood edn. Fla. State U., Tallahassee, 1969-71, program coordinator, academic advisor, 1971-72, asst. prof., 1974-78; mental health program analyst Fla. Dept. Health and Rehab. Services, 1978-79, tng. mgr., 1979-81, dir. staff devel. and tng., 1981—; curriculum specialist Wakulla County, Crawfordville, Fla., 1972-73; dir. evaluation and research Choctaw Reservation Project, Philadelphia, Miss., 1973-74; cons. Cherokee (N.C.) Reservation Evaluation and Research Project, 1973-74; cons. Metcor, Inc., Washington, 1973-74; mem. 25th anniversary commemoration com. Fla. State U., 1972; mem. Fla. Democratic Credentials Com., 1972; instr. Fla. Dem. Polit. Leadership Schs., 1974; mem. adv. bd. Sch. Social Work, Fla. State U., 1981—; mem. steering com. Ctr. for Pub. Affairs and Govt. Services, 1985—; mem. Leon County (Fla.) Dem. Com., 1979-81; del. Fla. Dem. Primary Conv., 1984. Mem. Fla. State U. Coll. Edn. Alumni Assn. (dir. 1976-78, 85—), Nat. Assn. Edn. of Young Children, Fla. Assn. Children Under Six, Nat. Council Social Studies, Assn. Childhood Edn., Am. Soc. Tng. and Devel., Internat. Reading Assn., Fla. State U. Alumni Assn. (dir. 1984—), Phi Kappa Phi, Kappa Delta Pi, Phi Delta Kappa, Alpha Gamma Delta. Democrat. Methodist. Contbr. bibliography, research papers in field. Home: 1206 Sarasota Dr Tallahassee FL 32301 Office: 1317 Winewood Blvd Bldg 3 Room 205 Tallahasse FL 32301

FRENCH, JOYCE NORTON, educational administrator; b. Buffalo, NY., Dec. 9, 1929; d. Thomas Lowell and Verna (Cutler) Norton; B.A., Wellesley Coll., 1951; M.S., U. Bridgeport, 1967; Ph.D., Columbia U., 1976; m. Donald F. French, June 11, 1951; children—Susan Linda French Falk, Richard Norton. Tchr., Greenwich (Conn.) Public Schs., 1965-70; head lower and middle schs. Greenwich Country Day Sch., 1970-76; dir. tchr. edn. Manhattanville Coll., Purchase, N.Y., 1977-85; vis. prof. Columbia U., N.Y.C., 1980-81; cons. pub. and pvt. schs. Research Inst. for Study of Learning Disabilities research fellow Columbia U., 1978-80. Mem. Am. Psychol. Assn., Internat. Reading Assn., N.Y. Acad. Scis., Internat. Platform Assn., Sigma Xi. Contbr. articles to profl. publs.; author books in field. Home: 185 Shore Rd Old Greenwich CT 06870 Office: Manhattanville Coll Purchase NY 10577

FRENCH, KAREN BONITA, real estate loan specialist; b. Conway, Ark., Sept. 12, 1952; d. Rudolph and Bernice Ruth (Gault) Wilson; m. Thomas John French, III, Sept. 10, 1974 (div. 1979); 1 son, Christopher Shane. B.A., Pittsburg U., 1974; postgrad. U. Kans. 1975-76, U. Mo.-Kansas City, 1982. Cert. real estate broker, Mo. Retail mgr., buyer Woolf Bros., Kansas City, Mo., 1976-79; tng. coordinator Minority Contractors, Kansas City, 1979-81; tng. coordinator Housing Devel. Corp., Kansas City, 1981-82, grants writer, 1979—, job placement officer, 1979-82; fin. mgr., 1982-83, chief loan officer, 1983—, grants writer minority contractors, 1979—, job placement officer, 1979-82; cons. Martin L. King Urban Ctr., 1978-80; EEO officer Community Services Adminstrn., 1979-81. Alt. del. Democratic Nat. Conv., 1984. Contbr. articles to profl. jours.; actress video drama Reflections - The Niles Home, 1984. Vice pres. communications Freedom, Inc., Kansas City, 1982-84. Mem. Nat. Tech. Assn. (v.p.) Kansas City C. of C. (cert. of appreciation 1983), NAACP, Alpha Kappa Alpha. Democrat. Methodist. Club: MC Players. Office: Housing Devel Corp 306 E 12th St Suite 535 Kansas City MO 64106

FRENCH, ROSEANN SODARO, communications company executive, real estate broker; b. Charleston, W.Va., Nov. 20, 1946; d. George Edward and Eloise (Neeley) Sodaro; m. George William French, May 6, 1967. Student Center Coll., Charleston, 1966, Morris Harvey Coll., Charleston, 1966-69. Lic. real estate broker, W.Va. Dist. sales mgr. Avon Products, Charleston, 1974-77; nat. sales mgr. Med-Pak Corp., Charleston, 1977-81; pres. French and Assocs., Charleston, 1982—; br. mgr. MCI Telecommunications, Charleston, 1984—. Mem. Nat. Assn. Realtors. Clubs: Quota (pres. 1980-82), Pilot. Home: 2050 Smith Rd Charleston WV 25314 Office: MCI Telecommunications 405 Capitol St Charleston WV 25301

FRENCH, STEPHANIE TAYLOR, arts administrator; b. Newark; d. William Taylor and Connie V. French; B.A., Wellesley Coll., 1972; M.B.A., Harvard U., 1978; m. Amory Houghton, III, Sept. 8, 1979; 1 dau., Christina French Houghton. Traffic mgr. Radio Sta. KFRC, 1973-74; dir. European Gallery, San Francisco, 1974-75; acct. exec. Young & Rubican, N.Y.C., 1978-79; acct. supr. Rives Smith Baldwin & Carlberg, Houston, 1980-81; mgr. cultural affairs and spl. programs Philip Morris Cos. Inc., N.Y.C., 1981—; free-lance on-air talent and prodn. San Francisco and Oakland cable TV stas., 1973-76. Bd. dirs. Twyla Tharp Dance Co., Art Table; co-chmn. producers council Bklyn. Acad. Music; co-chmn. Assocs. of Babies Hosp., Columbia Presbyn. Med. Ctr. Clubs: Harvard Bus. Sch., Wellesley. Home: 161 E 90th St Apt 2C New York NY 10128 Office: 120 Park Ave New York NY 10017

FRENGUT, RENEE HIRSCH, marketing research executive; b. N.Y.C., May 14, 1945; d. Erich F. and Eleanore F. (Kaplan) Hirsch; B.A., CCNY, 1966; M.A., Yeshiva U., 1968, Ph.D. (NIMH fellow), 1977. Instr. (part-time) dept. psychology N.Y. Inst. Tech., N.Y.C., 1968-69; clin. intern N.Y. State Psychiat. Inst., Columbia U. Coll. Physicians and Surgeons, 1969-70; staff psychologist Westchester County Community Mental Health Bd., 1970-71; staff psychologist Abbott House for Children, Irvington, N.Y., 1971-72, supr. exptl. therapeutic group homes, 1971-72; mem. faculty dept. psychology Montgomery Coll., Rockville, Md., 1972-74; staff psychologist Potomac Found. for Mental Health, Rockville, Md., 1973-75; pvt. practice clin. psychology, 1974-77; research cons. social research div. NBC, N.Y.C., 1976; qualitative media research cons. R.H. Bruskin Assocs., New Brunswick, N.J., 1976; lectr. (part-time) psychology Mercy Coll., Dobbs Ferry, N.Y., 1976-78; research group head The Nowland Orgn., Greenwich, Conn., 1977-78; pres. Qualitative Decisions Center, Inc., N.Y.C., 1978-84, Market Insights, Inc., Bronxville, N.Y., 1984—. Cert. psychologist. Mem. Am. Psychol. Assn., Am. Mktg. Assn. Office: 270 Bronxville Rd Bronxville NY 10708

FRENI, MIRELLA, soprano; b. Modena, Italy, Feb. 27, 1935; d. Ennio and Gianna F.; m. Leone Magiera, 1955; 1 dau., Micaela. Debut as Micaela in Carmen, Modena, 1955; since has appeared in major opera house throughout world, including La Scala, Royal Opera House, Covent Garden, Met. Opera, Vienna State Opera, Paris Opera, Salzburg Festival, Glyndebourne Festival; appeared in film Madame Butterfly and U.S. pub. TV broadcast of The Marriage of Figaro; major roles include: Nanetta in Falstaff, Mimi in La Boheme, Violetta in La Traviatta, Desdemona in Otello, Zerlina in Don Giovanni; appeared on numerous operatic recs., including Carmen (Grammy award for best opera rec. 1964). Office: care Hervert H Breslin Inc 119 W 57th St New York NY 10019*

FRERICHS, KATHRYN MARIE, nurse; b. Ransomville, N.Y., May 21, 1944; d. Gordon Douglas and Marie Lorraine (Faery) Goodman; m. Adrian E. Frerichs, Apr. 15, 1966; children—Tracey, Steven, Rebecca. R.N., Buffalo Gen. Hosp., 1965; U.B., SUNY, 1968; B.S.N. candidate Niagara U., 1984—. Cert. adminstr. Am. Nurses Assn. Staff nurse Buffalo Gen. Hosp., 1965-66; staff nurse New Fane Intercommunity Meml. Hosp. (N.Y.), 1966-68, supr., 1968-75, asst. dir. nursing services, 1975-78, dir. nursing services, 1978—. Active Wilson PTA, YWCA, 4-H Niagara County; softball coach Wilson Little League, 1980—. Niagara County Aux. Med. Assn. scholar, 1962; recipient Best Bedside Nurse award Class 1965 Buffalo Gen. Hosp., 1965. Mem. Alumni Assn. Buffalo Gen. Sch. Nursing, Dist. 1 N.Y. State Nurses Assn., Western N.Y. Nursing Service Adminstrs. Assn., Am. Hosp. Nursing Service Adminstrs. Assn. Roman Catholic. Club: Our Lady Rosary Altar and Rosary Soc. Home: 2707 Wilson-Cambria Rd Wilson NY 14172 Office: Intercommunity Meml Hosp 2600 William St Newfane NY 14108

FRESCOLN, KATHARINE PITMAN, emeritus history educator; b. Swarthmore, Pa., May 9, 1917; d. John Himes and Katharine Elsie (Anders) Pitman; m. Joseph Wright Frescoln, Jan. 6, 1942. A.B., Wittenberg U., 1965; M.A., W.Va. U., 1966, Ph.D., 1971. Social studies tchr. sch. Parsons, W.Va., 1963-65; instr., asst. prof., assoc. prof. history Shepherd Coll., Shepherdstown, W.Va., 1967-75, prof., 1975-85, prof. emeritus, 1985—. Contbr. articles to profl. jours. Samuel Sprecker scholar, 1959. Mem. Am. Hist. Assn., Am. Assn. for Advancement Slavic Studies, N.Am. Conf. on Brit. Studies, MidAtlantic Conf. on Brit. Studies, So. Conf. on Slavic Studies, DAR, Phi Alpha Theta (Internat. councillor 1980-82). Home: Heatherfield PO Box 683 Shepherdstown WV 25443

FRESKOS, ROSEMARY, journalist, editor, publisher, correspondent; b. Chgo., Aug. 24, 1934; d. Ralph and Rosalia (Armendariz) Diaz; m. John M. Freskos, Nov. 13, 1955; children—John, Elena. Student U. Calif.-Berkeley, 1952, Chgo. Art Inst., 1953-54, Cleve. Inst. Art, 1969-72, Kent State U., 1972-73. Cert. travel agt. Sec. various companies, Chgo., 1953-61; ski instr. The Ski Haus, Cleve., 1969-73; tchr. enameling Valley Art Ctr., Chagrin Falls, Ohio, 1973-74; travel agt. Chagrin Station, Chagrin Falls, 1974-75; free-lance writer Sun Newspapers, Cleve., 1973-76; pres., editor Ski Sun, Inc. Publs., Chagrin Falls, 1978—; midwest corr. The Ski Industry Letter, 1983—; contbr. Ski Magazine, 1979—, Ski Bus. Tabloid, 1983—, various ski trade jours., 1973—; editor, pub. Annual Directory Ohio Ski Clubs, 1979—. Mem. U.S. Ski Writers Assn. (pres. 1985—), Midwest Ski Writers Assn. (pres. 1978-81), Nat. Sportscasters and Sports Writers Assn., Assn. Internat. de la Presse Sportive, Outdoor Writers Assn., Chagrin Valley Art Assn. (First prize enameling 1977), Aircraft Owners and Pilots Assn. Roman Catholic. Club: Cleve. Press. Avocations: flying; cooking; tennis; golf; gardening; scuba diving; art. Home and Office: PO Box 943 Avon CO 81620

FREUND, CAROL LOUISE, social service agency administrator; b. Mineola, N.Y., Feb. 21, 1933; d. Warren Edwin and Dorothy Geraldine (Gilbrech) Darnell; m. Curtis B. Bennett, Jr., July 17, 1954 (dec. 1959); m. William O.H. Freund, Jr., Sept. 16, 1960; children—Carol Burnam, William O.H., 3d. B.A., Allegheny Coll., 1954; M.A., John Carroll U., 1982. Tchr. South Euclid Lyndhurst City Schs., Ohio, 1955-57; trainer Episcopal Diocese of Ohio, Cleve., 1972—; exec. dir. Hitchcock House, Cleve., 1983—. Mem. adv. com. Women and Alcohol Project, Cleve., 1983—; mem. council agy. execs. United Way Services, Cleve., 1983—; mem., v.p. Children's Services, Cleve., 1965-75; pres. Shaker Heights PTA, 1975-76, Cleve. Internat. Program, 1980-83; 1st v.p. Council Internat. Programs, 1984—. Recipient Outstanding Vol. Service award Cleve. Internat. Program, 1983, Founding Trustee award Edn. for Freedom of Choice in Ohio, 1982, Cert. Recognition, Council Internat. Programs, 1981. Episcopalian. Avocation: flower arranger. Home: 2850 Broxton Rd Shaker Heights OH 44120 Office: Hitchcock House 10917 Magnolia Dr Cleveland OH 44106

FREUND, EMMA FRANCES, medical technologist; b. Washington; d. Walter R. and Mabel W. (Loveland) Ervin; B.S., Wilson Tchrs. Coll., Washington, 1944; M.S. in Biology, Catholic U., Washington, 1953; cert. in mgmt. devel. Va. Commonwealth U., 1975; student SUNY, New Paltz, 1977, J. Sargeant Reynolds Community Coll., 1978; m. Frederic Reinert Freund, Mar. 4, 1953; children—Frances, Daphne, Fern, Frederic. Tchr. math. and sci. D.C. Sch. System, 1944-45; technician in parasitology lab., zool. div., U.S. Dept. Agr., Beltsville, Md., 1945-48; histologic technician dept. pathology Georgetown U. Med. Sch., Washington, 1948-49; clin. lab. technician Kent and Queen Anne's County Gen. Hosp., Chestertown, Md., 1949-51; histotechnologist surg. pathology dept. Med. Coll. Va. Hosp., Richmond, 1951—, supr. histology lab., 1970—; mem. exam. council Nat. Cert. Agy. Med. Lab. Personnel. Author: Instrumentation in Cytology and Histology, 1985. Asst. cub scout den leader Robert E. Lee council Boy Scouts Am., 1967-68, den leader, 1968-70. Cert. Nat. Cert. Agy. for Clin. Lab. Personnel. Mem. Am. Soc. Med. Technology (rep. to sci. assembly histology sect. 1977-78, chmn. histology sect. 1983-85), Va. Soc. Med. Technology (chmn. cytology sect. 1985-86), Richmond Soc. Med. Technologists (corr. sec. 1977-78, dir. 1981-82, pres. 1984-85), Va. Soc. Histology Technicians (dir. 1979—, pres. 1982—), N.Y. Acad. Scis., Am. Soc. Clin. Pathologists (cert. histology technician), Nat. Geog. Soc., Va. Govtl. Employees Assn., AAAS, Nat. Soc. Histotech. (by-laws com. 1981—; C.E.U. com. 1981—, program com. regional meeting 1984, 85), Am. Mus. Natural History, Smithsonian Instn., Am. Mgmt. Assn., Clin. Lab. Mgmt. Assn., Nat. Soc. Historic Preservation, Am. Biog. Inst. Research Assn. (life, medal of honor 1985), Sigma Xi, Phi Beta Rho, Kappa Delta Pi, Phi Lambda Theta. Home: 1315 Asbury Rd Richmond VA 23229 Office: Surgical Pathology Dept Med Coll Va Hosp 12th and Broad Sts Richmond VA 23298

FREUND, ROYLE LAUNCEY, investment and manufacturing exec.; b. Milw., June 14, 1930; d. Leroy and Anne (Edelman) Michel; children—Kim Glaser Selbert, Leslie Glaser Kanner. With Revell, Inc., Venice, Calif., 1958-82, pres., chief exec. officer, 1970-72, chairwoman bd., 1972-79, vice chairwoman bd., 1979-82; pres. R&M Investment Co.; pres. Avanzare; co-ptnr. RMC Holding Co.; dir. Merc. Nat. Bank, Los Angeles; video-tape participant UCLA mgmt. course, 1974. Mem. Toy Mfrs. Assn. (dir. 1975), Hobby Industry Assn. Am. (dir. 1974-75, sec. 1975, exec. com. 1975), Young Pres. Orgn. (exec. com. 1976-77), young Pres. Orgn.-Grads., World Bus. Council. Office: 1341 Ocean Ave Suite 371 Santa Monica CA 90401

FREVERT, JOYCE GLADYS, correctional administrator; b. Long Beach, Calif., Nov. 19, 1934; d. Arthur Christian and Bertha Esther (Culbertson) Modell; m. Richard Dean Frevert, July 14, 1956 (div. 1964); 1 child, Michael Dean. B.A. Calif. State U.-Long Beach, 1956; postgrad. U. Calif.-Riverside, 1970. Social worker Los Angeles County Bur. Pub. Assistance, Long Beach, Calif., 1956-61; probation officer Los Angeles County Probation Dept., El Monte, Calif. 1962-65; statis. mgr. Occidental Life Ins. Co., Los Angeles, 1966-67; probation officer San Bernardino County Probation Dept., Ontario, Calif., 1967-69, supervising probation officer, Chino, Calif., 1970-80, probation dir. I, San Bernardino, 1981-82, probation dir. II, 1983—; staff cons. San Bernardino County Juvenile Justice and Delinquency Prevention Commn., 1983—; mem. delinquency prevention com. Calif. Youth Authority, Tustin, 1984—, sec. regional citizens adv. council, 1985—. Past pres., bd. dirs. West End Family Counseling Service, Ontario, 1977—; bd. dirs. San Bernardino YWCA, 1985—, West End Toxic Abuse Service, 1985—. Mem. Calif. Probation, Parole and Correctional Assn., Am. Probation and Parole Assn. Presbyterian. Lodge: Altrusa Internat. Avocations: community service; reading; gardening; music. Office: San Bernardino County Probation Dept 175 W 5th St 4th Floor San Bernardino CA 92415

FREW, BARBARA, marketing researcher, educator; b. Newark, Nov. 22, 1944; d. Frank Edward and Phyllis O. (DeMeo) Leppo; m. James R. Frew, Jan. 5, 1980. B.A., Upsala Coll., 1966; M.S., U. Miami, 1976; postgrad., Purdue U., 1976-79, U. N.C., 1979—. Tchr. N.J. Sch. System, Old Bridge, 1966-69; asst. regional mgr. Aratex Services, Hialeah, Fla., 1970-74; asst. prof. U. N.C., Greensboro, 1979-84, Rollins Coll., Winter Park, Fla., 1984—; v.p. LuMar Research, Orlando, Fla., 1985—; cons. N.C. Real Estate Research Inst., Chapel Hill, 1981-83, Aratex Services, Fla., 1981, Nat. Assn. Econ. Edn., N.C., 1980-81, Sta. WFMY-TV, Greensboro, 1980-81. Contbr. articles to profl. jours. N.C. Real Estate Research Inst. grantee, 1981-83. Mem. Am. Mktg. Assn., Acad. Mktg. Sci., So. Mktg. Assn., Am. Mgmt. Assn., Winter Park C. of C. Avocations: raquetball; swimming; reading. Home: 651 Montego Bay Ct Winter Park FL 32792 Office: Rollins Coll Bus Studies Dep Winter Park FL 32789

FREY, AUDREY ETHEL, publishing company executive; b. India, Feb. 27, 1926; came to U.S., 1948, naturalized, 1953; d. Louis Percival and Marguerita Isabel (D'Silva) Spencer; S.C. honors degree, Cambridge (Eng.) U., 1942; student Govt. Sch. Art, 1942-47, Art Students League, 1949-50, 51-52; m. Eric Konstantin Frey, Jan. 21, 1961. With McGraw-Hill Pub. Co., N.Y.C., 1950—, prodn. mgr. Coal Age, also Engring. and Mining Jour., 1955-66, bus. mgr. Internat. Mgmt., 1966-69, U.S. mktg. services mgr. Internat. Mgmt. Network of Publs., 1969-76, service ops. mgr. Internat. Group of Publs., 1976-82, dir. U.S. internat. publs., 1983-84; mgr. pub. relations services McGraw-Hill Publs. Co., 1983—, mgr. mktg. communications, 1985—; speaker internat. mag. communications; panel mem. bus. seminars. Mem. Mus. Natural History, Nat. Wildlife Fedn., Art Students League. Recipient 3 first awards Printing Industries Met. N.Y. Home: 2860 Bailey Ave Apt 6A New York NY 10463 Office: 1221 Ave of Americas New York NY 10020

FREY, CHERYL MILLER, phys. chemist; b. Lorain, Ohio, Sept. 7, 1943; d. Louis Andrew and Margaret Louise (Metz) Miller; B.S. in Chemistry, Western Res. U., 1965; M.S. in Chemistry, Case-Western Res. U., 1968, Ph.D., 1971; m. Robert George Frey, Mar. 31, 1967. Sr. chemist B.F. Goodrich Chem. Co., Avon Lake, Ohio, 1974-78; asso. scientist Glidden Coatings & Resins, Strongsville, Ohio, 1978-81, scientist, 1981-82; tech. specialist 3M, St. Paul, 1982—; speaker women in sci. program Notre Dame Coll. Mem. Nat. Assn. Corrosion Engrs., Am. Chem. Soc., Cleve. Soc. Coatings Tech., Am. Paint Soc. Contbr. articles to Jour. Am. Chem. Soc., 1971-81. Home: 9650 Justen Trail White Bear Lake MN 55110 Office: 3M Center 236-2C Saint Paul MN 55144

FREY, JUDY WHITTER, social services supervisor; b. Jacksonville, Fla., June 3, 1950; d. Thomas Lytle and Cleo (Crews) Whitter; m. Robert Andrew Frey, Aug. 1, 1981. B.A. in History, Jacksonville U., 1972, M.B.A., 1985; postgrad. U. No. Fla., 1982—. Social worker State of Fla., Jacksonville, 1972-78, social rehab. services counselor II, 1978-82, supr., 1982—; spl. agent Naval Investigative Service Dept. Navy, 1978. Active March of Dimes Fund Drive, Jacksonville; vol. ofcl. Jacksonville Track Club. Mem. Jacksonville U. Alumni Bd. Govs. (pres. 1983-84), Jacksonville Alumnae Panhellenic Assn. (bd. dirs. 1972-76, 77-78, 81—), Zeta Tau Alpha (Zeta Day chmn. 1983; Key Woman 1982-83). Club: Civitan. Baptist. Home: 7419 Clinton St Jacksonville FL 32208 Office: Box 52239 111 Coastline Dr Jacksonville FL 32201

FREY, LINDA SUE, history educator; b. Toledo, Feb. 21, 1947; d. Henry H. and Dolores A. (Saionz) F. B.S. in Edn. summa cum laude, Ohio State U., 1967, B.A. summa cum laude, 1967, M.A., 1968, Ph.D., 1971. Asst. prof. U. Mont., Missoula, 1971-76, assoc. prof., 1976-82, prof., 1982—, chmn. history dept., 1983—. Author: A Question of Empire, 1983; Frederick I, 1984; co-compiler: Women in Western European Tradition, 1983, vol. 2, 1984. NEH grantee, 1977-78; Am. Council Learned Socs. grantee, 1981; faculty intern U.S. Office Edn., 1980. Mem. Am. Hist. Assn., Conf. on Slavic and East European History, Am. Assn. for Study of Hungary History (exec. com. 1982-84). Home: 100 Hillview Way Missoula MT 59803 Office: Dept History Univ Mont Missoula MT 59812

FREY, NORMA CLAIRE, psychiatric social worker; b. Buffalo, Apr. 15, 1929; d. Severn Michael and Antoinette (Langlois) Frey. B.A., Ursuline Coll., New Orleans, 1950; grad. Tulane U., Sch. Social Work, 1954; M.S.W., McGill U., Montreal, Que., Can., 1960. Cert. social worker, advanced clin. practitioner, Tex. Welfare visitor La. State Dept., Gretna, 1951-53; child welfare worker, dept. pub. welfare, Alexandria, La., 1954-56; case worker U. Tex. Med. br., Galveston, 1956-59; psychiat. social worker Tex. Research Inst. Mental Scis., Houston, 1960-85, ret.; pvt. cons. adv. council Adult Mental Health, Mental Retardation Authority, Houston, 1982—, chmn. com. to study homeless mentally ill, 1982—, chmn. com. to study goals of continuity of care; v.p., founding mem. Tex. chpt. Alliance Mental Recovery, Houston, 1980—; adj. faculty U. Houston Sch. Social Work, 1972—; bd. dirs. Houston/Harris County Coalition for Homeless. Recipient Honor Merit award adj. faculty, U. Houston, 1978—; Honor Merit award, Tulane U. Alumnae, 1974. Fellow Am. Orthopsychiat. Assn.; mem. Nat. Assn. Social Workers, Acad. Cert. Social Workers, Mental Health Assn., Mental Health Assn. of Harris County Continuity of Care Consortium. Republican. Roman Catholic. Club: Houston Opera Guild.

FREY, POLLY ANN, school administrator; b. Atlanta, Jan. 26, 1943; d. Archie Newton and Thelma Josephine (Walton) Powell; m. Robert Franklin Frey, July 14, 1962; children—Kimberly Ann, Robert Newton, Sara Allela. Student Women's Coll. Ga., 1961-62. Key punch operator Ga. Dept. Health, Atlanta, 1962-64; sec. Edward Chapel Bapt. Ch., Athens, Ga., 1976-77; receptionist, counselor Snelling and Snelling Employment, Athens, 1977-78; tchr. Prince Ave. Bapt. Ch., Athens, 1979-80, Watkinsville First Bapt. Ch., Athens, 1980-81; dir. Bridge to Learning Child Care Ctr., Athens, 1981—; tchr.'s aide Little Red Sch. House, East Point, Ga. Mem. Ga. Day Care Assn., Athens C. of C., Athens Pilot Club. Avocations: reading; music; crafts; fishing. Home: 455 Somerset Dr Athens GA 30606 Office: Bridge to Learning Child Care Ctr 1850 Timothy Rd Athens GA 30606

FREYBERG, JOAN TUTTLE, clin. psychologist; b. N.Y.C.; d. Herbert Wesley and Elizabeth Lorraine (Samuel) Tuttle; A.B., Barnard Coll., 1955; M.S. in Sch. Psychology, City U. N.Y., 1967, Ph.D. in Clin. Psychology, 1970; m. Michael Freyberg, Sept. 6, 1955; children—Mark Lawrence, Susan Jane. Lectr. psychology CCNY, 1969-70; psychotherapist Lincoln Inst. for Psychotherapy, 1970-72; asso. staff mem., lectr. Postgrad. Center for Mental Health, 1970-74, mem. staff, 1974—, mem. faculty, 1976—; mem. Group Project on Holocaust Survivors and Their Children, N.Y.C.; individual practice psychotherapy and testing, 1971—; adj. clin. supr. Yeshiva U., 1979—; cons. nursery schs. and media on devel. of imagination in children; psychol. cons. research projects in edn. disadvantaged learners U.S. Office Edn., 1965-69. Mem. Kappa Delta Pi. Co-author: Child's World of Make-Believe, 1973. Editor: Graduate Research in Education and Related Disciplines, 1966-68. Contbr. numerous articles on fantasy, disadvantaged children, children of Holocaust survivors, reading disabilities to profl. publs. Office: 125 E 87th St New York NY 10028 also 140 Lockwood Ave New Rochelle NY 10801

FREYER, ELLEN JACOBS, film producer; b. Los Angeles, Nov. 7, 1940; d. Lewis and Lillian (Wilentz) Jacobs; m. Stuart Freyer, July 30, 1961 (div. 1978); children—Daniel Benjamin, Adam Stephen. Student Brandeis U., 1957-59; B.A., Barnard Coll., 1961; M.A., NYU, 1971. Asst. film editor freelance, N.Y.C., 1972-76; adj. lectr. St. Peter's Coll., Jersey City, 1972-75, Hunter Coll., N.Y.C., 1980-83; freelance producer, writer, N.Y.C., 1976-83; project mgr. TeleCulture, Inc., N.Y.C., 1982-83; asst. project mgr. Wonderworks/PBS, N.Y.C., 1983-84, prodn. supr., 1984—; juror Am. Film Festival, N.Y.C., 1972-86; guest speaker, programmer Colls. and Univs., N.Y., 1972-83; U.S. rep. Internat. Film Festival, Hebrew U. Jerusalem Cinemateque, 1986; cons. Notable Am. Women, Cambridge, Mass., 1978. Producer, dir.: Marathon Woman, Miki Gorman, 1981, Girls' Sports: On The Right Track, 1976. Founding mem. Washington Square Day Care Center, N.Y.C., 1973; founder After School Workshops, N.Y.C., 1974. Grantee Women's Fund-Joint Found. Support, 1978, Hoso-Bunka Found. Japan, 1979, N.Y. State Council Arts, 1979, Mitsubishi Internat., 1980, NEH, 1981. Mem. N.Y. Women in Film, Nat. Acad. TV Arts and Scis. Home: 112 W 15th St New York NY 10011

FREYTAG, SHARON NELSON, lawyer; b. Larned, Kans., May 11, 1943; d. John Seldon and Ruth Marie (Herbel) Nelson; m. Thomas Lee Freytag, June 18, 1966; children—Kurt David, Hillary Lee. B.S. with highest distinction, U. Kans.-Lawrence, 1965; M.A., U. Mich., 1966; J.D. cum laude, So. Methodist U., 1981. Bar: Tex. 1981. Tchr. English, Gaithersburg (Md.) High Sch., 1966-70; instr. English, Eastfield Coll., 1974-78; law clk. U.S. Dist. Ct. for No. Dist. Tex., 1981-82, U.S. Ct. Appeals for 5th Circuit, 1982; assoc. in litigation firm Haynes and Boone, Dallas, 1983—, vis. prof. law Southern Meth. U., 1985-86. Editor-in-chief Southwestern Law Jour., 1980-81; contbr. articles to law jours. Mem. ABA, Tex. Bar Assn., Dallas Bar Assn., Dallas Mus. Fine Arts, Dallas Shakespeare Soc., Order of Coif, Barristers, Phi Delta Phi, Phi Beta Kappa. Lutheran.

FRIAS, ADA MILAGROS, management-employee development consultant, educator; b. N.Y.C., July 21, 1943; d. Rafael E. and Luz M. (Ortiz) F.; m. Raul Colon, 1967 (div. 1976); children—Raul Enrique, Ada Belen. B.A., U. P.R., 1966, M.A., 1977; Ph.D., Columbia Pacific U., 1981; postgrad. U. Miami (Fla.), 1977. Tng. program dir. Advanced Research and Mgmt. Co., P.R., 1975-77; v.p., Profl. Indsl. Services, P.R., 1978-80; prof. InterAm. U., P.R., 1977—; mentor Columbia Pacific U., Calif., 1982—; cons.; founder, dir. Fin. Trust Life Ins. Co., 1983—. Recipient performance awards, U.S. Interagency Tng., 1979, Personnel and Guidance Assn., 1980. Mem. P.R. Psychology Assn. Am. Soc. Personnel Adminstrn., Assn. Labor Relations Practitioners. Roman Catholic. Club: Lions (San Juan). Author: The Managerial Organizational Team Building Program, 1981; manual Work Book Organizational Devel.,

1983. Leader numerous seminars, workshops. Office: Management and Organizational Development Consulting Division PO Box 29754 65 Inf Sta Rio Piedras PR 00929

FRICK, DOROTHY MARY LES MONDE (MRS. RAY J. FRICK), artist, civic worker; b. Green Bay, Wis., Jan. 7, 1912; d. Desire Joseph and Olive Belle (Trask) Les Monde; pvt. study art; m. Ray J. Frick, Aug. 27, 1930 (dec. Aug. 1970); 1 son, William. One-man show at Rahr Civic Center, Manitowoc, Wis., 1963, 66; exhibited in group shows at Green Bay, Madison and Two Rivers, Wis.; sec. Little Gallery Inc., 1974-76, 79-80, pres., 1980-84, dir., 1974-84. Active fund drives ARC, Am. Cancer Soc.; pres. Little Gallery, Inc., Manitowoc, 1946-47, 66-67, sec., 1967-70, exhibit chmn., 1968-69; mem. City Council of Arts, 1970—. Bd. dirs. Rahr Civic Center, Manitowoc, 1960-68, vice chmn. mus. bd., 1960-68; bd. deacons First Presbyterian Ch., 1980-83. Mem. Fedn. Women's Clubs, Manitowoc County Hist. Soc. (pres. 1961-63, v.p. 1966-68), Palettiers (sec. 1966-67). Home: 815 Park St Manitowoc WI 54220

FRICON, TERRI MADELINE, music publisher, producer, consultant; b. Buffalo, July 19, 1943; d. Anthony Edward and Josephine Rose (D'Amico) F.; student San Jose (Calif.) State U., 1961; B.Mus., U. Miami (Fla.), 1963. Asst. to profl. mgr. Screen Gems Music, 1964; v.p., partner Wednesday's Child Prodns., 1967; pres. music group Filmways, also dir. music dept. Filmways TV and Filmways Motion Pictures, 1974-81; pres. Fricon Entertainment Co., Inc., Los Angeles, 1981—; mem. Calif. Copyright Conf., 1967—, pres. 1980-81; chmn. Music Pubs. Forum, 1979-81. Recipient Golden Staff award Music and Arts Found. Am., 1975—, Profl. Achievement award Soroptimist Club Los Angeles, 1977. Mem. ASCAP (pubs. adv. com. 1977—), Assn. Ind. Music Pubs., Nat. Acad. Rec. Arts and Scis., Nashville Songwriters Assn., Acad. Country Music, Black Music Assn., Nat. Music Pubs. Assn., Broadcast Music, Inc., Women in Film, Acad. TV Arts and Scis., Am. Fedn. Musicians. Address: 1048 S Ogden Dr Los Angeles CA 90019

FRIDLEY, SAUNDRA LYNN, internal audit manager; b. Columbus, Ohio, June 14, 1948; d. Jerry Dean and Esther Eliza (Bluhm) Fridley. B.S., Franklin U., 1976; M.B.A., Golden Gate U., 1980. Accounts receivable supr. Internat. Harvester, Columbus, Ohio, San Leandro, Calif., 1972-80; sr. internal auditor Western Union, San Francisco, 1980; internal auditor II, County of Santa Clara, San Jose, Calif., 1980-82; sr. internal auditor Tymshare, Inc., Cupertino, Calif., 1982-84, div. controller, 1984; internal audit mgr. VWR Scientific, Brisbane, Calif., 1984—. Mem. Internal Auditors Speakers Bur., Inst. Internal Auditors (pres.), Nat. Assn. Female Execs. Avocations: woodworking; gardening; crocheting. Home: 862 Bellflower St Livermore CA 94550 Office: VWR Scientific 3745 Bayshore Blvd Brisbane CA 94005

FRIED, ELAINE JUNE, business executive; b. Los Angeles, Oct. 19, 1943; grad. Pasadena (Calif.) High Sch., 1963; various coll. courses; m. Howard I. Fried, Aug. 7, 1966; children—Donna Marie, Randall Jay. Agt., office mgr. Howard I. Fried Agy., Alhambra, Calif., 1975—; v.p. Sea Hill, Inc., Pasadena, Calif., 1973—. Publicity chmn. San Gabriel Valley (Calif.) unit Am. Diabetes Assn.; past publicity chmn. San Gabriel Valley sect. Nat. Council Jewish Women, also tribute chmn. San Gabriel Valley sect.; past bd. dirs., personnel com. Vis. Nurse Assn. Pasadena and San Gabriel Valley; past membership, chmn. spl. events publicity Temple Beth Torah, Alhambra. Recipient Vol. award So. Calif. affiliate Am. Diabetes Assn., 1974-77. Clubs: B'nai B'rith Women, Hadassah, ORT (publicity chmn. region). Speaker on psycho-social aspects of diabetes, life and health ins. for diabetics.

FRIED, MAUREEN KESSLER, photography studio owner; b. Bronx, N.Y., July 26, 1944; d. David Isaac and Gertrude (Weiner) Kessler; m. Arthur Martin Fried, Oct. 16, 1965; children—Meredith Lynn, Jeffrey Scott, Laurel Beth. Student Hunter Coll., 1962-64, Am. Acad. Dramatic Arts, N.Y.C., 1962-63. With 1st Nat. City Bank, N.Y.C., 1963-65, Citadel Life Ins. Co., N.Y.C., 1965-67; bookkeeper/sec. Unique Table Cloth & Skirting Co., N.Y.C., 1978-80; bookkeeper Gilbert Frank Corp., N.Y.C., 1980-84; owner/ptnr. Azie Photographers, Wantagh, N.Y., 1984—. Writer children's stories. Pres., Meadowbrook PTA, East Meadow, N.Y., 1977-79; v.p. Sabra Hadassah, Long Beach, N.Y., 1968-70; pres. couples club Suburban Temple, Wantagh, N.Y., 1976-78. Recipient award Cerebral Palsy Assn. Nassau County, 1971; Leadership award Sabra-Hadassah, 1968-69; Founders Day award Meadowbrook Sch., 1980, N.Y. Writers award Queens County, 1958. Fellow Wantagh C. of C. Democrat. Jewish. Avocations: writing; theatre; photography; cooking; dancing; music. Home: 484 Clearmeadow Dr East Meadow NY 11554 Office: Azie Photographers 1943 Wantagh Ave Wantagh NY 11793

FRIED, RONNEE, marketing research company executive; b. N.Y.C., Dec. 16, 1947; d. Phillip Frank Fried and Gloria Edith (Pfeffer) Sandow; m. Gregory Wesley Pierce, Apr. 8, 1984. B.A., George Washington U., 1969. Field dir. AHF Mktg. Research, N.Y.C., 1969-73; project dir. Decisions Ctr. Inc., N.Y.C., 1973-76, Ogilvy & Mather Advt., N.Y.C., 1977; assoc. group mgr. Data Devel. Corp., N.Y.C., 1977-81; ptnr., exec. v.p. Brown Koff & Fried Inc., N.Y.C., 1981—; dir. Wats Interviewing Network Inc., Rutherford, N.J. Mem. speakers bur. Greater N.Y. Conf. Soviet Jewry, 1979—. Mem. Am. Mktg. Assn. (Effie Awards Judging co-chmn. 1982, membership com. 1981, Recognition award 1982), Advt. Women N.Y. Jewish. Club: Tarrytown Group. Avocations: 1948 Chrysler New Yorker. Home: One Fifth Ave New York NY 10003 Office: Brown Koff & Fried Inc 14 W 23d St New York NY 10010

FRIEDAN, BETTY, author, feminist leader; b. Peoria, Ill., Feb. 4, 1921; d. Harry and Miriam (Horwitz) Goldstein; B.A. summa cum laude, Smith Coll., 1942, D.H.L., 1975; m. Carl Friedan, June 1947 (div. May 1969); children—Daniel, Jonathan, Emily. Research fellow in psychology U. Calif. at Berkeley, 1943; lectr. feminism univs., bus. and profl. orgns., polit. groups in U.S. and Europe; founder NOW, 1st pres., 1966-70, chairwoman adv. com.; organizer Nat. Women's Polit. Caucus, 1971; organizer, dir. Womans First Woman's Bank; lectr. New Sch. Social Research, 1971; vis. prof. sociology Temple U., 1972, Queens Coll., 1975; vis. lectr. in sociology Calhoun Coll., Yale U., 1974; sr. research assoc. Ctr. Social Scis., Columbia U., 1979-81; fellow Inst. Politics, Kennedy Sch. Govt., Harvard U., 1982, research fellow ctr. Population Studies, 1982-83. Bd. dirs. NOW Legal Def. and Edn. Fund, Girl Scouts U.S. Recipient Humanist of Year award, 1975, Author of Yr. award Am. Soc. Journalists and Authors, 1982. Mem. P.E.N., Soc. Mag. Writers, Am. Sociol. Assn., Phi Beta Kappa. Author: The Feminine Mystique, 1963; It Changed My Life, 1976; The Second Stage, 1981; contbg. editor McCall's mag., 1971; contbr. Harper's, Social Policy, N.Y. Times mag.; editorial bd. Present Tense. Address: 1 Lincoln Plaza New York NY 10023*

FRIEDE, GRETCHEN PERAU, metal finishing company executive; b. Oswego, N.Y., Sept. 10, 1935; d. Karl W. and Hazel M. (Perau) Grulich; m. Walter R. Friede, (dec. July 1980); children—Lucinda, Sandra, Debra, Janis. B.S., Wagner Coll. Draftsman, Fairchild Engring., Long Island, N.Y., 1957-59; office mgr. Coastal Metal Finishing Co., Inc., Merrimac, Mass., 1969-79, gen. mgr., 1979-80, pres., 1980—. Mem. Am. Electroplaters Soc., Master Metal Finishers. Republican. Lutheran. Home: 7 Rawson Hill Rd Newburyport MA 01950 Office: Coastal Metal Finishing 2 Littles Court Merrimac MA 01860

FRIEDELL, JOANN, state agency administrator; b. Bklyn., Feb. 4, 1951; d. George and Edna F.; B.A. in Psychology, SUNY, Stony Brook, 1974; M.S. in Edl. Psychology, Coll. St. Rose, 1979. Auditor, N.Y. State Social Services, Albany, 1974-78, supr. computer piloting, 1978-79, supr. computer installation, 1979-81, mgr. computer ops., 1981—; renovator, mgr. income-producing property. Mem. Nat. Assn. Female Execs., Am. Pub. Welfare Assn. Club: Colonie Tennis (Albany). Office: 40 N Pearl St Albany NY 12207

FRIEDENBERG, JOAN ELLEN, language educator, educational consultant; b. N.Y.C., Dec. 2, 1951; d. Herbert and Faye (Gelman) Friedenberg; m. J. Ludwig Figueroa, Aug. 22, 1976. Student U. Madrid (Spain), 1970, Inst. Hispanic Culture, Madrid, 1972; B.A., Syracuse U.-Utica Coll., 1973; M.A., U. Ill., 1975, Ph.D., 1979. Tchr. elem. sch. Dept. Instrn., Guayama, P.R., 1973-74; curriculum specialist Danville (Ill.) Pub. Schs., 1978-79; lectr. linguistics U. Ill.-Chgo., 1979; instr. English as a 2d lang. Syracuse (N.Y.) U., 1979; asst. prof. bilingual edn. Fla. Internat. U., Miami, 1979-82, assoc. prof., 1982-85; research specialist/project dir. Nat. Ctr. for Research in Vocat. Edn., Ohio State U., Columbus, 1985—; cons. U.S. Dept. State, U.S. Dept. Edn., Washington; interpretor U.S. Immigration Service, Miami, 1980; cons. refugee agys., Miami, 1980—. Author: (with others) Foundations and Strategies for Bilingual Vocational Education, 1982; Instructional Materials for Bilingual Vocational Education, 1984; The Vocational ESL Handbook, 1984; Finding a Job in the United States, 1986; contbr. articles to profl. jours., chpts. to books. U.S. Dept. Edn. fellow, 1975-78; dissertation research grantee U. Ill., 1978. Mem. Tchrs. English to Speakers of Other Langs., Nat. Assn. Bilingual Edn., Am. Vocat. Assn., Phi Delta Kappa, Phi Kappa Phi. Jewish.

FRIEDENBERG, KAREN ROSEN, real estate associate; b. Savannah, Ga., May 3, 1949; d. Emanuel F. and Thelma Z. (Reed) Rosen; 1 child, Jodi. B.S. in Mass Communications, Emerson Coll., 1971; student U. N.C., summer 1968, Harvard U., summer 1967, U. Ga., 1967-69. Exec. trainee Jordan Marsh, Boston, 1974-76; broadcast dir. Rich's, Atlanta, 1976-78; mktg. dir. Northlake Mall, Atlanta, 1978-80, Lenox Square, Atlanta, 1980-82; retail leasing assoc. Trammell Crow Co., Atlanta, 1982-85, Kern & Co., Atlanta, 1985—. Bd. dirs. Atlanta Women's Network, Feminist Action Alliance, Atlanta, Atlanta chpt. Nat. Council Jewish Women; patron High Mus. Art, Ctr. for Puppetry Art; mem. Ga. Women's Polit. Caucus. Mem. Comml. Real Estate Women, Atlanta Advt. Club. Republican. Jewish. Lodge: Hadassah (Atlanta). Avocations: aerobics; bicycling; hiking; rafting. Home: Four Pendleton Pl Atlanta GA 30342 Office: Kern & Co 3520 Piedmont Rd Suite 300 Atlanta GA 30305

FRIEDLAND, BERNICE UDELLE, psychologist, educator; b. Akron, Ohio, June 18, 1935; d. Hymen H. and Ida S.; B.Sc., Ohio State U., 1956; M.Ed., Frostburg State Coll., 1969; Ed.D., W.Va. U., 1972; children by previous marriage—Holli, David Michael. Asso. prof. psychology Coppin State Coll., 1972-80; adj. prof. Bowie State Coll., Loyola Coll.; pvt. practice psychology, Balt., 1976—; psychologist Spring Grove State Hosp., Balt., 1978-83; chief psychology and psychiat. services Md. Correctional Instn. for Women, 1983—; bd. dirs. Blind Industries and Services of Md.; bd. advisors rehab. div. Balt. Goodwill Industries, 1979-83; cons., inservice trainer ednl. and vocat. rehab. agys. Bd. dirs. Alfred Adler Inst., Washington, 1984—. Mem. Am. Personnel and Guidance Assn., Am. Psychol. Assn., Nat. Rehab. Assn., N.Am. Soc. Adlerian Psychology. Author: (with W. McKelvie) Career Goal Counseling, 1978; editor Individual Psychologist, 1976-80; mem. editorial bd. Jour. Rehab., 1979-80; contbr. articles to profl. publs. Home: 6819 Cherokee Dr Baltimore MD 21209 Office: 101 W Read St Baltimore MD 21201

FRIEDLAND, LILLI, psychologist; b. Bad Gastein, Austria, Feb. 24, 1947; came to U.S., 1950, naturalized, 1956; d. Joseph and Marie (Bjerkenhejm) Rebhun; B.A., U. Oreg., 1966; Ph.D., U. So. Calif. 1975; m. David Lee Friedland, Feb. 22, 1969; children Jered, Elana, Ari. Research asst. Research Service Bur., Los Angeles, 1968-70; cons. to Council of Jewish Fedn., N.Y.C., 1969-70; research analyst Los Angeles Mental Health Dept., 1970-73; chief planning div. Office of Alcohol Abuse and Alcoholism, Los Angeles County, 1973-74, chief program and system evaluation, 1973-74; chief drug abuse planning Los Angeles County Dept. Health Services, 1973-76; dir. family devel. program Suicide Prevention Center, Los Angeles, 1975-77; pres. Friedland Psychol. Assos., Inc., Los Angeles, 1975—; cons. to pvt. secondary schs., Calif., 1973—; condr. workshops. Chairperson Devel. Disabilities Area Bd., Calif., 1977-79, Program Planning and Evaluation Com. Area Bd., 1975-77; mem. exec. com., community service com., leadership devel. com., mem. program planning and budgeting com. Jewish Fedn. Council, 1981—. Recipient certs. of appreciation Bd. Suprs. Los Angeles County, 1980, Los Angeles County Narcotics and Dangerous Drugs Commn., 1975. Mem. Am. Psychol. Assn., Calif. Psychol. Assn. (chair pub. info. com.), Los Angeles County Psychol. Assn. (pres. 1985), Los Angeles County Clin. Psychol. Assn. (dir. 1980—), Assn. for Media Psychology (sec.), Women in Bus., Women's Referral Service, Hadassah. Republican. Jewish. Home: 1216 Daniels Dr Los Angeles CA 90035 Office: 2080 Century Park E Suite 204 Los Angeles CA 90067

FRIEDMAN, BARBARA GLATT, human relations consultant, mental health counselor; b. Newark, May 13, 1937; d. Ben Harry and Sadie (Gudis) Glatt; B.A., Edison State Coll., 1979; postgrad. Trenton State Coll., 1979-80; M.S., U. Pa., 1982; m. Bernard Friedman, June 11, 1955 (dec.); children—Barry Jay, Ronnie Mark, Mitchell Ira. Cert. clin. hypnotherapist. Counselor, Am. Youth Crisis Center, Oberursel, W.Ger., 1972-74; career counselor VEST, Camden County, N.J., 1977-79; counselor Glassboro (N.J.) State Coll. Counseling Center, also cons., psychologist in pvt. practice, Cherry Hill, N.J., 1980—; cons., psychol. counselor Together, Inc., Glassboro, 1983—; tchr. continuing edn. program Gloucester County (N.J.) adult and community schs., 1982—; dir.-founder Alternatives in Direction, 1983; workshop facilitator; guest lectr. in field. Mem. Parents' Campaign for Handicapped Children and Youth; bd. dirs. Frankfurt (W.Ger.) Am. Jewish Community Chapel, 1969-72. Recipient cert. of recognition, Oberursel, 1973, presdl. cert. of honor Camden County Coll., 1978. Cert. Nat. Bd. Cert. Counselors. Mem. Am. Assn. Counseling and Devel., Am. Mental Health Counselors Assn., N.J. Profl. Counselors Assn., N.J. Career Guidance Assn., Arthritis Found., Cherry Hill C. of C. (chmn. edn. com. 1984—, cert. of recognition 1985, Speakers Bur. 1985—), Small Bus. Council, N.J. Assn. Women Bus. Owners. Home: 16 Dartmouth Rd Cherry Hill NJ 08034

FRIEDMAN, BARBARA SIEGEL, accountant; b. N.Y.C., Jan. 19, 1953; d. Philip and Laura (Gitlen) Siegel; B.S., Fairleigh Dickinson U., 1973, postgrad., 1974—; m. Bennett Friedman, June 1, 1975; children—Erica Brooke, Brett Ross (twins). Sr. auditor Benjamin Nadel & Co., N.Y.C., 1973-76; acctg. mgr. N.Y. Zool. Soc., Bronx, 1976-79; controller Vera Inst. Justice, N.Y.C., 1979-80; sr. acctg. coordinator Salomon Bros., N.Y.C., 1980-81; controller N.Y. Bot. Garden, 1981-83; controller, asst. treas. N.Y. Pub. Library, 1983—. Tech. asst. N.Y. State Council on Arts; asst. dist. leader 9th Ward Democratic Club, 1970-71; trustee Ctr. Preventive Psychiatry, White Plains, N.Y. Mem. Nat. Assn. Female Execs. Democrat. Jewish. Club: Racquetplaza Racquetball. Home: 58 Underhill Rd Scarsdale NY 10583

FRIEDMAN, COLLETTE SWEET, kitchen designer, interior designer; b. Los Angeles, Feb. 25, 1933; d. Maurice Paul and Ilona M. (Feld) Albert; student Los Angeles Valley Coll., 1961-63; student Calif. State U., Northridge, 1964, Pierce Coll., 1965-67, UCLA, 1968-70; children—Scott D., Brian C., Victoria A., Valaree L., Collette. Interior designer, North Hollywood, Calif., 1962-76; owner/designer Better Homes and Kitchens, Westlake Village, Calif., 1976—. Recipient award Bank of America, 1951. Mem. Nat. Kitchen and Bath Assn. (sec. So. Calif. chpt. 1979-82), Conejo Assn. Profl. Interior Designers, Am. Bus. Woman's Assn. (charter), Nat. Assn. Women in Constrn., Westlake Village C. of C., Conejo Valley C. of C., Zonta Internat. Office: 31121 Via Colinas 1004 Westlake Village CA 91362

FRIEDMAN, CONSTANCE JOY, electronic firm executive; b. Omaha, June 19, 1941; d. Philip and Sylvia (Goffstein) F. m. James Allen Schmerer, Nov. 13, 1966; (div. 1974); 1 dau., Pamela Anne. B.A., UCLA; M.B.A., Pepperdine U., 1982. Various positions in personnel Data Products, Woodland Hills, Calif., 1975-78; profl. specialist Transaction Tech., Santa Monica, Calif., 1978-79; personnel mgr. Micropolis Corp.; Chatsworth, Calif., 1979-81, dir. personnel, 1981-83, v.p. human resources, 1983—. Coordinator Jr. Achievement, Los Angeles, 1977, 78. Mem. Personnel and Incl. Relations Assn., Am. Soc. Personnel Adminstrn. Libertarian. Office: Micropolis Corp 21123 Nordhoff St Chatsworth CA 91311

FRIEDMAN, ELIZABETH ANN, educational administrator; b. N.Y.C., June 6, 1948; d. Aaron and Florence (Giatas) Zicherman; m. Paul Lawrence Friedman, May 25, 1975. B.A. cum laude, U. Pitts., 1970. Mgmt. analyst U.S. Dept. Commerce, 1970-73; tng. systems analyst Inst. Law and Social Research, Washington, 1973-78; dir. curriculum devel. and adminstrn. D.C. Bar (Unified), 1978-81; mgr. edn. programs Assn. Trial Lawyers Am., Washington, 1981-82; exec. dir. Inst. Profl. and Exec. Devel., Washington, 1982—. Mem. Friends of Jewish Council Aging Mem. Nat. Assn. Female Execs. Home: 3825 Ingomar St NW Washington DC 20015 Office: Inst Profl and Exec Devel 2300 M St NW Suite 260 Washington DC 20037

FRIEDMAN, ESTELLE YUDKIN, librarian; b. Bklyn., June 20, 1927; d. Isidore and Josephine (Kreditor) Yudkin; m. Izchak Friedman, Jan. 28, 1951; children—Jonathan, Wilma. B.A., Bklyn. Coll., 1947; M.L.S., Pratt Inst., 1969. Librarian, N.Y. Pub. Library, N.Y.C., 1969-72, sr. librarian, 1972-80, sr. br. librarian, 1980-83, supervising br. librarian, 1983—. Mem. ALA, N.Y. Library Assn. Home: 600 W 239th St Riverdale NY 10463 Office: NY Pub Library Fifth Ave and 42d St New York NY 10018

FRIEDMAN, EVELYN, chemical company executive; b. N.Y.C., Feb. 13, 1936; d. Hyman and Dora (Kirschner) F.; m. John L. Neumeyer, June 24, 1956; children—Ann M., David A., Elizabeth J. B.Sc., Northeastern U., 1978. Tchr. Meadowbrook Sch., Weston, Mass., 1978-80; admissions interviewer Wellesley Coll., Mass., 1980-81; pres. Research Biochems., Inc., Wayland, Mass., 1981—. Vice-chmn. Wayland Library Bldg. Planning Com., 1984—. Mem. LWV (officer 1966-72). Avocations: reading; classical music; skiing; hiking; travel.

FRIEDMAN, FRANCES FALLICK, public relations executive; b. Bklyn., Apr. 8; d. Aaron and Bertha (Itzkowitz) Fallick; m. Clifford Jerome Friedman, June 17, 1950; children—Kenneth, Jeffrey. B.B.A., CCNY, 1948. Editor, Decor mag., St. Louis, 1952-55; v.p. Conant & Co., N.Y.C., 1961-72; dir. pub. relations Melia Internat., N.Y.C., 1972-73; sr. v.p. Lobsenz-Stevens, Inc., N.Y.C., 1973-75; exec. v.p. Howard Rubenstein Co., N.Y.C., 1975-83; pres., prin. Frances Friedman Assocs., Inc., N.Y.C., 1983-84; chmn., pres. Greycom Inc. pub. relations subs. Grey Advt., N.Y.C., 1984—. Press sec. congl. candidate Nassau County Democratic Com. (N.Y.), 1964; mem. adv. bd. League for Parent Edn., N.Y.C., 1965-68; sec. City Coll. Fund, 1972-78. Mem. Women in Communications, Pub. Relations Soc. Am. Jewish. Club: City of N.Y. Home: 860 Fifth Ave New York NY 10021 also Appalachian Rd Kent CT 06757 Office: Greycom Inc 777 3d Ave New York NY 10022

FRIEDMAN, JO-ANN, health marketing consultant, author; b. Bklyn., Mar. 14, 1946; d. Leonard Noah and Frances (Siederer) Schwartz; m. Michael L. Friedman, May 31, 1970 (div. Aug. 1973). B.S., Bklyn. Coll., 1967; M.S., U. Mich., 1968. Chief speech pathology Albert Einstein Coll. Hosp., Bronx, N.Y., 1968-71; acctg. supr. Medcom, N.Y.C., 1972-75; pres. Health Mktg. Systems, Inc., N.Y.C., 1975—; clin. assoc. Columbia U., N.Y.C., 1970-72. Author: Home Health Care, 1986. Editor: Prevention Preview, 1977-82; To the Good Life, 1979-82. Bd. dirs. Am. Woman's Econ. Devel. Corp., N.Y.C., 1984—; chmn. Codanceco, N.Y.C., 1984—. Grantee NIH Neurol and Sensory Disease, Ann Arbor, Mich., 1968. Mem. Pharm. Advt. Council, Am. Woman Entrepreneurs. Avocations: swimming; tennis; dance. Home: 185 E 85th St New York NY 10028 Office: Health Mktg Systems Inc 18 E 48th St New York NY 10017

FRIEDMAN, LESLIE J., scriptwriter, businesswoman, author; b. N.Y.C., Oct. 12, 1948; d. Henry and Bernice A. Friedman; B.A., U. Cin., 1970; M.S., U. Ky., 1972. Children's librarian, then br. librarian trainee Public Library Cin. and Hamilton County, 1970-73; art librarian U. Ga., 1974-77; freelance lectr. women's media image, 1975—; producer: Mr. Whipple Groupies—Looking at Women's Advt. Image; Womanhood: A Pornographic Vision; author: Sex Role Stereotyping in the Mass Media, An Annotated Bibliography, 1977; owner Clarity Writing Service; v.p. JES Search Firm, Inc., Atlanta, 1983—. Mem. advisory bd. Atlanta Vocat. Counseling Center, Atlanta Council Battered Women. Mem. Women's Inst. Freedom Press, Women in Film, Art Libraries Soc. N.Am. (past regional pres.). Home: 20 26th St NW Atlanta GA 30309 Office: 1776 Peachtree St Suite 523 S Atlanta GA 30309

FRIEDMAN, LORRAINE (MRS. NORMAN B. FRIEDMAN), social worker, educator; b. Chgo., Sept. 24; d. Leon and Adele Weisman; A.B., U. Ill., 1944; M.A., Sch. Social Service Adminstrn., U. Chgo., 1947; children—Victor, Adele. Social caseworker State of Ill., Chgo., 1944-49; tchr. pub. schs., Chgo., 1960-66, sch. social worker, 1966-79, 81—; instr. field work Sch. Social Service Adminstrn., U. Chgo., 1971-79, cons. Ford Tchr. Tng. Program, staff mem. Grad. Sch. Edn., 1971-72, clin. asso. Sch. Social Service Adminstrn., 1974-79, coordinator bd. edn., 1979-80, acting coordinator, 1980-81; tchr. 1st course given on staff, human relations and social work Chgo. Bd. Edn., 1971-72. U.S. Children's Bur. fellow, 1945-47. Registered cert. social worker, Ill.; certified tchr.-social worker Chgo. Bd. Edn. Mem. Nat. Assn. Social Workers (workshop 5th Symposium 1977), Acad. Certified Social Workers. Contbr. articles to profl. jours. Address: 1236 E 57th St Chicago IL 60637

FRIEDMAN, MARIA ANDRE, public relations executive; b. Jackson, Mich., June 12, 1950; d. Robert Andre and Mary MacLean (Thompson) Hoving; m. Stanley N. Friedman, July 22, 1973; children—Alexandra, Adam. B.A. cum laude, U. Md., 1972, M.A., 1980. Writer, U.S. Bur. Mines, Washington, 1973-78; head writer Nat. Ctr. for Health Service Research and Health Care Tech. Assessment, DHHS, Rockville, Md., 1978-84, pub. affairs dir., 1984—; pres. Medi-Systems, Inc., Silver Spring, Md., 1980—; v.p. Metro Med. Assocs., Silver Spring, 1982—. Mem. Nat. Assn. Govt. Communicators, Pub. Relations Soc. Am., NOW. Home: 12535 Heurich Rd Silver Spring MD 20902 Office: Nat Ctr for Health Services Research and Health Care Tech Assessment 1-46 Park Bldg Rockville MD 20857

FRIEDMAN, MARNA WENDY, production coordinator, consultant; b. Pequannock, N.J., Jan. 13, 1959; d. Harold and Marcia Ruth (Nyman) F. Student Fairleigh Dickinson U., 1977-78; B.S., C.W. Post Coll., Greenvale, N.Y., 1981; M.A., New Sch. Social Research, N.Y.C., 1986. Sales mgr., Macy's, N.Y.C., 1981-82; traffic coordinator Direct Mktg. Agy., Stamford, Conn., 1982-83; prodn. coordinator The N.Y. Community Trust, N.Y.C., 1983—; v.p., dir. Prescriptive Promotions, Montville, N.J., 1984—; pres., bd. dirs. Baby Basket Co., Ltd., Montville, 1986—; cons. Friedman Enterprises, Montville, 1978—, Ferraioli, Wesdyk & Freifeld, Prompton Lakes, N.J., 1984-85. Mem. county com. Morris County Democrat, Montville, 1983-84; mem. Nat. Dem. Com., Washington, 1983—. Mem. Women in Communications, Internat. Communications Assn., Nat. Acad. TV Arts & Scis., Broadcasting Edn. Assn., Soc. Satellite Profls. Jewish. Avocations: music, traveling, gourmet cooking, calligraphy. Home: 2 Brittany Rd Montville NJ 07045 Office: The New York Community Trust 415 Madison Ave New York NY 10017

FRIEDMAN, ROCHELLE SAMUELS, lawyer; b. Pitts., Apr. 30, 1938; d. Leopold Weiss and Florence (Leipzig) Zimmerman; m. Irwin Mark Samuels, Aug. 23, 1959 (dec. 1968); children—Sharon Beth Samuels, Michele Lauren Samuels; m. Joseph Friedman, Nov. 25, 1970. B.A., U. Pitts., 1959, J.D., 1972. Bar: Pa. 1972. Dir. Gov.'s Justice Commn. Projects, Pitts., 1974-76; solicitor, clk. of cts. Allegheny County, Pitts., 1974-76; cons. criminal ct. tech. assistance Am. U. Law Sch., Washington, 1976; sole practice law, Pitts., 1972—; mem. faculty Grad. Sch. Pub. Health, U. Pitts., 1976-77; jud. law clk. Ct. Common Pleas, Allegheny County, Pitts., 1976—; bd. mem. SW Pa. Pre-Trial Services, Inc., Pitts., 1983—; mem. Exec. Women's Council, Pitts. Past chmn. legis. com. on juvenile justice Nat. Council Jewish Women, Pitts.; past mem. bd. dirs. C. Howard Marcy Hosp., Pitts., Big Bros. and Sisters of Greater Pitts., Community Day Sch., Pitts.; Republican candidate for clk. of cts., Pitts., 1975, for judge, 1977, 85; mem. B'nai B'rith Women, Orgn. of Rehab. through Tng. Mem. Allegheny County Bar Assn. (legal rights of women sect.), Pa. Bar Assn., Pa. Trial Lawyers Assn., Nat. Assn. Criminal Def. Lawyers. Office: 1125 Heberton St Pittsburgh PA 15206

FRIEDMAN, S. LILA, librarian; b. Bklyn., Sept. 25, 1926; d. Ephraim Eliezer and Naomi (Weisdorff) Ritter; m. S. Lester Friedman, Jan. 25, 1946; children—Matthew, Joel, Amy. B.A., Bklyn. Coll., 1948; M.L.S., L.I. U., 1975. Cert. library media specialist, secondary sch. tchr. library, N.Y. Librarian, Hunter Coll. High Sch., N.Y.C., 1973-74, Hawthorne (N.Y.) Cedar Knolls Sch., 1976, Samuel Tilden High Sch., Bklyn., 1978-79, Bellerose Jewish Ctr., Floral Park, N.Y., 1980—, dir. library, 1980—; librarian Katharine Gibbs Sch., Huntington, N.Y., 1984—. Area chmn. Queens United Cerebral Palsy, 1969, 71. Recipient 25th Anniversary award State of Israel Bonds, 1975, Youth Services award B'nai B'rith, 1983. Mem. ALA, Assn. Jewish Libraries, L.I. Assn. Jewish Libraries (charter mem.), Am. Assn. Sch. Librarians. Jewish. Home: 80 49 252d St Bellerose NY 11426 Office: Bellerose Jewish Center 254 04 Union Turnpike Floral Park NY 11004

FRIEDMAN, SALLY MAE, writer, editor; b. Phila., Dec. 17, 1938; d. Hymen and Lillian (Goldberg) Schwartz; m. Victor Friedman, July 3, 1960; children—Jill Meredith, Amy Elizabeth, Nancy Allison. B.S. in Edn., U. Pa., 1960. Freelance writer, 1968—; adj. prof. Burlington County Coll., Pemberton, N.J., 1982—; contract writer Syndicated Writers Group, Boyertown, Pa., 1984—. Contbr. articles to numerous publs., including N.Y. Times, Phila. Inquirer, Pa. Gazette, N.J. Monthly, Atlantic City Mag., Jersey Woman mag., Princeton Packet papers, Burling County Times, Welcomat; syndicated columnist Lifesounds; features editor Jersey Woman mag., 1982—. Bd. dirs. Foster Parents Burlington County, N.J., 1984-85, Cherry Hill unit Am. Heart Assn., N.J., 1985-86. Recipient Communicator of Yr. award N.J. Assn. Women Bus. Owners, 1984. Mem. N.J. Press Assn. (Best Column award 1981), Burlington County Press Assn. (Best Column award 1982). Democrat. Jewish. Avocations: antique collecting; sports.

FRIEDMAN, SUE TYLER, foundation executive, technical publications company executive; b. Nürnberg, W.Ger., Feb. 28, 1925; came to U.S., 1938;

d. William Theilheimer and Ann (Federlein) Tyler; m. Gerald Manfred Friedman, June 27, 1948; children—Judith Fay Friedman Rosen, Sharon Mira Friedman Azaria, Devora Paula Friedman Zewibach, Eva Jane Friedman Scholle, Wendy Tamar Friedman Spanier. R.N., Beth Israel Sch. Nursing, 1941-43. Exec. dir. Ventures and Publs. of Gerald M. Friedman, 1964—; owner Tyler Publications, Watervliet and Troy, N.Y., 1978—; treas. Northeastern Sci. Found., Inc., Troy, 1979—; treas. Gerry Exploration, Inc., Troy, N.Y., 1982—; office mgr. Rensselaer Ctr. Applied Geology, Troy, 1983—. Pres. Pioneer Women/Na'amat, Tulsa, 1961-64, treas., Jerusalem, Israel, 1964, pres., Albany, N.Y., 1968-70; bd. dirs. Temple Beth-el, 1965—, dir. Hebrew Sch., 1965-80. Jewish. Avocation: world travel. Home: 32 24th St Troy NY 12180 Office: Rensselaer Ctr Applied Geology 15 3d St Box 746 Troy NY 12181-0746

FRIEDMAN, SUSAN LYNN BELL, public relations specialist; b. Lafayette, Ind., May 23, 1953; d. Virgil Atwood and Jean Loree (Wiggins) B.; m. Frank H. Friedman, July 31, 1976. B.A., Purdue U., 1975; M.S., Ind. State U., 1981. Asst. dir. pub. relations Vincennes U. Jr. Coll., Ind., 1977-83; dir. Knox County C. of C., Vincennes, 1983-84; writer/editor VSE Corp., Alexandria, Va., 1984-85; pub. info. officer Am. Assn. Community and Jr. Colls., Washington, 1985—; cons., 1982-84. Bd. dirs. Knox County chpt. Am. Heart Assn., 1982-84; mem. exec. bd. Leadership Vincennes, 1982-84; local coordinator Common Cause, Fairfax County, Va., 1984—. Hoosier scholar, 1971, 72. Mem. Annandale Bus. and Profl. Women (treas. 1985-86), Am. Assn. Women in Community and Jr. Colls. (nat. liaison 1985—), LWV (chpt. v.p. 1982-84), Edpress, Nat. Press Club. Democrat. Home: 6565 Sand Wedge Ct Alexandria VA 22312 Office: Am Assn Community and Jr Colls One Dupont Circle NW Washington DC 20036

FRIEDMANN, EMILY MACCARO, accountant, company executive; b. N.Y.C., Nov. 9, 1949; d. William Anthony and Katherine Gladys (Butzgy) Maccaro; m. James Bernard Friedmann, Nov. 11, 1978; children—Katherine, Margaret. B.S., Syracuse U., 1971. Cost acct. Automatic Connectors, Commack, N.Y., 1971-76; sr. cost analyst Standard Brands, N.Y.C., 1976-77; asst. controller So. Calif. Carton, Gardena, 1977-79; mgr. fin. planning Dynachem Corp., Tustin, Calif., 1979-84; mgr. cost acctg. Targeted Coverage Inc., Pomona, Calif. Republican. Roman Catholic. Home: 716 Big Falls Dr Diamond Bar CA 91765 Office: 3200A Pomona Blvd Pomona CA 91768

FRIEDMANN, JANEE ARMSTRONG, civic worker; b. Wilkes-Barre, Pa., Jan. 11, 1937; d. F. Thoburn and Sara (Northrup) Armstrong; m. Paul Friedmann, Apr. 24, 1962; children—Pamela, Cynthia. A.B. magna cum laude, Bryn Mawr Coll., 1959; M.Ed., Temple U., 1962; M.A., U. Pa., 1967. Pres., Jr. League, Springfield, Mass., 1975-76, Early Childhood Ctrs., Springfield, 1975-77, Springfield Orch. Assn., 1983—, Adult Edn. Council, Springfield, 1984—; v.p. Richard Salter Storrs Library, Longmeadow, Mass., 1985—; trustee Library and Museums Assn., Springfield, 1984—; bd. dirs. Springfield Central Bus. Dist., 1980—. Republican.

FRIEDRICH, MARGRET COHEN, guidance counselor; b. Balt., June 4, 1947; d. Joseph Cohen and Judith (Kline) Cohen Roisman; m. Jay Joseph Friedrich, May 16, 1971; children—David Benjamin, Marc Adam, Samantha Lauren. B.Ed., U. Miami-Fla., 1969, M.Ed., 1970. Cert. alcoholism and addiction counselor. Grad. asst. U. Miami, Coral Gables, Fla., 1969-70; tchr. Balt. Bd. Edn., 1970; guidance counselor Ridgewood Bd. Edn., N.J., 1970—; alcoholism counselor Bergen County Dept. Health, Paramus, N.J., 1981-82; in-service tchr. Ridgewood Bd. Edn., 1983, supr., coordinator peer counseling program high sch., 1979—; with Assn. Mental Health and Counseling of No. N.J., 1985—. Author tech. papers. Exec. bd. Hadassah, Ridgewood-Glen Rock, N.J., 1971—; youth leadership com. United Jewish Appeal, Bergen County, 1974-75; sec. Bergen County Youth Com. Substance Abuse, Paramus, 1980—, conf. coordinating com., 1983; treas. Ridgewood Coalition Substance Use and Abuse, 1983-84; fundraiser, treas. United Parents/Safe Homes, Ridgewood, 1984; lectr./educator Passaic County Juvenile Conf. Com., Paterson, N.J., 1984. Reisman scholar, 1969; U. Miami teaching asst., 1970, recipient Recognition award, 1968. Mem. N.J. Assn. Alcoholism Counselors, Nat. Assn. Suicidology, N.J. Edn. Assn., Ridgewood Edn. Assn., Bergen County Edn. Assn., N.J. Task Force on Women and Alcohol, N.J. Personnel and Guidance Assn., Sigma Delta Tau. (exec. bd. 1983-85). Democrat. Jewish. Office: Assn Mental Health and Counseling No NJ Fairlawn NJ 07410

FRIEMAN, HILDEGARDE, special educator, consultant, diagnostician; b. Balt., Jan. 11, 1948; d. Maurice and Ethel (Belson) F. B.S., U. Md., 1970; M.S., Johns Hopkins U., 1975, Cert. Advanced Standing in Edn., 1976; cert. Minimum Brain Dysfunction, Temple U. Med. Sch., 1976. Cert. educator. Spl. educator Balt. City Schs., 1970—; mem. Council Exception Edn., Balt., 1970—. Guest lectr. in field sta. WEAA, Morgan State U., 1980. Cons. Spl. Olympics, Balt., 1983—; ednl. cons. city and state legislatures and dels., 1980—. Recipient Resolution for Outstanding Work, Balt. City Council, 1982; Cert. of Merit Parents Tchrs. Adv. Council Balt. City Schs., 1974, 75. Mem. NEA, Balt. Tchr. Union, Phi Lambda Theta. Democrat. Avocations: music, theater, health club. Home: 317 Lord Byson Ln Apt T1 Cockeysville MD 21030

FRIEND, MARION SKEATH, retired educator; b. Phila., July 18, 1922; d. William Charles and Marie (Hoffman) Skeath; B.A., Wellesley Coll., 1944; M.Ed., Coll. William and Mary, 1973; m. Edwin Abell Friend, Jr., June 29, 1946; children—Patricia, Marianna, Edwin Abell. Tchr. math. Miss Ellis Sch. for Girls, Pitts., 1944-46; sec., dean of women Pa. State U., College Park, 1946-47; tchr. math. Suffolk (Va.) City Schs., 1952-54; owner/operator The Yarn Barn, Suffolk, 1964-68; tchr. math. Nansemond County Schs., Suffolk, 1969-70, Nansemond-Suffolk Acad., 1970-73, dir. instrn./curriculum, 1973-81. Chmn. ecumenical comm. Meth. Ch., 1979-81, pres. Women's Soc., 1963-65. Mem. Nat. Council Tchrs. Math., Assn. Supervision and Curriculum Devel., Va. Assn. Supervision and Curriculum Devel., Tidewater Council Tchrs. Math., Council Basic Edn., Va. Consortium Social Studies Suprs. and Coll. Educators. Suffolk-Nansemond Hist. Soc., Suffolk Art League, Kappa Delta Pi, Kappa Delta Gamma. Address: 110-B 78th St Virginia Beach VA 23451

FRIEND, MIRIAM RUTH, personnel agency executive; b. Scranton, Pa., May 19, 1925; d. Benjamin and Etta (Weiss) Loewy; B.A., Syracuse U., 1947; cert. Inst. Public Welfare Tng., Cornell U., 1950; m. Sidney Friend, Aug. 27, 1950. Social worker child placing div. N.Y. State Dept. Welfare, 1948-52; v.p. Office Help Temporaries, Yonkers, N.Y., 1954-83; now pres. Friend and Friend Personnel Agy.; chmn. planning com. Pvt. Industry Council, 1979-80, pres., 1981-82. Bd. dirs. Yonkers Salvation Army, 1977—; bd. dirs. Yonkers Gen. Hosp., 1978—, pres., 1983-84; pres. Big Bros.-Big Sisters Yonkers, 1978-80, Work Opportunities Referrals for Kids; chmn. leadership dinner United Way; docent Hudson River Mus.; mem. vocat. adv. council Elizabeth Seton Coll. Recipient Yonkers Safari award for community service, 1978, Disting. Service award United Way, 1983, Yonkers Council Chs. award, 1984. Mem. Yonkers C. of C. (chmn. breakfast club 1978), Bus. and Profl. Women, Syracuse U. Alumni Assn., Psi Chi. Clubs: Soroptimists (pres. 1970-72), Racquet (Yonkers). Home: 11 Abbey Pl Yonkers NY 10701

FRIEND, SHARLEE FRIEDMAN BRUCHA, retired social worker; b. Chelm, Poland, Jan. 18, 1920; came to U.S., 1921; d. Abe Joseph and Minnie (Shtainman) Friedman; m. Leonard N. Friend, June 7, 1942 (dec.); children—Harold, Geraldine, David Lee, Francine, Barbara. M.S., Sam Houston State U., Huntsville, Tex., 1974; M.S.W., U. Houston, 1977. Cert. social worker. Caseworker, Dept. Pub. Welfare, Houston, 1963-76; social worker Harris County Children's Protective Service, Houston, 1976-85; cons. Women's Success Devel. Ctr., Houston, 1977-80. Tchr. Beth Yeshurun Synagogue, Houston, 1953-64; bd. dirs. Jewish War Veterans Shrine, Washington, 1980—; mem. nat. exec. bd., pres. Nat. Ladies Aux. Jewish War Veterans, 1985-86. Democrat. Lodges: B'nai B'rith Women (chpt. pres. 1961-63, council pres. 1964-65, state pres. 1966-67), Hanna Senesch Hadassah (pres. 1975-76).

FRIEND, SUSAN RAMONA, investigators' assistant; b. Burbank, Calif., June 4, 1958; d. Alden Emerson and Frieda (Rose) Friend. A.A., Moorpark Jr. Coll., 1984; postgrad. Calif. Luth. U. Actress/model White Oak Dinner Theatre, Granada Hills, Calif., 1977; pre-sch. tchrs. asst. Valley Jr. Coll. Pre-Sch., Van Nuys, Calif., 1976-77; med. asst. Valley Med. Clinic, Sepulveda, Calif., 1978-79; dep. clk. III (investigators' asst.) Marshal's Warrant div., Encino, Calif., 1979—; tour hostess Valley Travel Co., Van Nuys, Calif., 1985—. Mem. Assn. for Anorexia Nervosa and Other Disorders, Nat. Assn. Female Execs. Democrat. Office: Los Angeles County Marshal's Warrant Div 5767 White Oak Ave Encino CA 91316

FRIENDSHUH, JANET KAY, computer consultant, real estate broker; b. St. Paul, July 7, 1952; d. William Joseph and Helen Elizabeth (Cunningham) F.; m. Davis Rolland Schwartz, Mar. 4, 1976 (div. 1982). A.A., Normandale Community Coll., Bloomington, Minn., 1972; B.A. magna cum laude, U. Minn.-Mpls., 1976. Real estate agt. Pyramid Realty, San Francisco, 1978-81; computer specialist Berkeley Cons. Group, San Francisco, 1980-81; real estate broker Marin County Bd. Real Estate, San Rafael, Calif., 1981—; computer cons., trainer, San Francisco, 1983—; pres. Keystrokes, Bloomington, 1983—, v.p. ops. Terra Roofing System, Inc., Mpls. Mem. Minn. Office Systems Assn. (assoc. editor jour. 1984-85). Avocations: swimming, skiing, snowmobiling, backpacking, reading. Office: Keystrokes 9409 Grand Aves Bloomington MN 55420

FRIES, HELEN SERGEANT HAYNES (MRS. STUART G. FRIES), civic leader; b. Atlanta; d. Harwood Syme and Alice (Hobson) Haynes; student Coll. William and Mary, 1935-38; m. Stuart G. Fries, May 5, 1938. Bd. dirs. Community Ballet Assn., Huntsville, Ala., 1968—; mem. nat. nurses aid com. ARC, 1958-59; dir. ARC Aero Club, Eng., 1943-44; supr. ARC Clubmobile, Europe, 1944-46; mem. women's com. Nat. Symphony Orch., Washington, 1959—; vol. docent, sponsor Huntsville Mus. Art; vol. docent Weeden House of Twickenham Hist. Preservation Dist. Assn., Huntsville; bd. dirs. Madison County Republican Club, 1969-70; mem. nat. council Women's Nat. Rep. Club N.Y., 1963—, chmn. hospitality com., 1963-65; bd. dirs. League Rep. Women, 1952-61. Mem. Nat. Soc. Colonial Dames Am., DAR, Nat. Trust Hist. Preservation, D.C., Valley Forge (Pa.), Eastern Shore of Va. hist. socs., Nat. Soc. Daus. Am. Colonists, Assn. Preservation Va. Antiquities, Greensboro Soc. Preservation, Tenn. Valley Geneal. Soc., Huntsville Hist. Soc., English Speaking Union, Alliance Francaise. Clubs: Washington, Capitol Hill, Army-Navy Country (Washington); Huntsville Country, Heritage (Huntsville, Ala.); Garden (Redstone Arsenal), Redstone (Ala.) Yacht; Army-Navy (D.C.). Home: 409 Zandale Dr Huntsville AL 35801

FRIES, MAUREEN HOLMBERG, English literature educator; b. Buffalo, July 14, 1931; d. Howard Henry and Margaret Teresa (Wiley) Holmberg; children—Jeb Stuart, Howard Gordon, John Pelham, Sheila Maureen. A.B. magna cum laude, D'Youville Coll., 1952; M.A., Cornell U., 1953; Ph.D., SUNY-Buffalo, 1969. Advt. copywriter Eastman Advt. Co., Ithaca, N.Y., 1953-54, Coe Advt. Co., Syracuse, N.Y., 1954; free-lance journalist, Buffalo, 1964-69; teaching fellow SUNY-Buffalo, 1965-69; asst. prof. N.Y. State U. Coll. at Fredonia, 1969-73, assoc. prof., 1973-77, prof. medieval Brit. lit., 1977—; lectr. and cons. in field; participant, chmn. numerous confs. Contbr. articles to profl. jours., chpts. to books; Mem. editorial bds. Avalon to Camelot, 1984—, Interpretations, 1984—. Reader various publs. Recipient Chancellor's award for Excellence in Teaching, 1977, Callista Jones award, 1982; named to Kasling Meml. lectureship State U. of N.Y. Coll. at Fredonia, 1985; NEH fellow, 1975-76; grantee State Univ. of N.Y. Faculty Research awards, 72, 73, 79, 80, Am. Philos. Soc., summer 1978, Am. Council Learned Socs. travel grant, summer 1978, NEH, 1979—; Fulbright Research and Lecturing award, sr. professorship Universitat Regensburg, Fed. Republic Germany, Apr.-July 1984, other awards, grants, fellowships. Mem. Am. Classical League, Internat. Assn. Univ. Profs. of English Internat. Courtly Lit. Soc., Medieval Acad. of Am., MLA (chairperson Arthunàn Discussion Group ann. meeting Houston 1980, N.Y.C. 1981, mem. exec. com. 1978-82, organizer, chairperson other ann. meetings northeastern and southeastern chpts.), Société Internationale Arthurienne. Democrat. Roman Catholic. Office: New York State Univ Coll at Fredonia 254 Fenton Hall Fredonia NY 14063

FRIMML, JAYMEE JO, chiropractor, nurse; b. Watertown, S.D., Oct. 18, 1949; d. Rodney Elsworth and Marie Ruth (Musta) Dale; m. Steven James Frimml, July 1, 1984; 1 child, Richard Mark. A.S. in Nursing, So. Coll., Collegedale, Tenn., 1970; student U. Ariz., 1979-81; D. Chriopractic, Palmer Coll. Chiropractic, Davenport, Iowa, 1985. Registered nurse, Tenn., Tex., Okla., Mich., Ariz., Iowa, Idaho. Emergency room nurse Madison Hosp., Tenn., 1970-71; nursing supr. Wilson N. Jones Hosp., Sherman, Tex., 1972-74; neonatal nurse specialist Lansing Gen. Hosp., Mich., 1974-78; clin. nurse leader, pediatrics Tucson Med. Ctr., 1978-81, pulmonary nurse specialist, 1981-82; chiropractor Cramer Chiropractice Clinic, Boise, Idaho, 1986—; instr. lectr. Seventh-day Adventist Better Living Com., Caldwell, Idaho, 1986. Mem. Am. Chiropractice Assn., Internat. Chiropractic Assn., Council on Roentgenology, Idaho Assn. Chiropractice Physicians, Sigma Phi Chi. Seventh-day Adventist. Home: 3613 Juanita Way Nampa ID 83651 Office: Chiropractic Ctr 314 D Holly St Nampa ID 83651

FRISON, LINDA DIANE, physician; b. Portland, Oreg., Apr. 8, 1947; d. William Wendell and Jacy Claire (Austin) Frison; m. Robert Scott Glasser, Feb. 14, 1981. B.A., U. Oreg.-Eugene, 1969, M.D., Portland, 1974. Intern, Hennepin County Hosp., Mpls., 1974-75; resident U. Minn., Mpls., 1975-76, Stanford Hosp., Palo Alto, Calif., 1977-79; mem. Ob-Gyn staff Kaiser Hosp., Hayward, Calif., 1980-82; practice medicine specializing in Ob-Gyn, Fremont, Calif., 1983—; mem. staff Washington Twp. Hosp., Fremont, Calif., St. Rose Hosp., Hayward, Kaiser Hosp., Hayward, Stanford (Calif.) Hosp. Fellow Am. Coll. Ob-Gyn; mem. Am. Fertility Soc. Democrat. Methodist. Home: 3568 Bittern Pl Fremont CA 94536 Office: 2243 Mowry Ave Suite F Fremont CA 94538

FRITSCHNER, BEVERLY BACHMAN, training company executive; b. San Diego, July 9, 1946; d. Roy Francis and Alice (Treutlein) Bachman; m. Walter J. Fritschner, June 7, 1969 (div. Mar. 1972). B.A., San Diego State U., 1969; secondary cert. Calif. Western U., 1970; M.B.A., Nat. U., San Diego, 1973. Tchr. San Diego Pub. Schs., 1970-76; dir. product devel. Learnex Corp., San Diego, 1976-77; cons. Control Data Corp., San Diego, 1977-79, cons. mktg. edn., 1979-81, mgr. mktg. edn., Mpls., 1981-82; dir. edn. NBI, Boulder, Colo., 1982-83; pres. BBF & Assocs., Boulder, 1982—. Mem. Colo. State Adv. Council Vocat. Edn., 1982; chair Colo. State Council Vocat. Edn., 1983—; mem. Boulder Valley Vo-Tech Adv. Com., 1982—. Mem. Nat. Council Vocat. Edn. (com. council devel. 1983—, chair subcom. 1983—), Boulder C. of C. (legis. affairs com. 1983—), Inst. Mgmt. Cons. (assoc.), Sigma Kappa. Republican. Methodist. Clubs: PEO, ZLAC Rowing. Avocations: tennis; skiing; golf. Home: 2702 6th St Boulder CO 80306

FRITTER, GENEVIEVE DAVISSON, violinist, composer; b. Clarksburg, W.Va., Dec. 13, 1915; d. Dorsey Achilles and I. Maude (Wilcox) Davisson; B.Mus., Judson Coll., 1937; postgrad. Juilliard Summer Sch., 1937-38, Birmingham Conservatory of Music, 1939-40, Cin. Conservatory of Music, 1941-43; m. C. Eldon Fritter, Aug. 31, 1940 (dec. 1975); children—Jean Louise, Thelma Priscilla. Supr. music Lafayette (Ala.) Pub. Schs., 1937-39, Fairfield, Ala., 1939-40; violinist Birmingham Symphony, 1939-40; tchr violin and theory Quinn Sch. Music, Lakewood, Ohio, 1944-49; freelance violinist, Washington, 1959—; concertmaster Nat. Ballet Orch., 1965-70; music dir., resident composer Montgomery Ballet Co., 1960-80; violinist Kennedy Center Opera House Orch., Washington, until 1982, also Filene Center Orch., Wolf Trap Farm Park, Vienna, Va., 1971-82; lectr. on composition; compositions include: Sinfonietta No. 1, 1978; Poem for Flute and Orch., 1981; Theme and Variations for String Orch., 1976; String Quartet No. 2, 1982. Recipient 1st prize song div. Nat. Fedn. Music Clubs, 1940, Outstanding Alumna award Judson Coll., 1966. Mem. Am. Music Center, ASCAP, Am. Fedn. Musicians, Am. Women Composers, Inc., Friday Morning Music of Washington, Mu Phi Epsilon. Congregationalist.

FRITTS, LILLIAN ELIZABETH, nurse; b. N.Y.C., July 19, 1923; d. William Franklin and Elzora Jane (Hodge) Bowen; A.D.N., R.N., Central Peidmont Community Coll., 1969; m. Thurman Luther Fritts, Aug. 5, 1944; children—William Luther, Franklin Lee, George Allen. Emergency room nurse Lexington (N.C.) Meml. Hosp., 1953-58; office nurse James T. Welborn, M.D., Lexington, 1958-60; staff nurse Haven Nursing Center, Lexington, 1960-61; pvt. duty nurse, 1961-63; owner, partner Buena Vista Nursing Center, Lexington, 1964—; adult extension tchr. Davidson County Community Coll., 1978, adv. bd. nursing program, 1969-79. Mem. Am. Nurses Assn., N.C. Nurses Assn., Lic. Practical Nurse Orgn. (state sec. 1958-60), N.C. Lic. Practical Nurse Assn., Dist. 9 Nurse Assn. N.C., N.C. Health Care Facilities Services Assn., Gideons Internat. Baptist. Home: Everhart Rd PO Box 419 Lexington NC 27292

FRITZ, BARBARA HUGHES, lawyer; b. Rusk County, Tex., Feb. 11, 1928; d. Charles Allen and O'Dell (Harris) Hughes; m. Richard J. Fritz, June 14, 1952; children—Catherine, Maranda. B.B.A., U. Houston, 1974, J.D., 1977. Bar: Tex. 1977; cert. family law Tex. Bd. Legal Specialization. Product mgr. Johns-Manville Sales Corp., Houston, 1956-66; creative dir. copy Madison Advt., Inc., Louisville, 1968-71; store mgr. Spalding Services, Inc., Louisville, 1971-73; ptnr. Fritz & Fritz, Victoria, Tex., 1977—. Mem. Tex. Bar Assn., Assn. Trial Lawyers Am., Order Barons, Phi Kappa Phi. Address: PO Box 4626 Victoria TX 77903

FRITZ, DEBORAH LEE, health policy analyst, researcher; b. Denver, June 29, 1950; d. Curtis Lee and Shirley (Skelton) F. B.A., Duke U., 1972; M.P.H., U. N.C., 1976; M.Ph., Syracuse U., 1980, Ph.D., 1983. Sr. planner Central N.Y. Health Systems Agy., Syracuse, 1978-80, dist. dir., 1981-82; dir. planning Golden Empire Health Systems Agy., Sacramento, 1982-83; sr. mgr. for research policy and program devel. UMWA Health and Retirement Funds, Washington, 1984-85; exec. dir. Ctr. for Prepaid Health Care Research, Rockville, Md., 1985—; cons. Presbyn. Med. Services, Santa Fe, 1982. Founding mem., officer Sacramento Council of Occupational Health and Safety, 1982-83; mem. Met. Washington Area Council of Health Planning Agy., Washington, 1984—; chairperson Montgomery County Health Planning Commn., Md., 1986. Mem. Women in Govt. Relations, Am. Pub. Health Assn. Avocations: dance; performing arts. Office: Ctr for Prepaid Health Care Research 451 Hungerford Dr Suite 604 Rockville MD 20850

FRITZ, ETHEL MAE HENDRICKSON, writer; b. Gibbon, Nebr., Feb. 4, 1925; d. Walter Earl and Alice Hazel (Mickish) Hendrickson; B.S., Iowa State U., 1949; m. C. Wayne Fritz, Feb. 25, 1950; children—Linda Sue, Krista Jane. Dist. home economist Internat. Harvester Co., Des Moines, 1949-50; writer Wallace's Farmer mag., Des Moines, 1960-64; free-lance writer, 1960—. Chmn. Ariz. Council Flower Show Judges, 1983-85. Accredited master flower show judge. Mem. Women in Communications (pres. Phoenix profl. chpt.; nat. task force com. 1980—), Am. Soc. Profl. and Exec. Women, Am. Home Econs. Assn., Southwest Writers' Conf., Ariz. Authors Assn. PEO, Phi Upsilon Omicron, Kappa Delta. Author: The Story of an Amana Winemaker, 1984.

FRITZ, FORREST MAE, state official; b. Fulton, Ohio, Aug. 21, 1929; d. Clarence Robert and Anna Ella (Liggett) Skinner; m. Jerrold Eli Fritz, Aug. 20, 1954; children—Frederic Allen, Jeri Anne, Teri Anne. Student pub. schs., Cardington, Ohio. Sec. Hydraulic Press Mfg., Mt. Gilead, Ohio, 1947-53, Waring Enterprises, Delaware Water Gap, Pa., 1953-55; sec. Office Employment Security, Stroudsburg, Pa., 1962-69, claims interviewer, 1969, unemployment compensation supr., 1969—. Mem. Am. Mgmt. Assn., Bus. and Profl. Women of Stroudsburg (newsletter editor 1983-84, treas. 1984-85, 2d v.p. 1985-86). Republican. Methodist. Home: 181 Analomink St East Stroudsburg PA 18301 Office: Office of Employment Security 730 Phillips St Stroudsburg PA 18360

FRITZE, SHEILA KAY, librarian; b. Belleville, Ill., Oct. 31, 1949; d. Orel Emil and Louise Elizabeth (Zimmerman) Boos; m. James Ronald Fritze, June 17, 1972; children—Elizabeth Ann, Julia Louise. A.A., Belleville Area Coll., 1969; B.S., U. Ill., 1971, M.S., 1972. Librarian, Wellington Community Sch. Dist. (Ill.), 1972-74, Crescent City Pub. Library, 1975-82, Eagle Valley Elem. Sch. (Colo.), 1983—. Named Dist. Clubwoman of Yr., 8th Dist. Ill. Jr. Woman's Club, 1980. Mem. Colo. Ednl. Media Assn., Colo. Library Assn., ALA, Friends of the Library, Beta Phi Mu, Kappa Delta Phi. Republican. Lutheran. Clubs: Eagle Dandelion (pres. 1985-86), Crescent City Jr. Women's (sec. 1979-81). Home: 101 Short Horn Dr PO Box 985 Eagle CO 81631 Office: Eagle Valley Elem Sch PO Box 780 Eagle CO 81631

FRIZZI, VIRGINIA AGNES, college official, writer; b. Pitts., Nov. 20, 1953; d. Joseph Nicholas and Virginia Lourdes (Sheehan) Frizzi, Sr. B.A., Point Park Coll., 1975, M.A., 1984; postgrad. U. Pitts., 1977-81. Freelance writer, Pitts., 1975—; dir. media relations and pub. relations Point Park Coll., Pitts., 1976—; book reviewer Pitts. Press, 1981—. Contbr. articles and revs. to publs. including S.C. Monitor, Seventeen mag. Mem. pub. relations com. Am. Cancer Soc. of Western Pa. Mem. Women in Communications (pres. Pitts. 1982-83, Matrix award 1983), Am. Women in Radio and TV, Soc. Profl. Journalists (treas. Pitts. 1977—, rep. to Pitts. Press Club Golden Quill competition com. 1981-82, nat. freedom of info. and profl. chpt. devel. com. 1983—, asst. dir. for Western Pa.), Pitts. Press Club, Women's Press Club Pitts., Nat. Fedn. Press Women. Home: 1715 Chislett St Pittsburgh PA 15206 Office: Office of Media Relations Point Park Coll 201 Wood St Pittsburgh PA 15222

FROESCHNER, GWENDOLYN SUE, lawyer; b. Dexter, Mo., Apr. 10, 1945; d. David Franklin Pullam and Dorothy (McCollough) Mathews; m. Gary George Froeschner, May 22, 1965; children—Holly Rebecca, Brennan Theodore. A.B. in History, U. Mo.-Rolla, 1975; J.D., Washington U., St. Louis, 1978. Bar: Mo. 1978, Ill. 1979. Legal aid asst. Legal Aid-St. Louis, 1977; atty. Fed. Land Bank, St. Louis, 1978-81; sole practice, Columbia, 1981-82; ptnr. Shurtleff & Froeschner and predecessor firm Columbia, 1982—; atty. Heart of Mo. Sr. Games and Festival, Columbia, 1983—. Bd. dirs. YWCA, St. Louis, 1979-81; bd. dirs., past sec. Family and Children's Services Residential Adv. Bd., 1982—. Mem. Assn. Trial Lawyers Am., Mo. Assn. Trial Lawyers, ABA, St. Louis Bar Assn., Mo. Bar Assn. Democrat. Home: 603 Medavista St Columbia MO 65201 Office: Shurtleff & Froeschner 517 Guitar Bldg Columbia MO 65201

FROHMAN, CAROLE JOAN, interior designer, appraiser; b. Bklyn., July 22, 1930; d. Arthur and Shirley R. (Kaplan) Frohman; m. Harvey Wiener, May 22, 1955 (div. June 1964); 1 child, Byron. B.S. in Elem. Edn., Barnard Coll., 1950; postgrad. Ohio State U., 1957-58; student Frank LaForge, Estelle Liebling, William Herman, Alberto Digoristiaga. Child prodigy, performing most of maj. concert halls of world; apprentice Ruby Ross Wood-Billy Baldwin Interior Design Co., 1949-51, assoc. designer, 1951-53; now pres. Carole Frohman Interior Design, North Miami, Fla. Fund raiser Dem. party, Boston, 1946; entertainer USO, 1943-45, VA Hosp., Miami, Fla., 1972-75. Contbg. author, co-editor cook book to raise funds for ARC. Juilliard Prep. Sch. scholar, 1941; named Most Talented Newcomer Am. Motion Pictures, 1946. Mem. Nat. Home Fashions League (v.p. program com. 1982-85), Am. Soc. Interior Design, Profl. Antique Dealers Assn., Internat. Soc. Interior Design, Nat. Acad. Theater Arts and Scis., NOW, SAG, AGVA, AFTRA. Democrat. Avocation: voice coaching. Home: 11960 NE 19th Dr #15 North Miami FL 33181 Office: Carole Frohman Interior Design 11960 NE 19th Dr #15 North Miami FL 33181

FROHOCK, JOAN (WALTON), indsl. supply co. exec.; b. Des Moines, Aug. 6, 1939; d. John Martin and Dorothy (McCauley) Walton; A.A., Stephens Coll., Columbia, Mo., 1958; B.A., U. Wis., 1961; J.D., Drake U., 1964; m. Richard Wyman Frohock, June 27, 1964—children—Kent Martin, Trent Warren. With Standard Bearings Co. of Des Moines, 1956—, v.p., 1962-74, pres., 1974—, pres. Standard Bearing Co. of Mason City (Iowa), 1978—; pres. ICOM Systems, Inc., 1979—; pres. Standard Bearings Co. of Davenport, Inc., Standard Bearings Co. of Sioux City, Inc., Standard Bearings Co. of Cedar Rapids (Iowa), 1982—, Standard Bearings Co. of Tulsa, 1984—. Mem. Iowa State Bar Assn., Greater Des Moines C.of C. Republican. Episcopalian. Office: 2350 Hubbell Ave PO Box 823 Des Moines IA 50304

FROMM, ERIKA (MRS. PAUL FROMM), clinical psychologist; b. Frankfurt, Germany, Dec. 23, 1910; d. Siegfried and Clementine (Stern) Oppenheimer; came to U.S., 1938, naturalized, 1944; Ph.D. magna cum laude, U. Frankfurt, 1933; postgrad. child care program, Chgo. Inst. for Psychoanalysis, 1949-51; m. Paul Fromm, July 20, 1938; 1 dau., Joan (Mrs. Greenstone). Chief psychologist Apeldoorn State Hosp. (Holland), 1935-38, Francis W. Parker Sch., 1944-51; supervising psychologist Inst. for Juvenile Research, Chgo., 1951-53; asst. prof. to assoc. prof. Northwestern U. Med. Sch., 1954-61; prof. U. Chgo., 1961-76, prof. emeritus, 1976—, professorial lectr. Sch. Social Service Adminstrn., 1976—; mem. faculty Chgo. Sch. Profl. Psychology, 1980—. Diplomate Am. Bd. Examiners in Profl. Psychology, Am. Bd. Examiners Clin. Hypnosis. Fellow Am. Psychol. Assn. (pres. div. 30, 1972-73), Am. Orthopsychiat. Assn. (dir. 1961-63), AAAS, Soc. Clin. Exptl. Hypnosis (sec. 1965-67, pres. 1975-77); mem. Am. Bd. Psychol. Hypnosis (pres. 1971-74), Ill. Psychol. Assn. (council 1951-53, 55-57, bd. examiners 1959-62, v.p. bd. examiners 1960-61), Soc. Projective Techniques, Sigma Xi. Author: (with L.D. Hartman) Intelligence-A Dynamic Approach; (with Thomas M. French) Dream Interpretation: A New Approach, 1964, 2d edit., 1986; (with Ronald E. Shor) Hypnosis: Developments in Research and New Perspectives, 1972, 2d edit., 1979; (with Daniel P. Brown) Hypnotherapy and Hypnoanalysis, 1986; also numerous articles in profl. jours. Mem. editorial bd. Jour. Clin. and Exptl. Psychopathology, 1951-59; clin. editor Internat. Jour. Clin. and Exptl. Hypnosis, 1968—; mem. adv. bd. Jour. Imagination, Cognition and Personality, 1981—; assoc. editor Brit. Jour. Hypnosis, 1982—; cons. editor Psychoanalytic Psychology, 1983—. Home: 5715 S Kenwood Ave Chicago IL 60637 Office: Dept Behavioral Sciences U Chicago 5848 S University Ave Chicago IL 60637

FROMMELT, KATHERINE HELEN MURRAY, nurse; b. Lancaster, Wis., Sept. 7, 1947; d. William Roy and Ivanelle Patricia (Key) Murray; m. David John Frommelt, Jan. 25, 1969; children—Sean J., Jennifer L., Bridget A., Molly K. and Meghan C. (twins). R.N., Mercy Med. Ctr. Sch. Nursing, 1968; B.S.N., U. Dubuque, 1983, postgrad., 1984—. Staff nurse for psychol. mental health U. Wis. Hosp., Madison, 1968-69; instr. Sch. Nursing, Mercy Med. Ctr., Dubuque, Iowa, 1969-70, inservice edn. dir., 1969-70; nursing vol. instr., coordinator Hospice of Dubuque, 1982—, bd. dirs., 1983—, chairperson, 1986—; nurse of hope Iowa div. Am. Cancer Soc., 1983—; occupational health program dir. Frommelt Industries, Dubuque, 1985—. Bd. dirs., mem. pub. relations and legis. action com. Mercy Med. Ctr., Dubuque, 1983—; mem. St. Joseph's Sch. Bd. Edn., Dubuque, 1984—, pres., 1985—. Recipient Vol. Health Service award Iowa Med. Soc. Aux., 1985, Outstanding Vol. award Am. Cancer Soc., 1985, Mercy Med. Ctr. Disting. Alumni award, 1986. Roman Catholic. Clubs: Iowa State Mothers of Twins (state rep. 1982-83); Dubuqueland Mothers of Twins (pres. 1980-82, adv. bd. 1983—), Sertoma (Service to Mankind award Dubuque 1984). Home: 103 Cedar Ridge Rd Thunder Hills Estates Peosta IA 52068

FROMM-HARJES, LINDA SUSAN, nurse, hospital official; b. Elizabeth, N.J., Feb. 9, 1950; d. George Michael and Mildred Josephine (Hankh) Fromm; m. Oskar Harjes, July 12, 1974; children—Blake Ashley, Emilie Elisabeth. B.A. in Zoology, Physiology, Rutgers U., 1972; M.S., N.Y. Med. Coll.-Pace U., 1974. R.N., Conn. Nurse practitioner Greenwich Hosp., Conn., 1974-76; asst. dir. nursing, inservice tng. dir. Martha's Vineyard Hosp., Oak Bluffs, Mass., 1976-78; dir. nursing Sharon Hosp., Conn., 1978-79, asst. exec. dir., dir. patient care services, 1979—; cons. Fromm-Harjes Assocs., Salisbury, Conn., 1980—. Contbr. articles to nursing mags. Mem. Am. Hosp. Assn., Am. Nurses Assn., Am. Nurses Assn. Nurse Adminstrs., Conn. Hosp. Assn., Conn. Nurses Assn., New Eng. Hosp. Assn., Womens Dem. Club, Northwest Nuclear Disarmament. Roman Catholic. Clubs: Mothers, Garden (Salisbury). Avocations: writing; hiking; gardening; swimming; painting. Home: Box 343 Ravine Ridge Salisbury CT 06068 Office: Sharon Hosp W Main St Sharon CT 06069

FROMMOETHELYDO, DONNA LYNN, utility company executive; b. Lufkin, Tex., Dec. 15, 1953; d. Jessie James and Irma Jewel (Timmes) Lewis; m. Clydelho L. Frommoethelydo, Nov. 21, 1980; B.Adminstrn., Sacramento State U., 1979; M.Bus., Golden Gate U., 1983. Work assignment clk. Pacific Telephone Co., Sacramento, 1973-75, computer operator, Sacramento, 1975-78, systems analyst, Concord, Calif., 1978-80, prodn. support mgr., Concord, 1980-82, staff analyst, San Francisco, 1982—. Mem. Nat. Assn. Female Execs. Home: 1455 Corcoran St Vallejo CA 94590 Office: Pacific Bell Room 420 370 3d St San Francisco CA 94107

FROOKS, DOROTHY, lawyer, author; b. Saugerties, N.Y.; d. Reginald and Rosita (Siberez) F.; LL.B., Hamilton Coll., 1918, LL.M., 1919; spl. courses Harvard U., N.Y. U., St. Lawrence U., U. N.C. Law Sch., Tulane U., Duquesne U.; Ps.D., Nat. Inst. Psychology, 1946; student Indsl. Coll. Armed Forces, 1953. Admitted to N.Y. State bar, 1920, U.S. Customs Ct., 1932, U.S. Supreme Ct., 1934, Fed. bar P.R., 1925, Alaska bar, 1935, Calif. bar, 1926, La. bar, 1929, U.S. Ct. Claims, 1950, U.S. Ct. Mil. Appeals, 1954, Hawaii bar, 1958, C.Z. bar, 1959; atty. Salvation Army, N.Y.C., 1920-21; organizer Poor Man's Ct., 1921; atty. for com. U.S. Coast Guard, 1939-40; counsel N.Y. State Bd. Edn., 1940-41; owner, editor Public Service Record, N.Y.C., 1920-21; pub. Murray Hill News, Oyster Bay News, 1916-19; columnist N.Y. Evening World, 1929-32; del. 1st Inter-Am. Bar Conf., Havana, 1921, Internat. Law Conf., Oxford, Eng., 1932, Atty. Gen.'s Crime Congress, Washington, 1934, Gov.'s Crime Conf., Albany, 1935; candidate for Congress-at-large State N.Y., 1934; nat. judge adv. Vets. of World War I, Inc., 1969; arbitrator Small Claims Ct., 1970—. Served as chief yeoman U.S. Navy in charge woman enrollments and recruiting, World War I; served in Judge Adv. Office, U.S. Army, World War II. Recipient medal for patriotic service by Woodrow Wilson, 1918. Mem. Nat. Assn. Woman Lawyers (organizer, pres. 1921-22, chmn. mil. and naval law com. 1946), Nat. Aero. Assn., Am. Judicature Assn., Wis. Archaeol. Soc., Am. Bar Assn., N.Y. State Bar Assn., Westchester County Bar Assn., Inter-Am. Bar, Women of Greater N.Y. (pres.), Murray Hill Assn. (pres.), Iota Tau Tau, Epsilon Eta Phi. Presbyterian. Clubs: Westchester Jr. League, Eastern Star, Peekskill Country (dir.). Author: The American Heart, 1919; Civilization, 1922; Criminal Obscenity, 1923; Chronology of the Catholic Church; Loves Law, 1927; Wills and Estates, 1929; All in Love, 1932; Over the Heads of Congress, 1935; Portia on Horseback, 1943; The Olympic Torch, 1946; Girls Get Their Men, 1947; How to Use the Small Claims Court, 1979; Wills, 1981; Lady Lawyer, 1975; Labor Courts-Outlaw Strikes, 1984; Poisoned with Power, 1986. Office: Route 6 Lake Mohegan Peekskill NY 10547

FROSCH, HELEN NELL MORRIS, psychoanalytic psychotherapist; b. Bklyn., Feb. 3, 1943; d. Stanley Jerome and Sophye Morris; B.A., N.Y. U., 1965; M.S.W., Adelphi U., 1973; cert. Inst. for Study of Psychotherapy, 1978; m. Allan Frosch, June 30, 1974; 1 dau., Samantha Cassidy. Child psychotherapist, dept. child psychiatry Brookdale Hosp., Bklyn., 1973-75; chief psychiat. social worker Yonkers (N.Y.) Youth Services Agy., 1975-78; staff therapist Bklyn. Center for Psychotherapy, 1978-79; patient services coordinator Nat. Huntington's Disease Assn., N.Y.C., 1978-79, nat. patient services coordinator, 1979-83; pvt. practice individual, family, group psychotherapy, and treatment of individuals and families experiencing psychol. stress of illness, N.Y.C., 1977—; leader workshops on setting up practice, 1979, 81, 83. Mem. Nat. Assn. Social Workers, Acad. Cert. Social Workers, Soc. for Advancement of Psychoanalytic Devel. Psychology (past pres. N.Y.C.). Author: Huntington's Disease: Differential Clinical Care, 1982; sr. author (pamphlet) Support Groups for Huntington's Disease Families, 1982. Office: 100 Riverside Dr New York NY 10024

FROST, ARETA LUE, advertising agency executive; b. Seattle, June 10, 1938; d. Jesse Raymond and Carolyn Lee (Green) Hurley; B.A. magna cum laude in Speech and Hearing Pathology, U. Wash., 1960; m. June 11, 1960 (div. 1971); children—John, Jeff, Chris. Speech and hearing pathologist, Seattle, Spokane, and Everett, Wash., also Monmouth, N.J., 1960-71; communications-public relations dir. Mayor's Office, City of Everett, 1971-73; mktg. cons., tng. instr. Gen. Telephone Co., Everett, 1973-75; account exec. Investor's Diversified Services, Seattle, 1975; exec. recruiter, mgr. Seattle office Acme Personnel, Inc., Seattle, 1976-78; mktg. mgr. Home Savs. & Loan Assn., Seattle, 1978—, asst. v.p., 1979-80; asst. v.p., mktg. mgr. Umpqua Savs. & Loan Assn., Roseburg, Oreg., 1980-83; community relations dir. Umpqua Community Coll., 1983-85; owner Tremel-Frost & Assocs., 1984-86; vocat. rehab. cons. C.M. Carney & Assocs., 1985—. Pres. Greeters, Roseburg C. of C. (bd. dirs. 1983-86); 1st v.p. United Way 1982, pres., 1983, bd. dirs., 1981-86; bd. dirs. United Way of Oreg., 1982-86; mem. Regional Vol. Leaders Conf., 1982-86. Mem. Mortar Bd., Phi Beta Kappa. Contbr. articles to profl. publs. Home: 758 Cleveland Loop Dr Roseburg OR 97470

FROST, CAROL SHIRLEY, manufacturing company executive; b. Boston, Oct. 1, 1929; d. Charles J. and Agnes R. (Carroll) Popp; student Boston schs.; m. Donald Frost, Oct. 15, 1949 (dec.); children—Donald, Lorraine, Charles, Linda; m. 2d John M. Marenghi, Oct. 3, 1982. Pres., owner Klarmann Rulings, Inc., Waltham, Mass., 1960-76, Manchester and Litchfield, N.H., 1976—. Mem. Soc. Photog. Scientists and Engrs. Office: Bancroft Hwy Route 3A Litchfield NH 03108

FROST, FELICIA DODEE, brokerage firm executive; b. Oklahoma City, Oct. 19, 1956; d. Carl S. Frost and Mikki (Matheny) Marcus; m. Michael S. Nunally, Apr. 19, 1984. Student So. Meth. U., 1974-76. Gen. mgr. Keystone Readers Service, Dallas, 1976-80; adminstrv. mgr then asst. v.p. Merrill Lynch Pierce Fenner and Smith, Dallas, 1980—. Pub. Frost Reading and Math Program, 1979. Mem. Dallas Securities Dealers Assn., Nat. Assn. Securities Dealers (gen. securities prin., mcpl. securities rulemaking bd. prin., registered options prin.), Alpha Lambda Delta. Republican. Baptist. Home: 5590 Spring Valley St Unit C 207 Dallas TX 75240 Office: Merrill Lynch Pierce Fenner and Smith 200 Campbell Centre I 8350 N Central Expressway Dallas TX 75206

FROST, LUZ AURORA, physical sciences educator, bank teller; b. Zamboanguita, Philippines, Jan. 1, 1945; came to U.S., 1980; d. Benjamin C. and Jovita (Galicano) Corsino; m. George E. Frost, Dec. 18, 1976. B.S. in Chem. Engring., Adamson U., 1966; M.S. in Physics Edn., Ateneo de Manila U., 1972; Ed.D. in Sci. Edn., U. Va., 1981. Registered chem. engr., Philippines; cert. tchr., Calif. Physics instr. Andres Bonifacio Coll., Diplog, Philippines, 1967-69; asst. prof. physics. Silliman U., Dumaguete, Philippines, 1969-80, researcher, 1974, 77-79; bank teller Riverside Nat. Bank (Ill.), 1980-81, 82—. Author/researcher articles, author article; songwriter: Why, 1983, Those Smiling Eyes that Look at Me, 1983; author poetry. Leader Girl Scouts, Philippines, 1968-69, 71, camp coordinator physics camp, 1979. Fulbright-Hayes grantee Inst. Internat. Edn., Va., 1975-77; grantee Fund Assistance to Pvt. Edn., Ateno de Manila, 1971-72; cert. of excellence, Riverside Nat. Bank, 1983. Mem. Philippine Assn. Physics Tchrs. (editor 1979-80), Radioisotopes Soc. of Philippines, Philippine Inst. Chem. Engrs. Home: 39 Forest Apt 221 Riverside IL 60546 Office: Riverside Nat Bank 15 Riverside Rd Riverside IL 60546

FROST, MARY KATHERINE, mental health administrator; b. Windsor, Ont., Can., Nov. 13, 1928; came to U.S., 1951, naturalized, 1967; d. Philip Francis and Elizabeth Eppert; cert. in acctg. Windsor Bus. Coll., 1946; student Toronto Conservatory Music, 1946-47, Am. Inst. Banking, 1954-57; A.S., Wayne State U., 1967; m. William Max Frost, July 17, 1948; Teller, bookkeeper, asst. acct. Toronto Dominion Bank, Windsor, 1947-51; with Nat. Bank Detroit, 1951-54; mgr., customer relations officer City Nat. Bank Detroit, 1954-62; psychobiology research supr., adminstrv. asst. dept. mental health Lafayette Clinic, Detroit, 1964—; co-founder, coordinator, polysomnographer Lafayette Clinic Sleep Center, 1975—; also lectr. Mem. citizens adv. council Lafayette Clinic, chmn. membership, 1979-82, vice chmn., 1982—; bd. dirs. Travelers Aid Soc., 1973—, Casa Maria, 1974-81, Casgrain Hall, 1974—; trustee League Catholic Women, 1974—, mem. adv. bd., 1982—; co-founder Windsor Light Opera Co., 1948; mem. Project Hope League. Named Disting. Employee of 1981, Lafayette Clinic, 1982. Mem. Mich. State Employees Assn. (pres. mental health dept. Lafayette Clinic chpt. 1975-81), Assn. Polysomnography Technologists, Nat. Assn. Female Execs., Internat. Platform Assn., Mich. Mental Health Assn., Mich. Assn. Govt. Employees, Econ. Club Detroit. Republican. Clubs: Five o'Clock Forum, U. Detroit, U.S. Senatorial. Contbr. articles to profl. jours. Home: 1 Lafayette Plaisance Suite 1617 Detroit MI 48207 Office: Dept Psychobiology Lafayette Clinic 951 E Lafayette St Detroit MI 48207

FROWNFELTER, DONNA LEE, medical center physical therapy administrator, consultant, lecturer; b. S.I., Aug. 1, 1945; d. Orion Curtis and Lillian (Cumming) Larson; m. David Dell Frownfelter, June 16, 1967; children—Lauren Elyce, Daniel James, Kristin Joy. B.A. in Biology, North Park Coll., Chgo., 1967; cert. in phys. therapy Northwestern U., 1969; registered respiratory therapy U. Chgo., 1972; postgrad. Loyola U., Chgo., 1985—. Staff phys. therapist Northwestern Meml. Hosp., Chgo., 1969-71, chief chest phys. therapy, 1971-73; dir. chest phys. therapy Rush Med. Ctr., Chgo., 1973—; bd. dirs. Chgo. Lung Assn., 1978—, mem. exec. com., chmn. patient edn. com., 1983—; co-chmn. planning com. for surgeon gen.'s regional seminar on creating new options for ventilator dependent children and adults, 1984; co-chmn. coalition com. to follow-up on surgeon gen.'s regional seminar, 1984—. Editor: Chest Physical Therapy and Pulmonary Rehabilitation: An Interdisciplinary Approach, 1978. Contbr. articles, chpts. to profl. publs. Active Northbrook Covenant Ch., Ill., 1973—; mem. parent support team Nat. Assn. for Down Syndrome, Chgo., 1980—. Recipient cert. Youth for Easter Seals, cert. cardiopulmonary sect. Am. Phys. Therapy Assn., 1982; cert. Chgo. Lung Assn.; named to Outstanding Young Women Am., U.S. Jaycees, 1977. Mem. Am. Phys. Therapy Assn. (reviewer books and publs. for Physical Therapy jour. 1981—, program chmn. cardiopulmonary sect. 1982-86, vice chmn. sect. 1986—), Am. Assn. Respiratory Therapy (chmn. rehab. and continuing care com.), Beta Beta Beta (chpt. pres. 1967). Avocations: camping; swimming; sewing; children's programs. Home: 3349 Ralmark Glenview IL 60025 Office: Rush Med Ctr 1753 W Harrison Chicago IL 60612

FRUGARD, NAOMI L(NONIE) LEE, seeding and landscaping company executive; b. Norfolk, Va., July 7, 1942; d. Harry Melvin and Naomi Leigh (Robinson) Lee; m. William Noble Millikan, May 5, 1961 (div. 1975); children—Elizabeth Robin, William Noble, II, Jesse Lee; m. Roy Elwood Frugard, Oct. 9, 1982. Student pub. schs., Virginia Beach. Sales girl J.C. Penney Co., Norfolk, 1959-60; legal sec. pvt. law office, Norfolk, 1960-62; banker teller First Va. Bank, Norfolk, 1963-66; sec. to pres., owner Stafford Seeding, Inc., Norfolk, 1976—. Pianist Kempsville Ch. of Christ, Virginia Beach, 1970—; mem. Friends of Wesleyan Program, Virginia beach, 1982; lit. chmn. Met. Al-Anon Group, Norfolk, 1982, speaker various groups, 1976—. Mem. Am. Subcontractors Assn. (bd. dirs. Norfolk and Hampton 1980—, pres.-elect 1985—), Tidewater Utility and Heavy Constrn. Assn. (specification com. 1983—). Lodge: Eastern Star (chaplain 1984—). Avocations: dancing; reading; piano; bowling. Home: 1092 Northwood Dr Virginia Beach VA 23452 Office: Stafford Seeding Inc 904 Widgeon Rd Norfolk VA 23513

FRUHMANN, KAREN ANNE, laboratory administrator; b. Orange, N.J.; d. Robert Whitin and Anna (Harvey) Mullin; B.A. magna cum laude in Psychology and Biology, William Paterson Coll., 1974; cert. med. tech. St. Mary's Hosp., 1975; M.S. summa cum laude in Med. Tech., Fairleigh Dickinson U., 1977; Ph.D., Southeastern U., 1985. Biochemistry technologist Raritan Valley Hosp., Greenbrook N.J., 1975-76; asst. supr. enzymology, tech. writer quality assurance, diagnostic researcher, chemistry adminstr. Warner Lambert Gen. Diagnostics, Morris Plains, N.J., 1976-78; dir. lab. services Kessler Inst. for Rehab. W. Orange, N.J., 1979—. Mem. Am. Soc. Clin. Pathologists (affiliate mem.), N.Y. Acad. Scis., Am. Soc. Med. Tech., N.J. Soc. Med. Tech., Assn. for Women in Sci., Nat. Certification Agy. (clin. lab. scientist), Alpha Mu Tau. Presbyterian. Contbr. articles on hematology to profl. jours. Office: Kessler Inst 1199 Pleasant Valley Way W Orange NJ 07052

FRUM, DIANE INOLA, funeral home executive, owner art studio; b. Mpls., Aug. 11, 1932; d. Harold Lennard and Fern (Stegner) Hult; m. Eugene Lynch Frum, Aug. 21, 1954; 1 child, Geni Lynn. Owner, bookkeeper, cons. Frum Funeral Home, Lake Station, Ind., 1955—; artist, restorative specialist, tchr., cons. Inola Art Studio & Gallery, Lake Station, 1979—. Pres. PTA, Lake Station, 1968; treas. Band Boosters, Lake Station, 1974-78. Mem. Lake Station C. of C., Gary Artist League. Lodge: Order Eastern Star. Avocations: crafts; sewing; skiing; fishing. Home: 1307 Central Ave Lake Station IN 46405 Office: Art Studio 2679 Hamilton St Lake Station IN 46406

FRUMBERG, GLORIA, marketing executive; b. N.Y.C., Mar. 26, 1927; d. Joseph Morris and Ruth Sarah (Berlinger) Grossman; student public schs.; m. Ira Herbert Frumberg, May 15, 1949; children—Lawrence Lee, Charles Iver. Sec. public relations mfg. co., 1946-49; asst. advt. and promotions dir. mfg. corp., 1949-51; dist. mgr. World Book Ency., 1962-70; nat. mktg. mgr. Ency. Brit., Atlantic Beach, N.Y., 1970—. Pink Lady vol. Long Beach (N.Y.) Meml. Hosp., 1961-63; former pres. South Shore chpt. Kidney Found. N.Y. Mem. Women's Direct Response Group (pres. N.Y. chpt. 1980-81), Direct Mktg. Assn., Direct Mktg. Club of N.Y. Office: PO box 57 Atlantic Beach NY 11509

FRY, BARBARA ANN, government official; b. St. Charles, Ill., Nov. 10, 1937; d. Robert Nicholas and Marianne Eloise (Earhart) Wilford; B.S., U. Ill., 1959; M.B.A., Roosevelt U., 1976; m. Ronnie Darrel Fry, June 15, 1974; children—Kim Buskirk, Gena Buskirk. Budget analyst, then budget officer Navy Electronics Supply Office, Great Lakes, Ill., 1962-73; regional budget officer IRS, Chgo., 1973-75, Atlanta, 1975-76, regional fiscal mgmt. officer, 1976-83, regional mgmt. analysis officer, 1983—; former mem. adv. com. EEO. Past treas. Loch Lomond Property Owners Assn., PTA. Served with USAF, 1959-61. Mem. AAUW (past treas.), Federally Employed Women (past co-chmn. Inter-Agy. Council, past pres. Atlanta chpt.), Atlanta Assn. Fed. Execs. (treas. 1981-83), Am. Soc. Mil. Controllers (past v.p. North Shore chpt.), Decatur Bus. and Profl. Women (pres. 1986-87), U. Ill. Alumni Assn. (treas. Atlanta chpt. 1984-87), Sigma Kappa (treas. Atlanta alumnae 1985-87). Club: Zonta (bd. dirs. Atlanta). Home: 1511 Montevallo Circle Decatur GA 30033 Office: 275 Peachtree St NE Room 815 Atlanta GA 30043

FRY, KATHRYN MARIE, government official; b. Washington, Jan. 19, 1952; d. Bernard John and Angelina Carmela (Costantino) Beckmann. A.A., Montgomery Coll., 1972; student U. Md., 1972-76, postgrad., 1982; B.S., Am. U., 1979. With NIH, Bethesda, Md., 1973—, acct., 1979-80, budget analyst, 1980—, sr. budget analyst, 1982—. STRIDE intern, 1978-79. Mem. Assn. Govt. Accts. (chpt. pres. 1985-86), Am. Soc. Public Adminstrn. (chmn. fin. com. 1985-86), Am. Assn. Budget and Program Analysis, Nat. Assn. Female Execs., Phi Theta Kappa. Roman Catholic. Avocations: jazz and tap dancing. Home: 4801 Oxbow Rd Rockville MD 20852 Office: NIH 9000 Rockville Pike Bldg 1 Room 31K Bethesda MD 20892

FRYE, HELEN JACKSON, federal judge; b. Klamath Falls, Oreg., Dec. 10, 1930; d. Earl Clifford and Elizabeth Belle (Kirkpatrick) Jackson; children—Eric M., Karen Lynn, Heidi Elizabeth. Public sch. tchr., Eugene, Oreg., 1956-63; admitted to Oreg. bar, 1966; pvt. practice law, Eugene, 1966-71; judge Oreg. Circuit Ct., Eugene, 1971-80; judge U.S. Dist. Ct. Oreg., Portland, 1980—. Office: US Courthouse Portland OR 97205

FRYE, JUDITH ELEEN MINOR (MRS. VERNON LESTER FRYE), editor trade mag.; b. Seattle; d. George Edward and Eleen G. (Hartelius) Minor; student U. Cal. at Los Angeles, evenings 1947-48, U. So. Calif., 1948-53; m. Vernon Lester Frye, Apr. 1, 1954. Accountant, office mgr. Colony Wholesale Liquor, Culver City, Calif., 1947-48; credit mgr. Western Dist. Co., Culver City, 1948-53; partner in restaurants, Palm Springs, Los Angeles, 1948, partner in date ranch, La Quinta, Calif., 1949-53; partner, owner Imperial Printing, Huntington Beach, Calif., 1955—; editor New Era Laundry and Cleaning Lines, Huntington Beach, 1962—; registered lobbyist, Calif., 1975-84. Mem. Laundry and Cleaning Allied Trades Assn., Laundry and Dry Cleaning Suppliers Assn., Calif. Coin-op Assn. (exec. dir. 1975-84), Cooperation award 1971, Dedicated Service award 1976), Nat. Automatic Laundry and Cleaning Council (Leadership award 1972), Women in Laundry/Drycleaning (past pres.; Outstanding Service award 1977), Printing Industries Assn., Master Printers Am., Nat. Assn. Printers and Lithographers, Cleaning and Laundry Assn. Execs., Huntington Beach C. of C. Office: 22031 Bushard St Huntington Beach CA 92646

FRYE, LINDA BETH (HISLE), tchr.; b. Ada, Okla., Apr. 15, 1947; d. Roland Earl and Paralee M. (Jones) Hisle; B.A. in Art and Elem. Edn., E. Central State U., Ada, 1970; M.Ed. in Elem. Edn., E. Tex. State U., Commerce, 1975; m. Dennis Franklin Frye; 3 sons, Byron Franklin, Cody Earl, Matthew Cole. Tchr. Sherman (Tex.) Ind. Sch. Dist., 1971—. Mem. Tex. State Tchrs. Assn. (profl. rep. 1974-75), NEA, Classroom Tchrs. Assn. Cert. tchr., Tex.; specialist in lang., learning disabilities in special edn. Home: 401 Hidden Valley Trail Sherman TX 75090 Office: Dillingham Sch 2701 Log Lake Rd Sherman TX 75090

FRYER, CHRISTINE J., construction/supply company executive; b. Windsor, Ohio, July 21, 1933; d. Maurice Reginald and Florence Elizabeth (King) Rideout; m. Gaylord D. Fryer, May 9, 1953; children—Gaylinda D., Maurice Robert. Student Lakeland Community Coll., 1976—. With acctg. office Midland Ross, Painesville, Ohio, 1951-53, 55-57; exec. sec. Perry Local Schs. (Ohio), 1961-67; personnel office mgr. Lakeland Community Coll., Mentor, Ohio, 1967-78; adminstr. Casement Golf, Inc., Painesville, Ohio, 1978—; personnel office mgr. R.W. Sidley, Inc., 1978—. Mem. Am. Soc. Personnel Adminstrn. (sec. 1982-84, treas. 1984—), Am. Bus. Women. Episcopalian. Office: RW Sidley Inc PO Box 150 Painesville OH 44077

FRYER, GLADYS CONSTANCE, physician; b. London, Mar. 28, 1923; came to U.S., 1967; d. William John and Florence Annie (Dockett) Mercer; m. Donald Wilfred Fryer, Jan. 20, 1944; children—Peter Vivian, Gerard John, Gillian Celia. B. Medicine B. Surgery, U. Melbourne and Royal Melbourne Hosp., Victoria, Australia, 1956. Rotating resident Box Hill and Dist. Hosp., Victoria, 1956-57; med. registrar Queen Victoria Hosp., Melbourne, Australia, 1959-61; physician to pesticide program U. Hawaii, Honolulu, 1967-68; cardiologist Assunta Found., Petaling Jaya, Malaysia, 1961-64; physician, clin. research U.S. Army Med. Research Unit, Kuala Lumpur, Malaysia, 1964-66; internist Hawaii Permanente Kaiser Found., Honolulu, 1968-73; practice medicine specializing in geriatrics, Honolulu, 1975—; med. dir. Beverly Manor Convalescent Ctr., Honolulu, 1975—, Hale Nani Health Ctr., Honolulu, 1975—; hon. asst. clin. prof. medicine John Burns Sch. Medicine U. Hawaii, 1968—; med. cons. Salvation Army Alcohol Treatment Facility, Honolulu, 1975-81; physician to skilled nursing VA, Honolulu, 1984—; preceptor in geriatric nurse practitioner program U. Colo., Honolulu, 1984-85; mem. St. Francis Hosp. Clin. Staff; lectr. in field. Contbr. articles to profl. publs. Mem. adv. com. Honolulu Home Care, 1974—; mem. Long Term Care Task Force of Health and Community Services Council of Hawaii, 1978-84; adv. bd. Honolulu Gerontology Program, 1983—, Straub Home Health Program, Honolulu, 1984—; mem. sci. adv. bd. Alzheimer's Disease and Related Disorders Assn., Honolulu, 1984—. Recipient Edgar Rouse prize in Indsl. Medicine, U. Melbourne, 1955. Mem. AMA, Am. Coll. Physicians, Hawaii Med. Assn. (councillor 1984—), Honolulu County Med. Soc., World Med. Assn., Am. Geriatrics Soc., Gerontological Soc. Am., AAAS, N.Y. Acad. Scis. Avocations: reading, music, needlepoint, sewing, swimming. Office: Hale Nani Health Ctr 1677 Pensacola St Honolulu HI 96822

FRYER, MARIAN MCKNIGHT, government official; b. Jackson, Ga., May 16, 1938; d. Willie Louis and Sara M. (Merritt) Freeman; m. Leland Nichols Fryer, Dec. 11, 1969; children—Allicia Tandrea, Allen Dion; m. Allen McKnight, June 12, 1957 (div. 1967). Cert. USDA Grad. Sch., 1958, 61, 69, Georgetown U., 1979. Adminstrv. officer, bicentennial coordinator Redevel. Land Agy., Washington, 1973-76; women's program mgr. D.C. Dept. Housing and Community Devel., Washington, 1977—, EEO officer, 1979-83, tng. officer, 1982—. Adminstrv. asst. sec. Office Econ. Opportunity, Washington, 1965-68; program coordinator Redevel. Land Agy., Washington, 1968-71, ops. officer, 1971-73. Editor, pub. RLA Housing News, 1970; author, producer Audio Visual Show DHCD Women's Program, 1979. Del. Nat. Women's Conf., Houston, 1977; mem. Montgomery County Citizen's Adv. Com., 1982; v.p. Montgomery County Commn. for Women, 1985-86. Recipient Leadership award D.C. Women's Program Mgrs. Com., 1982, 20 Yr. Service award D.C. Govt., Washington, 1983, Outstanding Women's Program Mgr., 1983. Mem. NOW, D.C. Women's Program Mgrs. (chmn. 1979-82), Nat. Council Negro Women, NAACP, Washington Area Bowling Congress. Democrat. Home: 11221 Markwood Dr Wheaton MD 20902 Office: DC Dept of Housing and Community Devel 1133 N Capitol St NE Washington DC 20002

FRYM, JANET CAROLYN, travel agency executive; b. San Francisco, Oct. 30, 1946; d. Richard Kenneth Carmoney and Nancy Ruth (Doud) Brown; m. Roy W. Frym, Dec. 24, 1972 (div.); 4 stepchildren. Student Sonoma State Coll., 1964, Heald's Bus. Coll., 1965. Agt., asst. mgr. Santa Rosa Travel, Calif., 1966-67; agt. Small World Travel, Mill Valley, Calif., 1964-66, mgr., 1967-70, owner, mgr., 1970-75; outside sales from Kenya, E. Africa, Blue Marble Travel, Novato, Calif., 1976-77; co-owner, operator, Enterprises Unlimited, El Toro, Calif., 1977-81; mgr. Traveltime, Inc., Laguna Hills, Calif., 1980-83; gen. mgr. Bay Travel, Inc., Corona Del Mar, Calif., 1983—; adv. council Marin Savings & Loan Assn., Mill Valley, Calif. songwriter, lyricist under name J. C. Carmoney; designer restaurants. Recipient sales achievement awards from airlines, steamship companies, 1970-75. Mem. Orange County Travellarians, Orange County Sabre Club (v.p. 1983, founding bd. dirs. 1981-82). Republican. Presbyterian. Home: 2115 Arbutus Pl Newport Beach CA 92660 Office: Bay Travel Inc 2435 E Coast Hwy Corona Del Mar CA 92625

FRYMIRE, BRENDA ANN, nurse; b. Oklahoma City, Aug. 10, 1954; d. Gerald Maurice and Shirley Ann (Mitchell) Harrell; m. Charles Ray Frymire, Sept. 27, 1969; children—Mark Allen, Sharon Renee. B.S. in Nursing, Central State U., Edmond, Okla., 1983. R.N.; cert. advanced cardiac life support provider. Vol. coordinator, parent substitute tchr. Lee Elem. Sch., Oklahoma City, 1976-79; nursing technician Bapt. Med. Ctr. of Okla., Oklahoma City, 1982-83; staff nurse in orthopedics, 1983-86, coronary care unit, 1986—. Contbr. articles to profl. publs. Vol. S. Community Hosp., Oklahoma City, 1969. Recipient Appreciation of Service award Oklahoma City Pub. Schs. Helping Hands Orgn., 1979. Mem. Okla. Nurses Assn., Am. Nurses Assn. Democrat. Baptist.

FUCCI, LINDA DEAN, banker; b. Roanoke, Ala., July 2, 1947; d. Alton Hershall and Irma Nell (Trimble) Dean; A.S., So. Union State Jr. Coll., Opelika, Ala., 1974; spl. courses Am. Inst. Banking, Am. Inst. Real Estate, Auburn U., Air U., Lanett, Ala.; m. Bob Fucci, Aug. 1981; children—Allen, Debbie, Nicky, Mark. With Bank of East Ala., Opelika, 1968-72; adminstrv. asst. Auburn Nat. Bank (Ala.), 1972-80, asst. v.p., 1980-82, v.p., 1982-84, v.p., cashier, chief fin. officer, 1984—; recruiter, pilot Air Trans, Auburn, 1979-81. Treas. Lee County Heart Assn., 1979-81; crusade chmn. Lee County Cancer Soc., 1980, pres., 1980; mem. Auburn Heritage Soc. Cert. flight instr. Mem. Nat. Assn. Bank Women, Am. Heart Assn., Am. Inst. Banking (pres. East Ala. chpt. 1981, state com. 1982-84), Aircraft Owners and Pilots Assn., Pilots Lobby. Roman Catholic. Home: PO Box 592 Auburn AL 36830 Office: PO Box 711 Auburn AL 36830

FUCCI, MARIE LUCILLE, investment banking executive, author; b. N.Y.C., May 4, 1949; d. John Erve Ribelle and Edith Vincenza (Di Roberto) F. A.B., Smith Coll., 1970; Ph.D., U. Mich., 1976; M.B.A., Insead, Fontainebleau, France, 1978. Tchr., Eberhard Sch., Washington, 1974-76; research cons. fin. McKinsey & Co., London, Melbourne, Australia, 1976-79; mgmt. cons. Cresap, McCormick & Paget, Washington, 1979-80; sr. fin. analyst Hoffmann-LaRoche, Nutley, N.J., 1980-82; mgr. ops. analysis Am. Cyanamid, Wayne, N.J., 1983-84; mgr. bus. devel. cyanamid of Gt. Britain, 1984—. Author: Sweet Shipwreck (Hopwood award 1973); In My Backyard (Hopwood award 1973); Entr'acte, 1978; Sextet, 1986. Ford Found. fellow U. Mich., 1972-74. Home: 3601 Connecticut Ave NW Washington DC 20008 Office: MMG Patricof 24 Upper Brook St London W1Y 1PD England

FUCHS, ELINOR, theater critic, playwright; b. Cleve., Jan. 23, 1933; d. Joseph Fuchs and Lillian Kessler; m. Michael Oakes Finkelstein, May 3, 1962 (div. 1984); children—Claire Oakes Finkelstein, Katherine Eban Finkelstein. B.A. summa cum laude, Radcliffe Coll., 1955; M.A., Hunter Coll., 1975; M.Phil., CUNY Grad. Ctr., 1976. Research dir. Sextant Prodns.-ABC, N.Y.C., 1960-61; producer-writer Channel 13/WNET, N.Y.C., 1962-63; adj. lectr. SUNY-Stony Brook, 1975, 82; lit. mgr.-dramaturg Chelsea Theater Ctr., N.Y.C., 1978-79; staff theater critic Soho News, N.Y.C., 1979-82; contbg. critic Village Voice, N.Y.C., 1982—; dramaturg Women's Interart Theatre, N.Y.C., 1984—; cons. Nat. Endowment for Arts, Washington, 1982-83; mem. Plays-in-Process selection com. Theatre Communications Group, N.Y.C., 1983-84. Author play/book: (with Joyce Antler) Year One of the Empire (produced Odyssey Theatre, Los Angeles 1980, Drama-Logue Critic's award in playwriting 1980), 1973; contbr. numerous articles to periodicals, including Am. Theatre, Comparative Drama, Art and Cinema, Theatre Communications, Vogue, Ednl. Theatre Jour., Performing Arts Jour.; co-editor spl. issues on Am. theatre Alternatives théâtrales, Brussels, Nos. 9 and 10. Vice pres. Performing Artists for Nuclear Disarmament, N.Y.C., 1983-84. Scholar Swedish Inst., Stockholm, 1981; fellow MacDowell Colony, Peterborough, N.H., 1982; Rockefeller fellow, 1984-85; fellow Bunting Inst., Radcliffe Coll., 1985—; vis. prof. Emory U., 1987. Mem. Am. Theatre Assn., Dramatists' Guild, League Profl. Theatre Women, Phi Beta Kappa. Democrat. Office: care Lois Berman 250 W 57th St New York NY 10019

FUCHS, MARY ALLISON, hotel company executive; b. Detroit, Feb. 10, 1926; d. Lloyd H. and Mary (Peek) Allison; m. Arthur B. Fuchs, Oct. 31, 1948; 1 child, Gregory A. Student U. So. Calif.-Los Angeles. Asst. controller Anderson-Dunham, Los Angeles, 1947-56; paymaster Frontier Hotel, Las Vegas, 1956-57; asst. controller Tropicana Hotel, Las Vegas, 1957-73; paymaster MGM Grand Hotel, Las Vegas, 1973—, v.p., dir. Employees Credit Union, 1983—. Named Boss of Yr., Am. Bus. Women's Assn., 1985. Mem. Internat. Assn. Hospitality Accts. (Las Vegas chpt.; sec. 1981, treas. 1982, v.p. 1983, pres. 1984, chmn. bd. dirs. 1985, awards 1981, 84). Avocations: travel; reading. Office: Bally's Grand Inc 3645 Las Vega Blvd South Las Vegas NV 89109

FUCHS, NINA, moving company executive; b. N.Y.C., Sept. 8, 1953; d. Harry and Shirley (Hochreich) F.; student Franklin Pierce Coll., 1971-72, Nassau Community Coll., 1972-73. Mem. Kibbutz Adamit, Israel, 1975-76; with Century-Franklin Moving & Warehouse Corp., N.Y.C., 1976-81, sales mgr. in charge comml. storage and household moving sales, 1979-81; sales account exec. Air Couriers Internat., N.Y.C., 1981-82; exec. v.p., dir. Century-Franklin Corp., N.Y.C., 1982—. Mem. NOW, Nat. Women's Health Network, N.Y. Met. Moving and Storage Assn., Women Bus. Owners of N.Y., Assn. Record Mgrs. and Adminstrs., Women's Action Alliance N.Y. Office: Century-Franklin Corp 233-35 E 38th St New York NY 10016

FUCHS, OLIVIA ANNE MORRIS, lawyer; b. Louisville, May 2, 1949; d. H.H. Morris Jr. and Betty Jean Wills Saltkill; m. Robert Edward Fuchs, Dec. 27, 1969. B.A., U. Louisville, 1977, J.D. cum laude, 1980. Assoc. Brown, Todd & Heyburn, Louisville, 1981—. Notes editor Jour. Family Law, 1979-80. Vol. advocate R.A.P.E. Relief Ctr., Louisville YWCA, 1981—. Mem. ABA, Ky. Bar Assn., Louisville Bar Assn. (mem. profl. responsibility com. 1982—, mem. probate com. 1981—), Phi Alpha Delta. Democrat. Episcopalian. Club: Jefferson. Office: Brown Todd & Heyburn 1600 Citizens Plaza Louisville KY 40202

FUCHS, SARAH SHEILA, nurse; b. Ferndale, N.Y., May 18, 1922; d. Benjamin and Gussie (Fuchs) F.; children—Stephanie, Amy. R.N., Beth Israel Med. Ctr., 1942, R.N., N.Y., Calif., Fla. Head nurse Beth Israel Hosp., N.Y.C., 1943-46; staff nurse Mt. Sinai Hosp., N.Y.C., 1946-47; floating supr. Coney Island Hosp., N.Y.C., 1963-73; asst. team Dr. Edward Kahn, N.Y.C., 1945-85, Miss Green, R.N., N.Y.C., 1985—. Vol. nurse Civil Def., Queens, 1950. Mem. Alumni Beth Israel Med. Ctr. Sch. Nursing. Republican. Unitarian. Club: North Shore Gym and Health (Manhasset, N.Y.). Avocations: writing; music; art; swimming; dancing; Bible study. Home: 3070 Brighton First St Brooklyn NY 11235 Office: Miss Green RN 213-15 85th St Hollis Hills NY 11427

FUCHS, STEPHANIE KAREN, banker; b. Bklyn., Feb. 13, 1953; d. David and Helen (Yablon) Fuchs. B.S., Ithaca Coll., 1974; M.A., Adelphi U., 1976. Cert. fin. planner, 1983. Mobility instr. Indsl. Home for Blind, Bklyn., 1974-78; spl. edn. tchr. Fairmont Sch., N.Y.C., 1978-80; cert. fin. planner Welger/Siegel Fin. Group, N.Y.C., 1980-83; personal banker Chase Manhattan Bank, N.A., 1983—. Named Rookie of Yr., Welger/Siegel Fin. Group, 1980. Mem. Nat. Assn. Security Dealers, Nat. Assn. Life Underwriters, Women in Sales Assn. (pres. 1982-83), Nat. Assn. Female Execs. (network dir.). Jewish. Home: 184 Thompson St New York NY 10012

FUENTES, MARTHA AYERS, playwright, author; b. Ashland, Ala., Dec. 21, 1923; d. William Henry and Elizabeth (Dye) Ayers; B.A. in English (Ione Lester creative writing award), U. South Fla., 1969; m. Manuel Solomon Fuentes, Apr. 11, 1943. Author: (plays) The Rebel, 1970; Mama Don't Make Me Go To College, My Head Hurts, 1963; Two Characters in Search of An Agreement, 1970; contbr. articles to local, regional and nat. newspapers, feature articles and fiction to nat. mags. and jours.; author TV plays and feature articles for children and young adults; lectr., condr. workshops on drama, writing for TV. Recipient George Sergel drama award U. Chgo., 1969. Mem. Authors Guild, Authors League Am., Dramatists Guild, Soc. Children's Book Writers, Southeastern Writers Assn., Am. Theatre Assn., Internat. Women's Writing Guild. Roman Catholic. Club: U. South Fla. Alumni. Home and office: 102 Third St Belleair Beach FL 33535

FUGELBERG, NANCY JEAN, educator; b. Tarentum, Pa., Mar. 6, 1947; d. Stanley and Mary (Struhar) Homer; m. Darrell Marvin Fugelberg, Aug. 27, 1977. Cert. master piano classes and music lit. Mozarteum, Salzburg, Austria, 1968; B.Music Edn., Mount Union Coll., 1969; postgrad. Kent State U., 1976. Music tchr. Alliance Sch. Dist., Ohio, 1969-70, Minerva Sch. Dist., Ohio, 1970—; ch. organist First Imamnuel United Ch. of Christ, Alliance, Ohio, 1969-85. Pianist for musicals Carnation Players, Alliance, 1969-72. Recipient award for working with handicapped children Minerva Sch. Dist., 1981; Alumni Service award Mu Phi Epsilon, 1983, 84. Mem. Music Educators Nat. Conf., Minerva Tchrs. Assn., NEA, Mu Phi Epsilon (chpt. v.p. 1980-82, pres. 1982-84). Democrat. United Ch. of Christ. Lodge: Elks. Avocations: plants; flowers; traveling. Address: 345 S Rockhill Ave Alliance OH 44601

FUHRMAN, DEBORAH LYNN, petroleum industry executive; b. Minot, N.D., May 4, 1962; d. Kenneth Lester and Nancy Kay (Fowler) F. B.A., U. No. Iowa, 1983. Geol. sec. Placid Oil Co., Dallas, 1983-84; adminstrv. asst. Price Waterhouse, Dallas, 1984-85, communication community relations exec., 1985-86; now splty. group coordinator, petroleum industry. Mem. Bd. Evangelism-Our Redeemer, Dallas, 1984—; mem. com. Republican Party Fgn. Visitors, Dallas, 1984. Mem. Bus. Vol. Council, Mktg. Communications Execs. Internat. Republican. Lutheran. Avocations: synchronized swimming; reading; travel. Office: Price Waterhouse 1400 First City Ctr Dallas TX 75201

FUJITA, SANAE RISMA, designer, beautician; b. Osaka, Japan, Feb. 11, 1948; came to U.S., 1964, naturalized, 1983; d. Masao Chibu Fujita and Fumiko Yong Sik Sinkim. Ed. Shoin U., Osaka, 1965-67, Mayer Fashion Acad., N.Y.C., 1968-69, Fashion Inst. Tech., N.Y.C., 1969-70, Wilfred Acad. Beauty, N.Y.C., 1973-74. Fashion designer Sanae J.K., N.Y.C., 1971-73; silk screen painter Peter Gee, N.Y.C., 1973-74; hair stylist Vidal Sassoon, N.Y.C., 1974-75; make-up artist Louis Guy Dee, N.Y.C., 1975-76; hair stylist Zavier, N.Y.C., 1976-77; designer RISMA, N.Y.C., 1977—. Recipient Collaboration '80 award Interior Fabric Orgn., Met. Mus. Art, 1980. Office: RISMA 171 Duane St New York NY 10013

FUKUDA, HAROLYN GLENEICE, marketing coordinator, business educator; b. Honolulu, Nov. 2, 1945; d. Harold Toma and Gladys Yoshie (Morimoto) Shiroma; m. Keith Hideo Fukuda, Oct. 19, 1974. B.Edn., U. Hawaii, 1967, Instr. dept. adult edn. Hawaii Dept. Edn., Honolulu, 1967-71; with Meadow Gold Dairies, Honolulu, 1967—, personnel clk., 1967-68, sales dept. sec., 1968-74, sales and advt. coordinator, 1974-77, mktg. coordinator, 1978—. Named Jaycee of Yr., Honolulu Chinese Jaycees, Honolulu, 1980, Friend of 4-H, Coop. Extension Service, Honolulu, 1980; mem. Pres.' Honor Club Beatrice Foods Co., Chgo., 1980. Mem. Am. Mktg. Assn., Hawaii Food Mfrs. Assn. (sec. 1980-82, pres. 1982-84), Fashion and Products Assn. (sec./treas. 1980—), Hawaii Sch. Food Service Assn. Club: Ala Moana Toastmasters (v.p. 1983). Office: Meadow Gold Dairies Hawaii 925 Cedar St Honolulu HI 96814

FUKUSHIMA, BARBARA NAOMI, accountant; b. Honolulu, Apr. 5, 1948; d. Harry Kazuo and Misayo (Kawasaki) Murakoshi; B.A. with high honors, U. Hawaii, 1970; postgrad. Oreg. State U., 1971, 73, U. Oreg., 1972; m. Dennis Hiroshi Fukushima, Mar. 23, 1974; 1 son, Dennis Hiroshi Jr. Intern, Coopers & Lybrand, Honolulu, 1974; auditor Haskins & Sells, Kahului, Hawaii, 1974-77; pres. Book Doors, Inc., Pukalani, 1977—; pres. Barbara N. Fukushima C.P.A., Inc., Wailuku. 1979—; sec. treas. Target Pest Control, Inc., Wailuku, 1979—; internal auditor, acct. Maui Land & Pineapple Co., Inc., Kahului, 1977-80; instr. Maui Community Coll., Kahului, 1982—. Recipient Phi Beta Kappa Book award, 1969. Mem. Am. Inst. C.P.A.'s, Hawaii Soc. C.P.A.'s, Nat. Assn. Accts., Hawaii Assn. Public Accts., Bus. and Profl. Womens Club. Tenrikyo. Address: 270 Hookahi Suite 210 Wailuku HI 96793

FULDA, MARCIA, real estate broker; b. San Francisco, June 4, 1926; d. Nissim and Hazel (Chalfen) Aboudara; m. Robert W. Fulda, Nov. 6, 1948; children—Donald R., Laurel Ann. Exec. Sec. degree, Calif. Bus. Sch., San Francisco, 1946. Exec. sec. Santa Rosa Jr. Coll. (Calif.), 1950-53, Sta. KIEM TV, Eureka, Calif., 1956-59; broker assoc. House of Real Estate, Eureka, 1968-77, Century 21 Bob Fulda Realty, Eureka, 1977-83; broker Premium Properties, Eureka, 1983—; tchr. real estate Coll. Redwoods, Eureka, 1982—. Founder, United Way, Eureka, 1968; bd. dirs. Ferndale Repertory Theater, 1980, North Coast Repertory Theatre, Eureka, 1983. Mem. Humboldt County Bd. Realtors (pres. 1976-77, realtor of yr. 1978), Calif. Assn. Realtors (regional v.p. 1978), Nat. Assn. Realtors, Realtors Nat. Mktg. Inst. (cert. residential specialist). Republican. Office: Premium Properties 320 2d St Suite 2-C Eureka CA 95501

FULFORD, CHARLOTTE ANN, acct.; b. St. Petersburg, Fla., July 10, 1925; d. Percival Liden and Ruth (Stiles) Roberts; grad. St. Petersburg Public Schs., 1943; m. Fred Vernon Fulford, Jan. 30, 1944; children—Sue Ethel, Margaret Elizabeth, Rebecca Ann, Fred Vernon. With OPA, Pinellas County, Fla., 1946-47; bookkeeper P.L. Roberts Plumbing Co., St. Petersburg, 1952-58; with H.P. Hood & Sons, Dunedin, Fla., 1959-60; sec.-treas., office mgr., acct. So. Roofing Co., Inc., Clearwater, Fla., 1965-80; acct. D.&F. Warehouses Ltd., Pinellas Park, Fla., 1980—. Mem. Nat. Assn. Women in Constrn. (pres. St. Petersburg chpt. 1978-80, nat. dir. region 3 1980-82), Nat. Roofing Contractors Assn., Fla. Roofing, Sheet Metal and Air Conditioning Assn. Mem. Church of Christ. Home: 8638 10th St N Saint Petersburg FL 33702 Office: 4317 62d Ave N Pinellas Park FL 33526

FULKES, JEAN ASTON, author, musician; b. Chattanooga, Tenn., Mar. 21; d. Isaac David and Inez (Elder) Aston; m. James Sherman Fulkes, Jr. (dec. 1972); children—David, Duane, Marilyn. Student, So. Ill. U.; A.B., U. Tenn.; postgrad. Advanced French Inst., 1961, U. Mo.-Columbia, 1960-81. Asst. Presbyterian Ch., Mexico, Mo., 1958; tchr. French, English, creative writing Mexico High Sch., 1959-78; dir. vocal music and chapel activities Mo. Mil. Acad., 1978-82; free-lance writer, speaker, antique dealer, interior designer, composer, performer. Author: Forever, Forever; A Lovely Thing; New Road New Song; others. Contbr. articles, poetry to mags. Mem. com. Republican Party, Mo., 1950-60. Shakespeare fellow Yale U., 1961, recipient French award City of Centralia, Mo., 1985. Mem. Mo. State Tchr.'s Assn. (conv. speaker 1982), Presbyn. Women's Assn., Old Books and New Assn. (pres. 1973—), Delta Kappa Gamma (officer 1970's). Club: Silent Unity (Unity Village, Mo.). Avocations: travel, oil painting, music, cats. Home: 1605 Pollack Rd Mexico MO 65265 Office: Old Books and New Assn Route 4 White Birch 1605 Mexico MO 65265

FULLENWIDER, EILEEN J., medical administrator, nurse; b. Portland, Oreg., Oct. 4, 1942; d. Patrick Henry and Octavia Louisiana (White) Whalen; children—Matt, Pat, Maria, Clancy; m. 2d, Larry Fullenwider, Dec. 9, 1973; 1 dau., Heleen. R.N., Mercy Hosp., San Diego; A.A., Los Angeles Community Coll. Office and staff nurse, various locations; head nurse ICU and CCU, emergency room and records room, various hosps.; staff nurse operating room, hosp. in Idaho; adminstr. Rancho Surg. Plaza, Inc., Las Vegas, cons. Outpatient Surg. Ctrs. Calif., Orange. Mem. Assn. Operating Room Nurses. Republican. Mormon. Office: Rancho Surgical Plaza Inc 888 Rancho Dr Las Vegas NV 89106

FULLER, CECILIA, biotechnology company executive; b. N.Y.C., July 26, 1937; d. Cecil and Elizabeth (Williams) Randall; m. George Fuller, Mar. 12, 1955; children—Joi Denise, Steven George. B.A. in Psychology, SUNY-Old Westbury, 1976; M. in Human Resources, U. San Francisco, 1986. Exec. dir. Freeport Econ. Oppuntunity Commn., N.Y., 1972-78; regional personnel coordinator Trans World Airlines, 1978-81; employee relations specialist SmithKline, Burlingame, Calif., 1981-84; mgr. human resources Becton Dickinson, Mountain View, Calif., 1984—; cons. in field. Mem. Am. Soc. Personnel Adminstrs., Nat. Assn. Female Execs., No. Calif. Human Resource Council, Calif. Assn. Affirmative Action Officers. Avocation: fitness. Office: Becton Dickinson 2375 Garcia Ave Mountain View CA 94043

FULLER, DIANA L., lawyer; b. Morgantown, W.Va., Nov. 16, 1952; d. William Fleming and Amelia Marie (Lattanzi) F.; m. Robert Deeb Batey, July 21, 1979. B.S., W.Va. U., 1972, J.D., 1977. Bar: W.Va. 1977, U.S. Dist. Ct. (so. dist.) W.Va. 1977, Fla. 1978, U.S. Dist. Ct. (no., mid. and so. dists.) Fla., U.S. Ct. Appeals (5th and 11th cirs.). Law clk., ct. crier to presiding judge U.S. Dist. Ct. (mid. dist.) Fla., Tampa, 1977-79; shareholder Fowler, White, Gillen, Boggs, Villareal & Banker, P.A., Tampa, 1983-85; shareholder Smith & Fuller, P.A., Tampa, 1985—; lectr. on constrn. law. Contbr. articles to profl. jours. Mem. ABA (del. gen. assembly young lawyers div. 1984), Fed. Bar Assn., Am. Judicature Soc., Hillsborough County Bar Assn., W.Va. Trial Lawyers Assn., Greater Tampa C. of C., Phi Alpha Delta. Home: 2418 W Palm Dr Tampa FL 33629 Office: Smith & Fuller PA 201 E Kennedy Blvd Suite 201 Tampa FL 33602

FULLER, EMILY RUTGERS, artist; b. N.Y.C., Aug. 9, 1941; d. Stephen Dow and Emily Clarkson (Hurry) F.; m. Carl John Kingston, May 16, 1970 (dec. 1972); 1 son, Samuel Sayward Renwick; m. 2d, Newby Coleman Toms, June 11, 1983. Assoc. B.S., Garland Jr. Coll., 1962; student Sch. Mus. Fine Arts, Boston, 1962-66; B.S. in Art Edn., Tufts U., 1966; student Art Students League, 1968-69. One-woman exhbns. include: 55 Mercer, N.Y.C., 1972, 75, 78, 79, Webb & Parsons, Bedford Village, N.Y., 1977, Soho 20, N.Y.C., 1977, Frank Marino Gallery, N.Y.C., 1980, Cardet Gallery, Coral Gables, Fla., 1981; group exhbns. include: Webb & Parsons, 1972, 73, Living Arts Ctr. Gallery, Dayton, Ohio, 1975, Deson-Zaks Gallery, Chgo., 1975, Mus. Fine Arts Boston, 1977, UNESCO, Paris, 1977, Smithsonian Inst. Traveling Exhbn. Service, 1978, Mus. Modern Art, N.Y.C., 1978, 79, 79, Douglass Coll., Rutgers U., New Brunswick, N.J., 1979, Frank Marino Gallery, 1979, 80, 81, U. N.C.-Greensboro, 1979, C. Grimaldis Gallery, Balt., 1980, Dubins Gallery, Los Angeles, 1980, Wenniger Graphics, Boston, 1982, Alternative Mus., N.Y.C., 1982, 55 Mercer, 1983, Frauen Mus., Bonn. Fed. Republic Germany, 1984, AIR Gallery, N.Y.C., 1985; represented in permanent collections including Mus. Modern Art N.Y.C., Aldrich Mus. Contemporary Art, Ridgefield, Conn., Indpls. Mus. Art, Miami Dade Pub. Library System, Fla., Chase Manhattan Bank, N.Y.C., Prudential Ins. Co. Am., N.Y.C., IBM, N.Y.C., European Am. Bank, N.Y.C., 1st Nat. City Bank, N.Y.C., Elf Petroleum Corp., N.Y.C., Union Bank of Bavaria, N.Y.C., Owens-Corning Fiberglass Corp., Toledo, Amerada-Hess Corp., N.Y.C., Sidney Lewis Corp. Collection, Richmond, Va., Shearson-Am. Express, N.Y.C. Mem. Mayflower Descendants State of N.Y. Democrat. Episcopalian.

FULLER, M(ARY) CHRISTINE, personnel coordinator, management consultant; b. Ogden, Utah, Aug. 28, 1947; d. Ralph M. and Gladys Eola (Peavey) Fuller; A.A., Southwestern Coll., Chula Vista, Calif., 1972, A.A. in Photography, 1983; B.A., San Diego State U., 1974; M.P.A. in Finance and Personnel, San Diego State U., 1981. Program dir., student adv., asst. to chmn. dept. phys. edn., San Diego State U., 1975-79; founder, chmn. South Bay Cons., Chula Vista, Calif., 1978—; program and tng. coordinator United Way San Diego County, 1980—; spl. cons. to many civic orgns.; exhibited pictures Mus. Photographic Art, San Diego, 1983. Vice pres. devel. San Diego Civic Light Opera Assn./Starlight Women, 1980—; docent, editor, mem. Mus. Photographic Art, San Diego. Served with U.S. Army, 1968-70. Mem. Nat. Assn. Female Execs., Am. Assn. Pub. Adminstrs., Nat. Assn. Student Personnel Administrs., Am. Mgmt. Assn. Author: History of Student Activities: 1642-1900, 1978; California Dreams: A Collection of Poems, 1982; editor: Women at War: Woman's view (Gladys Fuller). Home and Office: 2142 N Ave National City CA 92050

FULLER, MARY MARGARET, editor; b. Lincoln, Nebr., Apr. 23, 1914; d. Ewald Ortwin and Marie Daisy (Douglass) Stiehm; m. Curtis G. Fuller, Sept. 24, 1938; children—Nancy Abigail, Michael Curtis. B.S., U. Wis.-Madison, 1938. Freelance writer, Wilmette, Ill., 1940-52; sec. Clark Pub. Co., Highland Park, Ill., 1949—; asst. editor Fate Mag., Highland Park, 1952-54, exec. editor, 1954-56, editor, 1956—, assoc. pub., 1977—; v.p. sec. Woodall Pub. Co., Highland Park, 1965-85. Mem. Ill. Soc. Psychic Research (pres. 1966-68), Soc. Psychic Research London, Theta Sigma Phi. Democrat. Universalist-Unitarian. Home: 815 E Deerpath Rd Lake Forest IL 60045 Office: 500 Hyacinth Pl Highland Park IL 60035

FULLER, NANCY FAY, librarian; b. Oxford, Miss., Sept. 23, 1945; d. Joe Bailey and Mattie Burris (Moore) F.; A.A., Wood Jr. Coll., 1965; B.A. in Edn., U. Miss., 1967, M.L.S. (NDEA fellow), 1968. Periodicals librarian George Peabody Coll. for Tchrs., Nashville, 1968-69; asst., asso. prof. and asst. librarian State Tech. Inst., Memphis, 1969-74, prof. and chmn. library dept., 1974-76; pharmacy librarian U. Miss., University, 1976—. Mem. ALA, Am. Assn. Colls. Pharmacy (membership chmn. libraries-ednl. resource sect. 1980-82, pres. elect 1983-84, pres. 1984-85, chmn. nominating com. 1985-86), chmn. acad. coordinating com. 1984-85, mem. adminstrv. bd. of council of faculties 1984-85, bd. dirs. 1984-85, mem. GAPS proposal rev. com. 1985-86), Southeastern Library Assn., Miss. Library Assn., U. Miss. Grad. Sch. Library and Info. Sci. Alumni Assn. (pres. 1979-80), U. Miss. Library Staff Assn. (pres. 1979-80), Med. Library Assn., Kappa Delta Pi. Baptist. Club: Pilot (dir. Oxford 1982-83). Office: Austin A Dodge Pharmacy Library U Miss University MS 38677

FULLER, NELL BENTON, medical librarian; b. Rock Hill, S.C., Apr. 6, 1917; d. James Newton and Annie Clementine (Bolling) Benton; A.B., U. N.C., Greensboro, 1940; M.S. in L.S., U. N.C., Chapel Hill, 1968; m. Henry Shepard Fuller, Dec. 15, 1962 (dec.). High sch. tchr., Stony Point, N.C., 1940-43; asst. librarian Bowman Gray Med. Sch., Wake Forest U., Winston-Salem, N.C., 1944-45, librarian, 1945-62; mem. faculty and staff Claude Moore Health Scis. Library, U. Va. Med. Center, Charlottesville, 1966-84, asst. prof., 1970-75, assoc. prof., 1975-84, head tech. services, 1970-84. Mem. Med. Library Assn. Democrat. Presbyterian. Home: 118 Dorset Ct Charlottesville VA 22901

FULLER, SHARON S., insurance agent; b. Hagerstown, Md., Sept. 6, 1946; d. Gerald Browning and Lillian Dorathy (Lane) Smith. Student schs. Hagerstown. Cert. ins. agt., Fla. With Washington Adventist Hosp., Takoma Park, Md., 1968-79; word processing coordinator Fla. Hosp., Orlando, 1979-84; info. systems adminstr. Broad & Cassel, Miami, Fla., 1984-85; ins. agt., Orlando, 1985—. Contbr. articles to profl. publ. Active Competency Evaluation Com. Orange County Pub. Schs., Orlando, 1984-85. Mem. Assn. Info. Systems Profls. (v.p. 1985), Nat. Assn. Female Execs. Seventh-day Adventist. Avocations: reading; travel. Home: 8712 Gopher Ln Orlando FL 32825

FULLER, SUE, artist; b. Pitts.; d. Samuel Leslie and Carrie (Cassedy) F.; B.A., Carnegie Inst. Tech., 1936; M.A., Columbia U., 1939. One-woman shows: Bertha Schaefer Gallery, McNay Art Inst., San Antonio, Norfolk Mus. Currier Gallery, Corcoran Gallery, Smithsonian Instn., Plum Gallery, Kensington, Md., others; exhibited in group shows: Aldrich Mus., Corcoran Gallery, Phila., Mus., Whitney Mus., Bklyn. Mus., others; represented in permanent collections: Addison Gallery Am. Art, Larry Aldrich Mus., Chgo. Art Inst., Des Moines Art Center, Ford Found., Met. Mus., Mus. Modern Art, Guggenheim Mus., Whitney Mus. Am. Art, Tate Gallery London, Library of Congress, All Souls Unitarian Ch., N.Y.C., Tobin Library, San Antonio. Recipient Alumni Merit award Carnegie Mellon U., 1974, Honor award for achievement in visual arts Women's Caucus for Art, 1986; Louis Comfort Tiffany fellow, 1948; John Simon Guggenheim fellow, 1949; Nat. Inst. Arts and Letters grantee, 1950; Eliot Pratt Found. fellow, 1966-68; Mark Rothko Found. grantee, 1973. Producer movies String Composition, 1970, 74. Patentee embedded string compositions. Home: PO Box 1580 Southampton NY 11968 Gallery: Chalette Internat 9 E 88th St New York NY 10028

FULLERTON, BETTY JANE, computer services executive; b. Los Angeles, Mar. 29, 1925; d. Melvin and Louise Katherine (Kuntz) Woldstad; B.A. cum laude, U. So. Calif., 1946, postgrad. in Asiatic studies, 1946-47; registered cert systems professional; m. Hal Bradford Fullerton, Jr., Sept. 7, 1944 (dec. 1974); children—Hal, Frances, Lorraine, Charlotte (dec.), Scott, Kent (dec.), Rhonda. Corp. sec. and dir. Kern Drilling Co. Internat., Ltd., Whittier, Calif., 1963-66, United Drilling Services, Inc., Whittier, 1964-75; local advt. rep. The Christian Science Monitor, 1967-70; staff asst. Brown & Root, Inc., Houston, 1975-77, office mgr. personnel tng. and devel. dept., 1977-78, industry rep. computer services div., 1978-82; systems analyst/engring. software adminstrv. mgr. AAA Tech., 1983—. Dist. precinct chmn. Republican Central Com. of Los Angeles County, 1960-64; mem. Republican State Central Com. of Calif., 1962-64; bd. dirs. Whittier area council Girl Scouts U.S., 1962-64, v.p. personnel, 1962-63; v.p. youth activities Freedom Found., Valley Forge women's div., Los Angeles County, 1964-66; bd. dirs. 1st Ch. of Christ, Scientist, Whittier, 1971-73; bd. dirs. Family YMCA, East Whittier, Calif., 1973-75; 1st reader 9th Ch. of Christ, Scientist, Houston, 1976-79, chmn. bd. trustees, 1979-83. Named Republican Woman of Yr., Whittier, 1972. Mem. Am. Soc. Tng. and Devel., Assn. Systems Mgmt., Project Mgmt. Inst. Engrs. Council of Houston (dir. tech. careers com.), Assn. of Inst. for Cert. Computer Profls. Home: 17406 Anvil Circle Houston TX 77090 Office: 3000 Rodgerdale St Houston TX 77042

FULLERTON, CHARRON ELIZABETH, business official; b. New Rochelle, N.Y., July 14, 1946; d. John Sudall and Lucille Josephine (Phillips) Fullerton. B.A., Fordham U. Editor-in-chief Pelham Sun (N.Y.), 1968-77; asst. editor MONY, N.Y.C., 1977-79, communication specialist, 1979-81, customer communications mgr., 1981-85, dir. internal and costumer communications, 1985—; freelance editor, N.Y.C., 1972—. Recipient Bicentennial award Pelham Bicentennial Com. (N.Y.), 1976. Fellow Life Mgmt. Assn. (bd. exam. reviewers 1983—), Life Advertisers Assn., Soc. Consumer Affairs Profls., Women in Communications (Outstanding Mem. award 1984). Democrat. Roman Catholic. Home: 312 W 88th St New York NY 10024

FULLERTON, DIANE CAROLINE, property mgmt. co. exec.; b. Mpls., Feb. 6, 1943; d. Carl and Mildred (Christensen) Hansen; student U. Minn.; children—Scott Anthony, Kristen Marie. Asst. to pres. Nat. Car Rental, Mpls.; asst. controller Imperial Oil Co., Los Angeles; profl. model and instr., Los Angeles; regional mgr. Alta Property Mgmt., 1978-80; exec. v.p. Mercury Property Mgmt., Irvine, Calif., 1980—; also cons. Mem. Community Assn. Insts., Bldg. Industry Assocs. Republican. Office: 4670 Barranca Pkwy Irvine CA 92714

FULLERTON, DORIS LILLIAN, company executive; b. Bklyn., Sept. 1, 1946; d. Kjell Norman and Marit (Tjersland) Andreassen; m. Andrew S. Fullerton, June 20, 1964; children—Dawn Leyanne, Tammy Annette. Student Career Acad., Milw., 1964-69, Centenary Coll., 1973-74, County Coll. Morris, 1975-76. Office mgr. J&N Laurora, M.D., P.A., Hackettstown, N.J., 1969-75; adminstr. Plaza Med. Assocs., Flanders/Hackettstown, N.J., 1975-83; pres. Practice Insight, Inc., Hackettstown, 1977—, Here to Help, Inc., Morristown, N.J., 1982—. Co-author: A Physician's Guide to Insurance Billing and Collections, 1980; author: Are Health Insurance Claims a Problem for You?, 1982; Guide to Collecting Health Insurance Benefits, 1983. Witness House Select Com. on Aging, Princeton, 1983, Adv. Council on Social Security, Washington, 1983, Pub. Hearing Designated Minority Bus. Devel. Authority,

1983. Mem. Am. Soc. Tng. and Devel., Med. Exec. Personnel Assn., Nat. Assn. Female Execs., Nat. Ins. Consumer Orgn., Hackettstown C. of C., Morris County C. of C., N.J. Assn. Women Bus. Owners (pres. Warren and Sussex chpt. 1983-84). Presbyterian. Club: Zonta. Office: Here To Help Inc 170 E Hanover Ave PO Box 1224R Morristown NJ 07840

FULLERTON, DOROTHY MALLAN, modeling agency executive; b. Ancon, C.Z., May 6, 1938; d. Daniel Harrington and Dorothy (Heintzelman) Mallan; m. Geoge Latimer Fullerton, May 31, 1957 (div. 1979); children—Daphne, Stuart, Nicholas. Student Women's Christian Coll., Madras, India, 1956, Corcoran Art Sch., 1960; Cours de Civilization certificate, Sorbonne, Paris, 1971, Ecole du Louvre, 1972. Antique dealer, Paris, 1970-73, antique sales rep., Heritage Place, San Francisco, 1979-81; fashion model Model Mgmt., Ford, N.Y., Brebner, San Francisco, 1980-85, talent dir., San Francisco, 1983-85. One man shows include Rohobath Art League, Del., 1965, Boston Visual Artists, Union, Mass., 1976, Artist Co-op, 1984, Castlebury Gallery, Arlington, Tex.; group shows include Leahy Hosp., Boston, 1976, Chez Henri, Warren, Vt., 1977, Artist Co-op of San Francisco, 1980-85; represented in permanent collections: Schueler, Boston, Latham, France, Frapier, France, McNally, Zena Jones, Ruth Assawa, Bea Kribs, San Francisco; also pvt. collections. Mem. Artist Cooperative Gallery (mem. bd.), Artist Cooperative Gallery (pres. 1982), Jr. League San Francisco, Nat. Mus. Women in Arts. Republican. Episcopalian. Avocations: music; fishing; hiking; traveling. Home: 2420 Leavenworth St San Francisco CA 94133 Office: Model Mgmt 1400 Castro St San Francisco CA 94114

FULLERTON, GAIL JACKSON, sociologist, university president; b. Lincoln. Nebr., Apr. 29, 1927; d. Earl Warren and Gladys (Marshall) Jackson; B.A., U. Nebr., 1949, M.A., 1950; Ph.D., U. Oreg., 1954; m. Snell Putney, July 28, 1950 (div. 1966); children—Gregory S., Cindy Gail; m. 2d, Stanley James Fullerton, Mar. 27, 1967. Lectr. sociology Drake U., Des Moines, 1955-57; asst. prof. sociology Fla. State U. at Tallahassee, 1957-60; asst. prof. sociology San Jose (Calif.) State U., 1963-68, assoc. prof., 1968-72, prof. sociology, 1972—, dean grad. studies and research 1972-76, exec. v.p., 1977-78, pres., 1978—. Bd. dirs. San Jose C. of C.; bd. govs. Santa Clara County region NCCJ; bd. dirs. EDUCOM, 1983—. Mem. Am. Sociol. Assn., Western Assn. Schs. and Colls. (sr. accrediting commn. 1985—), Phi Beta Kappa. Author: (with Snell Putney) Normal Neurosis, 1964, The Adjusted American, 1966; Survival in Marriage, 2d edit., 1977. Home: 226 Wave Crest Ave Santa Cruz CA 95060 Office: Office of Pres San Jose State U. San Jose CA 95192

FULLERTON, JO ANN, modeling agency/school executive; b. Oklahoma City, Mar. 3, 1934; d. Elof Rongwald and Laura Della (Francis) Bergstrand; children—Deborah Kay, Paula Ann. Grad. Ben Shaw Modeling Sch., 1959. Sec., Silberman Oil Co., Oklahoma City, 1953-58; reservationist Braniff Airways, Oklahoma City, 1956-59; co-owner Fullerton Ticket Agy., Oklahoma City, 1959-71; owner, founder, pres. Jo Ann Fullerton Modeling, Oklahoma City, 1971—. Producer 8 30-min. fashion specials for TV, 1979, 85. Pres. Okla. Bd. Pvt. Sch., 1984—; v.p. bd. dirs. YWCA, Oklahoma City, 1981; pres. Okla. Regional Fashion Group, 1972-73. Republican. Congregationalist. Avocations: writing; tennis; water sports. Home: 923 W Britton Rd Oklahoma City OK 73114 Office: Jo Ann Fullerton Modeling Agency 923 W Britton Rd Oklahoma City OK 73114

FULLERTON, PHYLLIS KAYE, educator; b. Wynnewood, Okla., Dec. 17, 1945; d. J.W. and Bernice (Collins) West; m. Gary Dale Fullerton, June 7, 1963; children—Dale, Rhonda, Jeremy. B.S. in Edn., E. Central U., 1968; postgrad. 1981—. Cert. elem. tchr., Okla. Elem. tchr. Davis Elem. Sch., Okla., 1968—, mem. gifted and talented program, 1983—, curriculum com., 1983-84, textbook rev. com., 1982-83. Tchr. Sunday Sch. Pentecostal Holiness Ch., Davis, 1982-84, art dir. vacation Bible Sch., 1982. Mem. Okla. Edn. Assn., Nat. Edn. Assn., Classroom Tchrs. Assn., Murray County Tchrs. Assn., Women's Auxillary (v.p. 1983-84, pres. 1984—). Democrat. Avocations: cross stitch; glass painting; sewing; tennis. Office: Davis Elem Sch Davis OK 73030

FULLING, KATHARINE PAINTER, educator, writer; b. Dodge City, Kans., Aug. 6; d. William George and Carrie (Lopp) Painter; B.A., Northwestern U., 1945; M.A., Columbia U., 1947; postgrad. Vassar Coll., 1948, San Marcos U., Lima, Peru, 1948-49, (fellow) Inst. Internat. Edn., U. Madrid, Spain, 1952-53; m. Virgil H. Fulling, Sept. 24, 1948. Asst. dir. Casa Panamericana, Mills Coll., 1944; asst. to dir. Fine Arts Dept., Columbia U., N.Y.C., 1945-47; tchr. public schs. Port Washington, L.I., N.Y., 1953-55; lectr. Global Edn., UN, N.Y.C., 1953-56; public relations dir. Nat. League Am. Pen Women, Washington, 1958-60; Non-Govtl. Orgns. rep. United Women of the Ams., UN, N.Y.C., 1959-62; lectr. Asia and Africa Halls, Smithsonian Inst., Washington, 1965-69; lectr. Folger Shakespeare Library, Washington, 1969-73; art reviewer Wyo., Denver Art Mus., 1974—. Mem. Wyo. Council for Humanities, 1979-80; bd. dirs. Am. Security Council, Washington. Mem. Asia Soc., Inter-Am. Center, AAUW, Nat. League Am. Pen Women (Woman of Achievement award 1973), LWV (pres. 1967-69), Nat. Mus. Women in the Arts (charter), Buffalo Bill Hist. Mus., Mark Twain Soc. (hon. mem.), Sigma Alpha Iota, Kappa Delta. Club: National Press (Washington). Author: The Cradle of American Art, 1948; Mantillas and Silver Spurs, 1952; contbr., columnist numerous jours. and mags. Address: 715 S Durbin St PO Box 1822 Casper WY 82602

FULLMER, LOIS MARIE, recreation center executive; b. Grandview, Iowa, Nov. 28, 1931; d. Charles and Margaret (Coder) Howell; student State U. Iowa, 1955-56, Mason City (Iowa) Jr. Coll., 1956-57; m. Edward E. Fullmer, Feb. 24, 1956; children—Sara, Jay Edward. Mgr. farm, 1956-64; sales rep. Russell Stover Candies, 1966-70; buyer Disneyland, Anaheim, Calif., 1970-79; buyer retail mdse. div. Walt Disney Co., Burbank, Calif., 1979—. Served with WAVES, 1951-52. Home: Monrovia CA Office: 500 S Buena Vista Burbank CA 91521

FULMER, (MARY) JEANNINE, broadcasting executive; b. Memphis, Feb. 10, 1945; d. Norman Elbert and Minnie Lee (Pruitt) F. B.S., Miss. U. Women, 1967; postgrad. diploma U. Bristol, Eng., 1969; M.A. in Journalism, La. State U., 1971. Asst. dir. info. services Brevard Jr. Coll., Cocoa, Fla., 1967; info. specialist U. West Fla., Pensacola, 1967-68; dir. info. services Averett Coll., Danville, Va., 1971-73; dir. pub. info. Miss. Authority Ednl. TV, Jackson, 1973-85, dir. programming and pub. info., 1985—; mem. task force TV is for Learning, 1977-80; pub. info. com. task force ThinkAbout agy. for instructional TV, 1977-79; chmn. pub. info. com. So. Edn. Communications Assn., 1982-83; adv. bd. Miss. Nat. Energy Edn. Day, 1983. Recipient numerous state and nat. awards for press kits and publicity materials. Mem. Miss. Press Women (treas. 1976-80, 82—; named Woman of Achievement 1983), So. Ednl. Communications Assn. Office: Miss Authority Ednl TV PO Box 1101 Jackson MS 39215

FULOP, JUDITH, insurance company executive; b. Budapest, Hungary, Sept. 21, 1934; came to U.S., 1956, naturalized, 1961; d. Laszlo and Reka (Lote) von Novak; m. Karoly Fulop, Nov. 28, 1953; children—Karoly Laszlo, Gabor Jozsef. A.S. in Acctg., Bentley Coll., 1979, B.S. in Econs. and Fin., 1983; M.S. in Fin., Boston Coll., 1986. Acct. Kodaly Musical Tng. Inst., 1974-77; bus. mgr., treas. Kodaly Ctr. Am., 1977-80; mgr. gen. acctg. Combined Ins. Co. Am., 1980-84, exec. staff-systems coordinator, 1984-85; sec., treas., chief fin. officer Life of Am. Ins. Corp. of Boston, Malden, Mass., 1985—; trustee, corp. mem., treas. Kodaly Ctr. Am., 1977—. Bd. dirs., past sec. Hungarian Soc. Mass., Boston. Mem. Am. Mgmt. Assn., Nat. Assn. Female Execs. Office: Life of Am Ins Corp of Boston 200 Pleasant St Malden MA 02148

FULTON, ETHEL MARGARET, college president, educator; b. Birtle, Man., Can., Sept. 8, 1922; d. Ernest Bain and Ethel Mary (Futers) F.; cert. Winnipeg Normal Sch., 1942; diploma, U. Minn., 1946; cert. U. Toronto, 1956, 61; M.A., U. B.C., 1960; Ph.D., U. Toronto, 1968; D. en Scis. of Edn. (hon.), U. Moncton. Pub. and secondary sch. tchr., Ont., 1948-53; head Eng. Coll. Inst., Thunder Bay, Ont., 1960-63; teaching fellow in English, U. Toronto, 1963-66; assoc. prof. English, Wilfred Laurier U., 1967-74; dean women U. B.C., 1974-78; pres., prof. English Mt. St. Vincent U., Halifax, N.S., Can., 1978—; dir. Fireman's Fund Ins. Co. of Can., North-South Inst. Ont. Decorated officer Order of Can. Grad. Fellowships; William P. Huffman scholar-in-residence, Miami U., Oxford, Ohio; hon. fellow Ryerson Poly. Inst. Mem. Interam. U. Assn. (dir.), Can. Congress Learning Opportunities for Women, Can. Assn. Univ. Tchrs., Assn. Can. Univ. Tchrs. English, Assn. Univs. and Colls. Can., Assn. Commonwealth Univs., Assn. Atlantic Univs., Assn. Can. and Que. Lit., Can. Council Tchrs. English, Can. Soc. Study Higher Edn., Victorian Studies Assn., Can. Research Inst. Advancement Women, Am. Assn. Higher Edn. Mem. NDP. Mem. United Ch. of Can. Clubs: Voice of Women, Univ. Women's, Zonta. Home: 12A Sherbrooke Dr Halifax NS B3M 1P6 Canada Office: Mount St Vincent University 166 Bedford Hwy Halifax NS B3M 2J6 Canada

FULTON, JOYCE ROSALIE, banker; b. Ware, Mass., Jan. 21, 1938; d. Joseph E. and Rose A. (Regin) Rabschnuk; student Clark U., U. Mass.; grad. Williams Coll. Sch. of Banking, 1971; m. Harlan W. Fulton, June 15, 1958; children—Catherine Joy, Margaret Beth. With Ware Trust Co. (Mass.), 1960—, v.p., 1973-75, exec. v.p., 1975-77, pres., 1977—, chmn. bd., 1980—. Bd. dirs. Mary Lane Hosp., Gilbertville (Mass.) Library Assn.; trustee New Eng. Sch. Banking at Williams Coll. Mem. Nat. Assn. Bank Women, Mass. Bankers Assn. (dir.), Bank Adminstrn. Inst. (pres. Western Mass. chpt., state dir. 1980-82, dist. dir.). Office: Ware Trust Co 73 Main St Ware MA 01082

FULTON, SUSAN E.O. BREAKEFIELD (MRS. RICHARD A. FULTON), fin. planner; b. Winthrop, Mass., Dec. 10, 1939; d. Durward Ellsworth and Annabelle (Owens) Breakerfield; B.A., Wilson Coll., Chambersburg, Pa., 1961; m. Richard Alsina Fulton, Apr. 13, 1971. Editor, Lititz (Pa.) Record-Express, 1961-62; account exec. Holyoke (Mass.) Transcript-Telegram, 1962-64; account exec. Washington Daily News, 1964-69; account exec. Sta. WASH, Metromedia Radio, Washington, 1969-73, local sales mgr., 1973-75, gen. sales mgr., 1975-77, v.p. and gen. mgr., 1977-81; registered rep. Linsco Corp., Alexandria, Va., 1981-82; fin. planner Manna Corp., Fairfax, Va., 1982-84, ptnr. Fulton, Lauroesch and Assocs., 1984. Trustee Wilson Coll. Cert. fin. planner Coll. Fin. Planning. Mem. Wilson Coll. Alumnae Assn., Internat. Assn. Fin. Planners, Woman's Network. Republican. Episcopalian. Club: Exec. Lodge: Soc. Companions of Holy Cross. Home: 3813 Garrison St NW Washington DC 20016 Office: Fulton Lauroesch and Assocs 4520 East-West Highway Bethesda MD 20814

FULWEILER, PATRICIA PLATT, civic worker; b. N.Y.C., Mar. 19, 1923; d. Haviland Hull and Marie-Louise (Fearey) Platt; A.B. cum laude, Bryn Mawr Coll., 1945; M.B.A., Columbia U., 1950; m. Spencer Biddle Fulweiler, Oct. 5, 1946; children—Marie-Louise Fulweiler Allen, Pamela Spencer, Hull Platt, Spencer Biddle. Jr. copywriter, asst. account exec. Dorland Internat. Pettingell & Fenton, N.Y.C., 1945-46; statistician, fin. staff treas.'s office Gen. Motors Corp., N.Y.C., 1950-52; asst. account mgr. investment dept. Fiduciary Trust Co., N.Y.C., 1953-61; bd. dirs. Chapin Brearley Exchange, Inc., N.Y.C., 1964-74, treas., 1966-71, pres., 1971-73; bd. dirs. Knickerbocker Greys, 1965—, treas., 1970-75; bd. dirs., treas. City Gardens Club, N.Y.C., 1974-79, chmn. ways and means com., 1974-81, treas., 1984—; bd. dirs. Nat. Soc. Colonial Dames State N.Y., 1973-82, asst. treas., 1973-82; mem. fin. com. Alumnae Assn. Bryn Mawr Coll., 1970-76; bd. dirs. Daus. of Cin., 1974-81, scholarship adminstr., 1976-81; Pres. Ladies Christian Union, 1982—; rec. sec. Women's Assn. St. James Ch., N.Y.C., 1972-75, treas., 1981-83, co-chmn. Spring Festival, 1974-75, chmn., 1975-76, mem. Altar Guild, 1975—; treas. Churchwomen's League for Patriotic Service, 1982-86; mem. scholarship com. Youth Found., 1981—, chmn., 1984-85; chmn. membership com. Huguenot Soc. Am., 1984-86, registrar, 1986—. Mem. Soc. Sponsers of U.S. Navy, Colonial Dames Am. Republican. Clubs: Colony, Wilson Point Beach Assn., Thursday Evening. Home: 158 E 83d St New York NY 10028

FUNDERBURK, ELEANOR JO, all terrain vehicle company executive, realtor; b. Monroe, La., Mar. 31, 1943; d. Hugh Franklin and Clotea Elizabeth (Mayes) Calhoun; m. Robert Andrew Heacock, Aug. 25, 1961 (dec. July 1963); m. 2d, Shelby Dean Funderburk, Dec. 29, 1964. Grad. Real Estate, Inst. Sales clk. S.H. Kress, Monroe, La., 1958-61; receptionist/sec. Dr. R.E. Harvey, Monroe, 1961-63; sec. Rivers Ford, Monroe, 1963-64; teller, sec. Ouachita Bank, Monroe, 1964-66; inventory control clk., sec. Olinkraft, Inc., West Monroe, 1966-70, sec., 1970-78; sec., treas. Funderburk 3-Wheeler, Monroe, 1980—; realtor Century 21 Roberts Realty, Monroe, 1978—. Patentee tire demounting device. Mem. Monroe West Monroe Bd. Realtors (Saleswoman award 1978, 79, Lister of Month, 1978-79), Monroe C. of C., La. Realtors, Nat. Realtors Assn. Democrat. Baptist. Clubs: Ouachita Tennis (Monroe); U.S. Tennis Assn. (N.Y.C.).

FUNDERBURKE, VANESSA CHRISTY, day care center director; b. Pageland, S.C., June 3, 1957; d. Craven DeWitt and Evangeline (Hough) Myers F. B.A., Claflin Coll., 1979; M.S., Bklyn. Coll., 1982. Sec. Rolando Realty Co., Charlotte, N.C., 1979; nurses asst. Presbyterian Hosp., Charlotte, 1979-80; computer operator Interim System, Inc., N.Y.C., 1980-81; bank teller CitiBank, N.Y.C., 1981; asst. tchr. East N.Y. Day Care Ctr., Bklyn., 1981-84; asst. dir., family day care coordinator, 1984—; adminstrv./personnel mgmt. tng. Fordham U., N.Y.C., 1985. Mem. Delta Sigma Theta (parliamentarian 1978-79). Democrat. Methodist. Avocations: bowling; bike riding; reading novels. Home: 713 Van Siclen Ave Brooklyn NY 11207 Office: East NY Day Care Ctr 2550 Atlantic Ave Brooklyn NY 11207

FUNDORA, RAQUEL (FERNÁNDEZ), poet, writer; b. Bolondrón, Cuba, May 19, 1924; came to U.S., 1959; d. Gerardo Francisco and Carolina (Fernández) Fundora; m. Roberto Rodríguez de Aragón, Sept. 14, 1951; children—Pepín, Lianne, Raquel Aurora. Grad. in Bus. Adminstrn., Immaculada Sch., Havana, Cuba, 1948. Collections of poems include: Nostalgia Inconsolable, 1973, El Canto del Viento, 1983; contbr. poems to Antologia Poetica Hispanoamericana, La Gota de Agua; contbr. poetry to lit. mags., 1970-84. Recipient Diploma of Honor Lincoln-Marti, HEW, 1973; Juan J. Remos, Cruzada Educativa Cubana, 1975; Cert. of Appreciation City of Miami, 1976, Miami Cuban Lions Club, 1980. Mem. Círculo de Cultura Panamericano (pres. Miami chpt. 1982-85, chmn. cultural congress U. Miami 1983-85), Grupo Artístico Literario Abril, Poets and Writers, Latin C. of C. of U.S.A. (founder, 1st dir. Camacol Library 1980). Roman Catholic. Club: Big Five (Miami, Fla.). Home and Office: 935 SW 24th Rd Miami FL 33129

FUNG, MINA HSU, advertising agency executive; b. Kwangsi, China, Feb. 14, 1947; came to U.S., 1966; d. Man-Tak and Yu-Wen (Chew) Hsu; divorced; 1 child, Daniel Fung. B.A., U. Ill., 1969; M.B.A., Loyola U., Chgo., 1972. Project dir. Conway/Milliken Corp., Chgo., 1969-73; research exec. Grey Advt., N.Y.C., 1976-77, asst. research dir., 1977-79, assoc. research dir., 1979-81, v.p., 1981—, sr. assoc. research dir., 1982-85, mgmt. planning dir., 1985—. Mem. Advt. Research Found., Am. Mktg. Assn. Home: 529 W 42d St New York NY 10036 Office: Grey Advertising 777 3d Ave New York NY 10017

FUNK, ELLA FRANCES, genealogist, author; b. Domino, Ky., Apr. 7, 1921; d. Roy William and Edna Rene (Cummins) Roach; B.Liberal Studies, Mary Washington Coll., Fredericksburg, Va., 1982; m. Eugene Boyd Funk, June 20, 1942; children—Susan Teresa, Eugene Boyd. Exec. sec. Lang. Labs., Inc., Bethesda, Md., 1969-70; office mgr. legal firm Donovan Leisure Newton & Irvine, Washington, 1970-76; genealogist, hist. researcher, writer, 1976—; vol. Assn. Preservation Va. Antiquities. Named Exec. of Week, Sta. WGMS, Washington, June 1975. Life mem. Nat. Geneal. Soc.; mem. Hist. Fredericksburg Found., DAR, Alpha Phi Sigma, Sigma Phi Gamma. Mem. Christian Ch. (Disciples of Christ). Club: Woman's (Fredericksburg, Va.). Lodge: Order Eastern Star. Author: Cummins Ancient, Cummins New, Vol. 1, 1978, Vol. 2, 1980; Joseph Funk, a biography, 1984. Address: Box 557 LOW Locust Grove VA 22508

FUNKE, JULIE A., graphics brokerage executive; b. Indpls., May 3, 1950; d. Paul R. and Rosetta A. (Freeman) Wheeler; m. William R. Funke, Jan. 25, 1969 (div. 1976); 1 son, Brian Dean; m. Benjamin H. Wolfenberger, Apr. 25, 1981. Student Ind. U. Exec. sec. City of Bloomington (Ind.), 1973-75; customer service rep. Herff Jones, Indpls., 1975-76; rep. trainee Maury Boyd & Assocs., 1976-77, customer service rep., 1977-82, v.p., 1983—. Mem. Women in Communications, Am. Soc. Assn. Execs., Coll. Fraternity Editors Assn., Profl. Fraternity Assn. (dir. 1982-86), Am. Bus. Women's Assn., Gamma Phi Beta (internat. officer). Republican. Home: 8018 Castle Lake Rd Indianapolis IN 46256 Office: Maury Boyd & Assocs Inc 5783 Park Plaza Ct Indianapolis IN 46220

FUNKE, ODELIA CATHARINE, political scientist; b. Washington, Sept. 30, 1947; d. Frederick Anton and Teresa W. (Dietrich) F. B.A., Catholic U., Washington, 1969; M.A., U. Va.-Charlottesville, 1971, Ph.D., 1974. Asst. prof. polit. philosophy U. Mo., Kansas City, 1973-79; social sci. analyst EPA, Washington, 1980-83, br. chief, 1983—; cons. Office of Tech. Assessment, Washington, 1980; prof. George Washington U., 1982, 83; guest lectr. U. Ind., Bloomington, 1983. Mem. editorial bd. Politics and Life Sci., 1983—; contbr. articles and revs. to profl. jours. Recipient Summer Seminar award NEH, 1977; spl. achievement award EPA, 1982, outstanding merit bonus award, 1983, 84, Bronze medal, 1985; Thomas Jefferson fellow, 1970-71; NDEA fellow, 1971; Dupont grantee, 1972-73. Fellow Royal Geog. Soc.; mem. Am. Polit. Sci. Assn., Assn. for Politics and Life Scis. (mem. council), Phi Beta Kappa, Delta Tau Kappa, Pi Gamma Mu. Roman Catholic. Office: EPA 401 M St SW Washington DC 20460

FURBUSH, MARY CHAPMAN, clubwoman; b. Danville, Va., Feb. 16, 1913; d. Fred L. and Martha L. (Hubbard) C.; student Goucher Coll., 1929-32; m. Spencer Sanderson Furbush, Aug. 24, 1940. N.H. state chmn. Flag of the U.S.A. com. DAR, 1959-62, state rec. sec. N.H., 1962-65, chpt. regent, 1960-62, state chmn. sch. com., 1974-77, nat. vice chmn. motion picture com., 1968-71, Constn. Week com., 1977-80; gov. N.H., Gen. Soc. Mayflower Descs., 1965-67, asst. gen., 1969-78, dep. gov. gen., 1978—; v.p. N.H. soc. Nat. Soc. Daus. Colonial Wars, 1968-71, pres. N.H. soc., 1971-74, nat. chaplain, 1974-77, nat. 1st. v.p., 1977-80; mem. Orders of Distinction com. Nat. Soc. Daus. of Barons of Runnymede. Mem. Sch. Bd. Somersworth (N.H.), 1946-49; trustee Trust Funds City of Somersworth, 1954-66, Forest Glade Cemetery, 1946-65. Recipient Valuable Service award Pres. U.S., 1948. Mem. Order of Americans of Armorial Ancestry, Nat. Hist. Soc., N.H. Hist. Soc., Somersworth Hist. Soc., Smithsonian Assos., N.H. Huguenot Soc. (state pres. 1984—), N.H. Soc. DAR (state program chmn. com. 1985-86), Mass. Huguenot Soc., Strawbery Banke, Nat. Soc. Daus. Am. Colonists, Huguenot Soc. N.H. (v.p.), Piscataqua Pioneers (v.p. 1970-75), Nat. Soc. Dames of Ct. of Honor (N.H. v.p. 1975-79, 82—), Jamestowne Soc., Nat. Soc. Colonial Dames XVII Century, Nat. Soc. Daus. Colonial Wars (nat. chaplain 1974-77, 1st v.p. 1977-80, nat. chmn. awards com. 1983—). Democrat. Episcopalian. Address: 20 Noble St Somersworth NH 03878

FURGASON, KIMBERELY ANNE, U.S. Army officer; b. Milw., Aug. 30, 1958; d. Richard Leo Furgason and Gwendolyn Dorothy (Dick) Wedor. student U. Nev.-Reno, 1976-78; B.S., U. Pacific, 1980. Commd. 2d H., U.S. Army, 1980, advanced through grades to capt., 1985; installation club officer U.S. Army, Ft. Ritchie, Md., 1984-85, asst. area club mgr., Kaiserslautern, Fed. Republic Germany, 1984-84. Mem. U.S. Republican Nat. Com. Mem. Club Mgrs. Assn. Am., Nat. Assn. Female Execs. Presbyterian. Lodge: Internat. Order of Rainbow. Avocations: cross-stitch, gourmet cooking and baking, sailing. Home: 5900 Watercrest Dr Fayetteville NC 28304

FURGIUELE, MARGERY WOOD, educator; b. Munden, Va., Sept. 28, 1919; d. Thomas Jarvis and Helen Godfrey (Ward) Wood; B.S., Mary Washington Coll., 1941; postgrad U. Ala., 1967-68, Catholic U. Am., 1974, 76, 80; m. Albert William Furgiuele, June 19, 1943; children—Martha Jane Furgiuele MacDonald, Harriet Randolph. Advt. and reservations sec. Hilton's Vacation Hide-A Way, Moodus, Conn., 1940; sec. Tenn. Valley Authority, Knoxville, 1941-43; adminstrv. asst., ct. reporter, Moody AFB, Valdosta, Ga., 1943-44; tchr. bus. Edenton (N.C.) High Sch., 1944-45; tchr. bus., coordinator coop. office edn. Culpeper (Va.) County High Sch., 1958-82; tchr. Piedment Tech. Edn. Center, 1970-81; co-owner Zinn Wood Antiques & Collectibles Shop, Culpeper, Va., 1980—. Co-leader Future Bus. Leaders Am., Culpeper, state advisor 1978-79, mem. state bd., 1978-82, exec. bd., 1978-81, Va. Bus. Edn. Assn. Com. chmn., 1978-79. Certified geneal. record Searcher. Mem. Nat., Va. bus. edn. assns., Am., Va. vocat. assns., Smithsonian Assocs. Club: Country (Culpeper). Home: 1630 Stonybrook Ln Culpeper VA 22701 Office: 1630 Stonybrook Ln Culpeper VA 22701

FURNESS, BETTY, broadcast journalist, consumer adviser, actress; b. N.Y.C., Jan. 3, 1916; d. George Choate and Florence (Sturtevant) F.; student Brearly Sch., N.Y.C., Bennett Sch., Millbrook, N.Y.; LL.D. (hon.), Iowa Wesleyan Coll., 1968, Pratt Inst., 1978; D.C.L. (hon.), Pace U., 1973, Marymount Manhattan Coll., 1976; m. John Waldo Green, Nov. 27, 1937 (div. Aug. 1943); 1 dau., Barbara Sturtevant; m. 2d, Hugh B. Ernst, Jr., Jan. 3, 1945 (dec. Apr. 1950); m. 3d, Leslie Midgley, Aug. 15, 1967. Movie actress, 1932-37; appeared stage plays Golden Boy, My Sister Eileen, Doughgirls; commls. for Westinghouse Corp., 1949-60; appeared on CBS-radio in Dimension of a Woman's World, Ask Betty Furness, 1961-67; spl. asst. to Pres. U.S. for consumer affairs, 1967-69; chmn. Pres.'s Com. Consumer Interests, 1967-69; exec. sec. Consumer Adv. Council, 1967-69; columnist McCall Mag., 1969-70, 72; chmn., exec. dir. N.Y. State Consumer Protection Bd., 1970-71; commr. N.Y. Dept. Consumer Affairs, 1973; now with NBC News, N.Y.C. Bd. dirs. Consumers Union, 1969—, Common Cause, 1971-75. Office: WNBC-TV 30 Rockefeller Plaza New York NY 10020

FURR, ANN LONGWELL, lawyer, judge; b. Jackson, Tenn., May 25, 1945; d. Thomas J. and Frances (Montgomery) F.; m. Olin F. Furr, Jr., 1967 (div. 1983); 1 dau., Sarah Shannon, B.A., U. S.C., 1967, J.D., 1976. Bar: S.C., 1976, U.S. Dist. Ct. S.C., U.S. Ct. Appeals (4th and 5th cirs.) 1977. Tchr. Columbia (S.C.) pub. Schs., 1967-79. U.S. Army, Fort Dix., N.J., 1969-70, social work supr. Saigon, Vietnam, 1970-71, tchr. Fort Jackson, S.C., 1971-73; clk. Richland County (S.C.) Pub. Defender's Office, 1974-75; instr. legal writing U. S.C. Law Sch., Columbia, 1975-76; ptnr. Furr and Delgado, Columbia, 1976—; asst. judge Columbia Mcpl. Ct., 1980—. Mem. ABA, S.C. Bar Assn., Richland County Bar Assn., S.C. Trial Lawyers Assn., Nat. Assn. Women Lawyers.

FURST, CARYN MELODY, public relations counselor; b. N.Y.C., Aug. 15, 1949; d. S. Robert and Ann (Bruder) Furst.; B.S., Cornell U., 1971. Asst. editor Madison Ave. mag., N.Y.C., 1971-73; assoc. editor Parade mag., 1973-74; features editor Women's Life mag., N.Y.C., 1974; v.p. The Softness Group, Inc., N.Y.C., 1974-78; sr. v.p., account group dir. Carl Byoir & Assocs., Inc., N.Y.C., 1978—. Recipient Thoth award Washington chpt. Public Relations Soc. Am., 1980; Silver Anvil, Public Relations Soc. Am., 1981, 82, 83. Home: 36 E 36th St New York NY 10016 Office: 380 Madison Ave New York NY 10017

FURST, RUTH ANN, escrow company executive; b. Newark, May 29, 1941; d. Lewis A. and Yetta M. Furst; B.A., U. Calif., San Fernando Valley, 1962. With Heritage Escrow Co., Encino, Calif., 1966—; with Pacific Coast Escrow Co., 1973—, Sunrise Co., developers country club communities; ptnr. Dress to Impress. Active Young Democrats; mem. Jewish Nat. Fedn. Mem. Calif. Escrow Assn., Calif. Escrow Inst. Club: Soroptomist. Office: 75-005 Country Club Dr Palm Desert CA 92260

FURSTMAN, SHIRLEY ELSIE DADDOW, advertising, public relations executive; b. Butler, N.J., Jan. 26, 1930; d. Richard and Eva M. (Kitchell) Daddow; grad. high sch.; m. Russell A. Bailey, Oct. 1, 1950 (div. Oct. 1967); m. 2d, William B. Furstman, Dec. 24, 1977. Asst. corp. sec. Hydrospace Tech., West Caldwell, N.J., 1960-62; sec. to pres. R.J. Dick Co., Totowa, N.J., 1962-63, Microlab, Livingston, N.J., 1963; asst. corp. sec. Astrosystems Internat., West Caldwell, N.J., 1963-65; corp. sec. Internat. Controls Corp., Fairfield, N.J., 1965-73; sec. Global Fin., Nassau, Bahamas, 1974, Internat. Barter Co., Nassau, 1975; corp. sec., sec. to pres. Haas Chem. Corp., Taylor, Pa., 1976-77; asst. to pub. and pres. Am. Home Mag., N.Y.C., 1977-78; adminstrv. supr. pub. relations Gilbert, Whitney & Johns, Whippany, N.J., 1979—. Address: 11A Foxwood Dr Morris Plains NJ 07950

FUSCO, JACQUELINE TECCE, management consultant; b. N.Y.C., Apr. 23, 1956; d. Sam L. and Lee M. (Malandri) Tecce; m. William Fusco, Apr. 7, 1984. A.A.S. in Bus. Adminstrn., St. Francis Coll., Bklyn., 1978, B.A. in Psychology, 1978. Cashier, Alexanders, Rego Park, N.Y., 1974; teller Chem. Bank, N.Y.C., 1975-78; new account dir. Macy's, Elmhurst, N.Y., 1978-79; asst. dir. lease adminstrn. Brooks Fashion Stores, N.Y.C., 1979-81; coordinator info. services Richard Kove Assocs., N.Y.C., 1981—; v.p. Bilco Mech. Corp., Port Washington, N.Y., 1985—. Mem. Anti-Vivisection Soc., 1978—, Save Our Strays, Bklyn., 1978—; vol. Rusk Inst., N.Y.C., 1982; mem. Citizens to Replace LILCO, 1985—. Mem. Nat. Assn. Female Execs., Ill. Mgmt. and Exec. Search Cons., Psi Chi, Chi Beta Phi. Republican. Roman Catholic. Home: 8 Guilford Rd Port Washington NY 11050 Office: Richard Kove Assocs 1 World Trade Ctr Suite 7967 New York NY 10048

FUSCO, LAURIE SMITH, art historian; b. Boston, Oct. 31, 1941; d. Byron Hobart Smith and Geraldine (Peterson) Smith Hershorn; B.A., Wellesley Coll., 1963; M.A., NYU, 1969, Ph.D., 1978; m. Peter Fusco, Apr. 28, 1972. Robert Lehman fellow Inst. Fine Arts, N.Y. U., 1969-72; Fulbright-Hays grantee to Rome, 1972-73; asst. prof. art history U. So. Calif., Los Angeles, 1975-76; head photo archives J. Paul Getty Mus., Malibu, Calif., 1976-78, dir. acad. affairs, 1978—. Contbr. articles on Italian 15th century art to profl. jours. Samuel H.

Kress grantee, 1974-75; Harvard U. fellow at Villa I Tatti, Florence, 1983. Mem. Coll. Art Assn., Renaissance Soc., Art Historians So. Calif. Home: 1356 N Ogden Dr Los Angeles CA 90046 Office: J Paul Getty Mus Box 2112 Santa Monica CA 90406

FUSILE, JEANETTE WALD, owner bridal boutique; b. Juneau, Alaska, Sept. 18, 1941; d. Carmel Catherine (Scheid) Wald; m. Ronald Phil Fusile, Aug. 31, 1963; children—Jeffrey P., Jill I., Dana L. Diploma Med. Sec., Rochester Community Coll. (Minn.), 1960. Med. sec. Mayo Clinic, Rochester, 1960-61; med. sec. Walter Reed U.S. Army Hosp., Washington, 1961-64; personal sec. U.S. Ho. of Reps., Washington, 1964-65; realtor, assoc. broker Long & Foster Realtors, Manassas, Va., 1973-76; realtor, assoc. broker Better Homes Realtors, Manassas, 1976-80; owner, mgr. Jeanette's Bride'N Boutique, Manassas, 1978—. Mem. No. Va. Bd. Realtors, Falls Church, Va., 1973-80, Prince William Bd. Realtors, Manassas, 1973-80. Recipient Superior Performance award U.S. Dept. Army, Washington, 1964. Club: Million Dollar Realtor Sales (both No. Va., Prince William Bd. Realtors). Office: Jeanette's Bride 'N Boutique 7833 Sudley Rd Manassas VA 22110

FUSILLO, ANNE M(ARIE), travel agency executive, consultant; b. Lansford, Pa., Sept. 12, 1921; d. Stephen Andrew and Mary Helen (Repko) Oracko; m. Frank Fusillo, June 28, 1947; children—Marianne, Merrie Beth. Student TV prodn. Columbia Coll., Chgo., 1960-62, Central Pa. Bus. Coll., 1941-42; also workshops on ins., bus. mgmt. and travel. Sec./supr. Bur. Vital Stats., Harrisburg, Pa., 1939-41; exec. sec. War Dept., Berwick, Pa., 1941-43, N.Y.C., 1943-45, Washington, 1945-47; exec. sec. Gary Diocesan and Pub. Schs. (Ind.), 1958-62, assoc. editor Gary Diocesan Publ., 1962-66; editor Fraternally Yours, First Catholic Slovak Ladies Assn., Beachwood, Ohio, 1966-80; travel cons., ptnr. Tour Desk One, Inc., Wheaton, Ill., 1979—. Editor, designer brochures, ann. report. Mem. press and pub. relations coms. United Fund, Gary, 1965-73; pres., sec.-treas Press and Pub. Relations sect. Nat. Frat. Congress Am., Chgo., 1968-77; pres. Ind. Frat. Congress, Indpls., 1974-75; pres. N.W. Ind. Visiting Nurse Assn., Hammond, 1965-69, editor newsletter, 1973-75; leader Girl Scouts U.S.A., 1957-60, 65-67; pres. Gary Diocesan Council Cath. Women, 1968-69; sec. N.W. Ind. Cath. Youth Orgn., 1963-74; pres. woman's aux. bd. Mundelein Coll., Chgo.,1967-70; tchr. cooking Wheaton Sch. Dist. Adult Edn., 1981-83; vol. Marianjoy Rehab. Hosp., Wheaton, 1981-83. Recipient Pro Deo et Juventute award, Cath. Youth Orgn., 1968. Mem. Cath. Press Assn., Pacific Area Travel Agts., Assn. Retail Travel Agts. Republican. Clubs: Gary Women's, Marianjoy Rehab. Hosp. Aux. Office: Tour Desk One Inc 404 S Main St Wheaton IL 60187

FUSILLO, LISA ANN, dance educator; b. Washington, Jan. 11, 1951; d. Matthew Henry and Alice Elbert (Zeigler) Fusillo; student Butler U., 1969-72; teaching cert. Royal Ballet Sch., 1975; B.S., George Washington U., 1976; M.A., Tex. Womans U., 1978, Ph.D., 1982; m. Robert Forshay Smith Jr., June 19, 1982. Dancer, Butler Ballet, Indpls., 1969-72; mus. asst. Royal Ballet, London, 1973-75; dancer Liz Lerman Group, Washington, 1975-76; teaching asst. Tex. Womans U., Denton, 1976-77, mem. adj. faculty, 1978, 81; choreographic asst. Leonide Massine, W. Ger., London, Paris, San Francisco, N.Y., 1976-78; instr. Skidmore Coll., Saratoga Springs, N.Y., 1978-80; asst. prof. ballet Tex. Christian U., Fort Worth, 1981-85, assoc. prof., 1985—; artistic cons., guest choreographer Chattanooga Civic Ballet, 1984; master tchr., artistic cons. San Angelo Civic Ballet, 1985; free lance choreographer, master tchr. in U.S. and Europe. Mem. AAHPER, Imperial Soc. Tchrs. Dancing, Royal Acad. Dancing, AAUP, Sigma Alpha Iota, Alpha Chi, Pi Lambda Theta, Chi Tau Epsilon. Office: Texas Christian Univ Division of Ballet and Modern Dance Box 32889 Fort Worth TX 76129

FUTCH, GRACE BONNER, real estate broker; b. Manchester, Ga., Sept. 24, 1924; d. Warner Augdon and Johnnye Grace (Brown) Bonner Harris; children by previous marriage—Lynda Futch Creed, Carol Futch Bores. Student Ga. State Coll. for Women, 1941-43, Woodrow Wilson Coll. Law, Ga. State U., 1954-55; grad. Realtors Inst. Pres. Realty Ctr. Assocs., Inc., Pensacola, Fla., 1960-85, Pensacola Beach Realty, Inc., 1970—; gen. ptnr. Lake Russell, Ltd., Pensacola, 1976—, Rockdale, Ltd., 1975—; trustee Turtle Lake Land Trust, 1974—. Pres., United Cerebral Palsy of Northwest Fla., 1971-73, United Cerebral Palsy, Fla., 1974. Mem. Pensacola Bd. Realtors, Fla. Assn. Realtors, Nat. Assn. Realtors, Pensacola C. of C. Republican. Baptist. Club: Zonta (pres. 1981). Office: Pensacola Beach Realty Inc 649 Pensacola Beach Blvd Pensacola Beach FL 32561

FUTRELL, KATHLEEN HUNT, educator; b. N.Y.C., Jan. 13, 1926; d. Robert Emmett and Margaret Mary (Fitzgerald) Hunt; B.A., Ladycliff Coll., 1947; M.A. in Edn., Goddard Coll.; diploma Washington Montessori Inst., 1967, 73; m. Alvin F. Futrell, June 5, 1946; children—Jonathan, David, Alison, Daniel. Dir., Aquinas Montessori Sch., Alexandria, Va., 1965—; lectr. Washington Montessori Inst., 1979—; cons. N.Am. Montessori Schs. Mem. N.Am. Montessori Tchrs. Assn., Assn. Montessori Internat. Author: The Normalized Child, 1967. Home: 3007 Cunningham Dr Alexandria VA 22309 Office: 8334 Mount Vernon Hwy Alexandria VA 22309

FUTRELL, MARY ALICE FRANKLIN HATWOOD, association executive; b. Alta Vista, Va., May 24, 1940; m. Donald Futrell, Oct. 8, 1977. B.A., Va. State U., 1962; M.A., George Washington U., 1968; postgrad. Md. U., 1965, U. Va., 1978-79, Va. Poly. Inst. and State U., 1979-80. High sch. tchr., Alexandria, Va., 1963-80; pres. Edn. Assn. Alexandria, 1973-75, Va. Edn. Assn., Richmond, 1976-78; sec.-treas. NEA, Washington, 1980-83, pres., 1983—. Office: NEA 1201 16th St NW Washington DC 20036

FUTTER, ELLEN VICTORIA, college president; b. N.Y.C., Sept. 21, 1949; d. Victor and Joan Babette (Feinberg) F.; m. John A. Shutkin, Aug. 25, 1974; 1 dau., Anne Victoria. Student U. Wis.-Madison; A.B., Barnard Coll., N.Y.C.; J.D., Columbia U., LL.D. (hon.), 1984; D.H.L. (hon.), Amherst Coll., 1984. Bar: N.Y. 1975. Assoc., Milbank, Tweed, Hadley & McCloy, N.Y.C., 1974-80; acting pres. Barnard Coll., 1980-81, pres., 1981—, also trustee; dir. Squibb Corp. Bd. dirs. Milbank Meml. Fund, The New York Blood Ctr.; mem. N.Y. State Gov.'s Council on State Priorities, 1982; trustee Ednl. Testing Service; mem., vice chmn. N.Y. Comm. Ind. Colls. and Univs.; bd. dirs. Regional Plan Assn.; mem. Helsinki Watch Com., N.Y. State Gov.'s. Com. Coll. and Univ. Pres.; mem. bus. adv. commn. Edn. Commn. States; mem. exec. com. Women's Coll. Coalition; mem. N.Y. State Gov.'s Council State Priorities, 1982; friend N.Y.C. Commn. Status of Women. Recipient Abram L. Sacher award Brandeis U., 1982; award Albert Einstein Coll. Medicine, Yeshiva U., 1984. Mem. Nat. Inst. Social Scis., Assn. Bar City N.Y., N.Y. State Bar Assn., ABA, NOW (mem. adv. bd. Legal Def. and Edn. Fund), Phi Beta Kappa. Club: Cosmopolitan (N.Y.C.). Office: Barnard Coll 3009 Broadway St New York NY 10027

FYFE, JANET HUNTER, library educator, historian; b. Blantyre, Scotland, Apr. 29, 1929; came to Can., 1963; d. James Stanley and Jean (Burleigh) F. M.A., U. Edinburgh, 1950; Ph.D., U. Guelph, 1977. Cert. ALA, 1956. Br. librarian Borough of Heston and Isleworth, Hounslow, Eng., 1956-58; sr. asst. librarian U. St. Andrews, Scotland, 1958-63; reference librarian U. Sask., Regina, Can., 1963-65, head dept. bibliography and book selection, Saskatoon, 1965-70; assoc. prof. Sch. Library and Info. Sci., U. Western Ont., London, 1970-81, prof., 1981—, mem. univ. senate, 1981-86, exec. com. faculty assn., 1982-84, chmn. status of women com., 1982-84; bd. mem. Internat. Inst. for Garibaldian Studies, Sarasota, Fla., 1982. Author, editor: Autobiography of John McAdam, 1980; author: Directory of Special Collections in Canadian Libraries, 1968; History Journals and Serials: An Analytical Guide, 1986; contbr. hist. articles to jours.; editor: Sask. Library, Saskatoon, 1966-70. Vis. research fellow Inst. for Advanced Studies in Humanities, U. Edinburgh, 1979; research grantee Social Scis. and Humanities Research Council Can., 1979, 83, 84. Fellow Library Assn.; mem. Sask. Library Assn. (councillor 1964-66), Saskatoon Library Assn. (pres. 1969-70), various hist. and library assns. Club: Internat. Toastmistress (pres. London 1982-83). Home: 432 Oak Park Dr London ON N6H 3N4 Canada Office: Sch Library and Info Sci Univ Western Ont London ON N6G 1H1 Canada

FYVOLENT, SUSAN GALE, lawyer; b. Orlando, Fla., May 11, 1954; d. David Bradley and Sally Aline (Felson) Fyvolent. B.A. in Journalism, U. Ga., 1976; paralegal Nat. Ctr. for Paralegal Tng., 1977; J.D., Woodrow Wilson Coll. Law, 1983. Bar: Ga. 1983. Paralegal Walter W. Furlong, Atlanta, 1977-83; sole practice, Atlanta, 1983—; dir. Profl. Uniform Apparel Co., Inc., St. Petersburg, Fla., Mem. Assn. Trial Lawyers Am., ABA, Ga. Assn. Women Lawyers, Atlanta Bar Assn., State Bar Ga. Democrat. Office: Susan G Fyvolent Atty at Law 1400 Bank South Bldg 55 Marietta St Atlanta GA 30303

GAARDER, MARIE, speech pathologist; b. New Britain, Conn., July 19, 1935; d. Nicholas and Clara (Sangeloty) Sarris; B.S., U. Ill., 1957; postgrad. U. Md., 1962-63, Our Lady of Lake U. Grad. Sch. Social Work, San Antonio, 1976-77; m. Kenneth R. Gaarder, Dec. 8, 1962; children—Jason, Galen. Founder speech therapy program Flossmoor (Ill.) Sch. Dist. 161, 1957-59; speech pathologist Prince George's County (Md.) Bd. Edn., 1959-65, Sidwell Friend's Sch., Washington, 1966-67, St. Maurice Sch. for Learning Disabilities, Potomac, Md., 1968-69; pvt. practice speech therapy, Chevy Chase, Md., 1967—; adminstrv. officer Gaarder Med. Corp., Chevy Chase, 1977—. Pres., Prince George's chpt. Council for Exceptional Children, 1963-64; mem. Florence Crittenton Circle, 1966-69, Hospitality and Info. Service for Diplomats, 1967—; chmn. activities com. Jr. Teens, 1979-80; chmn. publicity YWCA Internat. Fair, 1977-79, chmn. entertainment, 1983; mem. internat. com. Woman's Nat. Democratic Club; co-chmn. Adv. Com. for Quality Integrated Edn. in Montgomery County, 1977-78; bd. dirs. D.C. br. YWCA, 1981-82, Washington Ctr. Music Therapy Clinic, Cath. U. Am., 1983—, The Samaritans of Washington, 1984—; chmn. Career Day, Nat. Symphony Ednl. Activities, 1981—; chmn. oral history 65th Birthday Town of Chevy Chase; chmn. Mid-Atlantic regional adv. bd. Am. Found. for the Blind, 1984-85. Recipient cert. of appreciation Opera Guild San Antonio, 1977. Mem. Am. Speech, Lang. and Hearing Assn. (advanced cert.), Md. Speech, Lang. and Hearing Assn., Internat. Assn. Logopedics and Phoniatrics, World Affairs Council of Washington, Zeta Phi Eta. Greek Orthodox. Club: Capitol Speakers (sec. chpt. III 1983-84) (Washington). Contbg. author: San Antonio Cookbook II, 1976. Home and Office: 4221 Oakridge Ln Chevy Chase MD 20815

GABER, TINA MERRI, public relations specialist, counselor; b. Phila., Mar. 24, 1951; d. David and Iva (Bandes) G. B.A., U. Fla., 1974; M.Ed., U. Miami, 1976. Tchr. spl. edn. Dade County Pub. Sch. System, Miami, 1977; counselor dept. univ. family services U. Miami Med. Sch., 1977-80; counselor Fla. State Employment Service, Miami, 1980-85; dir. pub. relations Carriage House/Carriage Club, Miami Beach, Fla., 1985; dir. pub. relations Diabetes Research Inst., U. Miami Sch. Medicine, 1985; spl. projects coordinator Royal Palm Hotel, Miami Beach, Fla., 1985—. Mem. City of Miami Beach Adv. Bd. on Juvenile Problems, 1983-84; mem. City of Miami Beach Adv. Bd. on Recreational Ctrs. and Park Facilities, 1984—; trustee Ronald McDonald House of South Fla., Miami, 1984—, vol. coordinator, 1985, editor newsletter, 1985—. Mem. Greater Miami C. of C., Dade County Mental Health Assn., Dade County Assn. Retarded Citizens, Fla. Personnel and Guidance Assn., U. Miami Alumni Assn., Miami Beach Jaycee Women (pres. 1983-84). Avocations: sculpture, needlepoint, art, gardening.

GABLE, MARTHA ANNE, educator; b. Phila.; d. James F. and Stella (Gingrich) Gable; B.E., Ind. U., 1942; M.Ed., Temple U., 1935. Tchr. Phila. Public Schs., 1926-41, asst. dir. phys. and health edn., Phila., 1942-48, asst. dir. sch. and community relations, 1948-55, dir. radio-TV edn., 1955-66, dir. instrnl. materials, 1966-68; editor Am. Assn. Sch. Adminstrs., 1968-73; cons. ednl. tech., 1973—. Mem. Pa. Gov.'s Adv. Commn. Edn., 1956-58; mem. White House Conf. Edn., 1955; cons. Joint Council Ednl. TV, Washington. Del. Internat. Conf. Ednl. TV, London, 1954; judge Olympic Games, London, 1948, Helsinki, 1952, Melbourne, 1956, Rome, 1960, Tokyo, Japan, 1964; v.p. Women for Greater Phila. Recipient Temple U. Alumni award, 1964; named Disting. Dau. of Pa., named to Pa. Sports Hall of Fame, 1984. Mem. Phila. Public Relations Assn. (sec., Hall of Fame award), Am. Women in Radio and TV, NEA, Public Relations Soc. Am., TV-Radio Advt. Club, AAUW, Am. Assn. Sch. Adminstrs., Am. News Womens Clubs, Women in Communications. Presbyterian. Clubs: Cosmopolitan; Nat. Press (Washington). Home: 2601 Pkwy Philadelphia PA 19130

GABRIA, JOANNE BAKAITIS, information processing systems equipment company executive; b. Washington, Pa., Jan. 16, 1945; d. Vincent William and Mary Jo (Cario) Bakaitis. B.A. in English, U. Dayton, 1965, M.A. in Mktg. Communications, 1973, M.B.A., 1979. Advt. writer Dancer-Fitzgerald-Sample, Dayton, Ohio, 1969-72; advt. coordinator Monarch Marking Systems, Dayton, 1972-73; product tech. editor Frigidaire div. GM, Dayton, 1973-77; dir. tech. communications Mead Tech. Lab., Dayton, 1977-79; publs. mgr. NCR Corp., Dayton, 1979-81, internat. product mgr., 1981—; v.p., bd. dirs. Contact-Dayton, 1984-85. Author: Microwave Cooking in 3 Speeds, 1976, Communications Standards, 1978, Retail Operations, 1982; editor: Ivy Jour., 1980-82. Chair numerous coms. St. Leonard Community, Centerville, Ohio, 1978—; telephone vol. Contact-Dayton Crisis Intervention, 1982—; big sister Big Bros./Big Sisters, Dayton, 1985—. Recipient Disting. Achievement award Contact-Dayton, 1985. Mem. Nat. Assn. Female Execs., Dayton Soc. Natural History, Marianist Affiliates (co-chmn. 1981—). Democrat. Roman Catholic. Avocations: gardening, nature, classical music. Home: 7807 Graceland St Dayton OH 45459 Office: NCR Corp World Hdqrs-2 1700 S Patterson Blvd Dayton OH 45479

GABRIEL, BARBARA JAMIESON, educator; b. Pasadena, Calif., Jan. 21, 1929; d. Hamer Hershal and Hazel (Kendall) Jamieson; m. Albert Lawrence Gabriel, June 28, 1947; children—Sam Winston, Bryn Patricia Petersen. B.A. magna cum laude, Calif. State U.-Long Beach, 1971, M.A. in Ednl. Adminstrn., 1982; M.A. in Reading Edn., 1987. Cert. tchr., sch. adminstr., reading specialist, bilingual/cross cultural specialist, Calif. Bilingual tchr. Parkview Sch., 1973-78, minimum essential tchr., 1978-80; instructional materials specialist Mountain View Sch. Dist., El Monte, Calif., 1980—, bilingual program cons., 1985—. Mem. State Book Rev. Com., 1979, Four Dist. Task Force, 1979. Mem. Internat. Reading Assn., Assn. Supervision and Curriculum Devel., Nat. Council Tchrs. English, AAUW, Calif. Assn. Sch. Adminstrs., Am. Running and Fitness Assn., San Diego Zool. Soc., Phi Kappa Phi, Kappa Delta Pi, Phi Delta Kappa. Club: Alamitos Bay Yacht, (Long Beach, Calif.). Office: 2850 N Mountain View Rd El Monte CA 91732

GABRIEL, FANNIE ROCKEFELLER, secretary; b. Rutland, Vt., Aug. 17, 1922; d. Philip Stanard and Jessie (Stone) Rockefeller; m. George Evans Gabriel, Dec. 27, 1958 (dec. May 1968). A.B., U. Bridgeport, 1941; B.A., Beaver Coll., 1943. Social studies tchr. Canton Schs., Conn., 1943-45; underwriter Nat. Fire Ins. Co., Hartford, Conn., 1945-68; part-time sec. Gino L. Donato, Ins.-Real Estate, 1969—. Vice chmn. Bloomfield Republican Town Com., 1963-75; bd. dirs. Conn. Jr. Women, 1957, Bloomfield Commn. on Aging, 1960—; mem. Gov.'s Adv. Commn., 1971-75; coordinator Prosser Library, Bloomfield, Friends of Library, Cancer Soc.; sec. 250th Anniversary Bloomfield; coordinator House and Garden Tour. Named Woman of Yr., Jr. Woman's Club, 1972, Republican of Yr., Bloomfield, 1974. Mem. Huguenot Soc. Conn. (pres.). Clubs: Women's of Conn. (chmn. Women's Resource and Ednl. Ctr. 1982-86), Conn. Fedn. of Women's Clubs (pres. 1980-82). Home: 43 Prospect St Bloomfield CT 06002

GADE, DARLENE KAY, credit counselor; b. Hammond, Ind., Dec. 1, 1935; d. Cecil A. and Virginia M. (Normand) Stonecipher; m. Thor G. Gade, Sept. 28, 1973; children—Laura, Lisa, Russell. With Am. Furniture Stores, Inc., El Paso, Tex., 1965-85, credit mgr., 1972-81; dir. consumer credit counseling YWCA, El Paso; nat. panelist Alternatives to Bankruptcy. Mem. Leadership El Paso; chmn. adv. bd. Debit Counseling Service of YWCA. Named Credit Exec. of Yr., State of Tex., 1978-79, Woman of Yr. in Bus. and Fin., El Paso Women's Polit. Caucus, 1981. Cert. consumer credit exec. Mem. Internat. Consumer Credit Assn. (Disting. Service award 1980), Credit Mgmt. Assn., Tex., Credit women Internat., El Paso C. of C., El Paso Credit Women (Outstanding Mem. 1981), El Paso Bar Aux. Office: 1600 N Brown St El Paso TX 79902

GADOLA, NANCY LEE, political worker; b. Flint, Mich., Nov. 9, 1940; d. John Warner and Marion Helen (Lundsten) Brown; children—Deborah Helen, Diana Lee, Daniel N. Mem. Genessee County (Mich.) Bd. Commrs., 1977-83; exec. dir. Mich. Reagan-Bush Campaign, 1984. Del. Republican Nat. Conv., Kansas City, Mo., 1976, del.-at-large, Detroit, 1980; presdl. appointee White House Conf. on Aging; mem. Sarasota Rep. Exec. Com. (Fla.); bd. dirs. Sarasota County Big Bros./Big Sisters, Inc. Mem. Venice Area Bd. Realtors, Nat. Bd. Realtors, Fla. Bd. Realtors, Sarasota County Bd. Realtors. Home: 5416 Laurelwood Pl Sarasota FL 33582

GAERTNER, SARAH ANN, publications manager; b. Yoakum, Tex., Apr. 4, 1951; d. Rudolph Frank and Maureen (Barnett) Gaertner; m. David Alan Puntch, July 18, 1975. B.A., Sam Houston State U., 1972. Asst. editor Sam Houston State U. Newspaper, Huntsville, 1971-72; reporter Houston County Courier, Crockett, Tex., 1972; editor Tex. Edn. Agy., Austin, 1974-75; journalist Comptroller Pub. Accounts, Austin, 1978-79; info. coordinator Lower Colo. River Authority, Austin, 1980-82; writer Shoal Creek Hosp., 1982-84, publs. mgr. Horizon Health Corp., Dallas, 1984—. Recipient award of excellence for feature writing Internat. Assn. Bus. Communications. Mem. Women in Communication (exec. bd., treas. chpt.), Austin Writers League, Sigma Delta Chi, Pi Kappa Delta. Democrat. Roman Catholic. Office: Horizon Health Corp 2775 Villa Creek Dallas TX 75234

GAERTNER DORADO, MARIANNE, lawyer; b. Neptune, N.J., May 18, 1956; d. Wolfgang Wilhelm and Marianne Leopoldine (Weber) Gaertner; m. Richard Manuel Dorado, Oct. 1, 1982. B.A., Yale U., 1978; J.D., U. Mich., 1981. Bar: N.Y. 1982. Adminstrv. asst. W.W. Gaertner Research, Inc., Norwalk, Conn., 1972-79; assoc. Shearman & Sterling, N.Y.C., 1981—; dir. W. W. Gaertner Research, Inc., 1981—. Contbr. articles to profl. jours.; editor U. Mich. Jour. Law Reform, 1980-81. Extern Office Legal Advisor, Dept. State, 1980. Republican. Roman Catholic. Club: Yale. Home: 111 E 30th St Apt 12A New York NY 10016 Office: Shearman & Sterling 153 E 53d St New York NY 10022

GAFF, JOAN MCCLUSKEY, insurance official; b. Chelsea, Mass., Sept. 24, 1951; d. Joseph Francis and Eleanor Frances (Mortimer) McCluskey; m. Bradley John Clegg, Apr. 17, 1971 (div. Oct. 1978); children—Gretchen Anne, Andi Leigh, Grahm Bradley; m. 2d, Robert M. Gaff, July 7, 1984. A. Secretarial, No. Essex Coll., Haverhill, Mass., 1971; B.S. in Bus. Adminstrn., Suffolk U., Boston, 1983; M. Sci. Mgmt., Lesley Coll., Cambridge, Mass., 1985. Sr. sec. Mass. Gen. Hosp., Boston, 1976-79, exec. asst., 1979-81, ins. specialist, 1981-84, ins. mgr., 1984—. Mem. Risk Ins. Mgmt. Soc., Mass. Hosp. Risk Mgmt. Soc., Am. Soc. Hosp. Risk Mgmt. Roman Catholic. Office: Mass Gen Hosp MGH Box 135 Boston MA 02110

GAFFNEY, DOROTHEA FINNEN, retired federal employee, book company executive; b. Paterson, N.J., Aug. 19, 1918; d. Charles Christopher and Mary (Mitchell) Finnen; m. Harold R. Gaffney, Aug. 25, 1951; 1 child, Hale R. Student, Am. U., 1949-51. Asst. chief supply br. spl. services, U.S. Army, 1945-51; procurement officer Quartermaster Corp., U.S. Army, 1951-55; purchasing and contracting officer U.S. Air Force, 1956-59, U.S. Coast Guard, 1959-69; chief procurement br. 3d dist. U.S. Coast Guard, 1969-75; v.p. Am. Overseas Book Co., Norwood, N.J. 1975—. Recipient Silver medal for meritorious achievement U.S. Sec. Transp., 1974. Roman Catholic. Club: Garden Club (pres. 1980-84). Home: 22 Lambeth Ln Lakehurst NJ 08733

GAGE, DOROTHY JEAN, accounting technician; b. Howe, Okla., June 13, 1928; d. Seaman and Ruby Euretta (Phillips) Claborn; student pub. schs. Ark. and Calif.; m. Roy C. Gage, May 5, 1949; children—Roy Charles (dec.), Seaman Lynn, Christine, Terry Lee (dec.). Payroll clk. Saticoy Lemon Assn., Saticoy, Calif., 1946-48; comptometer operator Foremost Dairy, Ventura, Calif., 1948-57, Carnation Co., Ventura, 1957-67; acctg. technician Naval Ship Weapon Systems Engring. System, Port Hueneme, Calif., 1969-82; driver handicapped children, 1957-72. Charter mem. Ventura County Muscular Dystrophy Assn., 1955-82, officer or v.p., 1955-81, Ventura county chmn., 1958-82; bd. dirs. Ventura County Health Agys., 1968-80. Recipient award for service to Muscular Dystrophy Assn., Calif. Assembly, 1980, others; also named in Congressional Record. Mem. Ventura County Health Agy., Tri-Counties Muscular Dystrophy Assn., Jaycees. Democrat. Clubs: Eagles, Toastmistresses. Office: PO Box 1133 Port Hueneme CA 93041-6133

GAGE, NANCY ELIZABETH, college administrator, educator; b. Chgo., Aug. 22, 1947; d. Winfred Paul and Anne Ellen (Osbon) Rankhorn; m. Walter Howard Crane, June 14, 1969 (div. June 1977); 1 child, Patrick; m. James Lewis Gage, June 10, 1977 (div. Oct. 15, 1981); 1 child, Laura Anne. B.S., Ill. Inst. Tech., 1969; postgrad. Winona State U., 1978-80, U. Minn., 1981-82. Cert. tchr. math., Mich., Ill. Tchr. math. St. Bede Acad., Eau Claire, Wis., 1977; accounts specialist U. Minn., Mpls., 1981, asst. adminstr., 1981-82, assoc. adminstr., 1982-83; grants acct. Coll. of DuPage, Glen Ellyn, Ill., 1984, cash disbursements mgr., 1984—, chmn. supervisory com. Fed. Credit Union, 1985-86; mem. project team payroll/personnel systems implementation, 1985—. Contbg. author math. curriculum, 1972. Media contact coordinator Common Cause, Manistique, Mich., 1975-76; bd. dirs. pres. Manistique Coop. Nursery Sch., 1974-75; mem. Bicentennial program com. Manistique Jr. Women's Group, Manistique, 1975-76, Chgo. Tchrs. Against the Vietnam War, 1969. State of Ill. fellow, 1970; Ill. Inst. Tech. scholar, 1964. Mem. Nat. Assn. Female Execs., Coll. of DuPage Classified Personnel Assn., Kappa Phi Delta (treas. 1967-68). Democrat. Unitarian. Club: Manistique Extension Homemakers (treas. 1974-76). Avocations: macrame wall tapestries; embroidery; choral singing; gardening; camping; reading. Home: 7 S Whispering Hills Dr Apt A Naperville IL 60540 Office: Fin Office Coll of DuPage 22d St at Lambert Rd Glen Ellyn IL 60137

GAGNE, PAMELA BASHORE, lawyer; b. Harrisburg, Pa., Oct. 19, 1955; d. Charles Eicker and Helen Louise (Adams) Bashore; m. William Roderick Gagne, Aug. 26, 1978; 1 child, Roderick Bashore. B.A. cum laude, Vanderbilt U., 1977; student Inst. Internat. and Comparative Law, Sorbonne, Paris, 1978; J.D., Dickinson Sch. Law, 1980. Bar: Pa. 1980, Fla. 1982. Law clk. Pa. Dept. Environ. Resources, Harrisburg, 1978-79; jud. clk. to judge Gwilyn A. Price, Pitts., 1980-82; assoc. Marshall, Dennehey, Warner, Coleman & Goggin, Phila., 1982—; mem. Young Lawyers Child Abuse Com. Phila., 1983—; dir. Edwin L. Heim Co., Inc., Harrisburg. Mem. Lawyers for the Arts, Phila., 1983—; fundraiser, community organizer St. Christopher's Children's Hosp., Phila., 1983—; mem. Washington Mews Condominium Council, Phila., 1982-85. Recipient Am. Jurisprudence award, 1980; Merit award for Achievement in Advocacy, Dickinson Sch. Law, 1980. Mem. ABA, Pa. Bar Assn. (com. statutory constrn. 1985—; mem. com. youth edn. young lawyers div. 1985—), Fla. Bar Assn., LWV. Democrat. Presbyterian. Club: Acorn (Phila.). Home: 2210 Pine St Philadelphia PA 19103 Office: Marshall Dennehey Warner Coleman & Goggin 1515 Locust St Philadelphia PA 19102

GAGNON, EDITH MORRISON, ballerina, singer, actress; b. Chgo., Apr. 8; grad. Chalif Sch. Dancing, N.Y.C.; student Northwestern U.; voice student Forest Lamont of Chgo. Opera Co.; m. Alfred Gagnon, Feb. 3, 1977; children by previous marriage—Joyce, Morton. Premiere ballerina Pavley and Oukrainsky Russian Ballet of Chgo., performer with Chgo., Met., Ravinia Opera Cos.; appeared Birthday of Infanta, Greenwich Follies, The Five O'Clock Girl; founder, dir., instr. Sch. of Dance, St. Louis; singer in concert, Carnegie Hall; commentator radio programs Women on the Home Front, Sta. KSD, St. Louis, and CD program Sta. WEW, St. Louis U.; voice coach, producer, performer benefit performances, St. Louis, San Francisco area. Pres. Pets Unlimited, San Francisco; bd. dirs. Artists Embassy. Mem. Pacific Musical Soc. (v.p. San Francisco), Equity Guild. Clubs: Burlingame Country; International, Francisca Hillsborough CA 94010

GAGNON, LYNNE MARIE, nurse; b. Presque Isle, Maine, Aug. 1, 1951; d. Guilford Monroe and Caroline (Folger) Smith; m. Daniel Gale Gagnon, Dec. 29, 1971; children—Amber, Dawn, Beth. Nursing diploma Mercy Hosp. Sch. of Nursing, Portland, Maine, 1972; student St. Joseph's Coll., North Windham, Maine, 1969-72, U. Maine-Orono, 1980-84, SUNY-Albany, 1982—. Registered nurse, Maine; cert. emergency nurse. Staff nurse St. Agnes Hosp., Balt., 1972-73, Hartford Hosp., Conn., 1973-74; staff nurse, charge nurse A.R. Gould Meml. Hosp., Presque Isle, Maine, 1974-77; staff nurse I, emergency dept. Eastern Maine Med. Ctr., Bangor, Maine, 1979-82, staff developer, 1982—; mem. Gov.'s Adv. Bd. to Emergency Med. Services, 1983—, chmn., 1985—; chmn. 11th Ann. New Eng. Symposium on Emergency Nursing, 1985. Bd. dirs. Orono Vol. Rescue Service, 1985—; mem. Maine Seat Belt Coalition, 1986. Mem. Am. Nurses Assn., Maine State Nurses Assn., Emergency Dept. Nurses Assn. (chpt. pres. 1979-81), Maine Emergency Nurses Assn. (pres. 1984, 85-86). Democrat. Roman Catholic. Avocations: cross-country skiing; sewing; reading. Home: RFD 5 Box 260 Bangor ME 04401 Office: Eastern Maine Med Ctr Edn and Tng Ctr 489 State St Bangor ME 04401

GAGNON, YVONNE, public affairs specialist; b. Old Town, Maine, Feb. 3, 1946; d. Louis and Florence (Sirois) Gagnon. B.A., Albertus Magnus Coll., 1968; postgrad. Fgn. Service Inst., 1975, NYU. Tchr., Peace Corps, Fiji Islands, 1969-71, Colchester/W. Hartford, Conn., Woburn, Mass., 1968, 72-74; manpower tng. and planning advisor Pacific Arch. & Engrs., Jakarta, Indonesia, 1975-77; owner, dir. Transcultural Research Internat., W. Newton, Mass., 1977-80; pub. affairs mgr. Freeport Indonesia, N.Y.C., 1980-85.

Producer film documentary: Mining Challenge, 1981. Mem. Pub. Relations Soc. Am. Internat. Assn. Bus. Communicators.

GAGON, LYNNE LARSON, nursing administrator; b. Oakland, Calif., Nov. 24, 1944; d. Oakley Peter and Rhae (Thomas) Larson; m. Parker N. Downs, Nov. 26, 1964 (div. 1968); 1 child, Kimberly Christina; m. Kenneth W. Roberts, Jan. 23, 1971 (div. 1979); 1 child, Kendra Lynne Roberts; m. David Ira Gagon, Apr. 12, 1980. Assoc. degree Coll. of Desert, 1978; student St. Josephs Coll., since 1983—. Sec. orthopedic surgery Stanford Med. Ctr., Palo Alto, Calif., 1969-71; asst. to fiscal services Eisenhower Med. Ctr., Palm Desert, Calif., 1971-72; v.p. Roberts Constrn. Co., Palm Desert, 1973-79; staff nurse Uintah County Hosp., Vernal, Utah, 1979-80; patient care coordinator-obstetrics Ashley Valley Med. Ctr., Vernal, 1980-81, dir. nursing service, 1981—, mem. med. ctr. speakers bur., since 1985—; appt. Utah State Bd. Nursing, 1984—; chmn. practice com. Utah State Bd. Nursing, 1985—; chmn. Utah Entry into Practice Task Force, 1985—; mem. clin. faculty Weber State Coll., Ogden, Utah, 1984—. Pres. elect adv. council Uintah Basin Vocat. Ctr., Roosevelt, Utah, 1983—. Recipient Green Angel award Girl Scouts U.S.A., 1975. Mem. Am. Nurses Assn., Utah Nurses Assn. (past pres. elect Dist. 8). Republican. Avocation: ranching. Office: Ashley Valley Med Ctr 151 W 200 N Vernal UT 84078

GAIND, CONSTANCE MARY, laboratory services executive, chemist; b. Kirkwall, Orkney, Scotland, Aug. 6, 1941; came to U.S., 1968, naturalized, 1979; d. William and Rosetta Catherine (Bain) Groundwater; m. Arun Kumar Gaind, Nov. 30, 1968; children—Kiran Fiona, Anita Catherine, Sonia Frances. B.S. in Chemistry, U. Edinburgh, Scotland, 1963, diploma in edn., 1964. Tchr. Norfolk House Sch., Victoria, Can., 1964-65; research asst. Abbott Labs., Montreal, Que., Can., 1966-68; research chemist Sandoz Inc., Hanover, N.J., 1968-69, St. Regis Paper Co., West Nyack, N.Y., 1970-71; chemist Nanco Labs, Inc., Hopewell Junction, N.Y., 1975-78, pres., lab. dir., 1979—. Recipient Salute to Women and Industry award YWCA, Poughkeepsie, N.Y., 1985. Mem. Am. Chem. Soc., Water Pollution Control Fedn., Nat. Assn. Environ. Profls., ASTM, Assn. Ofcl. Analytical Chemists, Dutchess County Scottish Soc. Democrat. Presbyterian. Avocations: travel; writing. Office: Nanco Labs Inc PO Box 10 Unity St and Route 376 Hopewell Junction NY 12533

GAINER, RUBY JACKSON (MRS. HERBERT P. GAINER), educator, civic leader; b. Buena-Vista, Ga.; d. William B. and Lovie (Jones) Jackson; student Miles Meml. Coll., 1932-35; B.S., Ala. State Tchrs. Coll., 1939; M.A. in English and Social Studies, Atlanta U., 1953; postgrad. Fla. A&M U., 1962-63, Western Wash. State Coll., 1964, U. Conn., 1965, Okla. State U., 1968. H.H.D. (hon.) Selma U., 1968, Daniel Payne Coll., 1971; LL.D. (hon.), Birmingham Bapt. Coll., Faith Coll., Birmingham, 1976; L.H.D. (hon.), Bishop Coll., 1977; m. Herbert P. Gainer, June 2, 1946; children—Ruby Paulette, James H., Cecil F. Tchr. J.B. Turner High Sch., Milton, Fla., 1947-48, Pub. Schs. Birmingham, Washington Jr. High Sch., Pensacola, Fla., 1955-68; guidance counselor Wedgewood Jr.-Sr. High Sch., Pensacola, 1968—; tchr. English, Woodham High Sch. Brought 2 successful legal cases against Jefferson County (Ala.) Sch. Bd. for equalization of Negro tchr. salaries, 1946-47, re-instatement Negro tchrs. under Tchr. Tenure Act; organized 1st tchrs. union, Birmingham; organized local high sch. chpt. Future Tchrs. Am., local tchr. aide and teen service groups, local and county assns. edn.; local capt. Heart Fund, Mothers March of Dimes, Cancer Fund; active local PTA, past chmn. Fla. PTA Workshop, 1966; participant Fla. Gov.'s Conf. Edn., Tallahassee, 1967, Nat. Conf. Profl. Rights and Responsibilities, Arlington, Tex., 1968; participant, chmn. numerous profl. ednl. confs. So. U.S.; mem. Escambia County Guidance Council; mem., past officer Fla. Guidance Council. Bd. dirs. United Negro Coll. Fund, Pensacola, Partners for Progress, Pensacola, Escambia County Tb Assn.; mem. Pensacola Democratic Exec. Com., 1981—; area IV dir. Top Teens Am., 1981—; pres. Fla. Assn. Women's and Girls' Clubs with Boys' Aux. Named Tchr. of Yr., Dist. 1 Fla. State Tchrs. Assn., 1966, also recipient award meritorious service, Disting. Service award, 1966, DuShane Outstanding Service award, 1967; recipient DuShane Outstanding Dir. award Escambia County Tchrs. Assn., 1967, Disting. Service award civil, human, profl. rights, 1965; Outstanding Tchr. and Leader award Fla. Edn. Assn., honor award NEA Fla. State Tchrs. Assn., 1966, awards youth, community orgns.; Disting. Achievement in Edn. award, Outstanding Educator award, Honor award, Recognition Day award, Public Service award, Disting. Community Service award, Parent of Yr. award, Top Educator award (all 1970), human relations award Student Com. of Woodham High Sch., 1972, Polish award as outstanding tchr. of yr. 1981, others; cited Pitts. Courier, NAACP, 1946-47; Ruby J. Gainer Day proclaimed by mayor Pensacola, 1970, 81; Pensacola's Woman of Yr., Pensacola Voice Newspaper, 1974, awards Ala. State U., 1974, 75; Top Lady of Yr. as Disting. Am., 1981; Top Educator of Yr. award, 1981; Disting. Service award Five Flag Toastmasters Club, 1981; Human Relations in Edn. award Fla. Teaching Profession, 1981; Human Relations award S.E. Region Classroom Tchrs., 1981. Mem. Jefferson County (past. sec., past pres.), Escambia County (past sec., past pres,), Fla. (past bd. dirs. dist. 1, past pres. dist. 1, mem. tchr. edn. and profl. standards commn. and evaluation com., bd. advisers dept. classroom tchrs.), Ala. (past. chmn. secondary sch. tchrs.), Am. tchrs. assns., AAUW, Jefferson County Tchrs. Union (past pres.), NEA (v.p. assn. classroom tchrs. 1969-70), Nat. Council English Tchrs., Nat. Council Social Studies Tchrs., Escambia County League Justice, Future Tchrs. Am. Advisers Council, City-Wide Fedn. Women's Clubs (past officer), Internat. Platform Assn., LWV, Gen. Alumni Assn. Ala. State U. (exec. bd.), Top Ladies of Distinction (organizer, pres. Pensacola chpt., Pensacola Top Lady of Yr. 1980, Top Lady of Decade 1980, Area Top Lady of Yr. 1980), Nat. Gen. Alumni Assn. (v.p. 1981—), Alpha Kappa Alpha (Achievement award South Atlantic region 1970). Baptist (mem., pres. bd. ushers). Mem. Order Eastern Star. Clubs: Mary M. Bethune, New Idea Art and Study. (Pensacola). Composer: God Planted You Here, Talking to the Moon, It Is Better Not to Know, In the Quiet of the Day. Contbr. articles, poems publs. Address: 1516 W Gadsden St Pensacola FL 32501

GAINES, CHERIE ADELAIDE, lawyer; b. Queens, N.Y., May 17, 1935; d. Charles Oscar and Billie (Robinson) G.; children—Liana Jane, Eugene Michael, Elliott Mark. B.A., Barnard Coll., 1956; J.D., U. Pa., 1960. Bar: Calif. 1963, N.Y. 1981. Assoc. prof. law Golden Gate U., San Francisco, 1970-71; city atty. Berkeley (Calif.), 1971; asst. prof. law U. San Francisco Law Sch., 1971-73; asst. regional atty. U.S. EEOC, San Francisco, 1973-79, regional atty., N.Y.C., 1979-81; dep. gen. counsel N.Y.C. Housing Authority, 1981—; pvt. practice law, San Francisco, 1963-65; chief atty. Alameda County (Calif.) Legal Aid Soc., Oakland, 1965-70; asst. to asst. regional adminstr. HUD, San Francisco, 1970. Bd. dirs., chmn. mng. com., treas. Consumers Coop., Berkeley, 1972-76; bd. dirs. Berkeley-Albany chpt. ACLU, 1968, mem. San Francisco Regional Council, 1978. Recipient commendation plaque Alameda Affirmative Action Com., 1971, Assn. Real Estate Brokers, 1975, Alameda County Human Relations Commn., 1973. Mem. Calif. Bar Assn. (commn. profl. competence). Club: Charles Houston Law. Office: NYC Housing Authority 250 Broadway Rm 619 New York NY 10007

GAINES, KATHLYN ANNE, nursing educator; b. Florence, Colo., Dec. 20, 1934; d. William Cody and Estelle May (Smith) Gaines Rizk. B.S.N., Syracuse U., 1962; M.N., U. Fla., 1969; D.S.N., U. Ala.-Birmingham, 1981. Rehab. coordinator Ohio State U. Hosp., Columbus, 1965-67; asst. prof. Western Carolina U., Cullowhee, N.C., 1969-73; clinician Highland Hosp., Asheville, N.C., 1973-75; clin. specialist Bayfront Med. Ctr., St. Petersburg, Fla., 1976-77; mental health coordinator V.N.A. of Cleve., 1980-81; chmn. nursing div. Carson-Newman Coll., Jefferson City, Tenn., 1982—; mem. adv. com. Your Vis. Home Nurses, Knoxville, Tenn., 1982—. Mem. Am. Nurses Assn., Nat. League for Nursing, Assn. Rehab. Nurses, Advanced Council of Specialists in Psychiat. Mental Health Nursing, Century Club Am. Nurses Found., AAUW, LWV, Friends of Library, Beta Sigma Phi, Sigma Theta Tau, Omicron Delta Kappa. Episcopalian. Club: Les Amies of Carson-Newman. Office: Carson-Newman Coll Jefferson City TN 37760

GAINES, MARY JOSEPHINE, health care company data processing executive; b. N.Y.C., Feb. 22, 1939; d. Joseph Nathaniel and Mary Daisy (Pressley) Evans; m. George Joseph Gaines, June 30, 1963; 1 child, Jacqueline Maria. B.S. in Bus. Adelphi U., 1982. Data processing supr. N.Y. Times, N.Y.C., 1965-69; data processing operator Unified Sch. Dist., Los Angeles, 1969-72; sr. mgr. mini computer FISA, N.Y.C., 1977-83, also creator, developer all documentation and audit trails, 1977—; dir. data processing services Health/Hosps. Corp., N.Y.C., 1983—. Mem. N.Y. State Commn. on Status of Women, Albany, 1982—; mentor for unwed teenage mother Women in Partnership program N.Y. chpt. 100 Black Women, N.Y.C., 1983—; vol. Greater Harlem Guidance Ctr., Inc., N.Y.C., 1984—; mem. health care and govt. ops. coms. City Club N.Y., N.Y.C., 1984—. Mem. Nat. Assn. Female Execs., Data Entry Mgrs. Assn. Democrat. Avocations: flower arranging, reading, walking. Office: Health/Hosps Corp 230 W 41st St New York NY 10036

GAINES, PAMELA GAYE, corporate credit executive; b. Chgo., July 20, 1960; d. William J. and JoAnn (Stone) Helm; 1 child, Erica K. Diploma in Programming Computers for Bus., Devry Inst. Tech., 19. Clerk Oakbrook Marriott Hotel, Ill., 1981-82, credit supr., 1982-84; supr. Marriott Downtown Hotel Corp., Chgo., 1984-85; credit mgr. Executive House Hotel, Chgo., 1985—; corp. credit mgr. Mgmt. Group, Inc., Chgo., 1986—. Recipient Employee of Month award Marriott Oakbrook Hotel, 1983; Predsl. Honor Soc. Devry Inst. Tech., 1984. Assoc. mem. Chgo. Hotel and Motel Assn. (meeting hostess 1985—). Office: Ambassador West Hotel 1300 N State Pkwy Chicago IL 60610

GAINES, SUSANN FOSTER, retail executive; b. Gainesville, Ga., Jan. 31, 1947; d. George Almiran and Ann Ella (Foster) Gaines; student Pasadena Coll., 1965-67. Asst. mgr. Gaines Dept. Store, Riverside, Calif., 1967-69; dept. mgr. Broadway Dept. Stores, Montclair Plaza, 1969-70, buyer lingere, Los Angeles, 1970; buyer, office mgr., personnel mgr., part owner Gaines Dept. Store, Corona, Calif., 1970-82, also dir.; owner, pres. Astro Bus. Services, Corona, 1979-81; store mgr. Brooks Fashions, Anchorage, 1983—. Bd. dirs. Marching with Christ, Inc., 1976-80; election officer Riverside County Republican Com., 1980; bd. dirs. Corona Music Theater, 1974. Mem. Nat. Assn. Female Execs., Smithsonian Assos., Nat. Trust Hist. Preservation, Animal Protection Inst. Am., Am. Soc. Profl. and Exec. Women, AFTRA. Mem. Ch. Nazarene. Office: 800 E Diamond Blvd Suite 225 Anchorage AK 99515

GAIPTMAN, SHARON ANN, public relations firm executive; b. Phila., Aug. 30, 1948; d. Irving and Ruth (Sass) Gaiptman; m. Peter Kibble Freer, June 4, 1983. Asst. dir. programming Sta. KETC-TV, St. Louis, 1974-78; sta. mgr., program dir. KTOO-TV, Juneau, Alaska, 1978-81; dir. univ. relations U. Alaska-Juneau, 1982-85; owner, pres. Sharon Gaiptman Pub. Relations, Juneau, 1985—; exec. dir. Southeast Alaska Tourism Council, 1985—; vice chmn., dir. Sta. KTOO-FM TV, Juneau, Independent Pub. TV, Anchorage, 1984—; mem. media panel State Council on the Arts, Anchorage, 1982-83. Bd. dirs. Am. Cancer Soc., Juneau, 1981-83, Alaska Acquarium Soc., Juneau, 1984—, Alaska Fundraising and Devel. Council, Anchorage, 1984-85; co-chmn. Gov.'s Inaugural Ball (decorations), Juneau, 1983; pub. relations dir. United Way, 1985; mem. organizing com. Juneau Olympics, 1985—. Mem. Pub. Relations Soc. Am., Soroptimists Internat. (bd. dirs. 1979-83), AAUW (bd. dirs. 1985—). Democrat. Avocations: volunteer work; theatre-related activities. Home and Office: PO Box 385 Juneau AK 99802

GAISER, SHARON DARLENE, manufacturers representatives firm executive; b. Hazel Park, Mich., Nov. 9, 1945; d. Phillip Nelson and Mary Louise (Metcalf) Jourdan; m. Richard Eric Gaiser, June 3, 1967 (div. 1982); m. Ronald Revere Yerman, Aug. 3, 1984. Student Oakland U. Sec., D.P. Bros., Advt., Detroit, 1964-65, Gen. Motors, Warren, Mich., 1965-69; customer service rep. Consumers Power, Pontiac, Mich., 1977-79; sales engr. Infinity, Inc., Southfield, Mich., 1980—, pres. rep. div., 1985—. Creative participant Bi-centennial Floatable Boatable Community Affairs 1976 (award). Pres. Rochester Newcomers Club, Rochester Hills, 1978-79, PTA Peace Lutheran Sch., Utica, Mich., 1978-79; mem. Beautification Commn., Sterling Heights, Mich., 1972-73, Hist. Commn., Rochester Hills, 1976-77. Recipient sales awards, Pro Log Corp. and Infinity, Inc., 1982, 83, 84. Home: 400 Willow Grove Rochester Hills MI 48063 Office: Infinity Inc 29429 Southfield #5 Southfield MI 48076

GAISER, SHEILA MARIE, oil company executive; b. Elizabeth City, N.C., Nov. 17, 1944; d. Cyrus Newton and Ethel Marie (Herbig) G.; m. Curtis W. Bryan, May 5, 1967 (div. 1973); children—Richard M., Steven M. Student Tex. Tech U., 1962-64; B.S., North Tex. State U., 1966, postgrad., 1976-81. Tchr. Irving Ind. Sch. Dist. (Tex.), 1966-71; bookkeeper Arthur Andersen & Co., Dallas, 1972-75; staff acct. Bosco Fastening Service Ctr., Dallas, 1975-80; mgr. compliance dept. Maguire Oil Co., Dallas, 1980—. Auction co-chmn. KERA-TV, Dallas, 1977, mem., 1976—; active PTA, Farmers Branch, Tex., 1975—. Mem. AAUW (legis. com., chmn. Farmers br./Carrollton 1984-85, v.p. 1985-86, pres. 1986—, interbr. council rep. 1985—), Nat. Accts. Assn., Nat. Assn. Female Execs., Phi Chi Theta. Mem. Christian Ch. Office: Maguire Oil Co 4200 InterFirst One Bldg Dallas TX 75202

GAISSER, JULIA HAIG, classical educator; b. Cripple Creek, Colo., Jan. 12, 1941; s. Henry Wolseley and Gertrude Alice (Lent) Haig; m. Thomas Korff Gaisser, Dec. 29, 1964; 1 son, Thomas Wolseley. A.B., Brown U., 1962; A.M., Harvard U., 1966; Ph.D., U. Edinburgh (Scotland), 1966. Asst. prof. Newton Coll. (Mass.), 1966-69, Swarthmore Coll., (Pa.), 1970-72, Bklyn. Coll., 1973-75; assoc. prof. dept. Latin Bryn Mawr Coll. (Pa.), 1975-83, prof., 1984—, editor Bryn Mawr Commentaries, 1983—. Grantee Am. Philos. Soc., 1980-82, NEH, 1982-86. Mem. Am. Philological Assn. (dir. 1986—), Neo-Latin Soc. Office: Dept Latin Bryn Mawr Coll Bryn Mawr PA 19081

GAITER-MALONE, BETTYE MILTON, accounts receivable administrator; b. Houston, July 4, 1938; d. Linnell Milton and Lillie M. (Benjamin) Milton; m. Benjamin L. Gaiter, Sept. 13, 1961 (div.); children—Dwight, Lydia, Vincent, Martin; m. 2d, Phillip Malone, Sept. 5, 1982. Student Tex. Southern U., 1957-59. Cert. collection agy. exec. Soc. Cert. Collection Agy. Execs.; mgmt. cert. U. Colo. Ct. tech. asst. State of Colo., Denver, 1965-72, office mgr. IPA, 1975-76, accounts receivable adminstr., 1976—; ptnr., tax cons. Williamson Agy., Denver, 1965—. Chmn. allocation com. United Way, Denver, 1983, chmn. venture grant com., 1984; adv. bd. Vol. Ctr., 1981-83. Mem. Columbine Credit Women Internat. (adviser 1983-84), Colo. Fiscal Mgrs. Assn., Nat. Assn. Female Execs. Democrat. Club: Altruistic Civic & Social (Denver, pres. 1980-81).

GAJDICA, PAULINE MARIE, secondary educator; b. Dallas, Sept. 23, 1948; d. John Louis and Lillie Marie (Vlk) Trojacek; m. Daniel Robert Gajdica, Oct. 23, 1971 B.A., North Tex. State U., 1970; M.Ed., East Tex. State U., 1975, postgrad., 1976. Cert. ednl. diagnostician, Tex., secondary tchr., Tex. Secondary tchr. Dallas Ind. Sch. Dist., 1970—, chairperson spl. edn. and recreative arts dept., 1976—, participant Project LEAD, 1984-85. AAUW scholar North Tex. State U., 1966; So. Meth. U. scholar, 1966. Mem. Nat. Assn. Female Execs., Alpha Lambda Delta, Alpha Chi, Sigma Tau Delta. Democrat. Roman Catholic. Avocations: writing children's fiction, playing accordion and piano, photography, reading. Home: 11922 Audelia Rd Dallas TX 75243 Office: Dallas Ind Sch Dist TW Browne Middle Sch 3333 Sprague Dr Dallas TX 75233

GALANE, IRMA ADELE BERESTON, electronic engineer; b. Balt., Aug. 23, 1921; d. Dr. Arthur and Sarah (Hillman) Bereston; B.A., Goucher Coll., 1940; postgrad. Johns Hopkins, 1940-42, Mass. Inst. Tech., 1943, George Washington U., 1945, 65, 73, 77, 79, U. Md., 1958, Army Mgmt. Sch., 1964; 1 dau., Suzanne Felice Galane Duvall. Physicist, Naval Ordnance Lab., 1942-43; electronic engr. Navy Bur. Ships, 1943-49, Army Office Chief Signal Officer, 1949-51, Navy Bur. Aeros., 1951-56, Air Research and Devel. Command, USAF, 1956-57, FCC, 1957-60, NASA, 1960-62; supervisory electronic engr. USCG Hdqrs., 1962-64; sci. specialist engrng. scis. Library of Congress, 1964-65; project engr. Advanced Aerial Fire Support System, Army Materiel Command, 1965-66; engr. Naval Air Systems Command, 1966-71; electronic engr. Spectrum Mgmt. Task Force, FCC, 1971-76, sr. research engr. FCC, 1976—; Judge nat. capitol awards for engrs. and architects, 1975. Registered profl. engr., D.C. Mem. IEEE (sr.), Am. Inst. Aeros. and Astronautics, Nat. Soc. Profl. Engrs. (chmn. publs. com. 1959-60, co-chmn. civil def. com. 1965, spl. asst. to pres. 1965), Soc. Women Engrs. (sr. mem.; nat. membership chmn. 1952, nat. dir. 1953, mem. nat. scholarship com. 1958), Armed Forces Communications and Electronics Assn., Fedn. Profl. Assn., Am. Ordnance Assn., Johns Hopkins Alumni Assn., AAAS, U.S. Naval Inst., Marine Tech. Soc., Internat. Platform Assn., Smithsonian Inst. (assoc.), Mensa. Editor: The Met. Washington Profl. Engr., 1958-60. Home: 4201 Cathedral Ave NW Washington DC 20016

GALANTE, JANE HOHFELD, pianist, music historian; b. San Francisco, Feb. 14, 1924; d. Edward and Lillian (Devendorf) Hohfeld; A.B., Vassar Coll., 1944; M.A., U. Calif.-Berkeley, 1949; m. Clement Galante, Dec. 26, 1956; children—Edward Elio, John Clement. Instr., U. Calif., Berkeley, 1948-52, Mills Coll., Oakland, Calif., 1950-52; music editor Berkeley, A Jour. of Modern Culture, 1944-52; founder, dir. Composer's Forum of San Francisco, 1946-56; concert pianist German tours for USIS, 1952-54; Young Audience Concerts, San Francisco, 1963-70; now mem. Lyra Chamber Music Ensemble; trustee Morrison Chamber Music Center at San Francisco State U., ; hon. trustee San Francisco Conservatory of Music, 1970—. Transl.: Darius Milhaud (Paul Collaer), 1984. . Decorated chevalier de l'ordre des arts et des lettres. Mem. Am. Fedn. of Musicians, Women Musicians Club of San Francisco, Chamber Music Am.

GALANTE, MARY THERESE, nurse; b. Albany, N.Y., Nov. 25, 1956; d. Thomas Joseph and Anne Therese (Davis) Dunvar; m. Nicholas Thomas Galante, III, June 10, 1978; children—Elizabeth Nolan, Nicholas Thomas, Katharine Carey, James Davis. B.S. in Nursing, Catholic U. Am., 1978. R.N. Nurse pvt. office, Washington, 1975-77; nurse acute CCU, St. Peter Hosp., Albany, N.Y., 1979-80, profl. nurse Tri-Cities Nursing Registry, Albany, 1982—, patient care coordinator, 1983—. Vol., mem. fundraising com. Am. Cancer Soc., 1979—, Leukemia Soc., 1978—, M.S. Assn., 1983—; sec., chmn. provisional com. Jr. League, Troy, N.Y., 1983-85, bd. dirs., 1985-87, chmn. ways and means com., 1986-87. Author: Hold the Fort, 1984. Mem. Am. Nursing Assn., Nat. League Nursing. Democrat. Roman Catholic. Home: 10 London Heights N Loudonville NY 12211

GALAROWICZ, LINDA MARIE, editor, b. Antigo, Wis., Mar. 24, 1955; d. John Joseph and Ann (Drozdik) Galarowicz; m. Charles Ronald Gorchels, Aug. 21, 1982. B.B.A., U. Wis., 1976; M.B.A., Mich. State U., 1979. Copywriter, WAGO Radio, Oshkosh, Wis., 1974-75; adminstrv. asst. CPFA, Oshkosh, 1975-76; mktg. researcher Lear-Siegler, Inc., Zeeland, Mich., 1977; instr. U. Wis., Eau Claire, 1979-83, Cardinal Stritch Coll., 1985—; dir. mktg. research Wm. C. Brown Pub., Dubuque, 1983-84, bus. editor, 1984—, cons. Duo-Therm, Kalamazoo, Mich., 1978, Small Bus. Devel. Center, Eau Claire, Wis., 1979-83. Coordinator, Minority Internship Program, Eau Claire, 1982-83; faculty advisor Phi Sigma Epsilon, Eau Claire, 1982-83. Mem. Am. Mktg. Assn., Nat. Assn. Female Execs., Beta Gamma Sigma. Home: 4510 Windigo Trail Madison WI 53711 Office: Wm C Brown Pub Co Editorial Office 5712 Odana Rd Madison WI 53719

GALATZ, KAREN MICHELLE, White House fellow; b. Westbury, N.Y., May 15, 1954; d. Julius David and Dorothy (Kirschen) G. B.A. in Russian Area Studies, Barnard Coll., 1974; postgrad. Leningrad State U. (USSR), 1976, Pushkin Lang. Inst., Moscow, 1977; M.A. in Russian Area Studies, Georgetown, U., 1977. News reporter Las Vegas Sun newspaper, 1977-79; news reporter, anchor, producer Sta. KLAS-TV, Las Vegas, 1979-82; exec. aide, news sec. Nev. Gov.'s Office, Carson City, 1983-85, mem. subcom. on pub. broadcasting Nev. Legislature, 1983-85; White House fellow, assigned to Dept. State, Washington, 1985—. Mem. fund raising com. Channel 5 Pub. Broadcasting, Carson City, 1984. Mem. Nev. State Press Assn. Office: Office of Sec US Dept State 2201 C St NW Washington DC 20253

GALBRAITH, LILYAN KING, educator; b. Smithfield, Pa.; d. Jasper Thompson and Iona (Ewing) King; B.S., U. W.Va., 1927, M.S., 1946; Ed.D., Pa. State U., 1953; m. Carl Bennett Galbraith, April 28, 1923 (div. 1939). Tchr. home econs., Rivesville, W.Va. 1927-29, Clarksburg, W.Va., 1942-44; tchr. trainer W.Va. U., Morgantown, 1944-46; supr. home econs. edn. State Coll., Mansfield, Pa., 1946-53; head home econs. dept. Western Mich. U., Kalamazoo, 1953-55; prof., head home econs. edn. dept. S.D. State U., Brookings, 1955-68; prof. Western Ky. U., Bowling Green, 1968-70; prof. home econs. edn. W.Va. U., summers 1971, 72. Recipient citation of merit for meritorious and devoted service to vocat. home econ. edn. program in S.D., 1967; named S.D. Home Economist of Yr., 1968. Mem. Am. Home Econs. Assn., NEA, AAUP, Am. Vocat. Assn., Am. Ednl. Research Assn., AAUW (pres. Brookings br. 1961-63, Uniontown br. 1974-76, named Outstanding Woman of Yr. Uniontown Br. 1982), Bus. and Profl. Women's Club (pres. Brookings 1967-68, historian Uniontown 1974-76, chmn. legis. com. 1980-81, chmn. by-laws com. 1981-82, named Woman of Yr. 1980-81), Future Homemakers Am. (hon.), Fayette County Home Economics Assn. (pres. 1977-79, historian 1979—), Kappa Omicron Phi (chmn. nat. project com. 1954-60), Phi Lambda Theta, Delta Kappa Gamma (pres. chpt. 1964-66, 82-84, corr. sec. 1980-82), Kappa Delta Pi. Republican. Club: Uniontown Coll. (pres. chpt. 1981-82). Methodist (mem. ofcl. bd., trustee 1972-75, adminstrv. bd. 1972-84, chmn. 1978-82, v.p., pres. local unit United Meth. Women, 1971-81, dist. membership chmn. 1979-82). Contbr. articles to profl. publs. Home: 47 Water St Smithfield PA 15478

GALBRAITH, NORMA LUCILLE, investment counseling firm executive; b. Nelta, Tex., Nov. 9, 1938; d. Dennis Wayne and Pauline (Neal) Shrode; m. Lawrence C. Galbraith III, Aug. 23, 1957 (div. Apr. 1980); children—Sherri Lynn Galbraith Morgan, Lawrence C. IV. Student Eastfield Coll., 1977, Amber U., 1980—. Bookkeeper, H.E. Vaugan-Cotton, Dallas, 1966-70; sec., bookkeeper Dallas Christian Sch., Mesquite, Tex., 1970-75; sr. sec. Bonanza Internat., Dallas, 1975-77; trust portfolio asst. Mercantile Bank, Dallas, 1977-80; corp. sec., controller Mercantile Securities Corp., Dallas, 1981—Sec., Dallas Christian Sch. PTA, Mesquite, Tex., 1971. Mem. Nat. Assn. Female Execs. Mem. Ch. of Christ. Home: 9423 Gonzales Dr Dallas TX 75227 Office: Mercantile Securities Corp 1802 Main St Dallas TX 75201

GALBRAITH, RUTH LEGG, university dean; b. Lecompte, La., Nov. 5, 1923; d. Byron S. and Dora Ruth (Lindley) Legg; B.S., Purdue U., 1945, Ph.D., 1950; m. Harry W. Galbraith, June 16, 1950; 1 son, Allan Legg. Chemist, E. I. duPont de Nemours, Waynesboro, Va., 1945-46; textile chemist Gen. Electric Co., Bridgeport, Conn., 1946-47; teaching asst. chemistry Purdue U., 1947-48, research fellow, 1948-50; prof. textiles and clothing U. Tenn., Knoxville, 1950-55; asso. prof. U. Ill., Urbana, 1956-64, prof., 1964-70, chmn. textiles and clothing div., 1962-70; prof., head consumer dept. Auburn (Ala.) U., 1970-73, dean Sch. Home Econs., 1973—. Mem. Ala. Gov.'s Commn. on Status of Women, Ala. Commn. on Higher Edn., head home econs. research, 1973-85; mem. task force on quality of living Dept. Agr., 1967-68; mem. Carpet and Rug Inst. Consumer Action Panel, 1975; mem. nat. adv. com. Flammable Fabrics Act, 1971-73; mem. home econ. subcom. Agrl. Expt. Sta. Com. on Policy, 1975-79, 81-83, sec., 1977-79; mem. U.S. Dept. Agr. Com. Nine, 1981-83, sec., 1982, chmn., 1983. Recipient Disting. Alumni award Purdue U., 1970. Fellow Am. Inst. Chemists; mem. Am. Home Econs. Assn. (chmn. agy. mem. unit 1975-76, chmn. research sect. 1978-80), Am. Assn. Textile Chemists and Colorists, Am. Chem. Soc., ASTM (3d v.p. com. D-13 textiles 1975-79, hon. mem. 1980), Assn. Coll. Profs. Textiles and Clothing, Assn. Adminstrs. Home Econs., Nat. Council Adminstrs. Home Econs., AAUW, Ala. Home Econs. Assn. (pres. 1983-84), Sigma Xi, Omicron Nu, Phi Kappa Phi, Delta Kappa Gamma. Mem. editorial bd. Research Jour. Home Econs., 1973-77, chmn. policy bd., 1978-80; contbr. articles in field to profl. jours. Home: 368 Singleton St Auburn AL 36830 Office: Sch Home Econs Auburn U Auburn AL 36849

GALE, MARLA, clinical social worker; b. Uniontown, Pa., July 20, 1935; d. Saul and Sarah (Lisowitz) Krongold; A.B. magna cum laude, U. Miami, 1970; M.S.W., Barry Coll., 1972; m. Edward Gale, June 12, 1954; children—Jeffrey, Wendy, Lori. Research social worker VA Hosp., Miami, Fla., 1971; caseworker Jewish Family Service Broward County, Hollywood, Fla., 1971-81, supr. profl. staff, 1981—; mem. clin. faculty Barry U., Miami Shores, Fla.; parent effectiveness instr.; real estate investor. Mem. Nat. Assn. Social Workers, Acad. Cert. Social Workers, Common Cause, Project Newborn, Met. Mus., Animal Protection Soc., Diabetes Research Inst. Democrat. Jewish. Office: 4517 Hollywood Blvd Hollywood FL 33021

GALE, NAOMI, furniture design firm executive; b. Bklyn., Sept. 8, 1926; d. Emanuel H. and Jeannette (Greenfield) Gale; m. Bernard Silverman, Jan. 22, 1960; children—Moses, Emily, Daniel, Matthew. Student, Queen's Coll., 1943-44; Art cert., Traphaghen Sch. Design, 1945. Sr. designer Gimbels Bros., N.Y.C., 1948-50, W.A. Hathaway Co., N.Y.C., 1950-55; pres. Naomi Gale Design Studio Inc., N.Y.C., 1960—. Author: Book of Measurements, 1984. Recipient Daphne award Hardwood Inst., N.Y.C., 1982. Mem. Am. Soc. Interior Design (bd. dirs. 1983—, sec. 1984), Nat. Home Fashion League. Office: Naomi Gale Design Studio Inc 305 E 63d St New York NY 10044

GALE, SHIRLEY MCCLARD, travel agency executive, child psychologist; b. Clearlake, S.D., Jan. 19, 1931; d. George Marvin and Lillian Deloris (Beck) McClard; m. Kenneth Stanley Gale, Aug. 25, 1951; children—Kenneth, Lyndy, Kathy, David. A.B., Friends U., 1952; M.A., N. Mex. State U., 1967; Ed.S., Eastern N. Mex. U., 1978. Cert. tchr., sch. psychologist. Tchr. elems. schs. in Kans., Ariz., Va., New Mex., 1952-67; counselor, ednl. diagnostician

Portales Schs., New Mex., 1967-84, coordinator spl. edn., 1980-84; pres. Internat. Tours of Tucson, 1984—; chmn. New Mex. State Testing Commn., 1980-84; mem. New Mex. State Commn. Spl. Edn., 1976-80; chmn. New Mex. State Commn. Foster Care, 1982-84. Travel editor Cracker Barrel, 1985, Travel Trivia, 1984—. Sec. Altrusa Internat., 1978-84, LWV, 1966-80. Mem. Am. Bus. Women's Assn., Am. Soc. Travel Agts., Pacific Area Travel Assn., Cruise Lines Internat. Assn., Tucson Met. C. of C., NEA (life), AAUW (v.p. 1966-68), Resources for Women, Delta Kappa Gamma (pres. 1982-84), P.E.O. Avocations: music; sports. Home: 3150 N Avenida Del Conejo Tucson AZ 85749 Office: Internat Tours of Tucson 7181 E Speedway Tucson AZ 85710

GALEF, SANDRA RISK, county legislator, teacher; b. LaCrosse, Wis., May 7, 1940; d. William P. and Christine (Nay) Risk; m. Steven Allen Galef, Mar. 30, 1963; children—Gregory Todd, Gwendolyn. B.S., Purdue U., 1962; M.S. in Edn., U. Va., 1965. Tchr., Albemarle Schs., Charlottesville, Va., 1962-65, Scarsdale Schs., N.Y., 1965-67; mem. Westchester County Bd. Legislators, 1980—, minority leader, 1984—. Host cable TV show Westchester Today, 1982—. Bd. dirs. United Way No. Westchester, 1973—, pres., 1979-80, v.p., 1975-79; trustee Ossining Pub. Library, N.Y., 1975-80, Briarcliff Nursery Sch., N.Y., 1974-76; pres. chpt. LWV, 1973-75; chair Ossining Youth Employment Service, 1977-80; bd. dirs. Day Care Council Westchester, 1976-79; pub. affairs chair Jr. League Westchester-on-Hudson, Tarrytown, 1978-80, mem. tng. com., 1980-85; mem. adv. bd. Children's Village, Dobbs Ferry, N.Y., 1984—, Interfaith Council for Action, Ossining, 1983—; mem. Ossining Upward Bound Substances Abuse Council, 1984—, Ossining Restoration Com., 1975-77; mem. nominating com. White Plains chpt. ARC, 1985-86. Recipient Harold J. Marshall award United Way No. Westchester, 1981. Mem. N.Y. Assn. Counties (v.p. 1984—), Westchester Mcpl. Planning Fedn. (dir. 1982—), Westchester 2000 (task force 1985), Ossining C. of C. Democrat. Avocations: gardening; sewing; crafts; decorating. Home: 44 Orchard Dr Ossining NY 10562 Office: 800 County Office Bldg 148 Martine Ave White Plains NY 10601

GALER, MARY JANE, state legislator, librarian; b. Port Arthur, Tex., June 30, 1924; d. Harry F. and Clara Williams (Graham) Perkins; B.S.L.S., Carnegie Inst. Tech., 1947; B.A. in Edn., U. Pitts., 1945; m. Robert Fulton Galer, Nov. 7, 1951; children—Frank Fulton, Barbara Jean, Robin Robson. Librarian, U.S. Army, Korea, Japan and Calif., 1948-52, Ft. Benning, Ga., 1960-65, Mobile (Ala.) Public Library, 1966; asso. prof. library sci. Columbus (Ga.) Coll., 1967-76; mem. Ga. Ho. of Reps., 1977—. Co-founder, bd. dirs. Contact Teleministries, 1978-82; bd. dirs. Columbus Symphony, 1979-86; mem. Ga. Democratic Com.; del. Dem. Nat. Conv., 1980; adv. com. project Nat. Women's Edn. Fund, 1982-83. Recipient Columbus Public Service award, 1975; Women Helping Women award Soroptimist Internat., 1975; Maxine Goldstein freedom award Democratic Women, 1984; others. Mem. LWV, AAUP, Ga. Library Assn., AAUW (pres. 1975-79), Nat. Conf. State Legislatures (co-chmn. women's network 1982-83, exec. com. 1984—), Phi Delta Kappa, Alpha Delta Kappa. Presbyterian. Club: Soroptimist (public affairs chmn. 1977, dir. 1978). Indexer: (with others) microfilm collection Herstory; author: Women and State Pensions; Legislative Guide to Issues of Equity.

GALES, LESLIE SUE, management consultant; b. Winnipeg, Man., Can., Mar. 31, 1955; d. Donald H. and Ruth H. Gales. B.A. U. Man., 1977; M.B.A., McMaster U., 1980. Mgmt. cons., mgr. real estate div. Laventhol & Horwath, Toronto, Ont., Can., 1980—. Mem. leadership devel. com. United Jewish Cong. regations, Toronto, 1983-84. Mem. Toronto Home Builders Assn. (sales and mktg. council 1981-83), Urban Devel. Inst. (vice-chair assocs. group 1983), Am. Mktg. Assn., Profl. Mktg. Research Soc., Inst. Mgmt. Cons. Office: Laventhol & Horwath 20 Queen St W 3d Floor Toronto ON M5H 3R4 Canada

GALEY, MARY DUBOIS SCHAUB, architect; b. Washington, May 20, 1948; d. Benton Hall and Rosemary Duvall (Sands) Schaub; B.Arch., Tulane U., 1971; m. Gary Ray Galey, July 15, 1972. Cert. Nat. Council Archtl. Registration Bds. Intern architect Fed. Bur. Prisons, 1971-72; staff architect Hallmark Cards, Inc., Kansas City, Mo., 1972-74; with Office Facilities Devel., Fed. Bur. Prisons, Washington, 1974—, project mgr., architect, 1975—; co-owner Design Assos., Crownsville, Md., 1978—. Mem. AIA, Nat. Trust Historic Preservation, Smithsonian Assocs. Episcopalian. Clubs: Indian Landing Boat (pres. 1979-80), Soroptomists. Home: 1038 Plum Creek Dr Crownsville MD 21032 Office: 320 1st St NW Washington DC 20534 also Box 515 Crownsville MD 21032

GALINAT, LYNDA ANN, microcomputer consultant; b. Deadwood, S.D., Sept. 4, 1949; d. Lynn Haslip and Margaret Lucille (Corcoran) Farnham; m. Gary Lee Galinat, June 6, 1970; children—Christie Lyn, Bobbi Lee. B.S., Black Hills State Coll., 1971. Statis. clk. Donaldson's, Rapid City, S.D., 1971; acctg. clk. McBee Acctg., Rapid City, 1971-72; owner, mgr. Ceramic Yard, Harrold, S.D., 1973-75; sr. acct. Central Region Comprehensive Program, Pierre, S.D., 1978-81; sales rep., instr. Creative Circle, Pierre, 1982-83; systems analyst Applied Mgmt. Inc., Pierre, 1983—. Leader 4-H Club, 1974-76; pres. McKinley PTA, 1977-78; treas. Pierre PTA, 1978-79; bd. dirs. Am. Cancer Soc., Pierre, 1983—. Mem. AAUW (treas. 1981-84). Avocations: reading; camping; skiing. Home: 1903 E Sully Pierre SD 57501 Office: Applied Mgmt Inc 302 S Pawnee Pierre SD 57501

GALINDO, ERNESTINE, manufacturing executive; b. Plugerville, Tex., Jan. 23, 1931; d. Eliseo Barrera and Rita (Ortegon) Guajardo; m. Thomas Galindo II, Feb. 20, 1955; children—Thomas Eliseo III, Guillermo Eloy. Prodn. staff El Fenix, Austin, Tex., 1960-73; pres. El Galindo, Inc., Austin, 1973—. Recipient Businesswoman of Yr. award Mex. Am. C. of C., 1983. Home: 2911 Bowman Austin TX 78703 Office: El Galindo Inc 1601 E 6th St Austin TX 78702

GALKIN, FLORENCE, social worker; b. N.Y.C., Dec. 27, 1925; d. Victor and Sadie (Sobel) Greenwald; B.A., Hunter Coll., 1946; M.S.W., U. Pa., 1951; advanced cert. Columbia U., 1961, postgrad., NIMH fellow, 1962-64; m. Bernard Galkin, Dec. 18, 1948; children—Judith, William Seth. Caseworker, Jewish Child Care Assn., N.Y.C., 1951-57; field instr. community orgn. Bird S. Coler Hosp., 1968; cons. ombudsman program Community Council Greater N.Y., 1978—; research asso. Center Policy Research, 1980—; exec. dir. Community Action and Resources for the Elderly, 1976—; trainee leadership in public affairs Coro Found., 1981—. Bd. dirs. Nat. Coalition for Nursing Home Reform, 1978-79; trustee, mem. met. coordinating council, co-chmn. urban affairs commn. Am. Jewish Congress; mem. Met. Coordinating Council on Jewish Poverty. Recipient Louise Waterman Wise Humanitarian award Am. Jewish Congress. Mem. Nat. Assn. Social Workers. Jewish. Author: People and Nursing Homes, 1977; (with others) Neighborhood Information Center: A Study and Some Proposals, 1966; (with Hochbaum) The New York State Patient Advocacy Program, Patients and Their Complaints, 1978, Discharge Planning-No Deposit, No Return, 1982; Wanted: Nursing Home Patients: Those on Medicaid Need Not Apply. Home: 400 E 56th St New York NY 10022

GALL, ADRIENNE LYNN, managing editor; b. Long Branch, N.J., Jan. 25, 1960; d. Robert Conrad and Anna May (Critchfield) Gall. B.A., Hood Coll., Md., 1982. Editorial asst. Polo Mag., Fleet St. Corp., Gaithersburg, Md., 1982-83; assoc. editor Nat. Solid Wastes Mgmt. Assn., Washington, 1983-86; mng. editor Am. Soc. Tng. & Devel., Alexandria, Va., 1986—. Mem. Nat. Assn. Female Execs., Smithsonian Assocs., Nat. Trust Historic Preservation. Democrat. Avocations: equestrienne; historic preservation; environmental conservation. Office: Am Soc Tng & Devel 1630 Duke St Box 1443 Alexandria VA 22313

GALL, ELIZABETH BENSON, dating service executive; b. Williamson, W.Va., June 11, 1944; d. Thomas Jefferson Bluebaum and Ollie Mae (Moore) Bluebaum Walker; stepdau. Charles B. Walker; 1 child, Thomas Kontoleon. Ptnr., dir. Chicagoland Register, dating service, Chgo., 1974-84; cooking instr. Elizabeth Benson Internat. Cooking Lessons, 1978-84; owner Ethnic Party People Catering, 1981—, Phone-A-Friend Dating Service, Chgo., 1984—. Home and Office: 6314 N Troy St Chicago IL 60659

GALL, LENORE ROSALIE, educational administrator; b. Bklyn., Aug. 9, 1943; d. George W. Gall and Olive Rosalie (Weekes) Gall Bryant. A. Applied Sci., N.Y.U., 1970, Tng. and devel. cert., 1975, B.S. in Mgmt., 1973, M.A. in Counselor Edn., 1977; postgrad. Tchrs. Coll., Columbia U. Various positions Ford Found., N.Y.C., 1967-75; dep. dir. career devel. Grad. Sch. Bus., NYU, N.Y.C., 1976-79; dir. career devel. Pace Lubin Sch. Bus., N.Y.C., 1979-82; dir. career devel. Sch. Mgmt., Yale U., New Haven, 1982-85; asst. to assoc. provost Bklyn. Coll., 1985—; adj. lectr. LaGuardia Community Coll., Long Island City, N.Y., 1981—, Sch. Continuing Edn. N.Y.U., 1983-84; dir., sec. devel. workshop Coll. Placement Services, Bethlehem, Pa., 1978-81. Bd. dirs. Langston Hughes Community Library, Corona, N.Y., 1975-83, chairperson, 1975-79, 82-83; 2d v.p., chairperson awards com. Dollars for Scholars, Corona, 1976—. Mem. Assn. Black Women in Higher Edn. (exec. bd., membership chair), Am. Assn. Univ. Adminstrs., AAUW, Nat. Assn. Women Deans and Adminstrs., New Haven C. of C. (chmn. women bus. and industry conf. 1984), NAACP, Nat. Council Negro Women, Phi Delta Kappa, Kappa Delta Pi. Mem. A.M.E. Ch. Office: Bklyn Coll/CUNY 2231 Boylan Hall Bedford Ave and Ave H Brooklyn NY 11210

GALLAGHER, ANNE PORTER, business executive; b. Coral Gables, Fla., Mar. 16, 1950; d. William Moring Porter and Anne (Jewett) P.; m. Matthew Philip Gallagher, Jr., July 31, 1976; 1 child, Jacqueline Anne. B.A. in Edn., Stetson U., 1972. Tchr. elem. schs., Atlanta, 1972-74; sales rep. Xerox Corp., Atlanta, 1974-76, Fed. Systems, Rosslyn, Va., 1976-81; sales rep. No. Telecom Inc., Vienna, Va., 1981-84, account exec., 1984-85, dir. sales, 1985—. Mem. Nat. Assn. Female Execs. Episcopalian. Avocations: skiing; aerobics; needlepoint. Home: 7712 Kirkside Dr Alexandria VA 22306 Office: No Telecom Inc 8401 Old Courthouse Rd Vienna VA 22180

GALLAGHER, DOLORES ELIZABETH, psychologist; b. N.Y.C., Aug. 7, 1944; d. Joseph and Elizabeth (Goehringer) Ruebeck; B.S., Fordham U., 1965; M.A., Duquesne U., 1967; Ph.D. (NIMH fellow), U. So. Calif., 1979; m. William J. Gallagher, Aug. 27, 1966 (dec. 1979); m. 2d, Larry W. Thompson, Dec. 12, 1981. Rehab. psychologist Fedn. Handicapped, N.Y.C., 1965-72; staff psychologist Altoona (Pa.) Hosp. Community Mental Health Center, 1972-74; clin. psychologist Los Angeles County Occupational Health Services, 1975-77; intern Neuropsychiat. Inst. of UCLA, 1977-78; staff psychologist Adult Counseling Center, Andrus Gerontology Center, U. So. Calif., 1978-79, acting dir., 1980-81; adj. asst. prof. psychology U. So. Calif., 1978-80; co-dir. interdisciplinary team tng. program in geriatrics Palo Alto VA Med. Center, 1981-83, asst. dir. edn. and evaluation, 1983-85; assoc. dir. edn. and program evaluation Geriatric Research Edn. and Clin. Ctr., Palo Alto VA Med. Ctr., 1985—; pvt. practice Cognitive Therapy Assocs., Los Altos, Calif.; lectr. Stanford U. Sch. Medicine; clin. asst. prof. dept. psychiatry, instr. program in human biology, 1983—; research cons. aging projects in Los Angeles and San Francisco Bay areas. Trustee, Suicide Prevention and Crisis Center San Mateo County, 1981—; cons. Los Angeles County Suicide Prevention Center, 1981—. Recipient grants Nat. Inst. Aging, NIMH; lic. psychologist, Calif.; cert. Nat. Register Health Service Providers in Psychology. Mem. Am. Psychol. Assn., Soc. Psychotherapy Research, Gerontol. Soc. Am., Calif. Council Gerontology and Geriatrics. Democrat. Mem. Self-Realization Fellowship. Club: Sierra. Author: (with others) Depression in the Elderly: A Behavioral Treatment Manual, 1981; contbr. articles profl. jours. Home: 2049 Fallen Leaf Ln Los Altos CA 94022 Office: Geriatric Research Edn and Clin Center 182B Palo Alto VA Medical Center 3801 Miranda Ave Palo Alto CA 94304 also Cognitive Therapy Assocs 745 Distel Dr Suite F Los Altos CA 94022

GALLAGHER, IDELLA JANE SMITH (MRS. DONALD A. GALLAGHER), foundation executive, author; b. Union City, N.J., Jan. 1, 1917; d. Fred J. and Louise (Stewart) S.; Ph.B., Marquette U., 1941, M.A., 1943, Ph.D., 1963; postgrad. U. Louvain, Belgium, U. Paris, France; m. Donald A. Gallagher, June 29, 1938; children—Paul B., Maria Noel. Lectr. philosophy Marquette U., 1943-52, 54-56; instr. philosophy Alverno Coll., Milw., 1956-58; asst. prof. philosophy Villanova U., 1958-62; asst. prof. philosophy Boston Coll., 1962-68, asso. prof., 1968-69; asso. prof. philosophy U. Ottawa, 1969-71, prof., 1971-73; projects adminstr. DeRance Found., Milw., 1973-81, v.p. projects, 1981-85, sr. v.p., 1985—; vis. prof. philosophy Niagara U., 1976-81. Mem. Sudbury (Mass.) Com. for Human Rights, 1963-69; trustee Mt. Senario Coll., Ladysmith, Wis., 1976—. Recipient Sword and Shield award St. Louis U., Baguio City, Philippines, 1975; Disting. Service award Mt. Senario Coll., Ladysmith, Wis., 1984. Mem. Metaphys. Soc. Am., Am. Cath. Philos. Assn. (exec. council 1967-69), Am. Soc. Aesthetics, Assn. for Realistic Philosophy, Am. Assn. U. Profs., Brit. Soc. Aesthetics, Canadian Philos. Assn., Canadian Assn. U. Tchrs., Phi Alpha Theta, Phi Delta Gamma. Author: (with D.A. Gallagher) The Achievement of Jacques and Raissa Maritain, 1962; The Education of Man, 1962; (with D. A. Gallagher) A Maritain Reader, 1966; (with D.A. Gallagher) St. Augustine—The Catholic and Manichaean Ways of Life, 1966. Morality in Evolution: The Moral Philosophy of Henri Bergson, 1970. Gen. editor: Christian Culture and Philosophy Series, Bruce Pub. Co., 1965-68. Contbr. to New Cath. Ency., also articles to profl. jours. Home: 7714 W Wisconsin Ave Wauwatosa WI 53213 Office: DeRance Found 7700 W Bluemound Rd Milwaukee WI 53213

GALLAGHER, NANCY ELIZABETH, tax consultant, business executive; b. Ontario, Oreg., June 27, 1950; d. Martin Patrick Gallagher and Dorothy Ann (Bush) Turner; children—Susan Elizabeth, Sean Michael. Student U. Oreg., 1968-72. Lic. tax cons., notary pub. Bar mgr., Lamar's, Eugene, Oreg., 1972-73; tax preparer H & R Block, Eugene, Oreg., 1973-77; ptnr. Gallagher, Raven & Assocs., Eugene, 1977—; instr. Am. Inst. Taxation, Vancouver, Wash., 1984-85. Chairperson Aslan House Counseling Ctr., Eugene, 1976—; mem. external adv. bd. Lane Community Coll. Bus. Ctr. Mem. Internat. Assn. Fin. Planners, Assn. Tax Cons. (v.p. 1981-82, Disting. Service award 1979), Eugene Bus. Women (v.p.), Alliance for Career Advancement. Democrat. Home: 4560 Larkwood St Eugene OR 97405 Office: Gallagher Raven & Assocs 2833 Willamette St Suite A Eugene OR 97405

GALLAGHER, RITA J., real estate company executive. Comml. real estate broker, Ariz. Sch. Real Estate, 1983; Comml. appraiser, Lincoln Ctr., Phoenix, 1986. Lic. real estate broker, appraiser, Ariz. Real estate broker Century 21, Tempe, Ariz., 1976-79; comml. broker Realty Advisers, Tempe, 1979-83; v.p., designated broker Martorico div. Taurean Real Estate Group, Mesa, Ariz., 1984-86; broker, agt. Farwest Holdings, Internat., B.C., Can., 1980—; project mgr. Thayer Estates, Mesa, 1982-85, Friendly Cove, Mesa, 1982-85, Forest Knoll, Mesa, 1985—. Recipient Million Dollar award Bd. Realtors, 1983, Multi-Million Dollar award, 1984, 85; Prestigious Internat. award Farwest Holdings, 1985. Mem. Nat. Assn. Realtors, Mesa-Chandler-Tempe Realtors, Women Networking (dir. 1983-86), Nat. Assn. Female Execs., Mesa C. of C., Soroptimist Internat. Avocations: golf, tennis, aerobic workouts, reading. Home: 2718 S Rogers St Mesa AZ 85202 Office: Martorico Div Taurean Real Estate Group 1745 S Alma School Mesa AZ 85202

GALLANT, SANDRA KIRKHAM, psychologist; b. Dallas, July 15, 1933; d. Eugene Raley and Anita Bernice (Brandenburg) Kirkham; A.B., Hollins Coll., 1954; M.S., Va. Commonwealth U., 1956; m. Wade Miller Gallant, Jr., Sept. 15, 1979. Psychologist aide Lynchburg Tng. Sch. and Hosp., 1954-56, Rehab. Center of Rapides Parrish, 1956; clin. psychologist Bowman Gray Sch. Medicine, Wake Forest U., 1956-64, staff psychologist, acting dir. reading, speech and psychology center, 1962-64; staff psychologist Reading Speech and Psychology Center, part-time 1964-74; sch. psychologist Winston-Salem/Forsyth County Schs., part-time, 1974-75; clin. psychologist Child Guidance Clinic, Winston-Salem, N.C., 1975-82; ptnr. Triad Psychol. Assocs., 1982—; cons. to various community orgns. and agys. Bd. dirs. Family Services, 1964-66; bd. dirs. Little Theatre, 1963-66, pres., 1964-65; trustee to exec. com. Arts Council, 1965-68, v.p., 1967-68; bd. dirs. Mental Health Assn. Forsyth County, 1971-77, 79—, pres., 1974-75; bd. dirs. Mental Health Assn. N.C., 1975-82, sec., 1977-79, v.p., 1979-81. Named Vol. of Yr., Mental Health Assn. Forsyth County, 1976; co-recipient Forsyth Mental Health Bell award, 1981. Mem. Am. Psychol. Assn., N.C. Psychol. Assn. Episcopalian. Home: 2534 Warwick Rd Winston-Salem NC 27104 Office: Triad Psychol Assocs 840 W 4th St Winston-Salem NC 27101

GALLEANO, PAULA JOLENE, lawyer; b. Madera, Calif., Oct. 21, 1952; d. Joe and Lois Pauline (Astin) G. Student U. Redlands, 1970-71; B.A. in Psychology, U. Calif.-Davis, 1974; J.D., Cath. U., 1980. Bar: D.C. 1980. Assoc., Lane & Edson, P.C., Washington, 1979—; speaker, panelist continuing legal edn. Editor: Fundamentals of Municipal Bond Law, 1982, 83. Mem. D.C. Bar Assn., Women's Bar Assn. D.C., Nat. Assn. Bond Lawyers. Home: 1106 W Abington Dr Alexandria VA 22314 Office: Lane & Edson PC 2300 M St NW Washington DC 20037

GALLETT, JOHNNA LYNN, accountant, consultant; b. Dumas, Tex., May 11, 1952; d. Johnny Eugene and Laura Alice (Martin) G. B.S., No. Ariz. U., 1975. Accounting technician Dept. of the Army, Yuma, Ariz., 1978-82, operating acct., 1982-84, cost acct., 1984-85, supervisory operating acct., 1985—. Mem. Am. Bus. Women's Assn. (v.p. 1986—), Fed. Women's Program (asst. mgr. 1985—), Am. Soc. Mil. Comptrollers (treas. 1984-85), Assn. U.S. Army, Nat. Assn. Female Execs. Democrat. Methodist. Avocations: gourmet cooking, collecting books. Home: 1494 E 27th Pl Yuma AZ 85365

GALLIETT, CAROL SUE, transportation specialist; b. Chgo., Dec. 25, 1947; d. Emmerson William and Elfriede Christina (Schwerdtfeger) Munro; m. Peter Edward Galliett, Apr. 23, 1977; 1 dau., Kathryn Anne. B.M.E., Baker U., Baldwin, Kans., 1971; postgrad. Coll. of Advanced Traffic, Chgo., 1976-79. Tchr., Stanton County, Kans., 1971-73, Chgo. Bd. Edn., 1973; clk. F.P. Dow Co. Inc., Franklin Park, Ill., 1974; export saleswoman Midway Mfg. Corp., Franklin Park, 1975; asst. import mgr. Mitsui O.S.K. Lines, Chgo., 1975-77; regional mgr. Rail-Gate Piggyback, Schaumburg, Ill., 1977-85, Nippon Express U.S.A. (Ill.) Inc., 1986—. Mem. Nat. Republican Congl. Com., Washington, 1980. Methodist. Office: Nippon Express USA (IL) Inc 950 Edgewood Wood Dale IL 60191

GALLIGEN, AUDREY MARIE, educational administrator, educator; b. Bklyn., Feb. 4, 1929; d. Peter Francis and Matilda Mae G. B.A. in Elem. Edn., Bklyn. Coll., 1950, M.A. in Elem. Edn., 1953, M.S. in Guidance and Counseling, 1965, postgrad. diploma adminstrv. supr., 1967; Ed.D., Fordham U., 1976. Cert. sch. adminstr. Tchr., Bd. of Edn., Bklyn., 1950-61, guidance counselor, 1961-62, asst. prin., 1963—; asst. examiner Bd. of Examiners, Bklyn., 1966; instr. City Coll., N.Y.C., summer 1966, Bklyn. Coll., 1966-69. Contbr. articles to local newspapers; contbr. articles to profl. jours. Mem., chmn. edn. com. Community Planning Bd. #1, Bklyn., 1964-77; mem. Newtown Civic Assn., Elmhurst, N.Y., 1975-81, Citizens of Maspeth and Elmhurst, 1981—; pres. Mid-Queens Civic Assn., 1973-74. Recipient Service award Bklyn. Mental Health Assn., 1973; Named Educator of Yr., Assn. Tchrs. N.Y., 1984. Mem. Doctorate Assn. N.Y. Educators, N.Y. State Assn. Supervision and Curriculum Devel., Am. Assn. Sch. Adminstrs., Phi Delta Kappa, Kappa Delta Pi. Democrat. Roman Catholic. Clubs: Seneca, Continental. Avocations: cooking, reading, biographies. Office: PS 18 101 Maujer St Brooklyn NY 11206

GALLIN, PAMELA FRANCES, ophthalmologist; b. N.Y.C., Sept. 26, 1952; d. Martin and Saara (Lang) Gallin; m. Richard Matthew Cohen, Apr. 9, 1978; children—Laura, Abigail. A.B., B.S., Washington U., St. Louis, 1974, M.D., 1978. Diplomate Nat. Bd. Med. Examiners, Am. Bd. Ophthalmology. Med. intern NYU Med. Ctr., 1978-79; resident in ophthalmology Mt. Sinai med. Ctr., N.Y.C., 1979-82; fellow in pediatric ophthalmology, Children's Nat. Med. Ctr., Washington, 1982; vis. fellow in pediatric ophthalmology Johns Hopkins Med. Ctr., Balt., 1982; fellow in pediatric ophthalmology and oncology Columbia/Presbyn. Med. Ctr., 1983; fellow in pediatric ophthalmic oncology, N.Y. Hosp.-Cornell Med. Ctr., 1983; asst. in ophthalmology, Edward Harkness Eye Inst., 1983, Coll. Physicians and Surgeons, Columbia Presbyn. Med. Ctr., 1983; adj. asst. clin. prof. ophthalmology Mt. Sinai Med. Ctr., 1983; pvt. practice medicine specializing in pediatric ophthalmology, N.Y.C., 1983—. Contbr. articles to profl. jours. Exec. bd. Moprig, St. Louis, 1973, 79. Recipient Lange award for med. excellence Washington U., 1978. Fellow Heed Ophthalmic Found.; mem. Am. Acad. Ophthalmology, Phi Beta Kappa, Tau Beta Pi. Republican. Office: Edward Harkness Eye Inst 635 W 165th St New York NY 10032

GALLITERO, BETTY JO, manufacturing executive; b. Yakima, Wash., Sept. 27, 1933; d. Babe Frank and Maudie Lee (Mondier) Payton; B.S., Coll. Notre Dame, Belmont, Calif., 1979, Ryan credential, 1982, M.A.T. in History, 1985; m. William Harold Gallitero, Nov. 5, 1960 (dec. Dec. 1981); children—Paul William, David Joseph. Corp. sec. Rainbow Novelties, Inc., amusement machines, San Francisco, 1971-81, pres., owner, 1981—; pres. Future Enterprises Inc., 1982—; owner BG Leasing, 1983—. Mem. alumni bd. Coll. Notre Dame, 1979-83. Regent Merit scholar, 1978, 79. Mem. Calif. Coin Machine Assn. (assoc. dir. 1983—), AAUW, Delta Epsilon Sigma. Republican. Roman Catholic. Home: 12780 Dianne Dr Los Altos Hills CA 94022 Office: 1133 Mariposa St San Francisco CA 94107

GALLMEIER, TERRI MARIE, psychologist; b. Oklahoma City, Oct. 7, 1948; d. Seigmund H. and Ruth Pearl (Bunker) G., B.S. with honors, U. Tulsa, 1970, M.A., 1972; Ph.D., U Okla., 1978; m. Alan Cotton Schlessman, Mar. 8, 1980. Psychologist, dept. head Okla. Cerebral Palsy Center, Norman, 1973-75; teaching asst. U. Okla., Norman, 1975-76, teaching assoc., research center coordinator, 1977-78; hon. vis. fellow U. Sheffield (Eng.), 1976-77; dir. Child Guidance Center, Okla. Dept. Health, Miami, 1978-80, N.E. Okla. regional coordinator Child Guidance Clinics, dist. supervising psychologist Okla. Dept. Health, Tulsa, 1980-84, dir. spl. projects office of child abuse prevention, 1984—, chmn. peer rev. com., mem. ethics com.; chmn. Okla. adv. com. on child abuse and neglect, 1980—. Mem. Am. Psychol. Assn., Nat. Women's Polit. Caucus, NOW (treas. Tulsa 1979—, Okla. del. nat. conv. 1980), Okla. Public Health Assn. (mental health rep. legis. com. 1980—), Okla. Psychol. Assn., Phi Gamma Kappa. Democrat. Unitarian. Contbr. articles to profl. jours. Home: 2405 NW 56th St Oklahoma City OK 73112

GALLO, CAROLANN JEANETTE, educator; b. Northampton, Pa., Oct. 19, 1947; d. John Michael and Sophie (Romansky) Lelko; m. Dennis Joseph Gallo, Aug. 25, 1966; 1 child, Keith. B.S. in Elem. Edn., Glassboro State U., 1971. Elem. tchr. Mantua Twp. Pub. Schs., Mantua, N.J., 1974—. Mem. NEA, N.J. Edn. Assn., Gloucester County Edn. Assn., Mantua Twp. Edn. Assn. (sec. 1983-85), AAUW (treas. 1985-86). Roman Catholic. Club: Women's Internat. Bowling Congress (v.p.). Avocations: bowling; boating; skiing; sewing; crafts. Home: 501 Carew Ave Pitman NJ 08071

GALLO, MARY ELLEN, wholesale beverage distribution company executive; b. Allentown, Pa., May 2, 1957; d. Frank and Elizabeth Eugenia (Clark) Banko; m. Vincent James Gallo, Jr., Aug. 28, 1982; 1 child, Anthony James. B.S., Purdue U., 1979, B.A., 1980. Sec. Banko Beverage Co., Allentown, 1980-82, pres., 1982—. Bd. dirs. Bethlehem Musikfest Assn., Pa., 1983—, mktg. co-chmn., 1985; bd. dirs. Cities in Schs., Bethlehem, 1985—. Mem. U.S. C. of C., Bethlehem Area C. of C. (bd. dirs. 1985—), Nat. Beer Wholesalers Assn., Malt Beverage Distbrs. Assn., Pa. Importing Master Distbrs. Assn. Democrat. Roman Catholic. Avocations: eucharistic ministry; music; dancing; needlework. Home: 2201 Meadow Ln Dr Easton PA 18042 Office: Banko Beverage Co 2124 Hanover Ave Allentown PA 18103

GALLOWAY, DIANA MARIE, actress; b. Sculthorppe AFB, Norfolk, Eng., June 19, 1957; d. James E. and Eloise (Midgett) Galloway. Student theatre and music North Tex. State U., 1975-77; student music So. Meth. U., 1980-81. Office sec. DiscoVision Assocs., Los Angeles, 1978-80; mktg. specialist No. Telecom, Richardson, Tex., 1981—; freelance comedienne, actress and singer; treas., performer, skit writer Guava Bomblets Comedy Troupe, Dallas, 1981—; singer radio-TV commls., various sound studios, Dallas-Ft. Worth, 1983—. Mem. Chi Omega, Mu Phi Epsilon. Republican. Methodist. Office: Commonwealth Trading Co 8140 Walnut Hill Ln Suite 800 Dallas TX 75231

GALLOWAY, DIANE LENOIR, found. exec.; b. Phila., Aug. 24, 1941; d. Howard William and Florence Eleanor (Wagner) Galloway; B.A., Am. U., 1963, postgrad. 1963-64. Staff asst. Mfg. Chemists Assn., Washington, 1963-64; research asst. Federazione Italiana dei Consorzi Agrari, Washington, 1964; asst. Office of the Chief of Protocol, N.Y. World's Fair Corp., Flushing Meadow, N.Y., 1964-65; research asst. Population Office, Ford Found., N.Y.C., 1965-66, sr. staff asst. Office of the Pres., 1966-67, adminstrv. asst. Office of the Sec., 1967-68, exec. asst. Office of Sec. and Gen. Counsel, 1968-72, asst. adminstrv. officer 1972-78, asst. to gen. counsel and adminstrv. officer, 1978-83, asst. sec., 1983—. Mem. Women and Found./Corporate Philanthropy, Am. Soc. Profl. and Exec. Women, Nat. Assn. Female Execs., Alpha Chi Omega, Pi Sigma Alpha. Presbyterian. Clubs: Rockaway River Country, U.S. Senatorial. Home: 327 Morris Ave Boonton NJ 07005 Office: 320 E 43 St New York NY 10017

GALLOWAY, EILENE MARIE (MRS. GEORGE BARNES GALLOWAY), defense consultant; b. Kansas City, Mo., May 4, 1906; d. Joseph Locke and Lottie Rose (Harris) Slack; student Washington U., St. Louis, 1923-25; A.B., Swarthmore Coll., 1928; postgrad. Am. U., 1937-38, 43; m. George Barnes Galloway, Dec. 23, 1924; children—David Barnes, Jonathan Fuller. Tchr. polit. sci. Swarthmore Coll., 1928-30; editor Student Service, Washington, 1931; staff mem., edn. div. Fed. Emergency Relief Adminstrn., 1934-35; asst. chief info. sect., div. spl. info. Library of Congress, 1941-43, editor abstracts Legis. Reference Service, 1943-51, nat. def. analyst, 1951-57; specialist in nat. def., 1957-66; sr. specialist internat. relations (nat. security) Congl. Research Service, 1966-75; cons. internat. space activities, 1975—. staff mem. Senate Fgn. Relations Com., 1947; profl. staff mem. U.S. group Interparliamentary Union, 1958-66; cons. Senate Armed Services Com., 1953-74, Ford Found., 1958; spl. cons. spl. Senate Com. on Space and Astronautics, 1958; spl. cons. to Senate Com. on Aero. and Space Sci., 1958-77; cons. to Senate Com. on Commerce, Sci. and Transp., 1977—; chmn. com. edn. and recreation Washington, 1937-38; forum leader 1976-79; guest Soviet Acad. Sci., 1982, on adult edn. U.S. Office Edn., 1938; mem. Internat. Inst. Space Law of Internat. Astronautical Fedn., 1958—, U.S. mem. bd. dirs., v.p., 1967-79, hon. dir., 1979—, Fedn. ofcl. observer at sessions UN Com. on Peaceful Uses Outer Space, 1981-85, mem. com. for relations with internat. orgns., 1979—; mem. Am. Rocket Soc.'s Space Law and Sociology Com., 1959-62; mem. adv. panel Office Gen. Counsel, NASA, 1971; adviser outer space del. U.S. Mission to UN Working Group on Direct Broadcast Satellites, 1973-75, legal subcom., 1976; observer UN Conf. Exploration and Peaceful Uses of Outer Space, Vienna, 1982; lectr. Nat. Acad. Sci., 1973, U.S. CSC, Exec. Seminar Center, Oak Ridge, 1973, 74, 75, 76, 78; ednl. counselor Purdue U., 1974; lectr. Inst. Air and Space Law McGill U., 1975, Inter Am. Def. Coll., 1977, 78, U. Akron, 1984; mem. panel on solar power for satellites and U.S. space policy Office Tech. Assessment, 1979-80, 82-84, cons., 1982; cons. COMSAT, 1983, FCC Commn. on U.S. Telecommunications Policy, 1983-85. Pres., Theodore Von Karman Meml. Found., 1973—; mem. alumni council Swarthmore Coll., 1976-79; mem. organizing com., author symposium on Conditions Essential For Maintaining Outer Space for Peaceful Uses, Peace Palace, Netherlands, 1984; bd. advisers Students for Exploration and Devel. of Space, 1984—. Rockefeller Found. scholar-in-residence, Bellagio, Italy, 1976. Recipient Andrew G. Haley gold medal Internat. Inst. Space Law, 1968; award U.S. Air Force Space Command, 1984; Wilton Park fellow, Eng., 1968. Mem. LWV (chmn. study groups housing, welfare in D.C., 1937-38, mem. tech. com. on law and sociology task force on legal aspects 1979—), AIAA (tech. com. on legal aspects of aeros. and astronautics 1980—), World Peace Through Law Center, Am. Soc. Internat. Law, Am. Astronautical Soc., Lamar Soc. Internat. Law, Internat. Studies Assn., Internat. Acad. Astronautics (trustee, chmn. social scis. sect. 1982-87), Internat. Law Assn., Phi Beta Kappa, Delta Sigma Rho, Kappa Alpha Theta. Episcopalian. Author: Atomic Power: Issues Before Congress, 1946; (with Bernard Brodie) The Atomic Bomb and the Armed Services, 1947; History of United States Military Policy on Reserve Forces, 1775-1957, 1957; Guided Missiles in Foreign Countries, 1957; The Community of Law and Science, 1958; United Nations Ad hoc Committee on Peaceful Uses of Outer Space, 1959; Satellites: A Force for World Peace, World (trustee, chmn. social scis. sect. Security and the Peaceful Uses of Outer Space, 1960; International Cooperation and Organization for Outer Space, 1965; Space Treaty Proposals by the United States and U.S.S.R., 1966; Treaty on Principles Governing the Activities of States in the Exploration and Use of Outer Space, Including the Moon and Other Celestial Bodies: Analysis and Background Data, 1967; Remote Sensing of the Earth by Satellites: Legal Problems and Issues, 1973, 75; The Future of Space Law, 1976; Consensus as a Basis for International Space Cooperation, 1977; The Role of the United Nations in Earth Resources Satellites, 1972; Settlement of Space Law Disputes, 1980; Perspectives of Space Law, 1981; Conditions for Success of International Space Institutions, 1982; Space Manufacturing, 1981; U.S. Space Policy and Programs, 1982; Expanding Article IV of 1967 Space Treaty, 1982; History and Development of Space Law, 1982; editor: Space Law Symposium, 1958; The Legal Problems of Space Exploration, 1961; United States International Space Programs, 1965; International Cooperation in Outer Space: A Symposium, 1972; assoc. editor Advances in Earth Oriented Applications of Space Tech., 1978—; mem. editorial adv. bd. Jour. Space Law, U. Miss. Law Sch., Space Communication and Broadcasting. Home: 4612 29th Pl NW Washington DC 20008

GALLOWAY, PATRICIA DENESE, civil engineer; b. Lexington, Ky., June 14, 1957; d. John Howard and Lou Maudine (Jones) Frisby. B.S. in civil engring., Purdue U., 1978; M.B.A., N.Y. Inst. Tech., 1984. Registered profl. engr., N.Y., N.J., Ariz., Wis., Wyo. Project engr., inspector CH2M Hill, Milw., 1978-79, master program scheduler, 1979-81; sr. cons. Nielsen-Wurster Group, N.Y.C., 1981-83, sr. engr., 1983-84, v.p., 1984—; lectr. Columbia U., U. Wis.-Madison. Mem. Soc. Women Engrs., Project Mgmt. Inst., ASCE, Am. Assn. Cost Engrs., Am. Nuclear Soc. Sigma Kappa. Club: Toastmasters. Office: 180 Township Line Rd Belle Mead NJ 08502

GALLOWAY, VALERIE LYNNETTE, public relations officer; b. Dayton, Ohio, Oct. 26, 1957; d. George Henry and Barbara Gay (Holmes) G. B.A. in Communication Arts, U. Dayton, 1978; M.A. in Mgmt. and Supervision, Central Mich. U., 1983. Asst. community services dir. Sta. WDTN-TV, Dayton, 1978-79; pub. relations specialist Day-Mont W. Mental Health Ctr., Dayton, 1980-81; pub. info. officer Montgomery County Children Services, Dayton, 1981; pub. affairs specialist 2750th ABW/PA, WPAFB, Ohio, 1981-83, chief community relations AFLC/PAC, 1983—. Contbr. articles to jours. in field. Participant leadership devel. Class Dayton Urban League, 1983-84; publicity com. W. Area YMCA/YWCA, Dayton, 1981—; group sales ticket com. Dayton Contemporary Dance Co., 1984. Recipient Community Service award Black Woman Hall of Fame, Chgo., 1980; Outstanding Young Woman Am. award, 1980, 81; Dayton's Young Career Woman award Dayton Bus. and Profl. Women's Club, 1981-82. Mem. Women in Communications, Inc., Internat. Assn. Bus. Communicators (excellence newswriting award 1982). Baptist. Office: Air Force Logistics Command/PAC WPAFB OH 45433

GALLUP, JANE HARRINGTON, librarian; b. Great Barrington, Mass., Jan. 4, 1949; d. William Snyder and Frances Harrington (Smith) G. B.A., Boston U., 1970; M.S. in Library Sci., Simmons Coll., Boston, 1976. Cert. tchr., Mass. Librarian, Exploratory Project for Econ. Alternatives, Cambridge, Mass. and Washington, 1973-76; dir. info. Ctr. Community Econ. Devel., Cambridge, 1976-80; librarian Nat. Consumer Coop. Bank, Washington, 1980-81, Golembe Assocs., Washington, 1981—. Book reviewer Ctr. Community Econ. Devel. Newsletter, 1977-80, compiler bibliographies, 1977-80. Mem. Spl. Libraries Assn., Women in Housing and Finance. Home: 1301 S Scott St Apt 422 Arlington VA 22204 Office: Golembe Assocs 1025 Thomas Jefferson St NW Suite 301 Washington DC 20007

GALLUP, JANET LOUISE, business official; b. Rochester, N.Y., Aug. 11, 1951; d. John Joseph and Mildred Monica (O'Keefe) VerHulst; m. Robert Hicks Gallup, June 26, 1982 (div. Nov. 1985); 1 son, Jason Hicks. B.A., Hofstra U., 1973; M.A. (grad. asst.), Calif. State U.-Long Beach., 1979. Asst. trader E.F. Hutton, N.Y.C., 1973-75, Los Angeles, 1975, instr. Calif. State U.-Long Beach, 1978-79; fin. analyst Rockwell Internat., Seal Beach, Calif., 1979-85, coordinator mgmt. devel. and tech. tng., 1985—. Vol. Cedar House Ctr.-Child Abuse, Long Beach, 1976. Democrat. Roman Catholic. Office: Rockwell Internat 2600 Westminster Blvd Seal Beach CA 90740

GALLUP, JOYCE VIOLET, corporate controller, accounting administrator; b. Tampa, Fla., May 14, 1947; d. Eugene A. and Violet Olga Rowlands; m. Royce Lynn Gallup, Apr. 4, 1966; children—Randall L., Jeffrey B. B.A. in Bus. Adminstrn., Eckerd Coll., 1984. Cert. mgmt. acct.; notary public. Acctg. staff Jack Eckerd Corp., Largo, Fla., 1975-79, adminstrv. asst. tax dept., 1979-83, assoc. mdse. mgr., 1983-85; controller Johnson Sails, Inc., Pinellas Park, Fla., 1985—. Den leader Cub Scouts, Pinellas Area council Boy Scouts Am., St. Petersburg, Fla., 1978-83; active Neighborhood Assn. Mem. Nat. Assn. Female Execs., Am. Bus. Women's Assn., Suncoast Women in Mgmt. Democrat. Roman Catholic. Avocation: reading.

GALT, ELIZABETH ANNE, investment company executive; b. New Haven, Aug. 18, 1952; d. William Egleston and Alfreda (Sill) G.; m. John Arthur Hirsch, Nov. 2, 1981. B.A., Bennington Coll., 1975. Sales exec. Bear, Stearns & Co., N.Y.C., 1979-81; dir. mktg. The Leuthold Group, N.Y.C., 1981-84; v.p. Abel, Noser & Co., N.Y.C., 1984-85; investment policy com., dir. mktg. Sloate, Weisman, Murray & Co., Inc., N.Y.C., 1985—; owner E. Galt Ltd., N.Y.C., 1984—. Pres., bd. dirs., mem. exec. com. City Harvest, N.Y.C., 1986. Mem. Am. Investment Mgmt. Sales Execs., Fin. Women's Assn., Nat. Assn. Female Execs., Plan Sponsors & Money Mgrs. Club: Cosmopolitan. Avocations: tennis; skiing; photography. Home: 420 E 54th St New York NY 10022 Office: Sloate Weisman Murray & Co Inc 10 E 53d St New York NY 10022

GALVACH, PATRICIA SWELGIN, safety products company executive, consultant; b. Wilkes Barre, Pa., May 25, 1944; d. Herman G. and Jennie Theresa (Malkoski) Swelgin; m. James Joseph Galvach, Oct. 6, 1962 (div.); children—James, Theresa. B.S., Kean Coll., 1980; M.B.A., Montclair State Coll., 1983. Acctg. clk. N.J. Bell Telephone Co., Elizabeth, 1961-63; mem. office staff Bettman Nut Co., Rahway, N.J., 1970-73; accounts payable supr. Wing Co., Linden, N.J., 1973-76; asst. controller Falcon Safety Products, Mountainside, N.J., 1976-80; dir. acctg. Boyle Midway Internat., N.Y.C., 1980-81; controller Falcon Safety Products, Inc., Mountainside, 1981—. Advisor, Understanding Am. Bus. Project, N.J. Bus. and Industry Assn., Hillside, N.J., 1981, Westfield Day Care Ctr., 1980-82; chmn. Woodbridge council Boy Scouts Am. (N.J.), 1973-77; trustee North Princeton devel. ctr. N.J. State Dept. Human Services. Mem. Alpha Kappa Psi, Omicron Delta Epsilon. Office: Falcon Safety Products Inc 1065 Bristol Rd Mountainside NJ 07092

GALVAN, MARIA DE JESUS, educator, civic worker; b. Santo Domingo, Dominican Rep., Feb. 3, 1946, came to U.S., 1959; d. Jose Lucia and Marina (Medina) Galva; m. Carlos Antonio Romos, 1968 (div. 1984); children—Carlos Alberto and Lisandra Maria Ramos. B.A. in History and Polit. Sci., CCNY, 1972; M.A. in Social Studies, NYU and CCNY, 1979; M.A. in Supervision and Adminstrn., NYU; now postgrad. Bklyn. Law Sch. Asst. bilingual edn. N.Y.C. Bd. Edn., 1972-73, reading per diem tchr., 1973, bilingual profl. asst., 1974-75, bilingual social studies tchr. Louis D. Brandeis High Sch., N.Y.C., 1975—; owner Ga-Li-Lu Travel Network, N.Y.C. Compiler Tchrs. Writing Anthology of Writing Tchrs. Consortium, 1982-83. Pres. Dominican Cultural Civic Ctr., 1982-83; pub. relations sec. Club Juan Pablo Duarte, 1969-71; adviser Dominican Parade, 1984-85. Named Outstanding Mem. of Community, LaRazon, Corma, N.Y., 1983; del. Hispanic Women's Caucus, 1976, Hispanic Parade, 1972-73. Mem. United Fedn. Tchrs., N.Y. State United Tchrs., Nat. Assn. Female Execs., Nat. Council Social Studies, Com. Pro Monument Monte Cristi (Dominican Republic). Lodge: N.Y. Highbridge Lioness (pres. 1983-84, dist. sec. 1983-84, treas. 1985-86, dist. dep. v.p., award for outstanding dedication 1983, award for outstanding and dedicated service 1983, secretarial award 1984). Roman Catholic. Office: Louis D Brandeis High School 145 W 84th St New York NY 10024

GALVIN, MADELINE SHEILA, lawyer; b. N.Y.C., Jan. 31, 1948; d. Rod Sheil and Madeline (Twiss) G. B.A. cum laude with highest honors, Russell Sage Coll., 1970; J.D., Albany Law Sch., 1973. Bar: N.Y. 1974. U.S. Dist. Ct. (no. dist.) N.Y. 1974, U.S. Supreme Ct. 1978; lic. real estate broker; cert. parliamentarian. Staff atty. N.Y. State Dept. Law, Albany, 1973-74; sr. atty. Dormitory Authority State of N.Y., Elsmere, 1974-78; sole practice, Delmar, N.Y., 1974—. Mem. Stafford (Vt.) Hist. Soc., 1955—; active polit. campaigns, 1968—; del. N.Y. State Conv. Young Republican Clubs, 1969, asst. sec. 3d dist. N.Y. State Young Rep. Clubs, 1969-70; mem. Albany Inst. History and Art, 1976—; mem. Bethlehem Women's Rep. Club, 1974—, rep. in charge Teen-Age Club, 1976-79, del. N.Y. State Fedn. Women's Rep. Clubs, 1977, 84, corr. sec., 1978-80, legal adv. 1980—, 1st v.p., 1983—; mem. N.Y. Geneal. and Biog. Soc., 1977—; co-chmn. judiciary com. N.Y. State Legis. Forum, 1980-81; Rep. committeeman 15th Dist. Town of Bethlehem, 1980—; mem. Town of Bethlehem Rep. Com., 1980—, Albany County Rep. Com., 1980—; bd. dirs., chmn. endowment com., exec. bd. YMCA Albany, 1980—; bd. dirs. Mercy House (shelter for homeless and battered women), Albany, N.Y., 1980-83, v.p., 1981-82; mem. Town of Bethlehem Alcohol and Drug abuse Com., 1980; mem. fin. com. Ronald McDonald House, Albany, N.Y., 1981-83. Kellas scholar, 1967-70; recipient Corp. Law award Albany Law Sch., 1973, Estate Planning award, 1973; Edn. Found. Recognition award Albany br. AAUW, 1984, cert. of merit N.Y. State Rep. Com., 1985, cert. of appreciation N.Y. Assn. Vocat. Indsl. Clubs, 1985, others. Mem. ABA, N.Y. State Bar Assn. (real property law sect. com. real estate financing and liens 1974—, spl. com. pub. access to records 1980—), N.Y. State Women's Bar Assn. (legis. com. 1978-80), Albany County Bar Assn., Albany Law Sch. Alumni Assn., Nat. Assn. Parliamentarians, Russell Sage Coll. Alumnae Assn. (chmn. exec. bd., by-laws com. 1980-83, pres.-elect 1982-83, pres. 1983—). Zonta Club Albany (chmn. women com., fin. com. 1980-81, co-chmn. fin. com. 1981-82, dir. 1981-83, chmn. fin. com. 1982-83, rec. sec. 1983-84, treas. 1984—), AAUW (Albany br. membership com., legis. com. 1979-80, chmn. legis. com. 1980-81, 1st v.p., del. N.Y. state legis. forum 1981-83, del. N.Y. state div. conv. 1982, 83, chmn. decorations com. N.Y. state conv. 1983, pres. 1983-84 dir. 1984—; recognition cert. for work with high sch. students 1980), N.Y. State Trial Lawyers Assn., Albany Claims Assn., Nat. Fedn. Bus. and Profl. Women's Clubs (legis. com. chpt. 1980-81), Nat. Soc. DAR (chpt. 1st vice regent 1979-80, regent 1980-82, dir. 1982—, chmn., mem. numerous coms.), Phi Alpha Theta. Roman Catholic. Club: NYU (N.Y.C.). Office: 217 Delaware Ave Delmar NY 12054

GALVIN, MARYANNE, psychologist, educator; b. Worcester, Mass., Mar. 6, 1954; d. Stephen F. and Bernadette M. (McGinn) Galvin; B.S., Wheelock Coll., 1976; M.Ed. (Mass. Fedn. of Women's Clubs fellow), U. Mass., Amherst, 1978, Ed.D., 1980. Psychologist, Wellesley (Mass.) Public Sch., 1980-81, U. Mass. Med. Sch., Worcester, 1980-81; asst. prof. U. N.H., Durham, 1981-82; pvt. practice psychology, Durham, 1981-83, Boston, 1983—; clin. dir. sch. consultation program Tufts New Eng. Med. Ctr., Boston, 1982—; research psychologist Tufts Sch. Medicine, 1986—; cons. McBer and Co., Boston. Recipient of commendation UN, 1975; NSF grantee. Mem. Internat. Council Psychologists, Am. Psychol. Assn., Mass. Assn. for the Advancement of Individual Potential, Mass. Psychol. Assn., Physicians for Social Responsibility. Roman Catholic. Club: New Eng. Masters Competitive Swim. Contbr. articles on psychology to profl. jours. Home: 232 Newbury St Boston MA 02116 Office: McBer and Co 137 Newbury St Boston MA 02116

GAMBINO, ELAINE HELEN, banker; b. Milw., May 9, 1936; d. Harry Erhart and Mable (Krohn) Prokopf; m. Vito Gambino, Mar. 3, 1962; children—Frank, Harry. Student Northwestern U. Acctg. supr. Chgo. Eye, Ear, Nose Hosp., Chgo., 1970-75; exec. v.p. Capitol Fed. Bank for Savs., Chgo., 1975—; dir. Capitol Fed. Mortgage Corp., Chgo.; pres. Workshop Inc., Chgo., 1983—. Mem. Nat. Assn. Female Execs., Chgo. Council Fgn. Relations. Roman Catholic. Office: Capitol Fed Bank for Savings 4011 N Milwaukee St Chicago IL 60641

GAMBLE, BARBARA SUE, lawyer, journalist; b. Jacksonville, Fla., Feb. 18, 1946; d. John Orvin and Helen (Stutt) Yarwood; m. Eugene Bly Gamble, Sept. 10, 1966; children—Laura Marie, Melinda Sue. B.A., Baylor U., 1967; J.D., Memphis State U., 1981. Bar: Ill. 1982. News dir. Sta. WFTW-FM, Ft. Walton Beach, Fla., 1969-71; asst. editor U. Kans. Med. Center, Kansas City, 1973-74; asst. pub. relations dir. U. Ark. Med. Center, Little Rock, 1976-77; paralegal Callahan & Lavin, Chgo., 1981-82; asst. legal counsel Comprehensive Acctg. Corp., Aurora, Ill., 1982-83; sole practice law, Elgin, Ill., 1983—. Contbr. chpt. to book, brief to legal publ.; author news story (UPI Story of Month in Tex. 1967). Next friend counselor Shelby County Juvenile Ct., Memphis, 1980-81; v.p. PTA, Memphis, 1977-78. Judge, Moot Ct. Bd., Memphis State U., 1980. Mem. Women in Communications (parliamentarian 1974), Phi Delta Phi, Order Barristers, Beta Sigma Phi (woman of yr., pres. Memphis Eta Iota chpt. 1978, v.p. Little Rock 1976-77). Office: 707A Davis Rd Elgin IL 60120

GAMBLE, ELENA LYNN, advertising executive; b. Oklahoma City, May 23, 1956; d. Tuttle J. and Trecil M. (Wagnon) G. B.A. in Journalism, U. Okla., 1978. Outside claims adjustor Aetna Life & Casualty, Tulsa/Ft. Worth, 1978-79; copywriter/media planner Ottmann Advt., Ft. Worth, 1980-82; account service/media planner, copywriter pub. relations Goodman & Assocs., Ft. Worth, 1973—. Contbr. articles to profl. jours. Campaigner Republican Party, 1972-74. Mem. Direct Mktg. Assn. N. Tex., Alpha Delta Sigma. Repulican. Baptist. Office: Goodman and Assocs Advt 601 Penn St Fort Worth TX 76102

GAMBREL, MARCIA KAY, businesswoman, former state legislator; b. Omaha, Apr. 3, 1950; d. Robert Earl and Helen (Stuart) Gambrel; student Iowa Western U., 1976-77; children—Craig Justin, Melisa Kay. Adminstrv. asst. Iowa Ho. of Reps., 1974-80; mem. Iowa Ho. of Reps., 1980-82; v.p. Walter & Assocs., 1982-85. Pres., Pottawattamie County Democratic Women, 1972-75. Mem. Bus. and Profl. Women, Nat. Order Women Legislators, LaLeche League, Legis. Ladies League, YMCA Pumping Assn. Democrat. Congregationalist. Club: Des Moines Compass. Home: 221 24th St West Des Moines IA 50265

GAMBRELL, LUCK FLANDERS, executive; b. Augusta, Ga., Jan. 17, 1930; d. William Henry and Mattie Moring (Mitchell) Flanders; m. David Henry Gambrell, Oct. 16, 1953; children—Luck Gambrell Davidson, David Henry, Alice Kathleen, Mary Latimer. B.A., Duke U., 1950; diplome d'etudes français L'Institut de Touraine, Tours, France, 1951. Chmn. bd. LFG Co., 1960—. Mem. State Bd. Pub. Safety, 1981—; bd. dirs. Atlanta Symphony Orch., 1982-85; mem. Chpt. Nat. Cathedral, Washington, 1981-84; mem. World Service Council YWCA, 1965; elder First Presbyterian Ch., 1982-85. Trustee Student Aid Found., Atlanta, 1975—; trustes Tift Coll., 1982—; mem. steering com. Carter Presdl. Library, 1983—. Mem. Atlanta Jr. League, Alpha Delta Pi.

GAMBRELL, SARAH BELK, retail executive; b. Charlotte, N.C., Apr. 12, 1918; d. William Henry and Mary (Irwin) Belk; B.A., Sweet Briar Coll., 1939; D. Humanities, Erskine Coll., 1970, U. N.C.-Asheville; m. Charles Glenn Gambrell; 1 dau., Sarah Belk. Vice pres., dir. Belk Stores, various locations, 1947—, pres. 32 stores. Bd. overseers and bd. dirs. Sweet Briar (Va.) Coll.; trustee Princeton (N.J.) Theol. Sem., Johnson C. Smith U., Charlotte, N.C., Warren Wilson Coll., Swannanoa, N.C.; trustee nat. bd. YWCA; hon. bd. dirs. Parkinson's Disease Found.; bd. dirs. Charlotte Opera Assn., N.C. Symphony, Raleigh, Planned Parenthood, Charlotte, YWCA, Charlotte; hon. trustee Cancer Research Inst., N.Y.C.; hon. bd. dirs. YWCA, N.Y.C. Mem. Fashion Group, Inc., Jr. League N.Y.C., Nat. Soc. Colonial Dames, DAR. Home: 300 Cherokee Rd Charlotte NC 28207 Office: PO Box 31788 Charlotte NC 28234 also 111 W 40th St New York NY 10018

GAMER, TERRY ANN, newspaper publisher; b. Great Neck, N.Y., Nov. 27, 1943; d. Sidney and Shirley (Burros) Packales; m. Donald Fox Gamer, May 11, 1969; children—Tracey Paige, Jennifer Dale. B.S. in Edn., Tufts U., 1965; cert. Publicity Club N.Y., 1967. Sec., Grey Advt., N.Y.C., 1965-66; asst. pub. mgr. WNBC-TV, N.Y.C., 1966-68; co-owner Designing Women, Hartford, Conn., 1971-78; publicity mgr. Toby Moffett '78 Re-election, Hartford, 1978; dir. promotion Info-Dial, Hartford, 1978-79; pub. Hartford Woman, Fairfield County Woman, Conn. Bus. Rev. Hartford, 1979—; mem. adv. council U.S. SBA, Hartford, 1983—. Adv. bd. Elms Coll. (Mass.), 1982—, Am. Lung Assn., Hartford, 1982-83; bd. dirs. Greater Hartford Visitors and Conv. Bur., 1983—; corporator Inst. Living, Hartford, 1983—Mem. Hartford Women's Network, Capitol Region Bus. and Profl. women (Woman of Yr. 1982), Women in Communications, Hartford C. of C. (exec. women's task force). Democrat. Office: 595 Franklin Ave Hartford CT 06114

GAMESTER, SHARON VIRGINIA, med. technologist; b. Winchester, Ind., Feb. 18, 1941; d. John Earl and Lillymae (Matteson) Hardesty; M.T., Ball State Tchrs. Coll., 1962; m. Larry Eugene Gamester, Jan. 1, 1963. Med. technologist, blood bank Ball Meml. Hosp., Muncie, Ind., 1962-67; rotating med. technologist Jay County Hosp., Portland, Ind., 1967-68; rotating med. technologist Reid Meml. Hosp., Richmond, Ind., 1969-71, dept. chemistry, 1971-77; med. technologist Doctor C. Deckard, Lynn, Ind., 1972; sr. med. technologist, float technician Kino Community Hosp., Tucson, 1978—; co-owner, operator Gamester's Abbattoir, 1963-68, Gamester Restaurant, 1965-74, Pine Lane Acres, 1978—, Pine Lane Arabians, 1970—. Mem. Am. Soc. Clin. Pathology (cert. med. technologist), Half Arabian Assn. Ariz. Club: Order Eastern Star. Home: 4510 N Fairview St Tucson AZ 85705

GAMIN, JULIE ANN, educational author; b. Tampa, Fla., July 8, 1945; d. Elton and Mary Elizabeth (Turnbull) G. B.A., SUNY-Potsdam, 1967; postgrad. in theatre (fellow), U. So. Miss., 1970-71; Ed.M., Reading Specialist, SUNY-Buffalo, 1977. Tchr. English and reading, pub. schs., also Children's Psychiat. Ctr., N.Y. and Tex., 1969-77; itinerant resource tchr. Dallas Ind. Sch. Dist., 1977-78; dir. Better Reading Through Parents, Dallas, 1978—; staff writer Leonard's Learning Circus (Learning Prodns., Inc.), Dallas, 1979—. Author: Revised Better Reading through Parents Program, 1980, Program for Spanish-Speaking Parents, 1980, Program for Non-Reading Parents, 1980, Family Puppet Shows, Leonard's Learning Circus, 1980. Del. local and state Democratic presdl. convs. U.S. ESAA grantee, 1978-79, 79-80. Mem. Nat. Council Tchrs. English, Internat. Reading Assn., ALA, Nat. Conf. Parent Involvement, Nat. Com. Citizens in Edn., Nat. PTA. Office: 1602 S Buckner Blvd Dallas TX 75211

GANDHI, TERESITA PALAD, educator; b. Philippines, Feb. 20, 1932; came to U.S., 1968; d. Max and Isabel (Medina) Reyes; m. Armando Palad, June 5, 1962 (dec. 1974); m. Bomanjee G. Gandhi, Nov. 26, 1983; children by previous marriage—Armando R., Leroy, Chito, Allen; B.S. in Edn., U. Santo Tomas, 1955; M.Ed., U. San Francisco, 1980. Real estate agt. and businesswoman, Manila, 1965-68; tchr. Compton Unified Sch. Dist. (Calif.), 1970-72, Los Angeles Unified Sch. Dist., 1970—. Winner trophies in folk and ballroom dancing, Los Angeles, 1978-81. Mem. Los Angeles Educators Assn. (chmn.), U. Santo Tomas Alumni Assn. (rec. sec. 1981-84). Home: 237 N Carondelet St Los Angeles CA 90026

GANDOLF, DEBORAH SCHMALZ, nursing administrator; b. Bloominton, Ind., Feb. 10, 1948; d. Richard Harold and Sue (Corter) Schmalz; children—Jason Andrew, Joshua David, Adam Robert, Nicholas Paul and Anthony Scott (twins). B.S. in Nursing, Ind. U.-Indpls., 1970; M.S. in Nursing, Marquette U., Milw., 1981; cert. natural family planning practitioner Creighton U., Omaha, 1982. Registered nurse. Pediatrics nurse James Whitcomb Riley Hosp., Indpls., 1970-72; surgery nurse Dr. J.W. Wright, Jr., Indpls., 1972; supr. Mercy Hosp., Benton Harbor, Mich., 1973-74, Oaklawn Hosp., Marshall, Mich., 1975-76; instr. Lake Mich. Coll., Benton Harbor, 1973-74, Hackley Hosp. Sch. of Nursing, Muskegon, Mich., 1974-75, St. Michael Hosp., Milw., 1977-83, Marquette U., Milw., 1983, U. Wis.-Milw., 1983-84; emergency room nurse St. Alphonsus Hosp., Port Washington, Wis., 1977; adminstrv. supr. St. Michael Hosp., Milw., 1977-80; natural family planning practitioner-ovulation method St. Michael Hosp., Milw., 1980-83; dir. of nursing Plymouth Hosp., Wis., 1983-84; St. Joseph's Community Hosp. of West Bend, Inc., Wis., 1984—; lectr. in field. Chmn. pastor parish support team First Congl. Ch., Port Washington, Wis., 1985—. Mem. Am. Soc. Nursing Service Adminstrs., Am. Hosp. Assn., Wis. Soc. Nursing Service Adminstrs., Assn. Hosp. Nursing Adminstrs. of Greater Milw. Area, Southeastern Wis. Council Dirs. Nursing and Inservices, Greater Milw. Area Service and Nursing Edn. Adminstrs. Group, Marquette U. Post Grad. Conf. com. (chairperson elect 1984-85), Ind. U. Alumni Assn. (life mem), Sigma Theta Tau (Delta Gamma chpt). (chmn. awards and hall of fame). Avocations: aerobic exercise; antiques. Home: 1218 Port View Dr Port Washington WI 53074 Office: St Joseph's Community Hosp of West Bend Inc 551 Silverbrook Dr West Bend WI 53095

GANDOLFO, JANET ANN, lawyer; b. N.Y.C., Oct. 31, 1951; d. Peter Michael and Rose Virginia (Dente) G. B.S., U. Vt., 1973; J.D., New Eng. Sch. Law, 1976. Bar: Mass. 1977, N.Y. 1978, U.S. Dist. Ct. (so. and ea. dists.) N.Y. 1978, U.S. Dist. Ct. Mass. 1978. Legal asst. Chief Justice U.S. Ct. Internat. Trade, N.Y.C., 1976-78; sr. litigation counsel Legal Aid Soc., White Plains, N.Y., 1978-83; prin. Janet A. Gandolfo, Esq., North Tarrytown, N.Y., 1983—. Mem. adv. bd. N.Y. State Group Home for Mentally Retarded, 1982—; dep. mayor Bd. Trustees North Tarrytown, 1982-83, trustee, 1979-83; chmn. North Tarrytown Planning Bd., 1978-79; mem. legis. com. Village Ofcls. Westchester County, 1982. Editor: New Eng. Law Rev., 1975-76. Recipient Disting. Service award Village of Tarrytown, 1983, Cert. of award Pub. Schs. Tarrytown, 1982, Cert. merit Legal Aid Soc. White Plains, 1983. Mem. Bar Assn. Tarrytowns (pres. 1982-84), Bus. and Profl. Womens Club (1st v.p. 1984-85), Westchester County Bar Assn., ABA, Westchester County Womens Bar Assn., Tri Delta Alumni Assn., Hist. Soc. Democrat. Roman Catholic. Home: 61 Gory Brook Rd North Tarrytown NY 10591 Office: 35 Beekman Ave North Tarrytown NY 10591

GANDY, JOYCE ANN, business administrator, former dance educator; b. Picher, Okla., Feb. 2, 1937; d. Sheppard Levi and Naydeen Maxine (Phillips) G.; m. Bernard Diamond, Aug. 2, 1985. A.A., Parsons Jr. Coll., 1957; dance student of Thalia Mara, Gertrude Edwards Jory, Yurik Lazowsky, Robert Joffrey, Luigi, Frank Wagner. Cert. Cecchetti Council Am. Owner, tchr. Joyce's Dance Studio, Parsons, Kans., 1953-66; gen. sec. Nat. Acad. Ballet and Theatre Arts, N.Y.C., 1966-72; sec., adminstrv. asst. to office, convs. mgr. Am. Inst. Steel Constrn., N.Y.C., 1973-79, office mgr., Chgo., 1979-80, personnel adminstr., Chgo., 1980-81; bus. adminstr. Bernard Diamond, D.D.S., P.A., Edison, N.J., 1983—. Recipient various dance grants, 1949-66, Scholarship awards, Parsons Jr. Coll., 1954, 55, 57. Mem. Nat. Assn. Female Execs. Mem. Ch. of Christ. Avocations: drawing, music, dance, gardening. Office: Bernard Diamond DDS PA 42 Parsonage Rd Edison NJ 08837

GANEY, SUSAN CHARLINE, market research company executive, consultant; b. Buffalo, Mar. 10, 1944; d. Charles Bronson and Margaret Mary (Hewitt) Wall; m. M. James Ganey, Nov. 5, 1966; children—Christine, Charles. Student SUNY-Fredonia, 1962-63; innkeeper cert. Holiday Inn Tng. Sch., Memphis,

1963. Asst. innkeeper Holiday Inn, Hamburg, N.Y., 1963-66; owner, operator Goody Two Sue's, Hamburg, 1966-76; comptroller Niagara Frontier Mktg. Research Inc., Hamburg, 1976—; owner, cons. firm CMG Enterprises, Hamburg, 1984—. Troop leader Buffalo and Erie County council Girl Scouts U.S., 1976-78, field dir., 1978-80; pres., treas. Lakeshore Investment Club, Hamburg, 1979-85; campaign mgr., treas., town clk.'s office campaign, Hamburg, 1978, 83; ruling elder Wayside Presbyterian Ch., 1983-89, pres. women's assn., 1984-86. Mem. Buffalo Bus. and Profl. Women's Club (sec. 1977). Nat. Assn. Female Execs., Mktg. Research Assn. Republican. Club: Wanaka Country (pres. women's assn. 1972) (Hamburg). Home: 4944 Kennison Pkwy Hamburg NY 10475 Office: Niagara Frontier Mktg Research 5244 Lakeshore Rd Hamburg NY 14075

GANGLE, SANDRA SMITH, lawyer; b. Brockton, Mass., Jan. 11, 1943; d. Milton and Irene M. (Powers) S.; m. Eugene M. Gangle, Dec. 21, 1968; children—Melanie Jean, Jonathan Rocco. B.A., Coll. New Rochelle, 1964; M.A., U. Oreg.; J.D., Willamette U., 1980. Bar: Oreg. 1980. Instr. French, Oreg. State U., Corvallis, 1968-71, Willamette U., Salem, Oreg., 1971-74; instr. ESL, Chemeketa Community Coll., Salem, 1975-79; labor arbitrator Salem, 1980—; mem. Oreg., Idaho, Wash., Mont. Arbitration Panels; sole practice Salem, 1980—; clin. prof. Portland State U., 1981-84; cons. State Oreg., 1981. Contbr. articles to profl. jours. Land-use chmn. Faye Wright Neighborhood Assn., Salem, 1983-84; mem. Civil Service Commn., Marion County Fire Dist., Salem, 1983—; mem. U.S. Postal Service Expedited Arbitration Panel, 1984—; mem. Salem Neighbor-to-Neighbor Panel; mem. panel Fed. Mediation and Conciliation Service, 1986—. NDEA fellow, 1967. Mem. Am. Arbitration Assn. (arbitrator), Oreg. State Bar, Soc. Profls. in Dispute Resolution ABA, Oreg. Trial Lawyers Assn., Marion County Bar Assn. Office: 1156 Chemeketa NE Salem OR 97301

GANN, JEAN POPE, insurance agency executive, fine arts appraiser; b. Winfield, Ala., Dec. 5, 1917; d. Garvin and Clara (Couch) Pope; m. John Henry Gann, Apr. 6, 1935; children—John Garvin, W. Gerlad, Jean Gann Nelson. Student U. Howard Coll., 1949-52, U. Ala., 1964-68, Montevallo, Ala., 1983-84, Samford U., 1983-85. Lic. ins. agt.; cert. appraiser fine arts and antiques. Owner, mgr. Sylacauga Ins. Agy., Ala., 1952—; instr., trainer Sylacauga High Sch., 1960—; co-chmn. Citywide Sales Clinic, Sylacauga C. of C., 1972. Contbr. articles to profl. jours. Exec. bd. dirs. United Givers Fund, Sylacauga, 1978-81; charter mem. Sylacauga Mus. and Arts Ctr., 1982—; v.p. Sylacauga High Sch. PTA, 1961-62; chmn. edn. Am. Cancer Soc., South Talladega County, Ala., 1953-61; mem. Ala. Women's Polit. Caucus, 1978—; mem. Nat. Democratic Com., Ala. Dem. Com., Ala. Citizens for ERA; tchr. adult Bible class 1st Bapt. Ch., 1945—, mem. long range planning com., 1950-58; chmn. com. that established Ave. of Flags in Sylacauga, 1972; pres. Bapt. Women's Orgn., 1964-65, 76-80; chmn. prayer breakfast Nat. Bus. Women's Week, 1979-85. Named Woman of Achievement, Sylacauga Bus. and Profl. Women's Club, 1976, Sylacauga Woman of Yr., Sylacauga Exchange Club, 1961; recipient cert. in Christian tng. Howard Coll., Samford U., 1983; cert. of recognition 1st Bapt. Ch., 1985. Mem. Soc. Fine Arts U. Ala., Ala. Ind. Ins. Agts. (legis. com. 1978-79, 84-85), Nat. Assn. Ind. Ins. Agts., Ala. Fedn. Bus. and Profl. Women's (dist. chmn. for young careerists 1972-73, legis. chmn. Sylacauga chpt. 1983—, pres. 1962, 62, 73), Nat. Trust for Hist. Preservation, Sylacauga Antique Group, Alpha Lambda Delta, Sylacauga C. of C. (membership com. 1952—). Club: Coosa Valley Country (charter mem.). Avocations: antique buff-collector; historical sites and buildings. Home: 300 W Bay St Sylacauga AL 35150 Office: Sylacauga Ins Agy PO Box 598 Sylacauga AL 35150

GANN, JO RITA, association executive; b. Talihina, Okla., June 2, 1940; d. Herbert and Juanita R. (Fields) G. B.S., Okla. Baptist U., 1962; M.Theatre Arts, Portland State U., 1970. Tchr., Oklahoma City Pub. Schs., 1962-64; health edn. asst. dir. Oklahoma City YWCA, 1964-67; camp and teen dir. Porland YWCA, Oreg., 1967-72; program coordinator-asst. dir. Flint YWCA, Mich., 1972-75; exec. dir. Salem YWCA, Oreg., 1972—; chmn. United Way Agy. Execs., Salem, 1980-81, Northwest Region YWCA Staff, 1983; del. UN for Non-Govt. Orgns., 1984. Co-author: A New Look at Supervision, 1980. Pub. speaker Global Concerns, 1981-85; bd. dirs. Corp. Renewable Resources, Salem, 1980-82; mem. pres.'s council Salem Celebration. Mem. Exec. Dirs. YWCAs U.S., Nat. Orgn. Female Execs. Democrat. Christian Scientist. Avocations: photography; hiking; swimming; travel. Office: YWCA 768 State St Salem OR 97301

GANNETT, MARYE DECKER, government official; b. Mitchell County, Iowa, May 12, 1928; d. Bert George and Gertrude Grace (Haugen) Decker; m. Ellis Wells Hubbard, Mar. 18, 1950 (dec. Feb. 1960); children—David Wells, Steven Ellis; m. Arthur Chauncey Gannett, Apr. 4, 1970. B.A., U. Minn., 1949; M.S., George Washington U., 1973. Cert. systems mgr., data processor, bus. programmer. Asst. editor U. Minn. Press, Mpls., 1948-50; instr. English Tng. Inst., Tokyo, 1954-57; sec.-treas. Weissberg Bros. Realty, Arlington, Va., 1958-67; computer specialist GSA, Washington, 1968-75; mgr. U.S. Immigration and Naturalization Service, Washington, 1975-83, U.S. Dept. Def., Ft. Meade, Md., 1983—. Author: (anthology) Best Loved Poets, 1982. Editor Nat. Capital Communicator, 1983-85 (named to Top 10 1984). Sec. Prince Georges Hosp., Citizens Adv. Bd., Hyattsville, Md., 1974-77. Named Disting. Toastmaster Toastmasters Internat., 1983. Mem. Data Processing Mgmt. Assn., Assn. for Systems Mgmt., Assn. Computing Machinery, Bus. and Profl. Women. Episcopalian. Club: Toastmasters (dist. editor 1983-85). Avocation: volunteer scouts and senior citizens. Home: 6800 Baltimore Ave University Park Hyattsville MD 20782

GANNON, SISTER ANN IDA, educator, former college president; b. Chgo., 1915; d. George and Hanna (Murphy) Gannon; A.B., Clarke Coll., 1941; A.M., Loyola U., Chgo., 1948, LL.D., 1970; Ph.D., St. Louis U., 1952; Litt.D., DePaul U., 1972; L.H.D., Lincoln Coll., 1965, Columbia Coll., 1969, Luther Coll., 1969, Marycrest Coll., 1972, Ursuline Coll., 1972, Spertus Coll. Judaica, 1974, Holy Cross Coll., 1974; hon. degrees Rosary Coll., 1975, St. Ambrose Coll., 1975, St. Leo Coll., 1976, Mt. St. Joseph Coll., 1976, Stritch Coll., 1976, Stonehill Coll., 1976, Elmhurst Coll., 1977, Manchester Coll., 1977, Marymount Coll., 1977, Governor's State U., 1979, Seattle U., 1981, St. Michael's Coll., Vt., 1984, Nazareth Coll., N.Y., 1985, Holy Family Coll., 1986. Mem. Sisters of Charity; tchr. English, St. Mary's High Sch., Chgo., 1941-47; residence, study abroad, 1951; chmn. philosophy dept. Mundelein Coll., 1951-57, pres. coll., 1957-75, mem. faculty philosophy dept., 1975—; dir. NICOR. Mem. Adv. Bd. Sec. Navy, 1975-80, Chgo. Police Bd., 1979—; bd. dirs. Am. Council on Edn., 1971-75, chmn., 1973—; nat. bd. dirs. Girl Scouts U.S.A., 1966-74, nat. adv. bd., 1976-85; trustee St. Louis U., 1974—, Ursuline Coll., Cath. Theol. Union, 1983—; bd. dirs. Newberry Library, 1976—, WTTW Pub. TV, 1976—, Sears Roebuck Found., 1977-82; mem. Gannon-Proctor Commn. (Ill. gov.'s commn. on equity for women), 1982-84. Recipient Laetare medal, 1975; LaSallian award, 1975; Aquinas award, 1976; Chgo. Assn. Commerce and Industry award, 1976. Mem. Am. Cath. Philos. Assn. (exec. council 1953-56), Assn. Am. Colls. (dir. 1965—, chmn. 1969-70), Religious Edn. Assn. Am. (pres. 1973, chmn. bd. 1975-78), N. Central Assn. (commn. on colls. and univs. 1971-78, chmn. exec. bd. 1975-77, dir.), Assn. Governing Bds. Colls. and Univs. (dir. 1979—, vice chmn. 1986), AAUW, Metaphys. Soc. Am. Contbr. articles philos. jours. Address: 6363 Sheridan Rd Chicago IL 60660

GANNON, ANNE DURNEY, banker; b. Bethlehem, Pa., May 15, 1952; d. Joseph J. and Barbara J. (Graveline) Durney; B.A. in Polit. Sci. and History, Rosemont Coll., 1974; postgrad. in bus. adminstrn. Temple U., 1974-77, Stonier Grad. Sch. Banking, Rutgers U., 1977-80; m. Joseph H. Gannon, Oct. 11, 1980. Mut. fund adminstr. Provident Nat. Bank, Phila., 1974-76, mgr. fed. funds dept., 1976—, head Eurodollar trader Nassau br., 1980-86, div. head, facilities mgmt., 1986—. Mem. Greater Phila. Money Marketeers, Rosemont Coll. Alumnae Assn. (dir. and treas. 1978-80). Republican. Roman Catholic. Club: Cynwyd (Pa.). Home: 4 Meredith Rd Green Hill Farms PA 19151 Office: Provident Nat Bank Broad and Chestnut Sts Philadelphia PA 19101

GANNON, PHYLLIS RISUCCI, leasing industry executive, family therapist; b. Ossining, N.Y., Feb. 14, 1945; d. Philip and Josephine Marie (Grottola) Risucci; m. John F. Hallen, Feb. 20, 1971 (div. Feb. 1983); children—Melanie Rowe, Andrea; m. 2d, William J. Gannon, Feb. 1, 1986. B.A., Am. U., 1978; M.S.W., Catholic U., 1981. Orgn. cons. G.D. Searle Co., Skokie, Ill., 1973-74; v.p., mgmt. cons. Hallen Assocs., Inc., Rockville, Md., 1975-80; pvt. practice family and individual therapy, Rockville, Md., 1980-85; personnel and facilities mgr. Finalco, Inc., McLean, Va., 1981-84, contracts adminstr., 1984-85; equipment fin. analyst Electronic Data Systems, Southfield, Mich., 1985—; pvt. practice family and individual therapy, West Bloomfield, Mich., 1986—; bd. dirs. Spl. Approaches to Juvenile Assistance, Washington, 1981-82. Vol. St. Elizabeth Hosp., Washington, 1979. Mem. Nat. Assn. Social Workers, Nat. Assn. Female Execs., Phi Kappa Phi. Democrat. Roman Catholic. Avocations: fitness; tennis; canoeing; theater; literature; entertaining. Home: 2912 Moon Lake Dr West Bloomfield MI 48033

GANS, MARION EDELMAN, public relations consultant, author; b. Paterson, N.J., Mar. 16, 1929; d. Joseph George and Hattie (Alexander) Edelman; m. Irwin Gans, Aug. 27, 1950; children—Edward Matthew, Julie Ellen, Robert Fredrick. B.S. cum laude, Syracuse U., 1950; M.A. in Am. Studies, Fairfield U., 1973. Dir. speech therapy Clifton Pub. Schs., N.J., 1949-50; head nursery sch. Community Ctr., Stamford, Conn., 1954-56; tchr. English, speech and arts Rippowam High Sch., Stamford, 1957-58; dir. pub. relations BiCultural Day Sch., Stamford, 1972-78; pres. Gans Pub. Relations, Inc., Stamford, 1978—; cons. Cahill Assocs., 1983—; mem. faculty U. Conn., Stamford, 1984—; founding mem. profl. writer's program Grad. Sch. Communications, Fairfield U., 1976. Contbr. articles to profl. jours.; editor small bus. newsletters. Bd. dirs. Stamford Symphony Soc., 1983—; v.p. Interfaith Council, 1978-80; mem. task force Vol. Action Council, Stamford, 1983. Recipient awards First prize Women in Communications, 1982. Mem. Internat. Assn. Bus. Communicators (chpt. v.p. 1978-80), Conn. Press Women (1st prize 1979, 80, 83), Southwestern Area Commerce and Industry Assn. Home: 51 Caprice Dr Stamford CT 06902 Office: Gans Pub Relations Inc 126 Woodside Green Suite 2C Stamford CT 06905

GANZ, MARY KEOHAN, lawyer; b. Weymouth, Mass., Nov. 17, 1954; d. Francis Lawrence and Margaret (Quinn) Keohan; m. Alan H. Ganz, Sept. 7, 1980. B.A. magna cum laude, Emmanuel Coll., 1976; J.D., Suffolk U., 1979. Bar: Mass., N.H., U.S. Dist. Ct. Mass.; lic. real estate, cert. tchr., notary pub., Mass.; justice of peace, notary pub., N.H. Law clk., sec. Pullman & Weitzen, Boston, 1977-78; law clk. Law Office Alan H. Segal, Braintree, Mass., 1978-79; law clk., assoc. Law Office Michael J. Yerandi, Braintree, 1979-81; sole practice, Seabrook, N.H., 1981—; trustee U.S. Savs. Bank Am., Seabrook, 1982-84. Active Seacoast Community Women, Hampton, N.H., 1983—; Network of Emmanuel Women, 1983—. Mem. ABA, Mass. Bar Assn., N.H. Bar Assn., Rockingham County Bar Assn., Mass. Women Lawyers, Seabrook Bus. and Profl. Assn. (dir. 1983—, pres. 1986), Kappa Gamma Pi, Phi Delta Phi. Roman Catholic. Office: Seabrook Professional Bldg PO Box 238 549 Lafayette Rd Seabrook NH 03874

GAPEN, D. KAYE, library administrator; b. Mitchell, S.D., July 1, 1943. B.A. in Sociology, U. Wash., 1970, M.L.S., 1971. Gen. Cataloger Coll. of William and Mary, Williamsburg, Va., 1971-72; asst. head quick editing Ohio State U. Library, Columbus, 1972-74, head quick editing, 1974-77; asst. dir. tech. services Iowa State U. Library, Ames, 1977-81; dean libraries U. Ala., University, 1981-84; dir. gen. library system U. Wis., Madison, 1984—. Author: (with others) Cooperative Library Resources Sharing Among Universities Supporting Graduate Work in Alabama, 1982. Mem. OCLC (exec. bd. dirs., trustee 1980—, exec. com. bd. trustees 1981-82, fin. com. bd. trustees 1982—), Wis. library Assn., Ala. Library Assn., ALA, Southeastern Library Assn. Avocations: sailing; running. Office: 360 Memorial Library U Wis 728 State St Madison WI 53706

GARANT, CAROL ANN, management consultant; b. Fall River, Mass., Dec. 17, 1945; d. Joseph and Stella (Dobek) G. B.S.N., U. Pa., 1969; M.S.N., Yale U., 1973; M.B.A., Boston Coll., 1983. Instr. Mass. Gen. Hosp., Boston, 1969-70; staff nurse Hosp. St. Raphael, New Haven, Conn., 1971-72; adminstr. VA Hosp., Boston, 1973-74; cons. New Eng. Deaconess Hosp., Boston, 1974-84, Hillary O'Shea Assocs., N.Y.C. and Boston, 1985—; strategic planner and lobbyist, founding mem. Nurses United for Reimbursement of Services, Boston, 1975-79. Author, producer, dir. audio-visual presentation. Contbr. articles to profl. jours. NIMH traineeship, 1970-73, Insts. of Health traineeship, 1967-69. Mem. Am. Mktg. Assn. (research com. writer 1983—), Am. Psychomatic Soc., Sigma Theta Tau. Democrat. Roman Catholic. Clubs: Penn (bd. dirs. 1974-78), Yale (bd. dirs. 1979-80) (Boston). Avocations: squash; sailing; historic preservation; music.

GARBÁTY, MARIE LOUISE, art collector, patron of arts; b. Berlin, Ger., Mar. 9, 1910, widowed. Patron, Met. Opera, N.Y.C. Opera; patron, hon. mem. Allentown (Pa.) Art Mus.; mem. N.Y.C. Opera Guild; fellow in perpetuity Met. Mus. Art; life fellow Mus. Fine Arts, Boston; internat. centennial patron Mus. Fine Arts, Boston; benefactor, life mem. Chrysler Mus., Norfolk, Va.; assoc. mem. Solomon Guggenheim Mus., N.Y.C., co-founder Am. Shakespeare Festival Theater, Stratford, Conn.; friend N.Y.C. Library; mem. Am. Fedn. Art, China Inst. Am. Inc., N.Y.C., Asia Soc., N.Y.C., Art Mus., Palm Beach, Fla.; donations numerous museums, libraries, profl. socs., including Met. Mus. Art, N.Y.C., U. Wash., Cooper Union Mus., Boston U. Library, Calif. State Coll. Library, Fullerton, Yale U. Library, Hoover Library, Stanford U., Library of Congress, Art Inst., Chgo., Carnegie Inst. Art, others.

GARBER, CHARNA JANICE, wholesale shoe company executive; b. Lynn, Mass., Apr. 21, 1937; d. Saul William and Lena (Kline) Chalek; m. William Garber, Oct. 11, 1956; children—Holly Jeske, Ellise Garber. Student, U. N.H., 1960, 61, 62, Am. Inst. Banking, Lynn, Mass., 1954, 55. Mgr. customer services The Rochester Banks (N.H.), 1964-66; bus. mgr. computer dept. MIT, 1973-78; line builder, fashion coordinator Cole-Haan Footwear, 1978-80; sales rep. Internor Trade, N.Y.C., 1980-82; pres. C. G. Assocs. Inc., N.Y.C., 1982—; sec.-treas., owner N.E. Fashion Shoe Show, N.Y.C., 1976—; pres. d'Rossana Shoes. Bd. dirs. Dollars for Scholars, Mass., N.H., 1960-66. Mem. 210 Assn., Boot and Shoe Travelers Assn., Nat. Shoe Travelers Assn., Footwear and Accessories Council, NOW. Democrat. Jewish. Club: Hadassah. Home: 201 E 87th St Suite 21J New York NY 10128 Office: D'Rossana Co 12 W 57th St Room 801 New York NY 10019

GARBER, JUDITH ANN, health care cost containment company executive; b. Ville Platte, La., Dec. 6, 1949; d. Gordon Lee and Hazel (Pitre) Dardeau; m. Melvin Paul Garber, June 10, 1972; children—Raegan Dyane, Dustin Paul. B.S. in Nursing, U. Southwest La., 1972. Head nurse Rehab. Ctr., Ithaca, N.Y., 1973-74; charge nurse County Hosp., Ames, Iowa, 1975-76; nurse cons. pvt. industry, Tacoma, 1980-84; unit mgr. med. rev. Health Care Cost Containment, Orlando, Fla., 1984—. Speaker nat. edn. conf. Self Insured Inst. Am., San Francisco, 1985. Mem. Nat. Assn. Female Execs., Fla. Utilization Rev. Assn., Fla. Occupational Health Nurses Assn., Central Fla. Claims Assn. (bd. dirs.). Republican. Roman Catholic. Club: Seminole Soccer (Longwood, Fla.). Home: 251 Mounts Bay Ct Longwood FL 32779 Office: Intracorp 851 Trafalgar Ct Maitland FL 32751

GARBER, MARILYNN KAREN, registered nurse; b. North Kingston, R.I., Dec. 20, 1953; d. Cazimiro and Esther Mae (Coffey) Farria; m. William Edward Garber, Dec. 23, 1973; 1 dau., Kathryn Esther. A.S. in Nursing, Shenandoah Coll., 1974. Cert. ob/gyn nurse. Sec./bookkeeper Holly Acres Recreational Vehicle Storage, Woodbridge, Va., 1973—; staff nurse Alexandria Hosp., (Va.), 1974-75; staff nurse Potomac Hosp., Woodbridge, 1975—, also mem. nursing audit com.; office nurse Dr. M. Garvez, Woodbridge, 1976-82; emergency med. technician Prince William County, Woodbridge; mem. Potomac Hosp. Corp. Mem. Nurse's Assn. of Am. Coll. Obstetricians and Gynecologists, Prince William County C. of C. Baptist.

GARBETT, ROSEMARY SCHNEIDER, restauranteur; b. Houston, July 9, 1935; d. Rudolph George and Lorena (Boenker) Schneider; m. Thomas M. Garbett Jr., Jan. 30, 1954 (dec. 1976); children—Susan Garbett Kendrick, Thomas M. III, Katherine A., Michael S. Owner, ptnr. Los Tios Mexican Restaurants, Inc., Houston, 1970—, chief exec. officer, 1976—; dir. Westchase Corp., Houston, 1980. Bd. dirs. Greater Houston Conv. and Visitors Council, 1979—, mem. exec. com., 1983—; bd. dirs. Leukemia Soc., Houston, 1980—, Kidney Found., Houston, 1980-82; mem. Houston Com.; mem. Commn. for Clean Houston, 1983—; chmn. Clean Retailers Com.; mem. internat. and box seat com. Houston Livestock Show and Rodeo. Recipient Outstanding Restauranteur award City of Houston, 1980-81, Outstanding Women's award YWCA, 1985. Mem. Houston Restaurant Assn. (pres. 1982-83, dir. 1980-82), Tex. Restaurant Assn. (dir. 1982-83). Clubs: Warwick, Maxim, Univ., Bob Smith Yacht (charter mem.), Houston Livestock and Rodeo Show (life). Home: 7810 High Star St Houston TX 77036 Office: 10550 Westpark Houston TX 77042

GARCIA, JOSEFINA MARGARITA, dancer, nurse, educator; b. Mascota, Jalisco, Mex., May 2, 1906; came to U.S., 1923, naturalized, 1944; d. Manuel Garcia Perez and Margarita (Garcia) Flores; diploma Nat. Coll., Kansas City, Mo., 1933; tchrs. cert. State Tchrs. Coll., Queretaro, Mex., 1935; R.N., Bethany Hosp. Sch. Nursing, 1939; diploma in psychiat. nursing Inst. of Living, Hartford, Conn., 1941; B.S., Tchrs. Coll., Columbia U., 1943, M.A. in Health and Phys. Edn., 1945; Ph.D. in Dance and Related Arts, Tex. Woman's U., 1958. Elem. tchr. Meth. Normal Sch., Puebla, Mex., 1934-36; dir. religious edn., nurse, coordinator phys. edn. George O. Robinson Sch., San Juan, P.R., 1939-40; psychiat. nurse psychiat. div. N.Y. Okla. White Plains, 1941-43; tchr. health Poly. Inst., San German, P.R., 1943-44; charge corrective gymnastics Hosp. for Spl. Surgery, N.Y.C., 1944-45; nurse Bellevue Hosp., N.Y.C., 1945-50; tchr., performer La Meri's Ethnologic Center, N.Y.C., 1945-47; lectr., dancer Pearl Buck's East and West Assn., 1947-49; artist, tchr., nurse Jacob's Pillow U. of Dance, Lee, Mass., summers 1949-55; pvt. duty nurse Harkness Pavillion, N.Y.C., 1952-55; supr. psychiat. div. Parkland Meml. Hosp., Dallas, 1956-58; grad. asst. in dance Tex. Woman's U., Denton, 1956-58; chmn. health, phys. edn. and recreation dept. Okla. Coll. for Women, Chickasha, 1958-63 (on leave), instr., 1934-36, 39-40, prof., 1963-64; vis. prof. edn. Miami U., Coral Gables, Fla., 1963-64; dir. dance in dept. health and phys. edn., prof. phys. edn. Madison Coll., Harrisonburg, Va., 1964-67; tchr. English as secondary lang., bilingual edn. N.Y.C. Bd. Edn.; part-time staff Grady Meml. Hosp., Chickasha, 1962-63; numerous dance recitals and workshops, 1940—; tchr. Mexican and Latin Am. dance Tina Ramirez Dance Studio, N.Y.C.; cons. Sacred Dance Guild; choreographer on Mexican themes Alliance Latin Am. Arts, summers 1973-74; artist-in-residence Spelman Coll., Atlanta, 1978-79; relief night nurse, prof. geriatric health and exercises Williams Residence, N.Y.C. Vol., Channel 13 Public TV; founder Center for Internat. Security Studies; mem. Am. Security Council; bd. govs. N.Y. chpt. Arthritis Found. Fellow AAHPER; mem. Am., Okla., N.Y. State (dir.) nurses assns., Nat., So., Va. assns. phys. edn. coll. women, ANTA, Okla, Okla. Assn., Va. Assn. Health, Phys. Edn. and Recreation (chmn. 1962-63), AAUW, Chickasha Bus. and Profl. Women's Club (past chmn. internat. relations com.), Nat. Dance Tchrs. Guild, Nat. Council Arts in Edn., Mus. Natural History, Dance Notation Bur., Internat. Platform Assn., Pan Am. Women's Assn. (dir. 1967—, v.p.), Dance Film Library Assn. (dir. 1967—), Film Soc. (dir.), Profl. Dance Tchrs. Assn., Nat. Council Sr. Citizens, Met. Opera Guild, Cooper-Hewitt Mus., Nat. Geog. Soc., N.Y. YWCA, Kappa Delta Pi, Phi Sigma Iota. Contbr. articles on dance to profl. publs., Groliers Ency., Richards Ency. Home: 720 West End Ave Suite 1603 New York NY 10025

GARCIA, LOIS MARIE, public relations consultant, author; b. Mpls., Feb. 23, 1940; d. Robert Blaine and Lois Elaine (Whitesell) Christison; m. Alfredo Jorge Garcia, Jan. 28, 1961 (div. 1983); children—Michael, Theresa, Steven, Elizabeth. Licensed Practical Nurse, Vocat. Sch. Nursing, 1959. TV host, producer Channel 5, Butler, Pa., 1976-81; TV Telethon coordinator Cerebral Palsy, Steubenville, Ohio, 1980-81; pub. relations dir. King Prodns., Wintersville, Ohio, 1981-82; Telethon coordinator Arthritis Found., Steubenville, 1982; pub. relations cons., Pitts., 1983—. Author: Paul Gaudino Guide Fitness, 1985. Contbr. articles to profl. jours. Bd. dirs. YWCA, Butler, Pa., 1973-76, Human Relations Council, Butler, 1979-81, ARC, Butler, 1978-81; voters service chmn. League Women Voters, Pitts., 1985—. Recipient Promotion award United Way Am., 1979. Mem. Nat. Assn. Female Execs. Republican. Unity. Avocations: family history/research. Home: 2917 Shady Ave Pittsburgh PA 15217

GARCIA, MARGARITA, psychologist; b. Havana, Cuba, Sept. 7, 1942; came to U.S., 1960; d. Oswaldo and Alicia Margarita (Rodriguez-Alonso) Garcia-Brito; m. Guillermo A. Estevez; 1 dau., Victoria Margarita. B.S., Columbia U., 1965; M.A., 1967, Ph.D., 1972. Asst. prof. psychology Montclair State Coll. (N.J.), 1970-75, assoc. prof., 1975—; dir. spl. programs Internat. Rescue Com., Inc., West New York, N.J., part time, 1980—. Hispanic Research Ctr. scholar Fordham U., Bronx, 1978-79. Contbr. articles to profl. jours. Mem. Am. Psychol. Assn., Nat. Hispanic Psychol. Assn. Office: Dept Psychology Montclair State Coll Montclair NJ 07095

GARCIA, MARIA FRANCISCA, educator; b. Monterrey, Nuevo Leon, Mexico, Nov. 8, 1931, came to U.S., 1952; d. Hector P. and Margarita (Quiroz) Saenz; m. Juan P. Garcia, Aug. 17, 1974; children—John Michael, Naomi Lorea. B.A., Dominican Coll., 1974; M.S., Corpus Christi State U., 1981. Tchr., Houston Ind. Sch. Dist., 1974-75, Corpus Christi Ind. Sch. Dist. (Tex.), 1973-77, Am. Sch. Monterrey (Mexico), 1977-82; 4th grade tchr. Lamar Elem. Sch., Houston, from 1982, now tchr. De Zavala Elem. Sch., Houston. Leader Houston council Girl Scouts U.S., 1982—, Corpus Christi council, 1975-77; tchr. English, Houston Community Ctr., 1983; vol. Meml. Bapt. Hosp., Houston. Mem. Am. Fedn. Tchrs., Tex. Student Edn. Assn., NEA. Roman Catholic. Office: De Zavala Elem Sch Houston TX

GARCIA, MARY JANE MADRID, night club owner; b. Dona Ana, N.Mex., Dec. 24, 1936; d. Isaac C. and Victoria (Madrid) G. A.A., City Coll. San Francisco, 1957; B.Individual Study, N.Mex. State U., 1981, B.A. in Anthropology, 1983, M.A., 1985. Sec. USAF Acad., Colorado Springs, Colo., 1961-62; sec. to dep. city clerk and city mgr. City of Las Cruces, N.Mex., 1963-64; interpretor, translator Hotel Balboa (USAF), Madrid, 1972; adminstr. asst. RMK-BRJ Contractors, Saigon, Vietnam, 1966-72; owner, operator Billy the Kid Gift Shop, Old Mesilla, N.Mex., 1972-80, Victoria's Night Club, Las Cruces, 1980—; student archaelogist N.Mex. State Univ. Field Sch., Nuvaquetaka, Ariz, 1982, Peña Blanca Rockshelter, 1983, crew chief, Rollerskate Rockshelter (Organ Mountains, Las Cruces, 1984; dir. Sun Country Savs. Bank, Las Cruces. Sec., treas Lalo Garza for Dist. Atty., Las Cruces, N.Mex., 1976, Toney Anaya for U.S. Senate, 1978, Toney Anaya for Gov. N.Mex., 1981; mem. Dona Ana Ch. Conservation Com. Mem. Dona Ana Water Assn. (bd. dirs., sec., treas. 1983—), Mus. Anthropology N.Mex. State Univ. Democrat. Roman Catholic. Home: PO Box 22 Isaac Garcia Rd Dona Ana NM 88032 Office: Victoria's Night Club 2395 N Solano St Las Cruces NM 88001

GARCIA, MARY KATHERYN (PRUETT), clinical nurse specialist; b. Albuquerque, Mar. 9, 1954; d. Jasper Battles and Sarah Drucilla (Ridings) Pruett; m. Carl Edward Azbell, June 30, 1972 (div.); m. Rodolfo Torres Garcia, Sept. 21, 1979. B.S. in Nursing, Dallas Bapt. Coll., 1977; M.S. in Nursing, Tex. Woman's U., 1982. R.N. Tchr. kindergarten French's Sch., Bryan, Tex., 1973-74; office nurse Dallas Associated Dermatologists, Dallas, 1976-77; R.N., staff nurse St. Paul Hosp., Dallas, 1977-78; grad. adminstrv. asst. Tex. Woman's U., Dallas, 1981; staff nurse intensive care Charlton Meth. Hosp., Dallas, 1978-81; occupational health nurse Fireman's Fund Ins., Dallas, 1981-83; clin. nurse specialist NursCare, Dallas, 1983—; emergency med. technician Tex. Dept. Health, Dallas, 1979—; audiometric technician Council Accreditation in Occupational Hearing Conservation, 1983; spirometric technical NIOSH, Dallas, 1983; faculty Dallas Bapt. Coll., 1984. Editor corp. newsletter FireWire, 1982-83. CPR instr. Am. Heart Assn., 1981—; 1st aid instr. ARC, Dallas, 1981—. Mem. Am. Nurses Assn., Tex. Nurses Assn., Am. Assn. Critical Care Nurses, Council Nurse Researchers, Council Internat. Nursing, Sigma Theta Tau. Baptist. Club: Toastmasters.

GARCIA, MONTSERRAT GUBERN DE, hospital executive; b. Barcelona, Spain, Oct. 19, 1936; d. Carlos S. and Antonia (Barroso) Gubern; B.A. magna cum laude, U. P.R., 1964, M.H.A. magna cum laude (Best Student award), 1968; m. Felipe A. garcia, May 20, 1960; children—Mariana, Carlos Felipe, Maria Antonia. Admission sec. Gubern's Hosp., Fajardo, P.R., 1954-59, adminstr. from 1968, now exec. dir. Mem. Am. Coll. Hosp. Adminstrs., P.R. Hosp. Assn. (pres. 1983-84). Democrat. Roman Catholic. Club: Fajardo Civic. Home: E 16 5th St Fajardo PR 00648 Office: Gubern's Hospital 110 Antonio Rd Barcelo Fajardo PR 00648

GARCIA, ROXANN DEMENT, accountant; b. Dallas, Dec. 5, 1952; d. Hollis Eugene and Mary Francis (Reagan) Dement. B.A., North Tex. State U., 1975. Stenographer, Lone Star Gas Co., Dallas, 1975; acctg. office supr. Southwestern Bell Telephone Co., 1975-77, computer ops. supr., 1977-78, functional acctg. coordinator, 1978, asst. mgr. payrolls, 1978—. Advisor Jr. Achievement, Dallas, 1977-78. Democrat. Mem. Ch. of Christ. Office: Southwestern Bell Telephone Co 211 S Akard Dallas TX 75202

GARCIA, SUSAN BEDNER, human resource consultant; b. Monogahela, Pa., Nov. 24, 1947; d. Francis Ralph and Mary (Pelissero) Bedner; m. N. John Garcia, Apr. 27, 1974. B.S., U. Pitts., 1969; M.B.A., Fairleigh Dickinson U., 1982—. With Batus Retail, Pitts., N.Y.C., 1969-76; asst. v.p., employee mgr. First Union Nat. Bank, Charlotte, N.C., 1976-79; sales personnel mgr. M & M/Mars, Hackettstown, N.J., 1979-81; personnel mgr. Zayre Corp., Pitts.,

Northeastern zone mgr., Boston, 1981-85; cons. Acumen Resources, N.Y.C., 1985—. Mem. Nat. Assn. Female Execs., Women Execs. Charlotte (pres. 1977-79), Exec. Women Pitts., Pitts. Personnel Assn., Am. Soc. Tng. and Devel. Republican. Roman Catholic. Avocations: jogging; exercise; reading; bridge. Home: 303 W 80 St Apt 1A New York NY 10024

GARCIA-SWAIN, SUSAN ELAINE, emergency and weight management physician; b. Fresno, Calif., Feb. 3, 1947; d. Dick and Dorothy (Sauermilch) Garcia; m. John W. Swain, Mar. 22, 1968. B.A., U. No. Colo., 1974; M.D., U. Colo., 1978. Intern Tucson Hosp. Med. Edn. program, Ariz., 1978-79; resident Univ. Ariz., Tucson, 1979-80, Univ. So. Calif., Los Angeles, 1980-82; emergency physician Mountains Community Hosp., Lake Arrowhead, Calif., 1980—, Minor Emergency Med. Clinic, Fair Oaks, Calif., 1982—, Vacaville, Calif., 1982—, Lakecrest Walk-In Clinic, Sacramento, 1982—; pvt. practice medicine specializing in bariatrics, Sacramento, 1982—; mem. edn. com. Methodist of Sacramento Hosp., 1983—; mem. speakers bur. Sacramento Heart, Diabetes, Arthritis and Hypertension Found., 1983—. Pres. Coronado Riding Club, Inc., Sacramento, 1979—; mem. health and sports coms. Sacramento C. of C., 1983. Mem. Am. Soc. Bariatric Physicians, AMA, Am. Coll. Sports Medicine, U.S. Dressage Fedn. Office: Susan Garcia-Swain MD Inc 910 Florin Rd Suite 105 Sacramento CA 95831

GARD, BETSY ANN, educator; b. Detroit, May 1, 1951; d. Arthur W. and Nancy (Schiller) Schlesinger; B.A., U. Mich., 1972; Ph.D., Washington U., 1978; m. Steven J. Gard, Aug. 20, 1971. Clin. intern Meml. Hosp., U. N.C., Chapel Hill, 1975-76; cons. Judevine Center for Autistic Children, St. Louis, 1977-78, St. Louis State Hosp. Day Treatment Center, 1977-78; asst. prof. psychiatry Emory U. Sch. Medicine, 1978—; cons. in field. Lic. clin. psychologist, Ga. Mem. Am. Psychol. Assn., Ga. Psychol. Assn., Mortar Bd. Jewish. Contbr. articles to profl. jours. Home: Bryn Mawr Atlanta GA 30027

GARD, CONNIE RAE, data processing executive; b. Glasgow, Mont., Jan. 16, 1936; d. Arthur Alexander and Margaret (Crest) Oslund. Student Santa Rosa Jr. Coll., 1958-60; Cert., System Sci. Inst.-Los Angeles, 1980, Greenes Bus. Coll., 1966. Asst. ops. mgr. Sonoma County Data Processing, Santa Rosa, Calif., 1969—; office mgr. Anchorage Drug Supply, Alaska, 1963-67; cons. Chips & Bits Micros, Santa Rosa, 1984—. Served with USN, 1954-57. Mem. Data Processing Mgmt. Assn. (treas. 1981-83), Am. Mgmt. Assn., Nat. Assn. Female Execs. Democrat. Lutheran. Office: Sonoma County Data Processing 2615 Paulin Dr Santa Rosa CA 95405

GARDENIER, EDNA FRANCES, nurse; b. Teaneck, N.J., June 30, 1935; d. Andrew Cairns and Edna Frances (Manney) O'Neil; B.S. in Nursing, Seton Hall U., S. Orange, N.J., 1965; M.Ed., Columbia U., 1970; doctoral candidate in ednl. adminstrn. (grad. asst.) SUNY, Albany; m. Harvey James Gardenier, Aug. 25, 1961; children—Andrew, William. Staff nurse N.J. hosps., 1955-65; public health nurse, 1965-70; mem. nursing faculty Dutchess Community Coll., Poughkeepsie, N.Y., 1970—, program chmn. nursing, 1971-83, acting head dept. health technologies, 1979-80, head nursing dept., 1983—; mem. overall nursing faculty N.Y. State Regents Coll., 1981—; mem. nurse edn. com. SUNY; mem. Dutchess County chpt. Am. Heart Assn., 1974—; nutrition adv. council Dutchess County Coop. Edn., 1970-79. USPHS trainess, 1968-70. Mem. Am. Assn. Women in Jr. and Community Colls., N.Y. Asso. Degree Nurse Council, N.Y. State Nurses Assn., N.Y. State Two Year Coll. Assn. Home: RD 1 Box 85 Holsapple Rd Dover Plains NY 12522 Office: Dutchess Community Coll Pendell Rd Poughkeepsie NY 12601

GARDINE, JUANITA CONSTANTIA FORBES, retired educator; b. St. Croix, V.I., Aug. 6, 1912; d. Alphonso Sebastian and Petrina (Actien) Forbes; B.A., Hunter Coll., 1934; M.A., Columbia U., 1940; postgrad. U. Chgo., 1949, N.Y.U., summers 1960-66, Cheyney State Coll., summer 1967, U. Ill. at Chgo. Extension, St. Croix, V.I., 1980-82, Coll. Edn., 1982—, M.Ed., 1985; m. Cyprian A. Gardine, Apr. 23, 1942; children—Cyprian A., Vicki Maria Camilla, Letitia Theresa, Richard Whittington. Tchr. elem. schs., 1934-35; tchr. math. high sch., 1935-41, 48-49; acting asst. high sch. prin., 1941; jr. high sch. prin., 1941-47; substitute tchr. math., physics, Montclair, N.J., 1947-48; asst. supt. edn., 1949-55; assoc. dean, supr. elem. schs., Community Colls., 1955-57; high sch. prin., 1957-58; supr. ednl. stats., 1958-62; social worker Dept. Welfare, 1962-63; prin. Christiansted (St. Croix) Public Grammar Sch., 1963-74; tchr. math. evening session extension classes Cath. U. P.R., 1960-62; part-time instr. math. Coll. V.I., 1974-75, 80-81; partner St. Croix Tutorial Sch.; bookkeeper St. John's Ch.; testing supr. Ednl. Testing Service. Past sec. bd. dirs. St. Croix Fed. chpt. ARC; chmn. supervisory com., dir. St. Croix. Fed. Credit Union; past sec. St. Croix Sch. Health Com.; past pres. St. Croix (V.I.) Mental Health Assn. Pres., Tchrs. Assn., 1940, Municipal Employees Assn., 1942. Grammar sch. named in her honor. Mem. Am. Statis. Assn., Nat. Assn. Elem. Sch. Prins., V.I. Fedn. Bus. and Profl. Womens Clubs (past pres.), Episcopal Ch. Women of V.I. (past chmn. world affairs com., past pres.). Christiansted Bus. and Profl. Women's Club (treas., past pres., Woman of Yr. 1966), Daus. King (sec.). Home: 142 Whim Frederiksted VI 00840 also PO Box 1505 Christiansted St Croix VI 00820

GARDINEER, MARGARET VALLONE, librarian, English educator; b. N.Y.C., Apr. 26, 1953; d. Albert A. and Mary Jane (Kelly) Vallone; m. Richard Arthur Gardineer, Aug. 10, 1974; 1 child, Arthur Albert. B.A. magna cum laude, Dominican Coll., 1975; M.A., Fairleigh Dickinson U., 1977; M.S. with honors, Columbia U., 1980, postgrad., 1984—; postgrad. NYU, 1977-83. Cert. profl. librarian, tchr., N.Y. Teaching fellow Fairleigh Dickinson U., Teaneck, N.Y., 1975-77; reference librarian Blauvelt Free Library, N.Y., 1975-80, asst. dir., 1980-85; reference librarian Valley Cottage Library, N.Y., 1985—; adj. instr. English, Dominican Coll., Blauvelt, 1982—. Pres., St. Paul's Sch. Guild, Valley Cottage, N.Y., 1984-86. Brookdale Found. grantee, 1980. Mem. ALA, N.Y. Library Assn., Cath. Library Assn., Nat. Council Tchrs. English, Beta Phi Mu. Roman Catholic. Home: 193 S Harrison Ave Congers NY 10920 Office: Dominican College Blauvelt NY 10913

GARDIS, GILDA J., quality analyst; b. Jersey City, Jan. 16, 1944; d. William Patrick and Gilda Esther (Weber) Cornett; m. David Richard Gardis, Oct. 8, 1966 (div. 1981). Student Oceanside-Carlsbad Jr. Coll., Santa Monica City Coll. Prin. typist clk. UCLA, 1966-69, adminstrv. asst., 1969-73, acctg. asst., 1973-75, mgmt. services officer, 1975-79; mgmt. services officer U. Calif., San Diego, La Jolla, 1979-85; quality analyst Teledyne Kinetics, Solana Beach, Calif., 1986—. Active Oceanside High Sch. Booster Club, 1980-83. Recipient Tiffany award, Manpower, Carlsbad, Calif., 1985. Mem. Nat. Assn. Female Execs. Roman Catholic. Avocations: Tennis; bicycling; art; bowling. Home: 3559 Guava Way Oceanside CA 92054 Office: Teledyne Kinetics 410 S Cedros Solana Beach CA 92075

GARDNER, ANNE LANCASTER, lawyer; b. Corpus Christi, Tex., Aug. 19, 1942; d. Jack Quinn and DeWitte (Benton) Lancaster; B.A., U. Tex., 1964, LL.B., 1966; 1 son, Travis Gregory. Admitted to Tex. bar, 1966; asst. dir. continuing legal edn. State Bar Tex., 1966-67; law clk. to U.S. Dist. Ct. judge, 1967-71; partner firm Brown, Crowley, Simon & Peebles, Ft. Worth, 1971-78, Simon, Peebles, Haskell, Gardner & Betty, Ft. Worth, 1978-85, McLean, Sanders, Price, Mead & Ellis, P.C., Ft. Worth, 1985—. Fellow Tex. Bar Found.; mem. Am., Ft. Worth-Tarrant County (dir., v.p.) bar assns., State Bar Tex. (chmn. dist. 7 admissions com.), U. Tex. Law Sch. Assn. (dir.), Young Lawyers Assn. Ft. Worth, Kappa Beta Pi, Delta Zeta. Editor legal jours. Office: 100 Main Pl Fort Worth TX 76102

GARDNER, HOLLY HARTLEY, educational adminstrator; b. Mobile, Ala., Sept. 5, 1941; d. Julian O. and Mary E. (McKee) Hartley; m. Wayne Gardner, Aug. 1, 1981. B.S. in Edn., U. Ala., 1963; M.S. in Edn., Ga State U., 1976, postgrad., 1977—. Tchr. Atlanta Pub. Schs., 1963-68, Westminster Schs., Atlanta, 1968-77; prin. Joseph T. Walker Sch., Marietta, Ga., 1977-82; asst. prin., Pace Acad., Atlanta, 1982-84, prin. lower sch., 1984—; chmn. elem. prins. div. Atlanta Area Assn. Ind. Schs., 1980-82; mem. adv. bd. Ga. Youth Leadership Seminar, Hugh O'Brien Found., 1979-80, workshop leader. Bd. dirs. Met. Atlanta Crime Commn., Atlanta council Campfire Girls, Inc., Boys' Club Met. Atlanta, Jr. League Atlanta; active Atlanta Regional Commn. Task Force on Citizen Participation; speaker Ga. Conf. Volunteerism; vol. Atlanta Hist. Soc., Mus. Art, Humane Soc.; chmn. Community Bd. Inst. Republican. Methodist. Office: Pace Acad 966 W Paces Ferry Rd NW Atlanta GA 30327

GARDNER, INEZ MARIE, lawyer; b. Chgo., Aug. 17, 1948; d. Albert Jerome and Marie (Richards) Bernard; m. Isacc Gardner, Jr., Aug. 17, 1974. B.S., Chgo. State Coll., 1969; J.D., DePaul U., 1973; LL.M., U. Ill., 1974. Bar: Ill. 1975. Asst. state's atty. Cook County, Ill., 1976-80; sole practice trial atty. I.M. Gardner, Ltd., Chgo., 1981—; mem. fed. trial bar No. Dist. Ill.; panel atty. Community Law Project, Cook County Bar Assn., 1983-84. U. Ill. grad. fellow, 1974. Mem. ABA, Ill. Bar Assn., Chgo. Bar Assn., Cook County Bar Assn. Office: I M Gardner Ltd 6708 S Prairie Ave Suite 1 Chicago IL 60637

GARDNER, JANE KENDALL, state legislator; b. Montclair, N.J., Dec. 9, 1926; m. Walter H. Gardner; 3 sons, 3 daus. Student, Colby Jr. Coll. Vt. state rep., 1975-82; mem. Vt. State Senate, 1983—. Democrat. Episcopalian. Office: Vt State Capitol Bldg Montpelier VT 05602*

GARDNER, JEWELLE BAKER, business executive, interior design consultant; b. Ayden, N.C., May 23, 1925; d. Roland Ray and Helen Wingate (Jackson) Cannon; m. Paul Thomas Baker, July 25, 1956 (dec. 1963); children—Paula Jewelle, Paul Thomas; 1 stepdau., Blanche Baker Miller; m. Fred Calvin Gardner, Apr. 19, 1969 (dec. May 1983); 1 stepdau., Angela Gardner Jones. Student Woods Bus. Sch., New Bern, N.C., 1942-45; B.A., Am. Sch. Design, N.Y.C., 1948; B.F.A., U. N.C.-Greensboro, 1950. Dept. head Navy Supply, Cherry Point, N.C., 1941-45; ptnr. Cannons Paint & Wallpaper Co., Ayden, 1945-70; exec. v.p. Baker Furniture Co., Kinston, N.C., 1950-63; operator Cannon Farms, Ayden, 1956—; pres., treas. Baker Furniture Co., Kinston, 1963-69; owner Jewelle Baker Consultants, Kinston, 1969—; v.p. Gardner Homes, Elizabeth City, N.C., 1972-81; bus. cons. Gardner Constrn. Co., Kinston, 1975-81; bus. cons. Lenoir Plumbing & Heating Co., Kinston, 1975-81; chief exec. officer Gardner Homes, Elizabeth City, 1982—; chmn. bd., chief exec. officer Lenoir Plumbing & Heating Co., 1982—, Gardner Constrn. Co., 1982—; cons. Carolina Power & Light, 1963-65, N.C. Solar Energy Assn., 1977-79, Nutritional Therapy, Durham, 1979-81. Mem. Devel. Authority of Neuse River Council of Govts., 1984—. Columnist, Ayden Dispatch and Greenville News Leader, 1940-56; producer Performer Baker's commls., 1960-69. Mem. C. of C. Kinston (bd. dirs., v.p., chmn. retail mchts. div.), So. Retail Furniture Assn., Nat. Retail Furniture Assn., N.C. Mchts. Assn., Internat. Platform Assn., N.C. Farm Assn., Assoc. Gen. Contractors Am., N.C. Zool. Assn., N.C. Art Soc. Democrat. Mem. Ch. Disciples of Christ. Clubs: Kinston Country; Coral Bay, Pineknoll Golf and Country, Sea Water Marina (Atlantic Beach, N.C.). Home: 1708 Elizabeth Dr Kinston NC 28501 Office: Gardner Constrn Co PO Drawer 1278 Kinston NC 28501

GARDNER, LELA MARSHALL, speech pathologist; b. Wymore, Nebr., June 2, 1908; d. Virgil Ralph and Jeanie Mae (Warriner) Marshall; B.S. in Edn., U. Nebr., 1930; M.S. in Public Adminstrn., Washington U., St. Louis, 1932; postgrad. Columbia U., 1958-59, 60-61; m. John Hall Gardner, June 7, 1932; 1 dau., Marvel Jean Gardner. Speech pathologist Toledo Hearing League, 1959-60; grad. asst. Bowling Green (Ohio) State U., 1959-60; speech pathologist Bd. Edn., Newark, 1960-63, Johnstone Tng. Sch., Bordentown, N.J., 1963-66, Bd. Edn., Frederick County, Md., 1966-76, Western Md. Center, Hagerstown, 1976-77; free lance writer weekly Letters on nat. and internat. affairs, 1976—; cons. speech pathology State Home for Boys, Jamesburg, N.J., 1964-67. Mem. nat. adv. bd. Am. Security Council, 1973; Founding mem. Am. Media Network, 1985; life mem. Am. Conservation Union, 1973, John Birch Soc., 1973; founder Center for Internat. Securities Studies, 1977; sponsor Am. Council for World Freedom, 1972; pres. W.Va. Panhandle chpt. Eagle Forum, 1977; active Coalition for Peace Through Strength, Com. to Restore the Constn., 1974, Found. of Law and Soc., 1978; mem. bd. policy Liberty Lobby, 1973-81; bd. dirs. Northampton County (Pa.) Soc. for Crippled Children and Adults, 1951-55, dir. public relations, 1953-55. Recipient tchrs. cert., N.J., 1960, life cert., 1965, Advanced Profl. cert. in speech and hearing, Md., 1969. Mem. Am. Speech and Hearing Assn. (life mem., cert. clin. competence), AAUW (arts chmn. Easton, Pa. br., dir.), Mensa, Internat. Soc. Philos. Enquiry, Citizens for the Republic, Ams. Against Union Control of Govt., Com. to Restore the Constitution (bd. dirs.), Nat. Polit. Action Com., Jefferson County Rep. Club, Citizens Com. for Right to Keep and Bear Arms, Council Interam. Security, Nat. Rep. Congl. Com., Populist Conservative Tax Coalition, Internat. Platform Assn., Pi Lambda Theta. Republican. Club: Women's (music chmn. Easton). Home: Route 1 Box 240 Jefferson Terr Charles Town WV 25414

GARDNER, LINDA DIANE, elementary educator; b. Binghamton, N.Y., July 8, 1948; d. Ralph Douglas and Dorothy Alice (Pattillo) Smith; m. Jack E. Gardner, Apr. 10, 1971; 1 child, Chad Byron. B.A., Harding U., 1970; B.S.Edn., Henderson State U., 1973. Elem. sci. tchr. Glenwood Schs., Ark., 1971-85; tchr. math., sci., social studies Lake Hamilton Sch., Pearcy, Ark., 1985—; coordinator Sci. Fair, 1980-84. Pres., v.p. Jaycettes, Glenwood, 1972-73; treas. Glenwood Women's League, 1978-79. Mem. Ch. of Christ. Avocations: needlework; interior decorating; landscaping; reading. Home: PO Box 387 Glenwood AR 71943

GARDNER, LYNN SULLIVAN, public relations specialist; b. N.Y.C., Sept. 30, 1957; d. John Joseph and Christina Mary (Broderick) Sullivan; m. Randy Alan Gardner, Oct. 9, 1982. B.A., Boston Coll., 1978; postgrad. New Sch. Social Research, N.Y.C., 1985. Assoc. producer Miss Universe, Inc., N.Y.C., 1979-81, Time-Life Video, N.Y.C., 1981; script supr. RG Prodns./Warner Bros., N.Y.C. and Los Angeles, 1981-83; asst. Elite Model Mgmt., N.Y.C., 1983-84; pub. relations media specialist The Solomon Orgn., N.Y.C., 1984—; pres. Randalyn Prodns. Admission counselor Boston Coll., Chestnut Hill, 1979—; activist Associated Humane Socs., Newark, N.J., 1982—; foster parent Christian Children's Fund, Zambia, Africa, 1983—. Mem. Nat. Assn. Female Execs., Media Network (officer Boston Coll. Group), Am. Women in Radio and Television, Nat. Mus. Women in Arts, ASPCA. Democrat. Roman Catholic. Avocations: collecting crystal cats; acting; children's theatre; reading; traveling. Home: 35 Clark St #4-D Brooklyn Heights NY 11201 Office: The Solomon Orgn 18 E 48th St New York NY 10017

GARDNER, MAMIE ESOUBELL, child care administrator; b. Victoria, Tex., Feb. 1, 1940; d. George Dennis and Pearl Ella (Wade) Langley; m. Morris Eugene Gardner, Sept. 13, 1962; children—Marcerlein, Monica. Student Kent State U., Ohio, 1978. Owner, adminstr. Summit Lake Child Devel., Inc., Akron, Ohio, 1978—, Kandy Kane Christian Day Care, Inc., Akron, 1974—; cons. Performax, Inc., Akron, 1984—; trainer, presenter Akron Urban League, 1985—. Mem. child devel. adv. com. U. Akron, 1982, Akron Dept. Human Services, 1986; bd. dirs. Akron Police Community Dialogue Assn., 1986; v.p. Summit County Dirs. Assn. Recipient Christian Edn. award House of The Lord, Akron, 1980, Service to Children award, Summit County Dirs. Assn., 1980; named Bus. Woman of Yr., Negro Bus. and Profl. Women, 1985. Mem. Nat. Assn. Edn. Young Children, Nat. Assn. Female Execs., Black Child Devel. Assn., Assn. Excellence in Child Care. Democrat. Avocations: reading, travel, sports. Office: Kandy Kane Christian Day Care Inc 999 Copley Rd Akron OH 44320

GARDNER, MARIA EVRARD, pharmacist; b. Allentown, Pa., June 20, 1949; d. August E. and Helen Evrard; B.S. in Pharmacy, Phila. Coll. Pharmacy, 1972. Pharm.D., 1974; m. Lee Allan Gardner, July 5, 1975; children—Anne Christine, Megan Marie. Intern, Thomas Jefferson U. Hosp., 1972-73, resident in pharmacy, 1973-74, clin. pharmacist med. service, 1974-76, primary care pharmacist, 1974-76; adj. clin. instr. Phila. Coll. Pharmacy and Sci., 1974-76; outpatient clin. pharmacist Tucson VA Hosp., 1976-78; clin. pharmacist Tucson Gen. Hosp., 1978-85, Project AgeWell, 1986—; asst. prof. pharmacy practice U. Ariz., Tucson, 1977—. Mem. Am. Soc. Hosp. Pharmacists, So. Ariz. Soc. Hosp. Pharmacists (dir. 1979-80, sec. 1977-78), Ariz. Council Hosp. Pharmacists, Am. Assn. Colls. Pharmacy, Rho Chi. Republican. Roman Catholic. Contbr. articles on pharmacology to profl. publs. Home: 1432 N Sarnoff Dr Tucson AZ 85715 Office: College Pharmacy Univ Arizona Tucson AZ 85721

GARDNER, MARILYN LOUISE, journalist; b. Rockford, Ill., Oct. 30, 1942; d. Frederic Delwin and Camille Frances (Jensen) Utter; m. Paul Hunt Gardner, Nov. 6, 1965; 1 dau., Julie Stewart. B.A., Principia Coll., 1964. Editorial asst. Christian Sci. Monitor, Boston, 1964-65, copywriter, promotion dept., 1978-80, Living Page editor, 1980-83, Home and Family editor, 1984-85, staff wirter, 1986—; continuity writer Sta. WTVO-TV, Rockford, Ill., 1968-69; tech. editor Mitre Corp., McLean, Va., 1971; judge newswriting contest Pa. Women's Press Assn., 1984. Merit badge counselor for journalism, Boy Scouts Am., Metacom-Dist., Needham-Dedham, Mass., 1983—; mem. nat. adv. panel Harvard Family Research Project, 1984. Recipient Marjory Mills award New Eng. Woman's Press Assn., 1985. Mem. Phi Alpha Eta. Republican. Christian Scientist. Home: 14 Mann Ave Needham MA 02192 Office: Christian Sci Monitor One Norway St Boston MA 02115

GARDNER, MARJORIE HYER, chemist, educator; b. Logan, Utah, Apr. 25, 1923; d. Saul Edward and Gladys Ledingham (Christiansen) Hyer; B.S., Utah State U., 1946, Ph.D. (hon.), 1975; M.A., Ohio State U., 1958, Ph.D., 1960; cert. Ednl. Mgmt. Inst., Harvard U., 1975; m. Paul Leon Gardner, June 6, 1947; children—Pamela Jean, Mary Elizabeth. Tchr. sci., journalism and English high schs., Utah, Nev., Ohio, 1947-56; instr. Ohio State U., Columbus, 1957-60; asst. exec. dir. Nat. Sci. Tchrs. Assn., 1961-64; vis. prof. Australia, India, Yugoslavia, 1965; assoc. dean, dir. Bur. Ednl. Research and Field Service, College Park, Md., 1975-76; dir. Sci. Teaching Center, U. Md., College Park, 1976-77, prof. chemistry, 1964-84; dir. Lawrence Hall Sci., U. Calif.-Berkeley, 1984—; div. dir. NSF, 1979-81; cons. UNESCO, NSF. UNESCO grantee, 1970—; NSF grantee, 1964—. Fellow AAAS (council), Am. Inst. Chemistry; mem. Am. Chem. Soc., Chemistry Assn. Md. (pres.), Internat. Union of Pure and Applied Chemistry (exec. com.), Internat. Orgn. Chemistry in Devel. (edn. panel), Assn. Edn. of Tchrs. of Sci., Nat. Assn. Research in Sci. Teaching, Nat. Sci. Tchrs. Assn., Am. Assn. Higher Edn., Soc. Coll. Sci. Tchrs. (pres.), Fulbright Alumni Assn. (pres., dir.), Phi Delta Kappa, Phi Kappa Phi. Author: Chemistry in the Space Age, 1965; editor: Theory in Action, 1964, Vistas of Sci. Series, 1961-63; Investigating the Earth, 1968, Interdisciplinary Approaches to Chemistry, 1973, 1978-79; Under Roof, Dome and Sky, 1974, Toward Continuous Professional Development: Designs and Directions, 1976; contbr. articles in on chemistry and sci. edn. to profl. jours. Home: 517 Vista Height Rd Richmond CA 94805 Office: Lawrence Hall of Sci U Calif Berkeley CA 94702

GARDNER, MARY BERTHA HOEFT CHADWICK, businesswoman, former postmaster; b. Vernal, Utah, June 13, 1914; d. Edward and Hazel (Burgess) Hoeft; B.S. in Elem. Edn., Utah State U., 1950; m. Rulon Chadwick, Sept. 3, 1935 (div. July 1949); children—Mary Jo Chadwick Wight, Adriana Chadwick Forsgren; m. Leon D. Gardner, July 14, 1951 (dec. May 1974). Bookkeeper, Model Dairy, 1935-49, Weber Central Dairy, 1949-51, Bishops Storehouse, 1950-51; sch. tchr., Ogden, Utah, 1950-51; clk. Post Office, Honeyville, Utah, 1956-72, postmaster, 1972-81; ret., 1981; now propr. store and campground, Mantua, Utah. Pres., Relief Soc. Ch. Jesus Ch. of Latter-day Saints, mem. stake bd. relief soc., mem. stake bd. Sunday Sch., mem. stake bd. mut. improvement assn. orgn. Mem. Nat. League Postmasters (exec. v.p. state br., editor newsletter), Nat. Assn. Postmasters, AAUW (treas., rec. sec. 1983-84), Daus. Utah Pioneers, Bus. and Profl. Women's Club (treas. Brigham City), Women's Legis. Council Utah. Home: 8440 N Hwy 69 Honeyville UT 84314

GARDNER, MEREDITH LEE, speaker on aging issues, management consultant; b. Providence, Nov. 25, 1941; d. Leo and Gertrude Gloria (Ketover) Gleklen; m. Daniel Ezra Mahni, May 28, 1971 (div. 1980). A.A., Colby Sawyer Coll., New London, N.H., 1961; B.A., NYU, 1963; M.A. in Devel. Psychology, Columbia U., 1965. Dir. Office Student Activities, Hunter Coll., N.Y.C., 1965-66; dir. Internat. Office, Boston Coll., Chestnut Hill, Mass., 1966-72; dir. ret. sr. vol. program Commonwealth of Mass., Boston, 1972-74, dir. Office Citizen Participation, 1974-76; research assoc. Hadley Lackwood, N.Y.C., 1976-78; assoc. Gilbert Tweed Assocs., N.Y.C., 1978-80; sr. assoc. MBA Mgmt., Inc., 1980-81; pres. Too Young To Retire, N.Y.C., 1981—; condr. seminars, pub. speaker on aging. Author: My Friend Frank, 1985. Mem. Nat. Speakers Assn., Am. Assn. Ret. Persons, Council on Aging, Mature Outlook, Northeastern Gerontol. Assn., Understanding Aging. Republican. Jewish. Avocations: sailing; bicycling; flea market hunting; dancing; talking with older people. Home: 321 W 78th St New York NY 10024

GARDNER, NATALIE NELLIE JAGLOM, advt. agy. exec.; b. Cernauti, Rumania; came to U.S., 1939, naturalized, 1946; b. Abraham and Nadia (Shoenberg) Jaglom; student Ohio State U., 1943, N.Y. U., 1944, U. Calif., Berkeley, 1945; m. Ralph David Gardner, Apr. 9, 1952; children—Ralph David, John Jaglom, Peter Jaglom, James Jaglom. Dir. Ralph D. Gardner Advt., N.Y.C., 1955—; pres. Gardner Internat., Inc., 1981—; dir. N.Y. Commodities Corp., Saveurs, Inc., Overseas Barters, Inc. Vol., ARC, 1944; hosp. vol. Am. Women's Vol. Services, 1944-45; active UN Host Family Program. Home: 135 Central Park W New York NY 10023 Office: 745 Fifth Ave New York NY 10151

GARDNER, ORIN-JANE BRAGG, educational administrator; b. Mansfield, Ohio, May 8; d. Charles Treat and Orin-Dorio (Pearson) Bragg; m. Delvan Charles Gardner, Oct. 12, 1940 (dec.); 1 child, Dean Cameron James. B.A., Wayne U., 1930, cert., 1931, M.Ed., 1950, Ed.D., 1965. Cert. marriage and family counselor, Fla. Tchr. lit. Detroit Bd. Edn.; tchr. high sch., journalism and English; prin., pres. Shores Acad. Collegium, Miami Shores, Fla., 1968—; founder, pres. Sch. for Learning Inc. and The Spiral Learning Method. Author: Role of Teacher in Detroit Education from 1701-1965. Registrar Nat. Soc. Daughters of Am. Revolution, 1937, 72-78, regent, 1978-82; founder, pres. Quota Internat., Detroit, 1950-62; pres. Fla. Fedn. Republican Women, Biscayne chpt., 1978-80. Mem. Assn. of Career Tng. Schs. (bd. dirs. 1972, accreditation com.), Miami Shores C. of C., Fla. Ind. Schs. Assn. (charter mem.), Nat. Assn Secondary Sch. Prins., Alpha Gamma Delta (founder chpt. 1957), Sigma Sigma (founder, pres. Wayne State U.), Alpha Kappa Delta. Republican. Methodist. Club: Miami Shores Country. Avocations: curriculum study for gifted; genealogy; metaphysics study of light. Home: 100 NE 99 St Miami Shores FL 33138 Also: 2600 North Surf Rd Hollywood Beach FL 33019 Office: Sch for Learning Inc Shore Acad Collegium PO Drawer 1339-53 Miami Shores FL 33153

GARDNER, PHYLLIS CHRISTIE, state government program administrator, consultant; b. Winnsboro, S.C., Dec. 29, 1939; d. Lewis L. and Pauline (Bowers) Christie; m. Max Donovan Gardner, June 30, 1961; children—Max D., Paula Christie. B.S. in Bus. Adminstrn., U. S.C.-Columbia, 1975. Clk., S.C. Employment Security Commn., Columbia, 1957-70, manpower specialist, 1970-75; counselor S.C. Retirement System, Columbia, 1976-79, preretirement edn. mgr., 1979—. Editor: Systems Update, 1979—. Mem. com. S.C. Employees Suggestion Program for Budget and Control Bd., Columbia, 1982—. Mem. Am. Soc. Tng. and Devel., S.C. State Employees Assn. (dir. 1983—), Internat. Personnel and Mgmt. Assn. (com. chmn. 1983), Nat. Pre-Retirement Edn. Council (founder, bd. dirs. 1983—, sec. treas. 1983—). Club: Women's Profl. Orgn. (Columbia). Home: Route 2 Box 118-A Lexington SC 29072 Office: SC Retirement System PO Box 11960 Capitol Station Columbia SC 29211

GARDNER, TRUDI YORK, lawyer, insurance company executive; b. Portland, Oreg., Mar. 19, 1947; d. Harry and Martha (Gevurtz) York; m. Alan Joel Gardner, Dec. 19, 1971; 1 child, Jordan Casey. B.A., UCLA, 1969; M.S., Portland State U., 1971; postgrad. N.Y. Law Sch., 1975-76; J.D. Lewis and Clark Law Sch., 1977. Bar: Washington 1978, U.S. Dist. Ct. (we. dist.) Wash. 1979; cert. tchr. Calif., Oreg. Law clk. U.S. Atty.'s Office (so. dist.) N.Y.C., 1976, to law firm, Portland, Oreg., 1977; fin. relations specialist Puget Sound Power & Light Co., Bellevue, Wash., 1978-79; asst. atty. gen. Dept. Labor and Industries, State of Wash., Seattle, 1979-80; sole practice, Bellevue, 1980-81; regional atty. for Mont., Idaho, Wash. and Oreg., Ins. Corp. of Am., Houston, 1981—, regional v.p. for Mont., Idaho, Utah, Wyo., Wash. and Oreg., 1984—; curriculum cons. Portland (Oreg.) Pub. Schs., 1977. Assoc. editor: Multnomah Lawyer, Multnomah County Bar Assn., Portland, 1973. Contbr. articles, cover stories to Sunday supplement of The Oregonian, radio scripts for Am. Heritage Assn. to Sta. KWJJ; contbr. short stories to mags. Mem. King County United Way Conf. Panel for Developmentally Disabled, Seattle, 1978-79. Mem. Washington State Bar Assn. (pub. relations com. 1978-81), Seattle-King County Bar Assn., Portland City Club, Seattle Mcpl. League, Pi Sigma Alpha, Pi Lambda Theta. Clubs: Women's University (Seattle); Bellevue Athletic. Home: 2921 130th Pl NE Bellevue WA 98005 Office: Ins Corp Am 10604 NE 38th Pl Suite 118 Kirkland WA 98033

GARDNER-LANIER, PATRICIA ANN, accountant; b. Waukegan, Ill., July 27, 1958; d. Johnny Lee, Sr. and Mary Lee (Stackhouse) Gardner. B.S., So. Ill. U., 1980. C.P.A., Ill., Corp. auditor Baxter Travenol Labs., Deerfield, Ill., 1980-82, sr. auditor, 1982; real estate auditor Prudential Ins. Co., Houston, 1982-84, assoc. real estate and acctg. mgr., 1984—; Bd. dirs. Shiloh Baptist Ch. Fed. Credit Union, Waukegan, 1982-83; vol. counselor Campus Life div. Youth for Christ, Houston, 1983—. Mem. Am. Inst. C.P.A.s, Nat. Assn. Black Accountants (co-chmn. student chpt. com. 1983—), Delta Sigma Theta. Office: Prudential Ins Co 1100 Louisiana Houston TX 77002

GARELS, ANNE, television news correspondent, journalist. Student Middlebury Coll.; B.A., Harvard U., 1972. Editor Weidenfeld and Nicolson Pub. Co.,

Eng.; researcher/producer, prodn. assoc. ABC-TV News, N.Y., 1975-78, Moscow corr., 1979-82, State Dept. corr., 1982-84, Central Am. corr., 1984-85; State Dept. corr. NBC News, 1985—. Address: care NBC News 4001 Nebraska Ave NW Washington DC 20016*

GARFIELD, JOAN BARBARA, mathematics/statistics educator; b. Milw., May 4, 1950; d. Sol. L. and Amy L. (Nusbaum) G.; m. Michael G. Luxenberg, Aug. 17, 1980; children—Harlan Ross and Rebecca Ellen (twins). Student, U. Chgo., 1968; B.S., U. Wis., 1972; M.A., U. Minn., 1978, Ph.D., 1981. Asst. prof. math./stats. The Gen. Coll., U. Minn., Mpls., 1981—, coordinator research and evaluation, 1984—; created various tables on evaluations of coll. retention programs, 1979-82, 85; research interpreter Nat. Orgn. Mothers of Twins Club. Mem. Am. Statis. Assn., Am. Assn. Higher Edn., Am. Ednl. Research Assn., Assn. Study Higher Edn., Council on Adult and Experimental Learning. Jewish. Club: Mpls. Twins Topics (research chmn. 1984—). Research on teaching and learning stats. Avocations: violin; viola; running. Office: Div Sci Bus and Math 106 Nicholson Hall General College Univ Minnesota 216 Pillsbury Ave SE Minneapolis MN 55455

GARFUNKEL, SANDRA GREEN, sweater manufacturing company executive; b. Houston, Oct. 24, 1942; d. Sidney William and Shanal (Galperin) Turboff; m. Stephen L. Green, June 21, 1961 (div. July 1976); children—Daniel, Gary, Scott; m. George M. Garfunkel, Aug. 21, 1983; stepchildren—Jonathon, Jill Ann. Reporter Great Neck Newsmag., N.Y., 1973-75; regional dir. leasing Net Properties, Great Neck, 1975-78; pres. Paavia Fashions Ltd., N.Y.C., 1978—. Club: Beachpoint (Mamaroneck, N.Y.). Office: Paavia Fashions Ltd 512 7th Ave New York NY 10018

GARGANO, FRANCINE ANN, lawyer; b. Plainfield, N.J., Feb. 10, 1957; d. Rosalie Janice (Ferrin) Gargano. B.A., Seton Hall U., 1980; J.D. cum laude, Detroit Coll. of Law, 1983. Bar: N.J. 1983. Sole practice, South Plainfield, N.J., 1983—; dir. YWCA Legal Clinic, Plainfield, 1983—; Union County coordinator Haitian Pro Bono Projects, ABA, Plainfield, 1983—; research asst. prof. Detroit Coll. Law, Detroit, 1980-83. Trustee Plainfield Area YWCA, 1983-84; bd. dirs. Haifian Advancement Assn., Elizabeth, N.J., 1983-84. Recipient Internat. Legal Scholar award Detroit Coll. Law Internat. Law Soc., 1980-82, Jessup Internat. Law Competition award, 1982; H. Rakol Scholarship award Detroit Bar Assn., 1982. Mem. Union County Bar Assn., N.J. Bar Assn., ABA, Detroit Coll. Law Internat. Law Soc. (pres. 1980-82). Democrat. Roman Catholic. Office: Francine A Gargano Atty at Law 2101 Park Ave South Plainfield NJ 07080

GARGANO, JOAN CAROL, health physics technologist; b. Greenville, Miss., Nov. 24, 1955; d. George William and Barbara Louise (Harris) Zerkovich; m. William Louis Bruce Gargano, Aug. 5, 1984. A.A. in Life Sci., Yuba Coll., 1975; B.S. in Biochemistry, U. Calif.-Davis, 1977. Research assoc. U. Calif., Davis, 1978-82; asst. radiation safety officer U. Calif., Davis Med. Ctr., Sacramento, 1982—. Mem. Health Physics Soc., U.S. Parachute Assn. Democrat. Office: Univ Calif Davis Med Ctr Health Physics Office 2315 Stockton Blvd Sacramento CA 95817

GARIBALDI, MARIE L., state supreme court justice; B.A., Conn. Coll., 1956; LL.B., Columbia Law Sch., 1959; LL.M. in Tax Law, NYU, 1963; Bar: N.J., N.Y., D.C. With Office of Regional Counsel, IRS, N.Y.C., 1960-66; ptnr. Riker, Danzig, Scherer, Hyland & Perretti, Newark, 1966-83; assoc. justice N.J. Supreme Ct., Trenton, 1983—; lectr. NYU Tax Inst., N.J. Inst. Continuing Legal Edn., Seton Hall U. Tax Conf., N.J. State Bar Assn., Estate Planning Council of Central N.J., Jewish Community Found., LWV; dir. N.J. Bell Telephone Co., Washington Savs. Bank; acting mcpl. judge City of Weehawken (N.J.), 1973-75. Contbr. articles to profl. jours. Trustee St. Peter's Coll.; co-chair Thomas Kean's campaign for gov. of N.J., 1981; active Gov.-Elect Thomas Kean's Transition Team, 1981; active Gov. Byrne's Commn. on Dept. of Commerce, 1981; chair Weehawken Charter Commn., 1968-69. Recipient Disting. Alumni award NYU, 1982; Disting. Alumni award Columbia U., 1982. Fellow Am. Bar Found.; mem. N.J. State Bar Assn. (pres.), ABA (chmn. standards of tax practice com., sect. of taxation), Nat. Conf. Lawyers and C.P.A.s, N.J. C. of C. (bd. dirs.), Columbia U. Sch. Law Alumni Assn. (bd. dirs.). Office: NJ Old Hudson County Courthouse 500 Newark Ave Jersey City NJ 07306

GARISON, CATHY, banker; b. San Antonio, Aug. 14, 1951; d. Robert William and Vernell (Taylor) Bernhard; m. Richard L. Garison, Apr. 25, 1974. B.A., Trinity U., San Antonio, 1972. Editor Fox Stanley Photo Products Co., San Antonio, 1972; mgmt. trainee Nat. Bank of Commerce, San Antonio, 1972-74; publs. specialist United Services Automobile Assn., San Antonio, 1974-76; mktg. coordinator Frost Bank, San Antonio, 1976-78, asst. v.p., 1978-80, v.p. mktg., 1981—. Bd. dirs. Family Service Assn., San Antonio, 1982-85, Funding Info. Ctr., San Antonio, 1984—, Hospice San Antonio, 1985—. Mem. Pub. Relations Soc. Am. (accredited) Pub. Relations Found. Tex., Am. Mktg. Assn., Women in Communications, Conservation Soc. San Antonio, Sigma Delta Chi. Home: 122 Audrey Alene St San Antonio TX 78216 Office: Frost Bank PO Box 1600 San Antonio TX 78296

GARITY, JOAN PATRICIA, nurse, educator; b. Quincy, Mass., Apr. 29, 1944; d. Philip Francis and Virginia (Corcoran) Garity. B.S., Boston Coll., 1966; M.Ed., Northeastern U., 1971; Ed.D., Boston U., 1985. R.N., Mass. Vol. nursing clinic Mt. St. Joseph Acad., Mandeville, Jamaica, W.I., 1966-67; staff nurse Boston City Hosp., 1967-68; staff nurse Quincy City Hosp., Mass., 1968; dir. inservice edn. Quincy City Hosp., 1968-70, staff nurse recovery room, 1970-71; instr. staff edn. and nursing studies Mass. Gen. Hosp., Boston, 1971-80, coordinator mgmt. edn., staff edn. and nursing studies dept. nursing, 1980—; cons., lectr. in field. Contbr. articles to profl. jours. Mem. Gov.'s Adv. Council on Continuing Edn. for Nurses, Boston, 1985—. Am. Orgn. Nurse Execs. scholar Am. Nurses Found., 1984. Mem. Am. Nurses Assn., Mass. Nurses Assn. (mem. Council on Continuing Edn. 1980-81, co-chair Commn. on Continuing Edn. 1982-83, Cabinet on Continuing Edn. 1984), Sigma Theta Tau, Pi Lambda Theta, Alpha Gamma. Democrat. Roman Catholic. Avocations: novels; museums; art; concerts; traveling. Home: 9 Tingley Rd East Braintree MA 02184 Office: Mass Gen Hosp Fruit St Boston MA 02114

GARLAND, JOAN BRUDER, social worker; b. Cleve., Sept. 30, 1931; d. Henry Ignatius and Mary (Maher) Bruder; A.B., Mt. Holyoke Coll., 1952; postgrad. Wellesley Coll., 1952-53, U. Sao Paulo (Brazil), 1965-66; M.S., Sarah Lawrence Coll., 1974; M.S. in Social Work, Columbia U., 1977; m. Paul Griffith Garland, Aug. 28, 1954; children—Bonnie (dec.), Patrick, John, Cathryn. Grad. asst. chemistry dept. Wellesley (Mass.) Coll., 1952-53; chemist Polaroid Corp., Cambridge, Mass., 1953-54, 55-56; CAPES research fellow U. Sao Paulo, 1954-55; clin. instr. retardation N.Y. Med. Coll., Valhalla, 1978-80; social worker, psychiat. day treatment program Jewish Child Care Assn., Pleasantville (N.Y.) Cottage Sch., 1980; founder, Crime Victims Assistance Agy., Inc., 1981. Treas. council Girl Scouts, Sao Paulo, 1965-67; bd. dirs. PTA, 1972-73; bd. deacons Scarsdale (N.Y.) Congl. Ch., 1975; patient rep. White Plains (N.Y.) Med. Center, 1977; bd. dirs. Hudson Valley chpt. Leukemia Soc., 1981-83. Cert. in family therapy, Center for Family Learning, Phila. Child Guidance Clinic; cert. social worker, N.Y. State. Fellow Soc. Clin. Social Work Psychotherapists, Am. Orthopsychiat. Assn., Mem. Nat. Assn. Social Workers, Acad. Cert. Social Workers, AAUP, Nat. Soc. Genetic Counselors, N.Y. Acad. Scis. Clubs: Mt. Holyoke, Wellesley (Fairfield). Home: 139 Old Church Rd Greenwich CT 06830

GARLAND, JOAN DONAGHY, town administrator; b. Palmyra, N.J., Oct. 31, 1926; d. Atlee Burpee and Agnes Marie (Kempf) Donaghy; m. Carl Wesley Garland, July 30, 1955; children—Leslie, Andrew. B.S., Douglass Coll., 1948. Tchr. Thornton Acad., Saco, Maine, 1948-50; data processor Saco-Lowell Shops, Saco, 1950-53; data analyst Lincoln Lab., MIT, Cambridge, 1953-56; adminstr. Town of Belmont, Mass., 1975—; notary pub. State of Mass., 1978—. Mem. Rep. Town Meeting, Belmont, 1974—, Met. Boston Transit Authority Adv. Bd., Boston, 1975—. Mem. Mass. Mcpl. Mgmt. Assn., Internat. City Mgmt. Assn. Avocations: puzzles; reading; hiking. Home: 4 Edward St Belmont MA 02178 Office: Town Hall 455 Concord Ave Belmont MA 02178

GARLAND, LARETTA MATTHEWS, nurse, educator; b. Jacksonville, Fla., Sept. 23, 1920; d. Wilburn Louis and Clyde Marian (Chamberlin) Matthews; m. John B. Garland, Mar. 2, 1946; children—John B., Brien F., Amy Gwin. B.S. in Nursing, Emory U., 1950; B.A., U. Fla., 1951; M.Ed., Emory U., 1953; grad. study in counseling, 1968-70; Ed.D., U. Ga., 1975; grad. cert. in gerontology, Ga. State U., 1981. Staff nurse Lakeland Morrell Meml. Hosp. (Fla.), 1942; asst. prof. Med. Coll. Ga., 1965-67; instr. Emory U., 1952-54, assoc. prof. nursing, 1967-72, prof., 1972—, asst. dean, 1983—; ednl. psychologist, cardiovascular nurse specialist; gerontol. nurse, gerontologist. Author: Coping Behaviors and Nursing, 1982; contbr. articles to profl. jours., chpts. to textbooks. Served with AUS, 1942-45. Decorated Bronze Star, service medals. HEW fellow, 1966-67, research grantee, 1974-77; Nell Hodgson Woodruff grantee, 1978-80. Mem. Am. Nurses Assn., Nat. League Nursing, Am. Psychol. Assn., Am. Assn. Counseling and Devel., Am. Heart Assn., Gerontol. Soc., Council Nurse Researchers, Alpha Chi Omega, Sigma Theta Tau, Alpha Kappa Delta, Kappa Delta. Pi, Omicron Delta Kappa. Republican. Methodist. Office: Nell Hodgson Woodruff Sch Nursing Emory U Atlanta GA 30322

GARLAND, LINDA COOMBS, commercial producer; b. Glenridge, N.J., May 30, 1946; d. Samuel Holcomb and Ann (Thurman) Coombs; m. Robert Boaks, Mar. 15, 1968 (div. May 1970); m. 2d, Robert William Garland, July 16, 1976; 1 child, Skylar Delaney. B.A., Mich. State U., 1968. Sec., N. W. Ayer, Inc., Chgo., 1970-74, asst. producer, 1974-76; producer Post Keyes Gardener, Chgo., 1976-77, Foote, Cone & Belding, Chgo., 1977-79; sr. producer N. W. Ayer, Inc., Chgo., 1979-82; free lance producer, Chgo., 1982—.

GARLAND, SARA G., senatorial legislative assistant; b. New Rockford, N.D., May 1, 1946; d. John A. and Annabelle (Stephenson) G.; B.A., U. N.D., 1968, M.A., 1972; m. Kim E. Uhl, Aug. 10, 1979; children—Stephanie Garland, Joshua Edward, Jonathan Stewart. Reporter, Sta. KXJB-TV, Fargo, N.D., 1968-69; instr. speech, U. N.D., 1969-72; asst. dir. public affairs Corp. Public Broadcasting, 1972-76; legis. asst. to Rep. Margaret Heckler, 1976-77, to Sen. Quentin Burdick, 1977—; asst. Senate Appropriations Com. Mem. Capitol Hill Women's Polit. Caucus. Presbyterian. Home: 137 13th St NE Washington DC 20002 Office: Room 511 Hart Senate Office Bldg Washington DC 20510

GARLAND, SYLVIA DILLOF, lawyer; b. N.Y.C., June 4, 1919; d. Morris and Frieda (Gassner) Dillof; m. Albert Garland, May 4, 1942; children—Margaret Garland Clunie, Paul B. B.A., Bklyn. Coll., 1939; J.D. cum laude, N.Y. Law Sch., 1960. Bar: N.Y., 1960, U.S. Ct. Appeals (2d cir.), 1965, U.S. Ct. Claims, 1965, U.S. Supreme Ct., 1967, U.S. Customs Ct., 1972, U.S. Ct. Appeals (5th cir.), 1979. Assoc. firm Borden, Skidell, Fleck and Steindler, Jamaica, N.Y., 1960-61, Fields, Zimmerman, Skodnick & Segall, Jamaica, 1961-65, Marshall, Brater, Greene, Allison & Tucker, N.Y.C., 1965-68; law sec. to N.Y. Supreme Ct. justice, Suffolk County, 1968-70; ptnr. firm Hofheimer, Gartlir, Gottlieb & Gross, N.Y.C., 1970—; asst. adj. prof. N.Y. Law Sch., 1974-79; mem. com. on character and fitness N.Y. State Supreme Ct., 1st Jud. Dept., 1985—. Author: Workman's Compensation, 1957; Wills, 1959; Labor Law, 1962; contbg. author: Guardians and Custodians, 1970; editor-in-chief Law Rev. Jour., N.Y. Law Forum, 1959-60 (service award 1960); contbr. article to mag. Trustee N.Y. Law Sch., 1979—; pres. Oakland chpt. B'nai B'rith, Bayside, N.Y., 1955-57. Recipient Disting. Alumnus award, N.Y. Law Sch., 1978. Mem. ABA (litigation sect.), N.Y. State Bar Assn., Queen's County Bar Assn. (sec. civil practice 1960-79), N.Y. Law Sch. Alumni Assn. (pres. 1976-77), N.Y. Law Forum Alumni Assn. (pres. 1963-65). Jewish. Home: 425 E 58th St New York NY 10022

GARLICK, NANCY BUCKINGHAM, conductor, musician; b. White Plains, N.Y., Feb. 1, 1946; d. Robert and Betty (Bonnar) Buckingham; B.S., SUNY, Potsdam, 1968; M.M., Manhattan Sch. Music, 1970; postgrad. Ecoles Americaines des Beaux Arts, Fontainebleau, 1973, Tanglewood, 1974; m. D. Stevens Garlick, Aug. 30, 1980. Clarinetist, Am. Wind Symphony, 1969, Opera Orch. of N.Y., 1970, Nat. Orch. Assn., 1970, New Haven Symphony, 1971-75, Waterbury Symphony, 1974, Lakeside Symphony, 1976-81, Shenandoah Valley Music Festival of Am. Symphony Orch. League, 1977-78, Mo. Symphony Soc. Performing Arts Center, 1979, Am. Inst. Mus. Studies Orch., Graz, Austria, 1983; music dir. Wooster (Ohio) Symphony Orch., 1977-83; asso. prof. music Coll. Wooster, 1975-85; clarinetist Wooster Trio, 1980-83; music dir. Youth Orch. Charlottesville/Albemarle, 1986—; instr. clarinet U. Va., 1985—; prin. clarinetist Charlottesville Symphony, 1985—; N.Y. debut Wooster Trio, 1981; soloist Boston Pops Orch., in Weber's Concertino, New Haven Coluseum, 1973. Westchester Music Tchrs. Assn. grantee, 1964; Coll. Wooster Faculty grantee, 1977; recipient Nat. Orch. Assn. Accomplishment award, 1970. Mem. Internat. Clarinet Soc., Coll. Music Soc., Am. Fedn. Musicians. Home: 1202 Pinehurst Rd Staunton VA 24401 Office: Dept Music Old Cabell Hall U Va Charlottesville VA 22903

GARNER, CYNTHIA DIANNE, advertising executive; b. Baytown, Tex., Sept. 5, 1959; d. Robert Glenwood and Evelyn Inez (Inman) G. Student Southwestern Assemblies of God Coll., 1977-78, Blackburn Coll., 1979-80. Admitting clk. Carlinville Area Hosp., Ill., 1979-81; sr. receptionist Tex. Commerce Bank, Houston, 1982-84; v.p. Pronto Photo & Design-Works, Houston, 1983—. Avocations: music, aerobics. Home: 452 W 19th St Houston TX 77007

GARNER, GIROLAMA THOMASINA, educational administrator, educator; b. Muskegon, Mich., Sept. 15, 1923; d. John and Martha Ann (Thomas) Funaro; student Muskegon Jr. Coll., 1941; B.A., Western Mich. U., 1944, M.A. in Counseling and Guidance, 1958; Ed.D., U. Ariz., 1973; m. Charles Donald Garner, Sept. 16, 1944 (dec.); 1 dau., Linda Jeannette Garner Blake. Elem. tchr., Muskegon and Tucson, 1947-77; counselor Erickson Elem. Sch., Tucson, 1978-79; prin. Hudlow Elem. Sch., Tucson, 1979-85; cons. Tucson Unified Sch. Dist.; adj. prof. U. Ariz., 1973—, Pima Community Coll., 1981—; mem. Ariz. Com. Tchr. Evaluation and Cert., 1976-78; del. NEA convs. Active ARC, Crippled Children's Soc., UNESCO, DAV Aux., Rincon Renegades; bd. dirs. Hudlow Community Sch., 1973-76. Recipient Apple award for teaching excellence Pima Community Coll., 1982. Mem. Nat. Assn. Sci. Tchrs., Tucson Edn. Assn., Ariz. Edn. Assn., NEA, Assn. Supervision and Curriculum Devel., AAUW, Delta Kappa Gamma, Kappa Rho Sigma, Kappa Delta Pi. Democrat. Christian Scientist. Home: 6922 E Baker St Tucson AZ 85710

GARNER, MARY JANE, cosmetics company executive; b. Terre Haute, Ind., Oct. 6, 1916; d. Thomas Law and Myra (Short) Kemp; m. William Stanley Garner, Jan. 11, 1941 (div. Nov. 1965); 1 child, William Stanley. Student Lindenwood Coll. for Women, 1935, John Heron Art Sch., 1936-38; grad. Parsons Sch. Design, 1940, Planning for Preservation Inst. of Govt., U. N.C., 1972; student writers workshop Ind. U., 1967. Model made-to-order dept. Bergdorft Goodman, N.Y.C., 1940-41; asst. buyer Crystal Room, Indpls., 1965-66; proof cons. fact Inc., St. Louis, 1968-69; pres., founder Mary Jane Garner Cosmetics, Chapel Hill, N.C., 1985—. Sec. Chapel Hill Hist. Soc., 1973-74, bd. dirs., 1973-75; mem. N.C. Bicentennial Com., 1974-78, also mem. grants com.; mem. Chapel Hill Bicentenial Commn., 1974-76; Republican precinct chmn., Chapel Hill, 1972; co-chmn. Holshouser for Gov., Orange County, N.C., 1972; Rep. precinct registrar, Chapel Hill, 1973-75; pres. Rep. Women's Club, Chapel Hill, 1973-74; chmn. state conv. N.C. Fedn. Rep. Women, 1974, Bicentennial chmn., 1974-76, legis. chmn., 1976-77, area v.p., 1978-80, pub. relations chmn., 1981-83, mem. credentials com. for nat. conv., 1980; mem. U.S. Senate Minority Leader's Citizens Adv. Com., 1974-76; mem. nat. adv. bd. Am. Security Council, 1978-79; mem. bldg. com. N.C. Rep. Hdqrs., 1978. Recipient cert. appreciation Am. Revolution Bicentenial, 1976, Spl. Recognition award Am. Security Council, 1979, Presdl. Achievement award Pres. Reagan, 1982; named most improved golfer Golf Digest Mag., 1978. Club: Chapel Hill Country (bd. govs. 1975-76). Office: Mary Jane Garner Cosmetics 100 Howell Ln Chapel Hill NC 27514

GARNER, MARY MARTIN, lawyer; b. Little Rock, Ark.; d. Jared Owen and Mary Augusta (Conery) Martin; m. Meryl Everett Garner, Aug. 24, 1943 (dec.). J.D., George Washington U., 1942. Bar: D.C. 42, U.S. Supreme Ct. 1973. Atty. Office of Gen. Counsel, Div. Natural Resources, U.S. Dept. Agr., Washington, 1944-72, dep. dir., 1972-74; sole practice, Washington, 1975—; legal counsel Nat. Assn. Soil Conservation Dists., Washington, 1975—; mem. adv. task force on pollution in Great Lakes, U.S.-Can. Joint Commn., Windsor, Ont., Can., 1976-79; bd. dirs. Inter-Am. Bar Found., Washington, 1976—. Pres. Zonta Club Wash. Found., Washington, 1983-86. Recipient Citation for Outstanding Contbn. to Advancement of Human Rights, Capital Area div. UN Assn. of U.S., Washington, 1983. Mem. ABA (vice chmn. com. on agr., adminstrv. law sect. 1979-81), Fed. Bar Assn., Internat. Bar Assn. (mem. governing council 1976—), Washington Fgn. Law Soc., Inter-Am. Bar Assn. (asst. sec. 1978-85, mem. governing council 1985—), Bar Assn. D.C. (chmn. Inter-Am. relations com. 1976-77, Superior Service award 1977), Women's Bar Assn. of D.C. (pres. 1957-58), Phi Alpha Delta, Soil Conservation Soc. Am. Democrat. Roman Catholic. Clubs: Nat. Lawyers (bd. govs.), The Washington (dir.). Contbr. articles to profl. jours., chpt. to books, papers.

GARNER, OLLIE BELLE, contracting company executive; b. Waynesburg, Ky., Feb. 6, 1928; d. Rufus D. and Nettie B. (Hubble) Stonecypher; Rogers Bus. Coll., Somerset, Ky., 1947; m. Leo M. Garner, May 26, 1947. Sec., Pulaski County (Ky.) Extension Office, Somerset, 1948-50; bookkeeper W.C. Brass & Assos., Indpls., 1951-62; sec., bookkeeper Acme Constrn. Co., Indpls., 1963-65; sec., v.p., dir., co-owner J & O Contractors, Inc., Indpls., 1965—. Mem. Early Am. Soc., Marion County Art League, Nat. Assn. Women Bus. Owners, Network of Women in Bus., Nat. Assn. Women in Constrn., Internat. Platform Assn., Indpls. Mus. Art, YWCA. Club: Economic. Home: 7515 W Mooresville Rd Camby IN 46113 Office: 3906 W Washington St Indianapolis IN 46241

GARNHOLZ, CYNTHIA, lawyer; b. St. Louis, Oct. 4, 1953; d. Edward W. and Ivy A. (Gall) G.; m. William F. Eastman, Aug. 23, 1980; 1 child, Zachary. B.A. cum laude, Fontbonne Coll., 1976; J.D., Washington U., 1980. Bar: Mo. 1980. Law clk. 21st Jud. Cir. Mo., St. Louis, 1980-81; asst. county counselor St. Louis County (Mo.), 1981—. Mem. ABA, Mo. Bar Assn., Women Lawyers Assn. St. Louis, Met. Bar Assn. St. Louis, John Marshall Republican Club. Office: Office County Counselor 41 S Central St Clayton MO 63105

GARR, TERI, actress. Appeared in motion pictures including: Young Frankenstein, 1974, The Conversation, 1974, Won Ton Ton, The Dog Who Saved Hollywood, 1976, Oh God!, 1977, Close Encounters of the Third Kind, Mr. Mike's Mondo Video, 1979, The Black Stallion, 1979, Honky Tonk Freeway, 1981, Tootsie, 1982, One From the Heart, 1982, The Sting II, 1983, The Black Stallion Returns, 1983, Mr. Mom, 1983, After Hours, 1985; regular on TV series The Sonny Comedy Review, 1974; TV movies include: Law and Order, The Winter of our Discontent, To Catch a King. Office: care Press Relations William Morris Agy 151 El Camino Beverly Hills CA 90212*

GARRETT, BETTY RUTH, business consultant; b. Campbelton, Fla., Nov. 11, 1941; d. Malcolm Alex and Either Ida (Rich) Cushing; children—Michael, Charles, Richard, Greg, Gini. Student Tallahassee Community Coll. Cert. tchr., Fla. Adminstrv. asst. Leon County Sch. Bd., Tallahassee, 1971-81, bus. cons. Bus. Agy. Out-Reach, 1984—; office mgr. Fla. Tchrs. Assn., Tallahassee, 1981-83; asst. dir. Nat. Health Screening Council, Tallahassee, 1982-84; cons. in field. Mem. ASTD, Nat. Assn. Female Execs. Democrat. Baptist. Avocations: tennis; crossword puzzles; dancing; bridge. Home: 3829 Castleberry Dr Tallahassee FL 32303

GARRETT, CAROL ANN, speech-language pathologist; b. Danville, Va., June 24, 1940; d. James Claude Swanson and Hilma May (Hall) G.; A.A., Averett Coll., 1960; B.S. magna cum laude, Miss. U. for Women, 1962; M.Ed., U. Va., 1966. Speech-lang. pathologist Lynchburg (Va.) Public Schs., 1962—; pvt. practice speech-lang. pathology Lynchburg, 1963—; cons. in field. Mem. Am. Speech-Lang.-Hearing Assn. (com. on disorders of central auditory processing 1986), Speech and Hearing Assn. Va., Central Va. Speech-Lang.-Hearing Assn. (chmn. 1984-85), AAUW (life), Spl. Edn. Adv. Com. Lynchburg Public Schs., Beta Sigma Phi (life, pres. Lynchburg council 1964-65, pres. chpt. 1965-66, 68-71, 73-75, Girl of Yr. award 1969-71, 73-75), Methodist. Home: 723 Custer Dr Lynchburg VA 24502 Office: Lynchburg Public Schs 10th and Court Sts Lynchburg VA 24504

GARRETT, HELEN MARIE, state legislator; b. Paducah, Ky.; d. John Frank and Helen Eunice (Bean) Rickman; m. John Thomas Garret, 1952 (dec.); children—Tom, Carol. Mem. Ky. State Senate from Dist. 2, also majority whip. Recipient Conservation Service award Ducks Unltd. Mem. Bus. and Profl. Women. Democrat. Office: Ky State Capitol Bldg Frankfort KY 40601*

GARRETT, PAMELA DENISE, educator; b. Los Angeles, Nov. 2, 1954; d. Travis and Bette Jean (Perkins) G. B.A. in Child Devel. Calif. State U.-Los Angeles, 1976; A.A. in Psychology, West Los Angeles Coll., 1974. Tchrs. credential, Calif. Tchr.'s aide Los Angeles Unified Sch. Dist., 1975-76, tchr. Children's Ctr., 1977-79, tchr. Marcus Garvey Pre-Sch., Los Angeles, 1976-77; tchr. Compton Unified Sch. Dist. (Calif.), 1979—, Stephen C. Foster Elem. Sch., 1981—; cons. Mary Kay Cosmetics, Inc., 1975—; asst. dir., mem. bd. Creative Learning Inst., Compton, Calif., 1983—; travel cons. L.A. By Pam, sight seeing tours. Mem. Nat. Council Negro Women, Calif. Tchrs. Assn., Internat. Platform Assn., Research Council of Scripps Clinic and Research Found., Tau Gamma Delta, Phi Delta Kappa. Democrat. Baptist. Home: 2635 Vineyard Ave Los Angeles CA 90016

GARRETT, PATRICIA BEVERLY, lawyer; b. Billings, Mont., Dec. 25, 1939; d. George Dean and Elizabeth Mae (McNaught) Forney; m. Merrill Fredrick Garrett, June 21, 1959; children—Cleve Fredrick, Warren Merrill. A.B., U. Mont., 1961; J.D., Suffolk U., 1977. Bar: Mass. 1978, U.S. Dist. Ct. Mass. 1980. Tchr. French, English and Am. govt. Edison Jr. High Sch., Champaign, Ill., 1962-65; instructional systems analyst Honeywell Info. Systems, Wellesley Hills, Mass., 1969-74; instr. Honeywell Pty Ltd., Melbourne, Australia, 1974; ednl. cons. Honeywell Info. Systems, Wellesley Hills, Mass., 1975-80; counsel environ. issues Commerical Union Ins. Cos., Boston, 1980-84; cons. Litigation Systems, Inc., Boston, 1983—, assoc. gen. counsel, 1984—. Tchr., Mass. Corrections Instn., Norfolk, 1971-72, Martin Luther King Jr. Middle Sch., Dorchester, Mass., 1972-73. Mem. ABA, Mass. Bar Assn., Mass. Def. Lawyers Assn. Home: 90 Seaview Ave Marshfield MA 02050 Office: Litigation Systems Inc 100 5th Ave Waltham MA 02154

GARRETT, PAULINE, advertising executive; b. Muscatine, Iowa, July 5, 1933; B.S., U. Iowa, 1954. Personnel mgr. Musical Masterpieces div. Crowell Collier, N.Y.C., 1955-57; placement mgr. Coll. Grad. Agy., N.Y.C., 1957-60; personnel, office mgr. Seafarer Fiberglass Yachts, N.Y.C., 1960-61; account exec. Century Advt., N.Y.C., 1961-65, Edward Weiss Advt., N.Y.C., 1965-66; pres. Tempo Advt., Inc. (merged with World Wide Advt. Agy., Inc., 1976), N.Y.C., 1966-76; regional dir. World Wide Advt. Agy., Inc. (acquired as separate div. by J. Walter Thompson 1980), N.Y.C., 1976-82; sr. v.p. Thompson Recruitment Advt., N.Y.C., 1982; pres. Tempo Advt. Inc., 1983—. Home: 140 Riverside Dr New York NY 10024 Office: Tempo Advt Inc 5 W 37th St New York NY 10018

GARRETT, WILMA IDA, temporary employment agency executive; b. Santurce, P.R., June 9, 1938; d. Angel Luis and Verania (Morales) Lopez; B.A. in Psychology, U. P.R., 1959; m. Carlos Garrett; children—Rene Luis Aviles, Angel Luis Aviles. Sales mgr. Empresas Diaz, Rio Piedras, P.R., 1964-67; real estate broker Mackle Bros., Daytona, Fla., 1967-70; record mgr. San Juan (P.R.) City Hall, 1970-73; mgr. P.R., Kelly Services, Inc., Hato Rey, 1973—. Mem. Am. Soc. Personnel Adminstrs., P.R. C. of C., P.R. Mfrs. Assn., Sales and Mktg. Execs. Assn., Am. Bus. Women Assn., Zonta Internat. Republican. Roman Catholic. Office: Kelly Services Inc Scotiabank Plaza Suite 701 Hato Rey PR 00917

GARRISON, ALICE MARIE, real estate executive; b. Dallas, Aug. 26, 1932; d. George Clark and Thelma (Roberts) G. Student Hillsboro Jr. Coll., 1950-51, So. Meth. U., 1956-57, U. Tex., 1979-80, Univ. Coll., Oxford Univs., Eng., 1983. Mortgage banking officer Nat. Life & Accident Ins. Co., Dallas, 1952-60; real estate developer Sabre Realty, Inc., Dallas, 1962-65; pres. Am. Gallery of Sports Art, Dallas, 1966-80; exec. asst. to mayor City of Dallas, 1976-81; exec. v.p. Folsom Investments, Inc., Dallas, 1980—, dir., 1972—. Bd. dirs. Dallas Mus. Fine Art, 1981—; active Dallas Symphony League, 1980—, Dallas Opera Guild, 1983—; area leader United Way Dallas, 1980—. Mem. Am. Mgmt. Assn., Bus. and Profl. Women Dallas, Inc., Nat. Assn. Female Execs. So. Meth. U. Alumnia Assn. Republican. Presbyterian. Clubs: Bent Tree Country, Willow Bend Golf.

GARRISON, DOROTHY FRANCIS, city official; b. Norfolk, Nebr., Feb. 18, 1932; d. Leonard R. and Lena T. (Schafer) Doffin, m. Francis E. Garrison, Sept. 20, 1961; stepchildren—Judith A Hayes, Virginia K. Pedersen. Student Wayne State Coll., 1950-56. Cert. mcpl. clk. Tchr. Madison, Stanton, and Cumming counties, Nebr., 1950-57; housemother Luth. Childrens Service, Omaha, 1957-60; computer operator Consolidated Blenders, Inc., Fremont, Nebr., 1961-71; acctg. clk., dep. clk. City of Fremont, 1971-82, city clk. 1982—(first woman city clk. in Fremont); Sec. Mission Builders, Fremont, 1981—, Aid Assn. Lutherans Fraternal Br 5481, Fremont, 1985—. Mem. 3-Rivers Clk. Assn. (pres. 1984—), Internat. Inst. Mcpl. Clks. Republican. Home: 2052 E

19th St Fremont NE 68025 Office: City of Fremont 725 N Park St Fremont NE 68025

GARRISON, ELLEN BARRIER, archivist; b. Atlanta, Apr. 15, 1944; d. John Jacob and Lois (Trussell) Barrier; m. Edward Max Neal, Sept. 7, 1967 (div. Nov. 1978); 1 child, John Jacob Neal; m. Joseph Yates Garrison, July 6, 1979. B.A., Queens Coll., N.C., 1966; M.A., Stanford U., 1967, Ph.D., 1981. Tech. services archivist So. Hist. Collection, U. N.C.-Chapel Hill, 1975-79; assoc. archivist Ga. State U., Atlanta, 1979-82; dir. Archives of Appalachia, East Tenn. State U., Johnson City, 1982—; cons. Ga. Hist. Soc., U. Miss., Green County Records Commn. Editor: Provenance, 1982-84, Archives in Appalachia: A Directory, 1985. Contbr. articles to profl. dictionaries. Grantee Nat. Hist. Publs. and Records Commn., 1984-85, NEH, 1979-80, Rockefeller Fond., 1975-76. Mem. Soc. Am. Archivists (mem. del. People's Republic of China 1982), Appalachian Studies Conf. (treas. 1984—), Soc. Ga. Archivists (sec.-treas. 1980-82, dir. 1978-80), Tenn. Archivists, So. Hist. Assn., Ga. Hist. Soc. Episcopalian. Office: Archives of Appalachia East Tenn State U Johnson City TN 37614

GARRISON, KAREN GAIL, hospital administrator; b. Los Angeles, Jan. 21, 1944; d. Albert B. and Gertrude R. (Pew) Doran; student Santa Monica Coll., 1961-64, UCLA, 1963-64, Immaculate Heart Coll., 1964-66; B.S., Calif. State U., 1973; M.S., Loma Linda U., 1978; m. James Patrick Garrison, Oct. 20, 1978. Tchr. elem. grades public and parochial schs., Los Angeles, 1966-71; instr. critical care Glendale Adventist Med. Center, Glendale, Calif., 1974-76; critical care nurse Loma Linda U. Med. Center, 1976, nursing supr., 1977, dir. human resources devel., 1977-80; asst. adminstr. patient care services Feather River Hosp., Paradise, Calif., 1980-82; asst. adminstr. Mt. Diablo Hosp. and Med. Center, Concord, Calif., 1982—; cons. mgmt. and edn., 1978-82. Bd. dirs. San Francisco Lighthouse for the Blind. Mem. Am. Hosp. Assn., Nat. League Nursing, Am. Nursing Assn., East Bay Nursing Service Adminstrs. (sec.), Am. Assn. Critical Care Nursing, Nat. Critical Care Inst., AAUW, Calif. Soc. Nursing Service Adminstrs., Calif. Soc. Risk Mgmt., Sigma Theta Tau. Home: 22 Valley View Orinda CA 94563 Office: 2540 East St Concord CA 94520

GARRISON, WANDA BROWN, paper manufacturing company employee; b. Madison County, N.C., Sept. 16, 1936; d. Roy Lee Brown and Zella Arizona (Miller) Brown Hannah; m. Charles Mitchell Garrison, July 9, 1955; children—Roy Lee, Marsha Joan; 1 step-son, Charles Mitchell, Jr. Student air-line hostess Weaver Airlines, St. Louis, 1954-55; student Haywood Tech. Coll., Clyde, N.C., 1967-68; student IBM, Asheville, N.C., 1977; student data processing Agy. Record Control, Atlanta, 1978. Operator Day Co., Waynesville, N.C., 1954-57; driver Haywood County Schs., Waynesville, 1970-71; operator Am. Enka, N.C., 1972-75; bookkeeper L. N. Davis Ins. Co., Waynesville, 1975-80; with stock preparation dept. Champion Internat., Canton, N.C., 1980—. Sec./treas. James Chapel Baptist Ch., Haywood County, N.C., 1965-77; pres. Fire Dept. Aux., Crabtree, N.C., 1973—; pres. Women Mission Union, Crabtree Bapt. Ch., Haywood County, 1977-80; v.p. Gideon Aux., Haywood County, 1982-84, pres., 1984-86; state aux. follow-up rep., 1984. Recipient Life Saving plaque Lion's Club, Waynesville, 1972. Mem. AFL-CIO. Democrat. Home: Hwy 209 Route 1 Box 230A Clyde NC 28721

GARRISON-ARCHIE, ANDREA RENEE, television executive, consultant; b. New Haven, Apr. 1, 1956; d. James William and Mattie Pearl (Carr) Garrison; m. Keith Derrick Archie, July 22, 1982; 1 child, Keidera Monet. B.S. cum laude, Emerson Coll., 1978. Promotion asst. Sta.-WTNH-TV, New Haven, 1978-79, program asst., 1979, continuity dir., 1979-80; news ops. supr. ABC Network, N.Y.C., 1980-81, mgr. pub. service, 1981—. Bd. dirs. ABC Adopt A Sch. Program, 1986—. Mem. Nat. Assn. Female Execs., Am. Women in Radio and TV, Will Rogers Inst. (bd. dirs. health edn. com. 1982-86, award 1984), ABC Employee's Assn. (communications liaison 1985—). Democrat. Baptist. Avocations: writing poetry and lyrics. Home: 88-04 175th St Apt 2 Jamaica NY 11432 Office: ABC Network 1330 Ave of the Americas New York NY 10019

GARROTT, IDAMAE, state legislator; b. Washington, Dec. 24, 1916; A.B., Western Md. Coll., 1936, L.H.D. (hon.); married; 2 children. Mem. Md. Ho. of Dels., 1979—, mem. ways and means com., joint com. on energy. Mem. Montgomery County Council, 1966-74, chmn. planning com., 1970-74, pres., 1971; bd. dirs. Washington Met. Area Transit Authority, 1972-74; bd. dirs. Washington Suburban Transit Commn., 1971-74, chmn., 1972; bd. dirs. Met. Washington Council Govts., pres., 1974, chmn. land use com., 1969-74; bd. dirs. Solid Waste Mgmt. Agy. Met. Washington, 1969-74; pres. Montgomery County LWV, 1963-66, Montgomery County Humane Soc., 1976-77; bd. dirs. Wheaton Rescue Squad, 1982-84. Recipient John Dewey award, 1982; Humanitarian award Montgomery County Humane Soc., 1983; Cert. Appreciation, Montgomery County Edn. Assn., 1984, Horn Book award, 1985. Author: Paying Our Way, Maryland State Taxes and You, 1958. Office: 221 Lowe Bldg Annapolis MD 21401

GARSIDE, MARLENE ELIZABETH, advertising executive; b. Newark, Dec. 1, 1933; d. Abraham and Shirley (Janow) Carnow; B.S. in Commerce and Fin., Bucknell U., 1955; m. Stanley Kramer, Aug. 7, 1955 (dec. 1967); children—Deborah Frances, Elizabeth Anne; m. Martin Lutman, Aug. 27, 1969 (dec. 1981); m. Michael J. Weinstein, Apr. 9, 1983 (dec. Oct. 1984); m. Normand Garside, Apr. 5, 1986. Asst. research dir. Modern Materials Handling Co., Boston, 1955-57; econ. analyst, project adminstr. United Research Inc., Cambridge, Mass., 1957-58; free lance tech. writer, econ. analyst, 1958-66; asst. mgr. survey planning and market research IBM, White Plains, N.Y., 1967-69; mgr. research services McKinsey & Co., Cleve., 1969-72; past v.p., dir. Am. Custom Homes, Cleve., Liberty Builders, Inc., Cleve.; owner, v.p., dir. Am. Custom Builders Inc., Cape Coral, Fla., 1978—; partner, dir. Star Realty Inc., Cape Coral, 1980—; account exec. Media Graphics Inc., Naples, Fla.; now advt. mgr. Fox Electronics. Mem. Econ. and Indsl. Devel. Task Force, City of Cape Coral, 1979. Mem. Nat. Assn. Homebuilders, Nat. Bd. Realtors, Fla. Assn. Realtors, Bldg. Industry Assn., Constrn. Industry Assn. Home: 1482 Sautern Dr Fort Myers FL 33907 Office: Fox Electronics 6225 Presidential Ct Fort Myers FL 33907

GARWOOD, BARBARA ANN, psychologist, educator; b. Cleve., Jan. 7, 1936; d. Bradford Earl and Hazel Elizabeth (Obrock) Garwood; B.S. John Carroll U., 1963; M.A., Case-Western Res. U., 1968; Ph.D., Kent State U., 1973. Tchr., sr. high sch. English, Euclid (Ohio) Pub. Schs., 1966-68; cons. sch. psychologist Mayfield (Ohio) City Schs., 1973-76; sch. psychologist Cleve. City Schs., 1968-72; assoc. staff Richmond Heights Gen. Hosp.; pvt. practice psychology, Mentor, Ohio; prof. psychology Lakeland Community Coll., Mentor; mem. Ohio Bd. Psychology, 1976-81, pres., 1980-81. Mem. Lakeland Faculty Assn. (pres. 1980-81), Cleve. Psychol. Assn. (v.p. 1974-75), Ohio Sch. Psychologists Assn. (pres. 1976-77). Club: Pavilion Skating. Contbr. articles to profl. jours. Home: 6361 Candlewood Ct Mentor OH 44060 Office: 9853 Johnnycake Ridge Rd Mentor OH 44060

GARY, BEVERLY A. WILSON, govt. ofcl.; b. Uniontown, Pa., Oct. 6, 1942; d. Dorothy J. Wilson; B.S., Bowie State Coll., 1981; M.Ed., U. Mass., 1982; grad. Fed. Exec. Inst., 1984; m. James A. Gary, Feb. 24, 1962; 1 son, James A. With Bur. Public Rds., Dept. Commerce, 1960-65; with Equal Opportunity Commn., Washington, 1965—, dir. personnel, 1974—. Pres., Randolph Village Elem. Sch. PTA, 1969-70. Mem. Internat. Personnel Mgmt. Assn., Nat. Assn. Female Execs., Washington Urban League, Sr. Exec. Assn., Fed. Exec. Inst. Alumni Assn., NAACP. Baptist. Home: 901 6th St SW Apt 304A Washington DC 20024 Office: 2401 E St NW Room 330 Washington DC 20507

GARY, SHARON DELIGHT, psychological examiner; b. Decatur, Tex., June 14, 1951; d. Dorthea (Sommerville) Gary; B.S. with honors in Psychology, State Coll. Ark. (name changed to U. Central Ark.), 1973; M.S. in Clin. Psychology, Memphis State U., 1975. Liaison worker Foster Home and Group Home programs N.E. Community Mental Health Center, Memphis, 1975-76; psychol. examiner, asst. dir. Hutt Psychol. Group, Memphis, 1976-79; cons. psychol. examiner Sequoyah Center, Tenn. Psychiat. Hosp. and Inst., Memphis, 1976-77; coordinator, instr. foster care program U. Tenn., Memphis, 1978—; owner, psychol. examiner Psychol. Services of Memphis, 1979—; cons. St. Peter Home for Children, 1982-84, Holston Home, 1983—, West Tenn. AGAPE, 1980—; active workshops, seminars on learning disabilities and foster children's devel.; mem. Women's Resource Center, 1977-82, Multidisciplinary Child Abuse Rev. Team, 1979—, active NOW march for ERA; participant in lobbying for Ark. Assn. Children with Learning Disabilities; gov.'s appointee to Juvenile Justice Commn., 1985—, grant rev. com., 1986—. Co-author: Red Flays in the Development of the Foster Child; Parenting Happy Children: Coping with Destructive Behavior. Recipient Ark. Traveler cert., 1978; cert. of appreciation Tenn. Foster Care Assn., 1979, Tenn. Dept. Human Services. Mem. Am. Psychol. Assn., Tenn. Psychol. Assn., Memphis Psychol. Assn., Nat. Rehab. Assn., Council on Adoptable Children, Assn. for Children with Learning Disabilities, Psi Chi. Mem. Unity Christ Ch. Club: Zonta (corr. sec. 1983-84, dir. 1984—, del. internat. conf. Sydney, Australia, 1984, v.p. 1984-85, pres. 1985-86). Home: 3163 Highmeadow Dr Memphis TN 38128 Office: 1835 Union Ave Suite 215 Memphis TN 38104

GARZA, EILEEN ROSENDALE, occupational therapist; b. Balt., Oct. 29, 1958; d. Christopher Joseph and Mary Louise (O'Hare) Rosendale; m. Carlos Gerardo Garza, Oct. 15, 1983; 1 child, Sarah Catherine. Student Towson State U., 1976-78; B.S., Va. Commonwealth U. 1979; M.Occupational Therapy, Tex. Woman's U., 1982. Staff therapist St. Anthony Ctr., Houston, 1982-83, clin. coordinator, 1983, hand clinic supr., 1983-84; with home health dept. Logos, Houston, 1983; dir. Hand Rehab. Assocs., Houston, 1983—; patient care coordinator Houston Hand Rehab. Ctr., 1985—; cons. Houston Area Cancer Support Group, 1982. Contbr. articles to profl. jours. Vocalist Rice Catholic Student Ctr., Houston, 1983—. Recipient cert. of merit Houston Community Coll., 1983. Mem. Am. Occupational Therapy Assn., Tex. Occupational Therapy Assn. (editor newsletter), Houston Hand Interest Group (sec. 1986—), Gulf Coast East Dist. Occupational Therapy Assn., Pi Theta Epsilon. Home: 26307 Pin Oak Dr Magnolia TX 77355 Office: 17030 Nanes 208 Houston TX 77090

GARZA, LETICIA, educator; b. Del Rio, Tex., Dec. 5, 1949; d. Ramon Paredes and Virginia (Moreno) Garza. B.S. in Edn., Southwest Tex. State U., San Marcos, 1971; M.Ed., 1977; cert. adminstrn., Tex. Women's U., Denton, 1982. Tchr. elem. San Felipe Del Rio Consol. Ind. Sch. Dist., Del Rio, 1972-79; tchr. lang. arts Dallas Ind. Sch. Dist., 1979—. Recipient Ross Perot Excellence in Teaching award Ross Perot Found., Dallas Ind. Sch. Dist., 1983; Jim Lowe Found. Excellence in Teaching award, 1983; Tchr. of Yr. award Linda Hooe Elem. Sch., 1982. Mem. Assn. Supervision and Curriculum Devel. Dallas Assn. Bilingual Educators, Phi Delta Kappa, Delta Kappa Gamma. Democrat. Roman Catholic. Club: Les Bonne Amies (Del Rio) (sec.-treas. 1978-79). Home: 1923 Dennis St Irving TX 75062 Office: Lida Hooe Elem Sch 2419 Gladstone St Dallas TX 75208

GARZARELLI, ELAINE MARIE, economist; b. Phila., Oct. 13, 1951; d. Ralph J. and Ida M. (Pierantozzi) G.; B.S., Drexel U., 1973, M.B.A., 1977; doctoral candidate NYU, 1980. with A.G. Becker, N.Y.C., 1973—, v.p., economist, 1975-84, mng. dir., 1984; exec. v.p. Shearson Lehman Bros., 1984—; lectr. in field; Recipient award for bus. achievement YWCA, 1976. Mem. Nat. Assn. Bus. Economists, Women's Fin. Assn., Am. Statis. Assn., Women's Bond Assn. Author: Financial Techniques, 1976; contbr. articles to profl. jours. Developer Sector Analysis, econometric model for predicting industry profits and stock price movements. Home: 280 Butler Rd Springfield PA 19064 Office: 2 World Trade Ctr New York NY

GASKILL, DAWN LORRAINE, seminar and management consultant company executive; b. Lamar, Colo., Oct. 15, 1947; d. Robert Earl and Edna Lorraine (Southworth) Gaskill. A.A. in Fashion Merchandising, Tobe-Coburn Sch., N.Y.C., 1968; student bus. adminstrn. Ft. Lewis Coll., 1965-67. Head resource dept. Boyden Assocs., N.Y.C., 1968-70; corp. trainer U.S. Universal, Inc., San Rafeal, Calif., 1969-74; dir. mktg. and tng. i Natural, Nutrient, Inc. N.Y.C., 1974-75; owner Dawn & Co., Houston, 1975-78; v.p. merchandising Avacare Inc., Dallas, 1978-83; pres. Dawn Workshops, Dallas, 1983—; developer cosmetic line Treasures of Earth, 1978; mem. career bd. Mademoiselle mag., N.Y.C., 1968—. Cons., Cancer Counseling Ctr., Dallas, 1975-82. Mem. Fashion Group, Nat. Assn. Female Execs., Meeting Planners Internat., Dallas C. of C. Republican. Methodist. Lodge: Order Eastern Star. Office: Dawn Workshops 5440 Harvest Hill St Suite 209 Dallas TX 75230

GASKILL, LINDA ROSANNE, investment and property company executive, consultant; b. Long Beach, Calif., Sept. 14, 1952; d. Robert Edward and Patricia Jane (Horner) G. Student Saddleback Jr. Coll. Project acct. Leadership Housing Systems, Inc., Santa Ana, Calif., 1971-77; cost acct. Daon Corp., Newport Beach, Calif., 1979-81; chief acct. AHP Gen. Ptnr., Inc., Newport Beach, 1981-82; controller Creative Cons., Inc., Laguna Hills, Calif., 1982-83; co-propr. G&S Assocs., Costa Mesa, Calif., 1984—. Republican. Home and Office: 297 Lilac Ln Costa Mesa CA 92626

GASKIN, KATHLEEN ALICE, real estate brokerage executive; b. Lansing, Mich., Nov. 29, 1941; d. Roger J. and Mary A. (Lilly) Small; m. Karl A. H. Bohnhoff, Oct. 7, 1961 (div. 1970); children—Karl A., Kandice A.; m. Keith L. Gaskin, May 23, 1970; Student Grace Brethern coll., 1959-60, Mich. State U., 1961-62. Lic. broker, Mich. Customer rep. Xerox Corp., Buffalo, 1963-65; vehicle scheduler Ford Motor Co., Lansing, 1965-66; customer rep. Xerox Corp., Lansing, 1966-68; sales rep. Simon Real Estate, Lansing, 1968-77; pres. Century 21 Gaskin Realty, Lansing, 1977—; instr. in real estate sales Lansing Community Coll., 1975-82; dir. Capitol Nat. Bank, Lansing. Recipient Centurion award Century 21 Internat., 1983, 84; Gold Medallion award Century 21 Internat., 1983, 84. Mem. Lansing C. of C., Lansing Bd. Realtors (bd. dirs. 1978-80, sec. 1979, Life Mem. Million Dollar Club, First Woman to obtain Million Dollar Club). Republican. Club: Walnut Hills Country (Lansing). Avocation: golf. Home: 1424 Somerset Close East Lansing MI 48823 Office: Century 21 Gaskin Realty 1601 E Grand River St Lansing MI 48906

GASKINS, SANDRA RENE, government computer specialist, driving school executive; b. Suffolk, Va., Jan. 13, 1951; d. Johnnie Thomas and Irene (Turner) Williams; m. Gary McKenney Gaskins, Feb. 19, 1977; children—Kari Noel, Gary Jr., Craig Garrison. B.S. in Math., Morgan State U., 1973. Mathematician, U.S. Navy, Washington, 1973-79, computer specialist, 1979-82, computer systems programmer, 1982-83; computer programmer, analyst U.S. Dept. Treasury, Washington, 1983-84, computer specialist, 1984—. Mem. Pres. Commn. on Integrity and Efficiency, Treasury Microcomputer Users Group, Nat. Assn. Female Execs., Delta Sigma Theta. Democrat. Methodist. Avocations: taking field trips; reading; cooking. Home: 6915 Furman Pkwy Riverdale MD 20737 Office: Office of Sec Office Insp Gen ADP Staff 1201 Constitution Ave #7134 Washington DC 20423

GASKINS-DAVIS, JUNE CONSTANCE, financial consultant; b. Winchester, Va., Oct. 13, 1933; d. Kirk N. and Ella Virginia (Finley) G.; 1 child, Byron John. B.S., U. Md., 1975; M.B.A., Trinity Coll., 1979. Office mgr. U. Md., College Park, 1972-75; cons. JGD Assocs., Washington, 1975-81; regional dir. Classique Creations, Dallas, 1976-80; sr. sales Marshall Fields, Chgo., 1979-80; sr. fin. cons. Merrill, Lynch, Pierce, Fenner & Smith, Washington, 1980—. Contbr. articles to profl. jours. Recipient Black Achiever in Industry award Merrill Lynch, 1984. Mem. Nat. Council Career Women, Nat. Women's Econs. Alliance, Nat. Black Women's Polit. Congress, Nat. Assn. Female Execs. (dir. 1985-86), Exec. Club, Phi Chi Theta (v.p. 1978). Democrat. Avocations: travel; tennis; reading. Office: Merrill Lynch Pierce Fenner & Smith 1100 Connecticut Ave NW Washington DC 20036

GASPARI, LINDA ROCHFORD, patient relations specialist, consultant; b. Providence, Dec. 8, 1954; d. Allen Vallett and Marian Elsie (Smith) Rochford; m. Steven Jay Gaspari, Oct. 9, 1977 (div. July 1980). B.A. in Econs. summa cum laude, U. Mass.-Amherst, 1980; A.A. in Liberal Arts, Greenfield Community Coll., Mass., 1976. Group claims processor Aetna Life and Casualty, Springfield, Mass., 1976-80; bar mgr. Vibrations Lounge, Framingham, Mass., 1981-82; function coordinator Glen Ellen Country Club, Millis, Mass., 1982; dir. admissions Westwood Lodge Hosp., Mass., 1982-85; mgr. mem. services and enrollment MultiGroup Health Plan, Wellesley, Mass., 1985—; cons. ins. L. Gaspari, Gloucester, Mass., 1982—. Sponsor, Foster Parents Plan, Warwick, R.I., 1985. Commonwealth scholar U. Mass., 1980. Mem. New Eng. Soc., Relations Profls. (founder); Mass. Assn. Hosp. Admitting Mgrs. Avocations: aerobics; running; reading; hiking. Office: MultiGroup Health Plan 27 Mica Ln Wellesley MA 02181

GASPER, JO ANN, government official; b. Providence, Sept. 25, 1946; d. Joseph Siegleman and Jeanne VanMatre Shoaf; B.A., U. Dallas, 1967, M.B.A., 1969; m. Louis Clement Gasper, Sept. 21, 1974; children—Stephen Gregory, Monica Elizabeth, Jeanne Marie, Michelle Bernadette (dec.), Phyllis Anastasia. Adminstrv. asst. U. Dallas, 1964-68; dir., asst. adminstr. Britain Convalescent Center, Irving, Tex., 1964-68; pres. Medicare Centers, Inc., Dallas, 1968-69; bus. mgr., treas. U. Plano (Tex.), 1969-72; ins. agt., 1972-73; systems analyst Tex. Instruments, Inc., 1973-75; acctg. and bus. cons., 1976-81; editor, pub. The Right Woman—Congl. News for Women and the Family, also Register Report, 1980-81; dep. asst. sec. social services policy Office Asst. Sec. Planning and Evaluation, Dept. Health and Human Services, 1981-85, population affairs Office Asst. Sec. Health, Dept. Health and Human Services, 1985—; bd. dirs., treas. Council Inter-Am. Security, 1978-80; instr. George Mason U., Fairfax, Va., 1976. Mem. nat. family policy adv. bd. Reagan/Bush Campaign, 1980; del. White House Conf. Families, 1979-80; mem. Franklin Area Citizens Neighborhood Watch, McLean, Va., 1980-81, Fairfax County Citizens Coalition for Quality Child Care, 1980-82; co-chmn. St. John's Refugee Resettlement Com., 1975-77; U.S. adv. Inter-Am. Commn. Women, 1982—; U.S. del. XVI Pan Am. Child Congress, 1985—. Recipient award Eagle Forum, 1979, Wanderer Found., 1980; named Outstanding Conservative Woman, 1980-81, Bronze medal Health and Human Services, 1982. Mem. Exec. Women in Govt. Republican. Roman Catholic. Author articles in field, also columnist. Office: 330 Independence Ave SW Room 1351 Washington DC 20201

GASPER, RUTH EILEEN, real estate investor, property management company executive; b. Valparaiso, Ind., July 16, 1934; d. Reuben John and Effie (Wesner) Tenpas; m. Ralph L. Gasper, May 25, 1957. Student Purdue U., 1952-56; B.A., Govs. State U., 1982. Analyst computer systems Leo Burnette Advt., Chgo., 1958-69; nat. adminstr. registrars Sports Car Club Am., Denver, 1977-79; pres. Ainslie, Inc., Chgo., 1982—; mem. North River Commn. Housing Com., Chgo., 1982-83. Area coordinator Concerned Action Party, Lansing, Ill., 1977; chief race registrar Ind. Northwest Region Sports Car Club Am., 1969-80. Mem. Chgo. Property Owners Assn., Single Room Operators Assn. (bd. dirs.), Albany Park C. of C. Avocations: sports car racing; classical music.

GASPERONI, ELLEN JEAN LIAS (MRS. EMIL GASPERONI), real estate investments exec.; b. Rural Valley, Pa.; d. Dale S. and Ruth (Harris) Lias; student Youngstown U., 1952-54, John Carrol U., 1953-54, Westminster Coll., 1951-52; grad. Am. Inst. Banking; m. Emil Gasperoni, May 28, 1955; children—Sam, Emil, Jean Ellen. Real estate investments exec. Mem. Jr. Bus. Women's Club (dir. 1962-64). Presbyterian. Clubs: Sweetwater Country (Orlando, Fla.), Lake Toxaway (N.C.) Golf and Country. Home: 1126 Brownshine Ct Longwood FL 32779

GASSAWAY, MELINDA BROWN, newspaper editor; b. Hot Springs, Ark., Apr. 5, 1942; d. Joseph R. and Mary V. (Proctor) Brown. B.J., U. Mo., 1965. Reporter, Copley Newspapers, Los Angeles, 1965-67; feature writer States-Item, New Orleans, 1967-68; soc. co-editor Gulfport (Miss.) Daily Herald, 1968-69; reporter Hot Springs (Ark.) Sentinel-Record, 1974-76, soc. editor, 1977-78, assoc. editor, 1978-79, mng. editor, 1979-80, exec. editor, 1980—. Founding mem. Hot Springs Rape Task Force, 1980. Recipient Investigative Reporting award Sigma Delta Chi of Ark., 1977; Merit award Muscular Dystrophy Assn., 1977; column award AP Mng. Editors Assn., 1983, Ark. Press Assn., 1983; Woman of Yr. award Hot Springs Bus. and Profl. Women's Club, 1980; Champion award Dartmouth Coll./Champion Media Awards, 1981; citation Robert F. Kennedy Journalism awards, 1980. Mem. Hot Springs Med. Utilization Rev. Bd., 1979—. Mem. Ark. Press Assn., AP Mng. Editors Assn. (judge awards 1983-84), U. Mo. Alumni Assn. Lodge: Hot Springs Bus. and Profl. Women's (pres. 1979-80). Office: PO Box 580 Hot Springs AR 71901

GASTEYER, CARLIN EVANS (MRS. HARRY A. GASTEYER), cultural center administrator; b. Jackson, Mich., Mar. 30, 1917; d. Frank Howard and Marian (Spencer) Evans; student Barnard Coll., 1934-35; B.A., CUNY, 1983; m. Harry A. Gasteyer, Jan. 8, 1944; 1 dau., Nancy Catherine. Clk., First Nat. City Bank, 1939-42; statistician Bell Telephone Labs., 1942-45; dir. asst. S.I. Mus., 1956-61; bus. mgr. Mus. of the City of N.Y., 1961-63; mus. adminstr., 1963-66; asst. dir. Monmouth (N.J.) Mus., 1966-67, Mus. of City of N.Y., 1967-70; vice dir. adminstrn. Bklyn. Mus., 1970-74; dir. planning Snug Harbor Cultural Center, S.I., N.Y., 1975-79; cable TV Cons., 1980—; adj. lectr. mus. studies Coll. of S.I./CUNY, 1985—. Active Girl Scouts. Co-founder, pres. Jr. Mus. Guild, S.I. Mus., 1956-58. Mem. N.Y.C. Local Sch. Bd. 54, 1960-61. Mem. Am. Assn. Mus., Mus. Council of N.Y.C. Club: Cosmopolitan. Home: 50 Fort Pl Staten Island NY 10301

GASZTONYI, JULIA LINN, editor; b. San Pedro, Calif., June 27, 1956; d. Johannes Harrison and Barbara Ann (Barton) Shirley; m. Frank Gabor Gasztonyi, May 9, 1981. B.A., Calif. State U.-Long Beach, 1979. Asst news editor Anaheim Bull. (Calif.), 1979-81, tempo editor, 1981-82, mng. editor, 1982—. Mem. Orange County Press Club, Sigma Delta Chi. Office: Anaheim Bull 1771 S Lewis St Anaheim CA 92805

GATES, BARBARA LYNN, school administrator, educator; b. Billings, Mont., May 13, 1954; d. Joseph Isacc and Ima Evelyn (Daugherty) G. B.S. in Elementary Edn., Eastern Mont. Coll., 1976. Cert. tchr., Mont. Tchr., Union Sch., Lindsay, Mont., 1976-79, Greycliff Sch., Mont., 1979-80; supr. Alliance Christian Sch., Lewistown, Mont., 1981-83, prin., supr., 1983—. Christian Missionary Alliance.

GATES, CARLA LYNN, nurse; b. Lock Haven, Pa., Nov. 28, 1961; d. Lynn Alan and Joyce Alberta (Weaver) Robinson; m. David Clair Gates, Sept. 11, 1982; children—David Lynn, Michael, Johnathan. Diploma Philipsburg State Gen. Hosp. Lic. R.N., Pa. Nurses aide Lock Haven Hosp., 1980-81; staff nurse med.-surgical, 1982-85, Rehab Hosp., Pleasant Gap, Pa., 1985-86; med. surg. staff nurse Jersey Shore Hosp., Pa., 1986—. Am. Color and Chem. Co. scholar, 1982. Avocations: needlecrafts; cooking; gardening. Office: Jersey Shore Hosp Jersey Shore PA 17740

GATES, DEANNA L., insurance/pension fund executive; b. Omaha, Oct. 28, 1948; d. Robert C. and Kathryn L. (Adams) Gates; m. Robert E. Matthews, Jan. 3, 1970 (div.); m. 2d, Alan J. Sorem, Oct. 26, 1980. B.A., Wayne State Coll., 1971; M.B.A., Fordham U., 1981. Sec. Ark. Presbytery, Little Rock, 1975-76, United Presbyn. Ch., N.Y.C., 1976-77; adminstrv. asst. United Presbyn. Ch. hdqrs., N.Y.C., 1977-79; budget adminstr. United Brands Co., N.Y.C., 1979-82, treasury analyst, 1982-84; investment analyst Amalgamated Life Ins. Cos., N.Y.C., 1984—. Chairperson Planning Com., N.Y.C. Presbytery, 1984. Mem. N.Y. Cash Mgrs. Assn. (group leader 1983). Democrat. Home: 70 LaSalle St New York NY 10027

GATES, DOROTHY LOUISE, educator; b. National City, Calif., Feb. 21, 1926; d. Harold Roger and Bertha Marjorie (Lippold) Gates; B.A., U. Calif., Santa Barbara, 1949; M.A., U. Hawaii, 1963, Ph.D., 1975; postdoctoral student U. Uppsala (Sweden), 1976, Bedford Coll., London, 1978, Cuban Ministry of Justice, 1979. Dept. probation officer, Riverside County, Calif., 1950-54, 55-61; dir. La Morada, probation facility, Santa Barbara County, 1963-65; prof. sociology San Bernardino Valley Coll. (Calif.), 1965—; part-time tchr. criminology U. Redlands (Calif.), 1975—; chmn. Riverside County Juvenile Justice and Delinquency Prevention Commn., 1971—. Pres. Women's Equity Action League, Hawaii, 1972; mem. adv. group Riverside County Justice System, 1982. bd. dirs. San Bernardino County Mental Health Assn., Cooper Burkhart House, Riverside; mem. adv. council Ret. Sr. Vol. Program, San Bernardino. Recipient Cert. of Recognition, Riverside YWCA; named Citizen of Achievement, San Bernardino LWV, 1985; Nat. Endowment for Humanities fellow U. Va., 1977. Mem. Western Gerontology Assn., Am. Soc. Criminology, Calif. Probation, Parole and Correctional Assn. (award 1969), LWV. Address: 4665 Braemar Pl #212 Riverside CA 92501

GATES, JACQUIE KATHERINE, consultant; b. Birmingham, Ala., Apr. 11, 1938; d. John Warren and Inez (Pillar) Kirk; m. Charles James Gates, June 6, 1955 (div. Aug. 1970); 1 dau., Katherine Ann. Mgr. Chgo. Health Clubs, LaGrange, Ill., 1966-69; printing cons. Johnson Printers, Downers Grove, Ill., 1970-79; pres. Delegates, Inc., Mt. Prospect, Ill., 1980—; pres. Art/Temps, 1985—; host In Focus, weekly live cable show. Pub., editor The GraphiConnection, 1983. Town chmn. Am. Cancer Assn., Palatine, Ill., 1979-80; mem. Bensenville Cable Services. Mem. Nat. Fedn. Bus. and Profl. Women's Orgn. (pres. 1983-84), Breakfast Forum (founder 1982). Home: 802 S Addison St Bensenville IL 60106 Office: Delegates Inc Suite 101 S Pine Suite 2 Mount Prospect IL 60056

GATES, JOANNE FERRY, counselor; b. N.Y.C., Oct. 7, 1924; d. Joseph Rutherford and Constance (Riker) Ferry; B.A., Conn. Coll., 1946; M.A. in Counseling, St. Josephs Coll., 1981; m. Richard Judson Gates, Sept. 7, 1946;

children—Pamela, Cynthia, Suzanne, Rebecca. Mem. exec. bd. Jr. League Hartford, 1957-64; bd. dirs. Inst. Living Counselor, 1968-69; counselor Counseling Center, Hartford Coll. Women. 1981—; bd. dirs. Hartford Symphony, 1973-76, aux. v.p. nominating chmn., 1977; trustee Childrens Mus. Hartford, 1970-73, West Hartford Sch. Music, 1962-83. Centenary Coll. for Women, N.J. 1968—; pres. Jodik Found., 1977—; deacon 1st Ch. of Christ Congregational, 1977-79, tchr. religious edn., 1952-72, pres. women's guild, 1969-70; co-chmn. music and arts festival Trinity Coll., 1975; vol. Hartford Hosp., 1949-55, Meals on Wheels, 1977-80; v.p. women's bd., trustee Hartford Sem., 1978-84; mem. alumnae exec. bd., area chmn. capital fund drives Northfield (Mass.) Mt. Herman Sch.; sec., Smith Gates Corp., Farmington, Conn.; pres. Jodik Found.; trustee Centenary Coll., 1968—. Mem. Conn. Coll. (Hartford nominating chmn. 1964-65), Northfield Mt. Herman Sch. alumnae assns. Republican. Clubs: Seed and Weed Garden, Hartford Golf, Musical of Hartford, Watch Hill Yacht. Home: 108 Westmont West Hartford CT 06117 Office: Counseling Center Hartford Coll Women 50 Elizabeth St Hartford CT 06105

GATES, PAMELA JEAN, stagecoach company executive; b. San Bernardino, Calif., Oct. 11, 1946; d. Leo A. and Letha (Mead) Schatz; 1 child, Holly M. Student Valley Coll., 1965, U. Redlands, 1966-68. Chief exec. officer Atlas Travel Service, Redlands, Calif. 1963-69, Overland Butterfield Stagecoach, Inc., Redlands, 1974—. Writer newspaper column: Peoples Data Quiz, 1985—. Speech judge Calif. Native Sons, San Bernardino, 1985, 86. Mem. Am. Soc. Travel Agts. (awards 1965, 66), Nat. Assn. Female Execs. Republican. Home: Apt 133 1255 E Citrus Ave Redlands CA 92374 Office: Overland Butterfield Stagecoach Inc 419 San Jacinto St Redlands CA 92373

GATEWOOD, TELA LYNNE, lawyer; b. Cedar Rapids, Iowa, Mar. 23; d. Chester Russell and Cecilia Mae (McFarland) Weber; m. R.E. Gatewood, Mar. 18, 1982. B.A. with distinction, Cornell Coll., Mt. Vernon, Iowa, 1970; J.D. with distinction, U. Iowa, 1972. Bar: Iowa 1973, Calif. 1974, U.S. Supreme Ct. 1984. Instr., LaVerne Coll., Pt. Mugu, Calif., 1973; asst. city atty. City of Des Moines, 1973-78; sr. trial atty. and supervisory atty. EEOC, Dallas, also Phila., 1978—. Bd. dirs. Day Care Inc., Des Moines, 1975-78, sec., 1977, pres., 1978. Recipient Performance award EEOC, 1982, 84. Mem. ABA, Fed. Bar Assn., U.S. Supreme Ct. Bar Assn., Nat. Assn. Female Execs., AAUW. Office: EEOC 8303 Elmbrook Dr Dallas TX 75247

GATHINGS, MARY WOLFE, dental technology company executive; b. N.Y.C., Aug. 22, 1953; d. Hillard Hudson Wolfe, Jr. and Lillian (Cannon) Wolfe Queen; divorced. Assoc. Dental Hygiene, Midlands Tech. Coll., 1974. Registered dental hygienist. Hygienist, dental offices, Myrtle Beach, S.C., 1974-79, Atlanta, 1979-80; sales rep. Cleve-Dent/Cavitron, N.Y.C., 1980-81; mktg. and sales promotion mgr. Cavitron/Cooperlaser Sonics, N.Y.C., 1981—, tech. cons., 1981—. Mem. Am. Dental Hygienists Assn., S.C. Dental Hygienists Assn., N.C. Dental Hygienists Assn., Ga. Dental Hygienists, Nat. Assn. Female Execs. Home: 806 Abingdon Way Atlanta GA 30328 Office: Cavitron/Cooperlaser Sonics 11-40 Borden Ave Long Island City NY 11101

GATHMAN, ELIZABETH ANNE, human resources executive; b. Williamsport, Pa., Jan. 17, 1957; d. David William and Mildred Eleanor (Deihl) G. B.S. in Bus. Edn., Bloomsburg State Coll., 1979; postgrad. in mgmt. Villanova U., 1984—. Sales rep. Fidelity Union Life Ins. Co., King of Prussia, Pa., 1979-80; office mgr., asst. to pres. Comprehensive Benefits Service Co., Inc., Newtown Square, Pa., 1980-81, personnel dir., 1981-83, v.p. human resources, 1983—; co. rep. Self Ins. Inst. Am., 1983—, Self-Funding Assn. Pa., Harrisburg, 1983—. Vol. instr. Horizon, Inc., Delaware County, Pa., 1983—. Mem. Am. Soc. Personnel Administrs., Nat. Assn. Exec. Women, Newtown Sq. Bus. and Profl. Assn. (dir., sec. bd. 1983—). Republican. Office: Comprehensive Benefits Service Co Inc 90 S Newtown Street Rd Newton Square PA 19073

GATLING, ZINA ELAINE, personnel administrator; b. Bklyn., Dec. 8, 1960; d. Ralph Howard and Dorothy Lee (Willis) G. B.A., Spelman Coll., 1983. Adminstrv. asst. CIGNA, N.Y.C., 1983; personnel rep. East River Savs. Bank, N.Y.C., 1984—. Mem. Nat. Alumnae Assn. Spelman Coll. Democrat. Baptist.

GATSOS, ELAINE MARY, lawyer; b. Allentown, Pa., July 19, 1955; d. Stephen Louis and Zoe Ann (Hozion) G. B.A., Purdue U., 1977; J.D., Nova U., 1980. Assoc., Titone & Roarke, P.A., Lauderhill, Fla., 1980-82, Stuart & Walker P.A., Fort Lauderdale, Fla., 1982—; asst. city atty. City of Coconut Creek, Fla., 1982—. Pres., Young Democrats of Broward County (Fla.), 1982—; parliamentarian Fla. Young Democrats, 1984; bd. mem. Council of Pres. of Democratic Clubs, Broward County, Fla., 1984. Named Grad. of Yr., Phi Delta Phi, 1980. Mem. ABA, Nat. Assn. Women Lawyers, Broward County Bar Assn., Broward County Women Lawyers Assn. Democrat. Greek Orthodox. Office: Stuart & Walker PA 600 NE 3d Ave Fort Lauderdale FL 33304

GAU, MILDRED JOSEPHINE, business educator, college dean; b. Conover, Wis., Mar. 28, 1921; d. George Carl and Anna Linnea (Sandbeck) Dobbs; B.Ed., U. Wis., Whitewater, 1942, M.S., 1973; m. Donald Robert Gau, July 31, 1943; children—Robert Alan, Judith Ann Gau Hart. Tchr., Jefferson (Wis.) High Sch., 1942-44; clk. stenographer U.S. Civil Service, Miami, Fla., 1945-46; sec. Meyers Equipment Co., Milw., 1946-47; tchr. Spencerian Bus. Coll., Milw., 1947-48; tchr. Milw. Area Tech. Coll., 1955-80, secretarial sci. dept. chmn., 1971-75, supr. bus. and gen. edn. West Campus, 1980-81, dean bus. div., 1981—. Pres., S. 55th St. Sch. PTA, 1959. Recipient Wis. Outstanding Bus. Educator award, 1982. Mem. Word Processing Soc. (pres. 1979-80), Am. Vocat. Assn., Wis. Assn. Vocat. and Adult Edn., Nat. Bus. Edn. Assn., Wis. Bus. Edn. Assn. (pres. 1973), Wis. Vocat. Bus. Edn. Assn. (pres. 1970), Milw. Area Bus. Edn. Assn., Internat. Info./Word Processing Assn., Adminstrv. Mgmt. Soc., Data Processing Mgmt. Assn., U. Wis.-Whitewater Nat. Alumni Assn. (Disting. Alumni Service award 1982), Delta Pi Epsilon, Sigma Sigma Sigma. Lutheran. Clubs: Luther Manor Aux., Order Eastern Star. Columnist, The Word mag., 1979, 80; contbr. articles in field to profl. jours. Home: 6100 W Stonehedge Dr Milwaukee WI 53220 Office: 1015 N 6th St Milwaukee WI 53203

GAUDIO, MAXINE DIANE, biofeedback therapist, stress management consultant; b. Stamford, Conn., Oct. 7, 1939; d. Robert Fridolin and Doris (Altstadter) Goodman; m. Arthur Sebastian Gaudio, Oct. 7, 1962; 1 child, Dante Sebastian. Student Bryn Mawr Coll., 1959; B.S., NYU, 1960, M.S., 1972. Relaxation therapist The Biofeedback Clinic, New Canaan, Conn., 1970-73; chief EEG technologist St. Barnabas, Bronx, N.Y., 1973-75; biofeedback therapist Biofeedback Clinic, Stamford, Conn. and Winston-Salem, N.C., 1973—; clin. dir. Biofeedback Unltd. N.C., 1979—; clin. dir. Creative Mind Systems, Stamford, Conn., 1980—; tech. advisor Creative Mind Systems N.C., 1980-83; indsl. cons. major corps. U.S.A., 1976—; writer, creator stress video Hartley Prodns., Old Greenwich, Conn., 1984—; writer, creator, narrator Robert Gross Assocs., Stamford, Conn., 1984. Author, narrator video: Stress, 1984, Your Secret Energy Source, 1984; Author, narrator book and tapes: Creative Union, 1980; author: Land Within the Shadow, 1980. Mem. Am. Fedn. Press Women, Am. Soc. EEG Technologists, Am. Assn. Advancement Tension Control, Biofeedback Soc. Am., Biofeedback Soc. N.C. Avocations: swimming; fencing; flying; metaphysics; astrology; piano. Home: 3 Hackett Circle Apt 2 Stamford CT 06905

GAUGER, MICHELE ROBERTA, photographer, studio administrator; b. Elkhorn, Wis., Feb. 28, 1949; d. Robert F. and Christiane J. (Guiffaut) Marszalek; m. Richard C. Gauger, May 3, 1969. Student U. Wis.-Superior, 1967-69, U. Wis.-Whitewater, 1978-80, Winona Sch. Profl. Photography-Chgo., 1984-85. Wedding photographer Fossum Studio, Elkhorn, 1973-78; owner Photography by Michele, Whitewater, 1978-81; pres., photographer, mgr., Michele Inc. of Wis., Whitewater, 1981—. Contbr. articles to profl. jours. Mem. Nat. Arbor Found, Nebr., 1984—. Recipient 1st place Wedding Photography award Internat. Wedding Photography, 1983, 84, 2nd place award, 1985. Mem. Profl. Photographers Am. (Natl. Loan Collectional 1984), Wis. Profl. Photographer Assn., Wedding Photographer Internat., Whitewater C. of C. Republican. Roman Catholic. Avocations: world travel; big game hunting; horseback riding; cooking. Home: Gauger Rd Rt 2 Whitewater WI 53190 Office: Michele Inc Rt 2 Whitewater Lake Whitewater WI 53190

GAUGER, OTTILIE ERNSTINE, typesetting and computer services company executive, researcher, consultant; b. Milw., Sept. 8, 1917; d. William and Pauline (Krueger) Heinz; m. Charles Paul Gauger, May 31, 1941; children—Lynn, Charla Gauger Becker. Student various courses in bus. mgmt., behavioral sci. Milw. Area Vocat. Sch., 1959-60, Marquette U., 1961-62. Sec. purchasing agt. Blatz Brewery, Milw., 1936-39; sec. Riverside Lith Sch., Milw., 1939-43, Wis. Motor Corp., Milw., 1943-45; v.p. research Litho Compositors, Milw., 1950-60; v.p. prodn. C.P. Gauger Co., Milw., 1960-80; v.p., cons. Dataplex Services, Milw., 1980—, also dir.; tchr. typesetting various schs., Wis., 1954-76. Pres. Alpha Phi Mothers Aux., Milw., 1970; sec.-treas. Christ Lutheran Ch., Mequon, Wis., 1970-72, Wolf River Lakes Assn., White Lake, Wis., 1984-85. Mem. Nat. Cold Type Assn. (charter), Nat. Composition Assn. (charter). Republican. Lodge: Shriners Aux. Avocations: needlework, biking, shuffleboard, golf, fishing. Home: 8450 W Forest Ave Milwaukee WI 53228 Office: Dataplex Services and C P Gauger Co 8450 W Forest Ave Milwaukee WI 53228

GAUGHAN, PEARL MARY, former public health nurse, consultant; b. Reading, Pa., Apr. 9, 1921; d. Raymond Bucher and Lillian May (Fields) Fichthorn; m. Michael J. Gaughan, Jr., Feb. 14, 1946 (dec. 1985); children—Michael J., Patricia Ann. R.N., Reading Hosp. Sch. Nursing, 1943; student UCLA, 1965-83, U. So. Calif., 1965-83, Calif. State U.-San Bernardino, 1965—. Pvt. duty nurse, Reading, Pa., 1943-45; charge nurse U.S. Army Hosp., Richmond, Va., 1945-47; pvt. duty nurse, Roswell, N.M., 1947-48; charge nurse U.S. Indian Hosp., Winslow, Ariz., 1948-51; pvt. duty nurse, San Bernardino, Calif., 1951-62; asst. dir. Vis. Nurse Assn., San Bernardino, Calif., 1963-70; pub. health nurse San Bernardino County Health Dept., 1970-83; now ret.; student nurse cons. Calif. State U., others, 1965—. Author: Home Nursing Care Procedure, 1974. Instr. San Bernardino chpt. ARC, 1957-59; sec. Am. Lung Assn., 1975—; chmn. stroke com. Am. Heart Assn., 1977—; pres. Arrowhead Republican Women, 1958; active Boy Scouts Am., Girl Scouts U.S.A., 1955-67; comdr. Am. Legion Post 14, San Bernardino, Calif., 1974. Served as lt. Army Nurse Corps, 1945-47. Mem. Calif. Nurses Assn., So. Calif. Pub. Health Assn., Hosp. Discharge Planners Assn., Am. Assn. Continuity of Care, Bus. and Profl. Women of San Bernardino (committeewoman), Reading Hosp. Alumni Assn., Am. Nurses Assn., Nat. Orgn. World War Nurses. Republican. Roman Catholic. Lodge: Elks Wives Orgn. (sec. 1960-63). Home: 2870 Serrano Rd San Bernardino CA 92405

GAULDING, JULIA MILLER, marketing executive; b. Richmond, Va., Dec. 27, 1954; d. Ellison Parks Gaulding Jr. and Nelda Rose (Suites) Jernigan. B.A., U. South Fla., 1978; M.Internat. Bus., Fla. Internat. U., 1984; hon. degree in internat. trade Cambridge (Eng.) U., 1980, in internat. instns. U. Geneva, 1976. Mktg. adminstr. Miami Dept. Trade and Commerce (Fla.), 1980-81, Deloitte Haskins & Sells, Miami, 1981-84; pres. JMG Strategies, Miami, 1984—; dir. E.P. Supe Gaulding Import & Export, Inc., Miami. Team capt. March of Dimes Walkathon, Miami, 1982; mem. Com. of 100, Miami's for Me, 1982. Mem. Internat. Ctr. of Fla. (Pallot award 1978-84), Am. Advt. Assn., Am. Mktg. Assn. Methodist. Office: JMG Strategies 6511 Santona St Suite 8 Coral Gables FL 33146

GAULKE, MARY FLORENCE, library administrator; b. Johnson City, Tenn., Sept. 24, 1923; d. Gustus Thomas and Mary Belle (Dennett) Erickson; m. James Wymond Crowley, Dec. 1, 1939; 1 son, Grady Gaulke (name legally changed); m. 2d, Bud Gaulke, Sept. 1, 1945 (dec. Jan. 1978); m. 3d, Richard Lewis McNaughton, Mar. 21, 1983. B.S. in Home Econs., Oreg. State U., 1963; M.S. in L.S., U. Oreg., 1968, Ph.D. in Spl. Edn., 1970. Cert. standard personnel supr., standard handicapped learner, Oreg. Head dept. home econs. Riddle Sch. Dist. (Oreg.), 1963-66; library cons. Douglas County Intermediate Edn. Dist., Roseburg, Oreg., 1966-67; head resident, head counselor Prometheus Project, So. Oreg. Coll., Ashland, summers 1966-68; supr. librarians Medford Sch. Dist. (Oreg.), 1970-73; instr. in psychology So. Oreg. Coll., Ashland, 1970-73; library supr. Roseburg Sch. Dist., 1974—; resident psychologist Black Oaks Boys Sch., Medford, 1970-75; mem. Oreg. Gov.'s Council on Libraries, 1979. Author: Vo-Ed Course for Junior High, 1965; Library Handbook, 1967; Instructions for Preparation of Cards For All Materials Cataloged for Libraries, 1971; Handbook for Training Library Aides, 1972. Coordinator Laubach Lit. Workshops for High Sch. Tutors, Medford, 1972. Mem. So. Oreg. Library Fedn. (sec. 1971-73), ALA, Oreg. Library Assn., Pacific N.W. Library Assn., Delta Kappa Gamma (pres. 1980-82), Phi Delta Kappa (historian, research rep.). Republican. Methodist. Clubs: Lodge: Order Eastern Star (worthy matron 1956-57). Home: HC 1 Box 60 Canyonville OR 97417 Office: Roseburg Pub Schs 1419 Valley View Dr Roseburg OR 97470

GAUMER, OTIE LEONA, retired nurse; b. Ryan, Ky., Dec. 6, 1910; d. James Oscar and Gaythel (Hamilton) McKee; m. Lloyd Emil Gaumer, Jan. 23, 1937; children—Jane Arlene Gaumer Hoffman, Lloyd Emil, Jr. Grad. Nazareth Sch. Nursing, 1934; postgrad., Ohio State U., 1958, U. Mich., 1959. Lic. R.N., Ky, Ohio. Surgical nurse St. Joseph Hosp., Lexington, Ky., 1934; surgical nurse Mercy Hosp., Mt. Vernon, Ohio, 1934-37, part-time, 1948-52, full-time, 1952-57, pvt. duty nurse, 1937-40; pub. health nurse Mt. Vernon Health Dept., 1957-76. Bd. dirs. Knox County TB Health Assn., Mt. Vernon, 1957-65, Knox County Crippled Children Assn., Mt. Vernon, 1957-82; publicity, program dir. Knox County Heart Assn., Mt. Vernon, 1963-69; active numerous other vol. health agencies; helped establish Immunization Clinic, 1958, Home Health Agency, 1964, TB Skin Testing Clinic, 1959, Pediatric and Blood Pressure Clinics, 1973. Grantee Knox County TB Health Assn., 1958, Ohio Dept. Health, 1959, Knox County Crippled Childrens Assn., 1961. Mem. Am. Nurses Assn., Ky. State Nurses Assn., Ohio State Nurses Assn. Republican. Baptist.

GAUSE, JEANETTE NELSON, marketing consultant; b. The Dalles, Oreg., Aug. 28, 1934; d. Roy Vernon and Lillie Mae (Doughty) Bates; m. Richard Dale Nelson, Nov. 28, 1952 (div. Aug., 1975); children—Christine Anna Nelson Powell, Teresa Dale Nelson Chastain, Michael Alan; m. Jimmy Marshall Gause, Nov. 27, 1978. B.A., Portland State Coll.; postgrad. Universad de Puerto Rico. Editor, Sun Newspapers, Omaha, Nebr., 1969-72; staff mgr. C. of C., San Antonio, 1972-74; dir. pub. relations Trinity U., San Antonio, 1974-78; dir. mktg. Sani-Fresh Internat., San Antonio, 1980-82; co-owner, mgr. Gause & Assocs., San Antonio, 1979-84; chmn. bd., pres. J. Nelson Gause, Inc., San Antonio, 1984—; cons. Periodical Mgmt. Group, San Antonio, 1983—. Editor, Boys Town article, 1971-72 (Pulitzer Prize for Investigative Reporting-Weekly Newspaper 1972). Jury foreman Dist. Ct., San Antonio, 1972; nat. judge Internat. Assn. of Bus. Communicators, 1978; mem. Downtown Task Force, 1984, Bus. Prospect Task Force, 1984; lobbyist Periodical Mgmt. Group, 1984. Mem. Nat. Assn. of Female Execs., Am. Mgmt. Assn., Greater San Antonio C. of C. Avocations: gardening; tennis; swimming. Office: J Nelson Gause Inc 3223 Howard St Suite 11 San Antonio TX 78212

GAUSMAN, EDITH MARIE, treasurer; b. N.Y.C., Jan. 17, 1919; s. George and Eliza (Heuermann) G. Fiduciary acct. Sage Gray Todd & Sims, N.Y.C., 1950-64; asst. v.p. Scudder, Stevens & Clark, N.Y.C., 1964-72; asst. treas. Commonwealth Fund, N.Y.C., 1972-75, treas., 1975-81. Vice pres. bd. trustees Riverside Ch., N.Y.C., 1976-78; bd. dirs. Westside Ecumenical Ministry to the Elderly, Inc., 1979-84. Mem. Bus. and Profl. Women's Club. Home: 11 Riverside Dr New York NY 10023

GAUTHIER, LINDA KATHERINE, manufacturing company executive; b. N.Y.C., Oct. 4, 1947; d. Norman Leonard and Catherine (Layer) G.; student Pan Am Art Sch., 1966-69, Dutchess Community Coll., 1980—. Clk., Samberg Bros., Maspeth, N.Y., 1964; statis. clk. N.Y. Telephone Co., Bklyn., 1964-65; sec. Govt. Employees Ins. Co., 1965-66; adminstrv. asst. Rheingold Breweries, Bklyn., 1966-69; partner ARTvertising Agy., N.Y.C., 1969-71; reprographic services mgr. Singer Co., Stamford, Conn., 1971—. Mem. Union Vale Park Commn., 1977-78, Union Vale Bicentennial Com., 1975-76; chmn. publicity Union Vale Republican Club, 1977-78. Recipient citation of appreciation Am. Legion, 1967; award of merit Union Vale Bicentennial Com., 1976, cert. merit Dutchess Community Coll.; Mgmt. award The Singer Co., 1983. Mem. Bus. Forms Mgmt. Assn. (sec. N.Y. chpt.), Mgmt. Books Inst., Nat. Assn. Female Execs., Exec. Program. Roman Catholic. Office: 8 Stamford Forum Stamford CT 06904

GAUTREAUX, SHERRI HAYES, administrative operations assistant; b. Baton Rouge, Oct. 28, 1958; d. Judson William and Dorothy Mildred (Norris) Hayes; m. Mel Adam Gautreaux, Oct. 8, 1983. B.S., La. State U., 1980. Clerical and research work La. Atty. Gen.'s Office, Baton Rouge, 1980-84; ops. asst. La. State Senate, Baton Rouge, 1984—. Gymnastics scholar La. State U., 1976-79. Mem. Nat. Assn. Female Execs., La. State U. Alumni Club, Nat. Lettermen's Club, Alpha Gamma Delta. Republican. Avocations: gymnastics, racquetball, bowling, needlework, photography. Home: 3733 Byrd Dr Baton Rouge LA 70814 Office: La State Senate State Capitol PO Box 94183 Baton Rouge LA 70804

GAUTT, SANDRA WHAYNE, educator; b. Chgo., Nov. 12, 1943; d. Thaddeus Alonzo and Alyce Louise Whayne; B.Ed. cum laude, U. Mo., Columbia, 1964, M.Ed., 1966, Ph.D., 1975; m. Prentice Gautt, June 5, 1971. Tchr., Woodhaven Learning Center, Columbia, 1966-68; supr. Hosp. Sch., U. Mo., Columbia, 1968-69; tchr. supr. Spl. Sch. Dist., St. Louis County, Mo., 1969-71; instr. dept. spl. edn. U. Mo., 1971-76, asst. prof., 1977-81, assoc. prof., 1981—; cons., field reader spl. edn. program Div. Innovation and Devel. and Div. Personnel Preparation, U.S. Dept. Edn., U.S. Dept. Edn. grantee, 1978-85; ACE fellow in acad. adminstrn., 1984-85. Mem. Council for Exceptional Children, Pi Lambda Theta, Phi Delta Kappa, Kappa Delta Pi, Alpha Kappa Alpha. Office: Dept Spl Edn U MO 515 S 6th St Columbia MO 65211

GAVIN, VIDA REGINA, educational administrator; b. Birstonas, Lithuania, Aug. 12, 1941; d. Jurgis and Elena (Ciurlionis) Strazdas; came to U.S., 1948, naturalized, 1959; B.S., Northeastern U., 1968, M.Ed., 1973, postgrad., 1980—; m. Charles F. Gavin, June 26, 1965; 1 son, David. Dept. head, coordinator spl. services and reading Public Schs. Dedham (Mass.), 1971-81; dir. spl. services Scituate (Mass.) Public Schs., 1981—. Mem. Internat. Reading Assn., Council Exceptional Children, Assn. Supervision and Curriculum Devel., Adminstrs. Spl. Edn., New Eng. Coalition Ednl. Leaders, Mass. Reading Assn., Mass. Assn. Children with Learning Disabilities. Delta Kappa Gamma. Home: 141 Forest St Norwell MA 02061 Office: 606 Chief Justice Cushing Hwy Scituate MA 02066

GAVINS-BOLDS, BEATRICE BRENDA, government financial management specialist; b. Bklyn., Nov. 3, 1946; d. John Edward and Ellree (Williams) Gavins. B.S., CUNY, 1975. Adminstrv. asst. OEO, N.Y.C., 1967-73; adminstrv. asst. Social Security Adminstrn., HEW, N.Y.C., 1973-74, auditor, 1974-75, exec. asst. Office Child Support Enforcement, 1977-79, Health Care Financing Adminstrn., 1979-80, fin. mgmt. specialist Office Family Assistance, 1980—. Recipient Exemplary Employee award Social Security Adminstrn., N.Y.C., 1974; Spl. Achievement award Health Care Financing Adminstrn., N.Y.C., 1979; Disting. Performance cert. Office Civil Rights, N.Y.C., 1980. Mem. Federally Employed Women (chpt. pres. 1979-82, regional mgr. 1982-85, nat. v.p. for tng. 1985-86, Disting. Service award 1982), Coalition 100 Black Women, Nat. Assn. Female Execs. Avocations: tennis; skiing; bridge; backgammon. Home: 144 Lincoln Pl Brooklyn NY 11217

GAWEHN, DOROTHY JEANNE, retail sales company executive; b. Omaha, Jan. 20, 1931; d. Robert Floyd and Margaret Marie (Sitzman) Sealock; m. Kenneth Emil Gawehn, Apr. 17, 1951 (div. Jan. 1985); children Marilyn Gawehn Jeffries, Kenneth M., Eric M., Celeste Gawehn-Yates. Grad. high sch., Omaha, Nebr. Systems technician Nat. Welding Co., Richmond, Calif., 1926-63; lead data entry operator United Grocers Co., Fresno, Calif., 1964-68, data processing mgr., 1968-72, computer operator shift supr., Oakland, Calif., 1972-76, documentation specialist, 1976-82; mgr. adminstrv. systems Baddour, Inc., Memphis, 1983—. Reader for the blind Sta. WTTL, Memphis, 1983—; vol. worker Crisis and Suicide Intervention, Memphis, 1985—. Mem. Internat. Tng. In Communication (club del. 1985-86), Assn. Computing Machinery (sec., newsletter editor 1985—), Mensa. Republican. Roman Catholic. Avocations: backpacking; reading; writing; travel; hiking. Home: 6644 Elkgate Rd Memphis TN 38114 Office: Baddour Inc 4300 Getwell Rd Memphis TN 38118

GAY, BESSIE JEAN, computer software manager; b. Atlanta, Oct. 8, 1952; d. James W. and Lena (Sinkfield) Gay. Student Ga. State U., 1974. Supr. C & S Nat. Bank, Atlanta, 1970-74; systems engr. EDS, Dallas, 1975-77; mng. product cons. ISA, Atlanta, 1978-81; project mgr. Dyer, Wells & Assocs., Atlanta, 1981—. Chmn. Cascade United Meth. Ch. Evangelism Com., Atlanta, 1981-84; pres. Cascade United Meth. Ch. Singles Ministry, Atlanta, 1984—; mem. Big Sister Program, Atlanta, 1982. Mem. Am. Bus. Women Assn. (membership chmn. 1978-79). Office: Dyer Wells & Assocs 2251 Lake Park Dr Smyrna GA 30080

GAY, BONNIE LEWIS, lawyer; b. Newton Grove, N.C., Jan. 20, 1942; d. Clarence Henry and Patricia Lucile (Brock) Lewis; m. William Jan Gay, Mar. 10, 1962 (div. 1976); 1 child, Heather Laurie. B.A., Am. U., 1962, LL.B., 1964. Bar: Va. 1964, D.C. 1966, N.J. 1978, U.S. Supreme Ct., 1972. Law clk. U.S. Dist. Ct. D.C., 1964-66; sole practice, McLean, Va., 1966-68; project dir. Computer Retrieval Systems, Bethesda, Md., 1968-70; atty. opinion sect. office gen. counsel Dept. Treasury, Washington, 1970-73, tech. asst. to asst. gen. counsel, 1974-77; legal counsel Bur. Engraving and Printing, Washington, 1977-80; of counsel office chief counsel Office Revenue Sharing, Washington, 1980-84; asst. dir. Legal Edn. Inst., Dept. Justice, Washington, 1984—; mem. faculty U. Md., 1980-86; Contbr. articles to profl. jours. Bd. dirs., legal counsel Treasury Hist. Assn., 1973-76, 79-80, 81-83, 85-87; sec. Cleveland Terr. Owners Assn., 1981-82; mem. Treasury Women's Adv. Com., 1974-76; trustee Universalist Nat. Meml. Ch., 1969-75, chmn. music, 1969-71, chmn. fin., 1971-75; bd. dirs. Treasury Dept. Fedn. Credit Union, 1975-77; mem. Dean's Adv. Council Washington Coll. Law, 1982-85. Mem. ABA (corp. and banking subcom.), Fed. Bar Assn. (treas. D.C. chpt. 1982-83, bd. dirs. 1980-83, rec. sec. 1983-84, corr. sec. 1984-85, 2d v.p. 1985-86), D.C. Bar Assn. (sec. medico-legal com. 1973-75), Va. State Bar, Women's Bar Assn. D.C., Kappa Beta Pi (province pres. 1972-74). Home: 7008 Benjamin St McLean VA 22101 Office: Legal Edn Inst 1875 Connecticut Ave NW Room 1034 Washington DC 20530

GAY, CLAUDINE MOSS, physician; b. Alma, Ga., Nov. 30, 1915; d. Fred and Rosa (Mercer) Moss; B.S., Coll. William and Mary, 1935; M.D., U. Va., 1939; m. Lendall C. Gay, June 29, 1940 (dec. 1971); children—Gordon B., Spencer B.; m. J. Marion Bryant, 1974 (dec. 1986). Intern, Gallinger Mcpl. Hosp., Washington; practice medicine specializing in family practice, Washington, 1940—; mem. staff, exec. bd. Sibley Meml. and Capitol Hill Hosp., Washington; mem. Pres.'s Council on Malpractice, 1965; mem. health adv. commn. HEW, 1971-78; U.S. del. Med. Women's Internat. Congress, 5 times; del. Pres.'s Workshop on Non-Govtl. Orgn. Trustee Moss Charity Trust Fund, 1966—; adv. bd. Med. Coll. Pa., 1977; mem. president's council Coll. William and Mary. Fellow Am. Acad. Family Practice (del. 1971-81; alt. del. to ho. dels. 1964-71); mem. Assn. Med. Women Internat. (del. 1966-72, councillor 1978-84), Royal Acad. Medicine, Pan Am. Med. Soc., D.C. Acad. Gen. Practice (pres.), Am. Med. Women's Assn. (councilor orgn. and mgmt. 1972-73, v.p. 1974, nat. pres. 1977), D.C. Med. Women's Assn. (pres.), AMA, D.C. Med. Soc. (dir., exec. bd., past v.p., mem. nominating com. 1970, 81, relative value study com. 1970-72, house and bldg. com. 1971-72, legis., constn. and constn. bylaws com., sec. family practice sect. 1966, 69, 78). Clubs: Women's Roundtable for Health Issues, Washington Forum, Zonta (dir.). Home: 5030 Loughboro Rd NW Washington DC 20016 Office: 403 E Capitol St SE Washington DC 20003

GAY, DAWN VIRGINIA, executive recruiter, medical consultant; b. N.Y.C., Sept. 1, 1951; d. John and Grazina Lillian (Vizbara) G.; student St. Xavier Coll., 1969-71, Morraine Valley Community Coll., 1972-73, Rush U., 1974-75, DePaul U., 1975-77; grad. Way Internat. Ministry, Knoxville, Ohio, 1980; grad. fellows program in community and organizational systems Johns Hopkins U., 1981; B.A.A.BS., Nat. Coll. Edn.; cert. instr. ARC; 1 child, Christopher Alan. EKG technician, med. transcriber Christ Hosp., Oak Lawn, Ill., 1972-73; nursing asst. Rush Presbyn. St. Lukes Hosp., Chgo., 1974-75; adminstrv. asst. to Jean C. Alexandre, M.D., Broadview, Ill., 1975-78; clinic mgr. Chgo. Osteo. Hosp., 1978; cons. Med. Bus. Cons. & Assocs., LaGrange Park, Ill., 1979; pres. bd. dirs. CHIPS, Council for Health, Info. and Public Service, Inc., Maywood, Ill., 1979-80; pres., corp. officer Med. Practice Mgmt., Inc., Maywood, 1979-80; clinic mgr. Alma Comprehensive Med. Center, Ltd., Maywood, 1978-81; health care specialist Mgmt. Recruiters Internat., Frederick, Md., 1980-81; med. cons. and ptnr. Profl. Med. Services, Bensenville, Ill., 1982—; exec. recruiter Health Profls. Internat., Winnetka, Ill., 1982— sales and mktg. rep. Addison Med. Ctr. (Ill.), 1983-84 physician recruiter, cons. Profl. Search Internat., Addison, 1983; gen. mgr. Catalyst Health Care div. Catalyst Search, Ltd., 1984-86; med. cons. to osteo. physicians, 1986—; pres. Allister & Assocs., Inc. Mem. Am. Soc. Profl. and Exec. Women, Ill. Group Mgmt. Assn., Med. Group Mgmt. Assn., Am. Assn. Med. Assts. (cert.), Addison Indsl. Assn., Addison C. of C., Nat. Assn. Physician Recruiters. Office: PO Box 195 Bensenville IL 60106

GAY, ELIZABETH DERSHUCK, artist; b. Phila., Nov. 27, 1927; d. John Raymond and Marguerite Sloane (Bright) Dershuck; B.A., Sweet Briar Coll., 1949; postgrad. Nat. Acad. Fine Arts, N.Y.C., 1957-58; m. Frank Lipscomb

Gay, Jan. 8, 1955; children—Frank, Jack, Rutherford. One-woman shows include: Little Gallery, Katonah, N.Y., 1975, Mamaroneck Artists Guild, 1977, Hazleton (Pa.) Art League, Cassandra Gallery, White Plains, 1980, Sweet Briar Coll., Benedict Gallery, 1984; group shows include: Beaux Arts Finale, 1975, Westlake Gallery, White Plains, 1976, Lever House, 1977, Union Carbide, 1977, Knickerbocker Artists, 1976, 77, 79, 80-81, Nat. Arts Club, 1977, 79, New Eng. Exhbn. at Silvermine, 1977, Hudson Valley Arts Assn., 1975, 77, 79, Salmagundi Club, 1978, 81, NAD, 1980, Bergen County Mus. (N.J.), 1983, Westchester Community Coll., 1984; traveling exhbns. Nat. Assn. Women Artists, 1980-82; instr. Watercolor North Castle Adult Edn., 1974-77; instr., mem. adv. bd. Pelham Art Center, 1979—; Mem. Artists Equity Assn. N.Y., Knickerbocker Artists N.Y., Mamaroneck Artists Guild, Nat. Assn. Women Artists, Catherine Lorillard Wolfe Art Club N.Y. Republican. Clubs: Whippoorwill, Green Acres Garden. Home: 37 Round Hill Rd Armonk NY 10504

GAY, GRETCHEN M., nurse, administrator; b. Burlington, Kans., May 7, 1930; d. Donald Melvin and Millie Jane (Mattox) Remer; A.A. in Nursing, Johnson County Community Coll., 1973; student parapsychology under Joaquin Cunanan, Manila, 1978. Student, then grad. nurse Olathe Community Hosp. (Kans.), 1972-73; night supr. VA Hosp., Leavenworth, Kans., 1973-77; asst. dir. nursing Mid Continent Psychiat. Hosp., Olathe, 1978-84; supr. Western Mo. Mental Health Ctr., Kansas City, 1984—; dir. nursing Troost Nursing Home, 1980—; owner cons. firm Endless Horizons; co-writer grant and co-founder 1st Level Six Treatment Ctr. of Kans. for Wayward Children, Olathe, 1979; an organizer Nurse Adv. Tng. Program, Chgo., 1977. Lic. nursing home adminstr.; R.N. Mem. Metasci. Found., Soc. for Improvement Human Functioning, Mo. League for Nursing, Am. Holistic Nurses Assn., Martin Psychiat. Research Found., Brain Mind. Mem. Unity Ch. Home: 811 Layton Dr Olathe KS 66061 Office: Western Mo Mental Health Ctr 600 E 22d St Kansas City MO 64108

GAY, MARILYN FANELLI MARTIN, television talk show hostess, producer, writer; b. San Francisco, July 16, 1925; d. Louis and Gertrude (Dondero) Fanelli; m. Mel Raymond Gay, May 3, 1963. Student, U. Calif.-Berkeley, 1943-46, U. Oreg., 1946. Producer, hostess, writer "In God We Trust" (presented by Protestant Ch. Fedn.), Channel 5-KTLA, Los Angeles, 1954-55; "A Woman's World", TV talk show, Las Vegas, 1956, "Party with the Stars", KBIG Radio, 1958; writer TV film Passing Parade Films, ABC-TV, 1958; producer, hostess, writer "The Marilyn Gay Show", Dimension Cable TV, Group W Cable, Storer Cable TV, Los Angeles, 1982—; dir. spl. features, coordinator radio and TV "Invest in America", 1957. Contbg. feature writer Los Angeles Times, 1957. Past mem. Palos Verdes Christian Women's Club (Calif.), 1974-74, LWV, Rancho Palos Verdes, 1973-74. Recipient Outstanding Good Citizen award DAR, 1943. Mem. Nat. Fedn. Press Women, Calif. Press Women, U. Calif.-Berkeley Alumni Assn., Alpha Delta Pi. Mem. Ch. of Religious Sci. Home and Office: 2400 E Pleasant Valley Rd #98 Oxnard CA 93033

GAYDOS, LYNETTE ARLENE, optics manufacturing company executive; b. Phoenixville, Pa., Feb. 16, 1946; d. Joseph Garfield and Dorothy (Myers) Stanton; m. Paul John Gaydos, July 19, 1976; 1 dau., Elaine. Student Albright Coll., 1963-64, Ursinus Coll., 1972-73; cert. in Bus. Mgmt., Pa. State U., Reading, 1981. Acct., Stanley Tools, Royersford, Pa., 1973-76; gen. mgr. Sunset Mfg., Pottstown, Pa., 1976-79, contracts mgr., personnel mgr., sales and mktg. Plummer Precision Optics, Pennsburg, Pa., 1979—; adv. council Pa. Job Service, Pottstown, 1976-81. Bd. advisors Opportunities Indsl, Ctr., Pottstown, 1976-80; aux. mem. Mental Health Ctr., Pottstown. Mem. Instrument Soc. Am., Am. Soc. Personnel Adminstrs., Nat. Contract Mgmt. Assn., Upper Perkiomen C. of C. (v.p. 1983-). Republican. Lutheran. Home: 2419 Rosenberry Rd Gilbertsville PA 19525 Office: Plummer Precision Optics 601 Mongomery Ave Pennsburg PA 18073

GAYESKI, DIANE MARY, communications technology company executive; communications educator; b. Scranton, Pa., Feb. 14, 1953; d. Edward Charles and Alba (Lori) Gayeski; m. David V. Williams, Aug. 23, 1980. B.S., Ithaca Coll., 1974; M.A., U. Md., 1975, Ph.D., 1979. Instr., Montgomery Coll., Rockville, Md., 1977; instructional designer U. Md., College Park, 1978-79, dir. Ednl. Tech. Ctr., 1978; asst. prof. communications Ithaca Coll., N.Y., 1979-84, assoc. prof., 1984—, chmn. grad. studies, 1985—; prin. ptnr. OmniCom Assocs., Ithaca, 1979—. Author: Corporate and Instructional Video, 1984; (with D.V. Williams) Interactive Media, 1985; (with J. Arwady) Using Video, 1986. Contbr. articles to profl. jours. Dana scholar, 1982; grantee Ethnic Heritage Found. 1978. Mem. Internat. TV Assn. (chpt. pres. 1983-84), Assn. Ednl. Communications and Technology, Am. Soc. Tng. and Devel., Nat. Soc. Performance and Instrn. Office: OmniCom Assocs 407 Coddington Rd Ithaca NY 14850

GAYLORD, NELLIE WOLFE, retired educational administrator; b. Luthersville, Ga., Aug. 20, 1922; d. John Thomas and Madie (Jones) Wolfe; B.A. (scholar), Clark Coll., 1943; M.S. (scholar), Atlanta U., 1950; postgrad. Temple U., U. Pa.; m. Clyde Felton Gaylord, Jr., Aug. 2, 1953; 1 son, Clyde Felton III. Tchr., Atlanta Pub. Schs., 1944-46; tchr. Sch. Dist. Phila., 1946-69, tchr. on spl. assignment, 1969-70, adminstrv. asst. to dist. supt., 1970-72, vice prin., 1972-75, prin. secondary sch., 1975—; guest lectr. West Chester State Coll., Pa. State U. Vice chmn. Moorestown (N.J.) Zoning Bd. of Adjustment, 1981, chmn., 1982; vice chmn. Moorestown Shadetree Adv. Com., 1976, chmn., 1977; merit badge counselor Boy Scouts Am., 1974—; mem. Citizens Adv. Com. on Drug Abuse, 1970; bd. dirs. West End Community Center, Moorestown, N.J., pres. 1973; membership solicitor YMCA; vestryman Episcopal Ch. Recipient Meritorious Service award United Negro Coll. Fund, 1958; service award Cancer Crusade, 1969; NSF grantee, 1963-66. Mem. Phila. Assn. Sch. Adminstrs., Black Women Ednl. Alliance, Assn. for Supervision and Curriculum Devel., Phila. Clark Coll. Alumni, Alpha Kappa Alpha (N. Atlanta regional dir., past chpt. pres.). Republican. Clubs: Links (eastern area chmn. internat. trends and services 1983—), The Ems (Moorestown). Home: 405 Glen Ave Moorestown NJ 08057 Office: Sulzberger 48th and Fairmount Ave Philadelphia PA 19139

GAYMAN, PATRICIA GYNETH, chiropractor; b. San Pedro, Calif., Aug. 16, 1938; d. Norman Alan and Olive Delone (Jensen) Smith; m. Robert Dale May, Jan. 13, 1956 (div. Nov. 1968); children—Cheryl, Robert, Karla, Kym, Leland, Deirdre, Stacy; m. Merrill Gene Gayman, Mar. 29, 1969. Student Monterey Peninsula Coll., 1958-59, Shasta Coll., 1971-73; D.C., Palmer Coll. of Chriopractic, 1964. Chiropractor, Monterey, Calif., 1964; assoc. in chiropractice practice, Hayward, Calif., 1968-69, Redding, Calif., 1974-79; owner, operator Gayman Chiropractice Ctr., Redding, 1979—; founder Metaphys. Exploration Ctr., Redding, 1973-83; dir. Wellness Resource Ctr., Redding, 1979—; founder, sponsor Holistic Health Fair, 1979—. Contbr. articles to profl. jours. Personnel chmn. Family Planning Inc., Redding, 1972-77; regent Pacific States Chiropractice Coll., San Leandro, 1979-81; sec. Jazz Soc. and Festival, Redding, 1985-86. Mem. Nat. assn. Female Execs., Bus. and Profl. Women's Club, C. of C. (Bus. Woman of Yr. 1985). Lodge: Toastmasters. Avocations: continuing education; metaphysical studies; jazz. Home: 7252 Churn Creek Rd Redding CA 96001 Office: Gayman Chiropractic Ctr 1065 W Cypress Ave Redding CA 96001

GAYNOR, LEAH, publicist; b. Irvington, N.J.; d. Jack and Sophia Kamish; A.A., Miami Dade Community Coll., 1970; B.A., Fla. Internat. U., 1975, postgrad., 1975—; m. Robert Merrill, Mar. 27, 1954 (div.); children—Michael David, Lisa Heidi, Tracy Lynn. Owner, operator Lee Gaynor Assos., pub. relations, Miami, Fla., 1970-72; exec. dir. Ft. Lauderdale (Fla.) Jaycees, 1970-71; host interview program Sta. WGMA, Hollywood, Fla., 1971-73, Stas. WWOK and WIGL-FM, Fla., 1973-79; occupational specialist Lindsey Hopkins Edn. Center, Dade County Pub. Schs., with publicity-pub. relations dept., Miami, 1971—; producer/interviewer radio program Sta. WEDR-FM, 1985—. Mem. Northeast Citizens Adv. Com. Career and Vocat. Edn., 1973-79; mem. adv. com. North Miami Beach High Sch., 1977-79; mem. communications com. Council Continuing Edn. Women Miami, 1972—. Mem. Women in Communications, Am. Women in Radio and TV (dir. publicity Goldcoast chpt. 1974-76), Pub. Relations Soc. Am., Internat. Assn. Bus. Communicators (treas. chpt. 1983), Alliance Career Edn. (publicity chmn.), Nat. Schs. Pub. Relations Assn., Mus. of Sci., Ctr. Fine Arts, Women's C. of C. of South Fla. Democrat. Home: 1255 NE 171st Terr North Miami Beach FL 33162 Office: 750 NW 20th St Miami FL 33127

GAYNOR, MAGDALEN, lawyer; b. Nashville, Feb. 27, 1953; d. James William and Marion (Patterson) Gaynor. B.A., Simmons Coll., 1975; J.D., Fordham U., 1978. Bar: N.Y. 1979, Fla. 1979, U.S. Supreme Ct. 1979. Assoc. firm Buchman Buchman & O'Brien, N.Y.C., 1979-86, Baer Marks & Upham, N.Y.C., 1986—. Mem. ABA, N.Y. State Bar Assn., Estate Planning Council of N.Y.C. Clubs: Westchester Country (Rye, N.Y.); Liberty (N.Y.C.). Office: Baer Marks & Upham 805 3d Ave New York NY 10022

GAYNOR, SUZANNE MARIE, health care executive; b. Phila., Jan. 10, 1941; d. Howard Aloyousis and Irene Marie (Dunn) Gaynor; m. John Michael Hayes, May 26, 1962 (div. 1982); children—Marguerite, Jennifer, Christopher. Diploma in nursing Fitzgerald-Mercy Sch. Nursing, 1961; B.S., Marymount Coll. Va., 1977, M.B.A., 1981. R.N., Pa., Va. Service coordinator Upjohn Health Care, Washington, 1972-74, tng. coordinator, 1974-75; health intern U.S. Senate, Washington, 1977; health analyst Am. Blood Commn., Arlington, Va., 1977-79, dir. regionalization program, 1979-83, cons., 1983; dir. regional services Greater N.Y. Blood Program, N.Y.C., 1983—; mem. interagy. tech. com. Working Group on Blood Resources and Blood Substitutes, Dept. Health and Human Services, 1981-83; mem. subcom. on blood supply and blood services Com. on Pub. Health, N.Y. Acad. Medicine, 1984—. Contbr. articles to profl. jours. Discussion leader Jr. Great Books, Arlington, Va., 1974-75. Recipient Plaque for Recognition of Service, Am. Blood Commn., 1983. Mem. Am. Assn. Blood Banks, Nat. Assn. Female Execs., LWV (bd. dirs. 1973-76), NOW, Delta Sigma Epsilon. Democrat. Roman Catholic. Office: New York Blood Ctr 310 E 67th St New York NY 10021

GAYTON, BARBARA JEANNE, food co. official; b. Somerville, Mass., Oct. 8, 1948; d. Harold Russel and Sophia Eva Theresa (Minkiel) G.; A.A., Fairleigh Dickinson U., 1968, B.S., 1974, postgrad. With Thomas J. Lipton, Inc., Englewood Cliffs, N.J., 1968—, sales coordinator, 1974-75, asst. sales promotion mgr., 1975-79, asst. mgr. mktg. info., 1979-83, sales promotion adminstr., 1983—. Republican. Roman Catholic. Office: Thomas J Lipton Inc 800 Sylvan Ave Englewood Cliffs NJ 07632

GEANOULES, FRANCES CARMELA, cosmetics and pharmaceutical company executive; b. N.Y.C., July 14, 1945; d. Nicholas and Mary Josephine (Lombardo) Oliveri; m. Anthony Peter Geanoules, Oct. 8, 1967; children—Anthony Peter, Maria Claire. Sec., Equitable Life Assurance Soc., N.Y.C., 1963-64; wage and salary asst. Revlon, Inc., N.Y.C., 1965-68, compensation analyst, 1969-75, mgr. compensation, 1976-83, dir. compensation planning and adminstrn., 1984-85, dir. compensation planning and benefits adminstrn., 1986—. Mem. Am. Soc. Personnel Adminstrs., Am. Compensation Assn. Republican. Roman Catholic. Office: Revlon Inc 2147 Route 27 Edison NY 08818

GEANURACOS, ELSIE ADELAIDE DASILVA, foreign language educator; b. Bklyn., Dec. 29, 1922; d. John and Maria (Nascimento) DaSilva; m. George James Geanuracos, Jan. 28, 1945; children—Constance, Patricia, James, Joan, John. B.A., Hunter Coll., 1944; student Columbia U., 1944-47. Tchr. Portuguese lang. N.Y.C. Sch. System, 1945-50, Spanish tchr., 1945-50; prof. Spanish U. Bridgeport, Conn., 1969, 72, 73, Housatonic Community Coll., Bridgeport, 1970; founder, adviser Portuguese Scholarship Program, U. Bridgeport, 1973—, sec. Halsey Internat. Scholarship Program, 1974, mem. bd. advisers, instr. Spanish, Womens' Inst. U. Bridgeport; tutor Tutoring Ctr. Bridgeport. Com. mem. Womens' Aux. to Fairfield County Med. Assn., Am. Cancer Soc. Bridgeport chpt.; translator Bridgeport Hosp. Aux.; mem. bd. assoc. U. Bridgeport; mem. Bklyn. Hist. Soc., Bklyn. Recipient citation for community service Am. Cancer Soc. Bridgeport chpt.; citation as an internationalist UN Assn., 1975; 10-yr. service plaque Portuguese Scholar Ship Program of HISP, 1983. Mem. AAUW (treas. Fairfield chpt.), Judeo-Christian Women's Assn. (mistress of ceremonies first awards luncheon 1974), Alpha Delta Pi. Avocations: swimming; reading; drapery making; knitting; travel. Home: 102 Lu Manor Dr Fairfield CT 06432

GEARON, CATHLEEN, retired airline executive, computer consultant; b. Bay Shore, N.Y., Jan. 28, 1931; d. Joseph Michael and Oonagh Frances (Keown) Gearon; student SUNY, 1948-51; student Calif. State U., 1978—. Operator, N.J. Bell Telephone, Mount Holly, N.J., 1951-52; with Brit. Airways, 1955-84, supr. interline sales, N.Y.C., 1960-63, supr. reservations sales, Century City, Calif., 1969-72, computer troubleshooter and coordinator services, 1969-84, supr. tng., Los Angeles, 1972-84; faculty Los Angeles Trade-Tech. Coll., 1973-75, pvt. travel schs., 1979-80. Served with USAF, 1952-55. Mem. Am. Legion (post comdr. 1980-81, dist. comdr. 1984-85, vice comdr. Los Angeles County Council 1985-87), Nat. Assn. Female Execs., Air Force Sgts. Assn. Republican. Roman Catholic. Clubs: Past Comdrs., 20 and 4 Honor Soc. Women Legionaires. Home: 6153 Manton Ave Woodland Hills CA 91367

GEBBIE, KRISTINE MOORE, public health administrator; b. Sioux City, June 26, 1943; d. Thomas C. and G. Irene (Stewart) Moore; m. Neil Gebbie, June 18, 1966; children—Anna, Sharon, Eric. B.S. in Nursing, St. Olaf Coll., Northfield, Minn., 1965; M.Nursing, U. Calif.-Los Angeles, 1968. Lectr. nursing, UCLA, 1968-77; asst. prof. nursing St. Louis U., 1971-77, coordinator Ambulatory Care Hosp., 1974-76, asst. dir. Hosp., 1976-78; adminstr. Health Div. State Oreg., Portland, 1978—; adj. prof. Oreg. Health Scis. U., 1980—; cons. Nat. Inst. Mental Health Bur. Author: (with Grace Deloughery) Political Dynamics: Impact on Nurses and Nursing, 1975; (with Jeane Schweer) Creative Teaching in Clinical Nursing, 1976; (with Greace Deloughery, Betty Newman) Consultation and Community Organization in Community Mental Health Nursing, 1971. Bd. dirs. Luth. Family Services, Portland, 1970-84. Recipient Disting. Alumna award St. Olaf Coll., 1979. Mem. Am. Pub. Health Assn., Am. Nurses Assn., Oreg. Pub. Health Assn., Assn. of State and Territorial Ofcls. (pres., mem. exec. com. 1984), N. Am. Nursing Diagnosis Assn (treas. 1983—). Lutheran. Office: Oreg State Health Div 1400 SW 5th St PO Box 231 Portland OR 97207

GEBERT, CYNTHIA INGRID, nurse adminstrator; b. Newark, June 5, 1952; d. Donald Ralph and Elisie Elizabeth (Geise) G. B.S. in Nursing, Wagner Coll., S.I., N.Y., 1974; M.A. in Nursing, NYU, 1982. Cert. adult nurse practitioner; cert. in coronary care, intra-aortic balloon techniques, occupational health nurse. Staff nurse East Orange VA Hosp., N.J., 1974-77; nurse practitioner, 1977-79; supr., nurse practitioner Allied Corp., Morristown, N.J., 1979-83, regional nurse adminstr., 1984—. Bd. dirs. ARC, 1982—; fund raising com. Am. Cancer Soc., 1983-84. Mem. Am. Nurses Assn., Am. Assn. Occupational Health, Tri-County Nurses Assn. (v.p. 1983-85), Sigma Theta Tau. Home: 44 Center Grove Rd Apt M26 Randolph Township NJ 07869 Office: Allied Corp PO Box 2063R Columbia Rd Morristown NJ 07960

GEBHARDT, CAROL ANN, neuropsychologist; b. Phila., Oct. 24, 1952; d. Edwin James and Mildred Victoria (Holt) G.; B.A. with honors in Psychology (Nat. Merit scholar 1970-74, Phila. Bd. Edn. Merit scholar 1970-74), Allegheny Coll., 1974; A.M. (teaching fellow 1974-75, grad. scholar 1975-76, advanced teaching fellow 1976-77), Boston U., 1977, Ph.D. (advanced teaching fellow 1977, grad. scholar 1977-78), 1981; m. Abe Shliferstein, Feb. 9, 1980; 1 son, James Richard Shliferstein. Animal neuropsychology research asst. Boston VA Hosp., 1975-76; histology research technician Beth Israel Hosp., neurology unit Harvard U. Med. Sch., Boston, 1976; research asst in human neuropsychology Boston U. Sch. Medicine at Boston VA Med. Center, 1977-78; research asst , computerized tomography scan Boston VA Med. Center, 1978-79; Nat. Research Service Award trainee Boston U. Sch. Medicine, 1980-81; cons. neuropsychology, Leonardo, N.J., 1981—. Nat. Research Service awardee NIH, 1980-81. Mem. Internat. Neuropsychol. Soc., Am. Psychol. Assn. Research, publs. in field. Home: 19 Kelvin Ave Leonardo NJ 07737

GEDDES, ANN, talent agy. dir.; b. Evanston, Ill., Nov. 25, 1943; d. Robert Allen and Sara Elizabeth (Bonham) Geddes; student St. Petersburg (Fla.) Pub. Schs.; 1 son, Peter Allen, Profl. model, Chgo., 1963-67; owner, dir. Geddes Agy., Chgo., 1968—, Los Angeles, 1983—; cons. Am. Nat. Bank, 1969, 76, 77, Walter Heller Corp., 1977, Worldbook Child Craft Internat., 1978; dir. Chgo. Unltd., Inc. Mem. Chgo. Assn. Radio and TV Agents. Office: 875 N Michigan Ave Chicago IL 60611

GEDDES, JEAN LIONSDALE, author, playwright, journalist, lecturer; b. N.Y.C., Sept. 19, 1924; d. Alfred I. and Bernice B. Lionsdale; m. Glenn H. Geddes, Mar. 24, 1945; 1 child, Thomas Clinton. Student Columbia U., 1943-44; student The George Washington U., 1954-56. Author, playwright, editor, journalist, lectr., Washington, 1965—; lectr. various clubs, orgns., 1975—. Author: History of Northern Virginia, 1967, The Biography of an Actor, 1975; (play) Sally, 1977, Blossom, 1981, Baltimore Belles & Beaux, 1982. Contbr. articles to profl. jours. and mags. Chmn. Falls Church Friends of Library, 1978-80. Named Outstanding Vol., Va. State Parks, 1980. Mem. Nat. Press Club, Cherry Hill Writers (chmn. 1982-84). Clubs: Falls Church Woman's, Arlington Hosp. Aux., Avocations: gardening; hiking; piano; literary groups; creative writing. Home and Office: 411 Lincoln Ave Falls Church VA 22046

GEDDES, LANELLE EVELYN, nurse-physiologist; b. Houston, Sept. 15, 1935; d. Carl Otto and Evelyn Bertha (Frank) Nerger; B.S.N., U. Houston, 1957, Ph.D. (fellow), 1970; m. Leslie Alexander Geddes, Aug. 3, 1962. Staff nurse Houston Ind. Sch. Dist., 1957-62; instr. to asst. prof. physiology Baylor U. Coll. Medicine, 1972-75; asst. prof. nursing Tex. Women's U., 1972-75; prof., head Sch. Nursing, Purdue U., 1975—. Recipient teaching awards. Mem. Am. Nurses Assn., Nat. League Nursing, Am. Assn. Critical-Care Nurses, AAAS, N.Y. Acad. Scis., Phi Kappa Phi, Sigma Theta Tau, Iota Sigma Pi. Lutheran. Contbr. articles sci. jours., chpts. in books. Office: Sch Nursing Purdue University West Lafayette IN 47907

GEDDIS, AMELIA LOUISE, business civic worker; b. Northfield, N.H., Sept. 18, 1922; d. Albert Louis and Anna (Buczynski) Piszczek; m. James R. Geddis, Nov. 26, 1946; 1 child, John Robert. Student pub. schs., Tilton, N.H. Bookkeeper Gibson Woolen, Tilton, 1941-48; bookkeeper, office mgr. Canterbury Mills, Tilton, 1948-49; sec. to supt. Tilton-Northfield High Sch. Dist., Tilton, 1949-50; office mgr., acct. Tilton Leather Armour, 1950-55; acct., office mgr. Prescott Oil Co., West Franklin, N.H., 1955-85, bookkeeper Boynton & Robinson, P.C., Franklin, N.H., 1985—. Dep. town clk. Town of Northfield, 1960-65, mem. bicentennial com., 1979-80; chmn. hosp. lawn party Franklin Hosp., N.H., 1979-84; pres., chmn. bd. Franklin Regional Hosp. Assn., 1982-85; chmn. religious edn. com. Northfield-Tilton Congregational Ch., 1982-84. Named Woman of Achievement, Tilton-Northfield Bus. and Profl. Orgn., 1969. Mem. N.H. Fedn. Bus. and Profl. Women (state pres. 1969-70, Bus. and Profl. Woman of Yr. 1972), Nat. Fedn. Bus. and Profl. Women's Clubs Polish Home Assn. (pres. 1973-76). Democrat. Lodge: Granite (pres.). Avocations: travel; baking; walking. Home: RFD 1 Oak Hill Rd Franklin NH 03235 Office: Boynton & Robinson PC 10 Franklin St Franklin NH 03235

GEDEON-MARTIN, DIANE MARIE, marketing executive; b. Detroit, Oct. 4, 1957; d. Howard M. and Susan D. (Lalian) Gedeon; m. Roger J. Martin, Aug. 22, 1980. B.A., Oakland U., Rochester, Mich., 1979. Announcer WLAV-AM/FM, Grand Rapids, Mich., 1979-80; weathercaster WTOL-TV, Toledo, Ohio, 1980; announcer, prodn. dir. WMHE-FM, Toledo, 1980-82; mktg. dir. Food Service Enterprises, Inc., Port Clinton, Ohio, 1982-83; account exec. McCann-Erickson, Troy, Mich., 1983-84; advt./promotion mgr. WPBN/WTOM-TV, Traverse City, Mich., 1985—. Auctioneer WGTE-TV, Pub. Broadcasting Service, Toledo, 1981, 82, 83, 84. Recipient Appreciation award Ottawa Hills Schs., Ohio, 1982. Mem. Broadcast Promotion Mktg. Execs., Traverse City Ad Club. Club: German Shepherd (Toledo). Avocations: stained glass windows; equestrian show jumping; dog obedience training. Office: WPBN/WTOM-TV PO Box 546 Traverse City MI 49685-0546

GEE, IRENE, food stylist; b. N.Y.C., Aug. 17, 1950; d. Jimmy Set and Lin Fung (Ng) G.; B.A., Hunter Coll., 1971; M.S. in Family and Consumer Studies, Lehman Coll., 1974, M.S. in Guidance and Counseling, 1978; m. Oct. 17, 1981. Tchr., Olinville Jr. High Sch., Bronx, N.Y., 1971-75, Lehman Coll., Bronx, 1975-77, Harry Eiseman Jr. High Sch., Bklyn., 1978-80; food stylist, recipe developer Ladies Home Jour., 1977-78; food stylist, recipe developer Woman's Day Mag., 1979—, home economist, 1980—; owner, operator Irene's Catering, 1984—; food coordinator Evander Childs High Sch.; food cons. Corn Products Corp., 1978—; food stylist Nabisco, 1978, also Perdue Co.; developer recipe booklets various cos. including Progresso and Fla. Mushrooms; cons. food cos. and publs.; comml. model Mauna Loa Macadamia Nuts, Lewis & Neale. Contbr. articles to Forecast mag. Mem. Am. Home Econs. Assn., Home Economists in Bus., Am. Counseling Assn., Omicron Nu. Contbr. articles Woman's World mag.

GEE, JENNIFER, lawyer; b. San Francisco, Apr. 6, 1949; d. Bing Lai Won and Shuk Fong (Yee) Gee; m. Melvin Buck Sher Lee, Sept. 1, 1974; children—Michael David, Eric Robert, Katherine Anne. B.A. with honors U. Calif-Berkeley, 1971, J.D., 1974. Bar: Calif. 1974. Trial atty. EEOC, San Francisco, 1974-82; hearing officer Calif. New Motor Vehicle Bd., Sacramento, 1981—; adminstrv. judge U.S. Merit Systems Protection Bd., San Francisco, 1982—, Mem. Museum Soc., Chinese for Affirmative Action, both San Francisco, Action on Smoking, Health, Washington. John Woodman Ayer fellow U. Calif., 1974. Mem. ABA, Bar Assn. San Francisco, Asian Am. Bar Assn. Democrat. Clubs: Commonwealth (San Francisco), Prythanean Alumni (Berkeley) Office: US Merit Systems Protection Bd 525 Market St 28th Floor San Francisco CA 94105

GEE, MINNIE TOM, software engineer; b. San Francisco, July 17, 1950; d. Louis Tom and Lillian (Yee) G. A.B. in Computer Sci., U.Calif.-Berkeley, 1972, A.B. in Stats., 1972; M.S. in Elec. Engring. and Computer Sci., U. Santa Clara, 1979. Assoc. engr. Lockheed Missiles and Space Co., Sunnyvale, Calif., 1972-75, sci. programmer, 1975-80, sci. analyst, 1980-83, research specialist, 1983—. Mem. IEEE. Democrat. Mem. Bible Ch. Clubs: Tomadachi Tennis (sec. 1983-84) (San Jose, Calif.); Santa Clara Chinese Bowling (sec. 1975-76). Avocations: tennis, reading, crafts. Office: LMSC 1111 Lockheed Way Sunnyvale CA 94086

GEE, VIRGINIA C., university administrator; b. San Francisco, May 19, 1941; d. Hom Chew Wing and Sue (Jeong) Hom Chen; m. Herbert H. Gee, May 12, 1962; 1 son, Christopher. B.S. in Pub. Adminstrn., U. San Francisco, 1981. Bus. office supr. Pacific Telephone Co., San Francisco, 1959-63, pub. office mgr., 1963-66, mgmt. instr., 1966-68, urban affairs dir., 1968-70, personnel staff mgr., 1970-74; recruitment adminstr. Stanford U. (Calif.), 1974—; cons. Binghom Assocs., San Francisco, 1980—; arbitration panel Am. Intermediation Service, San Francisco, 1980-84. Cons. Asian Art Mus., San Francisco, 1982—; mediator, hearing officer San Francisco Human Rights Com., 1984—; appeals hearing officer Calif. Apprenticeship Council, San Francisco, 1974—, 1st woman chair, 1975—; mem. Fed. Com. Apprenticeship, Washington, 1975; dir. San Francisco Conservation Corps., 1984. Recipient Outstanding Service award Stanford Fed. Credit Union, 1978, Chinatown Resource Devel., 1974; Achievement award Chinese Inst. Engrs., 1975, Calif. Dept. Edn., 1984; Hon. Citizen Louisville, 1979. Mem. San Francisco Pvt. Industry Council (v.p. 1980-83), Calif. Community Coll. Placement Assn. (v.p. 1980), Asian Pacific Personnel Assn. (pres. 1980-82), San Francisco Women's Network. Republican. Roman Catholic. Clubs: San Francisco Squash, Commonwealth of Calif. Lodge: Chinese Am. Citizens Alliance (bd. officers 1979—).

GEFFEN, BETTY ADA, theatrical personal manager; b. Lachine, Que., Can., May 12, 1911; came to U.S., 1942, naturalized, 1945; d. Joseph and Minnie (Illievitz) Gottheil; student public schs., Montreal, Que.; m. Jacob N. Geffen, Dec. 23, 1944; 1 dau., JoAnn Merle. Sec., Saul Cohen/Trustee in Bankruptcy, Montreal, 1926-28, Maxwell Cummings Real Estate, 1928-30, Monroe Abbey, Atty., 1930-31; with Tic-Toc, Stanley Grill and Chez Maurice, Montreal, 1931-41; sec. H.L. Green, N.Y.C., 1941-44; pvt. personal mgr., casting cons., N.Y.C., 1950—; cons. Consab Assos. Corp., N.Y.C., 1966—. Trustee Israel Cancer Research Fund.; mem. cinema/radio/TV bd. B'nai B'rith. vol. Floating Hosp. Mem. Nat. Acad. TV Arts and Scis., Motion Picture Pioneers, Internat. Platform Assn. Democrat. Clubs: Variety Women N.Y. (v.p. 1977-81, pres. 1982-86, chmn. bd. 1986—), Brandeis U. Address: 17 W 71st St New York NY 10023

GEFFNER, DONNA SUE, speech pathologist, audiologist, educator; b. N.Y.C.; d. Louis and Sally (Weiner) G.; B.A. magna cum laude, Bklyn. Coll., 1967; M.A., N.Y.U., 1968, Ph.D. (NDEA fellow), 1970, postgrad. student Advanced Inst. Analytic Psychotherapy, 1973-75. Asst. prof. Lehman Coll., 1971-76; prof., chmn. dept. speech St. John's U., 1983—, dir. Speech and Hearing Center, 1976—, founder grad. program in speech pathology and audiology; cons. corp. communications; TV producer and hostess NBC, 1977-78, CBS, 1978-79. Emmy nominee for Outstanding Instrnl. Program, 1978; recipient award Pres.'s Com. on Employment of Handicapped; N.Y. State Edn. Dept. grantee, 1976-78; City U. N.Y. Research Found. grantee, 1972. Fellow Am. Speech, Lang. and Hearing Assn. (legis. councillor 1978—); mem. N.Y. State Speech and Hearing Assn. (pres. 1978-80), Audiology Study Group N.Y., Editor Monograph. Contbr. articles to profl. jours. and textbooks; issue editor Jour. Topics in Lang. Disorders, 1980. Office: St John's U Grand Central Pkwy Jamaica NY 11439

GEIGER, MARGUERITE PATRICIA, insurance broker; b. N.Y.C., Mar. 2, 1920; d. James Edward and Ethel (Reichert) C.; m. Walter Eugene Geiger, Sept. 5, 1937; 1 dau., Patricia Arleen Lehner. Lic. ins. broker Paterson State Coll. Profl. Sch. Bus., 1966. Lic. property, casualty and life ins. broker. Broker, office mgr. Motor Club Am., Englewood, N.J., 1963-76; broker, office mgr. Arthur Peterson Agy., Cliffside Park, N.J., 1976—. Mem. Housing Authority Commn., Edgewater (N.J.) Housing Authority, 1981—; exec. chmn. No. Valley chpt. ARC, 1984—; mem. St. Joseph's Guild for Boys and Girls. Mem. Ins. Women of No. N.J. (pres. 1975-76). Democrat. Roman Catholic. Clubs: Lioness (sec. 1980-82); Zonta (pres. 1981-83). Address: 1186 River Rd Edgewater NJ 07020

GEIL, BONNIE LOUISE, communications company executive, owner publication and directory guide, consultant; b. George AFB, Calif., July 9, 1954; d. Wayne Edgar and Marie Elizabeth (Thomas) Rhynard; m. Harry Earl Geil, Aug. 13, 1977. B.S. in Tech. Journalism with highest honors, Oreg. State U., 1976. Copy editor OSU Bull., Corvallis, Oreg., 1972-76; assoc. editor, editor Western Farmers Assn., Seattle, 1976-78, communications dir., 1978-80; cons., owner BRG Communications, Seattle, Bend, Oreg., 1980—; owner, pub. Our Town, Bend, 1984—; lectr., tchr. asst. Oreg. State U. Editor: Our World, 1983, also mags. Represented U.S. agrl. journalists Internat. Agrl. Fair, Berlin, 1979; judge Washington State Dairy Princess Pageant, Seattle, 1980. Mem. Coop. Editorial Assn. (chmn. 1979-81, moderator, panelist 1981), Women in Communications, Women Entrepreneurs (publicity dir.), Nat. Council Farmer Coops., Sigma Delta Chi, Sigma Kappa. Club: Quota Internat. Avocations: free lance writing, photography, travel, scuba, underwater photography, horseback riding, training, writing children's books, art, music, outdoor recreation. Office: BRG Communications Our Town Publications 1293 NW Wall Suite 1385 Bend OR 97701

GEISEL, ANN MARIE KELLNER, library director; b. Melrose, Mass., Dec. 28, 1947; d. John Paul and Irene (Liptrott) Kellner; m. Robert Carl Geisel, Jr., June 14, 1969; children—Stacy Ann, Todd Joseph, Courtney Lynn. B.A., Emmanuel Coll., 1969; M.L.S., Simmons Coll., 1972. Cert. media specialist, N.H. Br. librarian Waltham Pub. Library (Mass.), 1969-70; head librarian Hillsboro-Deering Schs., Hillsboro, N.H., 1970-74; librarian Stephenson Meml. Library, Greenfield, N.H., 1974-75; tchr. Adult Basic Edn., Hillsboro, 1972-75; dir. Peterborough Town Library (N.H.), 1975—. author weekly newspaper column: Library Corner, 1978—; editor pamphlet in field, 1983. Leader Girl Scouts U.S.A., Greenfield, 1978-85, community chairperson, 1985—; mem. adv. bd. Northeast Document Conservation Ctr., 1983—. ALA, New Eng. Library Assn., N.H. Library Assn. (rep. 1978-80), Nubanusit Library Coop. (treas. 1978—). Club: St. Patrick Women's Guild (treas., sec., v.p. Bennington, N.H. 1978—). Home: Bennington Rd Greenfield NH 03047 Office: Peterborough Town Library Main and Concord Sts Peterborough NH 03458

GEISENDORFER, ESTHER LILLIAN, nurse; b. Ferryville, Wis., May 18, 1927; d. Peter C. and Christie G. (Quamme) Walker; student U. Wis.-LaCrosse, 1944-45; R.N., Fairview Hosp. Sch. Nursing, Mpls., 1948; m. James V. Geisendorfer, Sept. 23, 1949; children—Jane, Karen, Lois. Staff nurse Worthington (Minn.) Clinic, 1948-50; pvt. duty nurse, Sioux Falls, S.D., 1950-51; obstet. nurse Fairview Hosp., Mpls., 1951-53; staff nurse St. Anthony Hosp., Rock Island, Ill., 1953-54; obstet. nurse Fairview Hosp., Mpls., 1954-58, post anesthesia recovery nurse, 1958-62, emergency room nurse, 1962-66, obstet. nurse, 1966-68, head nurse obstetrics, 1968-76; staff devel. instr. Bellin Meml. Hosp., Green Bay, Wis., 1976—; instr. in prenatal and Lamaze classes Ob-Gyn Assocs. of Green Bay Ltd. Mem. Wis. Assn. Perinatal Care, Nordfjord Laget in Am., Wis. Nurses Assn. (Disting. Service award 1981), Nurses Assn. Am. Coll. Obstetrics and Gynecology (cert.), Wis. Acad. Scis., Arts and Letters, Lutheran. Home: 1001 Shawano Ave Green Bay WI 54303 Office: 744 S Webster Ave Green Bay WI 54301

GEISLER, ROSEMARY P., computer dealer/lessor company executive; b. Chgo., Apr. 5, 1947; d. James Vincent and Raffaella Mary (DeSeno) Pastorello; student Triton Coll., 1970-72; B.A., DePaul U., 1981; m. Ervin R. Geisler, Aug. 17, 1968. Asst. market analyst Evans Products Co., Rolling Meadows, Ill., 1970-76; office services mgr., asst. market analyst Comdisco, Inc., Rosemont, Ill., 1976-78, asst. mktg. product mgr., 1978-80, dir. dealer relations, 1980-81, mktg. product mgr., market maker, 1981-83, asst. v.p., 1983-85, v.p., 1985—. Mem. Des Plaines (Ill.) Youth Commn. Mem. DePaul U. Alumni Assn. Home: 85 Brinker Rd Barrington Hills IL 60010 Office: Comdisco Inc 6400 Shafer Ct Rosemont IL 60018

GEISS, JANICE M(ARIE), lawyer, educator; b. St. Louis, July 20, 1950; d. Frank W. and Marcella M. (Schmidt) Carney; m. John Robert Geiss, Dec. 22, 1972; children—Michael John, Jeffrey Phillip. B.S. in Nursing, St. Louis U., 1971, J.D., 1982; M.A. in Edn., Washington U., St. Louis, 1977. Bar: Mo. 1983, U.S. Ct. Appeals (8th cir.) 1983, U.S. Dist. Ct. (ea. dist.) Mo. 1984. Mem. nursing staff St. Mary's Health Ctr., St. Louis, 1972-82, coordinator nursing inservice edn., 1974-79, asst. dir. nursing, 1979-82; assoc. Klutho, Cody, Kilo and Flynn Attys., Inc., St. Louis, 1982—; adj. prof. health law Maryville Coll., St. Louis, 1983—; presenter health law seminars, 1983—. Mem. Am. Soc. Law and Medicine, Mo. Bar Assn., Met. Bar Assn. St. Louis, ABA, Assn. Trial Lawyers Am., Mo. Assn. Trial Attys. Home: 2928 Yale Blvd Saint Charles MO 63301 Office: Klutho Cody Kilo and Flynn Attys Inc 5840 Oakland Ave St Louis MO 63110

GELBER, LINDA CECILE, lawyer, bank executive; b. Hackensack, N.J., Oct. 30, 1950; d. Melvin W. and Beverly E. (Gilman) Gelber. B.A., Ind. U., 1972, M.B.A., 1974, J.D., 1978; cert. fin. services counselor, Am. Bankers Assn. National Grad. Trust Sch., 1983. Bar: Ind. 1978, U.S. Dist. Ct. (so. dist.) Ind. 1978, U.S. Supreme Ct. 1983. Program analyst Indiana Legis. Services Agy., Indpls., 1978-80; trust officer First National Bank, Kokomo, Ind., 1980-82, v.p., trust officer, 1983—; part time instr. Indiana U., Kokomo, 1981-82, Ball State U., Muncie, Ind., 1979-80. Bd. dirs. United Way, Kokomo, 1983-85, div. chmn. fund raising campaign, 1983. Mem. Am. Inst. Banking (v.p. 1983—), Estate Planning Council Indpls., Howard County (Ind.) Bar Assn. (sec-treas. 1981), Indiana State Bar Assn., ABA. Club: Altrusa (Kokomo). Home: 5136 S Webster St Kokomo IN 46902 Office: First National Bank 322 N Main St Kokomo IN 46901

GELBERT, SARA IDA, travel agent, beauty products consultant; b. Mlawa, Plotzki, Poland, Aug. 19, 1926; came to U.S., 1951, naturalized, 1956; d. Isaac and Josephine (Berkovich) Mlawer; m. Sam Gelbart, Jan. 28, 1945 (div. 1966); children—Ellen, Irving. Avon products group leader Miami, Fla., 1962—; travel escort, cons. Nedras Travel Agy., Hallandale, Fla., 1977—. Democrat. Jewish.

GELBURD, DIANE ELIZABETH, archeologist; b. N.Y.C., Sept. 28, 1952; d. Irving and Margaret Beryl (Thorbes) G.; m. Stephen Robert Potter, June 22, 1980. B.A., George Washington U., 1974, M.A., 1978; postgrad. Am. U., 1982—. George Washington U. teaching fellow, 1975-77; archeologist/anthropologist Smithsonian Instn./George Washington U., Dobe/Botswana, 1976; archeologist Bur. Reclamation, Washington, 1977; archeologist Nat. Park Service, Washington, 1977-79, assoc. anthropologist, 1979-80; nat. cultural resources specialist Soil Conservation Service, Washington, 1980—. Contbr. articles to profl. jours. CPR instr. ARC, Arlington, Va., 1983—. Recipient Achievement award Bur. Reclamation, Washington, 1977; Cert. of Appreciation, Soil Conservation Service, 1984; Disting. Service award USDA, 1986; Am. U. Fellow, 1986-87. Mem. Am. Soc. Conservation Archeology, Am. Anthrop. Assn., George Wright Soc. (local chpt. treas. 1982), Soil Conservation Soc. Am. (vice chmn. human resources div. 1985-86, chmn. 1986-87, local chpt. sec. 1984, v.p. 1985, pres. elect 1986), Soc. Am. Archeology (exec. com. fed. archaeology 1979-84). Lutheran. Office: Soil Conservation Service US Dept Agr PO Box 2890 Washington DC 20013

GELFAND, JANICE ROHRS, marketing executive; b. Balt., Dec. 6, 1951; d. Frederick Vernon and Hazel Regina (Reid) Rohrs; B.S. in Chemistry with honors, U. Del., 1973; postgrad. in bus. adminstrn. Temple U., 1978—; children—Joshua Elliott, Jordan Michael. With Rohm and Haas Corp., 1973—, tech. sales rep., Bristol, Pa., 1974-79, asst. sales mgr. specialty chems., Phila., 1979-80, product mgr.-mktg., splty. chems., 1980-84, market mgr. detergent additives, 1984—. Mem. Am. Oil Chem. Soc., Cosmetic, Toiletries and Fragrances Assn., Chem. Spltys. Mfrs. Assn., Am. Mgmt. Assn. Home: 2 Jonathan Rd Cherry Hill NJ 08003 Office: Rohm and Haas Corp Indsl Chems N Am Independence Mall W Philadelphia PA 19105

GELHARDT, GHISLAINE MARIE ASTRID, concrete admixture company executive; b. Kuala Lumpur, Malaysia, Dec. 6, 1958; came to U.S., 1982; d. Herbert Grant, III, and Ernestine J.M. (Broddin) G. B.S., Fla. Atlantic U., 1984. Flight attendant Air Can., Toronto, 1978-82; model, Toronto, 1978-82; adminstrv. mgr. MAC-USA, Boca Raton, Fla., 1983-85; v.p. IAL, Inc., Boca Raton, 1985—. Office: IAL Inc 7777 Glades Rd #215 Boca Raton FL 33434

GELLER, JANICE GRACE, nurse; b. Auburn, Ga., Feb. 25, 1938; d. Erby Ralph and Jewell Grace (Maughon) Clack; student LaGrange Coll., 1955-57; B.S.N., Emory U., 1960; M.Sc., Rutgers U., 1962; m. Joseph Jerome Geller, Dec. 23, 1973; 1 dau., Elizabeth Joanne. Psychiat. staff nurse dept. psychiatry Emory U., Atlanta, 1960; nurse educator Ill. State Psychiat. Inst., Chgo., 1961; clin. specialist in mental retardation nursing Northville, Mich., 1962; faculty Rutgers U. Coll. Nursing, Newark, 1962-63, U. Mich. Coll. Nursing, Ann Arbor, 1963-64, Rutgers U. Advanced Program in Psychiat. Nursing, 1964-66, Teheran Coll. for Women, Iran, 1967-69; clin. specialist psychiat. nursing Roosevelt Hosp., N.Y.C., 1969-70; faculty, guest lectr. Columbia U., N.Y.C., 1969-70; supr. Dept. Psychiat. Nursing, Mt. Sinai Hosp., N.Y.C., 1970-72; pvt. practice psychotherapy, N.Y.C., 1972-77, Ridgewood, N.J., 1977—; faculty, curriculum coordinator in psychiat. nursing William Alanson White Inst. Psychiatry, Psychoanalysis and Psychology, N.Y.C., 1974-84; mem. U.S. del. of Community and Mental Health Nurses to People's Republic of China, 1983. Recipient 10th Anniversary award Outstanding Clin. Specialist in psychiat.-mental health nursing in N.J., Soc. Cert. Clin. Specialists, 1982. Fed. Govt. grantee as career tchr. in psychiat. nursing, Rutgers U., 1962-63; cert. psychiat. nurse and clin. specialist, N.J., N.Y. Mem. Am. Nurses Assn. (various certs.), N.J. State Nurses Assn., Soc. Cert. Clin. Specialists in Psychiat. Nursing, Council Specialists in Psychiat. Mental Health Nursing, Am. Group Psychotherapy Assn., Am. Assn. Mental Deficiency, World Fedn. Mental Health, AAAS, Friends of the Hermitage, LWV, Soc. of Valley Hosp. of Ridgewood, AMA Aux., Bergen County Med. Soc. Aux., Sigma Theta Tau. Club: Coll. Contbr. articles to profl. jours.; editorial bd. Perspectives in Psychiatric Care, 1971-74, 78—; author: (with Anita Marie Werner) Instruments for Study of Nurse-Patient Interaction, 1964. Address: 159 Fairmount Rd Ridgewood NJ 07450

GELLER, LINDA BERGER, software development corporation executive, financial executive; b. Bklyn., June 10, 1944; d. Nathan and Sylvia (Dombush) Berger; m. Richard Morton Geller, Sept. 4, 1966; children—Lisa, Deborah, Naomi. Student N.Y. U., 1962-64, New Sch. Social Research, 1964-65; B.S., SUNY-Old Westbury, 1977; M.A., N.Y. Inst. Tech., 1983; cert. advanced bus. mgmt. SUNY. Cert. tchr. N.Y. Bus. mgr. Tri-Tech., West Babylon, N.Y., 1967-72, treas., chief fin. officer, 1972-81, dir., 1981—; pres., chief exec. officer Am. Software Devel. Corp., West Babylon, 1981—; dir. Babylon Blueprint, Tri-Tech. Chairperson Long Island Div. Israel Bonds, Hicksville, N.Y., 1984; v.p. Oyster Bay Jewish Ctr., N.Y., 1980; trustee Wantagh Jewish Ctr., N.Y., 1970-76; chairperson Parents Assn. Solomon Schechter, Jericho, N.Y., 1976-80. Ednl. grantee L.I. Regional Edn. Ctr. Econ. Devel., 1983. Mem. Women's Ednl. and Counseling Ctr., Nat. Assn. Women Bus. Owners (founder Long Island chpt. 1985), Long Island Assn. Republican. Avocations: skiing, music, choir member. Office: Am Software Devel Corp 11 Farmingdale Rd West Bablon NY 11704

GELLER, MARGARET JOAN, astrophysicist; b. Ithaca, N.Y., Dec. 8, 1947; d. Seymour and Sarah (Levine) Geller. A.B., U. Calif.-Berkeley, 1970; M.A., Princeton U., 1972, Ph.D., 1975. Research fellow Center for Astrophysics, Cambridge, Mass., 1974-78; research assoc. Harvard Coll. Obs., Cambridge, 1978-80; sr. vis. fellow Inst. of Astronomy, Cambridge, Eng., 1978-82; asst. prof. Harvard U., 1980-83; astrophysicist Smithsonian Astrophys. Obs., Cambridge, 1983—. Contbr. articles to profl. jours. NSF fellow, 1970-73. Mem. Am. Astron. Soc. (councillor), Assoc. Univs. for Research in Astronomy (dir-at-large), AAAS, Internat. Astron. Union. Office: Center for Astrophysics 60 Garden St Cambridge MA 02138

GELLERSTEDT, MARIE ADA, manufacturing company executive; b. Davenport, Iowa, Oct. 19, 1926; d. Charles Beecher and Marie Elizabeth (Pasvogel) Kaufmann; m. Keith Orval Gellerstedt, Mar. 16, 1957; children—Lori Gellerstedt Doroba, Keith Todd, Jon Erik, Cory A. B.A., Augustana Coll., 1950. Pres., gen. mgr. Nixalite of Am., East Moline, Ill., 1957—. Mem. Internat. Exhibitors Assn., Nat. Pest Control Assn., Nat. Animal Damage Control Assn., Ill. Mfrs. Assn., Constrn. Specifications Inst., Moline Sr. High PTA (life). Republican. Lutheran. Lodges: Zonta, Masons. Home: 2711 17th Ave Ct Moline IL 61265 Office: Nixalite of Am 1025 16th Ave PO Box 727 East Moline IL 61244

GELLERT, GEORGIA MARRS, public relations executive; b. Denver, Oct. 8, 1917; d. William Middelton and Blanche (Boak) Marrs; student U. Denver, 1936-37; m. Winfield Turrell Barber, Jan. 18, 1941 (dec. May 1948); m. 2d, Nathan Henry Gellert, Mar. 12, 1954 (dec. Nov. 1959); m. 3d, James Kedzie Penfield, May 19, 1978. Soc. editor Denver Post, 1937-41; tech. writer, editor Consol. Vultee Aircraft, USN Radio and Sound Lab., San Diego, 1944-46; mgr. box office Central City Opera House Assn., Denver, 1948; soc. editor Denver Post, 1949-51; publicity dir. N.A.M., San Francisco, 1951-54; asst. exhibits dir. Seattle Worlds Fair, 1960-62; pub. relations dir. Seattle Center, 1962-64; free lance pub. relations, Seattle, 1964—; dir. Pacific Search Press, 1977—. Trustee Seattle Symphony Orch., 1960—, sec. bd., 1964-65, v.p., mem. exec. com., 1973-76, 79-83; dir. Allied Arts of Seattle, 1960—, treas., 1966-68; dir. Pottery N.W., Seattle, 1966-68; trustee Seattle Childrens Home, 1954-61, pres., 1959-61; trustee Found. Preservation Gov.'s Mansion, 1972—, mem. exec. com., 1975-80; trustee Seattle Ctr. Found., 1984—. Mem. Women in Communications, English-Speaking Union (dir. Seattle br. 1976—), Pi Beta Phi. Episcopalian. Clubs: Denver Womans Press, Seattle Tennis, Washington Athletic. Home: 1232 38th Ave E Seattle WA 98112 Office: 402 Grosvenor House Seattle WA 98121

GELMAN, ESTHER PAPER, county council member; b. Balt., June 14, 1931; m. Norman I. Gelman, 1951; children—Sharon Rachel, Judith Rebecca. B.A. in English, History and Philosophy cum laude, U. Colo.-Boulder, 1952. Council person, Montgomery County Council, Md., 1974—. Commr. Md.-Nat. Capital Park & Planning Commn., 1970-74; active Md. Assn. of Counties, pres. 1984, 1st v.p., chmn. Legis. Com., 1983, 2nd v.p., chmn., Conf. Planning Com., 1982, sec., 1981, treas., chmn. Budget and Personnel Com., 1979, 80, Liaison Com. to Nat. Assn. of Counties Conv., 1980-82; mem. UJAF Housing Corp. Adv. Council, 1976-78; hon. dir. Bd. dirs., Hebrew Acad. of Greater Washington, 1976—; bd. mem. Jewish Council for the Aging, 1978—, Jewish Community Ctr., 1983-84; mem. Adult Div. Com., Jewish Community Ctr. of Greater Washington, 1974—, Women's Polit. Caucus of Montgomery County, Ohr Kodesh Synagogue, Am. Planning Assn., Gray Panthers of Montgomery County, various coms. in the Montgomery County Council, Md. Assn. of Counties, Metro-Washington Council of Govs., Nat. Assn. of Counties. Recipient First Montgomery County "Disting. Woman in Local Govt." award Fedn. of Orgns. for Profl. Women, 1985, Spousal Abuse Award Montgomery County Govt., 1983, Am. ORT Fedn.'s Golda Meir award, 1984, Recognition award, Silver Spring YMCA, 1978. Mem. Hadassah, Pioneer Women, NAACP, AAUW, Bethesda-Chevy Chase C. of C. (pres.'s award 1980), Silver Spring C. of C. (life mem. 1980), Alpha Phi Alpha. Democrat. Jewish. Home: 8719 Postoak Rd Potomac MD 20854 Office: Montgomery County Council 100 Maryland Ave Rockville MD 20850

GELMAN, EVELYN GOLDSTEIN, bar association administrator, meeting planner and travel consultant; b. N.Y.C., May 2, 1939; d. Frederick E. and Lillian (Cohen) Goldstein; m. Milton Gelman, Apr. 16, 1961; children—Philip Ross, Melissa Marian. B.A., Barnard Coll., N.Y.C., 1959; postgrad. Middlebury Coll. (Vt.), 1959, Columbia U., 1960-62. Conf. officer, meeting coordinator UN, N.Y.C., 1960-62; exec. dir. Fed. Bar Council, N.Y.C., 1964—; pres. EG Travel Services, N.Y.C., 1978—; pres. Programme Assocs., N.Y.C., 1983—. Mem. adv. council Park Ave. Synagogue, N.Y.C., 1979-83, trustee, 1983—. Mem. Barnard Coll. Alumnae Council (Barnard Fund alumnae com.), N.Y. Soc. Assn. Execs., Nat. Council Jewish Women. Home: 49 E 96th St New York NY 10128 Office: Fed Bar Council 370 Lexington Ave New York NY 10017

GELORMINO, JOAN ANN, educator; b. Torrington, Conn., Jan. 3, 1939; d. Erminio and Jennie Rose Gelormino; B.S., Western Conn. State Coll., Danbury, 1960; M.S., U. Hartford, 1966; Ed.D., Nova U., Ft. Lauderdale, Fla., 1975. Tchr., Torrington Bd. Edn., 1960-62; tchr. Hartford (Conn.) Bd. Edn., 1960-68, tchr., dir., resource tchr. Early Childhood Learning Center, adj. faculty U. Hartford, 1969-71; dir. Lower Sch., Univ. Sch., Nova U., 1971—, assoc. dir. Sch. Center, 1973—; cons. Early Childhood Program, Waterbury, West Hartford, Farmington, Conn., 1970-72, Long Beach, N.Y., Half Hollow, N.Y., Merrick, N.Y., Learning Inst. N.C.; cons. migrant edn., Fla. Seminole Pre-Sch. Programs, Broward County, Fla., 1973-75; bd. dirs., v.p. United Way Child Care Centers, Broward County, 1975—, pres., 1976-78. Mem. Broward County Environ. Control Bd., 1979-80; sec. Kids in Distress, 1984—. Mem. Nat. Assn. for Edn. Young Children, Assn. for Childhood Edn. Internat., Soc. for Research Child Devel., Am. Montessori Assn., AAUW, Fla. Assn. for Children Under Six (conf. chmn. Hollywood 1980). Author: Pre-Number and Mathematic Skill Sequence With Activities, 1969; Constructing Games for Early Childhood Classrooms, 1974; Transactional Analysis For Parents and Teachers of Young Children, 1975. Home: 9800 SW 4th St Fort Lauderdale FL 33324 Office: 7500 SW 36th St Fort Lauderdale FL 33314

GELSHENEN, ROSEMARY ROBINSON, marketing executive; b. Queens, N.Y., Feb. 24, 1950; d. John Joseph and Ann (Doyle) Gelshenen; m. Dennis Berkholtz, Oct. 27, 1973 (div. 1980). B.A., Marquette U., 1972. Receptionist Atlanta Conv. Bur., 1974; sales mgr. Rodeway Inns, Atlanta, 1974; pub. relations dir. McDonald's Corp., Atlanta, 1975, McDonald & Little, Atlanta, 1976; dir. mktg. Ga. World Congress Center, Atlanta, 1976—. Banquet chmn. Beastly Feast, Zool. Soc., Atlanta, 1983, 84. Mem. Sales & Mktg. Execs. (dir.), Nat. Assn. Exposition Mgrs., Hotel Sales Mgmt. Assn., Profl. Conv. Mgmt. Assn., European Soc. Assn. Execs. (allied), Greater Washington Soc. Assn. Execs. (allied), Meeting Planners Internat. Roman Catholic. Home: 23110 Plantation Dr Atlanta GA 30324 Office: Ga World Congress Center 285 International St Atlanta GA 30313

GEMELLI, CHRISTINE LISA ANDERSON, real estate broker; b. Torrington, Conn., Sept. 18, 1951; d. Albond and Helen Bernice (Roman) A.; m. Wayne Allen Gemelli, June 24, 1972; children—Scott Allen, Brad Anderson. A.S., Northwestern Conn. Community Coll., 1971; student U. Conn., 1981-82. Clerk, Probate Ct., Litchfield, Conn., 1971-76; real estate sales person Monti Realty & Rit Zaharek Agy., Torrington, 1972-82; asst. to exec. dir. Conn. Jr. Republic, Litchfield, 1980-84, personnel adminstr., 1984-85; prin. Chris Gemelli Preferred Properties, Torrington, 1983—. Sec. Forbes PTO, Torrington, 1982-84; mem. Forbes Sch. Bldg. Com., Torrington, 1980-81. Mem. Nat. Assn. Realtors, Conn. Assn. Realtors, Litchfield County Women's Network, Conn. Assn. Sch. Bus. Officials; bd. dirs. Litchfield County Bd. Realtors, Litchfield County Multiple Listing Service. Democrat. Roman Catholic. Avocations: skiing, swimming; sailing. Office: Chris Gemelli Preferred Properties 60 Weed Rd Torrington CT 06790

GEMIGNANI, MARY KATHLEEN, educator; b. Pensacola, Fla., June 10, 1945; d. Frank Edward and Veryl (Laux) Meyer; m. John Felice Gemignani, Dec. 31, 1967; children—Christopher, Zachary, Anthony, Rebecca. B.A., St. Norbert Coll., 1967; M.Ed., U. Vt., 1975. Tchr., U.S. Peace Corps, Liberia, 1967-69; Lincoln Community Sch., Vt., 1970-75; dir. Lincoln Coop. Pre-Sch., 1975-83; cons. tchr./learning specialist Monkton Central Sch., Vt., 1984—; ednl. cons., 1980—. Author: A Bibilography of Non-Sexist Books for Parents and Educators, 1983—; dir. TV spl.: Spotlight on Monkton, 1985. Found. Parent Resource Library grantee, Nat. Home Library, 1984. Avocations: hiking; gardening; travel; reading. Home: RD 1 Box 660 Bristol VT 05443 Office: Monkton Central Sch Monkton VT 05469

GENCARELLI, JANE B., state legislator; b. Fall River, Mass., Apr. 28, 1929; d. Clement Stanley and Jane (Malone) Bradshaw; m. Francis Gencarelli, 1953; children—David, Ann Gencarelli Cruso, Lisa Jane, Francesca. Grad. New Eng. Conservatory of Music, Boston. Tchr. music Westerly U., 1956-76, Southeastern Mass. U., 1967-75; vice chmn. Westerly Sch. Com., 1981-83; mem. R.I. State Senate from Dist. 26, 1983—. Named Woman of Yr., Profl. Women's Club, 1983, Outstanding Profl. Woman, AAUW, 1985. Mem. Mu Phi Epsilon. Club: New England Conservatory. Roman Catholic. Republican. Office: RI State Capitol Bldg Providence RI 02903

GENCO, BARBARA ANN, librarian; b. Buffalo, Feb. 11, 1951; d. Joseph E. and Dorothy E. (Colmerauer) G.; m. Michael Rosenthal, July 27, 1974; 1 son, Andrew Joseph Genco. B.A. magna cum laude, Canisius Coll., 1973; M.L.S., Pratt Inst., 1975. Librarian Bklyn. Pub. Library, 1975-81, br. librarian, 1981-83, asst. to coordinator materials selection, 1983-84, asst. coordinator Office of New Books Selection, 1984—. Mem. N.Y. Library Assn. (co-chairperson union and roundtable 1983—), ALA (AFL-CIO com. service labor groups 1984-86, John Sessions Meml. award 1985—), Beta Phi Mu. Home: 170 Prospect Park W Brooklyn NY 11215 Office: Bklyn Pub Library Grand Army Plaza Brooklyn NY 11215

GENDLIN, FRANCES, association executive, editor; Staff mem. N.Y. State Council of Environ. Advisors, Aspen Inst. for Humanistic Studies, Bull. of Atomic Scientists, Psychotherapy; editor Sierra mag., 1975-84; dir. pub. affairs Sierra Club, 1977-84; exec. dir. Assn. Am. Univ. Presses, 1984—; pres. Am. Univ. Press Services, 1984—. Address: Assn Am Univ Presses 1 Park Ave New York NY 10016

GENGENBACH, MARIANNE S., chiropractic educator; b. West Chester, Pa., Oct. 24, 1956; d. Siegfried K. and Helga (Hunger) Schmidt-Gengenbach. B.A. cum laude, Washington U., St. Louis, 1978; D.C., Logan Coll. Chiropractic, 1983. Diplomate Nat. Bd. Chiropractic Examiners. Clinic dir. Logan Coll. Chiropractic, Chesterfield, Mo., 1983-85, instr. pediatrics, 1983—, instr. athletic injuries, 1984—, module edn. coordinator, 1984-85, postgrad. instr., 1986, dir. clin. edn., 1986—; gen. practice chiropractic medicine, St. Louis, 1983—. Mem. Am. Chiropractic Assn., Found. for Chiropractic Edn. and Research, Women's Sports Found., Mo. State Chiropractic Assn., Logan Coll. Alumni Assn. Democrat. Mem. Ethical Soc. Avocations: soccer; softball; running. Office: Logan Coll Chiropractic 1851 Schoettler Rd Chesterfield MO 63017

GENGOR, VIRGINIA ANDERSON, financial planning executive, financial services educator; b. Lyons, N.Y., May 2, 1927; d. Axel Jennings and Marie Margaret (Mack) Anderson; m. Peter Gengor, Mar. 2, 1952 (dec.); children—Peter Randall, Daniel Neal, Susan Leigh. A.B., Wheaton Coll., 1949; M.A., U. No. Colo., Greeley, 1975, 77. Cert. fin. planner. Chief hosp. intake service County of San Diego, 1966-77, chief Kearny Mesa Dist. Office, 1977-79, chief Dependent Children of C., 1979-81, chief child protection services, 1981-82; registered rep. Am. Pacific Securities, San Diego, 1982-85; assoc. Pollock & Assocs., San Diego, 1985—; cons. instr. Nat. Ctr. for Fin. Edn., San Diego, 1986—; instr. San Diego Community Coll., 1985—. Mem. allocations panel United Way, San Diego, 1976-79; chmn. com. Child Abuse Coordinating Council, San Diego, 1979-83; pres. Friends of Casa de la Esperanza, San Diego, 1980-85; 1st v.p. The Big Sister League, San Diego, 1985-86. Mem. Inst. Cert. Fin. Planners, Internat. Assn. Fin. Planning, Inland Soc. Tax Cons., AAUW, Nat. Ctr. Fin. Edn. Presbyterian. Avocations: community service; traveling; reading. Home: 6462 Spear St San Diego CA 92120 Office: Pollock & Assocs 2820 Camino Del Rio S #300 San Diego CA 92108

GENKINGER, LAUREN BETTIE, advertising agency executive; b. New Castle, Pa., June 4, 1949; d. Robert S. and Bettie (Davis) G. B.S. in Advt., 1971. Research asst. Campbell-Mithun, Inc., Mpls., 1972-73; research acct. exec., 1973-75, research acct. supr., 1975-78; assoc. research dir. McDonald and Little, Atlanta, 1978-79, v.p. research dir., 1979-81, sr. v.p. research dir. and mgmt. supr., 1981-84; sr. v.p. dir. strategic planning and research Burton-Campbell, Inc., Atlanta, 1984—; adv. advt. council U. Fla., Gainesville, 1981-83. Mem. Am. Mktg. Assn., Chi Omega. Republican. Avocations: tennis; water skiing. Home: 110 Verlaine Pl NW Atlanta GA 30327 Office: Burton-Campbell Inc 101 Colony Sq Atlanta GA 30361

GENOVA, DIANE MELISANO, lawyer; b. Yonkers, N.Y., Aug. 8, 1948; d. Joseph Louis and Ines (Fiumana) Melisano; m. Clyde Barry Schechter, Dec. 29, 1968 (div. Aug. 1981); m. 2d, Joseph Steven Genova, Jan. 15, 1983. A.B., Barnard Coll., 1970; postgrad. Harvard U., 1970-71; J.D., Columbia U., 1975. Assoc., Milbank, Tweed, Hadley & McCloy, N.Y.C., 1975-80, Tung, Drabkin & Boynton, N.Y.C., 1980-81; v.p., asst. resident counsel Morgan Guaranty Trust Co. N.Y., N.Y.C., 1981—. Harlan Fiske Stone scholar, 1972-75. Mem. Assn. Bar City N.Y., N.Y. State Bar Assn., ABA. Roman Catholic. Club: Montauk (Bklyn.). Office: Morgan Guaranty Trust Co of NY 23 Wall St New York NY 10015

GENTER, JOAN LEE, personnel executive; b. Corinth, Miss., Mar. 8, 1947; d. Henry Harry and Ruth Marie (Burcham) Hagen; m. Rodney William Genter, Apr. 15, 1968; children—Jeanette Marie, Brian William. B.A. in Liberal Studies, Calif. State U.-Northridge, 1976. Dir. human resources Las Encinas Hosp., Pasadena, Calif., 1979—; cons. in human resources Hosp. Corp. Am.; mem. adv. bd. vocat. edn. Pasadena Unified Sch. Dist. Served to sgt. USAF, 1976-79. Mem. Hosp. Personnel Mgrs. Assn., Personnel and Indsl. Relations Assn., Am. Soc. Hosp. Personnel Adminstrs., Am. Soc. Personnel Adminstrs., Pasadena C. of C. (chmn. mil. affairs com.). Republican. Roman Catholic. Office: Las Encinas Hosp 2900 E Del Mar Blvd Pasadena CA 91107

GENTILE, THERESE ANN, hospital coordinator, consultant; b. Phila., June 13, 1952; d. John Jules and Marie Agnes (De Haven) Mathias; m. Samuel Henry Gentile, June 6, 1981. R.N., Gwynedd-Mercy Coll., 1972, B.S. in Nursing, 1974; M.Ed., Temple U., 1980; M.S.N., Villanova U., 1984—. R.N., Pa. Part time charge nurse, team leader, North Penn Hosp., Lansdale, Pa., 1972-74, office nurse, Lansdale, 1976-81; asst. prof. Montgomery County Community Coll., Blue Bell, Pa., 1974-84; hospice coordinator Sacred Heart Med. Ctr., Chester, Pa., 1984—; active inservice edn. Montgomery Hosp., Norristown, Pa., North Penn Hosp., Lansdale, 1974—; pres. Nat. Med. Interpreters, Inc., 1984—. Editor manuscripts for textbooks Houghton Mifflin Co. Alumni rep. Gwynedd-Mercy Coll., 1980—. Roman Catholic. Home: 3815 Mill Rd Collegeville PA 19426

GENTILE, VALERIE ANN, lawyer; b. Cleve., Aug. 4, 1955; d. John Charles and Doreen Phyllis (Neale) G. B.L.S., Bowling Green U., 1977; J.D., Case Western Res. U., 1981. Bar: Ohio 1981. Summer assoc. Arter & Hadden, Cleve., 1980, assoc., 1981-83; assoc. Baker & Hostetler, Cleve., 1983—; sec. Royal Petroleum Properties, Inc., Cleve., 1982-83. Editor: Case Western Res. U. Law Rev., 1980-81, assoc. editor, 1979-80; assoc. editor Case Western Res. U. Jour. Internat. Law, 1978-79. Mem. Cleve. Citizens League, 1982-84; trustee Forest Hills Housing Corp., Cleve., 1982-84; mem. fgn. trade policy com. Cleve. World Trade Assn., 1982—. Mem. Ohio State Bar Assn., Cleve. Bar Assn., ABA, Alpha Epsilon Delta, Beta Beta Beta, Alpha Lambda Delta. Office: Baker & Hostetler 3200 National City Ctr Cleveland OH 44114

GENTLE, CARLA ALLEGRA, petroleum corporation executive, consultant; b. Colorado Springs, Colo., Feb. 27, 1955; d. John Edward and Rebecca (Lijavetsky) Gentle. B.A., Western State Coll., 1977; postgrad. U. Colo., 1979-81. Adminstrv. asst. Bldg. Owners and Mgrs., Inc., Washington, 1977-78; sales assoc. The Denver, Aurora, Colo., 1979; personnel asst. Occidental Fire and Casualty, Englewood, Colo., 1980-81; sr. employment specialist Petroleum Info. Corp., Littleton, Colo., 1981—; pvt. practice cons., Denver, 1983—. First vice chmn. Young Republicans, Jefferson County, Colo., 1983—; mem. Rep. Women's Task Force, 1983—. Western State Coll. athletic scholar, 1976. Mem. Colo. Soc. Personnel Adminstrn., Internat. Assn. Personnel Women, Women's Edn. Service Assn. Republican. Home: 9677-B W Chatfield Ave Littleton CO 80123 Office: Petroleum Info Corp 4100 E Dry Creek Rd Littleton CO 80122

GENTLE, MARGARET MARION, mayor; b. Cairn Brook, Pa., Oct. 19, 1920; d. John Joseph and Catherine Ann (Sefchik) Franko; m. James E. Gentle, Feb. 13, 1949. Student pub. schs., Gary, Ind. Mayor City of North Port, Fla., 1973—. Served to maj. U.S. Army, 1942-62. Democrat. Roman Catholic. Avocations: music; oil painting; golf. Home: 416 Payne St North Port FL 33596 Office: Mcpl Bldg 311 North Port Blvd North Port FL 33596

GENTLEMAN, JULIA B., state senator; b. Des Moines, Aug. 24, 1931; d. John and Marguerite Brooks; B.S., Northwestern U., 1953; m. Gregor Gentleman, 1954; 5 children. Formerly mem. Iowa Ho. of Reps., 1975-78; mem Iowa Senate, 1979—. Office: Iowa State House Des Moines IA 50319

GENTRY, JANICE ELISA, utility company executive; b. Alexandria, Va., Aug. 24, 1950; d. Marion E. (Mattonen) B.S., U. Va., Mary Washington Coll., 1972; M.Ed., U. Alaska, 1975. Tchr. physics Petersburg (Va.) High Sch., 1972-74; instr. physics U. Alaska, Fairbanks, 1974-75; instr. math. Big Bend Community Coll., Madrid, Spain, 1975, El Paso Community Coll., Madrid, 1976, City Coll. of Chicago, Madrid, 1977, Washington Tech. Inst., Madrid, 1978; service cons. So. Bell, Atlanta, 1979-80, account exec., 1980-81; staff supr. acctgs. staff AT&T Long Lines, Atlanta, 1982, staff supr. personnel, 1983, ops. mgr., 1984—. Big Sister United Way, Atlanta, 1979-82, campaign chairperson, 1982, co-chmn. gen. bus. unit, 1985. Mem. Nat. Assn. Profl. Women in Sales, Ga. Women's Exec. Network. Clubs: Women's Commerce (Atlanta); Atlanta Ski. Home: 603 Twin Brooks Way Marietta GA 30067 Office: AT&T 1950 W Exchange Pl Tucker GA 30084

GENTRY, JOYCE ANN, actress, dancer, promoter, producer stage plays; b. Mobile, Ala., Dec. 31, 1942; d. Travis A. Hicks and Marie (Morgan) Hicks Cash; m. Matthew A. Hayes, May 7, 1970 (div. June 1971); 1 child, Amy Sharae Hayes; m. Morris R. Gentry (dec. Feb. 1986). Student Los Angeles 20th Century Acting Sch., 1968-81; B.S. in Food Ops. and Theatre, U. Las Vegas, 1980. Prin., owner Encore Internat., Las Vegas, 1985—. Active St. Jude's, Las Vegas, 1981—; active George Wallace Campaign, Mobile, Ala., 1958, 59, 60, Gov.'s Luncheon, Las Vegas, 1980. Recipient Bronze medal Met. Police Dept. 9th Nev. Olympics, Las Vegas, 1984. Mem. Screen Actors Guild, AFTRA, AGVA, ASCAP, Broadcasters Union, Nat. Assn. Female Execs., Las Vegas C. of C. Avocations: boating; skiing; swimming; ice skating; collecting movie star photos. Home: 1103 S 6th St Las Vegas NV 89104

GENTRY, WANDA MARKHAM, utility executive; b. Franklin, Ky., Oct. 7, 1939; d. Thomas Harris and Edith Nell (Dinwiddie) Markham; student Bowling Green Bus. U., 1957-58; m. William Henry Gentry, Dec. 30, 1961; children—Jonathan Markham, Laura Leigh. Sec. to gen. mgr. N.H. Granite State Ins. Co., Jacksonville, Fla., 1958-60; sec. Ky. State Hwy. Dept., 1960-63; sec. to dir. of nurses East Ridge Community Hosp., Chattanooga, 1974, adminstrv. asst., 1974-76; adminstrv. asst. to pres. and chmn. bd. Tenn. Natural Resources Inc., and Nashville Gas Co., 1976—. Mem. Exec. Women Internat. (dir. Nashville chpt. 1978-82), Dream Makers. Republican. Baptist. Club: Cumberland. Home: 4502 Franklin Rd Nashville TN 37204 Office: 814 Church St Nashville TN 37203

GEORGE, BARBARA, publisher, author; b. Upper Darby, Pa., Nov. 15, 1942; d. John Adam and Betty Jean (Higgins) Wallace; m. Robert F. George, June 21, 1965; 1 child, Anna. B.A., Ind. U., 1964; M.A.T., Antioch Coll., 1969. Publisher, Velo-news, Brattleboro, Vt., 1972—, New Eng. Running, Brattleboro, 1984—. Author: Winning Bicycle Racing (with Jack Simes), 1976, Bicycle Road Racing, 1977, Bicycle Track Racing, 1977; (with Tom Doughty and Ed Pavelka) The Complete Book of Long-distance and Competitive Cycling, 1983. Mem. Phi Beta Kappa. Office: Velonews Corp Box 1257 Brattleboro VT 05301

GEORGE, BEVERLY ALICE, leasing company executive; b. Ft. Worth, Feb.12, 1945; d. William Barclay and Sylvia Vanda (Mazantini) George; m. John Joseph Richards, Jr., Jan. 6, 1966 (div. 1970); children—Amelie Barlow, John Joseph, Malcolm Chauvin. Student, U. St. Thomas, 1964-65, Loyola U. New Orleans, 1965-66. Project mgr. Anne Rozelle & Assocs., Houston, 1971-73; div. mgr. residential leasing Jim Tucker & Assocs., Houston, 1974-76; residential leasing cons. Woodway Locators, Houston, 1979-83; mng. ptnr., pres. Residential Locators, Houston, 1983—. Mem. Houston Apt. Assn., Houston Home Builders, Houston Assn. Apt. Location Services, Houston Bd. Realtors, Sales and Mktg. Execs., Meml. Exec. Breakfast Club. Republican. Episcopalian. Clubs: Harris County Heritage Soc. (hospitality chmn. 1975-79), Houston Mus. Natural Sci. Guild. Home: 5131 Torchlight Dr Houston TX 77035 Office: Residential Locators 3333 Bering Dr Suite 300 Houston TX 77057

GEORGE, KATHLEEN ELIZABETH, theatre educator; b. Johnstown, Pa., July 7, 1943; d. Richard Thomas and Catherine Ann (Abraham) G. B.A., U. Pitts., 1964, M.A., 1966, Ph.D., 1975. Asst. prof. Carlow Coll., Pitts., 1968-75; assoc. prof. theatre U. Pitts., 1976—. Author: Rhythm in Drama, 1981. Dir. numerous theatre prodns. Recipient Prodn. awards Pitts. Post-Gazette, 1978, 79, 81. Grantee Pa. Arts Council, U. Pitts., Mem. Am. Theatre Assn., Poets and Writers, Phi Beta Kappa. Democrat. Eastern Orthodox. Home: 6605 Rosemoor St Pittsburgh PA 15217 Office: Theatre B39CL Univ Pitts Pittsburgh PA 15260

GEORGE, LYNELLE, purchasing specialist; b. Los Angeles, Apr. 13, 1946; children—Kelli Rhondelyn, Damon Scott, Corey Bernard. B.A., Calif. State U.-Carson, 1985; A.A., W. Los Angeles Coll., 1982. Adminstrv. asst. Los Angeles County/MLK-Drew Med. Ctr., 1978-80; procurement mgr. Los Angeles County/Harbor-UCLA Med. Ctr., Torrance, 1980-82, Los Angeles County/Pub. Health Programs, Los Angeles, 1982-84; fixed asset coordinator Harbor-UCLA Med. Ctr., 1984; procurement specialist Los Angeles County/U. So. Calif. Med. Ctr., Los Angeles, 1984—. Corr. fin. sec. Assistance League of Stovall Found., Los Angeles, 1985-86, chmn. escort com., 1984-85; mem. Los Angeles Pub. Health Programs safety com., 1982-84, forms rev. com., 1982-84, supply com., 1982-84, others. Mem. Nat. Assn. Female Execs. Democrat. Avocations: travel, writing.

GEORGE, MARY SHANNON, state senator; b. Seattle, May 27, 1916; d. William Day and Agnes (Lovejoy) Shannon; B.A. cum laude, U. Wash., 1937; postgrad. U. Mich., 1937, Columbia U., 1938; m. Flave Joseph George; children—Flave Joseph, Karen Van Hook, Christy, Shannon Lowrey. Prodn. asst., asst. news editor Pathe News, N.Y.C., 1938-42; mem. fgn. editions staff Readers Digest, Pleasantville, N.Y., 1942-46; columnist Caracas (Venezuela) Daily Jour., 1953-60; councilwoman City and County of Honolulu, 1969-74; senator State of Hawaii, 1974—, asst. minority leader, 1978-80, minority policy leader, 1983-84, chmn. transp. com., 1981-82; mem. Nat. Air Quality Adv. Bd., 1974-75. Vice chmn. 1st Hawaii Ethics Commn., 1968; mem. budget com. Aloha United Fund, 1970; co-founder Citizens Com. on Constl. Conv., 1968; vice-chmn. platform com. Republican Nat. Conv., 1976, co-chmn., 1980; bd. dirs. Hawaii Planned Parenthood, 1970-72, 79-86, Hawaii Med. Services Assn., 1973-86; mem. adv. bd. Hawaii chpt. Mothers Against Drunk Driving. Recipient Jewish Men's Club Brotherhood award, 1974; Outstanding Legislator of Yr. award Nat. Rep. Legislators Assn., 1985; named Woman of Yr., Honolulu Press Club, 1969, Hawaii Fedn. Bus. and Profl. Women, 1970; Citizen of Yr., Hawaii Fed. Exec. Bd., 1973, 76. Mem. LWV (pres. Honolulu 1966-68), Mensa, Phi Beta Kappa, Kappa Alpha Theta. Episcopalian. Author: A Is for Abrazo, 1961. Home: 782-G N Kalaheo Ave Kailua HI 96734 Office: Hawaii State Capitol Honolulu HI 96813

GEORGE, PHYLLIS, sports broadcaster, wife of former gov. of Ky.; b. Denton, Tex., June 25, 1949; d. Robert and Louise G.; m. Robert Evans, Apr. 14, 1977 (div.); m. John Y. Brown, Jr., Mar. 17, 1979; children—Lincoln Tyler George, Pamela. Student, North Tex. State U., Tex. Christian U.; studied dance with Peter Gennaro, Ron Poindexter, studied drama under Darryl Hickman, Charles Conrad, Warren Robinson. Joined CBS Sports, 1975; sportscaster CBS NFL Today Show, 8 yrs., Super Bowl, 1979, 80, 81; co-anchor CBS Morning News, 1985; co-host Miss America Pageant, 1971-79, Candid Camera, People, Tournament of Roses Parade, 1978-82; guest host Good Morning America Show; appeared on Muppets Ann. Award Night, Charlie Brown's 30th Birthday Show, NBC's Tonight Show, CBS's Celebrity Challenge of Sexes, Hour Magazine, Mike Douglas Show, PM Magazine, Merv Griffin Show, Dinah Shore Show; lectr. Author: (with Bill Adler) I Love America Diet Book. Hon. chmn. Ky. Arts and Crafts Found., Save the Mansion, Inc.; charter mem. Com. of 200; chmn. Ky. Film Found.; bd. dirs. Appalachian Community Service Network, 1980-82; house tour chmn. Mus. Am. Folk Art, 1982; chmn. community affairs Spl. Olympics, 1977, 78, 79; hon. trustee United World coll.; originator Ky. Salute to Women of 80's Rally; sponsor Phyllis George Scholarships at U. Ky. and North Tex. State U. Named Texan of Yr., 1971; Named Miss America, 1971; recipient Ky. Gov.'s Disting. Service medal, 1982, Jack Quinlan award Notre Dame Club Chgo., 1983, Ida Lee Willis Preservation Project award, 1983; named Sportscaster of Yr. Washington Football Club, 1975; co-recipient Emmy award for NFL Today. Mem. Zeta Tau Alpha.

GEORGES, STACY ELAINE, engineering/manufacturing executive; b. East St. Louis, Ill., Apr. 4, 1957; d. Gus Anthony and Cleopatra (Carnegis) G. B.S. in Indsl. Engring., Gen. Motors Inst., 1980. Engr. Gen. Motors, Saginaw, Mich., 1980-81, systems analyst, 1981-83, sr. engr., 1983-84; engring. supr. electronic data systems, Detroit, 1984-85, engring./mfg. supr., 1986—; mktg. industry cons., 1985-86. Post adv. Explorers, Saginaw, 1982-85. Author: CAD/CAM in Product Engineering, 1980 (thesis honors distinction 1980). Mem. Inst. Indsl. Engrs. (v.p. programs 1984-85, bd. dirs. 1983-84), Soc. Automotive Engrs., Computer Automated Systems/Soc. Mfgr. Engrs. Republican. Mem. Greek Orthodox Ch. Avocations: travel, music, reading, crafts with seashells, scuba diving. Home: 1886 Allenway Ct Rochester Hills MI 48063

GEOVJIAN, LISA, veterinarian; b. Pontiac, Mich., Jan. 9, 1952; d. John and Helen (Hagopian) G.; m. Richard Herbert Crowley, Apr. 10, 1979; children—Bennet Geovjian Crowley, Shawn Geovjian Crowley. B.S., Mich. State U., 1973, D.V.M., 1975. Staff vet. Ark Animal Hosp., Pinconning, Mich., 1975, Rutland (Vt.) Vet. Clinic, 1975-77, chief of staff, 1977-84, owner, 1984—; state vet. chmn. Morris Animal Found., 1977-81; mem. Vt. Vet. Licensing Bd., 1985—. Crisis worker Herstory House shelter, Rutland, 1982; v.p., bd. dirs. Sugar Maple Day Care Ctr., Rutland, 1983-85; bd. dirs. Rutland Mental Health; incorporator Rutland Regional Med. Ctr. Mem. AVMA, Vt. Vet. Med. Assn., Am. Animal Hosp. Assn., Am. Soc. Avian Practitioners, Am. Assn. Women Vets. Home: Rural Route Box 252 East Wallingford VT 05742 Office: Rutland Veterinary Clinic North Main St Rutland VT 05701

GERACE, MARY ALICIA, property manager; b. Chgo., July 9, 1952; d. Josephil Louis and Mary Helen (Lupo) G. A.A.S., Ray Vogue Coll., Chgo., 1972; postgrad DePaul U., Chgo., 1980-81; B.A., Stephens Coll., 1985. Cert. resident mgr. Mgr. wholesale interior furnishings showrooms Merchandise Mart, Chgo., 1971-74, 79-80, 82; apt. rental property mgr., leasing agt., 1975-77; comml. property mgr., leasing agt., 1981; condominium property mgr., 1984-85; mgr. 666 N. Lake Shore Dr. Tower Residence, Chgo., 1986—; ptnr. Condo Concepts, Inc., 1986; co-founder Stop Sexual Abuse of Students Hotline, 1986—. Author: Battered Women: A Threepart Series, 1980. Co-founder, pres. Chgo. Council on Crimes Against Women, 1978-82; mem. Gov.'s Spl. Adv. Council on Women, 1979-82; mem. Cook County State's Atty. Task Force on Women's Issues, Chgo., 1981—; co-convenor Merchandise Mart Women's Network, Chgo., 1982; founding mem. women's com. 1992 Chgo. World's Fair, 1982. Unitarian. Address: 666 N Lake Shore Dr Apt #1720 Chicago IL 60611

GERAGHTY, LAURA LEE MARIE, state official, consultant; b. St. Paul, Sept. 5, 1944; d. John Charles and Leona Ann (Fahley) G.; m. Richard A. Beens, Aug. 9, 1974; 1 dau., Jennifer Lois Geraghty Beens. B.A., Coll. St. Catherine, 1966. Social worker Ramsey County Welfare Dept., St. Paul, 1966-70, vol. coordinator, 1970-75; dir. Minn. Office on Vol. Services, Dept. Adminstrn., St. Paul, 1975—; co-chair Vols. for Minn., 1982-84; mem. community faculty Met. State U., St. Paul, 1980—; mem. adv. com. M.A. in orgnl. leadership Coll. of St. Catherine, St. Paul, 1985—; mem. Action's Nat. Steering Com., Washington, 1980-81; mem. Human Resources Com. of Pres. Task Force on Pvt. Sector Initiatives, Washington, 1982-83. Chmn., Consumer Action Now, St. Paul, 1971-72; bd. dirs. Coalition to Advocate Pub. Utility Responsibility, Minn., 1972-73; mem. Metro Rate Authority, St. Paul, 1973. Recipient Woman of Achievement award West Suburban C. of C., Mpls., 1983; Pres. Vol. Action award Pres. Reagon, Washington, 1984; Outstanding Achievement award for govt./community devel. St. Paul YWCA. Mem. Assn. for Vol. Adminstrn. (pres. 1983-85), Minn. Assn. Vol. Dirs., Corp. Volunteerism Council. Roman Catholic. Office: Minn Office on Vol Services 500 Rice St Saint Paul MN 55155

GERAK, CHARLENE CORINNE, physical education educator; b. Cleve., Sept. 2, 1945; d. Charles William and Mildred Corinne (Mousson) G.; m. James Edward Boothe, Jan. 20, 1978 (div. Apr. 1979). B.S., Bowling Green State U., 1968, M.S., 1972; postgrad in ednl. law Kent State U. Cert. tchr., secondary sch. adminstr., supr. Tchr. health and phys. edn. Parma Sr. High Sch. (Ohio), 1968—, girls' and boys' tennis coach. CPR trainer Am. Heart Assn.; chem. dependency counselor. Mem. Ohio Edn. Assn., NEA, Parma Edn. Assn. Home: 4626 E 88th St Garfield Heights OH 44125 Office: Parma Sr High Sch 6285 W 54th St Parma OH 55129

GERARD, BARBARA, educator, visual artist; b. N.Y.C., Apr. 21, 1943; d. Arthur and Edith (Perrone) De Bernarda; B.S., N.Y.U., 1963, M.A., 1966, postgrad., 1972; profl. diploma, City Coll. of CUNY, 1975; postgrad. Columbia U., 1977-79; m. Marvin Hartenstein, Sept. 18, 1976; 1 son by previous marriage, David Gerard. Graphic designer C. A. Parshall Advt. Agy., N.Y.C., 1962; art tchr. Herman Ridder Jr. High Sch., N.Y.C., 1963-65; freelance designer Sam Muggeo Advt. Inc., N.Y.C., 1965-67; art chmn. Herman Ridder Jr. High Sch., 1967-70; program counselor recruitment and tng. of Spanish-speaking tchrs., N.Y.C. Bd. Edn., 1970-72, program coordinator bilingual pupil services Center for Bilingual Edn., 1972-75, dir. bilingual tchr.-intern program, 1975-79, dir. Center for Dissemination, 1979-81; owner, v.p. George Gerard Assocs., Inc., Port Washington, N.Y., 1981-83; cons. Yeshiva U., Pace U., 1973, Aspiria of N.Y., 1974, Children's TV Workshop - Sesame St., 1975; adj. lectr. CCNY, 1973-74, N.Y.U., 1974-75, Coll. New Rochelle, 1974-75; cons., participant WNBC-TV, 1970, 75, 79; one-woman shows: Lincoln Inst. Gallery, N.Y., 1968, Henry Hicks Gallery, Bklyn., 1976, Second Story Spring St. Gallery, N.Y., 1976, Viridian Gallery, N.Y., 1977, 79; exhibited in group shows Loeb Student Center Gallery, N.Y.C., 1962, 63, Riverdale Community Gallery, N.Y., 1965, Environment Gallery, N.Y.C., 1969, Metamorphosis, N.Y., 1970, Concepts II, N.Y.C., 1971, Union Carbide, N.Y., 1972, Lever House, 1973, Westchester Arts Soc., White Plains, N.Y., 1973, Gillary Gallery, Jericho, L.I., 1974, Manhattan Savs. Bank, 1976, Bklyn. Acad. Music, 1976, Pvt. Viewings/The Erlichs, The Colins, 1976, Gallery 91, Bklyn., 1976, Henry Hicks Gallery, Bklyn., 1975, 76, 77, Lincoln Center, Avery Fisher Hall N.Y., 1976, Second Story Spring St. Gallery, 1976, Bergdorf Goodman, White Plains, 1976, First Women's Bank, 1976, 80, Viridian Gallery, 1976, 77, 80, Womanart Gallery, 1976, Norman Kramer Gallery, Danbury, Conn., 1976, Mfrs. Hanover Bank, N.Y., 1977, Guild Hall Mus., East Hampton, N.Y., 1977, 80, Union of Maine Artists, Portland, 1977, Northeastern U., Boston, 1978, Vered Internat. Gallery, East Hampton, 1978, Women in the Arts Gallery, 1979, Rensselaer Inst., Troy, 1979, Marie Pellicone Gallery, 1981, Guild Hall Mus., 1982, 84, 85, Pace U., 1983, N.Y.C. Tech. Coll., 1983, N.Y. State Gov.'s Office/World Trade Ctr. Gallery, 1985; represented in permanent collections Mus. Contemporary Crafts, N.Y.C., BBD&O Advt., Inc., N.Y.C.; also pvt. collections. Chmn., Pres.' Task Force on Bilingual Edn., 1972; v.p. Viridian Gallery, 1976-77; bd. dirs. Nat. Assn. Italian-Am. Dirs., 1982; v.p. Italian Bilingual Bicultural Educators Assn., 1982; mem. N.Y.C. Bd. Edn., 1983—. HEW/Fed. Govt. ESEA Title VII grantee, 1975-79; recipient Nat. Scene Award for Achievement in Arts and Culture, 1979. Mem. NEA, Nat. Assn. Bilingual Edn., N.Y. State Assn. Bilingual Edn., Council Supervisory Adminstrs., NOW, Am. Council for Arts, Coalition of Women Artists Orgn., Assn. of Artist-Run Galleries, Women in the Arts, Advt. Women N.Y., Women Bus. Owners of N.Y. Contbr. articles to profl. jours. Home: 20 Waterside Plaza Apt 30E New York NY 10010 Office: 131 Livingston St Brooklyn NY 11201

GERARD, NANCY SHAPPELL, salon owner, employment agency owner; b. Oklahoma City, June 2, 1944; d. Nelson Harry and Helen Irene (Finigan) Shappell; m. James Alfred Darby, June 22, 1963 (div. Dec. 1976); children—Noma Darby, Jennifer Darby, Matthew Darby; m. Gary Len Gerard, Feb. 25, 1977. Student Los Angeles Valley Jr. Coll., 1962-64. Owner, mgr. Commercial Property, Amarillo, Tex., 1977-84; owner Shaw & Assocs., Amarillo, 1985, Illusions, Amarillo, 1984-85. Bd. dirs. Amarillo council Girl Scouts U.S.A., 1981-82, pres., 1982-85; sec. Amarillo Little Theatre Guild, 1982-84; bd. dirs. Lone Star Ballet, Inc., Amarillo, 1984-86. Mem. Nat. Assn. Personnel Cons., Nat. Personnel Assn., Inc., Tex. Assn. Personnel Cons. Republican. Presbyterian. Clubs: Lone Star Ballet Guild, Amarillo Symphony Guild, Art Alliance (Amarillo). Avocations: reading; music; travel. Home: 6815 Montague St Amarillo TX 79109 Office: Shaw & Assocs Tex Am Bank Bldg Suite 1007 Amarillo TX 79101

GERBER, ANN JADE, editor, columnist, author; b. Chgo., Sept. 17, 1930; d. Benjamin James and Henrietta (Rabin) G.; m. Alex Lustig, 1946 (div. 1947); m. 2d Robert Krit, 1955 (div. 1957); m. 3d Bernard James Kaplan, Apr. 23, 1966; children—Jeffrey, Blair. Student Wright Jr. Coll., Northwestern U., Mundelin U. Reporter, Lerner Newspapers, Chgo., 1945-46, assoc. editor, 1946-58, editor, 1958—; owner Panache Pub. Relations, Chgo., 1960-70; editor Tee Vee Guide, Chgo., 1955; pub. relations cons. Harlem-Irving Shopping Ctr., Chgo., 1955-56. Author: Chicago's Classiest Cuisine, 1983. Named Woman of Yr., Variety Club Women of Ill., 1983; recipient Editorial Excellence award Lerner Newspapers, 1982, hon. mention for columns, Ill. Press Assn., 1983. Jewish. Home: 5036 Fairview Ln Skokie IL 60077 Office: Lerner Newspapers 7519 N Ashland Ave Chicago IL 60625

GERBER, CHRISTINE NINER, counselor; b. Washington, Oct. 29, 1936; d. Paul Joseph and Anna M. (Wright) Niner; children—Thomas, Daniel, Anne. A.B., Dunbarton of Holy Cross, 1958; M.A., Ohio State U., 1982, Ph.D., 1985. Tchr./counselor Holy Cross High Sch., Rockville, Md., 1958-63; acct., mgr. Estate-Trust, Columbus, 1972-80; counselor Maryhaven, Inc., Columbus, 1980-81; exec. dir. Brookwood Recovery Ctr., Columbus, Ohio, 1982—; lectr., cons. in field. Bd. dirs. Maryhaven, 1980-83, Tri-Christian Ctr., 1982-84, others. Mem. Women in Communication, Ohio Assn. Alcohol and Other Drug Counselors, Nat. Assn. Alcoholism Counselors, Nat. Council on Alcoholism. Democrat. Roman Catholic.

GERBER, HADASSA, media executive; b. N.Y.C., Mar. 15, 1952; d. Benjamin and Rosalyn (Pollack) G. Student Hebrew U., Jerusalem, 1970-71; B.B.A. magna cum laude, Bernard Baruch Coll., 1973, postgrad., 1975-77; postgrad. Pratt Inst., 1973-74. Media planner Ted Bates & Co., N.Y.C., 1972-74; asst. media dir. Grey Advt. Inc., N.Y.C., 1975-78; v.p., asst. media dir. Batten, Barton, Durstine & Osborn, N.Y.C., 1978-80; sr. v.p., dir. media info. and new techs. McCann-Erickson Inc., N.Y.C., 1981—; lectr., instr. Bernard Baruch Coll., 1979-80, NYU, 1982, Parsons Coll., 1980—. Author: (booklet) McCann Reports Videotex, 1983. Mem. Videotex Industry Assn. (founding mem., dir. 1982—), Am. Assn. Adv. Agys. (new tech. com.).

GERBERDING, JOAN ELIZABETH, broadcasting company executive; b. Rockville Center, N.Y., July 29, 1949; d. Henry William and Edith Louise (Perry) G. Student West Chester State U., 1967-69. Asst. pub. relations dir. Conn. Heart Assn., Hartford, 1970-71; publs. editor Hartford Steam Boiler Ins. Co., 1971-72; asst. account exec. Wilson Haight & Welch, Inc., Hartford, 1972; copywriter Internat. Silver Co., Meriden, Conn., 1973-74; acct. exec. WCOD FM, Hyannis, Mass., 1975-76, gen. sales mgr., 1976-79, v.p., gen. sales mgr., 1979-80; sales devel. mgr. Nassau Broadcasting Co., WHWH AM/WPST FM, Princeton, N.J., 1980-82, gen. sales mgr., 1982-83, v.p. sales, 1983-85, corp. v.p., 1985—; cons. Woman's Newspaper of Princeton, 1984—; lectr., cons. Am. women in radio and TV, 1980—; lectr. Princeton YWCA/Women programs, Princeton, 1984—. Recipient YWCA TWIN award, Princeton, 1984. Mem. Am. Women in Radio and TV, N.J. Broadcasters Assn., Am. Bus. Assn., Inc., Princeton Bus. Assn., Radio Advt. Bur. Democrat. Episcopalian. Avocations: writing, music, running. Home: 3 Sunrise Ave Hopewell NJ 08525 Office: Nassau Broadcasting Co 221 Witherspoon St Princeton NJ 08542

GERBI, SUSAN ALEXANDRA, biology educator; b. N.Y.C.; Mar. 13, 1944; d. Claudio and Jeanette Lena (Klein) Gerbi; B.A. (N.Y. State Regents scholar), Barnard Coll., 1965; M.Phil., Yale, 1968, Ph.D. (NIH fellow), 1970; m. James Terrell McIlwain, April 10, 1976. NATO and Jane Coffin Childs Fund fellow Max-Planck Institut fur Biologie, Tubingen, W. Ger., 1970-72; asst. prof. biology Brown U., Providence, 1972-77, assoc. prof., 1977-82, prof., 1982—, dir. grad. program in molecular and cell biology; vis. assoc. prof. Duke U., Durham, N.C., 1981-82; mem. genetics research grants rev. panel NSF, 1979-81; mem. genetic basis of disease com. NIH, 1981-84. Dist. commr. Palmer River Pony Club, 1973-75. NIH research grantee, 1974—, research career devel. awardee, 1975-80. Mem. Am. Soc. for Cell Biology, Soc. for Devel. Biology, Genetics Soc., Sigma Xi. Contbr. articles to profl. jours. Office: Biomedical Div Brown U Providence RI 02912

GERDENICH, LINDA JANE WESTRICH, dance educator, choreographer; b. Delphos, Ohio, May 23, 1942; d. Melvin Franklin and Adelia I. (Wehinger) Westrich; m. Maten G. Gerdenich II, Aug. 8, 1964; children—Maten G. III, Wendy Kaye. B.A., Butler U., 1964, M.S., 1978. Lic. real estate salesman. Mem. ballet faculty Butler U., Indpls., 1972-84; artistic dir. Dancers Studio, Noblesville, Ind., 1972—; free-lance choreographer, 1978—; coordinator White River Arts Festival, Indpls., 1985—; dance chmn. Ind. Arts Commn., Indpls., 1980-84, mem. edn. panel, 1984—; entertainment dir. Middle Country U.S.A., 1986—; treas. Ind. Dance Alliance, Indpls., 1980-82. Choreographer: Peter and the Wolf, 1982, Faux Pas - Comedy of Errors, 1983, Dance Frivolities, 1984, A Day in the Park, 1984. Sec., Forest Hill PTO, Noblesville, 1975. Mem. Nat. Soc. Arts and Letters (dance chmn. 1982-84), Delta Gamma (alumnae pres., adv. bd. chmn., pledge trainer 1966-74, Nat. Cable award 1975), Sigma Rho Delta (nat. pres. 1984-85). Republican. Roman Catholic. Avocations: water and snow skiing; boating; bicycling; building dollhouses; sewing. Home: 500 Tamarack Ln Noblesville IN 46060

GEREAU, MARY C., consultant; b. Winterset, Iowa, Oct. 10, 1916; d. David Joseph and Sarah Rose (Stack) Condon; B.A., U. Iowa, 1939, M.A., 1941; student Mt. Mercy Jr. Coll., 1935-37; m. Gerald Robert Gereau, Jan. 14, 1961. Program dir. ARC, India, 1943-45; dean of students Eastern Mont. Coll., 1946-48; supt. pub. instrn. state of Mont., 1948-56; sr. legis. cons. NEA, 1957-73; dir. legislation Nat. Treasury Employees Union, 1973-76; legis. asst. to Senator Melcher, Mont., 1976-86. Mem. Council Chief State Sch. Officers (dir. 1953-56, pres. 1956), Rural Edn. Assn. (exec. bd. 1953-56), Nat. Women's Party (v.p. 1984—), Equal Rights Ratification Council (nat. chmn.), NEA. Named Conservationist of Yr., Mont. Conservation Council, 1952; recipient Disting. Service award VFW, 1951; Disting. Service award, Chief State Sch. Officers, 1956. Club: U.S. Congress Burro (pres. 1983-84). Contbr. articles on state govt., edn. to profl. jours. Office: 400 Madison Suite 401 Alexandria VA 22314

GERHARDT, LILLIAN NOREEN, editor; b. New Haven, Sept. 28, 1932; d. Victor Herbert and Lillian Angela (Beecher) G. B.S., So. Conn. State U., 1954; postgrad. U. Chgo., 1961-62. Asst. in reference New Haven Pub. Library, 1954-55; first asst. reference Meriden Pub. Library, Conn., 1955-58, head reference, 1958-61; assoc. editor Kirkus Service Inc., N.Y.C., 1962-66; exec. editor Sch. Library Jour. Book Rev./Bowker Juvenile Projects, N.Y.C., 1966-71; editor in chief Sch. Library Jour., N.Y.C., 1971—. Sr. editor: Best Books for Children, 1967-70, SLJ Book Review Cumulative, 1969-71, Children's Books in Print, 1969, Subject Guide to Children's Books in Print, 1970. Named Disting. Alumnus, So. Conn. State U., Div. Library Sci., New Haven, 1978. Mem. ALA (councilor 1976-80), Assn. Library Service for Children (pres. 1978-79), Women's Nat. Book Assn. (bd. mgrs. N.Y. chpt. 1972-75). Democrat. Baptist. Home: 39 Gramercy Park N Apt 8A New York NY 10010 Office: Sch Library Jour 205 E 42d St New York NY 10017

GERINGER, MARGARET MARY, consumer education educator; b. Summerville, N.J., Mar. 23, 1945; d. Harry Lee and Mary Margaret (Plock) Huff; m. John Carl Geringer, Dec. 15, 1973; children—Chris, Michelle, Michael. A.A., Antelope Valley Coll., 1965; B.S., Calif. State Poly. U., Pomona, 1967; M.S., Calif. Poly. State U., San Luis Obispo, 1972. Tchr. Charter Oak Unified Sch. Dist., Covina, Calif., 1967-69, Craven County Schs., N.C., 1970-71, Oak Grove Sch. Dist., San Jose, Calif., 1972—; assoc. prof. Calif. Poly. State U., 1971-72; in-service cons. County Office Edn., San Jose, 1983—. Author: Taking Care of Business, 1983. Editor OGEA Sounds, 1977-79. Instr. ARC, Santa Clara County, Calif., 1972—. Recipient Glenn Hoffmann Exemplary Program award; named Mentor tchr. Oak Grove Sch. Dist. Mem. Calif. Assn. Counseling and Devel., Oak Grove Tchrs. Assn. (faculty rep. 1977—), Calif. Tchrs. Assn. Republican. Roman Catholic. Avocations: golf; cooking; reading; writing; singing. Home: 326 Surber Dr San Jose CA 95123 Office: Herman Intermediate Sch 5955 Blossom Ave San Jose CA 95123

GERISCH, MARY ELISE, lawyer; b. Detroit, Apr. 21, 1950; d. Robert Albert and Betty Vivian (Gee) G.; m. John Francis Soghigian, Sept. 17, 1976; 1 son, Ben Robert Gerisch-Soghigian. B.A., Briarcliff Coll., 1972; postgrad. U. Detroit Bus. Sch., 1972-73; J.D., Detroit Coll. Law, 1977. Bar: Mich. 1981. Student atty. supr. Legal Aid, Detroit, 1974-76; assoc. Willford, Hanson & Pemberton, Gladwin, Mich., 1977-78; ptnr. Schneider, Handlon & Gerisch, Midland, Mich., 1978-82, Gerisch & Bourne, P.C., Midland, 1982—; adj. instr. Northwood Inst. Bd. dirs. Harbor House, Midland, 1984-85, Family/Children's Services, Midland, 1983—, Ctr. Against Sex Assault, Midland, 1982—, Fathers for Equal Rights, Southfield, Mich., 1983—, Women's Council Realtors, Midland, 1981-83, Sanford C. of C. (Mich.), 1981-83, Midland C. of C., 1982—. Mem. Women Lawyers Assn. (sec./treas. 1982—), Am. Trial Lawyers Assn., Mich. Bar Assn., ABA (fed. practice com. 1982—), Young Bus. Peoples Assn., Delta Theta Phi. Episcopalian. Club: Exec. 100. Home: 4914 Campau Dr Midland MI 49640

GERLICH, MARJORIE SHIELDS, laboratory supervisor, computer consultant; b. Baytown, Tex., Jan. 10, 1938; d. Earl Cleophas and Clara Velma (Morgan) Shields; m. Gilbert Martin Gerlich, Apr. 4, 1937; children—Michelle Marie, Gerald Shields, William James II, Kevin Joseph. A.A., Lee Coll., 1958. Sec., Humble Oil Co., Baytown, 1958-62; tchr. aide St. Joseph Sch., Baytown, 1972-75; sec. Exxon Co. U.S.A., Baytown, 1976-78; research technician Exxon Research & Engring. Co., Baytown, 1978-81, lab. supr. Exxon Chem. Co., Baytown, 1981—, mem. task force/integrated data base, 1981—, ASTM co. rep., 1983—. Author, editor: Testing Procedures Manual, 1981, edit., 1983. Roman Catholic. Home: 410 Briarwood Baytown TX 77520

GERLING, INGRID HELGA, nurse, social worker; b. Cottbus, Germany, Feb. 24, 1934; came to U.S., 1952, naturalized, 1958; d. Adolf and Herta (Lehmann) G.; B.S. in Nursing, U. Utah, 1964, M.S.W., 1967; R.N., Midstate Bapt. Hosp., Nashville, 1957; children—Christian A., Michael K. Generic social worker Bur. Indian Affairs, Fairbanks, Alaska, 1967-69; sch. social worker Pocatello Sch. Dist., 1969-76; nursing supr. Woodland Park Mental Health Center, Portland, Oreg., 1976-79; dist. nurse Estacada (Oreg.) Sch. Dist., 1979-84; pvt. practice mental health therapist, 1984—. Vol. group leader Parents Anonymous, 1984; mem. task force The Chem. People, Gladstone, Oreg., 1983-84; chmn. social com. Met. Youth Symphony, 1979-81. Recipient award for outstanding services Bur. Indian Affairs, 1967; registered clin. social worker. Mem. Nat. Assn. Social Workers (Fairbanks Area rep. 1968-69, treas. East Idaho br. 1971-74), Acad. Cert. Social Workers. Home and office: 7525 Springhill Dr Gladstone OR 97027

GERMAN, JOAN ALICE WOLFE, author; b. Phila., Feb. 9, 1933; d. Merrill Pierce Wolfe and Jeanette (Anderson) Evans; m. Donald Robert German, Sept. 4, 1954; 1 child, Donald Robert. Student Temple U., 1951-54. Adminstrv. asst. dept. pub. relations Vertol Aircraft Corp., Morton, Pa., 1958; freelance writer, 1964—. Author: (with D.R. German) Passkeys, 1967, Dividends, 1969, The Bank Teller's Handbook, 1970, rev. edit., 1981, Successful Job Hunting for Executives, 1974, Bank Employee's Marketing Handbook, 1975, Tested Techniques in Bank Marketing, vol. 1, 1977, vol. 2, 1979, Make Your Own Convenience Foods, 1979, How to Find a Job When Jobs Are Hard to Find, 1981, The Money Book, 1981, The Bank Employee's Security Handbook, 1982, Checklists for Profitability, 1983, The Only Money Book for the Middle Class, 1983, Money A to Z: A Consumer's Guide to the Language of Personal Finance, 1984; Ninety Days to Financial Fitness, 1986. co-editor Branch Banker's Report, 1968—, Bank Teller's Report, 1969—; contbr. to Banker's mag., Brides, Compass, Consumers Digest, Cosmopolitan, Dynamic Years, Easy Living, Money Maker, Nat. Enquirer, Tables, Woman's Day, poetry jours. Founder, dir. Community Craft Ctr., Hopkinton, Mass., 1968-69; bd. dirs. Berkshire Mental Health Assn. Pittsfield, Mass., 1981-82. Mem. Nat. League Am. Pen Women (br. pres. 1974-76, pres. Mass. 1976-78), Am. Soc. Journalists and Authors (dir.-at-large 1979-81, chmn. Berkshire Hills chpt. 1983—), Authors Guild, Boston Authors Club, Berkshire Poets Workshop (founder), Phi Gamma Nu. Unitarian. Address: West Mountain Rd Cheshire MA 01225

GERMI, KATHERINE NAVARRE, transformer manufacturing company executive; b. Lansing, Mich., Oct. 31, 1947; d. Frederick Earl and Mary Jane (Navarre) Tripp; B.A. in Bus. Adminstrn., Mich. State U., 1969; m. August Germi, Apr. 1, 1978. Asso. mgr. Mid-Am. Club, Chgo., 1973-77; corp. sec. Quality Transformers, Inc., Chgo., 1977-78, v.p., 1978-80, pres., chief exec. officer, 1980—, also dir. Mem. U.S. C. of C., Am. Nat. Standards Inst., Nat. Assn. Catering Execs. (cert.), Nat. Assn. Female Execs., Nat. Assn. Women Bus. Owners, Power Conversion Products Council Inc. Office: 3110 North Sheffield Ave Chicago IL 60657

GERNERT, ELEANOR TOWLES, editor, writer; b. N.Y.C., Sept. 7, 1928; d. Oliver Phelps and Cecile Helene (Long) Towles; m. J. Wayne Harris, Sept. 6, 1957 (div. 1967); m. Max Riley Gernert, July 4, 1970. Student Hofstra. U., 1946-48; B.A., Smith Coll., 1950; postgrad. U. Paris, 1954. Librarian, Huntington Library, San Marino, Calif., 1950-55, exec. sec. to dir., 1955-60; head Huntington Library Publs., San Marino, 1957-60; sr. research editor Rand Corp., Santa Monica, 1960-82; freelance editor/author, 1982—. Author: Anderson Rocky Mountain Journals (Western Hist. Assn. award 1967), 1967; Hoover Gold Rush Diaries, (in progress); (manual) Guide to Indexing, 1965; editor/author: Database Savvy: Programming in English, 1986. Editor, Notary Newsletter, 1967-68. Organizer John Anderson Calif. State Campaign, Pacific Palisades, 1980. Served to 2d lt. USMC, 1949-59. Named Am. Assn. Univ. Presses rep. Huntington Library, 1957. Democrat. Episcopalian. Clubs: French (Santa Monica) (head 1961-80); Avanti (so. Calif.). Avocations: bonsai; koi. Home: 958 Hartzell St Pacific Palisades CA 90272

GERNSBACHER, HELEN RUTH, food service equipment distributing company executive; b. Dallas, July 14, 1917; d. Robert and Sarah (Lynn) Stern; m. Harold Gernsbacher, Sr., Jan. 4, 1942 (dec. Aug. 1981); children—Sandra Gernsbacher O'Connor, Karen Gernsbacher Becker, Harold. Student U. Tex., 1933-36. Ptnr., Gernsbacher's, Fort Worth, 1946-82; pres. Gernsbacher's, Inc., Fort Worth, 1982—. Mem. Food Equipment Distbrs. Assn., Tex. Restaurant Assn. Democrat. Jewish. Avocations: books; antiques; travel. Home: 2916 Harlanwood Dr Fort Worth TX 76109 Office: PO Box 9090 Fort Worth TX 76107

GERONEMUS, DIANN FOX, social work consultant; b. Chgo., July 4, 1947; d. Herbert J. and Edith (Robbins) Fox; B.A. with high honors, Mich. State U., 1969; M.S.W., U. Ill., 1971; 1 dau., Heather Eileen. Lic. clin. social worker, lic. marriage and family therapist, Fla.; registered clin. social worker. Social worker neurology, neurosurgery and medicine Hosp. of Albert Einstein Coll. Medicine, 1971-74; prin. social worker ob-gyn and newborn infant service Rush-Presbyn.-St. Luke's Med. Center, Chgo., 1974-75; social worker neurology, adminstr. Multiple Sclerosis Treatment Center, St. Barnabas Hosp., Bronx, N.Y., 1975-77, socio-med. researcher (Nat. Multiple Sclerosis Soc. grantee), dept. neurology and psychiatry, 1977-79, dir. social service, 1979-80; field work instr. Fordham U. Grad. Sch. Social Service, 1979-80; mem. edn. com., med. adv. bd., cons. Nat. Multiple Sclerosis Soc., 1980—; clin. instr. social work program Fla. Atlantic U., 1982—; social work cons. long term care and rehab., home healthcare, 1980—; pvt. practice psychotherapy, 1984—. Mem. Acad. Cert. Social Workers, Nat. Assn. Social Workers, Soc. Hosp. Social Work Dirs., Am. Orthopsychiat. Assn., Adult Edn. Assn., Am. Assn. Sex Educators, Counselors and Therapists. Jewish. Contbr. articles to profl. jours. Home: 833 NW 81st Way Plantation FL 33324 Office: 833 NW 81st Way Plantation FL 33324

GEROULD, LESLEY CHAPMAN, utility company executive; b. Newark, July 15, 1929; d. Richard Dodge and Elinor (Chapman) Gerould; m. Beverly Charles Dunn, Jr., Oct. 1, 1954 (div. 1968). B.A., Smith Coll., 1950. Dir. legis. action dept. League of Women Voters of U.S., Washington, 1972-75; asst. sec. human services, spl. asst. Senate pres. Commonwealth of Mass., Boston, 1975-77; spl. asst. system communications Northeast Utilities, Berlin, Conn., 1977-78, dir. system community relations, 1978-81, dist. mgr., Norwalk, Conn., 1981-84, regional v.p., Stamford, Conn., 1984—. Pres. Greater Norwalk Community Council, 1984—; bd. dirs. George Washington Carver Found., Norwalk, 1982—, Greater Norwalk United Way, 1983—, Southwestern Area Commerce & Industry Assn., 1985—. Named Woman of Challenge, Southwestern Conn. Girl Scout Council, 1985. Mem. Nat. Assn. Female Execs., Women in Pub. Affairs Conn., Phi Beta Kappa, Sigma Xi. Democrat. Unitarian. Avocations: reading, music, gardening, needlework. Home: 275 Rowayton Ave Rowayton CT 06853 Office: Northeast Utilities PO Box 1337 Stamford CT 06904-1337

GERRING, CHERYL BUTLER, school librarian; b. Oceanside, Calif., May 15, 1949; d. Arthur Norris and Dorothy Louise (Raab) Butler; m. Alan Irwin Gerring, Oct. 15, 1978. B.A., Towson State U., 1971; M.L.S., U. Md., 1974. Tchr., English, Show Hill Middle Sch. (Md.), 1971-73; library media specialist Samuel Ogle Jr. High Sch., Bowie, Md., 1975-78; in-service program devel. specialist Prince George's Pub. Schs., Upper Marlboro, Md., 1978-79; library media specialist Benjamin Tasker Middle Sch., Bowie, 1979—; presenter Prevocat. Workshop, Upper Marlboro, 1977, Md. Middle Sch. Conf., Bowie, 1983; cons. Library Theater, Washington, 1979-81. Co-author: pamphlet/booklet Career Resource Center, 1977, Volunteer Handbook, 1978, Integrating Library Media Skills into the English Curriculum (guide), 1983. Oneg shabbat chmn. Jewish Community Ctr. Prince George's County, Greenbelt, 1979, librarian, 1980-83. Named Outstanding Young Educator, Bowie/Crofton Jr. C. of C., 1977, Outstanding Educator, Prince George's County, Upper Marlboro, 1983. Mem. Md. Ednl. Media Orgn., Ednl. Media Assn. Prince George's County (sec. 1981-82, Appreciation award 1980), Md. Middle Sch. Assn., Beta Phi Mu. Democrat. Office: Benjamin Tasker Middle Sch 4901 Collington Rd Bowie MD 20715

GERRINGER-BUSENBARK, ELIZABETH JACQUELINE, systems analyst; b. Edmund, Wis., Jan. 7, 1934; d. Clyde Elroy and Matilda Evangeline Knapp, student Madison Bus. Coll., 1952, San Francisco State Coll., 1953-54, Vivian Rich Sch. Fashion Design, 1955, Dale Carnegie Sch., 1956, Murray Sch. Modern Dance, 1956, Biscayne Acad. Music, 1957, Los Angeles City Coll., 1960-62, Santa Monica (Calif.) Jr. Coll., 1963; Hastings Coll. Law, 1973, Wharton Sch., U. Pa., 1977, London Art Coll., 1979, Ph.D., 1979; m. Roe Devon Gerringer-Busenbark, Sept. 30, 1968 (dec. Dec. 1972). Actress, Actors Workshop San Francisco, 1959, 65, Theatre of Arts Beverly Hills (Calif.), 1963, also radio; cons. and systems analyst for banks and pub. accounting agys.; artist, singer, songwriter, playwright. Pres., Environ. Improvement, Originals by Elizabeth, Dometrik's Jitmap, San Francisco, 1973—; ordained minister, 1978. Author: New Highways, 1967; Happenings—Impact-Mald, 1971; Seven Day Rainbow, 1972; Zachary's Adversaries, 1974; Fifteen from Iowa, 1977; Bart's White Elephant, 1978; Skid Row Minister, 1978; Points in Time, 1979; Special Appointment, A Clown in Town, 1979; Votes from the Closet, 1984; Man on the Stairway, 1984; Wait for Me, 1984. Address: PO Box 1640 7th and Mission Station San Francisco CA 94101

GERRISH, CATHERINE RUGGLES, food company executive; b. Winona, Minn., July 10, 1911; d. Clyde O. and Frances (Holmes) Ruggles; A.B., Radcliffe Coll., 1932, A.M., 1934; Ph.D., Harvard U., 1937; m. Hollis G. Gerrish, Sept. 10, 1946. Research asst. Harvard U., 1937-39; instr., asst. prof. econs. U. Ill., 1939-42; with Bur. Budget, Exec. Office President, 1943-45; assoc. prof. U. Ill., 1946; asst. editor Quar. Jour. Econs., 1951-69; treas., v.p. Squirrel Brand Co., Cambridge, Mass., 1966—. Mem. Am. Econ. Assn., Nat. Tax Assn. Home: 207 Grove St Cambridge MA 02138 Office: 17 Boardman St Cambridge MA 02139

GERSCHBACHER, CORINE MARIE, electronics company marketing executive; b. Whittier, Calif., Mar. 8, 1961; d. Frank Joseph Gerschbacher and Shirley Ann Stahl. B.A. in Mktg., Whittier Coll., 1983. Acctg. analyst Health Valley Foods, Montebello, Calif., 1982-84; mktg. coordinator Bland Contracting Co., Whittier, 1984-85; mktg. specialist Taxan Corp., City of Industry, Calif., 1985—; cons. computer systems, Whittier, 1985—. Milo Hunt Merit scholar Whittier Coll., 1980-83. Mem. M.B.A. Assn. (local activities dir. 1983-84), Calif. Scholarship Fedn. (life), Alpha Pi Delta. Home: 11611 Broadway Apt A Whittier CA 90601 Office: Taxan Corp 18005 Cortney Ct City of Industry CA 91748

GERSKE, JANET FAY, lawyer; b. Chgo., Nov. 14, 1950; d. Bernard G. Gerske and L. Fay (Knight) Capron; m. James P. Chapman, Dec. 5, 1982. B.S., Northwestern U., 1971; J.D., U. Mich., 1978. Bar: Ill. 1978, U.S. Dist. Ct. (no. dist.) Ill. 1978. Sole practice, Chgo., 1978-80, 84—; assoc. Jerome H. Torshen Ltd., Chgo., 1980-84. Chpt. chmn. Ind. Voters Ill./Ind. Precinct Orgn., Chgo., 1982—; co-chmn. Ill. Women's Agenda Com., 1985—. Mem. ABA, Assn. Trial Lawyers Am., Ill. Trial Lawyers Assn., Women's Bar Assn. Ill. (co-chmn. rights of women com. 1985-86), Chgo. Bar Assn. (co-chmn. legal status of women com. young lawyers sect.), Nat. Assn. Social Security Claimants' Rep., Ill. State Bar Assn. Democrat. Home: 850 W Oakdale Ave Chicago IL 60657 Office: 39 S LaSalle St Chicago IL 60603

GERSONI-EDELMAN, DIANE CLAIRE, author, editor; b. Bklyn., Apr. 16, 1947; d. James Arthur and Edna Bernice (Krinski) Gersoni; B.A. cum laude, Vassar Coll., 1967; m. James Neil Edelman, Oct. 5, 1975; children—Michael Lawrence, Sara Anne. Asst. editor, then asso. editor Sch. Library Jour. Book Rev., 1968-72; free lance writer, 1972-74, 77—; writer, editor Scholastic Mags., Inc., N.Y.C., 1974-77; author: Sexism and Youth, 1974; Work-Wise: Learning About the World of Work from Books, 1980; cons., speaker in field. Club: Vassar (N.Y.C.). Contbr. articles, book revs. to anthologies, newspapers, mags. Home: care Edelman 301 E 78th St New York NY 10021

GERSOVITZ, SARAH VALERIE, painter, printmaker; b. Montreal, Que., Can., Sept. 5, 1920; d. Solomon and Eva (Gampel) Gamer; student MacDonald Coll., Montreal Mus. Fine Arts, Ecole des Arts Appliques; diploma communication arts, M.A., Concordia U.; m. Benjamin Gersovitz, June 22, 1944; children—Mark, Julia, Jeremy. Tchr. painting and drawing Bronfman Centre, Montreal, 1972—; one-woman shows include Montreal Mus. Fine Arts, 1962, 65, Art Gallery Greater Victoria, 1966, U. Alta., 1968, Burnaby Art Gallery, 1969, Art Gallery Hamilton, 1969, Mt. St. Vincent U., 1971, Coll. St. Louis, 1972, Inst. Cultural Peruano, Lima, 1973, Confedn. Art Gallery, 1976, St. Mary's U., 1976, U. Sherbrooke, 1979, 83, Peter Whyte Gallery, 1982, London Regional Art Gallery, 1982, Holland Coll., 1982, Stewart Hall Art Gallery, 1984, U. Kaiserslautern (W.Ger.), 1984, others; represented in permanent collections Library of Congress, N.Y. Pub. Library, Nat. Gallery South Australia, Inst. Cultural Peruano, Lima, Am. Embassy, Ottawa, House of Humour and Satire, Gabrovo, Bulgaria, Israel Mus., Jerusalem, numerous Can. mus., univs. and embassies including Nat. Gallery Can., Montreal Mus. Fine Arts, Le Musée du Québec, Le Musée d'Art Contemporain; group exhbns. include 3d Internat. Play Group Exhbn., N.Y.C., 1973, Internat. Triennial, Grenchen, Switzerland, 1961, V, VI and X Internat. Biennial, Ibiza, Spain, 1972, 74, 82, II and III Internat. Biennial, Norway, 1974, 76, III and IV Internat. Biennial, Frechen, Germany, 1974, 76, 1st Internat. Bienal, Segovia, Spain, 1974, III Biennial Graphic, Cali, Colombia, 1976, 11th and 13th Biennale, Ljjubljana, Yugoslavia, 1975, 1979, ann. exhbn. NAD, N.Y.C., 1975, 11th Bienale Internat. d'Art de Menton, France, 1976, contemporary miniature Exhbn., U. Mich., 1977, XVIII and XXI Premio Internat. de Dibujo, Barcelona, 1979, 82, XV Internat. Bienal de São Paulo (Brazil), 1979, Bienal des Grabado, Maracaibo, Venezuela, 1977, Premio Internat. per l'Incisione, Biella, Italy, 1980, Internat. Biennale des Arts Grafiques, Brno, Czechoslovakia, 1980, 84, 1st and 2d Internat. Miniature Print Exhbn., Seoul, 1980, 82, Wesleyan Internat. Exhbn. Prints and Drawings, Macon, Ga., 1980, Salón Nacional de Grabado, Lima, Peru, 1981, Exhbn. Que. Graphics, Hong Kong, 1982, VI Biennale Internat. de Gabrovo, 1983; 4th Internat. Print Biennale, Seoul, Korea, 1983, VI Bienal Internat. de Arte, Valparaiso, Chile, 1983, 85, 3d Miniprint Internat., Cadaques, Spain, 1983, Internat. Print Exhibit, Taipei, Taiwan, 1984, 86; numerous others U.S. and abroad. Recipient 1st prize Seagram Fine Arts Expn., 1968; Graphic Art prize Winnipeg Art Gallery Bienial, 1962; Anaconda award Can. Soc. Painters-Etchers, 1963, 67; 1st prize Concours Graphique, U. Sherbrooke, 1977; purchase award Mus. de Que., 1966, Nat. Gallery South Australia, 1967, Dawson Coll., 1974, Thomas More Inst., 1977, Law Faculty U. Sherbrooke, 1979; hon. mention Miniature Painters, Sculptors, and Engravers, Washington, 1976; 1st prize and 2 gold medals Nat. Playwriting Competition, Ottawa, 1982, hon. mention awards, 1979, 80, 83; Travel award House of Humour and Satire, 1985; others. Mem. Royal Can. Acad. Arts (council 1981-82), Societe des Graveurs du Que., Dramatists Guild. Address: 5173 Mayfair Ave Montreal PQ H4V 2E8 Canada

GERST, ELIZABETH CARLSEN (MRS. PAUL H. GERST), university dean, educator, researcher; b. N.Y.C., June 10, 1929; d. Rolf and Gudrun (Wiborg) Carlsen; m. Paul H. Gerst, Aug. 3, 1957; children—Steven Richard, Jeffrey Carlton, Andrew Leigh. A.B. magna cum laude, Mt. Holyoke Coll., 1951; Ph.D., U. Pa., 1957. Instr. physiology Grad. Sch. Medicine, U. Pa., 1955-57, Cornell U. Med. Coll., N.Y.C., 1957-58; instr., asst. prof. physiology Columbia U. Coll. Physicians and Surgeons, N.Y.C., 1959-67, asst. dean for continuing med. edn., dir. Center Continuing Edn. in Health Scis., 1978—; team mem. Commn. on Higher Edn., Middle States Assn. Colls. and Schs., 1984—. Co-author: The Lung, Clinical Physiology and Pulmonary Function Tests, 1955, 62. Pres. Citizen's Ednl. Council Tenafly, 1972-73; vice chmn. Tenafly Environ. Commn., 1972-77; mem. Citizens Long-Range Planning Com., Tenafly Bd. Edn., 1971-72, mem. Tenafly Bd. Edn., 1973-77; trustee Tenafly Nature Center, 1972-80; bd. dirs., chmn. environ. quality Tenafly LWV, 1971-78; v.p. Bergen County LWV, 1973-75. Porter fellow Am. Physiol. Soc., 1956-57. Mem. Soc. Med. Coll. Dirs. of Continuing Med. Edn., Am. Physiol. Soc. (task force Women in Physiology 1973-75), N.Y. County Med. Soc. (com. on continuing med. edn. 1978—), Harvey Soc., Biophys. Soc., Alliance Continuing Med. Edn., N.Y. Acad. Scis., AAAS, Phi Beta Kappa, Sigma Xi, Sigma Delta Epsilon. Unitarian. Home: 141 Tekening Dr Tenafly NJ 07670 Office: Columbia Univ Coll Physicians and Surgeons 630 W 168th St New York NY 10032

GETMAN, THERESA RITA VALENTO, nursing educator, legal consultant; b. Phila., Jan. 27, 1949; d. Rosario Frank and Gelsomina (Pagliarulo) Valento; m. Edward T. Simonton, May 2, 1971 (div. Aug. 1983); children —Elizabeth, David, Danielle; m. Stewart M. Getman, Mar. 17, 1984. Assoc. Sci. in Nursing, Miami Dade Community Coll., 1969; B.S. in Nursing, Fla. Internat. U., 1974; M.S. in Nursing, U. Miami, 1978. Staff/charge nurse Larken Gen. Hosp., Miami, 1969-74; instr. Jackson Meml. Hosp., Miami, 1974; staff/charge nurse Williamsburg Meml. Hosp., Kingstree, S.C., 1974-75, instr. Jackson Meml Hosp., Miami, 1975—, home health nurse Fla. Home Health, Miami, 1979-81; legal cons. R.N. Expert, Inc., Miami, 1984—; instr. Miami Dade Community Coll., Miami, 1984—. Mem. profl. edn. com. Am. Cancer Soc., 1979. Serves as capt. Nurses Corps, U.S. Army, 1982—. Recipient Certs. Coral Gables Police Dept., 1978, Kiwanis Club, 1978, Am. Cancer Soc., Miami, 1979. Mem. Nurses Profl. Orgn., Am. Nurses Assn., Fla. Nurses Assn. Republican. Roman Catholic. Home: 418 Almeria Ave Coral Gables FL 33134 Office: Jackson Meml Hosp 1755 NW 12th Ave Miami FL 33136

GETTINGER, MIRIAM ELLEN, nurse, educator; b. Jersey, N.J., June 23; d. Charles LeRoy and Esther (Hersh) King; m. Kenneth Harold Gettinger, Nov. 28, 1953; children—Randy Craig, Neal Cory. A.A.Sci. (honors student), Dutchess Coll., 1970; vocat. certs. SUNY-Oswego, 1972, 73, Utica Rome Sch., 1975, 76, 77, NYU, 1978, Cornell U., 1983; grad. Labor Studies Program, Cornell U., 1985. Cert. tchr. Office mgr., Croton, N.Y., 1953-57; operating room technician Peekskill Hosp. (N.Y.), 1962-64; operating room nurse Butterfield Hosp., Cold Spring, N.Y., 1970-71, emergency room nurse, 1970-71; pvt. care infant nurse, Bklyn., 1971—; tchr. Bd. of Coop. Ednl. Services, Yorktown Heights, N.Y., 1971—, chmn. com. sch. pub. relations, 1981—; cons. Marr's Nursing Home, Mohegan, N.Y., 1982—; mem. adv. council Cornell U. Sch. Indsl. and Labor Relations. Com. leader Boy Scouts Am., Peekskill, 1961-63; advisor state senator Mary Goodhue, Albany, N.Y., 1980—, state assemblyman George Pataki; del. N.Y. tchrs. Retirement System, Albany, 1983; mem. geriatrics West County Mental Health Bd., White Plains, 1981-82. Mem. N.Y. State United Tchrs. Union (v.p., negotiator local 1978-82), N.Y. Tchrs. Retirement, N.Y. State Nurses Assn., United Staff Assn. (v.p. 1978-82). Independent Republican. Jewish. Home: 8 Foxhill Rd Peekskill NY 10566 Office: Bd of Coop Edn Services Pinesbridge Rd Yorktown Heights NY 10598

GETTLE, JUDY ANN, YWCA ofcl.; b. Lebanon, Pa., May 19, 1946; d. Warren George and Julia Harriet (Kreiger) G.; B.A. in Psychology, Lebanon Valley Coll., 1968; M.Ed. in Counselor Edn., Slippery Rock (Pa.) State Coll., 1973; Ph.D. in Counselor Edn., U. Pitts., 1985. Tchr., North Allegheny Sch. Dist., Pitts., 1968-73; coordinator adolescent and children's services No. Communities Mental Health/Mental Retardation, Pitts., 1974-80; dir. counseling and women's services YWCA Greater Pitts., 1980—; ind. counselor, 1975—. Grantee Henry Frick Found. Mem. Am. Assn. Counseling and Devel., Assn. Counselor Edn. and Supervision, Nat. Acad. Cert. Clin. Mental Health Counselors, Am. Mental Health Counselors Assn., Assn. for Psychol. Type, Pitts. Feminist Therapists. Home: 158 S Linwood Ave Pittsburgh PA 15205 Office: YWCA 4th and Wood Sts Pittsburgh PA 15222

GETTMAN, JUANITA M., genealogist; b. Des Moines, June 9, 1921; d. Marion Arthur and Achsah Amelia (Wulf) Comegys Beck; m. Wallace Alan Gettman, Oct. 29, 1955; children—Wallace Alan, James Ernest; m. Val B. Katzenberger (div. 1955); children—Eula Leon, Val Nita. Student Los Angeles City Coll., 1952-54. Office mgr. Anchor Screw Products, Los Angeles, 1950-56; temporary office help Brown's, Los Angeles, Dial Temporary, Whittier, Calif., 1969-78; chief fin. officer Drive In Locksmith, Pico Rivera, Calif., 1978—. Co-compiler, publisher Bridges Cemetery, 1980, Iowa Cousins, 1983. Democrat. Lutheran. Home: 9943 S Grovedale Dr Whittier CA 90603

GETTY, CAROL PAVILACK, government official; b. Wilmington, Del., Apr. 9, 1938; d. Frank Clifton McGraw and Maxine (Remaly) Fogarty; m. Lawrence Lee Pavilack, Aug. 18, 1960 (div. 1980); children—Douglas Brooks, Joann Clements; m. James John Getty, May 8, 1985. B.A., Wellesley Coll., 1960; M.S. in Criminal Justice, Ariz. State U., 1978; postgrad. Phoenix Coll., 1974, U. Oreg., 1975. Tchr. math. Beaver County Day Sch., Chestnut Hill, Mass., 1960-62; engring. aide Air Research, Phoenix, 1960-63; computer analyst Motorola, Phoenix, 1963; tchr. math. Phoenix County Day Sch., 1964-69; mem. Ariz. Bd. Pardons and Paroles, Phoenix, 1978-83; commr. U.S. Parole Commn., Washington, 1983—; tech. adviser Maricopa County Alts. to Incarceration Commn., 1980-83. Chmn. Annual Reports, Ariz. Bd. Pardons and Paroles, 1979, 80, 81, co-chmn. Rule Book, 1980. Treas., asst. treas., sec., impact community action, admissions & fin. Jr. League Phoenix, 1970-80; docent, treas. Phoenix Art Mus. League, 1968-79; vice chmn. Criminal Justice Adv. Com., Phoenix, 1973-78. Mem. Exec. Women in Govt., Nat. Fedn. Republican Women, Am. Correctional Assn., Am. Paroling Authority, Womens C. of C. Republican. Unitarian. Clubs: Soroptimist International; Wellesley (Kansas

City, Mo.). Home: 7709 NW Westside Dr Kansas City MO 64152 Office: US Parole Commn Dept of Justice 10920 Ambassador Dr Kansas City MO 64153

GETTY, LINDA SUE, advertising executive; b. Boone, Iowa, May 13, 1951; d. Lester LeRoy and Florine May (Wheeler) Weigel; m. Rikel Kent, Getty, July 25, 1976. B.A., Iowa State U., 1974; cert. German, U. Md., Augsburg, W.Ger., 1976. Camerawoman WOI-TV, Ames, Iowa, 1970-73; writer KEZT-FM, Ames, 1970-73; writer, studio prodn. KIRO TV/Radio, Seattle, 1974-75; photographer PCA Internat., Cologne, W.Ger., 1977; hostess radio program AFN Radio, Munich, 1980; account exec. Lessing Flynn Advt., Des Moines, 1982—. Tchr. sign lang. Ames pub. schs., 1980-81, United Community Sch., Boone, Iowa, 1981. Mem. Internat. TV Assn. (newsletter editor 1982-84, creative award 1982), Women in Communications. Roman Catholic. Home: 1129 Oklahoma St Ames IA 50010 Office: Lessing Flyn Advt 3106 Ingersoll Ave Des Moines IA 50312

GETTYS, NORINE ANNE, home health company executive; b. Cin., Sept. 27, 1940; d. William Charles and Anne (Dolvig) Muhiberg; m. John Wesley Gettys, Apr. 6, 1963; children—Stephanie, Wendy. R.N., Jewish Hosp. (Cin.), 1961; B.A., Coll. Mount St. Joseph, 1985. Asst. head nurse Jewish Hosp., Cin., 1961-72; dir. nursing Med. Personnel Pool, Cin., 1972-76; dir. nursing Am. Nursing Care, Cin., 1977-81, adminstr., 1981-84, regional adminstr., 1984-86, v.p. ops., 1986—, cons., 1985—. Mem. Buckeye State Nurses Orgn., Nat. Assn. Female Execs., Womanways Inc. Unitarian. Avocations: swimming, reading, racquetball. Home: 1277 Norman Ave Cincinnati OH 45231 Office: Am Nursing Care 110 Boggs Ln S-355 Cincinnati OH 45246

GETZENDANNER, SUSAN, judge; b. Chgo., July 24, 1939; d. William B. and Carole (Muehling) O'Meara; B.B.A., Loyola U., Chgo., 1966, J.D., 1966; children—Alexandra, Paul. Admitted to Ill. bar, law clk. U.S. Dist. Ct., 1966-68; assoc. firm Mayer, Brown & Platt, Chgo., 1968-80; judge U.S. Dist. Ct., Chgo., 1980—. Office: 219 S Dearborn St Chicago IL 60604

GEVERS, MARCIA B., lawyer; b. Mpls., Oct. 11, 1946; d. Sam and Bessie (Gottlieb) Fleisher; m. Michael A. Gevers, Sept. 13, 1970; children—Sarah Nichole, David Seth. B.A. with honors, Nat. Coll. Edn., 1968; M.A., Northeastern Ill. U., 1973; J.D., DePaul U., Chgo., 1980. Cert. tchr. and supr. K-12, Ill.; bar: Ill. 1980, U.S. Dist. Ct. (no. dist.) Ill. 1980. Tchr., Chgo. Bd. Edn., Harris Sch., North Suburban Spl. Edn. Dist., Highland Park, Ill., 1968-73; legis. asst. Ill. Rep. L.M. Getty, Dolton, Ill., 1974-79, campaign mgr., 1976, 78; cons. LWV Ill., Chgo., 1978; sole practice law, Park Forest, Ill., 1980-83; ptnr. Getty & Gevers, Dolton, 1983—. Treas. Park Forest Youth Commn., 1973-75; past v.p. South Suburban Child Care Coordinating Council; past bd. dirs. Far South Suburban Housing Service, South Suburban Housing Center; past human resource chmn., past bd. dirs. Park Forest-Park Forest South LWV; founder, chmn. Met. South Women's Polit. Caucus, 1975; pres. Ill. Women's Polit. Caucus, 1976; mem. steering com. Nat. Women's Polit. Caucus, 1976-80; alt. del. Democratic Nat. Conv., N.Y.C., 1980; past mem. bd. Congregation Beth Sholom; mem. Park Forest Equal Employment Opportunity Rev. Bd., 1975—, Fair Housing Rev. Bd., 1975—, Zoning Bd. Appeals, 1975—, Housing Bd. Appeals, 1975—; pres. South Suburban Community Hebrew Day Sch., 1982-85; mem. rotating panel of arbitrators Park Forest Cable Commn., 1982—. Mem. ABA, Am. Arbitration Assn., Ill. State Bar Assn., Chgo. Bar Assn., South Suburban Bar Assn., Decalogue Soc. Lawyers. Jewish. Lodges: Hadassah, B'nai B'rith Women. Office: Getty and Gevers 15000 Dorchester Ave Dolton IL 60419

GEVIS, LOUISE, search company executive; b. Jurbarkas, Lithuania, Oct. 7, 1938; came to U.S., 1948; d. Edmundas and Gabriele (Volodka) Korzonas; m. Albert Gevis, July 20, 1963; 1 child, Richard. B.A. in English, U. Ill., 1961; postgrad. Rockford Coll., 1972-76. English tchr. high sch., Chgo., 1961-66, Rockford, Ill., 1972-76; data processing recruiter Liberty Assocs., Chgo., 1976-80, Metricor, Inc., Oak Brook, Ill., 1980-81; recruiting mgr. Consumer Systems, Oak Brook, 1981-83; owner, mgr. Gevis, Koehler and Assocs., Oak Brook, 1983—. Mem. Women in Info. Processing (v.p. 1982-83), Assn. Women in Computer Careers (v.p. 1983-84). Home: 14 Kingsbury Ct Oak Brook IL 60521 Office: Gevis Koehler and Assocs 600 Enterprise Dr Suite 109 Oak Brook IL 60521

GEWIRTZ, GERRY, editor, publisher; b. N.Y.C., Dec. 22, 1920; d. Max and Minnie (Weiss) G.; B.A., Vassar Coll., 1941; m. Eugene W. Friedman, Nov. 11, 1945; children—John Henry, Robert James. Editor, Package Store Mgmt., 1942-44, Jewelry mag., 1945-53; freelance editor promotion dept. McCall's mag., Esquire, 1953-56; free-lance fashion and gifts editor Jewelers Circular Keystone, N.Y.C., 1955-71; editor, pub. The Fashionables, 1971-74, The Forecast, 1974—, Nat. Jeweler, Ann. Fashion Guide, 1976—, asso. pub., editor-in-chief Exec. Jeweler, 1980-83, editor, pub. Gerry Gewirtz Report, 1983—. Mem. exec. com. Cardinal Cooke's Inner City Council; trustee Marymount Coll., Tarrytown, N.Y.; bd. dirs. Israel Cancer Research Fund; exec. com. med. div. Greater N.Y. Campaign State of Israel Bonds; trustee Central Synagogue; mem. Am. Jewish Com., Nat. Interreligious Commn. Recipient Jewelry Industry Div. award Am. Jewish Com., 1978, (with husband) Tower of Hope award, 1981, cert. excellence for contbn. to jewelry industry, 1984. Mem. N.Y. Fashion Group, Nat. Home Fashions League, Women's Jewelry Assn. (pres. 1983—), Nat. Assn. TV Arts and Scis. Clubs: N.Y. Vassar; Overseas Press. Office: 420 Madison Ave New York NY 10017

GEYER, GEORGIE ANNE, columnist, author, speaker, educator; b. Chgo., Apr. 2, 1935; d. Robert George and Georgie Hazel (Gervens) G.; B.S., Northwestern U., 1956; postgrad. (Fulbright scholar) U. Vienna (Austria), 1956-57; Litt.D. (hon.), Lake Forest Coll., 1980, Mt. St. Joseph Coll., Cin., 1986, St. Mary's Coll., Notre Dame Coll., 1986. Reporter, Southtown Economist, Chgo., 1958; soc. reporter Chgo. Daily News, 1959-60, gen. assignment reporter, 1960-64, Latin Am. corr., 1964-67, roving world corr., 1967-75; syndicated columnist Los Angeles Times Syndicate, 1975-80, Universal Press Syndicate, 1980—; Spencer prof. journalism Syracuse U., 1976; John J. Fitzpatrick lectr. U. Utah, 1977; mem. bd. courses by newspaper project U. Calif., San Diego; speaker on trips to Africa, Asia and Iceland for Internat. Communication Agy., 1979, 81, 82; mem. steering com. Latin Am. governance project Aspen. Inst. Active Orgn. for S.W. Community Chgo., 1960—; trustee Am. U., Washington. Recipient 1st prize Am. Newspaper Guild, 1962; 2d prize Ill. Press Editors Assn., 1962; award for best reporting in Latin Am., Overseas Press Club, 1967; Alumni Merit award Northwestern U., 1968, Alumnae award, 1981; Maria Moors Cabot award Columbia U., 1971; Hannah Solomon award Nat. Council Jewish Women, 1973. Mem. Chgo. Council Fgn. Relations (dir.), Internat. Inst. Strategic Studies (London), Mortar Bd., Theta Sigma Chi. Author: The New Latins, 1970; The New 100 Years War, 1972; The Young Russians, 1975; Buying the Night Flight, 1983; contbr. articles to Atlantic Mag., Sat. Rev. Lit., Nat. Observer, New Republic, others. Address: 800 25th St NW Washington DC 20037

GEZELMAN, REGINA MARY JUNE, insurance company financial secretary; b. Bridgeport, Conn., Oct. 24, 1952; d. Samuel Benedicto and Antoinette (Morena) June; m. Ralph Lee Gezelman, III. B.A. in Journalism, U. Bridgeport, 1974. Supr. cashiers King Cole Stores, Bridgeport, Conn., 1970-76; dept. sec. U. Bridgeport, 1975-76; exec. sec. Glendinning Assocs., Westport, Conn., 1976-77; adminstrv. asst. Meredith Assoc., Westport, 1977-79; asst. to pres. Hiland Assocs., Westport, 1979; exec. mgr. Ponderosa Inc., Southington, Conn., 1979-85; fin. sec. Covenant Ins. Co., Hartford, Conn., 1985—. Roman Catholic. Home: 2 Woodside Ct Burlington CT 06013 Office: Covenant Ins Co 95 Woodland St Hartford CT 06105

GHAFFARI, AVIDEH BEHROUZ, design and construction company executive; b. Tehran, Iran, Apr. 17, 1943; came to U.S., 1975, naturalized, 1984; d. Zabih and Homa Behrouz; B.A., Art and Design Sch. Scotland, 1966; m. Abbas Ghaffari, Feb. 2, 1976; children—Narsi Azima, Borzou Azima. Founder, pres. Polydecor Co., Tehran and Paris, France, 1962-68; pres. Pakab Co. Ltd., Tehran, 1963-75, Avidecor Co., Inc., N.Y.C., 1979—, Avida Internat. Ltd., N.Y.C., 1985—; sec.-treas., dir. Metavi Inc., N.Y.C. Recipient Award of Merit, Imperial Govt. Iran, 1969. Mem. Am. Soc. Interior Designers, Internat. Soc. Interior Designers, Nat. Assn. Female Execs., Iran Inst. Interior Design. Home: 425 E 58th St New York NY 10022 Office: 790 Madison Ave New York NY 10021

GHANDHI, MADONNA STAHL, lawyer, judge; b. Robinson, Ill., Sept. 26, 1928; d. Lawrence Joy and Inez Lucille (Kennedy) Stahl; children—Khushro, Rustom, Behram. B.S., U. Ill., 1950; J.D., Albany Law Sch., 1973. Bar: N.Y. 1974, U.S. Dist. Ct. (no. dist.) N.Y. 1974, U.S. Ct. Apls. (2nd cir.) 1975, U.S. Supreme Ct. 1978. Atty. trainee N.Y. State Dept. Commerce, Albany, 1973-74; atty. Legal Aid Soc., Albany, 1974-76; ptnr. Powers, Ghandhi & Somers, and predecessor, Albany, 1976—; judge Albany City Ct., part-time, 1984—; mem. com. on character and fitness N.Y. State Supreme Ct. A.D. 3d Dept., Albany, 1980-86. Lobbyist Com. for Progressive Legislation, Schenectady, 1968-70. Mem. N.Y. State Bar Assn., Albany County Bar Assn., Women's Bar Assn. State N.Y. (Capital dist. pres. 1983-84). Democrat. Unitarian. Club: Altrusa. Office: Powers Ghandhi& Somers 230 Delaware Ave Delmar NY 12054

GHILERI, SIRLEEN JEAN, programmer analyst; b. Southgate, Calif., Mar. 7, 1943; d. Sirl and Dorothy Jean (Kaylor) Myhand; m. Richard Alan Wilson, Apr. 10, 1960 (div. 1972); children—Richard Alan Jr., Michael Dale; m. Norman Phillip Ghileri, Mar. 12, 1973. A.A., Golden West Jr. Coll., 1970. Peace Corps, vol., Ethiopia, 1971; eligibility worker Santa Cruz Co., Calif., 1972-76; rancher Ghigleri Ranch, San Juan Bautista, Calif., 1976-82; applications programmer Madic Corp., Santa Clara, Calif., 1983-85; programmer analyst Skyway Systems, Santa Cruz, 1985—. Chmn. Santa Cruz County Grand Jury, 1977-78. Mem. Prime Users Group, Mensa. Avocations: Physical fitness; quilting; investing.

GHIRALDINI, JOAN, financial company executive; b. Bklyn., Mar. 31, 1951; d. Robert and Anne (Centineo) G.; B.A., Smith Coll., 1972; M.B.A., U. Pa., 1975. Econ. specialist Western Electric Corp., N.Y.C., 1975-76; sr. fin. analyst Internat. Paper Co., N.Y.C., 1976-78, mgr. strategic planning, 1978-81; dir. fin. planning Executone, Inc., Jericho, N.Y., 1981-82, dir. strategic planning, 1982-83; dir. corp. analysis Equitable Life Assurance, 1983-84; asst. v.p. First Boston Corp., N.Y.C., 1985—. Mem. Fin. Women's Assn. N.Y., Am. Fin. Assn., Wharton Bus. Sch. Club N.Y., Smith Coll. Club N.Y. (bd. dirs.). Home: 155 E 38th St Apt 3G New York NY 10016 Office: 5 World Trade Ctr New York NY 10048

GHOLSTON, HELEN ALBERTA, educator; b. Lawrence, Mass., May 13, 1923; d. Albert Clinton and Helen Gertrude (Mitchell) McIlwain; B.A. in English with distinction, San Diego State U., 1976, M.A. in Edn., 1980; m. Andrew J. Gholston, Apr. 25, 1944; children—Andrea, Juanita, Corale, Wendy, Michael, Andrew J. Microfilm operator San Diego City Civil Service, 1957-58; engaged in real estate, 1961-70; tutor EEO program San Diego Community Colls., 1971-75; tchr. secondary div. San Diego Unified Sch. Dist., 1977—, tchr. English, Lincoln Sr. High Sch., 1979-86, chmn. dept., 1980-82, mem. textbook com. San Diego city schs., 1980-82 Mem. Nat. Council Tchrs. English, Assn. Supervision and Curriculum Devel., Nat. Council Negro Women, Am. Bus. Women's Assn., Browning Soc., San Diego State U. Alumni Assn. Baptist. Author articles, curriculum materials. Home: 5322 Hilltop Dr San Diego CA 92114 Office: San Diego City Schs 4100 Normal St San Diego CA 92103

GHORMLEY-GOIRAN, MARY VIRGINIA, sales executive; b. Oklahoma City, July 22, 1953; d. Luthur Wayne Ghormley and Jessica Ellen Van Vleck Stone; B.A., Stephens Coll., Columbia, Mo., 1974; m. Philip De La Hogue Goiran, Feb. 6, 1982. Salesperson, Gabrielle's, Denver, 1978; territory mgr. Wallace Berrie & Co., Van Nuys, Calif., 1978-79, dist. sales mgr., 1979-81, regional sales mgr., 1981-84; regional mgr. Applause div. Wallace Berrie & Co., Woodland Hills, Calif., 1984—; dir. sales SW div. Applause Co., 1984—. Named Rookie Salesperson of Yr., Wallace Berrie & Co., 1978. Mem. Nat. Assn. Female Execs., NOW, LWV, Am. Mgmt. Assn. Democrat. Roman Catholic. Home: 5200 Montview Blvd Denver CO 80207 Office: 6101 Variel St Woodland Hills CA 91364

GIANNONE, TONI LYNNE, speech pathologist; b. Bridgeport, Conn., Nov. 3, 1950; d. Peter Anthony and Eleanor Bridget (Scinto) G.; B.A., U. Conn., Storrs, 1972; M.A. with honors, Western Mich. U., Kalamazoo, 1973; m. Kenneth M. Nowak, Aug. 9, 1975. Speech pathologist Found. Sch., Orange, Conn., 1973-74; clin. coordinator Southeastern Conn. Hearing & Speech Center, Norwich, 1974-77; dir. speech pathology Lawrence and Meml. Hosp., New London, Conn., 1975-77; dir. primary unit Found. Sch., Orange, 1977—; prof. U. R.I., Kingston, 1976—; clin. supr., instr. accelerated program Post Coll., 1982—; speech pathologist Am. Cancer Soc., 1974-78; instr. Housatonic Community Coll., 1984—. Recipient DAR Good Citizen award, 1968. Mem. Am. Speech and Hearing Assn., Conn. Speech and Hearing Assn., Beta Phi Beta. Roman Catholic. Office: 719 Derby Milford Rd Orange CT 06477

GIANOLA, PATTI LEE, nursing educator; b. Worcester, Mass., Sept. 10, 1954; d. Harold Raymond and Edna Maude (Williamson) Thompson; m. James Howard Morse, Sept. 18, 1976 (div. June 1979); m. Peter Joseph Gianola, June 20, 1981; 1 son, Andrew Thompson. A.A., Quinsigamond Community Coll., 1976; B.S.N., Worcester State Coll., 1982. Gerontology nurse Westboro Nursing Home (Mass.), 1976-77; med.-surg. nurse Framingham Union Hosp. (Mass.), 1977-78, ICU nurse, 1978-81; instr. nursing sci. Central Maine Med. Ctr., Lewiston, 1982-83; instr. nursing edn. St. Mary's Gen. Hosp., Lewiston, 1983—; nurse vol. ARC Blood Mobile, Framingham, 1978-80; instr. basic life support Am. Heart Assn., Lewiston, 1983. Mem. Am. Assn. Critical Care Nurses. Democrat. Methodist. Lodge: Order of Rainbow Girls. Home: 57 Lafayette St Lewiston ME 04240 Office: St Marys Gen Hosp 45 Golder St Lewiston ME 04240

GIANUTSOS, ROSAMOND ROCKWELL, psychologist; b. Lawrence, Mass., Apr. 1, 1945; d. S. Forbes Rockwell and Ursula (Ingalls) Rockwell Hazen; m. John G. Gianutsos, Sept. 11, 1965; children—Gerasimos John, Matthew Nicholas. B.A., Barnard Coll., 1966; Ph.D., NYU, 1970. Lic. psychology, N.Y. Asst. prof. psychology Adelphi U., Garden City, N.Y., 1970-74, assoc. prof., 1974-83; sr. psychologist Bellevue-NYU Med. Ctr., N.Y.C., 1978-83; dir. Cognitive Rehab. Services, Sunnyside, N.Y., 1983—; adj. assoc. prof. neurology NYU Med. Ctr., N.Y.C., 1981—; allied health profl. Nyack Hosp., N.Y., 1985—; cons. to health facilities. Mem. editorial bd. Jour. Clin. and Exptl. Neuropsychology, 1984—. Contbr. articles to profl. jours. Fellow N.Y. Acad. Scis. (chmn. linguistics sect. 1974-76); mem. Nat. Head Injury Found. (mem. task force on edn.), Am. Psychol. Assn., Internat. Neuropsychol. Soc. Am. Congress Rehab. Medicine, N.Y. State Head Injury Assn., Psychologists for Social Action (nat. coordinator 1973-75). Office: Cognitive Rehab Services 38-25 52d St Sunnyside NY 11104

GIARRAPUTO, FRANCES MIRIAM, automotive maintenance management company executive; b. Chgo., Dec. 29, 1946; d. Edward James and Martha (Williams) McLaughlin; m. Leonard Giarraputo, Feb. 17, 1968; children—Laura, Christopher, Thomas. B.S. in Edn., Jacksonville U., 1968. Space salesperson Club Living Mag., Westchester, N.Y., 1980-81; dir. nat. accounts Gibraltar Transmission, Great Neck, N.Y., 1982-83; dir., v.p. Nat. Fleet Service, Jericho, N.Y., 1984—; model Saks Fifth Ave., 1980, Club Living Mag., 1981. Mem. Nat. Assn. Fleet Adminstrs., Nat. Assn. Female Execs., Long Island Businessmen Assn., Jacksonville U. Alumni Assn. Republican. Presbyterian. Clubs: Mill River (Upper Brookville, N.Y.), Syosset Racket (N.Y.). Avocations: real estate, skiing, aerobics, recreational flying. Office: Nat Fleet Service Inc 55 Jericho Tpke Jericho NY 11753

GIASOLLI, ROSE MARIE ANTOINETTE LEVATO, real estate company executive; b. Chgo., Mar. 14, 1939; d. Rosario A. and Carmella (D'Ambrose) Levato; student Chgo. Sch. Music, 1957, Santa Monica City Coll., 1960, South West Coll., 1965, student U. Hawaii, 1970, El Paso Community Coll., 1977-79; cert. U. Tex., 1975; grad. Real Estate Inst., 1979; m. Mero V. Giasolli, Aug. 10, 1957; children—Vincent S., Michael J., Anthony R., Robert M. Real estate sales agt. PDC Realty, El Paso, Tex., 1975-77; real estate broker DeWitt & Rearick Inc., El Paso, 1977-79; partner and prin. broker White-Giasolli-Hary Inc., El Paso, 1979-80, dir., 1980—; partner, pres. Remax West, El Paso, 1981—. Active performing mem. Ballet Folklorica, El Paso, 1978—; founder Ladies Mission Group, Kwajalein Island, Marshall Islands, 1968, pres., 1968-70; bd. dirs. Family Outreach, Shelter for Battered Women; 1st Woman pres. Investment Property Exchangors. 1985-86, 86-87. Cert. residential specialist. Mem. Tex. Assn. Realtors (profl. standards com.), Nat. Assn. Realtors, El Paso Bd. Realtors (chmn. Make Am Better program), Women's Council of Realtors (founder El Paso chpt. 1979, pres. 1979-81), Internat. Real Estate Fedn., El Paso C. of C., Soc. Arts and Letters, St. Matthews Guild. Roman Catholic. Clubs: Amici Italian (founder, pres. 1977-78), Tex. A&M Mothers (pres. 1979-80). Office: 250 Thunderbird El Paso TX 79912

GIATTINA, KAREN HELEN DETHLOFF, disability examiner, consultant; b. Mobile, Ala., Sept. 7, 1958; d. William Franklin and Helen (Mayes) Dethloff; m. Victor Andrew Giattina, July 20, 1984; 1 child, William Anthony. B.S., Mobile Coll., 1982; M.P.A., U. South Ala., 1986. Environ. health specialist Mobile County Health Dept., Ala., 1982-85; disability determination examiner Ala. Dept. Edn., Mobile, 1985—. Active Yellow Dog Democratic Club. Recipient letter of commendation Tulane U. Sch. Pub. Health, 1984, Continental Motors Aircraft Div., 1985, Judge Douglas Johnstone, 1985. Mem. Nat. Assn. Disability Examiners, Exec. Women's Forum, Ala. Environ. Health Assn. (S.W. chpt.) (v.p. and pres.-elect 1984-85), AAUW, Ala. State Employees Assn. Baptist. Avocations: white water rafting; antique collecting; current events.

GIBBONS, BARBARA, author, columnist, cooking educator; b. Newark. Writer nat. syndicated column The Slim Gourmet, United Features Syndicate, 1971—; organizer, instr. low-calories cooking classes, 1968—; guest on radio and TV programs including Today and Good Morning, America. Author: The Slim Gourmet Cookbook (Tastemaster award), 1976; The International Slim Gormet Cookbook (Tastemaster award), 1978; Family Circle Creative Low Calorie Cooking; The Consumer Guide Diet Cookbook; The Diet Watchers Cookbook; The Year-Round Turkey Cookbook, 1979; Lean Cuisine, 1979; The Light and Easy Cookbook, 1980; Calories Don't Count, 1980; Salads for All Seasons, 1982; Slim Gourmet Sweets and Treats, 1982. Mem. Am. Soc. Journalists and Authors, Authors League, Authors Guild, Nat. Fedn. Press Women, Newspaper Food Editors and Writers Assn. Club: Newswomen's (N.Y.C.). Address: 15 Wayland Dr Verona NJ 07044

GIBBONS, MRS. JOHN SHELDON (CELIA VICTORIA TOWNSEND), editor, publisher; b. Fargo, N.D.; d. Harry Alton and Helen (Haag) Townsend; student U. Minn., 1930-33; m. John Sheldon Gibbons, May 1, 1935; children—Mary Vee, John Townsend. Advt. mgr. Hotel Nicollet, Mpls., 1933-37; contbg. editor children's mags., 1935—; partner Youth Assos. Co., Mpls., 1942-65; pub., art dir. Mines and Escholier mags., 1954-65; founder Bull. Bd. Pictures, Inc., Mpls., 1954, pres., 1954—; founder Periodical Litho Art Co., Mpls., 1962-65, pres., 1962-65. Active St. Paul Internat. House, Friends of Inst., St. Paul Arts and Sci. Center. Republican chairwoman Golden Valley, Minn., 1950; alternate del. Hennepin County Rep. Conv., 1962. Mem. Mpls. Inst. Arts, Ft. Lauderdale Mus. Arts, Art Guild Boca Raton. Delta Zeta. Clubs: Woman's Minikahda; Woman's of Minneapolis; Woman's (Deerfield Beach, Fla.). Home: 1416 Alpine Pass Tyrol Hills Minneapolis MN 55416 Office: 1057 A1A Hillsboro Beach FL 33062

GIBBONS, JULIA SMITH, judge; b. Pulaski, Tenn., Dec. 23, 1950; d. John Floyd and Julia Jackson (Abernathy) Smith; m. William Lockhart Gibbons, Aug. 11, 1973; 1 dau., Rebecca Carey. B.A., Vanderbilt U., 1972; J.D., U. Va.-Charlottesville, 1975. Bar: Tenn. 1975. Law clk. U.S. Ct. Appeals (6th cir.), Nashville, 1975-76; assoc. Farris, Hancock, Gilman, Memphis, 1976-79; legal advisor to Gov. Lamar Alexander, State of Tenn., Nashville, 1979-81; circuit judge State of Tenn., Memphis, 1981-83; U.S. dist. judge U.S. Dist. Ct. for we. dist. Tenn., Memphis, 1983—. Fellow Am. Bar Found.; mem. ABA, Tenn. Bar Assn., Memphis and Shelby County Bar Assn., Nat. Assn. Women Judges, Am. Judicature Soc., Order of Coif, Phi Beta Kappa. Presbyterian. Clubs: Memphis Heritage, Zonta, Network (Memphis), Memphis Heritage. Office: US Dist Judge 1157 Clifford Davis Federal Bldg Memphis TN 38103

GIBBONS, SHEILA MARIE, aerospace company executive; b. N.Y.C., Mar. 31, 1931; d. Joseph Vincent and Edna Marie (McCarthy) MacAvoy; m. William James Gibbons, Feb. 14, 1953; children—Laura Cecile Burns, Philip Damian, Sally Honora Mc Mahon. B.A. in Art, Queens Coll., CUNY, 1952; J.D., St. John's U., 1976. Bar: N.Y. 1977, Calif. 1977. Assoc. Carnahan & Freeman, Woodland Hills, Calif., 1977; asst. sec. Northrop Corp., Los Angeles, 1978-80, sec., 1980-83, v.p., sec., 1983—; dir. Paramount Mut. Fund, Los Angeles. Honoree Tribute to Women in Internat. Industry, Nat. Bd. YWCA, Houston, 1983. Mem. ABA, Los Angeles Bar Assn., Am. Soc. Corp. Secs. (bd. dirs. 1985—, v.p. Los Angeles group 1984-85, adv. com. 1981-85, securities law com. 1981-84, ad hoc com. on tender offers 1984-85, securities industry com. 1985—). Office: Northrop Corp 1840 Century Park East Los Angeles CA 90067

GIBBS, ANN, chemist; b. Corpus Christi, Tex., May 19, 1941; d. Frank James and Elizabeth Ann (Setzer) G.; student Tulane U., 1958-59; B.A., U. Tex., Austin, 1961; M.S., U. Ark., 1964. Research asst. Inst. Marine Sci., U. Tex., 1960-62; chemist DuPont Co., Savannah River plant, Aiken, S.C., 1966—; mem. ad hoc com. NDA instrumentation U.S. Dept. Energy, 1980-82. AEC fellow, 1962-65. Mem. Am. Chem. Soc. (chmn. Savannah River sect. 1980), Am. Phys. Soc., AAAS, Am. Nuclear Soc., ASTM, Inst. Nuclear Materials Mgmt. Presbyterian. Research in nuclear spectroscopy and nondestructive instrumentation. Home: PO Box 6624 North Augusta SC 29841 Office: Bldg 247F Savannah River Lab Aiken SC 29808

GIBBS, BARBARA KENNEDY, art museum director; b. Newton, Mass., Feb. 15, 1950; d. Frederic Alexander and Jane (Ensinger) Kennedy. A.B. magna cum laude, Brown U., 1972; M.B.A., UCLA, 1979. Dep. dir. Portland Art Assn., Oreg., 1979-83; dir. Crocker Art Mus., Sacramento, 1983—. Guggenheim intern fellow, 1978. Mem. Assn. Art Mus. Dirs., Am. Assn. Mus. Home: 1036 56th St Sacramento CA 95819 Office: Crocker Art Mus 216 O St Sacramento CA 95814

GIBBS, DELENE G., city official; b. Montevallo, Ala., Aug. 6, 1938; d. Doyle R. and Nannie L. (Barnett) Gay; m. John Wesley Gibbs, Nov. 16, 1957; 1 child, John Wesley Jr. Grad. Birmingham Bus. Coll., 1957. Clk. City of Oneonta, Ala., 1958, asst. city clk., 1963-72, city clk., 1972—; clk. Register in Chancery, Oneonta, 1959-62. Methodist. Lodge: Order Eastern Star (conductress 1973-74). Home: 102 Hendrix St Oneonta AL 35121 Office: City Clk City Hall 202 3d Ave Oneonta AL 35121

GIBBS, JEWELLE TAYLOR, clinical psychologist; b. Stratford, Conn., Nov. 4, 1933; d. Julian Augustus and Margaret Pauline (Morris) Taylor; A.B. cum laude, Radcliffe Coll., 1955; postgrad. Harvard-Radcliffe Program in Bus. Adminstrn., 1959; M.S.W., U. Calif., Berkeley, 1970, Ph.D., 1980; m. James Lowell Gibbs, Jr., Aug. 25, 1956; children—Geoffrey Taylor, Lowell Dabney. Jr. mgmt. asst. U.S. Dept. Labor, Washington, 1955-56; market research coordinator Pillsbury Co., Mpls., 1959-61; clin. social worker Stanford (Calif.) U. Student Health Service, 1970-74, 78-79, research assoc. dept. psychiatry, 1971-73; asst. prof. Sch. Social Welfare U. Calif., Berkeley, 1979-83, acting assoc. prof., 1983-86, assoc. prof., 1986—; pvt. practice as clin. psychotherapist, 1983—; fellow Bunting Inst., Radcliffe Coll., spring, 1985. Bd. regents U. Santa Clara (Calif.), 1980-84; mem. Minn. State Commn. on Status of Women, 1963-65; co-chairperson Minn. Women's Com. for Civil Rights, 1963-65. NIMH fellow, 1979; Soroptimist Internat. grantee, 1978-79. Fellow Am. Orthopsychiat. Assn. (bd. dirs. 1985—); mem. Am. Psychol. Assn., Nat. Assn. Social Workers, Western Psychol. Assn. Democrat. Mem. editorial bd. Am. Jour. Orthopsychiatry, 1980-84; bd. publs. Nat. Assn. Social Workers, 1980-82; contbr. chpts. to books, articles to profl. jours. Office: Haviland Hall Sch Social Welfare U Calif Berkeley CA 94720

GIBBS, JUNE NESBITT, state senator; b. Newton, Mass., June 13, 1922; d. Samuel Frederick and Lulu (Glazier) Nesbitt; B.A. in Math., Wellesley Coll., 1943; M.A. in Math., Boston U., 1947; m. Donald T. Gibbs, Dec. 8, 1945; 1 dau., Elizabeth. Mem. R.I. Senate, 1985—. Republican nat. committeewoman, R.I., 1969-80; sec. Rep. Nat. Com., 1977-80; mem. def. adv. com. Women in Services, 1970-72, vice chmn., 1972; mem. Middletown Town Council, 1974-80, 82-84, pres., 1978-80. Served to lt. (j.g.) USNR, 1942-46. Home: 163 Riverview Ave Middletown RI 02840

GIBBS, KATHRYN LEE, author, educator, lecturer; b. Havre de Grace, Md., B.A., U. Pitts., 1954, A.M. in English (Owens fellow), 1957; Ph.D. in Modern Am. and Brit. Lit., Mich. State U., 1976. Mem. faculties St. Michael's Acad. (Tex.), Mich. State U. New Orleans U., Grove City Coll. (Pa.); editor, contbr.; Robert Frost: Studies of the Poetry, 1980; author book of poems (pen name Wilson Hayes): Ironwood and Ironwood II, 1973, 75; poems Chiascuro in Cathedral Poets II, 1976; Being Ourselves: Women Poets of North Carolina; contbr. poems, essays, revs. to jours.; editor, pub. Robert Frost Newsletter. Bd. dirs. St. Michael's Acad. Mem. Robert Frost Soc. (bd. dirs. 1975-84), MLA (presenter papers on Robert Frost, Hilda Doolittle Aldington, Katharine Anne Porter), South Central MLA, South Atlantic MLA, Coll. English Assn. (moderator "Women Writers' Portraits of Women" 1978), Soc. Study So. Lit. (talk on Katharine Anne Porter 1983), Popular Culture Assn. Home: 710 Park

Pl College Station TX 77840 Office: St Michaels Acad 2505 S College Ave College Station TX 77840

GIBBS, LELA VIRGINIA, psychiatric clinical specialist; b. Winston-Salem, N.C., Mar. 16, 1949; d. Selmer Gwyn and Daisy Truesdale; m. Will Yancey Tate, Jr., Mar. 6, 1966 (dec. Feb. 1981); children—Willette Virginia Tate, Melissah Elaine Tate, Will Yancey Tate. B.S.N., Winston-Salem State U., 1977; M.S.N., Med. Coll. Ga., 1986; Ph.D. candidate, U.S. Internat. U., 1986—. R.N., Calif., N.C., Ga. Instr., Forsyth Tech. Inst., Winston-Salem, 1977-78; staff nurse I, Forsyth County Mental Health, Winston-Salem, 1977-78; supr. Vista Hill Psychiat. Hosp., Chula Vista, Calif., 1978-82; staff nurse II, San Diego County Med. Instn., 1978-83; program coordinator Turner Job Corps, Albany, Ga., 1984; psychiat. clin. specialist Med. Coll. Ga., Augusta, 1984—. Mem. Calif. Nurses Assn., Nat. Assn. Female Execs., Sigma Theta Tau. Democrat. Baptist. Home: 1225 Lauriston Ave San Diego CA 92154

GIBBS-WATSON, AMELIA LOUISE, personnel specialist; b. Chester, Pa., June 14, 1952; d. Joseph and Eula (Teat) Gibbs; m. Michael Vincent Watson, Sept. 18, 1982. A.A., Pierce Jr. Coll., 1982. Statement teller Southeast Nat. Bank, Chester, 1970-71; personnel asst. Fidelity Bank, Phila., 1971-76; personnel specialist ARA Services, Inc., Phila., 1976-84; claim adjuster Allstate Ins. Co., 1986—. Nat. Assn. Female Execs. Office: ARA Services Inc Independence Sq West Philadelphia PA 19106

GIBBY, MABEL ENID KUNCE, psychologist; b. St. Louis, Mar. 30, 1926; d. Ralph Waldo and Mabel Enid (Warren) Kunce; student Washington U., St. Louis, 1943-44, postgrad., 1955-56; B.A., Park Coll., 1945; M.A., McCormick Theol. Sem., 1947; postgrad. Columbia U., 1948, U. Kansas City, 1949, George Washington U., 1953; M.Ed., U. Mo., 1951, Ed.D., 1952; m. John Francis Gibby, Aug. 27, 1948; children—Janet Marie (Mrs. Kim Williams), Harold Steven, Helen Elizabeth, Diane Louise (Mrs. Gregory Mappin), John Andrew, Keith Sherridan, Daniel Jay. Dir. religious edn. Westport Presbyn. Ch. Kansas City, Mo., 1947-49; tchr. elementary schs., Kansas City, 1949-50; high sch. counselor Arlington (Va.) Pub. Schs., 1952-54; counselor adult counseling services Washington U., 1955-56; counseling psychologist Coral Gables (Fla.) VA Hosp., 1956—; counseling psychologist Miami (Fla.) VA Hosp., 1956—, chief counseling psychology sect., 1982—, coordinator vocat. rehab. sect. psychology service, 1986—. Sec. bd. dirs. Fla. Vocat. Rehab. Found. Recipient Meritorious Service citation Fla. C. of C., 1965, President's Com. on Employment of Handicapped, 1965; commendation for meritorious service Com. on Employment of Physically Handicapped Dade County, 1965, 81, named outstanding rehab. profl., 1966, 81; named Profl. Fed. Employee of Year, Greater Miami Fed. Exec. Council, 1966; Outstanding Fed. Service award Greater Miami Fed. Exec. Council, 1966; Fed. Woman's award U.S. Civil Service Commn., 1968, Community Headliner award Theta Sigma Phi, 1968, Outstanding Alumni award Park Coll., 1968; certificate of appreciation Bur. Customs, U.S. Treasury Dept., 1969, Fla. Dept. Health and Rehab. Services, 1970. Mem. Am., Dade County (past sec.) psychol. assns., Nat., Fla. (past dir. Dade County chpt.) rehab. assns., Nat. Rehab. Counseling Assn. (past sec.). Patentee. Home: 10260 SW 56th St Miami FL 33165 Office: 1201 NW 16th St Miami FL 33125

GIBLETT, ELOISE ROSALIE, medical educator; b. Tacoma, Wash., Jan. 17, 1921; d. William Richard and Rose (Godfrey) G.; B.S., U. Wash., 1942, M.S., 1947, M.D. with honors, 1951. Mem. faculty U. Wash. Sch. Medicine, 1957—, research prof., 1967—; asso. dir., head immunogenetics Puget Sound Blood Center, 1955-79, exec. dir., 1979—; former mem. several research coms. NIH. Author: Genetic Markers in Human Blood, 1969. Editorial bd. Blood, Am. Jour. Human Genetics, Transfusion. Contbr. over 180 articles to profl. jours. Recipient fellowships, grants, Emily Cooley, Karl Landsteiner and Philip Levine immunohematology awards. Fellow AAAS; mem. Nat. Acad. Scis., Am. Soc. Human Genetics (pres. 1973), Am. Soc. Hematology, Am. Assn. Immunologists, Brit. Soc. Immunology, Internat. Soc. Hematologists, Am. Fedn. Clin. Research, Western Assn. Physicians, Assn. Am. Physicians, N.Y. Acad. Scis., Sigma Xi, Alpha Omega Alpha. Home: 6533 53d St NE Seattle WA 98115 Office: Puget Sound Blood Center Terry and Madison Sts Seattle WA 98104

GIBSON, ALTHEA, tennis player, golfer, state ofcl.; b. Silver, S.C., Aug. 25, 1927; d. Daniel and Annie B. (Washington) Gibson; m. Sydney Llewellyn, Apr. 11, 1983; B.S., Fla. A. and M. Coll., 1953; D.Pub. Service (hon.), Monmouth Coll., 1980; m. William A. Darben, Oct. 17, 1965. Amateur tennis player in U.S., Europe and S.Am., 1941-58; asst. instr. dept. health and phys. edn. Lincoln U., Jefferson City, Mo., 1953-55; appeared in movie in The Horse Soldiers, 1958; made profl. tennis tour with Harlem Globetrotters, 1959; community relations rep. Ward Baking Co., 1959; won world profl. tennis championship, 1960; joined Ladies Profl. Golf Assn. as profl. golfer, 1963; apptd. to N.Y. State Recreation Council, 1964; staff mem. Essex County Park Commn., Newark, 1970, recreation supr., 1970-71; dir. tennis programs, profl. Valley View Racquet Club, Northvale, N.J., 1972; tennis pro Morven, 1973—; athletic commr. State of N.J., 1975—; recreation mgr. City of East Orange (N.J.), 1980. Named Woman Athlete of Year, AP Poll, 1957-58; named to Lawn Tennis Hall of Fame and Tennis Mus., 1971, S.C. Athletic Hall of Fame, 1983. Mem. Alpha Kappa Alpha. Author: I Always Wanted to Be Somebody, 1958. Home: PO Box 768 East Orange NJ 07019

GIBSON, ELEANOR BEATRICE, artist, library consultant; b. London, Mar. 8, 1905; d. Harry Hepburn and Anne Elizabeth (White) G.; brought to U.S., 1905, derivative citizenship, 1914; grad. Loomis-Chaffee Sch., 1923; A.B., Cornell U., 1928; student St. Joseph Coll., West Hartford, 1937-38; M.S. in Library Sci., Syracuse U., 1957. With Aetna Life & Casualty Co., Hartford, Conn., 1928-42, librarian research div., 1933-42; librarian Logan Lewis Library, Carrier Corp. Research Center, Syracuse, N.Y., 1947-67, spl. adviser, 1967-70; tech. supr. computerized union catalogue project Conn. State Library, Hartford, 1968-71; now artist, library cons. Served from 1st lt. (WAAC) WAC, AUS, 1942-46; capt., 1950-51. Recipient Honors award Spl. Libraries Assn., 1968, named to Hall of Fame. Mem. Spl. Libraries Assn. (pres. Western N.Y. 1959-60; nat. chmn. metals materials div. 1961-62), Conn. Acad. Fine Arts (sustaining mem.), West Hartford Art League (hon. life), Alumni Assn. Syracuse U. Sch. Library Sci. and Info. (pres. 1967-68, Am. Legion, Nature Conservancy, Assn. on Am. Indian Affairs, Sierra Club, Pi Lambda Sigma (pres. 1958-59), Beta Phi Mu (local pres. 1959-60). Episcopalian. Editor: Guide to Metallurgical Information, 1965. Contbr. articles to profl. jours. Home: 23 Fernridge Rd West Hartford CT 06107 Studio: White Studio Leighton Hill Rd Newbury VT 05051

GIBSON, ELEANOR JACK, psychologist, educator; b. Peoria, Ill., Dec. 7, 1910; d. William A. and Isabel (Grier) Jack; B.A., Smith Coll., 1931, M.A., 1933, D.Sc. (hon.), 1972; Ph.D., Yale U., 1938; D.Sc. (hon.), Rutgers U., 1973, Trinity Coll., 1982, Bates Coll., 1985; L.H.D., SUNY-Albany, 1984; m. James J. Gibson, Sept. 17, 1932; children—James J., Jean Grier. Asst., instr., asst. prof. Smith Coll., 1931-49; research assoc. in psychology Cornell U., Ithaca, N.Y., 1949-66, prof., 1972—, Susan Linn Sage prof. psychology, 1972—; fellow Inst. for Advanced Study, Princeton U., 1959-60, Inst. for Advanced Study in Behavioral Scis., Stanford, Calif., 1963-64; vis. prof. M.I.T., 1973, U. Calif.-Davis, 1978, U. Minn., 1980, U. Pa., 1984; vis. scientist Salk Inst., 1979; vis. prof. U.Pa., 1984. Recipient Wilbur Cross medal Yale U., 1973; Disting. Service medal Columbia U. Tchrs. Coll., 1983. Guggenheim fellow, 1972-73; Montgomery fellow Dartmouth Coll., 1986. Fellow Am. Psychol. Assn. (disting. sci. contbn. award 1970, pres. div. 3 1977, G. Stanley Hall medal div. 7) AAAS (chmn. 1982); mem. Nat. Acad. Edn., Psychonomic Soc., Eastern Psychol. Assn. (pres. 1968), Brit. Psychol. Soc. (hon.), Soc. Exptl. Psychologists (Howard Crosby Warren medal 1977), Soc. Research in Child Devel. (governing council 1980—, disting. contbn. award 1981), Nat. Acad. Sci., N.Y. Acad. Scis. (hon.), Am. Acad. Arts and Scis., Phi Beta Kappa, Sigma Xi. Author: Principles of Perceptual Learning and Development (Century award), 1969; (with H. Levin) The Psychology of Reading, 1975.

GIBSON, ELISABETH JANE, educational administrator; b. Salina, Kans., Apr. 28, 1937; d. Cloyce Wesley and Margaret Mae (Yost) Kasson; A.B., Colo. State Coll., 1957; M.A., San Francisco State Coll., 1968; Ed.D., U. No. Colo., 1978; m. Harry B. Gibson, July 1, 1970. Tchr. various public schs., 1957-67; tchr. Central Kans. Diagnostic and Remedial Edn. Center, Salina, 1968-70; instr. Loretto Heights Coll., Denver, 1970-72, Regis Coll., Denver, spring 1973; instr. Met. State Coll., Denver, summer 1972, asst. prof., spring 1979; co-owner, v.p. Ednl. Cons. Enterprises, Inc., Greeley, Colo., 1974-77; exec. dir. Colo. Fedn. Council Exceptional Children, Denver, 1976-77; resource coordinator Mile High Consortium, Denver, 1976-77; cons. Mont. Dept. Public Instrn., Helena, 1978-79; spl. edn. dir. N.E. Colo. Bd. Cooperative Ednl. Services, Haxtun, 1979-82; elem./middle sch. prin., Elizabeth, Colo., 1982-84; cons. Colo. Dept. Edn., 1984-85; prin. elem. sch. Summit County Sch. Dist., Frisco, Colo., 1985—; mem. steering com. tchr./student tchr. evaluation project Mellon Found., 1984-85; mem. tchr. edn. adv. council Loretto Heights Coll., 1985—. Mem. Colo. Comprehensive Personnel Planning Com., 1977-82; mem. bd. dirs. MacIntosh Acad. for Gifted Children, Denver, 1977-79; mem. adv. council Denver Public Schs. Spl. Edn. Com., 1978-79, Colo. Title IV Council, 1980-82; acting co-chmn. Colo. Coalition for Edn. Handicapped Persons, Denver, 1978-79; pres. bd. dirs. Found. Exceptional Children, Reston, Va., 1980-81, bd. dirs., 1976-82; pres. bd. dirs. N.E. Colo. Services for Handicapped, Inc., Sterling, 1981-82; mem. Denver City and County Commn. Disabled, 1978-79; mem. coordinating com. Council of Adminstrs., 1982-84; mem. Colo. Data Acquisition Reporting and Utilization Com., 1983-84. Recipient Ann. Service award Colo. Fedn. Council Exceptional Children, 1981; Office of Edn. fellow San Francisco State Coll., 1967-68, grad. research fellow U. No. Colo., 1972-74. Mem. Colo. Assn. Sch. Execs., Nat. Assn. Elem. Sch. Prins., Council Adminstrs. Spl. Edn. Colo., Rural Edn. Assn., Am. Assn. Mental Deficiency, Colo. Assn. Gifted and Talented. Republican. Methodist. Club: Order of Eastern Star. Contbr. articles and ednl. minicourses to profl. publs. Home: 2443 S Colorado Blvd Apt 227 Denver CO 80222 Office: Summit County Pub Schs Frisco CO 80443

GIBSON, IRMA JEAN HILL, educator; b. Jacksonville, Fla., July 5, 1944; d. Daniel Willie and Thelma Lenore (Curry) Hill; m. Eddie Lee Gibson, May 22, 1981. B.S. in Soc. Sci., Fla. Meml. Coll., 1967; M.A. in Edn., Fla. A & M U., 1972. Cert. elem. tchr., Fla., Tex. Tchr., Alta Vista Elem. Sch., Polk County, Fla., 1968-70, Cedar Hills Elem. Sch., Jacksonville, 1970-72, Oak Hill Elem. Sch., Jacksonville, 1972-79, Dodson Elem. Sch., Houston, 1979—; cons. legis. publs. Parent Tchr. Orgn., Oak Hill Elem. Sch., 1972-79. Sponsor, Oak Hill Patrols, Jacksonville, 1973-79; mem. tchr. eval. com. Duval Bd. Pub. Instrn., Jacksonville, 1979. Named Tchr. of Yr., Oak Hill Elem. Sch., 1975, 77, 79. Mem. Zeta Phi Beta Phi Delta Kappa (Tchr. of Yr. 1979). Democrat. Baptist. Home: 3223 Woodmont Dr Houston TX 77045 Office: Dodson Elem Sch 1808 Sampson St Houston TX 77003

GIBSON, JACQUELYN JORDAN, electrologist; b. Phila., Aug. 2, 1924; d. Ira Andrew and Emma Ercyal (Brickley) Jordan; grad. Kree Electrologist Sch., 1946; m. Morgan Stone Gibson, Mar. 9, 1946; children—Bruce Morgan, Ronald Wayne, Jeffrey Jordan. Prin., Jacquelyn Jordan Gibson, electrologist, Balt., 1946-61, Salisbury, Md., 1961-81, Jupiter, Fla., 1982—. Numerous ch. activities including adminstrv. bd., sec. Council on Ministries, Altar Guild and Missionary Circle; vol. worker Bd. Elections; vol., mem. jr. bd. Peninsula Sem. and Hosp. Mem. Md. Electrolysis Assn. (charter), C. of C., Jupiter-Tequesta Bus. and Profl. Women. Republican. Methodist. Clubs: Elks Aux., Soroptimists (past chpt. pres., past chpt. treas.), Women of Moose. Home: 102 E Beverly Rd Jupiter FL 33458 Office: 390 Tequesta Dr Tequesta FL

GIBSON, MARJORIE BROOKS, mortgage banking executive; b. Durham, N.C., Dec. 23, 1948; d. Walker Saunders and Rebecca Lucinda (Andrews) Brooks; m. Philip Osborne, Mar. 1969 (div. 1973); 1 child, April; m. John F. Gibson, Aug. 20, 1973 (div. Aug. 1978); 1 child, Stacie. Student pub. schs., Silver Spring, Md. Sec. Weaver Bros. Inc., Washington, 1966-70; exec. sec. Office of Gustave Ring, Washington, 1970-73; real estate sales agt. Flaherty & Wing, Kensington, Md., 1975-76; mortgage counselor, customer service supr., loan examiner, loan closing supr., asst. sec. Weaver Bros. Inc., Chevy Chase, Md., 1977-84; loan officer, br. mgr. GMAC Mortgage Corp., Rockville, Md., 1984—; real estate agt. Frazee Realtors, Rockville, 1977—. Mem. Montgomery County Bd. Realtors (assoc.), Mortgage Bankers Assn. Republican. Mem. Christian Ch. (Disciples of Christ). Office: GMAC Mortgage Corp 11400 Rockville Pike Rockville MD 20853

GIBSON, MARTHA ALTHOUSE, savings and loan association executive; b. Orangeburg, S.C., Apr. 6, 1943; d. Woodrow Elie and Pearl (Wall) Rudd; student Patricia Stevens Finishing Coll., 1962, U. N.C., 1965, Foot Hill Coll., 1972; 1 dau., Robin Marie Althouse; m. Marvin McCall Gibson, 1982. With Chevy Chase Savs. Bank, Md., 1972-83 v.p., controller, 1977-83; sec.-treas. Glade Drive Devel. Co., North Ode Street Devel. Co., 1981-83; exec. v.p. Kingsley Savs. Assn., Gaithersburg, Md., 1983-84; asst. sec. Manor Investment Co. Mem. Fin. Mgrs. Soc. Savs. Instns. (editor chpt. newsletters, chmn. chpt. coms., nat. award of excellence 1977-78, treas. 1981-82, sec. 1982-83, v.p. 1983-84), Nat. Savs. and Loan League, Md. Savs. and Loan League, Women's Network, Republican. Clubs: Jr. Women's, Innerwheel of Greater Washington, Capital Speakers. Editor Inner Wheel Newsletter, 1984-85. Home: 9000 Clewerwall Dr Bethesda MD 20817

GIBSON, MARY ELIZABETH (PSEUDONYM MARALEE G. DAVIS), poet, novelist; b. Springfield, Mass., Jan. 9, 1924; d. Francis Clarence and Beatrice Grace (Tait) Gagnier; student, Bay Path Jr. Coll., 1941-42, Greenfield Community Coll., 1984—; m. Francis Charles Davis, July 18, 1942 (div. Aug. 1964); children—Beverley Tait Davis Clarke, Susan Olds Davis English, Maralee Ruth Dana Davis Chris; m. 2d, David Joel Thibault, Nov. 9, 1964 (div. Oct. 1967); m. 3d, William Carter Gibson, Jan. 21, 1970. Co-owner dairy farm, Amherst, Mass., 1951-60; with Amherst Jour., 1952-54; with Sta. WHMP, Northampton, Mass., intermittently 1955-73; owner Maralee G. Davis, real estate, Amherst, 1956-58; with Sta. WHYN Radio-TV, Springfield, Mass., intermittently, 1958-60; breeder Gt. Pyrenees dogs, 1959-62, Gt. Harlequin Danes, 1984; with Greenfield (Mass.) Recorder, 1958-62, WTTT, Amherst, 1963-64; free-lance advt. and writing, 1963—; asst. editor Sportsman's News, Northampton, 1963-64; founder, co-owner, pres., treas. Amherst Employment Service, 1968-69; asso. Heiser Real Estate, Northampton, 1973-74. Guest poet Sta. WMUL-TV series on poets for ednl. TV, 1971; guest poet and speaker Vt. Writers Seminar, U. Vt., 1970, Morris Harvey Coll., 1970-71. Treas. Hillcrest Cemetery Marker Service, Springfield, 1972—; bd. dirs. Franklin/Hampshire (Mass.) Community Mental Health Center, 1975-76; coordinator Sunrise art seminars, 1977. Recipient awards for poems Nat. Fedn. Poetry Socs., 1970; citation World Poetry Soc., 1970; citation Shenandoah Valley Acad. Lit., 1978, 79. Mem. N.H., W. Va. poetry socs., Martin County (Fla.) Writers Group, Poetry Soc. Am. Author: (under pseudonym Maralee G. Davis) Soliloquy's Virgin (poetry), 1964; The Valley of Self (poetry), 1969. Contbr. poems to various anthologies and lit. publs. including The Poetry Rev. Home: PO Box 301 North Amherst MA 01059

GIBSON, MELVERENE STEVENS, consultant; b. Bivins, Tex., Dec. 27, 1937; d. Muncie and Essie (Lavert) Stevens; m. Carroll Raymond Gibson, Feb. 12, 1962 (div. 1969); children—Denise Carol, Raymond LaVert. Student Griffin-Murphy Bus. Coll., Seattle, 1955-58, LaSalle Extension U., Chgo., 1967. Dressmaking instr., Seattle, 1960-62; typing instr., Seattle, 1960-62; owner, v.p. Carmark Transp. Co., Chgo., 1966-69; exec. sec. Am. Bar Endowment Orgn., Chgo., 1968-70, asst. adminstr., 1970-77, dep. dir., 1977-82; ins. cons. Eula Yates Agy., Chgo., 1982-83; adminstrv. mgr. Morton B. Stone & Assocs., Chgo., 1983-84; ins. agt. Equitable Assurance Soc. U.S., also Pioneer Life Ins. Co. of Ill., 1983-84; adminstr. Mack and Parker, Inc., Chgo., 1984; cons. Profl. Services Group, Chgo., 1984—; dir. Marcy-Newberry Agy., Chgo., 1979-80, sec. bd. dirs., 1980. Recipient Kizzy award for outstanding accomplishments personifying black women, 1979. Mem. Nat. Assn. Female Execs. Democrat. Home: 1616 E 50th Pl Apt 4E Chicago IL 60615 Office: Better Boys Found 407 S Dearborn St Chicago IL 60605

GIBSON, SAMANTHA LIVINGSTON, preventive maintenance specialist; b. Mesa, Ariz., Dec. 9, 1941; d. Burr and Gwendolyn (Porter) Webb; student No. Ariz. U., 1961, Coll. San Mateo, 1969, U. Ariz., 1977; m. David Kent Gibson, June 2, 1981; children by previous marriage—Laurence, Donald and Danielle Livingston. Pub. relations ofcl. Sahara Tahoe Hotel, Stateline, Nev., 1969-71; with South Lake Tahoe C. of C., 1972-75; mgr. Winslow C. of C., Ariz. 1975-76; preventive maintenance analyst S.W. Forest Industries, Snowflake, Ariz., 1976-82; cons. and writer. Mem. Snowflake Planning and Zoning Commn., 1977-78. Mem. Paper Industry Mgmt. Assn., Ariz. Assn. Indsl. Devel. (dir. 1975-76), Indsl. Devel. Endeavor Assn. (dir. 1975-76), Snowflake-Taylor C. of C. Republican. Research on trending in vibration analysis, analyzing mech. problems in rotating equipment. Home and Office: PO Box 997 Snowflake AZ 85937

GIBSON, TAMMY J., nurse; b. Laurel, Miss., Mar. 24, 1961; d. Edward Lewis and Doris Jean (Miller) Lowe; m. Anthony Kevin Gibson, July 11, 1982. A.A.S., Miss. Gulf Coast Jr. Coll., 1979-83; R.N., Singing River Hosp., 1985. Emergency room clk. Singing River Hosp., Pascagoula, Miss., 1978-79, nurse med. ICU, 1983—; with Hallmark Cards, 1978-83. Mem. Miss. Nurses Assn. Democrat. Baptist. Lodge: Order of Eastern Star. Home: 3501 Burroughs Ave Pascagoula MS 39567

GIBSON, VERNA KAYE, retail company executive; b. Charleston, W.Va., June 22, 1942; d. Carl W. LeMasters and Virginia E. (Meyers) LeMasters; m. James E. Gibson, Apr. 28, 1962; children—Kelly, Elizabeth. Grad with honors in fashion mktg. and retailing, Marshall U., Huntington, W.Va., 1962. Buyer, merchandise mgr. Smart Shops, Huntington, W.Va., 1965-71; trainee to asst. buyer Limited Stores, Inc., Columbus, Ohio, 1971-72, assoc. buyer to buyer, 1972-77, div. mdse. mgr., 1977-79, v.p. sportswear, 1979-82, exec. v.p. gen., mdse. mgr., 1982—, pres., 1985—; dir. Midland Mutual Life Ins. Co., Columbus, J. Duffy's. Recipient Harry L. Wexner award Limited Stores, Inc., 1983. Office: Limited Stores Inc 1 Limited Pkwy Columbus OH 43230

GIDDENS, MARY ELIZABETH, social service administrator; b. Miami, Fla., Sept. 9, 1948; d. William Ellis and Letty Josephine (Roberts) Giddens. A.A., S. Ga. Coll., 1970; B.S. in Edn., Ga. So. Coll., 1972. Tchr., Emanuel County Pub. Schs., Swainboro, Ga., 1970-71, Washington County Pub. Schs., Sandersville, Ga., 1971-72; supr. Polk Transp. Dept. (Fla.), 1972-78; dir. Student Traffic Safety, Lakeland, Fla., 1978-80; asst. dir. Fellowship Dining, Lakeland, 1980—; cattle rancher, Immokalee, Fla., 1982—. Chmn. Sr. Citizen's Day, Fla. Citrus Festival, 1977-78, Polk County Health-O-Rama, 1977; mem. adv. bd. scholarship house West Area Adult Sch., Polk County, 1983—; chmn. task force Bus. and Profl. Women's Fla. Edn. Found., 1983-85; mem. youth adv. council Heartland Employment and Tng. Adminstrn., 1978-80; bd. dirs. Coalition for Children and Youth, Polk County, 1978-80, Spouse Abuse Polk County, 1975-77; bd. dirs. Rape Crisis Ctr., Polk County, 1975-82, pres. bd., 1978-80; mem. Community Services Council Polk County, 1974-84, bd. dirs., 1982-83, pres., 1978, Disting. Service award, 1980. Mem. Bus. and Profl. Women (pres. Lakeland club 1983-84, Fla. Young Career Woman award 1976, state young careerist chmn. 1978, state lobbyist 1979-81, state legislation chmn. 1979-81, state program com. 1983-84, state chmn. future planning com. 1984-86). Democrat. Home: 4108 Wellington Dr Lakeland FL 33803 Office: Fellowship Dining 807 E Palmetto St Lakeland FL 33801

GIDDENS, ZELMA KIRK, broadcasting co. exec.; b. Lafayette, Ala.; d. James William and Eunice (Rice) Kirk; grad. So. Union Jr. Coll., 1932; student Auburn U., 1934-35; m. Kenneth R. Giddens, May 19, 1934; children—Annsley Giddens Green, Therese Giddens Greer, Sara Kay. With Sta. WKRG-AM, 1947-55; with Sta. WKRG-AM-FM-TV, Mobile, Ala., 1955—, pres., 1969—. Mem. English Speaking Union (v.p. 1964-76), Smithsonian Assos., Mobile Art Assn., Mobile C. of C.s Lion Aux., Nat. Press Club, Am. Newspaper Women's Assn. Home: 2555 N Delwood Dr Mobile AL 36606 Office: 555 Broadcast Dr Mobile AL 36616

GIDDINGS, LUCILLE CASSELL, nurse; b. Port Chester, N.Y., Jan. 30, 1947; d. Curtis Emmitt and Rose (Lucente) Cassell; R.N., St. Clare's Hosp., N.Y.C., 1969; B.A., Coll. Mt. St. Vincent, Bronx, N.Y., 1979; M.P.A., NYU, 1982; m. William Alfred Giddings, Apr. 2, 1977. Staff nurse hosps. in N.Y. State, 1969-71; elem. sch. nurse Port Chester-Rye Town Bd. Edn., 1971-82; dir. interdepartmental services Our Lady of Mercy Hosp. Med. Center, Bronx, N.Y., 1982-83, dir. admissions, 1984-86, asst. adminstr., 1986—; health services mgmt. cons. New Dimensions in Leadership, Inc., 1983-84; chmn. Port Chester br. ARC, 1978. Recipient Rev. Mother Jean Marie award, 1969. Mem. Am. Hosp. Assn., Am. Soc. Public Adminstrn., Nat. Assn. Female Execs., Am. Coll. Hosp. Adminstrs., NYU Alumni Assn., Coll. Mt. St. Vincent Alumni Assn. Home: 56 Hastings Ave Groton-on-Hudson NY 10520 Office: 600 E 233d St Bronx NY 10466

GIDEON, MIRIAM, composer; b. Greeley, Colo., Oct. 23, 1906; d. Abram and Henrietta (Shoninger) Gideon; B.A., Boston U., 1926; M.A., Columbia U., 1946; D.Sacred Music, Jewish Theol. Sem., 1970, D. Music (hon.), 1981; D.H.L. (hon.), Bklyn. Coll. CUNY, 1983; m. Frederic Ewen, 1949. Music faculty Bklyn. Coll., 1944-54, Coll. City N.Y., 1947-55, Cantors Inst., Jewish Theol. Sem., 1955—, Manhattan Sch. Music, N.Y.C., 1967—; vis prof. music City Coll., CUNY, 1971-76, prof. emeritus, 1976—; works performed in Europe, Far East, U.S. and S.Am. by Internat. Soc. Contemporary Music, League Composers, London, Tokyo, Zurich symphony orchs. Recipient Bloch prize for choral work, 1948; Nat. Fedn. Music Clubs and ASCAP award for symphonic music, 1969; Nat. Endowment of Arts grantee, 1974; commd. Library of Congress, 1979. Mem. Am. Acad. Arts and Letters, Am. Composers Alliance (bd. govs.), Internat. Soc. Contemporary Music (gov.). Composer: Fortunato (opera); Symphonia Brevis, Lyric Piece for Strings; String Quartet; Wood-wind Quartet; Viola Sonata; chamber settings of Hound of Heaven, Shakespeare Sonnets, Millay Sonnets; Biblical Masks; Cello Sonata; Songs of Voyage; The Condemned Playground; Questions on Nature; The Habitable Earth (cantata); Spiritual Madrigals; Rhymes from the Hill; Seasons of Time; Two Sacred Services; Fantasy on Irish Folk Motives; Nocturnes; Sonata for Piano; Songs of Youth and Madness, on Poems of Hölderlin for voice and orch.; Voices from Elysium; Spirit Above the Dust; Trio for Clarinet, Cello, and Piano; Suite for Clarinet or Bassoon and Piano; 2 song cycles on Hebrew poetry; Where Wild Carnations Blow (cantata); Wing'd Hour; orchestral, chamber, choral works recorded Westminster, Composers Recs., Inc., RCA Victor Records, Desto Records, Golden Crest Records, Serenus Records, New World Records. Home: 410 Central Park W New York NY 10025

GIDWITZ, BETSY R., aeronautics and political science educator, consultant; b. Chgo., Nov. 13, 1940; d. Joseph L. and Emily (Klein) G. B.A., U. Iowa, 1962; M.Ed., Boston U., 1965; Ph.D., U. Wash., 1976. Lectr. aeros. and astronautics, also polit. sci. MIT, 1974—; cons. in air transport and Soviet Union, Cambridge, 1976—. Author: The Politics of International Air Transport, 1980. Contbr. articles to profl. jours. Trustee Combined Jewish Philanthropies, Boston; mem. exec. bd. Jewish Community Relations Council, Boston; bd. dirs. Action for Soviet Jewry, Waltham, Mass., Union of Council for Soviet Jews, Washington. Mem. Am. Acad. Polit. and Social Sci., Am. Assn. Advancement of Slavic Studies, Am. Polit. Sci. Assn. Home: 975 Memorial Dr Cambridge MA 02138

GIEBEL, SHIRLEY FOSTER, public relations counselor; b. Avon Lake, Iowa, July 12, 1934; d. Darrel W. and Edna M. (Robson) Foster; m. Carl B. Giebel, July 12, 1953 (div. 1970); children—Gregory L., Gina. B.A., U. Mo.-St. Louis, 1975; student U. Mo.-Columbia, 1952-53, Washington U., 1953-54. Vice pres., partner Carl Giebel Landscape Architects and Nurserymen, Inc., Chesterfield, Mo., 1956-70; pub. relations counselor Gary Ferguson Inc., St. Louis, 1972—, partner, treas., 1976—. Bd. dirs. Open Space Council, St. Louis, 1965-68, Logos Sch., St. Louis, 1982—. Curators scholar, U. Mo., 1952. Mem. Advt. Women St. Louis (dir. 1975-76, newsletter editor 1976), Women in Communications (publicity chmn. 1982-83), Nat. Soc. Fund Raising Execs. Republican. Methodist. Home: 4551 McPherson St Saint Louis MO 63108

GIES, CAROL J(EAN), public relations agency executive, consultant; b. Detroit, Jan. 20, 1947; d. Stanley Paul Homer and Jean Rose Homer Turczyn; m. Craig Maurice Gies, Mar. 31, 1966; children—Jeffrey, Maureen. B.S., Wayne State U., 1971, M.A., 1972; M. B.A., Mich. State U., 1985—. Vice pres. civic affairs Detroit Conv. Bur., 1977-79, dir. pub. relations, 1975-77, dir. publs., 1973-75; exec. dir. host com. 1980 Republican Nat. Conv., 1979-80; exec. dir. 1982 Super Bowl Host Com., Detroit, 1981-82; sr. v.p. Anthony M. Franco, Inc., Detroit, 1982—. Bd. dirs. Mich. Thanksgiving Parade Found., Detroit; chmn. communications United Found., Detroit. Recipient Gold Quill award Internat. Assn. Bus. Communicators, 1976, Headliner award Women of Wayne, 1981; Wayne State U. grad. profl. scholar, 1970-71; Mem. Pub. Relations Soc. Am. (accredited 1979, Silver Anvil award 1981), Women in Communications (Clarion award 1977). Clubs: Women's Econ. (bd. dirs., program chmn.), Detroit Econ. Roman Catholic. Office: 400 Renaissance Ctr Suite 600 Detroit MI 48243

GIESSLER, EMILY SWEARINGEN, cosmetics sales ofcl.; b. Fort Wayne, Ind., Oct. 19, 1940; d. Milton Park and Sarah Lucile (Engle) Swearingen; B.A., Tex. Christian U., 1962; M.A., St. Francis Coll., 1966; children by previous marriage—James Hugh Engle, Melinda Sue Engle. Dir. edn. Am. Cancer Soc., Fort Worth, 1963; tchr. North Adams Community Sch., Decatur, Ind., 1963-79; sr. sales dir. Mary Kay Cosmetics Co., Decatur, Ind., 1978—. Treas. 1st United Meth. Ch., Decatur. Mem. Nat. Assn. Female Execs., Internat. Platform Assn., Tri Kappa. Republican. Address: 422 N 3d St Decatur IN 46733

GIEZENTANNER, DORIS PATTON, county official, civic worker; b. Alexander, N.C., Aug. 7, 1927; d. Oscar Jerome and Elizabeth Jane (Hunter) Patton; exec. sec. degree Blanton Bus. Coll., 1946; student U. Tenn., 1947-49; m. John Henry Giezentanner, Jan. 20, 1948; children—Debra Ann, John Henry. Sec., Interagy. Narcotic Squad, 1973-76; mem. Woodfin (N.C.) Bd. Aldermen, 1971-76; commr. Buncombe County, Ashville, N.C., 1976—, vice chmn., 1976—. Vice chmn. Blue Ridge Mental Health Bd.; bd. dirs. U. N.C. at Asheville Found., Western N.C. Health Systems Agy., Caring for Children, N.C. Gov.'s Working Group on Energy, Discovery Asheville; mem. Asheville Community Sch. Bd.; co-chmn. Yr. 2000 Historic Commn.; 2d v.p. Land of Sky Regional Council; mem. study commn. Alternatives for Asheville and Buncombe County; Vice-chmn. Buncombe County Bd. Commrs., 1984-85; mem. legis. study commn. Land of Sky, study commn. Preservation of N.C. Farm Land. Recipient spl. award Blue Ridge Mental Health Bd.; named one of Buncombe County's Outstanding Women, 1981. Mem. N.C. Assn. County Commrs. (dir.), Asheville Bus. and Profl. Womens Club, VFW Aux. Democrat. Baptist. Club: Asheville City. Address: Box 8462 Asheville NC 28804

GIFFEN, SALLIE ANN, university administrator; b. Warren, Pa., May 19, 1940; d. Edgar Louis and Glenna Marie (Tiedgen) G. B.S., U. Ala., 1962; M.B.A., Loyola U., Balt., 1975. Budget analyst U.S. Office Edn., Washington, 1962-68; asst. dean for adminstrn. Boston U., 1968-72; vice chancellor for adminstrv. affairs U. Md.-Balt. County Campus, Catonsville, 1972—. Mem. AAUW, Am. Council on Edn. Home: 1311 Biddle Ct Catonsville MD 21228 Office: Univ Maryland-Baltimore County Campus 925 Administration Bldg Catonsville MD 21228

GIFFIN, MARGARET ETHEL (PEGGY), management consultant; b. Cleve., Aug. 27, 1949; d. Arch Kenneth and Jeanne (Eggleton) G.; B.A. in Psychology, U. Pacific, Stockton, Calif., 1971; M.A. in Psychology, Calif. State U., Long Beach, 1973; Ph.D. in Quantitative Psychology, U. So. Calif., 1984. Psychometrist, Auto Club So. Calif., Los Angeles, 1973-74; dir. Equal Employment Opportunity Compliance Services div. Psychol. Services, Inc., Los Angeles, 1975—; mem. tech. adv. com. on testing Calif. Fair Employment and Housing Commn., 1974—, mem. steering com., 1978—. Mem. Internat. Personnel Mgmt. Assn. Assessment Council, Am. Psychol. Assn., Western Psychol. Assn., Personnel Testing Council So. Calif. (pres. 1980, chmn. bd. dirs. 1982). Club: Athletic (Los Angeles). Home: 330 S Westmoreland Ave Los Angeles CA 90020 Office: 100 W Broadway #100 Glendale CA 91210

GIFFORD, KAREN KOURY, investment banker; b. Hartford, Conn., July 11, 1944; d. Joseph Richard and Mary Margaret (Schwab) Koury; m. James P. Gifford, June 1, 1968. A.B., Smith Coll., 1966. Asst. v.p. First Boston Corp., N.Y.C., 1969-75; treas. Kaiser Found. Med. Care Program, Oakland, Calif., 1975-78; 1st v.p. Blyth Eastman, N.Y.C., 1978-80; mng. dir. Merrill Lynch, N.Y.C., 1980—; dir. Council on Mcpl. Performance, N.Y.C., 1984—; mem. mgmt. adv. group EPA, Washington, 1982-84. Trustee Kingswood-Oxford Sch., West Hartford, Conn., 1984—, Hunter Coll. Sch. Social Work. Club: Princeton (N.Y.C.). Office: Merrill Lynch Capital Markets 165 Broadway New York NY 10080

GIFFUNE, MAGDALENE ANN PONTOLILLO, educator; b. Ilion, N.Y., May 24, 1951; d. Frank Jerome and Frances Mary (Frank) Pontolillo; B.A., Syracuse U., 1973, M.S., 1974; Ed.D., Boston U., 1979; postgrad. Harvard U., 1985-86; m. Frank Paul Giffune, Dec. 28, 1975; children—Paul Vincent, Neille-Ann. Reading tchr. Warwick (N.Y.) Valley Central High Sch., 1974-75, Oriskany (N.Y.) Central High Sch., 1975-76, Seekonk (Mass.) High Sch., 1976-79; dir. fed. project for gifted and talented jr. high students Franklin (Mass.) Jr. High Sch., 1979-83; instructional resource tchr. Foxborough Pub. Schs. (Mass.), 1983-85, acting prin., 1984-85, adminstrv. asst. to supt., 1985—. Mem. Interstate Cert. Team. Mem. Internat. Reading Assn., Mass. Reading Assn., New Eng. Reading Assn., Assn. Supervision and Curriculum Devel., Am. Assn. Sch. Adminstrs., Mass. Assn. Advancement Individual Potential, Mass. Tchrs. Assn., NEA, Delta Kappa Gamma. Roman Catholic. Home: 31 Union St Foxborough MA 02035 Office: Igo Ctr Foxborough MA 02035

GIGANTINO, BETTY GENE, industrial educator; b. Bakersfield, Calif., Aug. 30, 1945; d. Roosevelt and Leona (Wilson) Gulley; m. Leonardo James Gigantino, Jan. 2, 1982; children—Terrence, Rachelle. Lic. Vocat. Nurse, Laney Coll., 1969; A.A., Contra Costa Coll., 1972; B.A., U. Calif.-Hayward, 1973. Tng. developer Pacific Telephone Co., San Francisco, 1966-77; tchr. Hayward Elem. Sch., 1973; postal clk. U.S. Post Office, Oakland, Calif., 1975; instr., developer tech. edn., tng. cons. Bell System Ctr., Lisle, Ill., 1977-79; instructional technologist AT&T, Altamonte Springs, Fla., 1984—. Author: (with others) Design/Development Standards, 1985; also tech. tng. courses, articles. Active Pioneers' Beep Ball for Blind, San Francisco, 1972; counselor AT&T Pioneers Spl. Olympics, Morristown, N.J., 1982; active Deltona Civic Assn., Fla., 1985—. Recipient cert. Spl. Olympic Com., Morristown, 1982; plaque, mktg. customer edn. dept. AT&T, N.J., 1983. Mem. Nat. Soc. for Performance Instrn., Am. Soc. for Tng. and Devel., Am. Express Centurion Council. Roman Catholic. Club: N.J. Ski (Basking Ridge). Avocations: golf, skiing.

GIGUIERE, MICHELE LOUISE, lawyer; b. Spokane, Feb. 11, 1944; d. Karl Earl and Mildred Elaine (Phillips) G.; B.A., U. Pacific, 1965; M.S., U. So. Calif., 1969; J.D., Lincoln Law Sch., 1980. Exec. trainee J.W. Robinson Co., Los Angeles, 1965-66; tchr. Novato (Calif.) Unified Sch. Dist., 1967-78; asst. dept. mgr. Emporium, San Rafael, Calif., 1970-74; admitted to Calif. bar, 1980, since practiced in Citrus Heights and Fair Oaks, Calif. Mem. ABA, State Bar Calif., Sacramento County Bar Assn., Calif. Women Lawyers, Women Lawyers Sacramento, LWV. Democrat. Presbyterian. Clubs: Network. Home: 4824 Minnesota Ave Fair Oaks CA 95628 Office: 6359 Auburn Blvd Citrus Heights CA 95621

GIKAS, CAROL SOMMERFELDT, museum director. Exec. dir. La. Arts and Sci. Ctr., Baton Rouge. Office: La Arts and Sci Ctr PO Box 3373 Baton Rouge LA 70821*

GILARDI, ANGELINA ANTOINETTE, real estate broker; b. Chgo., Aug. 9, 1956; d. Richard and Arcangela (Carparelli) G.; Grad., Ill. Real Estate Acad., Oak Lawn, 1976. Pvt. sec. Century 21-Mark Real Estate, Burbank, Ill., 1973-78, exec. dir., broker, 1978—; pvt. sec. Greene Internat., Chgo., 1974-77. Contbr. in field. Mem. Ill. Assn. Realtors (recipient Pres. Club Gold, Silver and Bronze Life award 1982), Southwest Suburban Bd. Realtors. Democrat. Roman Catholic. Office: Century 21-Mark Realty 8520 S Cicero Ave Burbank IL 60459

GILBERT, ALMA MAGGIORE, broadcasting exec.; b. Canton, Ohio; d. Vincent Dominick and Florence Antoinette (Manack) Maggiore; student pvt. sch., Canton, Ohio; m. Richard B. Gilbert, July 17, 1953; 1 son, Gary Richard. Dir., sec. Ariz. Aircasters, Inc., Scottsdale Broadcasting Co., 1955-58; program dir. Sta. KOPK, Scottsdale, Ariz., 1956-58; dir., sec. No. Ariz. Aircasters, Inc., 1957-59; program dir. Sta. KZOK, Prescott, Ariz., 1957-59; dir., v.p., sec. KYND Radio Corp., program dir. Sta. KYND, Tempe, Ariz., 1960-66; dir., v.p., sec. Aircasters, Inc., Scottsdale, Ariz., 1966-82; dir., v.p., sec. Ariz. Communications Corp., program dir. Sta. KXTC, Glendale/Phoenix, 1968-78; pres. Sta. KQST, Sedona, Ariz., 1982—; pres. Am. Aircasting Corp., Scottsdale, 1979—. Home and Office: Box 182 Scottsdale AZ 85252

GILBERT, ANN, advertising executive; b. Nashville, Mar. 24, 1944; d. Louis and Eleanore (Herts) Hersh; m. Frank Brandeis Gilbert, Apr. 8, 1973. B.A., U. Pa., 1966; postgrad. Temple U., 1968-70. Dir. lang. ctr. Chilton Books, Phila., 1966-68; sales promotion adminstr. Am. Foresight, Phila., 1968-69; advt. and sales promotion adminstr. Provident Mutual, Phila., 1969-73; communications specialist MONY, N.Y.C., 1974-75; v.p. mktg. Bankers Security Life, Washington, 1975-82; pres. Ann Gilbert Assocs., Chevy Chase, Md., 1982—. Instr. mktg., public relations, advt. Am. U., 1983—, instr. mktg. George Washington U., 1982-84. Bd. dir. Wider Opportunities for Women, Washington, 1983—. Mem. Women in Advt. and Mktg. (bd. dirs. 1980—, past pres., founder), Am. Mktg. Assn. Recipient Bronze plaque Fin. World, 1984. Avocations: travel; tennis. Home: 4701 Willard Ave #906 Chevy Chase MD 20815

GILBERT, ANNE MARIE BERTHE, writer; b. Paris, Oct. 31, 1921; came to U.S., 1946; d. Andre Louis and Marie Louise (Tribe) Lavoisot Rahou dit Roanne; stepdau. Pierre Renoir; m. Harry Edwin, May 5, 1945 (dec. Feb. 1972); children—Richard (dec.), Patricia, Bettina, Sabina. Student Lycee Maintenon, Fontainellean, 1937, Paris Conservatory, 1937, 40. Writer (movies) Le duchesse de Langeais, Les anges de la Mint, La Marseirlaire. Republican. Roman Catholic. Club: S' Cloud Golf (Paris); Everglades, Palm Beach Polo and Country (Palm Beach, Fla.). Avocations: swimming; riding; bicycling. Home: 13334 Polo Club Rd West Palm Beach FL 33414 also 8 Rue d'Artois Paris 75008 France

GILBERT, CAROL LYNN, librarian, educator; b. Chico, Calif., Sept. 19, 1951; d. Richard Perry and Emma L. (Knecht) Timmons. B.A. with honors, Calif. State U., Sacramento, 1978, postgrad., 1978-81; M.L.S. with honors, San Jose State U., 1983. Book repairer Calif. State U., Sacramento, 1979, library asst., 1979-80, reference asst., 1980-82, asst. librarian, 1983-85; collection devel. librarian Solano County, Fairfield, Calif., 1983-84; field services librarian Braille and Talking Book Library, Calif. State Library, 1984—; pres. Library Staff Assn., Calif. State U., Sacramento, 1979-80, library staff ombudsman, 1980-81. Compiler: Index to the Chicano Library Serials Set on Microfilm, 1982; Art History: A Selected Bibliography, 1983; book reviewer Lector, 1983-85. Library staff rep. Calif. State Employees Assn., Sacramento, 1980. Mem. ALA, Calif. Library Assn. Office: Calif State Library 600 Broadway Sacramento CA 95818

GILBERT, DIANA ZAJA, word processing executive; b. Hammond, Ind., Mar. 18, 1955; d. Clifford Frances and Corinthy Lucille (Kerr) Zaja; m. David Ellis Gilbert, Dec. 6, 1975; 1 son, Kyle Ellis. B.A., Purdue U., 1979. Receptionist, ABA, Chgo., 1973-75, sec. word processing, 1975-78, supr. word processing, 1978-81, dir. word processing, 1981—; council mem. client and adv. Norrell Temporary Service, Chgo., 1984; speaker, cons. Cahner's Exposition Group, 1983-84. Contbr. articles to profl. jours. Vol. women's bd. No. Ind. Arts Assn., Munster, 1982—. Mem. Assn. Info. System Profls. Democrat. Home: 8620 Greenwood St Munster IN 46321 Office: ABA 750 N Lake Shore Dr Chicago IL 60611

GILBERT, DIANE CHRISTINE, hospital administrator; b. Springfield, Mass., Apr. 10, 1945; d. Theodor Geisel and Dorothy Jean (Preston) Wallace m. Richard Barry Gilbert, June 27, 1970. A.B. in Govt., Bates Coll., 1967; postgrad. in managerial acctg. MIT, 1967. Mgmt. intern NASA Electronics Research Center, Cambridge, Mass., 1967-68, adminstrv. office, 1968-70; exec. asst. endocrine unit Mass. Gen. Hosp., Boston, 1972-81, asst. to chief medicine, 1981—; pvt. fin. mgr. Windham, N.H., 1979—. Active local community affairs. Republican. Office: Mass Gen Hosp Dept Medicine Fruit St Boston MA 02114

GILBERT, EDES POWELL, school administrator, educator; b. Bklyn., Mar. 25, 1932; d. Talcott Williams Powell and Helen Ann (Ranney) Anderson; m. Rexford Wilson, Aug. 18, 1954 (div. 1976); children—Timothy Rexford, Christopher Lawrence, Sarah Edes; m. Peter Gilbert, July 2, 1980. A.B., Vassar Coll., 1953; M.Ed., Lesley Coll., 1970. Cert. tchr., N.Y., Mass. Tchr. Tenacre Country Day Sch., Wellesley, Mass., 1966-70; dir. admissions, dir. studies Dexter Sch., Brookline, Mass., 1970-75; headmistress Mary Inst., St. Louis, 1976-83, Spence Sch., N.Y.C., 1983—. Trustee St. Louis Repertory Theatre, 1980-83; bd. dirs. Ensemble Studio Theatre, N.Y.C., 1985, St. David's Sch., N.Y.C., 1984—. Mem. Nat. Assn. Prin. Schs. for Girls, Headmasters Assn., Headmistresses of East, Nat. Assn. Ind. Schs. (v.p. 1983—). Democrat. Episcopalian. Avocations: travel; reading; walking; theatre. Office: Spence Sch 22 E 91st St New York NY 10138

GILBERT, HEATHER CAMPBELL, manufacturing company executive; b. Mt. Vernon, N.Y., Nov. 20, 1944; d. Ronald Ogston and Mary Lodivia (Campbell) G.; B.S. in Math. (Nat. Merit scholar), Stanford U., 1967; M.S. in Computer Sci. (NSF fellow), U. Wis., 1969. With Burroughs Corp., 1969-82, sr. mgmt. systems analyst, Detroit, 1975-77, mgr. mgmt. systems activity, Pasadena, Calif., 1977-82; mgr. software product mgmt. Logical Data Mgmt. Inc., Covina, Calif., 1982-83, dir. mktg., 1983, v.p. bus. devel., 1983-84, v.p. profl. services, 1984-85; mgr. software devel. Burroughs Corp., Lake Forest, Calif., 1985—. Mem. Assn. Computing Machinery, Am. Product and Inventory Control Soc., Stanford U. Alumni Assn. (life), Stanford Profl. Women Los Angeles County (pres. 1982-83), Nat. Assn. Female Execs., Town Hall. Republican. Home: 2020 Dacian Dr Walnut CA 91789 Office: 3 Burroughs Corp 19 Morgan St Lake Forest CA 92718

GILBERT, JOAN STULMAN, petroleum company public relations executive; b. N.Y.C., May 10, 1934; m. Phil E. Gilbert, Jr., Oct. 6, 1968; children—Linda Cooper, Dana, Patricia. Student Conn. Coll. for Women, 1951-53. Br. coordinator Vol. Service bur., Westchester, N.Y., 1970-72; dir. pub. relations Westchester Lighthouse, 1972-76; exec. dir. Westchester Heart Assn., 1976-77; community relations mgr. Texaco Inc., White Plains, N.Y., 1977—. Bd. dirs. Lend-A-Hand, Coll. Careers, Teatown Lake Reservation, Westchester Council for Arts, Youth Counseling League, pvt. industry council Westchester Coalition, Westchester County Med. Ctr., United Way of Westchester, Westchester Lighthouse; mem. pres.'s adv. council Coll. of New Rochelle, adv. council Westchester Community Coll.; former trustee Choate-Rosemary Hall, Wallingford, Conn. Mem. Pub. Relations Soc. Am. (pres. chpt. 1977), Women in Communications, Westchester County Assn. Home: The Croft Spring Valley Rd Ossining NY 10562 Office: 2000 Westchester Ave White Plains NY 10650

GILBERT, JUDITH ARLENE, lawyer; b. Los Angeles, Jan. 9, 1946; d. Beril B. and Dorothy Marilyn (Stern) Gilbert; student U. Calif.-Berkeley, 1963-64; B.A., UCLA, 1967; J.D., Harvard U., 1970; m. Joel Philip Schiff; children—Lauren Michelle Schiff, Jared Daniel Schiff. Bar: Calif. 1971. Practiced in Los Angeles; assoc. Rosenfeld, Meyer & Susman, 1970-72, Quittner, Stutman, Treister & Glatt, Los Angeles, 1972-73, Abeles & Markowitz, and predecessor, Beverly Hills, Calif., 1974-76; sr. counsel Bank of Am., 1977—; judge protem Beverly Hills Small Claims Ct., also Los Angeles County Mcpl. Ct., Los Angeles Superior Ct.; mem. arbitration panel Calif. Superior Ct.; atty. client disputes mediator, mem. arbitration com. Los Angeles Superior Ct. Mem. Los Angeles County Com. Human Resources; active Girl Scouts U.S.A., Cystic Fibrosis, City of Hope. Mem. Beverly Hills Bar Assn. (pres. 1985-86), Women Lawyers Assn. Los Angeles, Calif. Women Lawyers, Los Angeles County Bar Assn., Calif. State Bar (conv. del. 1975—), Thespians, Collegian Singers, Brick Muller Soc., Internat. Law Club (social co-chmn. 1970), UCLA Alumni Assn. (adv. com., scholarship com.), Tower and Flame, Phi Beta Kappa, Gamma Delta Epsilon, Pi Gamma Mu, Omega Delta Epsilon, Phi Chi Theta, Delta Phi Epsilon. Clubs: Merchants, Sutherland (sec.-treas. 1968-69). Office: Bank of America Dept 4017 555 S Flower St Los Angeles CA 90071

GILBERT, LUCIA ALBINO, psychology educator; b. Bklyn., July 27, 1941; d. William V. and Carmelina (Cutro) Albino; m. John Carl Gilbert, Dec. 18, 1965; 1 child, Melissa Carlotta. B.A., Wells Coll., 1963; M.S., Yale U., 1964; Ph.D., U. Tex., 1974. Lic. psychologist, Tex. Supr. research info. G.S. Gilmore Research Lab., New Haven, 1964-67; tchr. St. Stephen Sch., Austin, Tex., 1967-69; asst. prof. Iowa State U., Ames, 1974-76; asst. prof. U. Tex., Austin, 1976-81, assoc. prof., 1981-86, prof., 1986—. Author: Men in Dual Career Families, 1985; editor spl. issue Parenting, Dual Career Families. Recipient Excellence in Teaching award U. Tex., 1981-86. Fellow Am. Psychol. Assn. (rep. council 1980-83, 86-89); mem. Assn. Women in Psychology, Tex. Psychol. Assn. Avocations: swimming; progressive country music; ecology. Home: 4402 Balcones Dr Austin TX 78731 Office: U Tex Austin TX 78712

GILBERT, MYRNA JEAN, anthropologist; b. Boulder, Colo; d. Albert L. and Elizabeth (Goggin) Hall; B.A., Ariz. State U., 1957, M.A. in English, 1964; M.A. in Anthropology, U. Calif., Santa Barbara, 1974, Ph.D., 1980; m. Richard Leon Gilbert, Mar. 24, 1956 (dec. 1979); 1 dau., Lisa Anne. Research asso. Social Process Research Inst., U. Calif., Santa Barbara, 1974-76, Spanish Speaking Mental Health Research Inst., UCLA, 1976-78, scholar in Hispanic alcohol studies, 1984—; research project dir. Centro Familiar de Santa Barbara, 1978-81; program officer founds. and corp. relations Direct Relief Internat., Santa Barbara, 1981-84; research cons. Calif. Office Alcohol and Drug Programs, Sacramento, 1976-77, Calif. Commn. on Alcoholism for Spanish Speaking, Sacramento, 1978, Nat. Inst. on Drug Abuse, 1985—; researcher kinship networks in Mex., 1973-74. Bd. dirs. Zona Seca, 1984—, Santa Barbara Family Care Center, 1972-75, 82-84, Santa Barbara Mus. Art, 1970-72. NIMH grantee, 1978-81, 82-84; Nat. Inst. Alcohol and Alcohol Abuse grantee, 1982-84, also scholar in Hispanic alcohol studies; ; Office Child Devel. grantee, 1976-78. Mem. Am. Anthrop. Assn., Soc. Applied Anthropology, Santa Barbara Mus. Art (pres. docent council 1970-72). Contbr. articles on research in Hispanic communities, families and substance abuse to profl. jours. Home: 5254 Calle Morelia Santa Barbara CA 93111 Office: UCLA Spanish Speaking Mental Health Research Ctr Los Angeles CA 90024

GILBERT, PHYLLIS JO, dental educator; b. Mpls., Jan. 25, 1944; d. Philip Rod and Josephine Elsie (Korinek) Wicklund; m. Richard Earl Gilbert, Sept. 17, 1966; children—Scott Richard, Nicole Susan. B.S. cum laude in Dental Assisting Edn., U. Minn., 1981. Cert. dental asst., registered dental asst. Dental asst., office mgr. Dr. Ralph R. Nielson, Mpls., 1963-71; dental assisting instr. North Suburban Hennepin County Vocat. Sch., Mpls., 1971-73, Normandale Community Coll., 1976-78, 81—; dir. Mpls. Vocat. Inst., 1981—, China-U.S. Sci. Exchanges, Detroit, 1982-85. Contbr. articles to dental jours. Author, course curriculum Dental Office Mgr., 1983. Leader, first group of dental assts. to Peoples Republic China, 1982, returned to China with dental delegation, 1984. Mem. Am. Dental Assts. (chmn. membership com. 1982—, most valuable state member award, 1982), Minn. Educators of Dental Assts., Minn. Dental Assts. Assn. (pres. 1984-86), Mpls. Dental Assts. Soc. (pres. 1967-68). Republican. Lutheran. Clubs: Am. Needlepoint Guild, Minn. Alumni Assn. Lodge: Easter Star. Home: 3309 W 55th St Edina MN 55410

GILBERT, RACHEL SHAW, state legislator, real estate broker; b. Ottawa, Kans.; d. Herbert M. and L.C. Ferris (Pile) Shaw; B.A., U. Nebr., 1956; M.A., Coll. of Idaho, 1969; children—Cheryl Allison Gilbert Brady, Kimberly Lynn. Sch. tchr., Nebr., 1952-57; broker Walker & Co. Real Estate, Boise, Idaho, 1969-71; broker-owner Gilbert & Assocs. Realtors, Boise, 1972-82; mem. Idaho Ho. of Reps., 1980-83, Idaho Senate, 1984—. Bd. dirs. United Way, Boise, 1963-68, Boise Philharm. Orch., 1966-68; chmn. Idaho Legis. Dist. 15, 1980. Mem. Nat. Assn. Realtors (dir.), Idaho Assn. Realtors (dir. 1978-80), Idaho Assn. Commerce and Industry (dir.), Boise C. of C. (v.p. 1979). Republican. Home: 1111 Marshall St Boise ID 83706 Office: 1487 N Cole St Boise ID 83704

GILBERT, RITA K., lawyer; b. N.Y.C., Sept. 5, 1942; d. Emil and Esther (Screbranick) Katz; m. Bruce M. Gilbert, May 31, 1964; children—Lloyd H., Lonya Ann. B.A., Hunter Coll., 1963; M.A., Johns Hopkins U., 1966; J.D., Pace Law Sch., 1979. Bar: N.Y. 1980, Fla. 1981, U.S. Dist. Ct. (so. and ea. dists.) N.Y. 1980, U.S. Tax Ct. 1981. Atty., Campbell & Hyman, New Rochelle, N.Y., 1980-81, Hyman & Gilbert P.C., New Rochelle, 1982—. Author: Finding Your Way Through the UCC-Article 9, 1980; Paralegals and Successful Law Practice, 1981. Fulbright fellow Inst. Internat. Edn., 1964-65. Mem. ABA (trust and estates sect.), N.Y. Bar Assn., Westchester Women's Bar Assn. (chair trusts and estates, v.p.), Estate Planning Council Westchester, New Rochelle Bar Assn. (dir. 1983—). Republican. Jewish. Home: 150 Lyncroft Rd New Rochelle NY 10804 Office: Hyman & Gilbert PC 271 North Ave New Rochelle NY 10801

GILBERT, ROSE BENNETT, communications co. exec.; b. High Point, N.C., July 11, 1938; d. Ellis Howard and Sadie B. (Vernon) Bennett; B.A., Mary Washington Coll., 1960; postgrad. George Washington U., 1964-65; children—Scott Randolph, Bennett J. Reporter, Richmond (Va.) News-Leader, 1960-64; editor 1,001 Decorating Ideas Mag., N.Y.C., 1973-75; columnist Chgo. Tribune-Daily News Syndicate, 1975-77; v.p., partner Sweet & Co., N.Y.C., 1978-80; pres. Gilbert/Green Communications, N.Y.C., 1980—; asso. editor Country Decorating Mag., N.Y.C. Adult Sch. Maplewood/South Orange (N.J.) Adult Sch., 1975—; lectr. N.Y. Sch. Interior Design, 1985—. Mem. Mary Washington Coll. Alumni Assn. (v.p. 1966-67), Nat. Home Fashions League, Fashion Group. Episcopalian. Author: You-Do-It Book of Early American Decorating, 1978; Decorating Country-Style, 1980; Your Colors at Home, 1985. Home: 73 Jefferson Ave Maplewood NJ 07040 Office: 141 E 33 St New York NY 10016

GILBERT, RUTH LOUISE, tax mgr.; b. Hammond, Ind., Dec. 27, 1933; d. Alonzo Boyer and Eva Ella (Mills) Luyster; B.S. summa cum laude, in Acctg., U. Mo., 1972; m. Milton Caleb Gilbert, Jr., Mar. 10, 1951 (div.); children—David Donald, Steven Craig. Staff acct. Touche Ross & Co., St. Louis, 1973-75; sr. tax acct. Rubin, Brown, Gornstein & Co., St. Louis, 1975-77; mgr. tax research and planning Mallinckrodt, Inc., St. Louis, 1977—. C.P.A., Mo. Mem. Am. Inst. C.P.A.s, Nat. Assn. Accts. (dir.), Mo. Soc. C.P.A.s (sec. state taxation com. 1982-83), Beta Gamma Sigma (v.p. 1972-73), Beta Alpha Psi. Republican. Lutheran. Home: 503 Gatehall Ln Ballwin MO 63011 Office: 675 McDonnell Blvd PO Box 5840 Saint Louis MO 63134

GILBERT, SUSAN MARY, bank human resource executive; b. Milw., Dec. 8, 1954; d. Emil Warren and Lois Mae (Hill) Vogel. B.S., U. Wis.-Milw., 1977, M.S., 1979. Personnel mgr. Boston Store, Milw., 1980-81; corp. personnel mgr. Sakowitz, Houston, 1981-82; human resource program mgr. RepublicBank, Dallas and Houston, 1982-85, human resource mgr. corporate banking group, 1985—; adviser work study program Milw. Pub. Schs., 1980-81. Clin. asst. Planned Parenthood, Milw., 1973-74; vol. St. Mary's Hosp., Milw., 1975-76; adv. Assn. Retarded Citizens, Milw., 1977-79. Mem. Human Resource Systems Profls. (v.p. programs; bd. dirs.), Houston Personnel Assn., Dallas Personnel Assn., Internat. Immigration Assn., Assn. Corp. Relocators, Dallas Women's Found. Democrat. Roman Catholic.

GILBERT, SUZANNE HARRIS, advertising executive; b. Chgo., Mar. 8, 1943; d. Lawrence W. and Dorothea (Wilde) Harris; children—Kerry, Elizabeth, Gregory. B.S., Marquette U., 1965; postgrad. U. Chgo., 1983-84. Fin. planner Sci. Research Assocs., Chgo., 1965-67; fin. analyst Leo Burnett Co., Chgo., 1967-70; sr. v.p. fin. adminstrn., sec.-treas. Clinton E. Frank Inc., Chgo., 1975—. Office: Clinton E Frank Inc 120 S Riverside Plaza Chicago IL 60606

GILBERTSON, CATHERINE JO, veterinarian; b. Grand Forks, N.D., Dec. 30, 1948; d. Gordon Ladue and Alta Catherine (De Bey) Gilbertson; m. Richard Waller Stone, Nov. 2, 1972 (div. Dec. 1983). B.A. in English with high honors, Stanford U., 1971; B.S. in Vet. Sci. magna cum laude, Wash. State U., 1979, D.V.M. cum laude, 1981. Veterinarian, Burien Vet. Hosp., Seattle, 1981-83; sole practice vet. medicine, Bellingham, Wash., 1983—; lectr. Whatcom County Cat Fanciers, Bellingham, 1984—. Mem. AVMA, Wash. Vet. Med. Assn., Seattle Vet. Med. Assn., Am. Soc. Marine Mammology (assoc.), Am. Assn. Feline Practitioners, Tri-County Vet. Med. Assn., Am. Assn. Equine Practitioners, What com Women in Bus., Internat. Marine and Animal Trainers Assn. Home: 340 S Forest St Bellingham WA 98225 Office: Gene Poole Meml Cat Clinic 1214 Dupont St Bellingham WA 98225

GILBERTSON, JEAN BETH, radio station news director; b. Beloit, Wis., Mar. 8, 1954; d. James Thomas and Lucille (Lord) G. B.A. cum laude, U. Wis.-Whitewater, 1976. Weekend reporter Sta. WCLO/WJVL, Janesville, Wis., 1976; news dir. Sta. WFAW, Fort Atkinson, Wis., 1976-78; reporter, anchor Sta. WCLO/CJVL, Janesville, 1978-80, news dir., 1980—; lectr. communications dept. U. Wis.-Whitewater, 1985-86. Producer, writer radio interview shows: Farm Wives, 1977, Internat. Bus. Jargon, 1985. Mem. Radio-TV News Dirs. Assn., Sigma Delta Chi. Avocations: sailing; jogging; biking; music; cars. Home: 2804 Iroquois Ct Janesville WI 53545 Office: WCLO/WJVL Radio 1 South Parker Dr Janesville WI 53545

GILCHRIST, ELLEN, writer, journalist, radio commentator; b. Vicksburg, Miss., Feb. 20, 1935; d. William Garth and Aurora Louise (Alford) G.; children—Marshall Peteet Walker II, Garth Gilchrist Walker, Pierre Gautier Walker. B.A., Millsaps Coll., 1967. Commentator Nat. Pub. Radio, 1984-85. Author: The Land Surveyor's Daughter, 1979; In the Land of Dreamy Dreams, 1981; The Annunciation, 1983 (Book of Month alt. in U.S., Book of Month Club selection in Sweden); Victory Over Japan, 1984 (Am. Book award Assn. Am. Pubs. 1984). Contbr. short stories to Atlantic Monthly, Southern Living, Mademoiselle, Pushcart, Cosmopolitan, Prairie Schooner, New Orleans Rev.,

1978—. Contbr. poetry to quars., revs., mags. Recipient Sacifrage award, 1983, Fiction award of Miss. Acad. Arts and Sci., 1982, 85, Poetry award Miss. Arts Festival, 1968, Fiction award Prairie Schooner, 1981, Craft in Poetry award N.Y. Quar., 1978, Poetry award U. Ark. Grad. Sch., 1976, 2 Pushcart Prizes, Fulbright award U. Ark., 1985; In The Land of Dreamy Dreams named one of two honor books of La. Library Assn., 1981; Nat. Endowment Arts grantee, 1979. Mem. Authors Guild.

GIL DEL REAL, MARÍA TERESA, epidemiologist; b. Ccuta, Colombia, Jan. 5, 1941; came to U.S., 1962, naturalized, 1969; d. Antonio E. and Rosa (Calvo) Gil del R.; Asso., Bogotá Bus. Coll., 1961; B.A. in Anthropology, Rutgers U., 1979; M. in Pub. Health, Epidemiology, Columbia U., 1986; m. John R. Romano, Oct. 10, 1964; children—Christina M., John Alexander. Freelance translator, simultaneous interpreter, 1977-79; bilingual editor Princeton Internat. Translations, Princeton Junction, N.J., 1979-80; research asst. Robert Wood Johnson Found., Princeton, 1980-83; researcher U. Madrid, 1983-1984; cons. internat. pub. health. Mem. Am. Biog. Inst. Research Assn., Alpha Sigma Lambda. Home: 76 Princeton Ave Rocky Hill NJ 08553 Office: NJ Dept Health Div Epidemiology and Disease Control Cancer Epidemiology Program CN 369 Trenton NJ

GILDEN, NINA BETH, media and historical consultant, TV producer; b. St. Louis, May 27, 1957; d. Louis and Joanne Audrey (Bamberger) Gilden; m. Ormond Albert Seavey. Cert., Institut Ste. Andre, Tournai, Belgium, 1975; B.A., Washington U., St. Louis, 1978; postgrad. George Washington U., 1985-86. Dir. polit. action com. Coalition for New Fgn. and Mil. Policy, Washington, 1978; mil advisor Hon. Patricia Schroeder, U.S. Congress, Washington, 1979-80; spl. cons. women's affairs U.S. Dept. Def., Washington, 1980; pres. Nina Gilden Assocs., Washington, 1981—; historian, dir. oral history project COMSAT Corp., 1985-86; cons. Congresswomen's Caucus, U.S. Congress, 1979-80, Coalition on Women in Def., Washington, 1979-80. Producer TV show Jack Anderson Confidential, 1982, The Lawmakers, PBS-TV, 1984. Author articles on def. spending and strategic arms, 1979. Office mgr. McGovern for Pres., St. Louis, 1972; organizer United Farm Workers Union, St. Louis, 1973; vol. coordinator Morris Udall for Pres., St. Louis, 1976. Recipient Am. Youth Found. award Danforth Found., 1974; Am. Field Service scholar, 1974-75. Mem. Am. Hist. Soc., Phi Delta Gamma. Democrat. Jewish. Office: Nina Gilden Assocs 4214 Spruce Ave Takoma Park MD 20912

GILE, MARY STUART, educational executive; b. Montreal, Que., Can., Mar. 24, 1936; d. William Gillies and Hazel Irene (Stuart) Sinclair; m. Robert Hall Gile, Mar. 29, 1974; children—D. Christopher, Julia Mary, John, Robertson Sinclair. B.Sc., McGill U., 1957; M.Ed., U. N.H., 1971; Ed.D., Vanderbilt U., 1982. Specialist phys. edn. Protestant Sch. Bd. Greater Montreal, 1957-64, kindergarten tchr. White Mountains Sch. Bd., Littleton, N.H., 1965-67; dir. Open Door Kindergarten, Salem, N.H., 1967-69; coordinator State Follow Through, State of N.H., 1969-80, N.H. Right to Read, 1973-74, U.S. Sec.'s Initiative in Excellence chpt. 1 Edn. Consol. and Improvement Act, 1983-84; sr. cons. edn. N.H. State Dept. Edn., Concord, 1969-85; v.p. edn. and devel. Acad. Applied Sci., Concord, 1985—; state dept. staff assoc. to U. N.H., Durham, 1970-74; mem. Gov.'s Task Force on Sexual Harassment, Concord, 1981-83; chmn. Commr.'s Com. on Alt. Work Schedules, Concord, 1982-84; commr.'s rep. State Day Care Adv. Com., Concord, 1984-85. Contbr. articles to profl. jours. Pres., Concord Parents and Children, 1977-82; chmn. Citizens Adv. Bd. to Community Devel., 1978-82; bd. govs. Merrimack County United Way, 1983—; pres. N.H. Assn. for Mental Health, 1984—. Recipient Appreciation cert. Maine Dept. Edn., 1984, cert. outstanding achievement N.H. State Bd. Edn., 1985, Imperial Oil Ltd. scholar, 1953; U. N.H. early childhood fellow, 1969. Mem. N.H. Assn. for Edn. Young Children, State Employees Assn., Phi Delta Kappa. Congregationalist. Avocations: skiing; music; theatre; hiking.

GILES, LILLIAN EMILY, owner credit bureau; b. Boyd, Okla., Apr. 3, 1923; d. Roy and Anna (Dower) Claybrook; m. Ray L. Giles, May 23, 1940; 1 child, Maisie Giles Scanlan. Student Lamar Community Coll., 1983-85. Tchr. Pleasant Heights Sch., Lamar, Colo., 1944-45; credit mgr. Montgomery Ward & Co., Lamar, 1946-51; owner, operator Credit Bur. of Lamar, 1951—; pres. Assoc. Credit Burs. Colo., 1975-76, bd. dirs., 1983—, Sec. ofcl. bd. Methodist Ch., 1981-84, asst. treas., 1975—. Mem. Lamar C. of C. (bd. dirs. 1975-77, treas. 1976-77). Lodge: Zonta. Avocations: profl. football fan; basketball fan; hiking; camping. Office: Credit Bur of Lamar 203 W Olive St Lamar CO 81052

GILFORD, MARYE BLAND, business technology educator; b. Hot Springs, Ark.; d. Clarence Theodore and Naomi Frances (Hill) Andrews; m. Murrene Gilford, Feb. 18, 1961; children—Dexter Earl, Muriel Yvonne. B.A., Wiley Coll., Marshall, Tex., 1957; M.B.A., U. Tex., 1960; postgrad. St. Mary's U., 1964-65, Our Lady of Lake U., 1966, SW Tex. State U., 1974, N. Tex. State U., 1975, 76, 79, Tex. U., 1977. Lic. real estate broker. Mgr., Pythian Bath House, Hot Springs, 1949-55; sec. Grand Ct. Order of Calanthe of Tex., 1955-58; tchr. bus. Austin and San Antonio pub. schs., 1959-70; instr. acctg. tech. St. Philips Coll., San Antonio, 1970-74, asst. prof., 1974-82, assoc. prof., 1982—, chmn. acctg. tech., data processing, real estate programs, 1983-85, chmn. bus. tech. dept., 1985—. Chmn. supervisory com. Black Unity Coordinating Council Fed. Credit Union, 1976—. Mem. Am. Acctg. Assn., Tex Jr. Coll. Tchrs. Assn., Tex. Bus. Edn. Assn., Bus. Edn. Tchrs. Assn., Nat. Bus. Edn. Assn., Phi Delta Kappa, Delta Pi Epsilon, Zeta Phi Beta, Alpha Wives Aux. Club: Women's Coalition. Home: 3802 Willowwood St San Antonio TX 78219 Office: St Philips Coll 2111 Nevada St San Antonio TX 78203

GILFORD, ROSE MALETZ, travel agency executive, lawyer; b. Boston, July 18, 1920; d. Morris and Fannie (Priceman) Maletz; m. Warren S. Gilford, Nov. 26, 1944; 1 dau., Sarah Gilford Wolfe. Student Queens U., Ont., Can., 1938-40; J.D., Boston U. Sch. Law, 1943. Bar: Mass. 1943, D.C. 1945; Cert. travel agt. Law clk. Supreme Court Mass., Boston, 1943-44; editor Mass. Law Jour., Boston, 1945-47; legal counselor for students Boston U., 1947-59; founder, pres., chief exec. officer Chestnut Hill Travel Inc., Mass., 1955—; forum chmn. Inst. Cert. Travel Agts., Wellesley, Mass., 1981-82; mem. adv. bd. Pan Am. Airways, Boston, 1983—; mem. nat. adv. bd. Sonesta Internat. Hotels, Boston, 1982—; mem. adv. bd. Travel Edn. Ctr., Cambridge, Mass., 1981—. Assoc. editor in chief Boston U. Law Rev., 1942-43. Bd. dirs. Brookline Taxpayers Assn., Mass., 1965-67; govt. chmn. League of Women Voters-Mass., 1941-51; chmn. United Fund of Brookline, 1965-66; town meeting mem. Town of Brookline, 1945-67. Mem. Inst. Cert. Travel Agents, Am. Soc. Travel Agents, Mass. Assn. Women Lawyers. Clubs: Boston Yacht (Marblehead); University (Boston). Avocations: antiques, history, museums, gardens. Home: 135 Perkins St Jamaica Plain MA 02130 Office: Chestnut Hill Travel Inc 1210 Boylston St Brookline MA 02167

GILFOYLE, NATHALIE PRESTON, lawyer; b. Lynchburg, Va., May 4, 1949; d. Robert Edmund and Dorothea Henry (Ward) Gilfoyle; m. Christopher Y.W. Ma, Sept. 9, 1978; children—Olivia Otey, Rohan James. B.A., Hollins Coll., Roanoke, Va., 1971; J.D., U. Va., Charlottesville, 1974. Bar: Mass. 1974, D.C. 1977. Staff counsel Rate Setting Commn., Boston, 1974-76; ptnr. Peabody, Lambert & Meyers, Washington, 1976—; bd. dirs. Washington Lawyers Com. Civil Rights Under Law, Washington, 1982—; participating counsel Vol. Lawyers for Arts, Boston, 1974-76, Washington, 1978—. Bd. dirs. ACLU Nat. Capital Area, Washington, 1980-83, Filmore Early Learning Ctr., 1977-81. Mem. ABA, D.C. Bar Assn., Mass. Bar Assn., Women's Bar Assn. Episcopalian. Office: McDermott Will & Emery 1850 K St Washington DC 20006

GILHOOLEY, CATHERINE PATRICIA, social worker; b. Orange, N.J.; d. Patrick J. and Bridget T. (Farley) G.; B.S., Seton Hall U., 1953; M.S.W., Fordham U., 1973. Registered supr. for cert. of substance abuse counselors, N.J. Supr. N.J. Bell Telephone Co., Newark, 1946-69; social worker N.J. Div. Youth and Family Services, Elizabeth, 1969-71; asst. chief Drug Dependency Treatment Center, VA Med. Ctr., East Orange, N.J., 1973—. Mem. Nat. Assn. Social Workers, Acad. Cert. Social Workers, Nat. Assn. Social Workers Register of Clin. Social Workers, Seton Hall U. Alumni Assn., Fordham U. Alumni Assn. Home: 154 Freeman Ave East Orange NJ 07018 Office: VA Med Ctr Tremont Ave East Orange NJ 07018

GILKES, CHERYL LOUISE TOWNSEND, sociologist, minister; b. Boston, Nov. 2, 1947; d. Murray Luke, Jr., and Evelyn Annette (Reid) Townsend; B.A., Northeastern U., M.A., Ph.D. Lectr., Univ. Coll. Northeastern U., 1973-78, also instr. sociology Boston State Coll., 1974-78; asst. prof. sociology Boston U., 1978—; assoc. minister Union Baptist Ch., Cambridge, Mass., 1982—; vis. lectr. Tufts U., 1974; instr. sociology U. Mass., 1976; research assoc., vis. lectr. sociology of religion Harvard U. Div. Sch., 1981-82; vis. lectr. Afro-Am. studies Simmons Coll.; faculty fellow Bunting Inst., Radcliffe Coll., 1982-84. Sec. Cambridge Civic Unity Com., 1978—; mem. adv. com. Schlessinger Library, Racliffe Coll., 1984-86; pres. Cambridge Black Cultural and Hist. Assn., 1978—. Spivak Dissertation fellow Am. Sociol. Assn., 1977-78; Nat. Fellowships Fund dissertation fellow, 1977-78; Socialization Tng. fellow Northeastern U., 1970-73. Mem. Am. Sociol. Assn., Eastern Sociol. Soc., Mass. Sociol. Assn., Soc. Study of Social Problems, Assn. Humanist Sociology, Am. Acad. Religion, Soc. Study of Symbolic Interaction, Assn. Black Sociologists, Sociologists Women in Soc., Soc. Sci. Study of Religion, Soc. Study Black Religion, Urban League of Eastern Mass., Phi Kappa Phi, Delta Sigma Theta. Contbr. articles and revs. to profl. jours., chpts. in books. Office: 96 100 Cummington St Boston MA 02215

GILKES, MARTHA JANE WATKINS, government consultant, scuba diving educator, photographer, photojournalist; b. Aberdeen, Miss., Jan. 28, 1953; d. Robert McCluney and Martha Evelyn (Rye) Watkins; m. David Anthony Gilkes, June 1, 1981. B.A., Miss. State U., 1974, M.A., 1975. Served with U.S. Peace Corps, Grenada, 1975-77; cons. disaster relief Am. embassy, Barbados and Antigua, West Indies, 1977-85; free-lance scuba diving instr., 1979-85; owner, operator Fanta-Sea Island Divers, Antigua, 1985; Contbr. articles to mags. Photographer underwater postcards. Pres. Eastern Caribbean Safe Diving Assn., Barbados, 1984-86, Barbuda/Antigua Diving Club, Antigua, 1984-85. Mem. Alpha Zeta, Phi Mu. Republican. Baptist. Address: Dorchester House Half Moon Bay Antigua West Indies also PO Box 4680 Charlotte Amalie 00801 Saint Thomas Virgin Islands

GILKESON, SHIRLEY JEAN, educator; b. Standard, W.Va., July 10, 1937; d. Walter Edward and Velva (Patrick) Morrison; m. Roy Allen Gilkeson, Dec. 20, 1959; children—Connie Sue, Stephen Michael. B.A., W.Va. Inst. Tech., 1959; postgrad. W.Va. U., 1963-65, Marshall U., 1966-70. Cert. tchr. English and social studies, W.Va. Tchr., Kanawha County Schs., Charleston, W.Va., 1959-71, 81—; tutor Piedmont Elem. Sch., Charleston, 1976-83. Editor: (state newspaper) Children of American Revolution, 1981-83; Pioneer Post, 1980-85 (Best in State award 1983, 84, 85). Pres. Bona Vista Garden Club, Charleston, 1968-71; chmn. Parents Adv. Council, Piedmont Elem. Sch., 1976-83; bd. dirs. East End Soccer Council, Charleston, 1977-83. Recipient Martha Washington medal of honor SAR, 1984, cert. Merit Kanawha Juvenile Council, Ind., 1964. Mem. Kanawha County Tchrs. Assn., W.Va. Edn. Assn., NEA, Kanawha County Social Studies Council (sec. 1965-67), DAR (regent Kanawha Valley chpt. 1983—, award of merit W.Va. orgn. 1983), W.Va. Soc. Children of Am. Revolution (sr. state pres. W.Va. 1981-83), Nat. Soc. Children of Am. Revolution (sr. v.p. mid-so. region 1984-86), Nat. Soc. Children Am. Revolution Officers, United Daughters of Confederacy, Delta Kappa Gamma. Republican. Baptist. Lodge: Order of Eastern Star. Home: 1921 Oakridge Dr Charleston WV 25311

GILKISON, DANA DELANTY, banker; b. Glendale, Calif., Sept. 27, 1937; d. John Richard and Helen Talitha (Adams) Whitney; m. Edward Allen Gilkison, July 14, 1975; stepchildren—Dixie, Steve; m. William Hugh Delanty, Jr., June 22, 1957 (div. 1970); children—Patrice, James, Jennifer, Jeff. B.A., Marylhurst Coll., 1986; student Lewis & Clark Coll., 1955-56. Proof operator Fed. Res. Bank, Seattle, 1957-58; teller, note teller 1st Interstate Bank, Salem, Oreg., 1963-67; notes, loan sec. Western Security Bank, Salem, Oreg., 1969-73, personnel, tng. staff, 1973-78; bank mgmt. staff Oreg. Bank, Salem and Corvallis, 1978-83; personnel dir. Comml. Bank, Salem, Oreg., 1983—. Mem. Am. Inst. Banking (pres. 1980-81), Pacific Northwest Personnel Assn. Republican. Home: 265 SE Walnut St Dallas OR 97338 Office: Commercial Bank 373 Church St NE Salem OR 97301

GILL, BARBARA A., state legislator. Formerly mem. Maine Ho. of Reps.; now mem. Maine Senate. Republican. Office: Maine Senate State Capitol Augusta ME 04333*

GILL, CAROLE O'BRIEN, family therapist; b. Providence, R.I., Apr. 7, 1946; d. Charles Warren and Angelina (Carcieri) O'Brien; m. Frank Ralston Gill, Oct. 17, 1964, (div. 1975); children—Michael Patrick, Peter Ralston. B.A. in Edn., U. R.I., 1978, B.A. in Psychology, 1984, M.S. in Marriage and Family Therapy, 1986. Cert. tchr., marriage and family therapist. Tchr. East Greenwich Sch. System, R.I., 1978-79; counselor U. R.I., Providence, 1984, clin. asst., therapist Family Therapy Clinic, Kingston, R.I., 1984-86, family therapist, East Greenwich, 1985—; vol. Hotline/Sympatico, Wakefield, R.I., 1984; coordinator Women's Connection U. R.I., 1984; co-facilitator women's abuse group Women's Resource Ctr., Wakefield, R.I., 1985-86. Mem. Friends of East Greenwich Pub. Library, 1981—. Mem. R.I. Chpt. Nat. Com. for Prevention of Child Abuse, Nat. Council on Family Relations, Am. Assn. Female Execs., Inst. for Noetic Scis., Am. Assn. Marriage and Family Therapists, Am. Psychol. Assn., New Eng. Psychol. Assn. Avocations: archeology, anthropology, photography, needlework, music.

GILL, DIANA LEE, marketing communications executive, writer; b. Torrington, Conn., Oct. 14, 1954; d. David Thomas and Valerie (Morris) Gill. Student U. Conn., 1972-74; B.A. in English, U. Vt., 1976. Mng. editor Agri-Mark, Inc., North Andover, Mass., 1976-81; marketing communications and sales promotion specialist Data Gen. Corp., Westboro, Mass., 1981-84; mktg. communication mgr. Adelie Corp., 1984-85. Contbr. articles to various publs. Recipient First Place awards Nat. Milk Producers Fedn., 1980, second place award, 1980; Second Place award N.E. Advt. Assn., 1982; named Employee of Quarter, Data Gen. Corp., 1983. Club: Publicity of Boston (mem. edn. com. 1983—). Home: Four Village Way #12 Natick MA 01760 Office: Applix Inc 112 Turnpike Rd Westboro MA 01581

GILL, EVALYN PIERPOINT, editor, publisher; b. Boulder, Colo.; d. Walter Lawrence and Lou Octavia Pierpoint; student Lindenwood Coll., B.A., U. Colo.; postgrad. U. Nebr., U. Alaska, M.A., Central Mich. U., 1968; m. John Glanville Gill, Nov. 10, 1943; children—Susan Pierpoint, Mary Louise Glanville. Lectr. humanities Saginaw Valley State Coll., University Center, Mich., 1968-72; mem. English faculty U. N.C., Greensboro, 1973-74; editor Internat. Poetry Rev., Greensboro, 1975—; pres. TransVerse Press, Greensboro, 1981—. Bd. dirs. Eastern Music Festival, Greensboro, 1981—, Greensboro Symphony, 1982—, Greensboro Opera Co., 1982—, Weatherspoon Assn.; chmn. O. Henry Festival, 1985. Mem. Am. Lit. Translators Assn., MLA, N.C. Poetry Soc., Phi Beta Kappa. Author: Poetry By French Women 1930-1980, 1980; Dialogue, 1985; contbr. poetry to numerous mags. Home: 1501 Kirkpatrick St Greensboro NC 27408 Office: PO Box 2047 Greensboro NC 27402

GILL, JANE ROBERTS, clinical social worker; b. Boston, Dec. 6, 1923; d. Penfield Hitchcock and Cecilia (Washburn) Roberts; student Wellesley Coll., 1941-43; B.A., Boston U., 1954, M.S.W., 1956; m. Peter Lawrence Gill, Dec. 24, 1943 (div. 1973); children—Jonathan Penfield, Dorcas Pearson, Nicholas Brinton, Timothy Roberts. Social worker Beth Isreal Hosp., Boston, 1956-57, South End Family Program, Boston, 1957-58, Margaret Gifford Sch., Cambridge, Mass., 1963-65; Adams House Psychiat. Clinic, Boston, 1967—; coordinator outpatient clinic and cardiac rehab. program Faulkner Hosp., Boston, 1975—, sr. clin. social work supr., 1976—; staff The Headache Research Found., 1976—; pvt. practice social work, Brookline, 1970—; clin. instr. Simmons Coll. Sch. of Social Work, 1971-79. Mem. social service com. Am. Heart Assn., 1979—; program chmn. Mass. Mental Health Center, 1969-71; bd. dirs. Rutland Corner House, 1982—; mem. Democratic Town Com., Newton-Wellesley, 1959-64. Lic. ind. clin. social worker, Mass. Mem. Acad. Cert. Social Workers, Register Clin. Social Workers, Acad. Psychosomatic Medicine, Internat. Headache Soc., Peacham Hist. Assn. of Vt., Putney Sch. Alumni Assn. Contbr. papers to profl. meetings. Office: 318 Allandale Rd Chestnut Hill MA 02167 and Faulkner Hosp Center St at Allandale Rd Boston MA 02130

GILL, KATHY ELAINE, communications specialist, editor; b. Albany, Ga., Aug. 21, 1955; d. Edwin Earl and Ellen Janette (Dollar) G.; m. Daniel David Plinski, Apr. 27, 1984. A.A., Abraham Baldwin Agrl. Coll., Tifton, Ga., 1975; B.A., U. Ga., 1977; M.S., Va. Poly. Inst. and State U., 1979. Research asst. Va. Poly. Inst. and State U., Blacksburg, 1979-80; communications mgr. Inter State Milk Producers Coop., Southampton, Pa., 1980-84; asst. press sec. Pa. Dept. Agr., 1984—; publicity chmn. Md. Ag Week, 1982-83; dir. Pa. Young Farmer Found., 1981-84. Editor: Pennmarva, 1983 (2d place award 1982, 83), Asst. Dale Carnegie-Leadership Inst., 1982-84; mem. Pa. Ag Republicans, 1984. Recipient awards for writing Nat. Council Farmer Coops., 1984, Coop. Editorial Assn., 1982, 83, 84, Nat. Milk Producers Fedn., 1981, 82, 83; summer scholar Rotary of Oslo, Norway, 1975. Mem. Coop. Editorial Assn., Am. Agrl. Econs. Assn., Am. Agrl. Editors Assn., Internat. Assn. Bus. Communicators, Pa. Assn. Farmer Coops. (dir. 1981-84), Methodist. Club: Paek's Tae Kwon Do of Willow Grove, Pa. Home: 24 Eastwood Dr Carlisle PA 17013 Office: Press Office Pa Dept Agr 2301 N Cameron St Harrisburg PA 17110

GILL, KAY LYNN, editor; b. Rockford, Ill., Feb. 23, 1944; d. Ralph E. and Dorothy M. (Tilley) Geithman; m. Thomas Jeffrey Gill, Dec. 31, 1968; children—Samantha Jane, Matthew Scott. B.A. cum laude, Lindenwood Coll., 1967. Copy editor C.V. Mosby Co., St. Louis, 1967-68; assoc. editor Quinn Pub. Co., Boca Raton, Fla., 1968-69, freelance editor, 1974-79; from editorial asst. to assoc. editor, then editor Gale Research Co., Ft. Lauderdale, Fla., 1979-83, sr. editor, 1984—. Mem. Alpha Lambda Delta, Alpha Sigma Tau. Methodist. Avocations: reading; walking. Home: 671 NE 8th Ct Pompano Beach FL 33060 Office: Gale Research Co 1700 E Las Olas Blvd Fort Lauderdale FL 33301

GILL, REBECCA, engineer; b. Brownsboro, Tex., Sept. 17, 1944; d. Milton and Dona Mildred (Magee) La Losh; B.S. in Physics, U. Mich., 1965; M.B.A., Calif. State U., Northridge, 1980; m. Peter Mohammed Sharma, Sept. 1, 1965 (div.); m. James Fredrick Gill, Mar. 9, 1985; children—Eric, Melissa, Ben. Tchr., Derby, Kans., 1966; weight analyst Beech Aircraft, Wichita, Kans., 1966; weight engr. Ewing Tech. Design, assigned Boeing-Vertol, Phila., 1966-67, Bell Aerosystems, Buffalo, 1967; design specialist Lockheed-Calif. Co., Burbank, 1968-79; sr. staff engr. Hughes Aircraft Missile Systems, Canoga Park, Calif., 1979-82, project mgr. AMRAAM spl. test and tng. equipment, 1982-85, project mgr. IRGBU-15 ops/1R Navy Maverick ops., 1986—; sec. Nat. Cinema Corp. Com. chmn. Orgn. for Rehab. through Tng., 1971-75; active NOW; speaker ednl. and civic groups. Recipient Lockheed award of achievement, 1977. Mem. Soc. Allied Weight Engrs. (dir., sr. v.p., chmn. pub. relations com.), Aerospace Elec. Soc. (dir.), Nat. Assn. Female Execs. Republican. Contbr. articles to tech. publs. Office: Bldg 801 MSF6 Hughes Aircraft Missile Systems Tucson AZ 85734

GILLASPIE, DEBORAH LYNN, lawyer; b. Dallas, Oreg., Dec. 26, 1955; d. Rex Dale and Lois Jean (White) Gillaspie; m. Frederick Wienert Sturm, Jan. 15, 1982. A.B., Barnard Coll., 1977; J.D., Bklyn. Law Sch., 1980. Bar: N.Y. 1981, U.S. Dist. Ct. (so. and ea. dists.) N.Y. 1981. Researcher Legal Papers Aaron Burr, N.Y.C., 1976-77; law clk. Caruso & Caruso, P.C., Bklyn., 1978-80; vol. researcher Surrogate's Ct., Kings County, Bklyn., 1979; law clk. to trial judge Civil Ct., City of N.Y., Bklyn., 1980; assoc. Charles Berkman, Esq., Bklyn., 1981; sole practice, N.y.C., 1983—. Asst. to author: Biannual Supplements Fed. Estate and Gift Taxation, 1983-86; digester Jour. Taxation Digest, 1983-85, Partnership Tax Digest, 1984, Federal Estate and Gift Tax Digest, 1984. Mem. N.Y. State Bar Assn. (trusts sect., estates sect., young lawyers sect.), ABA, Women Bus. Owners N.Y., Bklyn. Law Sch. Alumni Assn., Phi Delta Phi (historian 1978-79, exchequer 1979-80, cert. of merit 1979). Office: Deborah L Gillaspie Atty at Law 187 Pinehurst Ave New York NY 10033

GILLEN, ADRIENNE KOSCIUSKO, librarian, researcher; b. Northampton, Mass., Jan. 7, 1947; d. Mitchell Fred and Gloria Theresa (Maynard) K.; m. William A. Gillen, May 24, 1986. B.A., U. Mass., 1969. Library asst. Hotchkiss Sch., Lakeville, Conn., 1971-72; grants mgr. Conn. Planning Com. on Adminstrn., Hartford, 1972-73; researcher Dept. Youth Service, Bridgeport, Conn., 1974-75, White House, Washington, 1976; librarian Republican Nat. Com., Washington, 1977-79; librarian U.S. Senate, Rep. Policy Com., Washington, 1979-82; library dir. White House, Washington, 1982—. Republican. Roman Catholic. Office: Library and Info Services Div Exec Office of Pres Room 308 OEOB Washington DC 20503

GILLENWATER, ANNE RIDINGS, maintenance planner; b. Detroit, Apr. 23, 1936; d. James Clarence and Mary Sue (Hughes) Ridings; B.S. in Bus. Adminstrn., U. Tenn., Knoxville, 1971, also postgrad. With Aluminum Co. Am., Alcoa, Tenn., 1962—, various secretarial positions, 1962-71, adminstrv. analyst, 1971-73, indsl. engr., 1973-75, systems analyst, 1975-76, systems design engr., 1976-80, maintenance planner, 1980—. Adviser Alcoa Jr. Achievement; chmn. plant savs. bond campaign, 1972, mem. Tenn. Commn. on Women, 1974-81, chmn., 1975, 80, 81; bd. dirs. Laurel Lake Youth Camp, treas., 1977—; co-sponsor White House Conf. on Domestic and Econ. Affairs, 1975; bd. dirs. Blount County Girls Club, 1980—. F.T. Bonham scholar, 1953-54. Cert. profl. sec. Mem. Am. Inst. Indsl. Engrs., Soc. Women Engrs. (sec., 1976, SE student activities coordinator, 1977-79, pres. Knoxville, 1979, nat. chmn. new student sects., 1979-80, dir., 1981), Am. Soc. Tng. and Devel. (pres. 1981 region IV conf. chair 1984), Tenn. Valley Personnel Assn. (TIPC chmn., 1981, treas. 1982, pres.-elect 1983, pres. 1984), Nat. Secs. Assn. (pres. 1972-74), AAUW, Smoky Mountain Passion Play Guild. Republican. Baptist. Clubs: Knoxville Club LeConte, Delta Zeta. Speaker workshops, seminars, confs.; instr. human relations and adminstrn. Home: Route 5 Box 200 24 Fairoaks Dr Maryville TN 37801 Office: PO Box 9158 N-40 Alcoa TN 37701

GILLER, RUTH EDNA, business association executive; b. Hampstead, London; Nov. 5, 1929; naturalized U.S. citizen, 1956; d. George and Judith (Gunzburg) Bradlaw; m. Marshall Giller, Jan. 27, 1952; children—Paul Bradlaw, Sara. Diplomate, U. London, 1950. Supr. Zool. Soc. London, 1950-52; mgr. better bus. div. Cape Kennedy C. of C., Cocoa, Fla., 1966-72; mgr. trade practice div. Better Bus. Bur. Eastern Pa., Inc., Phila., 1972-78; mgr. Better Bus. Bur. Western Mich., Inc., Grand Rapids, 1978—. Pres. Democratic Women's Club, Cocoa, Fla., 1960-63. Mem. Women in Communications, Soc. Consumer Affairs Profls. Jewish. Club: Torch (Grand Rapids). Office: Better Bus Bur Western Mich Inc 620 Trust Bldg Grand Rapids MI 49503

GILLERAN, DELLA ANDRESEN, graphic designer, instructor; b. Oakland, Calif., Nov. 22, 1955; d. Harold Burglin and LaVerne Frances (Spear) Andresen; m. Lyle Edward Gilleran, Aug. 13, 1978 (div. 1986). Designer, U. Calif.-Davis Com. for Arts and Letters, 1975-77, instr. extension, 1981—; artist Image Printing and Pub., Sacramento, 1977-78; graphic designer, Mktg. by Design, Sacramento, 1978-80; owner, designer Della Gilleran Design, Sacramento, 1980—. Bd. dirs. The Cammy Awards for Design Excellence, Sacramento, 1984-86; mem. Sta. KVIE Pub. Relations Adv. Com., Sacramento, 1984—. Mem. Art Dirs. and Artists Club (bd. dirs. 1982—, pres. 1984-85, chmn. Envision 11 Design Conf. 1984-85). Democrat. Avocations: windsurfing; golf. Office: Gilleran Design 2405 Capitol Ave #5 Sacramento CA 95816

GILLESPIE, ELAINE MARIE, real estate executive; b. Tiffin, Ohio, May 1, 1961; d. Charles James and Helen Elizabeth (Bork) G. B.A., Miami U., Oxford, Ohio, 1983. Interior space planner, designer, Cin., 1983-85; now comml. real estate sales person Coldwell Banker Comml. Group, Cin. Tchr., Head Start Program, Oxford, Ohio, 1984—. Mem. Cin. C. of C., Cin. Bd. Realtors. Avocations: drafting. Home: 2101 Grandin Rd Cincinnati OH 45208 Office: Coldwell Banker Comml Group 425 Walnut St Cincinnati OH 45202

GILLESPIE, ELSIE JULIANNA, business executive; b. Phila., Sept. 24, 1912; d. Julius Adelbert and Martha Amanda (Brunner) Kinderman; 1 son, Edward R. Buckalew. Student pub. schs., Phila. With menu and purchasing depts. Lintons Restaurants, Phila., 1930-42; cashier, mgr. accounts payable J.E. Caldwell Co., Phila., 1949-74; owner Gillespie Apts., Ocean City, N.J., 1974—; sec. Tourist Devel. Commn., 1982—. Mem. Guest and Apt. House Assn. Ocean City (pres. 1982-84), C. of C. Ocean City (dir. 1982-85, chmn. com. 1983). Republican. Presbyterian. Home and office: 3457 Asbury Ave Ocean City NJ 08226

GILLESPIE, MAUREEN ELIZABETH, telephone company public relations manager; b. Queens, N.Y., Sept. 10, 1945; d. John Francis and Ruth Irene (Bertschy) Hogan; children—Lauren Beth Alles, Kirsten Leigh Alles. Student Queens Coll., 1962-65, 70-72, Hunter Coll., 1977-79, NYU, 1976-77. Writer, N.Y. Telephone Co., N.Y.C., 1979-83, pub. relations mgr. product publicity and cultural advt., 1983-84, mgr. customer info., editorHELLO bill insert; guest lectr. New Sch. Social Research, Hunter Coll., NYU; freelance editor mags. and newspapers. Lobbyist various edn. orgns., 1977; founder, chmn. Clermont Tenants Assn., N.Y.C., 1976-81; campaign aide various state legislators, 1976-80. Recipient Andy award Advt. Club N.Y., 1984. Mem. Women in Communications, N.Y. Press Club, N.Y.C. Commn. Status of Women.

GILLESPIE, MINTIE (DENA), architectural drafting company executive; b. Vallejo, Calif., Dec. 14, 1945; d. John Junior and Mintie Jeanne Da Vee (Parker) Windsor; B.A., San Diego State U., 1967, postgrad., 1968; m. William John Gillespie, Aug. 29, 1965; children—Robert Windsor, Brock Bill, Taila Mintie. Tchr. English and modern dance Monte Vista High Sch., La Mesa, Calif., 1967-72, dean student activities, 1973-75; archtl. draftswoman Design Assos., El Cajon, Calif., 1976; owner, designer Gillespie Resdl. Drafting, El Cajon, 1976—. Active PTA, 1975-82; bd. dirs. El Cajon Girls' Club, 1977-78. Mem. Am. Inst. Bldg. Designers (home design award 1981, 82, 84, 86), Calif. Tchrs. Assn., AAUW, Aztec Alumni Assn., El Cajon C. of C. (mem. ambassador com. 1975-76). Office: PO Box 8136 Fairbanks Village Plaza Rancho Santa Fe CA 92067

GILLESPIE, RENA HARRELL, university administrator; b. Starkville, Miss., Oct. 26; d. Wardell and Rachel (Hogan) Harrell; m. Daryl Malcolm Gillespie, July 20, 1974 (dec. July 1977). B.S., Miss. State U., 1972, Ed.D., 1981; M.S., U. Cin., 1974. Resident counselor Cin. Pub. Schs., 1972-74; counselor Miss. U. for Women, Columbus, 1974-78; residence hall dir. Miss. State U., Starkville, 1979-81; assoc. dir. health careers enrichment program U. N.C., Chapel Hill, 1983—. Vice pres. United Meth. Women Soc., 1974-75. Recipient Recognition award United Meth. Ch., Starkville, 1980; Model Cities Counseling Project fellow U. Cin., 1972-74; univ. minority fellow Miss. U. for Women, 1978-81; Bur. Health Professions Health Careers Opportunity Program grantee, 1984. Mem. Nat. Minority Health Affairs, Black Faculty and Staff Caucus, So. Coll. Personnel Assn., Am. Personnel and Guidance Assn. Democrat. Avocations: jogging, tennis.

GILLESPIE, YVONNE LOUISE, financial company executive; b. Berkeley, Calif., July 26, 1951; d. Earl Richmond Gillespie, Jr. and Enid Claire (Miller) Herrera. Student Sacramento City Coll., 1970-72, Consumnee River Coll., 1971-72, Sacramento State U., 1972-74. Personnel analyst State of Calif., Sacramento, 1972-76; regional mgr. ops. ITEL Rail, San Francisco, also Atlanta, 1976-79; dir. ops. PLM, Inc., San Francisco, 1979-81; mktg. dir. F.S. Railcars, Northbrook, Ill., 1981-82; nat. mkgt. mgr. Chrysler Capital Corp. (formerly E.F. Hutton Credit Corp.), Greenwich, Conn., 1982—. Republican candidate for Stamford Bd. Reps., 1983. Recipient Ops. Excellence award ITEL Corp., 1978, Outstanding Achievement award E.F. Hutton Credit, 1984. Lodge: Order Eastern Star.

GILLETTE, ETHEL MORROW, columnist; b. Oelwein, Iowa, Nov. 27, 1921; d. Charles Henry and Myrne Sarah (Law) Morrow; student Coe Coll., 1939-41; B.A., Upper Iowa U., 1959; M.A., Western State Coll., 1969; m. Roman A. Gillette, May 6, 1944; children—Melody Ann, Richard Alan, William Robert. Stenographer, Penick & Ford, Cedar Rapids, Iowa, 1941-43, FBI, Washington, 1943-44; tchr. Fayette (Iowa) High Sch., 1959-60, Jordan Jr. High Sch., Mpls., 1960-64, Montrose (Colo.) High Sch., 1964-68; family living, religion editor The News-Record, Gillette, Wyo., 1977-79, columnist Distaff Side, 1979—. Mem. Wyo. Writers Assn., Western Writers Am. (assoc.), Nat. Writers Club. Contbr. articles to various mags. Home: 1804 E Locust St Montrose CO 81401

GILLEY, NANCY DEAN, data processing executive; b. Ft. Worth, Mar. 6, 1942; d. Harvey Lee and Minnie Lee (Jones) Elrod; m. Eddie Baker Gilley, Aug. 24, 1959; 1 son, Rockie Dean. B.S. in Computer Sci., North Tex. State U., 1971; B.S. in Computer Sci., Tex. Inst. Tech., 1971-73; B.S. in Bus. Mgmt., Electronic Computer Programming Inst., Dallas, 1977. Asst. data processing mgr. SMC Corp., Dallas, 1970-73; data processing mgr. H.P. Foley Co., Dallas, 1973-78; v.p. data processing Ft. Worth Pipe Co., 1978-81; dir. mgmt. info. systems Ryan Cos., Arlington, Tex., 1981-85, Tex. Soc. C.P.A.s, Dallas, 1985—; pres. Gilley & Assocs. data processing cons. and researcher, Ft. Worth, 1980—. Vol. Stars for Children, Arlington, 1984-85. Mem. Exec. Bus. Women Am., Am. Execs. in Constrn. Office: Gilley & Assocs PO Box 1486 Fort Worth TX 76101

GILLIAM, EARLENE RANSOME, welding company executive; b. Tarboro, N.C., Feb. 20, 1938; d. Wilbert Perry Draughn and Mary (Ransome) Jenkins; m. William Bernard Gilliam, Sept. 20, 1957; children—Michael, Mary, Andre, Sheldon. Student pub. schs. Battlesboro, N.C. Asst. dir. Zion Bapt. Ch., Newport News, Va., 1968-72; sec. Riverside Hosp., Newport News, 1972-76; pres. Gilliam Welding, Inc., Newport News, 1976—. Sponsor, Gilliam Welding Softball Team, Newport News, 1980-85. Mem. Am. Welding Soc., NAACP (life), Am. Assn. Black Women Entrepreneurs. Democrat. Avocations: reading; dancing; sewing; crafts. Home: 141 Pear Ave Newport News VA 23607 Office: Gilliam Welding Inc 419 45th St Newport News VA 23607

GILLIARD, SHERRY JEAN BROWER, industrial relations/personnel executive; b. Newark, Nov. 10, 1936; d. Sherman Eugene and Rose Elizabeth (Cook) Rapp; m. James David Brower, Sept. 3, 1960 (div. July 1980); children—Cindy Gilbreath, Mark Brower, Kim Brower; m. 2d Jimmy Del Gilliard, July 7, 1983. B.A., U. Ala., 1973. Exec. sec. to v.p. Sandoz Pharms., Hanover, N.J., 1958-60; office mgr. Personnel, Inc., Huntsville, Ala., 1973-76; personnel adminstr. Teledyne Firth, Grant, Ala., 1976-80; mgr. indsl. relations Webster Industries, Montgomery, Ala., 1980—; lectr. Mount Meigs Correctional Inst., Montgomery, Ala., 1982, State Ala. Vocational Schs., Montgomery, 1982, Acad. and Mgmt. Cons., Huntington Coll., 1982-83; guest lectr. U. Ala., Huntsville, 1985. Mem. Am. Soc. Personnel Adminstrs. (bd. dirs. 1986—), Sigma Kappa. Office: Webster Industries Inc PO Box 17318 Montgomery AL 36193

GILLICE, SONDRA JUPIN (MRS. GARDNER RUSSELL BROWN), personnel executive; b. Urbana, Ill.; d. Earl Cranston and Laura Lorraine (Rose) Jupin; B.S., Lindenwood Coll., 1958; M.B.A., Loyola Coll., 1982; m. Gardner Russell Brown, Jan. 12, 1980; 1 son, Thomas Alan Gillice. Div. tng. supr. Liberty Mut. Ins. Co., Chgo., N.Y.C., 1958-68; personnel officer N.Y. Citibank, 1968-70, 1st Nat. Bank of Chgo., 1970-72; mgr. human resources Potomac Electric Power Co., Washington, 1973-81; dir. personnel U.S. Synthetic Fuels Corp., Washington, 1981—. Mem. industry adv. bd. Behrend Coll., Pa. State U. Mem. Edison Electric Inst. (chmn. tng. and mgmt. devel. com.), AAUW (pres. Falls Church br. 1976-78), Am. Soc. Tng. and Devel., Am. Soc. Tng. and Devel., Am. Soc. Personnel Adminstrs., Washington Personnel Assn., Greater Met. Washington Bd. Trade. Republican. Clubs: Soroptimists (pres. Washington chpt. 1979-80), DAR, Army Navy Country, Soc. Magna Charta Dames. Club: Edgartown (Mass.) Yacht. Home: 309 N Maple Ave Falls Church VA 22046 Office: 2121 K St NW Washington DC 20568

GILLIGAN, MAUREEN FARQUHAR, lawyer; b. Newark, Jan. 21, 1954; d. William Charles Farquhar and Edith Janis (Cook) Falcone; m. Gerard Joseph Gilligan, Dec. 16, 1978; children—Meghann Mary, Eireann Christine. B.A., Boston Coll., 1976; J.D., Seton Hall U., 1979. Bar: N.J. 1981. Law clk. U.S. Dist. Judge H. Lee Sarokin, Newark, 1979-81; assoc. Ribis, McCluskey & Sweeney, Short Hills, N.J., 1981-82; atty. AT&T, Basking Ridge, N.J., 1983, Bell Communications Research, Inc., Basking Ridge, 1984—. Contbr. article, rev. to legal publ. Recipient awards Moot Ct. competitions, Seton Hall U., 1978. Mem. ABA, N.J. Bar Assn. Democrat. Roman Catholic. Home: 10 Parkview Dr Millburn NJ 07041 Office: Bell Communications Research Inc 295 N Maple Ave Basking Ridge NJ 07920

GILLIS, CHRISTINE DIEST-LORGION, financial planner, stockbroker; b. San Francisco; d. Evert Jan and Christine Helen (Radcliffe) Diest-Lorgion; B.S., U. Calif., Berkeley; M.S., U. So. Calif.; children—Barbara Gillis Pieper, Suzanne Gillis Seymour (twins). Account exec. Winslow, Cohu & Stetson, N.Y.C., 1962-63, Paine Webber, N.Y.C., 1964-65; sr. investment exec. Shearson Hammill, Beverly Hills, Calif., 1966-72; fin. planner E.F. Hutton & Co., Glendale, Calif., 1972—. Cert. fin. planner. Mem. Inst. Cert. Fin. Planners, Town Hall of Calif. (life, treas. 1974-75, dir., gov. 1976-80), Women Stockbrokers Assn. (founding pres. 1963), Women of Wall Street West (pres. 1979-84), Navy League (life; dir.), Assistance League Pasadena, AAUW (life; trustee Ednl. Found.), Bus. and Profl. Women, Phi Chi Theta (life). Episcopalian. Clubs: U. So. Calif. Town and Gown (life), Zonta (dir.). Home: 1495 Pegfair Estates Dr Pasadena CA 91103 Office: 225 W Broadway Glendale CA 91204

GILLIS, EILEEN FLEMING, educator; b. Boston, Dec. 9, 1930; d. James Joseph and Anna Theresa (Brosnahan) Fleming; A.B., Emmanuel Coll., 1946; M.Ed., Boston U., 1972; m. Joseph L. Gillis, June 17, 1948; children—Kathleen G., Joseph Leo, Julie Anne G. Dutcher, Daniel Edward, Michael Kerby, F. Brian. Math. researcher M.I.T., Cambridge, 1946-49; reading specialist Milton (Mass.) public schs., 1972-79, core evaluation chmn., 1979-82, resource tchr., 1982—, dir. inservice tng. program for secondary tchrs. in reading, 1978-79. Mem. Milton Town Meeting, 1975—; trustee Milton Pub. Library, 1976-85, rec. sec., 1981-82, chmn. computer study com., 1982-85; dir. Coll. Entrance Exam. Bd., Milton High Sch., 1980; chmn. Ann. Charity Ball, 1980; bd. dirs. Jr. Guild of Cath. Charities, Boston, 1979-82; asst. med. and patient edn. project, Center for Nutritional Research, M.I.T., summer 1977; cons. in field. Mem. Internat. Reading Assn., New Eng. Reading Assn., Mass. Reading Assn., S. Shore Reading Assn., Nat. Tchrs. Assn., Mass. Tchrs. Assn., Mass. Assn. Children with Learning Disabilities, Friends of Milton Library, Milton Hist. Soc., Mus. Fine Arts Boston, LWV, AAUW (pres. Milton area br. 1982-84, rec. sec. Mass. div. 1984-85), Friends of Boston Symphony Orch. Clubs: Milton Hoosic, others. Home: 1278 Canton Ave Milton MA 02186 Office: Milton Public Schs Milton MA 02186

GILLIS, PHYLLIS LESLIE, author; b. Cleve., July 3, 1945; d. Sidney and Joan (Greenis) Helper; B.A., Mich. State U., 1967; M.S.J., Northwestern U., 1968; m. David Gillis, Nov. 25, 1971; (div. Sept. 1984). 1 son, Jordon Clayton. Staff writer Urban Am., Inc., Washington, 1967; reporter Nat. Jour., Washington, 1968-70; staff asso. Office of Urban Affairs, CUNY, N.Y.C., 1970-72; exec. dir. Gallup Internat. Research Inst., Princeton, N.J., 1972-76; v.p. Louis Harris & Assocs., N.Y.C., 1976-78; mng. partner Carversville Inn, Inc. (Pa.), 1979-83; columnist Parents Mag., 1980-84; pres. Entrepreneurial Communications, Inc., 1985—. Mem. Am. Soc. Journalists and Authors, Authors Guild, Pub. Relations Soc. Am., Internat. Assn. Bus. Communicators. Author: The New Pregnancy, 1979; Entrepreneurial Mothers, 1984; Days Like This, 1986; contbr. articles to profl. jours. Address: 14 Pine St Princeton NJ 08540

GILLMOR, KAREN LAKO, state official; b. Cleve., Jan. 29, 1948; d. William M. and Charlotte (Sheldon) Lako; m. Paul E. Gillmor, Dec. 10, 1983; children—Linda D., Julie E. B.A. cum laude, Mich. State U., 1969; M.A., Ohio State U., 1970, Ph.D., 1981. Asst. to v.p. Ohio State U., Columbus, 1972-77, spl. asst. dean law, 1979-81; asst. to pres. Ind. Central U., Indpls., 1977-79; research asst. Burke Mktg. Research, Indpls., 1978-79; v.p. pub. affairs Huntington Nat. Bank, Columbus, 1981-82; fin. cons. Ohio Rep. Fin. Com., Columbus, 1982-83; chief mgmt. planning and research Indsl. Commn. Ohio, Columbus, 1983—. Legis. liaison Huntington Bancshares, Ohio, Ohio State U., Columbus. Grantee Andrew W. Mellon Found. 1978, Carnegie Corp. 1978. Mem. Women in Mainstream, Women's Roundtable, Ohio Fedn. Republican Women, Am. Assn. Counseling and Devel., Am. Assn. Higher Edn., Council Advancement and Support Edn., Phi Delta Kappa. Methodist. Clubs: Capital, University (Columbus). Office: Indsl Commn Ohio 78 E Chestnut St Columbus OH 43215

GILLUM, ELSIE FELTS (JUDY), engineering company executive; b. Jacksonville, Fla., June 16, 1930; d. Ethelbert Hayward and Elsie Maybeth (Gregory) Felts; m. Don Edwyn Massey, July 22, 1957 (div. Apr. 1966); m. Jimmie Corbett Gillum, June 30, 1968. Assoc. Sci., Hillsborough Community Coll., 1984. Cert. profl. sec. Sec., Rosenblum's, Jacksonville, Fla., 1948-50; exec. sec. Gibbs Corp., Jacksonville, 1950-60, Ryder Truck Lines, Jacksonville, 1960-62; asst. corp. sec. Greiner Engring. Scis., Inc., Tampa, Fla., 1962—. Mem. Profl. Secs. Internat. (pres. City Ctr. chpt. 1985-86, Sec. of Yr. 1985-86), Exec. Women Internat. (sec. 1984), Nat. Assn. Female Execs., League Women Voters, Greater Brandon C. of C., Greater Tampa C. of C. Democrat. Roman Catholic. Avocations: needlework; reading; gardening. Home: Route 1 Box 574 Dover FL 33527 Office: Greiner Engring Scis Inc PO Box 23646 5601 Mariner St Tampa FL 33630

GILMAN, BARBARA DIANE, contracts compliance administrator; b. Tacoma, Wash., Apr. 27, 1954; d. Richard Arthur and B. Janet (Settle) G. B.A., U. So. Calif., 1977; J.D., Loyola U., Los Angeles, 1980. Bar: Calif. 1981. Law clk. to justice Calif. Ct. Appeals, Los Angeles, 1980-81; assoc. in law firms, San Francisco, 1981-83; escrow officer San Francisco, 1983-85. Exec. editor Loyola of Los Angeles Internat. and Comparative Law Jour., 1979-80. Mem. State Bar Assn. Calif., Jr. League San Francisco. Office: DHL Airways Inc 333 Twin Dolphin Dr Redwood City CA 94065

GILMAN, CAROL ELIZABETH, lawyer; b. Detroit, Oct. 12, 1953; d. William Carpenter and Marilyn Ruth (Harris) Gilman; m. George O. Bertram, Dec. 27, 1975 (div. 1978). B.A., Stanford U., 1975; J.D., U. Denver, 1979. Bar: Colo. 1979. Assoc. Hall & Evans, Denver, 1979-80, Pryor, Carney & Johnson, Englewood, Colo., 1981; sole practice, Denver, 1982—; bd. dirs. Women Bus. Owners Assn., Denver, 1983-84. Deacon, Montview Presbyn. Ch., Denver, 1984. Recipient Am. Jurisprudence award Bancroft-Whitney, 1978. Mem. ABA, Denver Bar Assn., Colo. Bar Assn. Democrat. Office: 2005 E 20th Ave Denver CO 80205

GILMAN, ESTHER, artist, illustrator, set designer; b. Cleve., Aug. 13, 1925; d. Joseph and Bertha (Tenenbaum) Morgenstern; m. Richard M. Gilman, Sept. 1, 1949 (div. 1964); 1 son; Nicholas Alexander. B.S. in Design, U. Mich., 1961; M.A., NYU, 1981. Stage designer The Open Theater La Mama, N.Y.C., 1964-68; freelance illustrator, N.Y.C., 1964—; dir. Designers Workshop, N.Y.C., 1971—; visual cons. The Open Theater, 1964-68; bd. dirs., cons. The Feminist Press, Old Westbury, L.I., 1970-75; one woman shows at Razor Gallery, N.Y., 1978, Washington Sq. E. Gallery, N.Y.C., 1981, Americana in Soho, 1981, Salle Polyvalente, St. Amand Montrond, France, 1983; exhibited in group shows at Mus. Modern Art Young Printmakers, N.Y.C., 1956, Riverside Mus., N.Y.C., 1962, Nat. Acad. N.Y., 1965, Am. Water Color Soc., 1966; Illustrator books: Little Girl and Her Mother, 1964; Nothing But a Dog, 1972 Little Boat, 1974; I've Considered My Days, 1964; designer stage sets: Viet Rock, 1966; Keep Tightly Closed, 1966; It's Almost Like Being, 1964, Miss Nefertitti Regrets, 1965. Recipient medal of honor for watercolor, Painters and Sculptors Soc. N.J., 1958; first prize Robert Boardman award Painter Soc. N.J., 1956; Am. Inst. Graphic Art award, 1970. Fellow Va. Ctr. for Creative Arts, Cummington Community for the Arts; mem. Art Students League N.Y. Address: 160 Riverside Dr New York NY 10024

GILMER, JEROMEE SKEHAN, nurse, educator, therapist; b. Washington, Aug. 2, 1935; d. Jerome Francis and Edith Roberta (Worthington) Skehan; m. Frederick A.C. Baker (div.); children—Jeromee, Andrew, Jeffrey, Jennifer; m. 2d, Charles Frederick Gilmer, Jan. 8, 1984; stepchildren—Kimberly, Pamela, Gary. Student Hood Coll., 1953-55, Cornell U., 1956-57; B.S.N., Gwynedd Mercy Coll., 1979; M.S. in Nursing, U. Pa., 1986. R.N. Pa. Private duty nurse, Plymouth Meeting, Pa., 1967-68; bus mgr. surg. asst. for vet. clinics, 1975-81; instr. vet. econs. Harcum Coll., Bryn Mawr, Pa., 1978-79; v.p. Med. Adminstrn. Inc., Centre Sq., 1979-81; psychiatric staff nurse Eastern Pa. Psychiatric Inst., Phila., 1981, Northwestern Psychiatric Instn., Ft. Washington, Pa., 1982—; infection control practitioner Med. Coll. of Pa., Phila., 1982-83; instr. psychiat. mental health nursing Montgomery County Community Coll., 1982-84; nursing psychiatric cons., 1984—. Mem. Am. Nurses Assn., Pa. Nurses Assn. Republican. Home: 1078 Hemlock Dr Blue Bell PA 19442

GILMORE, MARJORIE HAVENS, lawyer, civic worker; b. N.Y.C., Aug. 16, 1918; d. William Westerfield and Elsie (Medl) Havens; A.B., Hunter Coll., 1938; J.D., Columbia, 1941; m. Hugh Redland Gilmore, May 8, 1942; children—Douglas Hugh, Anne Charlotte Gilmore Decker, Joan Louise. Admitted to N.Y. State bar, 1941, Va. bar, 1968; research asst. N.Y. Law Revision Commn., 1941-42; assoc. firm Spence, Windels, Walser, Hotchkiss & Angell, N.Y.C., 1942, Chadbourne, Wallace, Parke & Whiteside, N.Y.C., 1942-43; atty. U.S. Army, Washington, 1948-53. Sec., Thomas Jefferson Jr. High Sch. PTA, 1956-58; parliamentarian Wakefield High Sch. PTA, 1959-60, chmn. citizenship com., 1960-61; publicity chmn. Patrick Henry Sch. PTA, sec., 1964-65; parliamentarian Nottingham PTA, 1966-69; mem. extra-curricular activities com. Arlington County Sch. Bd.; area chmn. fund drive Cancer Soc., 1955-56; active Girl Scouts U.S.A., 1963-70; mem. '41 com. Columbia Law Sch. Fund. Recipient Constl. Law award Hunter Coll., 1938. Mem. Arlington Fedn. Women's Clubs (rec. sec. 1979-80), No. Dist. Va. Fedn. Women's Clubs (chmn. legis. com. 1986—, legis. chmn. No. Dist. 1986—), Columbia Law Sch. Alumni Assn., Alpha Sigma Rho. Presbyn. Club: Williamsburg Woman's of Arlington (corr. sec. 1970-72, 1st v.p. 1972-74, pres. 1974-76, chmn. communications 1981-82, chmn. legis. com. 1982-86). Home: 3020 N Nottingham St Arlington VA 22207

GILMORE, VHONDA LEAH, nurse; b. Monahans, Tex., Mar. 14, 1957; d. Bob Dean and Lois Elaine (White) Crouse; m. Peter Lee Gilmore, May 15, 1981. B.S. in Nursing, Tex. Woman's U., 1980. Registered nurse, Tex. Charge nurse St. Joseph Hosp., Bryan, Tex., 1980, 82-84, Womens and Children's Hosp., Odessa, Tex., 1981, St. Luke's Hosp., San Antonio, 1981-82; pediatric office nurse, Bryan, Tex., 1984-85; office nurse Samuell Clinic, Dallas, 1985—. Democrat. Baptist. Avocations: softball; racketball; volleyball; tennis. Home: 2066 Windchime Grand Prairie TX 75051 Office: Samuell Clinic 5940 Forest Park Rd Dallas TX 75206

GILROY, DEIRDRE HARNEY, nurse; b. Teaneck, N.J., June 16, 1956; d. Charles Joseph and Anna Lou (Taylor) Harney; m. Gordon Clay Gilroy, May 15, 1982. A.A., Green Mountain Coll., 1976; B.A. in Psychology, Syracuse U., 1979, B.S. in Nursing, 1980. R.N. Mary Hitchcock Hosp., Hanover, N.H., 1980-82, U. Wis. Hosp., Madison, 1982-85, Concord Hosp., N.H., 1985—. Mem. Neurosci. Nurses Assn. Home: RD 1 Box 726B Weare NH 03281

GILSON, JAMIE MARIE, writer; b. Beardstown, Ill., July 4, 1933; d. James Noyce and Sallie Anna (Wilkinson) Chisam; B.S. with honors in Speech, Northwestern U., 1955; m. Jerome Gilson, June 19, 1955; children—Tom, Matthew, Anne. Tchr., Thacker Jr. High Sch., Des Plaines, Ill., 1955-56; writer for ednl. radio, TV and film, producer div. radio and TV, Chgo. Public Schs., 1956-59; continuity dir. Sta. WFMT, Chgo., 1959-63; writer column and articles Chgo. Mag., 1977—; author children's books, including: Harvey, the Beer Can King (Merit award Friends Am. Writers 1979), 1978; Dial Leroi Rupert, D.J., 1979; Do Bananas Chew Gum (Carl Sandburg award Friends Chgo. Public Library 1981, Charlie May Simon award; Arkansas child-voted prize 1983), 1980; Can't Catch Me, I'm the Gingerbread Man, 1981; Thirteen Ways to Sink a Sub, 1982 (Okla. Sequoyah award 1985, Young Reader's Choice award Pacific Northwest Library Assn. 1985); 4B Goes Wild, 1983; Hello, My Name is Scrambled Eggs, 1985; tchr. creative writing 6th grade students, 1974—; lectr. on writing. Mem. Soc. Midland Authors, Children's Reading Round Table, Soc. Children's Book Writers.

GILSON, JUNE ELIZABETH, lawyer; b. Wilmington, Del., June 19, 1955; d. James William and Adele (Bukowski) Gilson; m. Arthur Thomas Donato, Jr., May 7, 1983. B.A. in Polit. Sci., U. Del., 1977; J.D., Del. Law Sch., 1980. Bar: Pa. 1980. Jud. clk. Judge Domenic D. Jerome, County of Del., Media, Pa., 1981-83; atty. Sereni & Lunardi, Broomall, Pa., 1983-84, German, Gallagher and Murtagh, Phila., 1984—; atty. Legal Clinic of Eugene Malady, Upper Darby, Pa., 1980-81. Recipient Am. Jurisprudence award Del. Law Sch., 1980. Mem. ABA, Pa. Bar Assn., Phila. County Bar Assn., Pi Sigma Alpha. Republican. Roman Catholic. Home: 620 S Devon Ave Wayne PA 19087 Office: German Gallagher & Murtagh 1818 Market St Suite 3100 Philadelphia PA 19103

GILTNER, DELORIS MARGARET, nurse; b. Princeton, Ill., Nov. 1, 1922; d. Hugh Verner and Margaret Elizabeth (Hess) G.; B.S. with spl. honors, U. Colo., Boulder, 1959; M.S., U. Calif., San Francisco, 1963; Ph.D., U. Denver, 1979. Supr., instr. Colo. State Hosp., Pueblo, 1949-56; clin. instr., nursing coordinator psychiat. unit St. Mary Corwin Hosp., Pueblo, 1959-64; asst. prof., acting dir. nursing So. Colo. State Coll., Pueblo, 1964-69; asso. prof., acting dir. nursing Met. State Coll., Denver, 1969-74; acting head dept. nursing Carroll Coll., Helena, Mont., 1975; dir. patient care, asst. adminstr. clin. services Boulder (Colo.) Psychiat. Inst., 1976-81; assoc. prof. U. Colo. Sch. Nursing, Denver, 1981—, assoc. dean student affairs, 1981-83; pvt. practice psychiat. counseling, Broomfield, Colo., 1984—; counselor support ctr., Nativity Parish, Broomfield, 1981—. Mem. Am. Nurses Assn. (mem. psychiat. mental health rev. team of nat. rev. com. for accreditation of nurse practitioner programs 1975-76), Nat. League Nursing (mem. forum for adminstrs. nursing 1977-81), Creative Ednl. Found., Am. Assn. Higher Edn., Western Soc. Research Nursing, Colo. Nurses Assn. (pres. 1973-74, 80-81, Nurse of Year 1974, Past Pres. award 1981), Colo. League Nursing, Colo. Soc. Clin. Specialists in Psychiat. Nursing, Sigma Theta Tau. Roman Catholic. Club: Denver Altrusa. Home: 36 Irene Ct Broomfield CO 80020 Office: 4200 E 9th Ave Box C288 Denver CO 80262

GIMOVSKY, ARLENE JOAN, biomedical engineer; b. Jamaica, N.Y., May 18, 1953; d. Gerald W. and Ethel (Friedman) Glaser; B.S. in Chem. Engring., Columbia U., 1973; M.S. in Bio Engring., N.Y.U., 1976; m. Martin L. Gimovsky, June 10, 1973; children—Alexis C. and Matthew D. (twins). With med. products div. Union Carbide Corp., Tarrytown, N.Y., 1973-80, project mgr. immunoassay systems, 1973-80; project mgr. urol. products Pharmaseal div. Am. Hosp. Supply Corp., Glendale, Calif., 1980-82, dir. spl. markets research and devel., 1982-84; pres. Maternal Learning Systems, 1984—. Recipient Creelman prize math. Williston Northampton Acad., 1969; Second Mile award for achievement through excellence Am. Pharmaseal, 1982; Ford Future Scientists of America honorable mention, 1967; grantee NSF summers 1968, 69. Registered profl. engr., Calif. Mem. Am. Inst. Chem. Engrs., Am. Assn. Clin. Chemistry, Nat. Soc. Profl. Engrs., Health Industry Mfrs. Assn. (com. on aids for ostomy and incontinence), Soc. Women Engrs. Author, patentee in field. Office: PO Box 1086 Upland CA 91785

GINALSKI, JUNE JOYCE IRENE HOUGLUND, mgmt. systems co. exec.; b. Kimberley, B.C., Can., May 6, 1938; came to U.S., 1961, naturalized, 1972; d. Charles A. and Elsie Joyce (Hartley) Houglund; A.S., Victoria Coll., 1958; B.S., U. B.C., 1959; Ph.D., Oreg. State U., 1963; postgrad. Harvard U., 1976; m. William Ginalski, Nov. 28, 1969; stepsons, Mark, Kevin. Dir. computing lab. Oreg. State U., 1961-66; cons. Gen. Electric Co., 1966-71; mgr. research and devel. Ramada Inns, Inc., Phoenix, 1972-73; asst. v.p. First Nat. Bank-Western Bancorp. Corp., Phoenix, 1973-78; v.p. planning Gt. Western Bank & Trust Co., Phoenix, 1978-80; asso. Continental Mgmt. Systems, 1980-82; managing partner, Am. Computing Co., 1982—. Mem. Nat. Assn. Bank Women (past dir.), Assn. for Research and Enlightenment, Futurist Soc. Democrat. Club: Harvard. Home: 5501 E Calle Tuberia Phoenix AZ 85018 Office: American Computing Co 845 N 3rd Ave Phoenix AZ 85003

GINSBERG, ELIZABETH, artist, educator; b. N.Y.C., 1942. B.F.A., R.I. Sch. Design, 1964. Instr., R.I. Sch. Design, Providence, 1970-71; mem. faculty Parson Sch. Design, N.Y.C., 1976-77; assoc. prof. art Moore Coll. of Art, Phila., 1971—; lectr. Kyoto Fujikawa Coll. Art, (Japan), U. Utah, Salt Lake City, R.I. Sch. Design; dir. travel/study program to Japan, Moore Coll. of Art, 1973; one-person shows: Chuo Gallery, Tokyo, 1965, Salt Lake Art Ctr., 1973, Susan Caldwell Gallery, N.Y.C., 1976, "Paintings and Works on Paper", U.S. Courthouse, N.Y.C., 1981, "Recent Monotypes", Marsha Mateyka, Washington, 1982, Mus. of Hudson Highlands, Cornwall-on-Hudson, N.Y., 1985, John Nichols, N.Y.C., 1985; group shows include: Kaigado Gallery, Tokyo, 1965, Fischman-Weiner Gallery, Phila., 1967, Providence Art Club, 1971, Del. Art Mus., Wilmington, 141 Prince St. Gallery, N.Y.C., Tweed Mus., Duluth, Minn., 1972, Henri Gallery, Washington, 1973, Moore Coll. of Art Gallery, Phila., Henri Gallery, 1974, Marion Locks Gallery, Phila., Harcus, Krakow, Rosen and Sonnabend Gallery, Boston, 1975, Del. Art Mus., 1976, Henri Gallery, 1976, Susan Caldwell Gallery, Pratt Manhattan Ctr., N.Y.C., Moore Coll. of Art Gallery, 1977, "Landscape, Abstract Landscape, Abstraction", U.S. Courthouse, N.Y.C., "New York, New York", Sebastian-Moore Gallery, Denver, Sargent Gallery, Eastern Ill., U., Charleston, Moore Coll. of Art Gallery, 1980, Judith Christian Gallery, N.Y.C., 1981, Ericson Gallery, N.Y.C., Heydt-Bair Gallery, Santa Fe, Marsha Mateyka Gallery, Washington, Lubbock Arts Festival (Tex.), Gallery 429 West Broadway, Okayama, Japan, 1983, John Christian Gallery, N.Y.C., 1984, numerous others represented in permanent collections: Chase Manhattan Bank, N.A., N.Y.C., Gallery Point, Tokyo, Union Carbide Corp., N.Y.C., First Nat. City Bank, N.Y.C., European-Am. Bank, N.Y.C., U.S. Steel Corp., N.Y.C., Am. Fedn. Savs., Orlando, Fla., First Options of Chgo., Port Authority of N.Y., Chuo Koron Sha Corp., Tokyo, Security Pacific Nat. Bank, Carmichal, Calif., Davis, Polk, and Wardwell, N.Y.C., A.P.F., N.Y.C., Cigna Collection, Phila. Carnegie grantee, 1963-64; Textron fellow, 1965; commd. work Parsippany Plaza Corporate Ctr., N.J., 1985. Moore Coll. of Art Faculty Research grantee, 1982. Office: 5 Great Jones St New York NY 10012

GINSBERG, JACQUELINE SARA FLORENCE, graphic arts and printing brokerage; b. N.Y.C., Nov. 6, 1933; d. Samuel Charles and Sylvia (Libin) Feldman; m. Edward Ginsberg, Mar. 23, 1957; children—Janice Ellen, Steven Fielding. B.S., SUNY-New Paltz, 1955. Buyer, Camp Millinery Buying Office, N.Y.C., 1955-61; with Edwards Graphic Co., Inc., N.Y.C., 1978-80, v.p., 1981-84, pres., 1984—. Chmn., Parents and Tchrs. Edn. Forum of Dist. 10, 1976-78. Recipient Nat. Cross award for Profl. Sales Achievement, 1984; The Morris & Fre Schlosser award Linden Meyr Paper Corp., 1983; Henry Kaufman Jr. Meml. award, 1985. Mem. Women's Bus. Owners of N.Y., Nat.

Assn. Profl. Sales Women (job bank dir. 1983-85), The Navigators of the Graphic Arts Industry. Republican. Hebrew. Avocations: dancing; swimming; horseback riding; reading. Office: Edwards Graphic Co Inc 3801 Hudson Manor Ter New York NY 10463-1199

GINSBERG, JANICE GORDON, marketing consultant, educator; b. Chgo., Feb. 13, 1950; d. David and Eunice (Wienshienk) Gordon; m. Marc David Ginsberg, Jan. 23, 1977; 1 son, Brian David. B.S.J., Northwestern U., 1971, M.B.A., 1973. With tennis mktg. dept. Wilson Sporting Goods Co., River Grove, Ill., 1973-76; advt. dir. Telemedia Inc., Chgo., 1976-78; sr. mgr. new products consumer products G.D. Searle Co., Skokie, Ill., 1978-82; mktg. cons., Wilmette, Ill., 1982—; prof. mktg. Kendall Coll., Evanston, Ill., 1982. Contbr. articles to profl. jours. Recipient Outstanding award Ill. Acad. Sci., 1967; Outstanding Woman of Yr. award Northwestern U., 1968. Mem. Am. Mktg. Assn., Chgo. Mktg. Assn., Assn. M.B.A. Execs., Assn. Nat. Advertisers, Chgo. Heart Assn. Home: 312 Central Park Wilmette IL 60091

GINSBERG, LINDA GARTNER, lawyer, author, lecturer; b. Jacksonville, Fla., Sept. 12, 1942; d. Samuel and Clara (Morgenstern) Gartner; m. Murray T. Ginsberg, June 27, 1965 (dec. 1976); children—Leslie, Marc, Tracy. B.S., Jacksonville U., 1963; J.D., John Marshall Law Sch., Atlanta, 1980. Bar: Ind. 1982, U.S. Dist. Ct. (no. and so. dists.) Ind. 1982. Sole practice, Indpls., 1982—; pres. Am. Practice Appraisers, Inc., Savannah Ga.; lectr. seminars in field. Author: Family Financial Survival, 1980; How to Succeed in Your Professional Practice, 1984; estate planning editor Dental Practice Mag., 1981-82; contbr. articles to publs. including Dental Mgmt. Mag., Dental Econs. Mag., Dental Student Mag., Podiatry Mgmt., Optometric Mgmt., ADA Jour., Ophthology Mgmt. Pres. Aux. to Ga. Dental Assn., Savannah, 1975-76. Recipient Good Samaritan award 1st Ch. Latter Day Saints, Savannah, 1977, Outstanding Woman award Savannah Bus. and Profl. Women, 1980, award Telethon for St. Jude's Children's Hosp., 1980. Mem. ABA, Ind. Bar Assn., Indpls. Bar Assn., Ga. Bar Assn. (assoc.). Republican. Jewish. Home: 125 E 45th St Savannah GA 31405 Office: 309 W Washington St Indianapolis IN 46104

GINSBERG, MARILYN KAPLAN, publisher; b. N.Y.C., Aug. 9, 1952; d. Samuel H. and Anne (Kuntz) Kaplan; m. Michael I. Ginsberg, Oct. 5, 1980. B.A., Queens Coll., CUNY, 1973; M.S., SUNY-Albany, 1974. Asst. to pub. World Press Rev., N.Y.C., 1976-77, circulation dir., 1977-82, assoc. pub., 1982-84, pub., 1984—. Mem. Direct Mktg. Club of N.Y. Office: World Press Rev 230 Park Ave New York NY 10169

GINSBURG, RUTH BADER, judge; b. Bklyn., Mar. 15, 1933; d. Nathan and Celia (Amster) Bader; B.A., Cornell U., 1954; postgrad. Harvard Law Sch., 1956-58; J.D. (Kent scholar), Columbia U., 1959; LL.D. (hon.), Lund (Sweden) U., 1969, Am. U., 1981, Vt. Law Sch., 1984, DePaul U., 1985, Georgetown U., 1985; m. Martin David Ginsburg, June 23, 1954; children—Jane Carol, James Steven. Bar: N.Y. 1959, D.C., U.S. Supreme Ct. Law clk. to dist. judge So. Dist. N.Y., 1959-61; research assoc. Columbia Law Sch. Project on Internat. Procedure, 1961-62, asso. dir., 1962-63; asst. prof. law Rutgers U., Newark, 1963-66, asso. prof., 1966-69, prof., 1969-72; prof. law Columbia, N.Y.C., 1972-80; U.S. circuit judge U.S. Ct. of Appeals for D.C. Circuit, Washington, 1980—; gen. counsel ACLU, 1973-80, bd. dirs, 1974-80. Mem. Am. Bar Assn. (bd. editors jour. 1972-78, council sect. individual rights and responsibilities 1975-81), Bar Assn. N.Y.C. (exec. com. 1974-80), Am. Law Inst. (council 1979—), Am. Bar Found. (dir. 1979—, exec. com. 1981—), Am. Acad. Arts and Scis., Council Fgn. Relations, Phi Beta Kappa (vis. scholar 1973-74), Phi Kappa Phi. Author: (with Anders Bruzelius) Civil Procedure in Sweden, 1965, The Swedish Code of Judicial Procedure, 1968; A Selective Survey of English Language Studies on Scandinavian Law, 1970; Constitutional Aspects of Sex-Based Discrimination, 1974; (with others) Sex-Based Discrimination, Text, Cases and Materials, 1974, supplement, 1978. Bd. editors Am. Jour. Comparative Law, 1966-72. Contbr. articles to books, encys., legal jours., mags. Home: 700 New Hampshire Ave NW Washington DC 20037 Office: US Ct of Appeals US Courthouse Washington DC 20001

GINTER, DOLORES DENA (DEDE), public relations consultant; b. Chgo., Aug. 22, 1929; d. Benjamin and Dorothy Vera (Doroshow) Henner; m. Edward M. Ginter, Nov. 22, 1950; children—Susan Allyn, Barbara Ann. Student Northwestern U., 1948-49. Dir. pub. relations and programming Muckenthaler Cultural Ctr., Fullerton, Calif., 1970-73; dir. pub. relations Rubin Advt. Inc., Fullerton, 1975-78; pres. Ginter Assocs., Fullerton, 1978—. Author chpts. in book. Contbr. articles to jours. in field. Active Nat. Women's Polit. Caucus, Orange County, Calif., 1975—; campaign dir. local, county, city, state candidates, jud. candidates, 1960-80; chmn. Fullerton Bicentennial Commn., 1974-76; trustee Girls' Clubs of Orange County, 1981-85; trustee Mus. North Orange County, 1978-82; 83, 84; council on extended edn. Calif. State U.-Fullerton, 1982—, profl. adviser pub. relations sequence, 1984—. Recipient Outstanding Citizen award City of Fullerton, 1976. Mem. Pub. Relations Soc. Am. (accredited, fellow counselor's acad., Protos award 1980, 81, 82, 83, 84; numerous awards of excellence, bd. dirs. 1980—, v.p. Orange County chpt. 1982-83, bd. dirs. 1984—), Democrat. Jewish. Club: Press of Orange County (Most Valuable Mem. award 1982). Office: Ginter Assocs 1816 Yermo Pl Fullerton CA 92633

GIOIA, KATHLEEN ROURKE, microbiologist; b. Waterbury, Conn., Jan. 7, 1933; d. James Michael and Kathleen Anetta (Classey) Rourke; B.A. in Microbiology, U. Conn., 1956; postgrad. Nova U. Grad. Sch., 1976-79; m. Anthony A. Gioia, Sept. 25, 1954 (div. 1966); children—Patrick, Kathleen, Michael. Intern Riverside (Calif.) Community Hosp., 1958-59, med. technologist, 1959-61; microbiologist, serologist Univ. Mo. Med. Center and Hosps., Columbia, 1961-64; supr. dept. microbiology St. Francis Hosp., Miami Beach, Fla., 1967-69; asst. to dir. research and quality control Gray Industries, Ft. Lauderdale, Fla., 1971-73; supr. dept. microbiology Fla. Med. Center, Ft. Lauderdale, 1973-75; microbiologist spl. testing North Ridge Gen. Hosp., Ft. Lauderdale, 1975—. Treas. Coral Springs Women's Club, 1975-77. Mem. Am. Soc. Microbiology, Am. Acad. Microbiology. Club: Coral Springs Women's. Office: 5757 North Dixie Hwy Fort Lauderdale FL 33334

GIOIA-CAMPBELL, MICHELE, publishing company supervisor; b. St. Louis, Sept. 26, 1954; d. Charles Louis and Patricia Ruth (Luck) Gioia; m. John Yockey Campbell, July 16, 1982; 1 child, Melissa Rose. B.A. in Liberal Arts with major Communications, St. Louis U., 1980—. Service order writer Southwestern Bell Telephone Co., St. Louis, 1980-81, directory composer, Southwestern Bell Pub., 1981-84; supr., 1984—. Mem. LWV, St. Louis, 1986. Recipient Sta. KTVI-Times Mirror scholarship, St. Louis, 1984. Mem. Nat. Assn. Female Execs., Am. Mgmt. Assn., Alpha Sigma Lambda. Roman Catholic. Avocations: reading, antiques, gardening, writing. Office: Southwestern Bell Pubs 1830 Craig Park Ct Saint Louis MO 63146

GIOPPO, NANCY JOY, ladies health club executive; b. Rockford, Ill., Sept. 28, 1953; d. Anthony Dominic and Nancy Dorothy (Raia) Arbisi; m. Michael Steven Gioppo, Sept. 29, 1973; children—Andrea, Peter, Michelle. Grad. high sch., Rockford. Owner, operator Capri Phys. Fitness Ctr. (formerly Shelly Lynn Health Club), Rockford, 1971—. Chmn. Am. Heart Assn. Dance for Heart, Rockford, 1984—. Democrat. Roman Catholic. Home: 3012 Latham St Rockford IL 61103 Office: Capri Phys Fitness Ctr 2416 S Alpine Rd Rockford IL 61108

GIORDANO, JUDITH LUCIA, publishing exec.; b. Bronx, N.Y., Feb. 11, 1954; d. Joseph Francesco and Elida Felicia (Buccino) G.; B.A. in Archaeology and Anthropology, Friends World Coll., 1976. Student archaeologist, Kyoto (Japan) Govt., 1973-74; free lance archaeologist, Rome, Italy, 1974-77; circulation clk. Natural History Mag., Am. Mus. Natural History, N.Y.C., 1978-79, fulfillment mgr., 1979-80; asst. circulation mgr. Bill Communications, N.Y.C., 1980, circulation mgr., 1981, dir. circulation plastics/chem. div., 1981-83, v.p. plastics/chem. div., 1983—; free lance cons. direct mail and circulation fulfillment. Recipient public service award Asahi Shimbun, Japan, 1974. Mem. Nat. Assn. Female Execs., Am. Bus. Press, Women in Communications, Fulfillment Mgr. Assn., Nat. Bus. Circulation Assn. Office: Bill Communications 633 3d Ave New York NY 10017

GIORGI, ELSIE AGNES, physician, educator b. N.Y.C., Mar. 8, 1911; d. Anacleto and Maria (Maserati) G. B.A., Hunter Coll., 1931; postgrad. Columbia U., 1943-45, M.D., 1949. Intern, Cornell 2d Med. Div., Bellevue Hosp., N.Y.C., 1949-50, asst. resident in medicine, Cornell Div., 1950-52, chief resident in medicine, 1952-53, chief of gen. med. clinics, 1953-59, assoc. attending physician, Bellevue Hosp., 1953-62; practice medicine specializing in internal medicine, N.Y.C., 1953-61, Los Angeles, 1962—; psychiat. trainee Cedars of Lebanon Hosp., Los Angeles, 1961-62, assoc. attending physician, 1962—; dir. div. home care and extended care Cedars-Sinai Med. Center, Los Angeles, 1962-66; chief of adolescent clinic, med. dir. clinics Mt. Sinai Hosp., Los Angeles, 1962-66, assoc. attending physician dept. medicine, 1962-69, attending physician, 1970—; med. dir., coordinator U. So. Calif. Family Neighborhood Health Services Center for Watts, 1966-67; attending physician Los Angeles County Hosp., U. So. Calif. Med. Center, 1966-71; assoc. mem. dept. internal medicine Orange County Med. Center, Orange, Calif., 1969—, dir. ambulatory care services, 1969-72; staff St. John's Hosp., Santa Monica, Calif., 1970—; adv. student health services State Coll., Dominguez Hills, Calif., 1967-73; asst. prof. clin. medicine Cornell U. Med. Coll., 1957-62; asst. prof. clin. medicine UCLA, 1962-66, guest lectr. Sch. Social Welfare, 1964—, assoc. clin. prof. medicine and community medicine Sch. Medicine, U. So. Calif., 1972—, PRIMEX, 1972-73; asst. prof. medicine Sch. Medicine, U. So. Calif., 1966-69, adj. assoc. prof. community dentistry Sch. Dentistry, 1970—; assoc. clin. prof. medicine, community medicine, family medicine Coll. Medicine, U. Calif., Irvine, 1969-72; cons. Martin E. Segal Co., 1969—, VA Hosp., Long Beach, Calif., 1972—, Washington, 1972—, Health Care Set. Social Security Adminstrn., Balt., Los Angeles County Health Dept., Calif. Council for Health Plan Alternative, Burlingame, Calif., Calif. Council for Health Plan Alternatives, Calif. Regional Med. Care Program, 1971-73, Tb and Health Assn. of Los Angeles; mem. nat. adv. bd. Nat. Council Sr. Citizens, Washington; mem. adv. com. USPHS, Calif. State Dept. Public Health, Vis. Nurse Assn. Los Angeles, 1976, Life Extension Inst., N.Y.C.; mem. edn. com. Am. Cancer Soc., San Francisco, cons. ednl. films. Active Town Hall, Los Angeles; vol., bd. dirs. South Central Child Care Centers for South Central Los Angeles. Recipient Achievement award AAUW, 1968; Better Life award for Patient Care in Medicine, Am. Nursing Home Assn., Washington, 1974; named to Hall of Fame, Hunter Coll. Alumnis Assn., 1976. Diplomate Am. Bd. Internal Medicine Mem. AMA, N.Y. County Med. Assn., Calif. Med. Assn., Los Angeles County Med. Assn., Los Angeles County Soc. Internists, Am. Public Health Assn. (med. care sect), Gerontol. Soc., Western Gerontology Assn., Nat. Council Sr. Citizens (nat. adv. bd. for legal research and services for elderly), UCI-21 Project Com. U. Calif., Irvine, Comprehensive Health Planning, Los Angeles, Nat. Acad. Scis., Inst. Medicine. Author sect. in textbook; contbr. articles to profl. jours.; presenter papers in fields of medicine, health care, aging, health benefits adminstr., women in stress to ednl. med. sci. govt. confs. Address: 153 S Lasky Dr Suite 3 Beverly Hills CA 90212

GIOSEFFI, DANIELA, poet, novelist, educator; b. Orange, N.J., Feb. 12, 1941; d. Daniel Donato and Josephine (Buzeska) G.; m. Richard J. Kearney, Sept. 7, 1965 (div.); 1 child, Thea D.; m. Lionel B. Luttinger, June 6, 1986. B.A., Montclair State Coll., 1963; M.F.A., Catholic U. of America, 1966. Cons., poet N.Y. Poets-in-the-Schs., Inc., N.Y.C., 1972—; free lance writer, lectr. at numerous univs. throughout U.S. and Europe, 1977—; novels include: The Great American Belly, 1977, 4th edit., 1979; collection of poems: Eggs in the Lake, 1979; non-fiction: Earth Dancing; Mother Nature's Oldest Rite, 1981; contbr. poetry, fiction and criticism to numerous periodicals and anthologies; performer stage presentations of work throughout U.S. and Europe; plays produced Off-Off-Broadway include The Golden Daffodil Dwarf, Care of the Body, The Sea Hag in the Cave of Sleep, N.Y.C., 1971-74. Vice-pres. Bklyn. Citizens for Sane Nuclear Policy, 1978-84; exec. bd. Writers and Pubs. Alliance for Disarmament, 1984—. Grantee NEA, 1972, N.Y. State Council on Arts, 1977; recipient Poetry/Fiction award Creative Artists' Pub. Service grantee N.Y. State Council on Arts. Mem. PEN Am. Ctr., Poetry Soc. America (poetry judge 1973-86), Actors' Equity Assn., Acad. Am. Poets, Author's Guild, Friends of Earth, Planetary Citizens at UN. Address: Earth Celebrations PO Box 197 Brooklyn Heights NY 11202

GIOVANNIELLO, MARGARET MONTGOMERY TORR, judge; b. Terre Haute, Ind., May 23, 1927; d. Raymond Osborne and Luella B. (Montgomery) Torr; m. Joseph Louis Giovanniello, June 10, 1951; children—Rocco, Raymond, Joseph, Earle. B.A., U. Wis., 1949; J.D., Bklyn. Law Sch., 1956. Bar: N.Y. 1957, U.S. Dist. Ct. (so. and ea. dists.) N.Y. 1962, U.S. Ct. Appeals (2d cir.) 1975, U.S. Supreme Ct. 1976. Copywriter W.T. Grant Co., N.Y.C., 1950; social worker N.Y. State Worker's Compensation Bd., N.Y.C., 1951; teller Chase Bank, N.Y.C., 1951; social investigator N.Y.C. Dept. of Welfare, 1949-50, N.Y.C. Dept. Hosps., 1952-53; asst. title search N.Y.C. Housing Authority, 1953-57; atty. Giovanniello & Giovanniello, Bklyn., 1957—; unemployment ins. administry. law judge N.Y. State Dept. of Labor, N.Y.C., 1977—; dir. Community Action for Legal Services, N.Y.C., 1980—. Mem. Bklyn. Women's Bar Assn. (past dir., rec. sec., treas., v.p., pres. 1982-84), Nassau Suffolk Women's Bar Assn. (treas. 1982-83), Bklyn. Bar Assn. (dir. 1983-86), Nat. Assn. Adminstrv. Law Judges (dir. 1984-85, pres.-elect 1985-86), N.Y. State Assn. Administrv. Law Judges (dir. N.Y.C. 1983-84, pres. 1984-85), N.Y. Women's Bar Assn., Bklyn. Women's Polit. Caucus, Kings County Criminal Bar Assn., Am. Judges Assn., Nat. Assn. Women Judges. Democrat. Roman Catholic. Clubs: Town Hall (N.Y.C.); Bklyn. Home: 718 1/2 President St Brooklyn NY 11215 Office: New York State Unemployment Ins Appeals Bd 2 World Trade Ctr New York NY 10048

GIOVE, BARBARA ANN JEAN, photographer; b. Bklyn., Aug. 6, 1954; d. Salvatore Thomas and Theresa Ann (Vitale) G.; student York Coll., 1972-73, Queens Coll., 1973-74. Freelance photographer, Jamaica Estates, N.Y., 1956—. Mem. Internat. Photography Soc., Photog. Soc. Am., Nat. Found. Ileitis and Colitis, Cousteau Soc., Animal Protection Inst., Nat. Audubon Soc., Fund for Animals, Nat. Wildlife Soc., Am. Mus. Natural History, Smithsonian Instn., Greenpeace. Democrat. Roman Catholic. Address: 182-04 80th Dr Jamaica Estates NY 11432

GIRARD, ELISA MICHELE, graphic artist; b. Paterson, N.J., May 3, 1953; d. Theodore Alsdorf and Estelle Ellen (Farley) Girard; m. Thomas Joseph Hernandez, Oct. 8, 1983. B.F.A., St. Mary's Coll., Notre Dame, Ind., 1975. Art asst. Tech. Pub. Co. div. Dun & Bradstreet Corp., Barrington, Ill., 1975-79; staff artist, 1979-81, art dir. for Power Engring. Mag. and Electric Light & Power mag., 1981—; propr., chief exec. officer EMG Enteprises, Barrington, 1978—. Mem. Nat. Trust for Historic Preservation, Lincoln Park Zoo, Brookfield Zoo, St. Mary's Alumni Assn., NOW. Democrat. Roman Catholic. Office: Technical Publishing Co 1301 S Grove Ave Barrington IL 60010

GIRARD, NETTABELL, lawyer; b. Riverton, Wyo., Feb. 24, 1938; d. George and Arranetta (Bell) Girard. Student Idaho State U., 1957-58; B.S., U. Wyo., 1959, LL.B., 1961. Bar: Wyo. 1961, D.C. 1969, U.S. Supreme Ct. 1969. Sole practice, Riverton, 1963-69, 84—; atty.-adviser on gen. counsel's staff HUD, assigned Office Interstate Land Sales Registration, Washington, 1969-70, sect. chief interstate land sales Office Gen. Counsel, 1970-73; ptnr. Larson & Larson, Riverton, 1973-84; guest lectr. at high schs.; condr. seminar on law for layman Riverton br. AAUW, 1965; condr. course on women and law; lectr. equal rights, job discrimination, land use planning. Editor Wyo. Clubwoman, 1966-68; bd. editors Wyo. Law Jour., 1959-61; writer Obiter Dictum column Women Lawyers Jour.; contbr. articles in law jours. Chmn. fund drive Wind River chpt. ARC, 1965, Citizens Com. for Better Hosp. Improvement, 1965; chmn. sub-com. on polit., legal rights and responsibilities Gov.'s Commn. on Status of Women, 1965-69, adv. mem., 1973—, rep. Nat. Conf. Govs. Commn., Washington, 1966; local chmn. Law Day, 1966, 67; state bd. dirs. Wyo. Girl Scouts U.S.A., sec., 1974-76, nat. bd. dirs., 1978-81; state vol. adviser Nat. Found., March of Dimes, 1967-69, 84—; bd. dirs. Am. Lung Assn. Wyo., 1984—; co-host Wyo. segment March of Dimes Teleton, 1984, 85; legal counsel Wyo. Women's Conf., 1977. Recipient Spl. Achievement award HUD, 1972; Disting. Leadership award Girl Scouts U.S.A., 1973; Franklin D. Roosevelt award March of Dimes, 1985; selected by Wonder Woman Found. and Girl Scouts U.S.A. one of five outstanding women in U.S. to make a unique and distinctive personal contbn. to women's history; spl. award Women's History Conf., 1982. Mem. Wyo. Bar Assn., Fremont County Bar Assn., D.C. Bar Assn., Women's Bar Assn. for D.C., Internat. Fedn. Women Lawyers, Am. Judicature Soc., Assn. Trial Lawyers Am., Nat. Assn. Women Lawyers (del. Wyo., nat. sec. 1969-70, v.p. 1970-71, pres. 1972-73), AAUW (br. pres.), Wyo. Fedn. Women's Clubs (state editor, pres. elect 1968-69, treas. 1974-76), Riverton Civic League, Kappa Delta, Delta Kappa Gamma (hon. mem. state chpt.). Clubs: Riverton Chautauqua (pres. 1965-67), Progressive Women's. Home: 224 W Sunset PO Box 687 Riverton WY 82501 Office: 513 E Main St Riverton WY 82501

GIRDEN, LISA JAN, family and marriage therapist; b. Stamford, Conn., Aug. 28, 1959; d. Eugene Lawrence and Charlene Margot (Tobin) Girden. B.A., Bucknell U., 1981; M.S., U. Pa., 1982, 84. Cert. in marriage and family therapy. Tchr., Internat. Sch. Paris, 1980-81; mental health worker Ctr. for Autistic Children, Phila., 1983; asst. dir., acting dir. Old Pine Community Ctr., Phila., 1984—; counselor Inst. for Learning, Phila., 1985—; pvt. practice psychology, family therapy, Rittenhouse Counseling Assocs., Phila., 1985—; asst. dir. aftersch. program Old Pine Community Ctr., Phila., 1985—. Mem. Am. Psychol. Assn. Club: Queen Village Racquetball. Avocations: skiing; horseback riding; needlepoint; gourmet cooking; travel. Office: Rittenhouse Counseling Assocs 2022 Locust St Philadelphia PA 19103

GIRIFALCO, SANDRA ANN, lawyer; b. Cin., Aug. 2, 1953; d. Louis Anthony and Catherine Ann (Lyons) G. B.A., U. Pa., 1975; J.D. (award), U. Pitts., 1980. Personnel mgr. Hosp. U. Pa., Phila., 1975-77; assoc. Stradley, Ronon, Stevens & Young, Phila., 1980—; instr. labor law La Salle Coll., Phila., 1983—. Editor U. Pitts. Law Rev., 1979-80. Litigation and labor atty. Mem. ABA, Am. Trial Lawyers Assn., Pa. Bar Assn., Phila. Bar Assn., AAUW (chpt. dir. 1984-85). Roman Catholic. Club: Phila. Bd. Women Ofcls. Office: Stradley Ronon Stevens & Young 1100 One Franklin Plaza Philadelphia PA 19102

GIRLING, BETTIE JOYCE MOORE, home health executive; b. Midlothian, Tex., Feb. 10, 1930; d. Robert and Florence Irene (Shaw) Moore; B.S. in Edn., Daniel Baker Coll., 1952; M.S.S.W., U. Tex., Austin, 1956; m. Robert George William Girling, III, Sept. 2, 1960; children—Robert George William IV, Maria Julia Anastasia Waggoner, Samuel Marcus Shaw, Katherine Susan Jane. Tchr., Clairemont (Tex.) Ind. Sch. Dist., 1952-53; caseworker Tex. Dept. Public Welfare, 1953-57, licensing supr., Dallas, 1960; caseworker Austin State Sch. for Mentally Retarded, 1957-60; with adoption intake Edna Gladney Home, Ft. Worth, 1961-65; researcher Child Welfare League Am., N.Y.C., 1966; organizer, exec. dir. Girling Home Care, Austin, 1967-69; asst. dir. agy. programs Girling Health Care, Inc., multi-state, comprehensive health care agy., 1967—; owner, operator child care facility, 1973-75; mem. long range planning com. Grad. Sch. Social Work, U. Tex.-Austin; mem. home health services adv. council Tex. Dept. Health; organizer, coordinator profl. workshops; Mem. Nat. Assn. Social Workers, Tex. Hosp. Assn., Tex. Home Health Agys., Nat. Assn. Home Health Agys., Women's Symphony League of Austin, Austin Symphony Orchestra Soc. (bd. dirs.). Democrat. Baptist. Office: 4902 Grover Ave PO Box 4294 Austin TX 78765

GIROD, JUDY, interior design firm executive; b. Alexandria, La., Aug. 24, 1948; d. John James and Lily (McKnight) Capdevielle; m. Jerold S. Girod, Aug. 22, 1970. B.F.A. in Interior Design, La. State U., 1971. Interior designer Bowles Inc., 1970-72; interior designer, mgr. dept. Clyde W. Smith Co., 1972-75; interior designer Blitch Architects, 1975-79; owner, pres. Judy Girod Interior Design Inc. (now Girod-Halley Design Group), New Orleans, 1979—. Contbr. series on interior design to Gambit Mag.Bd. dirs. Coliseum Sq. Assn., 1980—, St. Charles Ave. Bus. Assn., 1982, co-pres. Magazine St. Bus. Assn., 1984., Fashion Group of New Orleans, 1986, Crescent House, home for battered women, 1985, 86. Mem. La. State U. Alumni Assn. (dir. Greater New Orleans Met. chpt. 1979-80), Am. Soc. Interior Designers (pres. La. dist. chpt. 1982-83, nat. bd. dirs. 1985), Inst. Bus. Designers, Delta Zeta. Republican. Roman Catholic. Clubs: Spring Fiesta, Fashion Group, Preservation Resource Ctr. Home: 1402 Magazine St New Orleans LA 70130 Office: 1943 Magazine St New Orleans LA 70130

GIRON, JENNY M., educational administrator; b. Deming, N.Mex., July 8, 1956; d. Miguel and Manuela (Martinez) G. B.A., N.Mex. State U., 1978, M.A., 1980. Unemployment ins. specialist Dept. of Labor, Washington, 1980-81; instr. SER, Jobs for Progress, El Paso, Tex., 1981-82; supr. Kelly Services, Inc., El Paso, 1982-83; coordinator Worker Tng. Inst., El Paso Community Coll., 1983-85, coordinator off-campus credit program, 1986—. Contbr. article to profl. jour. Participant Si Se Puede Conf., El Paso, 1985. Mem. Bus. and Profl. Women, Am. Mgmt. Assn. (trainer 1986). Nat. Assn. Female Execs. Democrat. Club: Intercambios. Avocation: reading. Home: 200 Wallington 180 El Paso TX 79902

GIRONE, JOAN CHRISTINE CRUSE, county official; b. Kingston, Ont., Can., Aug. 30, 1927; naturalized U.S. citizen; d. Arthur William and Helen Wilson Cruse; m. Joseph Michael Girone, June 26, 1954; children—Susan, Richard, William. Buyer, Franklin Simon, Inc., N.Y.C., 1946-54; supr. Midlothian dist. Chesterfield County (Va.) Bd. Suprs., 1976—, vice chmn., 1976-82; Founding mem. Capitol Area Agy. on Aging, 1973—; commr., chmn. Richmond (Va.) Regional Planning Dist. Commn., 1976—, chmn. community edn. adv. com. Va. Bd. of Edn., 1972-79; mem. Va. Gov.'s Adv. Bd. on Aging, 1980-82; chmn. Richmond Met. Transp. Planning Orgn., 1981—; bd. visitors Va. State U., 1980-84; chmn. Chesterfield County Com. to elect John Warner and Paul Trible to U.S. Senate, 1979, 82, 84; Chesterfield chmn. Marshall Coleman for Gov., 1981—; chmn. Women for Reagan-Bush, 1984; state chmn. Va. Fedn. Rep. Women, 1985, mem. candidate recruitment com., 1985; mem. Central Va. River Basin com., 1985; chmn. evaluation task force United Way of Greater Richmond, 1985; bd. dirs. Maymont Found., 1982 . Recipient Good Govt. award Richmond First Club, 1985. Mem. Va. Assn. Counties (exec. bd. 1982—). Club: Huguenot Republican Woman's (Rep. Woman of Yr. 1983). Home: 2609 Dovershire Rd Bon Air VA 23235

GIROUARD, PEGGY JO FULCHER, ballet educator; b. Corpus Christi, Tex., Oct. 25, 1933; d. J.B. and Zora Alice (Jackson) Fulcher; m. Richard Ernest Girouard, Apr. 16, 1954 (div. Mar. 1963); children—Jo Linne, Richard Ernest. B.S. in Elem. Edn., U. Houston, 1970. Ballet Instr. Emmamae Horn Studio, Houston, 1951-81; owner, dir. Allegro Acad. Dance, Houston, 1981—; adminstrv. asst. Sugar Creek Homes Assn., Sugar Land, Tex., from 1979; artistic dir. Allegro Ballet Houston, from 1976. Choreographer (with Glenda W. Brown) Masquerade Suite, 1983, Sebelius Suite, 1983. Mem. Dance Masters Am. (dir. 1977-80), S.W. Regional Ballet Assn. (chmn. craft of choreography 1983—, coordinator to nat. assn. 1983), Am. Bus. Women's Assn. Democrat. Baptist. Home: 9925 Warwana St Houston TX 77080 *

GIROUARD, SHIRLEY ANN, nurse, municipal official; b. New London, Conn., Jan. 16, 1947; d. Maxime Albert Girouard and Irene Barbara (Arnold) Reid. Diploma in Nursing, Hartford Hosp. (Conn.), 1968; B.A. in Sociology, Eastern Conn. State Coll., Willimantic, 1972; M.A. in Sociology, U. Conn.-Storrs, 1974; M.S. in Nursing, Yale U., 1977; postgrad. Brandeis U. Cert. clin. nurse specialist, Am. Nurses Assn. Pub. health nurse Woodstock Pub. Health (Conn.), 1968-70; in service edn. coordinator Middlesex Meml. Hosp., Middletown, Conn., 1973-75; research asst. Yale U., 1976-77; clin. nurse specialist Mary Hitchcock Meml. Hosp., Hanover, N.H., 1977-83, nurse researcher, 1983—; cons. Profl. Devel. Cons., West Lebanon, N.H., 1983—; mem. N.H. Ho. of Reps., 1982-84; mem. West Lebanon City Council, N.H., 1985—. Contbr. chpts. to books and articles to profl. jours. Vice chmn. Lebanon Democratic Com., 1983; chmn. Health Caucus N.H. State Dems., Manchester, 1984. Grantee NIH, 1976-77, NIMH, 1983-84. Mem. Inst. Applied and Profl. Ethics, N.H. Nurses Assn. (dir. 1978-80), Sigma Theta Tau.

GIRTH, MARJORIE LOUISA, lawyer, educator; b. Trenton, N.J., Apr. 21, 1939; d. Harold Brookman and Marjorie Mathilda (Simonson) Girth; A.B., Mt. Holyoke Coll., 1959; LL.B., Harvard U., 1962. Admitted to N.J. bar, 1963, N.Y. bar, 1976, U.S. Supreme Ct. bar, 1969; pvt. practice, Trenton, 1963-65; research asso. Brookings Instn., 1965-70; assoc. prof. law SUNY Law Sch., Buffalo, 1971-79, prof., 1979—; vis. prof. U. Va. Law Sch., 1979-80. Bd. dirs. Buffalo and Erie County YWCA, 1972-76, Buffalo Unitarian Universalist Ch., 1981-84; mem. commn. on peace, justice and human rights Internat. Assn. Religious Freedom, 1976-79; chmn. Erie County Task Force Status of Women, 1985-86. Mem. ABA (consumer bankruptcy com. 1978—, chmn. consumer bankruptcy com. 1983—, mem. council of corp., banking, bus. law sect. 1985—), N.Y. Bar Assn. (exec. com. bus. law sect. 1980—; mem. bankruptcy law com. 1980—, chmn. bankruptcy law com. 1980-82), Erie County Bar Assn., N.Y. Women's Bar Assn., Mt. Holyoke Alumnae Assn. (Centennial award 1972). Author: Poor People's Lawyers, 1976; Bankruptcy Options for the Consumer Debtor, 1981; co-author: Bankruptcy: Problem, Process, Reform, 1971. Office: O'Brian Hall SUNY North Campus Buffalo NY 14260

GISCOMBE DAVIS, BEVERLY G, lawyer; b. East Orange, N.J., June 29, 1951; d. Ernest Davis and Mary Ellen (Irvin) Payne; m. Nov. 9, 1969 (div. Feb. 1974). B.A., Montclair State Coll., 1974, M.A., 1976; J.D., Seton Hall Coll., 1978. Bar: N.J. 1979, U.S. Dist. Ct. N.J. 1979. Tchr., Newark Bd. Edn., 1973-77; atty. All-State Ins. Co., Cranford, N.J., 1978-81, City of East Orange, 1981-83; sole practice law, East Orange, 1981—; ; atty., dep. counsel Essex County Bd. of Freeholders, Newark, 1982—; atty. NAACP of Oranges and Maplewood, Branch, N.J., 1982—. Mem. N.J. Student Assistance Bd. Higher

Edn., 1982—. Recipient award United Negro Coll. Fund, 1982. Mem. Am. Trial Lawyers Assn., Assn. Black Women Lawyers (N.J. dir. 1980-82), Negro Bus. and Profl. Women's Club (outstanding achievement woman in law award North Jersey unit 1982). Democrat. Baptist. Home: 175 Prospect St East Orange NJ 07018

GISH, DEBRA LEE, advertising executive; b. Washington, Feb. 26, 1954; d. Floyd Junior II and Nancy Lee (Hay) G. B.A. in Spanish and Linguistics, Ind. U., 1976. Nutrition supr. Peace Corps., Honduras, Central Am., 1976-78; radio broadcaster Sta. WBAA-Radio, Lafayette, Ind., 1978-79; account exec. Madison Ave., N.Y.C., 1979-82; mgmt. account supr. Sosa & Assocs., San Antonio, 1982—; mem. health steering com. Peace Corps, Washington, 1978—; counselor Teen Connection, San Antonio, 1985—; advtg. cons. Am. Cancer Soc., San Antonio, 1983—. Advisor United Way of San Antonio, 1982—, Ellis Island-Liberty Found., N.Y.C., 1985; mem. U.S. rep. Senatorial Task Force, 1984—. Named Outstanding Vol. of 1978 Peace Corps, 1978; Ind. U. grantee, 1974. Mem. Am. Mktg. Assn., Cert. Translators' Assn., Hispanics in Communications. Republican. Avocations: swimming; camping; hiking; racquetball. Home: 7810 Callaghan Rd #407 San Antonio TX 78229 Office: Sosa & Assocs 321 Alamo Plaza San Antonio TX 78205

GISH, LILLIAN, actress; b. Springfield, Ohio; d. James Lee and Mary (Robinson) Gishi; A.F.D., Rollins Coll.; H.H.D., Mt. Holyoke Coll.; D.F.A. (hon.), Bowling Green State U., 1976, Middlebury Coll. Debut on stage at 5; appeared in motion pictures, 1913—, including Birth of a Nation, Hearts of the World, Broken Blossoms, Way Down East, Orphans of the Storm, La Boheme, Scarlet Letter, Annie Laurie, The Wind, The Enemy, Night of the Hunter, The Cobweb, Miss Susie Slagle's, Duel in the Sun, Portrait of Jennie, Orders to Kill, The Unforgiven, 1960, Follow Me Boys, 1966, The Comedians, 1967, A Wedding, 1978, (TV) Thin Ice, 1980, Sweet Liberty, 1985; movies made in Italy: The White Sister, Romola; appeared in the theatre, 1930—, plays include Uncle Vanya, Camille, 9 Pine Street, Within the Gates, Ophelia in Hamlet, Star Wagon, Life with Father, The Marquise, Legend of Leonara, Crime and Punishment, 1948, title role in Miss Mabel, 1950, The Curious Savage, 1950, The Trip to Bountiful, Portrait of a Madonna, The Wreck of the 5:25, The Family Reunion, (Pulitzer Prize play) All the Way Home, 1960-61, nurse in Romeo and Juliet, 1965, Anya, 1966, I Never Sang for My Father, 1967, 68, Too True To Be Good, 1963, A Passage to India, 1963, Uncle Vanya, 1973, A Musical Jubilee, 1975; also many TV plays and movies including Twin Detectives, 1976, Sparrow, 1977, Hobson's Choice, 1983; Hambone and Hillie, 1984, Huckleberry Finn, 1984; documentary Jeanne Moreau, 1984. Toured Europe, Russia as lectr. on art films, 1969, 71-72, U.S.A., 1969-73; Royal Command appearance Queen Elizabeth the Queen Mothers, 1980. Recipient hon. Acad. Award, 1971; Handel medallion, City of N.Y., 1973; Medal of Arts and Letters, French Govt., 1983; Life Achievement award Am. Film Inst., 1984. Author: The Movies, Mr. Griffith and Me, 1969; Dorothy and Lillian Gish, 1973. Address: 430 E 57th St New York NY 10022

GITELSON, SUSAN AURELIA, business executive, civic leader; b. N.Y.C.; d. Moses Leo and Miriam Evelyn (Silverman) G. B.A., Barnard Coll., 1963; M.I.A., Columbia Sch. Internat. Affairs, 1966; Ph.D., Columbia U., 1970. Trainee Rockefeller Found., 1963-64; asst. prof. internat. relations Hebrew U., Jerusalem, 1970-75; research assoc. Columbia U., N.Y.C., 1975; dir. internat. affairs and third world World Jewish Congress, N.Y.C., 1976-80; pres. Internat. Cons., Inc., N.Y.C., 1980—; nat. dir. premiums and mail order Leifheit Internat., N.Y.C., 1981—; v.p. mktg. and sales Keter Plastic (USA), N.Y.C., 1982—. Author: Multilateral Aid for National Development and Self-Reliance, 1975; editor, author: Israel in the Third World, 1976; contbr. articles to profl. jours.; mem. editorial com. Jerusalem Papers on Peace Problems, 1973. Mem. nat. adv. council Center for Study Presidency, N.Y.C., 1979—; mem. Columbia U. seminars; mem. Internat. Relations Commn., Am. Jewish Com., 1985—. Recipient Outstanding Service award Columbia Sch. Internat. and Public Affairs, 1983; Alumni medal for conspicuous service Columbia U., 1984; sponsor Gitelson Essay Award for human values in internat. affairs and Gitelson Lectr. on human rights and U.S. fgn. policy Columbis U. Mem. Columbia Sch. Internat. and Public Affairs Alumni Assn. (pres. 1980-84), Soc. Internat. Devel. (pres. 1979), Columbia U. Alumni Fedn. (exec. com. 1981—), Internat. Studies Assn., Am. Polit. Sci. Assn., African Studies Assn., Am. Friends of Hebrew U. (exec. council Greater N.Y. 1984—), UN Assn. of N.Y. (adv. council 1977—). Jewish. Home: 303 E 83d St New York NY 10028 Office: International Consultants Inc 303 E 83d St New York NY 10028

GITMAN, ESTHER, jewelry manufacturing company executive; b. Sarayevo, Yugoslavia; came to U.S., 1972, naturalized, 1978; d. Gabriel and Hannah (Kaveson) Danon; m. Israel Gitman, Mar. 27, 1961; 1 child, Michal. Tchrs. diploma, Tchrs. Coll., Israel, 1962; B.A., Carleton U., Can., 1972; M.A. in Criminal Justice, L.I. U., 1975. Tchr., Ministry Edn., Haifa, Israel, 1962-67; tchr., Huntington, N.Y., 1972-77; dept. head fund raising Hadassah, N.Y.C., 1977-80; pres. IEG Sales Co Inc., N.Y.C., 1981—. Served as sgt. Navy, 1959-61. Republican. Avocations: painting; philosophy. Home: 1641 3d Ave Apt 30H New York NY 10028 Office: IEG Sales Co Inc 303 Fifth Ave New York NY 10016

GITT-EDWARDS, PATRICIA E., communications co. exec.; b. N.Y.C., Mar. 8, 1941; d. Michael A. and Cornelia K. (Cunn) Gitt; B.S. in Home Econs., U. Vt., 1962; M.B.A. in Mktg., Fordham U., 1980; m. Lee A. Edwards, Nov. 1, 1981. Acct. exec. The Rowland Co., Inc., 1968-71; account exec. Hill & Knowlton, Inc., N.Y.C., 1973-75; mgr. communications Life Savers, Inc., N.Y.C., 1976-80; owner, mgr. Patricia Gitt Co., N.Y.C., 1980—. Mem. Am. Women in Radio and TV (tres. N.Y.C. chpt. 1981-83, chpt. pres. 1984-86). Office: 305 E 24th St New York NY 10010

GITTELL, MARILYN, polit. scientist, educator; b. N.Y.C., Apr. 3, 1931; d. Julius and Rose (Meyerson) Jacobs; B.A., Bklyn. Coll., 1952; M.P.A., N.Y. U., 1953, Ph.D., 1960; m. Irwin Gittell, Aug. 20, 1950; children—Amy, Ross. Instr. polit. sci. Queens Coll., CUNY, 1960-62, asst. prof., 1962-65, asso. prof., 1965-67, prof., 1967-71, prof. urban studies, 1971-73, dir. Inst. Community Studies, 1967-73, chmn. dept. urban studies, 1971-73; prof. polit. sci. Bklyn. Coll., CUNY, 1973-78, asst. v.p. and asso. provost, 1973-78; prof. polit. sci. Grad. Center, CUNY, 1978—; cons. N.J. Dept. Higher Edn., Ford Found., Nat. Inst. Edn., UN. Mem. adv. bd. P.R. Research Center, Washington, 1971-75; mem. Queens Lay Advocate Service, 1972—; mem. community com. Met. Mus. Art, 1971—; mem. planning com. White House Conf. Children and Youth, 1970; mem. asso. task force on manpower U.S. Dept. Labor, 1970-74; mem. Nat. Study Commn. Undergrad. Edn. and Tchr. Edn., N.Y. State Regent Com. on Exams.; trustee Interface; mem. N.Y. State adv. com. Resource Center for Women; mem. Middle States evaluation teams Lafayette Coll., Inter-Am. U., U. P.R. Tax Found. fellow. Mem. Phi Beta Kappa. Author: Local Control in Education, 1972; (with Fantini) Decentralization: Achieving Reform, 1973; School Boards and School Policy, 1973; (with Cook and Mack) City Life: A Documentary History of the American City, 1973; What Was It Like: When Your Grandparents Were Your Age, 1976; Limits to Participation: The Decline of Community Organizations, 1980. Office: 33 W 42d St New York NY 10036

GITTLER, CAROL SPEAR, real estate broker; b. Chgo., Aug. 13, 1940; d. Louis L. and Esther (Katz) Spear; B.A., Roosevelt U., Chgo., 1978; m. Marvin Gittler, July 9, 1960; children—Michelle, Caryn, Susan, Mandy, Debra. Engaged in real estate, 1975—; real estate researcher U. Chgo., 1976-77; sec. Forus Investment Corp., Chgo., 1978—; pres. C.A.T.S. Realty, Chgo., 1980—. Mem. 5th Ward Citizens Com., Chgo., 1975—; bd. dirs. Hyde Park Community Conf., Chgo., 1981; cons. to Rep. Carol Braun, 1978—. Mem. Nat. Assn. Realtors, Hyde Park Hist. Soc., Franklin Honor Soc. Jewish. Home: 5458 Hyde Park Blvd Chicago IL 60615 also 10268 Apple Ave Union Pier MI 49129 Office: 120 W Madison St Chicago IL 60602

GIUFFRE, VIRGINIA M., banker; b. N.Y.C., Mar. 28, 1945; d. John M. and Mary J. (McLoughlin) McGovern; B.A., Coll. White Plains of Pace U., 1966; m. Joel G. Giuffre, Dec. 10, 1972. Mgmt. trainee Citicorp. Fin. Div., N.Y.C., 1970-73, data processing projects Services Mgmt. Group, 1975-77, asst. v.p. Personnel Group, 1977-78, v.p., dir. subs. Thrift Resources, Inc., 1978-82, dir. mktg. devel. and strategic planning Citicorp. Remittance Service, 1982-84; bus. mgr. investor services Citicorp Investment Bank, 1984—. Mem. Fin. Woman's Assn., NOW. Office: 153 E 53d St New York NY 10043

GIULIANI, MARY ELIZABETH, lawyer; b. Danville, Pa., Apr. 23, 1955; d. Emilio Romolo and Georgene May (Peterman) Giuliani; m. R. Gregory Stephens, June 9, 1984; 1 child, Jane Monroe. B.A. with distinction, U. Mich., 1977; postgrad. Cambridge (Eng.) U., 1979; J.D. cum laude, William Mitchell Coll. Law, 1981. Bar: Minn. 1981. Atty., Moore, Costello & Hart, St. Paul, 1981—. Staff mem. William Mitchell Coll. Law Rev., 1980. Mem. ABA, Minn. State Bar Assn. Office: Moore Costello & Hart 55 E 5th St Suite 1400 Saint Paul MN 55101

GIURGIU, ALEXANDRA MARIA, business executive, industrial engineer; b. N.Y.C., Mar. 28, 1958; d. Mircea Anthony and Lucia (Badescu) G.; m. Alessandro A. Piol. B.S., Sch. Engring. and Applied Sci. Columbia U., 1979, M.S., 1983. Registered engr. N.Y. Sr. officer for project fin. and adminstrn. Chemtex, Inc., N.Y.C., 1979-84; dir. internat. ops. Intersoft Corp. (doing bus. as Lifeboat Assocs.), N.Y.C., 1984; dir. strategy and corporate devel. Ing. C. Olivetti & C.S.p.A., N.Y.C., 1986—; freelance writer Defis mag., Paris, 1983—. Active Iuliu Maniu Rumanian Cultural Found., N.Y.C., 1976—. Recipient Prix du President, Lycee Francais de N.Y., 1976. Mem. Soc. Women Engrs., Nat. Assn. Female Execs., Alliance Francaise. Home: 7004 Blvd East Guttenberg NJ 07093 Office: Olivetti 535 Madison Ave 19th Floor New York NY 10022

GIVEN, ELAINE FORTNEY, librarian; b. Reading, Pa., Sept. 17, 1937; d. Stanley M. and Marie Daisy (Tomlinson) Fortney; m. William Todd Given, Nov. 17, 1962; 1 son, Scott William. B.S., Kutztown Coll., 1959; M.S., Villanova U., 1978. Librarian, Spring Grove Sch. Dist. (Pa.), 1959-60, Palmyra High Sch., Pa., 1960-62, Souderton Area Sch. Dist. (Pa.), 1969—, Franconia Sch., 1983—. Mem. ALA, Pa. Sch. Librarians Assn., Pa. Edn. Assn., NEA. Office: Souderton Area Sch Dist 366 Harleysville Pike Souderton PA 18964

GIVENS, CHARLENE KAY, business executive; educator; b. Lebanon, Ind., Oct. 6, 1947; d. John Robert and Anna Mildred (Bowers) Whittaker; m. Ralph A. Givens, June 19, 1969; 1 child, Maria Lynn. B.A., Ind. U., 1969. Lab. technician City of Carmel, Ind., 1972-75; lab. technician City of Noblesville, Ind., 1975-82, supt. of wastewater plant, 1982-85; ptnr., chief exec. officer Givens and Anthis Wastewater Co., Inc.; owner, mgr. Wastewater Plant Cons., Noblesville, 1982—; program chmn. Ind. Vocat. Tech. Coll., Indpls., 1983—. Mem. Nat. Environ. Training Assn. (Recognition of Training Devel. award 1984), Ind. Water Pollution Control Assn. (com. chmn. 1984—), Ind. Soc. of Cert. Operators (sec., treas. 1984—), Central Ind. Operator's Assn. (pres., founder 1983-84, Resolution award, 1983), Am. Bus. Women's Assn. (pres. 1980-81, Woman of Yr. award 1982). Avocations: knitting; reading; antiques; exploring out of the way rural areas. Office: 509 W Conner St Suite 104E-2 Noblesville IN 46060

GIVNISH, MEG, psychodramatist; b. Phila., 1939; B.A. in Speech and Drama, Chestnut Hill Coll., Phila., 1961; postgrad. U. Del., 1962-64; cert. psychodrama, Moreno Inst., Beacon, N.Y., 1971; M.A. in Humanities, Beaver Coll., Glenside, Pa., 1981; Ph.D. candidate Walden U., Mpls. Dir. community edn. Fairmount Inst., Phila., 1985—; dir., founder Problem Solving Theatre, Ambler, 1980—; pres. Moreno Inst./Acad. Psychodrama, 1982-83; editor Beacon House, Inc., Pubs., 1981—; cons. in field, 1969—. Fellow Am. Soc. Group Psychotherapy and Psychodrama (exec. council 1980-84); mem. Fedn. Trainers and Tng. Programs in Psychodrama (membership chmn. 1978-79), Phi Sigma Tau, Kappa Delta Pi. Author papers in field. Address: Problem Solving Theatre Inc PO Box 207 Ambler PA 19002

GIZA, MARIE THERESA, educator; b. Balt., May 1, 1931; d. Joseph Frank and Francis Theresa (Staniec) G.; B.A., Coll. of Notre Dame of Md., 1953; M.A., Cath. U. Am., 1960; Cert. Advanced Studies in Edn., Johns Hopkins U., 1972, M.S., 1982; postgrad. U. Oslo (Norway), 1973. Elem. tchr. St. Jerome's Sch., Balt., 1953-56; social studies tchr. Cath. High Sch. of Balt., 1956-62, guidance counselor, 1962; instr. evening coll. Essex Community Coll., 1975-77; primary and intermediate tchr. Balt. Highlands Elem. Sch., 1962—; instr. in-service creative writing course for tchrs. Sec. Polish Nat. Alliance, Group 692, 1975-78; treas. PTA, 1974-76; mem. ethnic adv. com. for Balt. City Sch. Tchrs., 1979—; pres. St. Stanislaus Parish Council, 1978-80, former pres. S.E. Area Council, Balt. Archdiocese; 1st sec. Archdiocesan Pastoral Council, Balt. Recipient Elinor Pancoast award for excellence in teaching econs., 1978; cert. of merit Joint Council on Econ. Edn. and Internat. Paper Co. Found., 1982; Balt. Polish Community award, 1980; Outstanding Tchr. award Baltimore County, 1983; NDEA fellow in lang. arts to Kutztown State Tchrs. Coll., 1956; Russian scholar, Georgetown U., 1963-64; recipient scholarships Jagiellonian U., Cracow, Poland, 1974. Cath. U. Lublin, Poland, 1976, Mikotaj Kopernik U., Torun, Poland, 1978. Mem. NEA, Md. State Tchrs. Assn., Tchrs. Assn. Balt. County, Md. Council Tchrs. of English, Smithsonian Assn., Eta Sigma Phi, Delta Epsilon Sigma. Democrat. Roman Catholic. Contbr. articles to Creative Teacher. Home: 321 E Lake Vista Circle Cockeysville MD 21030 Office: 4200 Annapolis Rd Baltimore MD 21227

GLACEL, BARBARA WARREN PATE, educator; b. Balt., Sept. 15, 1948; d. Jason Thomas and Virginia Forwood (Wetter) P.; B.A., Coll. William and Mary, 1970; M.A., U. Okla., 1973, Ph.D. in Polit. Sci., 1978; m. Robert Allan Glacel, Dec. 21, 1969; children—Jennifer Warren, Sarah Allane; Ashley Virginia. Tchr., Bel Air (Md.) Middle Sch., 1970-71, U.S. Army Dependent Schs., Germany, 1971-73; counselor U.S. Army Edn. Center, Germany, 1973-74; lectr. U. Md., Germany, 1973-74; teaching asst. U. Okla., Norman, 1974-75; instr. Suffolk U., Boston, 1975-77; adj. asst. prof. John Jay Coll. Criminal Justice, City U. N.Y., 1979-80, acad. coordinator West Point program, 1980; guest lectr. U.S. Mil. Acad., West Point, N.Y., 1978-80; adj. asst. prof. C.W. Post Center, L.I. U., 1980, St. Thomas Aquinas Coll., N.Y.C., 1981; acad. adv. Central Mich. U., 1981-82; human resource devel. cons., 1981—; lectr. St Mary's Coll., Lansing, Kans., 1981; asst. prof. U. Alaska, Anchorage, 1983-85; sr. cons. Leonard Lane Assocs., Anchorage, 1984; partner Pracel Prints, art cons., 1980-85; sr. mgmt. tng. specialist Atlantic Richfield Co., Anchorage, 1984-85; dir. Barbara Glacel & Assocs., Burke, Va., 1982—; 2d v.p. Chesapeake Broadcasting Corp.; participant profl. symposia. Recipient Comdr.'s award for pub. service Dept. of Army. AAUW Ednl. Found. fellow, 1977-78. Mem. Am. Soc. Tng. and Devel. (bd. dirs. Anchorage chpt.), Am. Polit. Sci. Assn., Nat. Mil. Families Assn. (bd. govs.), Am. Soc. Public Adminstrn., AAUW, Pi Sigma Alpha. Episcopalian. Author: (with others) A Sourcebook on Municipal, County and State Government, 1971; Regional Transit Authorities, 1983; 1000 Army Families, 1983. Home and Office: 5617 Tilia Ct Burke VA 22015

GLACKEN, AUDREY, retired educator, consultant; b. Colon, Panama, Sept. 20, 1919; s. Clay and Esta May (Kantro) Bernichon; m. Edward J. Speno, June 22, 1946 (Dec. Feb. 1971); children—Edward J., Jr., Sarah R., Thomas R., Amy Speno Geraci; m. Joseph F. Glacken, Oct. 22, 1977. B.S., Cornell U., 1942; M.A., Columbia U., 1946. Pvt. nursery sch. tchr. Brightside Day, N.Y.C., 1942-44; tchr. N.Y.C. Pub. Schs. and Nassau County Schs., 1944-54; pub. relations cons. Bankers Trust Co., N.Y.C., 1975-78. Trustee Molloy Coll., Rockville Centre, N.Y., 1976-78; mem. local library com. Recipient Hofstra Council award Hofstra U., 1973; citation of merit Assn. for Help of Retarded Children, 1976; named Kiwanis Woman of Yr., 1975. Mem. Kappa Delta. Republican. Roman Catholic. Clubs: Wheatley Hills Golf, Pine Tree Golf. Avocations: golf, theater, music.

GLAD, JOAN BOURNE, clinical psychologist, educator; b. Salt Lake City, Apr. 24, 1918; d. E. LeRoy and Ethel G. (Rogers) Bourne; m. Donald D. Glad, Sept. 10, 1938 (dec. 1980); children—Dawn JoAnne, Toni Ann, Sue Ellen, Roger Bruce. B.A., UCLA, 1953; M.A., U. Utah, 1960, Ph.D., 1965. Chief psychologist Utah State Dept. Health, Salt Lake City, 1955-65; dir., adminstr. Child and Family Guidance Clinic, Salt Lake City, 1965-68; dir. parent edn. Children's Hosp. Orange County, 1968-75; adminstr. Family Learning Ctr., Santa Ana-Tustin Community Hosp., Santa Ana, Calif., 1975-77; dir. Glad & Assocs., Tustin, Calif., 1977—; instr. Grad. Sch., Chapman Coll., Orange, Calif., 1970-73; cons. Calif. Assn. Neurologically Handicapped Children, Orange, 1970-77; lectr. self esteem Fullerton (Calif.) Coll., 1980-82. Author: Reading Unlimited, 1965. Mem. Assn. Holistic Health (a founder San Diego), Assn. Mormon Counselors and Psychotherapists, Calif. Assn. Neurologically Handicapped Children. Republican. Mem. Ch. of Jesus Christ of Latter-day Saints. Office: Glad & Assocs 1442 Irvine Blvd Suite 130 Tustin CA 92680

GLANTZ, GINA, consultant; b. N.Y.C., Apr. 3, 1943; d. Nathan L. and Lillian (Rosenbaum) Stritzler; m. Ronald A. Glantz, Oct. 17, 1968; children—Amy Samantha, Peter Samuel. B.A., U. Calif.-Berkeley, 1965. Chief of staff County Exec. Peter Shapiro, County of Essex, N.J., 1978-82; owner, mgr. Gina Glantz Cons., Springfield, N.J., 1982-83; sr. cons. Mondale for Pres., Washington, 1983-84; nat. field dir. Mondale/Ferraro, Inc., Washington, 1984; ptnr. Martin & Glantz, San Francisco, 1984—. Chmn. nat. edn. and tng. council Democratic Nat. Com., Washington, 1981-84. Home: 96 Ave Del Norte San Anselmo CA 94960 Office: Martin & Glantz 1840 Van Ness San Francisco CA 94109

GLANZMAN, LYNN ANN, credit union executive; b. Inglewood, Calif., May 9, 1962; d. Duane Marcus and Muriel Ann (Tarr) McIntire; m. Richard Allen Glanzman, Sept. 11, 1982. B.S. in B.A., Calif. State Poly. U., 1982. Teller supr. SGV Pub. Schs. Credit Union, El Monte, Calif., 1983-84, data processing mgr., 1984-85, ops. mgr., 1985—. Pres.'s scholar, Western State U., 1983. Mem. Fin. Ops. Assn., Credit Union Execs. Soc., Southern Calif. Credit Union Mgrs. Assn., Nat. Assn. Female Execs. Democrat. Christian. Avocations: riding; gardening; interior decorating. Home: 1784 Club Dr Pomona CA 91768 Office: SGV Public Schs Credit Union 11024 E Concert St El Monte CA 91731

GLASS, BARBARA BELL, bank personnel executive; b. Tulsa, Feb. 7, 1944; d. James Martin and Betty Lee (Johnson) Bell; m. William Albert Kidwell, Aug. 27, 1966 (div. 1977); children—Holly Lee, William Christopher; m. Ronald Roy Glass, Mar. 20, 1981. B.S., Okla. State U., 1966; M.A., U. Okla., 1979. Cert. profl. in human resources. Grad. asst. U. Okla., Norman, 1978-79, research asst., 1979-80; mgmt. trainee Fourth Nat. Bank, Tulsa, 1980-81, asst. cashier, 1981-82, asst. v.p., 1982-83, v.p., 1983—. Mem. profl. women's adv. bd. Tulsa Jr. Coll., 1982-83; mem. scholarship selection com. Patti Johnson Wilson Found.; mem. adv. bd. U. Tulsa Mgmt. Devel. Ctr. Mem. Am. Soc. Tng. and Devel., Am. Soc. Personnel Adminstrs., Tulsa Employee Benefits Group, Tulsa Equal Employment Opportunity Coordinators Assn. Democrat. Unitarian Universalist. Home: 3612 S Braden Pl Tulsa OK 74135

GLASS, ELIZABETH MARION, edn. cons.; b. Hartford, Conn., Aug. 24, 1922; d. Robert Anderson and Marion Gibson (Low) G.; student Hartford Coll. for Women, 1940-41; B.S., U. Conn., 1944, M.S., 1951. Tchr. math. and sci. Newington (Conn.) Jr./Sr. High Sch., 1945-50, Litchfield (Conn.) Jr./Sr. High Sch., 1951-52; asso. prof. math. edn. SUNY, Albany, 1952-62; edn. cons. Conn. Dept. Edn., 1965—; part-time faculty St. Rose Coll., Albany, Central Conn. State Coll., Eastern Conn. State Coll. Mem. Westbrook (Conn.) Zoning Commn. NSF fellow. Mem. Nat. Council Tchrs. of Math., Assn. State Suprs. of Math., Conn. Assn. Sch. Supts., U. Conn. Alumni Assn., Phi Delta Kappa. Republican. Author 5 math. textbooks, numerous articles. Home: 369 Linnmoore St Hartford CT 06106 Office: PO Box 2219 Hartford CT 06115

GLASS, MARILYN, advertising agency executive; b. Phila., July 10, 1940; d. Murray and Rebecca (Ash) Glass. B.A., U. Miami, Fla., 1961; student N.Y. Sch. Interior Design, 1965-66. Copy chief Chalek & Dryer, N.Y.C., 1964-65, Wyse Advt., N.Y.C., 1969-75; group creative dir. N. W. Ayer, N.Y.C., 1970-72; creative dir. E. Tal Advt., Tel Aviv, Israel, 1972-75; copywriter Kelly Nason Advt., N.Y.C., 1975-79; v.p., copy supr. Silberman Whitebrow Dolan, Inc., Phila., 1980—. Writer TV comml. for Ocean Spray, 1978, radio commercial for Progresso, 1967. Bd. dirs. Graham Home for Children, White Plains, N.Y., 1968, Anti-Defamation League B'nai B'rith, Phila., 1983-84. Democrat. Jewish. Office: Silberman Whitebrow Dolan 5 Penn Ctr Plaza Philadelphia PA 19103

GLASS, MARJORIE MILLS, art center administrator; b. Chgo., Oct. 8, 1923; d. James Edgar and Mabel (Leaf) Mills; m. Robert Louis Glass, Mar. 22, 1946; children—Daniel Brian, Michael James, Peter Kevin, Anthony Robert. Student U. Wis.-Madison, 1945, Met. U., Mpls., 1980, U. Minn., 1982. Pres. North Suburban Ctr. for Arts, Mpls., 1979-80, exec. dir., 1980—; art sect. program chmn. U. Minn. Faculty Women's Club, Mpls., 1979-80. Author newsletters, bylaws North Suburban Ctr. Arts. Editor: Art Lines, 1984—. Contbr. articles to profl. jours. Mem. Minn. Citizens for Arts, Minn. Pub. Radio, Minn. Pub. Tv, North Area C. of C., Sixth Dist. Arts Adv. Bd. Avocations: painting; gardening; writing. Home: 28 Oakwood Dr New Brighton MN 55112 Office: North Suburban Ctr for Arts Apache Plaza 37th and Silver Lake Rd Minneapolis MN 55421

GLASS, NAN LEWIS, town official; b. Hartford, Conn., June 7, 1929; d. Robert R. and Elizabeth (Mass) Lewis; children—Alan Lewis, Amy Suzanne, David Arthur, Mitchell Jonathan. B.A., U. Conn., 1950. Reporter, West Hartford News, Conn., 1971-73, columnist, 1973-75, mng. editor, 1978-79; clk. Town of West Hartford, 1979—. Mem. Town Council West Hartford, 1973-78; mem. steering com. Leadership Greater Hartford, 1976-78; bd. dirs. The Bridge, West Hartford, 1973-77, Noah Webster Found., 1984—, West Hartford Hist. Soc., 1984—, South Park Inn, Hartford, 1985—. Recipient Outstanding Service to Edn. award West Hartford Edn. Assn. Mem. Conn. Town Clks. Assn. (chmn. legis. com. 1982-84), New Eng. Town Clks. Assn., Internat. Inst. Mcpl. Clks. Democrat. Jewish. Avocations: reading, theater; music; arts. Home: 1086A Farmington Ave West Hartford CT 06107 Office: Town of West Hartford 28 S Main St West Hartford CT 06107

GLASS, WENDY DAVIS, art dealer; b. N.Y.C., Aug. 28, 1925; d. Aaron Wise and Helen Miller (Obstler) Davis; B.A., Bard Coll., 1948; children—Robin, Tim. Group worker with children Greenwich House, 1948, Mus. Modern Art, N.Y.C., 1958; owner, dir. Glass Gallery, N.Y.C., 1960—. Campaign worker Democratic candidates. Mem. Antiques Appraisers Assn. (registered), N.Y. Am. Women's Bus. Assn., Ukiyo-e Soc., Japan Soc., Asia Soc. Jewish. Address: 315 Central Park W Apt 8W New York NY 10025

GLASSCOCK, LANETTE HEILBRON, lawyer, oil company owner; b. San Antonio, May 26, 1911; d. Albert Edward and Annie (Wagner) Heilbron; m. Leon Donley Glasscock, Jan. 15, 1938 (dec. 1979); children—Lanette Glasscock Duperier, Leon Donley Glasscock, Albert Heilbron Glasscock. Student Incarnate Word Coll., 1927-28, San Antonio Coll., 1929. Bar: Tex. 1931. Ptnr., Heilbron & Heilbron, San Antonio, 1931-38, Glasscock & Glasscock, San Antonio, 1942-79; sole practice, San Antonio, 1979—; pres. Idaho Oil Co. Inc. First chmn. Mayor's Commn. on Status of Women, San Antonio, 1975; adv. bd. Salvation Army, San Antonio, 1975—. Recipient Headliner award Women in Communications, 1975. Mem. Ind. Petroleum Assn. Am. (dir. for SW Tex.), Nat. Assn. Women Lawyers, ABA, Tex. Bar Assn., San Antonio Bar Assn. Republican. Presbyterian. Club: Zonta (pres.). Home: 545 Elizabeth Rd San Antonio TX 78209 Office: Glasscock & Glasscock Law Offices 1802 N Saint Marys St San Antonio TX 78212

GLASSER, JEANNE ANNE (JANNA), lawyer; b. San Diego, Calif., Jan. 2, 1951; d. James Terry and Jeanne Familton (Stanton) Acuff; m. Morris Glasser, Sept. 2, 1972. Student, U. Corpus Christi, 1968-70; B.A., U. Tex., 1972; J.D., Benjamin N. Cardozo Sch. Law, 1979. Unit coordinator Flower and Fifth Ave. Hosps., N.Y.C., 1972-76; ptnr. Silfen & Glasser, P.C., N.Y.C., 1981—; adj. prof. Pace U. Sch. Law, 1983; lectr. in counselling clients in entertainment industry Practicing Law Inst., 1986—. Bd. advisors Entertainment Law Reporter, 1983—; bd. dirs. Westchester Sangueriters Guild,1986—. Mem. ABA (com. on entertainment and sports law), Westchester County Bar Assn. Office: Silfen & Glasser PC 545 Fifth Ave New York NY 10017

GLASSER, KAY ELBAUM, civic worker; b. Lawrence, Mass., July 24, 1918; d. Samuel and Anna Karass; B.A. magna cum laude, Radcliffe Coll., 1940; M.S.W., Simmons Coll., 1956; Ph.D., Brandeis U., 1967; m. Joshua B. Glasser, Nov. 22, 1972. Mental health educator Mass. Dept. Mental Health, 1956-62; asso. prof. social work U. Denver, 1967-73; mem. Sarasota County (Fla.) Sch. Bd., 1978—, also past chmn.; past mentor Eckerd Coll. Program Experienced Learners; citizens adv. bd. S.E. 1st Nat. Bank of Sarasota. Chmn. planning council United Way of Sarasota; trustee, sec. New Coll. Found.; bd. dirs. Taxpayers Assn. Saratota County, Sarasota County Civic League, 1977-78, United Way Found., 1980—; chmn. United Way Campaign and 1st vice chmn. bd. dirs. United Way of Sarasota; formerly active Mass. Republican Party; former mem. Newton (Mass.) Bd. Public Welfare; former vice chmn. Newton Rep. City Com.; mem. LWV, former v.p. Newton; bd. dirs. Community Coalition for Families, Sarasota County Informed Parents, L.I.F.E., Asolo Theatre Festival Assn.; mem. Fla. Adv. Council on Global Edn.; mem. task force on global edn. Nat. Sch. Bds. Assn. Mem. Acad. Cert. Social Workers, Nat. Assn. Social Workers, Council on Social Work Edn., Fla. Women's Network, UN Assn., Save Our Bays Assn., AAUW, AAUP, Phi Beta Kappa, Phi Beta Kappa Assocs. Clubs: Bird Key Yacht, Sarasota Women's Rep., Sarasota Bay Women's Rep. Office: 2418 Hatton St Sarasota FL 33577

GLASSMAN, CAROLINE DUBY, state supreme court justice; b. Baker, Oreg., Sept. 13, 1923; d. Charles F. and Caroline M. (Colton) Duby; m. Harry

P. Glassman, May 21, 1953; 1 child, Max Aaron. B.A., Eastern Oregon Coll.; LL.B., Wilamette U. Bar: Oreg. 1944, Calif. 1952, Maine 1969. Title ins. atty. Title Ins. & Trust Co., Salem, Oreg., 1944-46; assoc. Belli, Aske & Pinney, San Francisco, 1952-58; ptnr. Glassman, Beagle and Ridge, Portland, Maine, 1978-83; assoc. justice Maine Supreme Ct., Portland, 1983—. Address: Maine Supreme Ct 142 Federal St Portland ME 04112*

GLASSMEYER, EVELYN BROWN, counselor, therapist; b. Grant, Nebr., Jan. 20, 1945; d. Thomas Cartwright and Mildred Carrie (Wilkinson) Brown; m. Gerard E. Glassmeyer, Feb. 14, 1985. B.A. summa cum laude, Nebr. Wesleyan U., 1968; M.A. (Vocat. Rehab. Adminstrn. fellow, 1968-69), U. Nebr., 1970. Coordinator residential services Bexar County Mental Health/Mental Retardation, (Tex.), 1973-74; cons. 1980-83. San Antonio, 1974-80; vocat. rehab. counselor Mental Health Mental Retardation, Tex. Commn. for Blind, San Antonio, 1975-77; exec. dir. San Antonio Assn. Retarded Citizens, 1978-79; pvt. practice counselor, therapist, massage therapist, Austin, 1979-85, Pacifica, Calif., 1985—; seminar leader women's support groups. Co-founder, facilitator Crystal Chalice, 1980-83; mem. adv. bd. Tex. Assn. Child Care Workers, 1975—, adv. council Vol. Action Com., 1978-79. Mem. Austin Area Holistic Health Assn. (pres. 1980-83, networking dir. 1983-85), Assn. Humanistic Psychology (dir. 1983—), Found. Universal Unity, Human Unity Found., Health Freedom Council, Friends in Human Potential, Human Potential Inst., Tex. Assn. Child Care Workers, In-Ter Action Assocs. Columnist, HOLOS, 1980-83. Address: 844 Burns Ct Pacifica CA 94044

GLAVIN, A. RITA CHANDELLIER, lawyer; b. Schenectady, May 11, 1937; d. Pierre Charles and Helen C. (Fox) Chandellier; m. James H. Glavin, III, June 1, 1963; children—Helene, James, Rita, Henry. A.B. cum laude, Middlebury Coll., 1958; J.D., Union U. Albany Law Sch., 1961. Bar: N.Y. 1961, U.S. Dist. Ct. (no. dist.) N.Y. 1961, U.S. Tax Ct. 1965, U.S. Supreme Ct. 1978. Assoc. Eugene Steiner, Albany, N.Y., 1961-64, Helen Fox Chandellier, Schenectady, 1965-76; mem. Glavin and Glavin, Waterford, Schenectady, and Albany, N.Y., 1965—; del. 4th Jud. Dist. Nominating Conv., 1966-67; confidential law clk. presiding justices N.Y. State Ct. Claims, 1968-71. Bd. dirs., chmn. fin. com. Schenectady YWCA, 1979-81; tech. advisor HSA of Northeastern N.Y. Maternity and Pediatric Com., 1976; bd. dirs. Schenectady Jr. League, 1974, 76; del. N.Y. State Jr. League Pub. Affairs Com., 1976; bd. dirs., sec. Bellevue Maternity Hosp., Inc., 1966-83, bd. advisers, sec., 1984—; trustee Middlebury Coll., 1978—, vice chmn. bd. trustees, 1986-87, chmn. law com., 1982—; mem. council SUNY-Albany, 1985—. Mem. N.Y. State Bar Assn., Saratoga County Bar Assn. (exec. com. 1981—, pres. 1986), Schenectady County Bar Assn., Phi Beta Kappa, Kappa Kappa Gamma. Mem. editorial bd. Albany Law Rev., 1960-61. Address: 69 2d St PO Box 40 Waterford NY 12188

GLAZE, LYNN FERGUSON, development consultant; b. Oakland, Calif., May 24, 1933; d. Kenneth Loveland and Constance May (Pedder) Ferguson; m. Harry Smith Glaze, Jr., July 3, 1957; children—Catherine, Charles Richard. B.A., Stanford U., 1955, M.A., 1966. Devel. dir. Greenwich Acad., Conn., 1982-84; devel. cons. Brandywine Mus., Chadds Ford, Pa., 1984; fin. devel. dir. Del. Learning Ctr., Centreville, Del., 1985—; devel. cons. Opera Del. devel. com. Conn. Assn. Ind. Schs., Hartford, 1984. Pres. Darien-Norwalk YWCA, conn., 1973-76; sec. Darien Republican Town com., Darien, 1974-79; dist. chmn. Darien Rep. Meeting, 1974-76; vestry St. Luke's Ch., Darien, 1979-82; justice of the peace, Darien, 1981-84. Coro Found. fellow 1981. Mem. Nat. Soc. Fund Raising Execs. (Brandywine chpt.). Episcopalian. Club: Greenville Country. Avocations: reading, tennis, piano, swimming.

GLAZER, IRENE, special education pre-school executive, publisher, management-holding company executive, consultant; b. Bklyn., Feb. 6, 1944; d. Philip and Sophie Sylvia (Mitnitsky) Deutsch; m. Edward Allen Glazer, Nov. 3, 1962; children—T. Lawrence, Jason Charles. Student Brookdale Coll., 1982-83. Mgr., Healthmasters, Inc., N.Y.C., 1975-80; owner, operator Plantation, Englishtown, N.J., 1980-82; pres. Our P.L.A.C.E. Sch. Inc., S.I., N.Y., 1982—, also dir.; pres. Toddler/Infant Program for Spl. Edn. Inc., S.I., 1983—, also dir.; pres. Spl. Kids Intervention Program, Inc., Howard Beach, N.Y., 1985—, also dir.; v.p. I&N Mgmt., Inc., Englishtown, 1985—. Pub. Early Advantage for Your High Risk Child, Princeton, N.J., 1985—. Youth adviser Temple Shaari Emeth, Englishtown, 1980. Mem. Nat. Assn. for Deaf, Nat. Assn. Edn. Young Children, Organization Mondiale Pour L'Education Prescolaire, Nat. Assn. Pvt. Schs. for Handicapped. Democrat. Avocations: breeding west highland white terriers; cooking; reading; camping; travel. Office: Our PLACE Sch Inc 329 Norway Ave Staten Island NY 10335

GLAZER, JUDITH S., educational administrator; b. N.Y.C.; d. Max and Pauline V. Lager; B.A., Smith Coll., 1953; M.A., N.Y.U., 1973, Ph.D., 1981; children—Helen Marcy, George Douglas. Coordinator community services, coordinator spl. projects SUNY Coll., Purchase, 1970-72, asst. to v.p., 1972-73; asst. dean of community services Westchester (N.Y.) Community Coll., 1973-75; research asso. N.Y. State Temporary Commn. on Future of Postsecondary Edn., 1976-77; instr. higher edn. N.Y.U., N.Y.C., 1978-79; assoc. dir. Inter-Univ. Doctoral Consortia Project, N.Y.C., 1978-80; cons. ednl. and pub. affairs, 1975—; dir. N.Y. Alliance for Pub. Schs., N.Y.U., 1980-83; assoc. dean Sch. Edn. and Human Services, adj. assoc. prof. St. John's U., 1983—. Trustee, pres. Blind Brook-Rye Town Bd. Edn., 1963-72; bd. dirs. Westchester Nat. Council on Crime and Delinquency, 1978-80, Vol. Service Bur., 1974-79; bd. dirs. County Environ. Mgmt., 1973-80. Recipient NACO New County U.S.A. achievement award, 1975. Mem. Am. Assn. for Higher Edn., Assn. for Study Higher Edn., Nat. Assn. Women Deans and Adminstrs., Am. Ednl. Research Assn. Contbr. articles to publs. Home: 201 W 70th St New York NY 10023 Office: St John's U Grand Central and Utopia Pkwys Jamaica NY 11439

GLAZER, SHARON J., lawyer; b. Trenton, N.J., Feb. 7, 1953. B.A., Georgetown U., 1975; J.D., Catholic U., 1979. Dir. Office of Legal Affairs George Washington U. Med. Ctr., Washington, 1981-85; atty. Hayt, Hayt and Landau, Miami, 1985—; founder, chmn. In-House Hosp. Attys. of Washington, D.C., 1982-85. Mem. Nat. Health Lawyers' Assn., Am. Acad. Hosp. Attys. (speaker), ABA (young lawyers and health forum divs.), Fla. Assn. Women Lawyers. Office: Hayt Hayt and Landau 9100 S Dadeland Blvd 12th Floor Miami FL 33156

GLEASNER, DIANA COTTLE, author; b. New Brunswick, N.J., Apr. 26, 1936; d. Delmer Leroy and Elizabeth (Stanton) C.; m. G. William Gleasner, July 12, 1958; children—Stephen William, Suzanne Lynn. B.A., Ohio Wesleyan U., 1958; M.A., SUNY-Buffalo, 1965. Tchr. Kenmore (N.Y.) Sr. High Sch., 1958-64; instr. SUNY-Buffalo, 1970-76. Author: The Plaid Mouse, 1966; Pete Polar Bear's Trip Down the Erie Canal, 1970; Women in Swimming, 1975; Women in Track and Field, 1977; Hawaiian Gardens, 1978; Kauai Traveler's Guide, 1978; Oahu Traveler's Guide, 1978; Big Island Traveler's Guide, 1978; Maui Traveler's Guide, 1978; Breakthrough: Women in Writing, 1980; Illustrated Dictionary of Surfing, Swimming and Diving, 1980; Sea Islands of the South, 1980; Rock Climbing, 1980; Callaway Gardens, 1981; Inventions That Changed Our Lives: Dynamite, 1982; Charlotte: A Touch of Gold, 1983; Breakthrough: Women in Science, 1983; Inventions That Changed Our Lives: The Movies, 1983; Windsurfing, 1985; Florida Off the Beaten Path, 1986; contbr. numerous articles to mags., including Better Homes and Gardens, Field and Stream, Good Housekeeping, Am. Way, Brides mag., numerous others; monthly travel column Charlotte (N.C.) Observer, 1981—; Mem. Am. Soc. Journalists and Authors, Soc. Am. Travel Writers, Women in Communications, Outdoor Writers Assn. Am. Address: 132 Holly Ct Denver NC 28037

GLEASON, MABEL MALLENS, production executive, radio programmer; b. San Juan, P.R., Dec. 2, 1957; d. Victor Manuel and Mabel Betsy (Enriquez) Mallens; m. David Frackelton Gleason, May 31, 1980; 1 dau., Caroline Mallens. Travel agent Banking Programming Inst. 1977; Assoc. in Communications, Sacred Heart U., 1979. Teller, Comml. Exchange Savs. Citibank, N.A., San Juan, 1977-79; morning personality Sta. WQII-AM, San Juan, 1979-80; noon announcer, prodn. mgr. Sta. WHTT-AM, Miami, Fla., 1980-82; announcer, cons. Sta. WSUA-AM, Miami, 1982-83; v.p., cons., producer CYD Prodns., Miami, 1982—; cons. Sta. WUNO Radio, San Juan, 1983—; programmer Radio Omega, Lima, Peru, 1983—, programmer Sonorama 107, San Juan, 1982—, Radio Higo Sto. Domingo, Dominican Republic, 1982—. Collaborator, New Progressive Party/Youths, San Juan, 1975; vol. United Way, Citibank, San Juan, 1977, Muscular Dystrophy Marathon, 1978, Multiple Sclerosis Soc., 1984—. Nominee Female Disc Jockey Asociacion Criticos y Comentaristas De Arte, Miami, 1980; recipient Radio Telephone Operator Permit FCC, 1980. Mem. Nat. Assn. Female Execs., Nat. Assn. Women Bus. Owners (pub. relations com.). Republican. Roman Catholic. Home: 835 SW 134 Pl Miami FL 33184

GLEASON, NANCY STERLING, city public information official; b. Winchester, Mass., Mar. 5, 1958; d. Walter John and Elizabeth (Leary) Stelkovis; m. Michael John Gleason, Sept. 16, 1984. B.A. in Communications magna cum laude, Boston Coll., 1979; postgrad. in Broadcast Journalism, Boston U., 1981—. Asst. to mgr. Coveleigh Country Club, Rye, N.Y., 1975-79; assignment editor, series producer sta. WCVB-TV, Boston, 1979-82; assignment editor sta. WNEV-TV, Boston, 1982-84; planning editor sta. spl. events producer WOR-TV, N.Y.C., 1984-85; dir. informational services Boston Police Dept., 1985—. Editor: Medium Rare, 1986. Sch. liaison publicity coordinator Rye Youth Council, 1974-76. Winner various pub. speaking awards, 1970-76, Emmy award for news event, WCVB-TV, 1980. Mem. Writers Guild Am., Nat. Assn. Female Execs. Episcopalian.

GLEASON, ROBERTA ELLEN, real estate company executive; b. Boston, June 2, 1939; d. Lloyd Irbing and Ida May (Arnold) Toye; m. James R. Rundle, Nov. 10, 1957 (div.); children—Wendy L., Erika D.; m. Wesley S. Gleason, Jan. 11, 1977. Grad. Realtors Inst.; cert. real estate brokerage mgr. Sales assoc. Hamel Real Estate Co., North Conway, N.H., 1975-80, sales mgr., 1980-81, sales and office mgr., 1981-85, regional v.p., 1985—. Mem. Zoning Bd. Appeals, Conway, 1981-85. Mem. Real Estate Leaders Am., Nat. Assn. Female Execs., White Mountain Bd. Realtors (pres. 1985—). Home: RFD Duprey Rd North Conway NH 03860 Office: Hamel Real Estate Inc Main St North Conway NH 03860

GLEASON, VIRGINIA LEE, library administrator; b. Springfield, Mo., Sept. 7, 1923; d. Nathan Lee and Lulu Madge (Randolph) Casey; m. George Donald Gleason, Dec. 22, 1949; children—Barbara Jo, Anne Marie, Victoria Lu, George Randolph. A.B., W.Va. Wesleyon Coll., 1945; B.L.S., Columbia U., 1946; M.A., Northwestern U., 1949. Circulation librarian Northwestern U., Evanston, Ill., 1946-49; librarian Central High Sch., Superior, Wis., 1949-50; children's librarian San Diego Pub. Library, 1950-52; reference librarian U. Iowa, Iowa City, 1954-55; children's library supr. Springfield-Greene County Pub. Library, Mo., 1955—. Author: History of St. Paul United Methodist Church, 1983. Contbr. columnist to numerous newspapers. Chmn., library com. St. Paul Ch. Library, Springfield, 1972—; bd. mem. Children's Lit. Festival of the Ozarks, Springfield, 1982—; singer St. Paul Meth. Ch. choir, Springfield, 1970—; mem. reading is fundamental bd., Reading is Fundamental of Springfield, 1985; unit co-chair League of Women Voters, Springfield, 1984-85. Mem. Springfield Area Library Assn. (v.p. 1965-67), Mo. Library Assn., Children's Service Roundtable of the Mo. Library Assn. (chmn. 1970-71), ALA. Home: 1710 E Latoka St Springfield MO 65804 Office: Springfield Greene County Pub Library 397 E Central St Springfield MO 65801

GLEDHILL, CAROL ANN, physical education educator; b. Bonne Terre, Mo., Aug. 29, 1943; d. Kermit Warren and Jessie Jo (Dickson) Nations; m. John Theodore Gledhill, Jr., July 22, 1975. B.S. in Edn., S.W. Mo. State U., 1966; M.A.T., Wash. State U., 1973. Instr. phys. edn. High Sch. Dist. 113, Highland Park, Ill., 1966—, volleyball coach, 1973—; sponsor Penguin Synchronized Swim Club, 1966—; cross country ski instr. Lake Bluff (Ill.) Park Dist., 1982-83, Lake Forest High Sch. Adult Edn. (Ill.), 1984—. Producer-dir. slide show; Highland Park Phys. Edn. Curriculum, 1983, tchr. excellence award, 1983. Named to Athletic Hall of Fame, S.W. Mo. State U., 1981. Mem. AAHPER, U.S. Ski Assn., Ill. Assn. Health, Phys. Edn. and Recreation. Republican. Mem. Christian Ch. Club: Audubon. Lodge: Eastern Star. Home: 15710 W Woodbine Circle Mundelein IL 60060 Office: Highland Park High Sch 433 Vine Ave Highland Park IL 60035

GLEGHORN, LINDA LIPE, lawyer; b. Clarksdale, Miss., Jan. 10, 1948; s. William Ray and Gwendolyn (Strickland) Lipe; m. Larry L. Gleghorn, Feb. 15, 1983. B.B.A. in Accountancy, U. Miss., 1970, J.D., 1971. Bar: Miss. 1971, U.S. Dist. Ct. (no. dist.) Miss. 1971, Ark. 1976, U.S. Dist. Ct. (ea. dist.) Ark. 1976, U.S. Ct. Appeals (8th cir.) 1985. Sr. tax acct. Arthur Young & Co., San Jose, Calif., 1971-74; sr. tax acct. A.M. Pullen & Co., Knoxville, Tenn., 1975; legal counsel to gov. State of Ark., Little Rock, 1975-79; dep. pros. atty. 6th Jud. Dist. Ark., Little Rock, 1979-80, chief counsel Ark. Public Service Commn., Little Rock, 1980-83; asst. U.S. atty. Eastern Dist. Ark., Dept. Justice, Little Rock, 1983—. Mem. ABA, Miss. State Bar, Ark. State Bar Assn. Episcopalian. Office: US Attorney's Office 600 West Capitol PO Box 1229 Little Rock AR 72203

GLEICH, CAROL SUE, health professions education specialist; b. Kewanee, Ill., Jan. 18, 1935; d. Carl and Edna (Krause) Gleich; A.B., U. Iowa, 1958, M.S., 1967, Ph.D., 1972. Program dir. med. tech. program, asst. prof. dept. pathology U. Iowa, Iowa City, 1972-77; health manpower edn. specialist, div. assoc. health professions Bur. Health Professions, Health Resources Adminstrn., HHS, Rockville, Md., from 1977, now allied health cons. to Egypt; dir. Geriatric Edn. Ctrs. of PHS; adj. assoc. prof. U. Md. Sch. Medicine; mem. Iowa Health Manpower Com., 1976—; cons. U. Wis. System Acad. Affairs, 1976; panelist and participant workshops. Cert. clin. chemistry technologist, Nat. Registry Clin. Chemistry. Mem. Am. Soc. Allied Health Professions, Nat. Council for Internat. Health, Am. Soc. Clin. Pathologists (assoc.; cert. med. technologist; sec. Bd. Registry, 1975-77), Am. Soc. Med. Tech., D.C. Soc. Med. Tech. (Outstanding Med. Technologist of Yr. 1975), Beta Beta Beta. Assoc. editor Am. Jour. Med. Tech., 1974-83, Jour. Allied Health, 1982—; contbr. articles to profl. publs., papers to confs. Home: 5125 Norbeck Rd Rockville MD 20853 Office: Parklawn Bldg Room 8-103 5600 Fishers Ln Rockville MD 20857

GLEICHMAN, PAMELA WALTON, real estate developer; b. Rockford, Ill., May 8, 1944; d. Don Oliver and Charlotte E. (Walton) G.; m. John Thomas Scarcelli, Sept. 7, 1968 (div. 1978); children—Rosa Walton, Luigi John; m. Karl Swan Norberg, Dec. 31, 1980. B.E., No. Ill. U., 1967; M.F.A. in Painting, Pa. State U., 1969; student Spanish Lang. and Culture, Universidad de Barcelona, Spain, 1966. Instr. art U. Maine, Farmington and Gorham, 1970-73; dir. devel. and research Maine State Housing Authority, Augusta, 1974-77; founder, pres. Housing/State of the Art, Portland, Maine, 1977—; founder, pres. Gleichman & Co., Inc., Portland, 1979—; founder, pres. Franklin Oxford Maintenance Co., Portland, 1982—; dir. Council for Rural Housing and Devel., Washington, 1982—; mem. Gov's. Adv. Com. on Housing, Maine, 1980. State treas. Equal Rights for Maine, 1984; trustee, mem. exec. com. Waynflete Sch. dist., 1981—; bd. dirs. Portland Stage Co., 1985; state pres. Maine Women's Polit. Caucus, 1974-76; del. Dem. Nat. Conv., N.Y.C., 1974; trustee U. New Eng., 1985—; founder, exec. com. Uptown Revitalization, Portland, 1984-85. Recognized for demonstration of congregate elderly housing Bur. Maine's Elderly, 1981; HUD housing devel. grantee, 1984. Mem. Maine Real Estate Assn., Uptown Assocs. (Portland, co-founder, mem. exec. com.). Avocations: gardening; boating; skiing. Home: 223 Western Promenade Portland ME 04102 Office: Gleichman & Co Inc 45 Casco St Portland ME 04101

GLENN, BETTY JO, claims administrator; b. Poplar Bluff, Mo., Oct. 18, 1931; d. Linden Eldress and Julia Hazel (Leach) Berry; m. John Wiley Glenn, June 30, 1951; children—John Gary, Sharon Elaine, Karen Ann. Student S.E. Mo. State U., Cape Girardeau, 1950; Vista U., Oakland, Calif., 1983. Traffic clk. Pet Milk Co., St. Louis, 1951-54; sales analyst Dodson Jewelers, Spokane, Wash., 1955-60; assoc. in real estate Red Carpet Co., Fremont, Calif., 1972-75; claims adminstrv. exec. John Glenn Adjusters & Adminstrs., 1975—. Treas. Children's Med. Hosp. Br., Oakland, 1985-87; adv. bd. Shelter Against Violent Environments Inc., Fremont, 1982. Mem. Nat. Assn. Ins. Women, East Bay Assn. Ins. Women, So. Alameda (Calif.) Real Estate Bd. (million dollar award cert. 1974), Beta Sigma Phi (pres. Castro Valley, Calif.) (pres. 1964-65) Democrat. Methodist. Lodges: Eastern Star, Job's Daus. Council (1981-84) Home: 36601 Cuenca Ct Fremont CA 94536

GLENN, CLETA MAE, lawyer; b. Clinton, Ill., Sept. 24, 1921; d. John and Mattie Sylvester (Anderson) G.; B.S., U. Ill., 1947; J.D., DePaul U., 1976; m. Rex Eugene Loggans, Sept. 3, 1948 (div.); 1 dau., Susan. Bar: Ill. 1977. Real estate builder, developer, 1959-69; communications dir. Transp. Research Center, Northwestern U., Evanston, Ill., 1969-72; practice law, Chgo., 1977—; lectr. Assn. Trial Lawyers Am., John Marshall Law Sch. Served with U.S. Navy, 1943-59. Recipient Real Estate Humanitarian award Kislak Co., Miami, Fla., 1962. Mem. ABA (sect. chmn. 1980—, exec. mem. marriage and cohabitation div. family law sect.), Ill. Bar Assn. (assembly rep., standing com., council family law sect.), Chgo. Bar Assn., Assn. Trial Lawyers Am., Ill. Trial Lawyers Assn., Lex Leggio, Phi Alpha Delta. Editor: Collective Bargaining and Technological Change in American Transportation, 1979; contbr. articles to profl. publs. Home: 200 E Delaware Pl Chicago IL 60611 Office: 69 W Washington St Chicago IL 60602

GLENN, CONSTANCE W., univ. art mus. dir.; b. Topeka, Oct. 4, 1933; d. Henry A. and Madeline S. (Stewart) White; B.F.A., U. Kans., 1955; postgrad., U. Mo., 1964-69; M.A. in Art History, Calif. State U., Long Beach, 1974; m. Jack W. Glenn, June 19, 1955; children—Laurie Frances, Caroline Elizabeth, John Christopher. Prin. Constance W. Glenn Interiors, 1958-68; co-owner Jack Glenn Gallery, Corona del Mar, Calif., 1970-75; lectr., asst. prof., asso. prof., prof. art, Calif. State U., Long Beach, 1973—, dir. Univ. Art Mus., 1973—, dir. Mus. Studies Cert. Program; dir. Center for So. Calif. Studies in Visual Arts. Mem. Am. Assn. Mus., Assn. Art Mus. Dirs., Coll. Art Assn., Art Mus. Assn., Archives of Am. Art (chmn. So. Calif. adv. bd.), Friends of Photography (past trustee), Kappa Alpha Theta. Art cons. Architectural Digest; author books, catalogues, articles on contemporary art, design and architecture. Office: Calif State Univ Long Beach U Art Mus 1250 Bellflower Blvd Long Beach CA 90840

GLENN, DEBORAH ANN, communications manager; b. N.Y.C., Feb. 2, 1949; d. Anthony W. and Lillian (Rubin) G.; m. Michael Maver Gallaher, Oct. 10, 1982; 1 child, Aaron William. B.S., Temple U., 1971. Audiovisual coordinator Jack Morton Prodns., N.Y.C., 1973-75; multimedia producer Ted Colangelo Assocs., White Plains, N.Y., 1979-80; producer/dir. Marvin Lieberman Assocs., N.Y.C., 1980-81; communications mgr. Am. Express Co., N.Y.C., 1982-85; communications cons., N.Y.C., 1985—. Mem. Assn. for Multi-Image (dir. 1985—). Recipient Gold award for direction Internat. Film Producers Am., 1984; Silver medal Internat. TV and Film Festival, 1984; Crystal Apple award Assn. for Multi-Image, 1984. Home: 251 Oradell Ave Paramus NJ 07652

GLENN, DIANA JEAN, travel consultant, educator; b. Preston, Ga., Oct. 5, 1941; d. Rev. Daniel and Pearl (Robinson) Thomas; m. Charles Glenn, Jan. 8, 1964; children—Charles Christopher, Daniel Keith Glenn. A.B., Fort Valley State Coll., Ga., 1963; postgrad. Ga. Southwestern Coll., 1978—. Cert. tchr. Ga. Tchr., Glynn County Bd. Edn., Brunswick, Ga., 1966-67, 69-79, Americus Bd. Edn., Ga., 1967-69; sales rep. John Hancock Ins. Co., Atlanta, 1979-81; tchr. Dekalb Bd. Edn., Decatur, Ga., 1981-86; team mgr. Allure Natural Cosmetics Co., Atlanta, 1985—; dir. Tower High Sch., Decatur, Ga., 1982-83, 85-86. Mem. Bus. and Profl. Women (dir. membership 1984-86), Exec. Female Inc., Nat. Assn. Educators, Ga. Edn. Assn. (sch. rep. 1985), Delta Sigma Theta. Democrat. Am. Baptist. Clubs: Gospel Choir (pres. 1980-81), Courtesy Gill (pres. 1982-83). Avocations: church choir; sewing; home-maker; decorator. Home: 2645 Lantern Ln College Park GA 30349

GLENN, JUDY CAROLE, nurse, naval officer; b. Birmingham, Ala., July 2, 1946; d. Talmadge William and Maude Elizabeth (Steading) G.; diploma in nursing Univ. Hosp., Birmingham, 1967; B.S.N., Samford U., 1975; M.S.N. in Cardiovascular Nursing, U. Ala., Birmingham, 1978; Staff nurse Univ. Hosp., 1967-68; charge nurse CCU, Lloyd Noland Found., Fairfield, Ala., 1968-70; charge nurse Bessemer (Ala.) Carraway Med. Center, 1970-75, unit coordinator, 1975-76, cardiovascular clin. specialist, 1978-80; commd. lt. U.S. Naval Res., 1979; asst. charge nurse intermediate intensive care Naval Regional Med. Center, San Diego, 1981-83, staff nurse, charge nurse med. ward Naval Hosp., Long Beach, Calif., 1983-85; promoted to lt. comdr., 1984; chief nurse clin. investigation Naval Med. Research Unit 3, Cairo, 1985—; instr. CPR, corpsman cardiology course; mem. regional area CPR com. Ala. Heart Assn., 1979-80, CPR regional course coordinator, 1977-78. Camp nurse Assembly of God Ch., Montgomery, Ala., 1968, 77, 78. Recipient citation Ala. Heart Fund, 1975; USPHS Title II trainee, 1977-78. Mem. Am. Nurses Assn., Am. Heart Assn. (council on cardiovascular nursing), Am. Assn. Critical Care Nursing (tech. assistance panel 1978-79). Republican. Office: Naval Med Research Unit 3 Cairo FPO New York NY 09527-1600

GLENN, NAOMI, medical technologist; b. Venice, Ill., Apr. 26, 1942; d. Edward and Beatrice (Ratliff) Glasper; m. Nathaniel Glenn, Mar. 1, 1969. B.A., So. Ill. U., 1968, M.S., Chgo. State U., 1975. Med. technologist Washington U., St. Louis, 1962-69, Children's Meml. Hosp., Chgo., 1969-74; med. lab. technician instr. Central YMCA Community Coll., Chgo., 1975-76; med. technologist Mercy Hosp., Chgo., 1982—. Mem. Am. Soc. Clin. Pathologists (registered med. technologist). Home: 9124 Laflin Ave Chicago IL 60620 Office: Mercy Hosp and Med Ctr King Dr and Stevenson Expressway Chicago IL 60616

GLENN, PEGGY, writer, publisher; b. Haverhill, Mass., July 12, 1944; d. Joseph Flinn and Mildred (Leary) Flinn Mooradian; m. James C. Allison, Apr. 14, 1963 (div. 1969); children—Jane Marie, Michael J.; m. Gary A. Glenn, Sept. 27, 1975. Owner, Aames-Allen Pub. Co., Huntington Beach, Calif., 1977—. Author: How to Start and Run a Successful Home Typing Business, 1980; Word Processing Profits at Home, 1983; Publicity for Books and Authors, 1985; Kerosene Heaters, 1985; (with Gary A. Glenn) Don't Get Burned! A Family Fire-Safety Guide, 1982. Mem. edn. com. So. Calif. Fire Prevention Officers, 1984-85; mem. prevention com. Am. Burn Assn., 1984—. Mem. Women in Communications, Nat. Fedn. Press Women, Publicity Club Los Angeles, Am. Booksellers Assn., Pubs. Assn. So. Calif. (exhibits dir. 1983-86, bd. dirs. 1983—). Democrat. Avocations: sewing, camping, reading. Office: Aames-Allen Publishing Co 1106 Main St Huntington Beach CA 92648

GLESS, SHARON, actress; b. Los Angeles. Attended Gonzaga U., Spokane, Wash. Films: "The Star Chamber", 1983, "Airport 1975", 1974; TV films: "Palms", 1982, "Letting Go", 1985; TV series: "Cagney and Lacey" (Emmy nomination), 1982—, "House Calls, 1981-82. Address: care Creative Artists Agency Inc 1888 Century Park East Suite 1400 Los Angeles CA 90067

GLICK, BETTY JANE, accountant; b. Carlisle, Pa., Sept. 15, 1935; d. Benjamin Burns and Margaret Irene (Brinkerhoff) Bailey; student pub. schs., Carlisle; m. Carl Samuel Glick, Jr., Sept. 4, 1953; children—Elizabeth Rose, Carl Samuel III (dec.), John Robert, William Joseph. Sec., Bedford Shoe Co. div. G.R. Kinney Co., Carlisle, 1953-54, bookkeeper, 1956-57, lacer pre-fit room, 1959; acct. M.G. Riley, C.P.A., Kenai, Alaska, 1966-82. Program chmn. Kenai PTA, 1968-69, pres., 1969-70; mem. Kenai Planning & Zoning Adv. Com., 1974-76, chmn., 1976; mem. Kenai City Council, 1976-83, vice mayor, 1979-82; mem. Kenai Peninsula Borough Assembly, 1982—, v.p., 1984-85; parliamentarian Kenai Peninsula Borough Planning and Zoning Com., 1976-77, vice chmn., 1977-81, chmn., 1981-82; workshop speaker Kenai Peninsula Community Coll., 1984. Treas., Jr. Achievement, Kenai, 1978-81, chmn., 1981-82; bd. dirs. Jr. Achievement Alaska, 1982-85; bd. dirs. Cook Inlet Council on Alcohol and Drug Abuse, 1983-85; chmn. steering com. for sheltered workshop/residential care facility for handicapped People Count, Inc., 1983—. Named Citizen of Month, Kenai C. of C., 1977. Mem. Alaska Mcpl. League (dir. 1980-81, 2d v.p. 1981-82, 1st v.p. 1982-83, pres. 1983-84), Nat. League Cities (small cities adv. council 1983-84), Nat. Assn. Counties (bd. dirs. western region 1984—), Billiken Bus. and Profl. Women's Club (named Woman of Yr. 1978), LWV (parliamentarian Alaska ann. meeting 1983). Club: Peninsula Petroleum Wives. Home: 1601 E Aliak St Kenai AK 99611

GLICK, CYNTHIA SUSAN, lawyer; b. Sturgis, Mich. Aug. 6, 1950; d. Elmer Joseph and Ruth Edna (McCally) G. A.B., Ind. U., Bloomington, 1972; J.D., Ind. U.-Indpls., 1978. Bar: Ind. 1978, U.S. Dist. Ct. (no. dist.) Ind. 1981, U.S. Dist. Ct. (so. dist.) Ind. 1978. Campaign aide Ind. Republican Central Com., Indpls., 1972; adminstrv. aide to gov. State of Ind., Indpls., 1973-76; law clk. Ind. Ct. of Appeals, Indpls., 1976-79; dep. pros. atty. LaGrange County, Ind., 1980-83, pros. atty., 1983—. Named hon. speaker of Ind. House, speaker Ind. Ho. of Reps., 1972, Sagamore of Wabash, gov. Ind., 1974. Fellow Ind. Bar Found.; mem. Ind. Bar Assn., ABA, LaGrange County Bar Assn. (pres. 1983—), Am. Judicature Soc., DAR, Bus. and Profl. Women's Club. Republican. Methodist. Lodge: Order Eastern Star. Home: 113 W Spring St LaGrange IN 46761 Office: LaGrange County Pros Atty Courthouse LaGrange IN 46761

GLICK, HARRIET BRIER, theatre school director; b. Phila., Aug. 29, 1922; d. Ben and Gertrude (Lerner) Brier; m. Bernard Fine, May 23, 1942 (div. Mar. 1971); children—Diane Davids, Kenneth; m. Milton Glick, Mar. 19, 1971. Grad. Phila. Sch. Drama Art, 1940; student U. Pa., 1940-42, St. Joseph Coll., 1965, Barnes Found., 1969-76; postgrad. theater arts Villanova U., 1975. Practice tchr. creative dramatics Phila. Sch. System, 1962; dir. children's theater New Hope, Bucks County, 1963; dir. high sch. theater Cornelia Otis

Skinner Playhouse, Lower Merion Sch. System, 1967; instr. improvisational theater Harcum Jr. Coll., 1967, Main Line Sch., 1971; tchr. Lower Merion Sch. Dist., 1971-74; dir. children Bala Cynwyd Library, Narberth, Pa., 1964-74; instr. creative dramatics Merion Elem. Sch., 1971; dir. Belmont Hills Sch., Narberth, Pa., 1972—; instr. guides Bicentennial hist. tours Walnut St. Theater, Phila., 1975-76; instr. creative drama for children Main Line Center Arts, Haverford, Pa., 1975-79; dir. ednl. activities Walnut St. Theater, Phila., 1979; mem. staff Mainline Center Arts, Haverford, 1975-79; dir. theater workshop, dir. children's theater Royal Palm Theater, Boca Raton, Fla., 1979—. Author: What Makes An Actor and Artist and Not Just a Performer, 1969. Mem. Am. Ednl. Theater Assn. Home: 605 Conshohocken State Rd Penn Valley Narberth PA 19072 also 3400 Ocean Blvd Apt 1-1D Palm Beach FL 33480

GLICK, MARY ANN DRUCKER, accountant, educator; b. Cambridge, Mass., June 21, 1951; d. Jack and Evelyn (Sherer) Drucker; student piano Boston Conservatory Music, 1965-69; B.S., Boston U., 1973, M.B.A., 1974; postgrad. summer U. Calif. at Berkeley, 1972; m. Mark Glick, Sept. 1, 1973; children—Herman David, Jason Leon. Research asst. in accounting Boston U., 1973-74; sr. to supr. accountant Ernst & Whinney (formerly S.D. Leidesdorf & Co., C.P.A.'s), N.Y.C., 1974-79; asst. prof. acctg. C.W. Post Center of L.I. U., 1979-80, Hofstra U., 1980—; lectr. bus. adminstrn., tchr. advising accounting Marymount Manhattan Coll., 1977—. C.P.A., N.Y. Mem. Am. Inst. C.P.A.'s, Am. Women's Soc. C.P.A.'s, N.Y. State Soc. C.P.A.'s, Mensa, Mortar Board.

GLICK, RUTH BURTNICK, author, lecturer; b. Lexington, Ky., Apr. 27, 1942; d. Lester Leon and Beverly (Miller) Burtnick; m. Norman Stanley Glick, June 30, 1963; children Elissa, Ethan. B.A., George Washington U., 1964; M.A., U. Md., 1967. Author, 1973—; bd, dirs. Columbia Literary Assocs., Ellicott City, Md., 1981—; lectr. Romance Writers Am., Detroit, 1984, S.W. Writers Conf., Houston, 1984, Nebr. Writers Guild, Omaha, 1985, Romance Writers Am., Atlanta, 1985. Author: (with Nancy Baggett) Dollhouse Furniture You Can Make, 1977; Invasion of the Blue Lights, 1982; (with Buckholtz, Males and Titchener) Love Is Elected (one of best romances 1982), 1982; (with Louise Titchener) In the Arms of Love (romance best seller list), 1983; (with L. Titchener) Brian's Captive (romance best seller list), 1983; (with Buckholtz, Males, Titchener) Southern Persuasion, 1983; (with Titchener) Reluctant Merger (romance best seller list), 1983; (with Baggett and G. Greene) Don't Tell 'Em It's Good for 'Em, 1984; (with Buckholtz) End of Illusion, 1984; (with Titchener) Summer Wine, 1984; (with Buckholtz) Space Attack, 1984; Mission of the Secret Spy Squad, 1984; Mindbenders, 1984; (with Titchener) Beginners Luck, 1984; Hopelessly Devoted, 1985; Summer Stars, 1985; Doomstalker, 1985; Captain Kid and the Pirates, 1985; The Cats of Castle Mountain, 1985; More Than Promises, 1985; (with Baggett) Soup's On, 1985; (with Baggett and Greene) Eat Your Vegetables, 1985; Stolen Passion, 1986; In Search of the Dove, 1986; Flight of the Raven, 1986; others; contbr. articles to mags. and newspapers. U. Md. Am. Studies fellow, 1964-65. Mem. Soc. Children's Book Writers, Washington Ind. Writers, Authors' Guild, Romance Writers Am., Washington Romance Writers. Democrat.

GLICK-COLQUITT, KAREN LYNNE, college administrator; b. Bucyrus, Ohio, Sept. 2; d. Phillip Dole and Bernice Grace (Shasteen) Glick; B.S.J., Bowling Green State U., 1967, M.A., 1979; m. Michael Colquitt; children—M. Todd, K. Christine. Editor, Bowling Green (Ohio) State U., 1972-74; account exec. Howard E. Mitchell, Jr., Advt., Findlay, Ohio, 1974-77; asst. to dir. Student Devel. Program, Bowling Green State U., 1977-79; dir. pub. info. Bluffton (Ohio) Coll., 1980-83; asst. to v.p. for instl. advancement Findlay (Ohio) Coll., 1983—. Mem. Pub. Relations Soc. Am., Council Advancement and Support of Edn., Internat. Assn. Bus. Communicators (chpt. pres.). Episcopalian. Office: Findlay College 1000 N Main St Findlay OH 45840

GLICKENHAUS, SARAH BRODY, speech therapist; b. Mpls., Mar. 8, 1919; d. Morris and Ethel (Silin) Brody; B.S., U. Minn., 1940, M.S., 1945; m. Seth Morton Glickenhaus, Oct. 23, 1944; children—James Morris, Nancy Pier. Speech therapist, Davison Sch. Speech Correction, Atlanta, 1940-42; speech pathologist U. Minn., Mpls., 1945-46; speech therapist Queens Coll., N.Y.C., 1946-48; speech therapist VA, N.Y.C., 1949-50; pvt. practice, New Rochelle, N.Y., 1950-71; speech therapist Abbott Sch. United Free Sch. Dist. 13, Irvinton, N.Y., 1971—; tutor learning disabled children New Rochelle Public Schs., 1968-71. Mem. Am. Speech Hearing And Lang. Assn., N.Y. State Speech and Hearing Assn., Westchester Speech and Hearing Assn., AAAS. Club: Harvard (N.Y.C.). Jewish. Home and office: 100 Dorchester Rd Scarsdale NY 10583

GLICKFELD, CAROLE L., writer, editor; b. N.Y.C., July 20; d. Robert and Blanche (Mandelbaum) Lieber; student Syracuse U., 1957-58; B.A., CUNY, 1961; postgrad. Hunter Coll., 1962-63; cert. Grad. Sch. Bus., U. Wash., 1975. Communications aide Washington State Legislature, Olympia, Wash., 1970, 71, 72; press sec. U.S. Congress, Washington, 1972; community liaison Seattle City Light, 1975-76; dir. Mayor's Office for Sr. Citizens, Seattle, 1977-82; free-lance writer Proof Positive, Seattle, 1982—. Author: (novel) On The Cutting Edge, 1984; (screenplay) Name of the Game, 1979. Writer satirical polit. revues for fund-raising, Seattle, 1980, 82, 83. Contbr. articles to various publs. Office mgr. Wes Uhlman for Mayor, Seattle, 1969, 73; press sec. Norm Rice for Mayor, Seattle, 1985; bd. mem. Met. Democratic Club, Seattle, 1981-85; panelist NEH, 1981; mem. bd. Sr. Rights Assistance, Seattle, 1981-82, Community Home Health Care, Seattle, 1982-83. Mem. Pacific N.W. Writers Conf. Avocations: ballet student; films; theatre; politics. Home: 731 Broadway E Seattle WA 98102

GLICKLICH, LUCILLE BARASH, physician, child psychiatry; b. Fond du Lac, Wis., Jan. 10, 1926; d. Peter and Freda (Pevnick) Barash; m. Marvin Glicklich, Sept. 12, 1948 (div. Apr. 1983); children—Daniel, Anne, Peter, Lynn, Barry; m. John A. Rosenberg, Aug. 12, 1984. B.A., U. Wis.-Madison, 1947, M.D., 1950. Diplomate Am. Bd. Pediatrics, Am. Bd. Psychiatry and Neurology, Am. Bd. Child Psychiatry. Intern, Youngstown Hosp. Assn., Ohio, 1950-51; resident in pediatrics Milw. Children's Hosp., 1951-53, practice medicine specializing in psychiatry Marquette Med. Sch. Associated, Wis., 1967-69; child psychiatry fellow Marquette and Milw. Childrens Hosp., 1969-71; med. dir. children's div. Curative Workshop, Milw., 1959-63, Easter Seals Child Devel. program, 1963-67; chief med. cons. Milw. Pub. Schs., 1964-67; asst. prof. pediatrics Med. Coll. U. Wis., Milw., 1965-85, assoc. clin. prof., 1985—, asst. prof. psychiatry, 1971-85; dir. liaison psychiatry Milw. Children's Hosp., 1975-85; assoc. prof., vice chmn. dept. psychiatry U. Wis. Med. Sch., Milw. Clin. Campus, 1985—; hosp. staff appointments Milw. Children's Hosp., Milw. Psychiatric Hosp., Milw. County Med. Comples, Mt. Sinai Med. Ctr.; lectr. various colls. and univs.; cons. in field. Contbr. articles to profl. publs. Active mem. N'Shei group, Jewish Parenting, Communication for the 80's; Jewish Fedn. Women's div., Milw. Childrens Hosp. Jr. Aux. Target M.D. program U. Wis., Milw., 1981, congl. Emmanuel Yom Hashoah, 1982, Milw. Neonatal Nursing Consortium, Marquette U. panel Survivors of Holocaust, 1984; bd. dir. Milw. Bd. of Jewish Edn. Bd., 1971-78, pres. 1974-76, Milw. Jewish Fedn., 1977—; bd. trustees Congl. Beth Israel, 1975-77, youth commn. 1971-77; mem. Kesher Jewish Woman's network; mem. task force on teen pregnancies Planned Parenthood, 1984. Fellow Am. Acad. Child Psychiatry, Am. Psychiat. Assn., Am. Acad. Pediatrics (Wis. Br.); mem. Am. Soc. Adolescent Psychiatry, Wis. Council Adolescent and Child Psychiatry (sec. 1981-82, pres.-elect 1982-83, pres. 1983-85), Am. Orthopsychiatric Assn., Milw. Pediatric Soc., Soc. Adolescent Medicine, AMA, Wis. State Med. Soc. (del. 1978—, bd. dirs. 1985—, reference com. 1982—), Milw. County Med. Soc. (sec. treas. 1981, pres.-elect 1984, pres. 1985), Am. Med. Women's Assn. (Southeastern Wis. chpt. vice-dir. 1977-79), Women in Medicine in Wis. (bd. dirs. 1979-82, pres. 1979-80), Wis. Council Child and Adolescent Psychiatry (pres. 1984-86). Avocations: travel; bicycling; racquetball; walking; reading. Home: 3431 N Lake Dr Milwaukee WI 53211 Office: Mt Sinai Med Ctr 950 N 12th St PO Box 342 Milwaukee WI 53201

GLICKMAN, LAURA LEE, lawyer; b. Bklyn., Apr. 26, 1946; d. Daniel Bernard and Miriam K. (Friedman) Glickman; A.B. with honors, UCLA, 1967, J.D., 1970; m. James D. Leewong, Feb. 18, 1979; children—Andrea Jane, Hilary Anne. Bar: Calif. U.S. Supreme Ct., U.S. Ct. Appeals, U.S. Dist. Ct. Practiced in Pacoima, Calif., 1971-72, Los Angeles, 1972—; staff atty. San Fernando Valley Neighborhood Legal Services, Inc., Pacoima, 1971-72, directing atty., 1972; clin. supervising atty. Legal Aid Found. Los Angeles, 1972-74; adj. clin. prof. Loyola U. Sch. Law, Los Angeles, 1972-74. Mem. lawyers com. ACLU, 1972-74; chmn. young profl. leadership group Jewish Fedn. Council Greater Los Angeles, 1977-78, also mem. community relations com., 1978, leadership devel. com., 1978; referee bd. retirement Los Angeles County Employees Retirement Assn., 1975—. Recipient Bancroft-Whitney award, 1968, Appellate Advocacy award UCLA Law Sch., 1970. Mem. State Bar Calif., Los Angeles County Bar Assn., Women Lawyers Assn. Los Angeles, UCLA Law Alumni Assn. (dean's counsel), Calif. Women Lawyers Assn. Office: 911 Wilshire Blvd Suite 1070 Los Angeles CA 90017

GLODNEY, CAROLE SUE, property management company executive; b. Chgo., Dec. 6, 1944; d. Abe and Evelyn (Rosenthal) G. Student UCLA, 1963-65; B.S., U. San Francisco, 1983. Account clk. ABC, Hollywood, Calif., 1965-66; bookkeeper Laventhol & Horwath, Los Angeles, 1966-72; acct., controller, v.p. Goldrich & Kest, Culver City, Calif., 1972—. Mem. Assn. HUD Mgmt. Agts. (treas., bd. dirs.), Phi Sigma Sigma. Democrat. Jewish. Office: Goldrich & Kest 5150 Overland Ave Culver City CA 90230

GLOSSER, ELIZABETH BARBARA, business consultant; b. Plymouth, Pa., June 25, 1939; d. Charles B. and Elizabeth (Ruddy) G.; B.A., Coll. Misericordia, Dallas, Pa., 1961; M.Ed. (NDEA fellow), Rutgers U., 1965; M.B.A., Fairleigh Dickinson U., 1978. Tchr., Neptune High Sch., N.J., 1961-64; counselor, Westwood, N.J., 1965-69; tchr., River Dell, N.J., 1969-71; mgr. sales adminstrn. Xerox Corp., 1972-73, cons., 1971-72, product mgr., 1972, sales mgr., 1973-79; asst. prof. bus. and econs. Marymount Coll., Tarrytown, N.Y., also pres. Women at Work, 1979-81; mng. dir. The Exec. Exchange, Englewood Cliffs, N.J., 1981—; sec.-treas. Exec. Registry, Hackensack, N.J., 1983—; pres. Exec. Alternatives, Manasquan, N.J., 1986—. Fund raiser Multiple Sclerosis Soc., Am. Cancer Soc.; pres. Bergen County Friends of R.S.V.P., also trustee. Roman Catholic. Author: Moments Matter, 1977. Home: 17 Lincoln Ave Avon By The Sea NJ 07717 Office: 560 Sylvan Ave Englewood Cliffs NJ

GLOVER, BECKY JO, theatre manager; b. Green Bay, Wis., May 15, 1958; d. Robert Joseph and Mildred Marjorie (Arndt) Eisenreich; m. Ronald Leron Glover, Jan. 3, 1981. B.A. in Psychology, Tex. Lutheran Coll., 1980; postgrad. in psychology St. Mary's U., San Antonio, 1980. With Snelling & Snelling, San Antonio, 1981; asst. mgr. Santikos Theatres, Inc., San Antonio, 1982, gen. mgr. 4 plex, 1982-84, tng. dir., 1984-85, gen. mgr. 10 plex, 1985—. Recipient nat. achievement awards Snelling & Snelling, 1981; Friend of Freedom award Tex. Emancipation Day Com., 1983. Mem. Nat. Assn. Female Execs. (bd. dirs. San Antonio 1984—). Democrat. Lutheran. Avocations: playing guitar; song writing; psychology studies; reading; singing. Home: 9522 Bowen Dr San Antonio TX 78250

GLOVER, JUDITH (JUDY) ANN, banker; b. Holdrege, Nebr., Apr. 14, 1946; d. Charles Eugene and Nona Althea (Morris) Adcock; m. David Joseph Glover, Apr. 16, 1971 (div. Aug. 1976); 1 son, David Joseph V. Student Kearney State Coll., 1964-66, U. Colo., 1968-70; basic cert. Am. Inst. Banking, 1978; grad. in comml. banking Southwestern Grad. Sch. Banking at So. Methodist U., 1983. Sec. United Bank, Denver, 1969-70, Bank of Cripple Creek (Colo.), 1973-75, No. Hills Bank, San Antonio, 1975-77; ops. mgr. Metro Bank Dallas, 1977-78; cashier First Nat. Bank, Navasota, Tex., 1978-80; v.p. Bay Area Bank & Trust, Webster, Tex., 1980-84; exec. v.p., cashier Security Bank-Bay Area, Webster, 1984—. Mem. vestry St. Paul's Episcopal Ch. Navasota, 1979-80; mem. vestry St. Christopher Episcopal Ch., League City, Tex., 1983—, chmn. fin. com.; treas. Tex. Neurofibromatosis Found., Austin, 1980-82, bd. dirs., 1982—, state pres., 1983-84. Mem. Nat. Assn. Bank Women, Am. Mgmt. Assn. Bank Adminstrn. Inst. (bd. dirs. Bryan, Tex. chpt. 1978-80), Am. Inst. Banking. Republican. Club: Bay Area Episcopal Singles (Houston). Lodge: Order Eastern Star. Home: 614 Cole Webster TX 77598 Office: Security Bank-Bay Area 18333 Egret Bay Blvd Webster TX 77598

GLOVER, LAURICE WHITE, psychoanalyst, musician; b. Los Angeles, Oct. 15, 1930; d. Lawrence Francis and Alice Violet (King) White; B.A., Occidental Coll., 1951; M.S. in Social Work, Columbia, 1956; cert. in psychoanalysis and psychotherapy Postgrad. Center Mental Health, N.Y.C., 1971, cert. in supervision of psychoanalysis, 1975; student pipe organ Norman Wright, Robert Owen, Virgil Fox; m. Norman James Glover, Aug. 18, 1956 (div. 1963); remarried, Aug. 21, 1983; stepchildren—Valarie Scott, Norman James III, Susan Charlotte, John Thomas. Pvt. practice psychoanalysis, N.Y.C., 1968—; faculty and sr. supr. psychoanalysis Postgrad. Center Mental Health, N.Y.C., 1976—; asst. dean training, 1982—; asst. clin. prof. psychiatry Albert Einstein Coll. Medicine, Yeshiva, U., N.Y.C., 1975—; adj. asst. prof. psychology Bronx Community Coll., 1974; tng. analyst Nat. Psychol. Assn. for Psychoanalysis, 1974-76; psychoanalysis faculty Nat. Inst. Psychotherapies, 1978-83; faculty, sr. supr. psychoanalysis, tng. analyst Tng. Inst. Mental Health Practitioners, 1979—. Organist, choir dir. Throggs' Neck Lutheran Ch., Bronx, N.Y., 1964-67; jazz organist Hotel Barbizon for Women, 1965-66; organist, choir dir. 4th Ave. Meth. Ch., Bklyn., 1967—74. Mem. Psychoanalytic Soc., Postgrad. Ctr. Soc. Clin. Social Workers, Nat. Assn. Social Workers, Am. Group Psychotherapy Assn., Am. Guild Organists, Am. Theatre Organists Soc., Am. Fedn. Musicians. Contbr. articles to profl. publs. Office: 271 Central Park W New York NY 10024

GLOVER, LOIS YVONNE, state official; b. Cloverport, Ky., June 26, 1939; d. Ernest Everett and Mildred Alice (Brickey) Bohler; m. James Marshall Glover, Apr. 5, 1957 (div. June 1982). Ed. U. Louisville, 1964, Jefferson Community Coll., 1980. Lic. real estate broker. Exec. asst. West Ky. Coal Co., Louisville, 1957-64; mgr., buyer My Dear Watson, Louisville, 1965-69; exec. asst. KFC Corp., Louisville, 1969-71, office services supr., 1971-77; owner, operator Up Front, Louisville, 1977-79; events coordinator Ky. Dept. Parks, Frankfort, 1980—; bd. sec. Ky. Scottish Weekend, Carrollton, 1983—; com. mem. Heart of Parks Found., Louisville, 1984—; dir. Ky. Women's Softball Program, Louisville, 1979—; nat. coordinator women's softball U.S. Slo-Pitch Softball Assn., Richmond, Va., 1973-79. Author: Inky Trails, 1980 (Poet of the Yr.). Women's editor Softball News, 1979. Writer, performer Sweet Kentucky, 1978. Staff mem. John Y. Brown for Gov. Campaign, Louisville, 1979-80; fund raiser Shively Jay-Cees, Ky., 1983; com. mem. Heart of the Parks Found., Louisville, 1984; cons. J. Bruce Miller for County Judge, Louisville, 1985. Mem. U.S. Slo-Pitch Softball Assn. (nat. coordinator 1973-79, state dir. 1979—), Ky. Real Estate Commn. Democrat. Avocations: writing music; painting; cooking; softball; volleyball. Home: 7105 Pharris Ave Louisville KY 40258 Office: Ky Dept Parks Capital Plaza Tower Frankfort KY 40601

GLOWITZ, CHARLINE SILVIA, educational management consultant; b. N.Y.C., Oct. 8, 1951; d. Solomon Jacob and Claire Sara (Liker) G. Qualified dir. N.Y. State Edn. Dept. Human resources adminstr. Tech. Career Insts. (formerly RCA Insts.), N.Y.C., 1974-79; exec. dir. N.Y. State Assn. of Career Schs., N.Y.C., 1979-86; pvt. practice ednl. mgmt. consulting, N.Y.C., 1986—. Recipient Outstanding Achievement award N.Y. State Assn. Career Schs., 1985. Mem. Am. Soc. Assn. Execs., N.Y. Soc. Assn. Execs., Nat. Assn. Female Execs., N.Y.C. C. of C., Alpha Beta Kappa. Home: 175 W 87th St New York NY 10024

GLUCK, LOUISE ELISABETH, poet; b. N.Y.C., Apr. 22, 1943; d. Daniel and Beatrice (Grosby) Gluck; student Sarah Lawrence Coll., 1962, Columbia, 1963-65; m. Charles Hertz (div.); 1 son, Noah Benjamin; m. 2d, John Dranow, 1977. Vis. poet Goddard Coll., U. N.C., U. Va.; vis. poet U. Iowa; Elliston prof. U. Cin., 1978; vis. faculty Columbia U., 1979; faculty M.F.A. program Goddard Coll., 1976-80, Warren Wilson Coll., Swannanoa, N.C., 1981—; Holloway lectr. U. Calif., Berkeley, 1982; Scott prof. poetry Williams Coll., 1983; mem. faculty Williams Coll., 1984—; vis. prof. UCLA, 1985, 86. Recipient award for creative work Am. Acad. and Inst. Arts and Letters, 1981; Nat. Book Critics Circle award, 1985; Melville Cane award Poetry Soc. Am., 1986; Sara Teasdale Meml. prize Wellesley Coll., 1986; Rockefeller Found. grantee; NEA grantee, 1979-80; Guggenheim Found. grantee. Author: Firstborn, 1968; The House On Marshland, 1975; Descending Figure, 1980; The Triumph of Achilles, 1985. Address: Creamery Rd Plainfield VT 05667

GLUCK, RUTH RUBIN, lawyer; b. Frankfurt, Germany, Nov. 18, 1946; came to U.S., 1950, naturalized, 1956; d. Moses Mordecai and Anna (Kozulcyk) Rubin; m. Marshall J. Gluck, July 5, 1970; children—Abbe Rubin, Simon Ari. B.A., U. Pa., 1967; J.D., NYU, 1970. Bar: N.Y. 1970. Lawyer Met. Life Ins. Co., N.Y.C., 1970-77, asst. gen. counsel, asst. sec., 1977—. Mem. ABA, N.Y. State Bar Assn., N.Y. Women's Bar Assn. Democrat. Jewish. Club: Easthampton Tennis. Office: Met Life Ins Co 1 Madison Ave New York NY 10010

GLUSCHENKO, SHARON JEAN, financial services company executive; b. Los Angeles, May 27, 1947; d. George and Marion (Ratner) Veston; 1 son from previous marriage: Robert Brien. B.A., U. Calif.-Northridge, 1969. Personnel asst. Asia Found., San Francisco, 1971-72; with Honeywell, Inc., 1970-78, successively corp. field adminstrn., br. mgr., Sacramento, spl. projects mgr., specialist employee relations Process Control div. Phoenix, staffing specialist employee relations Def. Systems div., Mpls., dir. human resources Travelers Express Co., Inc., Mpls., 1979—. Bd. dirs. NAACP, 1976. Named EEO Employer of Yr., Nat. Urban League, Ariz., 1976, Handicap Employer of Yr., Mayor Phoenix, 1976, Mem. Chicanos Por la Casa, LULAC, Twin Cities Personnel Assn., Human Resources Exec. Roundtable (co founder). Democrat. Lutheran. Office: Travelers Express 5075 Wayzata St Minneapolis MN 55416

GLYNN (MASTERSON), CARLIN, actress; b. Cleve., Feb. 19, 1940; d. Guillford Cresse and Lois Carlin Wilks) G.; m. Peter Masterson, Dec. 29, 1960; children—Carlin Alexandra, Mary Stuart, Peter C.B. Student Sophie Newcomb Coll., 1957-58. Appeared in broadway plays Best Little Whorehouse in Texas, 1978-82; appeared in off-broadway plays Winter Play, 1983, Alterations, 1984, Outside WACO, 1985; films include Sixteen Candles, 1984, Three Days of the Condor, 1974, Continental Divide, 1980, The Trip to Bountiful, 1985; actress, resource dir. Sundance Inst., 1983-85; numerous appearances on T.V. Founder, exec. dir. Citizens Action Fund, N.Y.C., 1974-75; bd. dirs. Consumer Action NOW, N.Y.C., 1970-80. Recipient Theatre World award, 1978, Antionette Perry award, 1979, Lawrence Olivier award, 1981; named Actress of Yr. in musical Best Little Whorehouse in Texas. Mem. Actors Studio, Screens Actors Guild, Actors Equity Assn., AFTRA. Episcopalian.

GNADT, JOAN THERESE HARNEY, cardiologist, educator; b. Milw., July 20, 1949; d. Thomas Holland and Rose Caroline (Kriege) Harney; student Marquette U., 1967-68; B.S. in Zoology, U. Wis.-Milw., 1971; M.D., Med. Coll. Wis., 1976; m. Gregory James Gnadt, June 25, 1971; children—Geoffrey James, Victoria Rose. Intern, Martinez (Calif.) VA Med. Center, 1977-78, resident in internal medicine, 1978-80, fellow in cardiology, 1980-82, staff in cardiology, 1982, acting asst. chief cardiology, 1982—, dir. geriatrics/gerontology; asst. clin. prof. medicine U. Calif.-Davis, 1982—. Fellow Am. Coll. Cardiology; mem. ACP, Am. Med. Women's Assn. Roman Catholic. Home: 5745 Colton Blvd Oakland CA 94611 Office: 150 Muir Rd Martinez CA 94553

GNIPPE, SANDRA JOY, English and speech educator, librarian; b. Chgo., Aug. 7, 1937; d. Abraham Jacob and Jeanette (Rosenberg) G. B.S., Northwestern U., 1958; M.A.T., U. Chgo., 1972, A.M., 1972. Teaching cert., Ill. Library asst. U. Chgo. Lab. Sch., 1965-68; librarian Argo Community High Sch., Summit, Ill., 1969-70, T.F. North High Sch., Calumet City, Ill., 1970-81; reference librarian Roosevelt U., Chgo., 1973-76; librarian T. F. South High Sch., Lansing, Ill., 1981-83, tchr. English/speech, 1983—. Mem. Children's Reading Round Table, High Sch. Library Media Assn., Chgo. Library Club. Democrat. Jewish. Avocation: theater. Office: Thornton Fractional South High Sch 18500 Burnham Ave Lansing IL 60438

GO, SIAN TJING, hematologist; b. Amsterdam, Netherlands, Sept. 6, 1950; came to U.S., 1966, naturalized, 1971; d. Gam Ping and Olga Martha (Oostveen) Go. B.S. with honors in Biophysics, U. Calif.-Berkeley, 1972; M.D., U. Calif.-Davis, 1976; postdoctoral scholar, intern U. Calif.-San Francisco, 1978; honor baccalaureate U. Calif.-Berkeley, 1970-72. Resident in internal medicine N.Y. Infirmary-Beekman Hosp., 1980-81, Rockefeller-Meml. Sloan-Kettering Cancer Ctr., N.Y.C., 1981-82; hematology-oncology fellow Meml. Sloan-Kettering Cancer Ctr., 1982-83; staff attending physician Rockefeller U., N.Y.C., 1981-83; biochemistry-hematology fellow Harvard U., Cambridge, 1983—, Mass. Gen. Hosp., Boston, 1984—; clin. instr. in medicine U. Calif.-San Francisco, 1978-80. Editor: Chinese Character Dictionary, 1984. Am. Cancer Soc.; fellow. Mem. Am. Soc. Internal Medicine, Christian Med. Soc. Lutheran. Home: 33 Kingcrest Terr Randolph MA 02368 Office: Room 204 Byerly Hall Harvard U 8 Garden St Cambridge MA 02138

GOANS, JUDY SUSANNA WINEGAR, lawyer; b. Knoxville, Tenn., Sept. 27, 1949; d. Robert Henry and Lula Mae (Myers) Winegar; student Sam Houston State U., 1967-68; B.S. in Engring. Physics, U. Tenn., 1971, postgrad., 1971-74, J.D., 1978; m. Ronald E. Goans, June 18, 1971; children—Robert Henson, Ronald Earl. Teaching asst. dept. physics U. Tenn., Knoxville, 1971-74; instr. legal rights Women's Opportunities and Referrals of Knoxville, 1977-78; patent analyst nuclear div. Union Carbide Corp., Oak Ridge, 1978-79; atty. Office of Asst. Gen. Counsel for Patents, U.S. Dept. Energy, Washington, 1979-82; legis. and internat. intellectual property specialist Office Legislation and Internat. Affairs, U.S. Patent and Trademark Office, Washington, 1982—. Mem. Knoxville Women's Center, 1977-82; del. Nat. Women's Conf., Internat. Women's Year; mem. legal bd. Knoxville Rape Crisis Center, 1979; mem. Knox County Republican Exec. Com., 1978-79. Mem. ABA, Tenn. Bar Assn., NOW (dir. 1977-79), Govt. Patent Lawyers Assn. (sec. 1981-83), Am. Patent Law Assn., Sigma Pi Sigma, Tau Beta Pi. Methodist. Home: 2233 Pinefield Rd Waldorf MD 20601

GOBAR, SALLY ANN, school principal; b. Santa Maria, Calif., Nov. 27, 1933; d. Vernon Blythe Randall and Leona Margaret (Jackson) Batchman; m. Alfred Julian Gobar, June 17, 1957; children—Wendy Lee, Curtis Julian, Joseph Julian. B.A., Whittier Coll., 1955; M.A., Claremont Grad. Sch., 1967, Ph.D., 1979. Tchr., So. San Francisco High Sch., 1956-57, Santa Ana High Sch., Calif., 1957-61; counselor Sunny Hills High Sch., Fullerton, Calif., 1961-66; head counselor Troy High Sch., Fullerton, 1967-83; asst. prin. Buena Park High Sch., Calif., 1983-84; prin. Fullerton High Sch., 1984—; cons. Coll. Bd., N.Y., 1972-77. Mem. Pres.'s Assocs., Calif. State U.-Fullerton. Recipient Golden Book award Exchange Club, 1978, Outstanding Service award Calif. Personnel and Guidance Assn., 1980. Mem. Assn. Calif. Sch. Adminstrs., Whittier Coll. Alumni Assn., Claremont Grad. Sch. Alumni, Fullerton C. of C. Republican. Avocations: travel; classical music; piano. Home: 1100 Valencia Mesa Dr Fullerton CA 92633 Office: Fullerton Union High Sch 201 E Chapman Fullerton CA 92634

GOBER COSGROVE, RITAMAE ADELE, lawyer; b. New Britain, Conn., Oct. 7, 1950; d. Anthony William and Adele (Rita) Akronas) Gober; m. Gerald Paul Cosgrove, Sept. 10, 1982; 1 child, Sarah Adele. A.S. in Accounting, Greater Hartford Community Coll., 1970; B.A. in Econs., U. Hartford, 1977; M.A. in Econs., 1978; J.D., U. Tulsa, 1981. Bar: Conn. 1981. Prodn. and broadcast dir. Chirurg & Cairns, Farmington, Conn., 1968-71; media dir. Knudsen & Moore, Stamford, Conn., 1971-72; retail buyer G. Fox & Co., Hartford, Conn., 1972-76; prodn. analyst Conn. Dept. Transp., Wethersfield, 1977-78; hearing examiner Ct. Dept. Pub. Utilities, Hartford, 1979-81; atty. land dept. Arco Oil & Gas Co., Houston, 1981—; research asst. Nat. Energy Law and Policy Inst., Tulsa, 1979-81; adj. prof. U. Midland (Tex.), 1981-82, U. Houston-Downtown Campus, 1983—, Bates Coll. Law, U. Houston, 1984—; dir. Northwest Mcpl. Utility Dist. 9, Cypress/Houston, Tex., Tchr., cons. Project Bus./Jr. Achievement, Midland, 1981-82. Mem. ABA, Conn. Bar Assn., Nat. Soc. for Econs. Democrat. Roman Catholic.

GOCEK, MATILDA ARKENBOUT, library director, publisher; b. Hoboken, N.J., Feb. 18, 1923; d. Jacob Richard and Mathilde C. (Meyer) Arkenbout; m. John A. Gocek, Nov. 18, 1956; children—Ruth Ann Robinson, Dianne D. McKinstrie, John Jacob Gocek. A.A., Orange County Community Coll., 1961; B.A., SUNY-New Paltz, 1963; M.L.S., SUNY-Albany. Library dir. Monroe Free Library, N.Y., 1958-62, Tuxedo Park Library, N.Y., 1963-76, Suffern Free Library, N.Y., 1977—; ptnr. Library Research Assocs., Monroe, 1968-83, pres., 1984—. Author: Eden's END (Idiom award 1965), 1965; Benedict Arnold: Readers Guide, 1973; Orange County N.Y.: Readers Guide, 1973; Tuxedo Park Library: Social Aspects of Growth, 1978; Love is A Challenge, 1978. Mem. history and heritage com. Orange County Community Coll., 1975—; bd. dirs. Tuxedo Park Day Sch., 1971-80; pres. Mus. Village of Orange County, 1980-83; v.p. Montgomery Expdn. Meml. Observance, 1975—. Mem. Women's Club of Suffern, Orange-Sullivan Library Assn. (pres. 1967-70), Dirs. Assn. Romapo Catskill Library System (pres. 1971-73). Republican. Avocations: writing; needlepoint; guitar. Home: Dunderberg Rd Monroe NY 10950 Office: Library Research Assocs Inc Route 5 Box 41 Dunderberg Rd Monroe NY 10950

GOCHANOUR, MARY MARGARET, job placement officer; b. Boonville, Ind., May 28, 1920; d. William B. and Della Mae (Byers) Richardson; m. Charles E. Gochanour, Apr. 7, 1939; children—Dian Kelly, Robert, Randall, Richard, Kevin. Grad. secretarial program Ill. Bus. Coll., Springfield, 1938. Sec., Am. Nat. Red Cross Telecommunications, Springfield, 1954-56, Sangamon County Central Republican Com., Springfield, 1956-57; sec. Ill. Dept.

Labor, Decatur, 1957-61, interviewer, 1961-79, placement supr., 1979-85. Community speaker on labor issues. Republican. Baptist. Avocations: reading; teaching Sunday School. Home: 828 E Grandview St Mesa AZ 85203

GODDARD, JAN BARD, insurance analyst; b. Ft. Kent, Maine, Feb. 3, 1939; d. Hilaire and Emma (Dufour) Bard; m. Samuel N. Goddard, Aug. 11, 1961; children—Suzanne Goddard Clukey, Rebecca. Student Columbia U., 1957-59, U. Maine, 1979. With Western Union, Boston, 1956-60; with statis. dept. P. Lorillard Co., N.Y.C., 1957-59; with Goddard, Hodgdon, Mitchell Agy., Waterville, Maine, 1959—, ins. analyst, agt., 1980—. Chmn. bd. Park Street Nursery Sch., Waterville, 1971—; pres. Waterville Osteo. Hosp. Aux., 1978-80, bd. dirs., 1985; pres. Maine Assn. Hosp. Auxs., 1983—, North Kennebec area Am. Cancer Soc., 1976-78, Women's Union, 1st Bapt. Ch., 1967-68; com. chmn. United Way of Mid-Maine, 1979-80; chmn. Hains charity com. City of Waterville, 1978-79. Mem. Ins. Women of Central Maine (pres. 1965-66), Ind. Ins. Agts. Assn., Hist. (charter), Soc., China Hist. Soc. Republican. Baptist. Club: Antique of Waterville (pres. 1965-66). Waterville. Office: Goddard Hogdon Mitchell PO Box 748 Waterville ME 04904

GODDARD, ROSALIND KENT, librarian; b. Gadsden, Ala., Mar. 7, 1944; d. George and Nettye (Kent) G. B.A., San Francisco State Coll., 1965; M.L.S., UCLA, 1982. Research asst. IBM, San Jose, Calif., 1966-67; children's librarian Los Angeles Pub. Library, 1967-71, young adult librarian, 1972-73, sr. librarian Venice br., 1974-79, Robertson br., 1979—; ann. guest book reviewer Santa Monica Pub. Library, 1975—, Beverly Hills Recreation and Parks Dept., 1975—. Recipient Staff Commendation, Los Angeles Pub. Library, 1969; Exceptional Leadership award Los Angeles Brotherhood Crusade, 1973; award of appreciation Calif. Youth Authority, Nelles Sch., 1983. Mem. ALA, AAUW, Calif. Librarians Black Caucus. Democrat. Methodist. Home: 1960 S Shenandoah St Los Angeles CA 90034 Office: Robertson Br Los Angeles Pub Library 1719 S Robertson Blvd Los Angeles CA 90035

GODFREY, AGNES MULVEY, educator; b. N.Y.C., July 24, 1915; d. Charles Watt and Mary Elizabeth Mulvey; B.A. in Elem. Edn., Columbia U., 1937, M.A. in Child Devel., 1938; m. Raymond V. Godfrey; children—James Terrance, Raymond Michael, Lynn Ellen, Susan Marie. Teaching fellow Columbia U., 1936-37; research asst. Erpi Ednl. Films and Sci. Sch. of Air, 1937-38; tchr. Cranford, N.J., Rye, N.Y., 1938-41; staff div. cultural relations U.S. Dept. State, 1942; staff Nat. Cathedral Sch., Washington, 1943-44, Burroughs Sch., China Lake, Calif., 1947-50; curriculum coordinator Univ. Park Elem. Sch., Melbourne, Fla., 1961-68; dir. curriculum and materials center Brevard County (Fla.) Schs., Melbourne, 1968-69, dir. instrn., 1969-70, area reading clinician, 1971-77; curriculum coordinator, 1977—. Bd. dirs. Friends of Melbourne Library, 1968-70; docent Brevard Art Ctr. and Mus. Named Tchr. of Yr., 1961; recipient citation of merit Nat. Multiple Sclerosis Soc., 1976. Mem. Assn. Childhood Edn., AAUW, Am. Assn. Supervision and Curriculum Devel., Internat., Brevard County (dir.) reading assns., Ringling Art Mus., Delta Kappa Gamma. Author sch. publs.

GODFREY, LORETTA SACHS, advertising executive; b. Bloomfield, Ind., Dec. 19, 1946; d. Dennis Maurice and Betty Jean (Huber) Sachs; student Ind. U., 1964-69, postgrad., 1986—; B.A., Fordham U., 1983. Distbn. supr. Ednl. TV Stas. Program Service, Bloomington, Ind., 1967-69; mgr. traffic dept. Nat. Ednl. TV, N.Y.C., 1969-71; traffic mgr. Benton & Bowles Advt., N.Y.C., 1971; account exec. BBDO Advt., N.Y.C., 1973-76; supr. broadcast ops. and bus. affairs The Lever Media Group div. Lever Bros. Co., N.Y.C., 1976-82; advt. mgr. Publs. Clearing House, Port Washington, N.Y., 1982-85. Chmn. communications com. Country Club Estates Civic Assn., Hempstead, N.Y., 1980-81. Mem. NOW, AAUW, Phi Kappa Phi, Alpha Sigma Lambda. Club: Order Eastern Star.

GODFREY, MARY ROSE, business owner, financial planner; b. Medford, Mass., Nov. 27, 1942; d. Francis R. and Rose (Cuneo) Dittami; A.B., Regis Coll., Mass., 1964; m. William K. Godfrey, Oct. 15, 1966; children—Angela, James, Thomas. Auditor, IRS, Boston, 1964-67, group supr., 1968-69, field agt., 1969-70, instr., 1966-70; tax accountant, Holliston, Mass., 1970-73; treas. New Eng. Adv. Group, Inc., Newton, Mass., 1974-81, also dir.; pres., owner Suburban Airport Transit, 1981-84, owner, gen. mgr. Priority Express, 1983—; v.p., owner Marathon Lines, Framingham, Mass., 1984—. Mem. Sherborn Republican Town Com., Sherborn Yacht Club Race Com. Mut. Benefit Agts. Assn. (treas. 1977-79, dir.), Boston Life Underwriters. Club: Pres.'s. Home: 194 Maple St Sherborn MA 01770 Office: 196 Fountain St Framingham MA 01701

GODFREY, SARAH CAROLINE, educational administrator; b. Bryn Mawr, Pa., Aug. 19, 1951; d. Robert Duraine Godfrey, Jr. and Katharine (Krogness) McFalls. A.B., Vassar Coll., 1973; cert. Instituto Internacional, Madrid, Spain, 1972; M. Profl. Studies, Cornell U., 1976. Exec. housekeeper Hyatt Corp., Chgo., 1976-77; front office mgr., 1977-78; program adminstr. The Glenmede Trust Co., Phila., 1978-83; dir. devel. The Agnes Irwin Sch., Rosemont, Pa., 1983—, trustee, 1981-83; mem. bd. Health Systems Agy. S.E. Pa., Phila., 1980-82. Mem. Council for Advancement and Support of Edn., Nat. Soc. Fund Raising Execs., Advancement Delaware Valley Ind. Schs. (treas. 1983—), Phi Beta Kappa, Phi Kappa Phi. Club: Acorn (Philadelphia). Home: 250 Tanglewood Ln L-3 King of Prussia PA 19406 Office: The Agnes Irwin Sch Ithan Ave Rosemont PA 19010

GODFREY, TERRI POWELL, personnel director; b. Savannah, Ga., Jan. 13, 1950; d. Roderick Aaron and Elizabeth Ann (Hodges) Powell; m. Donald Elsworth Godfrey, July 5, 1969; children—Amanda Elizabeth, Christopher Donald. Student Draughon's Jr. Coll., 1968-69. Adminstrv. asst. personnel Chatham County Dept. Family and Children Service, Savannah, Ga., 1970-74; personnel dir., corp. asst. sec. John D. Carswell Co., Savannah, 1977—. Asst. to Chatham County Fund raising chmn. for Sanator Sam Nunn, 1977, 84; active United Community Services, 1977-84; pres., bd. dirs. Friends Savannah Ballet, 1984-85. Mem. Savannah Area C. of C., Nat. Assn. Ins. Women, Ins. Womens Savannah. Republican. Episcopalian. Club: Savannah Golf. Office: John D Carswell Co 112 E Bay St Savannah GA 31401

GODFREY, THERESE ANNE, business executive, professional lecturer; b. Wilson, N.C., Dec. 7, 1944; d. Edward Joseph and Frances Louise (Whitley) St. Amand; m. Howard Baptiste, Mar. 1968 (div. 1974); children—Frances, Therese, H. Thomas, H. Timothy; m. David John Godfrey, Feb. 14, 1979. Student in Home Econs., Our Lady of the Lake Coll., San Antonio, 1962-64; student Hawaii Entrepreneurship Tng. and Devel. Inst., Honolulu, 1980; B.S. in Bus. Adminstrn. Central Mich. U., 1985. Lic. pest control operator, Hawaii. Corp. sec., treas. Sure-Kill Termite Inc., Kailua, Hawaii, 1966-76; pub. relations, sales staff Island Termite Inc., Honolulu, 1976-78; pres., founder Pacific Pest Control Inc., Kailua, Hawaii, 1978-82; assoc. instr. Timemasters Inc., Honolulu, 1982-83; pres., founder Godfrey Enterprises Inc., Kailua, 1982—; dir. Fortunate Corp., Charlottesville, Va., 1982. Contbr. articles to profl. jours. Mem., Honolulu Status of Women Commn., 1979-81, U.S. Commerce Dist. Export Council, Honolulu, 1980-82, Am. Cancer Soc., Kiwanis Coast Guard; del. White House Conf. Small Bus., 1980; hon. mayor Kailua, 1980; co-founder Women's Prison Edn. Program, Kailua, 1983; del. White House Conf. Small Bus., 1986. Recipient Cert. of Merit, Honolulu, 1979; Cert. of Appreciation, U.S. Jr. C. of C., 1979; Outstanding Young Woman of Am., 1980; Cert. of Appreciation, Pres. Carter, 1980; Citizen of Week award Kailua, 1980, founder, 1980; Celebration of Children Day, Kailua, 1980, founder, 1980. Mem. Nat. Pest Control Assn. (dir. South Pacific region 1971-75, conv. chmn. 1979, Disting. Service award 1976), Nat. Speakers Assn., Toastmasters Internat. (area gov. 1984-85, Outstanding Toastmaster 1982, Disting. Toastmaster 1986), Assn. Women Toastmasters (founder 1981), Sertoma Internat., Hawaii Speakers Assn. (treas., charter mem. 1985—), C. of C. (Cert. of Appreciation), Hawaii Pest Control Assn. (exec. bd. 1971-75), Nat. Assn. Female Execs. Avocations: Triathlete; 1984 Ironman World Champion. Address: Godfrey Enterprises Inc 1169 Kahili St Kailua HI 96734

GODINEZ-TAYLOR, DORIS, lawyer; b. Mexico City, Dec. 8, 1946; came to U.S., 1965; d. Felipe and Dolores (Bolanos) Godinez; m. Raul A. Alarcon, Sept. 3, 1966 (div. 1970); m. 2d, Johnstone Latto Taylor, June 30, 1974; children—Raul, Yadira. A.A., Skyline Coll., 1977; B.A. summa cum laude, San Francisco State U., 1979; J.D., Boalt Hall, U. Calif.-Berkeley, 1982. Bar: Calif. Jud. extern Calif. Supreme Ct., San Francisco, 1981; div. chief Ct. Appeals (9th cir.), San Francisco, 1982-84; legal counsel Saga Corp., Menlo Park, Calif., 1984—. Contbr. article to legal rev. Bd. dirs. Planned Parenthood, San Mateo, Calif., 1984—, Alan Guttmacher Inst., Washington, 1985—; 1st v.p. MANA, San Mateo, 1983-84; mem. Berkeley Law Found., 1982. Recipient Best Brief award Moot Ct. Competition, U. Calif., Berkeley, 1980; mem. Calif. Law Rev., 1981. Mem. ABA, Calif. Bar Assn., San Francisco Bar Assn., San Mateo Bar Assn., Pi Sigma Alpha. Democrat. Roman Catholic. Office: Saga Corp 1 Saga Ln Menlo Park CA 94025

GODWIN, CHARLOTTE LOUISE, nurse; b. Glenmont, Md., May 5, 1921; d. Alfred Edward Jr. and Elizabeth (Walther) Linton; m. Jesse Granville Godwin, Aug. 22, 1943; 1 child, Sharon Louise Godwin Heimiller. Diploma Md. Gen. Hosp., 1942. Staff nurse Johns Hopkins Hosp., Balt., 1942-43, asst. head nurse, 1943-48, staff nurse, 1948-52, head nurse, 1952-56, nursing instr. supr., 1956-77, dir. radiology nursing, 1977—; lectr. in field. Editorial adv. bd. Applied Radiology; cons. Nursing '85. Contbr. article to profl. jour. Active Kingsville Civic Orgn., Mariners. Recipient Nursing Sci. Fair award Johns Hopkins Hosp., 1965, Cost Improvement cert., 1979, Service awards, 1958, 68, 78. Mem. Am. Radiol. Nurses Assn. (1st pres. 1981-83, chmn. nominating com. 1983, co-chmn. standards practice com. 1985), Md. State Nurses Assn., Nurses Alumni Assn. Md. Gen. Hosp. Presbyterian. Lodges: Order of Eastern Star; Order of Rainbow Girls (Masons). Avocations: sewing; crafts. Office: Johns Hopkins Hosp Dept Radiology 600 N Wolfe St Baltimore MD 21205

GOEBEL, JIL THERESE, electronics company executive; b. San Diego, Apr. 5, 1958; d. Robert Louis and Mary Kathryn (Beard) G. B.B.A., U. San Diego, 1980, M.B.A., 1982. Market researcher Central Fed., San Diego, 1980-81, Phillips Ramsey, San Diego, 1981; product promotion supr. LSI Products div. TRW, San Diego, 1981-85; mktg. communications mgr. Honeywell Inc., Colorado Springs, Colo., 1985—; programs com. San Diego Electronics Network, 1984-85. Moderator East San Diego Presbyn. Ch., 1984-85; com. mem. Women's Opportunities Week, San Diego, 1981-83; sec. Marina Park Condominium Assn., San Diego, 1983. Mem. Am. Mktg. Assn. (pres. 1984-85), Bus. and Profl. Advt. Assn. (charter), U. San Diego Alumni (com. mem. 1983-84), M.B.A. Alumni Assn., Delta Epsilon Sigma, Kappa Gamma Pi, Alpha Kappa Psi (v.p. 1980-84). Republican. Avocations: reading; music; dance; hiking. Office: Honeywell Inc 1150 E Cheyenne Mountain Blvd Colorado Springs CO 80906

GOEBEL, KATHLEEN DELORES CHRISTIAN, realtor; b. Elton, La., May 4, 1930; d. Herbert George and Ruth Wilodene (Pennington) Christian; m. Harvey Reynold Goebel, June 10, 1952; children—Kyle Kirk, Kurt Christian, Lores Kristen. B.S., Baylor U., 1950; student U. Colo.-Boulder, 1951; grad. Realtors Inst., La. State U., 1983. Lic. real estate broker, 1982. Chemist, Columbia So., Lake Charles, La., 1950-51; tchr. sci. Navasota (Tex.) High Sch., 1951-52; chemist Pantex Ordnance-AEC, Amarillo, Tex., 1952-53; tchr. Jefferson Davis Schs., Elton, La., 1954-78; realtor Mary Deshotel Realty, Jennings, La., 1978—; sec., exec. officer Rice Belt Bd. Realtors, 1980-81. Den mother Cahasieu Area council Boy Scouts Am., 1968-73; organist First Baptist Ch., Elton, 1945-47, 67-77. Mem. La. Realtors Assn. (dir. 1980—), La. Farm and Land Inst. (dir. 1983-86, state sec. 1983—), Women's Council Realtors (charter). Club: Entre Nous. Lodge: Order Eastern Star. Home: PO Box 447 Elton LA 70532 Office: Mary Deshotel Realty 215 N Cutting St Jennings LA 70546

GOEBEL, MARISTELLA, clinical psychologist, psychology educator; b. Racine, Wis., Sept. 10, 1915; d. James Nicholas and Henrietta Marie (Rademacher) Goebel. B.S., Edgewood Coll., 1944; M.A., Cath. U. Am., 1946, Ph.D., 1966. Diplomate in clin. biofeedback Am. Bd. Clin. Biofeedback. Mem. Dominican Sisters; tchr. English Cathedral High Sch., Sioux Falls, S.D., 1946-47, Heart of Mary High Sch., Mobile, Ala., 1947-49; assoc. prof. edn. Rosary Coll., River Forest, Ill., 1949-61, prof. psychology, 1966—; clin. psychologist Hines VA Hosp., Ill., 1970—; cons. Sinsinawa Dominican Sisters, Wis., 1966—. Author, editor tchr. guides Southeastern Curriculum Com., vols. Kindergarten-grade 8. Mem. editorial bd. Clin. Biofeedback and Health, Am. Assn. Biofeedback Clinics, Des Plaines, 1980—. Contbr. numerous articles to profl. jours. Mem. task force ch. related project Chgo. Heart Assn., 1979—. Recipient Outstanding Achievement in Psychol. Research, Ill. Psychol. Assn., 1982; Performance award Hines VA Hosp., 1983. Clin. fellow Am. Assn. Biofeedback Clinicians, Des Plaines, Ill., 1983. Fellow Am. Assn. Biofeedback Clinicians (bd. dirs. 1979—), mem. Am. Psychol. Assn., Soc. Clin. and Exptl. Hypnosis, Biofeedback Soc. Am., AAAS, Soc. Behavioral Medicine. Avocations: gardening; knitting, bicycling. Home: 7900 W Division River Forest IL 60305 Office: Hines VA Hosp Hines IL 60141

GOEDDEL, PAMELA FAYE, home health care organization administrator; b. Storm Lake, Iowa, Aug. 8, 1945; d. Merle Claude and Vera Maude (Van Buskirk) Pressel; m. Norval Bradley Goeddel, Feb. 4, 1966 (div. June 1983). B.S.B.A., U. Phoenix, 1983. Sec., Vis. Nurse Service, Denver, 1967-71, acctg. clk., 1977-78; acct. Rx Home Health, Wheat Ridge, Colo., 1978-80; adminstr. Ptnrs. Extended Care, Lakewood, Colo., 1981—; asst. adminstr. Ptnrs. Home Health, Lakewood, 1981-83, adminstrv./v.p., 1983—; cons. Health Care Ptnrs., Nashville, 1983—, also treas., dir. Author: You Can Get Well at Home, 1986. Chair, Denver Sch. Bilingual Com., 1976-77; del. Colo. Democratic Conv., 1976; mem. Alameda Music Boosters, Lakewood, 1986—, Alameda PTSA, 1986—. Mem. Am. Fedn. Home Health Agys. (regional dir. 1983-85), Exec. and Profl. Women's Council, Denver C. of C., Lakewood C. of C. Democrat. Methodist. Avocations: photography; cross-country skiing; reading, dancing. Home: 6215 W 1st Ave Lakewood CO 80226 Office: 7586 W Jewell St Lakewood CO 80226

GOELL, ABBY JANE, painter, appraiser; b. N.Y.C.; d. Stanley Mendel and Anne (Bellin) Wershof; B.A., Syracuse U., 1949; cert. N.Y. Sch. Interior Design, 1958; M.F.A., Columbia U., 1965; postgrad. Attingham Park, Shropshire, Eng., summer 1963, Pratt Graphic Art Center, 1966; 1 son, Mark Jordan. One-woman show: Automation House, N.Y.C., 1973; group shows include: Lumley-Cazalet, London, 1976; AAAL, 1977, Childe Hassam Purchase Exhbn., N.Y.C., 1977, U.S. Dept. State, Havana, Cuba, 1979, Sculpture Center, N.Y.C., 1981, Silvermine Ann., 1981, 82, TAGA Pratt Graphic Exhbn., Caracas, 1982; represented in permanent collections: Chase Manhattan Bank, Mus. Modern Art, N.Y.C., Atlantic Richfield Oil Co., Yale U., Sloane-Kettering Meml. Center, N.Y.C., Grafisches Kabinet, Munich, W.Ger., Neuberger Mus., Purchase, N.Y., Print Room, N.Y. Pub. Library; co-pub. Arcadia Press, N.Y.C., 1980—; tchr. Hunter Coll., 1967, Lab. Inst. Merchandising, 1967-70. Yaddo fellow, 1968; Va. Center for Creative Arts fellow, 1981. Mem. Am. Soc. Appraisers (sr.), Women's Caucus for Art, Victorian Soc. in Am., Nat. Trust Historic Preservation. Democrat. Club: Coffee House. Editor: English Silver 1675-1825, 1980. Home and office: 37 Washington Square W New York NY 10011

GOELTZ, JUDITH LENZ, corporate executive, writer; b. Boscobel, Wis., Nov. 23, 1940; d. Sheridan Lee and Bernice Angeline (Graf) Lenz; m. Francis S. Goeltz, Dec. 7, 1968; stepchildren—Marshall Link, Dianna, Shaun, Robert. B.S., U. Wis., 1962; postgrad. Adelphi U., Garden City, N.Y., 1963, U. San Francisco, Valencia, Spain, 1964, U. N.Mex., 1985. Cert. tchr. Spanish, Wis., N.Y. Tchr., Huntington (N.Y.) Schs., 1962-65; purser/flight attendant Pan Am. Airways, Miami and San Francisco, 1965-70; sales woman Castleton's Stores, Salt Lake City, 1971-72; mgr. organic farm Fightmaster Farms, Fairview, Utah, 1973-78; owner Tony B. Enterprises, San Francisco, 1980-83; asst. mktg. dir. Leach Research, Santa Fe, N.Mex., 1984—; corp. sec., treas., bus. mgr. Gibraltar, Inc.; hostess radio show Sta. KEST, San Francisco, 1980. Author: Beginner's Natural Food Guide, 1975; Jet Stress: What It Is & How to Cope with It, 1980; contbr. articles on health to profl. jours. Mem. Nat. Assn. Female Execs., Bus. and Profl. Women, Nat. Speakers Assn., Marin Self-Pubs., Orthomolecular Med. Soc., AAUW, Phi Beta Kappa, Phi Kappa Phi, Sigma Delta Pi, Pi Lambda Theta, Eta Kappa Lambda. Home: 2168 Candelero St Santa Fe NM 87505

GOEN, CYNTHIA DOLORES, nurse; b. Houston, Apr. 22, 1948; d. Simon and Consuelo Barbara (De La Garza) Elizondo; B.S. in Nursing, Dominican Coll., 1971; m. Herbert Don Goen, June 8, 1969; children—Anne Marie, Kelly Colleen, Philip Jeffery. Staff nurse med.-surg. unit St. Joseph Hosp., Houston, 1971-74; office nurse Michael K. O'Heeron, M.D., urologist, Houston, 1974; staff nurse CCU, Meml. Hosp. System-S.E. Unit, Houston, 1975-76, asst. head nurse med. unit, relief charge nurse duty emergency room, intensive care unit and CCU, 1976-80; cardiovascular nurse specialist, Coordinator Cardiology Lab., Kelsey-Seybold Clinic, Houston, 1980-85; dir. cardiovascular dept. Rosewood Med. Ctr., Houston, 1985—. Mem. Am. Heart Assn., ARC, Tex. A & M Assn. Profl. Women, Am. Cardiology Technologists Assn. Home: 8315 Glenalta St Houston TX 77061

GOETZ, THERESE ELIZABETH, orgnl. cons.; b. Orange, N.J., Nov. 23, 1950; d. Henry G. and Mathilde (Cornely) Goetz; B.A., Douglass Coll., Rutgers U., 1972; M.A., U. Ill., Champaign-Urbana, 1975, Ph.D., 1978; m. Ronald J. Lipinski, July 30, 1977; children—Valerie Anne, Kendra Jane. Teaching asst. U. Ill., 1972-77; asst. prof. psychology U. N.Mex., 1977-81, part-time, 1981-82, adj. prof., 1983—; orgnl. cons. Therese Goetz and Assos., Albuquerque, 1981—. U. N.Mex. research allocation grantee, 1977-80; NSF undergrad. research grantee, summer 1971. Mem. Profl. Orgn. for Women (exec. task force 1980-82, Am. Mgmt. Assn., Am. Psychol. Assn., Am. Soc. Tng. and Devel., Organizational Devel. Network, Sigma Xi, Psi Chi. Roman Catholic. Office: 1925 Juan Tabo NE Suite B Albuquerque NM 87112

GOFF, DONNA J., retail operations executive; b. Jan. 25, 1945; married; two children. B.B.A; postgrad. Harvard U., U. Oslo, Norway. Dept. head child devel. and family life edn. Children's Home Soc. Minn., 1971-80; dist. mgr. Kinder-Care Learning Ctr., Inc., 1980, region mgr., 1980-81, midwest zone mgr., 1981—.

GOFF, GIGI E., advt. agy. mgr.; b. Los Angeles, July 28, 1937; d. William Allen and Florence Roberta (Roberts) Glynn; student Central Oreg. Community Coll., 1954-55; divorced; children—Darrell, Dale, Nancy, Lynda, David. Partner, office mgr. Waco Auction House (Tex.), 1960-63; partner Goff & Assos., ins., 1963-75; mgr. Walter W. Cribbins Co., splty. advt., Beaverton, Oreg., 1976—. Recipient Creativity in Advt. awards (5), 1979-81. Mem. Sales and Mktg. Execs. Internat. (v.p.), Inst. Mangerial Women, Nat. Assn. Female Execs., Portland Advt. Fedn., Greater Portland Conv. and Visitors Assn., Portland C. of C., Beaverton C. of C. Office: Walter Cribbins Co 4175 SW Cedar Hills Blvd Beaverton OR 97005

GOFMAN, FEYGA, chemist; b. Kishinev, USSR, June 18, 1938; d. Khaim and Lea (Shtienberg) Rawitsky; student Kishinev State U., 1955-60; m. Semyon Gofman, Feb. 28, 1965; children—Yefim, Margarita. Chem. engr., Shoe factory, Zorile, Kishinev, USSR, 1960-63, mgr. chem. dept., 1963-79; chief chemist Davis Mfg. Co., Inc., San Antonio, 1979—. Jewish. Home: 518 Red Cliff San Antonio TX 78216 Office: 1023 Morales San Antonio TX 78285

GOFORTH, CATHLEEN HANLON, educator; b. Hastings, Nebr., Sept. 19, 1943; d. Arthur Crook and Patsy Ruth (Ratcliffe) G.; m. Joseph Matthew Hale, Dec. 6, 1977; 1 dau., Patricia Lucille Goforth Hale. B.S., U. Houston, 1965; M. Ed., Tex. So. U., 1975; postgrad. Customer rep. Xerox, Houston, 1966-71; tchr. Houston Schs., 1971-81; instr. U. Alaska, Fairbanks, 1981-82; honors tchr. Pasadena (Tex.) Schs., 1982—. Host parent Youth for Understanding, Houston, 1975—. Bd. sec. Kirkmont Mcpl. Utility Dist., Houston, 1983—; docent Houston Zool. Soc. Mem. Phi Beta, Chi Omega. Democrat. Methodist. Home: 10306 Kirkvale St Houston TX 77089 Office: Pasadena High Sch 206 S Shaver Pasadena TX 77506

GOFORTH-REED, MARIE, insurance agent; b. San Antonio, Oct. 24, 1946; d. Jose M. and Zapopan (Rodriguez) Pedraza; m. Richard C. Goforth, Dec. 18, 1965 (div. Apr. 1982); children—Jay Scott and Julie Marie (twins); m. Glenn Allen Reed, Jan. 24, 1985. Student San Antonio Coll., 1968-70, Our Lady of Lake U., San Antonio, 1981-82, Am. Coll., 1984-85. Adminstrv. asst. to pres. Leo Oppenheim & Co., securities, Oklahoma City, 1965-66; exec. sec. law firm Stone, Pigman, Walther, Wittman & Stone, New Orleans, 1966-68; owner Account Services, San Antonio, 1968-82; registered rep., agt. Prudential Ins. Co., San Antonio, 1982—. Mem. Million Dollar Round Table. Republican. Episcopalian. Avocation: tennis. Home: 16410 Ledge Park San Antonio TX 78232 Office: Prudential Insurance 9901 I-H 10 West 700 San Antonio TX 78230

GOGATE, SHASHI ANAND, physician; b. Indore, India, July 9, 1938; d. Kashinath M. and Manorama R.; M.B.B.S., M.G.M. Med. Coll., 1962; M.S., Ohio State U., 1969; m. Anand B. Gogate, June 20, 1962; children—Sangita, Soniya, Sanjay. Instr., research asso. Ohio State U., 1970-73, asst. prof. pathology, 1973-75, asst. clin. prof., 1975—; dir. lab. Columbus Pathology Lab., 1975-79, chief pathology, 1976—; pres. S.A. Gogate M.D., Inc., 1978—. Mem. adv. bd. Internat. Mediation Soc., Columbus. Fellow Coll. Am. Pathologists, Am. Soc. Clin. Pathologists; mem. AMA, Ohio Med. Assn., Franklin County Med. Soc., Fairfield County Med. Soc., Internat. Acad. Pathology, Republican. Hindu. Contbr. articles to profl. jours. Home: 6112 Sedgwick Rd Worthington OH 43085 Office: Lancaster Fairfield Community Hosp 401 N Ewing St Lancaster OH 43130

GOGGINS, PHYLLIS MORGAN ASHFORD, health care administrator; b. New Haven, Aug. 5, 1926; d. Daniel D. and Mildred R. (Hobbs) Morgan; B.S. in Nursing, Fla. Internat. U., 1974; M.S. in Nursing, U. Conn., 1979; m. William J. Goggins, May 8, 1971; children—Karen, Andrea, Christopher (dec.), Eric. Pub. health nurse, Fairfax County, Va., 1948-50; vol. clinic nurse, New Delhi, India, 1952-54, Asuncion, Paraguay, 1957-59, San Pedro Sula, Honduras, 1961-64; staff nurse Univ. Community Hosp., Tampa, Fla., 1969-71; evening charge nurse pediatrics Naples (Fla.) Community Hosp., 1971-73; public health nurse Collier County Health Dept., Naples, 1973-75; supr. Northwest Community Nursing and Health Service, Harmony, R.I., 1975-77, asst. dir., 1977-79, exec. dir., 1979—; clin. instr. community health nursing R.I. Coll., Providence, 1981-82, adj. faculty, 1983. Mem. R.I. Gov.'s Commn. Home Health Care Needs, 1981-82, Gov.'s Adv. Council on Zambarano Hosp., 1980-81 Gov.'s Commn. Long Term Care Hosps., 1983. Mem. Am. Pub. Health Assn., Nat. League Nursing, New Eng. Pub. Health Assn., R.I. Assn. Home Health Agys. (chmn. council dirs. 1980-82, pres. 1982-86), Glocester Bus. Assn., N. Providence Alumni Assn. Mass. Gen. Hosp. Home: 125 Smith Ave 6-D Greenville RI 02828 Office: PO Box 234 Harmony RI 02829

GOGICK, KATHY CHRISTINE, magazine editor; b. Passaic, N.J., Aug. 3, 1945; d. Joseph John and Emeline (Radwin) Wadowski; student Emmanuel Coll., 1963-64; B.S., Fairleigh Dickinson U., 1967; m. Robert Joseph Gogick, Feb. 24, 1968; 1 son, Jonathan. Asst. beauty editor Cosmopolitan Mag., N.Y.C., 1967-68; merchandising mgr. Co-ed Mag., 1968-69, editor-in-chief, 1976-80; editorial dir. Scholastic, Inc., 1980-86; creative mgr. Estee Lauder, Inc., N.Y.C., 1969-72; assoc. editor Town & Country Mag., 1972-76; pres., pub. Corp. Mags., Inc., 1986—. Trustee, Fairleigh Dickinson U., 1980—. Recipient Ednl. Press award, 1978, 79, 80, 82, 83; Trustee Alumni medal Fairleigh Dickinson U., 1984. Mem. Am. Soc. Mag. Editors, Women in Communications, Women's Econ. Roundtable. Office: 256 Columbia Turnpike Florham Park NJ 07932

GOLA, SANDRA VALENTINA, graphic designer, design educator; b. Passaic, N.J., Mar. 10, 1955; d. Henry Andrew and Ann (Skripak) G. B.F.A., Pratt Inst., 1978. Asst., Brodsky Graphics, N.Y.C., 1980-82; art dir. Cycles Peugeot, Carlstadt, N.J., 1982-83; owner, pres. Skylight Graphics, Hackensack, N.J., 1983—; instr. Art Ctr. of No. N.J., New Milford, 1983-85, Parsons Sch. of Design, N.Y.C., 1985—. Designer: Challenge tire tube packaging (Creativity award 1983), Johnson & Jonnson ultrasound sales kit (Art Dir. Club of N.J. award 1985), KLM stationery (Creativity award 1984). Mem. Art Dir.'s Club of N.J., Nat. Assn. Female Execs., Mensa. Avocations: bicycling; aerobics; nautilus. Home: 466 Boulevard Garfield NJ 07026 Office: Skylight Graphics 166 Main St Hackensack NJ 07601

GOLAN, MARGO ELIZABETH, business executive; b. Lafayette, Ind., Aug. 23, 1916; d. Charles Fenton and Sarah Elizabeth (Fisher) May; grad. high sch.; m. Samuel L. Golan, Dec. 2, 1944 (dec. Dec. 1969); 1 dau., Kim (Mrs. Marvin Chancellor Norton, Jr.); stepchildren—Leonard Walter, Frederick Joseph. With Kauffman & Wulf Dept. Store, Hammond, Ind., 1935-36; dept. head Goldblatt Bros., Inc., Hammond, 1936-42; with Holiday Inn, Key West, Fla., 1960—, gen. mgr., franchise holder, 1962—; dir. Key West & Lower Kays Devel. Corp., Key West Redevel. Agy., 1979-80. Chmn., Monroe County Advt. Commn., 1969-76; mem. Monroe County Master-Plan Adv. Council; bd. dirs. Monroe County Public Library; commr. governing bd. Lower Fla. Keys Hosp. Dist. Recipient Community Service award Lions Club, 1975; Outstanding Community Service award NAACP, 1975; Outstanding Service to Community award Fla. Keys Community Coll., 1976; Community Service award Key West Navy League, 1977; Outstanding Community Service award Fla. State Grand Lodge Masons, 1977; Outstanding Generosity and Service to Community award City of Key West, 1978; Jaycee award, 1980, 84; Appreciation award Boy Scouts Am., 1982, others; named to Bus. Hall of Fame, Key West C. of C., 1982. Mem. Key West C. of C. (dir., recipient Community Service award 1971), Internat. Assn. Holiday Inns (advt. com. 1971, reservation com. 1972), Tourist Devel. Commn., Founders Soc. Tennessee Williams Fine Arts Ctr.

(life), Key West Art and Hist. Soc. (benefactor). Club: Key West Women's (dir., recipient Outstanding Mem. award 1972). Home: 2 Go-Ln Key West FL 33040 Office: 1111 N Roosevelt Blvd Key West FL 33040

GOLD, LYNN ANNE, educator, consultant; b. Madison, Wis., May 26, 1945; d. Arthur John and Jean Marie (Colligan) Knabel; m. Richard Frank Gold, June 6, 1966 (div. May 1979). B.A., Purdue U., 1967; M.S., U. Bridgeport, 1974. Cert. tchr., Ind., Washington, Conn., N.Y. Tchr. Attica Pub. Schs. (Ind.), 1967-68, Richland Pub. Schs. (Wash.), 1968-69, Marymount Secondary Sch., Tarrytown, N.Y., 1969-70, Lakeland Pub. Schs., Shrub Oak, N.Y., 1970-73, Rye City Pub. Schs. (N.Y.), 1973-81, Norwalk Community Coll. (Conn.), 1982-83; cons. Silver Assocs., Springdale, Conn., 1979—; cons., lectr. Darien Pub. Schs. (Conn.), 1983; guest speaker Conn. Assn. for Gifted, Farmington, 1983. Author health care column, 1983. Conn. state coordinator Internat. Legion of Intelligence, Golden, Colo., 1983—. Mem. Am. Soc. Tng. and Devel., Assn. for Gifted, Assn. Productivity Specialists, Conn. Assn. Gifted Children, Flower Essence Soc., Huxley Inst., Nat. Assn. Gifted Children, Nat. Health Fedn., Soc. Accelerative Learning and Teaching, Purdue Alumni Assn., Mensa. Republican. Roman Catholic. Club: Nutmeg Curling (Darien). Home: 8 Little John Ln Springdale CT 06907 Office: Silver Assocs PO Box 4728 Springdale CT 06907

GOLD, SHIRLEY JEANNE, state legislator, labor relations specialist; b. N.Y.C., Oct. 2, 1925; d. Louis and Gussie (Lefkowitz) Diamondstein; B.A. in Music, Hunter Coll., 1945; M.A. in Behavioral Sci. (Crown-Zellerbach Corp. scholar), Reed Coll., 1962; m. David E. Gold, June 22, 1947; children—Andrew, Dana. Tchr., Portland (Oreg.) Public Schs., 1954-68; pres. Portland Fedn. Tchrs., Am. Fedn. Tchrs./AFL-CIO, 1965-72, pres. Oreg. Fedn. Tchrs., 1972-77; cons. labor relations to univs., coll., Portland, 1977-80; mem. Oreg. Ho. of Reps., Salem, 1980—, majority leader, 1985—, chmn. legis. rules, ops. and reform, mem. human resources com.; mem. Oreg. Tchr. Tenure Rev. Bd., 1965-72; mem. Nat. Multi-State Consortium, 1974; mem. Speak Out Oreg. com. to White House and Congress, 1978; mem. Oreg. Task Force on Tax Reform; AFL-CIO scholar George Meany Inst., 3 times, 1976-77; commr. Edn. Commn. of States; mem. Oreg. Commn. on Women. Chairperson precinct com., conv. del. Oreg. Democratic Party, 1960-80, dist. leader, chairperson edn. com., 1978-80; charter mem., mem. exec. bd., v.p. Oreg. Council for Cts., 1977-80. Named to Hunter Coll. Hall of Fame, 1985. Mem. Hunter Coll. Alumni Assn., Reed Coll. Alumni Assn., Pacific N.W. Labor History Assn., Portland Fedn. Tchrs., Oreg. Fedn. Tchrs., Oreg. Fedn. Dem. Women, Oreg. Coalition for Nat. Health Security, Oreg. Women's Polit. Caucus, ACLU, Coalition Labor Union Women. Jewish. Contbr. articles on labor relations to Willamette Week newspaper, 1977-80; editor Oreg. Tchr. newspaper, 1970-72. Office: H295 State Capitol Salem OR 97310

GOLD, SYLVIA, Canadian official. Pres. Can. Advisory Council on Status of Women, 1985—. Office: Can Adv Council on Status of Women 66 Slater St 18th Floor Ottawa ON K1P 5H1 Canada*

GOLDBERG, BARBARA SUE, educational administrator, counselor, clinical social worker; b. Bklyn., June 26, 1947; d. Norman Leonard Goldberg and Ray (Greenberg) Green. B.A. in English, L.I.U., 1967, M.S. in Guidance and Counseling, 1970; M.S.W., Hunter Sch. Social Work, 1973; postgrad. Baruch Coll., CCNY, Adler Inst. Cert. tchr., sch. social worker, counselor, N.Y. Tchr. English, Eastern Dist. High Sch., N.Y.C., 1967-72, dean of girls, 1970-72, supportive service counselor, 1977-80, coll.-bound counselor, 1973-76; caseworker Addiction Research and Treatment Corp., N.Y.C., 1972-73, group therapist, 1973; supportive service counselor Sarah J. Hale High Sch., N.Y.C., 1980-85; asst. project coordinator coll.-bound program, N.Y.C. Bd. Edn., 1985—. Contbr., editor guidance manuals. Mem. Register Clin. Social Workers, Acad. Cert. Social Workers, N.Y.C. Personnel and Guidance Assn., N.Am. Soc. Adlerian Psychologists, Phi Delta Kappa. Avocations: skiing; travel; camping; modern dance. Home: 200 E 28th St New York NY 10016

GOLDBERG, GAIL LOVELL, lawyer; b. Palmer, Mass., July 17, 1947; d. Lewis Jerome and Gertrude (Otis) Lovell; m. Henry Ronald Goldberg, Jan. 21, 1972; 1 dau., Sara Jane. B.A., Suffolk U., 1969, J.D., 1971. Bar: Mass. 1971. Legal intern, Mass. Defenders Com., Boston, summer 1969, Corp. Counsel City of Boston, 1969-70; consumer edn. asst. Mass. Consumers Council, Boston, summer 1970; atty., office gen. counsel Civil Service Commn., Washington, 1971-77, legal counsel to Civil Service Reform Task Force, 1977-78; chief legal counsel Fed. Personnel Mgmt. Project, Washington, 1977; atty. Office of Gen. Counsel, Office Personnel Mgmt., Washington, 1978-84, dep. asst. gen. counsel compensation div., 1984—; atty. adviser Pres.' Reorgn. Project, 1977; placement cons. Suffolk U. Law Sch. Placement Office, 1971—. Author, editor sects., chpts. fed. govt. publs. Commonwealth of Mass. scholar, 1965-66, 66-67; Suffolk U. scholar, 1965-66, 66-67; recipient Commr.'s Disting. Service award, Civil Service Commn., 1978. Gen. Counsel's award for Spl. Achievement, Office Personnel Mgmt., 1979. Mem. ABA, Mass. Bar Assn., Mass. Assn. Women Lawyers, Suffolk U. Law Sch. Alumni Assn. Club: Silver Spring Photo. Home: 6429 Deep Calm Columbia MD 21045 Office: Office Gen Counsel US Office Personnel Mgmt 1900 E St NW Washington DC 20415

GOLDBERG, GERALDINE ELIZABETH, clinical psychologist; b. Neptune, N.J., Mar. 22, 1939; d. Albert V. and Katherine Irene (Mulholland) McCormick; B.S. cum laude, East Stroudsburg (Pa.) U., 1967; M.A. in Psychology, Fairleigh Dickinson U., 1971; m. Arthur Goldberg, July 1, 1961. Staff clin. psychologist Youth Devel. Clinic, Newark, 1971-75; psychotherapist in clin. psychology Mental Health Consultation Center, N.Y.C., 1975—; human resources specialist Age Corp., Livingston, N.J., 1979—, v.p., 1980—, sec. bd. dirs., 1977—. Mem. Am. Psychol. Assn. (asso.), N.J. Assn. Profl. Psychologists (v.p. 1978-81, pres. 1982, 83), N.J. Psychol. Assn. (asso.).

GOLDBERG, JOCELYN HOPE SCHNIER, market research consultant; b. N.Y.C., Mar. 29, 1953; d. Alex and Eileen (Firstenburg) Schnier. A.B. in History cum laude, Princeton U., 1974; M.B.A. in Mktg., Harvard U., 1977. Statis. technician John Hancock Mut. Life Ins. Co., Boston, 1974-75; product mgr. Gen. Foods Corp., White Plains, N.Y., 1977-78; strategic bus. planner Bausch & Lomb Corp., Rochester, N.Y., 1979-80; mgmt. assoc., dir. key account mktg. Gordon S. Black Corp., Rochester, 1981—; pres., founder Gt. Outdoors, Honeoye Falls, N.Y., 1979—. Co-editor, co-pub. Net Present Value, 1976. Sr. advisor Jr. Achievement, Rochester, 1979-80. Mem. Am. Mktg. Assn., Profl. Ski Instrs. Am. Clubs: Princeton of Rochester (dir. 1978—, v.p. 1984-85), Harvard Bus. Sch. of Rochester (dir. 1983—, sec./treas. 1984-85). Home: 16 Ontario St Honeoye Falls NY 14472 Office: Gordon S Black Corp 1661 Penfield Rochester NY 14625

GOLDBERG, LEE WINICKI, retired furniture company executive; Laredo, Tex., Nov. 20, 1932; d. Frank and Goldie (Ostrowiak) Winicki; student San Diego State U., 1951-52; m. Frank M. Goldberg, Aug. 17, 1952; children—Susan Arlene, Edward Lewis, Anne Carri. With United Furniture Co., Inc., San Diego, 1953-83, corporate sec., dir., 1963-83, dir. environ. interiors, 1970-83; founder Drexel-Heritage store Edwards Interiors, subs. United Furniture, 1975; founding partner, v.p. FLJB Corp., constrn., 1976. Den mother Boy Scouts Am., San Diego, 1965; vol. Am. Cancer Soc., San Diego, 1964-69; chmn. jr. matrons United Jewish Fedn., San Diego, 1958; del. So. Pacific Coast region Hadassah Conv., 1960, pres. Galilee group San Diego chpt., 1960-61; supporter Marc Chagall Nat. Mus., Nice, France, Smithsonian Instn., Los Angeles County Mus., La Jolla (Calif.) Mus. Contemporary Art. Recipient Hadassah Service award San Diego chpt., 1958-59. Democrat. Jewish.

GOLDBERG, LOUISE BERNSTEIN, educator; b. N.Y.C., June 3, 1931; d. Joseph and Anna (Wainrober) Bernstein; B.A., Bklyn. Coll., 1965; M.S., Queens Coll., CUNY, 1968; m. Marvin Goldberg, May 2, 1953; children—Steven, Gary. Various secretarial positions, 1951-54; piano instr., 1961-62; tchr. 3d grade May Moore Sch., Deer Park, N.Y., 1965-86. Mem. NEA, PTA, Deer Park Tchrs. Assn., Am. Numis. Soc., High Sch. Music and Art Alumni Assn. Republican. Jewish. Home: 8 Belmont Pl Hicksville NY 11801 Office: 239 Central Ave Deer Park NY 11729

GOLDBERG, NATALIE ISAACS, advertising agency executive; b. Balt., May 6, 1953; d. David J. and Vera (Rifkin) Isaacs; m. Richard A. Goldberg, Jan. 5, 1975. B.S. in Advtg., U. Fla., 1974. Media dir. Multi-Media Advt. Co., Gainesville, Fla., 1975-76; v.p., creative dir. Drew Advt. Co., Tampa, Fla., 1978; mktg. coordinator Curtin & Assoc., Largo, Fla., 1979; promotion mgr. Fla. Trend mag., Tampa, 1979-81; v.p. Network 4 Mktg. Co., Tampa, 1983-85; pres. Creativity Plus, Longwood, Fla., 1980—; dir., cons. Tenski, Inc., Tampa, 1983-85. Editorial dir. Gainesville Mag., 1975 (creative writing award 1975). Promotion mgr. Fla. Trend Media Kit, 1979 (Best Promotion award Fla. Mag. Assocs. 1979). Recipient Pres.' Outstanding Service award Tampa Advt. Fedn., 1984. Mem. Bus. and Profl. Women's Network (pres. 1985, Disting. Leadership award 1984), Network of Exec. Women (v.p. 1983-84, Mem. of Yr. 1981-82), Advt. Fedn. (chmn. 1983-85), Nat. Assn. Female Execs. Democrat. Jewish. Club: Women's Am. O.R.T. (publicity chmn. 1982-84) (Fla.). Avocations: aerobics; poetry; photography. Home: 844 Maraval Ct Longwood FL 32750 Office: Creativity Plus PO Box 875 Longwood FL 32750

GOLDBERG, NORMA LORRAINE, state public welfare administrator; b. South Bend, Ind., May 6, 1929; d. James Albert and Minnie Sylvia (Kaplan) Seamon; m. Albert Goldberg, Apr. 19, 1959 (dec. Dec. 1976); children—Lisa Ann, Paul Ephraim. B.S., Ind. U.-Bloomington, 1950; postgrad. Sch. Social Work, Ind. U.-Indpls., 1950-52. Sch. social worker Indpls. Pub. Schs., 1951-53; with Marion County Dept. Pub. Welfare, Indpls., 1953-66, 71-73, asst. dir., 1961-64, dir., 1964-66, intake supr., 1971-73; asst. dir. Ind. Dept. Pub. Welfare, Indpls., 1973-79, dir., 1979—, now dir. Fraud and Investigative Div.; mem. steering com. Whitehouse Conf. on Children and Youth, Indpls., 1982-83; mem. program com. Gov.'s Conf. on Children and Youth, Indpls., 1982-83. Founder Welfare Service League, Indpls., 1968, pres., 1968-71, mem., 1968—. Mem. steering com. Indpls. sect. Nat. Council Jewish Women, 1982—; mem. steering com. Guardian ad Litem Project; mem. Republican Round Table, Indpls., 1983—; city chmn. adult bd. B'nai B'rith Youth Orgn., 1985. Recipient Gov.'s Voluntary Action Program Community Service award Gov. of Ind., 1980. Mem. Ind. Conf. on Social Concerns (state coordinator 1963-64), Network of Women in Bus., Indpls. Council of Women (program chmn. 1968-71). Lodge: Order Eastern Star. Office: State Dept Pub Welfare 100 N Senate Ave Suite 703 Indianapolis IN 46204

GOLDBERG, ROSLYN LENA, financial services company executive; b. Bklyn., Feb. 27; d. Hyman and Esther (Benchkofsky) G. B.A. magna cum laude in English, Hunter Coll., N.Y.C., 1971, postgrad., 1972; postgrad. Urban Acad., N.Y.C., 1979-80. Cert. tchr., N.Y. Office mgr. TOGS, N.Y.C., 1972-73; staff analyst Dept. Personnel, City of N.Y., 1973-77, dep. dir. personnel Fire Dept., 1977-78, dir. personnel Dept. Ports & Terminals, 1978-80; dir. human resources Fin. Info. Service Agy., N.Y.C., 1980-83, dir. internal control, 1983—. Campaign worker Village Ind. Democrats, N.Y.C., 1979, 80. Mem. Mcpl. Data Processing Council (vice chmn. 1982-83), Phi Beta Kappa, Sigma Tau Delta. Office: Fin Info Service Agy 111 8th Ave New York NY 10011

GOLDBERG, SUSAN SOLOMON, library administrator; b. N.Y.C., Mar. 18, 1944; d. Elias and Minnie (Barnett) Solomon; m. Eric A. Goldberg, Mar. 27, 1966; children—Evan, Jessica, Joanna. B.A., Harpur Coll. SUNY-Binghamton, 1965; M.S., Columbia U., 1966. Librarian N.Y. Pub. Library, 1966-67, br. librarian, 1967-68; reference librarian Bklyn. Pub. Library, 1971-72; reference librarian Finkelstein Meml. Library, Spring Valley, N.Y., 1975-76; coordinator adult services Tucson Pub. Library, 1977-80, dep. dir., 1980—; mem. adj. faculty Pima Community Coll., Tucson, 1978, U. Ariz., Tucson, 1978-79. Contbg. author: Critical Issues Conference 8, 1979; Public Librarianship, 1982; Reorganization in the Public Library, 1984. Vice pres. Cultural Alliance of Tucson, 1981-82; chmn. arts and culture com. Tucson Tomorrow, 1982—; mem. Ariz. Commn. on Arts, Phoenix, 1983—. Mem. ALA, Pub. Library Assn. (v.p./pres.-elect), Library Adminstrn. and Mgmt. Assn., Ariz. Library Assn., NOW (pres. Rockland County br. 1974-76). Home: 5450 E 6th St Tucson AZ 85711 Office: Tucson Pub Library PO Box 27470 Tucson AZ 85726

GOLDBERGER, BLANCHE RUBIN, sculptor, jeweler; b. N.Y.C., Feb. 2, 1914; d. David and Sarah (Israel) Rubin; m. Emanuel Goldberger, June 8, 1942; children—Richard N., Ary Louis. B.A., Hunter Coll., N.Y.C., 1934; M.A., Columbia U., 1936; Certificat d'Etudes, Sorbonne, Paris, 1936; postgrad. Westchester Arts Workshop Sculpture and Jewelry, White Plains, 1961-70, Silvermine Coll. Arts, 1962, Nat. Acad. Arts, N.Y.C., 1968. Tchr. French and Hebrew, N.Y.C. High Sch. System. One-woman shows include: Bloomingdale's, Eastchester, N.Y., 1975, Scarsdale Pub. Library, N.Y., 1976, Temple Israel, White Plains, N.Y., 1975, Greenwich Art Barn, Conn., 1972 Westlake Gallery, White Plains, N.Y., 1981; exhibited in group shows at Hudson River Mus., Yonkers, N.Y., 1978, Silvermine-New Eng. Ann., Silvermine, Conn., 1979; represented in permanent collection at Scarsdale High Sch. Library, N.Y.; also pvt. collections. Recipient award Beaux Arts of Westchester, White Plains, N.Y., 1967, First Prize, White Plains Art Show. Mem. Nat. Assn. Women Artists, Nat. Assn. Tchrs. French, Scarsdale Art Assn. (bd. dirs.; first prizes for sculpture). Jewish. Avocations: lecturing on sculpture; reading contemporary lit. in Hebrew.

GOLD-BIKIN, LYNNE ZAPOLEON, lawyer, educator; b. N.Y.C., Apr. 23, 1938; d. Herbert Ben and Muriel (Wimpheimer-Sarnoff) Zapoleon; m. Roy E. Gold, Sept. 20, 1956 (div. 1976); children—Russell, Sheryl, Lisa, Michael. B.A. summa cum laude, Albright Coll., 1973; J.D., Villanova U., 1976. Bar: Pa. 1976. Assoc. law firm Pechner, Dorfman, Wolffe, Rounick & Cabot, Norristown, Pa., 1976-81; ptnr. law firm Olin, Neil, Frock & Gold-Bikin, Norristown, 1981-82; pres. Gold-Bikin & Assocs., Norristown, 1983—; adj. prof. Temple Law Sch., 1978—. Contbr. articles to profl. jours. Mem. Pres.'s Council, Albright Coll., 1982—. Fellow Am. Acad. Matrimonial Lawyers; mem. Montgomery County Bar Assn. (chmn. family law sect. 1984—), ABA (mem. council family law sect. 1982—), Pa. Bar Assn. (mem. council family law sect. 1979—). Office: Gold-Bikin Derlin & Assocs One Montgomery Plaza Suite 400 Norristown PA 19401

GOLDEN, ESTHER OPHELIA, mobile home court executive; b. Harrisburg, Ark., Feb. 11, 1911; d. Robert G. and Hettie (Chamness) Costner; m. James F. Golden, Nov. 10, 1929; children—Roberta C., Stephen D. Student Jonesboro Bapt. Coll., 1929. Ptnr., Cleaning & Pressing Shop, Manilla, Ark., 1932-36; life ins. agt., Manila, 1941-44; real estate broker, 1944-67; owner, mgr. Golden Acres Mobile Home Park, House Springs, Mo., 1967—. Mem. Jefferson County Mobile Home Ct. Assn. (sec.). Clubs: Rock Twp. Democratic (pres.). Baptist. Home: 31 Golden Acres House Springs MO 63051

GOLDEN, EVELYN DAVIS, lawyer; b. Moultrie, Ga., June 1, 1951; d. Booker T. and Louise (Jordan) Davis; m. James T. Golden, Sept. 1, 1974; children—Vivian-Louise, Faye Jessica-Maurine. B.A. in Philosophy, CUNY, York Coll., 1972; J.D., U. Fla., Gainesville, 1976. Bar: Fla. 1978; cert. tchr. Fla. Dir. Lawyers' asst. program Valencia Community Coll., Orlando, 1977-79; mem. James T. Golden Law Office, Sanford Fla., 1978-79; asst. atty. gen. State of Fla., Daytona Beach, 1980—. Bd. dirs. Citrus council Girl Scouts U.S.A., 1979-80; vice chairperson Seminole County (Fla.) Program Adv. Com. Sta. WMFE-TV, 1976-79; mem. Volusia County Spouse Abuse Adv. Council, Daytona Beach, NAACP (life). Mem. ABA, Fla. Bar Assn., Fla. Assn. Women Lawyers (pres. Volusia chpt. 1981-82, pub. relations dir.) Democrat. African Methodist Episcopalian. Clubs: Girlfriends Inc. (Orlando Chpt.), Delta Sigma Theta (Daytona Beach) (parliamentarian 1983-85) Office: Dept Legal Affairs 125 N Ridgewood Ave 4th Floor Daytona Beach FL 32014

GOLDEN, LAURA LORETTA, educator; b. Lexington, Ky., June 11, 1940; d. Hubert Anthony and Caroline Garrard (Holt) G.; B.S., Fla. State U., 1964; M.Ed., Ga. Coll., 1971. Instr., Fla. State U., Tallahassee, 1964-70, Middle Ga. Coll., Cochran, 1971-73; asst. prof. Ga. Coll., Milledgeville, 1973-75; asst. prof., co-dir. athletics head coach women's basketball Colo. Coll., Colorado Springs, 1975-81; asst. prof. phys. edn., head coach womens basketball Central Mich. U., Mount Pleasant, 1981-84; head coach women's basketball U. Ill., Champaign, 1984—. Mem. Mich. Basketball Coaches Assn., Womens Nat. Basketball Coaches Assn. Office: Armory Bldg 505 E Armory Dr Champaign IL 61820

GOLDEN, LINDA LORRAINE, marketing educator, consultant; b. St. Petersburg, Fla., Nov. 3, 1949; d. Mack Joiner and Alva Lorraine (Finley) Golden. B.S.B.A., U. Fla., Gainesville, 1967-71, M.A., 1972, Ph.D. Bus., 1975. Asst. prof. U. Tex., Austin, 1974-79, assoc. prof., 1979-86, prof., 1986—; sr. study dir. Market Facts, Inc., Washington, 1980-81; cons. Lock Stock & Barrell, Austin, 1981—; cons. Sec. State, 1982, Tex. State Bar, 1980. Contbr. articles in field to jours. Mem. Allendale Neighborhood Assn., Austin. Grantee Inst. Constructive Capitalism, Austin, 1976, 81; fellow retailing U. Tex., 1982-83. Mem. Am. Mktg. Assn. (v.p. Austin chpt. 1979-80), Assn. Consumer Research, Am. Psychol. Assn. (div. 23 mem. chmn. 1981-82), SW Marketing Assn., Phi Kappa Phi. Republican. Baptist. Club: Yacht. (Austin). Office: Univ Tex Marketing Dept GSB 4 202 Austin TX 78712

GOLDEN, TERESA VITAGLIANO, business official; b. Mt. Vernon, N.Y., June 5, 1955; d. Vincent Jack and Audrey Mildred (Fabini) Vitagliano; B.A. in Econs., Coll. Mt. St. Vincent, 1975; M.B.A. in Corp. Fin., Pace U., 1979; m. George Patrick Golden, Jan. 3, 1976; children—Helen Marie, George Christopher. Accounts receivable mgr. ITEL Corp., White Plains, N.Y., 1975-78; fin. systems cons. Sci. Timesharing Corp., White Plains, 1978-79; systems analyst IBM, Poughkeepsie, N.Y., 1979-80, graphics mktg. rep., 1980-82, programming planner, 1982-83, mgr. graphics market support, White Plains, 1983-85, bus. planner, Armonk, N.Y., 1985—. Republican. Roman Catholic. Home: 14 Sarah Ln Hopewell Junction NY 12533 Office: IBM Armonk NY 10504

GOLDFIELD, EMILY DAWSON, finance company executive, artist; b. Bklyn., May 31, 1947; d. Martin and Renee (Solow) Dawson; m. Stephen Gary Goldfield, June 17, 1973; children—Stacy Rose, Daniel James. B.S., U. Mich., 1969; M.Ed., Pa. State U., 1971; Ph.D., U. So. Calif., 1977. Chmn. bd. Provident Mut. Escrow, Encino, Calif., 1982—; exec. v.p. Hanover Investment Services, Encino, 1982—; broker Oxford Home Loans, 1985—; dir. Investors Resale Services, 1985—, Hanover Consumer Fin., Encino, 1979—, United Reconveyance, Encino, 1980—; v.p. Rancho Campo de Oro. Minister Ch. Scientology. Author: The Value of Creative Dance, 1971; Development of Creative Dance, 1977. U. Mich. scholar, 1969; Pa. State U. fellow, 1970, U. So. Calif. fellow, 1972. Mem. Mortgage Brokers Inst., Calif. Consumer Fin., Am. Technion Soc., Encino C. of C., San Fernando Valley Bd. Realtors, Calif. Escrow Assn., Nat. Assn. Realtors, Calif. Assn. Realtors, Visual Arts Assn., Am. Horse Show Assn., Am. Paso Fino Owner and Breeders Assn., Bell Canyon Homeowners Assn., Sierra Club. Club: Ferrari Owners. Office: Provident Mutual Escrow Suite 832 15760 Ventura Blvd Encino CA 91436

GOLDIE-PETRAS, IRENE BARBARA, comptroller; b. Orange, N.J., May 3, 1939; d. Arthur and Eva Lea (Goldner) Goldie; m. George J. Petras III, Sept. 8, 1959; children—George J. IV, Laurence Stuart, Robyn Joy. Student Montclair State Coll., 1957-59. Comptroller Goldie Indsl. Supply Co., Hillside, N.J., 1973—, sec., treas., 1984—, also stockholder. Chmn. adult adv. com. Union Twp. Bd. Edn., 1980-83; trustee Temple Israel Union, 1981-85, mem. exec. bd., 1982—, mem. exec. bd. Sisterhood, 1975-85; mem. community betterment com. Union Twp. Mcpl. Govt., 1983-85, chmn. community relations com., 1985, treas., 1986; trustee Arthur Goldie Meml. Scholarship Fund; charter mem. Statue of Liberty Ellis Island Found., Inc. Recipient Meritorious Service award Temple Israel Union, 1982. Mem. Assn. Female Execs., Union County C. of C., Jewish Fedn. N.J. (bus. and profl. women's div.), Hillside Indsl. Assn., Phil Portnoy Humanitarian Assn. Clubs: B'nai B'rith, Hadassah (life). Home: 1113 Liberty Ave Union NJ 07083 Office: Goldie Indsl Supply Co 539 Sweetland Ave Hillside NJ 07205

GOLDIN, CYNTHIA EDITH, health care administrator; b. Phila., Mar. 3, 1954; d. Mayer Stuart and Pearl (Schechter) G. B.A., U. Pa., 1975; M.B.A., U. Va., 1980; postgrad. in pub. health U. Tex., Houston. Patient accounts asst. Methodist Hosp., Phila., 1975-76; Tb control specialist, U.S. Peace Corps, Korea, 1976-78; research asst. U. Va., Charlottesville, 1979; cons. U.Va. Med. Center, 1979-80; adminstrv. resident Riveredge Hosp., Forest Park, Ill., 1980-81; asst. adminstr. Houston Internat. Hosp., 1981-85; project specialist U. Tex. Health Sci. Ctr., 1985—; lectr. U. Houston, 1983—. Co-author tng. manual; author research study. Coordinator Returned Peace Corps Vols., Houston, 1983. Acad. scholar U. Va., 1978, 79; recipient Korea Music Festival Honors, 1978. Jewish. Home: 1732 Albans Houston TX 77005 Office: Harris County Psychiat Ctr U Tex Health Sci Ctr PO Box 20249 Houston TX 77225

GOLDING, CAROLYN MAY, government administrator; b. Essex County, N.J., July 1, 1941; d. Wesley Irwin and Florence Grace (Smith) G.; m. Gary Anthony Derosa, Oct. 18, 1975 (div. Sept. 1982). B.A., Duke U., 1963, postgrad., 1965-66. Tchr. English, Parkersburg High Sch. (W.Va.), 1963; asst. to registrar Duke U., Durham, N.C., 1963-65; mgmt. intern Dept. Labor, Washington, 1966-67, in various other positions, 1967-72, dep. assoc. regional adminstr. Employment and Tng. Adminstrn., San Francisco, 1972-77, comptroller, Washington, 1977-78, regional adminstr., San Francisco, 1979-82, dir. Unemployment Ins. Service, Dept. Labor, Washington, 1982—. Recipient Disting. Career Service award Dept. Labor, 1979, Fed. women's Career award Sec. Labor, 1983. Mem. Internat. Assn. Personnel in Employment Security, Nat. Assn. Female Execs., NOW, Pi Sigma Alpha. Episcopalian. Office: Unemployment Ins Service 601 D St NW Washington DC 20210

GOLDIZEN, CAROLYN SNYDER, nurse; b. Lahmansville, W.Va., Mar. 17, 1936; d. Lloyd Neil and Eva Lucretia (Parker) Snyder; R.N., Winchester (Va.) Meml. Hosp., 1956; B.S., St. Joseph Coll., North Winham, Maine; postgrad. Potomac State Coll., Keyser, W.Va., Parkersburg (W.Va.) Community Coll.; m. Lee Allen Goldizen, June 6, 1956; children—Lucretia Ann, Lee Allen (dec.), Cristina Leigh. Pediatric staff nurse Winchester Meml. Hosp., 1957; with Grant Meml. Hosp., Petersburg, W.Va., 1957—, beginning as head nurse med. surg. wing, successively staff operating room nurse, nurse cons. diet kitchen, med. and surg. supr., 1958-77, instr. area coal miners' emergency med. technician tng. program, 1977, emergency room supr., 1977—; dir. Grant County Ambulance Service, 1977—; mem. W.Va. Emergency Med. Service Testing Team; vocat. edn. instr. for emergency med. technicians Grant County Schs.; mem., sec. Northeastern W.Va. Regional Emergency Med. Services Council; bd. dirs. Area Regional Med. Services of W.Va.; mem. W.Va. Paramedic Curriculum Com.; cardiopulmonary affiliate faculty Am. Heart Assn.; advanced life support instr. Mem. Am. W.Va. Nurses Assn. (past pres. subdist. 6) Emergency Dept. Nurses, Nat. Soc. Registered Nurses, Nat. League Nursing. Methodist. Clubs: Home Demonstration, Hosp. Aux., Ladies Aide Soc., Eastern Star (past matron). Home: Knollview Star Route 1 Box 4 Lahmansville WV 26731

GOLDMAN, ALLENE TOWNSEND, marriage-family-child therapist, consultant; b. Roswell, N.Mex., Feb. 19, 1937; d. Thomas T. Mann and Allene (Ballard) M.; children—Emily, Justin. B.S., Colo. State U., 1959; M.S., Oreg. State U., 1965. Clin. trainee, tchr./therapist emotionally disturbed children Observation Clinic for Children, Los Angeles, 1960-63; tutor/therapist for emotionally disturbed and brain damaged children, Roswell, N.Mex., 1963-65; spl. edn. tchr., Roswell, 1964-65; dir., tchr., parent coordinator Midtown Sch., Los Angeles, 1965-66; dir. children's programs Ctr. for Early Edn., Los Angeles, 1966-69, instr., 1966-73; instr. Los Angeles Valley Coll., 1969-74; marriage and family therapist, Los Angeles and Dallas, 1970—; instr. Calif. State U.-Los Angeles, 1972, Santa Monica Coll., 1973-76; co-founder and pres. bd. Richstone Ctr., Los Angeles, 1974, dir., 1974-76; dir. Eastfield Parent/Child Study Ctr., Eastfield Coll., Mesquite, Tex., 1976-80; exec. dir. Parents Anonymous, Dallas, 1981—; cons.-therapist Recovery Assn.; mem. bd. Richardson Devel. Ctr. cons. The Family Place, Dallas; community speaker. Author: Are Mothers Always Awake?; contbr. articles to profl. jours. Interview com. Big Sisters, Van Nuys, Calif., 1974-76. Author: Are Mothers Always Awake? Contbr. articles to profl. jours. Mem. Nat. Assn. Edn. Young Children, So. Assn. Edn. Young Children, Tex. Assn. Edn. Young Children, Tex. Jr. Colls. Tchrs. Assn., Am. Assn. Marriage-Family Therapists, Tex. Assn. Marriage-Family Therapists, Dallas Assn. Edn. Young Children, Mental Health Assn. Dallas County (chmn. child and adolescent com., ann. parent conf. com., ann. child abuse conf. com.). Office: 5747 Morningside Dr Dallas TX 75206

GOLDMAN, ARLENE LESLIE, business consultant, troubleshooter; b. Paterson, N.J., July 7, 1956; d. Jacob and Bertha (Deck) G.; student Am. U., 1974. Asst. store mgr., asst. buyer Latt's Country Squire, Washington, 1976-77; ops. mgr. Complement, Washington, 1977-78; with Bidermann Industries, 1978-83, prodn. mgr. Jean-Paul Germain, div., N.Y.C., 1979-80, dir. ops., 1980-81, v.p., 1981-83; nat. sales mgr. Ralph Lauren div., 1983; ind. cons., 1983—. Mem. Whitney Mus., Nat. Assn. Female Execs., ORT. Home and office: 120 E 34th St Apt 3N New York NY 10016

GOLDMAN, ELIZABETH A., editor, writer; b. El Paso, Tex., June 22, 1949; d. Allan Edgar and Ruth Marjorie (Farkas) Goldman; m. Patrick Lon Clary; 1 son, Gabriel R. B.A., Ind. U.-Bloomington, 1972; Diplome, Alliance Francaise, Paris, 1979; M.A., Ind. U., 1977. Freelance abstractor Morningside Assn., Pleasantville, N.Y., 1973; asst. editor Dept. Game & Fish, Santa Fe, N.Mex., 1974-75; assoc. instr. religion dept. Ind. U., Bloomington, 1976-77; editor, writer Community Service Council, Bloomington, Ind., 1977-78; assoc. editor Am. Inst. Chem. Engrs., N.Y.C., 1980-81; editor, writer Am. Soc. Interior Designers, N.Y.C., 1981—1981-84; freelance writer, publicist, N.Y.C., 1984—; cons. ASID Computers Inc., 1982—, Moffat Communications,

1982—, both N.Y.C., 1982—, Oxford U. Press 1985. N.Y. State Arts Found. poetry fellow, 1983-84. Mem. Internat. Women Writers Guild. Home: 597 10th St Brooklyn NY 11215

GOLDMAN, ELIZABETH ANN, real estate executive; b. Great Falls, Mont., Feb. 23, 1954; d. Edmund B. and Barbara A. (Greene) G. Grad. high sch. Property supr. Moss & Co., Los Angeles, 1975-79; dir. property mgmt. Magna Properties, Houston and Los Angeles, 1979-81; v.p. in charge property mgmt. Ga. Income Properties Co., Atlanta, 1981-83; v.p. Ga.-CSM, Inc., Atlanta, then Los Angeles, 1983—; cons. distressed properties, 1980—. Mem. Nat. Assn. Female Execs., U.S. Senatorial Club. Republican. Jewish. Office: Ga-CSM Inc 12233 Olympic Blvd Suite 128 Los Angeles CA 90064

GOLDMAN, JANIS MERESMAN, lawyer, law firm executive; b. N.Y.C., Oct. 13, 1944; d. Harry and Helen (Chafets) Meresman; m. Michael David Goldman, Dec. 26, 1965; children—Melissa Lee, Lori Michelle. B.A. with honors in Psychology, U. Pa., 1965; J.D., Georgetown U. Law Center, Washington, 1969. Bar: D.C., Md. Sole practice, Washington, 1971-77; assoc. David Epstein, Esq., Washington, 1977-80; cons. Margolius, Davis & Finkelstein, Washington, 1980-82; pres. Lawyer's Lawyer, Inc., Washington, Chevy Chase, Md., 1983—, also chmn. bd. Co-author article in field. Chmn. U. Pa. Secondary Schs. Admissions Committee, Md., 1980—; trustee D.C. Bd. Library Trustees, 1972-74; bd. dirs. Washington Urban League, 1972-74. New York State Regents scholar, 1961. Mem. D.C. Bar Assn., Md. State Bar Assn., Montgomery County Bar Assn., Supreme Court Bar. Home: 3 Pinehurst Circle Chevy Chase MD 20815 Office: Lawyer's Lawyer Inc 1725 K St NW Suite 907 Washington DC 20006

GOLDMAN, JILL MINKOFF, pharmaceutical company information systems executive; b. Kansas City, Mo., July 12, 1953; d. Julius Burt and Eloise Joy (Shlensky) Minkoff; m. Barry Charles Goldman, Jan. 30, 1982; children—Joshua Scott, Elise Lynn. Certificat D'Assiduite, Université de Grenoble (France), 1968; B.A., Pomona Coll., 1974. Mktg. rep. IBM, Riverside, Calif., 1974-77, San Francisco, 1978-79; dir. store systems Neiman Marcus, Dallas, 1979-81; dir. end-user computing services. Marion Labs., Kansas City, Mo., 1982—. Sch. pres. ARC, Kansas City, Mo., 1966-67; v.p. chpt. B'nai B'rith Girls, Kansas City, 1968-69. Mem. Menorah Hosp. Aux., Nat. Council Jewish Women, Share, Inc., Guide Internat. Corp. Club: Toastmasters. Home: 5406 State Line Mission Hills KS 66208 Office: Marion Labs Inc 9300 Ward Pkwy Kansas City MO 64114

GOLDMAN, JOAN, lawyer, social worker; b. St. Louis, Mar. 4, 1938; d. Morris Albert and Regina (Aron) Greenberg; m. Michael Robert Goldman, Aug. 19, 1961; children—Tamara Ruth, Joshua Charles, Abigail Helaine. B.A., U. Ill., 1960; M.S.W., Loyola U., Chgo., 1982, J.D., 1982. Cert. social worker, Ill. Bar: Ill. 1982. Sole practice law, Chgo., 1982—; vis. lectr. Loyola U. Sch. Social Work, Chgo. Mem. Chgo. Bar Assn., Ill. State Bar Assn., ABA, Nat. Assn. Social Workers, Mortar Board. Jewish. Home: 247 Franklin Rd Glencoe IL 60022

GOLDMAN, PATRICIA ANN, govt. ofcl.; b. Newton, N.J., Mar. 22, 1942; d. Jacob Joseph and Miriam Louise (Cassiday) G.; B.A. in Econs., Goucher Coll., 1964; m. Charles A. Goodell, July 1, 1978. Research asst. Joint Econ. Com. of Congress, 1964-65; legis. asst. ad hoc subcom. on war on poverty, edn. and labor com. U.S. Ho. of Reps., 1965-66; research cons. U.S. C. of C., 1966, dir. manpower and poverty programs, 1967-71; legis. counsel Nat. League Cities, also U.S. Conf. of Mayors, 1971-72; exec. dir. The House Wednesday Group, U.S. Ho. of Reps., 1972-79; mem. Nat. Transp. Safety Bd., Washington, 1979—, vice chmn., 1982—; vis. prof. Woodrow Wilson Nat. Fellowship Program; lectr. Brookings Instn. Program for Sr. Govt. Execs. Chmn. bd. trustees Goucher Coll.; former treas. Nat. Women's Edn. Fund; former mem. adv. bd. Nat. Women's Polit. Caucus, also past chmn. Republican Women's Task Force; former chair governing bd. Ripon Soc. Fellow Kennedy Inst. Politics, Harvard U., 1978. Named Woman of Yr., Women's Transp. Seminar, 1982. Office: 800 Independence Ave SW Washington DC 20594

GOLDSMITH, BARBARA JANE, environmental consultant; b. Providence, Dec. 4, 1949; d. James and Marion (Jagolinzer) G.; B.A., George Washington U., 1971; M.CityPlanning, Harvard U., 1974. Asst. to dir. Met. Washington Coalition Clean Air, 1971-72; con. to environ. directorate OECD, Paris, 1974-75; sr. program mgr. Environ. Research and Tech., Inc., Concord, Mass. and Washington, 1973—. Mem. council Harvard Grad. Sch. Design Assn., 1980-83. EPA spl. fellow, 1972-74; fellow Dept. Transp., 1972. Mem. Air Pollution Control Assn. Club: Harvard (Washington). Author articles in field. Home: 282 Mt Auburn St Watertown MA 02172 Office: 696 Virginia Rd Concord MA 01742

GOLDSMITH, ELIZABETH BEARD, home economics educator; b. Buffalo, Nov. 24, 1949; d. Irving William and Betty Amelia Beard; B.A., Fla. State U., 1971; M.A., Mich. State U., 1972, Ph.D., 1977; m. Ronald Earl Goldsmith, July 31, 1971; children—David Scott, Andrew Patrick. Asst. prof. dept. home econs. N.Mex. State U., Las Cruces, 1976-78; asst. prof. Sch. Home Econs., U. Ala., Tuscaloosa, 1978-81; assoc. prof. dept. home and family life Coll. Home Econs., Fla. State U., Tallahassee, 1981—. Inst. Higher Edn. Research and Services postdoctoral scholar, 1980, U. Ala. grantee and fellow, 1977-80. Mem. Am. Assn. Housing Educators (state chmn.), Am. Home Econs. Assn., AAAS, Sigma Xi, Omicron Nu. Christian Scientist. Manuscript reviewer Prentice Hall, John Wiley, Allyn and Bacon and Houghton Mifflin, 1977—. Office: 215 Sandels Bldg Fla State U Tallahassee FL 32306

GOLDSMITH, GERTRUDE, wholesale co. exec.; b. Bremen, Ger., Nov. 10, 1909; came to U.S., 1939, naturalized, 1944; d. Emil and Selma (Mendel) Meyer; ed. in Ger., also Pittman's Coll., London; m. Henry R. Goldsmith, Sept. 28, 1938 (dec); children—Susan Lillian, Richard Michael. Founder (with husband) Compact Novelties, N.Y.C., 1945, now pres. Mem. C. of C. of U.S., Gifts and Decorative Accessories Assn. Jewish. Home: 85-15 Main St Jamaica NY 11435 Office: 303 Fifth Ave New York NY 10016

GOLDSMITH, JUDITH BECKER, association executive; b. Manitowoc, Wis., Nov. 26, 1938; m. Dick Goldsmith (div.); 1 dau., Rachel. B.A., U. Wis., M.A., SUNY-Buffalo. Prof. English, SUNY-Buffalo, then U. Wis.-Madison; mem. NOW, 1974-85, pres. Two Rivers-Manitowoc chpt. (Wis.), 1974-75, Wis. chpt., 1975-77, mem. nat. bd., 1977-78, v.p.exec., 1978-82, nat. pres., 1982-1985. Address: care NOW 1401 New York Ave NW Suite 800 Washington DC 20005

GOLDSMITH, KATHLEEN MAWHINNEY, accountant; b. Bklyn., July 16, 1957; d. James R. and Carmela (Ditria) Mawhinney; m. Marc Bruce Goldsmith, Oct. 7, 1979. B.S., Alfred U., 1979; M.B.A., U. Conn., 1986. C.P.A., Conn. Acct., Price Waterhouse, Stamford, Conn., 1979-83; controller OCE Bus. Systems Inc., Stamford, 1983—. Adv., Jr. Achievement, 1980-81. Mem. Am. Inst. C.P.A.s, Conn. Soc. C.P.A.s, Phi Kappa Phi, Delta Mu Delta. Home: 24 Lampost Dr West Redding CT 06896 Office: OCE Inc 1351 Washington Blvd Stamford CT 06902

GOLDSMITH, LEDA CARROLL, public relations executive; b. Los Angeles, May 1, 1936; d. Carroll and Norma Evelyn (Tobias) Carroll; m. Gerald P. Goldsmith, Aug. 2, 1957; children—Leslie Sara, Nicole K. Student Sarah Lawrence Coll., 1954-55. Asst. pub. relations dir. Bullocks Westwood, Los Angeles, 1956-57; copywriter SSC&B, N.Y.C., 1957-59; adminstrv. and legis. aide Hon. Benjamin Altman, N.Y.C., Albany, N.Y., 1965-69; community relations aide Hon. Herman Badillo, N.Y.C., Washington, 1969-73; v.p., dir. pub. affairs J. Walter Thompson, N.Y.C., 1973-82; v.p. communications/entertainment Barnum Secunda Assocs., N.Y.C., 1982-85, mktg. communications cons., 1985—. Author: (with G.P. Goldsmith) Boatfixit, 1958. Publicity chmn. LWV, Riverdale, N.Y., 1959-63, Benjamin Franklin Reform Democratic Club, Riverdale, 1959-63, Pub. Sch. 24, Riverdale, 1968-70; promoter Mcpl. Art Soc./Save Grand Central, N.Y.C., 1975-78. Mem. Pub. Relations Soc. Am., Advt. Women N.Y., Am. Women in Radio and Television, Women in Cable. Democrat. Jewish. Home: 3240 Henry Hudson Pkwy Bronx NY 10463 Office: 3240 Henry Hudson Pkwy Bronx NY 10463

GOLDSMITH, LYNN NATALIE, photographer, producer and director; b. Detroit, Feb. 11, 1948; d. Shakespeare Oliver and Edythe Victoria (Leader) Rubin. B.A., U. Mich., 1968, certificate in English, 1968. Publicist Elektra Records, N.Y.C., 1969-70; dir. Joshua TV, N.Y.C., 1970-72; creative cons. Grand Funk R.R., N.Y.C., 1972-76; photographer, video artist Goldsmith Inc., N.Y.C., 1977—; dir. ABC TV Calif. Jam, Los Angeles, 1973, WEA Promo Videos, N.Y., Los Angeles; recording artist Will Powers, Island Records, 1982—. Photographer (book): The Police, 1983; producer, writer, artist (album): Dancing for Mental Health, 1983; producer, dir. (videos): Adventures in Success, Smile, Kissing with Confidence. Mem. Dirs. Guild Am. (dir.), Am. Soc. Mag. Photographers, Am. Fedn. Musicians, Am. Fedn. TV and Radio Artists. Office: Lynn Goldsmith Inc 241 W 36th St New York NY 10018

GOLDSMITH, MARGIE, film director, writer, producer; b. San Francisco, Jan. 3, 1944; d. Eugene M. and Nancy Goldsmith; student Boston U., 1961-64; B.S., Columbia U., 1965. State mgr., summer stock and N.Y. Shakespeare Festival, 1962-65; asst. dir. off-Broadway and Broadway theatrical prodns. including Les Blancs, Boesman & Lena, People Are Living There, The Crucible, Othello, 1966-72; asso. producer, writer, dir. narration IS IS Christ, TV spl., 1972; sr. v.p. Planned Communication Services, film prodn., N.Y.C., 1973-83; founder, pres. MG Prodns. Inc., film and video prodn. and TV distbn., N.Y.C., 1983—. Author novel: Screw-Up, 1972; screenwriter Call It Sleep (Henry Roth), 1984; songwriter, Hanging on Hold, 1985; play wright SOS, 1973. Recipient Gold, Silver, Bronze awards Internat. Film and TV Festival N.Y., 1978, 79, 80, 81, 82, 83; Andy award for excellence Advt. Club N.Y., 1978, Cine Golden Eagle award, 1975, U.S. TV Commls. Festival, 1976, others. Office: 29 E 64th St New York NY 10021

GOLDSTEIN, AILEEN, investment company executive; b. Rosenberg, Tex., June 26, 1914; d. Cecil and Raye (Levine) Robinowitz; B.B.A., U. Tex., 1934; postgrad. in econs. Trinity U., San Antonio, 1959-61; m. Eli Goldstein, Jan. 27, 1935; 1 son, Gerald H. Cotton buyer R.B. Stores, Ft. Bend and Wharton Counties, Tex., 1934; legal sec., 1935-38; sec. Spl. Services, U.S. Air Force, Santa Maria, Calif., 1943; account exec. Dempsey-Tegler, San Antonio, 1961-66, E.F. Hutton, San Antonio, 1966-78; fin. cons. Shearson/Am. Express, San Antonio, 1978—; lectr., condr. seminars. Mem. investment com. Temple Beth El, 1979—; pres. San Antonio sect. Nat. Council Jewish Women, 1940-42; 1st pres. San Antonio chpt. Brandeis U. Women's Com., 1949-50, nat. bd. dirs., 1950-51; an organizer Vis. Nurse Service San Antonio, 1952, Sr. Citizens Center, 1958-62; mem. San Antonio Parks and Recreation Bd., 1960-64; mem. crusade com. Am. Cancer Soc.; charter mem. for San Antonio and Bexar County, Alamo Area Council Govts., 1968. Mem. Patrons and Friends of McNay Art Inst., Friends of San Antonio Library, San Antonio Mus. Assn., Smithsonian Assos., S.W. Research Found. Forum, Women's Aux. San Antonio Bar Assn. (charter), ACLU, Jewish Community Center, San Antonio Zool. Soc., Am. Jewish Com. Democrat. Clubs: San Antonio, Giraud. Home: 6803-B West Ave San Antonio TX 78213 Office: 110 E Crockett St San Antonio TX 78298

GOLDSTEIN, CHARLOTTE LIPSON, building inspection company executive; b. Boston, Aug. 1, 1929; d. George Lipson and Frances (Feldstein) L.; m. Norman R. Goldstein, Sept. 15, 1948; children—Sue, David, Julie. Student Mary Brooks Coll., 1945-47. Pres. Engineered Inspection System, Robbinsville, N.J., 1970—. Contbr. articles to profl. jours. Bd. dirs. Congregation Beth Chaim, 1977-82, Sunday Sch. tchr., 1952-69; charter mem. West Windsor Library Commn., 1981-85. Mem. Middlesex County (N.J.) Bd. Realtors (assoc.), Mercer County Bd. Realtors, Hunterdon County Bd. Realtors, So. Monmouth County Bd. Realtors, Somerset County Bd. Realtors, Burlington County Bd. Realtors, Pa.-Bucks County C. of C. Princeton C. of C., Mercer C of C. Republican. Jewish. Clubs: Hadassah (pres. 1952-53), B'nai B'rith (bd. dirs. 1968-70). Avocations: china painting; traveling; bridge; reading. Home: 10 Jeffrey Ln Princeton Junction NJ 08550 Office: Engineered Inspection System Inc 1200 Route 130 Robbinsville NJ 08691

GOLDSTEIN, DEBRA EDELSON, lawyer; b. Stamford, Conn., Oct. 5, 1950; d. A. Herbert and Sylvia (Gordon) Edelson; m. Jeffrey S. Goldstein, Aug. 11, 1974; children—Jennifer Alyss, Lisa Nicole. B.A., Wellesley Coll., 1972; J.D., Georgetown U., 1975. Bar: N.Y. 1976. Atty., Ogilvy & Mather Advt., N.Y.C., 1975-79, v.p., atty., 1979—. Mem. Lawyers Pro-Choice, Planned Parenthood, N.Y.C., 1982—. Mem. Am. Assn. Advt. Agys. (legal affairs com. 1985—), Am. Corp. Counsel Assn., Women in Law Depts., N.Y. State Bar Assn. (exec. com. corp. counsel sect. 1982-86, sec. 1984; mem. pub. relations com. 1983-86). Democrat. Jewish. Office: Ogilvy & Mather Advt 2 E 48th St New York NY 10017

GOLDSTEIN, DEBRA HOLLY, lawyer; b. Newark, Mar. 11, 1953; d. Aaron and Erica (Schreier) Green; m. Joel Ray Goldstein, Aug. 14, 1983; children—Stephen Michael, Jennifer Ann. B.A., U. Mich.-Ann Arbor, 1973; J.D., Emory U., Atlanta, 1977. Bar: Ga. 1977, Mich. 1978, D.C. 1978, Ala. 1984. Tax analyst atty. Gen. Motors Corp., Detroit, 1977-78; trial atty. U.S. Dept. Labor, Birmingham, Ala., 1978—. Sponsored exec. United Way, Birmingham, 1983; chairperson Women's Coordinating Bur., Birmingham, 1983-85. Recipient award for Meritorious Achievement U.S. Dept. Labor, 1981; B'nai B'rith Women Humanitarian award, 1981. Mem. Nat. Council Jewish Women, ORT. Jewish. Lodges: Hadassah (bd. dirs. 1979-83), Zonta (v.p. 1983-84), B'nai B'rith Women (mem. steering com. 1982-84, S.E. regional chmn. 1984-86) (Birmingham). Office: Office of Solicitor US Dept Labor Suite 201 2015 2d Ave N Birmingham AL 35201

GOLDSTEIN, HANNAH, import company executive; b. N.Y.C., Apr. 6, 1934; d. William and Cecil (Rock) Rosenblatt; A.A., U. Fla., 1953; B.S. in Bus. Adminstrn., N.Y. U., 1955; children—Joyce Dara, Mitchell Bruce, Stephen Elliott, Russell Jay. Self-employed, N.Y.C., 1954-65; with Equitable Life Assurance Soc., N.Y.C., 1962-65; with Creative Programs and Paul Breiff Assocs., N.Y.C., 1965-70; mem. N.Y. Mercantile Exchange and Nat. Stock Exchange, 1967-70; pres. J. Pierre Internat., N.Y.C., 1968-73, Discovery Internat. Ltd., Scottsdale, Ariz., 1972—, Goldwest Internat. Ltd., Scottsdale, 1980—; v.p. Southwest Ice Products, Inc., Scottsdale, 1984—, Mobile Ice Corp., Scottsdale, 1984—. Bd. dirs. Friends of Channel 8, Tempe, 1977—; mem. econ. devel. com. Scottsdale Town Enrichment Program, 1981-82; Democratic Precinct committeewoman, 1980—; State Dem. Committeewoman, 1981—; bd. dirs. Treatment Alts. for Street Crimes, Phoenix, 1983—, Phoenix Little Theatre; mem. econ. devel. com. Animal Welfare League, others. Mem. English Speaking Union, Ariz. World Trade Assn., Nat. Assn. Cable TV, Nat. Assn. TV Programming Execs., Am. Statis. Assn., Am. Mgmt. Assn., Nat. Acad. TV Arts and Scis., Alumni Assn. N.Y.U. Sch. Commerce, Beta Gamma Sigma. Clubs: N.Y. Univ.; Nucleus (Phoenix). Home: 8132 E Valley View Rd Scottsdale AZ 85253

GOLDSTEIN, MARCI-ANN F., health care executive, psychologist; b. Phila., Feb. 2, 1951; d. Howard M. Goldstein and Alayne (Abrams) Plotnick. B.S., Drexel U., 1972; M.A., Villanova U., 1974; Ed.D., Temple U., 1979. Research assoc. Pa. Hosp., Phila., 1972-73; dir. career counseling Delaware County Community Coll., Media, Pa., 1973-75; research assoc., dept. adminstr. adult edn. Temple U., Phila., 1976-79; dir. adult/continuing edn. Baruch Coll., N.Y.C., 1980-81; dir. tng. Am. Woman's Econ. Devel. Corp., N.Y.C., 1981-83; v.p. Med. Directions, N.Y.C., 1983—; mem. N.Y. Bus. Group on Health, 1983—; nat. bd. dirs. Roundtable for Women in Food Service, N.Y.C., 1981—; instr. Pa. State U.-Abington, 1976-79. Appointed mem. N.Y.C. Commn. Status of Women, 1981—. Recipient Outstanding Sr. award Drexel U., 1972, Key and Triangle award, 1972. Mem. Nat. Assn. Female Execs. (nat. adv. bd.), Key and Triangle Soc. (pres.). Jewish. Home: 10 Waterside Plaza #37H New York NY 10010 Office: Med Directions 171 Madison Ave New York NY 10016

GOLDSTEIN, MARSHA FEDER, tour company executive; b. Chgo., July 7, 1945; d. Charles S. and Geraldine (Shulman) Feder; m. Michael Warren Goldstein, Dec. 26, 1966; 1 child, Paul Goldstein. B.A., Roosevelt U., Chgo., 1967. Tchr. art Chgo. Pub. Schs., 1967-68; free-lance artist, Chgo., 1968-71; tchr. architecture Brandeis U., Northfield, Ill., 1974-80; tour guide My Kind of Town Tours, Highland Park, Ill., 1975-79, owner, 1979—; art cons. Randall Pub. Co., Inc., 1984—. Editor: Highland Park by Foot or Frame, 1980. Contbr. to book in field. Recipient Cert. of Completion, Chgo. Arch. Found., 1975; Cert. of Appreciation, Machinery Dealers Nat. Assn., 1982. Mem. Women's Exec. Network, Chgo. Assn. Commerce & Industry, Chgo. Conv. and Tourism Bd., Chgo. Soc. Assn. Execs., Milw. Conv. and Tourism Bd., No. Ill. Tourism Council. Republican. Jewish. Club: Brandeis U. Nat. Women (bd. dirs., v.p. 1977-84). Home: 266 Aspen Ln Highland Park IL 60035 Office: My Kind of Town Tours PO Box 924 Ravinia Sta Highland Park IL 60035

GOLDSTEIN, PATTI, public relations consultant, writer; b. N.Y.C., Dec. 5, 1932; d. Arthur J. and Shirley (Giberman) G. B.A., Hunter Coll., 1952. Publicist, CBS-TV, N.Y.C., 1955-57; mgr. mag. publicity NBC-TV, N.Y.C., 1957-60; writer features Show mag., N.Y.C., 1960-62; ptnr., owner Addison Goldstein Walsh Pub. Relations, N.Y.C., 1962-76; cons. to bus., 1980—. Author: Creature Comforts, 1983. Contbr. articles to mags. Avocations: film; gardening; travel. Office: Powers & Co 215 Park Ave S New York NY 10003

GOLDSTEIN, SANDRA, importing company executive; b. Chgo., Dec. 7; d. Jack Julius and Esther Judith (Glickman) Gilbert; student U. Wis., U. Ill., Champaign-Urbana; m. Seymour Leo Goldstein, Aug. 12, 1951; 1 dau., Jennie S. Co-founder, sr. v.p., sales mgr. Jennie G. Sales Co., Inc., Lincolnwood, Ill., 1961—; importer, designer accessory products. Mem. Nat. Assn. Convenience Stores, Nat. Oil Jobbers Assn., Ill. Petroleum Assn., Iowa Oil Jobbers Assn. Clubs: Carleton (Chgo.); Turnberry Yacht (Miami, Fla.); Internat. Club of Clubs. Office: 3770 W Pratt Ave Lincolnwood IL 60645

GOLDSTON, LINDA LEEBOV (MRS. EDWARD M. GOLDSTON), lawyer; b. Pitts., Aug. 17, 1942; d. Mike and Florence (Labovitz) Leebov; A.B., U. Pitts., 1964; student U. Seven Seas, fall 1963; J.D., U. Pitts., 1967; m. Edward M. Goldston, Apr. 12, 1969; children—Joseph Leebov, Samuel Morris. Admitted to Pa. bar, 1968; shareholder Baskin, Flaherty, Elliott and Mannino, P.C., Pitts., 1968—. Past pres. Temple Sinai. Mem. Am., Pa., Allegheny County bar assns., Nat. Assn. Women Lawyers, Nat. Council Jewish Women, Women's Am. O.R.T., Ladies Hosp. Aid Soc., Ladies Aux. Jewish Home for Aged. Lodges: B'nai B'rith, Hadassah. Home: 1309 Beechwood Blvd Pittsburgh PA 15217 Office: 2900 One Mellon Bank Ctr Pittsburgh PA 15219

GOLDSTON, SHARON RAFFERTY, financial planner; b. Salt Lake City, July 29, 1950; d. Kenneth G. and Phyllis (Devenport) Rafferty; m. Robert Wayne Thompson, May 14, 1971 (dec. Jan. 1975); m. 2d, Larry G. Goldston, Aug. 20, 1977; 1 son, Jeffrey James. B.B.A., Tex. Tech U., 1977. Cert. fin. planner; lic. real estate broker; registered securities rep., ins. agt. Trust asst. City Nat. Bank, Austin, Tex., 1973-75; planner, casewriter Assoc. Fin. Planners, Lubbock, Tex., 1977-83; fin. planner Pennington/Bass Co., Lubbock, 1983—. Contbr. weekly fin. column Lubbock Avalanche Jour., 1983. Mem. Internat. Assn. Fin. Planning (pres. 1982-83), Inst. Cert. Fin. Planners (cert. fin. planner), Lubbock C. of C. Baptist. Club: Lubbock Toastmasters. Home: 8504 Knoxville St Lubbock TX 79423 Office: Pennington/Bass Co 916 Main St Suite 706 Lubbock TX 79401

GOLDWYN, JUDITH S., typographer; b. N.Y.C., Apr. 1, 1940; d. Raymond B. and Rosetta (Van Gelder) Schlessel; B.A., N.Y.U., 1962; M.A., L.I.U., 1973; m. Ronald M. Goldwyn, Aug. 20, 1961; children—Ira D., Laura-Jill. Tchr., Gt. Neck, N.Y., 1972-77; owner The Word Factory, Gt. Neck, 1977—. Vice pres. pub. relations Gt. Neck United Community Fund. Mem. Gt. Neck Village Bus. Assn. (pres.), Gt. Neck C. of C. (dir.), Typographers Assn. N.Y. Office: 621 Middle Neck Rd Great Neck NY 11023

GOLICZ, PEGGY LOUISE, real estate appraiser; b. Washington, May 21, 1946; d. Ernest P. and Alicia A. (Peter) Erickson; student Wash. State U., Pullman, 1968; m. Lawrence J. Golicz, Aug. 3, 1968; children—Eric John, Karl Peter, Mark Joseph. Various secretarial and adminstrv. asst. positions, 1968-74; engaged in real estate, 1974—; broker, v.p. property mgmt., dir. Total Realty, Inc., Madison, 1978—; v.p. Am. Appraisal & Feasibility Corp., Madison, 1978—, also dir.; cons. in field. Mem. Nat. Center Housing Mgmt., Am. Inst. Real Estate Appraisers (candidate), Nat. Assn. Realtors, Greater Madison Bd. Realtors, Nat. Assn. Female Execs., Westmoreland Youth Hockey Assn., Alpha Phi. Club: Order Eastern Star. Author papers in field. Home: 1619 Elderwood Circle Middleton WI 53562 Office: 6506 Schroder Rd Madison WI 53711

GOLLIN, SUSANNE MERLE, cytogeneticist, cell biologist; b. Chgo., Sept. 22, 1953; d. Harvey A. and Pearl (Reiffel) G. B.A. in Biology, Northwestern U., 1974, M.S., 1975, Ph.D., 1980. Postdoctoral fellow U. Rochester Med. Ctr. (N.Y.), 1979-81; research assoc. in cell biology Baylor Coll. of Medicine, Houston, 1981-83, research assoc. in genetics, 1983-84; asst. prof. dept. pathology and pediatrics U. Ark. Med. Scis., 1984—; dir. cytogenetics lab. Ark. Children's Hosp., 1984—; mem. pediatric oncology group., mem. exec. com. Ark. Genetics Program. Vol. Lighthouse for the Blind, Houston, 1983. Mem. Am. Soc. Human Genetics, Am. Soc. Cell Biology, AAAS, Soc. Analytical Cytology, Sigma Xi. Contbr. articles to profl. jour. Office: Dept Pd Path Arkansas Childrens Hosp 800 Marshall St Little Rock AR 72202

GOLLNICK, REBECCA LEWIS, communications manager; b. Frankfurt, W. Germany, Sept. 10, 1957; d. Herbert Bruce and Marie (Losey) Lewis; m. Clayton Robert Gollnick, Oct. 22, 1983. B.B.A., U. Tex.-Austin, 1979. With Yaring's Austin, Tex., 1973-78; account exec. AT&T Long Lines, Houston, 1979-83; nat. account mgr. AT&T Communications, Houston, 1983-86. Mem. allocations panel United Way, Houston, 1981-86; advisor Jr. Achievement, Houston, 1980. Mem. Nat. Tex. Orgn. Profl. Saleswomen (treas.), U. Tex. Ex-Students Assn., Alpha Phi Alumnae. Roman Catholic. Club: Forum. Office: Am Tel and Tel Communications 333 Clay 18th Floor Houston TX 77002

GOLOMB, LYNNE ROOTH, educational psychologist; b. Chgo., Sept. 2, 1945; d. Eli and Florence (Goodman) Rooth; B.A., U. Pitts., 1966, M.S., 1968, Ed.D., Loyola U., 1980; m. Harvey Golomb, Dec. 28, 1965; children—Adam Simon, Sara Rooth. Grad. asst. Arsenal Family Childrens Center, Pitts., 1967-68; tchr., therapist League Sch., Boston, 1968-69; tchr., developer infant day care program Dept. Labor Nat. Capitol Area Day Care, Washington, 1969-71; cons. Programs for Handicapped, Chgo., 1974-78; pvt. practice ednl. psychology, Chgo., 1978—; adj. prof. Loyola U., Chgo., 1981—. NIMH fellow, 1966. Mem. Am. Psychol. Assn., Nat. Assn. Edn. Young Children, Council Exceptional Children, Ill. Sch. Psychologists Assn. Home and office: 5412 S Blackstone Ave Chicago IL 60615

GOLOWAY, FRANCES, geophysicist; b. Washington, Nov. 25, 1956; d. Edward Daniel and Phyllis (Strock) Goloway. B.S. in Chemistry magna cum laude, L.I. U., 1978; M.S. in Marine Geochemistry, U. R.I., 1981. Research chemist EPA, Narragansett, R.I., 1978-79; grad. asst. U. R.I., Kingston, 1979-80; seismic scientist Western Geophys. Co., Houston, 1981—. Contbr. articles to profl. jours. Mem. Am. Chem. Soc., Soc. Exploration Geophysicists (assoc). Office: Western Geophysical Co PO Box 18 455 London Rd Isleworth Middlesex England TW7 5AB

GOLTZ, SUSAN ACKERMAN, lawyer; b. Newark, Dec. 12, 1946; d. Morris and Ruth (Abend) Ackerman; 1 dau., Amanda Lauren. Student Beaver Coll., Glenside, Pa., 1964-66, City of London Coll., Eng., 1966-67; B.A., U. Mich., 1968, postgrad., 1968-69; J.D., NYU, 1971. Bar: N.Y. 1971, D.C. 1978. Asst. dist. atty. Bronx County, N.Y., 1971-74; legal officer U.S. Supreme Ct., Washington, 1974-78; assoc. Chapman, Duff & Paul, Washington, 1978-79; ptnr. DiSalle & Staudinger, Washington, 1979—; mem. adv. bd. Bur. Prosecution and Def. Service, State of N.Y., 1979; conferee Nat. Conf. Causes of Popular Dissatisfaction with Adminstrn. of Justice, St. Paul, 1976. Mem. ABA, NYU Law Alumni Assn. Home: 2472 Belmont Rd NW Washington DC 20008 Office: DiSalle & Staudinger 1919 Pennsylvania Ave NW Washington DC 20006

GOMEZ, ANA LYDIA MAS, ret. govt. ofcl., educator; ofcl.; b. San Juan, P.R., Sept. 30, 1913; d. Jose and Concepcion (Marti) Mas Nadal; B.A., U. P.R., 1937; M.A., Columbia, 1948; m. Edmundo Gomez, Dec. 24, 1934. Jr. econ. analyst U.S. Dept. State, 1945-48, agrl. econ. asst., econ. officer, 1948-52, asst. agrl. attache, 1952-54, econ. officer, attache, 1965-73; asst. agrl. attache U.S. Dept. Agr., 1954-65; lectr. econs. U. Ams., Mexico City, 1975—. Recipient Superior Service award U.S. Dept. Agr., 1956. Mem. Am. Econ. Assn. Home: Explanada 1210 Lomas de Chapultepec Mexico 10 DF Mexico

GOMEZ, EUGENIA PROVENCE, personnel executive; b. Waco, Tex., Sept. 14, 1939; d. Harry Mayo and Mary Frances (Bludworth) Provence; m. Vernon Joseph Gomez, May 29, 1976; 1 son—Gregory King McCown. Student Baylor U., 1957-59. Research asst. Tulane U., New Orleans, 1960-61; personnel asst. Gen. Tire, Waco, Tex., 1962-64; contact officer VA, Waco, 1968-70; cons. Ednl. Services, Inc., Waco, 1971-74; staffing mgr. Tex. Comptroller of Pub. Accts., Austin, 1975-84; personnel cons. Tex. Dept. Agr., Austin, 1983, dir. personnel and tng., 1984—. Chmn. decorations Laguna Gloria Art Mus., Austin., 1982-86; pres. Women of St. Matthias Ch., Waco, 1972-74; mem. awards com. Gov.'s Com. on Women, 1984—. Mem. Am. Soc. Personnel Adminstrn., Tex. Soc. Pub. Adminstrs., Coll. Placement Council. Democrat. Episcopalian. Home: 4603 Cliffstone Cove Austin TX 78735

GÓMEZ, MARÍA DEL CARMEN, architect; b. Camaguey, Cuba, Aug. 11, 1958; came to U.S., 1961, naturalized, 1980; d. Roberto and María del Carmen (Ramírez) G.; m. George Ravelo Díaz-Arrastia, Aug. 6, 1983. B.Arch. magna cum laude, U. Houston, 1982. With Spencer Herolz Architects, Houston, 1980-84, Peck Drennan Assocs., Houston, 1985; designer Haltner-Brooks & Co., Houston, 1985—. Mem. AIA (assoc.), Tex. Soc. Architects, Houston Chpt. AIA, Golden Key Nat. Honor Soc. Club: Beaver Creek (Colo.). Roman Catholic. Home: 5200 Weslayan A-207 Houston TX 77005 Office: Haltner-Brooks & Co 2200 W Loop S Suite 890 Houston TX 77027

GOMEZ, ROSE PONS, uniform company executive; b. Bethel, Conn., Aug. 26, 1932; d. Vincent A. and Constance E(Machado) Ballester; m. Pascual B. Gomez, Aug. 11, 1951; children—Lisa Ann, Lori Ann. Student pub. schs., New Britain, Conn. File clk. Magson Uniform Co., New Britain, 1950-51, billing clk., Kensington, Conn., 1951-55, bookkeeper, 1955-59, asst. office mgr., 1959-63, personnel dir., 1963-75, comptroller, asst. corp. sec., 1975—. Mem. Am. Mgmt. Assn. Republican. Roman Catholic. Clubs: Spanish Am. Culture (New Britain); Saint Matthews Ladies' Guild (Forestville, Conn.). Home: 208 Vera Rd Bristol CT 06010 Office: Magson Uniform Co 279 New Britain Rd Kensington CT 06037

GOMEZ-CARRION, YVONNE, physician; b. Bklyn., Feb. 6, 1957; d. William and Josephine (Aitcheson) Carrion. B.A., Princeton U., 1979; M.D., Columbia U., 1983. Intern, then resident in ob-gyn Columbia Presbyn. Med. Ctr.-Sloan Hosp. Women and Children, 1983—; ob-gyn instr., cons. Pre-Med. Research/Edn. Program, N.Y.C., 1979—. Mem. Coll. Ob-gyn. Democrat. Roman Catholic. Office: Dept Ob-Gyn Columbia Presbyn Med Ctr 622 W 168 St New York NY 10032

GOMORI FURST, ELISABETH, cardiologist; b. Budapest, Hungary, Feb. 7, 1954; d. Bela and Ibolya (Kovacs) Gomori; m. Michael L. Furst, Aug. 22, 1976; 1 dau., Jessica Rachel. M.D., Semmelweis Med. Sch., Budapest, 1977. Med. diplomate. Resident in internal medicine N.Y. Infirmary-Beekman Downtown Hosp., N.Y.C., 1980-83; fellow in cardiology Beth Israel Med. Ctr., N.Y.C., 1983—. Contbr. article, research papers to publs (1st prize 1976, hon. 1974). Mem. AMA, ACP (assoc.), Am. Heart Assn.

GONCHAR, ROSALIE JAMES, wholesale food company executive; b. Savannah, Ga., Sept. 9, 1927; d. Thomas Patterson James and Catherine Mae (Crider) Roberts James; m. Gershon Alexander Gonchar, Dec. 27, 1952. With IBM-code sect. Nat. Security Agy., Washington, 1943-45; computer operator So. States Iron-Roofing Co., Savannah, 1948-53; sales mgr., pres. Gonchar Produce Co., Savannah, 1955—. Mem. United Fresh Fruit and Vegetable Assn. Democrat. Jewish. Lodges: B'nai B'rith, Hadassah. Avocation: artist. Office: Gonchar Produce Co Inc US Hwy 80 Garden City GA 31408

GONCHER, SUSAN ELLEN, computer software executive; b. Herrin, Ill., Nov. 3, 1950; d. John and Doris Elaine (Cook) Grozik; m. Donald John Goncher, Oct. 20, 1973; 1 child, Andrew Joseph. B.S., So. Ill. U., 1972; M.S., Nat. Coll. Edn., 1981. Tchr. English, Bloomingdale Sch. Dist., Ill., 1973-74; personnel asst. Chgo. Pneumatic Tool Co., Bensenville, Ill., 1974-75; exec. asst. Bus. Appraisal Co., Oak Brook, Ill., 1975-76, System Devel. Corp., Oak Brook, 1976-77; office services mgr. Advanced System Applications, Inc., Bloomingdale, Ill., 1977-80, mger personnel adminstrn., 1980—. Contbr. articles to profl. jours. Ill. State scholar, 1968. Mem. Am. Soc. Personnel Adminstrn., Am. Mgmt. Assn., Alpha Omicron Pi. Russian Orthodox. Home: 117 Norton Dr Bloomingdale IL 60108 Office: Advanced System Applications Inc One Asa Plaza Bloomingdale IL 60108

GONSALVES, STEPHANIE ANN, lawyer; b. Honolulu, Oct. 11, 1955; d. Stephen and Josephine (Rivera) G. B.S. cum laude, U. San Francisco, 1977; J.D., Stanford U., 1981. Bar: Hawaii 1981. Atty., Cades Schutte, Fleming & Wright, Honolulu, 1981—. Bd. dirs. Big Bros./Big Sisters of Honolulu, 1981—, sec., 1984—. Mem. ABA, Hawaii State Bar Assn., Hawaii Women Lawyers (dir. 1984—), Hawaii Women Lawyers Found. (bd. dirs. 1984—), Alpha Sigma Nu. Democrat. Roman Catholic. Office: Cades Schutte Fleming & Wright 1000 Bishop St Honolulu HI 96813

GONYA, PATRICE YEAGER, ins. co. ofcl.; b. Bremen, Ga., Aug. 17, 1951; d. Forest William and Madge Moore (Cain) Yeager; B.S., U. Mo., Columbia, 1972, M.B.A., 1978; m. David E. Gonya. Devel. trainee State Farm Ins. Co., Columbia, 1972-73, jr. acct., 1973-74, acct., 1974-77, asst. acctg. mgr., Springfield, Pa., 1977-79, acctg. supt., 1979-83, acctg. mgr., Rohnert Park, Calif., 1983—. Vol. drives Heart Fund, 1975, 76; office co-chmn. United Way, 1979, chmn., 1980, mem. campaign effectiveness council, 1982. C.P.C.U. Mem. Nat. Assn. Accts., Nat. Assn. Female Execs. Office: 6400 State Farm Dr Rohnert Park CA 94926

GONZALES, LUCILLE CONTRERAS, educational administrator; b. Colton. Calif., Nov. 30, 1937; d. Antonio Colunga and Ramona (Arroyo) Contreras; A.A., San Bernardino Valley Coll., 1958; B.A., U. Calif., Santa Barbara, 1960; M.A., Claremont Grad. Sch., 1969; m. Enrique Gonzales, Aug. 27, 1960; children—Leticia Maria, Cecilia Maria. With Chino (Calif.) Public Schs., 1960-85, bilingual classroom tchr., 1970-74, bilingual coordinator, 1974-76, coordinator consol. application-intergroup relations, 1976-78, supr. spl. projects, 1978, adminstr. spl. projects, 1978-82, dir. spl. projects, 1982-85; dir. state and fed. programs Pomona Pub. Schs., Calif., 1985—; mem. State Supts. Regional Adv. Hispanic Council, State Supts. Middle Grade Task Force. Mem. Migrant Regional Exec. Bd.; mem. Bilingual Dirs. Task Force. Mem. Nat. Assn. Female Execs., San Bernardino County Assn. Compensatory Edn. Dirs. (pres., v.p.), P.E.O., Assn. Secondary Spl. Projects, Assn. Calif. Sch. Adminstrs., Los Angeles County Bilingual Dirs., Large Urban Dirs., Pi Lambda Theta, Delta Kappa Gamma, Phi Delta Kappa. Home: 4955 Tyler St Chino CA 91710 Office: 800 S Garey Pomona CA 91716

GONZALES, LYDIA ALCALA, technical services librarian, reference librarian; b. Balaoan, Philippines, Apr. 22, 1927; came to U.S., 1960; d. Gregorio Olay and Josefina (Zambrano) Orallo; m. Don C. Agtarap, June 1964 (div.); m. 2d, Leonard Martines Gonzales, June 17, 1972. B.S. in Edn., U. Philippines, 1951; M.Ed., Seattle U., 1962; M.L.S., U. Wash.-Seattle, 1970. Tchr. Manuel L. Quezon High Sch., Pasay City, Philippines, 1951-52, Philippine Sch. Arts and Trades, Manila, 1952-56; instr. Philippine Coll. Arts and Trades, Manila, 1956-59; tchr. St. Benedict's Sch., Seattle, 1965-67; librarian Woodbury U., Los Angeles, 1971—. Active Cath. Fgn. Mission Soc. Am., Inc., N.Y., 1964—. Mem. AAUP, ALA, Calif. Library Assn. Republican. Roman Catholic. Club: Filipino Community. Office: Woodbury U Library 1027 Wilshire Blvd Los Angeles CA 90017

GONZALEZ, CRISTINA, language educator; b. Gijón, Spain, Apr. 9, 1951; came to U.S., 1976; d. Cesar González and Maruja Sánchez; M.A., U. Oviedo, Spain, 1976; M.A., Ind. U., Bloomington, 1978, Ph.D., 1981; m. Richard A. Cohen, Aug. 8, 1979. Tchr. Spanish, Academia Clarín, Oviedo, Spain, 1976; asso. instr. Spanish, Ind. U., Bloomington, 1976-79; lectr. Spanish, Tufts U., 1980; asst. prof. Spanish, Purdue U., West Lafayette, Ind., 1981—. Ind. U. grantee, summer 1977; Purdue U. grantee, summer 1983; Am. Council Learned Socs. fellow, fall 1984. Mem. Société Internationale Arthurienne, Medieval Acad. Am., Semiotic Soc. Am., Am. Assn. Tchrs. Spanish and Portuguese, MLA, Centro Español de Documentación y Estudios. Author: Libro del Cavallero Zifar, critical edit., 1983; El Cavallero Zifar y el Reino Lejano, 1984, also articles; mem. editorial bds. Dieciocho, Third Woman. Home: 3332 Peppermill Dr West Lafayette IN 47906 Office: Dept Fgn Langs Purdue U West Lafayette IN 47907

GONZALEZ, DIANE KATHRYN, social worker; b. Cin., Aug. 20, 1947; d. Joseph Curtis and Kathryn Mary (Diskin) Gonzalez; B.A. in Social Work, U. Dayton, 1969; A.M. in Social Work, U. Chgo., 1973; m. Thomas Connolley Leibig, July 5, 1974; 1 dau., Abigail. Social worker Hamilton County Welfare Dept., Cin., 1969-71; social worker obstetrics dept. and prenatal clinic social service dept. St. Francis Hosp., Evanston, Ill., 1973-78; rap group leader Teen Scene, Planned Parenthood Assn., Chgo., part-time, 1979-80; social worker Chgo. Comprehensive Care Center, part-time, 1980—; chmn. adv. com. Evanston Continuing Edn. Center, 1978-80. Mem. landmark dist. com. Old Town Triangle, 1983—; co-chmn. Old Town Art Fair, 1984-85, gen. chmn., 1986. Cert. social worker, Ill. Mem. Nat. Assn. Social Workers, Acad. Cert. Social Workers. Roman Catholic. Home: 218 W Menomonee St Chicago IL 60614 Office: Chicago Comprehensive Care Center 3639 S Michigan Ave Chicago IL 60653

GONZÁLEZ, ELIZABETH RASCHE, medical journalist, medical editor and editorial consultant; b. Fairfax County, Va., Jan. 23, 1949; d. Herbert Herman and Gertrude Emma (Grether) Rasche; m. Robert Allen González, July 24, 975; 1 son, Matthew David. B.A., U. Wis.-Madison, 1972; postgrad U.N. Mex., 1973. Copy editor Am. Soc. Clin. Pathologists, Chgo., 1974-75; assoc. editor Comprehensive Therapy, Chgo., 1975-76; staff editor Hosp. Research and Edn. Trust, Chgo., 1977-79; assoc. editor Med. News Sect. Jour. of AMA, Chgo., 1979-83; nat. corr. Med. World News, Chgo., 1983-84, interim mng. editor Houston hdqrs., 1983; dir. div. health edn. Am. Acad. Pediatrics, Chgo., 1984—; invitee, discussant, vol. editorial cons. to mem. Philosophy Club of Dept. Psychiatry, Rush Med. Coll. and Rush-Presbyterian-St. Luke's Med. Ctr., Chgo., 1983—. Editor: Readings on Public-General Hospitals, 1978; author 300 med. news stories; editor 250 jour. articles and med. news stories. Recipient Award for Excellence in English, Nat. Council Tchrs. of English, 1966, first prize for prose U. Wis. Meml. Union Lit. Competition, 1968, Howard W. Blakeslee award in med journalism Am. Heart Assn., 1980, letter of commendation for report, exec. dir. Am. Acad. Pediatrics, 1982, internat. citation for researching and writing 1st public article on premenstrual syndrome. Mem. Am. Med. Writers Assn., Nat. Assn. Sci. Writers. Home: 4835 Lee St Skokie IL 60077 Office: Am Acad Pediatrics 141 Northwest Point Rd PO Box 927 Elk Grove Village IL 60007

GONZALEZ, SUSANA DORA, lawyer; b. Buenos Aires, Argentina, Oct. 5, 1953; d. Ovidio Salvador and Filomena (Charello) Gonzalez; m. Dennis A. Beesting, Nov. 24, 1979 (div. 1982). B.A., U. South Fla., 1976; J.D., Fla. State U., 1981. Scheduling Staff Alcoholism Services, Tampa, Fla., 1976-78; pvt. practice law, Tampa, 1981—; adj. prof. U. South Fla., Tampa, 1983-84, St. Petersburg Jr. Coll., 1984—. Selby scholar, 1972-76. Mem. Fla. Bar, ABA, Hillsborough Bar Assn., Homebuilders Assn., Network of Exec. Women. Republican. Roman Catholic. Office: 602 South Blvd Tampa FL 33606

GONZALEZ-MAJOR, JOANN PAULINE, telecommunications company executive; b. Port Newark, N.J., Mar. 21, 1956; d. Joseph Paul Major and Estellita (Gonzalez) Rainwater; m. Allen Charles Burch, June 2, 1973 (div.); children—Shjna Michelle, Cjadek Allen. B.S. in Indsl. Mgmt., Met. State Coll., Denver, 1983. Cert. advanced systems analyst. Programmer Mountain Bell Co., Denver, 1974-80, asst. mgr. personal subsystems, 1980-83; systems analyst AT&T Info. Systems, Morris Plains, N.J., 1983—. Author: Managers Training Guide for Order, 1982; User Guide for Order Processing System, 1984. Mem. Am. Mgmt. Assn. Republican. Roman Catholic. Avocations: racquetball; software design; reading. Home: PO Box 323 Columbia NJ 07832 Office: AT&T Info Systems 225 Littleton Rd Morris Plains NJ 07950

GONZALEZ-SUAREZ, ALINA MARIA, lawyer; b. Havana, Cuba, Aug. 14, 1955; came to U.S., 1961; d. Manuel Alberto and Maria Carmen (Arias) G.; m. Alfredo Suarez, Aug. 26, 1983. B.A., Valparaiso U., 1977; J.D., Boston Coll., 1980. Bar: N.Y. 1981, Mass. 1981, Fla. 1981. Summer assoc. Lincoln Nat. Ins. Co., Ft. Wayne, Ind., 1978, IBM, Armonk, N.Y., 1979; atty. Equitable Life Assurance Soc., N.Y.C., 1980-82; assoc. Beasley, Olle & Soto, Miami, Fla., 1983-84, Blank, Rome, Comisky & McCauley, Miami, 1984—. Mem. Equal Justice Found., Washington, 1980—; mem. admission com. Boston Coll., 1978-80. Mem. Am. Judicature Soc., ABA, Cuban Am. Bar Assn., N.Y. Bar Assn., Mass. Bar Assn., Fla. Bar Assn., Valparaiso U. Alumni Assn., Boston Coll. Law Sch. Recruiting and Alumni Assn. Republican. Roman Catholic. Home: 4801 NW 7th St Apt 606 Miami FL 33126 Office: Blank Rome Comisky & McCauley 4770 Biscayne Blvd Miami FL 33137

GONZLIK, PAMELA JOAN, cable television performer; b. N.Y.C., Apr. 20, 1948; d. John Martin and Regina (Cohen) Gonzlik; secretarial diploma, A.O.S. acctg. degree, Taylor Bus. Inst., 1975; student acctg. Pace U., 1975. Stock records clk. G. A. Saxton & Co., N.Y.C., 1970-71; sec., bookkeeper Acme Quilting Co., Inc., N.Y.C., 1971-73; acct., sec., office mgr. Alwyn Ptnrs., N.Y.C., 1975-77; treas. Independence Plaza Tenants Orgn. and Rent Strike Com., 1977-78; sec. Atalanta Corp., N.Y.C., 1978-80; legal sec. to chief tax counsel City of N.Y. Law Dept., 1980-86; sec. to gen mgr. splty. foods div. Atalanta Corp., 1986—; cable TV vol., producer, host, performer Musical Interludes cable TV show Exptl. TV Coop., Inc., N.Y.C., 1978-82; performer cabaret showcase Dangerfield's, 1984; vol., adminstrv. asst. ETC Studios, 1978-82; developer cable TV game shows. Mem. Nat. Council Geocosmic Research, Smithsonian Instn., Nat. Wildlife Fedn., Nat. Carousel Assn., Channel 13, and Channel 21 Pub. Broadcasting Service, Phi Chi Theta (rec. sec. Gamma Xi chpt. 1976-77). Home: 40 Harrison St Apt 38E New York NY 10013

GOOCH, PATRICIA CAROLYN, cytogeneticist; b. Michie, Tenn., Mar. 28, 1935; d. James Lide and Mary Frances (Hyneman) G.; B.S., U. Tenn., Knoxville, 1957. Tchr. sci. Knoxville (Tenn.) City Sch. System, 1957-58; biologist, biology div. Oak Ridge Nat. Lab., 1958-70, 73—; research asso. Grad. Sch. Biomed. Sci., U. Tex., Houston, 1970; sr. research analyst Northrop Corp., NASA-Johnson Space Center, Houston, 1970-72; organizing com. sci. confs. Named Outstanding Tenn. Woman, U. Tenn. Pan-Hellenic Assn., 1974. Mem. AAAS, Am. Genetic Assn., Genetics Soc. Am., Environ. Mutagen Soc., U. Tenn. Alumni Assn. (chpt. treas. 1980-81, chpt. sec. 1981-82, chpt. v.p. 1982-83, chpt. pres. 1983-84, bd. govs. 1984—), Oak Ridge Pan-Hellenic Assn. (benefit chmn. 1961), Delta Gamma Alumni Assn. (pres. Knoxville Area 1959-61, 67-69), Sigma Xi (chpt. admissions com. 1977-79). Democrat. Mem. Chs. of Christ. Club: Big Orange (sec. 1978-80, 82-84). Contbr. articles to profl. jours. Home: 226 Tusculum Dr Oak Ridge TN 37830 Office: Biology Div Oak Ridge Nat Lab PO Box Y Oak Ridge TN 37830

GOOD, ANNE LEEPER, civic worker; b. Jackson, Tenn., Nov. 10, 1923; d. Robert Allen and Ola (Crittenden) Leeper; A.B., B.S. cum laude, Lambuth Coll., 1944; m. John Carter Good, Oct. 28, 1945; children—John Robert, Carter Crittenden, William Allen. Co-chmn. Introduction to Washington com. The Hospitality and Info. Service, 1968-71, treas., 1971-75, v.p., 1975-77, pres., 1977-79, chmn. fin. com., 1983-85, exec. com., 1985-86; trustee Meridian House Internat., 1977-79, counselor, 1980—; membership chmn. Spanish Portuguese Study Group, 1968-69, v.p., 1969-70, pres., 1970-71; mem. ladies' bd. House of Mercy, 1970—, treas., 1972-74, trustee, 1986—. Bd. dirs. D.C. br. Nat. Capitol Area YWCA, 1971-78, 79-85, rec. sec., 1974, treas., 1974-76, 81-85; com. Hannah Harrison Career Sch., 1971-78, 79—, chmn., 1976-77, chmn. investment com., 1985—; bd. dirs. Nat. Capital Area YWCA, 1973-79, fin. com., 1978—; bd. dirs. Rosemount Infant Day Care Ctr., 1972-82, v.p., 1974-76; bd. dirs. Washington chpt. Achievement Rewards for Coll. Scientists, 1971-72, Alliance Francaise, Club d'Amitie Franco-Internationale. Clubs: St. Albans School Mothers (pres. Washington 1964-65), Air Force Officers Wives (mem. bd. Washington 1959-61).

GOOD, LINDA LOU, educator; b. Zanesville, Ohio, May 30, 1941; d. John Robert and Alice Laura (Fulkerson) Moore; B.S. in Elem. Edn., Ohio U., 1964; m. Larry Alvin Good, Jan. 11, 1964; children—Jason (dec.), Alicia and Tricia (twins), Amy Jo. Tchr., West Muskingum Sch. Dist., 1962-64; first grade tchr., Bellevue, Ohio, 1964-68, 2d grade tchr., Zanesville Sch. System, 1970—. Co-chmn. Zane Trace Commemoration. Mem. NEA, Ohio Edn. Assn., Zanesville Edn. Assn., Eastern Ohio Tchrs. Assn. Methodist.

GOOD, MARY JANE, temporary employment company executive; b. Indpls., Sept. 15, 1934; d. Street W. and Helen Blanche (Sarchet) Butler; student Public Relations Sch., Cleve., 1968, Real Estate Sch., Calumet Coll., Gary, Ind., 1976; m. Howard Ray, Dec. 5, 1952; children—Rae Jane Araujo, Eric Howard. Marketing mgr. Suburbs Ahead, Bolingbrook, Ill., 1972-73; dir. field services Am. Heart Assn., Cin., 1974-76; mgr. Norrell Services, Chgo., 1976-79, dist. mgr. Ohio-W.Va., Atlanta, 1979-84, regional mgr., 1984—, mem. Norrell Pres. Club, 1978, 81, 82, 83, 84, Leaders Panel, 1981. Ward com. chmn. Republican party, Strongsville, Ohio, 1967-69; chmn. Well Baby Clinic, Bolingbrook, 1972-73; com. mem. Strongsville Recreational Com. Library Com., 1968-69; chmn. Crown Point (Ind.) chpt. Am. Heart Assn., 1977-78, public relations chmn. Ind., 1978. Recipient Outstanding Citizen award Bolingbrook Women's Club, 1973; named hon. Ky. Col. Mem. Epsilon Sigma Alpha. Home: 1577 Pinehurst Dr Pittsburgh PA 15241 Office: 3092 Piedmont Rd NE Atlanta GA 30305

GOOD, MARY LOWE, chemist, research company executive; b. Grapevine, Tex., June 20, 1931; married 1952; 2 children. B.S., Ark. State Tchrs. Coll., 1950; M.S., U. Ark., 1953, Ph.D. in Inorganic Chemistry and Radiochemistry, 1955, LL.D. (hon.), 1979; D.Sc. (hon.), U. Ill.-Chgo., 1983. From instr. to asst. prof. chemistry La. State U., Baton Rouge, 1954-58; from assoc. prof. to prof. U. New Orleans, 1958-74, Boyd prof., 1974-81; v.p., dir. research UOP Inc., Des Plaines, Ill., 1981-84; pres. Signal Research Ctr., Inc., Des Plaines, 1985; mem. chemistry adv. panel NSF, 1972-75; mem., chmn. NIH, 1972-76; bd. dirs. Oak Ridge U. Assn., 1971-77; chmn. Pres.'s Com. Nat. Medal of Sci., 1979-82; mem. Nat. Sci. Bd., 1980-86. Recipient Honor Scroll La. chpt. Am. Inst. Chemists, 1974. Fellow Am. Inst. Chemists; mem. Am. Chem. Soc. (Garvan medal 1973). Address: Signal Research Ctr Inc PO Box 5016 Des Plaines IL 60017*

GOOD, SUSAN LUICK, hospitality industry executive; b. Cambridge, Mass., Aug. 23, 1947; d. Robert Burns and Evelyn (Pelletier) Luick; m. Frderick Lee Good, June 19, 1971; children—Caroline Paddock Good, Jessica Desloge Good. B.A., Manhattanville Coll., 1969; M.B.A., Harvard U., 1971. Corp. planning mgr. Howard Johnson Co., Quincy, Mass., 1972-74, budget mgr., 1974-75, cash mgr., 1975-80, dir. pub. relations, 1980-82, dir. strategic planning, asst. to pres., North Quincy, Mass., 1982—. Bd. dirs. Harvard Student Agencies Inc., Cambridge, 1972-82. Office: Howard Johnson Co 1 Monarch Dr North Quincy MA 02269

GOOD, SUSAN PAULINE, banker; b. Sanger, Calif., Aug. 17, 1953; d. Alfred Anton and Elsbeth (Grimm) Good; A.A., Reedley Coll., 1973; B.A. summa cum laude, Calif. State U., Fresno, 1975. Advt. asst. Bell Public Relations Agy., Fresno, Calif., 1976-77; account exec. Meeker Advt., Fresno, Calif., 1977-78; dir. advt. First Savs. and Loan, Fresno, Calif., 1978-81 (merger with Central Savs. and Loan 1981), asst. v.p., br. promotions mgr., br. mgr., regional asst., 1981—. Mem. mktg. com. U.S. League Savs. Assn., 1980-81; chmn. Fresno City-County Commn. on Status Women, 1979; chmn. Fresno County Democratic Central Com., 1985—; pres. Calif. State U. Fresno Alumni Assn., 1981. Recipient cert. of achievement Inst. Fin. Edn., 1982. Mem. Fresno Advt. Fedn. (pres. 1982—), Nat. Assn. Female Execs., Inst. Fin. Edn., Execs. Assn. Fresno, Fresno City-County C. of C. Roman Catholic. Club: Arthur Murray Dance. Office: 1930 E Shields Fresno CA 93726

GOODALE, HOPE KAUFMANN, educator; b. N.Y.C., Apr. 23, 1926; d. Charles Barnard and Nettie (Cramer) Kaufmann; A.B. with honors in Spanish, Bryn Mawr Coll., 1948, M.A., 1950, Ph.D., 1965; m. Robert Lincoln Goodale, Aug. 2, 1951. Music librarian Free Library of Phila., 1949-51; instr. dept. Spanish, Bryn Mawr Coll., 1952-59; asst. prof. modern langs. Widener Coll., Chester, Pa., 1964-67, assos. prof., 1967-71, prof., 1972—; corp. Internat. Inst. of Spain, Madrid. Fulbright fellow, Madrid, 1960-61. Mem. MLA, Phila. Vicinity MLA, Pa. MLA, Am. Assn. Tchrs. Spanish and Portuguese. Democrat. Contbr. articles to profl. jours. Home: 411 S Providence Rd Wallingford PA 19086 Office: LC 137A Widener Univ Chester PA 19013

GOODALE, KATHLEEN DOW, educational administrator; b. Laconia, N.H., Nov. 1, 1948; d. Ralph H. and Barbara E. (Spinney) Dow; m. A.J. Goodale, Aug. 2, 1968. B.S., Plymouth State Coll., N.H., 1970; M.Ed., La. State U., 1982. Msic tchr. Plymouth Area Schs., N.H., 1970-73; instrumental music dir., mem. adminstrv. team Gilford Middle-High Sch., N.H., 1974-78; supr. data processing Jimmy Swaggart Ministries, Baton Rouge, 1980-81; adminstr. Cornerstone Acad., Baton Rouge, 1982—; mem. eval. com. New Eng. Assn. Schs. and Colls., 1977; asst. prof. mentor program U.S. Sports Acad., Mobile, Ala., 1985-86. Mem. Nat. Assn. Secondary Sch. Prins., Assn. Supervision and Curriculum Devel. Home: 9444 W Darryl Pkwy Baton Rouge LA 70815 Office: Cornerstone Academy 1433 Sharp Ln Baton Rouge LA 70815

GOODALE, RONDA ANDELMAN, educator; b. Boston, June 16, 1949; d. Louis and Rose (Post) Andelman; B.S., Boston State Coll., 1967; Ed.M. in Spl. Edn., Northeastern U., 1968; Ph.D. in Ednl. Psychology, Boston Coll., 1982; children—Chandler Michael, Lara Faith. Spl. educator Boston public schs., 1968—, core evaluation team leader, 1976-77, support tchr., 1977-78, compliance specialist dept. spl. services, 1979—, a prin. planner for internat. high sch. program, 1980-82, mem. adv. bd. for internat. high sch. program, 1982; spl. educator Mass. Mental Health Center, 1969-72; ednl. dir. Boston-Brookline Collaborative Center, 1972-75; supr. student tchrs. Boston Coll., 1975-76; lectr. dept. psychology, U. Mass., Boston, 1968—, spl. edn. adv.; 1977—, lectr. spl. edn. Regis Coll., Weston, Mass., 1977-81; lectr. Tchr. Corps., 1979—. Mem. Council for Exceptional Children. Home: 42 Alton Pl Brookline MA 02146 Office: 26 Court St Boston MA 02108

GOODALE, TONI KRISSEL, development consultant; b. N.Y.C., May 26, 1941; d. Walter DuPont and Ricka Krissel; A.B. cum laude, Smith Coll., 1963; student U. Geneva, 1962-63; postgrad. Hunter Coll., 1964-65; m. James Campbell Goodale, May 3, 1964; children—Timothy Fuller, Ashley Krissel, Clayton Akiwenzie. Congl. intern Senator Keating, U.S. Senate, Washington, 1963; broadcast analyst FCC, Washington, 1963-64; adminstrv. asst., dir. grant research dept. Ford Found., N.Y.C., 1964-67, cons. public edn. dept., 1968-69; N.Y. rep. Smith Coll., N.Y.C., 1975-78, asst. dir. devel., 1978-79; pres. Goodale Assocs., N.Y.C., 1979—; mem. bd. advs. First Women's Bank. Mem. alumnae fund com. Smith Coll., chmn. 25th reunion; exec. com. Am. Council Arts, chmn. nat. patrons com.; trustee, alumnae fund chmn., mem. alumnae council Brearley Sch.; mem. exec. com. Parents Assn., St. Bernard's Sch.; trustee, bd. govs. Churchill Sch.; trustee N.Y. Inst. Child Devel.; mem. women's div. Legal Aid Soc.; mem. N.Y. com. Joffrey Ballet; mem. benefit com. Grosvenor House; vice chmn. N.Y.C. Opera Benefit; mem. N.Y. com. Sch. of Am. Ballet, Superskates. Mem. Nat. Soc. Fund Raising Execs., Am. Assn. Fund-Raising Counsel (bd. dirs.), Brearley Sch. Alumnae Assn., Smith Coll. Alumnae Assn. Clubs: Cosmopolitan, Doubles Internat., Smith Coll., Washington Tennis. Author preface Effective Corporate Fund Raising. Office: 3 W 51st St New York NY 10019

GOODE, BRENDA, social worker; b. Phila., Nov. 28, 1947; d. Joseph and Theadora (Clarke) G. B.S., Temple U., 1986. Youth service worker City of Phila., 1970-83, family service worker, 1983-85, social worker, 1985—; union steward council 33, Am. Fedn. State, County and Municipal Employees, Phila., 1971—. Mem. youth task force Mayor's Commn. on Sexual Minorities; mem. task force Teen Pregnancy in the Black Community. Mem. Nat. Assn. for Social Workers, Concerned Woman. Episcopalian. Home: 5703 N 13th St Philadelphia PA 19141 Office: 1401 Arch St Philadelphia PA 19102

GOODE, LOVETT DAVIS, insurance company executive, consultant; b. N.Y.C., Dec. 26, 1958; d. Dudley Anthony and Ivy Joy (Henry) Davis; m. Darrell C. Goode, Feb. 14, 1982; 1 child, Lyle Scott. Student Santa Monica Coll., 1980-82, Boston U., 1976-79; cert. Boston Coll., 1979. Lic. ins. broker, Calif. Personnel mgr. State Mutual Life of Am., Beverly Hills, Calif., 1980—; mktg. cons. Marsh & McLennan, Los Angeles, 1981—. Internship, Aid to Rep. Bunte Mass. State House, Boston, 1978, affirmative action dir. for State of Mass., 1979; vol. Friends of Tom Bradley for Gov., Los Angeles, 1986. Recipient citation for Exceptional Community Service, State of Mass., 1979. Mem. Nat. Assn. Female Execs. Democrat. Methodist. Home: 85 N Holliston #8 Pasadena CA 91106 Office: Marsh & McLennan Assocs 3303 Wilshire Blvd Los Angeles CA 90010

GOODE, RUTH ANN, hospital social work administrator, consultant; b. Louisville, Jan. 19, 1955; d. Charles Byron and Mabel (Shewmaker) G.; m. James Nicholas Chresos, June 29, 1985. B.S.W., U. Ky., 1978; M.S.S.A., Case Western Res. U., 1980; postgrad. Gestalt Inst. Cleve., 1983-85. Med. social worker Univ. Hosps., Cleve., 1980-83; dir. discharge planning Marymount Hosp., Cleve., 1983-84; psychiat. social worker Lutheran Med. Ctr., Cleve., 1984-85; sr. care coordinator Fairview Gen. Hosp., Cleve., 1985-86; dir. social work St. John Hosp., Cleve., 1986—; cons. Alzheimer's disease, geriatrics; mem. spaker's bur. Alzheimer's Disease Assn., Cleve., 1983—; mem. adv. com. Gestalt Inst. Cleve., 1986—. Author resource man. on Alzheimer's disease, 1982; also articles on geriatric social work. Recipient Outstanding Service award Alzheimer's Disease Assn., Cleve., 1982, 83. Mem. Ohio Soc. Hosp. Social Work Dirs., Am. Hosp. Assn.-Social Work Dirs., Gestalt Inst. Cleve., Nat. Assn. Social Workers, Acad. Cert. Social Workers. Democrat. Baptist. Avocations: racquetball; photography; movies; reading; collecting teddy bears. Home: 3729 Warrensville Center Rd Apt 7 Shaker Heights OH 44122 Office: St John Hosp 7911 Detroit Ave Cleveland OH 44102

GOODEN, BARBARA ANN, credit union executive; b. Waycross, Ga., July 14, 1946; d. James William and Juanita Christine (Davis) G. A.A. in

Psychology, A.A. in Bus. Adminstrn., A.A. in Edn., Waycross Jr. Coll.; grad. Sch. Fin. Counseling, Fla. State U., 1986. With Eli Witt Co., Tampa, Fla., 1968-80, credit union rep., 1974-80; credit card coordinator Waycross Seaboard System Fed. Credit Union, 1980-84, collection coordinator, 1984—. Contbr. articles on consumer credit to Waycross Jour. Herald, 1985. Women's rep. Southeast Area Employment and Tng. Council, Waycross, 1972-80. Mem. Waycross Credit Women (pres. 1984-85), Soc. Cert. Consumer Credit Execs., Ga. Soc. Credit Union Loan and Collection Coordinators (charter), League Credit Unions. Baptist. Club: Okefenokee Bus. and Profl. Women's (v.p. 1972-74). Avocations: reading, cake decorating, floral art, crafts, cooking. Home: 513 Riverside Dr Waycross GA 31501 Office: Waycross Seaboard System Fed Credit Union PO Box 1256 Waycross GA 31502

GOODEN, CHARLENE ADELIA, nurse; b. Suffern, N.Y., May 19, 1947; d. Charles Randall Gooden and Muriel Bernice (De Freese) Agnes; children—Thomas, Christopher. A.A.S., N.Y.C. Community Coll., Brooklyn, 1968. R.N., N.Y., Md. Charge nurse La Guardia Hosp., Rego Park, N.Y., 1969-71, U. Md. Hosp., Balt., 1977-79; asst. head nurse Drug Abuse Control Com., N.Y.C., 1973-76; Staff nurse Upjohn Healthcare, Balt., N.Y.C., 1978-82, Kimberly Nurses, Rego Park, N.Y., 1980-83, Sinai Hosp., Balt., 1983—. Den leader Greater N.Y. Council Pioneer Dist., Boy Scouts Am., 1980-83, troop leader, 1980-83; contbg. mem. Democratic Nat. Com., 1982—; sustaining mem. Republican Nat. Com., 1981—. Lutheran. Home: 3524 Carriage Hill Circle Randallastown MD 21133 Office: Sinai Hosp of Baltimore Belvedere and Greenspring Aves Baltimore MD 21215

GOODENOUGH, URSULA WILTSHIRE, cell biologist, researcher, educator; b. Queens Village, N.Y., Mar. 16, 1943; d. Erwin Ramsdell Goodenough and Evelyn (Wiltshire) Pitcher; m. Robert Paul Levine, Aug. 10, 1969 (div. 1980); children—Jason, Mathea; m. John Edward Heuser, July 29, 1980; children—Jessica, Thomas, James. Student Radcliffe Coll., 1960-61; B.A., Barnard Coll., N.Y.C., 1963; M.A., Columbia U., 1965; Ph.D., Harvard U., 1969. Asst. prof. biology Harvard U., 1971-76, assoc. prof., 1976-78; assoc. prof. Washington U., St. Louis, 1978-81, prof., 1981—; mem. study sect. NIH, Bethesda, Md., 1977-81. Author: Genetics, 1974, 3d edit., 1984; contbr. articles to profl. jours. Grantee NIH, NSF. Mem. Am. Soc. Cell Biology (assoc. editor jour. 1978-81). Democrat. Office: Dept Biology Washington U Saint Louis MO 63130

GOODEY, ILA MARIE, psychologist; b. Logan, Utah, Feb. 1, 1948; d. Vernal P. and Leona Marie (Williams) Goodey. B.A. with honors in English and Sociology, U. Utah, 1976; Grad. Cert. Criminology, U. Utah, 1976, M.S. in Counseling Psychology, 1984, Ph.D. in Psychology, 1985. Speech writer for dean of students U. Utah, Salt Lake City, 1980—, psychologist Univ. Counseling Ctr., 1984—; cons. Dept. Social Services, State of Utah, Salt Lake City, 1983—; pvt. practice psychology Consult West, Salt Lake City, 1985—; pub. relations coordinator Univ. Counseling Ctr., 1985—; cons. Aids Project, U. Utah, 1985—; writer civic news Salt Lake City Corp., 1980—. Author book: Love for All Seasons, 1971, play: Validation, 1979; musical drama: One Step, 1984. Contbr. articles to profl. jours. Chmn. policy bd. Dept. State Social Service, Salt Lake City, 1986—; campaign writer Utah Dem. Party, 1985. Recipient Creative Achievement award English SAC, U. Utah, 1978. Mem. Am. Psychol. Assn., Utah Psychol. Assn., AAUW, Internat. Platform Assn., Mortar Board, Phi Beta Kappa, Phi Kappa Phi, Alpha Lambda Delta. Mormon. Clubs: Mormon Theol. Symposium, Utah Poetry Assn. Avocations: theatrical activities; creative writing; travel; political activities. Office: University Counseling Center 450 SSB Utah Salt Lake City UT 84112

GOODFELLOW, JOAN BENNETT, building trade executive; b. Williamsport, Pa., Nov. 6, 1928; d. Kenneth Victor and Martha Emily (Covert) Bennett; m. John Goodfellow, May 30, 1955 (div. 1974); 1 child, John Charles, II. Student Ithaca Coll. Gen. mgr. Bennett Chem. Co., Hagaman, N.Y., 1948-65, Halifax Tile & Floor, Ormond Beach, Fla., 1967-70; office mgr. Service Paint & Glass, Daytona Beach, Fla., 1967; owner, pres. Halifax Tile & Floor Covering, Inc., Ormond Beach, 1970—; v.p. New Era, Inc., Ormond Beach, 1982—. Fellow Nat. Assn. Women in Construction (charter mem.), Nat. Assn. Home Builders Inc., Internat. Pilot Club, Inc., (internat. affairs dir.). Avocations: Golf; travel. Home: 2926 Anchor Dr Ormond Beach FL 32074 Office: Halifax Tile & Floor Covering Inc 275 Kenilworth Ave Ormond Beach FL 32074

GOODFELLOW, ROBIN IRENE, surgeon; b. Xenia, Ohio, Apr. 14, 1945; d. Willis Douglas and Irene Linna (Kirkland) G. B.A. summa cum laude, Western Res. U., Cleve., 1967; M.D. cum laude, Harvard U., 1971. Diplomate Am. Bd. Surgery. Intern, resident Peter Bent Brigham Hosp., Boston, 1971-76; staff surgeon Boston U., 1976-80, asst. prof. surgery, 1977-80; practice medicine specializing in surgery, Jonesboro, La., 1980-81, Albion, Mich., 1984—. Bd. overseers Case Western Res. U., 1977-82. Fellow AAUW, 1970; mem. AMA, Phi Beta Kappa. Republican. Methodist.

GOODGE, ANNE LOUISE, massage therapist, biofeedback therapist; b. New Castle, Pa., May 27, 1953; d. James Lloyd and Elizabeth Anne (Vigne) G. B.S., Westminster Coll., 1976; postgrad. U. N. Fla., 1986—. Registered massage therapist; cert. biofeedback therapist. Asst. buyer Movsovitz & Sons, Inc., Jacksonville, Fla., 1976-82; massage therapist Luna Clinic, Jacksonville, 1982-83; owner, massage therapist, biofeedback therapist A & G Clinic for Muscle Therapy, Jacksonville, 1983—. Mem. Fla. Massage Therapy Assn., Am. Massage Therapy Assn., Biofeedback Certifications Inst. Am., Nat. Assn. Female Execs., Inc. Roman Catholic. Avocations: golf, coaching softball, racquetball, volunteer for elderly. Office: A&G Clinic for Muscle Therapy 1859 Dean Rd Jacksonville FL 32216

GOODHUE, MARY BRIER, lawyer, state senator; d. Ernest and Marion H. (Hawks) Brier; B.A., Vassar Coll., 1942; LL.B., U. Mich., 1944; m. Francis A. Goodhue, Jr., May 15, 1948; 1 son, Francis A., III. Bar: N.Y. State 1945. Assoc. firm Root, Clark, Buckner & Ballantine, N.Y.C., 1945-48; asst. counsel N.Y. State Crime Commn., 1951-53, N.Y. State Moreland Commn., 1953-54; mem. firm Goodhue Banks Arons and Pickett, and predecessors, Mt. Kisco, 1955—; mem. N.Y. State Assembly from 93d Dist., 1975-78, N.Y. State Senate from 37th Dist., 1979—. Trustee, No. Westchester Hosp., Presbyn. Hosp., N.Y.C., Westchester Mental Health Assn.; N.Y. del. Nat. Women's Conf., Houston, 1977. Mem. Am. Bar Assn., No. Westchester Bar Assn., Westchester Bar Assn. Office: 126 Barker St Mount Kisco NY 10549

GOODKIN, DEBORAH GAY, internal management consultant; b. Oceanside, N.Y., Dec. 8, 1951; d. Harold and Rose (Mostkoff) Goodkin. B.A., Syracuse U., 1972; M. Urban Planning, NYU, 1977. Planner, Nassau-Suffolk Planning, Hauppauge, N.Y., 1972; asst. to treas. Nat. Assn. Savs. Banks, N.Y.C., 1973; planning aide Dept. City Planning, N.Y.C., 1973-79; planner, real property mgr. N.Y.C. Bd. Edn., 1979-81, dir. Capital Budget Bur., 1981-85; supervising mgmt. engr. Port Authority N.Y. & N.J., 1985—; cons. C. Corp., Los Angeles, 1983—. Security cons. Democratic Nat. Com., N.Y.C., 1980. Mem. Women in Govt. (guest lectr. 1983), Syracuse U. Alumni Assn., NYU Alumni Assn. Author: (zoning law) Bay Ridge Zoning Dist., 1978. Artist: Show of Selected Works, Sireuil, France, 1983. Office: Port Authority One World Trade Ctr New York NY 10048

GOODMAN, BERNICE EVELYN, psychotherapist; b. Hot Springs, Ark., June 27, 1927; d. Bernard and Dorothy (Neumann) G.; B.S., U. Wis., 1948; M.S., Columbia U., 1952. Dir. program city and country brs. Children's Aid Soc., N.Y.C., 1963-71; pvt. practice psychotherapy, N.Y.C., 1969—; cons. youth service systems Region II, HEW, 1971-72; co-founder, chairperson 1st bd. dirs. Inst. Human Identity, 1972-76; co-chairperson Nat. Task Force Lesbian/Gay Issues. Mem. Nat. Assn. Social Workers (co-chmn. task force gay issues 1979—), Acad. Cert. Social Workers. Author book and articles in field. Address: 32 E 3d St New York NY 10003

GOODMAN, CAROL, lawyer; b. Milford, Mass., Nov. 22, 1945; d. Louis and Ethel (Rosen) Goodman; m. John Peter Abramson, Jan. 9, 1972; 1 dau., Elizabeth Sarah Goodman Abramson. A.B. cum laude, Barnard Coll., 1966; J.D. magna cum laude, U. Maine, 1974; postgrad. Harvard U. Law Sch., 1973-74. Bar: N.Y. 1975, U.S. Dist. Ct. (so. dist.) N.Y. 1975, U.S. Ct. Appeals (2d cir.) 1975, Mass. 1978, U.S. Dist. Ct. (ea. dist.) Mass. 1978, U.S. Ct. Appeals (1st cir.) 1978, U.S. Supreme Ct. 1980, U.S. Ct. Appeals (10th cir.) 1986. Assoc., Paul Weiss Rifkind Wharton & Garrison, N.Y.C., 1974-77, Goodwin Proctor & Hoar, Boston, 1977-82; assoc. LeBoeuf, Lamb, Leiby & MacRae, N.Y.C., 1982-83, ptnr., Boston, 1984-86, Salt Lake City, 1986—; panel atty. Community Law Offices, Inc., N.Y.C., 1974-77. Mem. ABA (com. on fed. regulation of securities 1981—, subcom. on litigation 1983—), Mass. Bar Assn., Phi Beta Kappa. Democrat. Jewish. Office: LeBoeuf Lamb Leiby & MacRae 1000 Kearns Bldg 136 S Main Salt Lake City UT 84101

GOODMAN, ELLEN HOLTZ, author, columnist; b. Newton, Mass., Apr. 11, 1941; d. Jackson Jacob and Edith (Weinstein) Holtz; B.A. cum laude, Radcliffe Coll., 1963; 1 dau., Katherine Anne. Researcher, reporter Newsweek Mag., 1963-65; feature writer Detroit Free Press, 1965-67; feature writer columnist Boston Globe, 1967—; syndicated columnist Washington Post Writers Group, 1976—; radio commentator Spectrum, CBS, 1978—; commentator NBC Today Show, 1979—. Named New Eng. Newspaper Woman of Year, New Eng. Press Assn., 1968; recipient Catherine O'Brien award Stanley Home Products, 1971; Media award Mass. Commn. Status Women, 1974; Columnist of Year award New Eng. Women's Press Assn., 1975; Pulitzer prize, 1980; prize for commentary Am. Soc. Newspaper Editors, 1980; Nieman fellow, Harvard U., 1974. Author: Turning Books, 1979; Close to Home, 1979; At Large, 1981. Office: care Boston Globe Boston MA 02102

GOODMAN, GAIL BUSMAN, kitchen cabinet refacing company executive; b. N.Y.C., Feb. 8, 1953; d. Irving Laurence and Harriet (Topol) Busman; m. Laurence J. Goodman, July 17, 1979. B.S., Tufts U., 1975. Staff occupational therapist St. Joseph's Hosp., Yonkers, N.Y., 1975-77; sr. occupational therapist N.Y. Hosp., White Plains, 1977-79; chief occupational therapist Phelps Hosp., Tarrytown, N.Y., 1979-80; occupational therapy cons. Elmwood Manor Nursing Home, Nanuet, N.Y., 1982-83; dir. dealer ops. Facelifters, Bklyn., 1981-83, dir. franchising, asst. v.p. tng., research and devel., Bklyn., Chgo., 1983—; guest speaker Columbia U., N.Y.C., 1977, 78, 79, 82. Mem. Nat. Assn. Female Execs., Am. Mgmt. Assn., Am. Occupational Therapy Assn., Westchester Occupational Therapy Assn. (pres. 1979-81). Democrat. Jewish. Avocations: reading, movies, needlepoint, antique refinishing. Home: 28 Terrace Ave Suffern NY 10901

GOODMAN, LILLIAN RACHEL, nurse educator; b. Hanover, N.H., May 20, 1923; d. Benjamin and Anna (Tapper) G. R.N., Peter Bent Brigham Hosp. Sch. Nursing, 1947; B.S., Boston U. Sch. Nursing, 1950, M.S., 1954, Ed.D., Sch. Edn., 1969. Dir. nurses Boston State Hosp., 1955-63; asst. chief supr. psychiat. nursing Mass. Dept. Mental Health, Boston, 1963-69; prof., acting dean U. Mass. Sch. Nursing, Amherst, 1970-73; prof., chmn. Worcester State Coll. Dept. Nursing, 1973—; assoc. clin. prof. Boston U. Sch. Nursing, 1957-69; cons. VA Hosp., Brockton, Mass., 1960-67. Pres. Worcester Vis. Nursing Assn., 1982-85, co-chmn. program ops. com., 1980-82. Am. Jour. of Nursing fellow, 1967-68; recipient Mass. Nurses Assn. Leadership award, 1979. Mem. New Eng. Council on Higher Edn. for Nursing (mem. exec. com. 1974-76), Am. Nurses Assn., Mass. Nurses Assn., Nat. League Nursing, Mass. Assn. Colls. Nursing (chmn. 1985—), Sigma Theta Tau. Mem. editorial bd. Perspectives in Psychiatric Care, 1961-75, Nursing and Health Care, 1982—; author: Nursing Administration in Psychiatric Hospitals, 1983; co-author: The Schizophrenic's Mother, 1963; co-moderator videotape: Living with Dying, 1976. Home: 68 Topsfield Circle Shrewsbury MA 01545 Office: 486 Chandler St Worcester MA 01602

GOODMAN, LINDA GOLD, banker; b. Wallingford, Pa., Mar. 29, 1951; d. George and Rya Gold; B.A. in Econs., Goucher Coll., 1972. Research asso., project dir., bur. econ. research, disability and health div. Rutgers U., New Brunswick, N.J., 1972-73; corporate lending officer U.S. banking dept. Bankers Trust Co., N.Y.C., 1974-76, asst. treas. utilities div., 1976-77, asst. v.p. petroleum div., 1977-79, v.p., 1979—, head petroleum unit, 1981, sect. head coal, 1982-83, N.Y. nat. team leader, 1983, N.Y. nat. div. head, 1984—; N.Y. admission rep. Goucher Coll., Towson, Md., 1975, 76, career devel. rep., 1979-80; vol. worker, therapeutic activities div. Mt. Sinai Hosp., N.Y.C., 1977, 84—; mem. campaign com. N.Y. Young Republican Club, 1979—; mem. energy group Am. Jewish Com. Mem. N.Y. Real Estate Group (founder, pres. 1979—). Jewish. Home: 315 W 70 St Apt 15D New York NY 10023 Office: 280 Park Ave New York NY 10017

GOODMAN, LOIS ANN, librarian; b. Bklyn., Sept. 7, 1944; d. Nathan S. and Shirley (Lackowitz) G. B.A., Bklyn. Coll., 1965; M.L.S., Pratt Inst., 1967. Asst. reference librarian L.I. U., 1967-69; asst. librarian North Shore Community Coll., Beverly, Mass., 1969-72; art and photo librarian Rochester Inst. Tech., 1972-76, head pub. services, 1976-83, asst. dir. for info. services, 1983—. Mem. Brighton Theatre Guild, 1981-82, Animal Service League, 1983-85, Humane Soc. Rochester, 1983—, Lab. Ornithology, 1982—, Park-Meigs Neighborhood Assn., 1978—; bd. dirs. Hillel Found. of Rochester, 1986—, United Way Speakers Bur., 1985—. Mem. ALA, Beta Phi Mu. Office: Wallace Meml Library Rochester Inst Tech 1 Lomb Memorial Dr Rochester NY 14623

GOODMAN, PHYLLIS LOUISE, public relations executive; b. N.Y.C., Sept. 7, 1946; d. Bernard Jacob and Claire (Rosenberg) Goodman; B.S., Cornell U., 1967. Extension home economist Nassau County Extension Service, Mineola, N.Y., 1967-68; asst. editor Funk & Wagnalls, N.Y.C., 1968-69; sr. v.p. Glick & Lorwin, Inc., N.Y.C., 1969-80; sr. v.p. sci. and medicine div. Medicus Intercon Internat., Inc., 1981-82; v.p. Hill and Knowlton, Inc., N.Y.C., 1982-85; assoc. v.p. communications and pub. affairs St. Luke's Roosevelt Hosp. Ctr., 1986—. Mem. Home Economists in Bus. (chmn. N.Y.C. chpt. 1979-80, program chmn. nat. conv. 1981), Public Relations Soc. Am., Pharm. Advt. Council, Healthcare Businesswomen's Assn., Am. Hosp. Assn., Cornell U. Alumni Council (pub. relations com., steering com. on alumni leaders), Pi Lambda Theta. Home: 205 West End Ave New York NY 10023 Office: Amsterdam Ave at 114th St New York NY 10025

GOODMAN, TERRI WOOLRIDGE, public relations and marketing specialist; b. Oklahoma City, Jan. 23, 1955; d. Perry B. and Mayselle (Tidwell) Woolridge; m. Richard Stewart Goodman, May 29, 1981 (dec.). B.S., Okla. State U., 1977. Newspaper editor, 1977-79; dir. community relations South Community Hosp., Oklahoma City, 1979-84; community liaison dir. Bethany Pavilion, Healthcare Services Am., Inc., 1985—; pub. relations cons. Okla. Cancer Info. Line, 1983. Bd. deacons Presbyterian Ch., 1984—. Mem. Am. Soc. Hosp. Pub. Relations (cert., dir. region VII), Okla. Hosp. Assn. Pub. Relations Soc. (S.W. dist. dir.), Greater Oklahoma City Hosp. Pub. Relations Council (pres. 1982), Acad. Health Services Mktg., Am. Mktg. Assn., Okla. Mental Health Assn., Am. Assn. Suicidology. Office: 7600 NW 23d St Bethany OK 73008

GOODMAN, VIOLET LOWERY, realtor, investment counselor; b. Konawa, Okla., Sept. 10, 1913; d. Harvey Adell and Ruth Izora (Collins) Lowery; m. Orville C. Goodman, Dec. 24, 1934; children—Bruce Lowery, Alan Dale. Student in Bus., U. Okla., 1935-39; student in Nursing, Milw. Vocat.-Tech. U., 1943-47. Grad. Realtors Inst. Instr., Beauty Culture, Milw., 1940-47, Motor and Armature Repair, Norman, Okla., 1948-55; apt. mgr., Norman, 1970-75; real estate salesperson Acad. Realty, Inc., Norman, 1962—; instr. comml. and real estate investments, Okla. Real Estate Inst., 1970-74; counselor creative financing. Author instructor's manual: Commercial Real Estate, 1970. Mem. Nat. Assn. Realtors, Okla. Assn. Realtors (edn. com. 1970-76, dean of edn. 1972, state dir. 1968-76), Norman Bd. Realtors (pres. 1973, Realtor of Yr. 1972, Spl. Recognition award 1979), Realtor Nat. Mktg. Inst. (chmn. membership com. 1972-74), Norman C. of C., Bus. and Profl. Women (pres. 1968). Democrat. Presbyterian. Lodges: Order Eastern Star, White Shrine. Club: Altrusa. Home: 4321 24th Ave NW Norman OK 73069 Office: Academic Realty Inc 419 W Gray St Norman OK 73069

GOODMAN, YETTA M., educator; b. Cleve., Mar. 10, 1931; d. William and Dora (Shapiro) Trachtman; B.A. in History, Los Angeles State Coll., 1952, M.A. in Elem. Edn., 1956; Ed.D. in Curriculum Devel., Wayne State U., 1967; m. Kenneth S. Goodman, 1952; children—Debra, Karen Goodman Castro, Wendy Hood. Elem. and secondary tchr., public schs., Los Angeles, 1952-63; supr. pre-service teaching experiences Wayne State U., 1963-67; asst. to prof. U. Mich., Dearborn, 1967-75; prof. edn., co-dir. program in lang. and literacy U. Ariz., 1975—; speaker, cons. ednl. issues. Active in orgns. concerned with children's rights. Recipient Faculty Recognition award Tucson Trade Bur., 1978, Outstanding Tchr. Educator of Reading award Internat. Reading Assn., 1983. Mem. Nat. Council Tchrs. English (nat. dir. 1976—, pres. 1978-79), Center Expansion of Lang. and Thinking (dir. 1972—, pres. 1976-79), Internat. Reading Assn. (chairperson and active mem. various coms. 1962—), Assn. Supervision and Curriculum Devel., Am. Ednl. Research Assn., Assn. Childhood Edn. Internat. Jewish. Author books, including: (with C. Burke and B. Sherman) Reading Strategies: Focus on Comprehension, 1981; (with D. Watson and C. Burke) Reading Miscue Inventory: Alternate Procedures, 1986; contbr. numerous articles, chpts. to profl. publs.; also audio tapes scripts video, films. Home: 5649 E 10th St Tucson AZ 85711 Office: Program in Lang and Literacy Coll Edn U Ariz Tucson AZ 85721

GOODRICH, ELIZABETH ANNE, business educator; b. Seattle; d. Frank Allen and Hildegarde Anne (Hoffman) G.; secretarial cert. Western Mich. U., 1961, B.B.A., 1963; M.A., Mich. State U., 1968; Ph.D., U. Colo., 1975. Secretarial position Inst. Social Research, U. Mich., Ann Arbor, 1963-64, Downtown Kalamazoo Assn., 1964-66; instr. Lansing (Mich.) Community Coll., 1967; grad. asst., instr. bus. law and office adminstrn. dept. Mich. State U., East Lansing, 1966-68; tchr., chmn. bus. dept. Grand Ledge (Mich.) High Sch., 1968-72; instr., officer adminstr. dept. U. Colo., Boulder, 1972-75; prof. adminstrv. services and bus. tchr. edn. dept. Central Mich. U., Mt. Pleasant, 1975—. Cert. profl. sec. Inst. Cert. Secs.; permanent secondary teaching cert. bus. edn. Mich. Dept. Edn.; vocat. edn. permanent teaching cert. Mich. Bd. Edn. Mem. AAUW, NEA, Nat., N. Central bus. edn. assns., Profl. Secs. Internat., Adminstrv. Mgmt. Soc. Internat., Mich. Bus. Edn. Assn., Mich. Edn. Assn., Delta Pi Epsilon, Pi Omega Pi. Contbr. articles to profl. jours. Office: Sch Bus Adminstrn Central Mich U Mount Pleasant MI 48859

GOODRICH, GAIL LEE, personnel administrator; b. Nashville, June 17, 1947; d. Jack B. and Mildred A. (Redmon) G.; B.S., U. Tenn., 1969; M.B.A., U. Chgo., 1979. Tchr., Knox County Schs., Knoxville, Tenn., 1969-70; flight attendant United Airlines, Chgo., 1970-71, instr., 1971-73, field supr., 1973-76, tng. supr., 1976-77, indsl. relations rep., 1977-80, affirmative action mgr., 1980-81, mgr. human resources, 1981, personnel adminstr., 1982-86, mgr. personnel MIS div., 1986—; mem. Ill. Gov's. Grievance Panel, 1982—. Bd. dirs. No. Cook County div. Jr. Achievement, 1981—, officer, 1983—, mem. exec. com. project bus. div., Greater Chgo. area, 1983—; bd. dirs. N.W. Indsl. Council, 1986—. Mem. Am. Soc. Personnel Adminstrn., U. Chgo. Women's Bus. Group, U. Tenn. Alumni Assn., U. Chgo. Alumni Assn., Chi Omega. Republican. Methodist. Clubs: Women's Golf League, Management, Women's Bus. Group. Home: 2020 Lincoln Park W Chicago IL 60614 Office: PO Box 66100 Chicago IL 60666

GOODRICH, GRACE MARIE, sculptor, educator; b. Sioux Falls, S.D., Sept. 22, 1913; d. Edward Benjamin and Julia Margaret (Roache) G.; student U. Chgo., 1963-64; M.A. in Art Edn., Art Inst. Chgo., 1964; postgrad. Temple U., summer 1967; M.S. in Visual Design, Ill. Inst. Tech., 1968; M.F.A., Inst. Allende, San Miguel de Allende, Mexico, 1974; m. Edward W. Enthof, Aug. 31, 1940; 1 dau. Art educator, artist, 1932—; art dir. Lake Forest (Ill.) Public Schs., 1951-68; lectr. art edn. Lake Forest Coll., 1952-68; assoc. prof. art Dakota Wesleyan U., Mitchell, S.D., 1968-74; prof. history of art Inst. Allende, San Miguel de Allende, Guanajuato, Mexico, 1974—; exhibited drawings, paintings, printmaking and all media of sculpture, throughout U.S. and Mexico; one-woman shows include U. Calif., Berkeley, 1978, Galeria La Princesa San Miguel de Allende, 1978, Marin County Civic Center, San Rafael, Calif., 1981; represented by Artisans Gallery, Mill Valley, Calif., commd. six limestone panels at entrance for Deer Path Jr. High Sch., Lake Forest. Mem. Coll. Art Assn. Am., Civic Fine Arts Assn. Sioux Falls, Nat. Art Edn. Assn., Mus. Modern Art N.Y.C., Art Inst. Chgo., San Francisco Mus. Art, Ill. Inst. Tech. Alumni Assn., Phi Kappa Phi. Methodist. Club: Order Eastern Star. Author: The Ideal Art Center, 1968. Home: 387 S Morning Sun Ave Mill Valley CA 94941

GOODSELL, JOAN WALDRON, librarian; b. Bridgeport, Conn., May 19, 1949; d. Frederic and Elinor (Engels) G. B.A., U. Conn., 1971; M.S., Drexel U., 1973. Librarian, Laventhal, Kreckstein, Horwath & Horwath, Phila., 1978; catalog librarian Inter-Am. U., San German, P.R., 1974-78; cataloger, art librarian Info. Ctr., J. Walter Thompson Co., N.Y.C., 1978-83, collection devel. librarian creative library, 1983-85, asst. mgr. creative library, 1985—. Sustaining mem. Am. Shakespeare Theater Guild, Stratford, Conn., 1980—. Mem. ALA (editor Cognotes Jr. Mems. Round Table 1983-84, mem. Library and Info. Tech. Assn. 1984—, small libraries publs. series com.), Spl. Libraries Assn. (chmn. mus. arts and humanities group 1983-84), Library Adminstrn. and Mgmt. Assn. N.Y.C. Ballet Guild. Phi Beta Kappa. Episcopalian. Home: 502 Washington St Hoboken NJ 07030 Office: J Walter Thompson Co Creative Library 466 Lexington Ave New York NY 10017

GOODSON, CAROLE EDITH MCKISSOCK, technology educator; b. Des Moine, Dec. 31, 1946; d. William Thompson and Edith (Johnson) McKissock; m. Robert Wayne Peterson, July 1978; 1 son, David Shelby Peterson. B.S., U. Houston, 1968, M.Ed., 1971, Ed.D., 1975. Tchr., Spring Branch Ind. Sch. Dist., Houston, 1968-69; mem. faculty Coll. Tech., U. Houston, 1972—, instr., 1972-75, asst. prof., coll. counselor, 1975-78, assoc. prof., coll. counselor, 1978-81, assoc. prof., chmn. related courses tech., 1981—, assoc. dean, assoc. prof. tech. math., 1982—. Author: (with S.L. Miertschin) Technical Mathematics With Applications, 1983, 2d edit., 1986; Technical Mathematics with Calculus, 1985; Technical Algebra with Applications, 1985; contbr. articles to publs. Recipient Dow Outstanding Young Faculty award Am. Soc. Engring. Edn., 1982. Mem. Am. Soc. Engring. Edn. (vice chmn. 1985-86, sec.-treas. div. 1982-84, regional chair 1982-83), Nat. Council Tchrs. of Math., Math. Assn. Am., Phi Kappa Phi (chpt. pres. 1985). Presbyterian. Office: U Houston University Park Coll Tech 361-T2 Houston TX 77004

GOODSON, DOROTHY MOORE, English educator, counselor; b. N.C.; children—Regina L. Kane, Northington V. B.S., Hampton U., 1964, M.A., 1970; postgrad. Va. Poly. Inst. and State U., since 1972—. Lic. profl. counselor, Va.; nat. cert. counselor. English instr. Hampton City Schs., Va., 1964-69, counselor, guidance dir., 1969-83; asst. prof., profl. counselor Norfolk (Va.) State U., 1983—; English and reading instr. Upward Bound program Hampton U., 1968-76; English instr. Thomas Nelson Community Coll., Hampton, 1978-82; supr. Center '70, Coll. Admissions Testing Program, Hampton, 1976-81. Active Insight Enterprises, Hampton, 1985—. NDEA fellow, summers 1966, 68. Mem. Am. Assn. for Counseling and Devel., Assn. for Measurement and Evaluation in Counseling and Devel., NEA (life), Nat. Assn. for Female Execs., NAACP, Kappa Delta Pi. Baptist. Avocations: reading, listening to music, gardening. Home: 148 Settlers Landing Rd Hampton VA 23669 Office: Norfolk State U 2401 Corprew Ave Norfolk VA 23504

GOODSPEED, BARBARA, artist; b. Gardner, Mass., Sept. 1, 1919; d. George Daniel and Bernice (Lucas) G. Diploma Stoneleigh Coll., 1939, Famous Artist Schs., Westport, Conn., 1955. Free-lance photographer, N.Y.C., 1941-52, Christmas card designer, Sherman, Conn., 1952-69, oil and watercolor, fine arts artist, Sherman, 1969—. Illustrator: Forever Flowers, 1979. Recipient Merit award Sheffield Art League, 1979, 81, 83, others; named Artist of Yr., Art League of Harlem Valley, 1981. Fellow Am. Artists Profl. League; mem. Salmagundi Club, Hudson Valley Art Assn., Acad. Artists, Nat League Am. Pen Women, Kent Art Assn., Inc. (press. 1970-72, 80-83, 85—, medal of Merit 1979), Berkshire Watercolor Soc. (co-founder, sec. 1984—), Housatonic Art League (v.p., bd. dirs. 1977-83). Avocations: camping; crafts. Home and Studio: Holiday Point Rd PO Box 406 Sherman CT 06784

GOODSTEIN-SHAPIRO, FLORENCE, artist, art historian; b. N.Y.C., July 22, 1931; d. Philip and Cecelia (Pletchnow) Goodstein; m. Ivan Shapiro, June 1951 (div. 1957); 1 child, Lisa Jean; m. John Albert Walton, Sept. 30, 1968. B.S. in Art Edn., CCNY, 1952; student Cooper Union, 1950-52, Hans Hofmann Sch. Fine Arts, N.Y.C., 1956-58; M.S., U. Minn., 1972. Typorgrapher-designer U. Chgo. Press, 1953-54; art historian Lakewood Community Coll., White Bear Lake, Minn., 1970-72, Minn. Inst. Fine Arts, Mpls., 1972-73. One-woman shows: Aspects Gallery, N.Y.C., 1964, Cooper Union Gallery, 1967, Kipsbay Gallery, N.Y.C., 1968, Kiehle Gallery, St. Cloud, Minn., 1983; group shows include Roko Gallery, 1963-65, Kenkeleba Gallery, N.Y.C., 1985, Peter M. David Gallery, Mpls., 1984, 85, Art Banque, Mpls., 1985; represented in permanent collections Martin Luther King Mus., Kym Bonython Collection, Hon. Jose and Mrs. Agnes Cahacho Collection, U. Minn. Mus. Recipient award for excellence U. Chgo. Press/Chgo. Art Mus., 1953, Publ. award Expts. in Art and Tech., 1970. Mem. Archaeol. Soc. Minn. Democrat. Studio: 8066 Ruth St NE Minneapolis MN 55432

GOODSTONE, ERICA MAE, health and physical educator; b. N.Y.C., Apr. 16, 1946; d. Morris Goodstone and Muriel (Carnel) Goodstone Schaeffer. B.A., Queens Coll., 1966, M.A., N.Y. U., 1970, Ph.D., 1983. Cert. elem. and high sch. educator, N.Y. Primary tchr. Pub. Sch. 219, Queens, N.Y., 1966-67; exec. sec. Gotham Rec. Co., N.Y.C., 1967; tchr. 4th grade Pub. Sch. 106K, Bklyn., 1967-68; tchr. phys. edn., Women's tennis varsity coach, women's gymnastics varsity coach, Bayside High Sch., Queens, 1969-74; assoc. prof. health and phys. edn. Fashion Inst. Tech., N.Y.C., 1974—; women's athletic dir., women's varsity tennis coach Fashion Inst. Tech., N.Y.C., 1974-82. adj. lectr. Kingsborough Community Coll., Bklyn., 1971-73, Manhattan Community Coll., 1983-85; pvt. practice sexual counseling, mind/body therapy. Mem. AAHPER, AAUW, Nat. Council Internat. Health, Soc. Sci. Study Sex. Democrat. Jewish. Contbr. articles to mags. Home: 200 E 27th St New York NY 10016 Office: Fashion Inst Tech 227 W 27 St New York NY 10001

GOODWIN, BEVERLY B., lawyer, b. Fairmont, W. Va., Jan. 30, 1945; d. Joseph T. and Pauline (Stansbury) Brown; m. Richard E. Goodwin, June 28, 1968. B.A. in Zoology, W. Va. U., 1966, M.S. in Physiology and Biophysics, 1969; J.D. cum laude Fordham U., 1975. Bar: N.Y. 1976, U.S. Patent and Trademark Office 1978. Research assoc. Mt. Sinai Sch. Medicine, N.Y.C., 1970-72; assoc. Fish & Neale, N.Y.C., 1975-81, Darby & Darby, N.Y.C., 1981—. Assoc. editor Fordham Law Rev., 1975; contbr. articles on osteoporosis and enzymology, 1968-72, on patent Law, 1973-75. Mem. Fordham Law Alumni Assn. (dir.), ABA, Bar Assn. City of N.Y. (com. on patents), N.Y. State Bar Assn. Home: 340 E 64th St New York NY 10021 Office: Darby & Darby Chrysler Bldg 405 Lexington Ave New York NY 10174

GOODWIN, CARLA ANNE, educational psychologist; b. Torrington, Conn., Sept. 20, 1947; d. Albert and Anne (Salvadori) Banelli; m. Robert Douglas Goodwin, Aug. 15, 1970; children—Jenifer, Kelly. B.S. in Elem. Edn., Eastern Conn. State U., 1969; M.Ed., Univ. Bridgeport, 1970. Tchr. South Elem. Sch., Holbrook, Mass., 1970-72; guidance counselor Holbrook High Sch., 1972-74; pt. time psychometrist Silver Lake Regional Sch., Kingston, Mass., 1978-79; pt. time instr. Quincy Jr. Coll., Mass., 1980-82; group therapist, 1982-84; supr. practicum for M.A. Candidates in Family Therapy Eastern Nazarene Coll., Quincy, 1985; cons., guardian ad litem Mass. Trial and Family Court, Plymouth Div., Brockton and Plymouth, 1982-86; psychotherapist, South Easton, Mass., 1978—. Bd. dirs. League Women Voters of Mass., Boston, 1982, 83, 86; pres. League Women Voters, Easton, 1979-81. Fellow Am. Acad. Family Mediators; mem. Mass. Assn. for Marriage and Family Therapy, Soc. for Research and Family Therapy, Nat. Council for Children's Rights. Republican. Roman Catholic. Avocations: golf, gardening, skiing, travel. Office: 820 Washington St South Easton MA 02375

GOODWIN, ELEANOR, government agency administrator; b. Fayetteville, N.C., Apr. 12, 1941; d. Vernon F. and Edna Pauline (Rountree) Goodwin; B.A., U. N.C., 1963; M.Ed., Ga. State U., 1978; student Meredith Coll., 1959-61. With C & S Bank, Atlanta, 1963-64, Am. Oil Co., Atlanta, 1964-66; mgmt. intern U.S. Civil Service Commn., Atlanta, 1966; with U.S. Office Personnel Mgmt., Atlanta, 1966—, asst. regional dir. S.E. Region, 1980-83, mgr. Atlanta Area office, 1983, chief staffing services, div., 1983-85, chief policy analysis div. compensation group, Washington, 1985—; adv. bd. Atlanta Federally Employed Women. Active, Am. Heart Assn., Arthritis Found., Soc. Prevention Blindness. Mem. Am. Soc. Tng. and Devel., Atlanta O.D. Network, Internat. Personnel Mgmt. Assn., Atlanta Women's Network, Fed. Exec. Inst. Alumni Assn., Am. Soc. Pub. Adminstrn., So. Ctr. Govtl. Studies. Unitarian. Clubs: Sierra, Atlanta Sporting. Contbr. articles to profl. jours. Home: 2032 Derby Ridge Ln Siver Spring MD 20910 Office: 1900 E St NW Washington DC 20045

GOODWIN, KATIE MAXINE-AGIN, rehab. co. exec., realtor; b. Cleve., Feb. 26, 1952; d. Jerome and Cecile Sarah (Gray) Agin; B.S., Ohio State U., 1975. Occupational therapist Ga. Retardation Center, Atlanta, 1975-76; rehab. specialist Internat. Rehab. Assocs., Atlanta, 1976-78, account rep., 1978-79, Midwest regional mktg. mgr., Chgo., 1979-80, dist. sales mgr., Detroit, 1980-82, sales tng. tchr., 1979-84; mem. rehab. counseling adv. com. Mich. State U., 1982-85; rehab. cons. ConServ Co., Southfield, 1986—. Mem. Ga. Self-Insured Assn. (com. rep. 1978-79), So. Assn. Workers Compensation Adminstrn., Mich. Assn. Rehab. Profls. (membership chmn. 1981-82), Mich. Rehab. Assn. (chmn.), Am. Occupational Therapy Assn., Nat. Rehab. Assn., Detroit Adjusters Assn., Nat. Assn. Profl. Saleswomen (Mich. publicity com.), NOW. Home: 26100 W 12 Mile Rd #234 Southfield MI 48034

GOODWIN, MARY CAROLYN, educator; b. Dallas, Mar. 10, 1952; d. Joel Franklin and Betty (Mashburn) G. B.A., Baylor U., Waco, Tex., 1974; M.Ed., E. Tex. State U., 1980. Cert. elem. tchr., Tex. Tchr., Dallas Ind. Sch. Dist., 1974—. Asst. leader Girl Scouts U.S.A., Dallas, 1977—, asst. lead Day Camp, 1983. Finalist for H. Ross Perot award, 1986; named Tchr. of Yr., H.S. Thompson Elem. Sch., 1986. Mem. Alpha Delta Kappa. Republican. Baptist. Home: 6110 Sul Ross Ln Dallas TX 75214

GOODWIN, SHARON, nurse, psychiatric consultant, therapist; b. N.Y.C., Oct. 19, 1944; d. Orland and Grace (Doonan) G. R.N., St. Louis City Hosp., 1965; Psychiat. Assoc., Mo. Inst. Psychiatry, St. Louis, 1971. Staff nurse St. Louis City Hosp., 1965-66, head nurse isolation, 1966-67, head nurse psychiatry, 1966-68, community psychiatry developer, 1967-81; dir. nursing Fairground Nursing Home, St. Louis, 1970-71; asst. dir. med. program Community Placement Program, St. Louis, 1972-79; asst. dir., med. advisor Places for People, St. Louis, 1979-82; alcoholism nurse St. Joseph Hosp., Houston, 1982—; community psychiatry cons. Mo. Mental Health Div., St. Louis, 1979-82; community psychiatry trainer U. Mo. Social Work, St. Louis, 1981-82; presenter Washington U. Social Services Dept., St. Louis, 1976-81. Mem. Internat. Assn. Psychosocial Rehab. Centers (presenter 1977). Home: 5501 Valerie Houston TX 77081 Office: St Joseph Hosp 1919 LaBranch Houston TX 77002

GOOTEE, JANE MARIE, lawyer; b. Jasper, Ind., July 5, 1953; d. Thomas Herbert and Anne Marie (Dreifke) G. B.A., Ind. U., 1974; J.D. cum laude, St. Louis U., 1977. Bar: Ind. 1977, Mo. 1978, Mich. 1980, Ohio 1983. Dep. atty. gen. State of Ind., Indpls., 1977-79; corp. atty. Dow Chem. Co., Midland, Mich., 1979-81; div. counsel, Cleve., 1981-84, sr. atty., 1984—; chmn. epidemiology instnl. rev. bd. Dow Chem. U.S.A., 1984—; pro-bono def. counsel Midland Circuit Ct., 1980-81; adj. prof. Saginaw Valley State Coll., University Center, Mich., 1979-80. Bd. dirs. Big Sisters of Midland, 1979-81, 84—. Mem. Bar Assn. Greater Cleve., ABA, Mo. Bar Assn., Mich. Bar Assn., Ohio Bar Assn., Assn. Trial Lawyers Am., Nat. C. of C. (environmental law adv. com., nat. chamber litigation ctr. 1985—). Home: 1412 Brentwood Dr Midland MI 48640 Office: Dow Chemical Co 2030 Dow Center Midland MI 48640

GOOTNICK, MARGARET MARY, management consultant, trainer; b. Stamford, Conn., Oct. 14, 1951. Ptnr., assoc. dir. David Gootnick Assocs., N.Y.C., 1978—. Editor: The Insurance Primer for the Consumer, 1977; (with others) The Nonsexist Communicator, 1983; co-editor, contbg. author: The Standard Handbook of Business Communication, 1984. Columnist Electronic Buyers' News, 1982-84. Office: David Gootnick Assocs Internat Plaza Suite 23B 303 E 43d St New York NY 10017

GOOTNICK, MARGERY FISCHBEIN, lawyer; b. Rochester, N.Y., Oct. 24, 1927; d. Morris R. and Regina (Kroll) Fischbein; m. Lester T. Gootnick, Mar. 1, 1952; children—Jonathon, David, Amy. B.A., Harvard U., 1949; J.D., Cornell U., 1952. Bar: N.Y. 1952. Assoc. Stone & Hoffenberg, Rochester, N.Y., 1952-55; sole practice, Rochester, 1968—; permanent arbitrator United Airlines, Internat. Assn. Machine and Aerospace Workers System Bd. of Adjustment, 1975—, U.S. Steel, United Steel Workers Am., 1976-80, Nat. Treasury Employees Union, IRS Discipline Panel, 1980—; chmn. Fgn. Service Impasse Disputes Panel, Washington, 1983—. Bd. dirs. Upstate chpt. Nat. Kidney Found., Rochester, 1980—; mem. Rep. Jud. Screening Com., Rochester, 1976—. Mem. Nat. Acad. Arbitrators (bd. dirs.), Soc. Profls. in Dispute Resolution, Fed. Bar Assn., ABA (labor law sect. arbitration com.), N.Y. State Bar Assn. (labor law sect. arbitration com.). Republican. Jewish. Home and Office: 46 Knollwood Dr Rochester NY 14618

GOPLEN, DONNELLE, counselor; b. Loco, Okla., Nov. 5, 1936; d. Allen R. and Dorothy R. (Carmichael) Bean; B.A. with honors, U. N.Mex., 1974, M.A., 1977; postgrad. Family Therapy Inst., 1981-82; m. Bruce C. Goplen, Sept. 26, 1969; children—Stephen Harvey, Donald Harvey. State welfare worker State Welfare Agy., N.Mex., 1975-77; counseling intern Presbyn. Hosp., Albuquerque, 1977; social worker State of N.Mex., 1977-78; vol. mental health aide Prince William County (Va.) Community Mental Health Center, 1978-79, coordinator Social Activity Center, after 1979, now family therapist, also mental health counselor, cons. Mem. Am. Assn. Counseling AAUW. Home: 18414 Cedar Dr Triangle VA 22172 Office: Prince William Mental Health Center 8807 Sudley Dr Manassas VA 22110

GOPPERS, VELTA MANEKS, chemist; b. Gostini, Latvia, Feb. 28, 1915; d. Karlis and Milda (Udris) Maneks; came to U.S., 1949, naturalized, 1954; B.S., U. Riga, 1942, M.S., 1944; m. Sergejs Goppers, 1941 (div. 1947); 1 dau., Ilze Goppers Oredson. Asst., U. Riga, 1940-44; analytical chemist Farben Industries, Germany, 1944-45; instr. Tech. Sch., Stuttgart, Germany, 1945-47; mgr. Pharmacy and Chem. Preparation Lab., Esslingen, Germany, 1947-49; analytical chemist Twin City Testing & Engring. Lab., St. Paul, 1949-52; technologist sci. dept. U. Minn., 1952-53, jr. scientist dept. physiology, 1953-59, sr. scientist environ. health, 1959-68, sr. scientist Space Sci. Center, 1968-70, Environ. Health and Research Center, 1970—, tchr. microchemistry and chromatography dept. environ. health Grad. Sch. Recipient Recognition award planetary quarantine dept. NASA, 1974; U. Minn. Sch. Pub. Health award, 1983. Fellow Am. Inst. Chemists, AAAS; mem. Am. Chem. Soc., Am. Indsl. Hygiene Assn. (treas. 1966-68), Sigma Xi, Iota Sigma Pi (pres. Mercury chpt. 1973-74, research award in chemistry 1976), Sigma Delta Epsilon (treas. 1966-69). Lutheran. Contbr. research articles to profl. publs. Home: 5164 Abercrombie Dr Minneapolis MN 55435 Office: Dept Environ Health U Minn Minneapolis MN 55455

GORACKE, LORETTA JEANNETTE MAHANNA, audiologist; b. Riverhead, N.Y., Apr. 10, 1952; d. Robert Dean and Kathleen Lucille (McCutcheon) Mahanna; m. James Lynn Goracke, Nov. 2, 1985. B.A., U. Kans., 1974; M.A., Wichita State U., 1976. Audiologist I, Beatrice State Devel. Ctr., Nebr., 1976-78, audiologist II, 1978-80, dir. dept. pub. instrn. speech and hearing services, 1980—. Mem. Lincoln Civic Chorus, 1981-85; mem. Beatrice Arboretum Com., 1986. Mem. Am. Speech, Lang. and Hearing Assn., Nebr. Speech, Lang. and Hearing Assn. (clin. service east com.), U. Kans. Alumni Assn., Nat. Student Speech and Hearing Assn., AAUW, DAR, Sigma Kappa, Beta Sigma Phi. Republican. Methodist. Lodges: Eastern Star, Daus. of Nile. Avocations: sailing; reading; needlework, music. Home: Route 1 Box 85 Pickrell NE 68422 Office: Beatrice State Devel Ctr 3000 Lincoln Blvd Beatrice NE 68310

GORALSKI, PATRICIA JEAN, lawyer; b. Paynesville, Minn., June 16, 1923; d. Arthur and Lillian Constance (Hanson) Schwarz; m. Edwin Anthony Goralski, Sept. 4, 1947. B.S.E., U. Minn., 1947, M.A., 1956, Ph.D., 1964, J.D., 1981. Bar: Minn. 1982, U.S. Dist. Ct. Minn. 1982, U.S. Ct. Appeals (8th cir.) 1983. Engring. aide U.S. Govt., Dayton, Ohio, 1943-45; with Maple Lake State Bank (Minn.), 1941-42; teller 1st Nat. Bank, Mpls., 1942; with Mdse. Nat. Bank, Chgo., 1951-52; tchr. Lincoln Pub. Schs. (Nebr.), 1947-49; tchr. Whittier Jr. High Sch., Lincoln, 1948-51; tchr. Blackhawk Jr. High Sch., Park Forest, Ill., 1954-55; tchr. Stillwater Sr. High Sch. (Minn.), 1962-66; instr., supr. Off Campus Student Tchrs., coordinator U. Minn., Mpls., 1955-62; research coordinator Mpls. Pub. Schs., 1966-68; adminstr. Hosp.-Surg. Plan R.R. Donnelley and Sons Co., Chgo., 1953-54; dir. Professions Devel. Sect., Minn. State Dept. Edn., St. Paul, 1968-77; sole practice, St. Paul, 1981—. Mem. ABA, Minn. State Bar Assn., Minn. Trial Lawyers Assn., Ramsey County Bar Assn., Assn. Trial Lawyers of Am., Phi Beta Kappa, Phi Kappa Phi, Pi Lambda Theta. Contbr. articles to profl. jours.

GORDON, BLANCHE, marriage counselor; b. Poland, June 15, 1910; d. Abraham and Zelda (Cohen) Swatlo; came to U.S., 1917, naturalized, 1937; m. Dan M. Gordon, June 20, 1932; 1 dau., Suzanne. B.S., Wayne State U., 1938; M.A., Columbia U., 1969; grad. Inst. Religion, Health, 1974. Guidance counselor Mental Health and Religion Inst., Hamtrarch, Mich., 1932-39; dir. research on progressive edn. Hamtrarch Bd. Edn., 1939-42; teaching assoc. dept. psychology Tchr.'s Coll. Columbia U., 1968-69; family service cons. Guidance Clinic Am. Hebrew Synagogues, N.Y.C., 1970—; counselor dept. home and family life Payne Whitney Hosp., N.Y.C., 1971—; assoc. prof. Cornell U.-N.Y. Hosp. Recipient Merit award League Cath. Women Detroit, 1945; honored by Pres. Roosevelt for work in women's div. of Democratic Party, 1941; recipient Merit award Fedn. Jewish Charities, 1970, Save-A-Marriage Inst., 1972. Mem. Nat. Council Family Relations, Tri-State Council Family Relations, Am. Assn. Marriage, Family Counselors, N.Y. Assn. Marriage Family Counselors, Hadassah. Democrat. Jewish. Club: Fedn. Women's Clubs. Contbr. poems to mags., anthologies and newspapers. Home: 155 W 68th St New York NY 10023

GORDON, CARIN MAURINE, lawyer, writer; b. Salem, Mass., Oct. 6, 1953; d. Frank David and Syril Estelle (Freiberg) G. B.A. cum laude, Conn. Coll., 1975; J.D., U. Miami, 1978. Bar: Mass. 1979. Assoc., Springer & Langson, P.C., Boston, 1979, Lindauer & Gordon, Salem, Mass., 1979-82; ptnr. Pidgeon & Gordon, Salem, 1982—; substitute instr. Northeastern U., Boston, 1979-83; guest lectr. Salem State Coll., 1979-83. Columnist Beacon Newsletter, 1981; contbr. articles to Marblehead Mag., 1980-82. Mem. Women's Bus. Enterprise Adv. Bd., 1982; chmn. task force taxes and legislation Women's Bus. Devel. Council, 1983—. Recipient Disting. Service award Conn. Coll., 1975; Bodenwin prizes, 1974, 75; Roger Sorino award U. Miami, 1978. Mem. Fla. Bar Assn., Mass. Bar Assn., Salem Bar Assn., Essex Bar Assn., Boston Bar Assn. Club: Conn. Coll. of Boston (dir. 1979-81). Office: Pidgeon & Gordon 21 Front St Salem MA 01970

GORDON, CAROL ANNE, retail executive; b. N.Y.C., Sept. 13, 1956; d. Randal Hunter and Mary Alice (Novinger) Gordon. B.A., So. Meth. U., 1977. Salesperson Nieman-Marcus, Dallas, 1977-79; steel trader Comml. Metals Co., Dallas, 1979-81; asst. mgr. sales Concrete Works Co., Dallas, 1981; translator Putman Oil Co., Ardmore, Okla., 1981; pres. Calligraphy by Carol Anne, University Park, Tex., 1979—; asst. mgr. children's dept. Neiman-Marcus, Prestonwood, Dallas, 1981-83; pres. Camaran, Dallas, 1983—; owner, mgr. The Cheese Shop, Dallas, 1983—. Presbyterian. Office: The Cheese Shop 68 Highland Park Village Dallas TX 75205

GORDON, CAROL HANCOCK JOHNSON, telephone company manager; b. Flushing, N.Y., Mar. 21, 1947; d. Carl and Ophelia Lucille (Balkcom) Hancock; B.A., Radford U., 1969; postgrad. Brenau Coll., 1983—; m. A.J. Gordon III, Sept. 1986; 1 dau., Heather Lynn Johnson. Service rep. Ohio Bell Telephone Co., Cleve., 1969-72, S. Central Bell, Birmingham, Ala., 1972-77; service rep. So. Bell, Atlanta, 1977-79, mgr. Phone Ctr. Store, Atlanta, 1979-81; asst. mgr. Residence Service Ctr., Decatur, Ga., 1981-82, asst. mgr. residence staff, Atlanta, 1982-84, asst. staff mgr. hdqrs., Atlanta, 1984-86; asst. staff mgr. mktg. support BellSouth Services, 1986—. Active United Way. Republican. Presbyterian. Home: 3948 Cedar Circle Tucker GA 30084 Office: 675 W Peachtree St NE Atlanta GA 30375

GORDON, CAROLYN ROSE, interior designer; b. Kansas City, Kans., Apr. 9, 1939; d. Peter M. and Louise M. Bizal; B.S. in Art Edn., Pittsburg (Kans.) State U., 1961; postgrad. U. Wash., 1961-62; m. Robert L. Gordon, June 24, 1961; children—Michelle, Peter. Tchr. art, public schs., Burien, Wash., 1961-63, head dept. art Redwood Wash. Sr. High Sch., 1966-67; tchr. art Purahou Sch., Honolulu, 1967-68; instr. interior design Harper Coll., 1973-74; founder, owner, pres. Design Workshop Ltd., Northbrook, Ill., 1980—; tchr. interior decorating for adult edn. Pres., Panhellenic of Hawaii, 1972-73; troop leader Moraines council Girl Scouts U.S.A., 1973-74. Named Miss Pittsburg, Pittsburg Jaycees, 1959. Mem. Am. Soc. Interior Design, Women in Mgmt., Nat. Assn. for Self-Employed, Nat. Assn. for Future Women, Nat. Assn. Female Execs., Theater in the Rough, Alpha Gamma Delta (decorating cons.). Episcopalian. Home and Office: 19811 Gulfwind Ct Houston TX 77094

GORDON, DRUSILLA DELECE, educator; b. Geary, Okla., Aug. 13, 1927; d. Bryan Jack and Vanda Johnnie (Browning) Griffin; student UCLA, 1945, U. Tex., 1945-48; B.S., U. Ark., 1949, Ed.M., 1951; postgrad. Tex. Christian U., 1956-57, U. Ark., 1965-66; Ed.D., U. Miss., 1974; m. Richard Allen Gordon, Jr., Aug. 16, 1952; 1 son, Richard Allen, III. Tchr., Corpus Christi (Tex.) Ind. Sch. Dist., 1951-52, St. Ann's Sch., Midland, Tex., 1963-65; mem. faculty Westark Community Coll., Ft. Smith Ark., 1966—, chmn. dept. psychology and edn., 1979-80, 85-86. NSF grantee, 1967. Mem. AAUP (pres. 1975-77), Ark. Two-Yr. Coll. Tchrs. Assn., NEA, Ark. Edn. Assn., Phi Delta Kappa, Phi Kappa Phi, Alpha Gamma Delta. Office: Westark Community Coll PO Box 3649 Fort Smith AR 72913

GORDON, ELLEN RUBIN, candy company executive; d. William B. and Cele H. Rubin; m. Melvin J. Gordon, June 25, 1950; children—Virginia L., Karen D., Wendy J., Lisa J. Student Vassar Coll., 1948-50; B.A., Brandeis U., 1965; postgrad. Harvard U., 1968. Vice-pres. product devel. Tootsie Roll Industries, Inc., Chgo., 1974-77, corp. sec., 1974-77, sr. v.p., 1977-78, pres., 1978—. Active com. on resources Harvard Med. Sch., vis. com.; assoc. Northwestern U., Chgo. Mem. Nat. Confectioners Assn. (chmn. trade relations com.), Nat. Confectioners Wholesale Assn. (chmn. trade relations com.). Office: Tootsie Roll Industries Inc 7401 S Cicero Ave Chicago IL 60629

GORDON, GRISELDA, university administrator; b. Battle Creek, Mich., Feb. 7, 1938; d. Edward Daniel and Teritha (Faulce) Daniel Immerman; m. Henry Dell Gordon, Oct. 25, 1957; children—Cornell A., Gary L., Cheri A., Patrick H. B.S. magna cum laude, Western Mich. U., 1973, M.S. in Adminstrn., 1980. Surg. nurse Borgess Hosp., Kalamazoo, 1958-66; attendant nurse Kalamazoo State Hosp., 1966-70; counselor, trainer Coll. Gen. Studies, Western Mich. U., Kalamazoo, 1970-73, dir. Martin Luther King program, 1975-80, asst. to v.p. for acad. affairs/dir. spl. programs, 1980—; supr. packaging dept. Peter Echrich & Co., Kalamazoo, 1974-75; lectr. in field. Designer, developer Western Mich. U. Mentor Program, 1980. Recipient award for invaluable contbn. Upward Bound Program at Western Mich. U., 1982. Mem. NAACP, Am. Assn. Univ. Adminstrs., Nat. Assn. Female Execs., Nat. Consortium for Black Profl. Devel., Delta Kappa Gamma (Outstanding Contbn. to field Edn. award Kalamazoo 1981). Home: 42818 N 30th St PawPaw MI 49079 Office: Western Mich U W Michigan Ave Kalamazoo MI 49008

GORDON, GUANETTA STEWART, writer, poet; b. Kansas City, Mo.; d. Samuel Lewis and Minnie Anna (Brown) Stewart; ed. Baker U., U. Kan.; m. Lynell F. Gordon; children—Stewart Lynell, Krista Sharon. Radio dramatist sta. KMBC, Kansas City, Mo.; radio script writer, dramatist, lectr., book reviewer; free lance writer; author: Songs of the Wind, 1953; Under the Rainbow Arch, 1965; Petals From the Moon, 1971; Shadow Within the Flame, 1973; Above Rubies, 1976, Red Are the Embers, 1980; The Aurora Tree, 1982, also poetry various mags. Recipient feature writing awards Nat. League Am. Pen Women, 1954, spl. award for quantity of good articles submitted to 1956 contest; named Kans. Poet of Year, Midwest Fedn. Chaparrals, 1966, J. Donald Coffin Book award Kans. Authors Club, 1981, award of personal achievement in writing, 1982; Della Crowder Miller Meml. award for Petrarchan sonnet, 1982; numerous other nat. and internat. awards in prose and poetry. Mem. Nat. League Am. Pen Women (pres. Alexander br. 1956-58, nat. 1st v.p. 1970-72), Poetry Soc. Am., Nat. Fedn. State Poetry Socs., Internat. Mark Twain Soc. (hon.), World Poetry Soc. (distinguished service citation 1970), Poetry Soc. Va., Ariz., Phoenix (pres. 1973) poetry socs., Phoenix Writers Club, Fedn. Chaparral Poets, Eugene Field Soc. (hon.), Kans. Authors Club (hon.), DAR, Delta Delta Delta. Address: 11847 Hacienda Dr Sun City AZ 85351

GORDON, JANET HILL, lawyer; b. N.Y.C.; d. James P. Hill; m. William J. Gordon (dec.); 1 dau., Gail Gordon McCale. B.F.A., Syracuse U.; LL.B. magna cum laude, Bklyn. Law Sch. Bar: N.Y. Ptnr. William J. Gordon, 1941-67; commr. conciliation 6th Jud. Dist., N.Y. State Conciliation Bur., 1967-73; vice chmn. Com. on Marriage and Family Counseling and Conciliation, Family Law Sect., ABA, 1971-74; legal research asst. to Chenango County Family, Surrogates' and County Ct. Judge, 1973-75; mem. N.Y. State Assembly, 1946-58; mem. N.Y. State Senate, 1959-62; chmn. N.Y. State Joint Legis. Com. on Matrimonial and Family Laws, 1955-62; del. N.Y. State Constl. Conv., 1967; mem. N.Y. Statewide Com. for White House Conf. on Children and Youth; Mohawk Valley Regional Conf. on Children and Youth; 1970; Del. N.Y. Govs. Conf. on Children and Youth, 1970; mem. Temporary State Commn. to Recodify Family Ct. Act, 1979-83. Bd. dirs. Chenango County Soc. for Prevention of Cruelty to Animals. Mem. Bklyn. Law Rev. Assn., ABA, N.Y. State Bar Assn., Chenango County Bar Assn., Delta Kappa Gamma. Episcopalian.

GORDON, JOAN I., lawyer; b. N.Y.C., Nov. 1, 1945; d. Morris and Dora (Mittman) G. A.B., Vassar Coll., 1967; M.A., Brown U., 1969; J.D., Am. U., 1974. Bar: Md. 1974, D.C. 1975, U.S. Dist. Ct. 1976, U.S. Supreme Ct. 1978, N.Y. 1981. Intern, N.Y. State Pub. Adminstrn., Albany, 1969-70; adminstrv. asst. to asst. commr. N.Y. State Health Dept., Albany, 1970-71; staff counsel Washington Suburban San. Commn., Hyattsville, Md., 1975-80; legal counsel and govt. affairs officer Montgomery Community Coll., Rockville, Md., 1980-84, gen. counsel, 1984—; research cons. Inst. Studies in Justice and Soc. Behavior, Am. U. Law Sch., Washington, 1974. Contbr.: Maryland Criminal Jury Instructions and Commentary, 1975. Mem. prospective students com. Vassar Coll., Washington, 1975-83; Democratic precinct vice-chmn. Montgomery County, 1976-82; mem. archtl. control com. Redland Crossing Homeowners Assn., Derwood, Md., 1982-84, bd. dirs., 1984—. Recipient Am. Jurisprudence award, 1972, 73. Mem. Nat. Assn. Women Lawyers (legis. com. 1976, council of dels. 1977-83), D.C. Bar Assn. Md. Bar Assn. Women's Bar Assn. Md., Montgomery County Bar Assn., Women's Bar Assn. Montgomery County, Nat. Assn. Coll. and Univ. Attys. (com. arrangements, continuing legal edn. com., com. on nat. office), Am. Corporate Counsel Assn. (non-profit counsel com.). Jewish. Home: 15909 Yukon Ln Derwood MD 20855 Office: Montgomery Community Coll 900 Hungerford Dr Rockville MD 20850

GORDON, JUDITH RUTH, courseware development company executive; b. Bklyn., July 24, 1939; d. William and Goldie Freda (Levy) G. B.S., Pa. State U., 1961; M.S.W., Columbia U., 1963; J.D., Golden Gate U., 1971. Cert. community coll. tchr. Group worker Jewish Child Care Assn., N.Y.C., 1963-64; sr. child welfare worker San Francisco Dept. Social Services, 1965-67, child welfare supr., 1968-76; sales trainer Century 21 Office, San Jose, Calif., 1977-80; v.p. courseware devel. Pinnacle Courseware, Inc., San Jose, 1982—. Founder Bay Area Big Sisters, Inc., 1967; vol. Good Samaritan Hosp., San Jose, 1977-82; vol. English as a Second Lang. instr.; arbitrator Better Bus. Bur., San Jose, 1985—; vol. various profl. and little theater groups, Bay Area, 1966—; co-founder Placement Suprs. Assn., No. Calif., 1975. Mem. Nat. Soc. Performance and Instrn., Coordinators of Data Processing Edn. (assoc.), Nat. Assn. Realtors, Calif. Assn. Realtors. Democrat. Jewish. Avocations: hiking; photography; writing poetry; racquetball; collecting science fiction books. Home: 841 Blossom Hill Rd #215 San Jose CA 95118 Office: Pinnacle Courseware Inc 841 Blossom Hill Rd Suite 215 San Jose CA 95123

GORDON, JUDY BETH, public relations executive; b. Neptune, N.J., Feb. 3, 1952; d. Jack I. and Myrna (Turzanowky) G. B.S. in Pub. Communications, Syracuse U., 1974. Prodn. asst. Sta. KPIX-TV, San Francisco, 1974, Sta. KRON-TV, San Francisco, 1975; publicist The Rowland Co., Inc., N.Y.C., 1976-77; TV producer Minutes Plus Prodns., N.Y.C., 1977; assoc. dir. The Rowland Co., Inc., 1978-80; sr. v.p. Daniel J. Edelman, Inc., N.Y.C., 1981—; dir. G.N.G. Enterprises Inc., Old Tappan, N.J., E.M. Cons. Group Inc., N.Y.C. Lobby gallery assoc. The Whitney Mus. of Am. Art, N.Y.C., 1984. Office: Daniel J Edelman Inc 1775 Broadway New York NY 10019

GORDON, JUNE, psychology educator, consultant; b. Oshkosh, Wis., June 17, 1929; d. Felix and Harriet (Fero) Staerkel; m. Donald Emmanuel Gordon, Feb. 6, 1951; children—Bonita, Judy, Teresa, Thomas, Alexander, Philip. B.S., Rollins Coll., 1971, M.Ed., 1974; Ed.S., U. Fla., 1976; Ed.D., Fla. State U., 1979; advanced study Jung Inst., Switzerland, 1982, U. Wis., 1984; imagery tng., London, 1985. Cert. sch. psychologist, Fla.; lic. mental health counselor. Free lance artist, Calif., Fla., Wis., Ala., 1958-74; coordinator women's program Seminole Community Coll., Sanford, Fla., 1974-84; adj. prof. psychology Rollins Coll. and Seminole Community Coll., Winter Park, Fla., 1974-84; pvt. practice counseling mental health service Sanford, 1984—; bd. dirs. Project Wedge, Central Fla. Ednl. Consortium for Women, Orlando; cons. in field. Artist: painting Mother; Mother, The CIA is Coming (Wis. Blue Ribbon 1967). Author: (with others) Divorce, 1977; Legal Rights, 1979. Contbr. articles to profl. jours. Founder, Central Fla. Commn. on Status of Women, 1975; pres. Seminole County Mental Health Ctr., Inc., Fla., 1980-81; bd. dirs. Met. Alcohol Council, Orlando, 1981-83, Citrus council Girl Scouts U.S.; committeewoman Democratic Exec. Com. of Seminole County, 1981-84; gov.'s appointee East Central Fla. Regional Planning Council, 1983-85. Recipient Fannie Lou Hamers Human Rights award NOW, 1980. Mem. AAUW (pres. 1983-85), Nat. Wellness Assn., Jung Soc. North Fla., Fla. Assn. Community Colls., Future Soc. Avocations: all artistic and creative activities, designing, traveling, gardening. Home: 309 Idyllwilde Dr Sanford FL 32771

GORDON, LENORE DORIS, microbiology educator; b. Shenandoah, Pa., Nov. 23, 1931; d. Daniel and Betty (Mainker) G.; B.S. cum laude, Fairleigh Dickinson U., 1955; M.A. in Edn., Health Care, Central Mich. U., 1977. Microbiologist, Babies Hosp., Columbia U., N.Y.C., 1955-59, Belinson Hosp., Petah Tikva, Israel, 1960-72; head microbiology sect. Barnert Meml. Hosp.,

Paterson, N.J., 1972-75; instr. infection control U. Medicine and Dentistry N.J., Newark, 1977—; participant profl. confs. Mem. Am. Soc. Microbiology, Assn. Practitioners in Infection Control, Am. Soc. Med. Tech., Central Mich. U. Alumni Assn. Home: 215 Passaic Ave Apt 5-J Passaic NJ 07055

GORDON, LILLIAN PATRICIA, municipal corrections administrator; b. Lawrenceville, Va., Oct. 31, 1952; d. Wyatt and Marian Lee (Blackwell) Archer; m. Carroll Gordon, Feb. 23, 1981. B.S. in Bus. Adminstrn., Morgan State U., 1976. Lic. social work assoc., Md. Taxpayer service rep. IRS, Balt., 1975-76; community services specialist Balt. Mayor's Office, 1977-79; social worker Balt. City Jail, 1979-81, corrections classification supr., 1981-86, work release dir., 1986—; loaned exec. United Way Central Md., Balt., 1985. Mem. fin.-budget com. NAACP, Balt., 1985-86. Recipient Community Service award United Way, Balt., 1985. Mem. Nat. Assn. Female Execs., Am. Correctional Assn., Am. Jail Assn., Frat. Order Correctional Assocs. Democrat. Baptist. Avocations: reading; camping. Home: 1708 N Broadway Baltimore MD 21213 Office: Balt City Jail 729-31 Graves St Baltimore MD 21202

GORDON, LISA BRETT, helicopter company executive, aviation-airline maintenance, legal consultant; b. Tokyo, Nov. 19, 1957; came to U.S., 1958; d. Paul Lawerance and Suzy Eve (Aronson) Rosenberg; m. Andrew Pierre Gordon, Aug. 15, 1976 (div. Sept. 1980). Grad. Coll. Redwoods, 1979—; postgrad. Embry Riddle Aero. U., 1983-85, U. Tex.-Arlington, 1984—, Lewis and Clark Coll., 1984. Biomed. engr. Gen. Hosp., Eureka, Calif., 1975-77; bus. mgr. Eureka Aero, Inc., 1977-80; maintenance cons. West Air Airlines, Chico, Calif., 1980-81, Sierra West, Eureka, Calif., 1981-82; bus. mgr. Aircraft at Your Call, Hillsboro, Oreg., 1982-83; prodn. control adminstr. Heli-Dyne Systems, Ft. Worth, 1983—; legal researcher, asst. med. and aviation Dr. Richard Tilden, Portland, Oreg., 1984—; pilot instr. Redwoods Flying Club, Eureka, Calif., 1981-82. Author: (with Michael Cavanagh) Aircraft Inspection, 1980. Coordinator local aviation community Airshow, Eureka, Calif., 1982—. Mem. Helicopter Assn. Am. (cert. 1983), Aircraft Owners and Pilots Assn., Whirly Girls. Democrat. Jewish. Clubs: Alas Malamuk (Arlington, Tex.). Home: 1991 Wembley Pl Lake Oswego OR 97034

GORDON, MARYBETH, social worker, therapist; b. St. Louis, July 14, 1952; d. John and Marie Gordon; B.A. in Philosophy, So. Ill. U., Edwardsville, 1975; M.S.W., Washington U., St. Louis, 1980. With Southwestern Bell Telephone Co., St. Louis, plant staff evaluator, 1975-77, plant analysis supr., chief assigner, 1977-78, research asso., 1978, plant service evaluator, 1978-79; sch. social worker Community Sch. Dist. 9, Granite City, Ill., 1979-83, Kaskaskia Spl. Edn. Ctr., Centralia, Ill., 1983—. Mem. Nat. Assn. Social Workers, N.Am. Assn. Christian Social Workers, Assn. Women in Psychology, Ill. Assn. Sch. Social Workers, Am. Fedn. Tchrs. Address: care PO Box 86 Granite City IL 62040

GORDON, MARYLU TRACEWELL, lawyer, political scientist; b. Kansas City, Mo., Oct. 28, 1935; d. Arthur Nelson and Helen Louise (Boone) Tracewell; m. Dale O. Turner, Oct. 30, 1954 (div. 1961); m. 2d, James Dell Gordon, Sept. 11, 1963; children—Kevin Dell, Kent Tracewell, Tracy Helen, Kelly Claire. Student Lindenwood Coll., St. Charles, Mo., 1953-54, Washington U., St. Louis, 1963; B.A., Okla. U., 1965, M.A., 1966, postgrad., 1967-69; J.D., Oklahoma City U., 1975. Bar: Okla. 1975, U.S. Dist. Ct. (we. dist.) Okla. 1975, U.S. Ct. Appeals (10th cir.) 1976, U.S. Tax Ct. 1976. Instr. polit. sci. No. Okla. Coll., Tonkowa, 1966-67; tchr. history Moore (Okla.) High Sch., 1967-68; asst. prof. polit. sci. Oklahoma City U., 1969-75; asst. city atty., Oklahoma City, 1977-82; ptnr. Gordon & Gordon, Oklahoma City, 1982—; guest lectr. U. S.C., 1975, Central State U., Edmond, Okla., 1975, Taft Inst., Oklahoma City, 1972-76. Contbr. to Justice in America, 1973. Bd. dirs. New World Sch., 1972; pres. bd. dirs. Youth Services of Oklahoma County, 1984; mem. ACLU, NOW; resource person, lectr. Okla. Humanities Council, 1973-79. OEO grantee, 1971. Mem. ABA, Oklahoma County Bar Assn., Okla. Bar Assn., Pi Sigma Alpha. Club: Gourmet of Oklahoma City (chef). Home: 2501 NW 63d St Oklahoma City OK 73116 Office: Gordon & Gordon 1350 American First Tower Oklahoma City OK 73102

GORDON, MURIEL ANN CORRIGAN, librarian; b. Cleve., Dec. 14, 1930; d. Robert Paine and Florence Ann (Dittman) Corrigan; m. Gerald Charles Gordon, Aug. 15, 1959 (dec. Feb. 1979); children—Laura Anne, Robert Corrigan. B.S. in History, U. Rochester, 1953; M.S. in Edn., SUNY-Brockport, 1959. Cert. elem. tchr., N.J., N.Y., social studies tchr., N.J. Tchr., Durand-Eastman Sch., Irondequoit, N.Y., 1956-59, Lunnenburg (Mass.) Elem. Sch., 1959-60, Ludwigsburg Am. Elem. Sch., Germany, 1961-65; librarian St. Mary's Hall-Doane Acad., Burlington, N.J., 1980—. Mem. exec. bd. Parents and Friends Assn. Vineland Devel. Ctr. (N.J.), 1972—; adv. council Pub. Advt. for Developmentally Disabled, 1978—; ch. sch. supt. Christ the King Episcopal Ch., Willingboro, N.J., 1973—; bd. dirs. Burlington County (N.J.) chpt. ARC, 1966-72, Hawthorne Park PTA, 1977-80. Mem. ALA, AAUW, Burlington County Sch. Media Assn., Ind. Sch. Library Assn. Home: 83 Holstone Ln Willingboro NJ 08046 Office: Saint Marys Hall Doane Academy Riverbank St Burlington NJ 08016

GORDON, PAMELA ANN, pharmaceutical company executive, cytotechnologist; b. Bklyn., Feb. 17, 1953; d. Norman Anthony and Louise Regina (Cooper) G.; student Barry Coll., 1971-74; Cytotechnologist, U. Miami, 1975; B.B.A., Fla. Atlantic U., 1980. Staff cytotechnologist, instr. U. Miami (Fla.) Med. Sch., 1975-77; chief cytotechnologist Diagnostic Lab., North Palm Beach, Fla., 1977-78; sales rep. Glaxo Inc., N.C., 1981-85, dist. mgr., Ft. Lauderdale, Fla., 1985—; didactic and microscopic instr. U. Miami Sch. Cytotechnology, 1975-77. Mem. Am. Soc. Cytology, Am. Soc. Clin. Pathologists, Fla. Soc. Cytology, So. Assn. Cytotechnologists, Delta Sigma Pi. Home: 9933 Edelweiss Circle Shawnee Mission KS 66203 Office: 1900 W Commercial Blvd Fort Lauderdale FL 33309

GORDON, RITA SIMON, civic leader, former nurse, educator; b. Frederick, Md., Feb. 1, 1929; d. Jacob and Anna (Stein) Simon; m. Paul Perry Gordon, July 2, 1948; children—Stuart Yael, Hugh Ellis, Myla. R.N., Frederick Meml. Hosp., 1949. R.N., Md. Surg. staff nurse Prince Georges Gen. Hosp., 1949-50; pediatric staff nurse (part-time) Frederick Meml. Hosp., 1950-54; surg. office nurse, 1960-62; nurse blood program ARC 1954-83. Author: (with Paul P. Gordon) Textbook History of Frederick County. 1975. Mem. Frederick County Bd. Edn., 1975-85, pres., 1979-80, 83-84; mem. exec. com. Md. Assn. Bd. Edn., Annapolis, 1978-85, pres., 1983-84; bd. assocs. Hood Coll., Frederick, 1985—; mem. Md. Task Force on Ednl. Funding, Annapolis, 1983-84, Md. Values Edn. Com., Annapolis, 1979-83, Fed. Relations Network, Nat. Sch. Bd. Assn., 1978-82; bd. dirs. Community Commons, Frederick, 1983-85; area field rep. Am. Field Service, Frederick, 1970-75; assoc., mem. publicity com. 1973 Snow Ball, Frederick Meml. Hosp. Aux.; past bd. dirs., v.p. Beth Sholom, 1982-83, historian, past pres. Beth Sholom Sisterhood; past bd. dirs. Nat. Council Jewish Women, Frederick; vol. aide Frederick Waverly Elem. Sch.; officer, chmn. fund raising North Market St. Sch.; active Girl Scouts U.S.A.; past pres., v.p. Frederick Improvement Found. Editor, Town Crier. Named Woman of Yr., Bus. and Profl. Woman's Club, 1975; Frederick's Outstanding Woman, Internat. Woman's Yr., 1975. Mem. Md. Hist. Soc., Internat. Graphoanalysis Soc., Md. Jewish Hist. Soc., Frederick County Hist. Soc. Clubs: Woman's Civic (Frederick); Rotary Inner Wheel (Gaithersburg, M.D.) (v.p. 1975). Avocation: historical research. Home: 202 Meadowdale Ln Frederick MD 21701

GORDON, SUSAN AMBER, venture capital co. exec.; b. N.Y.C., Sept. 9, 1954; d. George S. and Jeanne Gordon Goldman; B.A. summa cum laude with honors in Psychology, Barnard Coll., Columbia U., 1976. Mng. editor TUBE Mag., Doubleday & Co., N.Y.C., 1977-78; with Boardroom Reports, N.Y.C., 1978-80, book mktg. dir., 1980; v.p. Weinrich-Zitzmann-Whitehead, 1980-81; v.p. Biotech Capital Corp., 1981—. Mem. Phi Beta Kappa. Office: Biotech Capital Corp 600 Madison Ave New York NY 10022

GORDON, VERONA CHRISTOFFERSON, nursing educator; b. Waubun, Minn., Oct. 3, 1923; d. Gunder and Clara (Sorenson) Christofferson; m. A.H. Gordon, May 17, 1947 (dec. 1982); children—Candace, Elizabeth, Christine, Susan, Robert. B.S. in Nursing Edn., U. Minn., Mpls., 1955, M.S. in Psychiatric Nursing, 1970, Ph.D. in Higher Edn., 1976. Psychiat. charge nurse VA Hosp., Mpls., 1966-67; instr. pediatrics Swedish Hosp. Sch. Nursing, Mpls., 1967-71; assoc. prof. psychiat. nursing Gustavus Adolphus Coll., St. Peter, Minn., 1971-78; prof. psychiat. nursing U. Minn., Mpls., 1978—. Author research studies and health care manuals. Trustee Met. Med. Ctr., Mpls., 1977—. Recipient edn. scholarship Finnish Ministry Edn., Helsinki, 1983, Edgar M. Clarkson award Gustavus Adolphus Coll., 1976, named Woman of Achievement, Minn. LWV, 1979. Mem. Royal Coll. Nursing Research London, Am. Nurses Assn., Minn. Nurses Assn. (mem. polit. bd. 1980-85, commn. on edn. 1981-83, named Nurse of Yr. 1985), Sigma Theta Tau, Sigma Xi, Phi Lambda Theta, Phi Delta Kappa. Democrat. Lutheran. Office: Univ Minn Sch Nursing 6-101 Health Scis Unit F 308 Harvard St SE Minneapolis MN 55455

GORE, CATHERINE ANN, social worker; b. Mullens, W.Va., Feb. 2, 1937; d. Bernard Joseph and Agnes Cecilia (Spradling) G.; B.A., Thomas More Coll., 1968; M.S.W., Ohio State U., 1971, M.A. in Pub. Adminstrn., 1983. Caseworker, Cath. Charities, Cin., 1967-69, 71-72; psychiat. social worker Mcpl. Ct. Psychiat. Clinic, Cin., 1973; mem. faculty Ct. Psychiat. Center, U. Cin., 1974-80, instr. psychiat. social work, social work supr., coordinator diagnostic and treatment services, 1974-77, asst. prof. psychiat. social work, coordinator consultation services, 1979-80; cons. Hamilton County Welfare Dept.; instr. No. Ky. U.; grad. research assoc. Ohio State U., 1981-85. Mem. Nat. Assn. Social Workers, Acad. Cert. Social Workers. Democrat. Roman Catholic. Home: 2599 Scioto View Ln Columbus OH 43221

GORE, CONNIE WALKER, lawyer; b. Oklahoma City, May 2, 1946; d. Bonham and Ruby (Damron) Walker; m. Richard J. Gore, Dec. 30, 1966; children—Jeffrey Matthew, Cara Allison. B.A. with distinction, U. Okla., Norman, 1967; J.D., 1975. Bar: Okla. 1975. Assoc., McAfee & Taft, Oklahoma City, 1975-84, stockholder, 1979-84; mem. Mahaffey & Gore, P.C., Oklahoma City, 1984—. Editor: Oklahoma Law Rev., 1973-75. Pres. Oklahoma Art Ctr. Assn., Oklahoma City, 1983. Mem. Order Coif, Phi Beta Kappa, Phi Delta Phi, Kappa Kappa Gamma. Episcopalian. Home: 1704 Camden Way Oklahoma City OK 73116 Office: Mahaffey & Gore 400 Main Pl 420 West Main Oklahoma City OK 73102

GORE, SAUNDRA SUE, nurse; b. Terre Haute, Ind., July 23, 1942; d. Robert Warren and Reba Louise (Burkholder) Guyer; diploma in nursing, Barnes Hosp., St. Louis, 1963; m. Neil Robert Gore, Mar. 4, 1967; 1 son, Vance Robert. Staff and head nurse cardiothoracic and coronary care Barnes Hosp., 1963-67, 70-71; mem. staff San Pedro (Calif.) Peninsula Hosp., 1968-70, 74—, dir. cardiology, 1979—; CPR instr. Cert. critical care nurse. Mem. Am. Heart Assn., Am. Assn. Critical Care Nurses, Am. Nursing Service Adminstrs., Nat. Mgmt. Assn. (pres. local chpt. 1983-84, nat. bd. dirs. 1984—). Contbr. articles to profl. jours. Home: 3534 Newridge Dr Rancho Palos Verdes CA 90274 Office: 1300 W 7th St San Pedro CA 90732

GORENA, MINERVA, educator; b. Edinburg, Tex., Mar. 30, 1943; d. Humberto and Eva (Benavides) Gorena; B.A., Pan Am. Coll., 1963; M.Ed., U. Tex., Austin, 1975. Tchr., Hidalgo County Common Sch. Dist., Runn, Tex., 1963-64, Mission (Tex.) Ind. Sch. Dist., 1964-67, Pharr-San Juan-Alamo Ind. Sch. Dist., Pharr, Tex., 1967-69; counselor Out-of-Sch. Neighborhood Youth Corps, asso. City County Econ. Devel. Corp., Edinburg, Tex., 1969-70; materials specialist Title VII Bilingual Edn. Program, Region XIII Edn. Service Center, Austin, Tex., 1970-74; cons. div. bilingual edn. Tex. Edn. Agy., Austin, 1974-77; mgr. user services Nat. Clearinghouse for Bilingual Edn./Inter-Am. Research Assos., Inc., Rosslyn, Va., 1978-81, asso. dir., 1981—, exec. asso. 1978—. NDEA fellow, 1967. Mem. Austin Area Assn. for Bilingual Edn. (sec. 1975-76), Nat. Assn. for Bilingual Edn. (del. 1979), Tex. State Tchrs. Assn. (Region XIII chpt. pres. 1973-74), Nat. Assn. Female Execs., Va. Assn. Bilingual Edn., Va. Assn. Hispanic Am. Democrats, Nat. Assn. Latino Elected Ofcls., YMCA, Phi Delta Kappa. Roman Catholic. Editor: Information and Materials to Teach the Cultural Heritage of the Mexican American, 1972, Resources in Bilingual Education: A Preliminary Guide to Government Agency Programs of Interest to Minority Language Groups, 1979; Sources of Materials for Minority Languages: A Preliminary List, 1979. Home: 2803 S Columbus St Arlington VA 22206 Office: 1555 Wilson Blvd Suite 605 Rosslyn VA 22209

GORENSTEIN, BERNA CECILLE,, political consultant; b. Chgo., May 21, 1941; d. Edward A. and Hilda (Goldblatt) Gorenstein; m. Lee W. Huebner, May 20, 1978; children—Charles Robert, David William. Researcher and writer staff of Nelson A. Rockefeller, 1964-77, mem. polit. staff, 1964-69, dir. research, 1973-75; asst. to Hugh Morrow, 1969-73; asst. to dir. communications N.Y. State, 1969-73; dir. research vice presdl. staff and press officer, 1975-76; study dir. Am. Conservation Assn. on Land Use Planning in Catskills, 1977-78. Trustee Am. Library in Paris, 1980—, Women's Inst. for Continuing Edn., 1980—; bd. dirs. Ripon Soc., 1971—; bd. trustees Vocat. Found., 1975—.

GORG, JANET TAIT, media buyer; b. St. Louis, Jan. 9, 1956; d. Wesley Ernest Bernard and Jane Cora (Tait) G. B.A., Bloomsburg State U., 1978; student Marshall U., 1978-79. Draftsman, Henkels & McCoy, Blue Bell, Pa., 1978-79; grad. asst. Marshall U., 1978-79; dir. mktg. Community Fed. Savs. & Loan, Blue Bell, Pa., 1979-81; media buyer Dallas, Leonard & Pease, Inc., Bala Cynwyd, Pa., 1982-84, media buyer/account coordinator, 1984—. Episcopalian. Home: 224 Forrest Ave Ambler PA 19002 Office: Dallas Leonard & Pease Inc Two Bala Plaza Suite 607 Bala Cynwyd PA 19004

GORGA, BARBARA ANNE, nurse; b. N.Y.C., Apr. 16, 1952; d. Frank William and Florence Alvina (Melville) Adamec; m. Peter Louis Gorga, Jr., Nov. 18, 1973. A.Nursing summa cum laude, No. Va. Community Coll., 1983; lic. practical nurse diploma, Misericordia Hosp., 1972. Lic. R.N., N.J. Lic. practical nurse Misericordia Hosp., Bronx, N.Y., 1972-74, Surg. staff nurse, 1976-80; gerontology nurse, clin. coordinator Rosemont Nursing Home, Pensacola, Fla., 1974-76; nurse Mountainside Hosp., Montclair, N.J., 1983—, counselor diabetes, 1983—. Mem. Nursing Policies in Govt. Coalition, N.J., 1984—; vol. cardiovascular screening Mason Dist. Park, Alexandria, Va., 1981-83. Mem. Council Med. Surg. Nursing, N.J. State Nurses Assn., Am. Nurses Assn., Phi Theta Kappa (ways and means com. 1982-83), Student Nurses Assn. Va. (treas. 1981-83). Republican. Roman Catholic. Avocations: painting; needleworking; refinishing furniture; swimming; skiing. Home: 15 Hawthorne Ave Bloomfield NJ 07003

GORLIN, CATHY ELLEN, lawyer; b. Shields Twp., Ill., July 25, 1953; d. Robert James and Marilyn (Alpern) G.; m. Marshall Howard Tanick, Feb. 20, 1982. B.A. (summer scholar), Wesleyan U., 1975; J.D., U. Minn., 1978. Bar: Minn. 1978. Law clk. Minn. Atty. Gen.'s Office, St. Paul, summer 1976, Mpls. and Bloomington City Atty.'s Office, 1977-78; assoc. Mullin, Weinberg & Daly, Mpls., 1978; law clk. to judges Hennepin County Family Ct., Mpls., 1979-80, temp. referee, summer 1980; assoc. Larkin, Hoffman, Daly & Lindgren, Ltd., Mpls., 1980-84; ptnr. Best & Flanagan, 1984—; sec. Hennepin Lawyer Mag., 1983—; chmn. Minn. Women Lawyers Appointments Com., Mpls., 1983—. Contbr. articles to legal publs.; guest appearances radio. Advance person Vice-Pres. Mondale, 1979, vol. various polit. candidates; del. 3d dist. conv., Minn., 1980-84. named Atty. of Month, Larkin, Hoffman, Daly & Lindgren, Ltd., 1983. Mem. ABA, Minn. Bar Assn. (chair elect 1984—), Hennepin County Bar Assn. (rep. to child support task force 1982, chmn. exec. com. family law sect., chmn. sect. 1982—), Minn. Trial Lawyers Assn., Jewish Bus. and Profl. Women's Group (dir., support group coordinator), Minn. Women's Network (dir.), Jewish Family and Children Service Counseling Com., West Suburban C. of C., Golden Valley Kennedy's Addition Women's Group. Democrat. Jewish. Home: 1230 Angelo Dr Golden Valley MN 55422 Office: Best & Flanagan 3500 IDS Tower Minneapolis MN 55402

GORLIN, WINIFRED CABITT, broadcasting company executive; b. Boston; d. Frank and Esta (Goldstein) Leifer; children—Stephen Mitchell Cabitt, Jill Ilene Cabitt. B.A., Emerson Coll., Boston, 1955; postgrad. in Communications, U. Chgo., 1968. Cert. tchr., Mass. Dir. radio-TV programs Mass. Heart Assn., 1966-71; commr. Mass. State Cable TV Commn., 1971-75; cons. State Charter Revision Commn., N.Y.C., 1976; sr. editor program practices CBS-TV, N.Y.C., 1977-78, mgr. adminstrn., 1978-81, dir. program practices, 1981—. Producer, dir. numerous TV commls. and programs in med. and ednl. fields. Editor: N.Y. Times Ency. of TV, 1977. Founder, trustee Heart Research Found., 1968—; mem. Mass. Consumer Council, Citizens Com. for Children of N.Y., 1974—, instructional TV bd. Archdiocese of N.Y., 1974—, Communications Com. Nat. Safety Council, 1980-84. Recipient Rome Betts award Am. Heart Assn., 1971—, Soc. Heart Assn. award, 1971. Mem. Internat. Radio and TV Soc. Address: CBS Broadcast Group CBS Inc 51 W 52d St New York NY 10019

GORMAN, FAYE ANNE, government relations specialist; b. Newton, Mass., July 29, 1954; d. Paul Francis and Grace Marie (Sweeney) Gorman. B.A., Trinity Coll., Washington, 1976. Asst. to mgr. state and local affairs Nat. Soft Drink Assn., Washington, 1976-80; govt. relations rep. Dow Corning Corp., Washington, 1980—, coordinator polit. action com., 1980—, dir. com., 1981—. Mem. Women in Govt. Relations, Am. League Lobbyists. Republican. Roman Catholic. Club: Capitol Hill. Home: 3804A Steppes Ct Falls Church VA 22041 Office: Dow Corning Corp 1800 M St NW Washington DC 20036

GORMAN, JACQUELIN AMBLER, lawyer; b. Balt., Feb. 8, 1955; d. Kenneth Aubrey and Jacquelin Ambler (Woods) Gorman; m. Kenneth Wayne Slutsky, Dec. 29, 1978. B.A. magna cum laude, Bowdoin Coll., 1976; J.D., UCLA, 1982. Bar: Calif. 1982. Account exec. So. Bell Mktg. Co., Atlanta, 1976-79; assoc. firm Gibson, Dunn & Grutcher, Los Angeles, 1981-83; staff atty. Centinela Hosp., Los Angeles, 1984-86. Articles editor Fed. Communications Law Jour., Los Angeles, 1981-82. James Bowdoin scholar Bowdoin Coll., 1975. Mem. Los Angeles Bar Assn. (hospice com. 1982—). Democrat. Episcopalian. Office: Centinela Hosp Med Ctr 555 E Hardy St Inglewood CA 90307

GORMAN, JEAN ANN, telecommunications company executive; b. Maracaibo, Venezuela, Nov. 29, 1957 (parents Am. citizen); d. Bernard Ellis and F. Jean (Guess) Hendricks; m. Gerald Joseph Gorman, Apr. 20, 1985. B.A., Smith Coll., 1981. Mktg. analyst Lifelab Corp., N.Y.C., 1981-83; copier sales specialist Pitney Bowes Inc., Woodside, N.Y., 1983-85; account exec. MCI Telecommunications, N.Y.C., 1985—. Mem. Nat. Assn. Female Execs. Home: 340 E 93 St Apt 6E New York NY 10128 Office: MCI Telecommunications 1301 Ave of Americas New York NY 10019

GORMAN, LILLIAN R., banker, indsl. psychologist; b. N.Y.C., July 4, 1953; d. Helmuth H. and Ida A. (Malitsch) Degen; B.A. in Psychology, Lehman Coll., City U. N.Y., 1975; M.A., Case Western Res. U., 1978, Ph.D. in Indsl. Psychology, 1979; M.B.A. in Corp. Fin., U. So. Calif., 1986; m. Mark R. Gorman, Oct. 23, 1976. Econ. benefits asst. Girl Scouts U.S.A., N.Y.C., 1971-75; staff cons. Personnel Research & Devel. Corp., Cleve., 1977-78; research asst. Case Western Res. U., 1975-79; v.p. human resource planning and info. systems First Interstate Bank Los Angeles, 1979-84; v.p., corp. mgr. human resources strategic planning First Interstate Bancorp., Los Angeles, 1985—; cons. psychology. Chmn. bd. dirs. INROADS/Los Angeles, 1986—. Mem. Am. Psychol. Assn., Personnel Testing Council So. Calif., Human Resource Planning Soc., Phi Beta Kappa. Lutheran. Home: 2305 Overland Ave Los Angeles CA 90064 Office: 707 Wilshire Blvd Los Angeles CA 90017

GORMAN, LINDA KORN, psychologist; b. Phila., June 1, 1953; d. Samuel and Muriel (Grass) Korn; B.A., Dickinson Coll., 1975; M.A., Temple U., 1978, Ph.D., 1980; m. Thomas Joseph Gorman, Jan. 7, 1979. Cert. sch. psychologist, N.J., Pa.; lic. psychologist, Pa. Clinic asst. Psychol. Services Ctr., Temple U., 1976-77, clinic supr., teaching asst., 1978-80; clin. psychology intern Norristown State Hosp., Pa., 1977-78; psychologist Program of Aux. Services for Students, non-pub. schs., Bala Cynwyd, Pa., 1980-83; psychologist St. Gabriel's Hall, Phoenixville, Pa., 1981, Phoenixville Psychol. Assocs., 1982-83, Hampton Psychol. Ctr., Huntingdon Valley, Pa., 1983; asst. dir. dept. psychology, dir. psychology internship program Eastern State Sch. and Hosp., Trevose, Pa., 1983—; pvt. clin. practice, Plymouth Valley, Pa., 1985—. Mem. Am. Psychol. Assn., Eastern Psychol. Assn., Pa. Psychol. Assn., Phila. Soc. Clin. Psychologists, Assn. Advancement Psychology, AAUW (lectr. 1982), Mensa, Dickinson Coll. Alumnae, Temple U. Alumnae, Phi Beta Kappa Alumnae, Pi Beta Phi Alumnae, Psi Chi, Alpha Psi Omega. Home: 352 Brighton Rd Norristown PA 19401 Office: 3740 Lincoln Hwy Trevose PA 19047

GORMAN, MARCIE SOTHERN, franchise executive; b. N.Y.C., Feb. 25, 1949; d. Jerry R. and Carole Edith (Frendel) Sothern; B.S., Memphis State U., 1970; m. N. Scott Gorman, June 14, 1969 (div.); children—Michael Stephen, Mark Jason. Tchr., Memphis City Sch. System, 1970-73; tng. dir. Weight Watchers of Palm Beach County and Weight Watchers So. Ala., Inc., West Palm Beach, Fla., 1973—, area dir., then pres., 1977—; pres. Markel Ads, Inc. Cubmaster Boy Scouts Am., 1984—; team sponsor Am. Youth Soccer Assn., 1983—. Hon. lt. col. a.d.c. Ala. Militia. Mem. Women' Am. ORT (program chmn. 1975), Optometric Soc. (sec. 1973), Weight Watchers Franchise Assn. (advt. com. 1983—), Am. Bus. Women's Assn., Nat. Assn. Female Execs., Exec. Women of Palm Beaches. Home: 3253 Hoy Lake Rd Lake Worth FL 33467 Office: 7597 Lake Worth Rd Suite 119 Lake Worth FL 33467

GORMLEY, PATRICIA ANN, government budget specialist; b. Monroe, Mich., Apr. 29, 1948; d. Matthew Leo and Hazel Luella (Hart) G.; m. Joseph Robert Garcia, Aug. 29, 1972 (div. Apr. 1981). Cert. gerontology U. Utah, 1980; B. Gen.Sci. in Psychology, Gerontology and Sociology, Weber State Coll., 1981. Tax examiner IRS, Ogden, Utah, 1967-69; with Hill AFB, Utah, 1969-83, adminstrv. asst. base ops. and tng. div., 1973-79, inventory mgmt. specialist wheels and brakes div., 1979-81, inventory mgmt. specialist Minuteman/Titan MX, 1981-83; inventory mgmt. specialist and supply systems analyst Minuteman/Titan/MX/MSL SPARES-Air Force Logistics Command/Investment SPARES Div. Hdqrs., Wright-Patterson AFB, Ohio, 1983—; tour guide hostess Fun Time Tours, Salt Lake City, 1983. Author: (poem) About Summer Love (Recorder award 1973), 1973; EEO investigator and counselor Ogden Air Logistics Command, Hill AFB, 1977-79. Recipient various govt. awards Hill AFB, 1974-83; Title IV A scholar, 1979-81; Bus. and Profl. Women scholar, 1982. Mem. Western Gerontol. Soc. Democrat. Roman Catholic. Home: PO Box 33153 Wright-Patterson AFB OH 45433 Office: MMMII Hdqrs Bldg 262 Wright-Patterson AFB OH 45433

GORRELL, NITA ROSENDAHL, lawyer; b. Fargo, N.D., Sept. 12, 1947; d. Glenn J. and Ardith M. (Johnson) Rosendahl; m. Douglas R. Bell, Feb., 1970; (div. 1975); m. 2d, John Jeffrey Gorrell, Oct. 25, 1975. B.A., U. Wash., 1969; postgrad. U. Fla., 1972-74, Nova U., 1974-75; J.D., Tulane U., 1978. Bar: La. 1978, U.S. Dist. Ct. (ea. dist.) La. 1980, U.S. Dist. Ct. (mid. dist.) La. 1980. Tchr., Duval County Sch. Bd., Jacksonville, Fla., 1970-74; ptnr. Morrison & Gorrell, Hammond, La., 1978-81, Mentz & Gorrell, Hammond, 1981-82, Tillery & Gorrell, Hammond, 1982-84; sole practice, Hammond, 1984—; dir. S.E. Legal Services Corp., 1985-86. Chmn. bd. Youth Service Bur., Hammond, 1978-82; sec.-treas., dir. Tangipahoa Council on Aging, Amite, La., 1981-82; vol. Crisis Phone, 1981; v.p. Mayor's Commn. Needs of Women, 1981—; mem. Southeastern Devel. Found., 1981—, sec., bd. dirs., 1985-86. Tulane U. scholar, 1977. Mem. La. Bar Assn., La. Trial Lawyers Assn., 21st Jud. Dist. Bar Assn., ABA. Home: 704 W Robert St Hammond LA 70401 Office: Nita R Gorrell PLC 112 W Morris St PO Box 1537 Hammond LA 70404

GORTON, LAURIE ANN, editor; b. Buffalo, Nov. 26, 1949; d. James Wallace and Doris Ida (Torke) G.; B.A. in Journalism cum laude, U. Wis., Madison, 1971. Asso. editor Cooking for Profit, Madison, 1971-74; editor, pub. dir. Baking Industry, Putman Pub. Co., Chgo., 1974-83; editor Bakers Digests 1983—, Baking Equipment, 1983—, assoc. editor Milling and Baking News, Sosland Pub. Co., 1983—. Mem. Inst. Food Technologists, Am. Assn. Cereal Chemists, Am. Soc. Bakery Engrs., Phi Beta Kappa. Christian Scientist. Office: Baking Equipment Sosland Publishing Co 9000 W 67th St Merrian KS 66202

GOSE, GRACE SMITH, wholesale lumber company executive; b. Burke's Garden, Va., Oct. 14, 1909; d. Tilden Hendricks and Margaret (Wynn) Short; m. Lionel Charles Smith, Oct. 30, 1927 (dec. Sept. 1956); children—Lionet Elizabeth and Hilah Mae (twins); m. John Paul Gose, Mar. 28, 1959. B.S. in Biology, Concord Coll., Athens, W.Va., 1954, B.S. in Vocat. Home Econs., 1956; lifetime cert. W.Va. U., 1976. Cert. tchr., W.Va. Elem. tchr., pub. schs., Sommers County, W.Va., 1954-61; supt. women's prison, Penoe Spring, W.Va., 1961-65; high sch. tchr., pub. schs., Raleigh County, W.Va., 1965-68, 70-79; owner, operator L. C. Smith Mine Timbers, Jumping Branch, W.Va., 1979—; active in real estate, Jumping Branch, 1945—. Mem. Internat. Assn. Chiefs of Police (life), Nat. Ret. Tchrs. Assn. Democrat. Methodist. Lodge: Order

Eastern Star. Avocations: selling real estate; travel in U.S. and Canada. Home and Office: PO Box 81 Jumping Branch WV 25969

GOSNELL, RUTH ELIZABETH ALLEN, civic worker, former educator; b. Balt., Apr. 12, 1909; d. William Thomas and Elizabeth (Van Huyck) Allen; m. Orville Thomas Gosnell, Nov. 23, 1944 (dec. 1974). Teaching cert. Towson State U., 1928; B.E., Johns Hopkins U., 1941, M.Ed., 1949, CASE cert., 1955, postgrad. profl. studies, 1951-71. Elem. tchr. Baltimore County Bd. Edn., Towson, 1928-49, elem. sch. prin., supr., 1949-74. Producer Cable TV programs for sr. citizens. Contbr. articles to profl. jours. Recreation and parks officer Liberty Rd. Recreation Council, 1950-73; mem. Baltimore County Recreation and Parks Bd., 1950—, chmn. 1974—; vol. staff Baltimore County Dept. Aging, 1979-82; trustee Baltimore County United Way, 1969-79; bd. dirs. Chesapeake council Camp Fire Girls, 1969-79; mem. council Woodstock Job Corps., 1974—; founder, adminstr. Ruth Gosnell Edn. Fund, 1980—; life mem. Md. State Congress PTAs, Nat. Congress PTAs. Mem. Women Educators of Baltimore County (past pres., sec.), Nat. Tchrs. Assn., Md. State Tchrs. Assn., Baltimore County Tchrs. Assn. (past pres.), Delta Kappa Gamma, Pi Lambda Theta. Democrat. Presbyterian. Avocations: reading; hiking; swimming. Home: 1 Giard Dr #11 Baltimore MD 21207

GOSS, JANELL JONES, voice message/mail service corporation executive; b. Arcadia, La.; d. Grady Edward and Ethel Jane (Peevy) Jones; B.S. in Social Scis., magna cum laude, La. State U., 1973; children—Frederick Stuart, Sherilyn Goss Short, Sharla Kathryn. Regional equipment order entry supr. Xerox Corp., Dallas, 1973-75, mgmt. info. system analyst, 1975-76, nat. systems devel. analyst, Rochester, N.Y., 1976-78, regional mgr. equipment order entry/commn. acctg., Dallas, 1978-81, nat. mgr. equipment planning/control, Office Products Div., Dallas, 1981-82; ptnr. Career Insights, Carrollton, Tex., 1982-83; mortgage lending rep. S.W. Heritage Fin. Corp., Richardson, Tex., 1983-84; nat. customer service mgr. U.S. Brass Corp., Plano, Tex., 1984-85; ops. mgr. Voice Retrieval Ctr., Dallas, 1986—. Recipient plaques for outstanding service Xerox Corp., 1978, 79, 80. Mem. Xerox Mgmt. Assn. (dir. 1975-76), Network Career Women, AAUW, LWV, Phi Kappa Phi, Phi Lambda Pi (pres. 1972-73). Baptist. Club: Order Eastern Star. Home: 2501 Winterstone Dr Plano TX 75023 Office: 17060 Dallas Pkwy Suite 213 Dallas TX 75248

GOSS, PATRICIA BELLAMY, missiles and space company official; b. Montreal, Que., Can., May 21, 1944; d. Clifford J. and May Glenn (Black) Bellamy; naturalized, 1966; A.B., UCLA, 1966, M.A., 1967; Ph.D., N.Y. U., 1978; children—Jennifer Suzanne, Geoffrey Bellamy. Lectr., dir. forensics UCLA, 1967-73; asst. prof. Lehman Coll., City U. N.Y., 1973-79; mgmt. cons. Lockheed Missiles and Space Co., Sunnyvale, Calif., 1980—. Named Debate Coach of Yr., Georgetown U., 1971; recipient H.A. Wichelns award for outstanding article in Free Speech Yearbook, Speech Communication Assn., 1975. Mem. Speech Communication Assn. Democrat. Office: Lockheed Missiles and Space Co 1111 Lockheed Way Sunnyvale CA 94086

GOSS-MOFFITT, NINA BESS, psychiatrist; b. Brookhaven, Miss., Aug. 13, 1926; d. Isaac Alanson and Aubrey Reid (Corban) Goss; B.S., Millsaps Coll., 1946; M.D., Tulane U., 1950; m. Ellis M. Moffitt, June 12, 1954; children—John Ellis, Virginia Ellen. Intern, St. Elizabeth's Hosp., Washington, 1950-52; staff physician Miss. State Hosp., Whitfield, 1952-53, 54-61; practice medicine specializing in family medicine, Natchez, Miss., 1953-55, Jackson, Miss., 1955-61; staff physician Western State Hosp., Staunton, Va., 1961-62; resident in psychiatry U. Louisville, 1962-64, U. Miss., 1965-66; cons. psychiatry Bur. Mental Health Services, Miss. State Bd. Health, Jackson, 1965-69, dir. bur., 1970-75; practice medicine specializing in psychiatry, Jackson, 1975-83; dir. outpatient psychiatry U. Miss. Med. Ctr., 1983—; mem. staff, asst. clin. prof. U. Miss. Med. Ctr.; mem staff, cons. alcohol and drug unit Doctors Hosp.; bd. dirs. Miss. Found. for Med. Care. Pres. PTA, Lester Sch., Jackson, 1968-70. Mem. Central Med. Soc., Miss. State Med. Assn., So. Med. Assn., Miss. Psychiat. Assn. (newsletter editor 1973-81, treas. 1981-86, pres. elect 1986), Am. Psychiat. Assn. Baptist. Office: Dept Psychiatry U Miss Med Ctr 2500 N State St Jackson MS 39216

GOTCH, LOU ANN MEYER, banker; b. Ft. Wayne, Ind., June 23, 1947; d. Donald LeRoy and Marjorie Ruth (Dyer) Meyer; m. John Raymond Gotch, Oct. 7, 1967; 1 child, Andrew John. Student, So. Ill. U., 1965-66, Am. Inst. Banking, 1979-81; cert. Sch. Bank Mktg., 1982. Teller Carbondale Savs. & Loan, Ill., 1974-76; customer service/advt. mgr. State Savs., Bowling Green, Ohio, 1976-78; mktg. asst. Pk. Nat. Bank, Newark, Ohio, 1978-79; dir. mktg. Central Trust Co., Newark, 1979-85; v.p. mktg. United Nat. Bank, Canton; Ohio, 1985—; cons. pub. speaking Bus. and Profl. women, Newark, 19; cons., mktg. Bldg. Better Bds., Newark, 1984. Newspaper columnist 1984-85. Loaned exec. United Way, Licking County, Ohio, 1978; bd. dirs. Am. Cancer Soc., Licking County, 1978-85, Named Outstanding Women of Am., 1983. Mem. Nat. Assn. Bank Women, Ohio Sch. Bank Mktg. Alumni Assn., C. of C. Licking County. Avocations: teaching aerobics, public speaking, music, Sunday Sch. Lit., sewing. Office: United Nat Bank PO Box 190 Canton OH 44701

GOTLIB, LORRAINE, provincial judge; b. Toronto, Ont., Can., May 13, 1931; B.A., U. Toronto, 1952; grad. Osgoode Hall; m. Christopher B. Paterson. Admitted to Ont. bar, 1959; former partner firm Kingsmill, Jennings, Toronto, also mem. Bd. Trade Met. Toronto, mem. house com., 1977-79, mem. council, 1979-83; group seminar instr. Bar Admission Course, 1968-72. Mem. council Ont. Coll. Art, 1976-79. Named Queen's Counsel, 1973; recipient Jubilee medal, 1977. Mem. Canadian Bar Assn. (nat. exec. com. 1976-78, pres. Ont. br. 1983-84), County of York Law Assn., Women's Law Assn. Ont., Med.-Legal Soc. Toronto, Univ. Coll. Alumnae Assn., Kappa Beta Pi (nat. dir. 1968-72). Clubs: Royal Can. Yacht, Lawyers of Toronto, Empire of Can. (dir.). Address: Court House 361 University Ave Toronto ON M5G IT3 Canada

GOTTESFELD, ILENE BURSON, nurse, educator; b. Kew Gardens, N.Y., Dec. 25, 1948; 2 children. Student U. Ala., 1966-67; B.S. in Nursing, Boston U., 1971; M. Nursing, U. Fla., 1974. R.N. N.Y. Staff nurse New Eng. Med. Ctr. Floating Hosp., Boston, 1971-72; pediatric community health nurse, emergency room coordinator, inservice instr. Columbia Point Health Ctr., Boston, 1972-73; teaching asst. Sch. Nursing, U. Fla., Gainesville, 1974; clin. nursing specialist in pediatrics L.O. Jewish-Hillside Med. Ctr., New Hyde Park, N.Y., 1974-75, specialist in pediatric cardiology, 1975-77; adj. clin. instr. Sch. Nursing Adelphi U., Garden City, N.Y., 1978-81; nurse clinician in pediatric cardiology North Shore Univ. Hosp., Manhasset, N.Y., 1982—; instr. continuing edn. program SUNY-Farmingdale, 1976; instr. CPR, Nassau Heart Assn., 1976-79. Mem. Am. Nurses Assn., Sigma Theta Tau. Address: 13 Norwood Rd Port Washington NY 11050 Office: North Shore Univ Hosp

GOTTFRIED, MARTHA ANN, real estate broker; b. Evansville, Ind., Apr. 21, 1937; d. Francis J. and Mildred E. (Schatz) Heines; student U. Evansville, 1958, Palm Beach Jr. Coll., 1971; m. Robert W. Gottfried, Nov. 13, 1970. Sec. production control Mead Johnson & Co., Evansville, 1956-61, sec., v.p. internat. div., 1961-63, sec., pres. internat. div., 1963-67, adminstrv. asst., chmn. bd., 1967-70; corp. sec.-treas., dir. Robert W. Gottfried, Inc., Palm Beach, Fla., 1970—; pres. Martha A. Gottfried, Inc., Real Estate, Palm Beach, 1977—; owner Gwen Fearing Real Estate, Palm Beach, 1979—. Mem. Internat. Fedn. Real Estate Fedn., Nat. Womens Council Realtors, Palm Beach Bd. Realtors, Palm Beach Civic Assn. Roman Catholic. Clubs: Poinciana, Govs. (Palm Beach). Home: 748 HiMount Palm Beach FL 33480 Office: 241 Worth Ave Palm Beach FL 33480

GOTTLIEB, ANITA BOBROW, blouse manufacturing company executive; b. N.Y.C., June 7, 1930; d. Max and Sylvia Estelle (Adlerstein) Bobrow; m. Merle Gottlieb, Jan. 12, 1969. Student UCLA, 1950; B.B.A., CCNY, 1951. Mem. exec. tng. program Kirby Block, 1949-50, asst. buyer, 1953-55; trainee to dept. mgr. Saks Fifth Ave, N.Y.C., 1950-51; fashion coordinator Donnybrook Coat and Suit Mfrs., 1951; asst. buyer Aaron Schwab, Los Angeles, 1951-53; assoc. buyer Frederick Atkins, 1955-67; operator June Bradlee, 1967-69; asst. to designer Alice Stuart, N.Y.C., from 1969, later sales and prodn. exec., asst. to pres., exec. v.p., now pres.; instr. seminars Fashion Inst. Tech. Mem. Nat. Blouse Assn. (gov.). Democrat. Jewish. Office: 525 7th Ave New York NY 10018

GOTTLIEB, ELIZABETH GEYER, choreographer, educator; b. N.Y.C., Nov. 22, 1951; d. Edward and Gertrude (Cohen) G.; m. Joseph Karpienia, Mar. 2, 1984. Student L.I.U., 1972-73; B.S., NYU, 1976. Dancer N.Y.C. Ballet Co., 1969-72; free-lance dancer, 1972-77; dir. E.G.G. & Dancers Inc., N.Y.C., 1977—; coach for profl. performers, 1977—. Producer, choreographer video films: Journey, 1980 (Bronze Internat. Filmfest award 1981), Videodances, 1982; choreographer (ballet) Choreotunes, 1980, 81, 82 (Criterion Found. grantee 1980, 81, 82). Vol. Crisis Intevention Ctr. C.W. Post Coll., Greenvale, N.Y., 1972-73; dir., founder Harvest, NYU, 1973-74. Mem. Dance Theater Workshop, Sutton Movement Shorthand Soc., NYU Alumni Assn. Democrat. Avocation: music. Office: EGG and Dancers 287 Broadway New York NY 10007

GOTTLIEB, LUCILLE MONTROSE FOX, retired state official; b. Hartford, Conn., May 30, 1929; d. Louis Paul and Rose Tomasina (Vignone) Montrose; student Cambridge Sch. Bus. Sci., 1948, Hillyer Jr. Coll., 1950; m. Francis R. Fox, Jr., June 26, 1954; m. Ralph Gottlieb, Sept. 28, 1979. Adminstrv. fiscal mgmt. officer Conn. Hwy. Dept., Hartford, 1950-61, asst. pub. relations dir., 1961-65, personnel asst., 1965-70; liaison officer Conn. Dept. Transp., from 1970; v.p. TV 58, Shoreline Communications Inc., 1976—. Chmn. Rocky Hill Park Com., 1968, Pool and Teen Center Com., 1976-77, Park and Recreation Adv. Bd., 1969; mem. Govs. Environ. Policy Com., 1972-74; chmn. Park and Recreation Adv. Bd., 1970; v.p. Gov's. Environ. Policy Panel on Travel and Transp.; trustee Council 13 Original States, 1978. Mem. NCCJ, Antiquarian Landmarks Soc. Conn., Fedn. Bus. and Profl. Women (chmn. pub. relations), Pub. Personnel Assn. Greater Hartford (v.p.), Conn. Employees Assn., Nat. Resources Council Conn., Great Meadow Conservation Trust, Conn. Pub. Health Assn., Women in Communications (v.p. Conn. chpt. 1978), Conn. Hist. Com., Conn. Italian-Am. Cultural Assn. (pres. 1978), Met. Opera Guild, Ft. Lauderdale Symphony Soc., Ft. Lauderdale Opera Guild, Audubon Soc., Am. Mus. Natural History, Internat. Platform Assn. Republican. Roman Catholic. Clubs: Lady Hilton VIP, Cosmopolitan Hartford, Officers of Conn. (sec.). Creator Gertie Glitter anti litter symbol. Home: 150 Crestview Rd Manchester NH 03104 also 3500 Galt Ocean Dr Fort Lauderdale FL 33308 also 16 Judd Rd Wetherfield CT 06109

GOTTSCHALK, JENNIFER LEIGH, lawyer; b. Bethesda, Md., Feb. 15, 1955; d. George Francis and Betty Jane (Butler) G. B.A., U. Del., 1976; J.D., Rutgers U., 1979. Bar: N.J. 1980. Jud. law clk. U.S. Bankruptcy Ct., Trenton, N.J., 1979-80; asst. prosecutor Monmouth County (N.J.), Freehold, 1980-82; assoc. Thompson & Stoller, Aberdeen, N.J., 1982-83; asst. counsel N.J. Casino Control Commn., Lawrenceville, 1983-84; dep atty. gen. N.J. Div. Criminal Justice, Trenton, 1984—. Mem. Monmouth Civic Chorus, Little Silver, N.J., 1981—; mem. Freehold Boro Women's Softball League, 1981—; mem. Aberdeen Twp. Women's Softball League, 1984—. Mem. N.J. Bar, Md. Bar, Monmouth Bar Assn., Phi Alpha Delta. Democrat. Christian Scientist. Home: 118 Strathmore Gardens Aberdeen NJ 07747 Office: Div Criminal Justice 25 Market St CN 085 Trenton NJ 08625

GOUDY, JOSEPHINE GRAY, social worker; b. Des Moines, Nov. 30, 1925; d. Gerald William and Myrtle Maria (Brooks) Gray; B.A., State U. Iowa, 1953, M.S.W., 1966; m. John Winston Goudy, June 5, 1948; children—Tracy Jean, Paula Rae. Child welfare supr. Iowa Dept. Social Services, 1960-68; psychiat. social worker Community Mental Health Center Scott County (Iowa), 1966-71; social work instr. Palmer Jr. Coll., Davenport, Iowa, 1967-70; psychiat. social worker, chief social services Jacksonville (Ill.) State Mental Hosp., 1971-74; coordinator community mental health outpatient services McFarland Mental Health Center, Springfield, Ill., 1974; exec. dir. Macoupin County Mental Health Center, Carlinville, Ill., 1974—; adj. instr. dept. psychiatry Sch. Medicine, So. Ill. U.; chmn. Human Services Edn. Council, Springfield, 1979-81; past exec. Davenport Community Welfare Council. Mem. Nat. Assn. Social Workers (registered clin. social worker; Social Worker of Yr. award Springfield and Central Ill. chpt. 1983), Nat. Assn. for Rural Mental Health, Acad. Cert. Social Workers, Am. Assn. for Counseling and Devel., AAUW (br. pres. 1964-66, mem. state bar 1966-68, br. grantee 1975), Internat. Fedn. U. Women, U. Iowa Alumni Assn., Carlinville Bus. and Profl. Women's Club (Woman of Yr. award 1983), Delta Kappa Gamma. Republican. Methodist. Club: Carlinville Women's (pres. 1975-77). Home: 364 W Tremont St Waverly IL 62692 Office: 100 N Side Sq Carlinville IL 62626

GOUGÉ, SUSAN CORNELIA JONES (MRS. JOHN OSCAR GOUGÉ), microbiologist; b. Chgo., Apr. 18, 1924; d. Harry LeRoy and Gladys (Moon) Jones; student Am. U., Washington, 1942-43, La. Coll., 1944-45; B.S., George Washington U., 1948; postgrad. Georgetown U., 1956-58, 66-69; M.A. in Pub. Health, Vt. Coll. of Norwich U., 1984; m. John Oscar Gougé, Aug. 7, 1943; children—John Ronald, Richard Michael, (dec.). Claudia Renée Gougé Carr. Med. technician Children's Hosp. Research Lab., Washington, 1948-49; bacteriologist George Washington U. Research Lab., D.C. Gen. Hosp., 1950-53; med. microbiologist Walter Reed Army Inst. Research, Washington, 1953-61; research asst. Dental Research, Walter Reed Army Med. Center, 1961-62; microbiologist antibiotics div. FDA, 1962-63; supr. quality control John D. Copanos Co., Pharms., Balt., 1963-64; research tng. asst., infectious diseases and tropical medicine Howard U. Med. Sch., 1964-65; research asso. Georgetown U. Lab. Infectious Diseases, D.C. Gen. Hosp., 1966-69; mycologist Georgetown U. Hosp. Lab., 1969-70; microbiologist The Research Found. of The Washington Hosp. Center, 1971-73; dir. quality control Bio-Medium Corp., Silver Spring, Md., 1973-76; microbiologist Alcolac, Balt., 1976-77; microbiologist div. of labs. Dept. Human Resources, Community Health and Hosps. Adminstrn., Washington, 1978-79; microbiologist div. ophthalmic devices Office Device Eval., Center Devices and Radiol. Health, FDA, 1979—. Sec. to exec. bd. Bethesda Project Awareness, 1970-71; cons. lead poisoning detection testing project D.C. Office Vols. for Internat. Tech. Assistance, 1970-71, recipient medal for community service; vol. Zacchaeus Free Med. Clinic, Washington, 1979-84; mem. Parish Social Concerns Com. Mem. Nat. Capital Harp Ensemble, 1941-65. Registered microbiologist Nat. Registry Microbiologists; specialist microbiologist, Am. Acad. Microbiology. Mem. AAAS, Am. Soc. for Microbiology, Am. Assn. Clin. Chemists, Am. Chem. Soc., Am. Inst. Biol. Scis., N.Y. Acad. Scis., Am. Public Health Assn., Albertus Magnus Guild, Capital Bus. and Profl. Women's Club (rec. sec. 1973-74, 1st v.p. 1974-75, pres. 1975-76), Pi Kappa Delta. Roman Catholic. Club: Toastmasters (sec. 1979-80). Home: Beth-Haran Route 5 Box 510 Winchester VA 22601 Office: Office Device Eval Ctr Devices and Radiol Health FDA 8757 Georgia Ave Silver Spring MD 20910

GOUGH, JESSIE POST (MRS. HERBERT FREDERICK GOUGH), ret. educator; b. Nakon Sri Tamaraj, Thailand, Jan. 26, 1907 (parents Am. citizens); d. Richard Walter and Mame (Stebbins) Post; B.A., Maryville Coll., 1927; M.A. in English, U. Chgo., 1928; Ed.D., U. Ga., 1965; m. Herbert Frederick Gough, June 30, 1934; children—Joan Acland (Mrs. Alexander Reed), Herbert Frederick. Tchr. English, Linden Hall, Lititz, Pa., 1930-32; tchr. Fairyland Sch., Lookout Mountain, Tenn., 1955-64; research asst. English curriculum studies center U. Ga., 1964-65; asso. prof. elem. edn. LaGrange (Ga.) Coll., 1965-73, prof., 1973-75; prof. N.W. Ga. area tchr. edn. services, 1969-71. Mem. Walker County (Ga.) Curriculum Council, 1959-61, Walker County Ednl. Planning Bd., 1958-60. Mem. Am. Ednl. Research Assn., Internat. Reading Assn., East Tenn. Hist. Soc., Nat., Ga. edn. assns., Delta Kappa Gamma. Home: 8111 Savannah Hills Dr Ooltewah TN 37363

GOUGH, MARGARET ELLEN, newspaper pub., editor; b. Boise, Idaho, Jan. 6, 1926; d. Everett Bancroft and Mabel Jean (Kennington) Knipe; student Coll. of Idaho, Caldwell, 1944-46; m. Theron McParlin Gough, Aug. 23, 1946 (dec. 1979); children—Teresa Ellen, Theron Thayne Timothy McParlin, Thomas Everett. Pub., editor Parma (Idaho) Rev., 1979—. Tchr. ch. sch., del. nat. women's conv., elder, youth leader United United Presbyterian Ch.; past pres. local PTA; organizer, past pres. West Canyon County Republican Women, Treasure Valley Toastmistress Club; bd. dirs. Caldwell Community Found., 1980—; adv. bd. Canyon County Soil Conservation Dist. 208; bd. dirs. Old Ft. Boise Hist. Soc., chmn. Old Ft. Boise Days, 1986; former Cub Scout leader; registrar of elections, head election judge, 1955-79. Recipient Jaycee Disting. Service award Parma Jaycees, 1955. Mem. Idaho Press Assn., Nat. Press Assn., Coll. of Idaho Alumni Assn., Parma C. of C. (pres.). Home: 4th and Tucker Sts Parma ID 83660 Office: Parma Review 2d St Parma ID 83660

GOUGH, PAULINE BJERKE, magazine editor; b. Wadena, Minn., Jan. 7, 1935; d. Luther C. and Zita Pauline (Halbmaier) Bjerke; B.A., U. Minn., Mpls., 1957; B.S., Moorhead (Minn.) State Coll., 1970; M.S., Ind. U., Bloomington, 1972, Ed.D., 1977; children—Mary Pauline, Sarah Elizabeth, Philip Clayton. Reporter women's page San Jose (Calif.) Mercury-News, 1957-58; with research dept. Campbell-Mithun Advt., Mpls., 1958-60; tchr. Univ. Elem. Sch., Bloomington, 1970-79; freelance writer Agy. Instructional TV, Bloomington, 1974-80; mem. adj. faculty Ind. U.-Purdue U., Indpls., summers 1976, 77; asst. editor Phi Delta Kappan, Bloomington, 1980-81, mng. editor, 1981—; mem. profl. staff Phi Delta Kappa, 1981—, also leader insts. on writing for publ. Recipient Disting. Alumna award Moorhead State U., 1982. Mem. Women in Communications, Phi Beta Kappa, Phi Delta Kappa, Pi Lambda Theta. Author articles in field. Home: 113 N Concord Rd Bloomington IN 47401 Office: Phi Delta Kappa PO Box 789 Bloomington IN 47402

GOULD, BONNIE MARIE, realtor; b. Cleve., Sept. 3, 1947; d. Edward Louis and Frances Dee (Pavlovich) Marincic; m. Wayne William Gould, June 7, 1969; 1 child, Scott Robert. Student John Carroll U., 1965-66, 76-78. Asst. prodn. mgr. Nelson Stern Advt., Cleve., 1966-73; sec. acctg. S. James Dubin & Assos., Eastlake, Ohio, 1976-78; sec., atty. James Todoroff, Andrews & Todoroff, Eastlake, 1977-78; realtor sales Century 21-Baur, Euclid, Ohio, 1978-82; relocations dir., mgr. Century 21, Euclid, 1979-82; realtor assoc., relocation dir. Century 21-Malone, Inc., Willowick, Ohio, 1982-83, Century 21-William T. Byrne, Euclid, 1983-84, Smythe, Cramer Co., Euclid, 1984-86; owner Acacia Realty Profls., Inc., 1986—; Mem. Realtors Polit. Action Com., Cleve., 1981—; vice chmn. local taxation and legislation com. Cleve. Area Bd. Realtors, 1983-84, chmn. home and flower, 1986, mem. enlarged legis. com., 1986—. Recipient Disting. Service award Cleve. Bd. Realtors, 1983. Mem. Cleve. Bd. Realtors (dir. 1984—), Ohio Assn. Realtors, Nat. Assn. Realtors, Women's Council Realtors, North East Roundtable (sec. 1980, chair 1981). Republican. Lutheran. Home: 293 E 266th St Euclid OH 44132 Office: Acacia Realty Profls Inc 21801 Lakeshore Blvd Euclid OH 44123

GOULD, JANET JETER, lawyer; b. Waco, Tex., July 29, 1952; d. Sidney Raymond and Betty Jane (Harmon) J.; m. Ronald Ray Gould, May 18, 1979; children—Jana Deanne, Victoria Lee. B.J. magna cum laude, U. Tex.-Austin, 1972, J.D. with honors, 1981. Bar: Ariz. 1981. Pub. info. officer City of Edinburg (Tex.), 1973-74; law clk. Office of State Comptroller, Austin, Tex., 1979-80; assoc. Streich, Lang, Weeks & Cardon, P.A., Phoenix, 1981—. Stumberg scholar 1978, Marshall Thomas Meml. 1979; recipient Judge Charles D. Betts award, 1981. Mem. Nat. Assn. Women in Comml. Real Estate, Ariz. Women Lawyers Assn., ABA, State Bar of Ariz., Phi Kappa Phi, Alpha Lambda Delta. Office: Streich Lang Weeks & Cardon PA 100 W Washington St Phoenix AZ 85003

GOULD, MAXINE LUBOW, law firm administrator; b. Bridgeton, N.J., Feb. 28, 1942; d. Louis A. and Bernice L. (Goldberg) Lubow; B.S., Temple U., 1962, J.D., 1968; m. Sam C. Gould, June 17, 1962 (div. 1984); children—Jack, Herman, David. Head resident dept. student personnel Temple U., 1962-66; dir., treas. Hilltop Interest Program, Inc., Los Angeles, 1973-74; law clk. law firms, Los Angeles, 1975-77; with Buffalo Resources Corp., Los Angeles, 1978-82, corp. sec., 1979-82; corp. sec., securities prin. Buffalo Securities Corp., Los Angeles, 1979-82; corp. sec. LaMaur Devel. Corp., Los Angeles, 1979-82; contracts analyst, land dept. Texaco Inc., Los Angeles, 1982-83; exec. dir. Sinai Temple, West Los Angeles, 1983-85; lawfirm adminstr., 1986—. Mem. Roscomare Valley Assn. Edn. Com., Bel Air, Calif., 1975-76; subcom. chmn. Roscomare Rd. Sch. Citizens Adv. Council, Bel Air; active various community drives. Recipient Joseph B. Wagner Oratory award B'nai B'rith, 1959, Voice of Democracy award, 1958-59, award Commentator Club, 1959. Mem. ABA, Los Angeles County Bar Assn., Nat. Assn. Female Execs. (network dir.), Calif. Women Lawyers, Women in Bus., Am. Assn. Petroleum Landmen, Los Angeles Assn. Petroleum Landmen, Nat. Assn. Exec. Dirs., Assn. Legal Adminstrs. of Beverly Hills and Los Angeles, Phi Alpha Theta, Alpha Lambda Delta. Jewish. Office: 2501 Roscomare Rd Bel Air CA 90077

GOULDER, DIANE KESSLER, lawyer; b. Columbus, Ohio, Apr. 27, 1950; d. Berry Lester and Shirley Lorraine (Goldstein) Kessler; m. Eric Alan Goulder, June 30, 1974; children—Jeremy, Joel, Anna Lisa. B.A., Ohio State U., 1972; J.D., Cornell U., 1975. Bar: Ohio 1975. Assoc., Mayer Terakedis & Weed, Columbus, 1975-76, Mayer, Terakedis & Blue Co. L.P.A., Columbus, 1976-79; sole practice, Worthington, Ohio, 1979-85; prin. Martin, Eichenberger & Baxter Co., L.P.A., 1985—. Active Twig 173, Women's Aux. of Children's Hosp., Worthington, 1980-85. Mem. ABA (adj. mem. taxation com. 1979—), Ohio State Bar Assn., Columbus Bar Assn. (employee benefits com. 1984—), Women Lawyers of Franklin County, Mortar Board, Phi Beta Kappa, Sigma Iota Lambda. Home: 6636 Plesenton Dr W Worthington OH 43085 Office: 6641 N High St Suite E Worthington OH 43085

GOULET, VICKY LYNNE, financial manager; b. Portsmouth, Va., Aug. 27, 1954; d. Lionel J. and Victoria T. (Makarczyk) G. B.S. in Acctg., Ariz. State U., 1975; M.B.A. candidate Duquesne U., 1983—. C.P.A., Pa. Audit supr. Coopers & Lybrand, Pitts., 1976-81; mgr. fin. policies and procedures Rockwell Internat., Pitts., 1981—. Mem. Am. Inst. C.P.A.s. Roman Catholic. Lodge: Toastmasters (pres. chpt. 1984-85, sec. 1985-86). Avocations: gardening; weights; decorating. Home: 813 Fruithurst Dr Pittsburgh PA 15228 Office: Rockwell Internat 600 Grant St Pittsburgh PA 15219

GOUW, JULIA SURYAPRANATA, accountant; b. Surabaya, Indonesia, Aug. 22, 1959; came to U.S., 1978; d. Moertopo Suryapranata and Indira (Koelani) Suryapranata; m. Ken Keng-Hok Gouw, June 1, 1981. B.S. with highest honors, U. Ill., 1981. C.P.A., Ill. Acct., Texaco, Inc., Los Angeles, 1981-83; from asst. acct. to sr. acct. Peat Marwick Mitchell Co., Los Angeles, 1983—. Mem. Youth Motivational Task Force, Los Angeles, 1982, Vol. Tax Assistance Program, Urbana, 1980. Mem. Chinese Am. C.P.A.s, Nat. Assn. Female Execs., Beta Alpha Psi. Home: 49 W La Sierra Arcadia CA 91006 Office: Peat Marwick Mitchell 725 S Figueroa Los Angeles CA 90017

GOWENS, VERNEETA VIOLA, journalist; b. South Holland, Ill., Mar. 19, 1913; d. William and Mary Cawthorne (Fowler) Gibson; ed. public schs., Bryant and Stratton Bus. Coll.; m. Albert Gowens, July 17, 1936; children—Victoria Ann Gowens Utke, Mary Ann Gowens Weiss. Clk., pub. relations worker Chgo. and Riverdale Lumber Co., Chgo., 1934-45; feature writer, women's editor Tribune Publs., Harvey, Ill., 1960-62; feature writer, women's editor Star-Tribune, Williams Press, Chicago Heights, Ill., 1963-78; freelance writer; script writer variety shows Ship Ahoy, 1963, Fair 'n' Square, 1964; contbr. to Internat. Altrusan, 1974, Church Herald, 1977. Sunday sch. tchr., youth leader 1st Ref. Ch., South Holland; mem. editorial council Ch. Herald, Ref. Ch. in Am., 1976-82; pres. Dist. 150 PTA, 1965-66; adv. com. program in ltd. occupation tng. Thornton High Sch., 1963-69; mem. South Holland Indsl. Commn., 1965-68; bd. dirs. Family Service and Mental Health Center of South Cook County, Ill., 1974-77; mem. South Holland unit Salvation Army, 1958—; judge Internat. Teen Pageant, 1969; mem. South Holland Community Chest, 1978—; adv. bd. Thornton Community Coll. nursing program, 1976-83; active South Holland Diamond Jubilee, 1969; mem. South Holland Cable Commn., 1984—. Recipient award South Holland C. of C., 1970, Genoa council K.C., 1974, Village of South Holland, 1969, 1st pl. in contest No. Ill. U., 1974, 75, award Suburban Press Found., 1969, 1st pl. award Ill. Press Assn., 1973, 50 other awards in writing. Mem. Ill. Women's Press Assn. (Woman of Yr. 1974, award 1978), Nat. Fedn. Press Women (1st pl. Sweepstakes award 1976). Home: 16830 S Park Ave South Holland IL 60473

GOWER, ALICE MARIE, educational administrator; b. Windsor, Mo., Aug. 28, 1922; d. Warren Leslie and Gladys Pearl (Whitesell) Beck; B.S. in Social Studies, Central Mo. State U., 1943, M.S. in Edn. and Library Sci., 1961, Ed.S., 1971; m. Henry D. Gower, Jan. 6, 1945; children—Henry D., Kolyn Nancy Gower Cochran, Phillip B. Tchr., various elem. schs., U.S.A., W.Ger., 1955-62; librarian Central Mo. State U. Residence Center, Independence, 1962-67, dean women, 1967-81, Warrensburg, dir. spl. student services, 1981—. Mem. Nat. Women in Higher Edn. Adminstrn., Nat. Assn. Women Deans, Adminstrs., and Counselors, Nat. Assn. Student Personnel Adminstrs., Mo. Student Personnel Assn., AAUW, Assn. for Women Students, Alpha Xi Delta. Presbyterian. Club: Order of Eastern Star. Home: PO Box 456 Warrensburg MO 64093 Office: Union 215 Warrensburg MO 64093

GOWIN, MARILYN J., financial and tax consultant; b. Morrisonville, Ill., May 20, 1939; d. Robert Edgar and Marjorie Lucille (Cloyd) G.; B.S., U. Ill., Urbana, 1961. With Price Waterhouse, N.Y.C., 1961-65, Arthur Andersen & Co., Tampa, Fla., and N.Y.C., 1965-72, Coopers & Lybrand, N.Y.C., 1972-78; fin. and tax cons., N.Y.C., 1978—. Vol. Community Tax Aid; mem. Ocean Beach Assn. C.P.A. Mem. Am. Inst. C.P.A.s, N.Y. State Soc. C.P.A.s, Am. Soc. Women Accts. (past dir. N.Y.C.), Am. Woman's Soc. C.P.A.s, Nat. Assn. Accts. (past dir. N.Y.C.), Mensa. Club: U. Ill. Alumni (past dir.) (N.Y.C.). Office: 240 Central Park S New York NY 10019

GOY, BARBARA ELAINE PERRY, music educator, consultant; b. St. Augustine, Fla., June 9, 1927; d. Alfred James and Nan (Klesmer) Perry; m. Robert William Goy, Nov. 13, 1948; children—Michael Frederick, Peter William, Elizabeth Ruth. Diploma High Sch. Music and Art, N.Y.C., 1944; student Eastman Sch. Music, 1947; B.A. in Music, U. Wis.-Madison, 1963. Pvt. piano instruction, Lawrence, Kans., 1954-61; music supr. Beaverton Sch. Dist., Oreg., 1964-71; founder, dir. Preschool of the Arts, Madison, 1971—; tchr. music U. Wis.-Madison extension, 1973-74; presenter music workshops to various ednl. and profl. groups. Recipient numerous awards for needlepainting, Wis. Regional Art Assn. Mem. Music Educators Nat. Conf., Wis. Music Educators Conf. Avocations: needlepainting; creative stitchery. Home: 1845 Summit Ave Madison WI 53705 Office: Preschool of the Arts Inc 3802 Regent St Madison WI 53705

GRABLE, MARTHA KAYE, pianist; b. Little Rock, May 4, 1955; d. James D. and Virginia Lee (White) G. B.Mus., Ark. State U., 1977. Music tchr., Portageville, Mo., 1967-77; dir., tchr. Yamaha Music Sch., Little Rock, 1977-79; keyboard artist, arranger The Common Good, Little Rock, 1977-80; mus. cons., arranger Loverock Prodns., Little Rock, 1979-80, personal sec., mus. advisor, 1980-81; profl. pianist, Dallas, 1981—; mgr., keyboard artist The Kaye Grable Trio; guest pianist with Lennon Sisters, 1981, with Phyllis Diller, 1981. Recipient 1st Pl. award Mo. State Music Festival, Columbia, 1973; named Girl of Yr., Bus. and Profl. Women's Club, Portageville, 1973; Lilly Peters Piano scholar Ark. State U., 1973-77. Home: 5919 Birchbrook Suite 221 Dallas TX 75206

GRACE, BARBARA JEAN, real estate company sales executive; b. Bremerton, Wash., Nov. 13, 1944; d. Arthur Elmer and Iva Gelene (Brasher) Swope; m. Wayne James Grace, Jan. 11, 1964 (div. June 1979); 1 dau., Pamela Ann. Grad. Real Estate Pre. Sch., Clayton, Mo., 1973; student Meramec Community Coll., Kirkwood, Mo., 1980-83. Lic. real estate broker, Mo. Receptionist/sec. Bi-State Machinery, St. Louis, 1979-80; sales rep., mgr. trainee Stratford House, Fenton, Mo., 1980; sales mgr. Holiday Inn, St. Louis, 1980-81; property mgr./leasing The Barn at Lucerne, Ballwin, Mo., 1981-83; dir. sales Park Tower condominium, asst. v.p. deRamco of Mo., Clayton, after 1983; now broker/sales assoc. Gundaker Realtors-Better Homes and Gardens. Com. mem. Recycling Ctr., Crestwood, Mo., 1975, Landmarks, Crestwood, 1975; chmn. bond issue City of Crestwood, 1976; chmn. Blood Bank for City Crestwood, 1978; bd. dirs. county League, Clayton, Mo., 1982-83. Mem. Am. Bus. Women's Assn. (speaker), Nat. Assn. Female Execs., West St. Louis County C. of C., Clayton C. of C., Regional Commerce and Growth Assn. Republican. Baptist. Club: Welcome Wagon (pres. 1967-79) Crestwood. Home: 1311A Prospect Village Ln Manchester MO 63011 Office: 12308 Manchester Rd Des Peres MO

GRACE, CHERYL JULANE, health club manager; b. Greensburg, Pa., Jan. 29, 1953; d. John R. Grace and Marjorie L. Harr; m. Lee Farber, Dec. 18, 1977 (div. 1981); m. Joseph Gabriel Marciano, Aug. 31, 1985. B.S. in Recreation, Temple U., 1975. Service coordinator European Health Spa, Chery Hill, N.J., 1975-76; dist. mgr. Spa Health and Fitness Ctrs., Springfield, Pa., 1976-81, Spa Lady, Falls Church, Va., 1981-82; regional mgr. Fitness America, Harrisburg, Pa., 1982—. Mem. Nat. Strength and Conditioning Assn., Internat. Dance-Exercise Assn. Found., Exercise-Safety Assn., Nat. Assn. Female Execs., NOW. Roman Catholic. Home: 804 Continental Dr Harleysville PA 19438 Office: Fitness America Rt 309 and Pumping Station Rd Quakertown PA 18951

GRACE, HELEN KENNEDY, foundation administrator; b. Beresford, S.D., Mar. 30, 1935; d. Walter James and Ethel Elvira (Soderstrom) Kennedy; B.S. in Nursing, Loyola U., Chgo., 1963; M.S. in Nursing, U. Ill., Chgo., 1965; Ph.D. in Sociology, Northwestern U., 1969; m. Elliott A. Grace, Nov. 20, 1961; 1 dau., Elizabeth Ann. Nursing adminstr. Ill. Dept. Mental Health, 1963-67; faculty Coll. of Nursing, U. Ill., Chgo., 1967-82, instr., 1967-69, asst. prof., 1969-71, assoc. prof., 1971-73, prof., assoc. dean for grad. study, 1973-77, dean coll. of Nursing 1977-82; program dir. W.K. Kellog Found., Battle Creek, Mich., 1982—. Recipient Disting. Alumnus award Loyola U., Coll. of Nursing U. Ill. Mem. Am. Nurses Assn., Nat. League for Nursing (governing bd. 1978—), Am. Acad. of Nursing (governing council 1976-80), Am. Sociol. Assn. Author: Mental Health Nursing: A Psychosocial Approach, 1977, 2d edit., 1981; Families Across the Life Cycle: Family Studies for Nursing, 1977; The Development of a Child Psychiatric Treatment Program, 1971; Current Issues in Nursing, 1981, 2d edit., 1985. Office: 400 North Ave Battle Creek MI 49015

GRADILLAS, JOSEPHINE, court reporter; b. Los Angeles, Oct. 6, 1942; d. Charles Brookman and Sara (Rascon) G. B.S., Woodbury U., 1960; student Bryan Coll., 1971. Cert. shorthand reporter; registered profl. reporter. Ct. reporter Nelson & Assocs., Los Angeles, 1972-75, Coleman, Haas Martin & Schwab, Los Angeles, 1975-77, Clark Shorthand, Los Angeles, 1977-83; ptnr. Kerns & Gradillas, Beverly Hills, 1983—. Author: Poems I Wrote, Borrowed-Stole, 1978; (with others) A Child is a Treasure, 1976. Mem. Nat. Shorthand Reporters Assn., Calif. Shorthand Reporters Assn., Los Angeles County Reporters Assn. Democrat. Roman Catholic. Avocations: cooking; racquetball; gardening; writing. Office: Kerns & Gradillas 400 S Beverly Dr Apt 306 Beverly Hills CA 90212

GRADISON, HEATHER JANE, government official; b. Houston, Sept. 6, 1952; d. David Lowe Stirton and Dorothy Johanne Flatt Cox; B.A., Radford U., 1975; postgrad. George Washington U., 1976, 78; m. Willis D. Gradison, Jr., Nov. 29, 1980; children—Maile Jo, Benjamin David. Summer intern So. Rwy. System, Washington, 1974, mgmt. trainee, 1975-76, market research asst., 1976-77, asst. rate officer, 1978-80, rate officer, 1978-82; mem. ICC, Washington, 1982—, vice chmn., 1985; mem. WTS Blue Ribbon Adv. Com., 1984. Mem. Exec. Level IV Presdl. Appointees Orgn., Rep. Congl. Wives Club. Republican. Office: 12th and Constitution Ave NW Room 4136 Washington DC 20423

GRADY, CAROL ANN, nurse; b. Lowell, Mass., June 6, 1942; d. Harry Ephrem and Rena Marion (Rondeau) Ayotte; m. Robert Joseph Grady, Sept. 5, 1964 (div. 1974); 1 dau., Sheryl Lynn. Diploma, Somerville Hosp. Sch. Nursing, 1963; grad. Lee Inst. Lic. real estate broker, Mass., N.H.; notary pub. Nurse, Central Hosp., Somerville, Mass. Mem. Nat. Wilderness Soc., Nat. Audubon Soc., Am. Nurses Assn., Nat. Assn. Female Execs., Am. Soc. Notaries, Mass. Nurses Assn., Mass. State Rifle and Pistol Assn., Nat. Rifle Assn., Nat. Trust for Historic Preservation. Lodge: Rosicrucians. Home: 126 Clifton St Malden MA 02148

GRADY, ELSIE MAE, educator, career consultant; b. Petersburg, Va., Jan. 14; d. Frank Thomas and Mary Anne (Drew) Harris; m. Gordon Edward Grady, Dec. 22, 1941 (div. June 1979); 1 child, Gloria Edwina. Student Minor's Tchrs. Coll., 1934-35; B.S. in Elem. Edn., Winston-Salem Tchrs. Coll., 1939; postgrad. Howard U., 1943-44, U. Pa., 1948-49. Elem. tchr. Pines Sch. Dist., Southern Pines, N.C., 1939-42, Berkley County, Berkley, Va., 1942-44; social worker Philadelphia County, Phila., 1944-45; elem. tchr. Phila. Sch. Dist., 1947-77; founder, dir. Harry Kravitz House, Phila., 1975—; owner Grady's Tutorial Service, Phila., 1980—; career counselor, Phila., 1983—. Block capt., 1976—; del. at large Eastern conf. United Methodist Ch., Phila., 1960-69. Recipient John F. Reynolds award P.T.A. John F. Reynolds Sch., Phila., 1969, 74, S.W. Citizens med Phila. Citizens, 1980. Mem. NAACP (life), Phila. Tchrs. Assn. (life), Zeta Phi Beta. Democrat. Methodist. Avocations: reading; research; crochet; Girl Scouts; chess.

GRADY, JOAN BUTTERWORTH, principal; b. N.Y.C., May 4, 1929; d. Roderick Gerard and Pearl (Levy) Butterworth; m. George Edward Grady, Nov. 24, 1954; children—Alicia Lynn, Glen Andrew. B.A., Hunter Coll., 1951; M.A., Columbia U., 1953; Ph.D., U. Colo., 1977. Tchr., dept. chmn., athletic dir. St. Mary's Acad., Englewood, Colo., 1963-75; asst. prin. Cherry Creek Schs., Englewood, 1975-82, prin., 1982—. Contbr. articles to profl. jours. Bd. dirs. Mile Hi council Girl Scouts U.S.A., Denver, 1980-83. Recipient Disting. Service award Nat. Assn. Student Councils, 1980; named Disting. Educator, Inst. Devel. Edn. Activities, 1983-85. Mem. Nat. Assn. Secondary Sch. Prins., Colo. Assn. Secondary Sch. Prins., Colo. Lang. Arts Soc., Colo. Assn. Middle Level Educators (past pres.), Phi Delta Kappa. Club: Aurora Stamp. Avocations: philately; genealogy.

GRADY-MCDONNELL, SHERRY ANN, engr.; b. Alexandria, Va., May 2, 1953; d. John David Jr. and Dorothy (Howard) Grady; m. Peter Daniel McDonnell, Sr.; 1 son, Peter Daniel Jr.; 1 stepdau., Melissa Margaret Ann McDonnell. B.S. in Engring., N.C. State U., 1977. Engr. in charge chem. lab. Contractors Engrs. Services Inc., Goldsboro, N.C., 1976—, engr. in charge engring. ops., 1978—, corp. sec., 1978—, design engr., 1979—, also dir.; mem. adv. panel Chem. Week Mgmt., 1981-82. Mem. N.C. Soc. Profl. Engrs., Soc. Am. Mil. Engrs. (nominating com. Goldsboro post), Soc. Women Engrs. (mem. N.C. sect.). Republican. Methodist. Club: N.C. State U. Women Engrs. (1st v.p.). Home: 203 N Slocumb St Goldsboro NC 27530 Office: PO Box 762 1304 N William St Goldsboro NC 27530

GRAEB, THELMA SAVARD, insurance agent; b. Rochester, N.Y., July 16, 1934; d. Basil Eugene and Thelma Lucile (Daus) Savard; B.S., Syracuse U., 1956, Ph.D., 1974; M.A., Northwestern U., 1958; m. Harold Sigfreid Graeb, Jr., July 19, 1958; children—Bruce, Jacqueline, Sharon, T. Randall. C.L.U. Supr., Hearing and Speech Center, Yale Sch. Medicine, New Haven, 1956-57; pvt. practice speech pathology, Newport, R.I., 1959-62; supr. hearing and speech Suffolk Rehab. Center for the Physically Handicapped, Inc., Commack, N.Y., 1963-66; asst. prof. spl. edn. N.J. State Coll., Jersey City, 1966-67; cons. speech and hearing dept. Mountainside Hosp., Montclair, N.J., 1967-69; dir., div. audiology Hearing & Speech Center of Rochester (N.Y.), Inc., 1969-71; U.S. Office Edn. fellow Syracuse U., 1971-73, dir. BOCES, 1973-75; ednl. cons. Organizational Change & Staff Devel., Manlius, N.Y., 1976; prin. Rockwell Elem. Sch., Nedrow, N.Y., from 1976; now agt. Donohue Mapstone Agy., Equitable Fin. Services; dir. Environ. Tech., Inc., Buffalo. Mem. Am. Assn. Sch. Adminstrs., Nat. Council for Exceptional Children, Am. Speech and Hearing Assn., Assn. Profl. Women in Mgmt., Nat. Assn. Women Bus. Owners, Million Dollar Round Table, Nat. Assn. Life Underwriters, Greater Syracuse C. of C. (pres.' cabinet), Phi Delta Kappa, Pi Lambda Theta, Zeta Phi Eta, Kappa Alpha Theta. Contbr. articles to profl. jours. Home: 7619 Glencliffe Rd Manlius NY 13104 Office: Donohue Mapstone Agy Equitable Fin Services Suite 1200 120 Madison St Syracuse NY 13202

GRAEFE, SUSAN WEBER, social worker, psychotherapist; b. New Britain, Conn., July 19, 1945; d. Samuel Lewis and Norma Margaret (Hein) Weber; m. Richard F. Graefe, June 17, 1967; children—Karin Elizabeth, Christopher William. B.A., Wilson Coll., Chambersburg, Pa., 1967; M.S.W., U. Pitts., 1969. Psychiat. social worker Western Psychiat. Inst. and Clinic, Pitts., 1969-71; clin. social worker St. Francis Hosp. Community Mental Health Center, Pitts., 1972-76; pediatric social worker R.I. Hosp., Providence, 1976; clin. social worker Providence Mental Health, 1976-78, coordinator elderly services, 1978-83; psychiat. social worker Family Inst. R.I., Pawtucket, 1983—. Leader R.I. council Girl Scouts U.S.A., North Kingstown, 1980-83; bd. dirs., v.p. Tockwotton Home, 1984—. Recipient Eleanor Slater award R.I. Coll. Gerontology Ctr., 1983. Mem. Nat. Assn. Social Workers (sec. R.I. chpt. 1982-85), Acad. Cert. Social Workers, Am. Group Psychotherapy Assn., N.E. Gerontol. Soc. Democrat. Unitarian-Universalist. Club: Wilson Coll. (sec. 1981—) (Boston). Home: 70 Meadowland Dr North Kingstown RI 02852 Office: Family Inst RI 351 East Ave Pawtucket RI 02860

GRAESCH, ALICE IRENE, banker; b. Maynard, Iowa, Mar. 8, 1930; d. George Edward and Irene Esther Trower; student public schs., Maynard; m. Walter R. Graesch, Mar. 11, 1951; children—Allan Lee, Marcia Ann. Graesch Hughson. With Oelwein State Bank (Iowa), 1947-50, 53—, asst. cashier, 1971-79, asst. v.p., 1979—; with Security State Bank, San Diego, 1951-52. Republican. Lutheran. Home: Rural Route 1 Box 66 Maynard IA 50655 Office: Oelwein State Bank Oelwein IA 50662

GRAF, DOROTHY ANN, business executive; b. Nashville, Mar. 21, 1935; d. Henry George and Martha Dunlap (Hill) Meek; student Montgomery Coll., 1979—; m. Peter Louis Graf, Oct. 28, 1971; children—Sidney E. Pollard, Deborah Lynn Pollard, Robert George Pollard, Michelle Joy Graf. Office mgr. Pa. Life Ins. Co., Miami and Dallas, 1957-72; exec. sec. to med. dir. Pitts. Children's Hosp., 1974; sec. G.E./TEMPO, Washington, 1974-76; adminstrv. asst. to sr. v.p. Logistics Mgmt. Inst., Washington, 1976-81, dir. adminstrv. services, 1981—; dir. KHI Services, Inc. Mem. Washington Tech. Personnel Forum. Democrat. Baptist. Home: 10000 Stedwick Rd Unit 303 Gaithersburgh MD 20879 Office: 6400 Goldsboro Rd Bethesda MD 20817-5886

GRAF, JENNY HINES, real estate executive; b. Somerset, Ky., July 7, 1933; d. Walter Bolen and Elta (Lester) Hines; student U. Miami, 1957-58, Broward Community Coll., Ft. Lauderdale, Fla., 1966-69; m. Jay J. Hammond, May 29, 1958 (div. Mar. 1966); children—Vivian, James, Robert, Heidi; m. 2d, Robert J. Graf, Aug. 30, 1969 (div. May 1974). Project mgr. W. Plantation Devel. Corp., Ft. Lauderdale, 1964-69; asst. to pres. Investment Co. Fla., Ft. Lauderdale, 1970-72; pres., dir. Wellington Realty Fla., also asst. sec., dir. Breakwater Housing Corp. and v.p. Bahamas Mortgage Co. (all Ft. Lauderdale), 1973-76; gen. partner Ideaction Inst., also Specific Markets Assos. (both N.Y.C.), 1976-77; v.p. Palm Beach Assos. div. Gould Inc., also broker/salesman Gould Realty Fla. and owner Specific Market, Inc. (all West Palm Beach, Fla.), 1977-85; broker-salesman Roy A. Glisson Realty Inc., 1986—; tchr. career counseling seminar Success Patterning, 1976-85; mem. mgmt. bd. First Am. Bank Palm Beach County, 1978—. Mem. Fla. com. Libertarian Party, 1976-80; mem. citizens adv. bd. Palm Beach Legis. Del., 1978-80; bd. dirs. Assn. Spl. Dists., 1979-85. Hon. mem. Inst. Residential Mktg.; mem. Am. Mktg. Assn., Nat. Assn. Home Builders (sales and mktg. council). Club: Zonta. Home: 12326 Westhampton Circle West Palm Beach FL 33414 Office: 12769A Forest Hill Blvd West Palm Beach FL 33414

GRAF, MARIE VIDMAR, communications executive; b. Cleve., Feb. 21, 1954; d. Stanley and Iva (Ovsenik) Vidmar; m. Mark G. Graf, Sept. 18, 1976; children—Philip Mark, John Francis. B.A. in Communications, Cleve. State U., 1976. Dir. pub. affairs Scripps-Howard Broadcasting, Cleve., 1974-83; dir. communications Ctr. Human Services, Cleve., 1983-84; regional mktg. mgr. Edward J. De Bartolo Corp., Cleve., 1984—; producer TV programs: Help Wanted/Help Found (Emmy award 1983), 1982; The Few, The Proud, The Women in the Military (Communicators award 1982), 1981. Mem. adv. bd. Cleve. Cath. Diocese, 1981—, Cleve. YWCA, 1981—; bd. dirs. River's Bend Parks Corp., 1982—. Recipient Above and Beyond award WomenSpace, 1982, Outstanding Pub. Service award United Cerebral Palsy Assn., 1983. Mem. Women in Communications (pres. Cleve. chpt.) Nat. Acad. TV Arts and Scis. (dir.), Cleve. Ad Club, Cleve. Press Club, Pub. Relations Soc. Am. (Lighthouse award 1981), Sales and Mktg. Execs. Club: Women's City (dir.). Home: 300 E 210th St Euclid OH 44123 Office: Edward J De Bartolo Corp 1 Randall Park Mall Cleveland OH 44128

GRAFT, ROSEMARY THOMAS NICHOLSON, government official; b. Meridian, Miss., Feb. 10, 1941; d. Roosevelt Ted and Mary Adeline (Burt) Thomas; m. Bobby L. Nicholson, Aug. 9, 1958 (div. Feb. 1969); children—Keith Wade, Sheila Kay, Glenn Alan; m. Donald R. Graft, Aug. 10, 1985. Student Ga. State U., 1976-77, Edison Community Coll., Ft. Myers, Fla., 1981. With Social Security Adminstrn., 1965—, beginning as claims clk., Baton Rouge, successively staff asst. Atlanta regional office, asst. dist. mgr., East Point, Ga., supr. regional commrs. inquiry unit, Atlanta, asst. dist. mgr., Lakeland, Fla., 1979-80, dist. mgr., Ft. Myers, Fla., 1980—. Mem. Ft. Myers Child Advocacy Group, 1982-84; bd. dirs. Lee County Community Coordinating Council, 1982-83, 85-86, rec. sec., 1983-84; mem. citizens adv. com. HUD Community Devel. Block Grant Program. Mem. Social Security Mgmt. Assn. (regional rep. mgmt. com. for nat. council), Am. Bus. Women's Assn. (Woman of Yr. S.W. chpt. 1978, v.p. Cape Coral chpt. 1981-82), Fla. Assn. Health and Social Services state v.p. 1983-84, chpt. v.p. 1981-84), Nat. Assn. Female Execs., Am. Soc. Profl. and Exec. Women. Democrat. Methodist. Club: Zonta (corr. sec. 1983-84). Office: Social Security Administration 3090 Evans Ave Fort Myers FL 33904

GRAGG, SARA ELIZABETH, motel executive; b. Malvern, Ark., Mar. 28, 1930; d. Alymer James and Martha Thelma (Cross) Wells; m. Glen E. Keller, Dec. 18, 1949 (div. 1964); children—Michael, Kathryn, Kim; m. Paris R. Green, Sept. 15, 1969 (dec. 1970); m. Billy Max Gragg, May 14, 1970. B.A., U. Ark., 1949, M.A., 1950, Ph.D., 1971. Exec. asst. dept. psychiatry U. Ark. Med. Ctr., Little Rock, 1951-56; asst. prof. English Ark. State U., Jonesboro, 1962-66; instr. English dept. U. Ark.-Fayetteville, 1966-69; asst. prof. U. Mo.-Rolla, 1969; pres. Gragg Motels, Inc., Fayetteville, 1970—. Author: The Artistic Unity of Carlyle's French Revolution, 1971. Pres. Ark. Med. Soc. Aux., Jonesboro, 1963-64; Republican county chmn., Jonesboro, 1962-63. Named Woman of Yr., Bus and Profl. Women, Mountain View, Ark., 1961. Mem. Ark. Motel Assn., Am. Hotel and Motel Assn., Ark. Retail Mchts. Assn., Fayetteville C. of C., Phi Beta Kappa, Lambda Tau, Psi Chi. Methodist. Avocations: writing; travelling. Home: Route 11 Smokehouse Rd Fayetteville AR 72701 Office: Gragg Motels Inc 215-229 N College St Fayetteville AR 72701

GRAHAM, ALISON, communications company executive; b. Palo Alto, Calif., Dec. 18, 1953; d. Arthur and Carol (Weiss) Graham; m. Richard J. Messina, Sept. 8, 1984. A.B., Harvard Coll., 1975; M.B.A., Stanford U., 1979. Exec. asst. Commonwealth of Mass., Boston, 1976-77; cons. McKinsey & Co., Washington, 1980-83; mgr. MCI Communications Corp., Washington, 1983-84; v.p. Am. TV Network, Inc., 1985—; cons. U.S. Dept. Commerce, Washington, 1978. Gov.'s scholar State of Calif., 1971. Mem. Charter 100 (founding mem.), Women in Communications, Stanford Bus. Sch. Alumni Assn. (dir., pres. 1980-81), Washington Mgmt. and Bus. Assn. Clubs: Harvard, Stanford (Washington). Home: 6155 Callista Ln McLean VA 22101 Office: Am TV Network Inc 1575 I St Suite 500 Washington DC 20005

GRAHAM, ANN MAUREEN, development company executive; b. Cass City, Mich., Aug. 14, 1938; d. John C. Zemke and Madeline M. Zemke Beaudry; m. Otis L. Graham, Sept. 5, 1959 (div. 1981); children—Lakin Kathryn, Wade Livingston. B.A., U. Hawaii, 1960; M.A. Stanford U., 1967; S.C.M.P., Harvard U., 1982; postgrad. U. So. Calif., 1984—. Vice pres. Greentree Realty, Santa Barbara, Calif., 1975-78, Littlestone Co., Santa Barbara, 1978-80; pres. Montec, Inc., Santa Barbara, 1980-82; pres. Grand Am. Inc., Santa Monica, 1982-85, vice chmn., 1985—. Mem. Malibu Twp. Council, 1982—. Danforth Found. fellow, 1965-67. Mem. Santa Barbara Symphony Assn. (past bd. dirs.), Santa Barbara Realtors Assn. (past. bd. dirs.), Am. Mgmt. Assn., Western Acad. Mgmt., Acad. of Mgmt. Home: 24402 Malibu Rd Malibu CA 90265 Office: Grand Am Inc 3008 Main St Santa Monica CA 90405

GRAHAM, ANNE, government official; b. Annapolis, Md., Dec. 28, 1949. Grad., Bradford Coll.; postgrad., Columbia U. Spl. asst. to dep. dir. for communications Republican Nat. Com., Washington, 1971; with White House News Summary Office, Washington, 1973, Office of Sec. of Treasury, 1974-75; press sec. to Senator Harrison Schmitt, Washington, 1976-79; asst. press sec. Reagan-Bush Campaign, 1980-81; dep. spl. asst. to Pres. for communications, Washington, 1981; asst. sec for legislation and pub. affairs Dept. Edn., Washington, 1981-85; mem. Consumer Product Safety Commn., 1985—. Office: Consumer Product Safety Commn 1111 18th St NW Washington DC 20207*

GRAHAM, CAROL ELIZABETH, psychology educator, administrator; b. Kingston, N.Y., Dec. 25, 1941; d. John Joseph Connors and Ellen Caroline (Ensign) Keresman; m. Alex Lon Graham, Mar. 19, 1964 (div. 1976); children—Alex Lon, Ellen Katherine. B.S., Troy State U., 1975, M.S., 1976, 83. Nat. cert. counselor. Coordinator prep. program Troy State U., Montgomery, Ala., 1975-76, acad. counselor and instr. psychology, 1976-78, dir. admissions and records, registrar European div., Wiesbaden, W.Ger., 1978-80, asst. prof. psychology, registrar, Ft. Benning, Ga., 1980—, coordinator Gen. Studies Program, 1986—. Mem. Troy State U. Personnel Assn. (faculty advisor student chpt. 1982—), Columbus Area Personnel Assn. (faculty advisor to Troy State U. student chpt. 1982—), Am. Assn. Counseling and Devel. (Ga. chpt.), Columbus Area Network Assn. Republican. Methodist. Home: 2840 Warm Springs Rd Apt B-1 Columbus GA 31904 Office: Troy State U PO Box 1656 Ft Benning GA 31905

GRAHAM, CELESTE MARILYN GOTCHER, business executive; b. Santa Monica, Calif., July 12, 1937; d. Leslie Louis and Winnie Viola (Miller) Gotcher; B.A. in Sociology, Calif. State U., Los Angeles, 1974; divorced; children—Leslie Dawn, Cindy Celeste, Wendy Ione, Linda Marie. Propr., C. Graham Graphics, Santa Monica, 1977—; editor Illumination mag., 1979—; pub. E-Z Interface, computer tech. newsletter; adminstrv. dir. Inst. Psycho-Dynamics, Inc., Fla., 1975—; pres. Hawk Diversified; dir. Celestial Visions Software Pub. Corp.; instr. Fla. Dept. Recreation, 1976-77; dir. info. mgmt. and graphics U. So. Calif. Sch. Music, Pres., Coll. Fin. Aid Found. Author: Layman's Guide to Enlightenment, or Cosmic Consciousness on the American Plan, 1980; Residential Treatment System for the Chronically Mentally Ill, 1981; The Utilization of Graying America, 1981; co-author: American Square Dancing, 1961. Originator techniques for meditation. Home and Office: 3175 S Hoover St 513 Los Angeles CA 90007

GRAHAM, FAIRY LOUISE LANIER, educational consultant; b. Hammond, La., Apr. 11, 1920; d. George Andrew and Louise Martha (Benson) Lanier; div.; children—Edward Benson, Leah Graham Meisel, Mark Howard. B.A., Southeastern La. U., 1948; M.Ed., Auburn U., 1966, student, 1968; cert. Ga. State U., 1982. Tchr. vocal music and domestic sci. Civil Service, Ft. Benning, Ga., 1948-50; tchr. Muscogee County Sch. Dist., Columbus, Ga., 1950-53, 61-69, coordinator, cons. gifted programs, 1969—. Title IVC/Gifted Edn. Early Childhood grantee, 1977-78, 81-82. Mem. Council Exceptional Children, Assn. for Gifted, Council Sch. Adminstrs. Spl. Edn., AAUP, Delta Kappa Gamma, Phi Delta Kappa. Republican. Methodist. Home: 3721 Oak Dr Columbus GA 31907 Office: Muscogee County Sch Dist 1200 Bradley Dr Columbus GA 31906

GRAHAM, KATHARINE, newspaper company executive; b. N.Y.C., June 16, 1917; d. Eugene and Agnes (Ernst) Meyer; student Vassar Coll., 1934-36; A.B., U. Chgo., 1938; m. Philip L. Graham, June 5, 1940 (dec. 1963); children—Elizabeth Morris, Graham Weymouth, Donald Edward, William Welsh, Stephen Meyer. Reporter San Francisco News, 1938-39; pres. Washington Post Co., 1963-73, chmn. bd., chief exec. officer, 1973—; dir. AP, Bowaters Mersey Paper Co. Ltd. Trustee Urban Inst., George Washington U., U. Chgo., Fed. City Council, Conf. Bd.; adv. com. Inst. Politics, John F. Kennedy Sch. Govt., Harvard U. Mem. Am. Soc. Newspaper Editors (adv. com.), Am. Newspaper Pubs. Assn. Clubs: Washington Press, 1925 F St., Nat. Press (Washington); Cosmopolitan (N.Y.C.). Office: 1150 15th St NW Washington DC 20071

GRAHAM, LAURA MARGARET (LAURA GRAHAM FORBES), artist; b. Washington, Ind.; d. Ray Austin and Eugenia Bruce (Winston) Graham; student Sacred Heart Convents (Grosse Pointe, Mich., Noroton, Conn., N.Y.C.) Westover and Nightingale Schs.; studied art Art Students League, with Bridgman and Frank du Mond; Grand Central Art Sch.; Traphagen Art Sch.; pvt. study with Mead Schaeffer, Henry Rittenberg, N.A. and Edward Dufner, N.A.; grad. Sch. Adult Edn., N.Y. U., 1965; m. Clifford Lee Forbes, May 4, 1940 (div.); 1 son. Exhibited paintings John Herron Art Mus., Indpls., N.Y. Water Color Club, Am. Water Color Soc., N.A.D. (youngest artist exhibiting Nov. 1932), Pa. Acad. Boston Art Club, Montclair Art Mus., World's Fair 1940, Contemporary Art Bldg., Conn. Acad. Fine Arts Exhibit, Allied Arts of Am., Ogunquit (Maine) Art Center, 50th Anniversary Celebration Westover Sch., Newport Art Assn., Nat. Arts Club. A sponsor N.Y. U. Chamber Music Concert, 1954—, concerts in Washington Sq. Park, 1954-55. Recipient Alexander Wall prize, 1943, Allied Artists Am. exhbn., N.Y. Nat. Arts Club, 1st prize for painting, 1939; 2d prize, 1940, 41, hon. mention, 1947, 48, 72; hon. mention Allied Artists, 1948, Art Assn. Ogunquit, Maine, 1947, 49; hon. mention and war bond, Terry Art Exhbn., Miami, Fla., 1952. Mem. Nat. Assn. Women Artists, Allied Artists of Am. (hon. artist mem.), Conn. Acad. Fine Arts (artist mem.), N.Y. U. Alumni Assn., N.Y. Hist. Soc., Museum City N.Y., Nat. Trust Historic Preservation, Victorian Soc. Am., English Speaking Union, Friends of the Philharmonic, Am. Artists Profl. League, Art Students League (life). Clubs: Nat. Arts, Pen and Brush, Women's Nat. Republican (N.Y.C.). Address: 10 Washington Sq N New York NY 10003

GRAHAM, LOLA AMANDA (BEALL) (MRS. JOHN JACKSON GRAHAM), photographer, author; b. nr. Bremen, Ga., Nov. 12, 1896; d. John Gainer and Nancy Caroline Idella (Reid) Beall; student Carroll State Normal Sch., 1914; m. John Jackson Graham, Aug. 3, 1916; children—Billy Duane, John Thomas, Helen (Mrs. D. Hall), Donald, Beverly (Mrs. Bob Forson). Tchr. elem. public sch., Centerdale, Ala., 1914, Eva, Ala., 1915; free lance photographer and writer, 1950—; editor poetry column Mobile Home News, 1968-69; designer jacket cover for Reader's Digest book Our Amazing World of Nature. Recipient numerous nat. prizes, 1950—; Crossroads of Tex. grand nat. in poetry for For Every Monkey Child, 1980; executed prize-winning Sioux Indian and heirloom photog. quilts. Mem. Ina Coolbrith Poetry Soc., Chapparal Poets. Author: (booklet) How to Recycle Ancestors and Grandcestors. Contbr. photographs to Ency. Brit., also numerous mags. and books. Address: 225-93 Mount Hermon Rd Scotts Valley CA 95066

GRAHAM, MARTHA, dancer, choreographer; b. Pitts., May 11, 1894; studied with Ruth St. Denis; LL.D., Mills Coll., Brandeis U., Smith Coll.,

Harvard, 1966, also numerous others. Soloist, Denishawn Co., 1920, Greenwich Village Follies, 1923; faculty Eastman Sch., 1925; debut as choreographer-dancer 48th St. Theatre, N.Y.C., 1926; founder, artistic dir. Martha Graham Dance Co., Martha Graham Sch. Contemporary Dance; Guggenheim, Fellow, 1932; choreographer 173 works including Primitive Mysteries, Appalachian Spring, Letter to the World, Clytemnestra Tragic Patterns, Frontier, Phaedra, Cortege of Eagles, Cave of the Heart, Scarlet Letter, Night Journey, Owl and the Pussycat, Acts of Light, The Rite of Spring, Flute of Pan, with music composed by Aaron Copland, Paul Hindemith, Carlos Chavez, Samuel Barber, Gian-Carlo Menotti, William Schuman, Edgar Varese, others: guest soloist leading U.S. orchs. in solos Judith, Triumph of St. Joan; Guggenheim fellow, fgn. tours with Martha Graham Dance Co., 1950, 54, 55-56, 60, 62-63, 67, 68, some under auspices U.S. Dept. State; U.S. tours, 1966, 70, sponsored by Nat. Endowment for Arts; 1st Am. modern dance co. to perform at Paris Opera House, 1984; ann. co. tours Europe, Asia, U.S. Mem. Nat. Council on Arts, 1985—. Recipient Aspen award, 1965; Creative Arts award Brandeis U., 1968; Disting. Service to Arts award Nat. Inst. Arts and Letters, 1970; Handel medallion City of N.Y., 1970; Presdl. medal of freedom, 1976; French Legion of Honor, 1984; Gold Florin' City of Florence, 1983; Capezio Dance award, 1960, 1st Presdl. Nat. Medal of Honor, 1985, also others. Mem. Am. Acad. and Inst. Arts and Letters (hon.). Author: Notebooks of Martha Graham, 1973. Address: 316 E 63rd St New York NY 10021

GRAHAM, NANCY KEOGH, psychotraumatologist, emergency medical services consultant; b. Chgo., July 12, 1932; d. Frank Belfort and Dorothy Elizabeth (Cavanaugh) Keogh; m. Edward Ralph Graham, May 12, 1956 (div. 1972); children—Scott, Ted, Sarah. Student Stanford U., 1949-51; B.S., Northwestern U., 1953; M.A., Azusa-Pacific U., 1978. Cert. marriage and family therapist, emergency med. technician. Copywriter, Young & Rubicam, N.Y.C., 1953-59; clin. assoc. Suicide Prevention Center, Los Angeles, 1971-74; med. social worker St. Francis Med. Ctr., Lynwood, Calif., 1974-76; psychotraumatologist, 1976—; asst. prof. grad. nursing program Calif. State U., Long Beach, 1979—; guest instr. Los Angeles County Paramedic Tng. Inst., Torrance, 1977—. Contbr. chpt. to book, articles to profl. jours. Mem. Psychosocial Clinicians in Emergency Medicine (dir.), Calif. Rescue and Paramedic Assn., Stanford Profl. Women. Democrat. Office: St Francis Med Center 3630 Imperial Hwy Lynwood CA 90262

GRAHAM, PATRICIA ALBJERG, university dean; b. Lafayette, Ind., Feb. 9, 1935; d. Victor L. and Marguerite (Hall) Albjerg; B.S., Purdue U., 1955, M.S., 1957, D.H.L. (hon.), 1980; Ph.D., Columbia U., 1964; D.H.L. (hon.), Manhattanville Coll., 1976; LL.D. (hon.), Beloit Coll., 1977, Clark U., 1978; D.P.A. (hon.), Suffolk U., 1978; LL.D. (hon.), Ind. U., 1980; P.Letters, St. Norbert Coll., 1980; D.H. (hon.) Emmanuel Coll., 1983; m. Loren R. Graham, Sept. 6, 1955; 1 dau., Marguerite Elizabeth. Tchr. high sch., Norfolk, Va., 1955-56, 57-58, N.Y.C., 1958-60; lectr., asst. prof. Ind. U., 1964-66; asst. prof. Barnard Coll. and Columbia Tchrs. Coll., N.Y.C., 1965-68, assoc. prof., 1968-72, prof., 1972-74; dean, v.p. Radcliffe Coll., Cambridge, Mass., 1974-77; prof. Harvard U., Cambridge, 1974-79, Charles Warren prof. history of edn., 1979—, dean Grad. Sch. Edn., 1982—; dir. Nat. Inst. Edn., HEW, Washington, 1977-79; dir. Northwestern Mut. Life Ins. Co., SRA. Bd. dirs. Dalton Sch., 1973-76, Beloit Coll., 1976-77, 79-82, Josiah Macy Jr. Found., 1976-77, 79—, Johnson Found., 1983—, Spencer Found., 1983—. Am. Council on Edn. fellow Princeton U., 1969-70; Guggenheim fellow, 1972-73; Radcliffe Inst. fellow, 1972-73; Woodrow Wilson Center fellow, 1981-82. Mem. History Edn. Soc. (pres. 1972-73), Am. Hist. Assn., Nat. Acad. Edn. (pres. 1985—), Phi Beta Kappa. Episcopalian. Author: Progressive Education: From Arcady to Academe, 1967; Community and Class in American Education: 1865-1918, 1974; (with W. Todd Furniss) Women in Higher Education, 1974. Home: 7 Francis Ave Cambridge MA 02138

GRAHAM, PAULA LEE, nurse; b. Genoa, Nebr., July 25, 1953; d. Arthur L. and Dorothy W. (Wheeler) Bourks; m. Richard R. Graham, Dec. 23, 1973. Student U. Nebr.-Omaha, 1971-73; A.S. in Nursing, Maria Coll., 1977; student Calif. State U.-Fresno, 1978-81; B.S. in Bus. Adminstrn., U. Phoenix, 1983. R.N. Staff nurse Valley Children's Hosp., Fresno, Calif., 1977-79, charge nurse pediatric intensive care unit, 1979-81; staff nurse pediatric intensive care unit Moffitt Hosp., U. Calif., San Francisco, 1981-82; pediatric supr. Kaiser Found. Hosp., Hayward, Calif., 1982-84; preceptor Alameda County Paramedics, Oakland, Calif., 1982-83; owner Headdress, 1985—. Mem. Am. Assn. Critical Care Nurses and Pediatrics spl. Interest Group, Am. Bus. Women's Assn. (corr. sec.), AAUW (chmn. internat. relations), Alpha Xi Delta. Home: 2525 Sherwood Dr Sherman TX 75090

GRAHAM, POLLY ANN, automobile dealership executive; b. Conway, S.C., Mar. 18, 1938; d. William David and Ina Mae (Hardee) Harrell; m. William Paul Graham, Feb. 29, 1956. Student pub. schs. Bus. mgr. Pinckney Volkswagen, Pensacola, Fla., 1972-75, Carroll Motors, Conway, 1975-79, Hewett Chevrolet Corp., Myrtle Beach, S.C., 1981—. Recipient cert. of excellence Chevrolet Corp., Charlotte, N.C., 1983-86. Fellow Am. Soc. Notaries. Baptist. Home: Route 1 Box 167 Conway SC 29526 Office: Hewett Chevrolet Corp Hwy 501 PO Box 425 Myrtle Beach SC 29578

GRAHAM, ROSEMARIE, personnel executive; b. McKeesport, Pa., Aug. 26, 1929; s. Charles Jalmer and Florence Ann (Carns) Isaacson; m. Melvin John Graham, Oct. 9, 1948; 1 child, Melvin John. B.S., U. Balt., 1972; cert. indsl. relations, U. Balt., 1968. Personnel dir. Farboil, A Beatrice Chem. Co. div. Beatrice Cos., Inc., Balt., 1969—. Mem. Am. Soc. Personnel Adminstrn., Am. Mgmt. Assn., Am. Mgmt. Assn., Personnel Assn. Greater Balt., People to People (del. to People's Republic of China 1984). Democrat. Roman Catholic. Office: Farboil A Beatrice Chem Co Div Beatrice Cos Inc 8200 Fischer Rd Baltimore MD 21222

GRAHAM, SHIRLEY RICHARDSON, court clerk; b. Rogersville, Tenn., Aug. 10, 1937; d. James Newton and Jessie (Johnson) Richardson; m. John P. Graham, Dec. 20, 1969; children—David, Kevin, Philip. Grad. Steed Coll. Tech., Johnson City, Tenn., 1955. Sec., bookkeeper, J. Mayes, Atty., Rogersville, Tenn., 1955-56, Hawkins Farmers Group Coop., Rogersville, 1960-61; dep. clk. Hawkins County Ct., Rogersville, 1961-73; dep. clk. Chancery Ct. for Hawkins County, Rogersville, 1973-79, clk., master, 1979—. Bd. dirs. Upper E. Tenn. Tourism Council, Jonesborough, 1984-85; mem. exec. com. Hawkins County Republican Party. Mem. Internat. Assn. State Ct. Clks., Tenn. Ct. Clks. Assn., East Tenn. State Ct. Clks. Assn. (v.p. 1984-85). Club: Hawkins County Rep. Women's (past pres.). Home: Steven St Rogersville TN 37857 Office: Hawkins County Courthouse Main St Rogersville TN 37857

GRAHAM, SYBIL ALLISON, public information specialist; b. North Massapequas, N.Y., June 14, 1958; d. Jack J. and Natalie F. (Friedman) Graham. B.S. in Communication, S.I. Newhouse Coll., 1980; M.B.A., Syracuse U., 1981. Entrepreneur, Creative Impact Co., Syracuse, N.Y., 1977-82; sales promoter Gen. Electric Co., Syracuse, 1977-78; product info. specialist Laubach Lit. Internat., Syracuse, 1981-82; sales promoter Blue Cross-Blue Shield, Syracuse, 1982—; owner The Typing Service, Syracuse, 1983—; cons. pub. relations SBA, Syracuse, 1977-82; pub. relations dir. Syracuse Women's Info. Ctr., 1981-83. Mem. fund-raising com. CNY Spl. Olympics, Syracuse, 1981—; fund-raising cons. CNY Cystic Fibrosis Found., Syracuse, 1983—; vol. counselor Am. Cancer Soc., Syracuse, 1984. Recipient Gov.'s Trophy award N.Y. State Hist. Soc., 1976, Archtl. Survey award, 1975; Spl. Olympics Coordinator Honor award, 1983, Internat. Bus. Communicator's award, 1984. Mem. Women in Communications, Bus. Profl. Advt. Assn., BIC. Democrat. Jewish. Home: 60 Presidential Plaza Syracuse NY 13202

GRAHAM, TERRY CLARK, nurse executive; b. Bluefield, W.Va., Feb. 24, 1952; d. Andrew Lewis and Theresa Caroline (Brown) Clark; m. Rickey Eugene Graham, Nov. 19, 1977; children—Alston Melissa, Justin Clark. B.S. in Nursing, W.Va. U., 1975; M.S. in Nursing, 1985. R.N., W.Va. Staff nurse med.-surg. unit Riverside Methodist Hosp., Columbus, Ohio, 1975-76; critical care nurse Ohio State U. Hosps., Columbus, 1976-77; nursing instr. A.D. program Bluefield State Coll., 1977-81; staff devel. instr., patient edn. coordinator Bluefield Community Hosp., 1981-82; assoc. exec. dir. nursing Humana Hosp. St. Luke's-Bluefield, 1982—. Mem. Am. Assn. Critical Care Nurses, W.Va. Soc. Hosp. Nursing Service Adminstrs., Sigma Theta Tau. Democrat. Episcopalian. Avocations: horseback riding, tennis, snow skiing, water skiing. Home: 1 Indian Rocke Boulder Park Princeton WV 24740 Office: Humana Hosp St Luke's Bluefield 1333 Southview Dr Bluefield WV 24701

GRAHAME, PAULA EASTER PATTON (MRS. ORVILLE FRANCIS GRAHAME), artist, writer; b. Clearfield, Iowa; d. Harry T. and Betsey J. (Jacobs) Patton; B.A., U. Iowa, 1926; m. Orville F. Grahame, Nov. 3, 1923; 1 dau., Sarah Grahame Cairns. Artist and sculptor exhibited at Ind. Artists, N.Y.C., Worcester Art Mus., Rockport Art Assn. Dir. Protective Ins. Assn. of Can., 1962-70; corporator Worcester Girls' Club; corporator, dir. Edward Street Day Nursery, 1954-60, Children's Friend Soc., 1963-67; pres. Unitarian Women's Alliance, 1966-68, dir. Youth Guidance Center, 1963-67; founder art scholarship fund U. Iowa, Distinguished Service award U. Iowa, 1969. Mem. Nat. Soc. Lit. and Arts, Worcester Hist. Soc., Worcester Sci. Center, DAR, State Hist. Soc. Iowa, Nat. Hist. Soc., Smithsonian Assocs., Assoc. Nat. Archives, Worcester Art Museum, Music Festival Assn., Nat. Trust Historic Preservation, Internat. Amigo Orgn. Am. States, Rockport Art Assn., AAUW (pres. Worcester br. 1959-61), Sigma Delta Chi. Unitarian. Author poems, short stories, Palimpsest hist. stories; editor Memorial Hospital News, 1951-54. Home: 6 Bancroft Tower Rd Worcester MA 01609

GRAINGER, JANET ELIZABETH, accountant; b. Houston, July 1, 1954; d. Oswald Joseph and Arline Elizabeth (David) G. B.B.A. in Acctg., Stephen F. Austin State U., Nacogdoches, Tex., 1976. Sec., bookkeeper Grainer, Inc., Houston, 1970-76; acct. Exxon Co. USA, Houston, 1976—. Home: 9630 Winsome St Houston TX 77063 Office: Exxon Co USA PO Box 2024 Houston TX 77001

GRAM, MARGARET HAMROCK, speech and lang. pathologist; b. Youngstown, Ohio, Apr. 5, 1951; d. Aloysius Thomas and Angela Marie (Salreno) Hamrock; B.S. magna cum laude, Kent State U., 1972, M.A. in Speech Pathology, 1973; m. George Richard Gram, Jan. 20, 1973. Speech and lang. pathologist Broward County (Fla.) Sch. Bd., 1973-74; co-owner Speech Pathology Assos., 1974-80; exec. sec. treas. Hamrock and Gram, P.A. Speech Pathology Assos., South Miami, Fla., 1980-81, pres., 1981-83; adminstr. Hamrock & Gram Rehab. Ctr. for Communication Disorders, Inc., 1983—; cons. speech and lang. pathology Mercy Hosp., Palmetto Gen. Hosp., South Miami Hosp., Hialeah Hosp., Coral Gables Hosp. Mem. South Miami C. of C., Am. Speech Lang. and Hearing Assn., Fla. Speech Lang. and Hearing Assn., Dade County Assn. Retarded Citizens, Internat. Assn. Logopedics and Phoniatrics. Roman Catholic. Contbr. Quality Assurance Manual, Fla. Assn. Home Health Agencies, 1979. Home: RFD #1 Pickpocket Woods Exeter NH 03833 Office: 10691 N Kendall Dr Suite 212 Miami FL 33176

GRAMDORF, MARILYN CAROL, nurse, accessory specialist; b. Watertown, Wis., Jan. 12, 1948; d. Harry Herman Joseph and Ruth Gertrude (Roth) G. Diploma in nursing Bellin Sch. Nursing, Green Bay, Wis., 1969; B.S., U. Wis.-Madison, 1981. Lic. nurse, Wis. Head nurse Bethesda Lutheran Home, Watertown, 1969-73, Lake Shore Manor, Madison, 1973-76; R.N. II, U. Wis. Hosp. and Clinic, Madison, 1976—; accessory specialist Home Interiors and Gifts, Madison, 1981—; sales person Tandy Leather Co., Madison, 1984-86; union rep. United Profls. for Quality Health Care, Madison, 1980-82, lobbyist, 1980—; chart auditor Clin. Sci. Ctr., Madison, 1985—; speaker, com. mem. Spl. Concerns of Elderly, Pre-Operative Teaching Conf., 1985. Author: (with others) teaching booklet If You're Having Surgery, 1984. Recipient Five Yr. Service award Ctr. Clin. Sci., U. Hosp., Madison, 1981. Mem. Home Interiors and Gifts Assn., Wis. Alumni Assn. Mem. Evangelical Free Ch. Avocations: leather crafter; reading; writing; gardening; music. Home: 409 W Broadway Monona WI 53716 Office: Clin Sci Ctr D4-6 600 Highland Madison WI 53704

GRAMM, WENDY LEE, government official; d. Joshua and Angeline (AnChin) Lee; m. Phil Gramm, Nov. 2, 1970; children—Marshall Kenneth, Jefferson Philip. B.A. in Econs., Wellesley Coll., 1966; Ph.D. in Econs., Northwestern U., 1970. Staff dept. quantitive methods U. Ill., 1969; asst. prof. Tex. A&M U., 1970-74, assoc. prof. dept. econs., 1975-79; research staff Inst. Def. Analyses, 1979-82; asst. dir. Bur. Econs., FTC, 1982-83, dir., 1983-85; adminstr. Office Info. and Regulatory Affairs, OMB, 1985—. Contbr. articles to profl. jours. Address: Office Mgmt and Budget Old Exec Office Bldg Room 246 Washington DC 20503

GRANADOS, CANDACE MICHELE, physical therapist; b. Albuquerque, Nov. 5, 1958; d. Lewis Ray and Pristina (Chavez) G. B.S. in Phys. Therapy, U. N.Mex., 1981. Chief phys. therapist CHI, Albuquerque, 1981; adminstr. Sports Phys. Therapy & Rehab., Albuquerque, 1982-83; v.p. N.Mex. Phys. Therapist Inc., Albuquerque, 1983—; v.p. Northeastern NMPT Inc.; mem. admissions com. U. N.Mex. Dept. Phys. Therapy, 1982—, mem. clin. edn. staff, 1985—; com. Bernallilo County Sports Medicine Com., 1986—. Mem. C. of C., Am. Phys. Therapy Assn., Nat. Assn. Female Execs., N.Mex. Phys. Therapy Assn., Albuquerque Medicine/Bus. Coalition, Am. Coll. Sports Medicine. Democrat. Roman Catholic. Avocations: water skiing; jogging; weight training; racquetball. Office: N Mex Phys Therapist Inc 2607 Wyoming Blvd NE Albuquerque NM 87112

GRAND, MARCIA, civic worker; b. N.Y.C., Aug. 9, 1933; d. Irving and Dorothy (Miller) Kosta; m. Richard Grand, Jan. 27, 1952; 1 child, Cindy Deborah. Docent, coordinator, docent trainer Tucson Mus. Art, 1965-71, chmn. edn. com. 1975-79, bd. dirs., 1972-79; v.p., sec. Richard Grand Found. for Legal Research and Edn., 1966-80, pres. 1980—; bd. dirs. Greenfields Schs., 1977-82, Tucson Mus. Art League, 1977-78; bd. dirs., sec. U. Ariz. Found., 1979—; bd. fellows Ctr. for Creative Photography, 1983—; mem. Tucson Airport Authority, 1986—. Recipient Disting. Citizen award U. Ariz. Coll. Fine Arts, YWCA Women on the Move award, 1982, Mortar Bd. Community Service award, 1978. Office: 127 W Franklin St Tucson AZ 85701

GRANDE, SARINA D'AMATO, designer, civic worker; b. N.Y.C., June 22; d. Francis and Maria D'Amato; pvt. tutors; numerous coll. courses; m. Frank Grande, Dec. 7, 1962. In various design and mfg. positions, garment industry, 1929-35; prin. design studio, clothing designs, N.Y.C., 1935-65; cons. to garment trade; cons. interior design; participant, coordinator Pageant of Lace for Ziegfield Club, 1941; cons. on synthetic fabrics I.E. DuPont de Nemours & Co., 1942-50; feature writer Italian Am. Rev. Active fund raiser for arts, charitable orgns., 1974—; mem. exec. bd., treas. Stanley Richter Assn. for Arts, Danbury, Conn., Scott Fanton Mus., Danbury, Hist. Soc. Danbury, Met. Opera Guild, N.Y.C., Am. Mus. Natural History, N.Y.C.; bd. dirs. Dante Found. Inc.; chmn. bd. Italian Am. Democratic Orgns. N.Y. N.Y.C., 1960-65; bd. dirs., founder, pres. D'Amato-Grande Scholarship Found. Inc.; mem. Danbury Cultural Commn., 1982-84; active Boys' Towns Italy, Girls' Towns Italy, Children's Day Treatment Ctr. and Sch. Recipient George B. DeLuca award Fedn. Italian Am. Dem. Orgns., 1959, Humanitarian award United Jewish Appeal and Friendship Internat., 1959; named Lady of Month, Italian Am. mag., 1962; cert. of recognition Vol. Bur. Greater Danbury, 1982. Mem. Ams. Italian Descent Inc. (chmn. bd. 1971-79), Am.-Italy Soc., French Alliance, Les Grands Vivants (founder and pres. 1974), N.Y. Mus. Modern Art, N.Y. Met. Mus., N.Y. Council Navy League of U.S. Roman Catholic. Club: Princeton (N.Y.). Designer for films: Three Men on a Horse, 1938; Black Magic, 1945; Power Unlimited, 1945; designer spl. garments for series This is America, 1945; patentee garment constrn., U.S., Can.; author Social Scene and Opera Scene columns Il Popolo weekly nat. newspaper, 1962-64. Home and Office: 400 E 56th St New York NY 10022

GRANDLE, LANNA CAROLE, construction company executive; b. Lewisville, Tex., Oct. 5, 1945; d. Henry Earle and Evelyn Elizabeth (Eason) Harris; m. Morris Charles Bollinger III, Dec. 3, 1966 (div. Jan. 1979); m. Edward Delong Grandle, June 27, 1980; children—Robert L., Elizabeth M., Bollinger. B.S., Washington U., St. Louis, 1971. Asst. mgr. office and personnel Fleetway Airlines, Tyler, Tex., 1964-68; office mgr., advt. dir. Harvey Little Assocs., Longview, Tex., 1971-74; exec. sec. Raymond Internat. Builders, Inc., Houston, 1975-80; v.p., owner Grandle Assocs., Inc., Houston, 1983—; breeder, owner Delongs Rare Treasures, 1980—. Mem. Houston Small Bus. Assn. Republican. Roman Catholic. Clubs: Chinese Shar-Pei of Am., South Central Chinese Shar-Pei (treas.). Home: 530 Bolton Pl Houston TX 77024 Office: Grandle Assocs Inc 530 Bolton Pl Houston TX 77024

GRANGER, NOELLE AUDREY, developmental biologist, anatomy educator; b. Bristol, Conn., Aug. 25, 1944; d. John Martin and Audrey Frances (LaCourse) Parsons; A.B., Mt. Holyoke Coll., 1965; Ph.D., Western Res. U., 1970; m. R. Eugene Granger, Aug. 19, 1967. Lectr. biol. scis. U. Calif., Irvine, 1971-77; research asso. dept. biol. scis. Northwestern U., Evanston, Ill., 1977-81; asst. prof. anatomy Med. Sch., U. N.C., Chapel Hill, 1981-85, assoc. prof., 1985—. Nat. Acad. Scis. exchange fellow Czechoslovak Nat. Acad. Scis., 1975-76; NSF grantee, 1976-81; Whitehall Found. grantee, 1976-81; NIH grantee, 1978—. Mem. Am. Women in Sci., Entomol. Soc. Am., European Soc. Comparative Endocrinologists, AAAS, Am. Soc. Zoologists. Democrat. Roman Catholic. Contbr. articles to profl. jours. Home: Route 8 Box 36I Chapel Hill NC 27514 Office: Dept Anatomy U NC Chapel Hill NC 27514

GRANLUND, BARBARA A., state legislator; b. Nebr. Mem. Wash. Ho. of Reps., Olympia, 1979-82, mem. Senate, 1983—, now chmn. human services and corrections standing com., mem. transp. and govtl. ops. coms. Democrat. Office: Wash State Capitol Bldg Olympia WA 98504*

GRANT, AUDRA LEE, real estate broker; b. Decatur, Tex., Dec. 13, 1907; d. Carl Curtis and Willie Mae (Golden) Smith; m. Elton Oran Grant, Aug. 22, 1941 (dec. 1957); 1 dau., Martha Linda. Prin., real estate broker Grant Agy., Ballinger, Tex., 1946—. Mem. Tex. Real Estate Bd., Nat. Real Estate Bd., C. of C. Ballinger (dir. 1957). Democrat. Baptist. Office: Grant Agy Tatum Bldg Ballinger TX 76821

GRANT, CHERYL, producer, syndicator TV; b. Phoenix, Mar. 1, 1944; d. William Edward and Mary Louise (Weldon) Grant; m. Louis Tancredi, Nov. 27, 1976; children—John Francis, Jennifer Grant. Student U. Fribourg, Switzerland, 1963-64; B.A., Coll. of Notre Dame of Md., 1965; M.S., Syracuse U., 1966. Assoc. producer Girl Talk ABC Films, N.Y.C., 1968-70, New Jersey Speaker for Itself, WNDT-TV, N.Y.C., 1966-68, Communications and Education, WNDT-TV, N.Y.C., 1967, The Virginia Graham Show, RKO, Los Angeles, 1970-71, Manhattan Townhouse, Source Internat., N.Y.C., 1971-72, Collision Course, Wolper Prodns., Los Angeles, 1972, Living Easy with Dr. Joyce Brothers, Capricorn Prodns., N.Y.C., 1972-73, Mike Douglas Show, Westinghouse, Phila., 1974, Beverly & Vidal Sassoon, Sta. KCOP, Los Angeles, 1975, Dinah, 20th Century Fox, Los Angeles, 1975; hostess A.M. Miami, Sta. WPLG-TV, Miami, Fla., 1972; exec. producer/pres. Carter-Grant Prodns., Inc., Los Angeles, 1976—, Sherry Grant Enterprises, Inc., Los Angeles, 1982—. Programs have been honored by the Freedom Found. award, Internat. Film and TV Festival of N.Y. Gold Award and Calif. Motion Picture Assn. Golden Halo award. Mem. Acad. T.V. Arts and Sci., Women in Bus., Women in Film, Am. Women in Radio and TV, AFTRA, Women in Cable. Roman Catholic. Home: 18120 Sweet Elm Dr Encino CA 91316 Office: Sherry Grant Enterprises 17915 Ventura Blvd Suite 208 Encino CA 91316

GRANT, CHRISTINE MARIE, lawyer; b. Grand Rapids, Mich., Aug. 27, 1947; d. Russell Joseph and Ruth Marie (Laird) G.; m. Michael David Halpern, Sept. 5, 1970; children—Ian Loren Halpern, Nathaniel Russell Halpern. B.A., Swarthmore Coll., 1969; M.B.A., Wharton Sch. Fin., 1973; J.D., Rutgers U., 1982. Bar: N.J. 1982, U.S. Dist. Ct. N.J. 1982. Program officer The Robert Wood Johnson Found., Princeton, N.J., 1973-79, sr. program officer, 1979; bus. mgr. Rutgers Law Rev., 1981-82; assoc. McCarter & English, Newark, 1982-84; dir. hosp. reimbursement program State of N.J., Trenton, 1984—. Trustee Assn. Advancement Mental Health, Princeton, 1984. Mem. N.J. Bar Assn.

GRANT, CYNTHIA ELIZABETH, museum director, teacher, consultant; b. Asheville, N.C., Oct. 4, 1948; d. Roger Alpine Grant, Jr. and Mary Elizabeth (Scott) Winterling. B.A., Salem Coll., 1970; M.A. in History, Wake Forest U., 1986. Cert. tchr. social studies. Tchr. Asheville City Schs., 1970-71; buyer Navy Exchange, U.S. Navy, Roosevelt Roads, P.R., 1971-72; staff asst. Tulane U., New Orleans, 1972-74; ombudsman Am. Bankers Assn., Washington, 1977-78; mus. dir. City of Alexandria, Va., 1978-81; dir. Hist. Columbia Found., S.C., 1981—; cons. Kensington Plantation, Eastover, S.C., 1985—, Hist. Beaufort Found., S.C., 1985; mem. resource com. Cultural Council, Columbia, 1983—. Bd. dirs. Young Profls. of Columbia Mus., 1984-85; com. chmn. Leadership Columbia, 1983—; event chmn. Champions of Children's Hosp., Columbia, 1984—; mem. stewardship com. Shandon Presbyn. Ch., Columbia, 1983—. Recipient Pres.'s prize Salem Coll., 1970; John H. Stibbs award Tulane U., 1973; named to Outstanding Young Women Am., 1985. Mem. Am. Assn. Mus., Southeast Mus. Conf., S.C. Fedn. Mus. (sec. 1983-84), Am. Assn. for State and Local History (award of merit for mus. 1984), Nat. Trust for Hist. Preservation, Columbia Forum. Democrat. Presbyterian. Avocations: photography, hiking, travel. Home: 1638 Greene St Columbia SC 29201 Office: Hist Columbia Found 1601 Richland St Columbia SC 29201

GRANT, GRETCHEN SUE, insurance agent; b. Westfield, Ohio, June 8, 1939; d. Paul David and Dorothy Gettinger; m. Victor R. Grant, Mar. 17, 1973; stepchildren—Kathleen, Victor J., Annemarie. Student, Adirondack Community Coll., 1982. Ins. agent B.V. Grant's Ins. Agy., Lake Luzerne, N.Y., 1971—. Mem. Warren City Republican Com., Glens Falls, N.Y. Mem. Ins. Women Assn. Roman Catholic. Club: Every Women's Council (Glen Falls). Lodge: Lioness (Hadley-Luzerne). Avocations: reading; gardening.

GRANT, HELEN LILLIAN, health spa chain exec.; b. Joliet, Ill., Jan. 2, 1925; d. Carmen and Lucia L. (Pistilli) Palleschi; student Met. Bus. Coll., 1943-44; student Budde Flying Sch., 1947-49, U. Houston, 1967-68; m. Michael D. Grant, June 20, 1958 (dec.); children—Laura Grant Chamblin, Mary Helen, Michael Daniel, Troy. Bookkeeper, acct., comptroller, v.p., cost clk. Am. Can. Co., Joliet, Ill., 1943-45; bookkeeper Aylin Advt. Agy. and Naman Hotel Supply, Houston, 1951-55; acct. Houston Bus. Service, 1955-65; comptroller Slenderbolic Health Spa, Houston, 1965-72, Dynamics Health Equipment Co., Houston, 1972-77; comptroller Figure World, Inc., San Antonio, 1972-79, v.p., 1980—; fin. advisor, dir. Lea Haller Internat., Inc., officer, M&L Oil and Gas Exploration, Inc., Mt. Calm Oil Devel., Inc., Somerset-Von Ormy Oil Devel., Inc. Active Blue Bird Aux., S.W. Tex. Meth. Hosp., San Antonio, 1980—. Served with WAVES, 1945-47. Roman Catholic. Club: Tex. A&M Mother's. Home: 200 Prinz St San Antonio TX 78213 Office: 508 W Rhapsody St San Antonio TX 78216

GRANT, ISABELLA HORTON, judge; b. Los Angeles, Sept. 24, 1924; d. John Daniel and Hannabelle (Horton) Grant. B.A., Swarthmore Coll., 1944; M.A., UCLA, 1946; J.D., Columbia U., 1950; LL.D., Molloy Coll., 1976. Jr. profl. asst. OSS, Washington, 1944-45; economist Inst. Indsl. Relations, UCLA, 1946-47, Office Price Stblzn., Los Angeles, 1951-52; assoc. Livingston, Grant, Stone & Kay, San Francisco, 1953-79; judge Mcpl. Ct., San Francisco, 1979-82, Superior Ct., San Francisco, 1982—. Bd. dirs. Advs. for Women, San Francisco, 1980—; adv. bd. Am. Conservatory Theatre, San Francisco, 1980—. Fellow ABA; mem. San Francisco Bar Assn. (bd. dirs. 1978-79), Acad. Matrimonial Lawyers (pres. No. Calif. chpt. 1976), Queen's Bench (pres. 1964), Phi Beta Kappa. Clubs: Met. (San Francisco); Calif. Tennis. Office: Superior Ct City Hall San Francisco CA 94102

GRANT, JUANITA G., librarian; b. Princeton, W.Va., July 25, 1930; d. William Randle and Cora (Fitch) Grant; B.S., Concord Coll., 1953; B.S. in L.S., U. N.C., 1955; M.Liberal Arts, Johns Hopkins U., 1970. Librarian, Spl. Services, U.S. Army, Germany, France, 1956-58; asst. librarian Carson Newman Coll., Jefferson City, Tenn., 1959-63; librarian Judson Coll., Marion, Ala., 1964-67; dir. Blount Library, Averett Coll., Danville, Va., 1967—; library adv. com. Va. Council Higher Edn., 1976-78; mem. adv. com. Danville Pub. Library; chmn. library com. Danville Mus. Fine Arts and History, 1976—. Mem. ALA, Southeastern Library Assn., Va. Library Assn., Am. Hist. Soc., Danville Hist. Soc., Phi Delta Kappa. Baptist. Club: Wednesday (Danville). Home: 126 Primrose Ct Danville VA 24541

GRANT, MARCIA JOY, property manager; b. Baton Rouge, Sept. 20, 1938; d. William Perry Crowell and Ida Mae (Meadows) Ferguson; m. Godfrey Ware Grant, Sept. 7, 1959 (div. 1981); children—James Godfrey, Stephen Everett. Student La. State U., Baton Rouge, 1958-59, U. Tex., 1956-57, North Tex. State U., Denton, 1957-58. Sec. to grad. dean U. Tex.-Austin, 1966-70; sec. Robert Britigan & Co., Kalamazoo, 1971-72; exec. sec. Prudential Ins. Co., Kalamazoo, 1972-78; bldg. mgr. Draper & Kramer Inc., Kalamazoo, 1978-82, property mgr., promotions dir., Des Moines, 1983—. Bd. dirs. Downtown Des Moines Inc., 1986—. Mem. C. of C. Kalamazoo (edn. com. 1982-83), C. of C. Des Moines chpt. (retention com. 1983), Bldg Owners & Mgrs. Assn (sec., governing council 1984, pres. 1986), Inst. Real Estate Mgmt. (mem. experience exchange com., v.p. 1986), Internat. Council Shopping Ctrs. Democrat. Episcopalian. Office: Draper and Kramer Inc 400 Locust Suite 690 Des Moines IA

GRANT, MARGARET ELLEN, psychiatrist; b. Clinton, Okla., July 5, 1948; d. Gilbert Richard and Bernice (Bledsoe) G.; B.A. in Biology, Rice U., 1970; M.D., U. Ark., 1975. Research asst. U. Ark. Sch. Medicine, Little Rock,

1970-72, intern, 1975-76; resident in psychiatry U. Colo., Denver, 1976-80; career resident Colo. State Hosp., Pueblo, 1978-79; practice medicine specializing in psychiatry, Denver, 1980—; psychiat. cons. Jefferson County Mental Health Center, Lakewood, Colo., 1980—; vol. U. Colo. Med. Center, 1980—; mem. staff Bethesda, Mt. Airy, St. Joseph hosps.; dir. Denver Women's Ctr. Diplomate Am. Bd. Psychiatry. Mem. Am. Psychiat. Assn., Colo. Psychiat. Soc., Colo. Women's Med. Assn. Democrat. Office: 3773 Cherry Creek Dr N Suite 225 Denver CO 80209

GRANT, RUBY JAYNE JOHNSON, insurance agent-broker; b. Glen Cove, N.Y., June 28; d. Alfred Lloyd and Ora Mae (Gibson) Pendleton; m. Nolan Eugene Grant, June 2; 1 child, Kristale Michelle. Grad. Glen Cove High Sch. Telephone operator N.Y. Phone Co., Roslyn, 1958-60; bookkeeper Town and Country, Roslyn, 1961-65; teller Meadowbrook Bank, Jericho, N.Y., 1966-67; ins. cons. Met. Life Ins. Co., Hicksville, N.Y., 1968-73; ins. agt. AllState Ins. Co., Glen Cove, 1973—. Active New Cassel Republican Club, Westbury, N.Y., 1985—; pres. Youth Club, Glen Cove, 1980-85. Mem. Nat. Assn. Negro Bus. and Profl. Women (life; rec. sec. 1985—), Nat. Assn. for Female Execs. Mem. 1st Ch. of God in Christ. Avocations: interior decorating, bicycling, roller skating. Home: 261 Brook St Westbury NY 11590 Office: Allstate Ins Co 75 Forest Ave Glen Cove NY 11542

GRANT, SARA CATHERINE, girl scouts training administrator; b. Johnstown, Pa., Mar. 28, 1950; d. James Walter and Bernetta (Bewak) G. B.S. in English, Lock Haven U., 1973; M.A. in Adult Edn., Ind. U. of Pa., 1978. Tchr. English sch. dist., Williamsport, Pa., 1973; adminstr., adult basic edn. sch. dist., Somerset, Pa., 1973-77; tng. dir. Girl Scouts U.S.A. Council, Harrisburg, Pa., 1977-79, adult devel. cons., N.Y.C., 1979-82, dir. tng., N.Y.C., 1982—. Contbr. articles to mags. Visitor for the elderly St. Patrick's Cathedral Social Services, N.Y.C., 1985—. Mem. Am. Soc. Tng. and Devel., Phi Delta Kappa. Democrat. Avocation: tennis. Home: 104-20 Queens Blvd Forest Hills NY 11375

GRANT, SYLVIA ORLENE, nursing administrator; b. Gary, Ind., Jan. 23, 1953; d. Benjamin Franklin and Juanita Zoe (Crone) Grant; m. Keith Wayne Bynam, Oct. 17, 1981. Student Fisk U., 1970-72, St. Louis U., 1973-74; B.S. in Nursing, Ind. U.-Purdue U., Indpls., 1976; M.S.N. in Psychiat. Mental Health Nursing, 1979. Staff nurse oncology unit Methodist Hosp., Indpls., 1976, discharge planner, 1976-77; psychotherapist LaPorte (Ind.) Mental Health Ctr., 1980-81; clin. coordinator Houston Internat. Hosp., 1981-82, asst. dir. nurses, 1982, acting dir. nurses, 1982-83; hosp. supr. West Oaks Hosp., Houston, 1983, asst. dir. nurses, 1984—; cons. Terry Stukalin Health Care Mgmt. Inc., Houston, 1982-83. Hoosier hon. scholar, 1970. Mem. Am. Nurses Assn. (co-coordinator Congl. dist. for Michael Andrews), Houston Area Psychiat. Nurse Mgrs. Assn. (pres., dir.), Tex. Nurses Assn., Nat. Nursing Adminstrn. Council. Democrat. Episcopalian. Club: Quintessence Social and Civic. Home: 12219 Lemon Ridge Houston TX 77035

GRANTHAM, CAROLYN R., association executive; b. Chgo., Nov. 15, 1947; d. Ernest and Bessie (Magee) G. B.A., Roosevelt U., 1975, M.P.A., 1979. Clk.-typist Naval Intelligence, Chgo., 1966-67; supr. support services Chgo. Title & Trust Co., 1971-75; office adminstr. Chgo. Health Manpower Consortium, 1975-78; asst. community dir. South Central Community Services, Chgo., 1980-81; staff adminstr. ABA, Chgo., 1981—; pvt. tutorer, Chgo., 1982—. Sec. NIA Comprehensive Ctr. for Devel. Disabilities, Inc., Chgo., 1982—; dir. Christian edn. Allen Temple Methodist Ch., Chgo., 1982—. Ill. State scholar, 1975. Mem. Nat. Assn. Female Execs. Clubs: Service Guild (treas. 1980—), Mayor's Civic (Chgo.).

GRANTHAM, MARGARET ETHEL, nurse; b. Manchester, N.H.; d. Alfred Joseph and Lena Margaret (Griffiths) Thibodeau; m. Arnold L. Grantham, Jan. 12, 1946; children—John, Robert, Michael, Christopher. R.N., Notre Dame Hosp., Manchester, N.H., 1941. Night supr. Notre Dame Hosp., Manchester, 1941-42; operating room supr. Newport Hosp. (N.H.), 1946-47; pub. health nurse, Newport, N.H., 1958-67; pub. health nurse Polk County Health Dept. (Fla.), 1970-75; central supply supr. Meth. Hosp., Hattiesburg, Miss., 1976-80; staff nurse Jones County Rest Home, Ellisville, Miss., 1980—. Served to lt. AUS 1942-46. Mem. Am. Nurses Assn., Am. Legion., Am. Legion Aux. Republican. Roman Catholic. Address: Route 2 Box 120 Moselle MS 39459

GRASSE, WANDA GENE, lawyer, writer; b. Baird, Tex., July 28, 1940; d. William Eugene and Alta Roberta (Dickerson) George; m. Weldon Morris Carriker, Jan 27, 1960; div. 1968; 1 son, Conrad Ray; m. 2d, John Lee Grasse, Mar. 28, 1970; 1 dau., Karen Diane. LL.B., LaSalle-Whittier Coll. Law, Los Angeles, 1977; postgrad. entertainment law studies, U. So. Calif., 1983. Bar: Calif. 1978, U.S. Tax Ct. 1981. Continuity dir. Sta. KLBK-TV and WTTN, Lubbock Tex., 1960-66; promotion writer, dir. KTTV and KCOP, Los Angeles, 1966-72; sole practice law, Los Angeles, 1978-81; assoc. Laurence E. Clark, Law Corp. Monterey Park, Calif., 1981—. Mem. Los Angeles County Bar Assn., San Gabriel Valley Bar Assn., ABA. Republican. Mem. Sci. Mind, Mensa. Club: Bus. and profl. Women's (v.p. 1980-81, woman achievement award 1980) (Los Angeles). Home: 1300 Fulton Ave Monterey Park CA 91754 Office: Laurence E Clark Law Corp 631 S Atlantic Blvd Monterey Park CA 91754

GRASSI, ELLEN ELIZABETH, photographic products company executive; b. N.Y.C., July 27, 1949; d. Dante J. and Mary D. (Olivieri) G. B.A. in Teaching, High Point Coll., 1971; postgrad. Brockport State Coll., 1972, C.W. Post Coll., 1978—. Cert. secondary tchr., N.Y. Tchr. Yonkers Bd. Edn., N.Y., 1971-76; electronic technician Canon U.S.A., Inc., Lake Success, N.Y., 1977-82, supr. ea. region, 1982-84, asst. mgr. electronic bus. equipment services nat., 1984-85, mgr. nat. service adminstrn., 1985—. Active, founding mem. Little Neck Hills Assn., N.Y., 1984; active Douglaston Civic Assn., N.Y.; tech. cons. N.Y.C. council Girl Scouts U.S.; polling booth elector N.Y.C. Bd. Elections. Mem. Nat. Service Mgrs. Assn., Nat. Assn. Female Execs. Avocations: racquetball; skiing; reading. Office: Canon USA Inc One Jericho Plaza Jericho NY 11753

GRASSO, DORIS TENEYCK (MRS. DOMINIC LAWRENCE GRASSO), artist; b. Sullivan County, N.Y., May 3, 1914; d. Eugene Oscar and Elsie (TenEyck) Teschner; student Ednl. Alliance, N.Y.C., 1957-57; student art centers and pvt. art tng.; m. Dominic Lawrence Grasso, Nov. 29, 1933; children—Robert Eugene, Virginia Ann. Art dir., instr. Doris Grasso Sch. Fine Arts, Bayonne, N.J., 1952-61; exhibited in numerous group shows, including Thomson Gallery, N.Y.C., Pen and Brush Club, N.Y.C., Terry Art Inst., Miami, Fla., Newark Art Mus., Montclair (N.J.) Art Mus., Lever House, N.Y.C., Nat. Arts Club, N.Y.C., Salamugundi Club, N.Y.C., Rockport Art Assn., North Shore Art Assn., also others; one man shows Burr Gallery, N.Y.C., Bennett Coll., Bayonne Pub. Library, others; represented in Paul Whitener Meml. Collection, Hickory (N.C.) Mus. Art, George B. Burr Permanent Collection, N.Y.C., Bambergers Collection Famous People N.J., Jersey City Art Mus. Trustee, Jersey City Mus. Art, 1955-57. Recipient Pauline Wick award, 1961, Windsor Newton awards, 1958, 61, Jersey City Mus. award, 1958; gold medallion Jersey Jour. award, gold medal Woman's Club, 1963; award for nat. achievement in art Amita, Inc., 1966; 1st award for sculpture Fedn. Women's Clubs, Ridgewood, N.J., 1971, Nat. Conv. Womens Clubs, Atlantic City, also others; 1st sculpture award Womens Club, Atlantic City, N.J., 1971; others. Fellow Am. Artists Profl. League, Internat. Arts and Letters (Switzerland); mem. Burr Artists, Hudson Artists (pres. 1960-62), Nat. Mus. Women in Arts (charter mem.), Jersey City Mus. Assn., N.J. Painters and Sculptors Soc. (dir., rec. sec.), Trailside Art Mus. (permanent mem.), Essex Watercolor Soc. Bayonne Mus. Arts, Whistler Art Soc., Burr Galleries, Village Art Center Galleries, Sarasota Mus. Art Assn., Hunterdon Art Center Assn., Newark Art Center, Hudson Artists (dir.), Gotham Painters Gotham Painters, Plainfield Art Assn., Rockport Artists Assn. (asso.), Elks Aux. (pres. 1950-52), Ch. Guild (pres. 1950-52). Club: Bayonne Women's (art chmn.). Address: Doris TenEyck Grasso Gallery 15 Langsford St Lanesville Cape Ann Gloucester MA 01930

GRATZ, PAULINE, emeritus human ecology educator; b. N.Y.C., Mar. 30, 1924; d. John and Rose (Berman) Gratz; B.A., Hunter Coll., 1945; M.A., Columbia, 1948, Ed.D., 1961; m. Sidney Aaronson, July 25, 1969. Jr. bacteriologist Queens (N.Y.) Gen. Hosp., 1945-47; research technician Jewish Hosp. Bklyn., 1947-48; instr. biol. and phys. scis. Bayonne (N.J.) Hosp. Sch. Nursing, 1948-51; sci. coordinator phys. and biol. scis. N.Y. Med. Coll. Sch. Nursing, 1951-56, New Rochelle (N.Y.) Hosp. Sch. Nursing, 1956-61; instr. nursing edn. Columbia U. Tchrs. Coll., 1961-62, asst. prof. natural scis. and nursing edn., 1963-65, asst. prof. natural scis., 1965-67, asso. prof., 1967-69; prof. human ecology Duke U. Sch. Nursing, 1969-85, prof. emeritus, 1985—; vis. prof. physiology N.C. Health Manpower Project, summer 1973; cons. Kingsborough Community Coll., Bklyn., 1967-68, Medi-Visuals, Inc., N.Y.C., 1968-72; bd. dirs. N.C. League Nursing, New Hope Audubon Soc. NSF fellow, 1965; Shell merit fellow, 1969. Fellow AAAS; mem. Durham Mental Health Assn., Kappa Delta Pi, Pi Lambda Theta, Iota Sigma Pi, Sigma Theta Tau (hon.). Author: Integrated Science: An Interdisciplinary Approach, 1966; (with Cornett) Human Physiology, 1986; Experiments in Physiology, 1986; Teachers Guide in Human Physiology, 1986; contbr. chpts. to books in field.

GRAU, MARCY BEINISH, investment banker; b. Bklyn., Aug. 7, 1950; d. Joseph Beinish and Gloria (Rosenbaum) Bennett; m. Bennett Grau, Nov. 19, 1978; 1 child, Shara. A.B. with high honors, U. Mich., 1971; postgrad. Columbia U. Grad. Sch. Russian, 1972, N.Y. Inst. Fin., 1973. Asst. to chef The Plaza Hotel, N.Y.C., 1972-73; asst. to chmn. Bancroft Convertible Fund, N.Y.C., 1973-75; precious metals trader J. Aron & Co., N.Y.C., 1975-81, mgr. metals mktg., 1981-83; v.p. Goldman, Sachs/J. Aron, N.Y.C., 1983—; bus. related translator Augustus Clothiers, N.Y.C., 1979—. Editor, contbr. Precious Metals Rev. and Outlook, 1980—. Assoc. The Child Devel. Ctr., N.Y.C., 1984-85; tutor Yorkville Neighborhood Assn., N.Y.C., 1984; vol. Yorkville Common Pantry, N.Y.C., 1984, Lenox Hill Hosp. Pediatrics, N.Y.C., 1978-79; asst. The Holiday Project, Hunger Project, N.Y.C., 1978-83. Mem. Assn. Profl. Women in Metals, Phi Beta Kappa. Democrat. Jewish. Club: Alliance Francaise (N.Y.C.). Avocations: interior design; fashion; cooking; swimming. Home: 445 E 80th St New York NY 10021 Office: Goldman Sachs & Co 85 Broad St New York NY 10004

GRAU, SHIRLEY ANN (MRS. JAMES KERN FEIBLEMAN), writer; b. New Orleans, July 8, 1929; d. Adolph and Katherine (Onions) Grau; B.A., Tulane U., 1950; m. James Kern Feibleman, Aug. 4, 1955; children—Ian, James, Nora Miranda, William, Katherine. Writer for Holiday, New Yorker, New World Writing, Mademoiselle, Sat. Eve. Post, Atlantic, The Reporter, 1954—. Author: The Black Prince and Other Stories, 1955; The Hard Blue Sky, 1958; The House on Coliseum Street, 1961; The Keepers of the House (Pulitzer prize for fiction 1965), 1964; The Condor Passes, 1971; The Wind Shifting West and Other Stories, 1973; Evidence of Love, 1977; Nine Women, 1986. Mem. Phi Beta Kappa. Office: 1314 First Nat Bank of Commerce Bldg New Orleans LA 70112

GRAUDONS, SALLY ANN, systems specialist; b. Little Falls, N.Y., Sept. 3, 1939; d. Arthur Marmaduke and Elizabeth Graudons; B.A. in Math., Syracuse U., 1960. Programmer trainee Mutual of N.Y., 1961; computer communications software programmer Univac, London, 1965-68; computer specialist Citibank, N.Y.C., 1968-71; edn. mgr. Basic Four Computer Co., N.Y.C., 1971-77; mktg. rep. Edutronics McGraw-Hill, N.Y.C., 1977-79; v.p. systems devel. N.Y. State Urban Devel. Corp., 1981-83; cons. in field. Mem. Data Processing Mgmt. Assn., Am. Soc. Tng. and Devel. Home: 440 E 79th St New York NY 10021

GRAUER, RHODA SHEILA, arts administrator, TV producer; b. Poughkeepsie, N.Y., Dec. 31, 1944; d. Paul Jacob and Ethel (Gingold) G. B.A., Vassar Coll., 1966. Prodn. asst. APA-Phoenix Repertory Co., N.Y.C., 1966-68; asst. to dir. Spoleto Festival, N.Y.C. and Spoleto, Italy, 1968-70, adminstrv. dir., 1970-74; exec. dir. Twyla Tharp Dance Found., N.Y.C., 1974-78, advisor, 1978-84, bd. dirs., 1984—; dir. dance program Nat. Endowment for Arts, Washington, 1978-82; dir. media devel. Am. Ballet Theatre, N.Y.C., 1982-84; assoc. dir. performance programs WNET/Thirteen, N.Y.C. 1984—; trustee Dance U.S.A., Washington, 1982-85; exec. producer TV spls.: The Catherine Wheel, 1983, Baryshnikov By Tharp, 1984 (3 nat. Emmy awards), Jerome Robbins and the New York City Ballet; assoc. producer TV spls.: Making Television Dance, 1976, Live from Studio 8H, An Evening with Jerome Robbins, 1980; producer: American Ballet Theatre at the Metropolitan, 1984. Recipient Maj. Achievement award Commune di Spoleto, 1973; Superior Achievement award Nat. Endowment for Arts, 1981.

GRAUL, ZOE ANN, sewing machine manufacturing company executive; b. Prairie du Chien, Wis., Mar. 17, 1950; d. Walter L. and Gretchen (Roth) G. B.S., U. Wis., 1973; M.Ed., Rutgers U., 1977, Sp.Edn. 1978. Tchr. home econs. Butler Middle Sch., Waukesha, Wis., 1973-76, N.Y.C. Public Schs., 1978-80; ednl. services coordinator Simplicity Pattern, N.Y.C., 1980-82; mgr. tng. and edn. Singer Co., Edison, N.J. 1982—; appearances on various TV talk shows, 1980—. U.S. Ednl. Profl. Devel. fellow, 1977-78. Mem. Am. Home Econs. Assn., Home Economists in Bus., Omicron Tau Theta. Home: 180 Mountainview Ave Nutley NJ 07110 Office: Singer Co 135 Raritan Center Pkwy Edison NJ 08837

GRAVES, DEBRA BERYL, tax accountant; b. Boston, Nov. 25, 1958; d. Berkley Edward and Driscilla (Thomas) G. B.A., Simmons Coll., 1980; cert. in acctg., Northeastern U., 1983. Career counselor Boston YMCA, 1979, Boston Employment and Econ. Policy Adminstrn., 1979, Boston State Coll., 1980, Wider Opportunities for Women, Boston, 1980; claims rep. Kemper Ins. Co., North Quincy, Mass., 1980-84; tax acct. John Hancock Mut. Life Ins. Co., Boston, 1984—. Mem. Nat. Assn. Female Execs., Urban League Ea. Mass., Third World Alliance (treas. Simmons Coll. chpt. 1985—). Democrat. Baptist. Avocations: photography; tennis; travel. Home: 12 Holborn St Boston MA 02121

GRAVES, MARTHA S., banker; b. Salina, Kans., Aug. 15, 1951; d. William H. and Helen M. (Mayo) Graves. B.A., Kans. Wesleyan U., 1974; M.B.A., U. Denver, 1975; grad. Colo. Sch. Banking, 1979, Am. Inst. Banking, 1983. Trust officer Jefferson Bank & Trust Co., Lakewood, Colo., 1975-79; Central Bank of Denver, 1979—. Trustee Kans. Wesleyan U., Salina, 1981—; adviser Jr. Achievement of Met. Denver, 1978—. Mem. Western Pension Conf. (Denver chpt.), Internat. Assn. Employee Benefit Plans, Denver Trust Officers Assn. (chmn. 1982-83), Foothills Credit Women Internat. (named Credit Woman of Yr. 1981, pres. 1983-84). Republican. Methodist. Home: 1777 Larimer #908 Denver CO 80202 Office: Central Bank of Denver 1515 Arapahoe St Denver CO 80202

GRAVES, MARY JO, landscape contractor; b. Beirne, Ark., Aug. 26, 1928; d. Wells Albert and Stella Mae (Baker) Wright; student Henderson (Ark.) State Tchrs. Coll., 1946-48, La. Landscape Sch., 1968-71; extension student Ark. State Tchrs. Coll. Conway, 1948; m. Cleve Verlon Graves, Mar. 5, 1949; children—Cleve Verlon, Sandra Lyn Graves Lindsay. Tchr., Glenrose, Ark., 1947-49, England, Ark., 1950; partner North Caddo Drug Co., Vivian, La., 1954—; propr. North Caddo Landscape, Vivian, 1973—; city horticulturist City of Vivian, 1973-79; mem. bd. Caddo-Bossier Conv. and Tourists Bur., 1975-83. Chmn. North Caddo Parish Bicentennial Com., 1973-76; renovations furnishings chmn. Redbud Mus., 1970-76; organizer Redbud Festival, 1964, pres., 1964-66; pres. Vivian Garden Club, 1962-64; designer promoter Bicentennial Fountain of Youth and Mini Park, 1976; organizer bicentennial covered-wagon train, 1976, wildflower trails La., 1979. Recipient award of appreciation from gov. La., 1974, 75; NW La. Beautification and Slogans Design award; 2d place award for Wildflower Trail, 1981; 1st place for rural projects, 1983; grantee La. Bicentennial Com., 1973; various other honors. Accredited master flower show judge. Mem. Landscape Design Critics Council, Council State Garden Clubs, La. Garden Club Fedn. (pres. 1979, judges council, chmn. roadsides 1981-83, wildflowers 1983—), N.W. La. Hist. Assn., La. Native Plant Soc. Presbyterian. Club: North Highlands Garden (pres. 1975-77). Co-author: Monterey?, 1973. Home: 311 W Mary St Vivian LA 71082 Office: 144 W Louisiana St Vivian LA 71082

GRAVES, MONICA RENEE, accountant; b. Chestertown, Md., June 3, 1958; d. Charles Henry and Hilda Virginia (Lively) Graves. B.S. in Acctg., Goldey Beacom, 1982, A.A. in Bus. Info. Systems, 1983. Taxpayer service rep. IRS, Washington, 1976-78; statis. analyst Am. Life Ins., Wilmington, Del., 1978-79; cost acct. E.I. DuPont de Nemours, Wilmington, 1979—; fin. ons. Dave Wooley Prodns., Wilmington, 1984—. Chmn. supervisory com. Delaware Valley Credit Union, Wilmington, 1980—; treas. Brandywine Profl. Assn., 1984-86. Named Outstanding Advisor, Jr. Achievement, Wilmington, 1984, 85. Mem. NAACP, Nat. Assn. Female Execs. Avocations: tennis; dancing; chess.

GRAVES, PIRKKO MAIJA-LEENA, clinical psychologist, psychoanalyst; b. Tampere, Finland, Jan. 20, 1930; came to U.S., 1957; d. Frans Vilho and Bertta Katariina (Katajisto) Lahtinen; Mag.Phil. (Finnish State scholar 1949-52), 1954; French Govt. scholar, U. Paris, 1954-55; Ph.D. (Fulbright scholar 1957-58, Lucy E. Elliott scholar 1958-59), U. Mich., 1964; postgrad. Washington Psychoanalytic Inst.; m. Irving Lawrence Graves, Dec. 31, 1969. Psychologist, U. Mich. Psychol. Clinic, 1960-63, asst. study dir. Survey Research Center, 1961-63, instr. psychology, 1964-70; asst. prof. Johns Hopkins U., 1970—, prin. investigator infant undernutrition, Calcutta, West Bengal and Katmandu, Nepal, Internat. Ctr. Med. Research, 1970-73, lectr., sr. research psychologist Precursors Study, Med. Sch., 1979—; clin. assoc. prof. U. Md., 1984—; dir. research Mental Health Study Center, NIMH, 1976-79; cons. in field. Fellow Md. Psychol. Assn.; mem. Am. Psychol. Assn., Am. Psychoanalytic Assn. Author articles in field, chpts. in books. Home: 2235 Kentucky Ave Baltimore MD 21213 Office: 550 N Broadway Baltimore MD 21205

GRAVES, SUSAN L. AKERS, marketing specialist; b. Garden City, Kans., Feb. 4, 1948; d. Riley D. and Clara F. (Pallissard) Akers. Student Ariz. State U., 1982-83; B.S., U. Calif.-San Diego, 1972; post-grad. in bus. Loyola Marymount U., 1977-80. Pub. info. dir. Coll. Medicine, U. Calif.-Irvine, 1974-77; dir. pub. relations and publs. Loyola Marymount U., Los Angeles, 1977-82; v.p. Ralph Jackson Assocs., Beverly Hills, Calif., 1980-82; dir. pub. affairs Ramada Inns, Inc., Phoenix, 1982-83; pub. relations mgr. Am. Med. Internat., Brea, Calif., 1983-84; mktg. mgr. indsl. real estate div. The Irvine Co., Newport Beach, Calif., 1984—; prin. Creative Consortium, mktg. firm. Active Scottsdale Arts Ctr. Assn., 1982-83, No. Ariz. Hist. Mus., Flagstaff, 1982, Los Angeles County Art Mus.; bd. dirs. Irvine Symphony Choir; mem. adv. bd. on mktg. Calif. Community Coll.; cons. LWV, Jr. Achievement, Phoenix, 1983. Co-recipient Silver Anvil award U. Calif.-San Diego, 1973; Council for Advancement and Support of Edn. grantee, 1976. Mem. Women in Communications, Inc. (Best Communications Student of Yr. 1970; editor regional newsletter 1970-72, regional student dir. 1970-72, v.p. 1982), Pub. Relations Soc. Am., Sigma Delta Chi. Democrat. Home: 20612 Reef Ln Huntington Beach CA 92646 Office: Irvine Co Newport Beach CA 92660

GRAY, ANN MAYNARD, broadcasting company executive; b. Boston, Aug. 22, 1945; B.A., U. Mich., 1967; M.B.A., N.Y.U., 1971; m. Richard R. Gray, Jr. With Chase Manhattan Bank, N.Y.C., 1967-68; with Chem. Bank, 1968-73, asst. sec., 1971-73; asst. to treas. ABC, Inc., N.Y.C., 1973, asst. treas., 1974-76, treas., 1976-81, v.p. corp. planning, 1979—; dir. Carteret Savs. Bank, F.A. Office: 1330 Ave of Americas New York NY 10019

GRAY, BETTY LOU GORDON, retail business owner; b. Jasper, Tex., Apr. 14, 1941; d. Walter Louis and Effie Marie (Hulett) Gordon; m. Walker Richard Gray Jr., May 13, 1961; 1 son, Walker Richard III. Teller, transit dept. Bank of SW, Houston, 1959-62; receptionist to pres. So. Nat. Bank, Houston, 1963-64; with cashiers dept. Maroney-Bishner Co., Houston, 1969-70; co-owner, dir. Tradewinds Corp., Houston, 1971—; co-owner, pres. House of Frames, Inc., Houston, 1971—; co-owner, dir. Skate City U.S.A., 1980—. Mem. Profl. Picture Framers Assn., Harris County Heritage Soc., Robertson County Hist. Soc., DAR, Daus. Republic of Tex. Republican. Baptist. Clubs: Greater Houston Pommeranian, Convertible of Houston. Address: House of Frames Inc 1833 W Alabama St Houston TX 77098

GRAY, CAROL GREVER, office temporary and personnel executive; b. Tulsa, July 20, 1940; d. Clyde M. and Merietta L. (Stroud) Grever; m. James Rowland Gray, Jan. 31, 1961; children—Stephen Scott, Gary Matthew. B.A. in Lang. Arts with honors, Phillips U., 1962; M.A. in English with distinction, Pacific U., Oreg., 1966; doctoral candidate Okla. State U., 1971-72. High sch. tchr., Fort Worth, 1961-62, Beaverton, Oreg., 1963; asst. prof. Phillips U., Enid, Okla., 1966-73; v.p., communications dir. Express Temp., Boulder, Colo., 1973—; tng. cons. Express Services, Inc., Oklahoma City, 1984—. Author: Sun of a New Dawn, 1983; writer/editor quar. newsletters, 1982—; contbr. articles to newspapers. Bd. dirs. Boulder YWCA, 1984, Community Food Share, 1985. Mem. Nat. Assn. Temp. Services, Colo. Assn. Personnel Cons., Bus. and Profl. Women, Boulder C. of C. (exec. council 1984—, dir. 1984—, pres.-elect 1986, chair ambassadors council 1983, grad. Leadership Boulder 1984). Republican. Clubs: Flatirons Country, Soroptimists (past pres.) (Boulder). Avocations: travel; writing; water sports; cats. Office: Express Services 2741 Mapleton Ave Boulder CO 80302

GRAY, CATHERINE GARRISON, personnel executive; b. Allen, Tex., Dec. 30, 1926; d. Larkin Guy and Ella Ruth (Keyworth) Garrison; m. Hoyle Mack Gray, June 6, 1945; 1 child, Jim Mack. Office clk. Tex. Bond Reporter, Dallas, 1944-45; acctg. clk. Dallas Title & Guaranty Co., 1946-48, sec., bookkeeper, 1949-70; personnel coordinator USLIFE Title Ins. Co., Dallas, 1971-75, v.p. personnel adminstrn., 1975-85; sr. v.p. human resources Title USA Ins. Corp., 1985—. Cert. graphoanalyst. Mem. Internat. Graphoanalysis Soc., Tex. Graphoanalysts, Dallas Personnel Assn. Mem. Ch. of Christ. Home: 208 Whisenant Dr PO Box 157 Allen TX 75002 Office: 580 Decker Dr Irving TX 75062

GRAY, DONNA KATHERINE, marketing analyst; b. Ravenna, Ohio, Nov. 16, 1956; d. Franklin Junior and Nancy Lou (Dean) G. B.A., Miami U., 1979; M.B.A., Am. U. 1982. Research asst. FTC, Washington, 1980-81; mktg. analyst World Trade Inst., N.Y.C., 1981-82; mktg. research analyst Adolph Coors Co., Golden, Colo., 1982-84, sr. mktg. analyst, 1984—; staff intern House Banking Com., U.S. Ho. of Reps., Washington, 1978. Active Young Republicans, Ohio, 1975; campaign asst. to Congressman William Stanton of Ohio, 1974-80. Mem. Am. Mktg. Assn., Assn. M.B.A. Execs., Soc. for Advancement Mgmt., Pi Sigma Alpha. Republican. Methodist. Clubs: Sierra, Am. Mountaineering. Home: 295 Zang St Apt 2946 Lakewood CO 80228 Office: Adolph Coors Co Ford St Golden CO 80401

GRAY, DORIS WILLIAMS, marriage and family counselor; b. Dodge County, Ga., Nov. 7, 1936; s. Harry Melton and Evelyn Louise (NeSmith) Williams; m. Robert Floyd Gray, June 14, 1959; children—Pamela, John, Karen. B.S., Ga. Coll., 1958; M.Ed., U. Ga., 1975. Cert. addiction counselor. Tchr. home econs., Quincy, Fla., 1958-61; extension home economist DeKalb County, Mo., 1963-65; tchr. adult edn. Milledgeville, Ga., 1970-73; psychologist Peachbelt Mental Health Center, Warner Robins, Ga., 1975-79; marriage and family counselor, addiction counselor Warner Robins, 1975—. Mem. Ga. Assn. Marriage and Family Therapists (pres. Middle Ga. chpt.), Ga. Addiction Counselors Assn. (bd. dirs., v.p. 1984, pres. 1985—), Nat. Fedn. Parents for Drug-Free Youth, Am. Assn. Marriage and Family Therapy, Nat. Assn. Alcohol and Drug Addiction Counselors (coordinator nat. counselor 1985, bd. dirs. 1985—). Democrat. Baptist. Office: 1764 Watson Blvd Suite 204 Warner Robins GA 31093

GRAY, ELIZABETH CHRETIEN, criminal justice educator, real estate salesperson; b. Lafayette, La., June 9, 1932; d. John Hiram and Caroline Ophelia (Ivey) Chretien; m. Noel Gray, Feb. 3, 1953 (div. Nov. 1962); 1 child, Mark Thaddeus. B.S., So. U. and A&M Coll., Baton Rouge, 1957; M.Ed. in Spl. Edn., Coppin State Coll., 1975; M.A. in Guidance-Psychology, Cath. U. Am., 1968; student Georgetown U., 1979, George Washington U., 1980, U. Md., 1982, Temple U., 1983—, SUNY, 1978. Tchr., adminstr. Lafayette Parish Pub. Schs., 1951-52; sec. So. U., Baton Rouge, 1953-56; sci. tchr. New Orleans Pub. Schs., 1956-58; reading-spl. edn. tchr. Montgomery County Pub. Schs., Rockville, Md., 1958-64; asst. prin. Washington Pub. Schs., 1964-72; assoc. prof. dept. criminal justice Coppin State Coll., Balt., 1972—; pres. Confidential Counseling Components, Balt., 1979-82; cons. delinquency prevention KO-BAR Mgmt. Cons. Assocs., Washington, 1980; speaker Md. Commn. on Women's Speakers Bur. Democratic candidate for Congress from Md. 7th dist., 1982, 84. Mem. Md. Assn. Tchr. Educators, Am. Assn. Counseling and Devel., Md. Mental Health Counselors Assn., NAACP (life), Urban League, Alpha Kappa Alpha. Work study grantee So. U., 1951. Presbyterian. Home: 4104 Belvieu Ave Baltimore MD 21215 Office: Coppin State Coll 2500 W North Ave Baltimore MD 21216

GRAY, ELIZABETH RINGHAM, artist, illustrator; b. Dallas, Aug. 28, 1952; d. Rodger Falk and Helen (Gavin) Ringham; m. Linwood Hursel Gray, Dec. 28, 1974 (dec. Nov. 1982). B.F.A., Stephens Coll., 1974. Drafting technician Gulf Oil Corp., New Orleans, 1974-75; free-lance artist for various clothing stores, New Orleans, also Houston, 1976-78; tech. illustrator Petroleum Learning Programs, Ltd., Houston, 1978-82; owner Beth Gray, Comml. Artist, Houston, 1980—. Artist, calligrapher: (cookbooks) Beginnings..., 1980; A Collection of Soups, Salads and Breads, 1981; A Collection of Entrees and Vegetables, 1982. Vol. artist for spl. events Houston Symphony League, 1982-83. Mem. AAUW, Stephens Coll. Alumnae Assn., Houston Mus. Fine Arts, Jr. Service League of North Houston (provisional 1985-86). Roman

Catholic. Club: Olde Oaks Women's (publicity chmn. 1980-81) (Houston). Home and office: 15811 Pebble Bend Dr Houston TX 77068

GRAY, GEAN CHATHAM, ceramicist; b. Bay City, Tex., Apr. 15, 1939; d. J.C. and Myra Carola (Hill) Chatham; m. James Wesley Kelly, May 15, 1956 (div.); m. James Carrell Gray, July 27, 1957; children—Joseph Allen, Clara Nell Gray Green, Myra Lee Gray Duke, Jennifer Marie Gray Smith. Student La. State U.-Eunice, 1968-69, Sam Houston State U., 1979-80, Lee Coll., 1980. PBX operator, Madison County Hosp., Madisonville, Tex., 1975-79; ceramicist Gray & Gray Enterprises, Madisonville, 1984—. Mem. Nat. Rifle Assn. Democrat. Baptist. Lodge: Order Eastern Star. Avocations: reading; sewing; swimming; cards and letters; writing poems. Home: Route 1 Box 171 Madisonville TX 77864 Office: Gray & Gray Enterprises Route 1 Box 170 Madisonville TX 77864

GRAY, GEORGIA NEESE, banker; b. Richland, Kans.; d. Albert and Ellen (O'Sullivan) Neese; A.B., Washburn Coll., 1921; D.B.A. (hon.), 1966; student Sargent's, 1921-22; L.H.D. (hon.), Russell Sage Coll., 1950; m. George M. Clark, Jan. 21, 1929; m. 2d, Andrew J. Gray, 1953. Began as actress, 1923; asst. cashier Richland State Bank, 1935-37, pres., 1937—; pres. Capital City State Bank & Trust Co., Topeka, 1964-74; dir. Capital City State Bank and Trust, Topeka; treas. of U.S., 1949-53; mem. Commn. Jud. Qualifications Supreme Ct. Kans. Del.-at-large nat. adv. com. SBA; Democratic nat. committeewoman, 1936-64; hon. chmn. Villages project C. of C. bd. dirs. Kans. A.A.A., 1950—; bd. dirs., former chmn. Kans. div. Am. Cancer Soc.; mem. bd. exec. campaign and maj. gifts com. Georgetown U.; bd. dirs. Seven Steps Found., Harry S. Truman Library; chmn. Alpha Phi Found., 1962-63; mem. nat. bd. Women's Med. Coll. Pa.; chmn. bd. regents Washburn U., 1975—; mem. bd., treas. Sex Information and Edn. Council U.S.; mem. White House Com. on Aging. Recipient Disting. Alumni award Washburn U., 1950. Mem. Am. Bus. Women's Assn., Topeka C. of C., Met. Bus. and Profl. Women's Club, Women in Communications, Alpha Phi (nat. trustee), Alpha Phi Upsilon, Alpha Delta Kappa. Clubs: Soroptimist (hon. life), Met. Zonta, Topeka Country. Address: 2709 W 29 St Topeka KS 66614

GRAY, HANNA HOLBORN, university president; b. Heidelberg, Germany, Oct. 25, 1930; d. Hajo and Annemarie (Bettman) Holborn; came to U.S., 1934; naturalized, 1940; A.B., Bryn Mawr Coll., 1950; Ph.D., Harvard U., 1957; M.A. (hon.), Yale U., 1971; LL.D., (hon.), Dartmouth Coll., 1978 Brown U., 1979, Wittenberg U., 1979 U. Rochester, U. Notre Dame, 1980, U. So. Calif., 1980; D.Litt. (hon.), Oxford U., 1979, numerous others; m. Charles Montgomery Gray, June 19, 1954. Instr., Bryn Mawr (Pa.) Coll., 1953-54; instr. Harvard U., 1957-59, asst. prof., 1959-60; asst. prof. U. Chgo., 1961-64, assoc. prof., 1964-72, pres., prof., 1978—, also trustee; prof. Northwestern U., Evanston, Ill., dean Coll. Arts and Scis., 1972-74; provost, prof. Yale U., New Haven, 1974-78, successor trustee, 1971-74, acting pres., 1977-78; Phi Beta Kappa vis. scholar, 1971-72; dir. Cummins Engine Co., Morgan Guaranty Trust Co., J.P. Morgan Co., Atlantic Richfield Co., Ameritech. Mem. Pulitzer Prize Com.; trustee Bryn Mawr Coll., Mus. of Sci. and Industry, Brookings Instn.; bd. dirs. Chgo. Council on Fgn. Relations, Andrew W. Mellon Found., Field Found. Ill., Nat. Humanities Ctr., Howard Hughes Med. Inst. Newberry Library fellow, 1960-61; Center for Advanced Study in Behavioral Scis. fellow, 1966-67; hon. fellow St. Anne's Coll., Oxford. Fellow Am. Acad. Arts and Scis.; mem. Am. Philos. Soc., Nat. Acad. Edn., Council Fgn. Relations, Renaissance Soc. Am., Phi Beta Kappa. Editor: (with Charles Gray) Jour. Modern History, 1965-70; contbr. articles to profl. jours. Office: Office of Pres U Chgo 5801 S Ellis Ave Chicago IL 60637

GRAY, KATHERINE, marriage and family counselor and support therapist; b. Los Angeles, July 6, 1941; d. Edward David and Marjorie (Graves) Ross; m. Daniel C. Gray, Feb. 5, 1965; children—Michael, Lisa. B.A., Calif. State U.-Sacramento, 1983, postgrad., 1983—. Instr. Shasta Coll., Redding, Calif., 1965-69; owner Water Ojai Valley Chapel, Ojai, Calif., 1971-77, Lipp & Sullivan, Marysville, Calif., 1978—; cons. and organizer various community outreach programs in edn. Contbr. articles to profl. jours., newspapers. County coordinator, bd. dirs. Am. Cancer Soc., Marysville, 1980—; bd. dirs., com. chairperson Gateway Projects, Yuba City, Calif., 1980—; bd. dirs. Mercy Guild, Yuba City, 1980—; past bd. dirs., com. chairperson Campfire Inc., Yuba City and Morro Bay, Calif., 1979-80; past pres. Ojai Valley-Oxnard Symphony Orch. Assn., Ventura County, Calif., 1975; Sacramento focus program coordinator 4-H, Yuba and Sutter Counties, 1985—. Grantee in field. Mem. Calif. Funeral Dirs. Assn., Calif. Assn. for Counseling and Devel., Sacramento Area Gifted Assn. Lodges: Soroptimists (bd. dirs.), Rainbow for Girls (bd. dirs. 1984-85). Avocations: music; art, travel; historical studies. Home: PO Box 611 Yuba City CA 95992 Office: PO Box 148 629 D St Marysville CA 95901

GRAY, KATHLEEN ANN, b. Reading, Pa., May 16, 1947; d. Sebastian and Helen Mary (Zajac) Vespico; m. George A. Gray, Oct. 22, 1966 (dec. July 1968). B.S. in Bus. Adminstrn., Drexel U., 1971, M.B.A., 1978; J.D., Wake Forest U., 1977. Bar: Pa. 1977. Computer programmer Ednl. Testing Service, Princeton, N.J., 1971-73, dir. data processing tng., 1973-74; assoc. Barley, Snyder, Cooper and Barber, Lancaster, Pa., 1977-83, ptnr., 1984—. Contbg. author: The Impact of Modern Non-Profit Corporations, 1977. Bd. dirs. Am. Lung Assn. of Lancaster, 1982—, Hist. Preservation Trust of Lancaster County, 1978—; sec., bd. dirs. Lancaster Integrated Specialized Transp. System, 1981—. Mem. ABA, Pa. Bar Assn., Lancaster Bar Assn., Pa. Sch. Bd. Solicitors Assn., Nat. Assn. Bond Lawyers. Republican. Office: Barley Snyder Cooper & Barber 126 E King St Lancaster PA 17602

GRAY, LINDA, actress; b. Santa Monica, Calif., Sept. 12; m. Ed Thrasher (div. 1983); children—Jeff, Kelly. Studied with, Charles Conrad. Worked as model appeared in over 400 television comms.; film appearances include Dogs; television films include The Two Worlds of Jenny Logan, Haywire, Chimps, Not in Front of the Children; appeared in: television series All That Glitters, 1977, Dallas, 1978—; other television appearances include Marcus Welby, M.D.; host CBS documentary: The Body Human: The Loving Process, 1981; co-host: Golden Globe awards, 1981. Emmy nominee for Dallas, 1981; recipient Bambi award for best actress Germany, 1982, Il Gato award for best actress Italy, 1983, 84; named Woman of Yr., Hollywood Radio and TV Soc., 1982. Office: care PMK 8336 W 3d St Los Angeles CA 90048

GRAY, LOIS JEAN TABBERSON, lawyer, instructor; b. Cokato, Minn., May 14, 1954; d. Kenneth Melvin and Inez May (Langehough) Tabberson; m. Richard Francis Gray, July 3, 1982. B.A. in Psychology/Social Work, Concordia Coll., Moorhead, Minn., 1976; J.D., U. Denver, 1980. Bar: Colo., 1981; real estate sales lic. With Realty World, Denver, 1980-81; mem. King, Wilkes & Scheffel, Denver, 1981-82; sole practice, Denver, 1982—; instr. Denver Paralegal Inst., 1982—. Author-editor: A Handbook of Referral Services for Wright County, Minnesota, 1975. Mem. Nat. Assn. of Counsel for Children, Am. Trial Lawyers Assn., ABA, Colo. Bar assn., Denver Bar Assn. Republican. Lutheran. Office: Lois Tabberson Gray Esq 2107 E Virginia Ave Denver CO 80209

GRAY, MARCIA TOMPANE, interior designer, consultant; b. Dover, N.J., Feb. 14, 1941; d. Albert Benton and Dorothea Mae (McGinnis) Tompane; m. John Dana Wise Jr., Dec. 23, 1962 (dec.); children—Anne Stuart, John Dana III; m. 2d, Horace Alfred Gray III (div.). B.A.A., Bennett Coll., 1961; postgrad. U. Va., 1970-72. Ptnr. TBH Ltd., Richmond, Va., 1970-76; pres. The Inside Job Ltd., Aspen, Colo., 1976-82, DIMA Group Ltd., Denver, 1982-85; pres. Gray Design Group, 1985—; pub. Denver Design Directory, 1986; v.p. Designers Market Place, 1984—. Guest editor Colo. Homes & Lifestyle, 1981. Bd. dirs. Belle Bryan Day Nursery, Richmond, Va., 1965-76, Valentine Mus., Richmond, 1970-76; alumnae rep. Bennett Coll., Millbrook, N.Y., 1969-71. Fellow Aspen Inst. Humanities; mem. Downtown Denver Inc., Historic Denver Inc. Republican. Episcopalian. Club: Oxford (Denver). Office: Gray Design Group 1900 Wazee St Suite 210 Denver CO 80202

GRAY, MARGARET ANN, management educator, consultant; b. Junction City, Kans., Sept. 19, 1950; d. Carl Ray and Mayme Louise (Kopmeyer) G.; m. Dennis Wayne Stokes, June 9, 1973 (div. July 1981). B.Ed., Pittsburg State U., Kans., 1972; M.B.A., Wichita State U., 1981. Tchr., Sch. Dist. 1, Kansas City, Mo., 1972-73; tchr. Haysville Sch. Dist., Kans., 1974-81, dist. coordinator, 1979-81; instr. mgmt. Wichita State U., 1981-85; mgmt. devel. rep. Beech Aircraft Corp. a Raytheon Co., Wichita, 1985—; cons. Dartnell Inst., Chgo., 1983—; assoc. dir. Ctr. for Entrepreneurship, Wichita State U., 1984-85. Bd. dirs. Kans. Found. for partnerships in Edn., 1986. Mem. ASTD, Beta Gamma Sigma. Democrat. Roman Catholic. Club: Turnip (Wichita). Avocations: ballet; cross country skiing; classical music. Office: Beech Aircraft Corp 9709 E Central St Wichita KS 67206

GRAY, MARGARET EDNA, nursing educator; b. Norfolk Va., June 11, 1931; d. William E. and Margaret E. (Smith) G.; diploma Norfolk Gen. Hosp. Sch. Nursing, 1952; B.S. in Nursing, Columbia U., 1956; M.S., U. Md., 1966; Ed.D., Va. Poly. Inst. and State U., 1980. Staff nurse Norfolk Gen. Hosp., 1952-55, asst. night supr., 1953-54, instr. med.-surg. nursing, 1956-58; instr. med.-surg. nursing Riverside Hosp. Sch. Nursing, Newport, Va., 1958-64; ednl. dir. Va. Bd. Nursing, Richmond, 1965-69; coordinator health technology Va. Dept. Community Colls., Richmond, 1969-72; asso. prof. nursing, dir. nursing program, Va. Appalachian Tricoll., Abingdon, 1972-78; grad. research asst. Va. Poly. Inst. and State U., Blacksburg, 1979; asst. prof. nursing grad. program U. Va. Sch. Nursing, Charlottesville 1980-82, mem. adj. faculty outreach grad. program, 1977-79; chmn. dept. nursing Va. State U., Petersburg, 1982—; cons. nursing programs various community colls. in Va., 1969—; mem. adv. com. ARC Health Systems Agy., Va. and Tenn. 1977-78. Mem. human rights com. Southside Tng. Ctr. and mem. adv. com. allied health programs John Tyler Community Coll., Chester, Va. Mem. Nat. League Nursing, Va. League Nursing (fin. com. 1981—, dir. 1982), Am. Nurses Assn., Va. Nurses Assn. (sec. 1976-79, com. mem. 1980—). Presbyterian. Contbr. articles on health care edn. to profl. publs. Office: Box 51 Va State U Dept Nursing Petersburg VA 23803

GRAY, MAURISSE TAYLOR, investment banking firm executive; b. Buffalo, July 25, 1954; d. James Graham and Joan Maurise (Fitzpatrick) G.; m. Salim Akbarali Valimahomed, Apr. 24, 1982; 1 dau., Zahra Gray Valimahomed. B.A., Mt. Holyoke Coll., 1976; M.P.A., NYU. Research asst. Rockefeller U., N.Y.C., 1976-77; assoc. Kidder, Peabody & Co. Inc., N.Y.C., 1977-80, asst. v.p., 1980-81, v.p., 1981—. Democrat. Roman Catholic.

GRAY, MIRIAM MARY, educator; b. Nevada, Mo., Nov. 29, 1905; d. Chester H. and Pearl (Welch) Gray; A.A., Cottey Coll., 1925; B.S., U. Mo., 1927; M.A., Columbia U., 1932, Ed.D., 1943. Tchr. phys. edn. high sch. and jr. coll., Moberly, Mo., 1927-30, jr. and sr. high sch., Chickasha, Okla., 1930-31, elem. and jr. high sch., Tulsa, 1934-41; phys. edn. dir. Knox Sch. for Girls, Cooperstown, N.Y., 1932-33; instr. phys. and health edn. U. Tex., 1943-46; asso. prof. health and phys. edn. Ill. State U., 1946-57, prof., 1957-72, emerita, 1972—, dance coordinator, 1946-69; dir. advanced study insts. in dance edn. U.S. Office Edn., summers 1968, 69; dir. Wayside Farm Inc., 1970—, pres., 1980-84. Dir., mem. adv. bd. Vernon County unit Ret. Senior Vol. Program, 1975-78, chmn. bd., 1977-78. Fellow AAHPERD (hon. fellow; life mem.; chmn. midwest dance sect. 1954-55, chmn. nat. sect. on dance 1958-60, editor dance div. 1966-70, program chmn. conf. on dance as a discipline 1965; chmn. dance div. 1970-73, dir. 1971-72, v.p. 1971-72, nat. dance assn. parliamentarian 1974-75, NDA Heritage award 1975, NDA scholar 1978-79, Centennial award 1985); mem. Nat., Ill. edn. assns., Ill. (hon. life), Mo. (hon. life) assns. health phys. edn. and recreation, Nat. (nat. editorial com. 1955-60, editor biennial publ. 1957-59), Midwest assns. for phys. edn. of coll. women, Internat. Assn. Phys. Edn. and Sports for Girls and Women, Nat. Found. for Health, Phys. Edn. and Recreation, Internat. Council Health, Phys. Edn. and Recreation, Am. Dance Guild, Sacred Dance Guild, Congress on Research in Dance (dir. 1969-73, parliamentarian 1973-74), Nat. Conf. Grad. Edn. (editorial com. 1967), Dance Notation Bur., Am. Dance Therapy Assn., Ill. Square Dance Callers Assn. (roving dir. 1955-57, central dir. 1960-62), Ill. Fedn. Square Dance Clubs (devel. chmn., editor newsletter 1955-57), Vernon County Hist. Soc. (dir. 1973—, corr. sec. 1974-76, pres. 1983, 84), AAUP (chpt. pres. 1953-54, Ill. conf. pres. 1955), Nat., Mo., Vernon County (sec.-treas. 1973-74, pres. 1974-76, dir. 1977-85) ret. tchrs. assns., Am. Assn. Ret. Persons, Ill. State U. Annuitants Assn., Bus. and Profl. Women's Club, AAUW (program topic chmn. 1975-77, dir. 1975-78, 80-84), Am. Cancer Soc. (v.p. Vernon County unit 1977, dir. 1977—), Delta Kappa Gamma (chpt. 2d v.p. 1964-66, pres. 1978-80, Mo. State Scrapbook-Photog. Com. 1983-85), Phi Theta Kappa (pres. 1924-25), Kappa Delta Pi, Pi Lambda Theta. Clubs: Idlers (pres. 1963-64), Nevada Camera (pres. 1976-78). Author: The Physical Education Demonstration, 1946; A Century of Growth, 1951; editor: Purposeful Action, Workshop Report of NAPECW, 1956; Focus on Dance V, Composition, 1969; co-editor; Designs for Dance, 1968; contbr. to profl., ednl. and lay publs. Dance dir. centennial pageants: The Past Is Prologue, Ill. Edn. Assn., 1955; With Faith in the Future, Ill. State U., 1957. Address: The Wayside Route 1 Nevada MO 64772

GRAY, NANCY JEAN, marketing and communications specialist, consultant; b. Waterbury, Conn., Nov. 29, 1939; d. William Vernon and Mearl Lauretta (Smith) Sigmon; m. Carl L. Gray, Mar. 14, 1976; stepchildren—Steven, Cheryl. B.S., Manchester Coll., 1966; M.A., U. Dayton, 1984. Tchr. Beavercreek Schs., Dayton, Ohio, 1962, New Madison Schs., Ohio, 1965-72; communication specialist Good Samaritan Hosp. and Health Ctr., Dayton, 1972-85, mktg. specialist, 1986—; producer, host Room to Grow cable TV and FM radio show, 1981—; workshop presenter Samaritan Ctr. for Youth Resources, Dayton, 1972-85; pres., founder Dayton Area Step-family Assn. Am., Inc., 1984—, nat. bd. dirs., 1986—. Vol. social service worker Brethren Vol. Services, 1962-64. Mem. Am. Orthopsychiat. Assn., Sigma Phi Gamma (corr. sec. Kappa Beta chpt. 1984, service sec. 1985). Democrat. Avocations: travel; photography; entertainment. Home: 405 Westview Pl Englewood OH 45322 Office: Room to Grow 2222 Philadelphia Dr Dayton OH 45406

GRAY, PEARL SPEARS, educational administrator; b. Selma, Ala., Aug. 19, 1945. B.A. in Sociology, Wilberforce U., 1968; M.A. in Secondary Edn., Antioch-Putney Grad. Sch. Edn., 1970; Ph.D. in Ednl. Adminstrn., Oreg. State U., 1986. Team leader Nathan Bishop Sch., Providence, 1971-72; exec. local ednl. adminstr. Providence Sch. System, 1981-83; assoc. dir. Portland Urban Tchr. Edn. program Oreg. State U., Corvallis, 1973-76, dir. Office of Affirmative Action, 1976-86, mem. faculty, 1973—; cons. Inter-Culture Assn., 1971-72, U.S. Civil Service, Portland, Oreg., 1971-73. Contbr. articles to profl. publs. Bd. govs. Oreg. State Bar, Portland, 1985—; bd. dirs. Nat. Human Relations Task Force, 1981—, Pub. Health Adv. Com., 1985—; chmn. Black Colls. Com., Inc., 1980—. Named to 100 Most Influential Persons, Black Jour., 1976; Boss of Yr., Oreg. State U., 1976-77; Rockefeller grantee, 1979; Am. Council on Edn. fellow, 1986—. Mem. Am. Mgmt. Assn., AAUW, Delta Sigma Theta. Avocations: art; jazz; reading.

GRAY, PENNY ULBRICHT, nursing adminstr.; b. San Antonio, Feb. 27, 1940; d. Hilmar August and Mary Elizabeth (Moore) Ulbricht; R.N., Seton Sch. Nursing, Austin, 1961; B.S. in Nursing, Incarnate Word Coll., 1963; M.S. in Nursing, U. Tex., Austin, 1973; m. Arnold Louis Gray, Nov. 22, 1969; 1 dau., Nicole Michelle. Float nurse Santa Rosa Hosp., San Antonio, 1962; staff nurse Guadalupe Valley Hosp., Seguin, 1963; asst. head nurse labor and delivery Nix Meml. Hosp., San Antonio, 1964-65; instr. L.V.N. Sch., Gary Job Corps, 1965-67; prof. San Jacinto Coll., 1967-77; dir. nursing support services St. Joseph Hosp., Houston, 1977—. Spl. lectr., Tex. Woman's U., Houston; cons. hosp. computers; adv. bd. Houston chpt. ARC. Mem. Nat. Assn. Nurse Recruiters, Nat. League Nursing, Tex. Nurses Assn., Tex. Assn. Nurse Recruiters, Houston Assn. Nurse Recruiters. United Methodist (chmn. council on ministries 1981). Home: 1701 Norwood St Deer Park TX 77536 Office: St Joseph Hosp 1919 LaBranch St Houston TX 77002

GRAY, ROXIE J., corporate field manager; b. Muleshoe, Tex., Sept. 4, 1935; d. Murray Luther and Jimmie B. (Kinney) McGuyer; m. Johnny Gray, Dec. 31, 1954 (div. 1967); children—Gary Gray, Miki Jo Gray. Student, Eastern N. Mex. U.; Cert. U. N.Mex. Safety engr. sec. ins. bus., Albuquerque, 1957-58; loan officer constrn. bus., Albuquerque, 1959-62; sales rep. Xerox Co., Seattle, 1970-72, service dispatcher, 1974-79, work support supr., Santa Clara, Calif., 1979-84, field mgr. customer services, 1984—, adv. council, Rochester, N.Y., 1983-84. Author: Poetry, 1953, book, 1954; songwriter demo, 1982. Mem. Calif. Country Music Assn. (sec. 1983-84). Democrat. Mem. Ch. of Christ. Avocations: play Do Bro; race car. Home: 1236 Rodney Dr San Jose CA 95118 Office: Xerox Corp 5000 Old Ironsides Dr Santa Clara CA 95050

GRAY, SALLY JEAN, corporate executive; b. Tonasket, Wash., Mar. 1, 1944; d. Wallace and Doris L. (Roeper) Bordeaux; m. James R. Gray, Aug. 22, 1964; 1 son, Jeffrey. Student U. Wash., 1961-65. Adminstrv. asst. Herron, Hooper & Co., Seattle, 1968-75; bus. mgr. Medicornea, Bellevue, Wash., 1975-81; v.p., controller CooperVision IOL, Bellevue, 1981—. Moderator 1st Congregational Ch., Bellevue, 1983; bd. dirs. Bellevue Philharm. Mem. Am. Mgmt. Assn., Bellevue C. of C. Home: 8809 NE 2d Pl Bellevue WA 98004 Office: CooperVision IOL 3190 160th St SE Bellevue WA 98008

GRAY, SHARON ANN THAUTE, lawyer; b. Palo Alto, Calif., May 8, 1951; d. Tanner E. and Lucy (Bradford) Thaute; m. David Rennie Gray, July 10, 1976. A.A., Cabrillo Coll., 1974; B.S. in Bus. Adminstrn., San Jose State U., 1976; M.B.A., U. Santa Clara, 1981, J.D., 1981. Bar: Calif. 1981. Legal sec. Rusconi & Foster, Morgan Hill, Calif., 1969-71; paralegal Murphy et al, Santa Cruz, Calif., 1971-74; corp. paralegal Toothman et al, San Jose, Calif., 1974-76; office mgr. Contemporaries, Los Altos, Calif., 1976-77; cons. mktg. research, legal research asst., 1977-81; assoc. firm Brobeck, Phleger & Harrison, San Francisco, 1982-85, Smith, Etnire, Polson & Scott, P.C., Pleasanton, Calif., 1985—. Mem. ABA, Calif. Bar, Alameda County Bar. Democrat. Club: Soroptimist Internat. Office: Foothill Profl Ctr Suite 200 5820 Stoneridge Mall Rd Pleasanton CA 94566

GRAY, SHEILA HAFTER, psychiatrist, psychoanalyst; b. N.Y.C., Oct. 19, 1930; M.D., Harvard U., 1958; cert. Washington Psychoanalytic Inst., 1969; m. Oscar Shalom Gray, Apr. 8, 1967. Intern, St. Elizabeths Hosp., Washington, 1958-59; resident McLean Hosp., Belmont, Mass., 1959-61; clin. and research fellow Mass. Gen. Hosp., Boston, 1961-62; staff psychiatrist Chestnut Lodge, Inc., Rockville, Md., 1962-64; practice medicine, specializing in psychiatry and psychoanalysis, Washington, 1964—; clin. asst. prof. psychiatry U. Md. Sch. Medicine, Balt., 1968-75, clin. assoc. prof., 1975-83, clin. prof., 1983—; instr. Washington Psychoanalytic Inst., 1971-75, teaching analyst, 1975—; mem. staff U. Md. Hosp., Balt.; physician mem. Commn. on Mental Health, Superior Ct. of D.C., 1972—; bd. govs. Nat. Capital Reciprocal Ins. Co., 1981—. Exec. com. Palisades Citizens' Assn., 1980—, treas., 1983-84, pres., 1984—; mem. D.C. Mayor's Adv. Com. Mental Health Services Reorgn., 1984; exec. com. D.C. Fedn. Civic Assns., 1984—, asst. rec. sec., 1985, rec. sec., 1986; v.p. programs Met. D.C. Women's Equity Action League, 1986. Fellow Am. Psychiat. Assn.; mem. Am. Psychoanalytic Assn. (diplomate Bd. of Profl. Standards), Washington Psychiat. Soc. (councillor 1981-83) Med. Soc. D.C. (exec. bd. 1982). Office: PO Box 40612 Palisades Station Washington DC 20016

GRAYSON, MARGARET MARION, association executive, anthropologist; b. Lynwood, Calif., Oct. 12, 1949; d. William Mac and Margaret Marian (Clark) Summerlin; m. Lawrence Marion Martin, June 18, 1967 (div.); 1 son, Jay Scott; m. 2d James Lee Grayson, Feb. 18, 1977. A.A. in Liberal Arts, Pasadena City Coll., 1972; B.A. in Anthropology, Calif. State U.-Los Angeles, 1975, M.A. in Anthropology, 1975. Dep. dir. L.S.B. Leakey Found., Pasadena, Calif., 1977-81; exec. dir. Santa Fe Trail council Camp Fire Inc., Temple City, Calif., 1981-83; assoc. exec. dir. Camp Fire Council Foothills, Inc., Pasadena, 1983—. Vol. United Way, Arcadia, Calif., 1981-83; mem. exec. bd. El Monte/South El Monte Community Coordinating Council (Calif.), 1983, rec. sec., 1984—. Mem. AAUW, Nat. Soc. Fundraising Execs., Women in Communications, Women in Mgmt. (corr. sec. San Gabriel Valley chpt. 1983-84, v.p. pub. relations 1984—), Camp Fire Assn. Profls. Democrat. Office: Camp Fire Council Foothills Inc 391 S Madison Pasadena CA 91101

GRAYSON, MARION LOU, art historian; b. English, Ind.; d. Raymond Francis and Ida Mae (Land) Spears; divorced; children—Jon Michael, Craig Martin. B.S., Columbia U., 1968, M.A., 1970, M.Ph., 1979, Ph.D., 1979. Lectr., cons. Mus. Fine Arts, St. Petersburg, Fla., 1979, curator, 1980-82; freelance lectr.-writer, 1982-83; asst. prof. art history, dir. Sewall Art Gallery, Rice U., Houston, 1983—. Author: (exhbn. catalogues) Paris in the Belle Epoque: People and Places, 1980, Fragonard and His Friends, 1982; contbr. articles to profl. jours. Mem. Coll. Art Assn., Historians Netherlandish Art, Phi Beta Kappa. Office: Dept Art and Art History Rice U PO Box 1892 Houston TX 77251

GRAZIANO, LAURA ELLEN, marketing executive; b. Suffern, N.Y., Nov. 22, 1955; d. Frank and Rose Mary (DiBenedetto) Campi; m. Joseph Robert Graziano, June 4, 1983; 1 child, Anthony Joseph. B.S. magna cum laude, Fairleigh Dickinson U., 1982, postgrad. 1983—. Adminstrv. asst. in mktg. Thomas J. Lipton, Inc., Englewood Cliffs, N.J., 1978-83; with mktg. dept. Good Humor Corp., Fairfield, N.J., 1983, brand asst., 1983-85, asst. product mgr., 1985-86; mktg. dir. Creative Computer Systems, Inc., Wayne, N.J., 1986—. Roman Catholic. Office: Creative Computer Systems Inc Wayne NJ 07470

GRAZIANO, MARY E, banker; b. Flushing, N.Y., June 23, 1929; d. Salvatore and Nina (Greco) Sisinni; m. Joseph John Graziano, May 30, 1948 (dec.); children—Joseph, John, Steven. Vice-pres. Hillside Contracting Co., New Hyde Park, N.Y., 1958-69; asst. v.p. Chem. Bank, Lake Success, N.Y., after 1969, v.p., Jericho, N.Y. Mem. Assn. Records Mgrs. and Adminstrs. (past pres.), Nat. Assn. Bank Women, Nat. Microfilm Assn. Roman Catholic. Club: Garden City Country. Address: Chem Bank 200 Jericho Quadrangle Jericho NY 11753

GREACEN, NAN, artist; b. Giverny, France, Mar. 6; d. Edmund and Ethol (Booth) G.; student Grand Central Sch. Art, 1926-30; m. Rene Bard Faure, Dec. 7, 1936; children—Nancy Faure Waesche, Renee Faure. Tchr., Grand Central Sch. Art, 1931-43; portrait painter, still life and landscapes; watercolor painter; tchr. pvt. art classes; works rep. Gateway Art Gallery (Palm Beach, Fla.), Grand Central Art Galleries, N.Y.C., Beeches Gallery (Carmel, Calif.), Balogh Gallery, Charlottesville, N.C. Recipient numerous awards for art, 1931-79, including: 1st prize Manhattan Savs. Bank exhibit Westchester Artists, 1963, Best in Show award Nat. Arts Club, 1964, purchase award and medal Montclair Mus., 1966, Landscape prize Nat. Arts Club, 1967, Kathleen Grumbacher medal 1969, Best in Show award St. Augustine Art Assn., 1972, Benedictine competition award, 1976, 1st watercolor prize St. Augustine Honor Show, 1977, 1st prize for oil, St. Augustine Mems., 1978, 1st prize for watercolor, St. Augustine Honor Show, 1979. Mem. NAD, Fla. Watercolor Soc. (awards 1973, 74, 1st prize 1983), Hudson Valley Art Assn. (Medal of Honor 1976, Gumbacher award 1968, John Newington award 1970), Allied Artists Am., Audubon Artists, St. Augustine Art Assn., Scarsdale Art Assn. Presbyterian. Clubs: Ponte Vedra, Sawgrass. Author: The Magic of Flower Painting, 1965; Still Life is Exciting, 1970. Studio: 184 San Juan Dr Ponte Vedra Beach FL 32082

GREAR, EFFIE CARTER, educational administrator; b. Huntington, W.Va., Aug. 15, 1927; d. Harold Jones and Margaret (Tinsley) Carter; Mus.B., W.Va. State Coll., 1948; M.A., Ohio State U., 1955; Ed.D., Nova U., 1976; m. William Alexander Grear, May 16, 1952; children—Rhonda Kaye, William Alexander. Band dir. Fla. A&M High Sch., Tallahassee, 1948-51, Smith-Brown High Sch., Arcadia, Fla., 1951-56; band dir. Lake Shore High Sch., Belle Glade, Fla., 1956-60, dean of girls, 1960-66, asst. prin., 1966-70; asst. prin. Glades Central High Sch., Belle Glade, Fla., 1970-76, prin., 1976—. Bd. dirs. Palm Beach County Mental Health Assn. Recognized for outstanding achievement by Fla. Sugar Cane League, 1985. Mem. Nat. Assn. Secondary Sch. Prins., Nat. Community Sch. Edn. Conf., Nat. Sch. Public Relations Assn., Assn. Supervision and Curriculum Devel., Fla. Assn. Secondary Sch. Prins., Palm Beach County Sch. Adminstrs. Assn., Belle Glade Assn. Women's Clubs (pres.), Belle Glade C. of C. (chmn. beautification Com., Phi Delta Kappa, Alpha Kappa Alpha. Clubs: Elite Community, Women's Civic. Office: Glades Central High School 425 W Canal St N Belle Glade FL 33430

GREASER, CONSTANCE UDEAN, research organization executive; b. San Diego, Jan. 18, 1938; d. Lloyd Edward and Udean Greaser; B.A., San Diego State Coll., 1959; postgrad. U. Copenhagen Grad. Sch. Fgn. Students, 1963, Georgetown U. Sch. Fgn. Service, 1967; M.A., U. So. Calif., 1968; Exec. M.B.A., UCLA, 1981. Advt., publicity mgr. Crofton Co., San Diego, 1959-62; supr. Mercury Publs., Fullerton, Calif., 1962-64; supr. engring. support services div. Arcata Data Mgmt., Hawthorne, Calif., 1964-67; mgr. computerized typesetting dept. Continental Graphics, Los Angeles, 1967-70; v.p., editorial dir. Sage Publs., Inc., Beverly Hills, Calif., 1970-74; head publs. Rand Corp., Santa Monica, Calif., 1974—. Mem. Women in Bus. (pres. 1977-78), Soc. for Scholarly Pubs. (nat. bd. dirs.), Women in Communication, World Future Soc., UCLA Exec. Program Assn. Co-author: Quick Writer—Build Your Own Word Processing Users Guide, 1983; Quick Writer—Word Processing Center Operations Manual, 1984; editor: Urban Research News, 1970-74; mng. editor Comparative Polit. Studies, 1971-74; contbr. articles to various jours. Home: 4735C La Villa Marina Marina Del Rey CA 90292 Office: 1700 Main St Santa Monica CA 90406

GREASER, PAULA MARIE, engineering manager, recruiter; b. Niagara Falls, N.Y., Feb. 14, 1955; d. Martin Aloysius and Catherine Isabelle (Dineen) Greaser; 1 dau., Larine Michelle. B.S. in Mech. Engring., Valparaiso U., 1977; postgrad. George Washington U., 1977-79. Engring. aide Hooker Chem. Corp., Niagara Falls, summer 1974, 75, Culatto's Mfg. Co., Niagara Falls, summer

1976; project mgr. Naval Ordnance Sta., Indian Head, Md., 1977—, recruiting subcom., 1977—; jr. profl. recruiter various univs. and colls., 1977—. Chmn., Equal Employment Opportunity Com., Indian Head, 1982. Recipient Valparaiso U. Achievement award, 1977; Community Action Program award Dept. Def.-Navy, 1982, 83, Jr. Profl. Recruiting award, 1983. Mem. ASME; (assoc.), Am. Soc. Performance Improvement (dir. 1978-79), Federally Employed Women (officer 1978-80), Soc. Women Engrs. (speaker, panel mem.), Assn. Hispanic Ams., Nat. Assn. Female Execs. Democrat. Roman Catholic. Home: 74 Oak Manor Dr Waldorf MD 20601 Office: Commanding Officer Naval Ordnance Sta Indian Head MD 20640

GREATHOUSE, LILLIAN ROSALEA, educator; b. St. Louis, Nov. 13, 1943; d. Ambrose and Rosalea Greathouse; B.A., Ouachita Baptist U., Arkadelphia, Ark., 1966; M.S., So. Ill. U., Carbondale, 1970, Ph.D., 1981. Tchr. bus. Acorn Consol. Schs., Mena, Ark., 1966-68; mem. faculty So. Ill. U., 1968—, asso. prof. tech. careers, 1982-86; assoc. prof. bus. Eastern Ill. U., Charleston, 1986—; asst. dean Sch. Tech. Careers, 1979-82; co-owner Career Assos., Carbondale, 1979—; cons. in field. Mem. Assn. Records Mgrs. and Adminstrs., Am. Vocat. Edn. Assn., Nat. Bus. Edn. Assn., Office Systems Research Assn., Midwestern Research Assn., Bus. and Profl. Women's Club, Delta Pi Epsilon. Author: Records Management, 1975; Time Management, 1979; also articles. Home: 2114 Sarah's Ln Charleston IL 61920 Office: Bus Edn and Adminstrv Office Mgmt Eastern Ill U Charleston IL 61920

GRECO, ANN FRANCES BREEN, lawyer; b. N.Y.C., Sept. 1, 1941; d. Joseph and Margaret (Purcell) Breen; B.A., Governors State U., Park Forest, Ill., 1979; postgrad. polit. sci., U. Ill.; J.D., Kent Coll. Law, Ill. Inst. Tech., Chgo., 1985; m. Frank Greco, Feb. 16, 1973; 1 dau., Colleen Lucia. Market research asst. Market Research Corp. Am., N.Y.C., 1964-67; field supr., market research asst. Cole Bender Assos., N.Y.C., 1967-69; clinic coordinator U. Chgo. Hosps., 1976-77; adminstrv. asst. Sta. WMAQ, Chgo., 1978; survey researcher U. Ill., 1979; legis. aide Congressman Gus Savage (Ill.), Washington, 1980-82; workshop leader, 1980—; with firm Rottman, Medansky, Elovitz, Chgo., 1985—. Mem. Women's Polit. Caucus (legis. chmn. Capitol Hill chpt. 1981), Chgo. Bar Assn., Ill. Women's Bar Assn. (student div.). Club: St. Bride's Women's (v.p. 1976). Home: 8453 S Colfax St Chicago IL 60617 Office: Rottman Medansky Elovitz 180 N LaSalle Chicago IL 60618

GREEN, ADELINE MANDEL (MRS. MAURICE L. GREEN), psychiatric social worker; b. St. Paul; d. Meyer and Eva Ulanove; B.S., U. Minn., 1933, M.S.W., 1955; m. Nathan G. Mandel, July 13, 1938 (div. July 1962); children—Meta Susan (Mrs. Richard Katzoff), Myra (Mrs. Jeffrey Halpern); m. 2d, Maurice L. Green, Aug. 31, 1969. Investigator, Ramsey County Mothers Aid and Aid to Dependent Children, Ramsey County Welfare Bd., St. Paul, 1933-37; psychiat. social worker Wilder Child Guidance Clinic, St. Paul, 1938; psychiat. social worker, supr. out patient psychiatry clinic U. Minn. Hosps., Mpls., 1955-68, supr., clin. instr. psychiatry social service, out patient psychiatry clinic, 1968-69; pvt. practice family and marriage counseling South Bay Clinic Pres. St. Paul sect. Council Jewish Women, 1950-54; chmn. Diagnostic Clinic for Rheumatic Fever-Wilder Clinic, St. Paul, 1952-54; assoc. Family and Child Psychiat. Med. Clinic. Lic. social Worker. Mem. Nat. Assn. Social Workers, Acad. Certified, Social Workers, Minn. Welfare Conf., Am. Assn. Marriage and Family Counselors, Brandeis U. Women. Democrat. Home: 2365 Oakcrest Dr Palm Springs CA 92264 Office: 14651 S Bascom Suite 225 Los Gatos CA 95030

GREEN, ALLISON ANNE, educator; b. Flint, Mich., Oct. 5, 1936; d. Edwin Stanley and Ruth Allison (Simmons) James; m. Richard Gerring Green, Dec. 23, 1961 (div. Oct. 1969). B.A., Albion Coll., 1959; M.A., U. Mich., 1978. Cert. tchr., Mich. Tchr. phys. edn. Southwestern High Sch., Flint, 1959-62; tchr. math. Harry Hunt Jr. High Sch., Portsmouth, Va., 1962-63; receptionist Tempcon, Inc., Mpls., 1963-64; tchr. phys. edn. and math. Longfellow Jr. High Sch., Flint, 1964-81, tchr. math., 1981—; chmn. Intervention Team Sch. Improvement Project, 1984. Mem. Fair Winds council Girl Scouts U.S.A., 1943—, leader Lone Troop, Albion, Mich., 1957, sr. tchr. aide adviser, 1964-67; mem. Big Sisters Genesee and Lapeer Counties, 1964-68; mem. adminstry. bd. Court St. United Methodist Ch.; treas. edn. work area, mission commn. United Meth. Women Soc. Christian Service (memorials chmn. 1985—, program chmn. endeavor circle 1985). Mem. NEA, Mich. Edn. Assn., Mich. Assn. Mid. Sch. Educators, United Tchrs. Flint (bldg. rep.), Delta Kappa Gamma (treas. 1982—, profl. affairs chmn. 1970-80, legis. chmn. 1980-82), Alpha Xi Delta (pres. Flint. alumnae, v.p., treas., corp. pres. Albion Coll., alumnae dir. province 1972-77, Outstanding Sr. Albion Coll. 1959), Phi Delta Kappa (historian 1985), Embroiderers Guild Am. (sec. 1977-80, maps rep. 1980-82). Home: 1002 Copeman Blvd Flint MI 48504 Office: 1255 N Chevrolet Ave Flint MI 48504

GREEN, AMANDA SUE, lawyer; b. Ardmore, Okla., Sept. 26, 1957; d. Jerry W. and Marilyn (Wilkenson) G. B.A., U. Tex.-Arlington, 1979; J.D., Tex. Tech. U., 1982. Bar: Tex. 1982. Chief law clk. Lubbock County Dist. Atty.'s Office (Tex.), 1981-82, asst. criminal dist. atty. Collin County Dist. Atty.'s Office, McKinney, Tex., 1983—, chief misdemeanor prosecutor, 1983—; cons. in field. Mem. ABA, Tex. Bar Assn., Tex. Dist. and County Attys. Assn., Nat. Dist. Attys. Assn., Kappa Delta Pi, Phi Alpha Delta. Republican. Episcopalian. Home: 3421 Scenic Hills Dr Bedford TX 76021 Office: Collin County Dist Attys Office Collin County Courthouse McKinney TX 75069

GREEN, ANDREA BETH, lawyer; b. Phila., Jan. 29, 1958; d. Barton Harvey and Arlene Faith (Gottman) G. A.B., Mt. Holyoke Coll., 1979; J.D., Fordham Law Sch., 1982. Bar: N.Y. 1983. Legal asst., pub. defender Montgomery County Pub. Defender's Office, 1980; legal asst. Kurzman Karelsen & Frank, N.Y.C., 1981; legal writing teaching asst. Fordham Law Sch., 1981-82; researcher, writer Corp. Mergers and Acquisitions, Byron & Eveanor Fox, 1981-82; assoc. Hahn & Hessen, N.Y.C., 1982—. Audio specialist, Boston (Mass.) State Ho. Press Office, 1977. Mem. ABA, N.Y. State Bar Assn., Assn. Comml. Fin. Attys., N.Y. County Bar Assn., Assn. Bar of City N.Y. Jewish. Club: Mt. Holyoke. Home: 345 W 58th St New York NY 10019 Office: Hahn & Hessen 350 Fifth Ave New York NY 10118

GREEN, BARBARA LYNN, lawyer; b. Bethesda, Md., Apr. 15, 1949; d. Baxter Davies and Lillian Mae (Bainbridge) Green; m. Howard Roy Eiden, May 27, 1973 (div. Feb. 1978); m. 2d George Leslie Vamos, June 28, 1978. A.B., U. N.C., 1970, J.D., 1973. Bar: Colo. 1973, U.S. Ct. Appeals (10th cir.) 1973. Sole practice, Denver, 1973-82; assoc. Hall and Evans, Denver, 1982—; mem. faculty Colo. Women's Coll., 1979-80; cons. to nurse practitioner programs. Mem. instl. rev. bd. Nat. Jewish Hosp., Denver, 1982-85; bd. dirs. Legal Aid Soc., 1978-79. Mem. ABA, Colo. Bar Assn. (treas. family law sect. 1980-81), Denver Bar Assn., Colo. Trial Lawyers Assn. (dir. 1979-81, bd. dirs. 1980-82, pub. relations chmn. 1981-82). Office: 1200 17th St Suite 1700 Denver CO 80202-5817

GREEN, BELVA JEAN, health association executive; b. Eaton County, Mich., Aug. 16, 1927; d. Phillip Clem and Gladys M. Green; student Mich. State Coll., 1945-47, Ind. U., 1959, Purdue U. Ins. Mktg. Inst., 1967. Sec. to pres. Rea Magnet Wire Co., Ft. Wayne, Ind., 1958-63; sec. to corp. purchasing v.p. Magnovox Co., Ft. Wayne, 1963-67; nat. exec. dir. United Cancer Council, Ft. Wayne and Indpls., 1967-71; exec. dir. Allen County Cancer Soc., Ft. Wayne, 1971-85; guest lectr. Ind. U., St. Francis Coll., IV-Tech. Coll., nursing, med. assts., LPN, 1971—; also lectr. Co-founder local unit Make Today Count, 1976, regional coordinator nat. group, 1980, nat. bd. dirs., 1985; nat. pres. United Cancer Council Staff Assn., 1982-83; vol. United Way of Allen County Bd., 1974-76, Speakers Bur., 1975—, mem. public relations com., 1975-76; v.p. adv. bd. Salvation Army, 1976—; charter mem. Friends and Families of Nursing Home Residents, 1978-81; vol. Mental Health Assn., 1978; mem. med. assts. adv. bd. Ind. Vocat. Tech. Coll., 1980-81; mem. No. Ind. Health Systems Agy. Hospice Panel, 1979; co-founder, bd. dirs. Hospice of Fort Wayne, Inc. Recipient Woman of Influence awards Toastmistress Clubs, Fort Wayne Club and Council #6, 1971, United Way Leadership awards, 1974, 76, Community Service award Seventh-day Adventist Ch., 1979, Community Leaders and Noteworthy Ams. award. Mem. Public Relations Soc. Am., Internat. Assn. Bus. Communicators, Women in Communication, Children's Book Writers (chmn. programs local soc.), Christian Writers (coordinator midwest writers Fort Wayne conf. 1986), Internat. Platform Assn., Allen County Social Service Agy. Adminstrs. Presbyterian. Clubs: Fort Wayne Press, Foster Park Lioness (charter mem., dir. 1980), World Wide Travel, Fort Wayne Toastmistress Internat., Order Eastern Star, Everywriter's. Editor (newsletters): Make Today Count, Soundoff. Contbr. articles to various publs. Office: Allen County Cancer Soc 2925 E State Blvd Fort Wayne IN 46805

GREEN, BETH SHAPIRO, photo editor, photojournalist; b. N.Y.C., May 31, 1949; d. Seymour and Doris (Kalman) Shapiro; m. Emmett Barry Green, Mar. 30, 1949; 1 son, Austin Bennett. B.S., Boston U., 1971. Photo asst. Imageworks, Boston, 1971-72; writer, photographer Ridgewood News, Ridgewood, N.J., 1972-74; photojournalist United Press Internat., Phila., 1974-78; photo editor Newsweek, Inc., N.Y.C., 1978—; adj. prof. photojournalism Fordham U., N.Y.C., 1980—. Mem. Women in Communications, Assn. Mag. Photographers, Press Photographers Assn. Home: 60 Riverside Dr New York NY 10024

GREEN, BRENDA JOYCE, state official; b. Phila., Jan. 16, 1944; d. Joseph C. Gordon and Flossie (Bedford) Gordon Boddie; m. Edmond W. Green, June 21, 1968 (div. Nov. 1978); 1 child, Christy. B.S., U. Md., 1966; M.S., Oreg. Coll. Edn., 1974; D.Edn., Wash. State U., 1982. Cert. elem. and secondary prin., secondary tchr., Wash. With Md. Nat. Bank, Balt., 1966-67; jr. high sch. tchr., Balt., 1967-68; supr., tng. instr. Boeing Co., Kent, Wash., 1968-69; research and evaluation analyst Seattle Model Cities Program, 1969-70; citizens' participation coordinator Portland Model Cities Program (Oreg.), 1970-72; coordinator Area II programs, manpower specialist Oreg. Dept. Edn., Salem, 1972-76; exec. asst. to supt. Salem Pub. Schs., 1976-78; edni. policy adminstrv. intern Washington U. (D.C.), 1978-79; personnel officer N.W. Regional Ednl. Lab., Portland, 1978-80; grad. teaching asst. dept. edn. Wash. State U., Pullman, 1980-82; asst. dir. personnel mgmt. Oreg. Dept. Human Resources, Salem, 1982—; mem. nat. council Adminstrv. Women in Edn., 1976-78; mem. Oreg. Bd. Edn. Intergroup Human Relations Commn., 1971-77, Oreg. Bd. Edn. Statewide Assessment Rev. Panel, 1973-74, 77-78; mem. Oreg. Gov.'s Council for Career and Vocat. Edn., 1977-78; mem. adv. com. schs. for cities Portland Pub. Schs., 1979. Pres. Salem chpt. Jack and Jill, Inc., 1983—; bd. dirs. YWCA, Pullman, 1980-82, Willamette chpt. ARC, 1977-78; mem. Oreg. Gov.'s Adv. Com. on Affirmative Action, 1975-77, Oreg. Gov.'s Task Force on Juv. Corrections, 1977-78, Oreg. Gov.'s State Law Enforcement Council, 1973-80. Recipient Oreg. Outstanding Citizen award United Negro Coll. Fund, 1979. Mem. Am. Soc. for Personnel Adminstrn., Oreg. Personnel Mgrs. Assn., Nat. Alliance Black Sch. Educators, NAACP (chpt. edn. chmn. 1976—), Alpha Kappa Alpha (Soror in My Life award 1973), Phi Delta Kappa. Mem. African-Methodist-Episcopal Ch. Office: Dept Human Resources 325 Public Service Bldg Salem OR 97310

GREEN, CAROL H., lawyer, journalist; b. Seattle, Feb. 18, 1944; B.A. summa cum laude in History and Journalism, La. Tech. U., 1965; M.Law (Ford Found. fellow), Yale U., 1977; J.D., U. Denver, 1979. Intern, Shreveport (La.) Times, 1964, reporter, 1965-66; reporter Guam Daily News, 1966-67; city editor Pacific Jour., Agana, Guam, 1967-68; reporter, editorial writer, Denver Post, 1968-75, legal affairs reporter, 1977-79, asst. editor editorial page, 1979-81, house counsel, 1980-83, labor relations mgr., 1981-83; assoc. Holme Roberts & Owen, 1983-85; v.p. human resources and legal affairs Denver Post, 1985—; cons. San Mateo County (Calif.) Criminal Justice Council; mem. corrections task force Colo. Criminal Justice Standards and Goals, 1985 speaker for USIA, India, Egypt. Bd. dirs. YWCA, Trans. Council, Denver C. of C. Recipient McWilliams award for juvenile justice, Denver, 1971; award for interpretive reporting Denver Newspaper Guild, 1979. Mem. ABA (forum on communications law), Colo. Women's Bar Assn., Colo. Bar Assn. (bd. govs. 1985-86, chairperson BAR-press com. 1980), Denver Bar Assn. (co-chairperson jud. selection and benefits com. 1982-85, 1st v.p. 1986). Clubs: Denver Press, Denver Athletic. Episcopalian. Office: The Denver Post 650 15th St Denver CO 80202

GREEN, CYNTHIA GAIL, insurance executive; b. Lansing, Mich., Nov. 2, 1947; d. Charles V. and Irene H. (CharKut) G., m. John P. Johnson, Dec. 7, 1968 (div. 1972); 1 dau., Lisa Michelle Green. Student Lansing Community Coll., 1965-66. Model, Lansing, 1965-75; sales cashier, sales sec. Story Olds dealership, Lansing, 1966-67, Phil Gordon's Williams Volkswagen, Inc., Lansing, 1967-70, Starnaman-Andres Oldsmobile dealership, Lansing, 1971-74, wholesale sales rep. AAMCO Transmissions, Lansing, part-time 1974-75; ins. agt. N.Y. Life Ins. Co., Grand Ledge, Mich., 1975—; owner, pres. MGM Service Corp., Grand Ledge, 1981—; registered rep. N.Y. Life Ins. & Annuity Corp., 1983—; coordinator seminars. Acting pres. Nat. Assn. Career Security, Inc., Grand Ledge, 1982—. Recipient numerous sales awards, 1978-83. Mem. Nat. Life Underwriters Assn., Women Life Underwriters Assn., Nat. Bus. Women's Assn. Roman Catholic. Club: University (Lansing). Office: MGM Service Corp 621 Saginaw Hwy Grand Ledge MI PO Box 265 Cedar Village MI 48837

GREEN, DIANA HUSS, publisher; b. Balt., Dec. 25, 1930; d. Albert B. and Lillian K. Huss; m. Sidney Green, Mar. 15, 1950; children—Claire Sidney, John Huss. Student Goucher Coll., Balt., 1948-50; B.A. in English, Tufts U., 1952; M.A., Boston U., 1959. Part-time instr. Boston U., 1969-70, Northeastern U., Boston, 1970-71, Middlesex Community Coll., Bedford, Mass., 1970-77, Radcliffe Coll., Cambridge, Mass., 1975-78; pub., editor Parent's Choice mag., Waban, Mass., 1977—; writer-in-residence Antioch Coll., 1971; speaker on children's literacy programs on nat. TV shows, cable network, profl. assns., comml. radio. Author: Lenny's Suprise Piano, 1965; Ski Country, 1966; The Lonely War of William Pinto, 1968; contbr. articles to mags. and anthologies. Pres., Parent's Choice Found., Waban, 1977—. Recipient award PAGES mag., 1982; fellow Bread Loaf Writers Conf., 1963, HEW, 1972. Jewish. Office: Parent's Choice Box 185 Waban MA 02168

GREEN, DOROTHY, broadcasting executive; b. Wakulla, Fla., Jan. 29, 1949; d. Marvin Green and Jessie (Douglas) Williams; 1 son, Keith Howard. Student Eckerd Coll., George Washington U. Lic. 1st class radio-telephone operator. Prodn. asst. Conn. Pub. TV, Hartford, 1971-74; staff dir., technician Sta. WLCY-TV, St. Petersburg, Fla., 1975-76; technician CBS Sta. WCAU-TV, Phila., 1976-80; studio supr. Sta. WHMM-TV, Howard U., Washington, 1980-81; tech. mgr. ABC Washington News Bur., 1981—; freelance producer/media cons., 1985—. Featured in cover story N.Y. Times Mag., Apr. 30, 1978, also in New Woman Mag., Mar.-Apr. 1975. Mem. Soc. Motion Picture and TV Engrs., Senate and House Radio TV Gallery (press mem.), Washington Women in Film, Washington World Affairs Council, Women in Arts Mus. (charter mem.), Am. Broadcast Employees Found. (co-founder, bd. dirs.). Club: Nat. Press. Office: ABC Washington News Bur 1717 DeSales St NW Washington DC 20036

GREEN, FRANCES HOPE, health care specialist; b. Mt. Vernon, Ill., Jan. 29, 1937; d. Walter Bryon and Myrtle Fern (Sulenski) Green. Student, Mt. Vernon Jr. Coll., 1956; diploma. Triton Coll., 1967. Registered respiratory therapist. Office mgr. De Sota Chem. Co., Chgo., 1965-66; therapist Hines VA Hosp., Hines, Ill., 1966-67, West Sub. Hosp., Oak Park, Ill., 1965-67; clin. instr. Rose Meml. Hosp., Denver, 1967-68; dir. respiratory therapy Children's Hosp., Denver, 1968-80, staff assoc. human resources, 1980—, dir. hosp. security, 1983—; cons. neonatal/pediatric respiratory care Aspen Valley Hosp., 1977-79, Respiratory Care, Inc., Arlington Hts., Ill., 1978-80; clin. instr. U. Stony Brook, N.Y., 1977-80; bd. advs. and clin. instr. Community Coll. Denver, 1969-77, Aurora Tech. Ctr. & St. Anthony Hosp., 1977-79; speaker in field. Designer, transport isolette for newborns, 1975, asst. designer, aircraft for transport of newborns, 1975; designer/evaluator, pediatric respiratory equipment, 1978-80. Bd. dirs., Fed. Credit Union (Mid-town), Denver, 1983, treas., 1983-84; pres., Mid-town Service Orgn., Denver, 1983-84. Served to AK2, USN, 1962-69, Memphis and San Diego, Calif. Recipient Outstanding service award U.S. Navy, San Diego, 1964. Mem. Am. Assn. Respiratory Therapy, Nat. Bd. Respiratory Therapists, Am. Lung Assn. Colo. Democrat. Lutheran. Contbr. article to profl. jour. Home: 2560 Field St Lakewood CO 80215 Office: The Children's Hosp 1056 E 19th Ave Denver CO 80218

GREEN, FREDI J. SANDY, educator; b. Jacksonville, Fla., Nov. 22, 1939; d. Homer Lee and Ella Lee (King) Jackson; m. John Daniel Green; children—Candace Landrea, Michael David. B.A., U. Calif.-Berkeley, 1970, M.A., 1972; postgrad. Portland State U. Cert. tchr., Oreg. Staff, Concordia Coll., Portland, Oreg., 1973-76; coordinator, vis. prof. East Carolina U., Greenville, N.C., 1978-80; counselor Exodus, Portland, 1982-83; tchr. Collins View Sch., Portland, 1984-85, Jefferson High Sch., Portland, 1985—; exec. dir. Day One Program, Portland, 1982—. Leader, Campfire Girls, Portland, 1982-85; care provider North/Northwest Mental Health Ctr., Portland, 1982-83; respite counselor Give Us This Day, Portland, 1984. Woodrow Wilson fellow, 1970-72; Heller Meml. scholar, 1968-70. Mem. Nat. Assn. Female Execs., Urban League of Portland, Portland Tchrs. Assn. (mem. minority/human rights com. 1984—), Oreg. Educators Assn. Democrat. Mem. Seventh-Day Adventists. Avocations: speaking; music. Home: PO Box 11073 Portland OR 97211

GREEN, GERALDINE DOROTHY, lawyer; b. N.Y.C., July 14, 1938; d. Edward and Lula M. (Albro) Chisholm; student CCNY, 1961-64; J.D., St. John's U., 1968. Bar: N.Y. 1968, Calif. 1972. Tax acct. Coopers & Lybrand, N.Y.C., 1966-68; staff atty. IBM, 1968-69, Gaithersberg, Md., 1969-71, Los Angeles, 1971-72; sr. atty., asst. corp. sec. Atlantic Richfield Co., Los Angeles, 1972-80; commr. corps. State of Calif., Los Angeles, 1980-83; ptnr. Rosenfeld Meyer & Susman, Beverly Hills, Calif., 1983-85; of counsel Burke, Robinson & Pearman, Los Angeles, 1985—. Bd. dirs. Los Angeles area USO, 1978—. Mem. NAACP, Nat. Bar Assn., ABA, Nat. Legal Aid and Defender Assn., Calif. Assn. Black Lawyers, Calif. Women Lawyers Assn., Black Women Lawyers Calif., Los Angeles World Affairs Council, Women Lawyers Assn. Los Angeles, U.S. Olympic Soc. Office: Burke Robinson & Pearman 1925 Century Park E Suite 350 Los Angeles CA 90067

GREEN, JO ANN ELIZABETH, financial service counselor; b. St. Louis, Oct. 21, 1954; d. John George and Pearl Marie (Randazzo) Lotzy; m. Millard Curtis Green, Oct. 6, 1973 (div. Sept. 1982). B.A., So. Ill. U., 1972, M.S., 1977. Mgr. Art Gallery, Belleville, Ill., 1978-80; art tchr. Webster Jr. High Sch., Collinsville, Ill., 1980; job developer So. Ill. U., Edwardsville, 1980-82; mgr. Art Gallery, St. Louis, 1983-84; fin. service counselor Savs. & Loan, San Diego, 1985—. Mem. Nat. Assn. Female Execs., Midwest Weavers Conf., St. Louis Weavers Guild, Phi Kappa Phi. Avocations: running; weaving and fiber-working; reading. Office: 1st Nationwide Savs 123 Camino de la Reina San Diego CA 92108

GREEN, JOAN SHAPIRO, banker; b. Hampton, Va., Nov. 7, 1944; d. Isaac and Doris (Mintz) Shapiro; A.B. in Math. with honors, Mt. Holyoke Coll., 1966; m. Franklin Lewis Green, June 26, 1966; children—Jeffrey, Julia. Statis. analyst instrumentation lab. M.I.T., Cambridge, 1966-68; from calculator applications specialist to dir. mktg. services copiers SCM Corp., N.Y.C., 1968-81; v.p. mktg. Bankers Trust, N.Y.C., 1981—; speaker in field. Bd. dirs. Henderson House Coop. Apt., N.Y.C., 1980-85, v.p., 1981-82, pres., 1983-85; friend Commn. Status of Women, N.Y.C., 1980—. Mem. Seven Colls. Careers Com. (a founder 1974, pres. 1975-81), Am. Mktg. Assn., Fin. Women Assn., Bus. and Profl. Women (chpt. dir. 1980-81). Club: Mt. Holyoke (dir. 1974-83) (N.Y.C.). Home: 535 E 86th St New York NY 10028 Office: Bankers Trust 280 Park Ave New York NY 10017

GREEN, JOYCE, book publishing company executive; b. Taylorville, Ill., Oct. 22, 1928; d. Lynn and Vivian Coke (Richardson) Reinerd; A.A., Christian Coll., 1946; B.S., MacMurray Coll., 1948; m. Warren H. Green, Oct. 8, 1960. Assoc. editor Warren H. Green, Inc., St. Louis, 1966-78, dir., 1978—; v.p. Visioneering Advt. Agy., 1972—; exec. sec. Affirmative Action Assn. Am., 1977—; pres. InterContinental Industries, Inc., 1980—; asst. to pres. Southeastern U., New Orleans, 1982-86, No. Utah U., Salt Lake City, 1986—. Mem. Am. Soc. Profl. and Exec. Women, Direct Mktg. Club St. Louis, C. of C. Democrat. Methodist. Clubs: Jr. League, Clayton Women's, Clayton, Media. Home: 12120 Hibler Dr Creve Coeur MO 63141 Office: 8356 Olive Blvd Saint Louis MO 63132

GREEN, JOYCE BROWN, nurse; b. Sanford, Fla., Feb. 3; d. Coley and Beatrice Dean (Christian) Brown; B.S.N., Meharry Med. Coll., 1961; M.A., Pepperdine U., 1981; children—Darryl, Luci. Asst. head nurse Rancho Los Amigos Hosp., Downey, Calif., 1962-65; sch. nurse Los Angeles City Schs., 1968-74; asst. nursing dir. Martin Luther King Jr. Hosp., Los Angeles, 1974—. Mem. Pentacostal Ch. Club: United Foursquare Women's Orgn.

GREEN, JOYCE HENS, federal judge; b. N.Y.C., Nov. 13, 1928; d. James Stanley and Hedy Emma (Bucher) Hens; B.A., U. Md., 1949; J.D., George Washington U., 1951; m. Samuel Green, Sept. 25, 1965 (dec. Oct. 1983); children—Michael Timothy, June Heather, James Harry. Admitted to D.C. bar, 1951, Va. bar, 1956, U.S. Supreme Ct., 1956; individual practice law, Washington, 1951-66; partner firm Green & Green, Washington, 1966-68; asso. judge D.C. Superior Ct. of D.C., 1968-79; U.S. dist. judge for D.C., 1979—. Chmn., Exec. Women in Govt., 1977, trustee D.C. div. Am. Cancer Soc., 1963-72. Recipient award Women's Legal Def. Fund, 1976, Alumni Achievement award George Washington U., 1975; Profl. Achievement award George Washington U. Law Alumni, 1978. Fellow Am. Bar Found., Am. Acad. Matrimonial Lawyers, mem. Am. Bar Assn., D.C. Bar, Bar Assn. D.C., Women's Bar Assn. D.C. (pres. 1960-62, Woman Lawyer of Yr. award 1979), Va. State Bar, Arlington County (Va.) Bar Assn., Phi Delta Phi, Kappa Beta Pi. Office: US Dist Ct Washington DC 20001

GREEN, JUNE LAZENBY, federal judge; b. Arnold, Md., Jan. 23, 1914; d. Eugene H. and Jessie T. (Briggs) Lazenby; J.D., Am. U., 1941; m. John Cawley Green, Sept. 5, 1936. Admitted to Md. bar, D.C. bar, U.S. Supreme Ct. bars; claims adjuster Lumberman's Mut. Casualty Co., 1942-43, claims atty., 1943-47; pvt. practice law, Washington, 1947-68, Annapolis, Md., 1950-68; judge U.S. Dist. Ct. D.C., Washington, 1968—; bar examiner, Washington, 1963-68. Fellow Am. Acad. Matrimonial Lawyers; mem. Bar Assn. D.C. (dir. 1966-68), Women's Bar Assn. D.C. (Woman Lawyer of Year 1965, pres. 1955-57), Inter-Am., Am., Md. bar assns., Zonta, Kappa Beta Pi. Club: Nat. Lawyers (Washington). Office: US Courthouse 3d and Constitution NW Washington DC 20001*

GREEN, KAREN, health executive, consultant; b. Milw., Apr. 18, 1940; d. Nathan and Myn (Apter) Paschen; m. Michael Leo Green; children—Charles, Roberta; m. Richard Tarney, Oct. 6, 1985. B.S. with honors, U. Wis.-Milw., 1978, M.S. in Nursing, 1982. In-service dir. Colonial Mayor, Milw., 1979; teaching asst. U. Wis.-Milw., 1982, lectr., 1984; v.p. Wis. div. Lifegain, Milw., 1978—; pres. Karen Green & Assocs., Milw., 1979—; instr. Med. Coll. Wis., Milw., 1984—; guest speaker, workshop creator-presentor. Reviewer: Applied Nursing Diagnosis, 1985; contbr. articles to profl. jours. Coordinator Congregation Emanu-El Program on Grief, Loss, Milw., 1979; tng./support group U. Wis. Extension-Grief and Loss, Milw., 1980-81; asst. dir. pub. relations Milw. Jewish Fedn., 1970-71; fundraiser Wis. Kidney Found., Milw. Mem. Am. Nurses Assn., Nat. League Nursing, Women's Welfare Bd., Wis. Nurses Assn., Wis. Speakers Assn. Club: Toastmasters (Milw.) (sec. 1980-81). Avocations: writing; bicycling; walking; swimming; travel. Office: 603 Mulberry Ct PO Box 17705 Milwaukee WI 53217

GREEN, KAREN BLEIER, advertising agency executive; b. N.Y.C., Apr. 18, 1945; d. Benjamin and Sally (Karger) Bleier; m. Joseph H. Green, Sept. 3, 1966; children—Jessica, Adam. B.A., Simmons Coll., 1967; M.B.A, Harvard U., 1969. Media planner Ogilvy & Mather Inc., N.Y.C., 1969-71, asst. media dir., 1971-74, v.p., account supr., 1974-79, v.p., mgmt. supr., 1979-82, sr. v.p., mgmt. supr., 1982—. Office: Ogilvy & Mather Inc 2 E 48th St New York NY 10017

GREEN, LAURA MARIE, communications executive; b. Balt., Aug. 31, 1961; d. Karl Mathias and Sue Emma (Harman) Green. B.A., U. Richmond, 1982. Federal lobbyist Nat. Right to Work Com., Washington, 1984-86; developmental sales rep. Procter & Gamble, Charlotte, N.C., 1983; legis. asst. Va. Retail Mchts. Assn., Richmond, 1983; legis. intern Va. Soc. Profl. Engrs., Richmond, 1982. Mem. Conservative Network, Washington, 1985—. Served with U.S. Army, 1981. Mem. AAUP, Women in Govt. Relations, Mortar Board, Omicron Delta Kappa. Republican. Presbyterian. Avocations: creative writing; painting; dance; horseback riding; weight lifting.

GREEN, LYNNE, stage director; b. Krsko, Yugoslavia, Oct. 16, 1944; came to U.S., 1949, naturalized, 1966; d. Robert and Albina (Schmuck) Prusak; m. Sam Robert Bass, Oct., 1974 (div. 1975). B.F.A. with honors in Directing, Webster Coll. Conservatory of Theatre Arts, 1979. Dir. stage shows including: Second Verse, N.Y.C., 1980, Button Button, N.Y.C., 1980, Atmosphere of Enforced Discipline, N.Y.C., 1981, Friend of a Friend, N.Y.C., 1982, The Other Women: A Farce Closing Saturday Night, N.Y.C., 1983, Question Marks and Periods, 1981, Mrs. Michaelangelo, N.Y.C., 1983, Crimes of the Heart, Las Cruces, N.Mex., 1984, Antigone, St. Louis, 1985, Vol., Harriet Woods Com., St. Louis, 1986. Recipient Best Dir. award Internat. Dirs. Festival, 1980. Mem. NOW, Ms. Found. for Women. Democrat. Avocations: photography; bicycling. Home: 4479 Weber Rd Saint Louis MO 63123

GREEN, MARIA LAPI, lawyer, consultant; b. Rochester, N.Y., Sept. 17, 1940; d. Louis L. and Edith (Harman) Lapi; children—Edith, Stella, Anna, Harry II, William, Margaret. B.A. in Econs., George Washington U., 1962; J.D., Syracuse U., 1979. Bar: N.Y. 1979, Fla. 1980. Sole practice, Canandaigua, N.Y., 1979—; cons. for small businesses; mem. 1st del. women attys. People's Republic of China, 1984. NEH fellow, 1980; named Bus. Woman of Yr., Bus. and Profl. Women, 1983. Mem. N.Y. State Bar Assn. (family bar sect.), ABA (family bar sect.), Fla. Bar Assn., Ont. County Women's Bar Assn. (founder, pres.) AAUW (chmn. by-laws com.). Democrat. Club: Bus. and Profl. Women (chmn. pub. relations com.). Home: 324 Gibson St Canandaigua NY 14424

GREEN, MARILYN M., nursing educator. B.S., Sch. Nursing, Ohio State U., 1957; cert. leadership parent discussion groups Sch. Nursing, Boston U., 1966, cert. supervision parent discussion groups, 1967; Ph.D. in Pediatric Nursing, U. Pitts., 1976, M.N.Ed. in Pediatric Nursing, 1982. Bd. dirs. Indpls. Settlements, Inc., 1978-83, Your House, 1977-79, Suemma Coleman Agy., Indpls., 1979—; active Adolescent Resource Council, 1979—, founder and chairperson group, 1979-81; mem. Marion County Prosecutor's Office Speaker's Bur., 1980-82; mem. child protection team Marion County Welfare, 1980-83; mem. Ind. Task Force, for White House Conf. on Children and Youth, 1981-82; mem. Child Abuse and Neglect Task Force, 1981, 82. Bd. dirs. chairperson personnel com., v.p., mem. coms. Girls Clubs Greater Indpls., 1980—. Named Employee of Month, Div. Pub. Health, Health and Hosp. Corp., 1980; recipient recognition award, 1980, Nurse of Yr. award Central Ind. chpt. March of Dimes, 1981, recognition award Pi Lambda Theta chpt., 1981, Hon. Alumni award Ind. U. Sch. Nursing, 1982, Outstanding Alumni award Ohio State U. Coll. Nursing, 1984. Mem. Am. Nurses Assn., Council Nurse Researchers of Am. Nurses Assn., Am. Pub. Health Assn., Soc. Adolescent Medicine, Torch Club, Sigma Theta Tau. Office: 610 Barnhill Dr Indianapolis IN 46223

GREEN, MARJORIE, automotive distribution, import and manufacturing company executive; b. N.Y.C., Sept. 27, 1943; d. Benjamin Maxon and Harriet (Weslock) Gruzen; m. Thomas Henry Green, May 31, 1964. Student Antioch Coll., 1961-63, CCNY, 1964-65. Adminstrv. asst. ednl. research U. Calif.-Berkeley, 1965-76; v.p., co-owner Automotion, Santa Clara, Calif., 1973—. Adv. bd. Import Car mag. Mem. Am. Fedn. State, County and Mcpl. Employees (pres. U. Calif. chpt. 1967), Porsche Club Am (v.p. Golden Gate region 1974, treas. region 1975). Home: 688 Cupples Ct Santa Clara CA 95051 Office: Automotion 3535 Kifer Rd Santa Clara CA 95051

GREEN, MARY JEAN MATTHEWS, French educator; b. Honesdale, Pa., July 27, 1944; d. Joseph Robert and Garnet Barbara (Bayly) Matthews; m. Ronald Michael Green, June 25, 1965; children—Julie Elisabeth, Matthew Daniel. A.B., Brown U., 1965; A.M., Harvard U., 1966, Ph.D., 1974. Teaching fellow Harvard U., 1966-68; instr. Colby Sawyer Coll., New London, N.H., 1969-72; instr. Franconia Coll. (N.H.), 1972-73; asst. prof. French, Dartmouth Coll., 1973-81, assoc. prof., 1981—, also co-chmn. Women's Studies Program. Author: Louis Guilloux: An Artisan of Language, 1980; Fiction in the Historical Present: French Writers and the Thirties; editor: Quebec Studies, 1983—. Vis. scholar U. Calif.-Berkeley, 1984—; Canadian Govt. Faculty Enrichment grantee, 1984. Mem. Am. Council for Que. Studies (pres. 1981-82), Assn. Can. Studies in U.S. (exec. councillor 1983—), MLA, Am. Assn. Tchrs. French, Northeast Modern Lang. Assn. Office: Dartmouth Coll Dept French and Italian Hanover NH 03755

GREEN, MELODYE LEIGH, real estate executive; b. Dallas, Nov. 14, 1955; d. Charles Lee and Ruth Avanel (Felty) Noland; m. Dewey Keith Green, Aug. 5, 1978. B.S., Tex. Technol. U., 1978; M.Ed., N. Tex. State U., 1981. Bus. tchr. Edgemead of Tex., Mineral Wells, 1978-80, Weatherford Jr. Coll., Tex., 1978-80; spl. edn. tchr. Garland Sch. Dist., Tex., 1980-82; real estate salesman Cardinal Am., Dallas, 1980-82, Real Invest, Inc., 1982-85, also pres.; pres. L.G.F., Inc., 1984—. Mem. Tex. Real Estate Commn., Tex. Quarter Horse Assn., Plano C. of C., Tau Beta Sigma. Republican. Mem. Christian Ch.

GREEN, NANCY JANE, paper company personnel executive; b. Detroit, Apr. 9, 1932; d. Orvice M. and Trema (Filbeck) Patton; m. Richard J. Green, Feb. 23, 1952 (div. Oct. 1982); children—Patrick W., Scott F., Karl D. Student public schs. Detroit. Adminstrv. asst. Kerr Mfg. Co., Detroit, 1950-52; payroll, sec. Thunder Bay Mfg. Co., Alpena, Mich., 1952-55; adminstrv. asst. Kerr Mfg. Co., Detroit, 1955-57; mgr., acct. No. Electric Co., Rogers City, Mich., 1957-59; personnel dir. Fletcher Paper Co., Alpena, Mich., 1960—. Mem. 4-Cs Citizens group Mich. State Police, 1975—; bd. dirs. Alpena Sr. Citizen Center, 1983—, Alpena United Fund, Alpena Jr. Achievement, 1985—. Mem. N.E. Mich. Personnel Assn., Nat. Assn. Accts., Posen C. of C. (pres. 1967-69, sec. treas. 1970-83). Lutheran. Home: 8920 US 23 S Ossineke MI 49766 Office: Fletcher Paper Co 318 W Fletcher St Alpena MI 49707

GREEN, NANCY LOUGHRIDGE, publisher; b. Lexington, Ky., Jan. 19, 1942; d. William S. and Nancy O. (Green) Loughridge; B.A. in Journalism, U. Ky., 1964; M.A. in Journalism, Ball State U., 1971; postgrad. U. Ky., 1968, U. Minn., 1968. Tchr. English and publs. adv. Clark County (Ky.) High Sch., Winchester, Ky., 1965-66, Pleasure Ridge Park High Sch., Louisville, 1966-67, Clarksville (Ind.) High Sch., 1967-68, Charleston (W.Va.) 1968-69; asst. publs. and public info. specialist W.Va. Dept. Edn., Charleston, 1969-70; tchr. journalism and publs. dir. Elmhurst High Sch., Ft. Wayne, Ind., 1970-71; student publs. adv. U. Ky., Lexington, 1971-82; gen. mgr. student publs. U. Tex., Austin, 1982-85; pres., pub. Palladium-Item, Richmond, Ind., 1985—; dir. Harte-Hanks urban journalism program, 1984; pres. Media Cons., Inc., Lexington, 1980; dir. urban journalism workshop program Louisville and Lexington newspaper pubs., 1976-82; sec. Kernel Press, Inc., 1971-82. Bd. dirs. Jr. League, Lexington, 1980-82, Manchester Center, 1978-82, pres., 1979-82. Recipient Ball State U. Journalism Alumnus award, 1975. Mem. Assoc. Collegiate Press, Journalism Edn. Assn., Nat. Council Coll. Publs. Advs. (pres. 1979-83; Disting. Newspaper Adv. 1976, Disting. Bus. Adviser, 1984). AP Mng. Editors, Columbia Scholastic Press Assn. (Gold Key 1980), So. Interscholastic Press Assn. (disting. service award 1983), Nat. Scholastic Press Assn. (Pioneer award 1982), Internat. Newspaper Advt. and Mktg. Execs., Sigma Delta Chi. Contbr. articles on journalism edn. to profl. publs. Home: 411 S 22d St Richmond IN 47374 Office: Palladium Item 1175 N A St Richmond IN 47374

GREEN, NANCYE LEWIS, business executive; b. Dec. 4, 1947; d. Robert Lewis and Ruth (Grad) Lewis Leebron; m. Michael P. Donovan, Oct. 3, 1981. Student in urban studies and polit sci. Newcomb Coll., Tulane U., 1965-68; student in environ. design Parsons Sch. Design, 1971-73. Pres. Donovan & Green, N.Y.C., 1975—. Editor: The Wood Chair in America, 1982. Bd. dirs. Harbor Shakespeare Festival, N.Y.C., 53d St. Assn., N.Y.C. Recipient awards Art Dir.'s Club Los Angeles, Ann. Advt. award Progressive Architecture; grantee Nat. Endowment for Arts, N.Y. State Council in Arts. Mem. Am. Inst. Graphic Arts (v.p., bd. dirs., various awards). Avocation: hunting. Office: Donovan & Green Inc One Madison Ave New York NY 10027

GREEN, NORMA FAY, journalism educator; b. Toledo, Ohio, June 14, 1947; d. George Warren and Pauline Green; m. John William Corbett, Sept. 4, 1982. A.A., Henry Ford Community Coll., 1967; B.A. in Journalism, Mich. State U., 1969; M.S. in Journalism, Northwestern U., 1972; Liberal Arts cert. U. Chgo., 1983. Reporter, copy editor State News, East Lansing, Mich., 1968-69; reporter Observer Newspapers, Plymouth, Mich., 1969-70; staff writer, copy editor Monroe Evening News (Mich.), 1971; reporter, editor Crain Communications, Chgo., 1972-79; mgr. mktg. services Follett Pub. Co., Chgo., 1980-83; dir. mktg. Crain Books, Chgo., 1983-85; instr. journalism Mich. State U. writing instr. Northwestern U., Evanston, Ill., 1979. Docent, Chgo. Architecture Found., 1978—, editor newsletter, 1978—; gallery guide Terra Mus. Am. Art, Evanston, 1981—; founding mem. women's com. 1992 Chgo. World's Fair, 1982—; bd. dirs. Preservation League Evanston, 1984—. Recipient Leadership cert. YWCA Met. Chgo., 1981; Creative award Chgo. Assn. Direct Mktg., 1984; Nat. Fedn. Press Women Helen Miller Mallock Scholar, 1986-87. Mem. Women in Communications (pres. Chgo. chpt. 1978-79; Appreciation cert. 1979, 80, Disting. Service award 1982), Soc. Profl. Journalists, Chgo. Women in Publishing, Internat. Assn. Bus. Communicators, AAUW. Office: Mich State U Sch Journalism Coll Communication Arts and Scis East Lansing MI 48824

GREEN, ROSE BASILE (MRS. RAYMOND S. GREEN), poet, author, educator; b. New Rochelle, N.Y., Dec. 19, 1914; d. Salvatore and Caroline (Galgano) Basile; B.A., Coll. New Rochelle, 1935; M.A., Columbia U., 1941; Ph.D., U. Pa., 1962; L.H.D. (hon.), Gwynedd-Mercy Coll., 1979, Cabrini Coll., 1982; m. Raymond S. Green, June 20, 1942; children—Carol-Rae (Mrs. Alfred Robert Hoffmann), Raymond Ferguson St. John. Tchr., Torrington (Conn.) High Sch., 1936-42; writer, researcher Fed. Writers Project, 1935-36; free-lance script writer Cavalcade of Am., NBC, 1940-42; assoc. prof., chmn. dept. English, univ. registrar Tampa (Fla.) U., 1942-43; spl. instr. English, Temple U., Phila., 1953-57; prof. dept. English, Cabrini Coll., Radnor, Pa., 1957-70, chmn. dept., 1957-70. Exec. dir. Am. Inst. Italian Studies; dir. lit. com. Phila. Art Alliance; bd. dirs. Phila. Opera Co.; bd. dirs., trustee Free Library of Phila.; v.p., dir. Nat. Italian-Am. Found.; chair Nat. Adv. Council Ethnic Heritage Studies; adv. bd. Women for Greater Phila.; dir. Balch Inst. Phila. Decorated cavalier Republic of Italy; named Woman of Yr. Pa., Sons of Italy, 1975, Disting. Dau. of Pa., 1978; recipient Nat. Amita award for lit., 1976; Nat. Bicentennial award for poetry DAR, 1976; Alumnae Achievement award Columbia U., 1986; other awards for contbns. to lit. and edn. Mem. Am. Acad. Polit. and Social Sci., Acad. Am. Poets, Acad. Polit. Sci., Am. Studies Assn., Ethnic Studies Assn., AAUW (dir.-at-large), Nat. Council Tchrs. English, Am.-Italy Soc. (dir. 1952—), Eastern Pa. Coll. New Rochelle Alumnae (pres. 1951-54), Kappa Gamma Pi. Club: Cosmopolitan (Phila.). Author: Cabrinian Philosophy of Education, 1967; (poetry) To Reason Why, 1971, Primo Vino, 1974, 76 for Philadelphia, 1975, Century Four, 1981, Songs of Ourselves, 1982; (criticism) The Italian-American Novel, 1974; (poems) Woman, The Second Coming, 1977; Lauding the American Dream, 1980; The Life of Mother Frances Cabrini, 1984; Songs of Ourselves, 1982; (poems) The Pennsylvania People, 1984; editor faculty jour. A-Zimuth, 1963-70. Home: 308 Manor Rd Philadelphia PA 19128

GREEN, RUTH NELDA (CUMMINGS), educator; b. Greenway, Ark., Aug. 25, 1928; d. William Harrison and Opal Lee (Davis) G.; B.S. in Edn., U. Omaha (now U. Nebr., Omaha), 1966, postgrad.; m. Robert C. Green, Jr., Apr. 22, 1951 (dec.); children—Dana Lynn Green Schrad, Lisa Jane Green Noon. Tchr., Public Schs. Greenway, 1948-51, Hancock County (Miss.), 1951-53, Bellevue (Nebr.), 1961—. Bd. govs. edn. com. Fontenelle Forest Nature Center. NSF scholar, 1968-73. Mem. NEA, Greater Nebr. Assn. Tchrs. Sci. (state pres. 1984-85), Nebr. Wildlife Assn., Nat. Audubon Soc. (Edn. award 1975), Omaha Audubon Soc., Bellevue Edn. Assn., Nebr. Edn. Assn., Inland Bird Banding Assn., Am. Birding Assn., Nebr. Ornithologists Union (state pres. 1982, state v.p. 1983-85, dir.), Alpha Delta Kappa. Mem. Ch. of Christ. Columnist for Audubon Soc. Omaha Newsletter, Nebr. Ornithologists Union Newsletter. Home: 506 W 31st Ave Bellevue NE 68005 Office: 700 Galvin Rd Bellevue NE 68005

GREEN, SELMA BLOCK, lawyer; b. N.Y.C., June 4, 1916; d. Abraham J. and Pauline (Hutner) Block; m. Emanuel Green, June 7, 1942; children—Lori, Frederick S., Nancy Green-Schieken. Student Cornell U., 1933-35; LL.B., NYU, 1938. Bar: N.Y. 1939. Spl. corp. counsel Corp. Counsel N.Y.C., 1939-40; asst. dir. Bur. Prevention Juvenile Delinquency, N.Y.C., 1940-42; atty. U.S. Army Legal Claims Div., Newport News, Va., 1943-44; assoc. Green & Green, N.Y.C., 1944—; owner, mgr. Plaza Pharmacy, Inc., N.Y.C., 1959—. Pres., Rego Park PTA, 1955; exec. bd. Halsey Jr. High Sch., Rego Park, 1956-57; commr. Girl Scouts U.S.A., 1955-57; dist. capt. Democratic Club, N.Y.C. and Forest Hills, N.Y., 1946-59; del. United Parents Assn., Rego Park, 1956-58; asst. sec., charter mem. Trylon Regular Dem. Club, Rego Park, 1956-69. Mem. N.Y. Women's Bar Assn. (v.p. 1940-41), Nat. Assn. Women Lawyers, ABA, Empire City Pharm. Assn., Nat. Assn. Retail Druggists. Club: Hadassah. Home: 15 Weaver St Scarsdale NY 10583 Office: Plaza Pharmacy Inc 1657 2d Ave New York NY 10028

GREEN, SHIA TOBY RINER, therapist; b. N.Y.C., July 1, 1937; d. Murray A. and Frances Riner; student CCNY, 1954-57; B.A., Antioch Coll., 1974, M.A., 1976; m. Gary S. Green, Sept. 4, 1957; children—Margot Laura, Vanessa Daryl, Garson Todd. Press. and legis. sec. U.S. Ho. of Reps., Washington, 1960-71; cons. Rehab. Services Adminstrn., Social and Rehab. Services, HEW, 1972-73; asst. dir. State of Md. Foster Care Impact Dmonstration Project, 1977-78; therapist Alexandria (Va.) Narcotics Treatment Program, 1979-84, Assocs. in Clin. Practice, Gaithersburg, Md., 1984—; mem. treatment com. Alexandria Case Mgmt. and Treatment of Child Sexual Abuse. Mem. exec. bd. Children's Adoption Resource Exchange, Washington; vol. worker Girl Scouts U.S.A., also Boy Scouts Am., 1970-74. Mem. Am. Psychol. Assn., Md. Psychol. Assn., Am. Assn. Marriage and Family Therapy, AAAS. Co-author: Permanent Planning in Maryland—A Manual for the Foster Care Worker. Home: 7609 Hackamore Dr Potomac MD 20854 Office: 9077 Shady Grove Ct Gaithersburg MD 20877

GREEN, SHIRLEY, marketing and advertising executive; b. Boston, Jan. 28, 1934; d. Maurice and Sophie Florence (Shindell) Betterman; m. Mort Green, Mar. 21, 1953; children—Susan, Pamela, Andrew. B.S., Boston U., 1967, M.S., 1968. Sci. tchr. Brockton High Sch. (Mass.), 1968-75; staff reporter Brockton Enterprise, 1975-77; asst. entertainment editor Hollywood Sun-Tattler (Fla.), 1977-79; news dir. Nova U., St. Lauderdale, Fla., 1979-81; mng. editor New Homes Guide, Pompano Beach, Fla., 1981; pres. Shirley Green Assocs., Deerfield Beach, Fla., 1982—. Contbr. articles to various publs. Publicity chmn. Broward's Friends of Chamber Music, Pompano Beach, 1981-83, bd. dirs., 1981—. Recipient Best Feature Story award Knight-Ritter Newspapers, 1980; named Woman of Month, Joy 107, Ft. Lauderdale, 1982. Mem. Mensa, Fla. Atlantic Builders Assn. (dir. 1982—, dir. sales and mktg. council 1982—, appreciation award 1983), Am. Mktg. Assn., Women in Communications, Ft. Lauderdale C. of C. (publicity com., winter festival task force), Sigma Delta Chi. Jewish. Office: Shirley Green Assocs 201 N Federal Hwy Deerfield Beach FL 33441

GREEN, VICKI LYNN, lawyer; b. Shreveport, La., Jan. 1, 1956; d. Charles Abner and Cleolis Cloteal (Hudson) G. B.A., La. Tech. U., 1977; J.D., Tulane U., 1980. Bar: La. 1980, U.S. Ct. Appeals (5th cir.) 1982, U.S. Dist. Ct. (we. dist.) La. 1982. Asst. dist. atty. Ouachita Parish (La.), Monroe, 1980-81; assoc. McLeod, Swearingen, Verlander & Dollar, Monroe, 1981-85, Sockrider, Bolin & Anglin, Shreveport, 1986—. Mem. ABA, La. Bar Assn. (legis. law reform com. family law sect. 1983—, ho. of dels. 1984-85), Trial Lawyers Assn. Am., N.E. La. Trial Lawyers Assn., La. Trial Lawyers Assn., 4th Jud. Dist. Bar Assn. (adv. bd. young lawyers sect. 1983-85, ethics com. 1983-85), Delta Theta Phi. Home: 47 Albert St Shreveport LA 71105 Office: Sockrider Bolin & Anglin 327 Crockett St Shreveport LA 71101

GREEN, YOLANDA ROCHELLE, special education educator; b. Lufkin, Tex., Oct. 11, 1958; d. Curtis Joe and Jo Emilie (Nelson) Jackson Green; 1 son, Kelby Jerod. B.S.N., Prairie View A&M U., 1981. Cert. spl. edn. tchr., Tex. Resource room tchr. Dallas Ind. Sch. Dist., 1981—. Mem. PTA, Dallas, 1983—. Mem. Council for Exceptional Children (pres. 1980-81), Assn. Childhood Internat.

GREENBERG, JEANNE LECRANN, corporate executive; b. N.Y.C., Dec. 23, 1935; d. Vincent and Anne LeCrann; student Fairleigh Dickenson U., 1959-60, Rider Coll., 1974-78, Princeton U.; m. Herbert M. Greenberg, July 30, 1969; children—Scott, Phillip, Holly. Dir. field ops., then v.p., dir. govt. services Mktg. Survey and Research Corp., Princeton, N.J., 1961-70, pres., 1975—; dir. placement and counseling OEO, New Opportunities Program, San Juan, P.R., 1965-66; dir. placement and counseling Social Research Corp., 1968-70; pres., gen. mgr. Progressive Communications, Inc., Sta. WIMG, Trenton, N.J., 1973-85; co-chmn., prin. Caliper Mgmt. Co., 1985—; chmn., chief exec. officer Caliper Co., Human Strategies Cons., 1985—; exec. v.p. Personality Dynamics, Inc., Princeton, 1970-83; founder, 1977, pres. N.J. Radio Network, 1977-81; workshop leader, speaker in field. Trustee Del. Valley United Way, 1978-80, chmn. publicity com., 1979—. Mem. Assn. Women in Radio and TV, Women's Equity Action League, Princeton C. of C. Democrat. Author articles in field. Home: 132 Hunt Dr Princeton NJ 08540 Office: PO Box 2050 Princeton NJ 08540

GREENBERG, JOYCE IRENE, investment banking firm executive; b. Annapolis, Md., Mar. 11, 1952; d. Edwin Gilbert and Anna (Eisenstein) G. B.A. with honors, Simmons Coll., 1973; M.B.A., Harvard U., 1978. Asst. treas. Chase Manhattan Bank, N.Y.C., 1973-76; v.p. Kidder, Peabody & Co. Inc., N.Y.C., 1978—. Mem. Hadassah Nat. Polit. Action Com. N.Y.C., 1983—. Recipient Tribute to Women in Internat. Industry award Nat. YMCA, 1984. Democrat. Jewish. Clubs: Harvard of N.Y.C., Harvard Bus. Sch. Club of N.Y.C., Simmons of N.Y.C. Office: Kidder Peabody & Co Inc 10 Hanover Sq New York NY 10005

GREENBERG, JUDITH LYNN, social worker; b. N.Y.C., Feb. 9, 1947; d. Sam Paul and Celia (Lidofsky) G. B.A. with distinction (Adelia Cheever scholar 1966), U. Mich., 1967; M.A., U. Chgo., 1970; postgrad. (univ. grantee) Adelphi U., 1979—. Elem. sch. tchr. Willow Run Pub. Schs., Mich., 1967-68; urban planner Chgo. Dept. Devel. and Planning, 1970-71; social worker Inst. Juvenile Research, Chgo., 1971; med. social worker St. Luke's Hosp., N.Y.C., 1972-73; social worker immigration and absorption dept. Jewish Agy., Jerusalem, 1973-74; social worker, student supr. Jewish Bd. Family and Children's Services, N.Y.C., 1974-82; dir. Queens Family Ct. Preventive Services, Jewish Bd. Family and Children's Services, Jamaica, N.Y., 1982—; instr. St. Joseph's Coll., Bklyn., 1979-82, Adelphi U. Sch. Social Work, Garden City, N.Y., 1985—; participant TV programs, family life edn. workshops. HEW fellow, 1968-70; NIMH fellow, 1979-80. Mem. Nat. Assn. Social Workers, Am. Assn. Sex Educators, Counselors and Therapists, Soc. Sex Therapy and Research, Acad. Cert. Social Workers, Clin. Social Workers Registry. Jewish. Home: 210 W 89th St Apt 1C New York NY 10024 Office: Queens Family Ct Preventive Services 89-14 Parsons Blvd Jamaica NY 11432

GREENBERG, LEAH, psychologist; b. Jan. 2; d. Laib and Hannah (Derman) G.; B.S., Johns Hopkins U.; B.H.L., Balt. Hebrew Coll.; M.A., Johns Hopkins U. Psychologist, Boys Village, Cheltenham, Md., 1963—. Mem. Am. Psychol. Assn., Eastern Psychol. Assn., Md. Psychol. Assn., Johns Hopkins Alumni Assn., Internat. Platform Assn., Phi Delta Kappa, Phi Delta Gamma. Contbr. articles to profl. jours. Home: 3812 Glengyle Ave Baltimore MD 21215 Office: Boys Village Cheltenham MD 20623

GREENBERG, ROSALIE, child psychiatrist; b. Bklyn., Dec. 21, 1950; d. Sam and Molly G.; B.A., N.Y.U., 1972; student Upstate Med. Center, Syracuse, 1972-73; M.D., Columbia U., 1976; m. Soly Baredes, Aug. 25, 1973. Intern, Overlook Hosp., Summit, N.J., 1976-77; resident in gen. psychiatry Columbia Presbyn. Med. Center, N.Y. State Psychiatric Inst., N.Y.C., 1977-80, fellow in child and adolescent psychiatry, 1979-81, dep. dir. pediatric psychiatry outpatient clinic, 1981-82; dir. child and adolescent outpatient services Fair Oaks Hosp., Summit, N.J., 1982—; instr. Columbia U., 1981—. Mem. Am. Psychiat. Assn., Am. Acad. Child Psychiatry, AMA. Office: Fair Oaks Hospital 19 Prospect St Summit NJ 07901

GREENBERGER, ELLEN, psychology educator; b. N.Y.C., Nov. 19, 1935; d. Edward Michael and Vera (Brisk) Silver; B.A., Vassar Coll., 1956; M.A., Harvard U., 1959, Ph.D., 1961; m. Michael Burton, Aug. 26, 1979; children by previous marriage—Kari Edwards, David Greenberger. Instr., Wellesley (Mass.) Coll., 1961-63, asst. prof., 1963-67; sr. research scientist Johns Hopkins U., Balt., 1967-75; prof. social ecology U. Calif., Irvine, 1975—, dir. program in social ecology, 1976-80. USPHS fellow, 1956-59; Margaret Floy Washburn fellow, 1956-58; Ford Found. grantee, 1979-81; Spencer Found. grantee, 1979-81. Fellow Am. Psychol. Assn.; mem. Soc. for Research in Child Devel., Contbr. articles to profl. jours. Office: Program in Social Ecology U Calif Irvine CA 92717

GREENBLATT, DEANA CHARLENE, educator; b. Chgo., Mar. 13, 1948; d. Walter and Betty (Lamasky) Beisel; B.S. in Edn., Chgo. State U., 1969; M.A. in Guidance and Counseling, Roosevelt U., 1973; m. Mark Greenblatt, June 22, 1975. Tchr., counselor Chgo. Pub. Schs., 1969-75, City Colls. of Chgo. GED-TV, 1976; tchr. Columbus (Ohio) Pub. Schs., 1976—; participant learning exchange, Chgo. Active B'nai B'rith; vol. Right-to-Read, Columbus; mem. Community Learning Exchange, Columbus. Certified tchr. K-9, Ill., Ohio; certified personnel guidance, Ill., Ohio; certified Chgo. Bd. Edn. Mem. Am. Personnel and Guidance Assn., Internat. Platform Assn. Democrat. Club: B'nai B'rith Women (chpt. v.p.). Home: 4083 Vineshire Dr Columbus OH 43227

GREENBLATT, HELLEN CHAYA, immunologist, researcher; b. Frankfurt am Main, W.Ger., May 15, 1947; came to U.S., 1948; d. Gedaljie and Sara (Glass) Greenblatt. B.A., CCNY, 1968; M.S., U. Okla., 1971; Ph.D., SUNY Downstate Med. Ctr.-Bklyn., 1977. Microbiologist, Walter Reed Army Inst. Research, Washington, 1978-80; sr. research immunoparasitologist Merck Sharp & Dohme, Rahway, N.J., 1980-81; assoc. Albert Einstein Coll. Medicine, Bronx, 1981-84; dir. research and devel. Clin. Scis. Inc., Whippany, N.J., 1984—; cons. Image Technology Corp., Deer Park, N.Y., 1983—. Contbr. articles to profl. jours. Recipient Outstanding Young Woman award Competitive Resident Research Council, Washington, 1978, Nat. Research Council award, 1978-80. Fellow N.Y. Acad. Scis.; mem. Assn. Women Scientists. Office: Clinical Sciences Inc 30 Troy Rd Whippany NJ 07981

GREENBLATT, JANE G., real estate developer; b. Paterson, N.J., Dec. 9, 1950; d. Nathan Edward and Anita (Samuels) G.; B.A., Syracuse U., 1972; M. in Urban Planning, N.Y.U., 1974. Devel. dir. N.Y.C. Office Devel., 1977-79; asst. mgr. Met. Life Ins. Co., N.Y.C., 1979-82; v.p. real estate devel. Howco Investment Corp., Livingston, N.J., 1982-85; exec. v.p. The Seltzer Orgn., Norwalk, Conn., 1985—. Mem. Hackensack Hosp. Women's Aux., 1978-85; mem. Mayor's Office for SRO, Elderly, Handicapped, N.Y.C., 1975-76. Mem. Nat. Assn. Indsl. and Office Parks (treas.), Real Estate Bd. N.Y., Urban Land Inst., Young Men's/Women's Real Estate Assn. N.Y. (mem. com.). Avocations: sports; cooking; travel. Office: The Seltzer Orgn 488 Main Ave Norwalk CT 06851

GREENBLATT, MIRIAM, author, editor, educator; b. Berlin; d. Gregory and Shifra (Zemach) Baraks; B.A. magna cum laude, Hunter Coll.; postgrad. U. Chgo., Spertus Coll.; m. Herbert Halbrecht (div. 1960); m. 2d, Howard Greenblatt, 1962 (div. 1978). Tchr., New Trier (Ill.) High Sch., 1978-81; editor Am. People's Ency., Chgo., 1957-58; editor Scott, Foresman & Co., Chgo., 1958-62; pres. Creative Textbooks, Evanston, Ill., 1972—. Vice pres. Chgo. Chpt. Am. Jewish Com., 1977-79, mem. nat. exec. council, 1980-84; treas. Glencoe Youth Services, 1981-83. Mem. Nat. Council Social Studies, Ill. Council Social Studies, Am. Hist. Assn., Chgo. Women in Publishing, Women in Mgmt. Jewish. Author: (with others) The American People, 1986; (with Jordan and Bowes) The Americans, 1985; (with Cox and Seaburg) Human Heritage, 1985; The History of Itasca, 1976; (with Larry Cuban) Japan, 1971; (with Don-chean Chu) The Story of China, 1968; edit. cons. Peoples and Cultures Series, 1976-78; contbg. editor A World History, 1979. Address: 550 Sheridan Sq Evanston IL 60202

GREEN-DORSEY, JEAN AUDREY, information systems executive; b. Cleve., Oct. 27, 1940; d. Sydney Howard and Bennie Irene (Blake) Green; B.A., L.I. U., 1962; m. William R. Dorsey, Nov. 1, 1980. With IBM, N.Y.C., 1966-72; mktg. mgr. office automation Olivetti, N.Y.C., 1972-80; dep. dir. N.Y.C. Mgmt. Info. Systems, 1981-85, computer systems mgr. Inter-agy. Task Force, 1985—; sr. cons. Inst. Mgmt. Devel., 1980—; adv. editor Hearst Pubs., 1981—, others; lectr. in field. Bd. dirs. Fair Harbor Community Assn., 1981—. Recipient cert. Fresh Air Fund, 1980. Mem. Assn. Computing Machinery, Assn. Info. Systems Profls. Clubs: Soroptimists Internat., The Club at N.Y. World Trade Center. Contbr. articles to profl. jours. Office: 137 Centre St New York City NY 10013

GREENE, ALICE HUBBARD, management consultant; b. San Juan, P.R., Sept. 10, 1957; d. Kenneth Lawrence Greene and Anna Gabriella (Wood) Peerbolt. B.S. in Mgmt., Speech and Indsl. Psychology, U. Minn., Mpls., 1984. Account rep. Sci. Computers, Inc., Minnetonka, Minn., 1984; field support specialist Mfg. Software Corp., Eagan, Minn., 1984-85, field support cons., 1985; mfg. mgmt. cons. Price Waterhouse, Mpls., 1985—. Mem. Am. Prodn. and Inventory Control Soc., (chpt. v.p. 1981-83, 84-86, region dir. 1985-86), Mpls. Women's Group (founder), Phi Kappa Phi. Avocations: art, swimming. Home: 3900 Blaisdell Ave S Minneapolis MN 55409 Office: Price Waterhouse 33 S 6th St Suite 3140 Minneapolis MN 55402

GREENE, AURELIA, state legislator; b. N.Y.C., Oct. 26, 1934; d. Edward Henry and Sybil Elaine (Russell) Holley; children—Rhonda, Russell; m. 2d, Jerome Alexander Greene, Apr. 18, 1975. B.A., Rutgers U., 1974. Dep. exec. dir. Morrisania Community Corp., N.Y.C., 1969-76; exec. dir. Bronx Area Policy Bd. No. 6, N.Y.C., 1980-82; mem. N.Y. State Assembly, 1982—. Dist. leader 76th Assembly Dist., Bronx, 1979-82; sec. Community Sch. Bd. No. 9, Bronx, 1980—; exec. mem. Bronx Unity Democratic Club; del. Dem. Nat. Conv., 1984. Mem. Morrisania Edn. Council, Bronx NAACP (Woman of Yr. award 1974). Democrat. Office: 1188 Grand Concourse Suite D Bronx NY 10456

GREENE, BEVERLY ANN, clinical psychologist; b. Orange, N.J., Aug. 14, 1950; d. Samuel and Thelma G.; B.A., N.Y.U., 1973; M.A., Adelphi U. 1977, Ph.D., 1983; postgrad. Marquette U., 1973-74. Lic. psychologist, N.Y. Psychologist div. child/adolescent psychiatry Downstate Med. Center, also clin. isntr. King County Hosp., 1973-74; psychology fellow Mental Retardation Inst., N.Y. Med. Coll., Valhalla, N.Y., 1974-76; cons. psychologist Williamsberg Child Devel. Center, Bklyn., 1976-78; research asst. N.J. Coll. Medicine and Dentistry, also VA Med. Center, 1979-80; psychology intern East Orange VA Med Ctr., 1978-79; psychology trainee Brookdale Hosp. and Med. Center, 1980; staff psychologist N.Y.C. Public Schs., 1980-84; sr. psychologist, dir. inpatient child and adolescent psychological services Kings County Hosp., 1984—; clin. instr., 1982-85, clin. asst. prof., 1985—. Downstate Med Ctr., acting dir. Children's Inpatient Unit 1985—. Fellow NIMH, 1976-77. Mem. Internat. Neuropsychol. Soc., Am. Psychol. Assn., Am. Orthopsychiatric Assn., Women in Psychology, N.Y. State Coalition of Hosp. and Instl. Psychologists; N.Y. Assn. Black Psychologists, N.Y. Neuropschology Group. Office: 606 Winthrop St Brooklyn NY 11203

GREENE, CYNTHIA LOU, lawyer; b. Miami, Fla., Oct. 14, 1950; d. Charles Kaye and Adelaide (Blum) G. B.A., U. Miami, 1975, J.D., 1979. Bar: Fla. 1979. Ptnr. Frumkes and Greene, P.A., Miami, 1979—. Contbr. articles to profl. jours. Mem. ABA, Fla. Bar (editor family law sect. jour. 1981—). Office: Law Offices of Frumkes and Greene PA 100 N Biscayne Blvd Miami FL 33132

GREENE, DOLORES EVANGELINE, university official; b. Pilot Grove, Mo., Sept. 21, 1929; d. David Hadley and Mary Esther (Chasteen) Simms; m. James Lincoln Greene, Nov. 18, 1950; children—Gary Alan, Jeffrey Warren, David Morgan. B.S., U. Wis., 1951, M.S., 1965. Cert. tchr., remedial reading tchr., notary pub., Wis. Tchr., Madison Area Tech. Sch. (Wis.), 1954-55, Milw. Pub. Schs., 1955-66; manpower specialist, supr., dir. Wis. Employment Service, Madison, 1967-72; area services specialist Wis. Dept. Health and Social Services, Madison, 1972-75; asst. to chancellor U. Wis. Extension, Madison, 1975-84; chmn. Milw. Reading Tchrs., 1962-63; cons. Milw. Urban League, 1957-60; support specialist Madison Pub. Schs., 1978-80; artist; actress stage and TV. Author: (with others) Ambidextrous (Natural) Tennis, 1979, 2d edit., 1982. Bd. dirs. Dane County Community Action Commn., 1969-72, Madison Urban League, 1974-76; del. Internat. Women's Yr., Houston, 1977; core council, dir. Coalition Minority Women, 1975-82; dir. Madison Civic Repertory Theatre, 1980-84; pres., sec. Brown St. PTA, 1960-64. Recipient Outstanding Pub. Service award Ethnic Heritage Award Com., 1978, award for advancement women's equality Wis. Women's Polit. Caucus, 1980, Meritorious Service award United Way of Dane County and YWCA, 1981, Affirmative Action/EEO Individual award Madison Urban League, 1982, state service award Gov.'s Affirmative Action Council, 1983. Mem. Internat. Reading Assn., Am. Assn. Affirmative Action, Wis. Assn. Affirmative Action and Equal Opportunity Profls., Madison Black Affirmative Action Officers Assn., Madison Minority Bus. Assn., Epsilon Sigma Phi, Delta Sigma Theta. Democrat. Methodist. Home: 302 S Bassett St Madison WI 53703

GREENE, EDEE, college administrator; b. Newark, Oct. 6, 1913; d. Henry Meyer and Emily (Sudworth) Nielsen; m. Thomas G. Greene, May 30, 1934 (div. Aug. 1951); children—Helen Reddy, Tom Jr., James B.; m. Joseph K. Rukenbrod, Jan. 15, 1955 (dec. June 1983). Women's editor Orlando Sentinel, Orlando, Fla., 1951-56; program dir. WABR Radio, Orlando, 1956-57; lifestyle exec. editor News/Sun Sentinel, Fort Lauderdale, Fla., 1957-76; dir. coll. relations Broward Community Coll., Fort Lauderdale, 1976—. Pres. United Way of Broward and Fort Lauderdale, 1977-78, Womens Advocacy/Majority Minority, Fort Lauderdale, 1976-79; bd. dirs. Community Service Council, Fort Lauderdale, 1965-76, v.p., 1985—; bd. dirs. Vol. Action Ctr., Fort Lauderdale, 1982-85; founding pres., life bd. dirs. Women in Distress, Fort Lauderdale, 1974—. Recipient Bell award Nat. Mental Health Assn., 1960, Penney Mo. awards U. Mo., Columbia, 1960, 63, 64, 67, awards Fla. Press Club, 1952-76; named Vol. of Yr., Vol. Action Ctr., 1978. Mem. Women in Communications (pres. 1966-67, Woman of Yr. 1976). Club: Fla. Press (bd. dirs., pres. 1951-76). Avocations: reading; traveling; walking. Office: Broward Community Coll 225 Elas Olas Blvd Fort Lauderdale FL 33301

GREENE, FRANCES, non-profit organization administrator; b. Sugarlock, Miss., Feb. 2, 1937; d. Willie and Frances (Moore) Jenkins; m. John Baptiste Greene, June 6, 1961; children—John Baptiste, Delores Green. B.A., Antioch West Coll. (Calif.), 1973, postgrad in early child devel., Mt. Diablo Coll., Calif. State U., Hayward, 1974. Nurses aide, Los Medanos Hosp., Pittsburg, Calif., 1961-69; instr., recreation supr. Pittsburg Unified Sch., 1971-72; community liasion Pre-Sch. Coordinating Council Inc., Pittsburg, 1972-73, program dir., 1973-84, exec. dir., 1972—. Vol. servant El Pueblo Sr. Citizens, Pittsburg, 1972—; pres. Black Polit. Assn., Pittsburg, 1979; trustee St. Mark Baptist Ch., Pittsburg, 1981—; co-mgr. Pittsburg City Council elections, 1982-84; pres. Delta Democrats, Antioch, Calif., 1982; com. coordinator Sch. Bd. Elections, Pittsburg; mem. Grand Jury, Marteniz, Calif., 1981; mem. Dem. Central Com. Mem. NAACP (chmn. com. 1960). Home: 56 Barrie Dr Pittsburg CA 94565 Office: Pre Sch Coordinating Council Inc 4 E 5th St Pittsburg CA 94565

GREENE, GAYLE JACOBA, English educator; b. San Francisco, June 23, 1943. B.A., U. Calif.-Berkeley, 1964, M.A., 1966; Ph.D. in English Lit., Columbia U., 1974. Edn. asst. Harper & Row Pub., 1967-68; lectr. English lit. Queens Coll., 1968-72, Bklyn. Coll., 1972-74; asst. prof. Scripps Coll., Claremont, Calif., 1974-80, assoc. prof. English lit., 1980—. Mem. MLA, Shakespeare Assn. Am., Nat. Women's Studies Assn. Co-editor: The Woman's Part: Feminist Criticism of Shakespeare, 1980; Making a Difference: Feminist Literary Criticism, 1985; contbr. articles to profl. jours. Address: Scripps Coll Claremont CA 91711

GREENE, IDA, educator; b. Minters, Ala., May 28, 1938; d. Willie O'Neal and Rosetta (Ulmer) Greene; 1 child, Christopher. B.A., San Diego State U., 1970, M.S., 1973; Ph.D. in Psychology; D.D. R.N., Calif.; lic. marriage family and child counselor. Charge nurse Univ. Hosp., San Diego, 1967, dir. nursing, 1971; sch. counselor San Diego State U., 1972; psychiatric nurse El Cajon Valley Hosp. (Calif.), 1973; sch. nurse O'Farrell Jr. High Sch., San Diego, 1975-84; tchr./counselor Lincoln Sr. High Sch., San Diego, 1981—; lectr. in field. Founder, Henry William Scholarship, 1973. Mem. Women in Mgmt., Women in Sales, Nat. Council Negro Women, Grow, Marriage and Family Child Counselors. Methodist. Club: Toastmasters. Author: Black Triumph, 1975. Address: 2910 Baily Ave San Diego CA 92105

GREENE, KAREN JANE, lawyer; b. Niagara, Wis., Mar. 8, 1951; d. Donald T. and Marjorie J. (Larson) Greene. B.A. with distinction, Cornell U., 1973; J.D., U. Pa., 1977. Bar: Calif. 1978. Staff atty. Am. Med. Internat., Inc., Beverly Hills, Calif., 1977-82, asst. v.p., 1982-83, v.p., sr. counsel, 1983—. Mem. Los Angeles County Bar Assn., Calif. Women Lawyers Assn., Am. Soc. Hosp. Attys., ABA. Republican. Office: Am Med Internat Inc 414 N Camden Dr Beverly Hills CA 90210

GREENE, KARIN CATHARINA, utility company executive; b. Hamont, Belgium, May 4, 1953; came to Can., 1977; d. Rene and Maria (Van Eyndhoven) Claessens; m. Godfrey B. Greene, Sept. 3, 1977. B.Com., U. Louvain (Belgium), 1973, M.Econs. with honors, 1976; M.B.A., U. Gent (Belgium), 1977. Departmental asst. Alta. Govt. Telephones, Edmonton, Can., 1978-79; mktg. research specialist, 1979-81; bus. planner, Calgary, 1981-83, market planning mgr. mobile communications, 1983—. Mem. Profl. Mktg. Research Assn., Am. Mktg. Assn. Roman Catholic. Club: Fit City (Calgary). Office: Mobile Communications Alta Govt Telephones 6620 36th St SE Calgary AB T2C 2G4 Canada

GREENE, KATHLEEN JAN, public relations consultant; b. Toledo, Feb. 18, 1949; d. Raymond Philip Greene and Joanne (Jorgensen) Greene Deatrick; m. Thomas Arne Olkkonen, May 24, 1980. B.A., Kent State U., 1972. Media dir. Gauge Public, Traverse City, Mich., 1973-74; copywriter Sta. WGTU/WGTQ-TV, Traverse City, 1974-78, asst. dir., 1978-79, dir. creative services, 1979-80; mktg. coordinator Sta. WPBN/WTOM-TV, Traverse City, 1980-82; pub. relations cons. KG Unltd., Traverse City, 1982—; media relations and sales Okerstrom Assocs., Traverse City, 1983—; pub. relations rep. N.Am. Vasa, Traverse City, 1983—; communications coordinator Grand Traverse Area United Way, 1983—. Co-producer/dir.: Central Lake (Am. Legion award), 1978; producer/dir.: Band Classics (music award), 1979, Reach Out (United Way award), 1980. Communications com. Grand Traverse Area United Way, 1977—; publicity com. Community Theatre Mich., 1983—, Traverse City Civic Players, 1975—. Mem. Women in Communications, Inc., Traverse Advt. Club (pres. 1978-79), Nat. Assn. Female Execs. Republican. Episcopalian. Home: 872 Indian Trail Traverse City MI 49684

GREENE, LUCIA MURRAY, writer; b. N.Y.C., Aug. 5, 1954; d. Philip M. and Constance (Clarke) G.; m. Thomas Girard Connolly, Sept. 20, 1980; children—Nora Clarke, Sophie Gordon. Student, U. Dijon, 1975; B.A. in English and French, Colgate U., 1975. Asst. editor E.P. Dutton Co., N.Y.C., 1976-78; photo researcher, editor, People Mag., N.Y.C., 1979-82, mgr. People Syndication, 1982-83, asst. editor, writer, 1983—; also freelance writer. Democrat. Roman Catholic. Address: 56 N Pease Rd Woodbridge CT 06525

GREENE, PHYLLIS ROSABONHEUR, handwriting analyst, questioned document examiner; b. Chgo., Mar. 9, 1913; d. Chester Holt and Helen Mary (Jones) Greene; m. John Waller Mattingly, Aug. 28, 1944; children—John Chester, James Robert, David Bruce. A.B., U. Chgo., 1938; M.S., Ill. Inst. Tech., 1940; cert. graphoanalyst Internat. Graphoanalysis Soc., 1975, master cert., 1977. Adminstrv. sec. Gen. Electric X-ray, Chgo., 1938-40; personnel mgr. Progressive Hotels, Chgo., 1940-44; tchr., dean girls Pensacola High Sch., Fla., 1945-48; owner Ft. Collins Welcome Lady, Colo., 1949-70; talk host KCOL Koffee Klub, Ft. Collins, 1950-60; owner Phyllis Mattingly Handwriting Services, Ft. Collins and Malibu, Calif., 1976—; instr. Colo. State U., Ft. Collins, 1980—. Pres. Friends of Ft. Collins Library, 1980-83, Internat. Ctr., Colo. State U., 1977-79; chmn. Council on Aging, Ft. Collins, 1975-76; rep. precinct committeeman, pres. Republican Women's Forum, Ft. Collins, 1965-74; exec. bd. dirs. Planned Parenthood, Denver, 1960-62; pres. Parents without Ptnrs., Ft. Collins, 1980-84. Named to 9 Who Care, Channel 9 television, 1982; U.S. Nat. Ballroom Dance champion, 1985; 1985 Roastee Ft. Collins Found., 1985. Mem. Internat. Graphoanalysis Soc. (instr. ann. congress 1983—), Colo. Graphoanalysis Soc. (Colo. Graphoanalyst of Yr. 1981, pres. 1984—), So. Calif. Graphoanalysis Soc. (exec. bd. dirs. 1980—, So Calif. Graphoanalyst of Yr. 1984), World Assn. Document Examiners, Nat. Assn. Document Examiners (sec. 1986—), Internat. Platform Assn. Republican. Christian Scientist. Avocations: dancing; bicycling; theatre; swimming; reading. Home and Office: 1113 Parkwood Dr Fort Collins CO 80525

GREENE, RENEE JUDITH, industrial psychology consultant; b. Charleston, S.C., Mar. 20, 1955; d. George and Sylvia R. (Ginsberg) Greene; m. Michael Fish, Mar. 29, 1986. B.S., U. Fla., 1976; M.S. in Human Services, Nova U., 1986. Dir. Dixie council B'nai B'rith Youth Orgn., Charleston, 1976-78; dir. youth activities Charleston Jewish Community Ctr., 1976-78; asst. dir. Fla. region B'nai B'rith Youth, Orlando, 1978-80; dir. Southeast region, dept. youth activities United Synagogue Am., Plantation, Fla., 1980-83; recruiting mgr. Office Specialists, Miami, Fla., 1983—. Recipient Star of Deborah award B'nai B'rith, 1973. Mem. Jewish Youth Dirs. Assn. (dir. 1981-82), S.E. Psychol. Assn. (assoc.), Nat. Alzheimer's and Related Diseases Assn. (assoc.), Nat. Assn. Temp. Services (chpt. pub. relations com., v.p. Fla. 1986), Nat. Assn. Female Execs. Jewish. Avocations. art; writing; jazz. Office. Office Specialists 1699 Coral Way Suite 500 Miami FL 33145

GREENE, SHARON LOUISE, business manager, editor; b. Washington, Sept. 8, 1960; d. Gary Edward and Lorna Sybil (Herzog) G. Student U. Colo., 1980-82. Office mgr. Irving Kerner Literary Agy., Boulder, 1979-81; bus. mgr. Alpha Micro Users Soc., Boulder, 1979—, editor, 1983—, meeting planner, 1984—, sec.-treas., 1983-86; cons. Club Mac, Boulder, 1984-85. Mem. Nat. Assn. Female Execs., Meeting Planners Internat., Colo. Press Assn. Democrat. Jewish. Avocations: fishing; camping; hiking; reading; sports. Office: Alpha Micro Users Soc 735 Walnut St Boulder CO 80302

GREENFIELD, JUDITH CAROL, librarian; b. Stamford, Conn., Feb. 16, 1935; d. Yale Jerome and Florence Janet (Cramer) Kweskin; m. Jay Greenfield, Sept. 8, 1957; children—Susan, Mark, Benjamin. B.A., Brown U., 1956; M.L.S., Simmons Coll., 1960; M.A., NYU, 1970. Cert. pub. librarian, library media specialist, N.Y. Head cataloging dept. Watertown Pub. Library (Mass.), 1959-60; cataloguer, bibliographer Nat. Library Medicine, 1960-61; reference librarian Queens Coll., Flushing, N.Y., 1966-70; library media specialist Washington Ave Sch., Greenburgh, N.Y., 1973-74; head children's room Rye Free Reading Room (N.Y.), 1974—; mem. children's services adv. bd. Westchester Library System, 1976-78, 80-82, mem. tech. services adv. bd., 1978—. Contbr. articles to profl. jours. Regional dir. alumni schs. program Brown U., 1978-81; chmn. regional screening com. Am. Field Service, Westchester, N.Y., 1981, 83; mem. Family Interest and Resource Service Team, Rye, 1981—. Mem. ALA, N.Y. Library Assn. (speaker children and young adult service sect. conf. 1981), Westchester Library Assn. (speaker panel on computers 1982). Democrat. Jewish. Club: Brown of Westchester (pres. 1984—). Home: 539 Oakhurst Rd Mamaroneck NY 10543 Office: Rye Free Reading Room Boston Post Rd Rye NY 10580

GREENFIELD, LOIS BRODER, educator; b. Chgo., Feb. 5, 1924; d. Samuel and Rose (Michel) Broder; B.S., U. Chgo., 1945, M.S., 1946; Ph.D., U. Calif., Berkeley, 1953; 1 dau., Ellen Beth. Faculty, U. Wis., Madison, 1956—, prof. engring., 1958—. Mem. Am. Soc. Engring. Edn., Am. Psychol. Assn., Am. Ednl. Research Assn., Soc. Women Engrs. Contbr. articles to profl. jours. Office: General Engineering Bldg U Wis Madison WI 53706

GREENFIELD, SUSAN COHEN, marketing specialist; b. Houston, June 27, 1943; d. Aaron J. and Felice W. Cohen; student U. Tex., 1963; B.S. in Psychology, U. Houston, 1965; systems engring. cert. IBM, 1967; children—Elizabeth Ann, Alysha Lynn. Br. mgr., fin. cons. FLC Fin. Services, Sherman Oaks, Calif., 1973-75; salesperson, ter. mgr. C.R. Bard Inc., Murray Hill, N.J., 1975-77; OEM mktg. specialist high tech. sales Honeywell, Inc., Los Angeles, 1977-86, Orange, Calif., 1986—. Bd. dirs. Orange County Easter Seal Soc., Rehab. Inst. Orange County, del. Calif. state conv., 1982; mem. Orange County Music Center. Named to Honeywell Pres.'s Club, 1980; recipient 1st place award for oil painting Orange County Fair, 1985. Mem. Mensa, Psi Chi. Photographs pub. in book of poetry, 1970. Home: 432 Roni Ln Anaheim CA 92807 Office: 721 S Parker Blvd Orange CA 92668

GREENFIELD, THELMA NELSON, English language educator; b. Portland, Sept. 11, 1922; d. Ivar Emanuel and Lulu Ruth (Maxwell) Nelson; B.A., U. Oreg., 1944, M.A., 1947; Ph.D., U. Wis., 1952; m. Stanley B. Greenfield, Jan. 22, 1951; children—Tamma L., Sayre N. Instr., Queens (N.Y.) Coll. Sch. Gen. Studies, 1955-56; mem. faculty U. Oreg., Eugene, 1963—, prof. English, 1972—, now also dept. head; vis. prof. U. Regensburg, 1974-75; guest lectr. Oreg. State Penitentiary. Mem. MLA, Shakespeare Assn. Am., Renaissance Soc. Am., Philol. Assn. Pacific Coast. Club: Shakespeare (Eugene). Author: The Induction in Elizabethan Drama, 1969; The Eye of Judgment, 1982; contbr. articles in field to profl. jours. Office: Department of English University of Oregon Eugene OR 97403

GREENLEAF, KATHERINE MAXIM, lawyer, retail food and drug company executive; b. N.Y.C., Oct. 28, 1948; d. George Lionel and Mildred Norris (Jameson) Maxim; B.A. with honors, Conn. Coll., 1970; J.D., Boston U., 1973; m. Peter Greenleaf, July 1, 1972; children—Julia Tyler, Robert Morgan. Admitted to Maine bar, 1973, Mass. bar, 1973; atty. Union Mutual Life Ins. Co., Portland, Maine, 1973-78, asso. counsel, 2d v.p. litigation, 1978-79, 2d v.p. benefits div., 1979-80, v.p. adminstrn., 1980-83, v.p. mktg., 1983-85; v.p. human resources Hannaford Bros. Co., 1975—; trustee Peoples Heritage Bank. Mem. Internat. Claim Assn., Maine Bar Assn., Maine Trial Lawyers Assn.

GREENLEE, BEVERLY ADELE, army officer, health care administrator; b. Lamesa, Tex., May 29, 1947; d. Cleo Wilson and Tommy Adele (Henley) Greenlee. B.S. in Nursing, Tex. Woman's U., Denton, 1970; M.S. in Health Care Adminstrn., Baylor U., 1976; grad. Comd. and Gen. Staff Coll., Ft. Leavenworth, Kans., 1978. Commd. 2d lt. U.S. Army, 1968, advanced through grades to lt. col., 1984—; staff nurse Ft. Benning Army Hosp., Columbus, Ga., 1970-71, U.S. Army Hosp., Bangkok, Thailand, 1971-72; staff nurse Walter Reed Army Med. Ctr., Washington, 1972, head nurse, 1973, supr., 1974; nursing methods analyst Madigan Army Med. Ctr., Tacoma, Wash., 1975-77, Hdqrs. 7th Med. Comd., Heidelberg, W.Ger., 1977-80; asst. chief dept. nursing Winn Army Hosp., Ft. Stewart, Ga., 1980-83; asst. inspector gen. Hdqrs. US Army Health Services Command, San Antonio, 1983-86; chief dept. nursing Fox Army Hosp., Redstone Arsenal, Ala., 1986—. Mem. Am. Nurses Assn., Tex. Nurses Assn., Sigma Theta Tau, Beta Beta Beta. Lodge: Order Eastern Star. Home: 5755 Spring Watch San Antonio TX 78247 Office: Office Inspector Gen Hdqrs US Army Health Services Comd Fort Sam Houston TX 78234

GREENMAN, ANTONIA MARGUERITE, lawyer; b. Niagara Falls, N.Y., Aug. 10, 1955; d. Morgan Andrew and Gloria Irene G. B.A. summa cum laude, Niagara U., 1977; J.D., U. Notre Dame, 1980; cert. London Sch. Econs., 1979. Bar: D.C. 1981. Bar: D.C. 1981. Assoc. dir. Am. Family Inst., Washington, 1980-81; legis. asst. Senator Al D'Amato, Washington, 1981; exec. dir. Hale Found., Washington, 1982-83; fgn. affairs specialist Republican Study Com., Ho. of Reps., Washington, 1983-84; spl. asst. office of Pub. Diplomacy, Dept. State, Washington, 1984—. Editor-in-chief U. Niagara Yearbook, 1976-77; research editor Jour. Legislation, 1978-79; contbr. govt. and fgn. affairs articles to jours. Recipient Sr. medal Niagara U., 1977, Fr. Duggan medal, 1977; Niagara U. scholar, 1974-77, U. Notre Dame scholar, 1978-80. Mem. ABA (internat. law sect.), Bar Assn. D.C., Phi Alpha Delta. Roman Catholic. Club: Capitol Hill. Office: Office Pub Diplomacy Dept State Washington DC 20520

GREENMAN, JILL DANFORTH, public relations executive; b. Lafayette, Ind., Oct. 9, 1947; d. Frederick Snow and Eugenie (Doran) Greenman. B.A., DePauw U., 1969; M.S.J., Northwestern U., 1976. Pub. relations specialist Harris Trust & Savs. Bank, Chgo., 1976-78; account supr. Burson-Marsteller, Chgo., 1978-81; v.p. Golin/Harris Communications, Inc., Chgo., 1982-84; dir. corporate relations Holiday Corp., Memphis, 1984-86; public relations cons., 1986—; pub. relations cons.; press relations mgr. for Ill. State Rep., 1978. Recipient award Internat. Assn. Bus. Communicators, 1978. Mem. Pub. Relations Soc. Am., Northwestern U. Alumni Assn., Alpha Phi. Republican. Roman Catholic. Home: 1683 Kimbrough Rd Germantown TN 38138

GREEN ROACH, ANTOINETTE VELORIES, fin. brokerage co. co. exec.; b. Meridian, Miss., July 8, 1931; d. Otha Lee and Ester (Mayatte) Ethridge; student public schs., Waco, Tex., Collinsville, Miss.; m. Billy J. Green, May 5, 1979; children—Carl Lowell Roach, Nan Roach Kurth, Mike Roach, Jackie Roach Pilkinton. Ins. and real estate salesperson, 1964-81; pres., owner, operator Lubbock Mortgage Co., Inc. (name now Guaranty Fin. Services, Inc.), Lubbock, Tex., 1976—; pres. Delta Cotton Co., 1977—; pres. Hunter & Roach Advt. Co., Lubbock, 1978—; founder Guaranty Constrn. of Miss. Inc., 1985—, Waveland, v.p., pres. Lubbock, Tex., 1985—. Mem. Nat. Assn. Fin. Cons., Nat. Assn. Female Execs. Inc., Better Bus. Bur., Sheriff Assn., Internat. Bus. Assn., Am. Alliance Small Bus. Club: Presidents of Tex. Home: 3013 78th St Lubbock TX 79423 Office: 1928 34th St Lubbock TX 79411

GREENSTEIN, RHONDA, lawyer; b. N.Y.C., Dec. 12, 1954; d. Zigmund and Annette (Berman) Greenstein; m. Spencer Adam Kravitz, Aug. 31, 1980. B.A. magna cum laude, CUNY, 1974; J.D. cum laude Temple U., 1977. Bar: N.Y. 1978. Asst. pub. defender Office of Monroe County Pub. Defender, Rochester, N.Y., 1977-80; sole practice law, N.Y.C., 1980-81; asst. atty. gen. N.Y. State Dept. Law, Office of Atty.-Gen., N.Y.C., 1981—; gen. counsel Automated Alternatives, Nassau County N.Y., 1983—. Counsel, Self-Help Community Services, N.Y.C., 1983—; legal cons. Pub. Interest Law Ctr., Phila., 1976; asst. coordinator Creedmore State Sch. and Hosp., N.Y.C., 1972-74. Mem. N.Y. State Bar Assn., ABA, Nat. Lawyers Guild, Phi Beta Kappa. Home: 23 Executive Dr Manhasset Hills NY 11040 Office: NY State Dept Law Office of Atty Gen 2 World Trade Ctr New York NY 11047

GREENSTEIN, RUTH LOUISE, lawyer; b. N.Y.C., Mar. 28, 1946; d. Milton and Beatrice (Zutty) Greenstein; B.A., Harvard U., 1966; M.A., Yale U., 1968; J.D., George Washington U., 1980; m. David Seidman, May 19, 1972. Bar: D.C. 1980. Fgn. service info. officer USIA, Washington and Tehran, Iran, 1968-70; adminstrv. asst. Export-Import Bank of the U.S., Washington, 1971-72; asst. dean Woodrow Wilson Sch. Public and Internat. Affairs, Princeton U., 1972-75; budget examiner U.S. Office Mgmt. and Budget, Washington, 1975-79; budget coordinator U.S. Internat. Devel. Coop. Agy., 1979-81; dep. gen. counsel NSF, 1981-84; assoc. counsel Genex Corp., Rockville Md., 1984-85, v.p., Gaithersburg, Md., 1985—. Mem. Am. Bar Assn., D.C. Bar Assn. Office: Genex Corp 16020 Industrial Dr Gaithersburg MD 20877

GREENWALD, DOROTHY I., art educator; b. Harrison, Ark., Sept. 22, 1920; d. George W. and Caroline (Brown) Neal; student Sch. of Cosmetology, Miami, Okla., 1938-39, Craft Students League, N.Y.C., 1938-62, m. Harry Greenwald, Apr. 17, 1949. Owner, operator beauty salon and ladies ready to wear stores, 1940-58; instr. ceramic dept. Craft Student League, N.Y.C., 1962-80, Queens Museum Sch. of Art, Flushing, N.Y., 1980—; past chmn. Craft Students League of YWCA of N.Y.; chmn. crafts dept. Rockland Ctr for Arts, West Nyack, N.Y.; treas. Greenwald Electro-Mech. Cons., Inc., Whitestone, N.Y. Recipient awards Rockland Center for Art, 1972, L.I. Guild of Craftsmen, 1972, Artist-Craftsmen N.Y., 1975. Mem. World Craft Council, Am. Craft Council, Artist-Craftsmen N.Y. (pres. 1972-75), L.I. Guild of Craftsmen, Queens Alliance for Artists. Republican. Home: 149-47 Powells Cove Blvd Whitestone NY 11357

GREENWALD, SUSAN, corporate executive; b. Long Beach, Calif., Aug. 7, 1945; d. Marinus and Anna (Mair) van Leeuwen; m. Kenton Lee Greenwald, Dec. 9, 1967 (div. June 21, 1977); 1 child, Julie Anna. Student Mt. St. Mary's Coll., 1963-64. Systems service rep. NCR Corp., Los Angeles, 1966-69; self-employed systems cons., Long Beach, Calif., 1969-72; controller Berney-Karp & Assocs., Los Angeles, 1972-78; v.p. mgmt. info. systems Century 21 Real Estate Corp., Irvine, Calif., 1978-82; dir. tech. mktg. support Microdata, Corp., Irvine, 1982-85; dir. tech. services McDonnell Douglas Field Service Co., Irvine, 1985—. Treas. Friends Irvine Pub. Library, Calif., 1982-86; dir. Orange County Camp Fire Council, Tustin, Calif., 1980. Mem. Data Processing Mgmt. Assn. (chpt. pres. 1980), MICRU Internat. (pres. 1980-82). Republican. Roman Catholic. Clubs: The 99's Incorporated (chpt. treas. 1974-75; chpt. chmn. 1976-77) (Long Beach, Calif.). Avocation: flying. Office: McDonnell Douglas Field Service Co 2361 McGaw Ave Irvine CA 92714

GREENWOOD, AUDREY GATES, librarian; b. Buffalo, Mar. 27, 1917; d. Marc Herbert and Genevieve Cecelia (Naab) Gates; B.A., D'Youville Coll., 1939; B.S. in Library Sci., Cath. U. Am., 1940, M.A., 1944; m. Clayton Edward Greenwood, Sept. 2, 1944; children—Mary Ellen, Nancy Jane, Susan Jean. Head librarian Gonzaga High Sch., Washington, 1940-45, Southeastern U. Evening Sch., 1941-45; reference librarian Cath. U. Am., evenings 1942-43; librarian St. Joseph's Collegiate Inst., Buffalo, 1945-46; head librarian Canisius High Sch., Buffalo, 1949-50; head librarian Eden (N.Y.) Central Schs., 1950—, coordinator state and fed. funds, 1969—, dir. adult edn., 1973—. Mem. Eden Tchrs. Assn. (pres.), Erie County Ednl. Assn. (v.p.), NEA, N.Y. State Tchrs. Assn., N.Y. State United Tchrs. (state del., legis. chmn. Western zone), Am. Fedn. Tchrs. (nat. del.), Sch. Librarians Assn. Western N.Y. (past pres.), N.Y. Educators Assn., Delta Kappa Gamma. (state legis. chmn.), Beta Zeta, Delta Kappa (state mem. legis. com.). Democrat. Roman Catholic. Home: 3688 Briarwood Ct Hamburg NY 14075 Office: 3150 Schoolview Eden NY 14057

GREENWOOD, HARRIET LOIS, environmental consultant, researcher; b. Detroit, Oct. 4, 1950; d. Samuel H. and Elizabeth Ann (Bode) G.; m. Michael E. Carlson, Aug. 23, 1981. B.A. in Biology, Antioch Coll., 1972; M.S. in Teaching, Antioch Coll. of New Eng., 1975; postgrad. U. Mich., 1985—. Dir. environ. studies Swanson Environ., Southfield, Mich., 1978-80; project mgr. ESEI, Ecol. Scis., Detroit, 1981-82; pres. Greenwood & Assocs., Detroit, 1982-83; mgr. environ. studies Environ. Research Group, Ann Arbor, Mich., 1983-85; environ. policy specialist Clayton Environ., Southfield, 1985—. Rec. clk. Detroit Friends Meeting, 1985-86. U. Mich. fellow, 1985-89. Mem. Soc. Risk Analysis, Internat. Assn. Bus. Communicators, Cranbrook Inst. Sci., Mich. Assn. Environ. Profls., Nat. Assn. Environ. Profls. Quaker. Avocations: English country dancing; cross country skiing. Office: Clayton Environ Cons 25711 Southfield Rd Southfield MI 48075

GREENWOOD, JANE, nursing educator; b. Portsmouth, Va., Feb. 18, 1930; d. Fabian Earle and Christine Virginia (Parker) Tew; m. Thomas Lee Greenwood, Jr., Sept. 14, 1957; children—Thomas Ward, William Lee. B.S. in Nursing, Med. Coll. Va., 1955. R.N., Va.; cert. coll. tchr., Va. Infirmary nurse Westhampton Coll., Richmond, Va., 1953-55; staff nurse Med. Coll. Va., Richmond, 1953-55; staff nurse Maryview Hosp., Portsmouth, 1955, 58-65, nurse instr. pediatrics, 1955-66; supr., nurse instr. med.-surg. OBICI Meml. Hosp., Suffolk, Va., 1956-58; clin. instr. Portsmouth Pub. Schs., 1968-71; dir., preclin. instr. Chesapeake (Va.) Schs., 1971—. Mem. Am. Nurses Assn., Nat. League Nursing, NEA, Vocat. Indsl. Clubs Am., Health Occupations Students Am., Am. Vocat. Assn. Baptist. Clubs: Elizabeth Manor Country (Portsmouth); Holiday Health (Chesapeake). Home: 1322 Hodges Ferry Rd Portsmouth VA 23701 Office: Chesapeake Technical Center 1617 Cedar Rd Chesapeake VA 23320

GREENWOOD, JANET KAE DALY, psychologist, educational administrator; b. Goldsboro, N.C., Dec. 9, 1943; d. Fulton Benton and Kelminy Ethel Esther (Ball) Daly; 1 child, Gerald Thompson. A.A., Peace Coll., 1963; B.S. in English and Psychology, East Carolina U., 1965, Ed.M. in Counseling, 1967; postgrad. N.C. State U., 1967-69, U. London, 1969; Ph.D. in Counseling and Higher Ednl. Adminstrn., Fla. State U., 1972. Tchr. English, Kinston City Schs., N.C., 1965-66, Goldsboro City schs., 1966-67; counselor and psychometrist primary and secondary schs. of Wake County, N.C., 1967-69; coordinator for Am. Inst. for Fgn. Study, 1969, supr. of student tours in Eng., France, Switzerland, Italy and Capri, 1969; counselor Fla. State U., Tallahassee, 1969-72; asst. dir. counseling Rutgers U., New Brunswick, N.J., 1972-73; cons. to v.p. for student services, 1973-74, lectr. in counseling psychology, 1972-74; coordinator and assoc. prof. counselor edn. U. Cin., 1974-77; adviser to grad. students, 1974—, vice provost student affairs, 1977—; cons. guidance South Plainfield Pub. Schs., 1973-76; adviser Parents Without Partners, 1976; pres. Longwood Coll., Farmville, Va., 1981—. Contbr. articles to profl. jours. Mem. Gov.'s Ad Hoc Edn. Com. on Tchr. Edn. and Counselor Edn., State of Ohio, 1975; mem. state planning commn. Nat. Identification of Women Project; chairwoman of Twin Rivers Tenants Rights Assn., 1972-74. Recipient Tchr. We Honor award Goldsboro City Schs., 1967, Stunt Night Dedication award, 1967, Black Arts Festival spl. award. Mem. Am. Coll. Personnel Assn. (editor chairperson media bd. 1975—), Am. Personnel and Guidance Assn., Cin. Personnel and Guidance Assn., Ohio Psychol. Assn., Cin. Psychol. Assn., Organizational Behavior Assn., AAUP, Am. Sch. Counselors Assn., Ohio Sch. Counselors Assn., Assn. for Women Faculty, Ohio Counselor Edn. and Supervision Assn., Kappa Delta Pi. Home: Longwood House Farmville VA 23901 Office: Pres Longwood Coll Farmville VA 23901

GREENWOOD, JANET L., college president. Pres. Longwood Coll., Farmville, Va. Office: Longwood Coll Farmville VA 23901*

GREENWOOD, KATY BROWN, educator; b. Wheeler, Tex., Jan. 24, 1935; d. Ray D. and Lena (Baker) Brown; B.S., W.Tex. State U., 1954; M.Ed., 1958; Ph.D., U. Minn., 1978; m. Jim D. Greenwood, July 11, 1954; children—Lisa Kay, Jim L., Joe Kelly, Lesley Ann. Dir. guidance Spearman Ind. Sch. Dist., Tex., 1968-71; vocat. cons. for handicapped Regional Ednl. Service Ctr., Amarillo, Tex., 1972; research assoc. U. Minn., 1973-77; asst. prof., coordinator grad. vocat. edn. Tex. A&M U., College Station, 1977-84, project dir. tech. assistance in vocat. edn. to Dominican Republic, 1981-82; ddir. Ctr. for Applied Tech., U. Houston, 1984—; cons. in policy devel., analysis, evaluation tng. in developing countries. Mem. Brazos Valley Devel. Council. Recipient Outstanding 1st Yr. Counselor award Tex. Edn. Agy., 1969; Leadership Devel. grantee U.S. Office of Edn., 1973-76. Mem. Tex. Vocat. Tchr. Educators Assn. (bd. dirs. 1979-81), Am. Vocat. Assn. (chmn. awards com. 1981-82), Phi Delta Kappa. Home: 15534 Weldon Dr Houston TX 77032 Office: Coll of Tech U Houston Houston TX 77004

GREENWOOD, NANCY LOUISE, insurance underwriter; b. Malden, Mass., Apr. 28, 1950; d. Donald Starrett and Barbara Louise (Cooley) G. B.S. in Elem. Edn., Lesley Coll., Cambridge, Mass., 1971; student Exec. Secretarial Sch., Newport, R.I., 1972; cert. in gen. ins. Ins. Inst. Am., 1978. Cert. profl. ins. woman. Tchr. aide Buckingham Sch., Cambridge, 1971; elem. tchr. Newport Sch. Dept., 1971-72; credit clk. W.T. Grant Co., Newport, 1972; sec., underwriter, customer service rep. Kirby, Inc., Newport, 1972-84; comml. lines underwriter, account mgr. James J. Reilly Agy., Inc. subs. Frank B. Hall & Co. R.I., Inc., East Providence, R.I., 1984—. Treas. Newport Food Coop., 1974-76; sec. Swanhurst Chorus, 1978-80; treas. Newport Bahai Community, 1975—. Mem. Nat. Assn. Ins. Women of R.I. (pres. 1983-85, dir. 1979-80, 80-82, 85-86). Office: James J Reilly Agy Inc 1990 Pawtucket Ave East Providence RI 02914

GREENWOOD, RUTH INGRID, financial executive, crafts retailer; b. Hanover, N.H., May 27, 1954; d. Carl Einar and Kathryn Elizabeth (Lorden) Carlson; m. Patrick Alan Greenwood, July 4, 1976; children—Tyson Everett, Tara Kate. B.S., Annhurst Coll., Woodstock, Conn., 1976. Acct., VA Med. and Regional Office Ctr., White River Junction, Vt., 1976-78; chief acctg. VA Med. Ctr., Manchester, N.H., 1978-82; auditor Northeast Consol. Services, Concord, N.H., 1982-85; controller Alice Peck Day Meml. Hosp., Lebanon, N.H., 1985—; propr. P & R Country Craft Shoppe, Canaan, N.H., 1983—. Mem. Health Care Fin. Mgmt. Assn., Nat. Assn. Female Execs., N.H. Hosp. Assn. (cost and acctg. task force 1985—). Republican. Roman Catholic. Avocations: cooking, music. Home: Rural Route 1 Box 4 High St Canaan NH 03741

GREENWOOD, SYLVIA RUTH, educator; b. Detroit, July 10, 1951; d. Lawson Cullen and Annie Alfreada (Smith) G. B.S., Central State U., 1973; postgrad. Wayne State U., 1977-79. Tchr., Detroit Bd. Edn., 1974—; producer Vol. Devel. of Youth Talent, Detroit, 1975—; mezzo soprano Brazeal Dennard Chorale, 1985—; producer mus. tour of Japan, Mich. Dept. Commerce. Choir dir. Youth Second Grace Ch., Detroit, 1977-85, Broadstreet Presbyn. Ch., Detroit, 1985—. Named Outstanding Tchr. in Area D, Detroit Pub. Schs., 1985, other honors. Democrat. Methodist. Avocation: sewing.

GREENWOOD-ROBINSON, MARGARET, writer; b. Quonset Point, R.I., May 24, 1952; d. Thomas Edward and Margaret (Ten Hagen) Greenwood; m. Jeffry Elliott, Oct. 8, 1983. B.A., U. Va., 1974; M.S., W. Va. U., 1978. Pub. relations asst. Aluminum Co. of Am., Massena, N.Y., 1978-80, communications mgr., 1980-85; owner MGR Communications; instr. continuing edn. program Ind. State U., Evansville, 1984. Contbr. articles to profl. jours. and nat. mags. Bd. dirs. Jr. Achievement S.W. Ind., Evansville, 1981—, Operation City Beautiful, Evansville, 1981—; treas. Warrick Alcoans Polit. Action Com., Newburgh, Ind., 1983—; 3d v.p. Massena C. of C., 1980; active Leadership Evansville, 1984-85. Named Young Careerist, Bus. and Profl. Women's Assn., 1980. Mem. Am. Bus. Women's Assn., Women in Communications, Internat. Assn. Bus. Communicators, Am. Assn. Med. Writers, Kappa Tau Alpha. Republican. Presbyterian. Club: Toastmistress (pres. 1979-80).

GREER, ANNE LINDSAY, food writer, menu and restaurant designer, consultant; b. Chgo., July 8, 1940; d. John Ralston and Elisabeth (Wood) Lindsay; m. Donald Merrill Greer, Jr., June 11, 1966 (div. 1979); children—Donald Merrill, William Wright. Student Foothill Jr. Coll., 1959-61, Morningside Coll., 1963-66; student bus. adminstrn. U. Calif.-Long Beach, 1966-67. Cons., Cuisinarts, Inc., Greenwich, Conn., 1975—; menu cons., 1776, Inc., San Antonio, 1983-84; concept and menu developer, Anatole Expansion Restaurants, and Verandah Club, Leows Anatole, Dallas, 1982, cons. restaurant and food concepts, 1982—. Author: (cookbooks) Culinary Renaissance, 1975; Cuisine of the American Southwest, 1983 (Book of the Month selection spring 1984 Tastemaker award). Active Jr. League, San Antonio and Dallas, 1973—; mem. Jr. Symphony. Mem. Internat. Assn. Cooking Schs. (charter), Am. Inst. Wine and Food, Maitre de Table Restauranteur - Confrerie de la Chaine des Rotisseurs (San Antonio and Dallas). Republican. Episcopalian. Clubs: Chandlers Landing, Verandah, Aerobic Center (Dallas). Home: 4321 University Blvd Dallas TX 75205

GREER, BERNA DEAN, accountant; b. Louisville, Miss., Aug. 17, 1957; d. A. J. and Mary (Miller) G. B.S., Jackson State U., 1979. C.P.A., Tex. Sr. acct. Coopers and Lybrand, Houston, 1981-83, supr., 1984—; vol. VITA, Internal Revenue Service, Houston, 1982—. Asst. treas. Sylvester Turner Campaign for County Commr., Houston, 1983-84; mem. Polit. Action League, Houston, 1983; campaign worker Kathy Whitmire Reelection Com., Houston, 1983. Mem. Am. Inst. C.P.A.s, Nat. Assn. Black Accts. (2d v.p. 1983-84), Nat. Assn. Accts. (com. chairperson 1983-84), Tex. Soc. C.P.A.s (com. chairperson Houston chpt. 1983-84), Bus. and Profl. Women's Club, Nat. Assn. Female Execs., Alpha Kappa Alpha. Democrat. Baptist. Home: 16126 Barbarossa Houston TX 77083 Office: Coopers & Lybrand 1100 Louisiana Suite 4100 Houston TX 77002

GREER, BONNIE BETH, educator; b. Toledo, Sept. 13, 1946; d. Therron Otto and Betty Mae Kleckner; A.B., Ind. U., 1968; M.Ed., Okla. U., 1969, Ph.D., 1971; m. John Garland Greer, July 9, 1977; children—Christopher John, Tiffany Maye. Instl. tchr. No. Ind. Children's Hosp., South Bend, 1968; tchr. 6th grade Blanchard (Okla.) public schs., 1968-69; successively grad. asst., spl. instr., lectr. Okla. U., 1969-72; program dir. Stone Belt Center Retarded, Bloomington, Ind., 1972-73; asst. prof. Bridgewater (Mass.) State Coll., 1973-74; mem. faculty Memphis State U., 1974—, asso. prof. spl. edn. and rehab., 1976—; lectr. edn. Ind. U., part-time, 1972-73. Mem. Council Exceptional Children, Am. Assn. Mental Deficiency, Delta Kappa Gamma. Author articles in field, chpts. in books; co-editor: Practical Strategies in Working with the Trainable Mentally Retarded, 1975. Office: Dept Spl Edn and Rehab Memphis TN 38152

GREER, DOROTHY LUCILLE LEECH (MRS. THOMAS KEISTER GREER), business executive; b. Fort Morgan, Colo., Nov. 5, 1921; d. Laurance Blakely and Lucille Otis (Gill) Leech; student Mills Coll., 1939-40; B.A., San Diego State Coll., 1943; m. Thomas Keister Greer, Jan. 9, 1943; children—Nancy Tallaferro Greer Alexander, Giles Carter, Celeste Claiborne. Tchr., Franklin County Schs., Rocky Mount, Va., 1944-45, 48-49, Roanoke (Va.) City Schs., 1949-51; dir., sec.-treas. Franklin County Times, Inc., Rocky Mount, 1968—; v.p. Greer Investment Corp., 1977-79. Mem. central com. Assistance League So. Calif., Los Angeles, 1952-54; nat. patron Met. Opera; mem. patrons com. Internat. Debutante Ball, 1969-71. Mem. DAR, Internat. Platform Assn. Christian Scientist. Club: Willow Creek Country (sec.-dir. Rocky Mount 1962-64). Home: The Grove Rocky Mount VA 24151

GREER, LAVERNE GRITTON, musician, retired educator; b. Penfield, Ill., June 12, 1916; d. Shelby Lylburn and Maudie Ann (Fetters) Gritton; B.A., U. Ill., 1937; student MacPhail Coll. Music, Mpls., 1951-53; m. E. Edward Greer, Mar. 25, 1937; 1 child, Lylburn. Tchr. music Woodbine (Kans.) pub. schs., 1944-45, schs. in Ill. and Minn., 1948-54, Rantoul (Ill.) pub. schs., 1954-76; pvt. music tchr., 1945—. Mem. Nat. Guild Piano Tchrs., Internat. Soc. Music Educators, Am. Choral Dirs. Assn. (life), Nat. Assn. Organ Tchrs., Internat. Platform Assn., AAUW (br. v.p. program). Mem. Christian Ch. Home: 513 Eden Park Rantoul IL 61866

GREER, SHARI BETH ROTHENSTEIN, software consulting firm executive; b. Reading, Pa., Mar. 1, 1959; d. Martin and Francine Rita (Gross) Rothenstein; m. Martin Brad Greer, Dec. 31, 1979; children—Shannon Leigh, Krista Heather. B.A. in Biochemistry, Wellesley Coll.-MIT, 1980; postgrad. in bus. adminstrn. Colo. State U., 1982-83. Lead thermal engr. Rockwell Internat. Space div., Downey, Calif., 1980-81; systems engr. Martin Marietta Aerospace, Denver, 1981-82, aerospace new bus. analyst, 1982-84; v.p. Miaco Corp. (Micro Automation Cons.), Lakewood, Colo., 1984—. Co-designer life systems monitor for Sudden Infant Death Syndrome, 1980. Recipient Recog. award for satellite work Martin Marietta Aerospace, 1982; VIP at 1st Space Shuttle landing, Rockwell Internat., Vandenberg, Calif., 1981. Mem. Intermountain Humane Soc., MIT Enterprise Forum of Colo. Democrat. Office: Miaco Corp 7112 W Jefferson Ave Suite 303 Lakewood CO 80235

GREESON, GAYLA LEE, accountant; b. Austin, Tex., Dec. 22, 1956; d. Howard Gaylon and Nancy Diane (Thomas) Brown; m. David Thomas Greeson, Aug. 25, 1979; children—Timothy David, Samantha Lea. B.B.A., U. Tex., 1979. C.P.A., Tex. Accounts examiner Office of State Comptroller, Austin, 1979-80; auditor Tyler, Willingham & Tuffly, C.P.A.s, Houston, 1981-82; adv. dir., comptroller Security Bank & Trust Co., Wharton, Tex., 1982—; treas. Security Capital Leasing Corp., Wharton, 1982—; treas. Wharton Capital Corp. Treas., Wharton Christian Sch., 1984-86. Mem. Am. Inst. C.P.A.s, Tex. Soc. C.P.A.s. Home: 600 Country Club Dr Richmond TX 77469 Office: Security Bank & Trust Co 112 N Fulton St Wharton TX 77488

GREGG, DOROTHY ELIZABETH, marketing, opinion research and public relations executive; b. Tempe, Ariz.; d. Alfred Tennyson and Mamie Elizabeth (Walker) G.; B.A., U. Tex., 1944, M.A. (grad. fellow), 1945; Ph.D. (all-univ. grad. fellow), Columbia U., 1951, L.H.D. (hon.), 1967; m. Paul Hughling Scott, 1952; children—Kimerly, Gregg. Lectr., Columbia U., 1946-52, asst. prof. econs., 1952-54; asst. dir. public relations U.S. Steel Corp., N.Y.C., 1956-74; dir. corp. communications Celanese Corp., N.Y.C., 1974-75, corp. v.p. communications, 1975-81, corp. v.p. external affairs, 1981-82; exec. v.p. Research & Forecasts Inc., 1983-84, sr. cons., 1984—. Mem. civilian public relations adv. com. U.S. Mil. Acad. Mem. Found. Public Relations Research and Edn., Women in Communications (Nat. Headliner award 1980), Nat. Com. U.S.-China Relations, Phi Beta Kappa, Pi Sigma Alpha. Clubs: Princeton, Zonta (N.Y.C.). Contbr. articles profl. mags., P.F. Collier & Son Ency. Home: 425 E 58th St New York NY 10022 Office: 110 E 58th St New York NY 10022

GREGG, NANCY LEE, military lawyer, army officer; b. Cin., Dec. 26, 1950; d. Robert Victor and Anna Mae (McWhirter) G. B.A. with distinction in Psychology, Southwestern at Memphis, 1972; J.D., U. Ark., 1978. Bar: Ark. 1978, U.S. Dist. Ct. (western dist.) Ark. 1978, U.S. Ct. Mil. Appeals 1978, U.S. Supreme Ct. 1982. Adminstrv. asst. to v.p. support ops. Sunstate Builders, Inc., Tampa, Fla., 1973-74; commd. capt. U.S. Army JAGC, 1978; def. counsel 2d Armored div., Ft. Hood, Tex., 1979-81, trial counsel, 1st Cav. div., Ft. Hood, 1981-82; chief adminstrv. law Hdqrs. V Corps, Office of Staff Judge Adv., Frankfurt, W.Ger., 1982—. Legal adviser Frankfurt Mil. Community, Child and Spouse Abuse Case Mgmt. Teams, 1983—. Decorated Army Commendation medal. Mem. ABA, Assn. Trial Lawyers Am., Phi Alpha Delta. Office: HHC V Corps SJA APO New York NY 09079

GREGOIRE, JEANNINE DIANE, radio station executive; b. Pocatello, Idaho, May 8, 1949; d. Edward Paul and Ruth Mardene (Nelson) Gregoire. B.S. in English Lit., Westminster Coll., 1972. Asst. sales promotion, advt. mgr. Sta. KTVX-TV, Salt Lake City, 1975-76, writer, producer, sales promotion/advt. mgr., 1976-78; writer, producer, asst. creative services mgr., audience promotion mgr. Sta. KPIX-TV, Channel 5, San Francisco, 1978-79; sales rep. Xerox Corp., Salt Lake City, 1979-80; dir. advt. and pub. info. Channel 7 Sta. KUED-TV, Salt Lake City, 1980-84; dir. mktg., sales and pub. relations Triad-La Caille Ventures and La Caille at Quail Run, 1984-86; account exec. sta. KDAB-FM, Salt Lake City, 1986—. Mem. pub. info. bd. dirs. Am. Cancer Soc., Salt Lake City; fundraiser Ballet West, 1985. Mem. Women in Communications, Broadcast Promotion Assn. Republican. Office: 400 E 350 S Salt Lake City UT 84111

GREGOR, HARRIET ELIZABETH WILSON, physician; b. Rock Island, Ill., Jan. 30, 1950; d. Harry Rex and Eleanor (Fisher) Wilson; m. Peter William Gregor, Aug. 12, 1972; children—Joel Alexander, Ian Russell, Neil Fraser. B.A. in Biology magna cum laude, Mt. Holyoke Coll., 1971; B.A. in Biology, St. Andrews U., Scotland, 1969-70; M.D., McMaster U., Hamilton, Ont., 1974. Diplomate Am. Acad. Family Practice, 1981. Intern, Hotel Dieu Hosp., 1974-75, Kingston Gen. Hosp., 1974-75; resident family medicine Queens U., Kingston, Ont., Can., 1974-76, anesthesia resident, Kingston, 1977, pediatric resident anesthesia, 1977-78, physician student health, instr. family medicine, 1978-79; physician Golden Clinic and Meml. Hosp., Elkins, W.Va., 1979-81; practice family medicine, Gilroy, Calif., 1980—; mem. staff Wheeler Hosp.; med. advisor Hillview Home Health, Gilroy, 1983-86. Sponsor, Gilroy Community Theatre, Gilroy, 1983-84; mem. Planned Parenthood Santa Clara County, 1983-84; mem. Hand Gun Control No. Calif., 1981-86. Fellow Am. Acad. Family Physicians; mem. Ont. Med. Assn., Can. Coll. Family Physicians, Can. Med. Assn., AMA, Phi Beta Kappa. Presbyterian. Home: 1570 Welburn Ave Gilroy CA 95020 Office: 7995 Princevalle St Gilroy CA 95020

GREGORIUS, BEVERLY JUNE, obstetrician and gynecologist; b. Ottawa, Ill., June 21, 1915; d. Henry Godfrey and Arline (Barry) Pruette; B.S., Madison (Tenn.) Coll., 1935; M.D., Loma Linda (Calif.) U., 1946, M.S., 1953; m. Hans Harvey Gregorius, Apr. 6, 1939 (dec.); 1 dau., Joan Gregorius Jones. Intern, Los Angeles County Gen. Hosp., 1946-47; resident in ob-gyn, White Meml. Hosp., Los Angeles, 1949-52; practice medicine specializing in ob-gyn, Burbank, Calif., 1953-77; assoc. clin. prof. Loma Linda U. Med. Sch., also U. So. Calif. Med. Sch., 1956—; clin. prof. ob-gym U. So. Calif. Med. Sch., 1985—; program dir. ob-gyn residency program Glendale (Calif.) Adventist Med. Center, 1977-81, chmn. dept. ob-gyn, 1981-83, cons., 1983—. Bd. dirs. Arroyo Vista Family Health Found. Diplomate Am. Bd. Ob-Gyn. Fellow Am. Coll. Ob-Gyn, ACS, Internat. Coll. Surgeons; mem. Los Angeles Ob-Gyn Soc. (council 1979-86, pres. 1984-85). Adventist (mem. adminstrv. bd. dirs. 1985—). Home: 10635 Landale St North Hollywood CA 91602 Office: 1530 E Chevy Chase Suite 101 Glendale CA 91206

GREGORY, ANDREA, personnel executive; b. Boston, May 23, 1938; d. Carmen and Rosa (Terrabassi) di Stefano; m. Bruce E. Gregory, June 2, 1984; children—Christopher Brian Alley, Nicholas Breakspear Alley, Jennifer Alley. B.S., N.H. Coll., 1979. Tchr., Montessori Sch., Mexico City, 1964; dir. SAT program Erich Lindeman Mental Health Ctr., Boston, 1973-74; dir. Castle Square Child Devel. Ctr., Boston, 1972-75; child care dir. Women Inc., Dorchester, Mass., 1975-78; coordinator, trainer Mass. Hort. Soc., Boston, 1978-79; personnel coordinator Mass. Trial Ct., Boston, 1979—; counselor Planned Parenthood, Boston, 1969-70; research asst. Mass. Superior Ct., 1979; coordinator Boston Archtl. Ctr., 1978-79; counselor for pre-sch. program for hearing impaired Boston pub. schs., 1976-77; cons. and lectr. in field. Hallmark Scholastic Art award, 1959. Mem. Nat. Inst. Cert. Scuba Divers. Clubs: Boston Harbor Yacht, U. Mass. Office: Mass Trial Ct Rm 317 Suffolk County Courthouse Office of Chief Adminstr Boston MA 02108

GREGORY, ANN YOUNG, editor, publisher; b. Lexington, Ky., Apr. 28, 1935; d. David Marion and Pauline (Adams) Young; B.A. with high distinction (Ky. Broadcasters Assn. scholar), U. Ky., 1956; m. Allen Gregory, Jan. 29, 1957; children—David Young, Mary Peyton. Sec., Ky. edit. TV Guide, Louisville, summer 1956; traffic mgr. Sta. WVLK, Lexington, 1956-61; part time tchr. adult basic edn. Wise County (Va.) Sch. Bd., St. Paul, 1966-72; adminstrv. asst. Appalachian Field Services, Children's TV Workshop, St. Paul, 1971-74; editor, co-pub. Clinch Valley Times, pres. Clinch Valley Pub. Co., Inc., St. Paul, 1974—. Vice pres. St. Paul PTA, 1970-73; trustee Lonesome Pine Regional Library Bd., 1972-80, chmn., 1978-80; chmn. com. to establish br. library in St. Paul, opened 1975; mem. adv. bd. Pro-Art (Wise County chpt. Va. Mus. Fine Arts), 1979—; co-leader Brownie troop Girl Scouts U.S.A., 1971-76, bd. dirs. Appalachian council; mem. adv. bd. Wise County (Va.) YMCA, 1977—; mem. Wise County Bd. Edn., 1975—, vice chmn., 1981—; mem. Va. Edn. Block Grants Adv. Com., 1981—; mem. exec. com. Va. High Sch. League; pres. Wise County Humane Soc., Inc.; bd. dirs. Va. Sch. Bds. Assn., 1979—, pres., 1985-86. Named Outstanding Clubwoman of Year, St. Paul Jr. Women's Club, 1964, 66; Outstanding Citizen, S.W. Va. dist. Va. Fedn. Women's Clubs, 1968. Mem. Va. Press Assn. (1st place award for editorial writing 1976), Nat. Press Women, Va. Press Women, Nat. Newspaper Assn., Women in Communications, Nat. Sch. Bds. Assn. (pub. relations com.), Mortar Bd., Delta Kappa Gamma (hon. mem. Alpha Psi chpt.), Phi Beta Kappa, Alpha Delta Pi. Democrat. Methodist. Editor, text writer The Flood of '77 in the St. Paul Area, 1977. Home: PO Box 303 Longview Dr Saint Paul VA 24283 Office: PO Box 817 Russell St Saint Paul VA 24283

GREGORY, BETTINA LOUISE, journalist; b. N.Y.C., June 4, 1946; d. George A. and V. Elizabeth (Elson) Friedman; m. John P. Flannery II, Nov. 14, 1981. Student Smith Coll., 1964-65; B.A., Pierce Coll., Athens, Greece, 1972; acting diploma Webber Douglas Acad. Dramatic Art, London, 1968. Reporter, Sta. WVBR-FM, Ithaca, N.Y., 1972-73, Sta. WCIC-TV, Ithaca, 1972; reporter, anchorwoman WGBB, Freeport, N.Y., 1973, Sta. WCBS, N.Y.C.; freelance reporter, writer AP, N.Y.C., 1973-74; freelance reporter N.Y. Times, 1973-74; with ABC News, 1974—, corr., Washington, 1977-79, White House corr., 1979—, sr. gen. assignment corr., 1980—. Recipient 1st Place award Nat. Feature News, Odyssey Inst., N.Y., 1978; Clarion award Women in Communications, Inc., 1979; hon. mention Nat. Commn. on Working Women, 1979; named Top 10 Investigative Reporters, TV Guide, 1983. Mem. White House Corr. Assn., Radio TV Corrs. Assn., Newswomen's Club N.Y. (Front Page award 1976), Washington Press Club. Office: ABC News 1717 De Sales St Washington DC 20036

GREGORY, CARMEDA OPHELIA, tax consultant; b. Saint Louis, Dec. 9, 1943; d. Murray C. and Maggie D. (Thornton) Rudasill; m. Lawrence J. Gregory, Aug. 14, 1966; 1 dau., Jessica. A.B., Harris Tchrs. Coll., 1965; postgrad. U. Mo., 1965-66, Ohio U., 1967-68, U. Ill. Extension, 1975—, No. Ill. U., 1974-81. Numerous clerical positions, 1960-65; tchr. Berkeley Pub. Schs. (Mo.); 1965-66, Athens Pub. Schs. (Ohio), 1966-68, Bedford Pub. Schs. (Mich.), 1968-69; counselor Towne Personnel Agy., Washington, 1969-70; research librarian Mortgage Bankers Assn., Washington, 1970; toy designer, DeKalb, Ill., 1973—; tax cons., acct., mgr. H & R Block, Newman's Acctg., DeKalb, 1974-81, pres., owner Gregory Acctg., DeKalb, 1981—, also owner 4 H&R Block offices; instr. Kishwaukee Jr. Coll., Malta, Ill., 1978—; mem. Kishwaukee Acctg. Rev. Bd., 1982—. Active Gurler Heritage Assn., DeKalb, 1981—, DeKalb Landmarks Commn. Mem. DeKalb Small Bus. Council, Nat. Assn. Enrolled Agts., Ill. Assn. Enrolled Agts., Nat. Assn. Income Tax Practitioners, Nat. Soc. Pub. Accts., Ind. Accts. Assn., Nat. Assn. Tax Cons., Nat. Assn. Female Execs., C. of C. Clubs: Altrusa DeKalb Women's (DeKalb). Home: 221 Delcy St DeKalb IL 60115 Office: Gregory Acctg 151 N 4th St DeKalb IL 60115

GREGORY, CLAIRE DISTELHORST, TV producer; b. Chgo., Mar. 6, 1926; d. Robert Henry and Genevieve (McCall) Distelhorst; student Cornell Coll., 1943-46; A.B., Ind. U., 1947, M.S., 1954, postgrad., 1959; children—Charles, Martha. Tchr. public schs., Bismarck and Rossville, Ill., 1947-50, Helmsburg, Ind., 1950-51; grad. asst. Audio Visual Center of Ind. U., 1953-55, lectr., dir. women's, children's and social service programs radio and TV, 1956-59; exec. dir. Community Service Council, Inc., Bloomington, Ind., 1971-75; asst. supr. instructional TV program devel. Ind. U. Radio and TV Service, 1975-81, dir. spl. projects, 1982—; chmn. Bloomington Telecommunications Council, 1975-80; writer, producer: Russian Revolution and Arts, Parts I and II, 1976; Teleconference on Mass Transportation, 1976; Transportation Briefing, 1977; videotapes on profl. devel. Internat. Devel. Inst., 1975-80; 16 videotapes on computer instrn., 1978-80; Getting There, 1980; Living Africa, 1979-82; Programming for Microcomputers, 1982; Negotiation, 1984; TV advisor Mostly Moliere Troupe, 1981—. Mem. United Way of Monroe County, 1982; treas. Blue Ridge Assn., 1978-81. Mem. Psi Iota Xi. Club: Univ. Office: 212 Radio and TV Bldg Indiana University Bloomington IN 47405

GREGORY, DELLA ARLENE ARLEDGE, educator; b. Martinsville, Ohio, Oct. 6, 1938; d. George and Lucille Irene (Shiverdecker) Arledge; B.A., Ohio State U., 1959, M.A., 1977, doctoral candidate, U. 1979—; student Ohio Wesleyan U., summers 1969, 70, 72, 74, 75, 77, 78; m. James Andrew Gregory, Dec. 20, 1959; children—James Andrew, Julie Ann, Janis Arlene. Tchr., Delaware (Ohio) City Schs., 1960—; part-time communications instr. Marion Tech. Coll.; also ednl. cons. Mem. adv. bd. Help Anonymous, 1974—; adv. 4-H Club, 1969—; adv. Am. Field Service, 1973-79, host mother, 1974-75; mem. edn. com. local Methodist ch., 1977—; publicity coordinator Delaware Arts Festival, 1977-79; vol. family outreach program Juvenile Ct. Annie Webb Blanton scholar Delta Kappa Gamma, 1979—, Louise and Marguerite Morse scholar, 1981; Lily Found. grantee, 1972; NEH grantee, 1983. Mem. United Teaching Profession, Ohio Council Tchrs. of English Lang. Arts (sec. 1973-76), Nat. Council Tchrs. of English (com. on poets in schs. 1974-76, judge writing awards 1975-79), Delaware City Tchrs. Assn. (pres. 1979-81), AAUW (charter pres. Delaware br. 1965-67), Delta Kappa Gamma (pres. Iota chpt.), Pi Lambda Theta. Editor: Hot Air. Contbr. articles to profl. jours. Home: 240 Homestead Ln Delaware OH 43015 Office: 289 Euclid Ave Delaware OH 43015

GREGORY, ELEANOR ANNE, artist, educator; b. Seattle, Jan. 20, 1939; d. John Noel and Eleanor Blanche G.; B.A., Reed Coll., 1963; M.F.A., U. Wash., 1966; M.Ed., Columbia U., 1978, Ed.D., 1978. Art tchr. Seattle Public Schs., 1970-75; instr. N.Y.C. Community Coll., 1977, Manhattan Community Coll., N.Y.C., 1978; asst. prof. N.Mex. State U., Las Crucas, 1978-79; asst. prof. art Purdue U., West Lafayette, Ind., 1979-82, W. Tex. State U., Canyon, 1982-84; lectr. Calif. State U.-Long Beach, 1985—; one woman shows: Columbia U. Tchrs. Coll., 1976, Watson's Crick Gallery, West Lafayette, 1980, 81, Gallery I, Purdue U., 1980, W. Tex. State U., 1983, Amarillo Art Ctr., 1984, Sch. Visual Concepts, Seattle, 1985; group shows include: El Paso (Tex.) Art Mus., 1979, Ind. State Mus., Indpls., 1980, Lafayette (Ind.) Art Mus., 1982; represented in permanent collection: Portland (Oreg.) Art Mus.; mgr. Watson's Crick Gallery, West Lafayette, 1982-83. Mem. Nat. Art Edn. Assn., N.Y. Soc. Scribes, Chgo. Calligraphy Collective, Internat. Soc. Edn. Through Art. Episcopalian. Home: 6347 Sand Point Way NE Seattle WA 98115

GREGORY, JEWELL KIRCHNER, personal services co. exec.; b. Carthage, Mo., Jan. 14, 1934; d. Carl Otto and Ruth Mildred (Jones) Kirchner; B.A., U. Pa., 1955; M.A., U. Ill., 1969; m. Edward Haig Gregory, May 31, 1953; children—Susan Faith, Jane Hope. Freelance newspaper columnist, club speaker, 1969-74; relocation specialist Equitable Relocation Service, Equitable Life Assurance Soc., N.Y.C., 1975-79, nat. mgr. home search services, N.Y.C., 1980-83; mgr. corp. relocation Carteret Home Services, Morristown, N.J., 1983—. Pres., Maine Twp. (Ill.) High Sch. Scholarship Fund, 1972-73. Mem. Assn. Alumnae U. Pa. (dir. 1961-64), Internat. Soc. Preretirement Planners. Democrat. Episcopalian. Club: Racquets of Short Hills. Contbr. articles to profl. jours. Home: 36 Elmwood Pl Short Hills NJ 07078

GREGORY, JUSTINA WINSTON, educator; b. Brattleboro, Vt., Sept. 24, 1946; d. Richard and Clara (Brussel) Winston; A.B., Smith Coll., 1967; M.A., Harvard U., 1972, Ph.D., 1974; m. Patrick Bolton Gregory, Aug. 2, 1969; children—Tobias, Nora. Asst. prof. classics Yale U., New Haven, 1974-75; asst. prof. classics Smith Coll., Northampton-Mass., 1975-80, asso. prof., 1980—. Fulbright fellow, 1967-68; Woodrow Wilson fellow, 1968-69; Am. Council Learned Socs. fellow, 1977. Mem. Classical Assn. New Eng., Am. Philol. Assn., Phi Beta Kappa. Translator: (with Patrick Gregory) Aesop's Fables, 1975; contbr. articles to scholarly jours. Office: Smith College Northampton MA 01063

GREGORY, MARY GIBSON, librarian; b. Tucson, Dec. 21, 1954; d. James A.B. and Helen Barbara (Eckey) Gibson; m. Dennis Clarke Gregory, Aug. 8, 1982. B.A. in English Lit. and Classics, U. Ariz., 1975, M.L.S., 1978. Library page and clk. U. Ariz., Tucson, 1975-76; library asst. Ariz. Daily Star Newspaper, Tucson, 1976-78; librarian Sells Elem. Sch. (Ariz.), 1978-80, Thornydale Elem. Sch., Tucson, 1980-83, Desert Winds Elem. Sch., Avra Valley, Ariz., 1983-85, Marana High Sch., Tucson, 1985—. Mem. ALA, Ariz. Ednl. Media Assn., NEA (local exec. bd. 1983-85, bldg. com.), Ariz. State Library Assn., Marana Edn. Assn. (com. chair). Democrat. Episcopalian. Home: 11020 W Ina Rd Tucson AZ 85743 Office: Marana High Sch 12000 W Emigh Rd Tucson AZ 85743

GREGORY, WANDA JEAN, court reporter, singer, musician; b. Little Rock, Sept. 7, 1925; d. John Albert and Angie (Thompson) Deming; student pub. schs. Little Rock; m. G. C. Gregory, Jan. 15, 1945 (div.); 1 son, Rex Carleton. Ofcl. ct. reporter, Nueces County, Tex., 1959-76, 36th Jud. Dist. Ct., San Patricio, Live Oak, McMullen, Aransas and Bee Counties, Tex., 1979-82; freelance court reporter, Corpus Christi, Tex., 1976-78, 82—, Honolulu, 1979. Vocalist with dance bands and jazz combos; pvt. tchr. jazz and pop singing; a founder Tex. Jazz Festival, 1958, appeared, 1961-82, master of ceremonies, 1983; soloist Corpus Christi Interdenominational Choir. Mem. Tex. Shorthand Reporters Assn. (cert.), Tex. Jazz Festival Soc. (founder 1969, past pres., now bd. dirs.), Am. Fedn. Musicians, LWV, Bus. and Profl. Women's Club. Democrat. Methodist. Home: 3926 Panama Apt 105 Corpus Christi TX 78415 Office: 615 Waco St Corpus Christi TX 78401

GREGORY-GOODRUM, ELLNA KAY, educator, artist; b. Houston, Oct. 3, 1943; d. A. N. and Harriet (Christensen) Gregory; m. Craig R. Goodrum, Aug. 11, 1983. B.F.A., U. Okla., 1965; M.F.A., North Tex. State U., 1979. Tchr., Dallas Ind. Schs., 1965-85; instr. art Richland Coll., Dallas, 1981—; lectr. in field; group exhibits include: Watercolor Soc. of Ala., 1979, Clifford Gallery, Dallas, 1982-83; Nat. Watercolor Soc., 1985, San Diego Watercolor Soc., 1985, Edith Baker Gallery, 1986; works represented in permament collections: Rockwell Internat., Brown Found. and Cons., Atlantic Richfield, Renaissance Ctr., Detroit, Southwestern Watercolor Soc. Recipient Cash awards Tex. Watercolor Soc., 1978, Dallas Art Mus., 1978, So. Watercolor Soc., 1979. Mem. Pastel Soc. Am. (best abstract 1979), Southwestern Watercolor Soc. (cash prize 1983), Coll. Art Assn., Nat. Watercolor Soc., Tex. Watercolor Soc., Women's Caucus on Art. Methodist. Home: 7214 Lane Park Dr Dallas TX 75225

GREICO, LINDA ANN, mathematics educator; b. Fergus Falls, Minn., Mar. 8, 1947; d. Maynard Sheldon and Dorothy Blanche (Schnetzer) Fletcher; m. William Warren Greico, Dec. 14, 1985; children by previous marriage—Fletcher, Zachary; stepchildren—Paul, Bobby, Maria, Warren. B.S., Moorhead State U., 1968; M.A., U. Ark., 1972; postgrad. U. South Fla., 1981—. Tchr. math. Leto High Sch., Tampa, Fla., 1972-78; prof. math. Hillsborough Community Coll., Tampa, 1974—; adj. prof. U. South Fla., Tampa, 1981—. Mem. Easter Seal Guild, Tampa, 1980—; bd. dirs. Symphony Guild, Tampa, 1978; mem. Red Cross Angels, Tampa, 1980—, Sword of Hope, Tampa, 1980—, Children's Home, Tampa, 1985—. NSF grantee, 1971-72. Mem. Nat. Council Tchrs. of Math., Math. Assn. Am., Fla. Assn. Community Colls., Nat. Assn. Female Execs. Republican. Roman Catholic. Avocation: tennis. Office: Hillsborough Community Coll PO Box 75313 Tampa FL 33675

GREIFER, JULIE LYNN, lawyer; b. N.Y.C., Apr. 4, 1958; d. Ira and Carol Felice (Lovell) G. B.A., Union Coll., Schenectady, 1979; J.D., Benjamin Cardozo Sch. Law, 1982. Bar: N.Y. 1983. With firm Shea & Gould, N.Y.C., 1982-84, Davis & Gilbert, N.Y.C., 1984-86, Skadden, Arps, Slate, Meagher & Flom, N.Y.C., 1986—. Contbr. Cardozo Sch. Law Rev., 1980-82. Mem. Hudson Group Young Democrats, N.Y.C., 1984—; mem. coordinating, recruitment coms. leadership devel. div. United Jewish Appeal-Fedn., N.Y.C., 1984—. Mem. ABA, Nat. Assn. Female Execs., Assn. of Bar City of N.Y. Avocations: writing, cooking, jazz exercising, knitting. Home: Apt 14-S 201 E 21st St New York NY 10010 Office: Skadden Arps Slate et al 919 3d Ave New York NY 10022

GRENN-SCOTT, DEBBI, public relations executive; b. N.Y.C., Oct. 20, 1951; d. Walter Joachim and Rita Rosalind (Kolb) Grenn; m. Charles B. Scott, Aug. 31, 1975. B.A. in Communications, San Francisco State U., 1971; postgrad. N.Y. Inst. Advt., Alliance Francaise, New Sch. Social Research. Jr. media buyer Richard K. Manoff Inc., N.Y.C., 1972-74; freelance writer/publicist, N.Y.C., 1974-78; account exec. Samuel Krasney Assocs., N.Y.C., 1978-81; asst. v.p. R.C. Auletta & Co., N.Y.C., 1981-83; sr. v.p. Howard J. Rubenstein Assocs., N.Y.C., 1983—. Active Temple Emanu-El. Mem. Fin. Women's Assn., Pub. Relations Soc. Am., Publicity Club N.Y., Les Amis du Vin. Office: Howard J Rubenstein Assocs Inc 1345 Ave of Americas New York NY 10105

GRENZEBACH, ELIZABETH STEWART, medical technologist; b. Richlands, Va., July 12, 1939; d. Frederick Fitzgerald and Margaret (Bronson) Stewart; student Mary Washington Coll., 1957-60; B.S., Med. Coll. Va., 1961; m. James Austin Grenzebach, May 12, 1973. With dept. pathology, Med. Coll. Va., Richmond, 1961-63, chief technologist Kidney Transplant Lab., 1963-66; research technologist Med. Coll. Wis., Milw., 1966-70, research asso. dept. environ. medicine, 1970-72; lab. dir. Silver Hill Found., New Canaan, Conn., 1973—. Mem. Am. Soc. Clin. Pathologists. Republican. Episcopalian. Club: Country of New Canaan. Home: 106 Elm Pl New Canaan CT 06840 Office: PO Box 1177 Valley Rd New Canaan CT 06840

GRESHAM, ANN ELIZABETH, retailer, horticulturist executive; b. Richmond, Va., Oct. 11, 1933; d. Allwin Stagg and Ruby Scott (Faber) Gresham. Student, Peace Coll., Raleigh, N.C., 1950-52, East Carolina U., 1952-53, Penland Sch., N.C., 1953-54, Va. Commonwealth U., 1960-64. Owner, prin. Ann Gresham's Gift Shop, Richmond, 1953-56; pres., treas. Gresham's Garden Ctr., Inc., Richmond, 1955-79; v.p. Gresham's Nursery, Inc., Richmond, 1959-73, pres., treas., 1973—; pres., treas. Gresham's Country Store, Richmond, 1964—; tchr., 1982—. Bd. dirs. Bainbridge Community Ministry, 1979; class agent Peace Coll., Raleigh, 1979, mem. alumnae council, 1983; Focus Group mem. Handworkshop, Richmond, 1983, bd. dirs., 1985-87. Fellow Am. Hort. Soc.; mem. Midlothian Antique Dealers (treas. 1975-79), Richmond Quilt Guild (chpt. v.p. 1983-84), Nat. Needlework Assn., Folk Art Mus., So. Highlands Folk Art Ctr. Episcopalian. Clubs: Chesmond Women's (v.p. 1979-80) (Richmond) James River Women's. Home: 2324 Logan St Bon Air VA 23235 Office: Gresham's Inc 6725 Midlothian Pike Richmond VA 23225

GRESS, ROSE MARIE, food companies executive; b. Scranton, Pa., Sept. 19, 1930; d. Harry Stephan and Oricia Elizabeth (Simco) Ezak; m. Edward James Gress, Feb. 28, 1950; children—James Michael, Jeffrey Paul, Gary Edward, Keith Stephan, Glenn Jay. Grad. tech. high sch. and comtometer sch., Scranton, Pa. With Am. News, Scranton, 1949-50; comptometer operator W.L. Maxsom Co., Old Forge, Pa., 1950-54; pres. J & R Inc., Clarks Summit, Pa., 1970—, Gress Poultry, Inc., Scranton, 1976—, Gress Frozen Foods, Scranton, 1980—; notary public, Scranton, 1970—. Bd. dirs. St. Francis of Assisi, Scranton, 1980—; mem. pres.'s circle U. Scranton, 1980—; v.p. St. Joseph's Ctr., Scranton, 1958; vol. Merch Hosp., Scranton, 1960. Club: Scranton Country (Clarks Summit, Pa.). Avocations: golf, swimming, gourmet cooking, travel, reading. Home: 145 Jermyn Dr Clarks Summit PA 18411 Office: Gress Poultry Inc 141 S Dewey Ave Scranton PA 18504

GRESSETTE, NANCY CAROLYN, advertising agency account executive; b. Meridian, Miss., Nov. 12, 1958; d. John Thomas and JoAnn (Adams) G. Student, Coll. of Charleston; B.S. in Mktg. and Mgmt., U. S.C., 1980, M.B.A., 1982. Adminstrv. assoc. Santee Cooper, Moncks Corner, S.C., 1982, pub. affairs specialist, Myrtle Beach, S.C., 1983-84; mktg. dir. Outlet Park at Waccamaw, Myrtle Beach, 1984-85; account exec. Fowler Communications, Columbia, S.C., 1985—. Pub. relations chmn. Am. Cancer Soc., Horry County, 1983-85; city chmn. Am. Heart Assn., Horry County, 1983-84; mem. industries com. United Way Horry County, 1983-84; pub. relations chmn. Multiple Sclerosis Soc., Columbia, 1986; participant Leadership S.C., 1984, Leadership Grand Strand, Myrtle Beach C. of C., 1983-84. Mem. Am. Bus. Women's Assn. (pres. 1984-85), Coastal Advt. Fedn., Pub. Relations Soc. Am., DAR, Grand Strand Panhellenic Alumnae Assn. (v.p. 1984-85, pres. 1985). Baptist. Home: 500 Zimalcrest Dr #3306 Columbia SC 29210 Office: Fowler Communications PO Box 50627 2725 Devine St Columbia SC 29205

GREVE, MADOLYN NAGLEY, menswear company executive; b. Columbus, Ohio, July 24, 1952; d. Kenneth Frye and Virginia (McDowell) N.; B.S., Adrian Coll., 1974; guest student Fashion Inst. Tech., 1973. Asst. buyer Abraham & Straus, Bklyn., 1974-75, Lord & Taylor, N.Y.C., 1975-80; merchandising analyst Asso. Merchandising Corp. Co., N.Y.C., 198 -82; v.p. sales Jonathan Bennett Neckwear, Inc., N.Y.C., 1982—. Vol. Bill Green for Congress; mem. futures com. Kingston (N.J.) Presbyterian Ch.; co-chmn. publicity Princeton Hosp. Fete. Mem. Women's Network of Fifth Ave. (pres.), Women's Assn. Fifth Ave., Phi Gamma Nu, Chi Omega. Republican. Office: 50 W 34th St New York NY 10001

GREWELL, GAIL ELAINE, oil company executive; b. Dover, Ohio, Oct. 10, 1955; d. Floyd Madison and Mary Catherine (Sica) Grewell; m. Larry Alan Fagley, Jan. 22, 1986; children by a previous marriage—John Paul Marino, Vanessa Marie Marino. Student Am. Inst. Banking, 1974, Kent State U., 1980-82. Land mgr. Penn-Ohio Energy Corp., New Philadelphia, Ohio, 1980-83; pres., Citi-Energy Ops. Inc., Dover and Vancouver, B.C., Can., 1983—. Mem. Sacred Heart Sch. Bd., New Philadelphia, 1985—. Mem. Eastern Mineral Law Found., Ohio and Gas Assn. (vice chmn. 1986—), Internat. Mgmt. Council youth and bus. chmn. 1985, one day seminar chmn. 1986), Ohio Petroleum Producers Assn., U.S. C. of C. Democrat. Roman Catholic. Avocations: water skiing; cooking; horses. Home: 219 N Cross St Dover OH 44622 Office: Citi-Energy Ops Inc 314 W Fourth St Suite 202 Dover OH 44622

GREWELL, MARY, oil and gas co. exec.; b. Dover, Ohio, Jan. 27, 1936; d. Paul and Maria E. Sica; student Inst. for Energy Devel., 1979-81; m. Floyd M. Grewell, Sept. 19, 1953; children—Brenda J., Gail E., Tammy K. Clk. bookkeeping dept. Reeves Steel & Mfg. Co., Dover, 1953-54; adminstrv. asst. prodn. and land dept. Resource Exploration, Inc., Dennison, Ohio, 1974-77, Canton, Ohio, 1977-79; land adminstr. Berea Oil & Gas Corp., New Philadelphia, Ohio, 1979-80, v.p. land, 1980-83; gen. mgr. Citi-Energy Ops., Inc., 1984—. Dist. chmn. Del. dist. Girl Scouts U.S.A., 1971-74; mem. bus. techs. adv. com. Kent State U., Tuscarawas, 1983—. Recipient Thanks badge Girl Scouts U.S.A., 1970. Mem. Am. Assn. Petroleum Landmen, Am. Right of Way Assn., Ohio Oil and Gas Assn., Ind. Oil and Gas Assn. W.Va. Mem. Moravian Ch. Club: Tuscarawas Valley Desk and Derrick, Internat. Mgmt. Council. Office: PO Box 660 Dover OH 44622

GREY, CONSTANCE KOHLER, real estate broker; b. Buffalo, Nov. 18, 1922; d. William David and Elizabeth Velma (Barnes) Kohler; student Buffalo State Coll. Tchrs. (now SUNY, Buffalo), 1944-48; m. Roger P. Grey, June 12, 1947; children—Roger Harland, Richard David, Cheryl Lynn. Salesperson, Dorothy Derby Realty, Frewsburg, N.Y., 1959-60; salesperson, then assoc. Realtor Marshall Dunn Realty Co., Jamestown, N.Y., 1960-69; owner Connie Grey Realty, Lakewood, N.Y., 1969—; mem. bd. assessment rev. Town of Ellicott (N.Y.), 1976; tchr. career edn. Frewsburg Central Sch.; sponsor weekly radio show. Bd. dirs. Chautauqua County (N.Y.) Women's Republican Club; trustee Village of Coloron (N.Y.), 1976. Mem. Nat. Assn. Realtors, Jamestown Bd. Realtors (chmn. multiple service), N.Y. Assn. Appraisers, Jamestown Area C. of C., Chautauqua County C. of C. (dir.), Chautauqua County Vacationlands Assn. (dir.), Nat. Council Women Realtors, Bus. Profl. Women's Club, Lakewood C. of C. (dir.), Nat. Fedn. Bus. and Profl. Women. Unitarian. Clubs: Zonta (publicity com., dir. 1982-83, 84-85), Lakewood Woman's. Address: 3005 Southwestern Dr Lakewood NY 14750

GREY, JEAN S., accountant, plastics company executive; b. N.Y.C., June 14, 1925; d. Isidore and Edithe (Sarette) Schwartz; B.B.A., CCNY, 1950; m. Charles Grey, Nov. 22, 1945; children—Scott, Shari. Pub. acct. Kipnis & Karchmer, C.P.A.s, N.Y.C., 1942-44; pub. acct., then asst. head tax dept. Clarence Rainess Co., C.P.A.s, N.Y.C., 1944-54; ind. tax specialist, estate acct., Syosset, N.Y., 1950—; organizer, 1952, since treas., dir. Cee-Jay Extruders, Inc., plastics co.; lectr., cons. in field. C.P.A., N.Y. Mem. Am. Soc. Women Accts. (pres.), Am. Women's Soc. C.P.A.s, N.Y. State Soc. C.P.A.s, Nat. Conf. C.P.A. Practitioners, Acctg. Inst. C.W. Post Coll. Art League, Bus. and Profl. Women's Club, U.S. Coast Guard Aux., Société des Vignerons. Clubs: Tappan Beach Yacht, Sagamore Yacht. Home: 9 Spruce Ln Syosset NY 11791 Office: 5 Sidney Ct Lindenhurst NY 11757

GREY, LINDA, book publisher. Pub., editor-in-chief Bantam Books Inc., N.Y.C. Office: Bantam Books Inc 666 Fifth Ave New York NY 10103*

GRIB, VALERIE JOSEPHINE, semiconductor production equipment company manager; b. Aberdeen, Md., Apr. 15, 1952; d. Walter R. and Josephine C. (Soboda) G. B.S. in Chemistry, Rensselaer Poly. Inst., 1974; M.B.A., 1983. Service mktg. mgr. GCA Corp., Andover, Mass., 1983—. Mem. Am. Mktg. Assn. Avocations: running; theatre; skiing; tennis; golf. Home: 107 Browne St #2 Brookline MA 02146 Office: GCA Corp 7 Shattuck Rd Andover MA 01810

GRIBIN, ELIZABETH ANNE, artist; b. London, Mar. 30, 1934; came to U.S., 1939; d. Jack and Margaret (Salomon) Poser; m. Nathaniel D. Griblin, June 17, 1956; children—Eric, Elisa, David. B.F.A., Boston U., 1956; student Art Students League, 1946-51, Mus. Modern Art, N.Y.C., 1944-46; student David Aronson, 1953-56, Margit Beck, 1979-80, Leo Manso, 1970-71, Paul Wood, 1971-84. One-woman show: Great Neck House (N.Y.), 1983; group shows include: City Hall Gallery, Boston, 1983, Knickerbocker Artists, N.Y.C., 1983, NAD, N.Y.C., 1984, Nat. Assn. Women Artists, N.Y.C., 1984, Long Beach Mus. (Calif.), 1984, Salmagundi Club, N.Y.C., 1984, Mussavi Gallery, N.Y.C., 1984.; represented in permanent collections; pvt. and corp. judge, lectr. L.I. Art Leagues; N.Y.C. coordinator Boston U. Visual Arts Com., 1982-84. Mem. Boston U. Alumni Schs. Com., 1979-84. Recipient award of Excellence, Suburban Art League, 1978; award of Excellence, Ind. Art Assn., 1980, hon. mention, 1982; hon. mention Nassau County Art Mus., 1982, Sole award Nassau County Art Ctr., Nat. League Am. Pen Women, 1982; Grumbach Gold medallion Knickerbocker Artists, 1982, award for oils and acrylics, 1983; 1st prize in acrylics Salmagundi Art Club, 1984. Mem. Nat. Assn. Women Artists (Doris Klein prize for oils and acrylics 1984), N.Y. Soc. Women Artists, Contemporary Artists Guild, Manhasset Art Assn. (First prize in oils and acrylics 1979, Grumbacher Art award 1982).

GRICE, BEVERLY ANN, administrative assistant; b. Hattiesburg, Miss., Aug. 28, 1950; d. John Walker and Annie (King) Little; m. Robert Michael Grice, Nov. 27, 1970 (div. 1984); 1 son, Preston Derek. Student U. So. Miss., 1968-70. Exec. sec. Sellers & Assocs., Cons. Engrs., Hattiesburg, Miss., 1970-75; sec./asst. Lowery Faler, D.M.D., Hattiesburg, 1975-77; administrv. asst. Landry Assoc. Architects, P.A., Hattiesburg, 1978—. Named Outstanding Woman in Constrn., Nat. Assn. Women in Constrn., 1974, Woman in Constrn. of Yr., 1979-80. Mem. Nat. Assn. Women in Constrn. (regional mem. nat. occupation research and referral com. 1985-86, regional mem. nat. edn. com. 1983-84). Republican. Episcopalian. Home: 315 S 15th Ave Hattiesburg MS 39401 Office: Landry Assoc Architects 711 Hardy St PO Box 510 Hattiesburg MS 39401

GRIDER, SYLVIA ANN, English educator; b. Pampa, Tex., Oct 21, 1940; d. R.C. and Huba Mildred (Holt) G.; B.A. in Latin, U. Tex., 1963, M.A. in History, 1967; Ph.D. in Folklore, Ind. U., 1976. Tchr., Tex. high schs., 1963-70; mem. faculty Tex. A&M U., 1976—, assoc. prof. English, 1979—, asst. dean Grad. Coll., 1981-84. Mem. Internat. Soc. Folk Narrative Research, Am. Folklore Soc., Children's Lit. Assn., Western Lit. Assn., Tex. Folklore Soc. (pres. 1982), Delta Kappa Gamma, Phi Kappa Phi. Office: English Dept Tex A&M U College Station TX 77843

GRIDLEY, DAILA SEFERS, microbiologist; b. Riga, Latvia, Jan. 16, 1944; came to U.S., 1949, naturalized, 1954; d. Videvuds and Marta (Snikers) Sefers; B.S., U. Oreg., 1966, M.S., 1971; Ph.D., Loma Linda U., 1978; m. Larry Brown Gridley, Mar. 9, 1968; children—Laila and Laura (twins), Lisa. Med. technologist U. Oreg., 1966-69; sr. med. technologist Loma Linda (Calif.) Med. Center, 1971-74; researcher assoc. Loma Linda U., 1978-81, asst. prof. microbiology, 1981—, asst. prof. radiation sci., 1983—; lectr. in field; lectr. Calif. Poly. U., 1982-84. Recipient Pres.'s award, Loma Linda U., 1978; Clinton Reed Brower scholar, 1978; Oreg. State scholar, 1962; Elsa U. Pardee Found. co-investigator, 1979-81, Nat. Dairy Council co-investigator, 1979-81. Mem. N.Y. Acad. Scis., Am. Soc. Clin. Pathology, Am. Soc. Microbiology, Nat. Registry Microbiologists, AAAS, Sigma Xi, Delta Gamma. Republican. Lutheran. Club: Mothers of Twins, Casa Colina. Contbr. articles to profl. jours. Home: 784 Hillcrest Dr Pomona CA 91768 Office: Loma Linda U Sch Medicine Dept Microbiology Loma Linda CA 92350

GRIER, BARBARA G. (GENE DAMON), author, editor, pub.; b. Cin., Nov. 4, 1933; d. Philip Strang and Dorothy Vernon (Black) G.; student public schs. Kansas City, Kans. Fiction, poetry editor The Ladder, Reno, 1966-67, editor, 1968-72; pub., 1970-72; dir. promotion NAIAD Press, Reno, 1973—, treas. NAIAD Press, Inc., 1976—, v.p., 1981—, also dir. Recipient President's award Gay Acad. Union, 1982. Author: (with Lee Stuart) The Lesbian in Literature, 1967, 3d edit., enlarged, 1981; chpt. in Sisterhood is Powerful, 1970; editor: (with Coletta Reid) Lesbian Lives: Biographies of Women from the Ladder, 1976; The Lesbian's Home Journal, 1976; The Lavender Herring, 1976; Lesbiana, 1976; Neither Profit Nor Salvation in the Lavender Culture, 1978; The Garden Variety Lesbian in The Lesbian Path, 1979, in The Coming Out Stories, 1980. Democrat. Address: PO Box 10543 Tallahasse FL 32302

GRIES, MARION WALTON (MRS. JOSEPH P. GRIES), occupational health and safety cons; b. Milw., Sept. 14, 1935; d. Ray Guy and Ruth (Schumann) Walton; R.N. cum laude, St mary's Hosp. Sch. Nursing, Milw., 1957; postgrad. Coll. Nursing, Marquette U., Milw., 1957-59, 75-76; B.S.N. (hon.), Alverno Coll., 1980; M.S.M. (hon.). Cardinal Stritch Coll., 1983; m. Joseph P. Gries, Aug. 22, 1959; children—Rita, Michael, Patrick, Robert, Lori. Staff nurse, supr. hosp., 1957-58; occupational health nurse, 1958-63; pvt. duty nurse, 1963-67; asst. dir. geriatric nursing, 1967-69; owner, mgr. HFM Textile Co., 1969-73; supr. occupational health nursing A.C. Spark Plug div. Gen. Motors Corp., Milw., 1973-78; occupational health and safety cons., v.p. Milw. Indsl. Clinics, 1978—; lectr. alcoholism-drug abuse, 1971—; edn. cons. Wis. Mental Health Assn., 1971-75; lectr. occupational health, 1974—. Chmn., United Cerebra Palsy campaign, 1966; leader, adviser Milw. council Girl Scouts U.S.A., 1968-73; chmn. Council on Drug Abuse, 1972-73; cert instr. ARC, 1973—, chmn. disaster nursing, 1974-78; mem. Inter-group Council Milw., Para-Medic Study Com.; campaign mgr. local dist. Democratic candidates, 1968—. Recipient Civic award Easter Seal Soc., 1965, 66, 67; C.A.R.O.L. award South Milwaukee, 1965, Oak Creek, Wis., 1966, West Allis, Wis., 1967; Leadership award United Cerebral Palsy, 1966; Distinguished Service award St. Mary's Alumni, 1969; Service award Milw. Safety Council, 1976; Citizen of Year, 1979. Mem. Am Assn. Occupational Health Nurses, S.E. Wis. Occupational Health Nurses (pres.-elect 1984, Shering award 1983), Milw. Assn. Occupational Health Nurses (treas.), Am. Assn Safety Engrs., Wis. Assn. Indsl. Hygrene, DAR,St. Mary's Alumni Assn., Wis. Jaycettes (life, v.p. 1967-68), Marquette U. Nursing Club (pres. 1957-58). Contbr. articles to profl. jours. Home: 7934 S Verdev Dr Oak Creek WI 53154 Office: 500 N 19 St Milwaukee WI 53233

GRIESER, MARSHA G., ice cream plant executive; b. Findlay, Ohio, Jan. 25, 1949; d. Enos Henry and Carolyn (Wittebort) Leass; m. Martin Luther Grieser, June 18, 1976; children—D. Shane, Christopher L. Gen. mgr. Plain View Dairy, Jenera, Ohio, 1976—. Mem. Nat. Assn. Female Execs., Arlington Area Bus. Assn. Republican. Lutheran. Avocations: reading; skiing; cooking; sewing; gardening. Office: Plain View Dairy 9534 State Route 103 Jenera OH 45841

GRIESSE, CAROLYN ANN, educational company executive; b. Imperial, Nebr., May 2, 1941; d. Richard Paul and Eleanor Mae (Bell) Griesse. B.S., U. Nebr., 1963; Ed.D., Nova U., 1979; postgrad. U. Nebr., 1963-66. Coordinator cons. services Behavioral Research Labs., Palo Alto, Calif., 1968-73; sr. project mgr. New Century Edn. Corp., Piscataway, N.J., 1973-78; author New Century Pubs., Piscataway, 1981; tchr. learning disabled Broward County Schs., Ft. Lauderdale, Fla., 1982-83; exec. Ind. Sch. Supportive Service, Inc., Ft. Lauderdale, 1982—; lectr. in field. Author: (with Jim Karas) The Raw Foods Diet, 1981; contbr. articles to profl. jours.; author: Games Manual, 1973. Mem. Women's Advocacy the Minority/Majority, Ft. Lauderdale, 1981—, Internat. Assn. Cancer Victims and Friends, 1981—, Metabolic Research Found., Niles, Ill., 1982—. Mem. Assn. Tchr. Educators, Assn. Supervision and Curriculum Devel., Am. Assn. Sch. Adminstrs. Episcopalian. Clubs: Ft. Lauderdale Christian Bus. Women, Daus. of King.

GRIEST, DOROTHY, college administrator, marketing consultant; b. Iota, La., Sept. 30, 1924; d. Henry R. and Dicie (Stakes) Hebert; B.S., U. Colo., 1945, M.B.E., 1951; Ph.D., La. State U., 1966; children—Gibson H. Sandham, Jennifer S. Guillory. Prof., Northeast La. U., 1973-76; prof. Coll. Bus. Adminstrn., U. Colo., Boulder, 1956-77, chmn. bus. environment and policy, 1978-81; head dept. mgmt., mktg. and adminstrv. studies U. Southwestern La., 1981—. Dir., Monroe Civic Center, 1973-76. Mem. Acad. Mgmt., Southwest Fedn. Adminstrv. Disciplines, Beta Gamma Sigma, Phi Kappa Phi, Pi Sigma Epsilon, Beta Sigma. Democrat. Presbyterian. Home: 601 Camellia Blvd Lafayette LA 70503 Office: Univ Southwestern LA PO Box 43570 Lafayette LA 70504

GRIEST, GUINEVERE LINDLEY, government official; b. Chgo., Jan. 14, 1924; d. Euclid Eugene and Marianna (Lindley) Griest; A.B., Cornell U., 1944; A.M., U. Chgo., 1947, Ph.D., 1961; postgrad. (Fulbright fellow) Cambridge (Eng.) U., 1953-55. Instr., U. Ill., Chgo., 1947-61, asst. prof., 1961-66, assoc. prof. English, 1966-72; program officer div. of fellowships and seminars Nat. Endowment for Humanities, Washington, 1969-73, dep. dir. div. of fellowships, 1973-85, acting dir., 1985-86, dir., 1986—. Mem. MLA, Phi Beta Kappa, Phi Kappa Phi. Episcopalian. Author: Mudie's Circulating Library and the Victorian Novel (MLA scholars' library award 1971), 1971; contbr. articles to profl. jours. Office: Div of Fellowships and Seminars Nat Endowment for Humanities 1100 Pennsylvania Ave NW Washington DC 20506

GRIEVER, ANN MAGNER, pathwork helper, computer systems consultant; b. St. Paul, Oct. 7, 1950; d. Thomas Freeman and Irma Ellen (Estes) Magner; m. William Louis Griever, Oct. 6, 1973; children—Paul Thomas, Ellen Vicket. B.S. in Computer Sci., Pa. State U., 1971; postgrad. in computer sci. George Washington U., 1972-75. Programmer, HumRRO, Alexandria, Va., 1971-72; programmer, analyst Am. Security Bank, Washington, 1972-73; sr. systems analyst FDIC, Washington, 1974-81; sr. cons. Analysas, Washington, 1981-82; computer specialist Exec. Office of Pres., Washington, 1982-85; v.p., pathwork helper Ctr. for the Living Force, Inc., Silver Spring, Md., 1983—; cons. Exec. Office Pres., Washington. Mem. Nat. Ski Patrol, Pa., Va., W.Va., 1969-74; bd. dirs. Washington Ethical Soc., 1977-78. Recipient Richard award Model 204 Users Group, 1982. Democrat. Club: Ikebana Internat. Avocations: Ikebana, sports. Home: 10220 Edgewood Ave Silver Spring MD 20901 Office: Ctr for the Living Force Silver Spring MD

GRIFFEE, CAROL MADGE, journalist; b. Washington, Dec. 30, 1937; d. John Franklin and Leda Mae (Woodruff) G.; B.A. with honors, U. Tulsa, 1959, M.A., 1966. Reporter. Ft. Smith (Ark.) Times-Record, 1955, Tulsa Daily World, 1958-60; news editor Annandale (Va.) Free Press, 1961-62; staff writer Washington Star, 1963-66; city editor No. Va. Sun, Arlington, Va., 1967-69, exec. editor, 1969-72; capitol reporter WEHCO Media, Camden, Ark., 1973; reporter Ark. Gazette, Little Rock, 1973-85; pres. Editorial Services, Inc., Little Rock, 1982—. Past pres. George Mason Republican Women's Club; past bd. dirs. Arlington chpt. ARC; past bd. visitors George Mason U., Fairfax, Va. Recipient Very Spl. Lady award Advt. Club Met. Washington, 1967, Spl. award Ark. Sanitarians Assn., 1977, Conservationist of Yr., Ark. Wildlife Fedn., 1985. Mem. Nat. Fedn. Press Women (dir. 1977-78, legislations-resolutions dir. 1978-80, award recipient), Ark. Press Women (pres. 1977-78, Woman of Achievement award 1977, 84), Mortar Bd., Phi Delta Epsilon, Phi Gamma Kappa, Phi Delta Theta, Pi Gamma Mu, Phi Mu, Sigma Delta Chi.-Soc. Profl. Journalists (v.p. 1980, 81, Region 12 deputy dir. 1984—).

Co-author, Horizons: 100 Arkansas Women of Achievement, 1980. Home and Office: 2610 N Taylor St Little Rock AR 72207

GRIFFES, DONNA BERSE, nurse, actress; b. Woodbridge, N.J., June 15; d. H. Benjamin and Mazie (Traiman) Berse; R.N., Mt. Sinai Hosp. Sch. Nursing, 1950; m. Arthur Raynes Griffes, Jr., Dec. 20, 1952 (div. 1972); children—Benjamin William, Susan Barbara, Peter Lynch. Head nurse pediatric div. Mt. Sinai Hosp., N.Y.C., 1950-52; free-lance fashion model Darcy Sheehan Agy., Ft. Lauderdale, Fla., 1971-75; asst. to pres. Internat. Yacht Brokerage, Ft. Lauderdale, 1975-79; asst. to pres. Burton Group, Culver City, Calif., 1979-80; exec. asst. Lonnie Dunn Co., Los Angeles, 1981; staff nurse St. John's Hosp., Santa Monica, Calif., 1981; pvt. duty nurse, Los Angeles, 1981—; actress in films, TV, comms., 1982—. Films include The Adventures kof Buckaroo Banzai, Homecoming, Fate, Dream for Me, It's Morning, Heart of the Matter, The Last Patch, The Information Explosion, Capitol, Hit Squad, Dawn's Dream. Mem. Mayor's Prayer Breakfast Com., Ft. Lauderdale, 1974-76; participant Presdl. Prayer Breakfast, Washington, 1976; campaign worker J.F. Kennedy, Broward City, 1962, Jack Eckerd for Gov., Broward County, 1976; vol. reader for the blind, 1968-70; bd. dirs. Community Concert Assn., 1970-78; mem. Ft. Lauderdale Symphony Soc., Ft. Lauderdale Mus. of Art. Recipient Total Family Recognition award 1st Presbyn. Ch., Ft. Lauderdale, 1963-64. Mem. Nat. Assn. Female Execs., Mensa, Screen Actors Guild, AFTRA, Republican. Presbyterian. Address: care DeNiro-Hardy Talent Agy 470 S San Vicente Blvd Suite 204-D Los Angeles CA 90048

GRIFFIN, BETTY JO ANN, goldsmith, conservator, consultant; b. Dallas, Sept. 22, 1935; d. James Frederick and Mary Audrey (West) G. B.B.A., So. Meth. U., 1957. Prodn. asst. Neiman-Marcus, Dallas, 1957-59; advt. dir. Ramsey Winch Mfg. Co., Tulsa, 1959-60; prodn. mgr. Bloom Advt. Co., Dallas, 1960-61; advt. dir. Swest, Inc., Dallas, 1965; self-employed goldsmith/conservator, Dallas, 1965—; objects conservator Dallas Mus. Art, 1976—; tchr. ptnr. Argent Jewelers Inst., Dallas, 1971—; tech. cons. Museo del Oro, Bogota, Colombia, S.Am., 1977—. presented paper 45th Congress of Americanists, Bogotá, 1985. Recipient Gold award Dallas Mus. Art, 1963; 1st award jewelry 18th Nat. Decorative Arts Exhibition, Wichita, Kans., 1964; Diamonds Today awards DeBeers-Diamond Info. Ctr., 1973, 74. Mem. Tex. Designer Craftsman, Am. Inst. Conservators, S.W. Assn. Conservators. Republican. Presbyterian. Home: 6206 Vanderbilt Ave Dallas TX 75214 Office: Dallas Mus Art 1717 N Harwood St Dallas TX 75201

GRIFFIN, EFFIE LENA, insurance agency executive; b. Boothbay, Maine, May 8, 1914; d. Austin Alpheus and Minnie Margaret (Murphy) Dodge; m. Roger Conant Clement, 1940 (div. Dec. 1941); 1 dau., Virginia Clement Glazier; m. 2d, James Clement Griffin, Feb. 14, 1945; 1 dau., Catherine Griffin Daigle. B.S. in Edn., U. Maine, 1969. Sec., J. Maxcy & Sons, Gardiner, Maine, 1932-64, owner, 1964-84, pres., 1964—. Mem. AAUW. Republican. Club: Augusta Zonta (treas. 1959-67). Home: 58 Harrison Ave Gardiner ME 04345 Office: J Maxcy & Sons Co 295 Water St Gardiner ME 04345

GRIFFIN, ELIZABETH LOOMIS, club woman; b. Chgo., Apr. 18, 1922; d. Eustis Holcomb and Elsie Violet (Cole) Loomis; student public schs., Bothell, Wash.; m. Samuel Walker Griffin, Apr. 18, 1967; children—James Loomis Ferguson, Thomas Eustis Wells. Bookkeeper, Bekins Moving Co., 1940-42, Keener's Meat Market, 1957-67. Mem. Northshore Bicentennial Com., Bothell, 1974-76; pres. Colonial Dames XVII Century, 1974-76; dist. pres. Vets. World War I Aux., 1977-78; state regent DAR, Wash., 1978-80. Recipient Americanism award VFW, 1978; medal of appreciation SAR, 1978. Mem. New Eng. Women, Am. Legion Aux., Daus. Brit. Empire, Bothell Hist. Soc., Wash. Gens., Freedom Found., Daus. Am. Colonists. Republican. Baptist. Clubs: Navy Mother's, Rebekahs. Home: 23816 2d Ave SE Bothell WA 98021

GRIFFIN, JEAN CHISHOLM, nursing administrator; b. San Francisco, Apr. 6, 1938; d. Roderick Alexander and Bertha F. (Mulcahy) Chisholm; m. Edward M. Griffin, Mar. 5, 1960; children—Patricia M., Theresa M., Joan M. B.S., U. San Francisco, 1960. Staff nurse St. Mary's Hosp., San Francisco, 1960; research nurse Stanford U. Hosp., Palo Alto, Calif., 1963-65; staff nurse Unity Med. Ctr., Fridley, Minn., 1973-80, nursing supr., 1980—. Mem. Democratic Farmer-Labor Party. Roman Catholic. Clubs: Austro-Am. Soc. (Salzburg, Austria); Totino-Grace GPO (Fridley, Minn.). Home: 3125 Ridgewood Rd Saint Paul MN 55112

GRIFFIN, JO ANN THOMAS, tax specialist; b. Dallas, July 20, 1933; d. John Baxton and Joan Marion (Ament) Thomas; m. John Barrett Brown, June 29, 1963 (div. 1972); children—John Barrett, Daniel Thomas; m. Thomas Reese Griffin, Jan. 25, 1976; stepchildren—Gregory Crawford, Kevin Bradley. B.A., U. Miss., 1955; B.S. magna cum laude, Lamar U., 1964; M.Edn., U. Del., 1972. Site mgr. Motivational Ctr., Inc., Wilmington, Del., 1976-78; asst. dir. Indochinese Social Services, Associated Cath. Charities, New Orleans, 1978-79; dir. continuing edn. St. Mary's Dominican Coll., New Orleans, 1979-80; with fin. mgmt. U.S. Dept. Agr., New Orleans, 1981; tax auditor IRS, New Orleans and Phila., 1981-86; tax specialist Horty & Horty, C.P.A.s, Wilmington, Del., 1986—. Docent Winterthur, New Orleans Mus. Art, Wilmington and New Orleans, 1966-85; sustaining mem. Jr. League of Wilmington, lay reader Episc. Ch. Dioces of Del., Wilmington, 1971—; regent DAR Vieux Carre chpt., New Orleans, 1985; bd. dirs. Neighborhood Watch, New Orleans, 1983-85. Recipient Grad. Scholarship award AAUW, 1971, Sustained Superior Performance award IRS, New Orleans, 1983. Mem. Nat. Assn. Female Execs. Democrat. Episcopalian. Club: Blue & Gold, Newark.

GRIFFIN, MARGARET MARIE, sales representative; b. N.Y.C., Jan. 15, 1950; d. John David and Margaret Mary (Dermody) Still; m. Charles Kenneth Griffin, Nov. 6, 1971 (div. 1980); 1 child, Bryan David Griffin. B.S., Fordham U., 1971; postgrad. N.Y. Inst. Fin., 1972. Lic. ins. agt., N.Mex. Media buyer Franklin, Spier & Co., 1971-72; adminstrv. asst. to sr. v.p. Smith, Barney & Co., 1972-73; analyst-banking and securities Am. Airlines, 1973-78; sec. to regional dir. of tax sheltered investments, asst. mgr., asst. v.p. E.F. Hutton & Co., Inc., 1979-83; asst. trader/adminstrv. asst. to exec. v.p. First City Investment Brokers Inc., (MONCOR), 1983; mktg. rep. John Hancock Fin. Services, 1984; asst. office mgr./sales agt. Ins. Mgmt. Corp., Albuquerque, 1984-85; sales rep. Compushop/Bell Atlantic, Albuquerque, 1985—; fin. cons. Westwind Winery, Bernalillo, N.Mex., 1984—. Mem. Nat. Assn. Female Execs. Republican. Roman Catholic. Avocations: gardening; baking; reading; exercise.

GRIFFIN, MARTHA ANNE, employee benefits specialist, consultant; b. Kings Moss, County Antrim, North Ireland, Oct. 15, 1944; came to U.S., 1962; d. William James and Norah (Webb) Murray; m. Ray Bogden, Oct. 20, 1962 (dec. 1967); children—Richard, Robert, Kelley, Karen; m. 2d, Jerry Lee Griffin, Mar. 26, 1982. B.A. in Psychology, U. B.C., 1962. Cert. employee benefits specialist. Group rep. Mass. Mut., San Francisco, 1973-80; benefits mgr. Port of Portland (Oreg.), 1980-82; benefits analyst Johnson & Higgins, Honolulu, 1982-83; account exec. Rollins, Burdick Hunter, Honolulu, 1983—; v.p. Benefits Council, Vancouver, B.C., Can., 1980. Advisor Jr. Achievement, Portland, 1981-82; mem. Child Abuse Program, Honolulu, Search for Talent, Honolulu, 1983. Served with USNR, 1978—. Mem. Am. Soc. Personnel Adminstrs. (com. Honolulu 1984), Hawaii Assn. Ins. Women, Employee Benefits Council (v.p. 1977-79), Naval Enlisted Res. Assn. (pres. Honolulu). Republican. Roman Catholic. Home: 511 Hahaione St Honolulu HI 96825 Office: Rollins Burdick Hunter 1221 Kapiolani Blvd Honolulu HI 96825

GRIFFIN, MARY ELIZABETH WILSON (MRS. DONALD F. GRIFFIN), metals manufacturer, educator, city official; b. Yuba City, Calif., May 24, 1932; d. Zacharias Walters and Mary (Nickerson) Wilson; A.A., Yuba Coll., 1952; A.B. cum laude (Calif. Congress PTA scholar), Chico State Coll., 1954; postgrad. Sacramento State Coll., 1956, San Francisco State Coll., 1957-58; m. Donald F. Griffin, Sept. 6, 1958; children—John Malcolm, Mimi Elizabeth, Zachary Paul. Tchr. pub. elem. schs., Santa Rosa, Calif., 1954-57; assoc. prof. edn. San Francisco State Coll., 1957-59, temporary tchr. Campus Elem. Sch., 1960-67; v.p. Griffin Metal Products, San Francisco, 1960-63, sec.-treas., 1963-80, pres., 1980—; tchr. South San Francisco Unified Sch. Dist., 1973—. Treas. library trust fund French-Am. Bi-Lingual Sch., San Francisco, 1965-67; active PTA, 1967—, dir. county parent edn. program, 1972-73; mem. Millbrae (Calif.) Beautification Com., 1971-78; bd. dirs. San Francisco Boys Chorus, until 1981; mem. Millbrae City Council, 1976—, mayor, 1980-81, 84-85; chmn. North San Mateo County Council of Cities, 1978-79; bd. dirs. San Mateo County Easter Seal Soc., 1977-82, 1st v.p., 1981-82; chmn. legis. com. San Mateo County Council of Mayors; 1st v.p. Peninsula div. League Calif. Cities, 1981-82, pres., 1982-83. Recipient appreciation cert. Cub Scouts Am., 1969, 70, 71, Hon. Service award Calif. Congress PTA, 1973; named Woman of Yr., Calif. Fedn. Women's Clubs, 1980. Mem. Millbrae C. of C. Democrat. Presbyterian. Club: Millbrae Woman's. Home: 67 Aura Vista Millbrae CA 94030 Office: 1320 Underwood Ave San Francisco CA 94124

GRIFFIN, MARY FRANCES, library media consultant; b. Cross Hill, Laurens County, S.C., Aug. 24, 1925; d. James and Rosa Lee (Carter) G.; A.B., Benedict Coll., 1947; M.S.L.S., Ind. U., 1957; student S.C. State Coll., summers 1948-51, Atlanta U., 1953, Va. State Coll., 1961. Tchr.-librarian Johnston (S.C.) Tng. Sch., Edgefield County Sch. Dist., 1947-51; librarian Lee County Sch. Dist., Dennis High, Bishopville, S.C., 1951-52, Greenville County (S.C.) Sch. Dist., 1952-66; library cons. S.C. Dept. Edn., Columbia, 1966—; vis. tchr. U. S.C., 1977. Recipient Cert. of Living the Legacy award Nat. Council Negro Women, 1980. Mem. ALA, Assn. Ednl. Communications and Tech. S.C., Assn. Curriculum Devel., AAUW (pres. Columbia br. 1978-80), Southeastern Library Assn. (sec. 1978-80), S.C. Library Assn. (sec. 1979), S.C. Assn. Sch. Librarians. Baptist. Home: PO Box 1652 Columbia SC 29202 also 1100 Skyland Dr Columbia SC 29210

GRIFFIN, OLETHA MARY, real estate agency executive, broker; b. Kiefer, Okla., Apr. 15, 1923; d. Clarence LeRoy and Alice Anna (Helbergh) Lloyd; m. Theodore William Griffin, July 27, 1941; children—Gary Lee, Bobby Dale, Genie Alice Griffin Allan. Student in real estate laws and mgmt. Tulsa U., 1967-68, in polit. sci. and religion Oral Roberts U., 1963-64; also real estate seminars. Sec., policy writer Landes, Seever & Thornton Ins., Tulsa, 1940-42, 48-50; exec. sec. Arthur Young & Assocs., Tulsa, 1950-51; secretarial asst., bookkeeper Dr. Fred Perry, Tulsa, 1951-53; broker, owner Tempo Realtors, Tulsa, 1968—. Pres., Highland Park Garden Club, Tulsa, 1964; area dir. Tulsa Community Chest, 1965. Recipient Spl. Youth Work award Okla. Palomino Exhibitors Assn., 1964. Fellow Nat. Assn. Real Estate Bds., Okla. Real Estate Bd., Met. Tulsa Real Estate Bd., Nat. Assn. Master Appraisers; mem. Met. Tulsa Home Builders Ladies Aux. (chmn. membership 1951-52), Nat. Assn. Realtors. Republican. Home: 5530 E 32 Pl Tulsa OK 74135 Office: Tempo Realtors 10976 E 23 St Tulsa OK 74129

GRIFFIN, PRISCILLA LORING (MRS. JOHN J. GRIFFIN), wax mfg. co. exec.; b. Winchester, Mass., Apr. 1, 1930; d. John Alden and Madeleine (Libby) Loring; student Pembroke Coll., Brown U., 1947-49, Katherine Gibbs Coll., 1949-50; m. John J. Griffin, Jan. 27, 1951; children—Patricia, Michael, Peter. Sec. to project Mass. Inst. Tech. (now Draper Labs.), 1950-52; adminstrv. asst., asst. treas. Roger A. Reed, Inc., Reading, Mass., 1971-72, pres., treas., 1972—; mem. corp. Massbank for Savs., 1977—, trustee, 1980—. Chmn., Camp Fire Girls of Reading, 1964-66, mem. state bd., 1966-68; mem. Reading Town Meeting, 1957-68; chmn. League Women Voters, Ipswich, 1969-70; trustee Roger A. Reed, Inc. Profit Sharing and Trust, 1968; mem. Small Bus. Task Force. Mem. New Eng. Women Bus. Owners Asso. Industries Mass., Small Bus. Assn. New Eng. Unitarian. Clubs: Ipswich Bay Yacht, E. Lake Woodlands. Home: Mountain Shadows PO Box 166 Melvin Village NH 03850 Office: 167 Pleasant St Reading MA 01867

GRIFFIN, RUTH LEWIN, state legislator; b. Fall River, Mass., July 9, 1925; d. Perez Otis and May Dorothy (Bailey) Lewin; m. John Kenneth Griffin, 1947; children—Joan Griffin Maloney, John Kenneth, Michael J., Joyce E., Timothy G. R.N., Wentworth Hosp. Sch. Nursing, 1946. Former mem. N.H. Ho. of Reps., now mem. N.H. State Senate from Dist. 24. Del., mem. platform com. N.H. State Republican Conv., 1972; 1st Dist. del., mem. platform com. Rep. Nat. Conv., 1972, del., 1976. Active Portsmouth Federated Rep. Women's Club. Mem. Order Women Legislators, Nat. Fedn. Rep. Women, DAR. Methodist. Office: NH State Capitol Bldg Concord NH 03301

GRIFFIN, SHEILA, marketing executive; b. Chgo., June 17, 1951; d. George Michael and Frances Josephine (Sheehan) Spielman; m. Woodson Jack Griffin, Dec. 30, 1972; 1 son, Woodson Jack, II. B.S., U. Ill., 1975, M.B.A., 1979. Personal banking rep. Am. Express Banking, Boeblingen, Germany, 1973-74; market research analyst Market Facts, Chgo., 1975-77; mgr. strategic research Motorola, Inc., Schaumburg, Ill., 1977-83, mktg. resource mgr., 1985—; gen. mgr. mktg. research and info. Ameritech Mobile Communications, Inc., Schaumburg, 1983-85. Trustee, Ill. Math. and Sci. Acad., 1986—. Recipient Disting. Alumni award U. Ill., 1985. Mem. Am. Mktg. Assn., Am. Demographic Inst., AAUW, U. Ill. Chgo. M.B.A. Alumni Assn. (pres. 1984—), U. Ill. Alumni Assn. (bd. dirs. 1984-86), Home: 53 Highgate Course St Charles IL 60174 Office: Motorola Inc 1301 E Algonquin Rd Schaumburg IL 60196

GRIFFITH, BEVERLY HUTCHESON, lawyer; b. Louisville, Dec. 26, 1954; d. Beverly Ray and Willie Edna (Trent) H. B.A. with highest honors, U. Miss., 1976; J.D., U. Ky., 1979. Bar: Ky. 1979, U.S. Ct. Appeals (5th cir.) 1983, U.S. Ct. Appeals (D.C. cir.) 1980, U.S. Supreme Ct. 1983. Sr. atty. Tex. Gas Transmission Corp., Owensboro, Ky., 1979—. Bd. dirs. Mary Kendal Home, Inc., Owensboro, 1983—, Tex. Gas Employees Credit Union, 1982—. Recipient Owensboro Young Career Woman award Bus. and Profl. Women's Club, 1983. Mem. ABA, Ky. Bar Assn. (dir. corp. house counsel sect.), Daviess County Bar Assn., Fed. Energy Bar Assn., Phi Kappa Phi, Alpha Lambda Delta, Alpha Omicron Pi. Democrat. Baptist. Club: Jr. League Owensboro. Home: 1855 Aspenwood Ct B-4 Owensboro KY 42301 Office: Tex Gas Transmission Corp 3800 Frederica St Owensboro KY 42301

GRIFFITH, DOROTHY AUBINOE, interior designer; b. Washington, Feb. 19, 1927; d. Alvin Love and Dorothy (Barron) Aubinoe; A.B., Rollins Coll., 1948; grad. teaching cert. U. Md., 1949; diploma Internat. Inst. Interior Design, 1958; children—June, Paul, Tod, Holly. Owner, interior designer Griffith Assos., Inc., Bethesda, Md., 1958-78; owner, dir. Griffith Gallery, Miami, Fla., 1978—; owner, pres. Griffith Investments. Mem. alumni council Rollins Coll., 1983—, trustee, 1983—, nat. dir. Coll. Fund, 1985-86 Mem. Am. Soc. Interior Designers. Club: Coral Gables Country. Home: 440 Giralda Ave Coral Gables FL 33134 also 322 Toll Gates Shores Blvd Islamorado FL

GRIFFITH, GWENDOLYN, lawyer; b. Memphis, July 21, 1957; d. John D. Griffith and Dorothy (Taylor) Lloyd; m. Jeffrey Lee Moench, Aug. 8, 1981. B.A., Rollins Coll., 1978; J.D., Stanford U., 1981. Bar: Calif. 1981, Tex. 1983. Research attache European Univ. Inst., Florence, Italy, 1981-82; assoc. Akin, Gump, Strauss, Hauer & Feld, Dallas, 1982—. Contbr. articles to legal jours. Editor-in-chief Stanford Jour. Internat. Law, 1980-81; assoc. editor Stanford Law Rev., 1980-81. Fulbright scholar, 1981. Mem. ABA, Tex. Bar Assn., Calif. Bar Assn., Dallas Bar Assn. Office: Akin Gump Strauss Hauer & Feld 2800 Republic Bank Bldg Dallas TX 75201

GRIFFITH, LINDA MARIE, curriculum consultant; b. New Bedford, Mass., Jan. 9, 1953; d. George Jesse and Helen Costa (Frias) Morris; m. Thomas Louis Dale Griffith, July 11, 1981. A. in Bus., Golden West Coll., 1974; B.A. in Liberal Studies, Calif. Poly. State U., 1977; M.A. in Ednl. Adminstrn., U. Las Vegas, 1982; postgrad. Brigham Young U., 1985—. Cert. elem. tchr., adminstr. Tchr. Clark County Sch. Dist., Las Vegas, 1977-79, 80-84, tchr. gifted children, 1979-80, curriculum cons., 1984—; instr. Clark County Community Coll., Las Vegas, 1978-79; mem. Com. for Profl. Standards, Las Vegas, 1984—. Author handbooks: News to Discuss, 1984; (with others) Crossroads, 1985. Mem. Nev. Women's Polit. Caucus, Las Vegas, 1983-85. Recipient Excellence in Edn. award Clark County Sch. Dist., 1984. Mem. Assn. for Supervision and Curriculum Devel., Internat. Reading Assn., So. Nev. Council of Math., Nat. Council Adminstrn. Women in Edn., Phi Delta Kappa. Republican. Roman Catholic. Avocations: gardening; swimming; cycling; music. Home: 7121 Tempest Pl Las Vegas NV 89128 Office: Clark County Sch Dist 2832 E Flamingo Rd Las Vegas NV 89121

GRIFFITH, LORI ANN, physical therapist; b. Detroit, July 16, 1957; d. Richard Gary and Mary Barbara (Vail) G.; m. Joseph Kurtyka, Nov. 22, 1980 (div. Sept. 1984); B.S., U. Mich., 1979. Phys. therapist Lansing Sch. Dist., Mich., 1979-81, Mich. Sch. for Blind, 1980-81, Ingham Med. Ctr., 1980-81; pediatric phys. therapist Toledo Hosp., 1981-84, Childrens Ortho Hosp. and Med. Ctr., Seattle, 1984-85; pediatric clin. specialist Kennestone Hosp., Marietta Ga., 1985—. Chmn. guided growth early intervention programs adv. com. YWCA, Cobb County, Ga., 1986. Mem. Am. Phys. Therapy Assn., Neurodevelopmental Treatment Assn. Avocations: stained glass; furniture refinishing; collection of Oriental art; backpacking; cooking. Home: 1712 Windcliff Dr Marietta GA 30067 Office: Kennestone Hosp Rehab Dept 677 Church St Marietta GA 30060

GRIFFITH, LYNN JOAN, lawyer; b. Newark, N.J., Apr. 19, 1949; d. Lambert Charles and Joan Marie (Schilling) Stadtman; m. Allan Thomas Griffith, Jan. 25, 1974; children—Charles Arthur, Valerie Lynn. B.A., Fla. So. Coll., 1971; J.D., Stetson U., 1974. Bar: Fla. 1974, U.S. Dist. Ct. (no. dist., mid. dist., so. dist.) Fla. 1982. Assoc., Friedman & Britton, Orlando, Fla., 1974-76; sole practice, Ft. Myers Beach, Fla., 1976-79; mng. ptnr. Griffith & Griffith, P.A., Ft. Myers, Fla., 1979—. Commr., Ft. Myers Beach Tax Dist. Bd., 1977-79; bd. dirs. Fla. Children's Home Soc., Daytona Beach, 1975-76. Recipient U.S. Law Week award Bur. Nat. Affairs, 1974. Mem. ABA, Fla. Bar Assn., Comml. Law League Am., Am. Bus. Women's Assn. (sec. Ft. Myers Beach 1978), Zonta Internat. Republican. Baptist. Office: Griffith & Griffith PA 5235 Ramsey Way Suite 17 Fort Myers FL 33907

GRIFFITH, MARIELLEN SHELLENBERGER, educator; b. Newton, Kans., Mar. 28, 1935; d. Peter Simon and Mabel Bertha (Deschner) Shellenberger; m. David Scott Griffith, July 15, 1961; children—Scott Whittier, Jon Peter. Ed.S., Butler U., Indpls., 1973; Ed.D., Ball State U., 1976. Mem. faculty Bluffton Coll., 1959-61; sch. counselor Western Boone Corp., Jamestown, Ind., 1971-74; mem. faculty Butler U., Indpls., 1975—, assoc. prof. marital and family therapy; cons. women and bus., stress mgmt., assertion tng. Mem. Am. Psychol. Assn., Am. Assn. Counseling and Devel., Acad. Psychologists in Family Psychology, AAUW, Am. Assn. Marriage and Family Therapy. Office: Butler U 4600 Sunset Ave Indianapolis IN 46208

GRIFFITH, MARY LOUISE KILPATRICK (MRS. EMLYN I. GRIFFITH), civic leader; b. Gadsden, Ala., Mar. 22, 1926; d. Lewis A. and Willie (Reid) Kilpatrick; A.B., Huntingdon Coll., 1947; m. Emlyn I. Griffith, Aug. 13, 1946; children—William L., James R. Pres. Evergreen Twig, hosp. charity group, Rome, 1966-67; bd. dirs. Rome Art and Community Center, 1967-72; mem. Bd. Edn. Rome City Sch. Dist., 1967-77; bd. dirs. Rome chpt. Am. Field Service, 1969-77; trustee Utica Coll. Found., 1974-80, George Jr. Republic, 1974—, Pub. Broadcasting Council Central N.Y., 1977—, 1st Presbyn. Ch., Rome, 1979-85; pres. Rome Home, 1973-75. Recipient Rose for Living award Rotary Club, 1973; Civic award for conspicuous service Colgate U., 1978. Presbyn. Mem. PEO (pres. 1965-66), AAUW, Nat. Soc. Lit. and Arts. Club: Wednesday Morning (pres. Rome 1968-70). Home: Golf Course Rd Rome NY 13440

GRIFFITH, REGINA M., financial consultant; b. Camden, N.J., Dec. 8, 1952; d. Lewis Kenneth and Mary Gertrude (Connors) Griffith. A.A., Camden County Coll., 1980; B.A., Glassboro State U., 1982. Paralegal Griffith & Burr, Phila., 1980-82; fin. cons. Cigna, Cherry Hill, N.J., 1983—; investment products coordinator Cigna, 1984—, fin. planner, 1984—. Mem. Nat. Orgn. Securities Dealers. Avocations: art; music; poetry. Address: Cigna 1800 Chapel Ave Suite 300 Cherry Hill NJ 08002

GRIFFITH, VALRIE QUARNBERG, electronic manufacturing company executive; b. Salt Lake City, July 17 1956; d. David Ray and Janice Robins Quarnberg; m. Robert Wayne Griffith, Jan. 4, 1975. Student public schs. Kearns, Utah. With MSI, Murray, Utah, 1973-75; prodn. mgr. SSC, Murray, 1973-75; v.p., mgr. Microtek of Utah, Salt Lake City, 1978-82, pres., West Valley City, Utah, 1982—. Recipient Speech award Sertoma Club, 1970. Avocations: Ceramics; quarterhorses. Office: M O U Inc 2465 S Progress Dr Salt Lake City UT 84119

GRIFFITHS, MARTHA W., lieutenant governor of Michigan, b. Pierce City, Mo., Jan. 29, 1912; m. Hicks G. Griffiths. B.A., U. Mo.; J.D., U. Mich.; 28 hon. degrees. Bar: Mich. 1941, U.S. Supreme Ct. 1955. Mem. Mich. Ho. of Reps., Lansing, 1949-52; judge, recorder Detroit Recorder's Ct., 1953; mem. Congress from 17th congl. Dist. Mich.; sole practice law. Romeo, Mich., 1976-82; lt. gov. Mich., 1983—; affirmative action officer State of Mich. Permanent chair Mich. Equal Employment and Bus. Opportunity Council; mem. Adminstrv. Bd., co-chmn. Mich. High Tech. Task Force; mem. Cabinet Council on Jobs and Econ. Devel.; chair State's Purchasing Task Force. Office: Office of Lt Gov State Capitol Lansing MI 48909

GRIFFO, ZORA JASINCUK, research administrator, physiologist; b. Prague, Czechoslovakia, Nov. 24, 1928; d. Illa and Domicela (Hupalo) Jasincuk; m. Joseph S. Griffo, June 19, 1954; children—Gordon G., Mark D. Asst. in anesthesiology Sch. Medicine, Washington U., St. Louis, 1958-61; grants assoc., div. research grants NIH, Bethesda, Md., 1969-70, br. and program chief Nat. Inst. Dental Research, 1971-73; spl. asst. to assoc. dir. extramural research and tng. NIH, Bethesda, 1973-75, spl. programs officer, 1975-83, appeals officer, 1983—. Recipient NIH Dir.'s award, 1978. Mem. AAUP, N.Y. Acad. Scis. Office: Office of Dir National Institutes of Health Bethesda MD 20892

GRIGGS, APRIL ROSINA, speech pathologist; b. Ventura, Calif., Apr. 20, 1946; d. Robert Dean and Margarite Terrill (Lyon) Smeltz; student Ventura Coll., 1964-66; B.A., Calif. State U., Fresno, 1968, M.A., 1971; postgrad. The Citadel, 1972-73, San Diego State U., 1977-78; 1 son, Jason. Grad. asst. Calif. State U., 1969-70; speech and lang. pathologist Fresno (Calif.) City Schs., 1969-70, Charleston (S.C.) Speech and Hearing Clinic, 1970-72; speech and lang. pathologist, supr. Charleston County Pub. Schs., 1972-76; speech and lang. pathologist, instr. Southwestern Coll., Chula Vista, Calif., 1976—; pvt. practice speech and lang. pathology, Chula Vista, 1978—. Lic. speech pathologist, Calif., S.C. Mem. Am., Calif. speech and hearing assns. Democrat. Office: 615 E Lexington El Cajon CA 92020 also 3d Ave Suite 103 Chula Vista CA 92011

GRIGGS, KATHERINE EILEEN, educator; consultant; b. Chico, Calif., Oct. 31, 1924; d. Thomas Mervyn and Nancy Fay (Orendorff) Kaney; m. David B. Morrison, July 3, 1945 (dec. 1954); children—Patricia E., John T., D. Paul; m. Charles V. Griggs, Nov. 19, 1960. B.A. in Psychology, San Jose State U., 1945. Owner, mgr. K&M Personnel, Sacramento, 1959-65; dir. personnel Mercy Hosps., Sacramento, 1965-75; dir. edn. and tng. Sutter Community Hosps., Sacramento, 1975-82, community health educator, 1982-85, trustee educator, 1985—; meeting plan cons. Griggs Assocs., Sacramento, 1984—. Contbr. articles to profl. jours. Active health com. Sacramento C. of C., 1983—. Recipient cert. of achievement KVIE-Channel 6 TV, 1984; Outstanding Contbr. award Vocat. Indsl. Clubs Am., 1985. Mem. Sacramento Soc. Assn. Execs., Meeting Planners Internat., Sacramento Women's Network, Sacramento Health Consortium for Cable. Republican. Roman Catholic. Avocations: golf; camping; handcrafts; bridge; spectator sports. Home: 2206 Landon Ln Sacramento CA 95825 Office: Sutter Health System 1111 Howe Ave Suite 600 Sacramento CA 95825

GRIGGS, RUTH MARIE, retired journalism educator, writer, publications consultant; b. Linton, Ind., Aug. 11, 1911; d. Roy Evans Price and Mary Blanche (Hays) P.; m. Paul Philip Griggs, Aug. 4, 1940. B.S., Butler U., 1933; postgrad. U. So. Calif., 1938, Northwestern U., 1939; M.A., U. Wyo., 1944. Cert. tchr. journalism, English, speech, bus. edn. Travel writer Indpls. Star, 1927-37; summer reporter Worthington Times, Ind., 1928-33; journalism, speech tchr. Warren Central High Sch., Indpls., 1937-37; tchr. bus. edn., journalism Greene Twp. High Sch., South Bend, Ind., 1937-38; tchr. journalism, English, bus. edn. Howe High Sch., Indpls., 1938-46; tchr. journalism Butler U., Indpls., 1946-48, evenings 1972-76; dir. publs. Broad Ripple High Sch., Indpls., 1948-77; summer journalism workshop instr. numerous univs. 1949-80. Author: History of Broad Ripple, 1968; co-author: Handbook for High School Journalism, 1951; Teacher's Guide to High School Journalism, 1965. Dow Jones Newspaper Fund fellow U. Minn., 1967; named Nat. Journalism Tchr. of Yr., Wall Street Jour., 1968, Woman of Achievement, Woman's Press Club of Ind., 1984. Mem. Journalism Edn. Assn. (v.p., pres. 1963-69, Towley award 1965), Women in Communications (pres. Indpls. 1969-70, Wright award 1969, Kleinhenz award 1978), Nat. Fed. Press Women (youth projects bd. 1979—), Columbia Scholastic Press Assn. (Gold Key award 1964, Golden Crown 1975, life mem. 1977), Ind. High Sch. Advisers Assn. (pres. 1972, Sengenberger award 1965), AAUW, DAR, Delta Zeta (Ind. Woman of Yr. 1984). Republican. Presbyterian.

GRILL, NANNETTE LOUISE, writer, producer, composer, educator; b. Los Angeles, Mar. 26, 1935; d. Raymond James and Ethel Mae (Rogers) G.; student Stanford U., 1952-55; B.A. summa cum laude, Immaculate Heart Coll., 1965; M.A., U. Calif., Los Angeles, 1969. Teaching sister Los Angeles Area Catholic Parochial schs., 1956-68; coordinator juvenile program Culver City (Calif.) High Sch., 1968-69; assoc. prof. English, Pasadena (Calif.) City Coll., 1969—; freelance writer, 1970-74; partner Scarecrow Publs., Los Angeles,

1971-73; co-founder So. Calif. chpt. Reading is Fundamental, 1972; cons. in field. Nat. Endowment for Humanities fellow, 1973-74; NDEA grantee, 1966. Mem. ASCAP, TV Acad. Arts and Scis., UCLA Alumni Assn., Stanford U. Alumni Assn. Author: (with Charonne Wali) Mister Abracadabra, 1971; Clothe the Naked, 1980; also papers. Interview guest on TV shows including Dinah's Place, Tom Snyder's Sunday Show. Designed and produced children's public service shows, 1972-73; producer, writer TV spl. Dear Bear's Christmas, 1980. Christmas (Emmy nominee 1982), Home: Brentwood CA Office: Pasadena City College Department of English 1560 E Colorado Blvd Pasadena CA 91106

GRILL, NINA DOINA, finishing school and modeling agency executive; b. Romania, Oct. 22, 1938; mother Am. citizen; d. Emil and Mary A. (Derloshon) Bendorfeanu; m. Edward E. Grill, Jan. 19, 1963; children—Theresa M., Sherri A. Student, Internat. Bus. Coll., Ft. Wayne, Ind., 1958, Ind. U., 1959. Tchr., Purdue U., Ft. Wayne, 1968-69, Huntington Coll., Ind., 1970-71, Internat. Bus. Coll., Ft. Wayne, 1971-72; dir., founder Charmaine Finishing Sch. and Model Agy., Ft. Wayne, 1969—; lectr. in field. Contbr. articles to profl. jours. Vol. Am. Cancer Soc., Ft. Wayne, 1973, Am. Diabetes Assn., Ft. Wayne, 1983; bd. dirs. Miss Ft. Wayne Scholarship Pageant, 1979—, Miss Allen County Pageant, 1984—; vol. bd. dirs. Allen County Crippled Children and Adults, Ft. Wayne, 1981—, United Cerebral Palsy, Ft. Wayne, 1981—. Named Tchr. of Month, Milady Pub. Co., 1969, 79. Mem. Advt. Assn. Ft. Wayne (bd. dirs. 1976-79), Women Bus. Owners Assn., Internat. Talent Modeling Schs. and Agys. Assn. (bd. dirs. 1979—), Ft. Wayne Bus. and Profl. Women Club. Avocations: reading; music; sports. Home: 10117 Stellhorn Rd Fort Wayne IN 46815 Office: Charmaine Finishing Sch and Model Agy 3538 Stellhorn Rd Fort Wayne IN 46815

GRILLS, CAROLINE MARGARET, micropublishing company executive; b. Washington, June 4, 1936; d. Silas Milo and Christine Irene (Donahue) Ransopher; m. Mervyn Joseph Grills, Mar. 27, 1968 (div. Nov. 1974); 1 child, George Glidden. B.A. cum laude in Radio-TV Prodn. and Directing, Kans. U., 1959; postgrad. UCLA, 1961. Head print prodn. NEA/Assn. Supervision and Curriculum Devel., 1974-76; editor Nat. Micrographics Assn., 1970-71; mgr. microforms and back issues Am. Chem. Soc., Washington, 1976-80; pres. Lasercom Prodns., Balt. and Washington, 1980—; mem. standards bd. color microfilm Nat. Micrographics Assn./Am. Nat. Standards Inst., 1978-81; mem. publs. bd. Internat. Micrographic Congress, 1979-81; del. White House Conf. Library and Info. Services, 1979. Author: Micropublishing in the 80's, 1980; A Buyer's Guide to Videodiscs, 1981; (with others) Micrographics Technology, 1976. Mem. Nat. Micrographics assn. (award), Am. Soc. Info. Sci., Assn. Info. Mgrs., Soc. Photog. Engrs. and Scientists, Am. Chem. Soc., Internat. Micrographic Congress, Columbia Assn. Democrat. Episcopalian. Office: Lasercom Prodns 8984 Watchlight Ct Columbia MD 21045

GRIMBAU, ROCHELLE, lawyer; b. Havana, Cuba, Jan. 20, 1946; came to U.S., 1949; d. David and Dora (Levin) Grimbau. B.A., U. Ill., 1968; M.A., Northeastern U., 1973; J.D., DePaul U., 1979. Bar: Ill. 1979. Tchr. handicapped children Spalding Sch., Chgo. Bd. Edn., 1968-80; assoc. Law Office Albert Weinberg, Chgo., 1980-83; ptnr. Wilcox & Grimbau, Chgo., 1983—. Mem. Chgo. Bar Assn., Woman's Bar Assn., Ill. Bar Assn., ABA, Nat. Assn. Women Bus. Owners. Office: Wilcox & Grimbau 127 N Dearborn Suite 720 Chicago IL 60602

GRIMES, ANTOINETTE LOUISE, managment consultant; b. N.Y.C., June 5, 1918; d. Julian Edward Stubbs and Ellen Louise (Grimes) Stubbs Grimes. B.A., CCNY, 1954. Office sec. Bloomingdale's dept. store, N.Y.C., 1958-61; office mgr. Litton Industries, N.Y.C., 1961-69; dir. ann. giving Little Red Sch. House, N.Y.C., 1969-74; dir. devel. Hewitt Sch., N.Y.C., 1974-77, bus. mgr., 1977-85; ind. mgmt. cons., N.Y.C., 1985—. Mem. N.Y. State Assn. Ind. Schs. (pres. bus. mgrs. council 1975-76), Ind. Schs. Bus. Officers Assn. (coordinator N.Y.C. 1984—), Nat. Assn. Ind. Schs., Met. Assn. Ednl. Services (bd. dirs. 1978-79), N.Y. Color Slide Club (pres. 1972-73). Democrat. Roman Catholic. Avocations: travel; reading; photography. Home and Office: 475 F D R Dr New York NY 10002

GRIMES, MARY ANNE, nurse; b. Kansas City, Kans., June 19, 1936; d. John Andy and Bertha Helen (Ball) G. R.N., St. Joseph's Hosp. Staff nurse St. Joseph's Hosp., Phoenix, 1957-61; office nurse Family Med. Clinic, Phoenix, 1961-62; pvt. duty nurse Central Registery, Phoenix, 1962-65; office nurse, mgr. Phoenix Urologic Clinic, 1965-79; sch. nurse Wilson Sch. Dist. 7, Phoenix, 1980-84, Balsz Sch. Dist. #31, 1984—. Primary fund raiser Classical Chorus Bach and Madrigal Soc., also sec., bd. dirs.; campaign worker Republican gubernatorial election, Phoenix, 1968, 70. Mem. Am. Bus. Women's Assn. (pres. 1974-75). Republican. Roman Catholic. Home: 1805 N 21st Pl Phoenix AZ 85006 Office: Balsz Sch Dist 31 4309 E Belleview Phoenix AZ 85008

GRIMM, KATHLEEN, lawyer; b. Troy, N.Y., Mar. 21, 1946; d. Frederick Henry and Helen (Johnson) G. B.A., Manhattanville Coll., 1967; J.D. cum laude, N.Y. Law Sch., 1980; LL.M. in Taxation, NYU, 1984. Bar: N.Y. 1981. Tchr., Colegio de Vera Cruz, Cd. Obregon, Son., Mex., 1967-68; social worker, adminstr. Menorah Home & Hosp., Bklyn., 1969-78; atty. U.S. Dept. Treasury, IRS, N.Y.C., 1981-83; assoc. Parker, Duryee, Zunino, Malone & Carter, N.Y.C., 1983-85; dep. commr. audit and enforcement N.Y.C. Dept. Fin., 1985—. Research coordinator casebook: Law, Medicine & Forensic Science, 1980. Alumni admissions rep. Manhattanville Coll., 1983—. Mem. ABA, N.Y. State Bar Assn., Nat. Task Force Income Tax for Estate Tax Attys., Assn. Bar City of N.Y., N.Y. Law Sch. Alumni Assn. (bd. dirs.). Roman Catholic. Club: Manhattanville of N.Y. (past pres.). Home: 333 E 69th St New York NY 10021 Office: NYC Dept Finance 345 Adams St Brooklyn NY 11201

GRIMMER, MARGOT, dancer, choreographer, director; b. Chgo., Apr. 5, 1944; d. Vernon and Ann (Radville) G.; student Lake Forest; 1963, Northwestern U., 1964-68. Dancer, N.Y.C. Ballet prodn. of Nutcracker Chgo., 1956-57, Kansas City Starlight Theatre, 1958, St. Louis Mcpl. Theatre, 1959, Chgo. TentHouse-Music Theater, 1960-61, Lyric Opera Ballet, Chgo., 1961, 63-66, 68, Ballet Russe de Monte Carlo, N.Y.C., 1962, Ruth Page Internat. Ballet, Chgo., 1965-70; dancer-choreographer Am. Dance Co., Chgo., 1972—, artistic dir., 1972—; dancer, choreographer Bob Hope Show, Milw., 1975, Washington Bicentennial Performance, Kennedy Center, 1976, Woody Guthrie Benefit Concerts, 1976-77, Assyrian Cultural Found., Chgo., 1977-78, Iranian Consulate Performance, Chgo., 1978, Israeli Consulate Concert, Chgo., 1980 Chgo. Council Fine Arts Programs, 1978—, U.S. Boating Indsl. Show, 1981—; dir.-tchr. Am. Dance Sch., 1971—; appeared in TV commls. and indsl. films for Libbys Foods, Sears, Gen. Motors, others, 1963—, also in feature film Risky Business, 1982; soloist in ballet Repertory Workshop, CBS-TV, 1964, dance film Statics (Internat. Film award), 1967; soloist in concert Ravinia, 1973. Ill. Arts Council grantee, 1972-74, 78, Nat. Endowment Arts grantee, 1973-74. Mem. Actors Equity Assn., Screen Actors Guild, Am. Guild Mus. Artists. Important works include ballets In-A-Gadda-Da-Vida, 1972, The Waste Land, 1973, Rachmaninoff: Theme and Variations, 1973, Le Baiser de la Fee and Sonata, 1974, Four Quartets, 1974, Am. Export, 1975, Earth, Wind and Fire, 1976, Blood, Sand and Empire, 1977, Disco Fever, 1978, Pax Romana, Xanadu, 1979, Ishmael, 1980, Vertigo, 1982, Eye in the Sky, 1984, Frankie Goes to Hollywood, 1986, others; dance critic Mail-Advertiser Publs., 1980-82; host cable TV show Spotlight, 1984-85. Home: 970 Vernon Ave Glencoe IL 60022 Office: 442 Central Ave Highland Park IL 60035

GRIMMS, LINDA J(EAN) DEVRIES, lawyer; b. Oakland, Calif., Apr. 29, 1954; d. James Floyd and Sybil Claire (Porter) DeV.; m. Douglas Howard Grimms, Aug. 10, 1985. B.A. in Environ. Scis., U. Calif.-Riverside, 1976; J.D., U. Oreg., 1982. Bar: Oreg. 1982, U.S. Dist. Ct. Oreg. 1983, U.S. Ct. Appeals (9th cir.) 1984. Law clk. U.S. Atty.'s Office, Eugene, Oreg., 1980-82; intern Sierra Club Legal Def. Fund, Juneau, Alaska, 1981; assoc. Stunz, Fonda, Pratt & Nichols, Nyssa, Oreg., 1982; comml. litigation atty. U.S. SBA, Portland, Oreg., 1983; asst. atty. gen. appellate div. Oreg. Dept. Justice, Salem, 1983—. Mem. ABA, Fed. Bar Assn. (pres. Oreg. chpt. 1985), Oreg. State Bar. Christian. Office: Dept Justice Justice Bldg Salem OR 97310

GRIMSLEY, JENNIE LEA, nurse; b. Shobonier, Ill., July 22, 1940; s. Walter Farthing and Rachel Ellen (Cohoon) Weaver; m. W. Duane Grimsley, Aug. 10, 1963 (dec. May 1967); 1 son, Michael Duane. R.N., Decatur Macon County Hosp., Decatur, Ill., 1960. Staff nurse Fayette County Hosp., Vandalia, Ill., 1960-63, staff operating room nurse, 1965-83, head nurse supr., 1983—; staff nurse Utlaut Meml. Hosp., Greenville, Ill., 1963-65. Co-chmn. Bond County Cancer Drive, Greenville, 1964; mem. Citizens adv. com. Vandalia Sch. Bd., 1972; v.p. Citizens Com. for Annexation to Lakeland Jr. Coll., Vandalia, 1973; lay religion tchr. Mother of Dolors Ch., Vandalia, 1973-80. Mem. Assn. Operating Room Nurses. Roman Catholic. Mem. Beta Sigma Phi. Home: Forrest Hills Estates Route 3 Vandalia IL 62471 Office: Fayette County Hospital 7th and Taylor Sts Vandalia IL 62471

GRIMSLEY, LYNN GRIFFIN, realtor; b. Fort Oglethorpe, Ga., Sept. 15, 1943; d. Homer Howard and Alice Cecelia (Hoopes) Griffin; student U. Tenn., Chattanooga, 1979-82; grad. Realtors Inst.; m. David Slater Grimsley, Aug. 25, 1962; children—Mary Lynn, Stephen Michael. Sec., Vol. State Life Ins. Co., 1961-62; sec. Pioneer Bank, 1962-63; legal sec. firm Strang, Fletcher, Carriger, Walker, Hodge & Smith, Chattanooga, 1967-71; exec. sec. Office Mayor Chattanooga, 1971-72, adminstrv. aide to mayor, 1972, adminstrv. asst., 1973-75; exec. dir. Allied Arts Fund Greater Chattanooga, and Chattanooga Arts Council, 1976-82; realtor Goodman Segar Hogan Residential Sales Corp., 1982—; mem. community devel. adv. panel Tenn. Arts Commn., 1979-82. Bd. dirs. Goodwill Industries, 1975-82; vice chmn. residential div. United Fund, 1979; mem. met. ministry com. Episcopal Commn. S.E. Tenn., 1979-82. Mem. Chattanooga C. of C. (central city council), Am. Council for Arts, Am. Coll., Univ. and Community Arts Adminstrs., Va. Assn. Realtors, Nat. Assn. Realtors, Women's Council Realtors (v.p. 1986), Newport News-Hampton Bd. Realtors. Office: 618 Denbigh Blvd Newport News VA 23602

GRINTER, PAULINE LINDA, computer company executive; b. Ardmore, Okla., July 30, 1947; d. Melville Edgar and Marie Josephine (Flogl) Malet; m. Thomas Charles Grinter, Oct. 2, 1982; children—Geoffrey Legler, Timothy Legler (from previous marriage). Student pub. schs., Tulsa. Adminstrv. clk. U.S. Marine Corps, Washington, 1965-68; sec. Am. Airlines, Tulsa, 1968-71 sec. Telex Computer Products, Tulsa, 1974-75, 77-81, supr., 1981-82, mgr. adminstrv., 1982-84, dir. field adminstrn., 1984—. Served with USMC, 1965—. Recipient Cert. of Appreciation, Hdqrs. Command, USAF, 1968; Cert. of Commendation, CG, 4th Marine Div., 1981; Meritorious Mast, Bn. Co. 4th Tank Bn., 1984. Mem. Nat. Assn. Female Execs. Democrat. Roman Catholic. Avocations: swimming; running. Home: 13308 E 32d Pl Tulsa OK 74134 Office: Telex Computer Products 6422 E 41st St Tulsa OK 74133

GRIPPER, SHERYL RILEY, broadcasting company executive; b. Waco, Tex., Dec. 16, 1951; d. Samuel Lawrence and Dolores (Posey) Harris; m. Edward Riley, Nov. 25, 1972 (div. Apr. 1979); 1 son, Edward Riley; m. 2d, Jefferey Lee Gripper, Oct. 9, 1982; 1 son, Jefferey Lee. B.A., Spelman Coll., Atlanta, 1972; M.Ed., Ga. State U.-Atlanta, 1977. Info. and research analyst Econ. Opportunity Atlanta, 1972-74; mgr. pub. info. Sta. WETV/30 and WABE-FM, Atlanta, 1974-81; v.p. community affairs WXIA-TV, Atlanta, 1981—; organizer, sponsor Woman in Balance-workshop to teach how to balance profl. and personal life, Atlanta, 1981. Producer: The Vanishing Middle Class, 1983, Murder by Neglect, 1982 (CEBA award 1982). Chmn. pub. relations United Negro Coll. Fund, Atlanta, 1981—; bd. dirs. Atlanta Area Services for the Blind, 1982—, Mental Health Assn., 1982—. Recipient Gabriel award Catholic Archdiocese, N.Y.C., 1981; hon. award Odyssey Inst., 1981; Pub. Awareness award Corp. of Pub. Broadcasting, 1981; Best of Gannett award Gannett Corp., Rochester, N.Y., 1982, 83. Mem. NAACP (chmn. membership 1981—), Nat. Assn. Media Women (v.p. 1981-83), Media Woman of the Yr. award 1982), Outstanding Atlanta (dir. 1982—). Baptist. Office: WXIA-TV 1611 Peachtree St NE Atlanta GA 30309

GRISEUK, GAIL GENTRY, financial consultant; b. Providence, Jan. 24, 1948; d. Marvin Houghton and Gertrude Emma (Feather) Gentry; student (Fla Power Corp. scholar), Fla. State U., 1966-70; grad. cert. fin. planner Coll. for Fin. Planning, Denver, Registry Fin. Planning Practitioners; m. Steven Paul Griseuk, Oct. 20, 1979; 1 dau., Christina Deborah. Asst. div. controller Mobile Home Industries, Tallahassee, 1968-70; owner, mgr. BDI Services, Tallahassee and Lake Charles, La., 1970-78; fin. cons. Aylesworth Fin., Inc., Clearwater, Fla., 1978-82; chief exec. officer, chmn. bd. Griseuk Assocs. Inc., St. Petersburg, Fla., 1982—; gen. securities and fin. and ops. prin. SEC; instr., dir. vet. outreach Angelina Coll., Lufkin, Tex., 1975-76. Vol., Sunland Tng. Center, 1970-72, George Criswell House, 1969-73; mem. Suncoast Better Bus. Council, Com. of 100. Mem. Nat. Assn. Security Dealers, Inst. Cert. Fin. Planners, Am. Assn. Fin. Planners, Internat. Assn. Fin. Planners, Pinellas County C. of C., Performing Arts Ctr. Theatre Assn., Am Kennel Club, Beta Sigma Phi. Methodist. Contbr. short stories to Redbook, McCall's, Christian Home. Home: 1024 Woodcrest Ave Clearwater FL 33516 Office: 6467 Central Ave Saint Petersburg FL 33707

GRISHAM, EDITH PEARL MOLES, librarian; b. Pinch, W.Va., Mar. 27, 1926; d. Edward Lawrence and Effie (Christy) Moles; m. Charles M. Grisham (div.). A.A., San Antonio Coll., 1958; B.B.A. cum laude, St. Mary's U., 1961; postgrad. Our Lady of the Lake, San Antonio, 1964; M.L.S., Tex. Woman's U., 1973. Billing, sales service asst. Uvalde Rock Asphalt Co., San Antonio, Tex., 1953-62; office mgr. Data Processing Ctr., Inc., San Antonio, 1962-64; serials librarian Houston Pub. Library, 1964-65, head lit. biography dept., 1966-68, head bus. and tech. dept., 1968-73; head Tech. Library Brown & Root, Inc., Houston, 1973-83; reference librarian Incarnate Word Coll., 1984—. Editor, compiler: Union List of Engineering Standards, Specifications, and Codes in Selected Texas Libraries, 1978. Served sgt. USAAF and USAF, 1944-53. Mem. Spl. Libraries Assn., Kappa Pi Sigma, Alpha Beta Alpha. Democrat. Lutheran.

GRISHAM, SANDRA ANN, district judge; b. Washington, Sept. 14, 1949; d. Wilber Glenn and Wyndoleen (McCarty) G.; m. Ronald Paul Ratkevich, Sept. 14, 1974 (div. 1982); m. 2d, Wayne Allen Jordon, June 4, 1983; 1 child, Addie Brieanne Jordon. B.A. in Polit. Sci., U. N.Mex., 1970, J.D., 1973. Bar: N.Mex., U.S. Dist. Ct. N.Mex., U.S. Ct. Appeals (10th cir.), U.S. Supreme Ct. Spl. asst. dist. atty. Bernalillo County, Albuquerque, 1973-77; sole practice, Albuquerque, 1973-78; mem. Durrett, Jordon & Grisham, P.C., Alamogordo, N.Mex., 1979-84; dist. judge State of N.Mex. 12th Jud. Dist., 1985—. Steering com. mem. Regional Resource Ctr. for Child Abuse and Neglect, Austin, Tex., 1979-82; chmn. Alamogordo City Charter Commn., 1982-83, Mayor's Com. on Alcoholism and Driving While Intoxicated, Alamogordo, 1983-84. Williston research fellow, 1972-73. Mem. ABA, N.Mex. Bar Assn., N.Mex. Trial Lawyers Assn., Otero County Bar Assn. Republican. Club: Arabian Horse Assn. N.Mex. (dir. 1978). Office: Dist Ct Div 1 PO Box 687 Alamogordo NM 88310

GRISKEY, PAULINE BECKER, university professor, researcher; b. Pitts., Oct. 30, 1933; d. William and Dorothy (Dzienis) Becker; m. Richard G. Griskey, June 11, 1955; children—Paula Louise, David Richard. B.S., Duquesne U., 1955; M.S., Radford U., 1966; ED.D., Nova U., 1985; postgrad. U. Denver, U. Del., Carnegie Mellon U. Tchr. Pitts. Pub. Schs., 1955-58; concertmistress Eastern Shore Symphony, Salisbury, Md., 1958-60; tchr. Blacksburg High Sch., Va., 1962-66; lectr. Arapahoe Jr. Coll., Littleton, Colo., 1966-68; head English dept. Mt. Pleasant High Sch., Livingston, N.J., 1968-71; acting dir., coordinator, lectr., researcher dept. learning skills U. Wis.-Milw., 1971—; reviewer Houghton, Mifflin, Boston, 1983—, Holt, Rhinehart Winston, N.Y.C., 1982—; adj. prof. Milw. Area Tech. Coll., 1981—. Author: Critical Reading, 1978; Speed Reading, 1982; editor Effective Study Strategies, 1978. Solicitor, Pub. TV Fund Raising, Milw., 1981, March of Dime, Milw., 1980, Univ. Sch. Milw., 1978-79. Recipient Outstanding Achievement award U. Wis.-Milw., 1975, Disting. Service award, 1980; U. Wis. System Minority Disadvantaged grantee, 1977; HEW fellow, 1964-66. Mem. Coll. Reading Assn., Western Reading Assn., Internat. Reading Assn., Adult Edn. Assn., MLA. Office: U Wis Dept Learning Skills PO Box 413 Milwaukee WI 53201

GRIVNA, MARY ALLENE, management services officer; b. Dexter, Minn., Sept. 30, 1942; d. Kenneth Ray and Lois Lorene (Schiefelbein) Coleman; student Des Moines Area Community Coll., 1975-78, Am. River Coll., 1984—; m. Donald Lee Grivna, Aug. 5, 1961; children—Mark Allen, Ellen Kay. Sec. dept. vet. physiology and pharmacology Iowa State U., Ames, 1972-77, adminstrv. asst. dept. biochemistry and biophysics, 1977-81; adminstrv. asst. dean's office Sch. Law, U. Calif.-Davis, 1982-85, mgmt. services officer, 1985—. Mem. Nat. Assn. Female Execs., Am. Bus. Women's Assn. Democrat. Lutheran. Home: 2600 Del Mar Ave Penryn CA 95663 Office: 1011 King Hall U Calif Davis CA 95616

GRIX, ANNE BOWDEN, U.S. Customs Service officer; b. Manchester, Eng., Oct. 2, 1940; d. Harold and Ethel (Ogden) Bowden; m. Robert John Grix, June 17, 1961; children—Mark John, Christopher Maximillian, Charlene Yvette. Grad. Miami Dade Community Coll., 1984, Community Coll. of the Air Force, 1984. Ptnr., Dist. Servicenter, Mt. Vernon, N.Y., 1961-63, Suffern, N.Y., 1963-65; v.p., treas. A&B Service Inc., Branford, Conn., 1970-73; exec. sec., R.E. Assocs., Tokyu Land Corp., Agana, Guam, 1974-76; tng. technician U.S. Air Force Reserves, Homestead, Fla., 1976—, career adv., 1981-83; acctg. technician U.S. Customs Service, Miami, Fla., 1980-81, import specialist, 1981-85, intelligence research analyst, 1985—, EEO counselor, 1981—; adminstv. asst., sec. Everglades Nat. Park, Homestead, Fla., 1977-80; mem. women's program council Miami Fed. Exec. Bd., 1978-79. Coordinator, United Way Campaign, 1978. Recipient Outstanding Performance award Dept. Interior, 1979; Air Force Spl. Achievement medal, 1983; Spl. Achievement award U.S. Customs Service, 1984; Bronze, Silver and Gold medals internat. ballroom dancing. Mem. Assn. Govt. Accts., Everglades Natural History Assn., VFW Aux., USAF Sgts. Assn., (life), Federally Employed Women (pres. 1979), Nat. Assn. Female Execs., Mus. Sci. and Planetarium, USAF Assn., USAF Non-Commd. Officers Assn. Republican. Roman Catholic. Home: PO Box 185 Tallahassee FL 32302

GRIZZLE, MARY R., state senator; b. Lawrence County, Ohio, Aug. 19, 1921; ed. Portsmouth Interstate Bus. Coll.; m. Ben F. Grizzle (dec.); children—Henry, Polley, Lorena, Mary Alice, Betty, Jeanne; m. Charles H. Pearson. Mem. Fla. Ho. of Reps., 1963-78; mem. Fla. Senate, 1978—, mem. econ. community and consumer affairs, appropriations, health and rehab. services, natural resources and conservation coms. Past chmn. Fla. Commn. on Status of Women; govt. rep. Nat. Conf. Women Community Leaders for Hwy. Safety; active P.T.A.; mem. Pinellas County (Fla.) Civil Service Com., Pinellas County Planning Com. Former town commr.; past pres. Women's Rep. Com. Named One of Ten Outstanding Women, St. Petersburg Times, 1966; recipient Achievement award Fla. Rehab. Assn., 1979; hon. life mem. Pinellas County Sch. Food Services, 1979; Largo Jr. Women's Club Woman of Year, 1980. Mem. League Women Voters, Largo Bus. and Profl. Womens Club, Altrusa, Woman's Club, Nat. Soc. Arts and Letters, Delta Kappa Gamma (hon. Alpha Phi chpt.). Episcopalian. Author: (with others) Thimbleful of History. Office: 2601 Jewel Rd Suite C Belleair Bluffs FL 33540

GROAH, LINDA KAY, nursing administrator and educator; b. Cedar Rapids, Iowa, Oct. 5, 1942; d. Joseph David and Irma Josephine (Zitek) Rozek; diploma St. Luke's Sch. Nursing, Cedar Rapids, 1963; student San Francisco City Coll., 1976-77; B.A., St. Mary's Coll., Moraga, Calif., 1978; B.S.N., Calif. State U.; m. Patrick Andrew Groah, Mar. 20, 1975; 1 dau., Kimberly; stepchildren—Nadine, Maureen, Patrick, Marcus. Staff nurse to head nurse U. Iowa, 1963-67; clin. supr., dir. operating and recovery room Michael Reese Hosp., Chgo., 1967-73; dir. operating rooms Med. Center Central Ga., Macon, 1973-74; dir. operating and recovery rooms U. Calif. Hosps. and Clinics, San Francisco, 1974-82, asst. dir. hosps. and clinics, 1982—; clin. instr. U. Calif. Sch. Nursing, San Francisco, 1975—; cons. to operating room suprs., to div. ednl. resources and programs Assn. Am. Med. Colls., 1976—; condr. seminars. Mem. Nat. League for Nurses, Am. Nurses Assn. (vice chmn. operating room conf. group 1974-76), Assn. Operating Room Nurses (com. on nominations 1979-84, treas. 1985-87), Center for Study Dem. Instns. Author: Perioperative Nursing Practice, 1983; contbr. articles on operating room techniques to profl. jours. and textbooks; author, producer audio-visual presentations; author computer software. Home: 5 Mateo Dr Tiburon CA 94920 Office: M423B 3d and Parnasus Sts San Francisco CA 94143

GROBE, KATHLEEN MADELINE, journalist; b. Dayton, Ohio, Sept. 12, 1949; d. John Nicholas and Rita Ellen (Shirden) Mauro; m. Timothy Alan Grobe, Sept. 16, 1972. B.S. in Journalism, Ohio U., 1971; M.A. in Journalism, Marshall U., 1984. Copy editor Huntington Pub. Co. (W.Va.), 1974-83, asst. news editor, 1983—. Explorer post adviser Tri State council Boy Scouts Am., 1978-80; vol. docent Huntington Galleries. Mem. Marshall U. Catholic Community, Sigma Delta Chi, Phi Delta Kappa (editor newsletter). Democrat Roman Catholic. Home: 515 Monroe Ave Apt 5 Huntington WV 25704 Office: Huntington Pub Co 946 5th Ave Huntington WV 25704

GRODE, RYKANDA (KANDY) DAWN, accountant; b. Detroit, Mar. 14, 1957; d. Gerald Henry and Nadine Gayle (Clifford) G. Student Schoolcraft Coll., 1977, Internat. Corr. Schs. Ctr. Degree Studies, 1982-84. Bookkeeping mgr. Hall Real Estate Group, Southfield, Mich., 1977-80; head acctg. clk. Edward Rose & Sons, Southfield, 1981; sr. acctg. supr. Mode O'Day, Burbank, Calif., 1981-84; user analyst, acctg. specialist Cardkey Systems, Chatsworth, Calif., 1984-86; cons.; owner, mgr. Kandy's Kounting Service, Tujunga, Calif., 1985—. Mem. Nat. Assn. Female Execs., Sunland Tujunga C. of C. Republican. Baptist. Avocations: cross-stitch; embroidery; dog breeding and raising. Home and Office: 10525 Las Lunitas St Tujunga CA 91042

GROESBECK, LAURE ANNE ELISE DE BRANGES DE BOURICA, artist; b. Versailles, France, Jan. 31, 1936 (parents Am. citizens); d. Vicount Louis de Branges de Bourcia II and Diane (McDonald) de Branges de Bourcia; student Phila. Coll. Art, 1954-55; m. James Richard Groesbeck, Oct. 3, 1958 (div. June 1969); children—Gretchen Atlee Bowes, Genevieve de Branges. One-man shows: The Agnes Irwin Sch., Rosemont, Pa., 1973, Phila. Cricket Club, Chestnut Hill, Pa., 1973. Recipient prize Rehoboth Beach Art League, 1944; Agnes Allen Art prize Agnes Irwin Sch., 1954. Republican. Episcopalian. Home: 3204 Leigh Rd Pompano Beach FL 33062 Office: Box 58 Pompano Beach FL 33061

GROESCHNER, MARY F., state employment agency administrator; b. LaCrosse, Wis., Aug. 5, 1948; d. Francis N. and Verneil (Holliday) Groeschner. B.A., Viterbo Coll., 1970. Placement interviewer Minn. Dept. Jobs and Tng., Grand Rapids, 1971-74, employment specialist, St. Paul, 1974-75, job service area mgr. I, Montevideo, 1975-78, mgr. II, Mora, 1978-81, mgr. III, Winona, 1981-84, dist. field ops. dir., Mpls., 1984—. Job service rep. S.E. Minn. Pvt. Industry Council, Rochester, 1983-84, City of Mpls. Pvt. Industry Council, 1984—; budget com., dir. employee devel. United Way Greater Winona, 1983, bd. dirs., 1984; bd. dirs. Am. Cancer Soc., Winona, 1982-84; dir. govt. affairs Winona Area C. of C., 1984; personnel com. YWCA, 1983-84. Mem. Am. Soc. Personnel Adminstrn. (sec. 1983-84), Twin Cities Personnel Assn., Nat. Assn. Women Bus. Owners (pub. affairs com. 1984—), Greater Mpls. C. of C. (legis. com. 1984—), Winona County Hist. Soc., Minn. Hist. Soc., Internat. Assn. Personnel in Employment Security (chpt. pres. 1977-78), AAUW, Bus. and Profl. Women's Club.

GROFF, JOANN, state legislator, banker; b. Ft. Leonardwood, Mo., Oct. 10, 1956; d. Barry T. Groff and Ann (Ferry) Ragsdale. Student Georgetown U., 1974-76; B.S. in Bus. Adminstrn., Babson Coll., Wellesley, Mass., 1978. Office mgr. Morgan Smith for Congress, Northglenn, Colo., 1978; fair and rodeo asst. Adams County Commrs., Brighton, Colo., 1979; mktg. devel. officer Columbine Title Co., Lakewood, Colo., 1979-80; express agt., loan officer Wells Fargo Credit Corp., Englewood, Colo., 1981-84; pub. banking rep. Central Bank of Denver, 1985—; mem. Colo. Ho. of Reps., Denver, 1983—, mem. audit com., fin. com. Mem. Colo. State Democratic Com., 1980—, Colo. State Exec. Com., 1983—, del. Nat. Conv., 1980. Mem. Met. North C. of C. Roman Catholic. Office: State of Colorado State Capitol Denver CO 80203

GROGAN, BETTE LOWERY, wholesale steel fastener distribution company executive; b. Seminole, Okla., Nov. 18, 1931; d. C.J. and Martha C. (Eakin) Lowery; m. Morris Rowell, Feb. 8, 1947 (div. Oct. 1960); children—Ronald Michael, Kathy D. Rowell Burkard; m. John Kenneth Grogan, Oct. 28, 1967. Student Del Mar Coll., 1949-51, So. Meth. U., 1963-65. Sec., office mgr. Carrigan Realty, Orlando, Fla., 1958-61; dist. sec. Tektronics, Inc., Orlando, 1961-63; legal sec. Jenkens, Anson, Spradley & Gilchrist, Dallas, 1963-67; real estate broker, Dallas, 1967-77; v.p. Grogan & Co., Dallas, 1972-77; pres. Fla. Threaded Products Inc., Orlando, 1977—; dir. Women's Bus. Ednl. Council, Inc., Orlando, pres., 1986. Mem. Planning and Zoning Commn., Carrollton, Tex., 1972-74; bd. dirs. Jr. Achievement, Orlando, 1981-83. Named Central Fla. Small Bus. Person of the Yr., SBA-C. of C., 1981. Mem. Women's Bus. Ednl. Confs. Fla. (bd. dirs. 1984-85, exec. v.p. 1985-86), Fastener Assn. (bd. dirs. 1980-84), Central Fla. Leadership Council (bd. dirs. 1984—), C. of C. Orlando, Nat. Fedn. Ind. Businesses, Fla. Exec. Women, Better Bus. Bur. Central Fla. (bd. dirs., mem. exec. com.), Beta Sigma Phi (pres. Orlando 1957-59). Republican. Episcopalian. Avocations: tennis; golf; reading. Office: Fla Threaded Products Inc 3060 Clemson Rd Orlando FL 32808

GROGAN, NANCY EDENS, interior designer; b. Jacksonville, Tex., Feb. 8, 1949; d. Terry Herland and Wanda (King) Edens; m. William Thomas Bailey, Jan. 3, 1970 (dec. 1975); m. 2d, Lamont Calvert Grogan, II, Apr. 1, 1977; 1 dau., Eden Katherine. B.S. in Math., U. Houston, 1971, B.F.A. in Environ. Design, 1978. Cert. interior designer. Internat. clk. Capital Nat. Bank,

Houston, 1970-72; Eudo-dollar trader Republic Nat. Bank, Dallas, 1972-74; internat. loan officer First Nat. City Bank N.Y., Houston, 1974-76; designer Michael Dale Interiors, Houston, 1978-80; owner, designer Edens Design, Houston, 1980—. Docent Bayou Bend Mus. Fine Arts, Houston, 1982-84. Mem. Am. Soc. Interior Designers (treas. Houston 1978). Republican. Clubs: Houstonian, Houston Livestock Show and Rodeo.

GROGAN, PAULA CATALDI, newspaper editor; b. Syracuse, N.Y., May 8, 1950; d. Peter Paul and Gilda Sarah (Ingano) Cataldi; m. John Patrick Grogan, June 24, 1978. B.A., Syracuse U., 1972. Reporter, Syracuse (N.Y.) Post-Standard, 1972-75; feature writer Ft. Lauderdale (Fla.) News, 1975-78; successively copy editor, lifestyle editor, assoc. features editor, exec. features editor Dayton (Ohio) Daily News and Jour. Herald, from 1978, now asst. mng. editor features; author column Paula Cataldi Grogan. Dir. Dayton YWCA. Mem. Ohio Newspaper Women's Assn. (2d place award 1983), Women in Communication. Office: Dayton Newspapers 4th and Ludlow Sts Dayton OH 45402

GROLL, JAYNE GORDON, law firm executive; b. Bklyn., Feb. 9, 1955; d. Robert and Minnie (Davis) Gordon; m. William A. Groll, May 17, 1986. B.A. in Music, U. Albany, 1976. Legal sec. Bouck Holloway & Kiernan, Albany, N.Y., 1977-78; litigation paralegal Weisen & Gurfein, N.Y.C., 1979-82; sr. litigation paralegal Golenbock & Barrell, N.Y.C., 1982-84; bond fund paralegal coordinator Davis Polk & Wardwell, N.Y.C., 1984-85, litigation support coordinator, computer specialist, 1985—; lectr. Weight Watchers Internat.; owner, cons. MacLean & Gordon, N.Y.C., 1983-84. Mem. ABA (legal tech. adv. council, litigation support working group 1986), Nat. Assn. Female Execs. Democrat. Roman Catholic. Avocations: theater productions; musical arrangements; tennis; baking. Home: 16 Juni Ct Staten Island NY 10314 Office: Davis Polk & Wardwell 1 Chase Manhattan Plaza New York NY 10001

GROOME, LINDA WILLIAMS, lawyer; b. Lynchburg, Va., June 9, 1952; d. Ernest McKinley and Iris Elmina (McCormick) Williams; m. Harvey Dean Groome, Dec. 28, 1974; children—Abby Marie, Molly Sue. B.S. in Sociology, Va. Poly. Inst., State U., Blacksburg, 1974; J.D., Marshall-Wythe Sch. Law, Coll. William & Mary, Williamsburg, 1978. Cert. tchr., Va. Bar: Va. 1979. Tchr. Sch. Bd. Lynchburg, Va., 1974-76; asst. commonwealth atty. City of Roanoke (Va.), 1980-81; asst. and dep. city atty. City of Chesapeake (Va.), 1981-85, groundwater com. 1981-85; mem. Legal Task Force Battered Women, Chesapeake, 1984. Mem. Multi-Discipline Team Child Abuse & Neglect Coordinating Council, Roanoke, 1980-81; tchr. Great Bridge Baptist Ch., Chesapeake, 1983—. Mem. ABA, Va. Bar Assn., Chesapeake Bar Ar Assn., Local Govt. Attys. Assn. So. Baptist. Home: 167 Holmes Circle Lynchburg VA 24501

GROOME, SALLY LUCYNTHIA, army officer; b. Pelham, N.C., Oct. 9, 1936; d. John Whitlock and Addie Estelle (Vass) G. B.A., Furman U., 1959; M.P.A., Shippensburg U., 1983; diploma Naval Coll. of Command and Staff, 1975, U.S. Army War Coll., 1981. Commd. 2d lt. U.S. Army, 1960, advanced through grades to col., 1982; mil. asst. to sec. of army Dept. of Army, Washington, 1977-78; exec. officer personnel info. systems dir. U.S. Mil. Personnel Ctr., Alexandria, Va., 1978-79; chief personnel actions bd., officer personnel mgmt. dir., 1979-80; dep. chief of staff U.S. Army War Coll., Carlisle, Pa., 1981-83; dir. nat. security studies dept. corr. studies, 1983-84; chief tng. Hdqrs. U.S.A. ROTC Cadet Command. Ft. Monroe, Va., 1984—. Mem. Assn. U.S. Army, Nat. Assn. Uniformed Services, Nat. Assn. Female Execs., Am. Soc. Pub. Adminstrn. Republican. Methodist. Avocations: animal welfare; animal conservation; travel; reading; music. Home: 354 Warrington Circle Hampton VA 23669 Office: C Tng Div Hdqrs USA Cadet Command Fort Monroe VA 23651

GROSE, EDITH (KATE) MARGARETHE, newspaper editor, printer; b. Scotia, N.Y., Mar. 7, 1917; d. Nelsen and Beatrice Edith (Yates) Geertsen; A.A., Schenectady Jr. Coll., 1937; m. Harold J. Hogan, June 17, 1938; children—David H., Charles J.; m. C.H. Grose, June 25, 1971; stepchildren—Lawrence C., Peter S., Susan K. Sec., Internat. Gen. Electric Co., 1937-41, 44-46; editor Scotia-Glenville Jour., 1960-80, Ballston Jour., Ballston Spa, N.Y., 1971-82; chmn. bd. Ballston Printing Co., Inc., 1978-82; sec. Jour. Newspapers, Inc., 1974—. Mem. N.Y. State Ednl. Conf. Bd., 1954-55; chair Schenectady County Ednl. Conf. Bd., 1956-57; mem. Scotia-Glenville Bd. Edn., 1957-63, v.p., 1958-60; mem. Schenectady County Child Guidance Bd., 1961-62; bd. dirs. N.Y. State congress Parents and Tchrs., 1950-53, legis. chmn., 1954-55, life mem. Fellow Internat. Conf. Newspaper Editors; mem. Saratoga County His. Soc. Presbyterian. Clubs: Pinehurst Country, Ballston Spa Country. Home: Box 461 Ballston Spa NY 12020

GROSFIELD, EVELYNN YBARRA, educator; b. Santa Paula, Calif., Nov. 13, 1955; d. Marcelino Sanchez and Minnie Genevieve (Rodriguez) Ybarra; A.A. in Liberal Arts, Ventura Coll., 1970; B.A., U. Calif., Santa Barbara, 1973; postgrad. Calif. State U., 1974-75; m. Robert Grosfield, Aug. 24, 1974; children—Elizabeth, Robert. Tchr., Fillmore Unified Sch. Dist., Ventura, Calif., 1973—; owner, pub. Lollipop Publs., Ventura, 1980—; newspaper columnist Lollipop Corner-Just for Kids. Mem. AAUW, Calif. Tchrs. Assn., Soc. Children's Book Writers, Ventura C. of C., Ventura Women's Network, Bus. and Profl. Women's Club. Democrat. Roman Catholic. Author booklets: How To Write A Book Report, 1980; Cookbook for Kids, 1982. Office: Lollipop Publs PO Box 6726 Ventura CA 93006

GROSH, SUSAN ELLEN, lawyer; b. N.Y.C., Sept. 1, 1958; d. Thomas Bayard and Eleanor Louise (Wangerin) Grosh. B.A. summa cum laude, Fordham U., 1979; J.D., Coll. William and Mary, 1982. Bar: Pa. 1982. Dir., Post Conviction Assistance Project, Williamsburg, Va., 1980-82; assoc. Wenger, Byler & Thomas, 1982-86, Blakenger, Byler, Grove, Thomas and Chillas, P.C., Lancaster, Pa., 1982. Mem. ABA, Pa. Bar Assn., Lancaster Bar Assn. Republican. Presbyterian. Office: Blakenger Byler Grove Thomas and Chillas PC 8 N Queen St Lancaster PA 17603

GROSINSKE, KAY MARIE, air force officer; b. Whitewater, Wis., Apr. 18, 1960; d. Donald Floyd and Joan Mary (Zenisek) G. B.S. in Engring., USAF Acad., 1982. Commd. 2d lt. U.S. Air Force, 1982, advanced through grades to 1st lt., 1986; base communications maintenance officer 1945 Info. Systems Group, Rhein-Main Air Base, Frankfurt, Fed. Republic Germany, 1983-84, maintenance control officer, 1984—. Mem. Armed Forces Communications-Electronics Assn. Roman Catholic. Avocation: skiing. Home: PSC Box 2101 APO New York NY 09057 Office: 1945 Info Systems Group/LGC APO New York NY 09057

GROSS, BARBARA LYN, librarian; b. Altoona, Pa., Oct. 9, 1943; d. Isaac Joseph and Betty Vivian (Diener) Lasser; m. Lawrence Gross, Dec. 26, 1965; children—Benjamin, Halley. B.S., Westchester State U., 1965; M.S. in L.S., Drexel Inst. Tech., 1968. Tchr., Upper Darby Sch. Dist. (Pa.), 1965-67; librarian, instructional materials ctr. specialist, 1967-70; pub. childrens librarian Free Library of Phila., 1970-71, vacation reading club librarian, 1973, 75-84; lower sch. librarian Baldwin Sch. Girls, Bryn Mawr, Pa., 1981—, trustee, 1983—. Bd. dirs. Merion Park Civic Assn., 1983—. Mem. ALA, Pa. Sch. Librarians Assn., Phila. Reading Round Table, Main Line Librarians Assn., Ind. Sch. Librarians Assn. (chmn. 1984-86). Republican. Jewish. Office: Baldwin Sch for Girls Morris and Montgomery Ave Bryn Mawr PA 19010

GROSS, CATHERINE THERESA, underwater research company executive, industrialist; b. Newark, Jan. 20, 1938; d. Dennis James and Kathryn Viola (Dalton) Donahue; m. Ralph L. Liguori, Sept. 7, 1956 (div. 1982); children—Kathryn Rose, Anthony, Lisa, Michael; m. John Charles Gross, Apr. 23, 1983. Student in Bus. Mgmt., Brookdale Community Coll., 1976-78. Exec. v.p. Artifacts Recovery Corp., New Smyrna Beach, Fla., 1982—; exec. v.p., dir. Merchandise Distbrs. Corp., Edgewater, Fla., 1982—; pres., dir. John C. Gross Investment Corp., Edgewater, 1982—; v.p., dir. Yacht Club Island Corp., New Smyrna Beach, Fla., 1982—; dir. Ponce deLeon Realty Corp., New Smyrna Beach, 1982—. Pres., Concerned Citizen's Conf., Ind., Edgewater, 1982—. Mem. Treasure Hunting Assn. Republican. Roman Catholic. Clubs: Halifax, Halifax Yacht, Oceans Racquet (Daytona Beach, Fla.); Fairgreen Country (New Smyrna Beach). Avocations: piano; tennis; golf; boating; treasure hunting. Home: 404 N Riverside Dr Edgewater FL 32032 Office: PO Box 596 New Smyrna Beach FL 32069

GROSS, HARRIET P. MARCUS, freelance writer, educator; b. Pitts., July 15, 1934; d. Joseph William and Rose (Roth) Pincus; A.B. magna cum laude, U. Pitts., 1954; cert. Religious Teaching, Spertus Coll. of Judaica, Chgo., 1962; 1972-73; children—Sol Benjamin, Devra Lynn. Asso. editor Jewish Criterion of Pitts., 1955-56; publs. writer B'nai B'rith Vocat. Service, 1956-57; leader recreation program for handicapped adults United Cerebral Palsy of Greater Chgo., 1957-58; group leader Jewish Community Centers of Met. Chgo., 1958-63; columnist Star Publs., Chicago Heights, Ill., 1964-80; public info. specialist Operation ABLE, Chgo., 1980-81; dir. religious sch. Temple Emanu-El, Dallas, 1983-86; tchr. creative writing Homewood-Flossmoor (Il.) Park Dist., Brookhaven Jr. Coll., Dallas; advisor journalism program Prairie State Coll., Chicago Heights, 1978-80; adv. bd. The Creative Woman quar. publ. Governors State U., Governors Park, Ill. Bd. dirs., sec. Family Service and Mental Health Center of South Cook County, Ill., 1965-71; mem. Park Forest (Ill.) Commn. on Human Relations, 1969-80, chmn., 1974-76; bd. dirs. Ill. Theatre Center, 1977-80, Park Forest Bus. and Profl. Assn., 1979-80, Greater Dallas sect. Nat. Council Jewish Women, 1981—, Jewish Family Service of Dallas, 1982—; mem. exec. com. Jewish Community Relations Council Dallas, 1983-85. Recipient Fellowship for Action Humanitarian Achievements award, 1974; Anti-Defamation League of B'nai B'rith Honor award, 1978; Dr. Charles E. Gavin Found. Community Service award, 1978. Mem. Nat. Fedn. Press Women, Ill. Woman's Press Assn. (named Woman of Yr. 1978), Intertel (pres. Gateway Forum of Dallas 1984-85), Nat. Assn. Temple Educators, Mensa, Sigma Delta Chi, Phi Sigma Sigma. Jewish. Developed 1st community newspaper action line column, 1966. Address: 8560 Park Ln #23 Dallas TX 75231

GROSS, KAREN, lawyer, educator; b. Highland Park, Ill., Apr. 27, 1952; d. Mitchel S. Rieger and Rena (White) Abelmann; m. 2d Stephen H. Cooper, Sept. 6, 1981; 1 son, Zachary Noel. Student Dartmouth Coll., 1972-73; B.A. cum laude, Smith Coll., 1974; J.D. cum laude, Temple U., 1977; student U. Chgo. Law Sch., 1976-77. Bar: Ill. 1977, N.Y. 1982, U.S. Dist. Ct. (so. dist.) N.Y. 1982, U.S. Dist. Ct. (no. dist.) Ill. 1977. Assoc. Arvey Hodes Costello & Burman, Chgo., 1977-80, Weil Gotshal & Manges, N.Y.C., 1980-84; assoc. prof. law N.Y. Law Sch., N.Y.C., 1984—. Rufus Choate scholar, 1973. Mem. ABA, Am. Bankruptcy Inst. (bd. dirs.), Comml. Law League Am., Met. Women Law Tchrs. Assn., Phi Beta Kappa. Democrat. Contbr. articles to profl. jours. Office: New York Law Sch 57 Worth St New York NY 10013

GROSS, LYNNE SCHAFER, communications educator, author; b. Pitts., Apr. 2, 1937; d. Elmer F. and Irene (Keefer) Schafer; m. Paul James Gross, Apr. 2, 1958; children—Kevin, Owen, Brian. Student Northwestern U., 1955-57; B.A., U. Pitts., 1958; M.A., Calif. State U.-Long Beach, 1962; Ed.D., UCLA, 1968. Instr., Met. Coll., Los Angeles, 1962-64; dir. telecommunications Long Beach City Coll., 1966-76; assoc. prof. communication arts Loyola Marymount U., Los Angeles, 1976-80; dir. programming Valley Cable TV, Encino, Calif., 1980-81; prof. communications Calif. State U., Fullerton, 1981—; producer Sta. KCET, Los Angeles, 1973-74; cons. Centre Films, The Pasadena Ctr. (Calif.), others. Author: Broadcast News, 1980; The Internship Experience, 1981; Telecommunications, 1986; New Television Technologies, 1986. Sunday sch. tchr. Manhattan Beach Community Ch. (Congregational), 1975—; puppeteer for handicapped KOLB Family Players, Manhattan Beach, 1977; team reporter Little League, Manhattan Beach, 1975-81; election clk., Manhattan Beach, 1980. Danforth assoc., 1978; recipient Student TV grant Mobil Oil Corp., 1979; NEH grantee, 1972; Disting. lectr. Calif. State U., 1983. Mem. Acad. TV Arts and Scis. (bd. govs.; treas. 1977-83), Consortium for Coll. TV (exec. council; chair com. 1970-76), Community Coll. TV Assn. (pres. 1972-73), Western Ednl. Soc. for Telecommunications (conf. chair 1975), Broadcast Edn. Assn. (com. vice-chair 1978), Film and TV Study Ctr. (adv. bd. 1975-77). Democrat. Club: Diploma Plus (adv. bd. 1980-82) (Los Angeles). Home: 1705 The Strand Manhattan Beach CA 90266 Office: Calif State U Nutwood St Fullerton CA 92634

GROSS, MIMI, sculptor, painter; b. N.Y.C. Ed., Bard Coll., 1957-59; Skowhegan Sch. of Painting and Sculpture, Maine, 1959; Kokoschka Sch. of Painting, Salzburg, Austria, 1960. Solo exhbns.: Castagno Gallery, N.Y.C., 1966; Area Gallery, N.Y.C., 1966; Collegiate Sch. for Boys, N.Y.C., 1978; group exhbns. (most recent): Postcards, N.Y.C., 1979, Italy, 1979, numerous others; commd. work: O'Neal's Restaurant, The New Room, N.Y.C., 1978-79, Vera List Graphics, Jewish Mus., N.Y.C., 1983, polychrome outdoor sculpture Wards' Island, N.Y.C., 1983; theater: sets, costumes Seven Days of Mourning, N.Y.C., 1977; costumes Douglas Dunn & Dancers, Foot Rules, 1979, backdrop Echo, 1980; performances: Il Piccolo Circo d'Ombra di Firenze, No. Italy, 1961; Berkeley Eruption, U. Calif.-Berkeley, 1968; Hippodrome Hardware, 1972; numerous films including; Ruckus Manhattan, 1975-76; vis. artist dept. painting Syracuse U., 1978; dept. painting Art Inst., Chgo., 1979; marathon workshop Time & Space Theater Ltd., N.Y.C., 1980. Author: Ruckus Manhattan, 1977. Nat. Endowment Arts grantee, 1977, 85; Am. Acad. and Inst. Arts and Letters grantee, 1981; N.Y. Found. Arts grantee, 1985.

GROSS, NANCY LYNN, accountant; b. St. Joseph, Mo., Nov. 2, 1952; d. Claude C. and Helen Fay (Oliver) Boner; B.S. in Acctg., U. Ky., 1975; M.B.A., U. Cin., 1980; m. Gary Lloyd Gross, May 29, 1976. With Armco Steel Corp., Kansas City, Mo. 1974-80, Middletown, Ohio, 1980, credit rep., Middletown, 1975-80; acct. Armco, Inc., Middletown, 1980-81, sr. acct., 1981-85, supr. acctg., 1985—; founder Miami Valley Acctg. Service, 1985—; lectr. Miami U., Middletown, 1980—. Mem. Beta Alpha Psi, Beta Gamma Sigma. Baptist. Home: 607 S Highview Rd Middletown OH 45042

GROSS, PRIVA BAIDAFF, art historian; b. Wieliczka, Poland, June 19, 1911; came to U.S., 1941, naturalized, 1955; d. Israel and Leopolda (Friedman) Baidaff; Ph.M., Jagellonian U., Cracow, Poland, 1937; postgrad. (N.Y. U. scholar 1945-47), N.Y. U. Inst. Fine Arts, 1945-48; m. Feliks Gross, July 25, 1937; 1 dau., Eva Helena Gross Friedman. Mem. faculty Queensborough Community Coll., CUNY, 1961-81, assoc. prof. art history, 1971-81, ret., 1981, co-chmn. art and music dept., 1966-68, chmn. art dept., 1968-74, dir. coll. gallery, 1968-77. SUNY grantee, 1967. Mem. AAUW (dir. 1972-76, 1980-82), Coll. Art Assn. Am., Soc. Archtl. Historians, Gallery Assn. N.Y. State (dir. 1972-73), N.Y. State Assn. Jr. Colls., AAUP, Polish Inst. Arts and Scis. Am., Council Gallery and Exhbn. Dirs. (dir. 1970-72). Contbr. articles, revs. to profl. publns. Home: 310 W 85th St New York NY 10024

GROSS, RUTH TAUBENHAUS, physician; b. Bryan, Tex., June 24, 1920; d. Jacob and Esther (Hirshenson) Taubenhaus; B.A., Barnard Coll., 1941; M.D., Columbia U., 1944; m. Reuben H. Gross, Jr., Aug. 22, 1942; (div. June 1952); 1 son, Gary E. Intern, Charity Hosp., New Orleans, 1944; resident in pediatrics Tulane U., New Orleans, 1945, Columbia U., N.Y.C., 1946, 47; instr. Radcliffe Infirmary, Oxford, Eng., 1949-50; instr. pediatrics Stanford (Calif.) U., 1950-53, asst. prof., 1953-56, asso. prof., 1956-60, prof., 1973—, acting exec. pediatrics, 1957-59, assoc. dean student affairs, 1973-75, dir. div. gen. and ambulatory pediatrics, from 1975, dir. Stanford-Children's Ambulatory Care Center, from 1980, nat. study dir. Infant Health and Devel. Program, 1983—; assoc. prof. pediatrics, co-dir. div. human genetics Albert Einstein Coll. Medicine, Yeshiva U., N.Y.C., 1960-64, prof. pediatrics, 1964-66; clin. prof. pediatrics U. Calif. Med. Center, San Francisco, 1966-73; dir. dept. pediatrics Mt. Zion Hosp. and Med. Center, San Francisco, 1966-73. Commonwealth fellow human genetics Instituto de Genetica, Pavia, Italy, 1959-60. Mem. Inst. Medicine, Nat. Acad. Scis., Am. Fedn. Clin. Research, Am. Pediatric Soc., Soc. Pediatric Research, Am. Acad. Pediatrics, Ambulatory Pediatric Assn., Soc. Research in Child Devel., Phi Beta Kappa, Alpha Omega Alpha, Sigma Xi. Contbr. articles to profl. jours. Office: Dept Pediatrics Stanford U Med Sch Stanford CA 94305

GROSS, SHERRI DENISE, marketing assistant, graphic artist, copy writer; b. Alhambra, Calif., Aug. 18, 1959; d. Burton and Lea Dee (Zorman) G. B.A. in Communications, Calif. State U.-Fullerton, 1982. Intern advt. dept. Nodstrom, Costa Mesa, Calif., asst. advt. mgr., 1978-81; advt. mgr. Designer Fashions/Anaheim Apparel (Calif.), 1981-82; graphics editor Daily Titan, Fullerton, Calif., 1982; account exec. The Englander Group, Newport Beach, Calif., 1982-83; mktg. asst. Bekins Moving & Storage Co., Glendale, Calif., 1983—. Mem. Nat. Assn. Female Execs., Gamma Phi Beta. Democrat. Jewish. Home: 18002 Prado Circle Villa Park CA 92667 Office: Bekins Moving & Storage Co 910 Grand Central Ave Glendale CA 91201

GROSS, SHIRLEY MARIE, farm manager, artist; b. Beardstown, Ill., Apr. 4, 1917; d. Robert Lee and Marie Elizabeth (Ellrich) Northcutt; A.A., Stephens Coll., 1936; B.A., Ill. Coll., 1938; m. Carl David Gross, Oct. 4, 1941; children—David Lee, Susan Jean Gross Conner. Med. technologist St. John's Hosp., Springfield, Ill., 1938-41, Schmidt Meml. Hosp., Beardstown, 1957-64; librarian Beardstown Public Library, 1970-76; pvt. practice farm mgmt., Beardstown, 1958—; dir. First State Bank Beardstown; exhibitor various art shows, Ill., 1969—. Bd. dirs. Beardstown Hosp., Head Start; trustee First Congregational Ch. Beardstown. Winner art awards various shows. Mem. Am. Soc. Clin. Pathologists (med. technologist), Beardstown Bus. and Profl. Women's Investment Club, Beardstown Restoration Soc. Jacksonville Area Artist League. Democrat. Clubs: Beardstown Woman's, Cass County Council for the Arts, Beardstown Bus. and Profl. Women's (pres., 1968-70). Home: 1116 Jefferson Beardstown IL 62618

GROSSBERG, ESTHER ROSENSTEIN, travel executive, radio commentator; b. Chgo., Mar. 28, 1924; d. Louis E. and Mae (Kazer) Rosenstein; m. Frederick S. Grossberg, Nov. 19, 1944; children—Michael Lee, David Alan. B.A., U. Miami, 1944, postgrad Law Sch., Coral Gables, 1945-46. Sales exec. Seitlin & Co., Miami, 1946-52, Tours & Travel, Houston, 1960-64, Travel Unltd., 1964-66; sales mgr. Houston Travel Ctr., 1966-68; dir. sales Diners Fugazy Travel, Houston, 1968-69; pres. Esther Grossberg Travel Inc., Houston, 1970—, Group Travel Ctr., 1970—. Travel columnist, Texan, Southwestern Argus, Westside News, Forward Times, Pioneer, 1972-79; host weekly radio show Ask the Expert, KTRH, 1970-76, Around the World with Esther, KTSU, 1984—. Mem. Assn. Retail Travel Agts. (nat. bd. dirs. 1980-82, v.p. Tex. region 1980-82), Soc. Incentive Travel Execs., Cruise Lines Internat. Assn., Pacific Area Travel Assn., Houston Exec. Women in Travel. Avocations: Needlepoint; dancing; gourmet cooking. Home: 5555 Del Monte St Apt 505 Houston TX 77056 Office: Esther Grossberg Travel Inc 6300 W Loop S Bellaire TX 77401

GROSSETETE, GINGER LEE, city official; b. Riverside, Calif., Feb. 9, 1936; d. Lee Roy and Bonita Beryl (Wheeler) Taylor; m. Alec Paul Grossetete, June 8, 1954; children—Elizabeth Gay Grossetete Blech, Teri Lee Grossetete Zeni. B.A. cum laude, U.N.Mex., 1974, M.P.A., 1978. Sr. ctr. supr. Office Sr. Affairs, City of Albuquerque, 1974-77, asst. dir., 1977—. Contbr. articles to profl. jours. Recipient Gov.'s Disting. Pub. Service award; Fellow award Nat. Recreation and Park Assn. Mem. Nat. Recreation and Park Assn. (dir. 1983-84), N.Mex. Recreation and Park Assn., Am. Soc. Pub. Adminstrn., Southwest Soc. Aging (pres. 1984-85), Chi Omega. Avocations: tennis; water skiing; snow skiing; jogging. Home: 517 La Veta NE Albuquerque NM 87108 Office: Office Sr Affairs 714 7th St SW Albuquerque NM 87102

GROSSHANS, MERILYN LA VONNE, librarian, consultant; b. Plaza, N.D., July 16, 1939; d. John Rudolph and Lillian (Erickson) Willey Peterson; m. Dennis Arthur Grosshans, June 20, 1942 (div. Sept. 1983). B.A., Northwestern Coll., Mpls., 1961; postgrad. Valley City State Coll., 1962; M.L.S., U. N.D., 1969. Tchr. Engish, Stanley (N.D.) High Sch., 1963-65, Williston (N.D.) High, 1965-67; children's librarian Los Angeles Pub. Library, 1969-70; librarian Vermillion (S.D.) High, 1970-72, Las Vegas (Nev.) High Sch., Clark County Sch. Dist., 1973—. Contbr. articles to profl. jours. Vol. worker Nev. State Prison, Jean and Indian Springs. Recipient Exceptional Tchr. award Clark County Bd. Sch. Trustees and PTA, 1983. Mem. ALA (com. best books for young adults, young adult div. 1970-82, mem. assn. Specialized and Coop. Agys.), Nev. Library Assn. (membership chair 1984-85), Nev. Assn. Sch. Librarians (pres. 1983), Am. Assn. Sch. Librarians (com. 1984—), Clark County Sch. Library Assn. (pres. 1976-77), LWV, Alpha Delta Kappa. Democrat. Home: 7129 Grasswood Las Vegas NV 89117 Office: Las Vegas High Sch 315 S 7th St Las Vegas NV 89101

GROSSMAN, BETTIE SILVERMAN, social worker, mental health center administrator; b. Springfield, Mass., Sept. 20, 1946; d. Sol S. and Sara (Cogan) Silverman; m. Barry Gene Grossman, June 20, 1971. B.S. with honors, U. Ill., 1968; M.S.W., Adelphi U., 1970. Psychiat. social worker Ill. State Psychiat. Inst., Chgo., 1970-71; Devel. Services Ctr., Champaign, Ill., 1971-72; treatment team leader Crisis Care Ctr., Danville, Ill., 1972-73; coordinator psychiat. social services Mercy Hosp., Urbana, Ill., 1973-77; asst. program dir. South Ctr. office Brevard County Mental Health Ctr., Inc., Melbourne, Fla., 1977-80; program coordinator Riverdale Mental Health Ctr., Bronx, N.Y., 1981; program dir. day hosp. and south county out-patient services Brevard Mental Health Ctrs. and Hosp. Inc., Melbourne, 1981—; field instr. Sch. Social Work U., Ill., Urbana, 1972-77; instr. in psychology Parkland Community Coll., Champaign, Ill., 1975-77; adj. prof. Sch. Social Work, U. Central Fla., Cocoa, 1977-78, Rollins Coll., Patrick AFB, Fla., 1978-80, 83—; field instr. Sch. Social Work, Fla. State U. 1979-80, 81—; pvt. practice clin. social work, Champaign and Urbana, Ill., 1974-77. Com. mem. N.W. Bronx Council on Aging (N.Y.), 1981, Council on Services to Aged, Bronx, 1981; reviewer Champus Peer, 1984—. Edmund J. James scholar, 1964; NIMH trainee Adelphi U., Garden City, N.Y., 1968; VA trainee Adelphi U. and VA, N.Y.C., 1969. Mem. Nat. Assn. Social Workers, Acad. Cert. Social Workers, Nat. Assn. Social Workers Register Clin. Social Workers, Am. Assn. Partial Hosps., Phi Beta Kappa, Psi Chi, Phi Kappa Phi. Home: 530 Sherwood Ave Satellite Beach FL 32937 Office: Brevard Mental Health Ctrs and Hosp Inc 400 E Sheridan Rd Melbourne FL 32901

GROSSMAN, ELIZABETH KORN, nursing adminstr., coll. dean; b. S.I., N.Y., May 15, 1923; d. George and Ethel (Elliot) Korn; B.A., Hunter Coll., 1944; M.N., Western Res. U., 1947; M.S. in Nursing Edn., Ind. U., 1960, Ed.D., 1972; m. Thomas Grossman, Feb. 23, 1952; 1 son, Theodore. Researcher, Columbia Carbon Corp., Bklyn., 1944; staff nurse, asst. head nurse, head nurse, supr. Univ. Hosp., Cleve., 1947-52; Instr. Mt. Sinai Hosp. Sch. Nursing, Cleve., 1952-53; supr. maternity nursing Meth. Hosp., Indpls., 1953-57; instr. maternity nursing, 1957-59; instr. DePauw U., Indpls., 1959-62; asst. prof., asso. prof., grad. maternity Ind. U., Indpls., 1959-66, chairperson grad.-undergrad. maternity nursing, 1966-73, dean Sch. Nursing, 1973—; civilian nat. cons. U.S. Air Force Nurse Corps, 1983—. Fellow Am. Acad. Nursing; mem. Am. Nurses Assn., Nat. League Nursing, Am. Assn. Colls. Nursing (treas. 1981-85), Nurses Assn. of Am. Coll. Ob-Gyn, Midwest Alliance Nursing (treas. 1979-81), Sigma Xi, Sigma Theta Tau (Disting. Service award 1977), Am. Assn. Maternal Child Health, Delta Kappa Gamma, Alpha Xi Delta. Republican. Roman Catholic. Contbr. articles to profl. jours. Home: 11201 Westfield Blvd Carmel IN 46032 Office: 610 Barnhill Dr Indianapolis IN 46223

GROSSMAN, GAIL LOUISE, county official; b. St. Louis, Feb. 1, 1955; d. Milton Sharp and Eleanor Louise (Gray) G. B.A., Washington U., St. Louis, 1977; J.D., Georgetown U., 1980. Bar: Fla. 1982. Law clk., bailiff 11th Jud. Circuit Fla., Miami, 1981-82; asst. state atty. State Atty.'s Office, Miami, 1982—. Contbg. editor Georgetown U. Law Weekly, 1979-80. Mem. ABA, Fla. Bar Assn., Dade County Bar Assn., Fla. Assn. Women Lawyers, Assn. Trial Lawyers Am., NOW. Office: State Atty's Office 1351 NW 12th St Miami FL 33125

GROSSMAN, LISA ROBBIN, clinical psychologist, lawyer; b. Chgo., Jan. 22, 1952; d. Samuel R. and Sarah (Kruger) G. B.A. with highest distinction and departmental honors in Psychology, Northwestern U., 1974, J.D. cum laude, 1979, Ph.D., 1982. Bar: Ill. 1981; registered psychologist, Ill. Jud. intern, U.S. Supreme Ct., Washington, 1975; pre-doctoral psychology intern Michael Reese Hosp. and Med. Center, Chgo., 1979-80; therapist Homes for Children, Chgo., 1980-83; psychologist Psychiat. Inst., Cir. Ct. Cook County, Chgo., 1981—; pvt. practice, 1984—; invited participant workshop HHS, Rockville, Md., 1981. Contbr. articles to profl. jours. Mem. Am. Psychol. Assn., Ill. Psychol. Assn., Chgo. Assn. for Psychoanalytic Psychologists (parliamentarian 1982), ABA, Ill. State Bar Assn., Chgo. Bar Assn., Mortar Bd., Phi Beta Kappa, Shi-Ai, Alpha Lambda Delta. Office Psychiat Inst Circuit Ct Cook County 2650 S California Ave Chicago IL 60608

GROSSMAN, ROBERTA ROCHELLE, oil company executive; b. N.Y.C., Dec. 27, 1944; d. Philip and Ruth (Brand) Silverstein; divorced 1980; children—Irene Beth, Adam Edward. B.A., Bklyn. Coll., 1965, M.A., 1967; postgrad. in bus. law Middlesex Community Coll., 1979. Office mgr. D. Dubin, Esq., N.Y.C., 1972-76; tchr. English and drama Woodbridge (N.J.) Bd. Edn. 1979-80; freight forwarder Southwestern Trading Co., Houston, 1981; facilities supr. Geosource Inc., Houston, 1981—; rep. Houston Bus. Council, 1982—. Vice pres. N.J. br Brandis U. Nat. Women's Com., 1976, editor cookbook, 1975. Fellow Bklyn. Coll., 1965. Mem. Adminstrv. Mgmt. Soc., Bus. Forms Mgmt. Assn., Internat. Facilities Mgmt. Assn., Purchasing Mgmt. Assn. Houston. Jewish. Home: 7702 Teal Run Houston TX 77071 Office: Geosource Inc 2700 Post Oak Blvd Suite 2000 Houston TX 77056

GROSSMANN, AGNES, orchestra conductor; d. Ferdinand Grossmann. Studied piano with Bruno Seidlhofer and Lili Kraus, touring N.Am. in 1972; studied conducting Hochschule fur Musik, Vienna, Austria. Formerly asst. condr. Vienna Jeunesse Choir, guest condr. Vienna Chamber Orch., condr. Vienna Singakademie choir; now condr. Chamber Players Toronto, Ont., Can., 1984—; vis. prof. U. Ottawa, 1981-83. Office: Chamber Players Toronto Town Hall St Lawrence Centre 24 Ryerson Ave Toronto ON M5T 2P3 Canada*

GROTE, E. ENID (MRS. JOHN HENRY GROTE, JR.), artist, librarian, editor; b. N.Y.C., Sept. 26, 1909; d. Lewis and Mary Katherine (Engle) Granath; student (Louise Graham Hinsdale scholar) Columbia U., 1928-31, Sch. Library Sci. and Sch. Journalism, 1933-35; m. John H. Grote, Jr., Dec. 28, 1935 (dec.). With Free Public Library, East Orange, N.J., 1932-37; mem. editorial staff fgn. and Washington news AP, N.Y.C., 1937-43; chief librarian, organizer news reference library Pan Am. World Airways, N.Y.C., 1943-44; organizer U.S. Info. Libraries, Office War Info., U.S. State Dept., N.Y.C. and Washington, 1944-45; chief librarian Hort. Soc. N.Y., N.Y.C., 1947-61; free-lance cons. editor to N.Y.C. pubs.; hort. manuscript evaluator, 1950-61; editor, contbr. book revs. and articles The Bulletin; group shows include: Woodstock Artists Assn., N.Y., Catskill Art Soc., Hurleyville, N.Y., also other art assn. shows, pvt. galleries; represented in pvt. collections. Mem. Spl. Libraries Assn., Woodstock Artists Assn., Catskill Art Soc., Internat. Soc. Artists, LWV, Internat. Platform Assn., Smithsonian Assocs., Nat. Trust for Historic Preservation, Nat. Mus. Women in Arts (charter). Republican. Presbyterian. Club: Woodstock Country. Home and Studio: 341 Tulip Blvd Port Saint Lucie FL 33453

GROTECLOSS, NONA LOUISE, ednl. adminstr.; b. Sayre, Pa., Jan. 23, 1925; d. Stanley Burton and Florence Kimmick (Bach) Severance; B.A., Syracuse U., 1945; M.A. in Guidance, U. South Fla., 1968, M.A. in Adult Edn., 1975; Ed.D., Nova U., 1979; m. Robert Grotecloss, Apr. 15, 1952; children—Robert, Gary, Steven, Bruce. Case Worker Dept. Vet. Assistance, Onondaga County, N.Y., 1945-50; social worker Fla. Welfare Dept., St. Petersburg, 1951-66; guidance coordinator St. Petersburg Vocat. Tech. Inst., 1969-77; counselor Pasco County Adult Edn., Dade City, Fla., 1977-80, supr. adult and community edn., Land-O'Lakes, Fla., 1980—. Mem. Am. Personnel and Guidance Assn., Fla. Personnel and Guidance Assn., Am. Vocat. Assn., Fla. Assn. Sch. Adminstrs., Adult Edn. Assn., Fla. Adult Edn. Assn., Commn. Adult Basic Edn., Pasco County Adminstrs. and Suprs. Assn., Tampa Bay Regional Planning Council, Phi Delta Kappa, Bus. and Profl. Women's Club, Alpha Chi Omega. Methodist. Home: PO Box 1661 Dade City FL 33525 Office: Pasco County Adult and Community Education 2609 US Hwy 41 N Land-O'Lakes FL 33539

GROTH, BETTY, conservationist, author, photographer; b. Oak Park, Ill.; d. Herman A. and Bertha L. (Luepke) G.; grad. Vassar Coll., 1932. Sec., Oak Park YMCA, 1935-42; sec. Ill. Commn. for Handicapped Children, 1943-46; pvt. sec. Chgo. Assn. of Commerce and Industry, 1947-53, Chgo. Heart Assn., 1953-75. Mem. Save-The-Dunes Council, North Central Audubon Council; sec., dir. Natural Resources Council of Ill., 1967-71, v.p., 1969-71; v.p., dir. Du Page County Clean Streams, 1967-69; founder, chmn. Northern Conservation Cabinet, 1971-75; landscape gardener Audubon Sanctuary, Wayne, Ill., 1977-79; color film nature lectr. Mem. Nat. Audubon Soc., Ill. Audubon Soc. (v.p. conservation, dir. 1962-73, sec. bd. dirs. 1973-74), Big Bluestem Audubon Soc. (dir., sec.), Du Page Audubon Soc., Nat. Wildlife Fedn., Conservation Explorers Club (pres. 1975-76), Morton Arboretum, Sarasota Jungle Gardens, Am. Bald Eagle Club. Baptist. Club: Wis. Vassar. Author: Open Spaces in Illinois, 1962; Surprise in the North Woods, 1966; Wildlife by John Burroughs Cabin, 1967; King's Ransom to Save a Prairie, 1968; Ivory Bills Found Alive in Texas Big Thicket, 1969; Great Swamp Wildlife Refuge Versus Jetport, 1970; The Fate of Thorn Creek Woods, 1971; Man's Dominion of the Green Earth, 1972; Country Estate, 1973; King of Sky, Land and Water, 1974; North Woods Shoreline, 1975; Vanished Illinois Prairie Returns, 1976; Florida Conservation and Environmental Survey, 3 vols. for Conservation Ctr., Univ. Wyo., 1983, 4 vols. for Vassar Coll. Library, 1984; Wisconsin Wilderness, 3 vols. for Conservation Ctr., Univ. Wyo., 1985; Yellowstone Park 1914; North with Springtime Florida to Maine, 4 vols. for Vassar Coll. Library, 1986. Contbr. articles to profl. jours. Home: Gull Shores Gills Rock Ellison Bay WI 54210

GROTTA, EMILY HARRIET, public information director; b. Newark, Jan. 27, 1946; d. John I. and Florence (Lieb) Slavin; m. James Charles Grotta, Aug. 22, 1968 (div. Oct. 1981); children—Amy, Jacob. B.A., U. Mich., 1968; M.A., U. Colo., 1977. Editorial asst. Coward-McCann, Inc., N.Y.C., 1967-68; reporter Neshoba Democrat., Philadelphia, Miss., 1972-74, Haverhill Gazette (Mass.), 1977-79, Houston Post, 1979-85; dir. pub. info. Harris County Hosp. Dist., 1985—; journalist-in-residence U. Houston, 1983. Mem. Edn. Writers Assn. (bd. dirs. 1983-84), Kappa Tau Alpha, Sigma Delta Chi (v.p., bd. dirs. Tex. Gulf Coast chpt. 1980-83). Jewish. Home: 5431 Paisley Houston TX 77096 Office: Harris County Hist Dist PO Box 66769 Houston TX 77269

GROTTA, SANDRA BROWN, interior designer; b. Detroit, June 7, 1934; d. John Leonard and Ada Victor Brown; student U. Mich., 1952-55, N.Y. Sch. Interior Design, 1964; m. Louis William Grotta, Sept. 8, 1955; children—Thomas Howard, Tracy Ann. Sr. partner s.g. Interiors, Maplewood, N.J., 1964—. Mem. Am. Soc. Interior Designers. Home: Maplewood NJ

GROTZINGER, LAUREL ANN, educator, univ. dean, b. Truman, Minn., Apr. 15, 1935; d. Edward F. and Marian Gertrude (Greeley) G.; B.A., Carleton Coll., 1957; M.S., U. Ill., 1958, Ph.D., 1964. Instr., asst. librarian Ill. State U., 1958-62; asst. prof. Western Mich. U., Kalamazoo, 1964-66, asso. prof., 1966-68, prof., 1968—, asst. dir. Sch. Librarianship, 1965-72, dean, chief research officer Grad. Coll., 1979—, interim dir. Sch. Library and Info. Sci., from 1982. Mem. ALA (sec.-treas. Library History Roundtable 1973-74, chair elect 1983—), Assn. Library and Info. Sci. Edn. Acad. Mgmt., Mich. Acad. Sci., Arts and Letters (v.p. 1980-81, pres.-elect 1981-83, pres. 1983—), Am. Assn. for Higher Edn., Council Grad. Schs., Nat. Council Univ. Research Adminstrs., Mich. Council Grad. Deans (chmn. 1983—), AAUP (sec. W.M. chpt. 1968-70), Phi Beta Kappa (pres. S.W. Mich. 1977-78), Beta Phi Mu (v.p., pres. Kappa chpt.), Pi Delta Epsilon, Alpha Beta Alpha. Author: The Power and the Dignity, 1966; mem. editorial bd. Jour. Edn. for Librarianship, 1973-77; contbr. articles to profl. publs.

GROVE, BEVERLY JONES, business executive; b. Kansas City, Mo., Sept. 9, 1932; d. Elmer George and Mildred L. (Coates) Jones; m. James Robert Grove, May 31, 1952; children—Hollis, Jay Robert, James A., Jeffrey J. B.S., Kans. State U., 1953; M.A., Goddard Coll., 1979. Cert. tchr., Kans., Tex., Okla. Tchr., Ashland (Kans) pub. schs., 1953-54, Oklahoma City pub. schs., 1954-55, Amarillo (Tex.) pub. schs., 1955-57; exec. v.p. JBH Assocs., Houston, 1978—, JBH Air Charter, Houston, 1978—; pres. JBH Travel, Houston, 1983—; dir. Interface. Contbr. articles to mags. and newspapers. Sec. bd. dirs. YMCA, Houston, 1974-76. Mem. Nat. Bus. Aircraft Assn., Airplane Owners and Pilots Assn., Chi. Omega. Republican. Presbyterian. Clubs: Houston Racquet, Braeburn Country. Home: 343 Knipp Forest Houston TX 77024 Office: JBH Air Charter 8402 Nelms St Houston TX 77061

GROVE, HELEN HARRIET, historian, artist; b. South Bend, Ind.; d. Samuel Harold and LaVerne Mae (Drescher) Grove; grad. Bayle Sch. Design, Meinzinger Found., 1937-39, Washington U., 1940-42; spl. studies, Paris, France. Owner studios of historic research and illustration, St. Louis, Chgo., 1943—; dir. archives, bus. history research Sears, Roebuck & Co., 1951-67; com. missions art and research for Northwestern U., Chgo.-Sears Roebuck & Co. Home: 6326 N Clark St Chicago IL 60626 Studio: 6328 N Clark St Chicago IL 60626

GROVE, JEAN DONNER, sculptor; b. Washington, May 15, 1912; d. Frederick Gregory and Georgia V. (Gartrell) Donner; m. Edward R. Grove, June 24, 1936; children—David Donner, Eric Donner. Student Cornell U., 1932, Hill Sch. of Sculpture, 1934-35, Corcoran Sch. Art, 1935-37, 42-44, Cath. U. Am., 1936-37, Phila. Mus. Art Sch., 1967; B.S., Wilson Tchrs. Coll., 1939. One-man shows: Wilson Tchrs. Coll., 1939, Grove Family Exhbns., Cayuga Mus. History and Art, Auburn, N.Y., 1964, Episcopal Acad. Gallery, Phila., 1966; group shows include: Pa. Acad. Fine Arts, Phila., 1947, 48, 51, 53, NAD, N.Y.C., 1949, 78, 81, 83, Nat. Sculpture Soc. at Archtl. League, N.Y.C., Topeka, 1957 and Lever House, N.Y.C., 1974, 75, Equitable Gallery, N.Y.C., 1976, 78, 83, Salmagundi Club, N.Y.C., 1985, Art U.S.A., Madison Sq. Garden, N.Y.C., 1958, Corcoran Gallery Art, Washington, 1943-47, Internat. Gallery, Washington, 1946, Phila. Mus. Art, 1955, 59, 62, Phil. Art Alliance, 1957, 60, 66, Phila. Civic Ctr., 1958, Flagler Art Ctr., West Palm Beach, Fla., 1972, Norton Gallery Art, West Palm Beach, 1974, 81; represented in permanent collections Rosenwald Collection, Phila., Ch. of Holy Comforter, Drexel Hill, Pa., Fine Arts Commn., City Hall, Phila.; numerous portrait commns., garden figures and fountains, 1940—. Recipient 1st prize sculpture Nat. Mus. Washington, 1946; 1st prize sculpture Arts Club, 1946, Portrait prize, 1947; Morris Goodman award John Herron Art Mus., Indpls., 1957; Competition prize for design and sculpture Artists Equity, Phila. award, 1960; Tallix Foundry award Nat. Sculpture Soc. Bicentennial Exhbn., Equitable Gallery, N.Y.C., 1976, Acad. of Italy with gold medal, 1979; Humane award Animal Rescue League Palm Beach, 1974, 80; Golden Centaur award Accademia Italia, 1982; others. Mem. Nat. Sculpture Soc., NAD (assoc.), Artists Equity Assn. (dir. Phila. chpt. 1964-66), Phila. Art Alliance, Soc. of Four Arts, Norton Gallery Art, Northwood Inst. (nat. women's bd. 1981—), Art for Olympia (adv. bd.), Soc. Washington Artists, Fedn. Internat. de Medaille, English Speaking Union, Animal Rescue League of Palm Beaches (com. chmn. 1972—, dir. 1975—), St. Mary's Guild of Episcopal Ch. Women (v.p. 1974-76), Kappa Delta Pi. Club: Poinciana (Palm Beach). Address: Sea-Lake Studio 3215 S Flagler Dr West Palm Beach FL 33405

GROVE, KATHRYN MOWREY (MRS. D. DWIGHT GROVE), church worker; b. Harrisburg, Pa., Jan. 11, 1914; d. D. Floyd and Eva (Shearer) Mowrey; A.B. cum laude, Lebanon Valley Coll., 1934; m. D. Dwight Grove, July 11, 1939; children—David, Carol (Mrs. Ronald W. Miller). Tchr. high sch., New Cumberland, Pa., 1934-39. Missionary, Evang. U.B. Ch., Sierra Leone, West Africa, 1939-41; mem. bd. Christian edn. East Pa. Conf., 1957-62, children's work council, 1957-62; v.p. Pa. Council Chs., 1964-68; mem. fgn. student com., dept. united ch. women Greater Phila. Council Chs., 1960-64; pres. Women's Soc. World Service, Phila. 3d Ch., 1964-67; pres. East Pa. Conf. br. Women's Soc. World Service, 1957-62, mem. gen. program com., 1957-62, mem. com. leadership edn., 1963-67, dept. health and welfare, 1963-67, mem. nat. council, 1963-68; pres. Gen. Women's Soc. World Service; sec. jud. council United Methodist Ch., 1968-76; trustee Eastern Pa. Conf. United Meth. Ch., 1976-82; mem. bus. and fin. com. Pa. Council Chs. Founder Jr. League, New Cumberland, 1936; pres. Phila. Story League, 1955-57; chmn. 20th biennial conv. Nat. Story League, Phila., 1964; pres. Birney Sch. P.T.A., Phila., 1960-61; speaker various ch. meetings, conv. confs. Mem. women's planning com. Japan Internat. Christian U. Found., Inc. Trustee, Lebanon Valley Coll., 1968—, Logan United Meth. Ch., 1971-79. Mem. AAUW, Pa. Folklore Soc., Elfreth's Assn. Republican. Mem. Order Eastern Star. Contbr. articles to religious publs. Home: 4639 Magnolia Commons Greensboro NC 27405

GROVE, PATRICIA LYNN, lawyer; b. Milw., May 8, 1949; d. George Hale and Audrey Edith (Moenschel) Grove. B.A., U. Wis., 1971; M.S.W., Wash. U.-St. Louis, 1972; J.D., U. Tulsa, 1981. Bar: Wis. Social worker Waukesha County Welfare Dept. (Wis.), 1973-76, Milw. County Hosp., 1976-77, Oak Creek Schs. (Wis.), 1977-78; judicial clk. Wis. Sup. Ct., Madison, 1981-82; mem. firm Walther & Halling, Milw., 1982—. Contbr. articles to profl. jours. Mem. ABA, Wis. Bar Assn. Home: 2562 N Prospect Ave Milwaukee WI 53211 Office: Walther & Halling 222 E Mason St Milwaukee WI 53202

GROVE, SUSAN HARRINGTON, wholesale and retail sales executive, political consultant; b. Chgo., Apr. 20, 1952; d. Edward Page and Mary (Denson) Harrington; m. Richard Vernon Clark, III, May 5, 1969 (div. 1974); m. William Franklin Grove, Aug. 21, 1982. B.A. in Polit. Sci., U. Chgo., 1973; postgrad. Republican Campaign Mgmt. Coll., Berlitz Sch. Langs., L'Ecole des Trois Gourmandes. Field dir. Com. to Re-elect the Pres., Nixon/Agnew campaign, 1972; Houston Flournoy for Gov. Calif., 1974; coordinator scheduling and fund raising Gerald Ford for Pres., 1975-76; dep. dir. advance scheduling, nat. dir. vols. Howard Baker for Pres., 1979-80; campaign mgr. Helen D. Bentley for U.S. Congress, 1980, Mick Staton for U.S. Congress, 1980; dir. caucus hearings Rep. Nat. Conv., Detroit, 1980, dep. dir. surrogate scheduling Reagan-Bush Presdl. Campaign Com., 1980; dir. cultural events Presdl. Inaugural Com., 1980-81; polit. cons., scheduling analyst Emory Follmar for Gov. Ala., 1981, Thompson for Gov. Ill., 1981; exec. asst. to v.p. Jamesway Corp., Secaucas, N.Y., 1977-79; owner, pres. Am. Arts, Lancaster, Pa., 1982—. Founder Students for Nixon, New Eng., 1967-68; jr. co-chmn. Feather Ball, N.Y.C., 1969-77, April in Paris Ball, N.Y.C., 1970-75; chmn. Atlanta Polo Ball, 1972, Tennis and Crumpets Charitable Benefit, Lancaster, 1984; bd. dirs. Lancaster Summer Arts Festival, 1983. Club: Lancaster Country. Avocations: tennis; squash; golf; painting.

GROVER, BEATRICE B., artist; b. Bklyn.; d. Jeremiah Robinson and Grace (Benedict) Bears; student NAD, 1920-22, Solon Borglum's Sch. Sculpture, 1923; studies lithography with George Miller; m. Allen Grover, Jan. 24, 1929; children—Loraine, Robinson Allen. Exhibited in one-man shows Contemporaries, 1955, 65, Guild Hall, East Hampton, 1978; exhibited in group shows Cin. Mus., 1950-56, NAD, 1951, Soc. Am. Graphic Artists, 1952-54, Bklyn. Mus., 1954, Nat. Assn. Women Artists, 1949-65, Inst. History and Art, Smithsonian Instn., 1965, Guild Hall, East Hampton, 1962-74, Ashawagh Hall, East Hampton, 1971-74, Benefit Auction Channel 13, 1974, Benefit Auction Parke-Bernet, 1975; mem. Art in Embassies program, 1968; represented in permanent collection Mus. Modern Art, N.Y.C. Mem. Nat. Assn. Women Artist. Author, illustrator: Broad Stripes and Bright Stars, 1941, External Infections of the Eye, 1963, 3d edit., 1984; Rhyming Word Games, 1964. Med. illustrator dept. ophthalmology N.Y.U.-Bellevue Hosp., 1956-63. Home: Box 81 Lily Pond Lane East Hampton NY 11937

GROVES, MILDRED, employment agency executive, consultant; b. Jersey City, June 30, 1927; d. Joseph James and Estelle (Di Paola) Patete; m. Richard Sage Groves, June 4, 1948; children—Richard, Gary. B.A., Rutgers U., 1977; cert. Fashion Inst. Tech., 1947. Sec. Ronson Corp., Newark, 1949-51; coop. advt. mgr., Woodbridge, N.J., 1956-58; personnel asst. Ingersoll Rand, East Brunswick, N.J., 1969-71; owner Network Employment, East Brunswick, 1977—; cons. in field. Sec. East Brunswick Women's Democratic Club, 1960-s, treas., 1970's. Mem. Assn. Bus. Women of Am., N.J. Women's Network, N.J. Assn. Personnel Cons. Roman Catholic. Avocations: boating; biking; painting. Home: 18-11 Civic Center Dr East Brunswick NJ 08816 Office: Network Employment 735 Route 18 East Brunswick NJ 08816

GROWE, JOAN ANDERSON, sec. state Minn.; b. Mpls., Sept. 28, 1935; d. Arthur F. and Lucille M. (Brown) Anderson; B.S., St. Cloud State U., 1956; cert. in spl. edn. U. Minn., 1964; children—Michael, Colleen, David, Patrick. Tchr. elem. pub. schs., Bloomington, Minn., 1956-58; tchr. for exceptional children elem. pub. schs., St. Paul, 1964-65; spl. edn. tchr. St. Anthony (Minn.) Pub. Schs., 1965-66; mem. Minn. Ho. of Reps., 1973-75; sec. of state State of Minn., St. Paul, 1974—; candidate U.S. Senate; mem. adv. com. Fed. Elections Commn.; participant exec. mgmt. program for state and local govt. Harvard U., 1979; mem. Minn. Bd. Investment, Jud. Planning Com. Recipient Minn. Sch. Bell award, 1977, Outstanding Achievement award YWCA, 1978. Mem. Nat. Assn. Secs. of State (pres. 1979-80), Bus. and Profl. Women's Club, Women's Polit. Caucus, Minn. LWV, Common Cause, Nat. Order Women Legislators, NOW, AAUW, Infact, Minn. Women's Network, Ams. for Democratic Action, Citizen's League, Democratic Statewide Elected Ofcls., Minn. Assn. for Retarded Citizens, Minn. Shares for Hunger, Urban Concerns. Mem. Democratic Farm Labor Party. Roman Catholic. Club: Zonta. Office: 180 State Office Bldg Saint Paul MN 55155

GRUBB, KITTY GOLDSMITH, lawyer; b. Bennettsville, S.C., July 29, 1952; d. Harry Simon and Carolyn (Davis) Goldsmith; m. Lawrence Logan Grubb, Aug. 6, 1972. A.B., U. Ala.-Tuscaloosa, 1974; J.D. cum laude, Cumberland Sch. Law, 1977; LL.M. in Taxation, NYU, 1981. Bar: Ala. 1977, U.S. Ct. Appeals (5th cir.) 1979, Tenn. 1981, U.S. Ct. Claims 1981, U.S. Tax Ct. 1981, U.S. Ct. Appeals (4th cir.) 1980, U.S. Dist. Ct. (ea. dist.) Tenn. 1982, U.S. Ct. Appeals (6th and Fed. cirs.) 1984, U.S. Ct. Mil. Appeals 1984. Staff atty. TVA, Knoxville, 1977-79; assoc. Lockridge & Becker, P.C., Knoxville, 1981-82; ptnr. Dunaway, Harrell, Grubb, Van Hook & Cotton, LaFollette, Tenn., 1982-85; assoc. Wagner & Myers, P.C., Knoxville, 1985-86; ptnr. McGehee, Grubb & Currier; P.C., Knoxville, 1986—; lectr. St. Mary's Hosp., Knoxville, Knoxville Women's Ctr., various other orgns.; mem. So. Pension Conf., Atlanta, 1981-82, Am. Pension Conf., N.Y.C., 1981-82. Assoc. editor Cumberland Law Rev., 1975-77. Chmn. fund drive, eastern Tenn. region Cumberland Sch. Law, 1979-80. Recipient Curia Honoris award Cumberland Sch. Law, 1978, cert. merit Cumberland Sch. Law chpt. Phi Delta Phi, 1977, cert. appreciation Knoxville Women's Ctr., 1983-86, Annie P. Selwyn award, 1986. Mem. Knoxville Bar Assn. (continuing legal edn. 1982—), ABA (Tenn. membership chmn. Young Lawyer's Conf. div.), Ala. Bar Assn., Tenn. Bar Assn., Assn. Trial Lawyers Am., Cumberland Law Sch. Alumni Assn., NYU Law Sch. Alumni Assn., U. Ala. Alumni (v.p. eastern Tenn. chpt. 1983, pres. chpt. 1984, merit awards eastern Tenn. chpt. 1982, 83, 84, nat. award 1984), AAUW, Knoxville Assn. Women Execs., Nat. Assn. Women Execs., Knoxville Zool. Soc., Polit. Button Collectors (Dixie chpt., Am. chpt.), Century Club of U. Ala. Alumni (eastern Tenn. chpt.), Omicron Delta Epsilon, Pi Sigma Alpha. Democrat. Methodist. Office: McGehee Grubb & Currier PC 1634 Plaza TowerKnoxville TN 37929

GRUBB, SHIRLEY MCCLURE, corporation executive; b. Belmont, N.C., Sept. 24, 1935; d. Woodrow D. and Emma (Austin) Ferguson; m. Donald Reid Grubb, July 31, 1954; children—Edwin Brian, Joy Donee. Grad. Sacred Heart Coll., Belmont, N.C., 1953. Tech. adminstr. Western Electric Co., Winston-Salem, 1958-62; adminstrv. asst. R.J. Reynolds Tobacco Co., Winston-Salem, 1964-66; adminstrv. asst. Admiral Hamilton Howe, Winston-Salem, 1966-69; adminstrv. asst. Smith Bagley, Winston-Salem and Washington, 1969-80; v.p. Musgrove Plantation, St. Simons Island, Ga., 1980—. Appointed mem. Lady Bird Johnson's Beautification Com., Washington; vol. Davidson County Democratic Party, Lexington, N.C., 1984. Mem. Am. Bus. Womens Assn. (sec. treas. 1969-72), N.C. Garden Club (dist. sec. 1965-67), Am. Found. Research in Medicine (pres. 1972-85). Methodist. Club: Village Garden (pres. 1964-65). Avocations: swimming; dancing; hydroponic gardening; flutist. Home: 431 Linda Ln Welcome NC 27374 Office: Musgrove Plantation 5720 Frederica Rd Saint Simons Island GA 31522

GRUBB, WILMA FAY, county official; b. Morehead, Ky., July 26, 1945; d. Noah E. and Pauline (Cordell) Buckner; m. Earl E. Grubb, Dec. 22, 1962; 1 child, Julie Anne. Student Concord Coll., Athens, W.Va. Sec. Butler Paper Co., Chgo., 1963-64, McCall Coal Co., Bluefield, W.Va., 1964-66; dep. clk. Clk. of the Circuit Ct., Mercer County, W.Va., 1967-79, clk., 1979—. Baptist. Clubs: Mercer County Democrat, Mercer County Women's Dem., Princeton Quota (1st v.p. 1984—). Avocation: camping. Office: Clk Cir Ct Courthouse Princeton WV 24740

GRUBBE, DEBORAH LYNN, chemical engineer; b. Chgo., Apr. 10, 1955; d. Jerome Walter and Domenica Veronica (Salce) G.; B.S. in Chem. Engring. with highest distinction, Purdue U., 1977; cert. (Winston Churchill fellow) U. Cambridge (Eng.), 1978. Registered profl. engr., Del. Chem. engr. E.I. duPont de Nemours & Co., Inc., East Chicago, Ind., 1978, services engr., Edge Moor, Del., 1978-80, area engr. constrn. div., Deepwater, N.J., 1980-81, div. engr., Wilmington, Del., 1981-84, sr. process engr., 1984-85, project engr., 1985—; mem. Nat. Council Engring. Examiners, 1985—. Mem. Am. Inst. Chem. Engrs. (career guidance com. 1985—), Nat. Soc. Profl. Engrs. (project mgr. Constrn. com.), Del. Soc. Profl. Engrs. (bd. dirs. 1985—), Del. Assn. Profl. Engrs. (council 1985—), Soc. Women Engrs., Wilmington Women in Bus. (bd. dirs. 1983-85, chmn. community involvement com. 1985-86), Del. Alliance Profl. Women (bd. dirs. 1983-87), Zeta Tau Alpha (pres. Wilmington alumnae chpt. 1980-82, province pres. Eastern Pa. region 1981-85), Tau Beta Pi, Phi Kappa Phi. Roman Catholic. Home: 103 Falcon Lane Wilmington DE 19808 Office: Project Div E I duPont de Nemours & Co Inc Louviers Bldg Wilmington DE 19898

GRUBBS, DEBRA ANN, real estate broker; b. Washington, Aug. 13, 1953; d. Jack Lewis and Marilyn Miller (McElroy) G.; student Old Dominion U., 1971. Real estate sales mgr. Long & Foster Real Estate, Inc., McLean, Va., 1976-79, real estate broker, 1979-84; pres. New Start Publs., Inc., Sterling, Va., 1981-84; pres. New Start Realty, Inc., Sterling. Mem. N.Am. Vegetarian Soc. PETA. Home: 1036 Riva Ridge Ct Great Falls VA 22066 Office: 100 Glenn Dr Sterling VA 22170

GRUBBS, JEWELL, environmental protection specialist; b. Valdosta, Ga., Feb. 12, 1956; d. Roy Grubbs and Betty Ruth (McFadden) Jenkins. B.A. in Polit. Sci., Clark Coll., 1977; postgrad. Ga. State U., 1985—. Clk.-typist EPA, Atlanta, 1975-78, environ. protection specialist, Atlanta, 1979-84, 85—, Washington, 1984-85; community planner HUD, Atlanta, 1978-79. Bd. dirs. Southeastern YMCA, Atlanta, 1985. Recipient cert. award Combined Fed. Campaign, 1977; Letter of Appreciation, 1977; cert. award EPA, 1976. Mem. Alpha Kappa Alpha. Democrat. Episcopalian. Avocations: reading; sewing; walking. Home: 620 Peachtree St NE 1115 Atlanta GA 30308 Office: EPA 345 Courtland St NE Atlanta GA 30365

GRUBE, REBECCA SUE, elementary educator, educational consultant; b. Lancaster, Pa., June 27, 1945; d. Warren Landis and Ruth Rebecca (Hackman) Newcomer; m. Terry Wayne Grube, Aug. 27, 1966; children—T. David, Joy Lynn, Matthew Warren. Student Juniata Coll., 1963-65; B.A., Franklin and Marshall Coll., 1976; M.Ed., Millersville U., 1979; postgrad. Temple U. Cert. spl. edn., neurolinguistic programmer. Grad. asst. Millersville U., Pa., 1978-79; tchr. gifted and learning disabled Sch. Dist. of Lancaster, Pa., 1979-80; tchr. pvt. sch., Lancaster, 1980-81; elem. tchr. Lancaster Country Day Sch., 1981-85, tchr. resource room, 1985—, chmn. elem. lang. arts curriculum, 1985—; pvt. practice ednl. cons., tutor, Lancaster, 1981—. Contbg. editor United Evangelical, 1975; contbr. articles to profl. quars.; author research report. Pres. bd. dirs. Contact Lancaster, 1986; Listening Ear, Parents of Adoptive Children Orgn., 1981-85. Recipient award Lancaster Assn. Retarded Citizens, 1978-79, Cert. of Appreciation, AFL-CIO Community Services, 1983. Mem. Assn. for Supervision and Curriculum, Nat. Council Tchrs. of English, Orton Dyslexia Soc., Assn. for Children with Learning Disabilities, Pi Lambda Theta (chmn. Lehman Home Project 1984-86). Republican. Lutheran. Avocations: tennis; walking; piano; drums; reading. Home: 18 Gordon Rd Lancaster PA 17603

GRUBER, EVELYN H., nurse, research administrator; b. Mt. Kisco, N.Y., Sept. 23, 1916; d. Harry Jaffy and Anne Singer; m. Malcolm Wein, Mar. 15, 1954 (dec.); m. George Gruber (dec.); children—Nancy, Lynne. B.S., U. Minn., 1939. R.N., Pa., N.Y. Nurse, Brooke Gen. Hosp., San Antonio, 1939-42; Staff nurse United Hosp., Port Chester, N.Y., 1943-46; lab. supr. St. Vincent's Hosp., Rye, N.Y., 1960-63; lab. supr. Burke Research Ctr., White Plains, N.Y., 1964-82; asst. research dir. Osborn Home, 1964—. Fund raiser Cerebral Palsy Assn., White Plains, 1967—, Kneses Tifereth Israel. Contbr. over 100 articles to med. jours. Patentee in research field. Mem. Am. Soc. Clin. Pathologists, Am. Soc. Med. Technologists. Home: 11 Carrollwood Dr Tarrytown NY 10591

GRUBER, KATHRYN CLINE (MRS. OWEN MARSHALL GRUBER), pianist, educator; b. Belton, Tex., Sept. 22; d. William Edwin and Permilla (Mitchell) Cline; B.A. in Latin, B. Music in Piano, U. Mary Hardin-Baylor, 1931; postgrad. U. Tex., Austin, 1938, 41, UCLA, 1957; pvt. studies in piano; pupil of Walter Gilewicz; m. Owen Marshall Gruber, Sept. 16, 1946. Tchr. Latin, Belton High Sch., 1931-46; concert and studio pianist, Los Angeles, 1946-55; accompanist for husband, concert baritone, 1946—; tchr. piano, Santa Monica, Calif., 1948-51, also San Fernando Valley; pianist various chs., Tex. and Calif. Recipient B. R. Stocking medal, 1931; Outstanding Alumna award Mary Hardin-Baylor U., 1977, named to Gilewicz Hall of Fame, 1984. Mem. Nat. Piano Guild, Music Tchrs. Assn. Calif., Music Tchrs. Assn. San Fernando Valley W., Palisades Fine Arts Soc. (v.p. 1950-54, pres. 1956-58), Opera Guild So. Calif., San Fernando Valley Symphony Assn., San Fernando Valley Community Concert Assn. (dir., v.p. publicity), Mary Hardin-Baylor U. Alumni So. Calif. (pres. 1960-64), DAR, Pi Gamma Mu, Alpha Chi, Sigma Alpha Iota. Composer musical settings for poetry of Horace. Home: 6450 Quakertown Ave Woodland Hills CA 91367

GRUBER, ROSALIND H., counseling psychologist; b. Bronx, N.Y., Feb. 10, 1943; d. Lazarus L. and Beatrice (England) G.; B.A. cum laude, SUNY, New Paltz, 1974; M.A., Suffolk U., 1978. Nat. Cert. Counselor; lic. clin. social worker. Sch. registrar Assn. Help Retarded Children, N.Y.C., 1970; counselor Neighborhood Youth Corps, Poughkeepsie, N.Y., 1971-73; liason Govt. Subsidized Housing, Cambridge, Mass., 1975-77; dir., counselor Aradia Counseling, Boston, 1978—; part-owner real estate investment co. Mem. Am. Personnel and Guidance Assn., Assn. Humanistic Edn. and Devel., Mass. Mental Health Counselors Assn., Assn. Women in Psychology, U.S. Power Squaron. Home: 2150 Old Kings Hwy PO Box 272 West Barnstable MA 02668 also 40 Atherton Rd Brookline MA 02146 Office: 520 Comm Ave Boston MA 02215

GRUBER, WENDY MARILYN, industrial engineer; b. Bronx, N.Y., May 28, 1959; d. Max and Felicia (Eisenbaum) G. B.I.E., Gen. Motors Inst., 1982; postgrad. Poly. U., Bklyn. Indsl. engr. Gen. Motors Co., Tarrytown, N.Y., 1982—. N.Y. State Regents scholar Gen. Motors Inst., Flint, Mich., 1977-82.

Mem. Am. Prodn. and Inventory Control Soc. (local pres. 1985-86, nat. Silver Circle award 1984), Am. Inst. Indsl. Engrs. (local bd. dirs. 1985-86), Soc. Mfg. Engrs., Soc. Women Engrs., Nat. Assn. Female Execs., Alpha Pi Mu. Jewish. Avocations: reading; travel; needlework. Home: 1109 Brown St Apt 4G Peekskill NY 10566 Office: CPC Div Gen Motors Corp 199 Beekman Ave North Tarrytown NY 10591

GRUE, LINDA DENISE, independent administrative research and career consultant; b. Mpls., Feb. 11, 1958; d. Merlin Curtis and Martha Marie (Wilcox) G. B.S. in Criminal Justice, East Tex. State U., 1981. Asst. to coordinator ednl. media and tech. East Tex. State U., Commerce, 1977-81; univ. housing security personnel Sam Houston State U., Huntsville, Tex., 1981-82; claims processor asst./underwriting billing control Nat. Health Ins., Grand Prairie, Tex., 1983—, staff writer The Talon, 1985—; ind. career cons. Renick Assocs., Fort Worth, 1984—; market researcher Kufta and Assocs., Houston, 1985—. Polit. campaign asst. Republican Women's club, Grand Prairie, 1976, Commerce, 1980; mem. Rep. Presdl. Task Force, 1984—; active U.S. Senatorial Club. Mem. Nat. Assn. Female Execs., Nat. Orgn. For Victim Assistance. Methodist. Avocations: horseback riding; racquetball; tennis; running. Home: 1313 Alexis Apt 304 Fort Worth TX 76112 Office: Renick Assocs PO Box 532784 Grand Prairie TX 75050

GRUEBEL, BARBARA JANE, internist, pulmonologist; b. Honolulu, May 12, 1950; d. Robert William and Elenor Jane (Perry) G.; B.S., Stephen F. Austin State U., 1971; M.D. (Robert Wood Johnson Found. scholar, Coll. Women's Club scholar), Baylor Coll. Medicine, 1974. Intern in internal medicine U. Rochester, 1974-75, resident in internal medicine, 1974-77; pulmonary fellow U. Mich., 1977-79; mem. med. staff Anthony L. Jordan Health Center, Rochester, N.Y., 1976-77, Univ. Health Service, Ann Arbor, Mich., 1978-79; med. dir. progressive respiratory care unit Meth. Hosp. of Dallas, 1979-80; asst. prof. medicine U. Tex. Health Sci. Center, Dallas, 1979-80; cons. in pulmonary disease, Dallas, 1980—; med. dir. pulmonary services Southeastern Meth. Hosp.; clin. asst. prof. medicine U. Tex. Health Sci. Center; nat. affiliate faculty Am. Heart Assn. Active TEXPAC. Recipient award for gen. excellence in pediatrics, 1974, Stanley W. Olson award for acad. excellence, 1974, John Richard Fox award, 1974, Stuart A. Wallace award in pathology, 1974; Welch Found. grantee, 1970; Am. Lung Assn. tng. fellow, 1977-79. Diplomate Nat. Bd. Med. Examiners. Fellow Am. Coll. Chest Physicians (named Young Pulmonary Physicians of Future 1979); mem. Am. Med. Women's Assn. (scholastic excellence award 1974), Am. Thoracic Soc., Am. Lung Assn., AMA, Dallas County Med. Soc., Tex. Med. Soc., Soc. Critical Care Medicine, Nat. Assn. Female Execs., Nat. Assn. Med. Dirs. Respiratory Care, Dallas Acad. Internal Medicine, Am. Cancer Soc. (dir. Oak Cliff area), Women Meeting Women, Dallas Acad. Medicine, Dallas C. of C., Oak Cliff C. of C., Alpha Omega Alpha, Beta Beta Beta. Office: 221 W Colorado St Suite 470 Dallas TX 75208

GRUEN, ERICA MARLENE, television producer, advertising executive; b. Chgo., May 15, 1951; d. Dieter Martin and Dolores (Colen) G. B.A., U. Mich., 1972; M.S., U. Wis., 1975. Sch. psychologist, Madison, Wis., 1975-76; concert mgr. U. Tenn., Knoxville, 1976-78; promotion dir. Aspen Music Festival, N.Y.C., 1978-80; mktg. dir. Rainbow Programming, Woodbury, N.Y., 1980-82; v.p., assoc. dir. electronic media Dancer Fitzgerald Sample, N.Y.C., 1982—; speaker New Sch. Social Research. Contbr. articles to advt. and cable TV publs. Retreat chmn. Soc. Advancement Judaism, N.Y.C., 1983-84. Mem. Am. Assn. Advt. Agys. (new technologies com. 1982—), Pinewoods Folk Music Club (edn. chmn. 1979-81), Sierra Club, Appalachian Mountain Club.

GRUEN, EVELYN JEANETTE, lawyer, accountant; b. Vancouver, B.C., Can., Oct. 13, 1956; came to U.S., 1960; d. Kurt and Mary Rose (Spörk) G. B.S., Calif. State U.-Northridge, 1977; M.Bus. Taxation, U. So. Calif., 1981, M.B.A., J.D., 1981. Bar: Calif. 1981. Law clk. Dreisen, Kassoy & Freiberg, Los Angeles, 1979-80, Katz, Simon, Weiss & Horwich, Los Angeles, 1980-81; assoc. Pepper, Hamilton & Scheetz, Los Angeles, 1981-83; mng. atty. Los Angeles office Reynolds, Hagendorf, Vance & Deason, 1983-84; sole practice, Simi Valley, Calif., 1984—. Mem. ABA, Calif. State Bar, Los Angeles County Bar Assn., Century City Bar Assn. (chmn. internat. law com.), Century City C. of C. (chmn. internat. bus. council, dir., exec. com.), Phi Alpha Delta, Phi Kappa Phi. Office: Plaza West Bldg 2720 Cochran St Suite 8B PO Box 202 Simi Valley CA 93062 also 1445 E Los Angeles Ave Suite 301 Simi Valley CA 93065

GRUENWALD, JANICE VALEE, public relations executive; b. Beaver Dam, Wis., Feb. 14, 1948; d. Kenneth Walter and Loira Magdelena (Radtke) Squires; m. Jon Ray Gruenwald, Jan. 25, 1969; 1 son, Jordan Jon. B.S. summa cum laude U. Wis.-Madison, 1970. Prodn. coordinator Research & Devel. Ctr. for Cognitive Learning, Madison, Wis, 1970-72; publs. design mgr. State Hist. Soc. Wis., Madison, 1972-73; media specialist Ednl. Resources for Health Scis., Madison, 1973-76; public relations mgr. Appleton Mills, Inc. (Wis.), 1976-80; community relations mgr. Calif. State U., Northridge, 1981-85; pub. relations cons., owner Image, Saugus, Calif., 1980—; ednl. media lectr. No. Ill. U., 1980; direct mail lectr. Mgmt. Inst. U. Wis.-Madison, 1978-79. Editor, designer: Listen to Yourself-Again, 1984; researcher, writer, producer PBSTV series Metrics Makes It Easy, 1975. Chmn. publicity and membership Appleton Taxpayers Assn. Wis.) 1977-79. Recipient Designer award Hist. Soc. Wis., 1973, Nat. 4H photography award Kodak Corp., 1965. Mem. Internat. Assn. Bus. Communicators, Pub. Relations Soc. Am., U. Wis. Alumni Assn. (life). Office: Image A Marketing Approach to Corporate Identity 27821 Fremont Ct Suite 9B Valencia CA 91355

GRUGER, AUDREY LINDGREN, county official; b. Minot, N.D., May 17, 1930; d. Swan Magnus and Mabel Johnson Lindgren; B.A., U. Wash., 1952; postgrad. U. Calif., Davis, 1966-67; m. Edward Hart Gruger, Jr., June 27, 1952; children—Sherri, Lawrence, Linda. Mem., Wash. State Ho. of Reps., 1977-82; mem. King County (Wash.) Council, 1981—. Chmn. ops. Police and Jud. Com., 1984—; chmn. Bd. of Health, 1984; chmn. Joint Policy Com. on Block Grants, Nat. Assn. Counties Community Devel., 1985. Mem. LWV, AAUW, Womens Polit. Caucus, Elected Wash. Women (dir. 1983—). Democrat. Mem. United Ch. of Christ. Home: 3727 NE 193d St Seattle WA 98155

GRUHL, ANDREA MORRIS, librarian; b. Ponca City, Okla., Dec. 9, 1939; d. Luther Oscar and Hazel Evangeline (Anderson) Morris; m. Werner Mann Gruhl, July 10, 1965; children—Sonja Krista, Diana Krista. B.A., Wesleyan Coll., 1961; M.L.S., U. Md., 1968; M.Liberal Arts Program, Johns Hopkins U., 1970; postgrad. U. Md., 1968, 70-73. Tchr., Broward County, Fla., Dept. Def. Montgomery County, Md., 1961-66; librarian Prince Georges County (Md.) Pub. Library, 1966-68, 81-83, U. Md., College Park, 1970-72; art history researcher Joseph Alsop, Washington, 1972-74; librarian Howard County Pub. Library, Columbia, Md., 1969-70, 74-79; European exchange staff Library of Congress, Washington, 1982—, processing dept. rep. women's program adv. com., 1983-86, mem. ofcl. del. Internat. Fedn. Library Assns. ann. conf., Munich, 1983, Chgo., 1985; state del. White House Conf. on Libraries, 1978. Indexer, editor: Learning Vacations, 3d edit., 1980; LCPA Index to Library of Congress Info. Bull., 1984. Trustee, Howard County Pub. Library, Columbia, Md., 1979-87; publ. chmn. LWV of Howard County, Md., 1974; citizen's rep. for Howard County and exec. bd. Balt. Regional Planning Council Library Com., 1976-79; bd. dirs. Friends of the Library, Howard County, Md., 1977-79, pres., 1976; vol. Nat. Gallery of Art Library, Washington, 1978-80. Mem. Art Libraries Soc. N.Am. (coordinator, pub. exhbn. 1980-82), ALA (mem. trustee assn. 1982—), Library of Congress Profl. Assn. (coordinator ann. staff art show 1982, 83, chmn. spl. interest group on library sci. 1985—), Md. Library Assn. (pres. trustee div. 1982-83), Kappa Delta Epsilon, Beta Phi Mu. Democrat. Methodist. Lutheran. Home: 5990 Jacob's Ladder Columbia MD 21045 Office: Library of Congress Washington DC 20540

GRUITS, PATRICIA BEALL, clergywoman, charitable corporation executive; b. Detroit, Feb. 22, 1923; d. Harry Lee and Myrtle D. (Monville) Beall; m. J. Peter Guits, June 15, 1946; children—Peter, Harry, Patrick, William. Student Central Bible Coll., 1944-45, Bethesda Bible Inst., 1950-53, Anchor Bay Coll., 1945-46; B. Theology, Nat. Bible Coll., 1951. Ordained to ministry, 1956; minister edn. Bethesda Missionary Temple, Detroit, 1955-83; founder, dean Minister Candidate Sch., Detroit, 1958-81; pres. founder RHEMA Internat. (Restoring Hope Through Ednl. and Med. Aid), Detroit, 1973-82, pres., 1984—; founder RHEMA Hosp. and Clinics, St. Marc, Haiti, 1983—, RHEMA-Galilean Med. Ctr., Mattheu, Haiti, 1986—. Author: Understanding God, 1972; Understanding God and His Covenants, 1985. Office: 1946 97th Terr NW Coral Springs Park FL 33071

GRUNER, VIRGINIA SHAW (MRS. GEORGE JOHN GRUNER), club woman; b. Chgo., Feb. 19, 1912; d. Neil John and Rose (Tenwick) Shaw; grad. Chgo. Tchrs. Coll., 1931; B.S., Northwestern U., 1932; Ph.D. (hon.), Colo. Christian Coll., 1973; m. George John Gruner, Nov. 6, 1935; children—Valerie Dale, Diane Rae. Tchr., Parker Practice Sch. of Chgo., Chgo. Tchrs. Coll., 1935-40. Active Girl Scouts Am., 1949-53; v.p. Factotums, Scarsdale (N.Y.) Woman's Club, 1953; mem. member's guild High Mus. Art, Atlanta. Recipient Civic Achievement award City of Chgo. Mem. Internat. Platform Assn., Pi Lambda Theta, Cui Bono, Alpha Omicron Pi. Republican. Presbyn. Clubs: Scarsdale Golf (chmn. women's golf assn. 1954-56); American Yacht (Rye, N.Y.); Druid Hills Golf (Atlanta). Home: 2609 174th Ave NE Redmond WA 98052

GRUSH, MARY ELLEN, computer company executive; b. Aurora, Ill., Oct. 28, 1947; d. Byron Edward and Olga Marion (Olson) Grush; m. Kenneth Takagi Takara, Oct. 25, 1981; 1 dau., Stephanie Suzanne Grush. B.A., Ft. Wright Coll., 1971; M.A., U. Denver, 1975. Mgr. met. info. retrieval network Bibliog. Ctr. for Research, Denver, 1975-77; customer services rep. tng. Lockheed Dialog Info. Systems, Palo Alto, Calif., 1977-78, computer ops. supr., 1978—. Mem. ALA, Spl. Libraries Assn., Beta Phi Mu, Pi Delta Phi. Home: PO Box 1378 Los Altos CA 94023

GRYCZ, ANNE ELIZABETH, values and ethics consultant; b. San Francisco, Apr. 7, 1944; d. Albert Winters and Elizabeth Gertrude (Bogle) Cunningham; B.A., U. San Francisco, 1965; 1965; M.A. Grad. Theol. Union, U. Calif.-Berkeley; m. June 25, 1966 (div.); children—Michal Joseph, Anastasia Christina. Tchr. Spanish, history Santa Clara (Calif.) Unified Sch. Dist., 1966-67; tchr. theology, in charge parish edn. programs and tchr. tng. Roman Cath. Archdiocese of San Francisco, 1970-76; sec. Behaviordyne, Inc., Palo Alto, Calif., 1976-78, asst. to pres., 1978-80, v.p. consumer services, 1980-84, v.p. spl. projects and long range planning, 1984—; condr. workshops in field; cons. handicapped children; assoc. Nat. Inst. Advancement of Career Edn., U. So. Calif. Bd. dirs. Palo Alto Adolescent Services Corp. Mem. AAUW, Nat. Assn. Female Execs., Corp. Planners Assn., Peninsula Exec. Group, Alpha Sigma Nu. Democrat. Roman Catholic. Author: The Guide Pak, 1978; contbr. articles to Migrant Echo, 1974-76. Home: 1142 Guinda St Palo Alto CA 94301

GUADAGNO, BETTY ANN, direct marketing executive, electrical contracting firm executive; b. N.Y.C., Jan. 6, 1955; d. Matthew Charles and Mary (Settembrini) Benincasa; m. Salvatore Joseph Guadagno III, Feb. 14, 1982. Student Pace U., 1982—. Coordinator RCA, N.Y.C., 1979-81, adminstr., 1981-82; mgr. bus. affairs RCA Direct Mktg., Inc., N.Y.C., 1982—. Avocations: piano; target shooting. Home: RFD 2 Box 341 Route 118 Yorktown Heights NY 10598 Office: RCA Direct Mktg Inc 1133 Ave of the Americas New York NY 10036 also: BSG Electric Inc PO Box 345 Hawthorne NY 10532

GUAJARDO, FRANCISCA, home school coordinator, educator; b. Laredo, Tex., June 30, 1946; d. Luis and Teresa G. A.A., Laredo Jr. Coll., 1966; B.S., Tex. Woman's U., 1968, M.Ed., 1973. Spl. edn. tchr. Denton (Tex.) State Sch., 1968-69; spl. edn. demonstration and supervisory tchr. Tex. Woman's U. Demonstration Sch., Denton, 1970-72; spl. edn. tchr. Denton Ind. Sch. Dist., 1972-74; early childhood spl. edn. tchr. Dallas Ind. Sch. Dist., 1974-76, home sch. coordinator/vis. tchr., 1976—, tchr. adult basic edn., 1982-83. Editor, author Parenting Newsletter, Child Chatter, 1977-79; editor Project Kids Parenting Newsletter, 1980-81, The Dispatch, 1980-81, The Cannon, 1981—; Newsletters for Dallas Assn. Home Sch. Coordinators/Vis. Tchrs. Treas., Familias Unidas, Denton, 1973-74. Recipient Scholarships, Mary Frances Doss Fund, Laredo, Tex., 1964, Paul Young Sr. Fund, Laredo, 1964, Laredo Jr. Coll. Choir, 1964-66, Assn. U. Women, 1966-68; Tex. Woman's U. sr. traineeship grantee, 1967-68, grad. fellow, 1969-70. Mem. Home Sch. Coordinator Assn. Tex. (pres. elect 1983-84), Dallas Assn. Home Sch. Coordinators/Vis. Tchrs. (pres. 1982-83, v.p. 1983-84), Phi Delta Kappa, Pi Lambda Theta. Democrat. Mem. Ch. of Christ. Home: 970 N Rustic Circle Dallas TX 75218 Office: Spl Edn Services 3434 S R L Thornton St Dallas TX 75224

GUARD, PATRICIA SPRUNGER, financial company personnel executive; b. Ft. Wayne, Ind., Sept. 26, 1953; d. John H. and Iris Stella (Butler) Sprunger; m. Neil R. Guard, May 18, 1974 (div. Sept. 1983); 1 dau., Heather Anne. B.S. in Psychology, U. Tex.-El Paso, 1975; M.A. in Indsl. Organizational Psychology, Ohio State U., 1980. Staff assoc. Applied Sci. Assocs., El Paso, Tex., 1976-77; research assoc. Ctr. for Human Resources Research, Columbus, Ohio, 1977-81; tng. dir. Gen. Homes Corp., Houston, 1981-83; v.p. human resources Commonwealth Fin. Group, Houston, 1983—; trainer organizational research, Columbus, 1978-79. U. Tex.-El Paso grad. scholar, 1975. Mem. Acad. Mgmt., Am. Soc. Tng. and Devel., Am. Psychol. Assn., Inst. Fin. Edn. (adv. gov. 1984). Republican. Methodist. Office: Commonwealth Financial Group 2223 W Loop S Houston TX 77027

GUARINO, FAUN D., advertising communications researcher; b. Astoria, N.Y., Nov. 26, 1954; d. Guy Xavier and Lucille Julia (Kouyoumjian) Witz; m. Kenneth Gary Guarino, Oct. 15, 1978. B.A. cum laude, Hofstra U., 1975, cert. in bus. studies, 1977; M.A., L.I. U., 1977; grad. advt. skills workshop Young & Rubicam, 1984. Grad. and research asst. C.W. Post Coll., L.I. U., Greenvale, N.Y., 1975-77; researcher and asst. to dir. tng. Franklin Stores Corp., Bronx, N.Y., 1977-78; sr. project dir. Mktg. Evaluations, Port Washington, N.Y., 1978-81; media research sr. analyst Young & Rubicam, N.Y.C., 1981-82, supr., 1982—. First v.p. Hofstra U. Alumni Coll. Senate, Hempstead, N.Y., 1978-81, chmn. ann. alumni art shows, 1976-78, chmn. undergrad. info. com., 1978-81, Alpha Theta Beta del., 1983—, mem. Hoftra U. 50th anniversary com., 1985-86; chmn. publicity com. Gray Wig, 1975-76, 80, mem. exec. bd., 1976, 80; prodn. assoc. Covent Garden Fair/My Fair Lady, 1985. Recipient Past Pres.'s award Hofstra Alumni Coll. Senate, 1981. Mem. Am. Mktg. Assn., Advt. Research Found. (bus. audience measurement com. 1986—), Alpha Kappa Delta (pres. chpt. 1976-77), Pi Gamma Mu. Office: Young and Rubicam 285 Madison Ave New York NY 10017

GUBERINA, CARMEN, ophthalmologist; b. Bjelovar, Yugoslavia, Apr. 1, 1943; d. Ivo and Nadja Guberina; B.A., Classical Gymnasium, Zagreb, Yugoslavia, 1962; M.D., U. Zagreb, 1967. Diplomate Am. Bd. Ophthalmology. Intern, Beth Israel Med. Ctr./Newark Coll. Medicine, 1970-71; resident in ophthalmology St. Vincent's Hosp. and Med. Ctr., N.Y.C., 1971-74, Univ. Eye Klinich, Munich, W.Ger., 1975; asst. attending surgeon Manhattan Eye Ear and Throat Hosp., N.Y.C., 1979—; assoc. attending surgeon St. Vincent's Hosp. and Cabrini Med. Center, N.Y.C., 1977—; fellow in oculoplastic surgery Manhattan Eye Ear Throat Hosp., 1976-77. Contbr. chpts. to books, articles to profl. jours. Fellow Am. Acad. Ophthalmology, Am. Soc. Ophthalmic Plastic and Reconstructive Surgery; mem. AMA, N.Y. County Med. Soc. Office: 30 E 60th St New York NY 10022

GUBSER, MARY DOUGLASS, cooking school executive, author, educator; b. Frederick, Okla., July 3, 1915; d. Walter and Winifred (Dodd) D.; m. Eugene Herbert Gubser, June 5, 1937; children—Nicholas James, Peter Anton, Michael Douglass. B.A., U. Okla, 1936. Owner, tchr. Cooking with Mary, Tulsa, 1972—; owner cooking schs. Oklahoma City, Enid, Okla., Houston, St. Louis, Dallas, Albuquerque, Sonoma, Calif., 1972—. Author: Mary's Bread-basket and Soup Kettle, 1975; America's Bread Book, 1985. Recipient Ocean Spray Spotlight on Women award, 1983. Mem. Shaker Soc. Ky., Culinary Historians of Boston, Preservation of Jonny Cake Assn. Democrat. Methodist.

GUEHL, JOHANNA CECILIA, accountant, lawyer; b. Pitts., Nov. 22, 1953; d. John J. and Fern M. (Lhota) Guehl; m. Edward A. McFarland, Oct. 29, 1983. B.A. in History, Vanderbilt U., 1975; J.D., U. Pitts., 1978; M.B.A., 1980. C.P.A., Pa. Bar: Pa. 1979. Tax mgr. Price Waterhouse, Pitts., 1980—. Mem. ABA, Allegheny County (Pa.) Bar Assn., Am. Inst. C.P.A.s, Pa. Inst. C.P.A.s Republican. Club: Pittsburgh Vanderbilt (v.p.).

GUERIN, JOAN HADWIN, banker; b. Portsmouth, Va., Jan. 20, 1951; d. Travis Ray and Mollie Mack (Riddick) Hadwin; m. Robert Edward McAllister, Mar. 28, 1971 (div. Feb. 1976); 1 child, Lisa Renee; m. Christopher Stuart Guerin, Feb. 4, 1984. Grad. Fla. Sch. Banking, 1982. Mcpl. securities prin. Ins. and acctg. Pensacola Home & Savs., Fla., 1968-71; acctg. officer Barnett Bank of Pensacola, 1973-80; portfolio adminstr. Barnett Banks of Fla., Inc., Jacksonville, 1980-82; compliance officer Barnett Bank of Jacksonville, 1982-83; investment devel. officer First Nat. Bank Atlanta, 1983-84; corr. banker First Wachovia, Atlanta, 1984—. Counselor, Jr. Achievement, Pensacola, 1975-80. Mem. Nat. Assn. Banking Women (mem. edn. com. 1985-86), Nat. Assn. Female Execs. Republican. Lutheran. Avocations: tennis, hiking. Office: First Wachovia MC352 2 Peachtree St NW Atlanta GA 30302

GUERNETTE, JOANNE GERDES, psychologist; b. Sacramento, Calif., Mar. 22, 1931; d. Fred Paul and Pauline Clements (Haines) Gerdes; B.A., Sacramento State U., 1954, M.A., 1966; Ph.D., Tex. A&M U., 1974; m. Gene Sutphen; children—Eric, Keslie. Speech pathologist, therapist Sacramento County Supt. of Schs. Office, 1957-60; sch. psychologist Sacramento County Office of Edn., 1960-66; staff psychologist St. Joseph Community Mental Health Center, Houston, 1967; clin. psychologist Hauser Neuropsychiat. Clinic, Houston, 1967-70; cons. Brazos County Mental Health Center also Milam County Mental Health Center, 1972-74; sr. psychologist, clin. dir. Devereux Found., Victoria, Tex., 1974-84; pvt. practice clin. psychology and neuropsychology, Victoria, Tex., 1979—; vol. cons. Brazos County Mental Health Center; Child Study Clinic, Victoria. Mem. Sacramento Area Sch. Psychologists Assn. (pres.-elect 1966), Calif. Assn. Sch. Psychologists and Psychometrists (dir. 1965), Am. Psychol. Assn., Tex. Psychol. Assn., Southwestern Psychol. Assn., Council for Exceptional Children. Home: 403 W Stayton Ave Victoria TX 77901 Office: BehavioraLearn Clinic 104 Kelly Dr Suite A Victoria TX 77904

GUERNSEY, LINDA JOYCE, cable television personnel executive; b. Elizabethton, Tenn., Sept. 19, 1957; d. Charles D. and Joyce Ann (Scott) Williamson; m. Mark Kevin Guernsey, Mar. 8, 1980. B.S. in Elem. Edn., Tenn. Tech. U., 1979. Sec., David Lipscomb Coll., Nashville, 1975-76; sec., librarian Tenn. Tech. U., Cookeville, 1976-78; area hostess Opryland, U.S.A., Nashville, summer, 1977; sales and service rep. CISCO, Lewisburg, Tenn., 1978-79; personnel mgr. Albuquerque Cable TV Co., 1979—; cons. careers U. N.Mex., Albuquerque, 1983. Tchr. church classes Ch. of Christ, Albuquerque, 1980—; mem. Neighborhood Assn., Albuquerque, 1983—; active Am. Lung Assn., N.Mex. affiliate Am. Heart Assn. Mem. N.Mex. Personnel Assn. (editor 1982 Newsletter, v.p. membership and publicity 1983, pres., 1984—), Am. Soc. Personnel Adminstrsn. (dir. hospitality for 1983 bi-regionl conf.), Women in Cable. Democrat. Office: Albuquerque Cable TV Inc 2633 Tennessee NE Albuquerque NM 87110

GUERNSEY, MARY LINDA, nurse; b. Wilmington, N.C., Mar. 13, 1945; d. Hugh Johnston, Jr. and Dorothy Margaret (Watson) Sloan; R.N., Miami Valley Hosp., Dayton, Ohio, 1966; postgrad. Wright State U., Dayton, Sinclair Community Coll., Dayton, Coll. Mt. St. Joseph, 1981-82, Miami U., 1983—; m. Donald Alan Guernsey, July 22, 1967; children—Michael Hugh, Kristina Nicole. Mem. nursing staff Miami Valley Hosp., 1966—, charge nurse self care hemodialysis piloted program Regional Artificial Kidney Center, 1980—. Sunday sch. tchr. Aldersgate United Methodist Ch., Huber Heights, Ohio, 1980—. Mem. Ohio Valley Council Nephrology Nurses and Technicians (sec. 1983-84). Republican. Clubs: Order Eastern Star, Order Rainbow Girls (Grand Cross of Color 1963). Author manuals in field; contbr. articles to profl. jours. Home: 5201 Beechview Dr Huber Heights OH 45424 Office: 1 Wyoming St Dayton OH 45409

GUERNSEY, NANCY PATRICIA, mechanical engineer; b. Newark, Oct. 12, 1955; d. Orville Wendell and Dorothy Elizabeth (Maccia) Guernsey. B.E. in Mech. Engring., Manhattan Coll., Riverdale, N.Y. 1977; M.S. in Nuclear Engring., Poly. Inst. Bklyn., 1986. Cert. aircraft single engine pilot. Asst. engr. systems engring. Grumman Aerospace Co., Bethpage, N.Y., 1977-83; engr. product support, Govt. Support Systems div., Harris Corp., Syosset, N.Y., 1983-86. Mem. Soc. Women Engrs., Am. Nuclear Soc., AIAA, ASME, The Ninety-Nines (sect. air age edn. chmn. 1982-84), Aircraft Owners and Pilots Assn., Pilots Internat. Assn., Nat. Rifle Assn. Republican. Episcopalian. Club: Long Island Early Fliers. Home: 14 3d St Ronkonkoma NY 11779

GUEST, BERNETTE PARKER, oil and gas company executive; b. Salt Lake City, May 18, 1952; d. Robert Farnsworth and Ilona Leiola (Wiebke) Parker; B.S. in Fin., Colo. State U., 1973; m. Russel Paul Guest, Sept. 15, 1973; children—Forrest Farnsworth, Robert Russel. Transfer agt., corp. sec.-treas. Am. Stock Transfer, Inc., Denver, 1969-70, v.p., dir., 1971-74; corp. sec., controller Golden Oil Co., Denver, 1974-78, treas., chief fin. officer, 1977—, v.p., 1978—, dir., 1976—; cons., sec.-treas., dir. G & S Service Co., Inc., Tulsa, 1977-79. Mem. Nat. Assn. Female Execs., Internat. Assn. Fin. Planning, Petroleum Accts. Soc. Colo., Ind. Petroleum Assn. Mountain States, Inst. Energy Devel., Ind. Petroleum Assn. Am., Nat. Fedn. Ind. Bus., Am., AAAS, Internat. Platform Assn. Office: 3650 S Yosemite 430 Denver CO 80237

GUEST, DEBRA DIANE, state official; b. Honolulu, June 19, 1951; d. Frederick Howard and Josephine Ann (Lech) G.; student Auburn (Ala.) U., 1969-70; M.S., U. South Fla., Tampa, 1972; Ed.D., Nova U., Ft. Lauderdale, Fla., 1980. Mem. staff MacDonald Tng. Center for Mentally Retarded, Tampa, 1972-74, acad. cons. Civitan pre-sch. program, 1973-74; with Fla. Dept. Health and Rehab. Services, 1974—, dir. dist. VI Diagnosis and Evaluation Center, Tampa, 1980-84, human services program adminstr., 1984—; mem. adj. faculty U. Tampa, 1973-75, Hillsborough Community Coll., 1976—. Chmn. promotion and entertainment com. dist. 8, Fla. Spl. Olympics, 1981—. HEW grantee, 1980-82. Mem. Am. Speech and Hearing Assn., Am. Assn. Mental Deficiency, Am. Soc. Profl. and Exec. Women, Nat. Assn. Female Execs., Fla. Speech and Hearing Assn., Network Exec. Women, Sons and Daus. Pearl Harbor Survivors (nat. v.p.). Author papers in field. Office: 4000 W Buffalo Ave Tampa FL 33614

GUIDO, ANNA MARIE, journalist; b. Salem, Ohio, Nov. 29, 1960; d. Paul Joseph and Lenna (Passi) G. B.A. in News-Editorial Journalism, Kent State U., 1983. Reporter, photographer The Morning Jour. Newspaper, Buckeye Pub. Co., Lisbon, Ohio, 1983—. Mem. Women in Communications, Inc. (Honored newspaper coverage spring 1983, fall 1982). Roman Catholic. Home: 366 Somer St Leetonia OH 44431 Office: Buckeye Pub Co 308 Maple St Lisbon OH 44432

GUIDO, JUDITH COOPER, seminary official, educator; b. Nyack, N.Y., d. Russell Seabury and Marjorie May (Osborne) Cooper; m. Fred J. Guido, Nov. 30, 1974. B.A. cum laude, Dominican Coll., N.Y., 1973; M.A. with honors, Manhattanville Coll., N.Y., 1974. Asst. to supt. for bus. Nyack Pub. Schs., N.Y., 1970-74; asst. to dean bus. program Dominican Coll., Orangeburg, N.Y., 1970-72; treas., bus. mgr. Elizabeth Seton Coll., Yonkers, N.Y., 1974-79; v.p. for fin. and adminstrn., treas. Union Theol. Sem., N.Y.C., 1979—. Mem., Friends Com., Mus. Am. Folk Art, 1978—; founding mem. Friends Union Theol. Sem. Burke Library, N.Y.C., 1982—; mem. trustee fin. com. The College Bd., N.Y.C., 1985—; mem. steering com. Friends of the Performing Arts, Wave Hill, Riverdale, N.Y., 1985—; mem. bd. dirs. Morningside Area Alliance, N.Y.C., 1981-85; mem. Pelham Art Ctr., N.Y., 1984—. Mem. Nat. Assn. Coll. and Univ. Bus. Officers (bd. dirs. 1984—), Eastern Assn. Coll. and Univ. Bus. Officers (bd. dirs. 1979—), Mgmt. Inst. for Religious Orgns. (adv. bd. 1983—), Am. Mgmt. Assn., Nat. Assn. Coll. Aux. Services, Am. Hist. Assn., N.Y. Geneaol. and Biog. Soc. Avocations: Ballet; jazz; reading; genealogical research; historical preservation. Office: Union Theol Sem 3041 Broadway at 120th St New York NY 10027

GUIDO, SHAREON CHRISTINE, mechanical contractor; b. Washington, Aug. 5, 1946; d. James Harold and Edna Louise (Mills) McCullough; m. Frank Michael Guido, June 7, 1975; 1 child, Craig Scott. Diploma, George C. Marshall Sch., 1964. Asst. corp. sec. First Charter Land, Falls Church, Va., 1969-70; sec. to v.p. Liberty Loan Corp., Falls Church, 1970-71; gen. mgr. Richards A/C Co. Inc., Falls Church, 1971-83; founder, pres. Precision Air, Inc., Falls Church, 1983—; sponser Va. Apprenticeship Program, Fairfax, 1983—. Contbr. articles to profl. jours. Bd. dirs. Boys Clubs of Am., Falls Church, Va., 1975-76; leader Boy Scouts Am. Falls Church, 1975-78; instr. religious edn. Diocese of Arlington, Va., 1976-77; counselor Telecommunications for the Deaf, 1982; guest lectr. Am. Lung Assn., 1983; notary pub. Va., 1971—; ofcl. Nat. Assn. Stock Car Auto Racing, 1972-74. Recipient Outstanding Service award Am. Lung Assn., 1983. Mem. Air Conditioning Contractors of Am., Falls Ch. Preservation Soc., Western Eastern Roadracers Assn., Plumbing, Heating, Cooling Contractors Assn., Am. Motorcyclist Assn. Roman Catholic. Avocations: pistol shooting; motorcycling; skiing; camping; reading. Office: Precision Air Inc 6048 Glen Carlyn Dr Falls Church VA 22041

GUIDROZ-GREEN, FAY THRASHER, psychologist; b. Wyhne, Ark., Dec. 17, 1935; d. Andrew Justin and Joy Maud (Charles) Thrasher; B.S., Miss. State U., 1958; M.Ed., McNeese State U., 1963; M.A., La. State U., 1968, Ph.D., 1970; m. Richard E. Green, Feb. 1978; children—Jeffrey Kane, Sidney Joseph.

Chief psychologist Lake Charles (La.) Mental Health Center, 1970-73; clin. psychologist VA Hosp., Salisbury, N.C., 1973-76; chief psychology service VA Outpatient Clinic, San Antonio, 1976-77; chief psychology service, coordinator research and devel. Alvin C. York Med. Ctr., Murfreesboro, Tenn., 1977—; asst. prof. dept. psychiatry Meharry Med. Coll., 1985—; regional trainer Tng. in Ind. and Group Effectiveness, 1974-76. Lic. psychologist. Mem. Am. Psychol. Assn., Menninger Found., Nat. Register Health Care Providers, N.Y. Acad. Scis., Oaklands Found., AMA Aux., Assn. Advancement Psychologists, Assn. VA Chief Psychologists. Home: 210 S College St Woodbury TN 37190 Office: Alvin C York Med Center Lebanon Rd Murfreesboro TN 37130

GUIDRY, MARY LEE, nursing educator, legal consultant; b. Glenmora, La., Nov. 25, 1928; d. James Thomas and Myrtle Lillian (Young) Walker; m. James Lawrence Guidry, May 29, 1961; children—Michael Wayne, James, Stephen Edward. B.S., Sacred Heart Dominican Coll., 1962; M.S., Tex. Woman's U., 1970. Staff nurse pediatrics St. Joseph's Hosp., Houston, 1950-55; staff nurse, head nurse, supr. VA Hosp., Houston, 1955-61; instr., coordinator Prairie View A. and M. Coll., 1963-70; supr., instr. M.D. Anderson Hosp., Houston, 1971-74; asst. prof. nursing U. St. Thomas, Houston, 1974—; asst. prof. nursing Prairie View Coll. Nursing, 1985—; coordinator R.N. sect. faculty devel. in nursing project So. Regional Edn. Bd., 1977-82; legal cons. Perdue, Turner, Berry, Law firm, Houston, 1980—. Instr. breast self exam. Am. Cancer Soc., Houston, 1979; mem. Cancer awareness Black Adv. Group, Cancer Info. Service, 1981-84, cert., 1982. Mem. Tex. Nurses Assn. (chmn. council on practice 1979-84, dist. bd. mem. 1983-84), Sigma Theta Tau, Sigma Gamma Rho. Democrat. Baptist. Home: 2418 Oakdale St Houston TX 77004

GUILD, LAUREL MARIE, lawyer; b. Santa Rosa, Calif., Dec. 12, 1953; d. George Prescott and Helen Elizabeth (Branker) Guild. B.A., Simmons Coll., 1975; J.D., Boston Coll., 1978. Bar: Mass. 1979, D.C. 1985. Law clk. Office Atty. Gen., Boston, 1977-78, Dept. Justice, Washington, summer 1977; atty. Fed. Commns. Com., Washington, 1978—. Assoc. editor UCLA Black Law Jour., 1978. Recipient Community Service award FCC, Washington, 1979, Women in FCC, 1983. Democrat. Roman Catholic. Home: 1220 East West Hwy Silver Spring MD 20910 Office: FCC 1919 M St NW Washington DC 20554

GUILFORD, ELIZABETH MCCLUNG, financial executive; b. Washington County, Va., Feb. 25, 1933; d. William Burns and P. Elizabeth (Rainey) McClung; m. William G. Grigg, June 11, 1954 (div. 1977); children—Elizabeth G., Margaret G., William G., Gordon G.; m. Richard Holden Guilford, Sept. 14, 1979. B.S., Longwood Coll., Va., 1954; postgrad. Va. Poly. Inst., 1969. Sr. planner Fifth Planning Dist., Roanoke, Va., 1968-70; sr. planner, exec. officer Commonwealth of Va., Richmond, 1970-74; sr. loan officer Va. Housing & Devel. Authority, Richmond, 1974-78; exec. v.p., prin. Corp. & Fin. Mgmt. Inc., Richmond, Va., Orlando, Fla., 1978—; dir. Mortgage Communication Systems Inc., Orlando, Fla., 1984—; dir. Allentic Industries Inc., Orlando, 1985—; cons. and lectr. in field. Author: (manual) Virginia Housing Manual, 1972. Editor: Housing Crises, 1973. Mem. Mortgage Bankers Assn. (state com. 1985-86). Avocations: sailing; tennis; reading. Office: Corp & Fin Mgmt Inc 7061 Grand Nat Dr Suite 100 Orlando FL 32819

GUILLEBEAU, JULIE GRAVES, public relations executive; b. Springfield, Mo., Apr. 3, 1948; d. Willard Lee and Winifred (Yadon) Graves; m. James Lester Guillebeau, Sept. 11, 1976; children—Christopher Lee, Thomas James, Julie Elizabeth. A.B., Drury Coll., 1969. Newscaster Sta. WRDW-TV-12, North Augusta, S.C., 1972-73; editor Med. Coll. Ga., Augusta, 1974-81; contbg. editor Healthcare, Springfield, Mo., 1983-84; dir. pub. relations Drury Coll., Springfield, 1981—; state chmn. Ga. Hosp. Assn., Augusta, 1978; seminar dir. Council on Ind. Colls., N.Y.C., 1984, 85; mediator Media-Pub. Relations Socs., Springfield, Mo., 1983-84. Writer Humpty Dumpty Syndrome, 1981; co-producer: Super Soybean, 1981; ILGA, 1983; exec. producer: Gradua Medicinae Doctoris, 1979. Dir., sec. Health Ctr. Credit Union, Augusta, Ga., 1980, 81; dir. Summerscape, Springfield, Mo., 1984—; vol. WINGS, Springfield, Mo., 1983, 84. Mem. Women in Communications, Inc., Am. Med. Writers Assn. Democrat. Presbyterian. Office: Drury Coll 900 N Benton Ave Springfield MO 65802

GUILLEMETTE, GLORIA VIVIAN, dressmaker, designer; b. North Attleboro, Mass., June 27, 1929; d. Wilfred Anthony Roy and Sylviana (Bonnoyer) King; student Nat. Sch. Dress Design, 1976; m. Thomas William Guillemette, Mar. 24, 1963; children—Sylvia Marie, Katherine Anne, John Thomas. Machine operator dress mfg. cos., 1945-60; asst. to dressmaker and designer, Windsor, Conn., 1960-63; owner Mrs. G's Studio, Enfield, Conn., 1963—; dir. Fashion Show, 1973, 76. Cub Scout commr. Boy Scouts Am., 1979-85; mem. Enfield Fair Rent Commn., 1979—; justice of peace Conn., 1979—; mem. Republican Town Com., 1976-85; sec. United Meth. Women, 1977-82; mem. Presdl. Task Force, 1982-83. Club: Republican Women.

GUILLERMO, LINDA SUE, social worker; b. Chgo., July 4, 1951; d. Triponio Pascua and Helen Elizabeth (Moskal) G.; B.A., U. Ill., Chgo., 1973, M.S.W., 1975, postgrad., 1980; postgrad. Jane Addams Coll. Social Work, 1980-82. Mktg. research interviewer Rabin Research Co., Chgo., 1970-73; mktg. research interviewer, coder Marcor Mktg. Research, Inc., Chgo., 1973-75; social work intern Child and Family Services, Chgo., 1973-74, Chgo. Bd. Edn., 1974-75; social worker, therapist child abuse and neglect, case investigator, case planning cons., social service program planner Ill. Dept. Children and Family Services, Chgo., 1975-78, social service program planner, contract negotiator, monitoring agt. Central Resources Contracts and Grants, 1978-79; sales person Sentry Realty, Chgo., 1978-80; social worker, therapist, program coordinator, casework supr. of child abuse assessment and intervention program, proposal writer Casa Central, Chgo., 1979-82, casework cons. of child abuse assessment and intervention program, proposal writer, program dir. and casework supr. of early intervention program, 1979-85; social worker Chgo. Bd. Edn., 1985—; tng. specialist City Coll. of Chgo., 1980; adj. asso. researcher Asher Feren Law Office, Chgo., 1980-81. Treas. Greenleaf Condominium Assn., Chgo., 1980-81. Lic. real estate salesperson, Ill. Mem. Nat. Assn. Social Workers, Acad. Cert. Social Workers, Ill. Cert. Social Workers, North Side Real Estate Bd. Home: 1510 W Greenleaf St Chicago IL 60626

GUIN, GRACE HUGHES, physician; b. Birmingham, Ala., July 23, 1912; d. Ernest Smith and Grace Allen (Hawkins) Hughes; B.S., Birmingham-So. Coll., 1938; M.D., Vanderbilt U., 1943; 1 dau., Grace Guin Schiff. Intern, Albany (N.Y.) Hosp., 1945-46; resident pathology Garfield Hosp., Washington, 1950-52, Children's Nat. Med. Center, Washington, 1952-53; fellow pathology Meml. Hosp., N.Y.C., 1953-54; assoc. dir. lab. Children's Nat. Med. Center, Washington, 1954-60, dir. lab., 1960-64; staff pathologist Arlington (Va.) Hosp., 1964-67; staff pathologist VA Med. Center, Washington, 1967-80, asst. to dir. pathology service VA Central Office, Washington, 1967—; clin. prof. pathology George Washington U. Med. Center, Washington, 1960—. Nat. Cancer Inst. postdoctoral fellow, 1952. Diplomate Am. Bd. Pathology (AP and CP). Mem. Internat. Acad. Pathology, Coll. Am. Pathologists, Washington Soc. Pathology, Med. Soc. D.C. Republican. Contbr. articles in field to med. jours. Home: 3600 N Abingdon St Arlington VA 22207 Office: VA Central Office 810 Vermont Ave NW Washington DC 20420

GULICK, BARBARA, public relations executive; b. Washington, Mar. 24, 1959; d. Hewitt Gaines and Violet Lea (Craig) Lewis; m. Randall Neil Gulick, May 21, 1983. B.S., Old Dominion U., 1984; postgrad. Am. U., 1986. Pub. affairs asst. U.S. Army C.E., Fort Belvoir, Va., 1977-83; customer service rep. Xerox Corp., Arlington, Va., 1983-84; pub. relations dir. Dynamac Corp., Rockville, Md., 1984—; recruitment vol. Old Dominion U., 1985—. Author, editor newsletters. Fellow Nat. Assn. Female Execs.; mem. Am. Mktg. Assn., Phi Mu. Avocations: reading; tennis; skiing. Home: 4920 Fran Pl 303 Alexandria VA 22312

GULIEX, E. ANN, savings association executive; b. Houston, May 9, 1947; d. David and Marjorie (Randle) Moten; m. Larry Eugene Guliex, Feb. 4, 1971; 1 dau., Jessica Elaine. B.S. in Bus. Adminstrn., Tex. So. U.; cert. in real estate, U. Houston, also cert. in small bus. adminstrn.; cert. Tex. Savs. and Loans, U. Tex.; diploma Mayo Hill Sch. Modeling, 1984. Exec. sec., Ethyl Corp., Houston, 1969-71, AMP Inc., Winston-Salem, N.C., 1972-76; adminstrv. asst. Westinghouse Electric, Houston, 1976-80; asst. v.p. Commonwealth Savs. Assn., Houston, 1981—. Mem. Am. Bus. Women's Assn. Democrat. Baptist. Home: 290 Wood Loop Houston TX 77015 Office: Commonwealth Savings Assn 2223 W Loop South Suite 700 Houston TX 77027

GULLETTE, ETHEL MAE BISHOP, pianist; b. St. Paul, Mar. 29, 1908; d. Clarence Eugene and Alma (Beckman) Bishop; m. William Brandon Gullette, Sept. 5, 1936; children—Ethel Mae, Charlene Ann. Mus.B., MacPhail Sch. Music, Mpls., 1928; B.A., U. Minn., 1931; diploma Juilliard Sch. Music, 1936; pvt. study piano with Donald N. Ferguson, James Friskin. Pianist and accompanist in concerts and radio appearances, Midwest U.S., 1925-33; voice accompanist Juilliard Sch. Music, also pvt. piano tchr., N.Y.C., 1934-48; duo-pianist, accompanist, Fairfield County, Conn., 1951—, also Hartford, Conn., N.J. and N.Y.C., 1967—; concert pianist, Eastern U.S., 1953—; 30 concerts Fairfield Hills Hosp., Newtown, Conn., 1957-71; concerts, Savannah, Ga., Hilton Head Island and Beaufort, S.C., 1972; accompanist Darien Troupers, 1968, 69, New Canaan High Sch. Summer Theater, 1972, 73; recent concert appearances include Dallas, 1983, Scottsdale, Ariz., 1985, Lebanon, Bridgeport, Greenwich, New Canaan, Norwalk and Darien, Conn., 1980—; mem. New Canaan Piano Quartet, 1960-68; mem. New Canaan Town Players, 1952—, accompanist, 1958-63, 73; mem., accompanist Nutmeg Music Theatre, 1957-61, Demi-Opera Co., Brookfield Summer Theatre, Conn., 1961, many others. Bd. govs., rehearsal pianist Norwalk Symphony Orch., 1955-62; bd. dirs. New Canaan Community Concerts Assn., 1961-69, membership chmn., 1967-69; active fund drives charitable orgns.; co-pres. New Canaan High Sch. Parent's Council, 1964-65. Recipient Hon. Golden Eaglet award Southwestern Coun. council Girl Scouts U.S.A., 1985; also citations for work in Am. Cancer Soc. and ARC drives. Mem. N.Y. Singing Tchrs. Assn., New Canaan Hist. Soc. (photographer gown exhibits 1968—), Darien Community Assn. (bd. dirs. 1982-84, chmn. duo piano group 1962-64, 82-84, sec. duo piano group 1984—), New Canaan Library, New Canaan Audubon Soc., Norwalk Symphony Orch. Women's Assn. (mem. bd. 1976-82), Am. Shakespeare Guild, AAUW (charter 1970—, named Outstanding Mem. Conn. 1980), Friends N.Y. Philharm. Orch. (New Canaan chmn. 1968-71), Fairfield County Panhellenic Council, Juilliard Alumni Assn., U. Minn. Alumni Assn. (past dir. N.Y.), New Canaan Community Concerts Assn. (hon. life, Membership and Service award 1974, hon. life mem. bd., citation for 25 yrs. outstanding achievements 1979), Mu Phi Epsilon (recognition as 50 yr. mem. 1977), Delta Zeta (alumni charter; pres. local alumnae chpt. 1961-63, treas. 1982-84, named Outstanding New Eng. Alumna 1980, Nat. Woman of Yr. 1982; Golden Rose 50 yr. mem. award 1981; ann. alumna service award established in her name by Fairfield County chpt. 1983). Congregationalist. Clubs: Schubert (St. Paul); Atlantic Beach (L.I., N.Y.); Schubert of Fairfield County (duo piano group sec. 1980-82). Home: 85 West Hills Rd New Canaan CT 06840

GULLIVER, ADELAIDE CROMWELL, sociologist, educator; b. Washington, Nov. 27, 1919; d. John Wesley, Jr. and Yetta Elizabeth (Mavritte) Cromwell; A.B., Smith Coll., 1940; M.A., U. Pa., 1941; cert. in social work, Bryn Mawr Coll., 1943; Ph.D., Radcliffe Coll., 1952; L.H.D., U. Southwestern Mass., 1972; 1 son by previous marriage, Anthony C. Hill. Mem. faculty Hunter Coll., 1942-44, Smith Coll., 1945-46; mem. faculty Boston U., 1951—, now prof. sociology emeritus. Mem. adv. com. vol. aid AID, 1964-80; mem. Nat. Council Humanities, 1968-70; adv. com. corrections Commonwealth Mass., 1955-68, mem. commn. instns. higher edn., 1973-74; adv. com. to dir. IRS, 1970-71, to dir. census, 1972-75. Mem. bd. Wheelock Coll., 1971-72, Nat. Center Afro-Am. Artists, 1970-80, African Am. Scholars Council, 1971-80, Sci. and Tech. for Internat. Devel., 1984—; mem. bd. Nat. Fellowship Fund, 1974-75, mem. bd. fgn. scholarships, 1980-84; mem. Bd. Sci. and Tech. for Internat. Devel., 1984—. Mem. African Studies Assn. (dir. 1966-68), Am. Acad. Arts and Scis., Am. Sociol. Assn., Council on Fgn. Affairs, Phi Beta Kappa. Home: 51 Addington Rd Brookline MA 02146 Office: 138 Mountfort St Brookline MA 02146

GULLO, DOROTHY, advertising agency executive; b. Jackson Heights, N.Y., Jan. 28, 1942; d. Basil John and Molly (Smilios) Siotkas; m. William Ronald Gullo, Nov. 26, 1963; children—Patricia Ann, Christine Marie, Audra Lynn. A.Applied Sci. in Mgmt., Queensborough Community Coll., 1977; postgrad. in communication arts N.Y. Inst. Tech.; cert. publicity and pub. relations Hofstra U., 1980. Adminstrv. asst. Ruder & Finn, N.Y.C., 1975-77; import mgr. Internat. Trading Group, Great Neck, N.Y., 1977-79; program coordinator Bio-Behavioral Psychiatry, Great Neck, 1979-81; pres. T.G. Advt., Inc., Roslyn, N.Y., 1981—. Mem. Nat. Assn. for Female Execs. (bd. dirs. L.I. chpt.), L.I. Advt. Club. Office: T G Advertising Inc 1800 Northern Blvd Roslyn NY 11576

GUMM, MARGARET R., lawyer; b. East Orange, N.J., June 25, 1940; d. John R. Gumm and Margaret M. (Clay) Wahl. B.A. with honors magna cum laude, William Smith Coll., 1962; J.D., NYU, 1969. Bar: NY 1970. Asst. to pub. relations officer Exec. Council Episc. Ch., N.Y.C., 1963-70; assoc. Ponzan & Goldblum, Queens, N.Y., 1970-73, Norman S. Reich, 1973-78; atty. Human Resources Adminstrn. Office of Legal Affairs, City of N.Y., 1978-83, assoc. atty., 1983—; counsel Episc. Women's Caucus, 1971-73, mem. Exec. Council, Episc. Diocese of N.Y., 1972-75, Mem. Canons Com., Episc. Diocese of N.Y., 1971-76; sr. warden St. Clement's Episc. Ch., N.Y.C., 1982—, mem. vestry, 1973—. Mem. Hobart and William Smith Club. of N.Y. (bd. govs. 1978-84), Phi Beta Kappa, Phi Sigma Iota. 356 E 78th St New York NY 10021 Office: Human Resources Adminstrn Office of Legal Affairs 220 Church St 6th Floor New York NY 10013

GUNDELFINGER, MARGARET ELLEN, construction company executive, real estate agent; b. Columbus, Ohio, Aug. 3, 1956; d. Boyd Allen and Juanita Melody (Sadler) G.; 1 dau., Justine Marie. B.A., Ohio Wesleyan U., 1977; postgrad. Miami U., Oxford, Ohio, 1979-80, Ohio State U., 1978, 80, 81, Columbus Tech. Coll., 1985. Adj. faculty mem. Ind. U., Richmond, 1980; exec. v.p. Boyd's Constrn. Co., Delaware, Ohio, 1980—; real estate agt. Dublin Realty, Ohio, 1985—; cons. Del. C. of C., 1986. Mem. Delaware Area Women's Network (founder 1984), Nat. Assn. Female Execs. (network dir. 1984—), Delaware Area Bus. and Profl. Women (Young Careerist 1985), Columbus Bd. Realtors, Delaware Area C. of C., Delaware Women's Republican Club, Alpha Gamma Delta. Roman Catholic. Avocations: dancing, cooking. Home: 440 S Section Line Rd Delaware OH 43015 Office: Boyds Constrn Co Inc 34 Reid St Delaware OH 43015

GUNDERSEN, ALICE MARSHALL, business executive; b. Groveton, N.H., Nov. 19, 1934; d. Daniel Weeks and Eleanor Marshall; student Fisher Jr. Coll., Boston, 1952-53, Boston U., 1956, Northeastern U., 1957-59, Madonna Coll., 1966; B.M., U. Mich., 1970; m. Carl A. Gundersen, Apr. 11, 1959; children—Daniel Carl, Scott M. Exec. sec. with New Eng. Colls. Fund, Boston, 1956-58, with John Hancock Mut. Life Ins. Co., Boston, 1958-59; office supr. dept. human genetics U. Mich., Ann Arbor, 1964-67; adminstrv. coordinator and mgr. brokerage adminstrn. Alexander Hamilton Life Ins. Co., Farmington, Mich., 1973-75; supr. data services Delta Dental Plan of Mich., Southfield, 1976-83; pres. AMG Computer Systems, Inc., Livonia, Mich.; cons. Nat. Med. Mgmt. Systems, Flint, Mich.; music dir. St. Timothy Presbyterian Ch., Livonia, Mich., 1964-72, Trinity Episcopal Ch., Farmington, 1975-77; CESA cons. Presbytery of Detroit, 1975-77, mem. task force on women, 1978—; mem. Livonia City Council, 1980-86; cons. women re-entering work force; systems cons. Adv. com. Livonia Sch. Bd., 1967-68; campaign coordinator City Council Candidate, 1970; active Livonia Com. for Better Human Relations, 1965-74. Cert. systems profl. Mem. Nat. Assn. Women Bus. Owners, Assn. Systems Mgmt. (publicity chmn. 1978, membership chmn. 1979-80, officer 1980-81, v.p., 1981-82, pres. 1983-84), Micro Mgrs. Assn., Women's Econ. Club Detroit (membership com., 1976, program com., 1977), Mich. Women's Polit. Caucus (polit. action chmn. 1979-81, state chmn. 1981-83), Nat. Women's Polit. Caucus (adminstrv. com. 1981-83). Home: 15715 Southampton St Livonia MI 48154 Office: 17177 N Laurel Park Dr Suite 116 Livonia MI 48152

GUNDERSEN, JOAN REZNER, history educator; b. Chgo., Nov. 9, 1946; d. Charles Louis and Lois Gladys (Baskin) Rezner; B.A., Monmouth Coll., Ill., 1968; M.A., Coll. William and Mary, 1969; Ph.D., U. Notre Dame, 1972; m. Robert P. Gundersen, Sept. 13, 1969; 1 dau., Kristina. Mem. assoc. faculty Ind. U., South Bend, 1971-74; vis. asst. prof. history Vanderbilt U., Nashville, 1974-75; asst. prof. history St. Olaf Coll., Northfield, Minn., 1975-82, assoc. prof., 1982—. Choir dir. All Saints Episcopal Ch., Northfield, 1975-81, mem. vestry, 1978-81, clk., 1981-85, bookkeeper, 1985—. Colonial Williamsburg research grantee, 1971, Newberry Library fellow in family history, 1973. Mem. Am. Hist. Assn., Orgn. Am. Historians, So. Hist. Assn., Women Historians Midwest, Minn. Hist. Soc., Northfield Hist. Soc. (pres. bd. dirs.), Phi Alpha Theta. Author: (with others) American History at a Glance, 3d edit., 1975, 4 edit., 1979, America: Changing Times, 1st edit., 1979, 2 edit., 1981; bd. editors Hist. Mag. of Episcopal Ch., 1977—; contbr. articles in field to profl. jours. Home: 315 Cherry St Northfield MN 55057 Office: Dept History St Olaf Coll Northfield MN 55057

GUNDERSON, JUDITH KEEFER, golf association executive; b. Charleroi, Pa., May 25, 1939; d. John R. and Irene G. (Gaskill) Keefer; student public schs., Uniontown, Pa.; m. Jerry L. Gunderson, Mar. 19, 1971; children—Jamie L., Jeff S.; stepchildren—Todd G. (dec.), Marc W., Lisa J. Bookkeeper, Fayette Nat. Bank, 1957-59, gen. ledger bookkeeper, 1960-63; head bookkeeper First Nat. Bank Broward, 1963-64; bookkeeper Ruthenberg Homes, Inc., 1966-69; bookkeeper, asst. sec./treas. Pennisular Properties, Inc. subs. Investors Diversified Services Properties, Mpls., 1969-72; comptroller, stockholder, pres. dir. Am. Golf Fla., Inc., dba Gulf and Tennis World, Deerfield Beach, 1972—; sec.-treas., stockholder, dir. Internat. Golf, Inc. County committeewoman, Broward County, Fla., 1965-66. Mem. Nat. Golf Found., C. of C., Beta Sigma Phi.

GUNDRUM, LAETTA JUNE, retired petrochemical company executive; b. East St. Louis, Ill., June 13, 1927; d. Norman Henry and Fern L. (Seibel) Gundrum; student Rockford Coll., 1943-44; B.S. in Chemistry, U. Chgo., 1947. Tech. editor U.S. Dept. Agriculture, Peoria, Ill., 1950-51; tech. writer E. I. DuPont deNemours & Co., Wilmington, Del., 1951-58; advt. mgr. Amoco Chems. Corp., Chgo., 1965-83. Named Person of Yr., Soc. Plastics Industry, 1977. Mem. Am. Chem. Soc.

GUNIN, LOUISE CAROL, banker; b. Jersey City, N.J., Aug. 12, 1951; d. David D. and Janet Naomi (Lichten) Gunin. B.A. in Sociology, Monmouth Coll., 1973; postgrad. in acctg. and fin., U. No. Fla., Jacksonville, 1976-77, U. Tex.-Dallas, 1978—. Campaign coord. Nat. Cystic Fibrosis Research Found., Totowa, N.J., 1973-75; adminstrv. asst. Barnett Winston Investment Trust, Jacksonville, Fla., 1975-78; asst. v.p. BancTex. Dallas N.A., 1978-83; v.p. InterFirst Bank Carrollton, Tex., 1984—. Bd. dirs. Glen Oaks Townhomes Homeowners Assn. Mem. C. of C. Democrat. Jewish. Office: InterFirst Bank Carrollton 1925 Beltline Rd Carrollton TX 75006

GUNN, CAROLYN, veterinarian; b. Tulsa, Oct. 30, 1949; d. Victor Lewis Gunn and Mary Carolyn (Aular) Chase. B.S., Okla. State U., 1971, D.V.M., 1978. Intern Angell Meml. Animal Hosp., Boston, 1978-79; resident U. Calif.-Davis, 1979-82; gen. practice vet. medicine, Salt Lake City, 1983, Montrose, Colo., 1985-86; vis. lectr. U. Calif.-Davis, 1983. Illustrator: Technique Guide to Fracture Fixation, 1981; contbg. author Canine and Feline Soft Tissue Surgery, 1984; contbr. articles to profl. jours. Biomed. research support grantee, 1981-82; recipient Dr. Helen Irwin award Okla. State U., Stillwater, 1978, Upjohn award, 1978. Mem. AVMA, Am. Animal Hosp. Assn., Okla. Vet. Med. Assn., Calif. Vet. Med. Assn., Mass. Vet. Assn., Vet. Cancer Soc., Phi Zeta, Phi Kappa Phi. Basecamp supr. NorthFace summit attempt China-Everest expdn., 1984; basecamp mgr., cook Rio Abiseo Nat. Park Research Project, Peru, 1985.

GUNN, REBECCA LOUISE, lawyer; b. Ft. Dodge, Iowa, Mar. 16, 1951; d. Ralph Barnett and Margaret Turner (Johnstone) G. B.A. in Elected Studies, U. Minn., 1976; J.D., Loyola Law Sch., Los Angeles, 1980; postgrad. Denver U., 1986—. Bar: Calif. 1980, Colo. 1981. Sole practice, Loveland, Colo., 1981-85; ptnr. Weatherill & Gunn, Loveland, 1986—; asst. mcpl. judge, Loveland, Colo., 1986—. Bd. dirs. Larimer County Vis. Nurse Assn., Loveland, 1981—. Mem. Loveland Legal Aid Assn. (pres. 1982), Colo. Bar Assn., Colo. Women's Bar Assn. (treas. 1986), ABA, ACLU. Home: 1105 W Shore Pl Loveland CO 80537 Office: Weatherill & Gunn 444 E 6th St Loveland CO 80537

GUNNERSON, MELISSA HARRIS, computer programmer; b. Itazuke, Japan, July 21, 1958 (parents Am. citizens); d. Monte Delano and Evelyn Lucille (Nations) Harris; m. Mark Avery Gunnerson, Aug. 4, 1981. B.S., U. So. Miss., 1981. Programmer, Texaco Inc., Houston, 1981-82, computer analyst Texaco USA, Bellaire, Tex., 1982-83, programmer Texaco Inc., Houston, 1983—. Republican. Mormon. Office: Texaco Inc 6464 Savoy St Houston TX 77036

GUNTER, ANNIE LAURIE, state ofcl.; b. Hollow Twp., N.C., June 23, 1919; d. Samuel Franklin and Daisy (Callahan) Cain; grad. Lake Wales (Fla.) High Sch., 1937; m. William Adams Gunter, Oct. 14, 1946; 1 son, William Adams. Sec., Lake Wales Public Schs., Lake Wales State Bank, 1942-45; apptd. coordinator Ala. Office of Hwy. and Traffic Safety, Montgomery, 1971-72, apptd. dir. Office of Consumer Protection, 1972-78; apptd. treas. State of Ala., 1978, elected treas., 1978—. Mem. Nat. Democratic Platform Com., 1972, 76; elected to Ala. Dem. Exec. Com. from Dist. 81, 1974-78; mem. career devel. adv. bd. U. Ala.; mem. adv. bd. Sch. Home Econs., Auburn U.; mem. president's adv. council Marion (Ala.) Inst. Mem. Soc. Consumer Affairs Profls., Am. Council Consumer Interests, Nat. Assn. Consumer Agy. Adminstrs., D.A.R., Daus. of Am. Colonists, Women in Communications. Presbyterian. Club: Soroptimist. Office: State Capital Bldg Room 111 Montgomery AL 36130*

GUNTER, BONNIE CAROLYN, realtor; b. Piggot, Ark., Apr. 2, 1941; d. William T. and Lema O. (Dixon) Bradshaw; m. Robert Sharp Gunter, Aug. 17, 1960; children—Michelle, Robert Jr., Lori. Student S.E. Mo. State U., 1959-60, Realtors Inst., 1979, 83. Realtor Rainey Realty Co., Little Rock, 1978-84, assoc. v.p., 1984—. Vice pres. Little Rock PTA, 1977, pres., 1979; pres. chpt. Nat. Kidney Found., Little Rock, 1982-83. Recipient numerous sales awards, 1979-84. Mem. Little Rock Bd. Realtors, Women's Council Realtors, Home Builders Assn. Little Rock. Republican. Presbyterian (elder). Club: Bus. Women (Little Rock). Home: #1 Northwest Court Little Rock AR 72212 Office: Rainey Realty Co 10515 West Markham St Little Rock AR 72205

GUNTER, GRETCHEN, beverage co. executive; b. Ft. Worth, Tex., Apr. 13, 1942; d. William Clinton and Frances Virginia (Spinks) Weeden; student Gulf Park Coll., 1960; B.A., Tex. Christian U., 1963; M.A., U. Denver, 1979; children—Garrett Edward, Holli Gretchen. Tchr., Ft. Worth (Tex.) public schs., 1963-64, Denver public schs., 1965-69; pub. relations dir. Classic Chorale, Denver, 1974-75; asso. producer Noonday-KOA-TV, Denver, 1978; with Mountain Bell, Denver, 1979; dir. Vols. Callaway for Senate, 1980; orgnl. dir. Bradford for Congress, 1980; producer Pub. Access, United Cable TV, 1980; local govt. lobbyist Adolph Coors Co., Denver, 1980-84, regional mgr. govt. affairs, 1984—. Mem. Women in Communications (pres-elect 1980-81), Leadership Denver Assn. (dir. 1984—). Republican. Episcopalian. Clubs: Mile High Republican Women's Forum (charter pres. 1982-84), Colo. Fedn. Rep. Women, Nat. Fedn. Rep. Women, Aurora Rep. Women's. Home: 10020 E Maplewood Ave Englewood CO 80111 Office: 303 E 17th Ave Suite 880 Denver CO 80203

GUNTER, LITRA O'LINA, government official; b. Bessemer, Ala., Oct. 3, 1952; d. Ailue O'Dell and Louise L. Gunter; B.A., Spelman Coll., 1974; postgrad. Atlanta U., 1974-78, Substitute tchr. Atlanta Bd. Edn., 1977; with IRS, 1977; collection agt. HEW, Atlanta, 1977-78, mgmt. analyst, Washington, 1978-80; mgmt. analyst Dept. Edn., Washington, 1980, asst. on-site monitor ADP contract, 1980-83, on-site monitor ADP contract, 1983—; dir. Diversified Investments Inc.; pres. Gunter Systems Inc. Mem. Nat. Assn. Female Execs. (network dir.), Ga. Assn. of Historians, Assn. Records Mgrs. and Adminstrs., Am. Forum for Internat. Study (bd. dirs.), Am. Soc. Profl. and Exec. Women, Nat. Assn. Corp. Dirs. Home: 200 Randolph Rd Silver Spring MD 20904 Office: 7th and D Streets SW Washington DC 20202

GUNTER, MARY ANN, wholesale broker; b. Ardmore, Okla., May 19, 1949; d. Deward Earl and Verna Mae (Toups) Bannister; student Oscar Rose Jr. Coll., 1978, U. Okla., 1981—; children—Brandon Joseph, Rebecca Ann. Bookkeeper, Webbs Office Supply, Ardmore, 1968; asst. mgr. Beneficial Fin. Co., Dallas, 1969-73; apt. reservationist U. Okla. Housing Programs, 1977-80, mgr., 1980-84; small bus. cons., wholesale broker Shaklee Corp., 1984—. Chairperson, Norman (Okla.) Fair Housing Resource Bd., 1981-82. Mem. Assn. Coll. and Univ. Housing Officers, Southwest Assn. Coll. and Univ. Housing Officers (state dir.), U. Okla. Managerial Staff Assn. (sec. 1982-83). Roman Catholic. Clubs: Trosper Archery, Okla. State Archery Assn. (sec. 1980-81), Fellowship of Robin Hood. Home: 510 Rambling Oaks Dr Norman OK 73069

GUNZER, BARBARA S., consulting actuary; b. N.Y.C., Oct. 31, 1944; d. Jack and Lee (Baron) Weiser; m. Theodore G. Gunzer, Apr. 30, 1972. B.A.,

Queen's Coll., 1965. Tchr. math. N.Y.C. High Schs., 1965-67; asst. actuary Buck Cons., N.Y.C., 1968-79, assoc. cons. actuary, Dallas, 1982—. Actuarial mgr. A.S. Hansen, Dallas, 1980-82. Mem. Am. Acad. Actuaries. Home: 2815 Welborn St Apt 106 Dallas TX 75219

GUNZER, SHIRLEY ANNE, travel industry executive; b. Rockville Centre, N.Y., Sept. 4, 1938; d. Charles Richard and Margaret Elizabeth (Sheridan) G. A.A., Centenary Coll., 1958; student NYU, 1960-61. Instr., Pan Am. Airways, N.Y.C., 1965-67, sr. sales instr., 1967-69, needs assessment project mgr., 1969-74, mgr. mgmt. devel., 1974-79, dir. tng. program devel., 1979-81; dir. tng. and communications Hertz Corp., N.Y.C., 1981—; client instr. Kepner Tregoe, Princeton, N.J., 1972-81, Xerox Corp., Stamford, Conn., 1975-81, Bus. Processes Inc., Denver, 1979-81, Air Transp. Travel Industry Tng. Bd. of Gt. Britain, London, 1979-81. Mem. Am. Soc. Tng. and Devel., Mensa. Democrat. Episcopalian. Home: 426 W 23d St New York NY 10011 Office: Hertz Corp 660 Madison Ave New York NY 10021

GURFEIN, HADASSAH NEIMAN, clinical psychologist; b. Bklyn.; d. Morris and Dorothy (Wagner) Neiman; B.A., Barnard Coll., 1960; M.A., CCNY, 1962; Ph.D., Fordham U., 1977; postgrad. in psychoanalysis and psychotherapy NYU, 1977, in hypnosis Inst. of Pa. Hosp., 1982; m. Elisha Gurfein, July 31, 1966; children—Joshua Noah, Jonathan Daniel, David Michael. Diplomate Am. Bd. Marital and Family Therapy. Clin. psychologist Hadassah Hosp., Israel, 1962-63; psychologist, clin. fellow Bklyn. Coll., 1963-64; cons. psychologist L.I. Consultation Center, 1963-64; psychologist Lynbrook and Fairfield Public Schs., 1964-67; adj., dept. psychology Fairleigh Dickinson U., Teaneck, N.J., 1977-78; psychologist, chmn. child study team Dumont (N.J.) Pub. Schs., 1977-83; cons. psychologist Tourette and Tic Lab., Mt. Sinai Hosp., N.Y.C., 1981—, clin. instr. psychiatry; pvt. practice clin. psychologist, N.Y.C., 1977—; mem. Fedn. of Jewish Philanthropies Task Force on Mental Health. Mem. Am. Psychol. Assn., N.Y. State Psychol. Assn., N.J. Psychol. Assn., N.Y. Assn. Clin. Psychologists, N.J. Assn. Psychologists, Soc. Clin. and Exptl. Hypnosis, Psi Chi, Phi Delta Kappa (Ph.D. dissertation award, 1976). Jewish. Home: 156 Sherwood Pl Englewood NJ 07631 Office: 1155 Park Ave New York NY 10128

GURKE, SHARON MCCUE, naval officer; b. Bklyn., Apr. 4, 1949; d. James Ambrose and Marion Denise (Coombs) McCue; B.A., Molloy Cath. Coll., 1970; M.S. in Systems Mgmt., U. So. Calif., 1977; m. Lee Samuel Gurke, Apr. 16, 1977; children—Marion Dawn, Leigh Elizabeth. Commd. ensign U.S. Navy, 1970; advanced through grades to comdr., 1979; aircraft maintenance duty officer Orgn.-Intermediate Maintenance Officer, Comdr. Naval Air Force U.S. Pacific Fleet, Naval Air Sta., North Island, San Diego, 1974-77; head quality assurance div. Intermediate Maintenance Dept. Supporting Aircraft, Naval Air Sta., Miramar, San Diego, 1977-78, avionics div. officer, 1978-80; officer in charge Naval Aviation Engrng. Service Unit Pacific Naval Air Sta., North Island, 1980-82; aircraft intermediate maintenance officer Naval Air Sta., Alameda, Calif., 1982-84; aircraft intermediate maintenance officer Naval Sta., Rota, Spain, 1984-86, comdr. Naval Air Systems Command Aviation Maintenance Policy Br., 1986—. Lic. pilot; first female naval officer selected for aero. engrng. tng.; recipient Capt. Winifred Q. Collins award USN, 1980, Naval Commendation medal, 1982, 84. Mem. Ninety Nines, San Diego Naval Women Officers Network (chmn.). Home: 2511 Londonberry St Alexandria VA 22308

GURNE, PATRICIA DOROTHY, lawyer; b. Phila., May 25, 1941; d. George Albert and Dorothy (Hammett) G.; B.A., MacMurray Coll., 1965; J.D., George Washington U., 1969; grad. Nat. Inst. Trial Advocacy, 1974. Bar: , pres. 1984), 1969, D.C. 1971. Law clk. to Judge Joyce H. Green, Superior Ct. D.C., Washington, 1969-71; assoc. Jackson, Campbell & Parkinson, and predecessors, Washington, 1971-75, partner, 1975—; mem. D.C. Ct. Appeals Jud. Conf., 1977—, D.C. Circuit Jud. Conf., 1979—; mem. U.S. Dist. Ct. Grievance Com., 1983—. Trustee, George Washington U., 1981—; bd. dirs. D.C. Women's Com. for Crime Prevention, 1978-79. Mem. ABA, Bar Assn. D.C. (exec. council young lawyers sect. 1974-77, vice chmn. young lawyers sect. 1976-77, dir. 1986—, Young Lawyer of Yr. award 1979), Women's Bar Assn. (pres. 1978-79, dir. 1980-83), Women's Bar Found. (dir. 1981—, pres. 1984—), D.C. Bar (sec., dir. 1978-79, ethics com. 1979-82, judicial evaluation com. 1986—), George Washington Law Assn. (dir.). Office: 1120 20th St NW Washington DC 20036

GURNEY, CAROL ANN, office expansion service executive; b. East Orange, N.J., June 1, 1949; d. William John and Lily May (Curran) G. Student Franklin Jr. Coll. (Mass.), 1967. Exec. sec. NL Industries, West Caldwell, N.J., 1972-73; v.p. personnel and office mgmt. Dancer Fitzgerald Sample, Inc., Torrance, Calif., 1973-83; prin., owner Carol Gurney Assocs., Office Expansion Services, Los Angeles, 1983—; Vol., Mary Manning Walsh Home, N.Y.C., 1972-74, Jr. Blind Assn., Los Angeles, 1980-81. Mem. Los Angeles Advt. Women (dir. 1981-82, Most Profl. award 1982). Office: Carol Gurney Assocs Office Expansion Services 10745 Ashton Ave Los Angeles CA 90024

GUSTAFSON, BARBARA ANN HELTON, lawyer; b. Washington, Ill., Apr. 26, 1948; d. Joseph and Marilou (Buckles) Balogh; m. Lee Alan Gustafson, Dec. 20, 1969. B.Music, So. Ill. U., 1969; M.Mus. Edn., Vandercook Coll., 1972; J.D., U. Chgo., 1983. Bar: Ill. 1983. Tchr. music Harrison Sch., Wonderlake, Ill., 1969-72, Cook County Dist. 125, Alsip, Ill., 1972-73; dir. orch. Kankakee Dist. III, Ill., 1973-80; atty. MidCon Corp., Lombard, Ill., 1983—. Asst. dir. Kankakee Youth Symphony (Ill.), 1973-76; violinist Kankakee Orch., 1977-80; musician Kankakee Valley Theater, 1976-80. Mem. Ill. State Bar Assn., Chgo. Bar Assn., AAUW, Mu Phi Epsilon (treas. 1968-69). Lutheran. Home: 176 Hickory Creek Dr Frankfort IL 60423 Office: MidCon Corp 701 E 22nd St Lombard IL 60148

GUSTAFSON, DOROTHY EVELYN, engineering search consultant; b. Parker's Prairie, Minn., July 1, 1910; d. William and Lillian (Bausman) Black; student Iowa State Coll., 1928-29; B.S., U. Minn., 1938; m. Durant A. Labrie, Nov. 3, 1934 (div. 1943); children—Wilhemine LaBrie Saucier, Mary LaBrie Peterson, Yvonne LaBrie Turner, Valeria LaBrie; m. 2d, Leo F. Touhey, Aug. 9, 1947 (dec. 1972); children—Virginia Touhey, Carol Touhey Burns, Phillip, Maureen Touhey Anderson; m. 3d, Peter S. Gustafson, Aug. 2, 1975 (dec. Nov. 1981). Social worker State of Minn., 1933-40; recruiter Mpls. and St. Paul U.S. Employment Service, 1941-48; personnel dir. St. Barnabas Hosp., Mpls., 1952-53; mgr. Central Personnel and Guardian Personnel, Mpls., 1953-60; engrng. cons. Der-Kel Employment Service, Mpls., 1960-75, Dunhill Personnel, San Diego, 1975-77, Westbrooke Search, Inc., San Diego, 1977-82, Profl. Resources, Inc., St. Louis Park, Minn., 1982—; cons. N. Hennepin County Community Coll., State of Minn. Dept. Vocat. Edn., U. Minn. Sch. Bus. and Grad. Sch. Continuing Edn.. Recipient Internat. Merit award and key, Adminstrv. Mgmt. Soc., 1973; WCCO Radio, NW Ford Dealers and NW Orient Airlines Good Neighbor award, 1973; first recipient Minn. and Nat. Employment Assn. Counselor of the Yr. award, 1973. Mem. Adminstrv. Mgmt. Soc. Internat. (chpt. dir. 1967-75), Calif. Employment Assn. (state dir. 1975-77), Acad. Cert. Personnel Cons., Am. Soc. Execs. and Profl. Women, Nat. Assn. Female Execs., Nat. Assn. Personnel Cons., U. Minn. Alumni Assn. Republican. Roman Catholic. Clubs: Univ. Minn. Alumni, Pilots Internat. Office: Profl Resources Inc 5354 Cedar Lake Rd Suite 102 Saint Louis Park MN 54426

GUSTAFSON, ROSE ELAINE, city ofcl.; b. Alta., Can., July 11, 1927; came to U.S., 1927; d. Albert Allen and Ronghild (Olsenberg) Olson; student Seattle Pacific U., 1964-65, Am. Inst. Banking, 1966-70, Inst. Fin. Edn., 1972-76; m. David E. Gustafson, Dec. 26, 1946; children—Gail Lynne, Shirley Jean, Jeffery David. With Rainier Bank, Seattle, 1957-70; v.p. br. ops. Queen City Savs. & Loan, Seattle, 1970-78; exec. v.p. Sound Savs. & Loan, Seattle, 1978-81; asst. city treas. Seattle, 1981—; regional mem. Pres.'s Commn. on White House Fellowships, 1979. Trustee Alki Found.; v.p. Small Bus. Council, Seattle C. of C., 1981—, trustee, 1979—; trustee Visitors & Conv. Bur., 1980-81; bd. dirs. Cardiopulmonary Research Inst., 1982—; mem. Virginia Mason Assos., 1982—. Mem. U.S., Wash., Seattle savs. leagues. Republican. Clubs: Zonta (pres. 1978-79), Women & Bus. (pres. 1980-81, trustee 1978-81). Office: 103 Municipal Bldg Seattle WA 98104

GUSTIN, ANN WINIFRED, psychologist; b. Winchester, Mass.; d. Bertram Pettingill and Ruth Lillian (Weller) G.; B.A. with honors in Psychology, U. Mass., 1963; M.S. (USPHS fellow), Syracuse U., 1966, Ph.D., 1969. Research asst., psychology trainee U. Mass., Tufts U., Harvard U., Syracuse U., 1961-66; psychology intern VA, Canandaigua, N.Y., 1967-68; asst. prof. psychology U. Regina (Sask., Can.), 1969-74, assoc. prof. psychology, dir. counseling services, head clin. tng., 1974-78; pvt. practice psychology, Carrollton, Ga., 1978—, Atlanta, 1983—; staff tng. cons. Frobisher Bay Dept. Social Services, N.W. Territories, Can., 1979-80; cons. staff Tanner Hosp.; ancillary staff West Paces Ferry Hosp.; psychiat. cons. Social Security Adminstrn., Ga. Dept. Human Resources, 1980—. Membership chmn. Carroll County Mental Health Assn., 1979-81. Registered psychologist, Sask.; lic. psychologist, Ga. Mem. Am. Psychol. Assn., Can. Psychol. Assn., Ga. Psychol. Assn., Sask. Psychol. Assn. (mem. exec. council 1971-72, registrar 1972-73). Office: 107 College St Carrollton GA 30117 also One Decatur Town Ctr 150 E Ponce de Leon Ave Suite 460 Decatur GA 30030

GUTHERY, GRACE MAXINE, educator, administrator; b. Athol, Ky., Aug. 24, 1934; d. Walker and Dora Belle (Chandler) McIntosh; children—James, Kenneth, Max. A.A., Lees Jr. Coll., 1973; B.A., McPherson Coll., 1978. Cook, sec. Oakdale Christian High Sch., Jackson, Ky., 1969-75, tchr., adminstr., 1979—; admissions sec., head resident Central Coll., McPherson, Kans., 1975-79. Author: (with Myrtle Anderson) The School in the Vale, 1985. Mem. Womens Christian Temperance Union, Christian Writers Club. Democrat. Methodist. Avocations: reading; sewing; traveling. Home: RR 1 Box 332 Jackson KY 41339 Office: Oakdale Christian High Sch RR1 Box 332 Jackson KY 41339

GUTHRIE, ANN GERTRUDE, health administrator physical therapist, consultant; b. Boulder, Colo., Aug. 4, 1943; d. John T. and Ruth I. Guthrie; B.S. in Phys. Therapy, 1966; M.S., U. Notre Dame, 1977. Phys. therapist Mass. Gen. Hosp., Boston, 1965-67, Univ. Hosp., Denver, 1967-70; dir. phys. therapy Mercy Med. Center, Denver, 1970-72, dir. allied services, 1972-76, patient rep., 1976-83, adminstrv. dir., 1979-83; dir. rehab. services Nat. Jewish Ctr. Immunology and Resp. Medicine, and Denver, 1983—; instr. U. Colo., 1967-70; cons. HEW, 1973-79, grant reviewer, Rockville, Md., 1979; acting dir., adminstr. McNamara Hosp. and Nursing Home, Fairplay, Colo., 1975; mem. State Bd. Phys. Therapy, 1973-76. Lic. phys. therapist, Colo. Democrat. Baptist. Contbr. articles on phys. therapy to profl. jours. Office: 1400 Jackson St Denver CO 80206

GUTHRIE, HELEN ANDREWS, educator; b. Sarnia, Can., Sept. 1925; came to U.S., 1946, naturalized, 1957; d. David and Helen Parker (Sweet) Andrews; B.S., U. Western Ont., 1946; M.S., Mich. State U., 1948; Ph.D., U. Hawaii, 1968; D.Sc., U. Western Ont., 1982; m. George M. Guthrie, June 4, 1949; children—Barbara, Jane, James. Asst. prof. nutrition Pa. State U., 1948-69, assoc. prof., 1969-72, prof., 1972—, head dept. nutrition Coll. Human Devel., 1979—; dir. Nabisco Brands Inc. Chmn., State College (Pa.) Bd. Health, 1978-82. Mem. Am. Inst. Nutrition (pres. 1987—), Soc. Nutrition Edn. (pres. 1979-80), Am. Dietetic Assn. Home: 1316 S Garner St State College PA 16801 Office: 106 Human Development University Park PA 16802

GUTHRIE, JANET, racing driver; b. Iowa City, Iowa, Mar. 7, 1938; d. William Lain and Jean Ruth (Midkiff) Guthrie; B.S. in Physics, U. Mich., 1960. Comml. pilot and flight instr., 1958-61; research and devel. engr. Republic Aviation Corp., Farmingdale, N.Y., 1960-67; publs. engr. Sperry Systems, Sperry Corp., Great Neck, N.Y., 1968-73; racing driver Sports Car Club Am. and Internat. Motor Sports Assn., 1963—; profl. racing driver U.S. Auto Club and Nat. Assn. for Stock Car Racing, 1975—. Recipient Curtis Turner award Nat. Assn. for Stock Car Racing-Charlotte World 600, 1976; First in Class, Sebring 12-hour, 1970; N.Atlantic Road Racing champion, 1973. Mem. Madison Ave. Sports Car Driving and Chowder Soc. First woman to qualify for and race in Indpls. 500, 1977, finished 9th, 1978.

GUTHRIE, MARILYN EDITH, association executive; b. Auburn, N.Y., Oct. 5, 1946; d. George Nelson and Marjorie Estelle (Field) G.; A.A.S., SUNY, Morrisville, 1966. Various secretarial positions, 1966-75; exec. asst. Northeastern Retail Lumbermens Assn., Rochester, N.Y., 1975-79, sr. v.p., Wellesley, Mass. and Rochester, 1979—. Mem. Meeting Planners Internat., Hotel Sales and Mgmt. Assn., Nat. Assn. Exhibit Mgrs. Republican. Office: 339 East Ave Rochester NY 14604

GUTHRIE, MYRNA JEAN, educator; b. Newton, Iowa, June 30, 1929; d. Frank Andrew and Hazel (Dolph) Guthrie; student Central Coll., 1947-49; B.A., Drake U., 1951, M.S., 1963. Child welfare worker State of Iowa, 1951-60; guidance counselor Newton Community Schs., 1960—, coordinator jr. high honors program; counselor Upward Bound, Central Coll., Pella, Iowa, 1967; cons. Jasper County Headstart program, 1968; coordinator Newton Achievement Motivation Project, 1971-72, Futures project Newton Community Sch., 1975. Past bd. dirs. Jasper County Community Action; past pres. RMR Soc.; past bd. dirs. Newton Community Orch; past pres. Iowa Future Problem Solving Bd. Recipient Maytag Found. Conv. award, 1965; named Nat. Future Problem Solving Coach of Yr., 1980. Mem. Internat. Platform Assn., NEA, Newton Edn. Assn., Am., Iowa personnel and guidance assns., Newton Bus. and Profl. Women's Club (past pres.), Jasper County Hist. Soc., Iowa Woman's Polit. Caucus, Newton Community Theater, Questers (past pres.), Alpha Xi Delta, Alpha Kappa Delta, Beta Sigma Phi. Republican. Methodist. Clubs: Soroptimist (past pres.) (Newton); Hazel Dell Acad., PEO. Co-pub. series Before the Colors Fade. Home: 326 E 4th St S Newton IA 50208

GUTMANN, BARBARA LANG, nurse, educator; b. Niagara Falls, N.Y.; d. Frank J. and Beryl (Tennant) Lang; m. James F. Gutmann, June 25, 1960; children—Carolyn P., Bennett J. Student SUNY-Cortland, 1952-53; B.S. in Nursing cum laude, Niagara U., 1956; cert. sch. nurse tchr. Syracuse U., 1962; M.S. in Nursing, SUNY-Buffalo, 1975. Cert. pub. health nurse, basic CPR instr., Calif., N.Y. Staff nurse VA Hosp., Syracuse, N.Y., 1956-58; pub. health nurse Syracuse City Health Dept., 1958-62, County Dept. Pub. Welfare, 1961-62; sch. nurse tchr. North Syracuse Central Schs., 1962-65; vol. Peace Corps, India, 1965-66; tchr. educable retarded North Syracuse Central Schs., 1966-67; staff nurse Stanford U. Hosp., Palo Alto, Calif., 1970-71; pvt. duty nurse, Buffalo, 1972-74; asst. prof. nursing Niagara County Community Coll., Sanborn, N.Y., 1975-77; dir. nursing services Homemaker Upjohn Contract Offices, Santa Barbara County Calif., 1977-78; project dir. Upjohn Health Care Services, Santa Barbara, 1978; dir. nursing Sansum Med. Clinic, Santa Barbara, 1979-81; dir. inservice edn. and staff devel. Pinecrest Hosp., Santa Barbara, 1981-82; dir. edn. Meml. Hosp., Santa Barbara, 1982-84; instr. nursing, health tech. and adult edn. Santa Barbara City Coll., 1984—; profl. adv. com. and utilization rev. com. Niagara County Health Dept., 1976-77; mem. Niagara Falls Regional Hypertension Bd., 1975-77, Buffalo Quality of Life Com., 1976-77; profl. adv. bd. upper div. nursing program Daemen Coll., Buffalo, 1975-77; ARC home nurse multiple sclerosis patients, 1978; substitute clin. nursing instr. Santa Barbara City Coll. Assoc. Degree Nursing Program, 1978; adv. com. Upjohn Health Care Services, 1979—; health occupations adv. com. med. assisting program Santa Barbara Community Coll., 1980; mem. Head Trauma Recovery Group, Santa Barbara, 1982-85. Adv. com. Friendship Ctr., Santa Barbara, 1977-79; bd. dirs. Friendship Sr. Day Care Ctr., Montecito, Calif., 1986—; basic CPR com. Am. Heart Assn., 1982-85; bishop's com. Diocese of Syracuse, 1965; bd. dirs. Onondaga County Health Assn., 1965; edn. com. Hillbrook Detention Home, 1967-70; mem. Inner City Bd. Dirs., Syracuse, 1968-70; sec. exec. com. bd. dirs. Onondaga Pastoral Counseling Ctr., 1967-70; asst. leader Girl Scouts/Cub Scouts, 1976-79; adult com. Boy Scouts Am., 1981—; bd. dirs. Jodi House, 1982-85. Mem. Assn. Rehab. Nurses, Nurses Christian Fellowship, Sigma Alpha Sigma. Roman Catholic. Home: 5474 Berkeley Rd Santa Barbara CA 93111 Office: Santa Barbara City Coll Dept Nursing 421 Cliff Dr Santa Barbara CA 93109

GUTREUTER, NANCY PAULY, pre-school operator; b. Chgo., Apr. 30, 1938; d. Carl H. and Helen Louise (Day) Pauly; m. Robert L. Gutreuter, Aug. 17, 1968 (div.). M.S., Marquette U., 1959; M.A., Northeastern Ill. U., 1970. Tchr. Northbrook Sch. Dist. 30, Ill., 1959-67, asst. prin., 1967-69, prin., 1969-70; owner, dir., tchr. Pre-Sch., Glenview, Ill., 1970-79, La Petite Ecole Pre-Sch., Northbrook, Ill., 1970—. Mem. DAR, Fairbanks Family In Am., NEA, Nat. Assn. for Edn. of Young Children, Ill. Assn. for Edn. of Young Chilren, Chgo. Assn. for Edn. of Young Children. Republican. Roman Catholic. Avocations: golf; walking; tennis; gardening; reading, travel. Home: 1425 Pebble Creek Dr Glenview IL 60025 Office: La Petite Ecole Pre Sch 2700 Willow Rd Northbrook IL 60062

GUTTERMAN-REINFELD, DEBRA ELLEN, physician, consultant; b. N.Y.C., Nov. 13, 1948; d. George and Nettie (Liss) Gutterman; m. Stuart Glenn Reinfeld, June 20, 1982; children—Alan Jeffrey, Naomi Rebecca. B.S., R.N. magna cum laude, SUNY Downstate Med. Ctr., 1972; postgrad. U. Auton, Guadalajara Sch. Medicine (Mex.), 1973-75; M.D., Coll. Medicine and Dentistry N.J., 1977. Intern, Boston City Hosp., 1977-78; resident in medicine Maimonides Med. Ctr., Bklyn., 1978-79, 79-80, Mt. Sinai Med. Ctr., Miami Beach, Fla., 1982-83; fellow Jackson Meml. Hosp., Miami, Fla., 1980-82; internist, cons. infectious diseases, chief dept. internal medicine Health Am., Ft. Lauderdale, Fla., 1983—. Fellow ACP. Jewish.

GUY, KARLA DANETTE, systems engineer; b. St. Louis, Aug. 17, 1955; d. Elmer and Charlotte (Robinson) G. B.S., Ga. State U., 1977. Supr. Travelers Ins. Co., Los Angeles, 1978-82; programmer Aerospace Co., Los Angeles, 1982-84; systems engr. IBM, Dallas, 1984—; gen. ptnr. Jewelry Connections, Etc.; cons. Exec. Motors, Los Angeles, 1983-84. Editor newspaper Inner Circle, 1983. Founder Reflective Changes, St. Louis, 1977; mem. Los Angeles Youth Motivation Task Force, 1983, Adopt-a-Sch., Dallas, 1986—. Mem. NAACP, Mortar Board (leadership award 1977).

GUY, LORA JANELLE, government official; b. Banner, Miss., Aug. 15, 1933; d. Willie Clark and Lora Allie (Moore) Wilson; A.A., Cochise Jr. Coll., 1976; B.S., SUNY, Albany, 1979; postgrad. U. Ariz., 1980; grad. Armed Forces Staff Coll., 1982; M.P.A., Golden Gate U., 1985; m. Bill A. Welch, Aug. 6, 1960 (dec. 1981); children—Karen Sue, Bill A., Richard; m. 2d, David R. Guy, Feb. 12, 1983. Exec. sec. various depts. within the govt. at numerous mil. installations, 1956-74; plans and programs specialist U.S. Army Air Traffic Control Activity, Fort Huachuca, Ariz., 1974-79, mgmt. analyst, comptroller office, 1979-82, chief mgmt. programs br., 1983—. Recipient Outstanding Alumnus award Ariz. Community Coll., 1985. Mem. Nat. Assn. Female Execs., Am. Soc. Mil. Comptrollers (past pres. Cochise chpt.), Soc. Am. Valuve Engrs., Aircraft Owners and Pilots Assn. Democrat. Home: Route 1 Box 121 Hereford AZ 85615 Office: US Army Communications Command Comptroller Office Fort Huachuca AZ 85613

GUY, MILDRED DOROTHY, educator; b. Brunswick, Ga.; d. John and Mamie Paul (Smith) Floyd; B.S. in Social Sci., Savannah State Coll., 1949; M.A. in Am. History, Atlanta U., 1952; postgrad. U. So. Calif., U. Colo.; m. Charles H. Guy, Aug. 18, 1956 (div. 1979); 1 dau., Rhonda Lynn. Tchr. social studies L.S. Ingraham High Sch., Sparta, Ga.; tchr. English and social studies North Jr. High Sch., Colorado Springs, 1958-84; ret., 1984; cooperating tchr. Tchr. Edn. Program, Col. Coll., 1968-72. Fund raiser for Citizens for Theatre Auditorium, Colorado Springs, 1979; bd. dirs. Urban League, 1971-75; del. to County and State Democratic Conv., 1972, 76, 80, 84; mem. Pike's Peak Community Coll. Council, 1976-83; mem. council of 500, Colorado Springs Opera; mem. nominating com. Wagon Wheel council Girl Scouts U.S.A., 1985—. Recipient Viking award North Jr. High Sch., 1973; Outstanding Black Woman of Colorado Springs award, 1975; named Pacesetter, Atlanta U., 1980-81, Outstanding Black Educator of Yr., Black Educators of Dist. II, Colorado Springs, 1981; Outstanding Achievement in Edn. award Negro Hist. Assn. of Colorado Springs, 1983, Outstanding Ednl. Service award Colo. Dept. and State Bd. Edn., 1983, Dedicated Service award Pikes Peak Community Coll., 1983; Outstanding Community Leadership award Alpha Phi Alpha, 1985; award Colo. Black Woman for Polit. Action, 1985, Sphinx award, 1986. Mem. NEA, (life mem.), Fedn. of Bus. and Profl. Women, AAUW, Colo. Council of Social Studies, Assn. for Study of Afro-Am. Life and History, Colo. LWV, Friends of Pioneers Mus. (life mem.), NAACP, Alpha Delta Kappa, Alpha Kappa Alpha (chpt. pres. 1984-86, award 1986). Baptist. Club: Elks. Home: 3132 Constitution Ave Colorado Springs CO 80909

GUY, ROXANNE JOSEPHINE, physician; b. Galesburg. Ill., Aug. 15, 1952; d. Robert Edward and Gertrude Josephine (Hoegg) Bowman; B.S., Ill. State U., 1974; postgrad. Salzburg Coll., 1973; M.D., So. Ill. U., 1977; m. Curtis Eugene Guy, May 17, 1980. Resident So. Ill. U. Sch. Medicine Affiliated Hosps., Springfield, 1977-81, chief resident gen. surgery, 1981-82, resident in plastic surgery, 1982-83, chief resident plastic surgery, 1983-84. Diplomate Am. Bd. Surgery, Nat. Bd. Med. Examiners. Mem. AMA, Am. Med. Women's Assn., Fla. State Med. Soc., Brevard County Med. Soc., So. Ill. U. Sch. Medicine Alumni Soc. Methodist. Contbr. articles to profl. jours. Home: 255 Paradise Blvd Indialantic FL 32903 Office: 1355 S Hickory St Melbourne FL 32901

GUYRE, JUDITH PITZO, industrial drive company executive; b. Phila., Nov. 27, 1945; d. Frank Joseph and Carolyn Marie (Miller) Pitzo; student parochial schs., spl. courses; m. Ronald T. Guyre, Aug. 19, 1978; children—Garrett M., Aubrey Eve. Sec. to pres. Alpha Lithograph, Camden, N.J., 1964-67; adminstrv. asst. Transam. Ins. Co., Phila., 1967-70; office mgr. Power Quip/C.J. Kitching Assocs., Pennsauken, N.J., 1972-78; v.p. Brisbane Indsl. Drive Co., Jim Thorpe, Pa., 1978—; seminar leader; mgr. distbn. sales. Asst. to dir. Voorhees Community, Edn. and Recreation Program; sec./treas. Top O'the Mountain Ecumenical Council for 8 area chs.; bd. dirs. community youth group. Mem. Nat. Assn. Female Execs., Power Transmission Reps. Assn. Republican. Roman Catholic. Home: Star Rt 2 Box 16A Blakeslee PA 18610 Office: Box 12 2d Star Rt Jim Thorpe PA 18229

GUZIEC, JOAN ANN, lawyer; b. Holyoke, Mass., Aug. 23, 1943; d. Joseph John and Ann Victoria (Zagrocka) Wdowiak; B.S., Am. Internat. Coll., 1967; M.Ed., Springfield Coll., 1969; J.D., Western New Eng. Sch. Law, 1976; m. Walter Paul Guziec, Jr., July 28, 1961 (div.); 1 dau., Joy A. Tchr., Minnechaug Regional High Sch., Wilbraham, Mass., 1967—; admitted to Mass. bar, 1977, U.S. Dist. Ct. bar, 1977; individual practice law, Springfield, Mass., 1977—. Mem. Am. Bar Assn., Mass. Bar Assn., Hampden County Bar Assn. Democrat. Roman Catholic. Home: 1715 Carew St Springfield MA 01104 Office: 31 Elm St Suite 651 Springfield MA 01103

GUZY, MARGUERITA LINNES, educator, consultant; b. Santa Monica, Calif., Nov. 19, 1938; d. Paul William and Margarete (Rodowski) Linnes; m. Stephen Paul Guzy, Aug. 26, 1962 (div. 1969); 1 child, David Paul. A.A., Santa Monica Coll., 1959; student U. Mexico, 1960; B.A., UCLA, 1966, teaching credential, 1967, M.A., 1973. Med. stenographer Santa Monica Hosp., Calif., 1957-58; keypunch verifier/lead Douglas Aircraft, Santa Monica, 1960-63; tchr. Inglewood Schs., Calif., 1967—, dept. chmn., 1971-81, state cert. lang. assessor, 1977—, tchr. assistance specialist, 1986—; tchr. Santa Monica Coll., 1976-77. Co-author: Curriculum Framework, 1978; Project Flores: A Bilingual Program, 1985; author: English Mechanics Workbook, 1986. Named Tchr. of Yr., Monroe Jr. High Sch., Inglewood, 1973. Mem. NEA, Calif. Tchrs. Assn., Inglewood Tchrs. Assn., UCLA Alumni Assn. (life), UCLA Prytanean Alumni Assn. Republican. Mem. Unity Ch. Club: Westside Alano (West Los Angeles, Calif.) (treas. 1982-83). Avocations: swimming; reading; travel; music; cooking. Office: Monroe Jr High Sch Inglewood Unified Sch Dist 10711 10th Ave Inglewood CA 90303

GUZY, MARY MARGARET, real estate appraiser; b. Staten Island, N.Y., Dec. 18, 1955; d. Frank and Ethel (Corcoran) G. B.A., Fordham U., 1977; appraisal cert. NYU, 1980. Library asst. Landauer Assocs., Inc., N.Y.C., 1977-78, sec., 1978-80, research assoc., 1980-82, assoc., 1982-84; sr. appraiser Real Estate Research Corp., N.Y.C., 1984; assoc. Krauser, Welsh, Sorich & Cirz, Morristown, N.J., 1984—. Mem. Rho Epsilon. Office: 182 South St Morristown NJ 07960

GWATHNEY, ROWEDA SUE, scaffold company executive; b. Henderson, Tex., Feb. 11, 1941; d. James Calvin and Fannie Juanita (Wiggins) McCaughey Slaughter; m. Franklin Leon Gwathney, Mar. 21, 1964; 1 dau., Tami-Shea. Student So. Meth. U., 1966-69. Western sec. treas. Western Window Cleaning Service, Dallas, 1964—; sec.-treas. Am. Equipment & Rental, Dallas, 1973-79; pres. A. L. Dennis Co., Dallas, 1979—; pres. Swing Scaffolds, Inc., Dallas, 1980—. Mem. Am. Subcontractors, Assoc. Gen. Contractors, Women in Constrn., Scaffold Industry Assn., Dallas Bldg. Owners and Mgrs. Club: Engineer (Dallas). Home: 1613 Merrimac Trail Garland TX 75043 Office: 4758 Gretna St Swing Scaffolds Inc Dallas TX 75207

GWIN, DAWN SIMMONS, graphic designer; b. Marshall, Tex., Aug. 23, 1951; d. Aura L. and Janette Fason (Ryan) Simmons; B.A., Trinity U., 1973; postgrad. U. Tex., San Antonio, 1978-80. Communications mgr. Frost Nat. Bank, San Antonio, 1976-80; editor San Antonio Mag., 1980-81; dir. mktg. 1776, Inc., San Antonio, 1981; owner The Drawing Room, San Antonio, 1981—. Mem. Internat. Assn. Bus. Communicators (awards of merit 1980, award of excellence 1978, dir. 1982), Women in Communications (award of excellence 1981), Am. Mktg. Assn. (dir.), San Antonio Press Club (1st v.p.), Chi Beta Epsilon, Kappa Delta Pi. Republican. Roman Catholic. Home: 14806

Gallant Fox San Antonio TX 78248 Office: 1100 NW Loop 410 Suite 402 San Antonio TX 78213

GYOR, HARRIET SUE, hypnotist, clinic director, author; b. Holbrook, Nebr., Dec. 25, 1942; d. William A. and Helen Joyce (Davis) Gardner; student Compton Jr. Coll., 1960-61, U. Calif., Berkeley, 1961-62; m. Jon Wesley Gyor, July 6, 1962 (div. 1979); children—Julie Ann, William Jon. Teaching asst. sign lang. elem. sch., Santa Fe Springs, Calif., 1971-74; dir. TERRAP, Orange County, Calif., 1976—; owner PGI Pub. Co., Westminster, Calif., 1980—. Vol., Norwalk State Hosp., 1965-67; asst. coordinator seminars for nurses, on phobias Golden West Coll., 1979, 81. Cert. leader TERRAP programs. Mem. Phobia Soc. Am., Am. Booksellers Assn. Mem. Ch. of Religious Sci. Author: Living in Hell: An Agoraphobic Experience, 1980; A.C.T.; Anxiety Control Techniques, 1982. Office: 14140 Beach Blvd Suite 204 Westminster CA 92683

HAAG, CAROL ANN GUNDERSON, marketing director; b. Mpls.; d. Glenn Alvin and Genevieve Esther (Knudson) Gunderson; B.J., U. Mo., 1969; postgrad. Roosevelt U., Chgo., 1975—; m. Lawrence S. Haag, Aug. 30, 1969; 1 child, Maren. Reporter, Waukegan (Ill.) News Sun, summers 1966-69; pub. relations writer, advt. copywriter Am. Hosp. Supply Corp., Evanston, 1969-70, also free-lance editor Lake County (Ill.) Circle weekly newspaper; asst. dir. pub. relations Rush-Presbyn.-St. Luke's Med. Center, Chgo., 1970-71; asst. mgr. pub. and employee communications Quaker Oats Co., Chgo., 1971-72, mgr. editorial communications, 1972-74, mgr. employee communications programs, 1974-77, also mem. corp. office planning com., 1972-77; dir. public relations Shaklee Corp., San Francisco, 1978-82; pres. CH & Assocs., 1982-84; dir. corp. communications BRAE Corp., 1984; dir. mktg. St. Francis Meml. Hosp., 1985—; cons., 1982—. Bd. dirs. Calif. League for Handicapped; adv. bd. San Francisco Spl. Olympics; mem. public relations com. San Francisco Recreation and Parks Dept., San Francisco Vol. Bur. Recipient 1st Place Cert. award Printing Industry Am., 1972, 74, 1st Place Spl. Communication award Internat. Assn. Bus. Communicators, 1974, First Place Citation for Outstanding Editorial Achievement award Chg. Assn. Bus. Communicators, 1974. Mem. Nat. Acad. TV Arts and Scis. (Chgo. and San Francisco chpts.), Indsl. Communication Council, Public Relations Soc. Am., San Francisco C. of C. (public relations com.), San Francisco Press Club. Presbyn. Home: 133 Fernwood Dr Moraga CA 94556 Office: Saint Francis Meml Hosp 900 Hyde St San Francisco CA 94109

HAAG, CARRIE A., association executive; b. Chgo., July 7, 1950; d. Arthur L. and Janice (Tidmarsh) H. B.A., Purdue U., 1972; M.A., Eastern Ky. U., 1977, Ed.S., 1978; postgrad. U. N.C.-Greensboro, 1978-79. Dir. nat. championships Assn. for Intercollegiate Athletics for Women, Washington, 1979-82; asst. dir. athletics Dartmouth Coll., Hanover, N.H., 1982-84; exec. dir. U.S. Field Hockey Assn., Inc., Colorado Springs, Colo., 1984—. Democrat. Avocations: running, sailing. Home: 405 Bear Creek Pl Colorado Springs CO 80906 Office: US Field Hockey Assn 1750 E Boulder St Colorado Springs CO 80909

HAAG, CINDY CHALK, state social service administrator; b. Vancouver, Wash., Feb. 27, 1943; d. Elmer Leroy and Faye (Cardon) Chalk; m. William Horace Gammell, Aug. 1, 1964 (div. Nov. 1972); 1 child, Michael W.; m. Max Leo Haag, Aug. 9, 1973; stepchildren—Shannon, Darin. B.S., Brigham Young U., 1964. With Dept. Social Service State of Utah, 1970—, eligibility specialist Assistance Payments Adminstrn., Salt Lake City, 1977-79, state eligibility coordinator, 1979-81, dir., 1981—. Mem. Am. Pub. Welfare Assn. Republican. Mormon. Office: Dept Social Services Assistance Payment Adminstrn 150 West N Temple Salt Lake City UT 84145

HAAR, ANA-MARÍ FERNÁNDEZ, advertising/public relations executive; b. Oriente Province, Cuba, Mar. 25, 1951; came to U.S., 1960, naturalized, 1970; d. Gilberto and Esmeralda Emiliana (Díaz) Fernández; m. Jerry N. Haar, June 1, 1984. Grad. Miami Dade Community Coll., 1971; student Barry Coll., 1972-78. Adminstrv. asst. thru asst. v.p. nat. accounts Flagship Bank, Miami Beach, Fla., 1971-77; v.p. comml. lending Jefferson Nat. Bank, Miami Beach, 1977-78; pres. IAC Advt. Group, Miami, 1978—; instr. Miami Dade Community Coll. Women in Mgmt. Program, 1980-81; hostess Sta. WPBT Program Viva. Mem. Dade County Commn. on Status of Women, 1979-82; chmn. Econ. Devel. Task Force of Commn. on Status of Women, 1979-82; bd. dirs. Downtown Miami Bus. Assn., 1979-82, Internat. Ctr. of Fla.; mem. Dist. Export Council; hostess (program) Viva, WPBT-TV. Recipient Gran Orden Martiana of Cuban Lyceum for excellence in community service, 1976. Mem. Advt. Fedn. Greater Miami, Greater Miami Advt. Fedn. (bd. dirs.), Asociación de Publicitarios Latino-Americanos (v.p.), Miami Beach C. of C. (hon. life), Greater Miami C. of C., Hispanic Heritage Festival Com.. Home: 2451 Brickell Ave Miami FL 33162 Office: 3050 Biscayne Blvd Suite 500 Miami FL 33137

HAARSGAARD, MARGARET LEE CLAYTON, interior designer; b. Durham, N.C., Mar. 15, 1952; d. Lonnie Lee and Mary (Moser) Clayton; m. Walter Joseph Haarsgaard, Oct. 29, 1983. B.F.A., Va. Commonwealth U., 1974. Dir. store planning and showroom display Horizons Inc., Hickory, N.C., 1974-75; freelance showroom display cons., High Point, 1975-76; sr. designer store planning dept. Drexel Heritage Furnishings Inc. (N.C.), 1976-79, store design coordinator, 1979-81, dir. display planning, 1979-82; owner, pres. Clayton Haarsgaard, design and advt. cons., Glencoe, Ill., 1982—. Mem. adv. council Western Carolina U. Mem. Am. Soc. Interior Designers (profl. mem.), Inst. Bus. Designers (profl. mem.), Nat. Trust Historic Preservation. Republican. Methodist. Home: 470 Greenwood Ave Glencoe IL 60022 Office: Clayton & Haarsgaard Ltd 1229 Greenbay Rd Wilmette IL

HAAS, CAROLYN BUHAI, writer, publisher, consultant; b. Chgo., Jan. 1, 1926; d. Michael and Tillie (Weiss) Buhai; m. Robert Green Haas, June 29, 1947 (dec. June 30, 1984); children—Andrew Robert, Mari Beth, Thomas Michael, Betsy Ann, Karen Sue. B.Ed., Smith Coll., Northampton, Mass., 1947; postgrad. Nat. Coll. Edn., Evanston, Ill., 1956-59; Art Inst. Chgo., 1958-59. Tchr., Francis W. Parker Sch., Chgo., 1947-49; tchr. art Glencoe Pub. Schs., Ill., 1967-68, substitute tchr., 1964-72; co-founder PAR Leadership Tng. Found., Northfield, Ill., 1969-81; pres., editor CBH Pub., Inc., Northfield, 1979—; cons. presch. sci. program Mus. Sci. and Industry, Chgo.; columnist Day Care and Early Edn. mag.; cons. in field. Author: (with Ann Cole and Betty Weinberger) I Saw a Purple Cow, 1972; A Pumpkin In A Pear Tree, 1974; Children Are Children Are Children, 1976; Backyard Vacation, 1978; Purple Cow to the Rescue, 1982; Recipes for Fun and Learning, 1982; author: The Big Book of Recipes for Fun, 1979; Look At Me: Activities for Babies and Toddlers, 1985. Contbr. articles to profl. jours. Pres., West Sch. PTA, Glencoe; pres. Jr. Bd. Scholarship and Guidance, Chgo.; bd. dirs. Family Counseling Service of Glencoe, Glencoe Human Relations Com.; pres., sec., bd. dirs. Glencoe Pub. Library; co-founder Glencoe Patriotic Days Com.; co-chmn. Frank Lloyd Wright Bridge Com., Glencoe; pres., bd. dirs. Chgo. League Smith Coll.; mem. women's bd. Northwestern U.; bd. dirs. Chgo. chpt. Am. Jewish Com.; mem. regional adv. bd. Am. Found. for Blind; mem. women's com. Chgo. Symphony Orch. Clubs. Mem. Soc. Children's Bookwriters, Children's Reading Roundtable, Nat. Assn. Edn. Young Children, Assn. Childhood Edn. Internat., IRA, NEA, Phi Delta Kappa. Democrat. Jewish. Club: Northmoor Country (Highland Park, Ill.). Avocations: art; reading; sports; travel. Office: CBH Publishing Inc 464 Central Northfield IL 60093

HAAS, DEBRA KAYE, nurse; b. Parkersburg, W.Va., Mar. 28, 1952; d. John Martin and Donna Jean (Grubb) Pugh; A.Nursing, Parkersburg Community Coll., 1977; m. Thomas Lee Haas, Aug. 21, 1975. Dir. nursing Christian Anchorage Nursing Home, Marietta, Ohio, 1977-80; rev. coordinator Area VIII Peer Rev., Zanesville, Ohio, 1980-81; dir. nursing Hickory Creek Nursing Center, The Plains, Ohio, 1981-82, Marietta Convalescent Center, 1982-83; owner, pres. PDQ Nursing, Inc. Reno, Ohio, 1983—. Mem. Belpre Area C. of C. Mem. Decatur Chapel Ch. Home: Rt #1 Box 234 Newport OH 45768 Office: PO Box 40 Reno OH 45773

HAAS, ELEANOR A., marketing and communications consultant; b. Jersey City, Mar. 12, 1932; d. Nicholas Mark and Eleanor (Cochran) Alter de Csanytalek; m. Peter Ralph Haas, Oct. 22, 1966. B.A., Smith Coll., 1953; cert. N.Y. Sch. Interior Design, 1960. Exec. sec. MCA Artists Ltd., N.Y.C., 1954-56; exec. sec. Young & Rubicam, Inc., N.Y.C., 1956-58; exec. sec. J. Walter Thompson Co., N.Y.C., 1958-59; exec. sec. Stanford Research Inst., N.Y.C., 1959, Deafness Research Found., N.Y.C., 1960, Earl Newsom & Co., N.Y.C., 1961-65; account exec. Ruder & Finn, Inc., N.Y.C., 1965-68; founder, pres. The Haas Group, Inc., N.Y.C., 1968—; co-founder, pres. DeNegris, Haas & England, Inc., 1978-79; adj. instr. dept. journalism N.Y. U., 1980-82; lectr. N.Y. U. Sch. Continuing Edn., 1981-85. Mem. Women in Communications, Public Relations Soc. Am., Women Execs. in Public Relations, Advt. Women N.Y., Internat. Radio and TV Soc., Council Communication Mgmt., N.Y. TV Acad. Club: Hajji Baba. Home: 171 W 79th St New York NY 10024 Office: 59 E 54th St New York NY 10022

HAAS, ELLEN R., employment consultant; b. N.Y.C., Oct. 28, 1942; d. Nathan and Lillian (Minkoff) Charney; m. Bert Robert Haas, Mar. 11, 1967 (dec. Sept. 1983); children—Caroline Audrey, Paul Edward. B.A., Hunter Coll., 1965. Tchr. speech improvement N.Y. Bd. Edn., Bklyn., 1965-69; mgr. Parker Finch Assocs., N.Y.C., 1978-81; permanent div. mgr. Towne Personnel, N.Y.C., 1981-82; office mgr. Harvey Marcus Personnel, N.Y.C., 1982; employment cons. Payson Ruby Agy., N.Y.C., 1982-85, D.J. Hertz & Assocs., N.Y.C., 1985—. Rep., Parents League, N.Y.C., Bentley Sch., N.Y.C., 1974-75, pres. Parents Assn., 1976-78; fund raising chmn. Rhodes Sch., N.Y.C., 1982-85, pres. Parents Assn., 1985—. Home: 315 E 86th St New York NY 10028 Office: D J Hertz & Assocs 270 Madison Ave New York NY 10016

HAAS, JACQUELINE CRAWFORD, lawyer; b. St. Louis, Nov. 9, 1935; d. Ernest Augustus and Nora (Fullard) Crawford; m. Karl Alan Haas, Jan. 27, 1962; children—James Andrew, Susan Jennifer, David Reid, Peter Crawford. A.B., Cornell U., 1957; LL.B., Harvard U., 1961. Bar: N.Y. 1962, Mass., 1972, U.S. Dist. Ct. (so. dist.) N.Y. 1963, U.S. Ct. Appeals (2d cir.), 1968. Corporate lawyer Lord, Day & Lord, N.Y.C., 1961-63; trial lawyer Family Ct. Div., Legal Aid Soc., Bklyn., 1964-66; examining atty. N.Y.C. Dept. Investigation, 1966-68; exec. asst. to commr. N.Y.C. Dept. Investigation, 1969-71; sole practice, Weston, Mass., 1971—; mem. Greater Boston Com., Harvard Law Sch. Fund, Cambridge, Mass., 1976—; mem. alumni student com. Harvard Law Sch. Council, Cambridge, 1980—. Del., Mass. Democratic Issues Conv., 1983, 85; del. Mass. Dem. Nominating Conv., 1984, 86; mem. Weston Democratic Town Com., 1984—; chmn. bd. Roxbury-Weston Programs, Inc., 1982—; mem. family com. Metco, 1973-75, mem. community coordinating council, 1982—. Mem. ABA (corp., antitrust and litigation sects., mem. com. on civil practice and procedure of antitrust sect.), Mass. Bar Assn., Assn. Bar City N.Y. Democrat. Episcopalian. Office: 42 Partridge Hill Rd Weston MA 02193

HAAS, RUTH SHERWOOD, librarian; b. Peoria, Ill., Nov. 28, 1937; d. Abijah Minor and Elizabeth Ida (Krumpe) Sherwood; m. Howard Wendell Dillon, July 27, 1957 (div.); children—Maureen Rachel, Jason Giles; m. 2d, Howard Clyde Haas, May 28, 1971. B.A., Knox Coll., 1959; M.S. in Library Sci., Ind. U., 1961. Adminstrv. asst. Ind. U. div. library sci., Bloomington, 1960-61; cataloguer Harvard Coll. Library, Cambridge, Mass., 1965-68, asst. head CONSER office, 1981-85, serials holdings specialist, 1985—; reference librarian Robbins Library, Arlington, Mass., 1976-81. Recipient Lawrence Latin prize Knox Coll., Galesburg, Ill., 1959; Mem. ALA (resources and tech. services div.), Soc. Scribes and Illuminators, Beta Phi Mu. Methodist. Home: 140 Pleasant St Arlington MA 02174 Office: Widener Library Harvard U Cambridge MA 02138

HABADA, PATRICIA ADELAIDE BREEDLOVE, textbook editor; b. Flint, Mich., Mar. 17, 1929; d. Robert Wiley and Lillie Savannah (Bowden) Breedlove; B.S., Kutztown (Pa.) State Coll., 1968; M.Ed., U. Pitts., 1976, Ph.D., 1982; m. Joseph Paul Habada, June 5, 1949; children—Shirley Dawn Habada Harvey, Beverly Kay, Paula Jo. Service rep. Heath Co., Benton Harbor, Mich., 1952-55; classroom tchr., Ohio and Pa., 1958-70; prin., Pa., 1970-73; research asst. U. Pitts., 1973-75; assoc. supt. schs. Pa. Conf. Seventh-day Adventists, Reading, Pa., 1975-79; sr. editor elem. reading textbooks Gen. Conf. Seventh-day Adventists, Washington, 1979—; leader family life seminars and workshops; cons. to sch. dists., colls., univs. Vice pres. Seventh-day Adventists Gen. Conf. Women's Aux.; v.p. edn., lay adv. bd. Pa. Conf. Seventh-day Adventists. Cert. in elem. teaching, adminstrn., supervision of instrn., Ohio, Pa., Seventh-Day Adventists. Mem. Internat. Reading Assn., Assn. Supervision and Curriculum Devel., N.Am. Div. Curriculum Com., Assn. Adventist Women. Writer family life curriculum materials, tchrs. guides to Pa. resources; contbr. articles to various jours. Office: General Conference of Seventh-day Adventists 6840 Eastern Ave NW Washington DC 20012

HABECK, GLORIA, farmer, former county official; b. Aitkin, Minn., Aug. 30, 1924; d. Carl H. and Tillie (Olson) Eklund; m. Carlyle F. Ogden, May 1947, 1 child, Robin J.; m. Walter Habeck, Oct. 30, 1953 (dec. May 1977); children—Rick A., Roy W., Ross C. Grad. high sch., Aitkin, Sec., various firms, Mpls., 1942-53; county commr. Mille Lacs County, Minn., 1977-84. Contbr. editorials to local newspaper. Chmn. East Central Regional Devel. Commn., Mora, Minn., 1977-84; leader 4H, Mille Lacs County, 1965-75; grey lady Fort Snelling VA Hosp., Mpls., 1944-46; chmn. Ladies Aid, Isle, Minn., 1960-77. Mem. Assn. Minn. Counties. Lutheran. Club: Homemakers (chmn. 1960-77).

HABER, AUDREY RUTH, psychologist, author; b. N.Y.C., Feb. 4, 1940; d. Eugene Jerome Friedman and Sally (Reit) Bremer, B.A., Adelphi U., 1960, Ph.D. (USPHS fellow), 1963; m. Jerome Jassenoff, Dec. 19, 1969; children—Laurie Beth, David Scott. Lic. psychologist, N.Y., N.J. Asso. prof. psychology C.W. Post Coll., Greenvale, N.Y., 1964-70; research psychologist UCLA, 1971-78; now dir. psychology Garden State Rehab. Hosp., Toms River, N.J. Author, 1967—; books include Business Statistics, 1982; Fundamentals of Behavioral Statistics, 5th ed., 1984; Fundamentals of Psychology, 4th edit., 1986; General Statistics, 3d edit., 1977; Psychology of Adjustment, 1984; contbr. articles profl. jours. Recipient Acad. of Distinction award Adelphi U., 1977. Mem. Eastern Psychol. Assn. Am. Psychol. Assn., N.J. Acad. Psychology, Psi Chi. Home and Office: 14 Hospital Dr Toms River NJ 08753

HABER, BARBARA LUBOTSKY, librarian; b. Milw., Apr. 1, 1934; d. John and Belle (Goldberg) Lubotsky; m. Herbert Robert Haber, Aug. 24, 1959; children—Jonathan Richard, Nicholas Edward. B.S., U. Wis., 1955; M.A., U. Chgo., 1957; M.L.S., Simmons Coll, 1968. Instr., Wayne State U., Detroit, 1961-63; instr. Highland Park Community Coll., 1964-66; curator books Schlesinge Library Radcliffe Coll., Cambridge, Mass., 1968—. Mem. adv. com., women's studies in religon Harvard Div. Sch., 1981—. Mem. trustees com. Bus. and Profl. Women Found., Washington, 1982—. Author: Women in America, 1980; editor: The Women's Ann., 1980—, American Women in the 20th Century Series 1982—, other books. Radcliffe scholar, 1979; Harvard U. grantee, 1979; fellow Harvard U, 1975, H.W. Wilson Co., 1967. Mem. Orgn. Am. Historians, Nat. Women's Studies Assn., Culinary Historians Boston, Women's Culinary Guild, 9 to 5. Democrat. Jewish. Avocation: culinary history. Home: 5 Woodside Rd Winchester MA 01890 Office: Schlesinger Library Radcliffe Coll 10 Garden St Cambridge MA 02138

HABERMANN, MARTHA MARIE, nursing home administrator, consultant; b. N.Y., Oct. 11, 1932; d. Anton and Martha (Schmidt) Schuierer; m. Joseph P. Habermann, Aug. 17, 1951; children—Joseph E., Elizabeth, Frances, Katharine. Student Fordham Hosp. Sch. Nursing, N.Y.C., 1950-51, CCNY, 1951-52, SUNY-Purchase, 1974-75, Dutchess Community Coll., 1974-75, Mercy Coll., 1981-82; nursing home adminstr. lic. Ithaca Coll., 1972. Bookkeeper Fox and Sutherland, Mt. Kisco, N.Y., 1968-70; office mgr., dir. admissions Waterview Hills Nursing Ctr., Purdys, N.Y., 1970-72, asst. adminstr., 1972-76; owner, operator Salem Hills Health Related Facility, Purdys, 1976—. Bd. dirs. Westchester Exceptional Children Sch., North Salem, 1979-82, sec., 1980; mem. Adv. Council to Disabled, North Salem, 1981—, Advisory Bd. for Group Homes, North Salem, 1981—; trustee North Salem Free Library, 1984—. Fellow Am. Coll. Health Care Adminstrs.; mem. N.Y. Acad. Sci., Am. Geriatric Soc., Gerontology Assn., AAAS, Westchester County Nursing Home Assn. (pres. 1982—), N.Y. State Health Facilities Assn. (bd. dirs. 1978—). Office: Salem Hills Health Related Facility Route 22 Purdys NY 10578

HABLUTZEL, NANCY ZIMMERMAN, lawyer educator; b. Chgo., Mar. 16, 1940; d. Arnold Fred and Maxine (Lewison) Goodman; m. Philip Norman Hablutzel, July 1, 1980; children—Margo Lynn, Robert Paul. B.S., Northwestern U., 1960; M.A., Northeastern Ill. 1972; J.D., Ill. Inst. Tech., 1980; Ph.D., Loyola U., 1983. Bar: Ill. 1980. U.S. Dist. Ct. (no. dist.) Ill. 1980. Speech therapist Northbrook Pub. Schs., (Ill.), 1960-61; audiologist Billings Hosp., Chgo., 1964-65; instr. Chgo. State U., 1972-76; legal clk. FDIC, Chgo., 1979-80; sole practice, Chgo., 1980—; asst. prof spl. edn., legal aspects of disability and juveniles Loyola U., Chgo., 1982—; dir. legal services Legal Clinic for Disabled, 1984-85, dir., 1985—. Mem. Ill. Gov.'s Com. on Handicapped, 1973-75. Mem. Council Exceptional Children, Am. Edn. Research Assn., ABA, Ill. Bar Assn. (standing com. on juvenil justice 1984), Chgo. Bar Assn. (corp. law and exec. coms.). Republican. Home: 214 W Menomonee St Chicago IL 60614 Office: Loyola U Chgo 820 N Michigan Ave Chicago IL 60611

HACH, LISA PETERS, investment consulting company exec.; b. N.Y.C., Dec. 31, 1943; d. Gilbert S. and Constance S. (Carpp) P. Student Hunter Coll. Bookkeeper, Hans Eichler Motor Cars, N.Y.C., 1967-70, Cars of France, Inc., N.Y.C., 1970-78; asst. controller Diversion Publs. Inc., N.Y.C., 1978-83; controller Upland Holdings, N.Y.C., 1983—; prin. Sheridan Bookkeeping Service, N.Y.C. Office: 60 E 42d St New York NY 10165

HACK, LINDA, lawyer; b. Chgo., Nov. 30, 1949; d. Paul K. and Lorraine B. (Johnston) Hack; m. Thomas E. Barnes, Nov. 30, 1967 (div.); m. Gary J. Derer, Aug. 15, 1979. A.A., Harper Coll., 1973; M.A., Roosevelt U., 1975; J.D., DePaul U., Chgo., 1979. Bar: Ill. 1979, Tex. 1980, U.S. Supreme Ct. 1983. Administrv. law judge Ill. Dept. of Labor, Chgo., 1980—; assoc. Law Offices F. Ward Steinbach, Dallas, 1981-83; staff atty., dir. N. Tex. Mediation Ctr., Inc., Dallas, 1983—; of counsel Hicks, Gillespie, James & Lesser, Dallas, 1983—; ptnr. Hack & Derer, Dallas, 1983—; mem. State Bar of Tex. Alt. Dispute Resolution Com., 1982-85. mem. Acad. Family Mediators, 1983—. Vice chair Dallas Area Woman's Polit. Caucus, 1983; bd. dirs. Choice, Dallas, TARAL 1983; mem. Oak Lawn Dems., Dallas, 1983. Mem. Dallas Women Lawyer's Assn. (pres. 1983-84), Tex. Fedn. Bus. and Profl. Women (treas. dist. 15 1984-85), Dallas Trial Lawyers' Assn., Assn. Trial Lawyers Am., ABA, Ill. Trial Lawyers Assn., Mediation Council of Ill., Ill. Trial Lawyers Assn., Tex. Trial Lawyers Assn., Am. Arbitration Assn., White Rock Bus. and Profl. Women (pres. 1985). Club: Zonta. Home: 2961 N Lincoln Chicago IL 60657

HACKER, HELENA, movie studio executive; b. San Antonio, Feb. 28, 1948; d. Harold Arthur and Pauline F. Shapiro; Am. Field Service exchange student, Sacre Coeur des Chartres, Lyons, France, 1965-66; B.A. cum laude, Stanford U., 1970. Editorial asst. New Yorker Mag., N.Y.C., 1970-72; copy editor Random House Pub. Co., N.Y.C., 1972-74; copychief The Village Voice, N.Y.C., 1974-75, assoc. editor, 1976, sr. editor, 1977; v.p. for prodn. Universal Pictures, 1978—. Mem. Women in Film (bd. dirs.). Office: Carr-Gershon 20th Century Fox PO Box 900 Beverly Hills CA 90213

HACKER, RANDI, magazine editor, humor writer; b. Bklyn., Dec. 13, 1951; d. Charles Herman and Sylvia (Sukoff) H. B.A. magna cum laude, U. Mich., 1973. Humor writer Nat. Lampoon, Ms. mag., Games mag., Muppet mag., Video, Savvy, Punch (with Jackie Kaufman); editor Electric Co. mag. Children's TV Workshop, N.Y.C., 1986—. Contbr. articles to numerous mags. Nominated for Nebula award, 1985. Mem. Writers' Guild Am. Office: Children's TV Workshop 1 Lincoln Plaza New York NY 10023

HACKETT, ANNE M., foreign service officer; b. Mass., Aug. 13, 1946; d. Edward F. and Mary (Fenton) Hackett; B.A., Coll. New Rochelle, 1968; M.A., NYU, 1970. Program coordinator Am. Field Service, N.Y.C. and Los Angeles, 1970-74; vice consul Am. Consulate, Istanbul, Turkey, 1976-78, Am. Embassy, Singapore, 1978-80; 1st sec., consul Am. Embassy, Djibouti, 1981-83; with African Bur., U.S. Dept. State, Washington, 1983—. Mem. Am. Fgn. Service Assn. Address: 1747 Q St NW Washington DC 20009

HACKETT, CAROL ANN HEDDEN, physician; b. Valdese, N.C., Dec. 18, 1939; d. Thomas Barnett and Zada Loray (Pope) Hedden; B.A., Duke, 1961; M.D., U. N.C., 1966; m. John Peter Hackett, July 27, 1968; children—John Hedden, Elizabeth Bentley, Susanne Rochet. Intern. Georgetown U. Hosp., Washington, 1966-67, resident, 1967-69; clinic physician DePaul Hosp., Norfolk, Va., 1969-71; chief spl. health services Arlington County Dept. Human Resources, Arlington, Va., 1971-72; gen. med. officer USPHS Hosp., Balt., 1974-75; pvt. practice family medicine, Seattle, 1975—; mem. staff, chmn. dept. family practice Overlake Meml. Hosp., 1985-86; clin. instr. U. Wash. Bd. dirs. Mercer Island (Wash.) Preschool Assn., 1977-78; coordinator 13th and 21st Ann. Inter-profl. Women's Dinner, 1978, 86, trustee Northwest Chamber Orch., 1984—. Mem. Wash., King County (chmn. com. TV violence) med. socs., Bellevue C. of C., NW Women Physicians (v.p. 1978), Seattle Symphony League, Eastside Women Physicians (founder, pres.), Sigma Kappa. Episcopalian. Club: Wash. Athletic. Home: 4304 E Mercer Way Mercer Island WA 98040 Office: 1128 112th Ave NE Bellevue WA 98004

HACKETT, LEILA LOUISE, publisher, editor, consultant, instructor; b. St. Thomas, V.I., Nov. 28, 1952; d. Lupercio Alvin and Cecile Estelle (Daniel) Wallace; m. Carlton Robert Hackett, Feb. 27, 1978; children—Keona Kishaun, Porshia Veronica, Celia Kimberly. A.A. in Computer Sci., NYU, 1977; A.A. in Bus. Mgmt., Central Tex. Coll., 1982; B.S. in Mgmt. Sci., Am. Tech. U., 1983, M.S. in Mgmt. Sci., 1984. Regional mgr. Cherry Hill Photography, Inc., N.J., 1981-83; coordinator computer based edn. Central Tex. Coll., Killeen, 1983-84; publisher, editor Hackett Publishing Co., Austin, 1984—, systems analyst dept. human services, 1985—; instr. Central Tex. Coll., 1983-85; cons. various orgns. Author: Island Puzzler, 1984; Fun in the Sun, 1985; Expressions, 1981; Marketing Yourself, 1983. Bd. dirs. NAACP Killeen, Tex. branch, 11984—, Central Tex. Health Systems Agy., Austin, 1981-83. Mem. Am. Mgmt. Assn., Am. Assn. Univ. Women, Nat. Assn. for Female Execs., Am. Bus. Woman's Assn. Republican. Seventh-day Adventist. Club: Toastmasters (Killeen). Avocations: photography, writing, travelling, tennis. Home: 6405 Crowley St Austin TX 78729 Office: Hackett Publishing Co PO Box 4773 Austin TX 78765

HACKETT, LOUISE, personnel services company executive, consultant; b. Sheridan, Mont., Nov. 11, 1933; d. Paul Duncan and Freda A. (Dudley) Johnson; m. Lewis Edward Hackett, June 24, 1962; 1 child, Dell Paul. Student U. Oreg., 1959-61; B.A., Calif. State U.-Sacramento, 1971. Legal sec. Samuel P. Friedman, Yreka, Calif., 1952-58, Barber & Cottrell, Eugene, Oreg., 1958-59; paralegal Elmer Sahlstrom, Eugene, 1959-62; legis. aide Calif. Legislature, Sacramento, 1962-72; owner Legal Personnel Services, Sacramento, 1973-78, corp. pres., 1979—; adviser dept. curriculum bus. Am. River Coll., Sacramento, 1974-79; founder, adminstr. Pacific Coll. Legal Careers, Sacramento, 1973-84; cons. legal edn. Barclay Schs., Sacramento, 1984. Designer, pub. Sacramento/Yolo Attys. Directory, 1974—. Contbr. articles to profl. jours. Adv. bd. San Juan Sch. Dist., 1975—. Mem. Sacramento Women's Network, Calif. Assn. Personnel Cons., Sacramento Council Pvt. Edn. (pres. 1976-77), Pi Omega Pi. Clubs: Sierra Sail and Trail, Soroptimist Internat. Lodge: Order of Rainbow. Avocations: skiing; sailing; sports car rallying. Office: Legal Personnel Services 1415 A 21st St Sacramento CA 95825

HACKLANDER, EFFIE HEWITT, university administrator; b. Walnut Grove, Minn., Oct. 10, 1940; d. Kenneth and Ruth (Weaver) Hewitt; B.S., U. Minn., 1962; M.A., Mich. State U., 1968, Ph.D., 1973; m. Duane Hacklander, Sept. 16, 1961; children—Jeffrey, Alan, Craig. Sec., spl. asst. Marriott Corp., 1962-66; lectr. Wayne State U., 1969; asst. prof. U. Md., College Park, 1973-79, asst. provost, div. human and community resources, 1979-80, asst. dean, 1982—; cons. Chmn. music com., trustee Congregational Christian Ch. of Fairfax County, 1975—. Mem. Assn. Consumer Research, Am. Home Econs. Assn., Am. Mktg. Assn., Eastern Econ. Assn., World Future Soc., Assn. Adminstrs. in Home Econs. (pres.-elect N.E. region). Office: 1100 Marie Mount Hall U Md College Park MD 20742

HACKLER, PATRICIA ANN, nursing administrator; b. Holyoke, Mass., May 5, 1948; d. Roger A. and Cecile M. (Martel) Hamel; m. Ronald Charles Hackler, Aug. 29, 1970; 1 child, Kristin Joelle. R.N., Providence Hosp., Holyoke, 1969. Charge nurse Providence Hosp., 1969-70; ICU staff nurse St. Mary's Med. Ctr., Knoxville, Tenn., 1970-72; edn. dir. operating room Meth. Med. Ctr., Oak Ridge, 1972-79; head nurse Smyrna Hosp., Ga., 1979-81, inservice dir., 1981-83, dir. nursing, 1983-86, risk mgr., 1986—. Mem. Nat. League Nursing, Assn. Nurse Execs., Am. Bus. Women's Assn. (chpt. pres. 1985; Woman of Yr. 1985). Office: Smyrna Hosp 3949 S Cobb Dr Smyrna GA 30080

HACKLER, RUTH NADINE, home economics educator, extension clothing specialist; b. Cloud Chief, Okla., Oct. 16, 1935; d. B.L. and Essie M. (Richey) Hackler. B.S. in Home Econs. Edn., Okla. A&M Coll., 1957; M.S. in Clothing, Textiles, Merchandising, Okla. State U., 1962. Vocat. home econs. tchr. pub. schs., Alva, Okla., 1957-61; instr. clothing and textiles Fla. State U., Tallahassee, 1962-69; asst. prof. home econs. U. Fla., Gainesville, 1969-74, assoc. prof., 1974-82, prof., 1982—. Recipient Past Pres.'s plaque Gamma Sigma Delta, 1981; Gen. Foods Fund fellow, 1961-62. Mem. Am. Home Econs. Assn., Fla. Home Econs. Assn., Assn. Coll. Profs. Textiles and Clothing, The Fashion Group, Am. Assn. Textile Colorists and Chemists, Assn. for Devel. of Computer-Based Instrl. Systems, Nat. Assn. 4-H Extension Agts., Internat. Fedn. Home Econs., Assn. for Devel. Computerbased Instrnl. Systems, ASTM, Okla. State U. Alumni Assn., Okla. State Home Econs. Alumni Assn., Epsilon Sigma Phi (cert. meritorious service 1980), Phi Kappa Phi, Gamma Kappa Omicron, Omicron Nu, Phi Upsilon Omicron, Delta Kappa Gamma. Contbr. numerous extension publs. on clothing and textiles. Office: U Fla 3002 McCarty Hall Gainesville FL 32611

HACKMAN, HELEN ANNA HENRIETTE, home economist; b. New Melle, Mo., Oct. 8, 1908; d. John Henry and Lydia Eliza (Meier) Hackman; A.B., Central Wesleyan Coll., Warrenton, Mo., 1929; B.S., U. Mo., 1942, postgrad., 1942; postgrad. U. Wis., 1934, U. Colo., 1953, 75, U. Ariz., 1975, 77. Prin., Wright City High Sch., 1929; home econs. tchr., Cape Girardeau, Mo., 1930-42; sr. extension adviser home econs. U. Ill., Pittsfield, 1942-78; sec. Pike County Health and Social Services Coordinating Com. Dietitian, buyer Oshkosh Wis. Camp Fire Girls Camp, summers 1935, 36, 37; sec.-treas. Western Ill. 4-H Camp Assn., 1952-54; mem. Western Ill. Fair Bd. Com., Griggsville, 1946—; v.p. Tri-county Assn. for Crippled, 1960—; tech. cons. White House Conf., 1960, 70; pres. Pike County Heart Assn., 1969, organizer Family Planning Centers, Diabetic and Blood Pressure Clinics, Pike County Health Dept., 1971; sec. Illini Hosp. Aux., 1978; Bd. dirs. Pike County Mental Health. Recipient Distinguished Service award Nat. Home Demonstration Agts. Assn., 1952; Meritorious Service award Heart Assn., 1960, 61. Mem. Ill. Home Advisers Assn. (sec. 1948), Nat. Assn. Extension Home Economists (3d v.p. 1951-53, pub. relations chmn. 1951-53), Am. Home Econs. Assn. (sec. Ill. nutrition com. 1967-69), Pittsfield Hist. Soc. Epsilon Sigma Phi (chief 1962), Gamma Sigma Delta. Clubs: Pittsfield Woman's (pres. 1979, 80, 81, 82), Pike County Bus. and Profl. (pres. 1970-71). Home: 230 S Illinois St Pittsfield IL 62363 Office: PO Box 227 Hwy 36 and 54th St E Pittsfield IL 62363

HACKMANN, KATHY ALENE, lawyer; b. Alton, Ill., Dec. 15, 1952; d. Alvin Harrison and Mildred Evelyn (Talbert) Petitt; m. William Sterling Hackmann, Dec. 22, 1973. B.A., U. Ill., 1973, M.S., 1974; J.D., Stanford U., 1980. Bar: Calif. 1980, Minn. 1983. Indsl. engr. Sears, Roebuck & Co., Chgo., 1974-77; research asst. Stanford U. (Calif.), 1978-80; law clk. Pacific Telephone Co., San Francisco, 1979, atty., 1980-85; atty. Pacific Telesis Group, 1985—. Mem. AAUW, Rochester, Minn., 1983—. Mem. ABA, Calif. Bar Assn., Minn. Bar Assn., Bar Assn. San Francisco. Republican. Home: 109 Minna #339 San Francisco CA 94105 Office: Pacific Telesis Group 140 New Montgomery Suite 1622 San Francisco CA 94105

HACKNEY, MARGARET HOWARD, encyclopedia publishing executive; b. Newport, N.C., Mar. 19, 1939; d. Jack Howard and Viola (Garner) Howard; m. Daniel Oliver Hackney, Aug. 10, 1958; children—Daniel, John, Gregory. B.A. in Edn. and History, U. N.C., 1961; postgrad. Wake Forest U., 1964, 65. Cert. tchr., history, English, humanities, N.C. Tchr., Winston-Salem/Forsyth Schs., N.C., 1962-66; chmn. depts. history and English Westchester Acad., High Point, N.C., 1968-75; free-lance sch. cons. with Fideler Pub. Co., Grand Rapids, Mich., 1975-77; div. promotions mgr. Ency. Britannica, Denver, 1978, western region promotions mgr., Denver, 1978-80, nat. promotions dir., Chgo., 1980-85, dir. spl. nat. promotions, Chgo., 1985—; coordinator Inst. Civic Edn., U. N.C., summers 1965, 66. Creator hist. and ednl. promotions. Editor: Promotions Profile Newsletter, 1979-85. Vice pres. Bus. and Profl. Women, High Point, 1974-75. R.J. Reynolds fellow, 1964, 65. Mem. Internat. Council Shopping Ctrs., Delta Kappa Gamma. Democrat. Presbyterian (elder). Avocations: piano; gourmet cooking; research. Office: Ency Britannica Nat Promotions Office 3333 Quebec Penthouse D Denver CO 80207

HACKWOOD, MARY-JEAN, state retirement system administrator; b. Turlock, Calif., Nov. 7, 1935; d. Arthur Wellesley and Gertrude Chandler (Stimson) H. B.A., U. Nev. 1958. Cert. and placement clk. Dept. Edn., Juneau, Alaska, 1958-59; benefit admnstr. Dept. Adminstrn., Juneau, 1959-72; dir. employee benefits Hughes Airwest, San Francisco, 1972-80; exec. dir. Mo. State Employees Retirement System, Jefferson City, 1981—; mem. Fin. Selected Seminars, Inc., Santa Barbara, Calif., 1983—; v.p. region III, Nat. Assn. State Retirement Adminstrs., 1983—. Mem. Internat. Found. Employee Benefit Plans, Nat. Conf. Pub. Employment Retirement Systems, Govt. Mcpl. Fin. Officers Assn., Midwest Pension Conf., Western Pension Conf. Phi Alpha Theta. Office: Mo State Employees' Retirement System PO Box 209 Jefferson City MO 65102

HADAS, PAMELA WHITE, author, educator; b. Holland, Mich., Oct. 31, 1946; d. James Floyd and Phyllis Elizabeth (Pelgrim) White; m. William Blattner, June 3, 1968 (div. May 1969); m. David Elkus Hadas, Dec. 31, 1970. B.A., Washington U., St. Louis, 1968, M.A., 1970, Ph.D., 1973. Assoc., vis. prof. Middlebury Coll., Washington U., Webster U., St. Louis, 1976-82; vis. prof. Columbia U., N.Y.C., 1985-86; staff assoc. Bread Loaf Writers' Conf., Middlebury, Vt., 1980—; prof. Bread Loaf Sch. English, Middlebury, 1982—; Roberta M. Holloway vis. prof. U. Calif.-Berkeley, 1984—. Author: Marianne Moore: Poet of Affection, 1977; Designing Women (Witter Bynner award Am. Acad. Arts and Letters 1980), 1979; In Light of Genesis, 1981, Beside Herself: Pocahantus to Patty Hearst, 1983. Poetry editor Webster Rev., St. Louis, 1981—. Crisis counsellor Reproductive Health Service, St. Louis, 1983-85. Fellow MacDowell Colony; mem. Poetry Soc. Am. (bd. mem. poetry rev. 1983-85), PEN, Am. Ctr. Avocations: music; flute and baroque flute; harpischord; figure drawing; dance.

HADDA, JANET RUTH, Yiddish language educator, lay psychoanalyst; b. Bradford, Eng., Dec. 23, 1945; came to U.S., 1948; d. George Manfred and Annemarie (Kohn) H.; m. Allan Joshua Tobin, Mar. 22, 1981; stepchildren—David, Adam. B.S. in Edn., U. Vt., 1966; M.A., Cornell U., 1969; Ph.D., Columbia U., 1975. Assoc. prof. Yiddish UCLA; research clin. assoc. So. Calif. Psychoanalytic Inst., Los Angeles, 1980—. Author: Yankev Glatshteyn, 1980; editorial bd. Prooftexts; contbr. articles to profl. jours. Mem. Assn. Jewish Studies, MLA, Phi Beta Kappa; affiliate mem. Am. Psychoanalytic Assn. Office: Dept Germanic Langs UCLA 310 Royce Hall Los Angeles CA 90024

HADDAD, EMILY TEMAME, turf supply company executive; b. Williamson, W.Va., Jan. 27, 1930; d. Michael and Amy (Abourezk) Abraham; m. George Abraham Haddad, Dec. 29, 1957; children—Amy, Mary, Leah. Student Morehead State Coll., 1949-50, Govs.' State U., 1980. Floral designer The Flower Nook, Williamson, 1950-55, Hilton Hotel, Columbus, Ohio, 1956-59; office mgr. Ind. Businessmen's Counselors, Peotone, Ill., 1970—; owner, office mgr. Bojo Turf Supply Co., Peotone, 1970—; chief designer visit of bishop of Canterbury, England, 1978. Floral and horticulture exhibitor Chgo. World Flower Show, 1972 (Blue ribbons). Republican. Anglican. Clubs: Peotone Women's (ways and means com. chmn. 1984—), Park Forest Women's (bd. dirs. 1971-72), Park Forest Garden (horticulture chmn. 1980—, fin. com. 1980—). Home: RR 1 Box 101 Peotone IL 60468 Office: Bojo Turf Supply Co RR 1 Box 101 Peotone IL 60468

HADDAD, JOSEPHINE SABBAGH, public relations consultant; b. Toledo, Dec. 16, 1943; d. George Morshed and Margaret Martha (Smith) Sabbagh; m. George Kalil Haddad, Jr., Jan. 29, 1966; 1 dau., Amy Jo Margaret. Tech. Degree, U. Toledo, 1964. Spl. events coordinator J.S. Haddad & Assocs., Cleve., 1967—, pub. relations cons., 1967—; dir., founder River's Bend Parks Corp., Cleve., 1981—; supr. Bailey Deardorff, Columbus, Ohio, 1980-81; promotion coordinator Mary Zunt & Assocs., Cleve., 1980; spl. events coordinator Meistergram, Cleve., 1984—. Mem. Mayor's Pub. Relations Adv. Com., Mayor's Waterfront Adv. Com.; former met. bd. mem. YWCA; former bd. dirs. WVIZ Women's Council; former trustee, publicity chmn. Cleve. Waterfront Coalition; trustee Riverbed Artists Assn.; former trustee, publicity chmn. Lebanese-Syrian Jr. Women's League; former community liaison com. mem. Cleve. Play House; mem. Greater Cleve. Com. Internat. Yr. of Child. Recipient Mayor's Recognition award City of Cleve., 1983, honored by Mayor with Joie S. Haddad Day, Mar. 12, 1984; Louis S. Pierce award sta. WVIZ Ednl. TV, Cleve., 1970; Ruth T. Lucas award Jr. League Cleve., 1982. Mem. Women in Communications, English Speaking Union. Republican. Eastern Orthodox. Club: Women's City, Jr. League (Cleve.). Lodge: Eastern Star. Home: 9274 Glenwood Trail Brecksville OH 44141 Office: Meistergram 5501 Cass Ave Cleveland OH 44102

HADDOCK, HELEN RUTH, county official; b. Breckenridge, Tex., July 12, 1933; d. Archie Albert and Mattie May (Speer) Airheart; children—Kerry Kim Haddock, Robin Dawn Haddock Bachman. Student Cisco Jr. Coll., Ranger Jr. Coll. Dep. county clk. Stephens County, Tex., 1952-75, sec. county atty., 1975-78, county clk., 1978—. Past pres. Stephens County Community Theatre, Breckenridge; mem. U.S. Congl. Adv. Bd. Recipient Outstanding Appreciation certs. Jud. Ct. Adminstrn., 1979-85. Mem. Tex. Assn. Counties, Internat. Assn. Clks. and Recorders, Stephens County Concert Assn. Tex., C. of C. County and dist. Clk. Assn. Tex., Tex. Polit. Caucus, Stephens County Law Enforcement Assn., Women's Aux. VFW. Democrat. Baptist. Lodge: Eady Elks. Home: PO Box 185 Breckenridge TX 76024 Office: Office County Clk Stephens County courthouse Breckenridge TX 76024

HADLEY, CAROLYN BETH, physician; b. Dallas, Nov. 22, 1945; d. Charles Franklin and Sadie Beth (Humphreys) Hadley; m. Richard G. Suchan, Dec. 28, 1985. B.A. with honors in Microbiology, U. Kans., 1968; M.S. in Clin. Microbiology, Columbia U. Coll. Physicians and Surgeons, 1974; M.D., U. Pa., 1981. Diplomate Am. Coll. Med. Examiners. Lab. technologist St. Joseph Mercy Hosp., Ann Arbor, Mich., 1968-70; sr. technologist, diagnostic microbiology service Columbia Presbyn. Med. Ctr., N.Y.C., 1970-73, sr. asst. supr., 1973-75; asst. microbiologist Hosp. of U. Pa., Phila., 1975-77, resident in ob-gyn, 1981-85, fellow in maternal fetal medicine, 1985—; teaching asst. in microbiology U. Kans., 1968; teaching fellow microbiology U. Mich. Med. Sch., 1969; lectr. dept. ob-gyn U. Pa. Sch. Medicine, 1984—. Recipient Undergrad. Research award U. Kans., 1967; Phillip Williams prize in obstetrics, 1984; S. Leon Israel prize in obstetrics, 1985; NSF fellow. Fellow Am. Coll. Ob-Gyn (jr. fellow); mem. Am. Soc. Microbiology (specialist in microbiology), Am. Soc. Clin. Pathologists (specialist microbiologist), Am. Soc. for Perinatal Obstetricians (assoc.), DAR, U. Kans. Alumni Assn., Phi Beta Kappa. Home: 1251 Dill Rd Havertown PA 19083 Office: Dept Ob-Gyn Hosp of U Pa Philadelphia PA 19104

HADLEY, JANE BYINGTON, psychotherapist; b. N.Y.C., Apr. 24, 1929; d. David and Ruth (Johnson) Millar; B.A., U. V., 1951; M.A., Columbia U., 1967; m. Arthur Twining Hadley, Feb. 24, 1979; children—Elisabeth Danish, Caroline Danish. Intern Queens Coll., 1969; pvt. practice psychotherapy, N.Y.C., 1971—; mem. Staff Met. Center for Mental Health, N.Y.C., 1976-79. Mem. Am. Psychol. Assn. Democrat. Episcopalian. Clubs: Cosmopolitan, Doubles, Edgarton Yacht.

HADLEY, KAREN MARIE, landscape contractor; b. Pasadena, Calif., May 1, 1945; d. Donald Russel and Virginia Frances (Jones) H.; student Los Angeles City Coll., 1967, Orange Coast Coll., 1973-84. Mail carrier U.S. Post Office, 1963-64; musician, singer, songwriter, 1964—; owner, operator Hadley Gallery, Newport Beach, Calif., 1968-72, Hadley Landscape Co., Costa Mesa, Calif., 1972-82. Mem. Am. Fedn. Musicians, Costa Mesa C. of C., Long Beach C. of C. Democrat. Office: PO Box 11082 Costa Mesa CA 92627

HADLEY, LEILA ELIOTT-BURTON, author; b. N.Y.C., Sept. 22, 1925; d. Frank Vincent and Beatrice Boswell (Eliott) Burton; m. Arthur T. Hadley, II, Mar. 2, 1944 (div. Aug. 1946); 1 child, Arthur T.; m. Yvor H. Smitter, Jan. 24, 1953 (div. Oct. 1969); children—Victoria C. Van D. Smitter Barlow, Matthew Smitter Eliott, Caroline Allison; m. William C. Musham, May 1976 (div. July 1979). Student, U. Witwatersrand, Johannesburg, S. Africa, 1954-55. Author: Give Me the World, 1958; How to Travel with Children in Europe, 1963; Manners for Children, 1967; Fielding's Guide to Traveling with Children in Europe, 1972, rev., 1974, 84; Traveling with Children in the U.S.A., 1974; Tibet-20 Years After the Chinese Takeover, 1979; A Journey with Elsa Cloud, 1987. Assoc. editor: Diplomat mag., N.Y.C., 1964-65, Saturday Evening Post, N.Y.C., 1965-67; editorial cons. TWYCH, N.Y.C., 1985—; book reviewer Palm Beach Life, Fla., 1967-72. Contbr. articles to various newspapers, mags. Mem. Soc. Woman Geographers (exec. council 1984—), Royal Soc. for Asian Affairs, Nat. Press Club. Republican. Presbyterian. Home: 300 E 75th St New York NY 10021 Office: care Peter Matson Literistic 264 Fifth Ave New York NY 10001

HADLOCK, DEBORAH JOYCE, veterinarian; b. Portland, Maine, Sept. 23, 1951; d. Edson Barry and Barbara (Whalen) H.; m. John Nevil Hawkins, June 18, 1977 (div. Jan. 1984). Student Purdue U., West Lafayette, Ind., 1969-71; B.S., U. Ill.-Champaign, 1974; V.M.D., U. Pa.-Phila., 1980. Intern in small animal medicine and surgery The Animal Med. Ctr., N.Y.C., 1980-81; assoc. veterinarian Gramercy Park Animal Clinic, N.Y.C., 1981-85; veterinarian cardiology cons. Cardiopet-Animed Roslyn, 1983—. Mem. The New Alliance Party, N.Y.C., 1983—. Mem. N.Y.C. Veterinary Med. Assn., N.Y. State Veterinary Med. Assn., AVMA, Acad. Veterinary Cardiology. Club: Century Rd. (N.Y.C.). Home: 330 W 56th St Apt 20H New York NY 10019 Office: Cardiopet 25 Lumber Rd Roslyn NY 11576-2105

HADLOCK, JUDITH PASAHOW, fashion marketing consultant, home furnishings consultant; b. Waterloo, Iowa, Nov. 17, 1944; d. Bernard David and Kathryn Elizabeth (Gaffney) Pasahow; m. John Matthew Hadlock, Aug. 31, 1969; 1 dau., Meghan Elizabeth. B.S., U. Wis., 1966; M.A., New Sch. Social Research, 1973. Copywriter, Sears Roebuck and Co., Chgo., 1966-68, copy chief, N.Y.C., 1968-72, apparel buyer, fashion dir., 1972-79; cons. Federated Dept. Stores, N.Y.C., 1979-80, Humphrey, Browning, Macdougall, N.Y.C., 1980—. Mem. Fashion Group Found., New Eng. Appraisers Assn., Fashion Group N.Y. Democrat. Presbyterian. Clubs: Southampton Bath and Tennis (N.Y.); Shinecock Golf. Home: 1136 Fifth Ave New York NY 10128 also 82 Main St Southampton NY 11968 also 39 Toylsome Southampton NY 11968

HADWYN, CAROLINE B., small business owner; b. Fayetteville, N.C., Apr. 19, 1961; d. James Clifton and Genevieve (Oulanoff) Hadwyn; m. Thomas Jay Batchelor, Jr., Dec. 26, 1984. B.B.A. in Fin., Augusta Coll., 1984, postgrad. Lic. real estate assoc.; life underwriter. Fin. counselor Talmadge Hosp., Augusta, Ga., 1980-83; real estate assoc. Crowell Co., Augusta, 1984-85; field underwriter N.Y. Life, Augusta, 1985-86; owner, day mgr. Paperworks, Martinez, Ga., 1986—; pres., editor Batchelor's Real Estate, Martinez, 1986—. Author/editor: Augusta, 1987; editor newsletter Soundbite, 1986. Active Cerebral Palsy Telethon, Augusta, 1985. Mem. Nat. Assn. Female Execs., C. of C. Republican. Episcopalian. Club: Ga. LWV. Avocations: golf; racquetball; biking; traveling; photography. Home: 4384 Shallowford Pl PO Box 828 Evans GA 30809 Office: Paperworks 4471 Columbia Rd B6 Martinez GA 30907

HAEGER, PHYLLIS M., management consultant; b. Chgo., May 20, 1928; d. Milton O. and Ethel M.; B.A., Lawrence U., 1950; M.A., Northwestern U., 1952. Midwest editor Tide Mag., Chgo., 1952-55; exec. v.p. Smith, Bucklin & Assos., Inc., Chgo., 1955-78; pres. P.M. Haeger & Assos., Inc., Chgo., 1978—. Mem. Nat. Assn. Women Bus. Owners, Am. Soc. Assn. Execs., Chgo. Soc. Assn. Execs., Inst. Assn. Mgmt. Cos., Chgo. Fin. Exchange, Chgo. Network. Office: P M Haeger & Assos Inc 500 N Michigan Ave Chicago IL 60611

HAERING, MARGARET ELAINE, lawyer; b. Columbus, Ohio, Mar. 3, 1947; d. Robert Lee and Mary E. (Brewer) H. B.A., Douglass Coll., 1969; J.D., George Washington U., 1975. Editor, atty. Bur. Nat. Affairs, Washington, 1975-78; ptnr. Cole Raywid & Braverman, Washington, 1978—. Mem. Women's Bar Assn. D.C., ABA. Office: Cole Raywid & Braverman 1919 Pennsylvania Ave NW Washington DC 20006

HAESSLY, JACQUELINE, peace education specialist, writer, consultant; b. Milw., Feb. 18, 1937; d. Jerome Francis and Janice (Ball) Haessly; m. Daniel G. Di Domizio, July 8, 1972; children—Michael, Ernest, Randolph, Francis, Kristyn. L.P.N., Sacred Heart Sch. Practical Nursing, Milw., 1958; student Alverno Coll., 1958-64; B.S. in Edn. U. Wis., 1971, M.S. in Edn., 1976. Staff nurse various local hosps., Milw., 1959-72; founder, dir. Milw. Peace Edn. Resource Ctr., 1974—; cons., facilitator Milw. Archdiocese, 1974—, Milw. Pub. Schs., 1974—; organizer prodn. Peace Child, Milw., 1985; cons. U. Wis., Milw., 1983—. Author: Peacemaking: Family Action for Justice and Peace, 1980. Editor Peacemaking for Children mag., 1983—. Contbr. numerous articles to profl. publs. Bd. dirs. Milw. Mental Health Agy., 1975-78; coordinator food policy conf. The Peace Ctr., Milw., 1975-77; mem. peace studies task force Milw. Pub. Schs., 1983—; chmn. peace studies com. Parent Tchr. Council, Milw., 1985—. Mem. Fellowship of Reconciliation (mem. bd., chmn. com. 1984-85), Parenting for Peace and Justice (mem. bd. 1981-84), Wis. Writer's Council, Nat. Writer's Club. Roman Catholic. Avocations: swimming; hiking; biking; knitting; reading. Office: Milw Peace Edn Resource Ctr 2437 N Grant Blvd Milwaukee WI 53210

HAFEN, ELIZABETH SUSAN SCOTT, physicist; b. Springfield, Mo., July 25, 1946; d. George William and Wealtha Belle (Chaplin) Scott; m. Clifford Henry Hafen, Jr., Sept. 27, 1970. B.S., Iowa State U., 1968, Ph.D., 1973. Instr. physics MIT, Cambridge, 1973-78, asst. prof., 1978-82, assoc. prof., 1982-83, prin. research scientist physics dept., 1983—. Contbr. articles to profl. jours. Mem. Am. Phys. Soc., New Eng. Hist. Geneol. Soc. Democrat. Methodist.

HAFER, MARY STEWART, museum curator; b. Newburgh, N.Y., Sept. 7, 1924; d. Thomas A. and Mary L. (Warden) Stewart; m. Frederick L. Hafer, June 8, 1946; children—Thomas F., John S., Abigail Ann. B.A. in Chemistry, Swarthmore Coll., 1945; M.S.L.S., Simmons Coll., 1968. Research Chemist Bartol Found., Franklin Inst., Phila., 1945-46; spl. instr. Patrick A.F.B., Fla., 1960-62; docent Nat. Gallery of Art, Washington, 1963-66; docent orgnr. Bedford (Mass.) pub. library volunteers, 1971—; curator Job Lane house, Bedford, 1980—, Bedford Hist. Soc., 1975—; mem. Historic dist. commn., Bedford, 1979—. Active library and mus. fund raising projects, Bedford, Lincoln, Mass., Boston, 1969-78. Mem. ALA, New Eng. Archivists. Republican. Home: 137 North Rd Bedford MA 01730 Office: Bedford Historical Soc 15 The Great Rd Bedford MA 01730

HAFEY, BARBARA ANN, public accounting firm executive, accountant; b. Los Angeles, Oct. 23, 1931; d. Elbert John Benton and Virginia Esther (Hurd) Benton Dingerson; children—Michael W. Aiken, Eric A. Aiken, Anita A. Aiken Brooks, H. L. Ted Aiken, W. Scott Aiken, Patrick T. Hafey. Acctg. diploma Bell and Howell schs., 1976; student St. Martin's Coll., Lacey, Wash. 1976, Centralia Coll., Wash., 1978. C.P.A., Wash. Staff acct. Arnold Gfeller & Co., Junction City, Kans., 1970-71; office mgr. Phillip T. Jorgensen, C.P.A., Lacey, 1971-76; prin. Barbara A. Hafey C.P.A., Centralia, 1976-82; pres. Bowen, Hafey & Pennington, C.P.A.s, Centralia, 1982—; instr. Centralia Coll., 1979-81; dir. Ken's Tire Service, Inc., Olympia, Wash., Web Joist NW Corp., Chehalis, Wash. Sec. Altrusa, Centralia, 1979-80, treas., 1980-81; treas. Lewis County Econ. Devel., Wash., 1984-85, Centralia Main St. Assn., 1984-85; bd. dirs. United Way Lewis County, 1984-85. Recipient Outstanding Achievement award Wash. Assn. Accts., 1978. Mem. Am. Inst. C.P.A.s, Wash. Soc. C.P.A.s. Home: 1026 Elm St Centralia WA 98531 Office: Bowen Hafey & Pennington CPAs Inc PS 120 W Magnolia Centralia WA 98531

HAFF, SANDRA A., legislative analyst; b. Troy, N.Y., Aug. 7, 1949; d. Samuel Tilden and Hilda Marie (Brown) Haff. R.N., Samaritan Hosp. Sch. Nursing, 1970; B.S.N., Russell Sage Coll., 1980, M.P.A., 1985. Emergency room nurse Samaritan Hosp., Troy, 1970-76, emergency room charge nurse, 1976-81, emergency room asst. head nurse, 1981-82; fellow N.Y. State Senate, Albany, 1983-84; assembly legis. analyst, research assoc. N.Y. State Assembly, Albany, 1985—, staff dir. assembly minority task force on sexual assault, 1985—. Contbr. to Political Action Handbook for Nurses, 1985. Mem. Legis. Forum N.Y. State, 1983-85. Fellow Soc. Shaeffer Library (assoc.); mem. N.Y. State Nurses Assn., Emergency Nurses Assn. Mem. Dutch Reformed Ch. Home: 7-4 Rose Garden Ct Latam NY 12110 Office: Office Research and Program Devel NY State Assembly Room 1000 99 Washington Ave Albany NY 12210

HAFFNER, MARLENE ELISABETH, physician, health care administrator; b. Cumberland, Md., Mar. 22, 1941. Student Western Res. U., 1958-61; M.D., George Washington U., 1965. Intern, George Washington U. Hosp., Washington, 1965-66; fellow in dermatology Columbia-Presbyn. Med. Ctr., N.Y.C., 1966-67; resident in internal medicine St. Luke's Hosp., N.Y.C., 1967-69; fellow in hematology. Albert Einstein Coll. Medicine, Bronx, 1969-71, asst. clin. prof. medicine, 1971-73; vis. asst. attending Bronx Mcpl. Hosp. Ctr. (N.Y.), 1969-71; clin. assoc. in family, community and emergency medicine U. N.Mex. Sch. Medicine, Albuquerque, 1974-83, clin. assoc. dept. medicine, 1974-83; acting clin. dir. Gallup Indian Med. Ctr. (N.Mex.), 1973-74, chief adult outpatient dept., 1971-74, chief dept. internal medicine, 1971-74; dir. Navajo Area Indian Health Service, Indian Health Service, Window Rock, Ariz., 1974-81; assoc. dir. for health affairs Bur. Med. Devices, FDA, Rockville, 1981-82, dir. Office Health Affairs, Ctr. for Devices and Radiol. Health, 1982—; asst. clin. prof. dept. medicine Uniformed Services Univ. of Health Scis., Bethesda, Md.; med. dir. USPHS. Home: 11616 Danville Dr Rockville MD 20852 Office: FDA Ctr for Devices and Radiol Health Office Health Affairs 8757 Georgia Ave Silver Spring MD 20910

HAFNER, CAROL NISHIMATSU, agricultural biologist; b. San Jose, Calif., Dec. 25, 1954; d. Rick and Matsuko (Nakamoto) Nishimatsu; m. Tye Terril Hafner, Dec. 20, 1980; 1 child, Erik Toshiro. B.A. in Botany, San Jose State U., 1978. Agrl. biologist Fresno County Dept. Agr., Fresno, Calif., 1979—. Mem. Nat. Assn. Female Execs., Calif. Women for Agr., Fresno County Farm Bur. Democrat. Buddhist. Avocations: crocheting; bowling; softball. Office: Fresno County Dept Agr 1730 S Maple Ave Fresno CA 93702

HAGAN, EILEEN, lighting co. exec.; b. Paterson, N.J., July 27, 1930; d. Thomas A. and Ruth J. (Conlon) H.; 1 son, Mark Fusco. Asst. to sales mgr. C. N. Burman Co., Paterson, 1955-61, asst. to pres., 1961-67, design coordinator, 1967-73, v.p. mktg. and design, dir., 1973—; dir. Heldak Lighting Products, Paterson Shade, Univ. Lamp, Cert. Shade Co. Bd. dirs. YWCA, Paterson, 1949-53. Mem. Decorative and Fine Arts Soc. Bergen County, Nat. Assn. Variety Stores, Internat. Platform Assn., Color Mktg., Assn. Gen. Mdse. Chains, Color Assn. U.S., Nat. Home Fashions League. Office: 781 River St Paterson NJ 07524

HAGAN, JENNY FAYE, purchasing agent; b. Louisville, Oct. 30, 1960; d. John Fraysure and Eula Mavis (Alsip) Deringer. B.A., Va. Commonwealth U., 1986; cert. in Acctg., Sullivan Bus. Coll., 1979. Bookkeeper Exec. Express, Louisville, 1978-79; typing clk. Philip Morris U.S.A., Louisville, 1979-80, acctg. clk., 1980-81, accounts payable coordinator, Richmond, Va., 1981-83, assoc. purchasing agt., 1983-86, purchasing agt., 1985—. Republican. Avocations: reading; aerobics and calisthenic exercises; painting. Home: 3111 Cottage Oaks Ct Midlothian VA 23113 Office: Philip Morris USA PO Box 26603 3601 Commerce Rd Richmond VA 23261

HAGAN, PATRICIA KITTREDGE, health services administrator; b. Milo, Maine, May 12, 1935; d. Milton Donald and Beatrice Alma (Ingalls) Kittredge; BS., U. Maine, 1976; M.P.A., Calif. State U., 1982. Food service mgr. U. Maine, Orono, 1961-62, Ind. U., 1962-64, U. Tex., Austin, 1965; adminstr. dietary services Cabrillo Med. Center, San Diego, 1965-69, adminstr. gen. services, 1969-70, adminstr. for ops., 1970-73, assoc. adminstr., 1973-76, adminstr., 1976-82; health services cons. CHSA, San Diego, 1982—; chief exec. officer Splty. Med. Clinic, La Jolla, Calif. 1986—. Served with USAF, 1954-58. Mem. Am. Coll. Hosp. Adminstrs., Am. Acad. Med. Adminstrs., Am. Hosp. Assn., Am. Dietetic Assn. Episcopalian. Club: Altrusa Internat. Home: 1275 Alexandria Dr San Diego CA 92107 Office: 351 Santa Fe Dr Suite 200 Encinotas CA 92024

HAGAN, SHIRLEY SMITH, med. technologist; b. Sherman, Tex., Apr. 20, 1936; d. J.B. and Frances Winnifred (Groce) Smith; diploma med. tech., Parkland Meml. Hosp., Dallas, 1961; B.S., Southeastern Okla. State U., 1977; M.S., Tex. Woman's U., 1981; m. George Phillip Hagan, Apr. 16, 1954; children—Philip Ray, Stephen Russell. Med. technologist hosps. in Tex., 1956-75; instr. med. lab. tech. Grayson County Coll., Denison, Tex., 1974—. Mem. Am. Soc. Clin. Pathologists (assoc.), Am. Soc. Med. Technologists, Tex. Soc. Med. Technologists, Tex. Jr. Coll. Tchrs. Assn. Baptist. Home: PO Box 684 Sherman TX 75090 Office: 6101 Grayson Dr Denison TX 75020

HAGANS, MICHELE VICTORIA, development and realty company executive, parking company executive; b. Washington, Oct. 16, 1949; d. Theodore R. and Dolores (Day) H. B.S. in Zoology, Howard U., 1973, M.E. in Bio-Environ. Engring., 1976. Vice pres. The Housing Ctr., Inc., Washington, 1981-82; exec. v.p. D&H Parking Systems, Inc., Washington, 1982—; pres. TRH Properties, Washington, 1984—, Ft. Lincoln Realty Co., Washington, 1984—, Ft. Lincoln New Town Corp., Washington, 1984—. Trustee, Fed. City Council, Washington, 1984; mem. Baseball Commn., Washington, 1984, Housing Prodn. Commn., Washington, 1985. Mem. Greater Washington Bd. Trade, Nat. Bus. League (treas. 1984—), D.C. Builders Assn. (mem. bd. dirs.), D.C. C. of C. (bd. dirs.), Heroes, Inc. (bd. dirs.). Avocations: skiing; music; photography. Office: Fort Lincoln New Town Corp 3298 Fort Lincoln Dr NE Washington DC 20018

HAGAR, DEBORAH RUTH, personnel executive; b. Milford, Mass., June 5, 1949; d. Dorothy M. Hagar Rafuse. B.S. in Bus., Calif. Western U., 1977, M.B.A., 1978. Adminstrv. sec. Martin Marietta Co., Denver, 1968-72, office mgr., 1972-74; dir. personnel Loma Linda Community Hosp., Calif., 1974—; seminar leader Am. Mgmt. Assn., 1980—; tchr. U. La Verne, Calif., 1983; accreditation coordinator Am. Soc. Personnel Adminstrn., 1983. Contbr. articles to profl. jours. Mem. scholarship com. Skadron Bus. Coll., 1979—; Yacaipa chmn. Mike Curb for Lt. Gov., 1976; party worker Reagan Campaign com., 1980. Mem. Am. Soc. Personnel Adminstrn. (Calif. state dir. 1986—), Personnel Indsl. Relations Assn., Am. Mgmt. Assn., Hosp. Personnel Mgmt. Assn. (sec. 1980-81). Republican. Seventh-day Adventist. Home: 36169 Senna Cir Yucaipa CA 92399 Office: Loma Linda Community Hosp 25333 Barton Rd Loma Linda CA 92354

HAGBERG, VIOLA WILGUS, lawyer, contracting officer; b. Salisbury, Md., July 3, 1952; d. William E. and Jean Shelton (Barlow) Wilgus; m. Chris Eric Hagberg, Feb. 19, 1978. B.A., Furman U., Greenville, S.C., 1974; J.D., U. S.C., 1978, U. Tulsa, 1978; DOD Army Logistics Sch. honor grad. basic mgmt. def. acquisition, def. small purchase, advanced fed. acquisition regulation, Fort Lee, Va., 1981-82. Bar: Okla. 1978, Va. 1979, U.S. Ct. Appeals (8th cir.). With Lawyers Com. for Civil Rights, Washington, 1979; pub. utility specialist Fed. Energy Regulatory Commn., Washington, 1979-80; contract specialist U.S. Army, C.E., Ft. Shafter, Hawaii, 1980-81; contract officer/supervisory contract specialist Tripler Army Med. Ctr., Hawaii 1981-83; supervisory procurement analyst and chief policy sect. Procurement Div. U.S. Coast Guard, Washington, 1983; contract officer and chief Avionics Engring Branch sect. engring., 1984; procurement analyst office of sec. Dept. Transp., 1984-85. Mem. Nat. Contract Mgmt. Assn., ABA (law student div. liaison 1977-78), Va. State Bar Assn., Okla. Bar Assn., Phi Alpha Delta, Kappa Delta Epsilon. Home: 4200 Ironwood Ave Seal Branch CA 90740

HAGE, ROSEMARY, computer systems analyst, soprano, actress, producer, director; b. Cortland, N.Y., Nov. 4, 1952; d. Nahra Abdo and Linda (Joseph) H. B.A., SUNY-Genesee, 1974, cert. secondary edn. in English and drama. Computer systems adminstr., analyst, operator, corp. legal dept. ABC, Inc., N.Y.C., 1981-85; freelance computer systems adminstr., analyst, operator, N.Y.C., 1985-86; computer systems adminstr., analyst, operator Law Sch., Columbia U., N.Y.C., 1986—; teacher and performer Middle Eastern dance, Washington and San Francisco. Performed with various opera cos. and other orgns., including N.Y. Opera Theatre, N.Y.C., N.Y. Gilbert and Sullivan Players, N.Y.C., Opera Theatre of Berkeley, Calif., The New Shakespeare Co. of San Francisco; appeared in various operas, operettas, and regional dinner theatre, theatre and summer stock prodns.; concert soloist; producer, dir. (operas) Don Giovanni, 1981, The Old Maid and the Thief, 1985, (concerts) An Evening of Amadeus, A Day in New York, a Night in Vienna, Offenbach's Birthday, An Evening of Gilbert & Sullivan, (summer stock) A Musical Revue, 1973, (concert series) Montauk Club's Operetta Concert Series, Bklyn., 1982-85, Operetta Concert Series, touring N.Y.C., 1982-86. Mem. Nat. Assn. Female Execs. Democrat. Roman Catholic. Home: 402 Bayridge Pkwy Apt 64 Brooklyn NY 11209 Office: Columbia U Law Sch Law Placement Office New York NY 10027

HAGEN, MARIE LOUISE, lawyer; b. Plainfield, N.J., Oct. 23, 1956; d. Richard A. and Mary Louise (Moore) H. A.B., Cornell U., 1978, J.D., 1981; student Oxford U. (Eng.), 1979. Bar: N.Y. 1981, Mass. 1982, U.S. Dist. Ct. (so. dist.) N.Y. 1982, U.S. Dist. Ct. (ea. dist.) N.Y. 1982. Assoc., Dickerson, Reilly & Mullen, N.Y.C., 1981-82; trial atty. U.S. Dept. of Justice, N.Y.C., 1982—; judge Philip C. Jessup Internat. Law Moot Ct. Competition. Mem. Maritime Law Assn., ABA, Am. Soc. Internat. Law. Democrat. Roman Catholic. Office: Dept of Justice 26 Federal Plaza Suite 36 100 New York NY 10278

HAGEN, RAEBURN ROSE, librarian; b. Wenatchee, Wash., Oct. 15, 1924; d. Raymond Redmond and Zelma (Reeves) Morrison; m. Wayne Delos Hagen, Sept. 14, 1946; children—Wendy, Raeburn Hagen McCauley, Wayne Delos. B.A. magna cum laude, U. Wash., 1946, M.Libr., 1975. Instr. English, Grays Harbor Coll., Aberdeen, Wash., 1969-72, 75-78, asst. librarian, 1977-78, asst. dean library and media services, 1978-85; dir. library Highline Community Coll., Des Moines, Wash., 1985—. Trustee Aberdeen Pub. Library, 1964-71, Timberland Regional Library, Olympia, 1971-76; bd. dirs. Grays Harbor Coll. Found., 1955-60, Girl Scout council, 1960. Mem. Wash. Library Assn. (bd. dirs. 1973-75), ALA, Assn. Coll. and Research Libraries, Wash. State Community Coll. Librarians and Media Specialists Library Media Dirs. Council (chmn.), Phi Beta Kappa, Beta Phi Mu, Chi Omega, PEO. Democrat. Episcopalian. Home: 1516 Bel Aire St Aberdeen WA 98520 Office: Highline Community College Des Moines WA 98198

HAGEN, UTA, actress; b. Gottingen, Germany, June 12, 1919; d. Oskar F. L. and Thyra A. (Leisner) H.; student U. Wis., Royal Acad. Dramatic Art, London; D.F.A. (hon.), Smith Coll., 1978, Wooster Coll., 1982; L.H.D. (hon.), De Paul U., 1981; m. Jose Ferrar (div.); m. Herbert Berghof, Jan. 24, 1951; 1 dau., Leticia. Played Ophelia, Dennis, Mass., 1937, Nina in Sea Gull, N.Y.C., 1938; appeared in Key Largo, 1939, Vicki, 1942, Othello, 1943-45, Whole World Over, Faust, Masterbuilder, 1947, Angel Street, 1948, Street Car Named Desire, 1948, 50, Country Girl, 1950, G.B. Shaw's Saint Joan, 1951-52, Tovarich, City Center, 1952, In Any Language, 1952, The Deep Blue Sea, 1953, The Magic and the Loss, 1954, The Island of Goats, 1955, A Month in the Country, 1956, Good Woman of Setzuan, 1957, Who's Afraid of Virginia Wolff, 1962-64, The Cherry Orchard, 1968, Charlotte, 1980 (also univ. tour 1981-82), The Other, 1972, The Boys from Brazil, 1978; TV appearances include A Month in the Country, 1956, Out of Dusk, 1959, A Doctor's Story, 1984; appeared in Mrs. Warren's Profession, off-Broadway, 1986; tchr. acting Herbert Berghof Studio, N.Y.C., 1947—. Recipient Antoinette Perry award, 1951, 63; N.Y. Drama Critics award, 1951, 63; Donaldson award best actress, 1951; London Critics award for best actress 1963-64 season; Outer Circle award; named to Theatre Hall of Fame, 1981. Author: Respect for Acting, 1973; Love for Cooking, 1976; Sources, 1982. Address: Herbert Berghof Studio 120 Bank St New York NY 10014*

HAGENER, ANTOINETTE RADER, county official; b. Buffalo, Nov. 22, 1926; d. Joseph G. and Angele (Van Wulpen) Rader; m. Louis W. Hagener, June 8, 1947; children—Louis I., Anne M., M. Jeffry, James F. (dec.). B.A., U. Denver, 1946. Tchr. sci. Westminster High Sch., Colo., 1946-47, South High Sch., Denver, 1947-49; lab. technician Vita Rich Dairy, Havre, Mont., 1954-69; mus. curator Hill County, Havre, 1964-81; county commr. Hill County, Havre, 1981—. Co-author Fossils of North Central Montana, 1973; Free for All, 1974. Mem. sch. bd. Sch. Dist. A16, Havre, 1969-71; mem. Park and Recreation Bd., City of Havre, 1970-79; mem. library bldg. adv. bd. City of Havre, 1975-80. Recipient Law Day award Havre Bar Assn., Mont., 1976, Contbn. to Edn. award Havre chpt. Mont. Edn. Assn., 1971; named Woman of Yr., Bus. and Profl. Women, Havre, 1975. Mem. Mont. Assn. Counties (2d v.p.), Mont. Hist. Soc. (pres. 1977-79), AAUW (pres. Mont. div. 1974-76). Democrat. Methodist.

HAGEN-LARSON, DEBRA LYNN, travel agency executive, consultant; b. Portland, Oreg., Oct. 19, 1952; d. Lowell Alden and Virginia Ruth (Powell) Hagen; m. Richard D. Larson, Jan. 1, 1981; 1 stepson, Matthew T. Cert. Inst. of Cert. Travel Agts., Wellesley, Mass., 1985. Mgr., Azumano Travel, Portland, 1981-83; dir. of mktg. Crossroads Travel, Portland, 1983-85; dir. sales Gelco Travel, 1985—. Home: Route 2 Box 139 Banks OR 97106 Office: 1515 SW 5th Ave Portland OR 97201

HAGERMAN, DORTHY JO, nursing home owner, administrator; b. Lexington, Okla., Apr. 12, 1945; d. Frank Robert and Willie (Greenway) Johnson; m. Fred Coburn, July 11, 1964 (div. 1975); children—Fred Christopher, Kip Harland, John Gregory; m. Franklin Thomas Hagerman, June 2, 1979; stepchildren—Dawna Barnes, Tom Hagerman, Deborah. Grad. Norman High Sch., 1963. Lic. nursing home adminstr., Okla., N.Mex. Mgr., El Reno Nursing Ctr., Okla., 1970-73, Timberlane Manor, Edmond, Okla., 1973-74; inspector Okla. Welfare Dept., Oklahoma City, 1974-75; dir. Masonic Charities of Okla., 1976-79; adminstr., cons. Oakridge Care Ctr., Wewoka, Okla., 1980, New Horizons Care Ctr., Konawa, Okla., 1980; cons. adminstr. Friendship Manor, Anadarko, Okla., 1981; sec., treas. Rainbow Health Mgmt. Inc., Pryor, Okla., 1982—; pres. Shady Rest Care Ctr. Inc., Pryor, 1982—, Colonial Terr. Care Ctr., Pryor, 1982—, Grand Valley Care Ctr. Inc., Pryor, 1982—; sec. treas. Shamrock Care Ctrs. of King Fisher, Stroud and Haskell, Okla., 1983—. Mem. Pryor C. of C., Okla. State Nursing Home Assn. Republican. Baptist. Avocations: reading; water skiing; decorating; cooking; flower arranging. Office: Rainbow Health Mgmt Inc 10 S Vann St Pryor OK 74361

HAGERTY, ELIZABETH ANNE, hotel executive, educator; b. Phila., Aug. 14, 1952; d. George Edward and Jacqueline (Olds) H.; 1 child, Margaret Murdock. B.S., Cornell U., 1977. Dir. housekeeping Westin Hotels, Inc., Seattle, 1977-83; exec. dir. housekeeping The Remington on Post Oak Park, Rosewood Hotels, Inc., Houston, 1983—; exec. asst. mgr. La Mansion del Rio Hotel, San Antonio, 1985—; adj. prof. Cornell U., Ithaca, N.Y., 1981—. Mem. Nat. Exec. Housekeepers Assn., Soc. Profl. Women, Cornell Alumni Assn., Cornell Soc. Hotelmen, Internat. Platform Assn. Democrat. Roman Catholic. Clubs: Historic Soc., Friends of the Arts, Houston Town and Country; Cornell (San Antonio). Office: 112 College St San Antonio TX

HAGGERTY, DONNA MARIE, public relations executive; b. Allentown, Pa., Aug. 30, 1953; d. Stanley Theodore and Emma Anna (Hendricks) Sosnowski; m. Terrence Bernard Haggerty, Mar. 3, 1979. B.S., West Chester U., 1975; M.Ed., Temple U., 1980. Cert. tchr. secondary edn. English, journalism. Teaching asst., curriculum planner West Chester U. (Pa.), 1973-75; sec., computer operator William Taylor Co., Allentown, 1975-76; tchr. English, Salisbury High Sch., Allentown, 1975-78; writer, edr.coordinator Morning Call Newspaper, Allentown, Pa. 1978-80, dir. edn. services, writer, 1980-85, pub. relations dir. Morning Call Newspapers, 1985—, ednl. cons., 1977-78; grad. level tchr. intermediate units, Allentown and Nazareth, Pa., 1979—. Bd. dirs. Lehigh Valley Child Care Assn., Allentown, Pa., 1983—. Author weekly edn. column, 1979—; author, editor teaching materials; editor: Headlines, Hometowns & History teaching guide, 1980. Mem. Pa. Newspaper Pubs. Assn. (chair 1981—), Nat. Fedn. Press Women (youth dir. 1983), Nat. Council Tchrs. of English, Phi Delta Kappa. Democrat. Roman Catholic. Office: Morning Call Newspapers 6th and Linden Sts PO Box 1260 Allentown PA 18105

HAGLER, MARY ANNE TYLER, physician; b. Nashville, Jan. 30, 1927; d. John Luck and Edythe (Belton) Tyler; B.S., U. Ga., 1947, postgrad. Sch. Medicine, 1947-48; M.D., Med. Coll. Ga., 1975; m. John Carroll Hagler, III, Oct. 16, 1948; children—Mary Anne, John Carroll IV, Richard B., Katharine W., Elizabeth T. Family practice resident Med. Coll. Ga., Augusta, 1975-78; med. dir. St. Joseph Hosp. Home Health Care and Hospice, Augusta, 1978-81; practice medicine specializing in family practice, Augusta; med. staffs St. Joseph Hosp., Univ. Hosp., Doctors Hosp. of Augusta. Diplomate Am. Bd. Family Practice. Fellow Am. Acad. Family Physicians; mem. AMA, Med. Assn. Ga., Richmond County Med. Soc., Ga. Acad. Family Physicians, Am. Geriatrics Soc., Women's Physicians Council Med. Coll. Ga., Historic Augusta, Inc., Ga. Trust for Hist. Preservation, Jr. League of Augusta, Nat. Soc. Colonial Dames Am. in State of Ga. Roman Catholic. Clubs: Augusta Country, Pinnacle. Home: 999 Highland Ave Augusta GA 30904 Office: 1417 Pendelton Rd Augusta GA 30904

HAGNER, COURTNEY STILLWELL, employment agency executive; b. Washington, July 29, 1942; d. Randall Hagner and Adlumia (Sterrett) H. Assoc. Sci. in Early Childhood, Garland Jr. Coll., 1963; B.S. in Spl. Edn., Boston U., 1965, M.Edn. in Spl. Edn., George Washington U., Washington, 1971; postgrad. U. Mass., 1983. Cert. spl. edn. tchr. Ednl. diagnostician Diagnostic and Evaluation Clinic and Growth and Devel. Ctr., Arlington County Dept. Human Resources, Arlington, Va., 1972-78; chmn. pub. awareness campaign D.C. Vol. Clearinghouse, D.C. Dept. Pub. Health, D.C. Immunization Pub. Awareness Campaign, Washington, 1978; handicapped services coordinator pre-sch. day care div. United Planning Orgn., Washington, 1978-80; sch. adminstr., spl. edn. coordinator Children's Hosp. Nat. Med. Ctr., Washington, 1981-83; pres. bd. dirs. Ind. Living for Handicapped, Inc., Washington, 1984—; pres. Nanny Placement Services, Washington, 1984—; team mem. Washington Met. Area Needs in the 80's, Jr. League Washington, 1981; cons. Mainstreaming Handicapped Preschoolers: A Guide for Parents, Washington Child Devel. Council, 1980. Recipient Vol. of Yr. award UN Assn. U.S.A., Capitol area div., 1979. Mem. Nat. Assn. Edn. Young Children. Republican. Episcopalian. Clubs: Chevy Chase (Md.); City Tavern (Washington). Office: Nanny Placement Services Inc 1621 Wisconsin Ave NW Washington DC 20007

HAGNER, JUDY, process service company executive, computer consultant; b. West Milwaukee, Wis., Dec. 31, 1946; d. Theodore Joseph and Esther (Fintak) H. A.A. in Bus. and Data Processing, Mil. Area Tech. Coll., 1974; cert. developing leadership skills, 1985; B.A. in Bus. Adminstrn., Fla. State U.-Orlando, 1980, B.A.S. in Bus. Adminstrn. and Mgmt., 1980. Computer console operator Marshall & Ilsley Bank, Milw., 1961-74; civil service temp. clk. 2 City Hall and Treasurer's Office, Election Commn., Milw., 1983-86, challenger election commr., 1985-86; congl. V.I.P. Congl. Election Com., Washington, 1984—; state process server, notary pub. State Process Services, Milw., 1986—; computer dir. Mell Leonard & Assocs., Orlando, Fla., 1979-80; computer mgr. and supr. Contract Programming Service, Milw., 1980-84; advt. dir. Assocs. Assistance Co., Cin., 1984—; computer cons. Computer Services, Milw., 1984—. Sponsor G.O.P. Victory Fund, Washington, 1984—; chmn.'s circle mem. 4th Congl. Dist., Republican party, Milw., 1986. Recipient cert. Recognition Congl. Election Com. NRCC and Pres. Ronald Reagan, 1985, R.I. Research-Beyonder Spl. Humane Being Lab., 1985. Mem. Nat. Assn. Female Execs., Am. Soc. Profl. and Exec. Women, Nat. Process Servers Assn., Smithsonian Assocs., St. Matthias Cadets Drum and Bugle Corps and Alumni Assn. (soloist 1958-68), Beta Sigma Phi. Republican. Roman Catholic. Avocations: sports, music; Indpls. and stock race cars; dining and dancing.

HAGUE, DEBORAH ANN, nursing educator; b. Steubenville, Ohio, May 15, 1950; d. James Richard and Ruth Eleanor (Heights) H. Diploma St. Vincent Hosp. Sch. of Nursing, Toledo, 1971; B.A., Ohio State U., 1975, B.S. in Nursing, 1980, M.S., 1981. Registered critical care nurse, Ohio. Staff, head nurse Univ. Hosp., Columbus, Ohio, 1971-75; staff nurse ICU, CCU Doctors Hosp., Columbus, 1975-76, nursing dir., 1976-80; grad. teaching assoc. Ohio State U., Columbus, 1980-81, instr. Coll. of Nursing, 1984—; asst. hosp. dir. nursing Armed Forces Hosp., Khamis, Saudi Arabia, 1982-84; program presenter Office of Continuing Edn. Ohio State U., Columbus, 1984—. Author: (with others) "Rena Fuller-An adult in renal system crisis, 1985. CPR instr. Central Ohio Heart Assn., Columbus, 1979-80. Mem. Am. Assn. Critical Care Nurses (pres. Central Ohio Chpt. 1980-81), Sigma Theta Tau. Republican. Roman Catholic. Avocations: interior decorating, reading. Office: Ohio State U Coll Nursing 1585 Neil Ave Columbus OH 43210

HAGY, LOIS EULALA, paralegal asst.; b. Bristol, Va., Oct. 22, 1950; d. William Kent and Shirley W. (Downs) Hagy; student U. Md., 1969-74, 76-78, Towson State Coll., 1974-76. Legal sec. O'Conor & Sweeney, Balt., 1968-72; asst. dir. mortgage fin. apts. and office parks div. Monumental Properties, Inc., Balt., 1972-75, project coordinator constrn. regional shopping mall div., 1975-76; with Wolpe Enterprises, Inc., Real Estate Developer and Comml. Leasing, Washington, 1976; office mgr. Stemmy & Tidler, C.P.A.s, College Park, Md., 1977; v.p., sec., treas. Metro Builders, Inc., Washington, 1977-80, also dir. residential and comml. renovation, constrn. mgmt., project mgr. condominium conversions; real estate broker David Bandy Real Estate, Washington, 1980-81; paralegal asst. firm Goodell, Landfield, Becker and Green, Washington, 1981—; dir. Capital Devel. Corp., Stemmy & Tidler, Metro Builders, Inc. Notary public. Mem. Washington Bd. Realtors. Office: Goodell Landfield Becker and Green 1220 19th St NW Washington DC 20036

HAHN, ANNA MARIE, nurse; b. Phila., Mar. 29, 1912; d. Joseph Conrad and Pauline (Willis) Hahn. B.A., N.J. State Coll., 1967. R.N., N.J. Head nurse Monmouth Med. Ctr., Long Branch, N.J., 1933-34, nursing arts instr., 1935-41; pvt. duty nurse, summers, 1950-79; sch. nurse Asbury Park High Sch. (N.J.), 1941-80; camp nurse Camp Blaisdell, Lake Sunapee, N.H., summer, 1946; ship nurse Am. Export Lines, N.Y. to Europe, summer, 1947, 48. Served to 2d lt. Nurse Corps, U.S. Army, 1944-45. Mem. Monmouth Meml. Nurses Alumnaea Assn. (life), Monmouth County Sch. Nurses Assn. (co-founder, various coms.). Democrat. Roman Catholic.

HAHN, BESSIE KING, library administrator; educator; b. Shanghai, China, May 14, 1939; came to U.S., 1959; d. Jen Fong and Wei (Lok) King; m. Roger Carl Hahn, June 1962 (div. 1983); children—Angela Yee-mei, Michael King-yau, Belinda Shee-wei. B.A., Mt. Marty Coll., 1961; M.L.S., Syracuse U., 1972. Librarian, Carrier Corp., Syracuse, N.Y., 1972; life scis. bibliographer Syracuse U. Libraries, 1973-75, head depts. sci. and tech., 1976-78; asst. dir. reader services Johns Hopkins U. Library, Balt., 1978-81; dir. library services Brandeis U., Waltham, Mass., 1981—; cons. Shanghai Jiao Tong U. Library, Shanghai, 1983—. Contbr. articles to profl. jours. Editor Jour. Ednl. Media and Library Scis., 1983—. Recipient Gold Cup award Johns Hopkins U. Class of 1980; named hon. prof. Shanghai Jiao Tong U., 1984; Hon. Benefactor award Brandeis Nat. Women's Com., 1986. Mem. ALA, Chinese-Am. Librarians Assn. (pres. 1982-83). Home: 82 Florence Rd Waltham MA 02154 Office: Brandeis U Library South St Waltham MA 02254

HAHN, CELIA FERNER, broadcaster; b. Sioux City, Iowa, Mar. 21, 1942; d. Arnold Erland and Celia Evelyn (Wright) Ferner; m. Curtis Henry Hahn, Feb. 6, 1966; children—Cathy Celia, Christopher Curtis. B.A., State U. Iowa, 1964. Asst. to pres. Cranbrook Ednl. Community, Bloomfield Hills, Mich., 1972-78; owner WLDM Radio, Westfield, Mass., 1978—. Mem. Greater Westfield Area C. of C. (pres. 1985), Ad Club, Valley Press Club. Episcopalian. Clubs: Westfield Woman's (program chmn. 1980-82); Williston Parents Assn. (v.p. 1983-84). Avocations: swimming; solar energy. Home: 28 Pineridge Dr Westfield MA 01085 Office: WLDM 249 Union St Box 1570 Westfield MA 01085

HAHN, DEBORAH KAY, nurse, home health agency director; b. Waco, Tex., Apr. 11, 1958; d. Edwin Arthur and Melva Irene (Michelsen) Hahn. B.S. in Nursing, Baylor U., 1980. Lic. R.N., Tex. Staff nurse Providence Hosp., Waco, Tex., 1980-81, head med. nurse, 1981-85; dir. services All Service Health Care, Waco, Tex., 1985—. Instr., mem. Am. Heart Assn., 1984—. Recipient Outstanding Young Women Am. award, 1984. Mem. Central Tex. Zool. Soc., Am. Nurses Assn., Tex. Nurses Assn. (bd. dirs. 1984—), Alpha Tau Delta (nat. v.p. 1981-83, pres. 1983-85), Sigma Theta Tau, Baylor U. Alumni Assn. (life). Lutheran. Avocations: snow skiing; needlework. Home: 2504 N 28th St Waco TX 76708 Office: All Service Health Care 3404 Bosque Blvd Waco TX 76710

HAHN, ELWANDA JEAN, educational administrator; b. Post, Tex., Mar. 8, 1933; d. Chris Veet O'Keefe and Aquie Pauline (Stewart) Price; m. Norman Earl Hahn, June 18, 1950; children—Holly, Dana, Janine, Erin. B.S., Tex. Tech. U., 1966; M.L.S., East Tex. State U., 1972. Cert. librarian, Tex. Tchr. Aspermont High Sch., Tex., 1966-67; librarian Jayton High, Tex., 1967-72; media specialist Jayton Girard Pub. Schs., Jayton, 1972—; dir. drama prodns., 1976—. Mem. Tex. Regional Arts Council (council), Tex. Ednl. Theatre Assn., Assn. Tex. Profl. Educators, Delta Kappa Gamma. Baptist. Avocation: artist. Home: Rt 3 Box 75 Jayton TX 79528 Office: Jayton Pub Schs Caliremont & Madison Jayton TX 79528

HAHN, HELENE HIRSH, graphics company owner; b. Balt., May 22, 1946; d. Allan T. and Eleanor (Rosenthal) Hirsh, Jr.; m. Joseph Edward Hahn, Aug. 4, 1968; children—Andrew Charles, David Stuart. B.S. in Early Childhood Edn., U. Md., 1968; M.Ed., U. N.C., 1972. Tchr. Gaston County Schs., Gastonia, N.C., 1969-72; instr. Gaston Community Coll., Dallas, N.C., 1972-76; dept. head Ottenheimer Pubs., Inc., Balt., 1979-80; owner Hahn Graphics, Inc., Balt., 1981—; supr. internship Md. Inst. Art, Balt., 1983—, Loyola U., Balt., 1984—; facilitator color reprodn. Port City Press, Balt., 1985. Author: Dictionary of Great Events in U.S. History, 1969, Learn About Animals, Birds, Flowers and Insects, 1973, Websters Vest Pocket Dictionary, 1977. Editor: Mischievious Kitten: Porky the Explorer, 1974. Chmn. Religious Sch., Temple Emanuel, Gastonia, 1975-79, pres. Sisterhood Hadassah, 1978-79, bd. dirs., 1975-78, sec., 1978-79; v.p. Gaston County Assn. Childhood Edn., Gastonia, 1969-73; mem. Children's 100 Inst. N.C., Durham, 1973-77, county survey chmn., 1973, mem. steering com., 1974-76; bd. dirs. Gaston County Headstart, Dallas, N.C., 1974-76, Jr. League Gaston County, Gastonia, 1976-79; v.p. Mid-Atlantic region Nat. Fedn. Temple Sisterhoods, 1977-83, pres., 1983-85; bd. dirs. Jr. League Balt., 1986-87; mem. Hadassah, Balt., 1979—, Nat. Council Jewish Women, Balt., 1981—, Walters Art Gallery, Balt., 1982—, Jewish Hist. Soc. Md., Balt., 1982—; mem. Sisterhood bd. Balt. Hebrew Congregation, 1982-85; bd. dirs. Women's Housing Coalition, Balt., 1984—, Assn. Jewish Charities-Womens div., Balt., 1985-88, Nat. Fedn. Temple Sisterhood, N.Y.C., 1985-89; mem. steering com. Md. Low Income Housing Coalition, Balt., 1985—. Mem. Printing Industries Md., Advt. Assn. Balt., Nat. Assn. Female Execs. Democrat. Jewish. Avocations: reading; travel; home decorating; tennis; bridge. Office: Hahn Graphics Inc 8422 Bellona Ln 101 Baltimore MD 21204

HAHN, JOAN CHRISTENSEN, drama educator, travel agent; b. Kemmerer, Wyo., May 9, 1933; d. Roy and Bernice (Pringle) Wainwright; m. Milton Angus Christensen, Dec. 29, 1952 (div. Oct. 1, 1971); children—Randall M., Carla J. Christensen Teasdale; m. Charles Henry Hahn, Nov. 15, 1972. B.S., Brigham Young U., 1965. Profl. ballroom dancer, 1951-59; travel dir. E.T. World Travel, Salt Lake City, 1969—; tchr. drama Payson High Sch., Utah, 1965-71, Cottonwood High Sch., Salt Lake City, 1971—; dir. Performing European Tours, Salt Lake City, 1969-76; dir. Broadway theater tours, 1976—. Dir. Salem City Salem Days, Utah, 1965-75; regional dir. dance Latter-day Saints Ch., 1954-72. Named Best Dir. High Sch. Musicals, Green Sheet Newspapers, 1977, 82, 84; recipient 1st place award Utah State Drama Tournament, 1974, 77, 78; Limelight award, 1982; Exemplary Performance in teaching theater arts Granite Sch. Dist., Salt Lake City, 1982. Mem. Internat. Thespian Soc. (sponsor 1968—, internat. dir. 1982-84, trustee 1978-84), Utah Speech Arts Assn. (pres. 1976-78), NEA, Utah Edn. Assn., Granite Edn. Assn., Profl. Travel Agts. Assn., Utah High Sch. Activities Assn. (drama rep. 1972-76), AAUW (pres. 1972-74). Republican. Mormon. Avocations: reading; travel; dancing. Home: 685 S 1st E Box 36 Salem UT 84653 Office: Cottonwood High Sch 5715 S 1300 E Salt Lake City UT 84121

HAHN, KANDRA, state official; b. Lincoln, Nebr., May 29, 1947; d. Kenneth Roy and Mildred Marie (Sedlacek) Bailey; m. Robert E. Hahn, Dec. 30, 1965 (div. 1967); 1 dau., Kandalyn; m. 2d, Donald L. Hunter, June 6, 1976. B.A., Nebr. Wesleyan U., 1970; M.B.A., U. Nebr.-Lincoln, 1982. Journalist, Lincoln Jour., 1974; clk. dist. ct. Lancaster County, Lincoln, 1975-82; media coordinator Kerrey for Gov. Campaign, Lincoln, 1982; dir. Energy Office, State of Nebr., Lincoln, 1983—. Office: Nebr Energy Office PO Box 95085 Lincoln NE 68509-5085

HAHN, KAREN VIRGINIA, holding company executive; b. Detroit, Jan. 9, 1947; d. A. Kurt and Virginia (Claspill) H. m. R. Eugene Neal, Jr., May 29, 1965 (div. 1973); children—Patricia, David. A.S., Sacred Heart U., 1975; B.A., Sarah Lawrence Coll., 1979. Legal asst. chems. group Comml. Olin Corp., Stamford, Conn., 1980-82; asst. to pres. H.K. James Co., Westport, Conn., 1982; asst. sec. Moore & Munger, Inc., Fairfield, Conn., 1983-85, dir. adminstrv. services, 1984—, sec. corp., 1985—. Mem. Choraliers (sec. 1982-83). Republican. Mem. United Ch. of Christ. Office: Moore & Munger Inc 140 Sherman St Fairfield CT 06430

HAHN, LIDA, healthcare services executive, hospital administrator; b. Oakland, Calif.; d. James Dyer and Cora Mildred (Helfrich) H.; m. Donald Richard Rasmussen (div.); children—Marina Ann, Donald Richard Jr.; m. Paul B. Henne, Jan. 12, 1974. R.N., Samuel Merritt Sch. Nursing, Oakland, 1941; student U. Munich (Germany), 1951, U. Calif.-Berkeley, 1969; student in bus. adminstrn., U. Calif-Santa Clara, 1970. Registered nurse. Chief nurse Oakland Army Base, Calif., 1944-48, Darmdstadt Infirmary, Germany, 1949-50; dir. nursing Civic Ctr. Hosp., Oakland, 1953-63, adminstr., 1960-63; sec., treas. and corp. owner Psychiat. Contract Services, Oakland, 1981—; v.p., exec. adminstr. E.A. Gladman Meml. Hosp., Oakland, 1967—; v.p. Telecare Corp., Oakland; dir. Telecare-Gladman. Organized 21 health care dispensaries in Oakland and Richmond, Calif., chief nurse Oakland Army Base. Mem. Calif. State Legislature Com. Mental Health, Sacramento, 1968, Alameda County Mental Health Assn., Oakland, Alameda County Comprehensive Health Planning Council, Oakland, 1974-76. Recipient Meritorious Service by a Civilian award U.S. War Dept., 1948; Woman of Yr. award Women's Health Care Execs. Fellow Am. Coll. Hosp. Adminstrs.; mem. East Bay Hosp. Conf. (pres.; Meritorious award 1981, bd. dirs.), Calif. Hosp. Assn., Women's Network (award of merit, life mem. exec. bd.), Assn. Western Hosps., Am. Hosp. Assn., ARC Nursing Service-1st Res., Hosp. Council No. Calif. (bd. dirs., govt. affairs com.). Club: Soroptimist. Office: Everett A Gladman Meml Hosp 2633 E 27th St Oakland CA 94601

HAHN, SHARON LEE, city official; b. Kenosha, Wis., Sept. 22, 1939; d. Vincent B. and Mary Lee (Vaux) McCloskey; m. Robert W. Hahn, Jan. 1967 (div. June 1977); 1 child, John V. Calhoun. Student Kent State U., 1983. Cert. mcpl. clk., notary pub., Ohio. Sec., Simmons Bedding Co., Columbus, Ohio, 1960-61; exec. sec. Westinghouse, Columbus, 1962-68; legal sec. Bricker Law Firm, Columbus, 1969-70; asst. to prosecutor Whiteleather Law Firm, Columbia City, Ind., 1970-77; legal sec. Metz, Bailey & Spicer, Westerville, Ohio, 1977-80; clk. of council, sec. to city mgr. City of Westerville, 1981—. Records mgr. City of Westerville, 1981—. Mem. Ohio Mcpl. Clks. Assn. (bd. dirs. 1984-86), Internat. Inst. Mcpl. Clks. (CMC award 1984). Presbyterian.

Avocations: golf; organ; rug hooking; interior decorating. Home: 382 Tradewind Ct Westerville OH 43081 Office: City of Westerville 21 S State St Westerville OH 43081

HAIGHT, DONNA GAY, editor; b. Afton, Iowa, Feb. 9, 1941; d. Leo Clark and G. Maxine (Tisue) Kaster; m. Dean E. Haight, July 10, 1960; children—Dena, Randall, Jeff, Vince. Personnel sec. Neodata Co., Boulder, Colo., 1962-69; news editor Afton Star-Enterprise, Iowa, 1969-80, editor/owner, 1980—. Mem. Iowa Newspaper Assn. Methodist. Home: Rt 1 Box 225 Ellston IA 50074 Office: Afton Star-Enterprise 274 N Douglas St Afton IA 50830

HAIKO, GERALDINE MAE, auto damage appraiser; b. Hartford, Conn., Nov. 5, 1940; d. Frank Joseph and May Lillian (Brandt) Haiko; m. Douglas Allen Gallant, May 27, 1961 (div. Mar. 1965); 1 child, Douglas Allen. A.A., Vt. Coll., 1960. Rating clk. Travelers Ins. Co., Hartford, 1961-65; teller, adminstrv. asst., Soc. for Savs., Wethersfield, 1965-69; teller, asst. head teller, customer service officer Coral Ridge Nat. Bank, Fort Lauderdale, Fla., 1970-74; with customer service dept. Bank Coral Springs, Fla., 1974-76; pres. Frank J. Haiko, Inc., Wethersfield, 1976—. Mem. Ind. Auto Damage Appraisers (sec. treas. NE region 1981—, nat. sec. 1985—), Wethersfield C. of C., U.S. C. of C. Republican. Avocations: cross country skiing; singing; dancing; spectator sports. Office: Frank J Haiko Inc 36 Silas Deane Hwy Wethersfield CT 06109

HAILI, RACHEL CHING, catering business executive, consultant; b. Honolulu, Apr. 17, 1918; d. Sing Kui and See Moi (Pang) Ching; m. Peter Davis Haili, Mar. 23, 1936 (dec.); children—Donna Pang, Sandra Antone, Roberta Ahnee, Rachel K., Lorraine Alo, Carol Hirayama. Waitress, Lau Yee Chai, Honolulu, 1939-45; waitress, mgr. Family Inn, Honolulu, 1946-49; owner Haili's Hawaiian Foods, Honolulu, 1949—; pres. Haili's Hale Aina Inc., Honolulu, 1981—. Mem. Honolulu Fish Dealer Assn. Democrat. Congregationalist. Office: Haili's Hawaiian Foods 1020 Auahi St Honolulu HI 96813

HAIMM, SHARLYNE, retail apparel company executive; b. Lithuania, Jan. 10, 1922; d. Morris and Sarah Sneider; children—Michael, Cindy. Pres., Michael's Discount Women's Apparel, Hallandale, Fla., 1972—. Mem. Broward Forum, Hallandale C. of C. (bd. dirs., pres. 1984). Clubs: Turnberry Yacht and Racquet, Jockey. Home: 3625 N Country Club Dr Penthouse 3 North Miami Beach FL 33180 Office: Michael's 383 NE 2d Ave Hallandale FL 33009

HAINE, CLARA JOSEPHINE, hospital administrator; b. Denver, Sept. 24, 1924; d. Frank Anthony and Eva (Gonzales) Lucero; m. Edward Rolen Haines, Oct. 17, 1959; children—Mark, Susan. B.A., U. Calif.-Berkeley, 1950; postgrad. U. So. Calif., 1951-57. Hosp. adminstr. Los Angeles County U. So. Calif. Med. Ctr., 1978-79, hosp. adminstr., assoc. exec. dir., 1979-85, chief ops. officer, assoc. exec. dir., 1985—; asst. clin. prof. U. So. Calif. Grad. Sch. Health Care Adminstrn., Los Angeles, 1980—; career advisor U. Calif.-Berkeley. Active LWV, So. Pasadena. Recipient Clin. Faculty Excellent Service award U. So. Calif., 1984. Mem. Am. Hosp. Assn., Calif. Hosp. Assn., Women in Health Adminstrn., Nat. Assn. Female Execs., CARES Aux. Los Angeles County-U. So. Calif. Med. Ctr., Flower Guild Aux. for Children. Democrat.

HAINES, CLARA ELIZABETH WARD, construction company and industrial park development executive; b. Balt., July 18, 1916; s. Arthur Thomas and Clara Louise (Eppler) W.; m. John Summer Haines, Jan. 14, 1939; children—Thomas W. W., Elizabeth L. Haines Sheldon. A.B., Goucher Coll., 1937. Asst. treas. Nat. Paving Co., 1949-54, v.p., 1954—; sec.-treas. Ward-Haines Industry, Balt., 1954-60, pres., 1960—; sec.-treas. Menlo Indsl. Park, Balt., 1960—. Officer Friends Am. Wing, Balt. Mus. Art, 1970-80, pres., 1981, 82; bd. dirs. Historic Hampton, Inc., Balt., 1982—. Democrat. Episcopalian. Clubs: Gibson Island (bd. mem. 1981); Balt. Country; Roland Park Garden. Avocations: antiques; gardening. Home: 25 Blythewood Rd Baltimore MD 21215 also Gibson Island MD 21056 Office: Ward Industries Inc 4200 Menlo Dr Baltimore MD 21215

HAINESWORTH, MARILYN BRYANT, accountant, consultant; b. Warren, Ohio, Feb. 27, 1947; d. William and Rovenia (Brogdon) Bryant; B.A. in Acctg., Hiram (Ohio) Coll., 1981; postgrad. Baldwin Wallace Coll.; m. Wayne Hainesworth, Mar. 28, 1964; children—Melani Lynn, Mario Dwayne. Acct., Packard Electric Co., Warren, 1965—; acct., mgr. Williams Electric Co., Warren, 1975—. Exec. adv. Warren Jr. Achievement. Mem. Nat. Assn. Female Execs., Distributive Edn. Clubs Am., Kent State U. Alumni Assn., Assn. M.B.A. Execs., Hiram Coll. Alumni Assn. Office: Quality Tng Ctr Packard Electric Co Plant 41 PO Box 431 Warren OH 44486

HAINLINE, GEORGIA RIVERS, satellite communications executive; b. Miami, Fla., Jan. 15, 1963; d. Eruith Dickinson and Marie (Bie) Rivers; m. Steven A. Hainline, Apr. 12, 1980; children—April Georgene, Robert Dee. A.A., Central Fla. Community Coll., 1982. Sec., Rivers Radio, Ocala, Fla., 1978-82; v.p. GRAM Corp., Ocala, 1982—, real estate advisor, 1982—; v.p. InterLace Communications, Ocala, 1984—; pres. Family Assoc. Bus., Ocala, 1982—. Author: (poetry) A Quiet Heart A Quiet Mind, 1985. Mem. Republican Presdl. Task Force, 1984. Mem. Am. Mgmt. Assn., Am. Women in Radio and TV, Fla. Assn. Broadcasters. Presbyterian. Club: Appaloosa Horse. Avocations: writing; poetry; horseback riding; boating; hunting. Home: 7660 S Magnolia Ave Ocala FL 32674

HAINSWORTH-STRAUS, CHRISTINE LOUISE, commercial real estate broker; b. Alton, Ill., Oct. 29, 1962; d. Joseph Richard and Nola Jo (Harwood) Hainsworth; m. Michael Wolcott Straus, Aug. 31, 1985. B.A. in Bus. Adminstrn., Principia Coll., 1983, B.A. in English Lit., 1983. Leasing agt. Murdoch & Coll., Inc., St. Louis, 1983-84, mktg. mgr., 1984-86; comml. real estate broker William D. Feldman Assocs., Culver City, Calif., 1986—. Editor Praxis, 1982, bus. mgr., 1983. Mem. Citizens for Light Rail Transit, St. Louis, 1984, 85; mem. telecommunications task force Los Angeles Central City Assn. Mem. Nat. Assn. Female Execs., Comml. Real Estate Women, Friends of Huntington Library, Principia Alumni Assn. Christian Scientist. Avocations: tennis; soccer; Japanese art and French Impressionist art. Home: 140 S Mentor Ave Apt 211 Pasadena CA 91106 Office: William D Feldman Assocs 5995 S Sepulveda Blvd Culver City CA 90230

HAIRSTON, BRENDA COLBY, insurance company executive; b. Biloxi, Miss., Aug. 23, 1947; d. Russell Sterling and V. Margaret (Allen) Colby; m. Robert E. Hairston, Jr., Sept. 4, 1971 (div. Apr. 1981). B.A., U. Fla., 1969. Adminstrv. asst. Mutual of Omaha, Miami, Fla., 1973-77; mktg. rep. Tab Products Co., Miami, 1977-80; 2d v.p. Mutual of Omaha, Miami, 1980-81, v.p., 1981—; 2d v.p. United of Omaha, Miami, 1980-81, v.p., 1981—; bd. dirs. Fla. Ins. Council, Tallahassee, 1981—; pres. Fla. Ins. News Service, Tallahassee, 1983-84, 1st v.p., 1984-86; dir. Fla. Life & Health Ins. Guaranty Assn., Jacksonville, 1983—. Bd. dirs. Jr. Achievement of Greater Miami, 1984—. Mem. YWCA Women's Network, LWV, Brickell Area Assn. (bd. dirs. 1981-83, treas. 1983-84, sec. 1984-85, v.p. 1985-86). Republican. Office: Mutual of Omaha Ins Co 1201 Brickell Ave Suite 601 PO Box 010711 Miami FL 33101

HAIST, NANCY MALONE, communication equipment manufacturing company executive; b. Nashville, Dec. 31, 1929; d. John Lain and Mary (Meek) Malone; m. Claude F. Linn, May 22, 1948 (div. 1960); children—Skip, Linda, Mike; m. Melval C. Haist, Mar. 8, 1962; children—Jay, Clark, Penny. Pres. House of Haist, Plantation, Fla., 1970-75, Buttercup, Inc., Delray Beach, Fla., 1976-82, Communication Equipment and Engring. Co., Plantation, 1982—; small bus. adv. mem. Fed. Res., Atlanta, 1985—. Mem. Plantation C. of C., Nat. Assn. Women Bus. Owners, Women in Electronics, Women's Advocacy Minority Majority, Women Bus. Owner's Council (dir. 1983-84, exec. v.p. 1986). Republican. Avocations: tennis, painting. Home: 6218 Tropical Way Delray Beach FL 33445 Office: Communication Equipment and Engring Co 1580 NW 65th Ave Plantation FL 33313

HAJEC, SUSAN HEFFRON, public relations executive; b. Eau Claire, Wis., Jan. 2, 1943; d. Anthony Noonan and Doris (Tanberg) Heffron; m. Thomas J. Hajec, June 19, 1965; children—Laura S., Kathleen M. B.A., Mich. State U., 1965, postgrad., 1981; postgrad. Western Mich. U., 1982, Kalamazoo Coll., 1982-83. Tchr. pvt. schs., Lexington, Ky., 1965-66, 69-74; pub. relations dir. Walnut Woods Golf Club, Gobles, Mich., 1977-83; v.p., sec. Argonauta Inc., 1977-84; regional corr. Kalamazoo Gazette, 1980—; pub. relations coordinator Health Circle, 1983—. Pub. relations cons. Gobles Schs., (Mich.), 1980—. Contbr. articles to profl. jours. Mem. Internat. Assn. Bus. Communicators, Nat. Fedn. Press Women, Women in Communications, Inc., Gobles Bus. Assn. Office: Health Circle 3624 S Westnedge Kalamazoo MI 49008

HAKIM, LOUISE ZALTA, import company executive; b. Mobile, Ala., July 14, 1922; d. Nouri L. and Zahda M. (Lizmi) Zalta; m. Albert S. Hakim, May 24, 1942; children—Saul, Betty, Theda, Eddie, Jack, Joseph, Shirley. Student Northeast U., Monroe, La., 1956-58. Mgr. York Children Shop, Monroe, La., 1942-60; importer, owner Tidy Ties Corp., Monroe, 1960-70, inventor, 1970—, developer, 1974—, researcher, 1980—, dir., 1960—. Designer, developer infant shoe ties, 1965, medicine container, 1965; inventor, designer, developer blanket holder, 1976, squeeze toys, 1976, pacifier, 1980. Mem. U.S. C. of C. Republican. Jewish. Avocations: tennis; golf; fishing. Home: PO Box 4826 Monroe LA 71211 Office: Tidy Corp 2813 DeSiard St Monroe LA 71201

HAKKARINEN, IDA MARIE, meterologist; b. Washington, Mar. 7, 1956; d. William and Vilma Helen (Pynnonen) H. B.S., U. Md., 1977, M.S., 1981. Meteorologist NOAA, Washington, 1978-79; grad. research asst. Inst. for Phys. Sci. and Tech., College Park, Md., 1978-81; research meteorologist Gen. Elec. Mgmt. and Tech. Services Co., Lanham, Md., 1981-82, Gen. Software Corp., Landover, Md., 1982—. Contbr. articles to profl. jours. Mentor summer inst. in sci. and tech. for jr. high girls NASA Goddard Space Flight Ctr., 1981-85; vol. speaker Washington Pub. Sch. System, 1983—. Mem. Am. Meteorol. Soc., Nat. Assn. Female Execs., Phi Beta Kappa, Sigma Xi, Phi Kappa Phi. Democrat. Lutheran. Avocations: sky-watching, genealogy. Office: Code 612 Goddard Space Flight Ctr Greenbelt MD 20771

HALBEDEL, JANE MARJORIE, consultant; b. Cleve., Jan. 22, 1947; d. John Forest and Edith Elaine (Brown) Stahl; m. Thomas Nicholas Halbedel, Dec. 27, 1969. B.S., Bowling Green State U., 1969; M.Ed., Cleve. State U., 1981. Cert. music edn. tchr., sch. counselor, alcoholism counselor. Lic. real estate agt. Cleary Realty, Seven Hills, Ohio, 1976-78; profl. soloist Unity Ctr. of Cleve., Cleveland Heights, 1976-79; choral dir. Jr./Sr. High Sch., Brooklyn, Ohio, 1969-70; secondary/elem. choral dir. Parma City Schs., Ohio, 1970-83; evaluation counselor locked unit Glenbeigh Adolescent Hosp., Cleve., 1982-83, outpatient assessment/admissions counselor, 1983, presenter-driver intervention program, 1984, pub. relations rep., 1983-85; instr. Metro Campus Cuyahoga Community Coll., Cleve., 1984; guidance counselor Padua Franciscan High Sch., Parma, 1985-86; pvt. practice cons., 1986—; pub. speaker, Cleve. area. Republican. Methodist. Home: 4 Laural Dr S Rocky River OH 44116

HALDEMAN, SHIRLEY, insurance company executive; b. Jenkintown, Pa., July 25, 1930; d. Oscar Allan and Helen Francis (Sensenbaugh) Frankenfield; m. Robert E. Haldeman, Nov. 23, 1946; 1 son, Robert E. Student schs. Abington, Pa. Asst. v.p. group service Inter-County Hospitalization Plan, Inc., Horsham, Pa., 1951—. Fellow Nat. Assn. Ins. Women; mem. Profl. Ins. Women Eastern Montgomery County (charter, dir. 1971-73). Republican. Episcopalian. Clubs: Soroptimist Internat. (pres. Old York Rd. 1974-76, 84). Office: Inter-County Hospitalization Plan Inc 720 Blair Mill Rd Horsham PA 19044

HALE, DAWN LOUISE, librarian; b. Reading, Pa., Nov. 19, 1950; d. Robert Harvey and Hilda Margaret (Ruth) Heinly; m. William C. Hale, Sept. 12, 1969 (div. Jan. 1983). B.S., Indiana U. of Pa., 1973; postgrad. U. Pa., 1974-76; M.Music, Temple U., 1978; M.L.S., Drexel U., 1980; postgrad. Columbia U., 1981-82; NYU, 1984—. Pvt. piano tchr., Phila., 1977-79; library asst. Drexel U., Phila., 1978-79; original monographic cataloger Columbia U. Tchrs. Coll., N.Y.C., 1981-83; cataloger NYU, N.Y.C., 1983—, NYU rep. to music program com. Research Libraries Group, Stanford, Calif., 1984—. Presser scholar Indiana U. of Pa., 1972-73. Mem. ALA (resources and tech. services div.), Library and Info. Tech. Assn. of ALA, N.Y. Tech. Services Librarians (sec.-treas. 1985-86), Assn. Coll. and Research Libraries (sec. Greater N.Y. met. area chpt. 1983-86), Music Library Assn. Democrat. Lutheran. Office: Bobst Library Catalog Dept New York Univ 70 Washington Sq S New York NY 10012

HALE, JANICE THOMAS, telecommunications account executive; b. Niagara Falls, N.Y., Nov. 15, 1954; d. James and Beulah Mae (Rose) Thomas; m. Bennie Hale, May 7, 1983; 1 son, Kenan Jarrett. B.S. in TV and Radio, Syracuse U. Radio reporter Sta. WEBR, Buffalo, 1976-78; pub. service dir. Sta. WGR-TV, Buffalo, 1978-80, morning news announcer, 1980-81, producer PM Mag., 1981-82; account exec. AT & T, Houston, 1982—. Communications dir. Windsor Village United Methodist Ch., 1983-84; bd. dirs. Erie Community Coll. Downtown, Buffalo, 1979-80. Minority Writers scholar Corp. Pub. Broadcasting, 1979; recipient Black Achievers award Sta. WGR-TV, 1981. Mem. Black Women's Alliance, Delta Sigma Theta. Democrat. Home: 13134 Bassford Dr Houston TX 77036

HALE, KATE MADDOX, educator, construction company executive; b. Elba, Ala., Feb. 17, 1930; d. James Waitus and Mellie (Thompson) Maddox; m. John Lafayette Parish, Mar. 15, 1951 (dec. July 1954); m. Edward Byron Hale, July 15, 1956; children—Mellie Claire, Susan Kate, Rebecca Ann, Edward Byron, Thomas Michael. B.S. in Edn., U. Ala., 1950, M.S. in Home Econs., 1956; postgrad. George Peabody Coll., 1968, 69, U. Ga., 1981, Albany State Coll., Ga., 1982. Tchr. Henry County Schs., Abbeville, Ala., 1950-51, Brewton City Schs., Ala., 1951-52, Wilcox County Schs., Camden, Ala., 1952-54, 66-68, Dougherty County Schs., Albany, Ga., 1968—. Mem. NEA, Ga. Assn. Educators, Dougherty County Assn. Educators, DAR (regent Chehaw chpt. 1981-83), UDC (chpt. pres. 1981-83), Delta Kappa Gamma, Phi Upsilon Omicron, Kappa Delta Pi. Baptist. Avocations: needlework; genealogy. Home: 3112 Alachua Ln Albany CA 31701 Office: Westover High Sch Albany GA 31701

HALE, LINDA DIANE, accountant, financial planning consultant; b. Balt., Apr. 24, 1953; d. John and Marian Louise (Wilson) Crawford; 1 child, Jaime Nicole. B.A., U. Md.-Baltimore County, 1975. Mdse. mgr. J.C. Penney Co., Balt., 1973-76; acct. TCOM Corp., Columbia, Md., 1976—; fin. planning cons. Hale's Fin. Services, Balt., 1980—. Democrat. Presbyterian. Home: 2659 Gatehouse Dr Baltimore MD 21207

HALE, MARSHA BENTLEY, mannequin historian, consultant; b. Santa Monica, Calif., Dec. 23, 1951; d. Douglas Eugene and Margery Edith (Hale) Marx. Student, U. Calif.-Santa Cruz, 1969-70, UCLA, 1977-79; B.F.A. in Film/Video, Calif. Inst. of the Arts, 1981. Co-owner Stanley Robert & Assocs., Beverly Hills, Calif., 1972-75, The Latticemakers, Westwood, Calif., 1975-76; instr. UCLA, 1983, 85; owner, designer Nat. Design Cons., Los Angeles, 1976—; cons. mannequin history Smithsonian Instn., Washington, 1985; curator, Fashion Mannequin, Security Pacific Nat. Bank, Los Angeles, 1981-82. Author: Mannequin Evolution, 1985. Director: film documentary Mannequin Market Week, 1982. Contbr. articles to profl. jours. Lectr., Art Ctr., Pasadena, Calif., 1984, Costume Soc. Am., Western Div., 1983, SEEDS Elem. Sch., Westwood, 1984. Mem. The Greater Los Angeles Press Club, The Costume Soc. Am., Am. Film Inst. Avocations: ocean; mountains; world travel; cultural arts. Home: PO Box 803 Forest Falls CA 92339 Office: Nat Design Cons 412 Palisades Ave Santa Monica CA 90402

HALE, MARY CARTER, life insurance company executive; b. Pittsfield, Mass., May 21, 1928; d. Stephen Hilliard and Mary Emma (Bull) Carter; m. Donald Bruce Hale, Apr. 10, 1948; children—M. Christine Hale Bienvenue, A. Stephen Hale. Mktg. asst. Berkshire Life Ins. Co., Pittsfield, Mass., 1963—. Sec.-treas. Tyringham Landowners Assn. (Mass.), 1977—; selectman Town of Tyringham, 1980—; v.p. Berkshire County Adv. Bd., 1984—; pres. v.p. Berkshire County Selectmen's Assn., 1984—; sec.-treas. Berkshire County Police Chief's Assn., 1984—; 2d v.p. Mass. Selectmen's Assn., 1985—; mem. local govt. adv. council to gov., 1985—. Episcopalian. Address: Main Rd Tyringham MA 01264

HALE, MARY HELEN PARKER, university administrator; b. Merryville, La., May 25, 1920; d. James Carroll and Mollie (Dear) Parker; B.A. in English (scholar), La. Coll., 1940, B.A. in Music, 1940; M.A. in English (fellow), La. State U., 1942; Ph.D. in Fine Arts (hon.), U. Alaska, 1965; m. George Erwin Hale, June 12, 1942; children—John Parker, James Milton, Nancy Anne. Instr., dir choral music, Boston 1944-45, Albany, N.Y., 1945, Washington, 1946-49, Anchorage, 1949-50; dir. Anchorage Community Chorus, 1951-59; founder, dir. Alaska Festival of Music, 1956-62; vice chmn. N.Am. Assembly Arts Agys., 1968-70; coordinator arts and community affiliates offices Anchorage Community Coll. and U. Alaska, Anchorage, 1970-76; dir. public services Anchorage Community Coll., 1977-81, asst. to pres., 1979-81. Founder Alaska Southcentral High Sch. Music Festival, 1950; mem. Alaska Centennial Commn., 1963-65; charter mem. Alaska State Council on Arts, 1966, chmn., 1967-71; founder, mem., sec. Alaska Humanities Forum, 1974-79; mem. adv. bd. No. TV, Inc., 1979—; trustee endowment trust. Anchorage Multi-Purpose Sr. Center; vice-chmn. citizens adv. council Anchorage Community Coll., 1981, mem. adv. council, 1981-86, founder Arts Fair and Women's Ctr. adv. com. Celebrating Alaska's Women, 1945-65. Recipient Mayor's Disting. Service award, Anchorage, 1965; 49'er award, elected to Hall of Fame, Alaska Press Club, 1970, 72; Outstanding Vol. award U. Alaska, Anchorage, 1976; Outstanding Alumni award La. Coll., 1979; President's citation Anchorage C. of C., 1979; Disting. Service award Anchorage Community Coll., 1983. Mem. Anchorage Arts Council (charter mem.), U. Alaska Anchorage Alumni Assos., Internat. Platform Assn., LWV, AAUW, Nat. Assn. Women Deans, Adminstrs. and Counselors, Mu Phi Epsilon, Beta Sigma Phi (hon.). Presbyterian. Clubs: Anchorage Woman's, Soroptimists (hon. mem., pres. 1956) (Anchorage). Home: 11501 Birch Rd Anchorage AK 99516

HALE, SANDRA JOHNSTON, state official; b. Glen Cove, N.Y., Dec. 9, 1934; d. Alexander Henry and Marian (Baker) Johnston; m. Roger Loucks Hale, June 10, 1961; children—Jocelyn, Leslie, Nina. B.A., Wellesley Coll., 1957. Asst. editor Little Brown & Co., Boston, 1957-61; office mgr., editorial assoc. Johns Hopkins Med. Sch., Balt., 1961-62; owner, mgr. The Book Tree, Mpls., 1968-70; assoc. prof. Met. State U., St. Paul/Mpls., 1973—(on leave); commr. adminstrn., chmn. exec. mgmt. sub-cabinet State of Minn., St. Paul, 1983—; cons. Nat. Endowment for Arts, Washington, 1976-79; host TV spls. KTCA-TV, St. Paul, 1978-79; book reviewer Mpls. Tribune, 1969-77; research project interviewer Johns Hopkins Med. Sch., Balt., 1963-68. Trustee. Macalester Coll., St. Paul, 1979—; past pres., past chmn. bd. dirs., Guthrie Theater, Mpls., 1980—; council mem. Nat. Council on Arts, Washington, 1979-80; commn. mem. 8th Circuit Ct. Appeals Nominating Com., St. Louis, 1978-80; chmn. Minn. Arts Bd., Mpls., 1976-79. Recipient Disting. Service award Minn. chpt. Am. Soc. Pub. Adminstrn., 1986. Office: Adminstrn Bldg Room 200 50 Sherburne Ave Saint Paul MN 55155

HALEVY, HILDA MARIA, physician, anesthesiologist; b. Havana, Cuba; d. Juan and Raimunda (Valdes) Cheng; B.S., Instituto de Segunda Enseñanza de la Habana, Havana, 1949; M.D., U. Havana, 1957; m. Simon Halevy, 1968; 1 son, Daniel A. Sr. house physician and surgeon Mother Cabrini Meml. Hosp., N.Y.C., 1957-58; resident in anesthesiology Met. Hosp., N.Y.C., 1958-60; fellow in anesthesiology, various hosps., N.Y.C., 1960-67; attending anesthesiologist Astoria (N.Y.) Gen. Hosp., 1967—; vis. scholar to Mexico, Holand, Israel. Mem. AMA (Physician's Recognition award), Am. Soc. Anesthesiologists, Med. Soc. State N.Y., N.Y. State Soc. Anesthesiologists, Med. Soc. County Queens. Democrat. Jewish. Office: Astoria Gen Hosp Dept Anesthesia 25-10 30th Ave Astoria NY 11102

HALEY, DEBRA ANN, educator; b. Wichita, Kans., June 14, 1953; d. Robert Gail and Anna Ellen H.; B.S. in Bus. Adminstrn. (acad. scholar), Kans. Newman Coll., 1975; M.B.A., Emporia State U., 1979; postgrad. Okla. State U., 1981—. News reporter KFH-Radio, Wichita, summer 1974; acct. Koch Oil Co., Wichita, 1975-78; instr. mktg., mgmt. Wichita State U., 1979-81, faculty adv. bus. and univ. students, 1980-81; instr. mktg. Okla. State U., Stillwater, 1981-84; asst. prof. U. No. Iowa, 1984—. Mem. Am. Mktg. Assn., Beta Gamma Sigma. Roman Catholic. Home: 3220 Neola Apt 6 Cedar Falls IA 50613 Office: Dept Mktg Sch Bus U No Iowa Cedar Falls IA 50614

HALEY, JOHNETTA RANDOLPH, musician, educator, university administrator; b. Alton, Ill., Mar. 19; d. John Alexander and Willye Ethel (Smith) Randolph; B.S. in Music Edn., Lincoln U., 1945; postgrad. U. Ill., 1947, Washington U., St. Louis, 1958; Mus.M., So. Ill. U., 1972; children—Karen Louise, Michael David. Tchr. piano, voice, choral dir. Lincoln High Sch., East St. Louis, Ill., 1945-48; tchr. music Turner Elem. Sch., Kirkwood, Mo., 1950-55, Turner Jr. High Sch., 1950-55, Nipher Jr. High Sch., 1955-72; prof. music So. Ill. U., Edwardsville, 1972—, dir. East St. Louis campus. Active St. Louis Met. YWCA; chmn. fund raising St. Louis council Girl Scouts Am.; dinner chmn. United Negro Coll. Fund, Inc., 1975-77; nat. chmn. Job Corp Com., Cleve. Job Corps for Girls, 1974-78; treas. Council of Lutheran Chs., 1975—; pres. bd. of curators Lincoln U., 1974—; bd. dirs. Luth. Mission Assn.; trustee Stillman Coll.; bd. dirs. Assn. Governing Bds. Universities and Colls. Recipient Disting. Citizen award St. Louis Argus Newspaper, 1970, Vol. Service award YWCA, 1968, Community Service award Alpha Kappa Alpha, Duchess of Paducah award Paducah, Ky. 1973, Key to City, Gary, Ind., Signal award St. Louis Sentinel Newspaper, 1974; Outstanding Service award Drifters, Inc.; Outstanding Community Service award So. Christian Leadership Conf.; Outstanding Leadership award YMCA, Ednl. Achievement award, 1985, Outstanding Achievement in Sci. award, 1985, Fred McDowell award for outstanding practitioner in higher edn., 1985, Outstanding and Dedicated Service award Ill. Com. on Black Concerns in Higher Edn., 1985, others; named Woman of Year, Greyhound Bus Corp., 1969, Woman of Year, Bus. and Profl. Womens Clubs, 1985. Mem. Coll. Mus. Soc., Nat. Choral Dirs. Assn., Artist Presentation Soc., AAUP, Ill. Music Edn. Assn., Nat. Assn. of Negro Musicians, NAACP, Mid-West Kodaly Music Educators, Urban League, Assn. Governing Bds. Univs. and Colls. (dir.), Mu Phi Epsilon, Pi Kappa Lambda, Alpha Kappa Alpha (nat. chmn. standards). Lutheran. Clubs: Las Amigas Social, Jack and Jill, Top Ladies of Distinction, Links Inc. Home: 30 Plaza Sq Saint Louis MO 63103 Office: Box 20B Southern Illinois U Edwardsville IL 62026

HALEY, PATRICIA (MAGILL), insurance company official; b. St. Louis, May 17, 1944; d. James Chauncey and Virginia Marie (Foley) Magill; m. Richard Bland Haley, Aug. 25, 1962; children—Michael Shawn, Timothy Shamus. Cert. Gen. Ins., Ins. Inst. Am., 1979; student Santa Ana Coll., 1979—, Marymount Coll., 1985—. Accredited personnel mgr., profl. in human resources. Teller, sec. Citizens Nat. Bank, Maplewood, Mo., 1960-64; sales sec. Statis. Tabulating Co., St. Louis, 1964-70; life sales sec. Home Ins. Co., Kansas City, Mo., 1971-73; sr. mgr. Am. States Ins. Co., Santa Ana, Calif., 1973—. Notary public, Calif., 1978—; team mother Little League Assn., Brea, Calif., 1975-86. Mem. Am. Soc. Personnel Adminstrn., Personnel Employee Relations Mgmt. Assn. (v.p., program chmn.). Roman Catholic. Club: Dana West Yacht. Home: 23336 Caminito Lazaro Laguna Hills CA 92653 Office: American States Ins Co 400 N Tustin Santa Ana CA 92705

HALEY-ASPNES, GRACE BERLENE, correctional center business administrator; b. Eastover S.C., Feb. 22, 1943; d. Hugh Wilder and Gladys Berlene (Hendren) Christmas; m. Thomas Ross Haley, Oct. 1, 1961 (div. June 1977); children—Tammy, Thomas Ross, Judy; m. Dale Jennings Aspnes, Mar. 9, 1983; children—Anita, Christopher. B.B.A., Eastern N.Mex. U., 1982. Profl. pub. buyer, 1980; cert. pub. purchasing officer, 1981. Mgr., Commonwealth Theatres, Inc., Gallup, N.Mex., 1970-76; bus. mgr. Roswell Correctional Ctr., Hagerman, N.Mex., 1976-85; bus. mgr. Western N.Mex. Correctional Facility, 1985—. Recipient Exemplary Performance award Dept. Corrections, Santa Fe, N.Mex., 1983. Mem. Am. Correctional Assn., Nat. Inst. Govtl. Purchasing, N.Mex. Correctional Assn. (corr. sec. 1983), Delta Mu Delta, Phi Kappa Phi. Republican. Baptist. Clubs: Moose (Belen, N.Mex.); Lions (Gallup, N.Mex.). Home: 1204 N 4th St Grants NM 87020 Office: PO Drawer 250 Grants NM 87020

HALF, MAXINE ELAINE, personnel agy. exec.; b. N.Y.C., Apr. 7, 1924; d. Alfred and Martha (Ernsthal) Levison; student N.Y.U., 1941-44; m. Robert Half, June 17, 1945; children—Nancy Half Asch, Peggy Half Silbert. Office mgr. Ry. Express Agy., N.Y.C., 1941-45; asst. export mgr. 20th Century Fox, N.Y.C., 1945-47; v.p. Robert Half of N.Y., Inc., N.Y.C., 1948; v.p. Robert Half Internat., Inc., franchisor of Robert Half and Accountemps offices in U.S., Can., and Gt. Brit., 1964—. Mem. Assn. Personnel Cons. N.Y., Nat. Assn. Personnel Cons., Nat. Assn. Female Execs. Office: 522 Fifth Ave New York NY 10036

HALFERTY, DIANE HARRIET, land developer, writer, consultant; b. Tacoma, Feb. 22, 1937; d. Benjamin and Lavina Eleanor (Simmons) Rosen; student U. Miami (Fla.), 1954-56; B.S., Willamette U., Salem, Oreg., 1958; Tech. Asso. of Law, A.A.S., Edmonds Community Coll. and U. Wash., 1976; m. Guy P. Halferty, III, Apr. 5, 1959; children—Geoffrey David, Denise Diane, Keary Douglas, Courtney Caryn. Pres., Creativity Unltd., Inc., Edmonds, Wash., 1966-73; pres. Great Pacific Devel. Co., Inc., Federal Way, Wash.,

1975—; corp. and consumer cons.; lectr. Mem. King County Housing Task Force, 1978—, King County Ordinance Adv. Com., 1979—; mem. Land Use Research Council; mem. council Shoreline Sch. Dist. Parent-Tchrs.-Student Assn., 1973, exec. bds. Lake Forest Park Sch., Kellogg Jr. High Sch., 1966-78; chmn. Lake Forest Park Safety Com., 1972; judge AAU, 1978—; mem. King County Juvenile Ct. Guardian ad Litem Program, 1981-82; mem. long-range planning com., action com. Univ. Prep. Acad., 1982-84; co-chmn. Consumers Against Gen. Motors, 1981-86. Mem. LWV, NOW, Assn. Mobile Home Park Owners (v.p. 1980, pres. 1981, bd. dirs. 1982-84, chmn. polit. action com.), Wash. State Hunter-Jumper Assn., Wash. State Horse Show Assn., Nat. Assn. Female Execs. Unitarian. Clubs: Wash. Athletic (assoc. mem., community affairs com.), Macauley Lahaina Yacht. Home: 2442 NW Market St Suite 88 Seattle WA 98107

HALICZER, BONNIE DIKMAN, reporter, editor; b. N.Y.C., Sept. 9, 1942; d. George Henry and Ruth (Hymes) Dikman; B.A. in English Edn., U. South Fla., 1968; m. Jonah Henry, Aug. 11, 1963 (div. 1986); children—Shera Lyn, Scott Harris. Feature and fashion writer St. Petersburg Times, Fla., 1956-64; writer Congl. Quar., Washington, 1961-62; fashion writer Tampa Tribune, Fla., 1977-84; fashion editor On Design mag., 1983—; pres. What's New, retail sportswear store; instr. journalism U. Tampa, 1979. Pres. Tampa Hadassah Group, 1974-76; founder Hillel Sch., Jewish Day Sch., Tampa. Recipient Men's Fashion Assn. Am. award 1980, 81, 83, award J.C. Penney, Mo., 1980. Mem. The Fashion Group, Sigma Delta Chi. Club: Palma Ceia Jr. Women's Westcoast editor Fla. Designer's Quar. mag., 1980—. Contbr. articles to profl. jours. Home: 4804 Culbreath Isles Rd Tampa FL 33609 Office: 12924 N Dale Mabry Tampa Fl 33618

HALIFAX, JOAN SQUIRE, anthropologist, foundation executive, author; b. Hanover, N.H., July 30, 1942; d. John and Eunice (Spillane) H.; m. Stanislav Grof, June 2, 1972 (div. 1976). Ph.D. in Med. Anthropology, Union Grad. Sch., 1973. Research asst. Columbia U. N.Y.C., 1964-68; researcher Com. du Film Ethnographique, Mus. of Man, Paris, 1968-69; faculty Dept. Psychiatry, Dept. of Pediatrics, U. Miami Sch. Medicine, Fla., 1970-72; New Sch. for Social Research, N.Y.C., 1977-79; research assoc. Md. Psychiat. Research Ctr., Balt., 1972-73; editor McGraw-Hill, N.Y.C., 1976-79; research asst. Joseph Campbell-Hist. Atlas of World Mythology, N.Y.C., 1976-79; dir. The Ojai Found., Ca., 1979—; anthrop. fieldwork, Africa, Asia, The Ams., 1955-85; lectr. in field. Author: Shaman The Wounded Healer, Shamanic Voices, The Human Encounter with Death. NSF fellow; hon. research fellow in med. ethnobotany Harvard U., 1980. Buddhist. Avocation: the wilderness. Office: The Ojai Found PO Box 1620 Ojai CA 93023

HALINA, MME. (HALINA JOZEFA LUTOMSKI, MRS. FLOYD MARTIN LUTOMSKI), dance educator, choreographer; b. Lwow, Poland, Feb. 4, 1930; came to U.S., 1947, naturalized, 1950; d. Adam and Katarzyna (Jezierska) Dziekan; student Warsaw Opera Ballet Sch., 1936-38, Wielke Theatre, Lwow, 1939-41; grad. Politechnik, Lwow, 1944; m. Floyd Martin Lutomski, Oct. 31, 1946; children—Norbert Michael, Ilona Maria, Kevin. Dancer, Warsaw Opera Ballet, 1938-39, World's Olympiade, Kiev, Russia, 1939, USO, Germany, 1945-46; producer Dance Capades, 1948—; owner, dir., resident choreographer Sch. of Dance Arts, Elmira and Corning, N.Y. tchr. Nat. Dance Tchrs. Orgns., U.S., P.R., 1950; choreographer children's and classical ballets Kimbo Dance Records, 1954—; founder, artistic dir., choreographer Elmira-Corning Ballet, Inc., 1955—, artistic dir. Nutcracker Suite, 1980 coordinator, also dir. ednl. programs; lectr.; producer, choreographer Four Seasons, 1950, Fairy Doll, 1951, Sleeping Beauty, 1953, 59, 65-67, Nutcracker, 1954, 78-82, Hansel and Gretel, 1955, Cinderella, 1957, 81-82, Les Ballet de Elements, 1958, Schlagobers. 1959, Gaite Parisienne, 1960-61, La Boutique Fantasque, 1961, adaptation of Les Sylphides, 1962, Swan Lake, 1952-64, Masquerade, 1962-63, Snow Maiden, 1964, Copelia, 1965, 68, 70, 77-78, Karnival Kontrasts, 1966, La Bayadere, 1966, Nutcracker, 1969, Aurora's Wedding, 1971, Wooden Prince, 1971, Americana, 1972, La Fille Mal Gardee, 1972, Vignette's Classique-Comedia, 1973, Sylvia, 1974, Cirque, 1975, Am. Alphabet Ballet, 1976, Magic Forest, 1978, Stars and Stripes, 1979, Stardust Trail, 1980, The Americas, 1981; dir., choreographer ballet Nutcracker for Elmira-Corning Ballet, 1963-66, also Red-White and Blue, Comedia del Arte, Masque; dir. Les Petits Riens, 1967; dir. Bicentennial ballet: Witching, Am. Gayeties, Peter and the Wolf, 1976, 80-83, Carnival, Snow White, 1977, Snow Maiden, 1980, Cinderella (Pro Kofiev), Jewels, 1982, Tale to Tale, 1983, The Magic Key, 1983; staged Once upon a Piper, Interplay, Openspace, 1979; staged, directed The Woodcutter's Tale, Fete de Jour, The Emperor's New Clothes, 1984; originated Pre Ballet album for presch. age Roper Records, 1977, now chmn. performing arts dept.; lectr. Steuben, Chenung, No. Pa. counties; tchr. ballet, Tokyo, 1983, Buenos Aires, Argentina and Rio de Janeiro, Brazil, 1984; supr. ballet records Roper label; rep. ballet dept. for Dance Educators Am. to Nat. Council Dance Tchrs' Orgns.; dir. Sch. Dance Arts, Elmira, N.Y., Corning, N.Y.; lectr. Elmira-Corning Sch. Dists., 1969-72, Schuyler County Schs., 1968-71. Recipient Steuben Crystal and Gold award Corning community. Mem. Dance Educators Am. (chmn. ballet exam., com. 1966-67, exec. bd. 1967-69, exec. dir. 1969-71). Roman Catholic. Recs. 36 ballet albums Roper Label, 41 ednl. records. Home: 933 Fassett Rd Elmira NY 14905 Office: 410-14 W Gray St Elmira NY 14905 also 258 Dennison Pkwy E Corning NY 14830

HALL, ALIX-MARIE, information industry executive; b. Newburgh, N.Y., July 30, 1941; d. William C. and Alix M. (de Saint Phalle) H.; B.A., Hunter Coll., 1965, M.A., 1972; M.B.A., NYU, 1984. Math. project editor Am. Book Co., N.Y.C., 1966-69; programming writer, analyst IBM, N.Y.C., 1969-72; sr. editor, sponsoring editor Gregg div. McGraw-Hill Book Co., N.Y.C., 1972-73, coordinator staff projects, exec. dept., 1973-74, editor-in-chief acctg., computing and data processing Gregg div., 1974-77; dir. adminstrn. McGraw-Hill Info. Systems Co., N.Y.C., 1977-78, v.p. adminstrn., 1978-83, v.p. adminstrn. and mktg., 1983-85; pres. AMH Assocs., N.Y.C., 1985-86; mgr. info. industry practice Coopers & Lybrand Mgmt. Cons., 1986—; conf. and seminar leader. Cert. in basic programming and system programming, IBM. Mem. Assn. Assn. M.B.A. Execs., Assn. Individual Investors, N.Y. Bus. Forum, Am. Mktg. Assn. Club: Knickerbocker Toastmasters (ednl. v.p. 1978-79, pres. 1979-80). Author: (with others) Introduction to Data Processing, 1977, 83, Data Processing Work Kit, 1977, 83. Address: 333 E 69th St Suite 5B New York NY 10021

HALL, ANN BERGIN, social work supervisor; b. Boston, Feb. 14, 1955; d. Joseph Thomas and Ann Claire (McKenna) Bergin; m. Robert MacLaren Hall, Feb. 14, 1980. B.A. in Psychology, Emmanuel Coll., 1976; M.Ed., Salem Coll., 1979; cert. advanced grad. study, Northeastern U., 1985, postgrad., 1985—. Lic. social worker, Mass. Case worker DARE, Inc., Boston, 1976-79; lab. instr. Emmanuel Coll., Boston, 1976-79; psychoednl. diagnostition North Shore Children's Hosp., Salem, Mass., 1979-83; dir. clin. and edn. services DARE, Inc., Boston, 1979-84, clin. supr., 1984—. Clin. cons. Community Group, Wakefield, Mass., 1980-83; bd. dirs. New Eng. Family Services, Newburyport, Mass., 1983—. Fellow Am. Psychol. Assn.; mem. Nat. Assn. Social Workers. Club: Thursday's (Beverly) (chmn. 1984—). Avocations: ice skating; swimming; gardening; travel by train. Office: DARE Inc 186 South St Boston MA 02111

HALL, BERTA SELLARDS, interior designer; b. Wayne, W.Va., Dec. 13, 1925; d. Harry and Edith (Jackson) Sellards; m. Harold Allan Hall, Mar. 10, 1946; children—Edith Hall Smith, Harold Allan II, Frank Andrew, Dan Richard, John Randolph, Patricia Jeanette Hall McRae, Susan Melinda. Student Marshall U., 1943-45, Coronado Sch. Fine Arts (Calif.), 1950-51, N.Y. Sch. Interior Design, 1964. Interior designer, Hurwitz Mintz, New Orleans, 1964-67; owner, interior designer Interiors by Berta Hall Sanford, Winter Park, Fla., 1967—. Founding pres. Friends of Mead Garden, Winter Park, 1982—. Recipient Community Service award Walt Disney World, 1983, Nat. Garden Club, 1983. Mem. Winter Park C. of C. (bd. dirs. 1978-83, v.p. 1982-84, named free enterprise businessperson of yr. 1982), Sigma Sigma Sigma. Democrat. Presbyterian. Club: 101 (Loch Haven). Office: Interiors by Berta Hall 2105 Park Ave N Winter Park FL 32789

HALL, BETTY JEAN, lawyer; b. Richmond, Ky., July 12, 1946; d. James Russell and Lillian Guy Hall; B.A., Berea Coll., 1968; J.D., Antioch Sch. Law, 1976; m. Thomas Michael Burke, Oct. 6, 1979; children—Timothy Michael and Tiffany Michelle (twins). Legal sec. firm Arent, Fox, Kintner, Plotkin & Kahn, Washington, 1968-70; asst. dir. youth program Appalachian Regional Commn., Washington, 1970-73; admitted to D.C. bar, 1977, Va. bar, 1977, Tenn. bar, 1979; assoc. firm James W. Lawson, Washington, 1976-77; exec. dir., gen. counsel Coal Employment Project, Oak Ridge, Tenn., and Dumfries, Va., 1977—. Bd. dirs. Highlander Research and Edn. Center, 1978—, Southeast Women's Employment Coalition, 1981—; mem. steering com. Appalachian Alliance, 1979-82; chmn. Appalachian Research and Edn. Assocs., 1979—; chmn. So. Appalachian Leadership Tng. Program, 1983—. Recipient Rockefeller Public Service award, 1981; John Hay Whitney fellow, 1978-80. Mem. Am. Bar Assn. Address: 16221 Sunny Knoll Ct Dumfries VA 22026

HALL, BEVERLY A., insurance company executive; b. Pomona, Calif., Dec. 27, 1952; d. Joseph Edward and Elaine (Lenser) H.; m. Clifford J. Dieterle, June 23, 1973 (div. Apr. 1975). B.S. in Acctg., Calif. State Poly. U., 1974; M.B.A., U. So. Calif., 1982. Cert. gen. ins. Staff acct. Auto Club of So. Calif., Los Angeles, 1974-76, sr. acct., 1976-80, acctg. systems coordinator, 1980-81, sr. fin. analyst, 1981-82, asst. mgr., 1982-83; treas. Redwood Fire & Casualty Ins. Co., Los Angeles, 1983—. Mem. Ins. Acctg. and Systems Assn. (pres. Los Angeles chpt. 1983—), U. So. Calif. M.B.A. Alumni, Beta Gamma Sigma. Home: 1831 S Summerplace Dr West Covina CA 91792 Office: Redwood Fire & Casualty Ins Co 815 Colorado Blvd Los Angeles CA 90041

HALL, BOBBIE MAUREEN, county treasurer; b. Shipley, Yorkshire, Eng., Sept. 17, 1927; came to U.S., 1948, naturalized, 1956. d. Ernest Wright and Amy (Jeffries) Wilson; A.A. in Bus. Adminstrn., Franklin U., 1980, A.A. on Pub. Adminstrn., 1982. Dir. Ohio Rep. Fin. Com., Columbus, 1972-74; exec. dir. Franklin County Rep. Fin. Com., Columbus, 1975-77; dep. treas. Franklin County, Columbus, 1977-84, treas., 1984—; chmn. Franklin County Budget Com., 1984—, Franklin County Data Processing Bd., 1984—; mem. Franklin County Microfilm Bd., 1985—; gov. rep. CMACAO, Columbus, 1985—. Pres. Bus. and Profl. Women, Columbus, 1979-81, Franklin County Forum, 1982-83; trustee Columbus Zoo, 1977-80; bd. dirs. Ohio Women's Polit. Caucus, 1980-83. Mem. Ohio County Treas. Assn., Govt. Fin. Officers Assn. Clubs: Canterbury Unit, Columbus Symphony. Avocations: knitting; opera; gardening; reading. Home: 5660 Olentangy River Rd Worthington OH 43085 Office: Franklin County Treasurers Office 410 S High St Columbus OH 43215

HALL, BRENDA YVONNE, lawyer; b. Shelbyville, Tenn., Sept. 26, 1957; d. William G. and Alene (Russell) Hall; m. Gary L. McDonald, Sept. 4, 1982. A.S., Columbia (Tenn.) State Community Coll., 1976; B.A., U. Tenn., 1978, J.D., 1980. Bar: Tenn. 1981, U.S. Dist. Ct. (ea. dist.) Tenn. 1981. Student atty. U. Tenn. Legal Clinic, Knoxville, 1980; law clk. Meares and Meares P.C., Maryville, Tenn., 1981; ptnr. Gamble & Hall, Wartburg, Tenn., 1981-82; ptnr. McDonald & Hall, Kingston, Tenn., 1982—; adv. bd. to bd. dirs. Rural Legal Services and Pub. Defenders Office, Oak Ridge, 1981-82. Research editor Tenn. U. Law Rev. 1979-80. Area dir. Knoxville Opera Co., 1982. Mem. ABA, Tenn. Trial Lawyers Assn., Tenn. Bar Assn., Knox County Bar Assn., Roane County Bar Assn., Gamma Beta Phi, Phi Kappa Phi, Pi Delta Phi., Alpha Gamma Rho, Phi Delta Phi. Democrat. Mem. Ch. Christ. Office: McDonald & Hall 104 Court Sq Kingston TN 37763

HALL, CYNTHIA HOLCOMB, judge; b. Los Angeles, Feb. 19, 1929; d. Harold Romeyn and Milded Gould (Kuck) Holcomb; m. John Harris Hall, June 6, 1970 (dec. Oct. 1980); 1 son, Harris Holcomb; 1 dau. by previous marriage, Desma Letitia. A.B., Stanford U., 1951, J.D., 1954; LL.M., N.Y. U., 1960. Bar: Ariz. 1954, Calif. 1956. Law clk. to judge U.S. Ct. Appeals 9th Circuit, 1954-55; trial atty. tax div. Dept. Justice, 1960-64; atty.-adviser Office Tax Legis. Counsel, Treasury Dept., 1964-66; mem. firm Brawerman & Holcomb, Beverly Hills, Calif., 1966-72; judge U.S. Tax Ct., Washington, 1972-81, U.S. Dist. Ct. for Central Dist. Calif., 1981-84, U.S. Ct. Appeals, Ninth Cir., 1984—. Served to lt. (j.g.) USNR, 1951-53. Mem. ABA. Office: PO Box 91510 Pasadena CA 91109

HALL, DORA VIOLA, bank executive; b. Hartford, Conn., July 19, 1946; d. A.C. Cannon and Viola Geneva (Davis) Cannon; m. Nathaniel Hall, Oct. 2, 1967; children—Gregory, Lawrence, Robert. Sec., Capitol Temporary Services, Hartford, 1964-74; customer service rep. Conn. Nat. Bank, Hartford, 1974—. Vol., Big Bros./Big Sisters, Hartford, 1980—. Avocations: reading; writing; collecting dolls. Office: Conn Nat Bank 410 Homestead Ave Hartford CT 06112

HALL, DOROTHY GAY NELL, homebuilder; b. Hatch, N.Mex., July 28, 1941; d. Samuel B. and Estelle R. (Lack) Luck; student Houston schs.; m. Donald A. Hall, July 30, 1958 (dec. 1984); children—Donna, Dean, David, Diana. Sec., dir. Superior Homes Custom, Inc., Houston, 1962-82, pres., dir., 1983—; pres., dir. United Thermal Insulators Co., 1980—; Active Leukemia Soc., Lung Assn. Recipient Spl. Ann. Appreciation award Nat. Assn. Women in Constrn., 1976, 77. Mem. Nat. Assn. Home Builders, Sales and Mktg. Council, Tex. Assn. Home Builders, Greater Houston Builders Assn. Democrat. Methodist. Office: PO Box 38547 Houston TX 77238

HALL, EDNA W., nursing home administrator; b. Tulsa, July 30, 1955; d. Jennings B. and Agatha Diane (Benson) Simmons; m. John Michael Hall, Nov. 20, 1980; children—Jason, Eugenie. B.S. in Nursing, Oklahoma City U., 1977; M.S. in Nursing Adminstrn., U. Okla., 1979. R.N., Okla. Nurse, Oklahoma City Methodist Hosp., 1977-78, in charge med. ICU, 1978-80; v.p. adminstrn. Werik Homes, Oklahoma City, 1984—. Mem. Am. Nurses Assn., Okla. Nurses Assn., Nat. Assn. Nursing Home Adminstrs., Friends of Pub. Library. Republican. Methodist. Address: Werik Homes 3532 NW 23d St Oklahoma City OK 73107

HALL, ELEANOR WILLIAMS, public relations executive; b. Boston; d. James Murray and Julia Eleanor (Williams) H. A.B cum laude, Radcliffe Coll., 1945. Exec. sec. Am. Express Co., N.Y.C., 1950-62, adminstrv. asst. corp. mktg., 1963-65, mgr. corp. mktg., 1965-69, mgr. corp. pub. relations, 1969-71; mgr. mktg. services Am. Express Internat. Banking Corp., N.Y.C., 1971-72, asst. treas. advt. and pub. relations, 1972-76, asst. v.p. advt. and pub. relations, 1976-82; pres. Eleanor Hall Assocs., Inc., 1982—. Club: Harvard. Home: 201 E 79th St New York NY 10021

HALL, ELIZABETH LEA, lawyer; b. Paducah, Ky., Dec. 20, 1954; d. Clarence Elton and Anna Kathryn (Humphrey) Hall. B.A. History, La. State U., 1976, J.D., 1981. Bar: La. 1982. Research assoc. La. State U., Baton Rouge, 1980-81; law clk. 14th Jud. Dist. Ct., Lake Charles, La., 1981-82; dir. Criminal Staff State La. 3d cir. Ct. Appeals, Lake Charles, 1982—. Mem. ABA, La. State Bar Assn., Southwest La. Bar Assn., Beta Sigma Phi. Republican. Mem. Ch. of Christ.

HALL, ELLA TAYLOR, clinical community psychologist; b. Macon, Miss., Nov. 30, 1948; d. Essex and Mamie (Roland) Taylor; B.A., Fisk U., 1971, M.A., 1973; Ph.D., George Peabody Coll., 1978; m. Alan Hall, Oct. 1, 1977; children—Banyikaai Monique (dec.), Motiqua Shante. Mental health specialist behavioral sci. div. Meharry Med. Coll., Nashville, 1976-77; asso. psychologist Bronx (N.Y.) Psychiat. Center, 1979; clin. psychologist Wiltwyck Residential Treatment Center, Ossining, N.Y., 1979-81; clin. cons. Abbott House, Irvington, N.Y., 1982-85; asst. psychologist Abbott Union Free Sch. Dist., 1985—. NIMH trainee; Crusade fellow; Kendall grantee. Mem. Am. Psychol. Assn., Delta Sigma Theta. Episcopalian. Research in field (lit.).

HALL, EVA LEE, roofing company executive; b. Heflin, Ala., Jan. 2, 1928; d. William Jackson and Flora Cleo (Hayes) Lambert; m. Joseph David Hall, Aug. 10, 1946 (dec. May 1979); children—David Lee, Ronald Gary. Owner, Hall Roofing Co. Inc., Anniston, Ala., 1979-84, sec.-treas., 1984—. Mem. Regional Med. Ctr. Aux., Anniston Meml. Found. Baptist. Home: 508 Chestnut Ave Anniston AL 36201

HALL, FRANCES HUNT, librarian; b. Panama City, July 14, 1919; came to U.S., 1919; s. Franklyn Evelyn and Ida Sue (Hunt) Hall. B.A., U. N.C.-Greensboro, 1940; M.A., U. N.C.-Chapel Hill, 1955, M.S.L.S., 1957, J.D., 1959. Bar: N.C. 1959. Asst. law librarian U. N.C.-Chapel Hill, 1959-63, asst. prof. Sch. Library Sci., 1968-72; reference librarian U. Chgo. Law Sch., 1963-66; documents librarian U. N.C.-Greensboro, 1966-68; assoc. prof., asst. law librarian U. Va., Charlottesville, 1972-73; assoc. prof., law librarian So. Meth. U., Dallas, 1975-77; librarian N.C. Supreme Ct., Raleigh, 1977—. Contbr. articles to profl. jours.; author: Cases and Materials on Librarianship and the Law, 1971. Bd. dirs. Badger-Iredell Found., Raleigh, 1983—, Triangle Area ARC, Raleigh, 1981—. Served to lt. comdr. USNR, 1942-54. Mem. N.C. Bar, N.C. Bar Assn., N.C. Library Assn., ABA, Am. Assn. Law Libraries, Spl. Library Assn., ALA. Democrat. Episcopalian. Home: 3939 Glenwood Ave Raleigh NC 27612 Office: NC Supreme Ct Library 2 E Morgan St Raleigh NC 27611

HALL, GEORGANNA, marketing consultant; b. Dallas, June 1, 1955; d. George Rufus and Vera Theresa (Shively) H. B.B.A., U. Tex., 1976; M.B.A., N. Tex. State U., 1981. Project dir. Southwest Research Inc., Dallas, 1976-78; field dir. The Media Assocs., Dallas, 1978-79; analyst Lone Star Gas Co., Dallas, 1979-80, mgr., 1980-84, dir., 1984; pres. The Value Exchange, Dallas, 1984—. Mem. Am. Mktg. Assn., Alpha Delta Pi. Presbyterian. Office: The Value Exchange Inc PO Box 190169 Dallas TX 75219

HALL, GLENDA KAY, automotive company executive; b. Thomasville, Ga., Sept. 27, 1956; d. Alvin Reece and Gladys (Brady) Hall, B.S. in Mktg., Fla. State U., 1981. Sales and service rep. West Bend Co., Houston, 1982-83; owner relations analyst, parts and service div. Ford Motor Co., Houston, 1983-84, parts zone mgr., 1984—. Mem. Fla. State U. Alumni Club. Democrat. Office: Ford Motor Co Parts and Service Div 2110 E Governors Circle Dr Houston TX 77092

HALL, GLYNDA MAYO, public administrator, social worker; b. Paris, Tenn., Mar. 30, 1950; d. Joseph Myles and Alma Heloise (Perry) Atkinson Mayo; m. Kennard Ray Hall, June 3, 1972; children—Kennard Jacquin, Eryck Nikkel. A.A., Southwestern Christian Coll., 1970; B.S., Abilene Christian U., 1972; postgrad. Redlands U., 1982—. Outreach counselor Hawaii Dept. Edn. Highlands Intermediate Sch., Pearl City, 1975-76; instr. Inter-Am. U., 1976-77; v.p. urban affairs Action Interprises Devel., San Diego, 1979; human services coordinator City of Chula Vista, Calif., 1979-83; social service dir., program dir. United Service Orgns., Washington, Ceiba, P.R., 1984-85, 77-78; exec. dir. Shelter House, Inc., Falls Church, Va., 1985—; cons. Ch. of Christ, 1979—; workshop facilitator, speaker Ch. of Christ, 1979—. Author: Christian Women's Tng. for Workshop and Ladies Days, 1984; author, editor: USO Senior Enlisted Advisory Council Manual, 1985. Editor: Human Services Directory, 1980. Mem., pres. South County Council on Aging, San Diego County, 1979-81; del. State House Conf. on Aging, Calif., 1981; mem. exec. bd. Calif. Women in Govt., San Diego, 1982-84; mem. Ladies Aux. for Christian Edn., San Diego, 1980-83; trustee Southwestern Christian Sch., San Diego, 1981-83. Named Boss of Yr., Am. Bus. Women's Assn., San Diego, 1981; recipient Outstanding Community Service award South County Council on Aging, San Diego, 1983, Spl. Recognition award Chula Vista C. of C., 1983. Mem. Nat. Assn. Female Execs., Inc., Nat. Naval Officers Assn. (assoc.), Supply Officers Wives, Nat. Mil. Family Assn. (bd. govs. 1985—). Democrat. Mem. Ch. of Christ. Home: 10215 Pumphrey Ct Fairfax VA 22032 Office: Shelter House Inc PO Box 1426 Falls Church VA 22041

HALL, HARRIET LOUISE, mental health center adminstr.; b. Los Angeles, Oct. 9, 1947; d. Donald Moore and Ethyl Louise (Hartsough) H.; B.A., Coll. Wooster, 1969; M.A., U. Wis.-Madison, 1971, Ph.D., 1973; m. Randy C. Stith, Nov. 26, 1977; children—Carolyn Annaliese Hall-Stith, Daniel Dag Hall-Stith, Timothy Vernon Hall-Stith. Psychologist, dir. inservice tng. Weld Mental Health Center, Greeley, Colo., 1974-78; child advocacy team mgr. Adams County Mental Health Center, Commerce City, Colo., 1978-80; dep. dir. clin. programs, 1980-81; asso. dir. programs Jefferson County Mental Health Center, Wheat Ridge, Colo., 1981-84, exec. dir., 1984—. Mem. Adams County Placement Alternative Commn., 1980-81, Adams County Child Protection Team, 1979-80, Jefferson County Community Corrections Bd., 1984—; mem. handicapped child subcom. Colo. Gov.'s Commn. for Children and Families, 1979-80; bd. dirs. Centennial Area Health Edn. Center, 1978, Partners Inc., Greeley, Colo., 1978; mem. Jefferson County Corrections Bd., 1984—, Jefferson County Placement Alternatives Commn., 1985—. Cert. psychologist, Colo. Mem. Colo. Assn. Community Mental Health Ctrs. and Clinics (sec. 1983-84, chmn. program com. 1984-85, chmn. budget com. 1985—), Colo. Psychol. Assn., Colo. Women Psychologists, NOW, Colo. Com. Status of Women in Mental Health (treas. 1981—). Home: 11205 E Vassar Dr Aurora CO 80014 Office: 6195 W 38th Ave Wheat Ridge CO 80033

HALL, HELENE W., educator; b. Centralia, Ill., Sept. 17, 1920; d. James O. and Gladys (Hosman) Lawrence; B.S., Emporia State U., 1966, M.S., 1969, E.D.S., 1974; m. William E. Hall, June 13, 1948; children—Ronald William, Steven Charles, Jerry Victor. Sec., asst. to physicians Medical Physicians & Dentists, Kansas City, Mo., 1966-69; tchr. Roosevelt Lab. High Sch., Emporia, Kans.; coordinator secondary sch. tchrs. Emporia State U., 1969-71, team leader Teacher Corps, 1971-73; instr., coordinator secretarial scis. Kansas City Community Coll., 1973—, also coordinator word processing. Mem. Nat. Bus. Edn. Assn., Am. Vocat. Assn., Kans. Vocat. Assn., Classroom Educators Assn., Kans. Bus. Edn. Assn., Nat. Secretaries Assn., Office Edn. Assn., Assn. Info. Systems Profls., Delta Pi Epsilon. Home: 403 S 6th St Osage City KS 66523 Office: Kansas City Kansas Community College 7250 State Ave Kansas City KS 66112

HALL, HILDA ADELINE, association executive; b. Humble, Tex., July 10, 1917; d. Robert George and Bertha Eugenia (Brown) Youngblood; m. Robert H. Hall, Aug. 26, 1934 (dec.); 1 child, Leslie Daline Head (dec.); m. 2d, Salvador Charles Clesi, Apr. 30, 1983. B.A., U. Houston, 1956. Asst. camp dir. United Way Tex. Gulf, Houston, 1937—. Bd. dirs. United Way, Houston, Boy Scouts of Am., Houston; bd. dirs. YMCA, v.p., 1981-82. Clubs: Jr. League, Theater Guild (v.p., treas. 1970), Flagg (v.p. 1971-72). Home: 12705 Alief Clodine Rd Houston TX 77082 Office: United Way of Tex Gulf Coast 1010 Waugh Dr Houston TX 77019

HALL, JACQUELINE YVONNE, lawyer, administrative law judge; b. Detroit, Jan. 8, 1953; d. William Hamilton and Evelyn Virginia (Callaway) Hall. B.Indsl. Adminstrn., Gen. Motors Inst., 1976; J.D., Detroit Coll. Law, 1980. Bar: Mich. 1980. Clk., coop. student Gen. Motors Corp., Detroit, 1971-76; trainee Ford Motor Co., Ypsilanti, Mich., 1976-78; corp. slection coordinator Ford Motor Co., Dearborn, Mich., 1978-80, position evaluation analyst, 1980-81, staff atty., 1981-84; adminstrv. law judge Mich. Dept. Labor, 1984—. Bd. advisors U. Detroit Nat. Black Alumni Assn., 1983—. Mem. Wolverine Bar Assn., Women Lawyers Assn., Nat. Bar Assn., Internat. Assn. Personnel Women, Mich. Assn. Adminstrv. Law Judges, Assn. Black Judges Mich., Nat. Assn. Women Judges. Founders Soc., NAACP, Delta Sigma Theta. Office: 1200 Sixth Ave 12th Floor Mich Plaza Bldg Detroit MI 48226

HALL, JENNIE V., educator; b. Nacogdoches, Tex., Feb. 21, 1927; d. Dock and Ola (Hayter) Anderson; m. George Hall, Oct. 21, 1957 (div. June 1965); 1 dau., Zenna Mae. A.A., S. Tex. Jr. Coll., Houston, 1972; B.S., Tex. So. U., 1974, M.S., 1976. Provisionally cert. elem. mid-mgmt. adminstr., Tex. Bookkeeper credit dept. Houston Fed. Credit Union, 1968-70; sec. New Macedonia Bapt. Ch., Houston, 1959—; tchr. North Forest Sch. Dist., Houston, 1974—. Mem. Adopt Black Children Com., Inc. Mem. Tex. Tchrs. Assn., NEA, Tex. Classroom Tchrs. Assn., Nat. Council Tchrs. of English, Greater Houston Reading Club, Kappa Delta Pi, Sigma Gamma Rho. Democrat. Baptist.

HALL, JOANN, publishing company executive; b. Auburn, Ky., Apr. 2, 1927; d. Everett Bluford and Geneva Mae (Maxwell) H.; student public schs., Detroit; m. Dec. 15, 1945 (div. 1964); 1 son, Mark Stephen Rudolph. With Daily News Broadcasting Co., Bowling Green, Ky., 1950-73, women's dir., dir. music and public affairs, 1960-70, ops. mgr., 1970-73; bus. mgr. Cockrel Corp., Bowling Green, 1974—, editor Back Home in Ky. mag., 1983-84. Hon. Ky. col.; recipient public service award USAF, 1971, Distbv. Edn. Clubs Am., 1970. Mem. Am. Bus. Women's Assn. (pres. 1967, Woman of Year award 1967), Bowling Green C. of C. Cumberland Presbyterian. Home: 2148 Walnut Ln Bowling Green KY 42101 Office: 5844 Scottsville Rd Bowling Green KY 42101

HALL, KATHLEEN JULIA, contractor, financial administrator; b. Detroit, Nov. 30, 1932; d. Daniel Joseph and Noreen Mary (O'Shea) O'Shea; m. Wendell George Hall, Sept. 20, 1969. Student Detroit Bus. Inst., 1954-57, Oakland Community Coll., 1980-81. Corp. staff Ex-Cello Corp., Detroit, 1964-69; staff asst. internat. div. Burroughs Corp., Detroit, 1969-77, Detroit Edison Co., 1979—; contractor VA, Detroit, 1983—. Vice-pres., Wensel Corp. to provide shelter for indigents, Detroit, 1982. Mem. Property Owners for Better Am. Living (sec. 1982—). Address: 2717 Ardmore St Royal Oak MI 48073

HALL, KATHRYN EVANGELINE, author, lectr.; b. Biltmore, N.C.; d. Hugh Canada and Evangeline Haddon (Jenkins) Hall; B.A., U. N.C., M.A.; diploma Adams Sch. Music, Montreat, N.C.; postgrad. Yale, U. London, Fla. Atlantic U. Author: The Papal Tiara, History of the Episcopal Church of Bethesda-By-The-Sea, 1964, The Architecture and Times of Robert Adam, 1969, The Pictorial History of the Episcopal Church of Bethesda-By-The-Sea, 1970-71, 86, Joseph Wright of Derby, A Painter of Science, Industry, and Romanticism, 1974, A History of English Architecture, 1976-82; Sir John Vanbrugh's Palaces and the Drama of Baroque Architecture, 1982-84; lectr. history, art and architecture, U.S., Eng. and Scotland, 1961—. Vice pres. The Jr. Patronesses, Palm Beach, Fla., 1964. Mem. Nat. League Am. Pen Women (Owl award 1972, 76, 77, pres. Palm Beach chpt. 1975-80), Palm Beach Quills (historian), Palm Beach County Hist. Soc. (gov.), Internat. Platform Assn., Nat. Soc. Arts and Letters, Soc. Four Arts, Cum Laude Soc., Palm Beach Civic Assn. Episcopalian. Clubs: Everglades (Palm Beach); English Speaking Union (Palm Beach and London). Home: Acadie PO Box 648 Palm Beach FL 33480

HALL, KAY MARGARET, nurse; b. Lima, Ohio, July 24, 1943; d. Harold Ray and Ruth (Gordon) H.; m. Robert G. Jarvis, Oct. 23, 1976 (div. 1983). Diploma Miami Valley Hosp. Sch. Nursing, Dayton, Ohio, 1965; student Wright State U., 1974-77, U. Dayton, 1971, Universidad Technologica De Santiago, Santo Domingo, Dominican Republic, 1985—. R.N., Ohio. Charge nurse recovery room Miami Valley Hosp., Dayton, 1965-66; indsl. nurse Harris Seybold Co., Dayton, 1966-68; office nurse to physician, Dayton, 1968-69, 80-82; coordinator nurse Mobile Unit Clinics, OEO, 1969-72; emergency nurse Kettering Med. Ctr., Ohio, 1972-80, radiology nurse, 1979-80; chair N.Am. del. of nurses to Council on Status of World's Children's Health, Geneva, 1985. Author: (manual) Procedures for Nursing Care in Radiology, 1977. Big sister Big Bros.-Big Sisters, Dayton, 1979-83. Mem. Miami Valley Hosp. Sch. Nursing Alumni, Critical Care Nurses Dayton. Home: PO Box 1961 Kettering OH 45429

HALL, KAYE, bus. exec., developer; b. Warnock, Ky., Oct. 29, 1944; d. Ermon Heinard and Ethel Aldean (Boggs) Bradley; m. Mark A. Youngren; 1 son, Keenan Lee Hall. Exec. sec. C&O/B&O Ry. Co., Russell, Ky., 1963-69; exec. Bus. Investment, Ltd., Honolulu, 1969-71, v.p., 1971—, corp. sec., 1975—, also dir.; v.p., corp. sec. West Coast Bus. Investment, Ltd., Portland, Oreg., 1971-77, also dir.; v.p. Calif. Bus. Investment, Ltd., Los Angeles, 1972-78, corp. sec., 1973-78, also dir.; pres. Gen. Mgmt. Corp., Honolulu, 1975—, also dir.; pres. Condominium Mgmt., Inc., Portland, 1972—, also dir.; sec., dir. Econ. Devel. & Cons. Engrs., Inc., Honolulu, 1975—. sec. Russell div. Ry. and S.S. Clks. Union, 1968-69. Bd. dirs. Mental Health/Mental Retardation Greenup County (Ky.), 1966-67, United Fund, Greenup County, 1966-67; chmn. USO Spl. Projects, Greenup County, 1967; adv. dir. Valley Christian Schs., Inc., Beaverton, Oreg., 1975-76. Appt. Ky. Col., 1969. Mem. Oreg. Homebuilders Assn. (multifamily housing council), Nat. Community Assns. Inst. (v.p., bd. dirs., program dir. Oreg. chpt., Edn. Council). Club: West Hills Racquet. Office: 278 SW Arthur St Portland OR 97201

HALL, LEE, painter; b. Lexington, N.C., Dec. 15, 1934; d. Robert L. and Florence (Fitzgerald) H.; B.F.A., U. N.C., 1955, D.F.A., (hon.), 1976; M.A., N.Y. U., 1959, Ph.D., 1965. Chmn. art dept. Drew U., Montclair, N.J., 1965-74; dean visual arts SUNY, Purchase, 1974-75; pres. R.I. Sch. Design, Providence, 1975-83; sr. v.p. Acad. for Ednl. Devel., N.Y.C., 1984—; dir. Old Stone Corp., Quinter, Inc., Gear Designs, Inc.; paintings exhibited Betty Parsons Gallery, Armstrong Gallery, N.Y.C., Montclair Mus. Bd. cons. Nat. Endowment Humanities, 1968-80. Recipient Scholar's award N.Y. U., 1965, Childe Hassam award Am. Acad. Arts and Scis.; Am. Philos. Soc. fellow U. London, Oxford, 1965, 68. Club: Cosmopolitan (N.Y.C.). Contbr. articles to profl. jours. Home: 15 Atwood Rd South Hadley MA 01075 Office: Acad Ednl Devel 680 Fifth Ave New York NY 10019

HALL, LESLIE CARLTON, artist, consultant; b. Rockville Centre, N.Y., May 14, 1952; d. Robert Wilson and Barbara Louise (Lyon) H. Student So. Conn. State Coll., 1970-72; B.A. in Psychology, U. Conn., 1975. Freelance artist PBC Advt. Co., New Canaan, Conn., 1978-80; graphics artist Stamford Weekly Mail, Conn., part-time 1978-80; art dir. Tru-Line Publs., Spring Valley, N.Y., 1974-80; owner Creative Intentions, Wilton, Conn., 1980—; cons. for creative design, logos. Editor Pipeline, 1980-83. Artist for cover Doberman World mag., 1985. Active Rescue and Placement of Abused or Stray Doberman Pinschers, Wilton, 1976—. Mem. Doberman Pinscher Club of Am., Doberman Pinscher Club of Tappan Zee (treas. 1976-82). Republican. Episcopalian. Home and Office: 341 Olmstead Hill Rd Wilton CT 06897

HALL, LISA LYNN, state official, auditor; b. Aurora, Ill., Oct. 13, 1948; d. Kenneth F. and Veva R. Hall; B.A. cum laude (Ill. State scholar, Sigma Lambda Sigma scholar, Helen R. Messenger, univ. grantee, High Ridge Sch. PTA scholar, Ill. PTA scholar), No. Ill. U., 1970; M.B.A. magna cum laude, Sangamon State U., Springfield, Ill., 1980; m. H. Huckaby, Oct. 12, 1980. Pres., owner Hall Real Estate Enterprises, Springfield, 1972—; mgr. internal audit Ill. Dept. Adminstrv. Services, 1977-79; mgr. audit and investigation Ill. Dept. Commerce, 1979-80, chief audits and investigations, 1980—; ptnr./owner H & L Investments Co., 1981—. Del., Ill. Republican Conv., 1980. Cert. info. systems and data processing auditor. Mem. Inst. Internal Auditors (internat. com. 1979—, charter pres. Springfield chpt. 1978; seminar instr. 1979—), No. Ill. U. Alumni Assn. (gov. 1979—), Nat. Assn. Female Execs., Ill. Audit Mgrs. Assn., Assn. M.B.A. Execs., Internat. EDP Auditors Assn., Am. Bus. Women's Assn., Cwens. Contbr. articles to profl. jours.

HALL, LUCILLE JONES GREY, city official, civic worker; b. Cuyahoga Falls, Ohio, Apr. 15, 1922; d. Mark Barber and Nellie (James) Jones; student U. Miami, 1939-41, Rollins Coll., 1941, U. Fla., summer 1942, Cornell U., 1942-43; m. Hugh Morton Grey, Jr., Sept. 27, 1943 (div. Apr. 8, 1977); children—Leslie Grey Harper, Hugh Morton Grey III, Roderic Marcus Upson, Helen Valerie; m. Daniel Luce Hall, II, Jan. 5, 1982. Mem. Venice (Fla.) City Council, 1980—, vice mayor, 1983. Organizing pres. Beaux Arts of Lowe Gallery, Coral Gables, Fla., 1952, Town and Country Garden Club, Concord, N.C., 1956; chmn. vol. guides Mus. Sci. and Natural History, Miami, 1952-54; guide Children's Mus., Charlotte, N.C., 1955-56; leader Girl Scouts U.S.A., Concord, Raleigh, N.C., Venice, 1954-68, Cub Scouts, Concord, 1956-57, 64-65, pres. Coll. Club of Venice Area, 1960-61, Band Parents Club, Venice, 1960-61; jr. chmn. Venice Garden Club, 1960-62; bd. dirs. PTA, Merrick Demonstration Sch., 1951-52, Miami Music Club, 1951-53, Sr. Friendship, Mental Health Assn. of Sarasota, Venice Little Theatre; mem. womens planning com. Venice Yacht Club, 1961-62; sustaining chmn. Sarasota Jr. Welfare League, 1967-68; bd. dirs. Family Service Assn. Sarasota, 1968-70; bd. dirs., rec. sec. Women's Library Assn. of New Coll., Sarasota, 1967-69; mem. adminstrv. bd. Grace United Meth. Ch. Mem. Jr. League Sarasota, DAR (regent Myakka chpt. 1973-75), Colonial Dames XVII Century (sec. William Bassett chpt. 1977-78), Daus. Am. Colonists (regent Venice on Gulf chpt. 1979—), Fine Arts Soc. Sarasota (charter), Upson Family Assn. Am., LWV, Bus. and Profl. Women, Friendly Sons and Daus. St. Patrick, Am. Assn. Ret. Persons, Fla. League of Cities, Venice Taxpayers League, Paperweight Collectors Assn., Kappa Kappa Gamma (organizing pres. Sarasota County chpt. 1962). Republican. Home: Bristol House 200 N Park Blvd #7 Inlets Blvd Nokomis FL 33555

HALL, LUCILLE WALSH, development company executive; b. Lenoir, N.C., May 4, 1942; d. Louis Sycho and Hazel Maie (Triplett) Hartley; m. Jerry Wilson Walsh, Sept. 30, 1961 (div. 1984); 1 child, Melissa; m. Calvin Odell Hall, Mar. 31, 1984. Student in acctg. Wilkes Community Coll. Lic. real estate broker; H & R Block tax cert., 1971. Legal sec. E. James Moore, Atty., North Wilkesboro, N.C., 1961; gen. office worker Town N. Wilkesboro, 1961; bookkeeper Duncan Elec. Co., N. Wilkesboro, 1961-67; librarian Wilkes County Library, N. Wilkesboro, 1967-71; pres. Horne Developers Inc., Triplett, N.C., 1971—. Jehovah Witness. Office: Horne Developers Inc Triplett NC 28686

HALL, LYNNE PETERSON, counselor, family therapist; b. Los Angeles, Jan. 23, 1942; d. Nelse Enoksen and June (Temple) Peterson; m. Robert T. Hall, July 11, 1964 (div. 1985); children—Michelle, Brian, Mark. M.A., Calif. State Coll., Bakersfield, 1978. Lic. marriage family child therapist. Extended opportunity program coordinator Bakersfield Coll., Calif., 1980-83, assessment coordinator, 1982—. Therapist, co-founder Westchester Counseling Ct., Bakersfield, 1981—; adj. prof. Sch. Edn. Calif. State Coll., Bakersfield, 1981—. Sec., Mental Health Assn. Kern County, 1984-85. Mem. Calif. Assn. Marriage Family Child Therapists, Calif. Assn. Counseling and Devel., Am. Assn. Counseling and Devel., Calif. Tchrs. Assn., NEA, Delta Kappa Gamma. Democrat. Lutheran. Office: Bakersfield Coll 1801 Panorama Dr Bakersfield CA 93305

HALL, MARGARET ANN, state official; b. Las Cruces, N.Mex., Sept. 19, 1945; d. John Lewis and Ethel Lee (Billings) Watts; m. Sanford Bradley Hall, Aug. 4, 1967. Student Oklahoma City U., 1965, 68; secretarial cert. Central State U., Edmond, Okla., 1968. Sec., Nat. Investors Life Ins., Oklahoma City, 1963-66; legal sec. W. Custer Service, Edmond, 1967; sec. Ho. of Reps., Oklahoma City, 1968, 69; legal sec. bill drafting State Legis. Council, Oklahoma City, 1968; legal sec. Davis, Austin, Carrier, Oklahoma City, 1969-71; asst. to lt. gov. Office of Lt. Gov., Oklahoma City, 1971-79; sec., sr. adminstr., asst. to gov. Office of Gov., Oklahoma City, 1979—. Bd. dirs. Donna Nigh Found., Oklahoma City, 1984—; mem. campaign staff George Nigh Campaign for Re-election Lt. Gov., Oklahoma City, 1974, George Nigh Campaign for Gov., 1978, George Nigh Campaign for Re-election Gov., 1982. Democrat. Methodist. Office: Office of Gov 212 State Capitol Oklahoma City OK 73105

HALL, MARY ANNE, nurse, civic worker; b. Nagoya, Japan, June 29, 1956; came to U.S., 1958, naturalized, 1971; d. John Lawrence and Asano (Honda) Knorpp; m. David Charles Hall, Nov. 28, 1980; children—Graham Charles, Richard Alan. B.S. in Nursing, Ind. U., 1981. R.N., Ind. Staff nurse, level-2 charge nurse post open-heart surg. unit Ind. U. Hosp., Indpls., 1981-83. Co-author: Post Open Heart Surgical Handbook. Chmn. Marion County Med. Aux. Bd., Ind., 1985—; 3d v.p. Marion County Med. Soc., 1985—; mem. Methodist task force bd. Meth. Hosp., Indpls., 1985—; Mem. Sigma Theta Tau. Republican. Avocations: sailing; windsurfing; gourmet cooking; traveling. Home: 4609 London Dr Indianapolis IN 46254

HALL, MARY CECILIA, oil company executive, data processing consultant; b. Springfield, Ohio, Apr. 30, 1946; d. Anthony and Angela (Wolbert) Ciavarella; m. James Henry Hall, July 9, 1968. B.S. in Math., U. Tex.-El Paso, 1971. Tchr. math. Aldine Ind. Sch. Dist., Houston, 1971-73; tchr. math., dept. chmn. Spring Branch Ind. Sch. Dist., Houston, 1973-75; systems analyst Foley's Dept. Stores, Houston, 1975-79; dist. tech. mgr. Time Sharing Resources, Houston and Dallas, 1979-81; systems cons. Charter Oil Co., Houston, 1981—; lectr. U. Houston, 1980-81; lectr. in field. Named Sponsor of Yr., YMCA, 1969; NSF grantee, 1974. Mem. Nat. Assn. Tchrs. Math. (nat. conv. publicity chmn. 1973), Sigapl, SIGAPL-Am. Computing Machinery (br. pres. 1983—), AAUW, Tex. Tchrs. Assn., Kappa Delta. Democrat. Roman Catholic. Home: 9510 Ravensworth Dr Houston TX 77031

HALL, MARY THERESA, naval officer, lawyer; b. Fort Belvoir, Va., Sept. 10, 1956; d. Robert Eric and Maude (Warden) Hall; B.A., Columbus Coll. (Ga.), 1976; J.D., U. Ga., 1978. Bar: Ga. 1978. Commd. ensign U.S. Navy, 1978, advanced through grades to lt., 1983; asst. staff judge advocate Naval Air Sta., Pensacola, Fla., 1979-80; head legal assistance Navy Legal Service Office, Pensacola, 1980-81; comdg. legal officer USS Proteus, Homeport, Guam, 1981-83; head claims Navy Legal Service Office, San Francisco, 1983-84, sr. def. counsel, 1984—; adj. prof. law Troy State U., Pensacola, 1980-81. Columnist, Waterfront Lawyer weekly, 1981. Recipient Navy Achievement medal, Navy Commendation medal. Mem. ABA, Bar Assn. San Francisco, Phi Alpha Delta. Office: Naval Legal Service Office Bldg 450-T I San Francisco CA 94130

HALL, NANCY ELDER, banker; b. Knoxville, Tenn., Apr. 7, 1938; d. J. Robert and Ethel B. (Bailey) Elder; grad. U. Fla. Sch. Banking; children—Robert Buren Hall, Lee Anne Hall. With Hamilton Nat. Bank, Knoxville, 1956-60, 1st Bank Clewiston (Fla.), 1962-64, Fla. Nat. Bank, West Palm Beach, 1964-69; with Mall Bank, West Palm Beach, Fla., 1969—, sr. v.p., 1978—. Mem. Nat. Assn. Bank Women, Am. Inst. Banking, DAR. Home: 5420 N Ocean Dr Apt 1901 Singer Island FL 33404 Office: 1801 Palm Beach Lakes Blvd West Palm Beach FL 33401

HALL, PAMELA S., environmental consulting firm executive; b. Hartford, Conn., Sept. 4, 1944; d. LeRoy Warren and Frances May (Murray) Sheely; m. Stuart R. Hall, July 21, 1967. B.A. in Zoology, U. Conn., 1966; M.S. in Zoology, U. N.H., 1969, B.S. in Bus. Adminstrn. summa cum laude, 1981. Curatorial asst. U. Conn., Storrs, 1966; research asst. Field Mus. Natural History, Chgo., 1966-67; teaching asst. U. N.H., Durham, 1967-70; program mgr. Normandeau Assocs. Inc., Portsmouth, N.H., 1971-79, marine lab. dir., 1979-81, programs and ops. mgr., Bedford, N.H., 1981-83, v.p., 1983-85, sr. v.p., 1986—. Mem. Conservation Commn., Portsmouth, 1977—. Graham Found. fellow, 1966; NDEA fellow, 1970-71. Mem. Water Pollution Control Fedn., Am. Fisheries Soc., Estuarine Research Fedn., Nat. Assn. Environ. Profls., ASTM, Sigma Xi. Home: 4 Pleasant Point Dr Portsmouth NH 03801 Office: Normandeau Assocs Inc 25 Nashua Rd Bedford NH 03201

HALL, PATRICIA DELAY, accountant; b. Texarkana, Tex., Dec. 24, 1930; d. Byron N. and Esther J. DeLay; B.B.A., Lamar U., Beaumont, Tex., 1981; m. Miles A. Hall, Apr. 16, 1969; children—Kathryn, Andrew. Bookkeeper, Am. Bridge div. U.S. Steel Corp., Orange, Tex., 1954-59; with du Pont Co., Orange, 1959—, accountant, 1976-79, acctg. specialist, 1979—. Mem. Am. Soc. Exec. and Profl. Women, Nat. Assn. Female Execs., Phi Kappa Phi. Beta Gamma Sigma. Home: 309 Sandy Dr Bridge City TX 77611 Office: PO Box 1089 Orange TX 77630

HALL, PHOEBE POULTERER, lawyer, judge; b. Watertown, N.Y., Dec. 4, 1941; d. William Taylor, Jr., and Betty (Bennett) Poulterer; m. Franklin P. Hall, July 26, 1969; children—Kimberly Ann, Franklin P. B.A., U. Del.-Wilmington, 1963; J.D., Georgetown U., 1969. Bar: Va. Assoc., Hall & Hall, Richmond, Va., 1969—; substitute judge Gen. Dist. Cts., City of Richmond, 1983—, commr. in chancery, circuit cts., 1981—; founding dir., Cardinal Savs. & Loan Assn., Richmond, 1978—. Bd. trustees, Va. Mus. Fine Arts, 1983—; commr. Human Relations Commn., Richmond, 1972-73; dir. Family and Children's Services, Richmond, 1976-78; mem. worship com. 1st Presbyterian Ch., Richmond, 1983—; mem. state central com. Democratic Party, Va., 1974-80. Recipient Outstanding Citizenship award Urban League, Richmond, 1983; first woman pub. defender, City of Richmond, 1970; designer, instr. first course for paralegals, Va. State Bar, 1974. Mem. ABA, Richmond Bar Assn., Met. Richmond Women's Bar (founding 1971—), Va. Trial Lawyers Assn., Assn. Trial Lawyers Am., Def. Research Inst., Bus. and Profl. Women's Assn., Am. Bus. Women's Assn. Lodge Soroptimists. Home: 9006 Cherokee Rd Richmond VA 23235 Office: Hall and Hall Suite One 700 Bldg Richmond VA 23219

HALL, REBA JANE, computerized freight auditing firm executive; b. Nanticoke, Pa., Nov. 27, 1937; d. Harry and Hannah (Davis) Reinholt; children—David, Suzanne, Beth, Gregory. Vice-pres. Tri-State Keypunch, Woodbridge, N.J., 1974-77; pres. T.A.R.I.F.F., Inc., Metuchen, N.J., 1977—. Named Woman of Yr. for Small Bus., Raritan Valley Regional C. of C., 1984. Democrat. Office: TARIFF Inc 16 Pearl St Metuchen NJ 08840

HALL, SANDRA KEARNEY, rest home administrator; b. Durham, N.C., June 23, 1949; d. Samuel Crawford and Mildred (Fuller) Kearney; m. James Edgar Hall, Aug. 28, 1965; children—James Edgar, John Michael, Teresa Gale. Student Durham Tech. Inst., Fla. Community Coll. Adminstrv. sec. N.C. Dept. Corrections, Raleigh, 1967-70; supr. Louisburg Nursing Ctr., N.C., 1979-83; adminstr. Carolina Rest Home, Durham, 1983—. Mem. N.C. Long Term Care Facilities Assn. Democrat. Baptist. Avocations: reading; candlewicking; cross-stitch. Office: Carolina Rest Home 3119 Colclough Ave Durham NC 27704

HALL, SANDRA RAE YATES, advertising executive; b. Youngstown, Ohio, July 22, 1937; d. Myron A. and Hazel V. (Bailey) Yates. Student El Camino Coll., 1955-57. Singer, actress various locations, 1958-68; acct. exec. Pacific Telephone, Los Angeles, 1968-75; mng. dir. Wahlstrom/West subs. Foote, Cone & Belding Co., Compton, Calif., 1975—. Mem. El Segundo Sister City Assn. (Calif.), 1976; mem. Children's Hosp. Aux., El Segundo, 1978; mem. Long Beach Community Players, 1982. Mem. Los Angeles Advt. Women. Office: Wahlstrom/West 2200 W Artesia Blvd Compton CA 90220

HALL, SHELLEY FLEMING, broadcasting executive; b. Hollywood, Fla., July 19, 1951; d. Paul Martin and Emma Ruth (Vasvary) Fleming; m. Richard Steven Hall, Apr. 28, 1973. B.A. in English, Stetson U., 1973. Library tech. asst. U. N.C., Chapel Hill, 1973-76; account exec. VIP Personnel Consultants, Durham, N.C., 1976-77; account exec. Sta. WDUR-Radio, Durham, 1977-78, sales mgr., 1978-79; account exec., dir. recruitment advt. Sta. WHDH-Radio, Boston, 1979-82; regional sales dir. Stas. WEAN & WPJB-Radio, Providence, 1983, nat. sales mgr., 1983—; media cons. Tile City Inc., Norwood, Mass., 1980-82. Mem. Women's Media Network (publs. com. 1981-82), Women in Communications (dir. 1981—, v.p. programming 1981-82, 83-84, chmn. job bank 1982-83), New Eng. Broadcasters Assn., R.I. Ad Club. Democrat. Home: 20 Robin Wood Rd Dedham MA 02026 Office: WEAN/WPJB Radio 290 Westminster Mall Providence RI 02903

HALL, SUE COLLIER, adult residential facility owner; b. Richmond, Va., Oct. 2, 1946; d. Wallace Rogers and Blanche Elizabeth (Turpin) Collier; m. Thomas Reece Roberts, Jr., Feb. 22, 1971 (div. 1982); children—Erin Christine, Jessica Collier, Thomas Reece III. B.S. in Occupational Therapy, Va. Commonwealth U., 1969. Cert. in occupational therapy. Occupational therapy aide Va. Home for Incurables, Richmond, 1966; asst. dir. Adult Devel. Ctr., Richmond, 1967; occupational therapist Med. Coll. Va., Richmond, 1969-72; adminstr. Richmond Mental Health Clinic, Richmond, 1973-82; owner, operator Collier's Home for Adults, Inc., Richmond, 1982—; cons. Orange County Mental Health Ctr., Va., 1975-76. Mem. Am. Occupational Therapy Assn., Va. Occupational Therapy Assn. (pub. relations chmn. 1971), Richmond Assn. Homes for Adults. Democrat. Baptist. Home: Route 2 Box 177A Montpelier VA 23192 Office: Collier's Home for Adults 3210 Chamberlayne Ave Richmond VA 23227

HALL, SYLVIA DUNN, entrepreneur; b. Kewanee, Ill., June 21, 1949; d. Martin Orrill and Elizabeth Jean (Boase) Dunn; m. James Vernon Hall, Jan. 14, 1977. B.A., Rockford Coll., 1971; M.L.S., N. Tex. State U., 1972; M.A., U. Tex., 1975; Ph.D.,U. Pitts. Library asst. Rockford Pub. Library (Ill.), 1966-71; librarian Holding Inst., Laredo, Tex., 1972-73; system coordinator San Antonio Pub. Library, 1973-76; tech. services librarian Corpus Christi Pub. Library (Tex.), 1976-78; asst. dir. So. Tier Library System, Corning, N.Y., 1978-81; devel. officer Pitts. Regional Library Ctr., 1981-85; pres. The Blue Bear Group, Inc., 1984—; cons. S.D. State Library, Pierre, 1981-83, State Library of Pa., Harrisburg, 1982-83, Dept. Def., Washington, 1983-84. Author: Retro Conversion for Major Libraries in South Central N.Y., 2 vols., 1979; History of Library Development in Pennsylvania, 1982; contbr. articles to profl. jours. U. Pitts. fellow, 1982. Mem. ALA (student staff award 1982), Pa. Library Assn. (dir. 1983-85), Am. Soc. Info. Scientists. Republican. Home: 3930 Old William Penn Hwy #313 Pittsburgh PA 15235 Office: The Blue Bear Group Inc 3930 Old William Penn Hwy Suite 311 Pittsburgh PA 15235

HALLANAN, ELIZABETH VIRGINIA, federal judge; b. Charleston, W.Va., Jan. 10, 1925; d. Walter Simms and Mary Imogene (Burns) H.; m. Harold Britton Kinison, July 24, 1948 (div. 1951). A.B., U. Charleston, 1946, LL.D. (hon.), 1971; J.D., W.Va. U., 1951. Bar: W.Va. 1951. Mem. W.Va. Bd. Edn., Charleston, 1955-57; asst. commr. W.Va. Pub. Inst., Charleston, 1958-59; mem. W.Va. Ho. of Reps., Charleston, 1957-58; judge Kanawha County Juvenile Ct., Charleston, 1959-61; exec. dir. W.Va. Assn. Colls. and Univs., Charleston, 1961-69; mem., chmn. Pub. Service Commn. W.Va., Charleston, 1969-75; mem. firm Dodson, Deutsch & Hallanan, Charleston, 1975-83; judge U.S. Dist. Ct. for so. dist. W.Va., Beckley, 1983—. Trustee U. Charleston, 1955—; bd. dirs., sec. Edn. Found., 1955—; mem. Human Right Commn. of Charleston, 1981-83. Recipient spl. citation Charleston Gazette, 1959; Meritorious Service to Community award Charleston Women's Club, 1959; Alumni Key award Morris Harvey Coll., 1968. Mem. ABA, Kanawha County Bar Assn., Nat. Assn. Regulatory Utilities Commrs. (sec. v.p. 1974), Gt. Lakes Conf. Pub. Utilities Commrs. (pres. 1973-74), Charleston Bus. and Profl. Womens Club (pres.). Club: Altrusa (Charleston). Office: PO Drawer 5009 Beckley WV 25801

HALLAS, SUSAN SEYMOUR, insurance marketing executive, civic worker; b. Louisville, July 10, 1942; d. George McClure and Florence Hooker (Leaning) Seymour; B.A. in Philosophy, Wellesley Coll., 1964; M.S. in Urban Edn., Central Conn. Coll., 1972; children—Katherine Seymour, Elizabeth McClure. Tchr., Hartford (Conn.) Bd. Edn., 1964-68; dir. city/suburb project U. Hartford, 1979-81; self-employed mgmt./devel. cons., 1981-84; asst. dir. mktg. Employee Benefit and Health Care Group div. CIGNA Corp., Hartford, 1984—. Second v.p. Jr. League of Hartford, 1973-75, pres., 1977-79; mem. area council Assn. of Jr. Leagues, N.Y.C, 1975-76, bd. dirs., 1980-82; chmn. Conn. Council of Jr. Leagues, 1978-79; bd. dirs. Hartford Hosp. Aux., 1971-74; mem. vestry Old St. Andrew's Episcopal Ch., 1975-78; bd. dirs. Wintonbury PTA, 1975-78, pres., 1976-77; bd. dirs. Conn. Valley council Girl Scouts U.S.A., 1979-82, Bushnell Park Found., 1982—; pres. Loomis Chaffee Alumni Assn., 1981-83; trustee Loomis Chaffee Sch., 1986—. Home: 635 Bloomfield Ave Bloomfield CT 06002 Office: CIGNA Corp Hartford CT 06152

HALLAS-GOTTLIEB, LISA GAIL, film director; b. Rahway, N.J., Feb. 22, 1950; d. Taras and Mary (Lapchinski) Hallas; m. David N. Gottlieb, May 2, 1980. B.A. in Broadcasting, Film and English with distinction, Stanford U., 1972. Second asst. dir. films: Opening Night, 1977, World's Greatest Lover, 1977, The Driver, 1977, Old Boyfriends, 1978, Just You and Me, Kid, 1978, A Small Circle of Friends, 1979; 2d asst. dir. TV show M*A*S*H, 1976; 1st asst. dir. TV shows Nobody's Perfect, 1979, Shirley, 1979, Hellinger's Law, 1980, Dynasty; 1980-81, Cagney and Lacey, 1983, Lottery $, 1983-84, Condor, 1984. Home: 1414 N Topanga Canyon Blvd Topanga CA 90290

HALLBAUER, ROSALIE CARLOTTA, business educator; b. Chgo., Dec. 8, 1939; d. Ernest Ludwig and Kathryn Marquerite (Ramm) Hallbauer; B.S., Rollins Coll., 1961; M.B.A., U. Chgo., 1963; Ph.D., U. Fla., 1973. Assoc. prof. bus. Fla. Internat. U., Miami, 1972—. C.P.A., Ill.; certified mgmt. accountant; cert. cost analyst. Mem. Am. Inst. C.P.A.s, Am. Accounting Assn., Nat. Assn. Accountants, Am. Woman's Soc. C.P.A.s, Ill. Soc. C.P.A.s, Inst. Mgmt. Accounting, Beta Alpha Psi, Pi Gamma Mu. Office: Florida Internat Univ Tamiami Trail Miami FL 33199

HALLBERG, NANCY LEVY, advertising agency executive; b. Englewood, N.J., Nov. 13, 1951; d. Israel and Gloria (Cutler) Levy; m. Howard Siskowitz, June 4, 1978 (div. Dec. 1983); m. 2d, Garth R. Hallberg, Mar. 23, 1984. B.A., U. Mich., 1973; M.A., U. Ill., Urbana, 1974; M.B.A., U. Pa., 1978. Properties supr. McCarter Theatre, Princeton, 1975-76; account exec. J. Walter Thompson, N.Y.C., 1978-80, v.p., 1980—, account supr., 1980-84, mgmt. supr., 1984—. Democrat. Jewish. Office: J Walter Thompson 466 Lexington Ave New York NY 10017

HALLEEN, SHIRLEY LOUISE KELLS, state legislator; b. Russell, Iowa, May 17, 1935; d. Ray Lester and Ruth Mae (Lewis) Kells; B.S., Wheaton Coll., 1957; m. Owen Halleen, June 8, 1957; children—Terri, Lynne, David. Tchr. secondary sch., Wurzburg, Ger., 1958-59; secondary and coll. tchr., St. Paul, 1963-68; mem. staff YWCA, Sheridan, Wyo., 1969-71; exercise cons. Sioux Valley Hosp., Sioux Falls, S.D., 1976; mem. S.D. Ho. of Reps., 1980—. Bd. dirs. United Way, Family Service, McCrossan Boys' Ranch, Girls Club, S.D. Symphony. Recipient YMCA Service to Youth award, 1970, Sioux Falls Leadership Luncheon award, 1978; named Outstanding Woman in Sports, 1978. Mem. AAUW, LWV, PTA, YWCA, Sioux Falls Coll. Faculty Folk. Democrat. Baptist. Club: P.E.O. Home: 1013 S Lyndale Sioux Falls SD 57105 Office: Ho of Reps State Capitol Pierre SD 57501

HALLIDAY, HARRIET HUDNUT (HOLLY), university administrator; b. Springfield, Ill., Dec. 7, 1941; d. William Herbert and Elizabeth Allen (Kilborne) Hudnut; B.A., Coll. Wooster, 1963; postgrad. McCormick Theol. Sem.; m. Terence C. Halliday, June 14, 1980; children—Tyler Hudnut Colman, Richard Terence, Kimberly Anne, Alastair Charles. Exec. sec. women's bd. Presbyterian Med. Ctr., San Francisco, 1965-68; editor Am. Bar Found., Chgo., 1968-70, asst. dir. publs., 1970-75, mng. editor Am. Bar Found. Research Jour., 1975-80; research asst. dept. philosophy Australian Nat. U., Canberra, 1980-82; mng. editor Chiron Publs., 1983-86; acad. asst. to dean social scis. U. Chgo., 1986—; dir. BCH Corp. Mem. exec. com. jr. governing bd. Chgo. Symphony Orch., 1969-70, 75-76; officer adv. bd. Unitarian Presch. Center, Chgo., 1974-77; mem. Assocs. Rush-Presbyn.-St. Luke's Med. Ctr., 1974-79; mem. alumni bd. Coll. Wooster, 1978-80, also chmn. pub. relations com., mem. nominating com., by-laws revision com.; bd. dirs. Children's Theatre of Winnetka, Ill., 1984-85; exec. com. Chgo. Bible Soc., 1983-86. Republican. Presbyterian. Home: 422 Rosewood Ave Winnetka IL 60093 Office: 400 Linden Ave Wilmette IL 60091

HALLORAN, ANNA MARIE, financial analyst; b. Chgo., Mar. 16, 1963; d. William Xavier and Catherine (Enright) H. B.A. in Econs. cum laude, U.

Calif.-Irvine, 1984. Adminstrv. intern U. Calif.-Irvine, 1982-83, coordinator adminstrv. intern program, 1983-84; auditor McDonnell Douglas, Huntington Beach, Calif., 1984, acct., 1985, fin. analyst, Long Beach, Calif., 1986—. Fundraiser U. Calif.-Irvine Newman Club, 1982-83. Mem. Nat. Assn. Female Execs., Fiscal Career Advancement Program, McDonnell Douglas Huntington Beach Mgmt. Assn. Avocations: traveling; tennis; snorkeling. Office: McDonnell Douglas Financial Controls 3855 Lakewood Blvd Long Beach CA 90846

HALPENNY, DIANA DORIS, lawyer; b. San Francisco, Jan. 18, 1951; d. William Frederick and Doris E. Halpenny; m. Gregory D. Prowell, Aug. 28, 1982. B.A., Calif. State Coll., 1973; J.D., Univ. Pacific, 1980. Bar: Calif. 1980. Bookkeeper/sales clerk Farmers Empire Drugs, Santa Rosa, Calif., 1971-73; activity dir. Beverly Manor Convalescent Hosp., Anaheim, Calif., 1973-74; instructional aide Los Angeles County Supt. Schs., Downey, Calif., 1974-76, sub. tchr., 1976-77; assoc. Littler, Mendelson, Fastiff & Tichy, San Jose, Calif., 1980-82, Walters & Shelburne, Sacramento, Calif., 1982-84, Kronick Moskowitz Tiedemann & Girard, Sacramento, 1984—. Mem. Calif. Bar Assn., ABA, Trayner Honor Soc., Order of Coif, Phi Alpha Delta, Pi Lambda Theta, Phi Kappa Phi. Republican. Lutheran. Office: Kronik Moskovitz et al 770 L St Suite 1200 Sacramento CA 95814

HALPERIN, CORRINE SANDRA, college administrator; b. Providence, Feb. 8, 1936; d. Barney and Rose Ruth (Bilsky) Gordon; student Behrend Coll., Wayne State U., U. Mich.; B.A., Mercyhurst Coll., 1980; children—Karen Halperin Shor, Micheal Jay, Amy Marlene. Freelance market researcher, 1968-72; exec. dir. Council Vols. Erie County, 1971-78; exec. dir. YWCA, Erie, 1978-81; unit dir. Am. Cancer Soc., Erie, 1982; adj. faculty Mercyhurst Coll., dir. spl. projects, 1982—; adviser Hospitality House for Women, 1975—. Sec., Erie Art Festival, 1973-74; chmn. Erie County Commn. Drug and Alcohol Abuse, 1978-80; bd. dirs. Pa. Women's Campaign Fund. Recipient Community Service award, 1977. Mem. Am. Soc. Tng. and Devel., AAUW, Nat. Council Jewish Women. Contbg. editor: Vol. Adminstrn., 1973-83. Home: 2948 Willow Wood Dr Erie PA 16506 Office: Mercyhurst Coll Glenwood Hills Erie PA 16546

HALPERN, AMY LYNN, marketing executive; b. Manhasset, N.Y., Sept. 8, 1957; d. Alvin and Ethel Joan (Weisblum) H. B.A. in Psychology, Syracuse U., 1979; M.B.A. in Mktg., Hofstra U., 1984. Asst. collection mgr. Harrington Righter & Parson, N.Y.C., 1979-80; promotion coordinator coop. advt. Elizabeth Arden, Inc., N.Y.C., 1980-81; dir. mktg. retail sales Bell & Halpern Pharmacy, Inc., Glen Cove, N.Y., 1981—. Mem. Nat. Assn. Female Execs., M.B. Assn., Am. Mgmt. Assn. Democrat. Avocations: sailing; traveling; photography. Home: PO Box 193 Sea View Dr Mill Neck NY 11765 Office: Bell & Halpern Pharmacy Inc 87 Forest Ave Glen Gove NY 11542

HALPERN, JO-ANNE ORENT, lawyer, legal assistant to county judges; b. Balt., Apr. 13, 1944; d. Max Howard and Marjorie (Ginsburg) Orent; m. M. David Halpern, Aug. 22, 1965; children—Hugh Nathanial, Lee Randall (dec.), Lauren Gail. B.A. Dickinson Coll., 1966; J.D., Dickinson Sch. Law, 1968. Bar: Pa. 1968. Law clk. Daupin County and Commonwealth Ct. Pa., 1965-68; assoc. Hurwitz Klein, Benjamin & Angino, Harrisburg, Pa., 1968-70; sole practice, Hollidaysburg, Pa., 1970—; legal asst. to Blair County Cts., Hollidaysburg, 1974—; solicitor Blair County Assn. Citizens with Learning Disabilities, 1979—, Family Violence Intervention, Inc., Altoona, Pa., 1980—; lectr., atty. Hospice Program of Home Nursing Agy. Blair County, 1979—. Adviser, bd. dirs. Agudath Achim Sisterhood, 1970—, pres., 1985-86. Mem. ABA, Pa. Bar Assn., Blair County Bar Assn., Am. Arbitration Assn. (arbitrator), Blair County Assn. Lawyers Wives, Phi Alpha Delta, Phi Mu. Republican. Jewish. Lodge: Hadassah. Home: 8 Hickory Hill Hollidaysburg PA 16648

HALPERN, PATRICIA, sales promotion and premiums company executive; b. San Francisco, Jan. 13, 1934; d. William and Alice (Dewey) O'Shaughnessy; student U. Ill., m. Harold Halpern, Apr. 1, 1951; children—Rebecca, Jay. Account exec., v.p. sales React Enterprises, N.Y.C., 1974—. Mem. Ad Specialty Assn., NOW. Home: 132 E 35th St New York NY 10016 Office: 15 E 26th St New York NY 10010

HALSBAND, FRANCES, architect; b. N.Y.C., Oct. 30, 1943; d. Samuel and Ruth H.. B.A., Swarthmore Coll., 1965, M.Arch., Columbia U., 1968, m. Robert Michael Kliment, May 1, 1971; 1 son, Alexander H. Architect with Mitchell/Giurgola Architects, N.Y.C., 1968-72; partner R.M. Kliment & Frances Halsband Architects, N.Y.C., 1972—; vis. critic archtl. design Columbia U., 1975-78, N.C. State U., 1978, Rice U., 1979, U. Va., 1980, Harvard U., 1981, U. Pa., 1981; mem. N.Y.C. Landmarks Preservation Commn., 1984—. Projects include: Computer Sci. Bldg., Columbia U., Gilmer Hall addition U. Va.; author: Annotated Bibliography of Technical Resources for Small Museums, 1983. Mem. Archtl. League N.Y. (exec. bd. 1975-81, v.p. arch. 1981-85, pres. 1985—), AIA (exec. bd. N.Y.C. 1979), Alliance Women in Architecture, Am. Assn. for State and Local History, Am. Assn. Museums, Catskill Center for Conservation and Devel., Gallery Assn. N.Y. State. Office: 255 W 26th St New York NY 10001

HALTER, FAITH LAURIE, environmental lawyer; b. Phila., Oct. 2, 1954; d. Arnold and Beverly (Hoffman) Halter. B.A., Pa. State U., 1975; J.D., U. Pa., 1978. Bar: Pa. 1978. Law clk. U.S. Dist. Ct., Tucson, 1978-79; spl. asst. to gen. counsel EPA, Washington, 1980-81, atty., Washington, Africa, 1980-84; atty. EPA, N.Y.C., 1984—; legal cons. U.N. Environment Program, Nairobi, Kenya, 1981-82; legal cons. World Wildlife Fund, Africa, 1983-84. Mem. Pa. Bar Assn., ABA, African Studies Assn. Jewish. Contbr. articles to profl. jours. Home: 44 Prospect Park W Brooklyn NY 11215

HALVERSON, CATHERINE VIRGINIA, production supervisor; b. LeMars, Iowa, Dec. 26, 1945; d. Leonard Allen and Doris Kathleen (Dickman) Brooks; m. Richard Francis McGee, Sept. 21, 1974 (div. 1978); 1 child, Chad Richard McGee; m. Dale Elliot Halverson, Apr. 5, 1985. B.S., U. No. Iowa, 1969, M.Ed., 1972. Mgmt. trainee Sears, Roebuck & Co., Waterloo, Iowa, 1969-71; dept. mgr. Montgomery Ward Co., Cedar Falls, Iowa, 1972-74; chem. analyst John Deere, Waterloo, 1974-78, prodn. supr., 1978—. Mem. Nat. Assn. Female Execs. Republican. Lutheran. Avocations: golf; aerobics. Home: 1525 W 3d St Waterloo IA 50701 Office: John Deere Component Works 400 Westfield Waterloo IA 50702

HALVORSON, DEBORA ANNE, actuary, consultant; b. Omaha, Jan. 16, 1951; d. Gordon Allen and Carolyn Ann (Visek) Johnston; m. Robert Jon Halvorson, Nov. 29, 1975. Student Stephens Coll., 1969-70; B.A., Gustavus Adolphus Coll., 1973. Actuary, Delta Dental Plan Minn., Mpls., 1974—, asst. v.p., 1984—; cons. actuary Pet Health Plan Minn., Inc., Mpls., 1983—. Chmn., Mpls. Aquatennial, 1979; bd. dirs. Shoreline Early childhood Devel. Ctr. Mem. Am. Acad. Actuaries (recognition award), Delta Dental Plans Assn. (chmn. nat. actuarial com 1982—). Republican. Lutheran. Home: 26170 Birch Bluff Rd Shorewood MN 55331 Office: Delta Dental Plan Minn 7807 Creekridge Circle Minneapolis MN 55440

HALWANI, CECELIA MARIE, anthropolist; b. Dallas, Feb. 24, 1951; d. Thomas Joseph and Mary Alice (Smith) Walter; m. Charles Michael Sibley, June 10, 1972 (div. Mar. 1978); 1 son, Thomas Mitchell; m. 2d, Nabil Ezzat Halwani, Mar. 18, 1978. A.A., Des Moines Area Community Coll., Ankeny, Iowa, 1974; B.S. with honors in Psychology, Iowa State U., 1979, M.A. in Sociology, 1986. Asst. dir. placement Empact, Inc., Des Moines, 1973-74; teaching asst. Day Care Services, Inc., Des Moines, 1974; telephone counselor Community Telephone Counseling, Des Moines, 1975-77; bus. coordinator, dir. Open Line, Inc., Ames, Iowa, 1979-80; teaching and research asst. dept. anthropology Iowa State U., Ames, 1978-82; personnel cons. Contax Career Cons., Dallas, 1982-84; mental health specialist Timberlawn Psychiat. Hosp., 1984-85, program asst., family genetic histories Dallas, 1985—. Treas. Story County Human Services Council, 1980-81; speakers bur. Polk County Rape/Sexual Assault Care Ctr., Des Moines, 1976-77; vol. Adapt Juvenile Facility, Des Moines, 1975-76; treas. United Native Am. Student Assn., Ames, 1978; vol. counselor Career Services, Richland Coll., Dallas, 1984; mem. parents adv. bd. YWCA, 1986—. Mem. Iowa State U. Alumni Assn., Des Moines Area Community Coll. Alumni Assn., Metroplex Assn. Personnel Cons., Nat. Assn. Female Execs., Psi Chi, Kappa Delta. Democrat. Moslim. Home: 1304 Timberlake Circle Richardson TX 75080 Office: Timberlawn Psychiat Ctr PO Box 11288 Dallas TX 75223

HAMALAINEN, LAUREL G., company administrator, author; b. Gaylord, Mich., Dec. 1, 1956; d. Eino Harold and Gloria Fern (Poynor) H. B.S., Central Mich. U., 1978. Instr. English Tecunseh Pub. Sch. (Mich.), 1978-79; asst. instr. Hope Coll., Holland, Mich., 1979; mktg. communications writer Shaw-Walker Co., Muskegon, Mich., 1979-83; writing assoc. Judd Perkins Pub. Relations, Muskegon, 1983; copy coordinator Haworth, Inc., Holland, 1983-84; communications mgr. Herman Miller, Inc., 1984—; dir., creative cons. Communications W., Muskegon, 1983—. Editor: The Top Drawer, 1981, The Leader, 1983, Striking Moments, 1983. Communications com. United Way Muskegon County, 1983, deferred giving com., 1983. Recipient "I Dare You" award St. Louis, 1974; Pres.'s scholarship No. Mich. U., 1974; Bd. Dirs. scholarship Central Mich. U., 1975-77. Mem. Women in Communications, Inc. (sec. 1983—), Profl. Women's Network, Assn. Creative Writers. Lutheran. Office: Herman Miller Inc 8500 Byron Rd Zeeland MI 49464

HAMAN, SHIRLEY ANN, retail exec.; b. Detroit, Sept. 11, 1921; d. William Harold and Grace Elizabeth (Hall) Tucker; student Wayne U., 1940-43; m. Edward A. Haman, Sept. 1, 1943 (dec.); children—Edward A., Ann Elizabeth. Account and bus. mgr., Mitchell Buick Sales, Mt. Clemens, Mich., 1945-53, sec.-treas., bus. mgr., 1973—. Mem. City Planning Commn., Mt. Clemens, Base Community Council. Roman Catholic. Home: 1212 Burlington Dr Mount Clemens MI 48043 Office: 165 N Gratiot Ave Mount Clemens MI 48043

HAMBLETON, BERNIECE CAMPBELL, nurse; b. Emerson, Ark., Feb. 9, 1926; d. Clarence Henry and Nellie Marie (Moore) Campbell; diploma, R.N., Warner Brown Sch. Nursing, El Dorado, Ark., 1948; m. Clarence Earl Hambleton, Jr., Dec. 23, 1947; children—Julianna Marie, Clarence Earl III. Nurse, Warner Brown Hosp., El Dorado, 1948-51, Alvin (Tex.) Meml. Hosp., 1963-65, St. Luke Episcopal Hosp., Houston, 1967-67, Alvin Gulfcoast Hosp., 1967-68; operating room supr. Caribou Meml. Hosp., Soda Springs, Idaho, 1969—. County chmn. Heart Fund, 1971. Mem. Am., Idaho nurses assns., Assn. Operating Room Nurses, Idaho Soc. for Nursing Service Adminstrs. Republican. Baptist. Home: 360 N 2d E Soda Springs ID 83276

HAMBLEY, SHARON L.R., nurse, government official; b. Mpls., Aug. 1, 1941; d. Walter Fred Rubinson and Blanche Loretta (Martindale) Clement; B.A., U. Minn., 1963, B.S., 1966; USPHS trainee Columbia U., 1968-69; M.P.A., Am. U. Coll. Govt. and Pub. Adminstrn. and Georgetown U. Sch. Medicine, 1982; cert. mental health adminstrn. (fellow) Washington Sch. Psychiatry, 1977; m. William A. Hambley, Jr., Sept. 10, 1965 (div. 1975). Sch. health nurse Arlington County (Va.) Schs., 1966-70; public health nurse Fairfax County (Va.) Health Dept., 1970-71; charge nurse splty. clinics Children's Hosp. Nat. Med. Center, Washington, 1971-72; primary nurse intensive care psychiatry Washington Hosp. Center, 1972-74; asst. to chief supervisory nurse forensic psychiatry Alcohol Drug Abuse and Mental Health Adminstrn., NIMH, Washington, 1974-80; program analyst Office Policy Devel. and Research, White House Conf. Aging, 1981; coordinator pre-trial forensic psychiatry Alcohol and Drug Abuse Adminstrn. NIMH, Washington, 1982—; health care planner Reston (Va.) Community Assn., 1970-73; chairperson D.C. Nurses Assn. Profl. Standards Review Orgn., 1976. Fellow Soc. Advanced Med. Systems; mem. Am. Assn. Med. Systems and Informatics (founding), Symposium on Computer Applications in Med. Care, Computer-assisted Psychiat. Evaluation and Research Systems, Am. Nurses Assn. (cert. excellence in practice in psychiatry 1977), Med. Soc. NIMH, Nat. Forensic Nurses Assn., Am. Public Health Assn., Am. Oceanic Soc., Am. Coll. Hosp. Adminstrs. Club: Sailing (Washington). Office: DHHS PHS ADAMHA NIMH CCS DFP Washington DC 20032

HAMBRICK, DENISE MARIE, research and development engineer; b. Gallipolis, Ohio, Nov. 17, 1956; d. Alvis Rupert and B. Marie (Lynch) H.; m. Samuel David Gee, Sept. 2, 1978 (div. 1983). B.S. in Metall. Engring., Ohio State U., 1980. Research intern Battelle Meml. Inst., Columbus, Ohio, 1978-80; mfg. engr. Gen. Dynamics Convair, San Diego, 1980-82; research and devel. engr. Avco Aerostructures Textron, Nashville, 1982—. Contbr. articles to profl. jours. Mem. Am. Soc. for Metals, Nat. Mgmt. Assn., Nat. Soc. Profl. Engrs. Club. Nashville Dog Tng. Avocations: dog training; sailing; travel; hiking. Office: Avco Aerostructures Textron PO Box 210 Nashville TN 37202

HAMBRICK, MARGARET REEVES, insurance and securities executive; b. Augusta, Ga., Sept. 19, 1928; d. William Robert and Neva Alice (Stewart) Reeves; m. Larry B. Smalley, July 5, 1946 (div. 1965); children—Larry Barton Smalley, Jr., Philip Dean Smalley; Barry Enoch Smalley; m. Robert Allen Hambrick, Feb. 10, 1968 (div. 1985). Mortgage loan assoc. Blanchard & Calhoun Realtors, Augusta, 1944-53; sec. personnel dept. VA Hosp., Augusta, 1955-70; personnel asst., 1970-74; incentive awards adminstr. Dept. Army, Fort Gordon, Ga., 1974-78; real estate assoc. Crowell & Co., Augusta, 1980; sales rep., regional v.p. A.L. Williams, Augusta, 1980—; real estate assoc. First Realty Group, Inc., Martinez, Ga., 1981—, regional v.p., 1982—; registered rep. First Am. Nat. Securities, Inc., 1985—. Recipient Outstanding Performance award VA Hosp., 1976, individual and divisional work performance awards A.L. Williams, 1981, 82, 83. Republican. Avocations: travel; reading; walking; Bible study and teaching. Home: 3106 Whaley Rd Augusta GA 30907 Office: AL Williams First Am Nat Securities Inc 3850 Washington Rd Martinez GA 30907

HAMBRICK, PATRICIA JUNE, mathematics educator; b. Richlands, Va., July 1, 1952; d. Cecil Gene and Lois (Thomas) Tatum; m. Ted Ray Hambrick; children—Tracey Ann, Tammy Lynn, Matthew Ray. A.B., Marshall U., 1974, M.A., 1976; M.A., Marshall U., 1985. Cert. elem. tchr., W. Va. Tchr. math Cabell County Schs., Huntington, W. Va., 1974, spl. math tchr., 1974-79, gifted math specialist, 1979-81, math specialist, 1981-83; asst. prof. Mt. Vernon Nazarene Coll., Ohio, 1983—; workshop presenter W. Va. Math Assn., 1974-82, Assn. Christian Schs. Internat., 1984—. Author: The Importance of Mathematics, 1985. Contbr. articles to profl. jours. Mem. Cabell County Math Assn., Nat. Council Tchrs. Math., W. Va. Council Tchrs. Math., Ohio Council Tchrs. Math., W. Va. Assn. Suprs. Curriculum and Devel., W. Va. Assn. Tchr. Excellence. Republican. Avocations: golf; swimming; bowling; tennis. Home: 6008 Johnstown Rd Box 442 New Albany OH 43054 Office: Mount Vernon Nazarene Coll 800 Martinsburg Rd Mount Vernon OH 43050

HAMBURGER, JODI M., brokerage firm executive; b. N.Y.C., Sept. 15, 1955; d. Lloyd Edward and Judith Ann (Tanney) H.; m. Robert Gordon Fately, Aug. 30, 1981. B.S., Syracuse U., 1977; M.B.A., Tulane U., 1979. Spl. summer intern Deloite Haskins & Sells, Los Angeles, 1978; mgmt. cons. Arthur Andersen & Co., N.Y.C., 1979-81; div. controller corp. resources group Prudential-Bache Securities, N.Y.C., 1981-82, mgr. registration dept., 1982-83, exec. asst to chmn., 1983—. Republican. Jewish. Club: Downtown Athletic (N.Y.C.). Office: Prudential-Bache Securities Inc One Seaport Plaza New York NY 10292

HAMBY, JACQUELINE, educator; b. Chandler, Ariz., Oct. 24, 1934; d. Jack Cookston and Lela Mae (Dunn) Henry; m. Marvin J. Hamby, Sept. 14, 1963; children—Rebecca Lynn, Joan Elizabeth, Russell Jay. B.A., Ariz. State U., 1957. Tchr. Gilbert (Ariz.) Elem. Sch., 1957-60, Kyrene Elem. Sch., Tempe, Ariz., 1960-64, Chandler (Ariz.) Jr. High Sch., 1966-68; tchr. Roxbury Elem. Sch., Solon, Ohio, 1968—, computer coordinator, 1982—. Recipient Freedom medal Freedoms Found., 1974; Jennings scholar, 1973. Home: 6894 Solon Blvd Solon OH 44139 Office: Roxbury Elem Sch 6795 Solon Blvd Solon OH 44139

HAMBY, JEANETTE, state legislator; b. Virginia, Minn., Mar. 15, 1933; d. John W. and Lydia M. (Soderholm) Johnson; m. Eugene Hamby, 1957; children—Taryn Rene, Tenya Ramine. B.S., U. Minn., 1956; M.S., U. Oreg., 1968; Ph.D., Oreg. State U., 1976. Vice chmn. Hillsboro High Sch. Dist. Bd., 1973-81; mem. Washington County Juvenile Services Com., 1980—; mem. suggested legis. com. Council State Govts., 1981—, Oreg. state rep., 1981-83; mem. Oreg. State Senate from 5th dist., 1983—. Mem. Oreg. Mental Health Assn., Am. Nurses Assn., Oreg. Nurses Assn., Am. Vocat. Assn., Oreg. Vocat. Assn., Oreg. Vocat./Career Adminstrs. Lutheran. Republican. Office: Oreg State Capitol Bldg Salem OR 97310

HAMED, MARTHA ELLEN, government administrator; b. Washington, Jan. 14, 1950; d. Rockford Morris and Dorothy Hope (Lough) H. Student in psychology and sociology George Washington U., 1972—, A.A., 1985. Command fed. women's program mgr. U.S. Atlantic Fleet, Norfolk, Va., 1978-79; fed. women's program mgr. Naval Ordnance Sta., Indian Head, Md., 1979-80; personnel mgr., EEO course dir. Naval Civilian Personnel Command, Arlington, Va., 1980-83; dep. EEO officer, site mgr. Ship Research and Devel. Ctr., Bethesda, Md., 1983-85, Naval Surface Weapons Ctr., Silver Spring, Md., 1985; command fed. women's program mgr. Naval Sea Systems Command, Washington, 1985—. Recipient Sustained Superior Performance award Naval Civilian Personnel Command, 1982, Spl. Achievement award, 1983; Sustained Superior Performance award Naval Surface Weapons Ctr., 1985; named to Outstanding Young Women Am., U.S. Jaycees, 1983. Mem. Federally Employed Women (chpt. pres. 1977-78, 79, registration chairperson nat. tng. program 1980), NOW. Democrat. Episcopalian. Avocations: geology; cats; salt-water fishing. Office: Naval Sea Systems Command FWPM Washington DC 22362

HAMEED, BETTE SAHIRAH, construction company executive; b. Chester, Pa., Jan. 4, 1947; d. Percy Cornelius and Mary (Wells) Johnson; m. Malachi Suluki Hameed, Mar. 29, 1977; children—Pharon Bashir and Malakeyah. B.S. in Edn., Cheyney U., Pa., 1968. Cert. tchr., Pa. Supr. State Farm Ins. Co., Santa Ana, Calif., 1970-72; tchr. Chester Upland Sch. Dist., Pa., 1978-79; distbr. Amway Corp., Ada, Mich., 1985—; v.p. Key-Ron Constrn. Co., Inc., Augusta, Ga., 1983—; asst. chmn. Am. Muslim Com. to Purchase 100,000 Commodities Plus, 1984-85. Mem. Nat. Assn. Female Execs. Democrat. Muslim. Avocations: tennis. Home: 1711 C Champagne Ave Augusta GA 30909

HAMEISTER, LAVON LOUETTA, social worker; b. Blairstown, Iowa, Nov. 27, 1922; d. George Frederick and Bertha (Anderson) Hameister; B.A., U. Ia., 1944; postgrad. N.Y. Sch. Social Work, Columbia, 1945-46, U. Minn. Sch. Social Work, summer 1952; M.A., U. Chgo., 1959. Child welfare practitioner Fayette County Dept. Social Welfare, West Union, Iowa, 1946-56; dist. cons. services in child welfare and pub. assistance Ia. Dept. Social Services, Des Moines, 1956-58, dist. field rep., 1959-64, regional supr., 1964-65, supr., specialist supervision, adminstrn, Bur. Staff Devel., 1965-66, chief Bur. Staff Devel., 1966-68, chief div. staff devel. and tng., 1968-73, asst. dir. Office Staff Devel. and Tng., 1973-78, continuing edn. mgr., 1978—; also co-mgr. farm. Active in drive to remodel, enlarge Oelwein (Iowa) Mercy Hosp., 1952. Mem. Bus. and Profl. Women's Club (chpt. sec. 1950-52), Am. Assn. U. Women, Nat. Assn. Social Workers (chpt. sec.-elect 1958-59), Am. Pub. Welfare Assn., Ia. Welfare Assn. Home: 1800 Grand Ave West Des Moines IA 50265 Office: Hoover State Office Bldg Des Moines IA 50309

HAMEL, JANE SEEGER, national seminar corporation executive; b. Winona, Minn., June 12, 1939; d. John Dunning and Dorothea Luse (Seeger) Tearse; m. Arthur Bernard Hamel, Jan. 30, 1965; children—John, James. B.S., Northwestern U., 1961. Tchr. kindergarten Jefferson Union Sch. Dist., Sunnyvale, Calif., 1961-62; tchr. kindergarten S. San Francisco Unified Sch. Dist., 1962-66; owner Sahara Motel & Pizza Inn, Modesto, Calif., 1966-72, Rumah Corp., San Jose, Calif., 1972—; owner, corp. officer Business Mktg. Corp., San Jose, Calif., 1975-82, pres., 1982—; sec., dir. Nat. Business-Fin. Corp., San Jose, 1980—, Nationwide Business Consultants, Inc., San Jose, 1981—, Arthur Hamel Bus. Brokers, Inc., San Jose, 1982—, Nat. Business Mktg. Corp., San Jose, 1981—. Editor: The Institute Business Newsletter, 1976-79; assoc. editor Arthur Hamel Business Report, 1980—. Bd. dirs., chmn. health welfare Foothill Family Faculty Club, Saratoga, Calif., 1979-80. Mem. Inst. Cert. Bus. Counselors (past sec.). Republican. Episcopalian. Office: Business Mktg Corp 1777 Saratoga Ave Suite 107 San Jose CA 95129

HAMEL, JUDITH ANNE, social worker; b. Boston, Sept. 10, 1954; d. Harvey Harding and Myrtle Elaine (Goldberg) H.; B.Social Work, N. Tex. State U., Denton, 1977; m. Jeffrey A. Kaufman, Sept. 5, 1982. From psychiat. counseling asst. to intensive psychiat. counselor Brookhaven Med. Center, Dallas, 1977-79; social worker, then dir. rehab. services Avodah Work Center, Dallas, 1979-82; child protective services worker Dallas County Child Welfare, Tex. Dept. Human Services, 1983-86. Mem. Nat. Assn. Social Workers, Assn. Jewish Vocat. Service Profls., Sigma Alpha Mu. Jewish. Club: B'nai B'rith (life). Home: 3815 Furneaux Carrollton TX 75007

HAMEL, VERONICA, actress; b. Phila., Nov. 20. Formerly model; first stage role The Big Knife, N.Y.C., other state appearances in Cactus Flower, The Miracle Worker; TV series, Hill Street Blues, 1981—; TV miniseries, Kane and Abel, 1985, 79 Park Avenue, 1977; movies-for-TV: The Gathering, The Gathering II, Sessions, 1983; films: Beyond the Poseidon Adventure, 1979, When Time Ran Out, 1980. Address: care Agy for the Performing Arts Inc 9000 Sunset Blvd Suite 1200 Los Angeles CA 90069*

HAMEL, VICKI OTTO, management analyst; b. Chgo., May 25, 1947; d. Earle W. and Paula Mae (Holman) Otto; m. Francis H. Hamel, July 7, 1969. Student Western Ill. U., 1965-66, Berlitz Sch. Langs., 1967, U. N.C.-Wilmington, 1984-85, Brunswick Tech. Coll., N.C., 1986. Office mgr. Admiral Coated Products, Inc., Skokie, Ill., 1966-69; paralegal law firm, Southport, N.C., 1972-74; credit mgr. Augusta Furniture Co., Staunton, Va., 1976-78; trust/tax clk. Franklin-Lamoille Bank, St. Albans, Vt., 1978-80; customs teller U.S. Customs Service, St. Albans, 1980-82; mgmt. analyst Dept. Army, Mil. Ocean Terminal, Southport, 1982—, fed. women's program mgr., 1983—. Mem. Boiling Spring Lakes Planning Bd., 1985—. Named Woman of Yr., Southport Jr. Women's Club, 1975; profl. awards U.S. Govt. Mem. Gen. Fedn. Women's Clubs, N.C. Fedn. Women's Clubs (dist. v.p. 1974-75), Am. Bus. Women's Assn., Nat. Assn. Female Execs. Republican. Roman Catholic. Clubs: Southport Jr. Women's (pres. 1975), Southport Women's (pub. affairs dept. 1984). Home: 257 Alcor Ln Boiling Spring Lakes Southport NC 28461 Office: Mil Ocean Terminal/Sunny Point Southport NC 28461

HAMELIN, DIANE MARIE, lawyer; b. Escanaba, Mich., Nov. 30, 1954; d. Duane Richard and Janet Margaret (Rice) Hamelin. B.B.A., U. Mich., 1977; J.D. cum laude, Thomas M. Cooley Law Sch., Lansing, Mich., 1982. Bar: Mich. 1983, Tex. 1984; C.P.A., Mich., Tex. Auditor, Ernst & Whinney, Lansing, 1977-79; securities examiner Corp. and Securities Bur., State of Mich., Lansing, 1980-82; assoc. gen. counsel Hall Fin. Group, Dallas, 1982—. Mem. Big Bros./Big Sisters. Fed. Bar Found. Edward H. Rakow scholar, 1981. Mem. Am. Inst. C.P.A.s, Tex. Soc. C.P.A.s, ABA, Mich. Bar Assn., Roman Catholic. Home: 6200 Swiss Ave Unit C Dallas TX 75214 Office: Hall Fin Group 10100 N Central Expressway Dallas TX 75231

HAMELINK, CRYSTAL MARY, human resources executive; b. Little Falls, N.Y., Dec. 6, 1947; d. Harold J. and Marian Louise (Hood) Settle; m. Drew R. Hamelink, Aug. 4, 1973; children—Craig A., Michael M. B.A., Wagner Coll., 1969; M.P.A., SUNY-Albany, 1984. Dir. employee advancement program N.Y. State Dept. Civil Service, Albany, 1984—. Treas., emergency med. technician Ballston Lake Emergency Squad, Ballston Lake, N.Y., 1979—. Mem. Internat. Personnel Mgmt. Assn., Pi Alpha Alpha. Unitarian. Home: 122 Westside Dr Ballston Lake NY 12019 Office: NY State Dept Civil Service Bldg 1 State Office Bldg Campus Albany NY 12239

HAMELMAN, HELAINE NICKUM, oil company executive; b. Akron, Ohio, May 10, 1939; d. Donatius John and Helen Mae (Smith) Nickum; m. William Eugen Hamelman, Nov. 14, 1969; stepchildren—Eugene Andreas, Christian Martin. B.B.A., U. Tex., 1961. Sec., First State Bank, Port Lavaca, 1961-62; sec. Atlantic Richfield, Dallas, 1962-73, supr. manuals adminstrn., 1973-82, dir. office services, 1982-86, mgr. office services, 1986—. Mem. citizens adv. council Am. Inst. Cancer Research, Washington, 1984—. Mem. Assn. Systems Mgmt., Internat. Word Processing Assn. (pres. 1980-81), Assn. Records Mgrs. and Adminstrs., Assn. Image and info. Mgmt., Adminstrv. Mgmt. Soc., AAUW, Nat. Assn. Female Execs. Avocations: travel; collecting military artifacts. Dallas TX Office: Atlantic Richfield Co PO Box 2819 Dallas TX 75221

HAMER, JEANNE HUNTINGTON, soprano, educator; b. Lovell, Wyo., Mar. 1, 1933; d. Edward Olney and Francine M. (Clavier) Huntington; Mus.B. with honors, U. Wyo., 1955, postgrad., 1976-82, M.A. with honors, 1984; postgrad. U. Denver, 1976; m. Roger F. Hamer, Aug. 19, 1955; children—Michael Edward, Kathryn Louise. Grad. teaching asst. U. Wyo., 1955-56; pvt. vocal tchr., Billings, Mont., 1957-58, Miles City, Mont., 1958-59, Grand Rapids, Minn., 1959-61, Torrington, Wyo., 1962—; instr. music Eastern Wyo. Coll., 1968—, chmn. dept. music, 1978—; lead roles in operas, including: The Medium, The Telephone, Cavalleria Rusticana, I Pagliacci, Baby Doe; soloist with Billings (Mont.) Symphony, Casper (Wyo.) Symphony, Scottsbluff (Nebr.) Symphony, Nebr. Panhandle Symphony, U. Wyo. Symphony; soprano Barta Trio, 1972—; adjudicator for music festivals, Wyo., Mont., Nebr.; organist, choir dir. All Saints Episcopal Ch., Torrington, 1974-82; dir. Torrington Community Chorus, 1975—. Mem. Nat. Assn. Tchrs. Singing (gov. Wyo.), Am. Choral Dirs. Assn., Music Educators Nat. Conf. Episcopalian.

Clubs: PEO, Order Eastern Star. Home: 515 E 23 Ave Torrington WY 82240 Office: 3200 W C St Torrington WY 82240

HAMER, SYLVIA JANE, ballet educator; b. Ann Arbor, Mich., July 9, 1900; d. Melvin Russel and Myrtle D. (Hilliker) Cole; m. Hazell King, Apr. 16, 1918; 1 child, Jay B.; m. Ellsworth Hamer (dec.). Student St. Mary's Abbey, Mills Hill, Eng.; Fellow Degree, Cacchitti Soc., London, 1972. Tchr. and trainer Sylvia Studio, Ann Arbor, 1934—. Founder, bd. dirs. Ann Arbor Civic Ballet, 1956—. Office: Ann Arbor Civic Ballet 525 E Liberty St Ann Arbor MI 48108

HAMID, LOUISE KATHERINE, clubwoman; b. Manchester, Conn., Jan. 18, 1951; d. Michael Alexander and Loretta Ruth (White) Kasevich; student U. Conn., 1969-71, 83—; m. Rashid Hamid, Aug. 14, 1971; children—Sophia Ann, Nadia Rashid. Mem. Greater Vernon Jaycee Wives, 1975-79, archivist, 1976-77, pres., 1977-79, chmn. bd. dirs., 1979-81; mem. Tolland County Spl. Olympics Track and Field Com., 1979—; leader Conn. Valley council Girl Scouts U.S.A., 1974, 80—; mem. Hockanum Valley Dept. Aging, 1978-79; mem. Maple Street Sch. PTO, 1980—, pres., 1980-82; mem. PTO Council, Vernon, 1982—, chmn., 1985. Democrat. Home: 113 Regan Rd Vernon CT 06066

HAMILTON, ANN STANLEY, marketing executive; b. Phila., Mar. 25, 1960; d. Russell and Helen Marcia (Brown) H. B.A. in Psychology, Temple U., 1982. Customer service rep. Continental Bank, Phila., 1977-82; mgr. pub. div. Hay Assocs., Phila., 1983-84; pres. Hamilton Assocs. mktg. cons., Phila., 1985—. Rep. Senatorial Inner Circle, Washington, 1986. Mem. Alliance Française de Philadelphie, Christian Endeavor, Nat. Assn. Female Execs. Republican. Presbyterian. Avocations: travel; reading; foreign cultures and languages.

HAMILTON, BARBARA, human services director; b. Hartford, Conn., Jan. 3, 1943; d. Harry and Rose Ida (Cohen) Karpman; m. Benjamin Theodore Sporn, Sept. 4, 1960 (div. 1967); children—Mindy Rebecca Sporn, Sarah Ann Sporn. B.A., Eckerd Coll., 1983; M.A., Norwich U., Vt., 1985. Asst. publicity mgr. Estee Lauder Inc., N.Y.C., 1972-74; owner, ptnr. Strongstarr Inc., N.Y.C., 1975-77; owner Barbara Hamilton Cons. Services, N.Y.C., 1977-81; co-founder The Life Ctr., Tampa, 1981-83; co-founder, co-dir. Project Rainbow, St. Petersburg, Fla., 1983—; cons., lectr. in field. Recipient Service to Mankind awards Sertoma Club, 1984-85. Mem. Assn. Care Children's Health, Forum Death Edn. and Counseling, Internat. Imagery Assn., Nat. Soc. Fund Raising Execs., Assn. Humanistic Psychology. Avocations: meditation. Home: PO Box 40261 Saint Petersburg FL 33743 Office: Project Rainbow Inc PO Box 47517 Saint Petersburg FL 33743

HAMILTON, BETTY JANE, maid service company executive; b. McAlester, Okla., May 12, 1924; d. William Oscar and Florence (Selby) Swales; m. Jess F. Hamilton, Oct. 16, 1953 (div. 1971); children—Russell (dec.), Paul. Pres. Maid-A-Day, Inc., San Antonio, 1967—. Club: Altrusa of San Antonio (pres. 1984-85). Avocations: bridge; reading; Bible study. Home: 3523 Well Springs Dr San Antonio TX 78230 Office: Maid-A-Day Inc 3523 Well Springs Dr San Antonio TX 78230

HAMILTON, BEVERLY LANNQUIST, technology company executive; b. Roxbury, Mass., Oct. 19, 1946; d. Arthur and Nancy L. B.A. cum laude, U. Mich., 1968; postgrad., Grad. Sch. Bus., NYU, 1969-70. Asst. trust officer Mfrs. Hanover, N.Y.C., 1970-72; prin. Auerbach, Pollak & Richardson, N.Y.C., 1972-75; v.p. Morgan Stanley & Co., N.Y.C., 1975-80, United Technologies, Hartford, Conn., 1980—; dir. Conn. Natural Gas Co. Trustee Hartford Coll. for Women, 1981—; bd. dirs. Inst. for Living, 1979-80. Mem. Fin. Women's Assn. Clubs: Hartford, Econ. N.Y. Office: United Technologies Main St Hartford CT 06101

HAMILTON, CAROLINE ALICE (CARRIE), real estate broker; b. Columbus, Ohio, Jan. 13, 1928; d. Herbert Samuel and Mabel Ione (Tussing) Erwin; m. Mark Justin Hamilton, July 1, 1947; children—Kimberly Hamilton Turner, Karolyn Hamilton Landon, Mark Jay. Grad. Realtor's Inst., 1979. Cert. residential specialist. Real estate salesman Barstow Realty Co. (Calif.), 1966-68, real estate broker, 1968-76; owner, broker Hamilton Realty Better Homes and Gardens, Barstow, 1976—. Pres. Rep. Women's Club, Barstow, 1966-67; chmn. United Fund, Barstow, 1978; 2d v.p. Barstow Devel. Corp., 1983. Mem. Barstow Bd. Realtors (dir. 1970-77, 77—, pres. 1970, 80), Calif. Assn. Realtors (dir. 1969-71, 79-80), Barstow C. of C. (dir. 1976—, chmn. legis. com. 1981—, pres. 1980). Republican. Home: 109 College Ct Barstow CA 92311 Office: Hamilton Realty Better Homes & Gardens 225 Barstow Rd Barstow CA 92311

HAMILTON, DAGMAR STRANDBERG, lawyer, educator; b. Phila., Jan. 10, 1932; d. Eric Wilhelm and Anna Elizabeth (Sjöström) Strandberg; A.B., Swarthmore Coll., 1953; J.D., U. Chgo. Law Sch., 1956; J.D., Am. U., 1961; m. Robert W. Hamilton, June 26, 1953; children—Eric Clark, Robert Andrew Hale, Meredith Hope. Admitted to Tex. bar, 1972; atty., civil rights div. U.S. Dept. Justice, Washington, 1965-66; asst. instr. govt. U. Tex.-Austin, 1966-71; lectr. Law Sch. U. Ariz., Tucson, 1971-72; editor, researcher Assoc. Justice William O. Douglas, U.S. Supreme Ct., 1962-73, 75-76; editor, research Douglas autobiography Random House Co., 1972-73; staff counsel Judiciary Com., U.S. Ho. of Reps., 1973-74; asst. prof. L.B. Johnson Sch. Pub. Affairs, U. Tex., Austin, 1974-77, assoc. prof., 1977-83, prof., assoc. dean, 1983—; vis. prof. Washington U. Law Sch., St. Louis, Spring 1982. Mem. steering com. Westlake Neighborhood Assn.; bd. dirs. ACLU. Mem. So., Am. polit. sci. assns., Tex. Bar Assn., Kappa Beta Phi (hon.), Phi Kappa Phi (hon.). Democrat. Quaker. Contbr. to various publs. Home: 403 Allegro Ln Austin TX 78746 Office: LBJ Sch Pub Affairs U Tex Austin TX 78712

HAMILTON, DEBORAH A., broadcast journalist, public relations consultant; b. Bryn Mawr, Pa., May 7, 1949; d. Perrin C. and Bette Jane H.; m. James K. Brengle, June 6, 1970; 1 son, Stephen Carpenter, Student Mary Baldwin Coll., Staunton, Va., 1967-69; B.S. in Polit. Sci., U. Santa Clara (Calif.), 1972. Talk radio producer Sta. KQED-FM, San Francisco, 1975; news reporter Nat. Pub. Radio, San Francisco, 1975-76, reporter, documentary producer, Washington, 1976-78; dir. pub. affairs and relations, producer, host Inside Phila., Stas. WPEN-AM and WMGK-FM, Phila., 1979-85; pres. Performance Plus, Haverford, Pa., 1982—. Bd. mgrs., chmn. pub. relations Jr. League Phila., 1979-81. Mem. Pub. Relations Soc. Am., Am. Women Radio and TV (bd. dirs. Phila. chpt. 1984, treas. 1985), Women in Communications, Nat. Soc. Colonial Dames, Sigma Delta Chi. Office: Performance Plus Box 65 Haverford PA 19041

HAMILTON, DEBORAH PRECHTEL, insurance company executive; b. Denver, Apr. 1, 1953; d. William Richard and Joyce (Covey) Prechtel; m. Gilbert D. Smith, Jan. 29, 1977 (div. July 1981); 1 son, Aaron Davis; m. James L. Hamilton, Jr. B.A., U. Colo., 1975. Cert. ins. counselor. Legal asst. Robert S. Berger, Denver, 1975-76; paralegal asst. Toedte & Sandblom, Denver, 1976-77; agt. Harry A. Lowe Agy., Ouray, Colo., 1978-81; property/casualty mgr. Ins. Design and Mktg., Boulder, Colo., 1982-83; personal and comml. lines mgr., Integrated Ins. Services, Inc., Denver, 1983—. Emergency med. technician Emergency Med. Services Ouray County, Ouray, Colo., 1980-81, Mountain Rescue Team, Ouray County, 1980-81. Mem. Profl. Ins. Agts., Boulder County Ins. Women. Democrat. Episcopalian. Home: 5550 W 80th Pl Unit 20 Arvada CO 80003 Office: J H Silversmith Inc 825 E Speer Blvd Denver CO 80218

HAMILTON, DOROTHY ELLEN, chemistry educator, researcher; b. Worcester, Mass., Aug. 31, 1957; d. Richard Paul and Irene Stella (Sirard) H. B.S. with distinction, Worcester Poly. Inst., 1979; Ph.D., U. Ill., 1985. Lectr. Smith Coll., Northampton, Mass., 1983-85, asst. prof. chemistry, 1985—. GTE focus grantee Smith Coll., 1984. Mem. Am. Chem. Soc., Sigma Xi, Phi Lambda Upsilon (sec. local chpt. 1978-79). Avocations: cooking; tennis; golf; racquetball. Office: Smith Coll Clark Sci Ctr Northampton MA 01063

HAMILTON, ELLEN MAE, lawyer; b. N.Y.C., Sept. 8, 1951; d. William Roland and Anita (Dyck) H.; m. Michael Arle Baugh, Sept. 18, 1976; 1 son, Michael Hamilton Baugh. B.A., Colo. Women's Coll., 1973; J.D., U. Tulsa, 1976. Bar: Tex. 1983, La. 1978, Okla. 1976. Assoc., Houston & Klein, Tulsa, 1976-78, Broadhurst, Brook, Mangham, Hardy & Reed, Lafayette, La., 1978-83, Rea & Archer, Houston, 1983—; dir. Acadiana Legal Services, Inc., Lafayette, 1982-83. Mem. Acadiana Women's Polit. Caucus, 1982-83; sec. Talent Bank, Lafayette, 1982-83. Mem. ABA, Tex. Bar Assn., Houston Bar Assn. (real estate sect.). Republican. Episcopalian. Home: 13411 Pebblebrook Dr Houston TX 77079 Office: Rea & Archer 11767 Katy Freeway Suite 200 Houston TX 77079

HAMILTON, JEAN CONSTANCE, judge; b. St. Louis, Nov. 12, 1945; d. Aubrey Bertrand and Rosemary (Crocker) H. A.B., Wellesley Coll., 1968; J.D., Washington U., St. Louis, 1971; LL.M., Yale U., 1982. Bar: Mo. 1971. Atty. Dept. of Justice, Washington, 1971-73, asst. U.S. atty., St. Louis, 1973-78; atty. Southwestern Bell Telephone Co., St. Louis, 1978-81; judge 22d Jud. Circuit, State of Mo., St. Louis, 1982—. Mem. ABA, Bar Assn. Met. St. Louis, Women Lawyers Assn. Met. St. Louis, Nat. Assn. Women Judges. Episcopalian. Office: 22d Judicial Circuit of Missouri 10 N Tucker Blvd Saint Louis MO 63101

HAMILTON, JOYCE KAY, marketing company executive; b. Indpls., Mar. 7, 1950; d. John Samuel and Agnes June (Stribling) McPheeters; m. Gary Roger Hamilton, Aug. 30, 1975 (div. 1981). B.S., U. Tex., 1983. Tax payer asst. IRS, Dallas, 1979-80; tech. asst. Dallas Dept. Edn., 1980-81 exec. adminstv. asst. Mass. Mutual, Dallas, 1981-82; v.p. Excalibur Mktg., 1983—. Served with USAF, 1974-77. Republican. Club: Toastmistress. Home: 2208 Tolosa St Dallas TX 75228 Office: Excalibur Mktg 9234 Arbor Trail Dallas TX 75243

HAMILTON, KATHLEEN O'CONNEL, banker; b. St. Louis, Aug. 11, 1940; d. Daniel Joseph and Helen (Galvin) O'Connell; m. Alan Andrew Hamilton, Nov. 17, 1962; children—Daniel O'Connell, Holly Tierney, Andrew Ashton. B.A. magna cum laude, Maryville Coll., St. Louis, 1962; M.A., Washington U., St. Louis, 1974. Cert. secondary tchr. Mo.; lic. real Estate agt. Instr. Trinity Coll., Washington, 1963, 64; secondary tchr. Acad. Sacred Heart, St. Louis, 1965-68; real estate agent Feinberg Real Estate Co., St. Louis, 1970-80; instr. St. Louis Community Colls., 1974-78; sr. v.p., dir., co-founder Central West End Savs. Bank, St. Louis, 1979—, also dir. Coauthor: History of City House-1827 to 1968; book reviewer, 1968-70; contbr. articles to profl. jours., local newspaper. Chmn. Arts & Humanities Commission, City St. Louis City Hall, 1983-84; bd. dirs. Villa Duchesne, City House Alumnae, Central West End Assn.; bd. dirs. Skinner De Baliviere Community Council, treas. 1981—. Recipient Profl. Achievement award, Maryville Coll., 1983. Mem. Women in Communications, Women's Info. Network. Democrat. Roman Catholic. Home: 6232 McPherson Saint Louis MO 63130 Office: Central West End Savings Loan 415 DeBaliviere Saint Louis MO 63112

HAMILTON, LAURA ANN, social worker; b. Cordele, Ga., Nov. 16, 1939; d. Herbert Williams and Janie LaVerne (Lumpkin) Hamilton; student Valdosta State Coll., 1957-58; B.S., Fla. State U., 1961, M.S.W., 1965; postgrad. U. Ga., 1961-62, U. Chgo., summer 1967, W. Ga. Coll., 1969, Ga. State U., 1970; postgrad. U. Tex.-Arlington, 1985—. Vis. tchr. Crisp County Schs., Cordele, 1961-63; social service worker Social Service Dept., Milledgeville (Ga.) State Hosp., 1963; med. social worker Crippled Children's Service, Birmingham, Ala., 1964; psychiat. social worker Fla. State Hosp., Chattahoochee, 1965, Milledgeville State Hosp., 1965-66; cons. for social work projects ESEA Title I, Ga. Dept. Edn., Atlanta, 1966-68, ESEA Title III, 1968-71; cons. program evaluations and audits Robert Davis Assos., Inc., Atlanta, 1971-72; chief Div. Planning, Evaluation, Monitoring and Analysis, S.C. Dept. Social Services, Columbia, 1973-76; regional dir. social services Regions 01 and 02, Tex. Dept. Public Welfare, Lubbock, 1976-77; partner Kaye Fleming Boutique and Bridal Corner, Ft. Worth, 1978-83; pvt. practice social work, Ft. Worth, Tex., 1978—; dir. Tarrant County Dept. Human Services, Ft. Worth, 1985—; field supr. Kirschner Assos., Inc., Albuquerque, 1972, 73; evaluator for edn. professions devel. act project Waycross (Ga.) City Schs., 1972, W. Ga. Ednl. Service Center, Carrollton, 1972; program auditor Clarke County Schs., Atlanta, 1972; instr. Human Resource Center, U. Tex., Arlington, 1977-79; lectr. in field. Mem. Acad. Cert. Social Workers, Am. Pub. Welfare Assn., Am. Soc. Pub. Adminstrn., Nat. Assn. Social Workers. Address: 1611 Trailridge Dr Arlington TX 76012

HAMILTON, LINDA KAY, publishing company executive; b. Waukegan, Ill., May 13, 1945; d. Lloyd Henry and Vida May (Harms) Fruth; B.A., Mich. State U., 1966; A.M. in Library Sci., U. Mich., 1968; M.B.A., Mich. State U., 1972; m. William Digby Hamilton, Nov. 5, 1966 (div. Dec. 1983); 1 dau., Arwen Elizabeth. Sect. head Mich. State U. Libraries, 1969-73; head catalog dept. Wayne State U. Libraries, Detroit, 1973-75, network coordinator, 1975-76, asst. dir. Mich. Library Consortium, 1976-77; mgr. bibliographic services Univ. Microfilms Internat., Ann Arbor, 1977-79, mgr. collections ops., 1979-82; v.p. acad. micropublishing Research Publs. Inc., Woodbridge, Conn., 1982-83, v.p. mktg., 1984—; dir. Research Publs., Woodbridge, Conn. Mem. Bethany Democratic Town Council. Mem. Friends of Bethany Library Assn. (treas. 1983—), ALA. Editor: MLA Intellectual Freedom Newsletter, 1974-75, Cort Cat News, 1974-77. Office: 12 Lunar Dr Woodbridge Ct 06525

HAMILTON, LISA JANE, advertising executive; b. Battle Creek, Mich., Nov. 29, 1953; d. Robert Philip and Beverly Gail (Pryor) Hamilton. B.A. in Social Sci., Mich. State U., 1975; postgrad. in advt. and mktg., Northwestern U., 1977. Account exec. J. Walter Thompson Co., Chgo., 1976-79, Henderson Advt., Greenville, S.C., 1979-80; v.p., account supr. McDonald & Little, Atlanta, 1980-83, Burton Campbell, Inc., Atlanta, 1984—. Recipient Young Turk award Ad Week, 1983. Office: Burton Campbell Inc 100 Colony Sq Atlanta GA 30361

HAMILTON, LISA TOMALYNN, lawyer; b. Columbia City, Ind., Apr. 9, 1958; d. Thomas G. and L. Anne (Biddle) Hamilton. B.A., Oberlin Coll., 1979; J.D. cum laude, Ind. U., 1982. Bar: Ind. 1982, U.S. Dist. Ct. (so. dist.) Ind. 1982, U.S. Dist. Ct. (no. dist.) Ind. 1983; U.S. Ct. Appeals (7th cir.) 1985, U.S. Supreme Ct. 1985. Jud. clk. to justice Ind. Ct. Appeals, Indpls., 1982-83; jud. clk. U.S. Dist. Ct., Ft. Wayne, Ind., 1983-85; assoc. Baker & Daniels & Shoaff, Ft. Wayne, 1985—. Mem. ABA, Allen County Bar Assn., 7th Cir. Bar Assn., Ind. Bar Assn. Republican.

HAMILTON, MARIAN ELOISE, city official; b. Salt Lake City, Mar. 21, 1931; d. Frederic William and Kathryn Eloise (Core) Wrathall; m. Stanley Keith Hamilton, Feb. 2, 1951 (dec. 1983); children—Edmond Scott, Perri Collette, Deena Kathryn. Student U. Utah, 1949-51, U. Calif.-Santa Barbara, 1951-52, U. Mont., 1952-53. Cert. pub. housing mgr. Field exec. Cross Timbers Girl Scouts, Denton, Tex., 1971-76; camp dir. Camp Kadohadacho, Pottsboro, Tex., 1971-75; acting dir. Wesley Pre-Sch., Denton, 1976-78; field dir. 1st Tex. Council, Campfire, Ft. Worth, 1979-81; housing mgr. Denton Housing Authority, 1981—; cons. on shared housing Tex. Agy. on Aging, Austin, 1984—; area rep. City of Denton Land Use Com., 1986—. Editor Heritage Highlights, 1981—. Mem. Nat. Assn. Housing and Redevel. Ofcls., Am. Assn. Homes for Aging, Nat. Council on Aging, Nat. Trust for Hist. Preservation, Nat. Assn. Female Execs. Democrat. Avocations: writing; travel; reading. Home: 900 Sierra Dr Denton TX 76201 Office: Heritage Oaks Denton Housing Authority 2501 Bell Ave Denton TX 76201

HAMILTON, MAURINE SMITH, tour agent; b. Galesburg, Ill., Dec. 9, 1906; d. Arthur Edgar and Grace Mabelle (Brown) Smith; m. David A. Hamilton, Aug. 4, 1930 (dec. Mar. 1961); m. Glen L. Scanlan, Nov. 30, 1975 (div. Aug. 1981). B.S., Knox Coll., 1929. Tchr., Galesburg pub. schs., 1929-31; farm mgr., farm nr. Galesburg, 1961—; owner, mgr. M. Hamilton Happiness Tour Co., Galesburg, 1956—, also Chgo., Sarasota, Fla., Treas., Knox County Council for Older Americans, 1986; mem. Republican Presdl. Task Force, 1982-86; life mem. Rep. Nat. Com.; past v.p. Knox Lombard Fifty Year Club, 1986. Named to Gallery of Ageless Achievers, Western Ill. Area Agy. on Aging, 1986. Mem. Bus. and Profl. Women, DAR (past sec., registrar), Children Am. Revolution (organizer chpt.), Newcomer Greeting Soc. (organizer), Pi Beta Phi. Congregationalist. Clubs: Altrusa, Oliver Wendell Literary. Home: 723 Warren St Galesburg IL 61401

HAMILTON, MILDRED, social services agency executive; b. Wilkes-Barre, Pa., Oct. 19, 1920; s. Maurice Williams and Rose (Bailine) Hamilton; m. Robert Hamilton, Apr. 26, 1946; children—Robert, Miriam, Rachel, B.A., U. Mich., 1941; M.S., Smith Coll., 1943. Social worker, marriage counselor. Psychiat. social worker ARC, 1943-46; caseworker Family Service, Youngstown, Ohio, 1947-48, caseworker, 1960-61, exec. dir., 1972—; asst. dir. Child Service Assn., Newark, 1961-72. Mem. profl. adv. com. Union County Mental Health, Elizabeth, N.J., 1982—. Mem. Internat. Platform Assn., Am. Assn. Marital and Family Therapy. Home: 186 Linden Ave Springfield NJ 07081 Office: Jewish Family Service Assn 500 Westfield Ave Elizabeth NJ 07208

HAMILTON, PAULA HAYDEN, library director; b. Bklyn., Aug. 11, 1946; d. Richard Alfred and Anne Frances (Keating) Hayden; m. Robert Earl Hamilton, Apr. 22, 1972; children—Hayden David, Michael Robert. Student Gonzaga U.-Florence, Italy, 1966-67; B.A., San Francisco Coll. for Women, 1968; M.L.S., U. Wis.-Madison, 1969. Circulation asst. head Northwestern U., Evanston, Ill., 1969-71, reference librarian newspaper and microfilm, 1971-72; reference and cataloging librarian U. Sci. and Tech., Kimasi, Ghana, 1972-73; br. librarian Chgo. Pub. Library, 1973-75; dir. Clackamas County Library, Oregon City, Oreg., 1975-76; dir. Marylhurst Coll. Library, (Oreg.), 1977—, dir. librarian's continuing edn. program Marylhurst Coll., 1980—, instr., 1982—; cons. USIS, Kumasi, 1972-73, Don Barney & Assos., Portland, Oreg., 1983. Campaigner various Democratic campaigns, 1972; eucharistic minister St. Clare Roman Catholic Ch., 1980, co-chmn. parish family life. Mem. ALA, NW Assn. Pvt. Coll. and Univ. Libraries (pres. 1982-83), Oreg. Library Assn. (com. 1980-83), Wash. Library Assn. (joint conf. com. 1985-87), Assn. Coll. and Research Libraries (Oreg. adv. bd. 1983-85), Library and Media Groups of Oreg. Home: 7110 SW Burlingame Ave Portland OR 97219 Office: Shoen Library Marylhurst Coll Marylhurst OR 97036

HAMILTON, RHODA LILLIAN ROSEN, educator; b. Chgo., May 8, 1915; d. Reinhold August and Olga (Peterson) Rosen; grad. Moser Coll., Chgo., 1932-33; B.S. in Edn., U. Wis., 1953, postgrad., 1976; M.A.T., Rollins Coll., 1967; postgrad. Ohio State U., 1959-60; postgrad. in clin. psychology Mich. State U., 1971, 76; postgrad. Yale U., 1972, Loma Linda U., 1972; postgrad. in computer mgmt. systems U. Okla., 1976; postgrad. in edn. U. Calif., Berkeley, 1980; m. Douglas Edward Hamilton, Jan. 23, 1936 (div. Feb. 1952); children—Perry Douglas, John Richard. Exec. sec. to pres. Ansul Chem. Co., Marinette, Wis., 1934-36; personnel counselor Burneice Larson's Med. Bur., Chgo., 1954-56 adminstrv. asst. to Ernst C. Schmidt, Lake Geneva, Wis., 1956-58; asso. prof. fin. aid Ohio State U., 1958-60; tchr. English to speakers of other langs., Istanbul, Turkey, 1960-65; counselor Groveland (Fla.) High Sch., 1965-68; guidance counselor and psychol. cons. early childhood edn. Dept. Def. Overseas Dependents Sch., Okinawa, 1968-85; pres. Hamilton Assocs., Inc., Groveland, Fla., 1985—; co-owner plumbing, heating bus., Marinette, 1943-49; journalist Rockford (Ill.) Morning Star, 1956-58, Istanbul AP, 1960. Vol. instr. U.S. citizenship classes, Okinawa, 1971-72. Mem. NEA, Okinawa Educators, Overseas Edn. Assn., Am. Personnel and Guidance Assn., Nat. Vocat. Guidance Assn., Assn. Measurement and Eval. in Guidance, Am. Fedn. Govt. Employees, Nat. Council Measurement in Edn., Am. Sch. Counselor Assn., Phi Delta Gamma. Episcopalian. Clubs: Order Eastern Star (organist Shuri chpt. 1); Ikebana Internat. Author poetry on Middle East, 1959-64; Career Awareness, 1978. Home and office: 255 E Waldo St Groveland FL 32736

HAMILTON, SHIRLEY SIEKMANN, arts administrator; b. South Bend, Ind., Aug. 31, 1928; d. George F. and Clarice B. (Rapp) Burdick; student St. Mary's Coll., 1946-47; B.A., DePauw U., 1950; postgrad. Ind. U., South Bend, 1951; m. Max R. Siekmann, June 23, 1951; children—Sheryl, Pamela, David; m. Keith L. Hamilton, Sept. 3, 1983. Tchr. public schs., St. Joseph County, Ind., 1950-51, Greencastle, Ind., 1951-52, Ft. Lauderdale, Fla., 1952-53; exec. dir. Michiana Arts and Scis. Council, Inc., South Bend, Ind., 1973-86; tech. asst. cons., adv. panelist Ind. Arts Commn.; treas. Ind. Alliance Arts Councils, 1982. Mem. St. Joseph County Parks and Recreation Bd., 1971-81; pres. Mental Health Assn. of St. Joseph County, 1972; bd. dirs. Century Center Found., South Bend, 1974-84, St. Joseph County Scholarship Found., 1977-82; pres., bd. dirs. United Way St. Joseph County, 1981-82. Recipient Community Service award Michiana Arts and Scis. Council, 1968. Mem. Ind. Arts Advs., Ind. Alliance Arts Councils, Nat. Assn. Arts Councils. Club: Jr. League South Bend (pres.). Producer 13 week TV series: Inside Our Schools (Jr. League of South Bend Outstanding Community Service award 1964), 1963. Office: 120 S St Joseph St South Bend IN 46601

HAMILTON, SUSAN OWENS, lawyer; b. Birmingham, Ala., Aug. 7, 1951; d. William Lewis Owens and Vonnette (Wilson) O.; m. Raymond Hamilton, June 8, 1974. B.A. in Polit. Sci., Auburn U., 1973; J.D. (Dean's award), Samford U., Cumberland Law Sch., Birmingham, Ala., 1977. Bar: Ala. 1977, Fla. 1982, U.S. Supreme Ct. 1981, U.S. Dist. Ct. (mid. dist.) Fla. 1982. Claim agt. Louisville & Nashville R.R., Birmingham, 1977-78, atty. Louisville, 1978-80, claims atty., 1980-81, asst. gen. atty. (merger Louisville & Nashville, and Seaboard Coast Line R.R.) Seaboard System R.R., Jacksonville, Fla., 1981-83, asst. gen. solicitor, 1983-84, gen. mgr. freight claim services dept., 1984-85; asst. v.p. adminstrn. Chessie System R.R., 1985—; lectr. in field. Contbr. articles in field to publs. Mem. ABA, Jacksonville Bar Assn., Assn. Am. R.R.s Legal Affairs (chmn. subcom. freight claims 1983-84), Jacksonville Bus., Profl. Women (pres. 1984-85), Fla. Fedn. Bus. and Profl. Women (named outstanding young career woman 1982), Louisville Bus. and Profl. Women (named outstanding young career woman 1980), Ky. Fedn. Bus. and Profl. Women (named outstanding young career woman dist. V 1981). Democrat. United Methodist. Club: Uptown Civitan (dir. 1983-85). (Jacksonville). Home: 12154 Hidden Hills Dr Jacksonville FL 32225 Office: CSX Transp 500 Water St PO Box 40466 Jacksonville FL 32202

HAMILTON, VIRGINIA (MRS. ARNOLD ADOFF), author; b. Yellow Springs, Ohio, Mar. 12, 1936; d. Kenneth James and Etta Belle (Perry) H.; student Antioch Coll., 1952-55, Ohio State U., 1957-58, New Sch. Social Research; m. Arnold Adoff, Mar. 19, 1960; children—Leigh Hamilton, Jaime Levi. Recipient Ohioana Lit. award, 1969; Boston Globe/Horn Book award. Author: (children's novels) Zeely (Nancy Block Meml. award Downtown Community Sch. Awards Com.), 1967; The House of Dies Drear (Edgar Allan Poe award for best juvenile mystery, 1969), 1968; The Time-Ago Tales of Jahdu, 1969; Planet of Junior Brown, 1971 (John Newberry honor book award 1982), W.E.B. Dubois: A Biography, 1972; Time-Ago Lost: More Tales of Jahdu, 1973; M.C. Higgins the Great (John Newbery medal 1974, Nat. Book award 1975), 1974; Paul Robeson: The Life and Times of a Free Black Man, 1974; Arilla Sun Down, 1976, Justice and Her Brothers, 1978, Dustland, 1980, The Gathering, 1980; Sweet Whispers, Brother Rush, 1982 (Coretta Scott King award 1983), The Magical Adventures of Pretty Pearl, 1983; Willie Bea and the Time the Martians Landed, 1983; A Little Love, 1984, Junius Over Far, 1985, The People Could Fly: American Black Folk Tales, 1985; editor: Writings of W.E.B. Dubois, 1975. Office: care Harper & Row Jr Books 10 E 53d St New York NY 10022*

HAMILTON, VIRGINIA VAN DER VEER, historian; b. Kansas City, Mo., Sept. 7, 1921; d. McClellan and Dorothy (Rainold) Van der Veer; A.B., Birmingham (Ala.)-So. Coll., 1941, M.A. (Ford Found. Fund for Adult Edn. fellow), 1961; Ph.D., U. Ala., Tuscaloosa, 1968; m. Lowell S. Hamilton, Aug. 4, 1946; children—Carol, David. Staff writer AP, Washington, 1942-46, Birmingham News, 1948-50; asst. prof. history U. Montevallo (Ala.), 1951-55; asst. prof., asst. to pres. for pub. relations Birmingham-So. Coll., 1955-65; lectr. in history U. Ala., Birmingham, 1965-68, asst. prof., 1968-71, asso. prof., 1971-75, prof., 1975—. U. Ala. at Tuscaloosa faculty research grantee, 1969; U. Ala. at Birmingham faculty research grantee, 1973-74, 74-75. Mem. So., Am. hist. assns., Orgn. Am. Historians, Soc. Am. Historians, Am. Assn. State, local History, Ala. Assn. Historians, Ala. Hist. Soc., Oral History Assn. Author: Hugo Black: The Alabama Years, 1972; Alabama: A History, 1977; The Story of Alabama, 1980; Your Alabama, 1980; Seeing Historic Alabama, 1982; editor: Hugo Black and the Bill of Rights, 1978. Home: 3246 Overbrook Rd Birmingham AL 35213 Office: Dept History U Ala Birmingham AL 35294

HAMILTON, ZELDA DELAIN, configuration manager; b. Minden, La., Nov. 6, 1956; d. Shelly and Mary Lee (Hamilton) Hewitt; 1 child, Rotonda. B.A., Grambling State U., 1978. Mfg. engr. Tex. Instruments, Dallas, 1978-80, configuration mgr., 1980-83; configuration mgr. Rockwell Internat., Richardson, Tex., 1983—. Active Dallas Urban League, Inc., Jr. Achievement. Mem. Nat. Mgmt. Assn., Alpha Kappa Alpha. Democrat. Home: 12314 Bellafonte Dr Dallas TX 75243

HAMLIN, MADGE TEMPERANCE SILLS, former educator; b. Newport News, Va., Sept. 27, 1897; d. James Everett and Fannie Montgomery (Smith) Sills; B.S., Greensboro Coll., 1920; M.A. in History, Columbia U., 1928; m. Paul Mahlon Hamlin, Feb. 18, 1927 (dec. Aug. 1968); 1 dau., Elizabeth Sills Hamlin Hill. Tchr. of English, Kobe, Japan and McIyeire Sch., Shanghai, China, 1921-22; lectr. Nat. Bd. YWCA, various U.S. colls., 1923-25; tchr. gifted children, Garden City, N.Y., 1928-30, Horace Mann Sch. Girls, N.Y.C., 1930-33; founder, benefactor, dir. Hamlin Country Day Sch. for Brilliant Children, Fair Lawn, N.J., 1933-66; organizer, dir. Orchard Sch. for Slow Learning Students, Fair Lawn, 1943-59. Mem. AAUW, DAR, Jamestown Soc.,

Nat. Soc. Colonial Dames in State N.J. Republican. Congregationalist. Clubs: Montclair Women's; Garden (Montclair and Rossmoor); Women's Nat. Rep. (N.Y.C.). Contbr. articles on travel and edn. to mags. and newspapers; lectr. on influence of Western civilization on Oriental culture, changing role of women. Address: 259 Old Nassau Rd Rossmoor PO Jamesburg NJ 08831

HAMM, ELEANOR JEANNE, electrical equipment manufacturing company executive; b. Vandergrift, Pa., 1921. Student Thompson Bus. Coll., 1940, Pa. State U. Sec. Oak Industries, Inc., Rancho Bernardo, Calif., Harper-Wyman Co., McCoy Electronics Co., Oak/Adec Inc., Oak Communications, Inc., Oak Materials Group, Inc., Oak Switch Systems, Oak Systems Inc., Oak Tech. Inc., Oak Media Corp., Nat. Subscription TV, Nat. Subscription TV of Chgo., Inc., Nat. Subscription TV of Ft. Lauderdale, Inc., Oak Broadcasting Systems, Inc. Mem. Am. Soc. Corp. Secs. Address: Oak Industries Inc 16935 W Bernardo Dr Rancho Bernardo CA 92127*

HAMMAN, NANCY ANN, health center executive; b. Toledo, Nov. 16, 1929; d. Raphael Lawrence and Helen Mary (Close) Nusbaum; m. Keith LaVern Hamman, Aug. 12, 1950; children—Kathleen, Robert, Lucina, Karen, Daniel, Edith, Eileen. R.N., Mercy Hosp., 1950; B.S., U. Toledo, 1981. Pvt. duty nurse Ofcl. Nurses's Registry, Toledo, 1950-52; charge nurse Flower Hosp., Toledo, 1952-55, St. Vincent Hosp., Toledo, 1956-70; supr. health services Bedford Sch., Temperance, Mich., 1970-80; exec. dir. Citizens Health Council, Temperance, 1980—; task force on family planning Mich. Dept. Health, Lansing., 1984; dir. First Am. Bank, Deerfield, Mich. Adv. bd. Sr. Nutrition Program, Monroe, Mich., 1975, Ret. Sr. Vol. Program, Temperance, 1980—, Bedford and Mason Nurses Aid Program, Temperance, 1975-80, Bedford Bus. Voc. Edn., 1980. Mercy Hosp. nursing scholar, 1947-50; recipient Service award Bedford Lions, 1978; Community Service award, Bedford Twp., 1979. Mem. Mich. Primary Care Assn. (bd. dirs. 1980—), Bedford Bus. Assn. (trustee 1983—), Bus. and Profl. Women's Club (v.p. 1978-80), Ladies Christian Benevolent Assn. (trustee 1955-60). Democrat. Roman Catholic. Club: Bedford Lioness (dir. 1983-85). Home: 955 Dempster St Temperance MI 48182 Office: Citizens Health Council 1575 W Temperance Rd Temperance MI 48182

HAMMER, EDNA, social worker; b. N.Y.C., Jan. 15, 1922; d. Meyer and Celia (Wainer) Rubinstein; B.S., N.Y.U., 1944; M.S.W., Adelphi U., 1959; m. Feb. 18, 1945 (div.); 1 son, Paul Gary. Caseworker, Jewish Community Services L.I., Far Rockaway, N.Y., 1959-62; psychiat. social worker W. Nassau Mental Health Center, Franklin Sq., N.Y., 1962-66; admissions interviewer Adelphi U. Sch. Social Work, Garden City, N.Y., 1966; adminstrv. supr. psychiat. social services Coney Island Hosp. Psychiat. Clinic, Bklyn., 1966-67; asst. prof., faculty advisor N.Y. U. Grad. Sch. Social Work, 1967, asst. prof., faculty field instr., faculty advisor, 1967-68; instr. psychiatry, co-dir. and adminstrv. supr. screening and evaluation clinic State U. N.Y. Downstate Med. Center, Kings County Hosp. Psychiat. Div., 1968-69; asst. dir. social service dept. Cancer Care, Inc., N.Y.C., 1969-74; asst. prof., exec. assoc. dir. social work dept. Mental Retardation Inst., N.Y. Med. Coll., Valhalla, 1974-76; dir. clin. services and program Bklyn. Psychiat. Centers, Inc., after 1976; pvt. practice social work; cons. Adelphi U. Sch. Social Work, 1980—; mem. adv. bd. Sch. Social Work, Adelphi U., mem. com. for protection human subjects, also mem. bd. Service Center. Bd. dirs. Inst. for Child Mental Health. Cert. social worker, N.Y. State Fellow Am. Orthopsychiat. Assn.; mem. Nat. Assn. Social Workers, Acad. Certified Social Workers. Home: 53 Passey Garden Long Branch NJ 07740 Office: 135 E 71 St New York NY 10021

HAMMIT, PAMELA KAY PORTER, personnel and administration director; b. Slaton, Tex., Jan. 8, 1956; d. James Richard and Marsa (Swope) Porter; m. John David Hammit, Dec. 31, 1976 (div. 1980). Student McMurry Coll., 1974-75; student in Bus. Mgmt., Tex. Tech. U., 1975-77. With pub. relations University City Country Club, Lubbock, Tex., 1976; adminstrv. asst. Permian Basin Regional Planning Commn., Midland, Tex., 1977-79, dir. personnel and adminstrn., 1981—; personnel asst. HNG Oil, Midland, 1979-80; mgmt. trainee U.S. CSC, Dallas, 1979. Panelist TV interview, 1983. Active United Way campaigns, Midland and Odessa, 1980-83; officer, coordinator Permian Basin Housing Fin. Corp., Midland and Odessa, 1982-83. Recipient certs. of achievement U.S. Civil Service, 1979-80, personnel dept. Midland Coll., 1981; Outstanding Achievement award Bd. Dirs. Permian Basin Regional Planning Commn., 1983. Mem. Nat. Assn. Regional Councils (fed. briefings Washington 1981, 82, 83), Tex. Assn. Regional Councils (conv. chmn. 1983), Bus. and Profl. Women (officer 1982-83, pres.-elect 1984; Best Speaker award 1983), Am. Bus. Women, Beta Sigma Phi, Xi Pi Kappa. Democrat. Methodist. Office: Permian Basin Regional Planning Commn PO Box 6391 Midland TX 79711

HAMMOND, CAROL ANNE, entrepreneur; b. Gainesville, Tex., Jan. 4, 1940; d. Charles Harvey and Alma Gladys (Proffer) Woolfolk; student North Tex. State U., 1957-58; mgmt. cert. Tarrant County Jr. Coll., 1981; children—Vanessa, Jaime, Christopher. Asst. to gen. supr. purchasing dept. Bell Helicopter/Textron, 1964-67; exec. sec. Paul R. Ray & Co., Inc., Ft. Worth, 1968-70, mgr. records and research, 1970-77, asst. corp. v.p., 1977; v.p. Gray & Assos., Inc., Dallas, 1977-78; sr. v.p., corp. sec., chief adminstrv. officer SE Assos. Corp., Dallas, 1978-83; pres., owner CH Research Services, Dallas, 1983—. Loaned exec. United Way of Met. Tarrant County (Tex.); sr. troop leader Circle T council Girl Scouts U.S.A., 1973-76. Recipient Women in Bus. Adv. award for Dallas dist. and Tex., SBA, 1986. Mem. Am. Bus. Women's Assn. (chpt. Woman of Yr. award 1980; pres. 1981), Nat. Assn. Female Execs., Assn. Women Entrepreneurs of Dallas (pres. 1986-87), Dallas Businessmen's Assn., Irving Network Career Women, WP Assoc. Network (asst. moderator), Dallas C. of C. Home: 112 Stonegate Ct Bedford TX 76022 Office: 1450 Empire Central Suite 121 Dallas TX 75247

HAMMOND, CYNTHIA CECELIA, optometrist; b. Dearborn, Mich., Sept. 1, 1957; d. Andrew and Angeline (Laorno) Kominksky; m. Theodore Glen Hammond. Student Oakland U., Rochester, Mich., 1976-77; O.D. magna cum laude, Ferris Coll. Optometry, 1981. Lic. optometrist, Mich. Intern, Optometric Inst. and Clinic of Detroit, 1980, Ferris State Coll., Big Rapids, Mich., 1980, Jackson Prison (Mich.), 1981; assoc. in pvt. practice, Warren, Mich., 1981-82; optometrist Pearle Vision Ctr., Sterling Heights, Mich., 1982-86, K Mart Optical Ctr., Sterling Heights, 1982—; provided eye care to nursing homes, Mt. Clemens, Mich. Inventer binocular low vision aid device. Avocations: music; sports, bicycling. Home: 47626 Cheryl Ct Utica MI 48087 Office: K Mart Optical Ctr 2051 18 Mile Rd Sterling Heights MI 48078

HAMMOND, DEANNA, educator; b. Terre Haute, Ind., Feb. 13, 1945; d. DeForest and Dorothy Illen (Spaulding) H. B.S. in Edn., U. Houston, 1970, M.Ed., 1983. Cert. tchr., reading specialist, Tex. Tchr., Gregg Elem. Sch., Houston, 1970, Fairchild Elem. Sch., Houston, 1970-77, Central Elem. Sch., Palacios, Tex., 1977-79, Foster Elem. Sch., Houston, 1979—, also grade chmn. Block capt. crime watch Huntington Village Civic Assn., Houston, 1982. Mem. Tex. State Council of Internat. Reading Assn., Greater Houston Area Reading Council, Congress Houston Tchrs. (bldg. rep. 1983, 85-86), Assn. Children with Learning Disabilities, Am. Assn. Ret. Persons, PTA. Republican. Clubs: Young Homemakers (Palacious); Christian Womens Fellowship (Houston). Home: 12426 South Dr Houston TX 77099 Office: ME Foster Elem Sch 3919 Ward St Houston TX 77021

HAMMOND, DEANNA LINDBERG, linguist; b. Calgary, Alta., Can., May 31, 1942; d. Albin William and Emma Lou (Thompson) Lindberg; m. Jerome J. Hammond, 1968 (div. 1980). B.A., Wash. State U., 1964; M.A., Ohio U., 1968; Ph.D., Georgetown U., 1977; student Summer Sch., U. Ariz., Guadalajara, Portland State U. With Peace Corps, Colombia, 1964-66; prof. English, Universidad Industrial, Bucaramanga, Colombia, 1966-67; tchr. English, Spanish, Pullman (Wash.) High Sch., 1969-74; lectr. Georgetown U., Washington, 1974-77, dir. summer sch. program Quito, Ecuador, 1977; head lang. services Congressional Research Service, Library of Congress, Washington, 1977—. Coordinator Combined Fed. Campaign, Congressional Research Service, 1978; vol. Washington Area Foster Parents Plan, vol. Support Group. Recipient Community Service Award Sec. Califano, 1978. Mem. Am. Translators Assn. nat. sec. Nat. Capital Area chpt., rep. Council Communication Socs., chmn. domestic liaison com., accreditation com., mem. legis. com.), N.E. Conf. Teaching Fgn. Langs., Assn. Tchrs. Spanish and Portuguese, Teaching English to Speakers Other Langs., Library of Congress Profl. Assn., Nat. Council Returned Peace Corps Vols, Returned Peace Corps Vols., Phi Beta Kappa, Phi Kappa Phi. Democrat. Editorial bd. Modern Lang. Jour. Home: 3560 S George Mason Dr Alexandria VA 22302 Office: Congressional Research Service Lang Services Library of Congress Washington DC 20540

HAMMOND, DOROTHY LEE, author, publisher, columnist; b. Fairfax, Mo., Sept. 24, 1924; d. Lee O. and Ella E. (Brunk) Martin; B.S., Maryville (Mo.) State Tchrs. Coll., 1949; m. Robert Byron, Sept. 1, 1944; children—Robert K., Kristy R., Byron K. Syndicated columnist Antiques and Collectibles, Columbia Features, Inc., N.Y.C., 1967—; assoc. editor Colonial Homes mag., 1980—; pres. Hammond Publs., Inc., pubs. The Country Calendar, Western Calendar, Wildlife Calendar, 1978—; author 11 books in field including: Confusing Collectibles, I-III; Mustache Cups; Collectible Advertising; Price Guide to Country Collectibles; The Pictorial Price Guide, Vol. I-VI; cons. Smithsonian Instn. Methodist. Office: PO Box 8212 Munger Sta Wichita KS 67208

HAMMOND, ELIZABETH EOLYNE, lawyer; b. Detroit, Sept. 6, 1957; d. Harry Richard and Constance (Landen) H. B.A., Kent State U., 1979; J.D., U. Akron, 1983, Bar: Ohio 1983. Adminstr., Alside, Inc. subs. U.S. Steel Co., Akron, Ohio, 1980-82; mgr. Columbus office Workers' Compensation Service Co., Cleve., 1982-84; atty. Weltman, Weinberg & Assocs., Columbus, 1985—; cons. in field. Musician, Arlington Civic Orch., Columbus, 1983—; advisor 4-H Club, 1974-78. Mem. ABA, Ohio Bar Assn., Eta Sigma Phi, Phi Alpha Theta, Phi Alpha Delta. Republican. Episcopalian. Home: 2563 N 4th St Columbus OH 43202 Office: Weltman Weinberg & Assocs 527 S High St Columbus OH 43215

HAMMOND, IDA B., educational administrator; b. Supply, Va., Feb. 21, 1931; d. Thomas and Lucille (Welch) Coleman; m. William Henry Hammond; children—Harolyn Terese, William Henry Jr. B.A., Thomas A. Edison State Coll., 1978; postgrad. U. Pa., 1982—. Coordinator adminstrv. services, Rutgers U., New Brunswick, N.J., 1970-72; program asst. office of program devel. N.J. Dept. Edn., Trenton, 1974-76, adminstrv. asst., 1979-81, edn. planner, 1981-83, edn. program specialist, 1983—; coordinator library services Edn. Improvement Ctr., Princeton, N.J., 1976-79; ptnr. William Hammond Contracting, Trenton, 1964—. Dept. chmn. N.J. State Heart Fund Campaign, 1985; mem. presdl. search com. Thomas A. Edison State Coll., Trenton, 1982, student counselor, 1984. Recipient Outstanding Services award Acad. Council Thomas A. Edison State Coll., 1985. Mem. Nat. Assn. Female Execs. Club: La Chaperones. Avocations: fashion design; dressmaking; reading; yoga; photography.

HAMMOND, JANE LAURA, librarian, lawyer; b. nr. Nashua, Iowa; d. Frank D. and Pauline (Flint) Hammond. B.A., U. Dubuque, 1950; M.S., Columbia U., 1952; J.D., Villanova U., 1965. Bar: Pa. 1965. Cataloguer, Harvard U. Law Library, 1952-54; asst. librarian Sch. Law, Villanova (Pa.) U., 1954-62, librarian, 1962-76, prof. law, 1965-76; law librarian, prof. law Cornell U., Ithaca, N.Y., 1976—; adj. prof. Drexel U., 1971-74; mem. depository library council to pub. printer U.S. Govt. Printing Office, 1975-78. Mem. Am. Assn. Law Libraries (sec. 1965-70, pres. 1975-76), Council Nat. Library Assns. (sec.-treas. 1971-72, chmn. 1979-80), Spl. Libraries Assn., ALA, ABA (accreditation com. 1982—, chmn. 1983-84; council sect. on legal edn. 1984—), Assn. Am. Law Schs. (exec. com. 1977), P.E.O. Episcopalian. Office: Cornell Law Library Myron Taylor Hall Ithaca NY 14853

HAMMOND, KARLA MARIE, writer and editor; b. Middletown, Conn., Apr. 26, 1949; d. Lester Arthur and Angelina (Lillian) Lorraine (Fusillo) H.; B.A., Goucher Coll., 1971; M.A., Trinity Coll., 1973. Freelance writer and editor, 1973—; research cons. Futures Group, Glastonbury, Conn., 1981; personnel cons. Barbara Chazan Assocs., Hartford, Conn., 1981; exec. staff adminstr. CT Student Loan Found., Hartford, 1982-83, Aetna Life & Casualty Co., 1983—; freelance book reviewer Sachem Pub. Assocs., Guilford, Conn., 1981-84. Recipient several prizes local colls. Democrat. Contbr. articles, essays, short stories, interviews, poems, fiction, and revs. to over 185 publs. in U.S.A., Eng., Can., Japan, Australia, Greece, Sweden and Italy. Home and office: Rural Route 7 12 West Dr East Hampton CT 06424

HAMMOND, NORA ELLEN, nurse; b. Hillsdale, Mich., Sept. 20, 1937; d. Wilford Randall and Mabel Dorothy (Lamb) Huffman; children—Susan Kay, Thomas Lauren. Diploma in Nursing, Henry Ford Hosp., Detroit, 1960; B.S. in Human Service, U. Detroit, 1981, M.S. in Health Service Adminstrn., 1984. R.N., Mich. Operating room supr. Branch County Community Hosp., Coldwater, Mich., 1961-72; clin. coordinator William Beaumont Hosp., Royal Oak, Mich., 1972-77; nursing dir. operating room Henry Ford Hosp., Detroit, 1977-84; dir. operating room service Wake County Med. Ctr., Raleigh, N.C., 1984—; cons. Kitch, Suhrheinrich, Saunbier & Drufchas, P.S., Detroit, 1982-84; group leader Alternative Health Service, Raleigh, 1985. Recipient Spirit of Detroit award, City Council, 1981, Human Service award U. Detroit, 1981. Mem. Nursing Council Operating Room Nurses (sec.-treas. 1980-84), Assn. Operating Room Nurses (legis. mem. region V 1978-80), Tarheel East Assn. Operating Room Nurses. Episcopalian. Avocations: swimming, golf, gardening. Home: 206 Oak Hallow Ct Raleigh NC 27612

HAMMOND, SUSAN, insurance company executive; b. Billings, Mont., Nov. 19, 1947; d. Sutton and Barbara (Thomas) Hammond. A.A., Coll. San Mateo, 1968; B.A. in Communications, U. Ariz., 1970. Cons. Conn. Gen. Life Co., San Francisco, 1973-76; asst. v.p. Transamerica Occidental Life Co., Los Angeles, 1976—; tchr. Foothill Coll., Portola Valley, Calif., 1977, U. Calif.-Berkeley, 1978-79. Mentor/tchr. Constitutional Rights Found., Los Angeles, 1980—; chairperson Transamerica Life Co. United Way Dr. Los Angeles, 1983; active Transamerica Involvement Corps, Los Angeles, 1980—. Recipient Top Renewed Sales of Yr. award, Conn. Gen. Life Co., 1974. Mem. Life Ins. Advertisers Assn., Los Angeles Jr. C. of C. Democrat. Episcopalian. Office: Transamerica Occidental Life Co 12th and Olive Sts Los Angeles CA 90015

HAMMOND, SUSAN CASAZZA, corporation executive, accountant; b. Hartford, Conn., Dec. 28, 1956; d. Stanley Anthony and Louise Anne (Martus) Casazza. B.S. in Bus. Adminstrn., Northeastern U., 1979; postgrad. Bentley Coll. C.P.A., Mass. Staff auditor Alexander Grant & Co., Boston, 1977-80; staff internal auditor Stone & Webster, Boston, 1981; fin. analyst KDT Industries, Inc., Newton, Mass., 1981-82; corp. fin. analyst XTRA Corp., Boston, 1982—; instr. Northeastern U., Boston, 1981-83. Fellow Mass. Soc. C.P.A.s, Am. Inst. C.P.A.s, Beta Alpha Psi (pres. Boston chpt. 1978). Roman Catholic. Office: XTRA Corp care XLCO 60 State St Boston MA 02109

HAMMOND, THERESA MARIE, librarian; b. Wilmington, Del., Jan. 26, 1944; d. Michael and Laura Stella (Mateuszczyk) Marroni; m. Thelbert Ray Hammond, Jan. 7, 1967; children—Thelbert Ray II, Christopher Michael. B.S., Villnova U., 1966, M.S. in Library Sci., 1971; postgrad. U. Md., 1970, Christopher Newport Coll., 1977-81. Br. librarian J. Lewis Crozer Library, Chester, Pa., 1965-67; adult services librarian Jervis Library, Rome, N.Y., 1968-69; librarian Prince Georges County Meml. Library System, Hyattsville, Md., 1970-72; head tech. services Auburn U., Montgomery, Ala., 1972-74; asst. librarian Va. Inst. Marine Sci., Gloucester Point, Va., 1975-77; dir. library services The Daily Press, Inc., Newport News, Va., 1977—. Chmn. trustees Newport News Public Library, 1982—; treas. Hampton Roads Acad. Community Assn., 1984; chmn. Christian edn. com. Our Lady Mt. Carmel Roman Catholic Ch., 1981—. Mem. ALA, Spl. Libraries Assn., Am. Soc. Info. Scis., Va. Library Assn., Am. Mgmt. Assn. Club: Peninsula Girls (sec. 1981—). Office: Daily Press Inc 7505 Warwick Blvd Newport News VA 23607

HAMMONS, MARJORIE MAGEE, personnel and marketing executive; b. Brookhaven, Miss., Sept. 18, 1925; d. James Hardy and Vera Gertrude (Davis) Magee; m. Jasper Glen Hammons, July 7, 1944; children—Marjorie Ann Hammons Lozes, Linda Hammons O'Connor, James, Robert, Catherine Hammons Gum, Mary Elizabeth. B.A., Northeast La. U., 1967, postgrad., 1971, 74, 78, 80. Mgr., owner Kelly Services, Inc., Monroe, La., 1970-80; gen. mgr. Hammons' Bus. Services, Inc., Monroe, 1980-84, pres., 1984—; Mem. Baton Rouge Health Coordinating Council, 1985—; pres. Quota Internat., Monroe, 1977-78; co-chmn. Vols. for Edwards, Monroe, 1983; active regional polit. campaigns. Named Outstanding Performance Br. Mgr., Kelly Services, Inc., 1974. Mem. La. Personnel Assn., Am. Soc. Personnel Adminstrs., Nat. Assn. Temporary Services. Democrat. Baptist. Avocations: reading, writing, travel, gardening. Home: 1901 Sherwood Ave Monroe LA 71201 Office: Hammons' Bus Services Inc 606 Louisville Ave Monroe LA 71201

HAMNER, MARVINE PAULA, cable TV executive, data processing consultant; b. Kansas City, Mo., Nov. 20, 1956; d. David Wilson and Sarah May (Brooks) Talbot; m. Robert Jefferson Hamner, Dec. 24, 1973; children—Erinn Nicole, James Robert. Student Oakton Community Coll., 1983—. Data entry operator Alexander & Alexander of Tex., Inc., Dallas, 1976-77; backup control operator Mobil Oil Corp., Dallas, 1977-79; self-employed in office systems, Dallas, 1979-80; EDP coordinator O'Donnell Wicklund, Pigozzi, Northbrook, Ill., 1981; specialist/periodic temporary, Glenview, Ill., 1981-82; spl. projects analyst Continental Cablevision, Chgo., 1982-83, materials mgr., 1983—. First woman pilot NAS Dallas Flying Club, 1977. Mem. Purchasing Mgrs. Assn. Chgo., Nat. Intercollegiate Flying Assn. (com. chmn. 1983-84), Exptl. Aircraft Assn., Aircraft Owners and Pilots Assn. Democrat. Methodist. Club: Ninety-Nines Inc. (librarian 1982-83) (Chgo.) Office: Continental Cablevision Inc 5725 E River Rd Suite 365 Chicago IL 60631

HAMON, CATHERINE LEBAR, retailer; b. Casper, Wyo., Feb. 16, 1949; d. John D. and Bette A. (Anderson) LeBar; m. Kenneth L. Hamon, II, Dec. 22, 1967; children—Morgan Kenneth, Clark David. Loan processing supr. Capitol Fed. Savs. & Loan, Denver, 1969-73; salesperson Towne & Country Realty, Grand Junction, Colo., 1978-79; broker assoc. Realty World/Monument Realty, Grnd Junction, 1979-83; pres., owner Capps Furniture, Inc., Grand Junction, 1983—. Bd. dirs. North Ave. Assn., 1983-84, Downtown Assn., 1985, Mus. Western Colo., 1985. Mem. Grand Junction Bd. Realtors (Realtor of Month 1980; dir. 1981-83), Colo. Assn. Realtors (dir. 1982), Colo. Furniture Dealers Assn. Club: PEO (chpt. pres. 1983-85). Home: 406 Stoneridge Ct Grand Junction CO 81503 Office: Capps Furniture 602 Main St Grand Junction CO 81502

HAMPSHIRE, SUSAN, actress; b. London, 1942; m. Pierre Granier-Deferre (dissolved 1974); 1 child; m. Eddie Kulukundis, 1981. D.Litt. (hon.), City U., London, 1984. Actress, stage appearances in Expresso Bongo, Follow That Girl, Ginger Man, Fairy Tales of N.Y., She Stoops to Conquer, On Approval, The Sleeping Prince, A Doll's House, The Taming of the Shrew, Romeo and Jeannette, Peter Pan, As You Like It, Man and Superman, Miss Julie, The Circle, Arms and the Man, Tribades, An Audience Called Edward, A Cruifer of Blood-Sherlock Holmes Mystery, Night and Day, The Revolt, House Guest; rôles in TV serials, KATV Andromeda, The Forsyte Saga, Vanity Fair, The First Churchills, The Pallisers, Dick Turpin, Barchester Chronicles, Leaving; films include During One Night, The Three Lives of Thomasina, Night Must Fall, Wonderful Life, Paris in August, The Fighting Prince of Donegal, Monte Carlo or Bust, Rogan, David Copperfield, Living Free, A Time for Loving, Malpertius, Neither the Sea Nor the Sand, Roses and Green Peppers, Bang. Winner Emmy award Best Actress in drama series, 1970, 71, 73. Author: Susan's Story; The Maternal Instinct; Lucy Jane at the Ballet. Address: care Midland Bank Ltd 92 Kensington High St London W8 England

HAMPTON, BEATRICE FLOWERS, educational administrator; b. Bradenton, Fla., Jan. 4, 1946; d. William Doby and Aldonia (Hadley) Flowers; children—Lee Royal IV, Thomas Joseph. B.S. in Pub. Adminstrn., Polit. Sci. and Biology, Fla. A&M U., 1978; postgrad. Fla. State U., 1979. Research asst. Bur. Intergovtl. Relations, Fla. Dept. Adminstrn., Tallahassee, 1975; legis. intern-analyst com. on regulated industries/licensing Fla. Ho. of Reps., Tallahassee, 1978-79; staff asst. to county adminstr. Leon County Bd. County Commrs., County Adminstrs. Office, Tallahassee, 1980-81; dir., spl. edn. tchr. devel. services program Gadsden County Day Care Services, Quincy, Fla., 1981-84; tchr. cert. specialist Fla. Dept. Edn., Tallahassee, 1984—. Mem. Leon County Democratic Women's Club, 1977-81, newsletter editor, bd. dirs., 1979-80; state del. Fla. Dem. Women's Conv., Naples, 1979; campaign aide Fla. Gubernatorial campaign, 1977-78; precinct capt. City Commr. Campaign, 1979-80. Bennett Coll. for Women acad. scholar, 1963-64; Carnegie exchange student scholar, 1972; HUD intern grantee, 1975. Mem. Nat. Assn. Female Execs. Baptist. Club: Gourmet Delites. Avocations: tapestries; French cuising; sailing; antiques; cycling. Home: 1222 Ford St Tallahassee FL 32303-5927

HAMPTON, CAROL MCDONALD, educator, administrator; b. Oklahoma City, Sept. 18, 1935; d. Denzil Vincent and Mildred Juanita (Cussen) McDonald; m. James Wilburn Hampton, Feb. 22, 1958; children—Jaime, Clayton, Diana, Neal. B.A., U. Okla., 1957, M.A., 1973, Ph.D., 1984. Teaching asst. U. Okla., Norman, 1976-81; instr. U. of Sci. and Arts of Okla., Chickasha, 1981-84; coordinator Consortium for Grad. Opportunities for Am. Indians, U. Calif.-Berkeley, 1985—; trustee Ctr. of Am. Indian, Oklahoma City, 1981—; vice chmn. Nat. Com. on Indian Work, Episcopal Ch., 1986—. Contbr. articles to profl. jours. Trustee Western History Collections, U. Okla., Okla. Found. for the Humanities, 1983—; bd. dirs. Okla. State Regents for Higher Edn., mem. adv. com. on social justice; mem. World Council of Chs. Program to Combat Racism, Geneva, 1985—; bd. dirs. Caddo Tribal Council, Okla., 1976-82. Francis C. Allen fellow, Ctr. fot the History of Am. Indian, 1983. Mem. Western History Assn., Western Social Sci. Assn., Orgn. of Am. Historians, Am. Hist. Assn., Okla. Hist. Soc., Assn. Am. Indian Historians (founding mem. 1981—). Democrat. Episcopal. Club: Jr. League (Oklahoma City). Avocation: travel. Home: 1414 N Hudson Oklahoma City OK 73103 Office: Consortium for Grad Opportunities for Am Indians Univ Calif 3415 Dwinelle Hall Berkeley CA 94720

HAMPTON, DOLORES H., army officer; b. Englewood, N.J., Oct. 18, 1946; d. Charles Milford and Kathleen (Steele) H. B.S., Fairleigh Dickenson U., 1971; M.A., Fla. A. &M. U., 1978; M.S., U.S. Army Command and Gen. Staff Coll., 1980. Enlisted in U.S. Army, 1965, advanced through grades to H. col., 1979; med. technologist Columbia Presbyn. Med. Ctr., N.Y.C., 1971-76; counselor Pensacola Community Mental Health Ctr., Fla., 1978-80; career devel. specialist Urban League, Englewood, N.J., 1980; personnel counselor Army Med. Dept. Recruitment, 1981-84, N.E. regional dir., 1984-85; Author/editor: U.S. Army Stress Management Training Program, 1979. Mem. 369th Vets. Assn., Assn. Mil. Surgeons U.S., Am. Legion, Res. Officers Assn., Psi Chi (chpt. v.p. 1976-77), Alpha Kappa Alpha. Democrat. Methodist. Avocations: poetry; theare; tennis; swimming; running. Home: 292 Liberty Rd Englewood NJ 07631

HAMPTON-KAUFFMAN, MARGARET FRANCES, corporate finance and banking consultant; b. Gainesville, Fla., May 12, 1947; d. William Wade and Carol Dorothy (Maples) Hampton; B.A. summa cum laude with honors in French, Fla. State U., 1969; postgrad. U. Nice (France), summer 1969; M.B.A. in Fin. (Alcoa Found. fellow), Columbia U., 1974; m. Kenneth L. Kauffman, May 12, 1973; 1 child, Robert Lee. Fin. analyst, economist Bd. of Govs. of Fed. Res. System, Washington, 1974-75; asst. v.p. corp. fin. Mfrs. Hanover Trust Co., N.Y.C., 1975-76; v.p., dir. corp. planning and research, sec. asset and liability mgmt. and strategic planning coms. Nat. Bank of Ga., Atlanta, 1976-81; sr. v.p. corp. planning and devel. Bank South Corp., Atlanta, 1981-85; mng. ptnr. Hampton Mgmt. Cons., Atlanta, 1985—; dir. Accent Enterprises, Inc., Atlanta, TOMAK, Inc., Atlanta. Trustee Leukemia Soc. Am., 1986—; trustee Ga. chpt. Leukemia Soc., 1980—, treas., 1981-82, 1st v.p., 1982-84. Recipient Outstanding Angel Merit award Angel Flight, 1968; named Trustee of Yr., Leukemia Soc., 1982, 85. Mem. Planning Execs. Inst., Inst. of Mgmt. Scis., Am. Inst. Banking, Inst. of Fin. Edn., Am. Fin. Assn., Downtown Atlanta C. of C., (govt. affairs subcom. 1976-77) Atlanta C. of C. (high tech. task force 1982-83), Ga. Women's Forum (sec./treas., bd. dirs. 1985-86), Ga. Exec. Women's Network (sec. 1982-83, dir. 1982-84), Mortar Bd., Alliance Française, Kappa Sigma Little Sisters (pres., treas., sweetheart), Phi Beta Kappa, Beta Gamma Sigma, Phi Kappa Phi, Alpha Lambda Delta, Pi Delta Phi, Alpha Delta Pi. Episcopalian. Club: Women's Commerce (charter mem., steering com. 1985-86). Office: 100 Galleria Pkwy Suite 400 Atlanta GA 30339

HAMRICK, JO ANNE, psychiatric program consultant, educator, psychometrist; b. Anniston, Ala., July 14, 1953; d. Euel Franklin and Mary Helen (Henderson) H. B.S. in Edn., Auburn U., 1973; M.A. in Edn., U. Ala.-Birmingham, 1976; A.A. in Edn., U. Ala.-Tuscaloosa, 1977. Primary emotional conflict tchr. Birmingham Schs., 1975-77, dir., head tchr., 1977-78; instr. U. Ala., Tuscaloosa, 1978-79; asst. dir., treatment coordinator Ga. Psycho-Ednl. Network, Griffin, 1979-81; tchr. coordinator Birmingham City Schs., 1982-85; ednl. specialist Brookwood Med. Ctr., Birmingham, 1981—; child and adolescent counseling, 1981—; psychiat. cons. Brookwood Psychiat. Ctr., Birmingham, 1985—. Editor (with D.M. Doleys and T.M. Vaughn) Assessment and Treatment of Development Problems. Active Ala. Symphony Chorus, Birmingham. Mem. Ala. Child Care Conf., Tourette Syndrome Assn., Nat. Soc. Children and Adults with Autism, Ala. Council Exceptional Children, Ala. Council Adminstrs. in Spl. Edn., Ala. Council Exceptional Children with Learning Disabilities, Ala. Council Children with Behavior Disorders, Council Adminstrs in Spl. Edn., Council Children with Behavior Disorders, Council Exceptional Children, Kappa Delta Pi, Phi Delta Kappa. Democrat. Baptist. Avocations: music; tennis; dancing; traveling; sports. Office: Birmingham Psychiatry PA 2018 Brookwood Med Ctr Dr Suite 304 Birmingham AL 85209

HAMROFF, ELLIE, records management company executive; b. N.Y.C., Apr. 17, 1933; d. Benedict Leo and Lillian Edith (Katzen) Lurie; m. Sheldon Hamroff, June 5, 1955; children—Robin Hamroff Boehler, Debra Hamroff Levi, Michael. Student Goucher Coll., 1950-51; B.A., Adelphi U., 1954. Social worker N.Y.C. Dept. Welfare, 1954-55; asst. adminstr. Kew Gardens Hosp., N.Y., 1975-78; pres. Comprehensive Archives, Inc., N.Y.C., 1978—. Pres., Naomi Hadassah, Jamaica Estates, N.Y., 1968-70; v.p. fund raising Hillcrest Hadassah, Jamaica Estates, 1971-73. Democrat. Office: Comprehensive Archives Inc 87-46 123d St Richmond Hill NY 11418

HANAS, SUZANNE ELAINE, manufacturing company sales executive; b. Pitts., July 27, 1950; d. George and Helen (Kalnicky) H. R.N. diploma Shadyside Hosp. Sch. Nursing, Pitts., 1971; B.S., Am. U., 1976. R.N., Ohio, Va., D.C. Head nurse cardio-vascular intensive care Cleve. Clinic Hosp., 1971-73; spl. duty nurse Georgetown U. Hosp., Washington, 1973-75; team coordinator Vis. Nurses' Assn. No. Va., Arlington, 1975-76; ter. mgr. Hollister Inc., Chgo., 1976-79; sr. account rep. 3M Co., West Caldwell, N.J., 1979—, sales trainer, 1984—; pres. Skyline Dance Studio, Inc., Falls Church, Va.; instr. Montgomery Coll., Rockville, Md., 1977-80. Del., Arlington County Civic Fedn. (Va.), 1978-81; v.p. Fairlington Citizens Assn., Arlington, 1978-80, pres., 1980-81; del. Va. Republican Conv., 1981; precinct chmn., mem. Arlington County Rep. Com. (Va.), 1982-83. Mem. Am. Cancer Soc., Am. U. Alumni Assn., Nat. Assn. Female Execs. Lutheran. Club: Arlington Rep. Women's Club Federated. Office: 15 Henderson Dr West Caldwell NJ 07006

HANAU, LAIA, educator; b. Boston, June 4, 1916; d. Samuel B. and Lucy A. (Greenwood) Pearlmutter; A.B., Smith Coll., 1937; M.A., U. Rochester, 1960; postgrad. U. Mich., 1942-45, U. Ky., 1951-53, U. Ariz., 1973-74; m. Richard Hanau, Jan. 2, 1941; 1 dau., Loren Michael. Copy editor Am. Horseman, Lexington, Ky., 1947-49; asst. editor pubs. Dept. Pub. Info., U. Ky., Lexington, 1949-50, editorial asst. dept. animal pathology, 1950-52; editorial cons. Optical Soc. Am., Rochester, N.Y., 1959; tchr. English, Lexington pub. schs. and Sayre Sch., 1960-66; instr. study methods U. Ky. Coll. Medicine, Lexington, 1967-69, asst. prof., 1970-73; cons. in field; tchr. Sayre Sch., 1974-76; contbr. Breadloaf Writers Conf., 1953; editorial cons. U. Ky. Coll. Medicine, 1963-66; tchr., cons. Hanau Method of Study and Writing Techniques. Recipient Avery and Jule Hopwood Award in nonfiction, 1942. Mem. Authors Guild. Author: The Study Game, How to Play and Win with —Statement Pie—, 1972, 73, 74; The Study Game Workbook: A Guide to Writing and Note Taking, 1976; The Study Game: How to Play and Win, 1979; Play the Study Game for Better Grades, 1985. Address: Route 4 Box 46 Stage Coach Rd Patterson NY 12563

HANBACK, HAZEL MARIE SMALLWOOD, management consultant; b. Washington, Sept. 19, 1918; d. Archibald Carlisle and Mary Louise (Mayhugh) Smallwood; A.B., George Washington U., 1940; M.P.A., Am. U., 1968; m. William B. Hanback, Sept. 26, 1942; 1 son, Christopher Brecht. Archivist, U.S. Office Housing Expediter, 1948-50; mgmt. engr. U.S. Archives, 1950-51; spl. asst.-indsl. specialist Sec. Def., 1951-53; dir. documentation div. Naval Facilities Engring., Alexandria, Va., 1953-81; mgmt. cons., 1981—. Pres., West End Citizens Assn., Washington, 1956-58; trustee George Washington U., 1979—. Nominee Rockefeller Public Service award, 1969, Fed. Woman's award, 1969; recipient cert. of merit Dep. Def., 1965. Mem. Mortar Bd., Phi Delta Gamma, Sigma Kappa. Democrat. Episcopalian. Clubs: George Washington U. (chmn. bd. 1971-75), Columbian Women (pres. George Washington U. 1967-69), Order Eastern Star. Author: Military Color Book, 1960; Status of Women in a Cybernetically Oriented Society, 1968; Worms Eye View, 1982. Home: 2152 F St NW Washington DC 20037 Office: 2154 F St NW Washington DC 20037

HANBERY, DONNA EVA, lawyer, writer; b. Framingham, Mass., July 15, 1952; d. Donald T. and Jacqueline J. Hanbery, B.A. summa cum laude, Hamline U., St. Paul, 1974; J.D. magna cum laude, U. Minn., 1977. Bar: Minn. 1977. Ptnr., Curtin & Mahoney, P.A., Mpls., 1976—. Columnist, New Homes Mag., 1979—; author: Why Cucumbers Are Better Than Men, 1983. Mem. Minn. Multi-Housing Assn., 1979—; sec., dir., counsel Crime Stoppers, Inc., Mpls.-St. Paul, 1979—; chairperson Loring Mall Bus. Assn., Mpls., 1980—. Mem. ABA, Minn. Bar Assn., Mpls. Bar Assn. Office: Curtin & Mahoney PA 4150 Multifoods Tower Minneapolis MN 55402

HANCOCK, DIANA ISON, artist, illustrator; b. Florence, S.C., Sept. 28, 1937; d. Franklin Miller and Virginia (Eaddy) Greene; m. Wade Hampton Ison III, Dec. 26, 1959 (dec. Feb. 1985); children—Virginia Ison Knox, Wade Hampton IV, Ison, Tirzah Kennedy Ison, David Miller Ison; m. Jerry Truman Hancock, June 29, 1985. A.A. in Advt., Central Piedmont Community Coll., 1976; B.A. in Econs., Queen's Coll., Charlotte, N.C., 1959. Cert. secondary tchr., S.C., Ga. Tchr. pub. schs., S.C., Ga., 1959-61; freelance designer, Charlotte, 1961-80; dist. collegiate dir. Phi Mu Nat. Frat., Charlotte, 1973-74; dir. publs. Winthrop Coll., Rock Hill, S.C., 1980-81; v.p. Jerry Hancock Agy., Charlotte, 1981-86; freelance artist, Catawba, N.C., 1986—; needlepoint designer Pat's Pointers, Field Enterprises, 1974-76. One-woman shows Florence Mus. Art, S.C., 1971; exhibited in group shows, including Internat. Needlepoint Exhbn., Monaco, 1974; represented in permanent collections Mint Mus. History, Charlotte. Del. Charlotte Panhellenic Council, 1974-76; bd. dirs. Charlotte Pops, 1984-85. Recipient First Place award in design and execution Internat. awards of Am. Needlepoint, 1974, First Place award PICA Awards, 1982. Mem. Nat. Soc. Tole Decorative Painters, DAR (chpt. sec. 1976), Charlotte Symphony Women's Assn., Phi Mu, Gamma Gamma chpt.) (chaplain 1958-59). Republican. Episcopalian. Lodge: Order Eastern Star (life mem. Rainbow Girls, Rainbow Girls worthy adviser 1955-56). Avocations: gardening; horseback riding. Home and Studio: Route 2 Box 151B Catawba NC 28609

HANCOCK, JOAN HERRIN, employment agency executive; b. Indpls., Apr. 16, 1930; d. Roy Silvey and Glenna Olive (Metsker) Herrin; m. John Newton Hancock, May 12, 1951 (div. Feb. 1976); children—Glenna Jill Hancock Smith, Jeri Lee Hancock Moore, John Norman. B.A., Butler U., 1953. Career counselor Career Cons. Inc., Indpls., 1974-82; counselor, corp. officer Unique Alternatives Inc., Indpls., 1982-84, Alternatives Plus Inc., Indpls., 1984—; pres. Herrin & Assocs., 1986—. Precinct Committeeperson Democratic Party, Indpls; pres. Sch. #59 PTA, C.W.F. Allisonville Christian Ch. Mem. Central Ind. Assn. Profl. Cons. (sec. 1984-85, ethics com. 1980-81), Am. Mgmt. Assn. (dir. membership 1986), Kappa Kappa Gamma (pres. Indpls. Assn.; province dir. 1970-74, Betty Miller Brown award 1982). Mem. Christian Ch. (Disciples of Christ). Club: Hoosier 500 Toastmistress (pres. 1963) (Indpls.). Home: 4127 Timber Ct Indianapolis IN 46250 Office: Alternatives Plus Inc 9135 N Meridian Suite A8 Indianapolis IN 46260

HANCOCK, PAMELA LYNETTE, computer programmer; b. El Paso, Tex., Jan. 20, 1961; d. John Allison and Karma Deane (Hill) H. B.S. in Computer Sci., U. Tex.-El Paso, 1983. Contract programmer Meridian Oil Inc., El Paso, 1984-85, assoc. programmer, 1985—. Mem. Nat. Assn. Female Execs., Alpha Kappa Alpha. Democrat. Methodist. Avocations: sketching; aerobics. Home: 4400 Wyoming Ave El Paso TX 79903

HANCOCK, PATRICIA JEAN, body shop owner; b. Norfolk, Nebr., Oct. 18, 1945; d. John Joseph Fagan, Jr. and Virginia Ruth (Simpson) Fagan Rauert; m. Robert Dale Hancock, Mar. 1, 1965; 1 child, Jennifer Lynn. B.S. in Math., U. Nebr.-Lincoln, 1967, tchrs. cert., 1967, M.A.T. in Math., 1971. Tchr. math., Palmyra, Nebr., 1967-68; grad. asst. U. Nebr., Lincoln, 1968-69; tchr. math. Pound Jr. High, Lincoln, 1969-74; sec.-treas. Bob's Body Shop, Grand Island, Nebr. Author articles. Bible sch. coordinator Trinity United Meth. Ch., 1983, 84, 85, mem. adminstrv. council ministries, 1984—; Leader 4-H, 1985—; tchr. Soc. Collision Repair Specialists; 4-H leader. Mem. Nebr. Auto Body Assn. (sec., newsletter editor, convention organizer 1981-83). Clubs: Riverside Golf (Grand Island) (treas., v.p., pres. Ladies Golf Assn.). Avocations: golf; tennis; swimming; sewing; organ. Home: Route 1 Box 185 Cairo NE 68824 Office: Bob's Body Shop Inc 1800 W Lincoln Hwy Grand Island NE 68803

HANCOCK, SUSAN HUNTER, educational administrator; b. Fresno, Calif., Apr. 3, 1944; d. Bertram Harry Jr. and Virginia Hawes (MacCracken) Hunter; m. Jack Edward Hancock, Sept. 15, 1979; 1 son, Craig. B.A., Calif. State U., Fresno, 1966; M.S., Oreg. State U., 1971. Dean women Boise State U., Idaho, 1971-72; asst. to dean students Humboldt State U., Arcata, Calif., 1972; asst. dean students, Calif. State U., Northridge, 1972-76; asst. statewide dean Chancellor's Office Calif. State U. System, 1976-80; dean students Chapman Coll., Orange, Calif., 1982—; Bd. dirs. ARC, San Fernando Valley, Calif., 1973-76; vol. guide Greater Los Angeles Zoo Assn., 1983-85. Recipient Service to Los Angeles City award Los Angeles City Planning Commn., 1968; named Bicentennial Woman of Yr., Los Angeles Human Relations Commn. 1976. Mem. Nat. Assn. Student Personnel Adminstrs. (bd. dirs. 1976-78, 1984-86, v.p. 1984-86, chmn. research div. 1976-78, editorial bd. jour. 1978-81), Calif. Coll. Personnel Assn., Nat. Assn. Women Deans Adminstrs. and Counselors, Phi Mu, Delta Kappa Gamma. Democrat. Home: 2320 E McCart La Habra CA 90631 Office: Chapman Coll 333 N Glassell Orange CA 92666

HANDAL, KATHLEEN A., physician; b. Bklyn., June 1, 1949; d. John and Evelyn Handal. B.S., St. Peter's Coll., 1970; M.D., Med. Coll. Pa., 1975. Intern Med. Coll. Pa., 1975-76, resident in emergency medicine, 1976-78; chmn. emergency dept. St. Rita Med Ctr., Lima, Ohio, 1978-79; dir. emergency service L.I. Jewish-Hillside Med. Ctr., New Hyde Park, N.Y., 1979—, emergency medicine residency dir, 1983—; chmn. tng. com. Emergency Med. Service, N.Y.C., 1980—, chmn. Trauma Ctr., 1981—; clin. asst. prof. SUNY, Stony Brook; cons. N.Y. Heart Assn., 1982—. Asst. editor Micro Medex, 1981. Fellow N.Y. Acad. Medicine; mem. Internat. Disaster Medicine, Am. Coll. Emergency Physicians (nat. EMS com., nat. steering com., bd. dirs. N.Y.). Office: LI Jewish-Hillside Med Ctr New Hyde Park NY 11042

HANDELMAN, ALICE ROBERTA, public relations official, freelance writer; b. Bklyn., Mar. 17, 1943; d. Ned Harlan and Margaret (Isaacs) Samuels; m. Howard Talbot Handelman, Aug. 29, 1965; children—Karen Leigh, Patricia Gail, Marjorie Lynn. B.J., U. Mo., 1965. Intern reporter Miami (Fla.) News, summer 1964; staff feature writer St. Louis Blues, 1968-77; freelance writer, St. Louis, 1967—; also community relations assoc. Jewish Ctr. for Aged, Chesterfield, Mo., 1981-85, dir. community relations and devel., 1985—; instr. hockey for women Meramec Community Coll., St. Louis, 1976-77; pub. relations cons. Jewish Family and Children's Service, St. Louis, 1983; adv. com. vis. prof. program JCA Assocs., 1981-83, Gerontol. Inst., St. Louis, 1981-83; freelance writer, contbr. to St. Louis Globe-Dem., St. Louis Post-Dispatch, St. Louis Jewish Light, Hockey News, Hockey World, Sporting News, Hockey Pictorial; author copy for Knight's Catalogue, 1983. Pub. relations chmn. Nat. Council Jewish Women, 1981-83, publicity chmn. fashion sale, 1985; pres. Weber Sch. PTA, Creve Coeur, Mo., 1982; mem. Women's Am. ORT, 1965—; life mem. Jewish Hosp. Aux., 1965—; pres. Young Women's Council on Edn. of Jewish Fedn. St. Louis, 1969; mem. central advancement team Pkwy. Central High Sch., 1985—. Recipient William Randolph Hearst award Hearst Found., Columbia, Mo., 1965; Besse Marks Meml. scholar, 1964-65. Mem. Mo. Press Women, Women in Communications (Ruth Philpott Collins award 1984). Republican. Jewish. Club: Meadowbrook Country (Ballwin, Mo.). Home: 12 Terryhill Ln Saint Louis MO 63131 Office: Jewish Center for Aged 13190 S Outer 40 Rd Chesterfield MO 63017

HANDELMAN, GLADYS, writer, editor; b. N.Y.C., Aug. 10, 1931; d. Max and Sophie (Urfirer) Braver; m. Stuart N. Handelman, Nov. 1, 1959; children—Kenneth, Robert. A.B. in English, Hunter Coll. Exec. sec. to merchandising editor Vogue Mag., N.Y.C., 1953-54; asst. to exec. producer Omnibus, N.Y.C., 1954-57; scriptreader CBS-TV, 20th Century Fox Studios, N.Y.C., 1957-58; writer, publicist Girl Scouts U.S.A., N.Y.C., 1958-61; editor Norwalk Trader, Westport, Conn., 1976-79; mag. editor Early Years Mag., Darien, Conn., 1981—. Author feature stories: Fairfield County Mag., 1980, Executive Mag., 1980, Columbia Mag., 1983. Publicity chmn. ORT, 1972-73; program chmn. Coleytown Elem. Sch., Westport, 1973-74; mem. sch. com. Temple Israel, 1979-80, coordinator job help, 1979—. Recipient Mademoiselle Coll. Bd. Rep. award, 1950; Prix de Paris award Vogue Mag., 1953. Mem. Women in Communications (bd. dirs. 1981-82). Home: 225 North Ave Westport CT 06880 Office: Early Years Mag 11 Hale Ln Darien CT

HANDLER, CAROLE ENID, lawyer, city planner; b. N.Y.C., Dec. 23, 1939; d. Milton and Marion Winter (Kahn) Handler; m. Peter U. Schoenbach, May 30, 1965 (div. Sept. 1979); children—Alisa, Ilana. A.B., Radcliffe Coll., 1957; M.S., U. Pa., 1963, J.D., 1975. Bar: Pa. 1975. Planner, Boston Redevel. Authority, 1959-61; head gen. plans sect. Phila. City Planning Commn., 1963-66; ednl. facilities planning cons. Phila. Sch. Dist., 1966-67, coordinator and dir. policy planning, 1967-69; instr. U. Pa., Phila., spring 1966, 68-69, U. Sao Paulo, Rio de Janeiro, Brazil, 1970-71; Cath. U., Rio de Janeiro, 1970-71; law clk. presiding judge Pa. Superior Ct., Phila., 1975-76; assoc. Goodman & Ewing, Phila., 1976-78, Schnader, Harrison, Segal & Lewis, Phila., 1978—. Bd. dirs. St. Peter's Sch., Society Hill Synagogue; panel mem. Thomas Jefferson U. (family law and psychiatry). Mem. Phila. Vol. Lawyers for the Arts (v.p.) Jewish. Home: 302 S Third St Philadelphia PA 19106 Office: Schnader Harrison Segal and Lewis 1600 Market St Suite 3600 Philadelphia PA 19103

HANDLER, EVELYN E., university president. Pres. Brandeis U., Waltham, Mass. Address: Office of the Pres Brandeis U Waltham MA 02254

HANDLER, JANICE, lawyer; b. Newark, July 9, 1945; d. Lester Robert and Rose Mildred (Reider) Handler; m. Norman Harry Ilowite, June 4, 1978. B.A., Douglass Coll., 1967; J.D., Rutgers Law Sch., 1970; LL.M., NYU, 1980. Bar: N.Y. Law clk. to presiding justice U.S. Dist. Ct. (so. dist.), N.Y.C., 1970-71; assoc. Fried, Frank, Harris, Shriver & Jacoboon, N.Y.C., 1971-72; atty. SEC, N.Y.C., 1972-74; counsel Thomas J. Lipton, Englewood Cliffs, N.J., 1974-77; mktg. counsel Lever Brothers Co., N.Y.C., 1977-83, asst. gen. counsel, 1983—; reviewer N.Y. Law Jour., N.Y.C., 1982—. Bd. dirs. Douglass Coll. Assoc. Alumnae, 1972-74. Mem. ABA (sect. on litigation's com. on corp. counsel), N.Y. State Bar Assn. (Corp. Counsel Sect.), Assn. Bar City N.Y. (advt. industry subcom. 1982—).

HANDLER-PENNINGTON, MARGARET ANGELA, financial consultant, art consultant; b. Birmingham, Ala., Sept. 20, 1942; d. George Frederick and Regina Angela (Moreno) Kirchoff; B.A., U. Tenn., 1963; M.S.W., Smith Coll., 1965; m. Gerald Lee Pennington. Faculty dept. psychiatry Emory U., Atlanta, 1966-69; asso. dir. St. Jude's House, Atlanta, 1969-72; asso. dir. public affairs Mental Health Assn., Atlanta, 1972-73; alcoholism cons. Ga. Dept. Human Resources, Atlanta, 1974-75; fine art cons. Rentar Industries, N.Y.C., 1975-85; sec. Shannsongs, Inc., 1985—; pres. Marpal, Inc., Nokomis, Fla., 1980—; dir. Penn-Products, Venice, Fla., 1982—. Bd. dirs. New Coll. Music Festival, Sarasota, Fla., 1982-86, Sarasota-Manatee Jewish Family Service, 1986—; sec. bd. dirs. women's div. Sarasota-Manatee Jewish Fedn., 1986—. Recipient awards, grants: Vocat. Rehab. Adminstrn., Nat. Found., Gen. Tire and Rubber Co., Wallace Silver Co., SCV. Mem. Nat. Assn. Social Workers, Acad. Cert. Social Workers, Am. Assn. Mus., Am. Craft Council, Am. Assn. Individual Investors, Nat. Assn. Female Execs., Smith Coll. Alumnae Assn., DAR, Colonial Dames XVII Century, Pi Beta Phi. Jewish. Club: Hadassah. Home and Office: 2207 Casey Key Rd Nokomis FL 33555

HANDLEY, JEAN MARY, telephone company executive; b. Manchester, Conn., Aug. 28, 1926; d. Francis P. and Margaret (Ivers) H.; B.A., Conn. Coll., 1948; M.A., Northwestern U., 1949. Public relations asst. So. New Eng. Telephone Co., New Haven, 1960, various positions in advt. and employee info., 1960-66, dist. mgr. employee info., 1966-72, gen. info. mgr., 1973-75, gen. advt. mgr., 1975, v.p. public relations, 1978-82, v.p. corp. relations and advt., 1982-83, v.p. personnel and corp. relations, 1984—; div. mgr. public relations dept., planning and press relations AT&T, N.Y.C., 1972-73, press relations dir., 1976-78; Vice-chair, dir. Sci. Park Devel. Corp., New Haven. Bd. dirs. Bus. Council Women, N.Y.C., 1978-80, Hospice Inst., New Haven, 1978-80, Newington (Conn.) Children's Hosp., 1978-83; v.p. New Haven Symphony Orch. 1981-86, dir., 1986—; mem. pres.'s adv. council Quinnipiac Coll., 1979-80; trustee Conn. Coll., New London. Mem. Public Relations Am., Public Relations Soc. N.Y., Women in Communications, Am. Women in Radio and TV, Greater New Haven C. of C. (women's steering com.). Office: So New Eng Telephone Co 227 Church St New Haven CT 06506

HANDLEY, MARGIE LEE, asphalt and aggregates manufacturing company executive, real estate development company executive, engineering contractor; b. Bakersfield, Calif., Sept. 29, 1939; d. Robert E. and Jayne A. (Knoblock) Harrah; m. Gordon Daniel Lovell, Feb. 17, 1956 (div. Sept. 1973); children—Steven Daniel Lovell, David Robert Lovell, Ronald Eugene Lovell; m. Leon C. Handley, Sr., Oct. 28, 1975. Grad. high sch., Willits, Calif. With Firco, Inc., Willits, 1955-57; legal sec. Galen Hathaway, atty. at law, Willits, 1957; receptionist, typist Remco Hydraulics, Inc., Willits, 1958-62; tchrs. aide Montague Sch. Dist., 1964, sec. to dist. supr., 1965-68; owner, operator Shasta Pallet Co., Montague, 1969-70; owner, operator Lovell's Tack 'n Togs, Yreka, Calif., 1970-73; v.p. Microphor, Inc., Willits, 1974-81; pres. Harrah Industries, Inc., Willits, 1981—, Hot Rocks, Inc., Willits, 1983—. Sec. Willits Community Scholarships, Inc., 1962; trustee Montague Methodist Ch., 1966-73; sec. Montague PTA, 1969; clk. bd. trustees Montague Sch. Dist., 1970-73; del. Calif. State Conf. Small Bus., 1984; alt. del. Republican Nat. Conv., Kansas City, Detroit, 1976, 80; 3d dist. chmn. Mendocino County Rep. Central Com., 1978-84; mem. Calif. State Rep. Central Com., 1985; charter mem. Senatorial Inner Circle, 1980—; mem. Rep. Congl. Leadership Council, 1980-82; Mendocino County chmn. Reagan/Bush, 1980, 84; Mendocino County co-chmn. Deukmejian for Gov., 1982; mem. Region IX Small Bus. Adminstrn. Adv. Council, 1982—; mem. Gov.'s Adv. Council, 1983—; del., asst. sergeant of arms Rep. Nat. Conv., Dallas, 1984; vice chmn. Mendocino County Rep. Central Com., 1985. Home: 16000 Hearst Rd Willits CA 95490 Office: Hot Rocks Inc 42 Madrone St Willits CA 95490

HANDY, LAELA EUGENIE, university administrator; b. Framingham, Mass., Oct. 17, 1940; d. Kalel George and Eugenie (Nassan) Handy; m. Kenneth Duane Jacobsen, Aug. 23, 1959 (div. Sept. 1965); 1 child, Christopher Daniel. B.A. in Mgmt., U. Redlands, 1983; postgrad. Claremont Grad. Sch., 1983—. Office mgr. Calif. State Poly. U., Pomona, 1959-66, 68-69; exec. sec. Disneyland, Anaheim, Calif., 1966-68; office mgr. Calif. State U.-Fullerton, 1969-71, adminstrv. asst., 1971-73, asst. dean Sch. Human Devel. and Community Service, 1973—, cons., 1980—; cons. Planning Instn. Execs., Los Angeles, 1983-84. Author: Foods of Lebanon, 1984. Fund raiser Tital Athletic Found., Fullerton, 1978-83, Orange County council Boy Scouts Am., 1973-78. South Coast Repertory Theatre, Costa Mesa, Calif., 1975-83; cadet comdr. air search and rescue CAP, Burbank, Calif., 1955-59. Named Outstanding Cadet of Yr. So. Calif. Region, 1959. Mem. AAUW, Internat. Assn. Personnel Women, Women's Network, Orange County World Affairs Council, Nat. Assn. for Female Execs., Phi Delta Kappa. Democrat. Melchite/Byzantine Catholic. Clubs: Balboa Ski (Network Beach, Calif.); Group Z (Anaheim); Playboy (Los Angeles); U.S. Ski Assn. Home: 2401 E Sommerset Dr Brea CA 92621 Office: Office of Dean Sch Human Devel and Community Service Calif State U Fullerton Fullerton CA 92621

HANEBERG, RISE ANN BLOCK, juvenile probation officer; b. Salina, Kans., Mar. 18, 1957; d. Harold Leslie and Wanda (Johnson) Block; m. Jeffrey Wayne Haneberg, Aug. 6, 1977; B.S. magna cum laude, Wichita State U., 1978. With 10th Jud. Dist. Ct., State of Kans., 1979—, supr. juvenile probation services, Olathe, 1984—. Mem. Kans. Assn. Ct. Service Officers. Democrat. Lutheran. Avocations: antiques, handcrafts. Office: Juvenile Probation Services PO Box 787 Olathe KS 66061

HANEX, TAYLOR ANNE, banker; b. Washington, Mar. 30, 1953; d. John Joseph and Eileen Mildred (Diamondson) H. B.Mus., Peabody Conservatory of Music, Johns Hopkins U., 1975, M.Mus., 1978; M.B.A., Fordham U., 1980; postgrad. student U. Nebr.-Lincoln, 1975, Conservatorio Municipal de Musica, Barcelona (Spain), 1976. Performer, royalty sales rep. G. Schirmer Music Publs., N.Y.C., 1977-78; research asst. Bill Communications, N.Y.C., 1978-79; account exec. Microband Corp. Am., N.Y.C., 1981-82, nat. accts. mgr., 1983-85; asst. v.p. for bus. ops. Irving Bank Corp., N.Y.C., 1986, asst. v.p., asst. sec., 1986—; guest lectr. Kean Coll., 1983—; solo concert pianist East and Midwest U.S.; performed with Orquesta Mcpl. de la Teatro de Barcelona, 1976. U. Nebr. teaching fellow, 1975; recipient Mabel H. Thomas award Peabody Conservatory of Music, Balt., 1970; Fordham U. grad. fellow, 1979; Joseph Mullan scholar Peabody Conservatory of Music, 1975. Mem. Am. Mktg. Assn. Republican. Roman Catholic. Club: Toastmasters Internat. Home: 233 E 69th St New York NY 10021 Office: Irving Bank Corp One Wall St New York NY 10005

HANEY, JACQUELINE TAYLOR, civic worker; b. Gilbertown, Ala., Feb. 10, 1940; d. Robert Long and Billie (Smith) Taylor; B.S., U. So. Miss., 1961; m. Harry Lee Haney, Jr., June 16, 1962; 1 dau., Jacqueline Lee. Tchr. sci. and phys. edn. T.R. Miller Sch., Brewton, Ala., 1961-62; tchr. sci. Freeport High Sch., Fla., 1966-67. Co-chmn., Am. Heart Assn., Clarke County, Miss., 1963, Young Reps., Clarke County, 1964; pres. Forestry Wives of Yale U., 1968-69, Yale Dames, 1969-70, Yale Women's Coordinating Council, 1970-71; participant Yale Polit. Union, 1969-74; mem. PTA bd. Ridge Rd. Elem. Sch., North Haven, Conn., 1973-74; vol. Harding Ave. Elem. Sch., Blacksburg, 1974-76, v.p. PTA, 1975-76; co-chmn. publicity Blacksburg Middle Sch. PTA, 1976-77, co-pres., 1977-78, pres., 1978-79; mem. LWV, Blacksburg, Va., 1975-76; parent rep. Roanoke Youth Symphony, 1976-79; mem. Roanoke Symphony Aux., Va., 1977-79; chmn. bd. dirs. Little Bros./Little Sisters, 1977-79; pres. adv. council for arts in Montgomery County Schs., 1979-81; dist. chmn. cultural arts New River Valley PTA, 1979-80; bd. dirs. Voluntary Action Ctr., 1979-80; sweetheart Alpha Phi Omega community service frat., Va. Inst. Tech., 1980-86. Recipient Vol. Service awards Harding Ave. Elem. Sch., 1975-76, Little Bros.:/Little Sisters, 1978, 79; Life Membership award Va. Congress of PTA's, 1979. Presbyterian. Address: 305 Franklin Dr Blacksburg VA 24060

HANEY, KIMBERLY LANGHAM, nursing administrator; b. Pitts., Apr. 20, 1960; d. Samuel Richard and Barbara (Mitchell) Langham; m. Kim R. Haney, Oct. 1, 1983. B.S. in Nursing, U. Pitts., 1982. Lic. R.N., Ark. Staff nurse Shadyside Hosp., Pitts., 1982-84; Rebsamen Regional Med. Ctr., Jacksonville, Ark., 1984-85, edn. coordinator, 1985—. Vol. ARC, Little Rock chpt., 1984—, instr. CPR, 1985—; sec. Protestant lay council Little Rock AFB Chapel, Jacksonville, 1985—. Mem. Ark. Soc. Hosp. Educators, Cental Ark. Nursing Devel. Orgn., Alpha Tau Delta (pres. Mu chpt. 1981-82), Kappa Kappa Gamma (Pitts. nominating com. chmn.). Club: Officers Wives (Little Rock AFB). Avocations: Needlecrafts; reading; swimming. Home: 130 Illinois Dr Jacksonville AR 70276 Office: Rebsamen Regional Med Ctr 1400 Brader St Jacksonville AR 72076

HANEY, MARY BELL, civil engineer; b. Miami, Fla., Nov. 10, 1946; d. James Bell and Suzanna (Allen) Trout; B.S.C.E., Clemson U., 1967, M.S. in Environ. Systems Engring. (USPHS trainee), 1968, postgrad. in mgmt., 1968-76; postgrad. in chemistry U. Tex., San Antonio, 1980-81; doctoral candidate Calif. Coast U.; m. Donald Lee Haney, Aug. 15, 1967; children—James Reuben, Donald Louis. Vis. lectr. and adj. prof. U. N.Mex., 1970-72; v.p. engring. Ruben Rodriguez Land Devel. Inc., Albuquerque, 1970-74; asst. project mgr. Pape-Dawson Cons. Engrs., Inc., San Antonio, 1976-78, project engr., 1978-82, project mgr., 1982—. Mem. properties com. Girl Scouts U.S.A., San Antonio; sec. Universal City Planning and Zoning Commn., 1985—. Registered profl. engr., Tex. Mem. Nat. Soc. Profl. Engrs., Tex. Soc. Profl. Engrs. (dir. 1980, treas. 1981, sec. 1982, mem. Speakers Bur. 1979—, dir. 1984, Outstanding Young Engr. of Yr. award Bexar chpt. 1982, Tex. 1982), Soc. Women Engrs., Assn. Women in Sci., Nat. Assn. Female Execs., Am. Statis. Assn., Water Pollution Control Fedn., Planetary Soc., ASCE, San Antonio Council Engring. Edn., NOW, YWCA, AAUW, Tau Beta Pi (Women's Badge 1965), Phi Kappa Phi, Sigma Tau Epsilon. Methodist. Clubs: Altrusa; Protestant Women of Chapel (pres. club 1975-76). Contbr. articles to profl. publs. Home: 318 Amistad Blvd Universal City TX 78148 Office: 9310 Broadway San Antonio TX 78217

HANEY, SHARON LORRAINE, restaurant company executive; b. Sacramento, May 6, 1942; d. Donald Leroy and Jacquelyn Delza (Woods) Glasson; m. Gaylon L. Haney, Mar. 10, 1963; children—Kathleen E., Kirk L. B.S., Fresno State U., 1964. Pres. Gaylon Haney, Inc., Salinas, Calif., 1966-78, Peninsula West, Inc., Monterey, Calif., 1978—. Chmn. benefit scholarship fund Santa Catalina Sch., Monterey, 1981-85; vol. Calif. Internat. Air Show, Salinas, 1981-85. Republican. Episcopalian. Avocations: tennis, coin collecting. Home: 12732 Sundance Lane Salinas CA 93908 Office: Peninsula West Inc 177 Webster St Suite 423 Monterey CA 93940

HANEY-JENKINS, TERILYN, sales executive; b. Maryville, Tenn., Oct. 30, 1956; d. Harold Ross and Glenda Marie (Duncan) Haney; m. Thomas Allan Jenkins, June 23, 1984. B.S.B.A., Appalachian State U., 1981. Sales rep. Van Heusen Co., Atlanta, 1981-84, Wrangler Co., Atlanta, 1985; v.p. mktg. and sales Logo House, Inc., Atlanta, 1986—; cons. Patter Prodns., Atlanta, 1984—; cons. promotional logos. Recipient sales awards Wrangler, Van Heusen. Mem. Nat. Assn. Female Execs., Young Republicans, Jaycettes. Avocations: golf, reading, skiing, aerobics, sailing. Home: 359 Sope Creek Ridge Marietta GA 30067 Office: Logo House Inc 2060 Bratton St NW Atlanta GA 30309

HANFT, RUTH S. SAMUELS (MRS. HERBERT HANFT), economist; b. N.Y.C., July 12, 1929; d. Max Joseph and Ethel (Schechter) Samuels; B.S., Cornell U., 1949; M.A., Hunter Coll., 1963; m. Herbert Hanft, June 17, 1951; children—Marjorie Jane, Jonathan Mark. Cons., Urban Med. Econs. Project, Hunter Coll., N.Y.C. and D.C. Dept. Health, 1962-63; health economist Office of Research and Stats., Social Security Adminstrn., Washington, 1964-66; chief grants mgmt., health div. OEO, Washington, 1966-68; sr. health analyst Office of Asst. Sec. Planning and Evaluation, HEW, Washington, 1968-71, spl. asst., asst. sec. health, 1971-72, dep. asst. sec. for health policy, research and stats., 1977-79, dep. asst. sec. for health research, stats. and tech., 1979-81, cons., 1981—; adj. prof. Dartmouth Med. Sch., 1976—. Sr. research assoc. Inst. Medicine-Nat. Acad. Scis., Washington, 1972-76. Fellow Hastings Inst. Bioethics; mem. Inst. Medicine of Nat. Acad. Sci. Jewish. Contbr. articles to profl. jours. Home: 3609 Cameron Mills Rd Alexandria VA 22305 Office: 2121 Wisconsin Ave NW Washington DC 20007

HANKIN, LOIS DUREITZ, management consultant, construction company executive; b. Cleve., Aug. 6, 1945; d. Arthur Frank and Ruth Gertrude (Renner) DuReitz; student (grantee) Mt. Union Coll., 1963-64, Ohio State U., 1964-65; B.S., Case Western Res. U., 1970; m. Norman Hankin, Oct. 31, 1976. Bookkeeper, Chem. Rubber Co., Cleve., 1965-70; office mgr. Importa Ltd., Washington, 1970-71; controller Nat. Coordinating Council on Drug Edn., Washington, 1971-72; v.p. fin. Am. Footwear Industries Assn., Arlington, Va., 1972-76; legal adminstr., controller Lane and Edson, P.C., Washington, 1977-81; pvt. practice mgmt. cons., 1976-77, 81—; pres. Hankin Constrn., Inc., 1984—. Treas., Sierra Villas Homeowners Assn., 1975; active Young Democrats, 1966-69, Stokes for Mayor campaign, 1968; nat. judge Distbv. Edn. Clubs Am., 1978. Recipient Service award Howard County Handicapped, 1977; resolution of appreciation for service, fin. mgmt. com. of Am. Footwear Industries Assn., 1976. Mem. Nat. Assn. Women in Constrn., ABA, Assn. Legal Adminstrs. (nat. and capital chpt.). Jewish. Home: 7165 Deer Valley Rd Highland MD 20777

HANKINS, SHIRLEY, state representative; b. Colby, Kans., Nov. 9, 1931; d. Mack Olif Williams and Florance (Wheaton) Williams Richard; m. Myron M. Hankins, Sr., Aug. 6, 1950 (dec.); children—Myron M., Jr., Shelley D., Sherrey A. Communications program coordinator UNC Nuclear Industry Inc., 1981-86; mem. Wash. Ho. of Reps.; mem. acad. adv. bd. Pa. Power and Light; bd. advisors Inst. for Regulatory Sci. Mem. Richland Republican Women; life mem. Richland Jr. Women's Club; past chmn. Tri-City Tech. Council. Mem. Richland Fedn. Women's Clubs, Richland Bus. and Profl. Women's Clubs, Health Physics Soc. (Columbia chpt.), Am. Nuclear Soc., Inc. (Richland sect.), Assns. Records, Mgrs. and Adminstrs. (Columbia Basin chpt.), Thomas County Hist. Soc., Am. Legion Aux. #71, U.S. Navy League (hon.), Washington Women, Tri-City Traditional Jazz Soc., UNC Nuclear Industries Mgmt. Assn. Methodist.

HANKS, BEATRICE JONES, magazine publisher; b. Washington, Mar. 2, 1950; d. Tiffany Millar and Virginia (Mithoff) Jones; m. Daniel N. Wood, Jan. 27, 1970 (div. Mar. 1972); m. Stephen Howard Hanks, Sept. 27, 1981. B.A., Bryn Mawr Coll., Pa., 1971; M.S. U. Pa., 1972. Coordinator, Praire-Dispatch Newspaper, Champaign-Urbana, Ill., 1973-75; account exec. Pubs. Clearing House, Port Washington, N.Y., 1976-77; account mgr. Sport Mag., N.Y.C., 1977-80, circulation mgr., 1980-81; circulation dir. Direct Mag., N.Y.C., 1981-83; founder, pub., pres. New York Sports Mag., Bklyn., 1983—; cons. in field; dir. New York Sports Inc. Avocations: backpacking; spelunking. Office: New York Sports 812 Carroll St Brooklyn NY 11215

HANKS, BEVERLY JOAN, accountant, town official; b. Middlebury, Vt., Mar. 7, 1934; d. Hugh Lewis and Dorothy Emeline (Crossman) Atwood; A.S., Becker Jr. Coll., 1954; B.S. magna cum laude in Bus. Adminstrn., Nathaniel Hawthorne Coll., 1980; m. John King Hanks, Dec. 26, 1954; children—John Hugh, Donna Lynn, Cynthia Jean, Bruce Barton. Bookkeeper to controller Semikron Internat., Hudson, N.H., 1977-79; controller Commonwealth Chem. Corp., Tewksbury, Mass., 1979-80, cons., 1981; town acct. Town of Hudson (N.H.), 1981-83; co-owner, treas., clk., Harbor's Head, Inc., Boothbay Harbor, Maine, 1983—. Town chmn. Reagan for Pres., 1976; treas. Town of Hudson, 1975-77, mem. budget com., 1976-77. Mem. Boothbay Harbor C. of C. (fin. advisor). Home and office: 7 Union St Boothbay Harbor ME 04538

HANKS, ELIZABETH ANN, city official; b. Lawrenceburg, Ky., Feb. 10, 1930; d. William Geoble and Myrtle Frances (Overstreet) Crossfield; m. Paul Wickliffe Hanks, Nov. 4, 1950; children—George Wickliffe, Brent Coleman. B.S., Bethel Coll., 1950. City clk. Lawrenceburg, Ky., 1957-58, 72—; substitute tchr. City of Lawrenceburg, 1958-60, bookkeeper Fashion Shop, Lawrenceburg, 1965-71. Home: 207 Gailane St Lawrenceburg KY 40342 Office: City of Lawrenceburg 201 Court St Lawrenceburg KY 40342

HANNA, INGA HAUGAARD, financial planner; b. Portland, Maine, Jan. 6, 1930; d. Ejnar Nielsen and Helene Martine (Buje) Haugaard; B.S., Simmons Coll., Boston, 1954; M.B.A., U. Mo., Columbia, 1973; m. John G. Hanna, July 2, 1949; children—Erik H., Charlotte H. Stock broker Putnam, Coffin & Burr, Portland, 1964-67; investment research officer Canal Nat. Bank, Portland, 1967-70; exec. dir. Treemont of Dallas, 1973-75, Portland YWCA, 1976-80; ind. fin. planner, Portland, 1980—; corporator Maine Savs. Bank. Mem. bd. World Affairs Council Maine, 1980-85. Recipient Thomas P. Weill award U. Mo., 1973; Danforth asso., 1981. Mem. Inst. Fin. Planners (cert.), Internat. Assn. Fin. Planners, Am. Soc. Profl. Cons., Maine Econ. Soc. (bd. dirs. 1983-85).

HANNA, LINDA HANNA WOHLGEMUTH, property management executive; b. Rochester, N.Y., Jan. 7, 1944; d. Basil Douglas Robinson and Charlotte Elizabeth (Toke) Robinson. B.S., Eastern Mich., 1967; M.A., Santa Clara, 1973. Tchr. English, Bellvue High Sch., Ypsilanti, Mich., 1967; tchr. English, Blackford High Sch., San Jose, Calif., 1967-70, dean of students, 1970-72; dean students Del Mar High Sch., San Jose, 1972-74; mktg. rep. QSP Inc., sub. Reader's Digest, Ridgefield, Conn., 1975-84; dir. sales Food Service Trade Ctr., San Francisco, 1985—; v.p. Instnl. Brokerage Co. Inc., Orinda, Calif., 1985—. Mem. Nat. Assn. Female Execs., Sierra Club. Club: Republican Women. Avocations: skiing; tennis; vocal; piano; photography; sailing; painting. Office: 1550 Bryant St San Francisco CA 94103

HANNAGAN, ANGELA MARIE, educator; b. St. Louis, Dec. 21, 1917; d. Edward Michael and Helen A. (Piechowski) H.; B.A., Fontbonne Coll., 1940; postgrad. Northwestern U., 1942-43, Ind. U. N.W., summers 1969, 70, 71. Dir. public relations Fontbonne Coll., 1940-41; with Famour-Barr Co., 1941-42, Employers Mut. Ins. Co., 1942; tchr. English, East Lansing (Mich.) High Sch., 1943-44; tchr. English, Lew Wallace High Sch., Gary, Ind., 1944—, chmn. English dept., 1965—. Recipient Viola Briley award local 4 Am. Fedn. Tchrs., 1974; named Lew Wallace High Sch. Outstanding Tchr. of Yr., Inland Steel Co., 1983. Mem. Nat. Council Tchrs. English (dir.), Ind. Council Tchrs. English (exec. bd. 1967—; E. H. Kemper McComb award 1981), Gary English Council (pres. 1960-61), Am. Fedn. Tchrs. (exec. bd. local 4, 1963—), Internat. Platform Assn., Fontbonne Coll. Alumnae Assn. (sec. 1940-42). Roman Catholic. Home: 430 S Grand Blvd Apt 415 Gary IN 46403 Office: Lew Wallace High Sch 415 W 45th Ave Gary IN 46408

HANNAH, MARY ELIZABETH, psychologist, educator; b. Bklyn., Sept. 8, 1940; d. Richards Wesley and Marie (Eitelbach) H.; B.A., Sweet Briar Coll., 1962; M.A., Alfred U., 1970; Ph.D., George Peabody Coll., Vanderbilt U., 1974. Sch. psychologist Rockford (Ill.) Public Schs., 1973-76; assoc. prof. psychology dept. U. Detroit, 1977—, also dir. sch. psychology program. NIMH trainee, 1971-72; faculty research grantee, U. Detroit, 1977. Mem. Am. Psychol. Assn., Nat. Assn. Sch. Psychologists (sec. 1979-81, presdl. service award 1981), Mich. Assn. Sch. Psychologists (regional dir. 1978-80), Psi Chi. Episcopalian. Editor: Challenge, 1976; Horizons, 1977; Tomorrow's Children, 1979; Celebrating Children, 1980, profl. conf. procs.; assoc. editor Acad. Psychology Bull.; contbr. articles to research publs. in field. Office: Psychology Dept U Detroit Detroit MI 48221

HANNEGAN, MARTHA MARIE, fraternity executive; b. Kansas City, Mo., Nov. 8, 1932; d. Joseph F. and Mayme A. (Overbay) Carolan; student Baker U., 1950-53; B.A., U. Wichita, 1959; m. Robert Eugene Hannegan, Aug. 30, 1958 (dec.); children—Lawrence David, Thomas Joseph, John Patrick. Elem. tchr. pub., schs., Wichita, Kans., 1954-58; vol. officer, alumna pres. Alpha Chi Omega, Lincoln, Nebr., 1963-65, province pres., Nebr. and Iowa, 1969-73, asst. collegiate v.p., Phoenix and Houston, 1973-76, nat. collegiate v.p., Houston, 1976-80, nat. pres., 1980-83; dir. devel. Alpha Chi Omega Found., 1983—. Democrat. Mem. United Ch. of Christ. Home: 5963 Preston Valley Dr Dallas TX 75240

HANNIBAL, ANGERLINE, elementary educator; b. Liberty, Tex., Dec. 22, 1931; d. Abie and Agnes (Prophet) Mosley; m. Marvin Dewitt Hannibal, June 6, 1954; children—Wendell Donovan, Wanda Rene. B.S., Tex. So. U., 1955, M.Ed., 1963. Cert. elem. edn. tchr., Tex., numerous other certs. Tray setter St. Theresa Hosp., Beaumont, Tex., 1950-51; cashier Wooten's Drugs, Houston, 1953-56; typist Neiman Marcus, Houston, 1957-59; tchr. Houston Ind. Sch. Dist., 1959—; faculty rep. Tex. So. U. Reading Council, Houston, 1979; rep. United Negro Coll. Fund, Houston, 1981-82. Block capt. Gruss Rd. Civic Club, Houston, 1979—, sec., 1979-80; leader neighborhood st. lights project, Houston, 1976. Recipient Service award Houston Ind. Sch. Dist., 1980, Excellent Edn. award, 1981-82, others. Mem. Houston Tchrs. Assn., Tex. State Tchrs. Assn., NEA. Democrat. Baptist. Club: Philoetts (Houston). Home: 4302 Cornell St Houston TX 77022

HANNIGAN, VERA SIMMONS, business executive, former White House official; b. Bklyn., Aug. 20, 1932; d. John Albert and Sadie Marion (Ziegler) Rogel; student U. Md., 1965-71; m. John J. Hannigan, June 15, 1974; children by previous marriage—Stephen F. Simmons, Vera Marifay Simmons Staup, Susan G. Simmons Bolle. Mem. staff Sen. William B. Saxbe of Ohio, 1972-74; confidential asst. Asst. Atty. Gen. for Legis. Affairs W. Vincent Rakestraw, Dept. Justice, 1974-75; with Office of Legis. Affairs, The White House, Washington, 1975-77; Washington rep. land devel. Union Pacific Corp., Washington, 1977—. Active local Va. politics, Republican Party. Home: 11220 Wedge Dr Reston VA 22090 Office: 1120 20th St NW Suite 600 S Washington DC 20036

HANNON, ELIZABETH HALL, information service co. exec.; b. Washington, Oct. 16, 1941; d. John Richard and Elizabeth Mae (Garber) H.; B.A., U. Md., 1963; m. Kevin Hayes Hannon, Sept. 12, 1964; children—Patrick Michael, Kathleen Anne, Megan Theresa. Reporter, Sci. Service, Washington, 1963-64; sci. reporter Syracuse (N.Y.) Post Standard, 1964-72; tech. editor Pacific Gas & Electric Co., San Francisco, 1973-74; mgr. Inforum, Atomic Indsl. Forum, Washington, 1974-80; pres. Utility Data Inst., Washington, 1980—. Office: 2011 I St NW Suite 700 Washington DC 20006

HANSEN, DIANA VICTORIA, communications company executive; b. Mobile, Ala., Feb. 25, 1947; d. LeRoy T. and Nella V. (Franz) H. A.A., San Antonio Jr. Coll., 1967; student U. of Ams., 1968, Am. Inst. Banking, 1971; B.A., U. Tex.-Austin, 1969. Curriculum writer SW Ednl. Research Lab, Austin, 1979-70; sec. First City Bank, Houston, 1971-72; secretarial stenographer SW Bell Telephone Co., Houston, 1972-74, dist. sec., 1974, asst. v.p., sec., Dallas, then Austin, 1974-77, exec. sec. Dallas, 1977-78, staff mgr., 1978-83; mgr. AT&T Communications, Inc., Austin, 1983—. Active Tex. Republican Party. Mem. Nat. Assn. Female Execs. (bd. dirs. 1983), Telecommunications Network in Tex. (founder, bd. dirs.), Community Assn. (bd. dirs.). Roman Catholic. Author: Bilingual Education, 1970. Home: 4159 Steck Ave Unit 103 Austin TX 78759 Office: AT&T Communications Inc 4412 Spicewood Springs Rd Suite 101 Austin TX 78759

HANSEN, DIANA WILLIAMS, home economist; b. Rushville, Ind., Feb. 26, 1937; d. John Thomas and Dorothy June (Jackson) Williams; B.S., Purdue U., 1959; M.B.A., Bellarmine Coll., 1982; m. Gunnar Oscar Hansen, Sept. 1, 1968; children—Christina Diana, Gunnar Thomas. Editorial home economist Gen. Mills, Inc., 1959-62; public relations home economist J. Walter Thompson Advt., 1962-65; range dept. specialist home economist Gen. Electric Co., 1965-70; freelance home economist, 1970-74; mgr. home econs. range dept. Gen. Electric Co., Louisville, 1974-80, mgr. cooking performance devel., 1980-84; food/microwave cooking cons., 1984—. Mem. Louisville Home Econs. Assn. (pres. 1970-71), Home Economists in Bus., Am. Home Econs. Assn., Internat. Microwave Power Inst. (chmn. membership, chmn. public relations cooking appliance sect. 1976-80) Inst. Food Technologists (bd. govs. 1982-83). Author: The Microwave Guide and Cookbook, 1977, 78, 79, 80, rev., 1982; The Combination Range Guide and Cookbook, 1980; The Grill-Griddle-Range Guide and Cookbook, 1981; Creative Microwaving, 1986; newspaper columnist The Microwave Way, Courier Jour., Louisville Times; NewWave Cooking, Los Angeles Times; also articles. Home: 91 Valley Rd Louisville KY 40204

HANSEN, FLORENCE MARIE CONGIOLOSI (MRS. JAMES S. HANSEN), social worker; b. Middletown, N.Y., Jan. 7, 1934; d. Joseph James and Florence (Harrigan) Congiolosi; B.A., Coll. New Rochelle, 1955; M.S.W., Fla. State U., 1960; m. James S. Hansen, June 16, 1959; 1 dau., Florence M. Caseworker, Orange County Dept. Pub. Welfare, N.Y., 1955-57, Catholic Welfare Bur., Miami, Fla., 1957-58; supr. Catholic Family Service, Spokane, Wash., 1960, Cuban Children's Program, Spokane, 1962-66; founder, dir. social service dept. Sacred Heart Med. Center, Spokane, 1968-84, adminstrv. supr., now dir. Spokane and Inland Empire Artificial Kidney Ctr., 1968—; bd. dirs. Family Counseling Service, 1981—. Asst. in program devel. St. Margaret's Hall, Spokane, 1961-62; mem. budget and planning div. United Way, 1964-77, chmn. projects com., 1972-73; mem. Spokane Quality of Life Commn., 1974-79; mem. kidney disease adv. com. Wash.-Alaska Regional Med. Program, 1972-75. Mem. Nat. Assn. Social Workers (pres. Inland Empire chpt. 1972-74, sec., mem. exec. bd. Wash. chpt. 1975-78), Acad. Cert. Social Workers (charter). Roman Catholic. Home: 5609 Northwest Blvd Spokane WA 99205 Office: Sacred Heart Med Center W 101 8th St Spokane WA 99204

HANSEN, HEIDI NEUMANN, advertising executive; b. N.Y.C., Feb. 2, 1955; d. Roy G. and Carolyn (Holmes) Neumann; m. Bruce Alan Hansen, Sept. 1, 1985. Student MIT, 1975; A.B., Colby Coll., Waterville, Maine, 1977. Benefits adminstr. Gen. Host Corp., Stamford, Conn., 1977-78; pres. Letterworks Internat., Portland, Maine, 1981—; dir. X-Press of Maine, Portland, Letterworks Internat., Portland. Editor Indsl. Report MIT, 1975. Dir., Maine Handicapped Skiing, Portland, 1984—; vol. Maine Med. Ctr., Portland, 1982—; mem. Maine Audubon Soc., Falmouth, 1984—, Nature Conservancy, Brunswick, Maine, 1984—. Mem. Ad Club of Greater Portland (dir. 1983-85, v.p. 1985-86), Colby Coll. Alumni Council. Club: Appalachian Mountain. Avocations: travel; hiking; sailing. Home: 313 Fowler Rd Cape Elizabeth ME 04107 Office: Letterworks Internat 10 Exchange St Portland ME 04101

HANSEN, INA, nursery co. exec.; b. Schiedam, Netherlands, Jan. 2 1937; d. Johan and Johanna (Bezemer) van den Berge; A.A., El Camino Coll., 1978; B.S. summa cum laude in Bus. Adminstrn., Calif. State U., Dominquez Hills, 1981; 1 dau., Valentina Kacani. Freelance med. sec., Rancho Palos Verdes, Calif., 1972-75; tchr. med. assisting Harbor Coll., Los Angeles, 1975, 76, So. Regional Occupational Center, Torrance, Calif., 1976-77, Cerritos (Calif.) Coll., 1977-78; owner, operator Marina Orchids, Marina Del Rey, Calif., 1978—. Dir., treas. Netherlands Social Service Orgn. (under auspices Consul Gen. of Netherlands in Los Angeles), 1981. Cert. Adminstrv. med. asst. Mem. Am. Orchids Soc., Bromeliad Soc., Apt. Owners Assn. (So. Los Angeles County). Republican. Office: Marina Orchids 800 Washington St Marina Del Rey CA 90291

HANSEN, JOAN VERONICA, licensing consultant; b. N.Y.C., July 8, 1943; d. Frederick W. and Edith (Hansen) Hansen; m. Stuart H. Mendelson, June 14, 1966; 1 child, Scott J. Student Mich. State U., 1961-63, Pratt Inst., 1963, N.Y. Coll. Music, 1951-61. Vice pres., sec. Botany Industries, Inc., N.Y.C., 1969-75, also pres. Botany Products Corp.; v.p. Fruit of the Loom, N.Y.C., 1975-78; owner, chief exec. officer Hansen & Co., N.Y.C., 1978—. Mem. The Fashion Group, Internat. Licensing Assn. Office: 1290 Ave of Americas Suite 1225 New York NY 10104

HANSEN, JOYCE KAY, accountant, tax consultant, educator; b. Cedar Springs, Mich., Sept. 26, 1946; d. Raymond A. and Mildred Ruth (Mc Intyre) Wesche; m. John Raymond Hansen, Sept. 3, 1966; children—James K., Jeffrey K. B.S. in Journalism and Edn., Central Mich. U., 1968, M.A. in Math., 1971. Instr. math Clare Pub. Schs., Mich., 1968-72; adj. prof. Davenport Coll., Grand Rapids, Mich., 1974-79; prof., head dept. Jordan Coll., Cedar Springs, 1978-79; founder, dir. Mich. Tax Cons., Lansing, 1979-83; adj. asst. prof. Aquinas Coll., Grand Rapids, 1979—; pres., acct. J & J Bus. Services, Inc., Cedar Springs, 1980—. Contbr. weekly column Cedar Springs Clipper, 1979-80. Treas. Cedar Springs Econ. Devel. Corp., 1982-85. Named 1st woman to 200 Club, Mich. Tax Cons., 1980. Mem. Nat. Assn. Enrolled Agts., Ind. Accts. Assn. Mich. (edn. co-chmn. 1985-86, edn. chairperson 1986—, vice chmn., chmn. Grand Rapids 1985—), Nat. Soc. Pub. Accts. (rules com. 1986), Accreditation Council for Accountancy, Cedar Springs Area C. of C. (co-founder 1980, dir., pres., v.p. 1980—). Republican. Methodist. Club: West Mich. Bus. (Grand Rapids). Avocations: reading; camping; travel; movies. Home: 4171 Indian Lakes Rd Cedar Springs MI 49319 Office: J & J Bus Services Inc PO Box 560 20 E Beech St Cedar Springs MI 49319-0560

HANSEN, KATHRYN GERTRUDE, former state official, association editor, author; b. Gardner, Ill., May 24, 1912; d. Harry J. and Marguerite (Gaston) Hansen; B.S. with honors, U. Ill., 1934, M.S., 1936. Personnel asst. U. Ill., Urbana, 1945-46, supr. tng. and activities, 1946-47, personnel officer, instr. psychology, 1947-52, exec. sec. U. Civil Service System Ill., also sec. for merit bd., 1952-61, adminstrv. officer, sec. merit bd., 1961-68, dir. system, 1968-72; lay asst. firm Webber, Balbach, Theis and Follmer, P.C., Urbana, Ill., 1972-74. Bd. dirs. Univ. YWCA, 1952-55, chmn., 1954-55; bd. dirs. Champaign-Urbana Symphony, 1978-81. Mem. Coll. and Univ. Personnel Assn. (hon., life mem., editor Jour. 1955-73, Newsletter, Internat. pres. 1967-68), Annuitants Assn. State Univs. Retirement System Ill. (state sec.-treas. 1974-75), Pres.'s Council U. Ill. (life), U. Ill. Alumni Assn. (life), U. Ill. Found., Campus Round Table U. Ill., Nat. League Am. Pen Women, Monday Writers, AAUW (state 1st v.p. 1958-60), Bus. and Profl. Women's Club, Champaign-Urbana Symphony Guild, Secretariat U. Ill. (life), Fortnightly Club Urbana, Delta Kappa Gamma (state pres. 1961-63), Phi Mu (life), Kappa Delta Pi, Kappa Tau Alpha. Lodge: Order Eastern Star. Author: (with others) A Plan of Position Classification for Colleges and Universities; A Classification Plan for Staff Positions at Colleges and Universities, 1968; Grundy Corners, 1982; Sarah, A Documentary, 1984; Ninety Years with the Fortnightly Club of Urbana, Illinois; editor: The Illini Worker, 1946-52; Campus Pathways, 1952-61; This is Your Civil Service Handbook, 1960-67. Author, lectr., cons., editor publs. on personnel practices. Home: 1004 E Harding Dr Apt 307 Urbana IL 61801

HANSEN, LORRAINE (SUNNY) SUNDAL, counselor educator; b. Albert Lea, Minn., Oct. 11, 1929; d. Rasmus O. and Cora B. Sundal; m. Tor Kjaerstad Hansen, Dec. 15, 1962; children—Sonja, Tor S. B.S., U. Minn., 1951, M.A., 1957, Ph.D., 1962; postgrad. U. Oslo, 1959-60. English tchr., St. Louis Park, Minn., 1951-53, Lab. Sch., U. Chgo., 1953-54; tchr. English and journalism Univ. High Sch., U. Minn., Mpls., 1954-57, counselor, dir. counseling, 1957-70; asst. prof., assoc. prof., prof. ednl. psychology, 1962—, dir. project BORN FREE; cons. schs. and colls.; lectr., dir. workshops on career devel. and career edn. Author: Career Guidance Practices in School and Community, 1970; An Examination of Concepts and Definitions of Career Education, 1976; (with others) Educating for Career Development, 1975, 80; Career Development and Planning, 1982. Editor: Career Development and Counseling of Women, 1978; numerous BORN FREE publs., videotapes. Contbr. articles to profl. publs., chpts. to books. Fulbright scholar, 1959-60. Fellow Am. Psychol. Assn.; mem. Am. Assn. for Counseling and Devel., Minn. Assn. for Counseling and Devel. (cert. recognition 1976), Nat. Career Devel. Assn. (pres. 1985-86), Internat. Assn. Ednl.-Vocat. Guidance, Am. Sch. Counselors Assn., Am. Coll. Personnel Assn., Assn. for Counselor Edn. and Supervision (Nat. Disting. Mentor award 1985). Democrat. Congregationalist. Clubs: Minn. Women's Consortium, WEAL. Office: 139 Burton Hall 178 Pillsbury U Minn Minneapolis MN 55455

HANSEN, LUISA FERNANDEZ, physicist; b. Santiago, Chile, May 23, 1927; d. Alberto Fernández and Esther Morales; B.S., U. Chile, 1949; M.S. in physics, U. Calif. at Berkeley, 1957, Ph.D., 1959; m. W. L. Hansen, Mar. 1, 1954; 1 son, George Albert. Came to U.S., 1955, naturalized, 1959. Laboratorist in cosmic ray U. Chile, Santiago, 1950-55, asst. prof., 1953-55; research asst. U. Calif. at Berkeley, 1955-59; sr. research physicist Lawrence Livermore Nat. Lab., U. Calif. at Livermore, 1959—, also coordinator and recruiting mem. affirmative action program. Mem. exec. com. Mt. Diablo Ednl. Project, 1972-75; chmn. com. Chileno, 1973-79. Mem. Am. Phys. Soc. (com. on internat. freedom of scientists, com. on status of women in physics), Am. Nuclear Soc., Bay Area Women in Sci. Network, Calif. Alumni Assn., AAUW, Sigma Xi. Contbr. over 100 articles to profl. jours. Home: 15 Avalon Ct Walnut Creek CA 94595 Office: PO Box 808 Livermore CA 94550

HANSEN, MARIE SABATA, former gas company executive, civic worker; b. nr. Bruno, Nebr.; d. Alois and Marie (Egr) Sabata; grad. Am. Bus. Coll., Omaha, 1929; ed. U. Nebr.-Omaha; m. Gilbert P. Hansen, Nov. 16, 1945 (dec. Mar. 1956). With No. Natural Gas Co. (now Enron Corp.), Omaha, 1931-72, dir. investor research and relations, 1969-72. Charter mem. Omaha Mayor's Commn. on Status of Women, 1969; bd. dirs., treas. Uta Halee Girls Village, Omaha, 1982—, chmn. policy and procedures com., 1984—; bd. dirs., parliamentarian Vols. Intervening for Equity, sr. citizens advocacy, Omaha, 1981-82. Mem. Nat. Assn. Parliamentarians (profl. registered), Nebr. Assn. Parliamentarians (treas. 1983-84, 1st v.p. 1984-86, pres.-elect 1986—), Cath. Daus. Am. (ct. parliamentarian 1981-82), Omaha C. of C. (past pres. women's div.). Clubs: Omaha Press (charter), Omaha Altrusa (pres. 1968-69, dist. treas. 1972-74, parliamentarian 1980-82).

HANSEN, MARILYN ELAINE, nurse; b. Pensacola, Fla., Feb. 13, 1941; d. Sylvester Arthur and Dorothy Elizabeth (O'Conor) Thomas; m. Ray Norman Hansen, Sept. 9, 1961; children—Randolph, Theresa, Michele, Ashley, Jeffrey. Diploma, St. Margaret's Sch. Nursing, Montgomery, Ala., 1961. R.N., Miss. Staff nurse Providence Hosp., Mobile, Ala., 1961-62; supr. Lakeland Nursing Ctr., Jackson, Miss., 1970-75; clin. educator Univ. Med. Ctr., Jackson, 1975-80; staff nurse Quality Care Nursing Service, Jackson, 1980-82, dir. nurses, 1982-85, adminstr., 1985—; cons. Mediplex, Inc., Jackson, 1976 78, PSRO, Jackson, 1975-77. Blood pressure screening nurse ARC, Am. Heart Assn., Jackson, 1980—. Recipient Nursing Dir. of Yr. award Quality Care Nat. Corp., 1983. Mem. Cath. Women's Assn. (bd. dirs. 1975-76, sec.-treas. div. 1976-79). Avocations: geneology; bridge; reading; music; handwork. Home: 5018 Canton Heights Dr Jackson MS 39211 Office: Quality Care Nursing Service 1050 C-1 N Flowood Dr Jackson MS 39208

HANSEN, MARY JACQUELINE, nurse; b. Maysville, Ky., May 5, 1956; d. Howard Lee and Mary Helen (Schuman) Kabler; m. Albert Edward Hansen, June 7, 1980; 1 dau., Marideth Anne. A. in Applied Sci., Maysville Community Coll., 1977. R.N., Ohio, Ky. Charge nurse St. Elizabeth Hosp., Covington, Ky., 1978-79; primary nurse Christ Hosp., Cin., 1979-80; supr. Clermont Convalescent Ctr., Milford, Ohio, 1977-78, 80-82; charge nurse Mt. Washington Care Ctr., Cin., 1982—; staff nurse Kelly Health Care, Cin., 1983—, on-call coordinator RN supr., 1984—. State Ohio chaplain DAV aux., 1977-78, musician, 1978-79, 81-82, 84-85, mem. unit 90, Ripley, Ohio. Mem. Ohio Nurses Assn., Republican. Roman Catholic. Home: 1051 Whitepine Ct Cincinnati OH 45230

HANSEN, PENELOPE MILLER, govt. ofcl.; b. Washington, July 4, 1938; d. David S. and Majorie (Taylor) Miller; student Skidmore Coll., 1956-58; B.S. cum laude, Johns Hopkins U., 1972; m. R. Brock Hansen, Nov. 18, 1972; children—Layne, David, Jared. Recycling coordinator, bd. dirs. Ecology Action, Balt., 1970-72; environ. protection specialist EPA, Washington, 1972-75, mgr. materials recovery program resource recovery div., 1975-78, mgr. state implimentation program Office Solid Waste, 1978-79, mgr. minerals and energy program, 1979-81, mgr. analysis and assessment program Indsl. Waste Div., 1981-84, chief Hazardous Waste Treatment br., 1984—. Recipient Bronze medal award EPA, 1975, Outstanding Service award, 1981. Mem. Am. Public Works Assn., Am. Polit. Sci. Assn. Author: Residential Paper Recovery, 1975; Decision-Makers Guide in Solid Waste Management, 1976; editor: National Recycling Directory, 1974; contbr. articles on hazardous waste treatment and waste recycling to profl. mags.; Home: 5158 Phantom Ct Columbia MD 21044 Office: EPA 401 M St SW Washington DC 20460

HANSEN, PHYLLIS JEAN, librarian; b. Ames, Iowa, Nov. 28, 1934; d. Elmer N. and Florence (Faust) H. A.B. with honors, U. Ill., 1960, M.S., 1961; M.A., Calif. Poly. State U., 1984. Librarian, Queens Borough Pub. Library, N.Y.C., 1961, San Leandro Community Library (Calif.), 1962-63, Calif. Poly. State U., San Luis Obispo, 1963—. Author bibliographies: Vitamin C, 1980, rev., 1984, Sex Role Stereotyping and Career Aspirations of Junior High and High School Students, 1983, Sex Role Stereotyping in Career Literature, 1984. Mem. ALA, Calif. Library Assn., Calif. Soc. Librarians, AAUW, County Hist. Assn. San Luis Obispo, Delta Kappa Gamma, Alpha Lambda Delta. Republican. Presbyterian. Club: Business and Professional Women (v.p. 1984-85) (San Luis Obispo). Home: 1241 Fredericks St San Luis Obispo CA 93401 Office: Calif Poly State Univ Library San Luis Obispo CA 93407

HANSENS, EUNICE DODD, civic worker; b. Vancouver, Wash., Nov. 11, 1919; d. William Wylie and Ada Eugenia (Wernette) Dodd; student Whitman Coll., 1937-39; m. Curtis Glenn Hansens, Feb. 6, 1948; children—Linda Yvonne, Glenn Elton, John Eric, Helen Aline. Exec. sec. United Way, Walla Walla, Wash., 1976-79; sec. Einan's Funeral Home, Richland, Wash., 1979-81;

office mgr. Richland Bell Furniture, 1981—; mem. economic devel. com. Walla Walla C. of C., 1977-78; pres. Republican Women of Walla Walla County, 1978-79; mem. Walla Walla Community Service Council, 1976—; mem. exec. com. Walla Walla Bicentennial Com., 1975-76; pres. Women's Guild of Walla Walla Symphony Soc., 1963, 73; mem. citizens study and adv. group, Walla Walla Regional Planning Com., 1974-81; mem. Walla Walla County Rep. Govtl. Conf., 1976-81. Mem. D.A.R. Republican. Lutheran. Mem. Order Eastern Star, P.E.O. (pres. Wash. chpt. 1971-72). Home: 507 Comstock St Richland WA 99352 Office: 714 Parkway Richland WA 99352

HANSFORD, NANCY GREER, city official, heating company executive; b. Kent, Ohio, Nov. 18, 1929; d. Redmond and Ruth (Gibson) Greer; m. Bruce William Hansford, Oct. 2, 1948; children—Susan, David. Student Kent State U. Bookkeeper Greer Heating, Inc., Kent, 1952-70, office mgr., 1970—; tax preparer H. R. Block Co., Kent, 1978-81, tax instr., 1980; mayor, pres. council City of Kent, 1982—; bd. dirs. Kent Downtown Corp., 1984—. Mem. care team Community Chem. Intervention, Kent, 1983—; chmn. campaign Portage County United Way, Ohio, 1985, trustee, 1985-87; moderator Eastern Ohio Assn. United Ch. Christ; gen. synod del. Ohio United Ch. Christ, 1983, 85; bd. dirs. Community Corrections Bd., Portage County Probation Dept., 1983—; trustee Portage County Alcoholism Service, 1983-86, Ohio Conf. United Ch. Christ, 1984-86. Mem. Ohio Mcpl. League Mayor's Assn., Nat. Assn. Parliamentarians (registered parliamentarian), Kent C. of C., Portage County Republican Women's Club, Chestnut Soc., Omicron Delta Kappa, Beta Gamma Sigma. Club: Coterie 111 (Kent). Lodge: Order Eastern Star (chpt. worthy matron 1962, Grand Ruth 1970, grand rep. 1975-77). Home: 1 Evergreen Dr Kent OH 44240 Office: City of Kent 319 S Water St Kent OH 44240

HANSON, ANN H., state legislator; b. May 10, 1935; m. Daniel J. Hanson, 1958; children—Julie, Jennifer, Rebecca, Erica. B.S., U. Vt., 1956. Mem. R.I. Ho. of Reps. from 88th Dist., 1980-83, dep. minority leader, 1983; mem. R.I. State Senate from 44th Dist., 1983—, dep. minority leader, 1983. Active Barrington Town Council, 1975-80, v.p., 1976-78, pres., 1978-80; active R.I. Save the Bay. Mem. LWV, R.I. Women's Polit. Caucus. Roman Catholic. Republican. Office: RI State Capitol Bldg Providence RI 02903*

HANSON, ANNE COFFIN, art historian; b. Kinston, N.C., Dec. 12, 1921; d. Francis Joseph Howells and Annie Roulhac (Coffin) Coffin; B.F.A., U. So. Calif., 1943; M.A. in Creative Arts, U. N.C., 1951; Ph.D., Bryn Mawr Coll., 1962; m. Bernard Alan Hanson, June 27, 1961; children by previous marriage—James Warfield Garson, Robert Coffin Garson, Ann Blaine Garson. Instr., Albright Art Sch., U. Buffalo, 1955-58; vis. asso. prof. art Cornell U., 1963; asst. prof. Swarthmore Coll., 1963-64, Bryn Mawr Coll., 1964-68; dir. Internat. Study Center, Mus. Modern Art, N.Y.C., 1968-69; adj. asso. prof. N.Y. U., 1969-70; prof. history art Yale U., New Haven, 1970—, John Hay Whitney prof., 1978—, chmn. dept., 1974-78, acting dir. Yale U. Art Gallery, 1985—; resident Am. Acad. Rome, spring, 1974; mem. Inst. for Advanced Study, Princeton, N.J., fall 1983. Nat. Endowment for Humanities fellow, 1967-68; Am. Council Learned Socs. grantee, summer 1963, fellow, 1983-84. Mem. Coll. Art Assn. Am. (pres. 1972-74), Comité Internationale de l'histoire de l'Art (nat. mem.). Author: Jacopo della Quercia's Fonte Gaia, 1965; Edouard Manet, 1966; Manet and the Modern Tradition, 1977; The Futurist Imagination, 1983; contbr. articles to profl. jours; editorial bd. The Art Bull., 1971—; editor monograph series Coll. Art Assn., 1968-70; governing bd. Yale U. Press, 1977—; editorial com. Art Jour., 1979-83. Office: Dept History Art 56 High St Yale U New Haven CT 06520

HANSON, FLORENCE COMFORTI, real estate broker; b. Cicero, Ill., May 17, 1923; d. Louis and Ida (Capalbo) Conforti; m. Elmer K. Fischer, Jan. 17, 1941 (div.); children—Linda Lou, James Louis, Louis; m. 2d, Herbert E. Hanson, Apr. 21, 1962; stepchildren—Lance, Patrice, Linda Ann, Craig, 1 son, David. Student Creighton U., DePaul U., 1957-59; grad. Real Estate Inst., Peoria, Ill., 1973. GRI, 1974; CRS, 1978. Sec., then exec. sec. Hotpoint Co., Chgo., 1957-60; exec. sec. to v.p. adminstrn. Goss Co., Cicero, Ill., 1960-62; real estate salesperson Dennis Realty, Berwyn, Ill., 1971-73; salesperson Pav-Hanson Realty, Berwyn, 1973-79; owner, prin. Hanson Realty, Berwyn, 1979—. Leader, Girl Scouts U.S.A.; organized Berwyn br. Am. Cancer Soc., 1972; sec. to pres. Emerson Sch. PTA, Berwyn, 1968-72; v.p. program women's aux. MacNeal Hosp., 1984. Mem. Women in Real Estate (recipient Flavia Marcucci Meml. award 1983, sec. 1975-76, 1st v.p. 1976-77, pres. 1977-78), Women Council Realtors (1st v.p. west suburban chpt. 1977-83, 1st v.p. Ill. chpt. 1982, pres. Ill. chpt. 1983, regional v.p. Ill., Wis. and Ind., 1984), West Town Bd. Realtors (sec., 1st v.p., pres. local bd. 1973-78), Ill. Assn. Realtors, RMNI Mktg. Soc. Ill. Assn. Realtors ($1 million producer 13 consecutive yrs.). Roman Catholic. Home: 2930 S Harlem Ave Riverside IL 60546 Office: Hanson Realtors 6500 W Cermak Rd Berwyn IL 60402

HANSON, JANET CURTIS, lawyer; b. Chgo., Jan. 9, 1948; d. Bruce B. and Marie Katherine (Marsh) Curtis. B.A. magna cum laude, Denison U., 1969; M.A., U. Minn., 1970; A.A., Edmonds Community Coll., 1978; J.D., Stanford U., 1981. Instr., So. Conn. State Coll., New Haven, 1973-74; parent edn. instr. N. Seattle Community Coll., 1974-76; paralegal George Wm. Cody, Lynwood, Wash., 1978, Davis, Wright, Todd, Riese & Jones, Seattle, 1977-78; assoc. Miller, Nash, Wiener, Hager & Carlsen, Portland, Oreg., 1981-84; assoc. gen. counsel N.W. Power Planning Council, Portland, 1984—. Contbr. articles to profl. jours. Bd. dirs., crime watch chmn., historic preservation chmn. Irvington Community Assn., Portland, 1982—. Mem. ABA, Oreg. State Bar, Multnomah County Bar Assn., Nat. Trust Hist. Preservation, Phi Beta Kappa, Sigma Xi, Psi Chi, Kappa Delta Pi. Presbyterian. Club: City (Portland). Home: 1631 NE Klickitat St Portland OR 97212 Office: Northwest Power Planning Council 850 SW Broadway Suite 1100 Portland OR 97205

HANSON, KAREN LINNEA, medical technologist; b. Moline, Ill., Sept. 8, 1936; d. Earl Henning and Rose Linnea (Anderson) Hanson; B.A., Augustana Coll., 1958; cert. med. tech. Rockford Meml. Hosp. Sch. Med. Tech., 1962. Med. technologist chemistry dept. Rockford (Ill.) Meml. Hosp., 1958-60, 1962-71, lab. Quad Cities Pathologist Group, Moline Luth. Hosp., 1971—. Aux. mem. Quad-City Symphony Orch., city chmn., 1978—, treas., 1984—, chmn., Moline City, 1977-78, vice chmn., 1976-77; mem. ch. council St. John's Luth. Ch., Rock Island, Ill., 1978-81, mem. worship and music com., 1978-81, chairperson program div., 1980-81, mem. altar guild, 1973—, mem. worship and music com., fine arts com., 1984—, tchr. Sunday sch., 1978-79. Mem. Am. Soc. Med. Technologists, Am. Soc. Clin. Pathologists (affiliate mem., cert med. technologist), Handel Oratorio Soc., P.E.O. Home: 3243 9 Ave Rock Island IL 61201 Office: Lutheran Hosp 501 10 Ave Moline IL 61265

HANSON, KAREN NOBLE, real estate financial company executive; b. Rochester, N.Y., June 17, 1943; d. Joseph L. and Kathryn C. Noble; children by previous marriage—Tammy C. Tobin, Scott R. Tobin, Robert L. Tobin; m. Thomas L. Hanson, May 7, 1977; 1 stepchild, Timothy. Student Syracuse U., 1961-63; B.A. cum laude, U. Rochester, 1971, postgrad., 1972; postgrad. Dept. Agr. Sr. Exec. Service Devel. Program, 1981. Teaching fellow U. Rochester, 1971, grad. teaching asst., 1971-72; dir. agrl. manpower Cornell U., Ithaca, N.Y., 1972-73; exec. dir. Program Funding, Inc., Rochester, N.Y., 1973-77; dir. Farmer's Home Adminstr., U.S. Dept. Agr., N.Y. and U.S. V.I., 1977-81, spl. asst. to adminstr., Washington, 1981; v.p. Genesee Mgmt. Inc., mgmt. holding co. for Wilmorite, Inc., Rochester, 1981—; chairperson N.Y. State Rural Housing Adv. Com.; mem. Monroe County Indsl. Devel. Com. Bd. dirs. United Way Greater Rochester, Genesee Valley Arts Theater, Rochester Philharmonic Orchestra, Nat. Child Labor Com., N.Y.C.; trustee St. Augustine's Coll., Raleigh, N.C.; trustee council U. Rochester. Recipient Disting. Service award United Way Rochester, 1976, Spl. Service award Nat. Assn. Farm Workers, 1982. Mem. Rural Am., N.Y. State Rural Housing Coalition. Democrat. Episcopalian. Club: Tower (Charlotte, N.C.). Office: 1265 Scottsville Rd Rochester NY 14624

HANSON, MARTHA, lawyer; b. Syracuse, N.Y., Dec. 8, 1941; d. Elmore W. and Martha (Hughes) Hagadorn; m. John A. Hanson, Apr. 5, 1973. B.A., Syracuse U., 1962; diploma X-Ray tech. Calif. Coll. Med. X-Ray and Lab. Sci., 1964; B.S. in Law, Valley U., 1978; B.S. in Law, Calif. Coll. Law, 1980, J.D., 1980. Bar: Calif. 1982, U.S. Dist. Ct. (central dist.) Calif. 1982, U.S. Ct. Appeals (9th cir.) 1984; cert. secondary tchr., Calif.; cert. X-Ray technician, Calif.; lic. Calif. Dept. Real Estate. High sch. sci. tchr. Los Angeles Unified Sch. Dist., 1969-80; sole practice, Los Angeles, 1984—; med.-legal cons. Central Valley Med. Clinic, Van Nuys, Calif., 1984—. Vol. tchr. children's unit Camarillo State Hosp. (Calif.), 1968. Recipient Service award Fairfax High Sch. Student League, Los Angeles, 1977; Community Service award Nat. Council Women, Los Angeles, 1978. Mem. Los Angeles Trial Lawyers Assn., Los Angeles County Bar Assn., ABA, Women Lawyers Assn., San Fernando Bar Assn., Attys. for Animal Rights, Cetacean Soc., Alpha Epsilon Delta, Zeta Epsilon Tau, Nu Beta Epsilon. Home: 7058 Bianca Ave Van Nuys CA 91406

HANSON, MARY LOUISE, banker, political worker; b. Bremerton, Wash., Apr. 24, 1944; d. Lawrence Grant and Ruth Louise (Johnson) Dix; student U. Wash., 1962-64, U. Colo., 1973-77; m. Michael Zabinski, Aug. 19, 1983. Adminstrv. asst. U. Pa., Phila., 1965-70, Provident Mgmt. Corp., Providence, 1970-72; with First Nat. Bank of Denver, 1972-80; v.p., exec. banking dept. United Bank of Denver, 1980—; dir. Integrated Media; mem. adv. bd. Network mag., 1984—; lectr.; chmn. adv. council Aton Found.; various state bd. positions Colo. Libertarian Party, 1976—; nat. vice chmn. Libertarian Party, 1977-81, mem.-at-large nat. com., 1981—, regional rep. on nat. com., 1977, nat. fin. chmn., 1980; Libertarian candidate for treas. of Colo., 1978. Bd. trustees AMC Cancer Research Inst., 1982—. Mem. Nat. Fedn. Bus. and Profl. Women, Colo. Fedn. Bus. and Profl. Women (1st v.p., pres. 1984-85), Downtown Denver Bus. and Profl. Women (pres. 1978-80, state legis. chmn. 1980-81), Robert Morris Assos. Office: United Bank 1700 Broadway Denver CO 80217 also 7887 Katy Freeway Suite 385 Houston TX 77024

HANSON, SANDRA J. MCKENZIE, educational administrator; b. Amery, Wis., Jan. 15, 1949; d. Earl Edward and Ariel Gloria (Benson) McKenzie; m. Craig W. Hanson, June 14, 1969; 1 child, Andrea McKenzie. B.A., U. Wis.-Eau Claire, 1970; M.P.A., U. Puget Sound, 1978. Instr. S.W. Wis. Tech. Inst., Fennimore, Wis., 1970-72; account exec. Ad Factors Advt., Spokane, Wash., 1972-74; dir. spl. projects Wash. Community Coll. Dist. 17, Spokane, 1974-76; instr., pubs. advisor Community Coll. Dist. 12, Olympia, Centralia, Wash., 1978-81; dir. coll. relations South Puget Sound Community Coll., Olympia, Wash., 1981-85; dir. coll. relations and devel. Fort Steilacoom Community Coll. Tacoma, Wash., 1985—; dist. rep. 2-yr. coll. com. CASE-Region VIII, Washington, 1982-83, 84-86; dir. Graphic Identity Program, 1984. Editor, creative dir. Admissions Brochure Series, 1984. Publicity vol. Am. Cancer Soc., Thurston County, Wash., 1985—; co-dir. N. Thurston Citizens for Schs., 1978-80. Recipient Award of Merit, Olympia Tech. Community Coll., 1980-81. Mem. Council for Advancement and Support of Edn. (dist. rep.), Wash. Community Coll. Adminstrs. Assn. (exec. bd. dirs., sec-treas.), Wash. Info. Council, Nat. Council for Community Relations, Wash. State Community Coll. Pub. Info. Com. Avocations: sailing; skiing. Office: Fort Steilacoom Community Coll 9401 Farwest Dr SW Tacoma WA 98498

HANSON, SUSAN JANE, real estate development controller; b. Columbus, Ohio, Dec. 21, 1958; d. Paul Edward and C. Jane (White) Hanson Van Hoose. B.A., Capital U., 1980, M.B.A., 1986. Staff acct. Vantage Properties Inc., Columbus, 1980-81, asst. controller, 1981-84, v.p. fin. 1984-86. Mem. Nat. Assn. Female Execs., Am. Mgmt. Assn., Nat. Assn. Office and Indsl. Parks. Methodist. Avocations: reading; writing; sewing; swimming; bowling. Home: 1738 Brice Rd Apt 10 Reynoldsburg OH 43068 Office: Vantage Properties Inc 100 E Campus View Blvd Suite 100 Columbus OH 43085

HANSON, WANDA KAY, hearing aid audiologist; b. Mason City, Iowa, Nov. 12, 1947; d. Chris J. and Ruby Marie (Christian) Oelberg; m. Douglas R. Hanson, Sept. 17, 1967; 1 child, Jana. Grad. high sch., Mason City. Cert. hearing aid audiologist Nat. Hearing Inst. Scis. Receptionist Beltone Hearing Aid Service, Mason City, 1970-76, lic. hearing aid specialist, 1976—, cert. hearing aid audiologist, 1980—, purchased bus. and changed name to Am. Hearing Aid Ctr., 1983—, opened 2d office of Am. Hearing Aid Ctr., Cedar Falls, Iowa, 1985—; former tchr. sign lang. N. Iowa Area Community Coll. Editor: The Sign Lang., publ. Iowa Assn. Deaf, 1976-83. Mem. Mason City C. of C., Cedar Falls C. of C., Iowa Hearing Aid Soc. (bd. dirs. 1980-82, sec. 1982-84, conv. chmn. 1984—), Nat. Hearing Aid Soc., Nat. Assn. Future Women (bd. dirs. 1984-85), Profl. and Bus. Women's Club. Home: 1819 Cerro Gordo Way Mason City IA 50401 Office: Am Hearing Aid Ctr 107 E State St Mason City IA 50401 also Am Hearing Aid Ctr 109 Black Hawk Village Cedar Falls IA 50613

HANWACKER, PATRICIA AILEEN LUDWIG, telecommunications engineer, computer systems engineering consultant; b. Bklyn., Mar. 22, 1951; d. Henry Raymond and Margaret Adelaide (Binz) Ludwig; m. Gerard Francis Hanwacker, July 11, 1971; children—Jessica, Jarrod. B.S. in Math., St. John's U., 1971; M.S. in Computer Sci., Stevens Inst. Tech., 1974. Planning, equipment engr. N.Y. Telephone Co., N.Y.C., 1971-74; computer systems engr. AT&T, N.Y.C., 1974-76; staff supr. market research and forecasting AT&T Long Lines, Bedminster, N.J., 1976-78, dist. mgr. fin. planning, 1978-80, dist. mgr. tech. sales support, Somerset, N.J., 1980-82; nat. account mgr. for ABC, AT&T Communications, N.Y.C., 1982—; cons. Curriculum Concepts, N.Y.C., 1976; v.p. Quantum Investment Corp., Millburn, N.J., 1978—. Mem. Soc. Women Engrs., Internat. Radio and TV Soc., Pi Mu Epsilon. Republican. Office: AT&T Communications 32 Ave of Americas Room 456 New York NY 10013

HANZEL, MARSHA WEINSTEIN, writer; b. Columbus, Ohio, Oct. 3, 1947; d. Marcus Leroy and Eleanor Frances (Reich) Weinstein; B.J., U. Mo., 1969; postgrad. U. Va., 1970-71; m. Jeffrey Sheldon Hanzel; children—Michael Brian, William Stephen. Staff writer Norfolk (Va.) Virginian-Pilot, 1969-70; editor Norfolk Naval Sta. newspaper, 1972-73; staff writer Hartford (Conn.) Courant, 1973-74; free-lance writer and photographer, 1974—; food editor Richmond Jewish News, 1981—. Mem. Chesterfield County Multidiscipline Team on Child Abuse and Neglect; mem. subcom. multidisciplinary teams Gov.'s Adv. Com. Child Abuse and Neglect; bd. dirs. Va. chpt. Nat. Com. Prevention of Child Abuse and Neglect (SCAN); state bd. dirs. Parents Anonymous. Mem. Women in Communications, Nat. Fedn. Press Women. Club: Bon Air Jr. Woman's. Home: 1613 Robindale Rd Richmond VA 23235

HAQUE, MALIKA HAKIM, pediatrician; b. Madras, India; came to U.S., 1967; d. S. Abdul and Rahimunisa (Hussain) Hakim; M.B.B.S., Madras Med. Coll., 1967; m. C. Azeez ul Haque, Feb. 5, 1967; children—Kifizeba, Masarath Nashr, Asim Zayd. Rotating intern Miriam Hosp., Brown U., Providence, 1967-68; resident in pediatrics Children's Hosp., N.J. Coll. Medicine, 1968-70; fellow in devel. disabilities Ohio State U., 1970-71; acting chief pediatrics Nisonger Center, 1973-74; staff pediatrician, pediatrician in charge community pediatrics and adolescent clinics. Children and Youth Project, Children's Hosp., Columbus, Ohio, also clin. asst. prof. pediatrics Ohio State U., 1974-80; clin. assoc. prof. pediatrics Ohio State U., 1981—; staff pediatrician Columbus Children's Hosp.; cons. Central Ohio Head Start Program, 1974-79. Mem. Republican Presdl. Task Force, 1982—, trustee, 1986—; mem. U.S. Senatorial Club, 1983. Recipient Physician Recognition award AMA, 1971-85, Gold medals in surgery, radiology, pediatrics and ob/gyn; Presdl. medal of Merit, 1982; diplomate Am. Bd. Pediatrics. Fellow Am. Acad. Pediatrics (mem. Ohio chpt., Prep fellow 1986); mem. Ambulatory Pediatric Assn., Central Ohio Pediatric Soc. Islam. Research on enuresis; contbr. articles to med. jours. Office: 700 Children's Dr Columbus OH 43205

HARANG, LINDA SUZANNA, lawyer; b. Louisville, Aug. 12, 1949; d. Edmund E. and Mary K. (Klemenz) H. B.S., La. State U., 1970, M.S., 1976; J.D., Tulane U., 1982. Tchr., Jefferson Parish Pub. Schs., Metairie, La., 1970-79; news copy editor The Times-Picayune, New Orleans, 1978-81; atty. Cummings & Gambel, New Orleans, 1982-83; atty., assoc. McGlinchey, Stafford, Mintz, Cellini & Lang, New Orleans, 1983—. Editor: Environmental Law (Thomas J. Schoenbaum), 1981. Vol. water safety instr. ARC, New Orleans, 1967-84; bd. dirs., chmn. com. on mktg. and cost recovery S.E. La. chpt. ARC. Mem. ABA, Assn. Women Attys., La. Bar Assn., Phi Alpha Delta. Republican. Roman Catholic. Office: McGlinchey, Stafford, Mintz, Cellini & Lang 630 Camp St New Orleans LA 70130

HARBAUGH, VIRGINIA WAYNE, govt. adminstr.; b. Savannah, Ga., Dec. 15, 1930; d. Adrian Bancker and Jeannette Butler (Strong) Talbot; B.A., Smith Coll., 1952; M. Planning and Urban Design, U. Va., 1971; m. William Henry Harbaugh, Aug. 15, 1953; children—Lyn Hartridge Harbaugh Brennan, William Talbot, Henry Richmond. Sr. planner Thomas Jefferson Planning Dist. Commn., Charlottesville, Va., 1973-79, exec. dir., 1979—. Pres. League of Women Voters, Mansfield, Conn., 1957-59, Lewisburg, Pa., 1964-66; pres. Va. Citizens Planning Commn., 1976-78. Mem. Am. Inst. Cert. Planners, Am. Planning Assn. Democrat. Unitarian. Home: 1930 Thomson Rd Charlottesville VA 22903 Office: 413 E Market St Suite 102 Charlottesville VA 22901

HARBINSON, KIMBERLY TAYLOR, lawyer; b. Durham, N.C., Feb. 19, 1955; d. Harold Lawrence and Frances Ruth (Smith) Taylor; m. Joel C. Harbinson, May 24, 1980. A.B. summa cum laude, Duke U., 1977; J.D. with honors, U. N.C., 1981. Bar: N.C. 1981. Ptnr., Harbinson, Harbinson & Parker, Taylorsville, N.C., 1981—. Pres., Democratic Women of Alexander County, Taylorsville, 1981—; mem. council of rev. N.C. Dem. Party, 1982—; bd. dirs. Alexander County Arts Council, Alexander County Youth Services, 1981—. Mem. ABA, N.C. Bar Assn., Assn. Trial Lawyers Am., N.C. Acad. Trial Lawyers, N.C. Assn. Women Attys., 22d Jud. Dist. Bar Assn. (pres. 1983-84), Order of Coif, Phi Beta Kappa. Office: Harbinson Harbinson & Parker 109 S Center St Taylorsville NC 28681

HARBISON, MARGARET WARLICK, physical education educator; b. Cleveland County, N.C., Dec. 19, 1935; d. Walter Theodore and Lessie Lawrence (Downs) Warlick; B.S., Appalachian State U., Boone, N.C., 1957, M.A., 1963; Ed.D., U. Miss., 1974; m. Clyde Hilton Waters, May 31, 1964 (div.); 1 son, Jack Hilton; m. Paul Dean Harbison, May 16, 1981. Instr. phys. edn. jr. high schs., N.C., 1957-61, Fla., 1961-62; asst. prof. health, phys. edn. and recreation U. Miss., 1963-67; asst. prof. phys. edn. Kennesaw Coll., Marietta, Ga., 1967-70; asst. prof. health, phys. edn. and recreation Delta State U., Cleveland, Miss., 1970-74; prof., assoc. coordinator phys. edn. and athletics dir. for women East Tex. State U., Commerce, 1974—; area coordinator Spl. Olympics, 1983-84. asst. recreation dir.; supr. summer playgrounds. Bd. dirs. United Way, 1977-80, treas., 1978-80; mem. Commerce Parks and Recreation Adv. Bd., 1982—. Recipient Presdl. citation AAHPER, 1974; Disting. Community Service award, 1981. Mem. Am. Alliance for Health, Phys. Edn., Recreation and Dance, Tex. Assn. Health, Phys. Edn. and Recreation, Tex. Assn. Coll. Tchrs., So. Assn. Phys. Edn. for Coll. Women, Nat. Assn. Phys. Edn. in Higher Edn., Nat. Assn. Intercollegiate Athletics (exec. com. 1980-83), C. of C. (dir., 1978-81), Delta Kappa Gamma, Kappa Delta Pi. Democrat. Baptist. Club: Psychology (pres., 1978-80), Sand Hills Golf and Country (dir. 1984—). Home: 2824 McCarley Dr Commerce TX 75428 Office: Dept Health and Phys Edn E Tex State U Commerce TX 75428

HARBOE, RUTH STEINFURTH, nursing educator; b. Springfield, Ohio, Aug. 3, 1922; d. Albert William and Hilda (Burghart) Steinfurth; m. Edward Miller Harboe, Sept. 28, 1946; children—Joyce Harboe Baldwin, William, Ronald, Kathryn Harboe Kalal, Sherrill. Student Wittenburg Coll., 1940-42; B.S., Carnegie-Mellon U., 1945; M.S., U. Colo., 1967. R.N. Various teaching and nursing service positions, Denver, 1947-62; instr. Presbyterian Hosp. Sch. Nursing, Denver, 1962-66; asst. prof. U. Md.-Balt., 1967-68; coordinator nursing N. Campus, Community Coll. Denver, 1968-74; asst. prof. U. No. Colo., Greeley, 1975-77; asst. prof. nursing Sch. Nursing, U. Colo. Health Scis. Ctr., Denver, 1977—; adv. bd. Practical Nurse Sch., Beth Israel Hosp.; cons. I.M. Injections, Venereal Disease Clinic, 1980; speaker; mem. nursing com. Colo. Cancer Soc., Denver, 1980-83. Author in field. Asst., Westland Health Fair, 1972-77; active Jefferson County Comprehensive Health Planning, 1970-73; adv. com. Continuing in Nursing, Red Rocks Campus Community Coll., Denver, 1974-76; mem. nursing and health programs com. Mile High chpt. ARC, 1973-76; mem. council, choir, women's orgn., Sunday/Sch. tchr. Lutheran Ch. of the Master, also mem. bldg. com., 1980-82; active Health and Wellness Ctr., Lakewood (Colo.) Dept. Parks and Recreation, 1983. Mem. Am. Nurses Assn., Colo. Nurses Assn. (dir. 1980-83, pres. Dist. 20, 1971-72, affirmative action com. 1977-79). Am. Cancer Soc., Oncology Nurses Soc., Sigma Theta Tau (pres. 1979-80, dir. 1980—), Delta Phi Alpha, Phi Kappa Phi. Home: 867 S Cole Dr Lakewood CO 80228 Office: U Colo Health Scis Ctr 4200 E 9th Ave C-288 Denver CO 80262

HARBOUR, EARTHA YVONNE, social worker; b. Corinth, Miss., June 11, 1955; d. Samuel Lee Harbour and Dorothy (Coman) Harbour-Cummings. B.A., Rust Coll., 1977; student So. Meth. U., Dallas, 1979, N. Tex. State U., 1980-81. Social worker Miss. Welfare Dept., Corinth, 1977-79; program dir. YWCA, Dallas, 1980-81; supr. family care Visiting Nurse of Dallas, 1981-82; human service specialist City of Dallas, 1983—. Mem. Ambassador of Friendship, 1974; pianist Bapt. Chs., Corinth, Miss., 1968-79; sec. Munger Ave. Ch. Singles II, Dallas, 1981. Named Outstanding Young Woman Am., 1981; Leontyne Price scholar, 1975. Mem. Nat. Assn. Music Therapy, Music Educator Nat. Conf., Delta Sigma Theta. Republican. Club: E.S. Bishop (Corinth) (v.p. 1978-79). Home: 6117 Melody Ln #1075 Dallas TX 75231 Office: City of Dallas 912 S Ervay St Dallas TX 75201

HARBOUR, NANCY CAINE, lawyer; b. Cleve., July 30, 1949; d. William Anthony and Bernadette (Frohnapple) Caine; m. Randall Lee Harbour, Sept. 29, 1979. B.A. magna cum laude, U. Detroit, 1970; J.D., Cleve. State U., 1978. Bar: Mich. 1978. Writer, Project Map, Inc., Washington, 1971-72; newspaper reporter Alexandria Gazette, Va., 1972-73, Times Herald Record, Goshen, N.Y., 1973-75; atty. Conklin, Benham, et al., Detroit, 1978-82, Miller, Cohen, Martens, and Ice, P.C., Detroit, 1982—. Mem. Am. Trial Lawyers Assn., Mich. Trial Lawyers Assn., Mich. Bar Assn., State Bar Mich. (mem. compensation council 1983-85), Gamma Pi Epsilon. Democrat. Office: Miller Cohen Martens & Ice PC 2400 First Nat Bldg Detroit MI 48226

HARDAGE, JEANNETTE, nutritionist; b. Vernon, Tex., July 30, 1933; d. Augustus and Pearl (Hobson) H.; B.A., Tex. Christian U., 1969; B.S., Tex. Woman's U., 1953, M.S., 1971, Ph.D., 1973; m. Olan S. Johnson, May 31, 1953 (div. May 1981); children—Layne Jeanette, Dean Olan; m. 2d, Edward Whitaker, Jan. 3, 1982. Tech. writer, mech. design draftsman Gen. Dynamics, Fort Worth, 1953-70; asso. prof. nutrition and food so. U., Baton Rouge, 1973-78; asso. prof. home econs., dir. food sci. and nutrition program Norfolk (Va.) State U., 1978-82; dir. dietetic programs Tidewater Community Coll., Virginia Beach, Va., 1983—; dietitian Manning Convalescent Home, Portsmouth, Va., 1979—. Mem. Women in Communications (pres., 1960, 77), Am. Dietetic Assn. (regional pres. 1980), Am. Home Econs. Assn., Internat. Food Service Execs. Assn., Va. Restaurant Assn., Va. Public Health Assn. Methodist. Home: 937 Leckie St Portsmouth VA 23704 Office: 1700 College Crescent Virginia Beach VA 23456

HARDAWAY, EVELYN RENEE, data processor; b. Columbus, Muscogee, Ga., Dec. 19, 1948; d. Roscoe and Vesta Mae (Mitchell) H.; student Johnson C. Smith U., Charlotte, N.C., 1967-68, Am. Inst. Banking, Columbus, Ga., 1969-70. Auditing clk. First Nat. Bank, Columbus, Ga., 1969-72; office mgr. Cagle, Inc., Omaha, 1972-74; account exec. Flair Personnel Service, Atlanta, 1974-76; tech. adv. Am. Mgmt. Services, Denver, 1976-80; data processing coordinator Katy (Tex.) Community Hosp., part of Lifemark Corp., Houston, 1981—. Recipient Operations Excellence award Am. Mgmt. Services, 1979. Mem. Nat. Assn. Female Execs., Internat. Platform Assn. Office: PO Box 656 Katy TX 77449

HARDAWAY-SHEPHERD, HURTICENE, lawyer; b. Detroit, Nov. 9, 1950; d. Rosco and Martha Jean (Harris) H.; m. Reginald B. Shepherd, Dec. 1985. B.A., Wayne State U., 1972; J.D., U. Mich., 1975. Bar: Mich. 1975. Prehearing atty. Mich. Ct. Appeals, Detroit, 1975-76; asst. corp. counsel City of Detroit Law Dept., 1976-83; mng. atty. UAW-GM Legal Services, Pontiac, Mich., 1983-85; gen. mgr. Axis Tech., Inc., Detroit, 1985—; treas. Pub. Attys. Assn., 1978-82. Trustee, treas., 2d vice-chmn. Ferris State Coll. Bd. of Control, Big Rapids, Mich., 1980-88; active NAACP, Detroit, 1983. Warren E. Bow scholar, 1969. Mem. Detroit Bar Assn., ABA, Assn. Trial Lawyers Am., Nat. Assn. Female Execs., Women Lawyers Assn. Mich., State Bar Mich., Mich. Law Alumni Soc. (dir.). Baptist. Office: UAW-GM Legal Services Plan 140 S Saginaw Suite 700 Pontiac MI 48058

HARDCASTLE, MILDRED TUCKER, civic worker, genealogist, historian; b. Warren County, Ky.; d. James Harvey and Mildred (Carpenter) Tucker; m. John Vernon Hardcastle. Student, Transylvania U., Lexington, Ky., 1930-32. Regent Samuel Davies chpt. DAR, Bowling Green, Ky., 1965-83; vice-chmn. Seimes Microfilm Ctr. nat. DAR, 1979-85, mem. membership com., 1975-78; librarian Ky. DAR, 1962-65, registrar, 1965-68, organizing sec., 1971-74; officer Ky. Officers Club, 1959-62, sr. state officer Children of Am. Revolution; chaired various state DAR coms., including protocol com., 1981-83, resolutions com., 1980-83; founder, contbr. vols. of records Geneal. Library, DAR, Bowling Green, 1984-86; organizer Western Ky. Waterland chpt. Daus. of Am. Colonists, 1980, regent, 1980-83; pres. Huguenot Soc. Ky., 1971-73, v.p., 1984-86; pres. Warren County Hist. Soc. (Ky.), 1965-68, v.p. 1969-86; charter mem. Mus. Assocs. and Century Club, Western Ky. U., 1983-86; bd. dirs. Hist. Hobson House Assn., 1977-83, hon. mem., 1984-86; organizer 7 DAR chpts., 1 SAR chpt.; DAR chmn. Jubilee 1984 Festival, Warren County, Ky. Compiler: Nat. Society DAR Yearbook (Nat. Soc. DAR Outstanding designation) 1981, 82, 83, 84, 85. Recipient Medal of Appreciation Nat. Soc. DAR, 1975; Medals of Appreciation, Nat. Soc. SAR, 1962, 68, 83, Good Citizenship medal, 1983; Ky. Col., 1984. Mem. Nat. Soc. Huguenots (charter), DAR (state pres. 1984-86, state pres. 50 Yr. Club 1985—), Chi Omega. Democrat. Mem. Christian Ch. (Disciples of Christ). Lodges: Magna Charta Dames and Barons, Colonial Dames, Founders and Patriots Am., Washington Family Descs., Washington's Army at Valley Forge.

HARDEN, ANITA JOYCE, nurse; b. Jackson, Tenn., May 17, 1947; d. Percy Lawrence and Marjorie (Robison) H.; B.S. in Nursing, Ind. U., 1968; M.S. in Nursing, Ind. U.-Purdue U., Indpls., 1973; 1 son, Brian Robison Weir. Staff nurse Indpls. hosps., 1968-71; instr. Ind. U. Sch. Nursing, 1973-75; dir. continuing care Gallahue Mental Health Center, Indpls., 1975-80; mgr. psychiatry Community Hosp., Indpls., 1980—; clin. asst. prof. Ind. U., 1977-82, clin. asso. prof., 1982—; product line mgr. for psychiatry and mental health, 1986—; clin. asso., trainer Suicide Prevention Service, Indpls., 1974-77; chmn. adv. bd. de-institutionalization project Central State Hosp., Indpls., 1978-79; mem. Ind. Council Community Mental Health Center, 1979-80. Recipient Outstanding Achievement in Professions award Center Leadership Devel., 1981. Mem. Ind. U. Alumni Assn., Christian Women's Fellowship, 500 Festival Assos., Sigma Theta Tau, Chi Eta Phi. Democrat. Mem. Christian Ch. (Disciples of Christ). Author articles in field. Home: 4057 Clarendon Rd Indianapolis IN 46208 Office: 7150 Clearvista Dr Indianapolis IN 46256

HARDEN, JEAN ANN, diversified industry executive; b. Traverse City, Mich., Nov. 6, 1948; d. Charles F. Long and Florence Margaret (Jarmuloski) Rendall; m. William R. Harden II, June 21, 1969 (div.); m. William J. Reid, Apr. 29, 1983. B.S. in Edn., Central Mich. U., 1970; M.B.A., Case-Western Res. U., 1979. Asst. librarian Harshaw Chem. Co. subs. Gulf Oil Corp., Cleve., 1974-76, market analyst, 1976-79, mgr. market research, 1979-80, mgr. planning and market research, 1980-83; mgr. Bus. Data Ctr., TRW, Inc., Cleve., 1984-86, mgr. bus. research, 1986—; cons. United Way, Cleve., 1983, Jr. Achievement, Cleve., 1980. Mem. Cleve. Bus. Economists Club (sec.-treas. 1979-80, pres. 1981-82), Nat. Assn. Bus. Economists, N.Am. Soc. Corp. Planning (v.p. Cleve. chpt. 1982-83), Chem. Mktg. Research Assn. Office: TRW Inc 1900 Richmond Rd Cleveland OH 44124

HARDER, HEATHER ANNE, child care center administrator; b. Henderson, Tenn., Mar. 2, 1948; d. Wendell Anderson and Anne (Gibbs) Stacks; m. Robert Alan Harder, Apr. 3, 1971; children—Kerry Anne, Stacie Elizabeth. B.S., Ind. U., 1970, M.S., 1974. Tchr., reading specialist Crown Point Community Schs., Ind., 1970-79; mem. adj. faculty Ball State U., Muncie, Ind., 1977-79, Purdue U.-Calumet, Hamond, Ind., 1981-82, Gov.'s Stte U., University Park, Ill., 1985; owner, exec. dir. Small World Child Care Ctrs., Valparaiso, Ind., 1983—, Merrillville, Ind., 1980—. Mem. adv. com. Purdue U.-Calumet, 1982—, Home Econ. Relations Occupations Crown Point High Sch., 1983—. Grantee Lake County Job Tng. Corp., 1984-85. Mem. Ind. Assn. Edn. Young Children (N.W. rep. 1984-86), Midwest Assn. Edn. Young Children, Nat. Assn. Edn. Young Children, So. Assn. Children Under Six, Resource for Infant Edn. Methodist. Avocations: Reading; painting; watching old movies. Home: 501 S Main St Crown Point IN 46307 Office: Small World Child Care Ctr 86 E 70th Ave Merrillville IN 46410

HARDER, NORMA JEAN, public health nurse; b. Thomas, Okla., Apr. 5, 1940; d. J. Roy and Helen Annabel (Frey) Eyster; m. Jack Allen Harder, Sept. 10, 1961 (div. Nov. 1977); children—Rebecca, Robert, Rhonda, Ranell, Royce. R.N., Okla. Gen. Hosp., Clinton, 1958-61; B.S. in Nursing, Southwestern Okla. U., 1980. Head nurse Okla. Gen. Hosp., Clinton, 1961-63; supr. nursing Southwestern Meml. Hosp., Weatherford, Okla., 1963-68; supr. nursing Deaconess Hosp., Oklahoma City, 1969-74; pub. health nurse Okla. State Dept. Health, Clinton, 1980-84, dist. supervising nurse, 1984; mem. citizens adv. bd., div. nursing Southwestern Okla. U., 1980—. Mem. Okla. Nurses Assn. (dist. pres.), Am. Coll. Ob-Gyn Nurses Assn., Okla. Pub. Health Assn., LWV. Democrat. Baptist. Club: Homemakers (past pres.). Office: Custer County Health Dept 3030 Custer Ave Clinton OK 73601

HARDER, SARAH SNELL, university administrator; b. Chgo., Sept. 9, 1937; d. Frank Wen and Margaret Louise (Bryne) Snell; student U. Iowa, 1955-58; B.A., B.S. cum laude, U. Wis., LaCrosse, 1963; M.A., Bowling Green State U., 1966; m. Harry R. Harder, Feb. 7, 1961; children—Richard, Bentley, Jennifer, Aaron. Mem. faculty in English, Bowling Green State U., 1967-68; mem. faculty English, U. Wis., Eau Claire, 1968, adv. to older students, 1975-77, asst. to chancellor for affirmative action, 1975-78, asst. to chancellor for affirmative action and ednl. opportunity, 1978—; mem. U. Wis. regents' task forces on basic skills, status of women, minority/disadvantaged students; cons. women's employment and equity, non-traditional programs in higher edn. Co-chmn. Nat. Women's Conf. Com., 1979—; trustee Eau Claire Public Library, 1980—, pres., 1984-85; chmn. bd. dirs. AAUW Ednl. Found., 1985—; founding bd. dirs. Wis. Women's Network; exec. Leadership Eau Claire, C. of C. Named one of 80 Leaders for the Eighties, Milw. Jour., 1979; 1st Excellence in Service award U. Wis.-Eau Claire, 1984. Dept. Edn. grantee, 1978—. Mem. AAUW (nat. dir., dir. legis. program, award, pres. 1985—), LWV, Nat. Women's Polit. Caucus (award Wis. br.), Wis. Women's Council (chairperson), Delta Kappa Gamma (chpt. pres.), Alpha Lambda Delta. Democrat. Co-designer Beyond ERA—an Action Plan, 1982; contbr. articles to Redbook, Grad. Woman, Stateswoman. Home: 463 Summit Ave Eau Claire WI 54701 Office: Library 2058 U Wis Eau Claire WI 54701

HARDESTY, MARY JANE, oil company personnel executive; b. Okemah, Okla., Apr. 21, 1937; d. Richard Floyd and Mary May (Hooley) Day; M. Edwin Eugene Hardesty, Oct. 31, 1953; children—Richard Scott, Bryan Eugene. B.A. in Bus. Adminstrn., Okla. Bapt. U., 1969. Secondary edn. tchr. Shawnee High Sch. (Okla.), 1969-70; personnel asst. Plantation Pipe Line Co., Atlanta, 1970-75; office personnel adminstr. Cities Service Corp., Houston, Tex., 1977-78; mgr. personnel Foreman Dyess Law Firm, Houston, 1978-79; sr. employee relations rep., Mitchell Energy & Devel. Corp., Woodlands, Tex., 1979-81, mgr. employee relations, 1981—, woman of yr. award, 1982. Mem. Tex. Exec. Women, Am. Soc. Personnel Adminstrs. Republican. Office: Mitchell Energy & Devel Corp 2002 Timberloch Pl PO Box 4000 The Woodlands TX 77380

HARDESTY, NANCY ANN, author, historian; b. Lima, Ohio, Aug. 22, 1941; d. Byron Tapscott and Ruth Lucille (Parr) H. A.B., Wheaton (Ill.) Coll., 1963; M.S.J., Northwestern U., 1964; Ph.D., U. Chgo., 1976. Editorial asst. Christian Century, Chgo., 1964-65; asst. editor Eternity mag., Phila., 1966-69; asst. prof. English, Trinity Coll., Deerfield, Ill., 1969-73; asst. prof. Am. ch. history Emory U., Atlanta, 1976-80; tchr. English, Gwinnett County Schs., Lawrenceville, Ga., 1980-82; ind. scholar, freelance writer/editor, 1982—; founder Evangelical Women's Caucus, 1973, nat. council rep.-at-large; founder Daus. of Sarah newsletter, Chgo., 1974. Author: (with Letha Scanzoni) All We're Meant to Be: Biblical Feminism Today (Eternity Book of Yr. 1974), 1974, rev. edit., 1986; Great Women of Faith, 1980; Women Called to Witness, 1984; contbr. articles to religious jours. Recipient Mile Jewett Prize, U. Chgo., 1976. Mem. Am. Soc. Ch. History, Wesleyan Theol. Soc., Publs. Services Guild, Coordinating Com. for Women in Hist. Professions. Democrat. Episcopalian. Home and Office: 2534 Bradford Sq NE Atlanta GA 30345

HARDESTY, SARAH JANE, violinist; b. Kansas City, Mo., Sept. 14, 1946; d. Egbert M. and Margaret E. H.; B.Mus. Drake U., 1967; postgrad. Ind. U., 1967-68. Mem. 1st violin sect. Dallas Symphony Orch. 1968—; lectr. in field; owner, breeder champion Gt. Danes and English Setters. Mem. Greater North Tex. Orchid Soc. (past sec.).

HARDIE, MARGO LYNNE, money management company executive; b. Birmingham, Ala., June 15, 1952; d. James Seymour and Myrtle Mae (Mercer) Hardie. Student Bethany Coll., 1970-71; B.A., Marymount Coll., 1975; postgrad. Inst. Fin., 1981. Registered rep. N.Y. Stock Market. Legal sec. Burns, Kennedy Schilling & O'Shea, N.Y.C., 1976-77, Wagman, Cannon, Musoff & Gallop, N.Y.C., 1977-79, James M. LaRossa, N.Y.C., 1979-80; head publs. Townsend-Greenspan & Co., Inc., N.Y.C., 1980-81; dir. instnl. services Bostian Research Assocs., Inc., N.Y.C., 1981—; cons. MultiMedia Mktg., N.Y.C., 1983—. Mem. Republican Presdl. Task Force, Washington, 1983. Contbr. chpts. to books, articles to newspapers; co-editor: Econ. Reports, 1980-81. Am. Women in Bus. scholar, 1973, 74; Nat. Def. Student Loan grantee, 1973-75. Mem. Nat. Assn. Bus. Economists, N.Y. Assn. Bus. Economists, Smithsonian Assn., Met. Mus. Art, Marymount Alumni Assn. Methodist. Club: N.Y. Health & Racquet. Office: Bostian Research Assocs Inc 360 Madison Ave New York NY 10017

HARDIMAN, THERESE ANNE, lawyer; b. Chestnut Hill, Pa., Mar. 2, 1956; d. Edward Joseph and Grace Joan (Shaw) Hardiman. B.A. in History, Mt. St. Mary's Coll., 1978, B.A. in Psychology, 1978; J.D., Thomas M. Cooley Law Sch., 1983. Bar: Pa. 1983. U.S. Dist. Ct. Pa. 1983, U.S. Ct. Appeals (3d cir.). Staff research asst. Internat. Brotherhood of Teamsters, Washington, 1978-79; law clk. Richard R. Rashid, Atty. at Law, Lansing, Mich., 1981-82; law clk. Pearlstine, Salkin, Hardiman & Robinson, Landsdale, Pa., 1981; staff asst. Employment Relations Bd., Mich. Dept. Civil Service, Lansing, 1982; mem. Pearlstine, Salkin, Hardiman & Robinson, Landsdale, 1983—. Editor-in-chief Pridwin, 1978, layout editor, 1977. Recipient Golden Key award, Delta Theta Phi, 1981; Outstanding Student award Student Bar Assn., Thomas M. Cooley Law Sch., 1982. Mem. ABA, Assn. Trial Lawyers Am., Pa. Assn. Trial Lawyers, Pa. Bar Assn., Montgomery County Bar Assn., Delta Theta Phi. Republican. Roman Catholic. Home: 306 Hughes Ave Sellersville PA 18960 Office: Pearlstine Salkin Hardiman & Robinson 1000 N Broad St Lansdale PA 19446

HARDIN, ANITA MILES, educational administrator; b. De Funiak Springs, Fla., Dec. 4, 1943; d. Ausphera Schubert and Daisy Belle (LeCroy) Miles; A.A., Chipola Jr. Coll., 1963; B.A., U. South Fla., 1965; cert. Bur. Studies in Adult Edn., Ind. U., 1977, 78, Behavioral Systems Inc., Atlanta, 1977, Personal Dynamics Inst., Adventures in Attitudes, Mpls., 1978, So. Personal and Profl. Devel. Co. Psychology of Winning Seminar, Auburn, Ala., 1981; M.Ed., Auburn U., Montgomery, Ala., 1978, Ed.D., 1983; 1 son, John William II. Tchr., Hillsborough County (Fla.) Bd. Edn., 1965-68, Escambia County (Fla.) Bd. Edn., 1968-73, Bullock Meml. Found., Union Springs, Ala., 1973-74; adminstr. Bullock County (Ala.) Bd. Edn., 1975-78; ESEA Title IV-C project dir. Auburn City Bd. Edn., 1978—, dir. ednl. services, 1978-83, asst. supt., 1983—; cons. Bullock County Bd. Edn., 1975. Recipient cert. of appreciation Auburn Lions Club, 1979, Ala. Reading Assn., 1980, Assn. Children with Learning Disabilities, 1981. Mem. Am. Assn. Sch. Adminstrs., Ala. Council Sch. Adminstrs. and Suprs., Assn. Supervision and Curriculum Devel., Phi Delta Kappa. Democrat. Methodist. Author grant proposals. Home: 1021 Eagle Circle Auburn AL 36830 Office: 855 E Samford Ave Auburn AL 36830

HARDIN, CHRISTINA FAY, city official; b. Ogden, Utah., Mar. 9, 1954; d. Abilino Antonio Gallegos and Colleen Kay (Bahr) Gallegos Stanglin; m. Francis Monroe Hardin, Jr., Sept. 4, 1975; 1 child, William Jason. A.B., Texarkana Coll., 1977. Exec. sec. W.W. Johnson Lumber, Texarkana, 1975-76; clk.-stenographer City of Texarkana, 1976, city mgr.'s sec., 1976-80, city sec., 1980—. Mem. Assn. City Clks. and Secs. of Tex., Internat. Inst. Mcpl. Clks. Republican. Methodist. Avocations: needlepoint; cross stitch. Home: 1608 W 16th St Texarkana TX 75501 Office: PO Box 1967 Texarkana TX 75504

HARDIN, DEBRA NELSON, construction company executive; b. Newport News, Va., Aug. 4, 1953; d. Claude Richard and Margaret Carol Lee (Briggs) Nelson; m. Thomas Vincent Hardin, June 14, 1975; 1 child, Ty Christopher. Student Marshall Real Estate, Hampton, Va., 1984. Reservation clk. Colonial Williamsburg, Va., 1970-72; nursing clk. Va. Health Dept., Williamsburg, 1972-74, chief clerical supr., 1976-80; med. sec. Dr. J. W. Musgrave, Williamsburg, 1974-76; sec., bookkeeper Marrich Constrn., Williamsburg, 1980-84, pres., 1984—. Baptist. Avocations: stitchery; aerobics; reading. Home: PO Box 98 Williamsburg VA 23187 Office: Marrich Constrn Inc 5525 Olde Towne Rd Williamsburg VA 23185

HARDING, KATHLEEN ANN, army officer; b. Olean, N.Y., Sept. 29, 1962; d. John Robert and Carol Ann (Miller) H. B.S., St. Lawrence U., 1984. Commd. 1st lt. U.S. Army, 1985; platoon leader U.S. Army, B Co 127th Signal Bn., Fort Ord, Calif., 1984—. Mem. Kappa Delta Sigma. Republican. Roman Catholic. Office: B Co 127th Signal Bn US Army 6th Ave Fort Ord CA 93906

HARDING, MARDI (MAUREEN) WELLS, real estate development company executive; b. Denver, Nov. 24, 1946; d. Jackson H. and Bernice M. Wells; B.A., U. Denver 1968, 1 son, Todd C. Property mgr. Bedford Properties, Inc., Lafayette, Calif. 1976-79, project mgr. 1979-82, v.p. property mgmt., 1982-83, v.p. spl. projects, 1983-85; v.p. acquisitions Kemper/Bedford Real Estate Inc., 1986—. Lic. real estate broker, Calif.; cert. property mgr. Mem. Inst. Real Estate Mgmt., Internat. Council Shopping Centers. Office: PO Box 1267 Lafayette CA 94549

HARDMAN, CAROL ANN KUNZ, international exchange organization program administrator; b. Newark, N.J., Jan. 19, 1943; d. Herman John and Adeline (Spinelli) K.; m. Willard M. Hardman, Apr. 16, 1983. B.S. in Edn., Montclair State Coll., 1964; M. in Internatl. Adminstrn., Sch. for Internat. Tng., Expt. in Internat. Living, 1978. Cert. tchr. grades 7-12, bus. edn., English. Tchr. Belleville Jr. High Sch., N.J., 1964-67; tchr. Dept. Def. Dependents Sch., Stuttgart, Germany, 1967-69, Izmir, Turkey, 1970-74, Seoul, Korea, 1974-77; program dir. Sister Cities Internat., Washington, 1978—; mem. grants panel Global Perspectives in Edn., N.Y., 1984—; cons. to various voluntary groups. Author, editor various publs. for Sister Cities Internat. Recipient Outstanding Performance awards Dept. Def. Dependents Schs., 1967-77. Roman Catholic. Avocations: theatre; reading; gardening; beachcombing. Office: Sister Cities International 1625 Eye St NW Suite 424 Washington DC 20006

HARDWICK, ELIZABETH, author; b. Lexington, Ky., July 27, 1916; d. Eugene Allen and Mary (Ramsey) Hardwick; A.B., U. Ky., 1938, M.A., 1939; postgrad. Columbia, 1939-41; m. Robert Lowell, July 28, 1949 (div. Oct. 1972); 1 dau., Harriet. Adj. assoc. prof. Barnard Coll. Guggenheim fellow, 1947; recipient George Jean Nathan award, dramatic criticism, 1966. Mem. Am. Acad. and Inst. Arts and Letters. Author: (novels) The Ghostly Lover, 1945, The Simple Truth, 1955, Sleepless Nights, 1979; (essays) A View of My Own, 1962; (essays) Seduction and Betrayal, 1974; (essays) Bartleby in Manhattan, 1983. Editor: The Selected Letters of William James, 1960; adv. editor N.Y. Rev. Books. Contbr. Partisan Rev., New Yorker, Harpers. Home: 15 W 67th St New York NY 10023

HARDWICK, JILL ALLISON WHITE, child care center owner; b. Jacksonville, Ill., Aug. 14, 1946; d. Berlyn Hugh and Lois Jane (Treadway) White; m. Gene Thomas Hardwick, Sept. 30, 1962 (div. June 1983); 1 child, Allison Jeayne. M.Ed. in Early Childhood Edn., U. Ill., 1976. Cert. early childhood edn., Ill. Dir. Orchard Downs Infant Day Care Ctr., U. Ill., Urbana, 1972-76; owner, dir. Early Learning, Champaign, Ill., 1976—; organizer, first pres. Directors' Group, Champaign-Urbana, 1976—; media rep. East Central Ill. Assn. for Edn. Young Children, 1984—; mem. Champaign-Urbana Spinners' and Weavers' Guild, 1978—. Mem. Nat. Assn. Edn. Young Children. Unitarian-Universalist. Avocations: weaving; reading. Home: 1115B Broadmoor Dr Champaign IL 61821 Office: Early Learning 809 W Kirby Ave Champaign IL 61820

HARDWICK, KAREN LOUISE, oil company executive; b. Ft. Worth, Mar. 14, 1949; d. Donald Nelson and Billie Louise (Peacock) Van Buren; m. David Randol Hardwick, Sept. 9, 1976; children—Blaine Nelson, Michele Lynn. Student Baylor U., 1967-69, Weatherford Coll., 1971-72. Acct., Am. Quasar Petroleum Co., Ft. Worth, 1976-78, Fultz Oil Co., Ft. Worth, 1978-79, R-K Oil & Gas Co., Ft. Worth, 1979—; asst. sec. Petroleum Basins Exploration, Inc., Ft. Worth, 1981—; v.p. Penn-Akron Corp., Ft. Worth, 1983—; cons. R-K Oil & Gas Co., Ft. Worth, 1979—, Kakel, Inc., Ft. Worth, 1979—, Cap Oil Co., Ft. Worth, 1983—, Spurline Oil Co., Ft. Worth, 1984—. Home: 6024 Westridge Ln Unit 315 Fort Worth TX 76116 Office: Petroleum Basins Exploration Inc 4100 Internat Plaza Tower II Suite 180 Fort Worth TX 76109

HARDWICKE, SANDRA DALTON, fashion model, design consultant; b. Asheville, N.C., July 31, 1945; d. Paul LeGrande and Sara (Bryson) Dalton. B.S. in Advt., U. Fla., 1969; cert. Barbizon Sch. Modeling, 1970. Model, design cons. Playtex, Paramus, N.J., 1970-71, Maidenform, Bayonne, N.J., 1971-79, Sears, N.Y.C., 1972-74, Donn Kenney, N.Y.C., 1972-74, Roxanne, N.Y.C., 1972-84, others; real estate investor, N.Y.C., 1981-85; product sales, N.Y., N.J., Conn., Fla., 1982-84; market researcher, 1985; design cons. to fashion industry, N.J., Conn., 1970-79, N.Y.C., 1970-84. Avocations: tennis; swimming; reading; music. Home and Office: 7855 Boulevard E Apt 23G North Bergen NJ 07047

HARDY, ELISA LEE, physical education educator, exercise physiologist; b. Ft. Worth, Tex., Nov. 2, 1953; d. Robert Lee and Betty Lois (Vaught) H. B.S. in Phys. Edn., U. Tex.-Austin, B.S. in History; postgrad. North Tex. State U., Denton. Cert. tchr., Tex. Tchr., coach middle sch. Dallas Ind. Schs., 1976-78, instr. aerobics, 1976-78, tchr., gymnastic coach high sch., 1979—, choreographer gymnastic workshops, 1976-83, coordinator aerobic workshops, 1984; instr. aerobics Aerobics Inst., Dallas, 1983—; grad. asst. North Tex. State U., 1984, fitness instr., 1984. Coordinator Jump for Your Life Am. Heart Assn., Dallas, 1984. Recipient Tchr. of Yr. award W.H. Gaston Middle Sch., 1976, Outstanding Support for Dallas Student award, 1978; Group Exercise Leadership award Aerobics Inst., 1983. Mem. Tex. Assn. Health Phys. Edn. Recreation and Dence, Dallas Cross Country Club, Dallas Assn. Health Phys. Edn. and Recreation, Tex. State Tchrs. Assn. Democrat. Baptist. Club: North Park Racketball (Dallas). Home: 48 S Bay Dr Bullard TX 75757

HARDY, GRACE HERVEY, elementary guidance counselor, language arts educator; b. Coffeeville, Miss., Feb. 3, 1940; d. Amos and Louella (Brown) Hervey; m. Willie Hardy, July 13, 1978; 1 child, Victor Kermit. B.A. magna cum laude, Miss. Indsl. Coll., 1961; M.Ed., Memphis State U., 1974. Tchr. English, Sand Flat High Sch., Mount Pleasant, Miss., 1961-62; sec. bus. edn. Tate County High Sch., Coldwater, Miss., 1963-73; tchr. Tate County Attendance Ctr., Coldwater, 1973-76; tchr. lang. arts, guidance counselor Coldwater Elem. Sch., 1976-84, tchr. French and lang. arts, guidance counselor, 1984—. Counselor, club leader Goodwill Boys Club, Memphis, 1974; mem. N.W. Miss. Regional Screening Team for Spl. Edn. Students, Hernando, Miss., 1977-81; mem., cons. to bd. dirs. for GED Test, N.W. Miss. Jr. Coll., Senatobia, 1984—; asst. sec. Truckers Caucus Assn., Memphis, 1979—; asst. sec. Rocky Mountain M.B. Ch., Water Valley, Miss., 1960-78; mem. Christian edn. bd., dir. Red Circle Missionary Soc.; pres. Improvement Circle, Sunday sch. tchr. Mt. Joyner M.B. Ch. Recipient Outstanding Performance award Mercury Bus. League of Rust Coll., Holly Springs, Miss., 1960. Mem. Tate Assn. Educators, Miss. Assn. Educators, NEA, N.W. Miss. Counseling Assn., Miss. Counseling Assn. Democrat. Baptist. Clubs: Memphis State U. Alumni; Le Cercle Francais (sponsor 1984-85). Avocations: traveling; interior decorating; reading. Home: 137 Sullivan Cove Memphis TN 38109 Office: Coldwater Elementary Sch PO Box F Coldwater MS 38168

HARDY, HELENE ANN, mechanical engineer; b. St. Louis, Sept. 26, 1960; d. Kenneth Burnham and Eileen Louise (Wolff) H.; m. Thomas Riley Pierce, Nov. 24, 1984. B.S. in Engring. Mgmt., U. Mo.-Rolla, 1983. Coop engr. Tamko, Joplin, Mo., 1981-83, corp. project engr., 1983-84, ops. analyst, 1984—; guest lectr. U. Mo.-Rolla, 1985. Instr. ARC, Joplin, 1981—, community service award, 1985. Mem. ASTM, TAPPI (assoc.). Republican. Roman Catholic. Avocations: reading; snow skiing; canoeing. Home: 1263 E Price St Springfield MO 65807

HARDY, JANE ELIZABETH, educator; b. Fenelon Falls, Ont., Can., Mar. 27, 1930; came to U.S., 1956, naturalized, 1976; d. Charles Edward and Augusta Miriam (Lang) Little; B.S. with distinction, Cornell U., 1953; m. Ernest E. Hardy, Sept. 3, 1955; children—Edward Harold, Robert Ernest. Garden editor and writer Can. Homes Mag., Maclean-Hunter Pub. Co., Ltd., Toronto, Ont., 1954-55, 56-62; contbg. editor Can. Homes, Southam Pub. Co., Toronto, 1962-66; instr. Cornell U., 1966-73, sr. lectr. in communication arts, 1979—; mem. Cornell U. Provost's Adv. Com. on Status of Women, 1977-81; lectr., condr. workshops on writing. Bd. dirs. Literacy Vols. of Tomkins County. Mem. Women in Communications, Inc. (faculty adv. Cornell chpt. 1977—adv. task force campus chpt.), Garden Writers Assn. Am., Royal Hort. Soc., Pi Alpha Xi, Phi Kappa Phi, Alpha Omicron Pi. Clubs: Toronto Garden, Ithaca Garden, Ithaca Women's. Contbr. numerous articles to mags.; author numerous other publs., including brochures, slide set scripts; editor pro tem Cornell Plantations Quar., 1981-82. Home: 215 Enfield Falls Rd Ithaca NY 14850 Office: 312 Roberts Hall Dept Communication Cornell U Ithaca NY 14853

HARDY, JANICE AUDREY, educator; b. Chester, Pa., Aug. 2, 1936; d. Arthur Bruno and Bertha May (Lawton) Neubert; m. Thomas Leon Hardy, Mar. 31, 1955; children—Cynthia Lou Hardy Blake, Timothy Kent (dec.), Amy Lee. B.A. magna cum laude, Glassboro State Coll., 1982; A.S., Delaware County Community Coll., 1978. Cert. elem. tchr., N.J. Elem. tchr., Aston, Pa., 1967-77; elem. tchr. Somers Point, N.J., 1977—, also testing coordinator. Active Girl Scouts U.S.A.; sec. Notre Dame Aux.; Eucharistic minister St. Joseph Ch., Somers Point, 1984—; extraordinary minister Shore Meml. Hosp. Mem. N.J. Council Math. Tchrs., Nat. Cath. Educators Assn. Republican. Roman Catholic. Avocations: ceramics; poetry; sewing; travel; reading. Home: 301 Bliss Ave Somers Point NJ 08144 Office: 580 Harbor Ln Somers Point NJ 08144

HARDY, JUNE DORFLINGER, portrait painter and photographer; b. N.Y.C., Feb. 2, 1929; d. William Francis Dorflinger, Jr. and Katheryn (Hait) Dorflinger Manchee; grad. Briarcliff Jr. Coll., 1949, student Parsons Sch. Design, 1949-50, N.Y. Sch. Interior Design, 1953-54, Nat. Acad. Art-Art Students League, 1966-85, Columbia U., 1963; m. John Alexander Hardy, Jr., May 26, 1956. Asst. tchr. Peck Sch., Morristown, N.J., 1950-51; with personnel dept. McGraw Hill, Inc., 1951-52; editorial asst., then asst. editor Better Homes and Gardens mag., 1952-57; editorial asst., then asst. editor Successful Farming mag., 1952-57; freelance portrait painter and photographer, 1969—; tchr. drawing and pastel painting Onteora Club, N.Y., summer 1977; mem. exhbn. com. Twilight Park Art Show, 1983-86. Nat. Home Fashions League scholar, 1953; recipient 1st prize portrait in oil Twilight Park Art Show, 1976, 79, 1st prize portrait photography, 1977, 2d prize pastel landscape, 1979, 2d prize for flower photography, 1982; 1st prize for flower photography Onteora Garden Club Show, 1982, 1st and 2d prizes for photography Twilight Park Art Show, 1985. Life mem. Art Students League. Republican. Episcopalian. Clubs: Colony (chmn. entertainment 1979-84), Wednesday (past pres.), Badminton, Onteora. Address: 14 Sutton Pl S New York NY 10022

HARE, NATHALIE FULLER, journalist, photographer; b. Detroit, Jan. 4, 1916; d. Burlie Joseph and Ann Marie (Lawson) Fuller; m. Robert Campbell Hare, Sept. 10, 1938 (dec.); children—Judith Hare Thorne, Andrew Campbell. A.A., Los Angeles City Coll., 1935. Soc./religion editor Angeles Mesa News, Los Angeles, 1952-53; editor Pico-Beverly Post, Beverly Hills, Calif., 1953-59; home editor, feature writer Valley News, Van Nuys, Calif., 1959-73; writer, copy editor, photographer Golden Rain/Leisure World News, Seal Beach, Calif., 1979—. Mem. Women in Communications, Calif. Press Women (12 awards), Valley Press Club (awards 1968-74), Los Angeles Press Club, Matrix Table. Republican. Home: 13981 Thunderbird Dr 2G Seal Beach CA 90740 Office: Leisure World News PO Box 2338 Seal Beach CA 90740

HARELSON, JUANITA, state senator; b. Stratford, Okla., July 4, 1923; d. Ivan and Callie (Phillips) Law; m. James Earl Harelson, 1947; children—Ted, Barry, Patrick, Rex. B.A., Ariz. State U., 1945. Mem. Ariz. Ho. of Reps., 1972-82; mem. Ariz. Senate from 27th Dist., 1983—. Republican. Address: 1756 El Camino Tempe AZ 85281*

HARGER, SUSAN JEAN, air force officer; b. Detroit, Oct. 23, 1947; d. Robert William and Barbara Bray (Bentley) H. B.A., Denison U., 1969; M.S. in Mgmt., Troy State U., 1976. Commd. 2d lt. U.S. Air Force, 1969, advanced through grades to lt. col., 1986; chief adminstrn. Columbus AFB, Miss., 1970-74; chief base adminstrn., San Vito di Normanni, Italy, 1974-77; chief adminstrn. Air Force Contract Mgmt. Div., Kirtland AFB, N.Mex., 1977-79; weapons dir., Wallace Air Sta., Philippines, 1979-80; weapons dir., staff officer Tactical Air Warfare Ctr., Eglin AFB, Fla., 1980-82; comdr. mission crew Airborne Warning and Control System, Tinker AFB, Okla., 1982—, chief ops. plans div., 1984—. Decorated Air medal, Meritorious Service medal. Mem. Air Force Assn. Republican. Presbyterian. Avocations: horseback riding; raising African violets. Office: 552 AWACW-DOX Tinker AFB OK 73145

HARGETT, SUZANNE JONES, medical technologist; b. Greenwood, Miss., Sept. 9, 1941; d. Theo Vivian and Katherine Roger (Wilson) Jones; m. Joseph Richard Hargett, June 9, 1960; children—Karen Melissa, Susan Elizabeth, William Robert. Student Cin. Conservatory Music, summers 1958-59; B.A. in Biology, Shorter Coll., 1963; diploma med. tech., Med. Ctr. Sch. Med. Tech., 1963. Staff technologist Med. Ctr., 1964-65; part-time technologist doctor's office, 1967-68; staff med. technologist Meth. Hosp., Dallas, 1969-70; supr. hematology and blood bank St. Francis Hosp., Columbus, Ga., 1971-72; supr. hematology and coagulation Med. Ctr., Columbus, 1972—; adj. asst. prof. med. tech. Columbus Coll., 1981—. Mem. Columbus Symphony Orch., 1963-68, 80-81, 1st Bapt. Ch. Orch., 1981—. Mem. Am. Soc. Clin. Pathologists (affiliate). Home: 4804 Allegheny Dr Columbus GA 31907 Office: 710 Center St Columbus GA 31902

HARGIS, CAROL JEAN LESLIE, publisher; b. Dallas, Dec. 25, 1951; d. John Conrad and Ollie May (Clay) Leslie; m. Glen Edward Hargis, Mar. 25, 1979. Student Southwestern U., 1970-72, So. Meth. U., 1972-74. Adminstrv. asst. Record Pub. Co., Dallas, 1973-74, v.p. and asst. pub., 1975—; auto ins. renewal clk. Roach, Howard, Smith & Hunter, Inc., Garland, Tex., 1974-75; adminstrv. asst. and underwriter Cravens, Dargan & Co. Ins. Mgrs., Dallas, 1975; lectr. in field. Former deacon Midway Hills Christian Ch., Dallas, soprano soloist and choir mem., past sec., treas., trustee, bd. dirs. Mem. N. Tex. Reenactment Soc. (sec.), Fedn. Ins. Women of Tex. (past polit. action chmn.), Dallas Assn. Ins. Women (pres. 1984-85, publicity chmn., bd. dirs.), Ins. Women of Dallas, Nat. Assn. Ins. Women (conv. com. 1981), Delta Zeta. Mng. editor The Ins. Record. Home: 9410 Crestedge Dr Dallas TX 75238 Office: PO Box 225770 Dallas TX 75265 also 2730 Stemmons Tower W Suite 507 Dallas TX 75207

HARGRAVE, CECILLE TERRY, interior designer; b. Paris, Tex., July 23, 1917; d. Carl C. and Una Lila (Sealy) Terry. B.A., East Tex. State U., 1938; postgrad. So. Meth. U. Downtown Coll., 1952-53, Little Sch. of Fine Arts, 1953; m. Glenn M. Hargrave, Oct. 9, 1937. Interior designer; specifiers-interior cons. Garland (Tex.) City Hall; guest editor Tex. Contractor, 1954, Furniture Age, 1956. Recipient Instns. Mag.'s award for Sam Rayburn Meml. Student Center, 1964; named Disting. Alumna, East Tex. State U., 1975. Mem. K.T. Ednl. Found. (hon.), East Tex. State U. Alumni Assn. (pres. Dallas county chpt.), Women in Architecture, Dallas Council World Affairs, Southwest Homefurnishing Assn. Alpha Alpha Gamma, Chi Omega. Episcopalian. Clubs: Park Cities Toastmistress (founder, past pres.) (Dallas); Merriman Park Women's (v.p.). Projects include Sam Rayburn Meml. Student Center, East Tex. State U., Commerce, Tex., Midway Park Elementary Sch., Euless, Tex., 1st Nat. Bank, Garland, 1st Security Nat. Bank Dallas, 1st Security Fin. Systems, Inc., Dallas, Parkdale State Bank, Corpus Christi, Tex., Dallas Mus. Fine Arts, Republic Bank Garland, Parkdale Bank, Corpus Christi. Club: Merriman Park Women's (pres. 1985-86). Home: 6938 Winchester St Dallas TX 75231

HARGRAVE, SARAH QUESENBERRY, corporate foundation executive; b. Mt. Airy, N.C., Dec. 11, 1944; d. Teddie W. and Lois Knight (Slusher) Quesenberry Stout. Student, Radford Coll., 1963-64, Va. Poly. Inst. State U., 1964-67. Mgmt. trainee Thalhimer Bros. Dept. Store, Richmond, Va., 1967-68; Central Va. fashion and publicity dir. Sears Roebuck & Co., Richmond, 1968-73, nat. decorating sch. coordinator, Chgo., 1973-74, nat. dir. bus. and profl. women's programs, Chgo., 1974-76, v.p., treas., program dir. Sears-Roebuck Found., Chgo., 1976—, program mgr. corp. contbns. and memberships, 1981-84, dir. corp. mktg., pub. affairs, 1984—; Bd. dirs. Am. Assembly Collegiate Schs. Bus., 1979-82, vis. com., 1979-82, fin. and audit com., 1980-82, task force on doctoral supply and demand, 1980-82; mem. Com. for Equal Opportunity for Women, 1976-82, chmn., 1978-79, 80-81; mem. bus. adv. council Walter E. Heller Coll. Bus. Adminstrn., Roosevelt U., 1979-82, 85—; co-dir. Ill. Internat. Women's Yr. Center, 1975. Named Outstanding Young Woman of Yr., Ill., 1976; Woman of Achievement, State St. Bus. and Profl. Woman's Club, 1978. Mem. Assn. Humanistic Psychology, Am. Home Econs. Assn., Nat. Fedn. Bus. and Profl. Women's Clubs, Eddystone Condominium Assn. (v.p. 1978—). Home: 421 W Melrose St Chicago IL 60657 Office: Sears-Roebuck Found Sears Tower Chicago IL 60684

HARGRAVES, EMILY RAINBOLT, artist; b. Bedford, Ind.; d. Lee Ellis and Katherine (Duncan) Rainbolt; student Chgo. Art Inst., 1932-33, Art Student's League, 1955; B.A., Ariz. State U., 1950, M.F.A., 1963; m. Howard Hargraves, 1935 (dec. May 1943); 1 dau., Martha Ellen. Tchr., painter Studio-Workshop & Gallery, Mesa, Ariz., 1957-67; exhibited Sally Robbins Gallery, East Orange, N.J., from 1959, Am. Gallery, Copehagen; tchr. life and anatomy Phoenix Mus. Sch., 1957—; one-man shows Phoenix Art Mus.; asst. prof. art Stephen F. Austin State U., Nacogdoches, Tex., 1967—. Hartford Found. fellow, 1955-56; Yaddo fellow, Saratoga Springs, N.Y., 1957-58; named Artist of Yr., City of Mesa and State of Ariz. Mem. Nat. Assn. Women Artists, Artists Equity, Ariz. Artists Guild (pres. 1957-58). Address: 911 Mocking Bird Ln Nacogdoches TX 75961

HARGRETT, CHERI, financial planner; b. Chgo., Mar. 24, 1954; d. McKinley and Constance (Long) Rounds; m. Fredrick Hargrett, Aug. 18, 1973. B.S. in Acctg., Calif. State U.-Long Beach, 1976; M.B.A. in Fin. Mgmt., West Coast U., 1980; Cert. fin. planner Coll. of Denver, 1985; exec. devel. cert. U. Ga., 1981. Cert. fin. planner. Acct., Conoco Oil/Douglas Oil Co., Costa Mesa, Calif., 1984-86; asst. controller Celanese Corp./Narmco, Costa Mesa, 1976-77; v.p. Pacific Savs. Bank, Costa Mesa, 1977-83; mgr., owner Innovative Fin. Planning Services, Ontario, Calif., 1983—. Mem. Internat. Assn. Fin. Planning, Registry of Fin. Planning Practitioners, Inst. Cert. Fin. Planners, Inst. Internal Auditors. Avocations: writing; music; community theater. Home: Box 1862 Tustin CA 92681 Office: Innovative Fin Planning Services 17542 E 17th Suite 400 Tustin CA 92681

HARGROVE, EARNESTINE CARNELIUS, banker; b. Goldsboro, N.C.; d. E.M. Hargrove and Esther (Edwards) Askew. B.S., Temple U., 1969; M.S. in Bus. Adminstrn., U. Mass., 1974; D.B.A., U. Ky., 1982. Instr. bus. edn. Phila. Pub. Schs., 1969-73, Morgan State U., Balt., 1975-77, U. Ky., Lexington, 1979-81; asst. prof. mktg. Ga. State U., Atlanta, 1981-83; sr. research analyst First Atlanta Bank, 1983-84, asst. v.p., 1984—. Fellow U. Mass., 1973-74, U. Ky., 1981. Mem. Am. Mktg. Assn., Assn. for Consumer Research, So. Mktg. Assn. Mem. African Methodist Episcopal Ch. Home: 1079 Oak St SW Atlanta GA 30310 Office: First Atlanta Bank 2 Peachtree St (MC 518) Atlanta GA 30310

HARGROVE, JERRY SUE, college administrator; b. Gulport, Miss., May 15, 1936; d. Augustus Woodcock, Jr. and Mabelle (Welford) Woodcock Ladnier; m. Hayward Thomas Hargrove, July 7, 1952; children—Gary Thomas, Hayward Timothy. B.S. summa cum laude, William Carey Coll., 1980, M.Ed., 1982. Tchr. bus. subjects Phillips Coll., Gulfport, Miss., 1969-77, tchr., dept. chmn., 1977-84, dir. acad. affairs, 1984—; guest speaker, instr. various companies and profl. groups. Named Outstanding Tchr. of Yr., Southwest Pvt. Comml. Schs. Assn., 1978, Southeast Bus. Colls. Assn., 1978. Mem. Nat. Bus. Edn. Assn., Miss. Bus. Edn. Assn. Club: Gulfport Yacht. Lodge: Shriners Lady. Avocations: reading; fishing; walking. Home: 2322 23d Ave Gulfport MS 39501 Office: Phillips Coll 0942 E Beach Blvd Gulfport MS 39501

HARGROW-SIMMONS, TERESA, communications company executive; b. Tuscaloosa, Ala., Feb. 23, 1951; d. William and Ethel B. (Oliver) Hargrow; m. Wandy Lee Simmons, June 20, 1981; 1 son, Quinn-Alexander. B.S. in Bus. Adminstrn., Tenn. State U., 1973. Data base analyst I Blue Cross Blue Shield, St. Louis, 1973-78; adminstrv. asst. Community Devel. Agy., City of St. Louis, 1978-80; staff supr. market mgmt. Southwestern Bell Telephone Co., St. Louis, 1980—. Advisor Jr. Achievement, St. Louis, 1975-78; vol., patron United Negro Coll. Fund, St. Louis, 1982. U.S. Supplemental Edn. grantee, 1969. Mem. Am. Statis. Assn., Delta Sigma Theta (sec. 1970-72). Democrat. Baptist. Home: 5683 Waterman #32 St Louis MO 63112 Office: Southwestern Bell Telephone Co 112 N 4th St Room 1420 St Louis MO 63102

HARING, GENE FRANCES, psychiatrist; b. San Francisco, Apr. 7, 1940; d. Arnold Walter and Esther Katherine (Huisman) H.; B.S., Jamestown Coll., 1961; M.D., Med. Coll. Pa., 1965. Intern, Med. Coll. Pa., Phila., 1965-66; resident Eastern Pa. Psychiatric Inst., Phila., 1966-69; staff psychiatrist, coordinator structured services, med. dir. Luzerne-Wyoming County Mental Health Center, Wilkes-Barre, Pa., 1969-79; practice medicine specializing in psychiatry, Kingston, Pa., 1979—; mem. staffs Wilkes-Barre Gen. Hosp.; clin. asso. prof. Hahnemann Med. Sch., 1974—. Bd. dirs. Mental Health Assn. of Luzerne County, 1969-82, Domestic Violence Center, 1981-82; chmn. adv. bd. Hospice of St. John. Mem. Am. Psychiatric Assn., Internat. Assn. Social Psychiatry, Am. Assn. Social Psychiatry, Am. Med. Womens Assn., Am. Group Psychotherapy Assn., Pa. Psychiatric Assn. Office: 841 Wyoming Ave Kingston PA 18704

HARING, PATRICIA ANN ZWER, legal assistant; b. L.I., N.Y., Mar. 31, 1944; d. Michael S. and Anna (Balchunas) Zwer; B.S., Hunter Coll., 1976; postgrad. New Sch. Social Research; grad. Paralegal Inst., Phila., 1972; 1 dau., Jill St. Jude. Legal sec. firm Davis Polk & Wardwell, 1966-69; adminstrv. asst. to press sec. and campaign mgr. N.Y. Mayoralty Campaign, 1969-70; system controller firm Skadden Aprs Slate Meagher & Flom, 1970-71; confidential asst. to pres. Webcor Electronics Corp., L.I., N.Y., 1972-73; office mgr. Frank L. Miller, N.Y.C., 1973-74; legal asst. environ. law Union Oil Co. Calif., 1976-77; asst. to treas. Mission Hills Property Corp., Palm Springs, Calif., 1977; pres. Palm Springs Resume Service & Career Counseling, 1977-78; office mgr. Freeman, Meade, Wasserman & Schneider, N.Y.C., 1978-80; freelance writer, 1980; legal asst. to gen. counsel Diamond Dealers Club of N.Y., Inc., 1981; legal asst. to corp. partner Pryor, Cashman, Sherman & Flynn, N.Y.C., 1981-82; legal asst. Weil, Gotshal & Manges, N.Y.C., 1982—. Vice pres. public relations Roosevelt Island (N.Y.) Residents Assn., 1980. Cert. scuba diver. Mem. Ind. Press Assn., Am. Soc. Profl. and Exec. Women, Am. Mus. Natural History (assoc.), Smithsonian Instn. (asso.), Internat. Platform Assn., Nat. Assn. Female Execs., HALT, City News Agy., Bus. and Profl. Women's Club, Nat. Assn. Female Execs., Am. Legion Ladies Aux. (John Eugene Wallace Post 1630). Roman Catholic. Contbr. articles to profl. jours. Home: 510 Main St No 724 Roosevelt Island NY 10044 Office: 767 Fifth Ave Suite 3201 New York NY 10153

HARITUN, ROSALIE ANN, clarinetist, music educator; b. Johnson City, N.Y., May 30, 1938; d. George and Helen (Ternosky) H.; B.Music Edn., Baldwin-Wallace Conservatory of Music, Ohio, 1960; M.S. in Music Edn., U. Ill., 1961; profl. diploma Tchrs. Coll., Columbia U., 1965, Ed.D., 1968, postdoctoral, 1971-72. Tchr. instrumental music elem. schs., Patchogue, L.I., N.Y., 1961-63, jr. high schs., 1963-65; instr. music edn. Sch. Music, Temple U., Phila., 1968-71; instr. instrumental music N.Y.C. Bd. Edn., 1971-72; asst. prof. music edn. Sch. Music, East Carolina U., Greenville, N.C., 1972—, del. to faculty assembly, Raleigh, N.C., 1981—; clarinetist/saxophonist Greenville Summer-in-the Park Orch., 1975-79; clarinetist Albemarle Players prodn. South Pacific, Elizabeth City, N.C.; cons. curriculum devel., 1976-82; adjudicator choral/instrumental festivals, solo/ensemble contests, 1975-82. Bd. dirs. pres.-elect Greenville Boys Choir, 1966—. Mem. Coll. Music Soc. (council mem. music edn. div. Mid-Atlantic chpt. 1982-84, sec./treas. 1984-86), Delta Kappa Gamma (chmn. exec. bd. 1980-82, pres. elect 1984-86), Sigma Alpha Iota (chpt. pres. 1966-68), Pi Kappa Lambda (chpt. pres. 1977-83). Democrat. Baptist. Contbr. articles on music edn. to prof. publs. Home: 206 N Oak St Greenville NC 27834 Office: Sch Music East Carolina U 10th St Greenville NC 27834

HARJAR, ANNE NICHOLSON, lighting fixture manufacturing company personnel executive; b. Durham, N.C., Nov. 30, 1936; d. William McNeal and Eunice (Stamey) Nicholson; m. Fayette Powers Grose, July 23, 1955 (div. Sept. 1978); children—James, Margaret, Mary Elizabeth, Kathryn, Alicia; m. 2d, Martin John Harjar, Sept. 1, 1979. Student Duke U., Lorain County Coll. Word processor Nordson Corp., Amherst, Ohio, 1976-77, employment asst., 1977-78; personnel asst. Invacare Corp., Elyria, Ohio, 1978-79; personnel mgr. Hi-Tek Comml. Lighting, Vermilion, Ohio, 1979—. Editor co. newspaper, 1978. Bd. dirs. Vermilion YMCA, 1982, 83. Mem. Am. Soc. Personnel Adminstrs., Erie County Personnel Assn., Vermilion C. of C. (bd. dirs. 1982, 83). Republican. Episcopalian. Office: Hi-Tek Comml Lighting 850 W River Rd Vermilion OH 44089

HARKAVY, MARY SUE, marketing researcher; b. N.Y.C., Nov. 10, 1936; d. Howard K. and Rochelle (Zeitlin) Rothenberg; m. Arnold Harkavy, Mar. 2, 1958; children—Ilene, Brad. B.S., U. Vt.-Montpelier, 1956. Sr. v.p. Yankelovich Skelly & White, N.Y.C., 1961-80; v.p., assoc. div. dir. Audits & Surveys, Inc., N.Y.C., 1981; exec. v.p. Lieber Attitude Research, N.Y.C., 1982—; research cons. Mus. Natural History, N.Y.C., 1981—. Trustee, Congregation Rodeph Sholom, N.Y.C., 1982—; chmn. sch. com. Rodeph Sholom Sch., N.Y.C., 1981-84. Mem. Am. Mktg. Assn. Home: 27 W 86th St New York NY 10024 Office: Lieber Attitude Research 1841 Broadway New York NY 10023

HARKER, DEBRA ANN, nurse; b. Hammond, Ind., Sept. 10, 1956; d. Zigy Wallace and Betty Frances (Small) Scott; m. Jay L. Harker, Aug. 2, 1980. B.S. in Nursing, Ball State U., 1978; M.S. in Adminstrn., Notre Dame U., 1985. R.N., Ind., Charge nurse operating room St. Margaret Hosp., Hammond, Ind., 1978-82; clin. dir. Calumet Surgery Ctr., Munster, Ind., 1983-85; dir. operating room, post-anesthesia recovery and out-patient services St. Margaret Hosp., Hammond, Ind., 1985—; cons. South Bend Clinic, Ind., 1984; instr. Am. Heart Assn., Merrillville, Ind., 1982—. Mem. Am. Orgn. Nurse Execs., Ind. Soc. Hosp. Nursing Adminstrs., N.W. Ind. Council Hosp. Nursing Adminstrs., Assn. Operating Room Nurses. Democrat. Roman Catholic. Avocation: tennis. Home: 8120 4th Pl E Highland IN 46322 Office: St Margaret Hosp 5454 Hohman Ave Hammond IN 46320

HARKER, DIANE ELIZABETH, business executive, consultant; b. Balt., Oct. 1, 1944; d. Hubert H. and Florence (Limpert) H. B.S. in Econs., U. Md., 1966. Supr., Am. Airlines, Los Angeles, 1970-73, sr. analyst, N.Y.C., 1973-75, group supr., 1975-78, mgr. mktg., N.Y.C., Dallas, 1978-81; staff v.p. sales Muse Air, Dallas, 1981-82, v.p. sales and services, 1982-83, v.p. mktg. services, 1983-85; pres. DEH Assocs., Dallas, 1985—. Mem. Assn. Women Entrepreneurs Dallas. Republican. Methodist. Office: PO Box 59031 Dallas TX 75229

HARKIN, CATHERINE (KAY) ROSE, insurance agent; b. Phila., Sept. 21, 1930; d. Albert James and Elizabeth Agnes (Callaghan) Walsh; m. John Harkin, May 24, 1969. Cert. profl. ins. woman. Jr. underwriter Gen. Accident Ins. Co., Phila., 1948-66; rater Conn. Nat. Am. Ins., Phila., 1966-69; adminstrv. asst. Frank B. Hall Ins., Phila., 1969-72; asst. property underwriter Paul Hertel Ins., Phila., 1972-75; adminstrv. asst. Johnson & Higgins, Phila., 1975-77; underwriting asst. Fireman's Fund Commercial Lines, Phila., 1979—; audit dept. Internal Revenue Service. Mem. Nat. Assn. Ins. Women (state legis. chmn.), Irish Soc., Derry Soc. (ball chmn., stewart), Irish Unity Group, Womens Ins. Soc. Phila. (sec., mem. various coms.), activities commn. Parish Ch. Democrat. Roman Catholic. Office: Fireman's Fund Ins 510 Walnut St Philadelphia PA 19106

HARKNESS, GAIL ANN, nursing educator; b. Rochester, N.Y., Mar. 14, 1939; d. Elmore Gibson Harkness and Doris (Wood) Harkness Kerbs; children—Michael D., Karen L. Hood Merrill. B.S. in Nursing, U. Rochester, 1961, M.S. in Nursing, 1963; Dr.P.H., U. Ill., 1981. Instr. Norfolk Gen. Hosp. Sch. Nursing, Va., 1963-64; instr. pediatrics Portsmouth Gen. Hosp., Va., 1965; instr. med.-surg. nursing Lankenau Hosp., Phila., 1966-68; adminstrv. asst. Reading Hosp. Sch. Nursing, Pa., 1969-72; assoc. prof. med.-surg. nursing No. Ill. U., DeKalb, 1972-85; research fellow U. Rochester Sch. Nursing, N.Y., 1983-85; assoc. prof., acting chmn. dept. research and doctoral studies Boston U. Sch. Nursing, 1985—. Author: Total Patient Care: Foundations and Practice, 4th-6th edits., 1984; Total Patient Care Workbook, 4th-6th edits., 1984. Bd. dirs. Health Systems Agy., 1978-83, pres., 1980-82; bd. dirs. Vis. Nurses Assn. Aurora, Ill., 1979-83. Recipient Nat. Research Service award HHS, 1977-80; nurse traineeship grantee HEW, 1961-62; Robert Wood Johnson Found. clin. nurse scholar U. Rochester Sch. Nursing, 1983-85. Mem. Am. Nurses Assn. (cabinet on nursing edn. 1980-86), Council Nurse Researchers, Ill. Nurses Assn. (bd. dirs. 1979-83), Sigma Tehta Tau, Delta Omega. Democrat. Presbyterian. Office: Boston U Sch Nursing 635 Commonwealth Ave Boston MA 02215

HARLAN, NANCY MARGARET, lawyer; b. Santa Monica, Calif., Sept. 10, 1946; d. William Galland and Betty M. (Miles) Plett; B.S. magna cum laude, Calif. State U., Hayward, 1972; J.D., U. Calif., Berkeley, 1975; m. John Hammack, Dec. 1, 1979; children—Laryssa Maria Rebello, Leea Elyce Harlan. Bar: Calif. 1975, U.S. Dist. Ct. (cen. dist.) Calif. 1976. Assoc., Poindexter & Doutré, Los Angeles, 1975-80; residential counsel Coldwell Banker Residential Brokerage Co., Fountain Valley, Calif., 1980-81; counsel for real estate subs., sr. atty. law dept. Pacific Lighting Corp., Santa Ana, Calif., 1981—; tchr., designer courses in real estate ethics, professionalism and law. Exec. v.p. student body U. Calif., Berkeley, 1974-75. Mem. State Bar Calif., ABA, Los Angeles County Bar Assn., Orange County Bar Assn. (dir. corp. counsel sect. 1982-84), Calif. Women Lawyers Assn., Orange County Women Lawyers Assn., Los Angeles Women Lawyers Assn., Nat. Assn. Female Execs., Saddleback Valley Bus. and Profl. Women's Club. Office: 48 Brookhollow Dr Santa Ana CA 92705

HARLAN, ROMA CHRISTINE, portrait painter; b. Warsaw, Ind.; d. Charles William and Fern (McCormick) Harlan; student Purdue U., Art Inst. Chgo.; pvt. study with Ralph Clarkson, Chgo., Francis Chapin, Chgo., Weyman Adams, N.Y.C., Marie Goth, Indpls. One-man shows Lake Shore Club Chgo., Little Gallery of Esquire Theater, Chgo., Purdue U. Gallery, West Lafayette, Ind., George Washington U. Gallery, Washington, Hoosier Salon, Indpls., All.-Ill. Soc. Fine Arts, Kaufmann's Gallery, Chgo., Lafayette (Ind.) Art Assn., Arts Club Washington; exhibited numerous group shows; represented in permanent collections at U.S. Supreme Ct., U.S. Capitol Bldg., SEC, D.C. Fed. Ct. House, Nat. Guard Bldg., Washington, Children's Hosp. Nat. Med. Ctr., Epis. Theol. Sem., Alexandria, Va., Nat. Fedn. Bus. and Profl. Women's Clubs, Washington, Lake Shore Club, Chgo., Purdue U., West Lafayette, Ind., Nat. Presbyn. Ch., Washington, St. Stevens Sch., Alexandria, Va., Walter Reed Army Med. Center. Art chmn. D.C. Fedn. Women's Clubs. Daus. of Ind. scholar. Mem. Ind. State Art Assn. Presbyterian. Clubs: Arts of Washington, Washington Forum, Zonta, D.C. Fed. Women's Clubs (Washington). Address: 1600 S Joyce St A-1607 Arlington VA 22202

HARLAND, MARY KATHRYN HOLTAN, business and economics educator; b. Forest City, Iowa, Mar. 3, 1946; d. Hans Oscar and Ruth (Hermanson) Holtan; m. Thomas Robert Harland, May 4, 1974. A.A., Waldorf Coll., Forest City, 1966; B.A., Wartburg Coll., Waverly, Iowa, 1969; M.A., Mankato State U. (Minn.), 1981. Instr., Chicago Lakes Area Schs., Minn., 1970-72, Suburban Hennepin Area Vo-Tech Inst., 1972-77, Albert Lea Area Vo-Tech Inst. (Minn.), 1977-80; asst. prof. bus. and econs. Waldorf Coll., 1980—; adj. faculty mem. Mankato State U., Minn., 1984; partime faculty Wartburg Coll., Iowa, 1986; cons., lectr. in field. Author ednl. materials. Mem. Bus. Communications Assn., Delta Pi Epsilon. Republican. Lutheran. Avocations: needlework, reading, bicycling. Home: RR 1 Box 44 Forest City IA 50436

HARLESS, KATHRYN FRANCES, staff assistant; b. Washington, Feb. 13, 1946; d. Joseph Sr. and Kathryn Winnifred (Ashley) Zagami; children—Angela Lynn, Joseph Anthony. Student Wheeling Coll., Montgomery Coll., Prince Georges Community Coll., ITT Bus. Inst. Sec., U.S. Parole Commn., Washington, 1968-74; with adminstrn. office, Burlingame, Calif., 1974-76; staff asst. to dir., Office of Mgmt. and Fin., U.S. Dept. Justice, Washington, 1976-77, mgmt. analyst, 1977-79, staff asst. to dep. asst. atty. gen. Office Personnel and Adminstrn., 1979—; notary pub. U.S. Parole Commn., 1974-76. Democrat. Roman Catholic. Avocations: boating; traveling; handicrafts; reading; computers. Home: 8521 Riggs Rd Adelphi MD 20783 Office: US Dept Justice Justice Mgmt Div Office Personnel Adminstrn Room 1116 10th and Constitution Ave NW Washington DC 20530

HARLEY, ANN, nurse, educator; b. San Juan, P.R.; d. Allen Gotwals and May Miller (Naile) H.; diploma in Nursing, Abington (Pa.) Meml. Hosp., 1954; B.S. in Nursing, U. Pa., 1960, M.S. in Nursing, 1962; Ed.D., Tchrs. Coll. Columbia U., 1978. Curriculum coordinator Presbyn. U. of Pa. Med. Center, Phila., 1968-74; asst. prof. CCNY, 1975-76; asso. prof. Coll. Nursing, U. Nebr. Med. Center, 1976-80; prof. nursing Western Wash. U., Bellingham, 1980—, chmn. dept. nursing, 1980—; cons. in field. Performing mem. Voices of Omaha, 1979. Mem. Am. Nurses Assn., Nat. League Nursing, Internat. Soc. Chronobiology, AAUW, Assn. Supervision and Curriculum Devel., Sigma Theta Tau, Pi Lambda Theta, Phi Delta Kappa, Kappa Delta Pi. Office: Western Washington University Bellingham WA 98225

HARLEY, ROSE MADELINE, training school executive; b. Paris, Ark.; d. Charles V.B. and Ella O. (McVay) H.; B.A. cum laude, Columbia U., M.A. in Adult Edn., 1976. Area mgr. N.Y.-L.I., Dale Carnegie orgn., 1960-63, instr. trainer internat. hdqrs., 1963-67, regional mgr. internat. hdqrs., 1967-76, mgr. Dale Carnegie Inst. of N.Y.C., 1976-79; pres. Harley Inst., Inc., presenting Dale Carnegie courses in No. N.J., Hackensack, 1979—. Bd. dirs. Council for Noncoll. Continuing Edn., now pres. Mem. Mensa, Internat. Platform Assn., Commerce and Industry Assn. N.J. (bd. dirs.), Columbia U. Alumni Assn., Sales Execs. Club N.Y.C. Club: Princeton. Home: 280 Prospect Ave Hackensack NJ 07601 Office: 25 E Salem St Hackensack NJ 07601

HARLOE, LINDA GAYLE, medical technologist, educator; b. Los Angeles, July 15, 1947; d. Rodney Theodore and Claire Rose (Grasser) H. B.S., U. Hawaii, 1969; M.A., Central Mich. U., 1983. Lic. med. technologist, Calif.; nationally registered med. technologist. Med. technologist St. John's Hosp., Santa Monica, Calif., 1969-72, Los Angeles County-U. So. Calif. Med. Ctr., Los Angeles, 1972-77; tech. rep. Coulter Electronics, Hialeah, Fla., 1977-80; med. technologist, lab. asst. dir. Hoag Meml. Hosp., Newport Beach, Calif., 1980—; instr. Orange Coast Coll., Costa Mesa, Calif., 1982—, Calif. State U.-Fullerton, 1986—. Contbr. articles to profl. jours. Mem. Calif. Assn. for Med. Lab. Tech. (state pres. elect 1985—, dist. cons. 1983-85), Mortar Bd. Republican. Roman Catholic. Avocations: tennis; reading. Office: Hoag Meml Hosp Clin Lab 301 Newport Blvd Newport Beach CA 92663

HARMAN, MARYANN WHITTEMORE, artist, educator; b. Roanoke, Va., Sept. 13, 1935; d. John Weed and Clifford Kelly Whittemore; B.A., Mary Washington Coll., 1955; M.A., Va. Poly. Inst., 1974; m. Roger Walke, Aug. 25, 1984; children—Mary Kelly, John Whittemore, Phillip Mears. Faculty, Va. Poly. Inst., Blacksburg, 1963—, prof. art 1981—; guest artist Emma Lake Art Workshop, U. Sask., 1985. One-woman shows: Andre Emmerich Gallery, N.Y.C., 1976, 78, Rubiner Gallery, Detroit, 1977, 78, Meredith Long Gallery, N.Y.C., 1980, Haber Theodore Gallery, N.Y.C., 1981-82, 84, 85, Osuna Gallery, Washington, 1982, 84; group shows include: Va. Mus. Art, Richmond, 1973, 74, 75, 80, 81, Southeastern Center for Contemporary Art, Winston Salem, N.C., 1963, 65, 67, 71, 76, Boston Mus. Fine Arts, 1981, 84, Roanoke (Va.) Mus., 1963-79, Butler Inst. Contemporary Art, Youngstown, Ohio, 1969, 72; represented in permanent collections: Boston Mus., General Motors, Detroit, Hunter Mus., Chattanooga, Roanoke Mus., Phillip Morris Corp., Richmond and N.Y.C., Mfrs. Hanover Trust, N.Y.C., Am. Can Corp., N.Y.C., Shawmut Bank of Boston, Mint Mus., CSX Corp., Ethyl Corp, others. Mem. Coll. Art Assn., Nat. Hon. Art and Architecture Soc., Tau Sigma Delta. Episcopalian. Home: 602 Landsdowne Dr Blacksburg VA 24060 Office: Va Poly Inst Blacksburg VA 24061

HARMON, ARTICE WARD, occupational therapist; b. Hughes, Ark., Oct. 2, 1940; d. William Oscar and Alice Williams (Turner) Ward; B.S., Ind. U., 1973; M.P.H., U. Ill., 1975; m. Luther Harmon, Dec. 5, 1959. Occupational therapy intern St. Elizabeth's Hosp., Washington, 1973, Helen Hayes Rehab. Hosp., W. Haverstraw, N.Y., 1973; staff occupational therapist Mercy Hosp. and Med. Center, Chgo., 1973-76; dir. occupational therapy program Westside Parents Center, of Retarded Children United, Chgo., 1976-77; head occupational therapy dept. Americana Health Care Center, Champaign, Ill., 1977-81; dir. occupational therapy program Chgo. State U., 1981—, acting dean Coll. Allied Health, 1985—; guest lectr. allied health curriculum U. Ill., Urbana-Champaign, fall 1975, grad. teaching asso. occupational therapy curriculum Coll. Asso. Health Professions, 1978-80, instr., 1980-81; chmn. steering com. Ill. Council Occupational Therapy Edn.; cons. in field. Mem. Am., Ill. occupational therapy assns., Am. Pub. Health Assn., Am., Ill. vocat. assns., Am. Soc. Allied Health Professions, People United to Save Humanity, Phi Delta Kappa, Kappa Delta Pi. Roman Catholic. Home: 5020 S Lake Shore Dr #806-N Chicago IL 60615 Office: Coll Allied Health Chgo State U 95th St at King Dr Chicago IL 60628

HARMON, BARBARA SAYRE, artist; b. Yerington, Nev., Aug. 8, 1927; d. Ruth (Barker) and Fred Grayson Sayre; student Bisttram Sch. Fine Art, 1947-49, Black Mountain Coll., 1950; m. Cliff Franklin Harmon, July 7, 1948; 1 son, Jonathan Henry. Founder, mgr. children's Gallery, Taos, 1963—, Children's Gallery Press, 1967—; paintings, graphics shown in pvt. galleries; author, illustrator: Tabbigail's Garden, 1967; Little People's Counting Book, 1968; This Little Pixie, 1969; Monday's Mouse, 1970; The Tumpfee Wood Acorn Book, 1977; Thimbly Hill, 1980; cover designer, illus. N.Mex. mag. Christmas story, 1981. Home: Box 202 Taos NM 87571

HARMON, CAROLE HELFERT, lawyer, educator; b. Dayton, Ohio, Aug. 1, 1948; d. Irving and Sylvia (Dinhofer) Helfert. B.A., Ind. U., 1970; J.D., Southwestern U.-Los Angeles, 1975. Bar: Calif. 1975. Assoc., Schwartz, Alschuler & Grossman (now Alschuler, Grossman & Pines), Century City, Calif., 1975-77; dep. city atty. Los Angeles, 1977-79; atty. Walt Disney Prodns., Burbank, Calif., 1979-81; assoc. counsel Lloyds Bank Calif., Los Angeles, 1982-83, counsel, 1983—; adj. prof. Southwestern U., Los Angeles, 1981, 82, 83. Mng. editor Southwestern U. Law Rev., 1974. Vol., Los Angeles Olympic Com., 1982-84; mem. The Dance Assn., Los Angeles County Mus. Art. Mem. ABA, Los Angeles County Bar Assn. (co-chmn. women in law com. 1983-84), Calif. State Bar. Republican. Jewish. Office: Lloyds Bank Calif 612 S Flower St #803 Los Angeles CA 90017

HARMON, LILY, artist; b. New Haven, Nov. 19, 1912; d. Benjamin and Bessie (Horowitz) Perelmutter; student Yale U. Sch. Art, 1929-31, Academie Colarossi Paris, 1931-32, Art Students League, 1932-33; m. Joseph H. Hirshhorn, 1945 (div. 1956); children—Amy, JoAnn; m. Milton Schachter, Oct. 1972. One-man shows Asso. Am. Artists Galleries, N.Y.C., 1944, 50, 53, 56, 57, Silvermine Art Assn., 1954, Westchester County Arts & Crafts, 1950, Ann Ross Gallery, N.Y.C., 1959, Selected Artists Gallery, N.Y.C., 1960, HCE Gallery, Provincetown, Mass., 1961, Yamada Gallery, Kyoto, Japan, 1963, Scargo Lake Gallery, Dennis, Mass., 1964, Tirca Karlis Gallery, Provincetown, Krasner Gallery, N.Y.C., 1966, Provincetown Group Gallery, 1966, Internat. Salon Palace of Fine Arts, Mexico City, 1973, U. Richmond, Marsh Gallery, George M. Modlin Fine Arts Center 1973, Krasner Gallery, N.Y.C., 1977, 81, others; 50-yr. retrospective exhbn. Wichita (Kans.), 1982-83; drawing show Summit Gallery, 1982-83; represented in permanent collections Butler Art Inst., Youngstown, Ohio, Whitney Mus. Am. Art, N.Y.C., Newark Mus., Ein Harod and Tel Aviv (Israel) mus., U. Mass. at Amherst, Kalamazoo (Mich.) Art Inst., Smithsonian Art Inst., Washington, St. Lawrence U. Mem. Provincetown Art Assn., Artists Equity Assn., Nat. Acad. Design, Provincetown Art Assn. Illustrator: Pride and Prejudice (Jane Austen), 1950; Sounds of a Distant Drum (Bill Martin, Jr.), 1967; (Japanese books) Buddenbrooks (Thomas Mann), 1965, Symphonie Pastorale (André Gide), 1965, The Counterfeiters (André Gide), 1965, Dirty Hands (Jean Paul Sartre), 1965, The Castle (Franz Kafka), 1965, Metamorphosis (Franz Kafka), 1965, Lafcadio's Adventures (André Gide), 1972; Therese (Francois Mauriac), 1972; House of Mirth (Edith Wharton), 1975; Short Stories of Guy de Maupassant, 1976; author: (autobiography) Freehand, 1981. Home: 151 Central Park West New York NY 10023 also 629 Commercial St Provincetown MA 02657

HARMON, NANCY CATHERINE, ophthalmic company customer relations manager; b. Seattle, Apr. 25, 1949; d. Thomas Wilson and Madeline (Winters) Doyle; 1 child, Melyssa April. B.S. in Bus., City U., Bellevue, Wash., 1984. Dist. sales coordinator Fluke Mfg., Everett, Wash., 1976-78; customer service mgr. Eldec Corp., Lynnwood, Wash., 1978-84; customer relations mgr. Coopervision 10L, Bellevue, 1984—; dir. Sound Investment Inc., Lynnwood, Wash., 1984-85. Mem. Nat. Assn. Credit Mgrs., Internat. Customer Service Assn. (charter), Credit Edn. Orgn. Republican. Avocation: philately. Office: Coopervision 10L 3190 160 Ave SE Bellevue WA 98008

HARMOUNT, CHARLENE ZENANA, principal; b. Fremont, Ohio, Apr. 18, 1951; d. Clarence Wesley and Zenana Jane (Holsinger) Warren; m. Terry P. Harmount, June 14, 1974; 1 dau., Charlotte Lynn. B.A., Heidelberg U., 1973; M.A. in History, U. Toledo, 1977. Sec., Heidelberg Coll., Tiffin, Ohio, 1970-73; clk. Mr. Wiggins, Tiffin, 1973-74; tchr. research history dept. U. Toledo, 1974-79; prin. St. Caspar Jr. High Sch., Wauseon, Ohio, 1979—. Cons., Campfire Girls, Wauseon, 1979—, St. Caspar Ch., Wauseon, 1979—; mem. steering com. PTA, Wauseon, 1980-82; coach soccer and softball Park and Recreation Dept. Wauseon, 1981—. Mem. Phi Alpha Theta. Republican. Roman Catholic. Club: Campfire (Wauseon) (1st v.p. 1980-83). Home: Route 2 Box 21 Wauseon OH 43267 Office: 1205 N Shoop Wauseon OH 43567

HARMSEN, MARYANNE J.,, insurance company executive; b. Bklyn., Dec. 22, 1945; d. Francis P. and Anne M. (Mannelli) Romano; student St. Peter's Coll., 1963, N.J. State Tchrs. Coll., 1964, Coll. Ins., 1977-78, Bergen Community Coll., 1979; children by previous marriage—Andrea Francesca and Jennifer Patricia Lamendola. Agt., Met. Life Ins. Co., Newark, 1974-76, Western World Ins. Co., Ramsey, N.J., 1977-80; account exec. Foxcroft Agy., Inc., Milford, Pa., 1980-83, asst. v.p. corp. risk analysis, 1984-85; sr. group rep. Met. Life Ins. Co., Hackensack, N.J. Bd. advisors Acad. St. Aloysius, 1973-74; charter mem., officer, dir. nat. chpt. Ladies of Unico, 1969-70. Recipient Leaders award Met. Life Ins. Co. Leaders Conf., 1975. Mem. Profl. Ins. Women, Risk and Ins. Mgmt. Soc. (asso.), Nat. Assn. Female Execs., N.J. Democratic Assn. Roman Catholic. Club: Franklin Lakes Newcomers (past pres.). Home: 22 Myrtle Ave Ramsey NJ 07446 Office: Two Univ Plaza Suite 500 Hackensack NJ 07601

HARNETT, JOYCE ROSALIA, industrial editor; b. Sheboygan, Wis., Nov. 10, 1926; d. Robert Joseph and Rosalia Bertha (Manthey) Werner; m. Richard Marion Harnett, Nov. 19, 1949; children—Mary, Timothy, John, Richard, Gerald, Eugene, James. Ph.B. in Journalism magna cum laude, Marquette U., 1948. Radio writer Sta. WHBY, Appleton, Wis., 1948; asst. editor Excavating Engr. jour., South Milwaukee, Wis., 1948-49; asst. info. officer San Mateo Union High Sch. Dist. (Calif.), 1974-76, proposal editor Guy F. Atkinson Co., South San Francisco, 1976—; editor Bd. News, San Mateo County Assn. Cath. Bds. Edn., 1973-76; cons. sch. brochures Cath. Schs., South San Francisco, 1972; writer, editor Archdiocesan Teen/Parent Handbook, 1968; newspaper weekly columnist on mother/child relationships, 1964-69. Mem. San Francisco Archdiocesan Bd. Edn., 1969-72, Serra High Sch. Bd. Edn., San Mateo, 1975-78; nat. exec. com. Nat. Assn. Bds. Edn., 1972-77; founding mem., pres. San Mateo County Assn. Cath. Bds. Edn., 1970-76; mem. San Mateo County Family Life Edn. Com., 1967-72; pres. San Mateo Parent-Tchr. Group, 1965-69. Mem. Women in Communications Inc., AAUW. Democrat. Roman Catholic. Office: Guy F Atkinson Co 10 W Orange St South San Francisco CA 94080

HARNETT, LILA BEVERLY (MRS. JOEL WILLIAM HARNETT), writer; b. Bklyn., Oct. 4, 1926; d. Milton Samuel and Claire S. (Merahn) Mogan; B.A., Bklyn. Coll., 1946; postgrad. New Sch. for Social Research, 1947-50; m. Joel William Harnett, Feb. 4, 1951. Personnel exec. Walter Lowen Agy., N.Y.C., 1947-52; pub. Bus. Atomics Report, N.Y.C., 1953-63; weekly columnist N.Y. State Newspapers, 1964-74; fine arts editor Cue mag., 1975-80; contbg. editor Mktg. Communications mag., 1979-83; pres. ArtTable Inc., 1980-84; cons. editor Phoenix Home & Garden Mag., 1980—. Mem. N.Y. State Council on Arts, 1983—. Club: Town Tennis. Home and Office: 2 Sutton Place S New York NY 10022

HARNSBERGER, THERESE COSCARELLI (MRS. FREDERICK OWEN HARNSBERGER), librarian; b. Muskegon, Mich.; d. Charles and Julia (Borrell) Coscarelli; B.A. cum laude, Marymount Coll., 1952; M.L.S., U. So. Calif., 1953; postgrad. Rosary Coll., River Forest, Ill., 1955-56, UCLA Extension, 1960-61; m. Frederick Owen Harnsberger, Dec. 24, 1962; 1 son, Lindsey Carleton. Free-lance writer, 1950—; librarian San Marino (Calif.) High Sch., 1953-56; cataloger, cons. San Marino Hall, South Pasadena, Calif., 1956-61; librarian Los Angeles State Coll., 1956-59; librarian dist. library Covina-Valley Unified Sch. Dist., Covina, Calif., 1959-67; librarian Los Angeles Trade Tech. Coll., part-time 1972—, Pasadena City Coll. Library, 1973—; librarian, evening instr. East Los Angeles Coll., 1970—; tumor registrar, med. librarian Alhambra Community Hosp., 1975-79; med. library cons., 1978—; pres. Research Unltd., 1980—; freelance reporter L.A.'s Best Bargains Newsletter, 1981—. Chmn. spiritual values com. Covina Cordinating Council, 1964-66; telephone chmn. Fremont Sch. PTA, Alhambra. Mem. Calif. Assn. Sch. Librarians (chmn. legis. com.), Covina Tchrs. Assn., Book Publicists of So. Calif., AAUW (historian 1972-73), U. So. Calif. Grad. Sch. Library Sci. (life), Nat. Tumor Registrars Assn., So. Calif. Med. Library Group (jobs com. 1977—), LWV, Am. Nutrition Soc. (chpt. Newsletter chmn.), Calif. State Poetry Soc., Pi Lambda Theta. Author poetry. Office: 2809 W Hellman Ave Alhambra CA 91803

HAROIAN, ROSE DOROTHY, audiologist, digital equipment company consultant; b. Waukegan, Ill., Nov. 18, 1923; d. Jacob and Gooleg (Toomasian) Haroian; divorced; children—David Danian, Gillis-Ann Haroian. B.A. in Speech and Drama, Marietta Coll., 1949; M.A. in Speech Communication, Boston U., 1951; Ph.D. in Ednl. Adminstrn., Boston Coll., 1981; student Columbia U., U. Mass., So. Conn. Coll., Marlboro Sch. Tufts U., 1950-70. Cert. spl. tchr., speech pathologist and audiologist, Mass. Nursing tng. Worcester City Hosp. (Mass.), 1942-44; med. tech. U.S. Navy, Long Beach, Calif., 1944-46; spl. edn. tchr. Worcester Pub. Schs., 1949-67; mem. faculty Worcester State Coll., 1967-79, adminstrv. dir. Communicative Disorders Clinic, 1970-72, prof. emeritus, 1979—; editor, writer Digital Equipment Corp., Maynard, Mass., 1981—; cons. Psychol. Therapeutic Learning Ctr., Worcester, 1970-73; diagnostic cons. regional nursing homes, Worcester, Holden, Clinton, Mass., 1973-79; mem. Congl. action com. Am. Speech-Lang.-Hearing Assn., Washington, 1973-79. Author various auditory diagnostic tests in Armenian lang. for children, also pamphlet for awareness of hearing problems in children; editor and writer major documents for use in office computer automation products; contbr. articles in field to profl. jours. Diagnostician, therapist Coll. Community Outreach Services, Central Mass. area, 1967-75; dir., supr. Neonatal Hearing Screening Program, Worcester City Hosp. (1st program of its kind); founder Communications Disorders Clinic, Worcester State Coll., 1967 (Gold Plaque award 1979). Mem. Phi Delta Kappa, Alpha Psi Omega. Mem. Armenian Apostolic Ch. Home: 630 Salisbury St Worcester MA 01609

HAROMY, KATHERINE ANN, lawyer; b. Lake Wales, Fla., June 19, 1957; d. John Carl and Barbara (Adams) H.; m. Richard Clinton Woltmann, Mar. 18, 1984. B.A., Fla. State U., 1978, J.D., 1982. Bar: Fla. 1983. Atty., sr. adv. Fla. Rural Legal Services, Bartow, 1983, Bay Area Legal Services, New Port Richey, Fla., 1983—. Mem. ABA, Fla. Bar (elderly law com. 1985-86), West Pasco Bar Assn. (co-chmn. legal aid com. 1985-86), Health Law Workgroup. Democrat. Unitarian. Avocations: travel; canoeing; biking; hiking. Office: Suite 102 Bay Area Legal Services Inc 5006 Trouble Creek Rd New Port Richey FL 33552

HARP, BEVERLY ANN, real estate broker; b. Little Rock, Dec. 11, 1942; d. Woodrow Wilson and Emma Lou (Weems) Utley; m. Robert Morris Wright, Jr., June 11, 1961 (div. Apr. 1969); children—Gary David, Karen Angela; m. 2d James William Harrison, Aug. 19, 1969; 1 son, James Wilson (div. 1985); m. 3d William T. Harp, Dec. 20, 1985. Student Henderson State U., 1960-61. Lic. real estate broker, Ark.; grad. Ark. Realtors Inst., 1981. Tenant selection officer North Little Rock Housing Authority (Ark.), 1966-69, 75-77; real estate salesperson Fausett & Co., Inc., Little Rock, 1979-82; relocation dir. Rainey Realty Better Homes & Gardens, Little Rock, 1983; assoc. broker ERA Collins Realty, Inc., Little Rock, 1983-84; sales assoc. Lakehill Realty Co., North Little Rock, 1984-85; broker, sales mgr. Gen. Properties, 1985—; owner BH Enterprises, Inc.; instr. Pike's Peak Community Coll. instr. real estate courses. Sec. Ark. Democratic Women, Little Rock, 1982; mem. North Little Rock Sch. Bd., 1978-81. Mem. Ark. Realtors Assn. (chmn. pub. relations 1982-84, liaison to Ark. Legislature 1982—), Greater Little Rock Women's Council Realtors (pres. 1981), Greater Little Rock Home Builders Aux. (pres.-elect 1983-84), North Pulaski Bd. Realtors (v.p. 1981), Nat. Bd. Realtors, Ark. Bd. Realtors, Nat. Home Builders Aux., Ladies Aux. United Transp. Union (local pres. 1975). Methodist. Home: 6313 Rolling Hills Dr North Little Rock AR 72118 Office: Gen Properties 4338 John F Kennedy Blvd North Little Rock AR 72216

HARP, JACQUELINE THERRESA, charitable executive, consultant; b. Stirling, N.J., May 29, 1935; d. William Henry and Huella Louise (Trappe) Ricci; m. Bobby Allen Harp, Dec. 6, 1952 (div. 1982); children—Jon Scott, Eric Alan, Vicki Lou. Student Santa Monica Community Coll., 1963, Abilene Christian U., 1967, U. Hawaii, 1970-73. Tchr. ednl. TV, Govt. Am. Samoa, Tutulia, 1965-70; tchr., asst. Assn. Retarded Citizens, Honolulu, 1971-75, dir. pilot project, Honolulu, 1975-76; exec. dir. Maui (Hawaii) United Way, 1977—; cons. Boy Scouts Am., Maui, 1978, Baldwin Found., Maui, 1983. Contbr. articles to newspapers. Rep., Vol. Leadership Devel. Program, Honolulu, 1981—, White House Conf. on Family, 1982; mem. adv. com., steering com. Halue Mahaolu, Maui, 1982. Named Queen Kaahamanu Outstanding Woman of Month, Kaahamanu Ctr., Maui, 1978. Mem. Am. Mktg. Assn., Nat. Assn. Female Execs., Harding U. Alumne Group, Hawaii Soc. Fund Raising Execs. Republican. Mem. United Ch. of Christ. Clubs: Runners (sec. 1982), Valley Isle (Maui); Runners. Office: Maui United Way 95 Mahalani St Wailuku Maui HI 96993

HARPER, ANNA LOUISE, entrepreneur; b. Little Rock, Nov. 26, 1960; d. Ernest Haven and Mary Louise (Suddreth) Harper. B.A., U. Little Rock, 1984. Staff asst. Office of Gov., Little Rock, 1982; fin. aid officer U. Ark. Med. Scis., Little Rock, 1982; receptionist Riley's Oak Hill Manor, Little Rock, 1982-83; adminstrv. asst. Beth Une for Senate, Little Rock, 1983-84; sales rep. Favorite Check Printers, Little Rock, 1984-86; owner, mgr. Harper's, Sherwood, Ark., 1986—. Mem. ladies aux. Ark. Children's Hosp., Little Rock, 1984—, Friends of Repertory Theatre, Little Rock, 1985—, Ark. Nature Conservancy, Little Rock, 1985—. Pulaski County Rep. Women; del Nat. Rep. Conv. of Ark., Little Rock, 1984. Mem. Nat. Assn. Female Execs., Planned Parenthood Ark., Quapaw Quarter Assn., Pi Beta Phi. Episcopalian. Office: 5500-A Landers Rd Sherwood AR 72117

HARPER, CARMELA ROSE, direct marketing company executive; b. N.Y.C., Feb. 8, 1919; d. Antonio and Assunta (Grenoi) Vergara; m. Rondel H. Harper, May 8, 1947. Student Coll. New Rochelle, 1936-38. Auditor, Liberty Mut. Ins. Co., N.Y.C., 1947-50; pres., chief exec. officer The Kleid Co. Inc., N.Y.C., 1950—. Contbr. articles to profl. jours. Named to Direct Mktg. Hall of Fame, 1983. Mem. Direct Mktg. Assn. (bd. dirs., chmn. 1981-82). Roman Catholic. Avocations: investments; animal causes; swimming. Office: The Kleid Co Inc 200 Park Ave New York NY 10166

HARPER, CATHY LORRAINE, medical technologist; b. Washington, Mar. 1, 1958; d. Samuel Aaron and Betty Delain (Onley) Harper. B.A. in Biochemistry, Mt. Holyoke Coll., 1980; M.A. in Sci. Edn., Atlanta U., 1986. Recreator Class I, Montgomery County Dept. Recreation, Rockville, Md., 1976-77; with Stuart's, Hadley, Mass., 1979-80; research asst. Emory/Grady Family Planning, Atlanta, 1980; med. technologist Grady Meml. Hosp., Atlanta, 1980—. Vol. Grady Meml. Hosp. Labor and Delivery Service, Atlanta, 1980-81; youth rep. Newton I. Steers, Montgomery County, Md., 1975-76. Atlanta U. grad. teaching assistantship, 1984-85; NIH grantee, 1982-84. Mem. Am. Soc. Clin. Pathologists, Southeastern Area Blood Bankers, Ga. Sci. Tchrs. Assn., Minority Women in Sci., AAAS. Democrat. Mem. A.M.E. Ch. Democrat. Clubs: Mt. Holyoke. Avocation: disc jockey. Home: 112 Summit Creek Dr Stone Mountain GA 30083 Office: Grady Meml Hosp 80 Butler St Atlanta GA 30309

HARPER, GLADYS COFFEY (MRS. THOMAS A. HARPER), health services agency adviser; b. Pitts.; d. Clarence William and India Anna (James) Jackson; B.A., U. Pitts., 1970, M.P.A., 1972, M.S.H., 1973; m. Thomas A. Harper, Jan. 21, 1968. With Allegheny County (Pa.) Health Dept., 1958—, chief office tng. and edn. adminstr., 1975-76, adv. curriculum devel. and health adminstrn., 1976—; health technician specialist office health affairs OEO, Washington, 1965; vis. lectr. Grad. Sch. Public and Internat. Affairs, U. Pitts., 1970—; panelist Sta. WQED-TV White House Conf. Food, Nutrition and Health; trustee Mayview State Hosp., 1975—, v.p. bd. trustees, 1978, trustee clin. pastoral edn. program, 1979-80; bd. dirs. United Mental Health, Inc. Program chmn. Law Day, Allegheny County Assn. Lawyers' Wives, 1975, v.p., 1978, pres., 1980; program chmn. Pa. Bar Assn. Wives Program, 1978; trustee Louis Little Meml. Fund, Allegheny County Bar Assn., 1979; founder Judge Thomas A. Harper Meml. Scholarship, Howard U. Sch. Law, 1984. Named Woman of Yr., Greyhound Corp., 1967, 1 of 25 Outstanding Pittsburghers, Wayfarer Mag., Chrysler Corp., 1967, Health Services award Pitts, Club United, 1970, Harold B. Gardner award-Md. Citizen Health award, Allegheny County Med. Soc., 1973, Drug Edn. recognition Pitts. Press, 1971, citation for environ. health curriculum devel. and supervision Chatham Coll., 1976; crowned Bahamas Princess Christmas Queen, Freeport, 1976. Mem. Am. Pub. Health Assn., Royal Soc. Health, Am. Soc. Pub. Adminstrn., Conf. Minority Pub. Adminstrs., Legis. Council Western Pa. (dir., v.p. elect 1982), Western Pa. Genealogy Soc. (pres. 1983), Legis. Council Western Pa. (pres. 1983), League Community Health Workers, AAUW, NAACP (Isabel Strickland Youth Advisor award 1967, Daisy E. Lampkin Human Rights award 1969), Hist. Soc. Western Pa. (trustee 1984), U. Pitts. Alumnae Assn. (Bicentennial scholarship com.), Program to Aid Citizen Enterprises. Co-producer documentary: What's Buggin' The Blacks?, Sta. KDKA-TV, 1968. Home: 5260 Centre Ave Coronada Apts 502 Pittsburgh PA 15232

HARPER, HELEN WOODARD, county court judge; b. Dublin, Ga., Nov. 26, 1945; d. James Ira and Addie Bell (Dixon) Woddard; m. Gurshen N. Baggett, June 29, 1963 (div. 1975); children—Neal Allen, Jeffery Gurshen; m. James Neal Harper, Sept. 11, 1980. Grad. high sch., Rentz, Ga. Legal sec. to presiding justice, Laurens County, Ga., 1964-68, clk. probate ct., 1968-80, judge probate ct., 1981—. Mem. adv. bd. Community Mental Health Ctr., Dublin, 1981—. Mem. Pilot Club of Dublin. Democrat. Baptist. Avocations: cross stitching; golf; walking. Home: PO Box 2129 Dublin GA 31021 Office: PO Box 2098 Dublin GA 31021

HARPER, JUDITH ANN, manufacturing company human resources executive; b. Chgo., May 23, 1940; d. William Louis and Lilien Eva (Kneisler) Barthel; m. Arthur F. Green, Jr., Apr. 4, 1959 (div. Dec. 1976); children—Dianne C., Lynda S.; m. Donald W. Harper, July 26, 1980 (div. Oct. 1984); B.S., Elmhurst Coll., 1985. Personnel asst. Velten & Pulver, Inc., Chicago Ridge, Ill., 1976-79; personnel mgr. Spring/Brummer div., Borg-Warner Corp., Frankfort, Ill., 1979-84; asst. mgr. Borg-Warner Corp., Chgo., 1984-86; vol. cons. Corp. Mgmt. Assistance Program, Chgo., 1984-86. Mem. Zoning Bd. Appeals, Palos Heights, Ill., 1974-76; sec. Hickory Hills Plan Commn., Ill., 1978-84, mem. Zoning Bd. Appeals, 1980-84. Mem. Midwest Personnel Mgmt. Assn., (pres. 1984-85, exec. bd. dirs. 1980-86), Am. Soc. Personnel Adminstrs., Employment Mgmt. Assn. Republican. Lutheran. Avocations: genealogical research; travel; reading. Home: 969 Clark Ave Mountain View CA 94040 Office: Borg-Warner Corp 200 S Michigan Chicago IL 60604

HARPER, LORETTA FINCHER, university purchasing director; b. Thomaston, Ga., Oct. 31, 1946; d. Robert Byron and Ethel Alberta (Brown) Fincher; m. James H. Harper, Jan. 29, 1966; children—Lara Kristel, Matthew Todd. A.A., Ga. State U., 1975, B.B.A., 1980, M.S., 1984. Sec. Ga. State U., Atlanta, 1972-74, buyer, 1974-75, asst. mgr. purchasing, 1975-77, mgr. purchasing, 1977-81, asst. dir. purchasing, 1981-82, dir. purchasing, 1982—, lectr., 1979—; mem. State of Ga. Purchasing Adv. Council, Atlanta, 1977—. Grade chmn. Lindley Middle Sch. PTA, Mableton, Ga., 1983-84; team mother S. Cobb Athletic Assn., Mableton, 1980. Mem. Nat. Assn. Purchasing Mgmt. (cert. purchasing mgr.), Am. Mgmt. Soc., Nat. Assn. Ednl. Buyers, Soc. Property Mgrs., In-Plant Printing Mgmt. Assn. Baptist. Clubs: Road Runners (Atlanta); Depression Glass (Marietta, Ga.). Office: Purchasing Dept Georgia State Univ University Plaza Atlanta GA 30303

HARPER, MARY RUDASICS, lawyer; b. Jacksonville, N.C., Sept. 18, 1950; d. James Eugene and Betty Jean (Lynn) Rudasics; m. Robert P. Harper, Nov. 20, 1981; 1 son, James Edward. B.A., Colo. State U., 1972; J.D., Valparaiso U., 1974. Bar: Ind. 1975. Dep. prosecutor Porter County Prosecutor, Valparaiso, Ind., 1975-78, chief dep. prosecutor, 1978-80; sole practice, Valparaiso, 1980-83; ptnr. Harper, Rogers & Harper, Valparaiso, 1983—. Author: Drunk Driving Arrest Procedures, 1979. Lectr. Valparaiso U. Rape Prevention Forum, 1978, Porter County Forum Child Abuse, Valparaiso, 1980; corp. dir. Porter County Boys Club, Inc., Valparaiso, 1979—; bd. dirs. Ind. Criminal Justice Commn., South Bend, Ind., 1976-79, South Haven Boys Club Bd., Valparaiso, 1979—; undercover narcotics agt. Porter County Drug Unit, 1979-80; Republican jud. nominee, 1984. Recipient Citation Community Service City of Valparaiso, 1980; Porter County Woman of Yr. award Gary Post-Tribune newspaper, 1978. Mem. ABA, Ind. Bar Assn., Porter County Bar Assn. (treas. 1982-83, sec. 1983—). Republican. Episcopalian. Office: Harper Rogers and Harper South Haven Sq Valparaiso IN 46383

HARPER, MARY SADLER, banker; b. Farmville, Va., June 15, 1941; d. Edward Henry and Vivien Morris (Garrett) Sadler; m. Joseph Taylor Harper, Dec. 21, 1968; children by previous marriage: James E. Hatch III, Mary Ann Hatch Czajka. Cert. Fla. Trust Sch., U. Fla., 1976. Registered securities rep., Fla. Dep. clk. Polk County Cts., Bartow, Fla., 1964-67; rep. Allen & Co., Lakeland, Fla., 1967-71; with First Nat. Bank, Palm Beach, Fla., 1971—, sr. v.p., 1984—; v.p. investments J.M. Rubin Found., Palm Beach, 1983—; mem. fin. com. Exec. Women of Palm Beaches, 1985—. Mem. adv. panel Palm Beach County YWCA, 1984—. Mem. Nat. Assn. Bank Women, Miami Bond Club, Fla. Securities Dealers Assn., Exec. Women of Palm Beaches, Palm Beach Martin County Med. Assn. (pres.'s club 1983—), Loxahatchee Hist. Soc., United Daus. of Confederacy, Lighthouse Gallery of Art. Democrat. Baptist. Clubs: Gov.'s, Jonathans. Avocations: reading, history. Home: 630 Ocean Dr Apt 103 Juno Beach FL 33408 Office: 1st Nat Bank in Palm Beach 255 S County Rd Palm Beach FL 33480

HARPER, MELINDA MARION, accountant; b. Vancouver, B.C., Can., Nov. 18, 1943; d. David Robert and Sadie Marion (White) Nichols. Student Colo. Women's Coll., 1962, U. Ariz., 1975-76; B.S.B.A., W.Va. U., 1977. C.P.A., Colo., W.Va. Asst. buyer Bon Marche, Seattle, 1965-68; office mgr. K-T Textiles, Denver, 1968-71; asst. to treas. U.S. Natural Resources, Menlo Park, Calif., 1973-74; mgr. KMG Main Hurdman, Denver, 1977—. Mem. Am. Inst. C.P.A.s (Sells award 1978), Alliance Profl. Women (co-founder 1984, pres. 1985—), Colo. Soc. C.P.A.s (chmn. litigation support services com. 1985—), Denver Women's Soc. C.P.A.s (founding bd. 1981, treas., bd. dirs. 1981-82), Am. Women's Soc. C.P.A.s, Colo. Optometric Soc. (bd. dirs. 1981-82). Avocations: Reading; travel; investing. Home: 274 Vine St Denver CO 80206 Office: KMG Main Hurdman 1675 Broadway Suite 1800 Denver CO 80202

HARPER, PAULA, art history educator; b. Boston, Nov. 17, 1938; d. Clarence Everett and Maura (Lee) Fish. B.A. in Art History magna cum laude, Hunter Coll., 1966, M.A. in Art History, 1968; postgrad. U. N.Mex., 1968-69; Ph.D. in Art History, Stanford U., 1976. Dancer, Munt-Brooks Modern Dance Co., N.Y.C., 1963-65; teaching fellow U. N.Mex., 1968-69; asst. prof. Calif. Inst. Arts, Valencia, 1971-72; dir. Hunter Arts Gallery, CUNY, 1977-78; vis. asst. prof. Mills Coll., Oakland, Calif., spring 1979, 1980-81; Stanford U. (Calif.), 1979-80; assoc. prof. art history U. Miami, Coral Gables, Fla., 1982—; art critic Miami News, 1982—; frequent lectr. mus., art galleries and univs. Author: Pissarro: (with R.E. Shikes) His Life and Work, 1980 (transl. into French and German); Daumier's Clowns, 1981; also contbns. to jours., books, exhbn. catalogues. Film Inst. fellow CUNY, 1966; Tuition fellow Hunter Coll., 1966-67; Ford Found. grantee Stanford U., 1969-73; research grantee French Govt., 1973-74. Mem. Coll. Art Assn. (founder Women's Caucus for Art 1972, pres. N.Y. chpt. 1977-78, mem. nat. adv. bd. 1977-80), Internat. Assn. Art Critics, Soc. Mayflower Descs. Office: Dept Art and Art History U Miami PO Box 248106 Coral Gables FL 33124

HARPER, PHYLLIS HAWKINS, journalist; b. Fawn Grove, Miss., Oct. 6, 1933; d. Edward Clinton and Mittie (Leslie) Hawkins; m. James Leverne Harper, Dec. 23, 1954 (div. May 1970); children—Lynn, Laurie, Leslie, Jamie, Beth Anne. Student Itawamba Jr. Coll., 1951-53, U. Miss., 1953-54. Proofreader, N.E. Miss. Daily Jour., Tupelo, 1969-72, reporter, 1972-77, feature editor, 1977—, speaker/lectr., 1977—; tchr. Tupelo City Schs., 1970-72. Bd. dirs. Tupelo Artists Guild, 1982—; co-chmn. March of Dimes Teamwalk, Lee County, Miss., 1984. Recipient Outstanding Pub. Service award St. Jude Children's Hosp., Memphis, 1979, Outstanding Service award Salvation Army of Tupelo-Lee County, 1982, 83, Battered Boot award March of Dimes, 1982; named Woman of Distinction, Altrusa Club, Tupelo, 1982; Service to God and Man award West Point Civitan Club, 1982; hon. dep. sheriff Lee County. Mem. Miss. Press Assn., Itawamba Hist. Soc. (Service award 1983), Tupelo Museum Assn., Community Devel. Found. Presbyterian. Office: NE Miss Daily Jour PO Box 909 Tupelo MS 38801

HARPER, SHARON ANDREA, revenue officer; b. Chgo., Nov. 15, 1950; d. Louis Jr. and Nearlean (Wilson) H.; 1 child, Dorian S. A.S., Kennedy-King Coll., 1978; B.A., Northeastern U., 1979; postgrad. Governor State U., 1980. Tchr.'s aide John Farren Sch., Chgo., 1975, Loretto Adult Ctr., Chgo., 1978-80; tng. specialist Chgo.-City Coll., 1980—; office asst. IRS, Chgo., 1980-81, revenue officer, 1981—, recrutier, 1982—. Poll watcher Anna Langford Orgn., Chgo., 1976. Recipient Social Service cert. Kennedy-King Coll., 1977, 78; Concerned Student cert. Northeastern U., 1978, 79. Mem. Nat. Assn. Female Execs. (network dir. 1984), Assn. Improvement Minorities. Democrat. Avocations: writing; drawing. Office: IRS 230 S Dearborn Chicago IL 60604

HARPER, WANDA CAVES, banking executive, homemaker; b. Ambrose, Ga., Oct. 21, 1939; d. Loran and Narciss (Harper) Caves; m. Clyde Lamar Harper, Aug. 19, 1961; 1 child, Christopher Lamar. Student Ga. Banking Sch., 1959-60; numerous banking courses and certs. Bank teller C&S Bank, Macon, Ga., 1959-60; exec. sec. Lott builders Supply Co., Douglas, Ga., 1960-75; asst. br. mgr. United Fed. Savs. Loan, Douglas, 1975-81, branch mgr., v.p., 1981-84; br. mgr., officer Anchor Savs. Bank, Douglas, 1984—. Mem. South Ga. Coll. Found. (mem. audit com. 1981-83), Douglas-Coffee County C. of C. Baptist. Home: Route 1 Box 521 Ambrose GA 31512 Office: Anchor Savs Bank 620 S Peterson Ave Douglas GA 31533

HARPHAM, VIRGINIA RUTH, violinist; b. Huntington, Ind., Dec. 10, 1917; d. Pyrl John and Nellie Grace (Whitaker) Harpham; A.B., Morehead State U., 1939; m. Dale Lamar Harpham, Dec. 25, 1938; children—Evelyn, George. Violinist, Nat. Symphony Orch., Washington, 1956—, prin. of second violin sect., 1964—; mem. Lywen String Quartet, 1960-69. Nat. Symphony String Quartet, 1973-82. Episcopalian. Home: 3816 Military Rd NW Washington DC 20015

HARRELL, CAROLYN HARDISON, nursing home administrator; b. Washington, N.C., Feb. 25, 1942; d. Dewey Jasper and Emma Blanche (Lilley) Hardison; R.N., Petersburg (Va.) Gen. Hosp., 1963; B. Nursing, Pacific Western U., 1981, D. Sc. in Health Care Adminstrn., 1982; m. Jerry W. Harrell,

Apr. 18, 1979; children by previous marriage—Natalie Dawn and John Michael Cameron. Staff nurse Petersburg Gen. Hosp., 1963-66; staff nurse, supr., inservice dir. Central State Hosp., Petersburg, 1963-73; owner, operator Cameron's Day Care Center, Colonial Heights, Va., 1973-74; dir. nurses Guarian Corp., Petersburg, 1974-76; adminstr. Am. Health Care Corp., Richmond, Va., 1976-77, Beverly Enterprises, Greenville, N.C., 1977-83, Pitt County Meml. Hosp., 1983-85, Britthaven, Inc., Kinston, N.C., 1985—. Vocat. adv. com. Martin Community Coll., 1979. Recipient Citizenship award, 1960; named Employee of Month, Guardian Corp., 1974. Mem. Am. Coll. Nursing Home Adminstrs., Va. Health Care Facilities Assn., N.C. Health Care Facilities Assn. Republican. Club: Bus. and Profl. Women. Home: 1403 Red Banks Rd Greenville NC 27834 Office: 317 Rhodes Ave Kinston NC 28501

HARRELL, MABEL JANET, medical technologist; b. Selma, N.C., Oct. 15, 1927; d. Joseph McNeil and Bessie Mabel (Greene) Butts; student Richmond Profl. Inst. of Coll. of William and Mary, 1945-47, 59-60, 60-61; M.T., Stuart Circle Hosp., 1948; m. Stewart Havens Harrell, June 3, 1967; children—Joseph Stewart, Diantha Rhea. Med. technologist Maria Parham Hosp., Henderson, N.C., 1950-58, Moses Cone Hosp., Greensboro, N.C., 1958-59, Richmond (Va.) Meml. Hosp., 1959-60; chief technologist Warren Gen. Hosp., Warrenton, N.C., 1960-62, 64; blood bank supr. Wake Meml. Hosp., Raleigh, N.C., 1962-63, 65-68; chief technologist Roanoke Rapids Hosp., Roanoke Rapids, N.C., 1969-72; med. technologist Halifax Meml. Hosp., Roanoke Rapids, 1980-85. Treas., Quankie Bapt. Ch., 1966-73, Sunday sch. tchr., 1967-81, dir. Women's Missionary Union, 1979-82, Vacation Bible Sch. dir., 1976-82, chmn. history com., 1976-82; dir. Women's Missionary Union and Vacation Bible Sch., S. Rosemary Bapt. Ch., 1982—. Mem. Am. Soc. Clin. Pathologists, Am. Soc. Med. Technologists, N.C. Soc. Med. Technologists. Address: Route 2 Box 409A Roanoke Rapids NC 27870

HARRELL, RUTH FLINN, psychologist; b. Americus, Ga., Apr. 19, 1900; d. Dan and Neva (Poley) Flinn; B.S., Wesleyan Coll., Macon, Ga., 1920; M.A., Columbia U., 1924, Ph.D., 1942; m. William Lee Harrell, Nov. 24, 1928; 1 dau., Ruth Harrell Capp. Psychologist, Norfolk (Va.) Schs., 1926-37; rehab. psychologist neuro-surgery Johns Hopkins Hosp., Balt., 1936-47; prof. psychology Old Dominion U., Norfolk, 1965-70, research prof., 1976—. Found. nutritional Advancement grantee, 1976. Mem. Am. Psychol. Assn., N.Y. Acad. Sci., Va. Psychol. Assn., NEA. Presbyterian. Author: Effect of Mothers Diets on the Intelligence of Offspring; Effect of Added Thiamin on Learning, 1943, Further Effects of Added Thiamin on Learning and Other Processes, 1947; co-author: Can Nutritional Supplements Help Mentally Retarded Children?: An Exploratory Study, 1981. Home: 3100 Shore Dr Virginia Beach VA 23451 Office: 801 W 46 St Norfolk VA 23508

HARRER, PEGGY LORRAINE, veterinarian, consultant; b. Ft. Sill, Okla., Apr. 6, 1943; d. Orin B. and Lorraine J. (Ueland) Tilley; children—Patrick Michael, Kelsie Ann; m. 2d, Roger Talbott Harrer, Jan. 14, 1975. Student U. Wash., 1961-64; B.S., Wash. State U., 1966, D.V.M., 1975. Assoc. veterinarian Valley Vet. Hosp., Lewiston, Idaho, 1975-78; owner, hosp. dir. Community Animal Hosp., Pocatello, Idaho, 1978—; cons. veterinarian Idaho State U., Pocatello, 1982—. Author weekly newspaper column Who's Who in the Zoo, 1981-82. Author, editor and star of weekly TV program Critter Catalogue, 1982-83. Sec. Pocatello Zool. Soc., 1981-82; bd. dirs. Zonta Internat., Pocatello, 1982-84. Recipient Woman of Yr. award Pullman Bus. and Profl. Women, 1972-73; Woman of Yr. award Wash. Bus. and Profl. Women, 1974-75; Pfizer Drug Co. vet. scholar, 1974-75. Mem. Am. Animal Hosp. Assn. (cert. hosp. dir.), AVMA, Idaho Vet. Med. Assn., Eastern Idaho Vet. Med. Assn. (pres. 1981-82). Republican. Office: Community Animal Hosp 833 N 12th Ave Pocatello ID 83201

HARRER, SUSAN ELLEN, county clerk; b. Winnemucca, Nev., Jan. 7, 1953; d. Roy Albert and Kathryn E. (English) H. A.A., Stevens Heneger Coll., 1973. Dep. county clk., Humboldt County, Winnemucca, Nev., 1973-77, commrs. sec., 1972-82, adminstrv. asst., 1981-83, county clk., 1983—; grants coordinator, 1980-82, welfare dir., 1983—. Mem. Nat. Assn. Bus. and Profl. Women's Clubs, Inc. (Nev. State rec. sec., 1984—), County Fiscal Officers Assn., Nev. Assn. County Ofcls. Democrat. Methodist. Office: Humboldt County 5th and Bridge St Winnemucca NV 89445

HARRIFF, SUZANNA ELIZABETH, advertising consultant; b. Vicksburg, Miss., Dec. 30, 1953; d. David S. and F. Suzanna (McElwee) Bahner; m. James R. Harriff, Sept. 10, 1977; 1 child, Michael James. B.A., SUNY-Fredonia, 1976; postgrad. Cornell U. Law Sch., 1981. Media asst. Comstock Advt., Syracuse, N.Y., and Buffalo, 1976-77; media buyer/planner G. Andre Delporte, Syracuse, 1979-81; media dir. Roberts Advt., Syracuse, 1982; dir. media services Signet Advt., Syracuse, 1982-84; owner, pres. MediaMarCon, Syracuse, 1984—. Music dir. Manlius United Methodist Ch., N.Y., 1983—, youth dir., 1983-85. Mem. Syracuse Advt. Club (dir. 1985-87, co-chmn. program com. 1985-86), Nat. Assn. Female Execs., Irish-Am. Cultural Inst. Syracuse, Phi Beta Kappa. Democrat. Avocations: music; theatre. Home: 7756 Newhope W Liverpool NY 13090

HARRIGAN, BEULAH SMITH, retired school library supervisor; b. St. Thomas, V.I., Aug. 10, 1922; d. James Henry and Clementine (Varlack) Smith; m. Albert Gomez, Dec. 7, 1942 (div. 1946); children—Jean Beverley, Eva Lorraine; m. 2d, Delvin Alestand Harrigan, June 27, 1951; children—Cheryl Eugenie, Deborah Charlene, Richard Delvin. Children's librarian Pub. Library, St. Thomas, 1945-71; librarian St. Thomas Dept. Edn., 1971-72, title II librarian, 1972-75, dist. librarian, 1976-79, acting dir., V.I., 1979-81, sch. libraries supr., St. Thomas and St. John, 1981-84, accreditation team mem., 1983-84; ret. 1984. Del., Gov.'s Conf., Virgin Islands, 1978; adv. bd. dirs. Ethnic Heritage Textbook, 1982-83, Emancipation Look, 1979-81; chmn. Gov.'s Library Adv. Council, St. Thomas, St. John and St. Croix, 1983; mem. Friends Library, St. Thomas, 1983—. Recipient Morris F. Decastro scholar award, 1974. Mem. St. Thomas Library Assn., V.I. Library Assn., ALA. Democrat. Roman Catholic. Home: PO Box 10272 Charlotte Amalie St Thomas VI 00801 Office: Dept Edn PO Box 6640 Charlotte Amalie St Thomas VI 00801

HARRIGAN, NANCY STAFFORD, lawyer; b. Albany, N.Y., Apr. 15, 1941; d. John Henry and Anne Ernestine (Stafford) H. B.A., Marymount Coll., 1963; J.D., Albany Law Sch., 1966. Bar: N.Y. 1966. Asst. counsel SUNY, 1966-70, assoc. counsel, 1970-74, asst. to chancellor, 1974-77, sr. assoc. counsel, 1977-79, dep. univ. counsel, 1979—; mem. Com. on Character and Fitness, N.Y. Supreme Ct., Appellate Div., 3d Jud. Dist., 1981—. Mem. ABA, N.Y. State Bar Assn., Nat. Assn. Coll. and Univ. Attys., N.Y. State Women's Bar Assn., Am. Soc. Pub. Adminstrn. Roman Catholic. Office: State Univ NY State University Plaza Albany NY 12246

HARRIMAN, PAMELA DIGBY CHURCHILL, political action committee administrator; b. Farnborough, Eng., Mar. 20, 1920; came to U.S., 1959, naturalized, 1971; d. Edward Kenelm and Constance Pamela Alice (Bruce) Digby; B. Domestic Sci.-Economy, Downham (Eng.) Coll., 1937; postgrad. Sorbonne, Paris, 1937-38; m. Randolph Churchill, 1939; 1 son, Winston Spencer; m. 2d, Leland Hayward, May 4, 1960; m. 3d, W. Averell Harriman, Sept. 27, 1971. With Ministry of Supply, London, 1942-43; with Churchill Club for Am. Servicemen, 1943-46; journalist Beaverbrook Press, Europe, 1946-49; mem. nat. fin. council Democratic Nat. Com.; mem. Democratic House and Senate Council; co-chmn. Democratic Congressional Dinner 1979; founder Democrats for the 80's, 1980—. Trustee Rockefeller U.; hon. trustee Menninger Found.; mem. adv. council Harriman Inst. for Advanced Soviet Studies; mem. trustees council Nat. Gallery Art; adv. com. World Rehab. Fund.; mem. adv. bd. Harriman Communications Ctr.; bd. visitors William and Mary Coll.; mem. bd. friends Kennan Inst. for Advanced Russian Studies; v.p. Hort. Soc. N.Y.; bd. dirs. Atlantic Council, Mary W. Harriman Found., also various philanthropic founds. Named Democratic Woman of Yr., Woman's Nat. Democratic Club 1980. Roman Catholic. Office: 3032 N St NW Washington DC 20007

HARRINGTON, SISTER NORA, college official; b. Holyoke, Mass., July 3, 1921; d. Maurice John and Mary T. (Courtney) Harrington; B.S., Coll. of Our Lady of Elms, 1944; M.S. in Chemistry, Fordham U., 1960. Joined Sisters of St. Joseph, Roman Catholic Ch., 1939; tchr. Sister Joseph's High Sch., Pittsfield, Mass., 1944-50; faculty Our Lady of Elms, 1950—, now assoc. prof. chemistry and physics, acad. dean, 1973-79, v.p., 1979—; mem. Sisters Senate, 1971-78, pres., 1972-74. NSF grantee Oak Ridge Summer Inst., 1968, Renssalaer Poly. Inst., 1970. Recipient Disting. Alumna award Coll. Our Lady of Elms, 1977; Nora Harrington Chemistry lecture established 1983. Mem. AAUP, AAUW, Am. Chem. Soc. Home and Office: 291 Springfield St Chicopee MA 01013

HARRINGTON, SANDRA MAY, educator, educational administrator; b. Geneva, N.Y., Sept. 21, 1948; d. James Jerome and Julia Mary (Deeb) H.; A.A., Niagara County Community Coll., 1968; B.S. in Secondary Edn., SUNY, Buffalo, 1970; M.S., Nova U., 1979. Tchr. trainable mentally handicapped Okeechobee (Fla.) Public Schs., 1971-79, tchr. educable mentally handicapped, 1979-81, dean of students Okeechobee High Sch., 1981-82, Okeechobee Jr. High Sch., 1982-83; tchr. Mt. Dora High Sch. (Fla.), 1983-85, Dabney Elem. Sch., Leesburg, Fla., 1985—. Recipient Entricy Herald Achievement award Niagara County Community Coll., 1968; Cert. of Appreciation, Okeechobee Cub Scouts, 1977; winner Fla. Learning Resources System/Alpha contest, 1979; Fla. Dept. Edn. grantee, 1976. Mem. Assn. Supervision and Curriculum Devel., Council Exceptional Children, Internat. Platform Assn., Dem. Women's Club of Lake County, Bus. and Profl. Women Mt. Dora (pres.). Democrat. Home: 1224 Palmetto Rd Eustis FL 32726

HARRIS, ALICE KESSLER, educator; b. Leicester, Eng., June 2, 1941; U.S. citizen; m. Bertram Silverman; 1 child. A.B., Goucher Coll., 1961; M.A., Rutgers U., 1963, Ph.D. in History, 1968. Tchr. pub. schs. Md., 1961-62; asst. prof. Hofstra U., 1968-74, assoc. prof., 1974-81, prof. history, 1981—, co-dir. work/leisure ctr., 1976—; dir. women's studies Sarah Lawrence Coll., 1974-76; sr. lectr. Ctr. Study Social History, U. Warwick, 1979-80; vis. prof. SUNY-Binghamton, 1985. Nat. Endowment for Humanities fellow, 1976-77, 85-86; Radcliffe Inst., Harvard U. fellow, 1977. Mem. Am. Hist. Assn., Orgn. Am. Historians, Am. Studies Assn., ACLU, Berkshire Conf. Women Historians. Author: Women Have Always Worked: A Historical Overview, 1980; Out to Work: A History of Wage Earning Women in the United States, 1982; co-editor: Women in Culture and Politics; A Century of Change, 1986. Address: Dept History Hofstra U Hempstead NY 11550

HARRIS, BARBARA GILLER, educational services company executive, educational consultant; b. N.Y.C., Aug. 10, 1929; d. Maurice and Dorothy Ruth (Steinberg) Giller; m. Harold Harris, Feb. 22, 1949; children—Richard Allan, Stephen Leigh, Carolyn Anne, Sharon Beth. A.B., Hunter Coll., 1950; M.S., Hofstra U., 1972. Classroom tchr. pub. schs., Conn., N.Y., 1956-69; adminstr. Hempstead Pub. Schs., N.Y., 1969-74; English/social studies chmn., Ridgefield, Conn., 1974-84; exec. dir. Global Edn. Outreach, Washington, 1983—; pres. Congl. Youth Leadership Council, Washington, 1985, Washington Ednl. Resources, 1982—. Bd. dirs. Pub. Library, Trumbull, Conn., 1957-59; com. chmn. Friends of Ridgefield Library, Conn., 1978; co-chmn. Youth Inaugural Conf., Washington, 1983-85. Japan Inst. Social and Econ. Affairs fellow, 1980; named Tchr. of Yr., Jr. C. of C., Ridgefield, 1982. Mem. Am. Enterprise Inst. (assoc.), Nat. Press Club, Nat. Council Social Studies, NEA. Avocations: travel; theatre; crossword puzzles; reading. Office: Washington Ednl Resources 1511 K St NW Washington DC 20005

HARRIS, BARBARA HULL (MRS. F. CHANDLER HARRIS), social agy. adminstr.; b. Los Angeles, Nov. 1, 1921; d. Hamilton and Marion (Eimers) Baird; student UCLA, 1939-41, 45-47; m. F. Chandler Harris, Aug. 10, 1946; children—Victoria, Randolph Boyd. Pres., Victoria Originals, 1955-62; partner J.B. Assocs., cons., 1971-73; statewide dir. vols. Children's Home Soc. Calif., 1971-75. Los Angeles County Heart Sunday chmn. Los Angeles County Heart Assn. (recipient Outstanding Service award 1965), 1965, bd. dirs., 1966-69; mem. exec. com. Hollywood Bowl Vols., 1966-84, chmn. vols., 1971, 75; chmn. Coll. Alumni of Assistance League, 1962; mem. exec. com. Assistance League So. Calif., 1964-71, 72-80, 83—, pres., 1976-80; bd. dirs. Nat. Charity League, Los Angeles, 1965-69, 75, sec., 1967, 3d v.p., 1968; ways and means chmn., dir. Los Angeles Am. Horse Show, 1969; dir. Coronet Debutante Ball, 1968, ball bd. chmn., 1969-70, 75, 84, mem. ball bd., 1969—; pres. Hollywood Bowl Patroness com., 1976; v.p. Irving Walker aux. Travelers Aid, 1976, 79; pres. So. Calif. alumni council Alpha Phi, 1961, fin. adviser to chpts. U. So. Calif., 1961-72, UCLA, 1965-72; benefit chmn. Gold Shield, 1969, 1st v.p., 1970-72; chmn. Golden Thimble III Needlework Exhbn., Hosp. of Good Samaritan, 1975; bd. dirs. UCLA Affiliates, 1976-78, KCET Women's Council, 1979-83, Region V United Way, 1980-83; pres. Jr. Philharmonic Com., 1981-82 bd. dirs. Los Angeles Founder chpt. Achievement Rewards for Coll. Scientists, 1980—, pres., 1984-85. Recipient Ivy award as outstanding Alpha Phi alumna So. Calif., 1969; outstanding alumni award for community service UCLA, 1978; Mannequin's Eve award, 1980. Mem. Hollywood C. of C. (dir. 1980-81). Home: 7774 Skyhill Dr Hollywood CA 90068

HARRIS, BARBARA IVEY, financial manager, budget analyst, accountant, management consultant, educator; b. Dothan, Ala., Oct. 19, 1951; d. Willie and Hattie Bell (Barnes) Ivey; B.S., Fla. A&M U., 1973. Internal revenue agt. IRS, Fort Lauderdale, Fla., 1974; adminstrv. asst. Internat. Paper Co., Panama City, Fla., 1974-77; sr. adminstr. fin. services, 1977-78, cost analyst, 1978-79; staff acct. S.W. Forest Industries, Panama City, 1979-82; office mgr. Panama City Devel. Ctr., 1982-83; adj. prof. Gulf Coast Community Coll., 1983—; mgmt. cons., acct. Macedonia Housing Authority, Panama City, 1983-84. Treas., Employees Mut. Benefit Assn., 1978-82; active United Way, recipient Outstanding Service award, 1975; mem. citizens' adv. council Am. Inst. Cancer Research. Ethel Vereen Meml. scholar, 1969, Union Carbide grantee, 1969. Mem. Nat. Assn. Female Execs., Nat. Notary Assn., Bay County Miracle Strip Jaycee Women (treas. 1984-85), Zeta Phi Beta. Democrat. Methodist.

HARRIS, BARBARA NELSON, librarian; b. Bridgeport, Conn., May 12, 1924; d. Carl Alexander and Helen Ella (Bodie) Nelson; m. John Donald Harris, July 12, 1946; children—John, Ralph, Lisa, Todd, Heather. Student Jr. Coll. Conn., Bridgeport, 1942-43; cert. Audio-Visual Inst. for Effective Communication, Bloomington, Ind., 1976; cert. pub. relations for libraries and info. service Simmons Coll., 1978, Circulation and reference asst. Groton (Conn.) Pub. Library, 1964-68, head adult services, 1969-72; reference asst., pub. relations Waterford (Conn.) Pub. Library, 1976—; mem. Groton Pub. Library Bd., 1976-77. Co-author: Reflexions in an Herb Garden, 1981. Sec., New London YWCA, 1970-71; pres. LWV Groton, 1976-77, Friends of Groton Pub. Library, 1975-76. Served with WAVES, USN, 1944-46. Mem. ALA, Conn. Library Assn. (chmn. publicity 1980-81, head pub. relations sect. 1981-82, treas. 1983—), New Eng. Library Assn. Democrat. Unitarian. Home: 230 Prospect Hill Rd Groton CT 06340 Office: Waterford Pub Library 49 Rope Ferry Rd Waterford CT 06385

HARRIS, BETH, journalist; b. Balt., Aug. 27; d. John J. and Pauline (Seligman) Mendes; m. Maurice Harris, Mar. 30, 1959. Writer, producer radio and TV, San Francisco and Los Angeles; advt. account exec., San Francisco; book reviewer Desert Sun, Palm Springs, Calif., 1977—. Program chmn. Friends of Library, Coll. of Desert. Mem. Nat. League Am. Pen Women, Palm Springs Women's Press Club (charter, Woman of Yr. 1982). Jewish. Address: PO Box 2569 Palm Springs CA 92263

HARRIS, BETTY COX, counselor; b. Los Angeles, Nov. 15, 1910; d. Joseph Harris and Mary Belle (Holt) Cox; student Occidental Coll., 1928-29; B.A., U. So. Calif., 1932; m. Gibson Olver Harris, Aug. 3, 1940 (dec. Aug. 16, 1984); 1 dau., Wendy Lynne Harris Replogle. Women's editor, gen. assignment reporter, ch. editor The Daily Report, Ontario, Calif., 1933-41; advt. columnist Pasadena Star News, 1955-59; ct. reporter, with woman's pages West Covina (Calif.) Daily Tribune, 1959-61; salesperson Calif. Dept. Real Estate, 1972-84; instr. real estate Mira Costa Coll., Oceanside, Calif., 1979; peer counselor Oceanside Sr. Citizens, 1981—. Mem. Women in Communications (dir. 1954-69), Nat. Assn. Realtors (women's council 1974-76), Alpha Gamma Delta, Republican. Presbyterian. Author: With Courage Adequate, with Dignity Intact, 1971. Address: 6711 Camino del Prado Carlsbad CA 92008

HARRIS, BEVERLY ANNE MICHIE, interior designer; b. Birmingham, Mich., Sept. 28, 1927; d. Bernard William and Frances Edith (Laursen) Schabot; m. Neil B. Michie (div.); children—Marijon, Jeanne, Francine, Robert, Ronald, Daniel; m. 2d Raymond Harris, Sept. 13, 1981. Owner Michie's Supper Club, Lauderdale-by-the-Sea, Fla., 1965-68; pres. 100 Condos, Ocean Bay Club, Ft. Lauderdale, Fla., 1968-73, owner Beverly Michie Interiors, Lauderdale-by-the-Sea, 1970-73, Lafayette-Walnut Creek, Calif., 1974—. Mem. Internat. Soc. Interior Designers, Lafayette C. of C., Working Women's Exchange, Bus. and Profl. Women (Concord, Calif.). Democrat. Lutheran. Clubs: Forest Lake Country, Sportsmen's (Mich.); Soroptomists (Lafayette). Home and Office: 3911 LeRoy Way Lafayette CA 94549

HARRIS, CAROL ANN, trucking company executive; b. Venus, Pa., Nov. 17, 1944; d. Lewis and Lulu Grace (Whitton) Ehrhart; m. William L. Chapman, Apr. 3, 1965 (dec. Apr. 1976); children—Jessica Grace, William C.; m. Ronald W. Harris, Aug. 22, 1976; 1 child, Jason Wayne. Comml. Art Design degree, Art Inst. Pitts., 1963. Design engr. Knox Glass, Inc., Pa., 1963-65; owner, mgr. Carol Chapman Antiques, Knox, 1975-76; v.p. W.H. Christie & Sons, Inc., Knox. 1976—; co-owner Clarion Antique Mall, 1985—; instr. antiques Clarion Vocat. Tech. Inst., Pa., 1984-85; co-founder Midwest Pa. Antique Assn., 1975; sec., bd. dirs. Sandford Gallery Assn., Clarion, 1984—. Chmn. Am. Cancer Soc., Knox, 1968-77. Mem. North Central Pa. Traffic Assn. (v.p. 1985—). Republican. Club: Clarion Civic. Avocations: antiques; painting; drawing.

HARRIS, CAROLE RIGGS, dance studio executive; b. Covington, Ky., Nov. 20, 1939; d. George William and Gladys Mildred (Griffin) Truitt; m. Melvin LeRoy Harris, Mar. 14, 1971. Grad. high sch. Ludlow, Ky.; pvt. lessons in piano, violin, drums, baton, and dancing. Owner, Carole Riggs Dance Studio, Lynchburg, Va., 1965-82, chmn., pres., 1982—, chmn., pres. Carole Riggs Franchise Devel. Corp., Lynchburg, 1985—; creator Little Miss Lynchburg Pageant, 1967-75, The Dancing Batons Marching Corps., Lynchburg, 1966-81, Harris Modeling Agy., Lynchburg, 1976—; judge numerous pageants Va., 1970—; founder The Carole Riggs System, method for children to learn the arts, 1965. Choreographer (ballet) The Dolle Shoppe Ballet, 1974, voice tng. aids for students in ballet, 1985; composer music for Barre and Center Floor in ballet and tap for dance students, 1985. Author ops. manual for Carole Riggs franchised studios, 1983-85. Fund raiser Crippled Children's Hosp., Greenville, S.C., 1973-83; choreographer Jr. Miss Pageant, Lynchburg, 1975-82; modeling instr. Miss Bronze Pageant, Lynchburg, 1972—; entertainment Lynchburg Tng. Sch. and Hosp., 1969-80. Mem. Dance Educators Am. Inc. (performing arts cert., ballroom dancing cert.). Republican. Christian Ch. Club: Guggenheimer Ladies Aux. (Lynchburg). Lodges: Eagles; Jobs Daughters (honored queen 1955-56). Avocations: restoring historic bldgs., tracing family tree, choreographing and composing music. Home: #10 Denver Ave Lynchburg VA 24503 Office: Carole Riggs Dance Studios Inc 416-420 Main St Lynchburg VA 24504

HARRIS, CATHERINE MARY, land surveyor; b. Dearborn, Mich., Sept. 19, 1961; d. Paul Charles and Catherine Helen (Friedman) Janshego; m. Mark Michael Harris, June 8, 1985. B.S. in Land Surveying, Mich. Tech. U., 1984. Computer-drafting technician Keith & Schnars, P.A., Ft. Lauderdale, Fla., 1984-85; project mgr., plat coordinator Craig A. Smith & Assocs., Pompano Beach, Fla. 1985-86; computer aided design technician Heller, Weaver & Cato, Inc., Margate, Fla., 1986—. Mem. Fla. Soc. Profl. Land Surveyors (assoc. rep. 1985—), Am. Congress on Surveying and Mapping (pres. Douglass Houghton chpt. Houghton, Mich. 1983-84). Republican. Roman Catholic. Avocations: diving; aerobics. Home: 4200 S Pine Island Rd Davie FL 33328

HARRIS, DALE HUTTER, judge; b. Lynchburg, Va., July 10, 1932; d. Quintus and Agnes (Adams) Hutter; m. Edward Richmond Harris, July 24, 1954; children—Mary Fontaine, Frances Harris Russell, Jennifer Richmond, Timothy Edward. B.A., Sweet Briar Coll., 1953; M.Ed. in Counseling and Guidance, Lynchburg Coll., 1970; J.D., U. Va., 1978. Bar: Va. 1978, U.S. Dist. Ct. (we. dist.) Va. 1978, U.S. Ct. Appeals (4th cir.) 1978. Admissions asst. Sweet Briar Coll. (Va.), 1953-54; caseworker Winchester/Frederick Dept. Welfare, Va., 1954-55; vis. lectr. Lynchburg Coll. (Va.), 1971; assoc. Davies & Peters, Lynchburg, 1978-82; substitute judge 24th Dist. Gen. Dist. and Juvenile and Domestic Relations Dist. Cts. Va., 1980-82; judge Juvenile and Domestic Relations Dist. Ct., Lynchburg, 1982—; lectr. law U. Va. Law Sch., 1986—. Vice chmn. bd. dirs. Sweet Briar Coll., 1976-86; vol. coordinator vols. in probation with Juvenile and Domestic Ct., 1971-73; chmn. steering com. for establishment Youth Service Bur., Lynchburg, 1972-73; chmn. bd. dirs. Lynchburg Youth Services, 1973-75; mem. adv. bd. Juvenile Ct., 1957-60, 62-68, sec., 1966-68; bd. dirs. Family Service Lynchburg, 1967-69; Lynchburg Fine Arts Ctr., 1965-67, Seven Hills Sch., 1966-73, Greater Lynchburg United Fund, 1963-65, Lynchburg Assn. Mental Health, 1960-61, Miller Home, 1980-82, Lynchburg Gen.-Marshall Lodge Hosps., Inc., 1980-82; v.p. Lynchburg Mental Health Study Commn., 1966; bd. dirs. Lynchburg Sheltered Workshop for Mentally Retarded Young Adults, 1965-69; bd. dirs. Lynchburg Guidance Ctr., 1959-61, v.p., 1970, pres., 1961; bd. dirs. Hist. Rev. Bd. Lynchburg, 1978-82. Mem. Nat. Council Juvenile and Family Ct. Judges, ABA, Va. State Bar, Va. Trial Lawyers Assn., Va. Bar Assn., Lynchburg Bar Assn., Phi Beta Kappa. Home: 1309 Crenshaw Ct Lynchburg VA 24503 Office: Lynchburg Juvenile and Domestic Relations Dist Ct PO Box 757 Lynchburg VA 24505

HARRIS, DEBRA LYNNE, jewelry sales company executive; b. Columbus, Ohio, Oct. 26, 1956; d. Conrad London and Ruth Evelyn (Bergglas) H. B.S. in Bus., Ind. U., 1978. Founder, owner Gold Connection, Inc., Chgo., 1978—. Mem. Jewelers Bd. of Trade, Jewelers of Am. Office: The Gold Connection Inc 2020 Lincoln Park W Chicago IL 60614

HARRIS, DIANA KOFFMAN, sociologist, educator; b. Memphis, Aug. 11, 1929; d. David Nathan and Helen Ethel (Rotter) Koffman; student U. Miami, 1947-48; B.S., U. Wis., 1951; postgrad. Tulane U., New Orleans, 1951-52; M.A., U. Tenn., 1967; postgrad. U. Oxford (Eng.), 1968-69; m. Lawrence A. Harris, June 24, 1951; children—Marla, Jennifer. Advt. and sales promotion mgr. Wallace Johnston Distbg. Co., Memphis, 1952-54; welfare worker Tenn. Dept. Public Welfare, Knoxville, 1954-56; instr. sociology Maryville (Tenn.) Coll., 1972-75; instr. sociology Fort Sanders Sch. Nursing, Knoxville, 1971-78; instr. sociology U. Tenn., Knoxville, 1967—. Chmn. U. Tenn. Council on Aging, 1979—; organizer Knoxville chpt. Gray Panthers, 1978; mem. Gov.'s Task Force on Preretirement Programs for State Employers, 1973; mem. White House Conf. on Aging, 1981; bd. mem. Knoxville-Knox County Council on Aging, 1976, Sr. Citizens Info. and Referral, 1979, Sr. Citizens Home-Aide Service, 1977; del. E. Tenn. Council on Aging, 1977. Recipient Meritorious award Nat. U. Continuing Edn. Assn., 1982. Mem. Am. Sociol. Assn., AAAS, Gerontol. Soc. Am., Popular Culture Assn., So. Sociol. Soc., So. Gerontol. Soc. (Pres.'s award 1984), N. Central Sociol. Assn. Clubs: London Competitor's; Nat. Contest Assn.; Knoxville Kontestars. Author: Readings in Social Gerontology, 1975; (with Cole) The Elderly in America, 1977, The Sociology of Aging, 1980; co-author: Sociology, 1984; Annotated Bibliography and Sourcebook: Sociology of Aging, 1985; contbr. articles to profl. jours. Home: 4505 Landon Dr PO Box 4247 Knoxville TN 37921 Office: Dept Sociology U Tenn Knoxville TN 37916

HARRIS, DIANE CAROL, optical manufacturing company executive; b. Rockville, Centre, N.Y., Dec. 25, 1942; d. Daniel Christopher and Laura Louise (Schmitt) Quigley; m. Wayne Manley Harris, Sept. 30, 1978. B.A. cum laude, Cath. U. Am., 1964; M.S., Rensselaer Poly. Inst., 1967. Analytical chemist Nat. Heart Inst., NIH, Bethesda, Md., 1964-65; with Bausch & Lomb, Inc., Rochester, N.Y., 1967—, line mgr. analytical products, 1976-77, v.p. planning and bus. devel. Soflens div., 1977-80, corp. dir. planning, 1980-81, v.p. corp. devel., 1981—; dir. Bausch & Lomb Ins. Co., 1977-80; dir. Delta Labs., Inc. Contbr. articles to profl. jours. Pres. Rochester Against Intoxicated Driving and Found., 1979-83, also chmn. polit. action com., 1979, 83—; bd. dirs. Nat. Council on Alcoholism, Rochester, 1980-84; mem. STOP-DWI (Adv. Council to Monroe County Legislature), 1982—; bd. dirs. Friends of Bristol Valley Playhouse Found., 1983—. Recipient Disting. Citizens award Monroe County, 1979, YWCA 1983 Tribute to Women in Industry and Service award, Rochester Area NCA Service award, 1984; Nat. Merit scholar, 1960; N.Y. State Regents scholar, 1960; NSF grantee, 1963. Mem. Am. Mgmt. Assn., Fin. Execs. Inst., Assn. Econ. Growth, Phi Beta Kappa, Sigma Xi, Delta Epsilon Sigma, Kappa Beta Gamma. Office: Bausch & Lomb Inc 1 Lincoln First Sq Rochester NY 14601

HARRIS, DONA LINDQUIST, educator; b. Blackfoot, Idaho, Jan. 27, 1945; d. Elvin Alexander and Irene (Ball) Lindquist; B.A. cum laude in Polit. Sci., U. Utah, 1967, M.A. in Ednl. Psychology, 1973, Ph.D. in Ednl. Psychology, 1975; m. E. Kent Harris, Aug. 24, 1968; children—Ashley Dawn, Ryan Kent. Congressional intern. U.S. Ho. of Reps., summers 1965, 66, 67; asso. for evaluation, sect. evaluation and methods devel. Intermountain Regional Med. Program, Salt Lake City, 1969-72, dir. sect., 1972-73; project dir. primary care preceptorship program dept. family and community medicine U. Utah, 1973-75, assoc. prof. family and community medicine, project dir. student programs in family medicine Sch. Medicine, 1975—, women's faculty liaison officer to Assn. Am. Med. Colls., 1982—. Mem. Soc. Tchrs. Family Medicine (bd. dirs. 1983-86, exec. com. 1984-86), Assn. Am. Med. Colls., Assn. Behavioral Scis. and Med. Edn. Research in evaluation edn., personality types of med. students, residents and faculty, determinants of career selections; editor edn. column. Family Medicine, 1981-83. Home: 2200 S 18th E Salt Lake City UT 84106 Office: IC 303 Med Center 50 N Medical Dr Salt Lake City UT 84132

HARRIS, DORIS LYNNE, college administrator, consultant; b. York, Pa., May 23, 1951; d. Benjamin F. Jr. and Cossie M. (Dickerson) Sexton; divorced; children—Kamal, Ahmed. B.S., U. Mass., 1977; M.Ed., Cambridge Coll., 1984. Ops. analyst Mass. Mut. Ins. Co., Springfield, 1979-81, Phoenix Mut. Ins. Co., Greenfield, Mass., 1981-82; dir. YWCA, Springfield, 1982-85; coordinator bus. div. Holyoke Community Coll., Mass., 1986—; cons. teenage pregnancy, Springfield, 1980—; facilitator time mgmt., Amherst, Mass., 1980—; researcher dept. pub. health U. Mass., Amherst, 1985-86; participant confs. Mem. community task force Am. Cancer Soc., Springfield, 1985—; bd. dirs. Upward Bound Program, Amherst, 1984—, A Better Chance Program, Amherst, 1985—. Mem. Mass. Assn. Women Deans, Adminstrs. and Counselors, Nat. Assn. Female Execs., Delta Sigma Theta. Avocations: sewing; tennis. Home: 92A Brittany Manor Dr Amherst MA 01002 Office: Holyoke Community Coll Bus Div 303 Homestead Ave Holyoke MA 01060

HARRIS, ELAINE DUBOW, non-profit organization executive; b. Montreal, Que., Can.; came to U.S., 1977, naturalized, 1981; d. Gerald Isadore and Anne Chazan (Elias) Nadler; B.A., McGill U., 1962; postgrad. Concordia U., 1969-70; Diploma in Electronic Media Broadcasting, Canadian Nat. Inst. Broadcasting, 1979; children—Wendy Debra, Douglas Brad, Jonathan David. Exec for Soviet Jewry, Can. Jewish Congress, Montreal, Que., 1974-75; owner, operator Galerie Innit, Eskimo Art Gallery, Montreal, Que., 1975-77; infor. counsellor Israel Council Soviet Jewry, Dept. Info., Tel Aviv, Israel, 1977-79; co-ordinator, speaker Nat. United Jewish Appeal, N.Y.C., 1979-81; co-founder, coordinator Jerusalem Women's Seminar, N.Y.C. 1979—; dir. devel. World Jewish Congress, N.Y.C., 1979—; panelist Second World Conf. Soviet Jewry, Brussels, 1976; host radio program Inside the Jewish World, 1982—; cons. United Jewish Appeal, 40th Anniversary Conv., 1978, Zionist Orgn. Am., Internat. Leadership Conf., 1979, Can. Govt. Commn. Soviet Jews, 1977-78; rep. Council Women for Christians and Jews, 1976-77; nat. exec. United Israel Appeal Can., 1979-80. Recipient Israel Bonds award Israel Bonds of Can., 1977; Nat. Film Festival awards for The Last Journey, 1982. Mem. Nat. Assn. Female Execs. Author: They Came to Stay, 1977; History of Project Renewal, 1979. Office: One Park Ave New York 10016

HARRIS, EMMA EARL, nurse, nursing home executive; b. Viper, Ky., Nov. 6, 1936; d. Andrew Jackson and Zola (Hall) S.; m. Ret Haney Henis Martin Harris, June 5, 1981; children—Debra, Joseph, Wynona, Robert Walsh. Grad. St. Joseph Sch. Practical Nursing. Staff nurse St. Joseph Hosp., Bangor, Maine, 1973-75; office nurse Dr. Eugene Brown, Bangor, 1975-77; dir. nurses Fairborn Nursing Home, Ohio, 1977-78; staff nurse Hillhaven Hospice, Tucson, 1979-80; asst. head nurse, 1980; co-owner Nu-Life Elderly Guest Home, Tucson, 1980—. Vol. Heart Assn., Bangor, 1965-70, Cancer Assn., Bangor, 1965-70. Mem. Nat. Assn. Female Execs., Assn. of Better Living for the Elderly (cons. 1983—). Democrat. Avocations: theatre; opera. Home: 1082 E Seneca Tucson AZ 85719

HARRIS, EVALYN BELLE BROOKSHIRE, veterinary laboratory and office services company executive; b. Ft. Worth, Dec. 17, 1946; d. Sidon and Evalyn Belle (Brookshire) H., IV. Student pub. schs., Ft. Worth. Office mgr., lab. asst. to Fred Soifer, D.V.M., Houston, 1973-75; cattle breeder Nathan's Acres Ranch, Brookshire, Tex., 1975-77; office mgr., lab. technician to James Hopper, D.V.M., Houston, 1977-79, Fondren Animal Clinic, Houston, 1979-83; owner, mgr. Temporary Vet. Service, Houston, 1983—. Recipient numerous awards various horse shows, 1956—. Mem. Tex. Hunter and Jumper Assn. (horse show sec. 1979-82), Tex. Palomino Assn., Tex. Horse Racing Assn., Am. Quarter Horse Assn., Jr. Quarter Horse Assn., Houston Zool. Soc., Mus. Fine Arts. Republican. Episcopalian. Home: PO Box 976 Brookshire TX 77423

HARRIS, FRANCES ALVORD (MRS. HUGH W. HARRIS), consultant, retired radio-television broadcaster; b. Detroit, Apr. 19, 1909; d. William Roy and Edith (Vosburgh) Alvord; A.B., Grinnell Coll., 1929; L.H.D. (hon.), Ferris State Coll., 1980; m. Hugh William Harris, Sept. 24, 1932; children—Patricia Anne (Mrs. Floyd A. Metz), Hugh William, Robert Alvord. With advt. dept. Himelhoch Bros. & Co., Detroit, 1929-31; broadcaster as Julia Hayes, Robert P. Gust Co., 1931-34, tng. and personnel dept. Ernst Kern Co., 1935-36; broadcaster as Nancy Dixon, Young & Rubicam, Inc., 1939-42; women's editor Sta. WWJ, Detroit, 1943-64, Sta. WWJ-TV, 1947-64, spl. features coordinator Sta. WWJ-TV-AM-FM, 1964-74; prin. Fran Harris & Assocs., cons. to social agys., instns., orgns., Detroit, 1974-85; pres., chief exec. officer I.C. Harris & Co., Detroit, 1982-84, chmn. bd., 1984-85. Mem. exec. bd. Wayne County chpt. Mich. Soc. for Mental Health, 1953-63; chmn. Mental Health Week, 1958-59; mem. Wayne County Commn. on Aging, 1975—, chmn., 1976-77; publicity com. YWCA, 1945, 2d v.p., 1963; mem. publicity com. Tri-County League for Nursing, 1956-61; publicity chmn. Met. Detroit YWCA Bd. Dirs., 1961-66, exec. com., 1962-67; campaign dist. chmn. United Found., 1959, unit chmn., 1960-61, chmn. speakers bur., 1974; exec. bd. United Found. Women's Orgn., 1962-64; governing bd. United Community Services Women's Com., 1961-66; bd. dirs. United Community Services, 1964-67, bd. dirs. Homemaker Service Met. Detroit, pres., 1969-70; bd. dirs. Vis. Nurse Assn., pres., 1974-76; bd. dirs. Camp Fire Girls of Detroit, mem. nat. council, 1967-72, mem. nat. bd., exec. com., 1970-72, pres., 1978-80; bd. dirs. Well Being Service Aging, 1969-74, Sr. Ctr., 1971-76, Friends Detroit Pub. library, 1972-77, Friends Children's Mus., 1972-74, Children's Mus., 1983—, Children's Ctr., 1985—; trustee Detroit Com. Alcoholism, 1961-64; mem. Mayor's Com. for Freedom Festival, 1959, chmn. women's activities, 1965; mem. Mayor's Com. for UN Week, 1959; mem. Gov.'s Commn. Status of Women, 1962-69, Mich. State Women's Commn., 1969-77; mem. nat. council Homemaker Service, 1970-73; mem. adv. com. to trustees Grinnell Coll.; mem. bd. control Ferris State Coll., 1968-78; mem. def. adv. com. Women in the Services, 1970-73, chmn., 1973; program chmn. Met. Detroit YMCA, 1973-75; sec.-treas. Mich. Assn. Governing Bds. State Colls. and Univs., 1975, v.p., 1976-77, pres., 1977-78; vice chmn. Detroit div. United Community Services, 1985—. Recipient Grinnell Coll. Alumni award, 1959, Mental Health Soc. Mich. award, 1958, Theta Sigma Phi Headliner award for Mich., 1951, nat., 1952; Women's Advt. Club of Detroit Civic award, 1957; named Advt. Woman of Yr., Detroit, 1958, 73, Soroptimist Woman of Yr., 1965; Fran Harris Day in her honor, Detroit, 1960; Vol. State of Mich., 1975; Heart of Gold award, 1976. Mem. Am. Women in Radio and TV (pres. Detroit chpt. 1957-58, gen. chmn. nat. conv. 1966, Outstanding Community Service award 1972), Nat. Assn. Women Bus. Owners (Community Service award Mich. chpt. 1982), Women's Advt. Club of Detroit (pres. 1959-60, mem. bd. 1974-77), UN Assn. U.S.A. (dir. Detroit chpt. 1962-65, Mich. div. bd. 1963-65), Advt. Fedn. (nat. v.p. women's activities 1964-67), Nat. Fedn. Press Women (hon.), Women in Communications (pres. Detroit 1950-51; del. to Asian-Am. Women in Broadcasting Conf. 1966, nat. 1st v.p. 1968-71, nat. pres. 1971-73, chmn. Communications Conf. Ams., 1968, del. III World Congress Women Journalists 1973), Pi Epsilon Delta. Episcopalian (communications com. local congregation and Diocese of Mich. 1965-66). Club: Women's Econ. (charter mem.; dir. 1975—, membership chmn. 1975, program chmn. 1976, pub. relations co-chmn. 1977, treas. 1978, sec. 1979, 1st v.p. 1980, pres. 1981-82; charter) (Detroit). Author, editor: Focus: Michigan Women, 1977. Home: 8120 E Jefferson Detroit MI 48214

HARRIS, FRANCES FLINTROY, university administrator; b. Monroe, La., Feb. 17, 1937; d. Mose Flintroy and Annie (Henry) Collins; m. Charles Blunt, July 11, 1955 (div. July 1967); children—Lorenzo, Alonzo, Sylvia Ann, Robert Earl; m. 2d, Roy L. Harris, Dec. 17, 1981. B.A., Tulane U., 1985. Sec., Grambling U., La., 1963-68, State Farm Ins., Monroe, La., 1968-75; rehab. dir. City of Monroe, La., 1975-81; asst. dir. tchr. edn. Tulane U., 1982—. Pres. Sickle Cell Anemia Found., Monroe, 1977-81. Mem. Nat. Assn. Female Execs., Nat. Assn. Negro Bus. and Profl. Women, Am. Legion Aux., Nat. Bowling Assn., New Orleans Women's Bowling Assn. Democrat. Baptist. Avocations: bowling; swimming; spectator sports; piano. Home: PO Box 56732 New Orleans LA 70156 Office: Tulane Univ 6823 Saint Charles St 211 Alcee Fortier New Orleans LA 70118

HARRIS, FRANCES SETTLE, nursing administrator; b. Rockingham, N.C., July 9, 1937; d. Hiriam Dixon and Nina Louise (Privett) Settle; m. Clarence Edward Harris, Mar. 28, 1958; children—Rebecca Louise, Philip Edward, Adrian Alan. B.A. in Math., U. N.C.-Greensboro, 1959, A.A.S. in Nursing, 1967; student nursing degree program East Carolina U., Greenville, N.C., 1985—. Cert. critical care nursing. Hemodialysis charge nurse Hendrick Hosp., Abilene, Tex., 1973-74; nursing instr. Mary Meek Sch. Nursing, Abilene, 1974-75; critical care in-service instr. Meth. Hosp., Memphis, 1977-79; staff nurse CCU, City of Memphis Hosp., 1979-80; patient edn. instr. St. Francis Hosp., Memphis, 1980-82; asst. dir. nursing Albemarle Hosp., Elizabeth City, N.C., 1982—. Mem. Am. Assn. Critical Care Nurses. Republican. Mem. Church of Christ. Avocations: canoeing; painting. Home: 20 Carter Rd Elizabeth City NC 27909 Office: Albemarle Hosp N Road St Elizabeth City NC 27909

HARRIS, GEORGIA, antiques dealer; b. Edna, Tex., Feb. 8, 1920; d. Lee Thomas and Lillie delilah (Walker) Jacobs; m. Volum Lawrence Harris, Mar. 16, 1938 (dec.); children—Patricia, Martha, Janice, Kathryn. Owner, operator antiques bus., Schulenburg, Tex., 1945-50, Weathervane Antiques, Columbus, Tex., 1950—; mgr. dir. Meml. City Antiques Show, Houston, 1972, Sharpstown Antiques, Houston, 1970-78, Magnolia Antiques Show, Columbus, 1964-68, LaGrange (Tex.) Fair Show, 1969-73; mgr. coordinator Columbus Antiques Show, benefit Am. Legion, 1975-80, Brenham (Tex.) Antiques Show, benefit Heritage Soc., 1979-82, Houston Antiques Show, benefit UN, 1981-82. Baptist. Home and Office: Hwy 90 W Box 187 Columbus TX 78934

HARRIS, HENRIETTA BUNDY HESTER, educational administrator; b. Jamestown, N.C., Mar. 9, 1926; s. Otis C. and Pearl (Barber) Bundy; m. Junnie T. Hester, Dec. 24, 1945 (dec. Mar. 1966); children—Susan R., Elizabeth Deblasio, J. Thomas; m. Cleo Harris, July 20, 1969; stepchildren—Ronald C. Harris, Brian K. Harris. B.S., High Point Coll., 1946; postgrad U. N.C. Greensboro; grad. Lausanne Sch. Montessori Tng. St. Nicholas Sch., London, 1976. Pres., owner Hester's Creative Schs., Inc., Greensboro, N.C., 1949—; v.p., owner Creative Ctr., High Point, N.C., 1972—. Mem. child care adv. com. Child Care Edn. div. Guilford Tech. Inst., 1969-76. Mem. City Council Pinehaven Village, 1985-86. Scholarship Fund named in her honor High Point Coll. Mem. N.C. Child Advocacy Inst. (charter), N.C. Day Care Assn. (state conv. chmn. 1986), N.C. Kindergarten Assn., N.C. Nursery Sch. Assn. Pvt. Operators, N.C. Assn. Edn. Young Children, Kingergarten Assn., Assn. Childhood Edn. Internat., Guilford County Nursery Sch. Assn. (past pres.), Greensboro Pre Sch. Tchrs. Assn., Child Devel. Assoc. Forum (v.p. 1983, treas. 1984-85), Guilford County Coalition. Democrat. Methodist. Home: 4 St Regis Ct Greensboro NC 27408 Office: Hester's Creative Schs Inc 2715 Pinedale Rd Greensboro NC 27408

HARRIS, ILENE BARMASH, educator; b. Chgo., Jan. 21, 1945; d. Charles and Shirley (Garfinkel) Barmash; B.A., U. Chgo., 1965, M.A. (Univ. fellow, Ford Found. fellow), 1972, Ph.D., 1979; m. Morton Edward Harris, July 9, 1967. Tchr. social studies Chgo. Public Schs., 1966-68; social studies test materials writer Sci. Research Assos., Chgo., 1969-73; instr. Rutgers U., New Brunswick, N.J., 1971, U. Chgo., 1973; research fellow U. Minn. Med. Sch., Mpls., 1973-78, research assoc., 1978-86, asst. prof., 1985-86, assoc. prof., sr. research assoc., 1986—, lectr. Coll. Edn., 1984-85, assoc. prof., 1986—, evaluation cons. Bush Found.; ednl. cons. Nat. Endowment for Humanities; faculty devel. cons. VA North Central Regional Med. Edn. Center; continuing med. edn. cons. Minn. Med. Assn.; curriculum cons. Southwestern Coop. Ednl. Lab. mem. Am. Ednl. Research Assn. (sec.-treas. profl. edn. div., invited speaker ann. meeting 1986), Am. Assn. Med. Colls., Nat. Soc. Study Edn., Assn. Supervision and Curriculum Devel., Evaluation Research Soc. Mem. editorial bd. Sch. Rev. 1969-71; cons. editor Jour. Curriculum and Supervision; contbr. articles to profl. jours. Home: 4375 Coolidge Ave S Minneapolis MN 55424 Office: 420 Deleware St SE Minneapolis MN 55455

HARRIS, JANINE DIANE, lawyer; b. Akron, Ohio, Jan. 12, 1948; d. Russell B. and Ethel Harriet (Smith) H.; m. Robert I. Coward, Sept. 14, 1968 (div. 1977); m. 2d, John Richard Ferguson, Feb. 1, 1980; children—Brigit Grace, Rachel Anna. A.B., Bryn Mawr Coll., 1970; J.D., Georgetown U., 1975. Bar: Va. 1975, D.C. 1976. Assoc. Baker & Hostetler, Washington, 1975-78, Pettit & Martin, Washington, 1979-80; assoc. Peabody, Lambert & Meyers, Washington, 1981-82, ptnr., 1983-84; lectr. Exec. Program La. State U., Baton Rouge, 1981—; pres. Nat. Found. Women's Bar Assns., 1985—. Mem. ABA, Fed. Bar Assn., Women's Bar Assn. D.C. (pres. 1984-85), D.C. Bar (bd. govs. 1985-88), Nat. Conf. Women's Bar Assns. (bd. dirs. 1985—). Club: Bryn Mawr (Washington). Home: 323 S St Asaph St Alexandria VA 22314

HARRIS, JEAN LOUISE, physician; b. Richmond, Va., Nov. 24, 1931; d. Vernon Joseph and Jean Louise (Pace) Harris; B.S., Va. Union U., 1951; M.D., Med. Coll., Va., 1955; D.Sc. (hon.), U. Richmond, 1981; m. Leslie John Ellis, Sept. 24, 1955; children—Karin Denise, Pamela Diane, Cynthia Suzanne. Exec. dir. Nat. Med. Assocs. Found., Washington, 1969-72; prof. family practice and dir. Center for Community Health Med. Coll. Va., Richmond, 1973-78; sec. human resources Commonwealth of Va., Richmond, 1978-82; v.p. state mktg. programs Control Data Corp., Mpls., 1982-86, v.p. bus. devel., 1986—; mem. President's Pvt. Sector Initiatives Task Force; mem. recombinant DNA com. NIH/HEW; mem. adv. bd. Women's Bank, Richmond; chmn. sickle cell adv. bd. NIH/HEW, 1978-79; mem. Dept. Def. adv. com. on women in the service, 1986-89. Named Woman of Yr., Richmond YMCA, 1980; recipient Disting. Service award Nat. Govs. Assn., 1981; named to list Top 100 Black Bus. and Profl. Women, Dollars and Sense Mag., 1986. Mem. Inst. Medicine/Nat. Acad. Sci., Richmond Acad. Medicine, So. Inst. Human Resources (pres. 1980-81), Am. Pub. Health Assn. (chmn. social policy bd. 1976-77), Continental Socs., Delta Sigma Theta. Episcopalian. Clubs: Links Inc., Jack'n Jill. Home: 10860 Forestview Circle Eden Prairie MN 55344 Office: 8100 34th Ave S Minneapolis MN 55440

HARRIS, JEAN NOTON, music educator; b. Monroe, Wis., Feb. 21, 1934; d. Albert Henry and Eunice Elizabeth (Edgerton) Noton; B.A., Monmouth (Ill.) Coll., 1955; M.S., U. Ill., 1975, adminstrv. cert., 1980, Ed.D., 1984; m. Laurence G. Landers, June 7, 1955; children—Theodore Scott, Thomas Warren, Philip John; m. Edward R. Harris, Nov. 27, 1981; stepchildren—Adrianne, Erica. Tchr. music schs. in Ill. and Fla., 1955-76; tchr. music Dist. 54, Schaumburg, Ill., from 1976. Named Outstanding Young Woman of Yr., Jaycee Wives, St. Charles, Mo., 1968. Mem. Music Educators Nat. Conf. (life) Ill. Music Educators Assn., NEA (life), Am. Choral Dirs. Assn., U. Ill. Alumni Assn. (life), Mortar Bd., Mensa, Sigma Omicron Mu., Kappa Delta Pi. Mem. United Ch. Christ. Home: 914 Roxbury Ln Schaumburg IL 60194

HARRIS, JENNIFER BROOME, public relations and advertising executive; b. Birmingham, Ala., Sept. 15, 1958; d. William Evan and Elizabeth Jean (Stinson) Broome; m. Sammy Ray Harris, Nov. 21, 1981. B.B.A., U. Montevallo, 1980. Communications analyst Rust Internat. Corp., Birmingham, Ala., 1980-81, mgr. pub. relations and advt., 1981—. Advisor, Jr. Achievement, 1982—; mem. adv. bd. Birmingham Better Bus. Bur., 1983; mem. exec. com. Boy Scouts Am., 1982—; mem. adv. bd. Birmingham Met. Devel. Bd., 1982. Mem Pub. Relations Council Ala., Internat. Assn. Bus. Communicators, Forum. Office: Rust Internat Corp 1130 S 22d St Birmingham AL 35205

HARRIS, JENNIFER LYNEEN, telecommunications official; b. Aurora, Colo., Nov. 6, 1962; d. Sedrick Paul Harris and Katharine Joan (Smith) Hellegaard. Student, pub. schs., Mt. Juliet, Tenn., 1978-80. Implementation coordinator M&SD Corp., Lyndhurst, N.J., 1980-81, telco coordinator, 1981-82; telco specialist No. Telecom, N.Y.C., 1982-83, supr., 1984—. Office: Northern Telecom Inc 40 W 57th St 17th Floor New York NY 10019

HARRIS, JERRY FRITZ, nurse; b. Camp Kilmer, N.J., July 1, 1952; d. John Bowdre Fritz and Mary Ellen (Hess) Fritz Meyn; m. Kenneth A. Harris, May 12, 1979; 1 child, Sarah Courtney. B.S., R.N., U. Wyo., 1975; M.A. in Rehab. Counseling, Seattle U., 1982. Staff nurse USPHS, Seattle, 1975-77; rehab. nurse Providence Hosp., Seattle, 1978; respiratory nurse specialist Vis. Nurse Service Seattle-King County, 1978-81; dir. nursing Exeter House, Seattle, 1982; nursing instr. Yakima Valley Community Coll., Ellensburg, Wash., 1983—; bus. office mgr. Kenneth A. Harris, M.D., Ellensburg, 1982—. Author: (with others) Disability Trap teaching game, 1982. Bd. dirs. Child Advocacy Council, Ellensburg, 1983—. Served to lt. (j.g.) USPHS, 1975-77. Mem. Western Geront. Soc., AAUW, AMA Aux., Central Wash. U. Scholarship Club. Republican. Episcopalian. Home: 609 E 4th St Ellensburg WA 98926 Office: Kenneth A Harris MD 702 E Manitoba St Ellensburg WA 98926

HARRIS, JESSIE G. (MRS. HUBERT LAMAR HARRIS), former educational administrator; b. Athens, Ga., May 12, 1909; d. Wiley Jackson and Dora (Hilley) Ginn; B.B.A., U. Ga., 1956; A.B., Ga. State U., 1960; m. Hubert Lamar Harris, Nov. 25, 1930; children—Mary Ann (Mrs. William Holley), Hubert Lamar, Dorothy (Mrs. Ronald Zazworksy), Martha Susan (Mrs. R. R. McCue, Jr.). Various secretarial positions, ins. and law offices, 1923-30; sec. div. gen. extension U. Ga., 1930-35, asst. dir. div. gen. extension, 1935-47; assisted with compilation survey Univ. System Ga., Atlanta, 1949-50, adminstrv. asst. to regents, 1951-63, asst. exec. sec., 1963-67, asso. exec. sec., 1967-72, asst. vice chancellor personnel, 1972-74, emeritus, 1974—. Asst. exec. dir. Ga. Scholarship Commn., 1965-66; asso. exec. sec. Ga. Med. Edn. Bd., 1952-72. Mem. AAUW (chmn. study group 1964-66, treas. 1972, 73), Atlanta Hist. Assn., So. Hist. Soc., Sandy Springs Arts and Heritage Soc., Crimson Key Honor Soc., Mortar Bd., Phi Chi Theta, Delta Mu Delta, Psi Chi. Club: Atlanta Writers. Home: Rosemont Route 4 Box 274 Monroe GA 30655

HARRIS, JOAN WHITE, arts administrator, TV producer; b. New Haven, Mar. 9, 1931; d. Louis and Martha (Rahm) White; m. Gerald Baumann Frank, Feb. 12, 1953 (div. 1974); children—Daniel Bruce, Jonathan White, Louise Blanche; m. Irving Brooks Harris, June 19, 1974. B.A., Smith Coll., 1952. Editorial asst. Oxford U. Press, N.Y.C., 1952-53, Ency. Brit., Chgo., 1953-54; TV producer, Chgo., 1976, 78, 80; pres. Chgo. Opera Theater, 1977-84, chair, 1984—, bd. dirs., 1975—; panelist, cons. Nat. Endowment for the Arts, 1980—; chair nat. bd. Aspen Music Festival, Colo., 1984-85; mem. adv. bd. U.S.-China Arts Exchange, 1985—. Bd. dirs. Harris Found., Chgo., 1976—; bd. dirs./trustee Mus. Contemporary Art, Chgo., 1976—, Hampshire Coll., Amherst, Mass., 1977-84, Chgo. Symphony Orch., 1978—, Nat. Inst. Music Theater, Washington, 1982—, Ind. Sector, Washington, 1983—. Clubs: Arts, Casino, Saddle and Cycle, Lake Shore, Standard (Chgo.). Home: 209 E Lake Shore Dr Chicago IL 60611 Office: Chicago Opera Theater 410 S Michigan Ave Chicago IL 60605

HARRIS, JOSEPHINE LYNEE, insurance company official, housing development fund executive; b. Pitts., Dec. 22, 1941; d. George Alvah and Ruth Elizabeth (Peoples) Brothers; m. William B. Harris, Jr., 1961 (div. 1968); 1 son, Lawrence George. A.A., Los Angeles City Coll., 1981. Bank teller Franklin Savs. Bank, N.Y.C., 1963-68, sr. service rep., 1968-73; contract rep. Equitable Life Assurance Soc., N.Y.C., 1973-74, service rep., 1975-77, adminstrv. assoc., 1978-82, guaranteed interest contract specialist, 1982—; pres., chmn. 464 W. 152d St. Housing Devel. Fund Corp.; bd. edn. Minority Interchange, N.Y.C., 1983—. Chorister Harlem Chorale Soc., Riverside Community Chorale, Trial Chorale. Mem. Black Women's Forum, Nat. Assn. Female Execs., Nat. Council Negro Women. Democrat. Baptist. Club: Media Women (Los Angeles). Home: 464 W 152d St Apt 4 New York NY 10031 Office: Equitable Life Assurance Soc 1271 Ave of Americas Suite 4350 New York NY 10019

HARRIS, JULIA HINES, elementary school principal; b. York, Pa., Oct. 20, 1940; d. Julius D. and Martha (Sellers) Hines; children—Richard E. Muldrow, Julius Hines Muldrow. B.S., Cheyney U., 1962; M.Ed., Millersville U., 1970; Ed.D., U. Pa., 1985. Tchr. mentally retarded York City Schs., Pa., 1962-65, 4th grade tchr., 1965-68, guidance counselor, 1968-70, reading tchr., 1972-83, elem. prin., 1983—; asst. prof. Millersville U., Pa., 1970-72. Bd. dirs. York Hosp., Martin Meml. Library, York; mem. adv. bd. Jr. League, York, Dem. Party, York, Voni Grimes Ctr.; bd. dirs. York br. Am. Cancer Soc., Crispus Attucks Ctr., 1980-83; minority advisor Penn Laurel Girl Scout Council; mem. Martin Luther King Scholarship Com. Mem. Nat. Assn. Sec. Sch. Prins., Assn. Supervision and Curriculum Devel., Phi Delta Kappa. Delta Sigma Theta. Baptist. Avocations: reading; travel; writing poetry; biking. Home: 335 W Springettsbury Ave York PA 17403 Office: Lincoln Elementary Sch 599 W King St York PA 17404

HARRIS, KAREN KOSTOCK, business executive; b. Chgo., Sept. 11, 1942; d. Kenneth P. and Elsie A. (Raffl) K.; student Mundelein Coll., Chgo., 1979—; m. Roy Lawrence Harris, Feb. 14, 1981. Clk. loan dept. Evanston Fed. Savs. and Loan (Ill.), 1960-63, mgr. collection dept., 1963-65; credit adminstr. Packaging Corp. Am., Evanston, 1965-72, adminstrv. asst. to v.p., 1972-74, credit mgr. trainee Am. Hosp. Supply Corp., 1974-75; cash mgr., asst. to treas. Pullman Standard, Chgo., 1975-76; nat. credit adminstr. Gen. Binding Corp., Northbrook, Ill., 1976-77; treas. C.H. Hanson Co., Chgo., 1977-79, sec.-treas., dir., 1980—; owner Stock Enterprises, Highland Park, Ill., 1980-82; partner Harris Enterprises, 1981—, pres. Sirrah Enterprises, Inc., 1982—, Cottage Keepers, Inc., 1985—. Founder Weekend Coll. Scholarship Fund, Mundelein Coll., 1981, charter mem. Mundelein Coll. Women's Network; mem. Venice Nokomis Republican Women's Club, 1982—. Recipient Cert. of Merit, Chgo. Assn. Commerce and Industry and Industry Youth Motivation Program, 1981, 85. Clubs: Swedish (sec., dir. 1981—), Mchts. and Mfrs. (Chgo.). Office: 303 W Erie St Chicago IL 60610

HARRIS, KATHARINE MOSES, broadcast executive; b. Albany, N.Y., Oct. 6, 1947; d. Laurence Raphael and Katharine Mason (Van Loan) Moses; 1 son, John Lory IV. B.A. in English and Edn., Syracuse U., 1969. Tchr., Phila. Pub. Schs., 1969-71; legal sec. pvt. law practice, Honolulu, 1971; dir. confs. U. Pa., Phila., 1972-76; account exec. Sta. WCHL, Chapel Hill, N.C., 1978-81, Sta. WRAL, Raleigh, N.C., 1981-84; gen. mgr. Stas. WBBB/WPCM, Burlington, N.C., 1984—. Dir. fundraising March of Dimes, 1977; fundraiser N.C. Kidney Found., 1985; bd. dirs. Falconbridge Homeowner's Assn., 1984-85. N.Y. Regents scholar, 1965. Mem. N.C. Assn. Broadcasters, Nat. Assn. Broadcasters, Chapel Hill C. of C. (publicity chmn. 1979), Triad Advt. Club, Triangle Advt. Fedn. Democrat. Methodist. Avocations: camping; horseback riding; antiques. Home: 1808 Inglewood Dr Burlington NC 27215 Office: WBBB/WPCM Radio Stas 1109 Tower Dr Burlington NC 27215

HARRIS, LOUISE, author; b. Warwick, R.I.; d. Samuel P. and Faustine M. (Borden) Harris; A.B., Brown U., 1926; pvt. study organ with T. Tertius Noble, N.Y., 1938-42. Sec., Samuel P. Harris, Inc., 1928-42; tchr. piano and organ, ch. organist, recitalist, Providence, 1928-46. Mem. corp. R.I. Hosp.; 1st founder Brown U. Med. Sch. Recipient World Culture prize Nat. Center Study and Research of Italy, 1984; listed in numerous directories (U.S., Eng., Italy); 3 medals minted in her honor Royal Mint, London. Fellow Internat. Biog. Assn. (life patron,), World Lit. Acad. (life), Anglo Am. Acad. (hon.); mem. Nat. Archives (assoc.), Am. Biog. Inst. Research Assn. (life patron, life dep. gov.), Am. Guild Organists, Hymn Soc. Am., Audubon Soc., Brown Alumnae Assn., Nat. Trust Historic Preservation, Nat., R.I., Western R.I., East Providence hist. socs. Am. Heritage Soc., Library of Human Resource of Am. Bicentennial Research Inst., Library of Human Resource of Am. Heritage Research Assn., Am. Mus. Natural History, Smithsonian Assocs. Author: A Comprehensive Bibliography of C.A. Stephens, 1965; None But the Best, 1966; A Chuckle and A Laugh, 1967; The Star of the Youth's Companion, 1969; The Flag Over the Schoolhouse, 1971, sequal Old Glory-Long May She Wave!, 1981; Our Great American Story-Teller, 1978; compiler: Under the Sea in the Salvador (C.A. Stephens), 1969; Louise Harris Looks at Norway, 1970; Charles Adams Tales (C.A. Stephens), 1973; Little Big Heart and Other Stories, 1974. Home: 395 Angell St Apt 111 Providence RI 02906 Office: Box 1926 Brown U Providence RI 02912

HARRIS, MARCELLA H. EASON (MRS. HARLEY EUGENE HARRIS, social worker; b. Augusta, Ark., Apr. 19, 1925; d. William Harvey and Hazel Faye (Haraway) Eason; B.A., Wilberforce U., 1947; M.S.W., Loyola U., Chgo., 1961; M.Ed. in Health Occupations, U. Ill., 1979; m. Harley Eugene Harris, June 15, 1952. Child welfare worker Ill. Dept. Pub. Welfare, 1952-54, caseworker Family Consultation Service, 1954-64; clin. social worker Winnebago County Mental Health Clinic, Rockford, Ill., 1964—, now coordinator emergency services Janet Wattles Mental Health Center. Mem. Rockford Bd. Edn., 1965—, sec., 1965-69. Recipient Francis Blair award Ill. Edn. Assn., 1970, Service above Self award Rockford Rotary Club, 1971. Mem. Nat. Assn. Social Workers (chpt. vice chmn. 1960-61), Ill. Welfare Assn., Acad. Certified Social Workers, Nat. Council Negro Women, Rockford Jr. League (hon.), Am. Assn. U. Women, Nat. Registry Health Care Providers in Clin. Social Work, Delta Kappa Gamma (hon.), Alpha Kappa Alpha. Club: Taus Sevice. Home: Cloisters Apt 1665 2929 Sunnyside Dr Rockford IL 61111 Office: 1325 E State St Rockford IL 61108

HARRIS, MARION HOPKINS, government official; b. Washington, July 27, 1938; d. Dennis Cason and Georgia (Greenlee) Hopkins; m. Charles E. Harris, July 1957 (div. 1964); 1 child, Alan E. M.P.A., U. Pitts., 1971; M.P.A., U. So. Calif., 1985, D.P.A., 1985. Dir. program planning Rochester Urban Renewal Agy., N.Y., 1971-72; exec. dir. Fairfax County Redevel. and Housing Authority, Fairfax, Va., 1972-73; dep. dir. housing mgmt. HUD, Detroit, 1973-75, sr. field officer for housing, Washington, 1979—; mng. auditor GAO, Washington, 1975-79. Bd. dirs. S.W. Neighborhood Assembly, Washington, 1979-80; commr. S.W. Adv. Neighborhood Commn., Washington, 1986; mem.

pub. adv. com. Washington Council Govts., 1985—. Recipient Outstanding Performance award HUD, 1984; Carnegie-Mellon mid-career fellow, 1970; Ford Found. travel-study awardee, 1970. Mem. Am. Acad. Soc. and Polit. Sci., U. So. Calif. Doctoral Assn., LWV (exec. bd. Washington 1983-84). Roman Catholic. Avocations: cross-country skiing; foreign travel; swimming. Home: 410 O St SW Apt 307 Washington DC 20024

HARRIS, MARITZA, nurse, medical administrator; b. Panama City, Panama, Oct. 6, 1947; came to U.S., 1966; d. Arnold and Lucilda (Forbes) Anglin Irons; m. Audley Leonard Harris, Jan. 17, 1970; 1 child, Lizette Ana Maria Harris. A.A. in Nursing, S.I. Community Coll., 1969; B.S., L.I. U., 1978; M.Health Care, C.W. Post Coll., 1986. R.N., N.Y. Psychiat. nurse Dept. Mental Health, Bklyn., 1972—; med. coordinator Addiction Research and Treatmant Corp., Bklyn., 1981—; cons., lectr. in field. Recipient appreciation award Urban Resources, 1983; Outstanding Achievement award UN, 1983. Fellow Am. Acad. Physician's Assts., N.Y. State Soc. Physicians Assts.; mem. Exec. Females. Democrat. Roman Catholic. Avocations: music; travel; fasion; computers. Home: 420 E 111th St Apt 2904 New York NY 10029 Office: Addiction Research and Treatment Corp 22 Chapel St New York NY 11201

HARRIS, MARY ELIZABETH, retired college official; b. St. Louis, Jan. 23, 1925; d. James R. and Mary B. (Harlan) Clayton; m. George E. Harris, July 4, 1944; children—Mary M. Harris Scott, George William. B.J., U. Mo., 1946; M.A. in Journalism and Pub. Relations, Ball State U., 1975. Soc. editor Muncie Morning Star (Ind.), 1946-47; reporter Muncie Evening Press, 1949-54, reporter, photographer, asst. women's editor, 1957-73; freelance reporter Universal Trade Press Syndicate, N.Y.C., 1953-57; sec. to assoc. dean Coll. of Bus., Ball State U., Muncie, 1974-75, M.B.A. coordinator, coll. editor, 1975-78, adminstrv. asst. to dean, M.B.A. coordinator, 1978-85, emeritus, 1985; coordinator grad. enrollment, 1983-85; editor Ball State Jour. Bus. Educators, Muncie, 1975-80, Ball State Bus. Rev., 1975-78. Author and editor: The Role of Women on Indiana Newspapers: 1876-1976, 1976. Recipient writing and photography awards UPI, Ind. Mng. Editors, Ind. AP Mng. Editors, Women's Press Club Ind., 1971-84; NEH/Ind. Arts Commn. grantee, 1976. Mem. Women in Communications, Del. County Hist. Soc., Muncie Jayshees (life), Beta Sigma Phi (Humanitarian award 1967), Delta Pi Epsilon (exec. bd. 1982-84), Sigma Delta Chi, Kappa Tau Alpha, Delta Theta Rho, Theta Sigma Phi (past pres.). Democrat. Methodist. Clubs: Altrusa (Muncie); Faculty Wives and Women Ball State U. (exec. bd. 1982-84), Women's Press Ind. (Kate Milner Rabb award 1978). Lodge: Order of Job's Daus.

HARRIS, MARY PAPAJOHN, business executive; b. Athens, Greece, Dec. 3, 1939; came to U.S., 1948; d. Harry M. and Alice (Anagnostopoulos) Papajohn; m. Andreas Harris, May 1, 1965 (div. 1981); children—Konstantine Philip, Alexander Scott. B.A., Marymount Manhattan Coll., 1971; M.P.A., Columbia U., 1984; cert. Sorbonne, 1962. Asst. to mayor City of N.Y., 1966-69; pres. MRC TV Network, N.Y.C., 1969-80; exec. v.p. Clipper Internat. Products, 1980-82; with Manhattan Bank, N.Y.C., 1983; dir. corp. relations Am. Standards Testing Bur., N.Y.C., 1984—; v.p. Am. Standards Bioscis. Corp., Reading, Pa., 1984—. bd. dirs. Ivy Club, 1983; chair Youth Against Cancer, 1979-82. Recipient Leadership award Met. Regional Council, N.Y.C., 1978; Outstanding Service award Am. Cancer Soc., 1980. Mem. AAUW, Women's Econ. Roundtable, LWV, Hellenic Am. C. of C., Council Greek Am. Affairs, N.Y. Acad. Scis. Greek Orthodox. Clubs: Princeton of N.Y., City (N.Y.C.). Home: 125 E 72d St New York NY 10021 Office: Am Standards Testing Bur 40 Water St New York NY 10004

HARRIS, MICALYN SHAFER, lawyer; b. Chgo., Oct. 31, 1941; d. Erwin and Dorothy (Sampson) Shafer; A.B., Wellesley Coll., 1963; J.D., U. Chgo., 1966. Bar: Ill. 1966, Mo. 1967, U.S. Dist. Ct. (ea. dist.) 1967, U.S. Supreme Ct. 1972, U.S. Ct. Appeals (8th cir.) 1974, N.Y. 1981. Law clk. U.S. Dist. Ct., St. Louis, 1967-68; atty. The May Dept. Stores, St. Louis, 1968-70, Ralston-Purina Co., St. Louis, 1970-72; atty., asst. sec. Chromalloy Am. Corp., St. Louis, 1972-76; sole practice, St. Louis, 1976-78; corp. counsel and asst. sec. CPC Internat., Englewood, Cliffs, N.J., 1978—. Contbr. articles to profl. publs. Mem. ABA (co-chmn. subcom. on counseling the mktg. function; subcom. on tender offers and proxy statements of fed. securities law com.), Chgo. Bar Assn., N.Y. State Bar Assn. (fed. securities law com.), Bar Assn. Met. St. Louis (chmn. TV com.), Mo. Bar Assn. (chmn. internat. law com.), Assn. Corp. Counsel of N.J. (exec. com. and chmn. sales, mktg. and distbn. law com.), ABA (fed. securities law subcom., vice chmn. counseling mktg. function subcom.). Address: 625 N Monroe Ridgewood NJ 07450

HARRIS, ORENE ELIZABETH, dance school administrator, educator; b. Sinton, Tex., Oct. 27, 1945; d. Orea Alvin and Norma Jean (Clendennen) Ehlers; m. Wayne Lee Harris, Sept. 28, 1979; 1 child, Lawrene Elizabeth. Student Del Mar Coll., Corpus Christi, 1964-65, 74-75. Dance instr. Sylvia Grey Sch., Corpus Christi, 1964-68, Hahn AFB and Bitburg AFB, W.Ger., 1968-70, Gwinn Ind. Sch. Dist., Mich., 1970-71; supr., dance instr. Corpus Christi Park and Recreation Dept., 1972-78; owner, instr. Cinderella Sch. Dance, Corpus Christi, 1972—; choreographer Encore Theatre, Corpus Christi, 1983, So. Charm, Panama City, Fla., 1986; Tex. dir. Am.'s Miss Charm, Jacksonville, N.C., 1985, So. Charm, Jackson, Tenn., 1986. Choreographer dance for TV comml., 1984. Beauty pageant judge; chmn. Dance-A-Thon, Cystic Fibrosis, Tex. Gulf Coast chpt., 1984-86. Recipient Best Prodn. dance award Regency Talent Competition, 1986; Best Prodn. dance award Encore Talent Competition, 1986; Most Outstanding Group Costume award Encore Talent Competition, 1986. Mem. Profl. Dance Tchrs.' Assn. Am., Nat. Assn. Female Execs., PTA, Encore Travel Club. Democrat. Methodist. Avocations: doll collecting; sewing and designing clothes; cake decorating. Office: Cinderella Sch Dance 4455 S Padre Island Dr Corpus Christi TX 78411

HARRIS, PATRICIA SKALNY, lawyer; b. Detroit, Mar. 28, 1949; s. John Francis and Sophie Skalny. A.B., U. Mich., 1970, J.D., 1974. Bar: Mich. 1974. Atty., Gen. Motors Corp., Detroit, 1974—. Mem. ABA, Mich. State Bar Assn. Office: Gen Motors Corp Room 15-139 3044 W Grand Blvd Detroit MI 48202

HARRIS, RHONDA DIAZ, telecommunications company executive, consultant; b. San Francisco, Aug. 29, 1958; d. Pedro Juan and Cecile Elizabeth (Walton) Diaz; m. Jim D. Harris, Apr. 19, 1980 (div. 1984); 1 child, Seth. B.A., Calif. State U.-Hayward, 1983; postgrad. U. Calif.-Berkeley, 1985—. Tax preparer, Fremont, Calif., 1981-83; sales rep. Fred Benedetti Co., Burlingame, Calif., 1982-83; acct. exec. AT&T, San Francisco, 1983—. Participant AT&T Charity Running Team, San Francisco, 1985—, U. Calif.-Berkeley/Stanford Spl. Olympics Fundraiser, Palo Alto, 1986. Recipient Regional Mktg. Leader award AT&T, 1984, Nat. Leaders Council award, 1985. Mem. Am. Hotel and Motel Assn., Calif. Hotel and Motel Assn., U. Calif. Bus. Alumni Assn., Nat. Assn. Female Execs. Republican. Club: Telegraph Hill (San Francisco). Avocations: outdoors; aerobics; running; sewing; tennis; art; music. Office: AT&T 333 Market St Suite 2508 San Francisco CA 94105

HARRIS, ROBERTA ELIZABETH BRUMMAGE, nurse; b. Keyser, W.Va., Oct. 9, 1947; d. Robert Leslie and Elizabeth Jane (Rotruck) Brummage; assoc. degree in nursing Fairmont State Coll., 1967; B.S cum laude in Nursing, W.Va. U., 1978, M.S. magna cum laude in Nursing, 1982; m. Howard Lee Harris, July 2, 1966; children—Troy Wayne, Todd Shawn. Staff nurse, intensive care unit W.Va. U. Med. Center, Morgantown, 1967-68; staff nurse, coronary care unit Fairmont (W.Va.) Gen. Hosp., 1969-71; surg. nurse practitioner, evening emergency room supr. Fairmont Clinic, 1971-77; paramedic instr., coordinator regions 6 and 7, Emergency Med. Services, Fairmont, 1977-80; cardiac rehab. nurse United Hosp. Center, Clarksburg, W.Va., 1980-81; assoc. inservice edn. coordinator Fairmont (W.Va.) Gen. Hosp., 1981-85, part-time, 1985—; med. nurse educator W.Va. U. Hosps., Inc., 1985—; pvt. practice nurse clinician, Fairmont, 1980—; mem. curriculum and tng. com. W.Va. Office of Emergency Med. Services, 1977-80; practical tester Nat. Registry Emergency Med. Technicians, 1979; speaker in field. Treas., United Methodist Women's Group, 1981-83. R.N., W.Va. Mem. Am. Nurses Assn. W.Va. Nurses Assn. (chmn. dist. gen. and economic welfare com., mem. com. 1978-81), Nurses Coalition for Action in Politics, Bus. and Profl. Women's Orgn., Am. Heart Assn. (basic cardiac support instr. 1978—, advanced cardiac life support instr. 1978—, faculty W.Va. affiliate 1979—, nursing com. W.Va. affiliate 1981—), Am. Diabetes Assn., Council Clin. Nurse Specialists. Republican. Club: Y-Sqs. Sq. Dance (pres. 1981-83). Contbg. author revision: Employment Standards for Registered Professional Nurses, 1981; developer stress mgmt. program. Home: Route 3 Box 383 M Fairmont WV 26554 Office: Fairmont Gen Hosp Locust Ave Fairmont WV 26554

HARRIS, ROBERTA LUCAS, social worker; b. St. Louis, Nov. 13, 1916; d. Robert Joseph and Clara Louise (Mellor) Lucas; A.B., St. Louis U., 1955, M.S.W. (NIMH grantee), 1964; m. William F. Sprengnether, Jr., Aug. 21, 1937 (dec. Aug. 30, 1951); children—Robert Lucas, Madelon Sprengnether Littlejohn, Ronald John; m. 2d, Victor B. Harris, Sept. 13, 1955 (dec. June 14, 1960). Field instr. Sch. Social Work St. Louis U., 1967-70; chief of domestic relations City of St. Louis, 1966—. Dir., Citizens' Housing Council, 1956-60; del. to Community Family Life Clinic, 1957; dir. Landmarks Assn., 1957-63; pres. Compton Heights Improvement Assn., 1973. Mem. Nat., Mo. assns. social workers, Assn. Family Conciliation Cts. (dir. 1968—), Greater St. Louis Probation and Parole Assn. (sec. 1976), St. Louis U. Sch. Social Service Alumni Assn. (sec. 1973), LWV (dir. 1956-61). Methodist. Club: Wednesday. Home: 3137 Longfellow St St Louis MO 63104

HARRIS, ROSALIE SHONFELD, writer, public relations and corporate communications executive; b. Chgo., Feb. 4, 1944; d. Paul A. and Esther M. (Schulman) Shonfeld. B.A., Antioch Coll., 1966. Acct. exec. Daniel J. Edelman, Chgo., 1966-67, Clinton E. Frank, Chgo., 1967-69, Genesis/BBDM, Chgo., 1969-75; acct. mgr. Container Corp., Chgo., 1975-79; mgr. pub. communications Motorola, Inc., Schaumburg, Ill., 1979-81; account supr. Golin/Harris, Chgo., 1981-82; owner Rosalie Harris: Creative Solutions, Chgo., 1982—. Contbr. articles to various publs. Bd. dirs. Chgo. String Ensemble. Recipient Headliner award Women in Communications, 1983. Mem. Women in Communications, Ind. Writers Chgo., Nat. Assn. Women Bus. Owners. Home and Office: 666 N Lake Shore Dr Suite 325 Chicago IL 60611

HARRIS, RUTH BERMAN, harpist, composer; b. New Haven, Nov. 3, 1916; d. Benjamin and Pauline Berman; m. Sydney I. Harris, Oct. 6, 1946; children—Mark (dec.), Kenneth, Susan. Student Inst. of Musical Art (now Juilliard), 1934-37, SUNY-Purchase, 1978-81; harp student with Marie Miller, Carlos Salzedo, Lucille Lawrence, Casper Reardom; composition student with Ronald Herder, 1978-81. Free lance orchestral harpist and soloist, NBC, 1938-42; CBS, 1942-50; staff harpist, soloist ABC, 1950-53; free lance harpist and soloist CBS Symphony Orch., NBC, ABC, radio and TV networks, movie and recording cos., 1953-82; harp tchr. pvt. practice and Westchester Conservatory, 1969—; guest of honor 8th Internat. Harp Contest, Jerusalem, 1982, 85. Compositions include: Requiem Mark Sumner Harris for chamber orch. and voices, 1981; String Quartet, 1982; Miniatures nos. 1, 2, 3, 1976, 77, 78; Collection of Harp Solos: O Holy Night (A. Adam), arranged with Sydney Harris, 1982; Passacaglia for Two Pianos, 1982. Active LWV, Jewish Community Center of White Plains. Recipient Madrigal award, 1933; Meet the Composer grantee, 1982, 84, 85, 86; Mem. Am. Harp Soc., Internat. League Women Composers, Music Tchrs. Council of Westchester (treas. 1981-83), Purchase Music Ensemble (v.p. 1983-85), Nat. Acad. Recording Arts and Scis. Home: 25 Ria Dr White Plains NY 10605

HARRIS, SANDRA LEE, corporate resources company executive; b. Memphis, Nov. 8, 1942; d. Jesse and Ina Faye (Odenbaugh) H. B.S.E., Memphis State U., 1972, M.A. in Communications, 1976. Acct. IBM, East Fishkill, N.Y., 1967-70; instr. Memphis State U., 1972-76; personnel mgr. Data Tech. Corp., Olive Br., Miss., 1976-78; mgr.-owner Clark & Assoc., Memphis, 1978-80; pres. Corp. Resources, Memphis, 1980—. Commr. City Beautiful, Memphis, 1984. Served to staff sgt. USAF, 1963-67. Democrat. Methodist. Avocations: golf; fishing. Home: 1284 E Raines Rd #11 Memphis TN 38116 Office: Corporate Resources Inc 3835 Viscount Suite 5 Memphis TN 38118

HARRIS, SHARON ELIZABETH, educator, child care administrator; b. Laurel, Miss., Sept. 14, 1954; d. Nukey and Mary Lee (Hudge) Harris. B.S., Alcorn A&M U., 1974; postgrad So. Miss. U., Hattiesburg, 1976. Learning disability tchr. Meridian Sch. System (Miss.), 1973-75; tchr. West End Elem. Sch., Meridian, 1975; deaf-blind multi handicapped tchr. Ellisville State Sch. (Miss.), 1975-76; spl. edn. tchr. Jones County Public Schs., Laurel, Miss., 1976-79; counselor Dallas County Juvenile Dept., Dallas, 1979-80; public info. officer Assn. Retarded Citizens Dallas, 1980-81; owner E's Profl. Cleaning Service, Dallas, 1982—; owner, dir. E's Haven Learning & Devel. Ctr., Dallas, 1983—, E's Haven Acad., Inc., 1985—; area coordinator for Dallas, Quality Child Care, Inc., 1983—; Leader Girl Scouts, Meridian, 1974-75; past mem. Internat. Year of Disabled, West Dallas Drug Center, Girls Club Dallas, Martin Luther King Center, Dallas, Community Youth Court, Laurel, Community Action Assn., Laurel, Citizens of Dallas. Served with AUS, 1969-71. Mem. Women in Communications, Female Execs., Alcorn Alumni Assn. (program chmn. 1982-83), Delta Sigma Theta (project chairperson 1977-79), Methodist. Lodge: Eastern Star.

HARRIS, SHELLEY RAENA, business executive; b. Miami, Fla., Apr. 11, 1951; d. Benjamin Loeb Harris and Lillian (Grossman) Nestler; m. Raymond Justin Shenfield, Dec. 23, 1972 (div. 1985); children—Melisa Adine, Robert Dustin. Student Northwestern U. Project coordinator Zink Pub. Co., Orlando, Fla., 1983-85; pub. Harris Pub. Co., Miami, 1985; adminstrv. dir. Med. Care Devel. Corp., Miami, 1985—, Doctor's Health Care Group, Inc., Miami, 1985—, Bayside Med. Equipment, Inc., Miami, 1985—, Heritage Health Care Group/PIU, Miami, 1985—, Utilization Mgmt. Services, 1985—; promotional asst. to Lillie Rubin, 1986—. Mem. Nat. Assn. Female Execs., Miami Beach C. of C., Coral Gables C. of C. Avocation: art. Home: 16546 NE 26th Ave Apt 3A North Miami Beach FL 33160

HARRIS, SHIRLEY G., personnel manager executive; b. Chgo., July 24, 1945; d. Henderson and Ruth (Johnson) Jackson; m. Arthur Lewis, May 3, 1968 (div.); children—Sam, Mike, LaChun. A.A., Malcolm X Coll., 1983; postgrad. Portland State U., 1975; postgrad. Nat. Coll. Edn., 1984—. Legal sec. Friedman Rochester, Chgo., 1974; clerical supr. Model Cities, Chgo. and Portland, Oreg., 1973-75; sec. Portland Met. Steering com., 1976-78; tchr. clerical Portland OIC, 1975-76; tchr. Yaun Youth Ctr., Portland, 1978-80; pres. Flexible Temps, Chgo., 1980—, cons., 1983—; cons. Personnel Plus, Chgo., 1983; typing tchr., Chgo., 1983; personnel recruiter, Chgo., 1974-75. Mem. Profls. Inc., Exec. Connections, Nat. Assn. Female Execs., MidAm. Mgmt. Assn. Democrat. Baptist. Clubs: Bus. Networking, Exec. Exchange (Chgo.). Office: Flexible Temps 323 S Franklin St 804 Chicago IL 60606

HARRIS, SHIRLEY ROLLINS, health plan administrator, actuary; b. Hustle, Va., Aug. 20, 1950; d. Charles David and Gladys Virginia (Sayles) Rollins; m. Winfred Alpheus Harris, Nov. 10, 1972 (div. 1982); children—Clifford Edward, Timothy Edward. B.S., Livingstone Coll., 1972. Actuary Office Personnel Mgmt., Washington, 1972-85; health plan adminstr. Nat. League Postmasters, Alexandria, Va., 1985—. Mem. Nat. Assn. Exec. Women, Delta Sigma Theta. Democrat. Methodist. Avocations: jogging; reading; swimming. Office: Nat League of Postmasters 1023 N Royal Alexandria VA

HARRIS, SUSAN JO, banker; b. Salem, Oreg., Jan. 4, 1955; d. Gordon Elroy Harris and Charlotte Joan (Dabner) Harris-Armstrong; 1 child, Charlotte Joan Armstrong Harris. Student Moorpark Jr. Coll., 1973-74. With Creditway of Am., Anaheim, Calif., 1974-75; chief teller Crocker Nat. Bank, Studio City, Calif., 1975-77; letter of credit adminstr. Lloyd's Bank Internat., Los Angeles, 1977-78; customer service Safeco Title Ins. Co., Ventura, Calif., 1978-81; adminstrv. asst. Gen. Amusement Co., Calabasas, Calif., 1981-83; asst. v.p. Gonejo Valley Nat. Bank, Thousand Oaks, Calif., 1983—. Bd. mgrs. Conejo Valley YMCA. Mem. Nat. Assn. Female Execs., Internat. Assn. Profl. Women. Republican. Avocations: reading, religion. Home: 221 Erbes Rd #101 Thousand Oaks CA 91360 Office: Conejo Valley Nat Bank 2060 Ave de Los Arboles Thousand Oaks CA 91360

HARRIS, VERA EVELYN,, personnel recruiting and search firm executive; b. Watson, Sask., Can., Jan. 11, 1932; came to U.S., 1957; d. Timothy and Margaret (Popoff) H.; student U. B.C. (Can.), Vancouver; children—Colin Clifford Graham, Barbara Cusimano Page. Office mgr. Keglers, Inc., Morgan City, La., 1964-67; office mgr., acct. John L. Hopper & Assos., New Orleans, 1967-71; office mgr. Elite Homes, Inc., Metairie, La., 1971-73; comptroller Le Pavillon Hotel, New Orleans, 1973-74; controller Waguespack-Pratt, Inc., New Orleans, 1974-76; adminstrv. controller Sizzler Family Steak Houses of So. La., Inc., Metairie, 1976-79; dir. adminstrn. Sunbelt, Inc., New Orleans, 1979-82, sec., dir., 1980—; exec. v.p. Corp. Cons., Inc., 1980-83, pres., 1984—; exec. dir. Nat. Sizzler Franchise Assn., 1976-79. Mem. Am. Bus. Women's Assn., Nat. Assn. Female Execs., La. Assn. Personnel Consultants (treas. 1985-86). Home: 2202 Caswell Ln Metairie LA 70001 Office: 806 Perdido St Suite 205 New Orleans LA 70112

HARRIS-LANGE, JANET ELLEN, manufacturing company executive; b. N.Y.C., June 7, 1946; d. M. Martin and Alma Regina (Roberts) Maglio; m. John Madison Harris, Dec. 19, 1970 (dec. Nov. 1981); m. 2d, Donald J. Lange, Sept. 8, 1984. A.A., Palm Beach Jr. Coll., 1966; B.S., Fla. Atlantic U., 1967, M.Ed., 1969. Tchr. French and Spanish, Palm Beach (Fla.) County Pub. Schs., 1968-73; pres., owner, chief exec. officer J & J Mfg. Corp., West Palm Beach, 1972—; pres., owner Branet Investments, Inc., West Palm Beach, 1982—; instr. entrepreneurship Palm Beach Jr. Coll.; del. White House Conf. Small Bus., 1986. Inventor measuring device, 1975, magnetic soap hook, 1983. Bd. dirs. Am. Diabetes Assn., Palm Beach, Fla., 1982—. Mem. Nat. Assn. Women Business Owners (v.p. 1982-84; nat. dir. 1982-84, 85-86, pres. 1984-85), World Trade Council, Nat. Housewares Mfr. Assn., Nat. Fedn. Ind. Businesses. Club: Forum (West Palm Beach). Office: J & J Mfg Corp Branet Investments Inc 1492 W 53rd St West Palm Beach FL 33407

HARRISON, ANNA JANE, chemist, educator; b. Benton City, Mo., Dec. 23, 1912; d. Albert S.J. and Mary (Jones) H.; student Lindenwood Coll., 1929-31, L.H.D. (hon.), 1977; A.B., U. Mo., 1933, B.S., 1935, M.A., 1937, Ph.D., 1940; D.Sc. (hon.), Tulane U., 1975, Smith Coll., 1975, Williams Coll., 1978, Am. Internat. Coll., 1978, Vincennes U., 1978, Lehigh U., 1979, Hood Coll., 1979, Hartford U., 1979, Worcester Poly. Inst., 1979, Suffolk U., 1979, U. Mo., 1983, Mt. Holyoke Coll., 1984, Russell Sage Coll., 1984, others. Instr. chemistry Newcomb Coll., 1940-42, asst. prof., 1942-45; asst. prof. chemistry Mt. Holyoke Coll., 1945-47, asso. prof., 1947-50, prof., 1950-79, prof. emeritus, 1979—, chmn. dept., 1960-66, William R. Kenan, Jr. prof., 1976-79. Mem. Nat. Sci. Bd., 1972-78. Recipient Frank Forrest award Am. Ceramic Soc., 1949; James Flack Norris award Northeastern sect. Am. Chem. Soc., 1977; AAUW Sarah Berliner fellow Cambridge U., Eng., 1952-53; Am. Chem. Soc. Petroleum Research Fund Internat. fellow NRC Can., 1959-60; recipient Coll. Chemistry Tchr. award Mfg. Chemists Assn., 1969. Mem. AAAS (dir. 1979—, pres. 1983-84, chmn. bd. 1984-85), Am. Chem. Soc. (chmn. div. chem. edn. 1971, pres. 1978, dir. 1976-79; award in chem. edn. 1982), Internat. Union Pure and Applied Chemistry (U.S. nat. com. 1978-81), Sigma Xi. Contbr. articles to profl. jours. Address: Dept Chemistry Mount Holyoke Coll South Hadley MA 01075

HARRISON, ANNE ELIZABETH, government official; b. Santa Maria, Calif., May 12, 1941; d. William Lee and Mary Hampton (Beveridge) H. B.S. cum laude, U. Calif.-Davis, 1964; M.S., U. Mich., 1966. Forest naturalist Coronado Nat. Forest, Forest Service, USDA, Tucson, 1966-72, dir. women's activities, regional office, eastern region, Milw., 1972-73, dir. regional visitor info. service, 1973-77, pub. info. officer Cleveland Nat. Forest, San Diego, 1977-81, pub. affairs officer Rocky Mountain Forest and Range Expt. Sta., Fort Collins, Colo., 1981-85, Pacific S.W. Forest Expt. Sta., Berkeley, Calif., 1985—; mem. environ. edn. adv. com. Ohio State U., Columbus, 1975-76; regional dir. S.W. region Assn. Interpretive Naturalists, Derwood, Md., 1979-81; project coordinator Seneca Rocks Visitor Ctr., W.Va., 1974-77. Editor, producer 6 tech. transfer modules Silviculture of Rocky Mountain Species, 1981-85 (Nat. Assn. Govt. Communicators nat. 1st place award for one title 1985). Contbr. tech. papers to symposia procs, bot. jours., 1960-80. Conservation chmn. Greenfield Jr. Women's Club, Wis., 1974; chmn. regional conf. S.W. Wis. Interpreter's Assn., 1975; active Christian Women's Clubs, Calif. Recipient 1st place award for exhibit Colo. State Forest Service, 1981, spl. act award USDA Forest Service, 1985. Mem. Nat. Assn. Female Execs. Avocations: weaving; hiking; camping; canoeing; cross-country skiing. Office: USDA Forest Service Pacific SW Forest and Range Expt Sta 1960 Addison St Berkeley CA 94704

HARRISON, CANDICE FREDRICA, association executive; b. Chgo., Dec. 16, 1948; d. Carl Fredrick Sperry and Betty Marie (Welch) Tapert. Student U. Ill.-Chgo., 1972-75. Asst. purchasing agent Am. Bakeries, Chgo., 1971-76; asst. office mgr. Am. Soc. Dentistry for Children, Chgo., 1976-78; supr. support personnel A.S. Hansen, Chgo., 1978-82; exec. dir. Aux. to the Am. Osteopathic Assn., Chgo., 1982—. Mem. Am. Soc. Personnel Adminstrs.

HARRISON, CARLA ISLEY, educator; b. Burlington, N.C., Dec. 13, 1948; d. Frederick Palmer and Elizabeth (Phillips) Isley; m. William Glenn Harrison III, June 17, 1973; children—Allison Palmer, William Glenn IV. B.S., Atlantic Christian Coll., 1971. Tchr. Chatham County Schs., Pittsboro, N.C., 1971-74, Alamance County Schs., Graham, N.C., 1974—. Treas. Haw River Elementary P.T.A., N.C., 1981-82; mem. Alamance County Arts Assn., Graham, N.C., 1982-86; precinct ofcl. Alamance County Bd. Elections, Graham, 1982-84; hon. mem. Service League Alamance County, Burlington, N.C., 1980. Mem. N.C. Assn. Sci. Tchrs., Alpha Delta Kappa, Phi Mu. Democrat. Methodist. Clubs: Burlington Jr. Women's (chmn. child identification project 1986) (N.C.); Brownies (food and entertainment dir. 1985-86) (Graham, N.C.). Lodge: Moose. Home: PO Box 381 Steelecrest Rd Graham NC 27253 Office: Alamance County Schs Haw River Elementary Route 2 Box 1 Haw River NC 27258

HARRISON, CAROLYN CASSELL, counselor; b. Waterbury, Conn., June 19, 1925; d. Kenneth Parker and Elizabeth Rachel (Emery) Wight; R.N., Mass. Gen. Hosp. Sch. Nursing, 1946; B.S in Nursing Edn., Catholic U., 1953; M.Ed. in Counseling, U. Md., 1969; m. Thomas Richard Harrison, June 16, 1973; children—Donna Cassell, Stafford Cassell, Jack Carlton Cassell. Nursing supr. Monadnock Community Hosp., Peterboro, N.H., 1947-49; staff nurse Doctors Hosp., VA Hosp., Washington, 1949-52; asst. dir. health services Am. U., Washington, 1949-50; dir. admissions Sch. Nursing, Washington Hosp. Center, 1957-67; dir. records office Coll. Edn., U. Md., College Park, 1968-70; counselor Prince George's Community Coll., Largo, Md., 1970-81; dir. career devel. Isothermal Community Coll., Spindale, N.C., 1981—. Trustee, sec. to bd. dirs. Gould Acad., Bethel, Maine, 1971—; bd. dirs. Task Force on Domestic Violence, Rutherford County, N.C., 1982-84; mem. adv. com. Statewide Assessment of Career Aspiration and Job Attainment Among Women Returning to Coll. in Md., 1978-80; bd. dirs. Prevention of Abuse in the Home, Rutherford County, N.C. Mem. NOW, Am. Personnel and Guidance Assn., N.C. Personnel and Guidance Assn., Nat. Assn. Women Deans, Adminstrs. and Counselors, Nat. Council Student Devel., NEA, Counseling and Personnel Assn.-U. Md. Methodist. Clubs: Faculty Women's (Am. U.), Pilot Internat. (dir. 1982-83). Home: 617 Brookwood Dr Spindale NC 28160 Office: Isothermal Community Coll PO Box 804 Spindale NC 28160

HARRISON, CHRISTINE DELANE, educational administrator; b. Dearborn, Mich., July 22, 1947; d. Walter Frederick and Marguerite Elaine (Champagne) Hancock; m. Charles Richard Bashawaty, Aug. 31, 1968 (div. 1972); 1 child, Brett Charles; m. Andrew David Harrison, June 14, 1980; 1 child, Andrew David, II. B.S., Eastern Mich. U., 1969. Cert. early elem. tchr., Mich. Tchr. Westland Schs., Mich., 1969-71, Dept. Army, Ansbach, Germany, 1971-72; prin. sec. chemistry dept. U. Mich., Ann Arbor, 1973-78; word processing mgr. Great Copy Co., Ann Arbor, 1978-79; dir. Great Lakes Apple Sch., Clawson, Mich., 1979—, also v.p. bd. dirs. Editorial asst. Herbal Extracts, 1984; Bull. of Thermodynamics and Thermochemistry, 1973-78. Bd. dirs. Perry Nursery Sch., Ann Arbor, 1976-77. Recipient Prodn. award and Dedication award Los Feliz Apple Sch. Mem. Clawson C. of C. Avocations: reading; bicycling; aerobics. Office: Great Lakes Sch 529 Grove St Clawson MI 48017

HARRISON, DELORES ANN, account representative; b. Phila., Feb. 20, 1952; d. William and Beulah (Price) Garrett; m. Thomas L. Harrison, July 31, 1971. Student pub. schs., Phila. Rater, Reliance Ins. Co., Phila., 1970-72; underwriter Clair Ins. Agy., Erdenheim, Pa., 1972-74, Cohen Setzer Inc., Elkins Park, Pa., 1974-77, S. Green & Co., 1977-80; surplus lines underwriter Bryson Assocs., Jenkintown, Pa., 1980-83; account rep. CIGNA Corp., Bala Cynwyd, Pa., 1983—; lectr. in field. Mem. Profl. Ins. Women of Eastern Montgomery (trustee 1979-82, treas. 1980-82, pres. 1982-84, Ins. Woman of Yr. 1983.). Democrat. Baptist. Home: Chestnut Hill Village 7720 A Stenton Ave Philadelphia PA 19118 Office: Cigna Corp 3 Bala Plaza W Bala Cynwyd PA 19004

HARRISON, DOROTHY GORDY, data processing administrator; b. Pittsfield, Mass., Jan. 1, 1939. B.A. in Chemistry, U. N.C., 1960; Cert. Info. Sci., Ga. Inst. Tech., 1962, M.S. in Info./Computer Sci., Indsl. Mgmt. and Engring., 1965; Cert. Physics, Math., Wake Forest U., 1964; M.Ln. in Adminstrn., Emory U., 1973. With tech. library and info. services Cone Mills Research and Devel., Greensboro, N.C., 1960-63; chmn. dept. physics Pittsfield High Sch., Mass., 1964; with sci. div. Pittsfield, Pub. Schs., 1964; research asst. Price Gilbert Meml. Library Ga. Inst. Tech., Atlanta, 1964-66, Engring. Expt. Sta.,

1965-66, Sch. Info. and Computer Sci., 1967; info. scientist and projects dir. Office Computing Activities, U. Ga., Athens, 1971-73; cons. info./computer sci. and administrn., 1962—; data processing dir. Clarke County, Ga.; bd. advs. Ga. Inst. Tech., Ga. State Archives, Athens Vocat.-Tech. Sch., Ga. NSF scholar, 1965-66; NSF fellow 1964-65; NSF grantee 1964; recipient citation Recording for the Blind, 1968-70, Young Info./Computer Scientist award, 1969, Outstanding Tchr. award, 1964; named Young Woman Engr. of Yr., 1964. Mem. Beta Phi Mu, Alpha Psi Omega.

HARRISON, EVELYN BYRD, archaeologist, educator; b. Charlottesville, Va., June 5, 1920; d. William Byrd and Eva (Detamore) Harrison; A.B., Barnard Coll., 1941; A.M., Columbia, 1943, Ph.D., 1952; postgrad. Bryn Mawr Coll., 1942-43. Instr. classics U. Cin., 1951-53; asst. prof. fine arts and archaeology Columbia U., 1955-59, assoc. prof., 1959-67, prof., 1967-70; prof. art and archaeology Princeton, 1970-74; prof. Inst. Fine Arts, N.Y. U., N.Y.C., 1974—; mem. Inst. for Advanced Study, 1961, 64. Guggenheim fellow, 1954-55; NEH, 1968-69. Mem. Am. Acad. Arts and Scis., Am. Philos. Soc. Archaeol. Inst. Am., Soc. Promotion Hellenic Studies, German Archaeol. Inst. Author: The Athenian Agora, I, Portrait Sculpture, 1953; XI, Archaic and Archaistic Sculpture, 1965. Contbr. articles to profl. jours. Home: 500 E 85th St New York NY 10028

HARRISON, GLORIA GAYE, sales executive; b. Phila., July 16, 1955; d. Joseph Alexander and Gloria Ida (Moore) H. B.S. in Mgmt., Widener U., 1979. Dept. mgr. Clover Dept. Store, Morton, Pa., 1979-80; acctg. technician Phila. Family Ct., 1980-85; sales mgr. ITC, Darby, Pa., 1985—. Bd. dirs. Walnut Hill Community Assn., 1980-83, Big Sisters, Phila., 1980-84. Recipient Big Sister Achievement award, Phila., 1981, 82, 83. Mem. Nat. Assn. Female Execs., Alpha Sigma Tau (v.p. Phila. chpt. 1979—). Democrat. Episcopalian. Home: 151 Bishop Ave I-9 Secane PA 19018 Office: Insulated Technologies Corp 140 Powell Ave Darby PA 19023

HARRISON, JEANNE, television producer and director; b. Phila.; d. David and Henriette (Ketchum) H.; m. Kurt Lassen, 1959 (div. 1980); children—Liza, Lydia. Dir., producer ZIV, N.Y.C., 1957-67; sr. producer J. Walter Thompson, N.Y.C., 1967-70; creative dir. Am. Home Products, N.Y.C., 1970-73; producer, dir., owner Harrison Prodns., N.Y.C., 1973—. Mem. Dirs. Guild Am. Home and office: Harrison Prodns 200 E 36th St New York NY 10016

HARRISON, JO A., film distributor, salon owner; b. Lee County, Ky., Mar. 31, 1934; d. Charles and Nannie Myrtle (Ashley) Ashcraft; m. William S. Harrison, Aug. 1, 1952; children—Billie Harrison Speigel, Kip Harrison Tannelli, Douglas C., Toni Lynn. Grad. high sch., Dayton, Ky. Office sec. 3M Co., Cin., 1952-53, John Van Range Co., Cin., 1956, Acme Newport Steel, Newport, Ky., 1956-58, Mead Corp., Cin., 1958-63, JMG Film Co., Cin., 1967-71; br. mgr. Bil-Ko Film Co., Cin., 1971-74; founder, president Myco Films, Inc., Cin., 1974—, Glitters, Inc., full service salon, Cin., 1985—. Mem. Cin. C. of C., Fedn. Ind. Businesses. Club: Altrusa of Clermont County (v.p. 1982—). Avocations: camping; reading; grandmothering. Home: 104 Saint Andrews Dr Cincinnati OH 45245 Office: Myco Films Inc PO Box 128 Amelia OH 45102

HARRISON, JOYCE VIRGINIA, advertising agency executive; b. Flin Flon, Man., Can., May 3, 1939; d. Peter V. and Amelia (Ohryn) H.; student U. Man., 1957-58, Laurentian U., 1968-69; children—Kim, Marley, Lindsay. Women's editor, program dir. Cambrian Broadcasting, Sudbury, Ont., Can., 1959-70; ops. mgr. Broadcast Services, Evanston, Ill., 1970-72; asso. creative dir. Arthur Meyerhoff & Assos. (now BBDO), Chgo., 1972-79; creative dir., sr. v.p. Draper Daniels, Chgo., 1979-80; creative dir., v.p. Bozell, Jacobs, Kenyon & Eckhardt, 1980—; pres. Rambull Inc., 1973-79; dir. Wax & Assos., Chgo., 1980-81. Mem. Nat. Acad. Rec. Arts & Scis., ASCAP. Republican. Roman Catholic. Composer songs. Home: 2762 Eastwood Evanston IL 60201 Office: Chicago IL

HARRISON, JUDITH ANN, hospital office manager; b. Roanoke, Va., Sept. 17, 1947; d. Mitchell Woodrow and Mary (Larimer) H. Cert. data processing Cornett Bus. Coll., Roanoke, 1967; cert. credit union mgmt., Va. Western Community Coll., 1983. Clk., Moore's Super Stores, Roanoke, 1967-68; bookkeeper Webb's Oil Corp., Hollins, Va., 1968-77; bus. office mgr. Roanoke Meml. Rehab. Ctr., Va., 1977—. Chmn. credit com. Roanoke Hosp. Assn. Employees Fed. Credit Union, 1981, 82, sec. bd. dirs., 1983, pres., 1984—; youth involvement rep. Roanoke Valley chpt. Credit Unions, 1983—. Big Sister, Big Bros./Big Sisters, Roanoke, 1983—. Named Vol. Yr. Roanoke Valley chpt. Credit Unions, 1984. Mem. Roanoke Network Profl. and Managerial Women, Southeastern Hosp. Accounts Receivable Personnel, Phi Beta Omicron, Beta Sigma Phi. Presbyterian. Home: 702 Arbutus Ave SE Roanoke VA 24014 Office: Roanoke Meml Rehab Ctr PO Box 13367 Roanoke VA 24033

HARRISON, LOIS COWLES, civic worker; b. Des Moines, Iowa, June 23, 1934; d. Gardner and Lois (Thornburg) Cowles; B.A., Wellesley Coll., 1956; m. John Raymond Harrison, June 24, 1955; children—Mark, Pat, Lois; m. Homer E. Hooks, Nov. 27, 1982. Dir., Cowles Media Co. (formerly Mpls. Star and Tribune Co.), 1975-85. Commr. Gov.'s Commn. on Status of Women, 1973-77, Fla. Ethics Commn., 1974-78; mem. Commn. on Fla. Constl. Revision, 1977-78; mem. Fla. Women's Polit. Caucus, 1973-75; v.p. LWV Fla., 1973-77, pres., 1977—, bd. dirs., 1982-83, dir. edn. fund, 1973-77, dir. LWV U.S. ERA chair, 1980-82; bd. dirs. ERAmerica, 1980-82; pres. Planned Parenthood Central Fla., 1982-85; dir. Fla. Fine Arts Council, 1972-80; mem. Mayor's Creative and Performing Arts Council, Lakeland, Fla., 1972-75; mem. Am. Bar Commn. on Evaluation of Profl. Standards, 1978-80; pres. Polk Mus. Art, 1985-86, The Hooks Group, 1985—. Episcopalian. Home: 2311 Nevada Rd Lakeland FL 33803

HARRISON, MARGIT GARTHE, pharmacist, fraternity executive, hand cream manufacturing company executive; b. Longmont, Colo., Apr. 28, 1916; d. Magnus E. and Hanna (Hagen) Garthe; m. Charles William Harrison, Oct. 7, 1942. B.S., Wash. State Coll., 1940. Pharmacist Harry Race Druggist, Ketchikan, Alaska, 1940-43, Higgins Drugstore, Pullman, Wash., 1943-45, Currin's for Drugs, Portland, Oreg., 1945-48; chief pharmacist hosp. of Nucleonics div. Gen. Electric Co., Richland, Wash., 1948-56; chief pharmacist Kadiec Methodist Hosp., 1950-64; pharmacist Visger Drug, Kennewick, Wash., 1964-66; dir. pharmacy service Kennewick Gen. Hosp., 1966-80; pres. Marcha Lab., Inc., Pasco, Wash., 1966—. Mem. Lambda Kappa Sigma (nat. pres. 1950-52, expansion chmn., 1950-54, Western dist. supr. 1954-56, nat. v.p. 1956-58, hon. advisor 1958-78, chmn. scholarship com. 1958-78). Address: 201 Easy St Pasco WA 99301

HARRISON, MARION FOX, violin company official, violin maker; b. Chattanooga, Sept. 1, 1911; d. Cicero Gaston and Lucy Mae (Catlett) Fox; m. Edwin Andrew O'Neal, June 4, 1932 (div. Apr. 1945); children—Anne E. O'Neal Langhaug, Sylvia I. O'Neal Nagel; m. 2d, Benjamin Frederick Harrison, Jr., Sept. 24, 1948; 1 dau., Marion Fredericka Harrison LaBounty. Grad. Ga. State Coll., Milledgeville. Tchr., Rossville (Ga.) Schs., 1930-35; chemist Hercules Powder Co., Tyner, Tenn., 1942-46, Chattanooga Medicine Co., 1946-49; mgr. Harrison Violins, Berkley, Mich., 1966—, lutheir, 1971—, mgr., part owner, 1966—; violin maker, 1971—. Sec., Oak Park Symphony Soc., 1968, dir., 1968; dir. Southfield (Mich.) Symphony Soc., 1981—. Mem. Violin Makers Assn. Ariz. (2d place in tone award 1976, 83). Home: 1415 Woodsboro Dr Royal Oak MI 48067 Office: Harrison Violins 2689 Coolidge St Berkley MI 48072

HARRISON, NEDRA JOYCE, surgeon; b. Buffalo, Apr. 16, 1951; d. Herman Lloyde and Gertrude (Newsom) H.; B.S., Rosary Hill Coll., 1973; M.D., SUNY, Buffalo, 1977. Diplomate Am. Bd. Surgery. Resident in surgery Millard Fillmore Hosps., Buffalo, 1977-82, mem. active attending staff in gen. surgery, 1983—; practice medicine specializing in gen. surgery, Buffalo, 1982—; clin. asst. in surgery SUNY at Buffalo Sch. Medicine; cons. staff Bry-Lyn Hosp., 1986—; provisional staff in gen. surgery St. Joseph Intercommunity Hosp., 1986—. Chmn. United Thank Offering, Episcopal Ch., Buffalo, 1982. Recipient Best Research Paper in Gen. Surgery award Millard Fillmore Hosps., 1978, 81. Mem. AMA, Am. Med. Women's Assn., Christian Med. Soc., N.Y. State Med. Soc., Med. Soc. Erie County, ACS (candidate), Delta Epsilon Sigma. Episcopalian. Office: 405 Linwood Ave Buffalo NY 14209

HARRISON, PATRICIA DE STACY, public relations company executive; b. N.Y.C.; d. Charles John and Marguerite (Andrews) de Stacy; m. Fred Spain (div. 1970); children—Christopher Charles, Claudia Christina, Courtney Catherine; m. Emmett Bruce Harrison. B.A., Am. U., 1967. Owner, sr. v.p. E. Bruce Harrison Co. Pub. Relations, Washington, 1973—. Author: America's New Women Entrepreneurs. Playwright: Cabbage Soup, 1980. Mem. Nat. Adv. Bd. Technology and Disabled, 1986; mem. White House Conf. on Small Bus., Mem. Nat. Women's Econ. Alliance (founder), Capital Press Women, Am. News Women's Club, Washington Opera Soc., Nat. Press Club, Internat. Club, Pub. Relations Soc. Am. (mem. counselors acad.). Republican. Methodist. Avocations: writing; public speaking. Office: E Bruce Harrison Co 605 14th St NW Washington DC 20005

HARRISON, SYLVIA MARIE, realtor, executive; b. Glens Falls, N.Y., Dec. 7, 1933; d. Louis Paul and Anna (Norton) Mayer; m. Bogue P. Harrison Oct. 1, 1955; (div. 1974); children—Ann, Helen. Attended schs. N.Y., Fla. Cert. real estate broker. Owner, pres. Condo World Realty Inc., Panama City Beach, Fla., 1975—, Condo World, Inc., 1975—. Active Anchorage Children's Home, Girls Club, Bay County; bd. dirs. United Fund, Panama City. Republican. Methodist. Home: 6905 Thomas Dr Panama City Beach FL 32407 Office: Condo World Inc 8815A Thomas Dr Panama City Beach FL 32407

HARRISS, CYNTHIA THERESE (CLARKE), retail chain executive; b. Huntington, W.Va., June 12, 1952; d. Forbes Richard and Arlene (Will) C. Student, St. Louis U., 1970-72. Buyer, Scripps McCartney, Canton, Ill., 1972-73; store mgr. Paul Harris Stores, Cin., 1973-75, dist. mgr., St. Louis, 1975-77, regional mgr., Chgo., 1977-82, v.p. stores operation, Indpls., 1982-85, v.p., divisional mdse. mgr., 1985—. Roman Catholic. Home: 3045 Daumcourt St Carmel IN 46032 Office: Paul Harris Stores 6003 Guion Rd Indianapolis IN 46268

HARRIS-WOOTEN, KATHLEEN RENEE, computer programmer, seamstress; b. Los Angeles, Nov. 30, 1954; d. William Rogiere Harris and IdaBelle (Norman) Rivers; m. James Robert Wooten, Sept. 4, 1976. A.A., Chabot Coll., 1980. Lic. pilot. Gen. clk. sec. Western Girl Temp. Agy., San Leandro, Calif., 1973-75; mag card II operator Bechtel Inc., San Francisco, 1975-76; data entry operator Bechtel Corp., San Francisco, 1976-79, office asst., 1979-80; administrv. asst. II Bechtel Power Corp., Walnut Creek, Calif., 1980-82, computer programmer I, San Francisco, 1982—; designer, seamstress, owner Feline Fit Weddings, Etc., Calif., 1984. Mem. Nat. Assn. Female Execs., Aircraft Owners and Pilots Assn., Bechtel Employees Club, Alpha Chi Phi Omega. Democrat. Lutheran. Clubs: Trojans Bowling, Aeromax Flying (Oakland, Calif.). Avocations: bowling; racquetball; flying. Home: 266 Smalley Ave Suite H Hayward CA 94541

HARRITY, BERNADINE TERESA, lawyer; b. Phila., Nov. 21, 1948; d. Bernard James and Eleanor Mary (McGoldrick) H. B.A., U. Pa., 1970; J.D., Duquesne U., 1974. Bar: Pa. 1974, U.S. Ct. Mil. Rev., 1974, U.S. Ct. Mil. Appeals 1975, U.S. Supreme Ct. 1978, U.S. Claims Ct. 1980. Atty. advisor Darcom, Alexandria, Va., 1979-80; contracts atty. VA, Washington, 1980—. Dir. Darcom Fed. Credit Union, 1980—, Terr. Townhouses of Annandale, 1981-82. Served as capt. JAGC, U.S. Army, 1974-79; maj. Res. Decorated Joint Services Commendation medal, Army Commendation medal with 2 oak leaf clusters. Mem. ABA, Pa. Bar Assn., D.C. Women's Bar Assn., Am. Legion, Amvets, Delta Theta Phi. Republican. Roman Catholic. Clubs: Falls Church (Va.) Bus. and Profl. Women's U. Pa. Alumni. Home: 6717 Perry Penney Dr Annandale VA 22003 Office: Veterans Administration 810 Vermont Ave NW Washington DC 20420

HARROD, JUDY ELIZABETH, nurse; b. Melbourne, Ky., July 31, 1948; d. Vernon C. and Mary (Benz) Reinert; m. Russell C. Harrod, June 15, 1985. Assoc. degree in Applied Sci., No. Ky. U., 1982, B.S. in Nursing, 1986. R.N. Cashier, typist Safeco Ins., Cin., 1967-74; med. sec. St. Elizabeth Med. Ctr., Covington, Ky., 1974-80, Good Samaritan Hosp, Cin., 1980-82; R.N., St. Francis St. George Hosp., Cin., 1983—. Tchr. religion to children; vol. St. Luke Hosp. Gift Shop, Ft. Thomas, Ky. Mem. Am. Assn. Occupational Health Nurses, NOW. Home: 217 Harrison Ct Cincinnati OH 45246

HARROLD, LOU ANN, home economist, farmer, educator, businesswoman; b. Findlay, Ohio, Dec. 9, 1935; d. Donald Layman and Carolyn Genevra (Mathews) Putnam; B.S. summa cum laude, Ohio State U., 1956; M.S. in Ednl. Adminstrn., U. Dayton, 1979, m. Clyde Ellis Harrold, June 10, 1977; children—Robert E. Spangler, Jr., Stacia Lee Spangler Westerhausen. Tchr., Alger High Sch., 1957-59; tchr., dept. head Kenton (Ohio) Jr. High Sch., 1964-79; tchr. home econs., dept. head Kenton St. High Sch., 1979-85; secondary coordinator Hardin County Dept. Edn., 1985-86, dir. curriculum, 1986—; farmer, dairy and hog, later grain, Ada, Ohio, 1957—; engaged in housing restoration and rental, 1977—; cons. Ohio Dept. Edn., 1974, 76, 82; dir. sch.-age parent project, 1981-83. State adv. bd. Ohio Coop. Extension Service, 1980—, Nutrition Edn. Tng. Program, 1981-83; sec. Cessna Twp. Bd. Zoning Appeals, 1974-85. Named Ohio Tchr. of Yr. in Home Econs., 1982; recipient service award Coll. Agr. and Home Econs. Ohio State U., 1982. Mem. Am. Home Econs. Assn., Ohio Home Econs. Assn. (state pres. 1980-81, Dist. A pres. 1978-79), Ohio Assn. for Supervision and Curriculum Devel., Internat. Fedn. Home Econs., Nat. Assn. Vocat. Home Econs. Tchrs., Nat. Assn. Female Execs., AAUW, Home Econs. Edn. Assn., Am. Vocat. Assn., Greater Toledo Dairy and Nutrition Council, Home Economists in Bus., Ohio Sch. Supervisors Assn., Delta Kappa Gamma, Phi Delta Kappa. Republican. Methodist. Club: University II (pres.). Supr. devel. Kenton Middle Sch. Home Econs. Curriculum, distributed nationally, 1981. Home: 8187 TR 90 Ada OH 45810 Office: Courthouse Kenton OH 43326

HARRON, PHOEBE ZASLOVE, investment banking firm executive; b. Knoxville, Tenn., June 12, 1953; d. Herbert James and Jean (Butler) Zaslove; m. Michael Fralinger Harron, Aug. 25, 1984. B.A. in Journalism, U. Ky., 1973; B.S.M. in Piano, Sch. Fine Arts, Boston U., 1975; postgrad. Inst. Fin., 1978-79. Registered rep., SEC, all exchanges, Nat. Assn. Securities Dealers. Instl. option sales trader First Boston, N.Y.C., 1978-80; v.p., head domestic and internat. instl. option arbitrage Morgan Stanley & Co., Inc., N.Y.C., 1980—; concert performances throughout New Eng., N.Y. and Europe, 1969-76. U. Ky. scholar, 1971-73; Swiss Govt. Tibor Varga Festival scholar, Sione, Switzerland, 1975-76. Mem. N.Y. Option Soc., Nat. Option and Futures Soc. (dir. 1979-80), Concert Artists Guild (dir. 1982-84). Episcopalian. Office: Morgan Stanley & Co 1251 Ave of Americas New York NY 10020

HARROP, NORMA (ELLINOR ROBERTS), public relations consultant, writer; b. Bklyn., Dec. 11, 1921; d. Frederick Warren and Nina Eliot (Paget) H. B.A., Hunter Coll., 1950; M.S. in Journalism, Columbia U., 1951; postgrad. Boston U., 1954, Western Res. U., 1955; M.S.W., U. Pitts., 1957. Publicity dir., Consumers Coop., N.Y.C., 1949-53; dir. Camp Fire Girls, Cleve., 1953-55; pub. relations account supr. Ketchum, MacLeod, Grove, Pitts., 1956-63; pub. relations account supr. BBDO, N.Y.C., 1963-66; dir. pub. relations Fedn. Jewish Philanthropies, N.Y.C., 1970-82; pvt. practice pub. relations, N.Y.C., 1966-70; dir. devel. pub. relations Jewish Theol. Sem., N.Y.C., 1983-84; gen. mgr. Kresh Communications, N.Y.C., 1984—. Author: One of the Great Cats, 1978. Contbr. articles to dailies and consumer mags. Founder, Pitts. chpt. Nat. Home Fashions League. Mem. Internat. Women Writers Guild, Internat. Assn. Bus. Communicators, Nat. Assn. Female Execs., Coop. Guild of USA, Am. Women in Radio and TV (bd. dirs. 1962-64), Am. Jewish Pub. Relations Soc. (bd. dirs. 1984—). Avocations: bike riding; ice skating; cross country skiing; photography. Office: 225 Park Ave S 17th Floor New York NY 10003

HARROUN, DOROTHY SUMMER, painter, educator; b. El Paso, Tex., Nov. 29, 1935; d. Daniel Stuart and Eleanor (Flowers) H.; B.F.A., U. N.Mex., 1957; postgrad. (Fulbright scholar) U. Paris, Sorbonne, 1957-58; M.F.A., U. Colo., 1960. One woman shows: The Gondolier Gallery, Boulder, Colo., 1961, 62, Sta. KAFE-FM Gallery, San Francisco, 1963, 64; Lovelace-Bataan Hosp., Albuquerque, 1976, 79; Eastern N.Mex. U., 1981, Rathaus, Kelkheim, W.Ger., N.Mex. State U. group shows include: Whitte Mus., San Antonio, 1960, shows in Hyannis, Mass., Waterbury, Conn., Newport, R.I., 1964-65, Mus. N.Mex., Santa Fe, 1966, Ogunguit (Maine) Art Ctr., 1977, Am. Watercolor Soc. 112th Ann., N.Y.C., 1979, Coos Art Mus., Coos Bay, Oreg., 1980, Western Slope Show, Montrose, Colo., 1981, 82, Ga. Watercolor Soc. Open, 1983, Western Fedn. Watercolor Socs., 1984, Sun Carnival Art Show, El Paso, 1984, Western Fedn. Watercolor Socs., 1984, 85, 86; represented in permanent collections U. N.Mex., U. Colo., Fine Arts Mus., Carlsbad, N.Mex., also pvt. collections in U.S., France, Italy, W.Ger.; art dir. Wood-Reich Advt. Agy., Boulder, 1960-61; lectr. U. Colo., Boulder, 1961-62; tchr. art Langley-Porter Neuropsychiat. Inst. U. Calif., 1963; lectr. San Francisco State Coll., 1964-65; tchr. Art Center Sch., Albuquerque, 1975-79; tchr. watercolor, drawing U. N.Mex., 1980-81. Mem. Artist Equity Assn. (pres. Albuquerque chpt. 1977-79), AAUW (state cultural dir.), Nat. League Am. Pen Women (pres. Albuquerque br. 1982—), N. Mex. Watercolor Soc. (v.p. 1984, pres. 1985). Author and illustrator: Take Time to Play and Listen, 1963, Phun-y Physics, 1975. Address: Star Route Box 982 Corrales NM 87048

HARSANYI, JANICE, singer, voice educator; b. Arlington, Mass., July 15, 1929; d. Edward Allen and Thelma (Jacobs) Morris; m. Nicholas Harsanyi, Apr. 19, 1952; 1 son, Peter. Mus. B., Westminster Choir Coll., 1951; postgrad., Acad. Vocal Arts, 1952-54. Voice tchr. Westminster Choir Coll., Princeton, N.J., 1951-63, chmn. dept. voice, 1963-65; lectr. Princeton Theol. Sem., N.J., 1956-63; voice tchr. U. Mich. Summer Sch., Interlochen, 1965-70; artist-in-residence Interlochen Arts Acad., 1967-70; voice tchr. N.C. Sch. Arts, Winston-Salem, N.C., 1971-78; music tchr. Salem Coll., Winston-Salem, 1973-76; prof. voice Fla. State U., Tallahassee, 1978—; soprano soloist Bach Aria Group, 1966-67, Princeton Chamber Orch., 1966-70, Piedmont Chamber Orch., 1974-76, Phila. String Quartet, 1965. Soprano soloist for major rec. cos., 1954—, maj. music festivals, 1959—, symphony orchs., 1958—. Recipient Merit of Achievement award Westminister Choir Coll., 1971. Mem. Nat. Assn. Tchrs. Singing, Music Tchrs. Nat. Assn., Riemenschneider Bach Inst., Sigma Alpha Iota (hon.). Presbyterian. Avocations: reading; poetry; writing; travel; bridge. Home: 725 Duparc Circle Tallahassee FL 32312 Office: Fla State U Sch Music Tallahassee FL 32306

HARSHAW, CONNIE MATTHEWS ROBINSON, government official; b. Savannah, Ga., Feb. 17, 1955; d. Slater B. and B. Lois (Floyd) Matthews; m. Calvin L. Robinson, Dec. 14, 1974 (div. Jan. 1981); m. James Michael Harshaw, Mar. 30, 1985; 1 son, Robert Matthew. B.S., Hampton Inst., 1977; postgrad. U. Md., 1978—. Adminstrv. asst. Nat. Bur. Standards, Gaithersburg, Md., 1977-81; personnel staffing asst. Dept. Air Force, Langley AFB, Va., 1981-83; personnel asst. Nat. Cancer Inst., NIH, Bethesda, Md., 1983-85; personnel staffing specialist Dept. Army Forces Command, Ft. Meade, Md., 1985—. Recipient Sustained Superior Performance award Nat. Bur. Standards, 1978. Mem. Internat. Personnel Mgmt. Assn., Nat. Assn. Female Execs., Nat. Polit. Congress of Black Women. Democrat. Roman Catholic. Avocations: camping; traveling; writing; public speaking. Home: 9470 Keepsake Way Columbia MD 21046 Office: Civilian Personnel Office Recruitment and Placement Br Fort George G Meade MD 20755

HARSNEY, JOHANNA MARIE OFFNER, registered nurse; b. Youngstown, Ohio, Oct. 15, 1914; d. Michael and Elizabeth (Untch) Offner; m. Theodore Harsney, Aug. 11, 1941; 1 son, Karl Michael. Grad. Youngstown Hosp. Sch. Nursing, 1939; B.A. in Fgn. Langs., Youngstown U., 1972. Staff nurse Youngstown Hosp., 1939-40; pvt. duty nurse Youngstown Profl. Nurse's Registry, Youngstown, 1940-84. Vol. Red Cross nurses. Mem. Am. Nurses Assn., Profl. Nurses Registry (dir.), Ohio Nurses Assn. (pres. pvt. duty sect. 1979-84), Am. Bus. Women Assn. (v.p. Gold Torch chpt. 1978, Nurse of Yr. Dist. 3, 1983), Phi Lambda Pi, Phi Lambda Pi (sec. 1973-74, pres. 1975). Office: Profl Nurses Registry 4011 Hillman Way Youngstown OH 44512

HART, ANGELA KATHERINE, lawyer; b. Radford, Va., May 10, 1949; d. William James, Jr., and Lina Elda (Filios) H. A.B., Trinity Coll., Washington, 1971; J.D., Loyola U., New Orleans, 1975. Bar: Md. 1975, D.C. 1981. Staff atty. Legal Aid Bur., Inc., Annapolis, Md., 1975-77; asst. county atty. Montgomery County, Md., Rockville, 1977—. Bd. dirs. Anne Arundel County chpt. ARC, 1983—. Mem. ABA, Md. Bar Assn., D.C. Bar Assn., Montgomery County Bar Assn., Anne Arundel County Bar Assn., St. Philip Neri Sodality. Democrat. Roman Catholic. Home: 323 Ardmore Rd Linthicum MD 21090 Office: County Attorneys Office 3d Floor Executive Office Bldg 101 Monroe St Rockville MD 20850

HART, BEVERLEY JEAN, child development official; b. Owego, N.Y., Aug. 23, 1936; d. George Francis and Dorothy Aline (Alexander) Williams, m. William Sylvester Hart (dec.); children—Robyn Hart Sheppard, Darryn, Karyn. Student Corning Community Coll., 1973. With Comprehensive Interdisciplinary Devel. Services, Inc., Elmira, N.Y., 1972—, urban unit assoc., 1976—; lectr. in field; mem. N.Y. State Med. Adv. Com., 1977—. Bd. dirs. United Community Services Chemung County, 1969-79, mem. zoning referral com. Chemung County Planning Bd., 1972-80; bd. dirs. Chemung County Neighborhood Justice Program, 1981-82; mem. Com. on Citizens' Goals for Chemung County, 1981-82; bd. dirs. Elmira YWCA, 1986—, mem. planning com., 1986, mem. latch key adv. com., 1986. Recipient numerous state, county and city awards, citations for pub. service. Mem. NAACP (exec. bd. Elmira-Corning br. 1973-81), LWV (bd. dirs., chmn. housing com., del. state conv. for Chemung County). Democrat. Roman Catholic. Home: 520 W 1st St Elmira NY 14901 Office: Comprehensive Interdisciplinary Developmental Services Inc Box EC 853 815 N Main St Elmira NY 14901

HART, EVELYN REESE, municipal official; b. Phoenix, Jan. 24, 1931; d. Marshall Leeman Reese and Velma (Springer) Bailey; m. William O. Mollison, Aug. 20, 1952 (div. 1960); children—Patti, Pam, Janet; m. J. Lynn Hart, May 27, 1961; stepchildren—Mike, James. With Harts Sporting Goods, Costa Mesa, Calif., 1961-80; mem. Newport Beach City Council, Calif., 1978—, mayor, 1982-84; chmn. Dist 5, Orange County Dept. Sanitation, 1980—; pres. Orange County League of Calif. Cities, Santa Ana, 1985—. Bd. dirs. YMCA Family Crisis Ctr., 1979—, Braille Inst., 1980—, Youth Employment Program, Orange County, 1985; mem. nominating com. Girl Scouts U.S.A. Republican. Home: 435 Redlands Newport Beach CA 92663

HART, JEAN CATHERINE, public relations executive; b. Oakland, Calif., May 14, 1948; d. Douglas Charles and Dorothy Caroline (Renner) Stahle; m. John Terry Hart, May 5, 1973 (div. Feb. 1982). B.J., U. Mo., 1971. Copywriter Tracy-Locke Co., Denver, 1971-72; Vista vol., South Providence, R.I., 1972-73; prodn. asst. Motherhood Maternity Shops, Santa Monica, Calif., 1973-76; creative dir. Boyce Advt., Santa Monica, Calif., 1976-78; art dir. Bryan Hardwick & Assocs., Palos Verdes Estates, Calif., 1978-80; owner One From the Hart, Palos Verdes Estates, Calif., 1980-81; art, prodn., pub. relations dir. Success Mag., Chgo., 1981-84; dir. corp. pub. relations Hal Publs., N.Y.C., 1984—; spl. events mgmt. Presdl. Inaugural Com.; project dir. Statue of Liberty Centennial Commn. Bd. dirs. St. Vincent Heart Assn., Los Angeles, 1978—; mem. Anchor, Chgo., 1983; mem. Atrium Playwright's Ctr., Chgo., 1983. Mem. Women in Communications, Women in Design, Publicity Club Chgo., Prodn. Club Chgo., Delta Delta Delta. Home: 3053 P St NW Washington DC 20007

HART, JOANNE MARIE, food service company executive; b. Boston, Jan. 9, 1931; d. Patrick Joseph and Josephine Hanna (Casey) Sullivan; student public schs.; m. Maurice Edmund Hart, Sept. 10, 1955; children—Charleen, Michael, Mary, Joseph, Brenda, Kathleen, Paul. Treas., mgr. Hart Bros. Caterers, Randolph, Mass., 1955—, Lantana Co., Randolph, 1971—; corporator Quincy (Mass.) Savs. Bank. Bd. dirs. Braintree Family Counseling and Guidance Center, South Shore Bus. and Indsl. Polit. Action Com., South Shore Polit. Action; bd. trustees South Shore Hosp., South Weymouth, Mass. Mem. Mass. Restaurant Assn., South Shore C. of C. (past dir.), Mass. Restaurant Assn. Roman Catholic. Club: Cohasset Golf; Jonathan's Landing Golf (Jupiter, Fla.). Home: 99 Atlantic Ave Cohasset MA 02025 Office: 43 Scanlon Dr Randolph MA 02368

HART, KITTY CARLISLE, arts adminstr.; b. New Orleans, Sept. 3, 1917; d. Joseph and Hortence (Holtzman) Conn; ed. London Sch. Econs., Royal Acad. Dramatic Arts; D.F.A. (hon.), Coll. New Rochelle; D.H.L. (hon.), Hartwick Coll., Manhattan Coll.; m. Moss Hart, Aug. 10, 1946 (dec.); children—Christopher, Cathy. Chmn. N.Y. State Council on Arts; panelist TV Show To Tell the Truth; actress on stage and in films, singer Met. Opera; TV moderator and interviewer. Assoc. fellow Timothy Dwight Coll. of Yale U.; bd. dirs. Empire State Coll.; formerly spl. cons. to N.Y. Gov. on women's opportunities; mem. vis. com., bd. overseers Harvard U. Music Sch.; mem. vis. com. for the arts M.I.T. Contbr. book revs. to jours. Office: 915 Broadway New York NY 10010*

HART, LAURA ROWSE, educator; b. Mineola, N.Y., Dec. 12, 1931; d. Edward Francis and Martha Scott (Stuart) Rowse; m. Humes Houston Hart, June 26, 1954 (div. 1972); children—William Allen. B.A. Goucher Coll., 1953. Tchr. Montgomery County Pub. Schs., Rockville, Md., 1953-72, Prince

George's County Bd. Edn., 1972—. Mem. NEA, Md. State Tchrs. Assn., Prince George's County Edn. Assn. (faculty rep.), Adelphi Elem. PTA (co-treas. 1985—, computer liasion 1984, 85—), Alpha Phi. Democrat. Presbyterian. Club: Gerrymanders Md. Square Dance (Chevy Chase, Md.) (treas. 1981—). Avocations: craft work; square dancing. Home: 121 Whitmoor Terr Silver Spring MD 20901 Office: Adelphi Elem Sch 8820 Riggs Rd Adelphi MD 20783

HART, MARA KIRK, librarian; b. N.Y.C., Dec. 25, 1933; d. George W. and Lucile D. (Dvorak) Kirk; B.A., Miami U., Oxford, Ohio, 1955; M.A., N.Y. U., 1957; M.A., U. Minn., 1973; m. Robert C. Hart, Aug. 1983; children by previous marriage—Steve Bauer, Jenny Bauer. Teenage dir. Central Br. YWCA, N.Y.C., 1957-58; tchr. English, Cleve., Mpls., 1958-61; dir. bibliography rm. U. Minn. Library, Mpls., 1964-65, Portuguese, Latin Am., Spanish bibliographer, 1965-69, acquisitions librarian, Duluth campus, 1973-84, head reference dept., 1985—; humanities bibliographer Claremont Colls., 1969-71; pub., editor Kirk Press Books. Manor Club scholar, 1956-57; Wis. Arts Bd. awardee, 1979. Democrat. Unitarian. Editor: Corn Village, 1971; poetry editor Plainsong, 1967-69, N. Country Anvil, 1971-77; translator various books from Spanish; author: (poetry) Some Yellow Flowers, 1979; pub.: Second Pond, 1980; Till Hope Creates, 1981. Home: 205 W Kent Rd Duluth MN 55812 Office: Univ Minn Duluth Library Duluth MN 55812

HART, NANCY INEZ, retail television, audio-visual executive; b. Miami, Fla., Oct. 6, 1954; d. John Henry Cain and Ruby Inez (Allen) Baker. A.A., Broward Community Coll. With vendor relations and accounts payable dept. Montgomery Ward Co./Jefferson Stores, Miami, 1973-77; office mgr. Luskin's High Fidelity, Hollywood, Fla., 1977-84, v.p. adminstrn., 1984—. Mem. Nat. Assn. Female Execs., Hollywood C. of C. (rep.). Avocations: music; dance; nautilus; gourmet food; cooking. Home: 20120-01 NE 3d Ct Miami FL 33179 Office: Luskin's High Fidelity 4150 N 28th Terr Hollywood FL 33020

HART, NINA MARIE, computing company executive; b. Lawrence, Mass., Feb. 4, 1955; d. John Angelo and Anita Mary (D'Andreta) Jaskot; m. Larry Calvin Hart, Sept. 3, 1982. B.S. in Bus. Adminstrn. magna cum laude, Merrimack Coll., 1977. With computer sales dept. Burroughs Co., Peabody, Mass., 1977-78; account rep. Xerox Corp., Lexington, Mass., 1978-83; software sales/account exec. Univ. Computing Co., Torrance, Calif., 1983—. Mem. Assn. Women in Computing, Nat. Fedn. Bus. and Profl. Women (del. 1981 nat. conf., Mass. Young Careerist award 1981). Club: Los Angeles Athletic. Home: 4000 Via Opata Palos Verdes Estates CA 90274 Office: Univ Computing Co 21515 Hawthorne Blvd Suite 1090 Torrance CA 90405

HARTENSTEIN, ROSLYN DAWSON, communications consultant, writer; b. Corpus Christi, Tex., Sept. 30, 1952; d. Joseph Turner and Melba Louise (Bruno) Dawson; B.A. in English, Journalism, Baylor U., 1973; M.A. in English Lit., Vanderbilt U., 1974; m. Darrel W. Hartenstein, Sept. 6, 1980; children—Diane Elizabeth, Stephen Dawson. News dir. Sta. KEFC-FM, Waco, Tex., 1972-73; news dir., announcer Nashville Public Radio, 1973-74; news dir., chief copywriter Sta. KEFC-FM, 1974-75; chief copywriter, producer WACO-AM, Waco, 1975; asst. mgr. Sta. KKIK-AM, 1976-77; instr. dept. English McLennan Community Coll., Waco, 1975-77; instr. dept. communications Baylor U., 1976-77; freelance writer and editor, Ft. Worth, 1978; dir. communications publs. Dallas C. of C., 1979-82; ind. communications cons., writer, 1982—; account exec. on contract to Carl Byoir & Assocs., Inc.; lectr. So. Meth. U., 1980. Chmn. publicity com. Dallas water utilities centennial 1981; chmn. publicity com. Martin Luther King, Jr. birthday celebration, 1980-81; bd. dirs. Auction for Cultural Arts, 1982-85; mem. women's com. Creative Learning Ctr.,1983-85, mem. publicity com. Vol. Ctr. Dallas, 1984-85; mktg. chmn. Met. Opera Centennial, Dallas, 1984; mem. pub. relations com. Dallas Women's Found., 1985, pub. relations chair, 1986—, bd. dirs., 1986—, pub. relations chair Jas. K. Wilson Awards, Dallas, 1986. Mem. Public Relations Soc. Am., Internat. Assn. Bus. Communicators, Women in Communications, Inc., Dallas Ad League, Press Club of Dallas, Am. Mgmt. Assn., Jr. League of Dallas. Publisher: Dallas mag., 1980-82. Home and Office: PO Box 190453 Dallas TX 75219

HARTER, JEAN ANN, architect, graphic art consultant; b. Kansas City, Kans., Sept. 28, 1959; d. Donald Lee Harter and Beth Arland (Hobbs) Stanley. B.Interior Arch., Kans. State U., 1983. Designer Michael Fox, Inc., St. Louis, 1983-85; interior architect Pabst Design Group, St. Louis, 1985; archtl. designer Interior Space Inc., St. Louis, 1985—; cons. CL Designs, St. Louis, 1985—. Mem. Inst. Bus. Designers (affiliate), Nat. Assn. Female Execs. Democrat. Avocations: graphic arts; music; dance.

HARTER, KATHLEEN BELL, real estate executive; b. Altoona, Pa., Mar. 9, 1953; d. William Mathias and Janet (Stultz) Bell; m. Bruce Carl Harter, May 18, 1973. Student Fla. State U.; B.S. in Acctg., U. South Fla., 1975. Staff auditor Arthur Andersen & Co., Tampa, 1975-77; from v.p., controller to div. pres. U.S. Home Corp., Clearwater, Fla., 1977-82; div. pres. Mason Homes, Orlando, Fla., 1982-86; regional mgr. Huckleberry-Lennau Corp., Orlando, Fla., 1986—. Mem. com. Orlando Growth Study Council, 1985, Seminole County Transp. Study, 1985. Mem. Home Builders Assn. Mid-Fla. (bd. dirs. 1984—, govt. affairs com. 1984—, chmn. Orange County affairs com. 1986—, Parade of Homes winners 1983, 85.). Republican. Roman Catholic. Avocation: Water skiing. Office: Huckleberry-Lennau Corp 12553 Lake Underhill Dr Orlando FL 32826

HARTH, ERICA, educator; b. N.Y.C. B.A., Barnard Coll., 1959; M.A., Columbia U., 1962, Ph.D. in French, 1968. Instr. French, NYU, 1964-66; from instr. to asst. prof. Columbia U., 1967-71; lectr. Tel-Aviv U., Israel, 1971-72; asst. prof. Brandeis U., 1972-75, assoc. prof. French, 1975-85, prof. French and comparative lit., 1985—. NEH fellow, 1970; Am. Council Learned Socs. fellow, 1978. Mem. MLA. Author: Cyrano de Bergerac and the Polemics of Modernity, 1970; Ideology and Culture in Seventeenth Century France; contbr. articles to profl. jours. Address: Dept Romance and Comparative Lit Brandeis U Waltham MA 02154

HARTLEY, EDITH WRIGHT, anatomist; b. Hancock, Mich., Nov. 23, 1946; d. Orrin Hughitt and Freddie (Tucker) Wright; m. Lawrence Edward Hartley, Dec. 18, 1976; children—Gregory Wright, Aaron Hughitt. B.S., Eckerd Coll., St. Petersburg, Fla., 1968; M.A., Duke U., 1972; Ph.D., U. South Fla., 1982. Apgar technician supr. Duke U. Hosp., Durham, 1969-71; substitute tchr. Polk County Schs. (Fla.), 1970-71; biol. lab. technician VA Hosp., Tampa, Fla., 1971-76; biostatis. cons. Tampa, 1977-82; clin. research assoc. dept. radiology U. South Fla., Tampa, 1982—. Author: (with H.N. Schnitzlein et al) A CT Atlas of the Head and Spine, 1982; contbr. articles to profl. jours.; numerous sci. presentations and demonstrations. Sec., Eckerd Coll. Alumni Council, St. Petersburg, 1971-81; bd. dirs., v.p. Lake Magdalene Restoration Assn., Tampa, 1977—; mem. Ft. Brooke Hist. Monument Commn., Tampa, 1981—; mem. local draft bd., 1984—. NSF trainee, 1968-71. Mem. Sigma Xi, Omicron Delta Kappa, Phi Kappa Phi. Democrat. Presbyterian. Lodge: DAR (organizing regent chpt. 1978-80, chpt. treas. 1980-82, regent 1982-84; state chmn. jr. membership 1974-76, state chmn. pages 1978-80, state organizing sec. 1980-82, state chmn. state conf. bd. 1982-84, state registrar 1984-86; nat. vice chmn. jr. membership, 1974-77; Outstanding Jr. Mem. Southeastern Div. 1982, Nat. Outstanding Jr. Mem. 1982; pres. Outstanding Jr. Club 1983-85).

HARTLEY, LODEMIA ROSE, nurse, nursing school administrator; b. Bagley, Iowa, Jan. 16, 1936; d. Charles Francis and Frances Lillian (Nelson) Dudley; m. William Burton Hartley, Jan. 19, 1957 (div. Dec. 1976); children—Julie Ann, Joni Marie, Jennifer Lynn, Jacqueline Beth. B.S.N., U. Colo., 1957; cert. in nurse anesthesia Mpls. Sch. Anesthesia, 1971; M.A. in Curriculum and Instruction-Allied Health, Coll. St. Thomas, 1984. Staff nurse Wardenburg Health Ctr., U. Colo., Boulder, 1957-60; staff nurse Herrick Hosp., Berkeley, Calif., 1960-61, VA Hosp., Madison, Wis., 1961-67; supr. Northfield Hosp., Minn., 1967-69; nurse anesthetist VA Med. Ctr., Mpls., 1971—, dir. Sch. Nurse Anesthesia. Mem. Am. Assn. Nurse Anesthetists, VA Nurses Assn. (sec. 1981-83), Minn. Assn. Nurse Anesthetists (treas. 1982-85). Democrat. Avocations: sailing; skiing; reading; knitting; gardening. Home: 4945 16th Ave S Minneapolis MN 55417 Office: Mpls VA Med Ctr Sch Anesthesia 112A 48th Ave S and 54th St Minneapolis MN 55417

HARTLEY-LINSE, BONNIE JEAN, college health nurse clinician, administrator, consultant; b. Chgo., July 26, 1923; d. Frank and Anna Kathleen (Koutecky) Kadlec; m. Robert William Hartley, June 23, 1949 (div. Feb. 1961); children—Robert Greig, Franklin James; m. Howard Albert Linse, June 10, 1978; stepchildren—Michael Howard, Janet Stokes. B.S. in Nursing, St. Xavier Coll., Chgo., 1945; cert. edn. Portland State Coll., 1965; M.S. in Nursing Edn., U. Oreg., 1972; cert. coll. health nurse practitioner program Brigham Young U., 1976. R.N., Oreg. Mem. faculty nursing St. Xavier Coll., 1945-47; head nurse U. Chgo. Clinics, 1947-48; nurse research newborn neurology U. Oreg. Med. Sch., Portland, summer 1961; coordinator dental assistant program, instr. biology Portland Pub. Schs., Oreg., 1965-67; health service clinician, adminstr. Clackamas Community Coll., Oregon City, Oreg., 1970-84; cons. Health Services Community Colls. of Oreg., 1972-84; pres. Coll. Health Nurses, State of Oreg., 1976-78. Mem. Northwest Oreg. Health Systems, Clackamas County Sub-Area Council, Oregon City, 1980—. Recipient Recognition for Outstanding Service award Clackamas Community Coll., 1984; USPHS grantee, 1968. Mem. Am. Nurses Assn., Oreg. Nurses Assn. (Clackamas County unit 26), Pacific Coast Coll. Health Assn. (ann. conf. program coordinator 1980), Oreg. Coll. Health Dirs. Assn. Avocations: travel; piano; choral singing; swimming. Home: 18633 Roundtree Dr Oregon City OR 97045

HARTMAN, ANNE CARLTON, banker; b. Charlotte, N.C., Sept. 24, 1942; d. Sigsby Carlton and Blannie (Lockamy) Tadlock; m. John Lewis Hartman III, June 7, 1964; children—Sally, Susan. B.S. in Bus. Adminstrn., U. Mo., 1976; M.B.A., Baldwin Wallace Coll., 1984. Adminstrv. asst. McDonnell Douglas Corp., St. Louis, 1977-78; mgmt. trainee Nat. City Bank, Cleve., 1978-79, ops. mgr., 1979-82, ops. officer, 1981, productivity officer, 1982, asst. v.p. productivity, 1983-85, v.p. corp. cash mgmt., 1985—, mem. speakers bur., 1983—. Mem. Am. Inst. Banking (edn. com. 1981—), Bank Adminstrn. Inst. (program com. 1982—). Republican. Baptist. Office: National City Bank 1900 E 9th St Cleveland OH 44114

HARTMAN, ARLENE, educational administrator; b. Pitts., Aug. 4, 1938; d. Edmund Arthur and Helen Frances (Waskowicz) H.; m. Walter John Miscavage, Aug. 5, 1970. B.S., Indiana U. of Pa., 1960, M.Ed., 1964; postgrad. Fairleigh Dickinson U., 1982—. Math. tchr. Gateway Union Schs., Monroeville, Pa., 1960-70; math. cons. Paramus Pub. Schs., N.J., 1970-77, elem. prin., 1977-78, 80-81, curriculum coordinator, 1978-80, 81-84, sch. adminstr., 1984—; referee Nat. Council Tchrs. Math., Reston, Va., 1975—. Author: Calculator Game Book, 1977; also monograph and articles. Mem. N.J. Assn. Sch. Adminstrs. (workshop conr. 1982—), Assn. for Supervision and Curriculum Devel., Nat. Assn. Elem. and Middle Sch. Prins. Office: West Brook Middle Sch Roosevelt Blvd Paramus NJ 07652

HARTMAN, CATHERINE RUDISILL, educator; b. Biscoe, N.C., Mar. 24, 1916; d. Jacob Andrew and Annie (Dietz) Rudisill; B.S., Appalachian State Tchrs. Coll., 1944; M.A., Columbia U., 1950, profl. diploma Tchrs. Coll., 1959; student U. London, Heidelberg U., summer 1953, NYU, summer 1954, UCLA, summer 1956; m. Harold R. Hartman, Dec. 26, 1962. Primary tchr. Park Grace Sch., Kings Mountain, N.C., 1936-39; elem., music tchr. Oakhurst Sch., Charlotte, N.C., 1939-44, Gary Sch., Tampa, Fla., 1945-47; elem. supr. schs. Gaston County Schs., Gastonia, N.C., 1947-55, dir. instrn., 1955-61, asst. supt. in charge instrn., 1961-63; assoc. prof. edn. William Paterson Coll. of N.J., Wayne, 1964-85, assoc. prof. emeritus, 1985—, chmn. gen. elem. program com. for curriculum revision, 1967-68, chmn. dept. secondary edn., 1972-78, chmn. dept. adminstrv., adult and secondary programs, 1979-85. Mem. Assn. Supervision and Curriculum Devel. of NEA (nat. dir. 1958-61), NCCJ (Carolinas regional dir. 1952-62), AAUW (dir. Charlotte 1953-55), Assn. Childhood Edn. (life, treas. N.C. 1955-57, adviser Gaston County br. 1955-63), William Paterson Fedn. Coll. Tchrs., Am. Assn. Sch. Adminstrs. (life), Kappa Delta Pi, Pi Lambda Theta. Presbyterian. Office: William Paterson Coll of NJ Wayne NJ 07470

HARTMAN, HEDY ANN, fund raising company executive, consultant; b. Sept. 24, 1954; d. Alan Stuart Hartman and Joan Marcia (Lederman) Hartman Goldsmith; m. Jon Abbott Mersereau, Nov. 27, 1976 (div. June 1981); m. William Bainbridge Everett, June 2, 1984. B.A. with distinction, U. Pa., 1975; M.A., U. Wash., 1982, Ph.C., 1983. Researcher Am. Mus. Natural History, N.Y.C., 1974; curatorial asst. Univ. Mus., U. Pa., Phila., 1974-75; instr. Children's Mus., Indpls., 1976; curatorial asst. Indpls. Mus. Art, 1975-76; program adminstr. statewide services S.C. State Mus., Columbia, 1977-80; pres. Hartman Planning & Devel. Group Ltd., Bellevue, Wash., 1980—; S.C. state rep. Southeastern Mus. Conf., 1979-80. Author: Funding Sources and Technical Assistance for Museums and Historical Organizations, 1979; Fund Raising for Museums, 1985. Editor: Official Museum Guide to Products and Services, 1980. Mem. Am. Assn. Museums, Am. Assn. State and Local History (bd. dirs. 1983—), Western Museums Conf. (bd. dirs. 1980-83), Wash. Mus. Assn. (bd. dirs. 1985—). Office: Hartman Planning and Development Group Ltd 14645 NE 34th St C-24 Bellevue WA 98007

HARTMAN, MYLITTA SUZANNE, writer, editor, educator, consultant in public relations; b. Seguin, Tex., Jan. 1, 1937; d. Julius Willard and Gertrude (Sweat) Forse; m. Franklin Lee Hartman, Aug. 25, 1959 (div. Aug. 1980); children—Tanya, Elisa, Lorien; m. Andrew Evans Byerley, Oct. 10, 1981. B.A., U. Iowa, 1958; M.A., U. Mich., 1964. Tchr. creative writing Case Western Res. U., 1968-80, Cuyahoga Community Coll., Cleve., 1984; editor New Day Press, Cleve., 1971—; dir. communication and devel. Coll. Urban Affairs Cleve. State U., Ohio, 1984—. Editor: Walk in My Footsteps, 1985. Contbr. short stories to popular mags. Fulbright scholar U. Heidelberg, Germany, 1964-65. Mem. Poets and Writers, Women in Communication. Democrat. Unitarian. Avocations: music; nature; urban affairs. Home: 3151 Scarborough Rd Cleveland Heights OH 44118 Office: Coll of Urban Affairs Cleve State U Corlett Bldg Cleveland OH 44115

HARTMAN, NANCY LEE, physician; b. Philipsburg, Pa., July 29, 1951; d. Richard Lee and Ann Hartman; grad. Barbizon Sch. Modeling, 1970; A.A., Harcum Jr. Coll., 1969-71; B.A., Lycoming Coll., 1974; M.S., L.I. U., 1977; M.D., Am. U. of Caribbean in Plymouth, Montserrat, W.I., 1981. Med. technologist Lock Haven (Pa.) Hosp., 1971-72, Williamsport (Pa.) Hosp., 1972-73, Renovo (Pa.) Hosp., 1974; microbiologist Jersey Shore (Pa.) Hosp., 1974, N.Y. Hosp. and Cornell Med. Center, N.Y.C., 1974-75, Drekter and Heisler Labs., N.Y.C., 1975, North Shore Labs., Inc., Syosset, N.Y., 1976-78. Allied Health Professions trainee, 1975-77; lab. technician North Shore Hosp., Manhasset, N.Y., 1981-82, Nat. Health Labs. Inc., Bethpage, N.Y., 1982; intern internal medicine program Interfaith Med. Ctr., Bklyn., 1983-84; med. cons. Shapiro, Baines & Saasto, Mineola, N.Y., 1985-86. Author: The Hand Pocketbook of Infectious Agents and their Treatments. Mem. Am. Soc. Clin. Pathologists (registered med. technologist), Am. Soc. Microbiology, N.Y. Acad. Scis., Internat. Platform Assn. Home: PO Box 98 Roslyn NY 11576

HARTMAN, SHARON ANN, medical technologist, marketing consultant; b. Salt Lake City, Apr. 6, 1951; d. Gerald and Patricia (Pearsall) H. B.S., Westminister Coll., Salt Lake City, 1975; M.A., Central Mich. U., 1982. Med. technologist St. Anthony Hosp., Denver, 1975-78, Children's Hosp., Denver, 1978—; instr. Colo. Assn. Continuing Med. Lab. Edn., Inc., Denver, 1980—; mktg. cons. non-profit orgns., Denver, 1981—. Co-contbr.: Marketability, 1982. Bd. dirs. Colo. Assn. Continuing Med. Lab. Edn., Denver, 1980-84. Recipient Vol. Recognition award Tech. Assistance Ctr., Denver, 1982-85. Mem. Am. Mktg. Assn., Am. Soc. Clin. Pathologists, Denver Jr. League (v.p. edn. 1983-84, v.p. mktg. 1984-85, chmn. 1988 U.S. figure skating championships 1984-88). Republican. Episcopalian. Club: Colo. Mountain (Denver). Avocations: skiing, tennis, windsurfing, reading, cooking.

HARTMAN-GOLDSMITH, JOAN, art historian; b. Malden, Mass., June 3, 1933; d. Hyman and Ruth (Hadler) Lederman; m. Alan Hartman, Jan. 10, 1952 (div.); 1 dau., Hedy Hartman; m. 2d, Robert Goldsmith, Aug. 12, 1976. Instr., coordinator, initiator art history program, China Inst. in Am., N.Y.C., 1967-77; lectr. sch. continuing edn. NYU, N.Y.C., 1976-77; exec. officer, dir. public info. Jewish Mus., N.Y.C., 1977-80; dir. Inst. for Asian Studies, Inc., N.Y.C., 1981—; lectr. Cooper-Hewitt Mus. of Design (Smithsonian Instn.), 1976, 83, Oriental Ceramic Soc., Tokyo, 1983, Hong Kong, 1985; lectr. mus. Los Angeles, St. Louis, Pitts., Indpls., Buffalo, Rochester, N.Y., Toronto, Can., Denver Art Mus., Seattle Art Mus., Asian Art Mus. San Francisco; spl. lecture tour for Archaeol. Inst. Am., 1977; condr. seminars on Chinese jade, Met. Mus. Art, N.Y.C., 1977, 83; fellow in perpetuity, mem. vis. com. slide and photograph library Met. Mus. Art; trustee Indpls. Mus. Art; mem. art com. China House Gallery, N.Y.C.; program chmn. ann. conf. MAR/Assn. Asian Studies, Bucknel U., 1974; guest speaker Pearl of Scandinavia cruise to China, 1983. Am. corr. Oriental Art mag., London, 1963—. Contbr. articles and book revs. to publs. in field. Guest curator, author catalogue: Ancient Chinese Jades from the Buffalo Museum of Science, China Inst. Am., 1975, Three Dynasties of Jade, Indpls. Mus. Art, 1971, Chinese Jade through the Centuries, China Inst. Am.. 1968-69, Chinese Jade of Five Centuries, 1969. Author slide survey: Introduction to Chinese Art, 1973. Nat. Endowment grantee, vis. specialist Buffalo Mus. Sci., 1972, Indpls. Mus. Art, 1971; reviewer Nat. Endowment for Humanities, div. public programs, 1978—. Mem. Am. Oriental Soc., Assn. for Asian Studies (founding mem. Mid-Atlantic Region, 1972, sec. 1973, adv. council, 1974-75), Oriental Club of N.Y. Treas., Upper Eastside Jewish Community Council, N.Y.C. Office: Inst for Asian Studies PO Box 1603 FDR Sta New York NY 10022

HARTNESS, SANDRA JEAN, venture capitalist; b. Jacksonville Fla., Aug. 19, 1944; d. Harold H. and Viola M. (House) H. A.B., Ga. So. Coll., 1969; post-grad., San Francisco State Coll., 1970-71. Researcher Savannah (Ga.) Planning Commn., 1969, Environ. Analysis Group, San Francisco, 1970-71; dir. Mission Inn, Riverside, Calif., 1971-75; developer, venture capitalist Hartness Assocs., Laguna Beach, Calif., 1976—; ptnr. Western Neuro-Care Ctr., Tustin Calif.; dir. Laguna Bd. Realtors, 1982—. Recipient numerous awards for community service. Republican. Club: Soroptimists (Riverside, Calif.). Home: 32612 Adriatic Dr Laguna Niguel CA 92677 Office: Hartness Associates 301 Forest Ave Laguna Beach CA 92651

HARTSHORN, BESSIE MAUDE, motion picture production company executive; b. Peculiar, Mo., June 9, 1941; d. Thomas Charles and Minnie Marie (Markham) Jensen; children—Diana, Donna, Donald, Kevin; m. Donald Bruce Hartshorn, May 2, 1972 (div. June 1979). Student acctg. Citrus Coll., 1982. Statis. clk. Lerner's Shops, Los Angeles, 1974-79; bookkeeper Kurley's Dept. Store, East Los Angeles, Calif., 1979-83; fin. load cons. Fin. Services, Orange, Calif., 1983-84; v.p. fin., dir., sec. Moore & Assocs., Beverly Hills, Calif., 1984—. Mem. Nat. Assn. Female Execs. Avocations: roller skating; bowling; cooking; sewing; dancing. Home: 549 Arrow Hwy Glendora CA 91740

HARTSOCK, JANE MARIE, nurse educator; b. Rock Island, Ill., Nov. 19, 1948; d. George Vincent and Patricia Anna (Holland) Woeber; m. Donald Lee Hartsock, Jan. 16, 1971; children—Cara Elizabeth, David Vincent. B.S. in Nursing, Marycrest Coll., 1977; M.A., U. Iowa, 1982. Head nurse U.S. Naval Hosp., Great Lakes, Ill., 1970-71; staff nurse Moline Pub. Hosp. (Ill.), 1971-72, instr. Sch. Nursing, 1977—. Song leader Blue Grass Ch., 1982—. Mem. Am. Nurses Assn., Nurse Educators Assn. (pres. 1984-85), AAUW. Democrat. Roman Catholic. Club: Pioneer (Blue Grass, Iowa, sec. 1983—). Contbr. chpt. in book. Home: Rural Route #2 #3 Village Oaks Blue Grass IA 52726

HARTSOOK, ELMA W., civic worker; b. Mt. Gilead, Ohio; d. Isaac W. and Maria (Ulrey) Wheeler; grad. public schs.; m. F.M. Hartsook, June 26, 1919 (dec. Jan. 1951). Treas., Morrow County's Med. Aux., 1958—, Morrow County Mental Health, 1956—; del. Rep. Nat. Conv., 1956; mem. finance commn. Methodist Ch. Mem. 40 and 8, Am. Legion Aux. Clubs: Ladies Oriental Shrine, Order White Shrine of Jerusalem, Order Eastern Star (past matron, past pres. dist.). Home: 133 E Main St Cardington OH 43315

HARTUNG, BARBARA WOLTER, journalism educator, writer, consultant; b. Redlands, Calif., June 23, 1934; d. William Jennings and Margaret Lucille (Hedrick) Wolter; m. James Stanton Hartung, June 19, 1959; children—James Stanton, Kathleen Marie. A.B. in Journalism, San Diego State Coll., 1956, M.S. in Mass Communications, 1976; Ph.D. in Human Behavior, U.S. Internat. U., 1981. Reporter San Diego Union, 1956-66, cons., 1983—; freelance writer/publicist, San Diego, 1966-76; asst. prof. journalism San Diego State U., 1976-81, assoc. prof., 1981-86, prof., 1986—, chmn. dept. journalism, 1985-86, exec. asst. to pres., 1986—. Writer syndicated column Decor Score, Copley News Service, 1968-86. Fellow Gannett Teaching Workshop, Ind. U., 1977, Danforth Found., 1982. Mem. Soc. Profl. Journalists Sigma Delta Chi (pres. San Diego chpt. 1981-82, bd. dirs. Sigma Delta Chi Found. 1981-84), Calif. Press Women (treas. so. dist. 1982-83), Women in Communications (nat. chmn. continuing edn. 1980, Woman of Achievement award Far West region 1982), Assn. for Edn. in Journalism and Mass Communications, Inter-Am. Press Assn. Republican. Presbyterian. Office: Office of Pres San Diego State U San Diego CA 92182

HARTWIG, CLEO, sculptor; b. Webberville, Mich., Oct. 20, 1911; d. Albert and Julia (Klunzinger) H.; A.B., Western Mich. U., 1932, D.F.A. (hon.), 1973; student Internat. Sch. Art, Europe, 1935; m. Vincent Glinsky, 1951 (dec. Mar. 1975); 1 son, Albert. Tchr. pvt. schs., N.Y.C., 1935-42; instr. Cooper Union, 1945-46; sculpture instr. Montclair (N.J.) Art Mus., 1945-71. First one man show, 1943; included group exhbns. Nat. Acad., Pa. Acad., Detroit Inst. Arts, Art Inst. Chgo., Met. Mus., Phila. Mus., Whitney Mus., Newark Mus., Phila. Art Alliance, Denver Art Mus., Boston Mus. Sci., N.Y. Zool. Soc., Nebr. Art Assn., State U. Iowa, U. Ark., Des Moines Art Center, So. Vt. Art Center, U. Conn., Smithsonian Instn. Natural History, USIA in Europe, Nat. Inst. Arts and Letters, U. Minn., Canton Art Inst., N.Y. Bot. Garden, others; traveling one-man show, Can., U.S.; represented in permanent collections; Brookgreen Gardens, S.C., Newark Mus., Detroit Inst. Arts, Pa. Acad., Montclair Art Mus., Mt. Holyoke Coll., Western Mich. U., Oswego (N.Y.) Univ., Chrysler Mus., Norfolk, Va., NAD, Nat. Mus. Am. Art, Smithsonian Instn., So. Vt. Art Center. Recipient Kamperman Haass prize Mich. Artists Annual, 1943; Anna Hyatt Huntington prize for sculpture, 1945; L. Reusch & Co. prize N.Y. Soc. Ceramic Arts, 1946; Nat. Assn. Women Artists 1st prize for sculpture, 1951, medal of honor, 1967; Audubon Artists prize for sculpture, 1952, Pres.'s award, 1972; Today's Art award and medal of merit, 1975; award mural and sculpture competition Munson-Williams-Proctor Inst., 1958; Feist Meml. prize, 1968. Salomone prize, 1972; Jeffrey Childs Willis Meml. prize, 1975, 82; Amelia Peabody award, 1976; Silver medal Nat. Sculpture Soc., 1969; C. Percival Dietsch prize, 1976; Ellin Pi Speyer prize NAD, 1979; Chaim Gross Found. award, 1986. Fellow Nat. Sculpture Soc. (Leonard Meiselman prize 1978, L.J. Liskin purchase prize 1980, Proskauer prize 1984); mem. Audubon Artists, Sculptors Guild, Nat. Assn. Women Artists, Nat. Acad. Design (academician). Home: 9 Patchin Pl New York NY 10011 Studio: 41 Union Sq New York NY 10003

HARTWIG, JUDY KAREN, heating company executive; b. Rapid City, S.D., Jan. 17, 1940; d. Wesley Philip and Margaret Sara (Arnold) Smith; m. Orville R. Hartwig, Apr. 13, 1956; children—Alan, Sharie, Mark, Scott, Brian, Dawn. Owner, sec., bookkeeper Hartwig Heating, Watertown, S.D., 1962—. Chmn. Muscular Dystrophy Assn. Mothers March, Watertown, S.D., 1969-74, chmn. telethon, 1975-79. Republican. Methodist. Clubs: Women's Bowling League (sec. 1980—), Mens Golf League (sec. 1983—), Couples Golf League (sec. 1983—), Am. Legion Baseball Assn. (sec.-treas. 1984-85). Avocations: golfing; bowling; crafts. Office: Hartwig Heating 107 4th St SW Watertown SD 57201

HARTY, MARY ANN, librarian; b. Holden, Mass., Oct. 28, 1949; d. Martin Christopher and Arlene Frances (Joyal) H.; student Salzburg (Austria) U., 1972-73; B.A. cum laude, U. N.H., 1974; postgrad. Johns Hopkins U., 1974-75; M.S., Simmons Coll., 1979; m. John Anthony Domini, Dec. 17, 1976; 1 child, Vera Lee. Cataloging asst. Widener Library, Harvard U., 1976-77, intern Baker Library, 1977-79; head tech. services Learning Resource Center No. Essex Community Coll., 1979-80; library project adminstr. Strategic Systems div. GTE Products Corp., Westboro, Mass., 1980-82; research coordinator Oreg. State U. Found., Corvallis, 1984-85, grad. bus. program Willamette U., Salem, Oreg., 1985—. Mem. Spl. Libraries Assn. (co-editor Boston chpt. News Bull. 1981-82), Am. Soc. Info. Sci., LWV of Corvallis (editor Bull. 1983-84), Beta Phi Mu (pres. Beta Beta chpt. 1981-82). Home: 310 SW 7th St Corvallis OR 97333

HARTZ, LUETTA BERTHA, insurance company executive; b. Stevens Point, Wis., Sept. 29, 1947; d. Alfred Bernard Carl and Bertha Martha (Stauffer) Janz; student Madison (Wis.) Bus. Coll., 1965-66; m. James Patrick Hartz, Dec. 31, 1975. With Employers Ins. of Wausau (Wis.), 1966-68; casualty rater Sentry Ins. Co., Stevens Point, Wis., 1968-70, casualty supr., 1970-71, casualty trainor, 1971-72, customer service corr., 1972-74, bur. technician, 1974-75, customer service and acctg. mgr., Concord, Mass., 1975-79, personal lines property processing mgr., 1979-81, personal lines casualty processing mgr., 1981-83, comml. lines underwriting services mgr., 1983-85, comml. lines ops. mgr., 1985—. Campaign treas. Republican Party county clk. candidate, Portage County, Wis., 1972. Mem. Nat. Assn. Ins. Women, Mass. Assn. Ins. Women, U.S. Golf Assn. (asso.). Lutheran. Clubs: Maynard (Mass.) Country (bd. govs. 1984-86); Emblem (1st asst. marshal 1980-81, treas. 1981-83) (Concord, Mass.). Home: 40 Drummer Rd Acton MA 01720 Office: Sentry Ins Co Old Road to Nine Acre Corner Concord MA 01742

HARTZELL, IRENE JANOFSKY, psychologist; b. Los Angeles, 1938; d. Leonard and Annelies Janofsky. Vor-Diplom, U. Munich, 1961; B.A., U. Calif.-Berkeley, 1963, M.A., 1965; Ph.D., U. Oreg., 1970. Lic. psychologist, Calif., Oreg., Wash. Psychologist, Lake Washington Sch. Dist., Kirkland, Wash., 1971-72; staff psychologist VA Hosp., Seattle, 1970-71, Long Beach, Calif., 1973-74; dir. parent edn. Childrens Hosp., Orange, Calif., 1975-78; clin. psychologist Kaiser Permanente, Van Nuys, Calif., 1979—; clin. instr. pediatrics dept. U. Calif. Med. Coll., Irvine, 1975-78. Author: Expert Student's Advantage, 1986; contbr. articles to profl. jours. Legis. intern Oreg. Legislature, 1974-75. U. Oreg. fellow, 1969. Mem. Am. Psychol. Assn., Pi Lambda Theta. Office: Kaiser Permanente Med Group 13746 Victory Blvd Van Nuys CA 91401

HARVEY, BARBARA, lawyer, legal educator; b. N.Y.C., Feb. 19, 1946; d. William and Sylvia (Abramson) Masin. Student Antioch Coll., 1962-65; B.A., Wayne State U., 1968, J.D., 1975. Bar: Mich., 1975. Law clk. to C.W. Joiner, U.S. dist. judge, Detroit, 1975-77; assoc. firm Barris, Sott, Denn & Driker, Detroit, 1977-79; asst. prof. Law Sch., Wayne State U., Detroit, 1979-82, adj. prof., 1982—; legal dir. ACLU of Mich., Detroit, 1983-86; practice labor law, Detroit, 1982—; mem. nat. adv. bd. Assn. for Union Democracy, N.Y.C., 1981—; mem. lawyers adv. com. Teamsters Rank and File Def. and Edn. Fund, Detroit, 1981-83. Article and book rev. editor Wayne Law Rev., 1975; contbr. articles to publs. Dir. Met. Detroit br. ACLU of Mich., 1977—, mem. lawyers com., 1979—, exec. sec., 1981-85, v.p., 1985—; hearing referee Mich. Civil Rights Commn., Lansing and Detroit, 1983—. Clin. program grantee U.S. Dept. Edn., 1980, 81; editor's scholar Wayne Law Sch., 1974-75; Law Sch. Fund scholar, 1973-75. Mem. ABA, State Bar Mich., Detroit Bar Assn., Assn. Trial Lawyers, Am., Mich. Trial Lawyers Assn. Office: One Kennedy Sq Suite 1930 Detroit MI 48226

HARVEY, BONNIE EILEEN, nurse, educational administrator; b. Homestead, Pa., Dec. 28, 1947; d. John Henry and Eileen T. (O'Leary) Boyle; m. James Wayne Harvey, May 23, 1967; children—Margaret, Timothy. R.N., Philipsburg State Gen. Hosp., Pa., 1977; B.S.N., U. Tampa, Fla., 1985. R.N. Fla., Pa. Dir. edn. Sun City Regional Med. Ctr., Hosp. Corp. Am., Sun City Center, Fla., 1983—; cons. Sandman Pre-sch. Sarasota, Fla., 1979—. Sec. PAC, 1984—. Mem. Am. Assn. Critical Care Nurses, Fla. Hosp. Assn. Republican. Roman Catholic. Home: 8279 Madonna Pl Sarasota FL 33580 Office: 4016 State Rd 674 Sun City Center FL 33570

HARVEY, BONNIE NEWCOME, chemistry and microbiology educator; b. Grafton, W.Va., Nov. 9, 1913; d. John Allen and Sallie (Marquess) Newcome; m. Wilson Ward Harvey, Oct. 24, 1941; children—John Calvin, Sarah Susan Harvey Haggerty. A.B., Fairmont State U., 1935; postgrad. W.Va. U., 1936-37, 68-69. Life teaching cert. in scis. Tchr. chemistry, physics, biology and history Flemington High Sch. (W.Va.), 1936-41; tchr. Am. history West Fairmont High Sch., Fairmont, W.Va., 1942-43; tchr. gen. sci. Benjamin Franklin High Sch., Parkersburg, W.Va., 1954-56; tchr. gen. sci. and geography Magnolia High Sch., New Martinsville, W.Va., 1958-61; instr. microbiology, clin. tech. biology and psychology, Potomac State Coll. of W.Va. U., Morgantown, 1966-76, counselor Potomac State Coll. Earth Week, 1969-84, mem. vis. com., 1979—. Counselor Tri High Y Girls, YMCA, New Martinsville, 1958-61; mem. W.Va. Nature Conservancy, 1966-84; Bible class tchr. 1st United Methodist Ch., Keyser, W.Va., 1961-84; treas. Ladies Oriental Shrine Club, Children's Hosps., 1980-84; sec. Romney dist. United Meth. Women, 1961-65, 79-83, group membership chmn.; historian Burlington Home for Children and Youth Aux., 1980-84; sci. fair judge Mineral County Bd. Edn., Keyser, 1967-84. Recipient counselor award Tri High Y, YMCA, 1961. Mem. West August Hist. Soc., W.Va. Acad. Sci. (life), W.Va. Edn. Assn., Mineral County Hist. Soc. (Order of Crozet 1978, mus. curator), DAR (regent Potomac Valley 1977-83), Alpha Delta Kappa (sec., historian 1974-84). Republican. Club: Mineral County. Lodge: Order Eastern Star.

HARVEY, CRETE BOWMAN, grain and livestock farmer, horse breeder; b. Butte, Ill., July 10, 1929; s. John D. and Crete (Dillon) Bowman; m. Douglas G. Harvey, Jan. 1, 1949 (div.); children—Crete B. Aldrich, Douglas G., Nicholas D.; m. Stanley C. Luhman, Dec. 15, 1979. Grad. high sch., Fairfax County, Va. Grain and livestock farmer, Arabian horse breeder Harvey Farms, Sterling, Ill. Trustee, Endowment Fund of YWCA; mem. women's aux. Community Gen. Hosp.; mem. bd. Mid-Continent Livestock Expo; co-founder Sterling Rock Falls Republican Women, 1964; mem. Nat. Resources Adv. Council, 1978-80; Ill. Rep. nat. committeewoman, 1976-80, 80-84; mem. Farm Credit Bd., 1984-86; active Blackhawk area council Boy Scouts Am., Civic Music Assn., Art Inst. Chgo., Whiteside County 4-H. Mem. Nat. Suffolk Sheep Assn., Red Angus Assn., Top Farmers Am. Assn., Am. Horse Council, World Arabian Horse Orgn., Internat. Arabian Horse Assn., Arabian Horse Registry (bd. trustees), Arabian Horse Trust (mem. bd.), Farm Bur. Assn. Ill., Whiteside County Port Producers, Sterling C. of C., Ill. Hist. Soc., Rock Falls C. of C. Presbyterian. Home and Office: Route 2 Fulfs Rd Sterling IL 61081

HARVEY, DIANE KADUSCWICZ, librarian, editor; b. Kearny, N.J., Dec. 18, 1952; d. Adam Stephen and Virginia (De Carlucci) Kaduscwicz; m. David John Harvey, Feb. 4, 1978; 1 child, Katherine Craven. B.A., Douglass Coll., 1974; M.L.S., Rutgers U., 1975; M.A., Johns Hopkins U., 1983. Planning librarian Middlesex County Planning Bd., New Brunswick, N.J., 1975-76; info. services librarian Rutgers U. Libraries, New Brunswick, 1976-79; head govt. publs. Eisenhower Library, Johns Hopkins U., Balt., 1979-83, mem. collection devel. staff Sch. Advanced Internat. Studies Library, 1985—; cons. New Sch. Social Research, N.Y.C., 1977. Assoc. editor Serials Rev., 1983-85; column editor Govt. Pub. Rev., 1983-85, editorial adv. bd., 1985—; contbr. articles to profl. jours. Mem. ALA, Documents Assn. N.J. Democrat. Roman Catholic.

HARVEY, DOROTHY MAY, newspaper editor; b. Bartlesville, Okla., Apr. 3, 1922; d. Paul and Vila May (Ray) H.; B.S. in Commerce, Okla. A&M Coll., 1950. Tech. asst. research dept. Phillips Petroleum Co., 1942-48; program dir., pub. relations dir. Topeka YWCA, 1950-55; asso. editor Capper's Weekly, Topeka, 1955-73, editor, 1974—. Mem. Women in Communications. Republican. Methodist. Home: 2311 Hazelton Ct Topeka KS 66606 Office: 616 Jefferson St Topeka KS 66607

HARVEY, ELAINE DEANE, data processing executive, consultant, systems analyst; b. San Antonio, July 14, 1945; d. Alvin Dean and Dorothy Jean Stratton. Student Ind. U., 1963-66. Systems analyst, programmer North Am. Reinsurance, N.Y.C., 1968-69; cons. Mauchly Mgmt. Services, Wayne, Pa., 1969-71; systems analyst, programmer Fidelity Mutual Life Ins., Phila., 1971-78; project leader Catalytic Inc., Phila., 1978-81; dir. tech. services Data Tek Inc., Phila., 1981-85; v.p. systems Chestnut Data Systems, Phila., 1985—. Mem. Network for Women in computer tech., North Eastern Region User Group. Republican. Episcopalian. Office: Chestnut Data Systems 1719 Delancey Pl Philadelphia PA 19103

HARVEY, KATHERINE ABLER, civic worker; b. Chgo., May 17, 1946; d. Julius and Elizabeth (Engelman) Abler; student La Sorbonne, Paris, 1965-66; A.A.S., Bennett Coll, 1968; m. Julian Whitcomb Harvey, Sept. 7, 1974. Asst. librarian McDermott, Will & Emery, Chgo., 1969-70; librarian Chapman & Cutler, Chgo., 1970-73, Coudert Freres, Paris, 1973-74; adviser, organizer library Lincoln Park Zool. Soc. and Zoo., Chgo., 1977-79, mem. soc.'s women's bd., 1976—, chmn. library com., 1977-79, mem. exec. com., 1977—, sec., 1979-81; mem. jr. bd. Alliance Française de Chgo., 1970-76, treas., mem. exec. com., 1971-73, 75-76, mem. women's bd., 1977-80; mem. Fred Harvey Fine Arts Found., 1976—; hon. life mem. Chgo. Symphony Soc., 1975—; mem. Phillips Acad. Alumni Council, Andover, Mass., 1977-81; mem. acad.'s bicentennial celebration com, class celebration leader, 1978, co-chmn. for Chgo. acad.'s bicentennial campaign, 1977-79; mem. women's bd. Northwestern Meml. Hosp., 1979—, treas., chmn. fin. com., 1981-84; mem. women's bd. Lyric Opera Chgo., 1979—, exec. com. 1980—, treas., 1983-84; mem. Guild Chgo. Hist. Soc., 1978—, Women's Assn. Chgo. Symphony Orch., 1979—; mem. aux. bd. Art Inst. Chgo., 1978—, life mem. Antiquarian Soc. of Art Inst. Chgo.; bd. dirs. Found Art Scholarships, 1982-83, Grant Park Concert Soc., 1986—; mem. Know Your Chgo. com. U. Chgo., 1981-84; dir. Glen Ellyn Children's Chorus, 1983—; founder, chmn. pres.'s com. Glen Ellyn Children's Chorus, 1983; mem. women's bd. Chgo. City Ballet, 1983; mem. 50th anniversary celebration Grant Park Concerts, 1984. Clubs: Arts, (Chgo.), Friday (corr. sec. 1981-83), Casino (gov. 1982—), (sec. 1984-85, 1st v.p. 1984—), Cliff Dwellers. Home: 1209 N Astor St Chicago IL 60610

HARVEY, LYNNE COOPER, broadcasting executive, civic worker; b. St. Louis County, Mo.; d. William A. and Margaret (Kehr) Cooper; A.B., Washington U., St. Louis, 1939, M.A., 1940; m. Paul Harvey, June 4, 1940; 1 son, Paul (Harvey) Aurandt. Broadcaster edni. program Sta. KXOX, St. Louis, 1940; broadcaster-writer women's news and WAC Variety Show, Fort Custer, Mich., 1941-43; gen. mgr. Paul Harvey News, ABC, 1944—; pres. Paulynne Prodns., Ltd., Chgo., 1968—, exec. producer Paul Harvey Comments, 1968—. Pres. woman's bd. Mental Health Assn. Greater Chgo., 1967-71, v.p. bd. dirs., 1966-71; pres. woman's aux. Infant Welfare Soc. Chgo., 1969-72 bd. dirs., 1969—; nominating chmn. Salvation Army Woman's Adv. Bd., 1967-69; reception chmn. Community Lectures. Bd., Oak Park-River Forest, Ill., 1963-69; pres. Mothers Council, River Forest, 1961-62; charter bd. mem. Gottlieb Meml. Hosp., Melrose Park, Ill.; mem. adv. bd. Nat. Christian Heritage Found., 1964—recipient Religious Heritage of Am. award, 1974; trustee John Brown U., 1980—. Mem. McGraw's Wildlife Found., Phi Beta Kappa, Kappa Delta Pi, Phi Sigma Iota, Eta Sigma Phi. Clubs: Chicago Golf, Woman's Athletic, Press (Chgo.); Nineteenth Century Woman's, Oak Park Country. Editor, compiler: The Rest of the Story, Destiny, 1983. Office: PO Box 77 River Forest IL 60305

HARVEY, MADELINE JEAN, public relations director, assistant hospital administrator; b. Phila., Nov. 2,; d. Arthur and Eva (Palermo) Viola; m. James Earl Harvey, Apr. 1; children—Arthur J., Alexis M. B.A., in Languages, U. Pa., 1955; student journalism Stockton Coll., 1976, pub. speaking, Atlantic Community coll., 1979. Asst. to med. dir. Phila. Gen. Hosp., 1956-60; dir. pub. relations and devel., asst. to adminstr. Children's Seashore House, Atlantic City, 1968—. Bd. mem. Atlantic County Homemakers, Atlantic Performing Arts Ctr., Atlantic City, 1980-83; hostess Miss Am. Hostess com., Atlantic City, 1978—; 1st v.p. Atlantic City Womens Chamber. Recipient Certification award Nat. Assn. Hosp. Devel., 1980, First prize, 1982; Named to People to Watch Atlantic City Mag., 1983. Mem. Am. Soc. Mktg. and Pub. Relations, Nat. Soc. Fund Raising Execs., N.J. Soc. Hosp. Pub. Relations, Nat. Soc. Hosp. Devel., Bus. and Profl. Women's Club (pres. 1980-81), Zonta Club Internat. (pres. 1978-80, pres., chmn. conf. 1977-78, nominated districtor dictor 1982), Greater Atlantic City C. of C. (pub. relations dir. 1978-80, dir. 1980-84), Atlantic City Women's C. of C. (1st v.p. 1985—). Republican. Roman Catholic. Home: 2701 Brigantine Ave Brigantine NJ 08203

HARVEY, MARY SHIELDA, cytotechnologist; b. Statesboro, Ga., May 31, 1949; d. James Kalip and Theatus (Kirby) Deal; m. Richard C. Harvey, June 30, 1968; 1 son, Sean Christian. A.A., Edison Community Coll., 1971; grad. Sch. Cytotech., U. Miami, 1974. Bench cytotechnologist, then sect. head cytology dept. Naples Community Hosp. (Fla.), 1974-81; cytotechnologist TBR Clin. Lab., Statesboro, Ga., 1981—, chief cytologist, 1981—. Mem. exec. bd. chpt. Am. Cancer Soc. Recipient Sword of Hope, Am. Cancer Soc., 1976. Mem. Am. Soc. Cytology, So. Assn. Cytotech., Am. Soc. Clin. Pathologists (assoc.), Ga. Soc. Cytotech. Democrat. Baptist. Home: 502 Zetterower Rd Statesboro GA 30458 Office: 303 Florence Ave Statesboro GA 30458

HARVEY, RHOBA JANE NEBLETT, clinical social worker, educator; b. Charlotte, Tenn., Nov. 7, 1928; d. John B. and Augusta Elizabeth (Tippit) Neblett; B.S., U. Tenn., 1952, M.S.S.W., 1968; postgrad. U. Chgo., 1957, U. St. Andrews (Scotland), 1978; 1 dau., Elizabeth Lee. Child welfare worker Tenn. Dept. Pub. Welfare, 1954-59, sr. child welfare worker, Gibson County, 1961-66, field supr., Shelby County, 1966-69; asst. prof. child devel. U. Tenn. Center for Health Scis., Memphis, 1969—, developer, dir. residential tng. program, 1970-76, clin. social worker, 1969—; supr. psychiat. social work Sequoyah Ctr., Memphis, 1981—; pvt. practice, 1966—. Licensed nursing home adminstr., Tenn. Mem. Nat. Assn. Social Workers (dir. Memphis chpt. 1976-78), Acad. Clin. Social Workers, Am. Assn. on Mental Deficiency, AAUP, Zeta Tau Alpha, Presbyterian. Club: D.A.R. Home: Box 112 St Paul Rd Charlotte TN 37036 Office: 865 Poplar Ave Memphis TN 38105

HARVEY, VANDA LEE, title company financial executive; b. Marietta, Okla., May 24, 1942; d. George Van and Anna Lee (Sanders) Burkhart; m. Jerry Don Harvey, Oct. 16, 1964 (div. 1970); children—Jeffrey Lynn, Kimberly Ann. Student Odessa Jr. Coll., 1960-61, So. Meth. U., 1975, Am. Mgmt. Assn. courses, 1980. Statistician, interviewer Tex. Employment Commn., Vernon, 1963-69; office and acctg. mgr. Metro Materials Mktg., Plano, Tex., 1969-75; staff acct. Sanger Harris, Dallas, 1976; office and acctg. mgr. Austin Shoes-Greenco Shoes, Dallas, 1976-79; asst. treas., controller Hexter Fair Title Co., Dallas, 1979—; dir., fin. adv. Witts & Wilson, Attys., Dallas, 1980—; controller Lawyers Title Agy. of Denton, Tex., 1980—; mem. state com. trust fund acctg., Tex. State Bd. Ins.; Speaker univ., high sch. Editor, collaborator: Parity (D.A. Witts), 1979, Theft (D.A. Witts), 1982. Club: Plaza Athletic (gov.). Office: Hexter Fair Title Co 1307 Pacific Ave Dallas TX 75202

HARVEY, VIRGINIA GRACE, oil water service company executive; b. Rockwood, Tenn., Sept. 27, 1920; d. Rufus Norman and Georgia Ann (Long) Erwin; m. Thomas Dexter Harvey, July 14, 1943 (dec. Dec. 1979); children—Georgia Ann, Pamela Lee, Michelle Virginia. Student U. Tenn., 1939. Sec.-treas. Pacific Airlines, Burbank, Calif., 1945-47; v.p. Thomas D. Harvey Co., Dallas, 1960-75; sec. Erwin Oil Water Service Co., Ft. Worth, 1980—. Pres., Central Tex. Ladies Golf Assn., Dallas, 1960, Dallas Womens Golf Assn., 1962; pres., tournament dir. Civitan Womens Golf Classic, Dallas, 1963, 66; chmn. ladies com. Byron Nelson Classic, Dallas, 1968-72; pres., chmn. Kidney Found. Tex., 1972; bd. dirs. ARC; precinct chmn. Dallas Republican Com., 1968. Recipient Golden award Exchange Club, Dallas, Sport award City of Dallas, 1966; Golf award Salesmanship Club, Dallas, 1976; charity award Civitan Club, Dallas, 1966. Home: 6222 Waggoner Dr Dallas TX 75230

HARVEY, VIRGINIA NICHOLSON, anesthesiologist; b. N.Y.C., Jan. 2, 1948; d. Edmund Newton and Sara Jeanette (Hickman) H. B.A., Conn. Coll., 1969; M.S., Boston Coll., 1972; M.D., Albany Med. Coll., 1977. Diplomate Am. Bd. Anesthesiology. Intern, UCLA, 1977-78; resident ob-gyn, 1978-80; resident anesthesia U. Calif.-Irvine, Orange, 1980-82; practice medicine specializing in anesthesiology Am. River Hosp., Carmichael Calif., 1982—. Mem. Am. Soc. Anesthesiologists, Physicians for Social Responsibility, Valley Anesthesia Soc., Calif. Soc. Anesthesiologists, Am. Med. Women's Assn., NOW. Home: 6125 Barker Elms Ct Carmichael CA 95608 Office: Am River Hosp 4747 Eagle Rd Carmichael CA 95608

HARVEY, VIRGINIA PEASELEY, organization consultant; b. Richmond, Va.; d. Gabriel B. and Florence V. (White) Peaseley; B.S., in Chemistry, U. Md., 1929; M.S. in Phy. Edn., U. Wis., 1932; Ed.D. in Ednl. Psychology, Western Res. U., 1963; postgrad. Temple U., 1966-67; m. E. W. Harvey, Apr. 8, 1939 (div. 1958); 1 dau., Virginia Lynn Harvey Schmitt. Instr. U. Mich., 1932-38; asst. prof. Kent (Ohio) State U., 1938-42, 44-46-54, assoc. prof., 1954-64, prof., 1964-76, prof. emeritus, 1976—, faculty senate vice chairperson, 1973-74. Vis. prof. group dynamics Temple U., summer 1967; mem. Nat. Tng. Lab. Inst. Applied Behavioral Sci.; pres. V. Harvey & Assocs. Recipient Disting. Tchr. award Kent State U., 1971, Service award Phi Delta Kappa, 1972. Amy Morris Homans fellow, 1962-63; licensed psychologist, Ohio. Mem. Am. Soc. Tng. and Devel., Orgn. Devel. Network, Kappa Kappa Gamma, Alpha Psi Omega, Delta Psi Kappa, Phi Delta Kappa, Omicron Delta Kappa. Home: 1315 Greenwood Ave Kent OH 44240

HARVITT, ADRIANNE STANLEY, lawyer; b. Chgo., May 15, 1954; d. Stanley and Maryln (Loye) H.; m. Donald M. Heinrich, Aug. 27, 1977. A.B., U. Chgo., 1975, M.B.A., 1976; J.D. cum laude, Ill. Inst. Tech./Chgo.-Kent Coll. Law, 1980. Bar: Ill. 1980, U.S. Dist. Ct. (no. dist.) Ill. 1980, U.S. Ct. Appeals (7th cir.) 1985, U.S. Supreme Ct. 1985. Fin. analyst Bell and Howell Co., Chgo., 1976-77; trial atty. U.S. Commodity Futures Trading Commn., Chgo., 1980-83; assoc. Hannafan & Handler, Ltd., Chgo., 1983-85; ptnr. Harvitt & Gekas, Ltd., Chgo., 1985—. Mem. ABA, Ill. State Bar Assn., Chgo. Bar Assn., U. Chgo. Women's Bus. Group. Office: Harvitt & Gekas Ltd 11 S LaSalle St Chicago IL 60603

HARWOOD, BETH MARGARET, communication consultant; b. Milw., July 2, 1952; d. James Richard and Lillian Lorraine (Sattler) H.; student Marquette U., 1970-72, postgrad. Law Sch., 1977-78; B.S., U. Wis., Milw., 1975, M.A., 1979; m. Stephen Charles Raymonds, May 27, 1978; children—Adam Harwood, Laura Rose, James Henry. Teaching asst. U. Wis., Milw., 1975-77, lectr., 1979-80, coordinator communication program, 1979-83; mgmt. cons., communication specialist, 1977—. Program coordinator Woman to Woman Conf., 1980-81, bd. dirs., 1980-82; class rep. Divine Savior-Holy Angels High Sch., 1970—. Mem. Am. Soc. for Tng. and Devel., Nat. Speakers Assn., Wis. Profl. Speakers Assn. Home: N85 W 14995 Knoll Terr Menomonee Falls WI 53051 Office: 929 N 6th St Milwaukee WI 53202

HARWOOD, ELEANOR CASH, librarian; b. Buckfield, Me., May 29, 1921; d. Leon Eugene and Ruth (Chick) Cash; B.A., Am. Internat. Coll., 1943; B.S., New Haven State Tchrs. Coll., 1955; m. Burton H. Harwood, Jr., June 21, 1944 (div. 1953); children—Ruth (Mrs. William R. Cline), Eleanor, James Burton. Librarian, Rathbun Meml. Library, East Haddam, Conn., 1955-56; asst. librarian Kent (Conn.) Sch., 1956-63; cons. to Chester (Conn.) Pub. Library, 1965-71. Served from ensign to lt. (j.g.) USNR, 1944-46. Mem. Am., Conn. library assns., Chester Hist. Soc. (trustee 1970-72), D.A.V., Am. Legion Aux., Soc. Mayflower Descs. Mem. United Ch. Author: (with John G. Park) The Independent School Library and the Gifted Child, 1956; The Age of Samuel Johnson, LL.D., 1959. sec., Home: Maple St Chester CT 06412

HARWOOD, LYNN CATHARINE, insurance agency owner; b. New Orleans, Mar. 19, 1941; d. John Michael and Marguerite Marie (Ferry) H.; B.A., La. State U., 1962. With Met. Life Ins. Co., New Orleans, 1968-78; mgr. Can. Life, Dallas, 1978—; owner, partner Ins. Service Center, Dallas, 1980—; v.p. Bohs-Harwood Co., Dallas, 1981—; pres. Invideo Prodns., Inc., Dallas, 1981—; partner B&H Investments; leader-trainer counselor selling, exec. mktg. skills. Recipient nat. quality award La. Life Leaders; C.L.U. Mem. Nat. Assn. C.L.U.s, Nat. Assn. Life Underwriters. Home: 5609 Del Roy Dr Dallas TX 75230 Office: 137 World Trade Center PO Box 581365 Dallas TX 75258

HASHIM, ELINOR M., librarian, government official; b. Pittsfield, Maine, Dec. 13, 1933. B.A., U. Vt., 1955; M.S., Conn. State Coll., 1970. Asst. mgr. corp. library Perkin-Elmer Corp., Norwalk, Conn., 1976-82; mem., chmn. Nat. Commn. on Libraries and Info. Sci., Washington, 1982—. Mem. ALA, Conn. State Library Bd. (chmn. 1976—). Address: Nat Commn on Libraries and Info Sci 7th and D Sts SW Washington DC 20024*

HASKELL, DARA, holography company executive; b. N.Y.C., Sept. 16, 1948; d. Harry C. and Juliet (Rosenthal) Robertson; m. Aug. 1976, (div. 1981); m. Bourveau Louis, Oct. 13, 1984. B.A., George Washington U., 1970; postgrad. Colgate U., 1970. Adminstr., Health Clinic, Dalhousie, India, 1970-73; minister Fellowship/Friends Ch., San Francisco, 1975-77; ptnr. Diamond Brokerage A. Haskell & Co., San Francisco, 1977-80; mktg. dir. Pathology Assoc. Lab., Los Angeles, 1981-83; pres., chief fin. officer Third Dimension Arts, Inc., San Rafael, Calif., 1983—. Author: San Francisco Bus. Jour., 1983. Mem. N.Am. Assn. Holographers (v.p. No. Calif. chpt. 1984—). Club: Les Amis du Vin (Mill Valley, Calif.). Avocations: gourmet cooking; wine appreciation; world travel. Home: 150 Monte Vista Mill Valley CA 94941 Office: Third Dimension Arts Inc 1414 4th St San Rafael CA 94901

HASKEW, JOYCE ANNETTE, engineering firm executive; b. Westerly, R.I., Mar. 7, 1942; d. John Victor and Isabella (MacGonegal) Biswurm, Sr.; m. Kenneth Lacy Haskew, Apr. 20, 1960; children—Kevin Dean, Scot Lacy. A.A., Am. River Coll., 1961. Delineator, State of Calif., Sacramento, 1961-66; engr. Kenneth L. Haskew, Ft. Bragg, Calif., and Ely, Nev., 1971-77; estimator, engr. Park Shah Abbas Co., Esfahan, Iran, 1977-78; civil drafter Pillsbury Engring., Reno, Nev., 1978-79; real estate saleswoman Preferred Equities, Reno, 1979-80; engr. Haskew Engring. Inc., Ely, Nev., 1979—; vice chmn. Regional Planning Commn., Ely, 1983-84; chmn. No. Nev. Pvt. Industry Council, Reno, 1983. Mem. Nat. Assn. Realtors, Ely C. of C. (co-chmn. legis. com. 1983). Republican. Baptist. Club: Sweet Adelines (Ely, Nev., and Valdez, Alaska). Office: 411 2d St Goldfield NV 89013

HASKIN, GRETCHEN CLAIRE, writer, photographer; b. Plainfield, N.J., Nov. 18, 1936; d. Harry Wolfe and Marguerite Cecilia (Granieri) Swartz; m. David Haskin, Jan. 1971; 1 dau., Claudia Leslie. B.A. with honors, U. Hawaii, 1958. Author: Imperial Affair, 1981; Fitness for Senior Citizens, 1985; contbr. articles and photographs to horse show mags., 1972—; editor for legal and med. publs.

HASLANGER, MARTHA LOUISE, filmmaker; b. Dearborn, Mich., Sept. 16, 1947; d. John Frederick and June (Loftsgordon) Anderson; A.B. with honors in Germanic Lit., Denison U.; M.F.A., Eastern Mich. U. Fellow in film, Bunting Inst., Cambridge, Mass.; film shows include; Whitney Mus. of Am. Art, N.Y.C., 1976, Berlin's (Germany) Arsenal, 5th Internat. Film Competition at Knokke-Heist, Belgium, London (Eng.) Filmmakers' Co-op, the Millenium, N.Y.C., The Collective, N.Y.C., Chgo. Filmgroup, and Munich (Germany) Stadtmuseum, Whitney Biennial, 1979, 81, 83, 3d Internat. Avant-Garde Film Festival, London, Festival Internat. du Jeune Cinema, Hyérès, France, Film as Art, Arts Council Gt. Britain, Internationale Filmfestspiele, Berlin, Edinburgh Film Festival; video shows include: Sao Paulo (Brazil) Biennial, Whitney Mus. of Art, Inst. of Contemporary Art, Phila.; judge numerous film festivals, panels. Recipient grant for video work, Nat. Endowment for the Arts, film grant Royal Film Archives of Belgium and the AGFA-GEVAERT Corp., grant Radcliffe Inst. and Harvard Corp., artist grant CAPS, N.Y. State; Jerome Found. grantee. Author: Memory Book, 1977; Goldy Dances 1978; contbr. works to numerous profl. mags. and jours. Films in collection of Am. Fedn. Arts, Royal Film Archives Belgium, Arts Council Gt. Britain, Internat. Forum of Young Cinema of Berlin, New Eng. Found. for Arts.

HASS, RUTH PEYSER, travel agency executive; b. N.Y.C., Jan. 12, 1927; d. Meyer Jacob and Dora (Haber) Peyser; m. Paul J. Hass, Mar. 30, 1946; 1 child, Jeffrey Karl. Student U. Vt., 1945; B.A., Hunter Coll., 1947; postgrad. NYU, 1963-65, Manhattan Coll., 1967. Tchr. pub. schs., N.Y.C., 1947, Yonkers, N.Y., 1963; v.p. Artful Inc., N.Y.C., 1971-75, G.S.S., N.Y.C., 1975-80; pres. All Tickets Inc., Ft. Lee, N.J., 1980—; cons. for audience devel. Mem. Am. Bus Assn., Nat. Tour Assn., Meeting Planners Assn., Ont. Motor Assn. Democrat. Jewish. Lodges: Hadassah, B'nai B'rith Women. Avocations: tennis; gardening; theatre attendance. Office: All Tickets Inc 2337 Lemoine Ave Fort Lee NJ 07024

HASSEL, ADELINE SUSAN SILVERI, arts publication executive; b. Mahanoy City, Pa., Feb. 16, 1938; s. Agabito Albert and Assunta Buzzeli Silveri; m. George Francis Hassel, July 5, 1958 (div. July 1972); 1 child, Holly Ann. Student Pa. State U., Schuylkill, 1972, Lehigh County Community Coll., 1975, Cedar Crest Coll., 1978. Salesperson Wolowitz Inc., Pottsville, Pa., 1964-66; sales mgr. Clothes Hut, Pottsville, 1973-74; sales Nan Carlby Inc., Allentown, Pa., 1975-77; pres., pub. Admar Assocs./Theatrical Faces Mag., Allentown, Pa., 1977—. Corr. sec. Pottsville Community Players, 1968-71, rec. sec., 1968-71, advt., publicity mgr., 1968-71, pres., 1968-71; co founder, bd. dirs. TheatrEast, Lehigh Valley, Pa., 1975-77. Recipient Disting. Sales award Sales & Mktg. Execs., Allentown, Pa., 1983. Fellow Sales and Mktg. Execs. Allentown, Nat. Assn. Profl. Sales Women. Republican. Roman Catholic. Avocations: choir; historical biographies; theatre. Office: Admar Assocs Theatrical Faces Inc 136 S 4th St Allentown PA 19102

HASSENPFLUG, KATHY COLLINS, human resource management executive; b. Washington, July 19, 1952; d. Gerald Sherman and Jane (Hampton) Collins; m. Dennis Harold Hassenpflug, June 19, 1982; children—Jennifer Ann, Kevin Michael. B.S., Va. Inst. Tech., 1974; postgrad. Nat. U., San Diego, 1978, U. Tex.-Arlington, 1981, U. Calif.-San Diego, 1977. Personnel adminstr. TRW Data Systems, San Diego, 1974-78, personnel supr. TRW Communications Systems and Services, Hawthorne, Calif., 1978-80, human relations facility mgr. TRW Customer Service, Grand Prairie, Tex., 1980—. Chmn. com. One Single Way of Calvary Temple, Irving, Tex., 1980-82; tchr. North County Christian Ctr. Sunday Sch., Escondido, Calif., 1974-76. Mem. Am. Soc. Personnel Adminstrn., Mid-Cities Personnel Assn., Metroplex Recreation Council, Nat. Employee Services and Recreation Assn., Tex. Computer Industry Council (edn. com.), Dallas Personnel Assn., Arlington C. of C., Va. Inst. Tech. Alumni Assn. (bd. dirs.), Delta Zeta (sec. 1975-76). Republican. Home: 1203 Hillcrest Dr Euless TX 76039 Office: TRW Customer Service Div 1301 Ave R Grand Prairie TX 75050

HASSETT, CAROL ALICE, psychologist; b. Bklyn., Apr. 19, 1947; d. Joseph and Anna (Portanova) Lusardi; B.S., St. John's U., 1968; M.Ed., Hofstra U., 1974, Ph.D. in Psychology (teaching asst.), 1981; m. John J. Hassett, June 29, 1968; 1 son, John J. Tchr. Day Elem. Sch., Bklyn., 1968-69; psychologist Nassau County Dept. Drug and Alcohol also Mental Health Assn. Nassau County, East Meadow, N.Y., 1981-84; supervising psychologist Queens Outreach Project, 1985—; pvt. practice clin. psychology, 1984—; adj. asst. prof. Hofstra U., 1980—. Bd. dirs. Malverne Vol. Ambulance Corps, 1976—;

bd. govs. Kings County Cadet Corps, 1966-72. Cert. advanced emergency med. technician, pre-hosp. critical care technician; permanently cert. tchr., N.Y. Mem. Am. Psychol. Assn. Republican. Roman Catholic. Contbr. articles profl. jours. Home: 105 Franklin Ave Malverne NY 11565 Office: 230 Hilton Ave Hempstead NY 11550

HASSETT, JACQUELYN ANN, nurse; b. La Crosse, Wis., Sept. 13, 1930; d. Frank Alois and Anne Helena (Milos) Spika; m. James John Hassett, Aug. 22, 1953; children—Barbara, Linda, Jean, Jane, Nancy, James David. Diploma in Nursing, St. Anthony de Padua Sch. Nursing, Chgo., 1951; B.S., Barat Coll., 1977; M.S., George Williams Coll., 1983. R.N., Ill., Wis. Operating room nurse VA Hosp., North Chicago, Ill., 1951-54; part-time nursing positions St. Therese Hosp., Waukegan, Ill., 1954-58, Johnson Motors, Waukegan, 1958-64, VA Hosp., North Chicago, Ill., 1964-71; dir. health services Coll. of Lake County, Grayslake, Ill., 1971—, co-chmn. Inst. Self-Study for Rehab. Act 1973, 1978. Mem. Project SUCCEED, No. Ill., 1980-81; com. mem. Health Systems Agy. Kane-Lake-McHenry Counties, 1978-80; vol. Lake County Cancer Soc., 1975—, Am. Heart Assn., 1975—; bd. dirs. Med. Service Adv. Com. Lake County Health Dept., 1980—, Lake County Tuberculosis Clinic, 1985—. Recipient Appreciation cert. Lake County Bd. Commrs., 1978; Meritorious Service award Am. Heart Assn., 1979-82; Outstanding award No. Ill. Council on Alcoholism, 1982. Mem. Am. Coll. Health Assn. (council of dels. 1978-80, 83—), Mid-Am. Coll. Health Assn. (v.p. 1981-82, pres. 1983-84), No. Ill. Coll. Health Nurses Assn., Am. Legion Aux., Altrusa Intern. Roman Catholic. Home: 42749 Washington St Winthrop Harbor IL 60096 Office: Coll of Lake County 19351 W Washington St Grayslake IL 60030

HASSLER, SANDRA LEE, controller; b. Allentown, Pa., Jan. 3, 1949; d. Harold Elmer and Ruth Eleanor (Dahlof) H.; A.A. in Bus. Adminstrn., Northampton County Community Coll., 1969; B.S. in Bus. Mgmt., Indiana (Pa.) U., 1971. Engaged in retail fin., 1971-77; corp. controller, asst. to chmn. bd. Apparel Affiliates, Inc., Quakertown, Pa., 1977-81; ind. fin. and retail cons. computer programming and internal auditing, Phila., 1981-82; div. controller Honeybee, women's retail apparel chain, Huntington Valley Pa., 1982-84; asst. controller Wall to Wall Sound & Video, Inc., Cinnaminson, N.J., 1984—. Mem. Am. Mgmt. Assn., Nat. Assn. Female Execs. Mem. Moravian Ch. Author ops. and retail manuals/booklets for design of data collection devices. Home: 800 Trenton Rd #275 Langhorne PA 19047 Office: 200 S Route 130 Cinnaminson NJ 08077

HAST, JOAN EILEEN, telecommunications engineer; b. Denver, Jan. 6, 1955; d. Bernard Arthur and Erma Ann (Pospisil) H. Student U. Denver, 1973-74, Goethe Inst., Munich, 1974-75; B.A. in Internat. Affairs, U. Colo., 1983, postgrad., 1983-85, M.S. in Telecommunications, 1985. Owner, mgr. Celebrity Slickers Custom Jackets, Boulder, Colo., 1978-80; shop mgr., monogram specialist Custom Monogramming, Denver, 1981; summer intern in telecommunications Horizon House Pub., Dedham, Mass., 1983; office mgr. Universal Fuels Oil Co., Denver, 1983-84; sr. engr. GTE-Midwestern Telephone Ops., Fort Wayne, Ind., 1985—. Advisor Jr. Achievement, Fort Wayne, 1985-86; vol. Fort Wayne Zoo, 1985; active YMCA, Fort Wayne. Research grantee U. Colo. Dept. Telecommunications, Honolulu, 1984, Las Vegas, 1984. Mem. IEEE, Nat. Assn. Female Execs. Avocations: foreign languages; travel; art; ballet; bicycling. Home: 1910 Woodhaven #6 Fort Wayne IN 46819 Office: GTE-Midwestern Telephone Operations 8001 W Jefferson Blvd Fort Wayne IN 46801

HASTE, BETTY GAYLE, sec.; b. Bedford, Ind., Nov. 15, 1957; d. Troy Nelson and June LaVonne (White) H. Perforator operator The Daily Reporter, Greenfield, Ind., 1977-80; sec. III, Purdue U., West Lafayette, Ind., 1980—. Methodist. Home: 506 N 11th St Lafayette IN 47904 Office: 688 Krannert Purdue U West Lafayette IN 47907

HASTINGS, SANDRA JEAN, ceramic artist; b. Cin., Apr. 8, 1942; d. Robert Joseph and Marian Jean (Eisert) Prinzo; m. Lynn Courtlandt Hastings, July 3, 1970 (div. 1972); 1 child, Derek Courtlandt; m. 2d, Roger Katen, Dec. 27, 1980. A.A. in Fine Arts, Miami-Dade Community Coll., 1982. Paralegal sec. firm Sams, Anderson, Miami, Fla., 1960-66, Adolfo del Castillo, Miami, 1970-71, Gautier & Ezell, Miami, 1971-72; design asst. Richard Plumer, Miami, 1967-69; design asst., v.p. Jeffrey Howard, Miami, 1972-77; designer William Maler, Ft. Lauderdale, Fla., 1977-78; free lance designer Burger-King Europe, 1978-79; owner Sandy Hastings Ceramics, Inc., Miami; owner, artist A Touch of Earth, Miami, 1979—. Artist ceramic sculpture. Mem. Am. Craft Council, Artists Equity, Fla. Craftsmen, Ceramic League Miami (chem. chmn. 1980-82). Republican. Roman Catholic. Office: 4438-36 SW 74th Ave Miami FL 33155

HATCH, ALLENE GATY (MRS. ALDEN R. HATCH), artist, author; b. Morristown, N.J.; d. Theodore Emmett and Jean (Gardner) Gaty; student Bard Coll., 1941-42, Fashion Acad., 1944-45, Columbia U., 1945, Art Student's League, 1963-64; m. Alden R. Hatch, Sept. 9, 1950. Asst. art dir. Allied Display Corp., 1945-47; artist N.Y. Daily News, 1947, Edwin Freed Advt. Agy., 1948-50; illustrator books Henry Holt & Co., Prentice Hall, Inc., Am. Heritage mag., Doubleday & Co., Inc., Crown Pubs., Inc., 1950—; asst. to pres. Scenic Hudson Preservation Conf., 1978-80; pub. relations cons. Travel Dynamics, Inc., 1980-81, York Co. & Gifford Wallace, 1982-85; articles and cartoons for Barrytown Explorer; public relations cons. Travel Dynamics, Aris Gloves; painter portraits in U.S., Europe. Mem. Colonial Dames Am. Republican. Episcopalian. Author, illustrator: Menopause Can Be Fun, 1972; author: Marjorie Merriwether Post, 1977. Home: Quartermile Germantown NY 12526

HATCH, ELAINE ANITA, trading company executive, financial educator; b. Bklyn., Nov. 3, 1946; d. Rudolph Newton and Marion (Palenik) H. Cert., Data Processing Schs., Inc., N.Y.C., 1965; student N.Y.C. Community Coll., 1976-78, Fordham U., 1980-83. Bookkeeper O.Z. Elec. Mfg. Co., Bklyn., 1964-69; office mgr. Met. Advt. Co., N.Y.C., 1969-73; asst. mgr. accounts receivable Thyssen, Inc., N.Y.C., 1973-76, supr. treasury ops., 1976-84, mgr. accounts receivable, 1984—, presenter tng. seminars for corp. staff, 1984. Contbr. articles to profl. publs. Tchr. Confraternity of Christian Doctrine classes Roman Catholic Ch., Bklyn., 1972. Mem. Nat. Assn. Female Execs., Mgmt. Women, Alumni Assn. John Jay High Sch. Democrat. Club: Matterhorn Sports (N.Y.C.). Avocations: theater; travel; reading; bowling; sketching. Office: Thyssen Inc 1114 Ave of Americas New York NY 10036

HATCH, MARY WENDELL VANDER POEL, non-profit organization executive, interior decorator; b. N.Y.C., Feb. 6, 1919; d. William Halsted and Blanche Pauline (Billings) Vander Poel; m. George Montagu Miller, Apr. 5, 1940 (div. 1974); children—Wendell Miller Steavenson, Gretchen Miller Elkus; m. Sinclair Hatch, May 14, 1977. Pres. Miller Richard, Inc., interior decorators, Glen Head, N.Y., 1972—, bd. dirs. Eye Bank Sight Restoration, N.Y.C., 1975—, pres., 1980—; bd. dirs. Manhattan Eye Ear and Throat Hosp., N.Y.C., 1966—, v.p., 1978—; bd. dirs. Cold Spring Harbor Lab., N.Y., 1985—; v.p. North Country Garden Club, Nassau County, N.Y., 1979-81, 1983-85; dir. Planned Parenthood Nassau County, Mineola, N.Y., 1982-84, Hutton House C.W. Post Coll., Greenvale, N.Y., 1982—. Republican. Episcopalian. Clubs: Colony (N.Y.C.), Church (N.Y.C.), Order St. John Jerusalem (N.Y.C.). Home: Mill River Rd Box 330 Oyster Bay NY 11771

HATCHER, JACQUELINE JEAN, sales executive; b. Hutchinson, Kans., Mar. 25, 1930; d. George Edgar and Hattie Lucille (Nesker) Crupper Woolworth; m. J.D. Hatcher, June 12, 1954; children—Kimberly Kay, Leanne. Student pub. schs., Wichita. Realtor. Office mgr. Penn Mut. Ins. Co., Wichita, 1952-56, David A. Dahl, M.D., Fremont, Calif., 1970-73; cons. Roundtree Homeowners, Fremont, 1973-75; mgr. sales Cordin Phase II, San Jose, Calif., 1978-80; v.p., dir. mktg. Unedus Mktg. Assocs., Los Gatos, Calif., 1980-82; dir., owner Nat. Toll Free Mktg., Oakland, Calif., 1982—; dir. Unedus Mktg. Assocs., 1980—. Friends U. scholar, 1948. Pres., Lutheran Ch. Women, 1968-69; chmn. Christ the King Luth. Ch., 1975-77. Mem. So. Alameda County Bd. Realtors, Nat. Assn. Female Execs., Am. Bus. Women (sec. ways and means 1978—), Nat. Assn. Profl. Saleswomen. Republican. Club: Toastmasters. Office: NTFM East Bay Regional Tng Center 333 Hegenberger Rd Suite 800 Oakland CA 94621

HATCHER, MARTHA OLIVIA TAYLOR (MRS. FRANK PRIDGEN HATCHER, SR.), biologist, educator; b. Birmingham, Ala., Feb. 17, 1920; d. Sanford Allia and Mary (McCullough) Taylor; B.S., Howard Coll., 1936-40; M.Ed. in Sci. Edn., U. Ga., 1966, Ed.D., 1973; tchrs. cert. Brenau Coll., 1964; m. Frank Pridgen Hatcher, Sr., Nov. 7, 1941; children—Frank Pridgen, Martha Elizabeth, Nancy Louise. Chief bacteriologist veterinary div. Ga. Dept. Agr., Atlanta, 1943-45; supr. surg. pathology lab. Jefferson Hillman Hosp., Med. Coll. Ala., Birmingham, 1945-46, research asst. in pathology, 1945-46; mgr. offices Fran Mar Farms, Inc., Gainesville, Ga., 1957-66; instr. biology Gainesville Jr. Coll., 1966-67, asst. prof. biology, 1967-74, assoc. prof., 1974-77, prof., 1977—, acting chmn. div. natural scis. and maths., 1968-74, chmn., 1974-82; prof. biology, adminstrv. asst. Brenau Coll., 1982—, dean student devel., 1986—; accompanist music dept. Brenau Coll., Gainesville, 1959-61. Chmn. Gray Ladies Vol. Services, Gainesville chpt. ARC, 1957-62; sec. Yohah council Girl Scouts U.S.A., 1959-61; bd. dirs. Community Concert Assn. Gainesville, 1968-70. NSF sci. faculty fellow in microbiology, 1970-71. Mem. AAUP, AAAS, Am. Guild Organists, Am. Inst. Biol. Scis., Nat. Assn. Biology Tchrs., Assn. S.E. Biologists, Nat. Assn. Research Sci. Teaching, Ga. Acad. Sci., Nat. Sci. Tchrs. Assn., Am. Legion Aux. (pres. 1948-50), Am. Soc. Zoologists, Southeastern Assn. Educators of Tchrs. Sci. (pres. 1983-84; editor Newsletter), UDC (chpt. pres. 1949-51), Am. Soc. Microbiology, AAUW, Kappa Delta Pi, Alpha Epsilon Delta, Delta Kappa Gamma, Phi Delta Kappa, Phi Theta Kappa, Delta Zeta. Clubs: Music (pres. 1950-52), Federated Music (sec. 1957-58) Phoenix Soc., Pilot Internat., (pres. 1983-84) (Gainesville). Home: 840 Memorial Dr NE Gainesville GA 30501 Office: Brenau Coll PO Box 4668 Gainesville GA 30501

HATELEY, ENID ELLEN, real estate broker; b. Guayaquil, Ecuador, Mar. 22, 1925; came to U.S., 1944, naturalized, 1948; d. Harry Hawkes and Silia (Blanco) Shephard; B.S., Colegio Guayaquil, 1942; B.A., U. So. Calif., 1946; m. James Charles Hateley, II, Aug. 24, 1946; children—James Charles, Robert, Donald. Asst. credit mgr. Bank of Calif., 1946-49; with IBEC, 1950-51, E.H. Imports, 1952-60; trust adminstr. Bank of Am., 1973-75; broker Coldwell Banker, Los Altos, Calif., 1976—; pres. City Resources, Inc., 1984. Named Miss Dominican Republic, 1946; named to Coldwell Banker Million Dollar Club, 1976, 77, 78; recipient Silver Circle award Coldwell Banker, 1979-81, Pres. Club award, 1983. Mem. Nat. Assn. Realtors, Calif. Assn. Realtors, Los Altos Bd. Realtors (life mem. Million Dollar Club). Republican. Roman Catholic. Club: Los Angeles Athletic. Home: 2175 Chuleta Ct Los Altos CA 94022 Office: 301 S San Antonio Rd Los Altos CA 94022

HATFIELD, NORMA JEAN, county government official; b. Marshall, Tex., Mar. 12, 1927; d. Allen Wilburn and Mary (Sikes) Nutt; m. Kenneth Allen Hatfield, Aug. 19, 1946; 1 child, Jodie Jean Hatfield Harris. A.A., U. So. Colo., 1982. Various positions with U.S. Army Post Exchange System, 1944-62; self-employed in bus., 1966-70: county clk., recorder Fremont County, Canon City, Colo., 1972—. Sec. Fremont County Dem. Central Com., 1971; pres. Canon City Altrusa, 1977-78; fin. chmn. Canon City Meals on Wheels, 1978-85; pres. Canon City United Way, 1985-86. Mem. Internat. Assn. County Clks., Recorders, Election Officials and Treasurers, Nat. Recorders Assn., Internat. Inst. Mcpl. Clks., Clk. and Recorders Assn. (pres. 1982-83), DAR (Colo. record sec. 1971-73). Baptist. Avocations: tennis, swimming, walking. Home: 2341 Melvina St Canon City CO 81212 Office: Fremont County Courthouse 600 Macon St Canon City CO 81212

HATHAWAY, JUANITA, nurse; b. Gonzales, Tex., Mar. 9, 1948; d. Ernest Chauncy and Effie Mae (Dyal) Hendershot; m. William John Hathaway, Jan. 14, 1972; children—William J., Jr., Kenneth Earl. Assoc. Degree Applied Sci., San Antonio Coll., 1971. Registered nurse. Charge nurse, Warm Springs, Gonzales, 1972-74, 74-81; charge nurse Davis Hosp., Luling, Tex., 1973-74, asst. dir. nursing, 1984—. Asst. den leader Capitol Area council Cub Scouts, 1984; vol. Luling Emergency Med. Service. Baptist. Home: 900 S Magnolia Luling TX 78648

HATHAWAY, ROBIN LEA, health resources company executive, consultant; b. Sioux Falls, S.D., Nov. 22, 1948; d. Eldon Lee Hathaway and Gladys Lee (Duley) Miller; m. Jerry Lee Bingham, May 16, 1970 (div. Apr. 1975). Student Ottawa U. R.N., Mo. Mgr. St. Luke's Hosp., Kansas City, Mo., 1976-78; occupational health nurse AT&T Long Lines, Kansas City, Mo., 1978-79; occupational health nurse, employee relations rep. Marion Labs., Inc., Kansas City, Mo., 1979-81; nurse cons. Crawford Rehab., Overland Park, Kans., 1981-82; mgr. St. Mary's Hosp., Kansas City, Mo., 1981-85; pres. Occupational Health Mgmt. Resources, Kansas City, Mo., 1985—. Co-author grant proposal Mo. Worksite Hypertension Screens, 1983 (award 1983, 85). Mem. industry com. ARC, Kansas City, Mo., 1985—; spl. events co-chmn. Dimensions Unltd., Kansas City, Mo., 1985—; mentorship program vol. Johnson County Bus. Women's Resource Ctr., 1986—; chmn. occupational health com. Mo. Safety Conf., 1986. Named Nurse of Month, Kansas City Nursing Jour., 1981. Mem. Mo. Assn. Occupational Health Nurses (bd. dirs. 1984-86), Nat. Assn. Women Bus. Owners, Health Promotion Council of Greater Kansas City, Am. Assn. Occupational Health Nurses, NOW, Interfaith Peace Alliance. Unitarian. Club: Feminine Alliance (Kansas City, Mo.). Avocations: power volleyball; racquetball; wallpapering; ballet; symphony. Office: Occupational Health Mgmt Resources 2727 Main Suite 201 Kansas City MO 64108

HATLEY, DOROTHY LEE RATLIFF, county official; b. Lometa, Tex., July 29, 1934; d. Robert Lee and Ethel Lucille (Dannheim) R.; m. Presley Lewis Hatley, May 15, 1951; children—Sandra Gwen, Gary Presley. Student Durham Bus. Coll., 1950-51. Abstract sec. Rocksprings Abstract Co., Tex., 1966-67; tax assessor dep. Rocksprings Tax Office, 1967-68, clk., dep., 1969-70; county and dist. clk. Edwards County, Rocksprings, 1970—. Sunday sch. primary tchr. First Bapt. Ch., Rocksprings. Home: PO Box 231 Rocksprings TX 78880 Office: County Clk Edwards County Seat County Courthouse Rocksprings TX 78880

HATTABAUGH, DOROTHY, vocational education educator, nutrition consultant; b. Cin., Sept. 14, 1930; d. Charles Everett Mitchell, Sr., and Mary Thomas (Farrow) Fleek; m. John Doyle Hattabaugh, Oct. 30, 1967 (dec. 1984); 1 child, John Allen. A.A., Orange Coast Coll., 1975; student in Vocat. Edn., UCLA, 1975—. Cert. tchr. Owner R.D.J. Catering, Huntington Beach, Calif., 1974-79; mgr. trainee Carl's Jr. Restaurant, Anaheim, Calif., 1975; mgr. Broadway Stores Restaurant, La Puenta, Calif., 1976; banquet mgr., cafeteria worker Orange Coast Coll., Costa Mesa, Calif., 1976-78; tchr. Coastline Regional Occupation Program, Costa Mesa, 1979-82, Los Angeles Regional Occupational Program, Pasadena, 1983-85. Mem. Nat. Assn. Female Execs., Council Hotel and Restaurant Instl. Edn. Republican. Methodist. Avocations: oil painting; ceramics. Home: 17371 Driver Collins Rd Mount Orab OH 45154

HATTAN, MARIE CANDICE, lawyer; b. N.Y.C., Sept. 23, 1951; d. William Joseph and Catherine (Mooney) H. B.A., Rutgers U., 1974, M.A., 1976; J.D., La. State U., 1978. Bar: La. 1979. Law clk. to judge Ct. Appeal, Lake Charles, La., 1978-79 assoc. firm Davidson, Meaux, Sonnier & Roy, Lafayette, La., 1979-82; ptnr. firm Roy & Hattan, Lafayette, 1982—. Editor, author Jour. Fine Arts Rutgers U., 1972, N.J. Fine Arts Jour., 1971-73. Atty. Hospice, Lafayette, 1983—; mem. Arts and Humanities Council Greater Baton Rouge, 1976—, Republican Caucas, Baton Rouge, 1976. Mem. ABA, La. State Bar Assn., La. Assn. Def. Counsel, Def. Research Inst., Am. Soc. Law and Medicine, La. Trial Lawyers Assn., Assn. Trial Lawyers Am., Acadiana Assn. Women Attys. (bd. dirs. 1981-84), Acadiana Bus. Womens Assn., Mu Sigma Rho. Roman Catholic. Office: Roy & Hattan PO Drawer 91850 556 Jefferson St Suite 401 Lafayette LA 70501

HATTON, CAROLYN S., dentist; b. El Campo, Tex., Nov. 26, 1946; d. Rene LaFayette and Gladys Vera (Trojcak) Mood; B.S. in Dental Hygiene, Baylor U., 1969, D.D.S., 1978; 1 son, Jeffrey Carter. Practice gen. dentistry and gnathology, asso. Dr. William L. Comcowich, Aspen, Colo., 1978—. Mem. ADA, Colo. Dental Assn., Western Colo. Dental Assn., Colo. Prosthodontic Assn., Aspen Dental Soc. (sec.), Soc. Occlusal Studies, Am. Equilibration Soc. Office: 420 W Main St Aspen CO 81611

HATVANY, NINA GABRIELE, real estate developer; b. Eng, Oct. 8, 1953; came to U.S., 1974; d. Baron Paul Bernard and Ingeborg (Kirchtag) H.; B.Sc. with 1st class honors, Bristol (Eng.) U., 1974; M.A. in Psychology (Univ. fellow), Stanford U., 1976, Ph.D. in Psychology, 1978. Asst. prof. bus. Grad. Sch. Bus., Columbia U., 1978-81; pres. Brit. Pacific Devel. Co., real estate devel., San Francisco, 1981—. Editor: (with D. Nadler and M. Tushman) Managerial Behavior, Concepts and Cases, 1982.

HAUCK, MARGUERITE HALL, broadcasting company marketing and research executive, art and antique dealer; b. Bayside, N.Y., June 30, 1948; d. Carlyle Washington and Anzonette Marguerite (Asmussen) Hall; student Syracuse U., 1966-67; B.A. summa cum laude, Queens Coll., U. City N.Y., 1974. Asso. producer Animatic Prodns., Ltd., N.Y.C., 1968-72; mktg. analyst BBDO, Inc., N.Y.C., 1974-75; mktg. analyst CBS, Inc., N.Y.C., 1975-76, mgr. mktg. and research FM nat. sales, Radio div. CBS, 1976-85; dir. research Christal Radio Sales div. Katz Communications, 1985—; pres. Lennon Hall Artsand Antiques, 1985—; mem. goals com. Radio Advt. Bur., 1979—. Bd. dirs. Queens Coll. Student Services Corp., 1973-74. Recipient Queens Coll. Disting. Service award, 1974. Mem. Nat. Assn. Female Execs., Radio Sta. Reps. Assn. Author: The $321 Billion Dollar Market, 1981; The Mid-day Myth Exploded; columnist TV/Radio Age mag., 1982. Home: 20 Continental Ave Forest Hills NY 11375 Office: Christal 919 3d Ave New York NY 10022

HAUER, MARCIA JODENE, financial administrator; b. Bryan, Ohio, Mar. 30, 1951; d. Richard Wayne and Daisy Josephine (Kelley) Short; m. Jerry Lee Salyer, Mar. 30, 1968 (div. 1973); 1 child, Sandra Lynn; m. Douglas Glen Hauer, Aug. 16, 1975; children—Tara Rebecca, Molly Jo. Student Baldwin-Wallace Coll., 1984—. Bookkeeper Lodge Floor Covering, Coldwater, Mich., 1972-78, Branch Area Career Ctr., Coldwater, 1978-80, Altenheim Nursing Home, Strongsville, Ohio, 1981-82; adminstrv. asst. Garfield Med. Care, Cleve., 1982-84; fin. dir. Amasa Stone House, Inc., Cleve., 1984—. Active Youth for Christ. Mem. Nat. Assn. Female Execs. Home: 5090 Grafton Rd Brunswick Hills OH 44212 Office: Amasa Stone House Inc 975 East Blvd Cleveland OH 44108

HAUGEN, MARILYN ANNE, nurse practitioner, health center director; b. Colorado Springs, Jan. 11, 1932; d. Arnold H. and Juanita P. (Porter) Miller; m. Halver Herbert Haugen, June 13, 1953; children—Steven Lee, Karen Elaine. B.A., Denver U., 1953; B.S. in Nursing, Miami U., Ohio, 1980. Cert. pediatric nurse practitioner; R.N. Tchr., Denver Pub. Schs., 1953-57; pediatric nurse Middletown Regional Hosp., Ohio, 1973-76, educator, 1976-77, pediatric nurse practitioner, 1978-82, project dir. maternal child health ctr., 1982—. Mem. adv. bd. Miami Valley Child Devel. Ctr., 1983—; chmn. Child and Family Health Services Consortium, 1986—; mem. adv. bd. Butler County Mental Health Assn. Mem. Nat. Assn. Pediatric Nurse Practitioners and Assocs. (treas., fin. chair 1982—, treas. Ohio chpt. 1980—), Am. Nurses Assn., Ohio Nurses Assn., Mortar Board, Kappa Delta. Republican. Home: 613 Regent Dr Middletown OH 45044 Office: Middletown Regional Hosp 105 McKnight Dr Middletown OH 45044

HAUGLAND, BRYNHILD, state legislator, farmer; b. Ward County, N.D., July 28, 1905; d. Nels and Sigurda (Ringoen) H.; B.A., Minot State Coll., 1956; LL.D. (hon.), N.D. State U., 1984. Mem. N.D. Ho. of Reps., 1939—, chmn. com. social services and vets. affairs, mem. com. industry, bus. and labor. Mem. Def. Adv. Com. Women in Services, 1955-58. Vice chmn. N.D. Gov.'s State Health Planning Com., 1944-75; mem. Ward County Zoning Commn., Minot City Planning Commn., N.D. Bicentennial Commn. Bd. dirs. Internat. Peace Garden, 1953—, Minot State Coll. Found., Minot Commn. on Aging. Named N.D.'s Outstanding Woman in Law, 1973; Outstanding Legislator, Nat. Assembly Govt. Employees, 1979; recipient Golden award for Outstanding Service, Minot State Coll. Alumni, 1968; Hon. Mem. Uniformed Fire Fighters N.D., 1976; Milky Way award Dairy Industry N.D., 1977; Disting. Service award Western N.D. Health Systems Agy., 1977-78; N.D. Water Wheel, N.D. Water Users Assn./N.D. Water Mgmt. Dists. Assn., 1981; Service to Mankind award Sertoma Clubs, 1983; Merit award Pub. Health Assn. N.D., 1983; Liberty Bell award State Bar Assn., 1983; Disting. Service award Mental Health Assn. N.D., 1983; award Minot Assn. Home Builders, 1984; Good Citizen Scouting award, 1984; Disting. Service award Am. Protestant Health Assn., 1985; others; inducted into Scandinavian Hall of Fame, 1984. Mem. Bus. and Profl. Women's Club (named Woman of Yr. 1956, 71), Am. Assn. Ret. Persons, Nat. Ret. Tchrs. Assn., Farmers Union and Farm Bur., Minot State Coll. Alumni Assn. (dir.), Delta Kappa Gamma. Lutheran. Club: Quota. Address: Box 1684 Minot ND 58701

HAUPT, CATHY, public housing adminstrator; b. Los Angeles, Dec. 21, 1950; d. Albert Paul and Xenia (Chernekoff) Lexin; m. Gary E. Haupt, 1973 (div. 1980); 1 dau., Melissa Ann. Student Downey, Calif., pub. schs. Adminstrv. asst. Fresno (Calif.) Housing Authority, 1973-79; dir. mgmt. services San Diego Housing Commn., 1979-82, dep. exec. dir., 1983—; editor ann. report San Diego Housing Commn., 1981. Active YWCA, San Diego council Pan-Asian Refugee Cooperative. Mem. Am. Soc. Personnel Adminstrs., San Diego Employers Assn., San Diego Apt. Assn. (best now property award 1982). Democrat. Molokan. Club: Toastmasters Internat. (San Diego). Home: 7226 Oakham Way San Diego CA 92139 Office: San Diego Housing Commn 121 Broadway St San Diego CA 92139

HAUPTFUHRER, BARBARA BARNES, corporate director; b. Greensboro, N.C., Oct. 11, 1928; d. J. Foster and Myrtle (Preyer) Barnes; B.A. cum laude, Wellesley Coll, 1949; m. George J. Hauptfuhrer, Jr., Sept. 9, 1950; children—George J. III, W. Barnes. Dir., Vanguard Group Investment Cos., Valley Forge, Pa., 1972—, Great Atlantic and Pacific Tea Co., Inc., Montvale, N.J., 1975—, Gen. Public Utilities Corp., Parsippany, N.J., 1976-79, Phila. Saving Fund Soc., 1976—, J. Walter Thompson Co., Inc., N.Y.C., 1977—, Knight-Ridder Newspapers, Inc., Miami, Fla., 1979—, Mass. Mut. Life Ins. Co., Springfield, 1979—, JWT Group, Inc., N.Y.C., 1980—, Owens-Ill., Inc., Toledo, 1981—; public mem. regional adv. com. on banking policies and practices 3d Nat. Bank Region, 1976-77; adv. bd. Phila. Fin. Assn., 1980—. Trustee, Wellesley (Mass.) Coll., 1970-85, Com. for Econ. Devel., 1979—; bd. dirs. John and Mary R. Markle Found., 1976—, Greater Phila. Partnership, 1975-85; bd. dirs. World Affairs Council Phila., 1977—, vice chmn., 1978-80; bd. dirs. Phila. United Fund, 1960-65, United Way Southeastern Pa., 1979—; trustee Salem Acad. and Coll., 1967-70, Eisenhower Exchange Fellowships, 1986—; mem. Harvard Vis. com. for Harvard and Radcliffe, 1972-78; mem. Presser Found., 1970-85; pres. Jr. League Phila., 1958-60, Meadowbrook Sch., 1962-63; mem. Phila. Orch. Council, 1979—; mem. Mayor's Commn. for Women, Phila., 1981-83. Recipient Disting. Alumna award Salem Acad., 1985. Mem. Wellesley Coll. Alumnae Assn. (pres. 1970-73). Lutheran. Home: 1700 Old Welsh Rd Huntingdon Valley PA 19006

HAUPTMAN, MARY MARGARET, court reporting agency executive; b. Queens, N.Y., May 18, 1955; d. Earl Edward and Margaret Frances (Struckman) H.; m. Ted John Doukas, Mar. 20, 1982. Grad. Verbatim/Stenotype Inst., Hicksville, N.Y., 1974. Court reporter, N.Y.C., 1975-79; pres., owner Hauptman Reporting, Syosset, N.Y., 1979—. Bd. dirs. Republican Party, Syosset-Woodbury, N.Y., 1983-85, committeewoman, 1984—. Mem. Nat. Shorthand Reporters Assn., N.Y. Shorthand Reporters Assn. Roman Catholic. Club: Syosset-Woodbury Republican. (bd. dirs. 1983-85). Home: 7 Evergreen Dr Syosset NY 11791 Office: 70 Split Rock Rd Syosset NY 11791 also: 150 Nassau St Suite 2000 New York NY

HAUSAFUS, CHERYL OLMSTEAD, home economics educator; b. Cin., Sept. 27, 1946; d. Ralph Maurice and Adelaide Louise (Schweninger) Olmstead; B.S., Fla. State U., 1968; M.S., Pa. State U., 1971; Ph.D., Iowa State U., 1978; m. John Earl Hausafus, May 26, 1973; children—Michael Todd, Tara Ann. Tchr. home econs. Taylor County High Sch., Perry, Fla., 1968-69; food service tchr. Gibbs Comprehensive High Sch., St. Petersburg, Fla., 1970; asst. prof. home econs. edn. E. Carolina U., Greenville, N.C., 1972-75; asst. prof. home econs. edn. Iowa State U., Ames, 1978—; mem. state adv. bd. Future Homemakers Am., 1980-85; mem. adv. council Des Moines Home Econs. Adv. Council, 1981—; cons. Grantee, Apple Edn. Found., 1980. Mem. Am. Home Econs. Assn., Am. Vocat. Assn., Council Vocat. Edn., Am. Ednl. Research Assn., Assn. Devel. Computer-Based Instructional Systems, Iowa Vocat. Assn. (dir.), Omicron Nu, Phi Delta Kappa. Democrat. Episcopalian. Contbr. articles to profl. jours. Home: 3700 Rollins Ave Des Moines IA 50312 Office: Dept Home Econs Edn Iowa State U Ames IA 50011

HAUSE, EDITH COLLINS, college administrator; b. Rock Hill, S.C., Dec. 11, 1933; d. Ernest O. and Violet (Smith) Collins; m. James Luke Hause, Sept. 3, 1955; children—Stephen Mark, Felicia Gaye Hause Friesen. B.A., Columbia Coll., S.C., 1956; postgrad. U. N.C.-Greensboro, 1967, U. S.C., 1971-75. Tchr. Richland Dist. II, Columbia, 1971-74; dir. alumnae affairs Columbia Coll., 1974-82, v.p. alumnae affairs, 1982-84, v.p. devel., 1984—. Named Outstanding Tchr. of Yr., Richland Dist. II, 1974. Mem. Columbia Network for Female Execs., Council for Advancement and Support Edn., Alpha Delta Kappa. Republican. Methodist. Home: Route 4 Box 760 Prosperity SC 29127 Office: Columbia Coll Devel Office Columbia SC 29203

HAUSER, JOYCE ROBERTA, public relations and marketing specialist; b. N.Y.C.; d. Abraham and Helen (Lesser) Frankel; B.A., SUNY, 1976; postgrad. Union Grad. Sch.; children—Mitchell, Mark, Ellen. Editor, Art in Flowers,

1955-58; pres. Joyce Advt., 1958-65; partner Hauser & Assocs., Pub. Relations, 1966-75; dir. broadcasting Bildersee Pub. Relations, 1973-75; pres. Hauser & Assocs., Inc., Pub. Relations, 1975-78, Hauser-Roberts, Inc., Pub. Relations/Mktg., N.Y.C., 1978-85, Mktg. Concepts and Communications, Inc., 1985—; moderator show Perceptions, Sta. WEVD, 1975-77, Speaking of Health, WNBC, 1977-80, 97 Health Line, Sta. WYNY, 1980-83, What's on Your Mind?, 1983-84, Talk-Net, 1985—, Conversations with Joyce Hauser, Sta. WNBC, 1975-86, Joyce Hauser Reports, Sta. WNBC, Speaking of Health, Sta. WNBC, 1985—; instr. Baruch Coll., CCNY, 1980-83; adj. prof. NYU, 1986—. Mem. Citywide Health Adv. Council on Sch. Health, 1970—, treas., 1980—; adv. bd. Sch. Continuing Edn., NYU Degree Program. Named one of 10 Top Successful Women, Cancer Soc., 1976; recipient Professionalism award Sta. WNBC, 1980. Mem. AFTRA, Am. Women in Radio and TV (corr. sec. 1973, chmn. coll. women in broadcasting 1974). Contbg. editor Alive, 1976-77. Home: 115 E 82d St New York NY 10028 Office: 20 E 53d St New York NY 10022

HAUSER, LAURETTE MARIE, public relations company executive; b. N.Y.C., Aug. 3, 1958; d. Kenneth James and Margaret (Bartro) H.; m. Carlos Guerrero Forcade, Aug. 29, 1981. B.A. magna cum laude, Columbia U., 1980; M.S., Rensselaer Poly. Inst., 1983. Editorial asst. N.Y. Acad. Scis., N.Y.C., part-time 1979-80; pub. relations research coordinator Albany Med. Coll., N.Y., 1980-81; communications specialist Matterson Assocs., Albany, 1981-82; account exec. Burson-Marsteller, N.Y.C., 1983-84; account supr. Daniel J. Edelman, Inc., N.Y.C., 1984-86, v.p. med./pharm. pub. relations, 1986—; adj. asst. prof. Fairleigh Dickenson U., Teaneck, N.J., 1985. Relief houseparent N.Y. State Div. for Youth, Albany, 1981-83; active Big Bros./Big Sisters, 1983. Mem. Am. Assn. Med. Writers, Internat. Communications Assn., Nat. Assn. Female Execs. Roman Catholic. Club: Sierra. Avocations: biking; cross-country skiing; travel; comparative literature; wildlife preservation. Home: 830 Howard Ave Staten Island NY 10301 Office: Daniel J Edelman Inc 1775 Broadway New York NY 10019

HAUSER, LYNN ELIZABETH, eye surgeon; b. Cleve., Apr. 11, 1951; d. Cavour Herman and Ruth Natalie (Lageman) H.; B.S. in Medicine, Northwestern U., 1974, M.D., 1976; m. Neil L. Ross, June 20, 1975; children—Michael Hauser Ross, Benjamin Hauser Ross. Resident in ophthalmology Northwestern U., 1976-80; practice medicine specializing in cataract surgery, Dekalb, Ill., 1980—; clin. asst. prof. ophthalmology U. Ill., Chgo.; lectr. in ophthalmology Northwestern U.; project ophthalmologist Nat. Eye Inst. Early Treatment Diabetic Retinopathy Study, 1982. Diplomate Am. Bd. Ophthalmology. Fellow Am. Acad. Ophthalmology, AMA, Dekalb County Med. Soc., Ill. Assn. Ophthalmology, Ill. State Med. Soc. Office: 8 Health Services Dr Suite 2 Dekalb IL 60115

HAUSER, PRISCILLA SUE, business executive, tole and decorative painting specialist, author; b. Tulsa, Mar. 11, 1940; d. Albert Logan and Dorothee (Langworthy) Wait; m. Gerald Maynard Hauser, July 31, 1959; children—Michael Timothy, Kimbelry Kay, Leslie Ann, Erich Von. Student U. Okla., 1957-58, U. Tulsa, 1958-59. Onwer-pres. Priscilla's Little Red Tole House, Tulsa, 1964—, Priscilla's Publs. and Products Inc., Tulsa, 1966-82, Priscilla's Studio by the Sea, Panama City Beach, Fla., 1985—; sec. Wait Sales Co. Tulsa, 1970—; cons. Martin F. Weber Co., Phila., 1982—. Mem. Nat. Soc. Tole and Decorative Painters (founder, pres. 1972-74, Silver Palette award 1978, pres.'s commendation 1984), Soc. Craft Designers, Nat. Art Materials Trade Assn., Hobby Industry Am. (craft div. good Egg award 1977, nat. Pres.'s award 1984). Republican. Home: 2150 Forest Blvd Tulsa OK 74114 Office: Priscilla's Little Red Tole House Inc PO Box 470730 Tulsa OK 74147

HAUSER, RITA E., lawyer; b. N.Y.C., July 12, 1934; d. Nathan and Frieda Abrams; A.B., Hunter Coll., 1954; Doctorate with highest honors, U. Strasbourg, France, 1955; Licence en Droit, U. Paris, 1958; LL.B., Harvard U.-NYU, 1959; m. Gustave M. Hauser, June 10, 1956; children—Glenvil, Patricia. Bar: D.C. 1960, N.Y. 1961. Sr. partner Stroock & Stroock & Lavan, N.Y.C., 1972—; dir. Israel Investors Corp., Wickes Cos. Inc. Trustee, Harvard U. Law Sch. Assn. of N.Y.C., Center for Inter-Am. Relations, Inst. for Internat. Edn., Freedom House; bd. dirs. Friends of the Hague Acad. Internat. Law, N.Y. Philharmonic-Symphony Soc.; mem. bd. govs., chmn. exec. com. Am. Jewish Com. Fellow Am. Bar Found. (life); mem. Am. Bar Assn., Am. Fgn. Law Assn., Assn. of Bar of City of N.Y. Office: Stroock Stroock Lavan 7 Hanover Sq New York NY 10004

HAUSKEN, SALLY ANN, educational counselor; b. Wahpeton, N.D., Aug. 10, 1934; d. Clyde Olaf and Lois Beatrice (Mc Michael) H.; B.S., Northwestern U., 1956; M.S., U. Colo., 1967; Sec. to pres. North Central Airlines, Mpls., 1958-59; service club dir. U.S. Army, Germany, 1959-61; tchr. bus., counselor Littleton (Colo.) High Sch., 1962-66; secondary counselor Detroit Lakes (Minn.) High Sch., 1967-68; secondary counselor Minnetonka West Jr. High Sch., Excelsior, Minn., 1968-82, Minnetonka High Sch., 1982—. Mem. Northwestern U. Alumni Admissions Council, 1972—. Mem. Am. Assn. for Counseling and Devel., Minn. Assn. for Counseling and Devel., Lake Area Counselors Assn., NEA, Minn. Edn. Assn., Minnetonka Tchrs. Assn. Episcopalian. Home: 1540 Skyview Dr Chaska MN 55318 Office: 18301 Hwy 7 Minnetonka MN 55345

HAUSMAN-SMITH, KATHRYN ELLEN, designer; b. Cleve., Oct. 9, 1949; d. Morris Hersh and Ruth Adele (Sablowitz) Hausman; student U. Wis., Madison, 1967-69; B.S., Fashion Inst. Tech., N.Y. U., 1971; m. David Smith, July 25, 1975; children—Trevor Leslie, Graham Morrison. Advt. dir. Sheffield Watch Corp., N.Y.C., 1971-72; owner, pres. designer Medusa's Heirlooms, N.Y.C., 1972—. Home: 154 E 89th St New York NY 10128 Office: 385 5th Ave Suite 501 New York NY 10016

HAVELOCK, CHRISTINE MITCHELL, educator; b. Cochrane, Ont., Can., June 2, 1924; d. William Waterson and Annie Margaret (Graham) Mitchell; B.A., U. Toronto, 1946; M.A., Harvard U., 1950, Ph.D., 1958; m. Eric A. Havelock, Nov. 21, 1962. Mem. faculty Vassar Coll., 1953—, prof. art history, 1967-78, Sarah Gibson Blanding chair, 1978-85, Mary Conover Mellon chair, 1985—, chmn. art dept., 1968-71, asst. to pres., 1972-73, dir. women's studies, 1978-80, curator class. collection. Recipient Charles Eliot Norton Fellowship award, 1950-51; NEH fellow, 1984-85. Mem. Coll. Art Assn., Archaeol. Inst. Am., Democrat. Author: Hellenistic Art, 2d edit., 1981. Office: Vassar Coll Box 358 Poughkeepsie NY 12601

HAVENS, DIANA LYNN, publishing company executive; b. Neptune, N.J., Jan. 25, 1958; d. Frederick Joseph Rible and Patricia Bernadette (Cwiakala) Rible Johnson; m. Lawrence Edward Havens, Jr., July 22, 1978. B.S., Kean Coll., 1981. Office asst. Standard-Keil Hardware, Allenwood, N.J., 1976-81; jr. customer service rep. McGraw-Hill, Inc., Hightstown, N.J., 1981-82, credit analyst, 1982-83, sr. credit analyst, 1983-84, asst. credit mgr., 1984—. Mem. Nat. Assn. Female Execs., Media Credit Assn. Club: McGraw-Hill Toastmasters (adminstrv. v.p. 1985, pres. 1986—) (Hightstown). Avocations: reading; writing; aerobics; parapsychology; public speaking. Home: RD 3 Box 367-F Jackson NJ 08527 Office: McGraw-Hill Inc Princeton-Hightstown Rd Hightstown NJ 08520

HAVERS, KATHERINE ARELENE, nursing educator, consultant; b. Baker, Oreg., July 5, 1952; d. Lynn R. and Elnora Margaret (Graham) Kandle; m. Perry Wayne Havers, Aug. 18, 1973 (div. 1985); children—Amber Cyrstal, Beverly Nell. B.S. in Secondary Edn., Phys. Edn. and Health, So. Oreg. State Coll., 1974; A.S. in Nursing, Bluemountain Community Coll., 1982. Tchr., coach Burnt River High Sch., Unity, Oreg., 1974-76; nursing asst. Corvallis Manor, Oreg., 1977, Good Samaritan Hosp., Corvallis, 1977-79; ward clk., nursing asst. Good Sheperd Hosp., Hermiston, Oreg., 1979-81; staff nurse to supr. Eastern Oreg. Hosp. and Tng. Ctr., Pendleton, 1981-84; nursing instr. Eastern Oreg. Psychiat. Ctr., Pendleton, 1984—; cons. Fed. Dept. Human Resources, Seattle, 1982—. Contbr. articles to profl. jours. Legis. liaison Assn. Deaf Awareness, 1979—, pres., 1981-84; pres. Oreg. Assn. Parents of Deaf, Salem, Oreg., 1984-85; rep. Oreg. Coalition Exceptional Children and Young Adults, Salem, 1983—; active Oreg. Adv. Com. Deaf, Salem, 1983. Recipient Outstanding Service and Achievement award Assn. for Deaf Awareness, Oreg. Tng. and Devel. Assn., 1984. Mem. Oreg. Nurses Assn., Oreg. Pub. Employees Union. Republican. Baptist. Club: 4-H; Campus Crusade for Christ. Avocations: sewing; gardening; fishing; camping; modern dance. Home: 605 Pomono Dr Umatilla OR 97882 Office: Eastern Oreg Psychiat Ctr 2600 Westgate Pendelton OR 97801

HAVIAN, VIVIAN VICTORIA, human resource development specialist, photographer; b. Peabody, Mass., Sept. 6, 1939; d. Izzy and Jennie Mary (Orzechowski) H. A.A., Goldey Beacom Jr. Coll., 1959; B.A. with honors, George Washington U., 1984. Sec., Hercules Inc., 1961-74; employee devel. specialist U.S. Secret Service, Washington, 1974—. Exhibited photographs Benttree Gallery, Tampa, Fla., 1983, George Washington U., 1983, No. Va. Photography Show, 1984, Colonnade Gallery, 1983-84, 1986 Internat. Platform Assn. Art Show, 1985, Artistic Touch, Brandon, Fla., 1985, 86, Fouquet's Fine Art Gallery, Orlando, Fla., 1986. Recipient Spl. Achievement award U.S. Dept. Treasury, 1982. Mem. Internat. Platform Assn., Am. Soc. Tng. and Devel. Home: 3701 S George Mason Dr 104N Falls Church VA 22041

HAVILAND, CAMILLA KLEIN, lawyer; b. Dodge City, Kans., Sept. 13, 1926; d. Robert Godfrey and Lelah (Luther) Klein; A.A., Monticello Coll., 1946; B.A., Radcliffe Coll., 1948; LL.B., Kans. U. Sch. Law, 1955, J.D., 1968; m. John Bodman Haviland, Sept. 7, 1957. Admitted to Kans. bar, 1955, Fed. bar, 1955; pvt. practice law, Wichita, Kans., 1955-56, Dodge City, 1956-57, 77—; judge Probate County and Juvenile Cts., Ford County, Kans., 1957-77. Mem. Kans. Atty. Gen.'s Youth Com., 1962-66; mem. probate law study com. Kans. Jud. Council, 1973, mem. probate forms com., 1975-79, mem. juvenile code com., 1979-82. Nat. committeewoman Young Democrats of Kans., 1948-54; v.p. Young Dem. Clubs Am., 1953-55. Mem. president's council St. Mary of Plains Coll., 1961-67; bd. dirs. Cascade (Colo.) Property Owners Assn., 1964-70, mem. adv. bd. Salvation Army, Dodge City, 1956—; mem. adv. council Kans. U. Sch. Religion, 1970—, Kans. U. Sch. Social Welfare, 1972—. Recipient Nathan Burkan Meml. award in copyright law A.S.C.A.P., 1955; cert. of recognition Nat. Council Juvenile Ct. Judges, 1966. Mem. ABA (mem. probate and real estate com. 1955—), Kans., Southwest Kans. (sec., treas. 1957-70, 1971-73; pres. 1970-71, Ford-Gray County (pres. 1979-80) bar assns., Kans. Probate Judges Assn. (pres. 1963-64), P.E.O., DAR, Am. Legion. Club: Soroptimists (Dodge City). Author: Poems by Camilla, 1948; also articles in Kans. Law Rev. Office: 203 W Spruce Dodge City KS 67801

HAVILAND, LEONA, librarian; b. Stamford, Conn., Nov. 10, 1916; d. Howard Brush and Ada Grace (Jewell) Haviland; B.S., U. Ala., 1940; M.S., U. Ill., 1951; postgrad. Columbia, 1943, 56-60; m. Warren John Burke, Sept. 10, 1973. Jr. asst. Ferguson Library, Stamford, 1936-37, summers 1938-39, sr. asst., 1940-44; student asst. U. Ala., 1937-40; asst. to cataloguer U.S. Nat. Mus. Library, Washington, 1944-48; librarian Arts and Industries Mus., Smithsonian Instn., Washington, 1948-50; reference librarian U.S. Mcht. Marine Acad., Kings Point, N.Y., 1952-77. Mem. council YWCA, Washington, 1945-47. Mem. A.L.A., Spl. Libraries Assn. (past group membership chmn.), L.I. Hist. Soc., N.Y. Geneal. and Biog. Soc., Smithsonian Assos., South Street Seaport Mus., Alpha Beta Alpha, Alpha Lambda Delta. Home: 809 Pennsylvania Ave Saint Cloud FL 32769

HAVIST, MARJORIE VICTORIA, librarian, educator; b. Johnstown, Pa., Nov. 6, 1931; d. Victor Dale and Lillie Mae (Bross) Mulhollen; m. George I. Melhorn, Aug. 8, 1953 (dec. Dec. 1962); children—Susan Lynn, Bradford George; m. Ewald Jack Havist, Aug. 7, 1969. B.S. in Edn., Bucknell U., 1953; M.L.S., U. Wash., 1966. Cert. librarian, Wash. Engr., Boeing Co., Seattle, 1955, 57-58; librarian Bellevue Community Coll., Wash., 1966-78; head librarian Seattle Central Community Coll., Seattle, 1978-80; assoc. dean library Skagit Valley Coll., Mt. Vernon, Wash., 1980—. Bd. dirs. ARC Skagit County, Mt. Vernon, 1982; loaned exec. United Way Skagit County, 1983-84. Mem. ALA, Community Coll. Librarians and Media Specialists (pres. 1977-78), Community Coll. Library Dirs. Council (pres. 1981-82), Phi Theta Kappa. Republican. Lutheran. Office: Skagit Valley Coll 2405 College Way Mount Vernon WA 98273

HAVOSTAL, MARJORIE PAINE, investment management company executive, writer; b. Mpls., Apr. 29, 1930; d. Franklin and Helen Paine; student U. Calif., Berkeley, 1948, George Washington U., 1960, U. Ariz., 1962-63; m. John J. Havostal, May 6, 1954 (div.); children—Ronald, Bruce, Wayne, Gloria. With Nat. Geog. Soc., Washington, 1950-52; personnel sec. U.S. Army, Ft. Myer, Va., 1952-54; exec. sec. Consol. Mut. Trust, Woodbridge, Va., 1980-82, exec. v.p., 1982-83; owner Greyhound Racers, Fla.; cons. animal rights. Contbr. articles to health mags.

HAWBAKER, DIANA SUE, software analyst, consultant; b. Des Moines, Jan. 6, 1953; d. Duane William and Pearl Jean (Zimmerman) H.; m. Gary David Perrin, Nov. 10, 1972 (div. 1974). Systems analyst Gen. Growth Devel., Des Moines, 1976-81, cons., 1981-82; project mgr. Mgmt. Controls, Des Moines, 1981-82; pres. Integrated Bus. Systems, Des Moines, 1982-83; project mgr. Gen. Instrument Corp., Des Moines, 1983-85, programming mgr., Balt., 1985-86; product mgr. software services Scan-Optics, Inc., East Hartford, Conn., 1986—; cons. Wallace-Homestead, Des Moines, 1982-84, Mental Health Assn.; Polk County, Des Moines, 1982-84, Miller Pub., Mpls., 1984-85. Author software packages. Mem. NOW, Am. Bus. Women's Assn. (pres. Challenge chpt. 1981-82), Digital Equipment Corp Users Soc., Nat. Assn. Female Execs. Brethren. Avocations: reading; camping; gardening; crafts; tennis. Home: 205 Vernon Ave Apt 152 Vernon CT 06066 Office: Scan-Optics Inc 22 Prestige Park Circle East Hartford CT 06108

HAWES, DEDRA WINIFRED, lawyer; b. Birmingham, Ala., Apr. 16, 1958; d. William and Precious (Williams) H. B.A., Fisk U., Nashville, 1979; J.D., U. Ala.-Tuscaloosa, 1982. Bar: Ala. 1982. Trial atty. EEOC, Birmingham, 1983—. Mem. ABA, Ala. Bar Assn., Ala. Trial Lawyers Assn., Ala. Lawyers Assn., Nat. Bar Assn., Alpha Kappa Alpha, Phi Alpha Delta. Democrat. Methodist. Home: 17 9th Ct SW Birmingham AL 35211

HAWES, GRACE MAXCY, archival specialist, author; b. Cumberland, Wis., Feb. 4, 1926; d. Clarence David and Mabel Hannah (Erickson) Maxcy; student U. Wis., 1944-46; B.A., San Jose State U., 1963, M.A., 1971; m. John G. Hawes, Aug. 28, 1948 (dec. 1977); children—Elizabeth, John D., Mark, Amy. Library asst. NASA, Langley, Va., 1948-49; archivist Hoover Archives Stanford U., 1976-80; writer Office of Devel., Stanford U., 1980-84, archival specialist Hoover Archives, 1985—. Mem. Soc. Am. Archivists, Writers Connection, Women in Hist. Research, Calif. Archivists Assn. Author: The Marshall Plan for China: Economic Cooperation Administration, 1948-1949, 1977. Home: 410 Sheridan Ave Apt 220 Palo Alto CA 94306 Office: Hoover Inst Archives Stanford CA 94304

HAWK, NANCY JO, educator; b. Billings, Mont., Mar. 13, 1925; d. Harry Hamilton and Montana Edith (Grady) Skaggs; B.B.A. in Bus. Mgmt., Nat. U., San Diego, 1978; M.B.A., 1979; postgrad. Point Loma Coll.; m. Frank H. Hawk, Aug. 17, 1945; children—Lenore Hawk Dale, Patricia, Stephen, Anthony. Owner, operator state beach concession, 1960-64; prin.'s sec., gen. office mgr. San Diego City Schs., 1964-79; tchr. bus. courses San Diego colls., 1976—; mem. Faculty Senate, Miramar Coll., Southwestern Coll.; condr. workshops in field of office edn. Pres., Wegeforth Sch. PTA, 1964-65; chmn. fundraising Tierrasant Little League, 1979; chmn. fund drive Am. Heart Assn. Mem. Nat. Assn. Female Execs., Am. Women in Community and Jr. Colls. (co-chmn. conf.); chmn. fund drive Am. Heart Assn., Alumni Assn. Nat. U., Bus. and Profl. Women's Club. Democrat. Office: Miramar Coll San Diego CA 92126 also Southwestern Colls Bonita CA 92010

HAWKE, SHARON LYNNE, lawyer; b. Terre Haute, Ind., June 14, 1945; d. Harold and Dorothy L. (Tygret) Hawke. B.A. in Govt. and Pub. Adminstrn., Am. U., 1968; J.D. cum laude, Baylor U., 1971. Assoc. Butler & Binion, Houston, 1972-76; corp. counsel Crystal Oil Co., Shreveport, La., 1976-78; officer, dir., shareholder Cohen Brame & Smith, P.C., Denver, 1978—; counselor Baylor U. Law Sch., Waco, Tex., 1975—. Editor-in-chief Baylor Law Rev., 1971. Big sister Big Sisters of Colo., Denver, 1978—; contbr. Denver Dumb Friends League, 1981—. Mem. ABA, Colo. Bar Assn., Tex. Bar Assn., Denver Bar Assn., Pi Sigma Alpha. Republican. Club: Colo. Elephant. Home: 7430 S Harrison Way Littleton CO 80122 Office: Cohen Brame & Smith 1670 Broadway Suite 3500 Denver CO 80202

HAWKES, GLORIA DAWN, consulting company executive; b. Batavia, N.Y., Mar. 7, 1934; d. Arthur Keating and Hazel A. (Laufer) Gore; m. Norman Harry Hawkes, May 7, 1955; children—Brett Allen, Guy Norman. Adminstrv. asst. Erdman Anthony & Hosley, Rochester, N.Y., 1958-59; office mgr. Tex. Instruments, Rochester, 1960-62; acting office mgr. P K Mgmt., Henrietta, N.Y., 1972-73; exec. dir. March of Dimes, Rochester, 1974-78; cons. G. Hawkes/Cons., McLean, Va., 1982-84; pres. H & H Cons. Co., Oakton, Va., 1984—. Mem. Rochester Women's Polit. Caucus, 1974-78, McLean Citizens Assn., 1980; mem., coordinating com. Genesee region Internat. Women's Yr., 1975-78. Mem. Fairfax County Bus. and Profl. Women's Club, Community Assns. Inst. (bd. contbg. editors 1986—, officer/dir. Washington Met. chpt. 1982—), Epsilon Sigma Alpha (life). Republican. Lutheran. Office: H & H Cons Co 10124 Oakwood Chase Ct Oakton VA 22124

HAWKINS, CARMEN DOLORAS, lawyer; b. Los Angeles, Sept. 17, 1955; d. Lenell Herman and Doloras (Mondy) Hawkins. B.A. in Polit. Sci., U. Calif.-Santa Cruz, 1977; J.D., Georgetown U., 1981. Bar: D.C. 1981, Calif. 1982. Assoc. Law Offices Thomas G. Neusom, Los Angeles, 1982-83; sole practice, Los Angeles, 1983—; sponsor Black Women's Forum, Los Angeles, 1983-85. Sec. Beverly Hills-Hollywood NAACP, 1982-84; asst. troop leader Girl Scouts Am., Los Angeles, 1983-84; mem. Black Am. Polit. Assn. Calif., Los Angeles, 1982-84; mem. Transafrica, Los Angeles, 1982-84, New Frontier Dem. Club, Los Angeles, 1982—; mem. Inglewood Dem. Club (Calif.), 1983-84. Recipient Community Service award Black Am. Law Students Assn., Washington, 1979. Mem. ABA, Los Angeles County Bar Assn. (exec. com. Barristers 1986-87), Langston Bar Assn., Lawyers Club Los Angeles, Black Women Lawyers Assn. (exec. com. 1984—), Assn. Trial Lawyers Am., Los Angeles Trial Lawyers Assn., Phi Alpha Delta. Democrat. Mem. African Meth. Episcopal Ch. Office: 1112 Crenshaw Blvd Los Angeles CA 90019

HAWKINS, CECELIA JONES, consulting and actuarial firm executive; b. Atlanta, Nov. 25, 1937; d. Griffin Oliver Jones and Blanche Roberta (Tallent) Jones Tanner; m. Wilburn Wesley Marbut, July 30, 1954 (div. Sept. 1970); children—Melanie Marbut Madden, Marcia Elaine; m. William Ewing Hawkins, Jr., June 12, 1976 (div. Aug 1979). B.S. in Gen. Studies, Columbus Coll., Ga., 1978. Ins. sec. Venable, Kent, Smith & Fargason, Columbus, Ga., 1966-69; legal asst. Page, Scrantom, Harris & Chapman, P.C., Columbus, 1969-78; assoc. cons. A.S. Hansen, Inc., Columbus, 1978-84; pres. C.J. Hawkins, Inc., Columbus, 1985—, also dir. Mem. Presdl. Task Force, Washington, 1984—, Small Bus. Council of Am., Inc., Washington, Columbus, 1985. Mem. AAUW (pres. elect 1985-87), Better Bus. Bur., Columbus, Chattahoochee Valley Bus. and Profl. Women (pres. 1982-83, adv. 1983—; Woman of Leadership award 1982), Nat. Assn. Legal Assts. (Cert. legal asst.; certifying bd. 1974-76), Columbus Area Network Profl. and Exec. Women (1st nominating com. 1981, bd. dirs. 1986—), Am. Bus. Women's Assn., Columbus C. of C. (sales team 1984—), Columbus Coll. Alumni Assn. (dir. 1985-88). Republican. Avocations: aerobic exercise, book store browsing, creative writing, bridge, computer programing. Office: C J Hawkins Inc PO Box 2646 Columbus GA 31902

HAWKINS, DIXIE LEE, public relations executive; b. Eugene, Oreg., Dec. 13, 1950; d. William Brevard and Jessie Irene (Qualls) H. B.J., U. Tex., 1970; postgrad. Trinity U., 1970. Copy writer and office mgr. Writers' Ink, Austin, Tex., 1971-72; news and pub. affairs adminstr. KTSA/KTFM Radio, San Antonio, 1972-74; news reporter KPRC Radio, Houston, 1974-76; pres. Hawkins Co., Houston, 1976-81; free-lance asst. editor Oil and Gas Digest, Houston, 1981; account supr. Bozell & Jacobs Pub. Relations, Houston, 1982—; cons. Assn. Women Attys., Houston, 1980. Contbr. articles to profl. jours. Media cons. various local election campaigns, 1978—; vol. Houston Council on Human Relations, 1977-82, Am. Heart Assn., Houston, 1984. Recipient Tex. Investigative Reporting award Tex. Associated Press, 1975. Mem. Soc. for Tech. Communication (awards competition co-chmn. local chpt. 1984, Meit award 1982-83, 83-84, Achievement award 1983-84, 84-85), Nat. Investor Relations Inst., Assn. Petroleum Writers, Forum Club of Houston, Aircraft Owners and Pilots Assn. Democrat. Club: Fondren Tennis (Houston). Avocations: flying; tennis; volleyball; reading; travel. Home: 3046 Las Palmas Houston TX 77027 Office: Bozell Jacobs Kenyon & Eckhardt Pub Relations 3300 Republic Bank Ctr Houston TX 77002

HAWKINS, GERI SUE, interior designer, real estate salesperson; b. Kansas City, Mo., Sept. 4, 1940; d. William S. McCune and Verla J. (Kempter) McCune Stoll; m. LeRay D. Long, Oct. 12, 1958 (div. Dec. 1961); 1 child, Lori Diane Long Seidl; m. Ray Eldon Hawkins, Oct. 9, 1964; children—Lynn M., John Ted; stepchildren—Celeste, Steve. Student Kansas City Bus. Coll., 1961-62, U. Mo.-Kansas City, 1974-75; A.A., Maple Woods Coll., 1974. Interior designer Carpenter Bros. Inc., Kansas City, 1975-77; pres., designer Gerry Hawkins Interiors, Kansas City, 1977-81; interior designer R. D. Mann Inc., Kansas City, 1981-83; owner-designer Designs By Geri, Kansas City, 1983—; realtor assoc. ERA Martin House, Platte City, Mo., 1984-85; interior designer Martin House Design, Platte City, 1984-85. Local theatrical appearances, 1972, 73. Leader Winding River council Girl Scouts U.S., 1966-71; mem. Grace Notes Singing Ensemble, Kansas City, 1980-85; fundraiser Muscular Dystrophy Assn., Platte City, 1985; trustee Park Hill Bapt. Ch., Parkville, Mo., 1983-85. Recipient Best Actress award Maple Woods Coll., 1972; arts grantee Maple Woods Coll., Kansas City, Mo., 1974. Mem. Platte County Bus. and Profl. Assn. (bd. dirs. 1980-81), Women in Bus. Republican. Baptist. Avocations: tennis; swimming; painting; theatre; gardening. Home: 8010 NW Mace Rd Kansas City MO 64152 Office: Design by Geri 8010 NW Mace Rd PO Box 14181 Kansas City MO 64152

HAWKINS, IDA FAYE, educator; b. Ft. Worth, Dec. 28, 1928; d. Christopher Columbus and Nannie Idella (Hughes) Hall; student Midwestern U., 1946-48; B.S., N. Tex. State U., 1951; student Lamar U., 1968-70; M.S., McNeese State U., 1973; m. Gene Hamilton Hawkins, Dec. 22, 1952; children—Gene Agner, Jane Hall. Tchr., DeQueen Elem. Sch., Port Arthur, Tex., 1950-54; tchr. Tyrrell Elem. Sch., Port Arthur, 1955-56; tchr. Roy Hatton Elem. Sch., Bridge City, Tex., 1967-68; tchr. Oak Forest Elem. Sch., Vidor, Tex., 1968—. Second vice-pres. Travis Elem. PTA, 1965-66, 1st v.p., 1966-67; corr. sec. Port Arthur City council PTA, 1966-67. Named Tchr. of Yr., Oak Forest Elem., 1984-85. Mem. NEA, Tex. State Tchrs. Assn., Classroom Tchrs. Assn., Am. Psychol. Assn., McNeese State U. Alumni Assn. Presbyterian (Sunday sch. tchr. 1951-53, 60-66). Home: 4075 Laurel Apt 73 Beaumont TX 77707 Office: Oak Forest Elem Sch 2400 Hwy 12 Vidor TX 77662

HAWKINS, KAREN FRANCES, banker; b. Portchester, N.Y., Nov. 30, 1947; d. George Lockwood, II and Helen Athena (Raftes) H.; B.A. in Math. and Spanish, Wells Coll., Aurora, N.Y., 1969; grad. Inst. Coop. Leadership, 1978. Asso. in corp. fin. Morgan Stanley & Co., N.Y.C., 1969-71; fin. analyst pvt. placements Travelers Ins. Co., Hartford, Conn., 1971-72; analyst corp. fin. and research Culverwell & Co., Inc., Springfield, Mass., 1972-74; asst. v.p., comml. loan officer Springfield Bank for Coops., 1974-80; group mgr. tng. comml. lenders Citizens & So. Nat. Bank, Atlanta, 1980-81, mgr. comml. br., 1982-84, v.p., comml. relationship mgr., 1984-86, mgr. Comml. Ctr., 1986—; tchr. classes in field. Mem. recreation com. Cross Creek Homeowners, 1984-85; mem. Gwinnett County Council Quality Growth. Mem. Am. Inst. Banking, Atlanta C. of C. (life), Nat. Assn. Bank Women. Republican. Episcopalian. Clubs: Cross Creek Ladies Twilight Golf League (chmn. 1981-82), Cross Creek Golf Assn. (treas. 1982, co-chmn. 1983), Civitan. Office: 3210 Holcomb Bridge Rd Norcross GA 30092

HAWKINS, KAREN LEE, lawyer; b. Central Falls, R.I., Oct. 17, 1945; d. Everett Yale and Kathryn Mary (Zagar) H.; m. Martin H. Rateau, Jr. B.A., U. Mass., Amherst, 1967; M.Ed., U. Calif.-Davis, 1976; J.D., Golden Gate U., 1979, M.B.A. in Taxation, 1981. Bar: Calif. 1979, cert. tax specialist 1985. Asst. dean student affairs U. Calif., Davis, 1973-76; tax cons. Touche Ross & Co., San Francisco, 1979-83; sole practice, 1983-84; ptnr. Berger & Taggart, San Francisco, 1985—; instr. Golden Gate U. Sch. Taxation, 1984—. Pres. Women's Rep. Assembly, Davis, 1974-75. Rockefeller Found. fellow, 1962-63; Mandarin Chinese grantee, 1962. Mem. ABA (com. taxation, litigation com.), Calif. Women Lawyers. Calif. Bar Assn., Bar Assn. San Francisco, Am. Trial Lawyers Assn., NOW, ACLU. Club: Sierra. Office: 100 Bush St 20th Floor San Francisco CA 94104

HAWKINS, LINDA SARAH COFER, entrepreneur; b. Long Branch, N.J., June 13, 1951; d. James H. and Marion D. (Willis) Cofer; children—Eldridge, Hillary. B.A. in Bus. Adminstrn., Upsala Coll., 1973; postgrad. Monmouth Coll., 1974-76. Adminstr. E. Hawkins Atty., East Orange, N.J., 1976—; pres. Cofer Hawkins Funeral Home, Inc., East Orange, 1981—; treas. Cofer Willis Corp., Red Bank, N.J., 1984—; pres. Lyn-El Corp., East Orange, 1985—. Founder Carl Lewis Fund, East Orange, 1984; dir. Ms. Essex County Sr. Citizen Pageant, East Orange, 1977-78. Named Outstanding Citizen City of Long Branch, 1974-75. Mem. Alpha Kappa Alpha. Clubs: Essex New Direction (treas. 1984—), Jack and Jill of Am. (North Jersey); Llewelly Park Ladies Assn. (rec. sec. 1984—). Avocations: classical piano; gardening. Home: Llewellyn Park West Orange NJ 07052 Office: Eldridge Hawkins Atty at Law 110 S Munn Ave East Orange NJ 07018

HAWKINS, MARY ELLEN HIGGINS, state legislator; b. Birmingham, Ala.; student U. Ala., Tuscaloosa, 1945-47; m. James H. Hawkins (div., 1971); children—Andrew Higgins, Elizabeth and Peter Hixon. Congl. aide to several mems. U.S. Ho. Reps., 1949-59; chmn. Sumter County (Ga.) Republican Com., 1970-72; vice-chmn. 3d Dist. Republican Com., 1970-72; community adv. council Sm. Bus. Adminstrn., Atlanta, 1970-72; mem. Fla. Ho. Reps., 1974—; dir., vice chmn. NAFCO Fin. Group Inc. and subs. including Naples Fed. Savs. and Loan Assn., Inc., 1979—. Mem. Fla. Adv. Council, U.S. Commn. Civil Rights, 1977-81; art instr. Sumter County Schs., Americus, Ga., 1971-72; staff writer Naples Daily News, Fla., 1972-74. Roman Catholic. Club: Zonta. Office: Fla Ho Reps State Capitol Tallahassee FL 32301

HAWKINS, MINNIE JEWEL, educator; b. Center, Tex., Nov. 28, 1930; d. Garfield and Pearl (Greer) Richards; m. Hezekiah Hawkins, Jr., July 11, 1953. B.A., Prairie View A&M Coll.; M.B.A., Tex. So. U. Cert. elem. and secondary tchr., bus. edn. adminstr., Tex. Tchr., Nacogoches (Tex.) Ind. Sch. Dist., 1952-60, Houston Ind. Sch. Dist., 1960—. Pres. Anna B. Kelso PTA, 1973-74; sponsor Camp Fire Girls, Houston, 1973—; mem. Crestmont Park Civic Club, 1968—, Precinct 132 Democratic Club, 1970—. Named Tchr. of Yr., Anna B. Kelso Elem. Sch., Houston, 1981-82. Mem. Houston Tchrs. Assn., Tex. Classroom Tchrs. Assn., Tex. Tchrs. Assn., NEA, Alpha Kappa Alpha. Methodist. Home: 5302 Tavenor Ln Houston TX 77048

HAWKINS, MURIEL ANNE, university administrator; b. Norfolk, Va., Apr. 22, 1946; d. George Hawkins and Frieda (Robinson) Hawkins Mitchell; 1 child, Jamal Scott. B.S. in Radiol. Scis., Chgo. Med. Sch., 1975; M.Ed., The Citadel, 1979. Lic. in radiography, Ill. Radiographer Meharry Med. Ctr., Nashville, 1967-70; clin. instr. Cook County Hosp., Chgo., 1971-76; instr. Med. U. S.C., Charleston, 1976-79; asst. prof. radiol. scis., coordinator student affairs Coll. Allied Health, Chgo. State U., 1980—; lectr. dept. radiography Malcolm X Coll., Chgo., 1976-77; instr. employee devel. Med. U. S.C., Charleston, 1977-79; mem. spl. faculty, div. allied health Nat. Coll. Edn., Evanston, Ill., 1982, 83, 84; cons. enrollment mgmt. West Chester U., Pa., 1985. Mem. adv. bd. radiol. sci. U. Health Sci., Chgo. Med. Sch., 1976-79; mem. adv. bd., allied health com. Am. Cancer Soc., Chgo., 1982—; bd. dirs., sec. Notre Dame Acad., Chgo., 1981-83; mem. adv. bd., radiography program Malcolm X Coll., Chgo., 1981—. Kellogg fellow, 1983-84. Mem. Am. Soc. Allied Health Professions, Ill. Assn. Allied Health Professions, Ill. Soc. Radiologic Technologists, Am. Assn. Higher Edn., Am. Ednl. Research Assn., Assn. for Supervision and Curriculum Devel., Ill. Com. on Black Concerns in Higher Edn., Phi Delta Kappa. Democrat. Methodist. Avocations: antique glassware. Home: 810 S Austin Blvd Oak Park IL 60304 Office: Coll Allied Health Chicago State University 9501 S King Dr Chicago IL 60628

HAWKINS, PAULA, U.S. senator; b. Salt Lake City, Jan. 24, 1927; ed. U. Utah, L.H.D. (hon.), 1982; m. Walter Eugene Hawkins, 1947; children—Genean, Kevin, Kelley. Mem. U.S. Senate from Fla., 1981—, chmn. Senate Drug Enforcement Caucus; mem. Republican Nat. Com., 1968—; co-chmn. platform com. Nat. Rep. Conv., 1984, co-chmn. rules com., 1980; v.p. AirFla., 1979-80. Mem. Fla. Pub. Service Commn., 1972-79, chmn., 1977-79. Mem. Fla. Fedn. Rep. Women; Nat. Fedn. Rep. Women. Recipient numerous awards including Guardian Small Bus., Nat. Fedn. Ind. Bus., 1982; Republican Woman of Yr. award Women's Nat. Rep. Club, 1981. Mem. Ch. Jesus Christ of Latter-day Saints. Office: 313 Hart Senate Office Bldg Washington DC 20510

HAWKINS, RUTH ANNE, university administrator; b. St. Louis, Mar. 31, 1947; d. James Henry and Hazel Marie (Snoddy) Wehmer; m. Van Ray Hawkins, May 17, 1969; 1 child, Warren Curt. A.A., Columbia Coll., Mo., 1967; B.J., U. Mo., 1969; M.A., Ark. State U., 1982; postgrad. U. Miss., 1984—. News reporter Sta. WVEC-TV, Hampton, Va., 1969-70; newspaper feature writer Ledger-Star, Norfolk, Va., 1970-74; coordinator pub. info. Newport News Pub. Schs., Va., 1974-78, legis. liaison, 1977-78; coordinator affirmative action Ark. State U., Jonesboro, 1978-79, dir. pub. relations, 1979-82, dir. pub. relations and devel., 1982—; mem. tech. rev. com. East Ark. Planning and Devel. Dist., Jonesboro, 1979—; U.S. Office Edn. del. Japanese Ministry Edn., 1977. Editor: Voices From State: An Oral History of Arkansas State University, 1984. Bd. dirs. United Way Greater Jonesboro, 1979-82. Recipient Penney-Mo. Nat. Fashion Writing award U. Mo., 1972, Slover News Writing award Ledger-Star, 1974. Mem. Council for Advancement Support of Edn., AAUW, Phi Kappa Phi. Home: 306 S Third St Paragould AR 72450 Office: Ark State U PO Box 1990 State University AR 72467

HAWKS, JANE ESTHER HOKANSON, nurse administrator, educator, researcher; b. Sac City, Iowa, Apr. 8, 1955; d. Charles Wesley and Esther Pearl (Langbein) Hokanson; m. Edward Harold Hawks, May 24, 1980; 1 child, Jennifer Jane. B.S. in Nursing, St. Olaf Coll., 1977; M.S. in Nursing, U. Nebr.-Omaha, 1981. Staff nurse Rochester Meth. Hosp., Rochester, Minn., 1977-78; instr. nursing Morningside Coll., Sioux City, Iowa, 1978-79, Jennie Edmundson Sch. Nursing, Council Bluffs, Iowa, 1979-81, U. Nebr. Med. Ctr. Coll. Nursing, Omaha, 1981-86; pvt. duty supr. Family Home Care, Omaha, 1986—; researcher Alcoholism Research Team, Omaha, 1982—. Recipient Rena Boyle award U. Nebr., 1980; named Nurse of Yr., Dist. 9 Iowa Nurses Assn., 1983. Mem. Iowa Nurses Assn. (pres. Dist. 9), Am. Nurses Assn., Sigma Theta Tau. Lutheran. Contbr. chpts. in books, articles to profl. jours. Home: 414 3d St Box 273A Rural Route 1 Underwood IA 51576 Office: Family Home Care 7500 Mercy Rd Omaha NE 68124

HAWLEY, ANNE, state arts administrator; b. Iowa City, Iowa, Nov. 3, 1943; d. Marshall Newton and Leone Ardith (Wilson) Hawley; m. Bruce Ivor McPherson, Sept. 4, 1977; 1 dau., Katherine Black. B.A., U. Iowa, 1966; M.A., George Washington U., 1969. Adminstrv. asst. Donald Mitchell, Washington, 1967-69; research assoc. Nat. Urban League, Washington, 1969-71, Ford Found. Study Leadership in Pub. Schs., Washington, 1971-73; exec. dir. Cultural Edn. Collaborative, Boston, 1974-77, Mass. Council Arts/Humanities, Boston, 1977—. Bd. dirs. New Eng. Found. for Arts, 1977—, Nat. Assembly/State Arts Agencies, Washington, 1981—. Recipient Design Travel Grant, Women's Travel Club, Boston, 1982. Mem. Nat. Endowment for Arts (museum panel, 1978-81, dance panel 1980-81). Office: Mass Council on Arts and Humanities 80 Boylston St Suite 1000 Boston MA 02116

HAWLEY, JILL KATHLEEN, government bank insurance company executive; b. Midland, Tex., Aug. 21, 1960; d. Samuel Olvin and Genevieve Frances (Douglas) H. B.B.A., Tex. A&M U., 1982. Petroleum landman DeVasto Energy, Tyler, Tex., 1982, Stubblefield & Assocs., Tyler, 1982; comml. account officer Fed. Deposit Ins. Corp., Midland, Tex., 1983-84, energy account officer, 1984-86, bank settlement officer, 1986—; judge Tex. Forensic Assn., Distributive Edn. Clubs Am. Mem. Nat. Assn. Female Execs. Methodist. Club: Tex. A&M (head promotions/Aggie Muster 1986). Avocations: horseback riding; swimming; aerobics; jogging; table tennis. Home: 5101 N Ave A #201 Midland TX 79705 Office: Fed Deposit Ins Corp PO Box 3148 303 Air Park Dr Midland TX 79702

HAWLEY, LINDA DONOVAN, advertising executive; b. Bryn Mawr, Pa., Nov. 1, 1946; d. John Donovan and Ann (Durnall) H.; diploma in advt. Charles Morris Price Sch. Advt., Phila., 1965. Sr. writer The Bulletin Co., Phila., 1968-72, The Advt. People, Inc., Bala Cynwyd, Pa., 1973-75, Elkman Advt. Co., Inc., Bala Cynwyd, 1975-77; sr. copywriter Mel Richman Inc., Bala Cynwyd, 1977-80; pres. Hawley & Matthews Inc., Valley Forge, Pa., 1980—; lectr. Charles Morris Price Sch., Pa. State U. Recipient various advt. awards including Neographics award. 1970, Addy award, 1976, Addy awards 2d Dist., 1980, Phila., 1981; Charles Morris Price Sch. Disting. Alumni Award, 1977; TRAC award, 1983, 84, 85. Mem. Phila. Club Advt. Women (pres. 1978-80), Phila. Women's Network (pres. 1983-84, dir. 1984—), Am. Advt. Fedn. (Pa. lt. gov. 1979-84, 2d dist. sec. 1981-82), TV and Radio Advt. Club. Roman Catholic. Office: Hawley & Matthews Inc PO Box 927 Davis Rd and Oakwood Ln Valley Forge PA 19481

HAWLEY, SANDRA SUE, electrical engineer; b. Spirit Lake, Iowa, May 7, 1948; d. Byrnard Leroy and Dorothy Virginia (Fischbeck) Smith; m. Michael John Hawley, June 7, 1970; 1 child, Alexander Tristin. B.S. in Elec. Engring., U. Dayton, 1981; B.S. in Math. and Statistics, Iowa State U., 1970; M.S. in Statistics, U. Del., 1975. Research analyst State of Wis., Madison, 1970-71; research asst. Del. State Coll., Dover, 1972-73; asst. prof. math. and statistics Wesley Coll., Dover, 1974-81, chmn. dept. math. and computer sci., 1978-80; elec. engr. Control Data Corp., Bloomington, Minn., 1982-85; sr. elec. engr. Custom Integrated Circuits, 1985—. Elder, Presbyterian Ch. U.S.A., 1975—, mem. session Oak Grove Presbyn. Ch., Bloomington, 1985—. NSF scholar U. Dayton, 1981. Mem. IEEE, Assn. Women in Sci., Am. Statis. Assn., Sigma Delta Epsilon. Home: 7724 W 85th St Circle Bloomington MN 55438 Office: Custom Integrated Circuits 5353 Wayzata Blvd Minneapolis MN 55416

HAWN, GOLDIE, actress; b. Washington, Nov. 21, 1945; d. Edward Rutledge and Laura (Steinhoff) Hawn; student Am. U.; m. Gus Trinkonis, May 16, 1969 (div.); m. 2d Bill Hudson (div.); children—Oliver, Kate Garry. Profl. dancer, 1965; 1st profl. acting in Good Morning, World, 1967-68; mem. company Laugh-In 1968-70; appeared in TV spl. Pure Goldie, 1971, Goldie and Kids—Listen to Us, 1982; appeared in films Cactus Flower (Acad. award best supporting actress), 1969, There's A Girl In My Soup, 1970, Dollars, 1971, Butterflies Are Free, 1971, The Sugarland Express, 1974, The Girl from Petrovka, 1974, Shampoo, 1975, The Duchess and the Dirtwater Fox, 1976, Foul Play, 1978, Seems Like Old Times, 1980, Best Friends, 1982, Swingshift, 1984; exec. producer and star Private Benjamin, 1980, Proctor, 1984, Wild cats, 1986. Office: care William Morris Agy 151 El Camino Dr Beverly Hills CA 90212*

HAWORTH, MIRIAM PLETCHER, psychologist; b. Abington, Pa., Dec. 1, 1931; d. Harry N. and Marie (Docherty) Pletcher; m. Donald Robert Haworth, Sr., Mar. 24, 1951 (div. Oct. 1976); children—Merry Jayne, Melodie Susan, Donald Robert. Student Purdue U., 1954-55; B.S., Okla. State U., 1958, M.S., 1963; Ph.D., U. Nebr., 1970. Instr., Okla. State U., Stillwater, 1963-66, U. Nebr., Lincoln, 1967-70; psychologist Nebr. Dept. Correctional Services, Lincoln, 1970—; cons. corrections, Lincoln, 1973—. Mem. adv. bd. Lancaster Office Mental Retardation, Lincoln, 1971-73; cons. Girl Scouts Am., Stillwater, Okla., 1963-66; mem. Mayor's Jail Study Com., Lincoln, 1974-75; mem. law enforcement com. Nebr. Drug Commn., Lincoln, 1973-79. Named Old Master, Purdue U., Lafayette, Ind., 1973; recipient Gov.'s award Ninety-Nines, 1973. Mem. Am. Psychol. Assn., Am. Correctional Assn., Nebr. Correctional Assn. (pres. 1973-75), Nebr. Soc. Profl. Psychologists, Nebr. Psychol. Assn. Republican. Club: Ninety-Nines. Office: Nebr Dept Correctional Services PO Box 94661 Lincoln NE 68509

HAWRYSH, ZENIA JEAN, food scientist; b. Edmonton, Alta., Can., Nov. 4, 1938; d. Onif and Pauline (Keaschuk) Lukianchuk; B.Sc. in Home Econs., U. Alta., Edmonton, 1959; M.Sc. in Foods, Mich. State U., 1960, Ph.D. in Food Sci., 1970. Lectr. foods, dept. home econs. U. Alta., 1960, asst. prof., 1962; grad. asst. dept. food sci. Mich. State U., 1969-70; asso. prof. foods, dept. home econs. U. Alta., 1976-80, prof., chmn. dept. foods and nutrition, 1980—. Gen. Foods Fund fellow, 1966-67; Thelma Porter fellow, 1967-68. Mem. Inst. Food Technologists, Can. Inst. Food Sci. and Tech., Am. Meat Sci. Assn., Am. Dairy Sci. Assn., AAAS, Am. Dietetic Assn., Can. Dietetic Assn., Can. Univ. Tchrs. Home Econs., Am. Home Econs. Assn., Central and East European Studies Assn. Can., Sigma Xi. Ukrainian Greek Orthodox. Club: Ukrainian Profl. and Bus. Office: 308C Home Economics Bldg University of Alberta Edmonton AB T6G 2M8 Canada

HAWTHORNE, BETTY EILEEN, educator, emeritus university dean; b. Seattle, Nov. 22, 1920; d. Harry Albert and Marcia (Thompson) Hawthorne; B.S., U. Wash., 1941, M.S., 1944. Ph.D., Mich. State U., 1954. Field nutritionist Pacific area ARC, Wash., 1943-44; instr., asst. prof. Oreg. State U., Corvallis, 1946-55, assoc. prof. foods and nutrition, 1955-62, prof., 1962-83, dean Sch. Home Econs., 1965-83; dir. Curtice-Burns, Inc., Rochester, N.Y.; chmn. home economics subcom., expt. sta. com. on orgn. and policy Nat. Assn. State Univs. and Land Grant Colls., 1977-80; dir. Pacific Corp., Portland. Bd. dirs. Good Samaritan Hosp., Corvallis, 1970-78, Children's Farm Home Found., Corvallis; hon. trustee Good Samaritan Hosp. Found. Served with ensign to lt. (j.g.). Supply Corps. USNR, 1944-46. Mem. Am., Oreg. (past pres.) dietetic assns., Am. Inst. Nutrition, Am. Home Econs. Assn. (past sect. chmn., pres. Found. 1985-86), Assn. Adminstrs. Home Econs. in Land Grant Colls. and State Univs. (pres. 1976-77), AAUW, Soc. Nutrition Edn., Western Gerontol. Soc., Am. Council Consumer Interests, Altrusa Internat. Phi Beta Kappa, Sigma Xi, Phi Kappa Phi, Omicron Nu, Iota Sigma Pi. Home: 144 NW 29th St Corvallis OR 97330

HAY, BETTY JO, civic worker; b. McAlester, Okla., June 6, 1931; d. Duncan and Kathryn Myrtle (Albert) Peacock; m. Jess Thomas Hay, Aug. 3, 1951; children—Deborah Hay Werner, Patricia Lynn. B.A., So. Meth. U., 1952. Bd. dirs. White House Preservation Fund, 1980—; bd. dirs. Nat. Mental Health Assn., 1978—, pres., 1986, mem. fin. com. and child adolescent com., 1978-79, mem. resource devel. com., 1980-83; v.p. fundraising Mental Health Assn. Tex., 1980, bd. dirs., 1974—, pres., 1983-84; bd. dirs. Community Council Dallas, 1984—, S.W. Family Inst., Dallas, 1984—; bd. dirs. Mental Health Assn., Dallas County, 1972—, pres., 1981-82; bd. dirs. United Way Met. Dallas, 1983—, Assn. Higher Edn. North Tex., 1980-82, vice chmn., 1982-83, chmn., 1984-85; mem. adv. bd. Sch. Social Work, U. Tex., Arlington, 1983—; mem. Dallas Council on World Affairs, Woman's Div., Dallas Symphony Orch. League, Historic Preservation League, March of Dimes Aux., 1982—, many past involvements in charitable orgns. Address: 7236 Lupton Circle Dallas TX 75225

HAY, ELIZABETH KERR, nurse, educator; b. N.Y.C., Apr. 11, 1943; d. Alexander Wilson and Elizabeth Ransom (Kerr) H.; A.B., Randolph-Macon Woman's Coll., 1965; B.S., Columbia U., 1967; R.N., Columbia-Presbyn. Med. Center, 1967; M.S.N., Vanderbilt U., 1976. Orthopedic staff nurse Presbyn. Hosp., N.Y.C., 1967-69; nursing supr., instr. Firestone Hosp., Harbel, Liberia, 1969; head nurse, supr. Rogosin Kidney Disease Treatment Center, N.Y. Hosp., Cornell Med. Center, 1970-74; staff nurse hemodialysis Nashville VA Hosp., 1974-75; clin. specialist adult neurosurgery/orthopedics, instr. med.-surg. nursing Vanderbilt U., Nashville, 1976-79, asst. prof. med.-surg. nursing, 1979-83, assoc. prof., 1983—, asst. to dean, 1983-84, interim assoc. dean for community service, faculty practice and internat. studies, 1984—, dirs. honors program; cons. profl. adv. bd., quality assurance reviewer Upjohn Health Care Services, 1979—; neurol.-neurosurg. cons. VA Hosp., Murfreesboro, Tenn.; neurol. cons. critical care program U. Tenn., 1981-83. Recipient Shirley Titus award Sch. Nursing, Vanderbilt U., 1981, 84, excellence in clin. instrn. award; Ellen Gregg Ingalls award Vanderbilt U., 1982. Mem. Am. Nurses Assn. (com. to develop standards of orthopedic nursing practice 1982-86), Nat. Assn. Orthopedic Nurses (pres. 1981-82), Tenn. Nurses Assn., Sigma Theta Tau. Office: Vanderbilt U Godchaux Hall 21st Ave S Nashville TN 37240

HAY, MAUREENE GRIFFOUL, advertising company executive; b. San Jose, Calif., May 17, 1946; d. Henry Maruice and Eileene (Durkin) Griffoul; m. Macgregor Bruce Hay, Feb. 19, 1966 (div. Mar. 1979); children—Alison Nicole, Morgan Andrew; m. Richard Philip Spencer, Apr. 30, 1983. Student San Jose State U. Acct., Honig Cooper & Harrington, San Francisco, 1966-67, media buyer, 1967-72; pvt. practice media buyer, planner, Oakland, Calif., 1972-79; v.p., media dir. Davis, Johnson, Mogul and Colombatto, San Francisco, 1979—. Mem. San Francisco Media Dirs. Council (pres.), San Francisco Ad Club. Republican. Roman Catholic. Club: Benefit Guild of the East Bay (v.p. 1977, pres. 1978). Home: 3938 Oakmore Rd Oakland CA 94602 Office: Davis Johnson Mogul and Colombatto 731 Market St San Francisco CA 94103

HAY, MILLICENT VICTORIA, writer; b. Long Beach, Calif., May 7, 1945; d. Glenn and Julie (DeLong) Gunnells; m. John Leonard Hay, Dec. 16, 1967; 1 son, Ian Daniel. B.A., U. Ariz., 1966; M.A., Ariz. State U., 1971, Ph.D., 1979. Instr. Ariz. State U., Tempe, 1969-73, editor Research News, 1979-82; freelance writer, Phoenix, 1982—; staff writer Phoenix Mag., 1983-84. Author: The Life of Robert Sidney, Earl of Leicester, 1984; editor: The Insomniac Reader, 1986; contbr. articles to various publs. Mem. Am. Soc. Journalists and Authors, Phi Beta Kappa, Sigma Delta Chi. Home and Office: 201 E Hayward Ave Phoenix AZ 85020

HAYDEN, VIRGINIA EVA, pharmaceutical company executive; b. Midland, Mich., May 20, 1927; d. Robert James and Altheda Mae (Wood) H.; B.A. in Acctg. and Econs., Mich. State U., 1949; m. Donald Conrad, Feb. 15, 1952 (div.). Stock inventory clk. Dow Chem. Co., 1949-50; budget clk., analyst, specialist, coordinator Upjohn Co., Kalamazoo, 1950-72, mgr. corp. budgeting, 1972-78, exec. devel. cons., 1978-85, sr. cons. exec. devel., 1985—, also co-founder, advisor Greater Opportunities for Women (GROW); speaker mgmt. classes; speaker on career planning and women in mgmt. to profl. orgns.; tchr. women in mgmt. Kalamazoo Coll. Chmn. adv. bd. Center for Women's Services of Western Mich. U.; bd. dirs. Kalamazoo Alcohol and Drug Abuse Council. Recipient W.E. Upjohn award, 1970. Mem. Kalamazoo Network (dir., co-founder), Am. Soc. Tng. and Devel., Kalamazoo Personnel Assn., Nat. Wildlife Assn., Kalamazoo Nature Center, Audubon Soc. Club: Kalamazoo Altrusa (past pres.). Home: 8207 Bruning St Kalamazoo MI 49002 Office: Upjohn Co 7000 Portage Rd Kalamazoo MI 49001

HAYE, MARY TERESSA, teacher, consultant; b. West Monroe, La., Oct. 31, 1953; d. Jackie R. and Carolyn (Russell) H. B.A., Northeast La. U., 1974, M.Ed., 1977, Edn. Specialist, 1982. Cert. tchr., La. Tchr. Swayze Elem. Sch., Monroe, La., 1974-81; mgr. Bonanza Steak House, Ruston, La., 1981-82; tchr. Jack Hayes Elem. Sch., Monroe, 1982; tchr. Drew Elem. Sch., West Monroe, 1982—, coordinator computer edn., 1984-86, dir. Social Studies Fairs, 1982-86; cons. Parent Tchr. Orgn., West Monroe, 1984-86. Author: Causes and Effects of Stress on Teachers, 1982. Coach Dixie Youth Softball, West Monroe, 1983, 85, umpire, 1984; umpire Amateur Softball Assn., Monroe, 1986. Mem. La. Fedn. Tchrs., Ouachita Fedn. Tchrs., Northeast La. Reading Council, La. Reading Council, Nat. Assn. Female Execs., Smithsonian Inst. Democrat. Baptist. Avocations: softball; basketball; horseback riding; jogging; photography; reading. Home: Route 2 Box 430 Farmerville LA 71241 Office: Drew Elem Sch Route 1 Arkansas Rd West Monroe LA 71291

HAYEK, CAROLYN JEAN, judge; b. Portland, Oreg., Aug. 17, 1948; d. Robert A. and Marion L. (DeKoning) H.; m. Steven M. Rosen, July 21, 1974; 1 son, Jonathan David. B.A. in Psychology, Carleton Coll., 1970; J.D., U. Chgo., 1973. Bar: Wash. 1973. Assoc. firm Jones, Grey & Bayley, Seattle, 1973-77; sole practice law, Federal Way, Wash., 1977-82; judge Federal Way Dist. Ct., 1982—. Task force mem. Alternatives for Wash., 1973-75; mem. Wash. State Ecol. Commn., 1975-77. Mem. ABA, Wash. Women Lawyers, Wash. State Bar Assn., AAUW (br. pres. 1978-80), King County Dist. Ct. Judges Assn. (treas., exec. com., com. chmn.), Elected Wash. Women (dir. 1983—), Nat. Assn. Women Judges (nat. bd. dirs., dist. bd. dirs. 1984—), Federal Way Women's Network (bd. dirs. 1984—, pres. 1985), Greater Federal Way C. of C. (dir. 1978-82, sec. 1980-81, v.p. 1981-82). Republican. Unitarian. Office: Federal Way Dist Ct 33506 10th Pl S Federal Way WA 98003

HAYEK, MARY ANNIE, psychologist; b. Paterson, N.J., Feb. 13, 1925; d. Anthony T. and Mary N. (Sara) Haddad; B.A. with distinction in Psychology, Fla. Internat. U., 1975, M.S. in Counselor Edn., 1978; Ph.D. in Clin. Psychology, Heed U., Hollywood, Fla., 1980; m. James Paul Hayek, Aug. 12, 1945; children—George Anthony, James Paul, Joanne Christine. Alcohol counselor, therapist South Miami Hosp., Miami, Fla., 1977-78; cons. psychologist, psychotherapist Victims Advocates for Sexually Abused Children, Miami, 1980-81; psychotherapist Counseling and Stress Control Center, Coral Gables, Fla., 1978-80, pvt. practice with Center, 1980—. Master and Johnson fellow, 1979-82. Mem. Am. Mental Health Counselors Assn., Am. Assn. Counseling and Devel., Am. Psychol. Assn., Fla. Assn. Practicing Psychologists, Fla. Assn. Profl. Hypnosis, Fla. Mental Health Counselors Assn., Nat. Rehab. Assn., Mental Health Assn. Dade County, Phi Theta Kappa, Phi Lambda Pi, Psi Chi. Author: Recovered Alcoholic Women With and Without Incest Experience, 1981. Home: 1801 SW 84th Ct Miami FL 33155 Office: 115 Madeira Ave Coral Gables FL 33134

HAYES, ALBERTA PHYLLIS WILDRICK, ret. health service exec.; b. Blakeslee, Pa., May 31, 1918; d. William and Maude (Robbins) Wildrick; diploma Wilkes Barre Gen. Hosp. Sch. Nursing, 1938-41; student Wilkes Coll., 1953-54, Pa. State U., 1969—; m. Glenmore Burton Hayes, Oct. 9, 1942; children—Glenmore Rolland, William Bruce. Nurse, Monroe County Gen. Hosp., East Stroudsburg, Pa., 1941-44; pvt. duty nurse, 1944-56; with White Haven (Pa.) Center, 1956-82, dir. residential services, 1966-82, ret., 1982. Pres. Tobyhanna Twp. Sch. PTA, 1948-49, Top-o-Pocono Women of Rotary, 1975-76; nurse ARC, 1955; adv. council Luzerne County Foster Grandparent Program, 1977—. Health Services Keystone Job Corps, Drums, Pa., 1977—. Mem. Am. Assn. Mental Deficiency, Am. Legion Aux. (unit pres. 1946-47). Club: Pocono Mountains Women's (Blakeslee). Home: PO Box 11 Blakeslee PA 18610

HAYES, ALBERTINE BRANNUM, educational consultant; b. Lake Providence, La.; d. William Anthony and Elizabeth (Hearns) Brannum; B.S., So. U., 1940; M.A., U. Mich., 1952; Ed.S., Peabody Coll., Nashville, 1961; Ed.D., U. Okla., 1964; m. James T. Hayes, June 2, 1950. Tchr. elem. level Natchitoches (La.) Parish Schs., 1940-41; tchr. math. Lake Charles (La.) City Schs., 1941-44, Caddo Parish Schs., Shreveport, La., 1944-58, supr. math. and sci. edn., 1964-73, asst. prin. instrn. and curriculum Booker T. Washington High Sch., Shreveport, 1958-64; asst. supt. community affairs Caddo Parish Sch. Bd., Shreveport, from 1973; now ednl. cons.; lectr. in edn. Centenary Coll., Shreveport, 1968-70; vis. prof. So. U., Baton Rouge, 1964-67, N.E. La. U., Monroe, 1968-70; mem. com. on state metric study La. Dept. Edn., 1973-74; mem. La. Adv. Com. on Math., 1966-70; cons. S.W. Ednl. Devel. Lab., 1965-69, S. Central Ednl. Lab., 1966-68. Mem. N.W. La. Health Planning Council, 1973—; mem. Mayor's Fact-Finding Com. for Youth Services, 1973—; mem. sr. choir St. Matthew A.M.E. Ch., 1960—, missionary soc., 1966—, fin. com. 1970—; bd. dirs. United Way, vice chmn., 1974-75, 78-79; bd. dirs. ARC, 1973—, Integrated Youth Services, Caddo Found. Exceptional Children, 1973—, Excel-Caddo, 1978-79, NCCJ, Vols. Am.; mem. Pelican council Girl Scouts U.S.; bd. dirs., treas. So. area Links, Inc.; mem. task force on edn. La. Priorities for Future; mem. steering com. Alliance for Better Community, 1978; mem. Caddo-Bossier Council on Alcoholism, Mayor's Correct Count Com., 1980. So. Edn. Found. fellow, 1962-64; recipient Outstanding Service award A.M.E. Ch., 1964, Educator of Yr. award Caddo Parish Schs., 1969, Outstanding Negro Woman of Yr., Nat. Daus. of Isis, 1975; named Woman of Yr., Zeta Phi Beta, 1965. Mem. La. Assn. Suprs. and Consultants (pres. 1968-73), Assn. Supervision and Curriculum Devel. (secondary edn. council 1969-71), Nat. Council Tchrs., Nat. Council Accreditation of Tchr. Edn. (evaluation bd. 1972), La. Edn. Assn., Nat. Assn. Secondary Sch. Prins., La. PTA (life), Nat. PTA (life), Delta Sigma Theta. Club: White Rose. Contbr. articles to profl. publs. Home: 3140 Milam St Shreveport LA 71103

HAYES, ALICE BOURKE, biologist, educator; b. Chgo., Dec. 31, 1937; d. William Joseph and Mary Alice (Cawley) Bourke; B.S., Mundelein Coll., Chgo., 1959; M.S., U. Ill., 1960; Ph.D., Northwestern U., 1972; m. John J. Hayes, Sept. 2, 1961 (dec. July 1981). Researcher, Mcpl. Tb Sanitarium, Chgo., 1960-62; mem. faculty Loyola U., Chgo., 1962—, chmn. dept. natural sci., 1968-77, dean natural scis. div., 1977-80, assoc. prof., 1974-79, prof., 1979—, assoc. acad. v.p., 1980-85. Fellow in botany U. Ill., 1959-60, NSF, 1969-71; grantee Am. Orchid Soc., 1967, HEW, 1969, NSF, 1975, NASA, 1980—. Mem. Am. Soc. Plant Physiology, Bot. Soc. Am., Soc. Ill. Microbiologists, Am. Soc. Microbiology, Internat. Soc. Human and Animal Mycology, AAAS, Am. Inst. Biol. Scis., Assn. Midwest Coll. Biology Tchrs. Roman Cath. Contbr. profl. publs. Home: 6190 N Indian Rd Chicago IL 60646 Office: 820 N Michigan Ave Chicago IL 60611

HAYES, ANN CARSON, art director; b. Hamlin, Tex. Apr. 25, 1941; d. Fred Elbert and Nona Faye (Riddle) Carson; m. Robert Lee Hayes, Nov. 15, 1975; m. James Russell Brown, May 7, 1959 (div. July 1973); children—James Allen, Daniel Russell, Robert Anthony, Debra Faye Mead. A.A.S., Howard Coll., Tex., 1972; student Regents Coll., N.Y.C., 1986. Freelance artist, Big Spring, Tex., 1956-76; real estate agt. Century 21, Littleton, Colo., 1976-78, Huntsville, Ala., 1978-79; art dir. Hayes and Co., Splendora, Tex. 1979—; lead drafter Tex. Eastern Corp., Houston, 1979—. Mem. Nat. Assn. Female Execs., Am. Bus. Womans Assn., LWV. Democrat. Episcopalian. Club: Toastmasters. Avocations: sculpting; glass etching; bowling; tennis. Home: 23 Pinemont Rd PO Box 761 Splendora TX 77372 Office: Tex Eastern Transmission Corp 1221 McKinney St PO Box 2521 Houston TX 77252

HAYES, ANNA, artist; b. Starkweather, N.D., Nov. 26, 1905; d. Axel and Carrie Anna (Hyman) Nelson; m. Clifford E. Hayes, Nov. 17, 1936; children—Robert C., Paul Richard. A.A., Long Beach City Coll., 1955; student of Robert Adams, 1960-61. Free lance artist, watercolor, India ink, Long Beach, Calif., 1954—. One man shows: Long Beach Mus. Art, 1962, Long Beach C. of C., 1965, Dana Library, Long Beach, 1972; participant exhbns. Newport Harbor Art Exhibit, 1960, Long Beach Art Assn. (Best of Show award), 1967, 73 (hon. mention), 1st Methodist Ch. 3d Ann. Lenten Art Festival, 1977 (hon. mention), Long Beach Art Assn. (best of show), 1967, 70, 73, 78, 79, 81, 85, Lakewood Artists Guild, 1973; represented in permanent collection Long Beach Mus. Art. Mem. Long Beach Art Assn. Republican. Methodist. Home: 1537 Armando Dr Long Beach CA 90807

HAYES, CAROL SWIFT, management analyst; b. Big Bear, Calif., Mar. 9, 1949; d. Alton Ray Swift and Joyce Irene (Gapp) Van der Maaten; married,

July 13, 1986. Student, LaVerne Coll., 1968-69; A.A., Southwestern Calif. Jr. Coll., 1971; student mgmt. U. Redlands, 1986—. Acctg. technician Navy Publs. & Printing, San Diego, 1975-77, purchasing agt., 1977-81, mgmt. asst., 1981-82; program analyst Marine Corp. Recruit Depot, San Diego, 1982-85, mgmt. analyst, 1985—. Active big sister for Big Bros. of Am., 1983-84. Recipient Outstanding Performance Rating, Navy Publs. and Printing Service, 1979, Superior Achievement award, 1981; Sustained Superior Performance award Marine Corp. Recruit Depot, 1984, Commendation cert., 1985. Mem. Am. Bus. Women's Assn. (pres. San Diego Charter chpt. 1985-86), Pres. Council (sec. 1985-86), Am. Soc. Mil. Comptrollers. Republican. Avocations: snow skiing; arts/crafts projects. Home: 1018 Devonshire Dr San Diego CA 92107 Office: MA Div Marine Corp Recruit Depot Bldg 31 Room 106A San Diego CA 92140

HAYES, DENISE LYNETTE, telephone company executive; b. Chgo., July 16, 1952; d. Jarrett Bernarr and Odelia Fianna (Griffin) Hayes. A.A., El Centro Jr. Coll., Dallas, 1973; B.B.A., So. Meth. U., 1978, M.B.A., 1984. Data examiner Info. Processing Corp., Dallas, 1976-78; supr. data entry Southwestern Bell Telephone Co., Dallas, 1978, supr. computer batch processing, 1978-80, asst. mgr. real time ops., 1980-81, asst. mgr. user adminstrn., 1981-84, asst. staff mgr. valuations, 1984—. Adviser, Jr. Achievement Dallas, 1979. Democrat. Church of Christ. Office: Southwestern Bell Telephone Co One Bell Plaza Room 2620 08 PO Box 225521 Dallas TX 75265

HAYES, EILEEN PATRICIA, opera theatre executive; b. Tillamook, Oreg.; d. Clemens and Martha Dandridge (Maddox) H.; m. Gale Southard Martin, Dec. 28, 1985. B.S., U. Oreg., 1968; B.A., U. Nev.-Las Vegas, 1985. Cert. tchr., Oreg.; cert. orch. mgr. Asst. to dir. Los Angeles Athletic Club, 1969-73; tchr. drama, music Tillamook Pub. Schs., 1973-74; mus. artist Portland Opera Co., Oreg., 1975-80, Oreg. Light Opera Co., 1977-78; mng. dir. Las Vegas Chamber Players, Las Vegas Symphony Orch., 1982-84; exec. dir. Nev. Opera Theatre, Las Vegas, 1985—; cons. theatre arts dept. U. Nev., Las Vegas, 1983; pub. relations dir. So. Nev. Mus. Arts Meml. Concert, Las Vegas, 1984. Newspaper writer, 1983; editor concert series program booklet, 1982-84; performance dir., artist Tribute to Vietnam Vets., 1975, Mus. Portrait (Nat. Endowment for Arts), 1986. Patron, Charleston Heights Art Ctr., Las Vegas, 1983—; com. mem. St. Rose de Lima Hosp. Aux., Henderson, Nev., 1983—; bd. dirs. Nev. Alliance for Arts Edn., 1986—; mem. Republican Women of Clark County, 1985—; soloist Christ Episcopal Ch., Las Vegas, 1985—. Recipient Internat. Thespian award Drama Dir. Tillamook, 1973. Mem. Am. Guild Mus. Artists, Nat. Assn. Female Execs., Met. Opera Guild, Internat. Assn. Bus. Communicators, Am. Symphony Orch. League, Assn. Calif. Symphony Orchs., Las Vegas C. of C. (nominating com. 1984). Episcopalian. Club: Los Angeles Athletic. Lodge: Order of Rainbow (worthy advisor 1963). Avocations: collecting antiques, rare books, gems, swimming, dancing. Office: Nev Opera Theatre care Clark, Green & Reeves 5606 S Eastern Ave Las Vegas NV 89119

HAYES, HELEN, actress; b. Washington, Oct. 10, 1900; d. Francis Van Arnum and Catherine Estell (Hayes) Brown; grad. Sacred Heart Acad., Washington, 1917; L.H.D., Hamilton Coll., Clinton, N.Y., 1939, Smith Coll., 1940; L.H.D., Elmira (N.Y.) Coll.; Litt.D., Columbia U., 1949 U. Denver, 1952; D.F.A., Princeton U., St. Mary's Coll.; m. Charles MacArthur, Aug. 17, 1928 (dec. Apr. 1956); 1 son, James. First appeared on stage at age of 6; mem. Columbia Players, Washington, 4 seasons; later toured with Lew Fields and John Drew; played in Old Dutch, Prodigal Husband, Pollyanna, Penrod; appeared with William Gillette in Dear Brutus; appeared in Clarence, Bab, To the Ladies, We Moderns, Dancing Mothers, Caesar and Cleopatra, What Every Woman Knows, Croquette, Mr. Gilhooley, Mary of Scotland, 1934, Victoria Regina, 1937-38, Ladies and Gentlemen, 1939-40, Twelfth Night, 1940-41, Candle in the Wind, 1941-42, Harriet, 1943-45, Happy Birthday, The Glass Menagerie, London, 1948, Farewell to Arms, Vanessa, The Wisteria Trees, 1950, Mrs. McThing, 1952, Mainstreet to Broadway, 1953, Skin of Our Teeth, Europe and U.S., 1955, Harvey, Long Days' Journey Into Night, 1971, others; appeared in motion pictures The Sin of Madelon Claudet, Arrowsmith, My Son John, 1951, Anastasia, 1956, Airport (Acad. award as best supporting actress 1971, 1970, Herbie Rides Again, 1974, Helen Hayes: Portrait of an American Actress, 1974, One of Our Dinosaurs is Missing, 1975, Candleshoe, 1978, Hopper's Silence, 1981; numerous TV appearances including series The Snoop Sisters, 1972-74; others; Mrs. Derth in TV revival of Barrie's Dear Brutus, 1956; mem. A.P.A. Phoenix Repertory Co., 1966—. Recipient best actress award Motion Picture Acad. Arts and Sciences, 1932, in The Sin of Madelon Claudet; Emmy award, 1954, Antoinette Perry award for best actress in Time Remembered, 1958; Medal of City N.Y.; Medal of Arts, Finland; Am. Exemplar medal Freedoms Found., 1978; Laetare medal U. Notre Dame, 1979. Hon. pres. Am. Theatre Wing; pres. Am. Nat. Theatre and Acad.; 2d v.p. Actors Fund, 1975—. Chmn. Women's activities Nat. Found. for Infantile Paralysis. Republican. Roman Catholic. Author: A Gift of Joy, 1965; On Reflection, 1968; (with Anita Loos) Twice Over Lightly, 1971; Star on Her Forehead, 1949.*

HAYES, JANET GRAY, former mayor San Jose (Calif.); b. Rushville, Ind., July 12, 1926; d. John Paul and Lucile (Gray) Frazee; A.B.. Ind. U., 1948; M.A. magna cum laude, U. Chgo., 1950; m. Kenneth Hayes, Mar. 20, 1950; children—Lindy, John, Katherine, Megan. Psychiat. caseworker Jewish Family Service Agy., Chgo., 1950-52; vol. Denver Crippled Children's Service, 1954-55; vol. Adult and Child Guidance Clinic, San Jose, 1958-59; mem. San Jose City Council, 1971-82, vice-mayor, 1973-74, mayor, 1975-82; trustee U.S. Conf. Mayors, 1977-82, mem. sci. and tech. task force, 1976-80; bd. dirs. League Calif. Cities, 1976-82, mem. property tax reform task force, 1976-82; chmn. State of Calif. Urban Devel. Adv. Com., 1976-77; mem. Calif. Commn. Fair Jud. Practices, 1976-72, client-community relations dir. Q. Tech., Santa Clara, Calif., 1983—; founder, adv. bd. Calif. Bus. Bank, 1982—. Mem. Democratic nat. campaign com., 1976; mem. Calif. Dem. Commn. Nat. Platform and Policy, 1976; del. Dem. Nat. Conv., 1980; bd. dirs. South San Francisco Bay Dischargers Authority; chmn. Santa Clara County Sanitation Dist.; mem. San Jose/Santa Clara Treatment Plant Adv. Bd.; chmn. Santa Clara Valley Employment and Tng. Bd. (CETA); past mem. EPA Aircraft/Airport Noise Task Group; bd. dirs. Calif. Center Research and Edn. in Govt., League to Save Lake Tahoe, 1984—, Alexian Bros. Hosp., 1985— bd. dirs., chmn. adv. council Public Tech. Inc. AAUW Edn. Found. grantee. Mem. Assn. Bay Area Govts. (exec. com. 1971-74, regional housing subcom. 1973-74, regional housing subcom. 1973-74), LWV (pres. San Francisco Bay Area chpt. 1968-70, pres. local 1966-67), Mortar Bd., Phi Beta Kappa., Kappa Alpha Theta. Democrat. Club: Century. Office: Q Tech 4701 Patrick Henry Dr Santa Clara CA 95054

HAYES, JENNIE HOWARD, educator; b. Baskerville, Va., Sept. 10, 1917; d. William Henry and Elizabeth (Jackson) Howard; m. James Henry Wright, June 28, 1942 (div. 1959); children—Joya Felicia, James Henry III; m. George Alexander Hayes, Aug. 20, 1960. A.B., Va. State U., 1940. Cert. tchr., Pa. Tchr., McKenney Tng., Dinwiddie, Va., 1940-41, Naked Creek, Elton, Va., 1941-42, Andrew Jackson, Luray, Va., 1942-43, Phila. Sch. Dist., 1953-81; ret., 1981. Author 2 books of poetry. Leader Girl Scouts U.S., Hartford, Conn., 1943-46, Phila., 1956-70; vice moderator bd. deacons Berean Presbyterian Ch., 1976-79 (Educator and Leadership Service awards 1976, 81-85). Recipient Vol. Service award Phila. Prisons, 1974; Girl Scouts leader award, 1968; Desegregation and Educator awards Kearney Sch., 1979, 81. Mem. Pa. Assn. Sch. Retirees, Phila. Pub. Sch. Ret. Employees Assn., Va. State U. Alumni Assn. Democrat. Avocations: writing; travel; reading poetry; swimming.

HAYES, JUDITH SLAYDEN, church association administrator; b. Nashville, Oct. 2, 1947; d. James Daniel and Oma Lee (Draper) Slayden; m. David Warren Hayes, Sept. 23, 1969. B.S., Middle Tenn. State U., 1969; M.B.A., Tenn. State U., 1982; postgrad., Scarritt Coll., 1983—. Art manuscript asst. Sunday Sch. Bd. So. Bapt. Conv., Nashville, 1969-70, editorial asst., 1970-76, asst. editor, 1976-82, editor, 1982—; minister youth and edn., Eastland Bapt. Ch., Nashville, 1985—; conf. leader Sunday Sch. Bd., Nashville, 1983—; spl. studies tchr. Bapt. Chs., Tenn., Ky., 1963—, pianist, organist, 1982—. Contbr. articles to profl. jours. Mem. So. Bapt. Religious Edn. Assn., Bapt. Pub. Relations Assn., Nat. League of Am. Pen Women, Mensa. Avocations: crafts; indoor gardening; piano and organ playing; travel. Home: 526 Idlewood Dr Mount Juliet TN 37122 Office: Bapt Sunday Sch Bd 127 9th Ave N Nashville TN 37234

HAYES, KATHLEEN ZIMMERMAN, retail store executive; b. Hammond, Ind., May 9, 1944; d. Warren Lee and Irene Rose (Glass) Zimmerman; B.S., Purdue U., 1967; M.B.A., U. Chgo., 1970; postgrad. in taxation DePaul U., 1979—. Pharmacist, various cos., Indpls. and Chgo., 1967-70; revenue agt. IRS, Des Moines, 1971-72; tax specialist McGladrey, Hendrickson & Co., Des Moines, 1972-75; tax mgr. Clow Corp., Oak Brook, Ill., 1975-79; tax compliance mgr. U.S. Gypsum Co., Chgo., 1979-82; tax mgr. Global Marine Inc., Houston, 1982-86; owner retail store, Houston; tax cons., 1976—. Pres. bd. Woman's Hosp. of Tex. Research and Edn. Found., 1986. C.P.A., Iowa, Ill. Mem. Tax Execs. Inst. (treas. Houston chpt., dir., chmn. internat. tax com.), Am. Inst. C.P.A.s, Iowa Soc. C.P.A.s, Ill. C.P.A. Found., Am. Women's Soc. C.P.A.s, Beta Alpha Psi. Home: 18203 Heaton Dr Houston TXOffice: 78 Woodlake Sq Houston TX 77042

HAYES, KRISTIN RAMAGE, lawyer; b. Syracuse, N.Y., Dec. 1, 1955; d. Peter Ramage and Rosemary (Ventura) H. B.A., Brown U., 1977, M.A., 1977; J.D., U. Pa., 1980. Bar: Pa. 1980. Assoc. Saul, Ewing, Remick & Saul, Phila., 1980—. Democrat. Office: Saul Ewing Remick & Saul 3800 Centre Sq W Philadelphia PA 19102

HAYES, MARY ESHBAUGH, newspaper editor; b. Rochester, N.Y., Sept. 27, 1928; d. William Paul and Eleanor Maude (Seivert) Eshbaugh; B.A. in English and Journalism, Syracuse (N.Y.) U., 1950; m. James Leon Hayes, Apr. 18, 1953; children—Pauli, Eli, Lauri Le June, Clayton, Merri Jess Bates. With Livingston County Republican, Geneseo, N.Y., summers, 1947-50, mng. editor, 1949-50; reporter Aurora (Colo.) Advocate, 1950-52; reporter-photographer Aspen (Colo.) Times, 1952-53, columnist, 1956—, reporter, 1972-77, asso. editor, 1977—; tchr. Colo. Mountain Coll., 1979. Mem. Nat. Fedn. Press Women (1st prizes in writing and editing 1976-80), Colo. Press Women's Assn. (writing award 1974, 75, 78-85, sweepstakes award for writing 1977, 78, 84, 85, also 2d place award 1976, 79, 82, 83, Woman of Achievement 1986). Mem. Aspen Community Ch. Photographer, editor: Aspen Potpourri, 1968. Home: PO Box 497 Aspen CO 81611 Office: Box E Aspen CO 81611

HAYES, MARY JANE, educational administrator; b. Cleve., July 25, 1929; d. Nicholas and Angela (Ratino) Danolfo; m. Anthony R. Drago, June 9, 1951 (dec. 1978); children—Kathleen, Thomas, Angela; m. Mathew Hayes, Dec. 19, 1978. B.S. in Edn., Bowling Green State U., 1951; postgrad. U. Calif.-San Diego, 1981, U. Nev.-Las Vegas, 1979. Tchr., Corlett Sch., Cleve., 1951-53, Howard Wasden Sch., Las Vegas, 1960-63; founder, tchr. Seton Acad., Las Vegas, 1963-75, dir., 1975—. Pres., Our Lady of Las Vegas Sch. Parents Club, 1960-61. Mem. Nat. Assn. Edn. Young Children, Comml. Child Care Providers of Nev., So. Nev. Assn. Edn. Young Children, Kappa Delta, Alpha Delta Kappa (sec. alumni 1984—). Republican. Roman Catholic. Club: PEO. Avocations: handwork; camping. Office: Seton Acad 1592 E Hacienda Ave Las Vegas NV 89119

HAYES, PATRICIA ANNE, government official; b. Chgo., Jan. 26, 1921; d. Frank Ambrose and Annabel (Fanning) Hayes; A.B., Coll. St. Teresa, 1942; B.S., U. Md., 1956; M.Ed., Coll. William and Mary, 1961; M.A., George Washington U., 1961; certificate in meteorology U. Chgo., 1945. Tchr. pub. schs., Chgo., 1942-44; meteorologist U.S. Weather Bur., Washington, 1945-49, climatologist U.S. Dept. Army, 1949-52; commd. 1st lt. U.S. Air Force, 1951, advanced through grades to maj., 1966; meteorologist A.F. Cambridge Research Center, Boston, 1952-54; base weather officer, Molesworth, Eng., 1954-57; team chief Forecast Center, Langley AFB, Va., 1957-58, asst. chief climatology div. hdqrs. 2d weather group, 1958-64; weather officer European Theater Forecast Center, 1964-67, aerospace scis. officer 8th Weather Squadron, Westover AFB, Mass., 1967-70, S.E. Asia Weather Center, 1970-71; wing climatologist 4th Weather Wing Ent AFB, Colo., 1971-72; claims rep. HEW, 1973—. Mem. Am. Meteorol. Soc., AAUW, Ret. Officers Assn., Kappa Gamma Pi. Home: 8145 N Harding St Skokie IL 60076

HAYES, PAULA FREDA, government official; b. Providence, Apr. 5, 1950; d. Ario Louis and Elena Marguerite (Gentile) Freda; m. Robert J. Hayes, Sept. 6, 1975; 1 child, Brendan Michael. B.A. magna cum laude, R.I. Coll., 1972; M.P.A., Maxwell Sch., Syracuse U., 1973. Criminal Justice planner City of Syracuse (N.Y.), 1973-75, asst. crime control coordinator, 1975-77; supervisory grants specialist Nat. Endowment Arts, Washington, 1977-78; criminal justice program analyst Dept. Justice, Washington, 1978-79, program mgr. arson discretionary grant program, 1979-80, sr. mgmt. analyst, 1980-81; dep. insp. gen. Community Services Adminstrn., Washington, 1981-82; dir. preventive analysis div. Office of Insp. Gen., Dept. Agr., Washington, 1982—. Recipient Outstanding Achievement awards Dept. Justice, 1979, 80, 81, 82; Spl. Achievement award Atty. Gen., 1981; Spl. Achievement Cash award HHS, 1982. Roman Catholic. Office: US Dept Agr Office of Insp Gen Room 447-E 12th and Independence Ave SW Washington DC 20250

HAYES, SANDRA LYNN, nurse; b. Trenton, N.J., Oct. 26, 1959; d. Joe Nathan and Agradean (Carter) H. Assoc. Sci., Northeastern Christian Jr. Coll., 1979; B.S.Nursing, Thomas Jefferson U., 1982; postgrad. U. Pa. Clin. nurse II, Thomas Jefferson U. Hosp., Phila., 1982—. Mem. Nat. Assn. Female Execs., Oncology Nursing Soc. Democrat. Mem. Ch. of Christ. Avocations: aerobics; ice skating; skiing. Home: 1000 Walnut St Philadelphia PA 19107

HAYES, SYLVIA RICHMOND, music educator; b. Lawrenceburg, Tenn.; d. Edward David and Blanche Audrey (Sells) Richmond; m. Gene Edwin Hayes; B.S., George Peabody Coll. Tchrs., M.Mus. Edn., 1968; postgrad. Tenn. State U.; postgrad. in data processing Columbia State Community Coll. Band dir., tchr. English, high sch., Loretto, Tenn.; dir. band, tchr. music Coffman Sch., Lawrenceburg, 1972—. Choir and music dir., sec. Immanuel Baptist Ch. Mem. Bus. and Profl. Women's Club (Career Woman of Yr. 1972), Lawrence County Edn. Assn., Midele Edn. Assn. (Tenn.), Tenn. Edn. Assn., NEA, Middle Band and Orch. Assn., Music Educators Nat. Conf. Democrat. Club: Lioness (pres. 1977-78).

HAYES, THELMA ANN, state official; b. Cleve., Dec. 4, 1918; d. Eugene and Beatrice (Thomas) Roberts; m. James Andrew Hayes, Mar. 27, 1963; children by previous marriage—K. Machuma Bondele, Yvonne Parker, Eugene Kilgore, Fabienne Goins. Student Franklin U., 1952. Dep. clk. supr. Cleve. Mcpl. Ct., 1966-79; sec. Zion Chapel Bapt. Ch., 1966—; audit cons. State of Ohio, 1979—. Mem. NAACP, Nat. Council Negro Women. Democrat. Baptist. Avocation: bowling. Home: 694 E 120 Cleveland OH 44108 Office: Zion Chapel Bapt Ch 4234 Lee Rd Cleveland OH 44128

HAYGOOD, DINA, real estate investor, consultant; b. Los Angeles; d. Betty (Brown) Robertson. A.S. in Criminal Justice, Compton Community Coll., 1977; B.S. in Adminstrn. of Criminal Justice, Calif. State U.-Long Beach, 1979. Adminstr., West Gastroenterology Group, Inglewood, Calif., 1980-82; cons. Joe Enterprise, Beverly Hills, Calif., 1983—; bd. dirs. Elevation Enterprise Inc., Beverly Hills, 1985—. Notary pub., Calif. Mem. Nat. Assn. Female Execs., Am. Congress on Real Estate, Nat. Notary Assn.

HAYMAN, JANE CAMERON, lawyer; b. Winter Haven, Fla., Feb. 28, 1948; d. Clyde Veryl and Charlotte Collins (Cameron) H. B.A. in Edn., U. Fla.-Gainesville, 1970, M.B.A., 1972; J.D., Fla. State U.-Tallahassee, 1980. Bar: Fla. 1981, U.S. Dist. Ct. Fla. 1981; cert. tchr. Fla. Dept. mgr. Maas Bros., Tampa, Fla., 1972; statistician II, Fla. Dept. Banking and Fin., Tallahassee, 1972-73; legis. research asst. Com. on Govt. Ops. Fla. Senate, Tallahassee, 1973-75, legis. analyst Com. on Edn., 1976-78, legis. intern Com. on Commerce, 1979-80, asst. Office of Pres., Office of Pres. Pro Tem, 1981, exec. asst. Office of Pres., 1982-84; mgmt. cons. Planned Mgmt. Corp., Tampa, 1975-76; intern Supreme Ct. Fla., Tallahassee, 1980, exec. asst. to chief justice, 1981-82; atty. Swann & Haddock, PA, Orlando, 1982—. Contbr. in field. Mem., supporter Nat. Multiple Sclerosis Soc., N.Y.C. and Tallahassee, 1975; organizer Carter Presdl. Campaign, Tallahassee, 1980. Mem. ABA, Fla. Bar, Phi Chi Theta, Alpha Omicron Pi (sec. 1968-69). Presbyterian. Home: 639-105 Laurel Oak Ln Altamonte FL 32701 Office: 135 W Central Blvd Orlando FL 32802

HAYNER, JEANNETTE C., state legislator; b. Jan. 22, 1919; m. Herman H. Hayner, 1942; children—Stephen A., James K., Judith A. B.A., U. Oreg., 1940, J.D., 1942. Atty., Bonneville Power Co., Portland, Oreg., 1943-47; mem. Wash. Ho. of Reps., 1972-76, Wash. Senate from Dist. 16, 1977—. Mem. Walla Walla Dist. 140 Sch. Bd., 1956-63, chmn. bd. 2 yrs.; mem. adv. bd. Walla Walla Youth and Family Services Assn., 1968-72; active YWCA, 1968-72; dist. chmn. White House Conf. on Children and Youth, 1970; chmn. Walla Walla County Mental Health Bd., 1970-72; former mem. Wash. Council on Crime and Delinquency, Nuclear Energy Council, Bonneville Power Regional Adv. Council, State Wash. Organized Crime Intelligence Adv. Bd.; former asst. whip Republican Caucus. Recipient Merit award Walla Walla C. of C. Mem. Oreg. Bar Assn., Delta Kappa Gamma (hon.), Kappa Kappa Gamma. Lutheran. Office: Wash State Capitol Bldg Olympia WA 98504*

HAYNES, JANET-LINDA, medical biologist, educator; b. Bklyn., Nov. 26, 1947; d. Fred Howard and Juliette Lillian (Dreifuss) H.; diploma in med. tech. (hosp. scholar) Beekman-Downtown Hosp. Sch. Med. Tech., N.Y.C., 1969; B.S. (N.Y. State Regents scholar, Empire State Assn. Med. Technologists scholar, N.Y. State Soc. Pathologists scholar), L.I.U., 1969, M.S., 1972; M.Phil., N.Y.U., 1982, postgrad., 1982—. Teaching fellow in scis. L.I.U., Bklyn., 1969-72, mem. faculty, 1973—, adj. asst. prof. biology, 1975-80, adj. assoc. prof. biology, 1980—, adj. mem. grad. faculty med. biology C.W. Post Coll., L.I.U., 1979—; research technologist Jewish Hosp. and Med. Center of Bklyn., 1972-77; faculty mem. Physician Asst. Program, Bklyn.-Cumberland Med. Center, 1976—; adj. asst. prof. biology Pace U., N.Y.C., 1977-78; teaching fellow in biology NYU, 1979-84; asst. prof., clin. coordinator dept. med. tech. Health Scis. Center, Sch. Allied Health Professions, SUNY-Stony Brook, 1981-83; adj. lectr. CUNY, 1973-81, N.Y.C. Tech. Coll., 1973, Borough of Manhattan Community Coll., 1984—; teaching fellow biology N.Y.U., 1979—; adj. lectr. Sch. Continuing Edn., NYU, 1984—; Active, Operation Baby Track, ARC, N.Y.C., 1981, Am. Cancer Soc., 1982—; mem. ad hoc. com. on status of women SUNY, Stony Brook, 1982. Recipient Charlotte Pann Meml. award N.Y.U., 1981; Phi Sigma grad. research awardee, 1972; Conn. State fellow, 1974-75; NIH trainee, 1974-75; N.Y.U. grantee in biology, 1980—; Sigma Xi grantee, 1981-82. Mem. Am. Soc. Clin. Pathologists (cert. med. technologist), Am. Soc. Med. Tech., Assn. for Women in Sci., AAUW, N.Y. Acad. Scis., AAAS, Sigma Xi, Alpha Epsilon Delta, Phi Sigma. Contbr. articles to profl. jours. Office: Dept Biology Long Island U University Plaza Brooklyn NY 11201

HAYNES, JEAN REED, lawyer; b. Miami, Fla., Apr. 6, 1949; d. Oswald Birnam and Arleen (Wiedman) Dow; m. William Rutherford Reed, Apr. 15, 1974 (div. Sept. 1981); m. 2d, Thomas Beranek Haynes, Aug. 7, 1982. A.B. with honors, Pembroke Coll., 1971; M.A., Brown U., 1971; J.D., U. Chgo., 1981. Bar: Ill. 1981. Tchr., facilitator open edn. St. Mary's Acad., Riverside, R.I., 1972-74; tchr., head lower sch. St. Francis Sch., Goshen, Ky., 1974-78; clk. to judge U.S. Ct. Appeals 7th Circuit, Chgo., 1981-83; assoc. Kirkland & Ellis, Chgo., 1983—. Mem. ABA (litigation sect.), Ill. Bar Assn., Chgo. Bar Assn., Am. Judicature Soc., Art Inst. Chgo. (aux. bd., sustaining fellow). Office: Kirkland & Ellis 200 E Randolph Dr Chicago IL 60611

HAYNES, MARGARET ELIZABETH, retired nurse, educator; b. Hopkinsville, Ky., Feb. 25, 1919; d. Philip E. and Marion (Bell) H.; A.A., Bethel Woman's Coll., 1939; B.S. in Nursing, Vanderbilt U., 1942; M.P.H., U. N.C., 1954. Staff pediatric nurse Vanderbilt U. Hosp., Nashville, 1942-43; head pediatric nurse John Sealy Hosp., Galveston, Tex., 1943-45, U. Colo., Colo. Gen. Hosp., 1947-48, U. Colo., Denver Gen. Hosp., 1948-52; asst. instr. obstet. nursing Vanderbilt U. Sch. Nursing, 1946-47, pub. health staff nurse Dist. Health Dept., Chapel Hill, N.C., 1954-58; asst. prof. U. N.C. Sch. Nursing, Chapel Hill, 1958-65; asst. prof. U. Tenn. Coll. Nursing, Memphis, 1967-69, assoc. prof. community health nursing, 1973-84, assoc. prof. emerita, 1984—, nursing cons. Child Devel. Center, U. Tenn. Med. Units, 1967-71; nursing cons. Arlington (Tenn.) Hosp. and Sch. for Retarded, 1970-71; dir. Coop. Community Health Nursing Edn. Project, 1972-73. Recipient Faculty award U. N.C. Sch. Nursing Class of 1965; John Runyan Community Nursing award, 1984. Mem. Am. Nurses Assn., Am. Pub. Health Assn., Vanderbilt U., U. N.C. nursing alumnae assns., Sigma Theta Tau. Baptist. Contbr. articles to profl. jours. Home: 730 Hedgegrove Dr Apt 4 Memphis TN 38117

HAYNES, MARTHA PATRICIA, astronomer; b. Boston, Apr. 24, 1951; d. William Veech and Louise Mary (Healy) Haynes; B.A., Wellesley Coll., 1973; M.A., Ind. U., 1975, Ph.D., 1978. Assoc. instr. Ind. U., 1974-76; jr. research assoc. Nat. Radio Astronomy Obs., Charlottesville, Va., 1976-78, asst. dir. Green Bank (W.Va.) Ops., 1981-83; instr. Piedmont Va. Community Coll., 1978; postdoctoral fellow Nat. Astronomy and Ionosphere Center, Arecibo Obs., P.R., 1978-80, staff research assoc., 1981; asst. prof. dept. astronomy Cornell U., Ithaca, N.Y., 1983-86, assoc. prof., 1986—. Mem. Am. Astron. Soc., AAAS, Internat. Astron. Union, Internat. Union Radio Sci., N.Y. Acad. Scis., Sigma Xi. Address: Space Scis Bldg Cornell Univ Ithaca NY 14853

HAYNES, PATRICIA, librarian; b. N.Y.C., Sept. 19, 1949; d. Clifford Nathaniel and Martha Carsue (Ford) Haynes. B.A., Bernard M. Baruch Coll., 1981; M.L.S., Columbia U., 1984. With Carlysle & Jacquelyn, N.Y.C., 1967-68; files asst. Carnegie Corp N.Y., N.Y.C., 1969-77, head of files, 1977-78, adminstrv. asst., 1978-84, supr. files and archives, 1985—. Mem. Consortium of Found. Libraries (chmn.) 1981—), INFORMED (treas. 1983-84, sec. 1984-85, chmn. 1985-86), ALA, Child Study Children's Book Com., New York State Library Assn., Bronx Teen Pregnancy Network, Coalition 100 Black Women. Home: 2954 Marion Ave Bronx NY 10458 Office: Carnegie Corp NY 437 Madison Ave New York NY 10022

HAYNES, PATRICIA SOMERVILLE, personnel management specialist; b. Leonardtown, Md.; d. Agnes Elizabeth (Stevens) Somerville. B.S., Howard U., 1980; M.S., Troy State U., 1983. Phys. therapist St. Francis Hosp., Columbus, Ga., 1980-81; personnel mgmt. specialist Communications-Electronics Command, Fort Monmouth, N.J., 1984—; condr. seminars on career devel. Co-author manual in field. Edn. coordinator Kelly Hill Chapel, Fort Benning, Ga., 1981-82. Named to Outstanding Young Women Am., U.S. Jaycees, 1985. Mem. Personnel Adminstrn. Soc., Alpha Kappa Alpha. Roman Catholic. Avocations: swimming; biking; tennis; flute.

HAYNICZ, LACY ANN, medical records administrator; b. Riverside, N.J., Sept. 12, 1950; d. Joseph Charles and Minnie May (Jones) Hale; student La. State U., 1968-70, Rider Coll., 1971-74; B.A. in Health Info. Mgmt., Stephens Coll., 1984; registered records adminstr.; m. Michael S. Haynicz, Dec. 21, 1974. Salesperson accessories dept. Pomeroy's, Willingboro, N.J., 1970; with Strawbridge & Clother, Cherry Hill, N.J., 1971-72; clk. typist R. M. Hollingshead Co., Camden, N.J., 1972-74; exec. sec. to corporate controller The Hibbert Co., Trenton, N.J., 1974-75; dir. med. records Cumberland Regional Health Plan, Vineland, N.J., 1975-78; asst. dir. med. records Phila. Coll. Osteo. Medicine, 1978; dir. med. records in care pavilion and Mt. Laurel Convalescent Centers, Geriatric and Med. Centers, Phila., 1979-80; dir. med. records, Vineland (N.J.) State Sch. Hosp., 1980-85; med. record adminstr. mgmt. Info. Systems unit Div. Devel. Disabilities, 1985—. Coach Little League cheerleading squad, 1972-73. Recipient Records Technician cert. Am. Med. Record Assn., 1977. Mem. N.J. Med. Record Assn., Hort. Soc., Alpha Chi Omega (pres.). Home: 267 Dogwood Ln Clarksboro NJ 08020 Office: 1 Capitol Pl 222 S Warren St Trenton NJ 08625

HAYNIE, MARY ELIZABETH, vol. services adminstr.; b. Atlantic City, N.J., Dec. 14, 1923; d. Edwin N. and Mary Rose (Dolan) Donaldson; ed. Atlantic City Bus. Coll., 1944-46, U. Del., 1982; m. John Francis Haynie, Oct. 29, 1944; children—Paul Stephen, Mark Christopher. Long distance supr. N.J. Bell Telephone Co., Atlantic City, 1942-65; dir. vol. services Children's Seashore House, Atlantic City, 1965—. Democratic state committeewoman, 1969-81; chmn. bd. trustees Woodbine Developmental Ctr., 1969-85; bd. dirs. Atlantic County chpt. ARC, 1973; vice chmn. gen. adv. com. Atlantic County Vocat. Sch.; chmn. Atlantic-Cape May County Traffic Safety Commn.; bd. dirs., mem. Atlantic County Council, So. N.J. Health Systems Agy., 1977—; mem. Atlantic County Bd. Chosen Freeholders, 1971-75, dep. dir., 1974. Recipient Clara Barton award ARC, 1985. Mem. Am. Soc. Dirs. Vol. Services, N.J. Assn. Dirs. Vol. Services, Council for Exceptional Children, Atlantic City Bus. and Profl. Women's Club, Common Cause (charter), N.J. Fed. Bus. and Profl. Women's Clubs (state pres. 1985-86). Roman Catholic. Home: 211 N Washington Ave Ventnor NJ 08406 Office: Children's Seashore House 4100 Atlantic Ave Atlantic City NJ 08401

HAYS, BONNIE LINN, county official; b. Silverton, Oreg., Aug. 21, 1950; d. Lacy Emmett and Ethel Marie (Hunt) Bowlsby; m. Robert Verne Hays, Mar. 21, 1972 (dec. Aug. 1976); m. Arthur J. Lewis, 1981. B.S., Oreg. State U., 1972; postgrad. Portland State U., 1973, 74, Rocky Mt. Inst., 1982, Lewis & Clark U., Northwestern U. Sch. Law, 1985—. Cert. tchr. secondary edn., Oreg. Tchr. high sch. Astoria Sch. Dist., Oreg., 1972-75; ins. agt. Equitable Life Assurance Co., Portland, Oreg., 1975-77; br. mgr. Transamerica Title Ins. Co., Beaverton, Oreg., 1977-82; county commr. Washington County, Hillsboro, Oreg., 1980—; dir. Washington County Community Corrections, Hillsboro, 1983—, State Job

Tng. Coordinating Council, Salem, Oreg., 1985—, Multnomah-Washington Pvt. Industry Council, Portland, 1983—. Bd. dirs. Un Lugar para Niños, Hillsboro, 1984—; bd. mgmt., chmn. YMCA of Washington County, Beaverton, 1983—; bd. dirs. Washington County Hist. Soc., Hillsboro, 1985—, pres., 1986—; mem. Young Republicans of Oreg., Salem, 1984—; mem. Oreg. Episc. Sch. Wetlands Adv. Com., 1986. Named One of Washington County's "10 Most Influential People", Valley Times Newspaper Poll, 1985. Mem. Am. Corrections Assn., Assn. Oreg. Counties (com. pub. safety and human resources 1982—, vice chmn. 1982, chmn. 1986). Republican. Roman Catholic. Club: Multnomah Athletic (Portland). Avocation: gourmet cooking. Home: 15540 SW Village Ct Beaverton OR 97007 Office: Washington County Courthouse 150 N First Ave Hillsboro OR 97124

HAYS, DARLEEN DAWN, real estate executive, rancher; b. Del Rio, Tex., May 14, 1946; d. Carl Edwin Yoas, Jr. and Virginia Dawn (Graves) Yoas Rounsaville; m. Curtis Lee Brookover, Sept. 4, 1964 (div. 1971); 1 child, Clinton Wade. Student Mountain View Coll., Dallas, 1978-79, North Lake Coll., Irving, Tex., 1979. Adminstrv. asst. pvt. law firm, Del Rio, 1964-65, USAF, Laughlin AFB, Tex., 1965-66; asst. to pres. Casey & Glass, Inc., Corpus Christi, Tex., 1966-68; beverage mgr. Pryor Entertainment Enterprises, Dallas, 1970-74; food and beverage mgr. Stemmons Inn, Dallas, 1974-78; owner Bachelor's Maid Service, 1977-79; co-owner Glasses by Rags, 1979-81; v.p. Inco, Inc., Dallas, 1978-81; exec. v.p. Real Realty Corp., Dallas, Amarillo and El Paso, Tex., 1978-81, Real Designs, Inc., Dallas, 1980-82; v.p. Real Condominiums, Inc., Dallas, 1978-81, Richland Condominiums, Dallas, 1983—; ptnr. Yoas Ranch Estate, exotic game preserve, Del Rio, 1983—; shareholder Hays/Hathaway Properties, Arlington, Tex., 1983-85; ptnr. Assn./Investor Mgmt. Partnership, Dallas, 1982—, Active Investment Mgmt., Inc., Dallas, Arlington and Ft. Worth, 1983—. Bd. dirs. Birchwood Manor Homeowners Assn., Birchbrook Homeowners Assn., Terr. Condominium Assn., Univ. Pl. Homeowners Assn., Cliffbrook Homeowners Assn., Routh & Welborn Homeowners Assn. (all Dallas), Thunderbird Homeowners Assn., El Paso, Willows at Shady Valley Homeowners Assn., Arlington, Exec. Mothers, Ft. Worth. Mem. Tex. Assn. Realtors, Greater Dallas Bd. Realtors, Dallas Apt. Assn., Apt. Assn. Tarrant County. Republican. Avocations: fishing, furniture design. Home: 2301 Ridgmar Plaza 11 Fort Worth TX 76116 Office: Assn-Investor Mgmt Inc 5065 Ridglea Ln 1011 Fort Worth TX 76116

HAYS, MARILYN PATRICIA, real estate company executive; b. Yarrow, Mo., Sept. 19, 1935; d. John Dewey and Ruth (McKim) H.; m. Harold Clifton Ledbetter, Dec. 13, 1953 (div. 1972); children—Latricia Lyn, Lisa Ledbetter Cerio, David Clifton, Laura Lizanne; Harold Clifton, Jr. B.S., Northeast Mo. State U., 1958; broker cert. U. Fla., 1976; M.A., U. Mo., 1983; J.D., Washburn U., 1987. Lic. real estate broker, Mo., Kans., Fla., Grad. Realtors Inst. Fashion coordinator Ashells, Regina's Co., Kirksville, Mo., 1951-54; instr. pub. schs., Crocker, Novinger, Kirksville and University City, Mo., 1954-61; real estate salestaff Goldman's Assocs., Daytona Beach, Fla., 1975-76; real estate broker Kellogg Century 21, Daytona Beach, 1976-78; pres. M.P. Hays Co., Olathe, Kans., 1978-82, Bucyrus, Kans., 1982—; cons. Goldman, Kellogg, Daytona Beach, 1975-78. Contbr. articles on real estate edn. to profl. jours. Pres. Fla. Osteopathic Med. Assn. Aux., Dist. 3, 1964-65, 73-74, pres.-elect, 1967-68; major chmn. Assn. of Jr. League, Daytona Beach, 1968-69, 72-73; Pan Hellenic del., 1972-78; adviser Ormond Beach Hosp. Guild, Fla., 1972-74. Scholar, Mo. Council PTAs, 1953, K.C., 1954; recipient Outstanding Sales Achievement award Kellogg Century 21, 1977. Mem. Miami County Bd. Realtors, Johnson County Bd. Realtors, Nat. Assn. Realtors, Kans. Assn. Realtors, ABA, Kans. Farm Bur., Women's Legal Forum, AAUW, Am. Quarterhorses Assn., Alpha Sigma Alpha. Republican. Roman Catholic. Clubs: Ormond Beach Woman's, Oceanside Country. Avocations: photography; cooking; horseback riding. Home: Route 1 Box 161 Bucyrus KS 66013 Office: M P Hays Co 223d St and State Line Rd Bucyrus KS 66013

HAYS, MARY, arts council administrator; b. Cleve., Apr. 9, 1943; d. Robert Louis and Lois (Mendelson) H. B.A., Cornell U., 1965, J.D., 1969; cert., Columbia U. Inst. Non-for-Profit Mgmt., 1978. Assoc., Rosenman, Colin, Kaye, et al, N.Y.C., 1969-70; dep. asst. dir. fiscal mgmt. N.Y. State Council on Arts, N.Y.C., 1970-72; assoc., Ende, Godsberg & Friedman, N.Y.C., 1972-73; dir. ops. Theatre Devel. Fund, N.Y.C., 1973-80; exec. dir. N.Y. State Council on Arts, N.Y.C., 1980—, cons., 1972-80; bd. mem. Mid-Atlantic States Arts Consortium, Balt., 1980—, Nat. Assembly State Arts Agys., Washington, 1983—; mem. selection com. Met. Life Found. Mus. Grants for Minority Artists, N.Y.C., 1984-86. Mem. Cornell Council, Ithaca, N.Y., 1983-85. Home: 256 W 10th St New York NY 10014

HAYS, MARY KATHERINE JACKSON (MRS. DONALD OSBORNE HAYS), civic worker; b. Flora, Miss.; d. Rufus Lafayette and Ada (Collum) Jackson; student U. Miss., 1925-26, Millsaps Coll., 1926-27, 43-44; grad. Clark Bus. Sch., 1934; student Columbia U., 1935, Strayer Bus. Coll., 1951; m. Halbert Puffer Oliver, Aug. 9, 1927 (dec. 1934); m. 2d, Donald Osborne Hays, Aug. 30, 1937. Sec. to pres. McCullough Box and Crate Co., Pharr, Tex., 1934-36; sec. to field supr. Miss. Unemployment Compensatio Commn., 1936-37; rep. Homes of Tomorrow, 1940 N.Y. World's Fair; sec. to head interior design Lord & Taylor, N.Y.C., 1940; sales dept. Knabe Piano Co., N.Y.C., 1941-43. Active, Little Theatre, Wilkes Barre, Pa., 1937-39; charter mem. and incorporator Conf. State Socs., Washington, 1952; vol. worker Am. Cancer Soc., Washington, 1956—; mem. Center City Residents Assn., Phila., 1956; mem. women's com. Nat. Symphony Assn., vol. worker USO, 1945-48, symphony sustaining com. drives, 1957-66; mem. women's com. Corcoran Gallery Art, Washington, 1957-62; mem. Pierce-Warwick Adoption Assn. of Washington Home for Foundlings; vol. Washington Heart Assn., 1959-66; mem. Nat. Capital Area chpt. United Ch. Women, 1957—; mem. D.C. Episcopal Home for Children, 1961—, D.C. Salvation Army Aux., 1962—. Mem. Miss. State Soc. D.C. (sec. 1950-53), Nat. Trust for Historic Preservation, Miss. Women's Club D.C., DAR (vice regent chpt. 1970-72, regent chpt. 1972-74, vice chmn. D.C. com. celebration Washington's birthday 1972-76, state librarian 1974-76), UDC (chpt. historian 1982—), Johnstone Clan Am. (exec. council 1976-81), First Families of Miss. Episcopalian. Club: The Washington. Home: 4000 Massachusetts Ave NW Washington DC 20016

HAYS, PAMELA RUTH, lawyer; b. Topeka, Jan. 18, 1957; d. Robert Fredrick and Marylee (Stauf) H. B.A., Washburn U., 1977, J.D. with honors, 1981; LL.M., So. Meth. U., 1983. Bar: Kans. 1981, Tex. 1983. Credit investigator Union Nat. Bank, Wichita, Kans., 1977-78; tax acct. Main Hurdman, Wichita, 1981-82; tax atty. Shell Oil Co., Houston, 1933—. Tech. editor Washburn Law Jour., 1980-81. Campaign worker Republican Party Kans., Topeka, 1978, Young Reps. Dallas, 1982; vol. Houston Area Women's Ctr., Rape Crisis Program. Recipient Law Scholarships, Washburn Law Sch. Alumnae Assn., 1980-81, So. Meth. Law Sch., 1982-83. Mem. ABA, Tex. Bar Assn., Houston Bar Assn., Phi Alpha Delta, Alpha Phi. Republican. Presbyterian. Club: PEO (Wichita). Office: Shell Oil Co PO Box 2463 Houston TX 77001

HAYS, SANDY MILLER, editor; b. Ft. Smith, Ark., June 25, 1955; d. Joe Warren and Nell Rae (Inklebarger) Miller; m. Mark Wayne Hays, Apr. 17, 1976. Student Ark. State U., 1973-74; B.A. magna cum laude, U. Ark., 1979. Entertainment writer Ark. Democrat, Little Rock, 1979-81, farm editor, 1981—, bus. editor, 1984—; regional v.p. Newspaper Farm Editors Am., 1983-84. Sec., mem. bd. dirs. Ark. Cystic Fibrosis Found., Little Rock, 1981—; participant European Community Visitors' Program, 1985. Recipient Agrl. Promotion award Ark. Press. Assn., 1983, 84, 85; Media Pub. Interest Reporting award WEHCO Media, Little Rock, 1983, 84. Mem. Council Agrl. Sci. and Tech., Newspaper Farm Editors Am. (regional v.p. 1983-84), Investigative Reporters and Editors, Sigma Delta Chi, Phi Kappa Phi, Kappa Tau Alpha. Home: 4015 W 10th St Little Rock AR 72204 Office: Arkansas Democrat PO Box 2221 Little Rock AR 72203

HAYSE, NELLIE, association executive; b. Louisville, Ky., Jan. 3, 1936; d. Joseph Murray and Nellie Armstrong (Stoess) H. B.A., Wellesley Coll., 1957; postgrad., U. Ky., 1960, John A. Logan Coll., 1978-79. Field dir. Malden council Girl Scouts, Mass., 1957-60, field exec. Pennyroyal council, Owensboro, Ky., 1960-64, camp dir. Bear Creek council, Paducah, Ky., 1964-69, field, asst. exec. dir. Pisgah council, Ashville, N.C., 1970-75, exec. dir. Shagbark council, Herrin, Ill., 1975-81, Colonial Coast council, Norfolk, Va., 1981—. Editor Administrative Manual, 1985. Charter pres. Friends of Women's Studies, Old Dominion U., Norfolk, 1986. Recipient Thanks badge Bear Creek council Girl Scouts, 1969, Trainer's award United Way, 1978, Pres.'s award Colonial Coast council Girl Scouts, 1985; named Seamen, U.S. Power Squadron, 1985. Mem. Assn. Girl Scout Exec. Staff. Episcopalian. Avocations: sailing; backpacking; classical music; reading. Office: Colonial Coast Girl Scout Council PO Box 268 415 St Paul's Blvd Norfolk VA 23501

HAYWARD, OLGA LORETTA HINES (MRS. SAMUEL E. HAYWARD), librarian; b. Alexandria, La.; d. Samuel James and Lillie (George) Hines; A.B., Dillard U., 1941; B.S. in L.S., Atlanta U., 1944; M.A., U. Mich., 1959; M.A. in History, La. State U., 1977; m. Samuel E. Hayward, July 12, 1945; children—Anne Elizabeth, Olga Patricia (Mrs. William Ryer). Tchr., Marksville (La.) High Schs., 1941-42; head librarian Grambling (La.) Coll., 1944-46; br. librarian br. nine New Orleans Pub. Library System, 1947-48; reference librarian So. U., Baton Rouge, 1948-73, prof. library sci., social scis. librarian, 1973-84, dir. collection devel., 1984—. Bd. dirs. La. Diocese Episcopal Community Services, 1972-78. Mem. ALA, La. Library Assn., Spl. Libraries Assn. (pres. La. chpt. 1978-79). Episcopalian. Author: Graduate Theses of Southern University 1959-71; A Bibliography of Literature By and About Whitney Moore Young, Jr., 1929-71, 1972; The Influence of Humanism on Sixteenth Century English Courtesy Texts, 1977; also other bibliographies. Contbr. articles to profl. jours. Home: 1632 Harding Blvd Baton Rouge LA 70807

HAYWARD, TERESA CALCAGNO, educator; b. N.Y.C., Jan. 28, 1907; d. Vito and Rosalie (Amato) Calcagno; m. Peter Hayward, Feb. 6, 1932; children—Nancy, Peter. B.A., Hunter Coll., 1929; M.A., Columbia U., 1931. Tchr. romance langs. Jr. High Sch. 164, N.Y.C., 1936-57, Jr. High Sch. 141, Riverdale, N.Y., 1957-71; tchr. English to Japanese women Nichibei Fujinkai, Riverdale, 1972-85. Chmn. Riverdale chpt. Nichibei Fujinkai, Riverdale, 1976-85; bd. dirs. Riverdale chpt. UN Assn., 1976-85. Democrat. Episcopalian. Avocations: concerts; piano; art lectures; travel.

HAYWORTH, KAREN MICHELLE, lawyer; b. Morristown, N.J., Sept. 21, 1956; d. Curtis Benjamin and Gerty Grace (Glaser) Hayworth; m. Richard A. Hainbach, Oct. 23, 1983. B.A., Brandeis U., 1977; J.D., NYU, 1980. Bar: N.Y. 1981. Assoc. law firm Parker Chapin Flattau & Klimpl, N.Y.C., 1980-84; assoc. Zellermayer & Gratch, P.C. N.Y.C., 1984—. Mem. N.Y. State Bar Assn., ABA. Home: 200 W 86th St Apt 19C New York NY 10024 Office: Zellermayer & Gratch PC 598 Madison Ave New York NY 10022

HAZALEUS, MARGARET BENNINGTON, univ. dean; b. Center, Colo., Mar. 8, 1919; d. Frank and Jessie Lynnanne (Scarff) Bennington; B.S. in Food Sci. and Nutrition, Colo. State U., 1941, M.S. in Sociology, 1960; m. Melvin Harp Hazaleus, Jan. 2, 1943; children—John Melvin, Susan Lynn. Dietitian sch. lunch program, LaJunta, Colo., 1941-42; tchr. chemistry and biology Del Norte High Sch., 1942-43; elem. tchr. Center Consol. Schs., 1945-46; asst. to dean Coll. Home Econs., Colo. State U., 1961-67, coordinator student programs, 1967-71, asst. dean Coll. Human Resource Scis., 1971—; conf. presenter. Mem. Poudre R-1 Citizens Com., Gov.'s Commn. Status of Women; vol. Reach to Recovery unit Am. Cancer Soc., 1974—; leader Cub Scouts, Brownie Scouts; mem. 4-H Devel. Com., Larimer County 4-H Scholarship Com. Named Outstanding Faculty Mem., Colo. State U. Coll. Home Econs., 1969; Outstanding Woman Adminstr., Colo. State U., 1973, Very Important Prof., 1980, recipient Disting. Service award in undergrad. advising, 1980. Mem. Am. Home Econs. Assn., Colo. Home Econs. Assn., Assn. Acad. Affairs Adminstrs., Nat. Council Family Relations, Coll. Home Econs. Alumni Assn., Colo. State U. Alumni Assn. (honor alumna 1977), Coll. Human Resource Scis. Alumni Council (pres. 1983-86), Coll. Home Econs. Alumni Council, Mortar Bd. Alumni Group, Gamma Sigma Delta, Delta Kappa Gamma, Phi Kappa Phi, Omicron Nu, Alpha Delta Kappa, Delta Delta Delta. Republican. Presbyterian. Club: PEO. Student patio on Gifford Bldg., Colo. State U. dedicated to biographee, 1982. Home: 1213 Green St Fort Collins CO 80524 Office: Gifford 100A Coll of Human Resource Scis Colo State U Fort Collins CO 80523

HAZARD, KAY JANELL, county financial official; b. Blair, Nebr., Feb. 22, 1942; d. Howard Frederick and Leola Vivian (Jensen) Kubie; m. Lloyd Eugene Hazard, June 17, 1961; children—Brenda Jean, Sheila Kay Hazard Stromberger. Student Wayne State Coll., Nebr., 1959-60, Dana Coll. Tech. clk. Western Electric, Omaha, 1960-62; tchr. aide Imperial Grade Sch., Nebr., 1970-73; county treas. Chase County, Nebr., 1975—. Ednl. v.p. Freedoms Found., Imperial, 1980-82; program dir. Democratic Women, Imperial, 1972-74; sec. United Meth. Women, Imperial, 1973-74; adminstrv. bd. United Meth. Ch., 1984—. Mem. Nebr. County Treas. Assn. (bd. dirs. 1984—), Nebr. County Ofcls. Assn. Lodge: Order Eastern Star (Martha 1983—). Avocations: reading; sewing. Home: PO Box 656 Imperial NE 69033 Office: Chase County Treas PO Box 398 Imperial NE 69033

HAZBOUN, VIVECA, psychiatrist; b. Ramallah, Jordan, Nov. 2, 1949; came to U.S., 1966; d. Albert Anthony and Helen (Kalaris) Hazboun. B.A. in Chemistry, Immaculate Heart Coll.-Los Angeles, 1970; M.D., U. So. Calif., 1976. Teaching asst. Grad. Sch. U. So. Calif., Los Angeles, 1970-72; intern in internal medicine Huntington Meml. Hosp., Pasadena, Calif., 1976-77; resident in adult psychiatry Los Angeles County-U. So. Calif. Med. Ctr., 1977-79, fellow in child and adolescent psychiatry, 1979-81, chief child resident, 1980-81, asst. prof. clin. psychiatry, 1981—, clin. instr. clin. psychiatry, 1980-81; practice medicine specializing in adult, child and adolescent psychiatry, Los Angeles, 1980—; ward chief children's inpatient service Los Angeles County-U. So. Calif. Med. Ctr. Psychiat. Hosp., 1981—; cons. staff Edgemont Psychiat. Hosp., Los Angeles, 1982—; asst. prof. clin. psychiatry U. So. Calif. Med. Sch., 1981—. Contbr. chpts. to publs. in field, film rev. to publ. Fellow Child Guidance Clinic, Los Angeles, 1980. Recipient Recognition awards Women in Data Processing, 1983, Child Guidance Clinic, 1980, Papal award, Rome, 1968. Mem. Am. Acad. Child Psychiatry, So. Calif. Psychiat. Soc., So. Calif. Soc. Child Psychiatry, Am. Arab Univ. Grads. Roman Catholic. Club: Los Angeles Athletic. Office: LAC-USC Med Ctr 1934 Hospital Pl Box 146 Los Angeles CA 90033

HAZELBAKER, EILEEN GENEVA, medical technologist; b. Decatur County, Kans., Nov. 2, 1928; d. Clint Leonard and Edith Helen (Vermilion) Huff; degree in gen. sci. Ft. Hays (Kans.) State Coll., 1953; m. Fred R. Hazelbaker, Oct. 5, 1974; 1 son by previous marriage, Wayne Leroy Wohler. Intern, Stormont-Vail Hosp., Topeka, 1953; med. technologist hosps. in Kans. and Wash., 1954-67; med. technologist Syringa Gen. Hosp., Grangeville, Idaho, 1967—. Mem. Am. Soc. Clin. Pathologists. Mem. Christian Ch. (Disciples of Christ). Clubs: Extension, Rebekahs. Home: PO Box 225 Grangeville ID 83530 Office: Syringa Gen Hosp Grangeville ID 83530

HAZELIP, EDWINA KAY, registered nurse; b. Louisville, Jan. 25, 1952; d. Edwin O'Neil and Lorraine Esta (Nicols) H.; grad. High Point (N.C.) Meml. Hosp. Sch. Nursing, 1975. Nurses aide Wilkes Gen. Hosp., North Wilkesboro, N.C., 1971-72; day care center worker Child's Kingdom, Wilkesboro, N.C., 1971-72; head nurse coronary and intensive care unit Wilkes Gen. Hosp., North Wilkesboro, 1972-82, pres. nurses' staff, 1976, 78; unit mgr. coronary and intensive care unit Wilkes Gen. Hosp., North Wilkesboro, 1982-84; staff nurse Med. Personnel Pool, Greensboro, N.C., 1982—. instr. cardiac defibrillation. Bd. dirs. Wilkes County unit Am. Heart Assn. Cert. instr. CPR. Mem. Am. Nurses Assn., N.C. Nurses Assn. Baptist. Home: 5112 Vickrey Chapel Rd Greensboro NC 27407

HAZELTON, LUCY REED, advt. writer, artist; b. St. Louis, Sept. 9, 1929; d. Ferdinand Maximillian and Elizabeth Emily (Benson) Schaeffer; student Washington U., St. Louis, 1947-48, St. Louis U., 1954-56; writers workshops, U. Colo., summer 1968, U. Houston, summer 1971; m. Burton W. Hazelton, Feb. 15, 1958 (dec.); children—Terence G. Reed (dec.), Deborah Lucy Reed, Ellen Frisch. Writer, artist for ednl. programming Webster Pub. Co., 1962-63; with Scharr Printers, 1966-67; advt. writer, artist Christian Bd. Publs., 1967-69; mgr. advt., public relations A.G. Edwards & Sons, Inc., brokerage, St. Louis, 1969-82; freelance writer/public relations, 1982—; monthly columnist Arts mag., Poetry Center Speaking. Bd. dirs. St. Louis Poetry Center, v.p., 1976-77, pres. bd. chancellors, 1980-84; bd. dirs. Big River Assn. Recipient 1st place E. Oscar Thalinger award for verse play, The Still Point, 1965, 2d pl. for verse play, The River Laughs, 1966; Merit awards Financial World mag., 1973-75, 76, 77, 78, 79; Bicentennial award St. Louis Poetry Center, 1975, Marianne Moore award, 1977. Mem. St. Louis Writers Guild (treas. 1975), Advt. Prodn. Club St. Louis, Acad. Am. Poets, ACLU, Women in Communications, Advt. Fedn. St. Louis. Author: Three Circles and the Princess, 1976; editor Poetry Center Speaking, 1973—; contbr. poetry to mags., revs. Home and Office: 668 Kirkshire Dr Kirkwood MO 63122

HAZELTON, NANCY TOLER, banker, culinary expert; b. Long Beach, Calif., July 11, 1949; d. Albert Eugene and Mary Olive (Fager) Toler; m. Charles Y. Hazelton, Mar. 1, 1969; children—Patricia, Christopher. Student Memphis State U., 1967-69, Sullivan Jr. Coll., 1983-84; diploma Inst. Fin. Edn., Chgo., 1977, cert., 1985. Mgmt. trainee Aristar, Inc., Memphis, 1968-76; loan officer Home Fed., Memphis, 1976-79; loan originator Future Fed. Savs. Bank, Louisville, 1979-85, v.p., mgr. residential lending/secondary mktg., 1985—. Adult edn. guest speaker Jefferson Community Coll., Louisville, 1984; active Jeffersontown Booster Club, Ky. Mem. Women's Council Realtors, Mortgage Bankers Assn., Louisville Bd. Realtors (assoc.), Homebuilders Assn. Louisville (assoc.), Ky. Assn. Profl. Mortgage Women (program chmn. 1985-86). Republican. Roman Catholic. Home: 3603 Pirogue Rd Jeffersontown KY 40299

HAZELTON, PENNY ANN, law librarian, educator; b. Yakima, Wash., Sept. 24, 1947; d. Fred Robert and Margaret (McLeod) Pease; m. Norris J. Hazelton, Sept. 12, 1971; 1 dau., Victoria MacLeod. B.A. cum laude, Linfield Coll., 1969; J.D., Lewis and Clark Law Sch., 1975; M.Law Librarianship, U. Wash., 1976. Admissions counselor Linfield Coll., 1969-71; serials librarian Lewis and Clark Law Sch. Law Library, Lewis and Clark Coll., 1972-75; admitted to Wash. bar, 1976; assoc. law librarian, assoc. prof. U. Maine, 1976-78, law librarian, assoc. prof., 1978-81; asst. librarian for research services U.S. Supreme Ct., Washington, 1981-85, law librarian U. Wash., Seattle, 1985—, prof. law, 1985—; tchr. legal research, law librarianship, Indian law, law and medicine; cons. Maine Adv. Com. on County Law Libraries. Mem. Law Librarians New Eng. (sec. 1977-79, pres. 1979-81), Am. Assn. Law Libraries (cert.; program chmn. ann. meeting 1984, exec. bd. 1984-87), Law Librarians' Soc. Washington (exec. bd. 1983-84, v.p., pres.-elect 1984-85), Am. Bar Assn. Fed. Bar Assn. Republican. Contbr. articles to Environ. Law. Office: 1100 NE Campus Pkwy Seattle WA 98105

HAZENFIELD, SUSAN LONG, speech pathologist; b. Akron, Ohio, Jan. 17, 1955; d. Ralph Patrick and Margaret Katherine (Thompson) Long; B.A., Ohio State U., 1977; M.A., Case-Western Res. U., 1979; m. John Erwin Hazenfield, Dec. 2, 1978; children—John Michael, Sarah Elizabeth. Speech pathologist Wicomico County Bd. Edn., Salisbury, Md., 1979-80, Roanoke-Chowan Hosp., Ahoskie, N.C., 1980, Summit County Bd. Mental Retardation and Developmental Disabilities, 1980— pvt. practice, Cuyahoga Falls, 1981-82; now with Weaver High Sch., Akron. lic. speech pathologist, N.C., Md., Ohio. Mem. Am. Speech, Lang. and Hearing Assn. (cert. clin. competence in speech pathology), N.C. Speech, Lang. and Hearing Assn., Md. Speech, Lang. and Hearing Assn., Akron Regional Speech, Lang. and Hearing Assn., Ohio State U. Alumni Assn., Ohio Speech, Lang. and Hearing Assn., Weaver Tchrs. Assn., NEA, Md. Tchrs. Assn., Wicomico County Edn. Assn. Home: 2384 Silver Spring Dr Stow OH 44224 Office: Weaver High Sch 140 E Market St Akron OH 44308

HAZLEHURST, JENNY MILLER, toy company manufacturers representative; b. Chattanooga, Dec. 11, 1946; d. Alfred Manuel and Virginia (Tarkington) Miller; m. Robert P. Hazlehurst, II, Apr. 30, 1977 (div.). Student U. Tenn.-Chattanooga, 1965-67, Middle Tenn. State U., 1964-65, Tenn. State U., 1973-75; B.S., Peabody Vanderbilt U., 1977. Office mgr., exec. sec. Mental Health Assn., Chattanooga, 1968-69; ins. agt. New Eng. Life, Chattanooga, 1969-71; fin. planner State Mut. Ins., Nashville, 1971-74; tchr. reading Nashville Schs., 1977-80; pres. sales Roadrunners Internat., Chattanooga, 1980—. Coordinator Hamilton County Suicide Prevention Service, Chattanooga, 1968-69; Mem. Southeastern Toy Travelers Assn., Juvenile Products Mfrs. Assn. Clubs: Westside Athletic, Nashville Tennis Assn., Nashville Striders. Avocations: tennis; hiking; whitewater canoeing. Home: 205 Pebble Brook Nashville TN 37221 Office: Roadrunners PO Box 8476 Chattanooga TN 37411

HAZLEWOOD, PHYLLIS JANE, school principal; b. Jefferson City, Tenn., Jan. 15, 1941; d. John Jacob and Mary Myrta (Yates) Buell; m. William Dean Hazlewood, July 8, 1960; children—Melissa Gail Hazlewood Ramsey, Steven Dean, John Austin. B.S., Lincoln Meml. U., 1971; M.S., U. Tenn., 1976, Ed.D., 1986. Tchr., Ellen Myers Elem. Sch., Harrogate, Tenn., 1971-76; asst. prin. New Tazewell-Tazewell Primary Sch., Tazewell, Tenn., 1976-77, prin., 1977-84; cons. reading and lang. arts Tenn. Dept. Edn., Knoxville, 1984-85; prin. Forge Ridge High Sch., Harrogate, 1985—; instr. grad. edn., curriculum Lincoln Meml. U., Harrogate, 1976—; in-service trainer for sch. systems throughout Tenn. Writer Tenn. Basic Skills First Language Arts curriculum, 1984. Organizer Claiborne County Hosp. Aux., 1983; v.p. Tenn. Baptist Woman's Missionary Union, 1983. Named Outstanding Woman of Yr., AAUW, Harrogate, 1983. Mem. Tenn. Edn. Assn., Claiborne County Edn. Assn., Tenn. Internat. Reading Assn. (local pres.), Tenn. Assn. for Supervision and Curriculum Devel., Nat. Council Tchrs. English, Nat. Assn. Elem. Sch. Prins., Tenn. Assn. Elem. Sch. Prins., Phi Kappa Phi, Alpha Chi. Club: Sodalitas Women's (pres. 1982-84). Avocation: vocalist at church and community gatherings. Home: PO Box 147 Harrogate TN 37752 Office: Forge Ridge High Sch Route 2 Box 164 Harrogate TN 37752

HAZZARD, MARY DWIGHT, writer; b. Ithaca, N.Y., May 3, 1928; d. Albert Sidney and Florence Bernice (Woolsey) H.; m. Peter Swiggart, Aug. 11, 1952 (div. 1981); children—William Field, Katherine Anne. B.S., Skidmore Coll., 1949; postgrad. Sch. Drama, Yale U., 1950-52, M.F.A., 1982. Playwright-in-residence Lehigh U., Bethlehem, Pa., 1983; dir. writers' workshops, lectr., poetry readings. Author (pseudonym Olivia Dwight): Close His Eyes, 1961 (scroll Mystery Writers Am. 1961); author novels: Sheltered Lives, 1980, Idle and Disorderly Persons, 1981, plays: Diary of the Seducer, 1981 (Molly Kazan playwriting award Yale U. 1981), Little Girls, 1985; author publ. poems. Editor in fiction and drama: Intro 15, 1985. Fellowship in fiction Mass. Arts and Humanities Found., 1977; MacDonald fellow, Yaddo, 1986. Mem. Authors Guild, Dramatists Guild, PEN, Assoc. Writing Programs. Democrat. Unitarian Universalist. Home: 452 Woodward St Waban MA 02168

HAZZARD, SHIRLEY, author; b. Sydney, Australia, Jan. 30, 1931; d. Reginald and Catherine (Stein) H.; ed. Queenwood Sch., Sydney, to 1946; m. Francis Steegmuller, Dec. 22, 1963. With Combined Services Intelligence, Hong Kong, 1947-48, U.K. High Commr.'s Office Wellington. N.Z., 1949-51, UN (Gen. Service Category), N.Y.C., 1952-62; Christian Gauss lectr. Princeton U., 1982; Boyer lectr., Australia, 1984. Trustee N.Y. Soc. Library. Recipient 1st prize O. Henry Short Story Awards, 1976; grantee in lit. Nat. Inst. Arts and Letters, 1966; Guggenheim fellow, 1974; Nat. Book Critics Circle award for Fiction, 1981. Mem. Nat. Inst. Arts and Letters. Author: Cliffs of Fall and Other Stories, 1963; (novel) The Evening of the Holiday, 1966; (fiction) People in Glass Houses, 1967; (novel) The Bay of Noon, 1970; (social history) Defeat of an Ideal: A Study of The Self-Destruction of the United Nations, 1973; (novel) The Transit of Venus, 1980; contbr. short stories to New Yorker mag. Address: 200 E 66th St New York NY 10021

HEAD, JANICE SELENA, lawyer; b. Mt. Olive, N.C., Feb. 26, 1951; d. Ross Wilson and Sara Ann (Kornegay) Head; m. M. Donnell Komegaz, Feb. 10, 1985. B.A., Wingate (N.C.) Jr. Coll., 1971; B.A., Wake Forest U., 1973, J.D., 1977. Bar: N.C. 1977, U.S. Dist. Ct. (mid. dist.) N.C. 1977, U.S. Dist. Ct. (ea. dist.) 1983., Assoc., Hatfield & Allman, Winston-Salem, N.C., 1976, 1977-80; atty., v.p. Alco Internat. Inc., Winston-Salem, 1980-82; assoc. Kornegay & Head, P.A., Mount Olive, 1983—; atty. Wayne County Juvenile Services, div. courthouse, Goldsboro, N.C., 1983—. Mem. So. Wayne Recreation Inc., Mount Olive. Mem. N.C. State Bar Assn., N.C. Acad. Trial Lawyers, ABA, Assn. Trial Lawyers Am., Wayne County (N.C.) Bar Assn., Coll. Trial Adv., Bus. and Profl. Women's Club (v.p. 1986). Democrat. Methodist. Home: Route 1 Box 145-B Mount Olive NC 28365 Office: Kornegay & Head PA 232 Smith Chapel Rd Mount Olive NC 28365

HEAD, LINDA KAY, videotape editor; b. Hollywood, Calif., Oct. 26, 1959; d. Karl and Barbara (Kahn) Bradlyn; m. Robert L. Head, Jr., Aug. 25, 1984. M.L.T. (A.S.), Ind. Voc. Tech. Coll., 1981; Cert. The Music Bus. Inst., 1983. Microbiology lab. tech. Wishard Hosp., Indpls., 1980-81; microbiology lab. tech. Providence Hosp., Mobile, Ala., 1982; ops. mgr. Henderson-Crowe Prodns., Atlanta, 1983-84; instr. The Music Bus. Inst., Atlanta, 1984—; ops. mgr. Moving Pictures, Inc., Atlanta, 1985—; videotape editor, Woodstock, Ga., 1984—; prodn. coordinator, Atlanta, 1985—; scriptwriter, 1984—. Prodn. mgr. TV show Pre-Awards Spl., 1984; scriptwriter TV show Vincent Price's Halloween Thriller, 1984; producer Kentucky Derby Weekend, 1985; prodn. mgr. music video Rumble Tonight, 1985. Mem. Nat. Assn. Female Execs., Nat. Assn. of Self-Employed, Nat. Acad. TV Arts and Scis. Episcopalian. Home:

401 Revere Ct Woodstock GA 30188 Office: The Music Bus Inst 3376 Peachtree Rd Atlanta GA 30305

HEAD, PAMELA ANN, interior designer; b. Humboldt, Tenn., Aug. 22, 1951; d. Otis O. and Margaret E. (Flowers) Milam; m. Robert W. Vanderdrift, Dec. 30, 1970 (div. 1977); m. 2d, R. Garland Head, Aug. 31, 1978; 1 son, Brandon Christopher. B.B.A. in Acctg. magna cum laude, North Tex. State U., Denton, 1973; A.A. in Interior Design, El Centro Coll., Dallas, 1980. C.P.A. Acct. tax dept. Peat, Marwick, Mitchell & Co., Dallas, 1973-74; acct. spl. projects FNB-Dallas, 1974-77; pvt. practice acctg., Dallas, 1977-79; instr. acctg. Am. Inst. Banking, Dallas, 1977-79; instr. interior design Bauder Coll., Arlington, Tex. 1980-82; prin., designer Interiors by Pam Head & Assocs., Dallas, 1979—. Vol. Dallas Symphony Orch. League-Innovators, 1983-84, March of Dimes, Am. Heart Assn., 1984; mem. Lakewood Presch. PTA, 1983-84. Mem. Tex. Doc. C.P.A.s, Am. Soc. Interior Designers (pub. chmn. students group 1979-80). Home: 5447 Glenwick Dallas TX 75209 Office: 2900 Turtle Creek Plaza Suite 230 Dallas TX 75219

HEAGARTY, MARGARET CAROLINE, physician; b. Charleston, W.Va., Sept. 8, 1934; d. John Patrick and Margaret Caroline (Walsh) H. B.A. summa cum laude, Seton Hill Coll., 1957; B.S., W.Va. Sch. Medicine, 1959; M.D., U. Pa., 1961. Rotating Phila. Gen. Hosp., 1961-62; resident in pediatrics St. Christopher's Hosp. for Children-Temple U., Phila., 1962-64; dir. Pediatric ambulatory care services N.Y. Hosp.-Cornell U. Med. Ctr., N.Y.C., 1969-78; dir. pediatrics Columbia U.-Harlem Hosp. Ctr., N.Y.C., 1978—; mem. select panel for promotion of child health HEW, Washington, 1979-80; mem. Surgeon Gen.'s Workshop on Maternal and Infant Health, HHS, Washington, 1980; mem. steering com. Inst. Medicine Planning Study, U.S. Health Goals for Year 2000, Washington, 1980, mem. com. on community oriented primary care, 1982; mem. Nat. Adv. Bd. Modern Medicine, Ohio, 1982; mem. Robert Wood Johnson's Found. Program for Prepaid Managed Health Care, Boston, 1984; mem. pediatric test com. Nat. Bd. Med. Examiners, Phila., 1978; mem. Robert Wood Johnson Health Policy Bd., Washington, 1976. Robert Wood Johnson Found. health policy fellow, Washington, 1975; Commonwealth Fund, grantee, N.Y.C., 1981; Robert Wood Johnson Found. grantee, N.Y.C., 1983; N.Y. State Dept. Health grantee, N.Y.C., 1984. Mem. Nat. Acad. Scis. (governing council inst. medicine), Inst. Medicine, Ambulatory Pediatric Assn. (past pres. 1976-77), Soc. for Pediatric Research, Am. Pediatric Soc. Office: Columbia U-Harlem Hosp Ctr 506 Lenox Ave New York NY 10037

HEAL, JOANNA MARY, physician; b. London, Jan. 28, 1943; came to U.S., 1972; d. John Christopher and Theresa Mary (Anstruther) H.; m. Neil Blumberg, May 2, 1981; children—David Anthony, Eric Lawrence. M.B., B.S., King's Coll. London U., 1966. House physician and surgeon Westminster Hosp., London, 1966-67; sr. house physician St. Stephens Hosp., London, 1967-68; sr. house officer Whittington Hosp., London, 1968-70; med. registrar Middlesex Hosp., London, 1970-71, Univ. Coll. Hosp., London, 1971-72; resident Georgetown U., Washington, 1972-73, fellow in hematology, 1973-75, Vincent Lombardi research fellow, 1975-78; blood bank fellow ARC, Washington, 1978-79, asst. med. dir., Rochester, N.Y., 1979-82, acting dir. blood services, 1982—; mem. ad hoc adv. group on nitrosourca research NIH, 1977-79; dir. Hemophilia Ctr. of Rochester & Monroe County, Inc., Rochester, 1980—; mem. adv. bd. N.Y. State Blood Council, 1983—; bd. dirs. Rochester Area Task Force on AIDS, 1985—. Contbr. to books and articles to profl. jours. Westminster Hosp. travelling scholar, 1965; grantee NIH, ARC, N.Y. State AIDS Inst., United Cancer Council, Inc. Mem. Royal Coll. Physicians (London), Am. Assn. Blood Banks, Internat. Soc. Blood Transfusion, Am. Soc. Hematology, Am. Fedn. Clin. Research, Am. Soc. Apheresis, Brit. Transfusion Soc., Am. Council on Transplantation. Home: 1519 East Ave Rochester NY 14610 Office: ARC Blood Service 50 Prince St Rochester NY 14607

HEALD, EMILY EASTHAM, civic worker; b. Lawrence, Mass., July 14, 1917; d. Ernest Eugene and Elsie (Eastham) H. Grad. Katharine Gibbs Sch., Boston, 1935. With Mass. Electric Co., 1935-81; ret., 1981; trustee First Essex Savs. Bank, Lawrence, 1977—. Mem. Girl Scout Council Greater Lawrence, Inc., 1935-63, pres. leaders assn., 1938-42, adviser sr. Girl Scouts planning bd., 1949-51, dir., 1951-63, sec. bd. dirs., 1952-53, v.p., 1957-61, pres., 1961-63, nat. council mem. 1949-61, 63-69, dir., pres. Merrimack River Girl Scout Council, Inc., 1963-70; dir. Methuen chpt. ARC, 1952-54, chmn., 1953-54, dir. Greater Lawrence chpt., 1954-81, sec., 1957-60, 1st vice chmn., 1961-63, chmn., 1963-65; sec. dist. 1 Mass. regional blood program, 1960-63, exec. com., 1963-66; chmn. Methuen div. Community Chest Drive, 1951; mem. budget com. United Fund, Lawrence, 1954-56, chmn. spl. gifts, Methuen, 1960; chmn. social action com. Greater Lawrence Council of Chs., 1959-61; sec. bd. dirs. Greater Lawrence Guidance Center; trustee Methuen Meml. Music Hall, Inc., 1949-81, sec., 1949-53, 55-56, 60-63, clk., 1951-55, 60-66, v.p., 1966-69, pres., 1969-73; pres. Gt. Harbors Residents Assn., East Falmouth, Mass., 1985—; vestryman St. Barnabas Meml. Episcopal Ch., Falmouth, Mass., 1985—. Clubs: Quota (Lawrence); Appalachian Mountain (Boston). Home: 54 Striper Lane E Falmouth MA 02536

HEALD, JANE DEWEY, non-profit organization executive; b. Evergreen Park, Ill., Mar. 19, 1931; d. Kirk Martin and Grace Gray (Thomas) D.; m. Mark Aiken Heald, June 9, 1952; children—Kathryn Grace, John Stanton, Charles Kirk. B.A., Oberlin Coll., 1952; B.S., New Haven State Tchr.'s Coll., 1953; M.S.L.S., Drexel U., 1970. Elem. tchr. New Haven Pub. Schs., Conn., 1953-54; research cons. Franklin Mint, Franklin Ctr., Pa., 1970-71; reference librarian J. Lewis Crozer Library, Chester, Pa., 1971-78; assoc. dir. Nat. Support Ctr. for Families of the Aging, Swarthmore, Pa., 1981-83, exec. dir., 1983—. Editor Change, 1982—; contbg. editor Photophile, 1976-78. Co-author: (with Carol Pierskalla) Help for Families of the Aging, 1982; Leaders' Manual, 1983. Author: Survey of Support Services, 1984. Mem. Am. Assn. Counseling and Devel., Phi Beta Kappa, Beta Phi Mu. Christian. Avocations: photography, sailing, camping. Office: Nat Support Ctr for Families of the Aging PO Box 245 Swarthmore PA 19081

HEALY, ANNE, sculptor; b. N.Y.C., 1939. B.A., Queens Coll., 1962. One-woman exhbns.: U.S. Theatre Technicians Symposium, 1971; Solow Bldg., N.Y.C., 1971; A.I.R. Gallery, N.Y.C., 1972, 74; CUNY Grad. Ctr., 1974; Hammarskjold Plaza Sculpture Garden, N.Y.C., 1974; 88 Pine St., N.Y.C., 1974-75; Zabriskie Gallery, N.Y.C., 1975, 78; Contemporary Art Ctr., Cin., 1976; Am.'s Cup Ave., Newport Art Assn., Susie Schochet Gallery, R.I., 1976; U. Mass., Amherst, 1976; A.I.R., N.Y.C., 1978; U. of South, Tex., 1979; group exhbns. include: Outdoor Installations, Basel, Switzerland, 1976, Paris, 1976; represented in permanent collections Solow Bldg., N.Y.C.; Mus. Contemporary Crafts, N.Y.C.; Dept. Cultural Affairs, N.Y.C.; N.Y. Cultural Ctr.; Mich. State U.; Allen Art Mus., Oberlin, Ohio; CUNY Grad. Ctr.; commns. include Wayne State U. Health Care Inst., Detroit, 1979; Springfield Mus. Fine Art, Mass., 1979; instr. sculpture St. Ann's Sch., Bklyn., 1973—; guest lectr. Mich. State U., 1973; vis. artist Mich. State U., 1973; guest lectr. U. Cin., 1974, 76, Smith Coll., Northampton, Mass., 1975, U. R.I., Kingston, 1975. Featured in numerous popular mags. and profl. jours.; contbr. articles to profl. jours. Address: 29 W 57th St New York NY 10019

HEALY, BERNADINE, cardiologist, educator; b. N.Y.C.; m. Floyd Loop, Aug. 17, 1985; 1 child by previous marriage, Bartlett Bulkley. A.B. summa cum laude, Vassar Coll., 1965; M.D. cum laude Harvard Med. Sch., 1970. Diplomate Am. Bd. Med. Examiners, Am. Bd. Cardiology, Am. Bd. Internal Medicine (bd. dirs. 1983-87); lic. physician, Md., D.C. Intern in medicine Johns Hopkins Hosp., Balt., 1970-71, asst. resident, 1971-72; staff fellow sect. pathology Nat. Heart, Blood & Lung Inst., NIH, Bethesda, Md., 1972-74; fellow cardiovascular div. dept. medicine Johns Hopkins U. Sch. Medicine, Balt., 1974-76, fellow dept. pathology, 1975-76, asst. prof. medicine and pathology, 1976-81, assoc. prof. medicine, 1977-82, asst. dean for postdoctoral programs and faculty devel., 1979-84, assoc. prof. pathology, 1981-84, prof. medicine, 1982-84; active staff medicine and pathology Johns Hopkins Hosp., 1976—, dir. CCU, 1977-84; dep. dir. Office Sci. and Tech. Policy, Exec. Office of White House, Washington, 1984-85; chmn. research Cleve. Clinic Found., Ohio, 1985—; co-dir. Mary Elizabeth Garrett Symposium, 1980; regional rep. com. admissions Harvard Med. Sch., Boston, 1974—, steering com., 1981—; co-dir. short course in Ischemic Heart disease, Internat. Acad. Pathology, 1977-81; chmn. Office of Tech. Assessment Panel in Devels. in Biotech., U.S. Congress, 1986—; bd. dirs. Stetler Research Fund for Women Physicians, 1979—; cons. Nat. Heart, Lung and Blood Inst., NIH, 1976—, cardiology adv. com., 1978-82, others. Editorial cons. numerous jours.; abstract reviewer; editorial bd. Jour. Cardiovascular Medicine, 1980—, Am. Jour. Medicine, 1976—, Am. Jour. Cardiology, 1981-82, Circulation, 1981—, Jour. Am. Coll. Cardiology, 1982—. Contbr. articles to profl. jours. Matthew Vassar scholar, 1962-65, Harvard Nat. scholar, 1965-70; Eloise Ellery fellow, 1965-66, Stetler Research fellow, 1976-77; recipient Ohio State award, Network for Continuing Med. Edn. Program, 1980; Nat. Bd. Ann. award for Medicine, Med. Coll. Pa., 1983; Spl. award for service, Am. Heart Ass., 1983, 84. Mem. Am. Fedn. Clin. Research (pres. 1983-84), Am. Heart Assn. (fellow Council on Clin. Cardiology, Council on Circulation, dir. 1983-84), Am. Coll. Cardiology (bd. govs. 1979-82), ACP, Assn. Am. Med. Colls., Internat. Acad. Pathology, Am. Med. Women's Assn., Assn. for Women in Sci., Am. Soc. Clin. Investigation. Office: Cleveland Clinic Research Div 9500 Euclid Ave Cleveland OH 44106

HEALY, JOAN MCDONOUGH, lawyer, nurse; b. Pitts., Aug. 7, 1955; d. Aloysius G. and Julia Ann (Connolly) McDonough; m. Patrick Kevin Healy, May 9, 1980. B.S. in Nursing, Georgetown U., 1977; J.D., Cath. U. Am., 1980. Bar: N.C. 1981, D.C. 1981. R.N. Staff nurse Georgetown U. Hosp., Washington, 1977-78; law clk. Aaron M. Levine, P.A., Washington, 1978-80, firm Jackson, Campbell & Parkinson, Washington, 1980-81; gen. counsel Forsyth Meml. Hosp. Found., Winston-Salem, N.C., 1981-84, corp. sec., 1981-84; gen. counsel, asst. sec. Carolina Medicorp Enterprises, Inc., 1984-86; corp. sec. Salem Health Services, Inc., Winston-Salem, 1982—, Found. Health Systems Corp., Winston-Salem, 1982-84; v.p. legal affairs Carolina Medicorp, 1986—. Mem. ABA, D.C. Bar Assn., N.C. Bar Assn., N.C. Acad. Trial Lawyers, N.C. Soc. Hosp. Attys., Nat. Health Lawyers Assn., Sigma Theta Tau. Office: Carolina Medicorp Enterprises Inc 3343 Silas Creek Pkwy PO Box 15025 Winston-Salem NC 27113

HEALY, JOYCE ANN KURY, banker; b. Pitts., Sept. 23, 1947; d. Andrew G. and Mary (Jacobs) K.; m. Donall Healy, May 17, 1969; 1 child, Brian. Student U. Toronto, 1965-68; B.A. in Sociology, U. Pitts., 1969; M.A. in Urban Studies, Boston U., 1973; postgrad. NYU and N.Y. Inst. Fin., 1974-75. Analyst, Boston Model Cities Adminstrn., 1969-71; mktg. research analyst Mfrs. Hanover Trust, 1971-72, sr. mktg. research analyst, 1972-73; asst. sec. 1973-74, asst. v.p., 1974-75, v.p., 1975-81, sr. v.p., 1981—; speaker in field. Contbr. articles to profl. jours. Trustee, YMCA Greater N.Y. Named Woman of Year, Nat. Kidney Found., 1984. Address: Manufacturers Hanover Trust Co Grand Central Tower 140 E 45th St New York NY 10017

HEALY, MARTHA LOUISE, jewelry company executive, jewelry designer and importer; b. Bethesda, Md., Feb. 23, 1947; d. Norman Clark and June (Ovenburg) H.; m. James Jeffrey Miller, Oct. 18, 1983. Account exec. Montgomery County Sentinel, Gaithersburg, Md., 1969-71; artist art dept. Rolling Stone Mag., San Francisco, 1971-72; owner, importer Somerset Silver Co., Ocean City, Md., 1976-80; owner, mgr., corp. v.p. Somerset Jewelers, Inc., Ocean City, 1980—. Mem. Ocean City C. of C., Downtown Improvement Assn., Nat. Assn. Female Execs., Nat. Geog. Soc. Republican. Avocations: jewelry design; sailing; tennis; travel; art projects. Office: Somerset Jewelers Inc 406 S Boardwalk PO Box 512 Ocean City MD 21842

HEALY, THERESA ANN, diplomat, former ambassador; b. Bklyn., July 14, 1932; d. Anthony and Mary Catherine (Kennedy) H.; B.A., St. John's U., 1954; L.L.D., St. John's U., 1985. Tchr. elem. and secondary schs., N.Y.C., 1951-55; with U.S. Fgn. Service, 1955—; ambassador to Sierra Leone, 1980-83; fgn. affairs fellow U. South Fla., 1983-84; Faculty advisor Nat. Def. U., 1984—. Mem. Am. Fgn. Service Assn. Roman Catholic. Home: 6800 Fleetwood Rd Apt 1002 McLean VA 22101 Office: care Foreign Service Lounge Dept of State Washington DC 20520

HEALY FOX, LINDA DEBORAH, mental health therapist; b. Chgo., July 8, 1952; d. Donn Merrill Healy Jr. and Joanne Louise (Ott) Healy Mathews; m. David Martin Fox, Oct. 11, 1977 (div. 1980); m. Michael Josef Schneider, Dec. 31, 1980. B.A., Valparaiso U., Ind., 1974; M.A., U. South Fla., 1981. Lic. mental health counselor, Fla. Counselor Health and Rehab. Services, State of Fla., Clearwater, 1981; counselor, cons. Sex, Health, Edn. Ctr., Clearwater, 1981-82; rehab. specialist Boley Manor, St. Petersburg, Fla., 1982; supervising counselor Alternative Human Services, pvt. non-profit instn., St. Petersburg, 1982-85; psycotherapist Cigna Healthplan of Fla., Inc., Tampa, 1985—; mental health therapist, cons., Largo, Fla., 1985—. Mem. Am. Assn. Counseling and Devel., Phi Kappa Phi. Avocations: violin, swimming, travel. Home: 303 Cedar St Clearwater FL 33515 Office: 1712 East Bay Dr Largo FL

HEAP, SYLVIA STUBER, civic worker; b. Clifton Springs, N.Y., Sept. 25, 1929; d. Stanley Irving and Helen (Hill) Stuber; B.A. cum laude, Bates Coll., 1950; postgrad. U. Conn. Sch. Social Work, 1952-54, Boston U. Sch. Social Work, 1953-54, SUNY, Brockport, 1979, SUNY-Potsdam, 1980, Syracuse U., 1980-83; m. Walker Ratcliffe Heap, June 9, 1951; children—Heidi Anne, Cynthia Joan, Walker Ratcliffe III. Dir. Y-Teens, YWCA, Holyoke, Mass., 1950-51; social group worker West Haven (Conn.) Community House, 1951-54; program dir. YWCA, Ann Arbor, 1954-55, part-time, 1955-59; mem. adv. bd. div. continuing edn. Jefferson Community Coll., 1965—, chmn. adv. bd., 1968—; pres. Jefferson County Med. Soc. Aux., 1971-72; bd. dirs. St. Lawrence Valley Ednl. TV, 1973-83, sec., 1976-80, treas., 1980-82; v.p., 1982-83, dir. Chem. People Project, 1983; bd. dirs. Watertown Lyric Theatre, 1973-83; bd. dirs. N.Y. State Med. Soc. Aux., 1974-80, 2d v.p. bd., 1979-80; fitness instr. Jefferson Community Coll., Watertown, 1977—; chmn. health projects N.Y. State Med. Soc. Aux., 1981-85. Named Citizen of Yr. Greater Watertown C. of C., 1975. Mem. Friends of Public TV, AAUW, Coll. Women's Club Jefferson County, Phi Beta Kappa. Unitarian Universalist. (UN office envoy 1978—).

HEAP, VIRGINIA SKINKLE, interior designer; b. Chgo., July 29, 1907; d. George Elliot and Blanche (Randolph) Skinkle; student Sorbonne, Paris, France, 1925-27; m. Sydney Heyworth Heap, Nov. 12, 1932; 1 son, Randolph Heyworth. Owner Virginia Heap Interiors, Los Angeles, 1940—. Precinct capt. Rep. Club, Los Angeles, 1945—; bd. dirs. Los Angeles unit Pro Am., v.p. edn., 1977-78; mem. Freedoms Found., Valley Forge, 1979—. Mem. Am. Assn. Interior Designers, Jr. League Los Angeles, English Speaking Union, Park LaBrae Republicans, Nat. Fedn. Republican Women, Bel Air Republicans. Author column In One Ear, 1933-35, Urban Phenomena, monthly mag. page, 1930-32. Address: 435 S Curson Ave Los Angeles CA 90036

HEARD, LYNNETTE MICHELLE, public relations specialist; b. Dayton, Ohio, Apr. 11, 1953; d. Edward Butler and Earnestine Yvonne (Lanier) Taylor; m. Gregory Eugene Heard, June 30, 1973; children—Gregory, Michael, Bryan. B.S. in Edn. and Communications, U. Cin., 1975; postgrad. Miami U., Oxford, Ohio, 1983—. Cert. secondary tchr., Ohio. Tchr., Chaminade-Julienne High Sch., Dayton, 1976-78; communications specialist Elder-Beerman Corp., Dayton, 1978; writer, editor NCR Corp., Dayton, 1978-80; pub. relations specialist NAACP, Dayton, 1980-82; pub. info. officer Montgomery County Children Services, Dayton, 1982-85; dir. pub. relations Planned Parenthood Miami Valley, Inc., 1985—. Editor, contbr. Pride Mag., 1980. Active Young Democrats, Top Ladies of Distinction, NAACP, United Negro Coll. Fund, Nat. Council Negro Women; vol. Action Center of United Way; bd. dirs. For Love of Children, Inc., Dayton, 1982—, Suicide Prevention Center, Dayton, 1982—; bd. dirs. YWCA, Dayton, 1982—, asst. treas., 1986-87; mem. Citizens Adv. Council, Daymont West Mental Health Center; grad. Black Leadership Devel. Program, Dayton Urban League; mem. Black Cultural Festival, Dr. Martin Luther King Jr. Celebration Com. Named Staff Mem. of Yr., Montgomery County Children Service, 1983; recipient Pathfinder award YWCA; Honor scholar U. Cin., 1971. Mem. Am. Women in Radio and TV, Women in Communications, Women Empowered, Internat. Assn. Bus. Communicators, Jack and Jill Am., Alpha Kappa Alpha (sec. 1973-81, Outstanding Soror 1981, nat. conv. press sec. 1980). Democrat. Episcopalian. Club: Silhouette (treas. 1980-82) (Dayton). Home: 4221 Belmore Trace Trotwood OH 45426 Office: Planned Parenthood Miami Valley 224 N Wilkinson St Dayton OH 45402

HEARD, ROSE MARIE, financial institution executive; b. Chgo., Nov. 30, 1930; d. William Horton and Mary Alice (Helm) Bradshaw; m. Eddie R. Heard, Jan. 1, 1976 (div.). B.A., U. Beverly Hills, 1981, M.B.A., 1981; Ph.D. in Bus. Adminstrn., 1983. Trust supr., asst. trust officer, trust officer then asst. v.p., Union Bank, Los Angeles, 1957-76; asst. dir. pension trust, asst. v.p. Beverly Hills Savings, Calif., 1976—; IRA/Keogh instr. Inst. Fin. Edn., Los Angeles, 1975-77; Served with WAF, 1948-52. Adj. mem. Beverly Hills Bar Assn. (mem. probate and trust com., retirement plans com., 1976—). Democrat. Christian Methodist Episcopalian. Lodges: Order of the Eastern Star (past matron, sec.); Heroines of Jericho (matron and grand dep.) (Los Angeles). Office: Beverly Hills Savings 1801 Ave of the Stars Los Angeles CA 90067

HEARN, JOYCE C., state legislator; d. J. C. and Carolyn (Carter) Camp; m. Thomas Harry Hearn; children—Theresa Hearn Potts, Kimberly Ann, Carolyn Lee. Grad. Ohio State U., 1957; postgrad. U. S.C. Former tchr. high sch.; mem. S.C. Ho. of Reps., 1975—, mem. labor and commerce com., joint legis. com. on alcohol and drug abuse, joint legis. com. on problems of handicapped in S.C., com. on structure of govt., asst. minority leader. Officer, S.C. Jud. Nominating Commn.; chmn. Richland County Republican party, 1972; mem. Richland County Planning Commn., 1973-76; 2d Congl. Dist. mgr. U.S. Census, 1970; legis. bd. S.C. Heart Assn.; officer Columbia Urban League; mem. Nat. Adv. Com. for Occupational Safety and Health, 1981-82, chmn., 1982-83; trustee Columbia Mus. Art, 1982-84. Recipient Outstanding Citizen award Columbia Rape Coalition, 1977; Disting. Service award Claims Mgmt. Assn. S.C., 1977, Nat. Fedn. Blind S.C., 1978; Outstanding Legislator of Yr. awards Alcohol and Drug Abuse Assn., 1980, Retarded Citizens Assn., 1982, S.C. Rehab. Assn., 1982. Republican. Baptist.

HEARON, SHELBY, writer, educator; b. Marion, Ky., Jan. 18, 1931; d. Charles Boogher and Evelyn Shelby (Roberts) Reed; m. Robert Hearon, Jr., June 15, 1953 (div. Mar. 1977); children—Anne Shelby, Robert Reed; m. Bill Lucas, Apr. 19, 1981. B.A., U. Tex., 1953. Disting. writer-in-residence Wichita (Kans.) U., 1984; writer-in-residence Clark U., Spring 1985; assoc. prof., vis. writer U. Houston, spring 1981; vis. lectr. U. Tex., spring 1978, 79, 80. Author: (novels) Armadillo in the Grass, 1968; The Second Dune, 1973; Hannah's House, 1976; Now and Another Time, 1977; A Prince of a Fellow, 1978; Painted Dresses, 1981; Afternoon of a Faun, 1983; Group Therapy, 1984; A Small Town, 1985; (non-fiction) (with Barbara Jordan) Barbara Jordan, 1979; also short fiction, articles, book revs. Pres., Jr. League Austin, 1970, Planned Parenthood Austin, 1959, Tex. Inst. Letters, 1980; chair lit. panel Tex. Commn. on Arts, 1980; mem. lit. panel N.Y. Council on Arts. Recipient NEA/PEN Syndication prizes, 1984, 85; Guggenheim fellow, 1982; Nat. Endowment Arts fellow, 1983. Mem. PEN, Authors Guild, Poets & Writers Inc., Women in Communications, Tex. Inst. Letters (Fiction award 1973, 78), Associated Writing Programs. Democrat. Presbyterian. Home: 5 Church St North White Plains NY 10603

HEARST, AUSTINE MCDONNELL, former columnist, feature writer, radio commentator; b. Boston, Nov. 22, 1928; d. Austin and Mary (Belt) McDonnell; grad. Notre Dame of Md., King-Smith Jr. Coll.; m. William Randolph Hearst, Jr., July 29, 1948, children—William Randolph III, John Augustine Chilton. Reporter, columnist Washington Times Herald, 1944-54; syndicated columnist King Features Syndicate, 1949-54; radio commentator CBS Mut. network. Active, North Salem Hist. Soc. Mem. Daus. Soc. Cincinnati, Nat. Soc. Barons of Runnemede, Soc. Descs. King William I the Conqueror and His Companions at Arm., Colonial Dames Am. Clubs: Nat. Press, Sulgrave (Washington); American Fox Hound; Colony, Cosmopolitan (N.Y.C.).

HEARST, GLADYS WHITLEY HENDERSON, writer; b. Wolfe City, Tex.; d. William Henry and Helen (Butler) Whitley; student Trinity U., 1924-26; B.A., U. Tex., 1928, M. Journalism, 1928, postgrad., 1938-40; m. Robert David Henderson, May 17, 1933 (dec. 1941); m. Charles Joseph Hearst, Oct. 30, 1943 (dec. Nov. 1980). Editor, Future Farmer News, Austin, Tex., 1930-33; dir. Service Bur., Tex. Congress Parents and Tchrs., Austin, 1933-36; dir. Student Union, U. Tex., 1939-42; freelance writer, 1945—; instr. U. No. Iowa, 1946-47. Instr. writing Waterloo YWCA, 1966-69. Vice chmn. Black Hawk County Democratic party, 1945-57; mem. County Extension Program Planning Com., 1965-68; past deaconess United Ch. of Christ, chmn. long range planning com., 1975-79; sec. Westminster Manor Residents Assn., 1983-85. Served to lt. WAVES, USN, 1942-45. Mem. AAUW (life, Iowa chmn. Status of Women 1954-56, past pres. Cedar Falls br.), Women in Communications (nat. pres., Disting. Service award 1962, 73, nat. chmn. by laws 1969-74, nat. citation 1969, Task Force Long-Range Planning Com. 1973-74; charter mem., v.p. NE Iowa chpt. 1978), PEO, Readers Guild, Ret. Faculty-Staff Assn., Zeta Tau Alpha, Kappa Tau Delta, Sigma Delta Chi (scholarship award). Clubs: Faculty Woman's Capital Gains Investment (past pres., treas. 1970-73) (Cedar Falls). A writer Cedar Falls Centennial Pageant, 1952; writer, editor hist. book Cedar Falls Naval Station 1942-45, Anthology Family Histories Northeast Iowa (Iowa Arts Council grant), 1978. Presbyterian. Address: 4100 Jackson St Apt 230 A Austin TX 78731

HEATER, SANDRA SUE, therapist, education consultant; b. Savannah, Mo., Apr. 29, 1942; d. Richard C. and Ethel E. (Boyer) Harvey; m. Joseph Paul Heater, Mar. 30, 1962; children—Tracy J., Kimberly. B.A., N.W. Mo. State U., 1964; M.S., U. Nebr.-Omaha, 1973; Ph.D., U. Nebr., Lincoln, 1983. Cert. Montessori trainer. Co-founder, dir. St. Paul's Montessori Sch., Council Bluffs, Iowa, 1965-68; program dir. Creighton U. Montessori Head Start, Omaha, 1968-71; program developer Glenwood State Hosp. Sch., Iowa, 1971-73; reading specialist, program coordinator Ralston Pub. Schs., Nebr., 1973-83; therapist eating disorders, Tucson, 1983—; ednl. cons. Mo. region Head Start, 1971-73, State of Iowa, 1971-73; founder eating disorder support groups, 1981—; cons. med. groups, 1983—. Author: Teaching Pre-school Reading, 1980; Am I Still Visible? A Woman's Triumph Over Anorexia Nervosa, 1983; contbg. author: Parents' Roles in Gifted Education, 1982. Founder Andrew County Young Democrats, Mo., 1956; pub. relations chair Greater Omaha Assn. Retarded Citizens, 1971-73. Named Educator of Yr., Ralston Pub. Schs., 1982. Mem. Authors Resource Ctr. (charter), Soc. Southwest Authors, Assn. Anorexia Nervosa and Allied Disorders (field cons. 1983—), Ariz. Reading Council (research com. 1985—), Romance Writers Am., Gamma Phi Delta (program chmn. 1974-76), Great Books Soc. Club: PEO (membership sec. 1976-78). Home: 7015 N Doane Tucson AZ 85718

HEATH, MAMIE EDITH SHARPE, mechanical contractor; b. Austin, Tex., June 27, 1958; d. Clyde Otto Sharpe and Althea Beatrice (Roberts) Sharpe Gross; m. Howard Claudy Heath, Nov. 25, 1977 (div.); children—Mamie Lynn, Howard Jr., Darla Denise, Donnie Ray. Student pub. schs., Tex. Lic. contractor, Tex. (1st woman licensed). Store mgr. U-tote-M, Austin, intermittently 1976-81; ptnr. H & M Contractors, Georgetown, Tex., 1979-83; pres. H & M Mech. Contractors, Inc., Georgetown, 1982-85; owner Master Heating & Air Conditioning, 1985—. Mem. Air-Conditioning Contractors Assn., Georgeton C. of C., Am. Bus. Women's Assn., Nat. Assn. Women in Constrn. Republican. Mem. Ch. of Christ. Avocations: bowling; skiing; fishing. Home: PO Box 426 Hutto TX 78634 Office: Master Heating and Air Conditioning PO Box 426 Hutto TX 78634

HEATH, MARIWYN DWYER, polit. cons.; b. Chgo., May 1, 1935; d. Thomas Leo and Winifred (Brennan) Dwyer; B.J., U. Mo., 1956; m. Eugene R. Heath, Sept. 3, 1956; children—Philip Clayton, Jeffrey Thomas. Mng. editor Chemung Valley Reporter, Horseheads, N.Y., 1956-57; self-employed freelance writer, speech writer, editor Tech. Transls., Dayton, Ohio, 1966—; cons. Internat. Women's Commn., 1975-76; ERA coordinator Nat. Fedn. Bus. and Profl. Women's Clubs, 1974—; mem. polit. and mgmt. cons. ERAmerica, 1976—; mem. Gov. Ohio Task Force Credit for Women, 1973; mem. Midwest regional adv. com. SBA, 1976—; chmn. Ohio Coalition ERA Implementation, 1974-75. Bd. dirs. Dayton YWCA, 1968-74. Recipient various service awards. Mem. AAUW (dir. Dayton 1965-72; Woman of Year award Dayton 1974), Nat. Fedn. Bus. and Profl. Women's Clubs (pres. Dayton 1967-69, Ohio 1976-77; Woman of Year award Dayton 1974, Ohio 1974), Ohio Women. Republican. Roman Catholic. Address: 10 Wisteria Dr Dayton OH 45419

HEATLEY, CAROLE JEAN, advertising agency executive; b. Piedmont, Calif., Mar. 13, 1940; d. Bernard Marion and Georgiana Margaret (Andrews)

Carter Jansse; m. Richard Adrien Heatley, Oct. 13, 1962; 1 child, Helene Adrienne. B.F.A., U. Ariz., 1964, postgrad., 1965-68. Tchr. English, Tucson High Sch., Ariz., 1965-70; media dir. Jeffers Advt., Tucson, 1970-75, Trustman Advt., Tucson, 1975-79; sales asst. KGUN-TV, Tucson, 1980-85; promotions dir. KDTU-TV, Tucson, 1985-86; v.p. Tucker-Heatley Advt., Tucson, 1986—. Recipient 1st place award Tucson Ad Club, 1985. Mem. Am. Women in Radio and TV (sec. 1985-86), Am. Mktg. Assn. (publicity com. 1985-86), Soc. Broadcast Engrs. (assoc. mem. 1983-86), Tucson Ad Club (bd. dirs. 1985-86). Republican. Episcopalian. Avocations: opera; drama; reading; stamp collecting. Home: 6300 N Camino Arco Tucson AZ 85718 Office: Tucker-Heatley Advt 4921 E 5th St Tucson AZ 85711

HEATON, JANE, religious educator; b. Centralia, Ill., Nov. 23, 1931; d. Wilbur Estle and Nina (Huddleston) Heaton; B.Music Edn., DePauw U., 1953; M.Religious Edn., Christian Theol. Sem., 1968. Sec., Div. Overseas Ministries, Christian Ch., Indpls., 1953-58, departmental assoc., 1958-61, dir. curriculum and edn. dept. ch. women Div. Homeland Ministries, 1961-72, dir. leadership devel., dept. ch. women, 1972-74; course adminstr. Pan-African Leadership Course for Women, Mindolo Ecumenical Centre, Kitwe, Zambia, 1975-78; asst. in curriculum and program sales Christian Bd. Publ., St. Louis, 1978-79, dir. curriculum and program sales, 1979-80, v.p. curriculum and program sales, 1980-85; dir. religious edn., Fort Belvoir, Va., 1985—; missionary in Zaire, 1959-60; ordained to ministry Christian Ch., 1970; tchr. Mindolo Ecumenical Centre, Kitwe, Zambia, 1973. Sec.-tres. Irvington Community Council, Indpls., 1972-75. Mem. Indpls. Radio Club, Theta Phi. Club: Zonta. Author: And What of Ourselves, Bible study guide on Hebrews, 1968; Journey of Struggle, Journey in Hope, 1983. Home: 4410-D Groombridge Way Alexandria VA 22309 Office: Office of Staff Chaplain Fort Belvoir VA 22060

HEATON, MONICA BAYER, communications executive; b. Louisville, Mar. 5, 1951; d. Ralph Joseph and Catherine Anna (Hanley) Bayer; m. Gary Howard Heaton, Oct. 8, 1977; children—Margeaux, Meredith. B.A., U. Iowa, 1973. Reporter, Times, Hammond, Ind., 1973, Herald-News, Joliet, Ill., 1973-74; city editor Compass, Hammond, 1974-75; asst. city editor Jour.-Register, Springfield, Ill., 1975-77; regional copy chief Globe-Democrat, St. Louis, 1978-80; dir. pub. relations Catholic Health Assn. U.S., St. Louis, 1980—. Recipient first place award Internat. Assn. Firefighters media awards, 1977. Mem. Women in Communications, Inc. (founding pres. Springfield chpt. 1977), Pub. Relations Soc. Am., Internat. Assn. Bus. Communicators (Gold Quill 1984, Bronze Quill 1985), Am. Soc. Assn. Execs. (Gold Circle 1985), Religious Pub. Relations Council (award of excellence 1984), Am. Soc. Hosp. Mktg. and Pub. Relations, Kappa Tau Alpha. Office: Cath Health Assn US 4455 Woodson Rd Saint Louis MO 63134

HEAVEY, IRENE ELIZABETH, personnel executive; b. Exeter, R.I., Dec. 10, 1932; d. Achilles Joseph and Eugenia Marie (Duguay) Carrier; student Boston U., 1952-54, Northeastern U., 1955-57, Am. U., 1978-80; m. Thomas Francis Heavey, Oct. 23, 1958; 1 child, Joan Marie. Advt. copywriter Parke Snow, Inc., Waltham, Mass., 1950-52; asst. buyer Star Market Co., Newton, Mass., 1952-59; adminstr. logistics Project Hope, Washington, 1960-61; adminstrv. mgr. Electronic Teaching Labs., Washington, 1961-63; exec. asst. to pres. Security Credit Corp., Silver Spring, Md., 1964-72, corp. sec., 1964-72; with Sperry, McLean, Va., 1972—, now mgr. employee benefits/services personnel dept. Election ofcl. Montgomery County, Md., 1970-74; treas. PTA, 1976; sec. Civic Assn., Silver Spring, 1974-78. Recipient award United Way, 1979, 80, 81, ARC, 1980, service award Sperry, 1977-79. Mem. Nat. Employee Services and Recreation Assn. (dir. 1980—, v.p. 1984-85), Washington Area Recreation and Employee Services Council (pres. 1980, 83, v.p. 1981-82), Am. Soc. Personnel Adminstrs., Am. Soc. Bus. and Profl. Women, Nat. Assn. Female Execs., Internat. Soc. PreRetirement Planners, Assn. Fitness in Bus. Republican. Roman Catholic. Office: 8008 Westpark Dr McLean VA 22102

HEBENSTREIT, JEAN ESTILL STARK, Christian Science teacher and practitioner; d. Charles Dickey and Blanche (Hervey) Stark; student Conservatory of Music; U. Mo. at Kansas City, 1933-34; A.B., U. Kans., 1936; m. William J. Hebenstreit, Sept. 4, 1942; children—James B., Mark W. Authorized C.S. practitioner, Kansas City, 1955—; chmn. bd., pres. 3d Ch., Kansas City, 1953-54, reader, 1959-62; authorized C.S. tchr., C.S.B., 1964—, former mem. C.S. Bd. Dirs.; bd. dirs. First Ch. of Christ Scientist, Boston, 1977-83, chmn. bd., 1981-82; mem. Christian Sci. Bd. of Lectureship. Bd. dirs. Principle Found., Religions and Cultures for Peace, Inc. Mem. Art of Assembly Parliamentarians (charter, 1st pres.), Internat. Platform Assn., Pi Epsilon Delta, Alpha Chi Omega (past pres.). Club: Carriage. Contbr. articles to C.S. lit. Home: 310 W 49th St Kansas City MO 64112 Office: 4849 Wornall Rd Suite 104 Kansas City MO 64112

HEBERT, THERESA MARIE, aircraft company executive, consultant; b. Renton, Wash., Oct. 3, 1950; d. Robert Joseph and Dorothy Darlene (Robbins) H. A.A. in Applied Arts and Scis. Transp., Green River Community Coll., 1970. Traffic rep. Indsl. Freight Traffic Services, Kent, Wash., 1970-71; traffic specialist Boeing Co., Seattle, 1972-85, traffic mgr., 1985—. Mem. com. transp. adv. group Green River Coll., Auburn, Wash., 1985—. Mem. Nat. Def. Transp. Assn., Aerospace Industries Assn. Am. (com.), Am. Soc. Transp. and Logistics (candidate), Boeing Mgmt. Assn. Home: 26219 172 Ave SE Kent WA 98042 Office: Boeing Co PO Box 3707 m/s 3N-65 Seattle WA 98124

HEBERT, YVONNE CECILIA, psychotherapist; b. Detroit, Apr. 20, 1936; d. Philip Joseph and Ruth Veronica (Ingalls) H. B.A., Calif. State U.-Los Angeles, 1971, M.A., 1975. With J. Walter Thompson, Detroit, 1954-59; office mgr., print prodn. mgr. Lewis & Assocs., Los Angeles, 1963-69; cost acct. Comprehensive Designers, Sherman Oaks, Calif., 1969-74; free-lance writer, artist, Los Angeles, 1962-77; counselor W. Los Angeles Coll., 1978-79; pvt. practice psychotherapist, marriage, family, child and rehab. areas, Long Beach, Calif., 1976—; frequent lectr. Author: Finding Peace in Pain, 1984; editor Wright Impact, 1979, Psyche, 1981-82. Mem. Assn. Christian Therapists, Nat. Rehab. Assn., Calif. Assn. Mental Health Counselors (dir. 1981-84), Calif. Assn. Marriage and Family Therapists. Roman Catholic. Office: 4182 Viking Way Suite 108 Long Beach CA 90808

HECHT, BARBARA ELIZABETH ROBERTS, lawyer; b. Kansas City, Mo., Oct. 29, 1946; d. Ralph Thomas and Margaret Naomi (Owen) Henderson; m. Scott William Hecht. B.A., U. Mo.-Kansas City, 1967, J.D., 1971. Bar: Mo. 1971. Gen. counsel, sec., asst. v.p. Oppenheimer Industries, Inc., Kansas City, Mo., 1971-81; dir., v.p., sec. Gunsight Inc., Kansas City, 1978-81; sole practice, Kansas City, 1981—; prin. Lowell Listrom & Co., Inc., Kansas City, 1984; pres. Cristobal Wine Co., Kansas City, 1981—; sec. Ft. McRae Corp., Truth or Consequences, 1983—; owner, pres. SERA II Corp., 1985—; ptnr. DeLago Assocs., 1985—, Lake Front Developers, 1985—. Instr. Elite Gym. Ctr., Overland Park, Kans.; pres. N.W. Mo. Citizens adv. bd.; vol. probation officer, 1974-81; bd. dirs. Engle Water Users Assn., 1985—; asst. sec. Sierra Water Users Assn., 1986. Recipient Vol. of Yr. award N.W. Mo. Probation and Parole Office, 1978; citation for meritorious service ABA, 1979. Mem. Mo. Bar Assn., ABA, Kansas City Bar Assn., Phi Alpha Delta. Republican. Home: 7334 Long Shaunee KS 66216

HECHT, DIANE MELESKI, interior designer; b. Kingston, N.Y., Oct. 17, 1945; d. Vincent J. and Rose S. (Fasce) Meleski; B.F.A., Boston U., 1967; m. Stephen S. Hecht, Aug. 17, 1968. Interior designer M. Brown & Co., Boston, 1966-67, Hans Krieks Assocs., Boston, 1967-68, F.A. Stahl & Assos., Boston, 1968-69, Interspace, Inc., Phila., 1969-70, William Sklaroff Design Assocs., Ardmore Pa., N.Y.C., 1970-81; now pres. D.M. Hecht & Assocs., Inc., N.Y.C. Recipient Outstanding Achievement in field of design award Women in Design Internat., 1981; honorable mention Hexter Design award, 1983. Mem. Archtl. League, Nat. Home Fashions League, Women in Design Internat., Preservation League N.Y. State, Westchester Preservation League (past trustee, v.p., dir. county wide archtl. survey), Mcpl. Art Soc., Nat. Trust Hist. Preservation, Classical Am. Democrat. Home: 30 Emerson Rd Larchmont NY 10538 Office: Hecht & Assocs 20 W 20th St New York NY 10011

HECHT, ETHEL MORELL, construction corporation executive; b. N.Y.C.; d. Louis and Lillie Morell; m. Al Hecht (dec. 1981); children—Randy, Kenneth, Eric; m. Aubrey E. Silver, May 19, 1985. Pres. Sands & Hecht Constrn. Corp., N.Y.C., 1968—. Avocations: writing poetry; tennis; golf; bridge. Office: Sands & Hecht Construction Corp 10 E 39th St New York NY 10016

HECHT, MARIE BERGENFELD, educator, author; b. N.Y.C., Oct. 21, 1918; d. Frank Falle and Marie (Trommer) Bergenfeld; B.A., Goucher Coll., 1939; M.A., New Sch. for Social Research, 1971; m. Morton Hecht, Jr., Dec. 17, 1937 (div.); children—Ann (Mrs. David Bloomfield), Margaret, Laurence, Andrew. Tchr. Am. history Mineola High Sch., Garden City Park, N.Y., 1960-80. Mem. Am. Hist. Assn., Orgn. Am. Historians. Author (with Herbert S. Parmet): Aaron Burr: Portrait of an Ambitious Man, 1967; Never Again: A President Runs for a Third Term, 1968; John Quincy Adams: A Personal History of An Independent Man, 1972; The Women, Yes, 1973; Beyond the Presidency: The Residues of Power, 1976; Odd Destiny: The Life of Alexander Hamilton, 1982. Address: 5 Hewlett Pl Great Neck NY 11024

HECHT, MARY, sculptor, educator; b. N.Y.C., June 23, 1931; d. Arthur Julius and Cecelia (Bartelstone) H. B.A., U. Cin., 1952; M.A., State U. of Iowa, 1957; student Art Acad. Cin., 1948-52, Art Students League, N.Y.C., summers 1949, 52, Columbia U., 1950, 52-53, Camberwell Sch. Art, London, 1958-60. Tutorial leader York U., Toronto, 1977—; tchr. Inner City Angels, Toronto, 1974—; illustrator Can. Mideast Focus, Toronto, 1978—, Wagner Notes, N.Y.C., 1979—, Reconstructionist, Phila. Sculptor; one woman shows include York U. McLaughlin Coll., Toronto 1980, 84, Heritage Ganaraska Found., Port Hope, Ont., 1980, Catholic Edn. Ctr., Toronto, 1982, 83, Gustaffson Gallery, Toronto, 1982, Drain Gallery, London, 1984, U. Toronto, 1985, also others; represented in pvt. collections. Ont. Arts Council grantee, 1976, 79, 85; Caterine Lorilard Wolfe grantee, 1983. Mem. Am. Medalic Sculpture Assn., Sculptors Soc. Can., Am. Soc. Contemporary Artists, Soc. Can. Artists. Democrat. Jewish.

HECK, GRACE FERN, lawyer; b. Tremont City, Ohio, Nov. 13, 1905; d. Thomas J. and Mary Etta (Maxson) H.; m. Leo H. Faust, May 25, 1977. B.A. cum laude, Ohio State U., 1928, J.D. summa cum laude, 1930. Bar: Ohio 1930, U.S. Dist. Ct. (so. dist.) Ohio 1932; U.S. Supreme Ct. 1960. Researcher, Nat. Commn. Law Observance and Enforcement, U.S. Dist. Ct. (so. dist.) Ohio, 1930-31, Ohio Jud. Council and Law Inst. Johns Hopkins U., 1931-32; pros.atty. Champaign County, Urbana, Ohio, 1933-37; assoc. Corry, Durfey and Martin, Springfield, Ohio, 1943-47; sole practice, Springfield, 1947-73, Urbana, Ill., part-time, 1973—, mcpl. judge Champaign County, 1954-58. Exec. sec. War Price and Rationing Bd., Urbana, 1941-43; bd. trustees Spring Grove Cemetery Assn., 1954—; sec. bd. trustees Magnetic Springs Found., Ohio, 1957-62; pres. Ohio State U., Coll. Law Alumni Assn., Columbus, 1971-72; mem. Nat. Council Coll. Law, Ohio State U. Columbus, 1971—, Champaign County Arts Council. Recipient Disting. Service award Ohio State U., 1971. Mem. Ohio State Bar Assn. (com. mem.), Champaign County Bar and Law Library Assn. (pres. 1965), Springfield Bar and Law library Assn. (sec. 1946-59, pres. 1963), ABA, Ohio State U. Alumni Assn. (2d v.p. 1956-58, adv. bd. 1962-73, Alumni Centennial award 1970, Springfield Art Ctr., Friends of Library of Ohio State U. (charter), Friends of Historic Costume and Textiles Collection of Ohio State U. (charter), Order of Coif, Phi Beta Kappa, Zeta Tau Alpha, Kappa Beta Pi, Delta Theta Tau (nat. v.p. 1939-40, nat. pres. 1941-42, bd. trustees 1942-45). Democrat. Methodist. Clubs: Springfield Country (Ohio); Troy Country (Ohio); Altrusa. Lodge: Order of Eastern Star. Avocations: fishing; hunting; travel; photography; gravestone rubbings. Home: 134 W Church St Urbana OH 43078

HECKART, EILEEN, actress; b. Columbus, Ohio, Mar. 29, 1919; d. Leo Herbert and Esther (Stark) Purcell; B.A., Ohio State U., 1942, L.H.D. (hon.), 1981; student Am. Theatre Wing, 1944-48; LL.D., Sacred Heart U., Bridgeport, Conn., 1973; D.F.A. (hon.), Niagara U., 1981; m. John Harrison Yankee, Jr., June 26, 1943; children—Mark Kelly, Philip Craig, Luke Brian. Actress Broadway plays, Voice of the Turtle, 1944, Brighten the Corner, 1946, They Knew What They Wanted, 1948, Stars Weep, 1949, The Traitor, 1950, Hilda Crane, 1951, In Any Language, 1953, Picnic, 1953, Bad Seed, 1955, A View From the Bridge, 1956, Dark at the Top of the Stairs, 1958, Invitation to a March, 1960, Everybody Loves Opal, 1961, Family Affair, 1962, Too True To Be Good, 1963, And Things That Go Bump in the Night, 1965, Barefoot in the Park, 1965-66, You Know I Can't Hear You When the Water's Running, 1967, The Mother Lover, 1968, Butterflies Are Free, 1969, Veronica's Room, 1973, The Effect of Gamma Rays on Man-in-the-Moon Marigolds, 1971, Remember Me, 1975, Mother Courage and Her Children, 1975, Mrs. Gibbs in Our Town, 1976, (one-woman show) Eleanor, 1976, Ladies at the Alamo, 1977, 'night Mother, 1985, 86; movies: Miracle in the Rain, Bad Seed, Somebody Up There Likes Me, Bus Stop, Hot Spell, Heller in Pink Tights, My Six Loves, 1962, Up the Down Staircase, 1966, No Way To Treat A Lady, 1968, Butterflies Are Free, 1972, Zandy's Bride, 1974, The Hiding Place, 1975, Burnt Offerings, 1975, Wedding Band, 1975; TV actress, 1947—, roles include series Trauma Center, 1983, Ptnrs. in Crime, 1984. Recipient Outer Circle award, 1953, Daniel Blum award, 1953, Sylvania TV award, 1954, Donaldson award, 1955, Oscar nomination, 1956, Hollywood Fgn. Press award, 1956, Film Daily citation, 1956, Variety Poll of N.Y. Drama Critics award, 1958; N.Y. Emmy for Save Me A Place at Forest Lawn, 1967; March Dimes award, 1970; Aegis award, 1970; Ohio State U. Centennial award, 1970; Acad. award for Butterflies Are Free, 1973; Straw Hat award, 1973, 75, 77; Gov.'s award of Ohio, 1977; Ohiana Library award, 1978. Mem. Pi Beta Phi. Office: Bauman Hiller & Assocs 250 W 57th St Suite 803 New York NY 10019

HECKERLING, AMY, film director. Dir. films Fast Times at Ridgemont High, 1982, Johnny Dangerously, 1984, National Lampoon's European Vacation, 1985. Address: Gersh Agy 222 N Canon Dr Beverly Hills CA 90210*

HECKERT, KENDRA LYNN, lawyer; b. Harrisburg, Pa., Oct. 12, 1947; d. Albert Kenneth and Spacha (Zaikoff) Dimond; m. Frederick Samuel Faber, June 21, 1969 (div. 1976); 1 dau., Elena Marie. B.A., Gettysburg Coll., 1969; M.A., Pa. State U., 1973; J.D., Dickinson Law Sch., 1979. Bar: Pa. 1979. Tchr. French, West Shore Sch. Dist., Lemoyne, Pa., 1969-73; asst. prof. Coll. Charlestown, Charleston, S.C., 1974-75; law clk. Commonwealth Ct., Harrisburg, 1979-80; dep. dist. atty. Dauphin County, Harrisburg, 1980-82; dep. atty. gen. Office of Atty. Gen., Harrisburg, 1982—, regional dir. Medicaid fraud control, 1985—. Mem. ABA, Pa. Bar Assn. (sec. criminal law sect.), Dauphin County Bar Assn., Dauphin County Women Lawyers. Republican. Eastern Orthodox. Home: 5202 Royal Dr Mechanicsburg PA 17055 Office: Office of Atty Gen Medicaid Fraud Control Sect 16th Floor Strawberry Sq Harrisburg PA 17120

HECKLER, MARGARET M. O'SHAUGHNESSY, government official; b. Flushing, N.Y., June 21, 1931; d. John and Bridget (McKeown) O'Shaughnessy; B.A. (scholar), Albertus Magnus Coll., 1953, LL.D., 1972; LL.B. (scholar), Boston Coll., 1956; postgrad. U. Leiden (Netherlands), 1953; L.H.D., Northeastern U., 1970, Emanuel Coll., 1969; D. Law and Letters, Stonehill Coll., 1969; LL.D. honoris causa, Regis Coll., St. Bonaventure U., 1975; m. John M. Heckler, Aug. 29, 1953; children—Belinda West, Alison Anne, John M. Bar: Mass. 1956. Mem. Mass. Gov.'s Council, 1962-66; mem. 90th to 97th Congresses from 10th Dist. Mass., mem. Agrl. Com., Joint Econ. Com., Vets. Affairs Com., Select Com. on Ethics, Sci. and Tech. Com.; founder, co-chair Congressional Caucus on Women's Issues; sec. HHS, Washington, 1983-1985; keynote speaker Nat. Women's Republican Conv., 1967. Mem. pres.'s adv. com. Wheaton Coll.; mem. corp. Madeira Sch.; mem. nat. adv. com. Hampshire Coll.; bd. dirs. March Dimes; hon. bd. dirs. Epilepsy Found. Am.; trustee Heart Research Found.; hon. trustee Newton Wellesley Hosp.; mem. U.S. Commn. on Observance of Internat. Women's Year. Recipient numerous civic and profl. awards. Mem. Am. Bar Assn. (com. on govt., legis. and public interest of food, drug and cosmetic law div.), Boston Bar Assn., Mass. Trial Lawyers, Mass. Women Lawyers, Catholic Women's Coll. Alumnae Assn. (past pres.). Club: Ninetieth (v.p.) (Washington). Office: Am Embassy care US Dept State Washington DC 20520

HECKMAN, JOANN, word processor; b. Newton, N.J., Feb. 23, 1950; d. James Richard and Frances Margaret (Bertram) H. A.S. in Communications, Centenary Coll., 1982, B.A. cum laude in Communications and Journalism, 1984. Freelance reporter, editorial asst. Daily Advance, Roxbury Twp., N.J., 1979-81; asst. mgr., pressperson Jag-Ton Print World, Hackettstown, N.J., 1985; owner, operator Words-Worth Word Processing Services, Budd Lake, N.J., 1984—; word processor MetLife Security Ins. Co., East Hanover, N.J., 1985—. Mem. Nat. Assn. Female Execs., AAUW, Phi Theta Kappa (Merit cert. 1982), Alpha Chi. Republican. Baha'i. Avocations: photography, graphic art and design, freelance writing, crafting. Home: 313 Shore Rd PO Box 114 Budd Lake NJ 07828 Office: MetLife Security Ins Co 72 Eagle Rock Ave East Hanover NJ 07936

HECKMAN, NORMA A., government official; b. Vinita, Okla., May 21, 1947; d. Norman A. and Dorothea Catherine (Loeffelholz) Maynard; m. Richard G. Heckman, Aug. 14, 1971. B.A., San Diego State U., 1974, M.A., 1977, postgrad., 1980—. Research psychologist Naval Health Research Ctr., San Diego, 1974-81; systems analyst Naval Ocean Systems Ctr., San Diego, 1981-84, computer tng. mgr., 1984—. Mem. Western Psychol. Assn., Nat. Assn. Female Execs. Democrat. Avocation: running. Home: 2004 Cecelia Terr San Diego CA 92110 Office: Naval Ocean Systems Ctr Code 9122-B San Diego CA 92152-5000

HEDGBETH, HARRIET BRIDGET, lawyer; b. Roanoke, Va., Jan. 3, 1950; d. Roger Albert and Linnae (Redd) Hedgbeth. B.A. with honors, Hollins Coll., 1971; M.Div., Princeton Theol. Sem., 1974; J.D., Whittier Coll., 1982. Bar: Calif. 1983. Minister United Meth. Ch., Syracuse, N.Y., 1975-78; assoc. Federman, Gridley, Mogab & Gradwohl, Los Angeles, 1983-85, Wasserman, Comden & Casselman, Tarzana, Calif., 1986—. Lead articles editor Whittier Coll. Law Rev., Los Angeles, 1981-82, case notes, comments editor, 1982. Mem. ABA, Los Angeles County Bar Assn.

HEDGE, CYNTHIA ANN, lawyer; b. LaPorte, Ind., June 7, 1952; d. John S. and Edith Rae (Badkey) H. A.B., Ind. U., 1975; J.D., Valparaiso U., 1978. Bar: Ind. 1978, U.S. Dist Ct. (no. dist., so. dist.) Ind. 1978. Staff writer Ind. Dept. Commerce, Indpls., 1975; pub. relations asst. Ravinia Festival, Chgo., 1976; freelance writer, LaPorte County, Ind., 1978—; dep. pros. atty. LaPorte County, 1978—; sole practice, Michigan City, Ind., 1978—; dir. Michiana Industries, LaPorte County. Chmn., Child Abuse Adv. Team, LaPorte County, 1982—; chmn. domestic violence task force La Porte County, 1985—; bd. dirs. Bethany Lutheran Ch., LaPorte, 1982—, Parents and Friends of the Handicapped. Mem. ABA, Ind. Bar Assn., LaPorte County Bar Assn., Michigan City Bar Assn., Christian Legal Soc., Ind. U. Alumni Assn., AAUW. Home: 2912 N Regal Dr LaPorte IN 46350 Office: 601 Franklin Sq Michigan City IN 46360

HEDGE, PATRICIA LYTGENS, environmentalist; b. Palo Alto, Calif., Feb. 19, 1940; d. Norman Julius and Ruth Ellen (Hemmer) Hedge; m. Charles Edward Weesner, Oct. 20, 1957 (div. 1973); children—Kathryn Ellen, James Reid; m. Richard Edwin Hammond, Apr. 8, 1978; children—Matthew Mills, Peter Edwin. B.S., U. Calif.-Berkeley, 1972; M.S., U. Calif.-Davis, 1974. Environ. planner Calif. Coastal Commn., San Francisco, 1974-77; real estate agt. Coldwell Banker Comml., Sacramento, 1977-79; pres., owner Hammond Designs, Sacramento and Mill Valley, Calif., 1979-82; regional dir. (Calif. and Nev.) The Wilderness Soc., San Francisco, 1982—; dir. Tuolumne River Trust, San Francisco, Planning and Conservation League, Sacramento; mem. com. Calif. State Bd. Forestry, Sacramento, 1978-79; mem. task force Bay Area Council, San Francisco, 1976. Contbr. articles to profl. jours. Regional dir. sta. KQED-TV Acution, San Francisco, 1969-70; docent Oakland Mus. (Calif.), 1968-70; leader Girl Scouts U.S.A., Berkeley, Calif., 1970-72; bd. dirs., officer John Muir Sch. Bd., Berkeley, 1967-70; Mem. Sierra Club, Smith River Alliance, Friends of the Earth, Friends of the River, Wilderness Soc., Phi Beta Kappa. Democrat. Club: Commonwealth (San Francisco). Home: 10 Heuter's Ln Mill Valley CA 94941 Office: Wilderness Soc 1791A Pine StFrancisco CA 94109

HEDGES, MINDY DAWN, advertising executive; b. Bklyn., Jan. 10, 1956; d. Marvin and Barbara Francis (Danziger) Schwartz; m. Donald David Hedges, Sept. 15, 1979; 1 child, Blair Danielle. B.A. in Communications, Ohio Wesleyan U., 1978. Cert. secondary tchr., Ohio. Research asst. Howard Swink Advt., Inc., Marion, Ohio, 1978-79; account exec. Scantland Communications, Marion, Ohio, 1979; mktg. asst. Floyd Browne Assocs., Ltd., Marion, 1979-81; mktg. research analyst Lord, Sullivan & Yoder Advt., Marion, 1981-83; media buyer/planner Ron Foth Retail, Columbus, Ohio, 1983—; prof. Marion Bus. Coll., 1980-81; lectr. Franklin U., Columbus, Ohio, 1982; Marion Tech. Coll. (Ohio), 1982. Youth group advisor Temple Isreal, Marion, 1978-79, Sunday sch. tchr., 1983-84. Mem. Am. Mktg. Assn. (dir. communications 1982-83, v.p. programming 1983-84, pres. 1984-85), Gamma Phi Beta (philanthropy chmn. 1977-78). Democrat. Home: 5203 Norton Rd Radnor OH 43066 Office: Ron Foth Retail 8100 N High St Columbus OH 43285

HEDGES, PHYLLIS IRENE, lawyer; b. Wichita, Kans., Sept. 27, 1948; d. Waldo Bass and Genevieve Lucille (Arnold) Wetmore; children—Allison T. Crist, Trevor A. Crist, David G. Hughes. B.A., U. Kans.-Lawrence, 1970; J.D., U. Denver, 1975. Bar: N.Mex., 1976. Assoc., Jones, Gallegos, Snead & Wertheim, P.A., Santa Fe, 1976-78; trust officer First Nat. Bank Santa Fe, 1978-81; sole practice, Los Alamos, 1981-85; asst. county atty. County of Los Alamos, N.Mex., 1985—. Democrat. Unitarian. Office: PO Box 30 Los Alamos NM 87544

HEDIEN, COLETTE JOHNSTON, lawyer; b. Chgo.; d. George A. and Catherine (Bugan) Johnston; m. Wayne E. Hedien; children—Mark, Jason, Georgiana. B.S. with honors, U. Wis., 1960; J.D., DePaul U., 1981. Bar: Ill. 1981. Tchr., Sch. Dist. 39, Wilmette, Ill., 1960-63, Tustin Pub. Schs. (Calif.), 1964-66; extern law clk. to judge, Chgo., 1980, U.S. Atty.'s Office, Chgo., 1980; sole practice, Northbrook, Ill., 1981—; atty. Chgo. Vol. Legal Services; mem. Chgo. Appellate Law Com., 1982-83. Chmn. Northbrook Planning Commn; founder Am. Women of Surrey (Eng.), 1975-77; founding dir. U. Irvine Friends of Library, 1965-66; guidance vol. Glenbrook High Sch., 1984—. NSF scholar, 1962. Mem. Chgo. Bar Assn., Ill. Bar Assn., ABA (com. on real property), Phi Kappa Phi, Kappa Alpha Theta.

HEDRICK, LOIS JEAN, investment company executive, political fundraiser; b. Topeka, Kans., Jan. 25, 1927; d. Arthur Lenard and Nellie Cecelia (Johnson) Lungstrum; m. Clayton Newton Hedrick, Apr. 26, 1949; 1 dau., Carol Beth. Cert., Strickler's Bus. Coll., 1947; student Washburn U., Topeka, 1980-863. Staff sec. Kans. State Senate, Topeka, 1946-65; staff sec./fundraiser Christian Rural Overseas Program, 1947-49; staff sec. U.S. Air Force Supply Depot, Topeka, Kans., 1951-54; co-owner Hedrick's Market, Topeka, 1963-67; exec. sec. to sr. legal counsel Security Benefit Life Ins. Co., Topeka, 1963-73; asst. corp. sec. Security Mgmt. Co., Topeka, 1973—, Security Distbrs. Inc., SBL Planning Inc., SBL Fund, Security Action Fund, Security Equity Fund, Security Investment Fund, Security Ultra Fund, Security Bond Fund, Security Cash Fund, Security Tax-Exempt Fund, Security Benefit Group, Ins., Security Mgmt. Co.; mgmt. cons. United Way of Greater Topeka, 1981—, mem. pub. relations staff, 1982—. Organizer, chmn. Topeka Crime Blockers, 1976—; chmn. Plant a Tree for Century III, 1976; mem. Greater Topeka Career Edn. Com., 1981—; vol. fundraiser Stormont-Vail Hosp., Am. Heart Assn., 1978—. Named Woman of Year, Am. Bus. Women's Assn., 1970; Sec. of Yr., Profl. Secs. Inc., 1975. Mem. Greater Topeka C. of C. (chmn. edn. com. 1981—, ambassador chmn. high sch. honors banquet, 1982—), Adminstrv. Mgmt. Soc. (dir., pres. 1976—). Am. Bus. Women's Assn. (Women of Yr. 1970, organizer chmn. Kans. chpt. 1970, pres. Echo chpt., career chpt., exec. chpt.), Topeka Women's Bowling Assn., Beta Sigma Phi. Republican. Home: 1556 SW 24th St Topeka KS 66611

HEEDING, MICHELLE ANNE, finance executive; b. Coral Gables, Fla., Nov. 24, 1953; d. Donovan and Wynona Mary (Sheleny) Macfarlane; m. William Carl Heeding, II, June 7, 1975. B.A. cum laude, U. Guam, 1974. Mail officer ARC, Agana, Guam, 1975; officer Lee-Wood Motors CO., Whittier, Calif., 1976-78; office mgr. Horizon Mazda Co., Lakewood Calif., 1979-80; bus. mgr. Astro Mgmt. Services Inc., Buena Park, Calif., 1980-81, v.p. fin., 1981—. Recipient numerous awards. Mem. Volkswagon of Am. Bus. Mgrs. Assn. (sec. 1984, excellence awards Mazda chpts. 1981, 82, 83, 84, 85, Nissan chpts. 1981-85). Republican. Mormon. Office: Astro Mgmt Services Inc 18707 Studebaker Rd Cerritos CA 90701

HEFFERNAN, PATRICIA CONNER, management consultant; b. N.Y.C., Oct. 11, 1946; d. Arthur S. and Catherine (Center) Conner; B.A., U. Va., 1968; M.B.A., Suffolk U., 1980; m. John Joseph Heffernan, Sept. 13, 1969. Office restaurant mgr. Wobbly Barn, Killington, Vt., 1968-72; bus. mgr. Woodstock Country Sch., Vt., 1972-74; bus. mgr., treas., assoc. dean Vt. Law Sch., Royalton, Vt., 1974-83; mgmt. cons. Heffernan & Assocs., Killington, 1982—, pres., 1982—; dir. Rutland div. Chittenden Bank. Trustee, pres. Killington Mountain Sch., 1978-85, pres., 1980-85; mem. Killington Planning Commn., 1975, vice chmn., 1976, chmn., 1977-79, 83—; mem. Killington Zoning Bd., 1979-84; mem. Vt. Epilepsy Assn., 1977—; mem. Vt. steering com. for ACE Nat. Identification Program for Women in Higher Edn., 1978-83; bd. dirs. Rutland Regional Med. Ctr. Mem. Assn. Mgmt. Cons., Inst. Mgmt. Accts., Women Bus. Owners Vt. (dir. 1983—, pres. 1984—), Inst. Mgmt. Cons., Am. Soc. Personnel Adminstrn., Adminstrv. Mgmt. Soc., Assn. Legal Adminstrs. Office Heffernan & Assocs 18 Elm St Woodstock VT 05091

HEFFERNAN, PATRICIA KATHLEEN, educational administrator; b. Wilkes-Barre, Pa., Apr. 26, 1946; d. Frank Charles and Katherine Camilla (Nareski) Heffernan; B.A., Pa. State U., 1968, M.Ed., (fellow), 1970; M.A. (fellow), Calif. State U., Northridge, 1977; Ed.D., SUNY-Buffalo, 1986. Speech and lang. cons. Head Start Bristol (Pa.) Twp. Sch. Dist., 1968-70; tchr. Pa. Sch. for the Deaf, Phila., 1968-69, 1970-71; supr. Child Hearing Therapy Program Pa. State U., University Park, 1969-70; tchr. Rochester (N.Y.) Sch. for the Deaf, 1971-76, supr. multihandicapped program, 1979-80, curriculum coordinator, asst. project dir. Title I, 1977-85; dept. head spl. edn. East High Sch., Rochester City Sch. System, 1985, Coordinating adminstr. spl. edn., 1985—study guide/caption writer U.S. Office Edn., Bur. Edn. for Handicapped/Conf. Execs. Am. Schs. for the Deaf, 1975-78, film evaluator/field evaluation coordinator, 1976-79, captioned films for the deaf; adv. The Caption Center, WGBH-TV, Boston. Mem. N.Y. State Assn. Educators of the Deaf, (past pres.), Conv. of Am. Instrs. of the Deaf, ACLU, Assn. Supervision and curriculum Devel., Nat. Ski Patrol System, NOW, Pa. State Coll. Edn. Alumni Soc. (dir. 1984—). Democrat. Unitarian. Contbr. articles in field to profl. jours. Home: 186 Trafalgar St Rochester NY 14619 Office: 1801 E Main St Rochester NY 14609

HEFFLEFINGER., CLARICE THORPE, real estate broker; b. Oregon, Ill., Oct. 5, 1937; d. Ralph Wayne and Wyota Anita (Nashold) Thorpe; A.A., Coll. Sequoias, Visalia, Calif.. 1967; m. Jack Kenneth Hefflefinger. Jan. 24, 1970; children—Kenneth, Jack, Deborah, Kevin. Various positions in banking and ins., 1956-76; real estate broker Hefflefinger Realty, Tulare, Calif.. 1977—; substitute tchr. Tulare City Schs., 1979—. Chmn. Tulare County SSS Draft Bd. Recipient Realtor of Year award Tulare Bd. Realtors, 1983. Mem. Nat. Assn. Realtors, Calif. Assn. Realtors (dir.), Tulare Bd. Realtors (dir., pres. 1982), Tulare C. of C. (dir. Crime Scope), Tulare Republican Women's Fedn., LWV. Amvets Aux. (pres. post 1982). Clubs: Toastmasters, Quota. Home and Office: 1351 Williams St PO Box 1213 Tulare CA 93275

HEFNER, CHRISTIE A., publishing/entertainment company executive; b. Chgo., Nov. 8, 1952; d. Hugh Marston and Mildred Marie (Williams) H.; B.A. summa cum laude in English and Am. Lit., Brandeis U., 1974. Free lance journalist, Boston, 1974-75; spl. asst. to pres. Playboy Enterprises, Inc., Chgo., 1975-78, v.p., 1978-82, dir., 1979—, pres., 1982—, chief operating officer, 1984—; bd. dirs. Playboy Found.-Playboy Enterprises, Inc. Vice pres. devel. Ill. chpt. ACLU. Mem. Brandeis Nat. Women's Com. (life); mem. Com. of 200, Young. Pres. Orgn., Mag. Pubs. Assn. (bd. dirs.), Voters for Choice, The Nation Inst., NOW (legal def. and edn. fund), Phi Beta Kappa. Democrat. Club: Economic. Office: 919 N Michigan Ave Chicago IL

HEFT, CAROLYN MAE, lawyer; b. Bklyn., Apr. 17, 1942; d. William and Pauline (Haselkorn) H. B.A., Skidmore Coll., 1962; postgrad. Hunter Coll., 1962-63; J.D., Columbia U., 1966. Bar: N.Y. 1967, U.S. Dist. Ct. (so. dist.) N.Y. 1971, U.S. Ct. Appeals (2d cir.) 1972, U.S. Supreme Ct. 1974. Staff atty. Inst. Pub. Adminstrn., N.Y.C., 1966-68; assoc. Shearman & Sterling, N.Y.C., 1968-70; adminstrv. dir. Manhattan Bowery Project, Vera Inst. Justice, N.Y.C., 1970-71; dir. litigation and test case unit M.F.Y. Legal Services, Inc., N.Y.C., 1971-75; sr. atty. Nat. Ctr. Social Welfare Policy & Law, N.Y.C., 1973-78, sole practice, N.Y.C., 1978—; cons. Legal Services Corp., Washington, Phila., 1978-81. Co-author: A New Mental Hygiene Law for New York State, 1968, also articles. Mem. Citizens Housing and Planning Council, N.Y.C., 1983. Bd. dirs. MFY Legal Services, Inc., 1980—, chmn. bd., 1986—; bd. dirs. Lorge Sch., N.Y.C., 1983—. Mem. ABA, N.Y. State Bar Assn., N.Y. County Lawyers Assn., Assn. Bar City N.Y. (moderator panel on foster care 1983), Nat. Legal Aid and Defenders Assn. (chmn. workshop and speaker Washington 1978), Gramercy Park Neighborhood Assn., Skidmore Alumni Assn., Columbia Law Sch. Alumni Assn. Democrat. Home: 70 Irving Pl New York NY 10003 Office: Carolyn M Heft Esquire 70 Irving Pl 3E New York NY 10003

HEGARTY, MARY FRANCES, lawyer; b. Chgo., Dec. 19, 1950; d. James E. and Frances M. (King) H. B.A., DePaul U., Chgo., 1972, J.D., 1975. Bar: Ill. 1975, U.S. Dist. Ct. 1975, Fed. Trial Bar 1984. Ptnr. firm Lannon & Hegarty, Park Ridge, Ill., 1975-80; sole practice, Park Ridge, 1980 . Mem. fin. com.'s revenue study com. Chgo. City Council, 1983-84; bd. dirs. Legal Assistance Found. Chgo., Historic Pullman Found.; v.p. Ill. Women's Agenda, 1984-85. Mem. Ill. Bar Assn., Women's Bar Assn. Ill. (pres. 1983-84), Chgo. Bar Assn., N.W. Suburban Bar Assn. Democrat. Roman Catholic. Clubs: Lake Point Tower (Chgo.), Park Ridge Women Entrepreneurs. Office: 22 S Washington St Suite 105 Park Ridge IL 60068

HEGE, LINDA CAROL, nurse; b. Lexington, N.C., Sept. 1, 1945; d. Olin Grady and Kate Vivian (Walser) Hege. B.S. in Nursing, Lenoir Rhyne Coll., 1967. Staff nurse Forsyth Meml. Hosp., Winston-Salem, N.C., 1967-69, 1974-75, asst. head nurse, 1969-73, 1975-80, nursing ednl. instr., 1980, clin. specialist, 1980-82, assoc. dir., 1982—; lectr. Forsyth Tech. Inst., Winston Salem, 1970-75, Mitchell Coll., Statesville, N.C., 1979-80, N.C. Lic. Practical Nurse Assn., Durham, N.C., 1982; mem. spl. ops. rescue team Forsyth County Emergency Med. Services, 1985—; instr. Forsyth County Heart Assn., Winston-Salem, 1983. Mem. Am. Nurses Assn., Dist. III N.C. Nurses Assn. (spl. projects chmn. 1984—). Methodist. Avocations: reading, swimming, candlewicking. Home: 1921 South St Winston-Salem NC 27107 Office: Forsyth Meml Hosp 3333 Silas Creek Pkwy Winston-Salem NC 27107

HEGEL, CAROLYN MARIE, farmer, farm bureau executive; b. Lagro, Ind., Apr. 19, 1940; d. Ralph H. and Mary Lucile (Rudig) Lynn; m. Tom Lee Hegel, June 3, 1962. Student pub. schs., Columbia City, Ind. Bookkeeper Huntington County Farm Bur. Co-op, Inc. (Ind.), 1959-67; office mgr., 1967-70; twp. woman leader Wabash County Farm Bur., Inc. (Ind.), 1970-73, county woman leader, 1973-76; dist. woman leader Ind. Farm Bur., Inc., Indpls., 1976-80, 2d v.p., 1980—, chmn. women's com., 1980—; farmer, Andrews, Ind., 1962—; dir. Farm Bur. Ins. Co., Indpls., 1980—, Ind. Farm Bur. Service Co., 1980—, dirs. Ind. Farm Bur. Found., Indpls., 1980—, Ind. Inst. Agr., Food and Nutrition, Indpls., 1982—, Ind. 4-H Found., Lafayette, 1983-86; com. mem. Hoosier Homestead Award Cert. Com., Indpls., 1980—. Women in the Field columnist Hoosier Farmer mag., 1980—. Organizer farm div. Wabash County Am. Cancer Soc. Fund Dr. (Ind.), 1974; pres. Bethel United Methodist Women, Lagro, 1975-81; bd. dirs. N.E. Ind. Kidney Found., 1984—, Nat. Kidney Found. of Ind., 1985—. Recipient State 4-H Home Econs. ward Ind. 4-H, 1960. Mem. Women in Communication, Inc., Ind. Agrl. Mktg. Assn. (bd. dirs. 1980—), Producers Mktg. Assn. (bd. dirs. 1980—), Am. Farm Bur. Fedn. (midwest rep. to women's com. 1986—). Republican. Home: Rural Route 1 Andrews IN 46702 Office: Ind Farm Bur Inc 130 E Washington St PO Box 1290 Indianapolis IN 46206

HEGENDERFER, JONITA SUSAN, public relations executive; b. Chgo., Mar. 18, 1944; d. Clifford Lincoln and Cornelia Anna (Larson) Hazzard; m. Gary William Hegenderfer, Mar. 12, 1971 (dec. 1978). B.A., Purdue U., 1965; postgrad. Calif. State U.-Long Beach, 1966-67, Northwestern U., 1969-70. Tchr. English, Long Beach schs., Calif., 1965-68; editorial asst. Playboy Mag., Chgo., 1968-70; communications specialist Am. Med. Assn., Chgo., 1970-72; v.p. Home Data, Hinsdale, Ill., 1972-75; mktg. mgr. Olympic Savs. & Loan, Berwyn, Ill., 1975-79; sr. v.p. Golin/Harris Communications, Chgo., 1979—. Editor directory, Fin. Info. Nat. Directory, 1972. Author: Slim Guide to Spas, 1984. Contbr. articles to profl. jours. Co-chmn. pub. relations com. Am. Cancer Soc., Chgo., 1984; com. mem. March of Dimes, Chgo., 1986. Recipient 3 Golden Trumpets, Publicity Club Chgo., 1983, 86, Silver Trumpet, 1984, 86; Spectra awards, Internat. Assn. Bus. Communicators, 1984, 85, Gold Quill, 1985; Silver Anvil, Pub. Relations Soc. Am., 1985. Mem. Am. Mktg. Assn., Publicity Club of Chgo. Clubs: Council on Fgn. Relations, Art Inst. Chgo. Avocations: travel; photography. Office: Golin/Harris Communications 500 N Michigan Ave Chicago IL 60611

HEGHINIAN, ELIZABETH ALBAN TRUMBOWER, artist, educator; b. N.Y.C., Jan. 11, 1917; d. Eli Cadwallader and Maria Lucas (Coyle) Trumbower; certificate dept. indsl. design Pratt Inst., 1938; B.S. magna cum laude, N.Y. U., 1950, M.A., 1952, Ph.D., 1957; postgrad. Bklyn. Inst. Arts and Scis., 1963-66, Bklyn. Mus. Art Sch., L.I. U., 1963-66, Fairleigh Dickinson U., 1970; studied under Richard Mayhew, Georgiana Brown Harbeson, Edith Fetterolf, Katheryn I. Young, Howard W. Arnold, I.-Ching Ku; m. Aram Lincoln Heghinian, Aug. 24, 1957; children—Elizabeth Alban, Marie Hunazant. Indsl. designer Belle Kogan Assos., 1938-40; art dir. Norcross Pubs., 1940-42; buyer for battle damaged U.S. naval vessels and equipment Arma Corp., 1942-45; dir. arts and crafts YWCA Camp Program, 1946; designer Cosmopolitan Crafts, Camp Fire Outfitting Co., 1946-47; faculty N.Y. U., 1947-61, asst. prof. edn., 1957-61; specialist consultation services nat. arts and crafts com. Boys' Clubs Am., 1949-65; research and practicum in remedial reading techniques N.Y.C. Pub. Sch., Bklyn., 1966-68; exhibited in group shows Pratt Inst., 1936-38, N.Y. U., 1948-52; represented in permanent collection Bklyn. Mus. Art Sch., pvt. collections. Mem. nat. adv. com. on recreation programs and activities arts and crafts sect. Nat. Recreation Assn., 1958-62; pres. Camp Jefferson, Inc., N.Y.C., dir. Camp Jefferson, Palisades Interstate Park, N.Y., 1945—; active town wide camping and sch. year program Girl Scouts U.S.A., 1969-73; mem. N.Y. Assn. for Brain Injured Children, 1963—. Recipient Founders Day certificate N.Y. U., 1950. Mem. Am. Watercolor Soc. (asso.), AAUW, Nat. Congress Parents and Tchrs., Tenafly Nature Center Assn., Palisades Interstate Park Camp Dirs.' Assn., Pi Lambda Theta, Kappa Delta Pi, Epsilon Pi Tau. Author: The Contribution of Craft Activities to the Philosophy and Objectives of Boys Clubs of America, 1957; (monograph) Crafts in Boys' Clubs, 1958. Address: 52 Howard Park Dr Tenafly NJ 07670

HEGLEY, NICKOLENA GRECO, car dealer; b. Syracuse, N.Y., Aug. 14, 1951; d. William James and Eileen (Knox) Greco; m. Robert B. Hegley, Dec. 27, 1974 (dec. 1983). Diploma, Gen. Motors Sch. Mdsing. and Mgmt., 1981, 82. Lead dancer Maori Polynesian Restaurant, W. Palm Beach, Fla., 1970-72; sales/mgmt. WJNO Radio, W. Palm Beach, 1970-76, WIRK & WNGS Radio, W. Palm Beach, 1976-80; truck/fleet mgr. Bob Hegley Inc., Clewiston, Fla., 1980-82; owner, pres. Nicky Hegley Chevrolet, Clewiston, Fla., 1983—. Sec., Airport Authority, Clewiston, 1983-86; bd. dirs. Actor's Community Theater, 1983-86; mem. Bus. Improvement Council, 1984-85. Mem. Nat. Assn. Female Execs., Sales Mktg. Execs., C. of C. Roman Catholic. Avocations: polynesian dancing; flying; reading; crafts; snow skiing. Office: Nicky Hegley Chrolet Pontiac Olds Inc 202 W Sugarland Clewiston FL 33440

HEGYELI, RUTH INGEBORG ELISABETH JOHNSSON, physician, government official; b. Stockholm, Aug. 14, 1931; came to U.S., 1963; d. John Alfred and Else Ingeborg (Sjogren) Johnsson; m. Andrew Francis Hegyeli, July 2, 1966 (dec. June 1982). B.A. in Scis., U. Toronto, 1958, M.D., 1962. Sr. research pathologist Battelle Meml. Inst., Columbus, Ohio, 1967-69; intern Toronto Gen. Hosp., 1962-63; med. officer Nat. Heart and Lung Inst., 1969-73; chief program devel. and evaluation Nat. Heart, Lung and Blood Inst., Bethesda, Md., 1973-76, acting dir. office program planning, 1975-76, asst. dir. internat. relations, 1976—; mem. sci. adv. bd. Giovanni Lorenzini Found., Inc., N.Y.C., Milan, 1982—. Coordinating editor Jour. Soviet Research in Cardiovascular Diseases, 1979—. Editor 10 sci. books. Contbr. poetry to nat. anthologies. Named Hon. Mem., Eagle Tribe of Haida Indians, Queen Charlotte Islands, B.C., Can., 1961; recipient Outstanding Scientist award Battelle Meml. Inst., Columbus, Ohio, 1966; Cert. for Superior Service, HEW, 1975. Fellow Acad. Medicine, Toronto; mem. Am. Soc. Cell Biology, Am. Soc. Artificial Internal Organs, World Affairs Council, Nat. Council Internat. Health, N.Y. Acad. Scis. Republican. Avocations: poetry; fiction writing; non-fiction writing; art; music; travel; hiking; singing; swimming; ecology. Home: 7063 Wolftree Ln Rockville MD 20852

HEIDEN, ANTONIETTE LOUISE (TONI), real estate broker; b. Santa Monica, Calif., Feb. 3, 1948; d. Donald Maurice and Marguarite Louise (Rosenberger) Mandrillo Torres; student Pierce Jr. Coll., 1967, San Fernando Valley State Coll., 1968, Mesa Coll., 1973-74, Colo. U., 1978-80; children—Chad Wesley, Trent Ashly. Owner, Clubhouse Crafts, Grand Junction, Colo., 1976-78; real estate broker Target Realtors, 1978-80, Home Owners Realty, 1980-81, Bray & Co., div. Better Homes & Gardens, 1981—. Mem. Nat. Assn. Realtors, Women's Council Realtors (ednl. chairperson), Colo. Assn. Realtors (trustee edn. found. 1983-86), Grand Junction Bd. Realtors. Roman Catholic. Home: 1015 N 7th St Grand Junction CO 81501 Office: Bray & Co 1015 N 7th St Grand Junction CO 81501

HEIDEN, PATRICIA ANN, investment company executive; b. Rochester, N.Y., Jan. 8, 1950; d. Patrick Ralph and Frances Lucy (DiMascio) Gifaldi; m. Christopher J. Farrell, III, Apr. 8, 1978; 1 child, Denise Leigh. Student Lesley Coll., 1983, Rochester Inst. Tech., 1978-84. Sec. to bus. mgr. U.A. Local 13, Rochester, 1972-74; asst. to pres. Allied Bldg. Trades Council, Rochester, 1974-78; fund adminstr. U.A. Local 13 Annuity Fund, Rochester, 1978-85; v.p. Housing Concepts, Inc., Hilton, N.Y., 1985—. Adminstrv. asst. Jobs & Energy Independence, Region 5, Central and Western N.Y., 1976-80; asst. to polit. coordinator election campaign Atty. Gen.'s Office, Central and Western N.Y., Atty. Gen. Robert Abrams; adminstrv. asst. Rochester Affirmative Action Program, 1974-78. Mem. Rochester Fund Mgrs. Assn., Nat. Assn. Female Execs., Internat. Found. Employee Benefit Plans. Roman Catholic. Avocations: photography; travel. Home: 8 Summer Haven Dr Hilton NY 14468 Office: Housing Concepts Inc 8 Summer Haven Dr Hilton NY 14468

HEIDENREICH, JOAN VICTORIA, lawyer; b. Houston, Feb. 24, 1944; d. John Ruess and Joan Frances (Lesinski) H. B.Sc. in Nursing, Marquette U., 1967; student Rosary Coll., River Forest, Ill., 1962-64; LL.B., McGill U., 1978. Bar: Calif. 1979; R.N., Calif., Wis. Staff nurse VA Ctr., Wood, Wis., 1967, Mt. Sinai Hosp., Milw., 1968-70, Queen Mary Vets. Hosp., Montreal, Que., Can., 1970-73; nursing instr. Dawson Coll., Montreal, 1973-75; assoc. Sedgwick, Detert, Moran & Arnold, San Francisco, 1979-82, Bostwick & Tehin, San Francisco, 1982-84, Law Offices C. Donald McBride, San Francisco, 1984-86; with Gooding, Heidenreich and Shinnick, san Francisco, 1986—. Mem. ABA, Calif. Trial Lawyers Assn. Home: 36 Iris St San Francisco CA 94118 Office: Gooding Heidenreich and Shinnick 535 Pacific St San Francisco CA 94111

HEIFETZ, SONIA, retired pharmacist; b. Rowne, Poland; d. Zise and Toiba (Ehrlich) Heifetz; came to U.S., 1929, naturalized, 1934; Ph.G., Temple U., 1933. Asst. chief pharmacist Grad. Hosp. U. Pa., Phila., 1937-49, dir. pharmacy services, 1949-77; formerly pharmacist-mgr. Rite-Aide Corp., now ret. Cert. tchr. of Russian, Phila. Bd. of Edn. div. sch. extension. Mem. Am. Soc. Hosp. Pharmacists, Del. Soc. Hosp. Pharmacists (hon.), Pa. Soc. Hosp. Pharmacists (hon.), Phila. Guild Hosp. Pharmacists (v.p. 1966, treas. 1967-77), AAUW. Home: 2665 Willits Rd Apt 324 Philadelphia PA 19114

HEIKES, MARY JANE, restaurant executive; b. Gettysburg, Pa., Apr. 2, 1922; d. Edward D. and Myana M. (Von Buskirk) Hudson; m. Andrew M. Heikes, Apr. 15, 1955 (div. 1960). Student pub. schs., York, Pa. Clk., U.S. Army, Eng. and France, 1943-45; hostess Hotel Gettysburg, 1952-55; hostess Howard Johnson's restaurant, Gettysburg, 1957-65, tng. supr., 1965-72, mgr., 1972—. Republican. Roman Catholic. Home: 700 Hills Dr Gettysburg PA 17325 Office: Howard Johnson's Restaurant 445 Steinwehr Ave Gettysburg PA 17325

HEIKKINEN, ELLEN JUNE, retail executive; b. Detroit, June 26, 1957; d. Floyd M. and Judith W. (Bartling) H.; m. Paul R. Schrier, Sept. 6, 1980. B.S. in Dietetics, Eastern Mich. U., 1979; postgrad. Amber U., Garland, Tex., 1981—. Registered dietitian. Clin. dietitian, St. Paul Hosp., Dallas, 1979-80, cost control mgr., 1980-81, asst. dir., 1981-83; pres. H & M Concessions, Grapevine, Tex., 1983—. Named Recognized Young Dietitian, Dallas Dietetic Assn., 1982. Mem. Am. Dietetic Assn., Dietitians in Bus. and Industry, Nat. Assn. Female Execs., Marina Assn. Tex. Home: 2203 Proctor Dr Carrollton TX 75007 Office: H & M Concession Inc PO Box 101 Grapevine TX 76051

HEILBRUN, CAROLYN GOLD, English literature educator; author; b. East Orange, N.J., Jan. 13, 1926; d. Archibald and Estelle (Roemer) Gold; m. James Heilbrun, Feb. 20, 1945; children—Emily, Margaret, Robert. B.A., Wellesley Coll., 1947; M.A., Columbia U., 1951, Ph.D., 1959; hon. degree U. Pa., 1984, Bucknell U., 1985, Rivier Coll., 1986. Instr., Bklyn. Coll., 1959-60; instr. Columbia U., 1960-62, asst. prof., 1962-67, assoc. prof., 1967-72, prof. English lit., 1972—, Avalon Found. prof. in the humanities, 1986—; vis. prof. U. Calif., Santa Cruz, 1979, Princeton (N.J.) U., 1981. Author: The Garnett Family, 1961; Towards Androgyny, 1973; Reinventing Womanhood, 1979; author 7 novels as Amanda Cross, 1964—. Guggenheim fellow, 1966; Rockefeller fellow, 1976; NEH fellow, 1984; recipient Nero Wolfe award, 1981; Alumnae Achievement award Wellesley Coll., 1984. Mem. MLA (pres. 1984), Mystery Writers Am. (exec. bd. 1982-84), Phi Beta Kappa. Office: Grad Dept English Columbia U 613 Philosophy Hall New York NY 10027

HEILBRUN, EMILY, lawyer; b. N.Y.C., Mar. 7, 1955; d. James and Carolyn (Gold) Heilbrun. A.B., Barnard Coll., 1977; J.D., Columbia U., 1981. Bar: Oreg. 1981. Sole practice, Eugene, Oreg., 1981—. Sec. bd. dirs. Mobility Internat. U.S.A., Eugene, 1982—; bd. dirs. Kids and Kin Head Start, Eugene, 1984—. Mem. ABA, Oreg. Bar Assn., Lane County Bar Assn. (chmn. young lawyers com. 1983-84, chmn. family law subcom. jud. adminstrn. com. 1984-86), Lane County Women Lawyers Assn., Oreg. Criminal Def. Lawyers Assn. Office: 915 Oak St Suite 204 Eugene OR 97401

HEILIG, MARGARET CRAMER, nurse; b. Lancaster, Pa., Jan. 17, 1914; d. William Stuart and Margaret White (Snader) Cramer; m. David Heilig, June 1, 1942; children—Judith, Bonnie, Barbara. B.A. in Psychology, Wilson Coll., 1935; M.S.W., U. Pa., 1940; AASci. in Nursing Delaware County Community Coll., 1970. Registered nurse. Caseworker Children's Bur., Lancaster, Pa., 1935-37, 39-42; group worker Ho. of Industry Settlement Ho., Phila., 1937-39; curriculum chmn. Upper Darby Adult Sch. (Pa.), 1958-68; health asst., camp mother Paradise Farm Camp, Downington, Pa., 1960-70, camp nurse, 1970-78, infirmary dir., 1978—; med. surg. nurse Crozer-Chester Med. Ctr., Chester, Pa., 1970; out-patient nurse Maternal Infant Care, Chester, 1971; coll. nurse Delaware County Community Coll., Media, Pa., 1971-76, dir. health services, 1976-84, writer coll. health newsletter, 1973—, health fair dir., 1979—. Author: First Aid Booklet, 1976; also articles and columns in health field. Nurse for health screening children's program Tyler Arboretum, Media, 1982—, Update on Personal Health, Broadmeadows Women's Prison, 1973, 82; former leader Delaware County Council Girl Scouts U.S.; mem. Upper Darby Recreation Bd., 1956-58, Upper Darby Adult Sch. Bd., 1956-68; provider host home for fgn. exchange students, 1965-75; participant Audubon Ann. Bird Count, 1970—; coordinator, dir. Ann. Soc. of Friends Ch. Retreat, 1970—. Mem. Am. Coll. Personnel Assn., Am. Nurses Assn., Pa. Nurses Assn., Delaware County Nurses Assn. (membership chmn. 1977-78), Southeastern Coll. and Health Assn., Southeastern Pa. Coll. Health Nurses Assn. (pres. 1983-85), Middle Atlantic Coll. Health Assn., Delaware Valley Soc. for Adolescent Health, LWV, Women's Internat. League for Peace and Freedom, Brandywine Conservance. Quaker. Home: 605 Mason Ave Drexel Hill PA 19026 Office: Delaware County Community Coll Media PA 19063

HEIMBOLD, MARGARET BYRNE, publisher, educator, consultant; b. Tullamore, Ireland, June 24; came to U.S., 1966, naturalized, 1973; d. John Christopher and Anne (Troy) Byrne; m. Arthur Heimbold, Feb. 26, 1984; 1 child, Eric Thomas Gordon. B.A., Queens Coll. Group advt. mgr. N.Y. Times, N.Y.C., 1978-85; pub. Am. Film, Washington, 1985-86, Nat. Trust for Hist. Preservation, Washington, 1986—. Recipient cert. Dale Carnegie, 1977, Psychol. Corp. Am., 1981, Wharton Sch., 1983. Mem. Nat. Assn. Female Execs., Women's Econ. Alliance. Club: Roughriders Speaking. Avocation: golf.

HEIMLICH, JANE MURRAY, journalist, author; b. N.Y.C., July 1, 1926; d. Arthur and Kathryn (Kohnfelder) Murray; m. Henry Jay Heimlich, June 3, 1951; children—Philip, Peter, Janet and Elizabeth (twins). B.A., Sarah Lawrence. Coll., 1948. Columnist Hartford Times (Conn.), 1967-70, Cin. Post., 1972-78, Cin. Enquirer, 1980—. Co-author: Homeopathic Medicine at Home, 1980; contbr. articles to publs. including Parents Mag., Americana, Writer's Digest, others. Mem. Authors Guild, Women in Communications.

HEIN, MARION RAMPEY, government aviation administration official, civil aviation security specialist; b. Memphis, Oct. 7, 1933; d. Ernest McWhite Rampey and Louise Selina (Harmon) Rampey Torreyson; m. William J. Fox., Nov. 18, 1950 (dec. Apr. 1959); children—William Robert, Jennings Ernest; m. 2d, Herbert J. Hein, Dec. 6, 1974. Student U. Tenn., 1961-65, Tex. Christian U., 1971-72. Aviation security asst. FAA, New Orleans, 1973-74, Houston, 1974-75, aviation security specialist, 1976-80, security specialist, 1980-82, civil aviation insp., 1982-83, spl. agt., 1983—; cons. Hazardous Material Transp. Cargo Assn., 1979—. Recipient letter of appreciation FAA, Ft. Worth, 1972, Spl. Achievement award, 1972, article of appreciation, 1980, letter of commendation, Houston, 1981. Mem. Women in Security, Am. Soc. Indsl. Security, Assn. Fed. Investigators. Republican. Club: Toastmistress (treas. 1972-73) (Ft. Worth). Office: FAA PO Box 60366 2800 Terminal Rd Houston TX 77205

HEINE, ELIZABETH, editor; b. S.I., Feb. 3, 1939; d. T.C. and Anne Meade Heine. B.A. in English and Math., Cornell U., 1960; A.M. in English, Radcliffe Coll., 1961; Ph.D., Harvard U., 1965. Resident fellow Radcliffe Coll., 1961-62; teaching fellow in English and gen. edn. Harvard U., 1962-65; instr. English, Bklyn. Coll., 1965-66; asst. prof. English, U. Hawaii, Manoa, 1966-71; lectr. humanities U. of Sci., Penang, Malaysia, 1972-73; assoc. prof. English, U. Tex., San Antonio, 1974-78; assoc. editor Abinger Edition, E.M. Forster, King's Coll., Cambridge, Eng., 1978-79, editor, 1980—. Editor: The Hill of Devi, and Other Indian Writings, 1983; The Longest Journey, 1984; co-editor: (with Oliver Stallybrass) Arctic Summer and Other Fiction, 1980. Contbr. articles and reviews to profl. jours. Woodrow Wilson fellow, Nat. Merit scholar. Mem. Phi Beta Kappa, Phi Kappa Phi. Address: King's Coll Cambridge England CB2 1ST

HEINEMAN, MRS. BEN W. (NATALIE), association executive. Past pres., now bd. dirs., mem. exec. com. Child Welfare League Am.; past pres., now bd. dirs., exec. com. Chgo. Child Care Soc.; past chmn. exec. com. United Settlement Appeal; past bd. dirs. Chgo. Fedn. of Settlements, past chmn. Citizens Com. of Adoption Info. Service State of Ill.; past bd. dirs. Council for Community Services in Met. Chgo.; bd. dirs., mem. exec. com. Erickson Inst. Advanced Study in Child Devel., United Way Met. Chgo.; past bd. dirs., exec. com. United Way Am.; mem. woman's bd. U. Chgo. Field Mus. Natural History, Northwestern U.; vis. com. U. Chgo. Sch. Social Service Adminstrn.; mem. citizens com. Juvenile Ct. Cook County; bd. dirs., mem. exec. com. Chapin Hall Ctr. Children U. Chgo. Address: 180 E Pearson St Chicago IL 60611

HEINEMANN, KATHERINE (KAKI), author; b. St. Louis; d. Herbert N. and Elsa S. (Straus) Arnstein; B.S., Washington U., St. Louis, 1950, M.A. (Arts and Scis. Faculty award 1950), 1956; m. Morton D. May, 1937; children—David A., Philip F.; m. Sol Heinemann, July 8, 1950; 1 dau., Kate Heinemann Taucher. Freelance writer, poet, 1960—; prof. English, U. Tex., El Paso, 1968-74; condr. poetry readings, workshops, 1968—; mem. El Paso Art Resources Dept. Bd., 1980-81; author: Brandings, 1968; Some Inhuman Familiars, 1983; taping for Poetry Collection of Library of Congress, 1982. Mem. PEN, Nat. Soc. Arts and Letters. Clubs: Coronado Country, El Paso Tennis, Sunset Heights Garden. Home: 4252 Ridge Crest Dr El Paso TX 79902

HEINS, MARILYN, college dean, pediatrics educator; b. Boston, Sept. 7, 1930; d. Harold and Esther (Berow) H.; m. Milton P. Lipson, 1958; children—Rachel, Jonathan. A.B., Radcliffe Coll., 1951; M.D., Columbia U., 1955. Diplomate Am. Bd. Pediatrics. Intern, N.Y. Hosp., N.Y.C., 1955-56; resident in pediatrics Babies Hosp., N.Y.C., 1956-59; asst. pediatrician Children's Hosp. Mich., Detroit, 1959-78; dir. pediatrics Detroit Receiving Hosp., 1965-71; asst., assoc. dean student affairs Wayne State U. Med. Sch., Detroit, 1971-79; assoc. dean acad. affairs U. Ariz. Med. Coll., Tucson, 1979-83, vice dean, 1983—, prof. pediatrics, 1985—. Author: Parenting, forthcoming. Mem. editorial bd. Jour. AMA, 1981—. Contbr. articles to profl. jours. Bd. dirs. Planned Parenthood So. Ariz., 1983—, mem. adv. com. Tucson Assn. Child Care, Inc., 1984—; mem. adv. bd. State Hosp., Office of Gov., 1985—. Recipient Alumni Faculty Service award Wayne State U., 1972, Recognition award, 1977, Women on the Move Achievement award YWCA Tucson, 1983. Fellow Am. Orthopsychiat. Assn., Am. Acad. Pediatrics; mem. Assn. Am. Med. Colls., Am. Hosp. Assn. (chmn. com. med. edn. 1985), Ariz. Med. Assn., Soc. Health and Human Values, Women in Sci. and Engring. U. Ariz. (bd. dirs. 1979—), Exec. Women's Council Tucson, Ariz. Med. Assn. (com. on med. service 1985—), Pima County Med. Soc., Pima County Pediatric Soc., Ambulatory Pediatric Assn., AAAS, Am. Pub. Health Assn., Assn. Am.

Med. Colls., Med. Soc. U.S. and Mex. Soc. Health and Human Values, Western Soc. Pediatric Research. Club: Second Tuesday (co-founder). Home: 6530 N Longfellow St Tucson AZ 85718 Office: Univ Ariz Med Coll 1501 N Campbell Ave Tucson AZ 85724

HEINSSEN, BARBARA ANNE, college textbook sales representative; b. Jamaica, N.Y., Feb. 17, 1960; d. Robert Kenneth and Jane (Koss) H. B.A. in English, Hofstra U., 1982. Prodn. intern CBS Coll. Pub., N.Y.C., 1981, free-lance proofreader, 1982, editorial asst., 1982-84, copywriter, 1984, sales rep., 1984—; guest lectr. Hofstra U., Hempstead, N.Y., 1983, 85. Mem. Nat. Assn. Female Execs., Women's Nat. Book Assn. (N.Y. chpt.), Smithsonian Assocs., Hofstra Alumni Assn., Phi Beta Kappa. Roman Catholic. Avocations: golf; skiing; travel; reading; dancing; enrichment courses. Office: CBS Coll Pub 521 Fifth Ave New York NY 10175

HEINZ, MARY JEAN EGYED, real estate appraiser; b. San Jose, Calif., Sept. 22, 1954; d. Frank and Charlotte Jean (Brown) Egyed; m. James T. Heinz, Sept. 23, 1980. B.A., Mills Coll., 1976. Chief appraiser Home Savs. of Am., San Mateo, Calif., 1979-83; owner Residential Valuation Service, Daly City, Calif., 1983—. Mem. Daly City C. of C. Democrat. Roman Catholic. Avocations: horseback riding, fishing, swimming, opera. Office: Residential Valuation Service 2790 Junipero Serra Blvd Daly City CA 94015

HEINZE, LINDA HOLLI, promotion agency executive, lecturer; b. N.Y.C., Dec. 31, 1939; d. Rudolf Ley and Jessica Mary (Babcock) H. A.A., N.Y.C. Community Coll., 1959; student in bus. adminstrn. Pace Coll., 1964-68, New Sch. Social Research, 1969, Baruch Coll. CCNY, 1970. Asst. mgr. advt. makeup Look mag., N.Y.C., 1959-64; prodn. mgr. McCall mag., N.Y.C., 1964-70; asst. promotion mgr. treasury div. J.C. Penney Co., N.Y.C., 1970-72; sr. v.p. Robert Brian Assocs., N.Y.C., 1972—. Mem. bus. games com. L.I. U.; bd. dirs. N.Y. chpt. Medic Alert, 1984-86. Mem. Am. Advt. Fedn. (Silver medal 1971), Advt. Women N.Y. (ELA award 1972), Sales Exec. Club. Office: Robert Brian Assocs 31 E 28th St New York NY 10016

HEINZERLING, BARBARA MANSFIELD, lawyer, educator; b. Pitts., Feb. 22, 1940; d. John Conrad and Mary Eleanor (Chinn) Mansfield; m. Paul Louis Heinzerling, June 16, 1962; children—Pam, Mark, Dan. B.S. summa cum laude, Ohio State U., 1962, M.S., 1963; J.D., U. Akron, 1979. Bar: Ohio 1979. Clk. typist U.S. Acctg. Office, Edwards AFB, Mojave, Calif., 1963-64; elem. tchr. Eastside Union Sch., Lancaster, Calif., 1964-65; substitute tchr. Hudson (Ohio) Schs., 1966-70; assoc. Nicely & Wagner, Akron, 1980—; assoc. prof. U. Akron, 1970—; mem. adv. bd. Family Ctr., Ctr. Nursing, 1980—; mem. adv. bd. State Dept. Edn., Vocat. and Home Econs., 1980—; mem. Major Appliance Consumer Action Panel, Chgo., 1983—; mem. adv. bd. consumer Credit Counseling Ctr., Akron, 1980—. Mem. ABA, Ohio Bar Assn., Akron Bar Assn., Am. Council Consumer Interests, Ohio Consumer Edn. Assn. Episcopalian. Office: U Akron Akron OH 44325

HEISE, ARDYS MARY, public relations and educational consultant; b. Upland, Calif., May 15, 1927; d. Ralph and Emma (Lenhert) Byer; m. Clarence Elmer Heise II, Aug. 22, 1948; children—Sherilin, Clarence Elmer III, Steven. B.A., in Social Sci., Upland, Coll., 1949; postgrad. San Diego State U., 1962, U. So. Calif.-Los Angeles, 1976-77. Spl. events mgr. Barnes Chase Advt. Agy. San Diego, 1962-65; owner, mgr. Ardys Heise and Assocs. pub. relations cons. San Diego, 1965-69; television, radio coordinator U. Calif.-San Diego, 1967-69, statewide television coordinator, 1969-71, pub. affairs officer Sch. Medicine, 1969-74; dir. communications services San Diego Community Coll. Dist., 1974-83; owner, founder Heise Internat., San Diego, 1983—; lectr., instr. numerous colls., 1952—. Candidate for Calif. State Legislature, 1972; mem. spl. San Diego Transit Review Com., 1976-77, San Diego County ad hoc com. on status of women, 1975—; v.p. Health Systems Agy, San Diego, 1977-78; mem. pub. relations adv. com. Children's Health Ctr., San Diego, 1970-83; mem. review panel Secondary School Recognition Program, U.S. Dept. Edn., 1984; mem. nat. adv. bd. Neurological and Communicative Disorders and Stroke Council, NIH, 1984-86; sec. So. Calif. Soc. Prevention Blindness, 1984-86, v.p., 1986—; mem. Western Ctr. Health Planning adv. bd., 1977-78; bd. dirs. Nat. Soc. Prevention Blindness, 1986—, chmn. San Diego br.; mem. clin. outcome com. U.S. Dept. Edn., 1985-86, mem. accreditation com., 1985—, site visitor secondary schs., 1985-86, elem. schs., 1986—; Author: Effective Public Relations, 1970; Successful Public Relations for Colleges and Universities, 1974; contbr. chpts., articles to profl. publs. Recipient Tribute to Women in Industry award YWCA, 1980. Mem. San Diego Council Adminstrv Women in Edn. (bd. dirs.), Pub. Relations Soc. Am. (Acredited, cert. of recognition 1981, Annual Silver Anvil awards 1981), Council for Advancement and Support of Edn. (chmn. 1982), Am. Assn. Community and Jr. Colls., Pub. Relations Club San Diego (named Profl. of Yr. 1974, Best Annual Report award 1980), Women in Communications (Best Pub. Service Programming award, Best Spl. External Publ. award, Matrix award 1981), Calif. Women in Govt., Internat. Assn. Bus. Communicators, C. of C. Office: Heise Internat 8340 Clairemont Mesa Blvd Suite 108 San Diego CA 92111

HEISE, DOROTHY AGNES, librarian; b. Erie, Pa., June 17, 1945; d. George William and Annette Genevieve (Forrester) Hilbert; m. Charles W. Heise, June 29, 1968. B.S. in L.S., Edinboro State U., 1968; postgrad. Cath. U., 1971-72, U. Md., 1984—. Cert. sch. librarian, Va., Md., N.J. Librarian Toms River Schs., N.J., Prince George's Schs., Md., Congl. Schs., Falls Church, Va., Consumer Prodn. Safety Commn., Bethesda, Md.; tech. info. specialist Raytheon Service Co., Crystal City, Va.; tech. info. specialist USDA/Econ. Research Service, Washington, now head ref. ctr., 1981—. Author report: Guide to Services of the Economic Research Service Reference Center, 1983. Mem. Gamma Sigma Sigma. Lutheran. Avocations: hobbies; needlecraft; painting. Home: 8569 Tyrolean Way Springfield VA 22153 Office: USDA/ERS Reference Ctr 500 12th St SW Washington DC 20250

HEISE, PATRICIA CATHERINE, travel agency owner; b. Rochester, N.Y.; d. John Benjamin and Wilma Ruth (Walzer) Watkins; m. William W. Heise, Jr., June 28, 1958; children—William, III, Wendy, Timothy, Tracy. B.A., Ind. U., 1956. Cert. travel cons., 1980. Pres. Around the World Travel, Inc., Palatine, Ill., 1974-82; pres., owner All Travel, Inc., Palatine, 1982—; dir. Internat. Travel Tng. Courses, Chgo., 1980-83. Pres. Buehler YMCA Woman's Aux., Palatine, 1972, Countryside Aux. Ill. Children's Home and Aid, Palatine, 1960-61. Mem. Am. Soc. Travel Agts., Pacific Assn. Travel Agts., Inst. Cert. Travel Agts., Travel Agts. Assn. Better Service (pres. 1975-77, ind. coordinator 1977—), Palatine C. of C. (pres. 1983-84). Republican. Presbyterian. Club: Palatine Jr. Woman's. Lodge: Rotary Wives (pres. 1963). Home: 375 Plymouth Dr Inverness IL 60067 Office: All Travel Inc 7 E Northwest Hwy Palatine IL 60067

HEISLER, BETTY, publisher, talk show host; b. Havana, Cuba, Aug. 27, 1941; came to U.S., 1960; d. Jaime and Pauline (Kantor) Tuchman; m. Charles Heisler, June 1, 1963 (dec. June 1978); children—Iliana, Steven. Student U. Havana, 1958-60, Miami-Dade Coll., 1973-75. Staff writer Spanish Good-housekeeping, Miami, Fla., 1975-77; asst. editor spl. edits. Spanish Cosmopolitan, Miami, 1977-78; editor Coqueta Miami, 1978-79; pub. Donde Mag., Miami, 1980—. Mem. Jewish Fedn. Profl. Women's Div., Profl. Women Orgn. Grove Isle (life), Hadassah. Republican. Avocations: travel; aerobics; tennis; gourmet cooking. Home: 7955 Biscayne Point Circle Miami Beach FL 33141 Office: Latin Am Publs Inc PO Box 41-4655 Miami Beach FL 33141

HEISSER, PATRICIA ANNE, psychologist, counseling center administrator; b. Los Angeles, May 15, 1946; d. Andrew and Charley (Smith) Johnson; m. Royal Heisser, July 16, 1976 (div. 1982); m. Luke Metoyer, Aug. 16, 1986. B.A., Calif. State U.-Los Angeles, 1966; Ph.D., U. Calif.-Irvine, 1976. Program mgr. Dept. Labor, Washington, 1969-70; psychology fellow UCLA, 1973-74; sr. staff psychologist Cedars-Sinai Med. Ctr., Los Angeles, 1974-85; owner, exec. dir. Crenshaw Counseling Ctr., Los Angeles, 1984—; mem. adv. bd. Ctr. for Study Trauma, Los Angeles, 1983-85; cons., trainer Headstart, Los Angeles, 1980—; instr. UCLA Extension, 1978-81; clin. supr. Calif. Sch. Psychology, Los Angeles, 1976-85; play and film producer. Contbr. articles to Howard U. Press. Mem. County Task Force on Mental Health, Los Angeles, 1982-85. USN grantee U. Calif.-Irvine, 1974; Video-film fellow Am. Film Inst., 1985-86. Mem. Am. Psychol. Assn., Assn. Black Psychologists, So. Calif. Assn. Black Psychologists, Women in Psychology, Crenshaw C. of C., Psi Chi, Alpha Kappa Alpha. Roman Catholic. Avocations: Yoga, painting, writing, dance, tennis.

HEISTER, ELLA, executive; b. Brasstown, N.C., Mar. 23, 1938; d. Gust and Opal Allene (Scroggs) Jorella; m. Paul Jay Heister, Aug. 6, 1960 (div. 1982); 1 dau., Michele Lynn. Student Wayne State U., 1958. Engring. sec. Detrex Chem. Co., Detroit, 1964-69; legal adminstrv. asst. Basil M. Briggs, P.C., Southfield, Mich., 1969-82; v.p. adminstrn., corp. sec. A.F. Campbell & Co., Inc., Dallas, 1982—; corp. sec. Murex Corp., Norcross, Ga., 1984—. Office: AF Campbell & Co Inc 2515 McKinney Ave Suite 1575 Dallas TX 75201

HEIZER, IDA ANN, real estate broker; b. Oxford, Colo., Mar. 14, 1919; d. Albert Henry and Ella (Engbrook) Ordener; m. Donald Heizer, Apr. 7, 1947; children—Robert John. Diploma, Brown's Bus. Coll., 1939; student Otero Jr. Coll., 1946-47, U. So. Colo., 1962; grad. Realtors Inst., Nat. Assn. Real Estate Bds., 1972. Cert. closer real estate, cert. residential specialist. Clk., Montgomery Ward Co., LaJunta, Colo., 1935-37; bookkeeper Colo. Bank & Trust Co., LaJunta, 1937-38; cashier/bookkeeper Fox Theatre, LaJunta, 1939-40; clk. Civil Service, LaJunta, 1940-45; stenoabstractor Deaf Smith Abstract Office, Hereford, Tex., 1948-50; sec. Otero County Agt. Office, Rocky Ford, Colo., 1953-55; real estate broker Pueblo Realty & Service Co., Inc., Colo., 1960—. Mem. Pueblo Bd. Realtors, Nat. Assn. Real Estate Appraisers, Nat. Assn. Realtors, Colo. Assn. Realtors, Women's Council Realtors, Beta Sigma Phi. Lodge: Quota Internat. Home: 331 Van Buren St Pueblo CO 81004 Office: Pueblo Realty & Service Co Inc 112 Colorado Ave Pueblo CO 81004

HEKHUIS, ELIN MARIE, college public information director; b. Newberry, Mich., Feb. 10, 1929; d. Jacob B. and Fannie E. (Sinko) Berglund; m. Clair Milan Hekhuis, Jan. 6, 1952; children—John, Elin, Julie, David. Student Macalester Coll., 1947-48; B.A., Mich. State U., 1951; M.P.A., Calif. Luth. Coll., 1980. Dir. promotion Sta. WTCN, Mpls., 1951-52; dir. community relations Marquette (Mich.) Job Corps, 1966; dir. News Bur., info. services and pub. info. Calif. Luth. Coll., Thousand Oaks, 1969—. Mem. ch. council Holy Trinity Lutheran Ch., 1980-83; mem. media com. Pacific S.W. Synod. Luth. Ch. in Am., 1982-85; mem. Am. Luth. Ch. Council for Advancement and Support of Edn. Mem. Women in Communications, Pub. Relations Adv. Council, Pub. Info. Officers Ventura County, Pub. Relations Assn. So. Calif. Colls. (charter), Mich. State U. Alumni Assn., Calif. Luth. Coll. Alumni Assn., Finlandia Found., Am. Scandinavian Found. Republican. Home: 1753 Hendrix Ave Thousand Oaks CA 91360

HEKTNER, CANDICE ELAINE, lawyer; b. Fargo, N.D., Apr. 22, 1948; d. Alfred G. and Hope E. (Posey) H.; 1 dau., Nicole Asha. B.A., Concordia Coll.-Moorhead, Minn., 1970; J.D., Valparaiso U., 1975. Bar: Minn. 1975, N.D. 1975, U.S. Dist. Ct. Minn., U.S. Dist. Ct. N.D., U.S. Ct. Appeals (8th cir.). Assoc. firm Ochs Larsen Klimek & Hektner, Edina, Minn., 1975-80; ptnr. firm Chadwick Johnson & Condon, Bloomington, Minn., 1980—. Contbr. writings to legal publs. Mem. ABA, Minn. State Bar Assn., Minn. Def. Lawyers Assn., Minn. Women Lawyers Assn. Lutheran. Club: Twin City Investment (pres. 1984-85). Office: Chadwick Johnson & Condon 7900 Xerxes Ave S Suite 2000 Bloomington MN 55431

HELBERG, SHIRLEY ADELAIDE HOLDEN, artist; b. Solvay, N.Y., Mar. 9; d. Isaac Edgar and Gladys Evelyn (Tucker) Holden; student Syracuse U.; B.E., Johns Hopkins U., 1969; M.F.A., Md. Inst. Art, 1975; m. Burton Edvard Helberg; children—Keir Holm, Kristin Vaughan, Kecia Tucker, Kandace Holden, Kraig Brownlee. Tchr. various schs. in N.J. and Pa.; tchr. Manchester (Pa.) Pub. Schs., 1965-84; one-woman art show U. Va., Charlottesville, 1974, Cayuga Mus. Art and History, Auburn, N.Y., 1974, Hist. Soc. York Mus., Pa., 1977, York Coll., 1984, Country Club of York; Bd. dirs. York (Pa.) Arts Council, 1964-66. Mem. Nat. League Am. Pen Women (Pa. State art chmn. 1972-74, pres. Pa. orgn. 1974-76, nat. scholarship chmn. 1976—, Disting. service award 1978, 80, 82, 84, 86), NEA, Pa. State Edn. Assn., Internat. Platform Assn., Harrisburg, York art assns. Republican. Methodist. Club: Johns Hopkins Faculty. Home: RD #4 Spring Grove PA 17362

HELBURN, JUDITH HORWITZ, library consultant; b. Milw., June 3, 1938; d. Harvey and Anne Levin Horwitz; m. I. B. Helburn III, Aug. 21, 1960; children—Graham David, Robin Lynn. B.S., U. Wis.-Madison, 1960, M.S.L.S., 1965. Sch. librarian Madison Schs., 1960-64; acting head children's librarian Madison Pub. Library, 1965; spl. projects librarian U. Tex. Tarlton Law Library, Austin, 1978-80; cons. dir. Library Mgmt. and Services, Austin, 1977—; sec., mem. Austin Library Commn., 1976-79; mem. adv. bd. Grad. Sch. Library and Info. Sci., U. Tex.-Austin, 1985—. Editor, pub. Practical Law Books Rev., 1978—; assoc. editor Checklist Human Rights Documents, 1978-79. Bd. dirs. LWV, Austin, 1968-72. Mem. Am. Assn. Law Libraries, Southwestern Assn. Law Libraries, Laguna Gloria Art Guild, Symphony Soc. Austin, Austin History Ctr., Sigma Epsilon Sigma, Pi Lambda Theta, Phi Kappa Phi, Beta Phi Mu. Democrat. Jewish. Avocations: travel; collecting American Indian art; music; reading. Home and Office: 5914 Highland Hills Dr Austin TX 78731

HELD, BARBARA SUSAN, psychologist; b. N.Y.C., Mar. 5, 1950; d. Milton H. and Harriette (Kornblum) H.; B.A. in Psychology, Douglass Coll., Rutgers U., 1972; Ph.D. in Psychology (NIMH tng. fellow), U. Nebr., Lincoln, 1979; m. David C. Bellows, Aug. 18, 1974. Intern in psychology Tex. Research Inst. Mental Scis., Tex. Med. Center, Houston, 1978-79; psychol. cons. Bath-Brunswick Area Mental Health Center, Brunswick, Maine, 1979-81; asst. prof. psychology Bowdoin Coll., Brunswick, 1979-85, assoc. prof., 1985—; Mellon Fund new course devel. grantee, 1980; pvt. practice clin. psychology, Brunswick, 1981—; supr., cons. specializing in family therapy for Maine mental health profls. Lic. psychologist, Maine. Mem. Am. Psychol. Assn., Phi Beta Kappa. Contbr. articles to profl. publs. Office: Psychology Dept Bowdoin Coll Brunswick ME 04011

HELD, CORINNE, clothing manufacturing company executive; b. N.Y.C., Jan. 22, 1947; d. Frank and Marjorie Edith (Goldberg) Held. Student Ball State Tchrs. Coll. Sales staff Geoffrey Beene, N.Y.C., 1970-71; sales mgr. Albert Capraro, N.Y.C., 1971-73, Richard Assatly, Ltd., N.Y.C., 1973-77; co-gen. mgr. Yves St. Laurent, N.Y.C., 1977-78; mng. dir. Christian Dior Sportswear, N.Y.C., 1978-82; pres. Ron Chereskin for Women, N.Y.C., 1982-85, Lisa Maghazeh Inc., 1985—. Mem. N.Y. Fashion Creators. Office: Lisa Maghazeh Inc 530 7th Ave New York NY 10018

HELDMAN, VICTORIA CLARE, lawyer; b. Dayton, Ohio, Aug. 28, 1949; d. Paul Frederick and Anne Frances (Thomas) Schmitz; m. Louis Marc Heldman, Sept. 23, 1971 (div. 1973); m. 2d John Askins, Feb. 28, 1975 (div. 1977). B.A., Ohio State U., 1972; J.D., U. Detroit, 1975. Bar: Mich. 1975, Colo. 1984. Assoc. firm Lopatin, Miller, Bindes & Freedman, Detroit and Denver, 1975-77; ptnr firm Schaden & Heldman, Detroit, 1977—; hearing referee Mich. Civil Rights Commn., Detroit, 1980—; hearing panelist atty. Discipline Bd. State of Mich., 1980—; arbitrator Am. Arbitration Assn., Detroit, 1982-86. Co-author: Product Design Liability, 1982; contbg. author: Women Trial Lawyers: How They Succeed in Practice and In the Courtroom, 1986; contbr. articles to legal publs. Mem. ABA (chmn. spl. com. on auto ins. legislation 1983-84), State Bar Mich., Assn. Trial Lawyers Am., Mich. Trial Lawyers Assn. (gov. 1979-80, 83-86), Women Lawyers Assn. Mich. (pres. Wayne Region, Detroit 1981-82), Colo. Trial Lawyers Assn., Colo. Bar Assn. also 1731 Emerson Denver CO 80218

HELENIC, RUTH ANN, health care training and development executive; b. McKees Rocks, Pa., Mar. 19, 1933; d. John John and Helen (Turis) Cobb Lychkoff; m. Michael J. Helenic, May 14, 1955; 1 son, Victor Helenic. B.A., Bethany Coll., 1954; M.B.A., U. Pitts., 1955. Continuity dir. Sta. WCMW, Canton, Ohio, 1956-58; advt. dir. Am. Assn. Med. Clinics, Charlottesville, Va., 1958-60; tchr. Waterloo Middle Sch., Ellicott City, Md., 1967-69; asst. prof. English, head dept. Daniel Webster Coll., Nashua, N.H., 1969-74; tchr. English, Merrimack (N.H.) Middle Sch., 1974-81; mgr. tng. and devel. Disneyland Hotel/Wrather Corp., Anaheim, Calif., 1982—. Bd. dirs., sec. Nashua Family Planning, 1977-80; adv. bd. adult div. North Orange County Community Coll. Named Outstanding Educator, New Eng. Aero. Inst., 1971, 73. Mem. Council Hotel and Restaurant Trainers, Nat. Assn. Female Execs., Am. Soc. Trainers and Developers, Internat. Platform Assn. Russian Orthodox. Republican. Home: 465 Fair Dr Apt 207 Costa Mesa CA 92626 Office: Hoag Meml Hosp Presbyn 130 Newport Blvd Newport Beach CA 92663

HELFER, JOANNE L., communications specialist; b. N.Y.C., Aug. 5, 1929; d. Isidore Lawrence and Frances Helen (Slobodin) Salomon; m. H. Lawrence Helfer, Dec. 22, 1956; children—Adam Daniel, Elizabeth Laura, Martha Blanche, Tamara Toby. B.A., Hunter Coll., 1950. Freelance writer and publicist, 1950-75; dir. communications Eastman Dental Center, Rochester, N.Y., 1976—. Bd. dirs. Enid Knapp Botsford Sch. Dance, Rochester, 1982—, Rochester Oratorio Soc., 1984; coordinator Rochester chpt. Common Cause, 1972-73; cons. Women's Career Center, Rochester, 1975—. Mem. Women in Communications (chpt. sec. 1977-78, v.p. 1983-84, pres. 1985-86), Pub. Relations Soc. Am. (chpt. dir. 1982—, v.p. 1984, pres. 1985), Internat. Assn. Bus. Communicators (Dist. One 1st Pl. Honors 1977), Rochester Women's Network, Phi Beta Kappa. Home: 30 Bradford Rd Rochester NY 14618 Office: Eastman Dental Center 625 Elmwood Ave Rochester NY 14620

HELIOFF, ANNE GRAILE, painter; b. Liverpool, Eng.; d. Max and Frances Elizabeth (Beilenson) H.; student Columbia U., Art Students League, N.Y.C.; m. Benjamin Michael Hirschberg. One-woman exhbns. include: Capricorn Gallery, N.Y.C., 1966-69, Phoenix Gallery, N.Y.C., 1972, 74, 76, 82, 85; group exhbns. include Milch Gallery, N.Y.C., 1940, Pepsi-Cola Nat., travelling show, maj. museums, U.S., 1947, Nat. Gallery Art, Washington, Pa. Acad. Ann., Art U.S.A., also bicentennial exhbn., 6 Americans in France, traveling show, 1976, museums in Florence and Naples, Italy; mem. U.S. del. 5th Congress Internat. Assn. Art, Tokyo, 1966; mem. Phoenix Gallery, N.Y.C., Ann Leonard Gallery, Woodstock, N.Y.; dir. exhbns. including 50 Yrs. of Woodstock Art (N.Y.), N.Y. State Tri-Centennial, 1959. Recipient Silver medal Albany (N.Y.) Mus. Art and Sci., 1957; Homer Boss scholar, 1939; Y. Kuniyoshi scholar, 1940-45. Mem. Woodstock Artists Assn. (life, past dir.), Art Students League (past dir.), Am. Soc. Contemporary Artists (past dir.; awards in oil, watercolor and acrylic), Nat. Assn. Women Artists, N.Y. Soc. Women Artists (past dir.), Archives of Am. Art, Smithsonian Mus. Home: 14 Neher St Woodstock NY 12498 Office: 340 W 28th St New York NY 10001

HELLENTHAL, LINDA BROUGHTON, psychologist; b. Seattle, May 22, 1947; d. Ray Munroe and Margret (Ryno) Broughton; m. Marc Edwin Hellenthal, June 10, 1967; children—Kristine Tara, Megan LaRue. B.A. with honors, Whitman Coll., 1969; M.A., Boston U., 1973, Ph.D., 1977. Lic. psychologist, Alaska. Lectr., Boston U., 1973-77; clin. psychologist Bear River Community Mental Health Ctr., Logan, Utah, 1978; asst. prof. U. Alaska, Anchorage, 1978-79; clin. psychologist, Anchorage, 1980—; cons. Standing Together Against Rape, Anchorage, 1980-81; treas., co-owner Hellenthal & Assocs., Anchorage, 1978—. Recipient Boston U. Grad. Scholarship award, 1971-77. Mem. Am. Psychol. Assn., Alaska Psychol. Assn. Congregationalist. Club: P.E.O. Home: 2220 Vanderbilt Cr Anchorage AK 99508 Office: 608 W 4th Suite 21 Anchorage AK 99501

HELLER, CHERYL CHRISTINE, advertising executive; b. Pitts., May 8, 1950; d. Robert B. and Adele (Dorazio) Yahner; m. Edwin H. Heller, Apr. 20, 1970 (div. 1972); m. 2d, Gary Nathan Scheft, Nov. 29, 1974. Student Boston Mus. Sch., 1972-73; B.F.A., magna cum laude Ohio Wesleyan U., 1972. Studio mgr. Giardin/Russell Agy., Watertown, Mass., 1972-74; design assoc. Gunn Assocs., Boston, 1974-80; v.p. design dir. Humphrey, Browning and MacDougall Agy., Boston, 1980—. Recipient numerous design awards. Mem. Am. Inst. Graphic Arts, Am. Soc. Typog. Arts. Democrat. Home: 191 Commonwealth Ave Boston MA 02116 Office: Humphrey Browning & MacDougall One Beacon St Boston MA 02108

HELLER, DENISE MARGARET, technical supervisor, computer programmer; b. Whittier, Calif., Apr. 30, 1957; d. Henry Edward and Joyce Elizabeth (Haubrich) H. B.S. in Computer Sci., Calif. State U., 1979. Data entry operator Beverly Hosp., Montebello, Calif., 1975-78; programmer ALS/Infotek, Anaheim, Calif., 1978; computer staging coordinator Decision Making Info., Santa Ana, Calif., 1978-79; programmer analyst Hughes Aircraft Co., Fullerton, Calif., 1979-81, tech. supr., 1981—. Adv. bd. Am. Security Council, Boston, Va., 1978—. Mem. Nat. Assn. Female Execs. Republican. Lutheran.

HELLMAN, SHEILA, cultural arts director; b. N.Y.C., July 8, 1928; d. Julius and Kate Almer; m. Harold Hellman, 1951; children—Jill, Jennifer. B.A., Marietta Coll., 1949; M.A., NYU, 1950. Dance tchr., performer, N.Y.C., 1955-77; cultural arts dir. YM-YWHA of N.J., Wayne, 1977—; dancer Nat. Endowment for the Arts, 1975-80. Home: 100 High St Leonia NJ 07470 Office: YM-YWHA North Jersey 1 Pike Dr Wayne NJ 07470

HELLMANN, NORMA JANELLE, cytotechnologist; b. Honolulu, Jan. 21, 1949; d. Norman Louis and Margaret Janelle (Baker) Hellmann; B.A., Carthage Coll., 1971; cert. Johns Hopkins Hosp. Sch. Cytotech., 1972. Asso. cytotechnologist Johns Hopkins Hosp., Balt., 1972-74; supr. cytology lab. Clin. Labs. of Nashville, 1974; ednl. coordinator Sch. Cytotech. Vanderbilt U., Nashville, 1974-76; supr. cytology lab. Clin. Labs. of Black Hills, Rapid City, S.D., 1976—; program coordinator CDC Workshops on Cytology, Rapid City, 1978. Mem. CAP, 1976-84, squadron comdr., 1982-83, dir. blood flight program S.D., 1976-83; exec. sec. Wonderland Homes Water and Service Co., 1979-80; founder, chmn. Literary Council of Black Hills, 1984—. Mem. Am. Soc. Cytology, Am. Soc. Clin. Pathologists (assoc.; cert. cytotechnologist), Internat. Acad. Cytology (cert.), Am. Soc. Cytotech., AAUW (S.D. UP-Program 1984—, v.p. program 1984-86, Woman of Worth award 1982), Aircraft Owners and Pilots Assn., 99s (S.D. chmn. 1984—), Beta Beta Beta, Alpha Mu Gamma. Republican. Lutheran. Home: Rt 1 Box 360 Black Hawk SD 57718 Office: PO Box 238 Rapid City SD 57709

HELLMER, MARY ANN, nurse educator; b. Bklyn., May 4, 1952; d. Raymond Joseph and Mary (Toporowsky) Hanson; m. George A. Hellmer, Jr., Aug. 29, 1979 (div.); 1 son, George A. III. A.A.S. in Nursing, SUNY, Agrl. and Tech. Coll.-Farmingdale, 1974; B.S. in Nursing, SUNY-Stony Brook, 1977; M.S. in Nursing, Adelphi U., 1979, Ph.D. in Nursing, 1986. Registered profl. nurse, N.Y. Asst. head nurse Brunswick Hosp., Amityville, N.Y., 1974-77, ICU staff nurse, 1977-80; instr. nursing Nassau Community Coll., Garden City, N.Y., 1978-83, asst. prof., 1983—, adj. instr. phys. edn., summers 1981, 82, 83. Co-chmn. health and safety com. Hawthorn Sch. PTA, Massapequa Park, N.Y., 1979-81, chmn. blood drive, 1979, 80; camp nurse Boy Scouts Am., Manorville, N.Y., 1982. Recipient Dept. Acad. award Dept. Nursing SUNY Agrl. and Tech. Coll.-Farmingdale, 1974; Nursing Achievement scholar Adelphi U., 1981-82. Mem. Am. Nurses Assn., N.Y. Assn. of Two Year Colls., AD Orgn. of Nurse Educators, Sigma Theta Tau (chpt. award; scholarship, eligibility and publicity coms.), Phi Theta Kappa. Contbr. chpts. in books, test materials; item writer Regents External Degree Program, 1981, 82, 85, 86. Office: Dept Nursing Nassau Community Coll Garden City NY 11530

HELMS, MARY ANN, nurse; b. Compton, Calif., Jan. 7, 1935; d. Raymond Whitfield and Amanda Zelpha (Hancock) Spencer; A.A. in Nursing, El Camino Coll., 1971; B.S. in Nursing, Calif. State U., Los Angeles, 1976; M.A. in Mgmt., St. Mary's Coll., 1978; M.S. in Nursing, Ariz. State U., 1985; m. Willard Ford Helms, Mar. 15, 1958; children—Michael Steven, Steven Allen. Med. sec., bookkeeper Palm Springs (Calif.) Med. Clinic, 1956-61; office mgr. William R. Stevens Ins. Agy., Santa Ana, Calif., 1961-63, I.J. Weinrot & Son Ins. Agy., Los Angeles, 1963-67; staff nurse Kaiser Found. Hosp., Harbor City, Calif., 1971-76; supr., coordinator pediatrics Maricopa County Gen. Hosp., Phoenix, 1976-80; critical care nurse Phoenix Baptist Hosp., 1980-81, critical care mgr., 1981—. Mem. Am. Nurses Assn., Am. Soc. Women Accts., Natural History Mus., Met. Mus. Art, Smithsonian Instn., Phoenix Zoo, Phoenix Art Mus., Cousteau Soc., Calif. State U. Alumni Assn., KAET Public Broadcasting System, Am. Assn. Critical Care Nurses, Ariz. Nurses Assn. Nat. League Nursing, Phi Kappa Phi, Alpha Gamma Sigma, Sigma Theta Tau. Republican. Mormon. Research on noise pollution on phys. and mental health of citizenry, phenylketonuria testing in Los Angeles, measurement of attitudes toward children in pediatric nurses, nursing practice. Home: 1007 E Michelle Dr Phoenix AZ 85022 Office: 6025 N 20th Ave Phoenix AZ 85015

HELMSLEY, LEONA MINDY, hotel executive; b. N.Y.C.; m. Harry B. Helmsley, Apr. 8, 1972. Vice pres. Pease & Elliman, N.Y.C., 1962-69; pres. Sutton & Towne Residential, N.Y.C., 1967-70; sr. v.p. Helmsley Spear, N.Y.C., 1970-72, Brown, Harris, Stevens, N.Y.C., 1970-72; pres. Helmsley Hotels, Inc., N.Y.C., 1980—. Named Woman of Yr., N.Y. Council Civic Affairs, 1970, Town and Country Condos and Coops., 1981, Internat. Hotel Industry, 1982; recipient Service award Ort Sch. Engring., 1981; Profl. Excellence award Les Dames E'Escoffier, 1981; spl. achievement awards Sales Exec. Club N.Y., 1981; Real Estate Industry-Good Scout award for outstanding community service Greater N.Y. Councils Boy Scouts Am., 1981; Internat. Humanitarian award Boys' Town of Italy, 1983. Home: 36 Central Park S New York NY 10019 Office: The Helmsley Palace Hotel 455 Madison Ave New York NY 10022

HELMS MCKENZIE, LYNN ALLISON, association executive; b. Brookville, Ind., Jan. 24, 1960; d. Donald Eugene and Mary Alice (McCarty) Helms. Student Purdue U., 1978-79. Sports dir. Sta. WRBI, Batesville, Ind., 1979-81; continuity dir. Sta. WSAL, Logansport, Ind., 1981-82; news dir. Sta. WOXY Radio, Oxford, Ohio, 1983-85. Del. Ind. Dem. Conv., Indpls., 1980, 84; mem. Jaycees. Mem. Bus. and Profl. Women (Young Careerist award 1981, 85), Oxford C. of C. (exec. dir. 1985—), Kappa Kappa Kappa. Lodge: DAR. Home: PO Box 20 Bath IN 47010 Office: Oxford C of C Park Place W Oxford OH 45056

HELOISE, syndicated columnist; b. Waco, Tex., Apr. 15, 1951; d. Marshal H. and Heloise (Bowles) Cruse; m. David L. Evans, Feb. 13, 1981; 1 child, Zinfandel. B.S. in Math. and Bus., Southwest Tex. State U., San Marcos, 1974. Office mgr. mother's column Hints from Heloise, San Antonio, 1974-77, sole column writer, 1977—; founder Nat. Smile Week; pres. Heloise, Inc.; idnternat. syndicated columnist affiliated King Features Syndicate, N.Y.C.; lectr. TV and radio. Author: Hints from Heloise, 1980; Help from Heloise, 1982; Heloise's Beauty Book, 1985; contbg. editor Good Housekeeping. Bailli (pres.), Confrere de la Chaine des Rotisseurs, 1980. Mem. AFTRA, Screen Actors Guild, Tex. Press Women, Women in Communications, Women in Radio and TV, Women in Bus. Clubs: Zonta, Les Amis du Vin, Mile High Pie in the Sky Balloon (co-founder, 1st pilot). Home: Box 32000 San Antonio TX 78216 Office: King Features 235 E 45th St New York NY 10017

HELPER, KIM RENE, radio station executive; b. Buffalo, Sept. 23, 1959; d. Donald F. and June M. (Will) Schweizer; m. Gerard M. Helper, Jr., June 13, 1981. A.S. with honors, Niagara Community Coll., 1979; B.A., SUNY-Buffalo, 1981. News dir. Sta. WUTV-29, Buffalo, 1979, Sta. WPHD-FM, Buffalo, 1979-82; weekend anchor, reporter Sta. WEBR, Buffalo, 1982; news dir. Sta. WBUF-FM, Buffalo, 1983—; mem. media adv. bd. Niagara Community Coll., Sanborn, N.Y., 1979—. Mem. Buffalo Bus. and Profl. Women (chmn. pub. relations 1984—, Young Careerist award 1985), Sigma Delta Chi, Beta Sigma Phi (city council pres. 1984—). Avocations: sports; travel. Office: Sta WBUF-FM 715 Delaware St Buffalo NY 14209

HELPERN, BEATRICE LIEBOVITZ NIGHTINGALE, civic worker; b. N.Y.C., July 23, 1907; d. Abraham L. and Hannah (Weinberg) Liebovitz; B.A. summa cum laude, N.J. Coll. for Women, 1928; m. 2d, Lester M. Nightingale, Dec. 1, 1935 (dec. 1951); children—William L., Stuart L.; m. 3d, Milton Helpern, Jan. 1, 1955 (dec. 1977); stepchildren—Nancy H. (Mrs. Edward Moldover), Susan H. (Mrs. Paul Nettler), Alice H. (Mrs. Elliot M. Gross). Vol. sec. to chief med. examiner City of N.Y., 1960-74, now vol. med.-legal archivist; sec. to Dr. Helpern, 1974-77; vol. sec. Milton Helpern Library of Legal Medicine, N.Y.C., 1962—, trustee, 1977—, asst. treas., 1978—; vol. sec. Inst. Forensic Medicine, N.Y. U. and City N.Y., 1968-74, dept. forensic medicine N.Y. U., 1960-72, vol. med.-legal archivist, 1974—. Mem. ladies organizing com. Internat. Meetings Forensic Medicine, N.Y.C., 1960, London, 1963; hon. chmn. women's com. 1st World Meeting Med. Law, Belgium, 1967; chmn. 2d World Meeting, Washington, 1970; hospitality com. Internat. Assn. Accident and Traffic Medicine, chmn., 1967-69; chmn. hospitality com. Symposia on Forensic Medicine, N.Y.C., 1962-74. Bd. dirs. N.Y. chpt. Am. Jewish Com., 1950—, League for Emotionally Disturbed Children, Hemophilia Found., 1961-63; bd. dirs. Womens Aux. Med. Soc. County of N.Y., 1973—, 2d v.p., 1979-80, pres. 1980, 81, chmn. symposium, 1976, 79, 81, 82. Recipient Silver medal Alliance Française, 1928; award Internat. Reference Orgn. Forensic Medicine, 1979. Mem. Mystery Writers Am. (hon.), Phi Beta Kappa. Home: 303 E 57th St New York NY 10022

HEMBY, DOROTHY JEAN, counselor; b. Greenville, N.C., Aug. 21; d. Samuel Emanuel and Queenie Ester H.; Student, Essex County Coll., 1971, Montclair State Coll., 1973-75, Kean Coll., N.J., 1975-77. Clk.-typist Remco Industries, Newark, IRS, Newark, 1963-66, VA Hosp., East Orange, N.J., 1966-71; part-time tchr. Newark Bd. Edn., 1973-76, coll. counselor/acad. adviser Kean Coll. N.J., Union, 1976-77; vol. job evaluator N.J. Vol. Employment Service Team, Newark, 1977-78; coll. counselor/adviser Passaic County Community Coll., Paterson, N.J., 1978—, also chmn. H.O.P.E. com. clk., East Orange Bd. Elections, 1971-72; v.p. Econ. Consumer's Community Aid, 1971-73, active local polit. orgn., 1973—, adv. Passaic County Gospel Choir and Christian Club, 1974. Mem. N.J. Assn. Black Educators, Assn. Black Women in Higher Edn., Am. Personnel and Guidance Assn., Am. Counseling Personnel Assn., N.J. Social Workers Assn., N.J. Behavioral Sci. Soc. Clubs: 700, PTL. Office: Passaic County Community Coll College Blvd Paterson NJ 07509

HEMINGWAY, BETH ROWLETT, author, columnist, lectr.; b. Richmond, Va., May 6, 1913; d. Robert Archer and Evelyn Lucille (Doggett) Rowlett; B.Mus., Hollins Coll., 1934; m. Harold Hemingway, Apr. 2, 1938; children—Ruth Hartley, Martha Scott. Writer, Richmond-Lifestyle mag.; columnist Artistry in Bloom, Richmond Times-Dispatch; author: A Second Treasury of Christmas Decorations, 1961; Flower Arrangement with Antiques, 1965; Christmas Decorations Say Welcome, 1972; Antiques Accented by Flowers, 1975; Beth Hemingway's No Kin to Ernest, 1980; Holidays with Hemingway, 1985; lectr. numerous states, also Australia, 1966, Eng., 1977. Vol., Hermitage Meth. Home, 1977-79. Mem. Nat. League Am. Pen Women, Va. Writers Club, Richmond Hort. Assn., Va. Fedn. Garden Clubs (book rev. chmn.), Richmond Council Garden Clubs (flower arrangement chmn.), Clay Spring Garden Club (pres. 1953-55), Barton Garden Club (pres. 1959-61, 74). Republican. Methodist. Home: 1604 Derek Ln Richmond VA 23229

HEMLOW, JOYCE, educator, author; b. Liscomb, N.S., Can., July 30, 1906; d. William and Rosalinda (Redmond) Hemlow; B.A., Queen's Coll., Kingston, Can., 1941, M.A., 1942; A.M., Radcliffe Coll., 1944, Ph.D., 1948; LL.D. (hon.), Queen's, 1967, Dalhousie U., 1972. Mem. faculty McGill U. from 1945, Greenshields prof. English lit. and lang., 1965-75, prof. emerita, 1975—. Guggenheim fellow, 1951-52, 66-67; recipient James Tait Black Meml. book prize for best biography in U.K., The History of Fanny Burney, 1958, also Gov. Gen. Can. medal for academic non-fiction, 1958, Rose Mary Crawshay prize Brit. Acad., 1960; Distinguished Achievement medal Radcliffe Coll., 1969. Fellow Royal Soc. Can.; mem. Internat. Assn. Univ. Tchrs. of English, Johnsonians, Phi Beta Kappa. Editor: Journals and Letters Fanny Burney (Madame d'Arblay), 12 vols., 1972-84. Home: 1521 Lemarchant St Apt 3-G Halifax NS B3H 3R2 also Liscomb NS Canada B0J 2A0

HEMPENIUS, PATRICIA ANN, motel management executive; b. Tampa, Fla., Nov. 5, 1936; d. Paul W. and Evelyn L. (Williams) Woodcock; m. Gerald E. Hempenius, Jan. 28, 1955; children—Sharyl L. Hempenius Britt, Jeffrey A. Student Valley Coll., 1952-54; R.N., Calif. State-Fullerton, 1956; postgrad. U. Calif.-Irvine, 1972-74. R.N., office mgr. Drs. Peterson and Wilson, Whittier, Calif., 1957-60; R.N., adminstr. Drs. Tyler, Irwin, and Hamilton, Whittier, 1960-76; vip. Com-Spec Properties, Inc., Morro Bay, Calif., 1976—; nurse cons. Emergency med. Services, San Luis Obispo, Calif., 1979—, San Luis Obispo Health Commn., 1979—. Active Morro Bay Republican Women., 1977—. Mem. Travelodge Internat., Inc., (v.p. 1985—), Quota Club (bd. dirs.). Methodist. Avocations: golf; reading; travelling. Home: 2075 Alturas Rd Atascadero CA 93422 Office: Com-Spec Properties Inc 645 Main St Suite D Morro Bay CA 93442

HEMPFLING, LINDA LEE, nurse; b. Indpls., July 28, 1947; d. Paul Roy and Myrtle Pearl (Ward) Hempfling; diploma Meth. Hosp. Ind. Sch. Nursing, 1968. Charge nurse Meth. Hosp., Indpl., 1968; staff nurse operating room Silver Cross Hosp., Joliet, Ill., 1969; charge nurse operating room Huntington (N.Y.) Hosp., 1969-73; night supr. operating room Hermann Hosp., Houston, 1973-76; unit. mgr., purchasing coordinator operating rooms, 1976-83; R.N. med. auditor Nat. Healthcare Rev., Inc., Houston, 1984—. Future Nurses Am. scholar, 1965; Nat. Merit scholar, 1965. Mem. Nat. League Nursing, Am. Nurses Assn., Assn. Operating Room Nurses. Office: 1130 Earle Houston TX 77030

HEMPHILL, HOLLY KINKADE, lawyer; b. Shawnee, Okla., Dec. 28, 1945; d. Hollis J. and Katharine Gail (Cotten) Kinkade; m. John Graham Hemphill, May 18, 1969. B.A., U. Okla., 1967; J.D., Georgetown U., 1977. Bar: Va. 1977, D.C. 1979. Mgmt. intern, personnel specialist Dept. Army, Washington, 1967-72, staff asst. civilian personnel policy, 1972-75, dir. office employment policy and grievance rev., 1977-78; specialist labor relations Labor Relations Council, Washington, 1975-77; asst. to sec. gen. bus. and industry adv. com. OECD, Paris, 1978-80; exec. asst. legal advisor Fed. Labor Relations Authority, Washington, 1980—. Editor Am. Criminal Law Rev., 1976. Mem. Jr. League Washington, 1983. Recipient Meritorious Civilian Service award Sec. Army, 1978; named Outstanding Young Career Woman in U.S., Nat. Fedn. Bus. and Profl. Women, 1967. Mem. ABA, Soc. Fed. Labor Relations Profls. Democrat.

HEMPHILL, KAY ELIZABETH, nurse; b. Thomas, Okla., June 27, 1952; d. Byron Frederick and Wilma Jean (Bickford) Mayfield; m. George Basil Hemphill, Aug. 9, 1974; children—David Andrew, Sarah Elizabeth. Student Oral Roberts U., 1970-71; B.S. in Nursing magna cum laude, Calif. State U.-Long Beach, 1975. R.N., Calif.; cert. pub. health nurse. Staff nurse pediatrics service Long Beach Meml. Hosp., 1974-75, Riverside (Calif.) Community Hosp., 1975-76, Parkview Community Hosp., Riverside, 1982-84; supervising pub. health nurse County Health Dept., San Bernardino, Calif., 1976—. Instr. Inland Counties chpt. Am. Cancer Soc., Riverside, 1977. Mem. Am. Pub. Health Assn. (co-author abstract 1986, coordinator hypertension worksite project, diabetes control project), Pub. Health Nurse Group (chmn. 1977-78, vice chmn. profl. preformance com. 1978, sec. peer rev. com. 1978), So. Calif. Pub. Health Assn., Pub. Health Advs. Democrat. Office: San Bernardino Pub Health Dept 320E D St Ontario CA 91764

HEMPHILL, MAUREEN LUCILLE, Canadian government official; b. Grand Forks, B.C., Jan. 26, 1937; d. Jim Leroy and Elaine Agnes Miller; children—Carol, Jim, Ross, Susan. R.N., Vancouver Gen. Hosp. Nurse, Vancouver Gen. Hosp., N. Vancouver Hosp., Good Samaritan Nursing Home, Edmonton; mem. Man. Legis. Assembly for Legan, 1981—. Minister of Edn., Govt. of Man., 1984—. Address: 168 Legislative Bldg Winnipeg MB R3C 0V8 Canada*

HEMPHILL-HAMMOND, BETTY, retired teacher, civic worker; b. Guthrie, Okla., Mar. 22, 1911; d. Rolla Kellogg and Bertha Louise Ferrier; m. Frederic Hemphill, May 23, 1936 (dec. 1978); 1 child, Patricia Steinke; m. Russell I. Hammond, Sept. 1, 1984. Student Kans. U., 1930-31, Coll. William and Mary, 1935, Midland Coll., 1942. Cert. elem. tchr., Kans., Okla. Tchr. Clay Ctr., Kans., 1928-30, 34-36, Merrimac, Okla., 1932-33; dir. Youth Art Contest, Tekamah, Nebr., 1942-65; milk technologist Fed. Milk Market, 1943-45; prodn. asst. weekly newspaper Tekamah, 1936-65; sec. Wyo. Vets. Affairs Commn., 1975—; chmn. for securing govt. and state grants for State Vets. Cemetery. Vol. local library and mus. Mem. Am. Legion Aux. (regional v.p., nat. historian), VFW Aux. (past pres.), Daus. of Nile, Eastern Star, Alpha Gamma Delta. Democrat. Methodist. Club: Laramie Woman's (pres. 1977). Avocations: art; fishing; handcrafts; china painting. Home: 816 S 17th Laramie WY 82070

HEMRIC, SHERYL JEAN, telecommunications executive; b. Salem, N.J., Oct. 11, 1954; d. Howard James and Thelma A. (Muhs) Hitcheer; 1 child, Rachel Lisa. A.S. in Computer Sci., Brevard Community Coll., 1984. Actuarial asst. William H. Collings Co., Jacksonville, Fla., 1974-76; asst. mgr. Gen. Fin. Corp., Dumfries, Va., also Satellite Beach, Fla., 1976-79; software engr. ITT Telecommunications, Cape Canaveral, Fla., 1980-84; test engr., lead data base adminstr. ITT Telecom. Raleigh, N.C., 1984-86; systems analyst, data base adminstr. No. Telecom, Research Triangle Park, N.C., 1986—. Mem. Nat. Assn. Female Execs., Nat. Mgmt. Assn., No. Telecom Mgmt. Assn. Roman Catholic. Avocations: music; gourmet cooking; modern and jazz dancing; walking; theater. Home: 7351 Sweet Bay Ln Raleigh NC 27609 Office: No Telecom Inc 4001 E Chapel Hill-Nelson Hwy Research Triangle Park NC 27709

HENDEE, ELLEN JACKSON, travel agency executive; b. Chgo., Jan. 5, 1925; d. Raymond F. and Jessie Lois (Miller) Jackson; m. Keith Alan Hendee, Mar. 22, 1945; children—James Cass, Bruce Alan. A.A., Colo. Women's Coll., 1945; B.A., Denver U., 1947. Tng. supr. Burdines, Ft. Lauderdale, Fla., 1949-52; tng. dir. Jordan Marsh, Miami, Fla., 1957-61; personnel dir. Britts Dept. Store, Ft. Lauderdale, 1962-69, pres. travel div., 1969-80; owner, pres. J J Travel, Fort Lauderdale, 1981—. Contbr. articles to Ft. Lauderdale News, 1972-82. Docent, Mus. Art. Mem. Am. Soc. Travel Agts. (bd. dirs. 1984-85, pres. So. Fla. chpt. 1976-78, chmn. Sch. at Sea, 1978-82), Ft. Lauderdale C. of C. (chmn. goodwill ambassadors 1975-76), Henderson Mental Health. Republican. Unitarian. Home: 1301 SE 5th Ave Pompano Beach FL 33060 Office: J J Travel 3034 E Commercial Blvd Fort Lauderdale FL 33308

HENDERSON, ANNE FORTUNE, educator, cattle farmer; b. Arrington, Va., July 25, 1928; d. Harry Pierce and Cecil Dorothy (Fortune) Henderson; diploma Va. Intermont Coll., 1948; B.S., Va. Commonwealth U., 1950; M.Ed., U. Va., 1958. Tchr., R.E. Lee Jr. High Sch., Lynchburg, Va., 1950-52, E.C. Glass High Sch., Lynchburg, 1952-62; asst. prof. health, phys. edn. and recreation Mary Washington Coll., Fredericksburg, Va., 1962-69; asst. prof. health, phys. edn. and recreation Lynchburg Coll., 1969-81, asso. prof., 1981—; owner, mgr. cattle farm, Nelson County, Va., 1969—. Mem. AAHPER, Va. So. assns. health, phys. edn. and recreation, Va. Angus Assn., Va. Beef Cattle Assn., Nelson County Farm Bur., U.S. Fencing Assn. Republican. Episcopalian. Club: Winton Country (Clifford, Va.). Home: Cherry Hill Arrington VA 22922 Office: Lynchburg College Lynchburg VA 24504

HENDERSON, BOBBIE ALLEN, child development and family relationship educator; b. Houston, May 30, 1940; d. Theodore Brown and Irma Lee (Hart) Allen; m. Robert Arthur Bingham, June 28, 1959 (div. 1967); children—Eric Courtland, Kevin Troy; m. John Ree Henderson, Jan. 4, 1968; 1 child, Shannon Aryana. B.A., Fisk U., 1959; M.A., Tex. So. U., 1973; Ph.D., U. Wis.-Madison, 1977. Cert. elem. tchr., Tex. Civil service position FBI, Washington and N.Y.C., 1961-65; pre-kindergarten tchr. Bunnyland Acad., Houston, 1965-66, 8th Ave Elem. Sch., 1972; social service coordinator Project Head Start, 1966-72; br. dir. YWCA, 1973-74; assoc. prof. Tex. So. U., Houston, 1973—, also dir. cons. in field. Contbr. articles to profl. jours. Chmn., Head State Policy Council, Houston, 1983—; bd. sec. Planned Parenthood, 1984—; affilaite rep. Tex. Assn. for Edn. Young Children, 1983—; bd. dirs. Family Service Ctr., 1982—; chmn. com. Mayor's Hearing Children & Youth, 1984-85. Recipient Humanitarian award Social Work Program Tex. State U., 1982, Community Service, Sta. KMJQ, 1984, Outstanding Service, Adopt Black Children, 1983, Outstanding Vol., Am. Heart Assn. Mem. Houston Assn. Edn. Young Children (pres., Outstanding Service award 1982), Nat. Assn. Edn. Young Children, So. Assn. Children Under Six (multi-cultural chmn.), Friends of Head Start, Phi Delta Kappa, Omicron Nu. Democrat. Episcopalian. Clubs: Delta Sigma Theta (sec.), Top Ladies Distinction, Coalition 100 Black Women. Home: 4203 Charleston St Houston TX 77021 Office: Texas So U 3100 Cleburne St Houston TX 77004 also Neighborhood Ctrs Inc 3401 Fannin St Houston TX 77004

HENDERSON, GERALDINE THOMAS, social security official; b. Luling, Tex., Jan. 7, 1924; d. Cornelius Thomas and Maggie (Keyes) Thomas; m. James E. Henderson, Feb. 9, 1942 (dec. Apr. 1978); children—Geraldine, Jessica, Jennifer. B.S., Fayetteville State U., 1967. Tchr. Cumberland County Schs., Fayetteville, N.C., 1966-67, Fayetteville City Schs., 1967-68; with Social Security Adminstrn., Fayetteville, 1968—, now claims rep. Pres. Fayetteville State U. Found., 1981-82, NAACP, Fayetteville br., 1983—; bd. dirs. Fayetteville Art Council, 1984—, Cumberland County United Way, 1983—. Named Woman of Yr. Zeta Phi Zeta, 1984, Citizen of Yr. Omega Psi Phi, 1985. Mem. Am. Legion Aux. (treas. 1981-83). Democrat. Presbyterian. Avocations: creative dress design; gardening; travel.

HENDERSON, JANE WHALEN, travel company executive; b. Fort Dodge, Iowa, June 24, 1913; d. William L. and Blanche (Tremaine) Whalen; m. Lon St. Clair Henderson, Oct. 16, 1946 (div.); children—Thomas, Clare, Anne. Student Fort Dodge Jr. Coll., Iowa, 1931-32, Fort Dodge Bus. Coll., 1932-33, Armstrong Coll., 1937-38. Travel cons. Peck Judah Travel Bur., San Francisco, 1942-48; mgr. World Travel Bur., Anaheim, Calif., 1955-56, Fullerton, Calif., 1958-60; mgr. Travel Advisers, Santa Ana, Calif., 1964-65; internat. travel adviser Anaheim Travel, 1960-64; v.p. sales Orange Empire Travel Bur., Anaheim, 1965-70; owner, pres. Jane Henderson Travel, Orange, Calif., 1970—; cons N.Am. Sch. Travel, Newport Beach, Calif., 1968—; mem. adv. bd. Orange Nat. Bank, Traveling Times, Valencia, Calif. Gold sponsor Miss Orange Pageant, 1976—; mem. street naming com. City of Orange, 1985—, mem. sister city program, 1985—. Named Orange Citizen of Yr., 1983. Mem. Am. Soc. Travel Agts., Assn. Retail Travel Agts., Pacific Area Travel Assn., Orange County Travel Agts. (pres. 1978), Cruise Lines Internat., Orange C. of C. (bd. dirs.). Roman Catholic. Lodge: Soroptimists Internat. Office: Jane Henderson Travel 1876 N Tustin Ave Orange CA 92665

HENDERSON, JANET LEE, diagnostics laboratory sales executive; b. Dallas, Aug. 12, 1946; d. William D. and Jane (Allen) H. B.S. in Med. Tech., North Tex. State U., 1969. Med. technologist Baylor U. Med Ctr., Dallas, 1969-72, Baptist Hosp., Miami, 1972-74, Sayet Lab., Miami, 1974-76; tech. sales rep. Electronucleonics, Inc., Fairfield, N.J., 1976-79; sales rep. Smith Kline Instruments, Sunnyvale, Calif., 1979-82, Beckman Instruments, Brea, Calif., 1982-83, Boehringer Mannheim Diagnostics, Indpls., 1983—. Mem. Am. Soc. Med. Technologists. Republican. Lutheran. Avocations: reading; dogs and cats. Home: 20643 SW 119th Pl Miami FL 33177

HENDERSON, JO ANN, banker; b. LaCompte, La., May 30, 1948; d. Joseph and Evalena (Hill) Tisino; m. Carl Edward Henderson, Oct. 1, 1970; children—Meagan Leigh, Ian Alexander. B.A., U. Wash., 1976, M.A., 1979. Co-founder Tiloben Pub., Seattle, 1969—; instr. Seattle Central Community Coll., Seattle, 1983-84; asst. v.p., personnel dir. Wash. div. Bank of Calif., N.A., Seattle, 1977—; cons. Mayor's Council for Aging, Seattle, 1981, Am. Heart Assn., Seattle, 1983—; co-founder, v.p. Catalyst III, 1983—; founder, chmn. Tisino-Henderson Enterprises (THE Corp.), 1984; advisor OFCCP Bank Liaison Com., Seattle, 1982, Seattle Community Coll. Dist., Seattle, 1982-84. Recipient First Citizen award Office of Mayor and Pacific N.W. Bankers Assn., Seattle, 1983. Mem. Nat. Assn. Urban Bankers (nat. rep. 1984), NAACP, Nat. Urban League (mem. com. 1982), Pacific N.W. Personnel Mgmt. Assn. (treas. 1980—), Am. Heart Assn. Wash. (chmn. 1982-83), Women's Profl. and Managerial Network. Democrat. Baptist.

HENDERSON, JOAN BLUST, lawyer, educator, writer; b. Paterson, N.J., July 7, 1936; d. Vincent M. and Ellen Kennedy (Adams) Blust; m. J. Eber Henderson, June 26, 1959 (div. 1976); children—Ian Scott, Heather Jo. B.A., Cedar Crest Coll., Allentown, Pa., 1958; M.A., U. Louisville, 1967, J.D., 1978. Bar: Ind. 1979, U.S. Dist. Ct. (so. dist.) Ind. 1979. Tchr. New Providence Sch. (N.J.), 1960-61, Army Sch., Ft. Campbell, Ky., 1961-62; tchr. chronically ill. Louisville Pub. Schs., 1962-65; exec. dir. Rauch Ctr. for Handicapped, New Albany, Ind., 1965-72; instr. Jeffersonville campus Webster U., St. Louis, 1983; sole practice, Jeffersonville, Ind., 1979—; lectr. various orgns. Author: A Good Worker, 1971; A Good Citizen, 1973; A Good Neighbor, 1976. Adv. com. on child abuse Clark County Welfare, Jeffersonville, 1980-84; edn. com. ARC, Louisville, 1982—. Recipient Jeffersonville United to Make Progress Bus. award, 1985. Mem. Ind. Bar Assn., Clark County Bar Assn., Assn. Trial Lawyers Am., Kappa Delta Pi, Phi Alpha Delta, Am. Bus. Women's Assn. (Jeffersonville chpt.). Home: 400 E Terrace Dr Jeffersonville IN 47130 Office: 521 E 7th St Jeffersonville IN 47130

HENDERSON, JOHNNIE MAE, nursing educator; b. McDonald, Ga., Feb. 6, 1926; d. Johnny Kyle and Ollie Mae (Thompson) Hardeman; m. Lorenza Henderson, Aug. 21, 1945; children—Lorenza II, Johnny Kenneth. B.S. in Nursing, B.A. in Sociology, Case Western Res. U., 1970, M.S., 1973; Ed.D., Nova U., 1979. Staff nurse Univ. Hosp., Cleve., 1966-67, charge nurse, 1967-69; instr. nursing Cuyahoga Community Coll., Cleve., 1970-74, asst. prof., 1974-77, assoc. prof., 1977-80, prof., 1980—. Bd. dirs. Cleve. Council Black Nurses, 1982—. Mem. Nat. League for Nursing, NAACP, Sigma Theta Tau, Alpha Kappa Alpha. Baptist. Office: Cuyahoga Community Coll 2900 Community College Ave Cleveland OH 44115

HENDERSON, MARIE CATHERINE, county official; b. Balt., Jan. 27, 1941; d. James Harrison Wilson and Marguerite (Jones) Wilson Campbell; m. Edward James Henderson, May 25, 1967; children—Michael Keith, Edward James, Jr. Student Howard U., 1960-62. Congl. corr. Scoial Security Adminstrn., Balt., 1961-67; program dir. Pub. Service Employment CETA Program, Balt., 1971-76; spl. asst. to mayor of Balt., 1976-78; administrv. asst. to county exec. Baltimore County, 1978-80; spl. asst. to dir. personnel Baltimore County Govt., 1980-81, spl. projects coordinator, 1981—. Campaign coordinator or mgr. for mayor Balt., 1977, Baltimore County exec., 1979, pres. Balt. City Council, 1983, incumbent judges, Balt., 1984; 1st female chairperson Md. Com. on Correctional Standards, Annapolis, 1981-85; mem. Md. Gov.'s Md. Heritage Commn., 1983-84; permanent chairperson United Way campaign, Balt., 1975—; pres., founder Md. Council for Cultural Progress, Balt., 1973—. Recipient Leadership award United Way Central Md.; Outstanding Service award NAACP, 1977-78, named among People to Watch in '84, Balt. Mag., 1984. Mem. Md. Assn. Affirmative Action Officers, Md. Assn. Personnel Officers. Democrat. Roman Catholic. Office: Baltimore County Govt 115 W Susquehanna Ave Towson MD 21204

HENDERSON, MARILYN ANN, research and engineering company executive; b. Scranton, Pa., Aug. 3, 1949; d. William Joseph and Mary Ann (Banick) Delorey; m. William Edgar Henderson, Oct. 23, 1971. Student U. Scranton, 1968; B.S., Pa. State U., 1970; M.B.A., Fairleigh Dickinson U., 1977. With AT&T, 1970-84, dist. mgr., various N.J. locations, 1977-83, div. mgr., Piscataway, N.J., 1983-84; div. mgr. Bell Communications Research, Piscataway, 1984—. Recipient various corp. awards and recognitions, 1976-85, Clements award Clements Found., 1967, 68, 69, 70. Mem. AAUW, Am. Mgmt. Assn., Assn. Computing Machinery, Nat. Assn. Female Execs., Morris County Hist. Soc., Frelinghuysen Arboretum, Omicron Nu. Roman Catholic. Avocations: power boating; cats; historical preservation. Home: Ten Pond Hill Rd Convent Station NJ 07961 Office: Bell Communications Research 444 Hoes Ln Piscataway NJ 08854

HENDERSON, MARY BIGELOW, health care executive, consultant; b. Barre, Vt., Jan. 29, 1950; d. Arthur Garfield and Dorothy Christine (Bartlett) Bigelow; m. Robert Wayne Henderson, Oct. 7, 1984. B.S., U. Vt., 1972. Discharge planning coordinator Arlington Hosp., Va., 1975-78; dir. nursing Carriage Hill Nursing Home, Arlington, 1978-79; dir. hosp. review No. Va. Found. Med. Care, Falls Church, 1979-80; profl. services dir. M.D.-IPA Health Plan, Rockville, 1980-83; health services dir., sr. assoc. Jurgovan & Blair, Rockville, 1983—; cons. Mohawk Valley Health Plan, Schenectady, 1983. Alumni advisor U. Vt., Burlington, 1980—. HMO Mgmt. fellow Group Health Assn. Am., 1983. Mem. Am. Med. Care Rev. Assn., Nat. Assn. Quality Assurance Profls. Avocations: racquetball; bike riding; cello; guitar; gardening. Home: 11605 Joseph Mill Rd Wheaton MD 20906 Office: Jurgovan and Blair Inc 7811 Montrose RdPotomac MD 20854

HENDERSON, MARY ELISABETH KENDALL, public relations administrator; b. West Berlin, W.Ger., Dec. 12, 1947 (parents American citizens); d. Sidney Sherman and Frank Andrews (Kelley) Kendall; m. Lindsey Patterson Henderson III, Mar. 22, 1969 (div. Feb. 1983); children—Daniel Hall, Frank Andrews Kelley, Elisabeth Sherman. Student Ga. So. Coll., 1968-69; B.A. in Social Sci., U. St. Thomas, Houston, 1971. Ward clk. Bulloch County Hosp., Statesboro, Ga., 1969-70, Diagnostics Hosp., Houston, 1970-71; asst. mgr. Ships Wheel Gallery, Savannah, Ga., 1971-73, Apogee Boutique, Houston, 1973-75; owner, mgr. Page 76 Bookstore, La Grange, Tex., 1975-77; info. coordinator Lower Colo. River Authority, Austin and La Grange, 1977—; prin. Creative Communicators, Consultants, La Grange, 1982—; cons. Creative Dance Studio, Columbus, Tex., 1979-82, Spectrum, Inc., La Grange, 1983—, Stafford Opera Ho. Theater Assn., Columbus, 1980—, Am. Aluminum Products, La Grange, 1981—, Le Petit Gourmet Shoppe, La Grange, 1980-83. Contbr. articles and photographs to various profl., trade and gen. publs. Chmn. steering com. Fayette County Republican Party, 1976-79; precinct chmn. Colorado County Republican Party, 1979-83; county sec. Rep. Party Tex., 1979-83, county coordinator various campaigns, 1978—; publicity chmn. Fayette County Kunstfest Assn., 1975-81, Fayette Meml. Hosp. Aux., 1975-77, Historic Savannah, Inc., 1971-73, Waterfront Assn., Savannah, 1971-73; docent Nat. Park Service, Ft. Pulaski, Ga., 1968-69, 71-73. Journalist, USNR, 1983—. Recipient Appreciation cert. SCV, Savannah, 1973, U.S. Dept. Interior, 1980; Presdl. Achievement award Republican Party, 1980. Mem. Pub. Relations Soc. Am., Tex. Profl. Photographers, Women in Communications, Pilot Internat. (local sec. 1982-83, dir. 1983-84), Alpha Xi Delta. Roman Catholic. Office: Lower Colorado River Authority PO Box 338 La Grange TX 78945

HENDERSON, MARY RUTH, educator, farmer; b. Sweetwater, Tenn., Oct. 25, 1951; d. Bill Hooper and Edna Lee (Largen) H.; B.S. in Home Econs., U. Tenn., 1973, M.S. in Agr., 1975. Asst. extension agt. U. Tenn. Agrl. Extension Service, Sequatchie County, Tenn., 1975-77; asst. prof. 4-H, state 4H specialist U. Tenn. Agrl. Extension Service, Knoxville, 1977—. Mem. Tenn. 4-H Alumni, Inc., Knoxville Area Home Econs. Assn., U. Tenn. Century Club. Mem. Nat. Assn. Extension 4-H Agts., Tenn. Assn. Extension 4-H Agts., Tenn. Assn. Agrl. Agts. and Specialists, Profl. Adminstrs. Vol. Services, Tenn. Livestock Assn., Epsilon Sigma Phi, Gamma Sigma Delta. Baptist. Editor The 4-H

Leader, 1977—; author 4-H publs., handbooks, visuals, newsletters. Home: Route 1 Box 112 Philadelphia TN 37846 Office: PO Box 1071 209 Morgan Hall Knoxville TN 37901

HENDERSON, MAXINE OLIVE BOOK (MRS. WILLIAM HENDERSON III), educational consultant, association executive; b. Rush, Colo., Apr. 22, 1924; d. Jesse Frank and Olive (Booth) Book; B.A., U. Colo., 1945; m. William Henderson III, Apr. 10, 1948; children—William IV, Meredith. Personnel adminstr. Gen. Electric Co., Schenectady and N.Y.C., 1945-54; asst. dir. placement Katherine Gibbs Sch., N.Y.C., 1967-70; v.p. William Henderson Cons., Inc., N.Y.C., 1969-83, pres. dir. 1983-86; dir. recruitment Girl Scouts U.S.A., N.Y.C., 1973-78, dir. human resources, 1978-82, dir. career devel., 1982—. Pres., Goddard-Riverside-Trinity Sch. Thrift Shop, N.Y.C., 1964-65, Trinity Sch. Mothers' Orgn., N.Y.C., 1965-66; treas. Brearley Sch. Parents Assn., N.Y.C., 1966-67. Episcopalian. Clubs: North Suffolk Garden, Nissequogue Beach, Nissequogue Platform Tennis Assn. (St. James, L.I., N.Y.). Home: 606 W 116th St New York NY 10027 also Nissequogue River Rd Saint James NY 11780 Office: 830 3d Ave New York NY 10022

HENDERSON, NAOMI HAIRSTON, market research company executive; b. Alexandria, La., Jan. 2, 1944; d. Joseph Henry and Anna Lee (Allen) Hairston; B.A. in Elem. Edn., Am. U., 1964, M.Ed. in Spl. Edn., 1968; m. Lucius Samuel Henderson, III, Aug. 8, 1964. Pres. Prism Corp., market research, Washington, 1978-81; dir. market research Goldberg/Marchesano & Assos., Inc., Washington, 1981-82; partner R.J. Sobus & Partners, Washington, 1982-83; pres. Riva Market Research, Washington, 1983—; focus group moderator; cons. in field; lectr. market research. Mem. Market Research Assn., Leadership Forum Washington (vice chmn. 1981-82), Am. Mktg. Assn., Washington Bd. of Trade, Nat. Assn. Women Bus. Owners. Address: 4417 Brandywine St NW Washington DC 20016

HENDERSON, PATRICIA MCGOVERN, state human rights agency executive; b. Mobile, Ala., Aug. 6, 1940; d. Thomas Joseph and Babe Hope (Lowery) McGovern; children—Thomas Bain, Patrick Sean. Student, Loretto Coll., Nerinx, Ky., 1958-61, U. So. Ala., 1965; B.A. in Psychology and Mgmt., Hawaii Pacific Coll., 1976; M.A., in Psychology and Mgmt., Antioch U., Honolulu, 1981. Cert. mgmt. Queen's Med. Ctr., 1977; cert. U. Ala. Sch. Medicine, 1979; cert. Neuropsychiat. Inst., UCLA, 1980. Dir. Mission and Youth Office for Catholic Diocese and Charities, Mobile, 1961-64; tchr. Ala. State Dept. Pub. Edn., Mobile, 1966-69; spl. edn. tchr., adminstr., social worker St. Peter Claver Sch. and Ctr., Tampa, Fla., 1970-72; chief adminstr., dir., prin., ednl. dir., social worker Salvation Army Kauluwela Corps, Kula Kokua Therapeutic Sch., Malama Makua Rehab. Ctr., 1973-77; exec. dir., chief exec. officer Protection and Advocacy Agy. of Hawaii and State Client Assistance Agy. of Hawaii, Honolulu, 1977—; cons. in field. Author, editor: A Self Advocate-You Have the Right to Speak for Yourself, 1978. Co-author, co-editor Legal Rights for Developmentally and Handicapped Citizens, 1981; The Answer Book for Parents on the Right to Education for the Handicapped Child, 1983. Bd. dirs. State Dept. Health Adv. Com., Honolulu, 1979—, Gov.'s State Planning Council on Developmental Disabilities, 1986; mem. Hawaii Women's Polit. Action, Honolulu, 1982—; co-chmn. Mayor's City and County Transp. for Handicapped/Elderly Task Force, 1984—. Recipient Disting. Service award Salvation Army, 1977; Keen, Dedicated, Outstanding Profl., Highest Calibre award Salvation Army, 1977; Spl. Contbns. Internat. Yr. of Disabled Persons award Gov. George Ariyoshi, 1981; Promotion and Advancement of Women award Hawaiian Telephone Co., 1984; Disting. American award Am. Biog. Inst., 1985; Outstanding and Disting. Service award Gov.'s Commn. on Children and Youth, 1986. Fellow Assn. Exec. Dirs. (dir. 1980), Nat. Legal Aide and Defender Assn.; mem. Am. Mgmt. Assn., Nat. Tourette Syndrome Assn. (exec. dir. 1984—), Nat. Assn. Protection and Advocacy Systems (dir. 1984—), Nat. Client Assistance Orgn. (dir. 1984—). Avocations: travel; theater; music; art collecting; photography. Home: 5567 Pia St Honolulu HI 96821 Office: Protection and Advocacy Agy of Hawaii 1580 Makaloa St Suite 860 Honolulu HI 96814

HENDERSON, SARAH COTHRAN, civic worker, former educator; b. Greenwood, S.C., Feb. 2, 1915; d. Thomas White and Willie Maude (Boswell) Cothran; A.B., Lander Coll., 1937; M.Ed., Furman U., 1963; postgrad. Clemson U., 1971-73, LaVerne Coll., 1971, Furman U., 1976; m. William Edward Henderson (dec. Jan. 1980); 1 child, William Edward Jr. Tchr., Greenville (S.C.) County Schs., 1950-78, S.C. Retired Educators Assn., 1978-86. Regent, Nathaneal Greene chpt. DAR, 1974-76, state chmn. public relations S.C. soc., 1976-79, state conf. chmn., 1982, dist. 1 dir., 1979-82, historian Palmetto State Officers Club, S.C., 1982-85, recording sec., 1985-88; rec. sec. Cornelius Keith chpt. Nat. Soc. Daus. Am. Colonists. Recipient Outstanding Ednl. Achievement award Friends of Edn. of Greenville County and Pleasantburg Rotary Club, 1974. Mem. Greenville Art Assn., Greenville Geneal. Soc. (charter, archivist 1980-83), Nat. Soc. Magna Charta Dames, Nat. Soc. Southern Dames Am., Plantagenet Soc., Order of Washington, S.C. Geneal. Soc., Greenville Hist. Soc., Ligon Family Assn., Huguenot Soc. S.C., Lander Coll. Alumni Assn., Furman U. Alumni Assn., Nat. Trust Hist. Preservation, Nat. Archives, Friends of S.C. State Mus., Friends of Greenville Library. Club: Greenville Woman's. Presbyterian. Home: 114 Woodruff Rd Route 6 Greenville SC 29607

HENDERSON-JAMES, NANCY LUCILE, librarian, researcher; b. Tacoma, July 13, 1945; d. Lawrence Wallace and Muriel May (Woods) Henderson; m. Douglas Henderson-James, June 8, 1968; children—Nathan, Noel. B.A., Carleton Coll., Northfield, Minn., 1967; M.L.S., Pratt Inst., Bklyn., 1974. Cert. in library sci. Librarian, Jordan High Sch., Durham, N.C., 1974-78, 79—; cataloging cons. Africa News, Durham, 1978-79; owner, data researcher Qwik-Search, Durham, 1984—, treas., 1984—. Treas., Morehead Sch. PTA, Durham, 1977-79, sec., 1984-86; sec. Friends of Durham Library, 1983-84, book sales chair, 1983-85. Mem. So. Assn. Colls. and Schs. (evaluator 1984), N.C. Library Assn., Durham County Library Assn. (newsletter editor 1982-83), Am. Assn. Sch. Librarians, N.C. Assn. Educators, NEA. Avocations: bicycling, gardening, reading. Office: C E Jordan High Sch 6806 Garrett Rd Durham NC 27707

HENDLER, MARSHA BECKY, hotel marketing executive; b. Temple, Tex., Dec. 7, 1951; d. Milton Bernard and Mary Elizabeth (Coker) H. B.S., U. Houston, 1973. Dir. catering Ky. Fried Chicken, Houston, 1972-73; dir. sales United Inns, Houston, 1973-75, Host Internat., Houston, 1975-79; asst. dir. sales Adam's Mark Hotel, Houston, 1979-81; dir. mktg. Century Mgmt., New Orleans, 1981-82, Sheraton Crest, Austin, Tex., 1982—; v.p. sales and mktg. Sidney Balman Properties, Inc., Dallas, 1984—. Mem. Hotel Sales Mktg. Assn. (chmn. pub. relations and govt. affairs Tex. chpt. 1984), Am. Bus. Women's Assn., Houston Livestock Show and Rodeo (life; com. chmn. 1983-84), Houston Soc. Assn. Mgmt. (dir. 1981), Hotel-Restaurant Mgmt. Soc. (pres. 1972). Democrat. Jewish. Office: Sheraton Crest Hotel 111 E 1st St Austin TX 78701

HENDREN, MERLYN CHURCHILL, furniture company executive; b. Gooding, Idaho, Oct. 16, 1926; d. Herbert Winston and Annie Averett Churchill; student U. Idaho, 1944-47; B.A., Coll. of Idaho, 1986. m. Robert Lee Hendren, June 14, 1947; children—Robert Lee, Anne Aleen. With Hendren's Furniture Co., Boise, 1947-69; co-owner, v.p. Hendren's Inc., Boise, 1969—. Bd. dirs. Idaho Law Found., 1978-84; chmn. Coll. of Idaho Symposium, 1977-78, mem. adv. bd., 1981—; pres. Boise Council on Aging, 1959-60, mem. adv. bd., 1984—; mem. Gov.'s Commn. on Aging, 1960, Idaho del. to White House Conf. Aging, 1961; trustee St. Luke's Regional Hosp., 1981—; mem. adv. bd. dirs. Boise Philharm. Assn., Inc., 1981—; bd. dirs. S.W. Idaho Pvt. Industry Council, 1984—. Mem. Boise C. of C. (bd. dirs. 1984-87). Republican. Episcopalian. Home: 3504 Hillcrest Dr Boise ID 83705 Office: 516 S 9th St Boise ID 83706

HENDRICK, LINDA FAYE, advertising agency casting executive; b. Bklyn., Sept. 15, 1948; d. Burton Ira and Rhoda (Goldberg) Mandel; m. James Tracey Hendrick, Apr. 21, 1971 (div. July 1979). B.S., U. Bridgeport, 1970. Substitute tchr. Farmingdale High Sch. (N.Y.), 1970-72; adminstrv. asst. Guinan Publs., Plainview, N.Y., 1972-74; asst. to head mktg. Thomas Cook Inc., N.Y.C., 1974-75; asst. to pres. W. Colston Leigh, N.Y.C., 1975-77; prodn. coordinator BCI Casting, N.Y.C., 1977-80; casting dir. Grey Lyon & King Advt. Inc., N.Y.C., 1980—; lectr. in field, 1980—. Mem. Nat. Acad. TV Arts and Scis. Jewish. Office: Grey Lyon & King Advt Inc 405 Lexington Ave New York NY 10174

HENDRICK, NANCY CROWELL, educator; b. Nashua, N.H., Feb. 4, 1914; d. Walter Andrew and Bertha Jane (Griffin) Crowell; m. Paul Hendrick, Nov. 29, 1941; children—Constance Jane Hendrick Post, Sandra Margaret Hendrick Adler, Peter Crowell Hendrick. A.B., Barnard Coll., 1935; postgrad. U. N.H., U. Maine, Boston U., Harvard U. Tchr. Alvirne High Sch., Hudson, N.H., 1953-57, West High Sch., Manchester, N.H., 1957-60, Nashua High Sch., N.H., 1960-68, Pinkerton Acad., Derry, N.H., 1969-71. Founding dir. N.H. Council World Affairs, Durham, 1979—; mission council rep. and vice chmn. Women's concerns team Presbyn. Synod of the Northeast, Syracuse, N.Y., 1980—; dir., past pres. N.H. Assn. Conservation Commns., Concord, 1974—; mem., past. chmn. Litchfield Conservation Commn., N.H., 1970—; state rep. N.H. Gen. Ct., Concord, 1978—; bd. dirs. Merrimack River Watershed Council, West Newbury, Mass., 1984—, Matthew Thornton Health Plan, Nashua, 1978-82; vice moderator No. New Eng. Presbytery, 1978—; founder, bd. dirs. Litchfield LWV. Mem. Orgn. Women Legislators. Democrat. Avocations: skiing; canoeing; theatre drama coach; choir director.

HENDRICK, ZELWANDA, educator; b. Rusk, Tex., Nov. 28, 1925; d. Lloyd Irvin and Viola Alice (McGuire) Hendrick; A.A., Lon Morris Coll., 1945; B.S., N. Tex. U., 1947; M.A., So. Meth. U., 1958. Tchr. theatre arts Overton (Tex.) High Sch., 1947-49, Nacogdoches (Tex.) High Sch., 1949-50, Boude Storey Sch., Dallas, 1950-53, Kimball High Sch., Dallas, 1953-62; tchr. theatre arts H. Grady Spruce High Sch., Dallas, 1962-78, chmn. fine arts dept., 1963-77, ret., 1978; drama and psychology tchr. Alexander Sch., 1978—; substitute tchr. Highland Park High Sch., Dallas, 1980—; part-time tchr. John Robert Powers Finishing Sch., 1951—; teaching fellow N. Tex. U., 1964-65; ptnr. Adventure II Miniature Horse Ranch, Rusk, Tex., 1985—. Active, Tyler (Tex.) Civic Symphony, 1949-50, Tyler Civic Theatre, 1949-50, Dallas Theatre Center, 1960-61; guest dir. Cherokee Civic Theatre, Rusk, 1983; mem. adv. com. Smithsonian Instn., 1975; co-sponsor U.S. Inst. Tech. Theatre; del. Democratic Dist. Conv., 1980; candidate Tex. State Legislature, 1980; chmn. Dallas County Transp. Bd., 1982—. Mem. Internat. Thespians (state dir.), Tex. Speech Assn. (sec. 1973—), Am. Assn. Ednl. Theatre, Dallas Ednl. Drama Assn. (governing bd.), Tex. Tchrs. Assn., Nat. Forensic League, AAUW, Classroom Tchrs. Dallas, Internat. Platform Assn., Ednl. Arts Assn., Tex. Congress Parent Tchr. Assn. (hon. life), DAR, Daus. Republic of Tex., N. Texas Collie Club, Nat. Assn. Royalty Owners, Tex. Ind. Producers and Royalty Owners Assn., Tex. Farm Bur., Am. Miniature Horse Assn., Delta Kappa Gamma. Club: Order Eastern Star. Contbr. to A Guide to Student Teaching in Music, 1968-70. Home: 204 E 4th St Rusk TX 75785

HENDRICKS, DOROTHY KAPROTH (KAPPY HENDRICKS), art gallery executive; b. Foley, Minn., June 28, 1935; d. Casper and Stella (Gapinski) Kaproth; student Coll. St. Scholastica, Duluth, Minn., 1952-54; B.S., U. Colo., 1956, postgrad., 1957-61; postgrad. U. Md., 1961-63, Naganuma (Tokyo Sch. Japanese Lang.), 1965-70; M.S. in Applied Linguistics, Japanese Lang., Georgetown U., 1973; m. Marshall L. Hendricks, Apr. 2, 1956; children—Jeffrey, Lisle. Food economist Safeway Stores, Denver, 1956-58; tchr. Denver Public Schs., 1958-61, Prince George's County Public Schs., 1961-63; prof. Jissen Joshi Daigaku, Tokyo, 1966-70; pres. The Hendricks Art Collection Ltd., Bethesda, Md., N.Y.C. and Tokyo, 1965—; lectr. in field. Mem. Am. Soc. Appraisers. Republican. Author: (with others) Tadashi Nakayama: His Life and Work, 1983; contbr. articles in field. Home and Office: 6502 Hillmead Rd Bethesda MD 20817

HENDRICKS, JUDITH ANN, physician; b. Staten Island, N.Y., Oct. 26, 1949; d. Albert B. and Rose (Galasso) Accettola; m. H. Keith Hendricks, Aug. 5, 1972; children—Pamela Elaine, Richard Reed. B.S. cum laude in Biology, Wagner Coll., 1971; M.D., U. Okla., 1975. Intern, med. resident S.I. Hosp., 1975-78, assoc. dir. emergency dept., 1978-79, chmn. cost containment com., 1980-82, chmn. cardiopulmonary resusitation com., 1980-84, assoc. attending physician, 1978-84, attending physician, 1984—; clin. instr. SUNY-Bklyn., 1982-84; med. dir. Chronic Disease Care Program, Staten Island, N.Y., 1980—; mem. N.Y.C. Subcom. on Emergency Cardiac Care In House Tng., 1980-81. Robert Wood Johnson Found. grantee, 1980-84. Mem. AMA, ACP, N.Y. State Med. Soc., Richmond County Med. Soc. Office: 1361 Hylan Blvd Staten Island NY 10305

HENDRICKS, MARY JO, electrical engineer; b. Steubenville, Ohio, Apr. 26, 1956; d. James Albert and Mary Joan (Dougherty) Deist; B.S. in Elec. Engring., W.Va. Inst. Tech., 1978; m. Michael K. Hendricks, June 3, 1978. Elec. design engr. Union Carbide Corp., Charleston, W.Va., 1978-82, lead elec. engr. energy systems Institute plant (W.Va.), 1982-86, sr. process engr. acetone unit, 1986—. Mem. IEEE (chmn. W.Va. sect. 1981-82; rep. Kanawha Valley Joint Tech. Council 1982-83), Nat. Fire Protection Assn. (nat. electric code panel 3), Eta Kappa Nu. Republican. Presbyterian. Home: 102 Green Dr Hurricane WV 25526 Office: Union Carbide Corp Box 2831 TRLR-12 Charleston WV 25330

HENDRICKS, PEARL NISLEY, nurse, clinical educator; b. Bennet, Nebr., July 19, 1922; d. Ray Marion and Laura Anna (Kayser) Nisley; m. Robert Dale Hendricks, Aug. 21, 1945; children—Robin Ann, Marcia Lou, Osa Ray, Alan Dale. Diploma, Lincoln Gen. Sch. Nursing, 1945; B.S., Nebr. Wesleyan U., 1946; M.S., U. Nebr.-Omaha, 1978. Head nurse tuberculosis floor Douglas County Hosp., Omaha, 1946, nursing instr. contagious diseases, 1946-47; nursing instr. Clarkson Hosp., Omaha, 1947-48; staff and intensive care nurse Meth. Hosp., Omaha, 1956-68, staff devel. nurse, 1968-75, instr. students, 1975—; guest lectr. Emergency Room Nurses, Omaha, 1982. Leader, co-leader 4-H Club, Bennet, 1936-40; active Girl Scouts U.S.A., 1955, 56, 59, 60, Boy Scouts Am., 1964, 65, 69, 70; instr. CPR, Nebr. Heart Assn., Omaha, 1968-76. Recipient Elliot award for outstanding instrn. Meth. Sch. Nursing, 1980. Mem. Am. Nurses Assn., Nat. League Nursing Edn., Assn. Operating Room Nurses. Democrat. Methodist. Home: 5406 Jaynes St Omaha NE 68104 Office: Meth Hosp 8303 Dodge St Omaha NE 68114

HENDRICKSON, LORRAINE UHLANER, business management educator, consultant; b. Washington, July 28, 1953; d. Julius Earl and Vera (Kolar) Uhlaner; m. Jack Reynold Hendrickson, Jr., Dec. 29, 1978; 1 son, Eric Benjamin. A.B., Radcliffe Coll., 1973; Doctorandus, U. Leiden (Netherlands), 1976; M.A., U. Mich., 1976, Ph.D., 1980. Research asst. U. Leiden, 1973-74; asst. study dir. Inst. for Social Research, Ann Arbor, Mich., 1974-78; instr., asst. prof. Mich. State U., East Lansing, 1979-81; asst. prof. dept. mgmt. Coll. Bus., Eastern Mich. U., Ypsilanti, 1981-86, assoc. prof., 1986—, dir. Ctr. for Entrepreneurship/Coll. Bus. Service Ctr., 1986—; cons. StarPak Solar Systems Corp., Novi, Mich., 1981-85, dir., treas., 1976-85; cons. Livingston County Sheriff's Dept., Howell, Mich., 1981; cons. personnel mgmt. and orgnl. devel.; del. White House Conf. on Small Bus., 1986; mem. adv. bd. Ann Arbor Innovation Ctr., 1986—. Contbr. book revs. to Personnel Psychology, 1983, 84, papers to profl. confs. Sec., co-chmn. Mich. Alliance Small Bus., Lansing, 1981-83; mem. innovation and tech. task force Gov.'s Conf. on Small Bus., 1981; candidate state Democratic primary, 1982. Council for European Studies pre-dissertation fellow, U. Pitts., 1975. Mem. Acad. Mgmt., Am. Mgmt. Assn., Mich. Assn. Indsl. and Organizational Psychologists, Ypsilanti C. of C. (small bus. council 1986—). Home: 5757 Pontiac Trail Ann Arbor MI 48105 Office: Dept Mgmt Coll Bus Eastern Mich Univ Ypsilanti MI 48197

HENDRIE, ELAINE, public relations executive; b. Bklyn.; d. David and Pearl (Saltzhauer) Kostell; m. Joseph Mallam Hendrie, July 9, 1949; children—Susan, Barbara. Asst. account exec. Benjamin Sonnenberg Pub. Relations firm, N.Y.C., 1953-57; pub. relations cons., writer, editor, 1957-72; dir. pub. relations and media Religious Heritage of Am., Washington, 1973-75; producer, interviewer Woman to Woman radio program, WRIV and WALK AM and FM, L.I., N.J., Westchester County, N.Y., Conn., 1974-77; exec. dir. Women in New Directions, Inc., Suffolk County, N.Y., 1974-77, cons. 1978; nat. media coordinator NOW, Washington, 1978; media dir. Am. Speech-Lang.-Hearing Assn., Washington, 1979-80; public info. officer, head media and mktg. Dept. Navy, Washington, 1980-81; pres. Triangle Enterprises, 1982, Hendrie & Pendzick, Pub. Relations, 1982—; resource person for media Nat. Commn. on Observance of Internat. Women's Yr., 1977; cons. Multi-Media Prodns. Inc., N.Y.C., 1978—, Women in New Directions, Inc., 1981—. Bd. dirs. Energy Edn. Exponents, 1982—; mem. adv. bd. Women's Ednl. and Counseling Ctr., SUNY-Farmingdale, 1982—. Mem. Am. Nuclear Soc. (exec. bd. L.I. chpt. 1985—). Club: Bellport Bay Yacht. Home: 50 Bellport Ln Bellport NY 11713

HENDRIKSEN, MARGIE, state senator; b. Henderson, Minn., Mar. 17, 1943; 1 child, Kara. B.A. cum laude, U. Minn., 1967; J.D., U. Oreg., 1975. Bar: Oreg. Asst. counsel Lane County, 1977-79, counsel, 1979-80; mem. Oreg. Ho. of Reps., 1980-82; mem. Oreg. Senate from 20th Dist. Vice-chmn. Democratic Platform Conv., 1980; committee-woman Dem. Precinct Com.; mem. Lane County Dem. Exec. Com. Mem. Oreg. Polit. Caucus, Nat. Women's Polit. Caucus, Assn. Trial Lawyers Am., Oreg. Bar Assn., Bus. and Profl. Women. Address: 2345 Patterson St #12 Eugene OR 97405

HENDRIX, KATHRYN ANN, trade association administrator; b. Olean, N.Y., July 6, 1934; d. George Tobias Whipp and Kathryn Elizabeth (Greene) H.; B.S., Carnegie Mellon U., 1955. Cert. assn. exec. Sec., NASA, 1955-57; with Forging Industry Assn., Cleve., 1957—, corp. sec., 1977—, asst. v.p. adminstrn., 1980—. Mem. Greater Cleve. Soc. Assn. Execs. (dir., sec.-treas., v.p., pres.), Cleve. Area Meeting Planners, Club: Women's City of Cleve. Lodge: Altrusa (bd. dirs.). Home: 4400 Clarkwood Pky #615 Warrensville Heights OH 44128 Office: 55 Public Sq Rm 1121 Cleveland OH 44113

HENDRIX, SHEILA MCMINN, computer retail store executive; b. Hendersonville, N.C., Mar. 20, 1944; d. Fred Mitchell Henry and Julia (McCrary) McMinn; m. Harry Glenn Dotson, Dec. 18, 1965 (dec.); children—Kelly Lynne; m. 2d, Benny Edward Hendrix, Feb. 21, 1981. B.S.E., Western Carolina U., 1966. Tchr. Gaston County Schs. (N.C.), 1966-67, Charlotte (N.C.)-McKlenburg Sch., 1967-68, tchr. Blue Ridge Tech. Inst., Hendersonville, part-time 1972-75, Henderson County Schs., 1975-82; mgr. Computer Alternatives of Hickory (N.C.), 1982—.

HENDRIX, SUSAN CLELIA DERRICK, civic worker; b. McClellanville, S.C., Jan. 19, 1920; d. Theodore Elbridge and Susan Regina (Bauknight) Derrick; m. Henry Gardner Hendrix, June 5, 1943; children—Susan Hendrix Redmond, Marilyn Hendrix Shedlock. B.A., Columbia Coll., 1941; M.A., Furman U., 1961; Ed.D. (hon.) Columbia Coll., 1985. Cert. tchr., S.C. Tchr. Whitmire Pub. Schs., 1941-43, Greenville Pub. Schs., S.C., 1944-46, 58-63, dir. Reading clinic, 1965-68; counselor Greenville Pub. Schs., 1963-65; supr. Greenville County Sch. Dist., S.C., 1965-68, dir. pub. relations, 1968-83; grad. instr. Furman U., 1967-69; cons. Nat. Seminar on Desegregation, 1973. Author: (with James P. Mahaffey) Teaching Secondary Reading, 1966; Communicating With the Community, 1979; editor: Communique, 1968-83. Contbr. articles to profl. jours. and mags. Chmn. bd. trustees Columbia Coll., 1969-70; chmn. Greenville County Rehab. Bd., S.C., 1974-76; vice chmn. bd. Jr. Achievement, Greenville, 1978-79; chmn. S.C. Commn. on Women, Columbia, 1982—; pres. United Methodist Women, Buncombe St. Ch., Greenville, 1956-57; mem. adminstrv. bd. Buncombe St. Ch., 1968—, bd. trustees, 1980—; mem. United Meth. Ch. Southeastern Jurisdictional Council on Ministries, 1984—; chmn. S.C. Conf. Council on Ministries United Meth. Ch., 1980—; mem. bd. Global Ministries United Meth. Ch., 1972-80, mem. Commn. Study of Ministry, 1984—. Recipient Medallion Columbia Coll., 1980; Alumnae Disting. Service award Columbia Coll., 1983; Disting. Achievement award Women's History Week, Greenville, 1984. Mem. S.C. PTA (life), Alpha Delta Kappa (pres. 1970-72), Columbia Coll. Alumnae Assn., Democratic Women, S.C. Women in Govt. Home: 309 Arundel Rd Greenville SC 29615 Office: SC Commn on Women 2221 Devine St Columbia SC 29205

HENEGAR, MARTHA, educational administrator; b. McMinnville, Tenn., July 9, 1937; s. Ulric Shaw and Lucile (Angel) H. B.A., George Peabody Coll., 1959, M.A., 1960. Tchr. English, Nashville pub. schs., 1959-68; promotion dir. Sta. WMCV-TV, Nashville, 1968-70; dir. pub. relations Nashville State Tech. Inst., 1970-84, head pub. affairs and devel., 1984—. Editor Print-Out, 1970—. Contbr. articles to profl. jours., travel mags. Vol. reader WPLN Talking Library for the Blind, Nashville, 1975—. Mem. Pub. Relations Soc. Am. (accredited in pub. relations; chpt. pres. 1980), Internat. Assn. Bus. Communicators (accredited bus. communicator, chpt. pres. 1976). Office: Nashville State Tech Inst 120 White Bridge Rd Nashville TN 37209

HENGEN, NONA LILLIAN, artist, author; b. Spokane, Wash., Mar. 28, 1934; d. Henry Caspar and Esther Dorothea (Knuth) H. B.A., Fort Wright Coll., 1956; M.A., U. Colo., 1960; Ph.D., Ind. U., 1968. Tchr. pub. schs. Kahlotus, Moses Lake and Spokane, Wash., 1956-60; TV tchr. Spokane Pub. Schs., 1960-65; tchr. U. Va., 1969, So. Oreg. Coll., 1969-70; with adminstrn., media services program Western Wash. U., Bellingham, 1970-76; with adminstrn., tchr. Grad. Sch., Ind. U., 1978-80; freelance artist, author, Spangle, Wash., 1980—; lectr. on art, regional history, painting of hist. themes. Author-illustrator: Max Leo: An Uncommon Cat, 1982; Plodding Princes of the Palouse, 1984. Mem. adv. bd. Spokanimal CARE (humane soc.), Spokane, Wash., 1985.

HENKALINE, SHARON TERUE, real estate broker; b. Greenville, Ohio, Dec. 5, 1946; d. Ronald Leroy and Francis Pauline (Daniel) Brown; MTI Bus. Sch., 1965; cert. in bus. adminstrn., U. Dayton, 1975; student Ohio State U., 1977; m. Jack Blaine Henkaline, Aug. 12, 1966; 1 son, Christopher Blaine. With aero. systems div. Wright Patterson AFB, Dayton, Ohio, 1965-66; with office adj. gen. U.S. Army, Fort Belvoir, Va., 1966-67; with purchasing and inventory control dept. Greenville (Ohio) Mfg., 1971-74; sales assoc. Paul Clark Realty, Van Wert, Ohio, 1974-76, office mgr., 1976-78; partner Newert Co., Van Wert, 1976-78; owner, broker King & Co. Realty, Van Wert, 1979-80; pres., owner, broker Sharron Realty Assos. Inc., Van Wert, 1980—; broker Van Cline Realty, Ft. Wayne, Ind., 1982—. Mem. Nat. Assn. Realtors, Am. Bus. Women's Assn., Ohio Assn. Realtors, Van Wert Bus. and Profl. Womens Club, Van Wert County Bd. Realtors (v.p. 1978-79), C. of C. Republican. Club: Elks. Home: 134 Boyd Van Wert OH 45891 Office: Shannon Realty Assos Inc 1043 S Shannon St Van Wert OH 45891

HENKE, ALICE MARIE, college administrator, archivist; b. Thorp, Wis., Oct. 30, 1923; d. Emil August and Anna Marie (Baldeschwiler) H. B.A., St. Thomas Coll., St. Paul, 1957; M.A., Loyola U., 1967. Joined Sisters, Servants of Mary, Roman Cath. Ch., 1943. Tchr., St. Paul Weirton, W.Va., Lannon, Wis., Ladysmith, Wis., Spooner, Wis., Washburn, Wis., Hillside, Ill., Carteret, N.J., 1946-68; instr. of history Mount Senario Coll., Ladysmith, 1968-71, asst. dir. of admissions, 1971-78, dir. of alumni, 1980—; archivist Sisters, Servants of Mary, Ladysmith, 1981—. Author: A Branch Amid the Pines, 1983. Contbr. articles to religious jours. Chmn. com. History of Rusk County, 1982-83; pres. Rusk County Hist. Soc., Ladysmith, 1970, 74-76, dir., bd. mem., 1976-79; chmn. Wis. Council of Local History, Northwestern Region, Ladysmith, 1976; mem. Ladysmith Centennial Com., 1985. Mem. Rusk County Hist. Soc., State Hist. Soc. of Wis., Soc. Am. Archivists, Midwest Archives Assn., Wis. Independent Colls. Alumni Assn. Avocation: historical research. Home: 1000 College Ave W Ladysmith WI 54848 Office: Mount Senario Coll Ladysmith WI 54848

HENKE, CECILIA THERESA, educational adminstator; b. Rice Lake, Wis., Aug. 1, 1930; d. Charles and Lucy Gagner; m. Charles Braun, Sept. 26, 1953 (div. 1975); m. William Henke, Jan. 11, 1986—; children—Cynthia, Corrine, Charles. Student Oshkosh State U., 1959-62; B.S., U. Ariz., 1972. Tchr., Rice Lake Pub. Schs., 1951-53; tchr. Portage Elem. Schs., Wis., 1955-57; remedial reading tchr. pilot program Green Lake Sch., Wis., 1958-60; dir. Swan Lake Day Activity Ctr., Windom, Minn., 1966-70; with Ariz. Tng. Programs, 1970-72; dir. Handicamp Inc., Tucson, 1972-74; dir. early childhood handicap program Gila River Indian Community, Sacaton, Ariz., 1974-78, spl. service program dir., community program developer, 1978—; community services worker Southeast Ariz.; cons. Southwestern Day Activity Assn. Mem. Council for Exceptional Children (chmn.), Nat. Assn. Retarded Citizens, Nat. Assn. Edn. Young Children. Roman Catholic. Home: 1165 Avenida Fresca Casa Grande AZ 85222 Office: PO Box 69 Sacaton AZ 85247

HENKE, SHIRLEY LYNN, state official; b. Ventnor, N.J., May 23, 1926; d. William Cruikshank and Ruth Amelia (Leyrer) Lynn; m. Dan F. Henke, June 10, 1950; children—Danferd William, Holly Lynn. B.A. in Econs. magna cum laude, Rutgers U., 1948; postgrad. Am. U., 1952; B.A. in Math., U.Calif.-Berkeley, 1967. Cert. secondary tchr., Calif. Bus.economist U.S. Dept. Commerce, Washington, 1948-49; fgn. affairs officer U.S. Dept. State, Washington, 1949-52; claims rep. U.S. Social Security Adminstrn., San Antonio, 1952-54; secondary sch. tchr. Piedmont, Acalanes, Orinda and Mt. Diablo, Calif., 1967-73; criminal justice planner Criminal Justice Agy. of Contra Costa County, Concord, Calif., 1973-76; founder, project adminstr. Crime Prevention Com. Contra Costa County, Concord, 1976-79; fire service tng. specialist Office State Fire Marshal, Sacramento. 1979-81; program analyst Calif. Dept. Social Services, Sacramento and Oakland, Calif., 1981—; instr. Calif. peace officer standards and tng. Crime Prevention Inst., Pomona, Calif., 1975-76; guest lectr. Diablo Valley Community Coll., Concord, 1975-76; mem. Calif. Crime Resistance Task Force, Sacramento, 1977-83; mem. County

Justice System Subvention Adv. Com., Concord, 1978-79; chmn. police services transition team for Orinda, Calif., 1985. Author: Alternative to Fear, 1975; also articles. Chmn. com. fundraising and resources, LWV, San Antonio, 1953-54; precinct organizer Contra Costa County Com. on Election Propositions, 1964; mem. Orinda Assn. on Crime Prevention, 1970-82, chmn., 1971-73; supervisorial appointee P-4 Adv. Com. on Police Services, 1982; bd. dirs. Friends Outside, Martinez, 1977-78. Recipient Hon. Mention, Nat. Crime Prevention Inst., 1979. Mem., Phi Beta Kappa. Home: 258 La Espiral St Orinda CA 94563

HENKEL, ELOISE ELIZABETH, writer, university information specialist, educator; b. Chgo., Apr. 23, 1923; d. Milford Franklin and Eloise Elizabeth (Lewis) H. B.S. in Journalism, Northwestern U., Evanston, Ill., 1944; M.A. in English, U. Chgo., 1964. Reporter, Battle Creek Enquirer-News (Mich.), 1944-45; pub. relations writer Office of Mil. Govt. U.S., Berlin, 1946-47; reporter, rewriter UP, Chgo. and Omaha, 1948; corr. Women's News Service, Paris, 1949; pub. relations officer Internat. Refugee Orgn., Bremen, W.Ger., 1950-51; fgn. corr. Worldwide Press Service, Europe, North Africa, Near East., 1952-54; test constructor Navy Project U. Chgo., 1955; freelance writer, India, Afghanistan, 1956-58, Tibet, China, 1983—; tchr. English Chgo. Bd. Edn., 1959-66, 72-75, 84-86; freelance corr., Vietnam, 1967-69; reporter Hammond Times (Ind.), 1971-72; media specialist U. Chgo., 1976-79, Ill. Inst. Tech., Chgo., 1980; developer Rainbow Condominium Assn., Chgo., 1981-82. Author: (with Dick Jones) How to Save Money in Paris, 1950. Recipient Best Feature Story award Ind. AP Mng. Editors, 1971, Best News Story award UPI Mng. Editors (Ind.), 1971, Stick-O-Type award for best feature story Chgo. Newspaper Guild, 1972. Mem. YWCA, YMCA; U.S. China Peoples Friendship Assn. Quaker. Club: Overseas Press. Home: 1454 W Hollywood Chicago IL 60660

HENKIN, PAULA L. S., marketing executive; b. N.Y.C., Aug. 17, 1956; d. Harold B. and Lois (Koppe) Schwartzapfel; m. Charles Jeffrey Henkin, July 3, 1983. B.A., SUNY-Binghamton, 1978; M.B.A., Temple U., 1980. Account mgr. JFY, Inc., Melville, N.Y., 1980-81; dir. mktg. Sureway Air Traffic, N.Y.C., 1981-84; mgr. healthcare industry mktg. Am. Express TRS Co., N.Y.C., 1984-86; asst. v.p. Citicorp Retail Services, 1986—. Mem. Am. Mktg. Assn., Advt. Women N.Y. Home: 16-66 Bell Blvd Bayside NY 11360 Office: Citicorp Retail Services 245 Old Country Rd Melville NY 11747

HENKIND, JANICE VERONICA, editor; b. N.Y.C., Feb. 3, 1951; d. William I. and Veronica A. Benjamin; B.A., Mercy Coll., 1972; M.Sc., U. Bridgeport, 1977; m. Paul Henkind, May 22, 1977; 1 son, Aaron Samuel. Electron microscopist Boyce Thompson Inst. Plant Research, 1972-74, dept. ophthalmology Montefiore Hosp. and Med. Center, 1974-76; exec. adminstr. Assn. for Research in Vision and Ophthalmology, New Rochelle, N.Y., 1977—; mng. editor Ophthalmology, Jour. Am. Acad. Ophthalmology, 1979—, Acta, 24th Internat. Congress Ophthalmology, 1982-83; v.p. Med. Dialogues, Inc. Contbr. chpts., articles to profl. publs. Bd. overseers Old Sturbridge Village (Mass.), 1984—; mem. corp. N.Y. Bot. Garden, 1984—. Recipient Martha Stone award in floriculture, 1983, 84. Mem. Assn. Women in Sci., Nat. Assn. Female Execs., Assn. for Research in Vision and Ophthalmology (hon.). Address: 276 Overlook Rd New Rochelle NY 10804

HENKLE, TERESA, writer; b. Baker, Oreg., Mar. 13, 1955; d. Ray and Ida Mae (Hall) Winn; children—Katy Lynn, Maxwell James. Student U. Oreg., 1973-75. Writer, co-founder Writers Assocs., Eugene, Oreg., 1975-77; writer KASH-KSND, Eugene, 1976-78; writer, creative dir. Brockett Real Estate, Eugene, 1978-82; creative dir. Sta. KVMT, Vail, Colo., 1982-84; writer Colle McVoy Advt., Denver, 1984—; writer, cons. to local companies. Author: Inside A Storm, 1981. Contbr. articles and poetry to various publs. Formerly active PTA, also Gifted Children Orgn., Eugene; pub. relations, advt. chmn. Jim Hale for County Commr., Eugene, 1982; hon. mem. Friends of the Library. Mem. Denver Advt. Fedn. Avocations: aerobics instruction; hiking; running; reading. Home: 6483 S Florence Way Englewood CO 80111

HENLEY, ANDREA LEVINSON, geologist, business executive, consultant; b. Pitts., Dec. 21, 1953; d. James Charles and Marilyn (Gasche) Levinson; m. Davis Clemens Henley, July 4, 1983. B.S., U.Cin., 1976; postgrad. U. Toledo, 1977-78; M.S., Bowling Green State U., 1979. Geologist, pres. Ranwell, Inc., Houston, 1980—; v.p. Airways Travel, Houston, 1983—, Jerusalem Touring Express, Inc., Houston, 1983—; mgr. Am. Med. Exporters, Inc., Houston, 1983—. Mem. Assn. Women Geoscientists, Houston Geol. Soc., Am. Assn. Petroleum Geologists, Soc. for Well Log Analysts. Republican. Jewish.

HENLEY, BETH, playwright, actress; b. Jackson, Miss., May 8, 1952; d. Charles and Lydy Henley. B.F.A., So. Meth. U., 1974; postgrad. U. Ill., 1975-76. Performed with Dallas Minority Repertory Theater, pageant Gt. American People Show, New Salem State Park, Ill., 1976; author plays: Crimes of the Heart (Broadway), 1981, The Wake of Jamey Foster (Broadway), 1982, Am I Blue, 1982, The Miss Firecracker Contest (off Broadway), 1984, The Debutante Ball (world premiere South Coast Repertory Theatre), 1985. Recipient awards for Crimes of the Heart including Pulitzer prize for drama, 1981, N.Y. Drama Critics Circle Best Play award, 1981, George Oppenheimer/Newsday Playwriting award, 1980-81. Address: care Gilbert Parker The William Morris Agy 1350 Ave of the Americas New York NY 10019*

HENLEY, HELEN MCTAGGART (MRS. W. BALLENTINE HENLEY), rancher; b. Pawnee, Ill., Mar. 20, 1910; d. Albert Thomas and Edith L. (Fallenstein) McTaggart; student Washington U., St. Louis, 1935-38; m. William Ballentine Henley, Dec. 15, 1942. Co-owner, mgr. Delmar Farm, Momence, Ill., 1943-58, Creston Circle Ranch, Paso Robles, Calif., 1958—; income property owner devel. and mgmt., 1955—. Mem. Am. Saddle Horse Assn., Am. Aberdeen-Angus Assn., Calif. Saddle Horse Breeder's Futurity (dir. 1945-48, 58-71). Home: 1224 Geneva St Glendale CA 91207 Office: Creston Circle Ranch Creston Star Route Paso Robles CA 93446

HENLEY, SALLIE HAMLET, artist, deaf interpreter; b. Norfolk, Va., Sept. 29, 1933; d. Charles McDowell and Sarah Speight (White) Hamlet; student pub. schs., Norfolk; m. William Franklin Henley, Jr., July 21, 1951; children—William Franklin III, Robert Matthew. Pub. speaker, Milw., 1968-71, Houston, 1971—; book dramatist, Milw., 1969-71, Houston, 1971-72; interpreter for deaf, Milw., 1969-71, Houston, 1971—; free-lance artist, Atlanta, 1963-65, Houston, 1975—; exhibited Sportsmans Gallery, Hanson Gallery, Town and Country Ctr., Houston, 1984, The Galleria, Houston. Interpreter to deaf Elmbrook Ch., Brookfield, Wis., 1969-70; vol. tchr. deaf retardate Fairview North Elementary Sch., Brookfield, 1970; narrator, interpreter Deaf Olympics, 1969; sec. Quail Valley Civic Assn., 1974-75; bd. dirs. Ephphatha, Inc., Milw., 1969-70. Mem. Registry Interpreters for Deaf. Republican. Home: 2806 E Pebble Beach Dr Missouri City TX 77459

HENLEY, SANDRA S., economist; b. Marion, Ill., Mar. 2, 1945; d. James Robert and Wilma S. (Johnson) Smithson; m. Robert C. Henley, May 5, 1965; children—Marjorie, Joseph. B.S., So. Ill. U., 1966, M.S., 1968; Ph.D. in Econs., U. Ind., 1970. Mem. faculty dept. econs. Governors State U., Park Forest, Ill., 1970-77; mem. exec. staff Indpls. Econ. Council, 1977—; cons. and lectr. in econs. and politics. Author: The Economic Development of Indiana, 1984; contbr. articles to profl. jours. Active, Girl Scouts Council, Indpls. Mem. Nat. Assn. Female Execs., Am. Econs. Assn., Ind. Assn. Social Scientists. Address: 635 E 6th St Seymour IN 47274*

HENLINE, FLORENCE, pianist; b. Ft. Wayne, Ind.; d. Samuel and Caroline Dorothy (Mollet) Henline; B.M., Chgo. Mus. Coll., 1928; m. Milson Jezek, Sept. 2, 1936. Made first concert appearance at age of 13; appeared with Ill. Symphony and Grant Park Orch., Chgo., Women's Symphony (ofcl. pianist); accompanist; staff pianist NBC network, 1930-32; pianist, soloist Chgo. Symphony String Ensemble, 1946-56, Chgo. Pops Symphonette; soloist Indpls. Symphony String Ensemble Symphonette, 1970, West Side Symphony of Chgo.; solo concert engagements throughout U.S.; faculty mem. Chgo. Conservatory, 1959; performer works by Chgo. composers Internat. Soc. Contemporary Music, 1960-61. Judge auditions piano solo contest 35th ann. Chicagoland Music Festival, 1964, ann. competition soloists Young Judea Symphony Orch. Chgo., 1965, 67. Fellow Internat. Inst. Arts and Letters (life); mem. Lake View Mus. Soc., Musicians' Club Women, Alliance Francaise (Chgo.), Ill. Opera Guild, Art Inst. Chgo., Chgo. Artists Assn., Mu Phi Epsilon (soloist at internat. conv. 1972). Club: Cordon. Home: 9715 S Vanderpoel Chicago IL 60643

HENN, SHIRLEY EMILY, retired librarian; b. Cleve., May 26, 1919; d. Albert Edwin and Florence Ely (Miller) Henn; A.B., Hollins Coll., 1941; M.S., U. N.C., 1966; m. John Van Bruggen, July 14, 1944 (div. May 1947); 1 son, Peter Albert (dec.). Library asst. Hollins (Va.) Coll., 1943-44, 61-64, reference librarian, 1965-84, ret., 1984; advt. mgr. R.M. Kellogg Co., Three Rivers, Mich., 1946-47; exec. sec. Hollins Coll. Alumnae Assn., 1947-55; real estate salesman Fowlkes & Kefauver, Roanoke, Va., 1955-61. Pres. Soc. for Prevention Cruelty to Animals, 1959-61, 69-72, bd. dirs., 1972-81. Mem. Am. Alumni Council (dir. 1952-54, dir. women's activities 1952-54), ALA, Va. Library Assn., Nat. DAR (librarian Nancy Christian Fleming chpt. Roanoke 1977-84, regent 1984—), Collie Club Am., Roanoke Bird Club, Roanoke Kennel Club. Club: Quota (chpt. pres. 1958-60) (Roanoke). Author and illustrator: Adventures of Hooty Owl and His Friends, 1953; editor: Hollins Alumnae Bull., 1947-56. Home: 6915 Tinkerdale Hollins VA 24019

HENNEBURY, MARION EDITH, educational administrator; b. Quincy, Mass., Jan. 27, 1937; d. John Henry and Edith Elizabeth (Danahy) Hennebury. B.S., Boston U., 1959; M.Ed., Fla. Atlantic U., 1969; Ed.D., U. So. Calif., 1978. Tchr., Barton Elem. Sch., Lake Worth, Fla., 1963-66, curriculum asst., 1966-69, dir. Head Start, summer 1968; asst. prin. Palm Beach Pub. Schs., Fla., 1969-78, prin., 1978-83; prin. Palm Springs Elem. Sch., Lake Worth, 1983—; curriculum writer Palm Beach County Sch. Bd., summers 1965-67, 71-74. Contbr. articles to profl. jours. Boston U. Dean of Women's scholar, 1955-59, Trustee scholar, 1955-59, News Bur. scholar, 1955-59. Mem. Nat. Assn. Elem. Sch. Prins., Palm Beach County Prins. Assn., Assn. for Supervision and Curriculum Devel., Nat. Assn. Sch. Adminstrs., Nat. Assn. Female Execs., Fla. Assn. Sch. Execs., Palm Beach County Jr. High Prins. Assn. (sec. 1978-79), Smithsonian Instn., Media (chpt. pres. 1959), Alpha Delta Kappa (nat. corr. sec. 1971, pres. 1973), Phi Delta Kappa. Avocations: bicycling; hiking; reading; writing; knitting. Home: 3145 Collin Dr West Palm Beach FL 33406 Office: Palm Springs Elementary Sch 3563 10th Ave N Lake Worth FL 33461

HENNECY, BOBBIE BOBO, English language educator; born Tignall, Georgia, August 11, 1922; daughter John Ebb and Lois Helen (Gulledge) Bobo; A.B. summa cum laude, Mercer University, Macon, Georgia, 1950; postgraduate (English-Speaking Union scholar) Oxford (Eng.) University, 1961; M.A. (NDEA fellow), Emory University, Atlanta, Georgia, 1962; m. James Howell Hennecy, December 28, 1963; 1 daughter, Erin. Adminstrv. asst. to pres., instr. Mercer U., 1950-1961, instr. English, 1961-1976, asst. prof., 1976—. A founder Tattnall Square Acad., Macon, Ga., 1968, sec. corp., 1968-1973, dir., 1968-1978. Bobbie Bobo Hennecy scholarship award given in her honor each year to valedictorian of Tattnall Square Academy; Bobbie Bobo Hennecy Scholarship Fund established in her honor, Mercer U., 1979. Mem. AAUW (chpt. pres. 1961), AAUP, MLA, South Atlantic MLA, So. Comparative Lit. Assn., Nat. Assn. Tchrs. English, Ga. Assn. Tchrs. English, English Speaking Union, Nat. Soc. Magna Charta Dames, Soc. Descs. of Colonial Clergy, Daus. Am. Colonists, Colonial Dames XVII Century, Jamestowne Soc., DAR (registrar 1980-1982), United Daus. 1812, United Daus. Confederacy, Middle Ga. Hist. Soc., Cardinal Key, Alpha Psi Omega, Sigma Tau Delta, Sigma Mu (past pres.), Phi Kappa Phi, Chi Omega (alumnae advisor 30 years). Baptist. Home: 1347-B Adams St Macon GA 31201 Office: Mercer Univ Macon GA 31207

HENNESSEY, ALICE ELIZABETH, building materials and paper company executive; b. Havenhill, Mass., May 24, 1936; d. H. Nelson and Elizabeth E. (Johnson) Pingree; A.B. with honors, U. Colo., 1957; cert. with distinction Harvard-Radcliffe Program in Bus. Adminstrn., 1958; m. Thomas M. Hennessey, June 13, 1959; children—Shannon, Sheila, Thomas N. With Boise Cascade Corp. (Idaho), 1958—, sec. to pres., 1958-60, adminstrv. asst. to pres., 1960-61, 65-71, corp. sec., 1971—, v.p., 1974-83, sr. v.p., 1983—. Mem. Boise Jr. League; trustee Boise State U. Found. Mem. Nat. Investor Relations Inst., Investor Relations Assn., Am. Soc. Corp. Secs., Phi Beta Kappa, Alpha Chi Omega. Office: Boise Cascade Corp 1 Jefferson Square Boise ID 83728*

HENNESSEY, CATHERINE, publishing executive; b. Newark, June 6, 1950; d. Bronislaw John and Anna Florence (Savrda) Szulc; m. Edward J. Hennessey, Oct. 29, 1972. B.A., Park Coll., 1972; M.B.A., Fairleigh Dickenson U., 1983. Advt. asst. Psychology Today, N.Y.C., 1974-76, advt. coordinator Cycle mag., N.Y.C., 1976-77; asst. rate and budget mgr. Ziff Davis Pub. Co., N.Y.C., 1977-78, corp. budget mgr., 1978-85; dir. bus. services CBS Mags., N.Y.C., 1985—. Tutor, Children's Aid Soc./Project Live, N.Y.C., 1986. Mem. Nat. Assn. Female Execs. Roman Catholic. Club: NYSC Yacht (City Island, N.Y.). Avocations: sailing; gardening; theatre. Office: CBS Mags 1515 Broadway New York NY 10017

HENNIGE, MARIANNE AMALIE, accountant; b. Stuttgart, Germany, Apr. 18, 1926; came to U.S., 1952, naturalized, 1956; d. Eugen Albert and Julie Pauline (Groezinger) H.; B.B.A. magna cum laude, Northwood Inst., Midland, Mich., 1981; children—Shirley I., Sharon C. Office mgr. Dept. Army, Europe, 1946-52; supr. acctg. dept. Mich. Farm Bur. Ins., 1953-58; sec. to prin. Peck (Mich.) Community Schs., 1958-61; asst. treas., mgr. acctg. dept. Proctor Homer Warren, Inc., 1961-77; chief acct., mgr. data processing dept. Mich. Products, Inc., distbrs. ednl. materials, Lansing, 1977-84; supr. cashier's office Clark County Community Coll., North Las Vegas, Nev., 1984-85, bursar, 1985—, fin. budget analyst, 1986—; officer, dir. Sanilac County Bd. Edn. Credit Union, Sandusky, Mich. Mem. Peck Library Bd.; chmn. com. for fgn. student exchange Greater Detroit Area YMCA. Mem. Nat. Assn. Female Execs., Am. Mgmt. Assn., Lansing Accts. Assn., AAUW (treas. Las Vegas br.), Phi Theta Kappa, Beta Sigma Phi (life; chpt. pres. 1962, 64, 69-70). Office: 3200 E Cheyenne Ave North Las Vegas NV 89030

HENNINGS, DOROTHY GRANT (MRS. GEORGE HENNINGS), educator; b. Paterson, N.J., Mar. 15, 1935; d. William Albert and Ethel Barbara (Moll) Grant; A.B., Barnard Coll., 1956; M.Ed. (NSF Acad. Yr. Inst. grantee), U. Va., 1959; Ed.D. (Field Enterprise grantee), Columbia, 1965; m. George Hennings, June 15, 1968. Tchr., Pierrepont Elementary Sch., Rutherford, N.J., 1956-58, Thomas Jefferson Jr. High Sch., Fair Lawn, N.J., 1959-64; prof. edn. Kean Coll. of N.J., Union, 1965—. Recipient Edn. Press. award, 1974; Author citation N.J. Inst. Tech., Div. Continuing Edn., 1982. Mem. Nat. Council Tchrs. English, N.J. Reading Assn., Internat. Reading Assn., Phi Beta Kappa, Phi Delta Kappa, Phi Kappa Phi, Kappa Delta Pi. Author: (with B. Grant) Teacher Moves, 1971; Content and Craft: Written Expression in the Elementary Sch., 1973; Smiles, Nods and Pauses: Activities to Enrich Children's Communication Skills, 1974; Mastering Classroom Communication: What Interaction Analysis Tells the Teacher, 1975; (with G. Hennings) Keep Earth Clean, Blue and Green: Environmental Activities for Young People, 1976; Words, Sounds, and Thoughts: More Activities to Enrich Children's Communication Skills, 1977; Communication in Action: Teaching the Language Arts, 1978, 2d edit., 1982; (with D. Russell) Listening Aids Through the Grades, 1979; (with G. Hennings) Today's Elementary Social Studies, 1980; Written Expression in the Language Arts, 1981; Teaching Communication and Reading Skills in the Content Areas, 1982; (with L. Fay) Star Show, 1986, Grand Tour, 1986, Previews, 1986; contbr. articles to Edn., The Record, Lang. Arts, Sci. Tchr., Tchr. to Tchrs., Sci. and Children, Early Years, others. Home: 21 Flintlock Dr Warren NJ 07060 Office: Kean Coll of NJ Morris Ave Union NJ 07083

HENNINGSON, KATHRYN AGNES, health science educator; b. Troy, N.Y., July 11, 1953; d. Walter Robert and Marion Munroe (Lawson) H. B.S. in Edn., Trenton State Coll., 1977, M.Ed., 1980; Ph.D. in Edn., So. Ill. U., 1984. Cert. in health edn., N.J. Phys. educator Isothermal Community Coll., Forest City, N.C., 1979-80; elem. tchr. Rutherford County Schs., N.C., 1979-80; health educator I, State of N.C., Yanceyville, 1981; grad. teaching asst. So. Ill. U., Carbondale, 1981-83, grad. adminstrv. asst., 1983-84; asst. prof. applied health sci. Ind. U., Bloomington, 1984—, coordination undergrad. tchr. preparation dept. applied health sci., 1984—; cons. Am. Cancer Soc., Indpls., 1984—; co-dir. worksite health promotion project Monroe County Community Schs. Corp., Bloomington, 1985—. Grant Addiction Research Found. grantee, 1983. Mem. Am. Pub. Health Assn. (council sch. health edn. and services sect. 1985-87), Am. Sch. Health Assn. (sch. health edn. study com. 1985—), Assn. Advancement Health Edn., Ind. Pub. Health Assn., LWV, Eta Sigma Gamma (chpt. pres. 1982-83, at-large mem. nat. exec. bd. 1984-86, John P. McGovern scholarship award 1983, project grantee 1982). Democrat. Methodist. Club: Alpine Ski (Bloomington). Avocations: water and snow skiing; racquetball; golf; running; weight lifting; fishing. Office: Ind U Dept Applied Health Sci HPER 116J Bloomington IN 47405

HENNION, CAROLYN LYN LAIRD, mutual fund executive, financial planner; b. Orange, Calif., July 27, 1943; d. George James and Jane (Porter) Laird; m. Reeve L. Hennion, Sept. 12, 1964; children—Jeffrey Reeve, Douglas Laird. B.A., Stanford U., 1965. Registered securities agt., tax preparer, Calif. Portfolio analyst Schwabacher & Co., San Francisco, 1964-66; adminstrv. coordinator Bicentennial Commn., San Mateo Council Calif., 1972-73; dir. devel. Crystal Springs Uplands Sch., Hillsborough, Calif., 1973-84; tax preparer Household Fin. Corp., Foster City, Calif., 1982, freelance, 1983—; sales promotion mgr. Franklin Distbrs., Inc., San Mateo, 1984-86, regional sales mgr., 1986—. Editor: Lest We Forget, 1975. Pres. South Hillsborough Sch. Parents' Group, Calif., 1974-75; sec. Vol. Bur. of San Mateo County, Burlingame, Calif., 1975; chmn. Community Info. Com., Town of Hillsborough, 1984-86; mem., subcom. chmn. fin. adv. com., Town of Hillsborough, 1984-86. Recipient awards Council for Advancement and Support of Edn., 1981, Exemplary Direct Mail Appeals Fund Raising Inst., 1982. Mem. Inst. Cert. Fin. Planners. Republican. Club: Jr. League (San Francisco). Home: 148 Greenway Circle Medford OR 97504 Office: Franklin Distbrs 130 E Main St #282 Medford OR 97501

HENRICH-ROSS, KATHLEEN BAKER, dental hygienist, consultant; b. Providence, Dec. 25, 1947; d. Daniel Ernest Baker and Virginia Mary (Furey) Bidle; m. Clarence Dean Ross, Oct. 11, 1985. B.S. in Dental Hygiene, U. R.I., 1970. Dental hygienist various dental offices, Mass., Fla., Mo., Minn., Ga., 1970—; research cons. Forsyth Dental Research Ctr., Boston, 1970-72; research cons. Monsanto Co., St. Louis, 1973-79; ednl. cons. Dental Sci. Systems, Reston, Va., 1982—, Teledyne Water Pik, Ft. Collins, Colo., 1977—, dir. continuing edn.; pres. Candy Baker, Inc., Atlanta, 1981—. Mem. Am. Dental Hygiene Assn., Ga. Dental Hygiene Assn., Internat. Dental Health Found. Home and office: 1603-L Post Oak Dr Clarkston GA 30021

HENRIE, BETTY COLLINS, high school principal, health science educator; b. Bloomsburg, Pa., June 17, 1922; d. Clease Ransom and Mary Margaret Alberta (Rhodes) Collins; m. J. Gilbert Henrie, Jr., June 19, 1948; 1 child, Betty June. B.S., East Stroudsburg U., 1944; M.A., Columbia U., 1947; postgrad. Pa. State U., 1953-72, Bucknell U., 1958-78; Ed.D., Nova U., 1981. Cert. tchr., prin., supt., Pa. Tchr. health and phys. edn. Sr. High Sch., Berwick, Pa., 1944-45, tchr., chmn., 1950-65, dean, asst. prin., 1965-78, prin., 1978—; prof. health sci., dir. phys. edn. Shimer Coll., Mt. Carroll, Ill., 1945-48. Author: Parachute Play, 1959, revised, 1964. Instr. first aid and home nursing ARC, 1952-73; council pres. PTA, Columbia County, Pa. Named Woman of Yr., Bus. and Profl. Women Orgn., 1979. Mem. Nat. Health and Phys. Edn. Assn., Pa. Health and Phys. Edn. Assn., NEA, Pa. Edn. Assn., Pa. Assn. Secondary Sch. Prins. (chmn. research and stats.), AAUW, Delta Kappa Gamma, Kappa Delta Pi. Republican. Club: Bus. and Profl. Women (pres. 1984-86). Lodges: Eastern Star, Amaranth. Avocations: travel; fishing; golf; reading; writing. Home: 801 E 3d St Berwick PA 18603 Office: Berwick Area Sr High Sch 1100 Fowler Ave Berwick PA 18603

HENRIQUES, PATRICIA ANN, management services executive; b. New Haven, Conn., Dec. 9, 1949; d. Walter Edward and Leontine Elizabeth (Marcus) Smith; m. Vico Emanuel Henriques, Jan. 12, 1981. B.A., Conn. Coll., New London, 1971; cert. Teaching English as a Second Lang., Paris, 1971. Exec. asst. Bank of Am. NT&SA, Brussels, London, 1971-73; account exec. Cunningham & Walsh, N.Y.C., 1973-76; adminstr. Law Office T.D. Naegele, Washington, 1977-78; dir. adminstrn. CBEMA, Washington, 1978-80; adminstr. Melrod, Redman & Gartlan, Washington, 1980-83; pres., chief exec. officer Mgmt. Alternatives, Inc., Washington, 1983—. Mem. Assn. Legal Adminstrs., Am. Soc. Assn. Execs., ABA (assoc.), Nat. Assn. Female Execs. Club: Soroptomist. Office: Mgmt Alternatives Inc 1015 20th St NW Washington DC 20036

HENRY, ANNE FREDERICK, needlework and gifts wholesaler and manufacturer; b. Cleveland, Miss., Apr. 25, 1954; d. Willie Holman and Gladys Elizabeth (Gray) Frederick; m. John Blanton Henry, Aug. 21, 1976; children—Beth, Jonathan, Jo Anne. B.S. in Biology, Delta State U., 1976, M.S. in Biology, 1978. Owner, operator Annie & Friends, Cleveland, Miss., 1983—. Recipient Heart-saver award Miss. affiliate Am. Heart Assn., 1981; Lifesaver award ARC, 1985; Safer Rural Miss. award Miss. Farm Bur. Fedn., 1985. Mem. Designers Guild, Bolivar County Farm Bur., Crosstie Arts Council Cleveland, Phi Kappa Phi, Phi Mu Alumnae (pres. Cleveland 1978-80). Methodist. Avocations: needlework; aerobics; swimming. Home: Route 2 Box 77 Cleveland MS 38732

HENRY, ANNETTE EMILY, state official; b. Bklyn., Feb. 13, 1941; d. Floyd and Clementine (Owens) Brown; m. Lankford R. Henry, Jan. 1, 1959 (div. 1981); children—Kevin L., Andre W., Craig M. Student York Coll., 1974-75, Bernard Baruch Coll., 1958-60. Sec. to dep. commr. N.Y.C. Highway Dept., 1970-71, sec. to commr., 1971-72; sec. to dep. adminstr. N.Y.C. Transp. Dept., 1972-74, sec. to spl. counsel, 1974-75; sec. to chmn. N.Y. State Thruway Authority, Albany, 1975-81, asst. sec. to bd. (1st woman and black apptd. to this position), 1981—, also mem. various standing coms., bd. dirs. Employee Relations Appeal Bd., 1981—. Troop leader Hudson Valley council Girl Scouts U.S.A., Albany, 1982, neighborhood chmn., 1984; mem. Hist. Albany Found., 1984, South End Hist. Soc., Albany, 1984; bd. dirs. South End Improvement Corp., Albany; notary public, N.Y. 1986—. Recipient Exec. Devel. Inst. award Ctr. Women in Govt., 1982; Self-Devel. Strategies for Black Adminstrs. in Pub. Sector award Am. Mgmt. Assn., 1982. Mem. Nat. Assn. Female Execs. Democrat. Roman Catholic. Club: Capital Dist. Polit. Action Com. Albany (exec. sec. 1983-85). Home: 46 Osborne St Albany NY 12202 Office: N Y State Thruway Authority 200 Southern Blvd Albany NY 12209

HENRY, BEVERLY SUSAN, public relations executive; b. Lexington, Ky., Nov. 3, 1948; d. Glenn Lacy and Elizabeth (Hurst) Lacy; m. John O. Henry, Aug. 28, 1970; 1 child, Leslie Paige. B.A. in Sociology, U. Ky., 1969; M.A. in Adult and Continuing Edn., 1972. Lic. social worker, Ky. County coordinator Ky. Youth Research Ctr., Frankfort, 1969-72, asst. area supr., 1972-75, social worker tng. specialist, 1975-78; med. social worker Berea Hosp., Ky., 1978-82, dir. pub. relations, devel., 1982—. Mem. Ky. Soc. for Hosp. Pub. Relations (numerous publ. awards 1978—, treas. 1985-86), Ky. Assn. for Hosp. Devel. (v.p. 1984-85, pres. 1985-86), Nat. Assn. for Hosp. Devel., Nat. Soc. for Hosp. Pub. Relations, Nat. Assn. Social Workers, Bus. and Profl. Women's Club. Democrat. Baptist. Home: PO Box 523 Berea KY 40403 Office: Berea Hosp Estill St Berea KY 40403

HENRY, CHERYL DARLENE, nurse; b. Kansas City, Mo., Oct. 12, 1951; d. William Pitt, Jr. and Clelia Delores (Lewis) H. B.S. in Edn., Kans. State Tchrs. Coll., 1973; M.S., Emporia Kans. State Coll., 1975; B.S. in Nursing, Pittsburg State U., Kans., 1982. Registered nurse, Kans. Tchr. physical edn., social studies Unified Sch. Dist. 253, Emporia, Kans., 1973-74, Unified Sch. Dist. 612, Shawnee Mission, Kans., 1975-76; instr., women's athletic trainer Emporia State U., Kans., 1976-80; staff nurse ICU, Newman Meml. County Hosp., Emporia, 1982—; outpatient cardiac rehab. coordinator Newman Meml. County Hosp., Emporia, 1983—. Contbr. articles to profl. publs. Instr. Neosho River Free Sch., Emporia, 1985; speaker Speaker's Bur., Newman Meml. County Hosp., Emporia, 1985; instr. ARC, 1975—; bd. mem., state del., instr., speaker Am. Heart Assn. Flint Hills Chpt., 1985—. Democrat. Avocations: reading, dancing. Office: Newman Meml County Hosp 12th and Chestnut Emporia KS 66801

HENRY, DIANA MARA, photographer; b. Cin., June 20, 1948; d. Carl and Edith Entratter) Henry. A.B., Harvard U., 1969. Gen. reporter S.I., Advance, 1970; originator, dir. community workshop program Internat. Ctr. Photography, N.Y.C., 1975-77, mem. faculty, 1976-79; owner Diana Mara Henry Photography, N.Y.C., 1972—; mem. exec. bd. Friends of Alice Austen, N.Y.C., 1977—; artist-in-residence N.Y. Found. Arts, 1985-86; one-woman shows: Ballard Mill Ctr. for Arts, Malone, N.Y., 1983, Overseas Press Club, N.Y.C., 1983, Brattleboro (Vt.) Mus., 1984, Catskill Cultural Ctr., Women's Studio Workshop, 1987; group shows include: Tyler Sch. Art Temple U., Phila., Fashion Inst. Tech., N.Y.C., Art Guild, Guilford, Conn.; represented in permanent collections Nat. Archives, Library of Congress, Smithsonian Instn., Washington, Schlesinger Library on History of Women in Am., Radcliffe Coll.; contbr. articles to So. Exposure. Ofcl. photographer First Nat. Women's Conf., Houston, 1977; Nat. Commn. on Observance of Internat. Women's Yr., Washington, 1978. Recipient Ferguson History prize Harvard U., 1967; grantee N.Y. State Council Arts, 1986. Mem. Soc. Photographic Edn. Home and Office: 1160 Fifth Ave New York NY 10029

HENRY, HARRIET PUTNAM, judge; b. Ashland, Ky., Sept. 28, 1923; d. Donald Hardie and Hannah Sheldon (Russell) Putnam; m. Merton Goodell Henry, Dec. 20, 1954; children—Donald, Douglas, Martha. B.A., Smith Coll., 1945; J.D., George Washington U., 1954; LL.D., Bowdoin Coll., 1984. Bar: Va. 1954, Maine 1955, U.S. Supreme Ct. 1958. Econ. analyst Office Q.M. Gen., Washington, 1945-46; research analyst Nat. Security Agy., Washington, 1946-57; sole practice, Portland, Maine, 1957-73; judge-at-large Maine Dist. Ct., 1973—; bd. dirs. Nat. Ctr. State Cts., 1985—. Chmn. Portland Housing Authority, 1967-68; pres. LWV, Portland, 1963-65; trustee Westbrook Coll., Portland, 1977-83; mem. Maine Status of Women Commn., 1968. Mem. ABA (exec. com. Nat. Conf. Spl. Ct. Judges, Maine Bar Assn. (pres. jud. div. 1984-85), Order of Coif. Author: Maine Law Affecting Marine Resources, 1969-70 (Vols. I-IV). Home: RR1 Box 640 North Windham ME 04062 Office: PO Box 1354 North Windham ME 04062

HENRY, JOANN, sales executive; b. Santa Barbara, Calif., Sept. 9, 1952; d. Fred and Elizabeth (Andrews) Ostermiller; m. Tony Lex Henry, July 29, 1972; (div. 1977). Student N.W. Community Coll., 1971-72. Editorial asst. High Country News, Lander, Wyo., 1968-71; asst. Wyo. State Jour., Lander, 1969-71; editor, pub. relations asst., asst. to graphics N.W. Community Coll., Powell, Wyo., 1971-72; graphic artist Case Thompson Printing, Albuquerque, 1972-74; art dir., sales rep. Starline Printing, Albuquerque, 1974-79; sales rep. Charles P. Young Houston, 1979—. Recipient 1st place award Mead Paper Show, 1978, also others. Mem. Houston Assn. Young Printing Execs., Bus. Profl. Advt. Assn., Houston Graphic Communications Council, Profl. Group, Internat. Assn. Bus. Communicators. Home: 3131 Hayes Rd Apt 1316 Houston TX 77082 Office: Charles P Young Houston PO Box 2622 Houston TX 77001

HENRY, JUDITH EULISS, retirement home owner; b. Hickory, N.C., May 25, 1940; d. Ned Hartwell and Lucille (Ford) Euliss; m. James Dewitte Henry, Mar. 19, 1983; children by previous marriage—Micheal Miller, Jennifer Miller. Student Clevenger Bus., 1958-60, Caldwell Community Coll. and Tech. Inst., 1980-82, U. N.C., 1985; various seminars and courses on aging. Owner, pres. Camelot Manor Retirement Home, Inc., Granite Falls, N.C., 1978—, Camelot Manor Nursing Care Facility, Inc., Granite Falls, 1985—; instr. therapy for the aged Caldwell Community Coll., 1970-78. Ch. treas., youth dir. St. James Episcopal Ch., Lenoir, N.C.; vol. Social Services, Rest Homes, Sr. Citizens Groups, Hickory Coop. Ministry, Fish, Bloodmobile, Heart Fund, Broughton Hosp., Morganton, N.C.; pres. Granite Falls Am. Field Service; bd. dirs., pres. PTA. Recipient Woman of Yr. award Granite Falls Bus. and Profl. Women's Orgn., 1984. Home: 117 Auld Farm Rd Lenoir NC 28645 Office: Camelot Manor Nursing Care Facility Inc 100 Sunset St Granite Falls NC 28600

HENRY, KAREN HAWLEY, lawyer; b. Whittier, Calif., Nov. 5, 1943; d. Ralph Henry and Dorothy Ellen (Carr) Hawley; m. John Dunlap, June 12, 1968 (div. Dec. 1974); m. 2d. Charles Gibbons Henry, Mar. 15, 1975; children—Scott Hawley, Alexander Gibbons, Joshua Kimball. B.S., So. Oreg. Coll., 1965; M.S., Iowa State U., 1967; J.D., Hastings Coll. Law, 1976. Bar: Calif. 1976. Tchr. Medford (Oreg.) Sch. Dist., 1965-66; dir. research program Calif. Nurses Assn., San Francisco, 1967-72; labor relations coordinator Affiliated Hosps. San Francisco, 1972-76, labor counsel, 1976—; ptnr. firm Little, Mendelson, Fastiff & Tichy, San Francisco, 1979—. Author: Healthcare Supervisors Legal Guide, 1984; Nursing Adminstration and Law Manual, 1985. Mem. ABA, Calif. State Bar, San Francisco Bar Assn., Calif. Soc. Healthcare Attys. (dir. 1984—), Order of Coif. Republican. Home: 2061 Casa Nuestra Box 379 Diablo CA 94528 Office: Littler Mendelson Fastiff & Tichy 650 California St San Francisco CA 94528

HENRY, KATHERINE SAVAGE, physician; b. Marietta, Ga., Aug. 30, 1944; d. James Ernest and Audrey Louise (Armstrong) Savage; B.A., Birmingham-So. Coll., 1966; M.D., Emory U., 1971. Intern, resident in internal medicine Ga. Bapt. Hosp., Atlanta, 1971-73; emergency room physician Baylor Med. Center, Dallas, 1973-74; family physician The Family Clinic, Garland, Tex., 1974; family practice medicine, Richardson, Tex., 1974—; chmn. dept. family practice Richardson Gen. Hosp., 1975; cons. health care Richardson YWCA; exec. com. Richardson Med. Center, 1975- 78; first physician, designer health service U. Tex., Dallas, 1974-76; chairperson med. adv. com. Dallas Hospice, Inc. Diplomate Am. Bd. Family Practice. Fellow Am. Acad. Family Physicians, Am. Coll. Cryosurgery, Am. Soc. Sports Medicine; mem. AMA (physicians recognition award), Am., Tex. acads. family practice, Dallas County Med. Soc., Tex. Soc. Sports Medicine, Tex. Med. Assn., Am. Med. Women's Assn. (charter pres. Dallas chpt. 1980). Home: 16007 Ranchita Dr Dallas TX 75248 Office: 721 W Arapaho Suite 2 Richardson TX 75080

HENRY, KATHLEEN MARIE, international marketing executive; b. Stillwater, Okla., Sept. 24, 1950; d. Irl Wayne and Hulda Mary (Duncan) Henry; B.S., Central State U. (Okla.), 1972. Community relations dir./account exec. Lowe Runkle Advt., Oklahoma City, 1972-74, account coordinator, 1975; sales promotion cons. McDonald's Corp., Houston, 1974; regional advt. supr. McDonald's Southfield (Mich.), 1975, regional advt. mgr., 1976-78, local store mktg. mgr., Oak Brook, Ill., 1978-80, staff dir., store mktg./sales promotion, 1980-82, home office dir. nat. sales promotion, 1982-84, dir. internat. mktg. services, 1984-85; dir. mktg. McDonald's Systems Europe, 1985—. Publicity chmn. Keep Okla. Beautiful, 1973-74; publicity chmn. Western Okla. chpt. Muscular Dystrophy Assn. Am., 1973-74; bd. dirs. Southfield Arts Council, 1976-78. Recipient Pres.'s award, McDonald's Corp., 1978; Chgo. YWCA Leadership award, 1978; Disting. Former Student award, Central State U., 1979, Outstanding Sr. Woman, 1972, Outstanding Greek Woman, 1972. Mem. Central State U. Alumni Assn. (dir. 1974), Nat. Assn. Female Execs., Women's Advt. Club Chgo., Sigma Kappa. Home: 11 Ave Emile Deschanel 75007 Paris France Office: McDonalds Plaza Oak Brook IL 60521

HENRY, LOIS HOLLENDER, human resources executive; b. Phila., Jan. 19, 1941; d. Edward Hubert and Frances Lois (Nesler) Hollender; m. Charles L. Henry, Oct. 24, 1964 (div. 1971); children—Deborah Lee, Randell Huitt, Andrew Edward; m. 2d Thomas C. Mosley, Jr., July 11, 1978 (separated Oct. 1983). B.A., Thomas A. Edison Coll., 1979; M.S.W., Fordham U., 1981. Cert. social worker, N.Y., N.J.; lic. service profl., Ariz. Personnel asst., sec. IBM, Paterson, N.J. and St. Louis, 1964-66; minister's asst. Grace Luth. Ch., St. Cloud, Fla., 1966-68; adminstr./tchr. Fla. Finishing Acad., St. Cloud, 1968-70; adminstrv. asst. Newark Book Ctr., 1972-77; intern, med. social worker Jersey City Med. Ctr., 1979-80; intern, psychiatric/med. social worker VA Med. Ctr., Lyons, N.J., 1980-81; sch. social worker Lakeview Learning Ctr., Budd Lake, N.J., 1981-82; mgr. human resources Terak Corp., Scottsdale, Ariz., 1982—; individual/family counselor/psychotherapist, speaker, Scottsdale, 1982; mem. employers com. Ariz. Dept. Econ. Security; cons. in field. Coordinator-vol. Job-A-Thon, Phoenix, 1983. Mem. Human Resources Council for Am. Electronics Assn., Am. Orthopsychiat. Assn., Nat. Assn. Social Workers, Am. Soc. Personnel Adminstrs., Phoenix Personnel Mgmt. Assn., Am. Compensation Assn., Ariz. Affirmative Action Assn. Home: 8628 E Granada Rd Scottsdale AZ 85257 Office: Terak Corp 14151 N 76th St Scottsdale AZ 85260

HENRY, MARTHA FRANCES, dietitian; b. Columbia, Mo., Sept. 19, 1920; d. James William and Martha Frances (Robinson) Shock; B.S., U. Mo., 1941; postgrad. Iowa State U., 1940, Tex. A&M U., 1973-74; m. Walter Keith Henry, Feb. 13, 1943; children—Stephen Allen, Dale Lee, Carl Bruce. County supr. Nat. Youth Adminstrn., Jefferson City, Mo., 1941-42; dietitian Mo. State Sanatorium, Mt. Vernon, 1942-43; cafeteria mgr. Scruggs-Vandervoort-Barney, St. Louis, 1943-45; dir. food service McQuay-Norris Mfg. Co., St. Louis, 1945; asst. dir. residence halls U. Mo., Columbia, 1946-47; lab. technician Tex. A&M U., College Station, 1965-71; dietitian Bryan (Tex.) Hosp., 1972-74; cons. dietitian Sherwood Health Care Facility, Bryan, 1974-75, Hennesey Nursing Home, Giddings, Tex., 1982-84; adminstrv., clin. dietitian St. Joseph Hosp., Bryan, 1976-78; pvt. cons. nutritionist College Station, 1978—; cons. Older Adults Nutrition Program. Flower chmn. A&M Methodist Ch., 1958—; active Brazos County chpt. ARC; mem. Brazos County Hist. Com., 1972—. Mem. Am. Dietetic Assn., Am. Diabetes Assn., Tex. Dietetic Assn., Mid-East Tex. Dietetic Assn., Brazos Valley Home Econs. Assn. (state pres.), Cons. Nutritionist-Pvt. Practice Group (past pres.), DAR, Daus. Am. Colonists (regent), Colonial Dames XVII Century, U.S. Daus. of 1812, Nat. Geneal. Soc., Brazos Valley Geneal. Assn., Magna Carta Dames. Republican. Club: Order Eastern Star. Home and Office: 1202 Caudill St College Station TX 77840

HENRY, PAMELA JANE, pharmacist; b. Greenville, Ohio, Nov. 3, 1954; d. John Harry and Juanita M. (Grilliot) H. B.S. in Pharmacy, Ohio No. U., 1978. Registered pharmacist, Ohio. Staff pharmacist Children's Med. Ctr., Dayton, Ohio, 1978-79; asst. mgr. Super X Drugs, Greenville, Ohio, 1979-84, Revco, Greenville, 1984—. Mem. Am. Pharm. Assn., Ohio Pharm. Assn., Darke County Geneal. Soc., Kappa Epsilon, Alpha Omicron Pi. Roman Catholic. Avocations: music; travel; collecting. Home: 134 W Harmon Dr Greenville OH 45331 Office: Revco DS 534 S Broadway Greenville OH 45331

HENRY, PAULA KATHALEEN, investment securities sales executive; b. Amarillo, Tex., Mar. 18, 1939; d. George Ralsey and Imogene Marie (Dumas) Stevens; m. Thomas Hinckson Becker, July 15, 1972 (dec. 1980); m. 2d, Robert Paul Henry, Oct. 13, 1984. Grad. high sch. Pres., Design Spectrum, Inc., Miami, Fla., 1973-81, S.R.I. Group, Inc., Sarasota, Fla., 1980-81, West Coast Tape Systems, Inc., Sarasota, 1979-85, Tri-State Mktg. Services, Inc., Sarasota, 1979-85, Specialized Mktg. Services, Sarasota, 1979-85, North Central Tape Mktg., Inc., Sarasota, 1979-85, Mobile Custom Systems, Inc., Sarasota, 1979-85, Memphis Custom Services, Inc., Sarasota, 1979-85, Hillsborough Custom Systems, Inc., Sarasota, 1979-85, Duval Customs Systems, Inc., Sarasota, 1979-85, Dade Custom Systems, Inc., Sarasota, 1979-85, Central Custom Enterprises, Inc., Sarasota, 1979-85, Broward Custom Systems, Sarasota, 1979-85, Sounds Personal, Inc., Sarasota, 1979-85, Investment Resources, Sarasota, 1980—, So. Resources, Sarasota, 1980—; salesman Henry Realty, Inc., Sarasota, 1980-81, owner, 1984—; salesman Stevens & Salt, Inc., Sarasota, 1982-84; registered rep. DHC Securities, Inc., N.Y.C., 1983—; registered rep., owner Diversified Security Investments, Inc., Sarasota, 1981-83. Mem. Nat. Assn. Securities Dealers, Inc.; former mem. Internat. Assn. Financial Planners, Inc. Republican. Episcopalian. Club: Cat Cay (membership com.) (Bahamas). Home: 6123 Willshire Circle Sarasota FL 33583 Office: Southern Resources Inc PO Box 21268 Sarasota FL 33583

HENRY, REGINA MARY GOFF, educator; b. St. Louis; d. Ward Wellington and Annabelle (Young) Goff; B.A. in Edn., Northwestern U., 1934; M.A., Columbia, 1940, Ph.D., 1948; m. Josiah F. Henry, Jr., Sept. 23, 1960. Dir. nursery sch., St. Louis, 1935; tchr. kindergarten, Kansas City, Kans., 1936-39; instr. Lincoln U., Jefferson City, Mo., 1940-46; dir. student teaching Stowe Tchrs. Coll., St. Louis, 1947-48; prof. child devel. Fla. A. and M. Coll., Tallahassee, also supr. Fla. Dept. Edn., 1949-50; mem. faculty Morgan State Coll., Balt., 1950-65, chmn. dept. edn., 1963-65; asst. commr., office of programs for disadvantaged U.S. Office Edn., Washington, 1965-71; prof. U. Md., 1971—; Union Grad. Sch., Union Exptl. Colls. and Univs., 1976—; cons. Ministry Edn. Iran, 1955-56. Mem. child welfare com. Md. Conf. and Welfare, 1960-62; pres. Urban League Md., 1961-63, bd. dirs., 1959-64; bd. dirs. UN of Md., Children's Guild Md., UNICEF of Md. Recipient Pub. Service in Edn. awards Urban League Balt., 1963, St. Louis Assn. Negro Women's Clubs, 1965, Nat. and Profl. Bus. Women's Clubs, 1966, Alpha Kappa Alpha, 1966; Rockefeller Found. fellow, 1945-46. Mem. Am. Psychol. Assn., Md. Assn. Tchr. Edn. (pres.), NEA, Pi Lambda Theta, Kappa Delta Pi, Psi Chi, Phi Delta Kappa, Alpha Kappa Alpha. Democrat. Roman Catholic. Contbr. articles on ednl. studies, cultural influence on personality devel. to ednl. jours. Home: 2306 Montebello Terr Baltimore MD 21214

HENRY, SANDRA KEDNOCKER, civic worker, small business investment corporation executive; m. Charles J. Henry; 2 children. B.A., U. N.C., 1959; postgrad. U. Cin., 1966-67. Pres. Intervest Group, 1984-85. Bd. dirs. North Shore Country Day Sch., Union League Found. Boys Clubs, Illinois Club, House of the Good Shepherd; mem. Consular Ball benefit com. of Library of Internat. Relations; chmn. Sept. Ball of the Children's Home and Aid Soc. Ill., 1984; bd. mgmt., v.p. sustaining membership, benefit chmn. Jr. League Chgo., 1984-85; mem. woman's bd., mem. ball com. Chgo. Heart Assn., 1985; mem. benefit com. Brookfield Zoo, 1985; history of active leadership in geneal. socs., pub. TV, archtl. preservation, community and ednl. organs., symphony orchs., convalescent hosp. for children. Mem. Nat. Soc. Fund Raising Execs., U. N.C. Alumni Assn., Nat. Soc. Daus. Am. Colonists, Nat. Soc. Daus. Founders and Patriots Am., Nat. Soc. Daus. Colonial Wars. Clubs: Fortnightly of Chgo., Woman's Athletic.

HENRY, SHIRLEY ANN, press executive; b. Los Angeles, Apr. 23, 1937; d. Austin Perry Shaver and Ann (Pitrucka) Wilhelm; m. Walter Sigman Henry, July 1, 1955 (dec. Oct. 1985); children—Debbie Henry Johnson, Shelly Henry Dozier, Derek Sigman. A.A. with honors, Contra Costa Coll., San Pablo, Calif., 1969. Lic. R.N., Calif. Nurse, VA Hosp., Martinez, Calif., 1970-73; chief exec. officer Lamorinda Press, Lafayette, Calif., 1976—. Baptist. Avocations: skiing; scuba diving. Office: Lamorinda Press 3409 C Mt Diablo Blvd Lafayette CA 94549

HENRY, SHIRLEY SHANNON, hardware company executive, architectural hardware consultant; b. Anacortes, Wash., Nov. 14, 1929; d. Thomas Marion and Alice Pauline (Gillespie) Shannon; m. Jaymes Francis Berg, Mar. 24, 1949 (div. Oct. 1955); 1 child, Thomas Andrew; m. Eugene W. Henry, June 24, 1960. Student U. Puget Sound 1947-49. Price clk. N.W. Builders Hardware, Seattle, 1949-59, office mgr., 1956-59; v.p. Builders Hardware & Supply Co., Seattle, 1959-84, pres., 1984—; archtl. hardware cons. Mem. Constrn. Specification Inst. (Pres.'s award 1973, Tech. Excellence award 1976, Albert E. Barnes award 1979, sec. 1974-76), Archtl. Hardware Cons. Republican. Presbyterian. Avocations: reading; gardening; sewing. Office: Builders Hardware & Supply Co 1516 15th Ave W Seattle WA 98119

HENSEL, SANDRA JEAN, museum executive; b. Akron, Nov. 8, 1948; d. Hubert Adam and Lucille Katrine (Rogers) H. B.A., Lake Erie Coll., 1970; M.A., Kent State U., 1980; student U. Madrid, 1969. Owner, producer World's Fare Rev., N.Y.C., 1972-78; producer/co-host Sta. WNEO-TV, Kent, Ohio, 1980-81; news reporter, producer Sta. WJAN-TV, Louisville, Ohio, 1981-82; producer. co-host Sta. WNEO TV, Kent, 1983-84; dir. pub. relations Akron Art Mus., 1982—; cons. ARC Press, Cleve., 1983, Kaleidoscope Mag., 1983. Mem. adv. bd. Akron Arts Festival, 1984, state meeting Ohio Arts Council, 1982. Mem. Pub. Relations Soc. Am., Akron Press Club, Actors Equity, AFTRA. Club: Lake Erie Coll. Office: Akron Art Mus 70 E Market St Akron OH 44308

HENSELMEIER, SANDRA NADINE, training and development consulting firm executive; b. Indpls., Nov. 20, 1937; d. Frederick Rost Henselmeier and Beatrice Nadine (Barnes) Henselmeier Enright; m. David Albert Funk, Oct. 2, 1976; children—William H. Stolz, Jr., Harry Phillip Stolz II, Sandra Ann Stolz. A.B., Purdue U., 1971; M.A.T., Ind. U., 1975. Exec. sec. to dean Ind. U. Sch. Law, Indpls., 1977-78; adminstrv. asst. Ind. U.-Purdue U., Indpls., 1978-80, assoc. archivist, 1980-81; program and communication coordinator Midwest Alliance in Nursing, Indpls., 1981-82; tng. coordinator Coll./Univ. Cos., Indpls., 1982-83; pres. Better Bus. Communications, Indpls., 1983—; adj. lectr. Ind. U.-Purdue U. at Indpls., 1971—, U. Indpls. Center Continuing Mgmt. Devel. and Edn., Indpls., 1984—. Contbr. articles to profl. jours. Mem. ASTD, Assn. Bus. Communication, Assn. Profl. Writing Cons., Ind. C. of C., Indpls., C. of C. Republican. Presbyterian. Avocations: traveling; walking; reading; learning new ideas. Office: Better Bus Communications 6208 N Delaware St Indianapolis IN 46220

HENSHAW, SIGRID MARGUERITE, lawyer, accountant; b. Des Moines, Aug. 19, 1932; d. Hadar Oscar and Marguerite (Gonda) Ortman; m. Peter S. Cascio; m. 2d, Harold W. Henshaw, Apr. 2, 1977. B.B.A. with distinction, Northwestern U., 1963; J.D., South Tex. Coll. Law, 1978. Bar: Okla. 1978; Fla. 1985; C.P.A., Ill., Tex., Okla. Managerial positions with C.P.A. firms and various corps., Phoenix, Chgo. and Los Angeles, 1955-71; asst. sec., dir. corporate tax Cordura, Inc., Los Angeles, 1971-73, Geosource, Ind., Houston, 1973-76; C.P.A. in individual practice, Tulsa, 1977—; sole practice law, Tulsa, 1978-80; mng. atty. Henshaw & Leblang, Tulsa, 1980—. Mem. ABA (tax sect.), Okla. Bar Assn., Tulsa County Bar Assn., Fla. Bar Assn., Assn. Am. Trial Lawyers (sustaining), Okla. Soc. C.P.A.s (mem. tax liaison com.), Tex. Soc. C.P.A.s, Tulsa County Bar Assn., Delta Mu Delta, Phi Alpha Delta. Republican. Roman Catholic. Home: 4406 E 82d St Tulsa OK 74137 Office: Henshaw & Leblang 7661 E 61st St Suite 251 Tulsa OK 74133

HENSLER, SONJA HOPE, school administrator; b. Bklyn., Apr. 26, 1943; d. John Norman Hope and Dorothy Ann (Hagan) Hope Anderson; m. Robert James Hensler, June 3, 1964; children—Eric Dylan, Kimberly Liesle. B.A. in History, Edn., Hofstra U., 1964; Ed.M. in Adminstrn. and Supervision, U. South Fla., 1980. Tchr. Patchegue High Sch., N.Y., 1965-67; tchr., prin. Clearwater-Largo Christian Sch., Fla., 1970-80; prin. St. Petersburg Christian Sch., Fla., 1980—. Mem. Flags (v.p. 1984—), Phi Alpha Theta, Phi Kappa Phi. Hofstra U. scholar, 1960-64. Republican. Avocations: reading; travel; sailing. Home: 11568 108th Ave N Largo FL 33544 Office: Saint Petersburg Christian Sch 2021 62d Ave N Saint Petersburg FL 33702

HENSLEY, JOANNA, talent management and tourist agency executive; b. Asheville, N.C., Dec. 9, 1939; d. Alice Gertrude (Bates); m. Olen Eugene Hensley, Sept. 22, 1955; children—Debra Jean, Michael Eugene. Ed., Anchorage Community Coll., LaSalle U. Owner-mgr. JoAnna's Diner, The Village Sq., Anchorage, 1971-73; sr. citizens programs dir. Salvation Army, Community YMCA, Anchorage, 1970-75; tour dir. Allways Travel, Anchorage, 1973-83; v.p., gen. ptnr. Jolido Agy. Ltd., Anchorage, 1982—. Resident services coordinator Alaska State Housing Authority. Home: 1701 Brink Dr Anchorage AK 99504

HENSLEY, MARGARET ANN, swimming pools distributing company official; b. Knoxville, Tenn., May 6, 1941; d. Herman Geissler and Carrie Lucille (Wilmoth) Ballard; children—Dennis Keith Logan, David Wayne Logan, John Ballard Pecora, Felicia Ann Pecora; m. Bill Clyde Hensley, Mar. 27, 1981. Student, Dale Carnegie Sch., 1969. Head subscriptions New Woman mag., Fort Lauderdale, Fla., 1974-75; med. asst. Medi Lab Systems, Fort Lauderdale, 1975-76; mgr. Swimming Pool Owners Assn., Fort Lauderdale, 1976-78; accts. receivable clk. Outdoor World Distbrs., Fort Lauderdale, 1978-81, purchasing agt., 1984—, asst. mgr., 1986—; credit mgr. Miller Assocs., Miami, Fla., 1981-83. Mem. Nat. Assn. Female Execs., Gold Coast Women in Credit. Avocations: golfing; bowling.

HENSON, GENE ETHRIDGE, legal administrator; b. Lawrenceville, Ga., Sept. 26, 1924; d. Fred Golden and Cora Jewell (Smith) Ethridge; student public schs., Lawrenceville; m. James Arthur Henson, May 2, 1948 (dec.); 1 dau., Gena Arlene. With Smith, Currie & Hancock, Atlanta, 1959—, adminstr., 1965—. Ofcl. hostess for State of Ga., So. Gov.'s Conf., Atlanta, 1971; past adult tchr. First Bapt. Ch., Lawrenceville; mem. adv. council Center for Profl. Edn., Ga. State U. Mem. Am. Bar Assn. (assoc.), Assn. Legal Adminstrs. (nat. v.p. 1979—, dir. 1979-83), Atlanta Assn. Legal Execs. (1st pres. 1975), Assn. Legal Adminstrs. (v.p. Atlanta chpt., pres.-elect 1986-87). Home: 74 Scenic Hwy Lawrenceville GA 30245 Office: Smith Currie & Hancock 2600 Peachtree Center Harris Tower Atlanta GA 30043

HENSON, OLEEN MAJORS, emeritus business educator; b. Winchester, Tenn., Mar. 19, 1922; d. James Thomas and Dora (Weaver) Majors; B.S., Tenn. Tech. U., 1943; M.A. in Edn. (grad. fellow), U. Ky., 1944; Ed.D., Temple U., 1964, M.Edn. Counseling, 1984; m. James Benjamin Henson, Aug. 8, 1946; children—David James, Cynthia Lynn. Asso. prof. Ga. State Woman's Coll., Valdosta, 1944-46; acctg. instr. Tenn. Tech. U., Cookville, 1946-49; instr. bus. edn. Temple U., 1963-65, asst. prof., 1965-69, asso. prof., 1969-75, prof., from 1975, now prof. emeritus; mem. project team Phila. Bus. Acads., 1972-78, adv. bd., 1982; study and evaluation teams Long Branch High Sch., Freehold Sch. Dist., Lakewood High Sch.; judge Future Bus. Leaders Am., Pa. state Leadership Conf., 1975, 77—; vol. counselor St. Peter's Episcopal Ch., Medford, N.J. Recipient Outstanding Service award St. Peter's Episcopal Ch., Medford, N.J., 1981, 82, Mem. Am. Vocat. Assn., AAUP Nat. Bus. Edn. Assn., Eastern Bus. Edn. Assn., Pa. Bus. Edn. Assn. (Post Secondary Educator of Yr. 1979), Phila. Bus. Tchrs. Assn., Am. Psychol. Assn., Am. Assn. Counseling and Devel., Delta Pi Epsilon (Achievement awards 1972, 78, 82), Phi Delta Kappa, Phi Beta Lambda (leadership award 1980). Democrat. Episcopalian. Club: Arrowhead Racquet. Author: (with others) Gregg Shorthand, Individual Progress Method, Diamond Jubilee Series, 1972, Series 90, 1982, Gregg Shorthand Dictation and Transcription, Individual Progress Method, 1974, Series 90, 1982; editor Delta Pi Epsilon Jour., 1978-82; co-editor Nat. Bus. Edn. Yearbook, 1974. Home: 38 Lenape Trial Medford Lakes NJ 08055 Office: 211 Ritter Annex College of Education Temple University Philadelphia PA 19122

HENTREL, BOBBIE KUYKENDALL, elementary school principal; b. Batesville, Miss., Sept. 9, 1938; d. James and Ethel Kuykendall; B.S., Tenn. State U., 1960; M.Ed., 1964; Ph.D., U. Mich., 1975; m. Percy Gonya Hentrel, Jan. 15, 1965; 1 son, Michael Lovell. Tchr., Memphis City Schs., 1960-69; tchr. Grand Rapids (Mich.) Public Schs., 1969-73; lectr. U. Mich., 1973-75; asst. prin. Southfield (Mich.) Schs., 1975-79, prin., 1979—; pres. Kuykendall Enterprises, pub. co. Co-author: Computers in Education—A Guide for Educators. Fulbright Hays award, Germany, 1975-76. Mem. Nat. Assn. Secondary Sch. Prins., Mich. Assn. Secondary Sch. Prins., Nat. Assn. Elem. Sch. Prins., Mich. Assn. Secondary Sch. Prins., Nat. Assn. Elem. Sch. Prins., Southfield Assn. Sch. Adminstrs., Mich. Assn. Elem. Sch. Prins., Nat. Assn. Supervision and Curriculum Devel., Delta Sigma Theta, Phi Delta Kappa. Democrat. Methodist. Home: 17577 E Goldwin St Southfield MI 48075 Office: 18575 W Nine Mile Rd Southfield MI 48075

HENTZ, MARIE EVA, real estate investor, manager, developer; b. Detroit, Sept. 27, 1920; d. Charles and Eva (Follman) Hentz. Student Detroit Bus. U., Wayne State U. Draftsman, Cadillac Motor Co., Detroit, 1941-44; stenographer Great Lakes Steel Co., River Rouge, Mich., 1945-46, Can. Nat. R.R., Detroit, 1946-49; sec. Union Oil Co. Calif., Los Angeles, 1950-72; real estate investor, mgr., developer, Burbank, Calif., 1950—; gen. ptnr. Hentz & Christensen, Ltd., South El Monte, Calif., 1953-85, Hentz Properties, Ltd., Burbank, 1971-85. Mem. Union Oil Women's Club. Republican. Avocations: gardening; reading; travel.

HENTZLER, JANET C., construction company executive; b. Memphis, June 21, 1948; d. Paul Martin and Oletta (Rowland) Aycock; children—Lynn Dale, Jenny Anne. Student Memphis State U., 1966-68, Midwest Ct. Reporters Sch., 1980-82, Houston Community Coll., 1984-86. Project sec. W-M Industries, Houston, 1981-83, Blazer Bldg. Co., Houston, 1983-84; exec. adminstrv. asst. Frontier Constrn. Co., Houston, 1984—. Organizer Community Election, Houston, 1983. Avocations: reading; tennis; school functions. Home: 17487 Red Oak Houston TX 77090 Office: Frontier Construction Co 6617 Flintlock Houston TX 77090

HENZE, GERALDINE LELA, educator, consultant; b. Newark, May 14, 1949; d. John Dean and Dorothy Althea (Daleske) H. B.A., Smith Coll., 1971. Instr. written and oral communication Harvard Bus. Sch., Boston, 1976-78; tech. editor United Engrs. and Constructors, Boston, 1978-80; dir. communications program Columbia Bus. Sch., N.Y.C., 1980—; cons. Author: From Murk to Masterpiece, 1984. Mem. Women in Communications, N.Y. Women in Communication, Internat. Assn. Bus. Communicators, Am. Bus. Communication Assn., Soc. Gen. Semantics, Mgmt. Communication Assn. Home: 788 Amsterdam Ave #4N New York NY 10025

HENZE, NANCY HARMEL, investent banker; b. Balt., July 7, 1946; d. Merel H. and Armide E. (Chilcoat) Harmel; m. Horace J. Caulkins, III, Sept. 21, 1968 (div. Mar. 1978); m. 2d, William F. Henze II, Oct. 3, 1980. A.B., Vassar Coll., 1968; M.B.A., NYU, 1977. Assoc., Bache Halsey Stuart Shields, N.Y.C., 1977-78, Dillon Read & Co., Inc., N.Y.C., 1978-82; sr. v.p. Shearson Lehman Bros., Inc., N.Y.C., 1982—. Office: Shearson Lehman Bros Inc Two World Trade Ctr New York NY 10048

HEPBURN, KATHARINE, actress; b. Hartford, Conn., 1909; d. Thomas N. and Katharine (Houghton) Hepburn; m. Ogden Ludlow (div.). Numerous appearances in motion pictures and theater including A Bill of Divorcement (film debut), 1932, Morning Glory, 1933; (Academy award for best actress), Little Women, Spitfire, The Lake (play), Alice Adams, Sylvia Scarlett, Mary of Scotland, Women Rebels, Quality Street, Stage Door, Bringing Up Baby, Holiday, Break of Hearts, Christopher Strong, The Philadelphia Story (play), Woman of the Year, 1942; Without Love (play), 1942; Keeper of the Flame, 1943; Dragon Seed, 1944; Undercurrent, 1946; Sea of Glass, 1946; Song of Love, 1947; State of the Union, 1948; Adams's Rib, 1949; As You Like It (play) (Rosalind), 1950; African Queen, 1951; Pat & Mike, 1952; The Millionairess (play Eng. and U.S.A.), 1952; Summertime, 1955 (award Acad. Motion Picture Arts and Scis. 1955); Iron Petticoat, The Rainmaker, The Desk Set, 1957; (plays) Taming of the Shrew, Merchant of Venice, Measure for Measure (Eng.

and Australia), 1955; Much Ado About Nothing, 1957 (plays); Suddenly Last Summer, 1959 (film); Long Days Journey into Night (motion picture), 1962; Guess Who's Coming to Dinner (motion picture), 1967 (Acad. award for best performance by actress 1968); Lion in Winter (Acad. award best actress 1969); Mad Woman of Chaillot, 1969; Trojan Women, 1971; appeared on stage in CoCo (musical), N.Y.C., 1970, on tour 1971; A Delicate Balance (movie), 1973; Glass Menagerie (TV movie), 1973; Love Among the Ruins (TV movie), 1975; A Matter of Gravity, N.Y. and tour, 1976-77; The Corn is Green (movie for TV), 1979; On Golden Pond (motion picture), 1981; The Ultimate Solution of Grace Quigley, 1985; Mrs. Delafield Wants to Marry (TV movie), 1986. Recipient gold medal as world's best motion picture actress, Internat. Motion Picture Expn., Venice, Italy, 1934; N.Y. Critic's award for performance in picture The Philadelphia Story, 1940; ann. award Shakespeare Club N.Y.C., 1950; Whistler Soc. award, 1957; Hasty Pudding Club's ann. Woman of Yr. award, 1958; Outstanding Achievement award for fostering finest ideals of acting profession, 1980; Lifetime Achievement award Council of Fashion Designers of Am., 1986. *

HEPNER, MARY LOUISE, ballet company director; b. Woodstock, Va., Feb. 22, 1949; d. Max Knighton and Kathleen (Mantz) H. B.F.A. in Art History, Old Dominion U.; postgrad. Wesleyan U. Cert. dance tchr. Dancer Jose Limon Co., Hartford Ballet, Conn., Virginia Beach Ballet Co., 1976-70; instr. Hartford Ballet, 1976-81; co-dir. Wilkes Barre Ballet Theatre Co., Pa., 1981—. Bd. dirs. Econ. Devel. Council, Wilkes-Barre, Fine Art Commn., Wilkes-Barre. Mem. Wilkes-Barre C. of C. (chmn. cultural affairs), Northeast Regional Ballet Assn. (chmn. membership). Avocation: acting. Office: Wilkes Barre Ballet Theatre 102-104 S Main St Wilkes Barre PA 18702

HEPTINSTALL, DEBRA LOU, newspaper executive; b. Tacoma, Mar. 5, 1952; d. Fred Bernard and June Isabella (Carter) H.; m. Michael Emory Smith, Sept. 26, 1980; m. Duval Meade McDaniel, Feb. 16, 1974 (div. Feb. 1978). Cert. Central Va. Community Coll., 1970, A.A.S. cum laude, 1973; student Longwood Coll., 1971-72. Advt. mgr. Times Record/Roane County Reporter, Spencer, W.Va., 1976-78; advt. clk., sales asst. The Washington Post, 1978-79, ind. sales contractor, 1980-81, advt. sales rep., 1981-85, mktg. analyst, 1985—; advt. mgr. The Reston Times, Va., 1979-80. Republican. Methodist. Avocations: playing classical piano. Home: 3927 Fairview Dr Fairfax VA 22031 Office: The Washington Post 1150 15th St NW Washington DC 20071

HERBERT, BARBARA RAE, librarian, educational media specialist; b. Neptune, N.J., Apr. 1, 1955; d. Raymond Louis and Grace Caroline (Freiermuth) Swan; m. Edward O. Herbert, Jr., June 7, 1986. A.A. cum laude, Ocean County Coll., 1974; B.A., Georgian Ct. Coll., 1976; M.L.S., Rutgers U., 1982. Ednl. media specialist, N.J., 1983. Substitute tchr. Brick Twp. Schs. (N.J.), 1976-77; dir. instructional materials/media ctr. Georgian Ct. Coll., Lakewood, N.J., 1977—; media cons. Lakewood Learning Ctr., 1980-81. Brick Twp. Fine Arts Guild drama scholar, 1972. Mem. ALA, N.J. Library Assn., Ednl. Media Assn. N.J., Nat. Audio Visual Assn., Assn. Audio-Visual Technicians, Ocean County Coll. Alumni Assn., Delta Tau Kappa, Gamma Sigma Sigma. Republican. Presbyterian. Club: Ocean County Alumnae of Georgian Ct. Coll. Office: Instructional Materials/Media Center Georgian Court Coll Lakewood Ave Lakewood NJ 08701

HERBERT, EUGENIA WARREN, history educator; b. Summit, N.J., Sept. 8, 1929; s. Robert Beach and Mildred (Fisk) Warren; m. Robert Louis Herbert, June 6, 1953; children—Timothy D., Rosemary, Catherine. B.A., Wellesley Coll., 1951; M.A., Yale U., 1953, Ph.D., 1957. Asst. prof. history Quinnipiac Coll., Hamden, Conn., 1970; lectr. history Yale U., New Haven, 1972-73, 76, collaborator with R.S. Lopez, 1971, research affiliate, 1976-79; asst. prof. history Mt. Holyoke Coll., South Hadley, Mass., 1978-82, assoc. prof., 1982-85, E. Nevius Rodman prof., 1985—; sr. assoc. mem. St. Anthony's Coll., Oxford U. (Eng.), 1978. Author: The Artist and Social Reform, 1961; (with Claude-Anne Lopez) The Private Franklin (Boston Globe award 1976), 1975; Red Gold of Africa, 1984; Red Gold: Copper Arts of Africa; film (with Candice Goucher and Carlyn Saltman) the Blooms of Banjeli, 1986; contbr. articles to profl. jours. Mem. Bethany Democratic Com., 1970-77; mem. Bethany Sch. Bd., 1964-68; pres. Ctr. for Ind. Study, New Haven, 1977. Fulbright fellow, Vienna, Austria, 1951-52; Mellon faculty fellow Mt. Holyoke Coll., 1982; Donner Found. fellow, 1982-85; NEH mus. grantee, 1984. Fellow Royal Geog. Soc.; mem. African Studies Assn., Am. Hist. Assn., Hist. Metallurgy Soc., Assn. Concerned African Scholars. Office: Dept History Mt Holyoke Coll South Hadley MA 01075

HERBERT, SALLY MARY, accountant; b. Grenada, Miss., Oct. 8, 1948; d. William Archie and Gladys Marie (Vance) H.; m. Gil Lewis Turchin, Jan. 1, 1981. B.B.A., U. Miss., 1973. C.P.A., Miss., Tex. Staff acct. Deloitte Haskins & Sells, Memphis, Tenn., 1974-79, supr., 1979-80, mgr., 1980-82, mgr., New Orleans, 1982-83, mgr., Dallas, 1983-84; pres. Pro Cons., Inc., 1984—. Mem. cast pub. TV film How to Reconcile Your Bank Account, 1977-79; mem. editorial bd. The Woman C.P.A., 1979-81. Chmn. coms. Provida; vol. Girls Clubs of Memphis, 1977-80; mem. budget coms. United Way, Memphis, 1976-78. Recipient Gold medal Miss. State Bd. Pub. Accountancy, Jackson, 1974. Mem. Am. Soc. Women Accts. (bd. dirs. 1977-81, v.p. 1978-79, pres. 1979-80), Am. Woman's Soc. C.P.A.s (nat. bd. dirs. 1980-81), Tenn. Soc. C.P.A.s (state council 1980-81), Bus. Adminstrn. and Acctg. Alumni Assn. U. Miss. (bd. dirs. 1983—), Assn. Women Entrepreneurs of Dallas. Office: Pro Consultants Inc 5750 Pineland Dr NE Suite 303 Dallas TX 75231

HERBORT, NOELIA SALDANA, journalist; b. Crystal City, Tex., Apr. 7, 1927; d. Herman and Sara (Delgado) Saldana; m. Manuel L. Martinez, Dec. 8, 1943 (div. 1957); children—Diana Noelia, Elizabeth, Manuel L.; m. Walter Henry Herbort, Jr., Jan. 7, 1972. Writer, editor Spanish page Zavala County Sentinel, Crystal City, 1954, soc. editor, proof reader, news writer, 1955-60; news corr. San Antonio Express News, 1960-64; news dir. Sta. KEPS, Eagle Pass, Tex., 1963; news dir. Sta. KBEN, Carrizo Springs, 1963—; news writer, editor Spanish sect. South Tex. Star, 1981—. Sec. Dimmit County Child Welfare Bd., Carrizo Springs, 1983-86, We Care Charitable Com., Carrizo Springs, 1983—; mem. Carrizo Springs Sch. Dist. Community Edn. Council, 1985—. Mem. Nat. Assn. Broadcasters, Tex. Assn. Broadcasters. Democrat. Roman Catholic. Club: Lioness (v.p.). Avocations: reading; needleworking; quilting. Home: 400 N 13th St Carrizo Springs TX 78834 Office: KBEN Radio PO Box 335 203 S 4th St Carrizo Springs TX 78834

HERD, CHARMIAN JUNE, educator, singer, actress; b. Waterville, Maine, June 1, 1930; d. Samuel Braid and Jennie (Lang) Herd; B.A., Colby Coll., 1950; M.Ed., U. Maine, 1964; postgrad. Boston U., 1951; ednl. cert. No. Conservatory, Bangor, Maine, 1954; also study voice with Roger A. Nye. Dir. music State Sch. for Girls, Hallowell, Maine, 1950-51; head English, French, dramatics dept. St. George High Sch., Tenants Harbor, Maine, 1951-52; dir. music pub. schs. Albion, Unity, Maine, 1952-54, Troy, Freedom, Maine, 1953-54; dir. music pub. sch. system Belgrade, Maine, Waterville Jr. High Sch., 1954-55; dir. vocal music Waterville Jr. and Sr. high schs., 1954-58; head English and dramatics depts. Besse High Sch., Albion, 1959-62; tchr. French, English and drama Skowhegan High Sch., 1962-69; tchr. French, Adult Edn. Sch., 1963—; dir. dramatic arts program Skowhegan Sch. Adult Edn., 1966-69; instr. French, Lawrence Sr. High Sch., Fairfield, Maine, 1969-71, chmn. dept. drama and speech, 1972-79; dramatics instr. U. Maine at Farmington 1969-70; soloist various chs., Maine, 1951—; soloist numerous club, ch., conv., coll. concerts, oratorios. 1st pres., performing mem. Waterville Theatre Guild, music dir., 1967—; performing mem. Theatre at Monmouth (Maine), Portland Lyric Theatre; chmn. bd. Augusta Players; mem. Camden Civic Theatre; mem. Titipu Choral Soc.; program chmn. Albion PTA; mem. Waterville Community Ballet Theatre, 1975—; bd. dirs. Waterville Opera House, 1975—; trustee Theater at Monmouth, 1970—, sec. bd. trustees, 1977—; 1st v.p. New Eng. Theatre Conf., 1976-77, fall conf. chmn., 1977; theatre chmn. Ann. Maine Festival of Arts, Bowdoin Coll., Brunswick, 1978. Mem. Waterville Friends Music, DAR (music chmn. Winslow (Maine) 1955-57, sec. 1957-59, vice regent 1959-61, regent 1961-62, Maine advt. chmn. 1958-60); Actors' Equity, Ednl. Speech and Theatre Assn. of Maine (state pres. 1972-74), Waterville Bus. and Profl. Women's Club (program chmn. 1957-58, v.p. 1958-59, pres. 1959-61, chmn. drama dept. 1961), Albion-Burnham Tchrs. Club. (sec. 1960-61), Bay State Post Card Club, R.I. Post Card Club, Pine Tree Post Card Club (chmn. Portland Mini-Show 1980-82, exec. bd. 1979-82, pres. 1983—), Internat. Platform Assn., New Eng. Theatre Council (dir. 1975—), NEA, Maine Tchrs. Assn., Theatre Assn. Maine (exec. bd. 1972-74, 2d v.p. 1973-74, exec. sec. 1975-76, state pres. 1976—), Actors Equity, Portland Lyric Theatre (sec. bd.), Vero Beach Ch. Soc., Riverside Theatre, Vero Beach theatre Guild, Treasure Coast Opera Co., Ft. Pierce, Fla., 1985—, others. Club: Cecilia (Augusta, Me.). Composer sacred music: Babylon, 1959, The Greatest of These is Love, 1961; Pan, 1963; Keep Not Thy Silence, O God; Remember Now Thy Creator; Slow, Slow, Fresh Fount; A Witch's Charm; Hymn to God The Father. Home: 12940 US Hwy I PO Box 714 Roseland FL 32957

HERLOCKER, MARY RYAN, nurse, administrator; b. Tonica, Ill., Jan. 3, 1934; d. Oliver H. and Dorothy (Hiltabrand) Ryan; m. J. Fred Herlocker, May 12, 1956; children—John F. Jr., Julia A. R.N., Evanston Hosp. 1955; B.S. with honors Nat. Coll. Edn., 1981, M.S., 1982. Head nurse emergency Evanston Hosp. (Ill.), 1955-57, trauma nurse, 1978-79, clin. coordinator, 1979-80; legis. aide. Ill. Sen. Bradley Glass, Northbrook, Ill., 1975-78; nurse cons. Weber Automated Systems, Chgo., 1980-82; nurse adminstr. The Mather, Evanston, 1982—; chmn. Health and Human Services Com. New Trier Twp., Winnetka, Ill., 1982-84. Pres. Women of Ch. of Holy Comforter, Kenilworth, Ill., 1968; co-dir. campaign Glass for State Treas., Northbrook, 1977; pres. New Trier Twp. High Sch. Caucus, Winnetka, 1978. Mem. Am. Nurses Assn.(council on gerontol, nursing, council on long-term care adminstrs.), Nat. Coll. Alumni Assn. Republican. Episcopalian. Home: 844 Boal Pkwy Winnetka IL 60093

HERMAN, CAROL KORNGUT, advertising agency executive; b. Atlantic City, Oct. 14, 1952; d. Richard F. and Regina (Kornblau) Korngut; m. Henry Lewis Herman, Dec. 30, 1972; children—Matthew, Gregory. B.A., U. Pa., 1972. Asst. account exec. Honig-Cooper and Harrington Advt., N.Y.C., 1973-74; asst. account exec. Grey Advt., N.Y.C., 1974-75, account exec., 1976-78, account supr., 1978-80, v.p., mgmt. supr., 1981-84, v.p., group mgmt. supr., 1985—. Office: Grey Advt 777 3d Ave New York NY 10017

HERMAN, EDITH CAROL, public relations executive; b. Edgewood, Md., July 1, 1944; d. Herbert and Thirza (Simmons) Herman; m. Leonard H. Wiener, June 16, 1974. B.A., Purdue U., 1966. Writer, reporter Hollister Pubs., Wilmette, Ill., 1966-68; reporter Chgo. Tribune, 1968-79, edn. editor, 1971-74; sr. editor TV Digest, Washington, 1980-83; media relations mgr. AT&T, Washington, 1983—. Recipient Journalism award Ill. Edn. Assn., 1969-70; Editorial award Ill. Automatic Merchandising Council, 1977. Mem. Sigma Delta Chi. Avocations: gardening; travel photography. Home: 5501 Burling Ct Bethesda MD 20817 Office: AT&T 1120 20th St NW Washington DC 20036

HERMAN, LISA LINN, meat merchandiser; b. Omaha, Nov. 11, 1961; d. Larry Lee and Judy Kaye (Ensminger) Herman. B.S.B.A., U. Fla., 1983. Cashier Publix Supermarkets, Gainesville and Lakeland, Fla., 1978-84; meat merchandiser Fleming Cos., Inc., Geneva, Ala., 1984—. Nat. Food Brokers Assn. scholar, 1983; George Jenkins Found. scholar Publix Supermarkets, Inc., 1980-83; Nat. Honor Soc. scholar, 1980. Mem. Nat. Assn. Female Execs., Phi Chi Theta, Alpha Xi Delta. Office: Fleming Cos Inc 1015 W Magnolia Ave Geneva AL 36340

HERMAN, LUCY-JO, public relations and advertising executive; b. Petersburg, Va., Nov. 5, 1935; d. Joseph John Malloy and Lucy (Powell) Malloy Miller; B.A., U. Pa., 1956, M.A., 1972; postgrad. Phila. Sch. Psychoanalysis, 1972-75; m. M. William Herman, Nov. 15, 1975; 1 dau., Emily Anne; children by previous marriage—Stephen Michael, Philip Joseph and Elisabeth-Jo Constantine Stephano. Exec. dir. Arts Found., 1967, C & B Toys, 1968-72; exec. cons., 1972-75; v.p. spl. projects Harriet Carter, Inc., Montgomeryville, Pa., 1975-84, charge Lynne's Miniature Treasures div., 1975-84; pub. relations and advt. dir. Pine Run Community Doylestown, Pa., 1984—. Mem. bd. Republican Women, 1966; publicity dir. County Reps., 1967, personnel dir., 1967-68. Mem. Nat. Assn. Miniature Enthusiasts, Miniature Industry Assn. Am., Delaware Valley Lyric Opera, Mensa (cert. of merit 1972). Contbr. articles to periodicals. Office: Pine Run Community Ferry and Iron Hill Rds Doylestown PA 18901

HERMANN, MARY KEVIN HOWARD, nurse, educator; b. St. Lawrence, Ky., Oct. 26, 1934; d. Charles Kevin and Mary M. Howard; R.N., St. Mary's Sch. of Nursing, Evansville, Ind., 1955; B.S. cum laude in Nursing, U. Evansville, 1970, M.A., 1972, M.S.N. in Nursing, 1974; Ed.D. in Higher Edn., Ind. U., 1984; m. Robert R. Hermann, Feb. 2, 1957; children—Michael R. (dec.), Barbara K., Leah M., Daniel J. Staff nurse St. Mary's Med. Center, Evansville, Ind., 1955-56, head nurse, 1956-58, asst. dir. nursing service, 1965-68; instr. nursing U. Evansville, 1970-73, asst. prof., 1973-76, assoc. prof., 1976-84, prof., 1984—, asst. dean baccalaureate program, 1974-80. Mem. adv. com. Am. Heart Assn. Program, Evansville, 1981. Mem. Am. Nurses Assn., Ind. Nurses Assn. (co-chmn. commn. on edn., chmn. task force on competencies, dir., dir. dist. 4 1982-84), Am. Assn. Critical Care Nurses. Home: 8011 Maple Ln Newburgh IN 47630 Office: 1800 Lincoln Ave Evansville IN 47702

HERMANOFF, SANDRA MARLENE, public relations administrator; b. Canton, Ohio; d. Max and Sylvia (Levin) Weisbrod; m. Michael Joel Hermanoff, Nov. 27, 1976; 1 son, Jeffrey Howard. B.A. in Journalism, Pub. Relations, Ohio State U., 1965. With Ont. Brewers Inst., Toronto, 1965; copywriter Miller Advt., Columbus, Ohio, 1965; asst. pub. relations dir. Huntington Nat. Bank, Columbus, 1965; pub. relations dir. Sta. CFTO-TV, Toronto, 1968-69; instr. pub. relations, journalism Humber Coll., Toronto, 1969-71; pub. relations adminstr. Liza Minnelli-Desi Arnaz Celebrity Tennis Tournament for Children's Asthma Research Inst. and Hosp., Denver, 1971, with Investor Relations, Toronto, 1972; with Continental Pub. Relations, Toronto, 1975-76; pub. relations dir. W.B. Doner and Co., Southfield, Mich., 1982-85; pres. Hermanoff & Assocs., Inc., 1985—. Mem. Pub. Relations Soc. Am. (accredited), Pub. Relations Soc. Am. Counselors Acad. (v.p.), Women in Communications, Detroit Press Club, Detroit Econs. Club. Office: Hermanoff & Assocs 31700 W 13 Mile Rd #202 Farmington Hills MI 48018

HERMANUZ, GHISLAINE, architect, educator; b. Lausanne, Switzerland, Apr. 28, 1942; came to U.S., 1968, d. Max and Manotte (Tauernier) H.; 1 child, Dahoud P. Walker. Architecture degree, ETH/L, Lausanne, 1967; student Harvard U., 1969; M.S. in Urban Planning, Columbia U., 1971. Registered architect, Switzerland. Architect, The Architects Renewal Com., Harlem, N.Y., 1971-72; urban designer Dept. City Planning, N.Y.C., 1972-73; lectr. Cornell U., Ithaca, N.Y., 1972-74; asst. dean for minority affairs, asst. prof. Columbia Sch. Architecture, N.Y.C., 1975-82, assoc. prof., 1982-84, dir. Community Design Workshop, 1984—; cons. in field; ptnr. PHD Assocs., N.Y.C., 1982—. Contbr. numerous articles to profl. jours. Fulbright scholar, 1968; fellow German Marshall Fund, 1979; grantee Nat. Endowment for Art, 1982, New York State Council on the Arts, 1984. Mem. Societe D'Ingenieurs et Architectes. Office: Columbia Univ Sch Architecture New York NY 10027

HERMENET, ARGELIA M. BUTTRAGO, psychologist, educator, radio and television producer, songwriter; b. Panama, Mar. 2, 1934; d. Samuel and Maxima (De Leon) Buitrago; m. Raymond A. Hermenet, Apr. 7, 1955; children—Raymond, Maxine Joy, Melinda, Melanie. Student U. Pacific, 1951-52, U. Panama Sch. Social Work, 1951, 52-54; B.S., Springfield Coll., 1958, M.Ed., 1960; Ed.D. (Acad. fellow), U. Mass., 1971. Exec. sec. Pan-Niram Shipping Co. (Marin, Inc.), Panama City, Panama, 1951-53, medico-social caseworker Inst. Interam. Affairs, Santo Tomas and Children's Hosp., 1953-55; med. sec. Geneva Gen. Hosp., N.Y., 1955-56;' night clk. IBM dept. Springfield-Monarch Life Ins. Co., Mass., 1956-57; social worker North End Area Ministry, Springfield Council Chs., 1959-61; developer Maestros & Amigos, home tutorial English as 2d lang. program, 1959-65; social caseworker Child and Family Service, 1962-72; assoc. prof. Springfield Coll., part-time 1969-72; dir. bicultural programs Springfield Tech. Community Coll., 1972-75; cons. psychologist Boston Sch. System, 1977; cons. nat. curriculum series Assn. Supervision and Curriculum Devel., HEW; lectr. in field; cons. to Pres. of Panama, 1983—, coordinator plans and programs, 1983—; mem. State Adv. Council on Bilingual Edn., 1971—, mem. steering com., 1972—, chmn. higher edn. com., 1972-76; chmn. linguistic minority access com. Mass. Adv. Council Vocat. and Tech. Edn., 1973—; founder, producer, dir. Latino, 1st bilingual TV program in New Eng., 1969—; incorporator New Eng. Spanish-Am. Regional Inst., 1970-74, mem. exec. com., 1970-74, sec., 1971-74, chmn. pub. relations, 1971-72; producer, hostess bilingual TV show Sta. WGGB, 1968—. Coordinator Mass. Juan Fiesta Com., 1960-61, 63; mem. Mayor's Minority Group Housing Com., 1962-64; mem. Mayor's Human Relations Commn., 1966-72, sec., 1967-70; sec. Springfield Area Mental Health Bd., 1967-76; mem. exec. com. Area Manpower System, 1970-71; mem. Mass. adv. com. U.S. Commn. on Civil Rights, 1971—, also mem. P.R. com.; mem. com. on rent control Springfield City Council, 1971-72; mem. Springfield's Mayor's com. to negotiate Springfield Plan with trade unions and mgmt. for more minority group participation, 1971-72; co-founder Springfield Free U., 1970; mem. Gov.'s Commn. on Status of Women, 1971-72; mem. exec. com. Gov.'s Comprehensive Health Planning Adv. Council, 1971-76, sec., 1973-75; mem. State Adv. Council Mental Health; founding mem. Hispanic-Am. House, 1963-64, sec., dir., 1963-71; bd. dirs. Casa Credit Union, 1967-75; bd. dirs., incorporator Interfaith Housing Corp.; incorporator, 1st v.p. 1st Hispanic Fedn. Springfield, 1970-71; bd. dirs., chmnn. pub. relations com. Vis. Nurses Assn., 1972-74; mem. steering com. Hartford-Springfield Edn.-Work Council. Recipient award community service Springfield Action Com., 1974; Mujer award for TV contbns., Hartford, 1977. Mem. Am. Guidance and Personnel Assn. (bd. dirs., exec. bd. Mass. chpt. 1972-74), Spanish Am. Union (bd. dirs., 1971-73, sec. 1971-73, co-chmn. 1972-73), World Affairs Council (bd. dirs. Connecticut Valley 1965-73), Sigma Lambda. Home: Vinamar Coco del Mar Apt 3-B Panama City Panama also 37 Westernview St Springfield MA 01108 Office: Presidence of the Republic Panama City Panama

HERMES, PATRICIA MARY, writer, educator; b. Bklyn., Feb. 21, 1936; d. Frederick Joseph and Jessie (Gould) Martin; m. Matthew E. Hermes, Aug. 24, 1957 (div. Oct. 1984); children—Paul, Mark, Tim, Matthew, Jennifer. B.A., St. John's U., 1957. Tchr., Rollingcrest Jr. High Sch., Takoma Park, Md., 1957-58, Delcastle Tech. High Sch. (Del.), 1972-73, Norfolk Schs. (Va.), 1981-82; author Harcourt Brace Jovanovich, Inc., San Diego, 1980—, also for Dell and Scholastic. Author: What If They Knew, 1980; Nobody's Fault, 1981; You Shouldn't Have to Say Goodbye, 1982; Who Will Take Care of Me, 1983; Friends Are Like That, 1984; (young adult novel) A Solitary Secret, 1985; contbr. articles to profl. jours. Mem. Soc. Children's Book Writers, Authors Guild. Democrat. Roman Catholic. Home: 1414 Melville Ave Fairfield CT 06430

HERMINGHOUSE, PATRICIA ANNE, educator; b. Melrose Park, Ill., Mar. 13, 1940; m. 1964, 2 children. B.A., Knox Coll., 1962; M.A., Washington U., 1965, Ph.D. in German, 1968. Asst. prof. German, U. Mo.-St. Louis, 1966-67, vis. lectr., 1968-69; asst. prof. Washington U., St. Louis, 1967-78, assoc. prof. German, 1978-83; Fuchs prof. German studies, U. Rochester, N.Y., 1983—, also chmn. dept. fgn. langs., lits. and linguistics; lectr. German, Fontbonne Coll., 1965-66. Internat. Research & Exchanges Bd. ad hoc grantee, 1976. Mem. MLA, Am. Assn. Tchrs. German (exec. council 1979-81), Soc. Study Multi-Ethnic Lit. U.S., Coalition Women German (coordinator 1974-75, nat. steering com. 1976-79). Contbr. articles to profl. jours.; editor or co-editor: Literatur der DDR in den Siebziger Jaren, 1983; Literatur und Literaturtheorie in der DDR, 1976; Frauen in Mittelpunkt/Focus on Women, 1985; editor GDR Bull.: Newsletter Lit. and Culture in German Dem. Republic, 1975-83. Address: Dept Fgn Langs Lits and Linguistics U Rochester Rochester NY

HERMUNDSTAD, SARA SEXSON, lawyer; b. Stuttgart, W.Ger., Mar. 29, 1955; came to U.S., 1956, naturalized, 1970; d. Julius Calvin and Coyla Jeane (Fields) Sexson; m. Mark Allen Hermundstad, Oct. 18, 1980; 1 child, Ann Michelle. B.A., Colo. State U., 1977; J.D., U. Colo., 1980. Bar: Colo. 1980. Law clk. NW Council of Govts., Frisco, Colo., 1979-80, assoc. Gerald B. Feather, P.C., Grand Junction, Colo., 1981-82; sole practice, Grand Junction, 1982—; mem. Selection Com. for Fed. Magistrate, Grand Junction, 1981. Speaker various orgns., including Women's Resource Center, 1981-83; mem. adv. bd. for day care for sick children Family Health West. Mem. ABA, Colo. Bar Assn., Mesa County Bar Assn., PEO, Altrusa (bd. dirs.). Home: PO Box 1513 Grand Junction CO 81502 Office: PO Box 2539 Grand Junction CO 81502

HERNANDEZ, GRISELLE CLAUDIA, hospital administrator, health field consultant; b. Havana, Cuba, May 18, 1953; d. Sabino and Maria (Vigoa) H. A.A., Miami Dade Jr. Coll., 1974; B.S., Fla. Internat. U., 1977; B.Pub. Adminstrn., Biscayne Coll., 1979. Ednl. services rep. Blue Cross of Fla., Miami, 1971-75, profl. relations rep., 1975-79; with fin. services dept. Mt. Sinai Med. Ctr., Miami Beach, Fla., 1979-83, asst dir. mktg., 1983—; cons. to various physicians, Miami, 1980—; cons. Humana Corp., Miami, 1980, Centro Medico de los Andes, Bogota, Colombia, 1983; guest educator Mil. Hosp., Bogota, 1983. Contbr. articles to profl. jours. Tchr. dance and cooking summer program YWCA, Miami, 1973, 74. Ford Found. scholar, 1968-70. Mem. Hosp. Fin. Mgmt. Assn., Nat. Assn. Female Execs., Profl. Women's Assn. Democrat. Home: 6101 N W 198th Terr Miami FL 33015 Office: Mt Sinai Med Ctr 4300 Alton Rd Miami Beach FL 33140

HERNANDEZ, KATHLEEN NYMAN, nurse; b. Chester, Pa., June 21, 1945; d. Ralph Henry and Beatrice Frances (Arico) Nyman; m. Alfred Joe Hernandez, Jr., July 18, 1970; children—Katelena Laura, Marc Andrew, Elizabeth Ann. B.S. in Nursing, U. Mich., 1967. R.N., Tex., Mich. Staff nurse Citizens Hosp., Houston, 1975; officer mgr., gastrointestinal asst. nurse A.J. Hernandez, Jr., M.D., P.A., Houston, 1976—. Served to lt. USNR, 1966-70. Mem. Soc. Gastrointestinal Assts., Tex. Med. Soc. Aux., Sigma Kappa. Presbyterian. Home: 12206 Clearfork Dr Houston TX 77077 Office: 1200 Binz Suite 650 Houston TX 77004

HERNÁNDEZ, NÉLIDA, banker; b. San Juan, P.R., Feb. 28, 1954; d. Adolfo and Nelida I. (González) Hernandez; 1 child, Luis Medina-Hernández. B.A. in Econs., U. P.R., 1971, M.B.A., 1982. Asst. prof. U. P.R., Río Piedras, 1971-72; cons. P.R. Planning Bd., Santurce, 1973-76; mgmt. trainee Chase Manhattan Bank, Hato Rey, P.R., 1976-78, mktg. researcher, 1978-80, mktg. research mgr., 1980-83, product devel. and research mgr., 1983-85, mktg. mgr., 1985—; prof. mktg. Am. Inst. Banking, San Juan, 1981—, Res. U. P.R., 1984—; dir. Revista de Economía, Río Piedras, 1971-73. Contbr. articles to profl. publs. Pres.'s grantee U. P.R., 1972. Mem. Am. Mktg. Assn. (chpt. com. dir. 1982-83), Asociación de Economistas de P.R., World Future Soc. Methodist. Home: 4F Apt 13 204 St Colinas de Fairview PR 00926 Office: Chase Manhattan Bank GPO Box 1990 San Juan PR 00936

HERNANDEZ, VICTORIA, youth organization executive; b. N.Y.C., Aug. 22, 1952; d. Guillermo and Victoria H. Student Syracuse U., 1970-72; B.A., Hampshire Coll., Amherst, Mass., 1975; M.Ed., U. Mass., 1981. Cert. tchr., Mass. Instr. English, N.E. Farmworker Council, Northampton, Mass., 1976-77; mem. faculty U. Mass., 1977-78; dir. Los Jardines del Barrio Inc., El Paso, Tex., 1979-80; instr. English, El Paso Community Coll., 1980-81; paralegal D.C. 37 Legal Services, N.Y.C., 1981-84; exec. dir. Aspira of Fla., Inc., Miami, 1984—. Co-founder Hispanic Coalition for Human Rights, Northampton, 1976-78; mem. Coalition of Hispanic Am. Women, Miami, 1985—; mem. hispanic leadership devel. program United Way, Miami, 1985—; sec. Orgn. Pub. Relations Democrats, 1984—. U. Mass. fellow, 1976-78. Mem. Greater Miami C. of C., Nat. Conf. Pub. Relations Women. Democrat. Roman Catholic. Avocations: jogging; dancing; photography; radio operator. Office: Aspira of Fla Inc 2902 NW 2d Ave Miami FL 33127

HERNANDEZ-BEASLEY, SILVIA, hair design and beauty business executive, cosmetic product developer; b. Guanajuato, Mex., Sept. 1, 1945; d. Jesus L. and Ezequiela (Sierra) H.; m. Kenneth Ray Beasley, Oct. 10, 1965 (div. 1982); children—Theresa Elizabeth, Kenneth Ray II. Lic. cosmetologist Rogers Beauty Sch., Detroit, 1963; Cert. in Gen. Esthetics, Internat. Sch. Aestheticians and Make-up Artists, N.Y.C., 1975; student Inst. Facial Design, Woodland Hills, Calif., 1978, Aestheticains Internat. Assn., Chgo., 1982; Advanced tng. Rockman's U.S.A. Ctr., N.Y.C., 1984. Owner, pres. Exotic Hair Design, Detroit, 1964—, Dearborn, Mich., 1971-77, Maeva Cosmetics, Detroit, 1981—, Ichiban Nails, Detroit, 1982—, Universal Nails Wholesaler, Detroit, 1983—, La Romana, Las Vegas, Nev., 1983—. Designer of mktg. concepts, packaging Maeva Cosmetics, Ichiban Nails, 1981—. Sec. Hispanic Orgn. Promoting Entrepreneurs, Detroit, 1979-80; mem. Gov. Blanchard's 1700 Club, Lansing, Mich., 1983—; officer Mex. Patriotic Com., Detroit, 1985—. Recipient Achievement award Redkin Labs., 1976; Product Packaging and Design 1st place award Aestheticains Internat. Assn., 1983. Mem. Nat. Aestheticians Nail Artists (pres. Mich. chpt. 1983—), Aestheticians Internat. Assn. (co-founder, v.p. Mich. chpt. 1981-83), Americoif, Sigma Pi Epsilon. Roman Catholic. Club: Fairlane Country (Dearborn). Avocations: Oil painting; ceramics; interior design; horseback riding. Office: Maeva Cosmetics 8529 W Vernor Hwy Detroit MI 48209

HERNDON, GLORIA ELAINE, insurance company executive; b. St. Louis, Aug. 9, 1950; d. Charles Dickens and Corine (Jackson) Bozeman; m. Brent Astaire Herndon, Apr. 16, 1977. A.A., Washington U., St. Louis, 1968; B.A., So. Ill. U., 1970; M.A., Johns Hopkins U., 1972; Ph.D., Ahmadu Bello U., Nigeria, 1980. Internat. economist USDA, Washington, 1973-75; economist, diplomat Dept. State, Washington, 1975-82; escort, interpreter, 1984-85; fin. planner Equitable Life Ins. Co., Rockville, Md., 1985—; trade cons. Kaduna C. of C., 1982-83, Dept. Commerce, 1983-84. Contbr. articles to profl. jours.

Active various civic orgns. Recipient Disting. Service award So. Ill. U., 1970. Mem. Nat. Assn. Life Underwriters, D.C. Life Underwriters Assn., D.C. C. of C., Nat. Assn. Economists, Johns Hopkins Alumni Assn., Mu Phi Epsilon. Avocations: piano; cello; organ; dance; handicrafts. Home: 642 F St NE Washington DC 20002

HEROLD, KATHLEEN FLYNN, city official; b. Fairbanks, Alaska, May 31, 1945; d. John Bernal and Helen Pauleen (McClain) Flynn; m. Gordon P. Heddell, Jan. 5, 1965 (div. June 1970); children—Gregory Peter, Luwana Marie. Student pub. schs. Anchorage. Cert. mcpl. clk. Mcpl. clk., Matanuska-Susitna Borough, 1967-69, City Bethel, Alaska, 1970-73, adminstrv. asst. Yupiktak-Bista, Bethel, 1973-75; owner Kathy's Bookkeeping, Anchorage, 1975-79; office mgr. Whitney Fidalgo Seafoods, Homer, Alaska, 1979-80; mcpl. clk. City Homer, 1980—. Den mother Boy Scouts Am., 1976-78; sec. St. Augustine's Episcopal Ch., 1983, sr. warden, 1985-86; treas. St. Mary's Playschool, Anchorage, 1978-79. Mem. Alaska Assn. Mcpl. Clks. (past pres., bd. dirs. 1984), Internat. Inst. Mcpl. Clks. (bd. dirs. 1985). Club: Kachemak Swim (v.p. 1983). Avocations: hiking; walking swimming; skiing.

HERPST, MARTHA JANE, artist, art educator; b. Titusville, Pa.; d. Henry Howard and Lou (Cupler) Herpst; student Pa. Acad. Fine Arts, Phila., 1931, Grand Central Sch. Art, N.Y.C. (medalist 1932), 1931-33; studied with Guy Pene DuBois, 1941. Began painting in oils at age of 9 yrs; sold first portrait at 12 yrs.; specializes in portraits; exhibited Nat. Arts Club, N.Y.C., 1933—, Butler Art. Inst., Youngstown, O., 1938, Ogunquit (Me.) Art Assn. Summer Show, 1951, 53, Catherine Lorillard Wolfe Art Club, 1954, 57, Am. Artist Profl. League, 1953—; represented in permanent collection Nat. Arts Club. Titusville (Pa.) Masonic Lodge, with portrait of Charles T. Evans, Titusville Woman's Club with portrait of Laura W. Luce, Titusville YWCA with portrait of Mrs. Fred B. Howland, USMC League with portrait of Capt. Robert Lee Green, Titusville Recreation Center with portrait of Mrs. Charles Burgess, Gannon Coll. with portrait of Archbishop John Mark Gannon, St. Benedict's Convent, Erie, Pa. with portraits of Sisters. Tchr. art St. Joseph Acad. High Sch., Titusville, 1955-69; portrait of Martha McKinney Fleming, McKinney Hall U. Pitts. Titusville Campus. Mem. Am. Artists Profl. League, Titusville Bus. and Profl. Women's Club. Clubs: Nat. Arts, Woman's Titusville Country. Republican. Roman Catholic. Home: 118 W Main St Titusville PA 16354

HERRICK, CAROLE LYNN, educator, trumpet player; b. Washington, June 16, 1949; d. Harold Colton and Doris Lorene (Cosper) H. Mus.B. with high honors, U. Tex., Austin, 1971, Mus.M., 1972; Ph.D. in Music Edn., North Texas State U., 1981. Trumpet player Midland (Tex.)-Odessa Symphony, 1966-67, Austin Symphony, 1967-73, Irving (Tex.) Symphony, 1974-76; Ark. Symphony, 1981—; band dir. Dallas Ind. Sch. Dist., 1973-76; mem. brass faculty, teaching fellow North Tex. State U., Denton, 1976-78; mem. brass faculty Brookhaven Coll., Dallas, 1978-80; assoc. prof. music Hendrix Coll., Conway, Ark., 1980—; clinician and adjudicator instrumental music, 1976—. North Tex. State U. research grantee, 1979-80; Hendrix Coll. research grantee, 1982. Mem. Music Educators Nat. Conf., Ark. Music Educators Assn., Ark. State Band and Orch. Assn., Ark. Elem. Music Educators Assn., Ark. Bandmasters Assn., Alpha Lambda Delta, Phi Kappa Phi, Pi Kappa Lambda, Sigma Alpha Iota, Pi Lambda Theta. Presbyterian. Office: Box 135 Hendrix Coll Conway AR 72032

HERRICK, DORIS EILEEN SCHLESINGER, sports association executive; b. Salina, Kans., Mar. 6, 1928; d. Jefferson Seligman and Jessie Merle (Nothern) Schlesinger; B.A., Ottawa (Kans.) U., 1949; m. William F. Herrick, June 5, 1948 (div. 1973); children—William Robert, David Michael, Susan Carol. Reporter, Arkansas City (Kans.) Daily Traveler, 1947; writer commls. Arkansas City Radio Sta., 1949; office mgr. Charlotte Finn Interior Design, White Plains, N.Y., 1973-78; exec. dir. Eastern Tennis Assn., White Plains, 1978—, Eastern Youth Tennis Found., 1979-83, Jr. Tennis Found., 1983—; mem. U.S. Tennis Assn., 1980—. Trustee, First Bapt. Ch. White Plains, 1979-83, pres., 1977-79, pres. woman's guild, 1960-64, 73; bd. dirs. Purchase (N.Y.) Community House, 1967-69; pres. Lake St. Sch. PTA, Harrison, N.Y., 1965-67, Purchase Sch. PTA, 1967-69; v.p. Met. Assn. Bapt. Women, 1962-64. Mem. AAUW (last v.p. Westchester br. 1966), N.Y. Soc. Assn. Execs. Democrat. Club: White Plains Woman's (pres. 1970-72). Home: 24 Fairview Ave White Plains NY 10603 Office: 202 Mamaroneck Ave White Plains NY 10601

HERRICK, KATHLEEN MAGARA, social worker; b. Mpls., Oct. 18, 1943; d. William Frank and Mary Genevieve (Gill) Magara; B.A. in Social Work and French, Coll. St. Benedict, St. Joseph, Minn., 1965; M.S.W. (Mildred B. Erickson fellow 1975), Mich. State U., E. Lansing, 1976; m. John Middlemist Herrick, Feb. 5, 1966; children—Elizabeth Jane, Kathryn Mary. Social worker II, Carver County Social Services, Chaska, Minn., 1965-70; therapist St. Lawrence Community Mental Health Center, Lansing, Mich., 1974-75; sch. social worker Ingham Intermediate Sch. Dist., Mason, Mich., 1975-76; home/sch. coordinator Eaton Intermediate Sch. Dist., Charlotte, Mich., 1976-81; caseworker St. Vincent Home for Children, Lansing, 1979-80; tchr. cons. for severely emotionally impaired, 1981-83; behavior disorder cons., 1983-85; sch. social work cons., 1985—. Vice chmn. bd. dirs. Eaton County Child Abuse and Neglect Prevention Council; Democratic precinct del.; bd. dirs. Catholic Social Services, Lansing. Mem. NEA, Mich. Edn. Assn., Okemos High Sch. Parent Orgn., Kinawa Parent Orgn., Nat. Assn. Social Workers, Nat. Assn. Retarded Citizens, Am. Orthopsychiat. Assn., Mich. Assn. Sch. Social Workers, Mich. Assn. Emotionally Disturbed Children, Eaton County Assn. Retarded Citizens, Feingold Assn. SE Mich., NOW, Nat. Women's Health Network, Amnesty Internat., Phi Kappa Phi, Phi Alpha. Democrat. Roman Catholic. Home: 2330 Shawnee Trail Okemos MI 48864 Office: 1790 E Packard Hwy Charlotte MI 48813

HERRICK, SUSAN KATHLEEN, computer company executive, design consultant; b. Duluth, Minn., Oct. 25, 1944; d. Lewis Carl and Gwendolyn Ann (Mohr) Erickson; m. Donald Richard Herrick, July, 1970; children—Ann Kathleen, Amy Laurel. B.A., Carleton Coll., 1966. Mgr. Analysts Internat. Corp., Mpls., 1974-79; cons. dir. Comtra Systems, Mpls., 1983—; pres. Cedar Cons., Inc., Mpls., 1980—, also dir. Republican. Avocations: reading; tennis; sports. Home: 12300 60th Ave N Plymouth MN 55442 Office: Cedar Cons Inc 5353 Wayzata Blvd Suite 401 Minneapolis MN 55416

HERRIN, CHARLENE ANN, educator; b. Bristol, Conn., Sept. 26, 1947; d. Charles E. and Margaret A. (Brondi) Maynard; m. John R. Herrin, Nov. 13, 1976 (div. 1981); m. Philip Sweeney, 1986. B.S., Central Conn. State Coll., 1969; M.A., U. Hartford, 1975. Instr., Palm Beach Prep. Sch., 1978-79; with Jordan Marsh Dept. Store, 1979, Gucci Shoppe, 1980, Lord & Taylor, West Palm Beach, Fla., 1981-82; primary resource tchr. learning disabilities Northboro Elem. Sch., West Palm Beach, 1980-82; programmer trainee electronic data systems, Dallas, 1982-83; instr. math., computer sci. Hockaday Sch., Dallas, 1983-85, Plano, Tex., 1985—; cons. Gifted and Talented Assn. Tex., Dallas, 1984—. Vol. hostess Young Republicans, Dallas, 1984—. Mem. Nat. Math. Assn., Nat. Reading Assn., Nat. Computing Orgn. Home: Apt 315 4055 Frankford Rd Dallas TX 75252 Office: Hughston Sch 2601 Cross Bend Plano TX 75023

HERRIN, DIAN, financial administrator b. San Diego, Oct. 16, 1932; d. Maurice Simpson and Lota Mitchell (Chambers) Todd; A.A. in Bus. Adminstrn., Soule Coll., New Orleans, 1952; student Calif. Lutheran Coll., Moorpark; B.S. in Behavioral Sci., UCLA; m. Richard Lee Herrin, May 7, 1955 (dec.); adopted children—Richard Lee, Dawn Lea. Various secretarial and office positions, 1950-75; dir. Tri Valley Alcohol Info. and Referral Center, Simi Valley, Calif., 1975-76, various temporary positions, 1976-85; lead facilitator Driving While Intoxicated Pilot Program, Ventura County, Calif., 1976-77; office mgr. Counselors of Alcohol Addictions and Related Disorders, Van Nuys, Calif., 1977-79; owner, operator Pet Experience, Simi Valley; fin. adminstr. Cal-Col Industries, Inc., Colorado Springs, Colo., 1985—; owner, breeder Rancho Capri Dobermans 1970-85; asst. project dir. ASSERT, Simi Valley, 1978-80; part-time crisis intervention counselor Interface Community, Newbury Park, Calif., 1978-81; adult edn. tchr., 1976—; chmn. Ventura County Alcoholism Adv. Bd., 1975-76; sec.-treas. Calif. Assn. Alcoholism Adv. Bds., 1976; agt., spl. services supr. Pa. Life Ins. Co. Mem. Doberman Pinscher Club Am., Counselors on Alcohol Addictions and Related Disorders, Nat. Assn. Alcoholism Counselors, Sierra Club. Republican. Office: 16027 Ventura Blvd Encino CA

HERRIN, KATHRYN KAY, broadcaster; b. Omaha, June 6, 1959; d. Harold George Jr. and Verda Lee (Bree) H. B.J. in Broadcasting, U. Nebr., 1982—. Announcer Sta. KIMB, Kimball, Nebr., 1978-82; program dir. Sta. KRLN, Canon City, Colo., 1982—; pres. AERHO (broadcasting hon.), 1981-82. Author/dir. (plays) Saga of the Good Gunfighter, 1981; Shame, 1982. Active Fremont Civic Theater, Canon City, 1982—; sec. Fremont County Chem. Abuse Steering Team, 1983—. U. Nebr. Regents scholar, 1977. Mem. AAUW. Republican. Methodist. Lodge: Eagles. Avocations: reading; horses; softball; rugby. Home: 1008 Macon St Apt B Canon City CO 81212 Office: Sta KRLN 1615 Central St Canon City CO 81212

HERRIN-BACKER, KAY, land company executive; b. Maryville, Mo., Mar. 16, 1942; d. Graham Harley and Nora Belle (Noakes) Edwards; m. Stanton Levelle Herrin, July 3, 1959 (div. 1977); 1 child, Kelly Joe; m. Hans O. Backer, Dec. 14, 1985. Grad. high sch., Wasco, Calif., 1960. Cotton broker asst. S.A. Camp Cos., Bakersfield, Calif., 1960-65; pub. relations mgr. Wismer & Becker, Sacramento, Calif., 1965-79, tng. dir., 1977-79, constrn. adminstrn. mgr., 1979-84; project mgr. Teichert Land Co., Sacramento, 1984-85, v.p., 1985—; lectr. Stanford U. Constrn. Mgmt. Inst., Palo Alto, Calif., 1982-83, Calif. State U.-Sacramento Constrn. Mgmt. Course, 1981-83. Author: W&B Management Manuel, 1979. Pres. bd. dirs. Sta. KXPR Pub. Radio, Sacramento, 1980, Jr. Achievement, Sacramento, 1976; bd. dirs. Eskaton, Sacramento, 1984-85, Salvation Army, Sacramento, 1981; mem. Gov. Deukmejians Efficiency Team, Sacramento, 1983. Named Disting. Businesswoman in Non Traditional Field, Sacramento Chamber, 1981. Mem. Urban Land Inst., Corp. Planners Assn., Sacramento Area Commerce and Trade Orgn. Avocations: skiing; sailing; interior design; music. Office: Teichert Land Co 3500 American River Dr Sacramento CA 95864

HERRING, DEBBIE LAJUAN, placement specialist; b. Gatesville, Tex., Apr. 10, 1952; d. John Thomas and Wanda Pearl (Ingram) H. B.S. in Criminal Justice, U. Houston, 1978, postgrad., 1983—. Transcript analyst Houston Community Coll., 1973-77, buyer, 1977-80, career assoc., 1980-81, interviewer, 1981-82, career specialist, 1982-84, women's support specialist, 1984; guest speaker Tex. Prison System Richmond, 1980-84; mem. adv. bd. Womens Support Services, Houston, 1983-86, Coll. Publs., 1983-84. Named Woman of Yr Houston Community Coll., 1983. Mem. Jr. Coll. Student Personnel Assn. Tex., Council Coll. Adminstrs., Coll. Office Personnel Assn. (sec. 1977-78). Office: Houston Community Coll Sam Houston Campus 9400 Irvington St Houston TX 77076

HERRING, DIANA LEA, corporation executive; b. Henderson, Tex., Dec. 7, 1944; d. Barney Lee and Julia Fay (Gentry) Waldrop; m. Franklin Herring, Nov. 29, 1961; 1 child, Clinton Franklin. B.S., U. Mich., 1975; A.S., Jackson Community Coll., 1972. Substitute tchr. C.C. High Sch., Brooklyn, Mich., 1975-77; tchr. Dickinson High Sch., Tex., 1977-79; pres. AnAid, Inc., Dickinson, 1979—. Mem. Local Polit. Action Group, Dickinson, 1981-83, Local Chpt. Nat. Women's Club, Brooklyn, 1967-70. Mem. Nat. Fedn. of Independent Bus., Dickinson C. of C., Friendswood C. of C., Clear Lake C. of C. Baptist. Club: Bayou Chantilly Civic. Lodge: Eastern Star. Home: 5101 Meadow Ln Dickinson TX 77539 Office: AnAid Inc PO Box 933 304B Tanglewood Dickinson TX 77539

HERRING, EVELYN MAE, leasing company executive; b. Portchester, N.Y., Apr. 13, 1936; d. Carl Gilman and Margaret Anna (Kersten) Wright; m. David Andrew Tilley, Aug. 7, 1965 (div. 1980); 1 child, David Andrew; m. Travis Carlie Herring, Dec. 27, 1981. B.S., Cornell U., 1958. Tchr. dept. home econs. Dept. Kings Park High Sch., Hauppauge, N.Y., 1958-62; real estate broker Jan Realty Co., St. James, N.Y., 1962-72; owner, operator The Village Tub, Plymouth, N.H., 1972-76; engraver, ptnr. The Trophy Shoppe, Sarasota, Fla., 1977-79; owner, mgr. The Plant Shed, Sarasota, 1979—. Mem., sec. Miller Place Fire Dept. Aux., N.Y., 1966-72; organist Trinity Methodist Ch., Plymouth, 1975, 76, Calvary Methodist Ch., Sarasota, 1979-82. Mem. Fla. Foliage Assn., Am. Bus. Women's Assn., Manasota Interiorscapers (founder). Republican. Club: Am. Contract Bridge League (Memphis). Lodge: Enterprise Rebekah. Avocations: band organist, duplicate bridge. Home: 2242 Shadow Lake Dr Sarasota FL 33582 Office: The Plant Shed 2242 Shadow Lake Dr Sarasota FL 33582

HERRING, FAYE, real estate and mortgage loan broker; b. Mexia, Tex., June 9, 1934; d. Carl Lee and Myrtle Inez (Sykes) Herring; children—Harvey Moody, Jr., Mickey Faye Reagan. Student Henderson County Jr. Coll., student real estate U. Houston; student property mgmt., Ky., La., Can. Cert. Nat. Assn. Ind. Fee Appraisers. Owner-operator Faye Herring Investments, Houston, 1967—. Office: 3408 Crawford St Houston TX 77004

HERRING, LUCY WOOTTEN, teacher, former marina owner, yacht captain; b. Durham, N.C., July 16, 1948; d. Edward Lewis and Calena (Brothers) H.; m. Allen John Gordon, Aug. 1, 1970 (div. Dec. 1977); m. Richard Daniel Champney, Dec. 8, 1980. A.B. in English Edn., U. N.C., 1970; Spl. Edn., U. Md.-College Park, 1975. Cert. tchr., Md. English, spl. edn. tchr. Prince Georges' County, Md., 1970-80; social studies tchr. St. Thomas Jr. High Sch., U.S. Virgin Islands, 1981; accounts payable clk. Am. Yacht Harbor, St. Thomas, 1981; charter captain, St. Thomas, 1981-82; owner, mgr. Yacht Haven, Carolina Beach, N.C., 1983-85. Mem. N.C. Marina Assn. (sec., treas. 1985). Democrat. Episcopalian. Avocations: sailing, reading, crocheting, horseback riding. Home: 18 Cathedral St Annapolis MD 21401

HERRING, PAMELA RHAE, advertising agency executive; b. Salina, Kans., Apr. 25, 1956; d. Rollin Leonard and Lucille Ann (Wolf) Johnson; m. Randall P. Herring, Sept. 9, 1979; 1 dau., Candess Rhae. B.S. in Journalism, Kans. State U., 1978. Bookkeeper, sec. Webb Johnson Electric, Salina, Kans., 1972-74; copy editor Kans. State Coll.-Manhattan, 1977-78; asst. advt. dir. Frontier Advt., Dallas, 1978-79; dir. pub. relations Square House Mus., Panhandle, Tex., 1979-80; account exec. McCormick Advt. Agy., Amarillo, Tex., 1980—. Mem. Republican Nat. Com., 1983. Mem. Bus. and Profl. Women, Kans. State Alumni Assn. Republican. Baptist. Office: McCormick Advt Agy 1000 Adams St Amarillo TX 79189

HERRINGTON, LOIS H., federal government official; b. Seattle, Dec. 6, 1939; married; 2 children. A.B., U. Calif.-Davis, 1961; J.D., U. Calif. Hastings Coll. Law, 1965. Pvt. practice law, 1967-76; dep. dist. atty. Alameda County, Calif., 1976-81; chmn. Pres.'s Task Force on Victims of Crime, 1981-83; asst. atty. gen. Office Justice Programs, Dept. Justice, Washington, 1983—; chmn. Crime Prevention Coalition; chmn. adv. bd. Crime Stoppers Internat.; mem. Fed. Coordinating Council on Juvenile Justice and Delinquency Prevention; mem. adv. bd. Nat. Inst. Corrections; mem. adv. com. on rape prevention and control HHS; mem. Nat. Adv. Bd. on Child Abuse and Neglect; mem. standards, ethics, edn. and tng. com. Nat. Sheriffs Assn.; U.S. del. 7th UN Congress on Crime Prevention and Treatment of Offenders, Milan, Italy. Del. UN Decade on Status of Women, Nairobi, Kenya. Mem. numerous profl. assns. Address: Dept Justice Office of Justice Programs Washington DC 20531

HERRINGTON-BORRE, FRANCES JUNE, state government human services executive, school executive; b. Austin, Tex., June 14, 1935; d. George Wilmas Neill and Mildred Lucille (Alexander) Williamson; m. Harold M. Herrington, June 6, 1953 (dec. Dec. 1978); children—Harold M., Cheryl Anne Herrington Martinez; m. Thomas Raymond Borre, Apr. 5, 1985. Student, U. Tex., 1967-71. With Tex. Dept. Human Services, Austin, 1961—, adminstrv. technician, 1967-71, field rep., 1971-81, asst. personnel dir., 1981—; free-lance profl. interpreter for deaf, 1964-85; dir. Austin Sign Lang. Sch., 1964-85; cons. in field; project dir. Gov.'s Office, 1980. Gov.'s appointee Joint Adv. Com. on Ednl. Services to Deaf, Austin, 1976-78; chmn. Tex. Commn. for Deaf Bd. Eval. of Interpreters, 1981-84; chmn. Tex. State Agy. Liaisons to Gov.'s Commn. for Women, 1985. Recipient Tex. Rehab. Commn. Merit award, 1977, Gov.'s citation, 1978; named An Outstanding Woman Central Tex., AAUW, 1982, Significant and Meritorious Service to Mankind award Capitol Sertoma Club, 1976, Disting. Service as Adv. and Interpretar award Dal-Tar Lions Club, 1977. Mem. Nat. Assn. of Deaf, Tex. Assn. of Deaf (Service citation 1967, Vol. Service award 1971, Interpreter of Decade award 1981), Nat. Registry Interpreters for Deaf, Tex. Soc. Interpreters for Deaf (pres. 1969-70), Austin Interpreters for Deaf. Mem. Ch. of Christ. Home: 2404 Laramie Trail Austin TX 78745 Office: Tex Dept Human Services 701 W 51st St Austin TX 78769

HERRMANN, NORMA CALLAWAY, airline executive; b. Atlanta, Oct. 3, 1935; d. Joseph Jennings and Frances Omega (Norman) Callaway; m. Ronald Alvin Herrmann, Dec. 31, 1963 (dec. July 1970); children—Scott Callaway, Mark Joseph Ronald. Student Emory U., 1955-56; B.S. in Edn., Ga. State U., 1959; postgrad. UCLA, 1971-72, Loyola U.-Los Angeles, 1970-71. Regional mgr. customer services Flying Tiger Line, Los Angeles and Chgo., 1970-76; regional mgr. sales and service Evergreen Internat. Airlines, Atlanta, 1978-79, dir. mktg., adminstrn., Tucson and McMinnville, Oreg., 1979; v.p. mktg., adminstrn. Pacific Alaska Airlines Co., Miami, Fla., 1980; exec. v.p. Azimuth Internat., Miami, 1980-83; exec. v.p. Caribbean Air Services, San Juan, P.R., 1984—; ind. cons., Atlanta, 1976-78. Mem. Conservative Caucus, Falls Church, Va., 1982—, Nat. Conservative Polit. Action Com., Washington, 1982—. Mem. Am. Mgmt. Assn., Nat. Mgmt. Assn., Bus. and Profl. Women's Orgn., World Future Soc. Episcopalian.

HERRON, ELLEN PATRICIA, Judge; b. Auburn, N.Y., July 30, 1927; d. David Martin and Grace Josephine (Berner) H.; A.B., Trinity Coll., 1949; M.A., Cath. U. Am., 1954; J.D., U. Calif., Berkeley, 1964. Asst. dean Cath. U. Am., 1952-54; instr. East High Sch., Auburn, 1955-57; asst. dean Wells Coll., Aurora, N.Y., 1957-58; instr. psychology and history Contra Costa Coll., 1958-60; dir. row Stanford, 1960-61; asso. firm Knox & Kretzmer, Richmond, Calif., 1964-65; admitted to Calif. bar, 1965; partner firm Knox & Herron, 1965-74, Knox, Herron and Masterson, 1974-77 (both Richmond, Calif.); Judge Superior Ct. Calif., 1977—; gen. partner Real Estate Syndicates, Calif., 1967-77. Active numerous civic orgns.; bd. dirs. Rhonoh Sch., Richmond, YWCA, Econ. Devel. Council Richmond; mem. alumni bd., Boalt Hall, U. Calif., 1980—. Mem. Am., Contra Costa (exec. com. 1969-74), Richmond bar assns., State Bar Calif., Nat. Women Judges Assn., Nat. Assn. Women Lawyers, Calif. Women Lawyers, Applicants Attys. Assn., Calif. Judges Assn. (ethics com. 1977-79, criminal procedure com. 1979-80), Queen's Bench, Nat. Women's Polit. Caucus. Democrat. Club: Commonwealth of Calif. Home: 51 Western Dr Point Richmond CA 94801

HERRON, JUDY ADELL, administrator; b. Jamestown, N.Y., June 16, 1939; d. Wilbur Eugene and Anna Ida Vivian (Carlson) North; m. James Otis Herron, Feb. 28, 1958 (div. 1978); children—David Eugene, Randall James, Tia Michele. A.A., Jamestown Community Coll., 1971; B.S., SUNY, 1973, M.S., 1976. Real estate agt. Connie Gray Realty, Lakewood, N.Y., 1968-73; tchr. Hurlbut Developmental, Chautauqua, N.Y., 1973-76, dir., 1976-80; sr. clk. Bur. Census, Jamestown, N.Y., 1980; agrl. dir. Reasor Farms, Russell, Pa., 1980-82; election data operator Bd. Elections, Mayville, N.Y., 1982—. Bd. dirs. PTA, Lakewood, N.Y., 1970; pres. Vol. Fire Dept. Aux., Lakewood, 1970; trustee Busti Lakewood Democratic Party, 1979. Mem. Chautauqua County Youth Bur., Parent Cooperative Pre-Schs. Internat., Chautauqua County Assn. Edn. Younger Children. Democrat. Methodist. Clubs: Lakewood Rod and Gun (Lakewood, N.Y.); Chautauqua Lake Power Boat (Stow, N.Y.).

HERRON, JULIE ANN, oilfield delivery service executive; b. Los Angeles, Oct. 4, 1960; d. Donald Eugene and Phyllis Mary (Norton) H.; cert. seminars Internat., France, Italy, 1980; student Nat. Coll., Rapid City, S.D., 1978-80, Dawson Coll., Glendive, Mont., 1983, Tour coordinator Jack Rabbit Bus. Lines, Rapid City, 1980; customer service rep. Big Sky Airlines, Glendale, 1981-83; pres. Road Runner Hotshot Service, Glendive, 1981—; gen. sec. B & H Welding & Machine, Glendive, 1981-85, treas., 1985—. Mem. All State Choir, Glendive, 1977, Glendive Forward. Republican. Methodist. Clubs: Chamber Chorale, Golf, Ducks Unltd. Lodge: Order of Rainbow for Girls (hon. mem.). Avocations: playing guitar, piano; writing poetry; swimming; camping; reading. Home: 412 Clay St Glendive MT 59330 Office: Road Runner Hotshot Services Inc C B Rt Glendive MT 59330

HERSHA, KATHRYN LOUISE JAMIESON, system and data analyst; b. Fort Wayne, Ind., Feb. 12, 1940; d. Norval Eugene and Dorothy Ellen (Turflinger) Jamieson; m. George William Hersha, July, 1964 (div. Sept. 1967). Student St. Francis Coll., Fort Wayne, 1964-65, Fort Wayne Art Inst., 1967-74; A.S., Ind. U.-Fort Wayne, 1973; student U. Evansville, 1977-79, Ringling Art Sch., 1984-86. Programmer Lincoln Nat. Bank, Fort Wayne, 1968-74; programmer, analyst Atlas Van Lines, Evansville, Ind., 1974-77; sr. analyst Nat. Sharedata, Evansville, 1977-79; project leader Fla. Software Services, Orlando, 1979-81; system cons. Anacomp, Sarasota, Fla., 1981—. Mem. Nat. Assn. Female Execs., Am. Mgmt. Assn., Sarasota Art Assn., Asolo Festival Theater Assn. Methodist. Avocations: art; sculpting. Home: PO Box 1235 Sarasota FL 33578 Office: Anacomp 33 N Pineapple Sarasota FL 33577

HERSH-COCHRAN, MONA SHEINFELD, university educator; b. Phila., Dec. 3, 1934; m. Kendall P. Cochran; children—Paula, Susan, Kenneth. B.A., Rutgers U., 1956; M.A., Temple U., 1968; M.A., So. Meth. U., 1964, Ph.D., 1966. Teaching asst. So. Meth. U., Dallas, 1961-64; vis. prof. State Coll. Ark., Conway, summers 1967, 68; prof. Tex. Woman's U., Denton, 1969—, prof. econs., 1965—; vis. research scholar London Sch. Econs., London Sch. Hygiene, 1981-82; acad. visitor U. York, Eng., 1981-82; visiting prof. U. Auckland, New Zealand, U. New Castle, New South Wales, Australia, 1985; cons. U.S. Dept HEW, Bur. Quality Assurance; econ. cons.; computer and systems analysis cons. Contbr. articles to profl. jours. Recipient Outstanding Profs. award Tex. Woman's U., 1969-71; Most Valuable Mem. award Ops. Research Soc. Am.; Tex. Woman's U. Research grantee, 1967, 76, Journalism award, 1973; Danforth Assoc. award, 1977-83; NSF award, 1981-82. Mem. Am. Econ. Assn., Assn. Social Econs. (assoc. editor Forum 1978-81, mem. nat. exec. council 1985-87); Southwestern Social Sci. Assn. (chmn. nominating com. 1978-81), Southwestern Econs. Assn. (sec.-treas. 1970-81), S.W. Soc. Economists, Western Soc. Economists, Western Social Sci. Assn., AAUW, Bus. and Profl. Women, Health Econs. Study Group United Kingdom, Omicron Delta Epsilon (nat. v.p. 1986-87). Home: 3765 Weeburn Dallas TX 75229 Office: Tex Womans U Dept Bus and Econs Denton TX 76204

HERSON, DIANE S., microbiologist; b. N.Y.C., Apr. 23, 1944; d. Morris A. and Esther K. (Goldman) H.; B.S., Cornell U., 1964; M.S., Rutgers U., 1966, Ph.D., 1968; m. Stephen H. Franklin, Oct. 21, 1973; children—Pamela Allison Franklin, Daniel Jonathan. Lab instr. Cornell U., Ithaca, N.Y., 1964; research asst. Rutgers U., New Brunswick, N.J., 1964-66, research asso., 1966-68; asst. prof. biol. scis. U. Del., Newark, 1968-74, assoc. prof. 1974—. Recipient research grants U. Del. Research Found., 1969-71, 75-76, Del. Inst. Med. Edn. Research, 1973-74, Water Resources, 1974-76, EPA, 1977-80, 82-85. Mem. Am. Soc. for Microbiology, AAAS, N.Y. Acad. Sci., Sigma Xi. Contbr. articles to profl. jours. Office: Sch of Life and Health Sci U of Del Newark DE 19716

HERTING, CLAIREEN LAVERN, personal financial planning executive; b. Chgo., Sept. 7, 1929; d. Ernst and Louise Caroline (Wagner) Molzan; m. Robert L. Herting, June 5, 1954; 1 son, Robert L., Jr. B.S., U. Ill.-Champaign, 1951; M.B.A., Northwestern U., Chgo., 1953; J.D., John Marshall Law Sch., 1960. Bar: Ill. 1960. C.P.A., Ill. With Cooper & Lybrands, Chgo., 1951—, dir. personal fin. planning, 1974—. Contbr. articles to profl. jours. Bd. dirs. Easter Seal Soc. Met. Chgo., 1974—, Chgo. Soc. Contemporary Composers, 1979-84; bd. trustees John Marshall Law Sch., Chgo., 1980—; com. mem. Ill. Dept. Registration and Edn., Springfield, 1984—. Recipient Disting. Service award John Marshall Alumni Assn., Chgo., 1983. Mem. Am. Inst. C.P.A.s, ABA, Ill. Bar Assn., Ill. C.P.A. Soc. (bd. dirs. 1974-76), Chgo. Estate Planning Council (past pres., bd. mem. 1976-84), Chgo. Bar Assn. Home: 1281 N Northwest Hwy Chicago IL 60068

HERTWECK, ALMA LOUISE, educator; b. Moline, Ill., Feb. 6, 1937; d. Jacob Ray and Sylvia Ethel (Whitt) Street; m. E. Romayne Hertweck, Dec. 16, 1955; 1 child, William Scott. A.A., Mira Costa Coll., 1969; B.A. in Sociology summa cum laude, U. Calif.-San Diego, 1975, M.A., 1977, Ph.D., 1982. Cert. sociology instr., multiple subjects teaching credential grades kindergarten-12, Calif. Staff research assoc. U. Calif.-San Diego, 1978-81; instr. sociology Chapman Coll., Orange, Calif., 1982—; instr. child devel. MiraCosta Coll., Oceanside, Calif., 1983—; instr. sociology U.S. Internat. U., San Diego, 1985—; exec. dir., v.p. El Camino Preschools, Inc., Oceanside, 1985—. Co-author: Handicapping the Handicapped, 1985. Mem. Am. Sociol. Assn., Am. Ednl. Research Assn., Nat. Council Family Relations, Nat. Assn. Edn. Young Children, Alpha Gamma Sigma (life). Avocations: foreign travel; sailing; bicycling. Home: 2024 Oceanview Rd Oceanside CA 92056 Office: El Camino Preschs Inc 2002 California St Oceanside CA 92054

HERWIG, JOAN EMILY, educational administrator; b. Chgo., Apr. 7, 1943; d. Roger Miles and Joyce Ivah (Mahlke) H.; student Merrill-Palmer Inst., 1964; B.S., U. Wis., Stout, 1965; M.S., Iowa State U., 1971; Ph.D. (David Ross fellow), Purdue U., 1978. Tchr. jr. high sch., Port Huron, Mich., 1965-69; dir.-tchr. Head Start, Port Huron, summers 1965-69; teaching asst. Iowa State U., 1969-70, assoc. prof. child devel., 1971—, chmn. dept., 1983—; research asst. Purdue U., 1976-78; cons. child devel., early childhood edn. Bd. dirs. Ames (Iowa) Presch., 1971-73, Pammel Nursery Sch., Ames, 1975-76; mem. governing bd. Episcopal Parish of Ames, 1982-85, sr. Warden, 1984-85. Recipient Amoco Outstanding Tchr. award, 1982-83; Disting. Alumni award U. Wis.-Stout, 1985. Mem. Soc. Research in Child Devel., Nat. Assn. Edn. Young Children, Midwest Assn. Edn. Young Children (Iowa rep. council 1985—, v.p. 1986—), Iowa Assn. Edn. Young Children (sec. 1979-82, v.p. 1982-83, pres. 1983-84), Am. Home Econs. Assn., Nat. Assn. Early Childhood Tchrs. Educators, Omicron Nu, Phi Delta Kappa. Contbr. chpts., articles to profl. publs.; research in cognitive devel. of young children, parent involvement. Office: 101A Child Devel Bldg Iowa State U Ames IA 50011

HERZBERG, DOROTHY CREWS, financial services administrator; b. N.Y.C., July 8, 1935; d. Floyd Houston and Julia (Lesser) Crews; A.B., Brown U., 1957; M.A., Stanford U., 1964; J.D., San Francisco Law Sch., 1976; m. Hershel Zelig Herzberg, May 22, 1962; children—Samuel Floyd, Laura Jill, Daniel Crews. Legal sec. various law firms, San Francisco, 1976-78; tchr. Mission Adult Sch., San Francisco, 1965-66; tchr. secondary and univ. levels Peace Corps, Nigeria, 1961-63; investigator Office of Dist. Atty., San Francisco, 1978-80; sr. adminstr. Dean Witter Reynolds Co., San Francisco, 1980-83; registered rep. Waddell and Reed, Oakland, Calif., 1983-84; fin. services rep. United Resources, Hayward, Calif., 1984-85, Ind. Planning Corp., San Francisco, 1985—; alt. for supr. San Francisco Mayor's Commn. on Criminal Justice, 1978. Bd. dirs. LWV, San Francisco, 1967-69; bd. dirs. Miraloma (Calif.) Improvement Club, 1977—, pres., 1980-81; pres. Council of Co-op Nursery Schs., San Francisco, 1969-71; active LWV Speakers Bur., 1967-69, 1977-79. Mem. Internat. Assn. Fin. Planning, San Francisco Bach Choir, San Francisco C. of C. Democrat. Unitarian. Club: West Portal Toastmistress. Editor Co-op Nursery Sch. Council newsletter, 1969-71, Miraloma Life newsletter, 1976-82, Democratic Women's Forum newsletter, 1980-81, Stanford Luncheon Club newsletter, 1984-85. Home: 238 Bella Vista Way San Francisco CA 94127 Office: 1255 Post St Suite 700 San Francisco CA 94109

HERZECA, LOIS FRIEDMAN, lawyer; b. N.Y.C., July 7, 1954; d. Martin and Elaine Shirley (Rapoport) Friedman; m. Christian Stefan Herzeca, Aug. 15, 1980. B.A. Harpur Coll., SUNY-Binghamton, 1976; J.D., Boston U., 1979. Bar: N.Y. 1980, U.S. Dist. Ct. (so. and ea. dist.) N.Y. 1980. Atty. antitrust div. U.S. Dept. Justice, Washington, 1979-80; assoc. firm Fried, Frank, Harris, Shriver & Jacobson, N.Y.C., 1980—. Editor Am. Jour. Law and Medicine, 1978-79. Mem. ABA, N.Y.C. Bar Assn. Democrat. Jewish. Office: Fried Frank Harris Shriver & Jacobson 1 New York Plaza New York NY 10004

HERZIG, MEG, sales and marketing executive; b. N.Y.C., Oct. 14, 1953; d. Leonard Adair and Doris Yvette (Fliegelman) H. B.A. cum laude, Rider Coll., 1975. Asst. buyer, buyer Korvette's, N.Y.C., 1975-77; asst. to v.p., salesperson, Halston V and VI, N.Y.C., 1977-78; salesperson Liz Claiborne, N.Y.C., 1978; N.Y.C. sales mgr. J.G. Hook, 1978-82; nat. sales and mktg. mgr. Arthur Winer, N.Y.C., 1982—. Mem. Nat. Assn. Female Execs., Cap and Crown, Alpha Kappa Delta. Democrat. Jewish. Office: Arthur Winer Inc 1290 Ave of the Americas New York NY 10104

HERZINGER, SONJA RAE, communications company manager; b. Twin Falls, Idaho, July 26, 1950; d. William A. and Faye N. (Krupp) Bergadine; m. Ranse L. Herzinger, Aug. 23, 1969 (div. Apr. 1978). B.A. in English, Boise State U., 1972. Office mgr. Mountain Bell, Boise, 1978, applications instr., Salt Lake City, 1978-80, tech. writer, Denver, 1980-83; tech. instr. gen. dept. AT&T, Basking Ridge, N.J., 1983, data administrator, 1984—, strategic planner, 1984—, cons. strategic info. systems planning, 1984—. Author tech. manuals. Scholar Boise State U., 1969. Mem. Nat. Assn. Female Execs. Democrat. Methodist. Avocations: collecting rare and out of print books; antiques; skiing. Home: 8 Ash Ln Morristown NJ 07960 Office: AT&T Communications 295 N Maple Ave Basking Ridge NJ 07920

HERZOG, DEBRA ELLEN, lawyer; b. Paterson, N.J., Dec. 15, 1954; d. Donald Arthur and Susan Lee (Kohlreiter) H. B.A. cum laude, Washington U., St. Louis, 1976, J.D., 1979. Bar: Mo. 1979. Asst. circuit atty. Circuit Attys. Office, St. Louis, 1979-82, assoc. Armstrong Teasdale, Kramer & Vaughn, St. Louis, 1981-83; asst. U.S. atty. U.S. Attys. Office Eastern Dist. Mo., St. Louis, 1983—; adj. prof. Sch. of Law, Washington U., St. Louis, 1986—; lectr. St. Louis Met. Police Acad. Mem. Nat. Dist. Attys. Assn. Office: US Attorneys Office 1114 Market St Saint Louis MO 63101

HERZOG, GAIL LOUISE, communications and marketing executive; b. Cape Girardeau, Mo., Nov. 10, 1949; d. Elliott Francis and Katherine Marie (Hotop) Mattingly; m. Ronald Joseph Herzog, May 30, 1970; children—Christopher Eric, Scott Matthew, Sarah Katherine. B.S., Southeast Mo. State U., 1971; M.A., So. Ill. U., 1980. Instr. Harris-Stowe State Coll., St. Louis, 1980-81, Lewis and Clark Community Coll., Godfrey, Ill., 1980-82, So. Ill. U., Edwardsville, 1979-85; dir. pub. relations and devel. River Bluffs Council Girl Scouts U.S., Edwardsville, 1982-84; exec. v.p. Multi-Media Services, St. Louis, 1984; pres. Herzog-Morris, Inc., East Alton, Ill., 1985—; cons. in field. Mem. Greater Alton Growth Assn., East Alton, 1985; mem. St. Kevin's Parents' Club, 1978-85. Mem. Pub. Relations Soc. Am., LWV. Am. Soc. Tng. and Devel., Democrat. Roman Catholic. Club: Greater Alton PR-Ad. Avocations: photography; reading; hiking; swimming; skiing. Home and office: 601 W Airwood St East Alton IL 62024

HERZOG, KATHRYN ROSE, health care administrator, hospice consultant; b. Des Moines, Nov. 10, 1955; d. Herman J. and Evelyn K. (Kempker) Wedel; m. Benjamin David Herzog, May 16, 1981. B.S.N., U. Iowa, 1978; M.S.N., U. Tex., 1980. Staff nurse U. Iowa Hosp., Iowa City, 1977-79; head nurse, supr. Seton Med. Ctr., Austin, Tex., 1980-83; asst. dir. nursing Sacred Heart Med. Ctr., Chester, Pa., 1983-84; Nat. Standard Seminar Instr., hospice surveyer Joint Commn. on Accreditation of Hosps., Chgo., 1983—; exec. dir. Del. Hospice, Wilmington, 1984-85; dir. nursing Bapt. Hosp., Beaumont, Tex., 1986—. Author of monthly continuing edn. program for nurses, Cancer Awareness, 1983; research presentation at Nat. Conf. on Nursing Adminstrn. Research, 1981; contbr. articles to profl. jours. Co-facilitator "I Can Cope" program, Am. Cancer Soc., Austin, 1981-83, instr. self breast exam Austin, Wilmington, Del., Houston, 1980—; CPR Instructor Am. Heart Assn., Austin, Wilmington, Houston, 1979—; lecturer on women and cancer to local hosp. and community groups, Austin, Wilmington, Houston, 1980—. Nominated for Outstanding Young Alumnus U. Iowa, 1983. Mem. Tex. Nurses Assn. (dist. 5 first v.p. 1981-82), Oncology Nursing Soc. (convention del. 1982), Del. State Hospice Orgn. (state rep. 1984—), Nat. Hospice Orgn. (nat. convention workshop instr. 1983—), Am. Nurses Assn., Wilmington Women in Bus., Phi Kappa Phi, Sigma Theta Tau. Avocations: china painting, reading, swimming. Home: 1504 Browning Orange TX 77630 Office: Bapt Hosp College and 11th St Beaumont TX 77706

HERZOG-ECOLIVET, BRIGITTE, lawyer; b. St. Sauveur Le Vicomte, Normandy, Jan. 11, 1943; came to U.S., 1970, naturalized, 1976; d. Roger and Berthe (Niobey) Ecolivet; m. Peter E. Herzog, June 29, 1970; children—Paul Roger, Elizabeth Ann. Licence en Droit with highest honors, Law Sch. Pantheon, Paris, 1967, Diplomes d'Etudes Superieures with highest honors, 1968; J.D., Syracuse U., 1975; hon. degree Acad. Internat. Law, The Hague, 1976. Bar: Paris 1968, N.Y. 1976. Assoc., Chardenon Law Firm, Paris, 1968-70, Cleary, Gottlieb, Steen & Hamilton, Paris, 1976-77; lectr. U. Paris Law Sch., 1968-70; staff atty. Carrier Corp., Syracuse, 1977-83, sr. atty., 1983-85, asst. gen. counsel, 1985—. Contbr. articles to profl. jours. Bd. dirs. Syracuse Stage Guild, 1974-77. Mem. ABA, N.Y. State Bar Assn., Am. Fgn. Law Assn. Roman Catholic. Home: 112 Erregger Rd Syracuse NY 13224 Office: Carrier Corp 6304 Carrier Pkwy Syracuse NY 13221

HESER, CATHERINE LUND, realtors board executive; b. Hartford, Conn., Jan. 7, 1946; d. Andrew Knudsen and Elly Emilie (Berg) Lund; m. Charles Lauren Heser, Dec. 3, 1966; children—Chaye Lauren, Casey Lorraine. Student various coll. courses. Cosmetologist Clinton Beach (Conn.), 1965-76; ins. clk. State Farm Ins. Co., Rockport, Tex., 1979-80; sec., receptionist Baker, Shaw Physicians, Rockport, 1980-82; exec. officer Rockport Bd. Realtors, 1982—. Mem. Clinton Women's Club (pres. 1975). Republican. Home: 109 Palm St PO Box 1834 Rockport TX 78382 Office: Rockport Area Bd Realtors POB 636 Rockport TX 78382

HESLIN, CATHLEEN JANE, designer; b. Bklyn., Feb. 24, 1929; d. Charles Jenkins and Katherine (Bauer) Hunter; A.A., Packer Collegiate Inst., Bklyn., 1950; postgrad. Duke U., Pratt Inst.; m. John Thomas Heslin, June 24, 1950. Sr. artist, designer Klopman Mills, Rockleigh, N.J., 1966-72; free-lance designer, 1972-78; propr. Quilters Corner, Tappan, N.Y., 1978—; historian Borough of Rockleigh (N.J.), 1973—, councilwoman, 1974—, chmn. environ. com., 1974, chmn. fin. com., 1977; chmn. Rockleigh Historic Adv. Com., 1978—. Trustee, Abram Demaree Homestead, 1982-84. Recipient various certs. of appreciation. Mem. Tappantown Hist. Soc. (dir.), Soc. Archtl. Historians, Am. Soc. Planning Ofcls., Bergen County Hist. Soc. (trustee 1984—), Historic Homes Assn. N.J. Republican. Author: History of Rockleigh, N.J., 1648-1973, 1973. Inventor Quilters Quarter, measuring device. Obtained Nat. Historic Dist. status for Borough of Rockleigh, 1976. Home: Piermont Rd Rockleigh NJ 07647 Office: 92 Main St Tappan NY 10983

HESLIN, DONNA LUCILLE, nurse; b. Bellingham, Wash., May 18, 1932; d. George David and Grace Winifred (Taylor) Rehberger Osier; m. Harris Wardner Heslin, July 6, 1951; children—Lawrence, Barbara, Carol, Jon, Gail, Kenneth, Craig, Dianna. A.A.S., Westark Community Coll., 1981, .A.A., 1985; L.P.N., R.N. Staff LPN, Drew Meml. Hosp., Monticello, Ark., 1977-79; staff nurse St Edward Med Ctr, Fort Smith, 1979-81; asst. dir. Beverly Enterprises, Fort Smith, 1982-85; head nurse Crawford Meml. Hosp., Van Buren, Ark., 1982—; adminstr. Hospice Area Agy. for Aging, 1985—. Pres., Relief Soc., Bastrop, La., 1974-75. Republican. Mem. Ch. Jesus Christ Latter-day Saints. Avocations: cooking, reading, sewing, geneaology. Home: 8312 Meadow Dr Fort Smith AR 72903

HESS, BETH BOWMAN, sociology educator; b. Buffalo, Sept. 13, 1928; d. Albert A. and Yetta (Lurie) Bowman; m. Richard C. Hess, Apr. 26, 1953; children—Laurence Albert, Emily Frances. B.A. magna cum laude, Radcliffe Coll., 1950; M.A., Rutgers U., 1966; Ph.D., Rutgers U., 1971. Research asst. Rutgers U., New Brunswick, 1964-69; asst. prof. County Coll., 1969-74, assoc. prof., 1975-79; prof. County Coll., Randolph, N.J., 1979—; adj. prof. CUNY Grad. Ctr., 1979; vis. prof. Boston U. Gerontology Ctr., 1980-81; lectr. Douglass Coll., 1981. Author: (with Elizabeth W. Markson) Aging and Old Age: An Introduction to Social Gerontology, 1980, Sociology, 1982, (with E. W. Markson and P. Stein), 2d edit., 1985; (with Matilda White Riley and Kathleen Bond.) Aging in Society: Selected Reviews of Recent Research, 1983; (with Myra Marx Ferree) Controversy and Coalition: The New Feminist Movement, 1985. Editor: Growing Old in America, 1976, 80, 85; (with Kathleen Bond) Leading Edges: Recent Research on Psychosocial Aging, 1981; assoc. editor Society, 1978-83, Research of Aging, 1980—, Contemporary Sociology, 1981-83; editor SWS Network, 1984—. Council mem. Morris County Council on the Aged, Morristown, N.J., 1975-80; bd. dirs. Planned Parenthood N.E. N.J., Morristown, 1980-84, Morris Shelter, Inc., Morristown, 1982-84; mem. Morris County Adv. Com. on Needs of Women. Fellow Gerontol. Soc. (sec. behavioral and social sci. sect. 1979-81, mem.-at-large 1984-86); mem. Soc. Study Social Problems (dir. 1981-84), Sociologists for Women in Soc. (treas. 1982-85), Am. Sociol. Assn. (nomination com. sect. on aging 1980, newsletter editor 1982-84), Assn. Humanist Sociology (pres.-elect 1986-87), Eastern Sociol. Soc. (v.p. 1984-85, Peter I. Gellman disting. service award 1982). Democrat. Jewish. Home: 2 Hampshire Dr Mendham NJ 07945 Office: County Coll of Morris Randolph NJ 07869

HESS, IRMA, university official, translator; b. Frankfurt, Germany, Feb. 5, 1939; came to U.S., 1957, naturalized, 1960; d. Frederick and Martha (Mahlert) Alban; 1 child, Harold Alban Hess. B.A., New Sch. for Social Research, 1977; B.S., SUNY-Albany, 1976; M.A., NYU, 1979, M.P.A., 1984, advanced profl. cert., grad. of bus., 1986. Asst. to spl. psychol. testing Bd. Edn., Mt. Vernon, N.Y., 1959-65, health chmn., 1959-66; ind. practice bookkeeping, 1959-65; translator N.Y.C. cts. and agys., 1959—, interpreter, 1959-77; counselor Family Ct., Criminal Ct. Youth Div., N.Y.C., 1976-78; tchr. New Rochell Bd. Edn., 1976-78; adminstr. NYU, N.Y.C., 1978—. Vice pres. PTA, Mt. Vernon, 1968-70; chmn. Mt. Vernon Community Chest, 1971-73; sec. N.Y.C. br. ARC, 1975-77. Recipient Mayor of N.Y. accomplishment cert., 1978; scholar State of N.Y., 1976, NYU, 1978. Mem. Am. Soc. Pub. Adminstrs., U.S. Exec. Women, Am. Translators Assn., Am. Pub. Health Adminstrs., Am. Polit. Sci. Assn., N.Y. Acad. Scis., New Sch. for Social Research Alumni Assn., NYU Alumni Assn. Avocations: golf; ballet; tennis; folk music. Office: NYU 33 Washington Sq W New York NY 10011

HESS, JEAN REISING, nurse; b. Ft. Wayne, Ind., Jan. 20, 1929; d. Peter Adam and Irene (McKenzie) Reising; m. Joe Ray Hess, Aug. 21, 1954; children—Francis Michael, Janet Marie, Mary Jo, Kenneth Robert. Student St. Vincent's Sch. of Nursing, Toledo, Ohio, 1949-51; nursing diploma Seton Sch. Nursing, Austin, Tex., 1954; student U. Tex., 1952-55. Registered nurse, Tex. Head nurse-pediatrics Spohn Hosp., Corpus Christi, Tex., 1959-61, shift dir. nursing service adminstrn., 1982—; head nurse-orthopedic neurosurgery Mem. Med. Ctr., Corpus Christi, 1964-71, night supr., 1971-75, surg. nursing supr., 1975-80, clin. nursing coordinator, 1980-82. Roman Catholic. Club: Cathedral Chorale (Corpus Christi). Avocations: classical music; choral singing; gardening; birdwatching; oil painting. Home: 3246 Austin St Corpus Christi TX 78404 Office: Spohn Hosp 600 Elizabeth St Corpus Christi TX 78404

HESS, LINDA LUCILLE, lawyer, educator, researcher; b. Arcata, Calif., Aug. 5, 1946; d. Carl Richard and Lucille Claire (Larson) Hutchins; m. Lloyd James Hess, June 7, 1969; children—Aaron, Melissa, Heidi, Rebecca. B.A., Calif. State Univ., 1967, M.A., 1969; J.D., W.Va. Univ., 1983. Bar: W.Va. 1983. Tchr. Eureka City Schs. (Calif.), 1969, San Andreas Schs. (Calif.), 1970-71, Delaware County Schs., Stamford, N.Y., 1972, Randolph County Schs., Elkins, W.Va., 1973-74; assoc. Cardot Law Office, Elkins, after 1983; now with Alphametrics Controls Corp., Citrus Heights, Calif. Bd. dirs. Meals on Wheels, Inc., Elkins, 1983-84, Birthright, Inc., Elkins, after 1982. Recipient Ambassador Jurisprudence award Sec. State, Charleston, W.Va., 1983. Mem. ABA, W.Va. Bar Assn. Democrat. Roman Catholic. Club: Rosary Guild (pres. 1983-84). Home: 8773 Via Alta Way Elk Grove CA 95624 Office: Alphametrics Controls Corp Bank of Am American River Dr Sacramento CA

HESS, MARGARET JOHNSTON, religious writer, educator; b. Ames. Iowa, Feb. 22, 1915; d. Howard Wright and Jane Edith (Stevenson) Johnston; B.A., Coe Coll., 1937; m. Bartlett Leonard Hess, July 31, 1937; children—Daniel, Deborah, John, Janet. Bible tchr. Community Bible Classes Ward Presbyn. Ch., Livonia, Mich., 1959—, Christ Ch. Cranbrook (Episcopalian), Bloomfield Hills, Mich., 1980—. Co-author: (with B.L. Hess) How to Have a Giving Church, 1974, The Power of a Loving Church, 1977, How Does Your Marriage Grow?, 1983, Never Say Old, 1984; author: Love Knows No Barriers, 1979; Esther: Courage in Crisis, 1980; Unconventional Women, 1981; contbr. articles to religious jours. Home: 16845 Riverside Dr Livonia MI 48154

HESS, NANCY OWENS, travel-study company executive; b. Cambridge, Mass., Nov. 22, 1947; d. Henry Edward and Christine Louise (O'Brien) Owens; m. Oliver Daniel O'Bryan, III, Jan. 3, 1967; m. Max Edwin Hess, Sept. 12, 1974; children—Charles Henry, Elizabeth Louise, William Richard. Student Wheelock Coll., 1965-67. U. Tex.-Austin, 1967-69; B.A., Northeastern U., Boston, 1972, M.A., 1975. Teaching asst. Northeastern U., Boston, 1973-75; ptnr. CET, Inc., Boston, 1979-81, pres., 1981—; cons. to advise Sen. Tsongas on Far Eastern Affairs, 1983—. Fgn. advisor Chinese docu-drama —Bright Eyes, 1985. Mem. U.S.-China Peoples Friendship Assn. (eastern regional coordinator 1976-80; nat. v.p. 1980-83); NOW. Democrat. Office: CET Inc 1110 Washington St Lower Mills Boston MA 02124

HESS, PAULA KAY, state legislative assistant; b. Hershey, Pa., Dec. 4, 1947; d. Paul Warren and Judith Alice (Morrett) H.; B.A., Lebanon Valley Coll., 1969; Ed.D., Pa. State U., 1980. Tchr., Cornwall-Lebanon (Pa.) Sch. Dist., 1969-77; fed. curriculum coordinator Joint Task Force New Arrivals, Ft. Indiantown Gap, Pa., 1975; grad. asst. dept. ednl. adminstrn. Pa. State U., 1977-79; dir. profl. devel. Pa. State Edn. Assn., Harrisburg, 1979-80; dir. govt. relations Pa. Assn. Sch. Adminstrs., Harrisburg, 1980-82; adminstrv. asst. to majority leader for legis. ops. Pa. Ho. of Reps., Harrisburg, 1982-83, legis. adminstr. office of Rep. whip, 1983—; presenter Edn.-Law Inst., Lehigh U., 1981. Registered Lobbyist, 1980-82. Mem. Nat. Orgn. Legal Problems in Edn., Nat. Assn. Female Execs., Pa. Assn. Sch. Adminstrs., Pi Gamma Mu, Phi Delta Kappa, Pi Lambda Theta. Republican. Home: 5428 Autumn Dr Harrisburg PA 17111 Office: PO Box 2 House Post Office Main Capitol Harrisburg PA 17120

HESS, VIRGINIA KRAUSE, retail executive, artist; b. New Carlisle, Ohio, Nov. 7, 1924; d. Albert Paul and Vadna (Gardner) Krause; m. Frederick Lee Hess, Oct. 19, 1946; children—Peter, Kristina, Victoria. Grad. Dayton Art Inst., 1961; B.F.A., U. Dayton, 1963. Artist-illustrator Wright-Field, Dayton, Ohio, 1942-43; fashion model Shillitos, Cin., 1945-46, Rikes, Dayton, 1946-51; tchr. art Springfield (Ohio) Art Center, 1966-70; free lance artist Am. Artists Group, N.Y.C., 1964-67; v.p. Hess Home Center, Inc., New Carlisle, 1970—. Mem. adv. bd. Hardware Wholesalers, Inc., Fort Wayne, Ind., 1979-81. Recipient numerous prizes, commns. and awards. Sculptor Portrait of Dr. Brinkman, 1983, Mother and Child, 1964, Eve, 1982, Seated Woman, 1983, Three Bronze Bats, Pitts., 1984. Mem. Trotwood-Madison (Ohio) Bd. Edn., 1967. Mem. Dayton Art Inst., Arts and Crafts Guild of Ohio. Clubs: Altrusa, Dayton Country. Home: 2230 S Patterson Blvd Kettering OH 45409 Office: Hess Home Center Inc 3310 S Dayton Lakeview Rd New Carlisle OH 45344

HESSE, MARTHA O., government official; b. Hattiesburg, Miss., Aug. 14, 1942; d. John and Jerry (Ossian) H. B.S., U. Iowa, 1964; postgrad., Northwestern U., 1972-76; M.B.A., U. Chgo., 1979. Research analyst Blue Shield, 1964-66; dir. div. data mgmt. Am. Hosp. Assn., 1966-69; v.p., chief operating officer SEI Info. Tech., Chgo., 1969-81; assoc. dept. sec. Dept. of Commerce, 1982; exec. dir. Pres.'s Task Force on Mgmt. Reform, 1982; asst. sec. mgmt. and adminstrn. Dept. Energy, Washington, 1982—. Vice chmn. Dean's Fund, Grad. Sch. Bus., U. Chgo., 1981—. Office: Dept Energy Mgmt and Adminstrn 1000 Independence Ave SW Washington DC 20585

HESSELBEIN, FRANCES RICHARDS, association executive; b. South Fork, Pa.; d. Burgess Harmon and Anne (Wicks) Richards; m. John Davis Hesselbein (dec. May 1978); 1 son, John Richards. Ed., U. Pitts. Exec. dir. Talus Rock Girl Scout council, Johnstown, Pa., 1970-74, Penn Laurel Girl Scout council, York, Pa., 1974-76; nat. exec. dir. Girl Scouts U.S.A., N.Y.C., 1976—; dir. Pa. Power & Light Co., Allentown, U.S. Fire Ins. Co. N., Morristown, N.J., River Ins. Co., Western Fire Ins. Co.; trustee Mut. of Am., N.Y.C. Bd. visitors Fairfield U. (Conn.); mem. adv. bd. Dyson Coll., Pace U., N.Y.C.; trustee Am. Humanics, Kansas City, Mo.; task group mem. Independent Sector, Washington, Pres. Com. on Employment of Handicapped. Recipient Ann. Achievement award Inter-Service Club Council Greater Johnstown (Pa.), 1976; God and Service Recognition award Ch. Commn. for Civic Youth Service Agys., N.Y.C., 1981; Entrepreneurial Women award Women Bus. Owners N.Y., U.S. Small Bus. Adminstrn., N.Y.C., 1984. Methodist. Clubs: Cosmopolitan, The Sky (N.Y.C.); The Pennsylvania Soc. (Waldorf-Astoria, N.Y.C.). Office: Girl Scouts USA 830 3d Ave New York NY 10022*

HESSELINK, ANN PATRICE, tax lawyer; b. Tokyo, July 20, 1954; d. Ira John Jr. and Etta Marie (Ter Louw) H.; m. Roland James Hicks, Jr., Jan 2, 1982. A.B., Hope Coll., 1975; J.D., St. Johns U., Jamaica, N.Y., 1980; advanced profl. cert. in fin. NYU Grad. Sch. Bus. Adminstrn., 1983. Bar: N.Y. 1981; C.P.A., N.Y. Tax mgr. Coopers & Lybrand, N.Y.C., 1980-82; asst. v.p. Bankers Trust Co., N.Y.C., 1982-83; mgr. internat. tax Pepsico, Inc., Purchase, N.Y., 1983—. Mem. ABA, N.Y. Women's Bar Assn., Am. Sch. in Japan Alumni Assn. (chmn. N.Y. region 1984). Democrat. Home: 440 W 24th St New York NY 10011 Office: PepsiCo Inc 700 Anderson Hill Rd Purchase NY 10577

HESSER, DANIELLE ELAN, aerospace company executive; b. Bklyn., May 19, 1949; d. William and Marie (Nelson) DiBella. Student Prince George's Community Coll., 1981-85. Jr. electronics technician Enviromarine, Inc., Laurel, Md., 1978-80; computer operator Bendix Field Engring. Corp., Columbia, Md., 1980-81; computer operator Ford Aerospace Co., College Park, Md., 1981-83, with command mgmt., 1983-84; satellite controller, obs. engr. OAO Corp., Greenbelt, Md., 1985—. Mem. Assn. for Humanistic Psychology. Republican. Avocations: cross-country skiing; hiking; reading; traveling; exercise. Office: OAO Corp 7500 Greenway Center Greenbelt MD 20770

HESTER, CAROLYN LAVAR, university official; b. Memphis, July 30, 1948; d. James Bateman and Boneta Elmaida (LeBeau) Fite; m. Jerry Dale Johnson, July 25, 1972 (div. 1977); m. Jimmy Noel Hester, May 22, 1980; 1 child, Matthew James. Student Technol. Inst. Monterrey, Nuevo Leon, Mex., 1968-69; B.S., Okla. State U., 1970. Social worker Okla. Dept. Welfare, Oklahoma City, 1970-72, instr. Pan Am. Airlines, Miami, Fla., 1972-74, Happy Time Sch., Richardson, Tex., 1975-77; sr. account exec. Fite-Davis Inc., Oklahoma City, 1977-80; dir. pub. relations Okla. State U. Tech. Inst., Oklahoma City, 1980—; dir. Fite-Hester Inc., Oklahoma City; advt. cons. Burl Holmes Ford, Oklahoma City, 1984—, Dodsons Cafeterias, Oklahoma City, 1984—, Sleepe Shoppe, Oklahoma City, 1984—. Author: Mary Lou Likes Blue, 1977; also song lyrics, poetry. Active cub scouting, local Boy Scouts Am. Recipient Appreciation plaque Oklahoma City Hort. Ctr., 1984. Mem. PTA (membership chmn. 1983, carnival chmn. 1984, Helping Hands award 1985), Oklahoma City Power Squadron (pub. relations officer 1985—), Oklahoma City Pub. Relations Assn., Oklahoma City Running Club (bd. dirs. 1985), Oklahoma City C. of C. (vice chmn. econ. devel. council). Democrat. Methodist. Avocations: sailing, camping, writing. Office: Okla State U Tech Inst 900 N Portland St Oklahoma City OK 73107

HESTER, EDITH GEORGE, college administrator; b. Evanston, Wyo., Apr. 8, 1940; d. Harold Glen and Phyllis Marie (Smith) George; m. Herschel G. Hester III, Dec. 26, 1969 (div. 1982), children—Dennis Lee Forsgren Jr., Shelleice Hester Stokes, Kristin Hester Coombs. B.S., Weber State Coll., 1969; postgrad. U. Utah, 1978-81. Sec. Sta. KLO, Ogden, Utah, 1958-62; artist, prodn. supr. Boise Cascade Printing Co., Idaho, 1962-65; with div. coll. relations Weber State Coll., Ogden, 1965—; pres. Edie Hester & Assocs., Ogden, 1981—; cons. to various orgns. Bd. dirs. Ogden Symphony Ballet Assn., 1981-82; info. rep. U.S. Mcht. Marine Acad., 1983—. Recipient Presdl. citation Weber State Coll., 1985; named Woman of Yr. in Edn., YWCA, Ogden, 1985. Mem. Am. Assn. Univ. Adminstrs. (regional coordinator 1981—), Am. Bus. Women (pres. Golden Spike chpt. 1981-82, name Woman of Yr., Golden Spike chpt. 1982), Ogden C. of C. (exec. com. Women in Mgt. 1983-84). Avocations: painting with acrylics; playing piano; golf; skiing; crocheting.

HESTER, NANCY ELIZABETH, county government administrator; b. Miami, Fla., Jan. 20, 1950; d. George Temple and Lorraine Patricia (Cluney) Hester; B.A., Bucknell U., 1972; M.I.A., Columbia U., 1974; M.B.A., Fla. Internat. U., 1979. Treasury rep. Westinghouse Elec. Co., N.Y.C., 1974-76; adminstrv. officer serving in bldg. and zoning, gen. services, and corrections and rehab. Met. Dade County, Miami, Fla., 1979—; adj. prof. Fla. Internat. U., Miami, 1980-83; realtor-assoc. Keyes Co., 1985—. Mem. network com. YWCA; mem. Bus. Vols. for Arts. Mem. Coral Gables Bd. Realtors, Zool. Soc. Fla., Ctr. for Fine Arts.

HESTON, JULIE LOU, physician; b. Columbus, Ohio, Aug. 13, 1939; d. Joseph Carter and Jane (Allen) H. B.A., DePauw U., 1961; M.D., U. Mich., 1965. Diplomate Am. Bd. Psychiatry and Neurology. Intern, Phila. Gen. Hosp., 1965-66; resident in psychiatry Johns Hopkins Hosp., Balt., 1966-69; resident in neurology Mass. Gen. Hosp., Boston, 1973-76; practice medicine specializing in psychiatry, Balt., 1969-73; instr. psychiatry Johns Hopkins Sch. Medicine, Balt., 1969-73; practice medicine specializing in neurology, Concord, N.H., 1976—. Episcopalian. Office: 10 Fayette St Concord NH 03301

HESTON, LYNNE KAREN, marketing consultant; b. N.Y.C., Dec. 30, 1951; d. Charles and Joan Heston; B.A., U. Pa., 1973; M.B.A., U. Hartford, 1980; m. Nicholas Paindiris, Oct. 26, 1975; children—Jessica Nicole, Charles Alexander. Research analyst The Futures Group, Glastonbury, Conn., 1973-77; mktg. research analyst Barclays Am./Bus. Credit, Inc. (formerly Aetna Bus. Credit, Inc.), East Hartford, Conn., 1977-79, mgr. mktg. research, 1979-81, asst. v.p. mktg. planning and research, 1981; mgr. mktg. research Conn. Gen. Life Ins. Co., Hartford, 1981-82; dir. mktg. research CIGNA, Hartford, 1982-83; ind. mktg. cons., 1984—; cons. in field. Mem. Am. Mktg. Assn. Home and office: 119 Butler Dr Glastonbury CT 06033

HESTOR, SUE CAROL, lawyer; b. Portland, Maine, Feb. 1, 1944; d. Kenneth and Harriet (Rose) Hestor; B.A., Wheaton Coll., 1965; J.D., Golden Gate U., 1976. Bar: Calif. 1977—, U.S. Dist. Ct. (no. dist.) Calif. Atty. San Francisco Unified Sch. Dist., 1977-80; environ. atty., San Francisco, 1981—. Founder, bd. dirs. San Franciscans for Reasonable Growth, 1979—; bd. dirs. San Francisco Consumer Action, 1981—, Regional Young Adult Project, 1982—, West Bay Health Systems Agy., San Francisco, 1976-82. Mem. Calif. Women Lawyers. Democrat. Baptist. Home: 4536 20th St San Francisco CA 94114 Office: 870 Market St Suite 1121 San Francisco CA 94102

HETER, MARTHA LOUISE, engineering manufacturing company administrator; b. Hutchinson, Kans., Nov. 3, 1949; d. Waid and Gladys (Richardson) H.; student Southwestern Coll., 1967-68; B.S., Kans. State U., 1971; postgrad. U. Kans., 1980-81. Adminstrv. asst. Gril-lite, Inc., Shawnee Mission, Kans., 1972-73, sales coordinator, 1973-75, mdse. coordinator, 1975-76; contract adminstr. Chgo. Heater Co., Inc. subs. Marley Co., Mission, Kans., 1976-80, purchasing agt., 1980—; pvt. piano instr., 1977-81. Mem. Lenexa (Kans.) Bicentennial Choir, 1976, Johnson County Republican Run, 1980, Mothers March of Dimes, Spl. Olympics, 1982. Mem. AAUW, Am. Home Econs. Assn., Nat. Assn. Purchasing Mgrs., Four Colonies Homes Assn., Kans. State U. Alumni Assn. Republican. Methodist. Clubs: Kansas City Racquet; Kansas City Ski. Home: 12224 W 79th Terr Lenexa KS 66215 Office: Chgo Heater Co Inc subs Marley Co 1900 Johnson Dr Mission Woods KS 66205

HETH, CHARLOTTE ANNE, music educator; b. Muskogee, Okla., Oct. 29, 1937; d. Woodrow Curt and Eula Jewel (Seabolt) Wilson; m. Linton LeRoy Heth, July 5, 1966 (div. Jan. 1970). B.A., U. Tulsa, 1959, M.Mus., 1960; Ph.D., UCLA, 1975. Tchr., Jal (N.Mex.) High Sch., 1960-61, Catoosa (Okla.) High Sch., 1961-62; Peace Corps vol. Maaraga Hiwot Haile Selassie I Sch., Ambo, Ethiopia, 1962-64; tchr. A.B.C. Unified Sch. Dist. Schs., Artesia, Calif., 1965-73; asst. prof., assoc. prof. music UCLA, 1974—, dir. Am. Indian Studies Ctr., 1976—; panel mem. for folk arts Nat. Endowment for Arts, 1980-82; bd. mem. Indian Ctrs., Inc., Los Angeles, 1977-78. Editor: Selected Reports in Ethnomusicology, 1980; American Indian Culture and Research Jour., 1982; record producer Songs of Earth, Water, Fire and Sky, etc., 1976; video producer Music of the Sacred Fire, etc., 1978. Ford Found. dissertation fellow, 1973-74; So. Fellowship Fund postdoctoral fellow, 1978-79; sr. postdoctoral award Newberry Library, Chgo., 1978-79, NRC, 1984-85. Mem. Soc. Ethnomusicology (council mem. 1977-84, council chmn. 1980-82), Nat. Indian Edn. Assn., Western Social Sci. Assn., Sigma Alpha Iota. Democrat. Baptist. Office: Music Dept Schoenberg Hall UCLA Los Angeles CA 90024

HETLAND, RUTH ELLEN, surgeon; b. Corpus Christi, July 9, 1952; d. Melvin James and Edith Lois (Rauchenecker) H.; m. Michael John Poccia, June 26, 1982; children—Rebecca Madeline, Thomas Albert. B.A., Cornell Coll., Mt. Vernon, Iowa, 1974; M.D., Washington U., St. Louis, 1976. Diplomate Am. Bd. Surgery. Intern, Barnes Hosp., St. Louis, 1976-77, resident in surgery, 1977-80, chief resident, 1980-81; assoc. in surgery U. Iowa Coll. Medicine, Iowa City, 1981-82; asst. prof. surgery U. Rochester, 1982—. Mem. Monroe County Med. Soc., Med. Soc. State N.Y., Assn. Acad. Surgery, Med. Women's Assn. Rochester, Phi Beta Kappa, Alpha Omega Alpha. Democrat. Roman Catholic. Office: The Genesee Hosp 220 Alexander St Rochester NY 14607

HETRICK, MICHELLE, truck parts company executive; b. Columbus, Ohio, Sept. 25, 1958; d. Saverio and Domenica Margaret (Zappia) Caruso; m. Lynn Paul Hetrick, Apr. 12, 1980; 1 dau., Vanessa Lynn. A.A., Stark Tech. Coll., Canton, Ohio, 1978. Vice-pres. Lynn Truck Parts Corp., Massillon, Ohio, 1979—. Mem. Massillon C. of C., Nat. Assn. Female Execs., Stark Tech. Alumni Assn., Internat. Truck Parts Assn. Republican. Roman Catholic. Clubs: Canton Jr. Woman's, Arboretum Garden, Timken Mercy Service League (Canton). Avocations: skiing; tennis; snowmobiling. Office: Lynn Truck Parts Corp 739 3d St SE Massillon OH 44646

HETTLER, MADELINE THERESE, data processing company executive; b. Phila., Feb. 3, 1949; d. Francis Joseph and Cecilia (Freisburg) H. B.S., U. Pa., 1986. With tech. support dept. Martin Marietta, Phila., 1976-84, Sundata, Phila., 1984-85; system support disaster recovery coordinator Nat. Liberties Corp., Frazer, Pa., 1985—. Home: 2217 Bond Ave Drexel HI-1 PA 19026 Office: Nat Liberties Corp Moores Rd Frazer PA 19355

HETU, JOAN LAFFORD, nursing administrator, business executive; b. Southbridge, Mass., Dec. 28, 1926; d. George William and Harriet (Delehanty) Tully; m. Malcolm Howard Lyle, Mar. 17, 1949 (dec. July 1952); m. Joseph Paul Hetu, June 8, 1955 (div. 1978); children—Christine Lyle Hamilton, George David, Jennifer, Wendy Clare, Martin Evan. Nursing diploma, The Meml. Hosp., Worcester, Mass., 1948; B.S. in Health Sci. Adminstrn., Chapman Coll., Orange, Calif., 1983. R.N., Calif., Mass. Asst. head nurse Boston City Hosp., 1949-50; nursing supr. Harrington Hosp., Southbridge, Mass., 1950-66; asst. head nurse Queen of Angels Hosp., Hollywood, Calif., 1970-72; head nurse Am. Med. Internat., Garden Grove, Calif., 1972-77, nursing supr., 1977-80; nursing adminstr. St. Joseph Health Systems, Yorba Linda, Calif., 1980—. Mem. Nat. Assn. Female Execs., Emergency Nurses Assn., AAUW. Democrat. Roman Catholic. Avocations: ballroom dancing; gourmet cooking. Office: Saint Joseph Health System Saint Jude Yorba Linda 16850 E Bastanchury Rd Yorba Linda CA 92686

HEUMAN, DONNA RENA, entrepreneur; b. Seattle, May 27, 1949; d. Russell George and Edna Inez (Armstrong) H. B.A. in Psychology, UCLA, 1972; J.D., U. Calif.-San Francisco, 1985. Owner, Heuman & Assocs., San Francisco, 1978—. Mem. Hastings Internat. and Comparative Law Rev., 1984-85. Mem. Nat. Shorthand Reporters Assn., Women Entrepreneurs, Calif. Shorthand Reporters Assn., Nat. Assn. Female Execs. Clubs: Commonwealth (San Francisco), World Affairs Council (San Francisco), Zonta (bd. dirs.) (San Francisco). Home: 365 Vallejo St Apt 6 San Francisco CA 94133

HEUN, GISELA MARIA, university administrator; b. Stuttgart, Ger., Aug. 4, 1944; came to U.S., 1968, naturalized, 1985; d. Wilhelm Otto and Else Klara Jaeger; B.B.A., U. Frankfurt/Main, 1964; student mgmt. seminars U. Mich., 1974; m. Hartmut Heun, Jan. 9, 1969. Exec. asst. export div. VDO Instruments, Frankfurt/Main, 1962-68, asst. to gen. mgr., Detroit, 1968-69; translator/editor Lang. and Lang. Behavior Abstracts Jour., U. Mich., 1971-72, adminstrv. asst. in Germanic langs. and lit., 1972-73, bus. mgr. Coll. Lit., Sci. and Arts Adminstrn., 1973-79, adminstrv. mgr. physiology Med. Sch., 1979—; cons. in fin. and personnel mgmt., grants mgmt.; translator and interpreter German/English, U. Mich. Mem. Am. Assn. Med. Colls. Club: German/Am. Cultural Exchange. Home: 3120 Pillar Dr Whitmore Lake MI 48189 Office: 1335 E Catherine St U Mich Ann Arbor MI 48109

HEWELL, GRACE L., educational administrator, government official; b. Atlanta, Dec. 18, 1918; d. John Lee and Josie (Harris) Hewell; A.B., Spelman Coll., 1940; M.S.W., Atlanta U., 1943; M.A., Columbia U., 1952, E.D., 1958, M.S. in Public Health Edn., 1954. Service club dir. U.S. Armed Forces Europe, 1945-50; public health educator Dept. Health, City of N.Y., 1954-60; program coordination officer Office of Asst. Sec. for Legis., HEW, 1961-65; edn. chief Com. on Edn. and Labor U. S. Ho. Reps., Washington, 1965-66; adult edn. program officer Office of Edn., N.Y. region, 1967-78; specialist ednl. telecommunications Dept. Edn., Washington, 1978—; commr. U. S. Nat. Commn. for UNESCO, 1975-80; cons. Job Corps Centers for Women, Pres.'s Task Force on War on Poverty, 1964-65; staff liaison rep. Pres. Kennedy's Commn. on Status of Women, HEW; cons. continuing edn. program Spelman Coll. Served with WAC, 1943-45; founder Acad. on Human Rights and Peace, 1977; Social Action Inst., 1975; U.S.A. del. to UNESCO Internat. Human Rights Congress, 1978. Recipient numerous awards in field of edn. including disting. service award for contributions in health, edn. and welfare, Commn. on Status of Negro Women of Greater N.Y., 1963. Fellow AAAS, Am. Public Health Assn.; mem. AAUW, Am. Assn. for Adult and Continuing Edn., Nat. Assn. for Public Continuing and Adult Edn. (recipient outstanding service award 1973, 81), Nat. Assn. Social Workers, N.Y. Acad. Scis., Nat. Council Negro Women, Kappa Delta Pi, Pi Lambda Theta, Phi Delta Kappa, Delta Sigma Theta. Baptist. Club: Altrusa, Inc. (chmn. internat. relations com., recipient citation for disting. contributions to human rights, Washington). Office: Dept Edn 400 Maryland Ave SW Washington DC 20202

HEWITT, ADRIENNE DEERE, lawyer; b. Moline, Ill., July 17, 1955; d. William Alexander Hewitt and Patricia (Deere) Wiman Hewitt. B.A. summa cum laude, Dartmouth Coll., 1977; J.D. cum laude, Georgetown U., 1982. Bar: D.C. 1983. Paralegal, Fidelman, Wolffe & Waldron, Washington, 1977-79; assoc. Milbank, Tweed, Hadley & McCloy, Washington, 1982—. Mem. Phi Beta Kappa. Episcopalian. Office: Milbank Tweed Hedley & McCloy 1825 Eye St Washington DC 20006

HEWITT, BASALINE HARRIS, educator; b. Fayette, Ala., Aug. 15; d. Robert and Zora (McConnell) Harris; m. Dempsey Hewitt, Aug. 23, 1943 (div. Dec. 1970); 1 dau., Miriam Ann. B.S., Ala. A&M Coll., 1954, postgrad. in adminstrn.; M.A., Atlanta U., 1971. Cert. tchr. exceptional children, Ga. Tchr. educable mentally handicapped children Atlanta Pub. Schs., 1955—, in-sch. chairperson Thomasville Heights Elem. Sch., 1978-82; cluster leader C.R. Drew Elem. Sch., 1983—; dir. Communication Skills Cons., Inc., Silver Spring, Md., 1983. Mem. Atlanta Fedn. Tchrs., Nat. Assn. Female Execs. Democrat. Clubs: Willing Workers, Gamnixs (treas. 1982—). Lodge: Order of Eastern Star (treas. 1982—). Home: 3125 Ivan Hill Dr SW Atlanta GA 30311 Office: Charles R Drew Elem Sch 409 E Lake Blvd SE Atlanta GA 30317

HEWITT, EMILY CLARK, lawyer; b. Balt., May 26, 1944; d. John Frank and Margaret Genevieve (Gray) Hewitt. A.B., Cornell U., 1966; M.Phil., Union Theol. Sem., 1975; J.D., Harvard U., 1978. Bar: Mass. 1978, U.S. Dist. Ct. Mass. 1979, U.S. Ct. Appeals (1st cir.) 1984. Ordained priest Protestant Episcopal Ch., 1974. Adminstr. Cornell and Hofstra U. Upward Bound Programs, N.Y.C., 1967-69; asst. minister St. Mary's Episcopal Ch., Manhattanville, N.Y., 1972-73; lectr. Union Theol. Sem., N.Y.C., 1972-73, 74-75; asst. prof. Andover Newton Theol. Sch., Newton Centre, Mass., 1973-75; assoc. firm Hill & Barlow, Boston, 1978-85; ptnr. firm Hill & Barlow, Boston, 1985—. Co-author: Women Priests: Yes or No?, 1973; contbr. works in field. Bd. dirs. Mass. Found. for Humanities and Pub. Policy, South Hadley, 1983—. Mem. ABA, Mass. Bar Assn. (council mem. real property sect., 1983—), Women's Bar Assn. Mass., New Eng. Women in Real Estate (bd. dirs. 1985—), Mass. Conveyancer's Assn. Office: Hill & Barlow 225 Franklin St Boston MA 02110

HEWITT, PATRICIA WIMAN (MRS. WILLIAM ALEXANDER HEWITT), agriculturalist; b. Chgo., Jan. 17, 1925; d. Charles Deere and Pattie (Southall) Wiman; student Conn. Coll. for Women, 1942-44, U. Calif. at Santa Barbara, 1944-45, George Washington U., 1946-47; m. William Alexander Hewitt, Jan. 3, 1948; children—Anna Hewitt Wolfe, Adrienne Deere, Alexander Southall. Asst. to mgr. Midvale Farms Corp., Tucson, 1945-47, dir., sec., 1945-80, half owner, 1963-80; owner, mgr. Friendship Farms, East Moline, Ill., 1955—; owner, joint mgr. Camelot Vineyards, Rutherford, Calif., 1960—; dir. Diagnostic Data Inc., Mountain View, Calif. Equestrian coach Japanese Self Def. Forces, 1967-68. Mem. Jr. League, San Francisco, 1951—; asst. to field dir. ARC, San Francisco, 1944-45, service cons., 1950-54; bd. dirs. YWCA, San Francisco, 1951-52, Moline Welfare Agy., 1959-69; governing mem. Arabian Horse Club Registry Am., 1963-64; trustee, pres.'s council Marycrest Coll., Davenport, Iowa, 1969-73; v.p. U.S. Modern Pentathlon Assn., 1971-76; mem. U.S. Olympic Games Com., 1970-76; mem. nat. bd. advisers Nat. Assn. for Retarded Children, 1967—; mem. Ill.-Iowa Assn. for Children with Specific Learning Problems, 1970-79; mem. Ill. State Adv. Council Edn. Handicapped Children, 1973-75; mem. exec. com. Nat. Reading Council, 1970-72; trustee Charles Deere Wiman Meml. Trust, Morris Animal Found., Lincoln Acad. of Ill., Rock Island Franciscan Hosp., Knox Coll., Galesburg, Ill., 1975—; chmn. bd. trustees Butterworth Meml. Trust; trustee Arabian Horse Owners Found., 1961-73, mem. adv. bd., 1973—; mem. women's bd. Field Mus. Natural History, Chgo., 1972-81; bd. dirs. Family YMCA, Rock Island, 1975-79; mem. service council United Way Rock Island, Ill. and Scott County, Iowa, 1973-76; bd. trustees Am. Farmland Trust, 1981—; governing life mem. Art Inst. Chgo., 1972—; mem. Nat. Com. on U.S.-China Relations, 1974—, Ill. Racing Bd., 1973-77, Nat. Assn. State Racing Commrs., 1973-77; mem. nat. bd. dirs. U.S. Equestrian Team, 1977—; mem. citizens com. U. Ill., 1974-77, animal sci. adv. com. Coll. Agr., 1974-77; mem. mental health adv. com. Rock Island County Pub. Health Bd., 1974—; mem. adv. bd. Assn. for Retarded Children and Adults Rock Island County, 1972—; mem. corp. vis. com. for dept. psychology M.I.T., 1977—. Mem. Internat. Arabian Horse Assn. (dir. 1964-67), Grayson Found., Arabian Horse Racing Assn., Am. Horse Show Assn. (life, mem. drugs and medications com.). Episcopalian. Clubs: Santa Barbara Yacht; Arts (Chgo.). Home: 3800 Blackhawk Rd Rock Island IL 61201 Office: Friendship Farms Rural Route 2 Box 612 East Moline IL 61244

HEWITT, SANDRA ELAINE STUARD, banker; b. Springfield, Tenn., May 30, 1951; d. Clarence Connell and Madge Delma (White) Stuard; B.S., Austin Peay State U., Clarksville, Tenn., 1973; grad. various banking courses; m. Richard W. Hewitt, Sept. 2, 1972; 1 dau., Lesley Elaine. With Commerce Union Bank, Nashville, 1973-82, asst. v.p., 1981-82, mgr. Madison br., 1980-82; v.p., dir. br. adminstrn. United So. Bank, Nashville, 1982-83; v.p. Union Planters Nat. Bank, 1983—; dir. Transaction Delivery. Chmn., Robertson County chpt. Am. Heart Assn., 1979-80, memls. chmn. Mid Tenn. chpt., 1980; mem. allocations com. Nashville Area United Way, 1978-79. Mem. Nat. Assn. Bank Women (nat. scholar 1983, treas. Met. Nashville, Tenn. awards and scholarship chmn., seminar and nat. workshop presenter), Am. Inst. Banking (counsel Nashville chpt. 1978), Rivergate Mall Mchts. Assn. (treas. 1979), Springfield Bus. and Profl. Women's Club (v.p., treas. 1979; Young Careerist award 1979, Bus. Woman of Yr. award 1979), Chi Omega. Club: Soroptimist (rec. sec. 1982-83). Home: Route 1 Cedar Hill TN 37032 Office: 200 4th Ave N Nashville TN 37219

HEWLETT-KIERSTEAD, NANCY CARRICK, psychologist; b. Schenectady, Feb. 19, 1927; d. Clarence Wilson and Mary Stephens (Carrick) Hewlett; B.F.A., Cornell U., 1949; M.A. (Univ. fellow), U. Mich., 1952; Ph.D. (Univ. fellow), U. Conn., 1972; registered clin. psychologist; m. Andrzej T. Romer, June 19, 1952 (div. 1969); children—Jan Edward, Anna Louise, Mary Helena; m. 2d, Henry A. Kierstead, July 26, 1981. Tchr. art Thomaston (Conn.) High Sch., 1960-63; freelance artist, potter, 1962-67; assoc. prof. psychology Eastern Conn. State Coll., Willimantic, 1969-34; clin. psychologist Effective Coping Strategies, Downers Grove, Ill., 1982—. Asst. clk. Storrs (Conn.) monthly meeting Soc. of Friends, 1978-80, clk., 1980. Mem. Am. Psychol. Assn., Ill. Psychol. Assn., Conn. Psychol. Assn., Sierra Club, AAUW, Clearwater. Office: ECS Greenbriar Med Ctr 6800 Main St Downers Grove IL

HEXNER, LILA M., entrepreneur, educator, consultant; b. Kimberly, Wis., May 14; d. Harold George and Florence Esther (McCabe) Fird; B.S. in Edn., U. Wis.; M.Phil.Ed., Boston Coll., 1973; m. Peter E. Hexner (div. 1986); children—Michael T., Holly A., Thomas S. Women's adv., mem. adminstrn. Middlesex Community Coll., 1971-78, founder, dir. women's center, 1971-75, founder dir. Widening Opportunity Research Center, 1975-78, founder, dir. div. community services, 1978; founder, Edn. for Commercialization div. No. Energy Corp., N.E. Regional Solar Energy Center Edn. Dept., Boston, 1978-82; founder, pres. Cons. Exchange, Inc., 1982—; mem. adv. com. Internat. Solar Renewable Energy Conf., 1981; chmn. Bus. Resource Ctr., Small Bus. Assn.; cons. in field. Mem. Mass. Adv. Council on Vocat. Tech. Edn., 1972-79; mem. Mass. Gov.'s Spl. Commn. on Youth Unemployment, 1978—; mem. exec. com. Mass. coordinating com. Internat. Women's Yr., 1978. Recipient Disting. Service award Middlesex Community Coll., 1973; grants include Fund for Improvement Postsecondary Edn., 1976-78. Mem. Women in Solar Energy (nat. adv. bd. 1980-82), Boston Computer Soc., Smaller Bus. Assn. New Eng. (chmn. first bus. conf.). Home: 105-1 Trowbridge Cambridge MA 02138

HEXT, KATHLEEN FLORENCE, corporate auditor; b. Bellingham, Wash., Oct. 7, 1941; d. Benjamin Byron and Sarah Debell (Youngquist) Gross.; m. George Ronald Hext, June 13, 1964 (div. 1972). B.A., Magna Cum Laude, Lewis & Clark Coll., Portland, Oreg., 1963; M.A., Stanford U., 1964; M.B.A., U.C.L.A., 1979. C.P.A.; cert. bank auditor; cert. info. systems auditor. Chief exec. officer Internat. Lang. Ctr., Rome, 1970-77; auditor Peat, Marwick, Mitchell & Co., Los Angeles, 1979-81; mgr. fin. audit Lloyds Bank, Los Angeles, 1981-83, mgr. EDP audit, 1983-85; dir. corp. audit First Interstate Bancorp, Los Angeles, 1985—; treas., Arcadia H.O. Assocs., El Monte, Calif., 1982-84, pres., 1985—. Recipient Edward W. Carter award UCLA, 1979. Mem. Am. Inst. C.P.A.s, Inst. Internal Auditors, EDP Auditors Assn., Data Processing Mgmt. Assn., Calif. Soc. C.P.A.s. Republican Episcopalian. Avocations: photography; microcomputers; reading. Home: 5331A N Peck Rd El Monte CA 91732 Office: First Interstate Bancorp 707 Wilshire Blvd Los Angeles CA 90017

HEYCK, GERTRUDE PAINE DALY (MRS. THEODORE R. HEYCK), club woman; b. Houston, Nov. 30, 1910; d. David and Gertrude (Paine) Daly; student Wellesley Coll., 1929, Pembroke Coll., 1931-34; B.A., Brown U., 1934; m. Theodore R. Heyck, May 1, 1935; children—Jane Peel (Mrs. Donald H. Gaucher), Theodore Daly. Dir., Union Stock Yards, San Antonio, 1961-64. Mem. Jr. League. Clubs: Wellesley, Brown-Pembroke (v.p.), Brown (Houston); Brown Faculty (Providence). Home: 1907 Bolsover Rd Houston TX 77005 also 400 Bellevue Ave Newport RI 02840

HEYDE, MARTHA BENNETT (MRS. ERNEST R. HEYDE), psychologist; b. New Bern, N.C., Jan. 31, 1920; d. George Spotswood and Katherine (McIntosh) Bennett; A.B., Barnard Coll., 1941; M.A., Columbia, 1949, Ph.D., 1959; m. Ernest R. Heyde, Aug. 17, 1946. Instr. psychol. founds. and services Tchrs. Coll., Columbia U., N.Y.C., 1953-60, research asst., career pattern study Horace Mann-Lincoln Inst., Tchrs. Coll. Columbia U., 1957-59, research asso., 1960-70, cons., 1970-73. Mem. Barnard Coll. Alumnae Council, 1956-61, 69—, pres. class, 1956-61. Trustee, Barnard Coll., 1974-78. Mem. Am. Psychol. Assn., Am. Personnel and Guidance Assn., Sigma Xi, Kappa Delta Pi, Pi Lambda Theta. Contbr. to research monograph The Vocational Maturity of Ninth Grade Boys, 1960, Floundering and Trial After High Sch, 1967; co-author Vocational Maturity during the High School Years, 1979. Home: 140 Cabrini Blvd Apt 109 New York NY 10033

HEYER, ANNA HARRIET, retired music librarian; b. Little Rock, Aug. 30, 1909; d. Arthur Wesley and Harriet Anna (Gage) H. A.B., B.Mus., Tex. Christian U., 1930; B.S. in L.S., U. Ill., 1933; M.S. in L.S., Columbia U., 1939; M.Mus. in Musicology, U. Mich., 1943. Elem. sch. music tchr. Ft. Worth Pub. Schs., 1931-32; high sch. librarian, 1934-38; cataloguer library, U. Tex.-Austin, 1939-40; music librarian, asst. prof. L.S., N. Tex. State U., Denton, 1940-65, librarian emeritus, 1976; cons. music library materials Tex. Christian U., Ft. Worth, 1965-79; ret., 1979. Author: A Check-List of Publications of Music, 1944; A Bibliography of Contemporary Music in the Music Library, North Texas State College, 1955; Historical Sets, Collected Editions and Monuments of Music: A Guide to Their Contents, 1957, 2d edit., 1969, 3d rev. edit., 1980; contbr. articles to profl. publs. Recipient citations for contbn. to music librarianship Music Library Assn., 1980, to music librarianship in Tex., 1983. Mem. ALA, Tex. Library Assn., Music Library Assn., AAUW, DAR. Mem. Disciples of Christ Ch. Clubs: Altrusa, Woman's Club Ft. Worth, Colonial Country. Home: 2538 Greene Ave Fort Worth TX 76109

HEYMANN, PATRICIA PEHLKE, container manufacturing company executive; b. Chgo., June 29, 1928; d. Frank Charles and Elsie (Oetting) Pehlke; m. John L. Heymann, June 17, 1950 (dec. 1980); children—Cynthia, William, Michael, Karen. B.A. Lake Forest Coll., 1950; M.A., U. Ill., 1985; postgrad. Harvard U., 1984. Sec. Encyclopedia Britannica, Chgo., 1950-53; pres. United Container Corp., Chgo., 1980—. Mem. Leed council New City YMCA, Chgo., 1983—. Office: United Container Corp 1350 N Elston St Chicago IL 60622

HEYN, EILEEN LEONE, aerospace company executive; b. Moose Lake, Minn., Mar. 9, 1945. A.A., Highline Coll., Des Moines, Wash., 1983; student in Bus. Adminstrn., City U., Bellevue, Wash., 1985—. Asst. br. mgr. Cascade Savs. & Loan Assn., Lynnwood, Wash., 1971-72; assoc. br. mgr. Avco Fin. Services, Everett, Wash., 1972-74; quality assurance tech. aide Boeing Co., Seattle, 1975-82; retrofit rev. bd. coordinator Boeing, Seattle, 1982-84, exec. placement specialist, 1984-85, integrated employee records systems analyst, 1985—; cons. and lectr. in field. Author-editor: (Bulletin) Illuminations, 1981-82; contbg. editor: Advisor, 1982. Mem., Seattle Repertory Orgn., 1982-86, Zonta Internat., 1983-85; v.p. Lake Heights Community Club, Bellevue, Wash., 1985-86, pres., 1986—. Recipient Extra Mile award Boy Scouts Am., Seattle, 1979; Boeing awards, 1980, 82. Mem. Am. Bus. Women's Assn. (pres. 1982-83, Member of Yr., 1982, Nat. Bus. Woman of Yr., 1983), Internat. Tng. in Communications Council (v.p. 1984-85), Seattle Profl. and Managerial Women's Network. Avocations: Public speaking; hiking; traveling; theatre-going.

HEYSER, HOLLY RUTH, interior landscaper; b. Norristown, Pa., Apr. 18, 1958; d. William Howard and Janice Marie (Knerr) H. B.S. in Mktg., Lehigh U., 1980. Mgr. Heyser Landscaping, Inc., Norristown, Pa., 1981—. Block chmn. Republican Party, Wayne, Pa., 1984—. Mem. Lehigh U. Alumni Orgn. (v.p. 1984—, Young Alumni award 1985). Presbyterian. Avocations: tennis; skiing; swimming; sailing; knitting. Office: Heyser Landscaping Inc 400 N Park Ave Norristown PA 19403

HEYWOOD, SANDRA RENE, video company executive; b. Ft. Richardson, Alaska, Dec. 31, 1946; d. William LeRoy Conant and Phyllis (Rogerson) Conant Colter; m. Kumen Leland Heywood, Sept. 3, 1965; children—Brian Kumen, Tori, Celia. Student Eastern Ariz. Jr. Coll., 1964-65, Utah Trade Inst. Tech., 1965-66, San Juan Coll., Farmington, N. Mex., 1973-75, Ariz. State U., 1978-79. Saleswoman, Farmington Realty, 1972-76; reading tutor and trainer Metra Reading Program, Mesa, Ariz., 1977-80; sales mgr. KDJI, Holbrook, Ariz., 1980-83; mgr. Rent-A-Flik, Holbrook, 1983; v.p. Heywood Video, Inc., Springerville, Ariz., 1983—. Pres. Young Women, Ch. of Jesus Christ Of Latter-day Saints, Holbrook, 1967-82, also dir. drama, speech and dance, other activities; den mother, coach Kit Carson council Cub Scouts Am., 1974-77; chmn. Holbrook Christmas Lights Com., 1982; mem. Planning and Zoning Commn., Edgar, Ariz., 1986. State of Ariz. grantee, 1964. Mem. Am. Video Assn. (bd. dirs. 1984-86). Republican.

HIATT, MARY POTT, English studies educator; b. Wusih, China; d. Walter Hawks and Elizabeth Washington (Fisher) Pott (parents Am. citizens); A.B., Elmira Coll.; M.A., Columbia U., Ph.D., 1971; m. Norman W. Storer, Feb. 1975; 1 son, Andrew Hiatt. Instr. English, Rutgers U., Newark, 1969-71; asst. prof. Baruch Coll., CUNY, 1971-75, assoc. prof., 1975-79, prof., 1979—, dept. chmn., 1981-85. Mem. Nat. Council Tchrs. English, MLA, Phi Beta Kappa. Author: Artful Balance: The Parallel Structures of Style, 1975; The Way Women Write, 1977. Office: Baruch College CUNY English Dept 17 Lexington Ave New York NY 10010

HIBBITTS, AGNES LOUISE, medical transport company executive; b. Snyder, Tex., Apr. 8, 1929; d. Thomas Daniel and Ruby Jewell (Tankersley) Malett; m. Jack Terry Hibbitts, Nov. 19, 1944; children—Terry Wayne, Danny LaMar, Ronnie Gene, Joyce Diane, Dickie Lynn. Machine knitting instr. Kitten Knitten, Midland, Tex., 1957-60; salesperson Avon, Tex., Calif., 1972-78; driver Medi-Van Service, Indio, Calif., 1978-79, owner, operator, 1979-84, exec. pres., 1984—, cons., 1984-85. Mem. Indio C. of C., Missing Children, Frat. Order Police. Democrat. Baptist. Lodge: Eagles (pres. local club 1974-75). Avocations: knitting; crocheting; latch hooking; needlepoint. Home: 1142 7th St Box 65 Coachella CA 92236 Office: Medi-Van Service 83-616 Ave 45 Suite 8 Indio CA 92201

HIBNER, JANET LOUISE, state legislator; b. Tippecanoe County, Ind., July 26, 1935; d. Harvey Delbert and Alta Pearle (Lucas) Nelson; A.B., Ind. U., 1957; children—Kevin C., Jill A. Assoc. microbiologist Eli Lilly & Co., Indpls., 1957-61; mem. Ind. Ho. of Reps., 1976—. Vice chmn. Wayne County Republican Com., 1974-76.

HICKCOX, BONITA ANN, nurse; b. Spring Green, Wis., Dec. 5, 1928; d. Sidney Hood and Mildred Veronica (Snyder) Runyan; R.N., Meth. Hosp. Sch. Nursing, 1950; student U. Wis., 1971, St. Petersburg Jr. Coll., 1976-77; m. Marvin Jackson Hickcox, Oct. 15, 1954; children—Kimberley, Jeffrey, Mark. Staff nurse Meth. Hosp., Madison, 1950-52, Reedsburg (Wis.) Hosp., 1952; supr. Meth. Hosp., Madison, 1952-53, asst. head nurse, 1953-55, emergency room nurse, 1956-58; staff nurse/head nurse Central Wis. Center, Madison, 1969-73; dir. nurses Extended Care Facilities, St. Petersburg, Dunedin and Largo, Fla., 1974-82; health care coordinator Abilities, Inc., Fla. Rehab. Center, 1982—. Home: 1729 Valencia Dr W Largo FL 33544 Office: 2735 Whitney Rd Clearwater FL 33520

HICKEN, GRACE DOROTHY, social worker; b. Milw., Sept. 15, 1919; d. Rudolph A. and Hildegarde Emma (Brandt) Maurer; m. Edward Oscar Schroeder, Sept. 2, 1942 (dec. 1962); children—David John (dec.), James Edward, John Frederick; m. William Stevens Hicken, Sept. 12, 1964. B.S.W. cum laude, Mt. Mary Coll., 1976. Sec. Slocum Straw Works, Milw., 1937-42; part time teller West Fed. Savs. & Loan, Milw., 1963-72; social worker Bradley Convalescent Center, Milw., 1977-78, St. Joseph's Hosp., Milw., 1978; dir. social work Community Meml. Hosp., Menomonee Falls, Wis., 1978-80, ret., 1980; vol. coordinator, facilitator Lifeline, support group for suicide prevention, Milw., 1981—; vol. worker refugee families and prison inmates; vol. speaker on suicide prevention; founder living apts. for elderly, 1976. Recipient Madonna medal Alumni Assn. Mt. Mary Coll. Mem. Am. Assn. Suidicology, Nat. Assn. Social Workers, Benedict Center for Criminal Justice, Kappa Gamma Pi. Lutheran. Home: 2869 N 58th St Milwaukee WI 53210

HICKEY, DELINA ROSE, state legislator; b. N.Y.C., Mar. 25, 1941; d. Robert Joseph and Marie (Ripa) H.; B.S. in Edn., SUNY, Oneonta, 1963; M.A., Manhattan Coll., 1967; Ed.D. in Counselor Edn. and Psychology, U. Idaho, 1971; m. David Andrews; 1 son by previous marriage, Jon Robert. Elem. sch. tchr., counselor, Westchester, N.Y., 1963-68; part-time instr. psychology St. Thomas Aquinas Coll., Sparkhill, N.Y., 1971-72; asst. prof. edn. Nathaniel Hawthorne Coll., Antrim, N.H., 1972-75; prof. faculty Keene (N.H.) State

Coll., 1975—, assoc. prof. edn., 1978—; mem. N.H. Legislature from 13th Dist., 1981—; mem. adv. council Title IV, 1979-82; fellow Nat. Ctr. Research in Vocat. Edn., 1984-85; assoc. in edn. Harvard U., 1984-85. Trustee, Big Bros./Big Sisters, Keene, 1978-80, Family Planning Services S.W. N.H., 1976—; mem. N.H. Juvenile Conf. Com., 1976-81. Mem. N.H. Order Women Legislators, New Eng. Research Orgn., Am. Vocat. Assn., N.H. Personnel and Guidance Assn. Democrat. Author articles in field. Office: Elliot Hall Keene NH 03431

HICKEY, JEAN ALICIA, state liquor control commissioner; b. Riverton, Vt., Dec. 7, 1927; d. William John and Elizabeth Julia (Culver) H. Bus. mgr. C Liquor Control Dept., Montpelier, Vt., 1969-73, commr., 1970-71, 71, liquor control bd. exec., 1973-79, commr., 1979, liquor control commr., 1979—. Mem. dean's adv. council Vt. Coll., Montpelier; mem. adv. bd. dirs. Vt. Fed. Savs. & Loan Assn., Montpelier. Mem. Nat. Alcoholic Beverage Control Assn. (new products and procedures, ethics and fair practices coms.). Roman Catholic. Club: Green Mountain Transp. (Burlington, Vt.). Office: Dept Liquor Control Green Mountain Dr Montpelier VT 05602

HICKEY, THERESA CAROLE, accountant; b. Jersey City, Dec. 18, 1949; d. Lawrence Anthony and Loretta Virginia (Edwards) H. Student, Jersey City State Coll., 1984. Accounts payable specialist Jonathon Logan Fin., Secaucus, N.J., 1981-83, contractors, freight accounts payable, collection coordinator, 1983—. Roman Catholic. Avocations: travel; reading; crochet.

HICKEY, WINIFRED ESPY, state legislator; b. Rawlins, Wyo.; d. David P. and Eugenia (Blake) Espy; children—John David, Paul Joseph. B.A., Loretto Heights Coll., 1933; postgrad. U. Utah, 1934, U. Chgo. Sch. Social Service, 1936. Dir., Carbon County Welfare Dept., 1935-36; field rep. Wyo. Dept. Welfare, 1937-38; dir. Red Cross Club, Europe, 1942-45; commr. Laramie County, Wyo., 1973-80; mem. Wyo. Senate, 1980—; dir. United Savs. & Loan Assn., Cheyenne, Wyo. Bd. dirs. U. Wyo. Found.; chmn. adv. council div. community programs Wyo. Dept. Health and Social Services; pres. county and state mental health assn., 1959-63; trustee U. Wyo., 1967-71; active Nat. Council Catholic Women. Named Outstanding Alumna, Loretto Heights Coll., 1959. Democrat. Club: Cheyenne Altrusa. Office: Wyo State Capitol Bldg Cheyenne WY 82002

HICKINGBOTHAM, BARBARA ANN, association executive; b. Eudora, Ark., Dec. 7, 1937; d. Herren Iveson and Marnette Sophia (Dardelle) Peacock; grad. Center Interior Design, 1964; cert. N.Y. Sch. Interior Design, 1965; cert. achievement Martin McDaniel Sch. Real Estate, 1977; m. Frank D. Hickingbotham, Aug. 21, 1955; children—Herren Curtis, Frank Todd. Interior decorator, Little Rock, 1965-68; with sales dept. Nat. Investor Life Ins. Co., Little Rock, 1968-70; co-organizer A. Q. Restaurants, Little Rock, 1970-72; mgr. restaurants Dogpatch USA, Harrison, Ark., 1972-74; dir. internat. affairs Ark. Sec. State, Little Rock, 1974-77; exec. dir. Nat. Soc. to Prevent Blindness, Little Rock, 1979-82, single parent program devel. Campus Crusade for Christ, 1982—; dir. pub. relations, area field suprs. Green Thumb, Inc., 1983—, also dir. field ops. Fund raiser March of Dimes. Mem. Ark. Health Assn., Ark. Vol. Coordinators Assn. Baptist. Clubs: Pleasant Valley Country, Altrusa (dir.) (Little Rock). Home: 17 Windsor Ct Little Rock AR 72212 Office: 200 S University Suite 100 Little Rock AR 72207

HICKMAN, ELIZABETH PODESTA, counselor, educator; b. Livingston, Ill., Sept. 30, 1922; d. Louis and Della (Martin) Podesta; B.E. summa cum laude, Eastern Ill. State U.; M.A., George Washington U., 1966; postgrad. U. Chgo., 1945, U. Va., 1964-66, (fellow) Northeastern U., 1967-68; Ed.D. (Exxon Found. grantee, Raskob Found. grantee), George Washington U., 1979; m. Franklin Jay Hickman, Mar. 17, 1944; children—Virginia Hickman Hellstern, Franklin. Tchr. public schs., Ill., Ohio, Va., Naples, Italy, 1944-64; dir. coll. transfer guidance Marymount Coll. of Va., Arlington, 1964-67, dir. Counseling Center, 1974-81, assoc. dean counseling and residence life, 1981-84; community counselor div. Mass. Employment Security, Newton, 1968-69; tchr. English conversation, Fuchu, Japan, 1969-73; placement dir., career counselor Coll. Great Falls (Mont.), 1973-74; lectr. Far East div. U. Md., Fuchu, 1971-73; spl. adv. Internat. Ranger Camps, Denmark and Switzerland, 1974-81; spl. cons. Internat. Quaker Sch., Wekhoven, Netherlands, 1959-63; mem. steering com. Pres.'s Com. on Employment of Handicapped, 1975—. Vol., ARC, 1967-78, Family Services, 1954-75. Served with WAVES, 1943-44. Recipient Disting. Alumnus award Eastern Ill. U., 1984. Lic. counselor, Va. Mem. Am. Personnel and Guidance Assn., Nat. Assn. Women Deans, Adminstrs. and Counselors (liaison to president's com.), Nat. Vocat. Guidance Assn., Am. Coll. Personnel Assn., No. Va. Counselors Assn., Delta Epsilon Sigma, Pi Lambda Theta. Roman Catholic. Home: 4708 38th Pl N Arlington VA 22207 Office: 2807 N Glebe Rd Arlington VA 22207

HICKMAN, GENEVA KILBURN, marriage and family therapist; b. Percilla, Tex., Nov. 12, 1922; d. Jessie Eugene and Cannie Bell (Adams) Kilburn; children—Sydnie Gene (dec.), Gail Denise, Georgia Ann. Cert. Austin Sch. Bus., 1940; B.A. with highest honors, Calif. State U., San Diego, 1964, postgrad., 1964-68; M.A. with high honors, Chapman Coll., 1974; Ph.D., Newport U., 1983. Sec. to asst. dist. atty. City of Austin (Tex.), 1939-40; asst. sec. to dir. Tex. State Employment Service, 1940-43; sec. to dean architecture U. Tex., Austin, 1943; asst. acct. Krueger Jewelers, Austin, 1945-48; partner Hickman & Hickman Public Accts., San Diego, 1950-59; tchr. Calif. Public Sch. System, 1964-73; head dept. bus. Lutheran High Sch., Orange, Calif., 1973-74; counselor Chapman Community Clinic, Orange, 1973-75; counselor Garden Grove Christian Counseling Center, 1974-75; therapist Human Services of Western Ark., Russellville, 1975-78; marriage and family counseling, Russellville, 1978-80; cons. psychologist Mental Health dept. State of Okla., Lawton, 1980; asst. psychologist Jim Taliaferro Mental Health Clinic, Lawton, 1980-82; pvt. practice, cons. in field, 1982—. Author articles in field. Organizer, leader Mothers March of Dimes, El Cajon, Calif.; active Better Water Com., National City, Calif.; mem. Calif. State PTA Mother Singers; youth dir., Sunday sch. tchr. Methodist Ch., El Cajon; lay reader, tchr. Sunday sch. Episcopal Ch. Recipient Sr. Woman's Honor award Calif. State U., San Diego, 1964; citation for outstanding work with youth Calif. State Assembly. Mem. Bus. Edn. Tchrs. Assn., Nat. Educators Fellowship, Am. Assn. Marriage & Family Therapists, Southwest Psychol. Assn., Christian Assn. Psychol. Studies, Internat. Acad. Profl. Counseling and Psychology (diplomate), Mortar Bd., Pi Omega Pi, Kappa Delta Pi, Beta Gamma Sigma. Republican. Address: 8035 La Mesa Blvd La Mesa CA 92041

HICKMAN, GRACE MARGUERITE, artist; b. Reno, Nev., Nov. 7, 1921; d. Charles Franklin and Jeannie (McPhee) Wolcott; m. Robert Frederick Hickman, Apr. 10, 1943; children—John Charles, Carol Ann Hickman Harp, David Paul. Student Emily Griffiths Opportunity Sch., Denver, 1968-71, Red Rocks Community Coll., Golden, Colo., 1974-75, Loretto Heights Coll., Denver, 1983-85. Tchr. art Aurora Parks & Recreation, Colo., 1979-81; instr. paint workshop Marine Resource Ctr., Atlantic Beach, N.C., 1981, 82; lectr. color theory Aurora Artists Club, 1985. One woman shows: Internat. House, Denver, 1974, Foothills Art Ctr., Golden, Colo., 1975, Greek Market Place, Denver, 1976, Marine Resource Ctr., Atlantic Beach, N.C., 1983, Depot Art Ctr., Littleton, Colo., 1984. group shows include: Wellshire Presbyn. Ch., Denver, 1975, Brass Cheque Gallery, Denver, 1978, Colo. Women in Arts, Denver, 1979, Garelick's Gallery, Scottsdale, Ariz., 1982; Bold Expressions, Littleton, Colo., 1983. represented in permanent collections: Augustana Luth. Ch., Denver, South Shores Ins. Agy., Huntington Beach, Calif., Texon Gen. Partnership, Englewood, Colo., others. Coordinator figure study Bicentennial Art Ctr., Aurora, 1986; pres. Depot Art Ctr., Littleton, Colo., 1980-82. Mem. Nat. Mus. for Women in the Arts, Artists Equity Assn., Colo. Artists Equity Assn. (chmn. publicity Colo. 1% for Art 1976-77), Pastel Soc. Am., Littleton Fine Arts Guild (pres. 1976-77). Democrat. Lutheran. Club: Aurora Athletic. Avocations: swimming; reading; art history. Home: 12361 E Bates Circle Aurora CO 80014

HICKMAN, JOLENE KAY, bank executive; b. Omaha, Sept. 5, 1954; d. Thomas Earl and Bernice Leona (McCoy) H. B.A., Otterbein Coll., 1977. Teller, Bancohio Nat. Bank, Columbus, Ohio, 1976-77, auditor, 1977-81; audit supr. Huntington Nat. Bank, Columbus, 1981-85, asst. v.p., mgr., 1985—. Mem. Victorian Village Soc., Columbus, 1983, Up Downtowners, Columbus, 1986. Mem. Nat. Assn. Bank Women (treas. 1985-86, Ohio state conf., chmn. Looking at Leadership series 1985-86), Nat. Inst. Auditors, Nat. Assn. Female Execs. Republican. Methodist. Avocations: softball; racquetball. Home: 895 Dennison Columbus OH 43215 Office: Huntington Nat Bank PO Box 1558 HC1010 Columbus OH 43216

HICKMAN, LINDA MARIE, nurse; b. Ada, Okla., Nov. 10, 1953; d. Charlie Lewis and Bertha Mae (Vinson) Phelps; m. Ronnie Clarence Hickman, May 26, 1972; 1 son, Dustin Jake. R.N., Cushing Mcpl. Hosp., Okla., 1974-75; Assoc. Sci., Okla. State U. Tech. Inst., 1974. Staff nurse Cushing Mcpl. Hosp., 1974-75; pub. health nurse Payne County Health, Cushing, 1975-78, 84-85; nurse cons. Care Manor, Stroud, Okla., 1982-83; house supr. Cushing Regional Hosp., 1982-83, asst. dir. home health service, 1983-84; communicable disease nurse Payne County Health Dept., Cushing, Okla., 1985—. Author: Cushing Regional Hospital Home Health Service Policy and Procedure Manual, 1984. Self breast exam. instr. Am. Cancer Soc., 1984—. Cushing Bus. and Profl. Women's Club sr. scholar, 1972, named Career Woman of Year, 1976. Mem. Okla. Pub. Health Assn. Democrat. Avocations: boating; skiing; camping; ceramics; woodworking. Home: Route 4 Box 13-AA Cushing OK 74023 Office: Payne County Health Dept 1001 E Cherry St Cushing OK 74023

HICKMAN, MARGARET CAPELLINI, advertising agency executive; b. Hartford, Conn., Sept. 21, 1949; d. Anthony Serafino Capellini and Mary Magdelan (Budash) Zanardi; m. Richard Lonnie Hickman, Nov. 6, 1982. B.A., U. Conn., 1971. Mktg. asst. Advo Systems, Inc., Hartford, 1971-72, mktg. analyst, 1972-75; mktg. asst. Cinamon Assocs. Inc., Brookline, Mass., 1975-77, prodn. supr., 1977-81, v.p. prodn., 1981-84, v.p. client services, 1984—; dir. Indian Head G.A.C., Inc., Manchester, Mass. Mem. New Eng. Direct Mktg. Assn. (past sec., treas., v.p.), Am. Legion Aux. Democrat. Roman Catholic. Home: 50 Centennial Ave Gloucester MA 01930 Office: Cinamon Assocs Inc 1 Boston Pl Boston MA 02108

HICKMAN, PAULA DIANE, lawyer, educator; b. Miami, July 24, 1947; d. Paul William Hickman and Eva Lena (McCampbell) Melvin; m. Arthur G. Wimer III, Apr. 1, 1973 (div. Apr. 1976). Student Longwood Coll., 1965-67; B.A. with honors, U. Tenn., 1969. Bar: Pa. 1980, N.H. 1981, Maine 1981, N.J. 1983. Flight attendant Pan Am. World Airways, N.Y.C., 1972-77; law clk. N.J. Superior Ct., Burlington, N.J., 1979-80; atty. Pub. Defender Program, Exeter, N.H., 1981-83; dep. clk. Rockingham County Superior Ct., Exeter, 1983—; instr. McIntosh Coll., Dover, N.H., 1984-85. Treas. bd. dirs. Rockingham Family Planning. Mem. ABA, N.H. Bar Assn., N.H. Trial Lawyers Assn., Rockingham County Bar Assn. (v.p.). Home: PO Box 711 Exeter NH 03833 Office: Rockingham County Superior Ct Exeter NH 03833

HICKS, CASSANDRA PAULINE, lawyer; b. Green Bay, Wis., Sept. 12, 1956; d. Paul Edward and Marjorie (Paine) H.; m. Jeffrey Stuart Weintraub, June 26, 1983. B.A. in Psychology and Polit. Sci., Ohio Wesleyan U., 1978; J.D., Am. U., 1981. Bar: Md. 1981, D.C. 1982. Assoc., Shapiro, Meiselman & Greene, Chtd., Rockville, Md., 1981—; dean's fellow LAWCOR, Washington Coll. Law, 1979-81. Mem. Md. Bar Assn., D.C. Bar Assn., Montgomery County Bar Assn. (chmn. Young Lawyers sect.; Chair of Yr. award 1986), Assn. Trial Lawyers Am. Democrat. Jewish. Club: Jewish Community Ctr. (Rockville). Office: Shapiro Meiselman & Greene Chtd 50 W Montgomery Ave Suite 230 Rockville MD 20850

HICKS, GRETA PATTERSON, accountant, lecturer; b. Aspermont, Tex., Oct. 14, 1940; d. Herman J. and Zina O'zella (Daniels) Patterson; children—Ted Aaron, Tina Marie. B.S.B.A., U. Tulsa, 1972. C.P.A., Tex., Okla. Revenue agt. IRS, Houston, 1973-79, dist. tng. and recruitment coordinator, 1979-80; tax mgr. Arthur Young & Co., Houston, 1980-81; prin. Greta P. Hicks, C.P.A., Houston, 1981—; lectr.; TV and radio appearances. Author/contbg. editor Money Talk column Houston Woman mag., 1982—; assoc. prof. U. Houston Sch. Optometry; mem. career devel. adv. com. Houston Ind. Sch. Dist., 1980—. Recipient letter of commendation IRS, 1975; cert. of merit U. Tulsa, 1972; named Woman of Yr., Fedn. Bus. and Profl. Women's Clubs, 1984; Am. Soc. Women Accts. scholar, 1972. Mem. Am. Inst. C.P.A.s, Tex. Soc. C.P.A.s, Am. Soc. Women Accts. (pres. Houston 1981-82), Am. Woman's Soc. C.P.A.s (charter), Fedn. Houston Profl. Women (treas. 1986). Office: 2855 Mangum Suite 303 Houston TX 77092

HICKS, GWENDOLYN ANN GROSS, educator; b. Roanoke, Ala., May 26, 1915; d. John Robert and Molly (Tomlinson) Gross; m. Curtis Alden Hicks, Dec. 26, 1940; children—Molly Ann, Martha Gwendolyn, Patsy Jane. B.S., Jacksonville State U., 1939; postgrad., George Peabody Coll.; M.A., Vanderbilt U., 1954. Cert. elem. tchr., Ala. Tchr. Wedowee Schs., Ala., 1936-40, Russellville, Ala., 1940-43, Cullman, Ala., 1943-45, Athens City Schs., 1931-77; tchr. Athens State Coll., 1964-68. Charter mem. Athens-Limestone Hist. Assn., 1968—; mem. Athens-Limestone Clean Community Commn., 1976—. Recipient Outstanding Vol. Work award Retired Sr. Vol. Program, Athens, 1981. Mem. NEA, Ala. Edn. Assn., Ala. Retired Tchrs. Assn., AAUW, Classroom Tchrs. Assn. (charter pres.) Athenian Study Club, Athens Garden Club, Magna Charta Dames, Order of Washington, Daus. Am. Colonist, DAR, Southern Dames of Am., numerous other patriotic orgns. Democrat. Methodist. Avocations: Geneology; bridge; swimming; travel. Home: 504 W Pryor St Athens AL 35611

HICKS, JANET ELLEN, lawyer, educator; b. Little Rock, Sept. 3, 1955; d. James Thomas and Joanne (Elliot) H. B.B.A., St. Mary's Coll., 1977; postgrad. London Sch. of Econs., Eng., summer 1978; J.D., DePaul U., 1980. Bar: Ill. 1980. Atty., asst. dir. Adminstrv. Office of Ill. Cts., Chgo., 1981-85; law clk. Ill. Appellate Ct., 1986—; legal writing instr. Loyola Law Sch., Chgo., 1983—. Mem. Chgo. Bar Assn., Ill. State Bar Assn., Women's Bar Assn. Ill., Cath. Lawyer's Guild Chgo., Ill. Club Catholic Women. Roman Catholic. Club: Univ. (Chgo.). Office: Room 3061 Richard J Daley Ctr Chicago IL 60602

HICKS, JOYCE BELLE, personnel administrator; b. Lebanon, Nebr., Nov. 30, 1934; d. Klee and Laura Losetta (Fisher) Bethel; m. Grover Ray Hicks, Dec. 18, 1980; children—Carmen, David. Student U. Nebr.-Lincoln, Opportunity Sch.-Denver, U. Mexico, U. El Paso. Purchasing clk. Chrysler Corp., Cape Canaveral, Fla., 1963-65, contract analyst, 1965-75, budget analyst, 1975-79, personnel adminstr., El Paso, Tex., 1979—. Volunteer, United Way of El Paso, 1979-83. Recipient Citation outstanding achievement, United Way of El Paso, 1979-83. Mem. Am. Soc. Personnel Adminstrn., El Paso Personnel Assn. Clubs: Discover El Paso, others. Home: 3313 Wayside El Paso TX 79936 Office: Chrysler Corp 11210 Armour Dr El Paso TX 79935

HICKS, JUDITH EILEEN, nursing administrator; b. Chgo., Jan. 1, 1947; d. John Patrick and Mary Ann (Clifford) Rohan; m. Laurence Joseph Hicks, Nov. 22, 1969; children—Colleen Driscoll, Patrick Kevin. B.S. in Nursing, St. Xavier Coll., Chgo., 1969; M.S. in Nursing, U. Ill.-Chgo., 1975. Staff nurse Mercy Hosp., Chgo., 1969-70, nursing supr., 1970-73; cons. continuing edn. Ill. Nurses Assn., Chgo., 1974-75; dir. obstetrics and gynecology nursing Northwestern Meml. Hosp., Chgo., 1975-81; v.p. nursing Children's Meml. Hosp., Chgo., 1981—; pres. Children's Meml. Home Health, Inc., 1986, Children's Meml. Nursing Services, 1986; dir. Near North Health Corp., Chgo., 1982—. Mem. Ill. Hosp. Assn. (chmn. Council on Nursing 1982-83), Inst. Medicine, Am. Soc. Nursing Adminstrs., Women's Health Exec. Network (pres. 1984-85). Roman Catholic. Home: 2206 Beechwood St Wilmette IL 60091 Office: Children's Meml Hosp 2300 Childrens Plaza Chicago IL 60614

HICKS, MARY CARVER, accounting executive; b. Moultrie, Ga., Mar. 8, 1941; d. James Edward and Sudie Mae (Holland) Carver; m. Paul Barnabus Hicks, June 12, 1964 (div. 1976); 1 son, Steven Edward. B.S. in Acctg., U. Houston, 1964. Bookkeeper, A&P Tea Co., Houston, 1955-64; with inventory control Houston Coca Cola Bottling Co., 1964-68, acctg. mgr., 1976—; auditor Moultrie Nat. Bank (Ga.), 1968-76. Mem. Nat. Assn. Profl. Women. Democrat. Baptist. Home: 8300 Sands Point Apt 905 Houston TX 77036 Office: Houston Coca Cola Bottling Co 2800 Bissonnet Houston TX 77006

HICKS, SUSAN LYNN BOWMAN, social worker; b. Flint, Mich., Mar. 24, 1952; d. Richard and Carol Joanne (Haney) Bowman; m. Duane James Hicks, Aug. 6, 1977. B.A., U. Mich., Flint, 1975; M.A., Central Mich. U., 1981. Med. social worker Flint Osteo. Hosp., 1974-77; dir. med. social work and patient relations Crittenton Hosp., Rochester, Mich., 1978—; mgmt. tng. and devel. cons. Buick, Oldsmobile, Cadillac div. Gen. Motors, Grand Blanc, Mich., 1985. Bd. dirs., chmn. com. Rochester Area Youth Guidance, Mich., 1986. Mem. Soc. for Hosp. Social Work Dirs. (Recognition award 1984, 85, pres.-elect 1985-86), Nat. Assn. Social Workers, Nat. Assn. Female Execs., Soc. Patient Representatives. Methodist. Avocations: tap dancing; writing. Home: 8080 Konczal Center Line MI 48015 Office: Crittenton Hosp 1101 W University Rochester MI 48063

HICKSON, CHARLOTTE ANN, librarian; b. Brownfield, Tex., Jan. 8, 1947; d. Rubert Alison and Bernice Viola (Doyle) Martin; B.A., Tex. Woman's U., 1968, M.L.S., 1969; m. Ronnie B. Hickson, Apr. 19, 1965; children—Kurt Leldon, Brandi Katrice. Reference librarian Tex. Tech. U., Lubbock, 1968-70, catalog librarian, 1970-75, acquisitions librarian monograph sect., 1975-79, dept. chmn., acquisitions librarian, 1979—. Bd. dirs. Mae Murfee PTA, Lubbock, 1979-80. Mem. NOW, Tex. Library Assn. Democrat. Methodist. Author articles in field. Home: 3412 74th St Lubbock TX 79423 Office: Texas Tech U Library Acquisitions Dept Lubbock TX 79423

HICKSON, SHARON FLORENCE, respiratory therapist; b. Los Angeles, Sept. 25, 1950; d. Robert David and Miriam Sue (Burwell) Hickson. A.A., Coll. of the Desert, 1973. Registered respiratory therapist. Supr. respiratory therapy dept. St. Marys Hosp., Reno, 1972-76, Rose Med. Ctr., Denver, 1976-78, Donald Sharp Meml. Hosp., San Diego, 1978-80; ednl. coordinator respiratory therapy dept. St. Francis Med. Ctr., Grand Island, Nebr., 1980-81; dir. cardio-pulmonary dept. Mary Lanning Meml. Hosp., Hastings, Nebr., 1981—; founder, instr. respiratory therapy program W. Nev. Community Coll., Reno, 1973-75; cert. clin. evaluator Calif. Coll. for Respiratory Therapy, San Diego, 1981—; cons. Hastings Respiratory Ctr., 1983—; coordinator asthma care tng. program Asthma and Allergy Found., Washington, 1985—. Mem. Am. Assn. Respiratory Therapy, Nebr. Soc. Respiratory Therapy (v.p. 1985-86), Am. Heart Assn., Am. Lung Assn. (coordinator Better Breathers program 1982—), Nat. Soc. Cardio-Pulmonary Tech. Democrat. Clubs: So. Hills Golf (Hastings), Monday Night Bowlers. Avocations: scuba diving; alpine skiing; oil painting; off road motorcycling; fishing. Office: Mary Lanning Meml Hosp 715 N St Joseph Ave Hastings NE 68901

HIDALGO, MARCI L., personnel administrator; b. N.Y.C., Apr. 6, 1960; d. Alfred and Nelly (Hernandez) Jimenez; m. Michael John Walczak, Dec. 21, 1985. B.A., Drew U.; postgrad. in law Seton Hall U.; postgrad. in pub. adminstrn. Fairleigh Dickinson U. Profl. asst. Office of Gov. of N.J., Trenton, 1981; emergency room unit sec. Overlook Hosp., Summit, N.J., 1980-83; office asst. Hellring, Lindeman et al, Newark, 1983-84; personnel adminstr. Olsten Corp., Edison, N.J., 1984—. Vol. worker Irvington Nat. Devel. Corp., N.J., 1978. Mem. Nat. Assn. Female Execs., Phi Alpha Delta. Democrat. Roman Catholic. Avocations: reading; writing; public speaking; foreign languages. Home: 510 Murray St Avenel NJ 07001

HIEATT, CONSTANCE BARTLETT, educator; b. Boston, Feb. 11, 1928; came to Can., 1968, naturalized, 1975; d. Arthur Charles and Eleonora (Very) Bartlett; student Smith Coll., 1945-47; B.A., Hunter Coll., City U. N.Y., 1953, A.M., 1957; Ph.D. (univ. and Lewis-Farmington fellow), Yale U., 1959; m. Allen Kent Hieatt, Oct. 25, 1958. Lectr. CCNY, 1959-60; asst. prof., asso. prof. Queensborough Community Coll., City U. N.Y., 1960-65; asso. prof., then prof. English, St. John's U., Jamaica, N.Y., 1965-68; prof. English, U. Western Ont., London, Can., 1968—. Recipient fellowships, grants Can. Council and Social Sci. and Humanities Research Council Can. Fellow Royal Soc. Can.; mem. Medieval Acad. Am., MLA, Soc. for Advancement of Scandinavian Studies, Internat. Saga Soc. (adv. bd.), Internat. Arthurian Soc., Anglo-Norman Text Soc., Children's Lit. Assn., Assn. Can. Univ. Tchrs. of English, Early English Text Soc., Internat. Assn. Anglo-Saxonists. Anglican. Editorial bd.: English Studies in Canada; author: The Realism of Dream Visions, 1967; Essentials of Old English, 1968; Karlamagnus Saga, vols. I, II, 1975, vol. III, 1981; (with Sharon Butler) Pleyn Delit: Medieval Cookery for Modern Cooks, 1976 Curye on Inglysch, 1985; eight children's books; translations and editions; contbr. articles to scholarly jours. Home: 1088 The Parkway London ON N6A 2X1 Canada Office: Dept English Univ Western Ontario London ON N6A 3K7 Canada

HIEBER, BARBARA E., railroad executive; b. East Chicago, Ind., Jan. 30, 1939; d. Fred H. Hieber and Barbara V. Jankauskas; children—Susan Poloncak Wilk, Steven M. Poloncak. Cert. in transp. mgmt. Calumet Coll., 1974; cert. in advt. studies Inst. Advanced Advt., Medill Sch. Journalism, Northwestern U., 1983; B.A. in Bus. Adminstrn., DePaul U., 1986. Mech. draftsman Combustion Engring. Inc., East Chicago, 1957-60; engring. technician Gen. Am. Transp. Corp., 1961-63, Pullman Standard Co., 1970-71, McKee Berger-Mansueto Co., 1971-72; traffic and transp. generalist Am. Maize, Hammond, 1973-74, Ind. Harbor Belt R.R., Hammond, 1974-78; traffic and transp. generalist Santa Fe Ry., Chgo., 1978-79, acct., 1979, splty. advt. coordinator Advt. Direction Inc., Chgo., 1979-83; cost and research analyst Santa Fe So. Pacific Corp., Chgo., 1983—, Am. Assn. Advt. Agys. fellow, 1983. Mem. Womens Advt. Club Chgo. (chmn. ethics legis. com. 1982-85), Am. Advt. Fedn., Cost Analysis Orgn. Assn. of Am. R.R.s, Am. Council R.R. Women. Home: 277 Stony Island Calumet City IL 60409 also Route 1 Box 267 Lake Bruce Kewanna IN 46939 Office: Santa Fe Ctr 224 S Michigan Ave Chicago IL 60604

HIEBERT, DIANE MARIE, nurse; b. Mpls., Jan. 30, 1955; d. Ailbe Patrick and Virginia S. (Zabukover) O'Donnell; m. Terry Ray Hiebert, June 11, 1977; children—Sean, Christopher. B.S.N., Marycrest Coll., 1977. R.N., Minn. Staff nurse Eitel Hosp., Mpls., 1977-78; cardiac rehab. R.N. Arlington Hosp., Va., 1984—, staff nurse, 1978-84, nursing supr., 1984—. Mem. ARC. Roman Catholic. Home: 4801 Bristow Dr Annandale VA 22003 Office: Arlington Hosp 1701 N George Mason Dr Arlington VA 22205

HIEBERT, ELIZABETH BLAKE, civic worker; b. Mpls., July 18, 1910; d. Henry Seavey and Grace (Riebeth) Blake; student Washburn U., 1926-30; B.S., U. Tex. 1933; m. Homer L. Hiebert, Aug. 29, 1935; children—Grace Elizabeth (Mrs. John E. Beam), Mary Sue (Mrs. Donald Wester), John Blake, Henry Leonard, David Mark. Sec. Topeka Regional Sci. Fair, 1958-60, bd. dirs., 1964—; bd. dirs. YMCA 1968-74, Topeka (Kans.) Friends of the 300; water safety instr. and swimming tchr. of handicapped; freelance writer; mem. Shawnee County Advocacy Council on Aging; Shawnee County chmn. Arthritis Found. Hon. fellow Harry S. Truman Library; recipient Paul Harris award Rotary, 1985. Mem. D.A.R., Daus. Am. Colonists, AAUW (dir. 1944-62, 65—), N.E. Hist. and Geneal. Soc., Tex. U. Alumni, Am. Home Econs. Assn., Shawnee County Med. Aux. (past pres.), Nat. Audubon, Met. Mus. Art, P.E.O. (past local pres. coop. bd.), Topeka Art Guild, Nat. Soc. Ancient and Hon. Arty., Nat. Trust Historic Preservation, Internat. Oceanographic Found., Nat. League Am. Pen Women (pres. Topeka 1970-72), Washburn Alumnae Assn., Am. Assn. State and Local History, Colo. Hist. Assn., Shawnee County Hist. Soc., Mont., Minn., Kans. hist. socs., Smithsonian Assos., Oceanic Soc., Internat. Platform Assn., Topeka Friends of the Library, Cousteau Soc., Am. Assn. Zookeepers, Nat. Assn. for Mature People, Am. Assn. Ret. Persons, K.U. Spencer Mus. Art, Conn. Soc. Genealogists, Nat., New Eng. geneal. socs., Topeka Beautification Assn. (sec.), Can Help, People to People, Archives Assos., Am. Space Found., Mus. Fine Arts Boston, Kans. Reading Assn., Am. Assn. Museums, SanDiego Zool. Soc., Nat. Space Inst., Oriental Inst., Delta Kappa Gamma (hon.), Delta Gamma, others. Club: Topeka Knife and Fork. Editor children's page Household mag., 1934-39. Home: 1517 Randolph Topeka KS 66604

HIEBERT, NANCY BRAMLEY, county official; b. Hutchinson, Kans., Dec. 4, 1941; d. Harold Leslie and Lois Daile (Kitch) Bramley; B.S. in Nursing, U. Kans., 1963, M.S. in Ednl. Psychology and Research, 1977, Ph.D. in Ednl. Psychology and Research, 1982; m. John Blake Hiebert, Aug. 25, 1962; children—Eric Blake, Rebecca Joan. Staff nurse U. Kans. Med. Center, 1962-63, nursing instr., 1963-65, 68; sch. nurse Shawnee Mission (Kans.) High Sch., 1965-67; nursing instr. new parent edn. Research Hosp. and Med. Center, 1970; Montessori presch. tchr. Johnson County Presch. and Kindergarten, 1971-73; teaching asst. dept. ednl. psychology and research U. Kans., 1976, grad. asst. Emily Taylor Women's Resource Center, 1978-80, vis. fellow Research Inst. Women's Public Lives, 1980-81; field coordinator Watkins campaign 3d Congl. Dist. Kans., 1980; dir. Century Club Builders' campaign Kans. Democratic Com., 1982—; project asst. Title IX Equity Workshop Project, Region VI, 1977; county commr., Lawrence, Kans., 1983—. Chmn. com. on women Kans. div. AAUW, 1979—; vice-chair local elected ofcls. bd. Job Tng. Partnership Act Program, S.D.A. II, Kans.; conv. adviser Intercollegiate Assn. Women Students, 1979, 80; co-chmn. steering com. UN Mid-Decade Conf. for Women Region VII, 1980; co-chmn. steering com. Kans. Women's Connection, 1981-82; chmn. Kans. Women's Polit. Caucus, 1981-82; fin. council Kans. Democratic Com.; mem. Victory Club Douglas County Dem. Party; mem. Kans. Tax Rev. Commn., 1983—. Named Outstanding Woman Staff Mem., U. Kans. Women's Recognition Com., 1979; vis. fellow Research Inst. Women's Public Lives, 1980-81. Mem. Nat. Assn. Women Deans, Adminstrs. and Counselors (exec. bd. 1981-82, Ruth Strang Research award 1981), Nat. Women's Polit. Caucus, Phi Delta Kappa, Pi Lambda Theta, Sigma Theta Tau. Home: 1521 Stratford Rd Lawrence KS 66044 Office: Courthouse 11th and Massachusetts St Lawrence KS 66044

HIENTON, DIANE DEBROSSE, lawyer; b. Fayetteville, Ark., Jan. 30, 1948; d. Joseph Denis and Opal Ruvena (Pitts) DeBrosse; m. James Robert Hienton, July 23, 1977. B.A., U. Hawaii, 1971; J.D., Ariz. State U., 1975. Bar: Ariz. 1975. Asst. atty. gen. State of Ariz., Phoenix, 1976-78, 84—; staff atty. Ariz. Ct. Appeals, 1978-81, 82-84; assoc. firm Jennings, Kepner & Haug, Phoenix, 1981-82. Contbr. articles to profl. jours. Mem. 1984 Phoenix Citizens Bond Com., Ariz. Theatre Guilde, Phoenix, 1982-84; founding life mem. Ariz. Mus. Sci. and Tech., 1984; bd. dirs. Ariz. Women's Town Hall. Mem. ABA, State Bar Ariz., Maricopa County Bar Assn., Jr. League Phoenix. Republican. Club: Soroptimist (editor Phoenix SOL Bull 1983-84). Office: Dept Law Office of Atty Gen 1275 W Washington Phoenix AZ 85007

HIERHOLZER, JOAN, artist; b. Grand Rapids, Mich.; d. Frank R. and Bernice H. (Cooper) H.; student Lindenwood Coll. for Women; B.F.A. U. Tex., 1952; M.F.A., Rutgers U., 1969; m. Harlan B. Pratt, May 3, 1980; children by previous marriage—Charles Cooper Bennett, David Pine Bennett. Fashion illustrator, San Antonio, 1947-56; tchr. art Summit (N.J.) Art Center and Public Schs., 1969-73; one-woman shows of paintings include: Exxon Refinery, Linden, N.J., 1975-82, Marion Koogler McNay Art Inst., San Antonio, 1959, Summit Art Center, 1964, 81, Ednl. Testing Service, Princeton, N.J., 1981, Allied Chem. Corp., Morristown, N.J., 1980, AT&T Galleries, Basking Ridge, N.J., 1983, Phoenix Gallery, N.Y.C., 1983, 85; group shows include: Bodley Gallery, N.Y.C., 1957, 58, Dallas Mus. Fine Arts, 1953, 54, 55, Equitable Life Assurance Co., N.Y.C., 1979, 80, Fairleigh Dickinson U., Madison, N.J., 1974, Lever House, N.Y.C., 1973, Montclair (N.J.) Art Mus., Mus. N.Mex., Santa Fe, 1956, NAD, N.Y.C., 1972, Nabisco, N.J., N.J. State Mus., Trenton, 1969, 82, Rutgers U. Art Gallery, New Brunswick, N.J., 1969, Witte Mus., San Antonio, 1952-55, N.J. State Mus. Art, Trenton, 1963, 82, Fed. Bldg., N.Y.C., 1981-85; mem. Phoenix Gallery, N.Y.C.; represented in permanent collections: Exxon Corp., Overlook Hosp., Summit, Schering Plough, Sentry Refining Inc., Chem. Bank., Juniata Coll., Pa., Hiram Coll., Ohio, Deloitte, Haskell & Sells, N.J., Diagnostic/Retrieval Systems, Inc., N.J., also pvt. collections. Trustee, Hunterdon Art Ctr. Mem. Nat. Assn. Women Artists, Artshowcase, Kappa Kappa Gamma, PEO. Republican. Christian Scientist. Address: RD 3 PO Box 380 Pittstown NJ 08867

HIERS, CONNIE LOUISE, plastic surgeon; b. Lubbock, Tex., July 3, 1955; d. Arlee Claud and May Belle (Bonner) Gowen; m. Darryl William Hiers, June 25, 1983. B.S. in Microbiology, Tex. Tech U., 1979; M.D., U. Tex.-Houston, 1979. Resident U. Hawaii, Honolulu, 1979-81, E. Tenn. State U., Johnson City, 1981-83; fellow plastic surgery U. Tenn.-Chattanooga, 1983-85; practice medicine specializing in plastic surgery, Jonesboro, Ark., 1985—. Recipient 2d pl. award Resident Research Day, Erlanger Med. Ctr., Chattanooga, 1985. Mem. AMA, So. Med. Assn., Crabhead County Med. Soc., Ark. Med. Soc., Plastic Surgery Assn., ACS (candidate). Office: 816 B Rains St Jonesboro AR 72401

HIETT, BETTY ANN, health educator, nurse; b. Buffalo, Aug. 20, 1949; d. Charles and Ruthie (Gresham) Terrell; m. Wendell Lee Saunders, Mar. 26, 1966 (dec. 1974); children—Kevin Lewis, Kenneth Lewis (dec.); m. 2d Ivan H. Hiett, June 23, 1979 (div. 1981). B.S., SUNY-Buffalo, 1976. R.N. Charge nurse Grady Meml. Hosp., Atlanta, 1976-77; staff nurse Hughes Spalding Hosp., Atlanta, 1977-78; staff nurse S.W. Community Hosp., Atlanta, 1978-80, asst. patient care mgr., 1980, patient edn. coordinator, 1980—, internal cons., 1980-82; cons. U.S. Penitentiary, Atlanta, 1982-83, Collections of Life & Heritage, Atlanta, 1983. Author tng. programs. Mem. Am. Nurses Assn., Nat. Black Nurses Assn., Atlanta Nurses Assn., Diabetes Assn. Atlanta, Diabetes Health Educators Assn. Democrat. Methodist. Home: 6650 Hidden Brook Trail College Park GA 30349

HIGBEE, FLORENCE SALICK, librarian; b. Milw.; d. Otto Thomas and Mary (Reiter) Salick; B.A., U. Wis., 1933; M.A. in Library Sci., Cath. U. Am., 1965; 1 dau., Joan Florence. Reference librarian Shirlington br. of Arlington County Public Libraries, Arlington, Va., 1965-67; br. librarian Glencarlyn br. Arlington County Public Libraries, Arlington, 1967, Columbia Pike br., 1967-73; translator, archivist. Mem. nominating com. Literacy Council No. Va., Inc., 1973-74. State of Va. Grad. fellow, 1964-65. Mem. ALA, Am. Malacological Union. Home: 13 N Bedford Arlington VA 22201

HIGDON, BARBARA, college president; b. Independence, Md., May 18, 1930; m. 1950; 3 children. B.A., U. Md., 1951, M.A., 1952, Ph.D. in Speech, 1961. Assoc. prof. English, speech, Tex. So. U., 1958-62; prof. Graceland Coll., Lamoni, Iowa, 1962-75, pres., 1984—; dean, v.p. acad. affairs Park Coll., 1975-84. Address: Graceland Coll Lamoni IA 50140*

HIGGINBOTHAM, DOROTHY HIGHTOWER, realtor; b. Guin, Ala.; d. John Norman and Nancy Leona (Burleson) Hightower; widowed; 1 child, Jennifer Lee. Student Birmingham Bus. Sch., 1955-58, South Coast Coll., 1960-62, correspondence U. So. Calif., 1971-73. Cert. realtor, Calif. Clk., U.S. Steel Corp., Birmingham, Ala., 1950-53; keypunch operator U.S. Treasury Dept., Birmingham, 1954-56; realtor R.E. Fair, Huntington Beach, Calif., 1970-72; owner, realtor Dot's Realty, Fountain Valley, Calif., 1972—; ptner., pres., J.D.L. Interiors, Fountain Valley, 1985. Vol. ARC, Orange County, 1984—; asst. Park Dept., Orange County, 1975—; vol. Republican Party, Orange County, 1980—. Mem. Huntington Beach-Fountain Valley Bd. Realtors (chmn. sales com. 1974-76), Hacienda Bd. Realtors (chmn. sales com. 1980), Apt. Assn., Drapery Assn. Orange County, Design. Assn. (bd. dirs.). Methodist. Avocations: bowling; golf; sewing; cooking; traveling. Home: 18400 Mt Stewart Circle Fountain Valley CA 92708 Office: Dot's Realty 9092 Talbert St Suite 2 Fountain Valley CA 92708

HIGGINBOTHAM, SARA, hospital education administrator, nurse; b. Hackensack, N.J., June 21, 1926; d. Donald and Theresa (DeLorenzo) Pepe; m. Manning E. Higginbotham, July 1, 1952; children—Nancy June, Miles Dudley. B.S. in Nursing, Alfred U., 1948; postgrad. Columbia U., 1950-52; M.S. in Personnel Counseling, Jacksonville State U., 1972. Staff nurse Hackensack Hosp. (N.J.), 1948-50, Meml. Ctr. Cancer and Allied Diseases, N.Y.C., 1950-51, supr., instr., 1951-55; dir. inservice edn. Bapt. Meml. Hosp., Gadsden, Ala., 1967-80, dir. edn. dept., 1980—; chmn. Inservice Edn. com. Ala. League Nursing, 1967-69. Mem. Am. Soc. Health Edn. and Tng., Am. Nurses Assn., Disabled Am. Vets. Aux. Club: Pilot of Gadsden (pres. 1983-84). Home: Route 2 Box 156 Gadsden AL 35903 Office: Bapt Meml Hosp 1007 Goodyear Ave Gadsden AL 35999

HIGGINS, LUCY MILLER, financial services company executive; b. Oklahoma City, Mar. 31, 1954; d. Charles Ferdinand and Marijo (Brigham) Miller; B.B.A., U. Okla., 1976; postgrad. So. Meth. U., 1981-83; m. Thomas Corlett Higgins, Jan. 28, 1978. Sales rep. Kerr-McGee Chem., Chgo., 1976-78, Western Omega Chem. Co., Los Angeles, 1978-79; sales rep. Celanese Corp., Los Angeles, 1979-80, field devel. engr., 1980; field devel. specialist Gen. Electric Corp., Dallas, 1980-82; product mgr. The Assocs. Corp., 1984-85, asst. v.p., 1985—. Mem. LWV, Nat. Assn. Female Execs., 500, Inc. (solicitations chmn. auction), Civic League Dallas, Chi Omega Alumnae (communications chmn.). Republican. Episcopalian. Clubs: Brookhaven Country, St. Mary's Guild. Home: 4230 Southcrest Rd Dallas TX 75229 Office: 250 Carpenter Freeway Dallas TX 75222

HIGGINS, MARGARET M., government agency administrator; b. Meriden, Conn., Dec. 11, 1944; d. Joseph C. and Katherine T. (Roche) H.; B.A., Albertus Magnus Coll., 1966; postgrad. Northeastern U., 1973. With U.S. Office of Personnel Mgmt., 1966—, mgr. Augusta (Maine) area office, 1970-72, personnel specialist, Boston regional office, 1972-74, mgr. Providence area office, 1974-79, chief adv. services office, Washington, 1979-82, chief recruiting, testing, and info. br., 1982-84, program analyst, 1984—. Bd. dirs. Opportunities for Women, Providence, 1977-79, Civil Service Employees Credit Union, 1982—. Recipient Office of Personnel Mgmt. Dirs. award for superior accomplishment, 1981, merit pay award, 1984. Mem. Internat. Personnel Mgmt. Assn., New Eng. Fed. Personnel Council (chmn. 1978-79), Am. Soc. Public Adminstrn. (chpt. pres. 1977-78).

HIGGINS, PAULINE EDWARDDS, savings association executive; b. Mandeville, Jamaica, W.I., Mar. 27, 1950; d. George Bazil and Doreen (Romans) Edwards; came to U.S., 1969; m. J. Aloysius Higgins, Aug. 10, 1973; 1 son, Nicholas Alexander. B.S., La. State U., 1977; postgrad. Rice U. Audit mgr. Coopers & Lybrand, Houston, 1978-83; v.p., chief fin. officer Benjamin Franklin Savs. Assn., Houston, 1983—. Author and editor tng. material for Coopers & Lybrand. Bd. dirs., asst. pres. Houston Women Employment and Edn., Inc., 1983 (Outstanding Fund Raiser award 1982); mem. Coalition 100 Black Women, Houston, 1983—; bd. dirs. Houston Area Women's Ctr. Mem. Am. Inst. C.P.A.s, Tex. Soc. C.P.A.s (savs. and loan com. 1983-84), Houston Soc. C.P.A.s, Fin. Mgrs. Soc., Nat. Assn. Female Execs. Episcopalian. Club: Christian Profl. Women's Assn. (Houston). Office: 5444 Westheimer at Yorktown St Benjamin Franklin Savs Houston TX 77056

HIGGINS, THERESE, college president; b. Winthrop, Mass., Sept. 29, 1925; d. James C. and Margaret M. (Lennon) H. A.B., Regis Coll., 1947; M.A., Boston Coll., 1957; Ph.D., U. Wis., 1963; D.H.L. (hon.), Emmanuel Coll., 1977; L.L.D. (hon.), Northeastern U., 1963. Joined Sisters of Congregation of St. Joseph, 1947. Area councilor Congregation of St. Joseph, Brighton, Mass., 1969-74; pres. Regis Coll., Weston, Mass., 1974—; bd. dirs. Council Ind. Colls., 1982-84; mem. exec. com. Women's Coll. Coalition, Washington, 1981-84; mem. nominating com. New Eng. Colls. Fund, 1982-84; mem. adv. bd. Pastoral Devel. Office, Archdiocese of Boston, 1981-84. Trustee, Newton Cath. High Sch., 1971-78, Cardinal Spellman Philatelic Mus., Weston, 1976; trustee, mem. exec. and nominating coms. Waltham Weston Hosp. Mem. AAUW, Assn. Ind. Colls. and Univs. (exec. com. 1975—), Conf. Small Pvt. Colls. (bd. dirs. 1980—). Home and Office: Regis Coll 235 Wellesley St Weston WA 02193

HIGGINS, SISTER THERESE, college president; b. Winthrop, Mass., Sept. 29, 1925; d. James C. and Margaret M. (Lennon) H.; A.B. cum laude, Regis Coll., 1947; M.A., Boston Coll., 1957; Ph.D., U. Wis., Madison, 1963; D.H.L., Emmanuel Coll., 1977 LL.D. (hon.), Northeastern U., 1983. Joined Sisters of St. Joseph, 1947; area councillor Sisters of St. Joseph, 1969-74; asso. prof. English, Regis Coll., 1968—, coll. pres., 1974—; trustee Cardinal Spellman Philatelic Mus., 1976—; adv. bd. pastoral devel. office Archdiocese of Boston, 1981-84. Mem. Gov.'s Commn. on Status of Women, 1977-79; trustee Waltham Hosp., 1978—; mem. nominating com. New Eng. Colls. Fund, 1982-84. Mem. AAUW, Assn. Ind. Colls. and Univs. Mass. (exec. com.), Conf. Small Pvt. Colls. (bd. dirs. 1980—), Council Ind. Colls. (bd. dirs. 1982-84), Women's Coll. Coalition (exec. com. 1981-84). Roman Catholic. Office: Regis Coll Weston MA 02193

HIGH, DOROTHY HELEN FRANK, city recreation administrator; b. Lincoln, Nebr., Feb 3, 1935; d. Theodore Ludwig and Lillian Winifred (Schellberg) F.; m. Duane High, Nov. 18, 1955; children—Ted Frank, Catherine Nadine. B.S. in Edn., U. Nebr., 1956; M.S. in Edn., Chadron State Coll., 1967. Instr. phys. edn. Lincoln Pub. Schs., Nebr., 1956-58, Alliance City Schs., Nebr., 1964-67, Scottsbluff Pub. Schs., Nebr., 1967-69, Hiram Scott Coll., Scottsbluff, 1969-71; asst. prof. edn., Tarkio Coll., Mo., 1971; recreation supr. City of Scottsbluff, 1973—. Mem. adv. bd. Nebr. Council Ednl. TV, Lincoln, 1968-70, Nebr. Dept. Edn., 1970; bd. dirs. Southeast Recreation Ctr., Scottsbluff, 1975-80, Jaycee Sr. Ctr., Scottsbluff, 1978-82; mem. adv. bd. Foster Grandparent Program, Scottsbluff, 1983—. Mem. Am. Assn. Leisure and Recreation (pres.-elect 1985-86, pres. 1986-87), Am. Alliance Health, Phys. Edn., Recreation and Dance (bd. govs. 1986-87, pres. central dist. 1982-84, Honor award 1975), Nebr. Assn. Health, Phys. Edn., Recreation and Dance (pres. 1972-73, Honor award 1970), Am. Soc. Aging. Republican. Lutheran. Club: Soroptimist Internat. of Scotts Bluff County (pres. 1978-79). Avocations: tennis; swimming. Home: 2210 7th Ave Scottsbluff NE 69361 Office: City of Scottsbluff 1818 Ave A Scottsbluff NE 69361

HIGH, SUZANNE IRENE, lawyer; b. Chgo., June 10, 1946; d. Jack G. and Irene (Sinko) H. A.B. cum laude, Syracuse U., 1968; M.A., Northwestern U., 1973; postgrad. Rosary Coll., 1974-75; J.D., DePaul U., Chgo., 1979. Bar: Ill. 1979, Fla. 1979, U.S. Sup. Ct. 1982. Tchr., Peace Corps, Wolisso, Ethiopia, 1968-70; researcher Compton's Ency., Ency. Brit., Chgo., 1970-72; ptnr. Renn & High, Chartered, Lisle, Ill, 1979—; dir. Lisle Savs. and Loan Assn. Bd. dirs. Little Friends, Inc. Mem. ABA, Fla. Bar Assn., Ill. Bar Assn., DuPage County Bar Assn., Women's Bar Assn. Ill., Fla. Women's Bar Assn., DuPage Assn. Women Lawyers, Ill. Trial Lawyers Assn., NOW, Lisle C. of C. Club: Women in Mgmt. (Oak Brook, Ill.). Home: Oak Brook IL Office: 4756 Main St Lisle IL 60532 also Suite 150 2805 Butterfield Rd Oak Brook IL 60521

HIGHSMITH, WANDA LAW, association executive; b. Cleveland, Mo., Oct. 25, 1928; d. Lloyd B. and Nan (Sisk) Law; student U. Mo., 1954-56; 1 dau., Holly. Legal sec., firms in Mo. and D.C., until 1960; various staff positions Am. Coll. Osteopathic Surgeons, 1960-72, asst. exec. dir., conv. mgr., Coral Gables, Fla., 1974—. Mem. Profl. Conv. Mgmt. Assn., Washington Soc. Assn. Execs., Am. Soc. Assn. Execs., Assn. Med. Soc. Execs., Nat. Assn. Female Execs. Republican. Methodist. Home: 1600 S Eads St Apt 1119-S Arlington VA 22202 Office: 122 C St NW Suite 875 Washington DC 20001

HIGHTO, GERALDINE GERRIE, writer, director, producer, citizens activist; b. Balt., Oct. 19, 1926; d. Jacob and Rose (Varsov) Bernstein; m. Martin Morris Highto, Apr. 18, 1948; children—Joan Ellen Highto Glasser, Gwen Carol. Student Strayers Bus. Coll., 1944. Dir. civic and philanthropic orgns., Balt., 1946—; citizen activist for grandparents' rights, 1980—; speaker in field. Contbr. articles to local and nat. newspapers. Lobbyist, Grandparents Found.; bd. dirs. Rogers Ave. Synagogue, 1955—, Greenspring Synagogue Amity Guild, 1955—, Jewish Convalescent Home, 1955—, Covenant Guild, 1955—, Sinai Hosp., 1984—. Democrat. Home: 622 Milford Mill Rd Baltimore MD 21208

HIGHTOWER, CAROLINE WARNER, arts institution executive; b. Cambridge, Mass., Feb. 22, 1935; d. William Lloyd and Mildred (Hall) Warner; children—Amanda Brantley, Matthew Lloyd. Student, Northwestern U., 1953-54, Cambridge U., 1954-55; B.A., Pomona Coll., 1958. Advt. mgr. U. Calif. Press., Berkeley, 1959-61; editor McGraw Hill Co., N.Y.C., 1961-64, Saturday Rev., N.Y.C., 1968-9; found. officer Carnegie Corp., N.Y.C., 1969-71; cons. Children's Television Workshop, Rockefeller Found., Ford Found., others, N.Y.C., 1971-77; dir. Am. Inst. Graphic Arts, N.Y.C., 1977—. Vice chmn. CAPS N.Y. State Council on Arts, N.Y.C., 1974-84; panelist NEA, Washington, 1979, 81, 83; scholarship juror art dept. Yale U., New Haven, 1982; bd. dirs. Pub. Ctr. for Cultural Resources, N.Y.C., 1984—, Documents of American Design, 1985—; mem. adv. bd. Lubalin Ctr., Cooper Union, Ctr. for the Book. Library of Congress, Innovative Design Fund, Coll. of Fine and Applied Arts, Rochester Inst. Tech., Documents of Am. Design. Office: Am Inst Graphic Arts 1059 3d Ave New York NY 10021

HIGHTSHOE, NANCY, expert on rape prevention and investigation; b. St. Louis, May 11, 1947; d. Edwin Jr. and Mary Ann (LaBarge) Kalbfleish. B.A. in Psychology magna cum laude, U. Mo., 1972; M.A. in Human Relations and Adminstrn. of Justice, Webster U., 1977. Commd. police officer sexual assault investigative unit St. Louis County, 1972-81; pres. Rape Prevention Seminars, Inc., St. Louis, 1982—; conv. speaker on rape cause, effect and prevention. Mem. Nat. Speakers Assn., Women's Crusade Against Crime, Women's Info. Network, Psi Chi. Office: PO Box 31339 Saint Louis MO 63131

HIGLEY, ROBERTA CATHRYN, lawyer; b. Detroit, Jan. 12, 1943; d. Robert Eugene and Mabel Kathleen (Cameron) Worms; m. Stephen Strong Higley, May 4, 1963; children—Donald S., Stephanie Robin, Jillian J. B.A., Hillsdale Coll., 1966; postgrad. U. Notre Dame, 1976-77; J.D., Case Western Res. U., 1979. Bar: Ohio 1979, Pa. 1981, U.S. Dist. Ct. (we. dist.) Pa. 1981. Tchr., pub. schs.; assoc. Reed, Luce, Good, Tosh & McGregor, Beaver, Pa., 1980-82; sole practice, Beaver, 1982—. Legal advisor People Who Care, Sewickley, Pa., 1983. Mem. ABA, Pa. Bar Assn., Allegheny County Bar Assn., Beaver County Bar Assn. Office: 855 2d St Beaver PA 15009

HILAND, CATHARINE CECELIA, investment firm executive; b. Darby, Pa., Oct. 17, 1947; d. Andrew Anthony and Catharine Marie (Bray) Hiland. B.A., West Chester State Coll., 1969. Registered rep. and prin., Nat. Assn. Securities Dealers. Advt. and pub. relations rep. Linton Food Services Inc., Phila., 1969-73; info. ctr. coordinator Nat. Liberty Corp., Valley Forge, Pa., 1972-73; editor Gino's Inc., King of Prussia, Pa., 1973-74; asst. to v.p. communications Wellington Mgmt. Co., Valley Forge, 1975-77; asst. v.p. Delaware Mgmt. Co. Inc., Phila., 1977—. Contbr. articles to profl. jours. Recipient Achievement award Soroptimists Internat., 1982. Mem. Mktg. Communications Execs. Internat. (editor Communicator 1980-81), TV and Radio Advt. Club. Republican. Roman Catholic. Home: 344 Avon Rd L338 Devon PA 19333 Office: Delaware Mgmt Co Inc 10 Penn Center Plaza Philadelphia PA 19103

HILBERT, IRMALEEN, international insurance company executive; b. Chgo., Nov. 5, 1931; d. Forest and Lucy Pearl (Howerton) Brame; children—George Edward Hilbert Jr., Janice Lynn Hilbert, John Forest Hilbert, Robert Louis Hilbert. Office mgr. Woodland Hills Ins. (Calif.), 1959-76; personal accounts mgr. Alexander & Alexander, Los Angeles, 1976-77, Wellington Agys., Los Angeles, 1977-80; v.p. Bayly, Martin & Fay Inc., Los Angeles, 1980—. Bd. dirs. Valley Hot Line Crises Intervention, Van Nuys, Calif., 1974-76. Mem. Woodland Hills Bus. and Profl. Women (pres. 1970-71, Woman of Yr. award 1974), Woodland Hills Chamber (freedom season sec. 1972), Women in Mgmt. (v.p. 1981, pres. 1982-83, pres. corp. bd. 1984—), So. Calif. Marine Underwriters, Ins. Women of Los Angeles, Democrat. Home: 9277 Florence Ave 25 Downey CA 90240 Office: Bayly Martin & Fay Inc 3200 Wilshire Blvd Los Angeles CA 90010

HILBY, PAULA BULLOCK, real estate syndication company executive, lawyer; b. Memphis, May 20, 1948; d. Leon and Robbie Lee (Stubblefield) Bullock; m. Bruce Titus Hilby, Oct. 28, 1975; 1 dau., Anne Titus. Student U. Miss., 1966-68; B.A., Southwestern at Memphis, 1971; J.D., Memphis State U., 1975; postgrad. Ariz. State U., 1977-78; grad. Pub. Utility Exec. Program, U. Mich., summer 1980. Bar: Ariz. Atty., law dept. Ariz. Pub. Service Co., Phoenix, 1976-79, mgr. gen. corp. services dept., 1980-81; asst. for intergovtl. programs, Gov.'s office, Phoenix, 1982-83; v.p. Tierra Assocs., Ltd., Phoenix, 1984—; exec.-in-residence Ariz. State U. Ctr. for Pvt. and Pub. Sector Ethics, Tempe, 1984—. Mem. Charter 100, sec., 1981; sect. chmn. New Dimensions Campaign, Phoenix, 1983; mem. Valley Leadership Alumnae Assn., 1981—, Jr. League of Phoenix, 1981—; bd. dirs. Phoenix Symphony, Valley Leadership, 1980-81. Mem. ABA, Maricopa County Bar Assn. (pres. elect, corp. counsel sect. 1981), Ariz. Pub. Service Polit. Action Com. (dir.). Democrat. Unitarian. Clubs: Phoenix Country, Plaza. Home: 114 E San Miguel Phoenix AZ 85012 Office: Tierra Associates Ltd 2700 N 3d St Phoenix AZ 85004

HILD, CHARLENE ETHEL, publishing company law editor; b. Murphysboro, Ill., July 9, 1958; d. Charles Henry Hild and Dorothy Mae (Porter) Gunn. B.A. in English, Loyola U., Chgo., 1981; postgrad. Chgo. Kent Sch. Law, 1982-83. Teller, teller supr. Devon Bank & Trust, Chgo., 1977-81; editorial asst.,law editor Commerce Clearing House, Inc., Chgo., 1981—; weekend proofreader supr. Skadden, Arps, Slate, Meagher & Flom, Corp. law firm, 1984—; freelance proofreader Scott Foresman & Co., Houghton Mifflin. Mem. Nat. Assn. Female Execs., AAUW, Greenpeace, ABA, Chgo. Women in Pub., NoSho Animal League. Office: Commerce Clearing House Inc 4025 W Peterson Ave Chicago IL 60646

HILDEBRANDT, CLAUDIA JOAN, banker; b. Inglewood, Calif., Feb. 12, 1942; d. Charles Samual and Clara Claudia (Palumbo) H. Student U. Colo., 1960-66, 79—. Head teller 1st Colo. Bank & Trust, Denver, 1969-70; asst. cashier 1st Nat. Bank, Englewood, Colo., 1975-79, asst. v.p., 1979-83, v.p., 1983—; owner, cons. CJH Enterprises, Inc., Breckenridge, Colo., 1980—. Mem. Nat. Assn. Bank Women, Am. Soc. for Personnel Adminstrn., Am. Inst. Banking. Roman Catholic. Club: SOA. Home: 6602 E Cornell Ave Denver CO 80224 Office: First Nat Bank 333 W Hampden Ave Englewood CO 80110

HILDEBRANDT, HILDE E., financial planner; b. Cortland, Ind., Oct. 24, 1933; d. Frank C. and Louisa A. (Krueger) Piel; m. Edward C. Metzger, Nov. 26, 1979 (dec. 1981); children—Shawna Batchelor, William Hildebrandt, Christine Hildebrandt. B.A. in Econs., U. Toledo, 1975; M.B.A., Capitol U., 1981. Internal auditor Owens Corning, Toledo, 1968-76, capital appropriations adminstr., Newark, Ohio, 1977-79; fin. planner IDS Fin. Services, Columbus, Ohio, 1979—; adj. instr. fin. planning Ohio State U.-Newark, 1981—. Mem. Inst. Cert. Fin. Planners, Bus. and Profl. Women, Nat. Assn. Female Execs. Republican. Lutheran. Home: PO Box 1205 Buckeye Lake OH 43008

HILDEBRANDT, KAREN CHRISTINE, maritime lawyer; b. N.Y.C., Feb. 3, 1954; d. William Edward and Catherine Teresa (O'Connell) H.; m. Ferdinando Antonio Marcucci, Oct. 15, 1983. B.A., Northeastern U., 1976; J.D., Suffolk U. 1979. Bar: N.Y. 1981. With personnel div. U.S. Civil Service, Boston, 1974-78; assoc., then ptnr. firm Kirlin, Campbell & Keating, N.Y.C., 1979—. Roman Catholic. Office: Kirlin Campbell & Keating 14 Wall St New York NY 10005

HILEMAN, SALLY JEAN, social worker; b. Ogden, Utah, Sept. 5, 1929; d. John A. and Molly Naomi (Arnovich) Sugar; B.S., Ariz. State U., 1971, M.S.W., 1973; children—Paul William, Jay Aron. Psychiat. social worker Riverside County Mental Health, Indio, Calif., 1973-76; dir. social service dept. Inter-Community Hosp., Covina, Calif., 1976-84; cons. police depts.; field instr. U. Calif., Long Beach; pvt. practice, Covina. Pres., Calif. Human Services Orgn., 1975-76; pres. bd. dirs. East Valley Free Clinic, 1978; trustee, sec. Hospice of East San Gabriel Valley, Inc.; bd. dirs. Handicapped Resource Center. Mem. Nat. Assn. Social Workers, Lic. Clin. Social Workers (Calif.), Nat. Assn. Clin. Social Workers. Address: 166-B W College St Covina CA 91723-2073

HILFSTEIN, ERNA, educator; b. Kraków, Poland; came to U.S., 1949, naturalized, 1954; d. Leon and Anna (Schornstein) Kluger; B.A., CCNY, 1967, M.A., 1971, Ph.D., CUNY, 1978; m. Max Hilfstein; children—Leon, Simone Juliana. Tchr. secondary schs., N.Y.C., 1968-84, 86—; vis. prof. Queens Coll., 1973; affiliate Grad. Sch./Univ. Center, CUNY NEH grantee, 1984-85. Mem. History Sci. Soc., N.Y. Acad. Sci., Polish Inst. Arts and Scis. in Am., United Fedn. of Tchrs. (chpt. chmn. 1978-84, 86—, del. 1980—). Jewish. Author: Starowolski's Biographies of Copernicus, 1980; collaborator English transl. Nicholas Copernicus' Complete Works, Vol. I, 1972, Vol. II, 1978, Vol. III, 1985; contbr. articles and revs. to profl. jours. Editor: Science and History, 1978. Address: 1523 Dwight Pl Bronx NY 10465

HILGEMAN, CHARLOTTE ANN, auditor; b. Sarasota, Fla., July 7, 1943; d. Joseph Lawrence Hilgeman and Margaret Eileen (Johnson) Hilgeman Lindsey; student San Francisco City Coll., 1962-63, San Francisco State Coll., 1963, Cumberland County Coll., 1969-71, Rutgers U., 1976. Vol., VISTA, Fla., 1965-66; N.J., 1966; propr. Wishing Well Motel, Vineland, N.J., 1971-77, Mario's Restaurant, Ocean City, Md., 1980-81, Harrison Hall, Ocean City, 1980-81; real estate salesperson Charles L. Scarani, Vineland, 1974-78; pres. Strawberry Enterprises, Ltd., Ocean City, Md., 1979—; night auditor Fairmont Hotel, New Orleans, 1980-83; owner Stirling City Hotel and County Store, Calif., 1986—; orientation dir. CETA, Cumberland County, 1974-75; state insp. multiple dwellings State of N.J., 1976-77, state compliance officer, 1977-78; cons. rural housing Farmworkers Corp., Vineland; also freelance writer. Mem. Cumberland County Democratic Exec. Com., 1973-76; v.p. Vineland Dem. Club, 1974-76; team capt. United Way, 1975; vol. worker Vineland Tiny Tim Fund, 1972-75; bd. dirs. Cumberland County Community Concerts, 1976-79. Mem. Cumberland County Bd. Realtors (asso.), Vineland C. of C., N.J. Assn. Notary Publics, NOW. Home and Office: 16975 Skyway Stirling city CA 95978

HILKEMEYER, RENILDA ESTELLA, nurse; b. Martinsburg, Mo., July 29, 1915; d. Henry Gerard and Anna Marie (Bertels) Hikemeyer. Diploma in nursing, St. Mary's Hosp., St. Louis U., 1936; B.S. in Nursing Edn., George Peabody Coll. for Tchrs., Nashville, 1947; postgrad. U. Minn., 1950, U. Tex. Sch. Nursing, 1981. Staff nurse operating room St. Mary's Hosp., Jefferson City, Mo., 1936-37; dist. pub. health nurse Mo. Div. Health, Jefferson City, 1937-40, cons. nursing edn., Mo., 1950-55; asst. dir. nursing Gen. Hosp. No. 1, Kansas City, Mo., 1947-49; asst. exec. sec. Mo. Nurses Assn., Jefferson City, 1949-50; dir. nursing U. Tex. System Cancer Ctr., Houston, 1955-77, asst. to pres. nursing resources, 1977-79, staff asst. to pres., 1979-84; mem. grant rev. com. NIH Nat. Cancer Inst, 1979-83, program rev. com., 1975-77, cons., 1982—; cons. NIH Nat. Heart, Blood and Lung Inst., 1983—, Worker's Inst. Safety, Health, 1983—; chmn., mem. scholarship and professorship com. Cancer Soc., 1980—, mem. nursing adv. com., 1963-80, profl. edn. com., 1984—; chmn. nursing adv. com., mem. adminstrv. bd. Renilda Hilkemeyer Child Care Ctr., U. Tex. Med. Ctr., 1969—; trustee Alice Lugy Nursing Found. Book reviewer Am. Jour. Nursing, 1982; contbr. articles to profl. jours. Recipient Outstanding Profl. Women's award Tex. Fedn. Houston Profl. Women, 1983, outstanding contbns. Award, Nat. Cancer Inst., 1983, Disting. Service award Am. Cancer Soc., 1981, Nurse of Yr. Award, Houston Area League Nursing, 1973, Matrix Award, Theta Sigma Phi, Houston, 1963, Disting. Merit award Internat. Soc. Nurses in Cancer Care, 1986; new child care ctr. at U. Tex. Med. Ctr. Houston, named in her honor, 1981 (1st ctr. established 1969); grantee HEW, 1974-77, Am. Cancer Soc., 1974-75, Tex. Fedn. and Profl. Women's Club, 1977-83. Mem. Oncology Nursing Soc., Am. Nurses Assn., Tex. Nurses Assn. (pres. 1962-64, dir. 1964-66, 71-75, Nurse of Yr. award 1979, dist. 9 service award 1970), Am. Med. Writers Assn. (Houston-Galveston sect. 1983-84), Sigma Theta Tau Club: Altrusa (pres. 1983-84) (Houston). Home: 3707 Murworth Houston TX 77025 Office: 6723 Bertner Ave Houston TX 77030

HILL, ANITA CARRAWAY, state legislator; b. Chatfield, Tex., Aug. 13, 1928; d. Archie Clark and Martha (Butler) Carraway; B.A. in Journalism, Tex. Woman's U., 1950; m. Harris Hill, Sept. 20, 1952; children—Stephen Victor, Virginia Evelyn. Reporter Garland (Tex.) Daily News, 1950-51; ednl. dir. First Meth. Ch., Garland, 1951-53; chemist Kraft Foods Co., Garland, 1953-56; legis. aide, Tex. Legislature, 1975-77; mem. Tex. Ho. of Reps., 1977—, mem. mcpl. bond and revenue sharing coms., 1971-74. Awards chmn. City of Garland Environ. Council; mem. City of Garland Park and Recreation Bd., 1971-77, chmn., 1976-77; life mem. PTA. Named Disting. Alumna, Tex. Woman's U., 1981. Mem. Garland C. of C., Rowlett C. of C., Bus. and Profl. Women's Club (Garland Woman of Year, 1980), AAUW, Tex. Assn. Elected Women. Republican. Methodist. Office: 203 Republic Bank Bldg 700 W Ave B Garland TX 75040

HILL, BARBARA ANNE, advertising agency executive; b. Chgo., Aug. 31, 1947; d. Spencer Franklin and Gladys Louise (Jones) Hill; m. John Donald Goullet, Jr., Sept. 25, 1982. A.A., Stephens Coll., 1967; B.S., U. Tenn., 1970. Media planner Foote, Cone & Belding, N.Y.C., 1971-73; media supr. Ted Bates, N.Y.C., 1973-76, account exec., 1976-78; account exec. Foote, Cone & Belding, 1978-79; sr. v.p., mgmt. supr. Avrett, Free & Ginsberg, N.Y.C., 1979—. Republican. Presbyterian. Office: Avrett Free & Ginsberg 800 3d Ave New York NY 10022

HILL, BARBARA MAE, librarian; b. Keene, N.H., Sept. 19, 1924; d. Gale Earl and Gertrude Wiseman (Reed) Hill; B.E., Keene Tchrs. Coll., 1946; M.S., Simmons Coll., 1952. Tchr. sci. and math. Thayer High Sch., Winchester, N.H., 1946-47; children's librarian Keene Public Library, 1947-52; asst. librarian Mass. Coll. Pharmacy and Allied Health Scis., Boston, 1952-58, asso. librarian, 1958-69, librarian, 1969—. Bd. dirs. Fenway Library Consortium, 1975—, coordinator, 1982-84. Mem. AAUP, Drug Info. Assn., Am. Assn. Colls. Pharmacy (ho. of dels. 1979-80, chmn. libraries-edn. resources sect. 1982-83), Med. Library Assn. (chmn. pharmacy group 1965-66, chmn. pharmacy and drug info. sect. 1985-86), Spl. Libraries Assn. (vice chmn. pharm. div. 1972-73, chmn. 1973-74), Kappa Delta Pi, Rho Chi. Office: Massachusetts College of Pharmacy and Allied Health Scis 179 Longwood Ave Boston MA 02115

HILL, BETTY JO, medical technologist; b. W. Liberty, Ky., Oct. 9, 1953; d. Arlyn Glen and Thelma Verna (Drake) Allen; m. Terrie Lee Hill, Sept. 22, 1979; children—Terrie Lee, Gaven Ryan. B.S. in Biology, Morehead State U., 1977. Med. technologist staff Licking Meml. Hosp., Newark, Ohio, 1976-81, med. technologist supr., 1981—. Republican. Methodist. Address: 500 Mill Race Rd Granville OH 43023

HILL, BEVERLY SAVORY, nurse; b. Concord, N.H., May 21, 1925; d. Fred Arthur and Florence Emma (Davis) Savory; m. John Reid Hill, July 25, 1948; children—Diane, Martha, Orton Fred. Diploma, Elliot Hosp., 1946. Staff nurse Margaret Pillsbury Meml. Hosp., Concord, 1946-47; head nurse Gifford Meml. Hosp., Randolph, Vt., 1947-48; office nurse to Dr. Edward Putnam, Warner, N.H., 1949-64; vol. Vis. Nurse Assn., New London, N.H., 1974—; staff Well Child Clinics, K.V.N.A., 1974—. Recipient Vol. of Year, Kearsarge Vis. Nurse Assn., 1976; Community Service award, Warner Men's Club, 1982, Gov.'s Steering Com. on Citizen and Community Involvement, 1982. Republican. United Ch. of Christ. Home: Route 2 Kirtland St Warner NH 03278

HILL, CAROLYN COLLINS, lawyer; b. Raleigh, N.C., Oct. 7, 1943; d. Edward Charles and Alma Lee (Tunstall) Collins; m. Peter Crawford Hill, Jr., Aug. 5, 1972. B.A., U. Va., 1965; LL.B., U. Richmond, 1968. Bar: Fla. 1968, D.C. 1972, U.S. Supreme Ct. 1981. Law clk. trainee FCC, Washington, 1968-69, gen. atty., 1969-72; sr. atty. United Telecommunications, Washington, 1972-78, asst. Washington counsel, 1978—. Trustee, Don Air Bapt. Ch., Arlington, Va., 1978—; mem. Stonewall Jackson Citizens Assn., Arlington, 1975—. Mem. ABA, Va. State Bar, D.C. Bar, Fed. Communications Bar Assn. (sec. 1979-80). Republican. Baptist. Home: 637 N Illinois St Arlington VA 22205 Office: United Telecommunications Inc 1875 Eye St NW Suite 1250 Washington DC 20006

HILL, DEBORAH JOAN, Spanish educator, researcher; b. Balt., Mar. 25, 1953; d. Jack Milton and Marie Rita (McLinden) Hill; m. Bret Martin Atkins, Aug. 21, 1982. B.A. in Spanish cum laude, Calif. State U., 1976; M.A. in Spanish, Fla. State U., 1981, Ph.D., 1983. Instr. Fla. State U., Tallahassee, 1982-83; instr. Ohio State U., Columbus, 1983—, undergrad. lang. coordinator, 1985, group leader Spanish lang. program, Madrid, 1985; co-dir. Teatro Unidad, 1985. Author: (genealogy) Little Heroes, 1984; (one-act play) El Voto (The Vote), 1985. Contbr. articles to profl. jours. Recipient Cert. of Commendation Fla. State U., 1982. Mem. Asociacion Internacional de Hispanistas, MLA, South Atlantic Modern Lang. Assn., Sigma Delta Pi, Lamda Iota Tau. Avocation: photography. Office: Ohio State U Dept Romance Langs 1841 Millikin Rd Columbus OH 43210

HILL, DEBRA LEE, gymnastics coach; b. Reno, June 27, 1952; d. Robert Darell and Alberta Lucille (Pollett) Stark; m. Rodney Cecil Hill, June 27, 1968; children—Troy Rodney, Lara Lee Marguerite. Student pub. schs. Wheatridge, Colo. Women's gymnastics coach Denver Sch. Gymnastics, Wheatridge, 1968-78, Brigham Young U., Provo, Utah, 1978—. Author: Women's Gymnastics, 1985. Mem. U.S. Nat. Women's Gymnastics Team, 1969-74, U.S. Worlds Games Team, 1970, U.S. Olympic Team, 1972, U.S. Pre-Worlds Games team, 1973. Named Most Inspirational Athlete, Denver YMCA, 1977; Outstanding Rocky Mountain Gymnast, Colo. AAU, 1974. Avocation: oil painting.

HILL, EDITH MARLENE, real estate investor, musician, songwriter; b. Oberlin, Kans., June 19, 1947; d. John Albert and Margaret Ann Louise (Germeroth) H.; m. Ricky Lee Brainard, Feb. 4, 1968 (div. 1972). B.S. in Elem. Edn., U. No. Colo., 1969; M.S. in Speech Pathology, Fort Hays (Kans.) State Coll.-Greeley, 1973. Speech therapist Kern County Schs., Bakersfield, Calif., 1973-75; staff speech pathologist Meml. Rehab. Found. Ctr., Santa Barbara, Calif., 1975-80; assoc. speech pathologist U. Calif.-Santa Barbara, 1977; speech pathologist pvt. practice, Santa Barbara, 1980-83; real estate acquisition, property mgmt., and partnership formation, Santa Barbara, 1977—. Author lyrics and music: Just a Baby, 1983, What Does Lonely Feel Like, 1985. Recipient 3rd in Best Bands award Ole-Time Fiddlers Conv., 1985. Club: Hoedowners (leader 1985—). Avocations: dancing; hiking. Home: Santa Barbara CA

HILL, EVELYN ARDEN (GRANDY), librarian; b. East Helena, Mont., Oct. 27, 1931; d. Arden Samuel and Ethel Knowles (Ten Eyck) Grandy; m. Elbert Bernard Hill, Nov. 14, 1952 (div. 1964); children—Mitchell D., Lynne R., Deborah F., Jonathan W. B.S., U. Mont., 1965; M.S., Troy State U., 1976. Librarian, U.S. Air Force, Glasgow AFB, Mont., 1965-67, Malmstrom, Great Falls, Mont., 1976-74, 79-81, Zweibrucken, W.Ger., 1974-79, West Berlin, W.Ger., 1982-83; reference librarian U.S. Air Force, Ramstein, W.Ger., 1984—. Mem. ALA. Democrat. Methodist. Club: Altrusa (treas. 1972). Office: 86th Combat Support Group SSL APO New York NY 09012

HILL, FRANCES CAROLYN, nursing service administrator, consultant; b. Decatur, Ala., Aug. 25, 1943; d. Patrick Joseph and Allene (Cross) Walsh; m. Robert Walter Hill, May 5, 1976. Diploma in nursing Grady Meml. Hosp.; B.S., Ogelthorpe U., 1973; M. Nursing Adminstrn., Med. Coll. Ga., 1977; D.Arts, Heed U., 1983. Adminstrv. head nurse Lakeland Regional Med. Ctr., Fla., 1964-71; staff nurse St. Joseph's Infirmary, Atlanta, 1971-72; registered profl. adult nurse practitioner Ga. Regional Med. Care Program, Atlanta, 1972-75; dir. nursing Ridgecrest Med. Ctr., Clayton, Ga., 1976-78; nursing service adminstr. Douglas Gen. Hosp., Douglasville, Ga., 1978-79; adminstrv. asst. Habersham County Med. Ctr., Demorest, Ga., 1979-84; v.p. nursing Parkview Episcopal Med. Ctr., Pueblo, Colo., 1984—; mem. faculty Hosp. Corp. Am. Ctr. Health Studies, Nashville; cons. mgmt. co., preceptor nursing exec. mgmt. program; clin. assoc. Brenau Coll., Gainesville, Ga.; data analyst, coordinator Atlanta Atty. Group. Author: The Role of the Director of Nursing: Sources of Conflict, 1983. Mem. commn. statewide master planning Gov. Ga. Mem. Am. Soc. Hosp. Nursing Service Adminstrs., Ga. Soc. Hosp. Nursing Service Adminstrs., Nat. League Nursing, Ga. State Nurses' Assn., Jr. Woman's Club, Am. Cancer Soc. (v.p. profl. edn. com.). Republican. Episcopalian. Home: PO Box 1405 Pueblo CO 81002 Office: Parkview Episcopal Med Ctr 400 W 16th St Pueblo CO 81003

HILL, HYACINTHE (VIRGINIA KAIN), poet; b. N.Y.C., May 24, 1920; d. Joseph Thomas and Angela Virginia (Bradley-Bruen) Cronin; B.A. cum laude with honors in English, Bklyn. Coll., 1961; M.A. in English and Comparative Lit., Hunter Coll., 1965; postgrad. Fordham U., 1965-69; Ph.D. (hon.), No. Pontifical Acad., Sweden, 1969; D.Arts and Letters (hon.), Gt. China Arts Coll., 1969; D. Hum., Coll. Alfred the Great, Hull, Eng., 1970; L.H.D. (hon.), L'Universite Libre d'Asie, India, 1974; m. Johan Anderson, July 15, 1940 (dec.); children—John Luke Anderson, Matthew Mark Anderson (dec.); m. 2d, John H. Kain, Dec. 28, 1978. Tchr. English, James Monroe High Sch., Bronx, N.Y., 1969-81; del. World Congress Poets, Manila, 1969, Taiwan, 1973; hon. v.p. Centro Studi e Scambi, Rome, 1974; Author: Shoots of a Vagrant Vine (Avalon Nat. Sonnets prize 1950), 1950; Promethea (Cameo Press book award 1957), 1957; Squaw, No More, 1975; also numerous individual poems; co-editor Diamond Year Anthology, 1970; editor North Atlantic edit. Great Am. World Poets Anthology, 1973; poems included in An Anthology of Women Poets from Deborah and Sappho to the Present. Recipient Poetry Soc. Am. prizes, 1958—; N.Am. Chapbook award, 1966; 1st prize Eleanor Otto award N.Y. Poetry Forum, 1969, 70; 1st prize Internat. Inst., 1970; York (Eng.) poetry prize, 1974; named champion Order United Religions, 1975; Keats Poetry prize London Lit. Edits., 1975; proclamation Mayor of Yonkers, 1975; named Dau. of Mark Twain for contbn. to modern Am. Poetry; numerous other awards. Mem. Acad. Am. Poets, Poetry Soc. Am., League Am. Pen-Women, Cosmosynthesis League (hon. life mem.), Alpha Delta Kappa. Quaker. Home: Merlin's Gleam Bell Hollow Rd Putnam Valley NY 10579

HILL, JUDITH DEEGAN, lawyer; b. Chgo., Dec. 13, 1940; d. William James and Ida May (Scott) Deegan; m. Dennis M. Harens, June 28, 1986; children by previous marriage—Colette M., Christina M. B.A., Western Mich. U., 1960; cert. U. Paris, Sorbonne, 1962; J.D., Marquette U., 1971. Bar: Wis. 1971, Ill. 1973, Nev. 1976, D.C. 1979. Tchr., Kalamazoo (Mich.) Bd. Edn., 1960-62, Maple Heights (Ohio), 1963-64, Shorewood (Wis.) Bd. Edn., 1964-68; corp. atty. Fort Howard Paper Co., Green Bay, Wis., 1971-72; sr. trust adminstr. Continental Ill. Nat. Bank & Trust, Chgo., 1972-76; atty. Morse, Foley & Wadsworth Law Firm, Las Vegas, 1976-77; dep. dist. atty., criminal prosecutor Clark County Atty., Las Vegas, 1977-83; atty. civil and criminal law Edward S. Coleman Profl. Law Corp., Las Vegas, 1983-84; sole practice, 1984-85; atty. criminal div. Office of City Atty., City of Las Vegas, 1985—. Bd. dirs. Nev. Legal Services, Carson City, 1980-84, state chmn., 1984—; bd. dirs. Clark County Legal Services, Las Vegas, 1980—; mem. Star Aux. for Handicapped Children, Las Vegas, 1986. Recipient Scholarship, Auto Specialties, St. Joseph, Mich., 1957-60; St. Thomas More Scholarship, Marquette U. Law Sch., Milw., 1968-69; juvenile law internship grantee Marquette U. Law Sch., 1970. Mem. ABA, Nev. Bar Assn., Woman's Bar Assn. of Ill., So. Nev. Assn. Women Attys., Ill. Bar Assn., Washington Bar Assn. Democrat. Club: Children's Village (pres. 1980) (Las Vegas, Nev.). Home: 1110 S 5th Pl Las Vegas NV 89104 Office: Office of City Atty 400 E Stewart St 6th Floor Las Vegas NV 89101

HILL, LARKIN PAYNE, real estate company data processing executive; b. El Paso, Tex., Oct. 30, 1954; d. Max Lloyd and Jane Olivia (Evatt) H.; m. J. Franklin Graves, July 12, 1975 (div. July 1979). Student Coll. Charleston, 1972-73, U. N.C., 1973. Lic. real estate broker, N.C. Sec., property mgr. Max L. Hill Co., Inc., Charleston, S.C., 1973-75, sec., data processor, 1979-82, data processing mgr., 1982—; resident mgr. Carolina Apts., Carrboro, N.C., 1975-77; sales assoc., Realtor, Southland Assocs., Chapel Hill, N.C., 1977-78; cons. specifications com. Charleston Trident Multiple Listing Service, 1985. Mem. Nat. Assn. Female Execs., Preservation Soc., Charleston Computer Users Group, N.C. Assn. Realtors. Republican. Methodist. Avocations: reading; crossword puzzles; furniture restoration; riflery. Home: 627 Bay Ct Mount Pleasant SC 29464 Office: Max L Hill Co Inc 632 Saint Andrews Blvd Charleston SC 29407

HILL, LYDA HUNT, health care and real estate executive, civic worker; b. Dallas, Sept. 17, 1942; d. Albert G. and Margaret (Hunt) H.; student Stanford U., 1960-61; B.S. in Math., Hollins Coll., 1964. With Seven Falls Co., tourist attraction, oil and gas and real estate co., Dallas and Colorado Springs, Colo., 1964—, sec., 1970-74, pres., 1974—; founder, chmn. bd. Hill World Travel, Dallas, 1968-73; pres. Hill Devel. Co., oil, gas, real estate investments, Dallas, 1974—. Chmn. Crystal Charity Ball, Dallas, 1975; bd. dirs. Dallas Soc. Crippled Children, Dallas; chmn. bd. Am. Heart Assn., Dallas, 1978-80, chmn. Tex. affiliate, 1986-87; mem. regional governing council Assn. Jr. Leagues, Dallas, 1975-76, 2d v.p. Jr. League of Dallas, 1975-76, treas., 1979-80, pres., 1982-83, editor Jr. League Mag., 1974; mem. Pres.'s Adv. Bd. for Pvt. Sector Initiatives, 1986-88; chmn. Vol. Connection, 1984—; bd. dirs. Arts Magnet High Sch., 1984—. Named an Outstanding Young Women Am., U.S. Jaycees, 1977, 79, Disting. Alumna Hockaday Sch., 1986; recipient Best of Am. award, 1985, Pres. Vol. Action award Vol. Connection, 1986. Mem. Young Pres. Orgn. Office: 5000 Thanksgiving Tower Dallas TX 75201

HILL, MARTHA ADELE, chemist; b. London, Ont., Can., Apr. 13, 1922; came to U.S., 1949, naturalized, 1956; returned to Can., naturalized, 1984; d. Rowland and Elsie (Wilkins) H.; B.S., Wheaton (Ill.) Coll., 1943; M.Sc., Rutgers U., 1945; Ph.D., U. Toronto, 1949. Chem. lab. asst. Wheaton Coll., 1942-43; grad. asst. N.J. Coll. for Women, Rutgers U., New Brunswick, N.J., 1943-45; demonstrator in chemistry U. Toronto, Ont., Can., 1945-48; analytical chemist Dow Chem. Co., Sarnia, Ont., summer, 1944; research chemist Eastman Kodak Co., Rochester, N.Y., 1949-56, research asso., 1957-64; faculty Engrng. Sci., U. Western Ont., 1973-80; exec. asst. VI Internat. Fermentation Symposium, 1978-80; ind. cons. chemist doing research for U. Tex., El Paso, 1981, Faculty of Engrng. Sci., U. Western Ont., London, 1982. Mem. Am. Chem. Soc., Sigma Pi Sigma. Club: London Christian Women's. Contbr. articles to profl. jours.; patentee in field. Home: 103 Wychwood Ct London ON N6G 1S6 Canada

HILL, MARY FRANCES, health care professional; b. N.J., Oct. 7, 1942; d. Ellsworth Roger and Frances (Carrubba) Hill; A.A., County Coll. of Morris, 1979; student Montclair State Coll., 1979—. Mem. staff Newton (N.J.) Meml. Hosp., 1964-66, St. Clare's Hosp., Denville, N.J., 1966-70, Chilton Meml. Hosp., Pompton Plains, N.J., 1972-79; asst. dir. PSRO, Wayne, N.J., 1979—; chmn. Passaic Valley PSRO med. record adv. com.; chairperson quality assurance coordinators N.J. PSRO. Served with USMC, 1961-63. Cert. med. record technician. Mem. Am. Med. Records Assn., Med. Record Assn. N.J., Nat. Assn. Quality Assurance Profls., Safe and Nuclear Free Environment, People for Am. Way, NOW, Greenpeace, Common Cause. Home: 289 Mount Hope Ave Apt B21 Dover NJ 07801 Office: 573 Valley Rd Wayne NJ 07470

HILL, MARY LUSAN, medical research scientist; b. Decatur, Ill., May 21, 1940; d. Carl McCrae and Mary Jayne (Ahrens) Hill; B.S., Webster Coll., 1962; M.T., Northwestern U., 1963. Cert. Am. Soc. Clin. Pathologists. Chief lab. instr. Clin. Pathology Course, Northwestern Med. Sch., Chgo., 1964, sr. research technologist, 1964-75; research assoc. dept. pathology, Duke U. Med. Center, Durham, N.C., 1975—; dir. Cell Diagnostics, Inc. Vol. Ind. Voters of Ill., Ind. Precinct Orgn., 1972; vol. tutoring program, 1969-71. Mem. Am. Soc. Clin. Pathologists. Roman Catholic. Clubs: Durham-Chapel Hill Ski and Sports (sec. 1978-79), Bus. and Profl. Women's (pres. 1977-78, legis. chmn. 1978-80). Contbr. articles to profl. jours. Home: 2800 Croasdaile Dr #J5 Durham NC 27705 Office: PO Box 3712 Durham NC 27710

HILL, MILDRED EVELYNNE, historical society executive, museum curator; b. Brazil, Ind., Jan. 24, 1912; d. George Wade and Bertha Ellen (Doran) LaBier; m. Harold Josef Hill, Sr., Jan. 1, 1930; children—Harold Joseph, Jr., Virginia Ellen, James Wade. Student Terre Haute Bus. Coll., 1929; B.A. equivalent, U. Chgo., 1941-42. Sec. to politician, Chgo., 1929; designer, dressmaker, 1928—; paramedic, 1951-66; house mother DePauw U., Greencastle, Ind., 1978-79; pres. Clay County Hist. Soc., Brazil, Ind., 1980-85, dir. curator mus., 1980-85, also chmn. bd. dirs., pres., 1980—. Editor monthly pamphlet House, 1937-39; editor, project dir. Clay County History, 1880-84, 1985. Bd. dirs. Stone Hills Shalsa, 1983-85, Brazil Pub. Library, 1984-86. Mem. Ind. Hist. Soc. Republican. Presbyterian. Avocations: sewing; knitting; lacemaking; cooking; travel. Home: 115 E Logan St Brazil IN 47834 Office: Clay County Hist Soc and Mus 100 E National Ave Brazil IN 47834

HILL, NOLANDA SUE, broadcast executive; b. Dallas, June 16, 1944; d. Nolan R. and Francile (Morrison) Butler; m. Sheldon K. Turner, Jr., Feb. 14, 1971 (div. 1975); m. 2d, Billy B. Hill, Jr., June 25, 1976; 1 son, Andrew Butler. B.A., B.S., Stephen F. Austin U., Nacogdoches, Tex., 1966. Exec. producer Doubleday Broadcasting, Dallas, 1968-70; pres. U.V. Sports, Los Angeles, 1970-71; chief exec. officer, chief fin. officer Nat. Bus. Network, Dallas, 1972-74; pres. Handel Pub., Dallas, 1974-76; chief exec. officer, chief fin. officer Nat. Bus. Network, Dallas, 1976-84; pres., chief exec. officer Ind. Am. Broadcasters, Dallas, 1984—; mem. bd. Tex. Bd. Archtl. Examiners, Austin, 1983—; moderator FCC/White House Symposium for Women Ownership in Telecommunications, 1983. Editor: National Directory of Performing Arts and Civic Centers, 1974, 75, 76; National Directory Arts/Canada, 1976. Mem. Speakers' Club Ho. of Reps., 1983; chmn. Women's Com. Speakers Club, 1984; mem. Dallas March of Dimes, Dallas Ballet Guild, Dallas Mus. Art. Mem. Nat. Assn. Broadcasters. Democrat. Home: 3507 Mc Farlin St Dallas TX 75205 Office: Independent American Broadcasters 1349 Empire Central Dr Suite 310 Dallas TX 75247

HILL, NORMA LOUISE, library administrator; b. Somerville, Mass., Oct. 27; d. Southern G. and Marguerite M. (Smith) Smallwood; m. George Forris Hill, Dec. 30, 1954; children—Gregory Harrison, Jonathan Smallwood. A.B., Wheaton Coll., 1952; M.S.L.S., Our Lady of the Lake Coll., 1975. Grad. asst. Our Lady of the Lake Coll., San Antonio, Tex., 1974-75; librarian Community Guidance Ctr., San Antonio, 1975, 86th Tactical Fighter Wing, Ramstein W.Ger., 1976-79; info. mgmt. specialist Exec. Office of the Pres., Washington, 1980; dept. head Howard County (Md.) Library, 1980-81, asst. dir., 1981—. Mem. Friends of the Howard County Library; mem. exec. bd. Howard County Assn. Community Services. Recipient Insp. Gen. Spl. Achievement award USAF, 1977, 78. Mem. Md. Assn. Pub. Library Adminstrs., Howard County Women's Network, Md. Library Assn. (chmn. nominations com. 1984-85, co-chmn. fed. relations subcom. 1985-86, 1st v.p., pres.-elect 1986—), ALA (pub. library div.), Nat. Assn. Female Execs., Alpha Kappa Alpha. Democrat. Office: Howard County Library 10375 Little Patuxent Pkwy Columbia MD 21044

HILL, PAMELA JEAN, pharmacist; b. Indpls., Nov. 4, 1958; d. Cecil Johnnie and Marguerite Alice (Budrech) Hill. B.S., Butler U., 1982; M.H.P., 1983—. Lic. pharmacist, Ind. Staff pharmacist Ind. U. Hosps., Indpls., 1983-85; dir. pharmacy services Care Mark Home Health Care of Am., Indpls., 1985—; nutrition cons. Care Mark Home Health Care of Am., 1985—. Contbr. articles to profl. jours. Author: Nutritional Handbook Indiana University Hospitals, 1985. Sec. music com. Southport Presbyn. Ch., Ind., 1985—. Mem. Am. Soc. Parenteral/Enteral Nutrition, Am. Soc. Hosp. Pharmacists, Ind. Pharmacists Assn., Ind. Soc. Hosp. Pharmacists, Nat. Assn. Female Execs. Butler U. Band Alumni Assn. (pres. 1985—). Republican. Presbyterian. Avocations: flautist; theatre; needlework; art. Office: Care Mark Home Health Care of America 5545 W Raymond St "J" Indianapolis IN 46241

HILL, PATRICIA A, lawyer, state legislator; b. Lima, Ohio, Dec. 10, 1945; m. Robert M. Hill, Dec. 30, 1974. B.A., Va. Poly. Inst., 1967; J.D., U. Houston, 1970. Bar: Tex. 1971, U.S. Ct. Appeals (5th cir.) 1972, U.S. Dist. Ct. (no. dist.) Tex. 1972, U.S. Dist. Ct. (so. dist.) Tex. 1976, U.S. Dist. Ct. (western dist.) Tex. 1977, U.S. Ct. Appeals (11th cir.) 1977, U.S. Dist. Ct. (ea. dist.) Tex. 1981, U.S. Supreme Ct. 1982. High sch. tchr. English, Lima, Ohio, 1967-68, law clk. U.S. Dist. Ct. (no. dist.) Tex., Dallas, 1971-72; assoc. firm Crouch and Nowell, Dallas, 1972-76; sole practice law, Dallas, 1976-83; dir., shareholder Baker, Smith & Mills, P.C., Dallas, 1984—; mem. Tex. Ho. of Reps., 1983—; vice chmn. state affairs com., mem. govt. orgns.; vice chmn. Sunset Adv. Commn., 1985-87. Monthly columnist Tex. Woman Mag., 1979-80. Sec., trustee Bette Claire McMurray and Gihon Founds., 1976—; mem. Charter 100 of Dallas, Dallas Assembly; treas. Exec. Women of Dallas, 1979; mem. adv. bd. Jr. League Dallas; mem. Mayor's Internat. Com.; mem. bd. mgmt. Downtown YMCA, 1982—. Mem. ABA (litigation sect.), State Bar Tex. (com. on adminstrn. of justice 1981-83), Dallas Bar Assn. (sec. 1979, dir. 1980-81), Dallas Women Lawyers (chmn. 1975), Am. Bar Found., Tex. Bar Found., Tex. Woman (dir.), U. Houston Law Sch. North Tex. Alumni Assn. (dir. 1981—). Episcopalian. Office: 1000 Pacific Pl 1910 Pacific Ave Dallas TX 75201

HILL, PATRICIA ARNOLD, government official; b. Balt., Oct. 29, 1936; d. George Henry and Mildred Mae (Kress) Arnold; student No. Va. Community Coll., part time 1966-76; m. Richard Denzil Hill, Oct. 24, 1970; children—Terry Marlene Fomby, Debra Michelle Hill. Sec. firm McEwan & Walker, Chattanooga, 1955; clk.-typist Bur. Aeros., Washington, 1956-58, security clk., 1958, security asst., 1959-62, security specialist Bur. Aeros. and Naval Weapons Washington, 1962-66; security specialist Bur. Naval Weapons, 1962-66, Naval Ordnance Systems Command, 1966-74; security specialist Naval Sea Systems Command, Washington, 1974-75, head classification mgmt. br., asst. dir. security div., 1975-80, dep. dir., head info. security br. security div., 1980-83, security mgr. and dir. security div., 1983—. Mem. Nat. Assn. Female Execs., Nat. Classification Mgmt. Soc., Ind. Sec. Assn., Va. State Soc., Profl. Bus. Women. Baptist. Home: 1003 Collingwood Rd Alexandria VA 22308 Office: Nat Center Bldg 3 Crystal City Arlington VA 22202

HILL, PATRICIA LISPENARD, insurance educator; b. N.Y.C., June 25, 1937; d. George Joseph and Elizabeth (Lispenard) H.; children—George, Christopher, Susan, Daniel, Frederic, Elizabeth. Student Barnard Coll., 1954-55, Pace U., 1972-74, Coll. of Ins., 1980. Lic. ins. broker, 1961—; owner, dir. Hill Sch. of Ins., N.Y.C., 1978—. Home: Ridgefield Ave South Salem NY 10590 Office: 93 Nassau St New York NY 10038

HILL, PATTY MAYNARD, nursing educator; b. Forsyth County, N.C., June 9, 1944; d. Ray and Etta Mae (Holleman) Maynard; diploma N.C. Bapt. Hosp. Sch. Nursing, 1966; B.S.N., U. N.C., 1969, M.Ed., 1973; Ed.D., N.C. State U., Raleigh, 1986; m. Gary P. Hill, Aug. 20, 1966; children—Gary P., Christopher, Caroline. Office nurse, 1967-69; instr. pediatric nursing Watts Sch. Nursing, Durham, N.C., 1970-74; instr. U. N.C. Sch. Nursing, Chapel Hill, 1974-77, asst. prof., 1977—; reviewer/cons. Duxbury Press; mem. rev. bd. Appleton Century Croft; condr. workshops. Bd. dirs. Chapel Hill Oasis, 1978-80, Chapel Hill Day Care Ctr., 1977—, Chapel Hill Service League, 1977—; del. St. Thomas More Sch., 1981-82, pres. Home-Sch. Assn. Mem. Am. Nurses Assn., N.C. Nurses Assn., AAUP, Nat. Assn. Adult Edn., Nat. Assn. Care of Hospitalized Child, Durham/Orange Dental Assn. (pres.), Sigma Theta Tau. Methodist. Co-editor, contbg. author: Development throughout Life: A Nursing Perspective, 1982; co-author: Human Development; contbr. articles in field. Home: 414 Sharon Rd Chapel Hill NC 27514

HILL, PRISCILLA GRANDIN, controller; b. Shaker Heights, Ohio, June 10, 1953; d. Robert Martin and Jean Culver (Grandin) H.; m. W.J. Weidman, Jr., Mar. 10, 1984. B.S., Stetson U., DeLand, Fla., 1975; grad. various banking, fin. and computer programming courses. With Mut. Bank Savs., Newton Centre, Mass., 1975-81, asst. comptroller, 1978-80, comptroller, 1980-81; fin. analyst Boston Fin. Data Services, Inc., 1981-82, asst. mgr., 1982, mgr., 1983-84, asst. controller, 1984—. Player, coach North River Women's Fastpitch Softball League, 1976-77, Quincy Women's Softball League, 1985. Mem. Savs. Bank Women Mass., Savs. Bank Assn. Mass. Officers Club, Duxbury Hist. Soc. Republican. Presbyterian. Home: 119 Buckboard Rd Duxbury MA 02332 Office: 2 Heritage Dr North Quincy MA 02171

HILL, ROSANNA, laboratory administrator; b. Macon, Ga., July 1, 1949; d. Henry and Julia (Chambliss) Hill; B.S., Clark Coll., 1971; postgrad. Howard U., 1971-72. Med. technologist Ga. Bapt. Med. Center, Atlanta, 1972-77, lab. mgr., 1977-81; lab. ops. mgr. Acculabs, Inc., Atlanta, 1981—, dir., partner, 1981—. Mem. Am. Public Health Assn., Clin. Lab. Mgmt. Assn., Nat. Assn. Female Execs. Mem. A.M.E. Ch. Home: 3110 Godby Rd Apt 21C College Park GA 30349 Office: 160 Boulevard NE Atlanta GA 30312

HILL, SARA LYNN, architect; b. Montclair, N.J., May 25, 1951; d. Lawrence and Mary (Allanson) H.; B.Arch. cum laude, Tulane U., 1974; B.F.A. magna cum laude, Newcomb Coll. Art, 1974. Chief designer Mathes, Bergman & Assocs., New Orleans, 1974-75; archtl. designer J. Buchanan Blitch & Assocs., 1975-76; archtl. cons. F. Monroe Labouisse Jr., 1976-79; staff architect, plans examiner Vieux Carre Commn., 1979-80; owner, partner V.C. Builders Gen. Contractors, 1980—; owner, mgr. Hill Co., 1980—; v.p. Robin Riley and Assocs., 1981-84; architect S. Stewart Farnet, Architect & Assocs., Inc., 1984—. Mem. AIA, La. Contractors Assn., Soc. Archtl. Historians. Club: So. Yacht. Office: 721 Louisa St New Orleans LA 70117 also 620 Louisa St New Orleans LA 70117

HILL, STEPHANIE HENSLEY, personnel executive; b. Cin., Jan. 6, 1955; d. Raymond Harold and Beverly Jane (Kunz) Hensley; m. Bradley Warren Hill, Aug. 2, 1980. B.A., U. South Fla., 1977. Br. mgr. Kelly Services, Inc., Savannah, Ga., 1977-79, nat. recruiting and retention mgr., Detroit, 1979-80, resident br. mgr., St. Louis, 1980-81, br. mgr., Pensacola, Fla., 1981—, tng. instr., 1983. Vol., Muscular Dystrophy Assn., Pensacola, 1982-83; fund raiser Ronald McDonald Houe, Pensacola, 1983; mem. fin. com. Trinity Presbyn. Ch., Pensacola, 1983. Named Outstanding Br. Mgr., Kelly Services, 1982, 83. Mem. Am. Soc. Personnel Assocs. (sec. 1983, dir. 1984), Bus. and Profl. Women (sec. 1978), Pensacola C. of C., Phi Kappa Phi. Republican. Presbyterian. Home: 6065 S Gulf Manor Pensacola FL 32506 Office: Kelly Services Inc 630 University Office Blvd Pensacola FL 32504

HILL, SUE WOODS, banker; b. Nashville, Mar. 14, 1936; d. Joseph Thomas and Marie (Woodward) Woods; m. Mac Hill, Aug. 21, 1953; 1 child, Joe Wallace. Student Columbia State Community Coll. Exec. sec. Judge Marshall County Ct., Lewisburg, Tenn., 1954-58; head credit dept. Venus Pen and Pencil Corp., Lewisburg, 1958-67; asst. v.p. First Nat. Bank, Lewisburg, 1967—. Active Cancer Fund, Lewisburg, 1978, Heart Fund, Lewisburg, 1979; mem. choir 1st United Methodist Ch., Lewisburg, 1962—. Mem. Nat. Assn. Bank Women, Bus. and Profl. Womens Club (sec. 1973-74, pres. 1974-75). Democrat. Lodge: Ladies of Elks (fellow). Avocations: tennis, needlepoint, crafts. Home: Route 2 1551 Mooresville Hwy Lewisburg TN 37091 Office: First Nat Bank 101 W Commerce St Lewisburg TN 37091

HILL, SUSAN RUTH, motel executive; b. Springfield, Ill., Dec. 14, 1924; d. Charles Albert and Laura Anna (Armstrong) Hamm; m. Frederick Thomas Hill, Jan. 29, 1955 (dec. Jan. 1980); 1 child, Ronald Gregory. Student Springfield Sec. Sch., 1941, United Airlines Tng. Sch., Chgo., 1943, Travelodge Tng. Sch., 1979; grad. Radio Electronics Inst., 1942, Jim Mort Real Estate Sch., 1978. Lic. real estate sales, Fla. Communications operator United Airlines, Chgo., 1941-43; sec. to pres. Witmer Rumsey Engring. Co., 1943-45; stenographer Am. Bridge Co., 1945-47, Union Pacific R.R., 1947-50; owner, opr. mgr. Travelodge, Salem, Oreg., 1979-81, Best Western Camelot Inn, Higginsville, Mo., 1983, Exec. Motel, Fond Du Lac, Wis., 1984—. Mem. Wis. Motel Assn. Republican. Avocations: cross-country skiing; cycling; reading; interior decorating. Office: Exec Motel 649 W Johnson St Fond Du Lac WI 54935

HILL, SUSAN SLOAN, safety engineer; b. Quincy, Mass., June 1, 1952; d. Ralph Arnold and Grace Elenore (Sloan) Crosby; m. William Loyd Hill, Dec. 16, 1973 (div. July 1982); m. William Joseph Graham, Sept. 10, 1983 (div. Feb. 1985). Assoc. Sci. in Gen. Engring., Motlow State Community Coll., Tullahoma, Tenn., 1976; B.S. in Indsl. Engring., Tenn. Technol. U., 1978. Intern, safety engr. Intern Tng. Ctr., U.S. Army, Red River Army Depot, Tex., 1978-79, Field Safety Activity, Charlestown, Idaho, 1979, system safety engr. Communications-Electronics Command, Ft. Monmouth, N.J., 1979-84, gen. engr., 1984-85; chief system safety Arnold Air Force Sta., USAF, Tullahoma, 1984; system safety engr. U.S. Army Safety Ctr., Ft. Rucker, Ala., 1985—. Recipient 3 letters of appreciation U.S. Army, 1982. Mem. Assn. Fed. Safety and Health Profls. (regional v.p. 1980-84), Soc. Women Engrs., Nat. Safety Mgmt. Soc., Am. Soc. Safety Engrs., System Safety Soc., Nat. Assn. Female Execs., Order Engr. Republican. Episcopalian. Avocations: bowling; needlework; sewing; cooking; golf. Home: 115 Liveoak Dr Enterprise AL 36330 Office: US Army Safety Ctr Attn PESCSE Fort Rucker AL 36362

HILL, SUZANNE, managment corporation executive, entertainment consultant; b. N.Y.C., Dec. 23, 1928; d. Isidore and Surah Tamara (Renert) Kamil; m. Stanley Martin Hiltzik, June 27, 1948 (div.); children—Marcie Bernette Strassner, Robin Leslie Levin, Richard David. Cert. in lang., Am. Sch., Rome, 1973; D.Music (hon.), Sch. for Performing Arts, N.Y.C., 1974. Performing artist Biltmore Hotel, N.Y.C., 1946-47; star program Suzanne Hill Sings, Mut. Network, N.Y.C., 1947-48; actress, singer TV and motion pictures, 1955—; co-owner, mgr. Englewood C.C., Englewood, N.J., 1959-65; exec. dir. Centex Corp., Cliffside Park, N.J., 1977-81; pres. Hill Mgmt. Corp., Edgewater, N.J., 1981—; entertainment dir. Roosevelt Hotel, N.Y.C., 1980—; entertainment cons. Centre Hotel, Abu Dhabi, United Arab Emirates, 1981-82; cons. Rose Assocs., N.Y.C., 1981, Sulzberger-Rolfe Assocs., N.Y.C., 1982—; dir. Palisadium, Cliffside Park, N.J., 1977-81. Organizer Am. Cancer Soc., N.J., 1979—, Fight for Sight, N.J., 1979—; performing artist USO, 1947-55. Recipient Meritorious Service award Am. Cancer Soc., 1980, Salvation Army, 1982. Mem. USO (Meritorious Service award 1950), Screen Actors Guild, Fedn. TV and Radio Artists, Guild Variety Artists. Home: 2 Horizon Rd Fort Lee NJ 07024 Office: Hill Management Corp 2 Horizon Rd Fort Lee NJ 07024

HILLBERRY, SHEILA MARIE STUEHRENBERG, microbiologist; b. Breckenridge, Minn., Apr. 19, 1945; d. Henry Ernest Fredrick and Marian Violet (Sandberg) Stuehrenberg; B.S., Moorhead State U., 1966; M.S., Purdue U., 1970; m. Joseph Hillberry, June 25, 1967; children—Russell Henry, Joseph Martin. Tchr. jr. high. sci. Wausau (Wis.) Public Schs., 1966-67; tchr. sci. Robert G. Cole High Sch., San Antonio, 1967-68; substitute tchr. Rapid City (S.D.) Schs., 1970-71; supr. clin. microbiology sect. Rapid City Regional Hosp., 1971—; adj. prof. S.D. Sch. Mines and Tech., 1979—. Organist, dir. choir, chmn. bd. edn. Lutheran Ch. Mem. Am. Soc. Clin. Pathology, Am. Soc. Microbiology, Black Hills Soc. Med. Technology. Home: 1309 38th St Rapid City SD 57701 Office: Laboratory 353 Fairmont Blvd Rapid City SD 57701

HILLEARY, ANNE MEGAN, government official; b. Washington, Nov. 1, 1951; d. Leo Paul and Sally Mary (Meenehan) H. B.S., George Mason U., 1974. Sec., GAO, Washington, 1974-76, budget analyst, 1976, mgmt. analyst, 1976-79, adminstrv. officer, 1979-80, program analyst, 1980-83, sr. evaluator, 1983—, instr. report writing course, 1984—. Recipient Certs. of Appreciation, GAO, 1975, 80. Roman Catholic. Office: US GAO 441 G St NW Room 3820 Washington DC 20548

HILLEN, VICTORIA EILEEN, nurse; b. Milford, Mass., Nov. 2, 1952; d. Richard Rhodes and Miriam Madeline (Wiggins) Sooley; m. James Patick O'Brien, Jr., Aug. 7, 1972 (div. Aug. 1977); children—Leslie, James; m. Robert Frank Hillen, Dec. 21, 1979. Student, S.E. Mo. State U., 1970-71; A.A. in Nursing, St. Mary's Coll., O'Fallon, Mo., 1978; student Maryville Coll., St. Louis, 1981. R.N., Mo. Staff nurse Barnes Hosp., St. Louis, 1978-79, 81-84, emergency mental health coordinator, 1979-81, asst. head nurse, 1979-81, problem-oriented med. record auditor, 1979-82, retrospective audit chmn., 1980-81; head nurse Hawthorne Children's Psychiat. Hosp., St. Louis, 1985—, treatment team coordinator, 1985—. Cheerleading coordinator, coach Bonhomme Jr. Football League, Ballwin, Mo., 1982-84; softball coach Manchester Athletic Assn., Mo., 1982-84; leader Greater St. Louis council Girl Scouts U.S.A., Manchester, 1982—, scout troop cons., 1984—; Cub Scouts vol. St. Louis Area council Boy Scouts Am., Manchester, summers 1983-85. Luth. scholar, 1976. Episcopalian. Home: 913 Queensbridge Rd Manchester MO 63021 Office: Hawthorne Children's Psychiat Hosp 5247 Fyler Ave Saint Louis MO 63139

HILLERS, VERA VERONICA, real estate executive, insurance executive; b. Pekin, Ill., Dec. 27, 1917; d. Fred and Frances (Pavalic) Vicich; m. Edwin R. Hillers, June 23, 1947 (dec. 1983); children—Edd H., Bradford J., Heidi K. Howard. Student Midstate Coll., 1937-41, Ill. Central Coll., 1967-68. Office worker Caterpillar Tractor Co., East Peoria, Ill., 1937-41; officer mgr. bookkeeper Peoria Candy Co., 1941-50; officer, owner, broker Hillers Realty & Ins., Inc., East Peoria, 1960-85. Charter mem. Fon Du Lac Golf League; active Little League and Pony League, East Peoria. Mem. Peoria Bd. Realtors, Nat. Bd. Realtors, Ill. Bd. Realtors, Am. Assn. Cert. Appraisers, East Peoria C. of C. (sec. 1970). Roman Catholic. Clubs: Mount Hawley Country, Sweet Adelines, Inc. Avocations: sports; golf; singing.

HILLERY, JUDITH ANN, county court Judge; b. Oneonta, N.Y., July 26, 1943; d. Joseph A. and Dorothea (McKeown) Hillery. B.A. in Psychology, SUNY-Buffalo, 1966; J.D., Buffalo Law Sch., 1967. Town justice Poughkeepsie, N.Y., 1975-78; family court judge Dutchess County, Poughkeepsie, 1978-83, county court judge, 1983—. Mem. ABA (jud. del. N.Y. conv. 1983), N.Y. State Bar Assn., N.Y. State Women's Bar Assn., Mid-Hudson Women's Bar Assn., County Court Judge's Assn. Clubs: Zonta, Bus. and Profl. Women (Poughkeepsie).

HILLERY, MARY JANE LARATO, editor; b. Boston, Sept. 15, 1931; d. Donato and Porzia (Avellis) Larato; Asso. Sci. (scholar), Northeastern U., 1950; B.S., U. Mass., 1962; m. Thomas H. Hillery, Feb. 25, 1961; 1 son, Thomas H. Sales agt., linguist Pan Am. Airways, Boston, 1955-61; interpreter Internat. Conf. Fire Chiefs, Boston, 1966; tchr. Spanish, YWCA, Natick, Mass., 1966-67; community relations cons., adv. bd. dirs., lectr. for migrant edn. project div. Mass. Dept. Community Affairs, Boston, 1967-69; editor-in-chief Sudbury (Mass.) Citizen, 1967-76; area editorial adviser Beacon Pub. Co., Acton, Mass., 1970-83; editor Beacon Publs., 1977-80; dir. public affairs com. Mass. Dept. Environ. Quality Engring., 1981-83. Mem. bus. adv. com. Town of Sudbury, 1972-77; mem. Sudbury Sch. Com., 1976-77; mem. Meml. Day Celebration Com., 1972—, master ceremonies, 1973-86, parade marshal, 1973, 74, 75, 82, chmn., 1974; panelist Internat. Women's Yr. Symposium, 1975; bd. dirs., incorporator Sudbury Nonprofit Housing Corp., 1973-74, chmn. Sudbury Town Report, 1969-72, mem., 1985. Served with USN, 1950-54; lt. col. U.S. Army Res. Named Editor of Yr., Beacon Pub. Co., 1970; recipient medal of appreciation DeMolay, 1969, Boy Scouts Am., 1974, CD Preparedness Agy., 1975, Mass. Bicentennial Commn., 1976, Woman of Achievement citation Mass. Senate, 1979, 82. Mem. Nat. Editorial Assn., Nat. Newspaper Assn., Internat. Platform Assn., New Eng. Press Assn., Res. Officers Assn. (life mem., sec. 1978-79, Outstanding Service award 1979), Bus. and Profl. Womens Club (1st v.p. 1973-74, pres. 1974-76, parliamentarian 1976-78, 82-86, mem. state elections com. 1976, state bylaws com. 1977-78, 79-81, chmn. state legis. com. 1979-81, Woman of Yr. 1979, Woman of Achievement award 1982), LWV (dir. 1964-68), Nat. League Am. Pen Women (exec. bd. Boston 1974-76, pres. 1976-78, master ceremonies 50th anniversary Boston br. 1977, parliamentarian 1978-86, auditor 1980-82), Omega Sigma. Contbg. editor Beacon, 1979-83, Towne Talk, 1975-79, Citizen's Forum, 1975-81. Home: 66 Willow Rd Sudbury MA 01776

HILLIARD, DONNA JEAN, nurse; b. Fairfield, Ill., Oct. 18, 1951; d. James F. and Norma Jean (Montgomery) Curry; diploma Burnham Hosp. Sch. Nursing, Champaign, Ill., 1972; m. Carroll Eugene Hilliard, Sept. 9, 1972; 2 daus., Melinda Suzanne, Megan Denise. Staff nurse Burnham City Hosp., Champaign, 1973; dir. nursing Scott County Nursing Center, Winchester, Ill., 1972—; coordinator Candy Striper program, Scott County. Instr., ARC; mem. Scott County Ambulance Bd. Republican. Mem. Christian Ch. Club: Bridge. Home: 201 E Cherry St Winchester IL 62694 Office: RR 2 Winchester IL 62694

HILLINGS, JENNIFER ANN, public relations consultant, government official; b. Washington, D.C., Oct. 7, 1954; d. Patrick Jerome and Phyllis Kaye (Reinbrecht) H.; B.A. in Pub. Relations, U. So. Calif., 1976. Account exec. Palisades Communications, Los Angeles, 1978-79; press dir. Calif. Senate Republican leader, Sacramento, 1979-81; press sec. Calif. Reagan-Bush campaign, Los Angeles, 1980; mem., press sec. Republican Nat. Com., Washington, 1981-83; pres. sec. White House Conf. Productivity, 1983; dep. dir. pub. affairs U.S. Dept. Commerce, 1983-84; media coordinator western states U.S. Dept. Interior, Washington, 1984-85; asst. sec. pub. affairs U.S. Dept. Transp., 1985—. Mem. Delta Gamma. Home: 2624 Woodley Pl NW Washington DC 20008 Office: US Dept Transp Washington DC

HILLIS, MARGARET, musician, choral conductor; b. Kokomo, Ind., Oct. 1, 1921; d. Glen R. and Bernice (Haynes) Hillis; B.A., Ind. U., 1947; postgrad. choral conducting, Juilliard Sch. Music, 1947-49; D.Mus. (hon.), Temple U., 1967, Ind. U., 1972, Carthage Coll., 1979, Wartburg Coll., 1981; D.F.A. (hon.), St. Mary's Coll., 1977, Lake Forest Coll., 1980. Dir. Met. Youth Chorale, Bklyn., 1948-51; asst. condr. Collegiate Choral, N.Y.C., 1952-53; mus. dir., condr. Am. Concert Choir, N.Y.C., 1950—, Am. Concert Orch., 1950—; condr., instr. Union Theol. Sem., 1950-60, Juilliard Sch. Music, 1951-53; dir. choral dept. Third St. Music Sch. Settlement, 1953-54; founder, music dir. Am. Choral Found., Inc., 1954—; choral dir. N.Y.C. Opera Co., 1955-56, Chgo. Mus. Coll. of Roosevelt U., 1961-62; condr., choral dir. Santa Fe Opera Co., 1958-59, Chgo. Symphony Chorus, 1957—; music dir. N.Y. Chamber Soloists, 1956-60; choral condr. Am. Opera Soc., N.Y.C., 1952-68; mus. asst. to music dir. Chgo. Symphony Orch., 1966-68; music dir., condr. Kenosha Symphony Orch., 1961-68; condr., choral dir. Cleve. Orch. Chorus, 1969-71; prof. conducting, dir. choral orgns. Northwestern U. Sch. Music, 1970-77; resident condr. Chgo. Civic Orch., 1967—; music dir. Choral Inst., 1968-70, 75; mus. dir., condr. Elgin (Ill.) Symphony Orch., 1971-85; condr. Do-It-Yourself Messiah, 1976—; vis. prof. conducting Ind. U., 1978—; dir. choral orgns. San Francisco Symphony, 1982-83; Guest condr. Chgo. Symphony, Cleve. Orch., Minn. Orch., Nat. Symphony Orch., others. Artists' adv. Nat. Fedn. Music Clubs Youth Auditions, 1966-70; mem. vis. com. dept. music U. Chgo., 1971—; chmn. choral panel Nat. Endowment for Arts, 1974-81; hon. mem. Roosevelt U. Council of 100, 1976—; adv. bd. Cathedral Choral Soc. Washington Cathedral, 1976—; mem. Nat. Council Arts, 1984—. Recipient Golden Plate award Am. Acad. Achievement, 1967; Alumnus of Yr. award Ind. U. Sch. Music Alumni, 1969; Steinway award, 1969; Chgo. YWCA Leader Luncheon I award, 1972; Friends of Lit. award, 1973; SAI Found. Circle of 15 award, 1974; Grammy award for best choral performance, 1977, 78, 79, 82, 83; Grand Prix du Disque, 1982; Leadership for Freedom award Women's Scholarship Assn. of Roosevelt U., 1978; award for contbn. to choral art Assn. Profl. Vocal Ensembles, 1980; named Woman of Yr., music category, Ladies Home Jour., 1978. Civilian flight instr., USN CAA, WTS, World War II. Mem. Nat. Fedn. Music Clubs (hon., citation for contbns. to music 1981), Am. Choral Dirs. Assn., Assn. Choral Condrs., Am. Music Center, Assn. Profl. Vocal Ensembles (exec. bd.), Am. Symphony Orch. League, Nat. Soc. Lit. and the Arts, PEO, Sigma Alpha Iota (hon.), Pi Kappa Lambda (hon.), Kappa Kappa Gamma (Alumni Achievement award 1978). Club: Musicians of Women (hon.). Office: 220 S Michigan Ave Chicago IL 60604

HILLMAN, CAROL ELLIS, speech-language pathologist, hosp. adminstr.; b. DuBois, Pa., May 5, 1953; d. Ralph Sheldon and Margaret (Girman) Ellis; B.S., Pa. State U., 1974, M.S., 1975; m. Robert Edward Hillman, Nov. 27, 1976; 1 dau., Sarah Ellen. Speech pathologist N.H. Easter Seal Soc., Manchester, 1975, Lawrence (Mass.) Gen. Hosp., 1975-76, Logansport (Ind.) Spl. Services, 1976-77; speech-lang. pathologist Lafayette (Ind.) Home Hosp., 1977-79; pvt. practice speech-lang. pathology, Stoneham, Mass., 1979-80; mgr. speech-lang. pathology dept. Beverly (Mass.) Hosp., 1980-81, dir. diagnostic/support services, 1981-84, adminstrv. dir. rehab. services and Sports Medicine Performance Ctr., 1984—; cons. speech-lang. pathology services Harbor Schs., Newburyport, Mass. Bd. dirs. United Cerebral Palsy, Lafayette, 1978-79. Recipient outstanding speech pathology student award Pa. State U., 1974. Mem. Am. Speech-Lang. and Hearing Assn. (cert. clin. competence), Mass. Speech-Lang. and Hearing Assn. Home: 27 Alan Rd South Hamilton MA 01982 Office: Beverly Hosp Beverly MA 01915

HILLMAN, ELSIE HILLIARD (MRS. HENRY LEA HILLMAN), political worker; b. Pitts., Dec. 9, 1925; d. Thomas Jones and Marianna (Talbott) Hilliard; student Westminster Choir Coll., 1944-45; hon. degrees Waynesburg Coll., 1979, Duquesne U., 1980; m. Henry Lea Hillman, May, 1945; children—Juliet (Mrs. J. Todd Simonds), Audrey (Mrs. Timothy O. Fisher), Henry Lea, William Talbott. Mem. 14th ward Republican Com., 1956, chmn. 1964-70; mem. Rep. Fin. Com., 1963; mem. Pa. State Adv. Com., 1963—; mem. Rep. State Exec. Com., 1963—; alt. del. Rep. Nat. Conv., 1964, del., 1968, 84, dep. del., 1976, del.-at-large, 1980; chmn. Rep. Exec. Com. Allegheny County, 1967-70; co-chmn. Re-elect Nixon Dinner, 1971; mem. Rep. Nat. Com., 1975—; co-chmn. Pa. Reagan-Bush com., 1984. Trustee, Ellis Sch., Pitts., 1951-66, hon. bd. mem. 1966—; trustee Carlow Coll.; bd. dirs., v.p. WQED Pub. TV, Pitts. Oratorio Soc.; bd. dirs., v.p. Pitts. Symphony Soc.; bd. dirs. Squirrel Hill Urban Coalition, 1972, v.p. 1972—; bd. dirs. Westminster Choir Coll. Named Women of Yr., Squirrel Hill Kiwanis, 1965, Pitts./Vectors, 1982; recipient Humanitarian award Guardians of Greater Pitts., 1973; Nat. Brotherhood award (with husband) NCCJ, 1973; Pa. Disting. Rep. award, 1974; Disting. Dau. of Pa. award, 1975. Mem. Urban League of Pitts. (past dir., 1st v.p. 1970). Episcopalian (mem. vestry 1976). Home: Holyrood Rd Morewood Heights Pittsburgh PA 15213

HILLMAN, LESLIE WIGINGTON, communications specialist; b. Pawhuska, Okla., Sept. 19, 1954; d. John Henry and Virginia Lee (Conger) Wigington; B.A. (H.H. Herbert hon. pub. relations scholar), U. Okla., 1976; m. Stephen Alan Hillman, May 23, 1976; children—Erica Michelle, Derek Thomas. News reporter Ada Evening News, Okla., 1977-78; editor Southside Times, Tulsa, 1978-79; wire editor Broken Arrow Daily Ledger, Okla., 1979-80; mng. editor Tulsalite mag., Tulsa, 1980-85; communications specialist, 1985—; editor Spotlite, Tulsa Performing Arts Ctr., 1980, 81. Recipient Irene Bowers Sells award, 1976, Service award Cystic Fibrosis Found., 1981. Mem. Women in Communications (2d v.p. Tulsa 1981-83, 1st v.p. 1983-84, sec. 1984-85). Office: 1308 S Indian Ave Tulsa OK 74127

HILLMAN, LUCILLE M., law school dean; b. Glens Falls, N.Y., Mar. 1, 1942; d. Albert R. and Martha A. (Hoag) H.; B.A., Chatham Coll., 1964. Fund raiser United Way of Allegheny County, Pitts., 1966-68; dir. alumnae fund Chatham Coll., 1968-70; dir. devel. Finch Coll., 1971-72; dir. WAIF/Travelers Aid Internat. Social Services of Am., N.Y.C., 1972-73; asst. dean N.Y. Law Sch., 1975—, asst. dean devel. and alumni relations, 1984—. Mem. Dutch Reformed Ch. Home: 201 E 25th St New York NY 10010 Office: 715 Broadway New York NY 10003

HILLMAN, SHEILAH ARCHAMBAULT, writer, publisher; b. Quincy, Mass., May 22, 1935; d. Alcide Joseph and Shirley Veronica (Griswold) Archambault; B.A. magna cum laude, Tufts U., 1957; m. Robert S. Hillman, Aug. 31, 1957; children—Kimberly Ann, Robert Joseph. Reporter, The Patriot Ledger, Quincy, 1954-57; mng. editor Gold Medal Books, Fawcett Pubs., N.Y.C., 1957-61; journalism tchr., public relations cons., 1972—. Mem. Women in Communications, Authors Guild. Author: Public Relations for Private Schools, 1976; (with Dr. Robert S. Hillman) Traveling Healthy: A Complete Guide to Medical Services in 23 Countries, 1980; The Baby Checkup Book, 1982; Cradle Kill, 1986

HILLMAN-JONES, GLADYS CORNELIA, educational administrator; b. Albany, N.Y., Jan. 15, 1938; d. Thomas Benjamin and Minnie Geneva (Colclough) Brooks; B.S., SUNY, Oneonta, 1960; M.A., Kean Coll. (formerly Newark State Coll.), 1970; m. Harold Jones, Apr. 19, 1980; 1 son by previous marriage, George I. Hillman III. Tchr. public schs., Albany, N.Y., 1960-64, Newark, 1964-69; vice prin. Chancellor Ave. Sch., Newark, 1969-76; prin. Marcus Garvey Sch., Newark, 1976-78, George Washington Carver Elem. Sch., Newark, 1978-81, Mt. Vernon Sch., 1984—; dep. exec. supt. Newark Public Schs., 1981-84; mgr. Cernitin Am. Inc. Recipient Disting. Alumnus award SUNY-Oneonta, 1983, named One in a Million, 1985. Mem. NAACP (life), Am. Assn. Sch. Adminstrs., Internat. Reading Assn., Assn. Supervision and Curriculum Devel., United Council Negro Women, N.J. Reading Assn., Essex County Council Sch. Adminstrs., Delta Sigma Theta (chmn. scholarship com. 1973-77). Baptist (chmn. Black coll. com. 1978-81, chmn. bd. Christian edn. 1982-85). Office: 142 Mt Vernon Pl Newark NJ 07106

HILL-ROWLEY, CHRISTINE FORCE, economic analyst; b. Brockton, Mass., Dec. 11, 1948; d. James Louis and Miriam Jesse (Carter) Force; m. Richard Hill-Rowley, Mar. 17, 1978. B.A., U. Mass., 1971; cert. in cartography Mich. State U., 1974; grad. in real estate Lansing Community Coll., 1979-82; postgrad. in hist. preservation Eastern Mich. U., 1984—. Cartographer dept. geography Mich. State U., East Lansing, 1975-76, Met. Area Planning Council, Boston, 1977, Camp, Dresser & McKee, Boston, 1977-78; free-lance Realtor assoc., Lansing, Mich., 1978-79; dept. analyst Mich. Dept. Transp., Lansing, 1979-82; econ. devel. analyst Mich. Dept. Commerce, Lansing, 1982—; aerial photographer. Asst. cartographic editor: Atlas of Michigan, 1977; cartographer various profl. jours., 1975-76. Active Women's Softball League, East Lansing. Mem. Nat. trust Hist. Preservation, People for Am. Way, Mich. Indsl. Developers Assn. (assoc., chairperson indsl. park com. 1982-83, gen. recognition award 1983), Soc. Archtl. Historians (Saarinen chpt.). Democrat. Avocations: foreign travel; sports; sewing; reading; photography; private pilot. Home: 146 Chesterfield Pkwy East Lansing MI 48823 Office: Mich Dept Commerce 525 W Ottawa St Lansing MI 48909

HILLS, ANNE, marketing executive; b. Beverly, Mass., Oct. 29, 1962; d. John Tenney and Nancy (Williams) Hills. B.S. in Bus. Adminstrn. cum laude, Colby-Sawyer Coll., 1983. Support analyst Wang Labs., Lowell, Mass., 1983-84, assoc. analyst, 1984-85, mktg. specialist, 1985—; lectr. Colby-Sawyer Coll., 1984-85. Sawyer fellow, 1982. Avocations: reading; skiing; racquetball. Office: Wang Labs Inc MS1903 One Industrial Ave Lowell MA 01851

HILLS, ARGENTINA SCHIFANO, editor, publisher; b. Pola, Italy, Oct. 4, 1921; d. Vincent and Argentina (Tomat) Schifano; student U.N.Y., 1940-42; hon. degree, Interam. U., 1969, Queens Coll., Charlotte, N.C., 1971, U. Miami (Fla.), 1978; m. Lee Hills, Oct. 31, 1963. Exec. Buitoni-Perugina, N.Y.C., 1941-51; editor, pub. El Mundo, San Juan, P.R., 1960—; pres. Radio Mundo, Angel Ramos Found. Pres. women's com. Detroit Art Inst., 1972-74; mem. women's com. Detroit Symphony, 1970-75; chmn. Dade County Council Arts and Scis., 1978-80; bd. dirs. ARC, 1961-65, Salvation Army, 1965-68, Americas Soc. N.Y., Miami Downtown Devel. Authority; trustee Barry U., Miami, Fla., 1979-83, U. Detroit, 1976-82. Recipient Maria Moors Cabot gold medal Columbia, 1968; Americas Found. award, 1977. Mem. Inter-Am. Press Assn. (dir., pres. 1977-78), Am. Soc. Newspaper Editors (dir. 1980-82), Am. Newspaper Pubs. Assn. Clubs: Surf, City, Bath (Miami); Bankers (San Juan); Grosse Pointe, Dorado Beach. Home: 4450 Banyan Ln Bay Point Miami FL 33137 Office: El Mundo Apartado 2408 San Juan PR 00936

HILLS, CARLA ANDERSON, lawyer, former secretary housing and urban development; b. Los Angeles, Jan. 3, 1934; d. Carl H. and Edith (Hume) Anderson; m. Roderick Maltman Hills, Sept. 27, 1958; children—Laura Hume, Roderick Maltman, Megan Elizabeth, Alison Macbeth. A.B. cum laude, Stanford U., 1955; student, St. Hilda's Coll., Oxford (Eng.) U., 1954; LL.B., Yale U., 1958; hon. degrees, Pepperdine U., 1975, Washington U., 1977, Mills Coll., 1977, Lake Forest Coll., 1978, Williams Coll., 1981. Bar: Calif. 1959, U.S. Supreme Ct. 1965, U.S. Ct. Claims, D.C. 1977. Asst. U.S. atty. civil div., Los Angeles, 1958-61; partner firm Munger, Tolles, Hills & Rickershauser, Los Angeles, 1962-74, Latham, Watkins & Hills, Washington, 1978—; asst. atty. gen. civil div. Justice Dept., Washington, 1974-75; sec. HUD, 1975-77; dir. IBM Corp., Corning Glass Works, Am. Airlines, Fed. Nat. Mortgage Assn., Signal Cos., Inc., Rand Corp., Standard Oil Co. Calif.; adj. prof. Sch. Law, UCLA, 1972; mem. Trilateral Commn., 1977—, Am. Com. on East-West Accord, 1977-79, Internat. Found. for Cultural Cooperation and Devel., 1977—, Fed. Acctg. Standards Adv. Council, 1978-80; bd. dirs. Internat. Exec. Service Corps.; mem. corrections task force Los Angeles County Sub-Regional; adv. bd. Calif. Council on Criminal Justice, 1969-71; mem. standing com. discipline U.S. Dist. Ct. for Central Calif., 1970-73; mem. Adminstrv. Conf. U.S., 1972-74; mem. exec. com. law and free soc. State Bar Calif., 1973; bd. councillors U. So. Calif. Law Center, 1972-74; trustee Pomona Coll., 1974-79, U. So. Calif., Brookings Instn.; mem. at large exec. com. Yale Law Sch., 1973—; mem. com. on Law Sch. Yale Univ. Council; Gordon Grand fellow Yale U., 1978; mem. Sloan Commn. on Govt. and Higher Edn., 1977-79; mem. advisory com. Princeton U., Woodrow Wilson Sch. of Pub. and Internat. Affairs, 1977—. Co-author: Federal Civil Practice, 1961; co-author, editor: Antitrust Adviser, 1971; contbg. editor: Legal Times, 1978—; mem. editorial bd.: Nat. Law Jour, 1978—. Trustee U. So. Calif., 1977-79, Norton Simon Mus. Art, Pasadena, Calif., 1976—, Lawyers Com. for Civil Rights under Law, 1978—, Urban Inst., 1978-80; chmn. Urban Inst., 1983—; co-chmn. Alliance To Save Energy, 1977—; vice chmn. adv. council on legal policy Am. Enterprise Inst., 1977—; bd. visitors, exec. com. Stanford U. Law Sch., 1978—; bd. dirs. Am. Council for Capital Formation, 1978—; mem. adv. com. M.I.T.-Harvard U. Joint Center for Urban Studies, 1978—; bd. govs. Nat. ARC, 1975—. Fellow Am. Bar Found.; mem. Los Angeles Women Lawyers Assn. (pres. 1964), ABA (chmn. publs. com. antitrust sect. 1972-74, council 1974, 77—, chmn. 1982-83), Fed. Bar Assn. (pres. Los Angeles chpt. 1963), Los Angeles County Bar Assn. (mem. fed. rules and practice com. 1963-72, chmn. issues and survey 1963-72, chmn. sub-com. revision local rules for fed. cts. 1966-72, mem. jud. qualifications com. 1971-72), Am. Bar Inst. Clubs: Yale of So. Calif. (dir.

1972-74); Yale (Washington). Office: 1333 New Hampshire Ave NW Suite 1200 Washington DC 20006

HILPERT, BRUNETTE KATHLEEN POWERS (MRS. ELMER ERNEST HILPERT), civic worker; b. Baton Rouge; d. Edward Oliver and Orvilla (Nettles) Powers; A.B., La. State U., 1930, B.S. in L.S., 1933; postgrad. Columbia U., 1937; m. Elmer Ernest Hilpert, Aug. 1, 1938; children—Margaret Ray, Elmer Ernest II. Cataloguer, La. State U. Library, Baton Rouge, 1930-36, La. State U. Law Sch. Library, 1936-38; librarian Washington U. Law Sch. Library, St. Louis, 1940-42; reference librarian Washington U. Library, St. Louis, 1952-54. Drive capt. United Fund, St. Louis, 1956; del. White House Conf. on Edn., St. Louis, 1962; trustee John Burroughs Sch., 1959-63; bd. dirs. Grace Hill Settlement House, 1957-63, v.p., 1960-62; bd. dirs. Internat. Inst., 1964-68; bd. dirs. Neighborhood Health Center, 1964-67, sec., 1964—; dir. Arts and Edn. Council, 1967—; pres., dir. Women's Assn. St. Louis Symphony Soc., 1969-71; exec. com., dir. St. Louis Symphony Soc., 1969—; bd. dirs. Miss. River Festival, 1969-74; dir. women's adv. bd. Continental Bank & Trust Co., 1970-77, 79—; bd. dirs. St. Louis Inst. Music, 1971-75; bd. dirs. St. Louis String Quartet, 1971-77, pres., 1975-77; bd. dirs. Community Music Sch., 1973-75, Little Symphony Concerts Assn., 1975-78, St. Louis Conservatory and Schs. for Arts, 1975-84, Dance Concert Soc., 1977-81, Women's Aux. Bd. Bethesda Gen. Hosp., 1981—. Recipient Woman of Achievement award St. Louis Globe Democrat, 1967. Mem. Nat. Soc. Arts and Letters (dir. 1964-65, 80-82), Delta Zeta. Republican. Presbyterian. Club: Wednesday (rec. sec. 1963-64). Home: 630 Francis Pl Apt 1-N Saint Louis MO 63105

HILTON, EVA (EVE) MAE, bank executive; b. Long Beach, Calif., Jan. 19, 1950; d. Albert Martin Wennekamp and Eva Geraldine (Hughes) Wennekamp Johnson; m. Charles H. Hilton, Jr., Nov. 30, 1968 (Div. 1982). Sr. teller Bank of Hawaii, Kailua, 1969-70; asst. mgr. ops. Ariz. Bank, Tucson, 1970-79; teller Valley Nat. Bank, Salome, Ariz., 1979-80; asst. v.p., supervisory br. mgr. Gt. Western Bank, Phoenix, 1980—; instr. Am. Inst. Banking, Tucson, 1981. Mem. Nat. Assn. Female Execs. Avocations: racquetball; water sports; reading. Home: 13233 N 25th Dr Phoenix AZ 85029 Office: Gt Western Bank and Trust 13651 N 35th Ave Phoenix AZ 85029

HILTON, MARY ELIZABETH, diaper service executive; b. Chgo., Sept. 20, 1937; d. Norman Fredrick Sorgenfrei and Frances Ellen (Smith) Schwab; m. William Merle Hilton, Sept. 8, 1956 (dec. 1978); children—Chris Reid, Andrew Reid, Molly Ellen. Student Mich. State U., 1956. Vice pres. Diapers Unlimited, Kalamazoo, 1962-78, pres., 1978—; pres. DyDee Service, Grand Rapids, Mich., 1978—, Cottontails Diaper Service, South Bend, Ind., 1980—, Cottontails Diaper Service, Chgo., 1980—; dir. First Fed. Savs. & Loan of Kalamazoo. Author consumer booklets on diaper service and related topics. Patentee DyDee Bear stuffed animal. Founder Wild Animal Release Program, Kalamazoo Nature Ctr., 1975; Sunday sch. tchr. Unity of Kalamazoo, 1970-78; mem. UN Nat. Yr. Child, 1980. Recipient Buckle Up Baby award Kalamazoo Jaycees, 1978; nominated Woman of Achievement, Kalamazoo YWCA, 1985. Mem. Nat. Assn. Female Execs., Textile Laundry Council, Nat. Assn. Diaper Services (mem. sales com. 1964—, nat. industry spokesperson 1977—, Auslander award 1979). Republican. Clubs: John Ball Park Zoo (Grand Rapids); Lincoln Park Zoo (Chgo.), Columbia Yacht. Avocations: scuba diving; cooking; sailing; ballet; flying. Home: 2125 Crane Ave Kalamazoo MI 49001 Office: Diapers Unltd 814 Nola St Kalamazoo MI 49007

HILTON-LEONARD, JEANNE, clinical social worker; b. Rockford, Ill., Sept. 1, 1934; d. Harry King and Caroline (Albers) Hilton; B.S. with honors, Ind. U., 1973, M.S.W. (Kappa Alpha Theta scholar), 1975; married; children—Stuart, Julie, Susan. Psychiat. social worker, then social work supr. LaRue D. Carter Meml. Hosp., Indpls., 1975-79; supr. counselors, then exec. dir. Family and Childrens Services, Ft. Wayne, Ind., 1979—. Cert. alcoholism counselor. Mem. Nat. Assn. Social Workers, Acad. Cert. Social Workers. Home: 1605 Old Lantern Trail Fort Wayne IN 46825 Office: 2712 S Calhoun St Fort Wayne IN 46807

HILTZ, DAWN PAPP, mail order company executive; b. Norwalk, Conn., Nov. 30, 1959; d. Frank Stephen and Elizabeth Madeline (Mola) Millard; m. Ellis Andrew Hiltz, Jr., Sept. 11, 1982. Student Norwalk State Tech. Coll., Sacred Heart U., Am. Inst. Banking. Clk. Union Trust Co., Norwalk, 1978-82; asst. mgr. Matthew's, Westport, Conn., 1982; asst. to pres. ISP, Inc., Norwalk, 1982—. Vol. Norwalk Seaport Assn., 1985. Mem. Nat. Assn. Female Execs. Republican. Roman Catholic. Club: South Norwalk Boat Club/Aux. Avocations: skiing; scuba diving; photography. Home: 45 Maple St Norwalk CT 06850 Office: ISP Inc 205 Liberty Sq Norwalk CT 06855

HILTZ, STARR ROXANNE, sociologist, educator; b. Little Rock, Sept. 7, 1942; d. John Donald and Mildred V. (Koons) Smyers; A.B., Vassar Coll., 1963; M.A., Columbia U., 1964, Ph.D., 1969; m. Murray Turoff, 1985; children—Jonathan David, Katherine Amanda. Prof. sociology, Upsala Coll., 1969—; assoc. dir. Computerized Conferencing and Communications Center, N.J. Inst. Tech., 1978—; pres. Computerized Conferencing, Inc., 1978—; cons. social impacts of computer systems. Mem. Am. Sociol. Assn., Assn. Computing Machinery, Internat. Communication Assn., Am. Soc. Info. Sci., World Future Soc. Unitarian. Author: Creating Community Services for Widows, 1976; (with M. Turoff) The Network Nation, 1978; (with E. Kerr) Computer-Mediated Communication, 1982; Online Communities, 1984. Home: 1531 Golf St Scotch Plains NJ 07076 Office: Upsala College East Orange NJ 07019

HILTZ-SCERBO, LEIZA ANN, designer, photographer; b. Farmington, Maine, Nov. 20, 1955; d. Raymond George and Florence Catherine (MacLeod) Hiltz; m. Justin Robert Francis Scerbo, Apr. 1, 1980; 1 child, Christopher Justin. Student Haystack-Hinkley Sch. Art., 1971, Brigham Young U., 1974-75, U. Maine-Farmington, 1975-77, Maine Photographic Workshops, 1977; B.F.A. magna cum laude, L.I. U. Southampton Coll., 1980. Darkroom technician pub. relations alumni office U. Maine-Farmington, 1975-76; asst. photographer Lilienthal Studios, Wilton, Maine, 1975-77; darkroom technician Southampton Coll., N.Y., 1979-80; artist layout lettering Assocs. & Ferren, Easthampton, N.Y., 1979-81; apprentice designer East Hampton Leather, 1979-81, owner, designer Leiza's Leather to Lace, Farmington, 1981—; free-lance photographer, N.Y., Maine, 1976—; cons. design, Maine, 1981—; tchr. color perception Kis-Western Mt. Photolab, Wilton, Maine, 1984—; customer trainer KIS Photo, 1985—. Vol. Anti-Nuclear Power Orgn. of Maine, 1981—; donator Sweatt Winter Day Care, Farmington, 1984; vol. Republican Women's Com., Farmington, 1972—. Haystack-Hinkley Sch. Art scholar, 1970, Farmington Elks scholar, 1974, Maine Photographic Workshops scholar, 1979. Presbyterian. Avocations: cross country skiing; swimming; hiking; botany. Home: 57 D Montgomery Rd Neshanic Station NJ 08853 Office: KIS Photo 35 Schoolhouse Rd Somerset NJ 08873

HIMLER, MARSHA SUE, information systems executive; b. Indpls., Mar. 26, 1943; d. John Milton and Ruth Devona (Burks) H.; B.S., Ind. U., 1964; postgrad. Syracuse U., 1968-72, Cornell U., 1969-72. With N.Y. State Dept. Labor, Albany, 1966—, now supervising adminstrv. analyst; owner Himler Data Services, Syracuse, N.Y., 1974-76. Mem. Duryea for Gov. campaign, 1979; charter mem. Republican Presdl. Task Force. Served to comdr. USNR, 1973—. Mem. Internat. Assn. Personnel in Employment Security, Nat. Assn. Female Execs. (network dir. Albany area), Mensa, Welsh Pony Soc. Am. (life), Am. Driving Soc. (recognized judge; nat. membership com.), Northeastern Welsh Pony Assn. (sec.-treas., dir. 1970—). Episcopalian. Home: 688 Gorge Rd Middleburgh NY 12122 Office: Bldg 12 State Campus Albany NY 12240

HIMMELBERGER, PATRICIA A. GROFF, nurse; b. Reading, Pa., Feb. 19, 1957; d. Harold T. and Nancy A. (Mangiolardo) Groff; m. Eugene D. Himmelberger, Sept. 29, 1984. Diploma St. Joseph Hosp., Reading, 1978; student Alvernia Coll., Reading, 1985—. Staff nurse operating room Community Gen. Hosp., Reading, 1981; staff nurse intensive care Reading Hosp.-Med. Ctr., 1978-80, 82-84; asst. dir. nursing Leader Nursing & Rehab., Reading, 1984-85; office nurse Dr. Eugene Shaffer, Reading, 1985—; staff nurse Reading Rehab. Hosp., 1985—; instr. CPR Am. Heart Assn., Reading, 1985—. Mem. Nat. Assn. Female Execs., Assn. Quality Assurance Profls. Roman Catholic. Avocation: needlework. Office: Reading Rehab Hosp RD 1 Box 250 Reading PA 19607

HIN, JUDITH, travel agency executive; b. Paterson, N.J., Jan. 28, 1954; d. Peter Andrew and Gertrude Patricia (Gavin) Hin. B.A., U. Vt., 1976; diploma, O'Brien's Travel Sch., 1979. Cert. travel cons. Asst. The Wilson Sch., Mt. Lakes, N.J., 1976-77; mgr. Garden State Travel, Teterboro, N.J., 1979-86; travel cons. Walker Travel, Ridgewood, N.J., 1986—; free lance watercolorist. Mem. Inst. Cert. Travel Agts., Ridgewood Art Inst. Republican. Roman Catholic. Avocations: watercolor painting; piano; skiing; flying; tennis; swimming; photography. Home: 284 Godwin Ave Carriage House Ridgewood NJ 07450

HINCHEE, RUTH JOAN, nurse, educator; b. Orlando, Fla., Oct. 28, 1926; d. Andrew Herbert and Ina Hattie (Hart) Tice; R.N. diploma Charity Hosp. Sch. Nursing, New Orleans, 1947; B.S.N., McNeese State U., 1974; M.S.N., U. Tex., 1976; m. Benjamin H. Hinchee, Feb. 4, 1948; children—Richard, Laura, Charles. R.N., La. Staff nurse hosps., Calif., Fla., La., 1947-53; hosp. nursing supr. Lake Charles (La.) Meml. Hosp., 1953-66; public health nurse Calcasieu Parish Health Unit, Lake Charles, 1966-74; instr. in nursing McNeese State U., 1975-77, asst. prof., 1977-82, assoc. prof., 1982—, community health nursing coordinator, 1975—, faculty adv. Student Nurses Assn., 1978—; chmn. nursing/health services Calcasieu-Cameron chpt. ARC, 1979—. Recipient Disting. Service award ARC, 1957, Kiwanis Internat., 1975. Mem. Am. Nurses Assn., Nat. League Nurses, La. State Public Health Assn., Am. Public Health Assn., La. State Nurses Assn., Lake Charles Dist. Nurses Assn. (treas. 1981—), Am. Bus. Women's Assn., Phi Lambda Pi, Sigma Theta Tau. Republican. Home: 735 Jefferson Lake Charles LA 70605 Office: McNeese State U Dept Nursing Lake Charles LA 70609

HINCKLEY, BARBARA PRENTISS, political scientist, educator; b. Boston, Aug. 12, 1937; children—Sandra, Karen. A.B., Mt. Holyoke Coll., 1959, LL.D. (hon.), 1984, Ph.D., Cornell U., 1968. Asst. prof. U. Mass., Amherst, 1968-70, Cornell U., Ithaca, N.Y., 1970-72; assoc. prof. polit-sci. U. Wis.-Madison, 1972-74, prof., 1974—; cons. house elections ABC News, N.Y.C., 1982, 84. Author: The Seniority System in Congress, 1971; Congressional Elections, 1981; Stability and Change in Congress, 3rd edition, 1983; contbr. articles to profl. jours. Guggenheim fellow, 1975; recipient Hawkins Prof. award U. Wis., 1983. Mem. Am. Polit. Sci. Assn. (v.p. 1975), Legis. Studies Group (pres. 1979-80). Office: Dept Polit Sci U Wis 1050 Bascom Mall Madison WI 53706

HINCKS, MARCIA LOCKWOOD, insurance company executive, lawyer; b. N.Y.C., July 3, 1935; d. John Salem and Dorothy Elinor (Tufts) Lockwood; m. John Winslow Hincks, June 14, 1958; children—Rebecca Towne, Jennifer Winslow, John Morris, Benjamin Lockwood. A.B., Bryn Mawr Coll., 1956; LL.B., Yale U., 1959. Bar: Conn. 1960. Atty., Aetna Life & Casualty, Hartford, Conn., 1961-64, 67-70, counsel, 1970-81, v.p., ins. counsel, 1981—; dir. Conn. Water Co., Clinton, 1983—. Trustee, Hartford Coll. for Women, 1979—; dir. Hartford Hosp., 1983—; chmn. United Way of the Capital Area, West Hartford, Conn., 1984-86. Recipient Community Service award United Way of the Capital Area, West Hartford, Conn., 1982. Mem. ABA, Assn. Life Ins. Counsel, Conn. Bar Assn. Congregationalist. Club: Hartford Golf (West Hartford, Conn.). Office: Aetna Life & Casualty 151 Farmington Ave Hartford CT 06156

HINDSON, PANSY HELEN LONG, chemistry educator; b. New Orleans, Feb. 9, 1907; d. Edward William and Louise (Mallet) Long; m. William Henry Hindson, May 1, 1940 (dec. July 1980). B.A., Tulane U., 1930, M.A., 1934; student Chemistry Inst. Mont. State, 1957, Chemistry Inst. U. South, 1962. With Orleans Parish Pub. Schs., New Orleans, 1925-70, tchr. math. and chemistry, 1948-58, tchr. chemistry, 1958-70; student tchr. advisor Tulane U., Loyola U., 1950-58. Contbr. articles to profl. jours. Archery dir. vol. New Orleans Recreation Dept., 1945-65; sec. Sci. Fair Bd. Dirs., 1973—; chmn. Jr. Acad. Scis., 1958-65, co-chmn. Regional Sci. Fair, 1958-65. Fellow Am. Inst. Chemists (cert. 1970); mem. Nat. Sci. Tchrs. Assn. (Disting. Service award 1968), C. of C. Women's Council, La. Ret. Tchrs. Assn., New Orleans Ret. Tchrs. Assn., La. Archery Assn. (Hall of Fame 1978), Delta Kappa Gamma (Tchr. of Yr. award 1959). Club: New Orleans Graden Guild (pres. 1977-79). Lodge: Order Eastern Star. Home: 5419 S Rocheblave St New Orleans LA 70125

HINE, DARLENE CLARK, history educator, administrator; b. Morley, Mo., Feb. 7, 1947; d. Levester and Lottie May (Thompson) Clark; m. William C. Hine, Aug. 21, 1970 (div. 1975); m. 2d, Johnny Earl Brown, July 25, 1981; 1 child, Robbie Davine. B.A. in Am. History, Roosevelt U., 1968; M.A., Kent State U., 1970, Ph.D. in Afro-Am. History, 1975. Teaching asst. Kent State U., Ohio, 1968-71, asst. prof. history, coordinator Black studies, S.C. State Coll., Orangeburg, 1972-74; asst. prof. Purdue U., West Lafayette, Ind., 1974-79, assoc. prof., 1980—, interim dir. African Studies and Research Ctr., 1978-79, vice provost, 1981—; v.p. 34d World Conf. Found., 1983—; mem. Ind. Com. for Humanities, 1983—; invited lectr. colls. and univs. including Harvard U., 1975, U. Ill., Chgo., 1981, St. Olaf Coll., 1981, Ind. U., 1982, U. Tex., Austin, 1983, So. Meth. U., 1983; grant rev. panelist NEH, 1979-80, Ford Found., NRC, 1980, 81, 82. Author: Black Victory, 1979; When the Truth is Told: A History of Black Women's Culture and Community in Indiana, 1875-1950, 1981; Black Women in the Nursing Profession: A Documentary History, 1984; contbr. chpts. to books, articles to publs., book revs. to jours. Ctr. assoc. Nat. Girls Club Am., Indpls., 1983—; mem. Ind. Com. for Humanities, Indpls., 1982—. Alumni fellow Kent State U., 1971-72; research awardee Africana Studies and Research Ctr., 1975, 78; faculty devel. grantee Purdue U., 1978-79; research awardee Rockefeller Archive Ctr., 1978; Rockefeller Found. fellow for minority group scholars, 1980; research grantee Eleanor Roosevelt Inst., 1980-81; project grantee Fund for Improvement of Post-Secondary Edn., 1980-82; NEH grantee, 1982-83; 1st place essay award Degolyer Inst., 1982. Mem. Assn. for Study of Negro Life and History (exec. council 1979), Orgn. Am. Historians, So. Hist. Assn., So. Assn. Women Historians (v.p. 1983—), Am. Hist. Assn., Assn. Black Women Historians, Phi Alpha Theta. Democrat. Baptist. Home: 154 N Navajo West Lafayette IN 47906 Office: Purdue Univ University Hall West Lafayette IN 47907

HINERFELD, RUTH J., civic organization executive; b. Boston, Sept. 18, 1930; m. Norman Hinerfeld, children—Lee, Thomas, Joshua. A.B., Vassar Coll., 1951; grad., Program in Bus. Adminstrn., Harvard-Radcliffe Coll., 1952. With LWV, 1954—, UN observer, 1969-72, chairperson internat. relations com., 1972-76, 1st v.p. in charge legis. activities, 1976-78, pres., 1978-82; dir. LWV Overseas Edn. Fund., 1975-76, trustee, 1975-86; chairperson LWV Edn. Fund, 1978-82; mem. White House Adv. Com. for Trade Negotiations, 1975-82; sec. UN Assn. of U.S., 1975-78, vice chmn., 1983—, bd. govs., bd. dirs., 1975—; mem. econ. policy council; mem. exec. com., dir. Overseas Devel. Council; mem. U.S. del. auspices of Nat. Com. on U.S.-China Relations and Chinese People's Inst. Fgn. Affairs, 1978. Mem. council Nat. Mcpl. League, 1977-80, 83—; del.-at-large Internat. Women's Year Conf., Houston, 1977; mem. exec. com. Leadership Conf. on Civil Rights, 1978-82; trustee Citizens Research Found., 1978—; mem. Nat. Petroleum Council, 1979-82; mem. U.S. del. to World Conf. on UN Decade of Women, 1980; mem. adv. com. Nat. Inst. for Citizen Edn. in the Law, 1981—; bd. dirs. Common Cause, 1984—; mem. vis. com. Harvard Bus. Sch., 1984—; bd. dirs. U.S. com. UNICEF, 1985—, vice chair, 1986—; mem. North South Roundtable, 1978—. Recipient Disting. Citizen award Nat. Mcpl. League, 1978; Outstanding Mother award Nat. Mother's Day Com., 1981; Aspen Inst. Presdl. fellow, 1981. Mem. Council on Fgn. Relations, Phi Beta Kappa. Office: 17 Oak Lane Larchmont NY 10538

HINES, DAISY MARIE, writer; b. Hanna City, Ill., Dec. 31, 1913; d. Frank W. and Edith Earl (Folger) Humphrey; m. Herbert Waldo Hines, Jr., Dec. 20, 1958; children—Grace Consuelo, Ruby Marie. Student Western Ill. U., 1955-57, So. Ill. U., 1956. Mem. staff advt. dept. Macomb Daily Jour. (Ill.), 1943-47; writer, exec., dir., promoter McDonough County Tb Assn., 1949-58; sec. U.S. Dept. Agr., Macomb, 1955-58; researcher, writer 1st Nat. Bank, Springfield, 1963; adminstrv. asst. to state legislator, 1964-69; newspaper columnist, free-lance writer, mem. survey staff Prairie Farmer Pub. Co., Oak Brook, Ill., 1965-79, Successful Farming, Des Moines, 1982; Springfield corr. Automotive News. Active Altar Soc. Blessed Sacrament Catholic Ch., Springfield; chmn. Illiopolis unit Univ. Ill. Home Extension; pub. relations dir. Springfield chpt. Am. Cancer Soc., 1961-68; 2d v.p. Ill. Conf. Tb Workers, 1952-53. Mem. Nat. League Am. Pen Women (pres. Springfield chpt. 1972-73, sec. Ill. br. 1974), Western Ill. U. Alumni Council (sec.; Disting. Alumni award 1982; com. mem. Coll. Applied Scis. Agr. rep. Alumni Council), Ill. Press Assn. USAF Air Def. Team (hon. life), Ill. Women for Agr., Civil War Round Table. Club: Republican Women's. Address: 2504 S Holmes Ave Springfield IL 62704

HINES, GLORIA CYNTHELIA, educational administrator; b. Los Angeles, Jan. 29, 1934; d. Earl and Hazel (Magnuss) Jones; m. William E. Hines, Jr., May 20, 1955; children—Tanya Gail, Payton Kevin, William Jones. B.A. in Edn. and English, Idaho State U., 1957; M.A. in Supervision and Adminstrn., Montclair State Coll., 1976. Cert. tchr., prin. Clk., Dept. Air Force, San Antonio, 1958-61, U.S. Air Force Acad., Colo., 1961-64, English tchr., 1964-66; sec. Dept. Air Force, Bentwaters AFB, Eng., 1967-68; tchr. English, Union Twp. Schs. (N.J.), 1969-75, supr. English dept., 1975-77, vice prin., 1977-83, prin., 1983—; bd. dirs. UTCAO, Inc., Vaux Hall, N.J., 1977-86. Recipient spl. award 1st Baptist Ch., 1983. Mem. NEA, N.J. Edn. Assn., Nat. Council Tchrs. English, Assn. Supervision and Curriculum Devel., Nat. Assn. Secondary Sch. Prins., N.J. Assn. Secondary Sch. Prins., Nat. Assn. Negro Bus. and Profl. Women (spl. award 1983), Phi Delta Kappa (rec. sec. 1977-79). Club: Soroptimist Internat. (pres. 1979-81, dir. 1981). Home: Hausman Ct Maplewood NJ 07040 Office: Kawameeh Jr High Sch Golf and David Terrs Union NJ 07062

HINES, MARY NELL, educator, educational administrator; b. Crowley, La., Apr. 12, 1932; d. Ernest and Beatrice (Daigle) Scott; m. Allen Joseph Hines, Sept. 16, 1952; children—Burnell Faye, Allene Beatrice, Carolyn Cecile. B.A., Tex. So. U., 1969, M.Ed., 1972; B. Theology, C.H. Mason Bible Coll., 1980; D.D., So. Union Bapt. Theology Coll. and Sem., 1985. Cert. tchr., counselor, Tex. Instr. English, C.H. Mason Bible Coll., Houston, 1958-60, dean of women, 1960-72, dean of academics, 1978-84; team tchr. reading Houston Ind. Sch. Dist., 1966-72; tchr. English, N. Forest Ind. Sch. Dist., Houston, 1972-78, counselor secondary edn., 1978—; Christian edn. counselor Gethsemane Ch. of God in Christ, Houston, 1978-84, N.E. Community and Sch. Inter-Active Orgn., 1980-84; dist. adv., state adv. Future Tchrs. Am., Tex., 1972-84. Author: The Role of the Christian Student, 1973; Code of Ethics for Pastors' Wives, 1976; Regulating Egos for Christian Enhancement, 1980; Counseling: Behavior Changes, 1982. Pres. Glenwood Forest Civic Assn., 1972. Named Woman of Yr., Diocese of Tex., S.E. Ch. of God in Christ, 1970; recipient LoveLady award Future Tchrs. Am., 1971. Mem. Tex. State Tchrs. Assn., NEA, Am. Assn. Counseling and Devel., Tex. Personnel Dist. Personnel and Guidance Assn., Nat. Assn. Secondary Prins. Democrat. Home: 8435 Sterlingshire St Houston TX 77078 Office: 7525 Tidwell St Houston TX 77016

HINES, PATRICIA, social worker; b. Watertown, N.Y., Nov. 4, 1947; d. Arthur and Bella (O'Neil) H.; B.S., SUNY-Oswego, 1969; M.S.W., SUNY-Buffalo, 1975; M.P.A., Fairleigh Dickinson U., 1982; labor relations cert. Rutgers U., 1984. Supr. social work Ocean County Bd. Social Services, Toms River, N.J., 1973-77, adminstrv. supr. social work, 1977-83, dep. dir., 1983—; social work cons. Medicenter and Rainbow Day Care, Lakewood, N.J., 1975—, Ocean County Vis. Homemaker Service, Inc., Toms River, 1975-80, Community Meml. Hosp., Toms River, 1978-79, Country Manor, Toms River, 1981—, Manchester Manor, 1983—, Toms River Convalescent Ctr., Garden State Rehab. Hosp., 1984—, Bartley Manor, 1985—, Barnegot Nursing Facility, 1986—, Ocean Convalescent Ctr., 1986—; prin. Sr. Care Planning Assocs.; instr. social work Georgian Court Coll., Lakewood, 1975—. Editor: Hospital, 1984-86. Chmn., Ocean County Title XX Coalition, 1977-82; bd. dirs. Ocean County Family Planning Program, Toms River, 1969-73; mem. Ocean County Mental Health Bd., 1983-84; bd. dirs. Ocean County United Way, 1984—. Cert., Dr. Thomas Gordon Parent Effectiveness Trainer. Mem. Acad. Cert. Social Workers, Nat. Assn. Social Workers. Home: 13 Bay Harbor Blvd Brick NJ 08723 Office: 1027 Hooper Ave Toms River NJ 08753

HINES, VC, newspaper marketing research executive; b. Los Angeles, Oct. 5, 1953; d. Bolden Eugene and Vivian Carrell (Burbridge) Hines; B.A., UCLA, 1975, M.B.A., 1977. With May Co., Los Angeles, 1977-84, regional newspaper advt. mgr., 1981-84; suburdan advt. coordinator Los Angeles Times, 1984—; bus. seminar instr. Inroads, Inc., 1982—. Mem. adv. bd. Dean's Council, UCLA Grad. Sch. Mgmt.; project bus. instr. Jr. Achievement, 1983-84; bd. dirs., chmn. communications com. Black Women's Network. Cert. community coll. instr. Mem. Nat. Black MBA Assn. (chair edn. com.). Club: Bradley Circle. Home: 3717 Bagley Ave Apt 111 Los Angeles CA 90034 Office: Los Angeles Times Market Research Dept Times Mirror Sq Los Angeles CA 90053

HINES CADY, MARY MARGARET, advertising executive; b. Deadwood, S.D., Feb. 3, 1947; d. Donald Philip Hines and Lois Elaine (Morrill) Watson; m. Frederic Lee Allen Cady, Mar. 29, 1980; children—Conrad, Christina. Student Augustana Coll., 1965-68. Writer, producer Sta. KSOO-TV, Sioux Falls, S.D., 1968-71; writer, producer Smith, Kaplan et al, Omaha, 1972-76; pres. Ferrari & Davidson Advt., Omaha, 1976-80; v.p. creative Smith, Kaplan Allen & Reynolds Advt., Omaha, 1980-83, v.p., creative dir. Rollheiser, Holland, Kahler Advt., Omaha, 1985—. Recipient Prominent Women in Advt. award H. Whitney McMillan, 1983. Mem. Am. Women in Radio TV (v.p. 1982-83, pres. 1983-84, dist. dir. 1985-86), Ad Club Omaha (bd. dirs. 1978-83). Republican. Episcopalian.

HINKLE, MURIEL RUTH NELSON, naval warfare analysis co. exec.; b. Bayonne, N.J., Mar. 17, 1929; d. Andrew and Florence Martha Ida (Nuber) Nelson; student Md. Coll. for Women, 1947-49; B.A., U. Md., 1951; m. David Randall Hinkle, June 5, 1954; children—Valerie Nelson, Janet Lee, Sally Ann. Mgr., Wildacres Thoroughbred Horse Farm, Waterford, Conn., 1960-70; illustrator Naval Warfare Predictions/Computer Simulated Naval Engagements, Analysis & Tech., Inc., North Stonington, Conn., 1970-73; pres. Sonalysts, Inc., Waterford, 1973—, also dir.; dir. Alpha Mortgage Corp., Beta Computer Corp., Command Engring. & Tech. Services Co.; cons. anti-submarine warfare cruise missile weapon systems Gen. Electric Co., 1974-76; cons. Def. Nuclear Agy. for Tactical Nuclear Effects in anti-submarine warfare, 1974-75; spl. edn. subsitute tchr. Waterford Pub. Schs., 1968-74. Bd. trustees Thames Sci. Center, 1979-82. Recipient commendation for services to submarine force Comdr. Submarine Squadron Ten, 1973. Mem. Conn. Thoroughbred Owners Assn., Nat. Audubon Soc., Submarine Devel. Group Two Wives Club (pres. 1968), Sigma Kappa. Republican. Baptist. Clubs: Westbrook Hunt, Navy Wives. Co-author: Scope of Acoustic Communications Systems in Naval Tactical Warfare, 1974; Non-Acoustic Anti Submarine Warfare, 1974; Nuclear Weapons Effects in Anti Submarine Warfare, 1974; Measures of Effectiveness, Naval Tactical Communications, 1975; co-author: Destroyer ASW Barrier, 1977. Home: RD 1 Box 168-A Stonington CT 06378 Office: Sonalysts Bldg 215 Parkway North Waterford CT 06385

HINMAN, MYRA MAHLOW, educator; b. Saginaw County, Mich., Jan. 11, 1926; d. Henry and Cynthia (Mims) Mahlow; B.S., Columbia U., 1946; M.A., U. Fla., 1954, Ph.D., 1959; m. George E. Olstead, 1948 (div. 1967); 1 son, Christopher Eric; m. 2d, Charlton, Hinman, 1968 (dec. 1977); 1 stepdau., Barbara. Asst. prof. Memphis State U., 1959-61; instr. U. Kans., Lawrence, 1961-63, asst. prof., 1963-68, asso. prof. English lit., 1968—. Travel grantee Am. Council Learned Socs., 1966. Mem. MLA, Internat. Arthurian Soc., Shakespeare Assn. Am., U. Va. Bibliog. Soc., AAUP, Kans. Folklore Soc., Midwest Modern Lang. Assn., S. Atlantic Modern Lang. Assn., United Burmese Cat Fanciers, Am. Shorthair Cat Assn., Phi Kappa Phi. Asst. editor: Hinman Text, Complete Works of Shakespeare. Contbr. articles to profl. jours. Home: 1932 Maine St Lawrence KS 66046 Office: Wescoe Hall Univ Kans Lawrence KS 66045

HINNRICHS-DAHMS, HOLLY BETH, educator; b. Milw., Oct. 31, 1945; d. Helmut Ferdinand and Rae W. (Beebe) H.; m. Raymond H. Dahms, June 11, 1983 (dec. Oct. 2, 1983). Student U. Wis.-Milw., 1963-64, 66, 79—, Chapman Coll., 1965, 67, Internat. Coll. Copenhagen, summer 1968, Temple U., summer 1970, B.A., Alverno Coll., 1971; postgrad. Marylhurst Coll., 1972, Chapman Coll. World Campus Afloat, summers 1973, 74, Inst. Shipboard Edn., 1978, 79. Vice pres. Hinnrichs Inc., Germantown, Wis., 1964-72; tchr. Germantown Recreation Dept., 1965; coach Milw. Recreation Dept., 1966-67; rep. for Wis., Chapman Coll., Orange, Calif., 1967; clk. Stein Drug Co., Menomonee Falls, Wis., 1967-72; tchr. Milw. area Catholic Schs., 1967-72, 83—; asst. mgr. Original Cookie Co. (Mother Hubbard's) Cookie Store, Northridge Mall, Milw., 1977-84, SAU-U Warehouse Deli, 1984-85, mgr. office, 1985—; substitute tchr. pub. schs. Milw. area, 1975-80, 83—; tchr. Indian Community Sch., Milw., 1971-72, Martin Luther King Sch., 1973-74, Crossroads Acad., Milw., 1974-75, Harambee Community Sch., 1980-83; Midwest rep. World Explorer Cruises, 1978—. Mem. Wis. math. Council, Nat. Council Tchrs. Math., Internat. Inst. Milw. Friends of Museum, Alpha Theta Epsilon. Christian Scientist. Traveled 63 countries; contbr. articles on travel to various publs. Home: W140 N9766 Hwy 145 Germantown WI 53022

HINOJOSA, BERTHA NORA, state rehabilitation commission administrator; b. Benavides, Tex., Aug. 31, 1944; d. Francisco and Gertrudis (Casas) Saenz; m. Jay Weldon Dwiggins, Nov. 23, 1968 (div. Dec. 1969); m. Narciso Hinojosa, Sept. 2, 1973. B.A., Tex. Woman's U., 1967; postgrad. Tex. Tech.

U., 1965-67; M.S., Abilene Christian U., 1976. Lic. profl. counselor, Tex. Counselor Tex. Rehab. Commn., Harlingen, 1967-70, Pharr, Tex., 1970-73, Dallas, 1973-74, area mgr., Dallas, 1974-78, Garland, 1978-81, ops. dir., Farmers Branch, 1981—. Mem. Tex. Rehab. Assn. (bd. dirs. 1975-77, Extra Mile award 1977), Tex. Rehab. Adminstrs. Assn. (pres. 1983-84), Tex. Quarter Horse Assn., Nat. Assn. Female Execs. Roman Catholic. Office: Tex Rehab Commn 13612 Midway Rd #530 Farmers Branch TX 75244

HINRICHS, GINA BURNS, agricultural implement company executive; b. Evanston, Ill., June 20, 1954; d. Martin Thomas and Judy (Holden) Burns; m. John Thomas Hinrichs, Apr. 22, 1978; children—Adam Paul, Julia Therese. B.A., Miami U., Oxford U., 1976; postgrad. St. Ambrose U. Mktg. rep IBM, Omaha, 1976-78; indsl. engr. John Deere, East Moline, Ill., 1978—. Cons. Ambrose Inst. Indsl. Engring., Davenport, Iowa, 1983. Mem. Inst. Indsl. Engring. (v.p. 1984-86, pres. 1986-87), Soc. Women Engrs. (program chmn. 1983-84). Roman Catholic. Club: St. Pius Renewal (Rock Island) (lay dir. 1984). Office: John Deere Harvester Works 1100 13th Ave East Moline IL 61244

HINRICHSEN, EVELYN ELIZABETH MERRELL (MRS. WALTER HINRICHSEN), corporate executive; b. Chgo., Nov. 30, 1910; d. Dwight Livingston and Julia (Dodd) Merrell; B.A., Mus.B., Mills Coll., 1938, M.A., 1940; cert. spl. teaching in music, Calif., 1941; m. Walter Hinrichsen, Aug. 2, 1946 (dec. July 1969); children—Martha Eleanor, Henry Hans. Asst. sec. to pres. Mills Coll., Oakland, Calif., 1942-44; sec. to chief asst. and librarian Library of Congress, Washington, 1944-46; v.p., sec. C.F. Peters Corp., N.Y.C., 1948-69, v.p., sec., owner, 1969-70, owner, pres., 1970-78, owner, chmn. bd., 1978—. Mem. AAUW, Met. Mus. Art, Mus. Modern Art, N.Y. Philharmonic, Alumnae Assn. Mills Coll., Sigma Alpha Iota. Home: 431 E 20th St New York NY 10010 Office: 373 Park Ave S New York NY 10016

HINSON, MICHELLE HALL, lawyer; b. San Antonio, Dec. 7, 1941; d. Arthur Lee and Dorothy Paulene (Haley) Hall; m. Hillord Hensley Hinson, Mar. 4, 1967; children—Michelle Lee, Travis Mark. B.S., Tex. Arts & Industries U., Kingsville, 1964; J.D., U. Houston, 1975. Bar: Tex. 1976. With Shell Oil Co., Houston, 1961-76; ptnr. Hinson & Hinson, Houston, 1976—; atty., counsellor U.S. Supreme Ct., Washington, 1980—. Editor Houston U. Law Rev., 1975. Bd. dirs. NW Forest Rep. Women's Orgn., 1983. Mem. Lawyers in Mensa (charter), Exec. Women's Network (dir. 1983-85), Order of Barons. Office: Hinson & Hinson Attys at Law 333 N Belt E Suite 1030 Houston TX 77060

HINSON, PEGGY MILDRED, educator; b. Thomaston, Ga., July 19, 1936; d. Robert LeGrand, Sr. and Mildred Sara (Keever) H.; B.S. in Edn., Auburn U., 1958; B.S. in Med. Adminstrn. and Supervision, Ga. State U., 1978. Head English dept. Faith Sch., Ft. Benning, Ga., 1958-61, Daniel Jr. High Sch., Columbus, Ga., 1961-63; tchr. Rothschild Jr. High Sch., Columbus, 1965-75, head English dept., 1976—; secondary English cons., Columbus, 1975-76; curriculum steering com. Columbus Coll. Named Star Tchr., 1975; recipient commendation Pres. of U.S., 1976, commendation U.S. Congress, 1976. Mem. Nat. Council Tchrs. of English, NEA, Ga. Assn. Educators, Muscogee Assn. Edn., Columbus Exec. Club, AAUW, Ga. Walking Horse Assn., Phi Delta Kappa, Alpha Delta Kappa, Delta Delta Delta. Home: 3312 Gail Dr Columbus GA 31907 Office: 1136 Hunt Ave Columbus GA 31907

HINTON-BRAATEN, KATHLEEN, violinist, writer; b. Ventura, Calif., Sept. 15, 1941; d. Jack C. and Adelaide (Hilford) McNeil; student Oberlin Coll., 1959-61; Calif. State U., Northridge, 1961-62, Calif. State U., San Francisco, 1962-63, Calif. State U., Fullerton, 1966, U. Md., College Park, 1977; 1 son, Randolph Phillip Hinton. Violinist, San Diego Symphony Orch., San Antonio Symphony, Cin. Symphony, Music in Maine String Quartet; co-founder, asst. personnel mgr., adminstr. 20th Century Consort, Nat. Symphony Orch., Washington, 1975-79; violinist Nat. Symphony Orch., 1969—; recitalist; freelance travel, performing arts, history and profile writer; contbr. to N.Y. Times, Washington Post, Symphony mag., Christian Sci. Monitor, S.W. Art mag., Orientations mag., Ceramics Monthly, Am. Craft, Internat. Musician, others. Mem. Washington Ind. Writers, Musicians Union Local. Home and Office: 4141 N Henderson Rd #304 Arlington VA 22203

HIPOLITO-GUERRERO, CORINE RODRIGUEZ, telecommunications company executive; b. Berkeley, Calif., June 17, 1945; d. Rudolph Perez Rodriguez and Teresa Romero; m. Francisco R. Hipolito, Mar. 2, 1964 (div. Dec. 1978); children—Francisco R., Richard R., Teresa Annette; m. Henry Adams Guerrero, Feb. 14, 1986. Student Austin Community Coll., 1977, U. Tex., 1980. Exec. adminstrv. asst. credit promotion dept., Foley's, Houston, 1968-72; adminstrv. asst. to pres. Viking Homes, Inc., Houston, 1972-74; asst. office mgr. Unit Fabric Corp., Houston, 1974-75; adminstrv. asst. MHMR-East 1st Human Devel. Ctr., Austin, Tex., 1976-77; adminstrv. asst. undergrad. Dean's Office, U. Tex. Coll. Bus. Adminstrn., Austin, 1977-81; adminstrv. asst. tax policy sect. office of State Comptroller, Austin, 1981-85; owner, pres. Best Communications, Inc., Austin, 1985—. Assoc. editor Editing and Info. Mgmt., 1985-86, State Comptrollers Newsletter, 1982-84. Campaign coordinator city, state and fed. elections, Austin, 1981—; mem. Travis County Grand Jury, Austin, 1983; mem. pres.'s com. and youth fair auction com. Austin Travis County Livestock Show, Austin, 1983—; participant U.S. Hispanic C. of C. Trade Fair, San Antonio, 1984; mem. recruiting com. Austin Aqua Festival, 1982-84. Mem. Nat. Assn. Female Execs., Austin Sisters Cities Assn. (bd. dirs. 1984-86, Mexican Am. Bus. and Profl. Women's Assn., Mexican Am. Comptroller Employees Assn. (exec. com. 1984—, chmn. recruiting com. 1983-85), Hispanic C. of C. (bd. dirs. 1985—, Service award 1985—), Image. Democrat. Roman Catholic. Club: South Austin Civic. Lodge: Lions. Avocations: snow skiing; tennis; swimming; horseback riding. Home: 500 E Riverside Dr Suite 243 Austin TX 78704 Office: Best Communications Inc 6012-A Manor Rd Austin TX 78723

HIPPS, DONNA MARIE (MRS. ROBERT O. HIPPS), librarian; b. Waterloo, Iowa, May 18, 1925; d. George Fred and Mamie Jean (Livingston) Westlic; B.S., Iowa State U., 1946; M.A., U. Minn., 1963; m. Robert O. Hipps, Aug. 9, 1946; Children—Alan, Margaret (Mrs. Douglas A. Peters), James. Tchr. pub. schs., Iowa, 1946-48; teaching asst. Univ. High Sch., U. Minn., Mpls., 1960-63; librarian Lincoln High Sch., Bloomington, Minn., 1963-70; library specialist Jefferson High Sch., Bloomington, 1970-74, dir. resource center, 1974-75, media dir., 1975—. Mem. Am. Fedn. Tchrs., NEA, LWV (state treas. 1958-59, dir. Edina 1955-58), Am. Field Service, AAUW, Sigma Kappa, Beta Phi Mu. Methodist. Home: 6604 Dakota Trail Edina MN 55435 Office: 4001 W 102d St Bloomington MN 55431

HIPSHIRE, LOUISE JOYNER, management consultant; b. Hampton, Va., Nov. 23, 1945; d. Odis B. and Nannie Leigh (Vick) Joyner; student Ga. State U., Mercer U.; m. James R. Hipshire, Sept. 12, 1980. With Peoples Bank and Trust Co., Rocky Mount, N.C., 1966-69, Avco Fin. Servies, Rocky Mount, 1969-72, Inventories Co., Garner, N.C., 1972-74; comptroller, officer mgr. Moffett and Henderson, P.C., attys.-at-law, Atlanta, 1974-83; mgmt. cons., Temple Terrace, Fla., 1984—; owner Preferred Bus. Services, Temple Terrace, 1984—, Spl. Arrangements, 1985—; sec.-treas. Charter Oak Mortgage Corp., 1975-83; cons. in acctg. systems. Soc. dir. Fulton County Young Rep., 1975; auditor Ga. Young Rep., 1975. Active local Big Sisters, 1979-83. Recipient Girl of The Year award, Beta Sigma Phi, 1970; mem. Nat. Assn. Legal Adminstrs., DeKalb County Bd. Realtors. Republican. Methodist. Office: PO Box 291365 Tampa FL 33687

HIRAHARA, PATTI, public relations agency executive; b. Lynwood, Calif., May 10, 1955; d. Frank C. and Mary K. Hirahara. A.A., Cypress Coll., 1975; B.A., Calif. State U.-Fullerton, 1977. Pub. affairs dir. United Television, Los Angeles, 1977-80; v.p. Asian Internat. Broadcasting Co., Los Angeles, 1980-81; mktg. cons. Disneyland, Anaheim, Calif., 1982; pub. relations agt. Japan External Trade Orgn., Los Angeles, 1982—; owner, pres. Prodns. By Hirahara, Anaheim, 1982—; comml. photographer Hirahara Photography, Anaheim, 1977-83; publicist Tokyo Met. Govt., 1981. Bd. dirs. Nisei Week Japanese Festival, Los Angeles, 1980-81. Nat. scholar Seventeen Mag. Youth Adv. Council, 1973; named Orange County Nisei Queen, Suburban Optimist Club, Buena Park, Calif., 1975. Mem. Soc. Profl. Journalists (bd. dirs. 1980-81), Nat. Assn. Female Execs., World Trade Ctr. Assn. Orange County, Japanese Am. Citizens League, Alpha Gamma Sigma.

HIRANO, JUNE YAMADA, education center administrator; b. Honolulu, Aug. 27, 1943; d. Harry Taketo and Aiko (Endo) Yamada; m. Michael James Hirano, Mar. 31, 1973. B.Ed., U. Hawaii, 1965, M.A., 1967. Instr., assoc. dir. for tng. Speech Communications Ctr., U. Hawaii, Honolulu, 1967-69, asst. to dir., grad./undergrad. coordinator univ. dept. speech communications, 196-70; asst. coordinator for participant activities East-West Ctr., Honolulu, 1970-73, selections adminstr., 1973-79, award service officer, 1979—. Co-author learning manuals: Speech Communication Learning System, vol. I and II, 1st edit., 1968, 3d edit., 1970, Speech Power Learning System, 1969. Mem. Am. Assn. Collegiate Registrars and Admissions Officers (rep. Nat. Council on Evaluation of Fgn. Ednl. Credentials 1985—), Nat. Assn. for Fgn. Student Affairs, Phi Kappa Phi. Avocations: Oriental art; contemporary prints; ceramics. Office: East-West Ctr 1777 East-West Rd Honolulu HI 96848

HIRASAKI, MARSHA PARRISH, manufacturing company executive; b. Sullivan's Island, S.C., Oct. 27, 1945; d. Louis August Rohde and Ruth Ann (Hynes) Nelson; B.S.M.E., Duke U., 1967; M.S.M.E., U. Houston, 1971; m. John Kiyoshi Hirasaki, Dec. 29, 1968; children—Kitt Nelson, Parrish Nelson. Aerospace engr. TRW Systems, Houston, 1967-72; design engr. Nat. Maritime Research Center, Galveston, Tex., 1972-74; sales mgr. Cooper Valve & Fitting, Inc., LaPorte, Tex., 1974-76; pres., gen. mgr. Eurasia Valve Corp., Houston, 1976-79; gen. mgr. Masoneilan div. McGraw Edison, Houston, 1979-84; gen. mgr. Dresser Valve and Controls, Houston, 1985; pres., gen. mgr. Nelson Controls, Inc., Deer Park, Tex., 1985—. Mem. Instrument Soc. Am. (pres. chpt. 1982-83), NOW (pres. Houston chpt. 1972-73), Portrait Artists Guild (pres. 1984-85). Home: 931 Shady Oak Dr Dickinson TX 77539

HIRD, ROZANNE, insurance underwriter; b. Shenandoah, Iowa, Apr. 19, 1951; d. John O. and Loretta Ann (Spiedel) H. B.S. in Fin., U. Mo.-Columbia, 1972. C.P.C.U. Casualty Underwriter Aetna Life & Casualty, St. Louis, 1973-76; sr. underwriter Hartford Ins. Co., Indpls., 1976-85; underwriting specialist CNA Ins., Phoenix, 1985—. Mem. Soc. C.P.C.U.s. Roman Catholic. Avocations: reading, sewing, knitting, traveling.

HIRD, SYDELLE D., interior designer; b. N.Y.C., May 23, 1925; m. Martin Hird, 1946; children—David, Pamela; m. Morris Kinzler, 1985. B.S., NYU, 1946; cert. N.Y. Sch. Interior Design; student Juilliard Inst. Music, N.Y.C. Designer, Gimbels, Yonkers, N.Y., 1961-65; freelance designer, N.Y.C., 1965-67; space planner-designer Thonet Industries, N.Y.C., 1967-73; chief interior designer MKDA Assocs., N.Y.C., 1973-80; prin. Sydelle D. Hird Ltd., N.Y.C., 1980—; project dir. ASID Design Service Corps, N.Y.C., 1979-80. Designer: Pro Bono Renovation for N.Y.C. Sanitation Dept. Bldg., 1979; Renovation of Pub. Lobby at N.Y. Design Ctr., 1982, Pub. Lounge and Mgmt. Offices, 1984. Mem. Inst. Bus. Designers (pres. N.Y. chpt. 1979-84, nat. bd. dirs. 1984-86).

HIRN, DORIS DREYER, health service administrator; b. N.Y.C., Dec. 3, 1933; d. James Howard and Dorothy Van Nostrand (Young) Dreyer; student Colby Jr. Coll., 1950-51, Hofstra U., 1953-56; m. John D. Hirn, Oct. 27, 1956; children—Deborah Lynn, Robert William. Owner, Dutchlands Farm, Albany, N.Y., 1957-62, Hickory Hill Farm, Galena, Ill., 1965-75; adminstr. Home Health Service, Chgo., 1972-74, exec. dir. Suburban Home Health Service, 1974—; pres. Hickory Hill Mgmt. Corp.; dir. Nat. Health Delivery Systems, Serengeti Prodns., Inc.; v.p. Compulease, Inc. Served with WAVES, 1951-52. Mem. Am. Fedn. Home Health Agys., Nat. Assn. Home Care (bd. dirs.), Ill. Council Home Health Agys. Clubs: Chgo. Yacht, East Bank. Contbr. articles to various periodicals. Home: One E Schiller Chicago IL 60610 Office: Suburban Home Health Service 2510 E Dempster Des Plaines IL 60016

HIRONO, MAZIE KEIKO, state legislator; b. Fukushima, Japan, Nov. 3, 1947; came to U.S., 1955, naturalized, 1957; d. Laura Chie (Sato) H. B.A., U. Hawaii, 1970; J.D., Georgetown U., 1978. Dep. atty. gen., Honolulu, 1978-80; house counsel INDEVCO, Honolulu, 1982-83; sole practice, Honolulu, 1983-84, Shim, Tam, Kirimitsu & Naito, 1984—; mem. Hawaii Ho. of Reps., Honolulu, 1980—. Del., State Democratic Party Conv., Honolulu, 1972-82; bd. dirs. Nuuanu YMCA, Honolulu, 1982-84, Moiliili Community Ctr., Honolulu, 1984, Mem. U.S. Supreme Ct. Bar, Hawaii Bar Assn., Phi Beta Kappa. Democrat. Office: Ho of Reps State Capitol Room 331 Honolulu HI 96813

HIROSHIMA, JUNE CLARA, retail executive; b. Osaka, Japan, Dec. 21, 1949; came to U.S., 1957; d. Koji Edmund and Shigeko Margaret (Ogata) H. B.A., in English Lit., U. Tex., 1972. Clk., salesman Don Juan Sportswear, N.Y.C., 1973-74, sales mgr., 1974-76; div. head Am. Argo, N.Y.C., 1977-79; product mgr. Federated Dept. Stores, N.Y.C., 1979-82, market mgr., 1982-83, mdse. adminstr., 1983—. Roman Catholic. Office: Federated Dept Stores 1440 Broadway New York NY 10018

HIRSCH, ELEANOR GULBIS, author, editor; b. Chgo., Nov. 26, 1923; d. Christian and Alvine Katherine (Bauman) Gulbis; B.A. in English, U. Ill., 1946; m. Fred W. Hirsch, Apr. 6, 1951; children—Leslie Kathleen, Melanie Ann. With Scott, Foresman and Co., Chgo., 1947-66, project editor, 1961-66; directing editor Ency. Brit. Ednl. Corp., Chgo., 1966-67; mng. editor Lyons and Carnahan, Chgo., 1967-73; editorial dir. Rand McNally, Skokie, Ill., 1973-75; exec. editor Holt, Rinehart and Winston, N.Y.C., 1975-77; editorial v.p. Scott, Foreman & Co., Glenview, Ill., 1977-78; v.p., dir. reading Ginn and Co., Lexington, Mass., 1978-80; author, ednl. cons., 1980—; author: The Principal's Resource, A Handbook, 1982; exec. editor monthly newsletter Principal's Principles, 1982—. Mem. devel. com. Chgo. Met. YWCA, 1981—; adv. bd. Youngperson. Honoree, Salute to Women in Bus., YWCA. Mem. Acad. Women Achievers (charter), Internat. Reading Assn., Nat. Assn. Elem. Sch. Prins., Assn. Supervision and Curriculum Devel., Nat. Council Tchrs. English. Unitarian. Address: 649 58th St Hinsdale IL 60521

HIRSCH, ELISABETH FEIST, philosopher, ret. educator; b. Mainz, Germany, Nov. 2, 1904; d. Sigmund and Toni (Rawicz) Feist; student U. Freiburg, 1924, U. Berlin, 1924-29; Ph.D., Marburg U., 1930; m. Felix Hirsch, Nov. 6, 1938; children—Roland, Thomas. Came to U.S., 1938, naturalized, 1944. Asst. prof. philosophy Bard Coll., Annandale-on-Hudson, N.Y., 1949-54; asst. prof. philosophy and modern langs. Trenton State Coll., 1956-64, asso. prof. philosophy, 1964-69, prof. philosophy, 1969-72, prof. emeritus, 1972—, chmn. dept. philosophy and religion, 1969-72. Rockefeller Found. award for studies in France, 1929-30; Sterling research fellow, Yale U., 1937-38; Gulbenkian Found. fellow, Lisbon, Portugal, summer 1960; Guggenheim fellow, 1960-61; prize Portuguese Acad. Internat. Culture, 1968. Mem. Renaissance Soc. Am., Am. Soc. Reformation Research, Heidegger Conf., AAUW (May Treat internat. fellow 1954-55). Author: Weltbild und Staatsidee bei Jean Bodin, 1930; Damião de Gois, The Life and Thought of a Portuguese Humanist (1502-1574), 1967. Editor: De Arte Dubitandi et Confidendi. Ignorandi et Sciendi (Sebastian Castellio), 1937, 2d edit., 1981; contbr. articles on history of ideas and philosophy of Martin Heidegger to books, scholarly and profl. jours. Home: Pennswood Village Apt L113 Newtown PA 18940

HIRSCH, IRMA LOU KOLTERMAN, nurse, association administrator; b. Clay Center, Kans., June 11, 1934; d. Arthur Henry and Mildred (Peterson) Kolterman; m. William A. Hirsch, June 8, 1958; children—David William, Brian Duane. B.S. in Nursing, U. Kans., 1957; M.Nursing, U. Washington, Seattle, 1961. R.N. Mo. Instr. Duke U., Durham, N.C., 1961-64; nurse clinician U. Kans. Med. Ctr., Kansas City, 1968-70; project dir., cons. Mo. Regional Med. Program, Kansas City, 1970-74; project dir., program coordinator Am. Nurses' Assn., Kansas City, 1974-79, dept. dir., 1981-83, dir. policy devel., 1983—; supr. VA Med. Ctr., Kansas City, 1979-81; cons. nursing edn. Joint Commn. on Accreditation of Hosps., Chgo., 1973; cons. for project devel. Am. Nurses Found., Kansas City, 1974; cons. nursing standards Health Standards Directorate, Ottawa, Ont., Can., 1978; trustee Presbyterian Manors of Mid-Am., Newton, Kans., 1979—. Editor: Guidelines for Review of Nursing Care at the Local Level, 1976; Nursing Quality Assurance Management/Learning System, 1982; Peer Review in Nursing, 1982; Issues in Professional Practice, 1985. Mem. Friends of Art, Kansas City, 1975—, Internat. Relations Council, Kansas City, 1980—, Historic Kansas City Found., 1982—; chpt. pres. Am. Field Services, Kansas City, 1978-79. Mem. Am. Nurses Assn., Mo. Nurses' Assn. (pres. Mo. dist. 1980-81), Kans. U. Nurses Alumni Assn. (pres. 1964-66), N.Am. Nursing Diagnosis Assn. (mem. task force 1973-77), Sigma Theta Tau. Club: P.E.O. (Kansas City). Avocations: home and financial management; walking; skiing. Home: 1035 W 57th Terr Kansas City MO 64113 Office: Am Nurses' Assn 2420 Pershing Rd Kansas City MO 64108

HIRSCH, JILL SUSAN, physician; b. Bklyn., Nov. 27, 1955; d. Arnold David and Vivian Honey (Agress) Hirsch; m. Randolph Jack Cohen, June 8, 1980. B.S., Columbia U., 1976; M.D., N.Y. Med. Coll., 1980. Diplomate Nat. Bd. Med. Examiners. Pediatric resident Brookdale Hosp., Bklyn., 1980-83, attending in charge pediatric emergency services, 1983-84. Fellow Am. Acad. Pediatrics (jr.); mem. Royal Soc. Arts (London), Tau Beta Pi, Phi Lambda Upsilon. Democrat. Jewish. Home: Liberty Manor Apts Crestview Dr and Route 52 Liberty NY 12754

HIRSCH, JOYCE APELIAN, banker; b. Paterson, N.J.; d. Samuel Apelian and Evelyn (Kordja) Orr; B.A., Vassar Coll., 1965; M.A., Columbia U., 1966; M.B.A., Fordham U., 1974; m. Jerome E. Hirsch, Aug. 7, 1966; children—Paul S., Alison Bick. Investment specialist Citibank NA, N.Y.C., 1966-76, manpower planning officer, 1976-77, v.p. ops., 1978-79, v.p., dept. head pvt. banking and investment div., 1979-84, dir. nat. expansion, 1984—. Fin. chmn. Jr. League of Scarsdale, 1982-83; treas. Jr. League of Central Westchester, 1984—. Chartered fin. analyst. Mem. Nat. Assn. Bank Women (pres. chpt. 1982-83). Inst. Chartered Fin. Analysts, N.Y. Soc. Fin. Analysts, Fin. Analyst Fedn., Am. Mgmt. Assn. Home: 64 Walworth Ave Scarsdale NY 10583 Office: 153 E 53d St New York NY 10043

HIRSCH, JULIA CAROL, management consultant; b. Freeport, Ill., Mar. 18, 1939; d. Muriel Woessner and Lois (Peterman) Woessner Hirsch; B.A., Stanford U., 1960. Program dir. Stanford (Calif.) Alumni Assn., 1960-68; exec. asst. to pres. Calif. Inst. Arts, Valencia, Calif., 1968-72; v.p. Nat. Center for Vol. Action, Washington, 1972-74; Calif. Gubernatorial campaign mgr. for Herb Haffif, San Francisco, 1974; pres. J. C. Hirsch and Assos., San Francisco, 1974-78; v.p. Boyden Assos., Inc., San Francisco, 1978-83, sr. v.p., 1983—. Mem. bd. Stanford Alumni Exec. Bd., 1973-76; trustee York Sch., 1979—. Mem. No. Calif. Human Relations Council, Econ. Round Table. Clubs: World Trade, St. Francis Yacht. Home: 2215 Beach St San Francisco CA 94123 Office: One Maritime Plaza Suite 1760 San Francisco CA 94111

HIRSCH, MICHELLE LINDA, psychiatrist; b. N.Y.C., June 12, 1947; d. Eli and Molly (Kinsler) H.; B.S. cum laude, CCNY, 1968; M.D., Upstate Med. Sch., Syracuse, N.Y., 1973; 2 children. Intern, Westchester div. N.Y. Med. Coll., 1974-75; resident in psychiatry, N.Y. State Psychiat. Inst., N.Y.C., 1975-79; fellow in child psychiatry Columbia-Presbyn. Hosp., 1978-80; asst. clin. prof. psychiatry Columbia U., N.Y.C., 1980—; staff Columbia-Presbyterian Hosp.; researcher, instr. U. Chgo., 1967-68. Diplomate Am. Bd. Psychiatry and Neurology. Mem. AMA, Am. Women's Med. Assn., Am. Psychiat. Assn., Am. Acad. Child Psychiatry, Phi Beta Kappa. Speaker profl. confs. in field. Office: 30 Lincoln Plaza New York NY 10023

HIRSCH, NORMA JEAN, neonatologist; b. Charles City, Iowa, Aug. 2, 1944; d. Milton Charles and Dorothy Leona (Lacour) H. B.S., Iowa State U., 1966; M.D., U. Iowa, 1970. Diplomate Am. Bd. Pediatrics. Intern pediatrics Children Med. Ctr., Dallas, 1970-71, resident, 1971-73; fellow in pediatric nephrology Ind. U., Indpls., 1973-74; asst. prof. pediatrics U. Tex., Dallas, 1974-75; fellow in neonatology Baylor Coll. Medicine, Houston, 1975-77; neonatologist, clin. asst. prof. Baylor U. Med. Ctr., 1977-79; clin. asst. prof. pediatrics U. Iowa, Iowa City, also staff Newborn Care Cons., P.C., Des Moines, 1979—; clin. asst. prof. pediatrics U. Iowa, Iowa City, 1979—; med. dir. Variety Club Newborn Intensive Care Nursery, 1981—. Author, editor numerous med. publs. Contbr. articles to med. jours. Bd. dirs. Sherman Hill Assn., 1983—. Named Woman of Achievement, YWCA, 1983. Fellow Am. Acad. Pediatrics; mem. AMA, Am. Med. Womens Assn., Iowa Med. Soc., Polk County Med. Soc. Republican. Lutheran. Club: Embassy. Office: Newborn Care Cons PC PO Box 4566 Des Moines IA 50306

HIRSCH, RUTH, architectural placement counseling and consulting firm executive; b. Cologne, Germany, Sept. 24, 1926; d. Emanuel and Citonia (Metzger) H. B.A., Hunter Coll., 1947; M.P.A., N.Y. U., 1951. Intern UN, 1947; audio-visual asst. Hunter Coll., 1949-51; profl. placement counselor N.Y. State Dept. Labor, 1951-64; archtl. placement counselor Career Builders, N.Y.C., 1964-69; pres., cons. Ruth Hirsch, Inc., N.Y.C., 1969—; lectr. seminar on archtl. employment opportunities AIA; lectr. on career guidance Columbia U., Fashion Inst. Tech.; condr. seminar Archtl. Employment Opportunities, Westchester chpt. AIA and N.Y. Soc. Architects. Named Outstanding Employee of Yr., N.Y. State div. Employment Services, 1964. Office: Ruth Hirsch Inc 400 Madison Ave New York NY 10017

HIRSCHMAN, ELIZABETH CALDWELL, marketing educator; b. Kingsport, Tenn., May 21, 1950; d. John Richard and Virginia (Carter) Caldwell; m. Raymond Hirschman, Mar. 3, 1973; children—Alixandra Chase, Anne-Nicole. B.A., U. Ga., 1971; M.B.A., Ga. State U., 1974, Ph.D., 1977. Advt. asst. Eastman-Kodak, N.Y.C., 1971; advt. writer J.C. Penney Co., N.Y.C., 1971-73; market research mgr. Rich's Dept. Stores, Atlanta, 1974-77; asst. prof. bus. adminstrn. U. Pitts., 1977-78; asst. prof. mktg. NYU, N.Y.C., 1978-81, assoc. prof. mktg., 1981—, editor Jour. of Retailing, 1980-83, assoc. dir. Inst. of Retail Mgmt., 1978-83; cons. AT & T, N.J., 1980; cons. NCR Corp., Ohio, 1979. Contbr. articles to profl. jours. Recipient George Malanos award Ga. State U., Atlanta, 1974. Fellow Am. Mktg. Assn. (v.p. edn. div. 1985-86); mem. Assn. Consumer Research (program chmn. 1984, treas. 1985), Am. Inst. of Decision Scis., Ops. Research Soc. Am., Phi Kappa Phi Beta Gamma Sigma, Kappa Tau Alpha. Democrat. Presbyterian.

HIRSON, ESTELLE, educator; b. Bayonne, N.J.; d. Morris and Bertha (Rubinstein) H.; tchr. credential UCLA; B.E., San Francisco State Coll.; student U. So. Calif., summers. Tchr., High St. Homes Sch., Oakland Calif., 1949-54, Prescott Sch., 1955-60, Ralph Bunche Sch., 1960-66, Lockwood Sch., 1966—; owner Puzzle-Gram Co., Los Angeles, 1946-49; pres. Major Automobile Co. Mem. NEA, Calif., Oakland, Los Angeles tchrs. assns., Sigma Delta Tau, Mt. Sinai-Duarte Nat. Med. Center (life mem.; parliamentarian, dir. 1946-50). Democrat. Mem. Order Easter Star, Scottish Rite Women's Assn. (v.p. Los Angeles 1982—, corr. sec. 1985). Home: 8670 Burton Way Los Angeles CA 90048

HIRST, WILMA ELIZABETH, psychologist; b. Shenandoah, Iowa; d. James H. and Lena (Donahue) Ellis; A.B. in Elementary Edn., Colo. State Coll., 1948, Ed.D. in Ednl. Psychology, 1954; M.A. in Psychology, U. Wyo., 1951; m. Clyde Henry Hirst (dec. 1969); 1 child, Donna (Mrs. Alan R. Goss). Elementary tchr., Cheyenne, Wyo., 1945-49, remedial reading instr., 1949-54; asso. prof. edn., dir. campus sch. Neb. State Tchrs. Coll., Kearney, 1954-56; sch. psychologist, head dept. spl. edn. Cheyenne (Wyo.) pub. schs., 1956-57, sch. psychologist, guidance coordinator, 1957-66; dir. div. of research, pub. relations, Cheyenne Schs., 1966-71; prin. investigator Coop. Research Study, U.S. Office Edn. project, dir. div. research and spl. projects, 1971-74; dir. research, spl. projects, also pupil personnel Laramie County Sch. Dist. 1, 1974-84; pvt. cons., 1984—. Vis. asst. prof. U. So. Calif., summer 1957, Omaha U., summer 1958; vis. lectr. U. Okla., summers 1959, 60, U. Nebr., summer 1961, U. Wyo., 1962, summer, 1964; extension asso. prof., Kabul, Afghanistan, 1970, Goiania, Brazil, 1974. Mem. Wyo. Bd. Psychology Examiners, 1965-74, sec.-treas., 1965-66, vice chmn., 1968-73; mem. adv. council div. exceptional children Wyo. Dept. Edn., 1974-84; mem. adv. bd. Cheyenne Transit Devel. Program, 1975-77; participant Russian seminar Internat. Fedn. Press Women, 1973, Kent State Comparative Edn. Seminar, South Africa, 1975. Mem. speakers bur., local mental health orgn.; active Little Theatre, 1936-70, Girl Scout Leaders Assn., 1943-50; mem., past chmn. bd. social devel. Cheyenne Model Cities; mem. S.E. Wyo. Mental Health Bd., 1968-69; v.p., bd. dirs. Wyo. Mental Health Assn.; bd. dirs. Wyo. Children's Home Soc., treas., 1977—; mem. exec. com. Wyo. Partners of Ams., 1973; mem. adv. bd. Stride Learning Center, 1975-77; elder 1st Presbyterian Ch., Cheyenne, 1978—; bd. dirs. Goodwill Industries Wyo., 1978—, chmn., 1981-82; mem. Friendship Force to Honduras, summer 1979, Child Protection Team, Laramie, County; co-chmn. Tech. Adv. Group Wyo. Dept. Edn., 1982-84; mem. allocations com. Laramie County United Way. Recipient Woman of Year award Cheyenne Bus. and Profl. Women's Club, 1974. Diplomate Am. Bd. Profl. Psychology. Fellow Internat. Council Psychologists (regional chair 1981—); mem. Am. Assn. State Psychology Bds. (sec.-treas. 1970-74), Nat. Fedn. Press Women (dir. 1979—), Wyo. Press Women, AAUP, Wyo. Psychol. Assn. (state sec.-treas. 1958-60, pres. 1962-63, exec. bd.) Am. Personnel and Guidance Assn., NEA (life mem.; mem. seminar People's Republic China 1978), AAUW, Assn. Supervision and Curriculum Devel., Cheyenne Assn. Prin. and Spl. Personnel (pres. 1964-65), Am. Assn. Sch. Adminstrs., Laramie County Council Social Agys. (sec.-treas. 1962), Nat. Assn. Gifted Children (state membership chmn., pres.), Internat. Platform Assn., Am. Ednl. Research Assn., DAR (chpt. vice regent 1976-78), Psi Chi, Kappa Delta Pi, Pi Lambda Theta, Alpha Delta Kappa (pres. 1965-66). Mem. Order Eastern Star, Daus. of Nile. Club: Zonta (pres. Cheyenne 1965-66, dist. treas. 1974-76). Author: Know Your School Psychologist, 1963; Effective Psychology for School Administrators, 1980; Contbr. articles to profl. jours. Home: 3458 Green Valley Rd Cheyenne WY 82001 Office: Sch Adminstrn Bldg Cheyenne WY 82001

HIRT, JANET ROSE, educator; b. Meadville, Pa., Mar. 14, 1942; d. Ira George and Gladys Gertrude (McLaren) H.; A.B., Eastern Coll., St. David's Pa., 1964; M.A. in English, Allegheny Coll., Meadville, Pa., 1969; M.A. in Counseling, Villanova (Pa.) U., 1973, postgrad. law sch., 1984; M.S. in L.S., Drexel U., Phila., 1977; postgrad. Oxford U., 1970, Sussex U., 1977. Copy editor Am. Bapt. Bd. Publs., Valley Forge, Pa., 1964; tchr. English, Springfield (Pa.) High Sch., 1964-73, 76—, counselor, 1973-75; reference librarian Villanova Law Sch., 1985. Cert. in comprehensive English, secondary sch. guidance, library sci., Pa. Mem. ALA, Modern Lang. Assn., Nat. Council Tchrs. of English (life), NEA, Pa. Edn. Assn., AAUW, Am. Assn. Law Libraries, Buten Mus. Wedgwood (life), English Speaking Union, Wedgwood Collectors Soc. (charter). Home: Aronimink Arms Drexel Hill PA 19026

HIRT-KRAVETSKY, PATRICIA CAROL, brokerage house executive; b. Jersey City, Apr. 16, 1948; d. Harold James and Gladys (Nitsch) Hirt; B.A., Upsala Coll., 1969; advanced cert. Am. Inst. Banking, 1973; M.B.A., Fairleigh Dickinson U., 1974. Asst. treas. Bank of N.Y., N.Y.C., 1975-77, asst. v.p., 1977-79, v.p., 1979-80; investment broker Garvin Guybutler, N.Y.C., 1980-83, asst. v.p., 1983—. Mem. Fin. Women's Assn. Clubs: Binghamton Racquet, Order Eastern Star. Home: 515 Forest Ct Rivervale NJ 07675 Office: 120 Broadway New York NY 10005

HIRYOK, KATHRYN ANN, fundraising organizer; b. Warren, Ohio, June 10, 1942; d. Edward J. and Mary K. (Namton) Lukco; m. Paul Joseph Hiryok, June 16, 1961 (dec. Apr. 1971); children—Janine Marie, Daniel Paul. B.F.A. candidate Kent State U., 1978—. Office mgr. Warren Otologic Group, Ohio, 1963-71, exec. asst., 1971-74, fin. dir., 1975—; property mgr. Northmar Ctr., Warren, 1984—; asst. nat. dir. Israel Tennis Ctrs., N.Y.C., 1975—. Founder/organizer Warren Women's Network, 1981-85; bd. dirs. Warren Family Service Assn., 1984—, chmn. pub. relations, 1985, v.p., 1986; trustee Trumbull County United Way, 1986—; mem. Trumbull Art Guild. Mem. Nat. Assn. Female Execs., Am. Assn. Editorial Cartoonists (hon.). Jewish. Lodge: Hadassah. Home: 160 Winter Ln Cortland OH 44410 Office: Israel Tennis Ctrs 3893 E Market St Warren OH 44484

HITCHCOCK, KAREN RUTH, developmental biologist, medical school dean; b. Mineola, N.Y., Feb. 10, 1943; d. Roy Clinton and Ruth (Wardell) Hitchcok. B.S. in Biology, St. Lawrence U., 1964; Ph.D. in Anatomy, U. Rochester, 1968. Postdoctoral fellow in Pulmonary Cell Biology, Webb-Waring Inst. Med. Research, 1968-70; asst. prof. dept. anatomy Tufts U. Sch. Medicine, Boston, 1970-75, assoc. prof. dept. anatomy, 1975-80, assoc. prof., acting chmn. dept. anatomy, 1976-78, assoc. prof., chmn. dept. anatomy, 1978-80, prof., chmn. dept. anatomy and cellular biology, 1980-82, George A. Bates prof. histology, chmn. dept. anatomy and cellular biology, 1982-85; prof. dept. cell biology and anatomy Tex. Tech U. Health Scis. Ctr., assoc. dean Tex. Tech U. Sch Medicine, Lubbock, 1985—; mem. adv. com. NIH, Nat. Bd. Med. Examiners, 1983-85. Mem. Am. Assn. Anatomy (chmn., exec. council 1979-81), Am. Assn. Anatomists (exec. com. 1981-85, v.p. 1986-88), Am. Assn. Anatomy Chmn. (nominating com. 1982-83). Home: 55 E Lakeshore Dr Ransom Canyon TX 79366 Office: Tex Tech Med Sch Lubbock TX 79340

HITE, CATHARINE LEAVEY, orchestra manager; b. Boston, Oct. 1, 1924; d. Edmond Harrison and Ruth Farrington Leavey; B.A., Coll. William and Mary, 1945; m. Robert Atkinson Hite, Aug. 28, 1948; children—Charles Harrison, Patricia Hite Rogers, Catharine Hite Dunn. Restoration guide Williamsburg Restoration, 1944-45; asst. edn. dept. Honolulu Acad. Arts, 1945-46; sec., tour guide edn. dept. office chief curator Nat. Gallery Art, 1946-48; opera liason/coordinator Honolulu Symphony, 1972-73, asst. to gen. mgr., 1973-75, community devel. dir./opera coordinator, 1975-77, dir. ops./opera prodn. coordinator, 1977-79, orch. mgr., 1979-84, mem. exec. com., 1965-69, pres. women's assn., 1965-66; com. chmn., opera assn. chmn. Hawaii Opera Theatre, 1966-69. Mem. W. R. Farrington Scholarship Com., 1977-82, chmn., 1983-84; mem. community arts panel State Found. Culture and the Arts, 1982, State Found. Music and Opera, 1984. Mem. Jr. League, Phi Beta Kappa. Episcopalian.

HITTSON, JO BETH, county official; b. Levelland, Tex., June 4, 1947; d. H.L. and Margaret (Goodman) Parks; m. Bill P. Fietz, June 17, 1967 (div. 1979); 1 child, Amber Elizabeth; m. Jesse Dan Hittson, Mar. 7, 1981. Student Tex. A&M U., 1983, 85. Mgr., King's Row Fireplace Shop, Lubbock, Tex., 1968-71; teller Tex. Am. Bank, Levelland, 1972-80; bookkeeper and office mgr. Community Coop Gin, Levelland, 1980-83; county treas. Hockley County, Tex., 1983—; mem. adv. com. Bookkeeping for County Govt., 1984. Chmn. Hockley County Sesquicentennial Com., 1986, March of Dimes, Levelland, 1984, Levelland High Sch. Execs. Assn., 1975, 85; sec. treas. Hockley County Early Settlers Day, 1984—. Mem. Levelland C. of C. (Marigold's div.). Democrat. Methodist. Home: 108 Capitol St Levelland TX 79336 Office: Box 4 Courthouse 800 Houston St Levelland TX 79336

HIVELY, EVELYN THOMAS HELMICK, association executive; b. McKeesport, Pa., July 20, 1928; s. Samuel Blair and Evelyn (Descaunets) Thomas; B.S. (Buhl Found. scholar 1946-50, Andrew Carnegie scholar 1948-50), Carnegie Mellon U., 1950; M.A., U. Miami, 1964, Ph.D., 1969; m. Robert William Hively, June 19, 1972; children—Jon Sommer Helmick, Jennifer Thomas Helmick, Melinda Blair Helmick. Tchr. French and English, Pub. Schs., New Wilmington, Pa., 1950-52; instr. humanities U. Miami, 1964-69, asst. prof., 1969-73, asso. prof. English, 1973-77, dir. Am. studies, 1975-77; acad. dean Salem Coll., Winston-Salem, N.C., 1977-81; v.p. acad. affairs Western Mont. Coll., Dillon, 1982-85; dir. Acad. Affairs Resource Ctr., Am. Assn. State Colls. and Univs., 1985—. Rockefeller Found. fellow, 1963-64. Mem. MLA, Am. Studies Assn., Fla. Coll. English Assn. Contbr. articles to profl. jours. Home: 21 S Fenwick St Arlington VA 22204 Office: Am Assn of State Coll and U 1 Dupont Circle Washington DC 20036

HIWA, LINDA FUSAKO, nurse; b. Honolulu, July 29, 1955; d. Albert Masaichi and Nancy Toyoko (Kinjo) H. B.S. in Nursing, U. Portland, 1979. Registered nurse, Oreg., Hawaii, Calif. On-call nurses aide Good Samaritan Hosp., Portland, Oreg., 1977-78; staff nurse Oreg. Health Scis. Ctr., Portland, 1979-80, Queen's Hosp., Honolulu, 1980-81, Pacific-Presbyn. Med. Ctr., San Francisco, 1981—. Mem. Am. Assn. Critical-Care Nurses, San Francisco Quilt Guild (historian 1983-84). Democrat. Avocations: quilting; cooking; rubber stamps.

HIX, MARSHA LUCILE, health care services administrator, nurse consultant; b. Oakland, Calif. Aug. 28, 1950; d. william E. and Beulah R. (Scott) Whitehouse; m. Lawrence J. Hix, Feb. 16, 1974. B.S. in Nursing, San Diego State U., 1972. Rev. coordinator San Francisco Peer Rev. Orgn., 1977; discharge planner Mary's Help Hosp., Daly City, Calif., 1977-80; home care coordinator Comprehensive Community Home Health, Daly City, 1980-83; dir. home care Linde Home Care, San Francisco, 1983-84; pres., dir. Discharge Resource Group, Brisbane, Calif., 1984—. Mem. service com. Am. Cancer Soc., San Mateo, Calif., 1984-85; mem. utilization rev. com. Comprehensive Community Home Health Hospice, Daly City, 1982-85; Avocations: travel; sailing; bicycling; skiing. Home: 224 Donahue St Sausalito CA 94965 Office: Discharge Resource Group 150 N Hill Dr Suite 19A Brisbane CA 94005

HIX, RITA ELAINE, banker; b. Hooker, Okla., July 30, 1947; d. Frank Emery and Elsie Gertrude (Brown) Loveland; m. Marion Arthur Crow, Aug. 8, 1962 (dec. Feb. 1965); 1 child, Roberta Sue Crow Jones; m. Clifford Porterfield, Jr., Nov. 13, 1965 (dec. Oct. 1978); children—Buddy Wayne, Paula Jean; m. Gary Gayle Hix, Feb. 14, 1985. Grad. Draughn's Bus. Coll., 1972. Office mgr. Millco Moving Service, Amarillo, Tex., 1973-77; bookkeeper Edwards Tires & Auto, Weatherford, Tex., 1977-78; computer operator Liberty State Bank, Tahlequah, Okla., 1981-83, asst. cashier, 1983-85, asst. v.p., 1985—. Co-chmn. Eastern Okla. March of Dimes, Tahlequah, 1984-86. Mem. Nat. Assn. Bank Women (chmn. edn. and tng. com. 1985-86), Nat. Assn. Female Execs., Ducks Unltd. Republican. Baptist. Club: Ladies Aux. Avocations: boating; camping; bowling. Office: Liberty State Bank 130 S Muskogee Tahlequah OK 74464

HIXON, CHRISTINE PRITCHARD, counselor; b. Wilcox County, Ala., May 13, 1918; d. Hoy Ellsworth and Rosa M. (Bridges) Pritchard; B.S., U. Ala., 1942; M.S., Samford U., 1967; advanced degree and AA cert. U. Ala., Birmingham, 1976; m. Daniel Alexander Hixon, June 14, 1942; children—Daniel Alexander, Charlotte Lisa Hixon Taylor. Tchr. public high schs. Alabama county systems, 1940-45, Birmingham (Ala.) Edn. Systems, 1962-80; guidance counselor Ramsay High Sch., Birmingham, 1967-72, Homewood (Ala.) High Sch., 1972-80; pvt. practice counseling, Birmingham, 1980—; cons. So. Assn. Accreditation, Birmingham, 1975. Student oratory sponsor VFW, Birmingham, 1970-72; student essay competition sponsor Freedom Found., Valley Forge, Pa., 1977-80; active Hoover Service Club, Birmingham; mem. ch. planning com., personnel com. Green Valley Baptist Ch., Birmingham, 1979—. Recipient cert. VFW, 1970, service recognition Am. Youth, 1981. Mem. Ala. Poetry Soc., Ala. Writers Conclave, Kappa Delta Pi (sec., scholarship chmn.). Contbr. poetry to Sampler; author: (poetry booklet) Yesterday, Today, Tomorrow, 1983. Home: 1827 Paulette Dr Birmingham AL 35226

HIXON, EVA MAE, real estate firm executive, broker, consultant; b. Borger, Tex., Sept. 21, 1932; d. Martin Bailey Mara and Mabel Catherine (Smith) Mara Davis; m. Richard Alvin Cross, June 5, 1976 (div. Dec. 1981); m. 2d Virgil Carl Hixon, Aug. 7, 1948; children—Gary Carson, Vickie Kay. Student Fresno Tech. Coll. 1951-53, Fresno City Coll., 1976-79. Lic. real estate salesperson and broker, Calif. Organizer, Hixon's Horse World, Clovis, Calif., 1962-75; salesperson Miracle Realty, Clovis, 1974-77; broker, owner C & H Realty, Clovis, 1977—; sales mgr. Stanley Co., Fresno, Calif., 1960-64. Pres., PTA, Clovis, 1968; v.p. LaCaballista de Fresno, 1975; sec. Ch. of Jesus Christ of Latter-day Saints Stake, Fresno, 1977-79, in-serivce work primary, 1974-77. Mem. Calif. State Horsemen Assn. (v.p. region 15 1972). Club: Fresno Appaloosa (sec. 1970). Office: C & H Realty 1924 Minnewawa Clovis CA 93612

HIXSON, SUSAN HARVILL, chemistry educator; b. Orange, N.J., Sept. 26, 1944; 2 children. B.S. in Chemistry, U. Mich., 1965; Ph.D. in Biochemistry, U. Wis.-Madison, 1970. Instr. chemistry Boston U., 1969-70; research assoc. U. Mass., Amherst, 1970-73; asst. prof. chemistry Mt. Holyoke Coll., South Hadley, Mass., 1973-79, assoc. prof. chemistry, 1979-86, prof., 1986—; vis. prof. dept. biochemistry U. N.C., Chapel Hill, 1980. NIH fellow, 1971-72. Mem. Am. Chem. Soc., Am. Soc. Biol. Chemists, AAAS, Council on Undergrad. Research, Assn. Women in Sci., Sigma Xi. Address: Dept of Chemistry Mount Holyoke Coll South Hadley MA 01075

HLOZEK, CAROLE DIANE QUAST, business executive; b. Dallas, Apr. 17, 1959; d. Robert E. and Bonnie (Wootton) Quast. B.S., Tex. A&M U., 1982, B.B.A., 1982. Internal auditor Brown & Root Inc., Houston, 1982-84; asst. controller Wilson Supply Co., Houston, 1984—. Mem. Houston Zool. Soc., Nat. Wildlife Assn., Nat. Geog. Soc., Am. Mus. Natural History, Nat. Assn. Female Execs., Soc. Advanced Mgmt., Assn. Former Students Tex. A&M U. Lutheran. Home: 8034 Log Hollow Houston TX 77040 Office: Wilson Supply Co PO Box 1492 Houston TX 77251

HMIELESKI, CAROL LYDIA, local government official; b. Perth Amboy, N.J., June 7, 1950; d. Alexander and Rose (Brozozowski) Shumny; 1 child, R.J. B.A., Rider Coll., 1972; M.A., Rutgers U., 1984. Tchr., South Amboy Bd. Edn., N.J., 1972-73, St. Stephens Sch., Perth Amboy, N.J., 1974-76, St. Theresa's Sch., Linden, N.J., 1976-80; ins. analyst The Children's Pl., Pinebrook, N.J., 1980-83; purchasing agt. Borough of Carteret, N.J., 1983—; notary public, State of N.J., 1983—; continuing edn. tchr. Woodbridge Bd. Edn., N.J., 1979—. Mem. Nat. Inst. Govtl. Purchasing (treas. 1984—), Govtl. Purchasing Assn., Carteret Police Athletic League. Roman Catholic. Avocation: antique collecting.

HO, JING-CHING SALLY, physical therapist; b. Taipei, Taiwan, Republic of China, Jan. 22, 1949; came to U.S. 1972, naturalized 1980; d. Tai-Kai and Shuck-Hing (Yau) Su; m. Larry Shiu-Bong Ho, July 20, 1974; 1 child, Ryan Ho. B.S. in Phys. Therapy, Nat. Taiwan U., 1971; M.S. in Phys. Therapy, Med. Coll. Va., 1974. Registered phys. therapist. Clin. instr. Med. Coll. Va. Hosp., Richmond, 1976-78; staff phys. therapist Retreat Hosp., Richmond, 1978-79; chief phys. therapist Ortho-Med. Surg. Group, Beverly Hills, Calif., 1979-81; dir., owner Ho Phys. Therapy, Beverly Hills, 1981—. Mem. com. Am. Lung Assn., Los Angeles, 1984-85. Mem. Am. Phys. Therapy Assn., So. Calif. Pvt. Practice Spl. Interest Group, Nat. Assn. Phys. Therapy & Rehab. Medicine, Beverly Hills Bus. and Profl. Women. Republican. Address: Ho Physical Therapy 435 N Bedford Dr Suite 412 Beverly Hills CA 90210

HOADLEY, IRENE BRADEN (MRS. EDWARD HOADLEY), librarian; b. Hondo, Tex., Sept. 26, 1938; d. Andrew Henry and Theresa Lillian (Lebold) Braden; m. Edward Hoadley, Feb. 21, 1970. B.A., U. Tex., 1960; A.M.L.S., U. Mich., 1961, Ph.D., 1967; M.A., Kans. State U., 1965. Cataloger Sam Houston State Tchrs. Coll. Library, Huntsville, Tex., 1961-62; head circulation dept. Kans. State U. Library, Manhattan, 1962-64; grad. asst. U. Mich. Dept. of Library Sci., 1964-66; librarian gen. adminstrn. and research Ohio State U. Libraries, Columbus, 1966-73, asst. dir. libraries adminstrv. services, 1973-74; dir. of libraries Tex. A. and M. U. Library, College Station, Tex., 1974—; dir. Higher Edn. Act Inst. Quantitative Methods in Librarianship, Ohio State U., summer 1969; instr. inst. U. Calif. at San Diego, 1970, summer; Mem. steering com. Gov's. Conf. on Library and Info. Services, Ohio, 1973-74, joint chairperson, 1974; mem. adv. com. Library Services and Constrn. Act Cuyahoga County Pub. Library, Cleve., 1973; mem. adv. com. Library Edn. Inst., 1984—; mem. sr. fellows program Council on Library Resources, 1984. Author: (with others) Physiological Factors Relating to Terrestrial Altitudes: A Bibliography, 1968; Editor: (with Alice S. Clark) Quantitative Methods in Librarianship: Standards, Research, Management, 1972; Contbr. articles to profl. jours. Recipient Scarecrow Press award for library lit., 1971; Distinguished Alumnus award Sch. Library Sci., U. Mich., 1976. Mem. ALA (Library Research Round Table, sec. 1984-86, com. on research 1985-88), Ohio Library Assn. (chmn. constn. com. 1967-68, chmn. election tellers cons. 1969, asst. gen. chmn. local conf. com. 1969-70, sec. 1970-71, v.p., pres.-elect 1971-72, chmn. budget advisory com. 1971-72, pres. 1972-73, bd. dirs. 1970-75), Tex. Library Assn. (com. on White House conf. 1975-77, vice chmn., chmn. coll. and univ. div. 1977-78, exec. bd. 1978-81), Assn. Research Libraries (bd. dirs. 1978-81, search com. for exec. dir. 1980, task force on library edn. 1981-85, staffing com. 1983-85, Midwest Fedn. Library Assns. (exec. bd. 1973-74, chairperson program com. 1974), Phi Kappa Phi, Phi Alpha Theta, Pi Lambda Theta, Beta Phi Mu, Phi Delta Gamma. Home: Route 5 Box 1048 College Station TX 77840

HOAGENSON, CONNIE LOU, practical nurse educator; b. Independence, Mo., Dec. 14, 1937; d. Kenneth John and Annabell (Bly) Smith Mosley; m. Evan Walter Seedorf, July 20, 1958 (div. Apr. 1970); m. Richard Eugene Hoagenson, Dec. 28, 1970; 1 son, Lloyd Walter. B.S., Coll. St. Francis, Joliet, Ill., 1982; R.N., Research Hosp., Kansas City, Mo., 1958. Cert. tchr., Mo. Inservice coordinator Jackson County Hosp., Kansas City, 1966-68; inservice instr. St. Joseph Hosp., Kansas City, 1968-70; surg. nurse Independence Sanitarium, 1970-71; instr. surg. technologists Health Occupations, Independence, 1971-81, instr. practical nurses, 1981—, coordinator daily activities, 1981—; author poetry. Mem. nurture com. Lutheran Ch. Mo. Synod, St. Louis, 1982—; tchr. midweek sch. St. Paul's Luth. Ch., Independence, 1981—; mem. Kansas City ARC, 1958—; bd. dirs. Beautiful Savior Home, Belton, Mo., 1980-82. Mem. Mo. State Assn. Health Occupation Educators (pres. 1985-86), Mo. Vocat. Assn. Democrat. Home: 1417 Millburn St Independence MO 64056 Office: Health Occupations 1509 W Truman St Independence MO 64050

HOAGLAND, PAMELA REDINGTON, ednl. adminstr.; b. Phoenix, June 2, 1937; d. George Appleton and Margaret Tweed (Rae) H.; B.A. with distinction, U. Ariz., 1959, M.Ed., 1965, Ed.D., 1973. Tchr., Tucson Unified Sch. Dist., 1959-73, dir. reading, lang. arts and library services, 1980—; curriculum specialist supr. Pima County Spl. Edn. Coop., Tucson, 1973-76; co-founder, co-dir. Learning Devel. Center, Tucson, 1970-74; pres. Redington Cons. Corp., Tucson, 1980—; lectr. U. Ariz., Tucson, 1965-66, U. Colo., Boulder, 1977, So. Oreg. Coll., Ashland, 1978. Bd. dirs. Behavior Assos., Tucson, 1969—, chmn., 1978-80; mem. adv. bd. Ariz. Right to Read Council, Phoenix, 1976-79, chmn., 1978-80; pres. U. Ariz. Coll. Edn. Alumni Council, 1986—; edn. supr. Grace Episcopal Ch., Tucson, 1965-67; bd. dirs. Tucson Westside Neighborhood Coalition, 1979-81; bd. dirs. Friends of Tucson Pub. Library, 1984—, v.p., 1985-86, pres. 1986—; bd. dirs. Tucson Adminstrs., Inc., 1985-86. Recipient Cert. of Recognition, U. Ariz., 1970, Disting. Service award Tucson Area Reading Council, 1986. Pi Delta Kappa Disting. Lecture Series award Hendrix Coll., Conway, Ark., 1978. Mem. Tucson Edn. Assn. (dir. 1967-73), Nat. Council Tchrs. of English, Internat. Reading Assn., (field cons. 1974—), Assn. Supervision and Curriculum Devel., LWV, Alpha Delta Kappa (chpt. pres. 1965-66), Pi Beta Phi Alumni Assn. Democrat. Episcopalian. Contbr. articles to profl. publs. Office: 2025 E Winsett St Tucson AZ 85719

HOANG, JOY GONZALES, hotel executive; b. Carmel, Calif., Dec. 30, 1949; d. Jose Quijano and Caridad Rodriquez (Martinez) Gonzales; m. Jack Minh Hoang, July 16, 1968; children—Jolene, Mario, Jack, Cherie. Student pvt. schs., Carmel and Monterey, Calif. Front desk mgr. Royal Inn, Monterey, 1972-74; asst. reservations mgr. Hyatt Hotel, Monterey, 1977-78; catering services rep. Casa Munras Hotel, Monterey, 1977-78; reservations mgr. Doubletree Hotel, Monterey, 1980-82, front office mgr., 1982-84, dir. catering, 1984—. Chmn. parent adv. council Monterey Sch. Dist., 1984-86; active Leadership Monterey Peninsula. Mem. Nat. Assn. Female Execs. Democrat. Roman Catholic. Home: 590 Harcourt Ave Seaside CA 93955 Office: Doubletree Hotel 2 Portola Plaza Monterey CA 93940

HOARD, ANN, court clerk; b. Georgiana, Ala., Nov. 7; d. Jimmy and Lena (Singer) Baggett; m. Gus Hoard, Jan. 12, 1951; children—Howard Dwayne, Stanley Marlon, Anita Elaine. Diploma in Cosmetology, Poro Coll. Beauty Art, Cin., 1945; cert. in IBM key punch Miami Jacobs Jr. Coll., Dayton, Ohio, 1962; A.A., Sinclair Community Coll., Dayton, 1983. Clk. typist Ohio Hwy. Patrol, Dayton, 1963-64; health technician Blairwood Sch., Dayton, 1964-65; procurement clk. typist Wright Patterson AFB, Fairborn, Ohio, 1966-68; dep. clk. of cts. Common Pleas Ct., Dayton, 1968—. Contbr. articles to Pride Mag., 1973-75. Recipient award Trinity Presbyn. Ch. U.S.A., Dayton, 1983, 84, cert. of appreciation Office Edn. Assn., Dayton, 1980. Clubs: Toastmistress (accredited skilled toastmistress, numerous positions, including pres. council 1981-82, 2d v.p. Mid-Am. region 1984-85, Gt. Lakes Region award for woman of influence 1978); Jet Aire (treas. 1974-75, v.p. 1975-76, pres. 1976-77. Home: 5221 Big Bend Dr Dayton OH 45427

HOARD, MARTHA LEE RHYAN, nurse, educator, administrator; b. Williams, Ariz., Feb. 22, 1925; d. Charles Walter and Ernestena (Busse) Rhyan; m. Harold Norvel Hoard, July 23, 1962 (dec. 1982); children—E. Gerry, Jeffrey S. Diploma in nursing Los Angeles County Med. Ctr. Sch. Nursing, 1947; B.A. in Nursing Edn., Calif. State U.-San Francisco 1951; M.A. in Edn., Stanford U., 1952; postgrad. U. Calif.-Berkeley, 1968-69; Ed.D., Calif. Coast U., 1985. R.N., Calif., Iowa; life teaching credential. Head nurse Spadra State Hosp. (Calif.), 1947; office nurse, Pomona, Calif., 1947-48; head nurse Outpatient Clinic and Hosp., Pomona, 1948-49; staff nurse Stanford U. Hosp., San Francisco, 1948-51; camp nurse Thousand Pines Camp, Crestline, Calif., summers 1950-52; dir. nursing edn. Sioux Valley Hosp., Sioux Falls, S.D., 1952-54, dir. sch. nursing and nursing services, 1954-60; charge nurse/supr. Immanuel Hosp., Mankato, Minn., 1960; instr., coordinator Mankato U., 1960-62; dir. nurses Flandreau Mcpl. Hosp. (S.D.), 1962-63; instr. Pasadena City Coll., 1963-64; instr. Fresno City Coll., 1964-65, dir. nursing edn., 1965-75, program dir. respiratory therapy, 1968-75, dir. emeritus nursing, 1975—; prof. Buena Vista Coll., 1986—; facilitator continuing edn. for nurses, Iowa Central Community Coll., Fort Dodge, 1979-81; accreditation visitor Calif. Bd. Nursing, 1970; mem. adv. com. Calif. San Joaquin Valley Health Consortium, 1970-75; mem. Calif. Western Council on Higher Edn. for Nurses, 1965-75. Contbr. articles to profl. jours. Sec., Pocahontas County Bd. Health, Iowa, 1979—; sec. bd. trustees, ch. treas. Presbyn. Ch., Rolfe, Iowa, 1981-84; sec. Pocahontas County Homemaker Home Health Aide Adminstrv. Bd., 1983—; chmn. Rolfe Ambulance Service Bd., 1980-82, numerous others. Mem. Nat. League Nursing, Am. Nurses Assn., Los Angeles County Med. Ctr. Nurses Alumni Assn., P.E.O., AAUW, Sioux Valley Hosp Sch. Nursing Alumni Assn. (hon.), numerous others. Clubs: Zonta, Tuesday, Sorosis (pres. 1978-80), Soroptomist. Address: 505 Locust St Rolfe IA 50581

HOBBS, JOAN PIZZO, data processing executive; b. Providence, Oct. 11, 1957; d. Ralph Edmund and Albina Margaret (Walsh) Pi.; m. Walter Romeo Hobbs III, Nov. 22, 1979; 1 child, Kelsey Mackensie. B.S., B.A., R.I. Coll., 1979; cert. Blake Programming Inst., 1980; postgrad bus. adminstrn. Providence Coll., 1981—. Lic. real estate broker, R.I. Substitute tchr., pub. schs., R.I., 1979-80; billing clk. Femic Inc., North Providence, 1980-81; software cons. I.P.L., Inc., Providence, 1981-84; programmer, analyst A.S.E. Services Inc., Woonsocket, R.I., 1984-85; mgr. data processing Builders Specialties, Pawtucket, 1985—. Mem. Am. Congress Real Estate Investors, Nat. Assn. Female Execs., R.I. Real Estate Investors, Elmwood Found. Archlt. and Hist. Preservation. Avocations: sailing; building restoration. Home: 1049 Smithfield Ave Lincoln RI 02865 Office: Builders Specialty Co 258 Pine St Pawtucket RI 02860

HOBBS, NILA ALENE, manufacturing company executive; b. Colorado Springs, Colo., Mar. 11, 1949; d. Harold Carl and Wilma Ella (French) H.; B.S. with high distinction, Colo. State U., 1971, M.B.A., 1973. Systems analyst Colo. div. Eastman Kodak Co., Windsor, 1974-80, sect. supr. systems devel., 1980-84, sr. systems analyst, 1984—. Mem. Am. Prodn. and Inventory Control Soc., Colo. State U. Alumni Assn., Phi Kappa Phi. Republican. Home: 1037 Parkview Dr Fort Collins CO 80525 Office: ISD Bldg C 42 Floor 3 Windsor CO 80551

HOBBY, GRETCHEN CLARK, civic worker; b. Washington, Apr. 22, 1939; d. Bruce Edmund and Phyllis Bryans (Wilson) Clark; B.A., Mary Baldwin Coll., 1960; m. William M. Hobby III, Oct. 12, 1962; children—Amy, William. Asst. to slide librarian, publs. supr., asst. chief publs. Nat. Gallery Art, summers 1957-59, 60-65; with art dept. Orlando (Fla.) Pub. Library, 1967-68; mgr. Loch Haven Art Center Shop, Orlando, 1969-76, docent, 1966-67; dir. fine arts div. Center Street Gallery, 1984—. Chmn. teenage vols. Orange Meml. Hosp. Aux., 1968-70; mem. Orlando Opera Gala Guild, 1967-72, Orlando Civic Theatre Guild, 1971-72; rec. sec. Loch Haven Art Center, 1970-71, dir., 1970-72, 75-77, mem. council of 101, asst. v.p. bd. dirs., 1975-77; commr. and corr. sec. Winter Park Sidewalk Art Festival Assn., 1970-79; bd. dirs., curator spl. events, product and shop devel. Maitland Art Center, 1978—. Named Outstanding Woman in the Arts, Orlando Downtown Bus. Assn., 1975. Mem. Orange County Bar Assn. Aux. (corr. sec., bd. dirs. 1975-76), Am. Assn. Museums, Mus. Store Assn. (chmn. conv. 1972, editor newsletter 1973-75, v.p., exec. com. 1973-76, pres. 1976-82), Mary Baldwin Coll. Alumnae Assn. (dir. 1974-79). Republican Unitarian. Home: 244 Sylvan Blvd Winter Park FL 32789 Office: 136 Park Ave S Winter Park FL 32789

HOBERMAN, MARY ANN, writer, consultant; b. Stamford, Conn., Aug. 12, 1930; d. Milton Gilbert and Dorothy (Miller) Freedman; m. Norman Hoberman, Feb. 4, 1951; children—Diane Hoberman Louie, Perry, Charles, Margaret. B.A. magna cum laude, Smith Coll., 1951; M.A., Yale U., 1985, postgrad. in English lit. Adj. prof. Fairfield U., Conn., 1980-83; program coordinator C. G. Jung Ctr., N.Y.C., 1981; speaker, cons. in field, artist-in-the schs., 1955—. Author children's books: All My Shoes Come in Two's, 1957; How Do I Go?, 1958; Hello and Good-by, 1959; What Jim Knew, 1963; Not Enough Beds for the Babies, 1965; A Little Book of Little Beasts, 1973; The Raucous Auk, 1973; The Looking Book, 1973; Nuts to You and Nuts to Me, 1974; I Like Old Clothes, 1976; Bugs, 1976; A House is a House for Me, 1978; Yellow Butter, Purple Jelly, Red Jam, Black Bread, 1981; The Cozy Book, 1982. Contbr. poems to So. Poetry Rev., Small Pond, Harper's Mag.; contbr. children's poems to numerous anthologies, textbooks, mags., U.S. and abroad; contbr. articles to N.Y. Times, Nutmegger Mag., Boston Globe, 1978-86. Active Greenwich Democratic Women's Club, Conn., 1963—, Greenwich Citizens for Nuclear Freeze, 1983—; founder, active mem. The Pocket People, children's theatre group, New Eng., 1968-75; trustee Greenwich Library, 1986—. Recipient children's Book Week Poem award Children's Book Council, 1976, Am. Book award, 1983. Mem. Author's League. Avocations: writing for, performing for, and attending theatre; travel; hiking; reading. Office: care Russell & Volkening Inc Literary Agts 50 W 29th St New York NY 10001

HOBGOOD, MARY BOB, real estate salesman, consultant, business executive; b. Toccoa, Ga., Jan. 11, 1924; d. Robert W. and Mary Sadie (Isbell) Acree; m. Noel Hayes Hobgood, Jr., Feb. 20, 1949; children—Mary Evans Hobgood Bannister, Robert Noel. A.B. in Edn. and Home Econs., Brenau Coll., Gainsville, Ga., 1945; Cert., lic. real estate sales Vocat. Edn. Fulton County, Atlanta, 1963. Corp. sec. Toccoa Tire & Recapping Co., Inc., Toccoa, 1960—, Acree Oil Co., Inc., Toccoa, 1963—; v.p. Modern Tire Co., Inc., Hartwell, Ga., 1962—; salesman Martin Realty Co., Inc., Toccoa, 1964—. Bd. dirs. Stephen County Hosp. Aux., Toccoa, 1960-62; bd. dirs. Salvation Army, Toccoa, 1965—, pres. 1969-70; pres. Women of Ch. First Baptist Ch., Toccoa, vice chmn. budget com, sec. pulpit com.; trustee Brenau Coll., 1970-72. Mem. Bus. Council Ga., Women Bus. Ownership Council Ga., Nat. Brenau Coll. Alumni Assn. (pres. 1968-70), Toccoa-Stephens County C. of C. (pres. 1982), Ga. State

C. of C., DAR, UDC. Democrat. Clubs: Toccoa Cotillion (pres. 1980-82), Toccoa Country and Golf (v.p. 1979-81), Toccoa Brenau (pres. 1967-70). Avocations: boating, swimming, horseback riding, bridge, tennis. Home: 441 North Blvd Toccoa GA 30577

HOBSON, ANNE GLEN, pharmacist; b. Lawrence, Mass., Apr. 11, 1925; d. William Harvey and Ina (Brown) Sparks; student Radcliffe Coll., 1942-43; B.A., Stanford U., 1946, M.A., 1947; postgrad. U. Houston, 1969-70; Ph.D., U. Tex., 1972, B.S. in Pharmacy, 1974; m. William C. Hobson, Jan. 9, 1960; children—Floyd, Bruce, Scott, William. Research asst. in preventive medicine U. Calif., San Francisco, 1947; research asso. in pharmacology Stanford Med. Sch., San Francisco, 1948; tchr. U.S. Army Dependents Sch., Manila, Philippines, 1949-51, Miss Harker's Sch., Palo Alto, Calif., 1951-53; med. lab. technician Palo Alto Clinic, 1953-54; tchr. Anglo-Am. Sch., Kifissia, Athens, Greece, 1954-56; chief lab. technician Dale County Hosp., Ozark, Ala., 1956-57; tchr. Bloomfield (N.J.) High Sch., 1957-58, Clark (N.J.) High Sch., 1958-59; asst. prof. Hellenika Anglaise Collegion, Athens, Greece, 1959-60; tchr. Molesworth AFB, Eng., 1960-61; asst. prof. Ashton Community Coll., Ashton-under-Lyne, Eng., 1961-62; tchr. Hartshead Sec. Sch., Ashton-under-Lyne, 1962-63, Droylsden (Eng.) Secondary Sch. for Girls, 1963-64; asst. coordinator Trenton Jr. 5 Exptl. Sch. program, for Disadvantaged, 1964-65; tchr. Trenton High Sch., 1965-66; research asso. Princeton (N.J.) U., 1966-67; tchr. Sam Rayburn High Sch., Pasadena, Tex., 1967-70; chief adult councilor Juvenile Drug Addiction, Pasadena, 1970-72; NSF grantee U. Tex., Austin, 1970-74; pharmacist, asst. mgr., mgr. Sommers Drug Stores, Austin, 1974-76; owner, pharmacist Hobson Pharmacy, Pflugerville, Tex., 1976—. Recipient Outstanding Alumna award U. Tex., 1977; registered pharmacist, Tex. Fellow Am. Coll. Apothecaries; mem. Am. Soc. Hosp. Pharmacists, Am. Pharm. Assn., Tex. Pharm. Assn., Capital Area Pharm. Assn., Am. Inst. History of Pharmacy (cert. of recognition 1973), Am. Tchrs. Assn., Tex. Tchrs. Assn., AAUW, Bus. and Profl. Women, Better Bus. Bur., Greater Pflugerville C. of C. (treas. 1985-86), Kappa Epsilon. Republican. Episcopalian. Clubs: Rainbow Girls, Am. Luth. Ch. Women's Assn. Contbr. articles to profl. jours; researcher in RH blood factor and leukemia, possible relationship with epilepsy, and mongolism, possible causal relationship between jaundice and hepatitis, others. Home: 18 Rowe Loop Pflugerville TX 78660 Office: 100 E Main St Pflugerville TX 78660

HOBSON, SHELLEY SMITH, television station executive; b. Greenville, S.C., Jan. 6, 1953; d. John Edwin and Elizabeth (Shelton) Smith; m. Walter Edmund Hobson, Apr. 30, 1983. B.A. in English, Furman U., 1974. Copywriter, Sta. WEZL, Charleston, S.C., 1975-77; copywriter, producer Sta. WCIV-TV, Charleston, 1977-79, promotion mgr., 1979-81; promotion mgr. Sta. WDSU-TV, New Orleans, 1981-84, dir. mktg., 1984—; mem. affiliate promotion com. NBC-TV, 1980-83, chmn., 1983-84. Bd. dirs. S.C. Lung Assn., Charleston, 1978-79; mem. mktg. com. New Orleans Symphony Orch., 1984-85. Recipient Addy awards, 1976-85. Mem. Broadcast Promotion and Mktg. Execs. Assn., Am. Women in Radio and TV. Republican. Presbyterian. Office: WDSU-TV 520 Royal St New Orleans LA 70130

HOCH, CORINNE MCLAURIN, telecommunications director; b. Dillon, S.C., Oct. 12, 1951; d. Daniel Lauchlan and Corinne Horne (Pate) McLaurin; m. Gregory Charles Hoch, Mar. 24, 1979; children—Daniel Lauchlan, Laurin Jennings. B.A. in Art History, Salem Coll., 1973; B.A. in Art Edn., U. N.C.-Boone, 1974. Asst. v.p. Citibank, N.Y.C., 1975-86; asst. dir. telecommunications Columbia U., N.Y.C., 1986—. Mem. Communications Mgrs. Assn., UDC (pres. James Henry Parker chpt. 1984—). Club: 200 (corr. sec. 1983-84). Home: 27 Glenridge Pkwy Montclair NJ 07042 Office: Columbia U 116th St and Broadway New York NY

HOCH, SUSAN CORRINNE, administrator; b. Hagerstown, Md., Apr. 19, 1949; d. Llewellyn Tom and Sybil (Brisentine) Coble; m. Richard M. Hoch (div.); 1 child, Karen. B.S., U. Md., 1972, postgrad., 1977-78. Owner/operator acctg. service, Silver Spring, Md., 1973-78; asst. controller Holiday Inn, Bethesda, Md., 1979-80; controller Internat. Personnel Mgmt. Assn., Washington, 1981-84; dir. fin. and adminstrn. Outdoor Power Equipment Inst., Washington, 1984—; producer/dir. Montgomery Community TV, Rockville, Md., 1986. Mem. Am. Soc. Assn. Execs., Greater Washington Soc. Assn. Execs., Am. Entrepreneurs Assn., ASAE Fin. Roundtable, Nat. Assn. Female Execs. Home: 16 Noblewood Ct Gaithersburg MD 20878 Office: Outdoor Power Equipment Inst 1901 L St NW Suite 700 Washington DC 20036

HOCHADEL, MARY EVELYN, real estate broker; b. Irvine, Ky., Feb. 12, 1929; d. Arthur and Martha (Johnston) Mansfield; m. Charles Bernard Hochadel, May 5, 1967; children by previous marriage—Stephen Tolliver, Myra Lou Tolliver, Keith Tolliver. Student Ind. Bus. Coll., 1965, St. Petersburg Jr. Coll., 1970. Mgr. telephone sales Sears Roebuck & Co., Muncie, Ind., 1956-58; with The Crisp Co., St. Petersburg, Fla., 1971-80; pres., broker Americana Properties, Inc., St. Petersburg, 1980—, chmn., gen. mgr., 1980—; sec. Century 21, Investment Soc., Fla., 1984-85. Newspaper columnist Pinellas County Rev., 1984. Mem. Small Bus. Council Ambassadors, St. Petersburg, 1982-85; mem. Pinellas County Com. of 100, 1982-85; mem. com. Zoning/Annexation, Cultural-Established Industries, Inc., 1985. Recipient Golden Dozen, Century 21, South Fla. Region, 1984, Top of the Century award, 1984. Mem. Nat. Assn. Realtors, Nat. Assn. Women Realtors, Fla. Assn. Realtors, Women Bus. Owners Network, St. Petersburg Bd. Realtors, The Century 21 Broker Roundtable. Club: Bardmoor Country. Avocations: writing; golfing. Home: 3888 Shore Acres Blvd NE Saint Petersburg FL 33703 Office: Century 21 Americana Properties Inc 5455 4th St N Saint Petersburg FL 33703

HOCHHEIMER, LAURA, musician; b. Worms, Germany, Apr. 18, 1933; came to U.S., 1938, naturalized, 1947; d. Otto and Trude Hochheimer; student Beaver Coll., 1951-52; B.M., Eastman Sch. Music, 1955; M.F.A., Ohio U., 1957; Ph.D., Ind. U., 1966. Tchr. strings and vocal music, conductor Bainbridge (N.Y.) High Sch., Jr. High Sch. Orchs., Bainbridge Elem. and Bainbridge High Sch., 1957-58; tchr. gen. music Chgo. Public Schs., tchr. mentally retarded and physically handicapped children Spalding Sch. for Handicapped Children, 1958-64; mem. Chgo. Chamber Orch., Northwestern U. Chamber Orch., Roosevelt U. Symphony, 1958-64; grad. asst. in violin Ind. U., Bloomington, tchr. strings and orch. Ind. U. Lab. Sch., 1964-66; tchr. music West Liberty (W.Va.) State Coll., 1968-70; vis. asst. prof. music U. B.C., Vancouver, 1970-71; tchr. music edn. Towson State Coll., 1971-73; asst. prof. music edn. U. Cin., 1973-76; asso. prof. music James Madison U., Harrisonburg, Va., 1976-81; asst. prof. music edn. Cin. Coll. Conservatory Music, mem. grad. faculty U. Cin., 1973-76; asso. prof. music Clemson (S.C.) U., 1981—; violinist Greenville Symphony Orch., 1984—; violinist solo, chamber music and symphony orchs; cons. music in spl. edn. Orff-Schulwerk and Kodaly approaches in schs. and state convs. throughout U.S. and Can. Recipient George Eastman award Eastman Sch. Music, 1955; Fulbright scholar, Vienna and Salzburg, Austria, 1966-67. Mem. Music Educators Nat. Conf., Am. Orff Schulwerk Assn., Coll. Music Soc., S.C. Music Educators Assn. Author: A Sequential Sourcebook for Elementary School Music, 1980; contbr. articles in field to profl. jours. Office: Strode Tower Box 48 Clemson U Clemson SC 29634

HOCHRON, BERYL JUDITH, marketing research consultant; b. N.Y.C., Jan. 2, 1947; d. Nathan and Marion (Freedman) Sadowsky; m. Joel Hochron, Jan. 2, 1981; 1 child, Matthew Noah. B.B.A. cum laude, CCNY, 1968; M.B.A., Baruch Coll., 1972. Staff acct. Haskins & Sells, N.Y.C., 1963-65; grad. asst. Baruch Coll., 1968-69; project dir. Batten, Barton, Durstine & Osborn Advt., N.Y.C., 1969-71; sr. project dir. AHF Mktg. Research Co., N.Y.C., 1971-74; mgr. RCA, N.Y.C., 1974-76; sr. research mgr. Clairol Inc., N.Y.C., 1976-83; group mgr. Lever Bros., N.Y.C., 1983-85. Mem. Am. Mktg. Assn. (asst. sec. N.Y. chpt. 1980-81, sec. 1981-82), Nat. Assn. Female Execs. Home: Union Valley Mahopac NY 10541 Office: 310 E 74th St New York NY 10021

HOCHSCHILD, CARROLL SHEPHERD, company administrator, educator; b. Whittier, Calif., Mar. 31, 1935; d. Vernon Vero and Effie Corinne (Hollingsworth) Shepherd; m. Richard Hochschild, July 25, 1959; children—Christopher Paul, Stephen Shepherd. B.A. in Internat. Relations, Pomona Coll., 1956; Teaching credential U. Calif.-Berkeley, 1957; M.B.A., Pepperdine U., 1985. Cert. elem. tchr., Calif. Elem. tchr. Oakland Pub. Schs. (Calif.), 1957-58, San Lorenzo Pub. Schs. (Calif.), 1958-59, Huntington Beach Pub. Schs. (Calif.), 1961-63, 67-68; adminstrv. asst. Microwave Instruments, Corona del Mar, Calif., 1968-74; co-owner Hoch Co., Corona del Mar, 1978—. Rep. Calif. Tchrs. Assn., Huntington Beach, 1962-63. Mem. AAUW, Nat. Assn. Female Execs. Republican. Presbyterian. Clubs: Toastmistress (corr. sec. 1983), Jr. Ebell (fine arts chmn. Newport Beach 1966-67).

HOCHSTADT, JOY, biochemist, microbiologist; b. N.Y.C., May 6, 1939; d. Julius Louis and Edith (Tabatchnick) Hochstadt; A.B., Barnard Coll., 1960; A.M. in Biol. Scis., Stanford U., 1963; Ph.D. in Microbiology, Georgetown U., 1969; m. Harvey L. Ozer, Feb. 3, 1960; 1 dau., Juliane Natasha Hochstadt-Ozer. Research fellow in devel. biochemistry Stanford U., 1961-62; instr. biology Coll. San Mateo (Calif) 1963; vis. fellow Karolinska Inst., Stockholm, Sweden, 1964-65; research fellow in biol. chemistry Harvard U., 1965-66; teaching asst. in microbiology Georgetown Med. Sch., 1967-68; NIH, USPHS postdoctoral fellow Nat. Heart and Lung Inst., Bethesda, Md., 1968-70; Am. Heart Assn. established investigator, 1970-75; sr. scientist Worcester Found. Exptl. Biology, Shrewsbury, Mass., 1972-76; research prof. N.Y. Med. Coll., Valhalla, 1977-81; dir. div. clin. biochemistry, dir. cell genetics research lab. Cath. Med. Center, Woodhaven, N.Y., 1981—; vis. scholar dept. biol. sci. Columbia U., 1984—; USPHS spl. trainee Cold Spring Harbor Lab., 1973; adj. prof. biochemistry Central New Eng. Colls., 1974-75; vis. prof. Weizmann Inst. Sci., Israel, 1976, U. R.I., 1976-77; dir. N.Y. Eldorado, 300 CPW Apts. Corp.; lectr., convener nat. sci. symposia, workshops, confs.; prin. investigator several research grants NIH, NSF; mem. postdoctoral fellowship evaluation panel NSF; mem. cell biology study sect., biomed. scis. rev. com. NIH; chmn. com. to distribute and administer instl. award Am. Cancer Soc., 1973-74. Mem. alumnae council Barnard Coll. Fellow Am. Acad. Microbiology, Am. Inst. Chemists (profl. opportunities com., legis. com.); mem. Am. Heart Assn. (basic sci. council 1970—), Am. Soc. Microbiology (com. on status of women 1970-73, sec. physiology div. 1972-74, nominating com. metabolism and physiology div. 1973—, internat. travel award), Genetics Soc. Am., Am. Soc. Biology Chemists, AAAS, Fedn. Am. Scientists, Am. Assn. Cancer Researchers, Assn. Women in Sci. (affirmative action rep. 1973-75), Profl. Women's Caucus (nat. policy com. 1970-73), N.Y. Acad. Scis., Harvey Soc., Am. Assn. Clin. Scientists, Am. Assn. Clin. Chemists. Contbr. research articles to profl. lit. Mem. editorial bd. Jour. Bacteriology, 1975-80. Discovered that penicillinase is involved in bacterial cell wall metabolism (differentiation to spore-wall in bacillus); elucidated mechanisms of utilization of several purines and pyrimidines in bacteria and animal cells; developed first cell-free vesicle system permitting study of nutrient transport across membranes isolated from mammalian cells in culture; identified that transport changes with growth, quiescence and reactivation involve membrane alterations. Home: 300 Central Park W New York NY 10024 Office: Cell Genetics Research Lab CMC St Anthony's Hosp Woodhaven NY 11421

HOCKETT, SHERI LYNN, radiologist; b. Cleburne, Tex., Apr. 20, 1953; d. Dale and Rosamond (Prater) Hockett; B.A., So. Meth. U., 1974; M.D., Southwestern Med. Sch., 1978; m. David Alexander Campbell, Apr. 22, 1978; children—Courtney Michelle, Jonathan David. Resident diagnostic radiology St. Paul Hosp., Dallas, 1978-81, chief resident, 1980-81; fellow, 198-82; staff radiologist Meml. Hosp. of Garland (Tex.), and Garland Community Hosp. Diplomate Am. Bd. Radiology. Mem. Am. Assn. Women Radiologists, Am. Coll. Radiology, Radiol. Soc. N.Am., Tex. Radiol. Soc., AMA, Dalls-Ft. Worth Radiol. Soc. Office: 2300 Marie Curie Dr Garland TX 75042

HODES, BARBARA, orgn. cons.; b. Chgo., Nov. 30, 1941; d. David and Tybe Zisook; B.S., Northwestern U., 1962; m. Scott Hodes, Dec. 19, 1961 (div. 1977); children—Brian, Valery; m. A. Bruce Schimberg, Dec. 29, 1984. Partner Just Causes, cons. not-for-profit orgns., Chgo., 1978—; Chgo. cons. Population Resource Center, 1978-82. Woman's bd. dirs. Mus. Contemporary Art; bd. dirs., vice chmn. Med. Research Inst. Council, Michael Reese Med. Center; bd. dirs., chmn. Midwest Women's Center; trustee Francis W. Parker Sch. Office: Just Causes 1405 N Dearborn Pkwy Chicago IL 60610

HODGE, ALICE MACNAUGHTON, retail advertising executive; b. Honolulu, Feb. 11, 1953; d. Malcolm and Winifred (Sperry) MacNaughton; A.B., Stanford U., 1975; postgrad. Foothill Coll., 1975, Golden Gate U., 1981; m. James Blythe Hodge, Jan. 3, 1981; stepchildren—Eric, Terra. With Emporium Capwell Co., San Francisco, 1975—, spl. events, public relations dir., 1979-81, broadcast advt. dir., 1981-86, dir. sales promotion mktg. and fin., 1986—. Mem. public relations com. Vol. Bur., San Francisco, 1980-83; mem. spl. events adv. com. Asso. Merchandising Corp., N.Y.C., 1978-81; area co-chmn. San Francisco chpt. Stanford Ann. Fund, 1975—; pres. jr. women's com. San Francisco Symphony, 1985-86; trustee Sacred Heart Schs., Menlo Park, Calif., 1986—. Mem. San Francisco Jr. League, Stanford Assocs. Republican. Episcopalian. Contbr. articles to profl. publs. Home: 2940 Lake St San Francisco CA 94121 Office: 835 Market St San Francisco CA 94103

HODGE, ANN FOREST, industrial company executive; b. Los Angeles, Aug. 17, 1949; d. Harry Carl and Violet (Howard) Calhoun; m. Thomas Michael Sanders (div. Feb. 1971); 1 child, Richard Dean; m. Robert David Hodge, May 15, 1982. B.A., UCLA, 1976. Legal adminstr. Cossack & Artz, Los Angeles, 1972-80; paralegal Mantt, Phelps, Rothenberg & Tunney, Los Angeles, 1980-82; tech. writer Galler Assocs., Houston, 1982-83; paralegal Mayor, Day & Caldwell, Houston, 1983-85; dir. govt. affairs Browning-Ferris Industries, Houston, 1985—; cons. non-profit groups, Houston, 1984—. Contbr. articles to profl. jours. Mem. Pub. Affairs Council, Pub. Affairs Roundtable, Tex. Assn. Bus., La. Assn. Bus. and Industry, Houston C. of C. Club: Forum. Lodge: Jobs Daughters (honored queen 1966-67). Avocations: reading; politics. Office: Browning Ferris Industries 14701 St Mary's Houston TX 77079

HODGE, DEANNA DEE, radio station executive; b. Ortonville, Minn., Nov. 20, 1939; d. August and Carrie Amanda (Monson) Witte; m. Don V. Versaevel; children—Jan, Jodi, Jill; m. Weldon Dean Hodge, Jan. 18, 1973. Ad layout Reminder, Montevideo, Minn., 1957-59; sec. Sta. KDMA, Montevideo, 1959-74, salesman, 1974-79, sales mgr., 1979-82, mgr., 1982—. Mem. Montevideo Police Res.; active Am. Cancer Soc., Montevideo, 1983; co-ambassador Fiesta, Inc., 1984, v.p., 1985; chmn. evangelism United Meth. Ch., Montevideo, 1985. Mem. C. of C. (chmn. adms. 1983-85), Montevideo Bus. and Profl. Women (2d v.p. 1985). Office: KDMA PO Box 738 Montevideo MN 56265

HODGE, DEBORAH ANN, nurse; b. Hamilton AFB, Calif., Feb. 19, 1953; d. Robert Rex and Wilhelmina Fredonia (Schindell) Walker; m. Ray Allen Hodge, May 27, 1985. Assoc. Applied Sci., Odessa Jr. Coll., 1972; student Tex. Tech U., 1973-74; nurse specialist Methodist Hosp., 1976. R.N., Tex. Staff nurse Baylor Med. Ctr., Dallas, 1972-73; staff nurse Meth. Hosp., Lubbock, Tex., 1973-75, cardiovascular nurse specialist, Houston, 1975-77; cardiovascular nurse specialist W.R. Gaston, MD, Houston, 1977-81; cardiovascular nurse specialist Baylor Coll. Medicine, Houston, 1981-85, adminstrv. asst., 1982-85; research nurse Baylor Coll. Medicine, Houston, 1985—. Mem. Am. Assn. Critical Care Nurses. Democrat. Baptist. Lodge: Order Eastern Star (Star Point 1980-81). Home: 1203 Bingle St Houston TX 77055 Office: Meth Hosp Clinical Research Center Houston TX 77030

HODGE, DORIS JEAN, educator; b. Chattanooga; d. Herman Van Buren and Motis Senetta (Hester) Davis; B.S., Wayne State U., 1965, Ed.D., 1980; M.A., U. Mich., 1971; 1 dau., Angela Karen. Reading coordinator Murray Wright, Detroit Public Schs., 1971-77; reading cons. Detroit Coll. Opportunities Program, U. Detroit, 1972-75; research asst. Office Research, Evaluation and Planning, Detroit Public Schs., 1977—, now evaluator ednl. programs. Pres., Episcopal Ch. Women of Grace Ch., 1980—; active Greater Opportunities Industrialization Centers voter registration drive, 1980; rec. sec. bd. govs. Wayne State U. Coll. Edn.; campaign worker local polit. campaign; participant Tng. Urban Educators for Linking Agt. Roles project Nat. Inst. Edn., 1980-81. Recipient Spirit of Detroit award, 1980. Mem. Am. Edn. Research Assn., Internat. Reading Assn., Assn. Sch. Curriculum Devel., Detroit Assn. Univ. Mich. Women, Mich. Alliance Black Sch. Educators, Mich. Council Tchrs. of English, Mich. Edn. Research Assn., Nat. Alliance Black Sch. Educators, Detroit Women Sch. Adminstrs., U. Mich. Alumni, Wayne State U. Coll. Edn. Alumni (bd. govs. 1981—), Alpha Kappa Alpha, Eta Phi Beta, Phi Delta Kappa. Democrat. Club: Jim Dandy Ski. Home: 1913 Hyde Park Dr Detroit MI 48207 Office: 5035 Woodward Detroit MI 48202

HODGE, MARY HARRISON, county official; b. Morristown, Tenn., Mar. 27, 1918; d. Baldwin Harle and Julia Elizabeth (Skeen) Harrison; m. Hubert leach Hodge Aug. 28, 1945 (dec. 1975); children—Nancy Elizabeth Hodge McGuire, Susan Janet Hodge Greene, Mary Hugh, Ruthelen. Student Morristown Sch. of Bus., 1977. Clk. and bookkeeper Dick's 5 & 10, Morristown, 1937-43; elementary tchr. Hamblen county, Tenn., 1943-45; bookkeeper and gen. office worker So. Furniture, Morristown, 1945-47; West Elem. Sch., Morristown, 1966-67; dep. clk. Register of Deeds, Morristown, 1960-66; bookkeeper and computer operator Bob Bales Ford, Morristown, 1967-76; register of deeds Hamblen County, 1978— (first woman elected to county-wide office in Hamblen County). Active Hamblen County Women's Democratic Club, First Bapt. Ch. Mem. Woman's Missionary Union. Home: 540 N Jackson St Morristown TN 37814 Office: Register of Deeds 511 W 2d N Morristown TN 37814

HODGE, MARY JO, health service administrator; b. Talladega, Ala., June 15, 1935; d. John Bowling and Martha Allene (Royal) McKinney; B.S., Auburn U., 1956; M.S. (fellow), U. Miss., 1958; D.Pub. Adminstrn., N.Y. U., 1978; m. Charles Cedric Hodge, Aug. 6, 1955; children—Donna, Holly. Psychometrist, Student Guidance Center, Auburn U., 1956-58; psychologist McGuffey Reading Clinic U. Va., Charlottesville, 1962-64, U. Va. Hosp., 1964-65; psychologist St. Lawrence Psychiat. Center, Ogdensburg, N.Y., 1966-73, mental hygiene treatment team leader, 1973-78; dir. Instn. Edn. and Tng., Gowanda Psychiat. Center, Helmuth, N.Y., 1978, dir. treatment services, 1979-81, dir. community services, 1981—. Bd. dirs. N.Y. Regional Geriatric Ctr., 1983-85. Mem. Am., Eastern psychol. assns., Gerontol. Soc. Am., Northeastern Gerontol. Soc., Acad. Polit. Sci., Assn. Mental Health Adminstrs. (treas. N.Y. chpt. 1985—), Am. Soc. Pub. Adminstrn., Assn. for Rural Mental Health, Kappa Delta Pi, Chi Delta Phi, Pi Tau Chi. Home: PO Box 234 Helmuth NY 14079 Office: Gowanda Psychiat Center Helmuth NY 14079

HODGE, SONIA, physician; b. Ponce, P.R., June 16, 1951; d. Vicente Rodriguez and Nieves Perez; m. Frank Lewis Hodge, Sept. 2, 1983. B.S., U.P.R., 1973; M.D., Nat. U. Pedro H. Urena, 1979. Intern, Damas Hosp., Ponce, 1979-80; gen. practitioner Juana Diaz Health Ctr., 1980-81; intern pediatrics Georgetown U. Hosp., Washington, 1981-82, resident in pediatrics, 1982-83; sr. resident in pediatrics Jackson Meml. Hosp., Miami, Fla., 1983-84; practice medicine specializing in pediatrics, Miami, 1984—; mem. staff Miami Children's Hosp., Broward Gen. Med. Ctr. Jr. fellow Am. Acad. Pediatrics; mem. AMA, Nat. Assn. Residents and Interns, Nat. Assn. Profl. Women, Fla. Med. Assn., Dade County Med. Assn. Republican. Roman Catholic. Avocations: reading; traveling; bicycle riding. Home: 2025 Brickell Ave Apt 1804 Miami FL 33129

HODGES, KAREN BEE, lawyer; b. Houston, Jan. 9, 1948; d. W. H. and Joyce Christine (McElveen) H. B.A., U. Tex.-Austin, 1969, Tchg. Cert., 1972; J.D., Tex. Tech. U., 1980. Speech pathologist Del Valle Ind. Sch. Dist., Austin, Tex., 1972-78; sole practice, Lubbock, Tex., 1981—. Bd. dirs. Women's Protective Services, Lubbock, 1982—, Women's Advocacy Project, Austin, 1983; del. Tex. State Dem. Conv., 1982, 84, 86; bd. dirs. E. Lubbock Neighborhood Assn., 1983; chancellor to vestry St. Stephen's Episcopal Ch., 1983-84; mem. steering com. Lubbock Catholic Worker Pilgrim House. Mem. State Bar of Tex., ABA. Democrat. Office: Law Office of Karen B Hodges 1515 13th St Lubbock TX 79401

HODGES, LAURA CLARK, lawyer; b. Munich, W.Ger., Sept. 19, 1957 (parents Am. citizens); d. George Atkinson Hodges, Jr. and Lynn (McMath) Hodges Dickey. B.A., Wellesley Coll., 1978; J.D., Harvard U., 1982. Bar: Mass. 1982. Litigation asst. Palmer & Dodge, Boston, 1977-79; assoc. firm Goodwin Procter & Hoar, Boston, 1982—. Mem. ABA, Mass. Bar Assn. Republican. Office: Goodwin Procter & Hoar 28 State St Boston MA 02109

HODGES, MARGARET ANN, television editor, newspaper columnist; b. McCamey, Tex., Sept. 7, 1928; d. Ernest Cornelius and Margaret Isabel (Wood) Haynes; m. Cecil Ray Hodges, July 2, 1954 (div. Nov. 1974); children—Craig McNeley, Elizabeth Ann. B.J., U. Tex., 1948. Reporter, Houston Chronicle, 1948-51; society editor The News, Mexico City, 1951-52; reporter Houston Chronicle, 1952-54, TV editor, columnist, 1962—; radio critic Sta. KIKK, Houston, 1981—. Mem. Critics Consensus (dir. 1965-75), TV Critics Assn. (founder, exec. bd., v.p., pres.). Club: Houston Press (pres. 1967-68). Office: Houston Chronicle Texas and Travis Sts Houston TX 77002

HODGETTS, VITALIA ESTEL, artist; b. Bronx, N.Y., Dec. 30; d. Victor Manuel and Maria Mercedes (Miura) Matamala; m. William Thomas Hodgetts, May 27, 1961; children—William Thomas, Jr., Robert Anthony. Art cert. Art Students League of N.Y., 1975-77; B.A., Montclair State Coll., N.J., 1979. One-Woman shows include Korby Gallery, Cedar Grove, N.J., AT&T World Hdqrs., Basking Ridge, N.J., 1981, Brandeis U., 1983; exhibited in group shows at Audubon Artists, 1973-83, State Mus., Trenton, N.J., Lever House, N.Y. exhibited in travelling exhibits Jesse Becker Mus., Alpena, Mich., Am. Cultural Ctr., Tel Aviv, Aknaten Gallery, Cairo. Recipient numerous awards for art; Ford Found. grantee, Art Students League of N.Y., 1975-78. Mem. West-Essex Art Assn. (pres. 1975-77), N.W. Essex Arts Council (bd. trustees 1978-80), Nat. Assn. Women Artists (fin. dir. 1981-83), Women's Caucus on Art, Artist Equity N.J., Audubon Artists. Avocation: photography. Home and Office: 469 Fairview Ave Cedar Grove NJ 07009

HODGKINS, SARA WILSON, former state official; b. Granite Falls, N.C., Nov. 25, 1930; d. Martin Morehead and Doris (Parker) Wilson; m. Norris L. Hodgkins, Jr., June 27, 1953; children—Caroline Eddy, Celeste, Grace. B.S. in Music Edn., Appalachian Coll., 1952. Music specialist Moore County Schs., Southern Pines, N.C., 1953-76; sec. N.C. Dept. Cultural Resources, Raleigh, 1977-84. Vice chmn. N.C. Arts Council, Raleigh, 1971-73; pres. N.C. Symphony Soc., Raleigh, 1972-74; mem. adv. bd. Duke Hosp., Durham, N.C., 1979-83; trustee N.C. Sch. of Arts, Winston-Salem; mem. Southern Pines Town Council, 1975-77. Democrat. Presbyterian. Office: 915 E Indiana Ave Southern Pines NC 28387

HODGKINSON, LOTTIE MAY, insurance company executive; b. Denison, Tex., Sept. 9, 1939; d. William V. and Jessie Lou (Dilbeck) Jones; m. Clinton S. Hodgkinson (div. Oct. 1982); children—Kathryn Lynn Hodgkinson Knagg, Kyle Stewart. Student So. Meth. U. Sec., Maxson Mahoney Turner Ins., Dallas, 1969-71; with Lundberg Pool, Dallas, 1971—, v.p., 1978-80, exec. v.p., 1980—; pres. LP Premium Funding, Dallas, 1980—; pres. Charter Gen. Agy., Dallas, 1983—. Mem. Fedn. Ins. Women Tex. (pres. 1982-83). Republican. Methodist.

HODGSON, AURORA SAULO, food scientist; b. Manila, Philippines, Feb. 24, 1950; came to U.S., 1973, naturalized, 1982; d. Serafin Bumanlag and Natividad David (Alfonso) Saulo; m. Laban Richard Hodgson, 1982. B.S. cum laude in Chemistry, Coll. of the Holy Spirit, Philippines, 1971; M.S. in Chemistry, U. Mass., 1977, Ph.D. in Food Sci., 1978. Flavor chemist, food processing engr. United Brands Corp. Research and Devel.-Quality Control Labs., Newton, Mass., 1978-81; food technologist/sr. food technologist Beatrice Cos., Fullerton, Calif., 1982-84; tech. advisor Orchards Hawaii, Ltd., 1985; food processing cons., 1985—; extension specialist in food tech. U. Hawaii at Manoa, 1985—. Sec., Christian Life Community, Manila, 1968-69, pres., 1969-70. Fulbright Hays scholar, 1973. Mem. Inst. Food Technologists, Am. Chem. Soc. Contbr. in field.

HODINKA, NANCY ELIZABETH, microbiologist; b. Yonkers, N.Y., July 1, 1953; d. Zoltan and Anna Elizabeth (Aitken) H. B.S., Pa. State U., 1974; M.S., L.I. U., 1977. Technologist, Analytab Products, Plainview, N.Y., 1976-78, lab supr., 1978-81; dir. research and devel. lab. IDS Inc., Atlanta, 1981-83, v.p. ops., 1981-83, v.p., co-owner, 1986—. Mem. Am. Soc. Microbiology, Soc. Indsl. Microbiology, Southeastern Assn. Clin. Microbiology, Internat. Fedn. Culture collections, NOW. Lodge: Order Eastern Star (assoc. matron 1982-83). Avocations: Piano; flute; skiing; needlework; dance. Home: 1150 Rankin St Apt A10 Stone Mountain GA 30083 Office: IDS Inc 3404 Oakcliff Rd C-1 Atlanta GA 30340

HODNETT, BARBARA MILTON, educatioinal counselor; b. Mobile, Ala., Mar. 31, 1942; d. Samuel and Mary Alice (Williams) Milton; student Dillard U., 1960-62; B.A., U. S.Ala., 1974; M.A. (Tchr. Corps fellow), Oakland U., 1976; m. Robert O. Hodnett, Sept. 2, 1967; 1 dau., Maki Danielle. Psychologist asst. Ala. Dept. Mental Health, Searcy Hosp., 1969-72; correctional counselor, Ala. Dept. Corrections, 1974; tchr. Clark County Sch. Dist., Las Vegas, 1976-78, elem. sch. counselor, 1978-81, 81—, participant spl. edn. conf. on parent involvement, 1981, chmn. ethnic adv. com., 1981—; parole and probation officer State of Nev., 1981; spl. edn. and learning disability tchr. high sch., 1983—; participant profl. confs. Mem. youth affairs com. NAACP; trustee Temporary Assistance for Domestic Crisis, 1984-85. Recipient Clark County Classroom Tchrs. Assn. service award, 1978, Excellence in Edn. award Clark County Sch. Dist., 1986. Mem. Am. Personnel and Guidance Assn., Nev. Personnel and Guidance Assn., Clark County Sch. Counselors Assn., Delta Sigma Theta. Methodist. Home: 4450 Buena Vista Las Vegas NV 89102 Office: 4291 W Penwood St Las Vegas NV 89102

HODNETT, ERNESTINE, personnel management specialist, reservist; b. Virginia Beach, Va., Feb. 1, 1949; d. David and Mary Elizabeth (Scott) H. B.S. in Bus. Adminstrn., Norfolk State U., 1978; postgrad. Valdosta State Coll., 1985—. Acctg. technician, Navy Pub. Works Ctr., Norfolk, 1967-78; personnel mgmt. specialist Naval Air Rework Facility, Norfolk, 1978-80, personnel staffing specialist, 1980-83, employee relations specialist, 1982-84; employee relations specialist Naval Submarine Base, Kings Bay, Ga., 1984-85, personnel mgmt. specialist, 1985—. Bd. dirs. United Way, Camden County, Ga., 1985. Mem. Black Profl. Women Club Inc. (chairperson scholarship com. 1983-84), Soc. Labor Relations Profls., Federally Employed Women, Personnel Mgmt. Soc., Phi Delta Kappa, NAACP. Democrat. Avocations: reading; golf; aerobics; camping. Home: 401 S Arizona St Kingsland GA 31548 Office: Naval Submarine Base Civilian Personnel N126 Kings Bay GA 31547

HODSON, BETH ANN, diversified manufacturing company executive; b. Muncie, Ind., Oct. 7, 1953; d. Ivan Ellis and Ruby Eleanora (Rhoades) H. Student Ball State U. Dance instr. Eleanor Coles Dance Studio, Muncie, Ind., 1969-76; supply clk. Marsha Supermarkets, Inc., Yorktown, Ind., 1972, offset press operator, 1972-77; tap dance instr. Gale Kim's Dance Studio, Muncie, 1977-80; graphic stripper-platemaker Ball Corp., Muncie, Ind., 1977-79, supr. reprographic services, 1979-80, supr. office services, 1980-84, mgr. office services, 1984—; bd. dirs. Ball Employees Credit Union, 1985—; mem. Ball Human Resource Devel. Team, 1980-84, team leader, 1983. Vol. Ind. Renaissance Fair, 1984; judge regional mktg. v.p. Jr. Achievement, 1984; actress, choreographer, costume coordinator, asst. dir., bd. dirs. Muncie Civic Theatre, 1984-85; vol. Salvation Army, 1979—; corp. vol. United Way Campaign, 1971—, grocery supplier team capt., 1983-85; judge printing contest Vocat. Indsl. Clubs Am. 1978, 82, 84; go-getter co-chmn. WIPB Telesale, 1983; chmn. 473 Postal Customer Council, 1982-84, bd. dirs., 1984—; program chmn. Am. Cancer Soc., 1985. Recipient Printing awards Ball Corp., 1979—, awards of merit Ball Corp., 1983, 85, Exceptional Achievement awards Ball Corp., 1982, 84, Gold award Ball Corp., 1984, Disting. Achievement award Ball Corp., 1984; certificates of Appreciation, Union City Kiwanis Club, 1983, Muncie Clean City, 1983, Channel 49's Telesale, 1983, Ind. Renaissance Fair, 1984, Women of Achievement award East Central Ind. profl. chpt. Women in Communications, Inc., 1985; named Outstanding Young Women in Am., 1983. Mem. In-Plant Printing Mgmt. Assn. (communicator mem. 1980—, exemplary mem. 1981—, pres. 1985—, mem. of yr. 1985), Advt. Club Muncie (bd. dirs. 1982-85), Muncie-Delaware County C. of C., Acad. Community Leadership. Club: Riley Jones Women's. Lodge: Elks. Avocations: bowling; dancing; snow skiing; tennis; golf; body building. Home: 1904 Duane Rd Muncie IN 47304 Office: Ball Corp 345 S High St Muncie IN 47305

HODSON, JAN CUNNINGHAM, university administrator; b. Athens, Ohio, Dec. 1, 1951; d. John Kientz and Donna Eileen (King) Cunningham; B. Interior Design, Ohio U., 1973; postgrad. Capital U., 1976-77; m. Thomas Scott Hodson. Paralegal, Lavelle & Yanity Law Firm, Athens, 1977-78, Yanity, DeVeau & Weisenberger, Athens, 1978-79, dir. planned giving Ohio U., 1979—. Mem. exec. com., treas. Athens County Democratic party; bd. dirs. Athens Met. Housing Authority. Mem. Council Advancement and Support of Edn., Athens LWV, Athens County Humane Soc. Office: 201 McGuffey Hall Ohio U Athens OH 45701

HOEFT, THEA MARIE, therapist, educator; b. Milw., Feb. 9, 1950; d. Peter Kazin and Renatte Katherine (Kaniewski) Zidonowitz. B.S. in Recreation, U. Wis.-LaCrosse, 1972; M.S. in Leisure Studies, U. Utah, 1973; Ed.D., Va. Poly. Tech. Inst. and State U., 1979. Playground dir. Watertown (Wis.) Dept. Parks and Recreation, 1969; dir. Bluffview playground LaCrosse Dept. Parks and Recreation, 1970; instr. Ind. State U., Terre Haute, 1973-74; day camp dir. Vigo County Extension Service, Terre Haute, Ind., 1974; instr. Radford (Va.) U., 1974-75; phys. edn. tchr. St. Patrick Cathedral Sch., Harrisburg, Pa., 1975; receptionist crisis worker Holy Spirit Hosp. Community Mental Health Center, Camphill, Pa., 1975; adj. faculty U. So. Miss., Hattiesburg, 1976; master recreational therapist Ellisville (Miss.) State Sch. for Mentally Ill and Retarded, 1976; instr. Radford U., 1976-77; mental retardation profl. Hearthside Rehab. Center, Brown Deer, Wis., 1979; asst. prof., coordinator therapeutic recreation curriculum Ariz. State U., Tempe, 1979-83; master therapist Mt. Sinai Med. Ctr. Geriatric Inst. Alzheimer Disease Day Hosp./Phys. Rehab. Hosp., Milw., 1983-84; asst. dir. evening coll. and extension programs Milw. Sch. Engring., 1985—; cons. 4-H, 1976, Crippled Children's Hosp., Va., 1978, others. Mem. Miss. Com. Spl. Olympics, 1976; rep. United Way Ariz., 1979; mem. Mayor's Adv. Drug Com., 1972; bd. dirs. Youth Treatment and Evaluation Center, Phoenix, 1979-82; mem. Phoenix spl. populations adv. council on recreation, 1980-82; vol. Phoenix Panhellenic Council, 1982; mem. Ariz. State U. Centennial Com., 1981-83, chairperson disabled students services adv. bd., 1981-83. Wis. Leadership grantee, 1968; recipient Disting. Service award Montgomery County Cardiac Therapy Center, 1979, United Way, 1980, Recreation Com. U. Wis., LaCrosse, 1971, 72; H. Roe Bartle Recruiting award, 1981. Mem. Am. Camping Assn., Ariz. Parks and Recreation Assn., Va. Parks and Recreation Assn., Nat. Recreation and Park Assn., Am. Assn. Adult and Continuing Edn., AAHPER and Dance (editorial bd.), Nat. Leadership Inst., Phi Delta Kappa, Sigma Kappa Sigma, Sigma Lambda Sigma, Gamma Sigma Sigma. Republican. Catholic. Contbr. articles to profl. jours. Home: 3279 N Cramer St Milwaukee WI 53211 Office: 1025 N Milwaukee St Milwaukee WI 53201

HOELSCHER, MILDRED BEATRICE, chemical company executive; b. West Point, Miss., Oct. 1, 1935; d. Homer Dell and Virginia Nina (Jackson) Blankenship; m. Robert Earl Hoelscher, Dec. 3, 1954; children—Sharon, Rebecca, Carla, Robin, Robert, William. Pres., chief exec. officer Safety Sealants, Inc., (formerly M & H Conversion Co.), New Castle, Ind.; sec. bd. dirs. Gen. Adhesives, Inc., New Castle, 1985—. Republican. Methodist. Home: 410 Crescent Dr New Castle IN 47362 Office: Safety Sealants Inc 1800 Troy Ave New Castle IN 47362

HOELTERHOFF, MANUELA VALI, editor, writer; b. Hamburg, W.Ger., Apr. 6, 1949; came to U.S., 1958; d. Heinz Alfons Martin and Olga Christine (Goertz) H. B.A., Hofstra U., 1971; M.A., Inst. Fine Arts, NYU, 1973. Assoc. editor Acad. Ency., Princeton, N.J., 1977-78, Portfolio mag., N.Y.C., 1978-79; editor-in-chief Art & Auction mag., N.Y.C., 1979-81; arts editor Wall Street Jour., N.Y.C., 1981—. Recipient Pulitzer prize for criticism, 1983. Office: Wall Street Jour 22 Cortlandt St New York NY 10007

HOEN, SHEILA ELIZABETH FLEETWOOD, lawyer, oil and gas company executive; b. Victoria, B.C., Can., Sept. 8, 1935; came to U.S., 1969, naturalized, 1983; d. William Leslie and Winnifred M. (Thomas) Hardie; m. Ernest Leon Wilhelm B. Hoen, Sept. 14, 1957; children—Liza, Margot, Zarah. B.A., U. B.C., 1957; M.B.A., Calif. State U., 1975; J.D., Okla. City U., 1981. Bar: Okla. 1981, U.S. Dist. Ct. (we. dist.) Okla., 1981. Biomed. librarian U. B.C., Vancouver, Royal Victoria Hosp., Montreal, Que., Can., 1959-60; tchr. South Peace High Sch., Dawson Creek, B.C., 1958-59, Brit. Sch., Tripoli, Libya, 1962-66; asst. to exploration mgr., scout Occidental Pet-Corp., Tripoli, 1968-69, econ. asst., sr. petroleum economist, Bakersfield, Calif., 1970-73, 1974-75; fin. analyst, mgr. gas contracts Grace Petroleum Corp., Oklahoma City, 1975-78; law clk. oil and gas atty. Andrews, Davis et al, Oklahoma City, 1979-83; v.p. land, gen. counsel Hoen Exploration Co., Oklahoma City, 1983—; cons. Okla. Zool. Soc., Oklahoma City, 1983-85. Mem. Women's Com. for Symphony, Oklahoma City, 1983—; commr. Edmond Arts and Humanities Council, 1985—; pres. Concerned Citizens for Captiva, Inc., 1985—. Recipient Am. Jurisprudence award, Bancroft-Whitney, Lawyer's Coop. Pub. Co., 1979; Equal Rights Amendment award, AAUW, 1981. Mem. Edmond C. of C., Women's Polit. Caucus (legislative chmn.), AAUW (legis. chmn.), ABA, Okla. Bar Assn., Internat. Bar Assn., Am. Assn. Petroleum Landmen, Natural Gas Assn. Okla., Internat. Assn. Energy Economists. Episcopalian. Home: 504 Clegern Dr Edmond OK 73034 Office: Hoen Exploration Co 1000 W Wilshire Blvd Suite 220 Oklahoma City OK 73116

HOENIG, JUDITH ANNE, nurse; b. Putnam, Conn., Nov. 11, 1943; d. Thomas Francis and Charlotte Zoe (King) Gorey; R.N., Joseph Lawrence Sch. Nursing, 1965; m. Michael J. Hoenig, III, Aug. 6, 1977. Supervising nurse Westview Convalescent Center, Dayville, Conn., 1968-73; asst. dir. nurses Stula Pavilion Nursing Home, Danielson, Conn., 1973-75; dir. nurses Westview Convalescent Center, Dayville, 1975-78, staff nurse, 1981-82; dir. nurses Beechwood Manor Convalescent Hosp., New London, Conn., 1982—; dir. nurses Norcliffe Rest Home, Inc., Brooklyn, Conn., 1979-81. Mem. profl. auditing com. Conn. Community Care, Inc., 1981—. Club: Bus. and Profl. Women's (sec. 1977). Contbr. poem to 1982 Anthology Twentieth Century Greatest Poems. Office: Beechwood Manor Convalescent Hosp 31 Vauxhall St London CT 06320

HOEVELER, DIANE LONG, English educator, researcher, writer; b. Chgo., Apr. 9, 1949; d. Vincent Leo, Jr., and Constance (Puglise) Long; m. John David Hoeveler, Jr., Jan. 29, 1972; children—John David, Emily Ann. B.A., U. Ill., 1970, M.A., 1972, Ph.D., 1976. Teaching asst. U. Ill., Urbana, 1970-72, 74-75; lectr. U. Wis.-Milw., 1972-73, 75-76; instr. Alverno Coll., Milw., 1976-78; asst. prof. English, U. Louisville, 1978-80; English tchr. King Coll. Prep., Milw., 1980—; project dir. Milw. Humanities Program, 1978-79. Editor: English Prose and Criticism in the Nineteenth Century, 1979; Milwaukee Women Yesterday, 1979; Milwaukee Women Today, 1979; contbr. book revs. and articles to publs. NEH grantee, 1978, 79, 81, 86. Mem. Alpha Lambda Delta, Phi Alpha Theta.

HOEWING, YVONNE MARIE, savings and loan executive; b. Keokuk, Iowa, Feb. 8, 1955; d. David Nathan, Sr. and Edna Marilyn (McIntosh) Phillips. m. Monty Leon Kearns, Sept. 27, 1972 (div. Mar. 1979); children—Bridie Lee, Brandie Lynn; m. Donald Wayne Hoewing, Feb. 14, 1982. GED diploma, Canton, Mo. Sec., teller Palmyra Saving & Bldg. Assn., Canton, 1975-78, mgr., 1979—. Bd. dirs. Planning and Zoning Commn., Canton, 1985, Indsl. Devel. Commn., Canton, 1985, Sun 'N Surf Pool Bd., Canton, 1985. Mem. Canton C. of C. (treas. 1983). Democrat. Baptist. Avocations: golf; softball. Home: 1306 White St Canton MO 63435 Office: Palmyra Saving and Bldg Assn 444 Lewis St Canton MO 63435

HOEY, JANE KOHRING, health center executive; b. Chgo., Sept. 4, 1940; d. Henry Carl and Jane Hamburg (Decker) Kohring; m. John Strong Hoey, Mar. 19, 1966; children—Anne Decker, John Wareham. B.A., Wells Coll., 1962; M.A., Wayne State U., 1979. Asst. art dept. J. Walter Thompson, Detroit, 1962-64, art buyer, N.Y.C., 1964-65; adminstrv. asst. United Found., Detroit, 1965; art asst. Franklin Siden Gallery, Detroit, 1965-66; counselor Macomb County Community Coll., Warren, Mich., 1979-80; mgr. cancer info. service Comprehensive Cancer Ctr. Met. Detroit, 1980—; dir. health edn. dept. Mich. Cancer Found., Detroit, 1986—; cons. service com. Am. Cancer Soc., Lansing, Mich., 1983-84. Bd. dirs., 1st v.p. Jr. League Detroit, 1982—; pres., bd. dirs. Family Life Edn. Council, Grosse Pointe, Mich., 1976-81; bd. dirs. Vis. Nurses Assn., Detroit, 1984—. Recipient Vol. award Jr. League Detroit, 1979. Mem. Mich. Pub. Health Assn., Mich. Health Council, Jr. League Detroit, Mich. Alliance for Info. and Referral Systems, Tau Beta Assn. Unitarian. Club: Ibex (Grosse Pointe). Office: Mich Cancer Found 110 E Warren Detroit MI 48201

HOFBAUER, DIANE LYNN, lawyer; b. Milw., July 8, 1957; d. Thomas Anton and Claudia Mary (Billig) Hofbauer. A.B., Duke U., 1979; J.D., Vanderbilt U., 1982. Bar: Fla. 1983, U.S. Dist. Ct. (no. dist.) Fla. 1983. Atty. aide Pub. Defender's Office, Nashville, 1980, Vanderbilt Legal Aid Soc., Nashville, 1981-82; assoc. firm Maguire, Voorhis & Wells, P.A., Orlando, Fla., 1982-84, Paul, Hastings, Janofsky & Walker, Washington, 1984—. Mem. ABA, Fla. Bar (communications com. 1982—), Orange County Bar Assn. (media and communications com. 1983), Fed. Communications Bar Assn. Republican. Roman Catholic. Office: Paul Hastings Janofsky & Walker 1050 Thomas Jefferson St NW Washington DC 20007

HOFER, JUDITH, retail company executive. B.A., Portland State U., 1962. Formerly with Meier & Frank Dept. Store, Portland, Oreg., Emporium-Capwell, San Francisco; v.p. Famous-Barr Stores (subs. The May Co.), 1978-81; pres. Meier & Frank, 1981-83; with parent co., Los Angeles, 1983-86, pres., chief exec. officer, St. Louis, 1986—. Address: Famous-Barr Co 601 Olive St St Louis MO 63101*

HOFERER, JEANNE, state legislator. Mem. Kans. Senate. Republican. Office: Kans Senate State Capitol Topeka KS 66612*

HOFF, LISI ANN, artist, educator; b. Copenhagen, Oct. 20, 1942; came to U.S., Sept. 4, 1963, naturalized, Sept. 20, 1978; d. Skjold Egmond and Agnes Emilie (Larsen) Petersen; m. Henry I. Hoff, Jr., Mar. 30, 1968 (div. 1976); children—Franz Erik, Elisja Andrea Kirstine. Diploma Danish Sch. Interior Architecture, 1961; A.A., Greenfield Community Coll., 1982; A.B. cum laude, Smith Coll., 1984. Printed circuit designer Sullivan & Cogliano Designers, Waltham, Mass., 1973-80, TAD Tech. Services, Cambridge, Mass., 1973-80; printed circuit designer-checker TAD Tech. Services, 1984-85; freelance artist, Erving, Mass., 1985—; art liason art dept. Smith Coll., Northampton, Mass., 1983-84. One woman show at Smith Coll., 1984. Bd. dirs. Franklin County Council Arts, 1985—. Ethel Dow grantee, 1981. Mem. Danish Soc. Mass., Smith Coll. Alumni Assn. Mem. Unitarian Ch. Avocations: piano; reading; redesigning and renovating of home. Home and Studio: 49 North St PO Box 127 Erving MA 01344

HOFF, VALERIE MARGARET KNECHT, lawyer; b. Tacoma, Nov. 9, 1946; d. Norbert Francis and Dorothy Margaret (Fawcett) Knecht; m. Mack Harrison Shultz, May 15, 1971 (dec. Mar. 1974); 1 son, Mack Harrison, Jr.; m. 2d David Daniel Hoff, Nov. 25, 1978; stepchildren—James Bradley, Paula J., Deana L. B.A., U. Puget Sound, 1969; M.A., Purdue U., 1975; J.D., U. Puget Sound, 1978. Bar: Wash. 1978, U.S. Dist. Ct. (wc. dist.) Wash., U.S. Ct. Appeals (9th cir.). Assoc. Manza, Moceri & Messina, Tacoma, 1978-79; ptnr. Rydberg, Hoff & Gagley, Kent, Wash., 1979-82; sole practice, Seattle, 1982—; speaker legal issues, 1983—. Mem. ABA, Wash. State Bar Assn., Seattle-King County Bar Assn., Wash. State Trial Lawyers Assn., Kappa Kappa Gamma Alumnae Assn. (pres. Seattle chpt.). Republican. Roman Catholic. Address: 4434 170th Ave SE Issaquah WA 98027

HOFFER, DIANE LYNN, psychologist; b. Coral Gables, Fla., Dec. 29, 1953; d. Harold Herman and Charlotte May (Bernstein) H.; B.A. in Sociology, U. Miami, 1974; M.Ed. in Psychology, Counseling and Psychol. Services, Ga. State U., 1975; Dr. Psychology, Nova U., 1981. Practicum student Community Mental Health S. Dade, Dade County, Fla., 1978-79; clin. psychology intern Univ. Health Services U. Mass., Amherst, 1980-81; psychologist in pvt. practice, Coral Gables, 1981—; co-owner Jazz Workout, dance and exercise studio, 1982-84; dance instr.; instr. Parent Effectiveness Tng. Lic. marriage and family therapist, mental health counselor, clin. psychologist. Mem. Am. Psychol. Assn., AAHPER, Nat. Dance Assn., Internat. Windsurfing Class Assn., Assn. Sex Educators, Counselors and Therapists, Fla. Psychol. Assn. Democrat. Jewish. Contbr. articles to profl. jours.

HOFFLEIT, ELLEN DORRIT, astronomer; b. Florence, Ala., Mar. 12, 1907; d. Fred and Kate (Sanio) H. A.B., Radcliffe Coll., 1928, M.A., 1932, Ph.D., 1938; D.Sc. (hon.) Smith Coll., 1984. Research asst. Harvard U. Obs., Cambridge, Mass., 1929-38, research assoc., 1938-43, astronomer, 1948-56; mathematician Aberdeen Proving Ground, Md., 1943-48; research assoc., sr. research astronomer Yale U., New Haven, Conn., 1956-84; dir. Maria Mitchell Observatory, Nantucket, Mass., 1957-78; tech. expert, cons. Ballistic Research Lab., Aberdeen Proving Ground, Md., 1948-61. Author: (catalogue) Yale Bright Star Catalogue, 1964, 82. Author: (booklet) Some Firsts in Astronomical Photography, 1950. Contbr. articles to profl. publs. Recipient Caroline Wilby prize Radcliffe Coll., 1938, Cert. Appreciation War Dept., Aberdeen Proving Ground, 1947, Grad. Soc. medal Radcliffe Coll., 1964, Alumni Recognition award Radcliffe Coll., 1983. Mem. Internat. Astron. Union, Am. Astron. Soc., AAAS, Meteoritical Soc. (past v.p.), Am. Assn. Variable Star Observers (past pres. chpt.), Am. Geophys. Union. Phi Beta Kappa, Sigma Xi (past pres.). Home: 255 Whitney Ave #14 New Haven CT 06511 Office: Dept Astronomy Yale U Box 6666 New Haven CT 06511

HOFFMAN, BARBARA A., state legislator; b. Balt., Mar. 8, 1940; d. Sidney Wolf and Eve (Simonoff) Marks; m. Donald Edwin Hoffman, 1960; children—Alan Samuel, Michael Stuart, Carolyn Mara. B.S., Towson State U., 1960; M.A., Johns Hopkins U., 1966. Secondary sch. tchr., Balt., 1960-63; supr. student tchrs. Morgan U., Balt., 1968-73; exec. dir. Md. Democratic party, 1979-84; mem. Md. State Senate from 42d Dist., 1983—. Co-author: Journeys in English, 1968. Recipient Appreciation cert. PTC Career Inst., 1984, Outstanding Contbns. to Party award Md. Dem. party, 1984. Mem. Md. Assn. Elected Women (exec. bd. 1985), Nat. Order Women Legislators, Balt. Blews Coalition Blacks and Jews, Md. Com. for Children (pres. 1983), Hadassah (group pres. 1980-82). Jewish. Office: Md State Capitol Bldg Annapolis MD 21401*

HOFFMAN, BETTY JANE, circuit court clerk; b. Mayville, Wis., Apr. 7, 1933; d. Theodore Henry and Henrietta Elizabeth (Luebke) Machmueller; m. Lyle Eugene Cole, May 12, 1956 (dec. Sept. 1977); children—David Allen, Nanette Rae Cole Mlodzik, Ritchie Brian; m. Clarence Carl Hoffman, May 30, 1981; stepchildren—Judith Ann Aldrich, Clarence Allen Hoffman. Student pub. schs., Ripon, Wis. Cashier Thorp Fin. Corp., Ripon, 1951-56; dep. clk. cir. ct. Green Lake County, Green Lake, Wis., 1968-78, clk. cir. ct., 1979—. Mem. Green Lake County Republican party, 1970—, Wis. Rep. party, 1979—, Green Lake County Rep. Women, 1975—. Mem. Green Lake Bus. and Profl. Women's Club (treas. 1970-72), Wis. Clk. of Cts. Assn., Tri-County Officers Assn. Lutheran. Avocations: sewing; cooking; travel. Home: 446 Scott St Green Lake WI 54941 Office: Clk of Cir Ct Courthouse 492 Hill St Green Lake WI 54941

HOFFMAN, DORIS JEAN, accountant; b. Rockford, Ill., June 7, 1929; d. Herschel Herbert and Ollie Mae (Sherlock) Wolfe; student LaSalle Extension U., 1950-51, Broward Community Coll., 1969-71; m. Rodney V. Hoffman, Feb. 14, 1949 (dec. 1968); children—Judith Hoffman Olson, Sandra Hoffman Hardy, Kurt Allyn. Operator, Ill. Bell Telephone Co., Rockford, 1946-49; acct., head tax dept. Fed. & State Tax Record Systems, Rockford, 1949-66, Ft. Lauderdale, Fla., 1966-69; pvt. practice acctg., Ft. Lauderdale, 1969-79; acct., pres. Hoffman & Assos., Inc., Ft. Lauderdale, 1979—; lectr. in field. Mem. bus. edn. adv. com. Fla. Dept. Edn., 1979—; chmn. Fla. del. to White House Conf. on Small Bus., 1979-80; mem. exec. bd., adminstr. adv. council SBA. Named Bus. Woman of Yr., Broward County Women in Communication, 1979; Woman of Yr., Am. Soc. Woman Accts., 1975; Soroptimist Woman of Yr. in Acctg., 1976, 77; Woman of Yr. in Acctg., Zonta, 1978; Bus. Person of Yr., FBLA, 1980; Broward County Bus. Leader of Yr., 1983. Mem. Fla. Accts. Assn. (pres. 1978-79), Nat. Soc. Public Accts., Internat. Platform Assn. Contbr. articles to profl. jours. Office: 3929 N Andrews Ave Fort Lauderdale FL 33309

HOFFMAN, ELLENDALE MCCOLLAM, psychologist, pastoral counselor; b. Alexandria, La., Apr. 3, 1951; d. William and Hope (Joffrion) McCollam; A.A., Briarcliff Coll., 1971; B.A., Manhattanville Coll., 1973; M.Div., Episcopal Div. Sch., 1976; D.Min., Andover Newton Theol. Sch., 1978; m. Charles L. Hoffman, Nov. 27, 1976. Ordained deacon Episcopal Ch., 1976, ordained priest, 1977; clin. supr. Pastoral Inst. for Tng. in Alcohol Problems, Cambridge, Mass., 1976-78; pvt. practice psychology and pastoral counseling, Falmouth, Mass., 1976—; dir. growth and learning center Marion (Mass.) Center for Human Services, 1978-79; clin. dir. Cape Counseling Center, Hyannis, 1979-82. Chmn., Commn. on Today's Families, Diocese of Mass., 1980-82. Named Woman of Yr., Falmouth Bus. and Profl. Women's Assn., 1982; Roothbert fellow, 1974-76; Episcopal Women's scholar, 1974-76; Robbins fellow, 1976-78; cert. alcoholism counselor, Mass. Fellow Am. Assn. Pastoral Counselors; mem. Am. Psychol. Assn., Am. Assn. Marriage and Family Therapists, Assn. Christian Therapists, LWV. Designer, writer driver's alcohol edn. curriculum, 1977. Home and Office: 78 Main St Falmouth MA 02540

HOFFMAN, JUDITH STOCKNER, advertising agency executive; b. Far Rockaway, N.Y., Oct. 25, 1950; d. Lester and Eileen (Stern) Stockner; m. David Lawrence Hoffman, Sept. 9, 1973; children—Jennifer Anne, Michael Stockner. B.A. in Psychology, Richmond Coll., Staten Island, N.Y., 1972. Direct mail mgr., Alexander Hamilton Inst., N.Y.C., 1972-75; circulation dir. Atlas World Press Rev., N.Y.C., 1975-76, Am. Home Mag., N.Y.C., 1976-77, Sheet Music Mag., Katonah, N.Y., 1978-81; mktg. dir. Maximum Exposure Advt., Scarsdale, N.Y., 1981-82; chief exec. officer, pres. Jenman Advt., Inc., South Salem, N.Y., 1982—. Mem. Nat. Assn. Female Execs. Office: Jenman Advt Inc Sabbath Day Hill South Salem NY 10590

HOFFMAN, KARLA LEIGH, mathematician; b. Paterson, N.J., Feb. 14, 1948; d. Abe and Bertha (Guthaim) Rakoff; B.A., Rutgers, U., 1969; M.B.A., George Washington U., 1971, D.Sc. in Ops. Research, 1975; m. Allan Stuart Hoffman, Dec. 26, 1971; 1 son, Matthew Douglas. Ops. research analyst IRS, Washington, 1970-72; research asst. George Washington U., 1972-75; asso. professorial lectr., 1978—; NSF postdoctoral research fellow Nat. Acad. Sci., Washington, 1975-76; mathematician Nat. Bur. Standards, Washington, 1976—; vis. asso. prof. ops. research U. Md., spring 1982; assoc. prof. systems engring. dept. George Mason U., 1985—; cons. to govt. agys. Recipient Applied Research award Nat. Bur. Standards, 1984, Silver medal U.S. Dept. Commerce, 1984. Mem. Ops. Research Soc. Am. (sec.-treas. computer sci. tech. sect. 1979-80, vice chmn. sect. 1981, chmn. sect. 1982, vis. professorial lectr. 1980—, chmn. tech. sect. com. 1983-86, council 1985—), Math. Programming Soc. (editor newsletter 1979-82, chmn. com. algorithms 1982-85, council 1985—). Club: Clifton Horse Soc. Contbr. articles on ops. research to profl. jours.; assoc. editor Internat. Abstracts of Ops. Research. Home: 6921 Clifton Rd Clifton VA 22024 Office: Center Applied Math Nat Bur Standards Washington DC 20234

HOFFMAN, LINDA M., chemist, educator; b. N.Y.C., Dec. 18, 1939; d. Theodore and Esther (Schaeffer) Weiss; B.S., Queens Coll., 1959; M.S., N.Y.U., 1967, Ph.D., 1970; m. Robert G. Hoffman; 1 child, Samuel A. Teaching fellow N.Y.U., 1965-68; postdoctoral fellow Sloan-Kettering Inst. Cancer Research, N.Y.C., 1972-73; research asso. Kingsbrook Jewish Med. Center, N.Y.C., 1973-77; mem. faculty Baruch Coll., CUNY, 1977—, prof. chemistry, 1982—. Recipient Moore award Am. Soc. Neuropathologists, 1980, 84. Mem. AAAS, Am. Chem. Soc., N.Y. Acad. Scis., Sigma Xi. Contbr. articles on glycolipids as related to cancer and Tay-Sachs disease to profl. jours. Office: 17 Lexington Ave New York NY 10010

HOFFMAN, MARGARET A., banking executive; b. Phila., Dec. 11, 1945; d. Raymond O. and Helen (Thomas) H. B.F.A., Phila. Coll. Fine Arts, 1967; M.Ed., Temple U., 1968; cert. in banking Am. Inst. Banking, 1976. Sr. analyst Glenmede Trust Co., Phila., 1971-75; credit mgr. Lincoln Bank, Phila., 1975-77; dir. credit div. Robert Morris Assocs., Phila., 1977-83; v.p. corp. tng. Barnett Banks of Fla., Inc., Jacksonville, 1983—; instr. Bank Lending Inst., 1985; adv. bd. Omega, San Francisco, 1984; instr. nat. workshop Robert Morris Assocs., Phila., 1984. Author: Credit Department Management, 1981; contbr. articles to banking jours. Assoc. mem. Robert Morris Assocs. Office: Barnett Banks of Fla Inc 100 Laura St 7th Floor Jacksonville FL 32231

HOFFMAN, MARGARET GROSS, community college administrator; b. Glassport, Pa., Jan. 14, 1940; d. Albert Frederick and Marguerite Bridget (Murphy) Gross; B.S., Slippery Rock State Coll., 1961; M.Ed., U. Pitts., 1972, Ph.D., 1980. children—Daniel Keith, Diane Lynn. Tchr. health and phys. edn. W. Mifflin Sch. Dist., Pa., 1961-63; tchr. Arroyo High Sch., Los Angeles, 1964-65; asst. prof. Community Coll. of Allegheny County, West Mifflin, Pa., 1970-75, athletic dir., 1975-76, asst. to v.p., exec. dean South Campus, 1976-82, asst. dean learning resources, 1982-83; exec. dir. Inst. for Bus., Industry and Govt., Orange County Community Coll., 1983; dd. dirs. Occupations, Inc. Mem. Am. Assn. Women in Community and Jr. Colls. (participant in Leaders for 80's Program), Am. Council on Edn. (instl. rep. Nat. Identification Program for Women, Pa., 1981-82), Nat. Council on Community Services and Continuing Edn., Women in Mgmt. Editor and writer: Data from the Dean. Home: 8 Crabapple Ln Middletown NY 10940 Office: 115 South St Morrison Hall Middletown NY 10940

HOFFMAN, MARJORIE NEGELE, nursing educator; b. Cleve., Sept. 1, 1941; d. Charles Frederick and Leah Virgil (Wettich) Negele; m. Walter William Hoffman, Feb. 10, 1968; children—Kevin William, Kimberly Ann, Kathryn Nicole. B.S.N., U. Mich., 1963; M.Nursing Edn., U. Pitts., 1967. Staff nurse U. Mich. Hosp., Ann Arbor, 1963-64; clin. instr. U. Mich., 1964-65; instr. Akron Children's Hosp., Ohio, 1965-66, Ill. Central Community Coll., East Peoria, 1968; clin. nursing specialist Columbus Children's Hosp., Ohio, 1978-80; asst. prof. Otterbein Coll., Westerville, Ohio, 1980—; participant project facilitating competency devel. Ohio site team of Midwest Alliance in Nursing, 1983-86. Deacon, elder Gahanna Mifflin Presbyn. Ch., Ohio, 1977-82; Sunday sch. tchr. Central College Presbyn. Ch., Westerville, 1984-85, deacon, 1985—; mem. adv. com. Ohio Edn. Program on Smoking and Health, 1982—; acting co-chmn., pres. acad. support group Westerville North High Sch., 1986. Mem. Am. Nurses Assn., Ohio Nurses Assn., Sigma Theta Tau. Avocations: crafts; sewing; cooking. Home: 605 Hackberry Dr Westerville OH 43081 Office: Grant-Otterbein Nursing Program Otterbein College Westerville OH 43081

HOFFMAN, MARY CATHERINE, nurse anesthetist; b. Winamac, Ind., July 14, 1923; d. Harmon William Whitney and Dessie Maude (Neely) H.; R.N.,

Methodist Hosp., Indpls., 1945; cert. obstet. analgesia and anesthesia, Johns Hopkins Hosp., 1949, grad. U. Hosp. of Cleve. Sch. Anesthesia, 1952; Staff nurse Meth. Hosp., 1945-49; research asst., then staff anesthetist Johns Hopkins Hosp., 1949-62; staff anesthetist Meth. Hosp., 1962-64, U. Chgo. Hosps., 1964-66; chief nurse anesthetist Paris (Ill.) Community Hosp., 1966-80; staff anesthetist Hendricks County Hosp., Danville, Ind., Ball Meml. Hosp., Muncie, Ind., 1981-86; instr.-trainer CPR, 1975-81; mem. Terr. 08 CPR Coordinating Com., 1975-80. Mem. Am. Assn. Nurse Anesthetists, Am. Heart Assn., Ind. Fedn. Bus. and Profl. Women's Clubs (Ill. dist. chmn. 1977-78, state found. chmn. 1978-79; found. award 1979). Republican. Presbyterian. Home: 1700 N Maddox Dr Muncie IN 47304

HOFFMAN, MERLE HOLLY, social psychologist, political activist, author; b. Phila., Mar. 6, 1946; d. Jack Rheins and Ruth (Dubow) H.; B.A. magna cum laude in Psychology, Queens Coll., 1972; postgrad. CUNY, 1972-75; m. Martin Gold, June 30, 1979. Founder, pres. Choices, Forest Hills, N.Y., 1971—; family planning cons. Health Ins. Plan, N.Y.C., 1973—; founder, pres. Center for Comprehensive Breast Services, N.Y.C., 1979—; speaker on women's issues; host TV talk show MH on the Issues. Bd. dirs. Found. for the Creative Community, 1979—; founder N.Y. Pro-Choice Coalition. Mem. Nat. Assn. Abortion Facilities (co-founder, pres. 1976-77), Nat. Abortion Fedn. (co-founder, sec. 1977-78), Am. Pub. Health Assn., Nat. Liberty Com. (founder, pres. 1981—), Phi Beta Kappa. Editor, Female Health Topics and Diagnostic Reporter, 1979-81; producer TV documentary on abortion; nat. spokeswoman and debater; editor, pub. ednl. jour. On the Issues; founder, dir. Project Outreach ednl. workshops for communities and instns.; contbr. articles in field to various publs. Office: Choices 97-77 Queens Blvd Forest Hills NY 11374

HOFFMAN, NANCY JOAN, history educator; b. Vallejo, Calif., May 22, 1948; d. Robert Edwin and Mary June (Hassett) H. B.A., San Diego State U., 1969, M.A., 1974; postgrad. U. de las Americas, Mexico City, 1969; Ph.D., U. Calif.-Santa Barbara, 1976. Teaching asst. U. Calif.-Santa Barbara, 1973-75; instr. Ventura Community Coll. (Calif.), 1975-76, Kauai Community Coll. br. U. Hawaii, 1976-78; asst. prof. history Pa. State U., DuBois, 1979—. Speaker, polit. cons. Hawaiian Pub. Com. for Humanities, Kauai, 1976-77. NEH fellow, summers 1978, 80, 81; research fellow Pa. State U., 1981. Mem. Am. Hist. Assn., Latin Am. Studies Assn., Middle Atlantic Council Latin Am. Studies, DuBois Hist. Soc. Office: Dept History Pa State U College Place DuBois PA 15801

HOFFMAN, NATHALIE R., lawyer; b. Pitts., Dec. 20, 1946; d. Herb and Rosella (Stein) Cohen; m. Stanley R. Hoffman, Dec. 21, 1969 (div. 1973). B.S., U. Mich., 1968; J.D., UCLA, 1973. Bar: Calif. 1973. Assoc. O'Melveny & Myers, Los Angeles, 1973-76, Mitchell, Silberberg & Knupp, Los Angeles, 1976-78; sole practice, Los Angeles, 1978-80; bus. affairs exec. 20th Century Fox, Los Angeles, 1980-81; ptnr. Graham & James, Los Angeles, 1981-83; of counsel Sidley & Austin, Los Angeles, 1983—. Trustee Brazil-Calif. Trade Assn. Mem. Calif. State Bd. Behavioral Sci. Examiners, ABA, State Bar Calif., Los Angeles County Bar Assn., Beverly Hills Bar Assn., Order of Coif, Phi Beta Kappa. Office: Sidley & Austin 2049 Century Pk E Los Angeles CA 90067

HOFFMAN, SHARON SMITH, account executive; b. Albany, N.Y., Nov. 6, 1958; d. Floyd Francis and Roberta Mary (Flood) Smith; m. Randy O. Hoffman, Sept. 1, 1984. B.S. in Telecommunications with honors, Ariz. State U. Asst. to program dir. Sta. KBBC and KTAR, Phoenix, 1978-80; nat. music coordinator Plough Broadcasting Co., Memphis, 1980-81; music dir. Friday Morning Quarterback, Cherry Hill, N.J., 1982; promotion dir. Sta. KCPX and KBUG, Salt Lake City, 1983-85; account exec. Sta. KLTQ-AM-FM, Salt Lake City, 1985, Sta. KSOP-AM-FM, Salt Lake City, 1986—. Editor co. newsletter On the Air, Price Broadcasting Co., 1983-85. Mem. Broadcast Promotion and Mktg. Execs., Utah Advt. Fedn. (3 gold awards 1984, silver award 1985). Roman Catholic. Avocations: music, aerobic dancing. Home: 5334 S Beacon Hill Circle Salt Lake City UT 84123 Office: KSOP Radio PO Box 25548 Salt Lake City UT 84125

HOFFMAN, SUSAN ANN, electronic product development specialist; b. Pasadena, June 10, 1953; d. James Alex Stewart and Shirley May (Eaton) Hoffman; m. Robert George Anderson, Jr., Dec. 21, 1975 (div. 1982). B.A. in English, Stanford U., 1975. Account exec. Mgmt. Recruiters, Cedar Rapids, Iowa, 1976-77; nat. accounts rep. Rand McNally Co., Chgo., 1977-79; product mgr. Marine Midland Bank, Buffalo, 1979-81, asst. v.p. corp. planning, N.Y.C., 1981-82; project dir. electronic distbn. Standard & Poor's Corp., N.Y.C., 1982—. Contbr. articles to profl. jours. Active Big Sis. of Am., 1983—. Calif. State scholar, 1971; Canfield scholar, 1974. Mem. Am. Mgmt. Assn., Info. Industry Assn. Club: NOW, Stanford Alumni Assn. Office: Standard and Poors Corp 25 Broadway New York NY 10004

HOFFMAN, SUSAN RONNIE, psychologist; b. Bklyn., May 5, 1948; d. Harold Abraham and Connie (Ellman) H.; B.S., Boston U., 1970, Ed.D., 1978. Asst. staff psychologist Judge Stone Child Guidance Center, Brockton, Mass., 1972-74; staff psychologist Dorchester Mental Health Center, Boston, 1974-76, Northeastern U. Counseling Center, Boston, 1976-81; psychologist Hurst Assos., P.C., Boston, 1979-82; pvt. practice psychology, Brookline, Mass., 1981—. Lic. psychologist Mass. Mem. Am. Psychol. Assn. Author articles in field. Office: 1180 Beacon St Suite 4C Brookline MA 02146

HOFFMAN, VICTORIA JUNE, lawyer; b. E. Lansing, Mich., Mar. 24, 1953; d. Ralph Alex and Lillian June (McVannel) Klawitter; m. John William Hoffman, Feb. 16, 1974; children—Thomas Clune, William Christopher, Veronica Irene. B.A. summa cum laude, Duquesne U., 1975; J.D. with honors, George Washington U., 1981. Bar: Va. 1981, U.S. Dist. Ct. (ea. dist.) Va. 1983, U.S. Ct. Appeals, 4th cir. 1983. Assoc. atty. Charles Kane Schanker, P.C., Fairfax, Va., and Washington, 1979—. Asst. den leader Boy Scouts Am., Burke, Va., 1982—; instr. CCD, Burke, Va., 1983-84. Mem. ABA, Assn. Trial Lawyers Am., Va. Trial Lawyers Assn., Fairfax Bar Assn., Am. Judicature Soc., Alpha Sigma Tau. Home: 6024 Meyers Landing Ct Burke VA 22015 Office: Charles Kane Schanker PC 1900 L St NW Suite 309 Washington DC 20036

HOFFMANN, FRANCES C., educator; b. Dunblane, Sask., Can., July 24, 1921; d. George Percy and Clara (Amerud) Carey; student Nebr. State Tchrs. Coll., 1943, 51-53; B.S., Iowa State U., 1955, M.S., 1956; m. Albert Theodore Hoffmann, Oct. 21, 1943 (dec. July 1951); children—Gerald Theodore, Thomas Gene. Library asst. Central High Sch., Sioux City, Iowa, 1938-39; dining room asst. St. Joseph's Hosp., 1940-41; underphotographer Elko Photo Co., Sioux City, 1941-42, U.S. Civil Service, 1943-44; grad. research asst. Iowa State U., 1955-56; home econs. instr. Whittier (Calif.) Coll., 1957-66, asst. prof., 1966—, chmn. dept. home econs., 1971-72, 76-81; home econs. dir. Saturday Programs and Summer Day Camps, Found. for the Jr. Blind, Los Angeles, 1964-78, cons. bldg. addition, 1966-68; judge The Greatest Sew on Earth, 1975. Mem. adv. com. Rio Hondo Coll., 1977-82, Rio Hondo Child Devel. Center; mem. costume council Los Angeles County Mus. Art, 1985—. Recipient Appreciation award Mchts. Club, 1975. Am. Home Econs. Assn.-Rehab. Services Adminstrn. fellow, 1969-70. Mem. AAUW Am. (mem. rehab. com. 1970-72, com. on coms. 1971), Calif. (adv. coll. chpts. 1968; profl. sect. chmn. coll. chpt. 1968-70 Foothill Dist. council, chmn. colls. and univs. com. 1979, pres. 1984-85, budget chair and counselor 1985—) home econs. assns., Internat. Fedn. Home Economists (chmn. 1980-82, chmn. scholarship com. 1982-83), AAUP, Calif. Tchrs. Assn., Am. Textile Chemists and Colorists, Whittier Coll. Assos., Assn. Coll. Profs. Textiles and Clothing, Nat. Assn. Edn. Young Children, Costume Soc. Am., Delta Phi Upsilon, Kappa Omicron Phi (chpt. adv. 1973-82). Methodist (adminstrv. bd. 1985—). Participant audio-visual documentary Out of Darkness-Light, 1971. Home: 5518 Adele Ave Whittier CA 90601

HOFFMANN, MARY ANN, data processing executive; b. Yonkers, N.Y., Nov. 19, 1946; d. Robert Augustus and Mary Margaret (Mansfield) Neary; B.A., Coll. Mt. St. Vincent, 1968; M.A., Fordham U., 1971; M.S., Fairleigh Dickinson U., 1978; m. Marvin W. Hoffmann, Mar. 9, 1968; children—Karri, Matthew. Project programmer IBM, Kingston, N.Y., 1977-82, devel. programmer, 1983-84, sr. programmer, 1984—. NSF fellow, 1968. Mem. AAUW, Kappa Gamma Pi. Roman Catholic. Home: RD 1 Box 386E Woodstock NY 12498 Office: IBM Neighborhood Rd Kingston NY 12401

HOFFMANN, NANCY LARRAINE, state legislator; m. Mark Hoffman; children—Eva, Anna, Gustav. B.A., Syracuse U.; M.S., U. Md. Former polit. organizer, Tenn., Miss., city councilor Syracuse, N.Y.; mem. N.Y. State Senate from 48th Dist., 1984—, mem. agr., crime and correction, fin., environ. conservation, local govt., tourism, recreation and sports coms. Mem. Gov.'s Council on Fiscal and Econ. Priorities. Democrat. Office: NY State Capitol Bldg Albany NY 12224

HOFFNER, MARILYN, university administrator; b. N.Y.C., Nov. 16, 1929; d. Daniel and Elsie (Schulz) H.; B.F.A., Cooper Union; m. Albert Greenberg, May 29, 1949; children—Doren Roe, Peter Cooper. Art dir. Printers' Ink mag., N.Y.C., 1953-63; art dir. Print mag., N.Y.C., 1960-62; corp. art dir. Vision, Inc., Latin Am., 1963-75; dir. alumni relations Cooper Union, 1975-82, dir. devel., 1982—. Bd. dirs. Art Dirs. Club N.Y., 1973-75, 79-82, exec. sec., 1973-75, exec. treas., 1979-82; mem. Citizens Adv. Cultural Arts Com. Dutchess County, 1978-80. Named Alumnus of Yr., Cooper Union, 1968; recipient Gold medal Art Dirs. Club, 1979. Mem. Cooper Union Alumni Assn. (editor-in-chief 1971-74, 1st v.p. 1974-75), Council Advancement and Support of Edn., Type Dirs. Club (numerous awards), Nat. Arts Club (exhbn. com.). Contbg. editor Print mag., 1960-62, Art Direction, 1959-64, Graphics mag., 1959-82; designer mags., advt., books. Home: 51 Fifth Ave New York NY 10003 Office: 41 Cooper Sq New York NY 10003

HOFFNUNG, AUDREY SONIA, speech-lang. pathologist, educator; b. N.Y.C., Mar. 15, 1928; d. Nathan and Gussie (Karp) Smith; B.A. cum laude, Bklyn. Coll., 1949; M.A., Columbia U., 1950; Ph.D., City U. N.Y., 1974; m. Joseph Hoffnung, Nov. 26, 1950; children—Bonnie Fern, Tami Lynn. Rehab. therapist Ridgewood Cerebral Palsy Center, 1949-50; dir. speech therapy Kingsbrook Med. Center, Bklyn., 1950-55; therapist and cons. Morris J. Solomon Clinic, Bklyn., 1956-58; therapist Speech and Hearing Center Bklyn. Coll., 1958-62, 63-64; pvt. practice speech therapy Hewlett (N.Y.) Med. Center, 1961-63; pvt. practice speech therapy, Oceanside, N.Y., 1964-71; cons. on staff for aphasic patients Phys. Medicine and Rehab. Center, South Nassau Communities Hosp., 1964-65; part-time lectr. Speech and Hearing Center, Queens (N.Y.) Coll., 1970-72; adj. lectr. dept. speech Bklyn. Coll., 1973-74, asst. prof. speech pathology, 1974-77; asst. prof. dept. speech communication and theatre St. John's U., Jamaica, N.Y., 1977-80, asso. prof., 1980—; guest lectr. N.Y. Orton Soc., 1979, Brookdale Med. Center, 1978; mem. profl. adv. bd. Vis. Home Health Services of Nassau County, 1973—. Cert. and lic. speech pathologist, N.Y. Mem. Am. Speech and Hearing Assn., N.Y.C. Speech, Hearing and Lang. Assn., N.Y. State Speech and Hearing Assn. (chairperson student activities 1978-79), L.I. Speech and Hearing Assn., Aphasia Study Group of N.Y.C., N.Y. Acad. Scis. Contbr. articles on speech pathology to profl. jours. Home: 3282 Woodward St Oceanside NY 11572 Office: Dept of Speech Communication St John's Univ Utopia and Grand Central Pkwys Jamaica NY 11439

HOFMAN, CHERYL JEAN, nurse; b. Culbertson, Mont., Apr. 22, 1951; d. Fred P. and Dorothy (Larsen) H.; 1 child, Robert Todd. B.S. in Nursing, Mont. State U., 1973. Charge nurse Roosevelt Meml. Hosp., Culbertson, 1973-74; office nurse, mgr. Dr. Reitzel's Office, Culbertson, 1974-77; charge nurse Roosevelt Meml. Hosp., 1978-81, supr., 1981-82, dir. nursing services, 1982-84, charge nurse, supr., 1985—, dir. nursing hosp. and nursing home, 1985—, infection control dir., 1982-84, coordinator fire and safety disaster, 1982-83. Vol. Red Cross Blood Drawing, Culbertson, 1984; treas. Ebenezer Lutheran ALCW, McCabe, Mont., 1985—. Recipient 10 Yr. award Roosevelt Meml. Hosp., 1983. Democrat. Lutheran. Club: Home Demonstration (pres. 1982, 83). Avocations: flower gardening; crafts; fishing; hunting. Home: Box 104 Culbertson MT 59218

HOFMAN, ETHEL GREENWALD, food columnist, author, food consultant; b. Glasgow, Scotland, Apr. 24, 1936; d. Harry and Jean (Segal) Greenwald; m. Walter Isaac Hofman, May 12, 1963; children—Andrew Lester, Michael Ross. Diploma in home econs., Glasgow Coll. Domestic Sci., 1959. Chief adminstrv. dietitian Michael Reese Hosp., Chgo., 1961-63; spokesperson to nat. cos., 1975-83; free lance journalist, food writer, 1978—. Author: Making Food Beautiful, 1982. Mem. Internat. Assn. Cooking Profls., Phila. Writers Orgn., Internat. Assn. Cooking Schs., Home Economists in Bus. Home: 707 S Bowman Ave Merion Station PA 19066

HOFMANN, BARBARA LEE, bus service company executive; b. Chgo., Jan. 11, 1953; d. Edward A. and Edith E. (Ely) H. B.A., Concordia Coll., River Forest, Ill., 1974; M.Music Edn., U. Chgo., 1976. Vehicle leasing agt. Internat. Harvester, Chgo., 1974; substitute tchr. South Suburban Dists., Met. Chgo., 1974-75; tchr. St. Paul Luth. Sch., Dolton, Ill., 1975-79; regional affairs rep. Regional Transp. Authority, Chgo., 1980-84; project mgr. Pace Suburban Bus Service, Chgo., 1984—; liaison Chgo. South Suburban Mass Transit Dist., Homewood, Ill., 1982-85; sub-regional advisor South Suburban Mayors' and Mgrs. Assn., Homewood, Ill., 1984-85. Republican. Lutheran. Home: 9242 Jill Ln Schiller Park IL 60176 Office: Pace Suburban Bus Service 550 W Algonquin Rd Arlington Heights IL 60005

HOFSTADTER, SARAH KATHERINE, lawyer; b. N.Y.C., July 22, 1952; d. Richard and Beatrice (Kevitt) H. B.A. magna cum laude, Princeton U., 1974; J.D., Stanford U., 1978. Bar: Calif. 1978, U.S. Dist. Ct. (no. dist.) Calif. 1978, U.S. Dist. Ct. (cen. dist.) Calif. 1981, U.S. Ct. Appeals (9th cir.) 1978. Law clk. U.S. Ct. Appeals (9th cir.), San Francisco, 1978-80; law clk. to Judge Marilyn Hall Patel, U.S. Dist. Ct., San Francisco, 1980-81; assoc. firm Howard, Rice, Nemerovski, Canady, Robertson & Falk, P.C., San Francisco, 1981—; dir. Stanford Pub. Interest Law Found., 1979-81; dir. Bay Area Lawyers for Individual Freedom, San Francisco, 1982-86; instr. New Coll., Calif. Sch. Law, San Francisco, 1979-80. Mem. Calif. Women Lawyers; San Francisco Women Lawyers Alliance, ABA, Bar Assn. San Francisco, Bay Area Lawyers for Individual Freedom, Phi Beta Kappa. Democrat. Office: Howard Rice Nemerovski Canady Robertson & Falk Three Embarcadero Ctr 7th floor San Francisco CA 94111

HOGAN, MARY ADELE DEASY, lawyer, educator, statistician; b. Columbus, Ohio, Dec. 29, 1912; d. Timothy S. and Mary A. (Deasy) H. B.A., U. Cin., 1932, B.Ed., 1933; M.Ed., Xavier U., 1953; LL.B., Chase Coll. Law, Cin., 1941; J.D., No. Ky. Coll. Law, 1967; student Sophia U., Tokyo, 1950-51, Trinity Coll., Dublin, 1969, U. Vienna, summer 1982. Cert. tchr., Ohio. Bar; Ohio 1941. Tchr., U.S. Govt., Ariz., 1947; edn. specialist Hdqrs. USAF, Tokyo, 1949-51; tchr. lit. Middle Eastern Tech. U., Ankara, Turkey, 1964-66, Peace Corps, Turkey, 1964-66; tchr. Cin. Pub. Schs., 193-7 1937-73; statis. asst. USPHS, Cin., 1976—. Mem. ABA. Home: 111 Garfield Pl Cincinnati OH 45202

HOGAN, PATRICIA ANNE, resale and thrift stores executive, educator; b. Denver, Oct. 24, 1936; d. Robert Joseph and Anne Louise (Hagel) Blaney; m. Thomas Emory Hogan, Oct. 12, 1957; children—Thomas, Christiane, Kerry, Constance, Katherine. B.S. in Edn., Loyola U., 1958. Cert. tchr. elem. edn., Mo. Tchr. pub. schs., Waynesville and Stoutland, Mo., 1958, 59. pres. Second Chance, Inc., Prospect Heights, Ill., 1972—. Mem. Nat. Assn. Re-Sale and Thrift Stores, Theta Phi Alpha (pres. alumni assn. 1968-72). Roman Catholic. Office: Second Chance Inc 692 Milwaukee Ave Prospect Heights IL 60070

HOGG, HELEN SAWYER, astronomer, emeritus educator; b. Lowell, Mass., Aug. 1, 1905; d. Edward Everett and Carrie (Sprague) Sawyer; A.B., Mt. Holyoke Coll., 1926, D.Sc. (hon.), 1958; M.A., Radcliffe Coll., 1928, Ph.D., 1931; D.Sc. (hon.) U. Waterloo, 1962, McMaster U., 1976, U. Toronto, 1977; D.Litt. (hon.), St. Mary's U., 1981; m. Frank Scott Hogg, Sept. 6, 1930; children—Sarah Longley Hogg MacDonald, David Edward, James Scott. Lectr., Smith Coll., 1927, Mt. Holyoke Coll., 1930-31, asst. prof. astronomy, acting chmn. dept., 1940-41; research asst. Dominion Astrophys. Obs., 1931-35; research asst. U. Toronto, 1936-41, lectr., 1941-50, asst. prof., 1951-55, assoc. prof., 1955-57, prof., 1957-76, emeritus, 1976—; program dir. astronomy NSF, Washington, 1955-56; astronomy columnist Toronto Daily Star, 1951-81; research assoc. David Dunlap Obs., Richmond Hill, Ont., Can., 1941—. Decorated companion Order of Can.; recipient citation Mt. Holyoke Coll., 1952, Rittenhouse Astron. Soc. medal, 1967, Centennial medal, 1967, medal of service, Order of Can., 1968, Klumpke-Roberts award Aston. Soc. of Pacific, 1983. Fellow Royal Soc. Can. (past pres. sect. 3); mem. Internat. Astron. Union (past pres. sub-com.), Royal Astron. Soc. Can. (hon. pres., service medal 1967), Am. (Annie J. Cannon prize 1950), Canadian (pres. 1971-72) astron. socs., Am. Assn. Variable Star Observers (past pres.), Women's Press Club, Royal Canadian Inst. (pres. 1964-65), Fedn. Ont. Naturalists, Phi Beta Kappa, Sigma Xi. Club: Univ. Womens (Toronto). Contbr. numerous articles to profl. jours. Office: David Dunlap Observatory Richmond Hill ON L4C 4Y6 Canada*

HOGG-WISE, SUSAN MARIE, physician; b. Lancaster, Pa., June 5, 1952; d. Norman Harry and Nancy Naomi (Longenecker) Hogg; m. Lawrence Norman Wise, Aug. 19, 1976. B.S., Muhlenberg Coll., 1974; M.D., Med. Coll. Pa., 1978. Resident in family practice Lancaster Gen. Hosp., Pa., 1978-81; physician Pub. Health Service, New Holland, Pa., 1981-83; practice medicine specializing in family practice, County Line Med. Ctr., Gap, Pa., 1983—; co-med. dir. Quality Care, Lancaster, 1984-85; adv. bd. Young Mother Program, Lancaster, 1982—. Mem. Lancaster City and County Med. Soc., Am. Acad. Family Physicians, Med. Soc. Pa., Phi Beta Kappa. Democrat. Avocations: sailing; cooking; gardening; knitting. Office: County Line Medical Center RD 1 Box 13 Gap PA 17527

HOGINS, MILDRED HOLDAR, medical technologist; b. Russelville, Ark., Jan. 18, 1939; d. Luther and Francess Eythl (Briscoe) Holdar; cert. in med. tech. Hillcrest Med. Center, Tulsa, 1963; B.S. in Biology, U. Mo., Kansas City, 1969; M.A. in Mgmt. and Supervision, Central Mich. U., 1976; m. Albert Gumbs; 1 son, Mark H. Hogins. Med. technologist St. Joseph Hosp., Tucson, 1964-66; bacteriologist Providence Hosp., Anchorage, Alaska, 1966-67; med. technologist St. Margaret Hosp., Kansas City, Kans., 1967-68, Providence Hosp., Kansas City, Kans., 1969-71; edn. coordinator Sch. Med. Tech., also asst. chief med. technologist Providence-St. Margaret Health Center, Kansas City, Kans., 1971-76, chief med. technologist, 1976—. Bd. dirs. Mill Creek Run Home Owners Assn., 1979-82, 85—, Plaza Acad., Kansas City, Mo., 1982-84. Mem. Clin. Lab. Mgrs. Assn. (bd. dirs. Kansas City chpt. 1985—) Am. Soc. Microbiology, Nat. Assn. Female Execs., Am. Soc. Clin. Pathologists, Kans. Soc. Med. Tech. (conv. chmn. 1975), Greater Kansas City Soc. Med. Tech. (treas. 1980), U. Mo. Kansas City Alumni Assn., Central Mich. U. Alumni Assn., Mensa (bd. dirs. Med-Am. chpt. 1983—). Home: 14076 W 88th Terr Lenexa KS 66215 Office: 8929 Parallel Pkwy Kansas City KS 66112

HOGSETTE, SARAH MARGARET, lawyer; b. Atlanta, May 18, 1948; d. Daniel Lawrence and Dorothy (Hayes) H. B.S., U. Ga., 1970; J.D., Emory U., 1981. Bar: Ga. 1981. Law clk DeKalb Superior Ct., Decatur, Ga., 1981-83, Supreme Ct. of Ga., Atlanta, 1983-84; atty. Life Ins. Co. of Ga., Atlanta, 1984—. Mem. Atlanta Pub. Affairs Council, 1984. Recipient award Bur. Nat. Affairs, 1981; Douglas Lee Peabody Meml. award, 1981. Mem. ABA, State Bar Ga., Atlanta Bar Assn. Corp. Counsel Greater Atlanta, Atlanta Pub. Affairs Council. Episcopalian. Office: Life Ins Co of Ga 5780 Powers Ferry Rd NW Atlanta GA 30365

HOGUE, SHARON LEA, music educator; b. Houston, Sept. 10, 1956; d. William Guy and Ethel Marie (Van Namen) Hogue, Jr. B.Music Edn., Sam Houston State U., 1980. Tchr. music elem. sch. Spring Branch Ind. Sch. Dist., Houston, 1980—; choir dir. Housman Elem. Harmonizers, Houston, 1980—; piano tchr., Houston, 1980, 81; choral condr. Cornerstone, 1984, Potter's Clay, 1985. Pianist, soloist, tchr. Candlelight Bible Ch., Houston, 1970—, asst. treas., 1984; ch. musician Spring Branch Community Ch., 1984. Mem. Tex. Music Educators Assn., Kodaly Educators Tex., Assn. Tex. Profl. Educators (local com. chmn. 1984), Nat. Assn. Christian Educators, Sigma Alpha Iota (pres. Sam Houston State U. chpt. 1979, scholastic award 1980), Kappa Delta Pi. Office: Housman Elem Sch 6705 Housman St Houston TX 77055

HOGYA, MARY GOLDING, government official; b. Newark, June 16, 1946; d. Wesley Irwin and Florence Grace (Smith) Golding. Certificate Universite de Grenoble, France, 1967; B.A., Lake Erie Coll., 1968. Editor, writer Bur. Labor Stats., Washington, 1968-72, Manpower Adminstrn., Dept. Labor, Washington, 1972-75; spl. asst. Employment and Tng. Adminstrn., 1975-78; budget, fiscal officer Interstate Commerce Commn., Washington, 1978—. Editor, author lit. jour. Nota Bene, 1967, Monthly Labor Rev., 1968-72. Mem. Friends of WETA, Washington, 1978—. Palisades Citizens Orgn., Washington, 1983—. Recipient Outstanding Performance award Dept. Labor, Washington, 1974, 78; Spl. Achievement Award, Interstate Commerce Commn., Washington, 1983, 85. Avocations: swimming; tennis; music; dancing, reading. Home: 5404 Carolina Pl NW Washington DC 20016 Office: Interstate Commerce Commn 12th and Constitution NW Washington DC 20423

HOHENER, BARBARA SANDE, interior decorating consultant; b. Twin Falls, Idaho, May 5, 1939; d. Einar and Pearl M. (Olson) Sande; m. Ernest Reinhardt Hohener, Sept. 3, 1961 (div. Sept. 1971); children—Heidi Catherine, Eric Christian. B.A., U. Idaho, 1961. Asst. mgr., buyer Home Yardage Inc., Oakland, Calif., 1972-76; cons. in antiques and antique valuation, Lafayette, Calif., 1977-78; interior designer Neighborhood Antiques and Interiors, Oakland, Calif., 1978—; cons., participant antique and art fair exhibits, Orinda and Piedmont, Calif., 1977—. Decorator Piedmont Christmas House Tour, 1983, Oakland Mus. Table Setting, 1984, Piedmont Showcase Family Room, 1985, Piedmont Kitchen House Tour, 1985. Bd. dirs. San Leandro Coop. Nursery Sch., 1967; health coordinator parent-faculty bd., Miramonte High Sch., Orinda, 1978, Acalanes Sch. Dist., Lafayette, Calif., 1978; bd. dirs. Orinda Community Ctr. Vols., 1979; originator Concerts in the Park, Orinda, 1979. Assoc. Am. Soc. Interior Design, Am. Soc. Appraisers; mem. Am. Decorative Arts Forum, De Young Mus., Nat. Trust Historic Preservation, San Francisco Opera Guild, San Francisco Symphony Guild. Democrat. Avocations: travel; hiking.

HOJNOWSKI, KAY LYNN, real estate investor; b. St. Louis, Sept. 27, 1948; d. Jean Fred and Maxine Florence (Ott) Kallmayer; m. Eugene Leo Hojnowski, Mar. 14, 1981; 1 dau., Jessica Ryan; m. Simon Peter Swarbrick, Apr. 17, 1971 (div. Jan. 1976). Forms analyst Northwestern Meml. Hosp., Chgo., 1970-72; mgr. retail Fabric World, Niles, Ill., 1972; account exec. UARCO Bus. Forms, Chgo., 1973-79, adminstr. health care mktg., 1980-85; real estate investor, Chgo., 1985—. Contbr. articles to trade jours. Named Regional rookie of Yr., UARCO, 1974. Mem. Nat. Assn. Female Execs. Democrat. Presbyterian. Club: Lake Shore Tennis. Co-founder Women in Transition, 1978-79, Chgo. Avocations: reading; writing; painting; crafts; upholstering.

HOKE-DAVID, LORETTE, educational administrator; b. Isola, Miss.; d. Ruble L. and Bertha Hoke; B.A., Greenville Coll., 1956; postgrad. Butler U., 1958, Ind. U., 1959; M.A., Fla. Atlantic U., 1969; Ed.D., Nova U., 1979; children—Leah Michelle, Monna Eileen. Tchr., Indpls. Public Sch. System, 1956-57, 60-63; tchr. Broward County Sch. System, Ft. Lauderdale, Fla., 1963-72, curriculum specialist, 1972-73, prin. Westchester Elem. Sch., Coral Springs, 1973-85, dir. elem. edn., 1985-86. Bd. govs. Nova U., 1975-84, sec., 1978, acting chmn., 1980, vice chmn., 1981-82, pres. Drill Team Parents Assn., 1980-81; chmn. Coral Springs Cultural Soc., 1981-82; mem. grants rev. com. Tourist Devel. Council, 1981-82; mem. Consumer Protection Bd., 1981-82; mem. Ft. Lauderdale Symphony Bd., Coral Springs 2000 Com. Named Outstanding Woman of Yr. in Edn., Women in Communications, 1979; Little Red Sch. House award, 1978, 80. Mem. Nat. Assn. Elem. Sch. Prins., Am. Assn. Sch. Adminstrs., Broward Assn. Elem. Sch. Prins., Fla. Assn. Sch. Adminstrs., North Area Elem. Prins. (chmn. 1979-81), Phi Delta Kappa, Delta Kappa Gamma, Club: Zonta. Office: Rickards Ctr 6000 NE 9th Ave Oakland Park FL 33334

HOLAHAN, PAULETTE HELDNER, court administrator; b. New Orleans, May 25, 1934; d. Knute and Colette (Pope) Heldner; m. John M. Holahan, Jan. 15, 1955; children—Shawn Louise, John Michael, Jr., Paulette Mary, Gregory Heldner, Odile Riley, Meghan Amy. Student Loyola U. of the South, New Orleans, 1953-55. Pub. info. officer Orleans Parish Prison, New Orleans, 1974-76; assoc. Ad-Vantage Pub. Relations, New Orleans, 1976-77; pub. info. officer La. Supreme Ct., New Orleans, 1977—. Editor Classroom Prescriptions for Learning Disabilities, 2 vols., 1974, La. Jud. Newsletter, 1977-84. Chmn. bd. New Orleans Pub. Library, 1979-83, La. State Library Commn., 1978-79, 82-84; mem. Nat. Commn. on Libraries and Info. Sci., 1979—; exec. bd. dirs. Urban Libraries Council, 1974—, v.p., 1984-86, pres., 1986—; del. White House Conf. on Libraries and Info. Sci., Washington, 1979. Recipient Modissette award La. Library Assn., 1981. Mem. La. Ct. Adminstrs. Assn. (co-founder, sec.-treas. 1982—), Nat. Assn. for Ct. Mgmt., Am. Judicature Soc. Democrat. Roman Catholic. Club: New Orleans Press. Avocations: reading; gardening; travel. Office: La Supreme Ct 301 Loyola Ave New Orleans LA 70112

HOLAMON, GLADYS MARIE AVERY, accountant; b. Halfway, Tex., Dec. 26, 1927; d. Samuel A. and Nova Ethel (Dudley) Avery; m. James Otis Holamon, May 19, 1951; 1 child: James Otis. Cert., Durham Bus. Coll., Ft. Worth, 1950, Nat. Iridology Assn., Tulsa, 1979, Internat. Inst. Natural Health Scis., Huntington Beach, Calif., 1980, Donsbach Herbal Inst., Huntington Beach, 1983. Journalist, Brady Standard, Brady, Tex., 1947-49; real estate broker, Ft. Worth, 1963-79; oil and gas acct. R.T. Roark, Ft. Worth, 1975—; owner health food store, Arlington, Tex., 1979-84; founder Health Alternatives Research Inst.; cons. and lectr. in field. Contbr. articles to profl. jours. Pres., North Tex. Herb Club, Dallas, 1986, treas. Greater Ft. Worth Herb Soc., 1986; docent Ft. Worth Bot. Gardens, 1986; mem. Wholistic Health Orgn., Headliners Club, Ft. Worth. Recipient Cert., Ctr. for Bldg. Better Health Naturally, 1981. Baptist. Avocation: health. Home: 1712 Robin Rd Arlington TX 76013

HOLAYTER, MARLENE C., school administrator, consultant; b. Butte, Mont., Nov. 11, 1939; d. James Martin and Domenica (Marietti) Troglia; children—Carly Marie, Kathy J. Calvin, Marianne; m. 2d, William J. Holayter, July 5, 1981. B.A., U. Wash., 1972, M.Ed., 1974; doctoral candidate Va. Poly. Tech. Inst. Cert. tchr., ednl. adminstr. Adminstr., tchr. Renton (Wash.) Sch. System, 1972-79; elem. prin. Issaquah (Wash.) Schs., 1979-81; assoc. prof. U. Wash., Seattle, 1978-81; cons. Seattle Post-In-telligencer, 1978-81; prin. Fairfax County Pub. Schs., Fairfax, Va., 1981-83, coordinator instrnl. services, 1983—; assoc. prof. Central Wash. U., Seattle, 1975-78, U. Wash., Seattle, 1978-81. Mem. Renton Human Rights Mcpl. Commn., 1979-81. Recipient Pulse Polit. award Wash. Edn. Assn., 1976, PTSA Community Service award, Issaquah, 1980; ednl. grantee Title I Office of Edn., 1974. Mem. AAUW, Assn. Supervision and Curriculum Devel., Renton Prins. Assn. (pres. elect), Wash. Assn. Secondary Sch. Prins., NEA, Wash. Edn. Assn., Nat. Assn. Elem. Sch. Prins., Am. Assn. Sch. Adminstrs., Phi Delta Kappa, Delta Kappa Gamma. Roman Catholic. Office: Fairfax County Public Schools 6525 Montrose St Alexandria VA 22312

HOLBERG, EVA MARIA, civic worker; b. Stralsund, Germany, Apr. 22, 1931; came to U.S., 1957, naturalized, 1962; d. Hans Herbert and Helene Wilhelmine (Engelhardt) Thieshen; student Free U. West Berlin, 1952-55; m. Dieter E. Holberg, May 28, 1955; children—Marion, Astrid. Mgr., Pathways to Music, Mt. St. Mary's Coll., Los Angeles, 1972-74; pres., mgr. Palisades Symphony, Pacific Palisades, Calif., 1974—; pres. Theatre Palisades, 1979-81, 82-83, v.p., 1983—, bd. dirs., chmn. ways and means, 1981—; mem. westside jr. com. Los Angeles Philharm., 1972-85, coordinator affiliates for youth programs and season tickets, 1979-81; cultural rep. Palisades Community Council, 1976; active Westside Jr. Philharmonic Com., 1971—, bd. dirs., 1972-85, pres., 1975-77, chmn. season ticket sales, 1977-83. Named Citizen of Yr. Pacific Palisades, 1981. Mem. Am. Symphony League. Home: 1081 Palisair Pl Pacific Palisades CA 90272 Office: Box 214 Pacific Palisades CA 90272

HOLBROOK, BARBARA CARR SAN, advertising agency executive; b. Roanoke, Va.; d. Louis James and Eleanor (Brophy) San; m. John Pinckney Holbrook, May 29, 1956; children—David Carr, Priscilla Mann. B.A., U. N.C. Copywriter Doherty, Clifford, Steers, Shenfield, N.Y.C., 1954-56, Doyle, Dane, Bernbach, N.Y.C., 1956-58, Ogilvy & Mather, N.Y.C., 1958-59; copy group head Benton & Bowles, N.Y.C., 1959-70; v.p., assoc. creative dir. Grey Advt. Inc., N.Y.C., 1970—. Bd. dirs. Nat. Assn. for Visually Handicapped. Named to Clio Hall of Fame, 1955; recipient Clio award, 1977. Hollywood Internat. Broadcast award, 1970, Andy award, 1970, 83, Grey Adv. Pres.'s award, 1985. Democrat. Episcopalian. Office: Grey Advt Inc 777 3d Ave New York NY 10017

HOLBROOK, NORMA JEANNETTE, nursing educator; b. Napton, Mo., Oct. 26, 1939; d. R. Milton and Thelma M. (Miller) Cochran; m. Ralph E. Holbrook, June 30, 1961; children—Tamara M., Jennifer L. B.S.N., Central Mo. State U., 1965; M.N., Kans. U., 1982. Staff nurse Menorah Med. Ctr., Kansas City, Mo., 1965-66, head nurse, 1966-67; instr. nursing Met. Community Coll., Kansas City, 1967-68; staff nurse Independence (Mo.) Med. Ctr., 1971-73; staff nurse St. Francis Hosp., Topeka, 1975-80, 84—; instr. nursing Washburn U., Topeka, 1981-85, asst. prof., 1986—; mem. nursing quality assurance com. Stormont Vail Regional Med. Ctr., Topeka, 1982-83, mem. task force for improved implementation nursing care plans, 1983. Chmn. nursing adv. com. ARC, Capital City chpt., Topeka, 1982-83, mem. nursing adv. com., 1980—. Contbr. articles to profl. jours. Mem. Am. Nurses Assn., Sigma Theta Tau. Republican. Methodist. Office: Washburn U 1700 College St Topeka KS 66621

HOLBROOK, PATRICIA ANN, architect; b. Greensboro, N.C., Nov. 28, 1940; d. Bulb Jackson and Pearl Ethylene (Angel) H.; student Coll. William and Mary, 1959-61, B.Arch., N.C. State U., Raleigh, 1967, M.B.A., Loyola Coll., Balt., 1980; m. William Minor May III, Nov. 4, 1961; children—Maria Siena, Jonathan Zwolle, Christopher London, Happy Savannah. Archtl. designer Leviatich & Miller, architects, Ithaca, N.Y., 1968-69, Wells & Koetter, architects, Ithaca, 1969-70; pvt. practice architecture, Balt., 1970-72; prin. architect, partner May & Holbrook, architects, Balt., 1972—; mem. faculty Catonsville Community Coll., 1976-77. Recipient NPS/APT historic preservation cert. Registered architect, Md.; cert. value engr. Mem. AIA (corp.), Md. Soc. Architects, Assn. Preservation Tech., Soc. Am. Mil. Engrs., Nat. Trust Historic Preservation. Office: 901 N Calvert St Baltimore MD 21202

HOLCOMB, DOROTHY TURNER, publicist; b. Roanoke, Va., June 15, 1924; d. Wiley Bryant and Lena Mae (Gray) Turner; m. Joseph E. Baxter, Aug. 1, 1944 (dec. Nov. 1944); m. 2d, G. William Holcomb, May 8, 1948 (div. 1962). Student Coronet Bus. Sch., Roanoke, 1943; interior decorator certificate N.Y. Sch. Interior Design, 1953; student U. Miami, 1962-63. Exec. sec. Am.'s Jr. Miss Pageant, Mobile, Ala., 1962; exec. asst. to pres. Gilbert Mktg. Group, Inc., N.Y.C., 1963-65; br. dirs. Heart Assn., Miami, Fla., 1965-66; publicist in charge on-air promotion Screen Gems, Hollywood, Calif., 1966-68; publicity dir. Mus. of Sci./Planetarium, Miami, 1968-71, Bryna Cosmetics, Inc., Miami, 1973-74; freelance publicist, 1971-73, 76—; pub. relations/communications ECKANKAR, Menlo Park, Calif., 1974-75. Mem. Publicists Guild, Internat. Alliance Theatrical Stage Employees, Moving Picture Machine Operators, Women in Communications. Home: 3727 Parliament Rd SW Apt 11 Roanoke VA 24014

HOLCOMB, ELIZABETH CARGILL, real estate broker; b. Orlando, Fla., Mar. 8, 1928; s. Theodore Ira Parrott and Lucy (Stimpson) Parrott Cargill; m. Edgar D. Holcomb, Jr., Dec. 9, 1946; children—Jane Elizabeth Purdy, Leslie Sherwood Bell, Melanie Ardath George, E. David III. Student Fla. State U., 1945-46, Avon Park Jr. Coll., 1966, U. Fla., 1970; grad. Realtors Inst. Salesperson Ed Schlitt Real Estate Agy., Vero Beach, Fla., 1970-71, F. Rickman Real Estate, Stuart, Fla., 1971-73; real estate broker, pres. Accent Realty, Inc., Stuart, 1973—; owner, buyer, mgr. Gingerbread House, Stuart, 1978—; agt. CP Chem. Sales, 1985—. Co-founder Holcomb Scholarship award U. Fla., 1972. Mem. Fla. State Hort. Soc., Fruit Crops Alumni and Friends U. Fla., Martin County and Fla. Farm Bur., Kappa Alpha Theta. Home: 2376 NW Fork Rd Stuart FL 33494 Office: Accent Realty Inc 215 W Ocean Blvd Stuart FL 33497

HOLCOMB, MARGUERITE KNOWLES, former city ofcl., shorthand reporting co. exec.; b. Dayton Twp., Mich., Apr. 9, 1913; d. Arthur Russell and Catherine (Biermeyer) Knowles; student public schs., Muskegon and Dayton Twp., Mich.; children—Joyce C. Holcomb Filius, John F., June A. Ofcl. circuit ct. reporter 14th Jud. Circuit, Muskegon, 1943-53; pres. Holcomb Reporting Service, Inc., Muskegon, 1953—; commr. City of Muskegon, 1975-84, vice-mayor, 1977-79, mayor, 1980-82; mem. econ. devel. com. U.S. Conf. Mayors. Mem. adv. council Ferris State Coll., Big Rapids, Mich. Named Businesswoman of Yr., Quadrangle Bus. and Profl. Women's Clubs 1970, State Small Businesswoman of Yr., Mich. Fedn. Bus. and Profl. Women's Clubs, 1973, Entrepreneur of Yr., County of Muskegon, 1984. Mem. Nat. Shorthand Reporters Assn., Mich. Shorthand Reporters Assn., Mich. Ct. Reporters Assn. (pres. 1967-68), Muskegon C. of C. (bd. dirs., pres. women's div. 1986-87). Republican. Clubs: Bus. and Profl. Women's (state pres. 1966-67), Zonta (dir. club), Century. Office: 1891 Lakeshore Dr Muskegon MI 49441

HOLDEN, ANNA MARIE, advertising and merchandising company executive; b. Hays, Kans., Jan. 31, 1954; d. Norbert Cyrille Benoit and Bernita Viola (Bellerive) Benoit Genter; m. James Dale Whitehead, Dec. 26, 1970 (div. 1978); children—Christopher James, Rebecca Sue; m. Richard Edward Holden, Jan. 18, 1979 (div. Apr. 1985). Grad. high sch., Wichita, Kans. Bakery mgr. Dillons Food Markets, Wichita, 1972-79; with Sta. KOAM, Pittsburg, Kans., 1980-82; pres., gen. mgr. Pro-Ad, Inc., Pittsburg, 1980-85; founder TBC, Inc., 1985—. Roman Catholic. Avocations: gardening; horseback riding. Office: TBC Inc Route 5 Box 311 Pittsburg KS 66762

HOLDEN, IVY MAY, lawyer, nurse; b. Betheltown, Jamaica, May 7, 1941; came to U.S., 1962; d. Clarence E. and Violet L. (Pryce) Lewis; m. T.D. Hilliard, Dec. 20, 1960 (div. 1967); m. 2d, Carl E. Holden, Nov. 13, 1967; children—Sherryetta, Carl Edward, Craig Eugene, Carla Marie. B.S. in Bus. Adminstrn., Calif. State U.-Dominquez Hills, 1975; J.D., Western State U., Fullerton, Calif., 1979. R.N., Calif., N.Y. Bar: Calif. 1980. Assoc. dir. nursing Kaiser Hosp., Inglewood, Calif., 1969-70; dir. nursing C.C. Ctr., Los Angeles, 1970-72; dir. nursing edn. W. Adams Hosp., Los Angeles, 1972-78; pvt. practice nursing cons., Los Angeles, 1979-81; assoc. Chase Rotchford Drukker & Bogust, Los Angeles, 1981-83, Bower Baraban & Kirkhimer, Los Angeles, 1983—; vol. atty. Family Law Project, Los Angeles, 1983. Black women lawyers rep. Jr. League of Women, Los Angeles, 1983; campaign worker Com. to Elect Mayor Bradley Governor, Los Angeles, 1983. Recipient 1st prize medicine Warrington Hosps. (Eng.), 1960; Black Women Lawyers Assn. grantee, 1978. Mem. So. Calif. Def., Los Angeles County Bar Assn., ABA, State Bar Calif., Fed. Bar Assn., Black Women Lawyers Assn. (mem. edn. com. 1983), Delta Theta Phi. Democrat. Roman Catholic. Office: Bower Baraban & Birkhimer 3200 Wilshire Blvd Los Angeles CA 90010

HOLDEN, JESSICA ANN, photographer; b. Hartford, Conn., Dec. 18, 1956; d. R. Stuart and Jean Elizabeth (Hanna) H. B.A. in Visual Arts, Mt. Vernon Coll., 1978. Salesman Cape Cod Photo, Orleans, Mass., 1976-77; salesman, Washington Gallery of Photography and Your Lab., Washington, 1977; photographer Friday Publs., Inc., Washington, 1977-78; photographer U.S. Senate, Washington, 1978—. Photographer: Good Housekeeping, 1984. Home: 5850 Cameron Run Terrace Apt 206 Alexandria VA 22303 Office: US Senate Photographic Studio Russell Senate Office 31B Washington DC 20510

HOLDEN, TAMMY LOU, computer consultant; b. Reading, Pa., July 18, 1958; d. Rawlins Warren and Emma Jeanette (Vanino) Bausher; m. Mark Raymond Holden, Aug. 14, 1982 (div. Oct. 1983). Student North Harris County Coll.; A.S. in Bus. Mgmt., Fisher Jr. Coll., 1981; student Boston Coll., Berklee Coll. Music, Pa. Gov.'s Sch. for the Arts. Teller, customer service Brookline Savs. Bank, Mass., 1978-79; computer operator Brookline Trust Co., 1979, Mast Industries, Woburn, Mass., 1979-80; 81; computer operator, programmer C. D. Burnes of Boston, 1980-81; programmer analyst Papa Gino's Needham, Mass., 1981; Computer cons. Computer Systems and Applications, Houston, 1981-84; computer cons., Houston, 1984—; pres., co-owner Sysware, Inc., Houston, 1984—. Reading Symphony Orch. scholar, 1976. Mem. Houston System 38 Users Group. Club: Fitness USA (Boston). Office: 5400 Adler Suite 3 Houston TX 77081

HOLDER, ANGELA RODDEY, lawyer, educator; b. Rock Hill, S.C., Mar. 13, 1938; d. John T. and Angela M. (Fisher) Roddey; student Radcliffe Coll., 1955-56; B.A., Newcomb Coll., 1958; postgrad. Faculty of Laws, King's Coll., London, Eng., 1957-58; J.D., Tulane U., 1960; LL.M., Yale U., 1975; div.; 1 son, John Thomas Roddey Holder. Admitted to La. and S.C. bars, 1960, Conn. bar, 1981; counsel Roddey, Carpenter & White, Rock Hill, 1960—; atty. criminal div. New Orleans Legal Aid Bur., 1961-62; counsel York County (S.C.) Family Ct., 1962-64; asst. prof. polit. sci. Winthrop Coll., Rock Hill, 1964-74; research assoc. Yale Law Sch., 1975-77, exec. dir. program in law, sci. and medicine, 1976-77; lectr. dept. pediatrics Yale Med. Sch., 1975-77, asst. clin. prof. pediatrics, 1977-79, assoc. clin. prof., 1979-83, clin. prof., 1983—; counsel for medicolegal affairs Yale-New Haven Hosp. and Yale Med. Sch., 1977—. Mem. Rock Hill Sch. Bd., 1967-68. Bd. dirs. Family Planning Clinic, chmn., 1970-73. Mem. Am., S.C. (medico-legal com. 1973—), La. bar assns., Am. Soc. Law and Medicine (exec. council, pres. 1986-87). Democrat. Episcopalian. Author: The Meaning of the Constitution, 1968; Medical Malpractice Law, 1975, 2d edit., 1978; Legal Issues in Pediatrics and Adolescent Medicine, 1977, 2d edit., 1985; contbg. editor Prism mag. AMA; editorial bd. IRB, Jour. Medicine and Philosophy; also articles. Home: 23 Eld St Apt B New Haven CT 06511 Office: Yale-New Haven Hospital 20 York St New Haven CT 06504

HOLDER, BRENDA JOYCE, oil company marketing analyst; b. Gadsden, Ala., Jan. 29, 1946; d. William A. and Norma D. (Helms) Grace; m. Robert N. Holder, Jr., June 24, 1967 (div. Aug. 1984). Grad. Ayers Sch. Bus., 1967, student U. Md., 1980-81, Community Coll. Denver, 1982-83. Sec., bookkeeper Sr. Citizens Services, Mobile, 1971-73, sec., receptionist Hook, Reed & Co., Denver, 1973-74, sec. Auburn Oil & Gas Co., 1974-75, Energy Minerals Corp., Denver, 1976-78; asst. mgr. Memmingen Non-Commd. Officers' Club, Fed. Republic Germany, 1978-81; crude mktg. analyst Meridian Oil Inc., Englewood, Colo., 1982—. Active Mobile United Way, 1971. Mem. Nat. Assn. Female Execs. Republican. Mem. Assembly of God. Club: Mile High Desk and Derrick (pres. 1986). Home: 9449 Briar Forest Dr #518 Houston TX 77063 Office: Meridian Oil Inc 2919 Allen Pkwy Houston TX 77019

HOLDER, LILLIAN LYDIA, nursing home administrator; b. Sand Draw, Wyo., July 17, 1936; d. Ezra G. and Lillian Lyon; student U. Wyo., 1955, Central Wyo. Coll., 1972-74; A.S. in Nursing, Casper Coll., 1976, student, 1977-79; student St. Joseph's Coll., 1980—; m. Willian Holder, Aug. 29, 1964 (div. 1983); children—Kim Marie (Mrs. Clyde Winckler), Mark Darrell. With Farnsworth Ins. Agy., Riverton, Wyo., 1954-55; bookkeeper Hagstrom Constrn., Riverton, 1955-62; supr. Maddox Well Service, Riverton, 1967-68; nursing asst. Bishop Randall Hosp., Lander, Wyo., 1970-72, Meml. Hosp., Riverton, 1973-74, Natrona County Meml. Hosp., Casper, Wyo., 1974-75; charge nurse, 1976-79; dir. nursing Geriatrics Inc. (name changed to ARA Living Ctrs.), Greeley, Colo., 1979-80; adminstr. Poplar Living Ctr., Casper, 1980—. Mem. Wyo. Am. Nurses Assn., Wyo. Health Care Assn. (bd. dirs.), Bus. and Profl. Women. Republican. United Methodist. Mem. Order Eastern Star. Home: 1710 S Elk Casper WY 82601 Office: 4305 S Poplar St Casper WY 82601

HOLDSWORTH, JANET NOTT, registered nurse, educator; b. Evanston, Ill., Dec. 25, 1941; d. William Alfred and Elizabeth Inez (Kelly) Nott; children—James William, Kelly Elizabeth, John David. B.S. in Nursing with high distinction, U. Iowa, 1963; M.Nursing, U. Wash., 1966; postgrad. U. Colo., 1981, U. No. Colo., 1982. Registered nurse, Colo. Staff nurse U. Colo. Hosp., Denver, 1963-64, Presbyn. Hosp., Denver, 1964-65, Grand Canyon Hosp., Ariz., 1965; asst. prof. U. Colo. Sch. Nursing, Denver, 1966-71; counseling nurse Boulder PolyDrug Treatment Ctr., Boulder, 1971-77; pvt. duty nurse Nurses' Official Registry, Denver, 1973-82; cons. nurse, tchr. parenting and child devel. Teenage Parent Program, Boulder Valley Schs., Boulder, 1980—; bd. dirs., treas. Nott's Travel, Aurora, Colo., 1980—; instr., nursing coordinator ARC, Boulder, 1979—, instr., nursing tng. specialist, 1980-82. Mem. adv. bd. Boulder County LaMaz Inc., 1980—; mem. adv. com. Child Find and Parent-Family, Boulder, 1981—; del. Republican County State Congl. Convs., 1972-86, sec. 17th Dist. Senatorial Com., Boulder, 1982—; vol. chmn. Mesa Sch. Parent Tchr. Orgn., Boulder, 1982—, bd. dirs., 1982—, v.p., 1983—. Mem. Am. Nurses Assn., Colo. Nurses Assn. (bd. dirs. 1975-76, human rights com. 1981-83, dist. pres. 1974-76), Soc. Adolescent Medicine, Council High Risk Prenatal Nurses, Council Intracultural Nurses, Sigma Theta Tau. Republican. Presbyterian (elder). Home: 1550 Findlay Way Boulder CO 80303 Office: Teenage Parent Program 3740 Martin Dr Boulder CO 80303

HOLIAN, GAIL CONCA, educator; b. Jersey City, Sept. 21, 1948; d. Samuel Joseph and Mariejoyce (Contey) Conca; B.A., Georgian Court Coll., 1970; M.A., St. Johns U., 1972; m. John F. Holian, Dec. 26, 1970. Instr. English, Neptune Twp. (N.J.) Bd. Edn., 1971-80; adj. instr. English, Ocean County Coll., Toms River, N.J., 1974—; teaching fellow English, NYU, N.Y.C., 1978-79; lectr. English, Georgian Court Coll., Lakewood, N.J., 1978-80, asst. prof. English, 1980—, dir. writing program, 1982—. Vol., ARC, 1972—; dir. media services and publs. Found. for Research in Optimal Living, Red Bank, N.J., 1984—. Georgian Court Coll. grantee, 1968. Mem. MLA, Nat. Council Tchrs. English (judge Achievement Awards in Writing 1984), AAUP, Sigma Tau Delta. Club: Soroptomists (v.p. 1983-84). Home: 65 Washington St Red Bank NJ 07701 Office: 9th St Lakewood NJ 08701

HOLIDAY, LOIS ANN, lawyer; b. Franklin, Ind., June 6, 1954; d. Dale Wesley and Helen Rosemary (Blaich) Jones; m. James Ernest Holiday, Aug. 5, 1978; 1 son, Wesley Ernest. B.S., Ind. State U., 1975; postgrad. Pepperdine U., 1977-78; J.D., Western State U., Fullerton, Calif., 1981. Bar: Ind. Staff atty. Ind. State Dept. Pub. Welfare, Indpls., 1981-83; dep. prosecutor Johnson County, Franklin, Ind., 1983—. Vice-pres. Hancock County Young Republicans, Greenfield, Ind., 1981—; precinct committeeman Sugar Creek Twp., New Palestine, Ind., 1984—; bd. dirs., past chmn. Interlocal Community Action Program, New Castle, 1982-86. Mem. Hancock County Bar Assn., Ind. State Bar Assn., Indpls. Bar Assn., Ind. Rural Lawyers Assn., Hancock County Republicans, Hancock County Republican Women. Congregationalist. Avocations: bowling; camping; antique collecting. Home: Rural Route 4 Box 270 New Palestine IN 46163 Office: Johnson County Prosecutor's Office Courthouse Annex Franklin IN 46131

HOLLAND, DENISE EDGECOMBE, psychiatrist; b. West Palm Beach, Fla., June 13, 1948; d. Erman Wilfred and Mildred Rose (Herndon) Edgecombe; B.S., Howard U., 1970, M.D., 1976; m. Elwood Samuel Holland, June 2, 1973. Adminstrv. asst. NASA, Washington, 1974; extern Alexandria (Va.) Hosp., 1976-78; resident in psychiatry George Washington U. Hosp., Washington, 1976-78, Howard U. Hosp., Washington, 1979-80; physician cons. Dept. Health and Human Services, Balt., 1980-82; physician analyst USPHS, Rockville, Md., 1982-83; fellow Howard U. Hosp., 1983; dir. geriatric program Crownsville (Md.) Hosp. Ctr., 1983—; cons. psychiatrist Bowie (Md.) State Coll., 1979-81, 84—, Palmer Park (Md.) Counseling Center, 1981-83, Prince George's County Dept. Mental Health, 1983—. Recipient awards Dept. Health and Human Services, 1980, Howard U. Hosp., 1979, D.C. Public Schs., 1981. Mem. AAUW, AMA, Am. Med. Women's Assn., Am. Profl. Practice Assn., Commd. Officers Assn., D.C. Med. Soc., Howard U. Alumni Assn., Howard U. Med. Alumni Assn., Nat. Assn. Residents and Interns, Nat. Med. Assn., Prince George's County Med. Soc., So. Med. Assn., Nat. Med. Assn. Aux. Democrat. Episcopalian. Club: Links (award 1979). Home: 7812 Lonesome Pine Ln Bethesda MD 20817 Office: Crownsville Hosp Center Cottage 11 Crownsville MD 21032

HOLLAND, DIANE KAY, oil company executive; b. Natchez, Miss., Dec. 23, 1951; d. Robert and Virginia (McCall) Holland. A.A., Copiah-Lincoln Jr. Coll., 1980; B.S. in Bus. Adminstrn., U. So. Miss., 1984. Sec. G.W. Gulmon, Petroleum Geologist, Natchez, 1969-78; office mgr. Domestic Oil/Rebel Drilling, Natchez, 1978-80; adminstrv. asst. Cornwell Exploration, Natchez, 1980-83, Petrovest, Inc., Natchez, 1983—. Del. Democrat Nominating Com., Natchez-Adams County, Miss., 1980. Mem. Desk and Derrick, Phi Theta Kappa. Home: 33 Cloverdale Dr Natchez MS 39120 Office: Petrovest Inc 329 Market PO Box 518 Natchez MS 39120

HOLLAND, GENE GRIGSBY (SCOTTY), artist; b. Hazard, Ky., June 30, 1928; d. Edward and Virginia Lee (Watson) Grigsby; B.A., U. S. Fla., 1968; pupil of Ruth Allison, Talequah, Okla., 1947-48, Ralph Smith, Washington, 1977, Clint Carter, Atlanta, 1977, R. Jordan, Winter Park, Fla., 1979, Cedric Baldwin Egeli Workshop, Charleston, S.C., 1984; m. George William Holland, Sept. 22, 1950; 3 children. Various clerical and secretarial positions, 1948-52; news reporter, photographer Bryan (Tex.) Daily News, 1952; clk. Fogarty Bros. Moving and Transfer, Tampa and Miami, Fla., 1954-57; tchr. elem. Schs., Hillsborough County, Fla., 1968-72; salesperson, assoc. real estate, 1984—; owner, operator antique store, 1982—. One-woman/group shows include: Tampa Woman's Clubhouse, 1973, Cor Jesu, Tampa, 1973, bank, Monks Corner, S.C., 1977, Summerville Artists Guild, 1977-78, Apopka (Fla.) Art and Foliage Festival, 1980, 81, 82, Fla. Fedn. Women's Clubs, 1980, 81, 82; numerous group shows, latest being: Island Gifts, Tampa, 1980-82, Brandon (Fla.) Station, 1980-81, Holland Originals, Orlando, Fla.; represented in permanent collections including Combank, Apopka, also pvt. collections. Vol., ARC, Tampa, 1965-69, United Fund Campaign, 1975-76; pres. Mango (Fla.) Elem. Sch. PTA, 1966-67; pres. Tampa Civic Assn., 1974-75; vol. Easter Seal Fund Campaign, 1962-63. Recipient numerous art awards, 1978-82. Mem. Internat. Soc. of Artists, Council of Arts and Scis. for Central Fla., Fedn. of Women's Clubs (pres. Hillsborough County 1974-75, v.p. Tampa 1974-75), Meth. Women's Soc. (sec. 1976-77), Nat. Trust for Historic Preservation, Nat. Hist. Soc., Central Fla. Geneal. and Hist. Soc., Am. Guild Flower Arrangers, Methodist Soc. Clubs: Internat. Inner Wheel (past chmn. dist. 696, pres. Tampa 1972-73), Musicale (1st v.p. bd. incorporators Tampa 1974-75), Apopka Woman's (pres. 1981-82, dir. 1983-85). Home: 1080 Errol Pkwy Apopka FL 32712 Office: PO Box 700 Plymouth FL 32768 also 1231 N Orange Ave Orlando FL 32804

HOLLAND, IRIS KAUFMAN, state legislator; b. Springfield, Mass., Sept. 30, 1920; d. Leo and Sadie Kaufman; grad. Rider Coll., Trenton, N.J.; m. Gilbert S. Holland, Jan. 1, 1941; children—Judy, Richard, Donald. Mem. Mass. Ho. of Reps. from 2d Hampden Dist., 1973—, Republican whip, 1979-82, asst. Republican floor leader, 1983—; columnist Your State Ombudsman; guest lectr. Mt. Holyoke, Smith, Springfield, Am. Internat., Western New Eng. colls.; Robert A. Taft lectr. Tufts U., U. Mass. Bd. corporators Baystate Med. Center, Goodwill Industries, Springfield Day Nursery; adv. bd. Mass. Comm. for Blind; trustee Willis Ross Sch. Deaf; adv. council, trustee Bay Path Jr. Coll.; bd. dirs. Pioneer Valley chpt. ARC; mem. spl. com. Pres. John F.Kennedy Meml. Named Woman of Yr., Women's Div., Greater Springfield C. of C., 1980; recipient Woman of Achievement award Mass. Fedn. Bus. and Profl. Women's Clubs; Outstanding Legislator of Yr. award Mass. League Cities and Towns; Disting. Citizen award Rep. Club of Mass. Mem. LWV, Mass. Caucus Women Legislators. Club: Zonta Internat.

HOLLAND, LISA ANN, real estate broker; b. Houston, Nov. 11, 1959; d. Robert Gene and Shirley Ann (Collins) H.; B.B.A., Southwest Tex. State U., 1982. Sr. property mgr. Century 21, San Marcos, Tex., 1980-83; v.p. Heritage Mgmt., Houston, 1983-84; exec. property mgr., broker U.S.A. Mgmt., Houston, 1984—. Mem. Gulf Coast AAU, Profl. Assn. Diving Instrs., Community Assn. Inst., Inst. Real Estate Mgmt. Home: 3400 Timmons St #1 Houston TX 77027

HOLLAND, PATTI ANNE, advertising executive; b. Balt., June 26, 1951; d. Harold Ray Holland and Shirley Anne (Rappoldt) Simmons; m. William Joseph Orr, Mar. 14, 1969 (div. 1972); m. 2d, Les Cockrell, Feb. 14, 1982. B.F.A., Middle Tenn. State U., 1976. Designer L.M. Berry, Nashville, 1976; designer Methodist Pub. House, Nashville, 1977-79; art dir. Parkhurst Pubs., Dallas, 1979-80; dir. advt. Bus. Pubs. Inc., Plano, Tex., 1980—. Mem. Art Dirs. Club (Silver award 1978), Nat. Assn. Female Execs. Home: 13433 Glenside Dr Farmers Branch TX 75234 Office: Bus Pubs Inc 1700 Alma Rd Plano TX 75075

HOLLAND, ROSETTA CLARE, dietitian; b. Flandrenau, S.D., Nov. 11, 1919; d. Stephen Elton and Josephine (Johnson) Perley; m. George Alfred Holland, June 24, 1950 (dec. 1980). B.S. in Dietetics, U. Minn., 1940; postgrad. U. Calif.-Berkeley, 1947-48, George Pepperdine Coll., 1952, Utah State U., 1970. Cert. tchr., dietitian, Calif. State supr. Sch. Lunch Program, S.D., 1940-43; dietitian VA, Gulfport, Miss., 1943-44, Cutter Lab., Berkeley, Calif., 1945-47; homemaking tchr. Elk Grove Sch. Dist., Calif., 1947-48; editor Western Home Econs., San Francisco, 1948-49; nutritionist Calif. State Dept. Edn., Berkeley, 1949-52; dir. food services San Jose Unified Sch. Dist., Calif., 1961—. Contbg. editor California School Lunch Guide and newsletters. Research grantee Calif. Dept. Edn., 1976-79, 79-82, U.S. Office Edn., 1982-86. Mem. Nat. Sch. Food Service Assn., Calif. Sch. Food Service Assn., No. Calif. Sch. Food Service Assn. (hon. life and pres.), Calif. Liaison Council Home Econs. (vice chmn. to program dir.), Calif. Assn. Urban Food Services Dirs. (pres.), Home Econs. Assn., AAUW, Nutrition Edn. Assn. Republican. Lutheran. Club: Quota (San Jose); League of Friends of Santa Clara Council Commn. on Status of Women. Avocations: piano; photography; reading; gardening; stamp collecting. Home: 1607 Koch Ln San Jose CA 95125 Office: San Jose Unified Sch Dist 706 W Julian St San Jose CA 95126

HOLLAND, SANDRA GUNTER, journalist, editor; b. Mount Airy, N.C., Jan. 12, 1952; d. Joseph Bernard and Rondalene Geralda (Stanley) Gunter; m. Gasper O. Holland, Feb. 14, 1981. B.S. in Journalism, Va. Commonwealth U., Richmond, 1973; postgrad. U. Tex., Austin, 1974, North Tex. State U., Denton, 1975-78. Report writer Va. Dept. Hwys., 1973; newsletter editor Tex. Employment Commn., Austin, 1977-80; former tchr. English and journalism; owner Holland Secretarial Services; Media contact Congl. candidate; office mgr., election coordinator Republican Party of Atascosa County, 1986; part-time reporter sta. KBOP, 1985—. Served with USAR; mem. Tex. Army N.G. Recipient Danforth award, 1973; Freedom Found. awards, 1980, 82. Mem. Am. Soc. Notaries, Mensa, UDC. Baptist. Home and Office: 529 Oakhaven Dr Pleasanton TX 78064

HOLLANDER, DORIS A., psychologist, consultant, businesswoman; b. St. Louis, Oct. 13, 1941; d. Samuel and Rose (Heller) H.; B.A., Washington U., 1964; M.A. with distinction, DePaul U., 1972; Ph.D., Loyola U., 1979; m. Jerrold Blumoff, June 9, 1963; children—Sam, Rebecca. Caseworker, Mo. Div. Welfare, St. Louis, 1964-65; research asso. Inst. Juvenile Research, Chgo.,

1967-68; instr. ednl. psychology Loyola U., Chgo., 1972-73; psychologist, program developer Women's Achievement Program, Hammond, Ind., 1976-78; pres. Whole Food & Grain Depot, Oak Park, Ill., 1972-78; asst. prof. psychology Webster Coll., St. Louis, 1979-83; pres. New Options, Inc., 1983—; co-chairperson psychology, sociology and anthropology, dir. adult learner project. Exec. v.p., program chmn. Oak Park Mental Health Bd., 1976-79. Mem. Assn. Community Mental Health Authorities Ill. (del.), Am. Psychol. Assn., Southeastern Psychol. Assn., Mo. Psychol. Assn. sec. 1985-87, chmn. women's issues com. 1983-84), St. Louis Network Women Psychologists coordinator women's issues com. 1982-84, bd. dirs. 1984-86), Am. Ednl. Research Assn., Am. Personnel and Guidance Assn., Am. Soc. Tng. and Devel., St. Louis Psychol. Assn. (pres.), Soc. St. Louis Psychologists (program chmn.). Editor: Missouri Psychologist. Home: 6330 Alexander Dr Saint Louis MO 63105 Office: 8600 Delmar Blvd Saint Louis MO 63130

HOLLANDER, ELLEN COLLINS, hospital personnel executive; b. Cambridge, Mass., Mar. 6, 1946; d. John Ambrose and Marjorie Emma (Merrifield) Collins; B.A., Boston Coll., 1967; M.A., Incarnate Word Coll., 1976; 1 child, Christopher Antony Botto. Teaching supr. dept. clin. adminstrn. Mass. Gen. Hosp., Boston, 1963-67; supr. radiology dept. Genesee Hosp., Rochester, N.Y., 1969-70; coordinator edn. S.W. Tex. Meth. Hosp., San Antonio, 1970-77, asst. dir. personnel, 1977—; adj. faculty Sch. Health Professions, S.W. Tex. State U., San Marcos, 1976—; bd. dirs. Santa Rosa Med. Ctr. Fed. Credit Union, 1986—. Mem. Am. Hosp. Assn., Am. Soc. Healthcare Edn. and Tng. (dir. 1977-80, Disting. Service award 1982), San Antonio Area Soc. Healthcare Edn. and Tng. (pres. 1972, 74-75), Tex. Soc. Hosp. Educators (Outstanding Service award 1981), Tex. Hosp. Assn. Author: Identifying Healthcare Training Needs, 1984; contbr. articles to profl. jours.; bd. dirs. Inservice Tng. and Edn. Mag., 1972-76. Home: 6123 Walking Gait Dr San Antonio TX 78240 Office: 7700 Floyd Curl Dr San Antonio TX 78229

HOLLANDER KING, CAROLE, editor; b. St. Louis, Jan. 21, 1949; d. Harry Emile and Vera Louise (Cobb) H.; m. Ahmad Abdulkadar Attallah, Dec. 21, 1970 (div. Aug. 1977); m. 2d, Cecil King, Jan. 25, 1980. B.A. magna cum laude, U. Mo.-St. Louis, 1978; M.S., So. Ill. U., 1983. Asst. editor Gateway Golfer, St. Louis, 1980-83; pres. KingSearcher Communications, St. Louis, 1983—, Webster U., 1984. instr. St. Louis Community Coll., 1983—. Author: St. Louis Is for Families, 1978; also numerous articles. Served with USAR, 1979-82. Mem. Internat. Assn. Bus. Communicators. Home: The Trapezium 3501 Arkansas Ave Saint Louis MO 63118

HOLLAND-OLSON, NANCY HUNTLEY, industrial relations executive, lawyer; b. Boise, Idaho, Jan. 7, 1941; d. Merle LeRoy and Isabel Hannah (Danielson) Huntley; m. Roger Gerald Olson, June 20, 1982; children—Stephen Roger, Carolyn Kay. B.S. in Bus. Adminstrn., Coll. of Idaho, 1964; J.D., U. Wash., 1972. Bar: Wash. 1973, U.S. Supreme Ct. 1979. Atty., Lane, Powell, Moss & Miller, Seattle, 1972-78; assoc. gen. counsel Gen. Telephone of N.W., Everett, Wash., 1978-81; lawyer Reed, McClure, Moceri & Thonn, Seattle, 1981-82; dir. indsl. relations Criton Technologies, Bellevue, Wash., 1982—; v.p. Bader & Olson, Seattle, 1983—. Bd. dirs. Spl. Olympics, Seattle, 1979. Mem. ABA, Wash. State Bar Assn., Seattle-King County Bar Assn., AAUW, Kappa Kappa Gamma. Republican. Mem. Ch. of Jesus Christ of Latter Day Saints. Home: 3110B Portage Bay Pl E Seattle WA 98102 Office: Criton Technologies 10800 NE 8th St Bellevue WA 98004

HOLLEB, DORIS B., urban planner, economist; b. N.Y.C., Oct. 26, 1922; d. Abraham and Rachel Bernstein; B.A., Hunter Coll., 1942; M.A., Harvard U., 1947; postgrad. U. Chgo., 1959-60, 65-66; m. Marshall M. Holleb, Oct. 15, 1944; children—Alan, Gordon, Paul. Economist Fed. Res. Bd., Washington, 1943-44; freelance journalist, 1945-63; econ. cons. Chgo. Dept. City Planning, 1963-64; research assoc. Center Urban Studies, U. Chgo., 1966-78, sr. research assoc., 1978—, dir. Met. Inst., 1973—, professional lectr., 1979—; chmn., Francis W. Parker Sch. Ednl. Council, 1965—; mem. adv. council Adlai E. Stevenson Center Inst., 1972-79; bd. dirs. Inter. Am. Found., 1980-84, Pacific Basin Inst., 1981—; mem. nat. adv. com. White House Conf. on Balanced Nat. Growth and Econ. Devel., 1978; mem. Northeastern Ill. Planning Commn., 1973-77; mem. Chgo. Met. Area Transp. Council, 1980-84; mem. adv. council to Nat. Ctr. Research on Vocat. Edn., Dept. Edn., 1979-82, Dept. state adv. com. internat. investment, tech. and devel., 1979-81. Mem. Am. Inst. Cert. Planners, Am. Planning Assn., Am. Econ. Assn., Phi Beta Kappa, Lambda Alpha. Clubs: Arts, Tavern Quadrangle, (Chgo.); Harvard (N.Y.C.). Author: Social and Economic Information for Urban Planning, 1968; Colleges and the Urban Poor; The Role of Public Higher Education in Community Service, 1972; contbr. articles to profl. jours. Home: 2650 Lakeview Ave Chicago IL 60614 Office: U Chgo 5828 S University Ave Chicago IL 60637

HOLLEY, KAREN COYETTE, lawyer; b. Montgomery, Ala., Nov. 16, 1953; d. James Coy and Virginia (Cardwell) H. B.A., Auburn U., 1976; J.D., Cumberland Law Sch., 1979. Legal asst. J. Formby Law Firm, Wetumpka, Ala., 1979-81; sr. claim rep. Travelers Ins. Co., Houston, 1981—. Mem. Tex. Bar Assn. Republican. Baptist. Home: 7500 Bellerive St Apt 516 Houston TX 77036 Office: Travelers Ins Co 4 Greenway Plaza E Houston TX 77046

HOLLEY, LAUREN ALLANA (MRS. WAYMAN TAYLOR HOLLEY), mental health consultant, family therapist; b. Balt., Oct. 9, 1948; d. Winston Willouby and Mary Elizabeth (Hart) Holley; B.S., Morgan State U., 1976; M.A., Antioch U., 1978. Staff Balt. City Schs., 1978—; night communications staff ARC, Balt.; outreach family therapist emergency services Rosewood State Ctr., Owings Mills, Md.; behavioral psychologist assoc. for mentally retarded and developmentally disabled. Recipient Award of Merit, Voter Registration Com., 1980, award outstanding achievement Jobs Project, Morris Goldseker Found., 1979-80. Mem. NAACP (membership com. 1980), Nat. Assn. Female Execs. Office: 4701 N Charles St Baltimore MD 21218 also Rosewood Ctr Owings Mills MD

HOLLEY, RONI MORGAN, insurance company executive; b. Okolona, Miss.; d. Romie Brown and Evelyn (Anderson) Morgan; m. Mickey Holley, Oct. 8, 1965 (dec. Sept. 1976); children—Scott, Burke, Leslie. B.S. in Bus. Edn., Troy State U., 1977. Sec. State Farm Ins., Enterprise, Ala., 1974-79, ins. agt., Dothan, Ala., 1979—. Active Kidney Found., United Way, March of Dimes. Recipient Nat. Quality award Nat. Assn. Life Underwriters, 1981; named Top Agt. Dothan Dist.-State Farm, 1985. Mem. Dothan Assn. Life Underwriters (1st v.p., pres. 1986-87), Women's Council of Realtors, Dothan Bd. Realtors, Dothan C. of C. Republican. Methodist. Lodge: Zonta Internat. (bd. dirs. 1985-86). Home: 1610 Haisten Dr Dothan AL 36301 Office: State Farm Ins 513 S Oates St PO Box 541 Dothan AL 35302

HOLLIDAY, BARBARA MIRIAM, journalist; b. Little River, Kans., Aug. 28, 1917; d. Ray Brooks and Nina Blanche (Cook) Brooks Gregg; m. Robert Breckenridge Holliday, Mar. 6, 1937 (dec. 1957); children—Nina, Robert Gregg, Mindy, Susan. A.A., Christian Coll., Columbia, Mo., 1937; B.A., U. Mo., 1939, M.A., 1967. Feature writer Columbia Daily Tribune, 1958-60; writer Detroit Free Press, 1960—, asst. mag. editor, 1966-69, feature, book page editor, 1970-80, book editor, 1980—; lectr. Oakland U., Rochester, Mich., 1979-83. Contbr. articles to popular mags., 1964-68. Recipient feature writing award Mo. Press Women, 1959-60, feature writing award Nat. Press Women, 1960, feature series award Mich. AP, 1963. Mem. Nat. Book Critics Circle, Soc. Profl. Journalists (treas. 1976-78), U. Mo. Alumni Assn. (communications com. 1968-83). Democrat. Methodist. Club: Detroit Press. Office: Detroit Free Press 321 W Lafayette Blvd Detroit MI 48231

HOLLIDAY, JENNIFER YVETTE, singer, actress; b. Riverside, Tex., Oct. 19, 1960; d. Oil Holliday and Genevieve Eaton. Began singing career in gospel music with Houston Bapt. Ch. choirs; appeared in Don't Bother Me, I Can't Cope, Houston, 1978, Your Arms Too Short to Box with God, Broadway, 1980-81, Dream Girls, Broadway, 1981-82, Los Angeles, 1983, Sing, Mahalia, Sing, 1985; recs. include Feel My Soul, 1983, Say You Love Me, 1985. Recipient Grammy award (Rhythm and blues vocal) for And I Am Telling You I'm Not Going, 1982; Tony award, Dream Girls, 1982. Address: care Geffen Records 9130 Sunset Blvd Los Angeles CA 90069*

HOLLIDAY, PATRICIA RUTH MCKENZIE, evangelist; b. Jacksonville, Fla., Nov. 17, 1935; d. Robert Irving and Leona Adele (Bell) McKenzie; student Massey Bus. Coll., 1969, Luther Rice Sem., 1976; D.D., Southeastern Sem., 1986; m. Jan. 20, 1965; children—Connie, Katheryn, Alexander. Sec., Delta Drug Corp., Jacksonville, 1965—; pres. Microfilm Center, Jacksonville, 1974—; pres. Miracle Outreach Ministry, Jacksonville, 1974—. Sec.. Four Found., Inc.; Republican candidate for Fla. Ho. of Reps., 1972; mem. Fla. Republican. Com., 1976-80; lobbyist Fla. Legislature, 1978-80; hostess Pat Holliday TV Show, Jacksonville. Clubs: Minutewomen of Fla. (founder), Univ., Women, Ponte Vedra Women's. Author: Holliday for the King, 1978; Be Free, 1979; Only Believe, 1980; Born Anew, 1981; The Walking Dead, 1982; Anointing Power, 1982; Signs, Wonders and Reactions, 1984; AIDS, 1985; Dealing with Heresies, 1986; columnist Christian Courier. Home: 9252 San Jose Blvd Apt 2804 Jacksonville FL 32217 Office: Miracle Outreach Ministry PO Box 10126 Jacksonville FL 32207

HOLLIDAY-BAKER, KAREN, hotel executive; b. Hollywood, Calif., Mar. 21, 1948; d. Frank A. Kelly Jr. and Dee A. (McWhorter) Kelly Archer; m. Kenneth J. Holliday, June 21, 1969 (div. Mar. 1978); 1 child, Tiffany Ann; m. Toby Evans Baker, June 8, 1980 (separated Sept. 1984). Student pub. schs., Woodland Hills, Calif. Mgr., Zane Grey Hotel, Avalon, Calif., 1969—, owner, 1975—. Chairperson Vehicle Rev. Bd., Avalon, 1982—. Republican. Club: Catalina Racquet (sec. 1972-80) (Avalon). Avocations: tennis; swimming; water skiing; needlework. Home: 199 Chimes Tower Rd Avalon CA 90704 Office: Zane Grey Pueblo Hotel PO Box 216 Avalon CA 90704

HOLLIES, LINDA HALL, pastor, workshop consultant; b. Gary, Ind., Mar. 29, 1943; d. James Donald and Doretha Robinson (Mosley) Adams; m. Charles H. Hollies, Oct. 14, 1962; children—Gregory Raymond, Grelon Renard, Grian Eunyke. B.S. in Adminstrn., Ind. U., 1975; M.A. in Communications, Gov. State U., 1980; M.Div., Garrett-Evang. Theol. Sem., 1986—. Tchr. Hammond Public Schs., Ind., 1975-77; supr. Gen. Motors Corp., Willow Springs, Ill., 1977-79; gen. supr. Ford Motor Co., East Chicago Heights, Ill., 1979-82; coordinator Women in Ministry Evangelical Theol. Sem., Evanston, Ill., 1984-86; pastor New Life Community Fellowship United Methodist Ch., Lansing, Mich., 1983—; founder, dir., cons. Church Aflame Workshops, Inc., Chgo., 1982—, Woman to Woman Ministries, Inc. Trustee Garrett Evang. Theol. Sem., 1984-86; appointee Mayor's Commn. on Role and Status of Women, Gary, 1982-83. Ford fellow, 1975, Benjamin E. Mays fellow, 1984; crusade scholar United Meth. Ch., 1984; Lucy Ryder Myer scholar, 1985-86. Mem. Bus. and Profl. Women Assn., Urban League, NAACP, Internat. Toastmistress Club (pres. 1976-77). Democrat. Avocations; reading; preaching; creative writing; latch hook. Home: 2725 Wabash Rd Lansing MI 48910 Office: Catherine McAuley Health Ctr 5301 E Huron River Dr PO Box 992 Ann Arbor MI 48106

HOLLINGER, PAULA COLODNY, state legislator; b. Washington, Dec. 30, 1940; d. Samuel and Ethel (Levy) Colodny; R.N. (Murry Guggenheim award 1961), Mt. Sinai Hosp., N.Y.C., 1961; m. Paul Hollinger, Sept. 16, 1962; children—Ilene, Marcy, David. Mem. Md. Ho. of Dels. from 11th Dist., 1978—. Mem. Commn. on Nursing Issues in Md., 1982, Gov.'s Task Force on Violence and Extremism, Gov.'s Task Force on AIDS, Gov.'s Task Force on Black Minority Health; mem. Joint Oversight Com. on Health Care Cost Containment; chmn. sci. and tech. resource com. Nat. Conf. State Legislatures, 1984; chmn. Acid Rain Workgroup Mem. Orgn. Rehab. Tng., Nat. Council Jewish Women, Women Legislators of Md. (v.p. 1984). Club: B'nai B'rith Women. Office: Room 310B House Office Bldg State Capitol Annapolis MD 21401

HOLLINGSWORTH, BARBARA D., lawyer, educator; b. Oak Grove, La., Jan. 19, 1945; d. James Vernon and Sarah Maurine (Black) H. B.S. in Phys. Edn., La. Tech. U., 1967, M.S. in Phys. Edn., 1969; Ph.D. in Motor Learning, Fla. State U., 1973; J.D., Campbell U., Buies Creek, N.C., 1983. Cert. tchr., N.C.; bar: N.C. 1983. Tchr., coach Port Allen (La.) High Sch., 1967-70, Cairo (Ga.) Middle Sch., 1971-72; assoc. prof. Mars Hill (N.C.) Coll., 1972-80; sole practice, Concord, N.C., 1983—. Author: Physical Activity for a Lifetime, 1978; contbr. articles to profl. jours., chpt. to book. Mem. ABA, N.C. Bar Assn., N.C. Assn. Women Attys., AAHPER, N.C. Assn. Health, Phys. Edn. and Recreation (adminstrv. chair), Omicron Delta Kappa, Delta Kappa Gamma. Democrat. Baptist. Home: 3257 C Shamrock Dr Charlotte NC 28215

HOLLINGSWORTH, MARTHA LYNNETTE, educator; b. Waco, Tex., Oct. 9, 1951; d. Willie Frederick and Georgia Cuddell (Bryant) J.; m. Roy David Hollingsworth, Dec. 31, 1971; children—Richard Avery, Justin Brian. A.A., McLennan Community Coll., 1972; B.B.A., Baylor U., 1974. Tchr., Connally Ind. Sch. Dist., Waco, 1974—; with Adult Edn. Night Sch., 1974-78; chairperson for Area III leadership conf. Vocat. Office Careers Clubs Tex., Waco, 1985—. Mem. Vocat. Office Edn. Tchr.'s Assn. Tex., Future Homemakers Am. Area VIII (hon.), Tex. Future Farmers Am. (hon.). Baptist. Office: Connally Vocat Dept 715 Rita Waco TX 76705

HOLLINSHEAD, ARIEL CAHILL, research oncologist, virologist, educator; b. Allentown, Pa., Aug. 24, 1929; d. Earl Darnell and Gertrude Loretta (Cahill) H.; student Swarthmore Coll., 1948; A.B., Ohio U., 1951, D.Sc., 1977; M.A., George Washington U., 1955, Ph.D., 1957; m. Montgomery K. Hyun, Sept. 27, 1958; children—William Cahill, Christopher Charles. Asst. prof., fellow in virology Baylor U. Med. Center, Houston, 1958-59; asst. prof. pharmacology George Washington U., Washington, 1959-61, asst. prof. medicine, 1961-64, assoc. prof. medicine, head lab. virus and cancer research, 1964-73, prof. medicine, dir. lab., 1974—. Named Med. Woman of Yr., 1976; decorated Star of Europe medal, 1980. Fellow AAAS, Am. Soc. Microbiology, N.Y. Acad. Sci.; mem. Internat. Assn. Comparative Leukemia Research, Internat. Assn. Study Lung Cancer, Am. Assn. Immunology, Soc. Exptl. Biology Medicine (Disting. Scientist award 1985), Am. Soc. Clin. Oncology, Am. Assn. Cancer Research, Washington Acad. Scis., Internat. Soc. Preventive Oncology, Internat. Agy Research on Cancer, Internat. Union Against Cancer, Grad. Women in Sci. (nat. pres. 1985-86). Washington Forum (pres. 1986—), Sigma Xi, Sigma Delta Epsilon. Clubs: Kenwood Country, Blue Ridge Mountain Country. Contbr. 200 articles to profl. jours., 30 book chpts.; discover specific active immunotherapy of cancer.

HOLLIS, MARY FERN CAUDILL, nurse, concert singer, author; b. Augusta, Ga., Mar. 13, 1942; d. Robert Paul and Ethel Fern (Alderton) Caudill; student Okla. Bapt. U., 1960-61, Memphis State U., 1961-62; B.Music Edn., U. Louisville, 1964; postgrad. George Peabody Coll. Tchrs., 1970-74, U. Tenn., Nashville, 1975-80; A.S. in Nursing, Tenn. State U., 1980; m. Harry Newcombe Hollis, Jr., Dec. 25, 1962; children—Harry III (dec.), Mary Melissa, Newcombe IV. Tchr. music, piano and vocal studies, 1962-75; profl. soloist, Louisville, 1962-69; concert soloist, Mid-South area, 1969—; mem., soloist Nashville Symphony Chorus and Orch., 1972-75; counselor Alive Hospice, Nashville, 1975—; registered nurse St. Thomas Hosp., Nashville, 1981-82; hospice nursice Alive Hospice, 1982—, pediatric program dir., 1984—. Historian, Middle Tenn. chpt. Oncology Nursing Soc., Nashville, 1981—. Mem. Nat. Oncology Nursing Soc., Children's Hospice Internat. (charter), Middle Tenn. Oncology Nursing Soc., Nashville Bonsai Soc., Sigma Alpha Iota, Gamma Phi Beta. Baptist. Author: My Hedges Were Down, 1982; Reflections of a Hospice Nurse, My Hedges Were Down. contbr. articles to profl. jours. Office: care ALIVE Hospice of Nashville 2313-21st Ave S Nashville TN 37212

HOLLIS-ALLBRITTON, CHERYL DAWN, retail paper supply store executive; b. Elgin, Ill., Feb. 15, 1959; d. L.T. and Florence (Elder) Saylors; m. Thomas Allbritton, Aug. 10, 1985. B.S. in Phys. Edn., Brigham Young U., 1981; cosmetologist Sch. Beauty Culture, Berwyn, 1981. Retail sales clk. Bee Discount, North Riverside, Ill., 1981-82, retail store mgr., Downers Grove, Ill., 1982, Oaklawn, Ill., 1982-83, St. Louis, 1983; retail tng. mgr. Arvey Paper & Supplies, Chgo., 1984, retail store mgr., Columbus, Ohio, 1985—. Mem. Nat. Assn. Female Execs. Republican. Mormon. Avocations: cosmetology; reading; travelling. Home: Columbus OH 43209 Office: Arvey Paper & Supplies 431 E Livingston Columbus OH 43215

HOLLISTER, MONICA A., cosmetics company executive; b. Chgo., Feb. 27, 1946; d. William J. and Joan Poetz; m. Thomas A. Manion, May 22, 1971 (div. 1975); m. 2d, Gary Lewis Hollister, May 6, 1978. Student No. Ill. U.; B.S. in Bus. Adminstrn., Northwestern U.-Chgo. Owner Merle Norman Studios, Hammond, Ind. and Merrillville, Ind., 1969-78; v.p. mktg. Merle Norman, Los Angeles, 1978-83; pvt. cons.

HOLLORAN, CECILIA MUELLER, shoe company executive, advertising educator; b. St. Louis; d. Anthony Louis Jungman and Ann Marie (Schnalzer) Jungman Mueller; stepdau. Frank Albert Mueller; m. Mark Richard Holloran, July 23, 1959 (div.); children—Michael Stephen Murdoch, Cara Lyn Schlotter, Cecilia Elizabeth. Student, Hadley Tech. Sch., 1949, Mo. U., 1954, Washington U.-St. Louis, 1957-59; B.A., St. Louis U., 1984. Pres., House of Holloran, Inc., St. Louis, 1963-65; advt. mgr. Weiss-Neuman Shoe Co., St. Louis, 1965-71; art dir. Venture, St. Louis, 1971-72, Famous-Barr, St. Louis, 1972-80; dir. advt. Boston Stores, Ft. Smith, Ark., 1980-81; dir. advt. Tober Industries, Inc., St. Louis, 1981—; instr. St. Louis Community Coll., 1971-80; cons. Expertise, St. Louis, 1978-80. Author poetry, 1949. Vice-chmn. Democratic Party Nat. Campaign, St. Louis, 1960; hdqrs. mgr. Dem. Party State/Senatorial, St. Louis, 1962; hdqr. mgr. Dem. Party City/Mayoral, St. Louis, 1964; area chmn. Easter Seal Soc.-March of Dimes, St. Louis, 1963-64, 1st prize, 1949. Recipient Restoration/renovation award Dutchtown Assn., 1979, Tower Grove Bank, 1978. Mem. Retail Advt. Conf. (awards 3), Nat. Assn. Female Execs., Internat. Press Assn., Internat. Platform Assn., Am. Film Inst., Nat. Trust for Hist. Preservation. Roman Catholic. Clubs: Advt. II, Press (St. Louis). Office: Tober Industries Inc 1520 Washington Ave St Louis MO 63103

HOLLOWAY, DIANE ELAINE, psychotherapist; b. Tulsa, Oct. 19, 1937; d. Lawrence Lynn and Helen May (Six) Hatcher; B.S., Tex. Woman's U., 1972, M.A., 1974, Ph.D., 1979; m. 1961; children—Brian, Kathleen; m. 2d, Bob Cheney, 1980. Brit. rep. Study Abroad, Inc., London, 1957-59; psychologist Presbyn. Hosp., Dallas, 1970-75, dir. psychol. services and asso. dir. continuing edn. in psychiatry, 1976-78; mental health/mental retardation cons. Drug Rehab. and Law Enforcement Offices, Dallas County, 1975-77; psychotherapist in pvt. practice, Dallas, 1978—; asso. Pain Therapy Assn., Dallas, 1979-81; pres. Security & Mgmt. Systems, Dallas, 1979-81, Mental Health Profl. Group, Dallas, 1980—. Hogg Found. grantee, Southwestern Med. Sch., 1972-73; lic. psychotherapist, Tex. Mem. Am. Med. Writers Assn., Tex. Psychol. Assn., Dallas Psychol. Assn., Am. Psychol. Assn., Tex. Police Assn., Internat. Assn. Chiefs of Police, Archaeol. Inst. Am., Soc. Police and Criminal Psychology, Mensa. Contbr. articles to profl. jours. Home: 11130 Cactus Dallas TX 75238 Office: Suite 619 8210 Walnut Hill Dallas TX 75231

HOLLOWAY, EDNA LARUE, county official; b. Hanover, Pa., July 28, 1942; d. Maurice Edward and Helen Viola (Smith) Wisner; m. Donald LeRoy Holloway, Dec. 29, 1963. B.A., Towson State U., 1964, M.Edn., 1972; cert. in vol. mgmt. U. Colo., 1981. Tchr. Balt. County Pub. Schs., Towson, 1964-74; bookkeeping asst. Gen. Bus. Systems, Parkton, Md., 1974-76; bookkeeper sec. Ret. Sr. Vol. Program, Grand Rapids, Mich., 1976-77, dir., 1977-79; vol. resources coordinator DeKalb County Health Dept., Decatur, Ga., 1981—; cons., liaison vol. DeKalb, Ga. and Atlanta, 1980-81; cons., trainer First Bapt. Ch. Atlanta, 1983; asst. conv. coordinator Balt. Life Ins. Co., 1974-76; sec., receptionist State Farm Ins. Co., 1980-81. Mem. Council Vol. Adminstrs. (bd. dirs. 1982—), Ret. Sr. Vol. Program (v.p. adv. council 1980—), Assn. Vol. Adminstrn. (regional liaison nat. assn.), Charg II. Republican. Club: Rivermist Women's (Lilburn, Ga.). Avocations: piano; tennis; gardening. Home: 3704 Shawnee Run Lilburn GA 30247 Office: DeKalb County Health Dept 440 Winn Way Decatur GA 30030

HOLLOWAY, (HELEN) JEANNETTE, accountant; b. Chilton, Tex., June 11, 1927; d. J.B. and Della Mae (Stussel) Roberts; B.B.A., U. Corpus Christi, 1955; m. May 27, 1950. Tax advisor to ind. oil operators, 1955-60; dealer John Deere indsl. equipment, Corpus Christi, Tex., 1960-64; owner, mgr. Dryden & Holloway Co., C.P.A.s, Corpus Christi, 1964—: Bd. dirs., sec.-treas. Coastal Bend Youth City, 1972-83; adv. dir. South Tex. Children's Heart Assn.; bd. dirs. YWCA, Tex. Research League. C.P.A., Tex. Mem. Am. Inst. C.P.A.s, Tex. Soc. C.P.A.s, Bus. and Estate Planning Council, Exec. Women Internat. Methodist. Office: Dryden & Holloway Co 700 Everhart Terr Corpus Christi TX 78411

HOLLOWAY, JUDY LAURIE, art director; b. Kannapolis, N.C., Nov. 21, 1942; d. Francis Duncan and Hazel Wilma (Baker) Dowless; children—William Clark, Jennifer Anne. B.F.A., Va. Commonwealth U., 1965; postgrad Sch. Visual Arts, N.Y.C., 1974, Fairleigh Dickenson U., 1981. Illustrator Venet Advt. Agy., Union, N.J., 1974-76; art dir. Lee/Baader & Rose, E. Orange, N.J., 1977-78, Robert H. Winters, Inc., East Brunswick, N.J., 1978-79; sr. designer Union Camp Corp., Wayne, N.J., 1979-84; art dir. Bozell, Jacobs, Kenyon & Eckhardt, Advt., Union, 1984—; freelance art dir., Scotch Plains, N.J., 1976-77; adj. faculty Kean Coll. N.J., Union, 1973; watercolor instr. Adult Sch., Grand Rapids, Mich., 1971. Campaigner Dems. for Gary Hart, 1984. Recipient Cert. of Merit, Art Dirs. Club N.J., 1983; Speakers Reporting award, Dale Carnegie Inst., 1985. Fellow Art Dirs. Club of N.J. Club: Franklin Green Ski Plus (historian 1982-83). Avocations: racquetball; skiing; biking; painting; white water rafting; canoeing. Home: 2381 Lake Park Ter Scotch Plains NJ 07076 Office: Bozell Jacobs Kenyon & Eckhardt 2700 Route 22 Union NJ 08073

HOLLOWAY, JULIA FRANCES, air force officer; b. Indianola, Miss., May 3, 1950; d. Harold Francis and Louise Isabelle (Hall) Holloway; B.A., Miss. State U., 1973; postgrad. U. Denver, 1978-80, St. Mary's U., 1983-84. Commd. capt. USAF, 1974; space surveillance officer Mill Valley AFS, Calif., 1974-77, Clear AFS, Alaska, 1977-78, missile warning officer Cheyenne Mt. Complex, Colo., 1978-79, chief MW Standardization/Evaluation Div., CMC, Colo., 1979-81, dep. dir. MW Ops. Directorate, 1981, MW Software Test/Integration mgr., 1981-82, 1st tech. tng. mgr. Air Force Space Systems Career Fields, 1982-84; space systems acquisition tng. mgr., Randolph AFB, Tex., 1984-85; action officer Joint Chiefs of Staff, Nat. Mil. Command System, Command and Control Div., Washington, 1985-86; tactical warning adviser to comdr.-in-chief European Forces Joint Ops. Directorate, Stuttgart, W. Ger., 1986—; cons. in field. Leader Girl Scouts U.S.A., 1975-76; disaster preparedness officer Mill Valley AFS, Calif., 1975-77; disaster preparedness evaluation officer Clear AFS, Alaska, 1977-78; acting chief disaster preparedness evaluation team Hdqrs. N. Am. Aerospace Def. Command, 1979-81. Mem. Air Force Assn., AAUW, Nat. Assn. Female Execs., NOW, Amnesty Internat., Smithsonian Inst. Home: APO New York NY Office: EUCOM/J-3 Patch Barracks Stuttgart Federal Republic of Germany

HOLLOWAY, LORINDA (JILL), advertising specialties executive; b. Sidney, Ohio, Sept. 3, 1952; d. J. Harold and Merry Edith (Cutlip) H.; m. John Conrad Heggblom, June 19, 1971 (div. Aug. 1981); children—Erin D'Lorah Holloway, Johanna Katherine. Student Scottsdale Community Coll., Ariz. State U. Mfr.'s rep. Holloway Sportswear, Ohio; owner, operator Hamer Promotions, Scottsdale, Ariz., 1983—. Bd. dirs. Christ Lutheran Sch., 1983—; mem. Las Rancheros Republican Women's Com., membership bd. dirs. Phoenix and Valley of Sun Conv. and Visitor's Bur.; leader Brownies, Girl Scouts U.S.A.; chmn. "Friends Program", State of Ariz., Phoenix, 1984. Mem. Specialty Advt. Assn. of Ariz. (social com., chairperson membership com., bd. dirs.), Phoenix Met. C. of C., Scottsdale C. of C. (co-chmn. com. 1984-85, chairperson Prospector's com., co-chmn. 1985 membership drive, Ambassador's com.). Republican. Lutheran. Avocations: golf; racquetball; swimming; horseback riding. Office: Hamer Promotions 3014 N Hayden Suite 113 Scottsdale AZ 85257

HOLLOWAY, MATTIE JEAN, social services administrator; b. Ft. Deposit, Ala., July 30, 1947; d. Freddie L. and Mattie (Johnson) Poole; m. Lister Holloway, Nov. 21, 1968; children—Derrick, Denise. B.A., Ala. A&M U., 1970; M.A., Kean Coll., 1978. Cert. tchr. English, French, social work/guidance and counseling. Team tchr. Newark Pub. Schs., 1970-72; tchr. English and drama Malcolm X Shabazz, Newark, 1972-78; mem. child study team Spl. Services, Irvington, N.J., 1978—; founder, exec. dir. Hope for Pregnant Teens, Inc., Hillside, N.J., 1980—; lectr. in field. Past chairperson Hillside Community Recreation Dept., 1978-84; chairperson Voter's Registration Drive, Union County, N.J., 1981-84; Black Com. for Re-Election of Gov. Kean, Union County, 1985. Recipient Outstanding Service award Hillside Recreation Dept., 1985, Outstanding Community Service award Citizens of Hillside, 1983, Outstanding Citizen award Lady "G", 1984, Certificate of Service award Hope, Inc., 1982. Mem. N.J. Edn. Assn., Irvington Edn. Assn., Am. Soc. Notaries, Internat. Black Women's Congress (sec. bd. dirs. 1984-85, Outstanding woman 1985). Avocations: tennis; aerobics; swimming; Bicycle riding; horseback riding.

HOLLOWAY, THERESA LEE, nurse; b. Claremore, Okla., Apr. 6, 1962; d. Sammy Price and Mary Joe (Johnson) Lagers; m. Mickey Wayne Holloway, July 16, 1982. Assoc. in Nursing, Northeastern Okla. A&M Coll., 1983. Lic. R.N., Okla. Sr. nurses aid St. Frances Hosp., Tulsa, 1982; R.N., Grand Valley Hosp., Pryor, Okla., 1983—, sec. patient quality assurance com., 1982—, mem. policy and procedures com., 1982—. Active ARC, Pryor, 1982—. Democrat. Mem. First Ch. of God. Home: Route 1 Box 23 Pryor OK 74361

HOLLY, JUNE S., fundraising executive; b. Houston, Nov. 27, 1920; d. Francis Harrison and Mabel Helen (Verlander) Siegert; m. Austin J. Holly, Nov., 1942 (div. 1971); children—Mary Melissa Holly Cadenhead, Douglas Rhodes, James Barbour. B.A., Rice U., 1942; M.A. in Sociology, U. Houston, 1974, D. Edn. (teaching fellow 1976-79), 1980. Dir. parish edn. St. Mark's Episcopal Ch., Houston, 1964-69; coordinator tng., vols. Houston Met. Ministries, 1969-71; acting exec. dir, 1971-72; cons. edn., bus., med., religious instns., 1972-77; exec. dir. Houston Ctr. Humanities, 1977-84; dir community relations Dexion Programs in Mental Health, 1984—; dir. devel. Harris County Heritage Soc., 1984—; adj. instr. behavioral, social scis., spl. edn. U. Houston, 1978—. Mem. Houston Mayor's Task Force Arts, 1982-83; mem. steering com., Leadership Houston, 1981-87, program chmn., 1981-84; bd. dirs. Nat. Assn. Community Leadership Orgns., 1983-85; chmn. adult edn. St. Mark's Episcopal Ch., Houston, 1982-83; trustee St. James Episcopal Sch., Houston, 1980-84; pres. Coalition Non-profit Orgns., 1984-85. Grantee Houston Ctr. Humanities, NEH, 1979-83, Tex. Com. for Ctr., 1977-84; mem. pub. relations com. Houston Archeol. Commn., 1985—. Mem. Am. Anthropol. Assn. (sec. treas. council anthropology, edn. 1980-83), World Future Soc., Cultural Arts Council Houston, Consortium Urban Edn. Houston, Houston Mus. Fine Arts, Tex. Assn. Museums (program com.), Nat. Soc. Fundraising Execs. Clubs: Houston Jr. Forum (pres. 1947-48), Bradford Townhome Assn. (pres. 1983-84, bd. dirs.). Office: Harris County Heritage Soc 1100 Bagby Houston TX 77002

HOLLY, MARCIA VIVIAN, business executive; b. Bklyn., Sept. 6, 1940; d. Edward Aaron and Mary (Silverman) H.; 1 dau., Alexandra Holly-Gottlieb. B.A., U. Miami, 1961, M.A., 1964; Ph.D., Wash. State U., 1969. Co-dir., founder Women's Studies, Quinnipiac Coll., Hamden, Conn., 1970-72; co-dir. Tng. for Urban Alternatives, New Haven, 1973-77; founder Belladonna Pub., New Haven, 1977-79; freelance med. writer, 1979-81; pres. Med. Communications Unltd., New Haven, 1981—. Contbr. articles to profl. jours. Mem. Pharm. Advt. Council, Am. Med. Writers Assn. (sec. 1982-83, exec. bd. 1983—). Jewish. Home: 214 Maple St New Haven CT 06511 Office: Med Communications Unltd 264 Amity Rd New Haven CT 06525

HOLLY, PATRICIA ANN, nursing educator; b. Ft. Wayne, Ind., Mar. 30, 1935; d. Jeremiah J. and Loretta M. (Borchers) H.; B.S. in Nursing, U. Dayton (Ohio), 1964; M.N., U. Pitts., 1970. Joined Franciscan Sisters, Roman Catholic Ch., 1951; supr., instr. pediatric nursing St. Elizabeth Hosp., Dayton, 1960-63, 65-68; med.-surg. nursing supr. St. Elizabeth Hosp., Covington, Ky., 1964; tchr. pediatric nursing Wright State U., Dayton, 1972-74; dir. nursing Franciscan Terr., Cin., 1975-79; asst. prof. nursing edn. U. Cin., 1981—; trustee Our Lady of Bellefont Hosp., Ashland, Ky., 1981-85, Schroder Manor Nursing Home, Hamilton, Ohio, 1975-84; speaker, cons. in field. Mem. Am. Nurses Assn., Nat. League Nursing. Home: 60 Compton Rd Cincinnati OH 45215 Office: 9555 Plainfield Rd Cincinnati OH 45236

HOLM, CAROLYN, graphic designer; b. Petaluma, Calif., Jan. 3, 1948; d. William Zartman Holm and Jean (Roy) Holm Shell. B.A., Scripps Coll., 1970; postgrad. Art Acad., San Francisco, 1978, Coll. Marin, 1978-80. Asst. mktg. mgr. Hurricane Internat., San Francisco, 1972-76; freelance writer and design coordinator, San Francisco, 1976-77; owner The Holm Group, graphic design firm, San Francisco, 1977—. Bd. dirs. Avanti House Inc., San Rafael, Calif., 1981-83, treas. bd. dirs. 1983—. Office: The Holm Group 405 Sansome St San Francisco CA 94111

HOLM, HANYA, choreographer, director, dancer, dance educator; b. Worms-am-Rhine, Germany; d. Valentin and Marie (Moerschel) Eckert; ed. pvt. schs., Germany; student of music Hoch Conservatory and Dalcroze Inst., Frankfurt-am-Main; grad. Dalcroze Inst., Hellerau; dance diploma Mary Wigman Central Inst., Dresden, Germany; D.F.A. (hon.), Colo. Coll., 1960, Adelphi U., 1969; married and divorced; 1 son, Klaus Holm. Came to U.S., 1931, naturalized, 1939. Chief instr., co-dir. Wigman Inst., Dresden, 10 yrs.; mem. original Wigman Co.; performer, dance dir., choreographer, Europe, until 1931; under auspices Sol Hurok, founder, dir. N.Y. Wigman Sch. Dance, 1931, which later became Hanya Holm Sch. Dance; began Am. concert career, 1936; major prodns.: Trend (N.Y. Times award from John Martin as best dance composition of year), 1937; Metropolitan Daily, 1938; Tragic Exodus (Dance Mag. award for best group choreography in modern dance), 1938; work with theatre; choreography, dir. Davey Crockett, one of Ballet Ballads, 1948; Kiss Me, Kate (Cole Porter) (best choreographer N.Y. Drama Critics award), 1948, Eng. prodn., 1951; Out of this World (C. Porter), 1950; choreographer, dir. The Golden Apple (Critics Circle citation best musical), 1954; staged dances for re-make of film Vagabond King, 1956; choreography for musical Reuben-Reuben, 1955-56; choreography and mus. numbers My Fair Lady (Tony nominee), 1955-56 (Israeli prodn. 1964), Where's Charley, My Fair Lady (English prodns.), 1958, Christine, and Camelot, 1960-61, Anya, 1965; choreographer television show Pinocchio, 1957, Dinner with the President, 1963, Metropolitan Daily (1st dance prodn. on TV), 1939; dir., choreographer world premiere opera The Ballad of Baby Doe, Central City, Colo. opera house, 1956; dir. dance dept. Mus. Theatre Acad., N.Y.C., 1962—. Pioneer Labanotation for copyright on dance scores musicals Kiss Me, Kate, 1948, My Darlin' Aida, 1952, My Fair Lady, 1956; dir. own sch., N.Y.C., until 1968; dir. summer sessions in dance Colo. Coll., 1941-83; mem. staff Alwin Nikolais/Murray Louis Dance Theatre Lab., N.Y.C., 1972—, Juilliard Sch., N.Y.C., 1975—; tchr., lectr. Bretton Coll., Eng., 1979; appeared on Am. Cancer Soc. series, Tactic (NBC), 1959; dir., choreographer opera Orpheus and Euridice (Gluck), Vancouver Internat. Festival, 1959. Recipient Capezio award, 1978; award Fedn. Jewish Philanthropies, 1959; Colo. Centennial award and Gov.'s award, 1973, 74; Heritage Honor award Nat. Dance Assn., 1976; award and medal of distinction in fine arts City of Colorado Springs, 1978; Samuel H. Scripps Am. Dance Festival award, 1984; cert. of Pres. and Fellows of Harvard Coll., 1983-84. Mem. Am. Arbitration Assn. (nat. panel arbitrators), Soc. Stage Dirs. and Choreographers (v.p.). Address: care Elsa Rainer Apt 6/5 145 W 12th St New York NY 10011

HOLMAN, MARY ALIDA, economist, educator; b. West Point, N.Y., June 26, 1933; d. Jonathan Lane and Anna Alida (Johnson) H.; B.A., George Washington U., 1955, M.A., 1957, Ph.D. (Thomas A. Edison fellow 1962), 1963; m. Theodore Suranyi-Unger, Dec. 15, 1962. Mem. faculty George Washington U., 1963—, prof. econs., 1973—; professorial lectr. Indsl. Coll. Armed Forces, 1965-85, Nat. War Coll., 1966-74, Naval Sch. Health Scis., 1979-86; cons. NASA, 1966-68, Pres.'s Cost of Living Council, 1971-73. Recipient Watson award Am. Patent Law Assn., 1964. Mem. Am. Econ. Assn. Author: The Political Economy of the Space Program, 1974; co-author: Price Theory and Its Uses, 1978. Office: Dept Econs George Washington U Washington DC 20052

HOLMBERG, JOYCE, state legislator; b. Rockford, Ill., July 19, 1930; m. Eugene Holmberg; 2 daus. B.A., No. Ill. U.; M.A., Alfred Adler Inst., Chgo. Mem. Ill. State Senate from 34th Dist., 1983—. Democrat. Office: Ill State Capitol Bldg Springfield IL 62706

HOLME, BARBARA SHAW, former state senator; b. Long Beach, Calif., May 24, 1946; d. Harry and Lillian (Walton) Shaw; student UCLA, 1962-63; B.A., Stanford U., 1967; m. Howard Holme, June 16, 1968; children—Timothy Peter, Lisa. Asst. dir. Met. Denver Urban Coalition, 1969-71; urban cons. Cogen Holt & Assocs., New Haven, 1968-69, 1971-72, Denver Housing Adminstrn., 1972-74; mem. Colo. Senate, 1975-85, Democratic caucus chmn., 1977-78, Dem. asst. minority leader, 1979-83. Co-pres. Colo. Young Dems., 1973-74; mem. Capitol Hill United Neighborhoods; mem. Colo. Colo. Environ. Coalition, Met. Air Quality Council; mem. Mayor's Adv. Com. on Youth, Denver, 1969-70; chmn. Colo. Women for Ida Nudel; bd. dirs. Colo. Common Cause. Recipient award for Outstanding Dem. Senator, Colo. Social Legis. Com., 1979, 80. Jewish.

HOLMES, AILEEN BELL, civic worker; b. Lumberton, N.C., May 6, 1926; d. James Edmond and Bertha (Brewington) Bell; m. Normie Holmes, July 27, 1946; children—Olivia Holmes Oxendine, Michael Holmes, Darlene Ransom, Edward. Cosmetology degree Fayetteville Cosmetology Sch., 1960, Doran Sch., 1961. Pres. Magnolia High Sch. Concerned Parents, Lumberton, 1972—; mem. Robeson County Bd. Edn., 1972-76; active LWV, Lumberton, 1975—; mem. adv. com. Robeson County Schs. Voc. Ctr., 1982—; mem. Lumber River Council Community Beautification, 1983—; bd. dirs. Robeson County Church and Community Ctr.; mem. long range planning bd. Robeson Tech. Coll., 1984—. Recipient Outstanding Service award Robeson County Sch. Dist., 1976, Outstanding Service award Robeson Tech. Coll., 1978. Mem. Nat. Hairdresser Assn., Nat. Sch. Bd. Assn., Nat. Ladies Aux. Assn., Alpha Omega Alumni Assn. Democrat. Baptist. Home: Route 10 Box 728 Lumberton NC 28388

HOLMES, BARBARA ANN KRAJKOSKI, educator; b. Evansville, Ind., Mar. 21, 1946; d. Frank Joseph and Estella Marie (DeWeese) Krajkoski; B.S., Ind. State U., 1968, M.S., 1969, specialist cert., 1976; postgrad. U. Nev., 1976-78; m. David Leo Holmes, Aug. 21, 1971; 1 dau., Susan Ann Sky. Acad. counselor Ind. State U., 1968-69, halls dir., 1969-73; dir. residence halls U. Utah, 1973-76; sales assoc. Fidelity Realty, Las Vegas, Nev., 1977-82. cert. analyst Nev. Dept. Edn., 1981-82; tchr. Clark County Sch. Dist., 1982—. Named Outstanding Sr. Class Woman, Ind. State U., 1969; recipient Dir's. award U. Utah Residence Halls, 1973, Outstanding Sales Assoc., 1977; Tchr. of Month award, 1983, Dist. Outstanding Tchr. award, 1984, Dist. Excellence in Edn. award, 1984, 86. Mem. Nev. Assn. Realtors, AAUW, Am. Assn. Women Deans, Adminstrs. and Counselors, Am. Personnel and Guidance Assn., Am. Coll. Personnel Assn., Nevadans for Equal Rights Amendment, Alumnae Chi Omega (treas. Terre Haute chpt. 1971-73, bd. officer Las Vegas 1977—), Clark County Panhellenic Alumnae Assn. (pres. 1978-79), Computer Using Educators So. Nev. (sec. 1983-86). Methodist. Clubs: Job's Daus., Order Eastern Star. Developed personal awareness program U. Utah, 1973-76. Home and Office: 3640 El Toro St Las Vegas NV 89121

HOLMES, BARBARA MARIE, publishing company executive; b. Petaluma, Calif., Sept. 22, 1950; d. Colin and Dorothy (Gamble) H.; spl. student in art Cuesta Coll., Calif., 1968-71; B.S. in Graphic Design, San Jose State U., 1974. Art cons., buyer, dir. holiday design Lee Wards, San Jose, Calif., 1974-75; tchr. art Peninsula Sch., Palo Alto, Calif., 1975-76; dist. mgr. sales Nat. Fedn. Ind. Bus., San Mateo, Calif., 1976-79; br. mgr. Datapro Research Corp. subs. McGraw Hill Co., Mountain View, Calif., 1979—, nat. account mgr., 1983-84; mktg. exec. E.W. Communications, Palo Alto, Calif., 1984—. Recipient cert. for dedication to underprivilaged children Cuesta Coll., 1969; Sales Achievement award Datapro Research Corp., 1979. Mem. Nat. Saleswomen's Assn., Delta Gamma (Sr. Achievement award 1975, v.p. 1975, rush adv. 1980—). Republican. Episcopalian. Office: EW Communications Palo Alto CA

HOLMES, CAROLYN THELMA, employee counselor, chemical addiction therapist; b. Augusta, Ga., Sept. 12, 1944; d. Hickman Leon and Thelma (McKie) H.; m. Wadsworth Lowell Bishop, Aug. 31, 1972 (div. 1980). Student Winston-Salem U., 1963-68; B.S. in Psychology, Rutgers U., 1973, postgrad. in Ednl. Counseling, 1983—. Cert. hypnotherapist, employee asst. counselor, literacy trainer in English. Spl. edn. instr. Planned Parenthood, Essex County, N.J., 1970-72; health and edn. specialist Nat. Urban League, N.Y., N.J., 1964-65; employee asst. counselor, Mcpl. Govt., Newark, 1977—; VISTA supr. Project Read, Newark, 1986—; tng. supr. Literacy Program, Newark, 1965—; addiction therapist Beth Israel Hosp., Passaic, N.J., 1984—. Art dir. Personnel Devel., 1977; mng. editor quar. newsletter. Choir dir. Methodist Ch., Dingmans Ferry, Pa., 1985-86; fundraiser United Negro Coll. Fund, 1982 (leadership award); chmn. U.S. Treasury, 1982-86. Recipient Citizen Activity award Bloomfield Civic Assn., 1976; Police Under Stress award Psychiat. Inst. St. Michael's Hosp., 1979; Employee Assistance Program award St. Joseph's U. and Lankenau Hosp., Phila., 1983. Mem. N.J. Alcoholism Assn., Laubach Literacy Internat. (dir. 1966-83, supr. 1980-85, Service award 1985), UN Assn. (UNICEF chmn. 1985, Service award 1982-85). Democrat. Methodist. Home: R D 1 Box 37 Dingmans Ferry PA 18328 Office: Municipal Government 920 Broad St Newark NJ 07102

HOLMES, CYNTHIA MISAO BELL, health services administrator; b. Yokohama, Japan, June 5, 1949; d. Isaac Walter Bell and Chihoko (Adachi) Bell Parker; m. Edward Theodore Holmes, Dec. 21, 1967 (div. Mar. 1973); children—Kenya K., Larik D. B.A., Columbia U., 1975; M.B.A., CUNY, 1977. Teller, N.Y. Bank for Savs., N.Y.C., 1968-69; sec., adminstrv. asst. Columbia U., N.Y.C., 1970-75; asst. day ctr. dir. N.Y. State Dept. Mental Hygiene, N.Y.C., 1976-77; planner, cons. Hosp. Affiliates, Inc., Nashville, 1977-79; program adminstr. Marion County Health Dept., Indpls., 1979—. Bd. dirs. Ind. Black Expo, Inc., 1981, 82; bd. dirs. chmn. Actors Ink Theatre Prodn. Co., Indpls., 1982—; organizer Health Fair, Ind. Black Expo, 1981, 82. Assoc. U. Programs in Health Administrn. scholar, 1975, 76. Mem. Met. Health Council Indpls. (bd. dirs., sec. 1980—), Ind. Primary Health Care Assn. (bd. dirs., treas. 1982—), Nat. Assn. Community Health Centers (com. mem. 1982—). Avocations: theatre; sweepstaking; real estate investment. Office: Marion County Health Dept 222 E Ohio St Indianapolis IN 46204

HOLMES, DANA CAROLINE, free-lance journalist, editor; b. Buffalo, Nov. 26, 1949; d. Volney Mason and Rivera Carmen (Ingle) H.; m. David Wayne Daniels, Oct. 9, 1982. A.A., Centenary Coll. for Women, 1970; B.A., Wichita State U., 1979; student Oxford U. (Eng.), 1984-85. Artist, Buffalo, 1970-74; media dir. Sullivan Higdon, Wichita, 1975-76; free-lance reporter and photographer, Wichita, 1976-77; pub. relations coordinator ARC, Buffalo, 1980-83; free-lance writer, Buffalo, 1981—. Editor Crosslink, 1980-83. Active Jr. League Buffalo, 1981. Recipient United Way award Excellence, 1983. Mem. Women in Communications. Democrat. Unitarian. Home: 555 Fillmore Ave East Aurora NY 14052

HOLMES, DEBORAH SUE, educational administrator; b. Topeka, Mar. 21, 1953; d. Robert G. and Virginia M. (Slingerland) H.; B.S. in Edn., U. Kans., 1974, M.S. in Curriculum Devel., 1979, cert. adminstrn. instructional tech., 1980. Elem. sch. tchr., Lawrence, Kans., 1972-73, 74-79; co-coordinator Green House Child Care Center, Lawrence, 1973-74; instr. U. Kans., 1973-75; curriculum developer media, literacy project Lawrence Public Schs., 1979-80; dir. fed. programs/curriculum projects University City, Mo., 1980-82; prin. Jackson Park Elem. Sch., University City, 1982-86, Brittany Woods Middle Sch., University City, 1986—; chmn. personnel com. Hilltop Child Devel. Center, Lawrence, 1975-80; cons. in field. Mem. adv. bd. English lang. sch. Recipient Vicki Larason Landman Non-Sexist Teaching award U. Kans., 1975, Jayhawk Tchr. award, 1976. Mem. Assn. Supervision and Curriculum Devel., Elem. Sch. Prins. Assn. Assn. Ednl. Communications and Tech., Conf., Edn., Ninety Nines, NOW, Phi Delta Kappa, Pi Lambda Theta. Author: Thumbs Up, 1978; Nature's Way, 1980; Daily Breaks, 1981, also articles; mem. adv. bd. Oasis mag. Home: 3537 Sidney St Saint Louis MO 63104 Office: 8125 Groby Rd University City MO 63130

HOLMES, DONNA CHRISTINE, telephone directory company executive; b. Oakland, Calif., Nov. 14, 1948; d. Michael Donn and Mary Christine (Woodward) Random; m. Horacio Ricardo Fonseca, Jan. 13, 1968 (div. July 1973); m. Wyndel Leon Holmes, July 14, 1973; stepchildren—Michael David, Matthew Jon. B.A. in Indsl. Psychology, Sierra U., 1986. Sales rep. Pacific Bell Directory, San Francisco, 1978-79; staff, tng. supr., 1979-80, telephone sales supr., Sacramento, 1983-86, bus. control mgr., 1986—; frame chief Pacific Bell, Berkeley, Calif., 1980-82. Named Master Sales mgr. Pacific Bell Directory, 1983, 84, 85, sales laureate, 1984, 85. Mem. Nat. Assn. Female Execs., Sacramento Women's Network. Democrat. Episcopalian. Avocations: reading; wine tasting; travel. Office: Pacific Bell Directory 8795 Folsom Blvd Room 200 Sacramento CA 95826

HOLMES, ETHELYN LIA, electronics engineer, consultant; b. Chgo., Nov. 22, 1953; d. James Turner and Ethyl Helena (Smith) H. B.S. in Math., Ill. Inst. Tech., 1969; A.A. in Electronics, DeVry Inst. Tech., 1980; B.S. in Elec. Engring., U. Dayton, 1986. Tchr. math. Chgo. Bd. Edn., 1970-74, communications cons., 1974; engring. aide Ill. Bell Telephone, Chgo., 1975-79; telecommunications engr. AT&T Long Lines, Chgo., 1980-83; engr., announcer CRIS-Radio, Chgo., 1983-85; chief engr. Northeastern Ill. U., Chgo., 1985—; broadcast engr. Sta. KEEF-AM, Skokie, Ill., 1980-81; civilian engr. U.S. Air Force, Dayton, 1987—. Contbr. articles to mags., profl. jours. Mem. Women in Telecommunications, Nat. Assn. Female Execs., Women Employed, IEEE. Roman Catholic. Avocations: fiction writing; ballet; foreign languages; weight lifting. Home: 5240 N Sheridan Rd #709 Chicago IL 60640

HOLMES, KAY ELIZABETH, health maintenance company executive, consultant; b. Chesapeake City, Md., Aug. 9; m. Clifton Wallace and Evelyn (Boyles) Morgan; m. Richard Holmes, Apr. 6, 1974 (div. Sept. 1977); children—Harold W. Dempsey, Sue J. Dempsey, Thomas C. Dempsey. Diploma Nursing Sch. Wilmington, 1969-72; A.S., Del. Tech. and Community Coll., 1975; student U. Del., 1972-80. R.N., Del. Head nurse A. I. DuPont Inst., Wilmington, 1973-76; utilization rev. coordinator Blue Cross/Blue Shield, Wilmington, 1976-77, mgr., 1977-85; assoc. exec. dir. Companion Healthcare, Columbia, S.C., 1985-86, v.p., Charleston, S.C., 1986—; cons. ins., health maintenance orgns. Mem. Group Health Assn. Am., Am. Mgmt. Assn., Am. Nurses Assn., Trident C. of C. (bd. dirs. 1985-86), LWV. Avocations: reading; music; American and English history. Home: 40A Montagu St Charleston SC 29401 Office: Companion Healthcare 3125 Ashley Phosphate Rd Charleston SC 29418

HOLMES, LOUISE MARIE GENOVESE, food management executive; b. Cleve., Nov. 17, 1937; d. Lorenzo and Louise H. (Salanetro) Genovese; m. James Arland Holmes, Dec. 30, 1983. B.S.H., Ohio U., 1959; postgrad. Mills Coll., 1959-60. With Stouffer Restaurant div. Stouffer Foods Corp., Cleve., 1960-68; dir. foods dept. Stouffer Food Service div., 1968-75; dir. food services Fono's Unltd., San Francisco, 1975-77; div. dietitian Servomation Corp., San Francisco, 1977-78; mgr. ops. purchasing Magic Pan, Inc., San Francisco, 1978-81; cons. on food service State of Calif. VA Home, Yountville, Calif., 1977-78, 80; coordinator quality assurance Greyhound Food Mgmt. Inc., div. Greyhound Corp., Phoenix, 1981—. Mem. women's bd. YWCA of San Mateo County, 1980-82. Mem. Am. Dietetic Assn., Ariz. Dietetic Assn., Bus. and Profl. Women's Assn., Cath. Alumnae Assn., Internat. Food Service Execs. Assn. (sec. Ariz. br. 1984-85), Mills Coll. Alumnae Assn. Republican. Roman Catholic. Club: Soroptimist (v.p. 1974-82). Contbr. articles to profl. jours. Office: Greyhound Towers Bldg 2 Sta 3113 Phoenix AZ 85012

HOLMES, LUCILLE MARTIN, florist; b. Tylertown, Miss., Jan. 9, 1921; d. Lawrence M. and Ella (Smith) Martin; m. Donald E. Holmes, Apr. 15, 1940; 1 child, Donette Holmes Titus. Student floral designing Am. Florist Assn., V. I., 1975, U. Miami 1976, Florist Trans World, London, 1980. Owner, operator Tylertown Florist, 1960—. Mem. Southeastern Florist Assn., La. Florist Assn., Ala. Florist Assn., Miss. Florist Assn. Democrat. Baptist. Clubs: Garden, Country. Avocations: tennis; camping; reading; traveling. Home and Office: Tylertown Florist 425 Beulah Ave Tylertown MS 39667

HOLMES, MARIA LEE, communication services executive; b. San Francisco, Mar. 2, 1944; d. Tracy Sherlock Holmes and Alda Maria (Baranzelli) Holmes-Lyddy. B.A., Calif. State U.-Long Beach, 1967; postgrad. Columbia Pacific U. Cert. tchr., Calif. Tchr., Los Angeles City Schs., 1967-80; cons. Maria Holmes Co., Harbor City, Calif., Maria Holmes Communication Services, Harbor City, 1980—; dir. bus. and program devel. TranSyn, Ltd., Cons., Venice, Calif., 1982; instr. bus. and psychology guest on radio and TV, Los Angeles; cons. Los Angeles County, Carson, 1980; instr. Long Beach State U. Free Coll., 1967. Mem. AAUW, United Tchrs. of Los Angeles, Women in Mgmt., Bus. Mgmt. Assn. Office: Maria Holmes Communication Services 760 W Lomita Blvd #144 Harbor City CA 90710

HOLMES, MARIAN MCGRATH, lawyer; b. Chgo., Apr. 1, 1934; d. Harmon Webber and Margaret Helen (Goodman) McGrath; children—Margaret Etta, Karen Chandler. B.A., Wellesley Coll., 1956; M.Ed., Nat. Coll. Edn., 1970; postgrad. Northwestern U., 1975; J.D., Tex. Tech U., 1982. Bar: Tex. 1982. Pres., Hartzell Corp., Evanston, Ill., 1969-70; tchr. North Shore Country Day Sch., Winnetka, Ill., 1970-76; headmistress Trinity Sch., Midland, Tex., 1976-79; assoc. atty. Lemon, Close, Shearer, Ehrlich & Brown, Perryton, Tex., 1982-85; assoc. Maxwell, Bennett, Thomas & Feldman, Dallas, 1986—. Author, editor Tex. Tech Law Rev., 1980-82. Mem. steering com. for Panhandle br. Women's Advocacy Project, Inc., Austin, 1983—; elder Trinity Presbyn. Ch., 1984-86. Centennial Fund grantee, 1972; recipient Oil and Gas law award, 1982. Mem. ABA, Tex. Bar Assn., Northeast Panhandle Bar Assn. (pres. 1984-86). Republican. Clubs: Bus. and Profl. Women's, Wheatheart Republican Women's (pres. 1983). Home: 4409 Colgate Dallas TX 75225

HOLMES, MARION, clothing designer, marketing consultant; b. N.Y.C., May 11, 1949; d. Tolbert Holmes and Carrie (Knights) Holmes; A.A.S., Fashion Inst. Tech., 1968; cert. fine arts Cooper Union, 1970; m. Richard Nadrich, Sept. 16, 1979 (div. 1984); 1 son, Garrett Richard. Stylist, Van Heusen Shirts, N.Y.C., 1970-74; mdse. mgr. Mann Mfg., Inc. (now Hortex), El Paso, Tex., 1975-76; gen. mdse. mgr. Metro/Pants Co., N.Y.C., 1976-81; pres. Marion Holmes Enterprises Co., apparel design and mktg. cons., N.Y.C., 1981—; designer, mktg. cons. Mem. St. Paulia Soc. (Eng.), Mensa. Patentee in field. Office: Marion Holmes Enterprises Inc 303 Fifth Ave New York NY 10016

HOLMES, MELISSA ANN, vocational consultant; b. Durham, N.C., Mar. 10, 1947; d. Austin and Gilda Ola (Gainer) Sampson; m. Larry Wayne Armstrong, Mar. 21, 1975 (div. 1981), 1 child, Nicholas; m. Glenn Holmes, Nov. 19, 1982. B.S. in Adminstrn. Justice, Wichita State U., 1978. Ops. clk. Boeing, Wichita, Kans., 1974-76; teller Kans. State Bank & Trust, Wichita, 1977-78; minority recruiter Big Bros. and Big Sisters of Sedgwick County, Kans., 1978-82; exec. dir. 1st Nat. Black Hist. Soc. Kans., Wichita, 1982-83, Work Options for Women, Wichita, 1984-85; pres. Holmes-Sampson Inc., Wichita, 1986—. Mem. Jr. League of Wichita, 1985—; bd. dirs. YWCA of Wichita, 1978-84; 1st v.p. Commn. Status of Women, 1983—; mem. adv. council Kans. Arts Commn., Topeka, 1985—; bd. dirs. Youth Devel. Services, Wichita, 1983—. Recipient Community Service award NAACP, 1985. Mem. Nat. Soc. Fund Raising Execs., Nat. Assn. Women Bus. Owners, Positive Black Networking (pres. 1983-85), Alpha Kappa Alpha. Democrat. Methodist. Avocations: counted cross stitch; bonsai culture. Home: 1455 N Ash St Wichita KS 67214

HOLMES, OPAL LAUREL, publisher; b. Laurens, Iowa, Oct. 14, 1913; d. Ila Laurel and Jessie Merle (Hesselgrave) Holmes; ed. pub. and pvt. schs.; m. Vardis Fisher, Apr. 16, 1940. Publisher, Opal Laurel Holmes, Pub. Co-author: Gold Rushes and Mining Camps of the Early American West. Recipient Golden Spur award, 1969. Mem. Authors Guild, Authors League Am., Nat. Soc. Lit. and Arts, Internat. Platform Assn. Office: PO Box 2535 Boise ID 83701

HOLMES-JOHNSON, ELIZABETH, psychologist; b. Boston, Sept. 2, 1951; d. Charles R. and Evelyn M. (Bedia) Holmes; B.S. in Psychology and Urban/Suburban Studies, U. Bridgeport (Conn.), 1974, M.S. in Sch. Psychology, 1976; Ph.D. in Clin. Psychology, Calif. Sch. Profl. Psychology, 1979; m. Frank C. Johnson, Aug. 2, 1974; children—Erin Kathleen, Adam Michael. Hall dir. U. Bridgeport, 1974-76; counselor Crisis House, San Diego, 1976-77, Tech. Research, Inc., San Diego, 1977-78; psychology intern County Mental Health, San Diego, 1978-79; commd. lt. (j.g.) Med. Service Corps, U.S. Navy, 1979; postdoctoral intern Nat. Naval Med. Center, Bethesda, Md., 1979-80; chmn. dept. behavioral psychology Nat. Naval Dental Center, Bethesda, 1980-84; cons. liaison psychiatry, faculty psychology intern U.S. Naval Hosp., Bethesda, 1983—; asst. prof. dept. psychiatry and med. psychology Uniformed Services U. Health Scis., 1984—; professorial lectr. Georgetown U. Sch. Dentistry, 1983—; psychol. cons. to dental div. Bur. Medicine and Surgery; trustee Calif. Sch. Profl. Psychology, 1977-79; cons. in field. Mem. Am. Psychol. Assn., Am. Assn. Dental Schs. Home: 1022 Moorefield Hill Pl Vienna VA 22180 Office: Naval Hosp Bethesda MD 20814

HOLMGREEN, MARIA LUISA KAHN, lawyer; b. Monterrey, Mex., Feb. 22, 1941 (parents Am. citizens); d. Henry Andres and Maria Luisa (Rangel) Kahn; m. W. Corbett Holmgreen, Aug. 11, 1962; children—Alan C., Celia L., Andrew W. B.A., So. Methodist U., 1962; M.A., Trinity U., San Antonio, 1976; J.D., St. Mary's U., San Antonio, 1982. Bar: Tex. 1982; cert. secondary tchr., Tex. Sole practice law, San Antonio, 1982—. Mem. ABA, Tex. Bar Assn., Delta Phi Alpha. Roman Catholic.

HOLOWEJ, OKSANA (SANDI), management training and consulting executive; b. Western Ukraine, Feb. 2, 1944; came to U.S., 1949, naturalized, 1957; d. Dmytro and Maria J. (Hadzaman) H.; B.S., U. Md., 1975. Acct., Edmund J. Bennett Assos., Bethesda, Md., 1964-67, Columbia (Md.) Parks and Recreation, 1967-70; asst. treas. Larsen Products Corp., Rockville, Md., 1970-74; controller Byron Motion Pictures, Washington, 1974-78; controller, fin. mgr. Sterling Inst., Washington, 1978—. Treas. Oxon Hill-Clinton unit Am. Cancer Soc. C.P.A. Mem. Assn. Women Govt. Contractors, Am. Inst. C.P.A.s, Md. Assn. C.P.A.s, AAUW, Am. Soc. Women C.P.A.s, Am. Bus. Women Assn., Women in Govt. Relations. Republican. Roman Catholic. Home: 113 Finale Terr Silver Spring MD 20901 Office: 1010 Wisconsin Ave NW Suite 700 Washington DC 20007

HOLSER, MARY ANN, human services agency executive; b. Detroit, May 21, 1928; d. Ray Ward and Ruth Belle (Ferguson) Harris; m. William Thomas Holser, Dec. 23, 1955; children—Thomas Dana, Alec Stuart, Margaret. B.A., U. Mich., 1950; M.S.W., Ohio State U., 1954. Young adult dir. YMCA,

Amarillo, Tex., 1950-51; recreation leader Columbus Recreation Dept., Ohio, 1951-53; cottage supr. Juvenile Diagnostic Ctr., Columbus, 1955; group work specialist Spl. Service for Groups, Los Angeles, 1955-56; psychiat. social worker Met. State Hosp., Norwalk, Calif., 1958-60, League of Latin Am. Citizens, Anaheim, Calif., 1965-67, Crisis Intervention Clinic, U. Calif., Irvine Med. Ctr., 1967-70; psychiat. social work cons. Los Angeles County Health Dept., 1970; clin. dir. Alcohol Traffic Safety Program, Eugene, Oreg., 1971-76; co-dir. Drinking Decisions, Eugene, 1977-78; dir. Behanna House, Eugene, 1978-79; exec. dir. Lane County Council on Alcoholism, Eugene, 1979-83; mid-career master Pub. Adminstrn., Harvard U., John F. Kennedy Sch. Govt., Cambridge, Mass., 1984-85; mental health examiner mental hearings State of Oreg., 1973—; vis. asst. prof. U. Oreg., Eugene, 1973-76; founder Orange County Free Clinic, 1969. Contbr. articles to profl. jours. Research grantee Max Planck Inst. for Psychiatry, Munich, Fed. Republic of Germany, 1976; winner Eugene Pub. Library Poetry Contest 1st prize, 1983. Mem. Nat. Assn. Social Workers, Acad. Clin. Social Workers, Oreg. Substance Abuse Assn., Lane County Affirmative Action Com. (chmn.), Oreg. Alcohol Program Mgrs. Assn. (sec.-treas.), Lane County Alcohol Program Mgrs. Assn. (sec.). Democrat. Home: 2620 Dresda de Ruta Eugene OR 97403 Office: 795 Willamette Eugene OR 97401

HOLSEY, TANYA CHAPPELL, banker; b. Cleve., Mar. 21, 1951; d. Isaac and Frances Lucille (Allen) C.; m. Alton Lewis Holsey, Feb. 12, 1983; 1 dau. (by previous marriage), Tanetia Ladese Sims. B.A., Howard U., 1972; M.B.A. (grad. asst.); Cleve State U., 1982. Notary pub., Ohio; lic. ins. salesperson, Ohio. Internat. trade asst. U.S. Dept. Commerce, Washington, 1971-73; traffic service rep. J.C. Penney Co., Columbus, Ohio, 1974-77; transp. analyst Diamond Shamrock Corp., Cleve., 1977-80; comml. mortgage adminstr. Central Nat. Bank, Cleve., 1982—; cons. World-Wide Services, Inc., Cleve., 1981—; trustee Hough Devel. Corp., Cleve., 1983—; lectr., condr. seminars in field. Fundraiser, Friends of Councilman Mike White, Cleve., Cleve. Orch., Julie Billiart Sch., Lyndhurst, Ohio. U.S. Dept. Commerce fellow, 1971-72; Ohio State U. fellow, 1973-74. Mem. Robert Morris Assocs., Urban Bankers Coalition, Am. Inst. Banking, Mortgage Banking Assn., Alpha Kappa Alpha. Democrat. Baptist. Club: Toastmasters. Office: Central National Bank 800 Superior Ave Cleveland OH 44114

HOLSMAN, DORENE ENOLA, banker; b. Kanona, Kans., Apr. 19, 1933; d. Darl Abraham and Lavina Gertrude (Anderson) Worley; m. Charley Frank Holsman, Mar. 22, 1950; children—Kelley Dee, Loree Gwendolyn. Student Highland Community Coll., 1982—. Sec. to county atty. Rawlins County, Atwood, Kans., 1950, 51; sec., asst. cashier, asst. v.p., v.p. ops. Bank of Horton (Kans.), 1963—, sec. to bd., 1977—. Ch. sec. United Methodist Ch., Horton, 1960-63, CR. treas., 1966-76. Mem. Horton C. of C. (women's div., officer 1976). Democrat. Methodist. Office: Bank of Horton 108 E 8th St Horton KS 66439

HOLSTON, SHARON SMITH, government official; b. Cleve., Dec. 15, 1945; d. Charles Coolidge and Eva Mae (Hall) Smith; m. Joseph Holston, Jr., Dec. 22, 1973; children—Joseph Ikaweba, Eve Denise. A.B., Columbia U., 1967; M.P.A., Harvard U., 1986. Personnel mgmt. specialist U.S. Commn. Civil Rights, 1967-70, HEW, 1970-72; EEO officer FDA, Rockville, Md., 1972-74, personnel mgmt. specialist, 1975-77, acting exec. officer, 1977-79, spl. asst. to assoc. commr. mgmt. and ops., 1979-80, dep. assoc. commr. mgmt. and ops., 1980—. Recipient Award of Merit, FDA, 1982, also commr.'s spl. citation, 1985. Mem. African Methodist Episcopal Ch. Club: Barnard-in-Washington (dir.). Office: 5600 Fishers Ln Rockville MD 20857

HOLT, BARBARA BERTANY, management consultant; b. Bridgeport, Conn., Nov. 4, 1940; d. Stephen Edward and Mary G. Bertany; student Regis Coll., 1958-59; B.A. in English, U. Bridgeport, 1962; m. Robert Holt, Dec. 5, 1971; children—Pamela Maren, Laura Kimbel, Mary Brooke. Instr. speech and theatre, U. Bridgeport (Conn.), 1962-69; gen. mgr. BFL Assos., Exec. Recruitment, N.Y.C., 1969-72; founder, pres. Barbara Holt Assos., mgmt. cons., N.Y.C., 1972—; mem. faculty New Sch. for Social Research. Chmn. bd. advisers Fine Arts Acad. Fairfield. Mem. N.Y. Fashion Group, Women in Mgmt. Club: Atrium (N.Y.C.). Developer, producer video career mgmt. series for public TV, 1976. Office: Barbara Holt Assos Box 713 Southport CT 06490

HOLT, BERTHA MARIAN, intercountry adoption agency executive; b. Des Moines, Feb. 5, 1904; d. Clifford Ai and Eva Eda (Sherman) H.; m. Harry Spencer Holt, Dec. 31, 1927 (dec. Apr. 1964); children—Stewart, Wanda, Molly, Barbara, Suzanne, Linda, Joseph, Robert, Mary, Christine, Nathaniel, Helen, Paul, Betty. B.S. in Nursing, U. Iowa, 1926; Doctorate (hon.), Choong Ang U., Seoul, 1968, Linfield Coll., 1977. Pvt. duty nurse, Des Moines, 1926-27; self-employed farmer, Firesteel, S.D., 1927-37, Creswell, Oreg. 1937-56; co-founder, pres. bd. Holt Internat. Children's Services, Creswell, 1956—. Author: Seed From the East, 1956; Outstretched Arms, 1956; Created for God's Glory, 1982; Bring My Sons from Afar, 1986. Named U.S. Mother of Yr., Am. Mothers Com., 1966, Woman of Yr., Soroptimist Internat., 1973, Moran medal for civil merit Republic of South Korea, 1974, Decade of the Child medallion Republic of Philippine Islands, 1981. Mem. Oreg. Mother's Assn. Organized passage of spl. Congl. bill for Korean orphans, 1955. Avocations: writing; traveling to visit children adopted through Holt Internat.; gardening. Office: Holt Internat Children's Services 1195 City View PO Box 2880 Eugene OR 97402

HOLT, BERTHA MERRILL, state legislator; b. Eufaula, Ala., Aug. 16, 1916; d. William Hoadley and Bertha Harden (Moore) Merrill; A.B., Agnes Scott Coll., 1938; LL.B., U. Ala., 1941; m. Winfield Clary Holt, Mar. 14, 1941; children—Harriet Wharton Holt Whitley, William Merrill, Winfield Jefferson. Admitted to Ala. bar, 1941; with Treasury Dept., Washington, 1941-42, Dept. Interior, Washington, 1942-43; mem. N.C. Ho. of Reps. from 22d Dist., 1975-80, 25th Dist., 1980—, chmn. select com. govtl. ethics, 1979-80, chmn. constl. amendments com., 1981, 83, mem. joint commn. govtl. ops., 1982-84, chmn. appropriation com. justice and pub. safety, 1985—. Pres., Democratic Women of Alamance, 1962, chmn. hdqrs., 1964, 68; mem. N.C. Dem. Exec. Com., 1964-75; pres. Episcopal Ch. Women, 1968; mem. council N.C. Episcopal Diocese, 1972-74, 84—; chmn. fin. dept., 1973-75, parish grant com., 1973-80, mem. standing com., 1975-78; chmn. Alamance County Social Services Bd., 1970; mem. N.C. Bd. Sci. and Tech., 1979-83; bd. dirs. Hospice N.C., State Council Social Legis. Recipient Outstanding Alumna award Agnes Scott Coll., 1978; Legis. award for service to elderly Non-Profit Rest Home Assn., 1985. Mem. Women's Forum N.C., Law Alumni Assn. U. N.C. Chapel Hill (dir. 1978-81), N.C. Bar Assn., NOW, English Speaking Union, N.C. Hist. Soc., Les Amis du Vin, Pi Beta Phi. Club: Century Book. Office: PO Box 111 Burlington NC 27215

HOLT, CHERYL ADAMS, archaeologist; b. Neodesha, Kans., Jan. 5, 1947; d. John Elvin and Pennie (Cobb) Adams; m. Herbert Allen Holt, July 15, 1967; 1 child Hillary Adams. B.A., George Washington U., 1976; M.A., Case Western Res. U., 1978; postgrad. Brandeis U., 1981. Lab. asst. Alexandria (Va.) Archaeology Lab., 1974-76; survey archaeologist Mus. Natural History, Cleve., 1976-77, field archaeologist, lab. asst., 1977, survey archaeologist, 1977; field archaeologist Western Ill. U., Macomb, 1978, Iroquois Research Inst., Fairfax, Va., 1979; sr. archaeologist Soil Systems, Inc., Alexandria, 1982-84, dir. analytical services for archaeologists, 1984—; reviewer NEH, Endowment for Humanities, 1979—. George Washington U. bd. trustees scholar, 1976; Brandeis U. anthropology scholar, 1979-81; Tannenbaum fellow, 1979-81. Mem. Am. Anthropol. Assn., Soc. Am. Archaeology. Contbr. articles to profl. jours. Home: 909 Cameron St Alexandria VA 22314

HOLT, EVE MAY, advertising agency executive; b. Bklyn., May 22, 1946; d. Harold and June (Mellon) Glicksman; m. Steven C. Holt, June 30, 1966; children—Edward, Jesse. Student Hunter Coll., 1964, U. Hawaii, 1980-83. Lic. real estate salesperson, Hawaii. Asst. converter Donson Fabrics, Inc., N.Y.C., 1965-68; mgr. Sutherland's, Inc., Portsmouth, N.H., 1973-75; gen. mgr. The Small Corp., Berwick, Maine, 1975-77; dept. mgr. Liberty House, Honolulu, 1977-79; account supr. Fawcett, McDermott, Cavanagh, Honolulu, 1979—; contbg. arts editor Portsmouth Herald, 1974. Pres. Portsmouth Parade Mall Mchts. Assn., 1975; choreographer Garrison Players, 1972-73; communications cons. to Hawaii state senator Wadsworth Yee, 1982. Recipient Pele award Honolulu Advt. Fedn., 1982, 24 Carat award Affiliated Advt. Agys., Inc., 1983. Mem. Network Mktg. Women (pres. 1984), Am. Mktg. Assn. (dir.), Honolulu Advt. Fedn. Office: Fawcett McDermott Cavanagh 1001 Bishop St Pauahi Tower 2300 Honolulu HI 96813

HOLT, JOANN LOUISE, nursing administrator; b. Brockway, Pa., Oct. 22, 1934; d. Herbert Samuel and Bertha Elizabeth (Henderson) H. Diploma, Presbyn. U., Pitts., 1955; B.S.N., U. Pitts., 1967, M.N.Ed., 1968. Supr., Magee Womens Hosp., Pitts., 1964-68, asst. dir. nursing, 1968-70; dir. nursing Lee Hosp., Johnstown, Pa., 1970-75; asst. exec. dir. Mercy Hosp., Pitts., 1975-78, assoc. exec. dir., 1978-80; v.p. nursing Akron Gen. Med. Center (Ohio), 1980—; cons. St. Alexis Hosp., Cleve., 1983; adj. prof. Akron U., 1981—, Kent State U., 1982—, U. Pitts., 1977-80. Bd. dirs. U. Pitts., 1978-80; trustee Western Pa. Leukemia Soc., 1975-80; mem. adv. bd. U. Akron Coll. Nursing, 1982-83. Mem. Am. Nurses Assn., Ohio Nurses Assn. (chmn. nursing service com. 1982), Nat. League Nursing, Forum Hosp. Nurse Adminstrs. (pres. 1977), Sigma Theta Tau. Republican. Presbyterian. Office: Akron Gen Med Center 400 Wabash Ave Akron OH 44307

HOLT, KAREN ANN, manufacturer; b. Seattle, Dec. 31, 1949; d. Phillip Edgar and Mavis Caroline (Johnson) Holt. Cert. in Dental Hygiene, Shoreline Community Coll., Seattle, 1971. Dental hygienist, Seattle, 1971-79; pres., owner K.A. Holt Co., Redmond, Wash., 1980-84, Colores Internat. Inc., Bellevue, Wash., 1981—. Recipient Bus. Excellence award Peoples Bank, Seattle, 1985. Avocations: reading; swimming; meditation. Home: 3415 W Lake Sammamish Pkwy Redmond WA 98052 Office: Colores Internat Inc 1405 132d Ave NE Bellevue WA 98052

HOLT, KATHLEEN MAGOUIRK, radio station executive; b. Dodge City, Kans., May 31, 1947; d. Lewis Glenn and Bernice Eleanor (Spence) Magouirk; m. Douglas Emerson Holt, July 22, 1967 (div. 1982); children—Matthew Douglas, Christopher Lewis. A.A., Cottey Coll., 1967; B.A., Bethel Coll., 1972. Tchr., pub. schs., Dallas, 1972-73; asst. adminstr. K Bar B Youth Ranch, La Combe, La., 1973-75; owner, operator Cimarron Hotel and Restaurant, Kans., 1977—; devel. dir. Sta. KANZ-FM, Pierceville, Kans., 1983—; cons. Sta. KZRA, Alamosa, Colo., 1985. Mem. Kans. State Assn. Foster Parents (regional v.p. 1980-82), Kans. Preservation Alliance (bd. dirs. 1980—). Republican. Avocations: historic renovation, reading. Home: 203 N Main Cimarron KS 67835 Office: KANZ-FM Pierceville KS 67835

HOLT, KATHRYN LYNN, lawyer; b. Panama City, Fla., Mar. 22, 1954; d. Joel Graham and Betty Lou (Sewell) Duncan; m. Mark Duren Holt, July 16, 1977. B.A. in Theatre Arts, Hendrix Coll., 1976; postgrad. So. Meth. U. Sch. Law, 1977-78; J.D., U. Ark.-Little Rock, 1980. Bar: Ark. 1980. Law clk. House, Wallace & Jewell, P.A., Little Rock, 1979-80, assoc., 1980—. Active Big Sisters Program Pulaski County (Ark.), 1983—; mem. fund raising com. Boy Scouts Am., 1981—. Recipient Am. Judicature award Am. Judicature Soc., 1980. Mem. ABA, Ark. Bar Assn. (mem. seminar com. labor law sect. 1983—), Ark. Assn. Women Lawyers (program chmn. 1982-83; scholarship chmn. 1983-84), Pulaski County Bar Assn. Methodist. Office: House Wallace & Jewell PA 1500 Tower Bldg Little Rock AR 72201

HOLT, MARJORIE SEWELL, congresswoman; b. Birmingham, Ala., Sept. 17, 1920; d. Edward Roland and Alice Juanita (Felts) Sewell; B.A., Jacksonville (Fla.) U., 1945; J.D., U. Fla., 1949; m. Duncan McKay Holt, Dec. 26, 1946; children—Rachel Holt Tschantre, Edward, Victoria Holt Stauffer. Admitted to Fla. Bar, 1949, Md. bar, 1962; practice law, 1950—; clk. Anne Arundel Circuit Ct., Annapolis, 1966-72; mem. 93d-99th Congresses from 4th Md. Dist., mem. budget com., 1975-80, mem. joint econ. commn., mem. armed services com. Supr. elections Anne Arundel County, 1963-65; mem. housing com. Anne Arundel County Human Relations Commn., 1964-67; bd. dirs. Office Technol. Assessment, 1976-77, vice chmn., 1977; chmn. Republican Study Com., 1975-76; del. Rep. Nat. Conv., 1968, 76, 80, 84. Recipient Disting. Alumna award U. Fla., 1975. ABA, Md. Bar Assn., Anne Arundel Bar Assn., LWV, Md. Fedn. Rep. Women, Bus. and Profl. Women's Club, Phi Kappa Phi, Phi Delta Delta. Presbyterian (elder 1959). Mem. staff Fla. Law Rev., 1947-49. Editor, co-author: The Case Against the Reckless Congress, 1976; Can You Afford This House, 1978. Office: 2412 Rayburn House Office Bldg Washington DC 20515

HOLT, MELVA RUTH, data processing executive; b. Lowes, Ky., Apr. 4, 1948; d. Robert Wilson and Mildred Frances (Leath) H.; B.S. in Bus. cum laude, Murray (Ky.) State U., 1973, M.B.A., 1983. Various secretarial positions, 1969-72; tchr. bus. Dixie Heights High Sch., Ft. Mitchell, Ky., 1973; exec. sec. to v.p. fin., then coordinator employment Murray State U., 1974-76; dental plan bus. mgr. U. Louisville Dental Sch., 1977, univ. budget analyst, 1978; fin. systems installment engr. HBO & Co., San Mateo, Calif., 1979; coordinator, mgr. user support fin. data systems Holy Cross Health Systems, South Bend, Ind., 1980-83; installation engr., tech. mktg. specialist Hewlett Packard Co., Andover, Mass., 1983—. Named Ky. Col. Cert. profl. sec. Mem. Nat. Secs. Assn. (membership chmn., pres.-elect), NEA, Nat. Assn. Female Execs., Hosp. Fin. Mgmt. Assn., Alpha Gamma Delta (treas., faculty adv.). Democrat. Baptist. Home: RFD 7 43 Old Nashua Rd Londonderry NH 03053 Office: 3000 Minuteman Rd Andover MA 01810

HOLT, MILDRED FRANCES, educator; b. Lorain, Ohio, July 30, 1932; d. William Henry and Rachel (Pierce) Daniels; B.S., U. Md., 1962, M.Ed., 1967, Ph.D., 1977; m. Maurice Lee Holt, Sept. 11, 1949 (dec.); children—Claudia, Frances, William, Rudi. Tchr. spl. edn. St. Mary's (Md.) County Public Schs., 1962-64, coordinator Felix Johnson Spl. Edn. Center, 1964-66; demonstration tchr. spl. edn. U. Md., College Park, summer 1970, instr. spl. edn. dept. Coll. Edn., 1969-73; supr. spl. edn. Calvert and St. Mary's (Md.) Counties, 1968-69; asso. prof. spl. edn. W. Liberty (W.Va.) State Coll., 1973-75; asst. prof. Eastern Ill. U., Charleston, 1975-77; supr. spl. edn. Warren County Public Schs., Front Royal, Va., 1977-85; spl. edn. tchr. Dallas Ind. Sch. Dist., 1985—. Mem. NEA, Warren County Edn. Assn., Council Exceptional Children, Assn. for Gifted, Assn. Supervision and Curriculum Devel., Va. Edn. Assn., Va. Council Exceptional Children, Blue Ridge Orgn. Gifted and Talented, Assn. Children with Learning Disabilities, Nat. Assn. Gifted Children, Phi Theta Kappa, Kappa Delta Pi. Contbr. articles to profl. jours.; author: Reach Guidebook, 1979. Home: 3712 Sugarberry Dr Mesquite TX 75150 Office: Joseph J Rhoads Elem Sch Dallas TX

HOLTON, ANNE LYSBETH, magazine advertising executive; b. Pitts., June 10, 1950; d. James Leo and Ruth Anna (Homan) H.; B.S. in Psychology, U. Bridgeport, 1972; postgrad. N.Y.U. Legis. aide to Congressman Henry Helstoski of N.J., 1973-74; asst. to advt. dir. New Times Mag., N.Y.C., 1974-75, sales rep., 1975; advt. sales rep. Rolling Stone Mag., N.Y.C., 1975-77; advt. sales rep. Ms. mag., N.Y.C., 1977-78, N.Y. adv. mgr., 1978-79, nat. advt. mgr., 1979, advt. dir., 1979-82; mktg. dir. Gentlemen's Quar. Mag., 1982-85; v.p., advt. dir. Parade Mag., 1985—. Mem. Mag. Pubs. Assn., Nat. Women's Polit. Party. Republican. Office: 350 Madison Ave New York NY 10017

HOLTON, PRISCILLA BROWNE, former educator; b. Hartford, Conn., Dec. 21, 1922; d. Edward Aston and Lucille J. (Ford) Browne; B.S., St. Joseph Coll., 1946; M.Ed., Antioch Coll., 1972; numerous spl. courses; m. John Lyle Holton, Dec. 24, 1944; children—Mary Frances, John Kingsley, Leslie Lucille. Dir., Women's League Day Care Center, Hartford, 1948-49; elementary tchr. Phila. Public Schs., 1954-62; head tchr. Green Tree Sch., Phila., 1963-67, prin., 1969-74; co-therapist parents group Green Tree Sch., 1966-67; dir. North Hill's Day Care Center, Pa., also head start coordinator Eastern Montgomery County, 1967-69; coordinator spl. edn. Antioch Grad. Sch. Edn., Phila., 1974-78, M.Ed. program adminstr., 1978-80, coordinator art exhibits, 1974-80; coordinator Head Start, City of Phila., 1980-83; cons. spl. edn. and early childhood edn.; lectr. chmn. adv. bd. Children's Village; bd. dirs. Mt. Airy Children's House, YWCA, Germantown. Recipient citation Gov. Schaeffer of Pa., 1946, plaque North Hills Day Care Bd., 1968, plaque Green Tree Sch., 1974, plaque V.I.P., 1980, award Chapel of Four Chaplains, 1980; named Outstanding Grad. of Class of 1946, Alumnae of St. Joseph Coll. for Women, 1981, recipient Disting. Alumnae award, 1983. Mem. Pa. Mental Health Assn., LWV, Pa. Tchr. Educators, Assn. Children with Learning Disabilities, Council Exceptional Children, YMCA, Black Women's Ednl. Alliance, Phila. Art Mus., Phila. Hort. Soc., Organisation Mondiale pour l'Education Prescholaire, Nat. Assn. Young Children's Edn., Delta Sigma Theta. Author: (with others) Teacher's Curriculum Guide, 1970; feature writer Hartford Chronicle, 1948. Home: 428 E Montana St Philadelphia PA 19119

HOLTSBERRY, BARBARA JEAN, manufacturing company executive; b. Coshocton County, Ohio, Aug. 26, 1938; d. William Raymond and Lena May (Ashcraft) Ramsey; student Ohio State U., 1958-65; B.Sc. in Bus. Adminstrn. summa cum laude, Franklin U., 1972; children—Rosemary, Theresa, Frederick. Sec., Battelle Meml. Inst., Columbus, Ohio, 1966-70; computer programmer Ohio Dept. Edn., Columbus, 1970-71; asst. acctg. supr. Westreco, Marysville, Ohio, 1972-78; supr. adminstrn. and planning, cost. engring. dept. Owen's Corning Fiberglas, Newark, Ohio, 1978—. Mem. Nat. Assn. Accts. (pres. Mid-Ohio chpt. 1982-83, 86-87, treas. Ohio council 1982-84). Republican. Mem. Ch. of Christ. Clubs: Land of Legend Singles, Cambridge (pres. 1981-82). Home: 651 Edgewood Dr Newark OH 43055 Office: Case Ave Newark OH 43055

HOLTZ, CHARLENE CUNNINGHAM, lawyer; b. Passaic, N.J., Oct. 14, 1948; d. Harrison Groome and Lillian Helen (Feltz) Cunningham; m. William Charles Holtz, Oct. 21, 1972; 1 dau., Kelsey Kristen. A.B. with honors, Rutgers U., 1970; J.D. cum laude, DePaul U., 1976. Bar: Ill. 1976; assoc. firm Coffield, Ungaretti, Harris & Slavin, Chgo., 1976-78, ptnr., 1978—. Ford Found. fellow 1970. Mem. ABA, Ill. Bar Assn., Chgo. Bar Assn., Women's Bar Assn. Ill. Presbyterian. Office: Coffield Ungaretti Harris & Slavin 3500 Three First Nat Plaza Chicago IL 60602

HOLTZCLAW, DIANE SMITH, educator; b. Buffalo, May 26, 1936; d. John Nelson and Beatrice M. (Salisbury) Smith; m. John Victor Holtzclaw, June 27, 1959; children—Kathryn Diane, John Bryan. B.S. in Edn. magna cum laude, SUNY-Brockport, 1957, M.S. with honors, 1961; postgrad. SUNY-Buffalo, 1960-65, Canisus Coll., 1979, Nazareth Coll., 1981-82. Tchr. Greece Central Sch., Rochester, N.Y., 1957-60; supr. SUNY-Brockport, 1960-64, assoc. prof. edn., 1960-64; dir. Early Childhood Ctr., Fairport, N.Y., 1968-80; tchr. Fairport Central Schs., 1971—; cons. in field. Music dir. Perinton Presbyterian Ch., Fairport, 1983—; pres. bd. dirs. Downtown Day Care Ctr., Rochester, 1974-83. Mem. Fairport Edn. Assn. (exec. bd. 1982-83, del. 1983), N.Y. State United Tchrs., AAUW (exec. bd. 1973-74, 77-79, 83-84, pres. Fairport br. 1971-73), Kappa Delta Pi. Home: 1455 Ayrault Rd Fairport NY 14450 Office: Fairport Central Schs 38 W Church St Fairport NY 14450

HOLTZMAN, ELIZABETH, district attorney; b. Bklyn., Aug. 11, 1941; d. Sidney and Filia (Ravitz) H.; B.A. magna cum laude, Radcliffe Coll., 1962; J.D., Harvard U., 1965. Bar: N.Y. 1966. Assoc. firm Wachtell, Lipton, Rosen, Katz and Kern, N.Y.C., 1965-67; asst. to mayor N.Y.C., 1967-70; assoc. firm Paul, Weiss, Rifkind, Wharton and Garrison, N.Y.C., 1970-72; mem. 93d-96th Congresses from 16th dist. N.Y.; dist. atty. Bklyn., 1982—; Democratic state committeewoman, dist. leader, Bklyn., 1970; del. Dem. Nat. Conv., 1972; founder Bklyn. Women's Polit. Caucus, 1971. Mem. nat. adv. council Hampshire (Mass.) Coll.; bd. overseers Harvard, 1976; mem. Nat. Commn. on Observance of Internat. Women's Year, 1977. Named 1 of 10 Women of Year, Mademoiselle mag., 1972, Woman of Year, United Hias Service, 1974; Outstanding Woman, Nassau region Hadassah, 1975; Annette Pinsky award ACLU, 1975; Woman of Year, Jewish War Vets., 1975; Spirit of Achievement award Albert Einstein Coll. Medicine, 1977; Distinguished Service award Fairleigh Dickinson U., 1977; recipient Alumnae Recognition award Radcliffe Coll. Alumnae Assn., 1973. Mem. Assn. Bar City N.Y. Democrat. Jewish. Office of the District Attorney 400 Brooklyn Municipal Bldg 210 Joralemon St Brooklyn NY 11201

HOLVEY, CAROLYN SUE, audit specialist, nurse; b. Weston, W.Va., Jan. 24, 1958; d. Billy Brown and Marjorie Carol (Hardman) Burke; m. William Anthony Holvey, Apr. 10, 1982; children—Burke Ashley, Samantha Carol. B.S. in Nursing, W. Va. U., 1980. R.N. Staff nurse Hermann Hosp., Houston, 1980-81; pvt. duty nurse Staff Builders, Houston, 1981; audit specialist, nurse, Republic Service Bur., Houston, 1981—. Mem. W.Va. Nurses Assn., Tex. Nurses Assn., Am. Soc. Post Anesthesia Nurses, W.Va. U. Alumni Assn., 4-H Allstars. Democrat. Baptist. Home: 9242 Beechnut Houston TX 77036 Office: Republic Service Bur Box 771967 Houston TX 77215

HOLZER, ESTELLE STARKMAN, insurance executive; b. Chgo., Jan. 27, 1930; d. Arthur J. and Beatrice (Shamberg) Starkman; m. Reginald J. Holzer, Aug. 27, 1950; children—Audrey Holzer Rubin, Bambi I. Ed.B., Chgo. Tchrs. Coll., 1951; M.A., Northwestern U., 1957. Tchr., Chgo. Bd. Edn., 1951-55; spl. agt. Prudential Ins. Co., Chgo., 1973-77, assoc. mgr., 1977-80, regional field cons., 1980-82, agy. mgr., gen. agt., 1982—. Author: Success Comes in Cans, 1980. Commr. Chgo. Housing Authority, 1983—; pres. Temple Bethel, Chgo., 1975-76. Mem. Chgo. Assn. Life Underwriters (pres. 1985-86), Life Underwriters Polit. Action Com., Gen. Agts. and Mgrs. Assn., Women's Life Underwriters Assn., Nat. Assn. Life Underwriters (Nat. Quality awards 1975—), Million Dollar Roundtable (life). Jewish. Office: Prudential Ins Co Am 5150 Golf Rd Skokie IL 60077

HOLZMAN, EILEEN FRANCES, insurance agency executive; b. Boston, Apr. 2, 1955; d. William Henry and Susan Bridgett (O'Connor) H. With J.F. Blum, C.L.U. & Assocs., Boston, 1978—. Now v.p.; v.p. B & V Ins. Agy., Inc., Boston, 1981—. Roman Catholic. Office: Boston MA 02114

HOMBS, KAREN KAY, financial planner; b. Denver, Aug. 3, 1942; d. Arthur Clark Eugene and Norma May (Urquhart) Ryman; grad. U. Denver/Colo. Women's Coll., 1984; m. Thomas Gibson Hombs, Apr. 12, 1978; 1 child, Timothy John. With Samsonite Corp., Denver, 1960-75, employee relations rep., supr., 1965-71, labor relations rep., 1971-75; labor relations rep. Climax Molybdenum Co. (Colo.) div. AMAX, 1975-78, prin. labor relations adminstr., 1978-83; registered rep. IDS/Am. Express, 1983—. Mem. council Lord of the Mountains Lutheran Ch., Summit County, Colo., 1979-80, founded women's chpt. Luth. Ch. Women, 1976, chpt. chmn., 1976-77, Sunday Sch. supt., 1976-81. Mem. Indsl. Relations Research Assn., Am. Mgmt. Assn. Club: Toastmasters (sec.-treas. 1984). Home: 7640 W 24th Ave Lakewood CO 80215 Office: IDS/Am Express Inc 1385 S Colorado Blvd Suite 620 Denver CO 80222

HOMER, TAMARA KUKRYCKA, advertising executive; b. Warsaw, Poland, Feb. 23, 1932; came to U.S., 1949, naturalized, 1953; d. Basil and Alexandra (Masiuk) Kukrycka; m. Edward John Homer, Sept. 6, 1954. B.A., Hunter Coll., 1954; postgrad. New Sch. for Social Sci., 1956-58. Pres. Sunwear, Inc., N.Y.C., 1964-66; exec. v.p. Allerton, Berman & Dean, N.Y.C., 1966-73; pres., owner Homer & Durham, N.Y.C., 1973—. Author travel guides for European countries. Trustee New Eyes for the Needy, Short Hills, N.J., 1982—; bd. dirs. March of Dimes, N.Y.C., 1983—. Recipient Matrix award Women Execs. in Communication, 1983, Extraordinary Service to Nation's Tourism, Republic of Ireland, 1976; named to Hall of Fame, Hunter Coll., 1983. Mem. Advt. Women of N.Y. (bd. dirs.; pres. 1983-85), Women Execs. in Pub. Relations, Fashion Group, Am. Advt. Fedn. (com. chmn. 1985—). Republican. Ukrainian Orthodox. Avocations: painting; tennis; fresh water fishing. Home: 1 Joanna Way Short Hills NJ 07078 Office: Homer & Durham Advt Ltd 115 Fifth Ave New York NY 10003

HOMESTEAD, SUSAN, psychotherapist, consultant; b. Bklyn., Sept. 20, 1937; d. Cy Simon and Katherine (Haas) Eichelbaum; m. George Gilbert Zanetti, Dec. 13, 1962 (div. 1972); 1 child, Bruce David; m. 2d, Ronald Eric Homestead, Jan. 16, 1973 (div. 1980). B.A., U. Miami-Fla., 1960; M.S.W., Tulane U., 1967. Lic. clin. social worker, Va., Calif. Pvt. practice, cons., Richmond, Va., 1971—; psychotherapist, cons. Family and Children's Services, Richmond, 1981—, Richmond Pain Clinic, 1983-84; cons. Health Internat. Va., P.C., Lynchburg, 1984-86, Santa Clara DDS, Calif., 1986—; co-dir. asthma program Va. Lung Assn., Richmond, 1975-79, Loma Prieta Regional Ctr.; chief clin. social worker Med. Coll. Va., Va. Commonwealth U., 1974-79. Contbr. articles to profl. jours. Active, Peninsula Children's Ctr., Morgan Ctr., Council for Community Action Planning, Community Assn. for Retarded, Comprehensive Health Planning Assn. Santa Clara, Mental Health Commn., Children and Adolescent Target Group Calif., Women's Com. Richmond Symphony, Va. Mus. Theatre, mem. fin. com. Robb for Gov.; mem. adv. com. Lung Assn.; mem. steering com. Am. Cancer Soc. Va. div. Epilepsy Found., Am. Heart Assn., Central Va. Guild for Infant Survival. Mem. Va. Soc. Clin. Social Work, Inc. (charter mem., sec. 1975-78), Nat. Assn. Social Workers, Soc. for Psychoanalytic Psychotherapy, Am. Acad. Psychotherapists. Jewish.

HOMRIGHAUSEN, LINDSLEY HARVEY, foundation executive; b. Wilkes-Barre, Pa., Aug. 30, 1945; d. Robert Burgess and Joan Lindsley (Blackman) Harvey Miner; B.A., Lake Erie Coll., Painesville, Ohio, 1967; m. David K. Homrighausen, Apr. 25, 1970; children—Sarah Harvey, Benjamin Burgess. With Mut. of N.Y., N.Y.C., 1967-71, Allied Temp. Service, N.Y.C., 1971-73; adminstr. grants Surdna Found., Inc., N.Y.C., 1973—. Office: 250 Park Ave New York NY 10177

HOMSEY, VICTORINE (MRS. SAMUEL E. HOMSEY), architect; b. Grosse Pointe Farms, Mich., Nov. 27, 1900; d. Antoin Bidermann and Ethel (Clark) duPont; A.B., Wellesley Coll., 1923; M.Arch., Cambridge (Mass.) Sch. Architecture, 1925; m. Samuel E. Homsey, Apr. 27, 1929; children—Coleman duPont, Eldon duPont. Practice as architect, 1926-82; mem. archtl. firm Victorine & Samuel Homsey; major works include Am. Embassy, Tehran, Iran. Mem. exec. com. Greater Wilmington Devel. Council; mem. adv. bd. Historic Am. Bldgs. Survey; mem. Commn. Fine Arts, Washington, 1976-81. Recipient 1st prize instl. architecture for Children's Beach House (Lewes, Del.), Pitts. Glass Inst.; regional, state awards for Cambridge Yacht Club, Md. Soc. Architects; hon. mention award for design Stubbs Elementary Sch., Wilmington, Del., Sch. Exec. mag. Fellow AIA; mem. NAD (asso.), Colonial Dames. Episcopalian. Club: Wilmington Garden. (Del.). Contbr. Archtl. Forum, Guide to Modern Architecture. Home: 602 Cokesbury Village Hockessin DE 19707 Office: 2003 N Scott St Wilmington DE 19806

HON, JEANNE ELIZABETH, school principal; b. Lawrence, Mass., Nov. 4, 1931; d. Andrew Paul Sorbo and Marjorie Elizabeth (O'Neill) Nichols; B.A., Calif. State U., Northridge, 1964, M.A. magna cum laude, 1969; Ed.D. with honors, Brigham Young U., 1973; m. Roy Charles Hon. Sr., June 20, 1949; children—Roy Charles, Jr., Kathleen Elizabeth. Sec. to supt. Duarte (Calif.) Unified Sch. Dist., 1959-61; tchr., coordinator, counselor Verdugo Hills Sch., Tujunga, Calif., 1966-75; asst. prin. North Hollywood (Calif.) High Sch., 1975-78; prin. Magnet Sch., Los Angeles Unified Sch. Dist., 1978-82, also pres. Prin. Orgn.; prin. Sun Valley (Calif.) Jr. High Sch., 1982—; lectr. grad. studies Calif. Luth. Coll., Thousand Oaks, Calif., 1979—. Chmn., United Fund, ARC; mem. coordinating council PTA; sponsor Mexican-Am. Youth Activities Group. Recipient Service award U. So. Calif. chpt. Phi Delta Kappa, 1982, Service Key award, 1983-84; DAV Aux., award, 1982; Outstanding Prin. of Year award Los Angeles C. of C. Mem. AAUW, Calif. Tchrs. Assn., NEA, Social Studies Assn., Phi Delta Kappa, Theta Sigma Tau. Democrat. Roman Catholic. Home: 6837 Estepa Dr Tujunga CA 91042 Office: 7330 Bakman Ave Sun Valley CA 91352

HONG, CAROL ANN, microbiologist; b. Altoona, Pa., Oct. 9, 1942; d. John Irwin and Lela Frances (Miller) Kleffman; B.A., Miami U., Oxford, Ohio, 1964; M.B.A., Cleve. State U., 1981; m. Philip Fernandez Ma, Sept. 15, 1965; 1 son, Michael; m. 2d, Jong Kyu Hong, Aug. 14, 1978; 1 dau., Elizabeth Soo Hyon. Teller, Akron (Ohio) Nat Bank, summers 1960-64; vol. Peace Corps, tchr. sci., math. and English, Philippines, 1964-66; bacteriology technologist Case Western Res. U. Hosps., Cleve., 1966; med. technologist, adminstrv. supr. microbiology Cleve. Clinic Found., from 1966, now also mgr. lab. services, microbiology, sec. subcom. infectious diseases, 1974-79, mem. safety com., 1979—. Registered med. technologist, registered specialist in microbiology Am. Soc. Clin. Pathologists. Mem. AAUW (chmn. hospitality 1975-77, dir. 1977-79), Am. Soc. Clin. Pathologists (council on microbiology 1977-83), Cuyahoga Women's Polit. Caucus, Am. Soc. Microbiology, Assn. for Practitioners in Infection Control (pres. Greater Cleve. chpt. 1975-76 chmn. nominating com. 1977, by-laws com., 1980, chmn. 1982-84, S. Central Assn. for Clin. Microbiology (sec. 1975, dir. area 1976-77, mem. nominating com. 1977-80, chmn. awards com. 1979-80, chmn. membership com. 1981, pres.-elect 1983, pres. 1984), Med. Group Mgmt. Assn., Clin. Lab. Mgmt. Assn. (pres. Cleve. chpt. 1975-76), Assn. M.B.A. Execs., Mensa, NOW. Club: Order of Eastern Star. Editorial bd. Lab. Medicine, 1978-80. Contbr. articles to profl. publs. Home: 374 Karen Dr Chardon OH 44024 Office: 9500 Euclid Ave Cleveland OH 44106

HONG, CHUNG-SOOK CHARLOTTE, librarian; b. Seoul, Apr. 15, 1940; came to U.S., 1963; d. Soon-Kyung and Un-Yun (Kim) Hong; m. Samuel Cynn-Sung Kang, Dec. 19, 1964 (div. Aug. 1978); m. Ben H. (Bong-Hyun) Kim, Nov. 17, 1985; children—Patricia Jean, Claudia Suk-Jin. B.A., Yonsei U., Seoul, 1962; M.Ed., Duquesne U., Pitts., 1967; M.L.S., U. Pitts., 1968; cert. mgmt. devel. program Pa. State U., 1978. Asst. librarian Whitehall Pub. Library, Pitts., 1965-66, children's librarian, 1966-67; asst. children's librarian Carnegie Library of Pitts., 1968-69, children's librarian, 1969-71, br. librarian, 1971-76, div. head., 1976-85; branch head Albany Park Br. Chgo. pub. Library, 1986—; prin. Korean Lang. Sch. Pitts., 1980-85. Deaconness Korean Central Ch. of Pitts., 1980-85, editor, 1983-84; historian Pitts. Folk Festival Pitts. Korean Assn., 1983-84; mem. panel Ams., NCCJ, 1984—. Mem. ALA, Pa. Library Assn. (co.-chmn. ann. conf. reception com. 1981, chmn. ann. conf. hospitality com. 1983, chmn. pub. relations com. S.W. chpt. 1981, program com. spring conf. 1984, chmn. pub., p.r. and NLW com. S.W. chpt. 1984). Democrat. Presbyterian. Club: Altrusa (chmn. internat. relations com. 1982-84) (Pitts.). Home: Hollywood Towers 5701 N Sheridan Rd Unit 25T Chicago IL 60660 Office: Albany Park Br Chicago Pub Library 5150 N Kimball Ave Chicago IL 60625

HONORÉ, ALYCE, wordprocessing director; b. Prairie View, Tex., May 19, 1948; d. John Clayborne and Priscilla Carrie (Jackson) Honore; B.A., Prairie View A&M U., 1969; M.Ed., Tex. So. U., 1976; postgrad. U. Houston, 1977—; 1 son. Research supr. reservoir behavior Exxon Co. U.S.A., Houston, 1970-76; word processing coordinator Vinson & Elkins Law Firm, Houston, 1977-86; dir. word processing Hargest Vocat. and Tech. Coll., 1986—. Vol. guidance counselor; polls vol. registration and sr. citizens transp.; vol. Julia C. Hester House; advisor Young People's Aux. of Mt. Horem Baptist Ch.; counselor Concerned Teens, Big Sister Exxon Vol. Program, 1974-76; bd. dirs., word processing advisor Houston Community Coll. Recipient VIP Profl. service award Exxon, 1975. Mem. Internat. Word Processing Assn., Am. Bus. Women's Assn., Nat. Assn. Negro Bus. and Profl. Women, Nat. Assn. Female Execs., Urban League, Nat. Council Negro Women, Operation Breadbasket, Nat. Assn. Black Women in Bus. and Industry, Eta Phi Beta. Democrat. Methodist. Club: Eastern Star. Home: 16223 Canaridge Dr Houston TX 77053 Office: 4608 Main St Houston TX 77002

HOOD, LOUISE B., state legislator; b. Windsor, Vt., Aug. 27, 1916; d. Albert E., Sr., and Gladys H. (Robinson) Buckman; student schs. Windsor; m. Lee B. Hood, Sept. 4, 1938 (dec.); children—L. Robert, Bonnie Lee, David John. Sec. to attys., payroll clk. Goodyear Tire and Rubber, Windsor, 1947-50; bookkeeper, sec., asst. town clk., justice of peace, notary public, Town of Windsor, 1950-68, treas., 1968-78; mem. Vt. Gen. Assembly, rep. from Dist. 3, 1979—. Trustee, Windsor Library; trustee, sec. Davis Home; sec. Salvation Army, 1975—; vice chmn. Rep. Town Com.; bd. dirs. Windsor Cemetery Assn., 1982—. Methodist. Office: State House Montpelier VT 05602

HOOD, TERESSA MARIE, insurance company executive; b. Lynchburg, Va., Dec. 25, 1951; d. Andrew Leroy and Augustine Louise (Hunter) H. A.A.S., Exec. Secretarial, Central Va. Community Coll., 1973. Cashier Shoppers Fair, Lynchburg, 1967-69, sec., payroll clk., 1969-74; with Nationwide Mut. Ins. Co., Lynchburg, 1973—, underwriter, 1981-83, auto services supr., 1983-85, fire services supr., 1985—; defensive driving instr., 1978-80. Active fellow and mem. Central Va. Community Choral Ensemble, 1978—, adminstr., 1983—; active fellow and mem. Civic Action Program, Lynchburg, 1979—; fellow, treas. ch. youth dept. New Vine Bapt. Ch., 1980—. Recipient Outstanding Performance and Outstanding Demonstrated Ability awards Dale Carnegie, Lynchburg, 1984. Democrat. Baptist. Lodge: Toastmistresses (local officer, 1980-85, regional treas. 1984-85, regional sec. 1985-86, regional 2d v.p. 1986-87). Avocations: singing; playing piano; trumpet; swimming; tennis. Home: Route 5 Box 582 Lynchburg VA 24501 Office: Nationwide Mut Ins Co 800 Graves Mill Rd Lynchburg VA 24506

HOOD, VALERIE LOGAN, university official; b. Kalispell, Mont., Nov. 3, 1937; d. William Regulous and Ione Montana (Swenson) Logan; B.A., Whitman Coll., 1960; M.A., George Washington U., 1963; m. Leroy E. Hood, Dec. 14, 1963; children—Eran William, Marqui Leigh. Tchr., Arcadia (Calif.) Unified Sch. Dist., 1963-67; vis. instr. Pacific Oaks Coll., 1974-78; gen. mgr. Fran W. Meyer Co., Glendale, Calif., 1978-80; mgr. mgmt. devel. Indsl. Relations Center, Calif. Inst. Tech., Pasadena, 1981-83, asst. dir., 1983-84, assoc. dir., 1984—. Bd. dirs. Women's Pub. Policy Research Ctr. Mem. Personnel and Indsl. Relations Assn. Club: Orgn. for Women-Caltech. Home: 1453 E California Blvd Pasadena CA 91106 Office: Calif Inst Tech 383 S Hill Ave I 90 Pasadena CA 91125

HOOD, VIRGINIA FORD (MRS. FREDERICK REDDING HOOD), civic worker; b. Vinita, Okla., May 1, 1905; d. William Thomas and Demmeria (Byrd) Ford; student Northeastern State Tchrs. Coll., 1920-21, 21-22; A.B., U. Okla., 1924; m. Frederick Redding Hood, Dec. 7, 1924; children—Frederick Frederick Redding, William Richard, Virginia Carol (Mrs. Kenneth Lee Pierce). Pres., Ladies Aux. Oklahoma County Med. Soc., 1937, co-chmn. Oklahoma City conv. So. Med. Conv., 1938, chmn. state conv. Okla. Med. Soc., 1950. Dist. chmn. Big One Drive, United Fund, Oklahoma City, 1953; chmn. Okla. Art Center Drive, 1957; capt. spl. gifts div. United Appeal, 1960-69, gen. chmn. Kappa Alpha Theta Found. Drive, 1964-65; chmn. Heritage Hills Hist. Home Tour, 1970-72; pres. Mothers Assn. U. Okla., 1957-58, Okla. Art League, 1960-61, Heritage Hills Aux., 1972-73; mem. Modern Classics, Oklahoma City; dir. YWCA, 1939-41, 66-72, met. bd. dirs., 1969-72, v.p., 1966-69, chmn. personnel com. 1966-68, 70-72, mem. dept. campus Christian life Okla. Assn. Christian Chs., 1964-68; pres. Heritage Hills Women's Com. of Hist. Preservation, 1973—. Mem. Kappa Alpha Theta (Okla. chmn. 1928-31, pres. Oklahoma City alumnae chpt. 1948-51, corp. bd. Alpha Omicron chpt. at U. Okla. 1954-57, 77-83, alumnae dist. pres. 1957-60, grand council 1960-64, v.p. service 1966-70, mem. bd. trustees found. 1966-70 Virginia Ford Hood Scholarship Fund created in her honor by Oklahoma City mems. 1984). Mem. Christian Ch. (deaconess bd. Oklahoma City 1954-57, 65-68, 72-75, 78-81, past chmn.; pres. Christian Women's fellowship Crown Heights Christian Ch., 1960-61, 61-62, tchr. bus. women's class, sponsor young married class, vice chmn. gen. bd. 1979-80, chmn. gen. bd. 1980-81, elder 1984-87). Club: Coterie Study (Oklahoma City).

HOOD JONES, BEVERLY ANN, lawyer; b. Little Rock, May 23, 1954; d. Chester Green and Dorothy Lee (Washington) Hood; m. Dennis Ray Jones, Oct. 16, 1976; children—Denise, Ebon, Deirdré. B.A., U. Ark., 1975, J.D., 1982. Bar: Ark. 1983. Atty., Central Ark. Legal Services, Little Rock, 1982—. Reginald Heber Smith Community Lawyer fellow Howard U., 1982-84. Mem. ABA, Ark. Bar Assn., Pulaski County Bar Assn., Am. Judicature Soc. Baptist. Office: Central Arkansas Legal Services 209 W Capitol Ave Hall Bldg Suite 36 Little Rock AR 72201

HOOK, ALICE PALO, librarian; b. Superior, Wis., Feb. 4, 1909; d. Elmer George and Helen (Payne) Palo; m. Norris M. Hook, June 21, 1945 (dec. 1946). B.S., U. Minn., 1930. Asst. in order dept. U. Minn., 1930; Taft order librarian U. Cin., 1931-37, head acquisition dept., 1943-46; order librarian Temple U., Phila., 1937-43; librarian Hist. and Philos. Soc. of Ohio, Cin., 1947-63; Cin. Art Mus., 1964-74. Mem. vol. canteen corps ARC, 1941-63; bd. dirs. Cin. Met. YWCA, 1957-70, rec. sec. bd. dirs. 1959-61, pub. relations chmn., 1961-64, centennial chmn., 1968; women's bd. dirs. Clovernook Home for Blind, 1974—, chmn., trustee, 1978-80. Mem. Am. Library Assn., Ohio Library Assn., Spl. Libraries Assn. (past pres. Cin. chpt., past chmn. nat. com. pub. relations, chmn. picture div. 1958-60), chmn. mus. div. 1964-66), Alpha Xi Delta. Clubs: Cin. Woman's (bd. dirs. 1974-77), College (bd. dirs. 1967-74, pres. 1983-84), Altrusa (gov. 5th dist. 1956-58).

HOOK, MARY JULIA, lawyer; b. Kansas City, Mo., Oct. 31, 1947; d. Vernon Anthony and Dula Mariah (Wood) H.; m. David Lee Smith, Dec. 30, 1972. B.A., So. Meth. U., 1967, M.A., 1969, J.D., 1972; LL.M., Harvard U., 1975. Bar: Tex. 1972, Colo. 1975. Trial atty. U.S. Dept. Justice, Washington, 1972-74, 75-76; assoc. Holland & Hart, Denver, 1976-81, ptnr., 1981—. Contbr. chpts. to Am. Law of Mining, 2d edit. Mem. ABA, Fed. Bar Assn., Tex. Bar Assn., Colo. Bar Assn., Denver Bar Assn., Assn. Trial Lawyers Am., Order of Coif, Phi Beta Kappa. Democrat. Methodist. Clubs: Denver, Denver Athletic. Home: 2036 Dexter St Denver CO 80207 Office: Holland & Hart 555 17th St Suite 2900 Denver CO 80202

HOOK, VIRGINIA MAY, marketing executive; b. Balt., Mar. 11, 1932; d. Arthur M. Monroe McClelland and Margaret (Shipley) McClelland Warfield; m. Donald F. Hook, Aug. 25, 1951 (dec. Dec. 1978); children—Donald F., Jr., Donna J. Hook Kellner. Grad. high sch. Teller, Central Savs. Bank, Balt., 1950-68, tng. dir., 1968-71; ops. mgr. Mature Temps, Inc., Balt., 1971-81; pres. VMH Mktg. Ltd., Glen Burnie, Md., 1982—. Mem. adv. council, sr. aides program D.C. Dept. Labor, 1980-81; active local Democratic party. Mem. Bank Personnel Assn. Md. (sec. 1969-71), Personnel Assn. Md. (sec. 1979-80), Exec. Women's Network, Market Research Assn., Am. Mktg. Assn., Nat. Assn. Women Bus. Owners. Methodist. Lodge: Order Eastern Star. Home: 3 Southerly Ct Towson MD 21204 Office: 8562-A Laureldale Dr Laurel MD 20707

HOOKER, LINDA ANN, microprocessor designer; b. Frankfurt, Ger., Sept. 26, 1955; came to U.S., 1957, naturalized, 1960; d. Winford Macon and Kathryn (Holt) Hooker. B.S. in Electronics Tech., U. Houston, 1984. Lic. in real estate, Tex.; cert. Reiki therapist. Exec. sec. to v.p. Fisk Electric, Houston, 1975-77; exec. sec. U. Houston, 1977-79, lab. teaching asst., 1979, electronics technician, 1979-81; microprocessor designer Stewart & Stevenson, Houston, 1981-84; staff engr. Hewlett Packard, Houston, 1984—. Named Student of the Year, IEEE, 1979. Mem. IEEE, Nat. Assn. Female Execs., Am. Internat. Reiki Assn., Tau Alpha Pi, Phi Kappa Phi. Republican. Christain Ch.

HOOKS, KAREN LEAH, accounting educator; b. Lakeland, Fla., Dec. 27, 1955; d. Wilbur Ocie and Frankie Emily (Grimes) H.; m. Stephen Srygley Walker, July 23, 1983. A.A., Polk Community Coll., 1974; B.A., U. S. Fla., 1976; Ph.D., Ga. State U., 1981. C.P.A., Fla. Asst. prof. acctg. U. South Fla., Tampa, 1979-85, assoc. prof., 1985—; staff acct. Touche Ross & Co., Tampa, 1976-77. Mem. Am. Woman's Soc. C.P.A. (v.p. nat. 1983-85, nat. dir. 1982-83), Nat. Assn. Accts. (dir. 1981-83), Fla. Inst. C.P.A.s, Am. Inst. C.P.A.s, Am. Acctg. Assn. Contbr. articles to profl. jours. Methodist. Office: Dept Acctg Coll Bus Univ South Fla Tampa FL 33620

HOOKS, LUCILLE T. BANKS, education specialist; b. Marion, Ala.; d. Judge Collie and Alice (Miles) Tubb; m. Arthur Lee Banks, Dec. 23, 1951; children—Myrtle K., Aldinea; m. Timothy Hooks, Jan. 7, 1978; 1 stepdau., Crystal Diane. Diploma, Selma U., Ala., 1947; B.S., Ala. State U., 1951; M.Ed., Tuskegee Inst. U., 1971; cert. in driver edn. U. Ala., 1969, Auburn U., 1970. Cert. tchr., Ala. Tchr. pub. elem. schs., Marion, Ala., 1951-61, Shorter, Ala., 1965-67; tchr. pub. schs., Tuskegee, 1967-77, edn. specialist, 1977—. Sec. Macon County Democratic Club, Tuskegee, 1979-80. Recipient service award Tuskegee Inst. Univ., 1975, Appreciation award Ala. Spl. Olympics, 1982, Leadership award Tuskegee Tchrs. Spl. Edn., 1983. Mem. NEA, Ala. Edn. Assn., Council Exceptional Children, Ala. Rehab. Assn., Nat. Assn. Female Execs., Kappa Delta Pi. Baptist. Lodge: Eastern Star. Avocations: travel; gardening; photography; antique collecting.

HOOKS, THERESA ANN, consulting firm executive, lawyer; b. Crestview, Fla., May 4, 1948; d. Edward M. and Doris V. (Coppage) Szarowicz; 1 dau., Joan Natalie Hooks. B.S., U. West Fla., 1970; M.S., Fla. State U., 1973, J.D., 1976. Staff analyst Fla. Ho. Reps., Tallahassee, 1974-76; atty. U.S. Dept. Commerce, Washington, 1976-78, U.S. Dept. Interior, Washington, 1978-80; cons. regulatory policy Hooks McCloskey & Assocs., Inc., Phila. and Westlake Village, Calif., 1980—; guest lectr. George Washington U., 1979, Villanova U., Pa., 1982. Mem. ABA (vice chmn. marine resources com. 1984-85), Fla. Bar Assn., D.C. Bar Assn., Pa. Bar Assn. Avocations: jogging; weight lifting; golf. Office: Hooks McCloskey & Assocs Inc 240 Lombard St #215 Thousand Oaks CA 91360

HOOKS, VANDALYN LAWRENCE, educator; b. Dyersburg, Tenn., Feb. 26, 1935; d. James Bridges and Mary Lucille (Anderson) Lawrence; m. Floyd Lester Hooks, June 15, 1952; children—Lawrence James, Steven Lester. B.A., Ky. Wesleyan U., 1967; M.A., Western Ky. U., 1970, Edn. Specialist, 1976; postgrad. U. Tenn., 1975. Tchr., Owensboro Bd. Edn., Ky., 1967-71, adminstr., 1976—; dir. career experience Western Ky. U., Bowling Green, 1971-73; dir. career edn. Owensboro Daviess County Sch. Dist., 1973-76; curriculum developer Career Experience Voc. Edn., Frankfort, Ky., 1971-76; cons. Motivation Workshop, Bowling Green, 1971-76, Decision and Goal Setting, 1971-76. Editor, Ky. Assn. Elem. Prin. Jour., 1977-81. Contbr. articles to profl. jours. Organizer, Ky. Council for Better Edn., Owensboro, 1984; legis. advisor Eagle Forum, Alton, Ill., 1976-85, leadership forum, Washington, 1985; legis. researcher Republican Party, Frankfort, 1984-85. Recipient Presdl. award, Ky. Wesleyan Coll., 1966. Mem. Concerned Edn. of Am., Nat. Council for Better Edn., Heritage Found., Pro Family Forum, Eagle Forum, Plymouth Rock Found.; Nat. Council Christian Educators, AAUW. Republican. Baptist. Address: 1302 Waverly Pl Owensboro KY 42301

HOOPER, ANDREA LAMMEY, city clerk; b. Des Moines, Nov. 24, 1937; d. Andy Newton and Gertrude Olive (Wright) Lammey; children—Dick Eugene, Kevin Mark, Craig Daniel. Student pub. schs. Tchr. aide Lynwood Sch. Dist., Calif., 1976-77; sec.-mgr. Lynwood C. of C., 1977-79; executor, dir. Lynwood-Compton Bd. Realtors, 1979-82; city clk. City of Lynwood, 1982—. Active Lynwood Welfare Bur., 1976-77; treas. Lynwood Community Coordinating Council, 1976-77, pres., 1978-79; precinct insp. city election, 1967-68, precinct worker primary, gen. elections, 1968-69; mem. ch. choir Lynwood United Meth. Ch., 1970-85; pack den mother Boy Scouts Am., 1965-74; chaperone Hosler Jr. High Sch. Band, 1972-74; chmn. dist. adv. council Lynwood Unified Sch. Dist., 1970-71; program chmn. Hosler Jr. High Sch., PTA, 1972-74; fin. sec., treas. Lynwood High Sch. PTA, 1971-72, pres., 1973-74; pres. Lindbergh Sch. PTA, 1969-70; PTA parliamentarian, 1975-78. Mem. Lynwood C. of C. (pres. 1983-84). Democrat. Club: Lynwood Women's (2d v.p. 1983-84). Avocations: sports; camping. Office: City Hall 11330 Bullis Rd Lynwood CA 90262

HOOPER, EDITH FERRY, museum trustee; b. Detroit, Nov. 30, 1909; d. Dexter Mason and Jeannette (Hawkins) Ferry; m. Arthur Upshur Hooper, June 22, 1945; children—Jeannette Williams, Kate Gorman, Queene Ferry. B.A., Vassar U. Indsl. design dept. asst. Mus. Modern Art, N.Y.C., 1939-40; clk. U.S. Procurement Office, Detroit, 1941-43; asst. Roeper City and Country Schs., Detroit, 1944; trustee Balt. Mus. Art., 1957—, pres. bd., 1973-75, accessions com., 1977—. Bd. dirs. Friends Art Gallery, Vassar Coll., Poughkeepsie, N.Y., 1974-76; pres. bd. trustees Bryn Mawr Sch., Balt., 1965-71, chmn. bldg. com., 1971-73; pres. DM Ferry Jr. Trustee Corp. (found.), Balt., 1973. Presbyterian. Clubs: Cosmopolitan (N.Y.C.), Hamilton St. (Balt.). Home: 1100 Copper Hill Rd Baltimore MD 21209

HOOPER, KATHY LAVERNE, manufacturing company executive; b. Timpson, Tex., Jan. 9, 1957; d. Bolden and Azzie Lee (Marks) H. A.A., Mo. Inst. Tech., 1977, B.S., 1978. Applications engr. Johnson Controls, Inc., Denver, 1978-80; customer engr. Hewlett-Packard Corp., Englewood, Colo., 1980-84, dist. customer engring. mgr., 1984—. Vol., ARC, Humana Hosp., Aurora, Colo., 1985—. Mem. Nat. Assn. Female Execs. Office: Hewlett-Packard Corp 24 Inverness Pl E Englewood CO 80112

HOOPES, MARIA SEGURA, librarian; b. Cananea, Mex., Jan. 16, 1945; came to U.S., 1954; d. Juan Segura Zabalza and Elvira (Garcia) Segura; m. F. Lance Hoopes, Dec. 26, 1964; children—Lance Patrick, Claire, Thomas. B.A., U. Ariz., 1975, M.L.S., 1978. Unit asst. Ariz. Health Sci. Ctr., Tucson, 1976-78; spl. agt. trainee FBI, Washington, 1980; librarian Donaldson Sch., Tucson, 1980-82; reference librarian U. Ariz. Tucson, 1982—; chmn. affirmative action com. Library Faculty Assembly, Tucson, 1983—. Mem. ALA, Ariz. State Library Assn., Reforma, Sigma Delta Pi. Democrat. Roman Catholic. Office: U Ariz Main Library Tucson AZ 85721

HOOSIN, JANICE LAUTT, social worker; b. Chgo., June 22, 1942; d. Herbert and Ruth Jean (Rubenstein) Lapine; B.A., U. Ill., 1964; M.S.W., Jane Addams Grad. Sch. Social Work, 1966; postgrad. U. Utah, summer, 1977. Cert. mental health adminstr., psychiat. social worker, Ill. Psychiat. social worker New Trier Twp. High Sch., East Winnetka, Ill., 1966-70; dir. day hosp. St. Vincent's Hosp., N.Y.C., 1970-73; psychotherapist (part-time) New Trier East High Sch., Winnetka, 1973-74; dir. psychiat. day hosp. dept. psychiatry Evanston (Ill.) Hosp., 1974-78, dir. partial hospitalization, 1978—; clin. assoc., field work supr. U. Chgo. Sch. Social Service Adminstrn., 1974—; cons. in field; pvt. practice marital and individual psychotherapy, specializing in chem. dependency, 1975—. NIMH fellow, 1964-66; cert. psychiat. social worker, Ill. Mem. Nat. Assn. Social Workers, Internat. Assn. Psychosocial Rehab., Assn. Mental Health Adminstrs. Jewish. Home: 2638 N Burling St Chicago IL 60614 Office: 2650 Ridge Ave Evanston IL 60201

HOOTKIN, PAMELA NAN, cosmetic company executive; b. N.Y.C., Nov. 14, 1947; d. Louis Arthur and Sally (Perlman) Mash; B.A., SUNY, Binghamton, 1968; M.A. in Econs., Boston U., 1970; m. Stephen Allen, Aug. 2, 1972; 1 dau., Julie Beth. Diversification analyst Champion Internat., N.Y.C., 1971-75; sr. fin. analyst Squibb Corp., N.Y.C., 1975-77, mgr. fin. analyst, 1977-79, dir. fin. planning, 1979-82; asst. controller Charles of The Ritz Group Ltd., N.Y.C., 1982-83, v.p., treas., 1983—; lectr. econs. U. York, Heslington, Eng., 1970-71. Mem. Fin. Women's Assn. of N.Y. Office: New York NY

HOOVER, BETTY-BRUCE HOWARD, educator; b. Wake County, N.C., Mar. 20, 1939; d. Bruce Ruffin and Mary Elizabeth (Brown) Howard; m. Herbert Charles Marsh Hoover, Sept. 3, 1961; children—David Andrew, Howard Webster, Lorraine VanSiclen. B.A., Wake Forest U., 1961; M.A., U. Fla., 1970. Tchr. English, Greensboro Sr. High Sch., N.C., 1961-62, Lindley Jr. High Sch., Greensboro, 1963, Berkeley Prep. Sch., Tampa, Fla., 1976—, chmn. English dept., 1977-85, dir., dean upper div., 1984—, chmn. curriculum com., 1982—. Pres., Suncoast Midshipmen Parents Club, Tampa Bay Area, 1983-84. Mem. Assn. Supervision Curriculum Devel., Nat. Council Tchrs. English, Wake Forest U. Alumni Assn., DAR, Hillsborough County Bar Aux., Cum Laude Soc. (sec. 1981), Nat. Honor Soc., Phi Beta Kappa, Phi Sigma Iota, Sigma Tau Delta. Republican. Episcopalian. Avocations: sewing; gardening. Home: 4504 Beachway Dr Tampa FL 33609 Office: Berkeley Preparatory Sch 4811 Kelly Rd Tampa FL 33615

HOOVER, LOLA MAE, communications company manager; b. Monticello, Ark., Apr. 1, 1947; d. Victor Arthur and Essie (Humphries) Piper; (div.); 1 child, Larry Wayne. With prodn. AT&T, West Chgo., 1963-78, 1st level shop mgr., 1978-83, warehouse mgr., 1983-84, office mgr., 1984—. Baptist. Home: 207 Briar Ln North Aurora IL 60542 Office: AT&T Info Systems 1700 Hawthorne Ln West Chicago IL 60185

HOOVER, MOLLY ANN, fashion/sales training consulting company executive; b. The Dallas, Oreg., May 17, 1948; d. Lile Wendell Hoover and Margaret Ernestine (Howard) Trullinger; m. Denny W. Homer, Mar. 28, 1970 (div. 1977). B.S., Oreg. State U., 1970, Ed.M., 1975. Tchr. bus. Aloha High Sch., Beaverton, Oreg., 1971-75; dental office mgr., Bridgeport, Wash., 1975-77; dist. sales mgr. Chrysler Corp., Portland, 1978-81; leasing mgr. Teague Motor Co., Salem, Oreg., 1981-83; nat. project mgr. A.D.P. Dealer Services, Portland, 1984-85; mng. dir. StyleRight Seminars, Portland, 1985—; word processing cons. Far West Fed., Portland, 1977; leasing cons. Pacific Coast Leasing, 1984. Comdr., Angel Flight ROCT Women's Aux., Corvallis, Oreg., 1968-70; treas., bd. dirs. Douglas Fed. Credit Union, Bridgeport, Wash., 1976-77; exhibit hall chmn. Small Bus. Adminstrn. Women's Conf., 1984. Named Salem Woman of 80's, Salem Spokesman Rev., 1982. Mem. Inst. Managerial and Profl. Women (v.p. 1985—, conf. dir. 1986), Nat. Assn. Female Execs., Zonta Internat., Kappa Alpha Theta, Phi Beta Lambda. Avocations: cross country skiing; painting; needlepoint; travel. Home: 3707 SW 52 Pl #1 Portland OR 97221 Office: StyleRight PO Box 6946 Portland OR 97228

HOPE, GERRI DANETTE, telecommunications specialist; b. North Highlands, Calif., Feb. 28, 1956; d. Albert Gerald and Beulah Rae (Bane) Hope. A.S., Sierra Coll., 1977; student Okla. State U., 1977-79. Admissions asst. Bass Meml. Hosp., Enid, Okla., 1978-79; instructional asst. San Juan Sch. Dist., Carmichael, Calif., 1979-82; telecommunications supr. Calif. Dental Service, San Francisco, 1982-85; telecommunications coordinator Farmers Savs. Bank, Davis, Calif., 1985—; cons. and lectr. in field. Mem. Women in Telecommunications, Nat. Assn. Female Execs. Republican. Avocations: writing; computers; ceramics; animal behavior; traveling. Home: 3025 U St North Highlands CA 95660

HOPE, MARGARET LAUTEN, civic worker; b. N.Y.C., Dec. 17; privately educated; m. Paul C. Debry, Jr., Nov. 9, 1943; m. 2d, Fred H. Hope, Jr., Mar. 30, 1959; 1 son, Frederick H., III. Bd. dirs. Nat. Leukemia Soc., 1974—; co-chmn. giftcom. Heart Ball, Palm Beach, Fla., 1967; mem. ball coms. various charity fund raising events. Mem. Jr. League N.Y.C. Clubs: Everglades, Sailfish (Palm Beach); Women's Nat. Republican (N.Y.C.); St. James (London, Eng.). Address: 236 Dunbar Rd PO Box 601 Palm Beach FL 33480

HOPKINS, BARBARA PETERS, public relations company executive; b. Santa Monica, Calif., Sept. 26, 1948; d. Philip Rising and Caroline Jean (Dickason) Peters; m. Philip Joseph Hopkins, May 23, 1981. A.A., Santa Monica Coll., 1971; B.S., San Diego State U., 1976; postgrad. UCLA, 1981, 82, 84. Gen. ptnr. Signet Properties, Los Angeles, 1971-85; tech. editor C. Brewer & Co., Hilo, Hawaii, 1975-76; editor Aztec Engineer, San Diego, 1976-77; regional publicist YWCA, San Diego, 1977-78; campaign cons. Republican Candidates, San Diego, 1978; pres. Humbird Hopkins Inc., Los Angeles, 1979—; pub. relations cons. ASCE, San Diego, 1975-76, Am. Soc. Mag. Photographers, San Diego, 1980. Author: The Layman's Guide to Raising Cane-A Guide to the Hawaiian Sugar Industry, 1976; The Student's

Survival Guide, 1977, 2d edit. 1978. Council mem. Mayor's Council on Libraries, Los Angeles, 1969; mem. Wilshire Blvd. Property Owners Assn., Los Angeles, 1972-78; docent Mus. Sci. and Industry, Los Angeles, 1970; founding mem. Comml. and Indsl. Properties Assn., Los Angeles, 1982—. Recipient Acting award Santa Monica Coll., 1970. Mem. Internat. Assn. Bus. Communicators, Sales and Mktg. Execs. Assn. Club: Santa Monica Athletic. Avocations: writing; travel; opera. Office: Humbird Hopkins Inc PO Box 49813 Los Angeles CA 90049

HOPKINS, CECILIA ANN (MRS. HENRY E. HOPKINS), educator; b. Havre, Mont., Feb. 17, 1922; d. Kost L. and Mary (Manaras) Sofos; B.S., Mont. State Coll., 1944; M.A., San Francisco State Coll., 1958, M.A., 1967; postgrad. Stanford U.; Ph.D., Calif. Western U., 1977; m. Henry E. Hopkins, Sept. 7, 1944. Bus. tchr. Havre (Mont.) High Sch., 1942-44; sec. George P. Gorham, realtor, San Mateo, Calif., 1944-45; escrow sec. Fox & Carskadon, realtors, 1945-50; escrow officer Calif. Pacific Title Ins. Co., 1950-57; bus. tchr. Westmoor High Sch., Daly City, Calif., 1958-59; bus. tchr. Coll. San Mateo, 1959—, chmn. real estate-ins. dept., 1963-76, dir. div. bus., 1976—; cons. to commr. Calif. Div. Real Estate, 1963—, mem. periodic exam. rev. com., 1974—; bd. advisers Glendale Fed./West Coast Fed. Savs. and Loan Assn. Vice chmn. Community Coll. Adv. Com., 1970-71, chmn., 1971-72; mem. adv. com. Chancellor's Community Coll. Endowment, 1975—; mem. Calif. Community Coll. real estate continuing edn. panel, 1979—. Recipient Woman of Achievement award Mateo-Burlingame Soroptimists, 1979. Mem. AAUW, Calif. Assn. Real Estate Tchrs. (state pres. 1964-65, hon. dir. 1962— named Outstanding Real Estate Tchr. 1979), Real Estate Certificate Inst. (cert. commendation), Calif. Bus. Edn. Assn. (Cert. of Commendation 1978), San Francisco State Coll. Guidance and Counseling Alumni, Theta Alpha Delta, Pi Lambda Theta, Delta Pi Epsilon (nat. dir. interchpt. relations 1962-65, nat. historian 1966-67, nat. sec. 1968-69), Alpha Gamma Delta. Co-author: Real Estate Principles in California; contbr. articles to profl. jours. Home: 504 Colgate Way San Mateo CA 94402

HOPKINS, DIANNE MCAFEE, state school library media administrator, consultant; b. Houston, Dec. 30, 1944; d. DeWitt Talmadge and Valda Lois (Baker) McAfee; m. Dale William Hopkins, July 7, 1982; children—Brent William, Scott McAfee. B.A., Fisk U., 1966; M.S.L.S., Atlanta U., 1967; Ed.S., Western Mich. U., 1973; Ph.D., U. Wis., 1981. Sch. librarian Houston Ind. Sch. Dist., 1967-71; sch. library specialist Dept. Edn., Lansing, Mich., 1972-73; library media specialist West Bloomfield Sch. Dist., Orchard Lake, Mich., 1973-74; library media cons. U. Mich., Ann Arbor, 1974-77; bur. dir. Dept. Pub. Instrn. Wis., Madison, 1977—. Contbr. articles to profl. jours., 1973—. Chmn. bd. outreach First Baptist Ch., Madison, 1981, mem. pulpit com., 1982, chmn. bd. edn., 1984. Recipient Exceptional Performance award Dept. Pub. Instrn. Wis., 1982. Mem. ALA (councilor 1982-86), Assn. Ednl. Communications and Tech. (bd. dirs. 1982-85, exec. com. 1984-85), Am. Assn. Sch. Librarians (rec. sec. 1976-77, parliamentarian 1986), Wis. Sch. Library Media Assn. (liaison 1977—, parliamentarian 1985), Wis. Library Assn. (chmn. intellectual freedom com. 1984), Delta Sigma Theta. Club: Links (Madison). Avocations: piano; reading; cross stitchery; museums; movies. Office: Dept Pub Instrn 125 S Webster PO Box 7841 Madison WI 53707

HOPKINS, ELIZABETH BALCH, tobacco company executive; b. Duluth, Minn., June 22, 1932; d. Richard Carlisle and Virginia (Finley) Balch; m. Dwight D. Hopkins, Oct. 23, 1954 (div. 1980); children—D. Douglas, Laura Clark, Timothy Balch. B.A., Wells Coll., 1954; M.A., SUNY-Buffalo, 1968. Tchr. English, Park Sch., Buffalo, 1968-69, Nottingham Acad., 1969; pres. Wonderwoman Employment, Inc., 1973-77; exec. dir. Everywoman Opportunity Ctr., Inc., 1977-80; adminstr. Philip Morris Inc., N.Y.C., 1981-83, mgr., 1983—. Chmn. adv. bd. N.Y. Displaced Homemaker Program, 1981-84; panelist Inter Arts Program, Nat. Endowment Arts, 1984. Mem. Women in Communications, Phi Beta Kappa. Democrat. Office: Philip Morris Inc 120 Park Ave New York NY 10017

HOPKINS, JEANNE SULICK, accountant; b. FairLawn, N.J., Oct. 14, 1952; d. Peter and Margaret Mary (McLaughlin) Sulick; B.S., Syracuse (N.Y.) U., 1974, M.B.A., 1975; m. Ronald T. Hopkins, Aug. 23, 1975. With Price Waterhouse, C.P.A.s, Syracuse, 1975-83, staff acct., 1975-78, sr. acct., 1978-80, audit mgr., 1980-83; mgr. cost acctg. United Techs./Carrier, Syracuse, 1983-85; ptnr. J.S. Hopkins & Co., C.P.A.s, Syracuse, 1985—; instr. in field. Mem. fund raising com. Syracuse Symphony Orch.; mem. Nat. Assn. Panhellenics. C.P.A., N.Y. Mem. Am. Inst. C.P.A.s, Planning Execs. Inst., Hosp. Fin. Mgmt. Assn., N.Y. State Soc. C.P.A.s, Syracuse U. Alumni Assn., Delta Delta Delta. Club: Zonta. Office: JS Hopkins & Co 5858 Molloy Rd Suite 164 Syracuse NY 13211

HOPKINS, LEANN ELISABETH, sales representative; b. Oklahoma City, Sept. 15, 1960; d. Donald Ray and Janyth Lee (Stanmire) H. B.A. in Motion Picture Journalism, U. Okla., 1982. Lic. ins. agt., Okla. Asst. dist. retail mgr. Fox-Stanley Photo, Inc., Oklahoma City, 1978-82; media cons. Okla. Horsemen's Assn., 1982; ter. mgr. ArtCarved Class Rings, Inc., Austin, Tex., 1982-85; sales rep. Met. Ins. Co., Oklahoma City, 1985—. Producer, asst. dir. and cinematographer: The Complete Works of Christopher Brandon (Silver award Okla. Internat. Film Festival), 1982. Mem. NOW, Am. Mensa, World Wildlife Fund, Greenpeace, Am. Film Inst., Nat. Assn. Female Execs. Democrat. Home: 1004 SW 84th #9 Oklahoma City OK 73139

HOPKINS, LINDA ANN, school psychologist; b. Bristol, Va., Aug. 23, 1937; d. James Robert and Trula Mae (Mink) Broce; A.B., King Coll., 1959; M.A., East Tenn. State U., 1977, postgrad., 1977-79; postgrad. Radford U., 1978-79; m. James Edwin Hopkins, Oct. 8, 1960; children—James Edwin, David Lawrence. Social worker Washington County Welfare Dept., Abingdon, Va., 1959-61; social worker Bristol (Va.) Welfare Dept., 1963-65, Washington County Welfare Dept., 1965-68, Bristol Meml. Hosp., 1968-72; psychologist Washington County Public Schs., Abingdon, 1978—; lectr. Va. Highlands Community Coll., Abingdon, 1981—. Mem. Nat. Assn. Sch. Psychologists, Va. Psychol. Assn., Va. Assn. Sch. Psychologists, Phi Kappa Phi. Methodist. Club: Dogwood Playhouse. Home: 436 Brookwood Dr Bristol TN 37620 Office: Washington County Pub Schs PO Box 1388 Abington VA 24210

HOPKINS, LYNETTE LANE, psychologist, educational therapist; b. Los Angeles, Sept. 12, 1934; d. Arthur Henry and LaVaughn Lorene (Beckwith) Lane; B.A., Whittier Coll., 1956; M.S.W., UCLA, 1966; M.S. in Spl. Edn., Mt. St. Mary's Coll., 1978; Ph.D., Internat. Coll., Los Angeles; m. Don J. Hopkins, Nov. 21, 1959; children—Kenneth, Scott, Richard. Elem. sch., jr. high music tchr. Fullerton, Calif., 1956-60; social worker Los Angeles County Dept. Public Social Services, 1960-66, staff devel. specialist, 1966-70; researcher Marianne Frostig Center, Los Angeles, 1974-76; master tchr., ednl. therapist Marianne Frostig Center, Los Angeles, 1976-84; dir. Ivalyn Ctr. Integrative Edn., 1984—. Registered social worker, Calif. Mem. Assn. Humanistic Psychology, Nat. Assn. Social Workers, Acad. Cert. Social Workers, Council for Exceptional Children, Holistic Educators Network. Baha'i. Home: 1144 N Jackson St Glendale CA 91207 Office: 221 S Kenwood St Glendale CA 91205

HOPKINS, PATRICIA FUOSS, architect, educator; b. Providence, May 14, 1935; d. Raymond Matthew Fuoss and Rose Elizabeth (Harrington) Spear; m. David Lawrence Hopkins, Aug. 27, 1957 (div. 1983); children—Steven Fuoss, Glenn William. B.Arch., Cornell U., 1957. Lic. architect, Colo. Project architect Gordon Sweet Architect, Colorado Springs, Colo., 1961-64, The Hopkins Architect-Planner, Aspen, 1964-82; project architect, cons. Bill Baker, Architect, Colorado Springs, 1983-84; assoc. prof., div. head solar engring. technology Colo. Tech. Coll., 1982—; prin. Pat Hopkins Architect and Planner, Colorado Springs, 1982—; cons. Robin Molny Architect, Aspen, 1981; instr., team leader Aspen Highlands Ski Sch., 1970-82. Teaching asst. Aspen pub. schs., 1969-81. Mem. Solar Energy and Conservation Assn. (charter), Nat. Assn. Home Builders, Energy Efficient Bldg. Assocs., Nat. Assn. Female Execs., Profl. Ski Instrs. Am., Alpha Alpha Gamma. Avocations: horseback riding, downhill skiing. Home: 4016 Goldenrod Dr Colorado Springs CO 80907 Office: Pat Hopkins Architect/Planner 4016 Goldenrod Dr Colorado Springs CO 80907

HOPKINS, PATRICIA MARGARET, marketing educator; b. Ilford, Essex, Eng., June 6, 1939; came to U.S. 1958, naturalized 1964; d. Edward George and Freda Miriam (Farront) Berg; m. McMillen Hopkins, Mar. 5, 1960 (div. 1981); children—Craig Edward, Keith Bryan. Secretarial diploma, Southwest Essex Tech. Coll., Walthamstow, Eng., 1955; A.A., Fullerton Jr. Coll., 1967; B.A., Calif. State U.-Fullerton, 1971, M.B.A., 1972; Ph.D., Claremont Grad. Sch., 1977. Sec. C.P.A., London, 1955-58; sec. Tidewater Oil, Los Angeles, 1958-63; statistician Rockwell Internat., Anaheim, Calif., 1965-69; prof. mktg. Calif. Poly. State U., Pomona, 1975—. Named Outstanding Educator Sch. Bus. Adminstrn., 1984. Mem. Acad. Mktg. Sci. (editorial bd.), Am. Mktg. Assn., Western Mktg. Educators Assn., Pi Sigma Epsilon, Phi Kappa Phi, Beta Gamma Sigma, Alpha Epsilon Omega, Mu Kappa Tau. Democrat. Home: 16326 Santa Bianca Dr Hacienda Heights CA 91745 Office: Calif State Polytech Univ 3801 Temple St Pomona CA 91768

HOPPE, LOUISE RUTH, government official; b. Alexandria, Va., Jan. 19, 1949; d. William G. and Ruth A. (Ehren) H. B.A., Va. Commonwealth U., 1971; postgrad. Am. U., 1972-73. Staff asst. to Dr. Henry A. Kissinger, Nat. Security Council, Washington, 1971-73; adminstrv. asst. Nat. Petroleum Council, Washington, 1973-75; profl. staff Senate Armed Service Com., Washington, 1976-81; spl. asst. Office of Legis. Affairs, Dept. of State, Washington, 1981-84, dep. asst. sec. of state Office of Legis. Affairs, 1984—. Republican. Lutheran. Avocations: cooking; gardening. Home: 403 Queen St Alexandria VA 22314 Office: Dept of State 2201 C St NW Washington DC 20520

HOPPE, MARY CLAIRE, marketing manager, health care company; b. Evanston, Ill., May 24, 1953; d. Paul P. and Lois M. (Wilson) H. B.S. in Nursing, Loyola U., Chgo., 1975; M.S. in Nursing, 1981. Instr. critical care St. Mary of Nazareth Sch. of Nursing, Chgo., 1975-77; nurse clinician St. Mary of Nazareth Hosp., Chgo., 1977-80; clin. nurse specialist Loyola U. Med. Ctr., Maywood, Ill., 1980-83; mgr. nursing practices Abbott Labs., North Chicago, Ill., 1983-85; mgr. partnership services Abbott Labs., North Chicago, 1985—; mem. Ill. Joint Practice Com., Chgo., 1982-83; dir.-at-large nursing Am. Soc. Parenteral and Enteral Nutrition, 1982-83. Mem. editorial bd. Jour. Parenteral and Enteral Nutrition, 1981-83, Nutrition Support Services Jour., 1983. Contbr. articles to profl. jours. Recipient Pres. award Abbott Home Care Div., 1984. Mem. Am. Soc. Parenteral and Enteral Nutrition (dir.-at-large nursing 1982-84), Sigma Theta Tau (chpt. pres. 1983-84). Clubs: Lake Shore Ski (communications dir. 1983-84, dir. beginners ski program 1985-86) (Chgo.). Avocations: skiing; sailing.

HOPPEN, MARILYN ROBERTA, insurance company executive; b. Seattle, Apr. 1, 1954; d. John and Ruth Karen (Dahlgren) Medley; m. Mark Edward Hoppen, June 19, 1976. B.A. in Bus. Adminstrn., U. Wash., 1976; M.B.A., Pacific Luth. U., 1981. Life underwriter United Pacific/Reliance Ins. Cos., Federal Way, Wash., 1977-78, adminstrv. asst.-human resources, 1978-81, asst. sec., asst. dir. human resources, 1981—, also dir. Mem. planning and allocations com. United Way Pierce County, Tacoma, 1979—. Mem. Pacific N.W. Personnel Mgmt. Assn., Sigma Kappa. Home: PO Box 160 Gig Harbor WA 98335 Office: United Pacific/Reliance Ins Cos 33405 8th Ave S C-3000 Federal Way WA 98003

HOPPER, ELLEN MARIE, editor; b. Elgin, Ill., Apr. 26, 1946; d. Edward Charles and Leona Joyce (Smith) Hubbard; stepdau. Robert Eugene and Joyce (Smith) Musall; m. Eugene Hopper, Oct. 22, 1969 (div. Dec. 1980). Writer, Daily Citizen, Cushing, Okla., 1976-78; society editor Derrick & Jour., Drumright, Okla., 1978-80, news editor, 1982—. Contbg. author: Cimarron Family Legends, 1978. Mem. Okla. Press Assn., Drumright C. of C. Democrat. Lutheran. Office: Drumright Newspapers PO Box 912 Drumright OK 74030

HOPPER, VIVIAN LINDA, training executive; b. Memphis, Tenn., June 8, 1947; d. Leslie Wright Hopper and Vivian Loraine (Beasley) Ray; m. Ben Claud Cook, Sept. 6, 1968 (div. 1976); m. Loyd Daniel Rainey, July 13, 1976. B.A. in Sociology, Memphis State U., 1973; postgrad., 1975; M. Gen. Adminstrn., U. Md., 1986. Instr., U. Pitts., 1975-78; media coordinator Amalgamated Clothing and Textile Workers' Union, Pitts., 1976-78; tng. coordinator Wider Opportunities for Women, Washington, 1979-83; tng. specialist Washington Met. Area Transit Authority, 1983-86; dir. tng. Internat. City Mgmt. Assn., Washington, 1986—; dir. D.C. Pvt. Industry Council; cons. No. Va. Info. and Counseling Ctr. for Women, Vienna, McKenna House, Washington; mem. speakers bur., program evaluation com. Pvt. Industry Council; workshop leader, panelist. Contbr.: Women into Trades and Technology, 1981. Mem. Am. Soc. Tng. and Devel., Nat. Assn. Female Execs. Home: 4770 N 25th St Arlington VA 22207 Office: Internat City Mgmt Assn 1120 G St NW Washington DC 20005

HOPPING, JANET MELINDA, educational administrator; b. Washington, Dec. 27, 1943; d. Russell Leroy and Janet L. (Cloud) H. B.S., Tex. Christian U., 1965; M.Ed., Ga. State U., 1977. Edn. cert., Ga. Tchr., Littleton, Colo., 1965-68, East Point, Ga., 1969, Atlanta, 1969-78; Title IVc coordinator Fulton County Schs., Atlanta, 1978-81, middle sch. project coordinator, 1981-82; asst. prin. West Middle Sch., East Point, 1982-83; prin. Holcomb Bridge Middle Sch., Alpharetta, Ga., 1983—; cons., trainer various sch. systems. Mem. Assn. Supervision and Curriculum Devel., Nat. Middle Sch. Assn., Ga. League Middle Grade Educators (pres. 1984-85), Prins. Inst. (adv. bd.), Atlanta Hist. Soc., Delta Kappa Gamma. Republican. Roman Catholic. Avocations: golf; tennis. Home: 720 Spring Creek Ln Dunwoody GA 30338 Office: 2700 Holcomb Bridge Rd Alpharetta GA 30201

HOPPOCK, D. LARUE, educator, antique appraiser; b. San Francisco, Mar. 27, 1933; d. Charles D. and Evelyn (Birdeen) H.; B.A., Western Wash. U., 1958; M.A., U. Calif.-Berkeley, 1962; M.A., Boston U., 1972; postgrad. U. Chgo., U. Md. Prin. high schs. Dept. Def., Paris, Naples, Italy, Istanbul, Turkey and Brunssum, Netherlands, 1963-75; tchr. high sch., Carlsbad, Calif., 1976-79, 83—, tchr. elem. sch., 1979-82; antique appraiser, 1981—; owner LaRue's Antiques; tchr. evening sch. Mira Costa Coll., 1977-82; prin. Mira Costa Adult High Sch., 1983—. Named Tchr. of Year, 1963, 65, 68, 69, 81. Mem. Carlsbad Unified Tchrs. Assn., Am. Personnel and Guidance Assn., Nat. Educators Fellowship, Delta Kappa Gamma, Assn. Calif. Sch. Adminstrs., Internat. Soc. Appraisers, Internat. Platform Assn. Contbr. articles in field to profl. jours. Home: PO Box 312 San Luis Rey CA 92068 Office: Carlsbad High Sch 3557 Monroe St Carlsbad CA 92008 also Mira Costa Coll Horne and Mission Sts Oceanside CA 92054 also LaRue's Antiques Past Times Mall 2922 State St Carlsbad CA 92008

HORAN, DOLORES VOLINI, lawyer; b. Chgo., Apr. 7, 1933; d. Italo Frederick and Marcella (Ringwald) Volini; m. Dennis John Horan, July 26, 1958; children—Cecilia, Matthew. B.S., Loyola U., Chgo., 1955; M.A., Columbia U., 1960; J.D., Northwestern U., 1965. Bar: Ill. 1965. Sole practice law, Chgo., 1965-76; ptnr. firm Barnes & Horan, Chgo., 1976—. Mem. legal com. Advocates for Handicapped, Chgo., 1978-83. Mem. ABA, Ill. Bar Assn., Chgo. Bar Assn., Appellate Lawyers Assn., Women's Bar Assn. Roman Catholic. Home: 6255 N Knox St Chicago IL 60646 Office: Barnes & Horan 180 N LaSalle St Chicago IL 60601

HORCHER, ANN-MARIE THERESE, system analyst; b. East St. Louis, Ill.; d. Linus Henry and Alice Marie (Leingang) Horcher; m. Donald Reid Martin. B.S. in Tech. Writing, Univ. Ill., 1979, M.S. in Info. Sci., 1981. Lab technician FAI-270 Archaeology Project, Urbana, Ill., 1978-79; instr. tech. writing Univ. Ill., Urbana, 1979-81; info. specialist Dow Corning Corp., Midland, Mich., 1981-83, sr. tools analyst, 1983-85, systems analyst, 1986—; cons. automation Midland Pub. Library, issue editor Am. Soc. for Info. Sci. bulletin, 1985. Contbr. articles to profl. jour. Mgt. Midland Music Soc. Bd., Mem. Am. Soc. for Info. Sci. (speaker annual meeting 1984, 85, mem. edn. com. 1983—), U.S. Dept. Edn. Accreditation Com., Am. Bus. Communication Assn. Avocations: ice skating, dance, folk music, theater.

HORELICK, MARY GAIL, physical therapist; b. Westport, Conn., Apr. 27, 1948; d. Michael and Rita (Hermenze) H.; B.S., Ithaca Coll., 1970; M.S., Hartford Grad. Ctr. Staff phys. therapist New Rochelle (N.Y.) Hosp. Med. Center, 1971-73, Misericordia Hosp. Med. Center, Bronx, 1974-77, chief phys. therapist/coordinator rehab. services, 1977-80; dir. rehab. services Newington (Conn.) Children's Hosp., 1980—. Mem. phys. therapy adv. council U. Conn. Mem. Am. Phys. Therapy Assn. (treas. Conn. chpt.), Am. Coll. Sports Medicine. Home: 24 Conestoga Way Glastonbury CT 06033 Office: 181 E Cedar St Newington CT 06111

HORENSTEIN, MURIEL CATHERINE, radio station executive; b. Bklyn., Nov. 15, 1919; d. Edward and Janette (Ehrmann) Mooney; m. Sol Horenstein; children—Eileen, Michael. Ed. NYU, Owner, Muriel Shop, 1940-43; with Matthew Exec. Search, N.Y.C., 1944-60, Staff Personnel, N.Y.C., 1948-60; co-owner, operator Sta.-WHYG, Babylon, N.Y., 1961—; faculty Sch. Bus., Columbia U., Suffolk City, N.Y., 1958-74. Pub. L.I. Club Woman. Trustee Dawling Coll., 1968-76, Suffolk County Park, 1969-74. Club: Overseas Press. Avocations: painting; golf. Home: 290 Farmingdale Rd West Babylon NY 11704

HORLOCK, DOROTHY GRAY, rancher, real estate developer; b. Tex., Feb. 8, 1931; d. John Edward and Lee G. Gray; student U. Houston, 1948-49, U. So. Calif., 1956-57; m. Roy M. Horlock, Nov. 22, 1966 (div. Jan. 1976); 1 son, Roy M. Exec. asst. to J. Heflin, Tex. State Rep., 1949-50; v.p. Seaport Realty Co., Inc., Houston, 1950-56; stewardess Trans World Airlines, Los Angeles, 1957-59; owner, operator Sugar Hill Ranch, Hallettsville, Tex., 1960—; property developer; investor; dir. 1100 South Post Oak, Inc., D.G.H. Investments, Inc. Bd. dirs. Houston Grand Opera, 1972-73, chmn. fund dr., 1972; trustee various pvt. trusts; fundraiser Mus. Fine Arts, Houston, Planned Parenthood, Houston. Mem. Tex. Longhorn Assn., Tex. Circle R. Republican. Methodist. Clubs: Houston City, Briar. Home: 6603 Torrey Pines Cove Austin TX 78746 Office: Sugar Hill Ranch Route 2 Box 225 Hallettsville TX 77964

HORN, DEBORAH SUE, organization administrator; b. Cin., July 14, 1954; d. Harry Robert and Helen (Ammann) H. B.S., Ball State U., 1977; postgrad. Calif. State U.-Fullerton, 1978-80. Asst. editor Scott Publs., Santa Ana, Calif., 1979-81; publs. mgr. Toastmasters Internat., Santa Ana, 1981-84, edn. mgr., 1984—, editor Toastmaster mag., 1981-84. Intern, Ind. Republican State Central Com., Indpls., 1976. Mem. Calif. Press Women (2d place mag. editing award 1982, 1st place mag. editing award 1983, pres. Orange County dist. 1984-85), Nat. Fedn. Press Women, Women in Communications, Soc. Profl. Journalists. Methodist. Club: Langlaufer Ski (corr. sec. 1985—, newsletter editor 1985—) (Downey, Calif.). Home: 2821 S Fairview Apt G Santa Ana CA 92704 Office: Toastmasters Internat 2200 N Grand Ave Santa Ana CA 92711

HORN, MARCIA T., public relations exec.; b. N.Y.C., Dec. 28, 1947; d. Jacob and Hilda (Savitt) Thomas; B.A., N.Y. U., 1969; A.A., Packer Jr. Coll., 1967; m. Donald Horn, Oct. 10, 1971. Public relations dir. Balmoral Hotel, Nassau, Bahamas, 1969-70; asst. to pres. Casey Assos., N.Y.C., 1970-71; editorial dir. The Design Store, Washington, 1973-75; asso. dir. public info. Investment Co. Inst., Washington, 1975—; contbg. editor The Exec. Female Digest, 1980. Judge, Graphic Arts Awards, 1980, 81; public relations vol. Washington Hebrew Congregation, 1980, 81; judge public relations competition AAUW, 1981. Mem. Women in Communications (pres. chpt. 1982—), Nat. Assn. Female Execs., Kappa Tau Alpha. Contbr. articles to profl. jours. Office: 1775 K St NW Washington DC 20006

HORN, MYRNA MOTTA, advertising executive; b. Glendale, Calif., June 17, 1939; d. Dominic Peter and Leona Dorothy (Wollmuth) Motta; m. Charles Glennon Horn, Aug. 22, 1959 (div. 1975); children—Melissa, Matthew; m. 2d, David Leroy Hill. B.S. magna cum laude in Edn., U. So. Calif.-Los Angeles, 1961. Cert. tchr. elem. edn., Calif. Tchr. elem. sch. Glendale Unified Sch. Dist. (Calif.), 1962-64, Hudson Sch. Dist., Hacienda Heights, Calif., 1964-66, Spring Branch Sch. Dist., Houston, 1966-67; media buyer, account executive Estey-Hoover, Newport Beach, Calif., 1976-78, account supr., 1978-81, v.p., account supr., 1981—, also dir. Recipient Achievement award Bank of Am., 1957; cert. of Excellence Orange County Ad Fedn., 1979; named Prominent Woman in Advt. H. Whitney McMillan Co., 1983. Mem. So. Calif. Women in Advt., Orange County Ad Fedn. (sec., treas. 1978-80), Phi Kappa Phi, Alpha Chi Omega (sec., treas., v.p. 1969-75). Republican. Office: Estey-Hoover Inc 3300 Irvine Ave #225 Newport Beach CA 92660

HORN, PAUL LOIS, educational training consultant, technical writer; b. N.Y.C., Jan. 20, 1947; d. Herman and Sadie Florence (Spiegelburd) H. B.A., Albany State U., 1969; M.S., Hofstra U., 1972; M.A., NYU, 1974; Ph.D., U. So. Calif., 1980. Reading cons. and specialist Seaford/Branford, N.Y. and Conn., 1971-74; instructional designer System Devel. Corp., Santa Monica, Calif., 1978-79; ednl. tng. cons. U So. Calif., Los Angeles, 1982-85; mktg. tng. cons. Xerox Corp., El Segundo, Calif., 1985-86; sr. tech. writer Ashton Tate Corp., Torrance, Calif., 1986—; cons. in field; advt. tng. cons. Nat. Tng. Systems, Santa Monica, 1979-80; ednl. tng. cons. Learning Systems, Encino, Calif., 1980-81; media tng. cons. Media Learning Systems, Pasadena, Calif., 1980-86; researcher Northridge U., Calif., 1984-85. Author: Economics Analysis for Business, 1982; instr., designer, editor: Consultants' Handbook, 1986. Mem. Nat. Soc. Performance and Instrn., Soc. Applied Learning Tech. (bd. dirs.), Assn. Tng. and Devel., Soc. Tech. Communication, Mensa, Phi Delta Kappa, Phi Delta Epsilon. Avocations: writing; reading; concerts; movies; theater. Home: 11023 Fruitland Dr #4 Studio City CA 91604 Office: Ashton Tate 20101 Hamilton Ave Torrance CA 90502

HORN, SALLY RUTH KUSNITZ, government official; b. Bridgeport, Conn., Nov. 19, 1946; d. H. Norman and Esther (Knepler) Kusnitz; m. Stuart Barry Horn, Mar. 15, 1969; children—Stephanie, Gayle. B.A. cum laude with high honors, Brown U., Providence, 1968; M.A., Yale U., 1969. Mgmt. intern Office Sec. of Def., Washington, 1969-70, Soviet, East Europe analyst, 1970-74, nat. security analyst, 1975-79, arms control analyst and negotiator, 1979-82, dir. verification policy, 1982—; legis asst. U.S. Congress, Washington, 1974-75; mem. U.S. del. Intermediate Nuclear Force Arms Control Talks, Geneva, 1981, U.S.-USSR Communications Talks, Washington, Moscow, 1983-84; chairperson U.S. Interagency Working Groups on Nuclear Arms Control Verification and Confidence Bldg. Measures, Washington, 1982—; del. White House Conf. on Youth, Washington, 1970. Contbr. articles to profl. jours. Unit chairperson League of Women Voters, Fairfax; v.p. Civic Assn., Fairfax. Recipient numerous honorary and cash awards Office Sec. Def., 1972—; Congl. and Fgn. Affairs fellow Office Sec. Def., 1974; Study in USSR grantee U.S. Govt., Kansas U., 1967. Mem. Council Fgn. Relations, Inst. Strategic Studies, Office Sec. Def. Sr. Profl. Women's Group, Dobro Slova, Phi Beta Kappa. Office: Office Sec of Def ISP Washington DC 20301

HORNBAKER, ALICE JOY, author; b. Cin., Feb. 3, 1927; B.A. cum laude and honors in Journalism, San Jose State U., 1949; children—Christopher Albert, Holly Jo, Joseph Bernard III. Asst. woman's editor San Jose Mercury-News, 1949-55; owner, mgr. Frisch Big Boy Restaurant, Cin., 1955-68; dir. pub. relations Children's Home Soc. Calif., Santa Clara, 1968-71; asst. dir. pub. relations United Fund Calif., Santa Clara, 1971—; editorial dir. Writers Digest Sch., Cin., 1971-75; columnist, critic, mag. writer, reporter, copy editor People Today sec. Cin. Enquirer, 1975—, also book editor and critic, columnist for Aging, feature writer Tempo sect.; reporter feature segments on aging WKRC-TV; tchr. adult edn. Forest Hills Sch. Dist., Thomas More Coll., 1973—; author: Preventive Care: Easy Exercise Against Aging, 1974; byline in People, Modern Maturity, Sr. Advocate, NATR Jour., and others; contbr. fiction to Enquirer mag.; freelance mag. writer. Recipient Bronze award in Am. health journalism, Am. Chiropractic Assn., 1977, 78; 1st place for feature writing Cin. Editors Assn., 1983. Mem. Blue Pencil of Ohio State U. (pres. 1981-82), Women in Communications, Ohio Newspaper Women's Assn. (v.p. 1981-83, 1st place human interest story, 1977-85, 2d place columnist award 1979, Tops in Ohio award 1982, M.M. McMullen 2d place award 1982, Recognition award 1985), Soc. Profl. Journalists (treas. 1981-82). Office: The Cin Enquirer 617 Vine St Cincinnati OH 45201

HORNBLOWER, AUGUSTA, state legislator; b. Boston, June 6, 1948; d. Henry Hornblower II and Dorothy (Shapard) Durphee. B.S. in Bus. Adminstrn., Babson Coll., 1971. Investments account exec. H.C. Wainwright & Co., Boston, 1973-77; fed. grant mgr. Exec. Office of Energy Resources, Boston, 1979-83; state fellow Nat. Gov.'s Assn., Washington, 1982-83; mem. Commonwealth of Mass. Gen. Ct., First Middlesex Dist., 1985—; gov.'s non-resident appointee Martha Vineyard Commn., Oak Bluffs, Mass., 1979-83; fundraiser, cons. Am. Tax Reform Found., Washington, 1983-84; nat. def. exec. reservist FEMA, Washington, 1981-84. Trustee Plimoth Plantation, Mass., 1981—, Schwamb Mill Preservation Trust, Arlington, Mass., 1973—; mem. Groton Republican Town Com., 1984—; dir. Reps. for Middlesex County, Wayland, Mass., 1979—; pres. Women's Rep. Club of Mass., Wayland, 1979-84, bd. dirs., 1984—. Named del. to Japan Am. Council for Young Polit. Leaders, 1980. Mem. Am. Legis. Exchange Council (state chmn. 1984—), Nat. Conf. of State Legislators (del.). Episcopalian. Office: Mass Gen Ct State House Room 26 Boston MA 02133

HORNBURGER, JANE MELVIN, educator; b. Fayetteville, N.C., Aug. 26, 1928; d. Roy Daniel and Ella (Carter) Melvin; B.S., Fayetteville State U., 1948; M.A., NYU, 1950, Ed.D., 1970; postgrad. UCLA, 1953, 55; m. Thomas Hornburger, Aug. 19, 1950. Tchr., Kinston (N.C.) Public Schs., 1948-54; tchr. Wilmington (Del.) Public Schs., 1954-66, supr. reading, 1966-69, dir. tchr. tng.,

1970-72; asst. prof. edn. Boston U., 1972-77, CUNY, 1977—; reading cons.; reviewer comml. publs.; editorial cons. Lang. Arts, 1976-78. Adv. bd. Early Childhood Center, N.Y.C., 1980—; exec. bd. Bronx Reading Council, 1980—, v.p.-elect, 1983-84. Named Women of Yr., AAUW, Wilmington, Del., 1968; Outstanding Delawarean, Sigma Gamma Rho, Wilmington 1970; N.Y.U. Honors scholar, recipient Founders Day award, 1971; U.S. Office Edn. grantee, 1969. Mem. Nat. Council Tchrs. of English (editorial bd.; com. classroom practices 1983—), Internat. Reading Assn. (com. chmn. 1981-83, exec. search com. 1983, nominating com. 1983, 84), Mass. Assn. Reading Educators (dir. 1976-77), N.Y.C. Reading Council, N.Y. State English Council, New Eng. Assn. Tchrs. English, AAUP, Phi Delta Kappa, Pi Lambda Theta, Kappa Delta Pi. Episcopalian. Author: So You Have an Aide, 1967; Teaching Multicultural Children, 1977; African Countries and Cultures, 1981; contbr. articles to profl. jours. Office: Bklyn Coll CUNY Bedford Ave and Ave H Brooklyn NY 11210

HORN-DALTON, KATHY ELLEN, rehabilitation center administrator; b. Latrobe, Pa., Apr. 12, 1952; d. William Irving and Stella Bertha (Denisiuk) Horn; m. Glenn Holbert Dalton, Aug. 4, 1973. B.S. in Social Work, W.Va. U., 1975, M.S. in Social Work, 1976; Ph.D. in Adminstrn., Columbia Pacific U., 1983. Counselor Womens' Info. Ctr., Morgantown, W.Va., 1973; psychiat. aide Torrance State Hosp., Pa., 1974; group home counselor Sommerset/Bedford Mental Health Ctr., Rockwood, Pa., 1974; shop foreman Southwest Wyo. Rehab. Ctr., Rock Springs, 1975-76, exec. dir., 1976-81, pres., adminstr., 1981—; grants adminstr. Sweetwater County, Wyo., 1982-83, liaison Nat. Orgn. Disability, 1984—; registered psychotherapist, 1982—; researcher emotionally disturbed, mentally retarded project Div. Vocat. Rehab., Cheyenne, Wyo., 1985—. Author: Develop and Design an Energy Efficient Sheltered Workshop, 1983. Mem. Wyo. Devel. Disabilities Council, 1978, Wyo. Pvt. Indsl. Council, 1983; state advisor U.S. Congl. Adv. Bd., Washington, 1984; mem. U. No. Colo. Adv. Bd., 1978. Recipient Cert. of support on Disabilities, Gov. of Wyo., 1983; named Boss of Yr., Wyo. Jaycees, 1978. Mem. Wyo. Assn. Rehab. Facilities (legis. chmn. 1981-83), Exec. Female, Bus. and Profl. Women, Nat. Assn. Social Workers. Avocation: sand drag racing.

HORNE, BLANCHE COBB GREENWAY, small business owner; b. Charleston, S.C., Mar. 3, 1937; d. John H. and Patsy P. (Pullin) Cobb; m. Jesse T. Greenway, Sr., Aug. 25, 1953 (div. Dec. 1970); children—Jesse Thomas, Kathleen Ann Greenway Davis, Sondra Leigh Greenway Sikes; m. Carey Wilson Horne, Jr., June 23, 1974. Grad. high sch. with honors. Cashier, Adler's Dept. Store, Savannah, Ga., 1953-56; cashier, stock clk. Fine's, Inc., Savannah, 1956-67; office mgr., bookkeeper Hillcrest Meml. Park, Savannah, 1967-82; owner, operator salesperson Gravel Hill Monument Co., Bloomingdale, Ga., 1982—; mgr., salesperson Meml. Gardens Cemetery, Bloomingdale, 1985—; sec. Pooler Athletic Assn., Ga., 1972. Mem. Nat. Bus. Women Assn., Ga. Bus. Women's Assn., Pooler Bus. Assn., Am. Legion Aux. Methodist. Avocations: family; helping others. Home: PO Box 313 Pooler GA 31322 Office: Gravel Hill Monument Co Rt 1 Box 118 Bloomingdale GA 31302

HORNE, CHARLOTTE ANN HOLCOMBE, real estate executive; b. Anniston, Ala., Feb. 5, 1938; d. Charlie Gardy and Ola Bell (Little) Holcombe; m. Robert (Bobby) Edward Horne, Nov. 6, 1954; children—Robbie Sheila Horne Owen, Gary Wayne, Shannon Michelle Horne Clarke. Cert. real estate appraiser, Ala. With credit dept. Hudson's, Anniston, 1971; sec. Super Valu Warehouse, Anniston, 1972; realtor Service Realty, Anniston, 1978-85, Howell Realty, Anniston, 1985—. Voter, dep. registrar, election poll worker, Anniston, 1970—. Mem. Women's Council of Realtors (v.p. 1984, pres. 1985), Calhoun County Area Bd. Realtors (Million Dollar Sales award 1983, 84, 85, Named to Sales Honor club 1980, 81, 82, bd. dirs. state and local 1985, chairperson grievance com. 1985), DAR. Baptist. Club: Christian Women's (exec. com.). Lodge: Elks (exec. sec. 1983). Home: 1113 Caswell Dr Anniston AL 36201 Office: 1325 Quintard St Anniston AL 36201

HORNE, D. SUE, school administrator; b. Milam, Tex., Oct. 19, 1945; d. Steve Jesse and Allie Exa (Wilson) H. B.S., Stephen F. Austin U., 1966, Ed.M., 1968; Ed.D., McNeese state U., 1977. Tchr., San Augustine Ind. Sch. Dist., Tex., 1967-70, asst. dean of women McNeese State U., Lake Charles, La., 1970-71; counselor, tchr. West Orange Cove Ind. Sch. Dist., Orange, Tex., 1971-81; prin. Lumberton Ind. Sch. Dist., Tex., 1982—; cons. Dupont, Gulf Oil, Orange, Tex., 1981-82, Owen Ill., Orange, 1981-82, S.E. Tex. Hospice, Orange, 1981-82. Author: Living Without Guilt, 1970. Recipient Nat. Sci. award U.S. Govt., 1968. Mem. Tex. Elem. Prins. Assn. (v.p.), Tex. Secondary Prins. Assn., Tex. Assn. for Reading Improvement, Daus. of Republic of Tex., Dalta Kappa Gamma. Republican. Roman Catholic. Home: 9 Dowlen Pl Beaumont TX 77706 Office: Lumberton Independent Sch Dist PO Box 8123 Lumberton TX 77711

HORNE, DONETTA CLAXTON, manufacturing company executive; b. St. Louis, Dec. 7, 1944; d. Donald Nathaniel and Wilma (Rue) Claxton; m. William George Horne, June 16, 1968 (div. Aug. 1983); 1 son, Yohance Salih. B.A., Harris Tchrs. Coll., 1966; postgrad. St. Louis U., 1968-71. Tchr., St. Louis Bd. Edn., 1966-71, Chgo. Bd. Edn., 1971-73; employment supr. Minority Info. Referral Ctr., Des Plaines, 1977-80; mgr. EEO, Keebler Co., Elmhurst, Ill., 1980—; dir. Habilitative Systems, Inc., Chgo., 1982—, Minority Econ. Resources Corp., Des Plaines, 1983—. Bd. dirs. United Way, Elmhurst, 1981-82, So. Christian Leadership Conf., Chgo., 1980-83, N.W. Suburban Girl Scout council, 1979-82. Recipient Black and Hispanic Achievers award YMCA Met. Chgo., 1980, Pub. Service award Networking Host Com., 1982, Youth Motivation Div. award Chgo. Assn. Commerce and Industry, 1980, 83, Ctr. Econ. Edn. award DePaul U., 1983. Mem. Am. Soc. Personnel Adminstrs., Nat. Urban Affairs Council, Ill. Affirmation Assn., Blacks in Philanthropy, Nat. Urban League, Alpha Kappa Alpha. Clubs: Jack and Jill Inc., Links. Home: 357 Rosalie Ln Palatine IL 60074 Office: Keebler Co 1 Hollow Tree Ln Elmhurst IL 60126

HORNE, GAY DAWN, lawyer; b. Laurel, Miss., Nov. 15, 1953; d. Raymond Llewellyn and Shirley Hope (Rowe) H. A.A., Jones County Jr. Coll., Ellisville, Miss., 1973; B.A. in Am. Studies, Anderson (Ind.) Coll., 1975; J.D., U. Miss., 1978; B.S. in Acctg., Belhaven Coll., Jackson, Miss., 1983. Bar: Miss. 1978; C.P.A. Dep. city atty. City of Jackson, 1979—. Mem. ABA. Mem. Ch. of God. Home: 1055-H Quinn St Jackson MS 39202 Office: City Attorneys Office PO Box 17 Jackson MS 39205

HORNE, KATHARYN, ballet director; b. Ft. Worth, June 20, 1932; d. William Sullivan and Catherine (Collie) Horn; student Tex. Christian U.; divorced; children—Collie MacCardell, Kirsi Enckell. Soloist, Am. Ballet Theatre, 1950-56; prin. dancer Met. Opera, 1957-65; prin. dancer, dir., tchr. Manhattan Festival Ballet, 1966-69; prin. dancer, tchr. Malmö (Sweden) Stadsteater, 1969-75; co-artistic dir., tchr. Omaha Ballet, 1975-80; artistic dir. Charlotte (N.C.) Ballet and New Reflections Dance Theater, 1981-83; faculty Central Piedmont Community Coll., 1983—; co-dir., choreographer Dance Central, 1983—; Choreographer; stager Classic ballets. mem. guest faculty Adelphi U., Garden City, N.Y., Cornell U., Creighton U., Omaha, No. Ill. U.; cons. to ballets on re-staging of classic ballets. Office: Dept Performing Arts Central Piedmont Community Coll Elizabeth at N King Sts Charlotte NC 28204

HORNER, BARBARA WARD, educator, library volunteer; b. Biltmore, N.C., Mar. 28, 1929; d. Waites Artemus and Ada (Shepherd) Ward; m. Theodore Wright Horner, Aug. 26, 1950; children—Thad, Ward. B.S., Meredith Coll., Raleigh, N.C., 1951; student Peace Coll., Raleigh, 1947-48, U. N.C., Chapel Hill, 1949-50. Caseworker, Wake County Pub. Welfare Dept., Raleigh, 1951-53; tchr. asst. reading dept. Montgomery County Pub. Schs., Rockville, Md., 1970-85; exec. dir. Friends of Library Montgomery County, Md., 1985—. Mem. Montgomery County Library Bd., 1976—, v.p., 1984-86; trustee Montgomery County Friends of the Library, 1983—, exec. dir., 1986—, chmn. speakers bur.; chmn. bd. Battery Park Citizens Assn., Bethesda, Md., 1975. Mem. ALA, Md. Library Assn., Md. Citizens for Pub. Library. Office: 99 Marylane Ave Rockville MD 20850

HORNER, KAREN SUE, tire manufacturing company executive; b. Ashland, Ohio, Feb. 5, 1953; d. Robert Eugene and Dora Louise (Camp) Brubaker; m. Russell Robert Horner, May 28, 1977. B.S. in Bus. Adminstrn., Ashland Coll., 1975; M.B.A., Bowling Green State U., 1976. Supr. tire ctr. ops. B.F. Goodrich Co., Akron, Ohio, 1976-77, supr. tire acctg., 1977-79, asst. product mgr. radial passenger tires, 1979-80, product mgr. broadline passenger tires, 1980-81, group product mgr. broadline passenger and light truck tires, 1981-83, mktg. mgr. T/A High Tech. radials, 1983—. Sect. chmn. indsl. div. United Way, Akron, 1983, 84, 85. Alpha Phi Clara Bradley Burdette scholar, 1975. Mem. Am. Mktg. Assn. (pres. Akron/Canton chpt. 1982-83, highest honors award 1983; v.p. bus. mktg. to nat. bd. dirs. 1984-86), Susan B. Anthony Soc., Nat. Assn. Female Execs., Beta Gamma Sigma, Omicron Delta Epsilon. Club: Zonta Internat. Home: 171 Granger Rd Granger Lake #130 Medina OH 44256 Office: Tire Group BF Goodrich Co 500 S Main St Akron OH 44318

HORNER, MATINA SOURETIS (MRS. JOSEPH L. HORNER), college president; b. Boston, July 28, 1939; d. Demetre John and Christine (Antonopoulos) Souretis; A.B. cum laude, Bryn Mawr Coll., 1961; M.S., U. Mich., 1963, Ph.D., 1968; LL.D., Dickinson Coll., 1973, Mt. Holyoke Coll., 1973, U. Pa., 1975, Smith Coll., 1979, Wheaton Coll., 1979; L.H.D. (hon.), U. Mass., 1973, Tufts U., 1976, U. Hartford, 1980; m. Joseph L. Horner, June 25, 1961; children—Tia Andrea, John, Christopher. Teaching fellow U. Mich., 1962-66; lectr. motivation personality U. Mich. at Ann Arbor, 1968-69; lectr. social relations Harvard U., 1969-70, asst. prof. clin. psychology dept. social relations, 1971-72, assoc. prof. psychology and social relations, 1972—, also cons. univ. health services; pres. Radcliffe Coll., 1972—; dir. Time, Inc., Fed. Res. Bank of Boston, Liberty Mut. Life Ins. Co. Trustee Twentieth Century Fund.; adv. council NSF, 1977—, chmn., 1980—; mem. President's Commn. for Nat. Agenda for the Eighties, 1979-80, chmn. Task Force on Quality Am. Life in Eighties; bd. dirs. Women's Research and Edn. Inst., 1979—, chmn. research com., 1982—; adv. com. Women's Leadership Conf. on Nat. Security, 1982—. Recipient Roger Baldwin award Mass. Civil Liberties Union Found., 1982; citation of merit NE region NCCJ, 1982; award outstanding services Nat. Inst. Social Scis., 1973. Mem. Phi Beta Kappa, Phi Delta Kappa, Phi Kappa Phi. Contbr. psychol. articles on motivation to profl. jours. Address: Office of Pres Radcliffe Coll 10 Garden St Cambridge MA 02138

HORNE'Y, CHRISTEL ADELE, dental laboratory proprietor, businesswoman; b. Munich, W.Ger., Nov. 1, 1938; came to U.S., 1959; d. Maxemillian and Marieluise (Stephan) Schmid; m. Richard Arlen Horne'y, Oct. 15, 1961 (div. 1979); children—Michaela Marieluise, Richard Eberhard. Student Dental Asst., U. Dentistry, Munich, 1955-57, student Dental Tech., 1957-59. Cert. dental technician. Founder Studio of Dental Ceramics, Indpls., 1967, owner, 1967—; cons., lectr. body chemistry, Indpls., 1975-79; dor. for Ind. Fund for Dental Health Assn., Chgo., 1983-84. Vol. Am. Legion, Lebanon, Ind., 1975—; pres. Med. Mission (div. Ch. Women United), Lebanon, 1976-79. Fellow Dental Lab. Assn. Ind. (bd. dirs. 1980-82). Republican. Roman Catholic. Avocations: Ballroom dancing; crossword puzzles; golf; travel; gin rummy; languages. Home: 2684 Lakeshire Ln Indianapolis IN 46268 Office: Studio of Dental Ceramics 9614 N College Ave Indianapolis IN 46280

HORNICK, DELORES MARIE, oil company executive; b. Binghamton, N.Y., Apr. 26, 1948; d. Jesse Oliver and Lula Vern (Simonds) Buchanan; m. Thomas Henry Hornick, Aug. 24, 1969; children—Thomas Joseph, Robert Andrew. B.S. in Social Sci., SUNY-Binghamton. Editor, investment adviser U.S. and Australia Mining Rev., 1983-84; v.p. Centex Oil and Gas Co., Binghamton, 1983—; cons. tng. Tri-Systems Cons. Co., Binghamton, 1984—; speaker, color cons. Beauty for All Seasons, Binghamton, 1984—. Mem. Republican Senatorial Inner Circle, Washington, 1986. Mem. AAUW, YWCA Women's Network. Avocations: yachting; gardening. Home: 104 Woodcrest Way Conklin NY 13748 Office: Centex Oil and Gas Co 230 Chenango St Binghamton NY 13901

HORNING, MARJORIE G., biochemistry educator; b. Detroit, Aug. 23, 1917; d. Herman and Nina Jane (Potter) Groothuis; m. Evan C. Horning, Sept. 26, 1942. B.A., Goucher Coll., 1938, D.Sc. (hon.), 1977; M.S., U. Mich., 1940, Ph.D., 1943. Research chemist NIH, Bethesda, Md., 1951-61; research assoc. prof. Baylor Coll. of Medicine, Houston, 1961-63, assoc. prof. biochemistry, 1963-69, prof., 1969—. Contbr. articles to profl. jours. Trustee Houston Mus. Fine Arts, 1975-80, 1983—. Recipient Warner Lambert award Am. Assn. Clin. Chemists, 1976, Alumnae Athena award U. Mich., 1980. Mem. Am. Soc. Pharmacology and Exptl. Therapeutics (sec.-treas. 1981-82, pres. 1984—), Am. Chem. Soc. (Garvan medal 1977), Soc. of Toxicology. Office: Baylor Coll Medicine 1 Baylor Plaza Houston TX 77030

HORNUNG, GERTRUDE SEYMOUR, art educator; b. Boston; d. Samuel Parker and Rose Anne Seymour; A.B., Wellesley Coll., 1929; M.A., Western Res. U., 1939, Ph.D., 1949; m. Robert M. Hornung, Oct. 31, 1932; 1 dau., Elizabeth Zimri Luce Smith. Lectr., instr., supr. adult programs Cleve. Mus. Art, 1937-60; lectr. Am. U., Rome, 1974-75; lectr. Tehran, Iran, 1975, Bangkok, Thailand, 1978, Dublin, Ireland, 1970; free lance lectr., Cleve., 1960—; lectr. Honolulu Acad. Arts, 1973-85. Mem. Nat. Art Educators Assn., Internat. Council Mus., Internat. Com. Mus. Edn., Am. Assn. Mus. Republican. Episcopalian. Home: 2240 Elandon Dr Cleveland OH 44106

HORNYACK-HILL, MARGARET LOUISE, epidemiologist; b. Rochester, Pa., Mar. 14, 1937; d. Thomas E. and Helen G. (Smith) Sopko; student U. Calif., Irvine, 1977-78; B.S. in Nursing, Calif. State U., Los Angeles, 1971; M.S. in Public Health, U. N.C., Chapel Hill, 1973; doctoral candidate U. Tex. Sch. Public Health, Houston, 1981—; married; children—James E., Timothy M. Occupational health nurse J & L Steel, Aliquippa, Pa., 1960 61, Hankins Med. Group, Azusa, Calif., 1961-66, Los Angeles Times, 1965-68, TRW Systems Group, Redondo Beach, Calif., 1968-71; cons. San Bernardino County Health Dept., 1971-74; environ. health and safety officer Calif. State Poly. U., Pomona, 1974-77; mem. occupational safety and health study sect. Nat. Insts. Occupational Safety and Health, 1976-79; research asso. Baylor Coll. Medicine, Houston, 1980-81 epidemiologist M.D. Anderson Hosp. Cancer Center, Houston, 1980—; also cons. Vice-pres., treas. Arlington High Sch. Booster Club, 1974-76. Mem. Calif. Assn. Occupational Health Nurses (v.p. 1977-78). Home: 155 Circle Dr Cleveland TX 77327

HOROSZEWSKI, KATHLEEN MARIA HAGERTY, telecommunications executive; b. N.Y.C., Mar. 5, 1942; d. George E. and Brigid (Doohan) Hagerty; B.A., Cambridge U., 1968, M.B.A., 1970; Ph.D., U. Mo., 1985; m. Roman D. Horoszewski, Aug. 3, 1963; children—Meredith, Roman. Asst. to v.p. fin. Olin Am., Dallas, 1973; staff Arthur Young & Co., Dallas, 1974-77; account exec. Southwestern Bell, 1977, data specialist, 1978, systems mgr., 1979; sales mgr., AT&T, Basking Ridge, N.J., 1980, nat. market mgr.-aerospace, 1981—; cons. in field. Recipient numerous Bell awards for outstanding contbns. to corp. Fellow AIAA (assoc.; mgmt. tech. com.); mem. Armed Forces Communications and Electronics Assn., Am. Mgmt. Assn., NOW, Am. Soc. Profl. and Exec. Women. Republican. Home: 2 Overbrook Rd Randolph NJ 07869 Office: 5212 A2 295 N Maple Ave Basking Ridge NJ 07920

HOROWITZ, FLORA BEGELMAN, secretarial service executive; b. N.Y.C., Feb. 18, 1915; d. Max and Celia (Allison) Begelman; widow; 1 child, Richard. B.A., Queens Coll., 1979. Pres., Empire State Repro Services, Empire State Bldg., N.Y.C., 1958—; instr. Drug Rehab. Program, N.Y.C., N.Y.C. Bd. Edn.; lectr. N.Y. Bus. Sch. Democrat. Avocations: tennis, choral group singing. Office: Empire State Repro Services 350 Fifth Ave New York NY 10118

HOROWITZ, LOUISE SCHWARTZ, lawyer; b. N.Y.C., Jan. 24, 1932; d. Charles and Bertie (Grad) Schwartz; m. David H. Horowitz, June 20, 1951 (div. 1976); children—Marilyn, Roger, Diana. B.A., Smith Coll., 1953; M.A., Columbia U., 1955, Ph.D., 1969; J.D., N.Y. Law Sch., 1981. Bar: N.Y. 1982. Lectr., Bklyn. Coll., 1966-67; assoc. prof. L.I.U., 1967-75, asst. dir. Learning Ctr., 1975-76; research fellow Wagner Coll., 1976-78; legal intern U.S. Atty.'s Office, Ea. Dist. N.Y., 1980-81; asst. corp. counsel Law Dept. City of N.Y., 1982—. Contbr. articles to profl. jours. Mem. N.Y. Woman's Bar Assn., Am. Philos. Assn., N.Y. State Bar Assn. Democrat. Jewish. Home: 50 W 70th St New York NY 10023 Office: Law Dept City NY 100 Church St New York NY 10007

HOROWITZ, NADIA, artist; b. Warsaw, Poland, May 12; came to U.S., 1951; d. Eli and Rose Bartowicz; B.A., Acad. Fine Art, Warsaw; B.A., Ecole Superieure des Arts Graphiques, Brussels, Belgium, 1933; grad. Acad. Fine Art La Grande Chaumiere, Paris, 1934; B.A., Rheiman Schule, Berlin. One-woman shows include: Clasemont Art Center, Haines Falls, N.Y., Gorline Gallery, N.Y.C., 1965, Herzl Gallery, N.Y.C., 1966, Anthroposophical Soc. Am., N.Y.C., 1967, Barsky Med. Center, 1978, Herzl Gallery, 1981, Channel 9, 1984; fgn. and U.S. group shows include: Jewish Mus., Gallery of Temple No. Westchester, Groton-on-Hudson, N.Y., 1961-66, Am. Pavilion, World's Fair, N.Y.C., 1964, Hudson Park Library, 1970, Artists Equity Assn., 1970, 78, New Age Gallery, 1978, Internat. Show, Zurich, 1973; works represented pvt. collection of Pablo Casals, also mus. in Ohio to honor Neil Armstrong's walk on moon; pvt. tchr. fine and comml. art. Recipient 1st prize The Gallery, Chgo., hon. mention City Center Group Show, 1st prize Conn. Show, 1978, Gold medal, Academia Italia delle Arti e del Lavoro, Parma, 1980; European Oscar, Italy. Mem. Artists Equity N.Y., Nat. Assn. Women Artists. Home and Office: 205 W 89th St New York NY 10024

HOROWITZ, SUSAN ALISON, data services company executive; b. Amsterdam, N.Y., May 16, 1946; d. Bernard and Helen Belle (Goldmeer) H.; B.A., Wheaton Coll., 1968; M.S., SUNY-Albany, 1969; Ed.D., Ind. U., 1982. Dir. fin. aid No. Essex Community Coll., Haverhill, Mass., 1969-76; coordinator fin. aid Mass. Bd. Higher Edn., Boston, 1976-77; asst. to chancellor, 1976-77; exec. dir. Tng. & Ednl. Data Services, Indpls., 1980—; resident staff trainer Inst. Fin. Aid Adminstrn., Bentley Coll., 1979-80, Southeastern Mass. U., 1977-78; cons. Mansfield Beaty Coll., Wilfred Beauty Coll., Boston, 1975-77. Author: Rationale for Colleges for Women, 1981; contbr. articles to profl. jours. Mem. adv. com. Permanent Charities Fund Boston, 1974-77. Raleigh W. Homstedt fellow Ind. U., 1979-80. Mem. Ind. and Indpls. Econ. Forum, Ind. C. of C., Indpls. C. of C., Assn. Computer Career Info. Systems, (chmn. publs. com. 1982—), Ind. Occupational Info. Com., Nat. Assn. Student Fin. Aid Adminstrs., Coll. Scholarship Service Assembly. Democrat. Jewish. Home: 3242 Braeside Dr Bloomington IN 47401 Office: Tng and Ednl Data Service Inc 150 W Market St Suite 503 Indianapolis IN 46204

HORRELL, EDNA RICHARDSON, elementary school principal; b. Leitchfield, Ky., Mar. 30, 1929; d. Lannie B. and Vonnie R. (Ramsey) Richardson; m. Billy B. Horrell, June 11, 1949; 1 child: Pamela Joy. B.S., Western Ky. U., 1952; M.A., Ind. U., 1966, postgrad., 1968-69. Cert. tchr., adminstr., Ky. Tchr. elem. sch. Grayson County, Fayette County, Ky., 1947-55; elem. tchr. Jefferson County, Louisville, Ky., 1955-67; curriculum coordinator Daviess County Schs., Owensboro, Ky., 1969-82; remedial reading tchr., 1982-83; prin. Daviess County Elem. Sch., Owensboro, 1983—. Mem. AAUW (sec. 1982-85), Delta Kappa Gamma (2d v.p. 1982-84). Club: Pilot Internat. (coordinator Owensboro, 1983-85). Home: 1901 Frederica St Owensboro KY 42301 Office: Daviess County Bd Edn Southeastern Pkwy Owensboro KY 42301

HORSLEY, PAULA ROSALIE, accountant; b. Smithfield, Nebr., Sept. 7, 1924; d. Karl and Clara Margaret (Busse) Fenske; m. Phillip Carreon (div.); children—Phillip, James, Robert, David, Richard; m. Norby Lumon, Apr. 5, 1980. Student AIB Bus. Coll., Des Moines, 1942-44, YMCA Coll., Chgo., 1944-47, UCLA Extension, 1974. Acctg. mgr. Montgomery Ward & Co., Denver, 1959-62; acct. Harman & Co., C.P.A.s, Arcadia, Calif., 1962-67; controller, officer G & H Transp., Montebello, Calif., 1967-78; comptroller Frederick Weisman Co., Century City, Calif., 1978-80; chief fin. officer Lutheran Shipping, Madang, Papua, New Guinea, 1980-82; prin. Village Bookkeeper, acctg. cons., Monreno Valley, Calif., 1982—. Mem. Riverside Tax Cons. Republican. Lutheran. Avocations: church activities; reading; cooking; physical fitness. Home: 1753 Sapphire St Perris CA 92370 Office: Village Bookkeeper PO Box 5 Monreno Valley CA 92388

HORSNELL, MARGARET EILEEN, history educator; b. St. Paul, Jan. 3, 1928; d. Kenneth George and Mary Elizabeth (Dowd) H.; B.A., U. Minn., 1961, M.A., 1963, Ph.D., 1967. Instr., U. Minn., Mpls., 1966-68, asst. prof. history Am. Internat. Coll., Springfield, Mass., 1968-76, assoc. prof., 1976-84, prof., 1984—. Author: Spencer Roane: Judicial Advocate of Jeffersonian Principles, 1986. Editorial bd. This Constitution, 1986—. Recipient award Tozer Found., 1966; McKnight Found. award, 1968; Am. Internat. Coll. Summer Research grantee, 1970; alt. postdoctoral fellow AAUW, 1974-75. Mem. Inst. Early Am. History and Culture, So. Hist. Assn., Soc. History of Edn., Am. Legal Studies Assn. Home: 15 Atwood Rd South Hadley MA 01075 Office: 24 Lee Hall Am Internat Coll Springfield MA 01109

HORST, JOSEPHINE MONACO, social worker; b. Easton, Pa., May 26, 1930; d. Carmelo and Carmela (Lizza) Monaco; B.A., Pa. State U., 1951; M.S.W., Rutgers U., 1971; m. Samuel L. Horst, Jan. 26, 1951; children—Jory Ann Horst Barone, Jeffrey C., David M. Caseworker, Berks County (Pa.) Bd. of Assistance, 1962-66; social services coordinator Econ. Opportunity Council of Reading and Berks County, 1966-67; social worker Correctional Instn. for Women, Clinton, 1967-69, supr. cottage life, 1969-76; ombudsman N.J. Dept. Corrections, 1976—; instr. Correction Officers Tng. Acad.; cons. Commn. on Accreditation for Corrections. Contbr. articles to profl. jours. Bd. dirs. Big Bros./Big Sisters of Hunterdon County, 1980-85. Mem. Nat. Assn. Social Workers, Am. Correctional Assn. (bd. dirs. N.J. chpt.), Acad. Cert. Social Workers. Club: Soroptimist (pres. Hunterdon County 1980-82). Home: Rural Delivery 2 Box 294 Stockton NJ 08559 Office: Whittlesey Rd PO Box 7387 Trenton NJ 08628

HORSTMANN, DOROTHY MILLICENT, physician; b. Spokane, Wash., July 2, 1911; d. Henry J. and Anna (Hunold) H.; A.B., U. Calif., 1936, M.D., 1940; D.Sc. (hon.), Smith Coll., 1961; M.A. (hon.), Yale U., 1961; Dr. Med. Scis. (hon.), Women's Med. Coll. of Pa., 1963. Intern San Francisco City and County Hosp., 1939-40, asst. resident medicine, 1940-41; asst. resident medicine Vanderbilt U. Hosp., 1941-42; Commonwealth Fund fellow, sect. preventive medicine, sch. medicine Yale U., New Haven, Conn., 1942-43, instr. preventive medicine, 1943-44, 45-47, asst. prof., 1948-52, asso. prof., 1952-56, asso. prof. preventive medicine and pediatrics, 1956-61, prof. epidemiology and pediatrics, 1961-69, John Rodman Paul prof. epidemiology, prof. pediatrics, 1969-82, emeritus, 1982—, sr. research scientist, 1982—; instr. medicine U. Calif., 1944-45; NIH fellow Nat. Inst. Med. Research, London, Eng., 1947-48, Master A.C.P.; hon. asso. fellow Am. Acad. Pediatrics; mem. Am. Soc. Clin. Investigation, Am. Epidemiological Soc., Am. Pediatric Soc., Am. Assn. Immunologists, Assn. Am. Physicians, Infectious Diseases Soc. Am. (pres. 1974-75, council 1971-77), Soc. Epidemiologic Research, Pan Am. Med. Assn., Internat. Epidemiological Assn., Royal Soc. Medicine (hon. mem. sect. epidemiology and preventive medicine), Conn. Acad. Sci. and Engring., European Assn. Against Virus Disease, Am. Soc. Virology (council 1983-84), South African Soc. Pathologists (hon. mem.), Nat. Acad. Scis. Home: 11 Autumn St New Haven Ct 06511 Office: Dept Epidemiology and Public Health 60 College St New Haven CT 06510

HORTON, ANN MITCHELL, health organization executive; b. Memphis, Apr. 14, 1949; d. Foy B. and Frances Louise (Mashbern) Mithcell; m. Steven Michael Horton, Dec. 20, 1970; children—Matthew William, Emily Frances. B.S., U. Tenn., 1970; M.A. in Speech Pathology, Memphis State U., 1972. postgrad. No. Ill. U., 1973, 74, Chgo. State U., 1974, Nat. Coll. Edn., 1975, U. Tenn., 1976, 84, U. Cin., 1984, 85. Lic. speech pathologist, Tenn., Ga.; cert. speech tchr., Tenn., Ill. Grad. asst. Memphis State U., Osceola, Ark., 1971-72, clin. supr., 1972; coordinator speech and lang. programs Northwest Suburban Spl. Edn. Coop., Palatine, Ill., 1972-75, coordinator reading programs, 1974-75; spl. services coordinator for handicapped children East Tenn. Children's Rehab. Ctr., Knoxville, 1975-76; speech pathologist cons. Nat. Health Corp., Athens, Tenn., 1976-83, eastern regional coordinator for communication disorders services, 1983—, corp. coordinator communication disorders services, 1986—, founder Athens Out-Patient Rehab. Program. Contbr. articles to profl. pubs. Mem. Nat. Assn. Female Execs., Nat. Health Corp. (co-chmn. quality assurance com. 1982—, co-chmn. supportive personnel com. 1985—), Am. Speech and Hearing Assn., Tenn. Speech and Hearing Assn. (peer rev. com. 1979—, adv. bd. to Blue Cross/Blue Shield 1980-84). Home: 404 Cutlas Rd Concord TN 37922 Office: Athens Health Care Ctr 214 Grove Ave Athens TN 37303

HORTON, JANICE SHIVER, state legislator; b. Barnesville, Ga., Jan. 23, 1945; d. Grover George and Sara (Zellner) Shiver; m. Charles Douglas Horton; children—Amy, Leigh. Tchr., Columbus and Forest Park, Ga., 1967-72; owner Horton Realty & Investment Co., Atlanta, 1973—; mem. McDonough City Council, Ga., 1974-78; commr. Henry County, 1977-79; mem. Ga. State Senate from 17th Dist., 1979—. Del., Democratic Nat. Conv., 1980. Baptist. Office: Ga State Capitol Bldg Atlanta GA 30334*

HORTON, THELMA WHITE, educational administrator, author; b. Blyesville, Ark., Feb. 7, 1949; d. William Soloman and Corrine (Carrigans) White; m. Charles D. Horton, May 20, 1970; children—Corrine Daniel, Tiffany Louise, Charles William. B.S.W., Boise State U., 1975; M.S.W., Barry Coll., 1978. Tchr., Community Coll., Miami, 1980-81; owner, dir. Hi School Day Care and Learning Center, Cutler Ridge, Fla., 1981—; tutor English, Perrine, 1982—; cons. Barr Industries, Perrine, 1981—. Mem. The Exec. Female, Childrens Advocates (pres. 1975-83), Alumni Assn. Boise State U., Inst.

Childrens Lit., Miami C. of C. Democrat. Baptist. Club: Spring Affairs (pres. Miami 1981-82). Home: 15905 SW 105th Ct Perrine FL 33157 Office: Hi Sch Day Care and Learning Center 114 SW 199th St Cutler Ridge FL 33157

HORVITZ, SHEILA SYLVIA, lawyer; b. N.Y.C., July 11, 1944; d. Morris and Evelyn (Hoffman) Epstein; m. Arthur Victor Horvitz, June 20, 1965; children—Sharin Risa, Marjorie Lisa. B.A., Queens Coll., 1965; M.A. in History, Northeastern U., 1969; J.D., U. Conn. Law Sch., 1977. Bar: Conn., 1977. Tchr. social sci. West Jr. High Sch., Brockton, Mass., 1965-68; clk. Conn. Legislature, Hartford, 1976-77; atty., ptnr. Brown, Jacobson, Jewett & Laudone, P.C., Norwich, Conn., 1978—; chmn. New London County Family Law Com., 1982—. Mem. Democratic Town Com., 1971—. Fellow Am. Acad. Matrimonial Lawyers; mem. ABA, Assn. Trial Lawyers Am., Conn. Bar Assn., Am. Assn. Women Lawyers, ACLU, Colchester Book Club (founder), Phi Beta Kappa, Kappa Delta Pi, Phi Alpha Theta. Jewish. Club: Hadassah (pres. 1979-80) (Colchester, Conn.). Office: Brown Jacobson Jewett and Laudone 22 Courthouse Sq Norwich CT 06360

HORWATH, LESLIE KATHLEEN, lawyer; b. Gt. Lakes, Ill., Oct. 12, 1953; d. John Adam and Patricia Ann (Lindholm) H. B.A., Northwestern U., 1975; J.D., Chgo.-Kent Coll. Law, 1978. Bar: Ill. 1978, U.S. dist. ct. (no. dist.) Ill. 1982. Assoc. Tim J. Harrington, Chgo., 1979; assoc. firm Querrey, Harrow, Gulanick & Kennedy, Ltd., 1979—. Mem. ABA, Ill. State Bar Assn., Chgo. Bar Assn., Assn. Trial Lawyers Am. Office: Querrey Harrow Gulanick & Kennedy 135 S LaSalle St Chicago IL 60603

HORYCZKO, REBECCA ANN, advisory marketing executive; b. Reading, Pa., Nov. 22, 1952; d. Frank Steven and Bernadine (Gaydos) Horyczko; student Rosemont Coll., 1970-71; B.S. in Math., Albright Coll., 1974; postgrad. in bus. adminstrn. St. Joseph's U. Adv. mktg. program adminstr. Valley Forge Regional Engring., Sci. and Indsl. Systems Ctr., nat. accounts div. IBM Corp. (Pa.). Mem. Am. Prodn. and Inventory Control Soc. (v.p. membership), Soc. Mfrs. Engrs. Office: 580 Swedesford Rd Valley Forge PA 19087

HOSEA, SANDRA DIANN, home economist, educator; b. Lincoln, Ala., June 13, 1948; d. Felice and Eva Arzella (Wills) White; B.S., Ala. A. and M. U., 1970, postgrad., 1980—; m. David Vernon Hosea, June 19, 1972; 1 child, Fresheda Chanteas. Tchr. gen. sci. Dallas County (Ala.) Bd. Edn., 1970-71; vocat. home econs. tchr. Mobile (Ala.) County Bd. Edn., 1971-72; extension home economist Ala. Coop. Extension Service, Russellville, 1973—. Sec., Family Planning Adv. Council, Tuscumbia, Ala., 1977-78. Recipient cert. and plaque Ala. Coop. Extension Service Employees' Orgn., 1977. Mem. Ala. Coop. Extension Service Employees Orgn. (rec. sec. 1979-81), Am. Home Econs. Assn., Ala. Farm Bur., Muscle Shoals Home Econs. Assn., Ala. Home Econs. Assn. Office: Ala Coop Extension Service Route 1 Box 110 Russellville AL 35653

HOSKINS, GERALDINE, hospital nursing administrator; b. Maysville, Ky., Aug. 15, 1940; d. Vernon Garrett Hoskins and Ivetti H. Hoskins Candy. Cert. Christ Hosp. Sch. Nursing, Cin., 1961; A.A., U. Cin., 1975. Staff nurse, evening supr. Adams County Hosp., West Union, Ohio, 1961-63; staff nurse, then head nurse, then supr. Christ Hosp., Cin., 1963-69; asst. supr., then supr. med. nursing Bethesda Hosp. Oak, Cin., 1969-70; dir. emergency and intensive care Bethesda Hosp. North, Cin., 1970-71, mgr., 1971-72, asst. v.p., 1972-80; self-employed securities salesperson, Fla., 1980-81; asst. v.p. Jewish Hosp., Cin., 1981, v.p., 1981—; ind. neighborhood nurse practitioner, Cin., 1972—; career counselor U. Cin.; mem. adv. bd. co-op. edn. dept. Coll. Mt. St. Joseph on the Ohio, 1982, mem. adv. bd. dept. bus., 1982—; presenter in field. Mem. Cin. Soc. Hosp. Nursing Adminstrs., Ohio Soc. Nursing Adminstrs., Nat. League Nursing, Ohio League Nursing, Am. Orgn. Nurse Execs., Ohio Co-op. Edn. Assn. Republican. Avocations: travel; spectator and participatory sports; swimming; reading; music. Home: 6542 Kentuckyview Dr Cincinnati OH 45230 Office: Jewish Hosp Cin Inc 3200 Burnet Ave Cincinnati OH 45229

HOSKINS, MARGARET ANN, physician assistant, nurse; b. Plainfield, N.J., Dec. 3, 1944; d. Howard Ellsworth and Emma Louise (Tote) Raymond; m. Robert William Sweatt, Sept. 17, 1966 (div. 1970); m. 2d, Samuel Gilbert Hoskins, Aug. 23, 1973; children—Matthew H., Andrew H. Diploma All Souls Hosp. Sch. Nursing, Morristown, N.J., 1965; A.A., U. Ala.-Birmingham, 1973. R.N., N.J., Ala. Operating room nurse Overlook Hosp., Summit, N.J., 1965-66, Valley Hosp., Ridgewood, N.J., 1966-71; nurse phlebotomist Bergen County Blood Bank, N.J., 1969-71; operating room nurse U Ala.-Birmingham, Med. Ctr. Hosp., 1971-72, emergency room nurse, 1973; physician asst. in surgery Mary Imogene Bassett Hosp., Cooperstown, N.Y., 1973—; supr. Surg. Outpatient dept., 1978—, coordinator med. edn. Surg. Outpatient dept., 1980—, dir. Pigmented Lesion Clinic, 1984—. Buyer, Cooperstown Natural Food Coop., 1980—; emergency med. technician Nat. Ski Patrol Systems, 1982—; patroller Deer Run Ski Patrol, 1983—; host parent Am.-Scandinavian Student Exchange, 1983-84. Mem. N.Y. State Soc. Physician's Assts., Am. Acad. Physician Assts., Otsego County Conservation Assn. Presbyterian. Club: Criterion (com. mem. 1980—), Avocations: motherhood; skiing; aerobic exercise; creative cooking; knitting; home renovation and decorating. Home: RD1 Box 93 Fly Creek NY 13337 Office: Mary Imogene Bassett Hosp Atwell Rd Cooperstown NY 13326

HOSLER, DORIS KELLER, librarian, educator; b. Berwick, Pa., Feb. 7, 1921; d. Jacob Leroy and Alma Bertha (Howard) Keller; m. Robert Clark Hosler, June 21, 1941. B.S. in Bus. Edn., Bloomsburg U. (Pa.), 1948; M.S. in L.S., Drexel U., Phila., 1967. Tchr. bus. edn. Penn Manor High Sch., Millersville, Pa., 1947-58, librarian, 1958-68; circulation librarian Millersville U., 1968-79, library instruction coordinator, 1979—, assoc. prof., 1977—, chmn. desegregation grievance com., 1980—; chmn. retirement com. Assn. Pa. State Coll. and Univ. Faculties, 1983—. Mem. Millersville Aux. to Lancaster Gen. Hosp., 1975—; Millersville Borough rep. Lancaster Redevel. Authority Regional Adv. Council, Lancaster, 1979—, mem. human services, 1980—; sec. Millersville Boro Planning Commn., 1981—. Grantee in field. Mem. Assn. Pa. State Univ. Faculty, ALA, NEA, Pa. State Edn. Assn., AAUP, Pa. Library Assn., Lancaster Library Assn., Pa. Assn. Higher Edn. (pres. region 1973-76). Democrat. Lutheran. Home: 560 Buttonwood Farm Rd Millersville PA 17551 Office: Millersville Univ Millersville PA 17551

HOSPITAL, JANETTE TURNER, writer, English language educator; b. Melbourne, Australia, Nov. 12, 1942; came to U.S., 1967, to Can., 1971; d. Adrian Charles and Elsie Evelyn (Morgan) Turner; m. Clifford George Hospital, Feb. 5, 1965; children—Geoffrey, Cressida. B.A. in English, U. Queensland, Brisbane, Australia, 1964; M.A. in English, Queen's U., Kingston, Ont., Can., 1973, postgrad., 1974-75. Cert. tchr., Australia, Ont. High sch. tchr., State Dept. Edn., Queensland, 1963-66; librarian Harvard U., Cambridge, Mass., 1967-71; teaching fellow Queen's U., 1971-74; lectr. in English lit. fed. penitentiaries, Kingston, 1975-76; writer, 1976—; lectr. lit. and writers, workshops various univs., 1982—; vis. writer-in-residence MIT, Cambridge, Mass., 1985-86; novels include: The Ivory Swing (Seal First Novel award), 1982; The Tiger in the Tiger Pit, 1983; Borderline, 1985; short stories include: Waiting (Atlantic First award Atlantic Monthly), 1978; Our Little Chamber Concerts (1st prize in mag. fiction Found. for Advancement Can. Letters), 1982; other short stories pub. in U.S., Can., U.K., Australia, 1976—. Named One of Can.'s Top Ten Younger Writers, 1986. Commonwealth scholar, 1961; Ont. grad. fellow, 1972-73; Can. Council doctoral fellow, 1974-75. Mem. Can. Writers Union, Authors League Am., P.E.N. Democrat. Methodist. Office: care Blanche C Gregory Lit Agent 2 Tudor City Pl New York NY 10017

HOSTETTER, MARGARET JONES, retirement community ofcl.; b. Louisville, Feb. 4, 1946; d. Harry W. and Doris (Morelend) Jones; B.A., Ind. U., 1978; postgrad. U. Tenn., 1978-80; m. Andrew Stuart Hostetter, Nov. 9, 1973 (dec.); 1 son, Erik Stuart. Nursing personnel hiring ofcl. Americana Healthcare, Indpls., 1976-78; mgr. Harding House Condominium, Nashville, 1978-79; dir. Deer Lake Retirement Community, Nashville, 1979—. Sec. Foster Grandparent Adv. Council, Social Action Group on Aging of Nat. Council Aging. Active ARC, Mental Health, Nat. Alliance Family Life, PTA, Am. Cancer Soc. Cert. nursing home adminstr. Mem. Bellevue Area C. of C., Am. Assn. Ret. Persons, Tenn. Health Care Assn., Nat. Citizens Coalition for Nursing Home Reform, Nat. Assn. Female Execs. Methodist. Home and Office: 368 Deer Lake Dr Nashville TN 37221

HOTALING, KAY CAROL, college administrator; b. Kingston, N.Y., Dec. 20, 1945; d. Kenneth LeGrand and Mary Louise (Straley) H.; B.S. in Math., SUNY, 1968, M.S. in Counseling Psychology, 1970, doctoral candidate, 1970—. Adminstrv. asst. office of v.p. student affairs SUNY, Albany, 1968-70, chief counselor, 1973-80, asst. dean, 1973-80, asst. vice chancellor alternative and continuing edn., central adminstrn., 1980—; counselor Adirondack Community Coll., 1970-73; cons. in field. Bd. dirs. Warren Washington Mental Health, Glens Falls, N.Y., 1970-73; bd. dirs. Glens Falls Youth Center, 1970-73; pres., bd. dirs. Vol. Action Center Albany, 1979-81; mem. Albany Council of Community Services, chmn. info. and research task force, 1973—; chmn. Task Force on Forced Career Change. Recipient Nat. Mental Health Assn. Ann. citation, 1973, ann. recognition award as outstanding woman Albany YWCA, 1979. Mem. Am. Assn. Adult and Continuing Edn., Continuing Edn. Assn. N.Y. (exec. bd. dirs. 1980—), AAUP, AAUW, Assn. for Continuing Higher Edn., Nat. Council Tchrs. Math., Chi Sigma Theta. SUNY Alumni Assn. (dir. 1976-83). Club: Jr. League of Albany (dir. 1977-80). Home: 18 Park Lane South Apt-10 Menands NY 12204 Office: SUNY State Univ Plaza S-311 Albany NY 12246

HOTCHKISS, ANITA RUTH, lawyer; b. East Orange, N.J., May 21, 1937; d. Carl Esward and Louise Charlotte (Francke) Kastner; m. 2d, Christopher Lawrence Martin, Dec. 24, 1976; m. Stephen Magowan Hotchkiss, June 18, 1960 (div. 1975); children—Kirsten Anne, Karl Elizabeth. B.A. magna cum laude, Bates Coll., Lewiston, Maine, 1959; M.L.S., Rutgers U., 1970; J.D. with honors, Rutgers U., 1975. Bar: N.J. 1975, N.Y. 1982, U.S. Supreme Ct. 1982. Research librarian Joint Free Pub. Library, Morristown, N.J., 1970-72; assoc. Porzio, Bromberg & Newman P.A., Morristown, 1975-79, ptnr., 1979—. Mem. Morris County (N.J.) Dem. Com., 1970-74; mem. ad hoc com. for Municipal Charter Study, 1971; mem. Morris County Chaplaincy Council, 1971-72; mem. exec. com. Morris City Fair Housing Council, 1970. Mem. ABA, N.J. Bar Assn., Trial Attys. N.J. (trustee 1982—), Phi Beta Kappa, Beta Phi Mu. Democrat. Presbyterian. Home: 31 Maxwell Ct Morristown NJ 07960 Office: Porzio Bromberg & Newman PA 163 Madison Ave Morristown NJ 07960

HOTES, ELIZABETH ANN, heavy equipment and land development company executive; b. Birmingham, Ala., Oct. 4, 1918; d. Richard and Florence (Ford) Oswald; m. Douglas N. Hotes; children—Richard, Elizabeth, John, Florence, Douglas. Student Hollins Coll., 1937-39, Phila. Sch. Indsl. Art, 1939-40, Art Inst., Chgo., 1941. Engring. draftsman Coast and Geodetic Survey, Washington, 1941-44; cartographer Aero Service, Phila., 1946-48; draftsman, artist C.E., Anchorage, 1968-71; sec., treas. T.E.R.R.A., Inc., Anchorage, 1971—; dir. Amstan, Inc., Anchorage, 1971—, pres., 1980—; dir. Alaska Diversified Digital, Anchorage. Home: 1900 W Hoteco Ave Anchorage AK 99502 Office: Amstan Inc PO Box 6046 Anchorage AK 99502

HOUCK, LINDA ROBINSON, home economist; b. Wadesboro, N.C., Sept. 30, 1949; d. George Jackson and Mattie Lois (Marsh) Robinson; m. Jacob Albert Houck, May 31, 1970. B.S.H.E., U. N.C.-Greensboro, 1971; M.Ed., Coll. William and Mary, 1978. Extension agt. in home econs. Va. Coop. Extension Service, Hampton, 1971—. Telephone crisis counselor, small group facilitator Contact Peninsula, Newport News, Va., 1978—. Mem. Am. Home Econs. Assn., Nat. Assn. Extension Home Economists, Peninsula Nutrition Council (chmn. 1984-86), Am. Assn. Counseling and Devel., Peninsula Women's Network. Avocation: reading. Home: 3 Redman Ct Hampton VA 23669 Office: Va Coop Extension Service 1320 LaSalle Ave Room 6 Hampton VA 23669

HOUCK, SUE BENNETT, computer software documentation writer; b. Fort Worth; d. William Sutton and Vera Kathryn (Yater) Bennett; m. Duane Roger Houck, May 21, 1965; children—Cindy, Carin, Michele. B.A., U. South Fla. 1980; postgrad., 1983-84. Tch. writer GTE Data Services, Tampa, 1981-84, publs. analyst, 1985—, IM sr. analyst-publs., 1985—. Vice pres. Lake Padgett Estates Civic Assn., Land O' Lakes, 1979-82; adult vol. Girl Scouts U.S., La. and Fla., 1971-79; v.p. Mcpl. Services Unit, 1981-85; exec. sec. Citizens Water Adv. Council, Pasco County, Fla., 1980-81. Mem. Soc. Tech. Communications (v.p. 1984-85), Alpha Mu Gamma. Methodist. Club: 99's. Avocations: flying; water sports; tennis. Office: GTE Data Services 111 Madison St Tampa FL 33602

HOUDE, DENISE CLAIRE, computer programmer, real estate and building industry cons.; b. Dover, N.H., Aug. 31, 1951; d. Raymond Arthur and Alice Mary (St. Cyr) H. Student McIntosh Coll., Babson Coll., U. N.H. Rater coder Liberty Mut. Ins. Co., Portsmouth, N.H., 1969-70, group leader, 1970-71, asst. clerical supr., 1971-73, clerical supr., 1973-74, staff asst., 1974-79, prodn. analyst for Mass. Automobile, 1979-80, prodn. analyst for Home Office Personal Risks, 1980-81, sr. prodn. analyst for Home Office Personal Risks, 1981-82, EDP trainer, 1982, div. coordinators trainer, 1981-82, sr. computer programmer, 1982—; owner, cons. Deni Service Ltd., Portsmouth, 1984-85; Organizer Horse of Different Color Rd. Race, Portsmouth, 1982, Clipper Rd. Race, 1983; coordinator profl. seminars, 1984, 85. Recipient trophy Alton Bay Rd. Race, 1981. Mem. Seacoast Women Network. Roman Catholic. Club: Off the Wall Racquetball. Avocations: running; bicycling; skiing; guitar; canoeing. Home: 370 Portsmouth Ave Greenland NH 03840 Office: Liberty Mutual Ins Co Borthwick Ave Portsmouth NH 03801

HOUDE, MARY JEAN, retail company executive; b. Chgo., Feb. 6, 1927; d. Edmund George and Muriel Alice (Staples) Mailloux; student Eureka Coll., 1945-47, Utah State U., 1971, U. Colo., 1973; m. Thomas R. Houde, Aug. 13, 1949 (dec.); 1 dau., Linda Jean Houde Marquie. Asst. to book editor Ziff-Davis Pub. Co., Chgo., 1947-48; reporter, feature writer, editor Kankakee (Ill) Daily Jour., 1948-71; chief vol. services Ill. Dept. Corrections, 1971-72; nat. dir. women's programs Sears, Roebuck and Co., 1972-82, mem. community relations, 1982—, also dir. nat. community improvement program; vice-chmn. Nat. Coalition to Prevent Shoplifting, 1978-80. Advisor, MW CARE; nat. dir. Jr. Women's Clubs, 1964-66; mem. Pres.' Com. on Employment of Handicapped. Mem. Women in Communications, Brain Research Found., Ill. Fedn. Women's Clubs (pres. 1970-72), Gen. Fedn. Women's Clubs (dir. 1960-84), Community Devel. Soc. (dir. 1973-76), Hands Up (founder; dir. nat. crime reduction program 1974-80). Republican. Roman Catholic. Club: Woman's of Kankakee, Woman's of Lisle. Author: The Clubwoman, 1970; The Organization Volunteer, 1972; co-author: Of the People, 1968; The Volunteer Organization Handbook, 1985. Home: 6371 Kindling Ct Lisle IL 60532 Office: Sears Tower D/703-40/5 Chicago IL 60684

HOUGH, BETTY MAE, administrative secretary; b. Pittsburg, Kans., Sept. 19, 1934; d. Bert H. and Edith Mae (Smith) Vanderpool; m. Glenn L. Hough, Aug. 18, 1956 (div. 1978); children—Gary Herbert, Gregory Glenn, Gordon Marion. Student, Kans. State Tchrs. Coll., 1952-54. Bank clk. Nat. Bank, Pittsburg, Kans., 1952-56; exec. sec. City Nat. Bank & Trust Co., Kansas City, Mo., 1956-57; corp. sec. Glenn L. Hough, Pittsburg, Kans., 1960-77; adminstrv. sec. Pitney-Bowes, Wichita, Kans., 1983—. Mem. Nat. Assn. Female Execs. Avocations: gourmet cooking; sewing; gardening; bicycling; swimming.

HOUGH, JANET GERDA CAMPBELL, research company scientist; b. Glen Ridge, N.J., Dec. 22, 1948; d. Ralph William and Gerda Lydia (Baarck) Campbell; m. John Harrison Hough, Oct. 1, 1966 (div.); 1 child, Laura Leigh. Student Temple U. and Tyler Sch. Art, Phila., 1970-72, Pa. Acad. Fine Arts, 1972, Camden County Coll., Blackwood, N.J., 1973-75; B.S., Thomas Jefferson U., 1977. Lab. animal technician Inst. Med. Research, Camden, N.J., 1972-75; research technician dept. biochemistry Thomas Jefferson U., Phila., 1976, phlebotomist, hematology technician, 1976-78, med. technologist spl. hematology, 1978-79, research technician dept. med. genetics, 1979-80; validation technician micromedic Rohm & Haas, Horsham, Pa., 1981-83; quality control technician micromedic Internat. Clin. Nuclear Inc., Cosa Mesa, Calif., and Horsham, 1983—. Collaborator, editor textbook Hematology for Medical Technology, 1984; poet, illustrator Thought Progressions, 1984. Democrat. Roman Catholic. Avocations: drawing; painting; long-distance walking. Office: Micromedic Systems Inc 102 Witmer Rd Horsham PA 19044

HOUGHTALING, PAMELA ANN, business machines company executive; b. Catskill, N.Y., July 8, 1949; d. Stanley Kenneth and Mildred Edythe (Fyfe) H. B.A., Princeton U., 1971; cert. Russian Inst., Columbia U., 1976, M.Internat. Affairs, 1974. Internat. relations analyst Library of Congress, Washington, 1974-75, U.S. Gen. Acctg. Office, Washington, 1976-77; pub. affairs specialist IBM Corp., Washington, 1977-81; sr. external programs analyst IBM World Trade Americas/Far East Corp., North Tarrytown, N.Y., 1981-82; mgr. labor affairs/bus. practices U.S. Council Internat. Bus., N.Y.C., 1982-84; communications specialist IBM Corp., Boca Raton, Fla., 1984—. Mem. Nat. Women's Polit. Caucus, Washington, 1983—, Municipal Art Soc. N.Y., N.Y.C., 1983-84, Scenic Hudson, Poughkeepsie, N.Y., 1983—, Westchester County Hist. Soc., Valhalla, N.Y., 1982-83. Mem. Women in Communications. Office: Entry Systems Div IBM Corp Boca Raton FL 33432

HOUGHTON, JUDITH DEAN, choreographer, consultant; b. Rawlins, Wyo., Dec. 4, 1939; d. Irvin C. and Dorothy H. (Ingram) Houghton. Student U. Tex., Austin, 1957-59. Faculty dance dept., So. Meth. U., Dallas, 1964-65; choreographer numerous themes parks, U.S., 1965-76, Miss Teenage America telecast, Dallas, 1964-80, Miss U.S.A. and Miss Universe Inc., telecasts, 1977—, numerous civic groups, Dallas, 1954—; sr. ptnr. Charles Meeker, Jr. and Assoc., Dallas, 1967-76; cons., meeting mgr., exec. producer Dr Pepper Co., Dallas, 1964—, producer centennial events, 1984-85; ptnr., choreographer Charlie's Place, Fort Worth, 1973-76, Incredible Charlie's Dinner Theatre, Dallas, 1976-78. Active Nat. Cheerleaders Assn., Dallas area orgns., 1965—. Mem. Meeting Planners Internat. (pub. relations com. 1982-84, edn. com. 1985-86, bd. dirs. 1986-87). Republican. Author: Miss Teenage America Tells How to Make Good Things Happen, 1976.

HOUGHTON, VIVIAN ANN, lawyer; b. Wilmington, Del., July 12, 1943; d. Edward S. and Amelia A. (Kaczur) Bobeck; m. William I. Houghton, May 21, 1971 (div.); 1 dau., Lucia Capodanno. B.A., U. Del., 1975; J.D., Del. Law Sch., 1979. Bar: Del. 1980. Program developer Seeda Program, Wilmington, 1977-78; law clk. Community Legal Aid, Wilmington, 1976-78; atty. for register of wills, New Castle, Del., 1979-82; ptnr. Boudart and Houghton, Wilmington, 1981—; asst. pub. defender Family Ct., Wilmington, 1983—, interim trustee bankruptcy ct. Dist. of Del., Wilmington, 1982—; instr. U. Del., Newark, winter 1984. Speaker equal rights NOW, Wilmington, 1977—, v.p., 1978-79; speaker women and law Commn. on Status of Women, Wilmington, 1977—; advisor Legacy for Del. Women, Wilmington, 1983-84; campaign mgr. Com. To Elect William I. Houghton, New Castle, 1978, Com. To Elect Karen E. Peterson, county council, 1980, Com. To Elect Mary C. Boudart County Council, New Castle, 1982; parliamentarian Women's Democratic Club, 1980-81. Recipient Woman of Yr. award Del. Bus. and Profl. Women's Club, 1982. Mem. Del. Bar Assn., Del. Women's Polit. Caucus (pres. 1979-80). Democrat. Roman Catholic. Home: 1514 Maryland Ave Wilmington DE 19805 Office: Boudart and Houghton 606 Market St Mall Wilmington DE 19801

HOULDEN, DEBORAH ANNE, marketing executive; b. Beverly, Mass., Oct. 8, 1957; d. Robert Curtis and Marcia Anne (Cloyd) H.; m. Steven Alan Barrett; 1 child, Krisanne; 1 stepchild, Alexandra. Student pub. schs., Manchester, Mass. Account exec. Agawam Assocs., Rowley, Mass., 1978-81; mktg. specialist Interactive Data Corp., Waltham, Mass., 1981-84; account supr., mgr. direct mktg. services Arnold & Co., Boston, 1984-85; pres., owner Mktg. Solutions, Manchester, Mass., 1985—. Mem. Nat. Assn. Female Execs., Am. Mktg. Assn. (healthcare subcom.). Office: Mktg Solutions 82 Pleasant St Manchester MA 01944

HOUREN, CAROL ADELAIDE, real estate broker; b. Dallas, Nov. 12; d. C.C. and Adelaide (Graham) Randle; children—Jay R., Laura M. B.B.A., So. Meth. U., 1959, postgrad., 1975-76. Vice pres. Cromwell Corp., Dallas, 1971-75; pres. Balanced Investment Securities Corp., Dallas, 1973-75; real estate broker, Dallas, 1965—. Mem. tax adv. com. City of Dallas, 1981—; mem. women's bd. Dallas Civic Opera, 1979—; bd. dirs. Dallas Ballet, 1978—, pres. women's com., 1984-85, exec. com., 1984—; pres. Bentwood Republican Womans Club, Dallas, 1981; bd. dirs. Dallas County Council Rep. Women, 1982; del. state and nat. women's convs. Rep. Party, numerous yrs. including 1984; charter mem. Republican Forum, Dallas. Mem. Nat. Assn. Realtors, Tex. Assn. Realtors, Dallas Bd. Realtors Nat. Assn. Security Dealers. Episcopalian. Clubs: Altrusa, Bentree Country, Dallas Charity Guild, others. Address: Henry S Miller Realtors 8300 Preston Rd Suite 111 Dallas TX 75248

HOUSE, CAROLYN JEAN, Realtor; b. Harlingen, Tex., July 14, 1949; d. Carroll Edward Stout and Betty Jean (Weber) Schindler; m. Lawson W. House, III, Apr. 3, 1969 (div. Feb. 1979); children—Christopher Steven, Jonathan Michael. Student Southwest Tex. State U., 1967-68, Harlingen Bus. Coll., 1968-69. Real estate broker, Okla. Substitute tchr. to migrant children, Harlingen, Tex., 1968-69; real estate salesperson Century 21 Despain Agy., Enid, Okla., 1977-82; broker, owner Century 21 American Homes Agy., Enid, 1982—; sec.-treas. Enid Bd. Realtors, 1981-82; treas. Century 21 Oklahoma City Brokers Council, 1984—, sec., 1985-86. Named Realtor Assoc. of Year, Enid Bd. Realtors, 1980. Mem. Enid C. of C., Nat. Assn. Realtors, Women's Council Realtors (sec. Enid chpt. 1985), Okla. Assn. Realtors, Enid Bd. Realtors (bd. dirs.), Beta Sigma Phi. Republican. Lutheran. Office: Century 21 American Homes Agy 424 S Van Buren Enid OK 73701

HOUSE, CAROLYN JOYCE, lawyer; b. Columbia, S.C., Nov. 11, 1952; d. George E. and Mary Frances (Green) Myers. B.A., U. South Fla., Tampa, 1974; J.D., U. S.C., 1977. Bar: Fla. 1978, U.S. Supreme Ct. 1983. Assoc. litigation counsel Jim Walter Corp., Tampa, Fla., 1977-80; asst. state atty. Hillsborough County, Fla., 1980-81; sole practice, Tampa, 1982—; continuing legal edn. com. Fla. Bar, 1983-84; speaker continuing legal edn. seminars. Dir. Tampa Orgn. Black Affairs, 1978-80, Hillsborough County Mental Health Ctr., 1980-81, Tampa Philharm. Soc., 1979-82. Mem. Nat. Bar Assn. (v.p. Fla. chpt. 1983-84; Mem. of Yr. award 1983), Hillsborough County Bar Assn. (chmn. membership com. 1984-85), George Edgecomb Bar Assn. (press sec. 1982-83, gen. counsel 1983-84). Democrat. Baptist. Office: 518 N Tampa St Suite 203 Tampa FL 33602

HOUSE, DARLENE LOU ARTHURNETT, advertising executive, consultant; b. Detroit, Mar. 18, 1958; d. David Louis and Allean (Hines) House. B.A. in Communications, Mich. State U., 1979. Research asst. Mich. State U. Coll. Urban Devel., East Lansing, 1977; asst. to producer Sta. WKAR-TV, East Lansing, 1978; market surveyor Mich. Interviews, Lansing, 1979; telephone campaign caller Mich. State U. Devel. Fund, East Lansing, 1979; sales promotion asst. Aeroquip Corp., Jackson, Mich., 1979-82; account adminstr. Ross Roy, Inc., Detroit, 1983-85, jr. copywriter, 1985—; pub. relations officer Amvets Aux. Post #55, Detroit, 1975-76; cons. and liaison Mich. State U. All Campus Radio Bd., 1975-77. Contbr. articles to mags. Intern, State Rep. Larry E. Burkhalter, Lansing, 1978, State Senator Jackie Vaughn, Lansing, 1979. Recipient YMCA Minority Achiever award. Mem. Women in Communications, Inc. (communicator of Yr. 1982, chmn. award com., publicity com. chmn. 1982), Nat. Writers Club, Poetry Resource Ctr. of Mich., DAZS Coalition Greek Women, Sigma Gamma Rho (advisor Gamma Omega chpt. 1980-82, pub. relations officer and historian 1983-84). Democrat. Baptist. Clubs: Nat. Pan-Hellenic Council (corr. sec., Greek week liaison 1978-79) (East Lansing); Allstates (corr. sec., program chmn. 1982—), Adcraft (Detroit). Home: 5811 Loraine St Detroit MI 48208

HOUSE, KAREN ELLIOTT, newspaper editor; b. Matador, Tex., Dec. 7, 1947; d. Ted and Bailey (McKeehan) Elliott; m. Arthur House, Apr. 5, 1975 (div. Oct. 1983); m. Peter Kann, June 2, 1984. B.J., U. Tex., 1970. Reporter edn. Dallas Morning News, 1970-71; corr. sta. WSHN, Washington, 1971-74; reporter regulatory agys. Wall Street Jour., Washington, 1974-75, energy reporter, 1975-78, diplomatic corr., 1978-83, fgn. editor, N.Y.C., 1984—; mem. adv. council Sch. Communications, U. Tex., Austin, 1984—, Johns Hopkins U., Washington, 1984—. Recipient Pulitzer prize, 1983; Edwin Hood award Nat. Press Club, 1982; Overseas Press Club award, 1983; Edward Weintal Diplomatic Reporting award, 1980. Office: Wall Street Jour 200 Liberty St New York NY 10007

HOUSE, LISA ELIZABETH, advertising account executive; b. Hartford, Conn., Sept. 16, 1958; d. Richard Bailey and Ruth (Broman) House; m. Michael Anthony Stanicak, July 18, 1981 (div.). Cert. Katharine Gibbs Sch., 1978, Life Mgmt. Inst. 1977; student Boston U., 1978-80. Policy analyst Security Conn. Life Ins. Co., Avon, 1975-77; sr. adminstrv. asst. Polaroid Corp., Cambridge, Mass., 1978-80; acct. exec. Keiler Advt., Farmington, Conn., 1980—. Mem. Ad Club of Greater Hartford. Lutheran. Home: 243 Brickyard Rd Farmington CT 06032

HOUSE, NADINE LEOLA, pilot; b. Kalispell, Mont., Jan. 18, 1942; d. Roy Bertrand and Nina Frances (Jones) Grant; m. Gordon Phillip Thompson, Oct. 3, 1958 (dec. Aug. 1965); children—Craig Allen, Scott Gordon, Larry Dale; m. David Gene House, June 14, 1966. Student Ag Aviation Acad., 1968. Cert. Comml. pilot, Alaska. Advanced ground instr. Round-Up Air Service, Pendleton, Oreg., 1969-72; claims, adjustments mgr. Shulton, Inc., Sparks, Nev., 1973-75; adminstrv. asst. Hydro-Search, Inc., Reno, 1975-79; free-lance house painter, Waldport, Oreg., 1979-83; adminstrv. asst. North Slope

Borough, Barrow, Alaska, 1983—; instr. rural edn. U. Alaska, 1983; written exam. adminstr. FAA, 1983—; advanced ground instr. various orgns., 1969—. Mem. Oreg. Pilots Assn. (sec. 1970), C.A.P. (aviation scis. instr.). Avocations: flying; fishing; bowling; horseback riding. Home: PO Box 3064 Barrow AK 99723

HOUSEMAN, ANN ELIZABETH LORD, educational administrator, arts administrator; b. New Orleans, Mar. 21, 1936; d. Noah Louis and Florence Marguerite (Coyle) Lord; m. Evan Kenny Houseman, June 25, 1960; children—Adrienne Ann, Jeannette Louise, Yvonne Elizabeth. B.A., Barnard Coll., 1957; M.A., Columbia U., 1962; Ph.D., U. Del., 1969. State supr. reading Del. Dept. Pub. Instrn., Dover, 1977-79; prin. M.L. King, Jr. Elem. Sch., Wilmington, Del., 1979-80; adminstr., exec. dir. Del. State Arts Council, Wilmington, 1980-84, acting dir. div. hist. and cultural affairs, Dover, 1983-84; prin. P.S. du Pont Elem. Sch., Wilmington, 1984—. bd. dirs. Mid-Atlantic States Arts Consortium, Balt., 1980-84; adv. bd. Rockwood Mus., Wilmington, 1981—; bd. dirs. Opera Del., 1984—, Del. Theatre Co., 1984—. Contbr. articles to profl. jours. Mem. Diamond State Reading Assn. (pres. 1977-79), Am. Assn. Mus., Assn. State and Local History, Del. Assn. Sch. Adminstrs., Assn. Supervision and Curriculum Devel., Psi Chi, Phi Delta Kappa. Republican. Presbyterian. Office: PS du Pont Elem Sch 34th and Van Buren Sts Wilmington DE 19802

HOUSER, LAINE ELIZABETH, project manager, designer; b. Los Angeles, Sept. 28, 1954; d. Wastell Hodgson and Barbara Murrison (Dunn) Dunham; m. Thomas Lloyd Houser, Dec. 15, 1973 (div. 1983); 1 dau., Katrina Leigh. B.A., Art Ctr. Coll. Design, Pasadena, 1981. Project designer The Only Co., North Hollywood, Calif., 1981-82, AVG Prodns., Valencia, Calif., 1982, Fredrick Hope & Assocs., Venice, Calif., 1982-84, Knott's Berry Farm, Buena Park, Calif., 1985—; cons. Knotts Berry Farm, Introvision Co., Broggie Elliott Animation, REC, Inc.; ptnr. The Works Partnership, Long Beach, Calif., 1983—. Mem. Nat. Assn. Female Execs., KBF Mgmt. Club. Democrat. Presbyterian.

HOUSER, LOUISE KELLEY, health care administrator; b. Bowman, S.C., Feb. 22, 1919; d. George Quillie and Byrdie Lucile (Stephens) Kelley; B.S., S.C. State Coll., 1941, M.S., 1959; m. John W. Houser, Jr., Sept. 18, 1943; children—John W., George D. Tchr. public schs., Marion County, S.C., 1941-44; tchr. sci. Ga. Sch. for Deaf, 1959-61; tchr. pub. schs., Rome, Ga., 1961-68; dir. personnel Brentwood Med. Care Home, Ga., 1967-71; adminstr. Brentwood Nursing Home, 1972-77; adminstr. Brentwood Park, Three Rivers Health Care Co., Rome, Ga., 1977—. Bd. dirs. Rome Girls Club. Mem. Rome Council on Human Relations, Ga. Health Care Assn., Am. Health Care Assn., Ga. Soc. Activity Dirs., Ga. Dental Soc. Aux. (past pres.), Am. Cancer Soc. (past pres. Floyd County div.), Aux. Nat. Dental Assn. (past pres., mem. exec. bd.). Home: 121 Jackson St Rome GA 30161 Office: Moran Lake Rd Rome GA 30161

HOUSEWORTH, LAURA JENNINGS, lawyer; b. Kansas City, Kans., Mar. 22, 1927; d. Frank Harvey and Lucile (Pollock) Jennings; m. Richard Court Houseworth, Nov. 1, 1952; children—Louise, Lucile, Court II. B.A. magna cum laude, Lake Forest Coll., 1949; M.Ed., U. Mo., 1951; J.D., Ariz. State U., 1975. Bar: Ariz. 1975. Nat. rep. Chi Omega, Cin., 1949-50; asst. dean women U. Kans., Lawrence, 1951-52; dep. county atty. Maricopa County, Phoenix, 1975—, juvenile div., 1979—, sr. trial atty., asst. supr. juvenile div., 1985—; lectr. Nat. Family Support Assn., San Diego, 1977. Founding bd., pres. Vol. Bur., Tucson, 1969; founding bd. Girl's Club Tucson, 1970; founding bd., 1st v.p. Crisis Nursery, Phoenix, 1978; exec. bd. United Way, Legal Aid, Family Service. Mem. Maricopa County Bar Assn., ABA, Am. Trial Lawyers Assn., Ariz. Women's Lawyers Assn., Ariz. Acad. Republican. Episcopalian. Club: Jr. League Phoenix. Home: Phoenix Towers 2201 N Central Ave 10F Phoenix AZ 85004 Office: Maricopa County Atty 101 W Jefferson St Phoenix AZ 85003

HOUSLEY, ELAINE A., telecommunications company executive; b. Chgo., Nov. 7, 1950; d. Bruce Emerson and Hedy (Feierfeil) Frankenfield; m. Phillip Lester Housley, May 20, 1972. B.S., U. Mo., 1972; M.B.A., Xavier U., 1976; M.S., Tex. Tech. U., 1979. Planning engr., Western Electric Co., Ballwin, Mo., 1972-73, indsl. engr., Columbus, Ohio, 1973-75; asst. prof. DeVry Inst. Tech., Columbus, 1976-77; planning engr. AT&T, Dublin, Ohio, 1977-79, dept. chief, 1979—. Mem. Inst. Indsl. Engrs., Soc. Women Engrs., Sigma Kappa. Episcopalian. Club: Presiding Ptnr. Profit Prophets (Columbus, Ohio). Avocations: sailing, bicycling, soccer. Home: 337 Glen Meadow Ct Dublin OH 43017 Office: AT&T 5151 Blaxer Memorial Pkwy Dublin OH 43017

HOUSTON, LESA RENEE, market sales executive; b. Fort Worth, Dec. 14, 1958; d. Louis Zeke Houston and Vivian Alpha (Brown) Drisdale. B.F.A., Tex. Christian U. Acct., Texaco Oil Co., Houston, 1981-83; mktg. rep. Allnet Co., Houston, 1983—. Mem. Girls' Service League, Ft. Worth, 1981, Big Sisters of Am., Houston, 1983; cons. Young Women Christian Club, Houston, 1981-82. Mem. Jaycees. Mem. Ch. of God in Christ. Club: The Assembly (Ft. Worth). Home: PO Box 740294 Houston TX 77274

HOUSTON, SHIRLEY MAE (MRS. THOMAS H. HOUSTON), ct. reporter; b. Jasper, Tex., Oct. 4, 1938; d. Walter Louis and Effie Marie (Hulett) Gordon; student U. Houston, 1957, South Tex. Jr. Coll., Houston, 1958; grad. Robert Krippner Sch. Reporting, 1965; m. Thomas Harold Houston, Aug. 3, 1957. Various secretarial positions, 1956-65; ct. reporter, owner Houston Reporting Service, 1965—; owner H-R-S, 1975—; v.p. Tradewinds Indsl. Park, Inc., 1974-83, dir., 1984—; partner Houston Video Service, 1977-84; dir. Skate City USA, 1980-83. Vol. juvenile counselor; advisor Houston Community Coll., 1976-78, Alvin Community Coll., 1980-84. Registered profl. reporter, cert. shorthand reporter, Tex. Mem. Greater Houston Ct. Reporters Assn. (pres. 1975, disting. service award 1983), Nat. Shorthand Reporters Assn. (state chmn. membership com. 1977-78 dir. 1979-80, placement com. 1980-82, ins. com. 1982-84, co-chmn. word processing com. 1981-83, seminar instr. nat. conv. 1978, 79, 81, 82, 83, 84, nat. membership award 1980), Tex. Shorthand Reporters Assn. (advt. chmn. conv. 1967, dir. 1978-80), Nat. Assn. Legal Secs., Tex. Assn. Legal Secs., Greater Houston Legal Secs. Assn. (dir. 1969), Legal Assts. Assn., DAR, UDC, Harris County Heritage Soc., Theatre Under the Stars. Baptist. Club: Cotillion (Houston). Address: 1001 Texas Suite 1100 Houston TX 77002

HOUX, SHIRLEY ANN, personal and business services company executive, consultant, researcher; b. Claremore, Okla., Nov. 1, 1931; d. George Warren and Alta Zena (Starkweather) Pritchard; m. William Dean Munson, June 1, 1951 (div. June 1962); children—Debra Kay, Diana Sue, Donna Lynn; m. Leonard Houx, June 22, 1963; 1 child, David Leonard. Student in bus. Okla. State U., 1949-50. Sec. Jack Gordon, P.A., Claremore, Okla., 1947-48; sec., personnel mgr. Gulf Oil Corp., Tulsa, 1950-51; exec. sec. to wing comdr. U.S. Air Force, Cocoa Beach, Fla., 1951-53; exec. sec. to gen. counsel Houston So., P.A., Stillwater, Okla., 1957-60; exec. sec. to exec. v.p. and sr. v.p. Williams Cos., Tulsa, 1962-64; owner, chief exec. officer Hallmark Exchange, Inc., Tulsa, 1981—; cons. small bus., Tulsa, 1981—; mem. small bus. adv. bd. Tulsa Jr. Coll., 1983—. Author: (drama) Wedding Rehearsal for the Bride of Christ, 1985. Contbg. editor The Chronicle, 1984. Co-creator, producer foot health program, 1967 (Am. Podiatry Assn. Outstanding award 1968); creator, advt. campaign for Cystic Fibrosis Found.: I'm One...Be One, 1978. Pres. women's aux. Okla. Podiatry Assn., Tulsa, 1966-82; sec.-treas. Okla. bd. examiners Okla. Podiatry Assn., 1969-76; nat. audio-visual chmn. women's aux. Am. Podiatry Assn., 1976; pres. Tulsa Cerebral Palsy Assn., 1977, Cystic Fibrosis Found. Aux., Tulsa, 1979. Named Miss Claremore, Claremore Bus. and Profl. Women, Okla., 1949; recipient Two-Star award Pure D'Lite Co., 1982. Mem. Nat. Assn. Female Execs., Tulsa C. of C. Democrat. Avocations: fashion design; the arts; writing. Office: 7404 E 98th St Tulsa OK 74133

HOWAR, BARBARA BELLE, nursing service administrator; b. North Platte, Nebr., June 8, 1934; d. Cecil Earl and Alice (Daly) Goodwin; m. Robert Alva Howar, Oct. 17, 1954; children—Rozanne, Cheryl, Mark, Lisa. Nursing degree Tex. Christian U., 1954. Staff nurse Creston Communty Hosp., Iowa, 1955, Fairfax Community Hosp., Mo., 1955-58; staff nurse Mahaska County Hosp., Oskaloosa, Iowa, 1958-62, supr., 1962-71, nursing service adminstr., 1971—; dist. chmn. nursing service adminstrn. Iowa Hosp. Assn., 1971-73; dist. rep. Iowa Assn. Quality Assurance Coordinators, 1978-79. Mem. Iowa Hosp. Assn. Nursing Service Adminstrs., Iowa Assn. Quality Assurance Coordinators (rep. 1978-79), Iowa Assn. Nursing Service Adminstrs. Republican. Disciples of Christ. Lodge: Kings Daughters (pres. 1980-82) (Oskaloosa).

HOWARD, CAROLE MARGARET MUNROE, public relations executive; b. Halifax, N.S., Can., Mar. 5, 1945; came to U.S., 1965; d. Frederick Craig and Dorothy Margaret (Crimes) Munroe; m. Robert William Howard, May 15, 1965. B.A., U. Calif.-Berkeley, 1967; M.S., Pace U., 1978. Reporter, Vancouver Sun (B.C.) 1965; editorial assoc. Pacific Northwest Bell, Seattle, 1967-70, employee info. supr., 1970-72, advt. supr., 1972, project mgr. EEO, 1972-73, mktg. mgr., 1973, info. mgr., 1974-75; dist. mgr. media relations AT&T, N.Y.C., 1975-77, dist. mgr. planning, 1977-78, dist. mgr. advt., 1978-80; media relations mgr. Western Electric, N.Y.C., 1980-83; div. mgr. regional pub. relations AT&T Info. Systems, Morristown, N.J., 1983-85; v.p. pub. relations and communications policy The Readers Digest Assn., Inc., Pleasantville, N.Y., 1985—. Author: (with Wilma Mathews) On Deadline: Managing Media Relations, 1985; contbg. author: A Communicator's Guide to Marketing, 1987, Experts in Action: Inside Public Relations, 2d edit., 1987. Editor newsletters Wash. State Republican Central Com., 1973-74; contbg. editor Pub. Relations Quar. Mem. Women in Communications (bd. dirs. Wash. state 1973), Internat. Assn. Bus. Communicators, Pub. Relations Soc. Am., Nat. Press Women, Wash. Press Women (bd. dirs. 1972), Pi Beta Phi. Angelican. Home: 31 Daniel Ct Ridgewood NJ 07450 Office: The Readers Digest Assn Inc Pleasantville NY 10570

HOWARD, JANE OSBURN, educator; b. Morris, Ill., Aug. 12, 1926; d. Everett Hooker and Bernice Otilda (Olson) Osburn; B.A., U. Ariz., 1948; M.A., U. N.Mex., 1966, Ph.D., 1969; m. Rollins Stanley Howard, June 5, 1948; children—Ellen Elizabeth, Susan (Mrs. John Karl Nuttall). Instr. U. N.Mex. Sch. Medicine, Albuquerque, 1968-70, mem. staff pediatrics, deaf blind children's program, Albuquerque, 1971-72, asst. dir. N.Mex. programs for deaf blind children, 1972—, instr. psychiatry, instr. pediatrics, coordinator deaf-blind children's program, 1972-76; ednl. cons., 1976—; publicity and pub. relations cons., 1983—; cons. Mountain-Plains Regional Center for Services to Deaf-Blind Children, Denver, 1971-74, Bur. Indian Affairs, 1974. Active Cystic Fibrosis, Mother's March, Heart Fund, Easter Seal-Crippled Children. Recipient fellowships U. N.Mex., 1965, 66, 66-67, 67-68, U. So. Calif. John Tracy Clinic, 1973. Fellow Royal Soc. Health; mem. Council Exceptional Children, Am. Assn. Mental Deficiency, Nat. Assn. Retarded Children, AAUW, Pi Lambda Theta, Zeta Phi Eta, Alpha Epsilon Rho. Republican. Methodist. Home: 615 Valencia Dr SE Albuquerque NM 87108

HOWARD, JANETTE (JAN) CROSS, probate paralegal and tax, real estate executive, consultant; b. Lebanon, Tenn., July 17, 1941; d. Carlie C. and Eva Lorene (Claywell) Cross; m. James D. Walker, Jan. 10, 1959 (div. Oct. 1966); children—James Scott Walker, Shari Lynne Schapson; m. Joseph B. Harris, Jan. 1, 1972 (div. Dec. 1980); 1 child, Brent Karsten L.; m. Orbin M. Howard, Feb. 5, 1983. Student Muncie Bus. Coll., 1964-65, Ball State U., 1965-67. Legal sec. Bingham, Summers, Welch & Spilmen, Indpls., 1969-72, Bose, McKinney, Evans, Indpls., 1976, Bowen, Cecere, O'Maley, Richmond, Ind., 1972-76; office mgr. Northwestern Mut. Life, Indpls., 1976-80; probate paralegal Campbell Kyle, Proffitt, Noblesville, Ind., 1980—; tax cons. in field. Mem. Ind. Paralegal Assn. (speaker, com. chmn. 1980-83, sec. 1983-84), Nat. Fed. Paralegal Assn. Democrat. Avocations: wood refinishing, boating, remodeling, snow skiing. Home: 207 Amhurst Circle Noblesville IN 46060 Office: Campbell Kyle Proffitt 198 S 9th St PO Box E Noblesville IN 46060

HOWARD, JENNIFER MAURY, management consultant; b. Montgomery, Ala., Mar. 18, 1951; s. Fontaine Maury and Janet Evelyn (Poole) Howard; m. Jonathan Alan Zimring, Oct. 6, 1979; 1 child, Maury Howard Zimring. Student Southwestern U., Memphis, 1969-70; B.A. in Psychology, U. Ala., 1972, M.A. in Clin. Psychology, 1974. Staff psychologist Indian Rivers Mental Health Ctr., Tuscaloosa, Ala., 1975-76, South Met. Children's Ctr., Atlanta, 1976-77; mgmt. cons. Behavioral Systems, Inc., Atlanta, 1977-79; v.p. Tarkenton and Co. Productivity Group, Atlanta, 1979-84; ptnr., v.p. L. M. Miller and Co., Atlanta, 1984—. Author: (with others) Teamwork: A Novel Learning Experience for Managers of Winning Teams, 1984. Bd. dirs Kutumi Sch., Atlanta, 1985. Mem. Atlanta Womens' Network, Am. Productivity Mgmt. Assn. Democrat. Methodist. Office: L M Miller & Co Perimeter Ridge 750 Hammond Dr Suite 100 Bldg 15 Atlanta GA 30328

HOWARD, JOANNE FRANCES, research analyst; b. St. Louis, Feb. 5, 1953; d. Frank Henry and Evelyn Julia (Haeckel) Spellazza; m. Claude Lorrain Howard, May 20, 1978. B.A., U. Mo.-St. Louis, 1975; M.S., Western Ill. U., 1976. Analyst, Streett Industries, Inc., St. Louis, 1977-78, research analyst Gallup & Robinson Co., Princeton, N.J., 1978-80, Jack Eckerd Corp., Clearwater, Fla., 1980-82, sr. research analyst, 1982—; cons. Anson Lee Rector Inc., Tarpon Springs, Fla., 1982-83, Med-Op Clinics, Tarpon Springs, Fla., 1983—. Editor monthly newsletter Florida West Coast chpt. Am. Mktg. Assn., 1982-83. Mem. Pinebrook Homeowners Assn., Largo, Fla., 1983-84. Mem. Am. Mktg. Assn. (past sec.-treas.). Democrat. Home: 7473 119th Ave N Largo FL 33543 Office: Jack Eckerd Corp PO Box 4689 Clearwater FL 33518

HOWARD, KATHLEEN, computer company executive; b. Norman, Okla., Nov. 3, 1947; d. Robert Adrian and Jane Elizabeth (Morgan) Howard; m. Lawrence W. Osgood, Aug. 10, 1968 (div. Sept. 1970); m. Norman Edlo Gibat, Oct. 15, 1971. Student U. Okla., 1966-68. Typesetter, Selenby Press, Norman, 1968-72; owner, pres. Noguska Industries, Fostoria, Ohio, 1973—; co-founder Home Wine Mchts., Chgo., 1976; cons. Bechtel Corp., Ann Arbor, Mich. and Gaithersburg, Md., 1980—; chairperson Am. Software Project, 1985. Co-author, illustrator: Lore of Still Building, 1972; co-author: Making Wine, Beer and Merry, 1973; also jours. and bus. mgmt. software. Recipient Disting. Service award Bechtel Corp., 1983; Founders award Home Wine and Beer Trade Assn., Chgo., 1976. Mem. Better Bus. Bur., Nat. Fedn. Ind. Bus., C. of C., Employer's Assn. Toledo, Altrusa Internat. (sec. Fostoria 1984-85). Avocations: painting, printing, travelling, reading. Home: 1030 Columbus Ave Fostoria OH 44830 Office: Noguska Industries 735-741 N Countyline Fostoria OH 44830

HOWARD, LINDA ANN, banker; b. Huntington, N.Y., June 6, 1953; d. Jack Francis and Catherine Dolores (Moon) Canino; m. William Harold Howard, Mar. 10, 1973. Student Suffolk County Community Coll., Selden, N.Y., 1971-72, L.I. U., 1977-80, SUNY-Westbury, 1986—. Teller, Chase Manhattan Bank, Great Neck, N.Y., 1972-74, gen. clk., teller, Douglaston, N.Y., 1974-78, platform asst., 1978, asst. mgr., Seaford, N.Y., 1978-79, br. mgr., asst. treas., Massapequa and West Islip, N.Y., 1979-85, 2d v.p., Melville, N.Y., 1985—. Treas., West Islip Mus., 1982-85; bd. dirs. West Islip Chamber Orch., 1982-85, Brentwood Family Health Ctr., N.Y., 1982-86; mem. 110/Action Bus. Assn., Melville, 1985—. Recipient Sr. Citizen Appreciation award Southside Hosp., Bayshore, N.Y., 1984, 85. Mem. Nat. Assn. Bank Women. Roman Catholic. Avocations: golf; gardening. Home: 20 Middleville Rd Northport NY 11768 Office: The Chase Manhattan Bank NA 135 Pinelawn Rd Melville NY 11747

HOWARD, LYNN MARSH, communications executive; b. Muskogee, Okla., Dec. 26, 1949; d. James B. Marsh and Marguerite H. Ross; student U. Okla., 1967-70; B.Ed. in Journalism, Northeastern State U., 1975; m. James K. Howard; 1 son, Marsh. Asst. women's editor Muskogee Phoenix, 1972-74; news editor Tahlequah (Okla.) Pictorial Press & Star-Citizen, 1976-80; mng. editor Tahlequah Daily Press, 1980-83; communications dir. Cherokee Nation of Okla., 1983—. Mem. Tahlequah Arts and Humanities Council, Fedn. Women Democrats; bd. dirs. Help in Crisis, Inc. Recipient H. & R. Block Public Service in Journalism award, 1973; 2d place award for feature Okla. Press Assn., 1981, 1st pl. typography, 1982. Mem. Tahlequah C. of C. Ambassadors (steering com. to revitalize bus. dist.), Okla. Press Assn., D.A.R., AAUW, Sigma Delta Chi, Delta Delta Delta. Episcopalian. Home: 714 Brentwood Dr Tahlequah OK 74464 Office: PO Box 948 Tahlequah OK 74465

HOWARD, MARGARET, lawyer, educator, consultant; b. Rocky Mount, N.C., Oct. 13, 1947; d. William Miller and Edith (Barnes) H. A.B., Duke U., 1969; M.S.W., Washington U., St. Louis, 1975, J.D., 1975; L.L.M., Yale U., 1981. Bar: Mo. 1975. Assoc. Lewis, Rice, Tucker, Allen & Chubb, St. Louis, 1975-77; asst. prof. law St. Louis U., 1977-80, assoc. prof. law, 1980-82; vis. assoc. prof. law Vanderbilt U., 1981-82, assoc. prof., 1982—; cons. Study Group on Internat. Adoption Minors, sec. State's Adv. Com. on Pvt. Internat. Law, Washington, 1983—. Contbr. articles to law publs. Recipient Breckenridge prize Washington U. Law Sch., 1975, Erna Arndt scholar, 1973-75. Mem. ABA, Mo. Bar Assn., Order Coif. Democrat. Methodist. 608 Kendall Dr Nashville TN 37209 Office: Vanderbilt U Law Sch Nashville TN 37240

HOWARD, MARGUERITE EVANGELINE BARKER, business executive, civic worker; b. Victoria, B.C., Can., July 30, 1921; d. Reuel Harold and Frances Penelope (Garnham) Barker; brought to U.S., 1924, naturalized, 1945; B.A., U. Wash., 1943; m. Joseph D. Howard, June 16, 1952; children—Wendy Doreen Frances, Bradford Reuel. Vice pres., dir. Howard Tours, Inc., Oakland, Calif., 1953—; co-owner, gen. mgr. Howard Travel Service, Oakland, Calif., 1956—, mng. dir. Howard Hall, Berkeley, Calif., 1964-74; co-owner, asst. mgr. Howard Investments, Oakland, 1960—; sec.-treas. Energy Dynamics, Inc. Bd. dirs. Piedmont council Campfire Girls, 1969-79, pres., 1974-79, nat. council, 1972-76, zone chmn., 1974-76, 77-83, nat. bd., 1976-83, bd. dirs. Alameda Contra Costa council, 1984—; bd. dirs. Oakland Symphony Guild, 1969—, pres., 1972-74; bd. dirs. Oakland Symphony Orch., 1972—, mem. exec. bd., 1972-74; 1st pres. East Oakland Inner Wheel, 1983-84. Recipient Wohelo Order, Campfire Girls, 1985. Mem. Oakland Mus. Assn., U. Wash. Alumni, East Bay Bot. and Zool. Soc., Am. Symphony Orch. League, Assn. Calif. Symphony Orchs., Young Audiences, Chi Omega Alumni Seattle, Chi Omega East Bay Alumni, Berkeley. Republican. Clubs: Womens University (Seattle); Women's Athletic (bd. dirs. 1986—) (Oakland). Home: 146 Bell Ave Piedmont CA 94611 Office: 526 Grand Ave Oakland CA 94610

HOWARD, MARILYN JOAN, advertising executive; b. N.Y.C., June 25, 1943; d. Edson John and Edna Emma (Witt) H.; m. Robert George Hammond, Jan. 17, 1976; children—Elizabeth, Kenneth. B.F.A., Syracuse U., 1964; postgrad. Sch. Visual Arts, 1965. Art dir. Grey Advt., N.Y.C., 1964-67, cons., 1967-68; founder, pres. Creative Freelancers, Inc., N.Y.C., 1969—. Mem. Advt. Women of N.Y., Am. Inst. Graphic Arts. Avocations: skiing; tennis. Home: 440 E 57th St New York NY 10022 Office: Creative Freelancers Inc 62 W 45th St New York NY 10036

HOWARD, MARY FRANCES, college administrator; b. Alton, Ill., Mar. 14, 1954; d. John Garfield and Frances Elnora (Banks) H.; B.A., U. Iowa, 1976, M.A., 1977. Research asst. spl. support services U. Iowa, Iowa City, 1976-77; asst. dir. developmental edn. U. Wis.-Oshkosh, 1978; dir. spl. services program, asst. dean services Coe Coll., Cedar Rapids, Iowa, 1978-84; assoc. dean students U.N.C.-Charlotte, 1984—. Mem. Cedar Rapids Civil Rights Commn.; mem. pres.'s council U. Iowa, 1983. Recipient Gwendolyn Brooks award, Alpha award, Penningroth award, J. Reed Delano award, Danforth award, Outstanding Young Profl. award Iowa Student Personnel Assn., Elliott Bryant award, Trio Achiever award Nat. Council Ednl. Opportunities Programs; named Outstanding Black Adminstr. Mem. Nat. Assn. Remedial and Spl. Programs in Postsecondary Edn., NAACP (past exec. bd.), Mid. Am. Assn. Ednl. Opportunity Program Personnel (pres. Iowa chpt. 1981-82, regional sec.), Am. Coll. Personnel Assn., Nat. Assn. Women Deans, Adminstrs. and Counselors, Assn. Black Women in Higher Edn., Iowa Student Personnel Assn., So. Assn. Coll. Student Affairs (editorial team jour.), Nat. Orientation Dirs. Assn., Nat. Assn. Student Personnel Adminstrs. (editorial team Coll. Affairs Jour.), Am. Assn. Counseling and Devel., AAUW, Charlotte Black Polit. Caucus, Women Adminstrs. in N.C. Higher Edn., Black Women's Civic Orgn. of Cedar Rapids, Delta Sigma Theta. Home: 4323 A Walker Rd Charlotte NC 28211 Office: UNCC Sta Charlotte NC 28223

HOWARD, PHYLLIS BERYL, former county commr.; b. Grand Rapids, Mich., Aug. 19, 1928; d. Cornielus George Swart and Helen Marie (Mullennix) Gleason; student public schs., Grand Rapids; m. Harvey W. Kelly, July 8, 1949 (dec.); m. 2d, James A. Yearnd, Mar. 14, 1964 (dec.); m. 3d, Joseph J. Howard, July 8, 1980 (dec. May 1981); children—Mary K. Kelly, Becky D. Kelly, Kimberly J. Yearnd. With Mich. Bell Telephone Co., Fremont, 1946-48, Gerber Products, Fremont, 1948-49; Newaygo County econ. investigator for Probate Ct. and Mich. Crippled Children Conveyor, 1956-58; partner Yearnd Funeral Home, Cadillac, Mich., 1964-79; Wexford County commr., 1975-80, vice chmn., 1977-80; chmn. 4-County Public Health Bd., 1979-80, 4-County Mental Health Bd., 1978-80, 7-County Substance Abuse Adv. Council, 1979-80; vice chmn. region 2, Mich. Assn. Counties, 1979-80; pres. Mich. Asso. Bd. Health, 1978-79; older workers community rep. N.W. Mich. Area Agy. on Aging, 1984—. Vol. coordinator Wexford County Dept. Social Services, 1982-83; mem. ch. council 1st Congregational Ch., Cadillac. Republican. Clubs: Cadillac Country, Women's Golf Assn.

HOWARD, REGINA V., county assessor; b. Louisville, Aug. 2, 1954; s. James G. and Virginia Jean (Hurlock) Holland; m. Michael A. Howard, Oct. 15, 1977 (div. 1984); 1 child, Stacy Lee; m. Larry Burrington, Nov. 28, 1985. B.S. in Math., Purdue U., 1976. With Hamilton County Surveyor's Office, Noblesville, Ind., 1972-75 (summers), dep. recorder Recorder's Office, 1976-78, county assessor, 1979—. Mem. Hamilton County Fed. Republican Women, 1976—. Mem. Ind. Assn. County Assessors. Home: 1143 Central Ave Noblesville IN 46060 Office: Hamilton County Assessor Court House Noblesville IN 46060

HOWARD, RUTH C., real estate broker; b. Shokan, N.Y., June 11, 1935; d. Hans J. and Hilde (Pfingst) Cohn; m. Morton Howard, Oct. 10, 1965 (div. 1977); 1 child, Mark S.; m. Thomas W. Slagle, Dec. 23, 1979. B.S., Columbia U., 1957. Free lance opera singer, 1957-72; dir. Info. and Referral Service, Abingdon, Va., 1976-77; realtor, owner Home Hunters III, Inc., Sarasota, Fla., 1980—. Mem. Sarasota Bd. Realtors (bd. dirs. 1984—, editor Newsreal mag. 1983—), Women's Council Realtors, Sarasota BBC. (bd. dirs. 1982—). Democrat. Jewish. Avocations: home remodeling, traveling. Home: 3137 Meyer Dr Sarasota FL 33579 Office: Home Hunters III Inc 3800 S Tamaimi Trail Suite 325 Sarasota FL 33579

HOWARD, SHARON JANEENE, lawyer; b. Ardmore, Okla., July 31, 1954; d. Eugene Francis and Wilma Louise (Smith) Howard. B.A. in Polit. Sci., U. Okla., 1976; J.D., 1981. Bar: Okla. 1982. Assoc. firm Linn & Helms, Oklahoma City, 1982—. Pres., Young Democrats Okla., 1975. Mem. ABA, Okla. Bar Assn., Oklahoma County Bar Assn., Nat. Assn. Female Execs., Phi Delta Phi. Home: 1914 Bar Dr Norman OK 73071 Office: Linn & Helms 400 Fidelity Plaza Oklahoma City OK 73102

HOWARD, SHIRLEY ANN, motel executive; b. Buffalo, July 10, 1936; d. Emil and Dorothy Louise (Osborne) Bohadlo; m. Merton Russell Howard, June 13, 1959; children—Roxanne Leslie, Lynn Rae. Student, Daemen Coll. Clk., typist Remington Rand, Buffalo, 1954-56, sec., 1956-58, supr., programmer, 1959-63; realtor Fred Koch, East Aurora, N.Y., 1967-75; owner, mgr. Aurora Motel, South Wales, N.Y., 1973—. Republican. Methodist. Club: Quota of East Aurora (v.p., bd. dirs.). Avocations: gardening; biking; walking; bowling; tennis. Office: The Aurora Motel 6421 Olean Rd South Wales NY 14139

HOWARD, SUSAN, actress; b. Marshall, Tex., Jan. 28; m. Calvin Cecil Chrane; 1 child, Lynn Elizabeth. Attended U. Tex.-Austin. TV films: Indict and Convict, 1974, Killer on Board, 1977, Superdome, 1978; appearances in various TV series; in series Petrocelli, 1974-76 (Emmy nomination for best supporting actress in drama series), Dallas, 1979—. Address: care Herb Tobias and Assocs Inc 1901 Ave of the Stars Suite 840 Los Angeles CA 90067*

HOWARD, VIRGINIA COLLINS, educational diagnostician; b. Dallas, Oct. 26, 1952; d. Maurice and Maudie B. (Jones) Collins; m. Lesley Gregory Howard, May 31, 1975; 1 child, Maury Sean. A.A., Mountain View Coll., 1973; B.S., Tex. Woman's U., 1975, M.Ed., 1980. Cert. counselor, Tex., diagnostician, Tex. Resource tchr. Irving Ind. Sch. Dist. (Tex.), 1975-80, lead resource tchr., 1981-86, diagnostician, 1986—; commencement speaker Mountain View Coll., Dallas, 1977. Mem. Assn. Profl. Educators, Alpha Kappa Alpha. Democrat. Mem. Ch. of Christ.

HOWATT, HELEN CLARE, library director; b. San Francisco, Apr. 5, 1927; d. Edward Bell and Helen Margaret (Kenney) H. B.A., Holy Name Coll., 1949; M.S. in Library Sci., U. So. Calif., 1972. Joined Order Sisters of the Holy Names, Roman Catholic Ch., 1945; cert. advanced studies Inst. Sch. Librarians, Our Lady of Lake U., San Antonio, 1966. Life teaching credential, life spl. services credential, Calif. Prin., St. Monica Sch., Santa Monica, Calif., 1957-60, St. Mary Sch., Los Angeles, 1960-63; tchr. jr. high sch. St. Augustine Sch., Oakland, Calif., 1964-69; tchr. jr. high math St. Monica Sch., San Francisco, 1969-71, St. Cecilia Sch., San Francisco, 1971-77; library dir. Holy Names Coll., Oakland, Calif., 1977—. Contbr. math. curriculum San Francisco Unified Sch. Dist., Cum Notis Variorum, publ. Music Library, U. Calif., Berkeley. NSF grantee, 1966; NDEA grantee, 1966. Mem. Cath. Library Assn. (chmn. No. Calif. elem. schs. 1971-72), Calif. Library Assn., ALA, Assn. Coll. and research Libraries. Home: 3500 Mountain Blvd Oakland CA 94619 Office: Holy Names Coll Library 3500 Mountain Blvd Oakland CA 94619

HOWE, DOROTHA ALMEDA, information and referral service executive; b. Jackson, Mich., Apr. 5, 1917; d. Frank Jonathon and Gertrude Alma (Saunt) Randall; 1 dau., Judith Ann Howe Klopfer. Diploma Jackson Bus. U., 1937; student Jackson Jr. Coll., U. Colo., U. Mich., U. Denver. Sales rep. Allstate Ins. Co., Jackson, Mich., 1941-42; sec., sales analyst, adminstrv. asst. Lederle Labs. div. Am. Cyanamid Co., Denver, 1946-72; owner Abortion Info. and Referral, Physician Info. and Referral Services, Denver, 1975—. Democrat. Unitarian Universalist. Club: Zonta (sec. 1951-70). Lodge: Order Eastern Star. Office: Profl Info and Referral Services Inc 1325 S Colorado Blvd Suite 408 Denver CO 80222

HOWE, MARIE ELIZABETH, state legislator; b. Somerville, Mass., June 13, 1944; d. William Andrew and Amelia Gertrude (McCauley) Howe; J.D., New Eng. Sch. of Law, 1969. Mem. Mass. Ho. of Reps., 1965—, asst. majority leader, 1973—. Mem. Somerville Sch. Com., 1965-68. Mem. Zonta. Home: 19 Pembroke St Somerville MA 02145 Office: State House Boston MA 02133

HOWE, PATRICIA MARY, investment banker; b. Chgo., Sept. 14, 1928; d. Harry Michael and Helen Mary (Maloney) Howe; student Barat Coll., Lake Forest, Ill., 1944-47, Goodman Theatre, Chgo., 1947; m. Ernest O. Ellison, Sept. 23, 1977. Instl. sales asst. Blyth & Co., 1954-55; with L.F. Rothschild & Co., 1957-82, mgr. San Francisco br., 1965-82, partner, 1968-82; pres. Ellmark Assocs., San Francisco, 1982—; chmn. Corp. Capital Investment Advisors, 1984—; mng. dir. Thrift Investment Services, 1984—; dir. Lear Siegler. Trustee U. San Diego, Women's Forum West. Mem. Securities Industry Assn., San Francisco Bond Club, Equestrian Order Holy Sepulchre, Opera Guild, San Francisco Symphony Found. Republican. Roman Catholic. Clubs: World Trade, Metropolitan, Bankers, Villa Taverna, Bankers (dir.), Bel Air Bay. Office: 550 Kearny St San Francisco CA 94108

HOWELL, DOROTHY COLVIN, home economist; b. Mansfield, La., June 17, 1922; d. Hardwick Joyner and Margeret Mellissa (Pickels) Colvin; B.S., La. State U., 1942; M.S., 1944; postgrad. Tex. Women's U., 1975; m. Sylvanus Thaddeus Howell, Jr., Apr. 10, 1945; children—Sylvanus Thaddeus III, Suzanne Antoinette. Research asst. La. Agr. Expt. Sta., Baton Rouge, 1944-45; tchr. home econs. Youree Drive Jr. High Sch., Shreveport, La., 1960-62; assoc. prof. foods and nutrition La. State U., Baton Rouge, 1962-84; freelance home economist, 1984—; asst. to dir. Sch. Home Econs., 1980-83. Recipient Service award La. State U. Alumni, 1975, Home Econs. Alumni award, 1983, also scholarships established in her honor. Mem. Coll. and Univ. Tchrs. of Food and Nutrition (pres. Tex., La. Ark. Okla. sect. 1980—), La. Home Econs. Assn. (pres. S. Central dist. 1979—), Am. Home Econs. Assn., PEO, Am. Bus. Women's Assn., DAR, Gamma Sigma Delta, Delta Kappa Gamma, Phi Upsilon Omicron, Phi Mu. Baptist. Author: (with others) Louisiana Tiger Bait, 1976. Home and Office: 877 Delgado Dr Baton Rouge LA 70808

HOWELL, HONOR SHARON, minister; b. Seguin, Tex, Oct. 12, 1947; d. Joe Milam and Mary Elizabeth (McKay) H. B.A., Austin Coll., 1970; M.Div., St. Paul Sch. Theology, 1973. Youth minister Key Meml. United Methodist Ch., Sherman, Tex., 1969-71, Second Presbyterian Ch., Kansas City, Mo., 1971-72; pastor Edwardsville United Meth. Ch., Kans., 1972-75; assoc. program dir. Council on Ministries, Topeka, 1975-80; v.p. St. Paul Sch. Theology, Kansas City, Mo., 1980-85; sr. pastor St. Mark United Meth. Ch., Overland Park, Kans., 1985—; pres. Commn. on Status and Role of Women in United Meth. Ch., Evanston, Ill., 1984—; chmn. personnel com. Council on Ministries, Topeka, Kans., 1984—. Mem. NOW, ACLU, Christian Educators Fellowship, Nat. Assn. Female Execs., Smithsonian Assocs., Internat. Assn. Women Ministers. Democrat. Home: 6600 Reeds Dr Mission KS 66202 Office: St Mark United Meth Ch 6422 Santa Fe Dr Overland Park KS 66202

HOWELL, JOY KAY, public relations consultant; b. Corpus Christi, Tex., Oct. 8, 1954; d. William Barnes and Orbyn Audrey (Smith) Howell. B.J., U. Tex.-Austin, 1976. Dir. pub. affairs Natural Gas Supply Assn., Washington, 1979-81; v.p., dir. media relations Hannaford Co., Inc., Washington, 1981-83; pres. Howell Communications, Washington, 1983—; instr. media and communication skills George Washington U., 1982-84. Mem. Women in Communications (D.C. chpt.), Nat. Assn. Female Execs. Democrat. Methodist. Home: 5130 Woodmire Ln Alexandria VA 22311 Office: Howell Communications 1140 19th St NW Suite 600 Washington DC 20036

HOWELL, MARIE LAUGHRIDGE, commercial printer; b. Marion, N.C., July 2, 1941; d. James Neil and Ernestine Mosley (Medlin) Laughridge; m. Frank Watson Howell, Jr., Dec. 20, 1958 (dec. Aug. 1978); children—Jennifer Marie, Barbara Leigh, Laurie Lynn. Student Western Carolina U., 1958, East Tenn. State U., 1959-60. Payroll clk. U. Miss., Iuka, 1960-61; exec. sec. SBA Promotions, Salisbury, N.C. 1968-71, Cooper Co., Salisbury, 1972-74; owner Marie's Print Shop, Salisbury, 1974—. Mem. Rowan County C. of C., Rowan County Merchants Assn. Democrat. Office: Marie's Print Shop PO Box 4307 124 N Church St Salisbury NC 28144

HOWELL, MARY LYNCH, diversified company executive; b. Springfield, Mass., July 10, 1952; d. Walter Edward and Mary Patricia (Landers) Lynch; m. John N. Howell, Oct. 27, 1980; 1 child, Patrick. B.A., U. Mass.; grad. advanced mgmt. program Harvard U. Dir. legis. affairs Health Industry Mfr.'s Assn., Washington; with Textron Inc., Washington, v.p. govt. affairs. Office: Textron Inc 1090 Vermont Ave NW Suite 1100 Washington DC 20005

HOWELL, WILMA JEAN, accountant; b. Sharp County, Ark., May 12, 1943; d. Raymond D. and Grace I. (Hughes) Carver; B.A. summa cum laude, Wichita State U., 1980; A.A., Butler County Community Coll., 1978; m. Kenneth Duane Howell, Aug. 26, 1961; children—Kenneth Dale, Kristopher Duane, Korey Dean. Sec., bookkeeper Durling-Richards Ins. Ajudsters, Wichita, Kans., 1961-62; staff acct. Alexander Grant and Co., El Dorado, Kans., 1980-85; individual practice acctg., Augusta, Kans., 1986—; instr. managerial acctg. Butler County Community Coll., 1981-83. C.P.A., Kans. Mem. Kansas Soc. C.P.A.s, Am. Inst. C.P.A.s, Beta Alpha Psi. Mem. Ch. of Christ. Home: Rural Route 1 Leon KS 67074 Office: 228 W Central St El Dorado KS 67042

HOWELLS, ELIZABETH JAEHNIG, public relations company executive; b. Hancock, Mich., June 8, 1928; d. Benjamin and Elizabeth (Campbell) Jaehnig; m. Robert E. Coulson, June 21, 1947; children—Steven E., David S., Elizabeth Coulson Jastrzebski; m. 2d Robert D. Howells, Aug. 12, 1972. Vice pres. Gerry J. Schnur Assocs., Chgo., 1966-70, Allen Rafalson & Assocs., Chgo., 1970-76; office mgr. Doremus & Co., Chgo., 1976-80, account supr., 1980-83, v.p., 1983—. Pres. Louisa May Alcott PTA, Chgo., 1962-64; bd. dirs., officer Park West Community Assn., Chgo., 1963-67; bd. dirs. Lincoln Park Conservation Assn., Chgo., 1967-70. Recipient Golden Trumpet, Publicity Club Chgo., 1981. Mem. Nat. Investor Relations Inst., Ill. Congress PTA (hon. life). Presbyterian. Home: 133 N Lombard Oak Park IL 60302 Office: Doremus & Co 500 N Michigan Ave Chicago IL 60611

HOWELLS, MURIEL GURDON SEABURY (MRS. WILLIAM WHITE HOWELLS), civic worker; b. White Plains, N.Y., May 3, 1910; d. William Marston and Katharine Emerson (Hovey) Seabury; student Chapin Sch., 1928; m. William White Howells, June 15, 1929; children—Muriel Gurdon Howells Metz, William Dean. Founder Brit. War Relief Soc., Madison, Wis., 1941, pres., 1941-43; apptd. visitor, dept. decorative arts and sculpture Boston Mus. Fine Arts, 1955-72, dept. Am. decorative arts, 1972—; ladies com. Inst. Contemporary Art, Boston, 1955-65, 67-68, asso., 1965-67; bd. dirs. Boston br. English-Speaking Union, 1955-80, v.p., 1973-74; a founder, trustee Strawbery Banke, Inc., Portsmouth, N.H., 1958-75, overseer, 1975-81, hon. overseer, 1981—; a founder, mem. steering com. Guild, 1959—; bd. dirs. Garden Club Am., 1959-62, nat. chmn. medal award com., 1962-65, judge flower arrangements; pres. Piscataqua Garden Club, 1952-54; mem. Harvard Solomon Islands Expdn., Malaita, 1968; chmn. Boston chpt. Venice Com., Internat. Fund for Monuments, 1970-71; vice chmn. Boston chpt. Save Venice Inc., 1971-77, mem. exec. com., 1971—. Recipient King's medal for Service in the Cause of Freedom (Britain), 1946; Historic Preservation award, zone 1 Garden Club Am., 1976. Mem. Nat. Soc. Colonial Dames N.H., Soc. Preservation New Eng. Antiquities (mem. Maine council 1976-78). Clubs: Women's Travel (pres. 1967-69), Chilton (Boston); Colony (N.Y.C.). Home: 274 Beacon St Boston MA 02116 also Kittery Point ME 03905

HOWES, PADDY (LILIAN B.) RUDD, writer/editor; b. Coventry, Eng., May 9, 1909; came to U.S., 1925, naturalized, 1941; d. John Alexander and Mary Elizabeth (Doherty) Rudd; student Liverpool Coll., Huyton, Eng., 1920-25; Oxford U., sr. sch. certificate, 1925; student U. Akron, 1934-35, U. Cin., 1941-42, Northwestern U., 1950; m. William R. Howes, Sept. 23, 1946. With Firestone Tire & Rubber Co., Akron, Ohio, 1926-36; sec. Children's Hosp. Research Found., Cin., 1936-42; sr. editor W.B. Saunders Co., Phila., 1942-46; fgn. corre. Country Gentleman Mag., Eng., 1946-48; manuscript editor Jour. Am. Dental Assn., Chgo., 1949-50, news editor, 1950-51; staff writer Survey of Med. Edn., Chgo., 1951-53; free lance writer, editor, publs. cons., Chgo., 1953-56, Phila., 1956-72, Harwich, Mass., 1972—. Bd. dirs. Cape Cod Family and Children's Service; corp. mem. bd. dirs. United Way of Cape Cod, 1978—; mem. Cape Cod Community Council, 1975—. Mem. Women in Communications (Chgo. chpt. pres. 1952-53 pres. Phila. chpt. 1962), Phila. Art Alliance, Asso. Country Women of World (life mem.; exec. com. 1946-48, press officer 1946). Writer-Collaborator Medical Schools in the United States at Mid-Century, 1953. Contbr. articles to mags., newspapers and profl. jours. Address: 17 Haromar Heath RFD 3 Harwich MA 02645

HOWINGTON, CAROLYN ANN, mfr.'s rep.; b. Wasco, Calif., Aug. 13, 1949; d. Calvin Verble and Pearline (Stutts) Worley; B.S. in Bus., N.E. La. State U., 1971; 1 son, Todd Eugene Howington. With Del-Tex Inc., Claremore, Okla., 1978-79, Oilfield Prodn. Equip., Kans., Okla., 1979-80; owner, pres. R & R Sales, Inc., Tulsa, 1981-83; mktg. rep. large scale computer systems Honeywell Info. Systems, 1983—. Mem. Nat. Assn. Female Execs., Okla. Minority Purchasing Council, NOW, Tulsa Theatre Drive. Republican. Presbyterian. Club: So. Hills Fitness Center. Home: 9732 Reeder Overland Park KS 66214 Office: PO Box 7809 Tulsa OK 74105

HOWITT, IDELLE ANNE, investment banker, lawyer; b. Providence, Dec. 4, 1949; d. Julius Harry and Shirley (Bertman) H. B.A., Boston U., 1971; J.D., Temple U., 1974; M.B.A., NYU, 1981. Bar: Pa. 1974, D.C. 1975, U.S. Supreme Ct. 1978, N.Y. 1983. Atty., Fed. Res. Bd., Washington, 1975-76; atty.-advisor U.S. Commn. on Civil Rights, Washington, 1976-79; mgr. pub. affairs Supermarkets Gen. Corp., Woodbridge, N.J., 1979-80; merger and acquisition assoc. Chase Manhattan Capital Markets Corp., N.Y.C., 1982-85; dir. bus. devel. and legal affairs Standard Research Cons., N.Y.C., 1985—; arbitrator Better Bus. Bur., N.Y.C., 1984. Bd. dirs. Mt. Vernon Coll. Sch. Bus., Washington, 1976-79. Recipient Silver Key award ABA, 1973. Mem. Women's Bar Assn. N.Y., Nat. Assn. Women Bus. Owners (dir. 1976-79).

HOWLAND, ANN, clin. psychologist; b. Cleve., Jan. 7, 1944; d. Richard Moulton and Natalie (Fuller) H.; stepfather—William F. Merrill, III; B.A., Goucher Coll., 1965; M.A., U. Fla., 1971, Ph.D., 1973; children—Andrea Merrill and Joshua Howland Sarver. VA trainee, 1971-72; treatment dir., therapy supr. Clin. Services Community Mental Health Clinic, Nelsonville, Ohio, 1973-75; pres. Athens (Ohio) Psychology Clinic, Inc., 1975-81; pres. Ann Howland, Ph.D. and Assos., Athens, 1981—; chief of staff psychology service O'Bleness Hosp., 1977-80; cons. W.Va. Head Start, 1975-78; instr. case mgmt. for mental health technicians Ohio U., 1975; cons. Athens County Probate Ct., 1975—; mem. Masters and Johnson Inst. Vol. Peace Corps, Colombia, S.A., 1966-68; active Athens Humane Soc., Animal Protection Inst., Save the Whales, Conservation of Endangered Species, NOW; bd. dirs. Ohio Hills Health Planning Agy. Mem. Am. Psychol. Assn., Ohio Psychol. Assn., Southeastern Ohio Psychol. Assn., Nat. Register Health Service Providers in Psychology, Nat. Acad. for Advancement Sci., Nat. Arbor Day Found., Common Cause, Ctr. for Environ. Edn., Nat. Audubon Soc., Greenpeace, Defenders of Wildlife, Am. Soc. for Prevention Cruelty to Animals. Club: Sawgrass (Fla.). Contbr. chpt. in book. Home and Office: Route 3 Box 163 Athens OH 45701

HOWLAND, BETTE, writer; b. Chgo., Jan. 28, 1937; d. Sam and Jessie (Berger) Sotonoff; m. Howard C. Howland (div.); children—Frank, Jacob. B.A., U. Chgo., 1955. Author: W-3, 1972; Blue in Chicago, 1978 (1st prize Friends of Am. Writers). Things to Come and Go, 1983. Fellow Rockefeller Found., 1969, Guggenheim Found., 1978, Nat. Endowment for the Arts, 1981, MacArthur Found., 1984. Jewish. Office: care Knopf Books 201 E 50th St New York NY 10022

HOWLAND, JUANITA MAE, fire protection equipment company official; b. Kirbyville, Mo., Sept. 7, 1929; d. Thomas Raymond and Ruth Marie (Rowley) Edwards; m. John David Howland, Mar. 24, 1949; children—Juanita Joan Howland Portier, John David, Jerri Ann. Various secretarial and office positions, 1947-72; adminstrv. asst. systems div. Edcor Safety Co., Kansas City, Mo., 1972-77; sales rep. B-H Electronics Co., Kansas City, Mo., 1977-78; pres. Able II Fire Protection Inc., Toledo, 1979—. Mem. Am. Bus. Women's Assn. (chpt. v.p. 1979-80, pres. 1981-82), Nat. Assn. Women in Constrn. (chpt. v.p. 1979-80), Toledo C. of C., Sylvania C. of C., Nat. Assn. Female Execs. (network dir.), Bus. and Profl. Women's Club. Methodist. Home: 7012 Orvieto Dr Sylvania OH 43560 Office: 709 S Bryne Rd Toledo OH 43609

HOWLE, JUDY DELINDA, broadcast official; b. Hartsville, S.C., May 28, 1951; d. James Joye and Lula (Hunter) Howle. B.A., U. S.C., 1973; postgrad. theology, Emory U., 1980-82. Adminstrv. asst. Cook, Ruef & Assocs., Columbia, S.C., 1975-77; program traffic mgr. Sta. WOLO-TV, Columbia, 1977-79; program ops. mgr. Turner Broadcasting System, Inc., Atlanta, 1979-82, media dir., 1982—. Republican. Presbyterian. Home: 2943 Appling Circle NE Atlanta GA 30341 Office: Turner Broadcasting System Inc 1050 Techwood Dr Atlanta GA 30318

HOWLETT, CAROLYN C., retired lawyer, civic worker; b. Millville, N.J., Aug. 28, 1915; d. R. Robinson and Carolyn Davidson (Abbott) Chance; m. Duncan Howlett, Apr. 26, 1943; children—Margaret (Mrs. Richard Spencer Hasty), Albert Duncan, Richard Chance, Carolyn Abbott (Mrs. Stephen Korth). Cert., Geneva Sch. Internat. Studies, Switzerland, 1934; A.B. magna cum laude, Mount Holyoke Coll., 1935; J.D., Yale U., 1938; L.H.D. (hon.) Meadville/Lombard Theol. Sch., Chgo., 1983. Bar: N.J. 1939, N.Y. 1942. Assoc., Kellogg & Chance, Jersey City, 1938-40, Hines, Rearick, Dorr & Hammond, N.Y.C., 1942-43; bd. dirs. Barney Neighborhood House, Washington, 1965-69, Western Maine Counseling Service, 1975-77, treas., 1976-77; treas. Lovell Library, Maine, 1981, pres., 1982—; bd. dirs. No. Cumberland Meml. Hosp., 1982—. Mem. LWV (bd. dirs. Boston chpt. 1953-57), Unitarian Universalist Women's Fedn. (bd. dirs. 1965-67, 2d v.p. 1967-69, treas. 1969-71), Unitarian Universalist Assn. (numerous coms., del.), Capital Area UN Assn. (bd. dirs. 1962-69), Leadership Conf. Civil Rights (bd. dirs. 1967-69), Washington Urban League (Service award 1967), Council Nat. Orgns. for Adult Edn., Internat. Assn. Liberal Religious Women (pres. 1969-78), Internat. Assn. Religious Freedom (exec. com. 1972-81, chmn. nominating com. 1974-75, pres. 1978-81, Outstanding Service award Am. chpt. 1980), Mt. Holyoke Coll. Alumnae Clubs (bd. dirs. Boston chpt. 1953-57, sec. Washington chpt. 1962-64, chmn. Maine Leadership fund drive 1975-78), Phi Beta Kappa. Home: RR1 Box 13 Center Lovell ME 04016

HOWLETT, PHYLLIS LOU, athletic conference administrator; b. Indianola, Iowa, Oct. 23, 1932; d. James Clarence and Mabel L. (Fisher) Hickman; m. Jerry H. Howlett, Jan. 2, 1955 (dec.); children—Timothy A., Jane A.; m. Ronlin Royer, Dec. 30, 1977. B.A., Simpson Coll., 1954. Psychometrist Drake U., Des Moines, 1956-57, asst. to men's athletic dir., 1974-79; asst. dir. athletics U. Kans., Lawrence, 1979-82; asst. commr. Big Ten Conf., Schaumburg, Ill., 1982—; mem. NCAA Football TV Com., 1980—, NCAA Women's Golf Com., 1983—. Chmn. Iowa Commn. Status of Women, 1976-79; pres. Vol. Bur. of Greater Des Moines, 1969-70, Arts and Recreation Council of Greater Des Moines, 1975, Iowa Children's and Family Services, 1973; nat. pres. Assn. Vol. Burs., Inc., 1972-73, service award. Recipient certs. of appreciation Des Moines C. of C., State of Iowa, Drake U. Mem. Nat. Assn. Dirs. of Collegiate Athletics, Council Collegiate Women Athletic Adminstrs. (bd. dirs.), Jr. League. Republican. Office: 1111 Plaza Dr Suite 600 Schaumburg IL 60195

HOWORTH, LUCY (SOMERVILLE), lawyer, international trade executive; b. Greenville, Miss., July 1, 1895; d. Robert and Nellie (Nugent) Somerville; A.B., Randolph-Macon Woman's Coll., 1916; postgrad. Columbia U., 1918; J.D. summa cum laude, U. Miss., 1922; m. Joseph Marion Howorth, Feb. 16, 1928. Asst. in psychology Randolph-Macon Woman's Coll., 1916-17; gauge insp. Allied Bur. Air Prodn., N.Y.C., 1918; indsl. research nat. bd. YWCA, 1919-20; admitted to Miss. bar, 1922; gen. practice Howorth & Howorth, Cleveland, Greenville, Jackson, Miss., 1922-34; U.S. commr. So. Jud. Dist. Miss., 1927-31; assoc. mem. Bd. Vet. Appeals, Washington, 1934-43; legis. atty. VA, 1943-49, v.p., dir. VA Employees Credit Union, 1937-49; assoc. gen. counsel War Claims Commn., 1949-52, dep. gen. counsel, 1952-53, gen. counsel, 1953-54; partner James Somerville & Assocs., overseas trade and devel., 1954-56; pvt. law practice, Cleveland, 1958—; atty. Commn. on Govt. Security, 1956-58; chmn. Miss. State Bd. Law Examiners, 1924-28; treas. com. for econ. survey, 1928-30; mem. Research Commn. Miss., 1930-34; mem. com. on fed. employment policies and practices Pres.'s Commn. on Status of Women, 1962-63; initiator oral history program Delta State U., 1973. Mem. Ho. of Reps., Miss. Legislature, Hinds County, 1932-36, chmn. com. public lands; keynote speaker White House Conf. on Women in Post-war Policy Making, 1944; at conf. on opening 81st Congress; mem. nat. bd. cons. Women's Archives, Radcliffe Coll.; mem. lay adv. com. study profl. nursing Carnegie Corp. N.Y., 1947-48; pres., trustee Monteagle Sunday Sch. Assembly, 1963—; dir. Monteagle Assembly Endowment Fund. Recipient Nellie Nugent Somerville award, 1975; Alumnae Achievement award Randolph Macon Woman's Coll., 1981; Lifetime Achievement award Radcliffe Coll., 1983; named Woman of Yr., Miss. State U., 1985. Mem. AAUW (nat. bd. dirs.; 2d. v.p., 1951-55, fellowship named in her honor 1973), Fed. Bar Assn., Nat. Assn. Women Lawyers, Am. Soc. Internat. Law (exec. council 1951-54), Am. Bar Assn., DAR, Daus. Am. Colonists, Am. Legion Aux. (past sec. Miss. dept.), Assembly Women's Orgns. for Nat. Security (chmn. 1951-52), Nat. Fedn. Bus. and Profl. Women's (nat. bd. dirs.; rep. Internat. Fedn., Trondheim, Norway, 1939; chmn. internat. conf., N.Y.C., 1946), Miss. Hist. Soc. (dir. 1982-85), Phi Beta Kappa, Pi Gamma Mu, Phi Delta Delta, Alpha Omicron Pi, Delta Kappa Gamma (hon.), Omicron Delta Kappa (hon., Wyman Founders award 1985), Phi Alpha Delta, Phi Kappa Phi (hon.). Democrat (del. nat. conv., 1932). Methodist. Clubs: Woman's Nat. Democratic; Soroptimist (Washington). Editor: (with W.M. Cash) Dear Nellie, the Civil War Letters of William L. Nugent, 1977; editor Fed. Bar Assn. News, 1944; assoc. editor Fed. Bar Assn. Jour., 1943-44. Contbr. articles to profl. jours. Address: 515 S Victoria Ave Cleveland MS 38732

HOWREN, LYDIA DELL, executive service company executive; b. Leesville, S.C., Dec. 26, 1944; d. Eligha Lutie and Dorothy D. (Hallman) Still; m. C. Gresham Howren, Oct. 31, 1963; children—Christopher Gresham, Desa Kathryne. Ed., Ga. State U., 1963-67. Mgr. br. office Adminstrn. Service Bur. Corp., Atlanta, 1963-69; pres., owner Howren Exec. Service, Inc., Atlanta, 1978—; adv. bd. Marietta-Cobb Vo-Tech, Marietta, Ga., 1982—. Sec. Republican Party Cobb County, Marietta, 1983-85; mem. Ga. Fedn. Rep. Women, Marietta, 1982—. Recipient Certs. of Merit, Service Bur. Corp., Atlanta, 1963-66; named New Jaycette of Yr., Jaycees of Smyrna, Ga., 1972. Mem. Ga. Secretarial Service Assn. (exec. com. 1979—), Nat. Assn. Secretarial Service, Cobb County C. of C. (outreach com. 1982—). Republican. Club: Atlanta Health and Racquet (Atlanta). Avocations: reading; sewing. Office: Howren Exec Services Inc 1800 Water Pl Suite 280 Atlanta GA 30339

HOWSON, AGNES WAGNER, nurse; b. Lebanon, Pa., May 9, 1940; d. Lester Frederick and Mary Elizabeth (Engle) Wagner; A.S., Becker Jr. Coll., 1960; A.A., Brookdale Community Coll., 1971, A.A.S., 1975, now student human services Edison State Coll.; m. Robert Douglas Howson, Mar. 25, 1961; children—R. Douglas, Geoffrey F., Eric M., Stephen M. Substitute sch. nurse Middletown (N.J.) Twp., 1976-82; staff nurse Riverview Hosp., Red Bank, N.J., 1977-78, 80-81; clinic supr., counselor Planned Parenthood of Monmouth County, Shrewsbury, N.J., 1978; staff nurse J.I.N.S. Shelter of Family & Children's Service of Monmouth County, Allenwood, N.J., 1979-80; office nurse Monmouth Pediatric Group, Red Bank, N.J., 1982; nurse, counselor Diet Inst., Matawan, N.J., 1982-83; staff community health nurse MCOSS Nursing Services, Red Bank, N.J., 1983—. Vice pres. PTA, River Plaza Sch., 1973-74; sec. High Sch. South Music Sponsors, 1979-80, parents council, 1978-79; bd. deacons Lincroft (N.J.) Presbyn. Ch., 1980-81. Registered nurse, N.J. Club: River Plaza Women's (treas. 1973-75). Home: 128 Bruce Rd Red Bank NJ 07701

HOWZE, KAREN AILEEN, newspaper editor; b. Detroit, Dec. 8, 1950; d. Manuel and Dorothy June (Smith) H. Student Madonna Coll., 1968-70; B.S., U. So. Calif., 1972; J.D., Hastings Coll. of Law, 1977. Reporter, San Francisco Chronicle, 1972-78; instr. Summer Program for Minority Journalist, U. Calif.-Berkeley, 1978; copy editor Newsday, Long Island, N.Y., 1978-79; asst. mng. editor The Times-Union, Rochester, N.Y., 1979-80; Sunday editor Democrat & Chronicle, Rochester, 1980-81; mng. editor systems USA Today, Arlington, VA., 1981—; prof. Howard U., Washington, 1982-83. Hon. chmn. Met. Washington Area Boys and Girls Clubs Awards; mem. task force on adoption D.C. Dept. Human Services, 1985. Mem. Nat. Assn. Black Journalists (regional dir., sec., parliamentarian 1976-83, bd. dirs. 1976-80), Women in Communications. Roman Catholic. Club: Nat. Press. Office: USA Today PO Box 500 Washington DC 20009

HOYLAND, JANET LOUISE, govt. ofcl.; b. Kansas City, Mo., July 21, 1940; d. Robert J. and Dora Louise (Worley) H.; B.A., Carleton Coll., 1962; postgrad. in music (Mu Phi Epsilon scholar 1966), U. Mo. at Kansas City, 1964-67; M.L.A., So. Meth. U., 1979. Policy writer Lynn Ins. Co., Kansas City, 1963-64; music librarian U. Mo. at Kansas City, 1966-68; benefit authorizer Social Security Adminstrn., Kansas City, Mo., 1969-75, tech. specialist, 1976-79, claims authorizer, 1980—; piano tchr. Leta Wallace Piano Studio, Kansas City, 1963, 68; piano accompanist Barn Players, Overland Park, Kans., 1972-75, Off Broadway Dinner Playhouse, Inc., Kansas City, 1973. Co-chmn. Project Equality work area, 1971; work area chmn. on ecumenism Council on Ministries, 1969-70; sec. fair housing action com. Council on Religion and Race, Kansas City, 1968; chmn. adminstrv. bd. Kairos United Meth. Ch., 1982; active ward and precinct work Democratic Com. for County Progress, 1968. Mem. Women's Div. Kansas City Philharmonic, Friends of Art Kansas City, Fellowship House Assn. Kansas City, Internat. Platform Assn., Kansas City Mus. Club (chmn. composition dept. 1967-68), Mu Phi Epsilon (v.p. Kansas City 1968, sec. 1971, pres. 1975-76), Pi Kappa Lambda. Home: 4322 Rockhill Rd Kansas City MO 64110

HOYLE, JOYCE BERG, airline sales executive; b. Chgo., July 1, 1937; d. Ole and Ovella (Proctor) Berg; m. Michael Gene Hoyle, May 31, 1958. Student W.Va. U., 1955; cert. Weaver Airline, Kansas City, 1957. Typist reservations The Greenbrier, White Sulphur Springs, W.Va., 1956-57; teletype operator Eastern Air Lines, Miami, Fla., Charlotte, N.C., 1957-72, agt. reservations and exec. sales, Charlotte, 1972—; pres. Eastern Teletype Operators Communications Workers Am., 1968-72. Co-chairwoman Ashley Dawn Wray Fund, Shelby, N.C., 1980; lobbyist Reyes Syndrome, 1980. Mem. Employee Involvement (chmn. task force 1984—, leader-facilitator tng. employee involvement 1984). Democrat. Presbyterian. Avocations: horticulture; swimming; skiing; golf; bees; fishing; teaching children to swim. Home: Route 2 Box 144 Cherryville NC 28021 Office: Eastern Air Lines 6010 Fairview Rd Charlotte NC 28210

HOYT, CHARLEE ILDORA, educator, consultant, former city official; b. Bluefield, W.Va., Mar. 21, 1936; d. Charles Ives Van Cleve and Kathryn Margarete (Harden) Perrow; m. Ronald Reiner Hoyt, Mar. 18, 1959 (div. Apr. 1983); children—Dean Christopher, Jason Allen. B.A. in Edn., U. Fla., 1959, M.Ed., 1962, postgrad., 1963-64. Cert. spl. edn. tchr. Tchr. Amherst County Schs., Elon, Va., 1958; tchr. spl. edn. Marion County Schs., Ocala, Fla., 1959-61; counselor Univ. Counseling Ctr., Gainesville, Fla., 1962-63, Sunland Tng. Ctr., Gainesville, 1963; mem. community faculty Minn. Met. State Coll., Mpls., 1972-83; mem. council City of Mpls., 1975-86; ptnr. Van Cleve Assocs., 1980—; mem. faculty Govt. Tng. Service, St. Paul, 1978—; pres. Minn. Women in City Govt., St. Paul, 1978-79; mem. Met. Land Use Adv. Bd., St. Paul, 1978-83; bd. dirs. Transp. Adv. Bd., St. Paul, 1979-81; mem. conf. faculty League of Minn. Cities, St. Paul, 1979-82; bd. dirs. Met. Council Criminal Justice Adv. Bd., St. Paul, 1979-82; pres. Women in Mcpl. Govt., Nat. League of Cities, Washington, 1980-81, founder minority caucus coalition, 1982, dir., 1982-84; curriculum cons. Nat. Women's Edn. Fund, Washington, trainer, 1982—. Presenter numerous workshops. Contbr. articles to profl. jours. Various offices with Republican Party, Minn., 1970—; pres. Burroughs Elem. Sch. PTA, Mpls., 1973-74; panelist White House Conf., 1981; chmn. Senator Durenburger's Task Force on Women's Issues, Mpls., 1981-84; bd. dirs. Nat. Conf. Rep. Mayors and Council Mems., 1984-85; mem. Senator Durenburger's Intergovtl. Relations Adv. Com., Mpls., 1984—; bd. dirs. Twin Cities Internat. Program, Mpls., 1983—; participant Women's Dialogue US/USSR, Moscow, 1985; trustee Council Internat. Programs, Cleve., 1985—; bd. dirs. At the Foot of the Mountain Theater, Mpls., 1985—; bd. dirs. GOP Feminists, Hamline U. Ctr. for Women in Govt.; mem. Nat. Women's Polit. Caucus, Hennepin County Women's Polit. Caucus. Mem. Minn. Women Elected Ofcls. (pres. 1983-85), Izaak Walton League. Methodist. Club: Remington Investment (pres. 1968-70)

(Mpls.). Avocations: lapidary; music; handwork; camping; gardening; science fiction. Home: 4921 Fremont Ave S Minneapolis MN 55409

HOYT, FRANCES WESTON, artist; b. Elizabeth, N.J., Nov. 15, 1908; d. Edward Faraday and Edith Ross (Parker) Weston; m. Malcolm Burrows Hoyt, June 1, 1944 (dec. Jan. 1984); children—Edith Hoyt Garrett, Edward Weston. Student Art Students League, N.Y.C., 1931-35. One-woman shows: Newark Art Club, 1942, Montclair Woman's Club (4), 1948-73, Pocono Lake Preserve, Pa., 1976; Montshire Mus., Hanover, N.H., 1986; exhibited in group shows: Nat. Arts Club, N.Y.C., 1943, Los Angeles Mus., 1946, Allied Artists Am., N.Y.C., 1980; represented in permanent collection: Bloomfield Art League N.J., Berkeley Sch., Bloomfield, N.J.; instr. Montclair Adult Sch., N.J., 1962-72; pvt. instr., N.Y.C., 1934-44. Recipient 1st prize Council Am. Artists Soc. N.Y.C., 1980. Fellow Am. Artists Profl. League (Gold medal Grand Nat. 1974); mem. Hudson Valley Art Assn. (bd. dirs. 1978—), Nat. Assn. Women Artists, Salmagundi, Acad. Artists Assn., Copley Soc. Boston.

HOYT, JANE KATHLEEN, television executive; b. Long Beach, Calif., Jan. 26, 1952; d. William Frances and Muriel Ann (Pennant) H.; m. Gary D. Daubert, Dec. 20, 1975. B.S. in Speech/Communications, Portland State U., 1975; student San Jose State U., 1971-72, U. So. Hampton-Eng., 1970-71. News reporter KOIN-AM & FM, Portland, Oreg., 1975-76; pub. affairs dir. KYTE-AM & FM, Portland, 1976-78; promotion dir. KEX-AM, Portland, 1979-80; creative services/promotion dir. KOIN-TV, Portland, 1980—; cons. Oreg. Health Div., 1984-85. Writer/producer 3 hr. spl. Barney's Farewell, 1979; editor, exec. producer TV features: Koin Capsules, 1984; writer producer, host talk show: Women's Viewpoint, 1976-79, Speaking of Everything, 1978. Promoter Loaves and Fishes, Portland, 1983-85; pub. relations advisor Gray Power, Portland, 1983-85; pub. relations bd. dirs. Oreg. Mus. Sci. and Industry, 1979; bd. dirs. The Dougy Ctr., 1985—. Recipient Award of Excellence, Am. Advt. Fedn., 1980, Portland Advt. Fedn., 1980, 81, 84, 85, Strathmore Graphics Gallery, 1980. Mem. Portland Advt. Fedn., Am. Fedn. TV and Radio Artists, Broadcast Promotion and Mktg. Execs., Portland C. of C. Roman Catholic. Avocations: reading; writing; acting; traveling; aerobics. Office: KOIN-TV 222 SW Columbia Ave Portland OR 97201

HOYT, MARCIA SWIGART, lawyer; b. Massillon, Ohio, Aug. 4, 1944; d. Robert William and Delores Jane (Swaney) Swigart; m. Kenneth Loyd Hoyt, Apr. 6, 1974. B.Ed., Ohio U., 1966, M.Ed., 1970; J.D., Ohio State U., 1979. Bar: Ohio 1979. Dir. Ohio State U., Columbus, 1970-76; assoc. firm Hahn, Loeser Freedheim, Dean & Wellman, Cleve., 1979-81; asst. counsel AmeriTrust Co., Cleve., 1981-84; atty. Roadway Services, Inc., Akron, Ohio, 1984-85; sole practice, Columbus, 1985—. Vice pres. Cleve. Independence Day Assn.; trustee Project Friendship, Inc., Cleve. Mem. ABA, Ohio Bar Assn., Bar Assn. Greater Cleve, Columbus Bar Assn. Republican. Lutheran. Home: 8345 Greyrocks Way Worthington OH 43085 Office: 51 N High St Suite 300 Columbus OH 43215

HOYTE, LENON HOLDER, curator; b. N.Y.C., July 4, 1905; d. Moses Emanuel and Rose Pari (Best) Holder; m. Lewis P Hoyte, Sept. 1, 1938. Diploma N.Y. Tng. Sch. for Tchrs., 1930; B.S. in Edn., CCNY, 1937, postgrad. to 1959; postgrad. Columbia U., 1937-40. Tchr., N.Y.C. Pub. Sch. Systems, 1930-70; established Aunt Len's Doll and Toy Mus., N.Y.C., 1970—; exhibited, lectr. Mus. Natural History, N.Y.; condr. workshop Workshop Center for Open Edn., CCNY. Recipient The Self Help Neighborhood Award, 1979-80; Awards in Black '72, 1972; award for Outstanding Contbns. in Black Culture, Kappa Sigma chpt. of Sigma Gamma Rho, 1981; Spl. Achievement award Harlem Week, 1982; others. Mem. Nat. Doll and Toy Collectors, Nat. Doll and Toy Collectors Club N.Y.C., United Fedn. Doll Clubs, Hamilton Terr. Block Assn., Upper Q Soc. Democrat. Episcopalian. Columnist: Doll News. Address: 6 Hamilton Ter New York NY 10031

HRANITZKY, JEANNE CROOKS, educator, consultant; b. New Rochelle, N.Y., Dec. 20, 1935; d. Henry Ervay and Irene Dorothy (McSherry) Crooks; m. Dennis Rogers Hranitzky, Dec. 19, 1959; children—Rachel, Dennis, Patrick. B.S., Midwestern U., Wichita Falls, Tex., 1957; postgrad. Yale U., 1959; M.Ed., Tex. Woman's U., 1979, Ph.D., 1981. Cert. elem., high sch., high sch. biology, elem. biology tchr., cert. in supervision, adminstrn. mid-mgmt., Tex. Research technologist S.W. Med. Sch., Dallas, 1957-58; tchr. biology Highland Park High Sch., Dallas, 1958-62; asst. prof. spl. edn., chmn. gifted edn. com. Tex. Woman's U., Denton, 1981—, cons. gifted edn., learning and problem solving; mem. ad hoc com. gifted and talented edn. Tex. State Bd. Edn.; evaluator various sch. dist. gifted programs; coordinator Tex. Woman's U. Young People's U., 1981; cons., instr. gifted and talented workshop Tex. Christian U., 1981; dir. Univ. Interscholastic League Sci. Competition, 4A Schs., Region XI, Tex., 1982. Trustee, Grapevine-Colleyville Ind. Sch. Dist. (Tex.), 1978—, v.p., 1982. NSF scholar Yale U., 1958, So. Meth. U., 1959. Mem. Tex. Assn. Gifted and Talented (dir.), Nat. Assn. Gifted and Talented, Nat. Assn. Sch. Bds., Tex. Assn. Sch. Bds., Pi Lambda Theta, Phi Delta Kappa, Beta Beta Beta, Alpha Psi Omega. Republican. Presbyterian. Office: Tex Woman's U Dept Spl Edn PO Box 23029 Denton TX 76051

HRINKO, JEAN AYR, retired educator; b. Goes, Ohio, Mar. 20 1923; married, 1 child. B.S. in Elementary Edn., Wittenberg Coll., Springfield, Ohio, 1968; postgrad. in spl. edn. U. Dayton, Kent (Ohio) State U. Cert. learning disabilities and exceptional children. Tchr., Mad-River Green Sch., Enon, Ohio, 1964-68; tchr. Springfield Pub. Sch., 1968-84; mem. Ohio Low Incidence Curriculum Com. Vol. info. desk Mercy and Community hosps., also St. John's Convalescent Home, Springfield. Mem. Civic Opera Guild, 1974—. Mem. NEA, Ohio Edn. Assn., Springfield Tchrs. Assn. Ohio Deaf Tchrs. Assn., Quota Internat. for Deaf, Theta Phi Gamma, Alpha Iota. Jennings scholar, 1970-71; named Tchr. of Yr., Springfield Pub. Schs., 1982. Cert. tchr., Ohio; specialist in field of hearing impaired, educable mentally retarded. Home: 3641 Troy Rd Springfield OH 45504 Office: 1600 N Limestone St Springfield OH 45502

HROMADKA, PAMELA J., corrections administrator; b. Friend, Nebr., Nov. 23, 1948; d. Frank and Elsie Mae (Stetina) Hromadka. B.S., U. Nebr., 1971, M.A., 1977; postgrad. U. S.C., 1981, U. Pa., 1980, Kearney State Coll., 1980. Tchr. home econs. Republican Valley Sch., Indianola, Nebr., 1971-72; social services worker York County div. Pub. Welfare, York, Nebr., 1972-73; social services worker Saunders County div. Pub. Welfare, Wahoo, Nebr, 1974; with Nebr. Ctr. for Women, York, 1974—, counselor, 1975-77, adminstrv. asst., 1977—; beauty cons. Mary Kay Cosmetics. Vol. York Community Theatre, 1980—. Mem. Nebr. Corrections Assn. (sec., conf. chmn.), U.Nebr. Alumni Assn., Am. Corrections Assn., Bus. and Profl. Women of York, LWV, Western Bohemian Fraternal Assn., York Home Econs. Club, Greater York Women's Council (sec. 1984—). Republican. Roman Catholic. Club: Toastmaster (sec. 1983-84). Avocations: reading; travel; horticulture. Home: 1208 Kiplinger Ave York NE 68467 Office: Nebr Ctr for Women Rural Route 1 Box 33 York NE 68467

HRONCICH, DIANE LUCILLE, nurse; b. Astoria, N.Y., Dec. 16, 1961; d. John and Marie Josephine (LeFace) H. B.S. in Nursing, Adelphi U., 1983. R.N., N.Y. Postgrad., Brookhaven Meml. Hosp., Patchogue, N.Y., 1983; nurse Upjohn Health Care, Hauppauge, N.Y., 1984—, U. Hosp. Stony Brook, 1984—. Roman Catholic.

HROVAT, VICKIE LYNN, computer pogrammer, analyst, speech therapist; b. Iowa City, Apr. 4, 1954; d. Marvin Lloyd and Dorothy (Whitmer) Beaver; m. Dale Michael Hrovat, Dec. 22, 1978; Student U. Nebr.-Lincoln, 1972-74; B.S., Ariz. State U., 1977, M.S., 1978; cert. Data Processing N. Am. Coll. Data Processing, 1983. Speech therapist Gilbert Pub. Schs., Ariz., 1978-79, Mesa Pub. Schs., Ariz., 1979-83; programmer analyst Motorola, Inc., Scottsdale, Ariz., 1983—. Named Woman of Year Iowa Bar Assn., 1972. Office: Motorola 8201 E McDowell Rd Scottsdale AZ

HRUBEC, JANE M., advertising executive; b. N.Y.C., Sept. 20, 1942; d. A. Andrew and Beatrice (Gaines) H. B.A., Briarcliff Coll., 1963. Copywriter, DeGarmo-McCaffery, Inc., 1966-69, Foote-Cone-Belding, Inc., 1969-71; copy supr. Ted Bates, Inc., 1971-73; assoc. creative dir. Ogilvy & Mather, N.Y.C., 1973—; conf. speaker Woman Bus. Owners N.Y., Inc., N.Y.C., 1983-84. Contbr. articles to mags. Bd. dirs. Friends of Parks, Chgo., 1976-79. Recipient Gold Medal award Art Dirs. Club, 1980, Silver award Internat. Radio's TV Festival, 1981, Gold and bronze, 1984; Adweek All-Am. Creative Team award, 1983 Clio Best Regional Campaign, 1984, Big Apple Best Humor Radio, 1984, Big Apple Best Music Radio, 1984. Democrat. Presbyterian. Home: 23 E 81st St New York NY 10028 Office: Ogilvy Mather 2 E 48th St New York NY 10017

HSU, HSIU-HSIANG, librarian; b. Taiwan, Republic of China, Jan. 2, 1938; came to U.S., 1965; d. A-hsien and An-mei (Lee) Wu; m. Chun-Fang Hsu, June 1, 1968; 1 son, Bruce. Diploma, Taiwan Norman U., Taipei, 1961; M.L.S., Villanova (Pa.) U., 1967; postgrad. Rutgers U., 1978, 82, Stockton Coll., 1982. Cert. profl. librarian N.J. Tchr. schs. Taiwan, 1956-65; student helper Drexel U., Phila., 1966-67; jr. librarian Cape May County Library, Cape May, N.J., 1967-74; supr. librarians 1975—, head tech. services, 1970—, network contact rep., 1983—. Mem. ALA, N.J. Library Assn.

HUANG, THERESA C., librarian; b. Nanking, China; m. Theodore S. Huang, Dec. 25, 1959. B.A., Nat. Taiwan U., 1955; M.S. in L.S., Syracuse U., 1958. Cataloger, Harvard U., Cambridge, Mass., 1958-60; with Bklyn. Pub. Library, 1960-78, regional librarian, 1978—. Joint compiler bibliography: Asia: A Guide to Books for Children, 1966; Nuclear Awareness, 1983; The U.S.A. through Children's Books, 1986. Mem. ALA, Assn. Library Service to Children, Pub. Library Assn., Chinese Am. Librarians Assn., Asia Pacific Am. Librarians Assn. Office: Brooklyn Pub Library 240 Division Ave Brooklyn NY 11211

HUBATCH, CONSTANCE JEAN, nurse; b. Janesville, Wis., May 17, 1936; d. Lawrence Hugo and Grace Elizabeth (Corts) Bruxer; m. James Edward Hubatch, Feb. 15, 1958; children—Kathie, David, Karen. R.N. diploma in nursing St. Mary's Sch. Nursing; B.S. summa cum laude in Nursing, Mt. Senario Coll., 1985. Staff nurse Langlade Meml. Hosp., Antigo, Wis., 1957-74, acting dir. nursing, 1978, evening supr., 1974-75, obstetrics supr., 1975-80, nurse primary care 1980—; ind. contractor Bodimetric Profiles Milw., Antigo, 1985—. Orgnl. leader Wislango Riders 4-H Club, Langlade County, Wis., 1983—, activity leader, 1969-83; flute player Antigo Community Band, 1976—. Mem. Am. Fedn. Nurses Health Profls. (sec. 1982-83, chmn. negotiations 1983-85 Local 5033), Firefighters Aux. (sec. 1974-78). Roman Catholic. Avocations: antiques; flute; horses. Home: W10475 County G Antigo WI 54409 Office: Langlade Meml Hosp E 5th Ave Antigo WI 54409

HUBBARD, ANNETTE M., nurse, counselor, psychologist; b. Blakely, Ga., June 19, 1934; d. Willie S. Hubbard and Senella E. (Wiggins) Pittman. Diploma in nursing Grady Meml. Hosp., Atlanta, 1955; B.S. in Nursing, Seton Hall U., 1965; M.A. in Guidance and Counseling, Jersey City State Coll., 1977. Cert. sch. psychologist. Staff nurse Pheobe Putney Hosp., Albany, Ga., 1955; charge nurse United Hosp. Med. Ctr., Newark, 1955-62, head nurse, 1962-71, supr., 1971-78, patient care coordinator, 1978—; cons. Sarcoidosis Found., Newark, 1985—; pvt. and orgnl. counselor. Mem. N.J. Women for Rainbow Coalition, Newark, 1984. Recipient Community Service award Roseville Coalition, Newark, 1984, Big Heart award Newark Anti-Hypertension Program, 1984; named to Women in Bethune Tradition, Nat. Council Negro Women, 1985. Mem. Concerned Black Nurses of Newark (founder, pres. 1978-82, v.p. 1974-78, advisor 1982), Am. Nurses Assn., Grady Nurses Conclave (alumni), Nat. Black Nurses Assn. Inc., Nat. Council Negro Women (bd. dirs. 1980—). Avocations: cooking; running; music. Home: 403 Stockton Ave Roselle NJ 07203 Office: United Hosps Med Ctr 15 S 9th St Newark NJ 07107

HUBBARD, ELIZABETH LOUISE, lawyer; b. Springfield, Ill., Mar. 10, 1949; d. Glenn Wellington and Elizabeth (Frederick) H.; m. A. Jeffrey Seidman, Oct. 27, 1974 (div. May 1982). Student Millikin U., 1967-69; B.A., U. Ky., 1971; J.D. with honors, Ill. Inst. Tech.-Chgo. Kent Coll. Law, 1974. Bar: Ill. 1974, U.S. Dist. Ct. (no. dist.) Ill. 1974, U.S. Ct. Appeals (7th cir.) 1976, U.S. Supreme Ct. 1984. Atty. Wyatt Co., Chgo., 1974-75, Gertz & Giampietro, Chgo., 1975-76, Baum, Sigman, Gold, Chgo., 1976-81, Elizabeth Hubbard, Ltd., Chgo., 1981—; legal counsel NOW, Chgo., 1978—, sec., 1977. Editor Chgo. Kent Law Rev., 1970. Bd. dirs., mem. The Remains Theatre, 1985—. Mem. Chgo. Bar Assn. (fed. civil procedure com.), Ill. State Bar Assn., Women's Bar Assn. Democrat. Office: 55 E Monroe Chicago IL 60603

HUBBARD, GERALDINE, wholesale drug company executive; b. Iola, Kans., July 30, 1932; d. James Clinton Nix and Esther Geraldine (Grindle) Wilson; m. Murray Dean, June 8, 1952 (div. May 1984); children—Kathy Johnson, Dan Hubbard, Cindy Hansen, Karen Bond, Monte Hubbard. A.A., Graceland Coll., 1952. Dir., owner Lazy H Kid's Ranch, Woodbine, Iowa, 1963-78; sales mgr., co-owner Apothecary, Inc., Woodbine, Iowa, 1979-84, pres., owner, 1984—. Author, editor: (poetry) Going Home, 1983; editor: Cooking with Beef, 1980. Sec. treas. Harrison County Cowbelles, 1979-81; sec. women's dept. Reorganized Ch. Jesus Christ Latter-day Saints, 1975-78, pres., 1972-73; reporter Am. Agrl. Movement, 1975—. Mem. Nat. Pharm. Alliance Generic Group (sec. 1984—). Democrat. Avocations: gardening; piano/organ; tennis; golf; horses; writing. Home: RR 2 Woodbine IA 51579 Office: Apothecary Inc RR 2 Woodbine IA 51579

HUBBARD, GLORIA KENDRICK, mfg. co. exec., advt. co. exec.; b. Folkston, Ga., Sept. 24, 1939; d. Grover Lee and Mildred Elizabeth (Wildes) Kendrick; A.B., Jacksonville U., 1959; B.S., Fla. State U., 1961; m. Samuel Walter Hubbard, Jr., June 10, 1967 (dec. 1976); children—Samuel Walter, Whitney Alexander. Vice-pres., Hubbard Co., Atlanta, 1977—; pres. J & J Advt., Inc., Atlanta, 1980—. Republican. Methodist. Office: 7N319A 250 Spring St Atlanta GA 30303

HUBBARD, MARSHA ANN, state government administrator; b. Utica, N.Y., June 28, 1947; d. John Field and Sally (Sinnott) H. Student Webster Coll., St. Louis, 1965-69, George Washington U., 1970-71, St. Louis U., 1972-73. Legis. asst. Congressman James Symington, Washington, 1969-72, Congresswoman Bella Abzug, Washington, 1973-74; adminstrv. asst. Senator Genie Chance, Alaska, 1974-76; budget analyst Health and Social Services, Juneau, Alaska, 1976-78; dir. mgmt. and budget, 1979-83, dir. budget and fin., 1983-84; mgr. lease processing U.S. Leasing Corp., San Francisco, 1979; spl. asst. Office of Gov. of Juneau, 1984-85; dep. commr. Alaska Dept. Adminstrn., Juneau, 1985—; commr. Medicaid Rate Commn., Juneau 1983-85; mem. Longevity Bonus Task Force, Juneau, 1984-85. Chmn. Women's Caucus-Alaska State Democratic Party, 1984—; mem. Women's Lobby, Alaska. Roman Catholic. Club: Juneau Golf and Country (bd. dirs. 1982). Home: 6737 Marquarite Juneau AK 99801 Office: Dept Commr PO Box C-0200 Juneau AK 99811

HUBBARD, ROWENA MCLEAN, consumer publicity agency executive; b. Winnipeg, Man., Can., July 7, 1935; came to U.S., 1953; d. Sydney Langille and Katherine (Meckling) McLean; m. George Marks, Dec. 28, 1962 (div. 1970); m. 2d, Scott Hubbard, June 30, 1972. B.Sc. in Home Econs., U. Man., Winnipeg, 1956; registered dietitian Mayo Clinic, 1957; postgrad. program for mgmt. devel. Sch. Bus., Harvard U., 1977. Adminstrv. dietitian Harriman Clinic, Long Beach, Calif., 1957-58; dist. home economist So. Calif. Edison Co., Santa Barbara, 1958-60; mgr. home econs. Spice Islands Co., San Francisco, 1961-70; dir. consumer affairs Castle & Cooke, San Francisco, 1970-80; cons., Portland, Oreg., 1980-82; mng. ptnr. Anderson/Miller & Hubbard, San Francisco, 1982—. Author: (cookbooks) California Cooks, 1970; The Thatched Kitchen, 1972; International Dining with Spice Islands, 1963. Recipient Rose award Seventeen mag., 1968; Time-Life Meals in Minutes—Eggs, Omelets and Souffles, 1983. Mem. Am. Dietetic Assn., Am. Home Econs. Assn., Soc. Nutrition Educators (dir. 1980-82). Republican. Office: Anderson Miller & Hubbard 846 California St San Francisco CA 94108

HUBER, CHERYL KATHLEEN, personnel/safety executive; b. Phila., Sept. 20, 1953; d. Elvin Arthur and Patricia Joan (Henry) Beyers; m. Dennis Joseph Huber, May 30, 1981; 1 child, Matthew Allen. Student Southwest Minn. State Coll., 1973; B.S. in Home Econs., S.D. State U., 1975. Housewares mgr. M & M Distbg. Co., Pipestone, Minn., 1975-77; customer service rep. Harker's Wholesale Meats, LeMars, Iowa, 1977-79; personnel dir. Ethyl-VisQueen, Manchester, Iowa, 1979—. Pres. Indsl. Relations Com., Manchester, Iowa, 1982-83. Mem. Delaware County Sheep Producers, NOW, Phi Kappa Delta, Phi Upsilon Omicron. Club: Mensa. Avocations: gourmet cooking; carpentry; horseback riding; water skiing; reading. Home: RR 2 Box 267 Manchester IA 52057 Office: Ethyl Corp VisQueen div Old Hwy 13S Manchester IA 52057

HUBER, JANET CLAIRE, publishing company executive; b. Indpls., Dec. 8, 1940; d. Charles Clark and Betty Ellen (Buser) McDermott; m. Eugene F. Huber II, May 16, 1964 (div. 1980); children—Christina A., Eugene F. III. A.A., Glendale Coll., 1960; B.S., UCLA, 1963; postgrad. Calif. State U., 1978. Cert. assn. exec. Dir., pres. Buena Park Parent Participation Nursery Sch., Buena Park, Calif., 1972-76; early childhood edn. dir., coordinator Centralia Sch. Dist., Buena Park, 1975-78; dir. membership Los Angeles County Med. Assn., Los Angeles, 1978-85; dir. membership, cons. Los Angeles Found. for Med. Care, 1985-86; assoc. pub. Universal Directory Pub. Corp., Buena Park, Calif., 1986—; lectr. Am. Soc. of Assn. Execs. Rep. Centralia Sch. Dist. Sch. Bd., Buena Park, 1977-78. Mem. Am. Assn. Med. Soc. Execs., Nat. Assn. Female Execs., AAUW (treas. 1972). Democrat. Roman Catholic. Home: 8810 Pierce Dr Buena Park CA 90620 Office: Universal Directory Pub Corp 6571 Altura Blvd Buena Park CA 90620

HUBER, JOAN ALTHAUS, university dean, sociology educator; b. Bluffton, Ohio, Oct. 17, 1925; d. Lawrence and Hallie (Althaus) H.; B.A., Pa. State U., 1945; M.A., Western Mich. U., 1963; Ph.D., Mich. State U., 1967; m. William Form, Feb. 2, 1971; children—Nancy Rytina. Steven Rytina. Asst. vis. prof., asst. prof. U. Notre Dame (Ind.), 1969-71; asst. prof. U. Ill., Urbana-Champaign, 1971-73, assoc. prof., 1973-78, prof., 1978—, head dept. sociology, 1979-83; dean Coll. Social and Behavioral Sci., Ohio State U., 1984—. NSF research grantee, 1978-81. Mem. Am. Sociol. Assn. (council 1975-78, v.p. 1980-83), Population Assn. Am. Author: (with W. Form) Income and Ideology, 1973; (with Paul Chalfant) Sociology of American Poverty, 1974; editor: Changing Women in a Changing Society, 1973; (with G. Spitze) Sex Stratification: Children, Housework, and Jobs, 1983. Home: 1439 London Dr Columbus OH 43221 Office: Coll Social and Behavioral Sci 164 W 17th Ave Ohio State U Columbus OH 43210

HUBER, JOAN MARIE, nurse, naval officer; b. Boston, Sept. 15, 1951; d. Fred Robert and Catherine Mary (Donovan) Huber; B.S. in Nursing, Villanova U., 1973; M.S. in Nursing, U. Calif.-San Francisco, 1982. Commd. in USN, 1971, advanced through grades to lt. comdr., 1980; staff nurse surg. ICU, Naval Regional Med. Center, Phila., 1973-76; head nurse critical care areas Naval Submarine Med. Center, Groton, Conn., 1976-78; head nurse surg. ICU, Naval Regional Med. Center, Okinawa, Japan, 1978-80; head nurse surg. unit Naval Regional Med. Center, Gt. Lakes, Ill., 1982-83; head quality assurance dept. Naval Med. Command, Northeast Region, Gt. Lakes, 1983-86, White House Med. Unit, 1986—. Decorated Navy Commendation medal, Nat. Def. Service medal, Meritorious Service medal. Mem. Am. Assn. Critical Care Nurses, Assn. Mil. Surgeons U.S., Nat. League Nursing, Am. Nurses Assn., Am. Assn. Nephrology Nurses and Technicians, Bus. and Profl. Womens Club (named Groton Young Career Woman of Yr. 1978), Sigma Theta Tau. Roman Catholic. Home: 12944 Tourmaline Terr Silver Spring MD 20904 Office: White House Washington DC 20500

HUBER, MARGARET ANN, college president; b. Rochester, Pa., July 27, 1949; d. Francis Xavier and Mary Ann (Socash) H. B.S. in Chemistry, Duquesne U., 1972; M.S.A., U. Notre Dame, 1975; Ph.D., U. Mich., 1979. Joined Sisters of Divine Providence of Pittsburgh, Pa.; jr. high tchr. St. Martin Sch., Pitts., 1971-72; asst. to acad. dean LaRoche Coll., Pitts., 1972-75; research assoc. U. Mich., Ann Arbor, 1978; dir. planning LaRoche Coll., 1978-80, exec. v.p., 1980-81, pres., 1981—. Mem. Am. Assn. for Higher Edn. Democrat. Roman Catholic. Office: LaRoche Coll 9000 Babcock Blvd Pittsburgh PA 15237

HUBER, PAULA ELESE, manufacturing company executive; b. Nampa, Idaho, July 18, 1938; d. William Clarence and Natalie (Pascoe) Towery; m. Don M. Huber, Feb. 19, 1959; children—Brenda, Joyce, Aaron, Louise, Lynette, Sharon, Sarah, Elese, Natalie, Kevin, Derek. Student U. Idaho, 1957-59, Mich. State U., 1959-60. Cons., DecaH Mfg., West Point, Ind., 1978-80, mgr. 1980-83, v.p., 1983—. Inventor in field., 1980. Pres., Relief Soc. Orgn., Moscow, Idaho, 1969-71; co chmn. Parents Adv. Com. TSC Sch. Corp., Lafayette, Ind., 1983—. Mormon. Avocations: swimming; reading; sports; sewing. Office: DecaH Mfg Route 1 Box 42H West Point IN 47992

HUBER, RITA NORMA, civic worker; b. Cin., July 16, 1931; d. Andrew Elwood and Mary Gertrude (Hille) Stewart; student Cin. Coll. Conservatory Music, 1949-50, Berlitz Sch., Cin., 1951-52; m. Justin G. Huber, July 17, 1954; children—Monica Ann, Sarah Marie, Rachel Miriam. Tchr. Russian lang. for officers' wives Ft. Sill, Okla., 1955-56; bd. dirs. United Community Services, Cedar Rapids, Iowa, 1969; founder, chairperson Linn County Consumers League, 1969-70; founder, public relations dir. Cedar Rapids Rape Crisis Services, 1974 ; owner/operator Hurber Janitorial Services; chairperson Linn County Democratic Womens Club, 1966-67, Linn County Com., Eugene McCarthy for Pres., 1967-68; campaign mgr. Delores Cortez for Iowa Legislature, 1968, Jan V. Johnson for Iowa Legislature, 1970, Stanley Ginsberg for county supr. Linn County, 1974, E.L. Colton for Cedar Rapids pub. safety commr., 1977; chairperson Linn County Dem. Central Com., 1976-77; state coordinator Jerry Brown for Pres., 1976; chairperson Pat Kane for Linn County Recorder, 1982; mem. Iowa and Nat. Women's Polit. Caucus; chmn. Linn County Bd. Health; instr. parliamentary procedures Cedar Rapids Women's Community Leadership Inst., 1975-77; lectr. local colls. and service orgns.; tchr. conversational Russian, Pierce Elementary Sch., Cedar Rapids, 1976; instr. Russian, Community Edn. div. Kirkwood Community Coll. Mem. Am. Inst. Parliamentarians. Roman Catholic (extraordinary minister of Eucharist). Composer: She is Risen, 1973. Home: 2050 Glass Rd NE Cedar Rapids IA 52402

HUBER, SISTER MARGARET, college president. Pres. La Roche Coll., Pitts. Office: La Roche Coll 9000 Babcock Blvd Pittsburgh PA 15237*

HUBER-LORE, DOLORES, nurse; b. Oceanside, N.Y., Sept. 23, 1953; d. Howard and Helen (Heu) Huber; m. Joseph A. Lore, Sept. 14, 1975; children—Erick, Jillian. Lic. practical nurse cert. Glen Cove Community Hosp. (N.Y.), 1974; A.A.S., R.N., diploma, SUNY-Albany, 1978. Staff lic. practical nurse Nassau Hosp., Mineola, N.Y., 1974-78; nurse, family planning counselor Nassau County Med. Ctr., East Meadow, N.Y., 1979—. Mem. Nurses Assn. of Am. Coll. Ob-Gyn (family planning counselor) Republican. Roman Catholic. Home: Massapequa NY

HUBLEY, DOROTHY GRAYBILL, musician, educator; b. Lititz, Pa., Sept. 9, 1921; d. Rufus Royce and Mary Elizabeth (Fink) Graybill; student Washington U., St. Louis, 1939, St. Louis Inst. Music, 1964, Ithaca Coll., 1959, Peabody Conservatory Music, 1977; cert. Am. Coll. Musicians; m. John A. Hubley, Jr., Aug. 6, 1943; 1 son, John A. III. Music tchr., Lititz, 1940-43, 59—. Bd. dirs. Lancaster County Youth Symphony, 1966-73. Mem. Lancaster (pres. 1971-73, 86—), Pa. (treas. 1971—, Distinguished Service award 1976) music tchrs. assns., Music Tchrs. Nat. Assn., Nat. Fedn. Music Clubs, Nat. Guild Piano Tchrs. (honor roll tchr.; chmn. Lancaster auditions center 1970—). Address: 413 S Cherry St Lititz PA 17543

HUCKABONE, ELIZABETH FRIED, real estate management executive; b. Buffalo, June 13, 1947; d. Martin B. and Isabel (Peek) Fried; A.B., SUNY, Coll. at Buffalo, 1979; postgrad. SUNY-Buffalo 1979-81; m. Darrell A. Huckabone, July 1, 1981; 1 child, Sara Elizabeth. Mgr., Belmont Mgmt. Co., Inc., Buffalo, 1976—; pres. Belmont Shelter Corp., Buffalo, 1977—; partner Belmont Housing Assos., Buffalo, 1981—. Registered apt. mgr. Mem. Nat. Leased Housing Assn. (dir., sec.). Office: 560 Delaware Ave Buffalo NY 14202

HUCKEBY, KAREN MARIE, graphic arts executive; b. San Diego, June 4, 1957; d. Floyd Riley and Georgette Laura (Wegimont) H.; student Coll. of Alameda, 1976; student 3-M dealer tng. program, St. Paul, 1975. Staff Huck's Press Service, Inc., Emeryville, Calif., 1968—, v.p., 1975—. Recipient Service award ARC, 1977. Mem. East Bay Club of Printing House Craftsman (treas. 1977-78), Internat. Platform Assn., Am. Film Inst., Nat. Assn. Female Execs., San Francisco Mus. Soc. Home: 509 Civic Center Richmond CA 94804 Office: 1311A 63d St Emeryville CA 94608

HUCKSTADT, ALICIA ANNETTA, nurse, educator; b. Garden City, Kans., Dec. 30, 1949; d. Allen Gilbert and Emma Catherine (Arends) Cole; B.S. in Nursing, Wichita (Kans.) State U., 1975, M.Nursing, 1978; Ph.D. in Edn., Kans. State U., Manhattan, 1981; m. Loren D. Huckstadt, Jan. 30, 1970. Staff nurse surg. ICU, St. Francis Hosp., Wichita, 1975-76; project coordinator, instr. alcohol edn. and tng. Wichita State U., 1975-76, instr. nursing, 1976-81, asst. prof., coordinator continuing edn., 1981-82, asst. prof., 1981-84, assoc. prof., 1984—; cons., speaker in field. Mem. Am. Nurses Assn. (council of nurse researchers 1985—), Midwest Nursing Research Soc., Kans. Nurses Assn., AAUP, Sigma Theta Tau (chpt. pres. 1982-84), Phi Kappa Phi. Roman

Catholic. Author articles, researcher in field. Office: Dept Nursing Box 41 Wichita State U Wichita KS 67208

HUDAK, CHRISTINE ANGELA, hospital official, nurse; b. Cleve., Dec. 13, 1950; d. Ernest John and Helen Marie (Orovets) H. B.S.N., Case Western Res. U., 1974; M.Ed., Cleve. State U., 1980. Staff nurse Vis. Nurse Assn., Cleve., 1974-75; clin. preceptor physicians asst. program Cuyahoga Community Coll., Cleve., 1975-77; staff nurse Sunny Acres Skilled Nursing Facility, Cleve., 1977-78; staff devel. instr. med. service Cleve. Met. Gen. Hosp., 1978-82, staff devel. instr. central programs/computers 1982-85, health care analyst/info. specialist, 1985—; cons. curriculum devel. Ctr. Health Affairs, Cleve., 1981—, Kidney Found. Ohio, 1979-85; instr. continuing edn. Cleve. State U., 1983—; instr. health care info. systems Capital U. Mem. women's com. Cleve. Orch., 1982—. Mem. Assn. Devel. Computer Based Instructional Systems, Ednl. Computer Consortium Ohio, Assn. Ednl. Communication and Tech., Mensa, Am. Assn. Artificial Intelligence, Phi Delta Kappa, Pi Lambda Theta, Sigma Theta Tau. Roman Catholic. Office: Cleve Met Gen Hosp 3395 Scranton Rd Cleveland OH 44109

HUDDLES, LINDA SUE, psychotherapist; b. Balt., July 5, 1939; d. Louis Cyrus and Beatrice (Freedman) Schwartz; B.S. summa cum laude, U. Md., 1962; M.S., Loyola Coll., Balt., 1980; grad. Jay Haley Family Therapy Inst., 1982; m. Gary Huddles, Dec. 16, 1961; children—John David, Kirk. Jr. exec. trainee Williams & Wilkens Med. Pubs., Balt., 1958-59; elem. tchr., Balt., 1962-63; vol. worker Sinai Hosp., Balt., 1970-71, Asso. Jewish Charities, Balt., 1970-75; counselor Planned Parenthood of Md., Balt., 1977-79; psychologist Northwestern Community Mental Health Center, Randallstown, Md., 1981—; pvt. practice psychotherapy, Towson, Md., 1981—. Former mem. Balt. County Arts Council; former chmn. div. Asso. Jewish Charities, award for service. Mem. Am. Psychol. Assn., Md. Psychol. Assn., Am. Personnel and Guidance Assn., Phi Kappa Phi, Kappa Delta Pi. Democrat. Jewish. Oil painter, works exhibited Balt. area, 1976-77. Home: 7 Swanhill Dr Baltimore MD 21208 Office: 28 Allegheny Ave Towson MD 21204

HUDDLESTON, FRANCES EMILY, retired guidance director; b. Pendleton, Ind., Jan. 27, 1900; d. Ulysses Grant and Estella May (Manifold) Taylor; A.B., DePauw U., 1922; A.M., N.Y.U., 1949; postgrad Catholic U. Am., 1934-35, Colo. U., 1936, Ind. U., 1948-50; m. Baron Emanuel Carol Fadda, 1929 (div. 1938); m. 2d, Earl R. Huddleston, June 18, 1938. Tchr., Portland (Ind.) High Sch., 1923-24, Huntington (Ind.) High Sch., 1925-29, Hammond (Ind.) High Sch., 1929, Lew Wallace High Sch., Gary, Ind., 1929-30; guidance dir. William A. Wirt High Sch., Gary, 1930-64; ret.; with Chgo. Travel Bur., 1964—. Mem. travel com. Gary YWCA; active Friends of Library. Mem. Alpha Phi, Delta Kappa Gamma. Club: Sebring (Fla.) Woman's (edn. com.). Home: 207 NE Lakeview Dr Sebring FL 33870

HUDDLESTON, MARILYN ANNE, business and financial consultant; b. Fayetteville, N.C., Jan. 28, 1953; d. Allen Paul and Julia Jewel (Hill) Miller; m. Roby Dwayne Huddleston, Sept. 13, 1946; children—Michelle, Christopher, Mathew, Danyel, Michael. B.A. in Real Estate and Fin., Central Tex. U., 1974; diploma Acad. of Coll. of Real Estate, 1977; postgrad. El Paso Community Coll. Owner, fin. cons. Cherokee Fin. Investments, Killeen, Tex., 1983—; owner, broker All Am. Ins. Agy., Killeen, 1984—; realtor, assoc. Exec. Fin., Austin, Tex., 1986—; owner Geodesic Homes of Tex., Killeen, 1984—. Author: Miracle Baby at Bracken Ridge Hospital, 1979; Financial Consulting Made Easy, 1983. Pres. Mil. Council of Catholic Women, Stuttgart, Fed. Republic Germany, 1980, Non-Commnd. Officers Wives, Stuttgart, 1980-82, Ciudad del Niño Orphanage Assn., Killeen, 1979—; instr. Christian Religion, Killeen, 1976—. Mem. Nat. Assn. Female Execs., Internat. Assn. Bus. and Fin. Cons. (hon.), Fort Hood Bd. Realtors, Nat. Assn. Realtors, Tex. Assn. Realtors Soc. Female Execs. (v.p. 1984-86). Republican. Roman Catholic. Avocations: singing; writing; tennis; golf; macrame. Home: Route 5 PO Box 67C Killeen TX 76541 Office: Cherokee Fin Investments PO Box 1299 Killeen TX 76540

HUDDLESTON, MARY LOUISE, bus company executive; b. Chattanooga, Dec. 28, 1945; d. Howard Pierce and Francis Louise (Talifereo) H.; m. Claude Herman, June 12, 1969 (div. 1976). B.S., U. Tenn., 1967. Tchr., Titusville High Sch., Fla., 1969-70, Bishop Byrne High Sch., Memphis, 1970-72; dir. sales Sea Life Park, Honolulu, 1972-74; v.p. sales Greyhound Royal Hawaiian, Honolulu, 1974-77; v.p. group sales Greyhound Lines, Phoenix, 1977-79; v.p. group sales Trailways, Inc., Dallas, 1979—. Named Travel Woman of Yr., Travel Industry Assn. Am., 1983. Mem. Am. Soc. Travel Agts., Am. Bus. Assn. (bd. dirs. 1980-85), Women in Transp. Dallas. Republican. Home: 9127 Valley Chapel Dallas TX 75220 Office: Trailways Inc 1500 Jackson St Suite 612 Dallas TX 75201

HUDDLESTON, TAMARA LYNNE, lawyer; b. Green Ridge, Mo., July 24, 1952; d. Wayne and Betty Jean (Fenley) H. B.S., Sch. Ozarks, 1974; J.D., U. Mo., 1977. Legal advisor Ariz. Criminal Intelligence System Agy., Phoenix, 1981-84; atty. Ariz. Pub. Service Co., 1984—. staff atty. Legal Aid Western Mo., Kansas City, 1977-78, Kans. Legal Services, Pittsburg, 1978-81. Vol., Tipton Legal Project, Kansas City, Mo., 1977; pres. bd. Safe House, Pittsburg, Kans., 1979-81. Mem. ABA, Legal Advisors Assn. (sec. treas. 1983), Mo. Bar Assn., Ariz. Bar Assn. Office: Ariz Pub Service Co Phoenix AZ 85036

HUDGINS, CATHERINE HARDING (MRS. ROBERT SCOTT HUDGINS, IV), business executive; b. Raleigh, N.C., June 25, 1913; d. William Thomas and Mary Alice (Timberlake) Harding; B.S., N.C. State U., 1929-33; grad. tchr. N.C. Sch. for Deaf, 1933-34; m. Robert Scott Hudgins, IV, Aug. 20, 1938; children—Catherine Harding, Deborah Ghiselin, Robert Scott V. Tchr., N.C. Sch. for Deaf, Morganton, 1934-36; sec. Dr. A. S. Oliver, Raleigh, 1937; tchr. N.J. Sch. for Deaf, Trenton, 1937-39; sec. Robert S. Hudgins Co., Charlotte, N.C., 1949-60, v.p., sec., treas., 1960—, also dir. Mem. Jr. Service League, Easton, Pa., 1939; project chmn. ladies aux. Profl. Engrs. N.C., 1954-55, pres., 1956-57; pres. Christian High Sch. PTA, 1963; program chmn. Charlotte Opera Guild, 1959-61, sec., 1961-63; sec. bd. Hezekiah Alexander House Restoration, 1949-52, mem. Hezekiah Alexander Found., 1975—, also aux., 1980—, treas., 1983-84, v.p., 1984-85, pres., 1985-86. Mem. N.C. Hist. Assn., English Speaking Union, Mint Mus. Arts (pres. drama guild 1967-69), Daus. Am. Colonists (N.C. chmn. nat. def. 1973-74), DAR (chpt. regent 1957-59, state program chmn. 1961-63, state chmn. nat. def. 1973-76, state rec. sec. 1977-79, state regent 1979-82, N.C. chmn. 1963-66, N.C. sr. pres. Children Am. Revolution 1963-66, nat. bd. mgmt. 1963—, sr. nat. corr. sec. 1966-68, sr. nat. 1st v.p. 1968-70, sr. nat. pres. 1970-72, sr. nat. chmn. fin. com., pres. nat. officers club 1979-82), Presbyterian (past chmn. home missions, annuities and relief Women of Ch., past pres. Sunday Sch. class). Clubs: Washington Arts, Charlotte City, Carmel Country (Charlotte); Tower. Home: 1514 Wendover Rd Charlotte NC 28211 Office: PO Box 220217 Charlotte NC 28211

HUDGINS, MARY DENGLER, writer; b. Hot Springs National Park, Ark., Nov. 24, 1901; d. Jackson Wharton and Ida (Dengler) Hudgins; B.A., U. Ark., 1924; student U. Wis., 1941, U. Chgo., 1940, Emory U., 1952, Rice Sch. of Spoken Word, 1925. Tchr., Waldo (Ark.) High Sch., 1924-25; free-lance writer, 1925-39, 60—; librarian Hot Springs Public Library, 1939-43; med. and gen. librarian Army and Navy Gen. Hosp., Hot Springs, 1943-59; articles pub. in encys., hist., lit., profl. and popular publs., radio, TV. Dir., Hot Springs Writer's Workshop, 1960-61, rep. to Fine Arts Council, Hot Springs, 1960—. Historian YWCA, Hot Springs. Mem. Ark. Hist. Assn. (dir. 1964-71, v.p. 1971-80), Ark. Geneal. Soc. (dir. 1965-73), D.A.R., Garland County Hist. Soc. (pres. 1962-63, program chmn. 1960, 61), ALA, Ark. Library Assn. (sec. spl. libraries div. 1959-60), Med. Library Assn., Southwest Library Assn., (Ark. reporter 1955), Ark. Folklore Assn. (1st v.p. 1958-59), AAUW (Ark. 1st v.p. 1929-30, pres. Hot Springs br. 1927, Ark. fellowship chmn. 1957-61, rep. to Fine Arts Council 1961-62), Med. Library Assn., Fine Arts Center (dir., incorporator 1961). Presbyterian. Clubs: Altrusa Internat. (pres. 1980-81), Sabina (pres. 1935), Current Book (pres. Hot Springs, 1952, 64, 68, 74). Author numerous mag. articles in field of Ark. composers and lyricists. Collector, donor to colls. and univs. Arkansiana in all fields; donor endowments for Ark. composers and hist. researchers U. Ark. Address: 1030 Park Ave Hot Springs AR 71901

HUDSON, ALICE PETERSON, chemistry consulting laboratory executive; b. Sherburn, Minn., Aug. 9, 1942; d. Robert Conner and Irene Helen (Danielson) Peterson; m. Donald E. Hudson, Aug. 31, 1963; children—Martha, Dana. B.S. in Chemistry, Iowa State U., 1963; M.S. in Chemistry, Fla. Atlantic U., 1977. Chemist, A.E. Staley Mfg. Co., Decatur, Ill., 1961-62, Pratt & Whitney Aircraft, West Palm Beach, Fla., 1963-64; med. technician A.G. Holley Hosp., Lantana, Fla., 1964-65; acct. John R. Haber, North Palm Beach, Fla., 1970-71; chemist, lab. dir. Surface Chemists of Fla., Inc., West Palm Beach, 1971-84, pres., owner, Riviera Beach, Fla., 1984—. Patentee laundry softener antistatic composition, ionomers as antistatic agts. Mem. Am. Chem. Soc. Avocation: marathon running. Home: 728 W Kalmia Dr Lake Park FL 33403 Office: Surface Chemists of Fla 328 W 11th St Riviera Beach FL 33404

HUDSON, DEBRA DARLENE, inventory control executive; b. Gallatin, Tenn., May 6, 1957; d. Gordan Browning and Joyce Marie (Suttle) Terry; m. Richard L. Hudson, June 15, 1974 (div. 1985); children—Richard Reid, Margaret Marie. Sec., Hendersonville, Tenn., 1978-79; inventory control mgr. Precious Metals Internat. and Nat. Refining Corp., Gallatin, 1980—, cons.; mktg. cons. various cos. Steering com. Aqua Tot, 1983—; pres. Women Jaycees Am., 1984; com. head Tenn. Homecoming '86, 1986; sec. county literacy council. Mem. Nat. Assn. Female Execs. Democrat. Baptist. Avocations: children's activities; aerobics; reading; traveling. Home: 1192 Meadowview Gallatin TN 37066 Office: Precious Metals Internat 554 W Main St Gallatin TN 37066

HUDSON, DONNA MICHELE, social worker; b. Newark, Oct. 20, 1956; d. Clarence Vernon and Barbara ANn (Patillo) Hudson. B.A., Douglass Coll., 1978; M.S.W., Rutgers U., 1981. Peer counselor Douglass Coll., New Brunswick, N.J., 1976-78, residential coordinator, 1978; grad. intern Douglas Coll., 1979-80, City of Elizabeth (N.J.), 1980-82; tchr. Bd. Edn., Newark, 1982-83; social worker Div. Youth and Family Services, Newark, 1983-85; supr. Cath. Community Services-Project Haven, Newark, 1985—. Mem. Nat. Assn. Social Workers, Douglas Coll. Alumni Assn., Rutgers Grad. Sch. Social Work Alumni Assn., Nat. Assn. Female Execs., AAUW. Democrat. Baptist.

HUDSON, DOROTHY MORGAN, businesswoman; b. Omaha, May 23, 1928; d. Glover and Maria Elizabeth Morgan; student U. Colo., 1967-68, Metropolitan State Coll., 1974-75; cert. EEOC Acad., 1975; m. Harrison Hudson, Aug. 29, 1964; 1 dau., Ronnette Marie Marshall Davis. Owner, propr. D.M.H. Enterprises; investigator, conciliator EEOC Denver, 1974-75, pay audit technician Air Force Fin. Center, Denver, 1956-74; pres. City Park Sundries. Committeewoman, Democratic party; del. Dem. nat. conv., 1984; neighborhood task force rep. Denver City Council. Recipient cert. of honor City of Denver, 1976, Colo. Centennial-Bicentennial Archivist Pin, 1976; named Colo. Outstanding Woman of Yr., 1979. Mem. Nat. Profl. Writers Club, Nat. Fedn. Bus. and Profl. Women's Clubs, Nat. Assn. Female Execs. (rep. Nat. Ind. Bus. Assn.), Denver LWV (dir. 1977-78, spl. events chmn. 1982-84, editor newsletter 1977-78), Colo. LWV (dir., editor newsletter 1984), Colo. Press Assn., Adult Edn. Council Met. Denver, Greater Park Hill Community, Inc., Women of Colo., Nat. Council Negro Women, Colo. Black Women for Polit. Action, NAACP, Nat. Assn. Ret. Fed. Employees, Sigma Gamma Chi. Baptist. Clubs: Denver Jane Jefferson, Denver Century.

HUDSON, ELISABETH HILDEGARDE (BETTY), banker; b. Albuquerque, Sept. 12, 1946; d. Clarence Fenton and Elisabeth Hildegarde (Scheele) Canoyer; m. David Kennedy Tudor, May 27, 1967 (div. 1974); children—Carlene Helene, Michael Reed. B.S., Calif. State Poly. Inst., 1968; postgrad. U. Calif-Berkeley, Sch. Mortgage Banking, Washington. Educator, San Ramon Valley Schs., Calif., 1970-73; mktg. agt. Bonanza Realty, Lafayette, Calif., 1973-76; loan rep. First Interstate Mortgage, Walnut Creek, Calif., 1976-82; sr. residential fin. officer Calif. Bay Mortgage, Pleasant Hill, 1982-84; mktg. dir. First Security Realty Services, Walnut Creek, 1984—; lectr. in field. Mem. AAUW, No. Calif. Mortgage Bankers Assn., Bay Area Mortgage Banking Assn., Calif. Residential Leaders Assn. Republican. Roman Catholic. Clubs: Roundhill Country (Alamo); Supreme Ct. Racquetball (Pleasant Hill). Avocations: singing; sailing; skiing; biking; photography. Home: 3147 Via Larga Alamo CA 94507 Office: First Security Realty Services 1575 Treat Blvd #125 Walnut Creek CA 94598

HUDSON, JACQUELINE, artist; b. Cambridge, Mass.; d. Eric and Gertrude (Dunton) H.; student Columbia U., Art Students League. One-woman shows: Burr Gallery, N.Y.C., Rockport Art Assn., Present Day Club, Princeton, N.J., Maine Art Gallery, Wiscasset, Moulson Union, Bowdoin Coll., 1979; group shows: NAD, Pa. Acad. Fine Arts, Library of Congress, Cin. Mus., Riverside Mus., Portland Mus. Art, Maine, Dayton Art Inst., Bixler Mus., Colby Coll., Maine Art Gallery, Wiscasset, Bowdoin Coll., Farnsworth Mus., Rockland, Maine, Vallombreuse Gallery, Palm Beach, Fla., Butler Inst. Am. Art (3d Graphic prize), 1983, Art Contemporain Cabinet des Dessins, Paris, 1986, many others; represented permanent collection Library of Congress; pvt. collections. Recipient Pennell Purchase prize Library of Congress, 1951; Allen Kander Found. award Rockport Art Assn., 1957, Edith Wengenroth Meml. prize, 1971, 75; Alice Standish Buell Meml. prize Nat. Assn. Women Artists, 1968, Helen Turner Graphic prize, 1974. Mem. Art Students League, Nat. Assn. Women Artists (Donna Miller Meml. prize 1980), Rockport Art Assn., Lincoln County Cultural and Hist. Assn., Monhegan (Maine) Assocs. (chmn. mus. com. 1963-67). Home: Monhegan Island ME 04852 also 81 Federal St Wiscasset ME 04578

HUDSON, JANE DUCLOS, management consultant; b. Great Barrington, Mass., Sept. 23, 1949; d. Edward Warren and Elaine Duclos (Connelly) H.; B.A. magna cum laude, Newton Coll. of Sacred Heart, 1971; postgrad. Syracuse U., 1971-72; M.A., George Washington U., 1975; m. Donald Lee Borod, Nov. 11, 1978; 1 son, James Hudson Borod. Social sci. analyst Fed. Hwy. Adminstrn., Washington, 1972-73; mgmt. intern GSA, Washington, 1973-74, mgmt. analyst, 1974-75; mgmt. analyst Nat. Archives and Records Service, Washington, 1976-78; program analyst Nat. Archives and Records Service, N.Y.C., 1978-80; mgmt. cons. Booz-Allen & Hamilton, N.Y.C., 1980-2, Price Waterhouse, Hartford, Conn., 1982-84; pvt. practice mgmt. cons., 1984—; lectr. public adminstrn. Southeastern U., Washington, 1975. Maxwell fellow Syracuse U., 1971-72; Herbert H. Lehman fellow, 1971-72. Roman Catholic. Office: PO Box 360 West Hartford CT 06107

HUDSON, JANE SMITHER, furniture manufacturing company executive; b. Altavista, Va., July 5, 1937; d. Victor Nelson and Elois Reynolds Smither; A.A.S. summa cum laude in Mgmt., Central Va. Community Coll., 1978; m. J. Lee Hudson, May 15, 1954; 1 son, Michael Edward. Adminstrv. asst. Altavista (Va.) High Sch., 1954-55; with Lane Co., Inc., Altavista, 1956—, exec. sec. to chmn. bd., 1976-81, exec. sec. to chmn. exec. com., 1981-81, spl. asst. for pub. relations communications, 1984-86, sales exec., spl. accounts, 1986—; realtor R. B. Carr & Co., Altavista, 1980—, assoc. broker, 1985—; mem. adv. bd. Am. Fed. Savs. and Loan, 1985—. Mem. town council Town of Altavista, 1980-86; sec. Altavista Community Improvement Council, 1981-82; mem. bd. deacons First Bapt. Ch., Altavista, 1980-83. Mem. Profl. Secs. Internat., Va. Assn. Realtors, Nat. Assn. Realtors. Corr. Lynchburg (Va.) News., 1966-72. Home: 1102 Commonwealth Dr Altavista VA 24517 Office: Lane Co Inc Franklin Ave Altavista VA 24517

HUDSON, KAREN ELIZABETH WAGNER, lawyer; b. Harriman, Tenn., Feb. 18, 1955; d. Theodore Franklin and Pauline Lucienne (Audette) Wagner; m. Roger Wilson Hudson, June 12, 1982. B.A., Ind. U., 1977; J.D., U. Tenn., 1980. Bar: Tenn. 1981. Asst. legal counsel 1st Fed. Savs. and Loan, Chattanooga, 1981-82; gen. counsel Nat. Savs. Life Ins. Co., Murfreesboro, Tenn., 1982—. Vol. Chattanooga Nature Ctr., 1981, Adult Edn., Murfreesboro, 1982—, Rutherford County Humane Soc., Murfreesboro, 1982—, Spl. Olympics. Mem. ABA, Rutherford County Bar Assn., Tenn. Bar Assn., Ind. U. Alumni Assn., Mortar Bd., Blue Key, Phi Delta Phi, Alpha Lambda Delta, Gamma Phi Beta. Republican. Christian Scientist. Home: 628 Rampart Ln Murfreesboro TN 37130 Office: Nat Savings Life Ins Co PO Box 1338 Murfreesboro TN 37133

HUDSON, MARGARET STOVER, educational administrator; b. Roanoke, Va., Sept. 27, 1947; d. Charles Marvin and Magdalene Virginia (Hobson) Stover; m. John David Hudson, Mar. 1, 1974; 1 stepchild, John David, Jr. B.B.A. cum laude, Roanoke Coll., 1971. Cashier, bookkeeper Roanoke Coll., Salem, Va., 1965-74, controller, 1974-79, dir. fin. and adminstrv. services, 1979-84, bus. mgr., 1984—; customer relations rep. Nat. Cash Register Co., Roanoke, 1974; trustee Diuguid-Spencer Trust, Salem, 1976—, Harold Harris Unitrust, Salem, 1983—, James W. Sieg Unitrust, Salem, 1984—, Lois C. Fisher Unitrust, Salem, 1984—, June Sheelsman Unitrust, 1984—, Rural and Thelma Meadors Annuity Trust, Salem, 1985—. Bd. dirs. Va. Choral Soc., Salem, 1974. Mem. Nat. Assn. Coll. and Univ. Bus. Officers, Nat. Assn. Accts., Coll. and Univ. Personnel Assn., So. Assn. Coll. and Univ. Bus. Officers. Methodist. Clubs: Va. Dressage Assn., U.S. Dressage Fedn., Roanoke Valley Figure Skating. Home: 6539 Laban Rd NW Roanoke VA 24019 Office: Roanoke Coll Salem VA 24153

HUDSON, MARIA THOMAS, advertising executive, public relations consultant; b. Gastonia, N.C., Feb. 12, 1949; d. Lester Ray and Fay Muriel (Slagle) Vause; m. 2d, Byron Malcolm Hudson, Apr. 5, 1980; 1 son, Buddy Thomas. B.A., U. N.C., 1973. Exec. sec. Belk Bros. Co., Charlotte, N.C., 1976-77; asst. program dir. WCCB-TV, Charlotte, 1977-78; creative services dir. WPCQ-TV, Charlotte, 1978-80; field reporter Westinghouse Broadcast Network, 1980; Stringer reporter/photojournalist Charlotte News, 1979, Charlotte Observer, 1980-81; dir. promotions and advt. Charlotte Coliseum, Ovens Auditorium, 1980—. Pres., Old Hickory Football Classic, N.C./S.C., 1979—; bd. dirs. Mecklenburg County Women's Commn., Charlotte, 1980—; mem. Gov.'s Conf. Women in Leadership, Raleigh, N.C., 1981, Gov.'s Conf. Women in the Economy, Raleigh, 1983; mem. exec. bd. U. N.C.-Charlotte Day for Women, 1981; publicity dir. Blueprint: Charlotte Women in the 80's, 1981-83; grad. Leadership Charlotte, 1983; nat. judge Award for Career Excellence, Women in Communication, Inc., 1982; publicity dir. Nat. 500, World 600 Races, 1983-84; active polit. campaigns. Mem. Internat. Platform Assn., Am. Women in Radio and TV (editor N.C. chpt. newspaper 1980-81), Nat. Assn. Female Execs. Democrat. Mem. Ch. of Jesus Christ of Latter-day Saints.

HUDSON, MARY, oil company executive; b. Athens, Tex., Sept. 30, 1912; d. John Thurmond and Lou Allie (Dewberry) H.; extension student U. Okla., U. Kans.; m. Cecil Wayne Driver, Sept. 20, 1939; 1 dau., Joyce Driver Cady; m. Frank Bane Vandgrift, June 2, 1945. Co-founder, 1932, since pres., chief exec. officer Hudson Oil Co., Kansas City, Kans.; pres., chief exec. officer Hudson Refining Co., 1977—; adv. com. Nat. Petroleum Council, 1976; counsel Republic Colombia in Kansas City, 1959—. Hon. bd. dirs. Rockhurst Coll., Kansas City, Kans. Named Hon. Citizen of Kansas City (Mo.), 1971, Ky. col., 1964. Mem. Soc. Ind. Gasoline Marketers Am. (a founder, pres. 1965-68), Ind. Gasoline Marketeers Council (a founder), Women's Kansas City Assn. Internat. Relations and Trade (pres. 1971-74), Am. Royal Assn. (gov.), Counsular Corps Greater Kansas City (dean), Am. Petroleum Inst., Am. Petroleum Refiners Assn., 25 Year Club Petroleum Industry, DAR. Clubs: Kansas City; Lauderdale Yacht (Ft. Lauderdale, Fla.); Order Eastern Star. Office: PO Box 907 Kansas City MO 64141*

HUDSON, PATRICE HOWELL, transportation planner, land development consultant; b. Painesville, Ohio, Oct. 31, 1954; d. Dale Harvey and Alexzenia (Norvell) Howell; m. Steve Hudson, Aug. 28, 1978 (div. 1981); 1 child, Tamara Nicole. B.A. in Sociology, Spelman Coll., 1977; M.City Planning, Ga. Inst. Tech., 1980. City planner City of Atlanta, 1976-77, Atlanta Regional Commn., 1977-80; transp. planner Wilms-Russell, John, Atlanta, 1980-84; chief planner Harrington, George & Dunn, P.C., Atlanta, 1985—. 701 grantee HUD, Atlanta, 1977. Mem. Am. Planning Assn., Conf. Minority Transp. Ofcls. (v.p. 1984), Nat. Assn. Female Execs., Spelman Coll. Alumni Assn. Presbyterian. Avocations: music; tennis; sewing. Office: Harrington George & Dunn PC 1401 Peachtree St Suite 120 Atlanta GA 30309

HUDSON, PAULA GOELDNER, lawyer; b. Lake Forest, Ill., Apr. 1, 1952; d. Paul and Mabel (Allan) Goeldner; m. James L. Hudson, Jr., Aug. 27, 1977; children—Ashley A., Whitney A. B.A. in French, U. Ill., 1976; J.D., John Marshall Law Sch., 1979. Bar: Ill. 1979, U.S. Dist. Ct. (cen. dist.) Ill. 1984, U.S. Ct. Appeals (7th cir.) 1985. Asst. state's atty. Office of State's Atty. of Champaign County, Urbana, Ill., 1979—. Mem. U. Ill. YWCA Networking, Urbana, 198486, Robeson's Career Council, Champaign, 1985-86, Broadlands Zoning Bd. Appeals, Ill., 1979-82, Colonial Williamsburg Found., 1982—, Thomas Paine PTA, Urbana, 1985—. Mem. Ill. State Bar Assn., Champaign County Bar Assn. (pres. elect 1986-87), Jr. League of Champaign-Urbana, Nat. Assn. Female Execs., Exec. Club of Champaign County, U. Ill. Alumni Assn., Chi Omega Bldg. Assn. (chmn. 1984-86), Chi Omega, Delta Theta Phi. Republican. Episcopalian. Clubs: Urbana Golf & Country, Quarterback, Illini Rebounders, Lincoln. Avocations: golf; bridge; antiques. Home: 2503 Slayback Dr Urbana IL 61801 Office: Courthouse 101 E Main St Urbana IL 61801

HUDSON, REBECCA BEALL GRAVES, resort executive; b. Charlottesville, Va., May 13, 1949; d. Henry Theodore Northcott and Rebecca Beall (Jackson) Graves; m. John Robert Hudson, Jr., June 28, 1969 (dec. Nov. 1980); children—Rebecca Beall, Mary Mathews. B.A., Hollins Coll., 1973. Asst. gen. mgr. Luray Caverns Corp., Caverns and Coach Restaurant, Car and Carriage Caravan, Luray Caverns Airport, Caverns Country Club Resort, Caverns Motel East, Caverns Motel West, Radio Stas. WLCC and WRAA, Luray Motor Co., Old Virginia Village, Oh Shenandoah Real Estate Devel., Luray, Va.; gen. mgr. Historic Car and Carriage Caravan, Bd. dirs. Shenandoah Arts Council, Winchester, Va.; Mem. DAR (outstanding Jr. Mem. 1978, chmn mag. com.), Va. Travel Council, So. Highlands Attractions, Va. Motel Assn., Nat. Caves Assn., Va. C. of C. Episcopalian. Clubs: Luray Garden, Caverns Country (Luray, Va.). Office: Luray Caverns Corp PO Box 748 Luray VA 22835

HUDSON, SANDRA STROTHER, publishing executive; b. Columbus, Ga., Sept. 3, 1947; d. Edmund Weyman and Lucile (Adkins) Strother III; m. Cecil Clifford Hudson, Jan. 1, 1982. B.A. cum laude, Hollins Coll., 1969. Prodn. mgr., edit. and prodn. asst. Winter House Ltd., N.Y.C., 1969-70; sr. designer, jr. designer, asst. to art dir., asst. to mng. editor Holt, Rinehart & Winston, N.Y.C., 1971-75; art dir. Book div. Curtis Pub. Co., Indpls., 1976-78; design and prodn. mgr. U. Ga. Press, Athens, 1980—. Recipient Book Design awards Am. Inst. Graphic Arts, Am. Assn. Univ. Presses, Print Mag., Chgo. Book Clinic, N.Y. Type Dirs. Club, Ind. Art Dirs. Club, Southeastern Library Assn., Printing Industries Am. Mem. Assn. Am. Univ. Presses (chmn. design and prodn. com. 1986), Am. Inst. Graphic Arts, Ga. Trust Hist. Preservation, Ga. Conservancy, Sierra Club. Episcopalian. Judge, 35th ann. book show Chgo. Book Clinic, 1984. Office: U Ga Press Athens GA 30602

HUESCHEN, HELEN JOAN, surgical nurse; b. Hemple, Mo., Feb. 6, 1941; d. William Cornelius and Agnes Marie (Halter) McLarney; m. Otto Raphael Hueschen, Aug. 31, 1974; children—Scott Andrew, Kurt William. Diploma, Sisters of Charity Sch. Nursing, Kansas City, Kans., 1961; B.S.Nursing, Avila Coll., 1980; M.Nursing, U. Kans., 1983. Cert. nurse-operating room. Staff nurse Providence Hosp., Kansas City, Kans., 1961; Papal Vols. for Latin Am. team mem. Our Lady of Guadalupe Hosp., Belem, Brazil, 1962-64; staff nurse operating room St. Joseph Hosp., Kansas City, Mo., 1965-77, ednl. coordinator operating room, 1977-80; research asst. U. Kans., Kansas City, 1981-83; dir. surg. services Research Med. Center, Kansas City, Mo., 1983—. Served to lt. col. USAFR, 1965—, chief aeromed. nursing 36th Aeromed. Evacuation unit Richards Gebaur AFB, Mo., 1983—. Decorated Sr. Flight Nurse badge, Chief Nurse badge, Air Force Commendation medal. Mem. Assn. Operating Room Nurses (chpt. pres. 1973-74, mem. nat. cert. bd. 1980-81, nat. com. on edn. 1983—), Res. Officers Assn., U. Kans. Alumni Assn., Avila Coll. Alumni Assn., Sigma Theta Tau. Democrat. Roman Catholic. Home: 1241 Romany St Kansas City MO 64113 Office: Research Medical Center 2316 E Meyer Blvd Kansas City MO 64132

HUEY, FRANCES COLLEEN, lawyer; b. Sacramento, Sept. 15, 1954; d. Francis Edward Huey and Gladys Colleen (Stone) Huey. A.A., Am. River Coll.; B.A., Calif. State U., Sacramento, 1977; J.D., Hamline U., St. Paul, 1980. Bar: Minn. 1980, Calif., 1982, U.S. Dist. Ct. (ea. dist.) Calif. Research asst. to assoc. dean Hamline U., 1978-80; assoc. editor Law Rev. Digest, Mpls., 1979-80; legal intern Freeman, Rishwain, Hall & Shore, Stockton Calif., 1982; sole practice, Sacramento, 1983—; mem. Indigent Criminal Def. Panel, Sacramento, 1983—. Author short stories. Rep. Sacramento County Council Folkdance Clubs, 1982—, v.p., 1985, 86. Mem. Asian ABA, ABA, Calif. State Bar Assn., Assn. Trial Lawyers Am., Calif. Trial Lawyers Assn., Fed. Bar Assn., Minn. State Bar Assn., Sacramento County Bar Assn. Democrat. Mem. Universal Freedom Ch. Home: 2017 Maryal Dr Sacramento CA 95864 Office: PO Box 61071 Sacramento CA 95860

HUEY, MARY EVELYN BLAGG, university president; b. Wills Point, Tex., Jan. 19, 1922; d. Henry H. and Melissa Evelyn (Manning) Blagg; B.S., Tex. Woman's U., 1942, M.A., 1943; M.A., U. Ky., 1947; postgrad. Harvard U., 1950; Ph.D., Duke U., 1954; Litt.D. (hon.), Baiko Jo Gakuin, Shimonoseki, Japan, 1981; m. Griffin B. Huey, Aug. 21, 1954; 1 son, Henry Griffin. Instr. English, Tex. Woman's U., Denton, 1943-45, dean Grad. Sch., 1971-76, prof. govt., 1971—, pres., 1976—; asst. dir. Bur. Pub. Adminstrn. U. Miss., 1946-47; instr. govt. North Tex. State U., 1947-51, asst. prof., 1954-63, assoc. prof.,

1963-66, prof., 1966-71. Mem. Bd. Adjustment, City of Denton, 1962-68, chmn., 1963-68; mem. regional exec. bd. North Central Tex. Planning Council for Hosp. and Related Health Services, 1969-70; mem. exec. bd. North Central Tex. Council Govts., 1970-71, pres. Tex. Woman's U. Demonstration Sch. PTA, 1970-71; exec. v.p. Fine Arts Soc. Tex., 1977, pres., 1977-79; mem. Denton Area War on Drugs Adv. Bd., 1981-84; mem. exec. com. Def. Adv. Com. on Women in the Services, 1981-83, nat. chmn., 1983; active First Presbyn. Ch., Denton, ruling elder, 1973-75, 81-84. Recipient Disting. Alumna award Tex. Woman's U., 1974; Otis Fowler award Denton C. of C., 1980; Women Helping Women award, Soroptimist Internat., 1980, pub. service commendation Comdt. U.S. Coast Guard, 1983, medal for outstanding pub. service Sec. Def., 1983; named to Tex. Women's Hall of Fame, 1984. Mem. AAUW (pres. Denton br. 1962-63, chmn. internat. cuisine and customs study group 1967-69) Am. Council Edn., Am. Polit. Sci. Assn., Am. Soc. Public Adminstrn. (v.p. N. Tex. chpt. 1968-69, pres. 1969-70), Assn. Tex. Coll. and Univs. (mem. exec. bd. 1977-80), Am. Assn. State Colls. and Univs.), So. Polit. Sci. Assn., Southwestern Polit. Sci. Assn., Southwestern Social Sci. Assn., Tex. Acad. Sci., Tex. Assn. Coll. Tchrs., Tex. Found. Women's Resources, Nat. Acad. Pub. Adminstrn., Nat. Commn. Coop. Edn. (trustee 1978—), Phi Alpha Theta, Delta Kappa Gamma, Phi Delta Gamma, Phi Kappa Phi, Pi Sigma Alpha, Sigma Alpha Iota. Republican. Contbr. in field. Office: PO Box 23925 Texas Woman's U Station Denton TX 76204

HUF, CAROL ELINOR, tax service company executive; b. Milw., Apr. 21, 1940; d. William Weiss and Florence H. (Melcher) Weiss Lange; m. Walter Franklin Huf, Sept. 9, 1961; children—Mardell Leslie, Walter Albert III. Student Valparaiso U., 1958-60, Waukesha County Tech. Inst., 1968-69. Tax preparer H & R Block, Milw., 1967-84, instr. tax sch., 1969-83; job service interviewer State of Wis., Waukesha, 1984; pres. Personalized Tax Service, Inc., West Allis, Wis., 1984—. Vol. worker Girl Scouts U.S.A., Waukesha, 1970-80, Boy Scouts Am., Waukesha, 1975—; swimming referee Wis. Interscholastic Athletic Assn., Milw., 1972-84. Recipient awards Boy Scouts Am. Mem. Wis. Assn. Accts., Met. Swimming Ofcls. Lutheran. Clubs: Edgewood Golf (Big Bend, Wis.) (pres. 1984—). Home: 17825 Westward Dr New Berlin WI 53151 Office: Personalized Tax Service Inc 10533 W National Ave West Allis WI 53227

HUFF, NANCY RUTH, citrus groves administrator, investments executive; b. Cin.; d. Norman Vincent and Marie (Voss) H.; m. William H. Brady, Sept. 9, 1961 (div. Apr. 1971); children—William Huff, Sherry Lynn. B.A., Newton Coll. of the Sacred Heart, Mass., 1961. Asst. to pres. Star Fruit Co., Lake Alfred, Fla., 1961-71; mgr., pres. Huff Groves, Winter Haven, Fla., 1971—; pres Star Investments, Winter Haven, 1980—; v.p. Allapattch Operating Co., Fort Pierce, Fla., 1982—, pres. Alpat Grove care Co., Fort Pierce, 1982—. Mem. Fla. Citrus Mutual, Indian River Citrus League (com. mem.), Women in Citrus, Fla. Citrus Women. Republican. Clubs: Lake Region Yacht and Country, Gardania Garden. (v.p. 1974-78) (Winter Haven); Citrus (Orlando, Fla.). Avocations: photography; dance; tennis. Office: PO Box 7167 Winter Haven FL 33883

HUFF, SUSAN LOUISE, real estate management consultant; b. Reading, Pa., July 4, 1950; d. Robert Eugene and Janet Louise (Miller) H. B.S. in Econs., U. Tampa, Fla., 1972. Salesperson, Provident Mut. Life Ins. Co., Tampa, 1972-73; v.p. Pearson Comml. Furnishings, S.I., N.Y., 1973—, pres. Susan James Assocs., S.I., 1980—; dir. Purchase Mgmt. Cons., S.I., 1984—. Cons., Jr. Achievement, N.Y.C., 1984. Mem. Nat. Assn. Female Execs., Internat. Facilities Mgmt. Assn., N.Y.C. C. of C. Republican. Home: 9 Shore Rd Edgewater NJ 07020 Office: Susan James Assocs 807 Castleton Ave Staten Island NY 10310

HUFFMAN, DEBORA LEE, educational administrator, musician; b. Newark, Sept. 10, 1943; d. George Christian and Hazel May (Bowers) Brix; m. Hughes McCoy Huffman Jr., Aug. 28, 1964; children—Jon Marc, Monica Lee. B.Mus. with high honor, Wheaton Coll., 1965; M.Mus., Northwestern U., 1968. Organist Christ Ch. of Oak Brook, Ill., 1965-77; founder, dir., tchr. DuPage Sch. Mus. Instrn., Wheaton, Ill., 1969-77; organist 1st Presbyn. Ch., Gastonia, N.C., 1977-80, Arcadia Presbyn. Ch. (Calif.), 1980—; tchr. piano, organ, Gastonia, 1977-80; exec. dir. Claremont Community Sch. Music, Calif., 1981—; dir. Claremont Girlchoir, 1981-83; music critic Gastonia Gazette, 1979; dir., accompanist Oak Brook Chorale, 1972-77; accompanist Chgo. Sunday Evening Club, sta. WTTW-TV, 1975-77. Organist recs. Christ Church Sings, 1075, Christmas at Christ Church, 1976, Peace on Earth, 1977. Rec. sec. Claremont Coordinating Council, 1982-84; mem. Mt. San Antonio Regional Arts Council, 1983-84. Recipient numerous scholarships, 1961-66. Mem. Presbyn. Assn. Musicians (cert. musician), Am. Guild Organists (registrar 1978-80), Music Tchrs. Assn. Calif., Calif. Fedn. Music Clubs (chmn. Pomona Valley Jr. Festival 1983, 84), Nat. Fedn. Music Clubs (chmn. So. Calif., Stillman Kelley scholar 1984, state chmn. jr. festivals 1984-85), Pomona Valley Musicians' Club, Suzuki Music Assn. Calif., Nat. Guild Community Schs. of Arts. Presbyterian. Clubs: Claremont Tennis; Gaston Country. Office: Claremont Community School of Music PO Box 53 Claremont CA 91711

HUFFMAN, HELEN HOBSON, finance officer; b. Raeford, N.C., July 30, 1944; d. Stacy Brown and Irene Catherine (Blue) Hobson; m. Linwood E. Huffman, Apr. 11, 1965; children—Kim, Chris, Jeff. Student U. N.C.-Greensboro, 1962-63, 1974—. Clk. inventory control House of Raeford, 1972-74; finance officer City of Raeford, 1974—. Treas., Hoke Swimming Assn., Raeford, 1983-85, Blazer Baseball Team, Raeford, 1983; pres. Fellowship Sunday School Class, Baptist Ch., 1980-85. Mem. Govt. Fin. Officers Assn., N.C. Pub. Fin. Officers Assn. (president's award 1984), N.C. Fin. Officers Assn. (bd. dirs. 1979-81, sec.-treas. 1981-82, pres. 1983—). Democrat. Avocations: Tennis; Baseball; Sewing; Woodcrafts; Painting. Home: 209 W Central Ave Raeford NC 28376 Office: City of Raeford PO Box 606 Raeford NC 28376

HUFFMAN, NONA GAY, investment and retirement specialist; b. Albuquerque, June 22, 1942; d. William Abraham and Opal Irene (Leaton) Crisp; m. Donald Clyde Williams, Oct. 20, 1961; children—Debra Gaylene, James Donald. Student pub. schs. Lawndale, Calif. Lic. ins., securities dealer, N.Mex. Sec. City of Los Angeles, 1960, Los Angeles City Schs. 1960-62, Aerospace Corp., El Segundo, Calif., 1962-64, Albuquerque Pub. Schs., 1972-73, Pub. Service Co. N.Mex., Albuquerque, 1973; rep., fin. planner Waddell & Reed, Inc., Albuquerque, 1979-84; broker Rauscher Pierce Refsnes, Inc., 1984-85; rep., investment and retirement specialist Fin. Network Investment Corp., 1985—; tchr. money mgmt. seminars for sr. citizens ctr. Mem. Profl. Orgn. Women (co-chmn.). Office: Fin Network Investment Corp 1418 Carlisle NE Suite A Albuquerque NM 87110

HUFFMAN, PATRICIA NELL, wholesale manufacturing company executive, designer, consultant; b. Springfield, Mo., Sept. 25, 1947; d. Rex Eugene and Helen Marie (Appleby) Riggs; m. Frank Dale Huffman, June 18, 1966; children—Chad, Heather, Tyler. Student Joplin Jr. Coll., 1966. Saleswoman Sta. KTVJ-TV, Joplin, Mo., 1972-77; designer, mktg. ADI-Comml. Interiors, Tulsa, 1983-84; pres., designer Bittersweet, Inc., Joplin, 1984—; cons. in field. Designer country gift items, 1978—. Vol., Mental Health Ctr., Joplin, 1965, Am. Heart Assn., Joplin, 1980, Family Self Help Ctr., Joplin, 1981—, United Way, Joplin, 1982; pres. Women's Support Group, Joplin, 1983-85. Mem. Nat. Assn. Female Execs. Avocations: golf; racquetball; bridge; creative writing. Office: Bittersweet Inc Route 8 Box 283 Joplin MO 64801

HUFFMAN, ROSEMARY ADAMS, lawyer, construction company executive; b. Orlando, Fla., Oct. 18, 1939; d. Elmer Victor and Esther (Weber) Adams; divorced; 1 child, Justin Adams Fruth. A.B. in Econs., Ind. U., 1959, J.D., 1962; LL.M., U. Chgo., 1967. Bar: Ind. 1962. Dep. prosecutor Marion County, Ind., 1963; ct. adminstr. Ind. Supreme Ct., 1967-68; pro-tem judge Marion County Mcpl. Ct., 1969-70; jud. coordinator Ind. Criminal Justice Planning Agy., 1969-70; dir. ctr. for Jud. Edn., Inc., 1970-73; pub. Jud. Xchange, 1972-73; instr. bus. law Purdue U., Indpls., 1962-63, Ind. U., Indpls., 1963-64; asst. Ind. Jud. Council, 1965; legis. intern Ford Found., 1965; sole practice, Indpls., 1962—; pres., owner Abacus, Inc., Indpls., 1980—. Mem. Ind. Bar Assn., Fla. Bar Assn., Indpls. Bar Assn. Home and Office: 6630 E 56th St Indianapolis IN 46226

HUFFMAN, TEELA LOUISE LEWELLEN, medical center administrator; b. Tulsa, May 17, 1948; d. Delmar Huron and Joliet Arlie (Russell) Lewellen; m. Clyde Dean Huffman, Sept. 30, 1980. Student, Okla. State Tech. Inst. Keypunch operator T.G.&Y. Co., Oklahoma City, 1966-68; keypunch supr. Nat. Sharedata Co., Oklahoma City, 1968-71; computer operator Insured Aircraft Title Co., Oklahoma City, 1972-74; prodn. supr. Computer Mgmt. Corp., Oklahoma City, 1974-79; acct. mgr. Automatic Data Processing Co., Tulsa and Chgo., 1979; ops. mgr. Baptist Med. Ctr., Oklahoma City, 1979-86; dir. info. mgmt. South Community Hosp., Oklahoma City, Okla., 1986—. Mem. Assn. for Computers Ops. Mgrs., Nat. Assn. Female Execs., Southwest Software Users Group. Republican. Baptist. Avocations: photography; travel; working with children. Home: 1617 College Ave Oklahoma City OK 73196 Office: South Community Hosp 1001 SW 44th St Oklahoma City OK 73109

HUFFMAN, VIRGINIA MCGUIRE, association executive; b. Renovo, Pa., Sept. 13, 1940; d. John Alfred McGuire and Virginia Elizabeth (Wolfe) McGuire Rothwell; m. Alfred John Beatty, Oct. 6, 1962 (dec. Feb. 1981); m. Robert J. Huffman, Nov. 16, 1984; children—John Alfred, Heather Lyn. Student U. Alaska, 1958-59; B.A., Fla. Atlantic U., 1966; M.A., Stetson U., 1978. Market rep. Villager, Inc., N.Y.C., 1965-70; dir. pub. relations Arts and Sci. Council, Charlotte, N.C., 1978-81; exec. dir. Am. Heart Assn., Charlotte, 1981-84. Mem. pub. relations com. Arts and Sci. Council, Charlotte, 1979-82; bd. dirs. Charlotte Pops Orch., 1981—; trustee United Community Services, Charlotte, 1981—. Mem. Charlotte C. of C. (uptown promotion com. 1980-84), Women in Communications, Women's Polit. Caucus, Pub. Relations Soc. Democrat. Roman Catholic. Home: 3931 Colony Crossing Dr Charlotte NC 28211 Office: 5601 Camelot Dr Matthews NC 28105

HUFFNUSS, BARBARA, health care executive; b. Chgo., Oct. 6, 1953; d. Klaus and Katharina (Gutti) Huffnuss. B.S. in Pharmacy, U. Ill.-Chgo., 1977. Registered pharmacist, Ill. Pharmacist, store mgr. Medicare Pharmacy, Chgo., 1977-78, Skokie, Ill., 1978-83; dist. dir. Medicare-Glaser Corp., Chgo., 1983—. Mem. Ill. Pharm. Assn., Am. Pharm. Assn. Democrat. Roman Catholic. Office: Medicare Pharmacy 2805 Devon Ave Chicago IL 60659

HUFNAGL, MARY FRANCES, radiography educator; b. Blue Island, Ill., Aug. 25, 1952; d. Darwin George and Dorothy F. (Sminchak) Hufnagl. A.A.S., Moraine Valley Community Coll., 1976; cert. health sci. mgmt. U. Ill.-Chgo., 1979. Staff technologist Central Community Hosp., Chgo., 1975-76, Holy Cross Hosp., Chgo., 1976-81; clin. instr. radiology U. Chgo. Hosps. and Clinics, 1981—; asst. coordinator Emergency Services Disaster Agy., Calumet Park, Ill., 1970-78; instr. first aid ARC, 1973-76. Mem. Ill. Soc. Radiologic Technologists (sec. dist. 1983, v.p., pres.-elect 1984—); Am. Soc. Radiologic Technologists, NOW (v.p. chpt. 1983—). Democrat. Roman Catholic. Home: 11801 Karlov St Alsip IL 60658 Office: Dept of Radiology U of Chicago 950 E 59th St Box 429 Chicago IL 60630

HUFNAGLE, BARBARA A., child care center executive; b. Brookville, Ohio, Apr. 18, 1939; d. Kenneth Harry and Gladys Iola (Lesher) Protzman; m. David R. Hufnagle, July 24, 1954 (div. June 1975); children—Eleanor Ruth, Julie Anne, Robert Walter. B.S. in Edn., Miami U., Oxford, Ohio, 1969, M.Ed. in Guidance and Counseling, 1972, M.Ed. in Curriculum and Supervision, 1975. Cert. ednl. adminstr. First grade tchr. West Carrollton Pub. Schs., Ohio, 1968—; pres., owner, mgr. Little Sch. Child Care Ctr., West Carrollton, 1976—. Author: Instructional Centers, 1983. Asst. band dir. West Carrollton High Sch. Band, 1983-85. Mem. NEA, Ohio Edn. Assn., West Carrollton Edn. Assn. (v.p. 1982—), Assn. for Supervision and Curriculum Devel., Nat. Assn. Edn. Young Children, U.S. Power Squadron, Ohio Assn. Child Care Providers, also yacht clubs and square dance clubs. Home: 6410 Blossom Park Dr West Carrollton OH 45449 Office: Little School Child Care Ctr 1049 Alex Rd Dayton OH 45449

HUFSTEDLER, SHIRLEY MOUNT (MRS. SETH M. HUFSTEDLER), lawyer; b. Denver, Aug. 24, 1925; d. Earl Stanley and Eva (Von Behren) Mount; B.B.A., U. N.Mex., 1945, LL.D., 1972; LL.B., Stanford U., 1949; LL.D. (hon.), U. Wyo., 1970, Gonzaga U., 1970, Occidental Coll., 1971, Tufts U., 1974, U. So. Calif., 1976, U. Pa., 1976, Georgetown U., 1976, U. Pacific, 1977, Columbia U., 1977, U. Mich., 1978, Rutgers U., 1981, Yale U., 1981, Claremont U. Center, 1981, Smith Coll., 1982, Syracuse U., 1983; H.H.D., Hood Coll., 1981; m. Seth Martin Hufstedler, Aug. 16, 1949; 1 child, Steven Mark. Bar: Calif. 1950; Pvt. practice Los Angeles, 1961, mem. firm of Beardsley, Hufstedler & Kemble, Los Angeles, 1951-61; mem. staff Stanford U. Law Rev., 1947-49, article and book rev. editor, 1948-49, judge Superior Ct., County Los Angeles, 1961-66; justice Calif. Ct. Appeal for 2d dist., 1966-68; circuit judge U.S. Ct. Appeals, 9th Circuit, 1968-79, U.S. sec. of edn., Washington, 1979-81; partner firm Hufstedler, Miller, Carlson & Beardsley, Los Angeles, 1981-85; dir. Hewlett Packard Co., U.S. West, Inc. Former bd. councilors Law Center U. So. Calif.; trustee Calif. Inst. Tech., Occidental Coll., Aspen Inst. Humanistic Studies, Colonial Williamsburg Found., John D. and Catherine T. MacArthur Found., Carnegie Endowment for Internat. Peace, 1985—, Inst. Advanced Studies, 1985-86; bd. overseers Inst. Civil Justice (Rand Corp.). Named Woman of Yr., Los Angeles Times, 1968, Ladies Home Jour., 1976; recipient UCLA medal, 1981. Mem. Am., Los Angeles bar assns., Women Lawyers Assn. (pres. 1957-58), Am. Judicature Soc. Council Fgn. Relations, Am. Law Inst. (council mem. 1975—), Inst. Jud. Adminstrn., Town Hall, Order of Coif. Office: 700 S Flower St Los Angeles CA 90017

HUGGARD, EILEEN ELISABETH, lawyer; b. N.Y.C., Apr. 12, 1957; d. Raymond Francis and Carol Jean (Kinsella) H. A.A.S., Agrl. and Tech. Coll. SUNY-Farmingdale, 1977; B.A. summa cum laude with highest honors in Communication Arts, Hofstra U., 1980; J.D., Georgetown U., 1983. Bar: D.C., 1983. Assoc. Pellegrin & Levine, Chartered, Washington, 1983—. Mem. ABA, Women's Bar Assn. of D.C., Women in Communications, Fed. Communications Bar Assn., D.C. Bar, Phi Beta Kappa, Pi Sigma Alpha. Roman Catholic. Office: Pellegrin & Levine Chartered 1140 Connecticut Ave Suite 312 Washington DC 20036

HUGGINS, CANNIE MAE COX HUNTER, former educator; b. Belton, Tex., July 16, 1916; d. Jesse Daniel and Mary Alice (Hamilton) Cox; B.S., Mary Hardin Baylor Coll., 1940; M.S., San Marcos Tchrs. Coll., 1942; postgrad. U. Tex., 1946-47, Tex. Tech U., 1956-70, U. San Diego, 1975, St. Mary's U., 1976; m. William Dudley Hunter, June 5, 1938 (div. 1967); children—Darline, Bob Roy; m. 2d, Bertrand Huggins, Aug. 4, 1979 (dec. July 19, 1980). Tchr. pub. schs., Belton, 1935-38, Galveston, Tex., 1938-42; mem. staff testing dept. U. Ariz., 1942-43; reading cons. Phoenix Pub. Schs., 1943-45; tchr.-counselor pub. schs., Killeen, Tex., 1946-54; classroom tchr., Lubbock, Tex., 1954-74; tchr. first grade bilingual lang. devel. Posey Elementary Sch., Lubbock, Tex., 1974-82; pres. CM Corp. First aid chmn. ARC, Lubbock County, 1960-63, first aid instr., 1956—; area dir. March of Dimes, 1958-63; tchr. high sch. dept. First Bapt. Ch., Lubbock, 1960—; state advisor U.S. Congl. Adv. Bd., 1985—. Recipient Outstanding Service award ARC, 1966; Bronze award CONTACT Lubbock. Cert. educator, Tex. Mem. Assn. Childhood Edn. Internat., NEA, Tex. Tchrs. Assn., Tex. Classroom Tchrs. Assn., Nat. PTA, Tex. Edn. Assn., Lubbock Educators Assn., Lubbock Classroom Tchrs. Assn., AAUW, Am. Bus. Women's Assn., S. Plains Writers Guild, YWCA, Lubbock, Killeen chambers commerce. Baptist. Club: University City (Lubbock). Home: 4626 30th St Lubbock TX 79410

HUGGINS, MYRTLE EVELYN, hotel executive; b. Childress, Tex., Feb. 16, 1925; d. Peter Abraham IV and Ida Rebecca (Hawkins) Deel; m. Jackson Huggins, Jr., June 24, 1941. Student Roswell Bus. Coll., 1948, Alaska Community Coll., 1978-83. Co-owner, sec. treas. Huggins, Inc., Anchorage, 1959-85; real estate agt. Marston Real Estate, Anchorage, 1960-64; real estate broker Huggins Realty, Inc., Anchorage, 1970-74, tchr., 1974-75; ptnr. Golden Lion Hotel, Anchorage, 1975—; com. mem. Anchorage Bd. Realtors Profl. Standards, 1972-73, 74; pres. Women's Council Bd. Realtors, 1970-74, mem. ex officio Bd. Realtors, 1970-75; mem. Multi Listing Service, 1970-75. Served to Pvt. WACS, 1945. Mem. AARP, Am. Legion, Anchorage Bus. and Profl. Women/USA (corr. sec. 1985-86, parlimentarian 1984-85), Spenard Bus. and Profl. Women (sec. treas., v.p., 1965-80), Alaska Fed. Bus. and Profl. Women U.S.A. (mem. coms. parlimentarian), Epsilon Sigma Alpha (sec.-treas., v.p., pres. 1965-85). Avocation: family history photographer. Home: 2820 Kempton Hills Dr Anchorage AK 95516-0056 Office: Best Western Goldon Lion Hotel 1000 E 36th Ave Anchorage AK 99508

HUGGINS, SARA COLLINS, lawyer; b. Shelbyville, Ky., June 13, 1954; d. Rudolph and Ruth Pauline (Stivers) Collins; m. Frederick George Huggins, June 28, 1981. B.A., Georgetown Coll., 1975; J.D., U. Ky.-Lexington, 1978. Bar: Ky. 1979. Law clk. Pub. Defender, Frankfort, Ky., 1979, atty., 1979-81; mem. firm Stewart & Roelandt, Crestwood, Ky., 1982-83; sole practice, Louisville, 1983-84; faculty Sullivan Jr. Coll., 1983, U. Louisville, 1984. Mem. Ky. Bar Assn., ABA. Club: Bus. and Profl. Women's. Democrat. Episcopalian. Home: 6110 N Washington Blvd Arlington VA 22205

HUGGINS, SARA ESPE, retired biology educator, researcher; b. Denver, June 29, 1913; d. Paul Albert and Ethel Maria (Benton) Espe; m. Russell Arno Huggins, Aug. 31, 1936; children—James Lee, George Raymond. A.B. Aurora U., 1934; M.S., U. Ill., 1936; Ph.D., Case Western Res. U., 1939. Instr. Payne Coll., Augusta, Ga., 1946-47; asst. prof., prof. U. Houston, 1947-78, prof. emerita, 1978—, chmn. biology dept., 1952-64; prof., acting chmn. biology dept. Mahidol U., Bangkok, Thailand, 1972-73; vis. prof. Fed. U., Pernambuco Recife, Brazil, 1979-80, 83. Contbr. articles to profl. publs. Mem. Am. Physiol. Soc., Soc. Exptl. Biology and Medicine, Assn. for Women Sci., Sigma Xi, Phi Kappa Phi. Avocations: swimming; genealogy. Home: 4811 Palmetto Bellaire TX 77401 Office: U Houston Houston TX 77004

HUGHES, ANN HIGHTOWER, economist; b. Birmingham, Ala., Nov. 24, 1938; d. Brady Alexander and Juanita Whitfield (Pope) Hughes; B.A., George Washington U., 1962, M.A., 1969. Internat. economist Dept. Commerce, Washington, 1963-77, dep. asst. sec. for trade agreements, 1981, dep. asst. sec. for western hemisphere, 1982—; mgr. U.S. tariff negotiations during multilateral trade negotiations for U.S. Trade Rep., Exec. Office of Pres., 1977-79; asst. U.S. Trade Rep. for Interagy. Coordination, 1979-80. Office: Dept Commerce 14th and Constitution Ave NW Washington DC 20230

HUGHES, BARBARA ANN, dietitian, public health administrator; b. McMinn County, Tenn., July 22, 1938; d. Cecil Earl and Hannah Ruth (Moss) Farmer; B.S. cum laude in Home Econs. Carson Newman Coll., Jefferson City, Tenn., 1960; M.S. in Instl. Mgmt., Ohio State U., Columbus, 1963; M.A. (Adonarium Judson scholar), So. Bapt. Theol. Sem., 1968; M.P.H. in Public Health Adminstrn., U. N.C., Chapel Hill, 1972; postgrad. in nutrition U. Iowa, 1974, U. N.C., 1975-85, Case Western Res. U., 1979, Walden U., 1986—; m. Carl Clifford Hughes, Oct. 13, 1962. Dietitian, instr. Riverside Meth. Hosp., Riverside Whitecross Sch. Nursing, Columbus, 1963-66; consulting dietitian eastern region N.C. Bd. Health, Raleigh, 1968-73; dir. Nutrition and Dietary Services br., div. Health Services, N.C. Dept. Human Resources, Raleigh, 1973—, also dir. Women-Infants-Children Program; cons. dietitian Mt. Holly Nursing Home, Louisville, 1967-68; adj. asst. prof. dept. nutrition Sch. Public Health, U. N.C., Chapel Hill; mem. adv. bd. Hospitality Edn. program N.C. Dept. Community Colls., 1974—, adv. com. Ret. Senior Vol. Program, Raleigh and Wake County, N.C., 1975-79, N.C. Network Coordinating Council for End-Stage Renal Disease, 1975, Nat. Adv. Council on Maternal, Infant, and Fetal Nutrition, Spl. Supplemental Food Program for Women, Infants, and Children, Dept. Agr., 1976-79, adv. com. Nutrition Edn. and Tng. program N.C. Dept. Public Instruction, 1978-80; coordinator undergrad. program in gen. dietetics East Carolina U.; adv. council N.C. Gov.'s Office Citizen Affairs; lectr., cons.; cons. dietitian Augusta Victoria Hosp. and Jerusalem (Israel) Crippled Childrens Center, 1968; witness U.S. congressional and Senate hearings in field. Active edn. programs Pullen Memorial Bapt. Church, Raleigh, deacon, 1976-80, area ministry capt., 1977-78, personnel com., 1978-80; dietitian/dir. food service archeol. expedition to Israel, 1978; bd. dirs. N.C. Literacy Assn. 1978-83, pres., 1981-83; v.p. Wake County Literacy Council, 1986-87; trustee Gardner-Webb Coll., Boiling Springs, N.C., 1979-82, chmn. curriculum com., 1981-82; chmn. Coalition Pub. Health Nutrition, 1983-85; del. various Democratic Convs., 1981-84, precinct sec.-treas., 1981-83, 1st vice chmn., 1983-85, chair, 1985-87; chmn. adv. bd. dept. home econs. Carson-Newman Coll. Named Woman of Yr., Wake County, 1975, N.C. Outstanding Dietitian of Yr., 1976, N.C. Outstanding Dietitian, Southeastern Hosp. Conf. for Dietitians, 1978; Disting. Alumna award Carson-Newman Coll., 1983. Mem. AAUW (life, pres. Raleigh br. 1971-75, pres. N.C. div. 1978-80, nat. bd. dirs. 1980-82, area rep. 1980-82), Am. Dietetic Assn. (del. 1971-74, pres. N.C. state assn. 1976-77, N.C. network legis. coordinator 1978-81, nat. nominating com. 1979-80, nat. chmn. council on practice 1982-83, chair legislation and pub. policy com. 1985-87), Am. Public Health Assn. (exec. com. So. br. 1977—, sec.-treas. 1979-80, 1st v.p. 1980-81), So. Health Assn. (pres. 1982-83, chair nominating com. 1985-86), Assn. State and Territorial Public Health Nutrition Dirs. (pres. 1977-79, dir. 1981—, liaison to Assn. Faculties Grad. Program in Pub. Health Nutrition, chair legis. com. 1984—), N.C. Council Foods and Nutrition (dir. 1976-78, chmn. membership 1975, nominating com. 1979). N.C. Council Women's Orgns., Am. Acad. Health Adminstrn., Soc. Nutrition Edn., Nutrition Today Soc., N.C. Acad. Public Health, Ohio State U. Alumni Assn., U. N.C. Gen. Alumni Assn. (life), U. N.C. Public Health Alumni Assn. (life), Altrusa Internat. (pres. Raleigh club 1973-74, dir. 1976-78, 1st vice gov. 1978-79, chmn. nomination com. 1980-82, gov. dist. Three, 1979-80, internat. vocat. services chmn. 1977-79, 1st v.p.), Altrusa Internat. Found. (1st v.p.), Women's Forum N.C. Co-author: Diet and Kidney Disease, Assn. for N.C. Regional Med. Program, 1969; contbr. numerous papers, articles to symposia, periodicals in field, vol. areas. Home: 4208 Galax Dr Raleigh NC 27612 Office: PO Box 2091 Raleigh NC 27602

HUGHES, BARBARA JEANNE, maritime company official, educator; b. Ft. Belvoir, Va., June 25, 1951; d. William Edward and Mary Barbara (Lydon) H. B.B.A., Chaminade U., Honolulu, 1973, M.B.A., 1978. Dir. travel study program Chaminade U., 1974, dir. summer programs, 1974-77, edn. counselor, 1977-79, dir. counseling center, 1979-80; market analyst Dillingham Maritime Pacific Div., Honolulu, 1980, pub. relations adminstr., 1980—; instr. mktg. and advt. Chaminade U., 1979—. Fund raiser Boy Scouts Am., 1982-84; vol. Aloha United Way, 1982—; pub. relations vol. Honolulu Marathon Assn., 1983. Mem. Pub. Relations Soc. Am., Nat. Def. Transp. Assn., Pacific and Asian Affairs Council. Roman Catholic. Office: Dillingham Maritime Pacific Div PO Box 3288 711 Nimitz Hwy Honolulu HI 96801

HUGHES, CANDACE SUZANNE, public relations writer; b. Delaware, Ohio, Feb. 19, 1952; d. George Richard and Martha Irene (Burroughs) Doland; m. Steven William Hughes, Sept. 15, 1973. B.A. in Journalism, Ohio State U., 1975; M.A. in Journalism, Ohio U., 1984. Cert. community coll. tchr., Ariz. Intern Ohio Ho. of Reps., Columbus, 1976; reporter Yuma (Ariz.) Daily Sun, 1977-79; asst. to med. info. dir., mng. editor Ohio D.O. alumni mag., Coll. Osteopathic Medicine, Ohio University, Athens, 1979-80; grad. assoc., Ohio U., 1980-81; reporter Scottsdale (Ariz.) Progress, 1981-84; writer Joanne Ralston and Assoc. Pub. Relations, Phoenix, 1984—; cons. Scottsdale Community Hosp., 1984—. Author: (with others) A Guidebook for Legislators, 1976. Mem. Arizona Presswomen's Assn., Soc. Profl. Journalists, Women in Communication, Internat. Assn. Bus. Communicators, LWV (dir. Athens chpt. 1981, newsletter editor Yuma chpt. 1978), Kappa Tau Alpha. Democrat. Office: Joanne Ralston and Assocs 3003 N Central Ave P MPhoenix AZ 85012

HUGHES, CAROL BRENDA, nurse administrator, educator; b. Atlanta, Jan. 7, 1949; d. Boyd Emory and Marilee (Johnston) H. A.D. in Nursing Ga. State U., 1973; B.S.N., Med. Coll. Ga., 1974, M.S. in Nursing, 1975. Staff nurse South Fulton Hosp., East Point, Ga., 1973-75, Grady Meml. Hosp., Atlanta, 1975-76; clin. nurse specialist Crawford W. Long Hosp., Atlanta, 1976-81, oncology clin. nurse coordinator, 1981—; hon. clin. instr. Ga. State U., Atlanta, 1982—; lectr. on cancer treatment to numerous profl. groups. Contbr. articles to tech. pubs. Nursing edn. vol. Am. Cancer Soc., 1980—. Recipient Cert. for Outstanding Preceptor, Ga. State U. Sch. Nursing, 1984. Mem. Am. Nurse's Assn., Oncology Nursing Soc., Clin. Oncology Assn. Ga., Ga. Nurses Assn. (joint practices com.), Nat. Intravenous Therapy Assn., Sigma Theta Tau. Methodist. Avocation: aircraft piloting. Home: 3050 Margaret Mitchell Dr NW Apt 18 Atlanta GA 30327 Office: Crawford W Long Hosp 35 Linden Ave NE Atlanta GA 30365

HUGHES, CHERI LYNN (CHERYL), modeling and television company executive; b. Cin., July 26, 1957; d. Harold Edward Hughes and Helen Marie (Miles) Perdue; Student N.Y. Inst. Art, 1974-75, Community Coll., Melbourne, Fla., 1973-75. Mem. dept. pub. relations Harris Corp., Melbourne, 1975-84; owner Cherie's/Casablancas, Indialantic, Fla., 1978—. Named Miss Galaxy Merritt Island, Fla., 1974; Miss Hemisphere, Cocoa Beach, Fla., 1974; Miss All Am., Melbourne, Fla., 1975. Mem. Melbourne C. of C., Palm Bay C. of C., Internat. Talent and Fashion. Democrat. Baptist. Club: Spanish (Melbourne). Avocations: designing; golfing; swimming; snow skiing; racquetball. Office: Cherie's/Casablancas Inc 404 5th Ave Suite A Indialantic FL 32903

HUGHES, CYNTHIA KENDALL, fashion designer, artist; b. Jackson, Miss., Jan. 18, 1957; d. Dudley Joe and Robbie Lou (Watson) H. B.S., Miss. State U., 1979. Pres., Erin Kendall of Ireland, N.Y.C., 1980-81, Cindy & Phil, Inc., N.Y.C., 1981-83, Cindy Hughes Designs, Inc., N.Y.C., 1983—; freelance fashion cons. and fashion show coordinator, Jackson, Miss. and regional area,

1977-79. Patron, Animal Rescue League, Nat., 1984—. Named Oustanding Mississippian Cancer Found., 1984. Republican. Baptist. Avocations: snow skiing; sailing; painting; cooking. Home: 2 Sutton Pl S #PhC New York NY 10022 Office: Cindy Hughes Designs Inc 405 E 72d St New York NY 10021

HUGHES, EDITH MARGARET, marketing executive; b. Denver, Mar. 21, 1949; d. Delmar Vern and Margaret Virginia (Smith) H.; m. Nicholas George Nonas, Sept. 11, 1983; children—Melanie Evelyn, Kathryn Irene. M.A., Ohio U., 1972. Dir. residence life Doane Coll., Crete, Nebr., 1972-73; v.p. Community Response of Colo., Denver, 1973-78; v.p., dir. research Entercom Inc., Denver, 1978-83; pres. Kinzley Hughes Inc., Denver, 1983—. Active Leadership Denver, Inc., 1983; co-chmn. AMC Women's Event, Denver, 1982; mem. mktg. com., United Way, Denver, 1982, 83. Mem. Am. Mktg. Assn. Republican. Greek Orthodox. Office: Kinzley-Hughes Inc 1623 Blake St Suite 475 Denver CO 80202

HUGHES, EDITH MARGARET, newspaper editor; b. Pitts., Dec. 9, 1931; d. Joseph Bernard and Marie Eglon (Harris) Hughes; children—Ronald, Sandra, Linda, Jeannine. B.A., U. Pitts., 1953. Corr., Pekin (Ill.) Times, 1959-61, Hammond (Ind.) Times, 1968-73; TV writer Gateway Publs., Monroeville, Pa., 1974, reporter, 1975-79, asst. editor east suburban papers, 1979-81, editor east suburban papers, 1981-83, mng. editor 17 newspapers, 1983—. Recipient 5 Keystone State awards, 1980, 82, 85, 86, Golden Quill award, 1980, Key art awards. Mem. Nat. Honor Soc. Republican. Episcopalian. Home: 1047 Harvard Rd Monroeville PA 15146 Office: Gateway Publications 610 Beatty Rd Monroeville PA 15146

HUGHES, ELAINE MARIE, social worker; b. Seattle; d. Arthur Thorvald and Magda Josefine (Mikaelsen) Kjellmann; A.A., Imperial Valley Coll., 1964; B.A., San Diego State Coll., 1966; postgrad Calif. State U.-Long Beach, 1966; M.S.W., U. So. Calif., 1977; m. Hugh Hugo Hughes, May 5, 1972. Cert. tchr., Calif.; lic. clin. social work, Calif. Sec., Bethlehem Steel Co., 1944-46, Nat. Auto Ins. Co., 1947-48, Zurich Inst. Co., 1948-49; clk. Home Indemnity, 1950-51; med. sec. U.S. Navy Hosp., Oceanside, 1952-54, VA Hosp., 1956; salesperson Turner Investment Co., 1962; sec. U.S. Dept. Agr., 1962-63; social worker adoption div. Imperial County Welfare Dept., El Centro, Calif., 1966-68, Orange County Dept. Social Service, Santa Ana, Calif., 1968-75; clin. social worker Human Services Agy., Orange County, Calif., 1977-79; social work cons., Santa Ana, 1980—, U.S. Navy Family Services, Long Beach, Calif., 1982-83; chief services USMC Air Sta., El Toro, Calif., 1983-84; clin. social worker Los Angeles County Dept. Children's Services, 1985—; mem. East Orange County Child Abuse Task Force, 1979. Mem. Acad. Cert. Social Workers, AAUW, Nat. Assn. Social Workers. Lutheran.

HUGHES, ELINOR LAMBERT, drama editor, critic; b. Cambridge, Mass., Mar. 3, 1906; d. Hector James and Elinor (Lambert) H.; ed. Buckingham Sch., Cambridge, 1915-20, May Sch., Boston, 1920-23; A.B., Radcliffe Coll., 1927; m. David D. Jacobus, July 14, 1957; stepchildren—David P. Jacobus, John H. Jacobus. Asst. in drama dept. Boston Herald-Traveler, 1929-34, drama and film editor and critic, 1934-66; lectr. on drama and film criticism. Mem. Soc. Preservation New Eng. Antiquities, Inst. Contemporary Art. Republican. Unitarian. Author: Famous Stars of Filmdom (Men) and Famous Stars of Filmdom (Women), 1932; Passing Through to Broadway, 1948. Blank verse rev. of Shakespearean prodns. included in Best News Stories of 1937-38. Home: 24 Academy Ln Bellport NY 11713

HUGHES, EMILY KARLA VOLLMAR, food scientist, nutritionist; b. Kansas City, Kans., Jan. 31, 1951; d. Emil Karl and Mildred (Harker) Vollmar; B.S. (Martha S. Pittman scholar 1972), Kans. State U., 1972, M.S., 1974; Ph.D., U. Tenn., Knoxville, 1978; m. L.R. Hughes, III. Grad. research asst., foods and nutrition, Kans. State U., Manhattan, 1973-74, asst. prof., state extension specialist, foods and nutrition, 1979; instr. human nutrition and foods Va. Poly. Inst. and State U., Blacksburg, 1974-76; grad. research asst. in food tech. and sci. U. Tenn., Knoxville, 1976-78; asst. prof., state extension specialist, human nutrition, foods, food systems mgmt. U. Mo., Columbia, 1980—, coordinator computer activities Home Econs. Extension, 1981—, mem. Mo. Coop. Extension Computer Com., 1982-84. Adv. com. home econs. curriculum Columbia Public Sch. System, 1981-82; mem. Super Shopper program Columbia-U. Mo. Columbia Chpt. Vet. Wives, 1980. Mem. Inst. Food Technologists, Am. Dietic Assn. (registered), Mo. Dietetic Assn., Central Mo. Dietetic Assn. (chmn. community nutrition com. 1980), Am. Home Econs. Assn., Mo. Home Econs. Assn., Assn. for Devel. of Computer-based Instructional Systems, Sigma Xi, Phi Kappa Phi, Phi Upsilon Omicron, Omicron Nu, Phi Tau Sigma (sec. U. Tenn. chpt., 1979), Gamma Sigma Delta. Contbr. papers to profl. confs.; coordinator com. for revision of Handbook of Food Preparation, Am. Home Econs. Assn., 1979; contbg. author to videotape and slide programs in field, articles to publs. in field. Home: 3421 St Charles Rd Columbia MO 62201 Office: 308 Gwynn Hall Univ Mo Columbia MO 65211

HUGHES, GRACE ANN, bus company executive; b. San Francisco, Nov. 19, 1937; d. William George and Ruth Grace (Plier) Melbern; m. Paul Heron Hughes (div. 1973) children—Jolie Anna, David Trevor. B.A., San Francisco State U., 1976. Fashion dir. Macy's Dept. Store, San Franciso, 1958-60; program dir. Coro Found., San Francisco, N.Y.C., 1978-80; pres., chief exec. officer Marin Airporter Co., Larkspur, Calif., 1984—. Chmn. bd. dirs. Marin County Mental Health Adv. Bd., Calif., 1979-80; bd. dirs Marin Symphony Bd., Big Bros., Mental Health Assn.; program dir. Democratic Nat. Com., N.Y.C., Washington, 1980-84. Mem. Am. Bus Assn., Calif. Bus Assn. (bd. dirs.), United Bus Owners Am. Club: Commonwealth (San Francisco). Office: Marin Airporter Co 300 Larkspur Landing Circle Larkspur CA 94939

HUGHES, JANE WOLFORD, educational administrator, speaker, writer; b. Detroit, June 8, 1920; d. Frank Ralph and Corinne Marie (Ouellette) Gerbig; m. Eugene Wolford, Sept. 23, 1944 (dec. Nov. 11, 1969); children—Diane, Maureen, Michael, John, James, Joseph, Marie Therese; m. 2d, John P. Hughes, June 1, 1972; 8 stepchildren. Student St. Mary Coll. and St. Cyril and Methodius Sem., Orchard Lake, Mich., 1972-73, St. Joseph's Coll., Cin., 1966-67, U. Detroit, 1965-68, Wayne State U., 1943-44; Ph.B., Marygrove Coll., 1942. Fashion copywriter J.L. Hudson Dept. Store, Detroit, 1942-44; dir. pub. relations Archdiocese of Detroit, 1959-62; chmn. pub. relations Nat. Council Cath. Women, Washington, 1960-64; dir. adult edn. Archdiocese of Detroit, 1966-85; mem. Nat. Think Tank, U.S. govt., Washington, 1972; chairperson leadership conf. Mich. Cath. Conf., 1977; mem. com. on edn. U.S. Cath. Conf., 1982—; mem. nat. adv. com. Adult Catechesis Exec. Com., 1974—; mem. faculty St. Mary Coll., Orchard Lake, 1977, 81, St. John Sem., Plymouth, Mich., 1981—; workshop and keynote speaker in field. Authors manuals; contbr. articles, chpts. to profl. publs.; writer, producer ednl. and tng. TV programs, 1968-72; editor: Working with Adult Learners, 1981. Mem. Round Table Christians and Jews, Detroit, 1962-68; mem. City of Detroit United Community Services, 1965-67; mem. Detroit Commn. on Human Relations, 1967-69; mem. Detroit Get Out and Vote Comm., 1968. Recipient Mother Domittala award Marygrove Coll., 1967, Key to City award City of Detroit, 1968; 1st place creativity award Adult Edn. Assn. Mich., 1968-69, creativity award hon. mention, 1970. Mem. Nat. Cath. Edn. Assn. (bd. dirs. 1967-76, Pres.'s award 1976), Religious Edn. Assn. U.S.A. and Can. (dir. 1976-80), Adult Edn. Assn. U.S.A. (chmn. religious sect. 1976-82). Clubs: Women's Economic, Press (Detroit). Office: Archdiocese of Detroit Dept Edn 305 Michigan Ave Detroit MI 48226

HUGHES, JUDI WATSON, oil company executive; b. Vicksburg, Miss., June 10, 1950; d. Lyman Thurston and Vivian Allene (Keyes) Watson; m. Dalton Lee Hughes, Apr. 20, 1985. B.A. in Journalism, La. State U., 1972. Lic. real estate broker, Tex. Salesman real estate Century 21, Houston, 1975-80; analyst contract Scurlock Oil Co., Houston, 1980-84; supr. contract and lease adminstrn., 1985—. Mem. Crude Oil Assn. Republican. Avocations: miniatures; doll collector; snow skiing. Home: 10701 Greenwillow Houston TX 77035 Office: Scurlock Oil Co Three Allen Ctr 29th Floor Houston TX 77002

HUGHES, JUDITH ANN, chemist; b. Denver, Dec. 27, 1941; d. William Leonard and Alice (Buckley) Reichwein; B.A. in Chemistry, Loretto Heights Coll., Denver, 1964; postgrad. U. Colo.; m. Roy A. Hughes, Oct. 15, 1971. With Public Service Co. of Colo., Denver, 1967—, supt. chemistry, 1974-81, dir. fuel forecasting and utilization, 1981-84, mgr. prodn. fuel and water, 1984-85, service mgr., 1985—; mem. exec. bd. Women and Bus. Conf., 1982—; pres., chmn. bd. Women and Bus. Enterprises, Inc., 1983—. Mem. Edison Electric Inst. (exec. com.), Am. Chem. Soc., Am. Entrepreneurs Assn., Nat. Assn. Female Execs., Exec. and Profl. Women's Council (co-founder, pres. 1980-81). Democrat. Home: 8097 Brook Dr Littleton CO 80123 Office: PO Box 840 Denver CO 80201

HUGHES, JUDITH MEEHAN, information systems executive; b. N.J., July 9, 1939; d. Joseph and Ellen (Raftery) Meehan; m. Thomas M. Hughes; children—Thomas, Dennis. B.A., Marywood Coll., 1960; M.S., U. Bridgeport, 1975. Cert. systems profl. Programming mgr. Johnson & Johnson, New Brunswick, N.J., 1969-72; account mgr., cons. Computer Assistance, Stamford, Conn., 1977-80; mgr. systems design Gen. Electric Co., Bridgeport, Conn., 1980-85; dir. info. systems Save the Children, Westport, 1985—. Contbr. articles to profl. jours. Recipient Bausch & Lomb Sci. award, 1957; Rutherford Women's Club scholar, 1957; Readers Digest scholar, 1957; Marywood Coll. scholar, 1957-60. Mem. Data Processing Mgmt. Assn., Assn. for Systems Mgmt., Assn. for Computing Machinery. Roman Catholic. Home: 8 Quintard Pl Westport CT 06880

HUGHES, KATHLEEN ANN, lawyer; b. Providence, Feb. 9, 1953; d. Paul Maurice and Bernadette Theresa (Sheehan) H.; m. James Nesbitt Dunlop, II, Sept. 1, 1979. B.A. cum laude, Carleton Coll., 1974; J.D. magna cum laude, U. Minn., 1979. Bar: to Minn. 1979, U.S. Dist. Ct. Minn., 1979. Mgmt. analyst Minn. Dept. Adminstrn., St. Paul, 1974-76; sr. mgmt. analyst Minn. Dept. Pub. Welfare, St. Paul, 1976, cons., 1976-77; research asst. U. Minn. Law Sch., Mpls., 1978-79; assoc. firm Fredrikson & Byron, P.A., Mpls., 1979-85, shareholder, 1985—; dir. Hennepin County Bar Assn. Legal Advice Clinics, Mpls., 1982—, mem. exec. com., 1982-83, 84—, treas., 1984-85. Co-author article in field. Precinct chmn. Democratic Farmer Labor Party, St. Paul, 1982-84, del. state conv., 1982. Mem. ABA, Minn. Bar Assn., Hennepin County Bar Assn., Order of Coif.

HUGHES, LINDA ELLEN, business executive; b. Noble County, Ohio, Mar. 15, 1938; d. Charles Franklin and Verna Ellen (King) Dotson; m. Clair Hughes, Aug. 27, 1955; children—Edward Wayne, Scott Anthony, Daniel Steven. Office mgr., realtor Reed Realty, Caldwell, Ohio, 1969-83; v.p., treas. Clair Hughes Trucking, Inc., Caldwell, 1972—; v.p., treas. Hughes Discount Truck Parts, Inc., 1978—. Mem. Amateur Trapshooting Assn. (life), Nat. Geneal. Soc., Ohio Geneal. Soc., Md.-Del. Geneal. Soc. Republican. Roman Catholic. Home: 811 Main St Caldwell OH 43724 Office: 810 Main St Caldwell OH 43724

HUGHES, LINDA GAYLE, marketing executive; b. East Chicago, Ind., Sept. 6, 1942; d. Walter O. and I.B. Pierce; B.A., UCLA, 1968; postgrad. Calif. State U., Los Angeles, 1970-72; M.B.A., Pepperdine U., 1974. Adminstrv. asst. Energy Scis., Inc., 1968-70; sales rep. E.R. Moore Co., Inc., 1971; product mgr. Creative Sound, Inc., 1972; sr. mktg. rep. Dun & Bradstreet, Inc., 1973-75, dist. sales mgr., 1976-80; corp. mktg. mgr. Kirk Paper Co., Inc., Los Angeles, 1981-82; asst. v.p. Wells Fargo Bank, Los Angeles, 1982-84; v.p. mktg. Calif. Fed. Savs. and Loan, 1985—. Mem. Sales and Mktg. Execs. Assn., Direct Mail Mktg. Assn., Am. Mktg. Assn., NOW, Republican. Home: 6121 Shoup Ave Apt 12 Woodland Hills CA 91367 Office: 5670 Wilshire Blvd Suite 1160 Los Angeles CA 90036

HUGHES, LINDA RENATE, lawyer, educator; b. Hanau, Germany, Oct. 25, 1947; came to U.S. 1950; d. J.A. and Ilga (Vankins) Eglite. B.A. magna cum laude, U. Minn., 1968; J.D. cum laude, Wayne State U., 1980. Bar: Mich. 1980, Ga. 1982, Fla. 1984. Human resource mgr. Browning Marine Co., St. Charles, Mich., 1973-76; law clk. to judge U.S. Dist. Ct. (ea. dist.) Mich., 1980-81; assoc. Miller, Cohen, Martens & Surgerman, Detroit, 1982, Thompson, Sizemore & Gonzalez, Tampa, 1984-85; asst. county atty. Hillsborough County, Fla., 1985—; instr. Valdosta State Coll. (Ga.), 1981; adj. prof. U. Detroit Law Sch., 1982; researcher comparative labor policy, Leigh Creek, Australia, 1983. Editor-in-chief Advocate, Wayne State U. Law Sch., 1979-80, also law rev. Vol. Community Mental Health Crisis Intervention, Saginaw, Mich., 1975-76, Ann Arbor, Mich., 1976-78, Clearwater Fla., 1984; dept. registrar Voter Registration Program, Pinellas County, Fla., 1983-84. Recipient Peace in our Time Essay Contest award Lions Club, Edina, Minn., 1968. Mem. State Bar Mich., Ga. State Bar, Fla. State Bar Assn. (exec. com. govt. lawyers sect.), Hillsborough County Bar Assn., Fla. Women Lawyers Assn. (officer, bd. dirs.), ABA, AAUW (Saginaw chpt. sec. 1974-75). Club: Tampa. Office: County Atty PO Box 1110 Tampa FL 33601

HUGHES, MARIE ANNE, nurse, dialysis director; b. Chicopee, Mass., July 8, 1948; d. Roland Joseph and Vivian Lorraine (Saurette) LaClair; m. James Frederick Hughes, Sept. 20, 1974. A.S., Holyoke Community Coll., 1972; B.S., Western Mich. U., Kalamazoo, 1982, postgrad., 1982-84. Staff nurse Mass. Gen. Hosp., Boston, 1972-73, Bay State Med. Ctr., Springfield, Mass., 1973-74; staff/charge nurse Biomed. Applications Dialysis, Oakland, Calif., 1974-78; nursing care coordinator Mercy Hosp., Benton Harbor, Mich., 1978-80, dir. dialysis, 1980—; mem. nurses speakers bur. Mich. Kidney Found., Ann Arbor, Mich., 1983—. Mem. Am. Assn. Nephrology Nurses and Technicians (nomination chairperson 1981-82, newsletter editor 1982-83, North Central v.p. 1984—), AAUW, Nat. Assn. Female Execs., Sigma Theta Tau. Roman Catholic. Home: 3938 Atherton Dr Coloma MI 49038 Office: Southwestern Mich Health Care Assn 960 Agard St Benton Harbor MI 49022

HUGHES, MARTHA HANNAH, educator; b. Pitts., Nov. 25, 1939; d. Jesse and Ethel May Foreman; B.S., Chgo. State U., 1972; postgrad. Pepperdine U., 1979, Calif. State U., Dominguez Hills, 1979-81, 84-86; m. John D. Thompson (dec.); m. 2d, Virgil Hughes, Nov. 27, 1971; children—Jewell Lee Johnson, Jawanna Lynn Thompson, Virgil Hughes. Sec., Allied Radio Corp., 1965-70; tchr. Chgo. Bd. Edn., 1972-78; tchr. Los Angeles Unified Sch. Dist., 1978—; receptionist Los Angeles County Sheriff's Dept., 1981—. Mem. Psi Alpha Theta. Roman Catholic.

HUGHES, MARY KATHERINE, lawyer; b. Kodiak, Alaska, July 16, 1949; d. John Chamberlain and Marjorie (Anstey) H.; m. Andrew H. Eker, July 7, 1982. B.B.A. cum laude, U. Alaska, 1971; J.D., Willamette U., 1974; postgrad. Heriot-Watt U., Edinburgh, Scotland, 1971. Bar: Alaska 1975. Ptnr., Hughes, Thorsness et al, Anchorage, 1974—; trustee Alaska Bar Found., pres., 1984—. Bd. visitors Willamette U. Coll. Law, Salem, Oreg., 1980—, mem. Willamette Law Fund Leadership Com., 1981-83; bd. dirs. Alaska Repertory Theatre, 1986—. Mem. Alaska Bar Assn. (bd. govs. 1981-84, pres. 1983-84), Anchorage Assn. Women Lawyers (pres. 1976-77), AAUW, Delta Theta Phi. Republican. Roman Catholic. Club: Soroptimists (v.p. 1981-83, pres. 1985—). Home: 2240 Kissee Ct Anchorage AK 99517 Office: Hughes Thorsness Gantz Powell & Brurdin 509 W 3d Ave Anchorage AK 99501

HUGHES, MICHELE JOAN, management consultant; b. Natick, Mass., Nov. 1, 1945; d. Harry G. and Mildred (Goldstein) Feldman; B.A. in English, U. Mass., 1967; postgrad. Oxford (Eng.) U., 1967; M.A. in English/Edn., Hofstra U., Hempstead, N.Y., 1972; m. Justin Peter Hughes, June 16, 1968. Secondary sch. tchr., Boston and N.Y., 1967-72; pres. Scott Parker Anderson, Inc., exec. search consultants, San Francisco, 1972-74, dir., 1973-74; pres. M.J. Hughes & Co., exec. search cons., San Francisco, 1974-76; partner William H. Clark Assos., exec. search cons., San Francisco, 1976-78; partner, shareholder, dir. Ward Howell Internat., San Francisco, 1978-86; pres. M.J. Hughes Internat., pub. Bon Voyage Travel Newsletter, 1986—; co-anchor cable TV show; producer radio series Sta. KSFO. Mem. bus. adv. bd. North Shore Community Coll. Sch. Bus.; mem. Bay Area Council, Internat. Hospitality Center. Named One of 25 Fastest Rising Execs. in San Francisco Bay Area, 1980, One of Top Ten Profl. Women, Glamour mag., 1980, One of All-time 10 Outstanding Working Women, 1984. Mem. Women's Forum West (dir. 1977-78, 86—, pres. 1986), Nat. Jr. Tennis League (dir., hon. trustee 1975—), San Francisco C. of C., Am. Mgmt. Assn., Am. Conservatory Theatre, Am. Mktg. Assn. (lectr.), Women in Bus. (speaker), Chi Omega. Club: Tiburon Peninsula. Home: 6 Rolling Hills Tiburon CA 94920 Office: 101 California St Suite 2780 San Francisco CA 94111

HUGHES, N. SUE, sch. counselor; b. Ballinger, Tex., Jan. 17, 1931; d. Hubert Edgar and Susie M. (Smith) Cothran; B.S., Centenary Coll. of La., 1951; M.Ed., So. Methodist U., 1971; m. Bennie Dee Hughes, Dec. 16, 1950; 1 dau., Vicki Lynn. Tchr. home econs. Caddo Parish Sch. Bd., Shreveport, La., 1951-54; tchr. elementary and jr. high sch. Refugio (Tex.) Ind. Sch. Dist., 1957-61; tchr. home econs. Assumption Parish, Napoleonville, La., 1962, Lafayette (La.) Parish Sch. Bd., 1963-68; tchr., counselor Richardson (Tex.) Ind. Sch. Dist., 1968—. Mem. Am., Tex., N. Central Tex. counseling and devel. assns., Richardson C. of C., Richardson Civic Art Soc., Southwest Watercolor Soc., Phi Delta Kappa, Chi Omega. Baptist. Home: 1217 Ashland Dr Richardson TX 75080Office: 1600 Spring Valley RD Richardson TX 75080

HUGHES, PAULA D., investment exec.; b. N.Y.C., Sept. 25, 1931; 1 dau., Catherine H. Benton. With Brown & Bigelow, N.Y.C., 1953-61; account exec. Shields & Co., N.Y.C., 1961-72; v.p. Thomson McKinnon Securities Inc., N.Y.C., 1972—, 1st. v.p., dir., 1979—; gov. U.S. Postal Service, 1980—; allied mem. N.Y. Stock Exchange; life trustee Cargenie-Mellon U., mem. fin. and exec. compensation coms.; dir. Com. for Corp. Support of Pvt. Univs.; lectr.-instr. Personal Investment Mgmt., N.Y.U.; lectr. various schs. and colls. including Vassar Coll.; speaker New Sch., N.Y.C., panel mem. Wall St. Conf., 1979, 82; speaker Securities Industry Assn. Conf., Wharton Sch., U. Pa., 1977. Panelist N.Y. State Casino Gambling Study, 1979; gov. Greenwich House, N.Y.C., 1961—. Recipient AMITA Golden Lady award in Fin., 1975; named Bus. Woman of Yr., Calif. Bus. Women, 1976. Mem. Women's Forum (dir. 1979—), Sales Execs. Club N.Y. (treas. 1977-79, dir. 1977—), Fin. Women's Assn., Am. Arbitration Soc., Internat. Assn. Fin. Planners. Republican. Clubs: Duquesne (Pitts.); Shenorock Shore (Rye); Yale (N.Y.C.). Featured cover articles in Fin. World, 1975, 78; featured articles in publs. including Fortune mag., Wall St. Jour., Pitts. Press, Ariz. Republic, N.Y. Times, N.Y. Post, Indpls. Star; guest on Wall St. Week. Office: Thomson McKinnon Securities Inc 200 Park Ave New York NY 10166

HUGHES, SHIRLEY MARGARET, life insurance company executive; b. Peterborough, Eng., Oct. 2, 1936 (came to U.S., 1964); d. John and Eliza (Lambley) Kisby; m. Peter Hughes, Mar. 12, 1960; children—Philip, Lisa. Student, Oxford U.; cert. computer sci., Peterborough Coll., 1956; Ed., UCLA, 1969, Santa Ana Coll., 1981. Key punch operator, Brit. Transp. Commn., Peterborough, 1953-61; personnel dir. South Bay Home Health Co., Hawthorne, Calif., 1968-79; tchr. Sawyer Coll. Bus., Los Angeles, 1970-74; admissions rep. Am. Coll. Paramed. Arts, Santa Ana, Calif., 1974-79; ins. mgr. Reserve Life Ins. Co., Tustin, Calif., 1979—; chmn. consumer edn. com. Nat. Assn. Life Underwriters. Active Rep. club, Daus. Brit. Empire. Champion, Brit. Transp. Commn. Western region table tennis league, 1954-58; recipient sales awards, Reserve Life Ins. Co., 1980—. Episcopalian. Home: 7520C Jerez Ct Rancho La Costa South Laguna CA 92677 Office: Reserve Life Ins Co 9620 Chesapeake Dr Suite 205 San Diego CA 92123

HUGHES, SUE MARGARET, librarian; b. Cleburne, Tex., Apr. 13; d. Chastain Wesley and Sue Willis (Payne) H.; B.B.A. with highest honors, U. Tex., Austin, 1949; M.L.S., Tex. Woman's U., 1960, postgrad., 1984—. Sec.-treas. several privately owned corps., Waco, Tex., 1949-59, asst. in pub. services Baylor U. Moody Library, Waco, 1960-64, acquisitions librarian, 1964-79, dir., 1980—. Mem. AAUP (pres. Baylor chpt. 1979-80), AAUW (pres. Waco br. 1974-76, state bylaws and resolutions chmn. 1977-79), ALA, (sec. RTSD Reprinting com., past chmn. duplicates exchange union com.), Southwestern Library Assn., Tex. Library Assn., (local chmn. dist. 3 meeting, 1975), Sigma Delta Pi, Beta Gamma Sigma, Delta Kappa Gamma (chmn. research com. 1976-78, rec. sec. 1978-80), Beta Phi Mu. Methodist. Clubs: Altrusa; Baylor Round Table (treas. 1974-75, sec. 1977-78), Waco Library. Office: PO Box 6307 Waco TX 76706

HUGHES, SUZANN, nurse, management consultant; b. Hartford, Conn., Aug. 21, 1948; d. James Edward and Mary (Durkin) Scanlon; m. Gerald David Hughes, June 3, 1972; 1 child, Chelsea Ayne. B.S. in Nursing, U. Conn., 1971, M.S. in Nursing, 1981. Instr. Curry Coll., Milton, Mass., 1979; recovery room staff nurse Boston Hosp. for Women, 1979-80; clin. nurse specialist St. Lukes Hosp., Phoenix, 1981-83; dir. nursing Valley Luth. Hosp., Mesa, Ariz., 1983-84; mgmt. cons., Mesa, 1984—; instr. U. Phoenix, 1985—; nursing cons. St. Luke's Hosp. Med. Ctr., Phoenix, 1985. Vol. Morris Udall Campaign for Pres., Boston, 1976. Mem. Ariz. Nurses Assn. (treas. polit. action com. 84-85, trustee 1984—), Am. Soc. Law and Medicine, Ariz. League for Nursing, Sigma Theta Tau. Home and Office: 813 N Robson Mesa AZ 85201

HUGHES, VICKY MARIE, university foundation fund raiser; b. Beaver Dam, Wis., Feb. 22, 1961; d. Donald Edward and Ferne Elaine (Riddle) Hughes. B.A., U. Fla., 1984. Student phonathon communicator U. Fla. Found., Inc., Gainesville, 1980-82, student phonathon dir., 1982-84, phonathon dir. Coll. Vet. Med., 1984, Coll. of Bus., 1984-85, asst. dir. ann. giving, 1985—; speaker. Mem. Speech and Debate Soc. (sec., treas. 1982-83, pres. 1983-84). Presbyterian. Avocations: reading; racquetball; swimming. Office: U Florida Found Inc Office Devel and Alumni Affairs 2012 W University Ave Gainesville FL 32603

HUGHES, VIRGINIA MARIE, electric utility public relations and communications executive; b. Faribault, Minn., Dec. 7, 1954; d. Alfred Thomas and Lenore Marie (Weum) Hughes; m. Charles Arnold Berg, June 23, 1984. B.S., Mankato State U., 1977. Registered cosmetologist, Minn. Acctg. asst. Steele Waseca Cooperative, Owatonna, Minn., 1974-77; owner Geraldine's Dress Shoppe, West Concord, Minn., 1977-78; mgr. Maurices, Inc., Faribault, Minn., 1978-79; mem. service asst. FROST-BENCO Electric, Mankato, Minn., 1979—, energy auditor, 1981—; chmn. Farm, Home and Energy Show, Mankato Minn., 1983; mem. mem. service adv. bd. Cooperative Power Assn., Eden Prairie, Minn., 1982—. Editor News of FROST-BENCO, 1981—. Organizer Minn. Women for Agriculture-Dist. 9, Southern Minn., 1982; sec., newsletter editor Mankato Area Christian Singles, Mankato, 1979-80. Mem. Am. Agri-Women, Rural Electric Mgmt. Assn. (service edn. com. 1982-86), Minn. Women for Agriculture (sec., treas. 1982-83, pub. relations com. 1984-86), Elec. Women's Round Table, Phi Kappa Phi, Phi Upsilon Omicron. Club: Goosedowners (Mankato, Minn.). Office: FROST-BENCO Electric Assn PO Box 8 Mankato MN 56002

HUGHES, WAUNELL MCDONALD (MRS. DELBERT E. HUGHES), psychiatrist; b. Tyler, Tex., Feb. 6, 1928; d. Conrad Claiborne and Bernice Oletha (Smith) McDonald; B.A., U. Tex. at Austin, 1946; M.D., Baylor U., 1951; m. Delbert Eugene Hughes, Aug. 14, 1948; children—Lark, Mark, Lynn, Michael. Intern VA Hosp., Houston, 1951-52; resident Parkland Hosp., Dallas, 1964-67; practiced gen. medicine in Tyler, Tex., 1952-64; acting chief psychiatry service VA Hosp., Dallas, 1967-68, asst. chief, 1968-73, chief Mental Hygiene Clinic and Day Treatment Center, 1973-82, unit chief acute inpatient psychiatry Med. Center, 1982—; clin. instr. psychiatry Southwestern Med. Sch., U. Tex. Health Sci. Center, Dallas, 1968—. Chmn. pre-sch. vision and hearing program Pilot Club, Tyler, 1960-64. Mem. Am. Med. Women's Assn. (pres. Dallas 1980-81), Am. Psychiat. Assn., Am. Group Psychotherapy Assn., (pres. Dallas chpt. 1984—), Dallas Area Women Psychiatrists (archivist 1985—), Alpha Epsilon Iota (pres. 1950-51). Home: 3428 University Blvd Dallas TX 75205 Office: 4500 Lancaster Rd Dallas TX 75216

HUGHEY, ELLEN MARIE, human resources consultant; b. Olean, N.Y., Dec. 3, 1954; d. James Fox and Janet Ellen (Taylor) H.; m. Robert I. Mackler, June 6, 1980 (div. Nov. 1983). B.A., Potsdam (N.Y.) Coll., 1975; cert. Inst. Paralegal Tng., Phila., 1976. Pension paralegal Harris, Beach & Wilcox, Rochester, N.Y., 1976-77; benefits cons. Alexander & Alexander, N.Y.C., 1977-78; sr. specialist pensions W.R. Grace & Co., N.Y.C., 1978-80, mgr. pension planning, 1980-82, mgr. acquisitions and spl. projects, 1982-84; benefits cons. Wm. Mercer-Meidinger, N.Y.C., 1984—. Editor, advisor: Old Age, Handicapped and Vietnam-Era Antidiscrimination Legislation 1980. Mem. Am. Pension Conf., N.Y. Personnel Mgmt. Assn. Republican. Presbyterian.

HUGHS, MARY GERALDINE, accountant, social service administrator; b. Marshalltown, Iowa, Nov. 28, 1929; d. Don Harold, Sr., and Alice Dorothy (Keister) Shaw; A.A., Highline Community Coll., 1970; B.A., U. Wash., 1972; m. Charles G. Hughs, Jan. 31, 1949; children—Mark George, Deborah Kay, Juli Ann, Grant Wesley. Asst. controller Moduline Internat., Inc., Chehalis, Wash., 1972-73; controller Data Recall Corp., El Segundo, Calif., 1973-74; fin. adminstr., acct. Saturn Mfg. Corp., Torrance, Calif., 1974-77; sr. acct., adminstrv. asst. Van Camp Ins., San Pedro, Calif., 1977-78; asst. adminstr. Harbor Regional Center, Torrance, Calif., 1978—; active bookkeeping service, 1978—; instr. math. and acctg. South Bay Bus. Coll., 1976-77. Sec. Pacific N.W. Mycol. Soc., 1966-67; treas., bd. dirs. Harbor Employees Fed. Credit Union. Recipient award Am. Mgmt. Assn., 1979. Mem. Beta Alpha. Republican. Methodist. Club: Holiday Spas. Author: Iowa Auto Dealers Assn. Title System, 1955; Harbor Regional Center Affirmative Action Plan, 1980; Harbor Regional Center-Financial Format, 1978—; Provider Audit System, 1979; Handling Client Funds, 1983; State Dept. Service, 1986. Office: 21231 Hawthorne Blvd Torrance CA 90509

HUGULEY, JENNIE REBECCA, welding supply company executive; b. Tupelo, Miss., Sept. 5, 1941; d. Leonard Forest and Lena Mae (Sheffield) Isbell; m. Robert C. Huguley, Nov. 1, 1960; children—Rebecca Lynn, Joseph Michael. Student Morton Coll., 1979-82. Keypunch operator, Victor Dana Corp., Chgo., 1965-68; tax cons. H & R Block, Berwyn, Ill., 1971-75; sec. Barton Welding Supply Co., Cicero, Ill., 1972—, bookkeeper, 1973—, cost acct., 1974-75, officer, personnel dir., 1975—; corp. officer, sec., treas. Cylinders & Equipment Co., Inc., Cicero, 1977—. Youth dir. Cicero-Berwyn Assembly of God, 1963-68, treas., 1965-71; trustee Morton East High Sch. Music Bd., 1978, 79-80. Mem. Welding Distbrs. Assn., Nat. Welding Supply Assn., Cicero Mfrs. Assn., Cicero C. of C. Home: 6714 W 41st St Stickney IL 60402 Office: Barton Welding Supply Co 5919 W Ogden Ave Cicero IL 60650

HUGUNIN, LYNN ANN, sports editor; b. Clinton, Iowa, May 17, 1947; d. Charles William and Evelyn Geraldine (Goers) Marr; m. Michael John Hugunin, Dec. 17, 1966; children—Timmothy Michael, Ted Alan, Travis John. Student Clinton Jr. Coll., 1965, Iowa State U., 1980. Sports editor Nevada (Iowa) Evening Jour., 1978—; columnist The Predicament, Emmetsburg, Iowa, 1981—; photographer Iowa State Cyclone, wrestling club Ames, 1983-84. Photographer: (book) Conditioning the Iowa Way, 1983. Mem. bd. Nevada Booster Club, 1982-84; mem. ex-ofcl. bd. Cyclone Wrestling Club, 1982-84. Mem. Iowa High Sch. Athletic Assn., Iowa High Sch. Girls Union. Democrat. Lutheran. Home: 1038 F Avenue Nevada IA 50201 Office: Nevada Evening Jour 1133 6th St Nevada IA 50201

HUIRAS, JEANNE MARIE, food service management and design consulting company executive; b. Deshler, Nebr., Jan. 23, 1941; d. Stephen Thomas and Jennie Eunice (Patterson) Davenport; m. Richard James Huiras, July 10, 1976. B.S. in Foods and Nutrition, Ariz. State U., 1963. Dietetic intern U. Oreg. Med. Sch. and Clinics, 1963-64; asst. dir. food service Good Samaritan Hosp., Phoenix, 1965-73; cons. dietitian, Phoenix, 1973-76; mem. faculty Mesa (Ariz.) Community Coll., 1973-74; nat. dietitian, sales staff 3M Co., St. Paul, Minn., 1974-78; corporate dietitian, food service cons. Lifemark Corp., Houston, 1978-80; food service cons., sales The Lemmons Co., Houston, 1980-82; v.p. HuMark Enterprises, Houston, 1982—; gourmet food demonstrator Marshall Fields Co., Galleria, Houston, 1983-85. Author: Study Guide for Food Service Suprs., 1973. Recipient Ariz. Dietitian of Yr. award 1976. Mem. Am. Dietetic Assn., Ariz. Dietetic Assn. (pres. 1972-73), Am. Soc. Hosp. Food Service Adminstrs. (chpt. pres. 1971-72), Dietitians in Bus. and Industry (nat. treas. 1977-78, nat. pres. 1980-81; chpt. pres. 1979—81), Tex. Dietetic Assn., South Tex. Dietetic Assn., Am. Home Econs. Assn., Tex. Home Econs. Assn., Home Economists in Bus., Greater Houston Home Economists in Bus. Clubs: Pairs in Squares (pres. 1980-81, sec., treas. 1981-82), Home: 13815 Ella Lee Ln Houston TX 77077 Office: HuMark Enterprises 13815 Ella Lee Ln Houston TX 77077

HUISMAN, DOROTHY L., financial executive; b. Oskaloosa, Iowa, May 21, 1950; d. Evert John and Cora Elizabeth (Jonker) Hol; m. John Martin Huisman, Aug. 21, 1971; children—Matthew Stephen, Lucas Evert. Student Trinity Christian Coll., 1968-72. Tchr., Berachah Music Acad., Toronto, Ont., Can., 1972-73; dir. devel. C.J.L. Found., Tor., 1973-80; v.p. adminstrn. Investors Leasing Co., Homewood, Ill., 1980-83; pres. Emerald Fin. Inc., South Holland, Ill., 1983—. Composer of contemporary Christian music. Office: Emerald Fin Inc 16042 Dobson Ave South Holland IL 60473

HULEN, MARJORIE JANE, association executive; b. Denver, Sept. 23, 1921; d. Perry E. and Garnet W. (Doty) Kellogg; student public schs., Redondo Beach, Calif.; m. Ray Romaine Hulen, June 10, 1950; 1 son, Lynn Robert. With A.O. Smith Corp., Los Angeles, 1948-60, sec., 1956-60; exec. sec. Sterling Electric Motors, Los Angeles, 1960-61; research sec. Pasadena (Calif.) Found. for Med. Research, 1961-65; exec. sec. Profl. Staff Assn., Los Angeles County/U. So. Calif. Med. Center, Los Angeles, 1965-70, office mgr., 1970-74, bus. mgr., 1974—, exec. dir., 1980—. Instl. rep. Los Angeles Regional Family Planning, 1977—. Mem. Nat. Secs. Assn., Soc. Research Adminstrs. (pres. So. Calif. chpt. 1982-83), Nat. Assn. Accts. (nat. pub. relations award 1979), Am. Soc. Assn. Execs., Nat. Assn. Female Execs., Assn. Ind. Research Insts. Democrat. Home: 2311 El Paseo St Alhambra CA 91803 Office: Los Angeles County/U So Calif Med Center 1739 Griffin Ave Los Angeles CA 90031

HULIN-SALKIN, BELINDA, writer; b. Lafayette, La., July 3, 1954; d. Adam Joseph and Audrey Mae (Breaux) Hulin; m. Richard Alan Salkin, Nov. 24, 1979. B.A. in Communications, Loyola U., New Orleans, 1975; M.S. in Urban Studies, U. New Orleans, 1983. Reporter, producer Sta. WYLD Radio News, New Orleans, 1975; entertainment editor Monroe Morning World, La., 1975-77; pub. info. dir. Mental Health Assn., New Orleans, 1978-79; asst. editor Focus Mag., Phila., 1980-82; freelance writer, Collingswood, N.J., 1982—; contbr. Money Mag., N.Y.C., 1982—, Advt. Age, Chgo., 1983—; contbg. editor Phila. Mag., 1986—. Editor: Home Improvement Workbook, 1979; Springhouse Report, newsletter, 1985. Counselor Crisis Line, New Orleans, 1979. Mem. Phila. Writers Orgn., Nat. Assn. for Female Execs., Women's Equity Action League, Sigma Delta Chi. Democrat. Roman Catholic. Home: 100 Woodlawn Ave Collingswood NJ 08108

HULKA, BARBARA SORENSON, physician, educator; b. Mpls., Mar. 1, 1931; d. Herbert F. and Mabel Adelia (Alquist) Sorenson; m. Jaroslav F. Hulka, Nov. 13, 1954; children—Carol Ann, Gregory Fabian, Bryan Herbert. B.S., Radcliffe Coll., 1952; M.S., Juilliard Sch. Music, 1954; postgrad. Columbia U., 1954-55, M.D., 1959. Diplomate Nat. Bd. Med. Examiners (preventive medicine and pub. health test com. 1985—). Intern, USPHS Hosp., S.I., 1959-60; USPHS fellow Columbia U. Sch. Pub. Health and Administrv. Medicine, 1960-61; asst. pub. health physician Pa. State Health Dept., Pitts., 1961-62; research instr. dept. obstetrics and gynecology U. Pitts., 1962-65, research asst. prof., 1966-67; research assoc. dept. preventive medicine Sch. Medicine, U. N.C.-Chapel Hill, 1967-68, asst. prof. dept. epidemiology Sch. Pub. health, 1967-71, asst. prof. dept. family medicine, Sch. Medicine, 1968-76, assoc. prof. dept. epidemiology, Sch. Pub. Health, 1972-76, prof., 1977—, clin. assoc. prof. dept. family medicine, 1977—, acting chmn. dept. epidemiology, 1982-83, chmn., 1983—; clin. assoc. prof. community and family medicine Duke U. Med. Center, Durham, N.C., 1976-82, adj. prof., 1982—; cons. in field; mem. Nat. Center for Health Services research Health Services devel. grants study sect., 1973-77, rev. com. for service fellow program, 1975-76; mem. com. on health services research Nat. Acad. Scis., Inst. Medicine, 1977-78, com. on epidemiology and vets. follow-up studies, 1979—; mem. epidemiology and disease control study sect. NIH, 1979-83, chmn., 1981-83; mem. bd. sci. counselors to div. resources, ctrs. and community activities, Nat. Cancer Inst., 1980-85, others. Contbr. articles to profl. jours. USPHS grantee, 1962-67; Nat. Ctr. for Health Services Research grantee, 1967-69, 69-76; Nat. Cancer Inst. grantee, 1970-72, 80—; Am. Cancer Soc. Instl. grantee, 1970-71; AID grantee, 1971-72; Ayerst Labs. grantee, 1976-78, 80-81; Nat. Inst. Occupational Safety and Health grantee, 1980-82. Fellow Am. Coll. Preventive Medicine; mem. Soc. Epidemiol. Research (pres. 1975-76, exec. com. 1973-77), Am. Pub. Health Assn. (chmn. epidemiology sect. council 1976-77, governing council 1976-78), Am. Epidemiologic Soc., Am. Soc. Preventive Oncology, Am. Coll. Preventive Medicine, Assn. Tchrs. Preventive Medicine, N.C. Pub. Health Assn., Delta Omega (chpt. pres. 1976-77, nat. soc. pres. 1979-81). Home: 2317 Honeysuckle Dr Chapel Hill NC 27514 Office: Dept Epidemiology Rosendau Hall 20 Univ NC Chapel Hill NC 27514

HULL, CATHERINE HOWARD, marketing executive; b. Paris, Tex., July 19, 1951; d. John Frank and Mary Charlene (Weaver) Howard; m. Ben Maron Bailey, Mar. 14, 1970 (div. 1973); 1 son, Harold E.; m. 2d, Robert Hardin Hull, Apr. 16, 1978. Student, U. Tex.-Arlington, 1969-72. Realtor, Red Carpet, Houston, 1975-77; sales rep. GSC/Six Flags Corp., Houston, 1978-79, mgr. mktg., 1979-81; bus. devel. CRS Constructors Managers, Houston, 1981-82, mgr. bus. devel., 1982-83, sr. mgr., bus. devel. dir., 1983-84; dir. mktg. interiors div. Pierce Goodwin Alexander, Houston, 1984—. Mem. DAR, Soc. Mktg. Profl. Services. Democrat. Methodist. Office: Pierce Goodwin Alexander 800 Bering Dr Houston TX 77019

HULL, CONSTANCE MAE, library administrator; b. Pitts., Nov. 29, 1928; d. Lysle L. and Lillian H. (Frahm) Gilman; m. Albert E. Ahrens, Jr., 1952 (div. 1958); m. 2d Howard Donald Hull, Oct. 13, 1960 (dec. Jan. 1984). Student MacAlester Coll., 1946-47, Miss Woods Tng. Sch., 1947-49; B.S. in Edn., Oreg. State U., 1966; postgrad. U. Oreg., 1968; M.S., Oreg. Coll. Edn., 1976. Cert. tchr., Minn., Mont. and Oreg. Tchr. Albert Lea Pub Schs. (Minn.), 1949-50, Saint Paul Pub. Schs. (Minn.), 1950-57, Missoula Pub. Schs. (Mont.), 1958; tchr. Sweet Homes Pub Schs. (Oreg.), 1961-65, librarian, 1965-78, library supr., 1978—, also instructional materials dir., adminstrv. asst. to supt.; instr. Linn-Benton Community Coll., Sweet Home, 1977-79; media cons. Contbr. articles to profl jours. Active Sportsmans Holiday Celebration; mem. Sweet Home Com. on Community Long-Range Plans. Grantee Title II Edn. program, 1968-70, 75-77. Mem. Assn. Bus. and Profl. Women (past officer), AAUW, Assn. Childhood Edn. Internat., Confedn. Oreg. Sch. Adminstrs., Northwest Women in Ednl. Adminstrn., Am. Assn. Sch. Adminstrs., Assn. Supervision and Curriculum Devel., Oreg. Assn. Supervision and Curriculum Devel., Oreg. Assn. Sch. Suprs., ALA, Oreg. Ednl. Media Assn., Am. Assn. Sch. Librarians, Assn. Ednl. Communications and Tech., Northwest Council Computer Edn., Delta Kappa Gamma Internat. (officer Beta chpt., media cons. Alpha Rho state chpt.). Republican. Presbyterian. Lodge: Order Eastern Star (worthy matron 1969). Home: 42899 Green River Dr Sweet Home OR 97386 Office: Sweet Home School Dist 55 1920 Long St Sweet Home OR 97386

HULL, DIANA, psychologist; b. Lawrence, N.Y., Aug. 13, 1924; d. Louis Albert and Rosalyn (Diamont) Jaffer; B.A., City U. N.Y., 1946; M.S.W., U. Mich., 1954; Ph.D., Sch. Public Health, U. Tex. Health Scis. Center, 1975; children—Marcy Ross Burton, Allison Langdon Boomer; m. 2d, David Pershing Hull, Dec. 27, 1969. Mem. clin. faculty Baylor Coll. Medicine, Houston, 1964-80; cons. cons. Tex. Inst. Family Psychiatry, Children's Psychiat. Clinic of Baylor Coll. Medicine. Fellow Am. Group Psychotherapy Assn. (nat. faculty), Houston Group Psychotherapy Soc. (pres. 1967, adv. bd. 1967-80); mem. Am. Psychol. Assn. (divs. health psychology and population and environment), Calif. Psychol. Assn. (pub. info. chmn., pres. div. VI), AAAS, N.Y. Acad. Scis., Assn. Media Psychology (bd. dirs., sec.), Sierra Club, So. Calif. Demographic Forum. Club: Birnam Wood Golf. Contbr. articles to profl. jours.; Am. contbr. to vol. on internat. migration problems. Home: 815 Cima Linda Ln Santa Barbara CA 93108

HULL, DORIS M., librarian; b. Quantico, Md., May 14, 1926; d. Orrensy and Lottie (Conway) Hull. B.S. in Edn., Va. State U., 1947; M.S. in L.S., Drexel U., 1951; M.A. in History, Howard U., 1957; Ph.D., Am. U., 1966. Tchr. librarian Salisbury (Md.) High Sch., 1947-50, Pomonkey (Md.) High Sch., 1951-52; head reference dept., supr. serials Founders Library, Howard U., Washington, 1952-64, reference librarian Moorland Spingarn Research Ctr., 1980—; UNESCO librarian Advanced Tchr. Tng. Coll., Ondo, Nigeria, 1964-66; exchange prof. Drexel U., Phila., 1967-68; head pub. service library Lagos (Nigeria) U., 1968-71; sr. history master Ministry of Edn., Oyo State, Nigeria, 1971-79; mem. faculty Grad. Sch., U.S. Dept. Agr., 1980—; cons. U.S. Dept. Agr. Grad. Sch., 1980—. Editor-in-chief Current Bibliography African Affairs, 1984—; contbr. articles to profl. jours. Recipient 10 Yr. Service award Howard U., 1962; Md. State scholar, 1943-51. Mem. African Studies Assn., Council of Library Technicians, Mid-Atlantic Regional Africanist Assn., ALA. Contbr. articles to profl. jours. Office: Moorland Spingarn Research Ctr Howard Univ Washington DC 20059

HULL, JANE LAUREL LEEK, nurse, adminstr.; b. Ontario, Calif., July 4, 1923; d. William Abram and Susan Bianca (Pethick) Leek; R.N., Columbia Presbyn. Sch. Nursing, 1944; B.A., Redlands U., 1977; ; m. James B. Hull, Oct. 10, 1944 (dec.); children—James W., William P., Kenneth D. Supr. obstetrics Sch. Nursing, Mid-Valley Hosp., Peckville, Pa., 1945-46; surg. nurse acute nursing Scranton (Pa.) State Hosp., 1947-52; nurse San Antonio Community Hosp., Upland, Calif., 1953-55; office nurse H.L. Archibald, Upland, 1965; vis. nurse Pomona West End Inc., continuity of care coordinator, Montclair, Calif., 1968-73, exec. dir., 1973—; tchr. ARC nursing course to high sch. students. Treas. PTA, Pomona, Calif.; vol. exec. dir. Inland Hospice Assn., 1979-80. Mem. Calif. Nurses Assn. (pres. dist. 53 1958), Calif. Assn. for Health Services at Home (dir.), Calif. League Nursing, Nat. Homecaring Council (dir.). Republican. Club: Zonta (Ontario, Upland, pres., 1976). Organizer Homemaker Dept. in Vis. Nurse Assn., 1972; developer (with Don Baxter Corp.) plugs for in-dwelling Foley catheters, 1963. Home: 543 W F St Ontario CA 91762 Office: 5156 Holt Blvd Montclair CA 91763

HULL, JOAN CAROL, society administrator; b. Newark, Apr. 13, 1932; d. Milton O. and Cemelia (Molitor) H.; B.A., St. Lawrence U., 1954; M.A., Montclair State Coll., 1962; degree in mus. adminstrn. Columbia U.; D. Hum. (hon.), Kean Coll., 1983. Tchr., Butler High Sch., 1958-63; dir. jr. hist. socs. N.J. Hist. Soc., Newark, 1963-69, asst. dir., 1969-79, acting dir., 1979, exec. dir., 1979—. Recipient Montclair State Coll. Alumni Bicentennial award; N.J. Hist. Commn. Pitcher. Mem. Am. Assn. State and Local History (chairperson regional awards 1981—), League Hist. Socs. N.J. (pres. 1978-82), AAUW (1st v.p. Essex county br. 1975-79). Clubs: Skytop, Downtown, Soroptomists (Newark). Office: 230 Broadway Newark NJ 07104

HULL, LOUISE KNOX, retired elementary educator, administrator; b. Springfield, Mo., May 24, 1912; d. William E. and Ruby Joe (Bradshaw) K.; m. Berrien J. Hull, Jan. 1, 1953. B.S. in Edn., Southwest Mo. State U., 1933; postgrad. Colo. U., 1939, Northwestern U., 1945; M.A., NYU, 1952. Cert. elem. and secondary tchr., Mo. Elem. tchr. R12 Sch. Dist., Springfield, 1936-70, supr. tchr., 1956-70, mem. adv. com. to supt., 1955-57. Chmn. Christian edn. com. Westminster Presbyn. Ch., 1953-66; pres. Women of Ch., 1970-73, pres. bd. trustees, 1983—; life mem. Wilson Creek Found., Springfield, 1954-67; sec. Greene County Hist. Soc., Springfield, 1960—; mem. Springfield Little Theater Guild, 1970—, Hist. Preservation Soc., Springfield, 1980—; docent Mus. Ozarks, Springfield, 1976; chmn. dist. Ill, John Calvin Presbterial, 1974-76, sec., 1977-80. Mem. Springfield Retired Tchrs. Assn. (life), Ozarks Genealogy Soc (sec. 1985—), Alpha Delta Pi (treas. house corp. 1932—), Alpha Delta Kappa (sec. 1965-67). Club: Sorosis (Springfield) (pres. 1980-82).

HULL, MARGARET RUTH, artist, educator, consultant; b. Dallas, Mar. 27, 1921; d. William Haynes and Ora Carroll (Adams) Leatherwood; m. LeRos Ennis Hull, Mar. 29, 1941; children—LeRos Ennis, Jr., James Daniel. B.A., So. Meth. U., 1952, postgrad., 1960-61; M.A., North Tex. State U., 1957. Art instr. W. W. Bushman Sch., Dallas Ind. Sch. Dist., 1952-57, Benjamin Franklin Jr. High Sch., Dallas, 1957-58; art instr. Hillcrest High Sch., Dallas, 1958-61, dean, pupil personnel counselor, 1961-70; tchr. children's painting Dallas Mus. Fine Art, 1956-70; designer, coordinator curriculm of visual art careers cluster Skyline High Sch., Dallas, 1970-71, Skyline Career Devel. Ctr., Dallas, 1971-76, Booker T. Washington Arts Magnet High Sch., Dallas, 1976-82; developer curriculum devel./writing art, 1971-82; artist, ednl. cons., 1982—; ednl. cons., 1982—; mus. reprodns. asst. Dallas Mus. Art, 1984—. Group shows: Dallas Mus. Fine Arts, 1958, Arts Magnet Faculty Shows, 1978, 79, 80, 81, 82, Arts Magnet High Sch., Dallas Art Edn. Assn. Show, 1981, D'Art Membership Show, Dallas, 1982, 83, represented in pvt. collections. Trustee Dallas Mus. Art, 1978-84. Mem. Tex. Designer/Craftsmen, Craft Guild Dallas, Fiber Artists Dallas, Dallas Art Edn. Assn., Tex. Art Edn. Assn., Nat. Art Edn. Assn., Dallas Counselors Assn. (pres. 1968), Delta Delta Delta.

HULL, MARY LOUISE, real estate broker; b. Kester, W.Va., Nov. 25, 1935; d. Howard Lee Alexander and Edith Mae (Smith) Rogers; m. Cecil Oliver Hull, Sept. 10, 1975 (dec. July 1984); children—Richard Wayne Tanner, Pamela Kay Wells. Student pub. schs., Grantsville, W.Va. Stenographer McCune & Co., Youngstown, Ohio, 1953-55, Moock Electric Co., Youngstown, 1955-56; receptionist Superior Industries, Youngstown, 1956-57; sec. Manpower, Inc., Akron, Ohio, 1957-61; sec., receptionist Mac Allied Tools, Tallmadge, Ohio, 1961-63; sec. Cornwell Tools, Mogadore, Ohio, 1963-64, Mac Allied Tools, Tallmadge, 1964-66; sec., bookkeeper Fla. Citrus Mut., Lakeland, 1966-76; real estate broker Mary Hull Real Estate, Lakeland and Howey-in-the-Hills, Fla., 1976—. Mem. citizen's com. Town of Howey-in-the-Hills, 1984. Mem. Lake County Bd. Realtors, Nat. Assn. Realtors. Republican. Club: Howey Garden (treas. 1982-84). Lodge: Eastern Star (electa 1980-81, chaplain 1985). Avocations: travel; walking. Home: 401 Camelia Way PO Box 237 Howey-in-the-Hills FL 32737 Office: Mary Hull Real Estate 109 W Central Ave Howey-in-the-Hills FL 32737

HULL, SUZANNE WHITE, institutional administrator; b. Orange, N.J., Aug. 24, 1921; d. Gordon Stowe and Lillian Fredonia (Siegling) White; m. George I. Hull, Feb. 20, 1943; children—George G., James R., Anne Hull Cabello. B.A. with honors, Swarthmore Coll., 1943; M.S. in L.S., U. So. Calif., 1967. Mem. staff Huntington Library, Art Gallery and Bot. Gardens, San Marino, Calif., 1969—, dir. adminstrn. and publ. services, prin. officer, 1972—; mem. adv. bd. Hagley Mus. and Library, 1984—. Author: Chaste, Silent & Obedient, 1982; Charter pres. Portola Jr. High Sch. PTA, Los Angeles, 1960-62; pres. Children's Service League, Los Angeles, 1963-64, YWCA, Los Angeles, 1967-69; mem. community adv. council Los Angeles Job Corps Ctr. for Women, 1972-78; mem. alumni council Swarthmore Coll., 1959-62, 83—; founder, chmn. Swarthmore-Los Angeles Connection, 1983-85; bd. dirs. Pasadena Planned Parenthood Assn., 1978-84, mem. adv. bd., 1984—. Mem. Monumental Brass Soc. (U.K.), Renaissance Soc., Brit. Studies Conf., Calif. Congress Parents and Tchrs. (hon. life), Beta Phi Mu (dir. U. So. Calif. br. 1982-84). Club: Athenaeum. Office: Huntington Library 1151 Oxford Rd San Marino CA 91108

HULLIN, SUSAN LEE, public relations executive; b. Walla Walla, Wash., May 22, 1944; d. Edward D. and Wilberta M. (Kirkman) Kanz; m. Tod Robert Hullin, May 6, 1967. B.A. in Polit. Sci., U. Wash., 1966. Exec. asst. to chmn. Garfinckel's, Washington, 1977-81; press relations/spl. events coordinator Emporium-Capwell, San Francisco, 1981-83; sr. account supr. Hill and Knowlton, Chgo., 1983—. Mem. San Francisco Symphony 500 Arts Council of Eureka Coll., Ill., bd. dirs. Hist. Alexandria Found.; jr. bd. dirs. Infant Welfare Soc. of Evanston. Mem. Pub. Relations Soc. Am. (accredited), San Francisco Bay Area Publicity Club, Fashion Group, Jr. League of Chgo. Republican. Presbyterian. Clubs: Commonwealth of Calif., Press of San Francisco (bd. dirs. 1983-84). Army-Navy Country (Arlington, Va.). Home: 634 Foster St Evanston IL 60201 Office: 111 E Wacker Dr Chicago IL 60601

HULME, DARLYS MAE, banker; b. Buckingham, Iowa, Apr. 2, 1937; d. Leland James and Dorothy Mae (Nation) Philp; m. Harlan Dale Hulme, Dec. 4, 1955 (div. Nov. 1971); children—Debra Jean Hulme Hanneman, Richard Dale. Student Iowa Sch. Banking, 1974, Sch. Bank Adminstrn. U. Wis.-Madison, 1982. Bookkeeper, Farmers Savs. Bank, Traer, Iowa, 1954-55, asst. cashier, 1962-72, v.p., 1973-83, sr. v.p., 1983—; acct. North Tama Housing, Inc., Traer, 1974—; sec. to bd. Traer Shares, Inc., Talen Aviation, Ltd., Traer; dir. Sunrise Hill Care Ctr., Traer. Mem. Iowa State Banking Bd., 1985—. Mem. Nat. Assn. Bank Women (group treas. 1980-81, group v.p. 1981-82, group pres. 1982-83, state membership chair 1983-84, regional membership chair 1984-85), Iowa Bankers Assn. (mem. edn. com. 1985—). Republican. Methodist. Club: PEO (Traer). Avocations: gardening; travel. Home: 701 S Main St Traer IA 50675 Office: Farmers Savs Bank 611 2d St Traer IA 50675

HULSEY, RUTH LENORA, state official; b. Athens, Ga., Nov. 28, 1927; d. Joseph Alonzo and Frances Rebecca (Bell) Johnson; student Pasadena Jr. Coll., 1938-40, San Bernardino Valley Coll., 1963-65; m. William A. Hulsey III, Mar. 28, 1958; children—William A., Stephen G., Alicia A. With State of Calif. Employment Devel. Office, 1960—, supr., San Bernardino Field Dept. Office, 1969-75, So. Region Office, Riverside, 1975-78, employment program mgr., asst. mgr. Ontario Field Office, 1979-80, employment program mgr., mgr. Fontana Field Office, 1980—; dir. Calif. State Employees Credit Union, 1972-75, mem. employer adv. council, 1978—. Mem. edn. com. Urban League, 1965, mem., 1965—; mem. Arrowhead Allied Arts Council, 1966-72; mem. Social Lites, 1963—, pres., 1964-66, 80-81, bd. dirs., 1980—, rec. sec., 1981—. Mem. Internat. Assn. Personnel in Employment Security, Calif. State Employees Assn., Bloomington C. of C., Fontana C. of C., Rialto C. of C., San Bernardino C. of C. Democrat. Methodist. Home: 1246 E Shamrock Ave San Bernardino CA 92410 Office: State of Calif Employment Devel Dept Office 17590 Foothill Blvd Fontana CA 92335

HULVEY, ALMA HOLWERDA, author, historian, poet; b. Holland, Mich., Jan. 13, 1922; d. Jan and Alberdena (Tillenga) Holwerda; m. Norris I. Hulvey (div.); 1 child, Bonnie E. Miller. A.A., Golden West Coll., Huntington Beach, Calif., 1976; B.S., Pepperdine U., 1978. In mgmt. Hughes Aircraft Co., Los Angeles, 1962-80; feature writer various newspapers, 1980—. Author. (hist. biography) Across the Cobwebs of the Years, 1983. Mem. Zeeland Hist. Soc., Friends of the Archives. Republican. Mem. Dutch Reformed Ch. Avocations: photography, world travel, stained glass windows, artwork. Office: PO Box 2235 Huntington Beach CA 92647

HUME, D. SUE, marketing executive; b. St. Louis, Dec. 26, 1946; d. James David and Mildred (Derickson) Fusselman; m. John Andrew Hume, Aug. 24, 1968. B.S. in Bus., S.W. Mo. State U., Springfield, 1968. Systems analyst McDonnell Douglas Corp., St. Louis, 1969-74; mgr. market research, Maritz, Inc., St. Louis, 1974-76; mgr. market info. Sherwood Med. Industries, St. Louis, 1976-79, staff specialist market research Southwestern Bell Co., St. Louis, 1979-82, staff mgr. rate adminstrn., 1982-84; dir. corp. strategic planning Southwestern Bell Publs., St. Louis, 1984—. Mem. Am. Mktg. Assn., Bus. Planning Bd., N.Am. Soc. Corp. Planning, Nat. Assn. Accts. Avocations: travel, wine. Home: 1352 Green Elm Dr Fenton MO 63026 Office: Southwestern Bell Publs 1625 Des Peres Rd Saint Louis MO 63131

HUMMEL, JOANNE, newspaper editor; b. Buffalo, May 13, 1949; d. Joseph S. and Genevieve A. (Walek) Grzelewski; m. John Edward Hummel, Oct. 21, 1972; 1 dau., Janna Elizabeth. B.A. magna cum laude, SUNY-Buffalo, 1971; M.L.S., SUNY-Geneseo, 1972. Asst. editor Evans Jour., Angola, N.Y., 1979-82, editor in chief, 1983—. Democrat. Roman Catholic. Mem. Phi Beta Kappa. Office: Evans Jour 19 Center St Angola NY 14006

HUMPHREY, BARBARA MYERS, nurse oncologist, clergywoman; b. Rochester, N.Y., Sept. 7, 1929; d. Ford Albert and Lois Julianna (Meyers) Myers; m. Paul Douglas Humphrey, Feb. 24, 1950; children—Margaret Jean, Paul Douglas, Catherine Blair. R.N., Rochester Gen. Hosp., 1950; postgrad. Colgate Rochester Croser Sem., 1978-82. Staff nurse, acting evening supr. Bethesda Hosp., Hornell, N.Y., 1950-51, operating room nurse Rochester Gen. Hosp. (N.Y.), 1951-54, nurse oncologist, 1973—; office nurse Robert McDonald, M.D., Webster, N.Y., 1955-64; research nurse oncology div. U. Rochester (N.Y.), 1970-73; bd. dirs. Genesee Valley Oncology Nurses, Rochester, 1983—. Assoc. rector Ch. of the Good Shepherd, Webster, N.Y., 1983-85; vicar St. Matthias Episcopal Ch., East Rochester, N.Y., 1985—; bd. dirs. Episc. Ch. Home, Rochester, 1983—, United Cancer Council, Rochester, 1983—; pres. bd. dirs. Am. Cancer Soc., Monroe County div., Rochester, 1983-85; cons. Episcopal Diocese Christian Edn., Rochester, 1980—. Mem. N.Y. State Cancer Programs Assn., Genesee Valley Nurses Assn. Home: 115 Iroquois St Webster NY 14580 Office: Rochester Gen Hosp 1425 Portland Ave Rochester NY 14621

HUMPHREY, JAYNE HULBERT, government official; b. Oakland, Calif., Apr. 1, 1947; d. Jack W. and Clare Roberta (Hittle) Hulbert; m. Donald James Humphrey, Nov. 11, 1983. Student Northwestern U., 1964-66, San Francisco State U., 1969-70. With various fed. govt. agencies, Washington, 1964-67; program asst. U.S. Dept. HUD, Washington, 1968, elderly housing program technician, San Francisco, 1969-70, housing rep., coordinator, 1970-75, dir. housing devel. div., 1975-83, dep. regional housing dir., 1983—; pres. Hulbert Humphrey, Inc., Fairfax, Calif., 1985—; instr. Calif. Mortgage Bankers Assn., Calif. Dept. Real Estate, Sacramento, 1985—; chief negotiator, mem. mgmt. contract with union HUD, San Francisco, 1983-84; mem. rev. bd. performance standards HUD, 1986—. Named Woman of Yr., U.S. HUD, 1985, recipient outstanding performance award, 1976, 78, 80, 81, 84, 85, Disting. Service nominee, 1979, spl. achievement award, 1972, 73, 75; hon. citizen City of Alameda, Calif., 1971. Mem. Fed. Mgrs. Assn., Nat. Soc. Female Execs., Am. Soc. Pub. Adminstrn. Democrat. Presbyterian. Avocations: music; computers. Office: Dept HUD 450 Golden Gate Ave Box 36003 San Francisco CA 94102-3448

HUMPHREY, LOUISE IRELAND (MRS. GILBERT W. HUMPHREY), civic worker, horsewoman; b. Morehead City, N.C., Nov. 1, 1918; d. R. Livingston and Margaret (Allen) Ireland; ed. pvt. schs.; m. Gilbert W. Humphrey, Dec. 27, 1939; children—Margaret (Mrs. K. Bindhart), George M. II, Gilbert Watts. Mem. corp., adv. bd. Tall Timbers Research Inc. Nurse's aide ARC, 1944—; past. dir. Nat. City Bank, Cleve., Nat. City Corp., Cleve., 1981-86; trustee Musical Arts Assn.; hon. trustee, past pres. Vis. Nurse Assn.; hon. trustee Lake Erie Coll., life trustee United Way Cleve., trustee Archbold Hosp., Thomasville, Ga.; hon. trustee Case Western Res. U.; bd. dirs. Monticello (Fla.) Opera House; mem., past trustee, 2d v.p. Jr. League; pres. bd. dirs. Met. Opera Assn.; bd. dirs. Thomas County Entertainment Found.; trustee No. Ohio Opera Assn.; treas., trustee Wildlife Conservation Fund Am.; former master foxhounds Chagrin Valley Hunt, Gates Mills, Ohio; dir., zone v.p. U.S. Equestrian Team, Inc.; mem. Garden Club Cleve.; bd. dirs., past pres. Nat. Homecaring Council; treas., bd. mem. Wildlife Legis. Fund Am.; bd. dir. Thomasville Cultural Ctr.; mem., vice chmn. Fla. Game and Fresh Water Fish Commn. Home: Woodfield Springs Plantation Miccosukee FL 32309

HUMPHREYS, BARBARA ANN, educator; b. Richmond, Va., May 1, 1934; d. James Currin and Agnes Elizabeth (Buttgen) Daniel; m. William Jared Humphreys, June 3, 1956; children—Kathryn Daniel Kotowski, William Jared

Jr., James Currin. Student, William and Mary Coll., 1952-56; B.A., Westhampton Coll., 1956. Cert. elem. and secondary tchr., Calif. Tchr., chmn. English dept. Perris Jr. High Sch., Calif., 1961-62; English tchr. Jurupa Jr. High Sch., Rubidoux, Calif., 1963-65; tchr., chmn. English dept. St. Michael's Prep. Sch., El Toro, Calif., 1974-75; tchr. Capistrano Sch. Dist., San Juan Capistrano, Calif., 1983—; founder, designer Sea Art, San Clemente, Calif., 1978—. Recipient several awards for fine arts and crafts Orange County (Calif.) Fair, 1979—. Republican. Avocations: boating; swimming; needlecraft; piano; designing.

HUMPHRIES, ELLEN THOM, bank officer; b. Oskaloosa, Iowa, Aug. 4, 1947; d. Theodore A. Thom and Catherine A. (Wilkes) Betts; m. Quinn F. Humphries, Jr., Dec. 4, 1965 (div. Feb. 1979); 1 child, Laura Amanda Kelly Humphries. Diploma, Killeen Comml. Coll., Tex. Banking officer, asst. mgr. First Nat. Bank, Metairie, La., 1967-78; banking officer Jefferson Bank & Trust, Metairie, 1978-80; banking officer, mgr. First Nat. Bank, Metairie, 1980-84; v.p. Gulf Fed. Savs. Bank, Metairie, 1984-85; account exec. First Fin. Bank, New Orleans, 1985—. Bd. dirs. New Orleans YWCA, 1982-85. Lutheran. Clubs: Metairie Central Bus. Dist. Assn. (sec. 1982-83, pres. 1983-84). Avocations: drama; dance; swimming; reading; youth counseling.

HUMPHRIES, JUDY LYNN, lawyer, nurse; b. Charleston, W.Va., Nov. 20, 1946; d. Robert Elmer and Arravelva Virginia (Davis) H.; m. Michael Allen Grant, Dec. 29, 1971; children—Susan Lindley, Christopher Allen, Elizabeth Davis. B.S. in Nursing, W.Va. U., 1968; M.S., U. Md.-Balt., 1970; J.D., Coll. of William and Mary, 1977. Bar: Va. 1977, W.Va. 1978, D.C. 1980. Instr. psychiat. nursing W.Va. U., Morgantown, 1970-72, asst. prof. Sch. Nursing, 1977-78; psychiat. nursing clin. specialist VA Hosp., Cin., 1972-73; vol. Newport News (Va.) Legal Aid, 1973-74; legal intern firm Frank, Nachman & Frank, Newport News, 1976; asst. pros. atty. Monongalia County, Morgantown, 1978-81; sole practice law, 1981-83, Fairmont, W.Va., 1983—; mem. faculty Fairmont State Coll. Bd. dirs. Monongalia County Youth Services Ctr., Morgantown, 1981-83, Vis. Homemaker Service, Morgantown, 1982-83, Hope, Inc., Fairmont. NIMH grantee, 1968-69, 69-70; scholar Marshall-Wythe Summer Law Sch., Coll. William and Mary at U. Exeter (Eng.), 1976. Mem. ABA, Assn. Trial Lawyers Am., W.Va. Sch. Nursing Alumni Assn. (pres. 1974-76, dir., 1974-82), LWV (sec. Marion County chpt. W.Va.), St. George Tucker Soc., Sigma Theta Tau. Episcopalian.

HUMPHRIES, LIN VERONICA, county official; b. Wheeling, W.Va., Mar. 11, 1938; d. Harry Edward and Helen Marie Humphries; m. William Edward Waress, Nov. 1956 (div. 1964); 1 child, Jolin Helen. B.A., Wheeling Coll., 1981. Office mgr. Hobbs Lumber Co., Wheeling, 1961-66, Penn Constrn. Co., Wheeling, 1966-76; magistrate Ct. of Ohio County, ct. clk. W.Va. Supreme Ct., Wheeling, 1977-83; circuit ct. clk. Ohio County, Wheeling, 1983—. Bd. dirs. YWCA, Wheeling, 1984—, Friends of W.Va No. Community Coll., Wheeling, 1984-85. Mem. W.Va. Assn. Circuit and County Clks. Republican. Avocations: reading, hand crafts. Home: 204 N Erie Wheeling WV 26003 Office: Ohio County Circuit Clk 1500 Chapline St Wheeling WV 26003

HUNGAR, JULIE YEARSLEY, educational administrator; b. Bismark, N.D., May 30, 1931; d. Julian Clayton and Gertrude Ethel (Bang) Yearsley; m. Gordon Earle Hungar, Aug. 30, 1953; children—Ann Alison, Susan Lynn, Thomas George Paula Jane. B.A. in English Lit., U. Wash., 1954, M.A. in English Lit., 1960; Ed.D. in Ednl. Leadership, Seattle U., 1982. News editor, traffic mgr. Sta. KBRC, Mt. Vernon, Wash., 1948-51; traffic and promotion mgr. KCTS-TV, Seattle, 1955-57; mem. faculty Seattle Central Community Coll., 1972-77, 80-82, devel. coordinator, 1978-80, chmn. div., 1982-84, vice chancellor Seattle Community Coll. Dist., 1984—; cons. Mills Cons. Assocs., Seattle, 1982—, Dr. William Berquist, Walnut Creek, Calif., 1981. Co-developer, moderator TV series: The Artist Among Us; contbr. articles to newspapers, mags. Founding chmn. Citizens for Quality Integrated Edn., Seattle, 1968-69; bd. dirs. Allied Arts of Seattle, 1965-68; v.p., bd. dirs. New Dimensions in Music, Seattle, 1968-71; bd. dirs., concert chmn. Seattle Symphony Family Concerts, 1963-65. Mem. Women in Communications, Wash. Assn. of Community Coll. Adminstrs., Wash. Community Coll. Humanities Assn., Seattle Econ. Devel. Commn., Seattle Urban League, Washington Council on Internat. Trade, World Affairs Council, Phi Delta Kappa, Phi Beta Kappa. Office: Seattle Community Coll Dist 300 Elliott Ave W Seattle WA 98119

HUNGATE, SUE CAROL, computer system account executive; b. San Antonio, Nov. 4, 1957; d. Joseph Irvin and Betty Lou (Hatzenbuehler) Hungate. B.A., U. S.C.-Columbia, 1978. Student asst. U. S.C., Columbia, 1975-78, research asst. Affiliated Computer, Dallas, 1978-79; media planner/buyer Bloom Advt., Dallas, 1979-81; customer service EDS/Cunadata, Dallas, 1981-82, regional rep., Charlotte, N.C., 1982-86; account mgr. Broadway & Seymour, Charlotte, 1986—. Named Employee of the Month, EDS/Cunadata, 1981. Mem. Am. Mgmt. Assn., Am. Bus. Women's Assn., Nat. Assn. Female Execs., AAUW, Pi Beta Phi. Methodist. Avocations: piano; reading; outdoor sports; sailing; water skiing. Home: 2709 New Hamlin Way Charlotte NC 28210 Office: Broadway & Seymour Inc 302 S Tryon St Charlotte NC 28202

HUNGERFORD, CONSTANCE CAIN, art educator; b. Chgo., Apr. 26, 1948; d. Craig John and Jocelyn Enid (Mason) Cain. B.A., Wellesley Coll., 1970; M.A., U. Calif.-Berkeley, 1972, Ph.D., 1977. Instr. to assoc. prof. history of art Swarthmore (Pa.) Coll., 1975—, chmn. dept. art, 1981—. Contbr. articles to profl. jours. Samuel H. Kress nat. fellow, 1973-75; Am. Council Learned Socs. grantee-in-aid, 1978; Am. Philos. Soc. grantee 1980. Mem. Coll. Art Assn. Am., AAUW (award 1983), Phi Beta Kappa. Office: Dept Art Swarthmore Coll Swarthmore PA 19081

HUNLEY, ANN BERNICE SUGGS, educational counselor; b. Balt., July 17; d. Isaac and Mary Elizabeth (Jones) Suggs; A.B., Morgan State Coll., Balt., 1954; M.S., Johns Hopkins U., 1975, Advanced Degree in Clin. Therapy, 1978. Nat. cert. counselor. Classroom and cooperating tchr. Balt. County Sch. System, 1955-73, ednl. counselor Parkville Middle Sch., 1973-84, Woodlawn High Sch., 1984-86; vol. div. instructional TV, Md. Dept. Edn., 1969. Past mem. bd. Md. div. Am. Lung Assn.; incorporator, past treas. Bar Belle-Field Neighborhood Assn.; pres. Our Lady of Lourdes Roman Cath. Ch. Parish Council, 1975-76, 86—; v.p. women's com. Balt., United Negro Coll. Fund, 1973; adv. world youth affairs UN, 1966; pres. aux, Echo House, 1975, pres. bd. dirs. Echo House Found., Inc., 1981—; mem. exec. com., bd. trustees Morgan Christian Center, Morgan State U., mem. president's com. for choir, 1982—; mem. Md. Task Force for Grad. Nursing Edn., 1975; phonathon vol. Johns Hopkins U., 1974—; pres. Md. women's com. for United Negro Coll. Fund., 1981-84; bd. dirs. Md. Conf. Social Concerns. Recipient citations for vol. work United Negro Coll. Fund, 1973, 74, Disting. Leadership award, 1980; Dedicated Community Service award Community Chest Balt. Area, 1982; Outstanding Women's award Philamathian, 1982; Community Service award Balt. Club Negro Bus. and Profl. Women, 1984; plaque for dedicated service and leadership Echo House Multi Service Ctr., 1984. Mem. NEA, Md. Tchrs. Assn., Tchrs. Assn. Balt. County, Balt. County Sch. Counselors Assn., Am. Assn. Counseling and Devel., Md. Assn. Counseling and Devel., Md. Assn. Multicultural Counseling and Devel. (parliamentarian), Balt. Urban League, NAACP (life), Mental Health Assn., YWCA, Md. League Women's Clubs, Nat. League Nursing, Md. League Nursing, Alpha Kappa Alpha (chpt. plaque 1973, Vivian J. Cook award Epsilon Omega chpt. 1982), Phi Delta Gamma (1st v.p. Gamma chpt. 1976-77, pres. 1979-80), Pi Lambda Theta (corr. sec. Chi chpt. 1983). Roman Catholic. Home: Baltimore MD Office: 1801 Woodlawn Dr Baltimore MD 21207

HUNLEY, W. HELEN, Canadian government official; b. Acme, Alta., Can., Sept. 6, 1920. Student Rocky Mt. House. Telephone operator, Carstairs, Acme, and Calgary, Alta.; operator farm; owner, operator truck dealership and ins. agy. (Internat. Harvester franchise), Rocky Mt. House, until 1968; owner, mgr. Helen Hunley Agy. Ltd., Rocky Mt. House, 1968-71; town councillor; mayor Rocky Mt. House; minister without portfolio, 1971; solicitor-gen., 1973; mem. Cabinet as minister of Social Services and Community Health, 1975-79; lt.-gov. Alta., Edmonton, 1985—. Active Alta. Girls Parliament and Provincial Mental Health Adv. Council. Office: Alta Govt Legislative Bldg Edmonton AB T5K 2B7 Canada

HUNSUCKER, TARA GAYLE, accountant; b. Kansas City, Mo., June 24, 1959; d. Robert D. and Majorie (Everet) H. B.B.A., U. Tex., 1981; M.S. in Human Resource Mgmt., Houston Bapt. U., 1986. Orientation advisor U. Tex., Austin, 1979-80; acct. Brown & Root, Inc., Houston, 1981—. Mem. spl. events com. U. Tex., 1979, mem. student com. on orientation procedures, 1979-80; vol. Juvenile Diabetes Found., Houston, 1977—; vol. UNICEF, Houston, 1973-77; vol. CPR instr. ARC, Houston, 1983—; camp counselor Disciples of Christ Ch., Houston, 1975, coastal plains area sec., 1976-77. Mem. Houston Payroll Tax Assn. Republican. Mem. Christian Ch. (Disciples of Christ). Office: Brown & Root Inc PO Box 3 Bldg 01 Room 204 Houston TX 77001

HUNT, ANITA M. HEARD, health care marketing executive, educator, consultant; b. Sayre, Okla., Oct. 14, 1943; d. William Lynn and Lydia Ethel (Boyer) Heard; m. Virgil Eugene Medley, Mar. 27, 1959 (div. 1970); children—Donald Eugene, Vicki Lea Medley-Wickham, Robert Lynn, Gary Duane. A.S. in Med. Tech., Sayre Coll., 1972; B.S. in Tech. Edn., Okla. State U., 1974; M.P.H. in Health Adminstrn., Okla. U., 1985; post-grad. Calif. State U.-Bakersfield, 1979. Cert. clin. lab. scientist, med. technologist. Profl. relations rep. Blue Cross & Blue Shield, Oklahoma City, 1977-78; med. technologist Kern County Hosp., Bakersfield, Calif., 1979; practice mgmt. cons. Med. Mgmt. Group, Oklahoma City, 1980-81; clin. lab. supr. South Community Hosp., Oklahoma City, 1982-85, hosp. services rep., 1985—; adj. asst. prof. Okla. U. Health Scis. Ctr., Oklahoma City, 1983-85. Editorial reviewer Jour. Med. Tech., 1984-86; author papers in field. Scouting coordinator Last Frontier council Boy Scouts Am., Oklahoma City, 1985. Sci. Products med. tech. grantee, 1973. Mem. Am. Med. Technologists (sec. bd. dirs. Inst. for Edn. 1976-77, nat. standards com. 1976-77, Disting. Achievement award 1978), Okla. Soc. Am. Med. Technologists (v.p. 1976-77), Nat. Assn. Female Execs., Am. Bus. Womens Assn., Okla. Pub. Health Assn., AAUW. Republican. Baptist. Clubs: Mensa, Toastmasters. Avocations: piano and vocal music; photography; water and snow skiing; yachting. Home: PO Box 95682 Oklahoma City OK 73143 Office: South Community Hospital 4200 S Douglas Medical Center Bldg Suite 101 Oklahoma City OK 73109

HUNT, ANN, college administrator, writer; b. Los Angeles, Feb. 17, 1927; d. Fred and Mollie (Diel) Hoffman; divorced; children—James Randolph, Lyndon Verle, Veronica Lyn, Florence Ann. Student, Western State Coll., Gunnison, Colo., 1944-48. Advt. mgr. The Bon Marche, Eugene, Oreg., 1954-59; writer Oreg. Jour., Portland, 1959-60; ptnr. Phil Hunt Pub. Relations, Portland, 1961-66; copy chief Jantzen Inc., Portland, 1966-76; dir. community service S.W. Oreg. Community Coll., Coos Bay, 1976—; writer scripts for documentary films, multi-image shows, TV programs. Contbr. articles to mags. and newspapers. Mem. State Travel Info. Council, 1972—, State Tourism Council, 1984—; bd. dirs. United Way Southwestern Oreg., 1980—. Mem. Oreg. Press Women, Oreg. Writers Colony, Bay Area C. of C. (sec., mem. exec. com.). Democrat. Roman Catholic. Home: 3893 Vista Dr North Bend OR 97459 Office: Southwestern Oregon Community Coll Coos Bay OR 97420

HUNT, CAROLYN ANN, paper company official; b. Amarillo, Tex., Dec. 12, 1931; d. Grover Cleveland and Leora (Britian) Elder; m. Charles Elmore Hunt, May 30, 1952; 1 son, Timothy Ray. B.S., U. Tex.-Dallas, 1978, M.S., 1984. Bookkeeper, Forrest Builders Supply, Lubbock, Tex., 1958-59, Modern TV Co., Ogden, Utah, 1959-65; office mgr. Austin Shoe Stores, Dallas, 1969-76; adminstrv. mgr. Slaughter Industries, Dallas, 1976-79; adminstrv. mgr. Internat. Paper Co., Dallas, 1979-80, office supr., 1980—. Chmn., United Way Internat. Paper Co., 1980-82. Mem. Am. Bus. Womens Assn. (v.p. 1983-84, woman of yr. 1982), Network Career Women (v.p. Dallas 1984-85), Am. Soc. Personnel Adminstrs., Dallas Personnel Assn., Vols. for Better Govt. Democrat. Baptist. Office: Internat Paper Co PO Box 809024 6700 LBJ Freeway Dallas TX 75380

HUNT, GLADYS MAE, writer; b. Moline, Mich., Oct. 23, 1926; d. Wilbur J. and Clara Jeanette (DeWeerd) Schriemer; B.A. in Journalism, Mich. State U., 1948, postgrad., 1958-59; m. Keith L. Hunt, Oct. 9, 1948; 1 son, Mark Earl. Author books: Does Anyone Here Know God?, 1967, Honey for a Child's Heart, 1969, Listen to Me, 1969, Focus on Family Life, 1970, How-to Bible Study, 1971. Don't Be Afraid to Die, 1971, Ms Means Myself, 1972, Family Secrets, 1985; co-author: Not Alone: The Necessity of Relationships, 1985, also Bible study guides; contbr. numerous articles for periodicals; asso. dir. Cedar Campus, a univ. student tng. center, 1954—; editorial bd. Today Mag., 1970—, Leadership Mag., 1979—. Mem. AAUW, Authors Guild. Baptist. Home: 1710 Saxon St Ann Arbor MI 48103

HUNT, JANET SUSAN, lawyer; b. Ft. Wayne, Ind., Mar. 28, 1951; d. Herbert Albert and Evelyn Louise (Prayther) Keller; m. Glenn Hunt, Mar. 20, 1976; children—Jennifer Janet, Sean Glenn. A.A., Orange Coast Coll., 1972; student U. Calif.-Riverside, 1969; B.S., Western State U., Fullerton, Calif., 1979, J.D., 1980. Bar: Calif. 1981; asst. ops. officer First Nat. Bank, Tustin, Calif., 1975-77; law intern Dist. Atty.'s Office, San Bernardino, Calif., 1979; law clk. Peterson & Moen, Fullerton, Calif., 1980; sole practice law, Mira Loma, Calif., 1981—. Mem. editorial bd. Western State Law Rev., 1980. Vol., Sch. Bd. Trustee Campaign, Orange County, Calif., 1981. Mem. Calif. State Bar Assn., ABA. Democrat. Lutheran. Clubs: Phoenix, Soroptimist. Address: 11100 Little Dipper St Mira Loma CA 91752

HUNT, JUDITH WAHNITTAH, feature writer; b. Phila., June 2, 1940; d. Carlee Gordon and Norma Ethlyn (Coe) Hunt; B.A. in Journalism, U. Wash., 1962; m. Neil C. Modie, Aug. 8, 1964 (div. 1975); children—Jonathan N., Claire E. Agrl./schs. reporter Lewiston (Idaho) Morning Tribune, 1963-64; gen. assignment reporter, makeup editor Vancouver (Wash.) Columbian, 1965-69; feature writer Seattle Post-Intelligencer, 1970—, furnishings editor, 1978—, also fashion editor. Winner, Spl. award, Penney-Mo. award, 1975; winner 14 state awards, Wash. Press Assn., 1974-81; 3d Pl. Nat. Hearst Papers award, 1977, others. Mem. Pacific N.W. Newspaper Guild (pres. 1979—), Wash. Press Assn., Nat. Press Women (3d place award 1979), Theta Sigma Phi, Kappa Delta. Democrat. Episcopalian. Clubs: Mazamas, Lumber Indian Tribe. Home: 13614 SE 232 St Kent WA 98031 Office: 521 Wall St Seattle WA 98121

HUNT, LENORE RUTH SISLER, nurse; b. Friendsville, Md., Jan. 24, 1926; d. Daniel C. and Ida Fay (Chidister) Sisler; m. John W. Hunt, Nov. 6, 1948 (dec.); children—John, George, Bruce. R.N., Lutheran Hosp. Md., 1948; B.S., Mt. St. Mary's Coll., 1977. Relief supr. Lutheran Hosp. Md., 1948-65; relief supr. Greater Balt. Med. Center, 1965-70, med. surg. coordinator, 1970—. Sec. White Rock Recreation Corp., 1975-78. Mem. Lutheran Hosp. Md. Alumnae Assn., Am. Nurses Assn., Md. Nurses Assn. Republican. Methodist. Club: Homemakers of Bel Air Acres. Home: 23 Idelwild St Bel Air MD 21014

HUNT, LINDA, actress; b. Morristown, N.J., Apr. 2, 1945. Student Interlochen Arts Acad.-Mich., Goodman Theatre and Sch. of Drama-Chgo. Off-Broadway theater debut in Down by the River, 1975; Little Victories, 1983; Top Girls, 1983; films include Dune, 1984, The Year of Living Dangerously, 1983 (Academy award for best supporting actress), The Bostonians, 1984, Eleni, 1985, Silverado, 1985, Popeye, 1980; Broadway appearance in Ah, Wilderness!, 1975, End of the World, 1984; in N.Y. Shakespeare Festival prodn. Aunt Dan and Lemon, 1985. Address: care Triad Artists Inc 10100 Santa Monica Blvd 16th Floor Los Angeles CA 90067*

HUNT, MYRTLE EVA, career devel. services exec.; b. Elberfeld, Ind., Jan. 20, 1927; d. John W. and Eva E. (Besing) Wilkison; B.A., U. Evansville, 1957; M.Ed., Colo. State U., 1964; m. Talmadege Hunt, Oct. 3, 1943; 1 son, Torrence L. Tchr. Evansville (Ind.)/Vanderburgh Sch. Corp., 1957-65; supr. Pinellas County Schs., Clearwater, Fla., 1965-71, dir., 1971—. Mem. Am. Assn. Sch. Adminstrs., Am. Vocat. Assn., Am. Home Econs. Assn., Fla. Assn. Sch. Adminstrs., Fla. Assn. Career Devel., Fla. Vocat. Assn., Fla. Home Econs. Assn., Am. Personnel and Guidance Assn., Fla. Personnel and Guidance Assn., Fla. Assn. Supervision and Curriculum Devel., Am. Personnel Assn., Fla. Personnel Assn., Pinellas Personnel Assn., Nat. Assn. Female Execs., Am. Assn. Supervision and Curriculum Devel., Bus. and Profl. Women, Program to Increase Minority Engring. Grads. (bd. dirs.). Democrat. Contbr. articles to profl. jours. Office: 1895 Gulf-to-Bay Blvd Clearwater FL 33515

HUNT, PATRICIA, real estate broker; b. Tyler, Tex., July 23, 1946; d. Alton Carter and Louise (Murphy) Ayers; divorced; 1 child, Christina. B.B.A., Tex. Tech U., 1965; M.A., U. Dallas, 1976. Lic. real estate broker. Model, Neiman-Marcus Co., Dallas, 1965-66, Kim Dawson Agy., Dallas, 1966-68; ind. real estate broker, Dallas, 1976—. Founder, 1st chmn. Cattle Barons' Ball for benefit Am. Cancer Soc., Dallas, 1974; active Young Republicans, Dallas, 1976—, Republican Assembly, Dallas, 1980—. Recipient 10th anniversary award Cattle Barons' Ball, 1984. Mem. Tex. Bd. Realtors, Dallas Bd. Realtors, Dallas Opera, Ballet and Symphony League, DAR, Daus. Republic Tex. Club: The 500 (Dallas). Home: 10517 Egret Ln Dallas TX 75230

HUNT, PATRICIA STANFORD, judge; b. Dunn, N.C., June 9, 1928; d. Lewis Knox and Florence Hibbette (Cooper) Denning; student Sweet Briar Coll., 1946-48; A.B., U. N.C., 1950, M.A., 1966, J.D., 1978; m. Donald M. Stanford, June 30, 1949 (dec. May 1970); children—Donald M., Randolph Lewis, Charles Ashley, James Cooper; m. Thomas M. Hunt, June 17, 1972. Tchr., Chapel Hill (N.C.) Carrboro Schs., 1963-69, counselor, 1969-73; admitted to N.C. bar, 1978; practiced in Chapel Hill, 1978—; mem. N.C. Gen. Assembly, 1972-81; dist. ct. judge, 15B Judicial Dist., Hillsborough, N.C., 1981—. Pres., Jr. Service League, 1960. Recipient Cert. of Appreciation, N.C. Autistic Soc., 1981, N.C. Assn. Attys., 1981, N.C. Acad. Trial Lawyers, 1981; Rockerfeller scholar, 1968-70; R. J. Reynolds fellow, 1970. Mem. Conf. Dist. Judges, N.C. State Bar Assn., N.C. Acad. Trial Lawyers, N.C. Assn. Women Attys. Democrat. Presbyterian. Co-author: (with Hugh Lefler) N.C. History, Geography and Government, 1970. Home: 100 Northwood Dr Chapel Hill NC 27514 Office: Clk Superior Ct Hillsborough NC 27278

HUNT, SUSAN ALICE, journalist; b. Cleve., Nov. 5, 1959; d. Warren H. and Rose Marie (Fulkerson) H. B.A., Miami U., 1982. Assoc. editor Herald Pub. Co., Barberton, Ohio, 1982-83; reporter News-Herald Newspapers, Wyandotte, Mich., 1983-84, Mellus Newspapers, Lincoln Park, Mich., 1984—; freelance photographer, 1982—; freelance writer, editor, 1984—. Pub. relations advisor Heritage Soc., Canal Fulton, Ohio, 1981-82; vol. Adult Creative Activities Program, Lincoln Park, 1983. Mem. Women in Communications Soc. Profl. Journalists, Miami U. Alumni Assn., Phi Mu. Office: Mellus Newspapers 1660 Fort St Lincoln Park MI 48146

HUNT, SUSANNE CAROL KRAFT, nurse; b. Plainfield, N.J., Dec., 25, 1943; d. Rudolph A. and Helen A. (Thomas) Kraft; diploma East Orange Gen. Hosp. Sch. of Nursing, 1964; cert. intravenous therapy technician; m. Kenneth G. Hunt, Oct. 29, 1965 (div.); children—Kenneth G., Kristen S. Nurse, Overlook Hosp., Summit, N.J., 1965-67; head nurse Woodbine Nursing Home, Alexandria, Va., 1967-68; staff nurse Circle Terrace Hosp., Alexandria, 1969-70; head intensive care Manassas (Va.) Manor Nursing Home, 1976-77, dir. nurses, 1977-79; charge nurse Martin Meml. Hosp., Stuart, Fla., 1979-85. Bd. dirs. Am. Cancer Soc., chmn. pub. edn. Cert. intravenous therapy technician; cert. chemotherapy nurse. Mem. Va. Nurses Assn., No. Va. Dirs. of Nursing Assn., Am. Heart Assn., Martin County Hist. Soc., United Meth. Women. Home: 6631 NW 21st St Margate FL 33063 Office: Hospital Dr Stuart FL

HUNT, WANDA HOLDER, state legislator; b. Bakersville, N.C., Mar. 22, 1944; d. Farrell Robert and Jane (Ledford) Winterhalter Holder; m. Robert Frank Hunt, Mar. 24, 1962; 1 dau., Donna Lynn. Student Appalachian State U. Asst. purchasing Appalachian State U., Boone, N.C., 1965-70; with purchasing/personnel Ceralon Mfg., Aberdeen, N.C., 1972-77; with purchasing office N.C. Dept. Transp., Raleigh, 1977-82; account exec. Pinehurst, Inc. (N.C.), 1984—; mem. N.C. Senate, 1983-86, vice-chair edn. com., 1983-84, chmn. sr. citizens com., 1985-86. Mem. bd. edn., Carthage, N.C., 1976-82; precinct chair Democratic party, Pinehurst, N.C., 1974-75; sec. Democratic party, Carthage, N.C., 1975. Recipient award Heart Fund; Disting. Service awards Moore County, 1983, Social Services Bd., Moore County, 1983; Vol. Service award Nat. Cystic Fibrosis, Pinehurst, N.C.; named Disting. Woman, State of N.C., Raleigh, 1984. Mem. Women in State Govt., N.C. State Govt. Employees Assn., N.C. Status of Women, N.C. Heart Fund Assn., Nat. Conf. State Legislatures (pensions com. 1985-86), State Legislators' Network (So. legis. conf. 1985-86), Travel Council N.C. (legis. com.), N.C. Council Hearing Impaired. Democrat. Presbyterian. Home: PO Box 1335 Pinehurst NC 28374

HUNTER, ANN GAIL, librarian; b. Milw., Nov. 8, 1949; d. Elmer Lester Herbert and Elizabeth Renatta (Bovee) Zaeske. B.A., U. Wis.-Madison, 1971, M.A., 1972. Asst. librarian U. Wis.-Wausau, 1972-73; cataloger, librarian MacMurray Coll., Jacksonville, Ill., 1973-76; corp. librarian Anheuser-Busch Co., Inc., St. Louis, 1976—; facilitator Anheuser-Busch Quality Circle, St. Louis, 1984—. Mem. Spl. Libraries Assn. (network liaison 1981-83, chmn. employment com., 1983-84, chmn. hospitality com. 1984-85), St. Louis Regional Library Network, AAUW (editor jour. 1981-84, scholar 1984, publicity chain 1985-86), Women in Bus. Network (adv. panel 1981-83, 86—). Avocation: stamp collecting. Office: Anheuser-Busch Co Inc One Busch Pl Saint Louis MO 63118

HUNTER, BETTY KATHERINE, executive search consultant; media personality; b. Los Angeles, May 28, 1945; d. Robert Cecil and B. Fay (McLean) H. B.S., U. So. Calif., 1967; postgrad., 1968. Ednl. cons. Los Angeles Unified Sch. Dist., 1968-80; exec. search cons. Korn/Ferry Internat., Los Angeles, 1980-81; pvt. practice exec. search consulting, Los Angeles, 1982—; dir. U. So. Calif. Commerce Assocs., 1974—; radio/TV personality various stas., 1982, 83, 84; career commentator Sta. KNBC News, Los Angeles, 1983-84. Contbr. articles to profl. jours. Mem. Town Hall of Calif., Los Angels World affairs Council. Recipient Hon. Life award in Excellence in Edn. PTA, 1976; Top Fund Raising award U. So. Calif. Grad. Sch. Bus., 1982-83. Mem. Internat. Platform Assn., Nat. Speakers Assn., U. So. Calif. Educare, Jr. League Los Angeles, Las Floristas. Home: 4201 Via Marina #265 Marina Del Rey CA 90292 Office: Betty K Hunter 2029 Century Park E Suite 580 Los Angeles CA 90067

HUNTER, BEVERLY CLAIRE, systems analyst, educator; b. Pitts., Apr. 19, 1941; d. Eldon Clare and Ethel Mae (Kamer) Roberts; B.A. cum laude (Nat. Merit scholar), U. Pitts., 1963; m. Harold G. Hunter, Jan. 7, 1966; children—Cynthia Claire, Gregory Shawn. Computer programmer U.S. Navy, 1964-65; systems engr. IBM Corp., 1965-66; dir. instructional programming Human Resources Research Orgn., Alexandria, Va., 1966-68, sr. staff scientist, 1970—; staff scientist Matrix Research, 1969; cons. U.S. Congress, U.S. Office Edn., Bell Labs., Telenet Communications; pres. Targeted Learning Corp.; v.p. Piedmont Research Center, 1979-80; peer reviewer NSF. NSF grantee, 1979—. Mem. AAAS, Nat. Sci. Tchrs. Assn., IEEE Computer Soc., Assn. Ednl. Data Systems, Assn. Computing Machinery, Union Concerned Scientists, Wilderness Soc., Nature Conservancy, Friends of the Earth, Rappahannock League Environ. Protection. Co-author: Learning Alternatives in U.S. Education: Where Student and Computer Meet, 1975; Computer Literacy, 1982; Author: My Students Use Computers, 1982; Guide to Learning Resources for Users of IBM Personal Computers; Scholastic U.S. History Data Bases, 1985; Scholastic U.S. Government Data Bases, 1985; Scholastic Life Science Data Bases, 1985; Scholastic Physical Sciences Data Bases, 1985; Scholastic World Geography Data Bases, 1986; Scholastic Poetry and Mythology Data Bases, 1986; Scholastic Literature Data Bases, 1986; contbr. articles to publs. Home: Route 1 Box 190 Amissville VA 22002 Office: Targeted Learning Corp Route 1 Box 190 Amissville VA 22002

HUNTER, CANDACE ELLEN, business executive, computer scientist, research chemist; b. Tampa, Fla., Feb. 9, 1936; d. Melville Gunby and Grace Florence (Robinson) Hunter; B.S. in Chemistry, Stetson U., DeLand, Fla., 1957; M.S. in Organic Chemistry, George Washington U., 1968; m. Robert Gene Plato, Dec. 17, 1955 (div. 1965). Public sch. tchr., Tampa, 1957-58; supr. chemistry labs. Stetson U., 1958-59; biochemist Nat. Inst. Arthritis and Metabolic Diseases, NIH, Bethesda, Md., 1960-66; analytical chemist pesticides standards FDA, Washington, 1966-74, computer systems analyst Bur. Foods, 1974-84, also com. chmn. Fed. Women's Program, fed. govt. project officer Low Acid Canned Food Filing Improvement Project; ptnr. Wiencke & Plato, Chevy Chase, Md., 1972—; pres. Semi-Custom Software Ltd., Chevy Chase, 1984—; tchr. seminars on differential scanning calorimetry U. Md. and George Washington U.; tchr. computer programming. Recipient awards from fed. govt. Mem. Am. Chem. Soc., AAAS, N.Y. Acad. Sci., Delta Delta Delta, Psi Chi, Gamma Sigma Epsilon, Sigma Pi Kappa. Republican. Office: Semi-Custom Software Ltd 6807 Brennon Lane Chevy Chase MD 20815

HUNTER, CHARLOTTE RAE, bank personnel officer, educator; b. Denver, Nov. 7, 1942; d. Ralph Emil and Edmae Marie (Landry) H.; m. Michael Eugene Waters, July 28, 1962 (div. 1977); children—Paige D., Michelle R. B.A., DePaul U., 1971; M.Ed., U. Ill., 1974, Ph.D., 1979. Cert. profl. in human resources. Pubs. editor Ill. Office Edn., Springfield, 1972-73; dir. research Triton Coll., River Grove, Ill., 1976-78; personnel dir. G.D. Searle & Co., Dallas, 1978-81, Saxon, Chgo., 1981-84; personnel officer World Bank, Washington, 1984—; adj. faculty Elmhurst Coll. (Ill.), 1983-84; mem. State Adv. Council on Adult, Vocat. Edn., Ill., 1977-79. Editor: Ill. Career Ednl. Jour., 1972; contbr. writings to publs. Commr. Ill. Commn. on Status of Women, 1975-79; bd. dirs. Nat. Assn. Commns. for Women, 1976-77; coordinating com. Internat. Women's Yr., Ill., 1977. EPDA fellow, 1973-75; recipient cert. of leadership YWCA Chgo., 1977. Mem. Am. Soc. Personnel

Adminstrs., Employment Mgmt. Assn., Phi Delta Kappa. Office: World Bank 1818 H St NW Washington DC 20433

HUNTER, DEBORAH JO, volleyball coach; b. Cape Girardeau, Mo., July 25, 1951; d. Joe Abner and Verniece (Carr) H. B.S. in Edn., SUNY-Cortland, 1973; M.S. in Edn., Memphis State U., 1975. Asst. volleyball coach Memphis State U., 1974-75; head volleyball coach So. Ill. U., Carbondale, 1975—; dir. Saluki Volleyball Camps; pres. Volleyball Tng. Network, Carbondale, 1984—; adviser U.S.A. Women's Nat. Volleyball Team, Coto de Casa, Calif., 1983-84; regional coordinator Prairie State Games, Champaign, Ill., 1984; coordinator U.S. Olympic Festival, Baton Rouge, La. and Houston, 1985-86. Mem. Collegiate Volleyball Coaches Assn. (charter), U.S. Volleyball Assn. (dir. 1981-83), Volleyball Am. (charter). Baptist. Avocations: travel; skiing; golf; flying; hiking. Home: 200 Brook Ln Carbondale IL 62901 Office: So Ill Univ Davies Gym Carbondale IL 62901

HUNTER, DELMA ELIZABETH, educator, consultant; b. Chgo., Oct. 13, 1952; d. Elbert and Mamie Lee (Trapp) H. B.S. in Edn., No. Ill. U., 1974; M.S. in Edn., Chgo. State U., 1980; M.B.A. in Fin., Loyola U., Chgo., 1985. Tchr., chmn. dept. trainable mentally handicapped Chgo. Bd. Edn., 1974—. Mem. Nat. Assn. Female Execs., Assn. M.B.A. Execs., Zeta Phi Beta. Baptist. Home: 8344 S Sangamon St Chicago IL 60620 Office: Spalding High Sch 1628 W Washington Chicago IL 60620

HUNTER, DIANNE MARY, health care products company executive; b. Mansfield, Ohio, July 29, 1946; d. William George Brooker and Helen B. (Hickey) Dickson; student in biology Mt. Union Coll., 1969. Asst. product mgr. Technicon Instruments subs. Revlon, Tarrytown, N.Y., 1976-77, product mgr. hematology, 1977-79; mktg. mgr. Ortho Instruments subs. Johnson & Johnson, Westwood, Mass., 1979-80; v.p. mktg./sales Genetic Diagnostics, Gt. Neck, N.Y., 1980—; mktg. and mgmt. cons.; co. dir. Mem. Biomed. Mktg. Assn., Nat. Assn. Female Execs. Home: Mamaroneck NY 10543 Office: 160 Community Dr Great Neck NY 11021

HUNTER, EDNA J., research psychologist; b. Danville, Ill., Mar. 25, 1923; d. John William and Nettie (Lee) Shank; B.A., U. Calif., Berkeley, 1946; M.S., San Diego State U., 1967; Ph.D., U.S. Internat. U., 1970; m. Daniel Bear Hunter, Apr. 28, 1924; children—Daniel, Robert, Ninah, Barbara. Tchr. adminstr. public schs., Stafford, Va., 1946-49; teaching asst., lectr. San Diego State U., 1964-67; clin. research psychologist Naval Health Research Center, San Diego, 1967-71; acting dir., adminstrv. dir. and head Family Studies Center for POW Studies, Naval Health Research Center, San Diego, 1971-78, dir. Family Research Center, U.S. Internat. U., San Diego, 1978—; disting. vis. prof. U.S. Mil. Acad.-West Point, 1985-86; owner Hunter Publs.; mem. congl. adv. bd. VA; mem. Nat. Adv. Bd. of Mil. Family Resource Center; cons. Devel. Assocs. Inc., Westinghouse Corp., William Beaumont Med. Ctr.; mem. Task Force on Families of Catastrophe; mem. Speakers' Bur.-Scientists in the Schs. Program. Fellow Am. Psychol. Assn. (named Disting. Mil. Psychologist 1983), Interuniv. Seminar on the Armed Forces; mem. Am. Assn. Marriage Family Therapy (cert. supr.), Nat. Council on Family Relations, Internat. Assn. Applied Psychology, Am. Women in Sci., Am. Bar Aux., Internat. Platform Assn., Internat. Council Sex Therapy. Republican. Club: Lioness. Author/editor: Family Separation and Reunion; Families in the Military System; Military Families: Adaptation to Change; One Flag, One Country; Black, White and Gray; Families Under the Flag; Professional Ethics and Law in the Health Sciences; Delusions of Clarity; editorial bd. Brunner/Mazel Psychosocial Stress Book series; editorial rev. bd. Armed Forces and Soc. Jour. contbr. articles to profl. jours. Home: PO Box A-81391 San Diego CA 92138 Office: BS&L US Mil Acad West Point NY 10996-1784

HUNTER, EMMA RUTH, educator; b. Crockett, Tex., Nov. 8, 1950; d. Viell Roland and Mary Etta (Jackson) H. B.S., Tex. So. U., 1971, M.Ed., 1974, postgrad., 1975-76. Tchr., Neff Sch., Houston, 1971-72, 72—; tchr. reading Tex. So. U., Houston, 1974-76. Reading adviser Shape Community Ctr., Houston, 1982-84. Named Outstanding Young Educator, Houston Ind. Sch. Dist., 1975, Tchr. of Yr., Neff Sch., 1980, 81. Mem. Internat. Reading Assn., Tex. So. Reading Council (corr. sec. 1973-74, rec. sec. 1975-76), Tex. Tchrs. Assn., Houston Tchrs. Assn., Delta Sigma Theta. Democrat. Home: 6233 Gulfton Apt 2219 Houston TX 77081

HUNTER, GEORGIA L., clergywoman, food service executive; b. Wiergate, Tex., June 14, 1938, d. George Clavert and Leila (Thomas) Spikes; m. LeRoy Hunter, Feb. 2, 1967; children—Balenda M. Spikes, Maria A. Spikes. Student Bible Moody Bible Inst. Ordained to ministry Christian Meth. Episcopal Ch., 1983. Counselor Ill. Dept. children and Family Services, Freeport, 1970-74; food service dir. Retirement Inc., Freeport, 1978—; pastor Christian Meth. Episcopal Ch., Madison, Wis., 1983—; corr. Jour. Standard, Freeport, 1982-83. Vice-pres. Freeport Bd. Edn., 1977—; pres. Ch. Women United, Freeport, 1970-83; asst. dir. youth Rockford and Vicinity Dist. Assn., 1980-82. Recipient Human Relations award City Council Freeport, 1974, Spiritual Achievement award Martin Luther King Ctr., Freeport, 1983, Good Neighbor award Freeport Jour. Standard, 1983, Achievement award Ch. Women United, 1983. Democrat. Avocations: bowling; researcher; reading; sewing; writing poetry. Home: 846 E Pleasant St Freeport IL 61032

HUNTER, JOAN WARD, academy administrator; b. Nashville, Dec. 8, 1939; d. Jim and Bessie Lucille (Hooper) Ward; m. Robert Hale Hunter, Dec. 31, 1959 (div. Oct. 1968); children—Robert Hale, Jeffrie Ward. Student pub. schs. Fin. mgr. Preston Lincoln Co., Nashville, 1966-68; v.p., co-owner Town/Country Uniform Rental Co., Nashville, 1968-71; sales mgr. Am. Housing Co., Nashville, 1972-74; pres., owner Contractors Constrn. Co., Nashville, 1974-78; 1st v.p. Acad. Fin. Tng., Altamonte Springs, Fla., 1979—. Bd. dirs. 1st Seventh-day Adventist Ch., Nashville, 1978-80, Sabbath Sch. supt., tchr., 1978-81; vol. worker with sr. citizens. Mem. Nat. Assn. Female Execs., Women's Network, Nat. Assn. Auctioneers, Fla. Assn. Auctioneers, Orange County Hist. Soc., Bus. and Profl. Women's Club (past pres. 1977-78). Avocations: gardening, interior design.

HUNTER, KATHRYN MOTZ, public relations executive; consultant; b. Akron, Ohio, July 5, 1925; d. Clarence Emery and Maud Marie (Rudy) Motz; m. John Barton Hunter, Aug. 31, 1946; children—David Motz, James Barton, Ann Rudy. A.B., Ohio Wesleyan U., 1946; M.S., U. Akron, 1969. Editor, Hudson Times, Ohio, 1957-63; editor, pub., 1956-63; editor, pub. Falls News, Cuyahoga Falls, Ohio, 1956-63; creator, coordinator spl. programs for women U. Akron, 1963-81; now v.p. pub. relations First Akron Corp., Valley Savs. & Loan, Akron. Contbr. articles to newspapers, mags. and profl. jours. Pres., Falls Family Service, Cuyahoga Falls, 1963-64; trustee Ohio Wesleyan U., Delaware, Ohio, 1974-83; bd. dirs. Akron Symphony Orch., 1965—, Summit County Hist. Soc., Akron, 1978—. Named Woman of Achievement, Knight-Ridder Newspapers, Akron, 1969, Ohio commodore, 1984; recipient Ohio Women's History Week award, 1984. Mem. Women in Communications, Ohio Hist. Soc. (treas. 1985—), Mortar Bd., Phi Beta Kappa, Pi Lambda Theta. Democrat. Congregationalist. Clubs: Akron City; Silver Lake Country; Farmington Country. Home: 3041 Silver Lake Blvd Cuyahoga Falls OH 44224 Office: First Akron Corp 611 W Market St Akron OH 44303

HUNTER, KIM (JANET COLE), actress; b. Detroit, Nov. 12, 1922; d. Donald and Grace Mabel (Lind) Cole; ed. pub. schs.; student acting with Charmine Lantaff Camine, 1938-40, Actors Studio; m. William A. Baldwin, Feb. 11, 1944 (div. 1946); 1 dau., Kathryn Emmett; m. 2d, Robert Emmett, Dec. 20, 1951; 1 son, Sean Emmett. First stage appearance, 1939; played in stock, 1940-42; Broadway debut in A Streetcar Named Desire, 1947; appeared in Two Blind Mice (tour), 1950; Darkness at Noon (N.Y.C.), 1951; The Chase, 1952 (N.Y.C.), They Knew What They Wanted (tour), 1952; The Children's Hour (revival) (N.Y.C.), 1952; The Tender Trap (N.Y.C.), 1954; Write Me a Murder (N.Y.C.), 1961; Weekend (N.Y.C.), 1968; The Penny Wars (N.Y.C.), 1969; And Miss Reardon Drinks a Little (tour), 1971-72; The Glass Menagerie (Atlanta), The Women (N.Y.C.), 1973; In Praise of Love (tour), 1975, The Lion in Winter (N.J.), 1975; The Cherry Orchard (N.Y.C.), 1976; The Chalk Garden (Pa.), 1976; Elizabeth The Queen (Buffalo), 1977; Semmelweiss (Buffalo), 1977; The Belle of Amherst (N.J.), 1978; The Little Foxes (Mass.), 1980; To Grandmother's House We Go (N.Y.C.), 1981, Another Part of the Forest (Seattle), 1981, When We Dead Awaken, (N.Y.C.), 1982, Ghosts (Garden City and Tarrytown, N.Y.), 1982; Territorial Rites, N.Y.C., 1983, Death of a Salesman, Stratford, Ont., 1983, Cat on a Hot Tin Roof, 1984, Life with Father, Coconut Grove, Fla., 1984, Sabrina Fair, Berkshire Theatre Festival, Mass., 1984, Faulkner's Bicycle, Yale Repertory and Joyce Theatre, N.Y.C., 1985, A Delicate Balance, Berkshire Theatre Festival, 1986; frequent appearances summer stock and repertory theater, 1940—; appeared Am. Shakespeare Festival, Stratford, Conn., 1961; film debut in The Seventh Victim, 1943; other motion pictures include: Tender Comrade, 1943, When Strangers Marry (re-released as Betrayed), 1944, You Came Along, 1945, A Canterbury Tale, 1949, Stairway to Heaven, 1946, A Streetcar Named Desire, 1951, Anything Can Happen, 1952, Deadline U.S.A., 1952, Storm Center, 1956, Bermuda Affair, 1957, The Young Stranger, 1957, Money, Women, and Guns, 1958, Lilith, 1964, Planet of the Apes, 1968, The Swimmer, 1968, Beneath the Planet of the Apes, 1970, Escape from the Planet of the Apes, 1971, Dark August, 1975, The Kindred, 1986; made TV debut on Actor's Studio program, 1948; numerous TV appearances include: Requeim for a Heavyweight, 1956, The Comedian, 1957 (both on Playhouse 90), Give Us Barabbas on Hallmark Hall of Fame, 1961, 63, 68, 69, Love, American Style, Colombo, Cannon, Night Gallery, Mission Impossible, The Magician, 1972-73, Marcus Welby, Hec Ramsey, Griff, Policy Story, Ironside, Med. Center, Bad Ronald, Born Innocent, 1974, Ellery Queen, 1975, Lucas Tanner, This Side of Innocence, Once an Eagle, Baretta, Gibbsville, Hunter, 1976, The Oregon Trail, 1977, Project: U.F.O., Stubby Pringle's Christmas, 1978, Backstairs at the White House, 1979, Specter on the Bridge, 1979, Edge of Night, 1979-80, F.D.R.'s Last Year, 1980, Skokie, 1981, Scene of the Crime, 1984, Private Sessions, 1985, Three Sovereigns for Sarah, 1985, Hot Pursuit, 1985, Martin Luther King Jr.: The Dream and the Drum, PBS, 1986; rec. From Morning 'Til Night (and a Bag Full of Poems), RCA Victor, 1961, Come, Woo Me: Unified Audio Classics, 1964; lectr. High Sch. for Performing Arts, N.Y.C., Friends Sem., N.Y.C., 1961, S.D. U., 1965, Lehigh U., 1965, ANTA In-Tchrs.-Service, N.Y.C., 1965, High Sch. Music and Art, N.Y.C., 1968, Brigham Young U., Provo, Utah, 1978. Recipient Donaldson award for best supporting actress in A Streetcar Named Desire, 1948, also on Variety N.Y. Critics Poll, 1948, for film, version, 1952; winner Acad. award, LOOK award, Hollywood, Fgn. Corrs. Golden Globe award; Emmy nominations for Baretta, 1977, Edge of Night, 1980, Carbonnell award for Big Mama in Cat on a Hot Tin Roof, U. So. Fla., 1984. Mem. Acad. Motion Picture Arts and Scis., ANTA, A.E.A. (council 1953-59), Screen Actors Guild. AFTRA. Author: Kim Hunter—Loose in The Kitchen, 1975.

HUNTER, MARLENE SELF, county legislative aide; b. Morganton, N.C., Feb. 9, 1934; d. Richard James and Azalee (Ritchey) Self; comml. cert. U. N.C., 1953; student U. Del.; m. Bill Roper Hunter, Nov. 28, 1953; children—Pamela Dawn, Charles Phifer, Gregory Scott, Susan Azalee. Adminstrv. asst. Charles County C. of C., La Plata, Md., 1974-78, mgr., 1978, exec. dir., 1978-84; legis. aide Prince Georges County Council, Md., 1985—. Pres. Charles County Democratic Club, 1976-78; bd. dirs. Charles County Handicapped and Retarded Citizens, 1978-80, sec., 1982; bd. dirs. Easter Seal Soc. for Disabled Children and Adults; mem. Charles County Career Edn. Adv. Council. Mem. Am. C. of C. Execs. (chmn. chpt. 1982), Md. C. of C. (legis. com.), Md. Assn. C. of C. Execs. (scholarship 1978), Bus. and Profl. Women, Md. Council Small Bus. Execs. Methodist. Clubs: Crescent Cities Jaycee-Ettes (pres. 1972); Zonta (pres. 1982-83) (Charles County). Home: Hunter Hill Farm Route 232 Box 148 Bryantown MD 20617 Office: Council Offices County Adminstrn Bldg Upper Marlboro MD 20772

HUNTER, MAUREEN LYNNELL, human factors engineer; b. Washington, Aug. 2, 1949; d. Herbert Bernard and Militza M. (Santin) Hunter Jr.; B.S.W., George Mason U., 1973; M.C., Ariz. State U., 1977. Counselor Maricopa County Community Coll., Mesa, Ariz., 1975-78; configuration mgmt. specialist Martin Marietta Aero., Yuma, Ariz., 1979-80; mem. tech. staff Hughes Helicopters, Inc., Culver City, Calif., 1980-81; human factors engring. cons. Xerox Corp., El Segundo, Calif., 1981-82; cons. human factors engring. Interface Engring. Systems, Inc., Tempe, Ariz., 1983—. Mem. Human Factor's Soc., Soc. Profl. Engrs., Am. Helicopter Soc., Soc. Women Engrs., IEEE, AAAS.

HUNTER, SUE PERSONS, former state official; b. Hico, Tex., Aug. 21, 1921; d. David Henry and Beulah (Boatwright) Persons; B.A., U. Tex., 1942; m. Charles Force Hunter; children—Shelley Hunter Richardson, Mary Hunter McCullough, Margaret Hunter Brown. Air traffic controller CAA (now FAA), San Antonio and Houston, 1942-52; writer Bissonet Plaza News, 1969-72; coordinator Goals for La., 1971-74; adminstrv. dir. Jeff Publs. Inc., 1974; press sec. Jefferson Parish Dist. Atty., 1972-75, communications cons., 1975-78; adminstr. Child Support Enforcement Div., 1979-85; contbg. editor The Jeffersonian, 1975-76. Pres. United Ch. Women East Jefferson (La.), 1938-39, LWV Jefferson Parish, La., 1961-64; pres. LWV La., 1967-71, also bd. dirs., 1962-67; mem. probation services com. Community Services Council, Jefferson, 1966-73, v.p., 1970-72; mem. Library Devel. Com. La., 1967-71, Nat. Com. for Support of Public Schs., 1967-72; mem. Goals Found. Council Met. New Orleans, 1969-75, sec. 1970, 72; mem. Goals La. Task Force State and Local Govt., 1969-70; pres. MMM Investment Club, 1969-72; bd. dirs. New Orleans Area Health Planning Council, 1969-75, Friends of Westminster Tower, 1986—; mem. adv. council La. State Health Planning, 1971-76; title I adv. council La. State Dept. Edn., 1970-72; vice chmn. Jefferson Women's Polit. Caucus, 1977-78, chmn., 1979, treas., 1980; bd. dirs. New Orleans Area/Bayou-River Health Systems Agy., 1978-82, pres., 1980, 81; mem. Task force for La. Talent Bank of Women, 1980; exec. bd. La. Child Support Enforcement Assn., 1980-86, pres., 1982-84; bd. dirs., legis. chmn. Nat. Child Support Enforcement Assn., 1983—; mem. Gov.'s Commn. on Child Support Enforcement, 1984—; mem. La. Statewide Health Coordinating Council, 1980-83. Recipient Outstanding Citizens award Rotary Club, Metairie, La., 1962; River Ridge award, 1976. Mem. Am. Assn. Individual Investors (pres. New Orleans chpt. 1986—), New Orleans Panhellenic (pres. 1956-57), Alpha Xi Delta. Presbyterian (elder). Home: 210 Stewart Ave River Ridge LA 70123

HUNTLEY, ALICE MAE, mfg. exec.; b. Atoka, Okla., May 9, 1917; d. Joseph LaHay and Lula May (Stapp) Howe; B.A., U. Okla., 1939; m. Loren Clifford Huntley, Nov. 7, 1942; children—Loren Lee, Marcia Lynn. Reporter, McAlester (Okla.) News Capital, 1939-41; sec., asst. to pres. and chmn. bd. N.Am. Aviation, Los Angeles, 1941-63; v.p., co-owner Tubular Specialties Mfg., Inc., Los Angeles, 1966—. Former sec. 1st Baptist Ch. of Westchester; sec. Westchester-Del Rey Republican Women, 1959-60; assoc. mem. Rep. State Central Com., 1973. Cert. profl. sec.; named Outstanding Sec. in So. Calif., So. Calif. chpt., 1954, Internat. Sec. of Year, 1955 (both Nat. Secs. Assn.). Home: 8238 Calabar Ave Playa del Rey CA 90293 Office: 13011 S Spring St Los Angeles CA 90061

HUNTLEY, LAURA ADACK, accountant; b. Schenectady, N.Y., Jan. 25, 1957; d. Konstanty and Bernadette (Slezak) Adack; m. Clarence Byrne Huntley, May 14, 1983. B.S. magna cum laude, Ind. U. of Pa., 1978. C.P.A., Pa. Audit sr. Peat, Marwick, Mitchell and Co., Washington, 1978-80; fin. analyst UNC Resources, Inc., Falls Church, Va., 1980-82; mgr. corp. fin. reporting MCI Communications Corp., Washington, 1982—. Mem. Am. Inst. C.P.A.s. Roman Catholic. Office: MCI Communications Corp 1133 19th St NW Washington DC 20036

HUNZIKER, KAREN LILLIAN, personnel administrator; b. Queens, N.Y., June 17, 1947; d. Frederick and Dorothy Lillian (Williams) Schmidt; m. Scott Esmond Hunziker, June 29, 1968; children—Candace Lillian, S. Brandon. B.S., SUNY-New Paltz, 1966; postgrad. Fairfield U., 1968, Sacred Heart U., Fairfield, Conn., 1980. Tchr., Wilton Bd. Edn., Conn., 1966-70; tchr., librarian Brookfield Bd. Edn., Conn., 1979-83; adminstrv. asst., office mgr. Safetyscope, Inc., Danbury, Conn., 1983-85; adminstrv. asst. Union Carbide, Danbury, 1985; personnel adminstr. Computrol, Inc., Ridgefield, Conn., 1986—. Mem. cultural com. Newtown PTA, 1978. Recipient Latin award New York Cultural Club, 1962. Mem. Personnel Mgmt. Assn. Western Conn., Nat. Assn. Female Execs. Methodist. Club: Newtown Square Dancing (v.p. 1977-79). Avocations: tennis; racquetball; jazzercise; reading; career development. Home: 16 Mountain Laurel Rd Newtown CT 06470 Office: Computrol Div of Kidde Industries 15 Ethan Allen Hwy Ridgefield CT 06877

HUPALO, KATHLEEN FIXSEN, lawyer; b. Sheridan Twp., Minn., Jan. 21, 1945; d. Orman Bernard and Margery Elizabeth (Swartz) Fixsen; m. Ivan Hupalo, May 24, 1964; 1 son, Peter. B.A. in Sociology, U. Minn., 1976, J.D., 1981. Bar: Minn. 1981, U.S. Dist. Ct. Minn. 1982, U.S. Ct. Appeals (8th cir.) 1982. Sole practice, St. Paul, 1981-84; atty. Am. Indian Health Agy., St. Paul, 1984; human rights law enforcement officer Minn. Dept. Human Rights, 1985—. Contbr. articles to legal jours. Atty. Nursing Home Rights, Mpls., 1982; den mother Boy Scouts Am., 1976; mem. West Side Neighborhood House, St. Paul, 1976—, West Side Citizens Edn., 1976. Mem. ABA, Minn. State Bar Assn., Ramsey County Bar Assn., Minn. Women Lawyers Inc., Minn. Alumni Assn., Lex Alumnae. Home: 684 Delaware Ave Saint Paul MN 55107

HUPALO, MEREDITH TOPLIFF, artist, illustrator; b. Tarpon Springs, Fla., Apr. 28, 1917; d. Walter and Maurine (Martin) Topliff; cert. in design Pratt Inst., 1938; m. Nicholas Hupalo, July 13, 1940 (dec. Sept. 1977); children—Walter Topliff, John Nicholas. One-woman shows: Tarpon Springs Public Library, 1945, Valley Stream (N.Y.) Mus., 1962, Contemporary Arts, Inc., N.Y.C., 1966, Jet Clubs Internat., N.Y.C., Henry Waldinger Library, Valley Stream, N.Y., 1977, East River Savs. Bank, Valley Stream, 1978; two-person show: Art League of Daytona Beach, 1986; represented in permanent collection Valley Stream Public Library, Tarpon Springs (Fla.) Public Library, Eastern Airlines Exec. Offices, N.Y.C.; tchr. printmaking Nassau County (N.Y.) Home Extension Service; art adviser Valley Stream Mus., 1962-64; illustrator Eastern Airlines, 1964-68; artist Shell Oil Co., 1968-70; designer Continental Can Co., N.Y.C., 1970-73; art tchr. Astor (Fla.) Community Center, 1980-82. Recipient spl. award oil painting 34th Nat. Spring Exhbn. Nat. Art League L.I., 1964, gold medal in oil painting 35th Membership Show, 1965; 1st pl. fine art Fla. Silver Springs Arts & Crafts Festival, 1980; 1st place award Umatilla Fall Festival (Fla.), 1983 merit award, 1985; merit award Tampa Realistic Artists, 1984; Best in Show award Nat. League Am. Pen Women, 1984. Mem. Fla. Watercolor Soc., Nat. Art League L.I. (treas. 1959-60), Tampa Realistic Artists, Art League of Daytona Beach, Fla. Watercolor Soc. (assoc.), Mus. Arts and Scis., DeLand Mus., Astor Area C. of C. (dir. 1981-82). Methodist. Works included Paintings with Markers, 1972. Home: Lot 37 Holiday Haven Astor FL 32002

HURCHALLA, MAGGY, county official; b. Miami, Fla., Dec. 11, 1940; d. Henry Olaf and Jane (Wood) Reno; m. James Hurchalla, Nov. 25, 1960; children—James, Robert, Jane, George. B.A., Swarthmore Coll., 1962. Mem. County Commn., Martin County, Fla., 1974—, chmn., 1978-79; mem. Speaker's Water Task Force Fla., 1982-84. Author: Woods and Bushes—Wild Places, 1985. Recipient Greening of Am. award Stuart Garden Club, 1977; named Conservationist of Yr., Fla. Audobon, 1984; Land and Water Conservationist, Fla. Wildlife Fedn., 1984. Democrat. Home: 5775 SE Nassau Terr Stuart FL 33494 Office: Martin County 50 Kindred St Stuart FL 33497

HURD, MAGGIE PATRICIANNE, electron microscopist; b. Atlanta, Mar. 6, 1940; d. Oscar James and Rubye (Chunn) Hurd; B.A., Spelman Coll., 1962; M.A., Atlanta U., 1967, Ph.D., 1976. Tchr. sci. Atlanta Public Schs., 1962-75; electron microscopist DeKalb (Ga.) County Sch. System, Fernbank Sci. Center, Atlanta, 1975—; adj. prof. Ga. State U., 1977—; adviser coop. ind. study program Agnes Scott Coll., 1978; adviser coop. grad. biology program Emory U., 1978; cons. sci. career seminar Spelman Coll., 1977; cons. NSF Workshop on Techniques in Preparing Sci. Projects for Sci. Tchrs., 1979; guest lectr. Malcolm X Coll., Chgo., 1980; participant Internat. Electron Microscopy Meeting, Hamburg, W.Ger., 1982; lectr. Janssen Pharmaceutica Research Lab., Beerse, Belgium, 1982. Mem. Ga. Acad. Sci., NEA, Am. Inst. Biol. Scis., AAAS, Assn. of Southeastern Biologists, Nat. Sci. Tchrs. Assn., SE Electron Microscopy Soc., Am. Phytopath. Soc., Electron Microscopy Soc. Am. (arrangements chairperson meeting southeastern chpt. 1981), Minority Women in Sci. (charter mem. Atlanta chpt. 1980, pres. 1983—), Phi Delta Kappa, Alpha Kappa Alpha, Beta Kappa Chi. Contbr. articles in field to profl. jours. Office: 156 Heaton Park Dr Atlanta Ga 30307

HURDLE, BESSIE M., civic worker; b. Reading, Pa., May 17, 1945; d. Frelton and Bessie Walker; student Reading Area Community Coll., 1975-78; m. James Hurdle Jr., Aug. 14, 1965 (separated); children—James W., Obai. Exec. dir. Berks County Welfare Rights Orgn., Reading, Pa., 1978-81; com. mem. Pa. State Food and Nutrition Com., 1979-81; Pa. coordinator Black Women in Polit. Action, 1979—; a coordinator Vol. Clearing House, Washington, nat. st. law program for adult edn. Shilo Bapt. Ch., nat. conv. Nat. Women of Color; active Wider Opportunities for Women, Birth Right; Women in Crisis; active several polit. campaigns. Bd. dirs. Berks Youth Counseling Center; adv. bd. J.B. Johnson Nursing Home, Washing, YWCA. Mem. Health Maintenance Orgn., NOW, Female Exec. Club, Internat. Readers Assn. (D.C. council). Home: 1338 Levis St NE Washington DC 20002

HURDLE, LOIS STOVALL, psychologist, researcher; b. Mocksville, N.C., June 1, 1936, d. Grady and Ruth (Mangrum) Stovall; div. 1979; children—Sonia, Renee Antoinette, Synlethia Latasha. B.S., Morgan State U., 1961; M.Ed., Loyola Coll.-Balt., 1967; Ph.D., U. Conn., 1980. Tchr. Balt. County Pub. Schs., 1961-65; counselor Howard County Pub. Schs., Howard City, Md., 1965-70, Deer Park Pub. Sch., N.Y., 1970-72; cons. psychology Virginia Beach Pub. Sch., 1973-74, Isle of Wight County Sch., Smithfield, Va., 1974; assoc. prof. psychology Norfolk State U., Va., 1974—. Contbr. articles to profl. jours. Del., Democratic Conv., Roanoke, Va., 1983; social ministry leader St. Matthews Cath. Ch., Virginia Beach, 1980-84; leader Community Outreach to Elderly, Tidewater Area, Va., 1982—, Girl Scouts U.S.A., Tidewater; active Am. Heart Assn. Recipient Am. Soc. Edn. Engrs. and Office Naval Research Cert. of Recognition; Norfolk State U. Service award, 1982-83; Girl Scouts cert. of appreciation, 1984; grants Norfolk State U. (Va.), Commonwealth U. Mem. Am. Psychol. Assn., Va. Psychol. Assn., Va. Assn. Counseling Psychologists, Va. Assn. Sch. Psychologists, Human Factor Soc., Tidewater Human Factor Soc., AAUP, Tidewater Mental Health Assn., Va. Social Sci. Assn., Kappa Delta Pi, Psi Chi, Phi Delta Kappa. Roman Catholic. Office: Norfolk State U 2401 Corprew Ave Norfolk VA 23504

HURLBUT, ROWENA JOSEPHINE, retail card and gift shop owner; b. Webster City, Iowa, May 20, 1917; d. Arthur C. and Eathel R. (Robinson) Bennett; m. Walter C. Hurlbut, June 10, 1942; (dec. 1973); children—Terrill C., Gary D., Cherie K. Student Morningside Coll. Pres., owner Ames News Agy. (Iowa), Inc., 1950—; gen. mgr. Walt's Hallmark Shops, Ames, 1952—, Boone, Iowa, 1969—, Jefferson, Iowa, 1975—, Des Moines, 1977—, Ames, 1978—, West Des Moines, 1983—. Bd. dirs. Story County, Am. Heart Assn., 1985-87. Mem. C. of C., Delta Zeta. Republican. Mem. Church of Christ (deaconess 1980—). Clubs: Ames Women's (chmn. group 1952-53). Lodge: Mem. Order Eastern Star. Home: 1421 Clark St Ames IA 50010 Office: Ames News Agy Inc 2110 E 13th St Ames IA 50010

HURLEY, ALLYSON KINGSLEY, dentist; b. Buffalo, June 15, 1949; d. Norman and Marion (Legler) Kingsley; m. Lawrence Joseph Hurley, May 28, 1977. Student Barat Coll. of Sacred Heart, 1967-68; R.D.H., Marquette U., 1970, B.S., 1971; D.D.S., Howard U., 1977. Pvt. practice dental hygiene, Washington, 1971-77; resident VA Hosp., Lyons, N.J., 1977-78; practice gen. dentistry, Chatham, N.J., 1978—; attending dentist Overlook Hosp., Summit, N.J., 1979—, dir. resident adminstrn., 1980—, mem. edn. com., 1981; clin. dental hygiene instr. Union County Tech. Inst., Scotch Plains, N.J., 1979-81; coordinator children's dental health program Chatham Boro Sch. System grades kindergarten-4, 1978—; active oral cancer screening program Chatham Boro Jr. Women's Club, 1980-82. Editor, contbg. author Word of Mouth newsletter, 1981—; author booklet: Your Child's Teeth, 1984. Alumni recruiter Marquette U., Morris County, N.J., 1977—; bd. dirs. Am. Cancer Soc., Morris County, 1981-83; chmn. Scholarship Found. of the Chathams, Inc., 1985—. Acad. Gen. Dentistry fellow, 1982. Mem. Columbia U. Dental Study Club (treas. 1980—), No. N.J. Women's Study Club (pres. 1980-82, sec. 1983—), Tri County Dental Soc. (dir. 1982-83), Acad. Gen. Dentistry, ADA, Internat. Platform Assn., N.Y. Acad. Scis. Republican. Roman Catholic. Clubs: Phase II (Chatham), Chatham Twp. Newcomer's. Office: Allyson Kingsley Hurley DDS PA 585 Main St Chatham NJ 07928

HURLEY, ANN MARIE, municipal official; b. N.Y.C., July 13, 1925; d. Timothy Charles and Mary Frances (Lacey) O'Neill; ed. N.Y.C. public schs., bus. courses and seminars; m. John D. Hurley, Jr., Aug. 24, 1947; children—John Edward, Patty Ann Hurley McGovern. Clk., bookkeeping supr. Guaranty Trust Co., N.Y.C., 1942-47; bookkeeping supr. Continental Bank & Trust Co., N.Y.C., 1947-48, N.Y. Trust Co., N.Y.C., 1948-49; head bookkeeper, prin. clk., dep. receiver of taxes Town of Huntington, N.Y., 1960-67, receiver of taxes, 1967—; spl. com. revision Suffolk County Tax Act, mem. Blue Ribbon com. to revise Suffolk County Tax Act, 1982; mem. adv. bd. N.Y. State Community Affairs. Pres. Heatherwood Civic Assn., South Huntington Democratic Club; exec. bd. Suffolk County Dem. Party; Dem. zone leader, Huntington Station, N.Y.; committeeperson Dem. Party, 1960—; mem. Spl. Com. on Women's Issues, 1983—; parish council St. Elizabeth Roman Catholic Ch.; grand marshal Huntington ann. St. Patrick's Day Parade, 1976. Named Woman of Yr., Nassau and Suffolk Bus. and Profl. Women's Clubs, 1983.

Mem. N.Y. State Receivers and Collectors of Taxes Assn. (v.p. 1979-82, pres. 1982), Suffolk County Receivers of Taxes Assn. (pres. 1969-83). Club: Soroptimist (grand pres. 1977-80, now bd. dirs.) (Huntington). Home: 2 Coe Pl Huntington Station NY 11746 Office: Huntington Town Hall 100 Main St Huntington NY 11743

HURLEY, JOAN ELIZABETH, marketing executive; b. St. Paul, Dec. 13, 1953; d. William Joseph and Delores Florence (Stevens) H. B.A., Coll. St. Benedict, 1975; M.B.A., U. Iowa, 1977. Membership analyst U.S. C. of C., Washington, 1978; advt. dir. Cliff Co., Houston, 1978-80; dir. marketing U.S. Home Corp., Houston, 1981-84; v.p. mktg. Randy Morine Homes, Austin, Tex., 1984-85; leasing Johnson/Randolph Devel. Co., Austin, 1985—. Mem. Bus. Profl. Advt. Assn., Greater Houston Builders Assn., Houston Advt. Fedn. (dir. 1980-81), Austin Assn. Homebuilders, Austin Retail Mktg. Assn., Office Leasing Brokers Assn. Roman Catholic. Home: 8114B Baywood Austin TX 78759

HURLEY, MARY KATHERINE, school system food service executive; b. Oakman, Ala., Mar. 27, 1933; d. William Isaiah and Abbie Eugenia (Carter) Allen; B.S., Blue Mountain (Miss.) Coll., 1955; M.S., U. Tenn., Martin, 1980; m. Lee L. Hurley, Jan. 30, 1970; 1 son, James. Food service supr. F. W. Woolworth Co., 1955-75; dir. food service Jackson City Schs. (Tenn.), 1975—. Mem. NEA, Tenn. Edn. Assn., Jackson Edn. Assn., Am. Sch. Foodservice Assn., Tenn. Sch. Foodservice Assn. (pres. 1983-84), Jackson City Sch. Foodservice Assn., Phi Delta Kappa. Republican. Baptist. Home: 106 Southshore Jackson TN 38305 Office: 201 E Deaderick St Jackson TN 38301

HURLOCK, ANN FOXWELL, railroad official; b. Balt., Sept. 10, 1948; d. Clarence Harlan, Jr. and Ruth (Singewald) H. B.A., U. Va., 1971; M.A.S. Johns Hopkins U., 1985. Dir. personnel, U.S. Security Services, Balt., 1971-72, Allegheny Pepsi Cola Co., Balt., 1972-73, Balt. Hilton Hotels, 1973-74; real estate assoc. Piper & Co. Realtors, Lutherville, Md., 1975-79; employee benefits officer Chessie Systems R.R.s, Balt., 1980-82, mgr. residential properties, 1982—. Mem. Greater Balt. Bd. Realtors, Nat. Assn. Realtors, Balt. Working Women. Democrat. Presbyterian. Home: 5308 Tilbury Way Baltimore MD 21212 Office: Chessie System RR 100 N Charles St Baltimore MD 21201

HURNYAK, CHRISTINA KAISER, lawyer; b. Noblesville, Ind., Dec. 22, 1949; d. Albert Michael and Lois Angie (Gatton) Kaiser; m. Cyril Hurnyak, June 24, 1972. B.A. Wittenberg U., 1972; J.D., SUNY-Buffalo, 1979. Bar: N.Y. 1980. Mem. support staff McKinsey & Co., Inc., mgmt. cons., Chgo., 1972-75; law clk. Justice Norman J. Wolf, N.Y. Supreme Ct., Buffalo, 1980-81; assoc. Dempsey & Dempsey, Buffalo, 1979-80, 81—. Mem. ABA, N.Y. State Bar Assn., Erie County Bar Assn., N.Y. Women's Bar Assn. (legis. com.), Women Lawyers of Western N.Y. Democrat. Lutheran. Home: 25 Fairview Ct Grand Island NY 14072 Office: Dempsey & Dempsey 561 Franklin St Buffalo NY 14202

HURREY, KATHARINE CARR, librarian; b. Washington, Jan. 5; d. William Arthur and Katharine Louise (Eckloff) Carr; A.B. in Psychology, Hollins (Va.) Coll., 1949; M.L.S., U. Md., 1967; m. Charles Lauder Hurrey, Feb. 21, 1951; children—Peter Laird, Earl Telford, Robert McGregor, Virginia Lee, Patrick Carr. Bookmobile librarian Calvert County (Md.) Public Library, 1962-65; adminstrv. asst., then children's coordinator So. Md. Regional Library Assn., LaPlata, 1965-68, dir., 1968—; mem. Library Practitioners, cons.; instr. Charles County Community Coll. Mem. Calvert County Bd. Edn., 1966-72, pres., 1968-72; mem. Republican State Central Com., 1982-86. Recipient Alumni of Yr. award U. Md. Coll. Library and Info. Sci., 1985. Mem. ALA, Am. Mgmt. Assn., World Future Soc., Md. Library Assn. (Disting. Service award 1978). Episcopalian. Home: Hurry Ln Port Republic MD 20676 Office: PO Box 1069 LaPlata MD 20646

HURST, ANN ELIZABETH, nurse, lawyer; b. Hartford, Conn., Apr. 6, 1952; d. William Lawrence and Alma Hurst; m. Charles Edward Latimer, July 13, 1981. B.S., Chapman Coll., 1978; J.D., McGeorge Sch. Law, 1982. Bar: Colo. 1982. Staff nurse St. Francis Hosp., Hartford, Conn., 1973-75; nurse Woodland (Calif.) Meml. Hosp., 1979-81, Swedish Med. Ctr., Englewood, Colo., 1981-83; staff nurse ARC, Clark Air Base, Philippines, 1984; legal counsel Pacific region Overseas Edn. Assn., 1984—. Served to capt. USAF, 1975-79. Mem. ABA, Colo. Bar Assn., Denver Bar Assn. Republican. Roman Catholic. Home: PSC 4 PO Box 17475 APO San Francisco CA 96408

HURST, DEBORA FAYE, industrial hygienist; b. Xenia, Ohio, Apr. 14, 1949; d. Marvin Eugene and Phyllis (Jones) H. B.S., Central State U., 1970; postgrad. in Biochemistry, U. Cin., 1971—, postgrad. in Indsl. Hygiene, 1979—. Research asst. U. Cin., 1970; substitute tchr. Xenia City Schs., Ohio, 1971; indsl. hygienist Dept. Indsl. Relations, State of Ohio, Cin., 1973-76; indsl. hygienist U.S. Dept. Labor OSHA, Cin., 1976—. Sponsor victory fund Nat. Republican Con., 1984—; active Ohio Rep. Party. Kettering fellow. Mem. Am. Indsl. Hygiene Assn., Am. Conf. Govtl. Indsl. Hygienists, AAAS, Nat. Assn. Female Execs., Beta Beta Beta. Avocation: manual communication. Office: US DOL OSHA 550 Main St Room 4028 Cincinnati OH 45202

HURST, LINDA LOUISE, constrn. exec.; b. Oakland, Calif., Mar. 9, 1941; d. John Frederick and Doris Ethel McGregor; student San Francisco public schs.; m. Timothy J. Hurst, May 18, 1968. Computer clk. U.S. Govt., San Francisco and Oakland, 1959-68; corp. sec. C & H Engring. Corp., Redwood City, Calif., 1968-71, Compass Engring. Corp., Phoenix, 1971-74; v.p. Hurst Constrn., Inc., Scottsdale, Ariz., 1974—; works include: preservation and conversion of hist. home to profl. office bldg., rehab. hist. home in Hist. Alvarado Area of Phoenix. Steering com. Hist. Alvarado Assn., 1981—, Scottsdale 5th Ave. Assn., 1980—. Recipient Environ. award City of Phoenix, 1975; named Miss Zero Defects, Oakland Army Terminal, 1966. Mem. Nat. Assn. Homebuilders, Smithsonian Instn. Republican. Club: Plaza (Phoenix). Home: 2233 N Alvarado Rd Phoenix AZ 85004 Office: 6840 E Indian School Rd Scottsdale AZ 85251

HURST, TONI, financial services company personnel executive; b. N.Y.C., Nov. 21, 1930; d. Otto Theodore Klotz and Pauline Sheffield; m. Douglas Ross Hurst, Jr., Aug. 18, 1951; children—Susan Ross Hurst Hall, Douglas Ross III. Ed. NYU, Mercy Coll. Office mgr. Madison Pub. Schs. (Conn.), 1971-77; personnel adminstr. Container Transport Internat., White Plains, N.Y., 1977-80; dir. personnel Litton Fin. Services, Inc., Stamford, Conn., 1980-82, dir. employee relations and adminstrn., 1980—. Mem. Republican Presdl. Task Force, Washington, 1983. Mem. Adminstrv. Mgmt. Soc. (chmn., dir. 1982-83, internat. membership award 1983), Am. Soc. Personnel Adminstrs. Lutheran. Office: MetLife Capital Credit Corp 10 Stamford Forum Stamford CT 06904

HURT, CHARLENE SCHMIDT, library administrator, consultant; b. St. Louis, Aug. 10, 1940; d. Lester John and Loretta Mary (Doyen) Schmidt; m. James E. Hurt, Aug. 22, 1959 (div. Oct. 1978); children—Andrew Pol, Lisa Jan. B.A., Culver-Stockton Coll., 1964; M.L., Emporia State U., 1974; M.P.A., U. Kans., 1979. Cataloger Washburn U., Topeka, Kans., 1974-76, asst. librarian pub. service, 1976-77, dir. library and media services, 1981-84; dir. libraries George Mason U., Fairfax, Va., 1984—; vis. lectr. library sci. Emporia State U., Kans., 1981. Contbr. articles to profl. jours. Author film script Battered Women: A Public or Private Problem, 1977. Commr. Mayor's Commn. on the Status of Women, Topeka, 1981-84; bd. dirs. YWCA, Topeka, 1982-84, Interfaith of Topeka, 1981-83; pres. Unitarian Universalist Fellowship of Topeka, 1981-83; mem. grantsmaking panel Unitarian Universalist Assn., Mpls., 1983—. Grantee Mt. Plains Library Assn., 1978-79, Kans. Com. on the Humanities, 1981. Mem. ALA (Olafson Meml. Novia 1979), Library Dir.'s Council, Consortium of Univs. Washington Area, D.C. Library Assn., Women Adminstrs. Discussion Group (co-chmn. 1981-82), Women Acad. Library Dirs., Phi Kappa Phi. Democrat. Avocations: research on women in religion; writing essays and poetry; walking. Home: 3714 Persimmon Circle Fairfax VA 22031 Office: Dir of Libraries George Mason U 4400 University Dr Fairfax VA 22030

HURWITZ, LINDA SUE, nursing administrator, clinical educator; b. Milw., May 6, 1948; d. Sidney Psyche and Marilyn (Safer) H. B.S., U. Wis., 1971, M.S., 1973; postgrad. U. Wis.-Milw., 1979. Nurse dir., chmn. Wis. Diabetes Assn. Camp Sidney Cohen, 1974-82; staff nurse Milw. Children's Hosp., 1973-74, clin. nurse specialist, clin. supr. metabolic and oncology, 1974-76; guest lectr. Marquette U., Milw., 1974-82; clin. nurse specialist, clin. supr. metabolic and acute medicine Milw. Children's Hosp., 1976-79, dir. nursing practice, 1980-81; clin. instr. pediatrics U. Wis.-Milw., 1976-79, adj. clin. asst. prof., 1979-81; asst. prof. U. Wis.-Milw. Sch. Nursing, 1981-84; assoc. dir. nursing Ctr. for Women and Children, Presbyn. Hosp., N.Y.C., 1984—; cons. St. Francis Hosp., Nursing Service, 1982-83, Sacred Heart Rehab. Hosp., Nursing Service Dept., 1982, Children's Hosp. of East Ont., 1985; pvt. practice nursing, 1982-83. Referee Quality Rev. Bull.: Quality Assurance, 1982—. Contbr. articles to profl. jours. Recipient Nurse of Yr. award Wis. Nurses Assn. and March of Dimes, 1980; Diabetes in Youth award Am. Diabetes Assn.-Wis. affiliate, 1981, Profl. Service award Am. Diabetes Assn.-Wis. affiliate. Mem. Am. Diabetes Assn. (bd. dirs. Wis. affiliate 1976-84, pres. Wis. affiliate 1979-80, chmn. Wis. affiliate 1980-81, camp advisor 1982-84, chmn. bylaws com. 1982-84, bd. dirs. N.Y. affiliate 1984—, nat. bd. dirs. 1982—, nat. v.p. health profls. 1985—), Am. Nurses Assn., Wis. Nurses Assn. (com. on quality assurance 1977), Sigma Theta Tau. Jewish. Avocation: aerobics. Office: Presbyn Hosp in City NY 622 W 168th St New York NY 10032

HUSAIN, SHAHEEN, management consultant; b. Khartoum, Sudan, Oct. 9, 1956; d. Syed Habib and Anis (Bano) Husain Rizvi. B.A., Pitzer Coll., 1978. Mgmt. cons., United Mo. Bank, Kansas City, 1979—. Cons., Jr. Achievement, 1982-83. Haynes Found. scholar, 1976-78; Calif. State scholar, 1974-78. Mem. Am. Bus. Women's Assn. (treas. 1981-82), Univ. Assocs. Avocations: reading; theatre; health and physical fitness.

HUSKISSON, C(YNTHIA) SUSAN, public relations and communication training company executive; b. Knoxville, Tenn., Mar. 21, 1950; d. Harry Clifford and Martha Elizabeth (Keaton) H. B.S., U. Tenn., Knoxville, 1972; M.B.A., Golden Gate U., 1982. Program asst. U.S. Dept. Transp., Washington, 1973, pub. affairs staff Dept. Energy, Washington and San Francisco, 1975-80; cons. pub. relations, Knoxville, 1973-74; dir. Western Fed. Regional Council San Francisco, 1980; prin. Huskisson & Assocs., San Francisco, 1980—; lectr., instr. mgmt. and communication Golden Gate U., San Francisco, 1983—; mem. Calif. Select Com. Small Bus., 1984—. Mem. City Celebration Performing Arts, San Francisco, 1984—. Recipient Exceptional Service award Exec. Office of Pres., Washington, 1977. Mem. San Francisco C. of C. (chmn. edn. com. 1984, bd. dirs. 1985—). Methodist. Club: San Francisco Tennis. Avocations: international travel, horseback riding. Home: 2340 Vallejo St San Francisco CA 94123 Office: Huskisson & Assocs 260 California St Suite 803 San Francisco CA 94111

HUSSELMAN, GRACE, innkeeper, educator; b. Paterson, N.J., July 24, 1923; d. Edward and Lydia (Kliphouse) Van Allen; B.A., William Paterson Coll.; m. Samuel Husselman, June 3, 1944; children—Samuel Glenn, Howard Lloyd. With personnel office Wright Aero. Corp., Fairlawn, Pub. 1942-45; library asst. Wyckoff (N.J.) Pub. Library, 1964-66; library dir. Allendale (N.J.) Pub. Library, 1967-81; elem. sch. tchr., assoc. ednl. media specialist, 1981-84; owner Ye Olde Buckmaster Inn, 1984—. Reading Merit Badge counselor Boy Scouts Am.; pioneer guide Pioneer Girls, nat. youth v.p., sec. friendship circle; sec. bookstore com. Christian Growth Ministries; sec. Ladies Aid Soc., Shrewsbury Community Ch.; bd. dirs. Shrewsbury Library, Vt. Mem. N.J., Bergen-Passaic library assns., Hist. Soc. of Shrewsbury (sec.), Kappa Delta Pi. Club: Captains and Mates Yacht. Home: Lincoln Hill Rd Shrewsburg VT 05783

HUSTED, GRACE SCHWENKER, librarian; b. Washington, Mo., Sept. 20, 1931; d. Edward Louis and Louise (Kossmann) Schwenker; m. John Lowell Husted, June 12, 1954; children—John Lowell, Jr., Michael Edward, Daniel David. B.A., Drury Coll., 1952; M.L.S., Drexel U., 1977. Tchr. English and drama Rolla High Sch. (Mo.), 1952-54; tchr. English Chattanooga Sch. System, 1955-56; library asst. Newark Library (Del.), 1970-76; dir. Hockessin Pub. Library (Del.), 1977—; pres. Del. Council Libraries, Dover, 1981-83; pub. library rep. LINCS Network, New Castle County, Del., 1981-83. Co-chairperson Legis. Com. Libraries, Dover, 1981—. Mem. ALA, Del. Library Assn. (pres. pub. libraries div. 1979-80), Beta Phi Mu. Republican. Office: Hockessin Pub Library Rd 1 Box 385B Hockessin DE 19707

HUSTON, BETTY LOU, nursing educator; b. Garretson, S.D., Dec. 5, 1938; d. Obert Bernard and Esther Betty Helene (Andersen) Ellefson; m. Lloyd Donald Haisch, Sept. 5, 1959 (div. Jan. 1977); m. Michael H. Huston, Sept. 1985; children—Donald Mark, Ann Marie. Diploma, Sioux Valley Hosp. Sch. Nursing, 1959; B.S. in Nursing cum laude, Upper Iowa U., 1982; M.A.E. in Ednl. Psychology and Teaching, U. No. Iowa, 1986. Supr. acute intensive treatment service Mental Health Inst., Independence, Iowa, 1959-62; head nurse Virginia Gay Hosp., Vinton, Iowa, 1962-65; office nurse G.A. Fry & Norman Reitzel, Vinton, 1965-70; instr. Mental Health Inst., Independence, 1970-81, Allen Meml. Hosp., Waterloo, Iowa, 1981—. Mem. curriculum com. Allen Meml. Hosp. Luth. Sch. Nursing, Waterloo, 1983—. Mem. Am. Nurses Assn. Home: 1601 2d St SW Independence IA 50644 Office: Allen Meml Hosp Sch Nursing 1825 Logan Ave Waterloo IA 50703

HUSTON, MARGO, journalist; b. Waukesha, Wis., Feb. 12, 1943; d. James and Cecile (Timlin) Bremner; student U. Wis., 1961-63; A.B. in Journalism, Marquette U., 1965; m. James Huston, Dec. 9, 1967 (div.); 1 son, Sean Patrick. Editorial asst. Marquette U., Milw., 1965-66; feature editor, reporter Waukesha Freeman, 1966-67; feature reporter Milw. Jour., 1967-70; reporter Spectrum, women's and food sections, 1972-79, editorial writer, 1979-84, polit reporter, 1984—, asst. picture editor, 1985—. Recipient Penney-Mo. award for consumer abortion series, 1975, Pulitzer Prize for investigation into plight of elderly, 1977, Clarion award, 1977, Knight of Golden Quill award, Milw. Press Club, 1977, Wis. AP writing award, 1977, special award Milw. Soc. Profl. Journalists, 1977, Penney-Mo. Paul Myhie award for excellence, 1978; By-Line award Marquette U. Coll. of Journalism, 1980; Wis. UPI best editorial award, 1982; Wis. Women's Network award for journalist achievement for women's issues, 1983 Mem. Nat. News Council (dir.), Investigative Reporters and Editors, Nat. Conf. Editorial Writers, Sigma Delta Chi. Club: Milw. Press. Home: 3289 N 50th St Milwaukee WI 53216 Office: 333 W State St Milwaukee WI 53201

HUTCHESON, PATRICIA RAY, retail service company executive; b. Honolulu, Aug. 13, 1959; d. Jack and Wanda (Tuck) H.; m. Donald Ray Walker, June 15, 1980 (div. Apr. 1981). A.A. in Mktg., Tenn. State Tech. U., 1980. Retail mgr. Sequoyah Pools, Knoxville, Tenn., 1976-78; v.p. HPC div. Pinco, Knoxville, 1978-82; pres. Prism Inc., Knoxville, 1982—, chmn. bd., 1983—. Mem. Better Bus. Bur., C. of C. Republican. Office: Prism Inc 5718 Kingston Pike Knoxville TN 37919

HUTCHESON, PEGGY GODWIN, career development and training consultant; b. Atlanta, Sept. 15, 1944; d. Clyde Lamar and Martha Josephine (Chaffin) Godwin; A.B.J. cum laude, U. Ga., 1965; M.Ed., Ga. State U., 1976, Ph.D., 1981; m. Ware Hutcheson, Jr., July 29, 1967; children—Anne Marie, Laura Ware. Editor, supr. employee activities and benefits Rich's, Inc., Atlanta, 1969-71, corp. tng. supr., 1971-73, mgr. corp. tng., 1973-75; ind. cons. career devel./training, Atlanta, 1976—; ptnr. Atlanta Resource Assocs., 1984—; cons. Career Devel. Research Project, Ga. State U., Atlanta, 1980—; mem. continuing edn. faculty Oglethorpe U., 1975-77, Ga. State U., 1975-79. Mem. adv. com. retailing and mktg. Atlanta Area Tech., Sch., 1972-75. Mem. Am. Soc. Tng. and Devel. (chpt. pres. elect 1981, Mem. of Yr., 1979, 80, regional rep. 1979-80, nat. bd. dirs. 1984—, editor nat. newsletter 1981; Torch award 1985). Presbyterian. Contbr. articles to profl. jours. Home: 216 Dijon Ct Riverdale GA 30296 Office: 100 Colony Sq Suite 200 Atlanta GA 30361

HUTCHESON, SHIRLEY JUNE ROBERTS, city official; b. Booneville, Miss., June 25, 1948; d. A.C. and Martha Geraldine (Houston) Roberts; m. Jerry Ronald Hutcheson, June 28, 1969; children—Dena Nicole, Joshua Allen. A.A., N.E. Miss. Jr. Coll., 1968; B.S., Miss. State U., 1972. Cert. city clk. Miss. Sec. to br. mgr. Bank of Miss., Booneville, 1970-72; acctg. technician Corinth Community Devel., Miss., 1973; mayor's sec. City of Booneville, Miss., 1973-75, mcpl. clk., 1975—. Mem. Miss. Mcpl. Clks. Assn., Internat. Mcpl. Clks. Assn. (cert.). Baptist. Avocations: reading; ceramics; needlework. Home: PO Box 187 Booneville MS 38829 Office: City of Booneville 203 N Main St Booneville MS 38829

HUTCHINGS, LEANNE VON NEUMEYER, communications executive, research consultant, freelance writer and lecturer; b. Los Angeles, Oct. 24, 1946; d. F. Louis and Greta Catherine (Clifford) von Neumeyer; m. Karl Hutchings, May 20, 1962 (div. 1986); children—Marc Lane, Kristin LeAnne, Michael Lane, Jamie Laird, Jeremy Leif, Bret Louis. Student Brigham Young U., 1962. Vice pres. Steenhoek Neeley von Neumeyer Assocs., Cons.; researcher, writer, owner Heritage Tree, Arcadia, Calif., 1970—; dir. pub. communications Ch. of Jesus Christ of Latter-day Saints, So. Calif., 1975—, dir. community relations, 1984—, asst. dir. area council, 1984—; seminar coordinator R.E.D.I., Inc., Los Angeles, 1982—, corp. relations dir., 1984—; design cons. H.M.J. Jewelers, Los Angeles, 1985—; adminstrv. dir. Pasadena Geneal. Library, Calif., 1977-82; dir., co-producer KBIG Radio, Los Angeles, 1979-80; regional cons. Latter-Day Sentinel Newspaper, Los Angeles, 1985—; dir. protocol Neeley Internat. Scholarship Found., Los Angeles, 1985—; artist. Author journalism series, 1978-80; also articles, collected works, stage trilogy. Pres. Daus. Utah Pioneers-Los Angeles County, 1983-85; instr. Arcadia chpt. ARC, Los Angeles, 1983-85; mem. Community Coordinating Council, Arcadia, 1983-86; mem. exec. bd. Calif. Utah Women, Los Angeles, 1977-79, 85-86. Recipient Mother of Yr. award Ch. of Jesus Christ of Latter-day Saints, Arcadia, 1979. Best of Exhibit award Sculptor's West Workshop, 1982. Mem. Assn. Latter-Day Media Artists (assoc. editor Voice of ALMA 1978-83, exec. bd. 1977-81, chmn. spl. events, 1985—, internat. bd. govs. fellow 1981-83), Nat. Assn. Female Execs., Bus. Industry Conf. (Earthquake Preparedness Project), Am. Film Inst., Deseret Bus. and Profl. Assn., Arcadia C. of C. (chmn. industry commn. of women's div. 1983-85). Republican. Avocations: sculpting; oil painting; violin; pistol marksmanship. Office: REDI Inc 112 W 9th St Suite 922 Los Angeles CA 90015

HUTCHINS, JANET M., environmental scientist; b. Washington, Aug. 16, 1947; d. James Otis and Lydia Merrick (Cummins) Taylor; children—Aaron Benjamin, Cristina-Marie, Ernst Frederick. A.A., U. N.D., 1974; B.S., Calif. State U.-San Bernardino, 1977; Cert., U.S. Coast Guard Pacific Strike Team, 1983, Calif. Spl. Tng. Inst., 1984, Monterey County Fire Tng. Officers Assn., 1984. Eviron. technician County of San Bernardino, Calif., 1974-77; environ. specialist U.S. Air Force Systems Command, Edwards AFB, Calif., 1978-82, U.S. Army, Ft. Ord, Calif., 1982-85; bioenviron. scientist HQ Forces Command, Ft. Gillem, Ga., 1985—. Author: Hazardous Waste in San Bernardino, 1976. Vol. firefighter Marina Pub. Safety, Calif., 1984-85; hazardous material spill coordinator, instr. Ft. Ord, Calif., 1982-85. Mem. Calif. Firefighters Assn., Nat. Assn. Environ. Profls. Avocations: photography; piano and synthesizer; hiking; canoeing.

HUTCHINS, JEANNE BAHN, town official; b. Rochester, N.Y., Mar. 12, 1922; d. Carl E. and Marie (Hall) Bahn; B.A., Wells Coll., 1943; M.P.A., SUNY, Brockport, 1980; m. Frank McAllister Hutchins, Aug. 24, 1945; children—Katharine H. Welling, Virginia H. Valkenburgh, Patricia H. Murphy, Constance H. Mills. Bacteriologist/chemist Manhattan Project Atomic Energy U. Rochester/Strong Meml. Hosp., 1943-45; library asst. Fort Benning, Ga., 1946-47, Dartmouth Coll., Hanover, N.H., 1947-48; town bd. legislator Town of Brighton, Rochester, N.Y., 1976—; notary pub., County of Monroe, 1976; trustee Monroe Savs. Bank, 1978—. Trustee, Wells Coll., 1977-86, adv. council bd. trustees, 1986—; trustee Colgate Rochester Div. Sch., 1984—; trustee Bexley Hall Episcopal Sem., 1984—, treas., 1986—; vestrywoman St. Paul's Episcopal Ch., 1977-83, treas., 1983—; bd. dirs. United Way of Greater Rochester, 1974-84; trustee Center for Govt. Research, 1979—; pres. Jr. League Rochester, 1957-59; bd. dirs. Vis. Nurse Service, Northaven Adoption Agy., 1965-69, Genesee Region Health Planning Council; bd. dirs. St. Ann's Home, 1982—, v.p., 1986—; pres. bd. dirs. Council Social Agys., 1969-70; bd. dirs. Nat. Com. on Social Work Careers, 1964-65, Monroe County Human Resources Council, 1975-81, Health Care, Rochester Gen. Hosp., 1985—, Family Service Am., 1985—; v.p. bd. dirs. Family Service Rochester, 1962-69, Planned Parenthood, 1960-69; mem. women's council Rochester Inst. Tech., 1970—, N.Y. State Communities Aid Assn., 1970—; pres. Rochester Female Charitable Soc., 1983-85, trustee, 1975—; bd. dirs. Rochester Area Found., 1973-76. Recipient Forman Flair award, 1973, Civic Medal award Rochester Mus. and Sci. Ctr., 1986. Grant Garvey award Am. Soc. Public Adminstrn., 1980; Shumway award Family Service of Rochester, 1983. Mem. Mo. County Bar Assn. (profl. rev. panel 1986—), Brighton C. of C., LWV, Compeer Inc. (bd. dirs. 1982—). Republican. Clubs: Mid Town Tennis, Rochester Dist. Golf, Western N.Y. Golf Assn. Home: 75 Indian Spring Ln Rochester NY 14618 Office: Brighton Town Hall 2300 Elmwood Ave Rochester NY 14618

HUTCHINSON, BETTY LEE, consulting editor; b. East Liverpool, Ohio, Jan. 26, 1927; d. Orville and Lillian (Parsons) Staats; m. Warner A. Hutchinson, Jan. 5, 1979; children—William, Cynthia, Keryn. Student Mountain State Coll., Syracuse U. Cons. editor Doubleday & Co., N.Y.C., 1985—; instr. New Sch. Social Research, N.Y.C., 1986—. Author Word Processing, 1983; Computer Typing, 1984; Business Letters, 1985; Secretarial Practices, 1985; The Displaywriters Users Guide, 1986; The Standard Manual of Office of Administrative Procedures, 1986. Club: Overseas Press (N.Y.C.). Avocation: quilting. Home and office: 62 Westervelt Ave Staten Island NY 10301

HUTCHINSON, DIANE WOOD, legal educator; b. Plainfield, N.J., July 4, 1950; d. Kenneth Reed and Lucille (Padmore) Wood; m. Dennis James Hutchinson, Sept. 2, 1978; children—Kathryn, David, Jane. B.A., U. Tex.-Austin, 1971, J.D., 1975. Bar: Tex. 1975, D.C. 1978. Law clk. U.S. Ct. Appeals, 5th Cir., 1975-76, U.S. Supreme Ct., 1976-77; atty.-advisor U.S. Dept. State, Washington, 1977-78; assoc. law firm Covington & Burling, Washington, 1978-80; asst. prof. law Georgetown U. Law Ctr., Washington, 1980-81, U. Chgo., 1981—; spl. cons. antitrust div. internat. guide U.S. Dept. Justice, 1986. Bd. dirs. Hyde-Park-Kenwood Community Health Ctr. Mem. ABA (chmn. internat. law sect. BIT Com. 1981-83), D.C. Bar, Am. Soc. Internat. Law. Democrat. Office: U Chgo Law Sch 1111 E 60th St Chicago IL 60637

HUTCHINSON, ELEANOR LOUISE, nurse; b. Mpls., Nov. 9, 1928; d. Paul Carl Theodore and Amanda Marie (Doell) Ewert; R.N., Swedish Hosp., Mpls., 1951; B.S. in Nursing Edn., U. Minn., 1956; m. Richard Westervelt Hutchinson, Mar. 6, 1965; children—David Henry, Susan Elizabeth. Instr., clin. supr. pediatrics Hennepin County Gen. Hosp., Mpls., 1956-60; supr. pediatric and young adult unit Fairview Hosps., Mpls., 1961-67; dir. nursing, staff devel. coordinator Indianola (Iowa) Long-Term Care Facility, 1973-80; dir. nursing Madison County Meml. Hosp., Winterset, Iowa, 1980—. Mem. Nat. League Nursing, AAUW, Madison County Nurses Assn., Simpson Coll. Guild. Presbyterian. Club: Order Eastern Star. Home: Box 397 Indianola IA 50125 Office: 300 Hutchings St Winterset IA 50273

HUTCHINSON, MARY JANE FOSTER, author; b. Tulsa, Feb. 8, 1924; d. William Henry and Carrie (Berry) Foster; m. William George Hutchinson, Oct. 30, 1954 (dec.); children—Mary Hollis, Margaret Giles, William Henry, George Winthrop. A.A., Monticello Jr. Coll., 1943; B.A., Wellesley Coll., 1945; M.A., Columbia U., 1947. Instr. English, Bishop Coll., 1970-71, Dallas Community Coll., 1972-79. Author: Red Ice, 1981; A Newcomer's Guide to the Wonderful World of Ice, 1975; contbr. numerous articles on figure skating to mags., newspapers. Nat. pub. relations committeewoman U.S. Figure Skating Assn., 1977-83, ofcl. judge, 1979—. Recipient Hermann Meml. Poetry prize, 1942, 43. Episcopalian. Clubs: Wellesley, Sierra. Home: 5709 Katydid Ln Austin TX 78744

HUTCHINSON, MIRIAM HODSON, nutritionist; b. Redlands, Calif., Feb. 28, 1936; d. John Adrience and Gertrude Enid (Scott) H.; m. Gerald William Hutchinson, June 8, 1982; children by previous marriage—Richard, Brian, James, Patricia. A.A., Los Angeles Pierce Coll., 1972; B.S., Calif. State U., 1974, M.S., 1975. Registered dietitian. Instr. home econs. Calif. State U., Northridge, 1975-76; nutritionist Weight Watchers, Los Angeles, 1976-77, City of Los Angeles Title VII Nutrition Program, 1976-78, Area Agy. on Aging, 1978—. Mem. Am. Dietetic Assn., Calif. Dietetic Assn., others. Democrat. Roman Catholic. Avocations: gardening; sewing; goat raising. Home: 35502 Voss St Agua Dulce CA 91350 Office: City of Los Angeles Dept Aging 207 S Broadway Los Angeles CA 90012

HUTCHINSON, PATTY S., insurance agency executive; b. Springfield, Mo., Mar. 25, 1933; d. Bernie E. and Macie W. (Israel) Armstrong; m. Robert O. Hutchinson, May 11, 1952 (div. 1975); children—Kevin D., Karen M. Student pub. schs. Pleasant Hope, Mo. Sec. various agts. and adjusters in Las Vegas, Nev., 1950-55; underwriter Peccole Ins. Agy., 1955-60; adjuster Key Adjustment Co., 1960-66; agent, office mgr. Harrington-Horsey Ins. Co., 1966-81; co-owner, agt. McFadden Ins. Agy., 1981—. Pres., Century Meadows Homeowners Assn., 1983-85. Mem. Ins. Women of Las Vegas (pres. 1983-84), Nev. Ind. Ins. Agents, Ind. Ins. Agents of So. Nev. (dir. 1982-83, pres. 1986—). Office: McFadden Ins Agy Inc 801 S Rancho #E-3B Las Vegas NV 89106

HUTCHISON, AGNES DIANA, cablevision executive, accountant; b. Monticello, Ky., Feb. 28, 1953; d. Stanley Ray and Zada Adarine (Stinson) Morgan;

m. David Earl Hutchison, Apr. 21, 1973; children John David, Kimberly. Student, Clinton County Vocat. Sch. Tchrs. aide Wayne County High Sch., Monticello, Ky., 1970-71; bookkeeper Twin Lakes Mobile Homes, Albany, Ky., 1971-74; bookkeeper, receptionist Monticello Cable Co., 1975-79; office mgr. Cumberland Valley Cablevision, Monticello, 1979—. Office: Cumberland Valley Cablevision Inc Route 3 Box 394E Monticello KY 42633

HUTCHISON, ALICE COLLEEN, lawyer; b. Tulsa, June 30, 1943; d. Grant G. and Billdana (Baxter) Forsythe; m. Donald Hutchison, July 31, 1971; children—Lisa, Grant. Student Okla. State U.-Stillwater, 1961-64; B.S. in Psychology, U. Tulsa, 1976, J.D., 1979. Bar: Okla. 1979, U.S. Tax Ct. 1981. Tax atty. Phillips Petroleum Co., Bartlesville, Okla., 1979-81, staff tax atty., 1981-83, sr. assoc. tax atty., 1983-85; tax atty. Shell Oil Co., Houston, 1986—. Bd. dirs. Phillips Found., Bartlesville, 1980-82. Mem. ABA, Okla. Bar Assn., Washington County Bar Assn., Tulsa Employee Benefits Group, Mensa, Phi Delta Phi. Republican. Methodist. Home: 12218 Normont Dr Houston TX 77070 Office: Shell Oil Co 4336 One Shell Plaza Houston TX 77001

HUTCHISON, CAROL LESLIE, healthcare consultant; b. Memphis, Oct. 5, 1951; d. Jack Ralph and Elizabeth Frances (Carey) Hutchison. B.A., So. Meth. U., 1973; M.B.A., U. Tex., 1978. Biochemistry research technician U. Tex. Health Sci. Ctr., Dallas, 1973-74; project rev. assoc. Tex. Area 5 Health Systems Agy., Irving, 1978-80; assoc. cons. Hamilton Assocs., Dallas, 1980-82; dir. planning Irving Community Hosp. (Tex.), 1982-83; sr. cons. Vol. Hosps. of Am. Enterprises, Irving, 1985—. Mem. Am. Hosp. Assn., Soc. Hosp. Planning, M.B.A. Execs., Nat. Assn. Securities Dealers, Beta Gamma Sigma, Delta Delta Delta. Presbyterian. Home: 3424 Haynie Dallas TX 75205

HUTCHISON, CAROL SUE, organizational specialist; b. Newark, June 17, 1946; d. James and Emma Suzanna (Bodner) Hutchison; B.S., Newark State Coll., Union, N.J., 1970; M.A., Montclair State Coll., Upper Montclair, N.J., 1972; 1 son, Frederick James. Tchr., coach schs. in N.J., 1967-74; field rep. N.H. Edn. Assn., 1975-76; asst. exec. dir. Pinellas Classroom Tchrs. Assn., 1976-78; field rep. Minn. Edn. Assn., 1978-81, organizational specialist membership and field services, Mpls., 1981—. Scottish Rite scholar, 1964; grad. fellow Montclair State Coll., 1970. Mem. Nat. Staff Assn., Nat. Assn. Female Execs., Profl. Staff Assn. of Minn. Edn. Assn., Montclair State Coll. Alumni Assn. Mem. Democrat-Farm-Labor Party. Presbyterian. Club: Order Eastern Star. Office: 4930 W 77th St Edina MN 55435

HUTCHISON, FLORENCE MELINDA, genealogist; b. Chgo., June 20, 1911; d. George and Nancy Melissa (Baker) Dressel; B.S. in Home Econs., Okla. State U., 1936; postgrad. U. Mo., 1949, So. Ill. U., 1957, Sangamon State U., Springfield, Ill., 1978-79; m. Sanford Elijah Hutchison, 1936; children—Nancy Ann, Richard Lee, Judy Margaret, Mary Ruth, Linda Kay. Tchr. home econs. and art in Mo. and Ill., 1949-59; founder, pres. Jacksonville (Ill.) Area Geneal. and Hist. Soc., 1972—; editor Jacksonville Geneal. Jour.; chmn. Morgan County Records Preservation Com., 1976—; lectr. on genealogy, heraldry and flag history; legis. promoter new Ill. state flag, 1964-70, re-designer 1970 flag. Mem. Morgan County Bicentennial Commn., 1975-77, Jacksonville Bicentennial Commn., 1975-77; adv. bd. Morgan County Cemetery, 1980—. Recipient award merit Ill. Hist. Soc., 1969, Jacksonville Mayor's disting. service award, 1982. Mem. AAUW, N.Am. Vexillological Assn. (corr. sec. 1978-80), Ill. Geneal. Soc. (Geneal. Service award 1975), Augustan Soc., Societas Octavianus, Colonial Daus. of XVII Century (John Rolfe chpt.), U.S. Daus. of 1812 (Sangamon River chpt.), Palatines to Am., Gen. Fedn. Women's Clubs (First Ladies recognition 1974). Methodist. Clubs: Morgan County Garden, Order Eastern Star, Jacksonville Women's. Author, pub.: Basics of Heraldry for Ancestral Knowledge, 1973, Constellatory Origins of the National Flag and Great Seal of the U.S.A., 1973, Helpful Hints for Genealogical Hopefuls, 1974, Am I May Mother's and Father's Lineage Keeper?, 1977, 800 G.A.R. Posts in Illinois, 1977; Documentary on the Life of Flagmaker Betsy Ross Claypoole, 1983. Address: 629 S Diamond St Jacksonville IL 62650

HUTCHISON, JANIE RUTH, artist, songwriter; b. Shreveport, La., Aug. 31, 1943; d. Rufus and Josephine (McGinthy) Martin; B.A., Columbia Coll., 1975; m. William E. Hutchison (dec.); children—William, Natalie Roxanne, Tamara Renee. Dir. Nightline, sales rep. Sta. WBBM-FM, Chgo., 1974-76, adminstrv. asst., communications dir. Chgo. Met. Council on Alcoholism, 1976-77; public affairs dir. Sta. WLOO-FM, Chgo., 1977-81. Chairperson adv. com. North Chgo. Sch. Dist. 64, 1974; office mgr. Jack Benny Center for Arts, Waukegan, Ill., 1968-70. Recipient Media/Communications Outstanding Leader award YWCA Lake County, 1980; Spl. Recognition award Ill. State Rep. John Matijevich, 1980. Mem. ASCAP. Baptist. Home: PO Box 5105 Evanston IL 60202

HUTCHISON, PAT, nurse, administrator; b. Omaha, Mar. 4, 1943; d. Earl Edward and Sylvia Lorraine (Kronen) Moore; m. James M. Hutchison, June 23, 1963; children—Michael, Danny. Diploma in nursing, St. Joseph's Sch. Nursing, 1968; student Central Ariz. Coll., 1976-82; B.S. in Health Service Adminstrn., U. Phoenix, 1983. R.N.; cert. in advanced cardiac life support, Ariz. Nurse Armish Maag Hosp., Teheran, Iran, 1969-71; supr. Hoemako Hosp., Casa Grande, Ariz., 1973-84; asst. dir. nursing Casa Grande Regional Med. Ctr., 1984—. Nursing chmn. ARC, Casa Grande, also bd. dirs., instr. disaster tng., 1982—; instr. cardiopulmonary resuscitation Am. Heart Assn., Casa Grande, 1978—. Recipient Care award Ariz. Hosp. Assn., 1984, Service and Appreciation award Bus. and Profl. Women's Assn., 1984. Mem. Ariz. Nurses in Mgmt., Emergency Nurses Assn. Democrat. Roman Catholic. Avocations: traveling; camping; boating; reading. Home: 1308 N Center St Casa Grande AZ 85222 Office: Casa Grande Regional Med Ctr 1800 E Florence Blvd Casa Grande AZ 85222

HUTCHISON, SUE JILL, retail store owner; b. Milw., Jan. 4, 1943; d. Robert Ernst and Irene June (Schloemer) Feldmann; m. Russell F. Moberly, July 8, 1963 (div. Sept. 1965); m. Vernon Laurence Hutchison, July 14, 1967; children—Peter M., Kristin A., Robert L. Student Marquette U., Milw., 1960-64. Tchr. nursery sch., Subic Bay, Philippines, 1969-71; nurse in doctor's office, Selma, Calif., 1971-75; owner, retailer T-Boutique & Athletics, Selma, 1975—; cons. in field. Mem. reader adv. bd. Impressions Mag., 1979—. Contbr. articles to profl. mags. (Outstanding Contbr. award 1983, Service to Industry award 1984). Bd. dirs. Kingsburg High Sch. Music Boosters, 1975, Athletic Boosters, 1975. Mem. Screen Printing Assn. Internat., Nat. Sporting Goods Assn., Fresno Dixieland Soc. Republican. Avocations: racquetball, swimming aerobics. Home: 14584 S McCall Ave Selma CA 93662 Office: T-Boutique & Athletics 2013 2d St Selma CA 93662

HUTH, SYLVIA TERESA, industrial engineer; b. Youngstown, Ohio, Mar. 25, 1945; d. John Patrick and Lois Virginia (Mirth) DeNicola; m. Robert Alexander Huth, Nov. 1, 1975. B.A., San Jose State U., 1967. Assoc. indsl. engr. Rockwell Internat., Downey, Calif., 1968-70; sr. adminstrv. analyst Chief Adminstrv. Office, County of Los Angeles, 1970-78; sr. mgmt. engr. Kaiser Permanente Med. Care Program, Los Angeles, 1978-81; dir. planning and devel. So. Calif. Permanente Med. Group, Los Angeles, 1981—; pres. MTM Assocs., also dir., v.p., conf. chmn., 1980, 82. Mem. Inst. Indsl. Engrs. (sr.), Am. Mgmt. Assn., Nat. Assn. Female Execs. Republican. Contbr. articles to profl. jours. Office: So Calif Permanente Med Group Walnut Ctr Pasadena CA 91188

HUTSON, GENEVA, refining company executive; b. Tyler, Tex., Nov. 6, 1923; d. Lonnie Frederick and Sylvia Louise (Allen) Wallace; student Sam Houston Tchrs. Coll., 1946, U. Houston, 1973, 74; m. Walter Murphy Hutson, May 23, 1941; children—Wayne Murphy, Mark Farrell. Stenographer Lone Star Def. Corp., Texarkana, Tex., 1942, Montgomery & Ward, Denver, 1943; sec.-bookkeeper William Steinkamp Lumber Co., Groveton, Tex., 1944-45; sec. to plant mgr. Continental Can Co., Houston, 1948-49; sec.-bookkeeper Wherry & Green Ind. Oil Co., Houston, 1951-59; exec. sec., bookkeeper, office mgr. Holmes Drilling Co., Houston, 1961-83; sec., treas. Hartcap Refining Corp., Houston, 1974-83; office mgr. Mildred M. Holmes Interests, Houston, 1983-86, Jameson & Jameson, Houston, 1986—. Lic. real estate broker, Tex.; cert. profl. sec. Mem. Profl. Secs. Assn. Republican. Episcopalian. Home: 4302 Sarong Dr Houston TX 77096 Office: 2626 Richmond Houston TX 77098

HUTTENSTINE, MARIAN LOUISE, journalism educator; b. Bloomsburg, Pa., Jan. 26, 1940; d. Ralph Benjamin and Marian Louise (Engler) H.; B.S., Bloomsburg State U., 1961, M.Ed., 1966; postgrad. (NDEA fellow, Newspaper Fund fellow), Rutgers U., 1962-63; Ph.D., U. N.C., 1985. High sch. English, journalism tchr., dept. chmn., 1961-66; asst. prof. Lock Haven (Pa.) State Coll., 1966-73, asso. prof. English, 1973-74; teaching asst., lectr. Sch. Journalism, U. N.C., Chapel Hill, 1974-76; cons., dir. Diener & Assos., Research Triangle Park, N.C., 1975-86; asst. prof. journalism Sch. Communication, U. Ala., Tuscaloosa, 1977—; cons. various publs., Ala., 1977—. Adult leader, vol. worker Luth. Ch., 1962—; bd. dirs. Ala. Civil Liberties Union. Mem. Assn. Edn. in Journalism, Internat. Communication Assn., Nat. Fedn. Press Women, Ala. Media Women, Nat. Assn. Female Execs., ACLU, Am. Advt. Fedn., AAUW, Kappa Tau Alpha. Clubs: Tuscaloosa Advt., Ala. SPJ-SDX. Contbr. papers to profl. lit. Home: K-1 Woodland Trace Tuscaloosa AL 35405 Office: Box 1482 Journalism Dept U Ala University AL 35486

HUTTNER, MARIAN ALICE, librarian; b. Mpls., Apr. 10, 1920; d. Frederick August and Hilda Christina (Anderson) H.; m. Russell R. Christensen, Apr. 15, 1950 (div. Mar. 1961). B.A. summa cum laude, Macalester Coll., 1941; B.S.L.S., U. Minn., 1942. Jr. librarian U. Minn., Mpls., 1941-42, librarian, 1942-43, sr. librarian, 1943-44, prin. librarian serials, 1944-46, prin. librarian archives, 1946-53; documents librarian Sioux City (Iowa) Pub. Library, 1953-54; serials librarian Hamline U., St. Paul, 1954-56; adult librarian Mpls. Pub. Library, 1956-60, research asst., 1961-64, adult group cons., 1964-67, head sociology dept., 1967-69, head main library subject depts., 1969-75; dep. dir. Cleve. Pub. Library, 1976-85, interim dir., 1986—. Author: Program for Branches 1976-1980 Cleveland Public Library, 1976. Mem. ALA (chmn. coop reference services com. 1973-76), Ohio Library Assn. (awards com. 1984—). Republican. Presbyterian. Home: 12700 Lake Ave Apt 2110 Lakewood OH 44107 Office: Cleve Pub Library 325 Superior Ave Cleveland OH 44114

HUTTON, CHARLOTTE COLES, biology educator, educational administrator; b. Troy, N.Y., Dec. 19, 1917; d. Andrew Dorsey and Erdin Maiden (Harder) Coles; m. David Lynn Hutton, Sept. 27, 1958; 1 dau., Charlotte Nettye Pauline. B.S., Livingstone Coll., Salisbury, N.C., 1943; M.S. in Botany, Catholic U. Am., 1953, postgrad., 1981-83. Diagnostic bacteriologist Walter Reed Army Med. Ctr., 1955-56; reference librarian Armed Services Tech. Info. Agy., 1957-61; tech. writer, editor Def. Documentation Ctr., U.S. Dept. Def., 1961-63, phys. scientist, 1961-64; tchr. sci. Garnet Patterson Jr. High Sch., Washington, 1964-67, Cardozo High Sch., Washington, 1967-74; program devel. specialist Washington Pub. Schs., 1972-74; curriculum devel. specialist, 1972-74, student affairs officer, 1974—; instr. urban ecology Howard U., 1973. Bd. dirs. Phyllis Wheatley YWCA, Washington, 1960-62, Big Sisters of Washington, 1960-63; pastoral enabler Plymouth Congl. Ch., Washington, 1983. Mem. Alpha Kappa Alpha (chmn. scholarship com. 1979—). Home: 6319 7th St NW Washington DC 20011

HUTTON, MARY MAGDELENE BOONE (MRS. RICHARD HUTTON), educator; b. Brownsville, Tenn., Nov. 1, 1925; d. George Alexander and Helen (Jones) Boone; student Wayne U., 1945-49, Tenn. Agrl. and Indsl. State Coll., 1946, Territorial Coll. Guam, 1954; A.A., Merritt Coll., 1962; student Laney Coll., 1967-68; B.A., Calif. State Coll. at Hayward, 1969; M.A. (Grad. Minority Program grantee), U. Calif. at Berkeley, 1971; Ph.D., Ind. U., 1975; m. Richard Hutton; children—Cozzette (Mrs. Richard Davis), Larry Keith, Jacqueline Yvonne. Timekeeper, Govt. Service, Agana, Guam, 1955-56; clk. typist Health Dept., Oakland, Calif., 1957-58, clk. III, 1958-59; clk.-typist Oakland (Calif.) Police Dept., 1960-64, div. sec. to capt. police, 1964-69; asst. instr. speech Ind. U., Bloomington, 1971-74; instr. Afro-Am. Studies, Milw., 1974-75; asst. prof. speech communication U. Ga., 1975-77, coordinator Black studies program, 1976-77; chairperson communications dept. Ala. State U., Montgomery, 1977-80, asso. prof. speech communication, 1980—. Bd. dirs. Rose St. Child Care Center, Berkeley, Calif., 1970-71. Served with WAVES, 1950-51. Econ. Opportunity fellow, 1971-72; Ford Found. fellow, 1973-74. Mem. Pi Kappa Delta, Pi Lambda Theta, Alpha Kappa Alpha. Mem. A.M.E. ch. Home: 3126 S Perry St Montgomery AL 36105 Office: Dept Communications Ala State Univ Montgomery AL 36101

HUXLEY, CAROLE CORCORAN, state education commissioner; b. Evanston, Ill., Jan. 1, 1938; d. Harold Francis and Angela Mary (Dawson) Corcoran; B.A., Mount Holyoke Coll., 1960; M.A. in Teaching, Harvard U., 1961; m. Michael Remsen Huxley, Mar. 27, 1971; children—Samuel Dawson, Ian Matthew Remsen. Tchr., Woodbury (Conn.) High Sch., 1961-62; area supr. to divisional dir. Am. Field Services, N.Y.C., 1962-71; program officer Nat. Endowment for the Humanities, Washington, 1971-79, dep. dir. state programs, 1979-80, dir. spl. programs, 1980-82; dep. commr. cultural edn. N.Y. Dept. Edn., Albany, 1982—. Trustee, Mount Holyoke Coll., 1982—, Albany Med. Coll.; mem. Commn. on Preservation and Access, Council on Library Resources. Mem. Am. Assn. Museums, Am. Assn. State and Local History, N.Y. Council on Humanities, Albany Tricentennial Commn. Roman Catholic. Office: State Education Dept Albany NY 12234

HWANG, CORDELIA JONG, chemist; b. N.Y.C., July 14, 1942; d. Goddard and Lily (Fung) Jong; m. Warren C. Hwang, Mar. 31, 1969; 1 son, Kevin. Student Alfred U., 1960-62; B.A., Barnard Coll., 1964; M.S., SUNY-Stony Brook, 1969. Research asst. Columbia U., N.Y.C., 1964-66; analytical chemist Veritron West Inc., Chatsworth, Calif., 1969-70; asst. lab. dir., chief chemist Pomeroy, Johnston & Bailey Environ. Engrs., Pasadena, Calif., 1970-76; research chemist Met. Water Dist. So. Calif., Los Angeles, 1976—; mem. Joint Task Group on Instrumental Identification of Taste and Odor Compounds, 1983-85, instr. Citrus Coll., 1974-76. Mem. Am. Chem. Soc., Am. Water Works Assn. (cert. water quality analyst level 3, Calif.-Nev.). Office: Met Water Dist So Calif 700 N Moreno St La Verne CA 91750

HYAMS, ALICE E., businesswoman, consultant, educator; b. N.Y.C.; d. Benjamin and Sophie (Cohen) Cooperman; m. Gerald T. Hyams; children—Sheri I., Ian D., Julie L. B.S., Drexel Inst. Tech.; M.Ed., D.Ed., Temple U., 1984. Owner, mgr. Alice E. Hyams Couturieres, Phila., 1970-77, Hot Number, Phila., 1977-79, Alice Industries, 1984—; gen. mgr. Limited Editions, Phila., 1975-77; instr. Barbizon Sch. Merchandising, Phila., 1979-81, Bucks County Coll., Newtown, Pa., 1981-83; prof. Phila. Coll. Textiles and Sci., 1984—, Pierce Coll., Phila., 1984—; cons., lectr. Phila., 1972—; dir. The Fashion Group, Inc., Phila., 1974—, com. chmn., 1980—. Active Child Abuse Prevention Effort, Phila., 1968—. Mem. Am. Mktg. Assn. Home and Office: 120 E Colonial St Philadelphia PA 19120

HYDE, BARBARA TAYLOR, educational administrator; b. Easton, Pa., Aug. 31, 1938; d. William H. and Mary (Dech) Taylor; m. James Patten Hyde, Jr., Dec. 24, 1960; children—Rebecca, Sarah. B.S. in Home Econs., Hood Coll., 1960; M.Ed., Rutgers U., 1969, Ed.D., 1983. Cert. tchr., prin., adminstr., N.J. Tchr. North Hunterdon High Sch., Annandale, N.J., 1960-74; tchr. Voorhees High Sch., Glen Gardner, N.J., 1974-78, asst. prin., 1979-81, prin., 1981—; asst. prin. North Hunterdon High Sch., 1979; adj. prof. Rutgers U., New Brunswick, N.J., 1978-81. Trustee Warren County Community Coll., Washington, N.J., 1982—. Mem. Am. Vocat. Assn., Am. Home Econs. Assn., Nat. Assn. Secondary Prins., Vocat. Home Econs. Edn. Assn. of N.J. (pres. 1980-81), Vocat. Edn. Assn. (pres. 1982-83), N.J. Interscholastic Athletic Assn. (pres. Mid-State Conf. 1985—), Epsilon Pi Tau, Omicron Nu, Omicron Tau Theta, Kappa Delta Pi. Club: Profl. Ski Instrs. Am. Avocations: skiing; sailing. Home: 900 Pennsylvania Ave Phillipsburg NJ 08865 Office: Voorhees High Sch Route 513 R D Glen Gardner NJ 08826

HYDE, CINDY LOUISE, geological and geophysical draftsperson; b. Houston, June 4, 1949; d. Robert Lloyd and Flossie M. (Dishman) H. B.S., Stephen F. Austin State U., 1971. Ptnr., drafter, G&G Mapping and Graphics, Houston, 1976-78; draftsperson Amoco Oil Co., Houston, 1978-80; sr. draftsperson Aminoil, USA, Houston, 1980-82; chief draftsperson Kriti Exploration, Houston, 1982-84; mgr. drafting services Gila Exploration, Inc., Santa Fe, 1985—. Mem. Am. Inst. Design and Drafting (sec. 1981-82, newsletter editor 1982-83, pres. 1984; Outstanding Service award 1981-82, Outstanding Mem., 1983-84. Avocations: fishing, reading. Office: Gila Exploration Inc Suite J 839 Paseo de Peralta Santa Fe NM 87501

HYDE, JO ANN MARIE, computer company official; b. Grand Rapids, Mich., Oct. 6, 1946; d. Joseph Charles and Lucille Irene (Lambers) Russo; B.A. magna cum laude in Lit., Central Mich. U., 1968; M.S. magna cum laude in Stats., U. Mich., 1970; m. Thomas W. Hyde, Feb. 17, 1979. Customer service rep. Westinghouse Elec. Co., 1968-69; with IBM Corp., 1969—, plans and controls asst., 1979-80, br. field engring. div., East Lansing, Mich., 1980-82, mgr. div. field ops., White Plains, N.Y., 1982-83, mgr. service support personnel, Franklin Lakes, N.J., 1983-85, orgn. adv., 1985—. Mem. bd. govs. United Way. Mem. Assn. Profl. and Exec. Women. Republican. Methodist. Home: 60 Cannonball Rd Wanaque NJ 07465 Office: 400 Parson's Pond Dr Franklin Lakes NJ 07417

HYDE, JUDITH ANN, newspaper editor; b. Bay City, Mich., Mar. 14, 1942; d. Harold John and Fern Elaine (Nutt) Padget; m. Jerry Carl Hyde, Oct. 20, 1962; children—Billie Jo, Vicki Lynn. Free lance writer, 1969-83; columnist N. Central Assoc. Pub., Durand, Ill., 1972-79; editor Stephenson County Scope, Lena, Ill., 1973-79; mng. editor Monroe Evening Times (Wis.), 1979—. Mem. Wis. Newspaper Assn. (J.C. Sturtevant Meml. award 1983), Ill. Press Assn., Monroe Bus. and Profl. Women, No. Ill. Newspaper Assn. Republican. Methodist. Club: Order Eastern Star. Home: 211 Townline St Lena IL 61048 Office: Monroe Evening Times 1065 4th Ave W Monroe WI 53566

HYDE, MARY MORLEY CRAPO (VISCOUNTESS ECCLES), author; b. Detroit, July 8, 1912; d. Stanford Tappan and Emma Caroline (Morley) Crapo; A.B., Vassar Coll., 1934; M.A., Columbia, 1936, Ph.D., 1947; D.Litt., Douglass Coll., 1964; Litt.D., Brown U., 1968, U. Birmingham (Eng.), 1969; D.H.L., Union Coll., 1979; m. Donald Frizell Hyde, Sept. 16, 1939 (dec. 1966); m. Viscount Eccles, Sept. 26, 1984. Trustee Pierpont Morgan Library, 1966—; trustee Johnson House, London, 1983—; mem. council Friends of Columbia U. Libraries, 1954—; mem. humanities vis. com. U. Chgo., 1956—; mem. English dept. and library adv. councils Princeton U., 1965—; mem. libraries vis. coms. Harvard U., 1966—; trustee Yale Libraries Assocs., 1970—. Decorated officer de l'Ordre de la Couronne (Belgium); Benjamin Franklin fellow Royal Soc. Arts, London; hon. fellow Pembroke Coll., Oxford U., 1986. Mem. Am. Philos. Soc., Johnson Soc. of Lichfield, Eng. (pres. 1957), Grolier Club (v.p. 1982), Bibliog. Soc. Am., Zamorano (Roxburghe, Eng.), The Johnsonians, Keats-Shelley Assn. Am. (dir. 1967—), N.Y. Hort. Soc., Association Internationale de Bibliophilie (v.p. 1983), Phi Beta Kappa. Author: Playwriting for Elizabethans, 1949; editor: (with E. L. McAdam and Donald Hyde) Johnson's Diaries, Prayers and Annals, 1958; Four Oaks Farm and Its Library, 1967; Impossible Friendship (Boswell and Mrs. Thrale), 1973; The Thrales of Streatham Park, 1977; Bernard Shaw and Alfred Douglas, A Correspondence, 1982. Mem. editorial com. Yale Works of Johnson, 1957, Private Papers Boswell, 1966—. Home: Four Oaks Farm 350 Burnt Mill Rd Somerville NJ 08876

HYDE, PAMELA S., mental health administrator, lawyer; b. Thayer, Mo., Nov. 7, 1950; d. Gaston Clark Hyde and L. Vineta (Cross) Hyde Sponsler; Student S.W. Baptist Coll., 1963-65; B.A., S.W. Mo. State U., 1972; J.D., U. Mich., 1976. Bar: Ohio. Staff atty. Ohio State Legal Services Assn., Columbus, 1976-77, staff atty. Ohio Legal Rights Service, Columbus, 1977-79, chief mental health unit, 1979-80, exec. dir., 1980-83; dir. Ohio Dept. Mental Health, Columbus, 1983—. Author: Patient's Rights Rules, 1978; Civil Commitment in Ohio, 1980. Treas., trustee YWCA, Columbus, 1980-83; gov.'s club mem. Ohio Democratic Party, Columbus, 1983-84; trustee, pres. Women's Music Union, Columbus, 1976-83; atty. Choices for Battered Women, Columbus, 1977; organizer Pro Se Divorce Clinic, Columbus, 1977. Recipient Edwin Rakow award Mich. Fed. Practice Bar, 1975; Community award S.W. Community Health Ctrs., Columbus, 1984; Citation of Young Women of Achievement, Nat. Council Women, N.Y., 1984, Mem. Ohio State Bar Assn., Columbus Bar Assn. (family law com. 1976-83, mental disorder law com. 1981-83), Nat. Lawyers Guild. Office: Ohio Dept Mental Health 30 E Broad St Room 1180 Columbus OH 43215

HYLANDER, BYRNA DEANE, banker, former software firm marketing executive; b. Bklyn., Nov. 4, 1939; d. Herman Adolph and Beatrice Bernardine (Zimpelman) Hylander. Asst. dept. head State Nat. Bank of Conn., Fairfield, 1958-66; dir. data processing Fairfield U., 1966-70; project mgr. Nestle, Inc., White Plains, N.Y., 1970-74; project mgr. Ethan Allen, Inc., Danbury, Conn., 1974-75; mgmt. cons., 1975-78; supr. systems and programming Central Vt. Public Service, Rutland, 1978-79; dir. mgmt. info. systems Internat. Coins and currency, Montpelier, Vt., 1979-80; mgmt. cons. to gen. bus. and data processing, 1980-83; mktg. support cons. Tarkenton Software Inc., Atlanta, 1983-84; asst. v.p./mgr. corporate systems First Am. Nat. Bank, Nashville, 1984—. Mem. faculty Fairfield U. Sch. Continuing Edn., 1967-74. Spl. police officer, Redding, Conn., Randolph, Vt.; dep. sheriffs Vt. Mem. Assn. Systems Mgmt., Vt. Computer Users Group (sec.-treas. 1979-80), Am. Mgmt. Assn., Computer Security Inst. Republican. Roman Catholic. Office: 1st Am Center Corporate Systems Nashville TN 37237

HYLE, NANCY ELIZABETH, educator; b. Cin., July 28, 1949; d. John Arthur and Ida Mae (Mause) Shoemaker; m. Francis Michael Hyle, June 24, 1972; children—Robyn Michelle, Katie Christine. B.A. in Edn., Thomas More Coll., 1971. Lic. elem. tchr., Ohio. Tchr. St. Jude Sch., Cin., 1971-73, St. William Sch., Cin., 1973—. Coordinator Cath. Engaged Encounter of Cin., 1983—; mem. com. Outline Task Force of Engaged Encounter, 1985; Brownie leader Girl Scouts U.S., Cin., 1984—. Democrat. Roman Catholic. Avocations: tennis; gardening; decorating. Home: 2840 Kleeman Rd Cincinnati OH 45211

HYLTON, TERRIE ELLERY, union executive; b. Detroit, Sept. 22, 1955; d. George Leroy and Hannah Belle (Mack) Ellery; m. Kenneth Niles Hylton Jr., 1 child, Kenneth Niles III. B.A. with honors, Wayne State U., 1975, M.A., 1984. Asst. juvenile ct. officer State of Mich., Detroit, 1978-79; counselor Wayne State U., 1979-80; admissions coordinator Detroit Inst. Tech., 1980-81; placement dir. Internat. Transp. Inst., Dearborn, Mich., 1981-82; program coordinator Mich. State AFL-CIO, Detroit, 1984—. Mem. Theatre Hospitality Enterprise, Detroit, 1980, editor newsletter, 1982, 83; vice chmn. Friends of Detroit Youtheatre, 1984, chmn., 1985; Democratic precinct del., Detroit, 1984. Mem. Am. Assn. Counseling and Devel., Nat. Employment Counselors Assn., Am. Coll. Personnel Assn., Assn. Specialists in Group Work, Founders Soc. Detroit Inst. Arts. Avocations: traveling; reading. Club: Econ. of Detroit. Office: Metro-Detroit AFL-CIO 2550 W Grand Blvd Detroit MI 48208

HYMAN, PAULA E(LLEN), history educator; b. Boston; d. Sydney Max and Ida Frances (Tatelman) H.; m. Stanley Harvey Rosenbaum, June 7, 1969; children—Judith Hyman Rosenbaum, Adina Hyman Rosenbaum. B.J.Ed., Hebrew Coll., Brookline, Mass., 1966; B.A., Radcliffe Coll., 1968; M.A., Columbia U., 1970, Ph.D., 1975. Asst. prof. Columbia U., N.Y.C., 1974-81; assoc. prof. history Jewish Theol. Sem., N.Y.C., 1981-86, dean Sem., Coll. Jewish Studies, 1981-86; Lady Davis vis. assoc. prof Hebrew U. of Jerusalem, 1986; Lucy Moses prof. history Yale U., New Haven, 1986—. Series editor Ind. U. Press. Bloomington, 1982—; contbg. editor Sh'ma Mag., N.Y.C., 1977—; author: From Dreyfus to Vichy, 1979; co-author: The Jewish Woman in America, 1976; co-editor: Perspectives on the Jewish Family, 1986. Contbr. articles to publs. Vice chmn. Zionist Acad. Council, N.Y.C., 1982-83. NEH summer grantee, 1977; Am. Council Learned Socs. fellow, 1978; grantee N.Y. Council for Humanities, 1980. Mem. Am. Hist. Assn. (com. 1983), Assn. for Jewish Studies (bd. dirs. 1978-81, 83—), Leo Baeck Inst. (bd. dirs. 1979—), Yivo Inst. for Jewish Research, Phi Beta Kappa. Jewish. Office: Dept History Yale U New Haven CT

HYMAN, SYLVIA GERTRUDE, artist, designer, craftsman, educator; b. Buffalo, Sept. 9, 1917; d. Norman Nathan and Ida (Diamond) Risman; m. Maurice Hyman, Oct. 25, 1944 (dec. Dec. 1979); children—Paul Maurice, Jackie Diamond Hyman Wilson; m. Arthur Gunzberg, Sept. 8, 1985. Diploma in fine arts, Albright Art Sch., Buffalo, 1937; B.S. in Art Edn., State Tchrs. Coll., Buffalo, 1938; M.A. in Art, Peabody Coll., 1963. Tchr. art Buffalo Pub. Schs., 1937-43, Jefferson County Schs., Middletown, Ky., 1957-60; asst. prof. art George Peabody Coll., 1964-71; chmn. planning bd. Internat. Ceramic Symposium, Memphis, 1973; cons. in field. One woman shows: Tenn. Fine Arts Ctr., 1983, numerous others; group shows include: Mus. Contemporary Crafts, N.Y.C., 1964, 65, Mint Mus. Art, Charlotte, N.C., 1964, 71, 73, Speed Mus., Louisville, 1968, 72, Brooks Gallery, Memphis, 1969, 77, Met. Mus. and Art Ctr., Miami, Fla., 1976, SEECA, Winston-Salem, N.C., 1979, Smithsonian Instn., Washington, 1980; numerous pub. and pvt. collections; exhibitor 1st World Triennial, Muzejski Prostor, Zagreb, Yugoslavia, 1984; contbr. articles to profl. jours. Chmn. adv. com. Tenn. Arts Commn., Nashville, 1968-72; mem. Century III Commn., Nashville, 1977-79; mem. Mayor's Task Force for Community Excellence, Nashville, 1981-82; Chmn. Internat. Ceramic Symposium, Appalachian Ctr. Crafts, 1985. Recipient Commendation Outstanding Service award ARC & U.S. Army, 1944; Best in Clay award Arts Festival Arts Ctr, Oak Ridge, Tenn., 1979; numerous other awards. Mem. Tenn. Artist-Craftsmen's Assn. (co-founder), Tenn. Ann. Crafts Fair (bd. chmn. 1971-74), Am. Craft Council N.Y., Internat. Acad. Ceramics. Democrat. Jewish. Club: Nashville Artist Guild (pres. 1964-66), Tri-Arts (pres. 1972-74).

HYMEL, FRANCES M., physician; b. White Castle, La., Dec. 3, 1914; d. Lulovic Paul and Agnes (LeGlue) Hymel; M.D., La. State U., 1949. Head nurse Charity Hosp., New Orleans, 1935-36; staff nurse La. State Dept. Health, New Roads and Franklin, 1936-42; intern Charity Hosp., New Orleans, 1949-50, resident, 1950-51; practice gen. medicine, New Orleans, 1951—; mem. hon. staff Hotel Dieu Hosp., New Orleans. Charter fellow Am. Acad. Family Physicians (life mem.); mem. Orleans Parish, La. med. socs., AAUW, Am. Legion Aux., Alpha Epsilon Iota. Home: 1241 N Hagan Ave New Orleans LA 70119 Office: 1239 N Hagan Ave New Orleans LA 70119

HYTIER, ADRIENNE DORIS, French educator; d. Jean and Katharine (Matson) H.; B.A. summa cum laude, Barnard Coll., 1952; M.A., Columbia U., 1953, Ph.D., 1958. Instr. French, Vassar Coll., Poughkeepsie, N.Y., 1959-61, asst. prof., 1961-66, assoc. prof., 1966-70, Louise Boyd Lichtenstein Dale prof. French, 1970—; vis. assoc. prof. Columbia U., 1966, U. Calif., 1968-69. Guggenheim fellow, 1967-68. Mem. MLA, Am. Assn. Tchrs. French, Am. Soc. 18th Century Studies, Internat. Soc. 18th Century Studies, N.E. Soc. 18th Century Studies, Middle Atlantic Soc. 18th Century Studies, Phi Beta Kappa. Editor: French Literature, The 18th Century: A Current Bibliography, 1970—; author: Les Dépêches diplomatiques du Comte de Gobineau en Perse, 1959; Two Years of French Foreign Policy 1940-42, 1958, 2d edit., 1974; La Guerre, 1975, 2d edit., 1985; contbr. articles to profl. jours. Office: Vassar Coll Poughkeepsie NY 12601

IACHETTI, ROSE MARIA ANNE, educator; b. Watervliet, N.Y., Sept. 22, 1931; d. Augustus and Rose Elizabeth Archer (Orciuolo) Iachetti; B.S., Coll. St. Rose, 1961; M.Ed., U. Ariz., 1969. Joined Sisters of Mercy, Albany, N.Y., 1949-66; tchr. various parochial schs. Albany (N.Y.) Diocese, 1952-66; tchr. Headstart Program, Troy, N.Y., 1966; tchr. fine arts Watervliet Jr. and Sr. High Sch., 1966-67; tchr. W.J. Meyer Sch., Tombstone, Ariz., 1968-71, Colonel Johnston Sch., Ft. Huachuca, Ariz., 1971-78; tchr. Myer Sch., Ft. Huachuca, 1978—, coordinator program for gifted and talented, 1981-85. Ann. chmn. Ariz. Children's Home Assn., Tombstone, 1973-74; trustee Tombstone Sch. Dist. #1, 1972-80; active Democratic Club; mem. Bicentennial Commn. for Ariz., 1972-76, Tombstone Centennial Commn., 1979-80, chmn. Centennial Ball, 1980; pres. Tombstone Community Health Services, 1978-80; mem. Tombstone City Council, 1982-84; governing bd. Southeast Ariz. Area Health Edn. Ctr., 1985—. Mem. Ariz. Edn. Assn. (so. regional dir. 1971-73), Ft. Huachuca Edn. Assn., Tombstone Dist. 1 Edn. Assn. (pres. 1969-71), Ariz. Sch. Bd. Assn., NEA (del. 1971-73), Ariz. Classroom Tchrs. Assn. (del. 1969-71), Internat. Platform Assn., Tombstone Bus. and Profl. Womens Club, Am. Legion Aux., Tombstone Assn. Arts, Pi Lambda Theta, Delta Kappa Gamma, (pres. 1982-84), Phi Delta Kappa (historian 1979-82, 2d v.p. 1982-83). Home: Round Up Trailer Ranch Box 725 Tombstone AZ 85638 Office: Myer School Fort Huachuca AZ 85613

IBA, BARBARA JEAN YOUNG, government agency administrator; b. Ellwood City, Pa., Oct. 18, 1937; d. Robert Harold and Ellen Lucille (Newton) Young; R.N., Presbyn.-Univ. Hosp., Pitts., 1958; student Bethany (W.Va.) Coll., 1958-59; B.S. in Nursing, U. Pitts., 1961; postgrad. Am. U., 1980; m. Edward Toshikatsu Iba, Oct. 23, 1965; children—Jennifer Emi, Robert Yoshio. Staff nurse Presbyn.-Univ. Hosp., 1958-59, Bethany Coll., 1958-59; nursing instr. Presbyn.-Univ. Hosp., 1959-64; nurse, population genetic researcher Nat. Inst. Dental Research, NIH, Bethesda, Md., 1964-74, equal opportunity coordinator, 1974-80, acting fed. women's program mgr., 1980-84, fed. women's program mgr., 1984—, chief of staff Equal Opportunity Evaluation Task Force, 1979-80; mem. Woodside Child Care Program Task Force, Silver Spring, Md., 1973-79; vice chmn. NIH Child Care Program Adv. Coms., 1973-74. Chmn., Parents of Preschoolers, Inc., 1974-75; mental retardation adv., Washington. Fed. nurse trainee, 1960. Recipient Equal Opportunity Achievement award Nat. Inst. Dental Research, 1978; Dir.'s award NIH, 1980. Mem. Women's Equity Action League, Federally Employed Women, Kensington Bus. and Profl. Women (1st v.p. 1985-86). Home: 8716 Milford Ave Silver Spring MD 20910 Office: 40 NIH Bethesda MD 20892

IBANEZ, SILVIA SAFILLE, financial consultant; b. Havana, Cuba, Nov. 3, 1952; came to U.S., 1961; d. Eduardo and Alicia (Martin) Safille; m. Juan Antonio Ibáñez, July 5, 1974; children—Juan-Carlos and Christina (twins). B.B.A., U. Miami, Fla., 1973, M.S. in Acctg., 1974; J.D., U. P.R., 1981. Bar: Fla. 1983; C.P.A., Fla. Auditor, Coopers & Lybrand, Miami, Fla., 1974-75, tax specialist, 1977-81; prof. U. Católica Mad. & Meastra, Santiago, Dominican Republic, 1975-76; tax mgr. Main Hurdman C.P.A.s, St. Petersburg, Fla., 1981-84; fin. planner Interstate Securities Co., Fort Myers, Fla., 1985; fin. cons., Silvia S. Ibañez, Fort Myers, 1985—; investment broker FSC Securities Corp., Fort Myers, 1985—; mem., lectr. S.W. Fla. Tax Council, Fort Myers, 1985—. Mem., Lee County Med. Soc. Aux., Fort Myers, 1986—. Mem. ABA, Am. Inst. C.P.A.s, Internat. Assn. Fin. Planning, Fla. Inst. C.P.A.s (Outstanding Grad. 1974), Fla. Bar Assn., S.W. Fla. Estate Planning Council, Nat. Assn. Female Execs., Women's Network. Republican. Roman Catholic. Avocations: reading; singing; piano; family. Home: 14556 Aeries Way SE Fort Myers FL 33912 Office: Silvia S Ibañez CPA 4066 Evans Ave Suite 8 Fort Myers FL 33901

ICE, GLENDA SUE, nurse; b. Anderson, Ind., May 13, 1960; d. Glenn Randolph and Vivian Irene (Craft) Reasor; m. Tommy Joe Ice, Aug. 25, 1979; children—Jessica Lynn, Christine Marie. A. in Nursing, Anderson Coll., 1982. Lic. R.N., Ind. Nurses aide Parkview Convalescant Ctr., Elwood, Ind., 1978-79; staff nurse St. John's Med. Ctr., Anderson, Ind., 1982-83, Mercy Hosp., Elwood, 1983—. Methodist. Avocations: neddle craft; reading; jogging. Home: Alexandria IN 46001

ICHIKAWA, CHRISTIE OZAWA, nursing educator; b. Sacramento, Apr. 4, 1928; s. Walt Wataru and Pauline Kikuye (Tamura) Ozawa; m. Robert Setsuto Ichikawa, Oct. 22, 1950; children—Robert D., Ross A., Laura A. R.N., Los Angeles County Gen. Hosp., 1950; B.S., U. So. Calif., 1950; M.A., Calif. State U.-Dominguez Hills, 1973. Cert. women's health care nurse practitioner, Calif. Staff nurse Seaside Hosp. (now Long Beach Meml. Hosp.), Long Beach, Calif., 1950-52; office nurse Donald J. Crawford, M.D., Long Beach, 1952-54; operating room nurse Los Angeles County Harbor-UCLA Med. Ctr., Torrance, 1955-56; sch. nurse Los Angeles Unified Sch. Dist., 1956-68; prof. nursing Los Angeles Community Coll. Dist., Wilmington, 1968-79; chairperson div. nursing Los Angeles Harbor Coll., Wilmington, 1979—; chairperson Assoc. Degree Nursing Program Dirs. Los Angeles Community Coll. Dist., 1981-83. Vol. Little Tokyo Health Fair, Los Angeles, 1979-82; bd. dirs. Torrance Sister City Assn., Calif., 1982-86; vol., mem. Am. Cancer Soc., Long Beach, 1983—; mem. Leadership Edn. for Asian Pacifics, Los Angeles, 1984, Los Angeles County Mus. Art; pres. DeMolay Mothers Club, 1961. Recipient DeMolay Top Hat award, 1962; named South Bay Woman of Yr., Torrance YWCA, 1982. Mem. Calif. Nurses Assn., Nat. League for Nursing, Am. Fedn. Tchrs., Coll. Guild, Delta Kappa Gamma (2d v.p. Eta Gamma chpt. 1976-78, pres. 1978-80, parliamentarian 1980-84, chmn. fin. and budget com. 1984—). Republican. Office: Los Angeles Harbor Coll 1111 Figueroa Pl Wilmington CA 90744

ICHINO, YOKO, ballerina; b. Los Angeles; student of Mia Slavenska, from 1967. Mem. City Center Joffrey Ballet, N.Y.C., 1973-75, Stuttgart Ballet, W. Ger., 1975-76, Am. Ballet Theatre, N.Y.C., 1977—; internat. guest artist and tchr., including 2d World Ballet Festival, Japan, 1979, 4th World Ballet Festival, 1985; prin. Nat. Ballet Can., 1982—. Recipient Bronze medal Moscow Competition, 1977.

IDDINS, MILDRED, retired librarian; b. Fountain City, Tenn.; d. Joseph Franklin and Lucy (Chandler) I.; A.B., Carson-Newman Coll., 1936; B.S., George Peabody Coll., 1941. Tchr., Bell House Sch., Knoxville, Tenn., 1936-37; tchr. Roane County High Sch., Kingston, 1937-41; librarian Dandridge (Tenn.) High Sch., 1941-43; Army librarian, Ft. Oglethorpe, Ga., 1943-44; librarian Carson-Newman Coll., Jefferson City, Tenn., 1944-81. Former mem. ALA, Southeastern, Tenn. library assns.; mem. AAUW (br. treas. 1964-66). Baptist. Clubs: Monday Literary, Modern Literary. Home: 403 Russell St Jefferson City TN 37760

IDLEWINE, SHERRY LYNN, business management educator; b. Indpls., May 24, 1959; d. Lenord George and Mary Walteen (York) I. B.A., Ind. Central U., 1981, M.A., M.B.A., 1984. Dept. mgr. Target Corp., Indpls., 1976-81; job placement coordinator Lockyear Coll., Indpls., 1981—, instr. secretarial work, 1981-83, instr. computer sci., 1983-85, instr. mgmt., 1985—; cons., mem. Partners 2000, Indpls., 1984—; cons. Foremost Ins. Co., Indpls., 1985. Active Indpls. Alliance for Jobs, 1984—; judge Jr. Miss Pageant for Ind., Brownsburg, 1985. Mem. Nat. Assn. for Female Execs., Mu Phi Epsilon (co-organizer internat. conf. 1980, Sterling Staff award 1981, 1st v.p. 1982-83, mag. chmn. 1982-83). Republican. Baptist. Club: Ind. Central Univ. M.B.A. Alumni. Avocations: music, art, writing, travel, tennis. Office: Lockyear Coll Bus Dept 5330 E 38th St Indianapolis IN 46218

IGLESIAS, MARIA ADELA, educational specialist; b. Sancti Spiritus, Las Villas, Cuba, Oct. 3, 1950; came to U.S., Nov. 1960; d. Jorge Antonio and Adela (Orizondo) I. B.A., Fla. State U., 1972; M.Ed., Fla. Atlantic U., 1976; postgrad. U. Mass., 1985—. Spl. edn. dept. head, tchr. Palm Beach County Schs., Boynton Beach, Fla., 1976-80, Dade County Pub. Schs., Coral Gables, Fla., 1980-84; bilingual spl. edn. tchr. Boston Pub. Schs., Jamaica Plain, Mass., 1984-85; ednl. specialist III, Mass. State Dept. Edn., Wellesley, 1985—; cons. Fla. Career Coll., Miami, 1982-83; tutor S.W. Miami Boys Clubs, 1983-84. Mem. Council Exceptional Children, Am. Fedn. Tchrs., Boston Tchrs. Union. Democrat. Roman Catholic. Avocations: tennis; biking; jogging. Office: Commonwealth Mass Dept Edn Greater Boston Regional Edn Ctr 27 Cedar St Wellesley MA 02181

IHDE, JANET KAY, surgeon, educator; b. Barstow, Calif., July 13, 1952; d. Ralph H. and Jean Holderby (Laidley) I. B.S., Loma Linda U., M.D., 1977. Diplomate Am. Bd. Surgery. Resident in surgery Loma Linda U., to 1982; mem. faculty Oral Roberts U., 1983-84; asst. prof. surgery Loma Linda U. (Calif.), 1984—. Recipient Harold J. Hoxie award, 1977, Sandoz award, 1976-77; Janet M. Glasgow achievement citation Am. Med. Women's Assn. Mem. Soc. Critical Care Medicine, Alpha Omega Alpha. Office: Loma Linda U Med Ctr Dept Surgery Loma Linda CA 92354

IKEDA, NAOMI, gemologist, gem and jewelry institute administrator; b. San Diego, May 22, 1949; d. Frank Yoshiharu and Jeanne Haruko (Masuda) I. Grad., Buena Park Beauty Sch., Calif., 1967, Gemological Inst. Am., Santa Monica, Calif., 1970. Cosmetologist, Blossom Hair Fashions, Buena Park, 1967-68, Nikko Wig Fashions, Orange, Calif., 1969-70; sales clk. Pacific Gem Cutters, Los Angeles, 1971-72; mgr. Nikko Gem & Jewelry Inst. Inc., Honolulu, 1972—, v.p., 1979—; lectr. U. Hawaii, 1980—. Mem. Gemological Inst. Am. Alumni Assn. (treas. Hawaii chpt. 1984-86, v.p. 1986). Buddhist. Office: Nikko Gem & Jewelry Inst Inc 512 Atkinson Dr Honolulu HI 96814

IKLE, DORIS MARGRET, energy conservation corporation executive; b. Frankfort, Germany, May 28, 1928; came to U.S., 1937, naturalized, 1945; d. Richard and Sonia (Pappenheimer) Eisemann; m. Fred Charles Ikle, Dec. 23, 1959; children—Judith, Miriam. B.A., NYU, 1949, M.A., 1953; postgrad. Columbia U., 1957. Economist, Nat. Bur. Econ. Research, N.Y.C., 1949-56, Rand Corp., Santa Monica, Calif., 1957-60, Inst. Energy Analysis, Washington, 1976-77; cons. U.S. Dept. Commerce, Washington, 1975-76; pres. Conservation Mgmt. Corp., Bethesda, Md., 1977—; adv. council Am. for Energy Independence, 1985—; cons. in field. Author: The Complete Energy Audit Book, 1980, (software) RCS and CACS Audit Systems, 1984. Contbr. articles to profl. jours. Home: 7010 Glenbrook Rd Bethesda MD 20814 Office: Conservation Mgmt Corp 101 Millburn Ave Millburn NJ 07041

IKNER, ARDELLA WARDRISHA, government official; b. Wiergate, Tex., Feb. 25, 1930; d. Fred Eddie and Hattie Rella (Shankle) Simmons; m. Rufus Louis Ikner, Apr. 19, 1949; children—Ronnie Derricothe, Wayne Demarr, Louis Drandon, Neva Wardrisha. B.A., U. Colo.-Denver, 1969, M.P.A., 1976; cert. Jones Sch. Real Estate, Denver, 1978. L.P.N. Nursing asst. VA Hosp., Denver, 1956-67; statis. clk. Bur. of Mines, Denver, 1967-69, sociologist, 1969-71, personnel mgmt. specialist, 1971-76; personnel mgmt. specialist SBA, Denver, 1976-79, personnel officer, 1979—, employee counselor, 1978—. Probation counselor Denver Probation Services, 1967; guardian Camp Fire Girls, Denver, 1967; sec. Denver Adv. Council, 1975-78. Named Career Woman in Community Services, Assn. Fed. and Profl. and Adminstrv. Women, 1975. Mem. Internat. Personnel Mgmt. Assn., Classification and Compensation Soc., Personnel Council (vice chmn. 1980-81), Iota Phi Lambda. Democrat. Club: Fed. Foothills Toastmistress of Denver (v.p. 1970). Lodge: Eastern Star (awards 1975, 80). Home: 55 S Albion St Denver CO 80222

ILCHMAN, ALICE STONE, college president, former government official; b. Cin., Apr. 18, 1935; d. Donald Crawford and Alice Kathryn (Biermann) Stone; B.A., Mt. Holyoke Coll., 1957; M.P.A., Maxwell Sch. Citizenship, Syracuse U., 1958; Ph.D., London Sch. Econs., 1965; hon. degrees: Mt. Holyoke Coll., Franklin and Marshall Coll.; m. Warren Frederick Ilchman, June 11, 1960; children—Frederick Andrew Crawford, Alice Sarah Crawford. Asst. to pres., mem. faculty Berkshire Community Coll., 1961-64; asst. research polit. scientist Inst. Govtl. Studies, U. Calif. at Berkeley, 1966, lectr., program dir. Center for South Asia Studies, 1966-68, 69-70, dir. Profl. Studies Program, India, 1968-69, lectr., asst. prof., dir. Pakistan Edn. Program, Sch. Edn., 1971-73; prof. econs. and edn., dean Wellesley (Mass.) Coll., 1973-78; asst. sec. ednl. and cultural affairs Dept. State, 1978; asso. dir. ednl. and cultural affairs Internat. Communications Agy., 1978-81; advisor to sec. Smithsonian Instn., 1981; pres. Sarah Lawrence Coll., Bronxville, N.Y., 1981—; intern, asst. to Sen. John F. Kennedy, 1957; seminar leader, dir. Peace Corps Tng. Program for India, 1965-66; chmn. com. on women's employment Nat. Acad. Scis. Trustee Mt. Holyoke Coll., The Experiment in Internat. Living, East-West Center, Honolulu, Markle Found.; mem. Econ. Policy Council, UN; mem. control bd. City of Yonkers (N.Y.); mem. Smithsonian Council. Mem. Nat. Acad. Public Adminstrn., Council Fgn. Relations. Clubs: Cosmopolitan (N.Y.C.); Field (Bronxville, N.Y.). Author: The New Men of Knowledge and the New States, 1968; (with W.F. Ilchman) Education and Employment in India, The Policy Nexus, 1976. Home: 935 Kimball Ave Bronxville NY 10708 Office: Sarah Lawrence Coll Bronxville NY 10708

IMERGOOT, LYNN CAROL, educator; b. Bronx, Dec. 29, 1948; d. Bernard Jack and Selma (Goldberg) Stockman; m. Michael Harris Imergoot, Dec. 23, 1973; children—Douglas Elliot, Jennifer Hope. A.B., Lehman Coll., 1969; M.S., U. Ill., 1970. Grad. teaching asst. U. Ill., Urbana, 1969-70; phys. edn. tchr. White Plains (N.Y.) High Sch., 1970-72; instr. phys. edn. Washington U., St. Louis, 1972-77, women's tennis coach, 1975—, coordinator women's sports, 1977-84, asst. athletic dir., 1984—; v.p. Midwest Camp Cons., Maryland Heights, Mo., 1978—. Contbr. articles to profl. jours. Mem. St. Louis Post-Dispatch Scholar-Athlete adv. com., 1978-84; vol. Channel 9 Auction, St. Louis, 1981-84; solicitor United Way Campaign, St. Louis, 1983-84. Thomas Hunter scholar, 1965; recipient A. W. Neidhart award Lehman Coll., 1969. Mem. Intercollegiate Tennis Coaches Assn., Women's Phys. Edn. Club St. Louis (pres. 1976-78), Mo. Assn. Health, Council Collegiate Women Athletic Adminstrs., Internat. Assn. Physical Edn. Sports for Girls and Women, Phys. Edn., Recreation and Dance (Helen Manley award 1984), AAHPERD. Democrat. Jewish. Home: 1785 Red Coat Dr Maryland Heights MO 63043 Office: Washington U PO Box 1067 Saint Louis MO 63130

IMPELLIZZERI, ANNE ELMENDORF, insurance company executive; b. Chgo., Jan. 26, 1933; d. Armin and Laura (Gundlach) Elmendorf; m. Julius Simon Impellizzeri, Oct. 12, 1961; children—Laura, Theodore. B.A., Smith Coll., 1955; M.A., Yale U., 1957. C.L.U.; chartered fin. cons. Tchr., Amity Regional High Sch., Woodbridge, Conn., 1957-58; adminstrv. and editorial asst. East Europe Inst., N.Y.C., 1958-59; health educator Met. Life Ins. Co., N.Y.C., 1959-62, 71-76, adminstrv. asst. pub. affairs, 1976-78, asst. v.p., 1978-80, v.p., 1980-85, v.p. group ins., 1985—; dir. Elmendorf Research, Inc., Minority Equity Capital Co., N.Y.C.; chmn. bus. urban issues council Conf. Bd., 1983-85. Chmn. summer jobs adv. com. N.Y.C. Partnership, 1980-82; pres. Am. Assn. Gifted Children, 1975-85, chair, 1985—; bd. dirs. Nat. Safety Council, 1974-80; trustee Lakeland Bd. Edn., Westchester County, N.Y., 1967-71, pres., 1970-71. Named to Acad. of Women Achievers, YWCA N.Y., 1978; Fulbright grantee, 1955-56. Mem. Assn. Yale Alumni (bd. govs. 1985—), Phi Beta Kappa. Office: Metropolitan Life Insurance Co One Madison Ave New York NY 10010

IN, RACHEL CHIANG, newspaper editor and publisher, researcher; b. China, Mar. 10, 1938, came to U.S., 1960; d. Jen Kwei and Kwei-In (Ling) Chiang; m. Yu-Wei In, June 15, 1960; children—Yee-Liu, Wei-Yee, Thomas, Peggy, Yee-Pao. B.A., Tamkang U., China, 1959; M.A., CUNY, 1967. Pub., exec. editor Orient Times, N.Y.C., 1979—; mgr. coll. text John Wiley & Sons, N.Y.C., 1967-81; research dir. Editor and Publisher, N.Y.C., 1982—; dir. Overseas Chinese Soc., 1979—; tchr. of Chinese. Contbr. articles to profl. jours. Producer benefit concert Com. to Aid Indochinese Refugees, 1979; dir. UN Boat People Rally, 1979; advisor Congl. Adv. Bd., Washington, 1983. Office: Editor and Publisher 11 W 19th St New York NY 10011

INAN, CZATDANA, publishing company executive; b. Leningrad, Russia, Apr. 16, 1943; B.S., U. Minn., 1965; M.B.A., U. Chgo., 1971; married; 1 child, Zaba. Research dir. Telephony Pub. Corp., Chgo.; editor Telecom Mktg. Newsletter. Contbr. articles to profl. jours.; author ann. telecommunications industry forecasts; cons. U.S. Telecommunications Suppliers Assn. Office: Telephony Pub Corp 55 E Jackson Blvd Chicago IL 60604

INCAGNOLI, THERESA MARIE, clinical neuropsychologist; b. N.Y.C., June 22, 1949; d. Thomas Marcel and Marie Incagnoli. B.A. cum laude, Bklyn. Coll., 1970; Ph.D., St. John's U., 1978. Diplomate in clin. neuropsychology Am. Bd. Profl. Psychology. Psychologist, St. Vincent's Med. Ctr., N.Y.C., 1973-79; postdoctoral fellow in clin. neuropsychology U. Okla. Health Scis. Ctr., 1979-80; clin. neuropsychologist VA Med. Ctr., Northport, N.Y., 1981—; asst. prof. dept. psychiatry (psychology) Sch. Medicine SUNY-Stony Brook, 1982—. Editor textbook: Clinical Application of Neuropsychological Batteries, 1986. NIMH fellow, 1979-80. Mem. Am. Psychol. Assn., Internat. Neuropsychol. Soc., Nat. Acad. Neuropsychologists, N.Y. State Psychol. Assn. Home: 240 Central Park S New York NY 10019 Office: VA Med Center Psychology Dept Northport NY 11768

INDICK, JANET, sculptor, educational administrator; b. Bklyn., Mar. 3, 1932; d. Charles and Sarah (Goldsmith) Suslak; m. Benjamin Philip Indick, Aug. 23, 1953; children—Michael Cory, Karen Leigh Indick Maizel. B.S. in Art, Hunter Coll., 1953, postgrad., 1953; postgrad. New Sch., 1961-62. Tchr. kindergarten pub. schs., Elizabeth, N.J., 1953-54; dir. nursery sch. Teaneck Jewish Ctr., N.J., 1964—. Executed commd. sculpture works Teaneck Jewish Ctr., 1974, Temple Beth Rishon, Wyckoff, N.J., 1981, 82. Advisor Teaneck Arts Adv. Bd., 1982—. Recipient sculpture prize Nat. Assn. Painters and Sculptors, 1978-80; N.J. State Council Arts fellow, 1981. Mem. Modern Artists Guild Paramus (v.p. sec. 1983-84), Sculptors Assn. N.J., Sculptors League Internat., Nat. Assn. Women Artists (juror; sculpture prize 1974), N.Y. Soc. Women Artists (juror), Women's Caucus Art (juror). Democrat. Jewish. Home: 428 Sagamore Ave Teaneck NJ 07666

INFANTE, ISA MARIA, political scientist, educator; b. Santo Domingo, Dominican Republic, Sept. 8, 1942; came to U.S., 1945; d. Rafael Infante and Dolores Nieves; student Woodbury Coll., 1960-61; B.A., U. Calif.-Santa Cruz, 1973; M.A. in Comparative Polit. Systems, Yale U., 1975; postgrad. U. Santa Clara Law Sch. and People's Coll. of Law, 1975-77; Ph.D. in Polit. Sci. (Ford Found. fellow), U. Calif.-Riverside, 1977; 1 child, Ninette Maria. Mgmt. trainee Calif. Savs. and Loan Assn., Los Angeles, 1960-61; asst. fgn. corr. Los Angeles Times, Mexico City, 1961-62; bus. enterprise officer, Los Angeles, 1962-64; regional mgr. advt. Strout Realty, Pasadena, Calif., 1964-66; dir. ops. Branford, Inc., N.Y.C., 1966-68; entrepreneur retail stores, Los Angeles, Lake Elsinore, Calif., Anaheim, Calif.; exec. dir. coll. adult rehab. program U. Calif., Riverside, 1970-71; research asso. U. Calif., Santa Cruz, 1972-73; dir. human resources project SUNY, Binghamton, 1973-75; instr. social scis. div. Riverside (Calif.) Community Coll., 1976; dir. nat. immigration bd. Nat. Lawyers Guild, Los Angeles, 1977; acad. adv. and exec. asst. to provost Antioch Coll. West, Antioch U., San Francisco, 1977-78; sr. devel. officer U.S. Human Resources Corp., San Francisco, 1978; mem. profl. staff Interdepartmental Task Force on Women, White House, Washington, 1978-79; policy fellow and program officer Inst. for Ednl. Leadership/Fund for Improvement of Postsecondary Edn., HEW, Washington, 1978-79; assoc. dean Labor Coll., Empire State Coll., SUNY, N.Y.C., 1979-81; pres. I. Infante Assocs., internat. cons., 1980—; prof. polit. sci., dir. Latin Am. studies dept. Jersey City State Coll., 1983—; cons. to various ednl. orgns. and govt. agys. Pres., Nat. Hispanic Coalition, Washington, 1978-80; notary public, 1980—; mem. Am. Council on Edn., 1980—, Community Bd. 12, Borough of Manhattan, N.Y., 1980—; bd. dirs. Nagle House Co-op, N.Y.C., 1980—, Solidaridad Humana, Inc., N.Y.C., 1980—; trustee Center for Integrative Devel., N.Y.C., 1979. P.R. Legal Defense and Edn. Fund scholar, 1975-77, Pease Barker scholar, 1972-73, Council on Legal Edn. Opportunity scholar, 1975-76. Fellow Am. Polit. Sci. Assn.; mem. Soc. for Internat. Devel., Internat. Polit. Sci. Assn., Am. Ednl. Research Assn., Latin Am. Studies Assn., Univ. and Coll. Labor Edn. Assn., Nat. Women's Polit. Caucus, Nat. Women's Health Network, Nat. Assn. Female Execs. Club: Yale of N.Y.C. Author: (with others) Field Preparation Manual, 1973; contbg. author: Voices From the Ghetto, 1968; The Politics of Teaching Political Science, 1978; Labor Studies Jour., 1981; Black Studies Jour., 1983; Political Affairs, 1984. Address: 239 37th Ave North Nashville TN 37209

ING, JANET, rare book librarian, researcher; b. San Francisco, May 26, 1948; d. John N., Jr., and Ladene (McGregor) Thompson; m. Dexter Ing, Dec. 26, 1970 (div. 1976). B.A., Occidental Coll., 1970; M.L.S., U. Calif.-Berkeley, 1977, Ph.D., 1985. Asst. librarian Calif. Coll. Arts and Crafts, Oakland, 1977-78; acting instr. U. Calif., Berkeley, 1982, 85; spl. collections librarian, lectr. in letters, Mills Coll., Oakland, 1982-85; librarian The Scheide Library, Princeton U., 1985—. Contbr. articles to jours. including Brit. Library Jour., Fine Print, Papers of Bibliog. Soc. Am. AAUW fellow, 1981-82. Mem. Bibliog. Soc. London, Bibliog. Soc. Am., Printing Hist. Soc. London, Am. Printing History Assn. Club: Grolier (N.Y.C.). Office: The Scheide Library Princeton U Princeton NJ 08544

INGALLS, CAROL BETH, insurance agency executive and agent; b. Long Beach, Calif., Jan. 23, 1948; d. Robert E. and Mary Louise (Butterbaugh) Myers; m. Dennis Edward Ingalls, Dec. 18, 1976; children—Jed Edward, Andrew Dennis. B.S., U. Nev.-Reno, 1970. Comml. underwriter Kemper Ins., Chgo., 1971-75; comml. underwriter Fireman's Fund, Reno, 1976-80; pres., agt., ptnr. Truckee Meadows Ins., Reno, 1980—. Pres., Women of the Ch. of God, Sparks, Nev., 1983-84; mem. Republican Women Reno; state coordinator Spl. Olympics. Mem. Profl. Ins. Agts. (pres. No. Nev. chpt. 1983-84). Profl. Ins. Agts. Calif. and Nev. (dir. 1983-85). Ins. Women of Reno. Office: Truckee Meadows Ins PO Box 20727 Reno NV 89515

INGALSBE, LILLIAN CAROLINE (MRS. CHARLES KREIGER), real estate broker, judge; b. Donald, Washington, Mar. 27, 1932; d. Wiley Claude and Lillian (Graham) Close; student Centralia Jr. Coll., 1970—; m. Charles Kreiger, Sept. 22, 1947; children—Sherry, Charles E., Roger, Tony, Shane. Justice peace, Morton, Wash., 1961-67; police judge, 1963-75; real estate salesman Rainier Real Estate, 1966-67; broker, br. mgr. Forrester Realty, Morton, after 1968; now owner, broker Mountain Realty, Morton. Sec., Eastern Lewis County Democratic Club. Agt., Dept. Licensing, Dept. Transp. Mem. Women of Moose. Home: Box 130 Morton WA 98356 Office: 2d St and Airport Way Morton WA 98356

INGLE, JOAN MARIE, family nurse practitioner; b. Balt., Nov. 2, 1943; d. Edgar Allen and Mary Virginia (Reese) Peppler; m. Elbert L. Fisher, Nov. 12, 1966 (div. Mar. 1975); children—Heather Marie, Todd Perry; m. 2d, William Kenneth Ingle, Dec. 25, 1979. R.N., Bon Secours Sch. Nursing, Balt., 1964; student U. N.C., 1979-82. Staff nurse Doctors Hosp., Coral Gables, Fla., 1965-68, charge nurse CCU, 1976-78; staff nurse CCU, South Miami Hosp., Miami, Fla., 1978-79; home care supr. Med. Personnel Pool, Asheville, N.C., 1980-81, dir. nurses, 1981-82, dir. home health, 1982. Mem. N.C. Nurses Assn. (chmn. legis. com. 1983-84). Democrat. Baptist. Club: Altrusa (Asheville). Home: PO Box 15434 Asheville NC 28813 Office: Med Personnel Pool 155 Biltmore Ave Asheville NC 28801

INGOLD, WANDA GAIL, city finance director, town clerk; b. Burlington, N.C., Sept. 29, 1952; d. Floyd Lee and Irene (Boswell) I. A.B. in Bus. Edn., Elon Coll., N.C., 1974. Asst. town clk. Town of Siler City, N.C., 1974-75, asst. clk., treas., 1975, town clk., 1975—, fin. dir., 1982—. Mem. Internat. Inst. Mcpl. Clks., N.C. Assn. Mcpl. Clks., N.C. Fin. Officers' Assn., Mcpl. Fin. Officers Assn., Siler City Bus. and Profl. Women's Club (corr. sec. 1977-78, 80-81, 81-82). Republican. Baptist. Avocations: photography, travel, tennis. Home: 112 White Oak Dr Siler City NC 27344 Office: Town of Siler City 311 N 2d Ave Siler City NC 27344

INGRAHAM, TERRY JO, public relations-advertising executive; b. Balt., Dec. 29, 1954; d. Clayton Bailey and Sheila (Ominsky) Hobbs; m. Dan Robert Ingraham, Dec. 17, 1977. A.A. in Journalism, Gulf Coast Community Coll., 1974; B.A. in Journalism with high honors, U. Fla., 1976. Dir. pub. relations Bay Med. Ctr., Panama City, Fla., 1974-77; mktg. dir. Bay Point Yacht Club, Panama City, 1978-80; owner New Dimensions Pub. Relations and Advt., Panama City, 1980—; cons. in field. Chmn. pub. info. Bay County chpt. Am.

Cancer Soc., 1979-83; mem. Muscular Dystrophy Adv. Bd., Home Health of Panama City Adv. Bd., Bay County United Way Adv. Com. mem. Fla. div. Am. Cancer Soc. Pub. Info. Com., Tampa, 1981-85. Named Vol. of Yr., Am. Cancer Soc., 1982; Outstanding Journalist award Gulf Coast Community Coll., 1974. Mem. Bay County C. of C. Methodist. Avocations: creative writing; oil painting; reading; bird training. Address: New Dimensions Public Relations and Advt 714 Grace Ave PO Box 2022 Panama City FL 32402

INGRAHAM-DIETZEN, CAROLYN ANNE, lawyer; b. Jacksonville, N.C., Dec. 16, 1947; d. Robert Edward and Evelyn Anne (Hymel) Ingraham; m. Gary H. Dietzen, Aug. 17, 1985. B.A., U. New Orleans, 1974, M.A., 1977; J.D., Loyola U. of New Orleans, 1979. Bar: La. 1979. Dental asst. Raymond Rocker, Metairie, La., 1966-67; clk. Shell Oil Co., Metairie, 1967-69; sr. clerk Shell Chem. Co., Geismar, La., 1969-71; sole practice, New Orleans, 1979-80; assoc. Keaty, Keaty, & Garvey, New Orleans, 1980-81; sole practice, Lafayette, La., 1981—; dir. Acadiana Open Channel TV, Lafayette, 1984—. Co-author pamphlet: A Guide to Patents, Trademarks and Copyrights for Louisiana Attorneys, 1981, Protecting Your Business through the Use of Patents, Trademarks, Copyrights and Trade Secrets, 1982. Mem. Lafayette Fine Arts Found., 1982—. New Orleans English Speaking Union scholar, Oxford U., 1974. Mem. Acadiana Assn. Women Attys., (v.p. 1981-84), Lafayette Parish Bar Assn. (dir. 1983-84), ABA, Am. Intellectual Property Law Assn., La. Trial Lawyers Assn. Democrat. Episcopalian. Office: Carolyn Ingraham-Dietzen Atty at Law PO Box 54044 Lafayette LA 70505

INGRAHAM-PARSON, VIVIAN JUNE LOWELL, fed. program adminstr.; b. Omaha, June 1, 1922; d. John Calvert and Pearl Mabel (Whitscell) Lowell; student schs. Omaha; m. Clarence Parson, Sept. 7, 1969; children—Richard D. Ingraham, Leroy Lowell Ingraham, John Edwin Ingraham, Jeffrey Scott Ingraham. Supr. customer service Met. Utilities Dist., 1940-46; news reporter Sta. KBON, Omaha, 1962-67; med. transcriber VA Hosp., Omaha, 1971-73; exec. dir. Gt. Plains council Girl Scouts U.S.A., Omaha, 1973-75; job developer City of Omaha, 1976-81; employment coordinator Iowa CETA, 1981—. Exec. com. Mid-Am. council Boy Scouts Am., 1960—, Fontenelle Dist. Boy Scouts Am., 1958-76; youth coordinator Douglas County ARC, 1965-70; dist. II dir. Nebr. State PTA, 1964-68; v.p. Omaha PTA Council, 1966-68; pres. Walnut Hill Sch. PTA, 1958-60, Monroe Sch., 1965-67, Fontenelle Schs., 1962-64; dist. del. Republican Party. Recipient hon. life membership award, nat. and state PTA, 1972; Good Neighbor award Ak-Sar-Ben, 1970; Brotherhood Week-Good Neighbor award NCCJ, 1967; Service award ARC, 1968; nat. officer (Stewards) Nat. Presbyn. Mariners, 1960-66; hon. adm. Nebr. Navy. Mem. Profl. Assn. Girl Scout Execs. Presbyterian. Panelist: Discrimination and Its Effect on Children, 1970; author booklet: A Look at PTA, 1966; contbr. articles to religious mags. Office: 521 S Main St Council Bluffs IA 51501

INGRAM, ARBUTUS BOYD, manufacturing company executive; b. Ferrum, Va., Mar. 29, 1930; d. Ted Lee and Gladys (Spencer) Boyd; student Ferrum Coll., 1947, Cornett Bus. Sch., 1947-48; m. Alexander Fountin Ingram, Jr., Nov. 16, 1948. Sec. to v.p. Clover Creamery, Roanoke, Va., 1948-50; sec. to pres. Double Envelope Corp., Roanoke, Va., 1954-75, v.p., asst. to pres., 1975-78, asst. to chmn., 1977-84; now with Bear Enterprises. Sec. North Roanoke Civic League. Mem. Profl. Secs. Internat. (dir.). Episcopalian. Clubs: Jefferson, Alpine Garden (pres.). Home: 7823 Alpine Rd Roanoke VA 24019 Office: 2115 Crystal Spring Ave Roanoke VA 24014

INGRAM, DONNA GAE, heavy equipment manufacturing company executive; b. San Angelo, Tex., May 25, 1947; d. Wharton Dewain and Edna Mae (Davenport) Dallas; m. Victor Burton, Nov. 11, 1967 (div. 1968); m. Curtis Oneal Ingram, Apr. 1, 1971. Student Brookhaven Coll. Personnel mgr. Searle Optical Co., Dallas, 1967-79, Ferguson Mfg. and Equipment Co., Inc., Dallas 1979—. Mem. Am. Soc. Personnel Adminstrn., Dallas Personnel Assn., Am. Compensation Assn. Republican. Home: 11839 High Meadow Dallas TX 75234 Office: PO Box 1369 Dallas TX 75221

INGRAM, JO LINDA, nurse, office coordinator; b. Osaka, Japan, Aug. 6, 1950; d. William Jennings Bryan and Juanita (Kennemer) Paxton; m. Gene Almontie Ingram, Dec. 22, 1968; 1 son, Jacob Gene. B.S., Tex. Woman's U., Denton, 1972. R.N., Tex.; registered cardio pulmonary technician-invasive cardiology, Tex., Staff nurse, Veteran's Hosp., Dallas, 1972-74; supr. ICU, Garland Community Hosp. (Tex.), 1974-77; office nurse Jack C. Shelton, M.D., Garland, 1977-80, Phoebus Koutras, M.D., Garland, 1981-82; cardiac catherization lab. technician, nurse Baylor U. Med. Ctr., Dallas, 1980-83; office coordinator Robert G. Stone, M.D. Assocs., Dallas, 1983—. Active Circle Ten council Boy Scouts Am., Dallas, 1983. Mem. Am. Assn. Med. Assts. (pres. Garland chpt. 1983, Service award 1980, chaplin Garland chpt. 1980, Service award 1982, Mem. of Yr. award 1983), Nat. Soc. Cardio Pulmonary Technology, Sigma Theta Tau. Home: 11706 Featherbrook Dr Dallas TX 75228

INGRAM, MARY ELLEN, town official; b. Bryson City, N.C., Oct. 8, 1931; d. John Wright Higdon and Mary Ellen (Crisp) Higdon Christopher; m. Herbert Dewitt Ingram, Jr., June 6, 1953; children—Melanie, DeWitt. Student George Washington U., 1950-53. Cert. mcpl. clk. Sec., librarian U.S. Govt., Washington, Alaska and Taiwan, 1950-63; sec. Frank Briscoe Co., Leesburg, Va., 1971-75; town clk. Town of Herndon, Va., 1975—; sec. The White House, Washington, 1977-78. Active Loudoun County Republican Women, 1975—, Episcopal Women, St. James Ch., Leesburg, Va., 1974—. Mem. Bus. and Profl. Women (Woman of Yr. 1981), DAR, Internat. Inst. Mcpl. Clks., Va. Mcpl. Clks. Assn. Home: 104 Morven Park Rd SW Leesburg VA 22075 Office: Town of Herndon 730 Elden St Herndon VA 22070

INGRAM-EDMONDS, BARBARA JEAN, union official, writer; b. Mineola, N.Y., May 13, 1960; d. William L. and Evor (Jarvis) I. B.S. in Pub. Policy, Cornell U., 1982. Cert. microcomputers, database systems, word processing. Pub. relations asst. Cornell U., Ithaca, N.Y., 1981-82; legis. aide Nat. Hosp. Union 1199, N.Y.C., 1981, occupational safety cons., 1982, research asst., 1982, contract coordinator, 1982-84; asst. dir. research and negotiations dist. council 37 AFSCME, AFL-CIO, N.Y.C., 1983—. Co-editor The Cornell Exchange, 1979-80; contbg. editor Community Weekly Newspaper, Westbury Times, 1981, 84; contbg. poet student publs., 1981, Presstime Poets Corner, 1983, 83 (Semi Final Poet award 1983, 84). Labor union coordinator Nat. Mobilization March on Washington, 1983; mem. Lawyers and Legal Workers for Working Women, Coalition of Labor Union Women, N.Y.C. Mem. Women in Communication, Cornell Alumni Assn. Home: 162 E 2d St Apt 2B New York NY 10009 Office: Dist 37 AFSCME 125 Barclay St New York NY 10004

INGRAO, GLORIA D'ANGELO, clothing manufacturing company executive; b. N.Y.C., Apr. 2, 1929; d. Nicholas A. and Angela Marie (Rossello) D'Angelo; m. Joseph A. Ingrao, Sept. 1, 1952; children—Nannette Ingrao Conners, Anthony G., Angela I. Ingrao Powers. B.S. with honors in Commerce, Coll. of Mt. St. Vincent, 1950; M.A. in Edn., NYU, 1968. Acct. Smith Ranscht, Mitchell and Croake, Attys., White Plains, N.Y., 1950-54; substitute tchr. Pelham Schs., N.Y., 1968-75; adminstr. D'Angelo Suits and Coats, N.Y.C., 1975-77; adminstr., pres. d'Angelo Originals, Ltd., N.Y.C., 1978—. Vice pres. Chester Heights Women's Club, Eastchester, N.Y., 1955-60; solicitor ARC, Community Chest, Catholic Charities, others; vol. Mother Socs. of Iona Prep Holy Child Sch., Good Counsel Acad., 1960-76; publicity chmn. St. Catharine's-Mothers Soc. Coll. Mt. St. Vincent scholar, 1946-50. Mem. Nat. Orgn. Italian Am. Women, Am. Assn. Cloak and Suit Mfrs., Coll. Mt. St. Vincent Alumnae Assn. (fund agent, mem. fund for 80s), Ladies of Charity. Republican. Lodge: Columbiettes. Home: 15 Archer Dr Bronxville NY 10708 Office: D'Angelo Originals Ltd 575 8th Ave New York NY 10018

INIE, RUTH JENIFER, retail mail order company executive; b. York, Eng., Mar. 3, 1953; came to U.S., 1980; d. Victor and Doreen (Buttery) I.; m. H. David Richards, Mar. 15, 1980. C.Q.S.W., Stevenage Coll., Eng., 1976; B.S., Empire State Coll., 1982; M.B.A., Simmons Coll., 1983. Dep. prin. Ukia Girls High Sch., Kenya, 1972-73; project coordinator Lambeth Borough Council, Eng., 1979-80; pub. mgr. Small Bus. Found. Am., Boston, 1984; pres. Abilities Internat., Elizabethtown, N.Y., 1984—; cons. Automated Assemblies Corp., Clinton, Mass., 1983, Parker Bros., Beverly, Mass., 1983. Prodn. mgr. book: Exportise, 1983. Mem. Nat. Assn. Female Execs., Champlain Valley Bus. and Profl. Women, Adirondack North Country Assn. Avocations: gardening; tennis. Home: PO Box 398 Elizabethtown NY 12932 Office: Abilities Internat Old Forge Rd Elizabethtown NY 12932

INKELES, ELLEN-JANE OPAT, design account executive, promotion specialist; b. N.Y.C., Aug. 24, 1953; d. David S. and Ami Winifred (Sear) Opat; m. Bennett Evan Inkeles, Feb. 20, 1983. B.A., Douglas Coll.-Rutgers U., 1975. Asst. editor Print Mag., N.Y.C., 1975-77; supr. coll. advt. Prentice-Hall, Englewood Cliffs, N.J., 1977-78; asst. mgr. direct mail Cambridge U. Press, N.Y.C., 1979-81; advt. and promotion mgr. Franklin Watts, Grolier, N.Y.C., 1981-83; trade sales adminstr. Random House, N.Y.C., 1983-84; prin. Opat Ink, 1983—. Asst. editor: 37 Design and Environment Awards, 1977; Print Casebooks 2, 1977. Mem. Assn. Reform Zionists Am., N.Y.C., 1980—, Handgun Control, Inc., 1981—. Mem. Nat. Assn. Female Execs., Pubs. Ad Club. Democrat. Jewish. Office: 170 Van Buren Ave Teaneck NJ 07666

INMAN, LINDA ROOP, computer career consultant executive; b. Knoxville, Tenn., Aug. 10, 1949; d. James Kyle and Anna Lee (Hulen) Roop; m. Benjamin Fox Inman, Nov. 1, 1975. B.S. in Bus. Adminstrn., Knoxville-U. Tenn., 1972. Acctg. analyst Union Carbide Corp., Oak Ridge, 1972-75; systems analyst Tenn. Dept. Revenue, Nashville, 1975-77, systems analyst dir., 1977-78; adminstrv. aide polit. campaign, Nashville, 1978; BMS territory mgr. Burroughs Corp., Nashville, 1978-80, ter. mgr., 1980-82, mktg. mgr., 1982-84; acct. rep. Wang Labs., Nashville, 1984; dir. Computer Career Cons. Inc., Nashville, 1984—. Mem., Nat. Democratic Women's Club, Nashville, 1976-86; vol. WDCN-TV Action Auction, Nashville, 1984; vol. YWCA, Nashville, 1985-86; v.p. Davidson County Democratic Women's Club, Nashville, 1986, numerous other civic activities. Recipient numerous awards for profl. excellence including: Achievement Club, Computer Career Cons. Inc., 1985. Mem. Nat. Assn. Female Execs., Nat. Assn. Profl. Saleswomen (hospitality com. 1983-86), Seminars Chairmen Assn. of Systems Mgmt. Democrat. Baptist. Office: Computer Career Cons Inc 2 Brentwood Commons Suite 103 Brentwood TN 37027

INNES, GEORGETTE MEYER, real estate and insurance broker; b. Wilmington, Del., Mar. 20, 1918; d. George and Flora Sue (Saunders) Meyer; m. Andrew T. Innes, Jr., Nov. 26, 1947 (dec.). Grad. high sch.; cert. appraiser Villanova Coll, 1974. Lic. Realtor, Pa.; ins. broker. Realtor, Phila., 1945—; ins. broker, Phila., 1946—, also appraiser. Mem., speaker Juniata Park Civic Assn., Phila., 1984. Mem. Phila. Women's Realty Assn. (pres. 1949-51; Woman of Yr. 1972-73; pres. bd. govs. 1949-85), Am. Bus. Women's Assn. (chpt. v.p. 1971), North Phila. Realty Bd. (v.p. 1975, 76, pres. 1977, Gustav A. Wick award 1979), Delaware Council Realty Bds. (sec. 1974), Real Estate Multiple Listing Burs. (treas. 1972-76), Nat. Assn. Realtors (sec.-treas. and v.p. chpt. 1975-80), Phila. Bd. Realtors (v.p. residential div. 1975), Sigma Lambda Soc. (chpt. pres. 1948). Avocations: golf; dancing; gardening; cooking; embroidery. Home: 1367 Woodland Rd Rydal PA 19046

INNIS, PAULINE, author, newspaper company executive; b. Devon, Eng.; came to U.S., 1954; m. Walter Deane Innis, Aug. 1, 1959. Student U. Manchester, U. London. Author: Hurricane Fighters, 1962; Ernestine or the Pig in the Potting Shed, 1963; The Wild Swans Fly, 1964; The Ice Bird, 1965; Wind of the Pampas, 1967; Fire from the Fountains, 1968; Astronumerology, 1971; Gold in the Blue Ridge, 1973, 2d edit., 1980; My Trails (transl. from French), 1975; (with Mary Jane McCaffery) Protocol, 1977; Prayer and Power in the Capital, 1982. Bd. dirs. Washington Goodwill Industries Guild, 1962-66; membership chmn. Welcome to Washington Club, 1961-64; co-chmn. Internat. Workshop Capital Speakers' Club, 1961-64; pres. Children's Book Guild, 1967-68; dir. Ednl. Communications; bd. dirs. Internat. Conf. Women Writers and Journalists; mem. criminal justice com. D.C. Commn. on Status of Women; founder vol. program D.C. Women's Detention Center; chmn. women's com. Washington Opera, 1977-79; mem. Liaison Com. for Med. Edn., 1979-85; nat. trustee Med. Coll., Pa., 1980—; bd. dirs. Kahill Gibran Found., 1983—; mem. Edn. Council for Fgn. Med. Grads., 1986—. Named Hoosier Woman of Yr., 1966. Mem. Soc. Woman Geographers, Authors League, Smithsonian Assocs. (women's bd.), English-Speaking Union (dir.), Spanish-Portuguese Group D.C. (pres. 1965-66), Brit. Inst. U.S. Clubs: Am. Newspaper Women's (pres. 1971-73), Nat. Press. Home: 2700 Virginia Ave NW Washington DC 20037 also Skipper's Row Gibson Island MD

INSELBERG, MARCIA BERNSTEIN, rehabilitation counselor, civic worker; b. Peoria, Ill., 1948; d. Stanley and Bettye (Miller) Bernstein; m. Carl David Inselberg, Aug. 31, 1969; 1 child, Robert Frederick. Student, U. Mo., 1966-68; B.A. in Bus. Adminstrn., Bradley U., 1970; M.S., DePaul U., 1977; postgrad. No. Ill. U., 1977. Cert. rehab. counselor. Service mgr., asst. floor supr., Famous Barr, St. Louis, 1969-71; adjudicator VA, St. Louis, 1970-71; community worker Ill. Inst. for Soc. Policy, Peoria, 1971-72; rehab. counselor III, office mgr. Vocat. Incentive Program, Peoria, 1972-78; supr. work eval., counselor alt. employment program, counselor work adjustment Vocat. Guidance and Rehab. Services, Cleve., 1978-80; workmen's compensation specialist Hand Surgery Assocs. of Ind., Indpls. Clinic vol. Planned Parenthood, 1973-74, mem. legis. awareness com., 1974-77; mem. hospitality com. Lakeview Ctr. for Arts and Scis., 1973, chmn., 1974-75, mem. Muse bd., 1974-76, arts and scis. del., 1976; mem. Peoria Panhellenic, 1973-78, v.p., 1974, pres., 1975; campaign worker United Way, 1974-75, team leader, 1975, allocation panel mem., 1975-78; speakers bur. chairperson Peoria Child Abuse Consortium, 1974-75; program chmn. Organ. Rehab. through Tng., 1974, council del., 1976; campaign worker Jewish Community Council, 1973-75, del. at large, 1974-75; mem. pub. relations com. Peoria Easter Seals, 1976-78; bd. dirs. Peoria Multiple Sclerosis, 1977-78; steering com. mem. Access Peoria, 1977-78, publ. relations. com., site-selection com.; adv. com. mem. Access Cleve., 1979-81, vol. tng. coordinator, 1980, distbn. com. adv. bd., 1981; mem. Nat. Council Jewish Women, 1979—, lunch bunch vol., program survey com., emergency shelter care vol., 1980-82, bd. dirs. 1981, asst. to v.p. community service, Cleve. Shalom vol., 1981-82, bd. dirs., 1983—, co-chmn. retail ops., 1983-85, fin. sec., 1985, mem. fin. com., 1984-85, collectors choice-set-up com., 1984; chmn. Las Vegas Night Solicitations, 1980-81, fundraising com., 1981-82; bd. dirs., workshop adv. com., personnel adv. com. United Cerebral Palsy, 1981-82; post partum caller BORN Line, 1980-82, ad hoc adminstrv. com., 1981; co-chmn. Young Peoples Congregation membership, 1979-80, religious sch. com., 1981-82; mem. Suburban presch. PTA, 1980-83, newspaper chmn., 1981-82; Pepper Pike del. to Internat. Yr of Disabled Persons, Fedn. for Community Planning, 1981, audio-visual com., 1981-82; alumni bd. Bradley U., 1977-78, parents/alum recruiting com., 1978-82; writer Jr. League of Indpls., 1983-85, contbr. to annual report, 1984, ad salesperson for Review, 1985, pub. relations com., 1984—, vol. for children's day at Connor Prairie; calendar treas. Hadassah, 1984-85, bd. dirs., membership chairperson, 1985-86; mother's council, room mother, library asst. Park Tudor Sch.; mem. welcome com. Columns connection Alpha Epsilon Phi; bd. dirs., program chairperson, Indpls. Hebrew Congregation Sisterhood, 1985-87; registrar Indpls. Youth Hockey Assn. Recipient award of merit United Jewish Appeal, 1975. Mem. Ill. Rehab. Assn. (chpt. pres., state conv. chmn. 1976, state pres. elect 1977-78), Counselor Adv. Com.-State of Ill. div. Vocat. Rehab. (alternate 1976-77, del. 1977-78), Ill. Rehab. Counselor Assn., Peoria Client Assessment Team Consortium (del. 1977-78), Ohio Rehab. Assn. (state constitution com. 1978-79), Northeast Ohio Rehab. Assn. (sec. 1979), Ohio Rehab. Counseling Assn. (awards com. chmn. 1979-80), Nat. Rehab. Assn., Nat. Rehab. Counseling Assn. Avocations: needlework, reading. Home: 10387 Briar Creek Pl Carmel IN 46032

INSELMAN, LAURA SUE, pediatrician; b. Bklyn., Nov. 2, 1944; d. Alexander M. and Rae (Bloom) Inselman. B.A., Barnard Coll., 1966; M.D., Med. Coll. Pa., 1970. Intern St. Lukes Hosp. Ctr., N.Y.C., 1970-73; fellow in pediatric pulmonary disease Babies Hosp., N.Y.C., 1973-76; chief pediatric pulmonary div. Interfaith Med. Ctr., Bklyn., 1976-81; chief pediatric pulmonary div. North Shore Univ. Hosp., Manhasset, N.Y., 1981—; asst. prof. pediatrics Cornell U. Med. Coll., N.Y.C., 1981—; mem. staff Good Samaritan Hosp., West Islip, N.Y. Bd. dirs. Am. Lung Assn. Nassau-Suffolk, East Meadow, N.Y., 1983—. Fellow Am. Acad. Pediatrics, Am. Coll. Chest Physicians; mem. Am. Thoracic Soc., Am. Fedn. Clin. Research, N.Y. Acad. Medicine, Harvey Soc. Office: North Shore University Hosp 300 Community Dr Manhasset NY 11030

INTVELDT-WORK, SUSAN MARIE, psychologist, consultant; b. Waverly, Iowa, Oct. 14, 1948; d. Frederick Durand and Lucille Hazel (Erbes) Infelt; m. Mitchell Robert Work, Mar. 9, 1979; children—Jessica Olney, Emily Christine. B.A. magna cum laude, Wartburg Coll., 1971; M.S., U. Fla., 1976; Ph.D., U. Pa., 1983. Dir. spl. services Central Coll., Pella, Iowa, 1976-78; psychologist U. Pa., Phila., 1979-82, Del. Valley Psychol. Clinics, Phila., 1982—. Cons., bd. dirs. Women's Network, Inc., 1980-83; mem. adv. bd. Stepping Stones program Bucks County Community Coll., Pa., 1982-83; cons. Bucks County Adv. Council on Women, 1983—. Mem. Am. Psychol. Assn., Pa. Psychol. Assn., Phil. Soc. Clin. Psychologists, Kappa Alpha Theta Alumnae Assn. Democrat. Lutheran. Avocations: antiques; decorating; travel; reading. Home: 853 Crown St Morrisville PA 19067 Office: Del Valley Psychol Clinics 1536 Pratt St Philadelphia PA 19124

IOANES, JOYCE, lawyer, social worker; b. Washington, Feb. 23, 1944; d. Raymond Andrew and Irma Elizabeth (Blazo) I.; B.A. in French Lit., Dunbarton Coll., Washington, 1965; M.S. in Psychiat. Social Work, Simmons Coll., 1971; J.D. cum laude, Suffolk U., 1983. Bar: R.I. 1983, U.S. Cts. 1984, Mass. 1985; cert. Acad. Cert. Social Workers, 1978. Social caseworker R.I. Dept. Social and Rehab. Services, Cranston and Providence, 1968-74, casework supr., Cranston and Johnston, R.I., 1974-77; therapist Northwestern Mental Health Clinic, Greenville, R.I., 1974-75, Washington County Mental Health Clinic, Charlestown, R.I., 1977-79; mental health profl. R.I. Mental Health Advs. Office, Cranston, 1977—, atty., 1983—; sole practice, Jamestown, 1983—; field instr. R.I. Coll., Roger Williams Coll., 1975-77, Providence Coll., 1975-81; mem. Gov.'s Task Force Community Placement of Geriatric Patients, 1977-81. Recipient Am. Jurisprudence award, 1980-81. Mem. Nat. Assn. Social Workers, ABA, R.I. Bar Assn. Home: 78 Columbia Ave Jamestown RI 02835 Office: Rhode Island Mental Health Advocates Office RIMC Cottage 405 Cranston RI 02920

IOANNIDIS, LESLIE PAMELA COOK, mathematics educator, researcher; b. Kingston, Ont., Can., Aug. 23, 1946; came to U.S., 1956; d. Leslie G. and Alfreda M. Cook; m. George A. Ioannidis, Nov. 26, 1972; children—Alexander, James. B.A., U. Rochester, 1967; M.S., Cornell U., 1969, Ph.D., 1971. NATO postdoctoral fellow U. Utrecht (Netherlands), 1971-72; research assoc., instr. Cornell U., Ithaca, N.Y., 1972-73; asst. prof. UCLA, 1973-80; assoc. prof. math., 1980—; assoc. prof. math. U. Del., Newark, 1983—. Author: Transonic Aerodynamics. NDEA Title IV fellow Cornell U., 1967-70; NSF grad. fellow, 1970-71; NSF grantee UCLA, U. Del., 1977—. Mem. Soc. Indsl. and Applied Math. (council 1984—), Am. Math. Soc., Am. Phys. Soc. Office: Math Dept Ewing Hall U Del Newark DE 19716

IORFIDA, DIANE MARY, personnel administrator; b. Chgo., Sept. 21, 1954; d. Boleslaus and Genevieve Marie (Sumara) Laskowski; m. Samuel Joseph Iorfida, Sept. 13, 1975. B.A. in English, DePaul U., 1975, postgrad. 1975-76; M.S., Notre Dame U. (Ind.), 1984. Lic. tchr., Ill., Ind. Tng. coordinator Saxon Home Care Ctrs., Chgo., 1971-75; reading specialist Dept. Spl. Edn., LaGrange, Ill., 1975-76; tng. coordinator LaGrange State Bank, 1976-78; dir. tng. and personnel Garatoni & Assocs., South Bend, Ind., 1978; asst. dir. personnel Elkhart Gen. Hosp. (Ind.), 1978-80, dir. personnel, 1980—. Editorial bd. Am. Soc. Personnel Adminstrn., 1980-84; contbr. to profl. jour. Mem. Ind. Soc. Hosp. Personnel Adminstrn. (bd. dirs. 1980—, pres. 1983-84), Am. Compensation Assn., Ind. Personnel Assn., Am. Soc. Personnel Adminstrn., Michiana Soc. Personnel Adminstrn., Greater Elkhart Personnel Assn., Ind. Hosp. Assn., Am. Hosp. Assn., Am. Soc. Hosp. Personnel Assn. Office: Elkhart Gen Hosp Dept Personnel 600 East Blvd Elkhart IN 46514

IRBY, LEILANI JUNE, nursing educator; b. Idaho Springs, Colo., Feb. 26, 1939; d. Robert C. and Bernice M. (Reimer) McClain; R.N., Grace-New Haven Sch. Nursing, New Haven, 1958; B.S.N., U. Okla., 1967, M.S., 1974, Ph.D., 1983; m. Michael Eugene Irby, Aug. 27, 1966; children—Michelle, Michael. Staff nurse/supr. Presbyn. and Mt. Sinai hosps., N.Y.C., Good Samaritan Hosp., Phoenix and Cedars-Sinai Hosp., Los Angeles, 1958-66; chief nurse Central Okla. Mental Health Center, Norman, 1967-72; nurse epidemiologist, asst. dir. nursing St. Anthony Hosp., Oklahoma City, 1974-77; instr. Central State U., Edmond, Okla., 1977-81, asst. prof., 1981-85, assoc. prof., 1985—. Active public edn. and screening for diabetes and hypertension; resource person Redlands council Girls Scouts U.S.A., local PTA; Sunday sch. tchr. New Convenant United Methodist Ch., 1968—. Mem. Am. Nurses Assn., Okla. Nurses Assn., Phi Delta Kappa, Sigma Theta Tau. Democrat. Club: Edmond Garden. Edmond Soccer. Home: 616 S Firelane Rd Edmond OK 73034 Office: 100 N University Dr Edmond OK 73034

IRBY, TERRY RENEE, adult basic education specialist, educator; b. New Orleans, May 23, 1949; d. John Duddley and Alice Paerl (Leonard) McEwen; B.S. in Edn., So. Ill. U., 1970, M.S. in Rehab. Counseling, 1973, Ph.D. in Edn., 1978; m. Harry J. Irby, Aug. 22, 1970; children—Harry Vincent, James Courtland, Traci Donayle. Tchr., A.O. Marshall Sch., Joliet, Ill., 1970-71, counselor Office of Off Campus Housing So. Ill. U., 1971-73, counselor Counseling Ctr., 1972-73, admissions coordinator Med. Sch., 1973-78; asst. dir. acad. and health affairs Bd. Higher Edn. State of Ill., Springfield, 1978-81; asst. dean, dir. office student services U. Ill. Coll. Nursing, 1981-82; career vocat. specialist, instr. Joliet Jr. Coll., 1983-84, dir. adult edn., instr., 1984—; evaluator AMA, 1979—, Ill. State Bd. Edn., 1980—, Nat. Accrediting Commn. of Cosmetology Arts & Scis., 1980—, North Central Accrediting Assn. of Colls. and Schs.; mem. Gov.'s Task Force of Voluntary Citizen Participation, 1981. V.p. League Women Voters, Springfield, 1980-81. Nat. Edn. Policy Fellows program fellow, 1979-80. Mem. Am. Personnel and Guidance Assn., AAUW, Nat. Assn. Women Deans and Counselors, Alpha Kappa Alpha. Baptist. Author: Craigs New Haircut, 1969, Renee & the Devil, 1969; contbr. poetry and essays. Home: 511 Wheeler Ave Joliet IL 60436

IRELAND, PAIGE VALENTINE, institutional director; b. Englewood, N.J., Apr. 28, 1954; d. Lloyd Owen and Frances (Valentine) I. B.S., Cornell U., 1976, M.B.A., 1983. Research specialist, v.p. research Cornell U., Ithaca, N.Y., 1974-79; research planning assoc. Instl. Planning and Analysis, Cornell U., Ithaca, 1979-83; dir., 1983—. Product sales chmn. Camp Fire, Ithaca, 1983, bd. dirs., 1983. Mem. Soc. Coll. and Univ. Planners, Assn. Inst. Research, North East Assn. Instl. Research, Kappa Kappa Gamma. Home: 1036 East Shore Dr Ithaca NY 14850 Office: Cornell U 235 Day Hall Ithaca NY 14853

IRELAND, PAMELA WOODHULL, department store buyer; b. Englewood, N.J., May 14, 1957; d. Lloyd Owen and Frances Woodhull (Valentine) I. B.A. magna cum laude, Hobart and William Smith Coll., 1979. Asst. buyer B. Altman & Co., N.Y.C., 1979-80, sr. asst. buyer, 1980-82, buyer children's accessories and sleepwear, 1982-83, buyer infants and toddler apparel, 1983—. Mem. St. Bartholomews Community Club, N.Y.C., 1985-86. Mem. Phi Beta Kappa. Avocations: tennis; travel. Office: B Altman & Co 361 5th Ave New York NY 10016

IREY, CHARLOTTE YORK, educator; b. Oklahoma City, Arp. 29, 1918; d. Charles William and Annie Charlotte (Upsher) York; B.S. with honors, U. Wis., 1940; M.A., U. Colo., 1965; m. Eugene Floyd Irey, June 10, 1942; 1 dau., Susan Gail. Instr. dance Stephens Coll., Columbia, Mo., 1940-43; prof. dance U. Colo., Boulder, 1945—, chmn. dance div., dept. theatre and dance, 1973—. Recipient Robert L. Steans award U. Colo., Boulder, 1973, Thomas Jefferson award, 1980; Mem. Nat. Dance Assn. (pres. 1975-76, Scholar of Yr. 1982-83), AAHPERD, Am. Coll. Dance Festival, Council Dance Adminstrs., Congress Dance Research, Am. Dance Guild. Episcopalian. Author: (with Frances Bascom) Costume Cues, 1952. Charlotte York Irey Studio/Theatre at U. Colo., Boulder named in her honor, 1984. Office: U Colo Box 261 Boulder CO 80309

IRLAND, LORRAINE, systems consultant; b. Newark, Dec. 21, 1946; d. Allen Robert and Evelyn (Lusardi) Zensen; m. Michael Joseph Berger, Feb. 13, 1966 (div. 1971); 1 child, Michael Louis Berger; m. James Frederick Irland, Dec. 28, 1983; 1 child, Kevin Frederick. A.A. in Bus. Mgmt., Diablo Valley Coll., 1979; B.A. in Bus. Adminstrn., Upper Iowa U., 1983; M.S. in Corp. Planning, U. Pa., 1986. Communications cons. Pacific Telephone & Telegraph Co., San Francisco, 1969-80; industry cons. AT&T, Basking Ridge, N.J., 1981-84; systems cons. Pitney Bowes, Inc., San Antonio, 1985-86. Mem. Nat. Assn. Female Execs., Inc., AAUW. Republican. Roman Catholic. Clubs: Goebel Collector's (N.Y.); Model A Ford (Calif.). Avocations: antiques; needlepoint; fashion design; antique Model A cars; floral arranging. Home: 5801 Spring Village San Antonio TX 78247 Office: Pitney Bowes Inc 231 W Cypress St San Antonio TX 78231

IRONS, PATRICIA DOUBLEDAY, magazine editor; b. N.Y.C., Mar. 25, 1934; d. George Chester and Mary (Kelley) Doubleday; m. Henry Clay Irons, July 10, 1954; children—Henry Clay, G. Chester, Carol Irons Ross. B.A., Vassar Coll., 1956. Asst. editor Ladies Home Jour., N.Y.C., 1952-54; assoc. editor Baby Talk Mag., N.Y.C., 1957-76, editor-in-chief, 1976—. Mem. Am. Soc. Mag. Editors. Republican. Roman Catholic. Office: Baby Talk Mag 185 Madison Ave New York NY 10016

IRSCH, CAROLYN RUTH, personnel executive; b. Chgo., Dec. 31, 1953; d. Paul Edward and Adele Loraine (Schultz) I.; m. Kenneth Edward Condy, Nov. 15, 1980. B.A. in Psychology, U. Ill., 1976. Office mgr. Greyhound Personnel, Chgo., 1976; personnel rep. Stewart-Warner, Chgo., 1976-79; supr. compensation ITT, Des Plaines, Ill., 1979-81; supr. personnel Long John Silvers, Des Plaines, 1981; mgr. employment and compensation Ben Franklin Stores, Des Plaines, 1981—. Mem. personnel com. Chgo. YWCA, 1983-84. Mem. Am. Soc. Personnel Adminstrs., Women in Mgmt., Internat. Assn. Personnel Women, Nat. Assn. Female Execs., Women's Ednl. Service Assn., Internat. Platform Assn. Club: Des Plaines Toastmasters (ednl. v.p.). Home: 4234 W Nelson St Chicago IL 60641 Office: Ben Franklin Stores div Household Merchandising Inc 1700 S Wolf St Des Plaines IL 60018

IRVIN, GEORGIA KENNEDY, consulting executive; b. Williston, S.C., June 27, 1932; d. Quincy Adolphus and Kate Baxter (Boylston) Kennedy; m. Henry Stuart Irvin, Dec. 27, 1957; children—Henry Stuart, Kate Kennedy. B.A., U. S.C., 1955. Tchr. Md. Pub. Schs., Leonardtown, 1958-60; v.p. Q.A. Kennedy, Inc., Williston, S.C., 1963-82; dir. admissions, fin. aid Sidwell Friends Sch., Washington, 1969-84; pres., chief exec. officer Georgia K. Irvin & Assocs., Inc., Chevy Chase, Md., 1984—; cons. Nat. Assn. of Ind. Schs., Boston, 1984—; lectr. Ednl. Workshops, 1975—. Trustee, The Black Student Fund, Washington, 1980—; bd. dirs. Sch. Scholar Service, Princeton, N.J., 1975-79. Mem. Secondary Sch. Admissions Test Bd. (com. chmn. 1981—), Ind. Ednl. Counselors Assn. Democrat. Episcopalian. Home: 5507 Center St Chevy Chase MD 20815 Office: Georgia K Irvin and Assocs 4701 Willard Ave Suite 227 Chevy Chase MD 20815

IRVIN, KATHRYN JEANETTE, educator; b. Tallahassee, Nov. 16, 1947; d. LeRoy Clinton and Lilly Mae (Pope) Sneed; m. Willie James Irvin, June 24, 1965 (div. Nov. 1975); children—Angela Kay, Cynthia Lillette. B.A., Fla. A&M U.; M.Ed., Fla. Atlantic U. Tchr., Palm Beach County Schs., West Palm Beach, Fla., 1969—, head tchr. adult spl. edn., 1985—, media rep. adult edn., 1985—. Author: Black, Brown and Amber, 1979, Comes a Riderless Horse, 1983, reading home tutoring system Tutor Your Child, 1983. Dir. Kambi Youth Theatre, West Palm Beach, 1979-82; tech. dir. Performing Arts Summer Sch., Palm Beach Gardens, Fla., 1983-84, 85. Recipient 1st place award Cleveland Creative Arts, Tenn., 1981, Walter Bogle award Creative Arts Guild, 1983. Mem. Nat. Writers Club (hon. mention 1983), NEA, Fla. Freelance Writers (1st pl. awards 1984, 85), Classroom Tchrs. Assn. Club: Sisterhood Palm Beach Women. Avocations: drawing, painting, collecting art objects. Home: 312 Baker Dr West Palm Beach FL 33409

IRVINE, EVELYN ADAMS, cosmetologist; b. Stanley County, N.C., Mar. 8, 1928; d. Lee Jerome and Carrie (Brooks) Walters; student Thomas Nelson Community Coll., Hampton, Va., 1978-79; m. Gerald W. Irvine, June 5, 1983; 1 son, James Glenn Adams. Hairdresser, Charlotte, N.C., 1942-52; owner Grant's Beauty Salon, Newport News and Hampton, 1953—, Jan Mar of Norfolk and Williamsburg, Va., 1953—, Laines House of Beauty, Newport News, 1953—, Hayes Beauty, Inc., Newport News and Hayes, Va., 1978—; owner Jan-Mar Beauty, Inc., Jan-Mar Beauty Acad., 1968—; mem. Va. State Bd. Cosmetology, 1982—. Mem. Nat. Assn. Cosmetology Schs. (sec. 1974), Tchrs. Ednl. Council (pres. 1975-77), Am. Bus. Women's Assn., Nat. Hairdressers Assn., Va. Hairdressers Assn. Democrat. Jewish. Address: Tchrs Ednl Council 411 Jan Mar Dr Newport News VA 23606

IRVING, AMY, actress; b. Palo Alto, Calif., Sept. 10, 1953; student Am. Conservatory Theatre, London Acad. Dramatic Art. Films include Carrie, The Fury, Voices, Honeysuckle Rose, The Competition, Yentl, Mickey and Maude; TV appearances include: The Rookies, Policewoman, Happy Days, Panache, I'm A Fool, Dynasty, Voices, Once An Eagle; appeared as Juliet in Romeo and Juliet, Seattle Repertory Theatre, 1982-83; appeared on Broadway in Amadeus, 1981-82; on Broadway in Heartbreak House, 1983-84, on Showtime, 1985. Office: David Hunter Kimball Parseghian Rifkin 7319 Beverly Blvd Los Angeles CA 90036*

IRWIN, MIRIAM DIANNE OWEN, miniature book publisher, writer; b. Columbus, Ohio, June 14, 1930; d. John Milton and Miriam Faith (Studebaker) Owen; m. Kenneth John Irwin, June 5, 1960; 1 child, Christopher Owen Irwin. B.S. in Home Econs., Ohio State U., 1952, postgrad. in bus. adminstrn., 1961-62. Editorial asst. Am. Home Mag., N.Y.C., 1953-56; salesman Owen Realty, Dayton, Ohio, 1957-58, Clevenger Realty, Phoenix, 1958-59; home economist Columbus and So. Ohio Electric Co., 1959-60; pub. Mosaic Press, Cin., 1977—. Author: Lute and Lyre, 1977; Forty is Fine, 1977; Miriam Mouse's Survival Manual, 1977; Miriam Mouse's Costume Collection, 1977; Miriam Mouse's Marriage Contract, 1977; Miriam Mouse, Rock Hound, 1977; Silver Bindings, 1983. Editor: Tribute to the Arts, 1984. Illustrator: Corals of Pennekamp, 1979. Daytime crew chief Wyoming Life Squad, Ohio, 1965-70. Mem. Internat. Guild Miniature Artisans, Miniature Book Soc. (bd. dirs. 1983—), Am. Philol. Assn. Republican. Presbyterian. Avocation: book collecting. Home and Office: 358 Oliver Rd Cincinnati OH 45215

IRWIN, NAN KELLY, real estate executive; b. Lubbock, Tex., May 15; d. Samuel Edgar and Molly (Stratton) Kelly; m. Raulie Lee Irwin, Oct. 6, 1945 (dec.); children—Raulie Lee Jr., Lenora Mae. Grad. Real Estate Inst. Cashier, Humble Oil & Refinery Co. (now Exxon), Ingleside, Tex., 1941-49; Irwin Real Estate, ptnr. Irwin & Irwin Devel. Co., Rockport, Tex., 1955—; sec.-treas. Brashear-Irwin Industries, Inc., 1959-66, Irwin Industries, Inc., 1972-80; v.p. Aransas-San Patricio County Bd Realtors, 1960-61, sec.-treas., 1967-68. Republican. Methodist. Club: Ingleside Woman's (pres. 1954-55). Office: Irwin Properties & Investments Hwy 35 S Rockport TX 78382

IRWIN, NANCY BARBARA, chemical company executive; b. Cleve., Apr. 16, 1944; d. L.M. and Barbara L. (Boer) I.; m. Joseph Wilson Prejean, Jr., June 2, 1979; 1 son, Lawrence Kapaekukui Irwin Prejean. B.A., Miami U., Oxford, Ohio, 1965; M.B.A., Cleve. State U., 1977. Internat. mktg. mgr. The Harshaw Chem. Co., Cleve., 1975-79; regional mgr. AKZO Chemie Americas, Houston, 1980-83; treas. The KIP Co., Cleve., 1983—; cons. in field. Served to capt. WAC, U.S. Army, 1965-72. Mem. 1st Spl. Forces Group (hon.), Chem. Mktg. Research Assn., Sigma Kappa. Episcopalian. Office: The KIP Co 1925 Lakeview Ave Cleveland OH 44116-2413

ISAAC, MARGRETHE GLORIA, educator; b. Chgo., May 6, 1927; s. Merle J. and Margrethe D. (Lehmann) I.; B.E., Chgo. Tchrs. Coll., 1947; M.A., Northwestern U., 1950, Ph.D., 1962. Tchr., Chgo. Pub. Schs., 1947-58; instr. TV Tchrs. Coll., WGN-TV, Chgo., 1958-59; asst. prof. Chgo. Tchrs. Coll., 1959-61; assoc. prof. Northeastern Ill. U., Chgo., 1961—, assoc. chmn. dept. early childhood edn., 1968-71, 73-80, chmn., 1980—; vis. faculty Northwestern U., summer 1964. Mem. exec. com. elem. sch. sect. Nat. Safety Council, 1972-81, vice-chmn., 1975-76, chmn., 1976-77, mem. exec. com. sch. and coll. div., 1976-81, bd. dirs., 1977-80; book reviewer Ill. Reading Service, 1971-76; mem. adv. com. Child Safety Club, 1977—. Recipient Outstanding Service award Nat. Safety Council, 1977. Mem. Chgo. Pub. Schs. Kindergarten-Primary Assn. (pres. 1954-56), Ill. Edn. Assn. (pres. Chgo. div. 1964-65, Disting. Service award 1967), Ill. Assn. Higher Edn. (pres. 1968-69), Assn. Childhood Edn. Internat. (chmn. various coms. 1954—, v.p. Chgo. area br. 1973-77), NEA, AAUP, AAUW, Assn. Tchr. Educators, Nat. Assn. Edn. Young Children, Alpha Delta Kappa (Pres. Ill. Alpha Epsilon chpt. 1957-59, Ill. historian 1958-60, Ill. rec. sec. 1964-66), Pi Lambda Theta (rec. sec. Alpha Zeta chpt. 1965-67, corr. sec. Chgo. area chpt. 1973-77, pres. Chgo. area chpt. 1977-81), Delta Kappa Gamma (chpt. music chmn. 1972-76), Phi Delta Kappa (chpt. historian 1977-79). Research on profl. problems of beginning tchrs. Home: 700 Victoria Rd Des Plaines IL 60016 Office: Northeastern Ill U Bryn Mawr at St Louis Ave Chicago IL 60625

ISAAC, SHARON LEE, educational administrator; b. Covington, Ky., Dec. 7, 1943; d. Clyde Estle and Sarah Elizabeth (Hollis) Haynes; m. Ronald Gene Isaac, Aug. 28, 1964. B.S.N., Ind. U. Sch. Nursing, 1968, M.S.N., 1971, Ed.D., 1979. Instr. Marion County Gen. Hosp. Sch. Nursing, Indpls., 1964-65; charge nurse Morgan County Meml. Hosp., Martinsville, Ind., 1965-67; relief charge nurse Bloomington Hosp., Ind., 1967-68; assoc. prof. Ind. U. Sch. Nursing, Indpls., 1971-75, coordinator continuing edn. Meth. Hosp. Ind., Indpls., 1975-79, dept. head, 1979—; workshop presenter, 1975—. Contbr. articles to profl. jours. Bd. dirs. Meth. Hosp. Fed. Credit Union, 1982-83. Mem. Ind. State Nurses Assn. (pres. 1981-83), Sigma Theta Tau, Pi Lambda Theta. Home: 5435 N Central Ave Indianapolis IN 46220 Office: Meth Hosp Ind 1604 N Capitol Ave PO Box 1367 Indianapolis IN 46206

ISAAC, TERESA ANN, lawyer, educator; b. Lynch, Ky., July 3, 1955; d. Samuel Thomas and Barbara Ann (Thomas) I.; m. James Isaac Lowry, IV, Dec. 30, 1978; children—Oran Jacob Isaac-Lowry, Alicyn Lyle Isaac-Lowry. B.A., Transylvania U., 1976; J.D., U. Ky., 1979. Bar: Ky. 1979. Legis. staff U.S. Senate, Washington, 1974; law clk. to county prosecutor, Lexington, Ky., 1977-79, Ky. Legal Services, Lexington, 1977; sole practice law, Lexington, 1979—; asst. dir. paralegal programs Eastern Ky. U., Richmond, 1983-84; asst. Fayette County Atty., 1986; lead counsel Ky. Civil Liberties Union, Louisville, 1983-84, Haitian Refugee Def. Com., Lexington, 1981-84; vol. lawyer Lexington Council of Arts, 1982-84. Bd. editors Ky. Bar Assn. Jour., 1983-84; editor Lexington Forum Jour., 1984. Bd. dirs. Displaced Homemaker Bd., Lexington, 1982-84, Human Resources Bd., Lexington, 1982-84; mem. steering com. Collins for Gov. campaign, 1983, Goals for Lexington, 1983-84. Recipient Bicentennial Service award Transylvania U., 1980; mem. Moot Ct. Bd., U. Ky. Law Sch., 1978. Mem. ABA (6th cir. lt. gov. 1977-79, Silver Key award 1979), Fed. Bar Assn., Ky. Bar Assn., Nat. Assn. Women Lawyers, Lexington Women in Communications, Omicron Delta Kappa. Democrat. Roman Catholic. Clubs: Eastern Ky. U. Women's, Phi Mu Alumnae (house corp. v.p. Lexington 1983-84). Home: 335 Garden Rd Lexington KY 40502 Office: PO Box 22163 Duke Rd Sta Lexington KY 40522

ISAAC, YVONNE RENEE, architecture company executive; b. Cleve., Apr. 13, 1948; d. Leon Warren and Vernice (Hallom) Isaac; m. Robert Frank McMillan, June 15, 1971 (div. Aug. 1975); m. 2d, Harold Erian Rhynie, Dec. 30, 1983. B.A. in Liberal Arts, Sarah Lawrence Coll., 1970; M.S. in Urban and Environ. Sci., Rensselaer Poly. Inst., Troy, N.Y., 1973; M.S. in Transp. Engring., Poly. Inst. N.Y., Bklyn., 1976. Market research analyst Gen. Electric Co., Phila., 1971-72; sr. assoc., cons. Perkins & Will, Chgo. and N.Y.C., 1972-76; supply assoc. Mobil Oil Corp., N.Y.C., 1976-78; project mgr. Perkins & Will, N.Y.C., 1978-80; project mgr. The Ehrenkrantz Group, N.Y.C., 1980—; assoc. prof. Pratt Inst., Columbia U., 1977-80; dir. Operation Open City, N.Y.C., 1977—. Dir., co-founder Black Woman Collaborative, 1977; mem. Ill. Bicentennial Commn., 1975; mem. Nat. Housing Task Force, Chgo., 1975-76. UMTA fellow, 1975. Mem. Inst. Transp. Engring., Am. Real Estate and Urban Econs. Assn., Sarah Lawrence Coll. Black Alumni Orgn. Democrat. Home: 649 Saint Marks Ave Brooklyn NY 11216 Office: The Ehrenkrantz Group 19 W 44th St New York NY 10036

ISAACS, FLORENCE, writer; b. Bklyn., July 2, 1937; d. Joseph and Sylvia (Tanklow) Satow; m. Harvey A. Isaacs, Sept. 1, 1962; children—Jonathan, Andrew. B.B.A., Baruch Sch., CCNY, 1957. Copywriter Fisher Radio Corp., Long Island City, N.Y., 1957-58, Cosmair Inc., N.Y.C., 1958-59; advt.-promotion mgr. mag. div. Dell Pub. Co., Inc., N.Y.C., 1960-71; free-lance writer specializing in health and medicine, marriage and family, N.Y.C., 1971—, contbr. articles to Reader's Digest, Family Circle, N.Y. Times, N.Y. News Sunday Mag., Family Weekly, Parade, Newsday, Cosmopolitan, Good Housekeeping, Mademoiselle, Rx: Being Well; free-lance pub. relations writer. Mem. membership com. The New Mus., N.Y.C., 1983-84; mem. fund raising com. Nat. Found., for Ileitis and Colitis, N.Y.C. 1983-84. Mem. Am. Soc. Journalists and Authors (program chmn.).

ISAACS, HELEN COOLIDGE ADAMS (MRS. KENNETH L. ISAACS), artist; b. Flushing, N.Y., Jan. 17, 1917; d. Thomas Safford and Martha (Montgomery) Adams; student Miss Hewett's classes, N.Y.C., Miss Porter's Sch., Farmington, Conn., Fontainbleau (France) Sch. Art and Music, 1935, Art Students League, 1936; m. Kenneth L. Isaacs, Mar. 10, 1949; children—Kenneth Coolidge, Anne Isaacs Merwin. Agt., Child's Gallery, Boston; one-woman shows at Child's Gallery, 3 times exhibited in group shows Allied Artists, N.Y., Boston Arts Festival; portraits of various prominent persons; murals in various public bldgs., Boston, Rochester, N.Y., Pittsfield, Mass., Daytona, Fla.; represented in painting and drawing collections Fogg Mus., Cambridge, Mass. Mem. Colonial Dames Am. Clubs: Colony (N.Y.C.); Chilton (Boston). Home: 68 Beacon St Boston MA 02108

ISAACS, MARY JO, educational administrator; b. Winston-Salem, N.C., June 27, 1931; d. James Spurgeon and Era (Brookshire) Isaacs; student Mars Hill Jr. Coll., 1949-51; A.B. cum laude, Meredith Coll., 1953; M.Ed., U. N.C. at Greensboro, 1958. Tchr., Sedge Garden Elem. Sch., Winston-Salem/Forsyth County Schs., 1953-59, supr. elem. edn., 1959-71, prin. Diggs Intermediate Sch., 1971-76, Brunson Elem. Sch., 1976—; tchr. Western Carolina U., Cullowhee, N.C., summers 1964, 65. Pres. Winston-Salem Maids of Melody, 1957; v.p. Winston-Salem Altrusa Club, 1967-68, pres., 1968-69; bd. dirs. Forsyth Singers' Guild, 1959, 60, Group Homes Forsyth County, 1976—, Children's Theatre, 1977-81. Mem. Assn. for Childhood Edn., N.C. (pres. div. suprs. and dirs. instrn. N.C. 1970-71), Winston-Salem/Forsyth County (pres. 1959-61) edn. assns., Forsyth County Elem. Prins. Assn. (sec.-treas. 1973-74, 84-85), Forsyth County Prins. Assn. (pres. 1986—), N.C. Assn. Educators (dir. div. prins. 1984—), N.C. Prins./Asst. Prins. Assn., N.C. Assn. Sch. Adminstrs., N.C. Assn. for Childhood Edn. (sec. 1965-67), Assn. Supervision and Curriculum Devel., Phi Delta Kappa, Delta Kappa Gamma. Democrat. Baptist. Home: 4240 Mashie Dr Grandview Route 1 Pfafftown NC 27040 Office: 155 N Hawthorne Rd Winston-Salem NC 27104

ISAACSON, ARLINE LEVINE, restaurant executive; b. Bklyn., Jan. 28, 1946; d. Harry and Sally (Fogelman) Levine; m. Leslie Robert Isaacson, Oct. 31, 1964 (div. July 1970); 1 child, Eric Michael. A.A.S. in Hotel and Restaurant Mgmt., N.Y.C. Tech. Coll., 1983. Restaurant and lounge mgr. Holiday Inn, N.Y.C., 1982-83; mgr. Astors, St. Regis Hotel, N.Y.C., 1983-84; banquet and conf. mgr. Mariner 15 Conf. Ctr., N.Y.C., 1984-85; dir. banquets, confs. and sales Sardi's Restaurant Corp., N.Y.C., 1985—. Democratic vol. Koch Relection Campaign, N.Y.C., 1985. Mem. Food and Beverage Mgrs. Assn. (sec. 1984—), Roundtable for Women in Food Service (treas. 1986—), Meeting Planners Internat., Soc. Incentive Travel, Hotel Sales and Mktg. Assn., Internat. Food Service Execs., N.Y.C. Tech. Coll. Alumni Assn. (bd. dirs. 1986—). Jewish. Avocations: dancing; travel; theatre; gourmet cooking. Home: 1836 E 18th St Brooklyn NY 11229 Office: Sardi's Restaurant Corp 234 W 44th St New York NY 10036

ISAKI, LUCY POWER SLYNGSTAD, lawyer; b. Jersey City, Oct. 21, 1945; d. Charles Edward and Ann Mary (Power) Slyngstad; m. Paul S. Isaki, Aug. 26, 1967. B.A. summa cum laude, Seattle U., 1973; J.D. cum laude, U. Puget Sound, 1977. Bar: Wash. 1977. Case worker San Joaquin County Welfare, Stockton, Calif., 1968-70, Alameda County Welfare, Oakland, Calif., 1971-73; law clk. to justice Wash. Supreme Ct., 1977-78; ptnr. Bogle & Gates, Seattle, 1978—; cons. Region X, HHS, 1975. Bd. dirs. King County Family Services, Seattle, 1982—, Wash. State Council Crime and Delinquency, 1981; trustee U. Puget Sound; vice chmn. law bd. Visitors U. Puget Sound, 1984—. Dean's scholar, 1976-77. Mem. Wash. Women Lawyers (pres. Seattle-King County chpt. 1982), ABA, Wash. State Bar Assn., Wash. Women Lawyers (v.p. 1984), U. Puget Sound Law Alumni Soc. (pres. 1979). Democrat. Home: 2018 Federal Ave E Seattle WA 98102 Office: 2200 Bank of California Center 900 4th Ave Seattle WA 98164

ISALY, SHARON MARTIN, real estate developer, contractor; b. Columbus, Ohio, July 31, 1946; d. John W. and Patricia M. Martin; student in edn. No. Ariz. U., 1964-66; m. Charles W. Isaly, Nov. 5, 1966; children—Jeffrey Scott, Bradley William. Interior designer John Martin Constrn., Phoenix, 1967-72; interior designer Martin Devel. Co., Missoula, Mont., 1972-79; v.p., partner Security-West Devel. Co., Missoula, 1979-82; dir.; pres., owner SMI Interiors, Missoula, sec.-treas. Prospect Assos./Devel. Co., Missoula, 1979-82, also dir.; v.p. Martin Constrn. Co., Phoenix and San Antonio, 1983—. Vice pres. Missoula Civic Symphony, 1977-78; bd. dirs. Missoula Children's Theatre, 1977-78. Mem. Am. Soc. Interior Designers, LWV, Delta Delta Delta. Republican. Methodist. Home: 4701 E Marston Dr Paradise Valley AZ 85253 Office: 10439 N Cave Creek Rd Phoenix AZ 85023

ISBELL, VIRGINIA, state legislator; b. Chinook, Mont., May 8, 1932; d. Domenico Renda and Bessie M. (Newton) Renda; cert. med. sec. No. Mont. Coll., 1953; m. Donald D. Isbell, Oct. 11, 1953; children—David, Daniel, Mahealani, Iwalani, Richard. Tchr., Kona (Hawaii) Schs., 1962-72; mgr. Wilmot Boone, M.D., Allan Hubacker, M.D., Kona Coast Med. Group, Inc., Kailua, Kona, Hawaii, 1978—; mem. Hawaii Ho. of Reps., 1980—. Bd. dirs. Kona Family YMCA; active ARC. Named Woman of Yr., Mayor's award, 1980. Republican. Mem. Ch. of Jesus Christ of Latter-day Saints. Club: Soroptimist (pres.).

ISELY, MARGARET, nutritional consultant; b. Orion, Ill., Aug. 13, 1921; d. John Henry and Sadie Mae (Durman) Sheesley; m. Henry Philip Isely, June 12, 1948; children—Zephyr, LaRock, Lark, Robin, Kemper, Heather. Student Antioch Coll., 1941-46. Acting dietitian Antioch Coll., Yellow Springs, Ohio, 1942; nutritional cons. Vitamin Cottage, Lakewood, Colo., 1955—; pres. Nat. Found. for Nutritional Research, Lakewood, 1982—. Mem. Rocky Mountain Nutritional Foods Assn. (pres. Denver 1978-82), Nat. Nutritional Foods Assn. (dir., mem. exec. council 1978-83), Orthomolecular Med. Soc. Home: 241 Zephyr Ave Golden CO 80401 Office: Vitamin Cottage 8800 W 14th St Lakewood CO 80215

ISERMAN, C. JOANNE, management consultant, nurse; b. Paducah, Ky., Aug. 21, 1932; d. John Grigsby and Velma Grace (Russell) Page; m. B.J. Iserman, Nov. 21, 1951; children—Randall W., Richard C., Elizabeth G., Russell J. A.S., Henry Ford Community Coll., 1965; B.B.A., Pacific Western U., 1982. R.N., Mich. Charge nurse pediatrics Botsford Hosp., Farmington, Mich., 1965-70; bus. analyst Blue Cross Blue Shield, Detroit, 1976-82; v.p. Med. Affairs Mgmt. Group, Inc., Rochester, Mich., 1982—. Contbr. articles to profl. publs. Mem. Am. Mgmt. Assn., Internat. Platform Assn., Soc. Tech. Communication. Lutheran. Pres., Cross of Christ Women, Bloomfield Hills, Mich. Home: 1623 Dennett Ln Rochester MI 48063 Office: Medical Affairs Mgmt Group Inc PO Box 758 Troy MI 48099

ISHAM, BERNICE JEAN, musician, educator; b. Salem, Oreg., Mar. 30, 1929; d. Earl and Tillie Charlotte (Kildahl) I.; B.Mus., Willamette U., 1950; M.Mus., U. Oreg., 1957, D.M.A., 1976. Tchr. music Taft (Oreg.) High Sch. and Elem. Sch., 1950-56, Beaverton (Oreg.) High Sch., 1956-59, Elmhurst Jr. High Sch., Oakland, Calif., 1959-60; instr. music West Hills Community Coll., Coalinga, Calif., 1960-84; condr.; ch. choir dir.; dir. opera workshop; dir. ann. Christmas madrigal feast. Musician, various community orgns. Recipient disting. services citation Sec. Treasury, 1944, community services award Masons, 1974. Mem. Music Assn. Calif. Community Colls. (state sec. 1970-72, sr. v.p. 1972-74), Am. Choral Dirs., Music Educators Nat. Conf., Nat. Assn. Tchrs. of Singing, Delta Kappa Gamma. Lutheran. Home: 800 Hummingbird Rd Cave Junction OR 97523

ISHERWOOD, HELEN CURL, librarian; b. Edgerton Ohio, Mar. 28, 1915; d. George R. and Hortense (Gillis) Curl; m. William Isherwood June 26, 1946; 1 dau., Anne Marie. B.A., U. Chgo, 1937, M.A., 1938; M.L.S., Columbia U., 1971. Personnel technician U.S. Govt., Chgo., Washington and N.Y.C., 1941-55, Westchester County, N.Y., 1956-58; librarian N.Y. Inst. for Edn. of Blind, Bronx, N.Y., 1971—. Mem. ALA, Bronx Library Assn. Club: Lake Isle Country (Eastchester, N.Y.). Office: NY Inst for Edn of Blind 999 Pelham Pkwy Bronx NY 10469

ISLES-SPEAR, DEIRDRE LOUISE, nurse; b. New Orleans, Mar. 7, 1961; d. Raymond Isles and Alice Lisa (Gant) Kennedy; m. John Russell Spear, Dec. 23, 1983; 1 child, Johnathan Michael. B.S. in Nursing, Dillard U., 1983. Lic. nurse, La. Staff nurse Touro Infirmary, New Orleans, 1983—. Mem. Am. Nurses Assn., La. State Nurses Assn., New Orleans Dist. Nurses Assn. Democrat. Roman Catholic. Avocations: reading; aerobics; jogging. Home: 3420 Palmyra St Apt B New Orleans LA 70119 Office: Touro Infirmary Hosp 1401 Foucher New Orleans LA 70115

ISON, GEORGIE LOU (JOY), insurance agency executive; b. Bryn Mawr, Pa., June 4, 1949; d. Malvin Harland and Georgie Lou (Easterling) I.; B.S. in Mktg., U. Ala., 1971. Sr. asst. buyer Mercantile Store, Inc., N.Y.C., 1971-72; rep. coordinator Coll. Mktg. & Research, Inc., Chgo., 1972-74; sales rep. Revlon, Inc., Chgo., 1974-76; v.p. Ison Ins. Agy., Mobile, Ala., 1976—. Tutor, Mich. Ave. Presbyn. Ch., Chgo., 1975. Mem. Internat. Platform Assn., Nat. Assn. Female Execs., Ins. Women Mobile (edn. chmn., by-laws chmn., mem. exec. bd., Rookie of Yr. 1979), Mobile Assn. Ind. Ins. Agts. (bd. dirs.), Ala. Assn. Ind. Ins. Agts. (chmn. personal lines com.), U. Ala. Alumni Assn. Baptist. Club: Career. Home: 5917 Cricket Ln Mobile AL 36609 Office: PO Box 6623 Mobile AL 36660

ISRAEL, BARBARA, fundraising consultant, corporate events specialist; b. N.Y.C., Dec. 14, 1942; d. Emanuel and Betty (Ostrow) Lapidus; m. Stanley Israel, June 28, 1965 (div. 1978); m. Stanley Merrill Gortikov, Feb. 28, 1980; children—Jacquelyn, Johanna. B.A., Queens Coll., CUNY, 1963. Assoc. dir. edn. UN Assn., 1963-65; geriatrics social worker N.Y.C. Dept. Aging, 1965-68; devel. dir. AMC Cancer Research Center-Eastern Region, N.Y.C., 1972-78; spl. events producer, fundraising cons. Barbara Israel Assocs., Inc., N.Y.C., 1978—; cons. Lincoln Ctr. for Performing Arts, 1986—; founder, nat. advisor High Priority: the Breast Cancer Research/Info. Network, 1983—. Mem. adv. bd. Center for Def. Info., Washington, 1984—; advisor, cons. Calhoun Sch., N.Y.C., 1972—; advisor Gay Men's Health Crisis, 1985—. Mem. Women Bus. Owners N.Y., Sales Execs. Club. Home: 90 Riverside Dr New York NY 10024 Office: Barbara Israel Assos Inc 250 W 57th St New York NY 10107

ISRAEL, MARGIE OLANOFF, psychotherapist; b. Atlantic City, Apr. 30, 1927; d. Herman and Mary (Salter) Olanoff; student U. Miami, 1945-46, 50, Am. Acad. Dramatic Arts, 1946-47; B.A. in Psychology cum laude, Hunter Coll., 1970; M.S.W. with honors in fieldwork, Hunter Sch. Social Work, 1972; psychoanalytic tng. N.Y. Soc. Freudian Psychologists, 1965-70, Manhattan Center for Advanced Psychoanalytic Studies, 1972-74, 76; m. Allan Edward Israel, Sept. 20, 1953; 1 dau., Janet. Celebrity interviewer Lunchin' with Marge radio show Sta. WFPG, Atlantic City, 1947-48; co-host Steel Pier Midnight radio show, 1949; publicity writer Hy Gardner Astor Hotel, N.Y.C., 1948; writer theatrical interviews Miami (Fla.) Daily News, 1950-51; sec. to exec. dir. Hebrew Old Age Center, Atlantic City, 1951-55; sec. to dir. TV-films and radio Nat. Office, Am. Cancer Soc., N.Y.C., 1959-66, asst. to dir. TV-films and radio, 1966-70; social worker Bellevue Hosp., N.Y.C., 1972-76; field instr. social work N.Y. U., 1975-76; practice psychotherapy, N.Y.C., 1973—. Certified social worker, N.Y. Fellow N.Y. State Soc. Clin. Social Work Psychotherapists, Am. Orthopsychiat. Assn.; mem. Nat. Assn. Social Workers, Acad. Cert. Social Workers, N.Y. Acad. Scis., Psi Chi. Office: 201 E 28th St Suite 1F New York NY 10016

ISRAEL, NANCY DIANE, lawyer; b. Fall River, Mass., Apr. 20, 1955; d. David Joseph and Charlotte Millicent (Epstein) I. A.B. magna cum laude, Harvard U., 1976, J.D., 1979. Bar: Mass. 1979. Assoc. Hale and Dorr, Boston, 1980-83; atty. Harvard U., Cambridge, Mass., 1983—; competition judge Ames Moot Court, Harvard Law Sch., Cambridge, 1981—. Mem. ad hoc com. Coalition for Better Judges, Boston, 1971-72; bd. dirs., nominating com. Mass. Council for Pub. Justice, Inc., Boston, 1971-76; Southeastern Mass. coordinator Dukakis Gubernatorial Campaign, New Bedford, Mass., 1974, mem. energy and environ. issues task forces. Boston, 1982; bd. dirs. devel. com. Ctr. House, Inc., Boston, 1980—. Mem. Mass. Bar Assn. (bd. dirs., com. chairperson young Lawyers div. 1982—, regional del. 1984—), Am. Corp. Counsel Assn. (Univ. counsel com. chairperson 1983—), ABA (del. young lawyers div. 1982—), Radcliffe Alumnae Assn. (participant various panels 1983—), Women's Bar Assn., Boston Bar Assn., Middlesex Bar Assn., Assn. Trial Lawyers Am., Mass. Assn. Women Lawyers, Nat. Assn. Coll. and Univ. Attys. Democrat. Clubs: Harvard (Boston schs. and scholarship com. 1980—), Radcliffe (Cambridge, Mass.), New Bedford Yacht (South Dartmouth, Mass.). Office: Office of Gen Counsel Harvard U 1350 Massachusetts Ave Cambridge MA 02138

ISRAELOV, RHODA, financial planner, writer; b. Pitts., May 20, 1940; d. Joseph and Fannie (Friedman) Kreinen; divorced; children—Jerome, Arthur, Russ. Student Herzlia Hebrew Tchr.'s Coll., N.Y.C., 1959-61; U. Mo.-Kansas City, 1965. Tchr. Hebrew, various schs., 1961-79; ins. agt. Conn. Mut. Life, Indpls., 1979-81; fin. planner E. F. Hutton, Indpls., 1981—, v.p., 1986—; instr. for mut. fund licensing exams. Pathfinder Securities Sch., Indpls., 1983—; cons. channel 7 News, 1985. Weekly fin. columnist Indpls. Bus. Jour., 1982—; bi-weekly fin. columnist Jewish Post & Opinion, 1982—. Mem. Inst. Cert. Fin. Planners, Nat. Assn. Life Underwriters, Women's Life Underwriters' Conf. (treas. Ind. chpt. 1982, v.p. chpt. 1983), Internat. Assn. Fin. Planning (v.p. Ind. chpt. 1983—), Nat. Speakers Assn. (v.p. Ind. chpt. 1985—), Registry Fin. Planning Profls. Lodge: Toastmasters (chpt. ednl. v.p. 1985—). Avocations: piano; folk and square dancing; needlepoint; theatre; racquetball. Office: E F Hutton One American Sq Suite 180 Indianapolis IN 46282

ISSAKHANIAN-STONER, ALICE, civil engineer; came to U.S., 1973, naturalized, 1977; d. Bartooghemyus and Sima (Masihi) Issakhanian; m. Stephen Earl Stoner, Mar. 5, 1973; 1 child, Armineh. A.A., Chiba U., Japan,

1970, B.S. in Archtl. Engring., 1973. Registered profl. engr., 1982. Interior designer, architect Nikken Sekkel Ltd., Tokyo, 1973; structural engr. City of Sacramento, 1978, civil engr., 1978-83, assoc. civil engr., 1983—. Univ. scholar Japanese Govt. Ministry Edn., 1968-73. Mem. Western Council Engrs. Republican. Avocations: oil painting; water colors; piano; languages. Office: City of Sacramento 915 "I" St Sacramento CA 95814

IVANAJ, DRITA A., information systems administrator, consultant; b. Novara, Italy, June 15, 1933; came to U.S., 1952; d. Martin and Giuseppina (Pogliotti) I. Sci. degree, Sci. Lyceum, Mortara, Italy, 1951; B.A., Hunter Coll., 1960; certs. in Mgmt. Devel. Program, Assn. Systems Mgmt., 1974-85 ; spl. cert. IBM Systems Sci. Inst., 1982. Cert. systems profl. With Fiat U.S., N.Y.C., 1954-69; program analyst Columbia U., N.Y.C., 1969-71, project leader, 1971-74, DP ops. mgr., 1974-79, mgr. adminstrv. systems control ops., 1979-83, adminstrv. and planning mgr., 1983-85, mgr. computer ctr., 1985—. Author procedural and operational manuals for computer installations, 1982-83, research projects reports depts., 1984-85. Mem. Assn. Systems Mgmt. (research chairperson 1982-83, pres.-elect 1983-84, pres. 1984-85, long-term planning chair 1985-86), World Future Soc. (sec. 1982-83, bd. dirs. 1984), Am. Mgmt. Assn., Assn. Computer Operator Mgrs., Nat. Assn. Female Execs. Republican. Roman Catholic. Office: Columbia U Ctr for Computing Activities 119th St and Broadway New York NY 10027

IVANYI, MAGDA IRENE, controller; b. Sopron, Hungary, Feb. 17, 1931; came to U.S., 1954, naturalized, 1960; d. John and Emilia (Urbasik) Mandak; m. Louis Szathmary, Jan. 20, 1953 (div. Feb. 1960); 1 child, Magda; m. 2d, Andrew John Ivanyi, Oct. 15, 1960; children—Andrea, Eniko. B.S., Nat. Inst. Commerce, Hungary, 1949. Full charge bookkeeper Wilson, Ryan & Leigh, Inc., Westport, Conn., 1969-76; chief acct. Don Hansen Advt., Inc., Westport, 1976—, controller, 1977—. Mem. Republican Nationalities Council, Washington, D.C., 1972; bd. dirs. Am. Hungarian Fedn., Washington, D.C., 1977; pres. Hungarian Com. Norwalk and Vicinity (Conn.), 1982—; mem. Nationality Broadcasting Network, Cleve., 1980—. Roman Catholic. Club: Pannonia (pres. 1959-61) (Bridgeport). Home: 82 Chestnut Hill Rd Norwalk CT 06851 Office: Don Hansen Advt Inc 21 Bridge Sq Westport CT 06880

IVENS, J(ESSIE) LOREENA, science editor, writer; b. nr. Mt. Carmel, Ill., Apr. 5, 1922; d. Elisher and Gertrude Arletta (McKibben) Moudy; m. Creighton Carl Webb, Dec. 24, 1946 (dec. 1950); m. 2d, Ralph Wilson Ivens, Sept. 30, 1950. B.S., U. Ill.-Urbana-Champaign, 1945, M.S., 1947. Instr. rhetoric U. Ill.-Urbana-Champaign, 1947-48, asst. editor Inst. Aviation, 1950-51; instr. English-journalism Ill. State U., 1948-50; newspaper editor Chanute AFB, Rantoul, Ill., 1951-60; tech. editor Ill. State Water Survey, Champaign, 1960-80, head communications unit, 1980—; interim exec. dir. Soc. Ill. Sci. Surveys, 1984. Assoc. editor Man-Made Lakes: Their Problems and Environmental Effects, 1973; author, co-author, editor NSF reports, Water Survey Report, 1977, 81, 83. Served with USNR, 1943-44. Recipient YWCA Achievement award, 1984; Rotary Paul Harris fellow, 1983. Mem. Soc. Tech. Communications, Nat. League Am. Pen Women, AAAS, Women in Communications. Republican. Club: Altrusa Internat. (past pres., past dist. sec.). Home: 802 S Busey St Urbana IL 61801 Office: Ill State Water Survey 2204 Griffith Dr Champaign IL 61820

IVENS, VIRGINIA RUTH, veterinary educator; b. Decatur, Ill., July 27, 1922; d. John Raymond and Dessie Lenora (Underwood) I.; B.S., U. Ill., 1950. Tracer blueprints Caterpillar Mil. Engine Co., Decatur, 1941-45; mem. faculty Coll. Vet. Medicine, U. Ill., Urbana, 1950—, assoc. prof. vet. parasitology, 1979—, chmn. curriculum com. dept. vet. pathobiology, 1976-78; chmn. 9th Ann. Conf. Coccidiosis, 1972. Mem. Am. Soc. Parasitologists (transl. com. 1963-71, 80-85), Soc. Protozoologist, Am. Inst. Biol. Scis., Entomol. Soc. Am., LWV, Sigma Xi, Phi Zeta. Translator Russian articles on parasitology; contbr. articles to profl. jours. and co-author 4 monographs; sr. author: Principal Parasites of Domestic Animals in the U.S., 1978, 81. Home: 608 S Edwin St Champaign IL 61821 Office: 2603 Basic Sci Bldg U Ill 2001 S Lincoln Ave Urbana IL 61801

IVERSON, KAREN MARIE, lawyer; b. Urbana, Ill., June 16, 1946; d. Leroy Cook and Evelyn Mae (Wright) I.; m. Daniel Brook Bartlett, Feb. 16, 1980. B.A., Stephens Coll., 1968; J.D., U. Mo., 1972. Adminstrv. asst. U. Mo., Columbia, 1968-69; asst. atty. gen. State of Mo., Jefferson City, 1972-77; assoc. firm Lathrop, Koontz, Righter, Clagett & Norquist, Kansas City, Mo., 1977-83, ptnr., 1983—; curator Stephens Coll., Columbia, 1973-76, 77—. Bd. dirs. Univ. Assocs., Kansas City, Mo., 1983-86. Named Outstanding Woman of Yr., Mo. Bus. and Profl. Women, 1974. Mem. ABA, Mo. Bar, Kansas City Bar Assn. Republican. Office: Lathrop Koontz Righter Clagett & Norquist 2345 Grand Ave Suite 2600 Kansas City MO 64108

IVERSON, PATRICIA ANN, insurance company administrator; b. Mpls., Jan. 7, 1952; d. Clarence Robert and Dorothy Ada (Cocroft) Tietze; m. Ronald Charles Oren, Oct. 23, 1971 (div. 1980); m. 2d, Donald Christ Iverson, Feb. 14, 1982; 1 dau., Chelsa Dawn Oren. B.S., U. Minn., 1980. Tchr. Children's Place, Rochester, Minn., 1976-78; counselor Katahdin, Mpls., 1978-79; personnel sec. Am. Hardware Mut. Ins. Co., Mpls., 1979-81, employment asst., 1981, employment supr., 1981-83, asst. personnel mgr., 1983—. Author/editor: Child Care Pamphlet, 1981; Employee Handbook, 1983; Study on Flextime, 1982. Task force mem. Youth Outreach Alliance, Mpls., 1978-79; com. mem. Employee Research Adv. Com., Mpls., 1981—; active Chart, Mpls., 1984. Mem. Twin City Personnel Assn., Am. Soc. Personnel Adminstrn. (profl. in human resources). Office: Am Hardware Mutual Ins Co 3033 Excelsior Blvd Minneapolis MN 55416

IVES, KATHLEEN SUSAN, videotex executive, developer; b. Pasadena, Calif., Apr. 16, 1955; d. Richard King and Patricia Jeanne (Kurtz) I.; m. Bruce David Matzner, Aug. 16, 1980 (div. June 1984). B.A., U. Calif.-Davis, 1977; M.A., U. So. Calif., 1980. Staff writer Apparel News Group, Los Angeles, 1977-79; cons. Edwards, Inc., Sierra Madre, Calif., 1980; cons. printing systems div. Xerox Corp., El Segundo, Calif., 1980; prodn. supr. CBS Teletext Project, Los Angeles, 1980-82; mgr. graphic ops. CBS Videotex Project, Fairlawn, N.J., 1982-83; asst. staff mgr. AT&T Info. Systems, Parsippany, N.J., 1983-84, mgr., 1984—. Mem. Women in Communications, Am. Women in Radio and TV, Inc., Nat. Assn. Female Execs., Inc., AAUW. Office: AT&T Info Systems 5 Wood Hollow Rd Parsippany NJ 07054

IVES, PHYLLIS ENID, executive search agency executive; b. N.Y.C., Jan. 31, 1944; d. Paul and Rose (Shernow) Langsam; m. Ira Ives, May 30, 1965; children—Robin Lynn, Andrew Steven. B.S. in Edn., NYU, 1965. Owner, operator Gift 'N' Stitch, Columbus, Ohio, 1973-79; recruiter Fortune Personnel, Columbus, 1979-81; pres. Ives & Assocs., Columbus, 1981—. Treas. Congregation Beth Tikuah, Columbus, 1982. Mem. Am. Mktg. Assn., Ohio Assn. Personnel Cons., Columbus Area C. of C., Sales Execs. Club Columbus. Lodge: B'nai B'rith women (pres. Columbus 1972). Avocations: tennis; needlepoint; swimming. Home: 288 S Drexel Ave Columbus OH 43209 Office: Ives & Assocs 520 E Rich St Columbus OH 43215

IVEY, ALVENA LEE, nurse; b. Saginaw, Mich., Jan. 6, 1914; d. James Burgess and Julia Jane (Sutton) I. R.N., Takoma Hosp. and Sanitarium, 1937; cert. Berlitz Sch. Lang.; student Union Coll., 1939; cert. U. Cin., 1959. Surg. nurse U.S. Army Res., 1943-74, commd. 2d lt., 1943, advanced through ranks to lt. col., 1968; ret., 1974; nurse, Cin., 1939—; registered medico-legal reporter. Author: Episode TV series Mash; editorial asst. med. articles and books. Decorated Award of Merit U.S. Army, 1969, Nat. Def. award, 1946. Mem. U. Cin. Alumni, Adminstrv. Mgmt. Soc. (pres. 1983-84; Diamond Merit award 1980, Merit award 1970, 300 Merit award 1985), Am. Nurses Assn., Ohio Nurses Assn., Nat. Shorthand Reporters Assn., Ohio State Shorthand Reporters Assn. Republican. Club: Am. Legion-Nurses (pres. 1947-49). Home: 609 McAlpin Ave Apt #9 Cincinnati OH 45220 Office: Medico-Legal Reporting Service 609 McAlpin Ave Cincinnati OH 45220

IVEY, PATRICIA MELGIE, author/photographer; b. Omaha, Mar. 5, 1941; d. Wilbur and Mabel Gertrude (Morton) Ward; student Colo. State U., 1959, U. Alaska, 1976-80; children—Perry Gene Vaughn, Jr., Stephen Michael Vaughn. Various secretarial positions, 1966-69; exec. asst. to v.p. indsl. mktg., sales div. Spartan Mills Inc., Spartanburg, S.C., 1969-74; freelance writer, photographer, 1976—; profl. model, 1977-78; sec., then adminstrv. sec. Alaska Coop. Extension Service, U. Alaska, Fairbanks, 1975-83, exec. officer univ. assembly, 1983—; condr. workshops, speaker, lectr. in field. Public relations chmn. Fairbanks chpt. Am. Heart Assn., 1978. Mem. Am. Film Inst., Nat. Fedn. Press Women, Alaska Press Women (pres. No. region 1977-79), Alaska Heritage Writers Assn. (exec. sec.). Home: PO Box 60634 Fairbanks AK 99706

IVEY, SARA ANNE (LEE), editor, publisher; b. Atlanta, Mar. 20, 1936; d. Hubert Floyd and Margaret Embry (Morris) Lee; student public schs., Ga.; m. William F. Ivey, Dec. 14, 1968; children—Alecia Lee Cash Styles, Tresia Anne Ivey. With Harverty Furniture Co., 1955-56, First Nat. Bank, 1956, Scottdale Mills, 1957-61, Fry/Southeastern Carbon Paper, 1962-64, Airway Hydraulics, 1964-68; sec., bookkeeper MKD Industries, Decatur, Ga., 1974-76; bookkeeper Decatur Clinic, 1976-77; sec. Morgan Equipment Co., Decatur, 1977-78; editor, pub. Dixie Bus. Mag., Decatur, 1978—; ins. assoc. Presbyr. Ch. in Am., 1982-84. Pres., Midway Manor Community Orgn., Decatur, 1979—. Named hon. Ky. col. Presbyterian. Clubs: Atlanta Advt., Colony Sq. Bus. and Profl. Women's, Atlanta PBX Club, Atlanta Press. Home: 1420 Catherine St Decatur GA 30030 Office: 4592 Covington Rd Decatur GA 30035

IVEY, VALERIE KAY, modeling agency executive; b. Oklahoma City, Mar. 27, 1961; d. Charles Samuel and M. Faye (Price) Ivey. B.A. in Acctg., Central State U., Edmond, Okla., 1982, postgrad. in bus., 1982—. Bookkeeper, Scrivner, Inc., Oklahoma City, 1979-84; owner, pres. John Casablancas Model Mgmt., Oklahoma City and Tulsa, 1984—; choreographer fashion shows for bus. and charity benefits. Mem. Okla. Film and Tape Profls. Assn., Tulsa Ad Club. Republican. Avocations: scuba diving, travel. Home: 611 Ridgecrest Rd Edmond OK 73013 Office: John Casablancas Model Mgmt 1034 NW 65th St Suite 201 Oklahoma City OK 73116

IVIE, DOROTHY ANNE, city clerk, realtor; b. Richmond, Ky., Oct. 26, 1941; d. David Pryse and Eleanor Henry (Best) Azbill; m. Thomas Garner Ivie, Sept. 10, 1960; children—Karen Elaine, Kathleen Margaret, David Reid. A.A., Eastern Ky. U., 1960; B.A., No. Ky. U., 1984. Lic. real estate salesperson, Ky. Reporter, Campbell Co. News, Newport, Ky., 1975-76; fin. clk. City of Ft. Thomas, Ky., 1976-79, city clk., 1979—; realtor assoc. Jim Huff Realty, Highland Heights, Ky., 1982—. Poet, writer anthology pamphlet Collage (Poet of Yr. award 1975). Editor, writer: Mcpl. News, Cannon Cues, From the Fountain. Treas., Ft. Thomas Jr. Woman's Club, 1972-73; chmn. com. Youth Haven Guild, Ft. Thomas, 1973-74; sec. Ky. Profl. Firefighters, 1983-85. Mem. Ky. Mcpl. Clks. Assn., Ft. Thomas Heritage League (sec. 1983-85), Internat. Inst. Mcpl. Clks. (pubs. relations com. 1985—), Kenton Boone Bd. Realtors, Cambell County Bd. Realtors, Democrat. Methodist. Club: Circle #11 (Ft. Thomas). Lodge: Order of Eastern Star. Avocations: swimming; golfing; writing. Home: 115 Garden Way Fort Thomas KY 41075 Office: City of Fort Thomas 130 N Ft Thomas Ave Fort Thomas KY 41075

IVORY, LORETTA CAROL, nurse-midwife, writer, educator; b. Wooster, Ohio, Oct. 12, 1946; d. Martin and Elizabeth (Basche) Cermely; m. Thomas Martin Ivory, III, Sept. 22, 1972; 1 child, Kelly Elizabeth. B.S., U. Cin., 1968; M.S. in Nursing, U. Utah, 1973; D.D. (hon.), Ch. of Seven Arrows, Denver, 1982. Cert. nurse-midwife. Staff nurse Cin. Gen. Hosp., 1968; nurse-midwife McKeesport Hosp., Pa., 1973-74; instr. U. Colo., Denver, 1975-78; dir. nurse-midwifery Denver Birth Ctr., 1978—; clin. instr., cons. U. Utah, 1979—; birth ctr. cons., instr., 1978—. Author: Obstetric Nursing, 1980; Contemporary Obstetric and Gynecologic Nursing, 1980; Cooking Naturally; also teaching modules for U. Colo., 1976-77. Patentee rocking cradle; writer TV show Meeting of Young Minds with Steve Allen, 1983, 85. Mem. Colo. Perinatal Care Council, 1978-82, legis. chmn., 1980-82. Served to lt. USN, 1968-71, Vietnam. Nat. Nurse Practice Act scholar, 1971-73; research grantee U. Utah, 1972-73. Mem. Am. Coll. Nurse-Midwives (legis. chmn. 1978-80, mem. nat. legis. com. 1978-83), TRIDEA (chmn. 1984-85). Democrat. Avocations: gardening; gourmet cooking. Home: 6263 S Niagara Way Englewood CO 80111 Office: Denver Birth Ctr 1201 E 17th St Suite 202 Denver CO 80218

IWAMASA, FUMIKO, state ofcl.; b. Honolulu; d. W.G. and Sho (Muraoka) Kimura; B.A., U. Hawaii, 1933; m. Haruto W. Iwamasa, Apr. 2, 1937. Social work Dept. Social Services, Hilo, Hawaii, 1939-47, asst. supr., 1947-54, supr., 1954-62, Hawaii br. adminstr., 1962-75, ret., 1975. Adviser, Big Island Presch. Assn., 1965-75. Mem. disaster council County of Hawaii, 1960-75; mem. eviction com. Hawaii Housing Authority, 1962—; mem. county com. Children and Youth, 1954-75; mem. Gov.'s Com. Mental Health, proceedings chmn., 1962-63, mem. Com. Aging, 1962—; mem. Big Island Council on Addiction, 1963-75; mem. Big Island adv. com. Law Enforcement Adv. Agy., 1969-75; cons. com. Hawaii County Comprehensive Health Planning Advisory Council, 1968-75. Bd. dirs. ARC, Hilo, 1962-78, Am. Cancer Soc., 1962-77, Salvation Army, Hilo, 1963-80, YMCA, 1963-70, Hawaii County Econ. Opportunity Council, 1965-75, Hawaii Fed. and State Employees Fed. Credit Union, 1966-71, Hawaii Island United Way, 1975—; mem. Hawaii County Rural Devel. Com., 1970-75. Mem. Hawaii Govt. Employees Retirement Assn. (state long-range com., chmn. edn. com.). Club: Zonta. Home: 52 Puuko St Hilo HI 96720

IYER, HOLLY HENDERSON, telephone company executive; b. Glen Cove, N.Y., Jan. 11, 1949; d. George Devine and Genevieve (Manning) Henderson; B.A. in Math., Bucknell U., 1971; M.Stats., U. Fla., 1973; M.B.A., Pace U., 1981; m. Harihar K. Iyer, Apr. 14, 1974; children—Janna, Tamra. Asst., U. Fla., 1971-73; engr. So. Bell Tel. & Tel. Co., 1973-77, forecaster, Atlanta, 1982-83; strategic planner BellSouth, 1983—; corp. planner AT&T, Basking Ridge, N.J., 1977-82. Coordinator fund raising drive Bucknell U.; bd. dirs. First Montessori Sch. Atlanta. Mem. Nat. Assn. Female Execs. Office: 41A63 So Bell Center 675 W Peachtree Atlanta GA 30375

IZEN, AFTON JANE, lawyer; b. Fort Worth, Dec. 16, 1948; d. Joe Alfred and Faye Jeanene (Nycum) I. B.A., U. Houston, 1972; J.D., S. Tex. Coll. Law, Houston, 1982. Office mgr. Pasadena ENT Clinic, P.A., Tex., 1970—. Mem. ABA, Young Lawyer's Assn., Assn. Trial Lawyers, Am. Judicature Soc., Tex. Bar Assn. Avocations: traveling; studying; helping underprivileged. Home: 15 Greenway Plaza Apt 2G Houston TX 77046 Office: 8191 Southwest Freeway Suite 117 Houston TX 77074

IZZO, FRANCES SUSAN, nursing educator; b. Glen Cove, N.Y., Aug. 11, 1947; d. Joseph Lawrence and Angeline Marie (DeMaio) Belfiore; m. Joseph May, 13, 1979 (div. May 1983). A.A.S., Nassau Community Coll., 1968; B.S.N., Adelphi U., 1973, M.S.N., 1978. Adult nurse practitioner cert. Am. Nurses Assn. Staff nurse, asst. head nurse Community Hosp., Glen Cove, N.Y., 1965-77; nurse practitioner St. Francis Hosp., Roslyn, N.Y., 1978-81; instr. nursing Molloy Coll., Rockville Centre, N.Y., 1982-85; adj. faculty Adelphi U., Garden City, 1975-82; adj. faculty Nassau Community Coll., 1981-85, instr. nursing, 1985—; cons., instr. continuing edn. SUNY-Farmingdale/N.Y. State Nurses Assn. Dist. 14, Bklyn., 1981—. Corr. sec. Glen Cove Republican Club, 1979-81. N.Y. State Regents scholar, 1965. (USPHS trainee, 1972-73, 77-78). Mem. N.Y. State Nurses Assn., Alpha Omega Sigma Theta Tau. Roman Catholic. Contbr.: Assess Test, 1982-85. Office: Nassau Community Coll Dept Nursing Garden City NY 11530

IZZO, MARY MADELYN, psychiatric social worker; b. White River Junction, Vt., Dec. 12, 1923; d. Dominic and Jennie (Izzo) I. B.A., Boston U., 1945; M.S.W., Columbia U., 1962. Cert. social worker. Psychiat. social worker Silver Hill Psychiat. Ctr., New Canaan, Conn., 1962-68; sch. social worker Town of Greenwich, Conn., 1968—. Mem. Nat. Assn. Social Workers.

JABALEY, SELMA ANN, petroleum engineer; b. LaGrange, Ga., Sept. 7, 1952; d. Raymond Philip and Yolanda Marie (Katter) J. B.C.E., Ga. Inst. Tech., 1974. Facilities and constrn. engr. Chevron USA, New Orleans, 1974-76; project engr. Atlantic Richfield, Dallas, 1976-79; facilities, constrn. engr. Mobil Exploration Norway, Stavanger, Norway, 1979-82; petroleum engr. Gaffney, Cline & Assocs., Dallas and Singapore, 1982-85; Mass Rapid Transit Corp., Singapore, 1985—. Mem. Soc. Petroleum Engrs. (chmn. Singapore chpt. 1986), Soc. Women Engrs. (past pres. Dallas chpt. 1978-79, univ. advisor, 1975-76), Ga. Tech. North Tex. Alumni Assn., Alpha Xi Delta. Roman Catholic. Home: 79 Farrer Dr #06-04 Singapore 1025 Republic of Singapore

JACK, DIANE MARIE, automotive dealer financial executive, consultant; b. Brookline, Mass., Sept. 3, 1950; d. Henry and Evelyn Gertrude (Morrel) Serra; m. Ronald Francis Jack, Nov. 10, 1969; 1 son, Marshall Francis. B.S. in Bus. Adminstrn. cum laude, U. Balt., 1982. Bookkeeper/mgr. E. V.'s, Brockton, Mass., 1965-70; accounts receivable clk. Hendries Frozen Foods, Inc., Southboro, Mass., 1970-72; bookkeeper/troubleshooter Smithy-Douglass Fertilizer Co., Seaford, Del., 1973-75; acct. Seaford Head Start (Del.), 1973-75; fin. analyst Profl. Bus. Mgmt., Inc., Balt., 1975-78; controllr K & M, Inc., Balt., 1978-82; acctg. mgr. Everbest Corp., Balt., 1982-83; controller Heritage Chevrolet, Owings Mills, Md., 1983—; owner, operator Misty Blue Kennels. Mem. Am. Prodn. and Inventory Control Soc. Office: Heritage Chevrolet 11234 Reisterstown Rd Owings Mills MD 21061

JACKER, CORINNE LITVIN, author; b. Chgo., June 29, 1933; d. Thomas Henry and Theresa (Bellak) Litvin; student Stanford U., 1950-52; B.S. (Lovdedale scholar, Univ. scholar), Northwestern U., 1954, M.A., 1955, postgrad., 1955-56; m. Richard Jacker, July 1, 1956 (div. Apr. 1959). Assoc. editor Liberal Arts Press, 1959-60, trade sci. dept. Macmillan Co., 1961-63; assoc. editor sci. book dept. Charles Scribner's Sons, N.Y.C., 1963-65; writer, researcher NET Playhouse, WNET, 1971-73; story cons. CBS Playhouse 90, 1973-74; script editor Bicentennial Minutes, CBS, 1974-75; head writer Best of Families, PBS, 1976-77, Another World, NBC, 1981-83; adj. assoc. prof. NYU, 1976-78; vis. asst. prof. Yale U., 1979-81. Recipient Obie award, 1974, 75, Ciné Golden Eagle, 1975, award Am. Film Inst. Video Features Fest, 1985, Rotterdam Film Fest, 1985; Rockefeller fellow, 1979-80. Mem. Authors League, Dramatists Guild, PEN, Writers Guild Am., Zeta Phi Eta. Author: (books) Man, Memory, and Machines, 1964; Window on the Unknown, 1966; Black Flag of Anarchy, 1968; The Biological Revolution, 1971; (off-Broadway and regionally produced plays) Pale Horse, Pale Rider, 1958; A Happy Ending, 1959; Terminal; Jennifer, Jemima and the Machine, 1970; Scientific Method, 1970; Project Omega, Lillian, 1971; Bits and Pieces, 1973; Travellers, 1974; Night Thoughts, 1974; Harry Outside, 1974; My Life, 1976; Other People's Tables, 1976; Later, 1978; After the Season, 1979; Domestic Issues, 1981; In Place, 1982; This Thing Called Love, 1985; (TV plays) Actors Choice Series, 1970; The Anatomy of Love; When This You See, Remember Me; A Singular Man; Brewsie and Willie, 1972; Boxes, 1972; Secrets, 1973; The Adams Chronicles, 1976; Best of Families, 1977; Loose Change, 1978; The Jilting of Granny Weatherall, 1979; Overdrawn at the Memory Bank, 1983; various poems published in Spectrum, Fiddlehead, Carleton Miscellany, Riverside Poetry III, Mutiny. Office: 110 W 86th New York NY 10024

JACKSON, ALICE MAUD, association executive; b. Trelawny, W.I., Feb. 1, 1952; came to U.S., 1970, naturalized, 1985; d. Howard Richard and Rebecca (Mongal) Hines; m. Donald Arthur Jackson, Mar. 30, 1974; children—Janine, Kevin. B.A., Howard U., 1980, M.P.A., 1983. Adminstr. Nat. Assn. Community Health Ctrs., Washington, 1983-85, policy analyst, 1985—. Bd. dirs. Coalition for Human Needs, Washington, 1986. Mem. Am. Soc. Pub. Adminstrn., Nat. Assn. Female Execs., Pi Sigma Alpha, Pi Alpha Alpha. Presbyterian. Home: 7009 Freeport St Hyattsville MD 20784

JACKSON, ANDREA CARROLL, public relations executive, writer, photographer; b. Lockesburg, Ark., Jan. 8, 1945; d. Jake Charles and Lola Evelyn (Hale) Carroll; m. Ronald William Jackson, Dec. 23, 1967 (div. Jan. 1978). B.S. in Edn., Henderson State U., 1967; postgrad. in journalism La. State U., 1981-82. Phys. edn. tchr. Lamar Consol. Schs., Ark., 1967-68; field advisor Ark. Post council Girl Scouts U.S.A., Pine Bluff, 1969-74, pub. relations dir. Ouachita council, Little Rock, 1974-79; program and pub. relations dir. Baton Rouge Area YWCA, 1979-81; editor Bayou Country Publs., Plaquemine, La., 1981-83; communications dir. Am. Lung Assn. of Ark., Little Rock, 1984—; freelance writer, photographer. Editor: (tng. manual) Safe Homes Project for Battered Women, 1981; Ark. Women's Rights OURS newspaper, 1985—. Recipient Excellence in color slide photography awards Ouachita Girl Scout Council and Girl Scouts U.S.A., 1978; Outstanding Service award Baton Rouge Area YWCA, 1980. Mem. Ark. Press Women (feature writing awards, 2 in 1982, 3 in 1983, 2 interview awards 1984, 2 broadcast awards 1984), Congress of Lung Assn. Staff, Sierra Club (state conservation chair, state media chair, Central Ark. group chair, So. Plains regional conservation com. del.). Avocations: horticulture, reading, racquetball, hiking, whitewater rafting. Home: 511 E 8th St Apt 3 Little Rock AR 72202 Office: Am Lung Assn of Ark 412 W 7th St Little Rock AR 72201

JACKSON, ANN(I)E LOU STINGLEY, librarian; b. Blevins, Ark.; d. William Henry and Nina (Duke) Stingley; A.B., Henderson State Tchrs. Coll., 1951; M.L.S., Tex. State Coll. for Women, Denton, Tex., 1954; m. Joseph Jackson, Sept. 4, 1922; children—Joseph Lyle, Andrew Stingley, Kenneth Edwin. Tchr., librarian Washington (Ark.) High Sch., 1940-46; asst. librarian Ouachita Coll., Arkadelphia, Ark., summer 1944; head librarian Arkadelphia City and Clark County Library, 1946-53; cons. for high sch. and public libraries Ark. Library Commn., 1953-65; state sch. library supr. Ark. Dept. Edn., 1965-72; library cons., 1972-74; dir. Elem. and Secondary Edn. Act, Title II; mem. adv. bd. Southwest Ark. Regional Archives, 1977-78. Active Community Chest Bd., Arkadelphia, UN Speakers Bur. in Ark.; mem. adult edn. coordinating bd. YWCA. Mem. Commr. Edn.'s Adv. Com. on Sch. Libraries; chmn. state com. on sch. library study So. States Work Conf. on Edn., 1957-60; vol. chmn. library services Second Bapt. Ch. in Little Rock, 1979—; sec. Pulaski County Chapter UN, 1964; exec. dir. Nat. Library Week for Ark., 1963. Recipient cert. merit, Ark. Jaycees, 1956; cert. merit for disting. service to library sci. Mem. Am. Assn. Sch. Libraries (state pres., rep. for Nat. Library Week 1959-60), Am. (chmn. Ark. membership com. Audio-Visual div. 1956), Ark. Student (librarian's council), Ark. library assns., Nat. Adult Edn. Assn., Ark. Hist. Assn., Nat. Assn. State Sch. Library Suprs. (pres. 1972-73), AAUW (1st v.p. 1970-72), Vets. World War I Aux. (state conductress 1973-74, chaplain 1974-75, state pres. 1976-77), UN Assn. (pres. state div. USA for Ark. 1969-70), Clark County Hist. Soc., NEA, Ark. Edn. Assn., Nat. Soc. Arts and Letters (pres. Little Rock 1974-76, asso. nat. chaplain 1976), Internat. Platform Assn., Women's Nat. Book Assn. (chmn. U. Ark. Personal Library Contest 1972-73, chpt. pres. 1976-77), Greater Little Rock Fedn. Womens Clubs (sec. 1974-75), Ark. Geneal. Soc., Ark. Pioneers, Delta Kappa Gamma (2d v.p. Gamma chpt. 1966-68), Kappa Delta Pi, Alpha Chi, Alpha Beta Alpha. Democrat. Baptist. Mem. Order Eastern Star. Clubs: Altrusa (bd. dirs. Little Rock 1965-74, 1st v.p. 1968-69, pres. 1971-72, internat. relations chmn. internat. dist. 8 1970-72), Fine Arts. Mem. ALA editorial subcom., compiling Basic Book Collection for High Schs., 1957; adviser and assisted editing Handbook for the Student Assistant in the School Library, 1959; rev. bibliography Arkansiana for High Schools, 1960, 1964; editorial com. for bibliography Ethnic Groups: Their Cultures and Contbns.; chmn. com. compiling bibliography on Black Ams.; author, compiler Stingleys: Then and Now, 1983. Contbr. World Book Ency., 1960, 72. Home: 4 Rhinehart Ln Apt 317 Little Rock AR 72205

JACKSON, ARLENE L., family therapist; b. Rockford, Ill., July 16, 1943; d. John E. and LaVern R. (Hazzard) J.; divorced; children—Jan Arlene, James Paul. A.A., Rock Valley Coll., 1978; B.A. summa cum laude in Clin. Psychology and Eng. Lit., Beloit Coll., 1979; postgrad. Ill. State U., 1981-82; M.S. in Community Mental Health, Mo. Ill. U., 1985, postgrad., 1986—. Advocate, coordinator Ill. Status Offender Service, Rockford, 1979-80; dir. Pathways, Inc., Rockford, 1980-81; therapist Family Life Ctr., Rockford, 1982—; exec. dir. Youth Services Network, Inc., Rockford, 1982—; prin. J & J Cons., 1986—; cons. in field. Chmn. task forces Youth Services Network, Inc., 1982—; mem. Peace and Justice Commn., Rockford, 1982—; bd. dirs. Knights Community Complex, Rockford, 1984—. Bingham fellow Beloit Coll., 1979. Mem. NOW, Nat. Assn. Social Workers, Rockford Network, Nat. Assn. Women Bus. Owners, Rockford C. of C., Phi Beta Kappa, Psi Chi. Unitarian. Avocations: writing poetry; dancing; interior decorating; travel; theater. Office: Youth Services 4402 N Main St Rockford IL 61105

JACKSON, ARTHURLENE THERESA, psychologist, liaison to probate court; b. Fort Worth, May 19, 1944; d. John Arthur and Millie Theresa (Bolden) Lee; m. Jesse Wallace Jackson, Jan. 24, 1963; children—Maria Terez, Jesse Wallace III. B.S., Tenn. State U., Nashville, 1969, M.S., 1973. Psychologist spl. services Houston Sch. Dist., 1974-75; psychologist Mental Health, Mental Retardation Agy., Houston, 1975; dir. mental retardation Services, Houston, 1975-77; dir. geriatric service, Mental Health Agy., Houston, 1977-79, dir. alcohol services, 1979-81, liaison to Probate Ct., 1981—. Community organizer Democratic Party, Nashville, 1971; active Houston Dem. campaigns, 1981—. Mem. Am. Assn. Mental Deficiency, Coalition 100 Black Women, Links, Inc. (pres. 1977-80), Delta Sigma Theta. Baptist. Clubs: Coterie, Chama (Houston). Home: 3330 Charleston St Houston TX 77021 Office: Mental Health and Mental Retardation 6125 Hillcroft Houston TX 77081

JACKSON, BERNICE ESSIC, educator; b. Arlington, Ga., Sept. 26, 1927; d. Dock and Lillian (Allen) Essic; m. Arthur H. Jackson, Jan. 12, 1949 (div.); children—Arthurene, Bernard, Paulette. B.S. in Elementary Edn., Albany State

Coll., 1955; postgrad. Atlanta U., 1963-65; Interdenominational Theol. Ctr., 1978. Elementary tchr. Dougherty County, Albany, Ga., 1957-70, Fulton County, Atlanta, 1970—. Recipient Cert. of Spl. Achievement, Am. Red Cross Youth Service, Met. Atlanta chpt., 1983. Mem. NEA, Ga. Assn. Educators, Fulton County Assn. Educators. Democrat. Methodist. Avocations: reading; watching TV; traveling. Office: Utoy Springs Elementary 4001 Danforth Rd SW Atlanta GA 30331

JACKSON, BETTY EILEEN, music educator; b. Denver, Oct. 9, 1925; d. James Bowen and Fannie (Shelton) J. B.Mus., U. Colo., 1948, M.Mus., 1949, B.Mus. Edn., 1963; postgrad. Ind. U., 1952-55, Hochschule fur Musik, Munich, 1955-56. Cert. educator Colo., Calif. Tchr., accompanist H.L. Davis Vocal Studios, Denver, 1949-52; grad. asst. Ind. U., Bloomington, 1952-55; teaching assoc. U. Colo., Boulder, 1961-63, vis. lectr., 1963-69; tchr. Fontana Unified Sch. Dist., Calif., 1963—, pvt. studio, 1966—; lectr. in music Calif. State U., San Bernardino, 1967-76; performer, accompanist, music dir. numerous musical cos. including performer, music dir. Fontana Mummers, 1980—, Riverside Community Players, Calif., 1984—; performer Rialto Community Theatre, Calif., 1983—. Performances include numerous operas, musical comedies and oratorios. Judge, Inland Theatre League, Riverside, 1983—. Fulbright grantee, Munich, 1955-56; named Outstanding Performer Inland Theatre League, 1982-84. Mem. AAUW (bd. dirs., cultural chair 1979—), Nat. Assn. Tchrs. Singing (exec. bd. 1985—), NEA, Music Educators Nat. Conf., Calif. Tchrs. Assn., Fontana Tchrs. Assn., Music Tchrs. Assn., Kappa Kappa Iota (v.p. 1977-85). Lodge: Eastern Star. Avocations: Community theater and opera; travel; collecting Hummels and plates. Home: PO Box 885 Rialto CA 92376

JACKSON, CAROLE DOWDLE, designer, artist, nursing registry administrator; b. Safford, Ariz., Sept. 22, 1937; d. Edward David and Leota (Hazeltine Foster) Dowdle; m. Edward Britton Jackson, Oct. 2, 1954 (div. Mar. 1976); children—Daniel Edward, Henry Earl, Stephen James. A.S.N., Alvin Jr. Coll., 1975. Cert., Art Instrn., Inc., Chgo., 1955. Sales rep. Cornett realty, Fremont, Calif., 1969-70; supr. Kimberley Nurses, Houston, 1977-80; supr. med. dept. Hughes Tool Co., Houston, 1980-85; owner, mgr. CJ Designs, Houston, 1979—; owner, dir. Burns Nurses Registry, Houston, 1985—; design cons. Carousel Crafts Co., Houston, 1980—, Nat. Syndications Inc., Ramsay, N.J., 1983—, Adams Properties, Houston, 1985—. Designer line of needlework and soft sculpture kits, shuttlebug tatting shuttle Areacpt. Republican Com., Milpitas, 1964, pollwatcher, Houston, 1980, 84; vol. READ, Houston, 1985; chmn. Bicentennial Com., Alvin, Tex., 1976. Mem. Occupational Health Nurses Tex., Am. Entrepreneurs Assn., Hobby Industries Assn. Am. (assoc.), Phi Theta Kappa. Episcopalian. Avocations: community theater, antique collection; bicycling, museums; fine art collection. Office: Burns Nurses Registry 8950 Westpark Suite 101 Houston TX 77063

JACKSON, CAROLE EDYTHE, computer software firm executive; b. Bloomfield Hills, Mich., Apr. 20, 1956; d. William Carlton Warrick and Joan Ruth (Hessler) Jackson. B.A. in Art History, U. Mich., 1976, M.B.A., 1978; postgrad. Harrington Inst. Interior Design, 1985—. Lic. real estate broker, securities sales. Corp. research analyst Ill. Bell Telephone Co., Chgo., 1978-81; mktg. account mgr. Dun & Bradstreet Corp., Chgo., 1981-83; dir. mktg. Monchik Weber Corp., Chgo., 1983-85; v.p. mktg. Walsh Greenwood & Co., Chgo., 1985—; mktg. cons. Triton Coll., River Grove, Ill., 1982-83, Roeper City and Country Sch., Bloomfield Hills, 1984. Artist/designer water color, pencil drawings. Com. mem. Ann Arbor City Planning Commn., 1976-77. Mem. Am. Mktg. Assn., Am. Mgmt. Assn., Am. Assn. Individual Investors, Option Soc. (asst. chmn. selection com. 1984-85), Nat. Assn. Women Bus. Owners. Presbyterian. Home: Coach House 2618 N Orchard Chicago IL 60614 Office: Wang Fin Info Services Co 440 S LaSalle St Suite 1915 Chicago IL 60605

JACKSON, CONSTANCE CORDICE, reading cons.; b. Winchester, Mass.; d. Conrad and Florence (Smith) Cordice; B.S. in Elem. Edn., Boston U., 1963, M.Ed. in Reading, Lang., Elem. Edn., 1966, Ed.D. in Reading, Elem. Edn., 1974; m. Eugene B. Jackson. Tchr. Scituate (Mass.) Public Schs., 1963-64; tchr. Marshfield (Mass.) Public Schs., 1964-68, reading cons., 1968—; teaching fellow Boston U., 1972. Dir. Marshfield Right to Read Effort, 1973-76. Mem. NEA, Internat. Reading Assn., Mass., Marshfield tchrs. assns., Mass. Reading Assn., Delta Kappa Gamma, Pi Lambda Theta. Home: PO Box 126 North Marshfield MA 02059 Office: Eames Way Sch Marshfield MA 02050

JACKSON, DELLA ROSETTA HAYDEN, civic worker, educator, author; b. Mill Spring, N.C., Mar. 2, 1905; d. Robert Twitty and Amanda (Petty) Hayden; B.A., Johnson C. Smith U., 1948; M.A., N.C. Coll., 1956; m. G. Franklin Davenport, Sept. 28, 1930 (dec. Jan. 1936); children—Evelyn Frances Davenport Petty, Amanda Elizabeth Davenport Gray, Robert Franklin; m. 2d, Clarence Eugene Jackson, Oct. 30, 1943 (dec. Mar. 1951); children—Mae Carolyn Jackson Williams, Clarence Stinson. Tchr., Stony Knoll Sch., Polk County, N.C., 1927-30, Tryon Sch., 1930-31, Pea Ridge Sch., 1932-39, Union Grove Sch., 1939-48, Edmund Embury Sch., 1949-51, Cobb Elementary Sch., Tryon, N.C., 1951-65; tchr. adult edn. Isothermal Community Coll., Mill Spring, N.C., 1971-77; organizer, librarian Stony Knoll Community Library, 1937—, pres., 1972—, also chmn. bd. trustees; spl. edn. tchr. Polk Central High Sch., Mill Spring, 1966-69; resource person Polk County Community Schs., 1982—. Mem. Central Highlands Health Council, 1968-70; 2d v.p. Polk County Homemakers Council; pres. Polk County Extension Homemakers, 1974-75; sec.-treas. Polk County Community Devel. Council; mem. Polk County Family Life Study Com., 1978-79; mem. Ancillary Manpower Planning Bd., Region C, 1972-82, mem. exec. com., 1976-83; leader 4-H clubs, 1965-85; v.p. Polk County Child Devel. Council, 1971-75, Eastern Appalachian Children's Council, 1971-73; chmn. Polk County Child Care Com., 1971-73; mem. Polk County Emergency Med. Service Adv. Com., 1973-75, Polk County Commn. on Aging, 1974—, N.C. Child Care, N.C. Children's 100; bd. dirs. Isothermal Health Council, sec., 1972-76; bd. dirs. Polk County Mental Health Council, 1972-73, St. Luke Hosp. Aux., 1970-77, 85—, Regional Health Council Eastern Appalachia, 1970-77, Polk County unit Am. Cancer Soc., 1979-82; bd. govs., mem. exec. com. Western N.C. Health System Agy., 1977-81, mem. resource devel. com., 1978-81; steering com. Gov.'s Regional Conf. on Leadership Devel. for Women, 1978-79; mem. Region C Employment and Tng. Adv. Com., 1978-83, Polk County Interagy. Council, 1978-81, Polk County Family Life Council, 1978; club rep. Polk County Community Resource Council, 1986—. Named Mother of Year, Afro, 1948, Mother of Year, Homemakers Council Polk County and Western Dist. N.C., 1971; recipient cert. service N.C. Recreation Soc., 1962; cert. leadership for service Western N.C. Community Devel. Program Asheville Agrl. Devel. Council, 1962; award for outstanding leadership and service Western N.C. Devel. Assn., 1979, Woman of Year, 1979; cert. of appreciation Western N.C. Health System Agy., 1981; cert. of award Polk County Hist. Assn., 1980; Sunday Sch. Tchr. of Yr., Stony Knoll C.M.E. Ch., 1980. Mem. LWV (dir. 1970—), Stony Knoll Recreation Soc., Polk County Hist. Assn. Clubs: Order of Calanthe (worthy counselor), Stony Knoll Community (pres. 1959-62). Author: Special Approaches for Sunday School in Small Churches, 1981; Poems of Experience and Emotion, 1981; Twenty Little Prayers, 1981; Let My People Go, 1982. Home: Box 95 Mill Spring NC 28756

JACKSON, DENISE VARNELL, educator; b. Cleve., Sept. 5, 1952; d. Walter Alvin and Margaret (Scott) Wolff; m. Eugene Jack Jackson, Jr., June 6, 1976; 1 dau., Denise Daniele. B.A., Tex. So. U., 1974, M.A. 1978. Tchr. English, Houston Ind. Sch. Dist., 1974-81, 82—; instr. English Houston Community Coll., 1974-75, 78-79; personnel asst. Union Carbide, Houston, 1981-82; mem. French Fgn. Lang. Curriculum Com., Houston, 1975; guest speaker Houston Ind. Sch. Dist. In-Service, Houston, 1980. L'Alliance Francaise scholar, Houston, 1972; Ford Ednl. Found. grantee, Houston, 1983. Mem. Assn. Supervision and Curriculum Devel. Nat. Council Tchrs. English, Houston Area Council Tchrs. English, Tex. Assn. Supervision and Curriculum Devel. Democrat. Roman Catholic. Home: 3723 Grapevine Dr Houston TX 77045 Office: Houston Ind Sch Dist 1700 Dumble St Houston TX 77025

JACKSON, EVELYN ARDETH, nurse; b. Great Falls, Mont., Feb. 11, 1929; d. Henry and Esther Lillian (Morris) Bergdorf; m. Elmer Donald Jackson, May 16, 1952; children—Donita Jo, Jenice Evelyn. Student Gonzaga U., 1947-48; R.N., St. Luke's Sch. Nursing, Spokane, Wash., 1950; postgrad. St. Joseph's Coll., Roanoke, Va., 1983—. Staff nurse in doctors' offices, Spokane, 1950-55, Houston, 1956-68; 76-78; supr. M.D. Anderson Hosp. and Cancer Inst., Houston, 1968-76; nursing supr. Austin Steel Co., Houston, 1978-80; charge nurse Reed Rock Bit Co., Houston, 1980—. Mem. Houston Occupational Health Nurses Assn. (documentation com. 1980-81, telephone com. 1981-82, nomination com. 1982-83, dir. 1982—), Am. Occupational Health Assn., Tex. Occupational Health Assn. (dir. 1986—), Nat. Mgmt. Assn., Profl. and Bus. Women, ARC (instr. 1980—), Am. Security Council. Republican. Methodist. Club: U.S. Senatorial (presdl. task force 1985) (Washington). Home: PO Box 325 Bellaire TX 77401 Office: Reed Rock Bit PO Box 2119 Houston TX 77252

JACKSON, FRANCES D., accounting technician; b. Coldspring, Tex., May 19, 1952; d. James and Margarett L. (Washington) Jackson. Student U. Houston, 1971, 80; Cert., U.S. Postal Service, 1981. With Neighborhood Youth Co., Coldspring, Tex., 1970; ward clk. St. Joseph Hosp., Houston, 1971-72; with Exxon Co., USA, Houston, 1972-73, keypunch operator, 1973-74; keypunch operator Occidental Petroleum, Houston, 1974-75; acctg. technician U.S. Postal Service, Houston, 1975—, key word processing operator, 1985—. Pres., San Jacinto County 4-H Club, Coldspring, 1969. Recipient Spl. Achievement award U.S. Postal Service, Houston, 1981, named Employee of Mo., 1981; Gold Star award, Tex. A&M U. 4-H Club, 1969. Mem. Nat. Assn. Female Execs. Avocations: sewing; cooking; macrame; fishing; sports. Office: US Postal Service 401 Franklin Houston TX 77071

JACKSON, FRANCES HANLEY, telephone company administrator; b. Bluefield, W.Va., Nov. 6, 1941; d. Ralph Keys and Rosa Jane (Ferguson) Hanley; 1 child, Sylvia Evette Mahan. B.S., Bluefield State Coll., 1962. With So. Bell Telephone Co., 1968-69, 78—, asst. mgr., Decatur, Ga., 1979—; v.p. RKH & Assocs., Decatur, 1982—. Recipient I Made the Difference award So. Bell Telephone, 1985. Mem. Democratic Club Dekalb County (dir. 1984), Southeastern YMCA Women's Club (pres. 1978—), Nat. Bus. and Profl. Women's Club Am. (treas. 1975—), Am. Bus. Women (sec. 1982-85). Baptist. Avocations: piano playing; cooking. Home: 1981 Ethel Ln Decatur GA 30032 Office: So Bell Telephone 5147 Peachtree Industrial Blvd Chamblee GA 30058

JACKSON, FREDA LUCILLE, clergywoman, church administrator, editor; b. Sikeston, Mo., Sept. 15, 1928; d. Jesse Freda and Ruby Lucille (Carter) Andres; student Three Rivers Jr. Coll., 1969, Central Bible Coll., Springfield, Mo., 1973; B.S., Drury Coll., 1980; M.A. in Bibl. Lit., Assemblies of God Theol. Sem., 1986; m. Thomas Lowell Jackson, Oct. 2, 1947; children—Stephen Andres, Elizabeth Ann, Thomas Dean. Bookkeeper, Aduddel Wholesale Auto Parks, Sikeston, 1947-48; pvt. sec. to v.p. So. Ice & Coal Co., Memphis, 1948-49; sec. firm Bailey & Craig, Sikeston, 1950-56, firm Blanton & Blanton, 1956-57; ordained to ministry Assemblies of God Ch., 1983; promotions coordinator, editor deferred giving and trusts dept., gen. council Assemblies of God, Springfield, Mo., 1974—; tchr. English, Central Bibl. Coll., 1986—. Mem. Alpha Sigma Lambda, Womens Ministries, Maranatha Aux. Editor: New Dimensions, 1979—, Maranatha newsletter, 1977; contbr. articles to denominational publs. Home: 2407 W Atlantic St Springfield MO 65803 Office: Office: 1445 Boonville Ave Springfield MO 65802

JACKSON, GERALDINE MCMILLAN, mathematics educator; b. Lubbock, Tex., Feb. 15, 1949; d. Thawather and Lenora (Morrison) McM.; m. Fabian Wallace Jackson, Dec. 19, 1973; children—Africia, Kafricia. B.S., M.S., Prairie View A&M U. Mgr., Nat. Convenience Stores, Houston, 1972-77; tchr. North Forest Ind. Sch. Dist., Houston, 1977—, curriculum writer, 1979—, mem. textbook com., 1983. NSF scholar, 1980. Mem. Delta Sigma Theta, Kappa Delta Pi. Office: North Forest Ind Sch Dist 7525 Tidwell St Houston TX 77018

JACKSON, HELEN RUTH, retail executive; b. Little Rock, Feb. 21, 1952; d. Raymond Warren and Georgia Pearl (Cavanah) Jackson. B.F.A., U. Okla., 1976, postgrad. in bus. adminstrn., 1977. With Sanger Harris dept. stores, Dallas, 1978-83, sr. asst. buyer lingerie, 1980-81, sr. asst. buyer bath accessories, 1981, buyer stationery, 1981-83; gift buyer, mdse. mgr. Bennett Card Shops, Inc., Arlington, Tex., 1983-84; gift, accessory and ready-to-wear buyer Aeroplex div. Zale Corp., Irving, Tex., 1984—. Republican. Methodist. Home: 6108 Abrams St Apt 405 Dallas TX 75231 Office: Zale Corp PO Box 152765 Irving TX 75015

JACKSON, HOLLACE DAWNE, physician; b. Lakewood, N.J., Jan. 6, 1944; d. William Ward and Rae Muriel (Applegate) J.; m. Jeffrey Stephen Tullman, Dec. 12, 1970; children—Matthew Leigh, Gillian Blythe. B.A., Conn. Coll., 1965; M.D., N.Y. Med. Coll., 1970. Diplomate Am. Bd. Ob-Gyn. Intern dept. surgery Met. Hosp./Flower Fifth Ave Hosp., N.Y.C., resident dept. ob-gyn, 1971-75; practice medicine specializing in ob-gyn, Huntington, N.Y., 1975—. Fellow Am. Coll. Ob-Gyn (mem. com. on patient edn. 1981—); mem. Martin L. Stone Soc. Ob-Gyn, Med. Soc. N.Y., N.Y. Med. Coll., Suffolk County Med. Soc., Suffolk County Ob-Gyn Soc. (mem. exec. com. 1976). Club: Huntington Bay (Huntington, N.Y.). Office: 161 E Main St Huntington NY 11743

JACKSON, JEANNE ANNE, educational consultant; b. Lakewood, Ohio, Aug. 21, 1922; d. Edward Adam and Elsa Wilhelmina (Stengel) Roege; A.B., Hiram Coll., 1944; M.A., Kent State U., 1962; Ph.D., Case-Western Res. U., 1970; m. Stuart Ray Jackson, July 12, 1946; children—Stuart Clinton, Philip Clay. With Nat. City Bank Cleve., 1944-47, Geneva Savs. & Trust Co. (Ohio), 1947-52; tchr. Geneva Area City Schs., 1954-68; tchr., guidance counselor Kirtland (Ohio) Middle Sch., 1969-70; adminstrv. asst. Ashtabula (Ohio) County Joint Vocat. Sch., 1970-75; prin., adminstrv. asst. Geneva Area City Schs., 1975-82; pres. Curriculum and Supervision Services, Inc., 1982—; asst. prof. Kent (Ohio) State U., 1980—. Past pres. United Way Ashtabula County; trustee Ohio Citizens Council, Ashtabula Arts Ctr., Overlook House, Cleve.; trustee 1st Ch. of Christ Scientist, Ashtabula. Recipient Status of Women award Zonta 1981; Outstanding Citizen award Ashtabula C. of C., 1982. Mem. AAUW, Women's Service League Ashtabula, LWV, Assn. Supervision and Curriculum Devel., Am. Assn. Sch. Adminstrs., Internat. Reading Assn., Mensa, Nat. Council Tchrs. English, Delta Kappa Gamma. Republican. Clubs: Eastern Star (past matron), Zonta. Home: 1634 Highland Ln Ashtabula OH 44004

JACKSON, JEWEL, state youth authority official; b. Shreveport, La., June 3, 1942; d. Willie Burghardt and Bernice Jewel (Mayberry) Norton; m. Edward James Norman, May 17, 1961 (div. Nov. 1968); children—Steven, June Kelly; m. Wilbert Jackson, Apr. 6, 1969; children—Michael, Anthony. With Calif. Youth Authority, 1965—, group supr., San Andreas and Santa Rosa, 1965-67, youth counselor, Ventura, 1967-78, sr. youth counselor, Stockton, 1978-81, treatment team supr., program mgr., Whittier and Ione, 1981—, affirmative action adv. mem., Sacramento, 1976-78, equal employment adv. mem., 1978-79; speaker U. Pacific Youth Motivational Project, Stockton, Calif., 1985-86. Mem. Women in Criminal Justice-North (co-chair 1974-76), Nat. Assn. for Female Execs., Assn. Black Correctional Workers (chpt. v.p. 1979, editor newsletter 1978-80). Avocations: reading, horseback riding, writing poetry and short stories, designing clothing. Office: CYA-Preston Sch Industry 201 Waterman Rd Ione CA 95640

JACKSON, JOE ANN, medical association administrator; b. Brewton, Ala., Feb. 13, 1949; d. William Joseph and Missouri (Stokes) J. B.S., Northwestern U., 1986. Program adminstr. AMA, Chgo., 1974—. editor directories: Opportunity Placement Register, Physician Placement Register. Mem. Am. Mktg. Assn. Mem. Pentecostal Ch. Home: 5050 S Lake Shore Dr 2708 Chicago IL 60615 Office: AMA 535 N Dearborn Chicago IL 60610

JACKSON, JOSLYN DELA HOUSSAYE, fashion designer, manufacturer; b. New Orleans, June 15, 1943; d. Clyde Greig and Joslyn Louise (Anderson) de la Houssaye; m. Robert Bruce Jackson, Dec. 12, 1974; children—Robert Bruce, Melissa Lyn. m. Carl Sidley Craine, Dec. 18, 1964 (div. Apr. 1974); 1 child, Saunders Paul Jones. B.A., Newcomb Coll., 1965. Tchr., Rugby Acad., New Orleans, 1965-67; pres. Lynley Designs, Jefferson, La., 1968—. Republican. Episcopalian. Avocations: tennis; walking; reading. Office: Lynley Designs 2628 Jefferson Hwy Jefferson LA 70121

JACKSON, JOY JUANITA, educator; b. New Orleans, Oct. 8, 1928; d. Oliver Daniel and Oneida Christina (Drouant) Jackson; student La. State U., 1946-49; B.A., Tulane U., 1951, M.A., 1958, Ph.D., 1961. Feature writer New Orleans Times-Picayune, 1951-56; instr. Nicholls State Coll., Thibodaux, La., 1961-62, asst. prof., 1962-66; asst. prof. Southeastern La. U., Hammond, 1966-68, asso. prof., 1968-73, prof. history, 1973—, dir. Center for Regional Studies and univ. archives, 1982—. AAUW Irma E. Voight fellow, 1960-61. Mem. Am., La. (dir. 1966-68, pres. 1977-78), So. Hist. Assn., S.E. La. Hist. Assn. (pres. Hammond 1978), Oral History Assn. Author: New Orleans in the Gilded Age, 1969. Home: 1411 University Dr Hammond LA 70401

JACKSON, JOYCE ANITA, deputy sheriff; b. Commerce, Tex., Feb. 8, 1935; d. James Monroe and Ada Ann (Graham) Newell; student Abiline Christian Coll., 1978-79; cert. dental asst. Baylor Dental Coll., 1958; children—Kathy Ann Jackson, Jack E. Jackson, James Edward Jackson, Laura Jo Crabb. Dental asst. bus. mgmt. Drs. Swords and Miranda, Dallas, 1954-67; pres., owner Breakaway Enterprises, Dallas, 1967-69; v.p. Emergency Info. Systems, Dallas, 1970-77; part-time dep. U.S. marshall, Dallas, 1978; dep. sheriff Dallas County Sheriffs Dept., 1977—. Asst. coordinator charity for handicapped children of Dallas-Ft. Worth area. Mem. Republican Nat. Com., 1980-82. Mem. Am. Dental Asst. Assn., Profl. and Businesswomen's Assn., Dallas County Sheriffs Assn., Beta Sigma Phi. Republican. Office: Dallas County Sheriffs Dept 600 Commerce Dallas TX 75202

JACKSON, JOYCE ELIZABETH MITCHELL, government official; b. Washington, Aug. 21, 1935; d. Clarence Hural and Flora Elizabeth (Washington) Mitchell; m. William I. McAdoo, Feb. 4, 1955; 1 child, Gregory Michael; m. Leo Jackson, June 23, 1962; 1 child, Gary Leo. A.A., Univ. of D.C., 1983, B.A. cum laude, 1985. Exec. sec. Voice of Am., Washington, 1975-81, staff asst., 1981-82; paralegal USIA, Washington, 1982, personnel specialist, 1982-85, research specialist, 1985—. Block leader Ft. Lincoln Civic Assn., Washington, 1980-81. Mem. Nat. Assn. Female Execs., Am. Polit. Sci. Assn. (assoc.), Nat. Assn. Realtors (assoc.), Washington Bd. Realtors, Nat. Capitol Area Paralegal Assn., Delta Sigma Theta. Democrat. Episcopalian. Avocations: piano, organ, travel. Home: 240 M St SW Apt E-507 Washington DC 20024 Office: USIA 301 4th St SW R562 Washington DC 20547

JACKSON, KAREN SUE, electrical engineer; b. Wrightstown, N.J., Apr. 15, 1958; d. Lloyd William and Olivia Bernice (Pickens) Jackson. B.S.E.E., U. Okla., 1981. Engr. I, Pub. Service of Okla., Tulsa, 1981-83, elec. engr., Jenks, 1983—. U. Okla. scholar, 1975. Mem. IEEE, Nat. Assn. Female Execs., Nat. Soc. Black Engrs. Democrat. Baptist. Home: 1610 N Cheyenne Tulsa OK 74106 Office: Public Service Co of Okla Riverside Sta 116th St and Arkansas River Jenks OK 74037

JACKSON, KATE, actress; b. Birmingham, Ala., Oct. 29; d. Hogan and Ruth J.; m. Andrew Stevens, Aug. 23, 1978. Grad. Am. Acad. Dramatic Arts, 1971; student U. Miss., Birmingham U. Worked as model; TV series: Dark Shadows 1966-71, The Rookies, 1972-76, Charlie's Angels, 1976-79; other TV appearances include: Movin' On, The Jimmy Stewart Show; TV movies include: Death Cruise, 1974, Killer Bees, 1974, Death Scream, 1975, Charlie's Angels, 1976, The New Healers, 1972, James at 15, 1977; film appearances: Dark Shadows, Limbo, Thunder and Lightning, Dirty Tricks, 1979; exec. producer, star TV movie Topper, 1979; star TV series: Scarecrow and Mrs. King, 1983—. Nominated 3 times for Emmy award. Address: care Creative Artists Agency Inc 1888 Century Park E Suite 1400 Los Angeles CA 90067*

JACKSON, KATHLEEN LYNN, sales executive; b. Winamac, Ind., Mar. 20, 1954; d. Stanley Clark and Darlene Jeanette (Muffley) Chaney; m. Douglas Wayne Jackson, June 4, 1976. B.A., Drake U., 1976, M.A., 1983. Sales assoc./dept. mgr. Younkers, Des Moines, 1976-77; brokers asst./sec. Kidder Peabody, Kansas City, Mo., 1977-78; editor newsletter, exec. sec. The Weitz Co., Des Moines, 1979-82; creative writer P.S. Writes, Des Moines, 1982—; scriptwriter Am. Media, Inc., Des Moines, 1983-84; account exec. advt. Sales Sta. KJJY, Des Moines, 1984—. Editor newsletter Women in Communications, 1983-84. Mem. Women in Communications. Republican. Home: 2914 Hillsdale Dr Urbandale IA 50322

JACKSON, LADY LOYD APPLEBY, personnel executive; b. Toccoa, Ga., July 8, 1946; d. Samuel Cecil and Lillian Loyd (Collins) Appleby; m. Joseph Howard Torrence, July 27, 1968 (div. 1973); 1 dau., Katherine Loyd; m. Thomas Houston Jackson, May 3, 1974; children—Thomas Houston, Jr., John Andrew. B.A., Mary Baldwin Coll., 1968. Cert. profl. in human resources. Exec. trainee Sears, Roebuck & Co., Phila., 1968-69; tng. adminstr. Genesco, Inc., Nashville, 1969-72; adminstrv. asst. State Tenn. Dept. Human Services, Nashville, 1972-73, dir. office services, 1973-77, dir. personnel, 1977-80; dir. personnel ARC, Nashville, 1980-81; asst. dir. personnel Nashville Electric Service, 1981—; sec.-treas. The Guide Co., Inc., 1984—. Vice chmn. bd. Mcpl. Auditorium Bd., Nashville, 1976-77; sec., treas. Tenn. Personnel Adv. Council, Nashville, 1978-79; mem. Outlook Nashville Personnel Com. bd. dirs. United Methodist Neighborhood Centes, Nashville, 1984—, chmn. personnel com., 1985; cons. Jr. Achievement, 1986. Recipient Laurel Soc. award Mary Baldwin Coll., 1968. Mem. Indsl. Personnel Assn. (chmn. operating com. 1982-83), Indsl. Personnel Assn. (sec. treas. v.p. 1984, pres. 1985), Am. Soc. Personnel Adminstrs. (program com. chmn. 1984, sec. 1986), Internat. Assn. Quality Circles (co-founder, dir. Central Tenn. chpt. 1982-83). Democrat. Mem. Church of Christ. Office: Nashville Electric Service 1214 Church St Nashville TN 37246

JACKSON, LELA EVELYNE, company executive; b. Mesilla Park, N.Mex. Feb. 11, 1941; d. Willie L. and Ruth (Boggess) Ashworth; m. Robert C. Jackson, Apr. 21, 1969; children—Cinthia Sams, Edward Taber, Elizabeth Baker; adopted children—Shiela Prokuski, Robert Jackson, Regina Jackson. B.A. in Acctg., Bakersfield Coll., 1970; cert. fed. taxation Tex. A&M U., 1983. Ptnr., Personalized Bookkeeping, Bakersfield, 1969-71, Jackson & Jackson, Vivian, La., 1977-79; pres. Le Jac Inc., Vivian, 1979—. Subsect. mem. Nat. Republican Com., Washington, 1982—. Mem. North Caddo C. of C. (co-founder, sec. 1980-81), Profl. Cons. Baptist. Avocations: fishing; gardening; reading. Home: PO Box 747 Vivian LA 71082 Office: Le Jac Inc 611 S Pine Vivian LA 71082

JACKSON, LINDA ELAINE, nurse; b. Los Angeles, Mar. 12, 1945; d. Gordon Leslie and Rose Elaine Jackson; m. Robert B. Baxter, Nov. 1966 (div. 1971); m. James P. Wood, Feb. 20, 1971 (div. Aug. 1975); m. William Ernest Paul, Oct. 6, 1984; 1 child, Loree Elaine. R.N., Samuel Merritt Hosp. Sch. Nursing, Oakland, Calif., 1966; B. Health Scis., Chapman Coll., 1978. Cert. ins. rehab. specialist. Staff nurse, inservice dir. Sierra View Dist. Hosp., Porterville, Calif., 1966-76; asst. prof. nursing Kern Community Coll. Dist., Bakersfield, Calif., 1976-82; rehab. nurse. Indsl. Indemnity Co., Bakersfield, 1983—; instr. IV therapy Kern Nursing Edn. Assocs., Bakersfield, 1982—. Mem. Golden Empire Safety Soc., Occupational Health Nurses Group. Republican. Avocations: gardening; swimming; traveling; flying. Office: Industrial Indemnity 2200 19th St Bakersfield CA 93301

JACKSON, LOIS ANN, rehabilitation facility program administrator; b. Clinton, Iowa, Aug. 23, 1948; d. Alvin E. and Vera Miranda (Barnes) Roberts; m. Darrell John Jackson, Jan. 1, 1972; children—Vanessa Ann, Brian Nicholas, Valerie Rose. B.A., U. No. Iowa, 1970. Cert. tchr. mental retardation, elem., Iowa. Tchr. trainable mentally retarded Pottawattamie County Schs., Council Bluffs, Iowa, 1970-72; head tchr. Skyline Ctr., Inc., Clinton, Iowa, 1972-76, program mgr., 1976—. Mem. Nat. Assn. Female Execs., Smithsonian Assocs. Lutheran. Avocations: reading; antique and auto shows. Home: 832 3d Ave S Clinton IA 52732 Office: Skyline Ctr Inc PO Box 3064 Clinton IA 52732

JACKSON, LOIS THIGPEN, county official; b. Bailey, N.C., May 28, 1935; d. George Washington and Lillie B. (Temple) Thigpen; m. Osco Kermit Jackson, Sept. 21, 1957; 1 child, Elsie Yvonne. Grad. Hradbarger Bus. Sch., Raleigh, N.C., 1956; student Carson-Newman Coll., Walters State Community Coll. Cert. tax preparer, IRS. With Wachovia Bank & Trust Co., Raleigh, 1953-56; exec. sec. N.C. Dairy Products Assn., Inc., Raleigh, 1956-57; legal sec. Daniel & Daniel, Rutledge, Tenn., 1957-69; clk. and master Grainger County Chancery Ct., Rutledge, 1969—. Vice-chair Grainger County Vocat. Adv. Com., 1983-85; chair Grainger County Council on Aging, 1980—, Grainger County Republican Women, 1970—; sec. Grainger County Rep. party, 1970—; vol. Ridgeview Terr. Nursing Home, 1980—; mem. adv. council Walters State Community Coll. Found., 1970-83; chair Grainger County Heart Assn., 1982-83, Grainger County Cancer Drive, various times. Mem. Tenn. County Ofcls. Assn., State Ct. Clks. Assn. Baptist. Avocations: sewing; decorating; gardening; catering. Home: Route 4 Box 77 Rutledge TN 37861 Office: Courthouse Rutledge TN 37861

JACKSON, LORA RUTHE THOMPSON, parliamentarian, corporate executive; b. Ft. Worth, Oct. 29, 1920; d. John Lyle and Florence (Ector) Thompson; student Ft. Worth Christian Coll., 1960, Christian Coll. of Southwest, 1969, bus. courses; m. Vernon Jackson, Sept. 10, 1944; children—Xanna Yvonne Jackson Young, Jorja Annette Jackson Clemson. Mail and advt. clk. Mut. Benefit Ins. Co., 1940-42; clk. to exec. sec. N. Am. Aviation, 1942-45; exec. sec. TEMCO Mfg., 1945-47, Luscombe Aircraft, 1947-50; sec., gen. office supr. SA-SO Sign Mfg. Co., 1950-53; co-owner All-Quality Sign Co., 1953-59; co-owner, v.p., office supr., public relations dir. Jackson Vending Supply, Inc., Grand Prairie, Tex., 1959—; dir. DeSoto First Nat. Bank; tchr., judge parliamentary law. Mem. Dallas County Sch. Bd., 1974—, Dallas County Hist. Commn., 1974—; chmn. Grand Prairie Arts and Hist. Preservation Commn., 1976—; chmn. Grand Prairie Bi-Centennial, 1974-76; mem. Grand Prairie Civil Def. Commn., 1959—; mem., past chmn. Grand Prairie Community and Home Improvements Commn., 1964—; mem. spl. funds com. Grand Prairie Ind. Sch. Dist.; active local, council and dist PTA's; regional v.p. Tex. PTA. Recipient Mrs. Lyndon B. Johnson environ. award Keep Am. Beautiful, 1977; hon. life mem. Nat. Congress Parents and Tchrs., Tex. Congress Parents and Tchrs.; recipient Tex. Bluebonnet state award Beautify Tex. Council, 1978, award in conservation Tex. Forest Service, 1976; named Woman of Yr., Grand Prairie Daily News, 1979. Registered profl. parliamentarian. Mem. Grand Prairie Friends of the Library (pres. 1978-80), Grand Prairie C. of C. (Women of Year Women's div. 1967, Citizen of Year, 1969, pres. chamber 1982—), Tex. Assn. Parliamentarians (state pres. 1974-75), Nat. Assn. Parliamentarians, Beautify Tex. Council (state pres. 1976-78), Grand Prairie Hist. Orgn., (life, sec., founding pres.), Grand Prairie Hosp. Aux. (life). Democrat. Mem. Ch. of Christ. Clubs: Grand Prairie Bus. and Profl. Women's (treas., Woman of Year 1976, 82, pres.-elect 1982-83), Grand Prairie Garden (pres., Woman of Year 1975), Soroptimist of Grand Prairie (corr. sec.), Soroptomist Internat. (regional parliamentarian). Contbr. articles on parliamentary law, beautification and community improvement, and cultural arts to mags.; co-host, co-dir. cable TV show It's Happening in Grand Prairie, 1981—. Home and Office: 200 Meyers Rd Grand Prairie TX 75050

JACKSON, MAE FRANCES, human resources development specialist; b. Butler, Ala., Aug. 24, 1942; d. Henry Barnett and Lennie Toreatha (Morse) J.; m. Charles Walter Williams, July 16, 1962 (div. 1984); children—Derrick Kenneth Williams, Charles Henry Williams, Monique Janeen Williams. B.A., Fisk U., 1963; M.S.W., Hunter Coll., 1968. Cert. social worker, N.Y. Asst. prof. Utica Coll. of Syracuse U., 1979-83; exec. v.p. IGT Travel, Hollis, N.Y., 1984—; pres. Mae Jackson Assocs., St. Albans, N.Y., 1983—; sr. human resource devel. specialist Fed. Express Corp., Memphis, 1986—; cons. in field. Named Woman of Yr., Nat. Fedn. Bus. & Profl. Women's Clubs Inc., Utica, N.Y., 1982. Mem. AAUW, Am. Assn. Female Execs., Am. Soc. Travel Agts., Nat. Assn. Social Workers, Nat. Council Negro Women, Nat. Urban League, NAACP, N.Y. Assn. Social Work Educators (pres. 1983), Alpha Kappa Alpha (chpt. pres. 1982). Avocations: traveling; lecturing; walking. Address: PO Box 171305 Memphis TN 38117

JACKSON, MARIE-THERESE OLIVER, judge; b. Pitts., Aug. 14, 1947; d. Warren Joseph and Nettie Marie (Wall) Oliver; m. Peter Jackson, July 8, 1972 (div.); children—Vincent, Alphonso. B.A., Mt. Holyoke Coll., 1969. Bar: Mass. 1973, U.S. Dist. Ct. Mass., 1973. Assoc. Cambridge & Somerville Legal Services, Mass., 1972-74; atty. Mass. Commn. Against Discrimination, Boston, 1974, dir. investigation, 1974-76; adminstrv. judge Div. Hearing Officers, State of Mass., Boston, 1976-77; gen. counsel Exec. Office Adminstrn. and Fin., Boston, 1977-80; judge Cambridge Dist. Ct. (Mass.), 1980—; mem. Juvenile Justice Com., Gov.'s Anti-Crime Commn., 1983—; teaching faculty Mass. Continuing Legal Edn., Mass. Judicial Inst. Bd. dirs. Adolescent Consultation Service, Cambridge, 1981—, Cambridge and Somerville Mental Health Bd., 1981-84, West Medford Community Ctr. (Mass.), 1979-84; mem. Mass. Commn. on Correction Alternatives; mem. Gov.'s Com. on Foster Care, 1986; bd. dirs. Nat. Conf. Christians and Jews, 1985—, Boston Youth Symphony Orch., 1984—. Named one of Ten Outstanding Young Leaders, Boston Jr. C. of C., 1981; recipient citation for advocacy for foster parenting Boston City Council, 1985, Mass. Senate, 1985; Juvenile Justice award. Mem. Nat. Assn. Women Judges (dir. 1982-84) ABA (del. commn. courts, community, Nat. Conf. Spl. Ct. Judges 1983), Nat. Assn. Bus. and Profl. Women (Boston & vicinity group 1st v.p. 1979-80, leadership award 1981, Sojourner Truth Leadership award 1984), Mass. Black Lawyers Assn. (dir. 1978-79, leadership award 1980), Alpha Kappa Alpha. Baptist. Office: Cambridge Dist Ct 40 Thorndike St Cambridge MA 02141

JACKSON, MARY CLARE LOKKEN, jeweler, educational/advertising consultant; b. LaCrosse, Wis., July 28, 1949; d. Clayton Marvin and Marian Lucille (Knutson) Lokken; m. William Thomas Jackson, Oct. 2, 1970; 1 dau., MaryJune Lokken. Student St. Olaf Coll., 1967-68; B.S. in Journalism, Iowa State U., 1971. Tchr., Portage (Wis.) Pub. Schs., 1972-76; pres., owner Magi Jewelry Ltd., Ames, Iowa, 1976—; salon coordinator/advt. cons. Finesse Imagemakers, Ames, 1976—; ednl. cons. Profl. Cosmetology Inst., Ames, 1978—. Mem. Iowa Jewelers and Watchmakers Assn. (dir.), Jewelers Am., Nat. Hairdressers and Cosmetologists Assn., Iowa Cosmetology Schs. Assn. Republican. Lutheran. Clubs: Altrusa, Order Eastern Star. Home: 4712 West Bend Dr Ames IA 50010 Office: Magi Jewelry Ltd 707 24th St Ames IA 50010

JACKSON, (MARY) RUTH, orthopaedic surgeon; b. Jefferson, Iowa, Dec. 13, 1902; d. William Riley and Carolyn Arabelle (Babb) J.; B.A., U. Tex., 1924; M.D., Baylor U., 1928. Gen. intern Meml. Hosp., Worcester, Mass., 1928-29, resident in orthopaedic surgery, 1930-31; intern in orthopaedic surgery Univ. Hosps., U. Iowa, 1929-30, resident in orthopaedic surgery Tex. Scottish Rite Hosp. for Crippled Children, Dallas and asst. at Carrell-Driver-Girard Clinic, Dallas, 1931-32; pvt. practice medicine specializing in orthopaedic surgery, Dallas, 1932—; clin. instr. in orthopaedic surgery Baylor U., Dallas, 1936-43; hon. cons. orthopaedic surgeon Baylor U. Med. Center, Dallas, Parkland Meml. Hosp., Dallas; hon. asst. clin. prof. orthopaedic surgery Southwestern Med. Sch. of U. Tex., Dallas; lectr. in field. Diplomate Am. Bd. Orthopaedic Surgery. Fellow ACS, Internat. Coll. Surgeons; mem. Dallas County Med. Assn., Tex. Med. Assn., So. Med. Assn., AMA, Tex. Orthopaedic Assn., Tex. Rheumatism Assn., Southwestern Surg. Congress, Am. Acad. Orthopaedic Surgeons, Am. Orthopaedic Foot Soc., Am. Assn. for Study Headache, Am. Trauma Soc., Am. Assn. Automotive Medicine, Am. Soc. Contemporary Medicine and Surgery, Western Orthopaedic Assn., Law-Sci. Acad. Am., Pan-Am. Med. Assn. (diplomate sect. orthopaedic surgery), Royal Soc. Medicine (assoc.), Nat. Assn. Disability Examiners, Dallas C. of C., North Dallas C. of C., Kaufman C. of C., Ruth Jackson Soc. Republican. Methodist. Club: Zonta Internat. Author monograph: The Cervical Syndrome, 1956, 4th edit., 1977, Japanese transl, 1967; contbr. articles to profl. jours. Office: 3629 Fairmount Dallas TX 75219

JACKSON, MAXINE ALLEN, city official; b. Chesterfield, Va., Jan. 11, 1945; d. Norman R. and Kathleen (West) Allen; m. Carl L. Jackson, June 20, 1964; children—Resnoquila, Carolyn, Carroll L., Richard, Kim, Marilyn, Demetrian. A.S., John Tyler Coll., 1972; B.Individualized Study, Va. State U., 1981, M.Ed., 1986. Social worker Chesterfield Social Service, 1976-78; case mgr. Mental Retardation, Chesterfield, 1978-79; tchr. Chesterfield Sch. System, 1979-81; eligibility worker Petersburg Social Service, Va., 1981—. Scholar Brown and Williamson U., 1985. Fellow NAACP, Nat. Eligibility Workers Assn., Va. Council Social Workers, Alpha Phi Alpha. Mem. African Methodist Ch. (sec. sr. missionary soc. 1983—; pres. young adult missionary soc. 1984—). Avocations: tennis; Softball, Bowling. Home: 13429 Bradley Bridge Rd Chester VA 23831 Office: Petersburg Social Services 35 W Fillmore St Petersburg VA 23803

JACKSON, MICHELLE EILEEN ROBERTS, lawyer; b. Orlando, Fla., Sept. 12, 1955; d. Sanford B. and Selma (Witte) Roberts; m. Patrick K. Jackson, Sept. 2, 1979; 1 child, Rachel Lauren. B.A. in Psychology cum laude, U. Miami, 1975, J.D., 1978. Bar: Fla. 1978, La. 1979, U.S. Ct. Appeals (5th cir.) 1980, U.S. Dist. Ct. (ea. dist.) La. 1980. Law clk. Friedman & Britton, Miami, Fla., 1976; legal intern State's Atty.'s Office, Dade County, Miami, 1977-78; asst. dist. atty. Orleans Parish Dist. Atty.'s Office, New Orleans, 1978-80, Dist. Atty.'s Office 15th Jud. Dist., Lafayette Parish, Lafayette, La., 1980—; bd. dirs. Acadiana Legal Services, Lafayette, 1982-84. Treas. Lafayette Talent Bank of Women, 1980—; friend of commn. Mayor's Commn. on Needs of Women, 1980-84, mem., 1984—; advisor Law Explorers Post 610, Boy Scouts Am., Lafayette, 1982-84; walkathon chmn. Lafayette chpt. Women in Mainstream, 1983; mem. Temple Rodelph Shalom Sisterhood. Mem. ABA (sect. criminal justice), Fla. Bar Assn., La. Bar Assn., Lafayette Parish Bar Assn., La. Trial Lawyers Assn., Acadiana Assn. Women Attys., La. Dist. Attys. Assn. (dir. 1983-86, pres. asst. dist. atty. sect. 1985-86), Nat. Dist. Attys. Assn., Phi Kappa Phi, Omicron Delta Kappa, Tau Epsilon Rho. Democrat. Club: Altrusa. Office: Dist Attys Office PO Box 3306 Lafayette LA 70502

JACKSON, MURIEL GRACE, university official; b. Wood-Ridge, N.J., Apr. 21, 1929; d. John David and Lillian Grace (Rogers) Kappeler; B.A., Keuka Coll., 1950; M.S., Columbia U. Sch. Journalism, 1952; grad. U. Mich. Inst. Acad. Adminstrv. Advancement, 1973, Oreg. Mgmt. Devel. Program, 1974; m. Rudolph Lorenz, Mar. 27, 1955 (dec. Nov. 1965); children—John Martin, Tracy Ann, Andrea Grace; m. 2d, Ross E. Jackson, June 10, 1967. Pub. relations asst. St. Lawrence U., 1950-51; editorial asst. Ridgewood (N.J.) News, 1952-53; reporter Binghamton (N.Y.) Press, 1953-56; adminstrv. asst. to pres. San Jose State Coll., 1966-69; asst. to pres. U. Oreg., 1969-75, dir. univ. relations, 1974-79, asst. for adminstrn., 1979-85, asst. v.p. for adminstrn., 1985—, dir. univ. bookstore, 1977-84. Troop leader Western Rivers Council Girl Scouts U.S.A., 1973-74; troop treas. Oreg. Trails Council Boy Scouts Am., 1973-74; sr. warden Episcopal Ch. of the Resurrection, Eugene, Oreg., 1973-74; chmn. Central Convocation Episcopal Diocese of Oreg., 1974-76; spl. events chmn. Lane County (Oreg.) United Way, 1976, 77; bd. dirs. Lane County Cancer Soc., 1978-80; bd. dirs. Lane Meml. Blood Bank, 1979-86, pres., 1984-85. Recipient Disting. Alumna award Keuka Coll., 1975. Mem. Council Advancement and Support of Edn., Eugene C. of C. (chmn. univ. affairs com. 1978, 81, 82), Lane County Rubicon Soc. Republican. Home: 401 Brae Burn Dr Eugene OR 97405 Office: 204 Johnson Hall U of Oreg Eugene OR 97403

JACKSON, NANCY ALICE, lawyer, educator; b. Findlay, Ohio, May 28, 1943; d. Charles Alfred and Margaret (Palmer) Jackson; m. Andre Ezis, Sept. 10, 1966; children—Katherine, Jenna. B.A. in English, Ohio State U., 1965, J.D. 1969; M.S., U. Detroit, 1983; postgrad. in criminal justice Wayne State U. Bar: Mich. 1970. Adminstrv. law judge Mich. Dept. Social Service, Detroit, 1970-72; asst. U.S. atty. U.S. Dept. Justice, Detroit, 1972-74; adminstrv. law judge Bur. Workers Compensation, Detroit, 1977-79. Mem. ABA, Mich. Bar Assn., Women Lawyers Assn. Mich. (founding mem.), Chi Delta Phi. Democrat. Home: 23235 W River Rd Grosse Ile MI 48138

JACKSON, NANCY LYNN, retail manager; b. Dallas, May 11, 1957; d. Eugene Laverne and Marcelene J. (Lamb) J. B.B.A., Baylor U., 1979; M.B.A., U. Tex.-Arlington, 1981. Lic. Realtor, Tex. Sales rep. Chemline, Inc., Plano, Tex., 1980-82; dept. mgr. Sanger-Harris, Dallas, 1982—; also real estate sales assoc. Campaigner Dallas Area Rapid Transit, 1983; outreach leader Grace Temple Baptist Ch.; mem. Dallas Mus. Fine Arts. Mem. Internat. Customer Service Assn., Baylor Alumni Assn. Republican. Clubs: Dallas Baylor, Southwest Baylor Bear. Office: Sanger-Harris 7600 Ambassador Row Dallas TX 75247

JACKSON, NORMA WHITEHEAD, educator; b. Houston, Aug. 14, 1937; d. Oliver and Lucy (Smith) Whitehead; m. William Cullen Jackson, July 28, 1962; children—Bristol Bouvier, William Cullen. B.A., Calif. State U.-Los Angeles, 1959; M.A., Loyola Marymount U., Los Angeles, 1981. Tchr., English, Carver Jr. High Sch., Los Angeles, 1961-64; tchr. English, San Fernando (Calif.) Jr. High Sch., 1964-72, dept. chmn., 1967-70, master tchr., 1968-71; tchr. English, Henry Clay Jr. High Sch., Los Angeles, 1972-81, dean students, 1981—, dept. chmn., 1973-78; pres. Norma Jackson & Assocs. Travel Consultants, partnership coordinator UCLA, Westwood, 1978-80. Mem. Choice, Van Nuys, Calif., 1978—, Force, Van Nuys, 1980—. Recipient Career Guidance award U. Calif.-Westwood, 1979; named Tchr. of Yr., Henry Clay Jr. High Sch., 1979; writing fellow, 1979. Mem. Calif. Tchrs. Assn., Los Angeles Pupil Personnel Assn. Democrat. Baptist. Home: 1924 W 108th St Los Angeles CA 90047 Office: Henry Clay Jr High School 12226 S Western Ave Los Angeles CA 90047

JACKSON, PATRICIA LEE (MRS. CLIFFORD L. JACKSON), psychologist; b. N.Y.C.; d. Albert George and Lisbeth P. (Lee) Scharf; B.A., Barnard Coll.; M.A., Ph.D., Tchrs. Coll. Columbia U.; m. Clifford L. Jackson. Dir. psychol. testing R. H. Macy & Co., Inc., 1941-49; employment dir. Alexander's Dept. Stores, Inc., Bronx, N.Y., 1949-52; asst. prof. psychology Hunter Coll., N.Y.C., 1951-66, asso. prof., 1966-77, coordinator of counseling services, 1959-71; research dir. Klein Inst. for Aptitude Testing, Inc., N.Y.C., 1953-59, asst. v.p., 1957-59; pvt. practice in psychotherapy, 1964—. Trustee Alfred Adler Inst.; v.p. bd. trustees Ch. of Healing Christ (Emmet Fox Ch.), N.Y.C. Mem. AAAS, Am. Personnel and Guidance Assn., Am. Psychol. Assn., Am. Statis. Assn., Am. Group Psychotherapy Assn., N.Y. Soc. Clin. Psychologists. Author articles in field. Home: 129 E 35th St New York NY 10016

JACKSON, PAULETTE WHITE, nursing administrator, home health agency executive; b. New Orleans, Jan. 19, 1949; d. Lawrence III and Velma (Jones) White; m. Robert Wardell Tate, June 30, 1964 (div. 1969); children—Robert Jr., Detra Jeanene; m. Tommy Lee Jackson, July 20, 1974; 1 child, Byron. B.S. in Nursing, Southeastern La. U., 1980. Staff nurse Capitol Home Health, Baton Rouge, 1980-81; dir. nursing service Hill Haven Nursing Home, Baton Rouge, 1981; nephrology nurse BMA Baton Rouge, 1981-82; staff nurse Ammon's Home Health, Baton Rouge, 1981-83; supr. Greenwell Springs Hosp., La., 1983; owner, adminstr. Faith Home Health Services, Baton Rouge, 1983—. Recipient Outstanding Bus. Achievement award Wybirk & Assocs. Inc., 1984. Mem. Beta Beta Beta. Democrat. Avocations: reading; skating; swimming. Home: 5589 Monarch Ave Baton Rouge LA 70811 Office: Faith Home Health Services 2034 Wooddale Blvd Suite A Baton Rouge LA 70806

JACKSON, PHYLLIS RUTHERFORD, interior designer, consultant; b. Bristol, Va., Apr. 18, 1950; d. James Simon and Ruby Marie (Arnold) Rutherford; m. Wendal Douglas Jackson, Sept. 12, 1975; 1 child, Melissa; stepchildren—Julie, Ted. A.A., Va. Intermont Coll., 1970; B.S., U. Tenn., 1976. Cert. interior designer. Mgmt. trainee Dominion Bank, Bristol, Va., 1970-72; head purchasing design dept. Camara Inns, Inc., Bristol, 1972-74; freelance designer, Eastern Tenn. area, 1974-78; interior designer Taylors, Inc., Johnson City, Tenn., 1978-79; owner, designer Jackson Interior Design, Blountville, Tenn., 1979—. Bd. dirs. Theatre Bristol, 1984—. Mem. Am. Soc. Interior Designers (assoc.), Greater Bristol Area C. of C. (bd. dirs. 1984—). Democrat. Methodist. Avocations: water skiing; softball. Home: Route 1 Box 344F-1 Piney Flats TN 37686 Office: PO Box 1117 TCAS Suite 116 Tri-city Airport Blountville TN 37617

JACKSON, RUTHIE FAY, govt. ofcl.; b. Wynne, Ark., June 2, 1948; d. Tyree and Ruth (Perry) Weaver; A.A.S. in Secretarial Sci., Seattle Community Coll., 1968; student U. Wash., 1971; m. Charles M. Jackson, July 6, 1974; children—Vanessa Marie, Casey Nathaniel. Receptionist Mobil Oil Corp., Seattle, 1969; clk., stenographer HEW (now Dept. Health and Human Services), Seattle, 1970-74, equal opportunity specialist, 1974-78, child support specialist, 1978-80, dep. regional rep. child support office, 1980-81, regional rep. Office Child Support Enforcement, Region X, Seattle, 1981—. Recipient Cert. of Merit, Dept. HHS, 1980, cash award, 1984, Merit award, 1985, 86. Mem. Nat. Assn. Female Execs., Am. Soc. Pub. Adminstrs., Seattle Urban League, NAACP. Mem. Church of God in Christ. Home: 12734 SE 73d St Renton WA 98056 Office: 2901 3d Ave M/S 415 Seattle WA 98121

JACKSON, SHARON PATRICE, research analyst; b. Washington, Feb. 4, 1958; d. Archibald and Frances (Armwood) J. B.A., Catholic U., 1980; M.A., Johns Hopkins U., 1982. Pub. info. specialist White House Council on Environ. Quality, Washington, 1980-81, research analyst NAACP, Washington, 1981-82, U.S. Dept. Def., Washington, 1982—. Mem. Network of Women in Slavic Studies, Nat. Assn. Female Execs., Johns Hopkins U. Alumni Assn. Avocation: reading.

JACKSON, SHIRLEY ANN, theoretical physicist; b. Washington; d. George Hiter and Beatrice (Cosby) J.; m. Morris A. Washington; 1 son, Alan. B.S. in Physics, M.I.T., 1968, Ph.D., 1973. Research assoc. Fermi Nat. Accelerator Lab., Batavia, Ill., 1973-74, 75-76; vis. scientist European Orgn. for Nuclear Research, Geneva, 1974-75; mem. tech. staff AT & T Bell Labs., Murray Hill, N.J., 1976—; visitor Stanford Linear Accelerator Center, 1976, Aspen Center for Physics, 1976, 77; mem. com. edn. and employment women in sci. and engring. NRC, 1980—; cons. NSF, 1977, NRC, 1977—; dir. N.J. Resources Corp. Mem. ednl. council M.I.T., 1976-80, trustee, 1975-85, mem. corp., 1975—; trustee Lincoln U. (Pa.), 1980—; mem. N.J. Commn. on Sci. and Tech. Recipient Candace award Nat. Coalition 100 Black Women, Salute to Policy Makers award Exec. Women of N.J., 1986, Black Achievers in Industry award Harlem YMCA, 1986; Martin Marietta Corp. scholar, 1964-68; Prince Hall Grand Masons scholar, 1964-68; NSF trainee, 1968-71; Ford Found. fellow, 1971-73; grantee, 1974-75; Martin Marietta Corp. grad. fellow, 1972-73. Mem. Am. Phys. Soc. (com. on status of women in physics 1986—), AAAS (com. on sci. freedom and responsibility), N.Y. Acad. Scis., Nat. Inst. Sci., Nat. Soc. Black Physicists (pres. 1979—), MIT Alumni Assn. (v.p. 1986—), Sigma Xi, Delta Theta Sigma. Editorial adv. bd. Jour. Sci. Tech. and Human Values, 1982—; contbr. numerous articles to physics jours. Office: Room ID-337 AT&T Bell Labs 600 Mountain Ave Murray Hill NJ 07974

JACKSON, SHIRLEY CRITE, government agency administration; b. Memphis, June 4, 1940; d. Golden and Lucinda (Berry) Crite; B.A. in Elem. Edn., Northeastern U., 1961, M.A. in Applied Linguistics and English Lang., 1966; postgrad. U. Chgo., George Washington U., 1967-77; Ed.D. in Curriculum and Instrn., Cath. U. Am., 1982; m. Allen D. Jackson, July 5, 1969; 1 son, Dewyane Anthony. Tchr., Chgo. Public Schs., 1961-66, high sch. English cons., 1966-68, coordinator reading, lang. arts, high sch. English programs, 1968-72; communication skills and math. cons., program coordinator D.C. Health Pub. Co., Lexington, Mass., 1972-75; prof. U. Maine, Portland/Gorham, 1975-77; tech. asst. to state depts. edn. Right to Read Program, U.S. Office Edn., Washington, 1975, program devel. br. chief Right to Read Program, 1975-77, dep. dir. program, 1977, dir. program, 1977-78, dir. Nat. Basic Skills Improvement Program, 1978-81, dir. basic edn. programs, 1979-81, acting dep. asst. sec. ednl. support programs, 1981-82, dir. state and local ednl. programs, 1982; asso. dir. Teaching and Learning Research Programs Nat. Inst. Edn., 1982—; dir. analysis and data collection service Office Civil Rights, Washington; mem. Nat. Brain Trust on Edn. of Congressional Black Caucus; mem. adv. council Nat. Center for the Book, Library of Congress; mem. nat. adv. council ERIC Reading/Communication Skills; mem. exec. devel. council Horace Mann Learning Center, also mem. exec. resources bd.; mem. task panel Pres.'s Commn. on Mental Health; mem. literacy task panel White House Conf. on Libraries; speaker. Sr. Usher, missionary Allen Chapel A.M.E. Ch., Washington, 1975—; developer, chairperson Operation Cell. Bound: Hosts, 1980-82; active Boy Scouts Am.; v.p. Shugart Jr. High Sch. PTA, 1976; mem. Prince George's County Parents Integration Task Force, 1975-76. Cert. tchr., Ill.; recipient profl. certs. U.S. Dept. Edn., 1976, 78, 80, 81; Recognition cert. U.S. Office of Edn., 1981; others. Mem. Internat. Reading Assn., Assn. Supervision and Curriculum Devel., Am. Ednl. Research Assn., Nat. Council Negro Women, NAACP, Nat. Urban League, Alpha Kappa Alpha, Phi Delta Kappa. Author Manuals and articles in field. Home: 2120 Keating St Temple Hills MD 20748 Office: 330 C St SW Washington DC 20202

JACKSON, THELMA MARIE, educator; b. Shreveport, La., Aug. 25; d. Robert and Gertie Lee (Harrison) J.; B.S., Grambling U., 1957; M.A., Eastern Mich. U., 1968; postgrad. Northwestern U., 1972-74, La. State U., 1973-74. Tchr., Northside Elementary Sch., 1957-68; tchr. Forest Hill Elementary Sch., Shreveport, La., 1968-81, elementary lang. arts coordinator, 1968-70, 79-80, now mandated inservice faculty chmn., curriculum demonstration tchr.; active staff devel. Caddo Parish Sch. Bd., 1981. Mem. Nat., State, Local tchr. assns., Nat., State, Local (pres.-elect) reading assns., Assn. for Supervision and Curriculum Devel., Nat. PTA, La. PTA, Caddo Dist. PTA (awards 1979-81), Delta Sigma Theta (Shreveport Alumnae, social action chmn. 1977-78, public relations chmn. 1981-82, awards 1978-80), YMCA (nominating com.). Baptist. Contbr. revision local social studies guide, 1980-81; lang. arts textbook critic, 1981-82. Home: 3833 Lisa Ln Shreveport LA 71109

JACKSON, THERESA PATRICIA, physician; b. Bronx, N.Y., Oct. 15, 1952; d. Pat Howard and Genevieve (Glover) Jackson. B.A., Hunter Coll, City U. N.Y., 1974; M.D., Cornell U. Med. Coll., 1978. Diploma Am. Bd. Pediatrics. Intern Montefiore Hosp., Bronx, 1978-79, resident, 1979-81, clin. instr., attending pediatrician, 1981-85; assoc. dir. clin. devel. Lederle Labs./Am. Cyanamid, Pearl River, N.Y., 1985—. Louis-Simon scholar, 1970-74; Nat. Med. fellow, 1974-76. Mem. Nat. Med. Assn., Susan Smith McKinney Stewart Found. Democrat. Roman Catholic. Home: 59 Alan Rd Spring Valley NY 10977 Office: Lederle Labs/Am Cyanamid Middletown Rd Pearl River NY 10965

JACKSON, WILMA (DARCY DEMILLE), columnist, public relations consultant; b. Chgo., Dec. 17; d. R.L. and Sophia O. Littlejohn; B.S. in Urban Studies/Sociology, U. Mich., 1977; cert. in urban studies Mich. State U., 1977; m. Gordon Chester Jackson, July 1, 1959; children—Carole Harris, Linda Luten, Jill, Shelley Bethay. Feature writer and columnist Sepia Mag., Fort Worth, 1961-81; columnist Hip Mag., 1963-81, Soul-Teen Mag., 1973-81, Bronze Thrills Mag., 1957—, also feature writer, 1956—, Chgo. Daily Defender, 1959-61; columnist, feature writer Flint Jour. (Mich.), 1981—; pub. relations cons. A. Gail Mazaraki, cons., 1982—; syndicated columnist Associated Negro Press, 1959-64, women's editor, 1959-61; reporter and feature writer Negro Press Internat., 1964-65; market research interviewer Barlow Survey Service, Chgo., 1958-59; owner, mgr. Medi-Rary Lit. Agy., 1963—; assoc. editor Vines mag., 1980—; instr. Jordan Coll., 1982—, Mott Community Coll., 1984—; guest lectr. creative writing U. Mich., Flint, 1977-78; adv. Black Fashion Mus., N.Y.C., 1979-80; public relations dir. The Links, Inc., 1979—, also chmn. internat. trends and services; eval. specialist and instr. The Kennedy Center, Flint, 1979-83; bus. liaison rep., tchr. Flint Community Schs.; cons. Manulife Ins., Timeshares, Inc. Mem. public affairs com. YWCA; bd. dirs., mem. adv. council Mich. League for Human Services. Recipient Woman of Year awards (3), 1983, Media Women Humanitarian award, 1983. numerous writing awards. Mem. Nat. Assn. Media Women (Woman of Yr. award 1978, pres. 1978-80), Flint Writers Club (v.p. 1973-74), Greater Flint Art Guild, U. Mich. Alumni Assn., Paint and Palette Art Group, Grand Blanc Arts Guild, Flint Inst. Arts, Phi Delta Kappa. Democrat. Office: 615 Lippincott Blvd Flint MI 48503

JACOB, DELIA LEGGETT, personnel executive; b. Los Angeles, Sept. 16, 1950; d. Charles William and Delia (Marin); B.A. with honors, Stanford U., 1972; M.A., U. Mich., 1975; student U. So. Calif., 1968-70; m. John Edward Jacob, Feb. 14, 1979; 1 son, Jonathon Michael. Study coordinator Soc. Psychol. Study of Social Issues-Am. Psychol. Assn., Ann Arbor, Mich., 1973; teaching fellow U. Mich., Ann Arbor, 1974, 75-76; research asso. Survey Research Center, Ann Arbor, 1977-78; acad. counselor Coll. Lit., Sci. and Arts, U. Mich., 1978-79; administrv. mgr. Rackham Grad. Sch., U. Mich., 1979-80; personnel asst. Martec Services, Los Angeles, 1981; asst. dir. personnel Cox, Castle & Nicholson, Century City, Calif., 1981-82; staffing mgr. applied tech. div. TRW, Redondo Beach, Calif., 1982-85, personnel policies mgr. ops. and support group, 1985—. Mem. career mktg. bd. Mademoiselle mag.; mem. program council Women for Richstone. Ford Found. fellow, 1972-77; Calif. State scholar, 1970-72; recipient Book award Calif. State Employees Assn., 1968-69; Gov.'s scholar, Calif., 1968. Mem. Am. Psychol. Assn., Women in Communication, Nat. Network Hispanic Women, Chicano Student Psychol. Assn., Theta Sigma Phi. Democrat. Contbr. articles to profl. jours. Home: 718 Indiana Ct Apt 2 El Segundo CA 90245 Office: TRW One Space Park Dr MS S/2746 Redondo Beach CA 90278

JACOB, LOIS MARIE, toxicologist, consultant; b. Chgo., Mar. 24, 1950; s. James Christian and Mary Agnes J.; m. Merle G. Galbraith, Jr., Mar. 25, 1978. B.A. with honors in Chemistry, U. Ill., 1971; M.S. in Environ. and Indsl. Health, U. Mich., 1974. Research asst. U. Mich., Ann Arbor, 1974-76; toxicologist Office of Pesticides and Toxic Substances EPA, Washington, 1976-78, toxicologist and sci. advisor Office of Enforcement, 1978-81; sr. health specialist Mich. Toxic Substance Control Commn., Lansing, 1981-85; prin. Environ. Health Cons. Internat., Chgo., 1985—; resourse person for univ. and profl. women's sci. career devel. groups; guest speaker at profl. confs., civic groups and colls. Author: Research Results and Recommendations for Environmental and Occupational MBOCA Levels, 1982. Tech. dir. Citizen's Guide for Community Health Studies, 1985. Founder and pres. Ann Arbor chpt. of Am. Youth Hostels, 1973-76; fundraiser for NOW, Women's Campaign Fund and Local Shelters. Fellow NIH, AEC; recipient Cert. Appreciation Mich. Assn. Environ. Professionals; nominee for Capital Area Mich. Pub. Service award. Mem. N.Y. Acad. Sci., AAAS, Mich. Soc. Toxicology, Am. Chem. Soc., Am. Pub. Health Assn., Women in State Govt., Mich. Women in Sci. Clubs: North Cape Yacht, Seven Seas Cruising Assn. Home: 9820 S Hamilton Ave Chicago IL 60643 Office: PO Box 2096 Chicago IL 60690

JACOB, NANCY LOUISE, university administrator; b. Berkeley, Calif., Jan. 15, 1943; d. Irvin Carl and Ruby (Roberts) Feustel; m. George B. Fotheringham, Dec. 22, 1972. B.A. magna cum laude, U. Wash., 1967; Ph.D. in Econs. magna cum laude, U. Calif.-Irvine, 1970. Summer research staff Ctr. Naval Analysis, Arlington, Va., 1969; mem. faculty U. Wash., Seattle, 1970—, chmn. dept. fin. and bus. econs. Schs. Bus. Adminstrn., 1978-81, dean Sch. Bus. Adminstrn., Grad. Sch. Bus. Adminstrn., 1981—, prof. fin., 1981—; trustee Coll. Retirement Equities Fund, N.Y., 1980—; dir. Puget Sound Power & Light Co., Bellevue, Wash., Rainier Nat. Bank, 1985—. Contbr. articles to profl. jours. Bd. dirs. Jr. Achievement, Seattle, 1982-84, Wash. Council Internat.

Trade, Seattle, 1981—. Recipient Wall St. Jour. Achievement award U. Wash., 1967; NDEA Title IV fellow, 1968-70. Mem. Am. Econ. Assn., Am. Fin. Assn., Western Fin. Assn., Seattle Soc. Fin. Analysts, Phi Beta Kappa. Clubs: Rainier, Nat. League Am. Pen Women, Columbia Tower. Office: U Wash Schs Bus Adminstrn DJ 10 Seattle WA 98195

JACOB, RUTH ANN, beauty business owner; b. Flint, Mich., Nov. 14, 1945; d. Theodore Sargis and Charlotte (Isaac) J. A.A., Flint Jr. Coll., 1968; B.F.A., San Francisco Art Inst., 1971; M.F.A., U. Mich., 1974. Asst. buyer, clk. Saks Fifth Ave, Evanston, Ill., 1974-75; receptionist Gazebo Salon, Park Ridge, Ill., 1975-76; receptionist, asst. mgr. Mark Benaim Salon, Chgo., 1976-77; mgr. salon Drake Hotel Salon, Chgo., 1977-78; br. coordinator Glemby Internat., Chgo., 1979-81; owner, bookeeper Mark/James Inc., Chgo., 1981—; instr. fine arts North Shore Arts, Winnetka, Ill., 1975-76, Goddard Coll., Plainfield, Vt., 1974-75; co-owner Creations & Things, Flint, Mich., 1975-76; teaching asst. U. Mich., Ann Arbor, 1973-74. Mem. Old Town Art League, Chgo., 1983. Recipient award Craft Commitment Exhbn., Rochester, Minn., 1974, Scholarship, Assyrian Am. Nat. Exhbn., Chgo., 1974, Plaque, Metro-Help, Chgo., 1981; grantee San Francisco Art Inst., 1971, Kiwanis Club, Flint, 1971. Mem. U. Mich. Alumni Assn. Republican. Presbyterian. Club: Women's Workout (Chgo.). Avocations: painting; sewing. Office: The Hair Salon of Mark/James Inc 1652 N Wells St Chicago IL 60614

JACOBI, ANGELA MARIA, nursing educator, lactation consultant; b. Camden, N.J., Apr. 7, 1947; d. Thomas Edward and Rita Marie (Feifer) Jacobi; m. James Hollahan, Aug. 17, 1968 (div. 1977); 1 son, Michael James; m. 2d, Burleigh Paul Angle, Dec. 17, 1977; children—John Edward, Thomas Martin. B.S. in Nursing, Loyola U., 1970; M.N. in Nursing, U. Pitts., 1977. Cert. CPR instr.; cert. lactation cons. Staff nurse U. Ill. Hosp., Chgo., 1970-71; pvt. med. office nurse, Chgo., 1972-74; neonatal staff nurse Magee Women's Hosp., Pitts., 1974-75, inservice instr., 1975-77; nursing supr. Northwestern Meml. Hosp., Chgo., 1978-79; mem. faculty Loyola U., Chgo., 1979-82; practitioner-tchr., asst. prof. nursing Rush Presbyn. St. Lukes Med. Ctr., Chgo., 1982—. Mem. editorial staff, contbg. columnist Jour. Human Lactation, 1985—. Mem. nursing adv. council Chgo. Chpt. March of Dimes, 1978—; mem. Rogers Park Community Council, Chgo., 1981—; chmn. Cub Scout Pack, Chgo., 1984—. Mem. Nurses Assn. Am. Coll. Obstetricians and Gynecologists (Purdue-Frederick fellow 1977), Am. Assn. History of Nursing, LaLeche League, Internat. Lactation Consultants Assn., Met. Ill. Lactation Consultants, Sigma Theta Tau. Roman Catholic. Office: Rush Presbyn St Lukes Med Ctr 1743 W Harrison St Chicago IL 60612

JACOBI, MARY JO, investment banker; b. Bay St. Louis, Miss., Dec. 7, 1951; d. Lawrence John and Delta Mae (Lizana) Jacobi. B.B.A., Loyola U., 1973; M.B.A., George Washington U., 1976; student Cath. U. Am., 1969-70. Chief adminstr. U.S. Senate Commerce Com., 1973-76; dir. mktg. regulations and govt. ops. NAM, 1977-79; mgr. regulatory affairs 3M Co., 1979-81; bus. liaison U.S. Dept. Commerce, Washington, 1981-83; spl. asst. to the Pres. of U.S., The White House, Washington, 1983-85 ; corp. v.p. Drexel Burnham Lambert, Inc., 1985—; v.p. Nat. Energy Resources Orgn., Washington, 1983—. Contbg. author: Mandate for Leadership, 1980. Mem. Republican Women's Fed. Forum, others. Mem. Women in Govt. Relations, Nat. Women's Econ. Alliance, Acad. Polit. Sci. Roman Catholic. Home: 44 Gramercy Park New York NY 10010 Office: Drexel Burnham Lambert Inc 60 Broad St New York NY 10004

JACOBOWITZ, RUTH SCHERR public relations consultant; b. Pitts., Apr. 12, 1933; d. Irving and Claire (Chernoff) Scherr; m. B. Paul Jacobowitz, Jan. 19, 1952; children—Jan, Jody, Julie. Student, U. Pitts., 1951-53, Cuyahoga Community Coll., 1960-63, Ursuline Coll., Cleve., 1978. Free-lance writer Cleve. Plain Dealer, 1965-67, book reviewer, 1978-82; pub. relations dir. Mt. Sinai Med. Ctr., Cleve., 1967-73, v.p. pub. affairs, 1973-84; mem. pub. relations com. Univ. Circle, Cleve., 1976—; regional chmn. Am. Assn. Med. Colls., Washington, 1978-79; pub. relations dir. spl. event Women's Wellness Day, 1983; mem. pub. affairs com. Ctr. for Health Affairs, Cleve., 1983-85. Mem. Pub. Relations Soc. Am., Internat. Assn. Bus. Communicators (editor quar. mag. Caring, 1974-85), Nat. Assn. Female Execs., Greater Cleve. Hosp. Assn. (chmn. pub. relations com. 1980-82), Womenspace, NOW. Jewish. Clubs: Playhouse, Communicators, University (Cleve.); Elyria Country; Avon Oaks Country. Office: Ruth Jocabowitz & Assocs Inc 381 Statlor Office Tower Cleveland OH 44115

JACOBOZZI, VIVIAN MARIE, retail store executive; b. Montenero, Italy, Apr. 24, 1933 (parents Am. citizens); d. Andrea and Adelia Z. (Tornincasa) Iacobozzi; student public schs., Lorain, Ohio. Acct., Caravan Inn, Phoenix, 1963-67; office mgr. AME Food Service, Scottsdale, Ariz., 1967-70, v.p., 1970-78, pres., 1978-81, also dir.; new pres. retail store; treas. Arcos Dress Shop, Sun City, Ariz., 1973—. Recipient plaque March of Dimes, 1978. Mem. Nat. Assn. Meat Purveyors (hon.), Livestock Mktg. Assn. (trustee). Republican. Roman Catholic. Home: 2836 N 76th Pl Scottsdale AZ 85251 Office: 7129 6th Ave Scottsdale AZ 85251

JACOBS, AGNES JACQUELINE EVERINGTON, retired wildlife federation executive; b. Wilkinsburg, Pa., June 17, 1923; d. James Pate and Agnes Kathleen (Scurry) Everington; A.B., Coker Coll., Hartsville, S.C., 1944, D.Letters (hon.), 1986; M.S, U. S.C., 1961, Ph.D. in Biology, 1968; m. Harold Weinberg Jacobs, May 11, 1947; children—Patricia Francyl, Janet Carolyn, James Cecil. Tchr. pub. schs., Columbia, S.C., 1957-64, 71-73; instructional TV specialist S.C. Dept. Edn., 1968-71; coordinator Inst. Environ. Studies, U. S.C., The Citadel, Clemson U., summers 1972-77; exec. dir. S.C. Wildlife Fedn., Columbia, 1974-83; mem. exec. com. S.C. Gov.'s Overall Recreation Plan Exchange Council, 1975—; charter mem. S.C. Environmental Edn. Assn., 1976—. Lectr. to various civic orgns., garden clubs, Rotary clubs, Scouts; mem. choir St. Michael and All Angels' Ch., Columbia, lay reader, 1980, mem. vestry, 1980-83, sr. warden, 1983; trustee Coker Coll., 1971-77, pres. Alumni Assn., 1975-77; bd. visitors Coker Coll., 1977-80; vice chmn. citizens' environ. planning com. Central Midlands Regional Planning Council, 1976-83; mem. S.C. Coastal Council, 1976-77; mem. citizens' adv. com. Riverbanks Zoo, Columbia, 1979—; mem. Russell Dam Task Force, 1979-83; bd. dirs. Yr. of Coast, 1980—; mem. S.C. Forestry Study Group, U.S. Dept. Agr., 1979; Wildlife adv. com. Coll. Agrl. Scis., Clemson U., 1976-82; bd. dirs. Harry R.E. Hampton Wildlife Meml. Fund; mem. Wildlife and Marine Resources Commn., 1983—; co-chmn. Gov.'s Council Natural Resources and the Environment, 1983-85; exec. com. S.C. Marine Sci. Mus., 1986—. Served with USMC Women's Res., 1944-46. Decorated Letter of Commendation; recipient Conservation Educator of Year award S.C. Wildlife Fedn., 1970, F. Bartow Culp award, 1975, Conservationist of Yr. award, 1983; S.C. Conservation of Year award Woodmen of World, 1975; Outstanding Service award Nat. Wildlife Fedn., 1977, Disting. Service award, 1983; Outstanding Alumni award Coker Coll., 1980; S.C. Wildlife and Marine Resource Dept. and Commn.'s Meritorious Service award, 1983; Gov.'s Order of Palmetto; S.C. Trappers Assn. cert. appreciation, 1983; Environ. Edn. Assn. S.C. citation meritorious service, 1983. NSF fellow, summers 1959-60, 63-65, W. Gordon Belser fellow U. S.C., 1964-65; Belle W. Baruch Found. grantee U. S.C., 1967-68; EPA film grantee, 1980. Mem. AAAS, Am. Inst. Biol. Scis., Assn. Southeastern Biologists, Nat. Assn. Biology Tchrs. (Outstanding Biology Tchr. award for S.C. 1963), S.C. Assn. Biology Tchrs. (pres. 1965), S.C. Acad. Sci. (pres. 1973), S.C. Edn. Assn. (life), Richland County Legal Aux. (charter), Wildlife Soc. (charter mem. S.C. chpt.), S.C. Wildlife Fedn. (life bd. dirs. 1986, trustee Ednl. Found. 1986), Sigma Xi. Episcopalian. (layreader). Author: Life Science-Teacher's Guide to ITV Courses, 1970; also sci. papers. Producer-tchr ITV Life Science series, 1969-70. Producer films The Loggerhead Turtle Story, 1971, South Carolina Coastal Nesting Birds, 1971, Life in the Coral Reef, 1971, The Russell Dam—A Question of Values, 1977; One Percent, 1980. Home: 5 Northlake Rd Columbia SC 29223

JACOBS, ANITA HALL, mathematics educator; b. Indpls., July 7, 1960; d. Edward Lee and Mia (Takahata) Hall; m. William Alex Jacobs, Nov. 19, 1983. B.S. in Edn. (Future Tchrs. Scholar), Stephen F. Austin Coll., 1981. Math. tchr. pub. schs., Houston, 1982—. Mem. NEA, Tex. State Tchrs. Assn., Spring Branch Tchrs. Assn., Nat. Council Math. Tchrs., Spring Branch Council Math. Tchrs. (sec. 1982-83). Republican. Methodist.

JACOBS, ANN ELIZABETH, lawyer; b. Lima, Ohio, July 28, 1950; d. Warren C. and Virginia E. (Lewis) Jacobs. B.A., George Washington U., 1972; J.D., Catholic U. Am., 1976. Bar: Ohio 1977, Calif. 1977, U.S. Ct. Appeals (D.C. cir.) 1980. Asst. atty. gen. office of Atty. Gen. of Ohio, Columbus, 1977-78; trial atty. EEOC, Miami, Fla., 1978-80; sole practice, Lima, Ohio, 1980—. Trustee Pathfinder House, Lima, 1981—; adv. bd. Women's Crisis Ctr., 1983-85. Recipient Recognition award U.S. Naval Air Sta., Jacksonville, Fla., 1979. Mem. ABA, Assn. Trial Lawyers Am, Allen County Bar Assn., Ohio Bar Assn., Columbus Bar Assn., D.C. Bar Assn., LWV. Presbyterian. Home: 1540 Walnut Ct Lima OH 45805 Office: 618 National Bank Bldg Lima OH 45801

JACOBS, ANNIE LEE, lawyer; b. Washington, Aug. 25, 1948; d. Harry Thomas and Sarah Rachel (May) Jacobs; m. Mark Henderson Congdon, Apr. 2, 1971 (div. Nov. 1980); m. 2d Charles Kirk Pilkington, Aug. 18, 1984. B.A. in Polit. Sci., U. Richmond, 1969; J.D., U. Va., 1976; postgrad. in polit. sci. Emory U., 1970-71. Bar: Va. 1976. Tchr. Belle Haven Elem. Sch., Accomack County, Va., 1969-70, Columbia Dist. Sch., Palmyra, Va., 1971-72, Buford Middle Sch., Charlottesville, Va., 1972-73; instr. Piedmont Community Coll., Charlottesville, 1976—; sole practice, Charlottesville, 1976; litigation atty. Lowe and Jacobs, Charlottesville, 1977—; commr. in Chancery Circuit Ct. Albemarle County, Va., 1984—. Mem. adv. council Shelter for Help in Emergency, 1980-82, bd. dirs., 1983—; organizational steering com. Community Mediation Ctr. for Charlottesville-Albemarle, 1984, bd. dirs., 1985—, sec., 1986. Mem. Va. Bar Assn. (child custody com.), Va. State Bar (domestic relations com.), Va. Trial Lawyers Assn., ABA, Charlottesville-Albemarle Bar Assn., Charlottesville Criminal Bar Assn. (treas. 1983-84), Va. Women Attys. Assn., Charlottesville Area Women's Bar Assn., Phi Beta Kappa, Pi Sigma Alpha. Lodges: Hadassah, Soroptimist (past treas.). Office: Lowe and Jacobs Ltd 100 Court Sq Charlottesville VA 22901

JACOBS, AUGUSTA ADELLE, educator, recycling company executive; b. Portsmouth, Ohio, Nov. 25, 1925; d. Jacob Harry and Rose (Levine) J. B.S., U. Cin., 1947; postgrad. Ohio U., Ohio State U.; grad. Kathleen Bushe and Dody Howard Sch. Modeling, 1954. Tchr. bus. East High Sch., Portsmouth, 1947-51, Green High Sch., Franklin Furnace, Ohio, 1951—; office sec. Eagle Iron Co., Portsmouth, 1957-75, v.p., purchasing agt., 1975-77, v.p., asst. mgr., ptnr., 1977—. Mem. NEA, Southestern Ohio Tchrs. Assn., Ohio Bus. Tchrs. Assn., Green Local Tchrs. Assn., Portsmouth C. of C., AAUW (past pres. Portsmouth, rec. sec. Ohio div. 1956-58, bd. dirs. Ohio div. 1956-60), Bus. and Profl. Women's Club Portsmouth (pres.), Delta Kappa Gamma. Sec., Am. Cancer Soc. Scioto County, also bd. dirs.; tchr. Sunday Sch., Temple Beneh Abraham, also bull. editor, pres. Jewish Temple Sisterhood; capt. fund drives United Way. Republican. Home: 2840 N Hill Rd Portsmouth OH 45662 Office: Green High Sch Bobcat Circle Franklin Furnace OH 45629

JACOBS, ELEANOR ALICE, clinical psychologist; b. Royal Oak, Mich., Dec. 25, 1923; d. Roy Dana and Alice Ann (Keaton) Jacobs; B.A., U. Buffalo, 1949, M.A., 1952, Ph.D., 1955. Chief psychology service VA Med. Center, Buffalo, 1954-83, equal employment opportunity counselor, 1962-79; clin. prof. SUNY, Buffalo, 1950—. Speaker on psychology to community orgns., clubs, 1952—. Past mem. adult devel. and aging com. NICHD, Dept. Health, Edn. and Welfare. Recipient Outstanding Superior Performance award Buffalo VA Hosp., 1958; Spl. Recognition award State U. N.Y. at Buffalo, 1971, Disting. Alumni award, 1983; Adminstrs. commendation VA, Washington, 1974; Dirs. commendation VA Med. Center, Buffalo, 1978, 83; named Woman of Year, Bus. and Profl. Women's Club Buffalo, 1973. Mem. Am., Eastern, N.Y. State psychol. assns., Am. Group Psychotherapy Assn., Am. Soc. Group Psychotherapy and Psychodrama, Nat., Western N.Y. leagues nursing, Psychol. Assn. Western N.Y. (Disting. Achievement award 1976), Group Psychotherapy Assn. Western N.Y., Undersea Med. Soc., N.Y. Acad. Sci., Assn. Advancement Women in Sci. Research and publs. on hyperbaric medicine, hyperoxygenation effect on cognitive functions in aged. Home: 221 Pleasant Ave N Ridgeway ON L0S 1N0 Canada

JACOBS, ELLEN WINEMAN, travel agency executive; b. N.Y.C., Nov. 25, 1934; d. Joseph Marx and Suzanne (Frenkel) Wineman; m. J. Kenneth Jacobs, Aug. 14, 1956; children—Margaret Louise, Thomas Wineman, William Edward. B.A., Conn. Coll., 1956. Cert. tchr., Ind. Elem. sch. tchr. Met. Schs., Nashville, 1957-60; case worker ARC, Nashville, 1957, 58; Ambassador Travel Agy., Nashville, 1975-83, sales dir., 1983-84; pres. Sailair Travel Agy., Nashville, 1984—; mem. commn. on tourism Nashville Tech. Sch., 1985—; seminar leader Assn. Retail Travel Agys., 1984-85; mem. group travel authority Travel Authority, N.Y.C., 1984—. Mem. auction commn. Cheekwood Swan Ball, Nashville, 1984-85. Mem. Nat. Council Jewish Women (pres. 1970-72, pres., inst. leader 1973), NCCJ (sr. co-chmn. 1974-76, bd. dirs. 1976—). Avocations: tennis; amateur stage productions. Home: 4500 Malone Pl Nashville TN 37205 Office: Sailair Travel Agy 28 White Bridge Rd Nashville TN 37205

JACOBS, GLORIA MARGARET, state official; b. Colfax, Wash., July 28, 1924; d. Merle Haley and Kathryn Lois (Shoemaker) Price; A.A., Western Wash. U., 1972; m. Nile Harvey Vande Mark, July 3, 1941 (div. 1951); children—David B., Cassandra Mae Van de Mark Lown, William Nile, Kathryn Rose Van de Mark Binkley; m. George Henry Jacobs, Sr., Oct. 16, 1954 (dissolved 1981); children—Lois A. Jacobs McKee, Alice Lynne Jacobs Baxter, Mildred Bernice Jacobs Baxter, George Henry. Checker, Chroma-Crystalike Photo Finishing Co., Tacoma, 1961-63; community counselor trainee Community Mental Health Clinic, Tacoma, 1966; community counselor Make Opportunity Rehab. Econs. Inc., Puyallup, Wash., 1966-67; br. mgr. Rural Econ. Opportunity Inc., Parkland, Wash., 1967-68, acting dir., 1968, field rep., asst. to dir., 1968-70; social service asst. III, Office of Econ. Opportunity State of Wash., Olympia, 1970-73, community affairs asst., 1973-74, community affairs cons. I, 1974-80, community program developer II, 1980—. Baha'i. Home: PO Box 5459 Lacey WA 98503 Office: Dept Community Devel 9th and Columbia Bldg Olympia WA 98504

JACOBS, HELEN DEBORAH, film production company executive; b. Los Angeles, July 4, 1952; d. Max and Sarah (Feder) J. B.A., UCLA, 1974, J.D., 1977. Bar: Calif. 1977. Pres., First Artist Prodn., Los Angeles, 1983—, Hanover Equities, Los Angeles, 1981—, Mazel Investments, Los Angeles, 1980—, Hanover Properties, Los Angeles, 1984—, Spirit of Nev., Las Vegas, 1985—; exec. dir. New Century, Beverly Hills, Calif., 1984—. Mem. ABA, Los Angeles Bar Assn., Beverly Hills Bar Assn., Order of the Coif, Phi Beta Kappa. Democrat. Jewish. Avocations: snow skiing; windsurfing; scuba diving. Office: Firanha Security Systems 8671 Wilshire Blvd Beverly Hills CA 90211

JACOBS, JANE, author; b. Scranton, Pa., May 4, 1916; d. John Decker and Bess Mary (Robison) Butzner; m. Robert Hyde Jacobs, Jr., May 27, 1944; children—James Kedzie, Edward Decker, Mary Hyde. Author: Downtown Is For People in The Exploding Metropolis, 1959, The Death and Life of Great American Cities, 1961, The Economy of Cities, 1969, The Question of Separatism, 1980, Cities and the Wealth of Nations: Principles of Economic Life, 1984. Address: care Random House 201 E 50th St New York NY 10022

JACOBS, KAREN LOUISE, medical technologist; b. Kingston, N.Y., May 7, 1943; d. William Charles and Vera Elizabeth (Kelly) Jacobs; B.S. in Applied Tech., Empire State Coll., 1976; M.S. in Public Service Adminstrn., Russell Sage Coll., 1982. Sr. lab. technician, hosp. lab. supr. City of Kingston (N.Y.) Labs., 1962-68; sr. research asst. Dudley Obs., Albany, N.Y., 1972-75; lab. adminstr. Albany Med. Coll., 1976—, mem. faculty, 1982—. Bd. dirs. chpt. Leukemia Soc. Am., 1983. Mem. Clin. Lab. Mgmt. Assn., Blood Banks Assn. of N.Y. State, Am. Soc. Clin. Pathologists, Nat. Speleological Soc., Helderberg-Hudson Grotto, Sierra Club, Earthwatch. Home: 37B Picotte Dr Albany NY 12208 Office: Albany Med Coll Div Oncology 47 New Scotland Ave Albany NY 12208

JACOBS, LINDA CARROL, systems analyst, computer consultant; b. Long Beach, Calif., June 26, 1946; d. Scott Willard and Darlene Ell (Wolfe) Busselle; m. Albert Stickley Jacobs, June 6, 1981; stepchildren—Bruce, Kenneth, Don, Randy, Kevin, Cynthia; m. George Henry Martin, Nov. 6, 1963 (div.); 1 child, Michael. Student Pierce Community Coll., 1971-73. Cert. systems profl. programmer, Olga Co., Inc., Van Nuys, Calif., 1971-75; programmer analyst Idaho Power Co., Inc., Boise, 1975-78; systems analyst Morrison-Knudsen Co., Boise, 1978—; computer cons., Boise, 1981—, Macintosh cons., 1985—. Mem. publicity staff Republican senatorial campaigna, Boise, 1979-80. Mem. Assn. Systems Mgmt. Republican. Methodist. Avocations: sailing; skiing. Home: 64 Horizon Dr Boise ID 83702 Office: Morrison-Knudsen Co Inc One Morrison-Knudsen Plaza Boise ID 83729

JACOBS, LINDA LEE, hospital administrator; b. Lincoln, Nebr., Apr. 18, 1949; d. Jacob and Darleen Rose (Worster) J.; B.S., U. Nebr., 1971. Gastrointestinal asst. Bryan Meml. Hosp., Lincoln, Nebr., 1972-78, chief gastrointestinal asst., 1978-81, supr. gastrointestinal lab., 1981-85, mem. employee adv. com., 1973-74; dir. Jacobs Constrn. Co., Inc., Lincoln; clin. instr. Cooper LaserSonics, Inc., Santa Clara, Calif., 1985. Active Vols. in Probation. Mem. Nat. Soc. Gastrointestinal Assts. (pres. 1980-81, chmn. nominating com. 1981-82, ex officio dir. at large 1981-84, editor jour. 1981-84), Am. Soc. Lasers in Medicine and Sci., U. Nebr. Alumnae Assn., Nat. Assn. Female Execs., Am. Assn. Tng. and Devel., Am. Legion Aux., Gamma Phi Beta Alumnae (corp. bd. pres. 1983-85). Club: Does (Lincoln, Nebr.). Home: 2624 Austin Dr Lincoln NE 68506 Office: 4848 Sumner St Lincoln NE 68506

JACOBS, LOLA CHARLENE, Realtor, real estate franchise coordinator; b. Denver, Mar. 28, 1950; d. Charles Alfred and Patsy Ellenor (Jellison) J.; m. Dana Alfred Wurdemen, Jan. 16, 1981 (div. Feb. 1983). Student, Nebr. Western Coll., 1978-80. Sec., Colo., Nebr., 1968-73; tech. writer Lockwood Corp., Gering, 1973-78; coordinator, Realtor, ERA-Atkinson & Assocs., Scottsbluff, Nebr., 1979-80; Realtor, Winterer Realty, Scottsbluff, 1980-82; dep. county assessor Scotts Bluff County (Nebr.), 1982-83; Realtor, coordinator ERA-LeBlanc Realty, Scottsbluff, 1983—. Mem. Bus. and Profl. Women, Christian Women's Assn., Scottsbluff C. of C., Nat. Assn. Realtors. Office: ERA-LaBlanc Realty & Auctions Inc 123 W 17th Scottsbluff NE 69361

JACOBS, MARIAN BECKMANN, chemical market research analyst, former geologist; b. Teaneck, N.J., Dec. 20, 1935; d. Frederick J. and Marguerite J. (Thoma) Beckmann; B.A. cum laude (Grace Potter Rice fellow), Barnard Coll., 1957; M.A. (Columbia scholar, Quincy Ward Boese fellow, James Furman Kemp fellow), Columbia, 1959, Ph.D., 1963; m. Warren R. Jacobs Jr., Sept. 5, 1959 (dec.); children—Laura Diane, Anita Michelle; m. 2d, Donald H. Norman, Jan. 9, 1975 (dec.). Research asst. mineralogy dept. Columbia, N.Y.C., 1960-63; research asso. Lamont-Doherty Geol. Obs. of Columbia, Palisades, N.Y., 1963-76; asst. prof. oceanography Ramapo Coll. of N.J., Mahwah, 1974-76; sr. analyst market and industry research for polyolefins and spl. chems. ARCO Chem. Co., Inc. subs. Atlantic Richfield Co., 1976—. NSF grantee, 1965-66, 66-67, 69-71, 71-72, 72-73. Mem. Soc. Plastics Engrs., Am. AAAS, Mineral. Soc. Am., Geol. Soc. Am., Clay Minerals Soc., Phi Beta Kappa, Sigma Xi. Contbr. articles to profl. jours. Research X-ray diffractions and fluorescence studies deep-sea sediments and particulate matter in sea water. Home: 7 Robin Rd PO Box 572 Mahwah NJ 07430 Office: Arco Chem Co 1500 Market St Philadelphia PA 19101

JACOBS, MARY LEE, lawyer; b. Pitts., June 29, 1950; d. George Joseph and Mary Jane (Swinderman) Jacobs. B.A. in History, Wellesley Coll., 1972; J.D., Boston U., 1975. Bar: Mass. 1975, U.S. Dist. Ct. Mass. 1976, U.S. Ct. Appeals (1st cir.) 1978, U.S. Supreme Ct. 1981. Assoc. Moulton & Looney, Boston, 1978-80; assoc. Nutter, McClennen & Fish, Boston, 1980-84; gen. counsel Tufts U., Medford, Mass., 1984—. Mem. ABA, Boston Bar Assn., Women's Bar Assn. Mass. Office: Gen Counsel Tufts Univ Ballou Hall Medford MA

JACOBS, MARY SHARRON, librarian; b. Endicott, N.Y., June 19, 1947; d. John Arnold and Evelyn Grace Jacobs; student U. Buffalo, 1965-68, M.L.S., SUNY, Geneseo, 1971. Dir., David A. Howe Public Library, Wellsville, N.Y., 1972—. Librarian, Sovereign Grace Ch., 1978—, coordinator women's activities, 1980—, trustee, 1983. Mem. Allegany County Library Assn. (v.p. 1981-83), N.Y. State Library Assn., ALA. Republican. Office: 155 N Main St Wellsville NY 14895

JACOBS, ROSEMARIE, management consultant; b. Lincoln, Nebr., Oct. 25, 1943; d. Jacob Jr. and Darleen Rose (Worster) J.; children—Michael Jacob Schwabauer, Douglas Henry Schwabauer. B.S., U. Nebr., 1965. Staff med. technologist Shawnee Mission Hosp., Kans., 1965-66, Pediatric Profl. Assn., Shawnee Mission, 1971-73; med. technologist Shawnee Mission Med. Ctr., 1976-77, lab. mgr. 1977-84; cons. Profl. Mgmt. Services, 1984—; dir. Jacobs Constrn. Co., Inc. Bd. dirs. Kansas City Mothers' Milk Bank, Mental Health Assn. Johnson County, 1986—; internal coordinator United Way campaign, 1980, 81; mem. adminstrv. bd. Valley View United Meth. Ch., 1981-83, chmn. worship com., mem. Council on Ministries, 1981-83; pres. Shawnee Mission Women's Chorale, 1974-76, program chmn., 1985-86. Mem. Am. Soc. Tng. and Devel., Am. Soc. Med. Technologists, Kans. Soc. Med. Technologists, Nat. Assn. Women Bus. Owners, Nat. Assn. Female Execs., Johnson County Businesswomen, Lenexa C. of C., U. Nebr. Alumni Assn., AAUW Alpha Xi Delta. Address: Profl Mgmt Services 9202 W 90th St Overland Park KS 66212

JACOBS, SHERRY RAPHAEL, lawyer; b. Weehawken, N.J., June 29, 1943; d. Leon L. and Fay (Silverstein) Raphael; B.A., Fairleigh Dickinson U., 1967; J.D., Loyola U., Chgo., 1970; m. Stephen E. Jacobs, Jan. 4, 1976; children by previous marriage—Jeremiah Raphael and Deborah Feinsmith. Admitted to Ill. bar, 1970, N.Y. State bar, 1974; asso. firm Weil, Gotshal & Manges, N.Y.C., 1972-75, Wachtel, Lipton, Rosen & Katz, N.Y.C., 1975-76; asso. counsel Este Lauder, Inc., N.Y.C., 1976-77; v.p. legal R.H. Macy & Co., Inc., N.Y.C., 1977-79; v.p., gen. counsel Saks Fifth Ave., N.Y.C., 1979-83, v.p., gen. counsel, dir. loss prevention, 1983-84, v.p., gen. mgr., 1984-86; mng. ptnr. Eolis & Jacobs, N.Y.C., 1986—; dir. Guilford Mills, Inc. Mem. ABA, N.Y. State Bar Assn., N.Y. County Bar Assn., Assn. Bar City N.Y. Home: 180 East End Ave New York NY 10128 Office: 215 E 31st St New York NY 10016

JACOBS, SUE CAROL, lawyer; b. N.Y.C., June 21, 1940; d. Harry and Harriet (Rosenblatt) Braunstein; m. Robert A. Jacobs, Aug. 21, 1961; children—Jacqueline Anne, Michelle Keri. B.A. with honors, Hunter Coll., 1960; M.A., Am. U., 1966; J.D., Pace U., 1979; postgrad. New Sch. Social Research, N.Y.C., 1960-62. Bar: N.Y. 1980, U.S. Dist. Ct. (so. dist.) N.Y. 1980. Tchr., N.Y.C. Bd. Edn., 1960-61, 62-64, Arlington County Bd. Edn., 1963-67; atty. Siff & Newman PC, N.Y.C., 1980—; law guardian Family Ct., Westchester, N.Y., 1980—. Bd. dirs. LWV, East Manhattan, Scarsdale, N.Y., 1967-76; founder Hunter Coll. Call for Action, N.Y.C., 1975-77. Alvin Johnson fellow New Sch. for Social Research, N.Y.C., 1960. Mem. ABA, N.Y. State Bar Assn., Westchester Women's Bar Assn. Democrat. Jewish. Home: 88 Catherine Rd Scarsdale NY 10583 Office: Siff & Newman PC 233 Broadway New York NY 10279

JACOBSEN, DOROTHY HELEN CALDWELL, occupational therapist; b. Algona, Iowa, Aug. 19, 1935; d. Harry Vincent and Beulah Ramona (Larsen) Caldwell; B.A. in Occupational Therapy, U. Iowa, 1957; m. Eric Kasner Jacobsen, Mar. 30, 1957; 1 son, Steven Keith. Occupational therapist St. Louis County (Mo.) Spl. Dist. of Edn. for Severely Handicapped Children, Brentwood, 1960-64; dir. occupational therapy St. Luke's Hosp., St. Louis, 1964-69; instr. U. Kans., 1970-71; pvt. practice occupational therapy, phys. dysfunction and sensory dysfunction, Chargrin Falls, Ohio, 1971—; cons. in field. Lic. profl. therapist. Mem. Am., Ohio occupational therapy assns., Center for the Study of Sensory Integrative Dysfunction. Presbyterian. Home: 16 Louise Dr Chagrin Falls OH 44022

JACOBSEN, PAMELA, special education educator, consultant, counselor; b. Cleve., June 25, 1947; d. Michael Antony and Mary (Pappas) Hoty; m. William Henry Jacobsen, Aug. 21, 1971 (div. 1982). B.S. in Elem. Edn., Baldwin-Wallace Coll., 1969; postgrad. in learning disabilities, Akron U., 1971-72; M.Ed. in Educating Handicapped, Adams State Coll., 1976. Tchr. Strongsville Schs., Ohio, 1969-71, lang. disabilities tchr., 1971-73; educationally handicapped itinerant tchr. Dist. 60, Pueblo, Colo., 1973-74, educationally handicapped lab. educator, 1974-77, educationally handicapped resource tchr., 1977-79, emotional/behavior disorder educator, 1979—; educator Summer Champ Camp for Asthmatics, Woodland Park, Colo., 1983-86. Author: Correct and Effective Use of Placement and Procedures for Emotionally Disordered Students, 1985. Active Pueblo Nature Ctr., 1981—; area chmn. Channel 8 Pub. TV Auction, 1982—; bd. dirs. Altrusa Club of Pueblo, 1986; nominating com. Columbine Girl Scout Council, 1984-86. Recipient Hon. Mention award Gov. Colo., 1985; Service award Champ Camp Program, 1984, 85. Mem. Nat. Assn. Female Execs., Bus. and Profl. Women, Phi Delta Kappa. Greek Orthodox. Club: Pueblo Country. Avocations: golf; hiking; reading. Home: 2810 7th Ave Pueblo CO 81003 Office: Sunset Park Elem Sch 110 University Circle Pueblo CO 81005

JACOBSON, ANN KATHERINE, nursing administrator; b. Mpls., June 30, 1942; d. Stanley Vincent Jacobson and Marian Lucille (Tronson) Jacobson Hoke; m. Stephen W. Ballou, Feb. 6, 1965 (div. Mar. 1977); children—Emily, Rachel, Sarah; m. Anthony J. Schnarsky, June 19, 1981. Student Macalester

Coll., 1960-61; Nursing diploma Madison Gen. Hosp., 1964; B.S.Nursing, U. Wis.-Milw., 1968, M.S.Nursing, 1980. Instr. nursing U. Wis., Milw., 1968-74, 75-77, 81-83; coordinator nursing edn. Planned Parenthood Wis., Milw., 1978; psychiat. clin. specialist, psychotherapist Mt. Sinai Med. Ctr., Milw., 1983-85; nurse mgr., clin. specialist psychiat. unit Columbia Hosp., Milw., 1985—. Contbr. articles to profl. jours. Mem. Am. Nurses Assn. (cert. specialist psychiat. and mental health nursing Council Psychiat. and Mental Health), Sigma Theta Tau. Office: Columbia Hosp 2025 E Newport Ave Milwaukee WI 53211

JACOBSON, BONNIE BROWN, utility company executive, statistician; b. Annapolis, Md., Feb. 15, 1952; d. Albert Robert and Ruth Marie (Puhak) Brown; m. Peter Roy Jacobson, Apr. 28, 1979. B.S. cum laude, LaRoche Coll., Pitts., 1974; M.S., U. Pitts., 1976. Research scholar U. Pitts., 1974-76; research assoc. Squibb Inst. Med. Research, Princeton, N.J., 1976-78; assoc. statistician N.E. Utilities Service Co., Hartford, Conn., 1978-80, statistician, 1980-82, sr. statistician, 1982-83, mgr. consumer research, 1983—; cons. stats., Hartford, 1976—; adviser Electric Power Research Inst., Palo Alto, Calif., 1978—. Research plan developer Conn. Energy Assistance Study Project, Hartford, 1983-84. Mem. Am. Statis. Assn., Am. Mktg. Assn., Nat. Assn. Female Execs., Electric Utility Market Research Council. Club: Sport and Leisure (Wallingford, Conn.). Avocations: golf; skiing; racquetball; gardening; reading. Home: 45 Stephen Dr Meriden CT 06450 Office: NE Utilities Service Co PO Box 270 Hartford CT 06141

JACOBSON, CAROLE RENEE, lawyer, educator; b. N.Y.C., Feb. 10, 1935; d. Daniel and Sally (Leader) Gold; m. David S. Jacobson, Jan. 28, 1962; children—Robin, Mark, Brad. B.S. with honors, U. Pa., 1956; M.A. English with honors, Columbia U., 1957; J.D., Rutgers U., 1979. Bar: Pa. 1980, Fla. 1982, N.J. 1983; cert. English tchr., N.J. Tchr. Manhasset (L.I., N.Y.) High Sch., 1958-62, Westfield (N.J.) High Sch., 1962; dir. social services South Brunswick (N.J.) High Sch., 1976; asst. counsel N.J. Casino Control Commn., Lawrenceville, 1981—. Editor N.J. Voter, 1974-75. Mem. Hunterdon (N.J.) Central Bd. Edn., 1983—, v.p., 1986—; mem. Raritan Twp. (N.J.) Bd. Adjustment, 1979-82; chmn. legis. subcom. State Consumer Affairs Adv. Com., 1976—; mem. N.J. State bd. LWV, 1974-75, pres. Hunterdon County, 1972-74, Plainfield, 1968-70; pres. Vol. Bur. Hunterdon County, 1974-76; trustee Hunterdon County Housing Council, 1972-76; mem. Citizens Housing Corp. Raritan Twp. 1971-72; chmn. Hunterdon County Coalition Better Pub. Schs., 1971-72. Recipient resolution of appreciation Bd. Adjustment, Raritan Twp., 1982. Democrat. Home: RD 6 Box 149 A Flemington NJ 08822 Office: Princeton Pike Office Park Lawrenceville NJ 18625

JACOBSON, CYNTHIA JANE, real estate executive; b. Denver, July 9, 1945; d. Gale Milan and E. Jean (Johnson) J. Student U. Nebr., 1963-65. Employment counselor H.S. Placement, Green Bay, Wis., 1969-72; gen. mgr. Northland Inn Keepers, Green Bay, 1972-79; pres. Realty Services, Inc., Green Bay, 1979—. Mem. Nat. Leased Housing Assn. (asst. sec., bd. dirs. 1983—). Office: Realty Services Inc 130 E Walnut St Green Bay WI 54301

JACOBSON, DEBRA ANN, lawyer; b. Kingston, N.Y., Mar. 20, 1952; d. Charles and Esther (Tasker) Denkensohn; B.A. summa cum laude in Environ. Studies, U. Rochester (N.Y.), 1974; J.D. with honors, George Washington U., 1977; m. David Edward Jacobson, Aug. 10, 1975; 1 son, Andrew Scott. Admitted to N.Y. bar, 1979, D.C. bar, 1985; congressional legis. asst., 1977-79; counsel subcom. on oversight and investigations, com. energy and commerce U.S. Ho. Reps., 1979—; dir.-at-large Women's Council Energy and Environ., 1981-83. Recipient award Delta Labs., 1972. Mem. Nature Conservancy, NOW, N.Y. State Bar Assn., Nat. Spinal Cord Injury Assn. Author govt. report. Office: 2323 Rayburn House Office Bldg Washington DC 20515

JACOBSON, GLORIA NADINE, coll. adminstr.; b. Jewell, Iowa, July 12, 1930; d. Christian Frederick and Amanda M. (Englebart) Larson; B.B.A., U. Iowa, 1974; m. Richard T. Jacobson, July 22, 1951; children—Richard Thomas, Douglas L., William Andrew. Mem. adminstrn. staff U. Iowa, Iowa City, 1950—, asst. to the dean Coll. of Pharmacy, 1981—. Mem. Phi Gamma Nu, Kappa Epsilon. Republican. Lutheran. Home: 415 Ridgeview Iowa City IA 52240 Office: U of Iowa Coll of Pharmacy Iowa City IA 52242

JACOBSON, HELEN G. (MRS. DAVID JACOBSON), civic worker; b. San Antonio, Tex.; d. Jac Elton and Rosetta (Dreyfus) Gugenheim; B.A., Hollins Coll.; m. David Jacobson, Nov. 6, 1938; children—Elizabeth, Dorothy (Mrs. Sam Miller). News, spl. events staff NBC, N.Y.C., 1933-38. First v.p. San Antonio, Bexar County council Girl Scouts U.S.A., 1957-63; Tex. State rep. UNICEF, 1964-69; bd. dirs. U.S. com. UNICEF, 1970-80, hon. bd. dirs., 1980—; bd. dirs. Nat. Fedn. Temple Sisterhoods, 1973-77, Temple Beth-El Sisterhood, Youth Alternatives, Inc.; bd. dirs. Community Guidance Center, chmn. bd., 1960-63; bd. dirs. Sunshine Cottage Sch. for Deaf Children, chmn. bd., 1952-54; pres. Community Welfare Council, 1968-70; pres. bd. trustees San Antonio Pub. Library, 1957-61; trustee Nat. Council Crime and Delinquency, 1964-70, San Antonio Mus. Assn., 1964-73; bd. dirs. Cancer Therapy and Research Found. South Tex., 1977—, sec., 1977-83; pres. S.W. region Tex. Coalition for Juvenile Justice, 1977-79; chmn. Mayor's Commn. on Status of Women, 1972-74; del. White House Conf. on Children, 1970; mem. Commn. on Social Action of Reform Judaism, 1973-77; chmn. Foster Grandparent project Bexar County Hosp. Dist., 1968-69; sec. Nat. Assembly for Social Policy and Devel., 1969-74; pres. women's com. Ecumenical Center for Religion and Health, 1975-77; mem. criminal justice planning com. Alamo Area Council of Govts., chmn., 1975-77; mem. Tex. Internat. Women's Yr. Coordinating Com., 1977; co-chmn. San Antonio chpt. NCCJ, 1980-84; chmn. United Negro Coll. Fund Campaign, 1983, 84; v.p. Avance; trustee Target 90/Goals for San Antonio. Recipient Headliner award for civic work San Antonio chpt. Women in Communications, 1958; named Vol. Woman of Yr., Express-News, 1959; honoree San Antonio chpt. NCCJ, 1970, Nat. Jewish Hosp., 1978; Nat. Humanitarian award B'nai B'rith, 1975; Hannah G. Solomon award Nat. Council Jewish Women, 1979, others. Mem. San Antonio Women's Fedn., Nat. Council Jewish Women, Symphony Soc. (women's com.). Club: Argyle. Home: 207 Beechwood Ln San Antonio TX 78216

JACOBSON, JANICE OSBORNE, hospital business office manager; b. Birmingham, Ala., July 29, 1950; d. Charles Norman and Margarita Myrtle (McFarland) Osborne; m. Joseph Lee Miller, July 12, 1970 (div. 1976); children—Joseph Bryan, Margarita Marie; m. Jon Richard Jacobson, Apr. 21, 1978 (div. 1980). A.A., St. Petersburg (Fla.) Jr. Coll., 1975. Mgr. bus. office Medfeild Corp., St. Petersburg, 1976-79; accounts receivable cons. Nat. Med. Enterprises, Tampa, Fla., Los Angeles, 1979-81, Am. Med. Internat., Atlanta also Los Angeles, 1981-82; mgr. patient accounts St. Joseph's Hosp., Atlanta, 1982-83; mgr. bus. office North Fulton Med. Ctr., Am. Med. Internat., Atlanta, 1984—. Mem. Am. Bus. Women's Assn., Hosp. Fin. Mgrs. Assn. Democrat. Methodist. Office: North Fulton Med Ctr 11585 Alpharetta St Roswell GA 30076

JACOBSON, JOYCE AUSTIN, insurance agency executive, dairy farm and cattle exporter; b. Harmony, Minn., Mar. 3, 1927; d. Oscar George and Helma Josephine (Gulbranson) Austin; m. George Harley Milne, June 22, 1947 (div. 1971); 1 child, Jeffrie Lee; m. Murrell James Jacobson, Dec. 26, 1971. B.S., Winona State U., 1960; M.S., U. S.D., 1965, Ed.S., 1968. Tchr. Harmony Elem. Sch., Minn., 1947-60; reading cons. Harmony High Sch., 1960-70, Mankato Schs., 1970-72; summer sch. cons. U. S.D., Vermillion, 1968-71; owner, agt. Jacobson Agy., Harmony, 1973—. Sec., treas. Harmony Hosp. Assn. 1980—; pres. Root River Conf. Luth. Women, S.E. Minn., 1983—; sec. Independent Republicans, Fillmore County (Minn.) 1950s; mem. Minn. Internat. Trade Travel Group Sec. of Agr., 1983. Mem. Ind. Ins. Agts., Minn. Assn. Mut. Ins. Agts., Minn. Purebred Livestock Breeders (bd. dirs. 1980—), Purebred Dairy Cattle Assn. (bd. dirs. 1980—), U. Minn. Adv. Council, Minn. Assn. Farm Mut. Ins. Cos. (sec. treas 1983—), Fillmore County Extension Services (bd. dirs. 1982—). Avocation: giving speeches and lectures. Home: Box 656 Harmony MN 55939 Office: Jacobson Ins Agy 25 Main Ave S Harmony MN 55939

JACOBSON, JUDITH HELEN, state senator; b. South Bend, Ind., Feb. 26, 1939; d. Robert Marcene and Leah (Alexander) Haxton; m. John Raymond Jacobson, 1963; children—JoDee, Eric, Wendy. Student U. Wis.-Milw. and Madison, 1957-60. Mem. Mont. Senate, 1980—. Mem. Nat. Conf. State Legislators (human resources com. 1981—, del. Mont. Med. Aux. (legis. chmn. 1981—). Democrat. Lutheran. Office: Mont Senate State Capitol Helena MT 59620*

JACOBSON, JUNE, psychotherapist; b. Worcester, Mass., June 6, 1929; d. James Allen and Agnes May (Cunningham) Fusca; B.A., Mich. State U., 1965, Ednl. Specialist, 1976; children—David, Matthew, Paul. Coordinator, Listening Ear Crisis Center, East Lansing, Mich., 1969-72; counselor Mich. State U. Counseling Center, East Lansing, 1973-76; social worker, ptnr. Psychol. and Behavioral Consultants, East Lansing, 1976—; cons. Child Abuse and Neglect Council. Recipient public service citation East Lansing City Council, 1972. Mem. Am. Psychol. Assn. (assoc.), Am. Personnel and Guidance Assn., Phi Kappa Phi. Office: 5020 Northwind Dr Suite 201 East Lansing MI 48823

JACOBSON, MARGARET, bank executive; b. Chgo., Aug. 11, 1944; d. Leon Christian and Kathleen Eileen (Brennan) Eschbach; m. Herbert Jacobson, Dec. 8, 1972. B.S., U. Ill., 1967. Mgmt. trainee Harris Trust, Chgo., 1967-69; asst. to dir. advt. Velsicol Chem. Co., Chgo., 1969-70; account exec. Gardner, Stein & Frank, Chgo., 1970-74; v.p. consumer mktg. Budget Rent-a-Car, Chgo., 1974-82; sr. v.p. Bozell & Jacobs, N.Y.C., 1982-85; v.p. Citibank U.S.A., N.Y.C., 1985—; guest lectr. AMR, Inc., N.Y.C., 1975-76. Treas., bd. dirs. Profl. Women for Brain Reearch, Chgo., 1973-75. Named Mktg. Warrior of Yr., AMR, Inc., 1980; selected finalist as Advt. Woman of Yr., Women's Advt. Club, Chgo., 1978, 79. Avocations: Chinese cooking; travel; racquetball.

JACOBSON, MARIAN SLUTZ, lawyer; b. Cin., Nov. 10, 1945; d. Leonard Doering and Emily Dana (Wells) Slutz; m. Fruman Jacobson, Sept. 21, 1975; 1 dau., Lisa Wells. B.A., Ohio Wesleyan U., 1967; J.D., U. Chgo., 1972. Bar: Ill., 1972. Assoc. Sonnenschein Carlin Nath & Rosenthal, Chgo., 1972-79, ptnr., 1979—; research dir. Ctr. for Studies in Criminal Justice, Law Sch. U. Chgo., 1973-74. Mem. ABA, Ill. Bar Assn., Chgo. Council Lawyers. Home: 1640 E 50th St Chicago IL 60615 Office: Sonnenschein Carlin Nath & Rosenthal 8000 Sears Tower Chicago IL 60606

JACOBSON, MARILYN AMY HAAS, casino marketing representative; b. St. Louis, Aug. 28, 1932; d. Roy and Edith (Bowman) Haas; m. Garen Elwood Parker, Sept. 29, 1965 (div. 1968); m. Howard Lee Jacobson, Nov. 25, 1973. B.S., Boston U., 1954; student Washington U., St. Louis, 1950-51. Artist, New Eng. Tel. & Tel., Boston, 1954-55; prodn. artist Wohl Shoe Co., St. Louis, 1955-57; artist, ad designer Edison Bros. Stores, St. Louis, 1957-73; owner New Dimensions in Travel, Norfolk, Va., 1978-84; casino rep. Travel Enterprises, Norfolk, Va., 1976—. Jewish. Avocations: sculpture, ballet, figure skating, crafts. Home: 963 Colonial Meadows Way Virginia Beach VA 23454 Office: Travel Enterprises Inc 403 Plaza One Bldg Norfolk VA 23510

JACOBSON, NANCY HELEN, registered nurse, consultant, educator; b. Lansdowne, Pa., Nov. 16, 1947; d. Homer Pierce and Helen Irwin (Duffy) Tillotson; m. Philip William Jacobson, Dec. 11, 1976; children—Jeneane Renee, Abbe Nicole. Diploma Chester County Hosp., 1968; B.S.N., U. Pa., 1973, M.S.N., 1978. Lic. R.N. Staff nurse Hosp. of U. Pa., Phila., 1968-79, head nurse, 1970-73, staff devel. instr., 1973-79; instr. Holy Family Coll., Phila., 1979-83; cons. nursing, Phila., 1983—; curriculum specialist Med. Coll. Pa., Phila., 1985—; cons. 1982-85; cons. United Home Health Services, Phila., 1984—, Springhouse Corp., Phila., 1984—; guest lectr. continuing edn. various agys., 1977—. Contbr. articles to profl. jours. Instr. ARC, Phila., 1985, cons. needs assessment, 1985, coordinator student project, 1985. Recipient Profl. Nurse Traineeship award Dept. HEW, 1977. Mem. Am. Nurses Assn., Pa. Nurses Assn., League of I.V. Therapy Edn. (guest lectr. at 1985 conv.), Pa. Assn. for Gifted Edn., Sigma Theta Tau. Home: 617 Elkins Ave Elkins Park PA 19117 Office: Med Coll Pa 3300 Henry Ave Philadelphia PA 19111

JACOBSON, PATRICIA ANNE FITTS, lawyer; b. Buffalo, N.Y., Dec. 1, 1946; d. Francis Michael Fitts and Ruth Marie (Condon) Fitts Hawkins; m. Carl Whitney Jacobson, June 7, 1969; children—Berit Elissa Jacobson; Matthew Michael Fitts Jacobson. B.A. in Polit. Sci. and Econs., Rosary Coll., River Forest, Ill., 1968; M.A. in Polit. Sci., Boston U., 1973, J.D., Case Western Res. U., Cleve., 1980. Bar: Ohio 1980. Seminar dir. UN Assn./U.S.A., N.Y.C., 1968-69; tchr. English, Chinese Middle Sch. and Chinese U. Hong Kong, 1971-73; continuing edn. planner cons. U. Mich., Ann Arbor, 1973-77; research assoc. Case Western Res. U., 1978-79; assoc. Hahn, Loeser, Freedheim, Dean & Wellman, Cleve., 1980-82, ptnr. Wickens, Herzer & Panza Co., L.P.A., Lorain, Ohio, 1982—; chairperson Com. on Goals of Mich. Edn. State Dept. Edn., Lansing, 1976-77. Editor: Volume 30 Case Western Res. Law Rev., 1979-80. Consulting lawyer, mem. devel. adv. com. Nord Ctr. for Mental Health, Elyria/Lorain, Ohio, 1982—; mem. lawyers adv. com. ACLU, Cleve., 1981—, bd. dirs., Oberlin, Ohio, 1982—. mem. Com. of Concerned Asian Scholars (mem. editorial bd. 1969-71), ABA, Lorain County Bar Assn., Nat. Health Lawyers Assn. Home: 336 Reamer Pl Oberlin OH 44074 Office: Wickens Herzer & Panza Co LPA 1144 W Erie Ave Lorain OH 44052

JACOBSON, PATRICIA OLENCHALK, banker; b. Luzerne, Pa., Oct. 17, 1939; d. John Joseph and Mary Ann (Skerut) Olenchalk; student pvt. and pub. schs., New Britain, Conn.; m. Nicholas Jacobson, Jan. 11, 1975; 1 son, Albert J. Moseley; stepchildren—Karla Pelletier, Kris Jacobson. Clk. typist Household Fin. Corp., New Britain, Conn., 1956-70, asst. mgr., 1970-71, mgr., Nashua, N.H., 1971-74, Atlanta, 1974; inventory clk. Montgomery Ward, Newington, N.H., 1974; mgr. Burgher Haus Restaurant, Manchester, N.H., 1976-77; loan counselor Manchester Bank, 1977-78, mcht. devel. rep., 1978 79, sr. loan counselor and personal banking officer, 1979; mgr. mortgage processing Bank East Mortgage Corp., Manchester, 1979-82, asst. v.p. ops., 1982-83; v.p. First N.H. Mortgage Corp., 1983-86; asst. v.p. First Bank Mortgage Corp., 1983—; v.p. Peterborough Savs. Bank, 1986—. Mem. Greater Manchester Bus. and Profl. Women's Club (past treas.), Nat. Assn. Bank Women, Nat. Assn. Female Execs., YWCA. Republican. Congregationalist. Home: 35 N Reading St Manchester NH 03104 Office: 35 Main St Peterborough NH 03458

JACOBSON, SUE, financial executive; b. Ft. Smith, Ark., Aug. 13, 1940; d. Ray Bradley and Joy Anna (Person) McAlister; m. Lyle Norman Jacobson, Nov. 23, 1958; children—Lyle Michael, Daniel Ray, Julie Anne, Eric Joseph. Degree, Coll. for Fin. Planning, 1984. Cert. fin. paraplanner. Office mgr. Twin Cities Lithographic Inst., St. Paul, 1963-66; sec., St. Paul, Mpls., 1971-78; asst. to pres., office mgr. Planners Fin. Services, Mpls., 1978-85; fin. paraplanner McAlmont Investment Co., Mpls., 1985—; dir. Planners Fin. Services; mem. bd. advisors Coll. for Fin. Planning, Denver, 1982—; speaker various orgns. Co-creator Paraplanning Profession Advisor. Del., Dem. Farmer Labor Party, St. Paul, 1980; campaign chmn. mayoral election, Roseville, Minn., 1983, county commr., city council election, Roseville, 1980, 84; local chmn. for passage of E.R.A., Minn.; chmn. Am. Lung Assn., St. Paul; past. pres. PTA, Minn. Recipient Volunteerism award Gov. State of Minn., 1981; Cert. of Appreciation, Minn. Bicentennial Com., 1976; named 1st place winner Indianhead council Boy Scouts Am., 1981. Mem. Internat. Assn. Fin. Planning, Twin Cities Assn. Fin. Planners, Internat. Assn. Bus. and Profl. Women (bd. dirs. 1977-86, pres. 1980-82, named Woman of Yr. 1982), Concordia Acad. Booster Club, Beta Sigma Phi Nu Phi Mu Chpt. Democrat. Lutheran. Avocations: tennis; riding; reading; piano; fencing. Home: 2171 Dellwood Ave N Roseville MN 55113 Office: McAlmont Investment Co Shelard Plaza N Minneapolis MN 55426

JACOBSON, SUSAN CURTIS, lawyer; b. Bklyn., Sept. 27, 1946; d. Edwin Arthur and Mathilde Anne (Nettels) Charles; m. W. James Tillett, June 13, 1969 (div. June 1976); m. 2d, Arvid Victor Jacobson, Feb. 28, 1976. B.A., U. Kans., 1978, J.D., 1980. Bar: Kans. 1980, U.S. Dist. Ct. Kans. 1980. Exec. editor Nat. Orgn. on Legal Problems in Edn., Topeka, Kans., 1974-78; assoc. Robertson & Jacobson, Junction City, Kans., 1980-82; ptnr. Jacobson & Jacobson, Junction City, 1982—. Editor: Contemporary Legal Problems in Education, 1974; New Directions in School Law, 1975; editor Nolpe Sch. Law Jour., 1974-77; mem. U. Kans. Law Rev., 1980; contbr. articles to legal jours. Bd. dirs. United Way of Junction City, 1984—, ARC, Junction City, 1984, 85, Armed Forces YMCA, Junction City, 1983-84, Crisis Ctr., Manhattan, Kans., 1980-84; bd. dirs. Geary County Council Social Agys., Junction City, 1981-84. Mem. Geary County Bar Assn. (1981 Law Day chmn., award of Merit 1981), Kans. Bar Assn., Kans. Trial Lawyers Assn., Assn. Trial Lawyers Am., Junction City C. of C. (young ambassadors 1981-84, old trooper regiment 1983-84, bd. dirs. 1985-86), Assn. U.S. Army. Republican. Episcopalian. Home: 1012 Kingsbury St Junction City KS 66441 Office: Jacobson & Jacobson 526 W 6th St Junction City KS 66441

JACOBY, CAROL LYNNE, physical education educator, coach; b. Chgo., Apr. 11, 1956; d. George Edward and Leota (Rebout) Jacoby. B.S. in Edn., Northern Ill. U., 1978; M.S. in Edn., George Williams Coll., 1984. Tchr. archery Community Park Dist., LaGrange Park, Ill., summers 1978-80; tchr. volleyball Villa Park (Ill.) Park Recreation, summers 1981-83; tchr. Willow Brook High Sch., Villa Park, 1978—, head volleyball coach, 1978-84, head track coach, 1978—. Mem. U.S. Volleyball Assn., Delta Psi Kappa. Roman Catholic. Competitive roller skater, 1978-82, Ill. State champion, 1979. Home: 1021 Newberry Ave LaGrange Park IL 60525 Office: Willowbrook High Sch 1250 S Ardmore Villa Park IL 60181

JACOBY, PATRICIA DAVIS, anesthetist; b. Roanoke, Pa., Oct. 13, 1951; d. Ernest E. and Clara (Stiller) Davis; m. Leslie Howard Jacoby, May 30, 1972 (div. 1976); 1 child, Jennifer Robyn. Diploma in nursing, Polyclinic Med. Ctr., 1972; cert. in nurse anesthesia, Harrisburg Sch. Anesthesia, Pa., 1980; B.A. in Bus., Pa. State U., 1984. R.N., Pa.; R.N. Anesthetist, Pa. Anesthetist, Community Gen. Osteo. Hosp., Harrisburg, 1981—. Bd. dirs. Community Concern for Nursing Home Residents, Harrisburg, 1984—; mem. pub. affairs and advocacy coms. Harrisburg Jr. League, 1984—. Mem. Pa. Assn. Nurse Anesthetists (edn. com. 1983—). Republican. Home: RD Box 189 Hummelstown PA 17036 Office: Community Gen Osteo Hosp Londonderry Rd Harrisburg PA 17105

JAEGLY, PEGGY JANE, public relations executive; b. Toledo, Dec. 6, 1953; d. Daniel Francis and Elsie Fern (Getz) Perch; m. Robert Thomas Jaegly, Aug. 30, 1975; children—Jennifer Kristen, Robert Paul, Jason James. Student U. Salzburg, 1973-74; B.A., Carthage Coll., 1975; postgrad. in bus. adminstrn. U. Toledo, 1982—. Teller, proof supr. Mid-Am. Nat. Bank, Bowling Green, Ohio, 1975-76, 76-77; asst. br. mgr., Toledo, 1977-78, tng. dir., 1978-79, br. mgr. Rossford, Ohio, 1979-80, wage and salary adminstr., Bowling Green, 1980-81; freelance writer United Way Greater Toledo, 1981-84; editor Toledo Alive mag., 1984; pub. relations asst., guest relations dir. Mercy Hosp., 1984—; instr. Am. Inst. Banking, Toledo, 1978, 79. Mktg. rep. Community Planning Council, Toledo, 1983-84; mem. fin. com. Good Shepherd Ch., Toledo, 1979, 80. Recipient Outstanding award Ohio Sch. Banking, 1980. Mem. Women in Communications (treas. 1982-83), Writers Forum of N.W. Ohio (v.p. 1984—), Am. Inst. Banking, Am. Mgmt. Assn. (chmn. assessment ctr. Toledo 1978), Psi Chi, Alpha Lambda Delta. Republican. Roman Catholic. Home: 1980 Rose Arbor Dr Toledo OH 43614 Office: Mercy Hosp 2200 Jefferson Ave Toledo OH 43604

JAEKEL, BARBARA DOROTHY, public relations and marketing company executive; b. San Mateo, Calif., Apr. 9, 1958; d. Ralph Carl and Dorothy Willene J. B.S., Syracuse U., 1978; M.S., U. Tenn., 1983. News anchor, dir. pub. affairs Sta. WOLF, Syracuse, N.Y., 1977-78; news dir., investigative reporter Sta. WSKG, Endicott, N.Y., 1978-81, news dir., Knoxville, Tenn., 1981-83; freelance pub. relations cons., Knoxville, 1981-83; sr. account exec. Campbell & Co., Detroit, 1983-86, exec. v.p. Target Mkfg. Group, 1986—; account exec. Ford-Lyn St. James Program, 1983—, Lincoln-Mercury Cellular Communications Program, 1982—. Mem. Nat. Assn. Broadcast Engrs. and Technicians, Soc. Profl. Journalists, Am. Bus. Women's Assn. Avocations: running; swimming; writing. Home: 13236 Joslin Lake Rd Gregory MI 48137 Office: Campbell & Co PO Drawer 490 Dearborn MI 48121

JAFFA, AILEEN RABY, retired librarian, poet, artist; b. Oakland, Calif., Apr. 26, 1900; d. Myer Edward and Adele Rosa (Solomons) J.; A.B., U. Calif., Berkeley, 1922, cert. in librarianship, 1928; m. Milton Jerome Katzky, June 21, 1922 (div.); children—Lawrence Marvin, Joan Elizabeth (dec.). Jr. asst. U. Calif. Library Agrl. Reference Service, Berkeley, 1928-33, agrl. librarian, 1933-62; head Agr. Library, U. Calif., Berkeley, 1956-62, ret., 1962; poet, artist; books include: Three Sonnets, 1939; Trondheims, 1960; Three Dragons Easily, 1963; Word Out of Time, 1965; Tiptoe To the Wind, 1967; Let the Star Shine, 1973; The Forty-First Day, 1978; When Sailors Used Potatoes, 1984; paintings and sculpture exhibited in Berkeley, Richmond, Modesto and San Francisco, Calif., New Eng. Mem. Calif. Writers Club, Calif. State Poetry Soc., Calif. Fedn. Chaparral Poets, (chmn. North chpt. 1983—, pres. Poets Corner chpt. 1982—), Central Calif. Art League, Ina Coolbrith Circle (pres. 1971-72), Nat. League Am. Pen Women, San Francisco Browning Soc., San Francisco Mus. Soc., Modesto Arts Adv. Council, Am. Assn. Ret. Persons, Ret. State Govt. Employees Assn. Calif., U. Calif.-Berkeley Sch. Librarianship Alumni Assn., Phi Beta Kappa. Republican. Club: U. Calif. Berkeley Women's Faculty. Home: 1105 Wellesley Ave Modesto CA 95350

JAFFARIAN, SARA, retired library and media services director, consultant; b. Haverhill, Mass. Sept. 7, 1915; d. Mugerdich and Quhar (Nalbandian) J. B.A., Bates Coll., 1937; B.S., Simmons Coll., 1947; M.Ed., Boston U., 1957; postgrad. U. N.C.-Greensboro, 1955-56; postgrad. in Edn., Harvard U., 1963-70. Cert. tchr., librarian, media specialist. Library asst. Haverhill Pub. Library (Mass.), 1937-42; tchr. Ossipee High Sch. (N.H.), 1942-43; librarian, Quincy Jr. High Sch. (Mass.), 1943-53; dir. libraries Greensboro Pub. Schs., (N.C.), 1953-60, Seattle Pub. Schs., 1960-61; dir. library, media, Lexington Pub. Schs. (Mass.), 1961-78; cons. media programs sch. dists. and sch. library design; cons. and adviser to book pubs. and book wholesalers and architects planning sch. libraries; lectr., cons. various regional and state profl. assns., New Eng., Southeast, West Coast; grad. library sch. instr. Queens Coll., L.I., N.Y., summer 1959; dir. sch. library workshop, U. Oreg. Grad. Sch., Eugene, summer 1956; dir. sch. library workshop U.S. Office Edn., U. Hawaii, summer 1968, instr. Grad. Sch. Edn., U. N.H., Durham, summers 1964-71. Editor: Every School Needs a Library, 1952; contbr. chpt. to text series (transl. Japanese); guest editor Jr. Libraries, 1957; contbr. articles to library and ednl. jours. Recipient Britannica Sch. Library award, ALA and Ency. Britannica, 1964; U.S. Govt. grantee Grad. Sch. U. So. Calif., 1969. Mem. ALA (council 1962-66, dir. Nat. Library Week, State N.C. 1958-59), Am. Assn. Sch. Librarians (dir. 1954-56, sec. 1956, Newberry-Caldecott award com.), New Eng. Sch. Library Assn. (v.p. 1950-53, dir.), New Eng. Library Assn. (dir. 1962-66), Am. Sch. Library Suprs. Assn. (sec. treas. and pres. 1954-62), Mass. Sch. Library Assn. (pres. 1964-66), NEA (joint com. on libraries 1959-60), Mass. Tchrs. Assn. (publicity dir. 1950-52), Assn. for Supervision and Curriculum Devel., Assn. for Ednl. Communications and Tech., Simmons Alumni Assn. (dir. 1963-64), Bates Key, Pi Lambda Theta (Boston U. Alumni chpt.), Phi Delta Kappa (Harvard Alumni chpt.), Delta Kappa Gamma. Republican. Lodge: Order Eastern Star. Home: 58 Bateman St Haverhill MA 01830

JAFFE, AMY EILEEN, marketing manager, consultant; b. Schenectady, N.Y., May 3, 1961; d. Samuel Ellis and Laurie Ellen (Rothstein) J. B.S. in Econs., SUNY-Albany, 1982; postgrad. in bus. Rennsalear Poly. Inst. Account exec. Retail Mktg. Cons., Albany, 1981-83; regional mktg. mgr. The Pyramid Cos., Glens Falls, N.Y., 1983-84; mktg. mgr. The Rouse Co., Springfield, Mass., 1984—; cons. Childsplay Mag., Springfield, 1984—; dir. Sharper Edge Advt. Co., N.Y.C. Mem. steering com. Young patrons of the Quadrangle Mus., Springfield, Mass., 1984—; bd. dirs. Leukemia Soc. Am., Springfield, 1984—. Mem. Bus. and Profl. Women's Club (Young Careerist award 1984), New Eng. Mktg. Dirs. Council, Advt. Club Western Mass., Pub. Relations Soc., Women in Communications. Democrat. Jewish. Club: Appalachian Mt. (Hartford, Conn.). Home: 26 Forest Hills Ln West Hartford CT 06117 Office: The Rouse Co 1655 Boston Rd Springfield MA 01129

JAFFE, BARBARA GEFEN, financial advisor; b. Jacksonville, Fla., Mar. 21, 1948; d. Sidney J. and Lois (Isaac) Gefen; m. Lawrence L. Jaffe, Nov. 30, 1980; children—Bradley, Sanford. Student U. Fla., 1966-68, Jacksonville U., 1968-70. Newspaper reporter Fla. Times Union, Jacksonville, 1966-74; sr. v.p. investments, asst. mgr. Prudential-Bache Securities, Jacksonville, 1979—. Vice-chair Jacksonville Mayor's Adv. Com. on Status of Women, 1976-80; mem. council Jacksonville U., 1983—; chair Women and the Law, 1978. Democrat. Jewish. Lodge: Hadassah (pres. 1976) (Jacksonville). Avocations: golf; art. Office: Prudential-Bache 1300 Gulf Life Dr Suite 508 Jacksonville FL 32207

JAFFE, ELAINE, financial executive; b. N.Y.C., Feb. 24, 1928; d. Elias and Rose (Weicholz) Blau; m. Wallace Alvin Jaffe, June 20, 1948; children—Rhonda Marian, Amy Dianne. B.A. cum laude, Bklyn. Coll., 1948; M.S., Hofstra U., 1967. Lic. commodities broker; lic. life ins. agt. Account exec. Wood Walker, Woodbury, N.Y., 1972-74; account exec. Dean Witter Reynolds, Garden City, N.Y., 1974-83, assoc. v.p. investments, 1983-84, v.p. investments, 1984—. Avocations: bridge; photography; golf; watercoloring. Office: Dean Witter Reynolds 1075 Franklin Ave Garden City NY 11530

JAFFE, LOUISE, English language educator, creative writer; b. Bronx, N.Y., May 17, 1936; d. Joseph and Anna (Movitz) Neuwirth; m. Steven Jaffe, Aug. 26, 1962 (div. 1975); 1 child, Aaron Lawrence. B.A., Queens Coll., 1956; M.A.,

Hunter Coll., 1959; Ph.D., U. Nebr., 1965. Instr. Kingsborough Community Coll., Bklyn, 1965-67, asst. prof., 1967-70, assoc. prof. English, 1970—. Atuhor: Hyacinths and Biscuits, 1985. Author numerous poetry and fiction stories. Mem. editorial bd. Community Review CUNY, 1984—; faculty adv. student lit. mag., 1983—. Recipient First prize N.Y. Poetry Forum, 1980, First prize, First honorable mention Shelley Soc. N.Y., 1983, 84, and others. Mem. Mensa, Poets and Writers Inc., Shelley Soc. of N.Y., Writers Union, Feminist Writers Guild, Democrat. Jewish. Avocations: creative writing; scrabble; crossword puzzles; people-watching; attending and giving poetry readings. Home: 2411 E 3rd St Brooklyn NY 11223 Office: Kingsborough Community Coll Oriental Blvd Manhattan Beach Brooklyn NY 11223

JAFFE, NORA CROW, educator; b. Los Angeles, Feb. 12, 1944; d. Thomas J. and Helen E. (Beshears) Crow; A.B. magna cum laude in English and Classics (Univ. scholar, Ford Found. fellow), Stanford U., 1965; A.M., Harvard U., 1968, Ph.D. (Grad. Prize fellow), 1972; m. Arthur M. Jaffe, July 24, 1971. Tutor, teaching fellow Harvard U., 1968-70; asst. prof. English, Smith Coll., Northampton, Mass., 1971-79, assoc. prof., 1979—. Ford Found. fellow, 1965; Harvard U. travel grantee, 1969; Hyder Rollins Found. grantee, 1975. Mem. Am. Soc. 18th-Century Studies, MLA (exec. com. div. Restoration and early Eighteenth-Century English lit.), Phi Beta Kappa. Author: The Poet Swift, 1977; co-editor: The Evil Image. Two Centuries of Gothic Short Fiction and Poetry. The Literary Art of Terror from Daniel Defoe to Stephen King, 1981; contbr. articles to profl. jours., chpts. in books. Home: 27 Lancaster St Cambridge MA 02140 Office: English Dept Smith College Northampton MA 01063

JAFFE, PHYLLIS SHELLEY, lawyer; b. N.Y.C., Feb. 13, 1925; d. Robert and Jessie (Sinick) Shelley; m. Frederick Stanley Jaffe, Aug. 7, 1947 (dec. Aug. 1978); children—Paul, David, Richard. B.A., Queens Coll., 1944; J.D., Columbia U., 1949. Bar: N.Y. 1949, U.S. Dist. Ct. (so. dist.) N.Y. 1981, U.S. Ct. Appeals (2d cir.) 1984. Sole practice, Ossining, N.Y., 1953-69; editor Prentice-Hall, Englewood Cliffs, N.J., 1969-71; labor relations specialist N.Y.C. Bd. Edn., 1971-72; staff atty. Bd. Coop. Ednl. Services, Yorktown Heights, N.Y., 1972-75; ptnr. Plunkett & Jaffe, P.C., White Plains, N.Y., 1975—. Mem., pres. Ossining Bd. Edn., 1964-69. Served as sgt. WAC, U.S. Army, 1944-46. Mem. Westchester County Bar Assn., Women's Bar Assn. N.Y. State. Jewish. Avocations: tennis; gardening. Office: Plunkett & Jaffe PC 1 N Broadway White Plains NY 10601

JAFFE, RONA, author; b. N.Y.C., June 12, 1932; d. Samuel and Diana (Ginsberg) J.; B.A., Radcliffe Coll., 1951. Sec., N.Y.C., 1952; asso. editor Fawcett Publs., N.Y.C., 1952-56. Author: The Best of Everything, 1958, Away From Home, 1960, The Last of the Wizards, 1961, Mr. Right is Dead, 1965, The Cherry in the Martini, 1966, The Fame Game, 1969, The Other Woman, 1972, Family Secrets, 1974, The Last Chance, 1976, Class Reunion, 1979; Mazes and Monsters, 1981; After the Reunion, 1985. Office: care Delacorte Press Dell Pub Co Inc One Dag Hammarskjold Plaza New York NY 10017*

JAFFE, SYLVIA SARAH, art collector, former medical technologist; b. Detroit, May 16, 1917; d. Sam and Rose (Rosmarin) Turner; B.S. in Med. Tech., U. Wis., 1940; m. David Jaffe, Nov. 8, 1942. Med. technologist Watts Hosp. Lab., Durham, N.C., 1940-45; research hematology technologist in leukemia Sloan Kettering Meml. Hosp. Lab., N.Y.C., 1946-47; chief med. technologist in hematology Arlington (Va.) Hosp. Lab., 1948-55; chief technologist in diagnostic hematology Georgetown U. Hosp., Washington, 1959-70; collector 19th century and 20th century art, 1970—. Mem. Am. Soc. Med. Technologists, Am. Soc. Clin. Pathologists (assoc.), Am. Women in Sci., Corcoran Gallery Art, Pa. Acad. Fine Arts, Nat. Trust Hist. Preservation, The Washington Print Club, U. Wis. Alumni Assn., Boston Mus. Arts, Nat. Mus. Women in Arts (charter). Democrat. Jewish. Club: Pioneer Women. Contbr. articles to profl. socs. Address: 1913 S Quincy St Arlington VA 22204

JAHDE, JUDY ANN, health care educator; b. Beatrice, Nebr., July 23, 1949; d. Harry Lee and JoAnne Roberta (Heble) Scott; m. Marv John Jahde, Apr. 15, 1972; children—Jennifer D., Sarah A., Matthew J. Diploma in nursing Bryan Meml. Sch. Nursing, 1970; student in nursing U. Nebr., 1970-72, Marquette U., 1981, Coll. St. Francis, Joliet, Ill., 1981—. R.N., Nebr., Iowa, Wis. Staff nurse, clinic nurse U. Nebr. Student Health Ctr., Lincoln, 1970-71; clin. instr. med.-surg. nursing Lincoln Gen. Sch. Nursing, 1971-72; patient teaching coordinator Deaconess Hosp., Milw., 1972-73; edn. coordinator, patient tchr., nurse recruiter Family Hosp., Milw., 1973-80; nursing edn. coordinator Norrell Home Health Services, West Des Moines, IA, 1986—; cons., speaker in field. Author teaching guides, articles on women's health issues. Mem. Metro Maternal Child Steering Com., Des Moines, 1985—; speaker Iowa Luth. Hosp., 1985—. Mem. Nat. Assn. Female Execs., Met. Women's Network Des Moines (speakers bur.), Resolve Orgn., Exec. Circle Des Moines, Continuing Inservice Educators of Iowa, Iowa Nursing Assn. (commn. on nursing practice), Greater Des Moines Chamber Fedn. (health and human services com.). Republican. Lutheran. Home: 501 45th St West Des Moines IA 50265 Office: Norrell Home Health Services 3636 Westown Pkwy Suite 215 West Des Moines IA 50265

JAHN, BILLIE JANE, nurse; b. Byers, Tex., Dec. 12, 1921; d. Thomas Oscar and Molly Verona (Kennemer) Downing; student Scott and White Sch. Nursing, 1941-42, U. Mich., 1973-75; B.S. in Nursing, Wayne State U., 1971; M.S., East Tex. State U., 1976, Ph.D., 1982; m. Edward L. Jahn, Dec. 6, 1942; children—Antoinette R., James T., Thomas L., Edward L., Janette E. Staff nurse Warren Meml. Hosp., Centerline, Mich., 1957-61; supr. nursing service Mich. Dept. Mental Health, Northville, 1962-71, Franklin County (Tex.) Hosp., 1972-74; instr. nursing Paris (Tex.) Jr. Coll., 1975-80; nurse educator VA, Waco, Tex., 1981-82; exec. v.p., dir., sr. nursing cons. Dos Cabezas, Inc., Mt. Vernon, Waco and Temple, Tex., 1981—; adj. faculty U. Tex.-Arlington, 1985—; mem. dept. phys. medicine and rehab. Scott and White Hosp., Temple, Tex., 1985—; cons. East Tex. State U., Texarkana, 1978—. adj. faculty U. Tex.-Arlington; staff dept. rehab. medicine Scott and White Hosp., Temple, Tex. Vol., ARC, 1971—; den mother Boy Scouts Am., 1960-62; sec. PTA, Warren, Mich., 1960-62; v.p., Temple, Tex., 1957-58. Mem. AAAS, Nat. League Nursing, Nat. Assn. Rehab. Nurses (rev. bd. Rehab. Nursing Inst. 1986—), Tex. League Nursing, AAUP, Nat. Assn. Female Execs., Am. Assn. Curriculum and Supervision, Phi Delta Kappa, Kappa Delta Pi. Home: PO Box 594 Mount Vernon TX 75457 Office: PO Box 340 Nount Vernon TX 75457 also 2024 S 15th St Temple TX 76501 also 2024 S 15th St Temple TX 76501

JAI, JONI, automatic tube cleaner mfg. co. exec.; b. Des Moines, Feb. 15, 1936; d. Mahlon Alonzo and Mary Jane (Cooper) Baldwin; student Orange Coast Coll., U. Minn.; m. Ken Jai, Apr. 24, 1967; children—Robert, Cindy, Troy, Aubrey, Mitchell, Tonya. Owner tax cons. and bookkeeping service, Calif., 1969; owner Global Heat Exchanger Inc., Beaumont, Tex., 1970—, sec.-treas., chmn. bd., 1970—; developer Riverside Marina seminar leader boiler maintenance. Mem. Republican Nat. Com. Mem. Tex. Assn. Bus., Tex. Mfrs. Assn. (life), U.S. Automobile Club, Nat. Assn. Stock Car Autoracing. Roman Catholic. Patentee automatic tube cleaner, clean and brush cleaning tool. Address: PO Box 1127 Beaumont TX 77704

JAIDINGER, JUDITH CLARANN, wood engraver, painter; b. Chgo., Apr. 10, 1941; d. John Henry and Charlotte Violet (Anton) J.; m. Gerald Szesko, June 27, 1970; 1 dau., Loralee C. Kolton. B.F.A. in Drawing, Painting and Printmaking, Sch. Art Inst. Chgo., 1970. Represented in permanent collections including: Ill. State Mus., Kemper Group, Eastern Ill. U., Charleston, Brand Library Art Ctr., Glendale, Calif., Washington and Jefferson Coll., Washington, Pa., Minot State Coll. (N.D.), Prairie State Coll., Chicago Heights; group shows include: NAD, N.Y.C., Boston Printmakers, Needham, Mass., J.B. Speed Art Mus., Louisville, Soc. Wood Engravers and Relief Printers, Eng. Included in portfolio: Face to Face, 1985. Recipient awards including 1st graphics Okla. Art Guild, Oklahoma City, 1974, N.Mex. Art League, Albuquerque, 1974, Okla. Mus. Art, Oklahoma City, 1975, Smithsonian Traveling Exhbn., 1971-74, Norfolk Biennial, 1971. Home: 6110 N Newburg Ave Chicago IL 60631

JAKAB, IRENE, psychiatrist, educator; b. Oradea, Rumania; came to U.S., 1961, naturalized, 1966; d. Odon and Rosa A. (Riedl) Jakab; M.D., Ferencz Jozsef U., Kolozsvar, Hungary, 1944; lic. in Psychology, Paedagogy, Philosophy cum laude Hungarian U., Kolozsvar, 1947; Ph.D. summa cum laude in Psychology, Paedagogy, Gen. Lit., Pazmany Peter U., Budapest, 1948; D. honoris causa, U. Besancon, France, 1982. Rotating intern Ferencz Jozsef U., Kolozsvar, 1943-44; resident in psychiatry Univ. Hosp., Kolozsvar, 1944-47, resident in neurology, 1947-50; resident in internal medicine Univ. Hosp. of Internal Medicine, Pecs, Hungary, 1950-51; chief physician Univ. Hosp. for Neurology and Psychiatry, Pecs, 1951-59; staff neuropath. research lab. Neurol. Univ. Clinic, Zurich, Switzerland, 1959-61; sect. chief Kans. Neurol. Inst., Topeka, 1961-63; dir. research and edn., 1966; resident psychiatry Topeka State Hosp., 1963-66; asst. psychiatrist McLean Hosp., Belmont, Mass., 1966-67, asso. psychiatrist, 1967-74; prof. psychiatry U. Pitts. Med. Sch., 1974—, dir. John Merck program, 1974-81; mem. faculty dept. psychiatry Med. Sch., Pecs, 1951-59; asst. Univ. Hosp. Neurology, Zurich, Switzerland, 1959-61; asso. in psychiatry Harvard Med. Sch., Boston, 1966-69, asst. prof. in psychiatry, 1969-74, lectr. psychiatry, 1974—; dir. planning Children's Treatment and Ednl. Center, John Merck Found., 1970; program dir. grad. course in mental retardation NIMH, 1970—. Fellow Menninger Sch. Psychiatry, Topeka, 1963-66. Recipient Prinzhorn prize, 1967, Ernst Kris prize, 1973. Diplomate Am. Bd. Psychiatry. Mem. AMA, Am. Psychol. Assn., Am. Psychiat. Assn. (Gold award for sci. exhibit 1980), Société Medico Psychologique de Paris, Internat. Rorschach Soc., Internat. (v.p. 1959—), Am. (chmn. 1965—) socs. psychopathology of expression, Internat. Soc. Child Psychiatry and Allied Professions, Deutschsprachige Gesellschaft fur Psychopathologie des Ausdrucks (hon.). Author: Dessins et Peintures des Alienes, 1956; Zeichnungen und Gemalde der Geisteskranken, 1956. Editor: Art and Psychiatry, Proceedings of the Fourth International Colloquium of Psychopathology of Expression, 1968, Art Interpretation and Art Therapy, 1969; Conscious and Unconscious Expressive Art: Theories, Methodology and Pathographies, 1971; Transcultural Aspects of Psychiatric Art, 1975; co-editor: Dynamische Psychiatrie (Berlin), 1968; mem. editorial bd. Confinia Psychiatrica (Basel), 1968, now editor-in-chief. Reviewer, Annales Medico-Psychologiques, 1957—, Acta Paedo Psychiatrica, 1963—. Contbr. articles to publs. Home: 228 Parkman Ave Pittsburgh PA 15213 Office: 3811 O'Hara St Pittsburgh PA 15213

JAKOBI, SHARON MARIE, insurance agent; b. Berwyn, Ill., Mar. 7, 1940; d. Arthur H. and Christine A. J.; C.P.C. U. cert. Am. Inst. Property and Casualty Underwriters, 1976; asso. in risk mgmt. cert. Ins. Inst. Am., 1979; student in ins. Golden Gate U. Sec., personnel asst. Ceco Steel Corp., Chgo., 1959-65; with Dinner Levison Co., San Francisco, 1965-78, account coordinator, 1973-77, dept. mgr./ednl. coordinator, 1977-78; v.p., dept. mgr., tng./ednl. coordinator Andreini and Co., San Mateo, Calif., 1978-80; v.p., account exec. Poulton Assos., Oakland, Calif., 1981-83; ins. agt. Nationwide Ins. Co., Walnut Creek Calif., 1983—. Sec. Meadlowland Homeowners Assn., Fairfax, Calif., 1977-79; sec. Montcarle Townhouse Homeowners Assn., 1981-82, pres., 1982-84. Mem. Am. Soc. C.P.C.U.s (columnist The Retro 1977-79, ednl. v.p., candidate devel. No. Calif. chpt. 1978-79, sec. chpt. 1979—, v.p. ops. 1980, chmn. bylaw com. 1981-82, chmn. internship com. 1981-82, pres. 1984-85, membership com. 1985-86, Ins. Profl. of Yr. No. Calif. chpt. 1985), Peninsula Assn. Life Underwriters, Nat. Assn. Life Underwriters, Calif. Assn. Life Underwriters, Ins. Ednl. Assn. (C.P.C.U. rep. to industry liaison com. 1980-82), Ins. Forum San Francisco (ednl. chairperson 1978-79), Golden Gate Alumni Assn. (council, mem. chpt. devel. com. Peninsula-South Bay chpt. 1980-82, v.p. Peninsula chpt. 1986). Club: Commonwealth (San Francisco). Office: 1070 6th Ave Suite 305 Belmont CA 94002

JAKOBS, NANCY MARTHA, manufacturing company executive; b. Los Angeles, Nov. 23, 1940; d. F. George and Mildred C. (Ramsey) Herlihy; m. Robert W. Belk, June 25, 1966 (div. 1978); m. 2d Frederick Herman Jakobs, 1978. B.A., U. Ariz., 1962; M.A., U. So. Calif., 1963. Asst. prof. Calif. Luth. Coll., Thousand Oaks, 1963-69; personnel mgr. Bechtel Corp., San Francisco, 1973-78; dir. personnel Materials Research Corp., Orangeburg, N.Y., 1978-83, v.p., 1983—; dir. Rockland County Job Service, Nanuet, N.Y. Mem. Rockland County Future, Pomona, N.Y., 1982-83. Named Outstanding Jr. Mem., Calif. and Western region DAR, 1974. Mem. Am. Compensation Assn., Am. Soc. for Personnel Adminstrn. (founder, treas., dir. Bergen-Rockland chpt. 1976—), Alpha Omicron Pi (regional dir. 1971-73, regional v.p. 1973-74). Office: Materials Research Corp Route 303 Orangeburg NY 10962

JAKUBOWSKI, KAREN SUE, manufacturing company executive; b. Lorain, Ohio, Sept. 27, 1955; s. James Joseph and Matilda Christina (Tammaro) J. B.A., Kent State U., 1977, postgrad. Bowling Green State U., 1979, Lorain County Community Coll., 1982-83; M.B.A., Baldwin Wallace Coll., 1985. Counselor, tchr. Lorain County Domestic Relations Ct., Elyria, Ohio, 1977-80, 81-82; sales asst. RKO Radio Sales, Atlanta, 1980; youth enrichment specialist Lorain County Domestic Relations Ct., Ohio, 1982-84; dep. dir. Youth devel. Ctr., Lorain, 1984-85; dir., 1985-86; personnel mgr. Western Enterprises div. Scott & Fetzer Co., Avon Lake and Westlake, Ohio, 1986—. Eucharistic minister St. Mary's Ch., Lorain, 1979—. Mem. Assn. M.B.A. Execs., Nat. Assn. Female Execs., Am. Soc. Personnel Adminstr., Kent State U. Alumni Assn., Baldwin Wallace Coll. MBA Alumni Assn. Roman Catholic. Club: Scandinavian Health Spa (Westlake). Avocations: theatre; ballet; travel. Office: Western Enterprises 875 Bassett Rd Westlake OH 44145

JAMBOR, MARGARET MARY, lawyer; b. Cleve., July 28, 1948; d. Stephen Joseph and Mary Jane (Gernat) J. B.A. cum laude, Cleve. State U., 1970, J.D., 1973. Bar: Ohio 1973. Gen. atty. Immigration and Naturalization Service, U.S. Dept. Justice, Los Angeles, 1973—, acting naturalization program mgr., 1982-83; trial litigation atty., 1983—. Vol., St. John's Hosp., Santa Monica, Calif.; singer St. John's Cathedral Choir, Cleve., 1970-73, St. Monica's Adult Choir, 1979-81, St. Paul the Apostle Schola Cantorum Choir, 1981—. Woodrow Wilson Scholar nominee, 1967; named Outstanding Woman of Yr., Cleve. State U., 1969-70; Dean's List, Cleve. State U., 1967-70; recipient Dept. Justice commendation, 1976; Cert. of Achievement, Immigration and Naturalization Service, 1981, Outstanding Performance rating, 1980. Mem. ABA, Los Angeles County Bar Assn., Cleve. Bar Assn., U.S. Figure Skating Assn. (preliminary and bronze dance medalist 1982, 83, pre-silver medalist, 1984, Southwest, Pacific Coast, Puget Sound internat. Gold medalist Adult Precision Team Competitions 1985-86), Los Angeles Figure Skating Club, Santa Monica Figure Skating Club (1st place award 1982, 2d place 1983, 3d place 1983), Wing and Torch Soc. (life), Phi Alpha Delta (past chief justice Meck chpt.), Beta Sigma Omicron. Roman Catholic. Mailing Address: US Immigration and Naturalization Service Los Angeles CA 90012

JAMES, ALICE HOWRY, educator; b. Evanston, Ill., Apr. 9, 1918; d. Henry Burney and Edyth (Wornall) H.; A.B., U. Louisville, 1939, M.Ed., 1974; m. Thomas James II, July 15, 1941 (dec.); children—Thomas III, Edyth MacMillan, David Buchanan. Tchr., St. Mark's Presch., Louisville, 1959-61; asst. dir., tchr. Crescent Hill Meth. Presch., Louisville, 1961-66; kindergarten tchr. Louisville Bd. Edn., 1966-75; kindergarten tchr. Jefferson County Bd. Edn., Louisville, 1975-79; assoc. prof. early childhood edn. Jefferson Community Coll., Louisville, 1979—. Chmn., Peterson-Dumesnil Restoration Com., 1978; mem. Crescent Hill Community Council Edn. Com., 1979; bd. dirs. Home of the Innocents, 1980-86; mem. career devel. com. Head Start, 1980, chmn. policy council, 1983-84; bd. dirs. Peterson-Dumesnil Found., 1983-85, Community Coordinated Child Care. Mem. Am. Assn. Community Coll. Early Childhood Educators, Nat. Assn. Edn. Young Children, Ky. Assn. Edn. Young Children, Louisville Assn. for Children Under Six, LWV, Phi Delta Kappa. Episcopalian. Clubs: Pendennis Club, Louisville Country. Home: 240 S Peterson Ave Louisville KY 40206 Office: Jefferson Community Coll 109 E Broadway Louisville KY 40202

JAMES, BARBARA ANN, hospitality industry executive, interior design consultant; b. Owensboro, Ky., Feb. 14, 1936; d. J.T. and Thelma (Newman) Woodward; m. William E. James, Feb. 19, 1951 (div. June 1953); 1 child, Keith Douglas. Vice pres., Fla. Containers Inc., Sebring, 1978-81; v.p. Barda Services Inc., Tampa, Fla., 1981—; v.p., gen. mgr. BJ's of Tampa, Inc., 1982—. Democrat. Roman Catholic. Office: Barda Services Inc PO Box 24247 Tampa FL 33623

JAMES, BARBARA DEAN, psychiatric social worker; b. Augusta, Ga., Apr. 21, 1951; d. James Elvia and Susie Mae (Thomas) Walden; m. Oscar Neil James, Dec. 26, 1981; children—Malik Karif, Oscar Sydney II. A.S., Essex County Coll., Newark, 1972; B.A., Jersey City State Coll., 1974. Social caseworker Div. Pub. Welfare, State of N.J., Newark, 1974-75; mental health specialist Univ. Medicine and Dentistry N.J., Newark, 1975—. Vice-pres. parent council Rutgers Chen Sch., Newark, 1985. Mem. Sharpe James Civic Assn., N.Y. Theater Club (v.p. 1979-80). Democrat. Presbyterian. Club: Social (Newark). Lodge: Eastern Star. Avocation: sewing. Office: Univ Medicine and Dentistry NJ 100 Bergen St Newark NJ 07103

JAMES, BETTY NOWLIN, university administrator; b. Athens, Ga., Feb. 16, 1936; d. William F. and Marie (Davis) Nowlin; children—Beth Marie Morris, Dewey Douglas Morris. Francis James, Dec. 12, 1981. B.A., Fisk U., 1956; M.A., U. Houston, 1970, Ed.D., 1975. Tchr., Houston Ind. Sch. Dist., 1958-72, tech. asst., 1972-73, basic skills evaluator, 1974-76; Coordinator program evaluation U. Houston-Downtown, 1976-81, dir. instl. research, 1981-83, dir. instl. services/personnel-instl. services, 1983—. Mem. allocations panel United Way, Houston, 1980-83; vol. United Negro Coll. Fund, 1983-84. Jesse Jones scholar, 1954-55; Rockefeller Found. grantee, 1956-57. Mem. Personnel Assn. Tex. Colls. and Univs., Tex. Assn. Instl. Research, Coll./Univ. Personnel Assn., Nat. Assn. Equal Opportunity, Fisk Alumni Assn. (chpt. pres. 1980-83), Alpha Kappa Alpha. Home: 3301 Oakdale Houston TX 77004 Office: One Main St Houston TX 77002

JAMES, CATHERINE BENNETT, investment banker; b. Boston, Sept. 5, 1952; d. Robert Gregory and Ardis (Butler) J. B.A. with distinction, Carleton Coll., 1974; M.B.A., Harvard U., 1976. Vice pres. Dean Witter Reynolds Inc., N.Y.C., 1976-82; v.p. Morgan Stanley & Co., Inc., N.Y.C., 1982-84, prin., 1984—. Trustee Carleton Coll., Northfield, Minn., 1984—. Club: Harvard (N.Y.C.). Office: Morgan Stanley & Co Inc 1251 Ave of Americas New York NY 10020

JAMES, CLAUDIA JOYCE, transportation company executive; b. Oklahoma City, Aug. 10, 1953; d. Harvey C. and Betty Joyce (Thomas) Barber; m. Scott Allan Serbin, Feb. 19, 1971 (div. Apr. 1974); m. Paul Melton James, Apr. 15, 1975; children—Phillip Benjamin, Richard Clint. Grad. Chilton Corp., Dallas. Sales staff Amway Co., Dallas, 1971-73; owner S & S Maintenance Co., Dallas, 1974-77, S.W. Sign Co., Richardson, Tex., 1977-79, Profl. Budget Mgmt. Co., 1985—; chief exec. officer, chmn. bd. James Transp. Inc., Irving, Tex., 1979—; ptnr. H.C. Barber Enterprises, Gulf Western Mortgage and Loan, 1985—. Campaign worker Republican Party, Greenville, Tex., 1979; fund raiser Children's Med. Ctr., Dallas, 1981, Hunt County Com. on Aging, Greenville, 1982. Recipient awards Amway Co., Dallas, 1971-73. Republican. Mormon. Avocations: woodworking; stained glass making; decorating; stonework; painting. Home: 216 Iron Bridge Pl Euless TX 76040 Office: James Transp Inc 8420 Sterling St Irving TX 75063

JAMES, CURTIA LYNNE, editor; b. Columbus, Ohio, Oct. 28, 1958; d. Curtis and Jean (Fulton) J. B.A., Howard U., 1980. Adminstrv. asst. John Wiley & Sons, N.Y.C., 1980-81; intern The Bulletin Newspaper, Phila., 1981; asst. editor Essence mag., N.Y.C., 1981-84, assoc. food editor, 1984, contemporary living editor, 1984—. Mem. Delta Sigma Theta. Home: 411 State St Brooklyn NY 11217 Office: ESSENCE Communications Inc 1500 Broadway New York NY 11217

JAMES, GENEVA BEHRENS, educator; b. Marietta, Minn., Mar. 23, 1942; d. Siegfried and Dora (Schoenrock) Behrens; B.S., Mankato State U., 1963; m. Howard James, Aug. 2, 1963; children—Scott, Dawn. Tchr. English high schs., Minn., 1964-65; instr. acctg., Adult Continuing Edn., Bellevue, Nebr., 1971-75, dir. Adult Basic Edn. Center, 1974—, vol. coordinator, 1983—, instr. computer literacy, 1984—. Mem. exec. com. Boy Scouts Am., 1974-80. Mem. AAUW, Nat. Assn. Public and Continuing Adult Edn., Adult and Continuing Edn. Assn. Nebr., NEA, Nat. Council Tchrs. English (dist. curriculum com. 1985—). Republican. Lutheran. Home: 1314 Hansen Ave Bellevue NE 68005 Office: 2221 Main St Bellevue NE 68005

JAMES, GLEDA JO, mineral water company executive; b. Atlanta, Jan. 17, 1929; d. Oscar Lee and Jewell Odessa (Hancock) Brown; m. William Edward James, Jan. 6, 1951 (dec. Oct. 1982); children—Jennifer James Camp, Gregory, Susan. Art student, Naples, Italy, 1962-65; student, Wilmington Coll., 1966-67. Owner, James House Restaurant, Lithia Springs, Ga., 1971-84; real estate sales agt. Finch Realty, Lithia Springs, 1984-85; owner, pres., chmn. bd. Lithia Springs Mineral Water Co., Inc., 1983—, also Cave Spring Pure Water Co., Inc. Pres., Lithia Springs Civic Club, 1978; curator Family Dr. Mus., 1984—; mem. Ga. Trust for Hist. Preservation, 1985—. Recipient Best Painting in Show award Jacksonville Artists Club, N.C., 1966, Homemaker of Yr. award Congl. Dist. Ga. Homemakers, 1970. Mem. Internat. Bottled Water Assn. (pub. relations com. 1984, Pub. Relations award 1984, 85), Sweetwater Hist. Soc. (pres. 1979-85), Atlanta Hist. Soc. Methodist. Avocations: collecting medical memorabilia; historical preservation. Home: 2973 Skyview Dr PO Box 713 Lithia Springs GA 30057 Office: Lithia Springs Mineral Water Co Inc 2910 Bankhead Hwy PO Box 713 Lithia Springs GA 30057

JAMES, JEANNIE HENRIETTA, educator; b. Greenville, S.C., Dec. 5, 1921; d. Portice J. and Essie Virginia (Ross) J.; B.S., Berea (Ky.) Coll., 1945; M.S., U. N.C., 1949; postgrad. Iowa State U., 1955-56; Ed.D., Pa. State U., 1965. Tchr. home econs. Stowe (Vt.) High Sch., 1945-48; asst. prof., asso. prof. home econs. Lincoln Meml. U., Harrogage, Tenn., 1949-59; asst. prof., asso. profl. Ill. State U., Normal, 1959-75; asso. prof. early childhood edn. U. S.C., Columbia, 1975-79, Spartanburg Meth. Coll., 1980; mem. Ill. White House Conf. on Children and Youth, 1969-70. Mem. Nat., S.C. assns. for edn. young children, Soc. for Research and Child Devel., AAUP, World Orgn. for Edn. Children, S.C. Home Econs. Assn., So. Highlands Handicraft Guild, Am. Home Econs. Assn. (program chmn. sect. 1977-79), AAUW, Phi Kappa Delta, Zeta Tau Alpha. Contbr. articles to profl. jours. Home: Belmont Estates #205 Fountain In SC 29644

JAMES, KAREN KING, medical technology administrator; b. Houston, Oct. 28, 1951; d. Jack Edison and Mary Lou (Hudson) King; m. George Cunningham James, Dec. 17, 1977; children—Benjamin, Andrew. Cert. in med. technology Hermann Hosp., 1973; B.S. in Biology, U. Houston, 1973. Med. technologist Hermann Hosp., Houston, 1972-76; evening supr. Meml. City Gen. Hosp., Houston, 1976-80, lab. mgr., 1980—. Mem. Clin. Lab. Mgmt. Assn., Am. Soc. for Med. Tech., Delta Zeta. Republican. Methodist. Club: Houston Dive. Home: 2706 Quincannon Houston TX 77043 Office: Meml City Gen Hosp 920 Frostwood Houston TX 77024

JAMES, KATHERINE A., educational administrator; b. Washington, Oct. 17, 1942; m. Lawrence E. James, Jr., Apr. 7, 1977; children—Jennifer, Juliette. B.A., Am. U., 1964; M.A., Pacific Western U., 1985. Dir. fgn. students Temple Sch., Washington, 1964-69; lectr. in Spanish, Am. U., Washington, 1964-65; instr. Internat. Lang. Inst., Washington, 1971, 75, U. D.C., Washington, 1969-81; upper sch. head Barrie Sch., Silver Spring, Md., 1981—; instr. (contract) GAO, Washington, 1968-69, NEA, Washington, 1974; cons. to pres. Transemantics, Inc., Chevy Chase, Md., 1971. Author textbook: Dialogues in English for the Foreign Born, 1965. Elder, tchr. Northminster Presbyterian Ch., Washington, 1961—; newsletter editor Carole Highlands Civic Assn., Takoma Park, Md., 1977-80; pres. Carole Highlands PTA, 1980-82; pres. Ki-Wives of Shepherd Park, Washington, 1982—. Mem. Nat. Assn. Female Execs., Phi Delta Kappa (sec. 1982-84, v.p. 1984-85, pres. 1985-86, chpt. Service award 1985). Republican. Avocation: ballroom dancing. Home: 1508 Erskine St Takoma Park MD 20912 Office: Barrie School Upper School 2400 Bel Pre Rd Silver Spring MD 20906

JAMES, LEONA KAY, city official; b. Wichita, Aug. 14, 1940; d. Murrell Kennedy and Byrness Leone (Belden Hunter; m. Philip Sidney James, June 14, 1964; children—Philip S. II, Todd L., Kirk K. A.A., Colo. Womans Coll., 1960; student Colo. U. Extension, 1964, Mesa Coll., 1985, Denver U., 1962. Acct., Eyl's Animal Hosp., Montrose, Colo., 1957-58; asst. prof. Colo. Woman's Coll., Denver, 1959-60; sec. to controller Am. Motors Sales Corp., Denver, 1960-66; mgr. Day Care Ctr., Aurora, Colo., 1968-75; fin. dir. City Montrose, Colo., 1975—. Alt. del. Republican Con. Colo., 1984; acting chmn. bd. dirs. Gt. Am. Summer Salute, Montrose, 1983—; chmn. com. Montrose Centennial, 1982. Recipient Best of Show award oil painting Colo. Western Slope Art Show, 1973. Mem. Colo. Govt. Fin. Officers Assn. (pres., v.p., treas. 1982—), Nat. Govt. Fin. Officers Assn. (state rep. 1984—), Colo. Mcpl. League (sales tax task force, policy com. 1984-85), Montrose C. of C., Alpha Pi Epsilon, Tri Chi. Club: Altrusa. Avocations: skiing; painting; archeology. Home: 67793 Colina Dr Montrose CO 81401 Office: City of Montrose PO Box 790 Montrose CO 84102

JAMES, LORRAINE ANDRESS, city official, accountant; b. Kalamazoo, Mich., Mar. 16, 1949; d. Basil John and Anna Viola (Manchip) Andress; m. John Allan Miedema, Feb. 20, 1971 (div. 1978); children—John Basil, Leigh Ann; m. Dean Allen James, Aug. 2, 1985. A.A.S., Ferris State Coll., 1969, B.S., 1973; M.A., Central Mich. U., 1977. Plant acct. Ferris State Coll., Big Rapids, Mich., 1975-78, grant acct., 1978-82, acctg. instr. (part time), 1974-83; city treas. City of Big Rapids, 1982—; owner, operator Miedema's Tax Service, Big Rapids, 1976—. Judge Mecosta County Bus. Woman of Yr., 1979; active Parent Tchrs. League, St. Peter's Lutheran Sch., 1976—, St. Peter's Luth. Ch., 1976—, Mecosta County Hosp. Aux., 1978-79; Cub Scout parent vol., 1980; fundraiser United Fund, Am. Cancer Soc., Femur Follies, Jerry Lewis Muscular Dystrophy Telethon; panel mem. Student Bus. Dialogue Day, 1979-80, others. Mem. Mich. Treas. Assn., Mcpl. Fin. Officers Assn., Big Rapids Intermediate Women's Club (first v.p. 1978-79), Big Rapids Woman's Softball Assn. (treas. 1982—), Delta Zeta (collegiate dir., 1978-80). Home: 1017 Loudon St Big Rapids MI 49307 Office: City of Big Rapids 226 N Michigan Ave Big Rapids MI 49307

JAMES, MARIE RUPPERT, financial consultant; b. N.Y.C., Sept. 13, 1942; d. John Arthur and Nellie (Huber) Ruppert; m. Michael Joseph James, Jr., June 5, 1976. B.B.A., Baruch Coll., CCNY, 1979; A.A., Alfonsus Coll., 1963. C.L.U.; chartered fin. cons. Tchr., St. John's Villa, Santiago, Chile, 1963-67; dir. head start Archdiocese of N.Y., Bronx, 1967-68; officer mgr. Frederick B. Ayer & Assocs., Inc., N.Y.C., 1968-77; fin. cons. N.Y. Life, Westchester, N.Y., 1979—. Civilian patrol liaison Woodlean Taxpayers Assn., Bronx, 1984. Mem. Nat. Assn. Life Underwriters, Women's Life Underwriters, Am. Soc. C.L.U.s, Life Underwriters of Westchester (dir.), Beta Gamma Sigma Alumni. Republican. Roman Catholic. Club: Westchester Chorale. Avocations: choral singing; trapshooting. Home: 318 E 242d St Bronx NY 10470 Office: Marie R James & Assocs 411 Theodore Fremd Ave 3d Floor Rye NY 10580

JAMES, MILDRED HANNAH, hypnotist; b. Hopewell, Va., Oct. 18, 1918; d. Charles and Fannie (Enoch) Feldman; student Sch. Tech. Hypnosis, Ethical Hypnosis Tng. Center, Am. Inst. Hypnosis, Am. Guild Hypnotherapists; m. Albert W. James, Dec. 31, 1965; children by previous marriage—Shiela, Leslie, Andrea, David, Valerie, Kelly. Apprentice in hypnosis, 1959-60; practicing hypnotist, 1961—; pres., chmn. bd. Mildred H. James, Inc., Kent, Wash., 1976—; lectr., condr. seminars. Mem. Am. Inst. Hypnosis, Am. Guild Hypnotherapists, Hypnotists Union. Author weight reduction methods and smoking control methods; producer cassette tapes. Address: 322 Hibiscus Trail Melbourne Beach FL 32951

JAMES, REBECCA LOU, educator, consultant; b. Houston, Mar. 4, 1938; d. Ben Allen and Julia Corinth (Wainscott) J.; m. William Fabian Kitchell, June 10, 1961 (dec. Nov. 1982); 1 dau., Julie Ann. B.S., U. Houston, 1959, M.Ed., 1976, Ed.D., 1982. Tchr., Houston Ind. Schs., 1959-73; asst. supr. Timbergrove Christian Acad., Houston, 1974-75; grad. fellow U. Houston, 1975-78; cons. region 4 Edn. Service Ctr., Houston, 1978-79; student tchr. supr. U. Houston, 1979-80; gifted/talented instr. Galena Park Schs., Houston, 1980-84; pres. The Whole Brain Experience, Inc., 1984—; Bibl. counselor 700 Club, Houston, 1982—, dir. tng. programs, 1982-83; mem. task force, Tex. Council for Personnel Preparation for Handicapped, Austin, Houston, 1976-77; mem. evaluation com. So. Assn. Colls. and Schs., Houston, 1982; cons. region 4 Edn. Service Ctr., Houston, 1979—. Cons., Hope Ctr. for Youth, Houston, 1980-82; counselor rape victims, parents of gifted or handicapped children Evangelistic Temple, 1980—; co-dir. Evangelistic Temple Sch. of Bible, Houston, 1979-82. Internat. Order Alhambra scholar, 1976; Grad. Scholarship Endowment grantee U. Houston, 1980. Mem. Council Exceptional Children, Tex. Council Exceptional Children, Tex. Assn. Gifted and Talented Soc. Accelerated Learning and Teaching, Phi Delta Kappa, Kappa Delta Pi, Delta Delta Delta. Home: 2008 Woodhead St Houston TX 77019

JAMES, SHERIDAN FRANCES, licensing corporation executive; b. Bakersfield, Calif., July 3, 1937; d. Chester A. and Bettye Lou (Short) J. B.S., UCLA, 1959; postgrad. Harvard Bus. Sch., 1960. Dept. mgr. Filene's, Boston, 1960-64, I. Magnin & Co., San Francisco, 1964-68; v.p. licensing Determined Prodns., Inc., San Francisco, 1968-82; pres. Claremont Internat., Inc., N.Y.C., 1983—. Republican. Episcopalian. Clubs: Harvard, Radcliffe. Home: 903 Park Ave New York NY 10021 Office: Claremont Internat Inc 12 W 27th St 18th Floor New York NY 10001

JAMES, SHIRLEY FAY, cosmetics company executive; b. McAlester, Okla., Oct. 27, 1939; d. Sam Jay and Ruby Jewel (Line) Hamilton; 1 child, Sandra Jean Armstrong. Grad. Bus. Coll., Modesto, Calif., 1969. Sec., bookkeeper, office mgr. Long Drug Stores, 1969-73; dist. dir. Jafra Cosmetics, Modesto, 1973-80; dir. retail devel. Am. Dream Internat., Santa Barbara, Calif., 1980-81, dir. mktg., 1981-84; formed James, McDuffie and McDuffie, Inc., 1983; owner, chmn. bd. Subtle Images Cosmetics, Ltd., Irvine, Calif., 1984—. Named No. Calif. Top Sales Person, Top Br. Builder, recipient Dorothy Gordon award, Jafra Cosmetics. Mem. Christian Bus. and Profl. Womens Assn. Republican. Office: 17945 Sky Park Circle Irvine CA 92714

JAMES, SUSAN LYNN, personnel management consultant, educator; b. Oklahoma City, Oct. 14, 1951; d. Roy and Florene (Wright) Pickens; m. Barry C. James, Aug. 5, 1972. B.S., Central State U., Edmond, Okla., 1972, M.B.A., 1979. Cert. human resources profl. Staff asst. Univ. Hosp. and Clinics, Oklahoma City, 1973-78; asst. dir. employee relations Baptist Med. Ctr., Oklahoma City, 1978-83; prof. mgmt. Central State U., Edmond, Okla., 1981—; pres., owner James Assocs., Oklahoma City, 1983—. Recipient Vol. Cost Containment award Baptist Med. Ctr., 1979. Mem. Assn. M.B.A. Execs., Soc. for Advancement of Mgmt., Okla. Hosp. Personnel Assn., Oklahoma City Personnel Assn., Am. Soc. for Personnel Adminstrn., Okla. Women Bus. Owners, Alpha Chi, Kappa Delta Pi. Republican. Presbyterian. Office: James Assocs 4045 NW 64 Suite 680 Oklahoma City OK 73116

JAMES, SUSAN OLIVIA, engineer; b. Balt., Apr. 14, 1951; d. Joseph Edward and Frances Marlene (Kolodziejski) Schmidt; student Community Coll. R.I., 1977-83, Western New Eng. Coll., 1984—; m. Alan R. James; children—Eileen, Karen. With Victor Corp., West Warwick, R.I., 1971-83, cost estimator, 1973-76, process engr., 1976-79, applications engr., 1979-81, process engrng. supr., 1981-82, process engrng. mgr., 1982-83; product engr. Mold Con div. K&M Electronics, West Springfield, Mass., 1983-84; harness engr. Am. Electric Cable Co., Holyoke, Mass., 1984—. Mem. Wire Assn. Mem. Soc. Friends. Home: 133 Old Farm Rd Springfield MA 01119 Office: 181 Appleton St Holyoke MA 01040

JAMES, VIRGINIA CRYSTELL, nursing educator; b. Cumberland, Va., June 30; d. Charles and Virginia (Fowler) Anderson. B.S.N., Fairleigh Dicksinson U., 1965; M.Ed., Rutgers U., 1974; M.S.N., Hampton Inst., 1981. Instr., City Hosp. Sch. Nursing, Newark, 1964-65, Somerset Hosp. Sch. Nursing, Somerville, N.J., 1965-70; instr. Muhlenberg Hosp. Sch. Nursing, Plainfield, N.J., 1970-76, med.-surg. coordinator, 1976-79, level coordinator, 1981-83, asst. dean, 1983—, advisor to minority students, 1982—; clin. asst. prof. Union County Coll., Cranford, N.J., 1975—. Bd. dirs. Vis. Nurses Assn., Plainfield, N.J., 1983-85; mem. Watson Ave. Block Assn., Plainfield, 1975—. Mem. Nat. League Nursing, AAUW, N.Y. Acad. Scis., N.J. State Nurses Assn. Democrat. Baptist. Home: PO Box 2771 Plainfield NJ 07062 Office: Muhlenberg Hosp Sch Nursing Park Ave Plainfield NJ 07061

JAMESON, DOROTHEA, sensory psychologist; b. Newton, Mass., Nov. 16, 1920; d. Robert and Josephine (Murray) Jameson; B.A., Wellesley Coll., 1942; M.A. (hon.), U. Pa., 1973; m. Leo M. Hurvich, Oct. 23, 1948. Research asst. Harvard, 1941-47; research psychologist Eastman Kodak Co., Rochester, N.Y., 1947-57; research scientist N.Y.U., 1957-62; vis. scientist Venezuelan Inst. Sci. Research, 1965; research asso. to prof. Psychol. and Inst. Neurol. Scis., U. Pa., 1962-74, Univ. prof. U. Pa., 1975—; vis. prof. Center Visual Sci., U. Rochester, 1974, Columbia U., 1974-76; cons. in field. Mem. Nat. Acad. Sci.-NCR Commn. on Human Resources, 1977-80, chmn. com. on vision, 1980-80. Recipient I.H. Godlove award Inter-Soc. Color Council, 1973; Alumnae Achievement award Wellesley Coll., 1974; Deane B. Judd award Assn. Internationale 'de Couleur, 1985; fellow Center for Advanced Study in the Behavioral Scis., 1981-82. Mem. Soc. Exptl. Psychologists (Howard Crosby Warren medal 1971), Am. Psychol. Assn. (Distinguished Sci. Contbn. award 1972), Nat. Acad. Scis., Am. Acad. Arts and Scis., AAAS, Assn. Research in Vision and Ophthalmology, Biophys. Soc., Internat. Brain Research Orgn., Internat. Research Group Color Vision Deficiencies, Optical Soc. Am. (Tillyer medal 1982), Psychonomic Soc., Soc. Neurosci., Sigma Xi. Co-author: The Perception of Brightness and Darkness, 1966; co-author introduction and English translation: (E. Hering) Outlines of a Theory of the Light Sense, 1964. Co-editor, author chpt.: Visual Psychophysics: Handbook of Sensory Physiology, vol. VII/4, 1972. Contbr. articles to profl. jours. Office: 3815 Walnut St Philadelphia PA 19104

JAMESON, PATRICIA MARIAN, government agency administrator; b. Pitts., Mar. 17, 1945; d. Vernon L. and Dorothy Leam (Wilson) J.; B.A., Northwestern U., 1967; M.A., Ohio State U., 1969, with HUD, 1970—, project mgr., Detroit, 1976-77, acting dir. housing mgmt., 1978, dep. area mgr. Milw. Area Office, 1978-85, acting area mgr., 1979-80, 82, regional dir. adminstrn. Chgo. Regional Office, 1985—. Counselor, Women's Crisis Line. Recipient Quality Performance award HUD, 1973, 75, 80, Outstanding Performance award, 1980, 85; NDEA fellow, 1967-69. Mem. Am. Mgmt. Assn., Nat. Assn. Female Execs., NOW, ACLU, Phi Beta Kappa, Pi Sigma Alpha. Office: 300 S Wacker Dr Rm 2237 Chicago IL 60606

JAMESON, PHYLLIS ANN, county coroner; b. Milford, Ill., Sept. 25, 1931; d. Elmer John and Annette H. (Frerichs) Breymerer; m. Dale W. Jameson, Jan. 5, 1952 (dec. Nov. 1977); children—Douglas Alan, Susan D. Jameson Odenthal, Daniel Earl, Sally Ann Jameson Allhands; m. Raymond Paul Gibson, July 8, 1984. Student No. Ill. U., 1979-80, U. St. Louis Sch. Medicine, 1981. County coroner Iroquois County, Watseka, Ill., 1977—. Precinct committeeman Iroquois County Republicans, 1977—; sec. Iroquois County Central Com., 1978-82. Mem. Internat. Assn. Med. Examiners and Coroners, Iroquois County Mental Health Bd., Iroquois County Law Enforcement Assn., Ill. Coroners Assn. (pres. 1985—), Watseka Bus. and Profl. Womens Club, Am. Legion Aux. Lutheran. Office: Iroquois County 550 S Tenth Watseka IL 60970

JAMIESON, FRANCES JEAN KENTOR, psychologist; b. Denver, Apr. 8, 1922; d. Charles and Hazel (Dietrich) Kentor; A.B., U. Denver, 1943; M.A., Stanford, 1950; postgrad. U. Calif. at Berkeley, 1959-60, Nova U., 1977-82; m. Robert Howard Jamieson, Nov. 2, 1946 (dec. June 1953); 1 dau., Nancy Rose. Supr. attendance Office Edn., Modesto, Calif., 1944-46; tchr. pub. schs., Stockton, Calif., 1943-44; prin. Mountain View Sch., Stanislaus County, Calif., 1948-49; supr. guidance, Richmond, Calif., 1949-50, tchr., Sacramento, 1950-58; dean girls, head English dept., Crockett, Calif., 1958-60; coordinator psychol. services Monterey County Office Edn., Salinas, Calif., 1960-64; pvt. practice as psychologist, Sacramento, 1956-58, Salinas, 1963-68, South San Francisco, 1976—; psychologist Diagnostic Sch. for Neurologically Handicapped Children No. Calif., San Francisco, 1968-70, dir. ednl. and psychol. services, 1970-77, asst. supt., 1977—. Sec. Monterey County Democratic Central Com.; mem. Calif. Dem. Com., 1966-68. Mem. Am. Personnel and Guidance Assn., NEA, Council for Exceptional Children, Nat., Calif. assns. parliamentarians, Calif. Assn. for Measurement and Evaluation in guidance, Calif. Employees Assn., Calif. Fedn. Bus. and Profl. Women's Clubs (state pres. 1973-74), Am. Legion Aux., San Francisco Bus. and Profl. Women's Club, Phi Lambda Theta. Presbyn. (deacon). Clubs: Order Eastern Star, White Shrine, South San Francisco Democratic (pres.). Home: 849 W Orange Ave Apt 2011 South San Francisco CA 94080

JAMISON, DARLENE MARY, university administrator; b. Kansas City, Mo., Nov. 24, 1928; d. Joseph and Caroline E. Broyles; B.A. in Sociology, U. Mo., Kansas City, 1963, M.A., 1969; m. Homer C. Jamison, Feb. 12, 1971; 1 dau., Carolyn Suzanne Love. Mem. adminstrv. staff U. Mo., Kansas City, 1967-74, dir. affirmative action-academic, 1973-74; adminstrv. assoc., affirmative action officer Sch. Optometry, U. Ala., Birmingham, 1974-81, asst. to dean, 1981—. Mem. Am. Soc. Personnel Adminstrs., Coll. and Univ. Personnel Assn., Nat. Council Adminstrv. Women in Edn., Ala. Assn. Women Deans, Adminstrs. and Councelors, Personnel Assn. Birmingham, Nat. Conf. Women in Chambers of Conf. (del. 1979-81), Women's Jr. C. of C. Birmingham (pres. 1981-82), Birmingham Met. Bus. and Profl. Women's Club (v.p. 1979-80), Am. Bus. Women's Assn. (chpt. pres. 1984-85, chpt. Woman of Yr. 1986). Editor various univ. publs. Home: 3586 Rockhill Rd Birmingham AL 35223 Office: Sch Optometry U Ala Birmingham AL 35294

JAMISON, EDITH, charitable association executive; b. Columbia, S.C., July 14, 1948; d. Wendell Neal and Lue Ella (Ward) Jamison Neal. B.S., U. Md., 1981. Youth supr. I, Md. Govt., Balt., 1969-70, youth supr. II, 1970-71; project coordinator consumer edn. United Communities Against Poverty, Inc., Fairmount Heights, Md., 1971-72, project coordinator, 1972-73, asst. dir., 1973-75, exec. dir. Prince George's County Community Action Agy., Capital Heights, Md., 1975—; mem. Md. Assn. Community Action Agys., Salisbury, 1978—; mem. S.E. Rural Community Assistance Project, Roanoke, Va., 1981—, convener Prince George's County Anti-Hunger Coalition, Capitol Heights, Md., 1982-83; pres. Prince George's County Sesame St. Fire Safety Project Task Force, Capitol Heights, Md., 1981-83. Recipient Outstanding Community Service award United Communities Against Poverty, Prince George's County, Md., 1974; Unselfish Community Service award Model Neighborhood Interest Group, U. Md., 1978; award for disting. service rendered Pi Omicron Rho Omega, 1980; award for service to ch. and community Far East Ministerial Assn., 1981; Outstanding Community Service award Nat. Hook-up Black Women, 1983. Mem. Nat. Community Action Agys. Dirs., So. Bus. and Profl. Women's Club. Democrat. Baptist. Office: United Communities Against Poverty Inc 1400 Doewood Ln Capitol Heights MD 20743

JAMISON, NADINE TREADWAY, county official; b. Paragould, Ark., Dec. 17, 1938; d. Lawrence Nelson and Mariam Inas (Williams) Treadway; m. Jacksie Gene Jamison, Nov. 16, 1956; children—Jacksie Dean, Darron Gene. Degree Jonesboro Bus. Coll., 1968. Cert. Am. Inst. Banking. With Jamison Real Estate, Paragould, 1970-74, Security Bank, Paragould, 1974-76, G. Collier, M.D., Paragould, 1976-78; county clk. Greene County, Ark., 1979—. Bd. dirs. Ark. Pvt. Industry council, 1983—; v.p. Crowley's Ridge Devel. Council, Jonesboro, Ark., 1984—. Mem. Assn. Ark. Counties (bd. dirs. 1983—), Ark. County Clks. Assn. Home: Route 2 Box 86F Paragould AR 72450 Office: County Clk Box 62 Paragould AR 72450

JAMISON, SUSAN CLAPP, library director, English educator; b. Pitts., Mar. 21, 1929; d. Harlan Luther and Irene Julia (Krause) Clapp; m. Robert Beatty Jamison, Dec. 19, 1947; children—Linda F., Stephen R. B.A., Richmond Coll., 1971; M.A., U. Del., 1972, 74; M.L.S., U. Md., 1979. Dir. Corbit-Calloway Meml. Library, Odessa, Del., 1975—; asst. dir. Dover Pub. Library, Dover, 1980-85; mem. faculty Wilmington Coll., New Castle, Del., 1975—, adj. prof. English, 1975—; pres. Central Del. Library Consortium, Dover, 1981-84; pres. Kent Library Network, Dover, 1984-85; speaker Speaker's Bur., Del. Humanities Forum, 1982—; project dir. Multi-Media Library Series, Del., 1979-81, 83-85. Chmn. pub. relations Kent County Tricentennial Commn., Dover, 1983; founder Septemberfest, 1982. Recipient Facts on File award for reference pub. ideas, 1985. Mem. ALA, Del. Library Assn. (pres. 1986-87, div. pres. 1979-80), Del. Computer Output Microform Union (catalogue com.), Libraries in New Castle County Network, AAUW, Del. Fedn. Women's Clubs. Home: Starr-Lore House Main St Odessa DE 19730 Office: Corbit-Calloway Meml Library Odessa DE 19730

JAMISON, VIRGINIA WRAY, environmental microbiologist; b. Phila., Oct. 11, 1924; d. Robert Weir and Elizabeth (Wray) J.; student Juniata Coll., 1942-44; B.S., U. Pa., 1969. Technician, Sun Oil Co., Marcus Hook, Pa., 1944-63, asst. scientist, 1964-69, assoc. scientist, 1969-75, scientist Sun Tech, Inc. subs., 1975-81, sr. research scientist, 1981-83; founder Environ. Biol. Services, Inc., 1983—. Recipient Charles Porter award Soc. Indsl. Microbiology, 1975. Mem. Am. Chem. Soc., ASTM, Am. Soc. Microbiology, Soc. Indsl. Microbiology. Republican. Baptist. Contbr. articles to profl. jours.; patentee in field. Home: 521 11th Ave Prospect Park PA 19076

JAMISON-WILLIAMS, ANITA LOUISE, telephone sales executive; b. DeSoto, Mo., July 27, 1946; d. Oswald Arthur Curtis and Alice Ruth (Coffman) Jamison; m. Jon-Pierre Williams, May 7, 1983. A.A., Jefferson Coll., 1966; B.S.E. (summa cum laude), U. Mo., 1968, M.Mus., 1969. Cert. pub. sch. tchr., Mo. Vocal mus. tchr. Ritenour Schs., St. Louis, 1969-76, dept. coordinator, 1971-74; mktg. rep. IBM Corp., St. Louis, 1976-78; systems rep. Honeywell, Inc., St. Louis, 1978-80; staff specialist Southwestern Bell, St. Louis, 1980-82, sales mgr., 1983—. Founder Hoech Jr. High pom-pom squad, 1971. Mem. Bus. Services Profls. (sec. 1981-82), Working Ptnrs., Inc. (co-founder, sec.), NEA, Phi Theta Kappa, Sigma Alpha Iota.

JANECEK, LENORE ELAINE, business executive, chamber of commerce executive; b. Chgo., May 2, 1944; d. Morris and Florence (Bear) Picker; M.A.J. in Speech Communications (talent scholar), Northeastern Ill. U., 1972; postgrad. (Ill. Assn. C. of C. Execs. scholar) Inst. for Organizational Mgmt., U. Notre Dame, 1979-80; M.B.A., Columbia Pacific U.; m. John Janecek, Sept. 12, 1964; childen—Frank, Michael. Adminstrv. asst., exec. dir. Ill. Mcpl. Retirement Fund, Chgo., 1963-65; personnel mgr. Profile Personnel, Chgo., 1965-68; personnel rep. Marsh Instrument Co., Skokie, Ill., 1971-73; restaurant mgt. Gold Mine Restaurant and What's Cooking Restaurant, Chgo., 1974-76; pres., owner Secretarial Office Services, Chgo., 1976-78; founder, exec. dir. Lincolnwood (Ill.) C. of C. and Industry, 1978—; rep. 10th dist. U.S. C. of C., 1978—; pres. Lenore Janecek & Assocs. Ltd. Mem. mktg. bd. Niles Twp. Sheltered Workshop; pres. Lincolnwood Sch. Dist. 74 Sch. Bd. Caucus; bd. mem., officer, founder Ill. Fraternal Order Police Ladies Aux.; bd. mem., officer Lincolnwood Girl's Softball League, PTA, United Way; mem. sch. curriculum com. Lincolnwood Bd. Edn.; candidate for state rep. 1st dist. Ill.; presdl. appointee Selective Service Bd. Mem. Am. C. of C. Execs., Ill. Assn. C. of C. Execs., Women in Mgmt., Nat. Assn. Female Execs., Am. Notary Soc., Ill. LWV, Nat. Council Jewish Women, Hadassah, City of Hope. Jewish. Home: 6707 N Monticello St Lincolnwood IL 60645 Office: PO Box 46217 Chicago IL 60646

JANEWAY, ELIZABETH (HALL), author; b. Bklyn., Oct. 7, 1913; d. Charles H. and Jeannette F. (Searle) Hall; student Swarthmore Coll.; A.B., Barnard Coll., 1935; D. Litt., Simpson Coll., 1972, Cedar Crest Coll., 1974, Villa Maria Coll.; D.H.L., Russell Sage Coll., 1981; m. Eliot Janeway; children-Michael, William. Author: The Walsh Girls, 1943; Daisy Kenyon, 1945; The Question of Gregory, 1949; The Vikings, 1951; Leaving Home, 1953; Early Days of the Automobile, 1956; The Third Choice, 1959; Angry Kate, 1963; Accident, 1964; Ivanov Seven, 1967; Man's World, Woman's Place, 1971; Between Myth and Morning: Women Awakening, 1974; Powers of the Weak, 1980; Cross Sections from a Decade of Change, 1982; contbr.: Comprehensive Textbook of Psychiatry, 2d edit., 1980; Harvard Guide to Contemporary American Writing, 1979; also short stories and critical writing in periodicals and newspapers. Judge, Nat. Book Award, 1955, Pulitzer Prize Com., 1971. Trustee Barnard Coll.; bd. dirs. N.Y. State Council on Humanities. Named Disting. Alumna, Barnard Coll.; recipient Medal of Distinction, Barnard Coll., 1981. Mem. Authors Guild Inc. (council), Authors League Am. (council), PEN, NOW (bd. dirs. legal def. and edn. fund), Phi Beta Kappa. Home: 15 E 80th St New York NY 10021

JANICKE, PATRICIA ANN, technical writer, editor; b. Milw., Aug. 28, 1932; d. John Harold and Dorothy Ellen (Lappen) Carney; student U. Wis., 1950-51; B.A. in Speech, Radio and Dramatics, Mt. Mary Coll., 1954; postgrad. Moorpark Coll., 1974-76; m. Joseph E. Janicke, Jan. 13, 1962 (dec. 1976); 1 dau., Julia Ellen. Exec. sec. Acad. Motion Picture Arts and Scis., Beverly Hills, Calif., 1959-63; computer operator Litton Industries, Van Nuys, Calif., 1969-72; acct. Vetek Computer Systems, Inc., Westlake Village, Calif., 1974-75, Datex, Oxnard, Calif., 1975-76; tech. writer, editor Vitro Labs., Oxnard, 1976-80; tech. writer, logistics analyst Raytheon Service Co., Ventura, Calif., 1980-82; tech. writer L.I. Dimmick Corp., Oxnard, 1982-84; sr. systems analyst System Devel. Corp., Camarillo, Calif., 1984-85, sr. logistician support mgmt. services, Oxnard, 1985-86; sr. tech. writer/editor McLaughlin Research Corp., Camarillo, Calif., 1986—. Pres. Westlake Village (Calif.) chpt. One Again, Inc., 1977-79, bd. dirs., 1977-79; bd. dirs. Am. Contract Bridge League, Oxnard, 1978-80; v.p. Raytheon Activities Club, 1980-82. Recipient Masque and Gavel award Mt. Mary Coll., 1954. Mem. Am. Soc. Women Accts., N.W. Indsl. Editors Assn., Ventura County Heart Fund Guild. Republican. Roman Catholic. Club: Sweet Adelines. Home: 42 Margarita Camarillo CA 93010 Office: 555 Hueneme Rd Oxnard CA 93034

JANKO, MAY, graphic artist; b. N.Y.C., Feb. 27, 1926; d. Jacob and Clara (Schupler) J. B.A., Hunter Coll., 1946, M.A., 1952; student Art Students League, 1949-53. Tchr. art N.Y.C. Pub. Schs., 1953-60; textile designer M. Lowenstein Corp., N.Y.C., 1967-84. Exhibited in group shows: Library of Congress, Washington, 1956, 63; Albany, 1959; Whitney Mus. Am. Art, N.Y.C., 1959; Pa. Acad., Phila., 1959; Bklyn. Mus., 1960; Taipei Nat. Mus. (Taiwan), 1984; represented in permanent collections: Met. Mus. Art, N.Y.C., Rockefeller Collection, N.Y.C., Cin. Mus. Art, Nat. Gallery, Washington. Recipient Achievement award Hunter Coll., 1956; I.B. Markell award in graphics Audubon Artists, N.Y.C., 1961; Leo Meissner award NAD, N.Y.C., 1984; Louis Comfort Tiffany Found. fellow, 1959. Mem. Soc. Am. Graphic Artists (life; mem. council 1977, Henry B. Shope award 1954, Graphic Chem. award 1985), Boston Printmakers, Am. Color Print Soc., Art Students League (life).

JANKOWSKI, JANET MARIE, speech pathologist; b. Worcester, Mass., Nov. 5, 1949; d. Chester Joseph and Sophie Mary (Modzelewski) Jankowski; B.A. in French, Anna Maria Coll., 1971; M.S. in Speech, Emerson Coll., 1974; m. John Paul Chmielowiec, May 16, 1981. Tchr. French, St. Mary's High Sch., Worcester, Mass., 1974; vol. speech pathologist Mercy Center, Worcester, 1974; speech and lang. pathologist Stamford (Conn.) Public Schs., Mem. Am. Speech and Hearing Assn. (cert. clin. competence), Alpha Mu Gamma. Christian Ch. Home: 34 Huntington Ct Bethel CT 06801

JANNEY, MARY DRAPER, social and educational service organization executive; b. Bklyn., May 28, 1921; d. Ernest Gallaudet and Mary White (Childs) Draper; B.A. in Sociology, Vassar Coll.; M.A. in Sociology, Yale U.; m. Frederick Wistar Morris Janney, Jan. 15, 1944; children—Peter Wistar, Christopher D. Tchr. Am. history Potomac Sch., McLean, Va., 1961-64, head history dept., student adviser, 1961-64; founder, pres. Wider Opportunities for Women, Inc., Washington, 1966—; exec. dir. Planned Parenthood of Met. Washington. Mem. Washington Commn. on Status of Women, 1973—; bd. dirs. The Madeira Sch., Greenway, Va., 1969-72, Potomac Sch., McLean, 1966-72, Common Cause; trustee Vassar Coll., 1975—, chmn., 1981—; trustee Fed. Woman's Award. Named One of 1975's Washingtonians of Year. Home: 2960 University Terr Washington DC 20016 Office: 1108 16th St NW Washington DC 20016

JANOUSEK, JUDITH ANN, savings and loan association executive; b. Chgo., July 25, 1940; d. Anton C. and Emily R. (Bajza) J. A.A. in Bus. Morton Coll., 1960; B.S. in Bus. Mgmt., Elmhurst Coll., 1981; postgrad. U. Ill., 1981-82, U. Ga., 1984-85; A.A. in Paralegal Studies, MacCormac Coll., 1984. Lic. real estate broker, Ill. Supr. Olympic Fed. Savs. and Loan Assn., Berwyn, Ill., 1960-65; corp. asst. sec. Clyde Fed. Savs. and Loan Assn., North Riverside, Ill., 1965-75, Proviso Fed. Savs. and Loan Assn., 1975-79; mgr. acctg. dept. Fidelity Fedn. Savs. and Loan Assn., Berwyn, 1979-80; asst. v.p. lending collections Security Fed. Savs. and Loan Assn., Chgo., 1980—. Mem. Soc. Loan Underwriters, Soc. Fin. Mgrs., Nat. Comml. Soc. Fin. Mgrs., Nat. Assn. Female Execs., AAUW, Catholic Alumni Club, Dialogue for Blind, Bus. and Profl. Woman's Club (local and dist. sec. 1968-70). Roman Catholic. Home: Westchester IL Office: Security Fed Savs and Loan Assn 1209 N Milwaukee Ave Chicago IL 60622

JANSCH, LUCILLE WOOD, court clerk; b. Victoria, Va., Oct. 20, 1925; d. William Bernard and Vetra Bertha (Faris) Wood; m. Warren Walter Jansch, Sept. 16, 1942; children—Sharon Jansch Carter, Sheila Jansch Huddle, Deborah Warren Jansch. Student pub. schs. Victoria, Clk., U.S. Postal Service, Chesterfield, Va., 1956-58, Juvenile and Domestic Relations Ct., Chesterfield, 1958—. Mem. com. Supreme Ct., Richmond, Va., 1985. Mem. Govt. Va. Employees Assn., Dist. Ct. Clks. Assn. (3d v.p. 1983, edn. officer 1985), Chesterfield Hist. Soc. Lodge: Eastern Star. Methodist. Avocations: swimming; golf; handwork; gardening. Office: Chesterfield Juvenile and Domestic Dist Ct 9600 Krause Rd PO Box 20 Chesterfield VA 23832

JANSEN, DIANE LYNN, weight loss center executive; b. Bay City, Mich., July 11, 1963; d. Donald Warren and Dorothy (Fenske) Jansen. A.B., Delta Coll., 83. Face designer Merle Norman, Saginaw, Mich., 1979-82; salesman Wiechmans, Essexville, Mich., 1982-83; v.p. mktg. PatLyne Fiberglass, Flint, Mich., 1984-85; asst. dir. Weight Loss Clinic Internat., Saginaw, 1983-85; mgr. Bariatrix, Midland, Mich., 1985, Doctors Family Weight Loss Ctr., Saginaw, 1985—; cons., 1986—. Mem. Nat. Assn. Female Execs., Midland C. of C. Avocations: sailing; cross-country skiing; camping. Home: 700 N Walnut Apt 2 Bay City MI 48706 Office: Doctors Family Weight Loss Ctrs 4040 Bay Rd Saginaw MI 48603

JANSEN, ISABEL, civic worker; b. Phlox, Wis., May 26, 1906; d. Mose A. and Clara K. J.; R.N., Marquette U., Milw., 1927. Surg. asst. to prof. oral and maxillofacial surgery Marquette U., 1927-52; ret., 1954; chmn. Antigo Freedom Com., 1960—. Recipient Liberty award Congress of Freedom, Inc., annually 1972-78, Keeper of the Flame award Woman Constitutionalist, 1974, cert. of appreciation Nat. Police Officers Assn. Am., 1973. Roman Catholic. Research on heart deaths in Antigo, Wis., 1974; research on cancer deaths in Antigo,

1930-80; inventor Jansen Ray Pen, 1947. Home: 608 Gowan Rd Antigo WI 54409

JANSEN, PATRICIA GAIL, television producer; b. Bronxville, N.Y., July 3, 1946; d. Patrick Frank and Rita (Twohig) Curry; B.A. in Journalism/Broadcasting, Fordham U., 1968. Exec. producer Skyline series WNET, N.Y.C., 1978-79; coordinating producer Alexander the Great, Time-Life Films, N.Y.C., 1979-80, FYI with Hal Linden, ABC/Network, N.Y.C., 1980-81; assoc. dir. documentary programming HBO Cable, N.Y.C., 1981-83; sr. producer Why in the World series WNET/PBS, 1984—. Recipient Emmy award FYI series ABC-TV, 1980. Mem. Women in Film, Am. Acad. TV Arts and Scis. Home: 430 W 24th St New York NY 10011

JANSSEN, CAROL ANN, retail company executive; b. Ellensburg, Wash., Dec. 12, 1949; d. Jack Vernon and Margaret (Williams) Hall; m. Thomas Lee Janssen, Dec 27, 1969; children—Joel G., Jarrad J. Student Oreg. State U., 1968-69. Sales staff Lipman Wolfe & Co., Corvallis, Oreg., 1968-69, J.C. Penney Co. Chula Vista, Calif., 1970-71, Lipman Wolfe & Co., Portland, Oreg., 1971-73, personnel mgr., 1973-77, exec. dept. mgr., 1977-78; asst. personnel mgr. Portland Willamette Co., Oreg., 1978-79; personnel mgr. Norm Thompson Outfitters, Portland, 1979—. Dir. Sunset Sci. Park Fed. Credit Union, 1980-84, mem. credit com., 1985-86. Mem. pacific Northwest Personnel Mgrs. Assn., Adminstrv. Mgmt. Soc. (pres. 1984-85). Avocations: Water and snow skiing; racquetball; aerobic dance. Office: Norm Thompson Outfitters Inc 137000 NW Science Park Dr Portland OR 97229

JANUARY, MARY A., sports marketing and public relations consultant; b. Dallas, Feb. 25, 1949; d. Alvin Eugene and Mae Elizabeth (Robinson) Patterson; 1 child, Mariah January. Student, North Tex. State U., 1967-68, Coll. of Marin, 1973-75. Pvt. practice fine arts cons., San Francisco, 1974-78, Dallas, 1978-79; assoc. dir. Allrich Gallery, San Francisco, 1980-81; account exec. Platt Communications, San Rafael, Calif., 1981-82; account exec. and promotions Sta. KFTY-TV, Santa Rosa, Calif., 1982-83; v.p. Sears Point Internat. Raceway, Sonoma, Calif., 1983-86; owner Auto/Sports Internat., 1986—; cons. Personal Resources Systems, La Jolla, Calif., 1983—. Fellow North Bay Advt. and Communications (bd. dirs.), Am. Advt. Fedn. Home: PO Box 1821 Sausalito CA 94965 Office: 210 Miller Ave Mill Valley CA 94941

JANZEN, NORINE MADELYN QUINLAN (MRS. DOUGLAS MACARTHUR JANZEN), medical technologist; b. Fond du Lac, Wis., Feb. 9, 1943; d. Joseph Wesley and Norma Edith (Gustin) Quinlan; B.S., Marian Coll., 1965; med. technologist St. Agnes Sch. Med. Tech., Fond du Lac, 1966; M.A., Central Mich. U., 1980; m. Douglas MacArthur Janzen, July 18, 1970; 1 son, Justin James. Supr. med. technologist Mayfair Med. Lab., Wauwatosa, Wis., 1966-69, Dr.s Mason, Chamberlain, Franke, Klink & Kamper, Milw., 1969-76; supr. med. tech. Hartford-Parkview Clinic, Ltd., 1976—. Substitute poll worker Democratic com., Fond du Lac, 1964-65; mem. Dem. Nat. Com., 1973—. Mem. Wis. South Eastern Suprs. Groups (co-chmn. 1976-77), Milw. Soc. Med. Technologists (pres., 1971-72, dir. 1972-73 chair nominations com. 1985-86), Wis. Assn. Med. Tech. (treas. 1977-81, chmn. awards com. 1976-77, 84-85, 86-87, dir. 1977-84, 85-87, pres.-elect 1981-82, pres. 1982-83, past pres. 1983-84, Med. Technologist of Yr. award 1982), Am. Soc. Med. Tech. (awards com. 1984—), LWV, Am. Mgmt. Assn., Alpha Delta Theta (nat. dist. chmn., 1967-69; nat. alumnae dir. 1969-71). Methodist. Home: N 98 W 17298 Dotty Way Germantown WI 53022 Office: 1004 E Sumner St Hartford WI 53027

JAPAR, SUSAN ELIZABETH, nurse, obstetrical nurse practitioner; b. Bronx, N.Y., Jan. 8, 1949; d. Romeo and Susan (Kuklish) Japar; B.S. in Nursing, Hunter Coll., 1970; ob/gyn nurse practitioner cert. U. Kans. Med. Center, 1975; M.S., U. Calif., San Francisco, 1977. Med.-surg. staff nurse Albert Einstein Hosp., Bronx, 1970-72; staff nurse USAF Hosp., 1972-74; nurse practitioner, Grand Forks AFB, N.D., 1974-75; USAF Hosp., Clark AFB, Philippines, 1977-78; course supr. USAF, 1978-83; gynecol. nurse practitioner USAF Hosp., Myrtle Beach AFB, S.C., 1983—; ob-gyn nurse practitioner cons. to surg. gen. USAF, 1982; vis. lectr. U. Okla. Health Scis. Center. Served with USAF, 1972—. Mem. Nurses Assn. of Am. Coll. Ob-Gyn (chmn. Armed Forces Dist. 1983-85). Lutheran. Author: Diagnosis and Treatment of Vulvovaginitis, 1982; 4-part series on contraception, 1983.

JAPENGA, LAURENA BOOKER, pediatrician; b. Greensboro, N.C., Nov. 6, 1927; d. William Gray and Nina Emmaline (Park) Booker; m. Jack Wallace Japenga, Nov. 1, 1952; children—William Martin, Ann Theresa, Charles Albert, Diana Katherine. Student U. N.C., 1944-47; M.D., Duke U., 1951. Resident U. Chgo. Hosps., 1951-53; resident in pediatrics Mt. Zion Hosp., San Francisco, 1953; physician Alameda County Health Dept. (Calif.), 1953-55, U. Chgo.-LaRabida Hosp., 1956-59; practice medicine specializing in pediatrics, Glendora, Covina and San Dimas, Calif., 1961—; chief of staff San Dimas Hosp., 1984; mem. staff Foothill Presbyn. Hosp., Inter-Community Hosp., Queen of Valley Hosp. Mem. AMA, Calif. Med. Assn., Los Angeles County Med. Assn., Am. Acad. Pediatrics. Home: 2452 N Cameron Ave Covina CA 91724 Office: 1330 W Covina Blvd San Dimas CA 91773

JAQUET, ADA CHARLOTTE, piano teacher, writer; b. Chgo., Aug. 17, 1912; d. Harry Irving and Bertha Mae (Broom) Thomas; m. Eugene S. Tanner, June 20, 1935 (dec. 1970); children—Joanne Elizabeth, Jane E., Malin, John E., Julie E. Smith; m. Roy R. Hewitt, Mar. 8, 1973 (dec. 1976); m. Felix W. Jaquet, Nov. 14, 1980. B.E., Nat. Coll. Edn., 1933; postgrad. U. N.D., 1935-37, Juillard Sch. Music, 1939, U. Tulsa, 1942-44, Syracuse U., 1969; M.A.T., Coll. of Wooster, 1971. Cert. tchr., Ill. Tchr. Pub. Schs., Libertyville, Ill., 1933-35, Country Day Sch., Tulsa, 1937-42; founder, dir. Women's League Play Sch., Grand Fork, N.D., 1935-37; owner, dir., tchr. Musical K, Tulsa, 1942-54; tchr., dir., mgr. Piano Studio Musical K., Wooster, Ohio, 1954-62; private instr. piano, Jaquet Piano Studio, Wooster, 1953—; freelance reporter Chautauqua Daily, N.Y., 1965-73, Wooster Daily Record, 1970-73. Dir. childrens choir Westminster Presbyterian Ch., Wooster, 1959-60, 1st Presbyn. Ch., Wooster, 1960-62; leader vol. poetry wookshop Community Ctr., Wooster, 1979-84. Author: (poetry) Gleaning, 1972. Mem. Wooster Poetry Soc. (sec. 1964-65), Nat. League Am. Pen Women (pres. Central Ohio branch 1982-84), Monday Club (pres. 1967-68), MacDowell Club; AAUW, Nat. Kindergarten Assn. (field sec. 1935-37), Nat. Writers Club, Verse Writers Guild. Democrat. Avocations: Ecology; water coloring; RV travel. Home: 1607 Burbank Rd Wooster OH 44691

JARAMILLO, MARI-LUCI, university official; b. Las Vegas, N.Mex., June 19, 1928; d. Maurillo and Elvira (Ruiz) Antuna; B.A. magna cum laude, N.Mex. Highlands U., 1955, M.A. with honors, 1959, Ph.D., 1970; m. J. Heriberto Jaramillo, Jan. 3, 1972. Prof., chmn. dept. elem. edn. U. N.Mex., 1972-74, prof. edn., 1974-77, spl. asst. to pres., 1981-82, assoc. dean Coll. Edn., 1982-85, v.p. student affairs, 1985—; ambassador to Honduras, 1977-80. Recipient N.Mex. Disting. Public Service award, 1977. Mem. Mex. Am. Women's Assn. Democrat. Roman Catholic. Address: U NMex Scholes 122 Albuquerque NM 87131

JARRELL, IRIS BONDS, educator, business executive; b. Winston-Salem, N.C., May 25, 1942; d. Ira and Annie Gertrude (Vandiver) Bonds; m. Tommy Dorsey Martin, Feb. 13, 1965; 1 child, Carlos Miguel; m. 2d, Clyde Rickey Jarrell, June 25, 1983; stepchildren—Tamara, Cris, Kimberly. Student U. N.C.-Greensboro, 1960-61, 68-69, 74-75, Salem Coll., 1976; B.S. in Edn., Winston-Salem State U., 1981; postgrad. Appalachian State U., 1983. Cert. tchr., N.C. Resource person Winston-Salem Dental Health Plan; substitute tchr. Winston-Salem/Forsyth County Schs., 1967—; tchr. Rutledge Coll., Winston-Salem, 1982-84; owner, mgr. Rainbow's End Consignment Shop, Winston-Salem, 1983-85; tchr. lang. arts Winston-Salem/Forsyth County Sch. System, 1985—. Contbr. poetry to mags. Mem. Assn. of Couples for Marriage Enrichment, Winston-Salem, 1984-86, Forsyth-Stokes Mental Health Assn., 1985-86. Mem. Internat. Reading Assn., N.C. Assn. Adult Edn., Forsyth Assn. Classroom Tchrs., Nat. Assn. Female Execs. Democrat. Baptist. Avocations: singing; writing; sewing; crewel embroidery; gardening; reading. Home: 1008 Gales Ave SW Winston-Salem NC 27103

JARRETT, JOYCE CRISCOE, media relations executive; b. Greensboro, N.C., Oct. 13, 1938; d. Langester Clayton and Lillian Louise (Joyce) Criscoe; A.A., Guilford Coll.; m. Ralph R. Jarrett; 1 dau., Patti Lee Jessup Finney. Tech. publs. writer Celanese Corp., Asheville, N.C., 1962-65; exec. sec. Lorillard, Inc., Greensboro, 1965-75, mgr., editor employee publs., mgr. community media relations, 1975—. Del. N.C. Gov.'s Conf. for Women, 1982, 83; chmn. United Way, 1983. Named Outstanding Greensboro Businesswoman, 1982. Mem. Internat. Assn. Bus. Communicators (Piedmont chpt., compleat communicator awards 1981, 1982). Carolinas Assn. Bus. Communicators, Greensboro C. of C. (council on bus. communications 1985-86), The Bd., A Profl. Women's Consortium, Quill and Scroll (bd. dirs.), N.C. Human Genetics Assn. (bd. dirs. 1983-84). Republican. Baptist. Home: 122 Pineburr Rd Greensboro NC 27408 Office: 2525 E Market St Greensboro NC 27401

JARVIS, BARBARA ANNE, lawyer; b. Kansas City, Mo., Apr. 14, 1934; d. Herman Edward and Marjorie Maude (Graber) Spitzenfeil; A.A., Kansas City Jr. Coll., 1953; B.S. in Polit. Sci. magna cum laude, Ariz. State U., 1976, J.D., 1979; m. Thomas B. Jarvis, Sept. 9, 1965; 1 son, Kenneth Mark. Technologist Menorah Med. Center, Kansas City, Mo., 1955-56, Ariz. State U. Student Health Service, 1960-62, Scottsdale (Ariz.) Bapt. Hosp., 1962-65; chief technologist Skyline Lab., Globe, Ariz., 1967-72; practice law, Phoenix, 1979—. Sec. Globe Planning and Zoning Commn., 1970-75; assoc. coordinator Women's Polit. Caucus Ariz.; 1st vice chmn. Ariz. Democratic Com.; mem. Dem. Nat. Com. from Ariz.; chmn. neighborhood rehab. com. Phoenix Urban Form, 1976-77, mem. steering com., 1976-79; mem. Phoenix Bd. Adjustment, 1977-82, chmn., 1980-81; chmn. Village 4 Planning Com., City of Phoenix; chmn. citizens adv. com. Ariz. Dept. Corrections, 1983-85, Paradise Corridor, 1986—; bd. dirs. Salvation Army, Globe, Gila Pueblo campus Eastern Ariz. Coll., Gila County Guidance Clinic. Mem. Am. Bar Assn., State Bar Ariz., Maricopa County Bar Assn. (co-chmn. alternatives to sentencing com. 1980-81), Ariz. Women Lawyers, Women in Law (chmn.), Ariz. State U. Law Sch. Alumni Assn., Charter 100, Pi Sigma Alpha, Phi Kappa Phi. Address: 7015 N 4th Pl Phoenix AZ 85020

JARVIS, JEAN, market research executive; b. Kansas City, Kans., Feb. 7, 1927; d. Charles Frederick Schmitz and Irene Mary (Wetzel) Schmitz-Dailey; m. Raymond E. Jarvis, May 1, 1948; children—Greg, Mike, Jeff, Chris, Becky, Laurie. Student, Kansas City Jr. Coll. (Kans.), 1945; A.A., Kansas City Jr. Coll. (Mo.), 1946; student Ohio Dominion Coll., 1966. With Western Auto, Kansas City, Mo., 1944-45, Harzfeld's Kansas City, Mo., 1945-46; merchandiser Hallmark Cards, Kansas City, Mo., 1946-48; owner Jarvis Surveys of Columbus (Ohio), 1955-75; co-owner Columbus Research Center, 1975—. Contbr. articles to mktg. publs. Mem. Market Research Assn., Am. Mktg. Assn. (officer), Jefferson Twp. Fire Assn. Aux. (pres.), Gahanna Hist. Soc. (v.p. 1979-80), Jefferson Bus. Assn. (sec. 1984—). Republican. Roman Catholic. Home: Rt 1 Blacklick OH 43004 Office: Columbus Research Center 700 Morse Rd Suite 201 Columbus OH 43214

JARVIS, RITA CAROL, real estate relocation consultant; b. Ottumwa, Iowa, June 1, 1949; d. Ted and Martha Ellen (Fetters) Gundy; m. Richard Lee Mathes, Apr. 20, 1978 (div.); 1 dau., Danielle Paige; m. David Alan Jarvis, Sept. 25, 1981; 1 son, David Nathaniel. Student Northeast Mo. State Tchrs. Coll., 1967. Cert. Topeka Bd. Realtors; lic. real estate agt., Kans., Nebr. Houseparent Chaddock Boys Sch., Quincy, Ill., 1970-72, The Villages, Inc., Topeka, Kans., 1972-74; sec. to pres. Griffith & Blair Real Estate, Topeka, 1974-75; salesperson, relocation dir. John F. Robb & Co. Real Estate, Topeka, 1975-81; relocation dir. Brosius & Meyer Real Estate, Topeka, 1981-84; relocation cons. TransEquity, Inc., Omaha, 1984—, group move cons., 1985, rep. to conv., Dallas, 1985, seminar dir., Omaha, 1986; speaker nat. seminar Cons. in Relocation, Washington, 1985. Author, editor: Your Relocation (workbook), 1984; author Relocation Department policy manual, 1983. Solicitor, United Way Greater Topeka, 1978; mem. social concerns com. Most Pure Heart Ch., Topeka, 1975-76; active mem. Joslyn Art Mus., Omaha, 1985—, Omaha Friends of Zoo, 1985—. Recipient Outstanding Performance award Electronic Realty Assn., 1984; named to Million Dollar Club Topeka Bd. Realtors, 1984, ERA Brosius & Meyer Realtors, 1984. Mem. Nat. Assn. Female Execs., Nat. Assn. Realtors, Topeka Bd. Realtors (mem. realtor assoc. com. 1982). Republican. Roman Catholic. Club: New Neighbors. Avocations: needlework; swimming; golf; reading; collecting Hummel figures and carousel horses. Home: 14812 Monroe Omaha NE 68137 Office: Byron Reed/TransEquity Inc 600 Continental Building Omaha NE 68137

JARVIS-KIZILARMUT, KATHRYN ANN, insurance company sales executive; b. Royal Oak, Mich., Nov. 16, 1953; d. Victor Edwin and Mona Lucy (Parnham) Jarvis; 1 son, Cihan Victor. Student Schoolcraft Coll., 1978-82. Clerical worker Guardian Industries, Novi, Mich., 1970-74; from adminstr. to acting br. mgr. Am. Internat. Group, Southfield, Mich., and Chgo., 1974-79; resident sales mgr. CNA Spl. Risks Div., Birmingham, Mich., 1979—. Mem. Mich. Group Reps. Assn. (treas. 1983—, 1st v.p. 1984), Nat. Assn. Female Execs. Republican. Roman Catholic. Home: 20275 Woodhill Dr Northville MI 48167 Office: CNA Spl Risks Div 30200 Telegraph Rd Suite 300 Birmingham MI 48010

JASPER, JOANNE BABLITZ, management analyst; b. Lexington, Ky., Sept. 15, 1938; d. Frederick William and Elizabeth (Turpin) Bablitz; m. Jack Newton Jasper, Oct. 11, 1974; children—Karen Elizabeth, Shari Lynn, Ronda Kay, David Otha. A.A., Albany Jr. Coll., 1981. Sec. Lexington Army Dept., 1956-61, U.S. Army Signal Communication Agy., Lexington, 1961-63, U.S. Army Logistics Ctr., Lexington, 1963-73, U.S. Army TMDE Activity, Lexington, 1973-78, Marine Corps Logistics Base, Albany, Ga., 1978-81, mgmt. analyst, 1981—. Recipient Outstanding Performance awards Marine Corps Logistics Base 1978, 80, Outstanding Performance awards Lexington Army Dept. 1965, 66, 67, 72, 73, 74, 75, 78, Sustained Superior Performance award Lexington Army Dept. 1975-76, Spl. Act award Marine Corps. Logistics Base 1981, 15 yr. Safety award Lexington Army Dept. 1972. Mem. Am. Bus. Womens Assn. (recording sec. 1984-85). Baptist. Avocations: cooking; volunteer work. Home: 2712 Westgate Blvd Albany GA 31707 Office: Marine Corps Logistics Base Albany GA 31704

JAWIN, MICHELE RODIN, lawyer; b. Bklyn., Nov. 18, 1955; d. Bernard Martin and Gloria Toby (Shluker) Rodin; m. Paul Gregory Jawin, Jan. 22, 1983; 1 child, Alixandra. Student U. London, 1975; B.A. magna cum laude, Hofstra U., 1977; J.D., Benjamin N. Cardozo Sch. Law, 1980. Bar: N.Y. 1981. Dep. asst. atty. gen., State of N.Y., N.Y.C., 1980-81; assoc. firm Booth, Lipton & Lipton, N.Y.C., 1981-82, firm Dreyer and Traub, N.Y.C., 1982—; asst. sec. J&B Mgmt. Corp., Ft. Lee, N.J., 1983-86; sec., dir. 27 E 65th Street Owners Corp. Mem. ABA, Assn. Bar City N.Y., English Speaking Union (N.Y. br.). Democrat. Home: 27 E 65 St New York NY 10021 Office: Dreyer and Traub 101 Park Ave New York NY 10178

JAY, ANITA KAYE, county clerk; b. Durant, Okla., Nov. 28, 1943; d. William Irving Sykes and Elsie Virginia (Fehr) Mills; m. Donald Roy Jay, Oct. 29, 1965; children—Geoffry Todd, Karri Dawn. Clk., typist State Hwy. Dept., Oklahoma City, 1961-65; stenographer Conoco, Ponca City, Okla., 1965-73; owner, operator Jay's Tastee Freez, Tonkawa, Okla., 1973-76; legal sec. Mike McLaughlin, Cherokee, Okla., 1980—; county clk. Alfalfa County, Cherokee, 1981—. Vol. Alfalfa County Republican Party, Cherokee, 1981—; pres. Band Boosters Club, Cherokee, 1985—. Mem. N.W. County Officers Assn., Okla. County Officers Assn., Okla. County Clks. Assn., Beta Sigma Phi (pres. 1983-84). Methodist. Club: Bus. and Profl. Women (treas. 1985—) (Cherokee). Avocations: reading; travel; fishing. Home: 405 S Grand Cherokee OK 73728

JAY, E. DEBORAH, research institute executive; b. Detroit, Dec. 27, 1950; d. David J. and Shirley A. (Shapiro) Jay; m. Hugh Anthony Levine, Feb. 14, 1981; 1 dau., Pamela Beth. B.A. magna cum laude, UCLA, 1972; M.A., U. Calif.-Berkeley, 1973, Ph.D., 1981. Research assoc. Survey Research Ctr., U. Calif.-Berkeley, 1973-77; lectr. dept. polit. sci. U. Calif.-Davis, 1978-79; polit. cons. Teknekron, Inc., Berkeley, 1978-80, The Pub. Sector, San Francisco, 1979-80; sr. social scientist Stanford Research Inst., Menlo Park, Calif., 1981—. Mem. Am. Pub. Opinion Research Assn., Am. Mktg. Assn., Am. Polit. Sci. Assn., Am. Stats. Assn., Phi Beta Kappa. Office: Stanford Research Inst Survey Research Program 333 Ravenswood Ave Menlo Park CA 94025

JAY, NANCY SISEMORE, radio executive; b. Kansas City, Mo., June 4, 1955; d. Sam S. and Poppy LaRue (Hammond) Malosky; m. Don Michael Sisemore, Nov. 21, 1982. B.A., U. Okla., 1976; postgrad. Grad. Sch. Speech, West Tex. State U., 1977. News anchor, reporter, assignments editor Sta. KFDA-TV, Amarillo, Tex., 1976-77; exec. asst. Sta. KNUS Radio, Dallas, 1977-78; morning news anchor Sta. WBAP/KSCS Radio, Forth Worth, 1978-79; news, pub. affairs dir. Sta. KAFM/KAAM, Radio, Dallas, 1979—; lectr. to high schs., colls., Dallas, Fort Worth, San Antonio, 1979—; cable TV co-host Fashion Today and Dallas Today, 1981—; free-lance actress. Writer mag. articles. Chmn. media adv. bd. March of Dimes, Dallas, 1980-82; mem. radio publicity com. Cystic Fibrosis Found., Dallas, 1981—; host, auctioneer TACA Charity for Arts, Dallas, 1981—; auctioneer PBS-KERA TV, Dallas, 1982; mem. adv. bd. Safety Council Greater Dallas, 1983—; co-founder, vol. coordinator DWI Hotline, Dallas, Fort Worth, 1982-84. Recipient Media award Safety Council Greater Dallas, 1983; Outstanding Media Contbn. award Dallas Soc. for Crippled Children. Mem. Radio and TV News Dirs. Assn., Am. Women in Radio and TV, Chi Omega. Republican. Office: KAFM/KAAM Radio 15851 Dallas Pkwy Suite 1200 Dallas TX 75248

JAY, NORMA JOYCE, artist; b. Wichita, Kans., Nov. 11, 1925; d. Albert Hugh and Thelma Ree (Boyd) Braly; m. Laurence Eugene Jay, Sept. 2, 1949; children—Dana Denise, Allison Eden. Student Wichita State U., 1946-49, Art Inst. Chgo., 1955-56, Calif. State Coll., 1963. Illustrator Boeing Aircraft, Wichita, Kans., 1949-51; co-owner Back Door Gallery, Laguna Beach, Calif., 1973—. One-woman shows Milcir Gallery, Tiburon, Calif., 1978, Newport Beach City Gallery, 1981; group shows include Am. Soc. Marine Artists ann. exhbns., N.Y.C., 1978-86, Peabody Mus., Salem, Mass., 1981, Mystic Seaport Mus. Gallery, Conn., 1982, 85, Mongerson Gallery Ltd., Chgo., 1984, Mariners' Mus., Newport News, Va., 1985-86; represented in permanent collections including James Irvine Found., Newport Beach, Niguel Art Assn., Laguna Niguel, Calif., Deloitte, Haskins & Sells, Costa Mesa, Calif., M.J. Brook & Sons Inc., North Hollywood, Calif., others. Recipient Best of Show award Ford Nat. Competition, 1961, First Place award Traditional Artists Exhbn., San Bernadino County Mus., 1976, Artist award Chriswood Gallery Invitational Exhbn., Rancho California, Calif., 1973. Fellow Am. Soc. Marine Artists; mem. Niguel Art Assn. (first pres. 1968, hon. life mem. 1978), Artists Equity, Am. Artists Profl. League, Laguna Beach C. of C. Republican. Office: Back Door Gallery 325 N Coast Hwy Laguna Beach CA 92651

JAYARAM, SUSAN ANN, professional secretary; b. Stockton, Calif., Nov. 23, 1930; d. George Leroy and Violet Yvonne (Rushing) Potter; student Pasadena Coll., 1951-52; Woodbury Coll., 1961; A.A., Long Beach City Coll., 1979; m. M. R. Jayaram, July 2, 1960. Sec. to mgr. First Western Bank, Los Angeles, 1953-56; sec. to pres. Studio City Bank (Calif.), 1957-60; sec. to exec. v.p. Union Bank, Los Angeles, 1962-81; with Amex Systems, Inc., Hawthorne, Calif., 1981-82; personal sec. to Howard B. Keck of W.M. Keck Found., Los Angeles, 1982—. Sec., bd. advisors Citizens for Law Enforcement Needs, 1972-74; dir. Los Angeles, Bombay Sister City Com. Cert. Profl. Sec. Mem. DAR, Assistance League So. Calif., Windsor Square/Hancock Park Hist. Soc., League of Ams. (dir.), Freedoms Found. at Valley Forge, Beverly Hills Council, U.S. Navy League. Republican. Club: Los Angeles Club (dir., sec. 1967-83). Editor: Los Angeles Club Panorama, 1979-80; California Clarion, 1978-80. Office: 555 S Flower St Los Angeles CA 90071

JAYNE, LOUISE MARGARET, lawyer; b. Pitts., June 30, 1929; d. Reuel Curtis and Margaret May (Fry) J.; m. Chester S. Kurzet, June 30, 1951; children—Reuel Kurzet, Jay Kurzet. B.A., U. Pa., 1948; LL.B., Yale U., 1951. Bar: N.Y. 1952, Oreg. 1953, U.S. Supreme Ct. 1970. Assoc. Sullivan & Cromwell, N.Y.C., 1951-52; dep. dist. atty. Multnomah County Dist. Atty.'s Office, Portland, Oreg., 1954; sole practice, Portland, 1954—. Mem. ABA, N.Y. State Bar Assn., Oreg. State Bar Assn., Met. Women's Club (legal counsel 1973, pres. 1975), Phi Beta Kappa, Pi Gamma Mu. Republican. Episcopalian. Avocations: reading; tournament bridge; gourmet cooking. Office: 610 SW Alder Suite 705 Portland OR 97205

JEBENS, PATRICIA S., medical occupations educator; b. Berkeley, Calif., July 5, 1936; d. Wesley James and Constance Lord (Brady) Smith; m. Donald R. Jebens, Sept. 15, 1957; children—David Scott, Mark Alan. B.S. in Nursing, Calif. State U.-Fullerton, 1980; M.A., Calif. State U.-Long Beach, 1982. R.N., Calif.; lic. pub. health nurse, Calif. Staff nurse Providence Hosp., Oakland, Calif., 1957; nurse, team leader Garden Park Hosp., Anaheim, Calif., 1961-70; instr. Nurses Tng. Inst., Fullerton, Calif., 1970-73; med. occupations educator North Orange County Community Coll. Dist., Fullerton, 1974—, program coordinator health occupations, 1983—, guest lectr., 1980-83. Active Orange County council Boy Scouts Am., 1964-75; mem. vestry St. Joseph's Episcopal Ch., Buena Park, Calif., 1982; counselor, vol. Orange County Dept. Mental Health, 1978-81. Mem. Am. Soc. Aging, Orange County/Long Beach Nursing Consortium, Phi Kappa Phi. Office: North Orange County Community Col Dist 1800 W Ball Rd Anaheim CA 92804

JECKLIN, LOIS U., art corporation executive, consultant; b. Manning, Iowa, Oct. 5, 1934; d. J.R. and Ruth O. (Austin) Underwood; m. Dirk C. Jecklin, June 24, 1955; children—Jennifer Anne, Ivan Peter. Student State U. Iowa, 1953-55, 60-61, 74-75. Residency coordinator Quad City Arts Council, Rock Island, Ill., 1973-78; field rep. Affiliate Artists, Inc., N.Y.C., 1975-77; mgr., artist in residence Deere & Co., Moline, Ill., 1977-80; dir. Vis. Artist Series, Davenport, Iowa, 1978-81; pres. Vis. Artists, Inc., Davenport, 1981—; cons. writer's program St. Ambrose Coll., Davenport, 1981, 83, 85; mem. com. Iowa Arts Council, Des Moines, 1983-84; panelist Chamber Music Am., N.Y.C., 1984, Pub. Art Conf., Cedar Rapids, Iowa, 1984; panelist, mem. com. Lt. Gov.'s Conf. on Iowa's Future, Des Moines, 1984. Trustee Davenport Art Gallery; mem. steering com. Iowa Citizens for Arts, Des Moines, 1970-71; bd. dirs. Tri-City Symphony Orchestra Assn., Davenport, 1968-83; founding mem. Urban Design Council, HOME, City of Davenport Beautification Com., all Davenport, 1970-72. Recipient numerous awards Izaak Walton League, Davenport Art Gallery, Assn. for Retarded Citizens, Am. Heart Assn., Ill. Bur. Corrections, many others; LaVernes Noyes scholar, 1953-55. Mem. Am. Council for Arts, Ptnrs. for Livable Places, Ann. Coll. Univ. Community Arts Adminstrs., Iowa Assembly Local Arts Agys. (state exec. com.), Nat. Assembly Local Arts Agys., Am. Assn. Mus.Republican. Episcopalian. Club: Outing, Crow Valley Golf. Home: 2717 Nichols Ln Davenport IA 52803 Office: Vis Artists Inc 106 E 3rd St Suite 220 Davenport IA 52801

JEFFERIS, LU ELLEN, personnel executive; b. Little Rock, Oct. 2, 1952; d. Charles Wesley and Eva Louise (Elmore) Walton; m. Michael Jefferis, Oct. 1, 1982; 1 son, Russell Walton. B.A., Miss. State U.-Starkville, 1973; postgrad. U. So. Miss., 1983. Personnel mgr. Ferro Corp., Jackson, Miss., 1973-83, cons., 1983—. Chmn., Rankin County Job Service Improvement Program, Pearl, Miss., 1980-84; panelist Miss. Job Service Job-A-Thon on Ednl. TV, 1983. Recipient Miss. Gov.'s Meritorious Service award, 1980. Mem. Am. Soc. Personnel Adminstrn., Capitol Area Personnel Assn. (com. chmn. 1979-82), Miss. Psychol. Assn., Activity Vector Analysis Assn. Republican. Methodist. Home: 506 Dixton Dr Jackson MS 39208 Office: Personnel Consultants 506 Dixton Dr Jackson MS 39208

JEFFERS, BARBARA CLARK, learning clinic administrator, owner; b. Washington, Jan. 9, 1938; d. E. Kent and Catherine Reagan (Groseclose) Clark; m. John Herrick Jeffers, June 22, 1957; children—David Kent, Jennifer Lee. B.A., U. South Fla., 1969, M.A., 1971. Tchr. Hillsborough Pub. Sch., Tampa, Fla., 1969-70, U. South Fla., Tampa, 1970-71; clinician Tampa Reading Clinic, 1971-83; owner, dir. Brevard Learning Clinic, Melbourne, Fla., 1983—. Bd. dirs., personnel Bayshore Presbyn. Apts., Tampa, 1977-83, Sharahome. Mem. AAUW (v.p. 1984—), Assn. Children Learning Disabilities (pres. 1984—), Internat. Reading Assn., Orton Dyslexia soc. (legis. rep. 1984—, bd. dirs. 1984—), Melbourne C. of C., Delta Kappa Gamma (grantee 1984, leader workshops). Republican. Lodge: Soroptimist Internat. (sec. 1984—). Avocations: sailing; needlework; antiques. Office: Brevard Learning Clinic 1900 S Harbor City Blvd Melbourne FL 32901

JEFFERS, DONNA M., budget analyst; b. Milton, N.D., July 30, 1931; d. John and Josephine (Johnson) Lundgren; m. Ray J. Jeffers, Aug. 4, 1952 (dec. Mar. 1980); children—Pamela, Gregory Ray. B.S., Calif. Coast U., 1983; postgrad. St. Leo Coll., 1984—. Acctg. technician U.S. Govt., U.S. Navy, Norfolk, Va., 1969-81, budget, acctg. analyst, Virginia Beach, Va., 1981-83, budget analyst, Norfolk, Va., 1983—; ptnr. Ray, Ltd. Recipient Semi-Ann. Civilian Excellence award U.S. Navy, 1982. Home: 2400 Jenan Rd Virginia Beach VA 23454 Office: Commander Operational Test and Evaluation Force Norfolk VA 23511

JEFFERS, JUDITH, lawyer; b. Greeley, Colo., Sept. 14, 1945; d. Theadore Russell and Leila Margaret (Anderson) J.; m. Wayne H. Tsuji, Sept. 16, 1983. B.A., Colo. State Coll., 1969; M.A., U. No. Colo., 1971; J.D., Tex. Tech U., 1974. Bar: Wash. 1975, U.S. Dist. Ct. (we. dist.) Wash. 1975; cert. family law mediator Ctr. for Dispute Resolution, Denver, 1984. Law clk. to judge King County Superior Ct., Seattle, 1974-76; assoc. Bangs & Castle, Seattle, 1976; sole practice, Seattle, 1977—; mem. Pacific Family Law Inst., 1984-85; lectr. Colo. State Coll., Greeley, 1970-71, Edmonds Community Coll., Lynnwood, Wash.,

1977, U. Puget Sound, Seattle, 1977, Nat. Inst. Trial Advocacy Tng., 1979. Editor: Communication for the Working Lawyer, 1978. Fundraiser Community Home Health Care Honolulu Marathon; bd. dirs. Wash. Assn. for Retarded Citizens. Mem. Wash. State Bar Assn., Wash. Women Lawyers (v.p. Seattle chpt. 1985), Seattle-King County Bar Assn., Japanese Am. Citizens League (Seattle chpt.), Wash. State Trial Lawyers Assn., Assn. Trial Lawyers Am., Soc. Profls. in Dispute Resolution, NW Women's Law Ctr. (fundraiser). Democrat. Congregationalist. Club: Wash. Athletic. Home: 1721 Evergreen Pl Seattle WA 98122 Office: 300 Grand Central on the Park 216 1st Ave S Seattle WA 98104

JEFFERS, JUNE MCLAURIN, funeral home owner; b. Reidsville, N.C.; d. Lorenzo Houston and Lillian (Harrison) McLaurin; m. Albert Henry Clark, III, Dec. 18, 1954 (div. 1971); children—Albert Henry, III (dec.), Anthony L., Ashton McLaurin; m. Leonidas Michael Jeffers, May 27, 1977. B.S. in Edn., Wayne State U., 1955; grad. Simmons Sch. Mortuary Sci., Syracuse, N.Y., 1958; M.Ed., U. N.C.-Greensboro, 1970. Tchr. Rock County Bd. Edn., Wentworth, N.C., 1956-57, 62-72; mgr., ptnr. McLaurin Funeral Home, Reidsville, N.C., 1972-79, owner, operator, 1979—. Contbr. articles to profl. publs. Trustee N.C. Central U., Durham, 1977—; sec. Rockingham County Democratic Women, N.C., 1980—; co-chmn. State Dem. Unity Com., Raleigh, 1984. Recipient Order of Long Leaf Pine award State of N.C., 1984. Mem. N.C. Funeral Dirs. Assn., Nat. Funeral Dirs. Assn., Funeral Dirs. and Morticians Assn. N.C. (pres. 1982-84, chmn. bd. 1984—; Woman of Yr. 1974), Nat. Funeral Dirs. and Morticians Assn. (pres. 1984-85, chmn. bd. 1985—; Women of Yr. 1974), Nat. Assn. Nergo Bus. and Profl. Womens Clubs, Inc. (Community Service award Reidsville Club 1975, Outstanding Leadership award Greensboro club 1982), Nat. Assn. Bus. and Profl. Women (pres. Reidsville 1976-78), Reidsville C. of C. (bd. dirs. 1972-76, 80-84), Omega Psi Psi (Outstanding Leadership award 1978). Methodist. Clubs: Girl Friends (pres. 1974-76), Home Beautiful (pres. 1979-81), Royal Coterie Larks (treas. 1980-82). Lodges: Order of Eastern Star, Order of Golden Circle, Dau. of Isis. Home: Route 8 Box 138 Wentworth St Reidsville NC 27320 Office: McLaurin Funeral Home 721 E Morehead St Reidsville NC 27320

JEFFERS, KAY AUDRA, sales executive; b. Ft. Wayne, Ind., Nov. 10, 1953; d. Howard Ben and Audra Mildred (Dalton) Tenny; m. Ronald Thomas Jeffers, May 12, 1979. B.S. in Indsl. Mgmt., Purdue U., 1976. Asst. buyer Block's Dept. Sotre, Indpls., 1976-77, buyer, 1977-79; sales analyst Ford Motor Co., Indpls., 1979-80, zone mgr., Houston, 1980—, light truck merchandising mgr., 1986—; dist. sales mgr. Jaguar Cars, 1986—. Home: 701 Bering Apt 704 Houston TX 77057

JEFFERS, SUZANNE MIDDLETON, actress; d. A.H. and Rita Eileen Middleton; B.S., Calif. State Poly. U.; M.A., U. Calif., Berkeley, 1976; m. Michael B. Jeffers, Aug. 14, 1977; 1 dau. Flight attendant TWA, 1970-75; instr. Marymount Manhattan Coll., N.Y.C., also ind. bus. cons., 1974-75; TV journalist, also cons. to corps. in tng. and devel., 1976-79; pres. Corp. & Media Cons., Inc., N.Y.C., 1979-83; actress, 1983—; lectr. in field. Chmn. bd. Children's Oncology Soc. N.Y., 1977-83. Named an outstanding working woman of U.S., 1981. Mem. Nat. Acad. TV Arts and Scis., Nat. Acad. TV Program Execs., Assn. Women Bus. Owners, U. Calif. Alumni Assn., Jr. League N.Y., Actors Equity Assn., AFTRA. Episcopalian. Clubs: West Side Tennis, River (N.Y.C.). Address: 993 Park Ave New York NY 10028

JEFFERSON, GERALDINE HAILSTOLK, psychotherapist, communications consultant; b. N.Y.C., June 4, 1951; d. Frank Linwood and Bessie (Andrews) Hailstolk; student Hunter Coll., 1970, Bklyn. Coll., 1969; B.S., Empire State Coll., 1982; M.S.W., valedictorian, NYU, 1984; 1 dau., Lisa Lynn. Prodn. coordinator Great Am. Dream Machine, Feeling Good Health Show, N.Y.C., 1972, 75; program supr. ABC-TV Entertainment Div., N.Y.C., 1973-74; features editor Soap Opera Digest, N.Y.C., 1977-79; writer/producer Law and the Disabled radio series, N.Y.C., 1979-80; radio cons. Center for Ind. Living, N.Y.C., 1981-83; psychotherapist, 1984—; consumer columnist Elan Mag., 1982; grants evaluator U.S. Dept. Edn., 1980-81; panel mem. Nat. Acad. TV Arts and Scis. Emmy Awards, 1980. Crisis Counselor, N.Y. Women Against Rape Center, 1978. Recipient Award for Excellence in TV Prodn., Bklyn. Coll./Central Bklyn. Model Cities, 1971, Nat. Acad. TV Arts and Scis., 1972. Mem. Nat. Assn. Social Workers Authors Guild, Nat. Acad. TV Arts and Sci. Club: N.Y. Press. Contbr. articles to profl. and consumer jours.; also poetry. Address: 35 Midwood St Brooklyn NY 11225

JEFFETT, NANCY PEARCE, tennis administrator, foundation executive, b. St. Louis, July 16, 1928; d. Charles Frederick and Lillian (Schaefer) Pearce; m. Frank A. Jeffett, Dec. 29, 1956; children—Wiliam F., Elizabeth. B.S. in Edn., Washington U., St. Louis, 1951. Co-founder Tyler (Tex.) Tennis Assn., 1954; chmn. jr. devel. com. Tex. Tennis Assn., Dallas, 1963—, chmn. Virginia Slims Dallas Tennis tournament, 1970—, MCB Internat. Teams, U.S. and Gt. Britain, 1973—; chmn., pres. Maureen Connolly Brinker Tennis Found., Dallas, 1968—; mem. Women's Internat. Profl. Tennis Council, 1974-83; chmn. Davis Cup Tie, U.S. vs. Mex., 1965; capt. U.S. Fedn. Cup Tennis Team, 1983; chmn. Wightman Cup and Fedn. Cup Com., 1976-84. Mem. bd. YMCA, Tyler, 1956, Dallas, 1962; Recipient Caswell award Tex. Tennis Assn., 1970; Service Bowl award U.S. Tennis Assn., 1970; World Championship Tennis Service to Tennis award, 1983; named Tex. Mus. Tennis Hall of Fame, 1983. Mem. Jr. League Dallas, Dallas Tennis Assn. (dir.), Tex. Tennis Assn. (dir.), U.S. Tennis Assn. (exec. com.). Republican. Episcopalian. Home: 5419 Wateka Dr Dallas TX 75209 Office: Maureen Connolly Brinker Tennis Found 5419 Wateka Dr Dallas TX 75209

JEFFORDS, JEAN GARRETT, county official; b. Waycross, Ga., Feb. 8, 1921; d. Quillian Lemuel and Glenn Antoinette (Allen) Garrett; A.B., U. Ga., 1942; M.A. in Polit. Sci. (Univ. fellow), 1944; m. William Quintillus Jeffords, Jr., Oct. 15, 1954 (dec.); 1 son, Lawrence Garrett. With fgn. service Dept. State, Guatemala, 1945-48; asst. to dean Coll. Spl. and Continuation Studies, U. Md., College Park, 1948-49; prin. planner Jacksonville (Fla.) Area Planning Bd., 1965-74; planning dir. Central Fla. Regional Planning Council, Bartow, 1974-79; planning cons., after 1979; now supr. aging programs Collier County, Fla. Mem. Alpha Delta Pi. Republican. Episcopalian. Author reports in field. Home: 4054 Bayshore Dr Naples FL 33962 Office: Collier County Govt Complex Naples FL 33962

JEFFREY, MARGIE SUE, transportation company executive; b. Evansville, Ind., June 19, 1935; d. James Andrew and Eula Madeth (Tucker) Baughn; student McHenry County Coll., 1977-79, Coll. Advanced Traffic, Chgo., 1977; m. Joseph W. Jeffrey, Nov. 28, 1981; children from previous marriage—Dan Market, Tony Market, Lee Ann Market. With Market Produce Trucking, Evansville, 1959-70; gen. ops. mgr. Farm Service & Supplies Inc., Marengo, Ill., 1970—, v.p., 1980—; pres. MLB Mktg. Services, Marengo 1981—; admitted to practice transport law ICC, 1977. Mem. Marengo Union C. of C., Am. Soc. Traffic and Transp., Assn. ICC Practitioners (nat. com. motor fleet supr. tng.), Am. Assn. Handwriting Analysts, Women's Traffic Club Evansville, Soc. Integrative Graphology (founding mem.), Internat. Platform Assn., Notaries Assn. Ill., Central States Women's Traffic Conf. (dir.), No. Ill. Transp. Club (founding mem.), Mid-West Trucking Assn., Delta Nu Alpha, Traffic Clubs Internat. Home: 9505 Elm Ln Crystal Lake IL 60014 Office: 21606 W Railroad St Marengo IL 60152

JEFFREY-SMITH, LILLI ANN, biofeedback specialist, educator, administrator; b. Bedford, Ind.; d. Charles Constantine and Adelai (Malon) Jeffrey-Smith. Grad. Ind. Bus. Coll., 1963; B.S., Ind. U., 1973; postgrad. Albert Einstein Coll. Medicine. Cert. biofeedback specialist. Project assoc., stress mgmt. clinician City of Indpls., 1973-79; cons. Airport Med. Clinic, Indpls., 1981; outreach coordinator Abbot-Northwestern Hosp., Mpls., 1981; dir. biofeedback dept. Sister Kenney Inst., Mpls., 1979-81, Noran Neurol. Clinic, Mpls., 1981-83; instr., dir. Biofeedback Tng. and Treatment Ctr., Edina, Minn., 1979—; pres. Biofeedback Research and Devel. Co. Ltd., Edina, 1983—; cons. to biofeedback depts. St. Joseph Hosp., Mankato, Minn., 1984—, Lakeview Clinic, Waconia, Minn., 1983, Psychiat. Clinic of Mankato, 1983—. Author, narrator health and wellness tape series. Mem. Republican Presdl. Task Force, 1984-85, NSC, 1985; co-chmn. Mayor's Handicapped Task Force, Indpls., 1975; founder, pres. Miss Wheel Chair of Ind., Inc. Named Hon. Lt. Gov., State of Ind., 1978; given Key to the City of Indpls., 1973, Flag of the City of Indpls., 1975. Mem. Am. Inst. Stress, N.Y. Acad. Sci., AAAS, Edina C. of C., Minn. Women's Network, Biofeedback Soc. Am., Biofeedback Soc. Minn., Am. Assn. Control Tension, Am. Assn. Biofeedback Clinicians, Nat. Assn. Women Bus. Owners, Soc. Open Focus and Tng. Research, Assn. Trainers in Clin. Hypnosis, Internat. Stress and Tension Control Assn., Minn. Assn. Rehab. Providers, Nat. Assn. Exec. Women. Avocations: music; stamp collecting; shooting; poetry. Office: Biofeedback Tng & Treatment Ctr Southdale Med Bldg Suite 158 6545 France Ave S Edina MN 55435

JELINSKI, JANE MARY, county official; b. Minocqua, Wis., Apr. 17, 1942; d. Lyle Franklin and Rosalie Julia (Wolk) Schilling; m. Jack B. Jelinski, Aug. 24, 1968; children—Kristina, Adam. B.A., Fontbonne Coll., St. Louis, 1966; postgrad. Mont. State U., 1980—. Cert. tchr., Mont. Tchr. pub. grade sch., Kansas City, Mo., 1966-67, St. Charles Sch., Bloomington, Ind., 1968-69; exec. dir. Gallatin Advocacy, Bozeman, Mont., 1978-84; county commr. Gallatin County, Mont., 1984—; mem. Job Tng. Partnership Act Council Commrs., Mont., 1985—. Author monograph: Sex-Role Stereotyping in Grade School Readers, 1976. Vol. United Way, Bozeman, 1980-83; Mont. Democratic committeewoman, 1983—; v.p. bd. dirs. Mont. Advocacy Program, Helena, 1984—; bd. dirs. Consumer Counseling Service, Bozeman, 1984-85. Grantee United Way, Bozeman, 1980-84, Pub. Welfare Found., 1981-82, Developmental Disabilities Planning and Adv. Council, 1983. Mem. Bus. and Profl. Women, Friends of Music. Roman Catholic. Avocations: piano; camping; writing. Home: 433 N Tracy Bozeman MT 59715 Office: Gallatin County Courthouse PO Box 1905 Bozeman MT 59715

JELTEMA, JUDITH LOUISE, construction company executive; b. Grand Rapids, Mich., Oct. 9, 1946; d. Wesley G. and Maxine C. (Dutema) J.; B.S., Western Mich. U., 1969; postgrad. Mich. State U., 1974-76. Tchr., girls athletic dir. Lakeview Schs., Battle Creek, Mich., 1969-74; dir. edn. and safety Asso. Gen. Contractors, Lansing, Mich., 1974-76; corporate mgr., human resources and safety Townsend & Bottum, Inc., Ann Arbor, Mich., 1976-84; v.p. First Southwest Constrn. Corp., Temple, Tex., 1984—. Mem. Am. Soc. Personnel Adminstrs., Am. Soc. Safety Engrs., Constrn. Personnel Execs., Gamma Phi Beta. Office: First Southwest Constrn Corp 200 W Calhoun Temple TX 76502

JENKINS, ANNE ELIZABETH GREEN, pediatric therapist; b. Richmond, Va., May 18, 1944; d. John P. and Dorothy Mae (Williams) Green; B.S., (Rehab. Service Adminstrn. scholar), N.Y.U., 1972; M.A. (Minority Student grad. fellow), Columbia Tchrs. Coll., 1975, Ed.M., 1976; Ph.D. candidate, U. N.C.-Greensboro; m. Earnest Jenkins, June 1, 1964; children—Frederick Anthony, April Kaché, August Kali. Occupational therapist Harlem Hosp., N.Y.C., 1972-74, Blythedale Children's Hosp., Valhalla, N.Y., 1974-77; developmental disabilities specialist Amos Cottage Bowman Gray Sch. Medicine, Winston-Salem, N.C., 1977; dir. Early Intervention Program, Forsyth/Stokes counties, Winston-Salem, N.C., 1977-80, learning disabilities specialist, 1980-84; pvt. practice; 1984—; mem. faculty N.Y.U. Sch. Edn., N.Y.U. Med. Sch., U. N.C.-Chapel Hill, Winston-Salem State U., 1984—; cons. pre-schools and developmental day-care centers. Mem. Am. Occupational Therapy Assn., Smithsonian Instrn., Assn. Retarded Citizens (dir.), Center Study Sensory Integrations, Am. Burn Assn. Liberal. Roman Catholic. Designer hand orthotics, adaptive equipment for the handicapped. Home: 2931 Springhaven Dr Winston-Salem NC 27103

JENKINS, AUDREY LOVELESS, health care corporation executive; b. McCormick, S.C., Sept. 19, 1924; d. James Wilson and Eula Mae (McMahan) Loveless; m. Joseph Bradford Roberts, May 26, 1945 (dec. 1966); children—Kathy Jo, James Bradford, Susan Roberts Millsap, Thea Frances; m. Winford Lee Jenkins, Dec. 10, 1977. Grad. Anderson Hosp. Sch. Nursing, 1945; postgrad. Mo. U., 1973-74, Lincoln U., 1973-75. Asst. supr. med. floor Vets. Hosp., Fayetteville, Ark., 1947-49; adminstr. Phelps County Health Dept. and Home Health Agy., Rolla, Mo., 1964-73; dir. Waynesville Pub. Sch. Practical Nursing, Mo., 1973-75; pub. health nurse cons. Bur. Pub. Health Nursing Mo. Div. Health, Jefferson City, Mo., 1975-78; cons. community health nurse Bur. Maternal and Child Health, 1978-79, Bur. Hosp. Licensing and Cert., 1979-84; pres. Mo. Health Care Mgmt. Services, Inc., Jefferson City, 1984—; mem. Mo. State Bd. Nursing, 1975-79. Mem. Mo. Pub. Health Assn., Mo. Heart Assn. (bd. dirs. 1972—, chmn. 1968-72), Mo. Assn. Home Health Agys., Beta Sigma Phi. Baptist. Avocations: antiquing; walnut Victorian furniture; crocheting; gardening. Home: Route 3 Box 32 California MO 65018 Office: Mo Health Care Mgmt Services 915-M Southwest Blvd Jefferson City MO 65101

JENKINS, BRENDA GWENETTA, early childhood education specialist; b. Durham, N.C., Aug. 11, 1949; d. Brinton Alfred and Ophelia Arden (Eaton) Jenkins. B.S., Howard U., 1971, M.Ed., 1972, Cert. Spl. Edn., 1973-75; postgrad. Trinity Coll., Am. U., U. D.C., 1976—. Cheerleader coach Howard U., Washington, 1971—, aerobics instr. D.C. Pub. Schs., 1982—, tchr., 1972—; v.p. Nerdlich Corp., Washington, 1985—; ptnr. Jenkins, Trapp-Dukes and Yates Partnership; aerobic instr. for handicapped Council for Exceptional Children, Washington, 1982. Recipient Conscientious Service award D.C. Pub. Schs., 1985; Outstanding Recognition award Howard U. Alumni Cheerleaders Assn., 1984; Outstanding Service awards Kappa Delta Pi, 1978, 79, 81, 82, 84; citation Washington Tchrs. Union, 1985; Appreciation cert. D.C. Dept. Recreation, 1985, others. Mem. Am. Fedn. Tchrs., Theta Alpha chpt. Kappa Delta Pi (exec. com.), Howard U. Alumni Cheerleaders Assn. (co-founder 1977) Democrat. Avocations: fashion design; cooking; dancing; poetry writing.

JENKINS, CHARLA R., public relations executive; b. Emporia, Kans., Sept. 18, 1947; d. Charles Raymond and Christine L. (Bonczkowski) Jenkins. B.S. in Journalism, U. Kans., 1969. News service mgr. Emporia State U. (Kans.), 1970-72; info. writer U. Kans., Lawrence, 1972-74; asst. pub. relations dir. Kans. Turnpike Authority, Wichita, 1974-75; pub. relations dir. Kans. Wesleyan Coll., Salina, 1975-77, Kans. U. Performing Arts, U. Kans., Lawrence, 1977—. Media coordinator Manning for Sec. of State, Topeka and Lawrence, Kans., 1972. Mem. Women in Communications, Kans. Press Women, Kans. U. Alumni Assn. Democrat. Methodist. Home: 2532 Ousdahl Rd Lawrence KS 66044 Office: Univ Theatre Kansas U 317 Murphy Hall Lawrence KS 66045

JENKINS, CLARA BARNES, teacher educator; b. Franklinton, N.C.; d. Walter and Stella (Griffin) Barnes; B.S., Winston-Salem State U., 1939; postgrad. N.Y.U., 1947-48, U. N.C.-Chapel Hill, 1963; M.A., N.C. Central U., 1947; Ed.D., U. Pitts., 1965; postgrad. N.C. Agrl. and Tech. State U., summer 1981; m. Hugh Jenkins, Dec. 24, 1949 (div. Feb. 1955). Tchr. pub. schs., Wendell, N.C., 1939-43, Wise, N.C., 1943-45; mem. faculty Fayetteville State U., 1945-53, Rust Coll., Holly Spring, Miss., 1953-58; asst. prof. Shaw U., 1958-64; prof. edn. and psychology St. Paul's Coll., Lawrenceville, Va., 1964—; vis. prof. edn. Friendship Jr. Coll., Rock Hill, S.C., summer 1947, N.C. Agrl. and Tech. State U., 1966-82. Former mem. bd. dirs. Winston-Salem State U. Notary pub., N.C.; United Negro Coll. Fund Faculty fellow, 1963-64; Am. Bapt. Conv. grantee, 1963-64. Mem. AAUP, Nat. Soc. for Study Edn., NEA, AAUW, Am. Hist. Assn., Va. Edn. Assn., Am. Acad. Polit. and Social Sci., AAAS, Internat. Platform Assn., Assn. Tchr. Educators, History Edn. Soc., Doctoral Assn. Educators, Am. Assn. Higher Edn., Acad. Polit. Sci., Am. Psychol. Assn., Soc. Research in Child Devel., Marquis Biog. Library Soc., Jean Piaget Soc., Philosophy of Edn. Soc., Soc. Profs. Edn., Phi Eta Kappa, Zeta Phi Beta, Phi Delta Kappa, Kappa Delta Pi. Episcopalian. Home: 920 Bridges St Henderson NC 27536 Office: St Paul's Coll Lawrenceville VA 23868

JENKINS, ELIZABETH GARDNER, trade school executive; b. Burkeville, Ala., Apr. 26, 1926; d. William and Roberta (Carson) Gardner; m. Edwin C. Jenkins, Aug. 30, 1947 (dec. 1982); 1 child, Carol A. Student Ala. State U., 1939-41; A.A., Booker T. Washington Jr. Coll. Bus., 1943; student Tuskegee Inst., 1943-44. Registrar, Booker T. Washington Jr. Coll. Bus., Birmingham, Ala., 1944-47; adminstr. Printing Trades Sch., N.Y.C., 1950-80, pres., 1981—. Recipient Disting. Leadership Bus. Edn. award Booker T. Washington Coll. Bus., 1984. Mem. Nat. Assn. Trade and Tech. Schs. (Outstanding Community Service award 1976), Nat. Rehab. Assn. (Disting. Service award 1978), Ala. State U. Alumni Assn. (Outstanding Service award 1982), Nat. Assn. Printers and Lithographers, N.Y. State Assn. Career Schs. (pres.), Women in Prodn. Assn., Nat. Minority Bus. Council, Office: Printing Trades Sch 229 Park Ave S New York NY 10003

JENKINS, E(THEL) VALERIE, retired media specialist; b. Amherst, Ohio, Sept. 7, 1913; d. Frank A. and Ethel E. (Dute) Eppley; student Hiram Coll., 1932; B.A., Baldwin-Wallace Coll., 1936; postgrad. Western Res. U., 1936, 41, 66, State U. Iowa, 1938-39, Ohio State U., 1960; M.A., Kent State U., 1962; m. William J. Jenkins, Aug. 13, 1944 (div. May 1964). Dir. dramatics Baldwin-Wallace Coll., Berea, Ohio, 1936-38; tchr. English and speech St. Elmo (Ill.) High Sch., 1939-42; tchr. English, speech, dir. dramatics Clearview-Lorain (Ohio) High Sch., 1942-57, librarian, 1949-57; library coordinator Amherst (Ohio) Pub. Schs., 1957-80, drama dir., 1957-60, 75-77; instr. Kent State U., 1963-66; instr. speech Cleve. State U., 1966-70; lectr. costumes for theatre; owner, operator children's theatre, also costume rental; cons. Amherst Pub. Library Bldg. Program, 1972-73. Founder Workshop Players, Inc., 1948, trustee, 1948—, pres., 1949-49, 56-58, 60, 75-80, now vol. worker; mng. dir. Workshop Theatre, 1980—; mem. bd. Amherst Pub. Library, 1962—, pres., 1963-65, 83-85. Recipient Alumni Merit award Baldwin-Wallace Coll., 1986; Paul Harris fellow Rotary Internat., 1985. Mem. Nat., Ohio (life) edn. assns., Am. Theatre Assn., ALA, Ohio Ednl. Library Media Assn. (dir. NE chpt. 1974-76), Amherst Tchrs. Assn. (pres. 1962-64), Internat. Platform Assn., Delta Kappa Gamma, Phi Mu. Republican. Conglist. Home: 439 Shupe Ave Amherst OH 44001

JENKINS, GEORGANN KLAUS, librarian; b. Pitts., Oct. 9, 1950; d. Francis William and Mary Ida (Steingraber) Klaus; m. Robert M. Jenkins, Jr., Aug. 24, 1974; children—Andrew Klaus, Jeffrey Robert. B.S. in Edn., Edinboro (Pa.) U., 1972; M.L.S., U. Pitts., 1977; postgrad. suprs. program U. Pitts., 1986—. Cert. sch. librarian, Pa. Librarian grades 5-8, Pitts. Pub. Schs., 1972-74; librarian grades K-6, dist. audio-visual coordinator Baldwin-Whitehall Sch., Pitts., 1974—; guest lectr. Sch. Sociology, U. Pitts., 1982. Contbr. book revs. to profl. jour. Mem. ALA, Pa. Edn. Assn., Am. Assn. Sch. Librarians, Council Sch. Librarians (Southwest Pitts. chpt.), Pa. Sch. Librarians Assn., Beta Phi Mu. Democrat. Roman Catholic. Home: 1038 Thornwood Dr Pittsburgh PA 15234 Office: Whitehall Elem Sch Curry Rd Pittsburgh PA 15236

JENKINS, GLORIA DELORES, former airline official; d. David and Johnnie Sue (Smith) Barnes; extension student City U. N.Y.; cert. fund raising N.Y. U., 1982; m. John Elmo Jenkins, 1960 (dec.); children—Gloria Susan, Melanie Yvette Treadwell, Carol Lynn, Jonathan Edward. With Pan Am. World Airways, 1955-82, mgmt. prodn. planning aircraft service control maintenance and engring. JFK Airport, N.Y.C., 1979-82, mgmt. powerplant planning A/C engine maintenance and engring., 1982; mem. FAA Speakers Cadre. Exec. bd. Hansel & Gretel Inc., 1977-79; pres. Addisleigh Park Civic Orgn., 1960; mem. John E. Jenkins Meml. Scholarship Fund, 1980; mem. exec. bd. Queens council Boy Scouts Am. Recipient various service awards. Mem. Nat. Assn. Female Execs. (network dir.), NAACP (br. exec. bd.). Mem. A.M.E. Ch. Clubs: Hansel and Gretel (past nat. pres.), Toastmistresses.

JENKINS, JO ANN VIRGINIA, journalist; b. Cin., Feb. 14, 1930; d. Herbert Francis and May Frieda (Steidle) Jeffries; m. Vincent Howard Jenkins, Apr. 15, 1967; 1 child, John. B.A., Am. U., 1954. Staff asst. U.S. Senate and Ho. of Reps., Washington, 1955-65; congl. asst. Fed. Maritime Commn., Washington, 1965-69; news editor Catoctin Enterprise, Thurmont, Md., 1981—. Mem. Democratic Central Com., Thurmont, 1983; officer Frederick County Council PTAs, 1981-83, Thurmont PTA, 1980—. Mem. Md. Press Women, Nat. Fedn. Press Women. Episcopalian. Home: 111 Tacoma St Thurmont MD 21788 Office: Catoctin Enterprise 10 N Church St Thurmont MD 21788

JENKINS, KATHLEEN KAY, lawyer; b. Mpls., 1952; d. Grover Eugene and Beatrice (Cramer) Fanning; divorced; children—Scott, Laurie. B.A., Fayetteville State U., 1975; J.D., U. Mo.-Kansas City. Bar: Mo. 1979. Copy editor, columnist Korea Herald, Seoul, 1972-73; eligibility supr. N.C. Dept. Social Services, Fayetteville, 1974-76; copywriter Richard P. Mills Advt., Lee's Summit, Mo., 1976; law clk. U.S. Dist. Ct., Kansas City, Mo., 1979-82; assoc. Hillix, Brewer, Hoffhaus & Whittaker, Kansas City, Mo., 1982-86, ptnr., 1986—; mem. expedited arbitration panel Reynolds Metals Co.-United Steelworkers, Kansas City, Mo., 1983—. Mem. exec. com., bd. dirs. Legal Aid Soc. Western Mo., Kansas City, 1982—; chmn. bd. trustees Jackson County Mental Health Levy Bd., Kansas City, Mo., 1982-84. Mem. Kansas City Bar Assn. (pres.-elect young lawyers sect. 1986), Mo. Bar Assn., ABA, Lawyers' Assn. Kansas City. Democrat. Episcopalian. Office: Hillix Brewer Hoffhaus & Whittaker 2700 Commerce Tower PO Box 13367 Kansas City MO 64199

JENKINS, MADGE MARIE, management educator, consultant; b. Dearborn, Mich., Oct. 19, 1938; d. Lem and Margaret Mary (Tulloch) VicKroy; m. Robert Eugene Brennan, Dec. 28, 1958 (div. 1965); 1 child, Richard; m. George Henry Jenkins, Aug. 15, 1967. Student Systems Inst., Detroit, 1965, Henry Ford Community Coll., 1965-67; B.A. cum laude, U. Mich., 1976; M.P.A., Wayne State U., 1978. Ops. mgr. Custom Lab., Dearborn, Mich., 1967-68; mgr. Jenkins Wedding Studies, Dearborn, 1968-74; unit dir. dept. recreation City of Dearborn, 1976-78; enumerator Dept. Agr., Seattle, 1978-79; coordinator Stillaguamish Ctr., Arlington, Wash., 1979-80; asst. prof. mgmt. Lima Tech. Coll., Ohio, 1980—; mem. Adv. Bd. Continuing Edn., Bellingham, Wash., 1978-80, Marysville, Wash., 1979-80; mgmt. cons. Jenkins & Jenkins, Cario, Ohio, 1984—; cons. Ctr. for Bus. and Econ. Research, Western Wash. U. 1979-80. Elder, Columbus Grove Presbyterian Ch., Ohio, 1982-83. Mem. Acad. Mgmt., Am. Mgmt. Assn., Am. Assn. Pub. Adminstrn., Am. Soc. Tng. and Devel., Am. Assn. Personnel Adminstrn. Republican. Club: 8-16 Cine (Detroit). Lodge: Toastmasters (v.p. local chpt. 1981-82). Office: Lima Tech Coll Ohio State U Campus Lima OH 45804

JENKINS, MARGARET AIKENS, educational administrator; b. Lexington, Miss., May 14, 1925; d. Joel Bryant and Marie C. (Threadgill) Melton; m. Daniel Armstrong, May 21, 1944 (div. 1950); children—Marie Cynthia, Marsha Rochelle; m. Gabe Aikens, June 29, 1954 (div. 1962); m. Herbert Jenkins, May 21, 1966. Student, Chgo. Conservatory of Music, 1959, Moody Bible Inst., Chgo., 1959, Calif. State U.-Northridge, 1984; H.H.D. (hon.), Payne Acad., 1984. Clk., U.S. Signal Corp., Chgo., 1943-44, Cuneo Press., Chgo., 1948-52, Ford Aircraft, Chgo., 1952-58, Corp of Engrs., Chgo., 1958-64; progress control clk. Def. Contract Adminstrn. Service Region, Los Angeles, 1966-73; founder, adminstr. Celeste Scott Christian Sch., Inglewood, Calif., 1976—; founder, pres. Mary Celeste Scott Meml. Found., Inc., Inglewood, 1973—; pub., writer, founder Magoll Records, Chgo., 1958-64. Recipient Cert. Appreciation, Mayor of Inglewood, 1984, Mayor of Los Angeles, 1980, State Senator, 1975, State Rep., 1976; named Women of Yr., Los Angeles Sentinel, 1982, Inglewood C. of C., 1982. Mem. Broadcast Music Inc., Am. Fedn. TV and Radio Artists, Nat. Assn. Pentecostal Women and Men Inc. Avocations: religion, writing music, recording music. Home: 11602 Cimarron Ave Los Angeles CA 90047 Office: Celeste Scott Christian Sch 930 S Osage Ave Inglewood Ca 90301

JENKINS, MARY BARNES, lawyer; b. Danbury, Conn., July 5, 1946; d. Charles Thomas and Helen Eva (Bakanau) Barnes; m. Richard Thomas Jenkins, Aug. 7, 1974; 1 child, Elizabeth Alexandra Barnes Jenkins. A.B., Barnard Coll., 1968; B.S. in Nursing, Columbia U., 1974; J.D., Fordham U., 1979. Bar: N.Y. 1980. Litigation asst. Sullivan & Cromwell, N.Y.C., 1968-72; pediatric nurse, ICU, Babies Hosp., Columbia-Presbyn. Med. Ctr., N.Y.C., 1974-76; assoc. Paul, Weiss, Rifkind, Wharton & Garrison, N.Y.C., 1979-83; counsel Revlon, Inc., N.Y.C., 1984-85, sr. counsel, asst. sec., 1985—. Mem. ABA, Am. Soc. Corp. Secs. Democrat. Episcopalian. Home: 24 Prospect Dr Greenwich CT 06830 Office: Revlon Inc 767 Fifth Ave New York NY 10153

JENKINS, MYRA ELLEN, historian, archivist; b. Elizabeth, Colo., Sept. 26, 1916; d. Lewis Harlan and Minnie (Ackroyd) Jenkins; B.A. cum laude, U. Colo., 1937, M.A., 1938; Ph.D., U. N.Mex., 1953. Instr. pub. schs., Climax, Colo., 1939-41, Granada, Colo., 1941-43, Pueblo, Colo., 1943-50; fellow U. N.Mex., 1950-52, asst., 1952-53; free-lance historian and hist. cons., Albuquerque, 1953-59; archivist Hist. Soc. N.Mex., Santa Fe, 1959-60; sr. archivist N.Mex. Records Center and Archives, 1960-69, dep. for archives, 1968-70; N.Mex. state historian, 1967-80; ret., 1980; instr. St. Michael's Coll., 1962-63, Coll. of Santa Fe, 1966-74, 81-82; adj. assoc. prof. N.Mex. State U., 1983; assoc. adj. prof. U.N. Mex., summer 1982, 84, 86. Mem. Western History Assn., Hist. Soc. N.Mex., Phi Beta Kappa, Phi Kappa Phi, Phi Alpha Theta, Kappa Delta Pi. Democrat. Episcopalian. Author: (with Albert H. Schroeder) A Brief History of New Mexico, 1974; Guides and Calendars to the Spanish, Mexican and Territorial Archives of New Mexico; contbr. articles to profl. jours. and book revs. Home: 1022 Don Cubero St Santa Fe NM 87501

JENKINS, SALLIE ALLISON, publisher; b. San Antonio, Mar. 1, 1936; d. Carroll H. and Jessie M. (Lucky) Allison; m. Travis Jenkins, Feb. 12, 1955; children—Earlyn, Debbie, Dawn, Wayne. Sec. to pres. Broadway Nat. Bank, San Antonio, 1953-56; sec.-treas. C.H. Allison Paving, Inc., San Antonio, 1969-80, office mgr., 1972-78; owner Mandolin Publs., San Antonio, 1978—, also writer, sales dir. Mem. San Antonio Advt. Fedn. Mem. Christian Ch. Club: San Antonio Garden. Home: 5000 Enterprise San Antonio TX 78249 Office: Mandolin Publs Rt 2 Box 708 San Antonio TX 78249

JENKINS, SANDRA GOTHAM, advertising and marketing executive, consultant; b. Tokyo, June 9, 1948; d. Fred Calvin and Evelyn (Dirr) Gotham; m. James P. Jenkins, June 15, 1970 (div. 1982). Student Stanford-in-France, Tours, 1968-69; B.A., Stanford U., 1970, M.A., 1971. Account exec. Young & Rubicam Inc., N.Y.C., 1972-78, account supr., 1978-80; pres., Gotham Prodns., N.Y.C., 1980-85; v.p., mgmt. supr. Ogilvy & Mather Ptnrs., 1982-85; v.p. Steuben Glass, N.Y.C., 1985—; cons. Congl. coms., FDA, FTC for exec. program Am. Assn. Advt. Agys., Washington, 1978-80; cons. Ctr. Arctic Studies Sorbonne, Paris, in U.S. and Can., 1980-82; seminar dir. N.Y. chpt. Women in Bus., N.Y.C., 1983-84. Writer and editor 4-part TV documentary script Invit! The Universal Cry of the Eskimo People, 1981. Writer speeches for Georgetown Ctr. Strategic and Internat. Studies, also newsletter for Am. Assn. Advt. Agys. Fund raiser Stanford U., N.Y.C., 1982-84; promotion coordinator of benefits and advt. Medic Alert, N.Y.C., 1983-84; mem. exec. com. Youth Counseling League, N.Y.C., 1984. Named to dean's list Stanford U., 1966-70. Mem. Writers Guild Am., Young Profls. Group of Fgn. Policy Assn. (organizing chmn. 1980-81), N.Y. Women in Communications. Club: Stanford (N.Y.C.). Home: 210 E 73d St New York NY 10021 Office: Steuben Glass Fifth Ave and 56th St New York NY 10022

JENKINS, SUZANNE CLARA, museum official; b. Washington, Sept. 2, 1951; d. Edward James and Floy Ethel (McLaughlin) J.; 1 child, Christopher Alex Smith. Registrar Nat. Portrait Gallery, Smithsonian Instn., Washington, 1974—. Home: 9250 Canterbury Riding Laurel MD 20707 Office: Nat Portrait Gallery 8th and F Sts NW Washington DC 20560

JENKINSON, JUDITH ELLEN, librarian; b. Monroe, Mich., Apr. 9, 1943; d. Robert Henry Williams and Caroline (Pardee) Stephenson; m. Arnold Apsey, July 1, 1962 (div. 1977); 1 child, Amy Lou; m. Leif Jenkinson, May 21, 1977, 1 stepchild, Karl J. A.A., Alpena Community Coll., 1964; B.A., Mich. State U., 1966; Arts M.L.S., U. Mich., 1969. Elem. tchr., Lincoln, Mich., 1966-68, high sch. librarian, 1969-72; elem. librarian, Ketchikan, Alaska, 1972-75, high sch. librarian, 1975—. Mem. Ketchiken Community Coll. Council, 1980-84, pres., 1984-85; del. Alaska Democratic Conv., 1982; dir., producer, actress, mem. stage crew First City Players, 1972—. Mem. ALA, NEA, AAUW, NOW, LWV, Ketchikan Edn. Assn., NEA-Alaska, Women's Internat. League for Peace and Freedom, Alaska Library Assn. VFW Aux., Swinging Kings Square Dancers (pres. 1985-86). Lodge: Eagles. Home: Box 5342 Ketchikan AK 99901 Office: 2610 4th Ave Ketchikan AK 99901

JENKS, MARY ELLEN, food products company executive; b. Milw., 1933. Student U. Wis., 1956, 57. Vice pres. consumer affairs Pillsbury Co., Mpls. Dir. Better Bus. Bur. of Minn. Mem. Am. Women in Radio and TV, Am. Home Econs. Assn., Grocery Mfrs. of Am. (consumer affairs com.). Office: Pillsbury Co The Pillsbury Ctr 200 S 6th St Minneapolis MN 55402*

JENKS, SARAH ISABEL, retired nursing administrator; b. Springfield, Mo., May 5, 1913; d. George S. and Mary (Laing) Cuckie; diploma St. Joseph Mercy Hosp., 1934; student U. Calif. Extension, 1959-70, West Coast U., 1974, 78; m. Dean F. Thompson, June 16, 1936 (dec. 1949); 1 son, Dean F.; m. 2d, Kermit Jenks, June 17, 1951. Staff nurse Calif. Hosp., Los Angeles, 1936-37, head nurse, 1937-38, supr., 1938-40; indsl. nurse May Co., Los Angeles, 1940-43; office nurse, Burbank, Calif., 1944-45, Fort Dodge, Iowa, 1946-57; office mgr. Inglewood Med. Clinic ret., 1985; 1957-58; occupational health nurse, Hawthorne, Calif., 1958-72; supervising nurse Occupational Health Service, Los Angeles County, 1972-75; chief occupational health nurse Naval Regional Med. Center, Long Beach, Calif., 1975-81; adminstrv. nurse Occupational Health Center, U. Calif.-Irvine, 1981-85, ret., 1985; nursing chmn. ARC, 1964-70. Recipient Schering Occupational Health Nurse award, 1979; named Nurse of Yr., Harbor Area Assn. Occupational Health Nurses, 1985; Sarah I. Jenks scholarship established in her honor U. Calif.-Irvine, 1985. Mem. Am. Nurses Assn. (chmn. occupational health nurse forum 1968-72), Calif. State Nurses Assn. (pres. Centinela Valley 1963-65), Calif. State Occupational Health Nurses Assn., Am. Assn. Occupational Health Nurses, United Scottish Soc. Democrat. Presbyterian. Home: 17700-88 Avalon Blvd Carson CA 90746 Office: Southern Occupational Health Center Univ Calif Irvine 19722 MacArthur Blvd Irvine CA 92717

JENNER, KATHERINE ANN, construction rental company executive; b. Lufkin, Tex., June 30, 1945; d. John B. Whitehead and Velma G. (Reeves) Whitehead Ballard; children—Kimberly, Debbie. Student U. Mich., 1982. Ins. salesperson Rite Lambret Kelly, Detroit, 1973-75; real estate salesperson Bonk Real Estate, Mt. Clemens, Mich., 1975-79; owner, mgr. Recreational Vehicle Campground, Destin, Fla., 1979-83; owner, mgr. Jenner Enterprises, Inc., Destin Rental Ctr., 1983—. Sec., treas. Preservation of Destin; sec. Destin Theatre Group. Mem. Destin C. of C., Am. Bus. Women Assn., Am. Rental Assn. Republican. Baptist. Avocation: golf. Office: Jenner Enterprises Inc Destin Rental Ctr 110A Palmetto St Destin FL 32541

JENNESS, DEBRA DIANE, medical office administrator; b. Portland, Oreg., Sept. 12, 1954; d. Byron Edward and Emma Bessie (Ghilliasa) McDonnell; diploma Western Bus. U., 1973, Univ. Acad. Music, 1973; cert. Med. Sch. U. Oreg., 1975; m. Gordon D. Jenness, Dec. 31, 1975. Adminstrv. sec., Hydronics, Inc., Portland, 1973; exec. sec., claims processor CNA/Ins., Portland, 1973-74; claims analyst Aetna Medicare, Portland, 1973-76; tchr. math. S. Albany High Sch., Albany, Oreg., 1976; exec. sec. Plywood Components, Albany, 1977; exec. sec., office mgr. Wise Personnel, Corvallis, Oreg., 1977-78; sr. loan processor, 1st Nat. Bank Oreg., Salem, Oreg., 1978-83; loan shipping dir., secondary mktg. asst. State Fed. Savs. and Loan Assn., Corvallis, Oreg., 1983-85; med. sec. James R. Price, D.P.M., Albany, Oreg., 1985—; exec. sec. for div. mgr. Automation Tech. div. Intelledex, Inc., Corvallis, Oreg., 1986—; owner, operator Elf Express. Mem. Am. Inst. Banking, Nat. Secs. Assn., Am. Bus. Women's Assn., Christian Business Women's Assn., Benton Hospice Service, Beta Sigma Phi. Home: 4176 Durillo Pl SE Albany OR 97321 Office: 4565 SW Research Way Corvallis OR 97333

JENNINGS, B. JOELLE, educator; b. Phila., Nov. 8, 1944; d. John Joseph and Foresta (Cianfrogna) Rodgers.; m. James T. Jennings, Sept. 25, 1971 (div. 1981). B.A., Holy Family Coll., Phila., 1966; postgrad. in edn. Immaculate Heart Coll., Los Angeles, 1977. Cert. tchr., Calif. Intake worker Mental Health Devel. Ctr., Los Angeles, 1966-69; adminstrv. asst. Los Angeles Mut. Ins. Co., 1969-70; sec. med. staff Queen of Angels Hosp., Los Angeles, 1970-76; tchr. sci. Los Angeles Unified Sch. Dist, 1977-79; chmn. New Jewish High Sch., Los Angeles, 1980-83; research mgr. Heidrick & Struggles, Los Angeles, 1983—; cons. ednl. pvt. psychotherapist, Woodland Hills, Calif., 1979—. Hospice vol. St. Joseph Med. Ctr., Burbank, Calif. Mem. NEA, Calif. Tchrs. Assn. Office: 445 S Figueroa St Suite 2330 Los Angeles CA 90071

JENNINGS, BARBARA MIDGETT, health care administrator; b. Phila., May 24, 1938; d. Lucy A. Midgett and Etta Gurganus (Baum) Midgett; m. Fletcher H. Carr, Aug. 30, 1956 (div. 1964); children—Alton B. Carr, Moira Lynne Goldsworthy; m. Joseph E. Jennings, Sept. 28, 1972; children—Donnette, Karen, Pam, Jennifer. Nursing degree Norfolk Gen. Hosp., Old Dominion U., Va., 1973—. Cert. med. records adminstr. Quality assurance coordinator Portsmouth Psychiat. Ctr., Va., 1973-77; exec. dir. Colonial Va. Found., Virginia Beach, 1977-84; med. records cons., 1984—; owner small bus.; mem. clin. faculty Joint Commn. Accreditation of Hosps., 1977—; Co-author: Interqual Nursing Audit Series, 1979; JCAH Psychiatric Audit Seminars, 1980; JCAH Alcohol Treatment Series, 1981. Mem. Norfolk City Planning Commn., 1985—. Mem. Am. Med. Peer Rev. Assn., Am. Med. Records Assn., Nat. Assn. Female Execs., Am. Nurses Assn., Am. Bus. Women's Assn. Democrat. Methodist. Avocation: sailing. Home: 1300 E Ocean View Ave Norfolk VA 23503

JENNINGS, BETTY JEAN MCDONALD, educational administrator; b. Houston, May 10, 1930; d. Ernest Bois and Jessie Leah (Tullis) McDonald; m. James N. Jennings (div.); 1 dau., Lesajean McDonald Jennings. B.S., Prairie View U., 1949; M.Ed., 1958, vocat. cert., 1964, 70, 79, 82; student costume design Pratt Inst., 1951. Instr. home econs. Wiley Coll., Marshal, Tex., 1956; tchr. adult edn. Houston Ind. Sch. Dist., 1957-60, tchr. needle trades, 1956-79, vocat. counselor 1979-81, specialist vocat. counselor, 1981-83, asst. dir. bus. industry coordination, 1984—; instr., cons. Prairie View U., 1975-78; freelance model, Houston, 1956—; fashion show coordinator for community and ch. orgns., 1956—. Advisor modeling post Boy Scouts Am., Houston, 1975-82; judge Tex. local and state Blue Bonnet Beauty Contest, 1978—. Named Woman of Yr., Fashion Guild Houston, 1976; recipient Outstanding Adminstrv. Service award Yates Faculty, Houston, 1979, Outstanding Models award Tom Kato Models Found., 1976; Mary Gibbs Jones scholar Jones Found., 1946-49. Mem. Houston Profl. Assn., NEA, Tex. Tchrs. Assn., Am. Vocat. Assn., Houston Tchrs. Assn., Tex. Indsl. and Vocat. Assn., Delta Sigma Theta, Iota Lambda Sigma, Epsilon Phi Tau. Democrat. Baptist. Home: 1317 Live Oak St Houston TX 77003 Office: Occupational and Continuing Edn Div 3830 Richmond Ave Houston TX 77027

JENNINGS, CHERYL DENISE, history educator, program administrator; b. Sopchoppy, Fla., Aug. 13, 1954; d. Norman Jefferson and Lueberta (Godbolt) Jefferson; m. Larry Darnell Jennings, Sept. 21, 1976. B.S., Fla. A&M U., 1976. Tchr. Leon County Schs., Tallahassee, Fla., 1977—, program dir., chmn. gifted program Lincoln High Sch., 1983—. Vol., Assn. Retarded Citizens, 1982-85; co-race dir. Leon County Sickle Cell Found., 1983, 84, 85, Big Bend 4-C Council, 1985. Recipient Tchr. of Month award Lincoln High Sch., 1984, 85; 1985 Grand Prix Champion award Gulf Winds Track Club, 1983, 84, 85. Mem. Leon County Sch. Gifted Adv. Council, Leon Assn. Gifted Children. Democrat. Baptist. Avocation: competitive distance running. Home: 2708 Oak Ridge Rd Tallahassee FL 32304 Office: Leon County Schs Lincoln High Sch 3838 Trojan Trail Tallahassee FL 23201

JENNINGS, KAREN LYNN, lawyer; b. Mt. Holly, N.J., Nov. 14, 1956; d. Duane Merville and Lois (Harrison) Jennings. B.A. in Econs. cum laude, Wells Coll., 1978; J.D., U. N.Mex., 1982. Bar: N.Mex. 1982. Asst. dist. atty. 10th Jud. Dist. Dist. Atty.'s Office, Tucumcari, N.Mex., 1982-84; asst. dist. atty. adult felony div. 11th Jud. Dist., Farmington, N.Mex., 1984-85; assoc. firm Moeller and Burnam, Farmington, 1986—; law enforcement lectr., 1983-84. Editorial bd. Natural Resources Jour., 1981-82. Bd. dirs. Econ. Council Helping others, Farmington, 1985. Mem. ABA, N.Mex. Bar Assn. (criminal law sect.), N.Mex. Trial Lawyers Assn., San Juan County Bar Assn., Quay County Bar Assn. (treas. 1982-84, pres. 1984). Office: PO Box 210 Farmington NM

JENNINGS, LINDA GAIL, information services executive; b. Torrance, Calif., June 15, 1945; d. Herbert Chandler and Olive (Doench) Jennings; m. Kirby Jones, May 21, 1980. B.A. in English, Coll. of Wooster, 1967; M.A. in Ednl. Devel., Ohio State U., 1975. With dept. preventive medicine Ohio State U., Columbus, 1967-71, research found., 1971-73; with MCI Communications Corp., 1976-81, mgr. mktg. services, 1981-82, mgr. cop. devel., 1982-84, sr. mgr. corp. info. services, Washington, 1985—. Mem. Assoc. Info. Mgrs., Soc. Consumer Affairs Profls., Nat. Alliance for Women in Communications Industries. Avocations: travel; scuba diving; photography. Office: MCI Communications Corp 1133 19th St NW Washington DC 20036

JENNINGS, MADELYN PULVER, communications company executive; b. Saratoga Springs, N.Y., Nov. 23, 1934; d. George Joseph and Martha (Walsh) Pulver; B.A. in Bus. and Econs., Tex. Woman's U., 1956. Asst. dir. pub. relations Slick Airways, Dallas, 1956-58; asst. dir. radio-TV promotion VIP Service, Inc., N.Y.C., 1958-60; bus. mktg. planning Gen. Electric Co., Bridgeport, Conn., 1960-68, mgr. manpower planning, 1968-71, mgr. environ. support operation, 1971-73; v.p. human resources Standard Brands, Inc., N.Y.C., 1976-79; v.p. human resources Gannett Co., Rochester, N.Y., 1979-80, sr. v.p. personnel, Arlington, Va., 1980—. Trustee Russell Sage Coll., Gannett Found. Mem. Human Resources Planning Soc., Human Resources Roundtable; Newspaper Personnel Relations Assn., Am. Soc. Personnel Adminstrn., Am. Press Inst. (bd. dirs.), Conf. Bd., Yaddo Nat. Council. Office: Gannett Co PO Box 7858 Washington DC 20044

JENNINGS, MARCELLA GRADY, rancher, investor; b. Springfield, Ill., Mar. 4, 1920; d. William Francis and Magdalene Mary (Spies) Grady; student pub. schs.; m. Leo J. Jennings, Dec. 16, 1950 (dec.). Pub. relations Econolite Corp., Los Angeles, 1958-61; v.p., asst. mgr. LJ Quarter Circle Ranch, Inc., Polson, Mont., 1961-73, pres., gen. mgr., owner, 1973—; dir. Giselle's Travel Inc., Sacramento; fin. advisor to Allentown, Inc., Charlo, Mont.; sales cons. to Amie's Jumpin' Jacks and Jills, Garland, Tex. investor. Mem. Internat. Charolais Assn., Los Angeles County Apt. Assn. Republican. Roman Catholic. Home and office: 509 Mt. Holyoke Ave Pacific Palisades CA 90272

JENNINGS, MARY FRANCES, jewelry company executive, gemologist; b. Fairbanks, Alaska, Nov. 18, 1958; d. Robert L. and Billye H. (Barton) Corran; m. Gary R. Jennings, Apr. 3, 1979. Student U. Tex.-Austin, 1976-78, U. Tex.-Arlington, 1978, Eastern N. Mex. U., 1985, Gemologist Inst. Am., Sales rep. Snyder-Chenards, Austin, Tex., 1971-76; bank teller City Bank, Austin, 1977-78; exec. asst. Aspen Co., Dallas, 1978; ops. mgr. Golden Silver Mfg., Dallas, 1979-84; v.p. The Gold Source, Inc., Roswell, N.Mex., 1984—. Mem. Profl. Oriented Women, Aerobics and Fitness Assn. Am., Gemologist Inst. Am. Avocations: aerobics; swimming; snow skiing; water skiing; tennis; bowling. Office: Gold Source Inc 1400 W 2d St Roswell NM 88201

JENNINGS, SANDRA CHARLENE, retail store executive, designer; b. Dallas, Apr. 4, 1939; d. Charles Otis and Eula Mae (Williams) J.; children—Charles Haws, Amy Haws Jeffrey, Jay Haws, Larry Haws. Coordinating dir. Zales Corp., Dallas, 1976-77; pres. Fleming & Fleming, Inc., Dallas, 1977-78; sales mgr. Cockrell Wholesale, Dallas, 1979-80; pres. Jael Industries, Inc., Dallas, 1980—; organizer workshops. Trustee Suicide Prevention, Dallas, 1979-81; bd. dirs. Laos House, Austin, Tex., 1983—. Office: 2067 N Central Expressway Richardson TX 75080

JENNINGS, SISTER VIVIEN, college president; b. Jersey City; d. Eugene Oliver and Mary Alice (Smith) J. B.A., Caldwell Coll., 1960; M.A., Cath. U. Am., 1966; Ph.D., Fordham U., 1972; D.H.L. h.c. Caldwell Coll., 1975; Joined Sisters of St. Dominic, 1954; Superior Gen. 1969. Tchr. elem. and secondary schs., 1954-59; asst. prof. English, Caldwell Coll., 1959-69, now pres. Nat. chmn. Dominican Leadership Conf., 1974; chmn. region III, Leadership Conf. of Women Religious, nat. bd. 1974-76; founder Project Link, Newark, hon. D.Ed. Providence Coll.; del. Call to Action Conf., Detroit, 1976; mem. Dominican Leadership Conf., 1973-74. Author: The Valiant Woman at the Heart of Reconciliation, 1974. Address: Caldwell College Ryerson Ave Caldwell NJ 07006*

JENNINGS, TONI, state senator, construction company executive; b. Orlando, Fla., May 17, 1949; d. Jack C. and Margaret (Murphy) J. B.A., Wesleyan Coll., Macon, Ga., 1971; postgrad., Rollins Coll., 1972-73. Tchr. Killarney Elementary Sch., Winter Park, Fla., 1971-73; sec.-treas. Jack Jennings and Sons, Inc., Gen. Contractors, Orlando, 1973—; mem. Fla. Ho. of Reps., 1976-80; mem. Fla. Senate, 1980—, Republican leader pro tempore, 1982—, Rep. leader, 1984, mem. coms. personnel, retirement and collective bargaining, fin., taxation and claims, transp., exec. bus., rules and calendar. Active Sr. Citizens Adv. Council, Sea World, Winter Park Rep. Women's club, Leadership council, Rep. Women's Federated Club of Winter Park. Recipient Appreciation award Fla. Med. Assn. and Physicans of Fla., 1983, Legis. award Fla. Chiropractic Assn., 1983, Outstanding Service award Retail Grocers Assn. of Fla., 1983, Outstanding Efforts award Tampa Missing Children Help Ctr., 1983, Support of Law Enforcement award Fla. Sheriffs' Assn., 1983, Freedom award Women for Responsible Legis., 1982, Disting. Alumni award Wesleyan Coll., 1981, Outstanding Service award Homebuilders Assn. Mid-Fla., 1980, Spl. Commendation award Fla. Restaurant Assn., 1979, Meritorious Service award Fla. Fedn. Humane Socs., 1979; named Legislator of Yr. Fla. Assn. Realtors, 1984, Outstanding Rep. Woman of Yr. Orange County Rep. Exec. Com., 1983, Legislator of Yr. Orange County Young Rep. Club, 1980-81, Legislator of Yr. Assn. Builders and Contractors of Fla., 1978, Outstanding Woman in Govt. Orlando C. of C. Central City Com., 1977. Mem. Orlando-Winter Park Bd. Realtors, Assn. Builders and Contractors, Central Fla. Builders Exchange, Delta Kappa Gamma, Phi Kappa Phi, Kappa Delta Epsilon. Office: Fla Senate Dist #15 1032 Wilfred Dr Orlando FL 32803

JENNINGS, VIVIEN LEE, bookstore management and licensing organization executive; b. Little Rock, Ark., Mar. 7, 1945; d. Loron and Mildred Louise (Wright) Bolen; m. Richard Walker Jennings, Sept. 1, 1967; children—Geoffrey, Alison. B.A., Rhodes Coll., Memphis, 1967. Women's fiction cons. Ballantine Books, Inc., N.Y., 1981-82, Berkeley Pub. Group, N.Y., 1982-83; pres. Rainy Day Books, Inc., Fairway, Kans., 1975—. Editor nat. weekly market trend letter Boy Meets Girl. Exec. editor serialized women's fiction project Universal Press Syndicate, 1984. Author: The Romance Wars. Contbr. articles to profl. publs. Featured on nat. pub. radio and nat. TV programs. Mem. Greater Kansas City Booksellers Assn. (pres. 1980-82), Romance Writers Am., Inc. (bd. dirs.), Am. Booksellers Assn. (Abacus Group). Episcopalian. Club: Carriage (Kansas City). Home: 5413 Norwood Rd Fairway KS 66205 Office: Rainy Day Books Inc 2812 W 53d St Fairway KS 66205

JENNINGS-PURNELL, ANN SMITH, physician; b. Yemassee, S.C., Aug. 11, 1938; d. Benjamin and Hattie Smith; m. Albert Jennings (div. 1971); m. George Purnell, Mar. 25, 1978; children—William, Daniel, Albert, Eric. B.S., Sarah Lawrence Coll. 1975; postgrad. Med. Sch., Rutgers U., 1975-77; M.D., NYU, 1979. With U.S. Post Office, 1962-71; clk. Grassland Hosp., 1972-73; intern and resident Harlem Hosp., N.Y.C., 1979-82, asst. attending emergency room, 1981—, preceptor with physician assts. Community action bd. mem. CAP, 1981—. Democrat. Methodist. Office: Harlem Hosp 135th and Lenox New York NY 10037

JENSEN, ANNE TURNER, automobile service company executive; b. Upper Providence Twp., Pa., Sept. 15, 1926; d. Ellwood Jackson and Elizabeth Addis (Downing) Turner; student Hood Coll., 1944-45, Phila. Coll. Pharmacy and Sci., 1945-46, 47-48; m. Harry Frederick Jensen, Jr., Apr. 13, 1946; children—Frederick Howard, Richard Jordan, Peter Hielm. Legal sec. Robertson & Turner, Media, Pa., 1950-51; sec. Luncheon-is-Served, Media, 1951-53; asst. sec., treas. Delvale Realty Corp., Media, 1955-59; bookkeeper Turner Realty Co., 1960-64, William H. Turner, Atty., 1960-64, Media Auto Service, 1957-74; sec. Media Auto Service, Inc., 1957-84. Capt. Heard Fund Dr., 1958-60. Republican. Presbyterian. Clubs: DAR (chpt. regent 1971-74, state corr. sec. 1977-80, nat. chmn. 1974-77), Daughters of Am. Colonists, Daughters of Colonial Wars (state treas. 1974-77, 80-83), Magna Carta Soc., Daus. of 1812, Navy League U.S. (N.Y. Council). Home: Still Pond MD 21678

JENSEN, DORIS J., educational administrator; b. Sterling, Colo., Aug. 10, 1939; d. Clarence J. and Lillian Lucille (Lawrie) Buckley; m. R. Blair Jensen, Aug. 28, 1960; children—Steven J., Cheryl B. A.A., Graceland Coll., 1959; B.S., Central Mo. State U., 1961, M.A. in English, 1964; postgrad. in Ednl. Adminstrn., U. Mo.-Kansas City, 1986—. English instr. Central Mo. State U., Independence, 1969-74, U. Mo., Kansas City, 1974-80; registrar Cleveland Chiropractic Coll., Kansas City, 1980-81, dean student affairs and admissions, 1981—. Mem. Am. Assn. Coll. Registrars and Admissions Officers, Mo. Assn. Coll. Registrars and Admissions Officers, Phi Lambda Theta. Office: Cleveland Chiropractic College 6401 Rockhill Rd Kansas City MO 64131

JENSEN, ELOUISE HENRIE, civic worker; b. Manti, Utah, Jan. 20, 1932; d. Irven Lund and Orlene (Larsen) Henrie; m. Clayne R. Jensen, Mar. 14, 1952; children—Craig R., Michael H., Blake Jensen, Christian Jensen. Student Brigham Young U., 1950-53, Utah State U., 1958-62. Pres., Brigham Young Univ. Women, 1982, Utah Valley Symphony Guild, Utah, 1983-84; mem. housing bd. Brigham Young U., 1976-82. Mem. U.S. Tennis Assn., Utah Valley Symphony Bd. Republican. Mem. Ch. of Jesus Christ of Latter Day Saints. Clubs: Cleafon (pres. 1981), Etien (pres. 1979), Riverside Country (program chmn. 1985), Ridge Tennis (tournament chmn. 1984). Address: 1900 N Oak Ln Provo UT 84604

JENSEN, HELEN, musical artists management company executive; b. Seattle, June 30, 1919; d. Frank and Sophia (Kantosky) Leponis; student public schs., Seattle; m. Ernest Jensen, Dec. 2, 1939; children—Ernest, Ronald Lee. Co-chmn., Seattle Community Concert Assn., 1957-62; sec. family concerts Seattle Symphony Orch., 1959-61; hostess radio program Timely Topics, 1959-60; gen. mgr. Western Opera Co., Seattle, 1962-64, pres. 1963-64; v.p., dir., mgr. public relations Seattle Opera Assn., 1964—, preview artists Coordinator, 1981-84; bus. mgr. Portland (Oreg.) Opera Co., 1968, cons., 1967-69; owner, mgr. Helen Jensen Artists Mgmt., Seattle, 1970—. First v.p. Music and Art Found., 1981-84, pres., 1984-85. Recipient Cert., Women in Bus in the Field of Art, 1973. Mem. Met. Opera Guild, Friends of Opera, Am. Guild Mus. Artists, Music and Art Found., Seattle Opera Guild (pres., award of distinction 1983), Ballard Symphony League (sec.), Seattle Civic Opera Assn. (pres. 1981-86), Portland Opera Assn., Portland Opera Guild, Seattle Opera Assn. (Pub. service and Outstanding Civic Support award 1974), 200 Plus One, Lyric Preview Group, Past Pres. Assembly (pres. 1977-79) North Shore Performing Arts Assn. (pres. 1981). Club: Kenmore Community. Home: 19029 56th Ln NE Seattle WA 98155 Office: 716 Joseph Vance Bldg Seattle WA 98101

JENSEN, JOY DOLORES, real estate broker; b. Cushing, Okla., Jan. 30, 1938; d. J. D. and Nancy Grace (Franklin) Raper; m. Darrel F. Kuhlmann, June 1, 1958 (div. 1967); children—Kirsta Kae, Kari Gae; m. 2d, Victor Robert Jensen, Dec. 6, 1969. Student pub. schs. Legal pvt. sec. Pure Oil Co., Wichita, Kans., 1957-59; builder sec. Hudson Co., Boulder, 1960—, real estate property mgr., 1971; closings broker Time Unlimited, Boulder, 1971-76; real estate broker Remax of Boulder, Colo., 1976-80, Joy Jensen Realty, Boulder, 1980—. Mem. Colo. Real Estate Assn., Nat. Real Estate Assn., Boulder Bd. Realtors, North Suburban Bd. Realtors, Farm and Ranch Inst. Republican. Lutheran. Office: Joy Jensen Realty 3120 Folsom St Boulder CO 80302

JENSEN, KAREN KRISTINE, engineering administrator; b. Bklyn., Oct. 12, 1943; d. Peter Spangaard and Kathryn Mary (Kelleher) Jensen. B.S. in Personnel, Northeastern U., 1981; M.S. in Mgmt., Lesley Coll., 1982. Adminstrv. asst. Saxon Paper Corp., Brighton, Mass., 1963-70; exec. asst. M.S. Govt., Boston, San Francisco, 1970-72; engring. adminstr. Polaroid Corp., Cambridge, Mass., 1972—. Mem. Personnel bd. City of Winchester (Mass.), 1983—. Mem. Am. Soc. Personnel Adminstrn., Sigma Epsilon Rho. Roman Catholic. Office: Polaroid Corp 38 Henry St Cambridge MA 02139

JENSEN, LINDA SMERNOFF, financial and estate planner; b. Bingham Canyon, Utah, Sept. 23, 1942; d. Hyman and Norrene (Andreason) Smernoff; student U. Utah, 1960-63; m. Frank Jensen, Mar. 28, 1973; 1 son, Gary Bryan Fessenden. With Prudential Fed. Savs. & Loan Assn., Salt Lake City, 1965-68; office mgr. Knight Adjustment Bur., Salt Lake City, 1968-73; owner, mgr. LDR Profl. Billing, Salt Lake City, 1973-79; asst. dir. Phoenix Inst., 1982-84; v.p. Septre Group Ltd., Salt Lake City, 1980—; owner, operator Yes I Will, Inc., Salt Lake City, 1979—. Recipient WIN award Women's Info. Network, 1981, 83, 84; Pathfinder award Women in Bus. Conf. Com., 1986. Mem. Nat. Assn. Female Execs., Life Underwriters Assn. Salt Lake, Women's Life Underwriters Conf., Internat. Assn. Fin. Planners, Inst. Cert. Fin. Planners, Salt Lake Area C. of C. (speakers bur.), Women's Info. Network (founder, past pres.); Bus. and Profl. Women, Profl. Mortgage Women, Utah Profl. Sales Women's Assn. Office: 350 E 5th St S Suite 200 Salt Lake City UT 84111

JENSEN, MALCYE WISDOMA, health consultant, nursing educator; b. New Haven, June 4, 1930; d. James Wisdom Jones and Malcye Heros (Collins) Toney; m. James Alfred Bush, Apr. 25, 1954 (div. 1981); children—Michael, Kevin, Michele; m. 2nd Kurt Alan Jensen, June 21, 1981. B.A., Calif. State U., 1957; M.S., B.S., Loma Linda U., 1964, 52; Ph.D., Calif. Grad. Inst., 1983. R.N.; registered psychol. asst. Nursing instr. Orange Coast Coll., Costa Mesa, Calif., 1963-67; asst. prof. Loma Linda U., Calif., 1967-71; rehab. nurse Fireman's Fund Ins. Co., Los Angeles, 1973-76; nursing instr. Calif. Med. Ctr., Los Angeles, 1976-77; occupational health cons. Dept. Indsl. Relations, Los Angeles, 1977—; co-trainer State of Calif., 1983-85; lectr. Med. Media Assocs., East Hanover, N.J., 1984—; faculty sponsor Calif. Med. Ctr., 1976-77; mental health practitioner Pasadena Family Service, Los Angeles, 1984—. Author book chpt.; contbr. articles to profl. jours. Mem. sch. bd. San Gabriel Acad., Calif., 1984—; workshop facilator community chs., Altadena, Los Angeles, 1983—, lectr., 1983—. Mem. So. Calif. Assn. Black Psychologists, Nat. Assn. Black Psychologists, Research Council of Scripps Clinic, The Menniger Found., Nat. Assn. Female Execs., Oakwood Coll. Alumni, Loma Linda Alumni, Rose Soc. Avocations: reading; traveling. Home: 427-42E Mission Rd Alhambra CA 91801 Office: State of Calif Dept Indsl Relations 3560 Wilshire Room 304 Los Angeles CA 90010

JENSEN, MARSHA KAY, printer; b. Audubon, Iowa, Feb. 11, 1957; d. Delbert Dean and Elizabeth Ellen (Oliver) J.; Student Westmar Coll., 1975-76. Mgr., Carroll Copy Ctr. & Print Shop, Inc., Iowa, 1978-80, owner-mgr., 1980—. Mem. Carroll C. of C., Carroll Jaycees. Lutheran. Avocations: painting; yardwork; aquaria. Office: 504 N Clark St Carroll IA 51401

JENSEN, MARY LORENE, lawyer; b. Topeka, Kans., Apr. 6, 1949; d. John M. and Lorene M. (Rollheiser) Davis; m. Paul W. Jensen, June 12, 1971 (div. Mar. 1978). B.B.A., U. Mo.-Kansas City, 1971, J.D. with distinction, 1980. Bar: Mo. 1980; C.P.A., Mo. Revenue agent IRS, Kansas City, 1971-77; law clk. Linde Thomson, Kansas City, 1978-80, assoc., 1980-82; ptnr. Husch, Eppenberger, Donohue, Cornfeld, Kansas City, 1982—. Bd. dirs. John Knox Village, Lee's Summit, Mo., 1982—, chmn. bd. dirs., 1985—; trustee John Knox Village Found., Lee's Summit, 1983—. Mem. ABA, Mo. Bar Assn., Jackson County Bar Assn., Kansas City Bar Assn., Bench and Robe Soc., Beta Gamma Sigma. Office: Husch Eppenberger et al 2500 City Ctr Square Kansas City MO 64105

JENSEN, MYRTLE TAYLOR, accountant; b. Kelso, Wash., July 20, 1917; d. Perry Edward and Ada May (Hubbard) Taylor; student U. So. Calif., U. Calif. at Los Angeles; m. Walter P. Jensen, May 20, 1936. Prin., M.T. Jensen, C.P.A., Los Angeles, 1947—. C.P.A., Calif. Mem. Am. Inst. C.P.A.'s, Calif. Soc. C.P.A.'s Soc. Calif. Accountants, Nat. Soc. Pub. Accountants. Republican. Home: 912 E Windsor Rd Glendale CA 91205 Office: 4201 Wilshire Blvd Suite 218 Los Angeles CA 90010

JENSEN, PATRICIA ANN, lawyer; b. Osage City, Kans., Apr. 27, 1942; d. Warren G. and Velma Louise (Evans) Glenn; m. Richard Henry Passman, Sept. 2, 1961 (div. Feb. 1977); children—Ramona Jean, Richard Henry, John Patrick; m. 2d, Carl Arthur Jensen, June 14, 1977. B.A. in Psychology, Coll. St. Catherine, St. Paul, 1974; J.D., William Mitchell Coll. Law, St. Paul, 1978; grad. Dartmouth Inst., 1982. Bar: Minn. 1978, U.S. Dist. Ct. Minn. 1979. Researcher, Minn. State Senate, St. Paul, 1975-76; ptnr. Jensen & Jensen, Sleepy Eye, Minn., 1977-79; spl. asst. to Gov. of Minn., St. Paul, 1979-81; dir. govt. relations Pillsbury Co., Mpls., 1981-85; shareholder, sr. atty., legis. counsel firm Popham, Haik, Schnobrick, Kaufman & Doty, Ltd., Mpls., 1985—; dir. Pillsbury Polit. Action Com., 1983-85; exec. dir. Nat. Adv. Council on Women's Ednl. Programs, 1984-85. Nat. adv. bd. Council Am. Pvt. Edn., 1983-84; bd. dirs. Urban Concerns Workshop, 1983-84, Chem. Dependency Appeals Bd., 1983-84, Ramsey County Abuse Council, 1985—, Pillar Credit Union, Minn. Battered Women's Task Force, 1980-81; adv. bd. St. Paul YWCA, 1983-84. Mem. ABA, Minn. Bar Assn., Ramsey County Bar Assn., Pi Gamma Mu. Republican. Roman Catholic. Club: Midland Hills Golf (Arden Hills, Minn.). Home: 3530 Ridgewood Rd Arden Hills MN 55112 Office: 4344 IDS Center Minneapolis MN 55402

JENSEN, SENTA HELLA, speech pathologist, translator, writer; b. Hamburg, Ger., Sept. 17, 1920; d. John Henry and Martha Erna (Wiering) Poock; cert. Webster Bus. Coll., Jersey City, 1938; B.A., Hunter Coll., 1950; M.A. in Speech Pathology, 1953; m. Christian T. Jensen, June 26, 1943 (dec.); children—Lenore Christina Jensen Simon. Fgn. lang. sec., N.Y.C., 1938-42; co-owner John Poock Constrn. Co., Ridgefield Park, N.J., 1942-52; pvt. practice speech pathology, N.Y.C., 1953-61; dir., owner Bergen Speech Clinic, Ridgefield Park, 1953-61; speech pathologist Cornell U., N.Y. Hosp., dir. plastic surgery cleftpalate speech clinic, 1953-61; chief speech clinician Einstein Med. Center, Phila., 1964; speech pathologist Pennsauken (N.J.) Public Schs. and Bucks County (Pa.) Public Schs., 1965-68; speech pathologist, hearing clinician De La Warr Sch. Dist., New Castle, Del., 1968-72; free-lance learning disability cons., 1972-74; coordinator, cons. N.J. Dept. Mental Retardation, 1974-75; adminstrv. dir. Betty Bacharach Rehab. Hosp., Pomona, N.J., 1975-78; founder, dir. 1st cleftpalate speech clinic and aphasia clinic in S. Jersey, 1976-78. Mem. Legis. Task Force Com. Am. Speech and Hearing Assn., Washington, 1978-80. Fund raiser Easter Seals. Lic. speech pathologist, Md., Del. Mem. Am. Speech, Lang. and Hearing Assn. (cert.), N.Y. Acad. Scis., Lit. Soc. Found. (hon.), Am. Scandinavian Found., Internat. Council Exceptional Children, Delta Phi Alpha, Sigma Epsilon Phi. Office: The Spoken Word PO Box 724 Haddonfield NJ 08033

JENSEN, VIVIAN NELSON, educator, state legislator; b. Redmond, Utah, Apr. 16; d. Franklin Theodore and Annette Christine (Willardson) Nelson; m. Moroni Lundby Jensen, Mar. 8, 1934; children—Moroni Leon, Jerold Lynn. B.S., Columbia U., 1950; postgrad. U. Utah, 1952-55. Tchr. Sevier Sch. Dist., Salina, Utah, 1940-50; librarian Granite Sch. Dist., Salt Lake City, 1950-56, tchr., 1956-59, counselor, 1959-76; mem. Utah Senate, 1980-81; mem. Utah Ho. of Reps., 1982-84. Named Woman of Achievement, Bus. and Profl. Womens Club Utah, Salt Lake City, 1983. Mem. Order Women Legislators. Democrat. Mormon. Avocation: writing. Home: 2940 Filmore St Salt Lake City UT 84106

JENSEN, WILMA, superintendent of schools; b. Choteau, Mont., Dec. 12, 1918; d. Robert and Edith Olive (Watson) van Scherpenzeel; m. John L. Jensen, Jan. 17, 1942 (div. 1967); 1 child, Dorothy Marie Backland. B.S., No. Mont. Coll., 1966; M.Ed., U. Mont., 1981. Tchr., Baker Sch. Dist., Dutton, Mont., 1939-40, Agawam Sch. Dist., Mont., 1940-45, Erickson Sch. Dist., Conrad, Mont., 1945-46, Pendroy Sch., Mont., 1949-52, 55-64, Troy Sch., Mont., 1964-67, Dutton Sch., Mont., 1967-78; county supt. schs. Teton County, Choteau, 1979—; sec. Big Sky Spl. Edn. Co-op, Conrad, 1981—. Mem. Soroptimist Internat. Choteau & vicinity, 1981—; sec. Teton County Women's Republican Club, Choteau, 1979—; mem. Teton County Rep. Central Com., Choteau, 1978—. Mem. Mont. Assn. County Sch. Supts., Sch. Adminstrs. Mont., Am. Assn. Sch. Adminstrs., Assn. Supervision and Curriculum Devel., Delta Kappa Gamma. Methodist. Home: PO Box 292 15 3d Ave SW Choteau MT 59422 Office: Teton County Supt Schs Courthouse Choteau MT 59422

JEPPESEN, SUSAN QUANDT, marketing executive; b. Milw., Sept. 8, 1954; d. Raymond W. and Ruth M. (Sievers) Quandt; m. Edward Aloes, Kersten (div.); 1 dau., Jennifer Elizabeth; m. 2d, Eric David Jeppesen; 1 dau., Katherine Joan. B.S. in Acctg., Valparaiso U., 1976; M.B.A., U. Wis., 1978. Acct. E.C. Hicks & Assocs., Merrillville, Ind., 1976-77; market research analyst Wis. Telephone Co., Milw., 1979, S.C. Johnson & Son Inc., Racine, Wis., 1980; sales fin. cons. Wis. Telephone Co., Milw., 1981-82; mgr. sales support AT&T Info. Systems, Chgo., 1983; comptroller Ameritech Communications Inc., Chgo., 1984, dir. product mgmt., 1984—; prof. mktg. Alverno Coll., Milw., 1982; instr. mktg. Milw. Area Tech. Coll., 1982. Mem. Am. Mktg. Assn. (pres. Milw. chpt. 1982-83, pres. elect 1981-82, v.p. communications 1980-81), Chgo. Zool. Soc., Am. Statis. Assn. Home: 44 Golf Ave Clarendon Hills IL 60514 Office: Ameritech Communications Inc 300 S Riverside St Chicago IL 60606

JERNIGAN, JEAN ALLEN, business official, newspaper reporter; b. Brookline, Mass., May 26, 1923; d. Langdon and Dorothy (Talbot) Allen; A.A., Garland Jr. Coll., 1942; m. Roger R. Jernigan, May 31, 1943; children—Roger, Jeffrey, Bruce, Linda. Fashion and beauty editorial asst. Boston Herald Traveler, 1942-44; news editor Sun Newspapers, Contra Costa County, Calif., 1958-64; aide to county supr. Contra Costa County, 1964-66; dir. public relations Children's Hosp. Med. Center, Oakland, Calif., 1966-68; women's editor, feature writer Berkeley (Calif.) Gazette, 1968-78; dir. public relations, asst. exec. dir. Berkeley-East Bay Humane Soc., 1978-81; adminstrv. asst. to v.p. fin Cetus Corp., Berkeley, 1981-83; group exec. asst. Triad Systems Corp., 1983—; freelance reporter Contra Costa Suns, Lafayette, Calif., 1979-80. Mem. Women in Communication, East Bay Press Club, Contra Costa Press Club. Republican. Office: 1252 Orleans Dr Sunnyvale CA 94088

JEROME, ARDIS DIANE, sales and operations director; b. Glasgow, Mont., Nov. 22, 1943; d. Hartvik Palmer and Agnes Christine (Buen) Garsjo; m. Roy E. Jerome, Mar. 17, 1962 (div. 1980); 1 child: Vincent Roy Jerome; m. Bernhard C. Uiterwijk, Nov. 30, 1985. Student, Spokane Community Coll. Mgr., Kwik Print, Missoula, Mont., 1967-70; owner, mgr. Econo Print, Billings, Mont., 1970-76; sales and ops. dir. Goodwill Industries, Spokane, Wash., 1977-81; mtkg. dir. Big Sky Airlines, Billings, Mont., 1982-83; mktg. dir. Easter Seals/Goodwill, Great Falls, Mont., 1983-85; sales and ops. dir. Goodwill Industries, San Francisco, 1985—; 1st v.p. Downtown Bus. Council, Gt. Falls, Mont., 1983-84. Recipient DAR Good Citizenship award, 1961; You've Earned Your Spurs award Easter Seals/Goodwill, 1984; Leadership award Gt. Falls C. of C., 1984. Mem. Sales and Mtkg. Execs. (bd. dirs. 1986-88), Mont. Mfg. and Mktg. Assn. (charter mem. 1983), Gt. Falls Advt. Fedn. Lutheran. Home: 10 Mabrey Ct San Francisco CA 94124 Office: Goodwill Industries 980 Howard San Francisco CA 94103

JEROME, BETTE, actress, speaker; b. Newport News, Va.; d. Elias and Sophie (Harris) J.; m. Samuel M. Bialek, June 26, 1960; children by previous marriage—Alan Craig Rafel, Lisa Rafel Himelfarb. Stage and radio actress, concert artist, choral condr., TV producer/moderator, writer, 1953—; narrator govt. and industry tng. films; actress, spokesvoice commls.; pres., exec. dir. BJB Prodns., Ltd.; producer radio programs including Mind's Eye Theatre, Foggy Bottom, Interact; tchr. dynamic speech for TV and radio newscasters, announcers; condr. speech and spokespersons workshops. Recipient Emmy award, AAUW award, Dept. Indian Affairs award, Gold Mike award McCalls. Mem. Am. Women in Radio and TV (pres. Washington chpt. 1971-72), AFTRA (pres. Washington/Balt. local 1973-75), Nat. Acad. TV Arts and Scis., Screen Actors Guild, Actors Equity Assn. Home: 2737 Devonshire Pl NW Washington DC 20008 Office: 445 Fifth Ave New York NY 10016

JERRIS, MILDRED CAROL, mathematics educator; b. Buffalo, Feb. 17, 1928; d. Philip J. and Ida P. (Incavo) Scaffidi; B.A., U. Buffalo, 1948; M.A., N.Y. State Coll. Tchrs., 1955, postgrad., 1970-72; postgrad. Nova U., 1984-86; m. Richard Jerris, Apr. 10, 1950; children—Robert, Janice, Keith, Karen. Tchr., Buffalo Pub. Schs., 1948-53, Amherst (N.Y.) Jr. High Sch., 1957-58, DeLand (Fla.) Jr. High Sch., 1967-72; tchr., dept. head math. Nova Middle Sch., Ft. Lauderdale, Fla., 1972—; mem. curriculum devel. com. Broward County Schs., 1980-85; tchr. cons. Mathematics 6, 1983; coach math. competition teams. Treas., DeLand Children's Mus., 1969-71. Stetson U. scholar, 1967; NSF grantee SUNY, 1970. Mem. NEA, Fla. Edn. Assn., Classroom Tchrs. Assn., Nat., Fla. (dir. dist. VII 1983-85), Broward County (south central dist. dir. 1985-87); councils tchrs. of math., Delta Kappa Gamma (v.p. 1980-82, 84-86), Gamma Beta Chi (pres. 1986—). Home: 8550 SW 26th Pl Ft Lauderdale FL 33328 Office: 3602 SW College Ave Ft Lauderdale FL 33314

JERSON, CAROL ANNE, industrial engineer, management consultant; b. Worcester, Mass., Feb. 17, 1957; d. Samuel Albert and Anne Rose (Shablin) Alukas; m. Jack Ted Jerson, Sept. 16, 1983. B.S. magna cum laude, Emerson Coll., 1979, M.S., 1982. Loss prevention rep. Liberty Mut. Ins. Co., Boston and Miami, 1980-81, Am. Gen. Fire and Casualty, Houston, 1982-83; mgmt. cons. Boeing Mil. Airplane Co., Wichita, Kans., 1984-85, Patricia Stevens Career Coll., 1984-85; cons. Liberty Mut. Ins. Co., Boston, John Hancock Ins. Co., Boston, Am. Inst. Banking, Boston, 1979-80. Host cable TV Carol Alukas Show, 1974-75; co-host radio show That's Life, 1974-75. Recipient Gold Key award Emerson Coll., 1977; vol. Wichita Radio Reading Service. Mem. Assn. Safety Engrs., Soc. Advancement Mgmt. (sec. 1980), Am. Helicopter Soc., North Dade C. of C., Houston C. of C., Gamma Sigma Sigma.

JERVIS, JANIS WILLIAMS, public service organization executive; b. Wilmington, N.C., Apr. 5, 1924; d. R. Saunders and Thelma J. (Pickard) Williams; m. Frederick Martin Jervis, Sept. 23, 1947; children—Bruce Martin, Ellen Day, Jane Winfield. B.A., U. N.C., 1947; postgrad. U. N.H., 1947-49. Freelance writer, Durham, N.H., 1960-71; co-founder, seminar leader, dir. publs., co-dir. Ctr. for Constructive Change, Durham, 1971—; mgmt. cons., 1974—; treas., dir. Delphi Mgmt. Systems, Durham, 1981-85. Trustee, Gruber Found., 1981—; active City/Town Planning Forums, 1975—. Saul O. Sidore Found. grantee, 1979-80. Author: Change: Piecemeal or Comprehensive, 1975; contbr. numerous articles to profl. jours. Office: Center for Constructive Change 16 Strafford Ave Durham NH 03824

JESSEE, VIRGINIA MAE, collections service executive; b. Shawnee, Okla., Nov. 22, 1948; d. Roy Albert Akers and Ruby Lee (Moore) Akers Smith; m. Kenneth Hugh Jessee, Apr. 12, 1968; children—Katherine Gail, Michele Lynnette. Grad. high sch., Woodland, Calif. Sales clk. Sprouse Reitz, Woodland, 1966-68; clerical worker Doctors and Mchts. Collections Service, Woodland, 1968-76; qualified mgr. Yolo County Collections, Woodland, 1977-80, co-owner, operator 1980—. Mem. Calif. Assn. Collectors (sec. unit 2, 1984—), Woodland Women's Bowling Assn. (bd. dirs. 1983—), Woodland Women's 500 Club (v.p. 1983—). Avocations: auto racing; fishing; bowling; camping. Office: Yolo County Collections 313 4th St Suite 6 Woodland CA 95695

JESSOP, JANICE SUZANNE, educational administrator; b. Yuma, Ariz., Dec. 12, 1937; d. Jack Baker and Rosemary Emmaline (Madden) J. B.A., San Diego State U., 1959, M.A., 1967. Cert. secondary tchr., Calif., ednl. adminstr., Calif. Tchr. Rosary High Sch., San Diego, 1958, Grossmont Union High Sch. Dist., La Mesa, Calif., 1959-77; adminstr. Calif. Interscholastic Fedn.-San Diego Sect., 1977—; counselor Montecito-Sequoia Camps, Santa Barbara, Calif., 1959; cons. rules com. Nat. Fedn. State High Sch. Assns., Kansas City, Mo., 1978-82. Dir. Ward Sports-Camp div. Ch. of Jesus Christ of Latterday Saints, La Mesa, Calif., 1967-68, Stake Sports Camp, 1969-70. Recipient Outstanding Achievement award Calif. Athletic Dirs. Assn., 1977. Mem. San Diego Council for Adminstrv. Women in Edn., Nat. Council for Adminstrv. Women in Edn., Calif. Assn. Health, Physical Edn., Recreation and Dance (cons. badminton 1970; Service Recognition award 1980), NOW, Women's Equity Action League. Democrat. Mormon. Avocations: golf; motorhome travel. Home: 3040 Udall St San Diego CA 92106 Office: Calif Interscholastic Fedn-San Diego Sect 6401 Linda Vista Rd San Diego CA 92111

JESSUP, MARY FROST, retired survey statistician, social and economic researcher; b. N.Y.C., June 18, 1902; d. David Stuart Dodge and Maud Ogden (Heath) J. A.B., Vassar Coll., 1925; M.A., Columbia U., 1930. Cert., U.S. Civil Service Commn. Surveyor, City of N.Y., 1925-26; research asst. Inst. Social and Religious Research-Rockefeller Found., N.Y.C., 1929-32; asst. dir., field dir. consumer purchase study U.S. Depts. Labor, Agri. 1936-37, 42; researcher div. hist. studies, U.S. Dept. Labor, 1943-44, Field Progress Br. U.S. Dept. Army, 1944-46; spl. asst. gen. dir. AAUW, Washington, 1954-56; research analyst Office of Equal Opportunity, U.S. Dept. Labor, 1971-73; research assoc. social research br., U.S. Dept. of Human Resources, Washington, 1973-76; mem. staff Women's Ednl. Research AAUW, Washington br., 1983-86; cons. and lectr. in field. Contbr. articles to profl. jours. Area chmn. United Way, N.W. sect., Washington, 1960's; bd. dirs., pres. All Souls Housing Corp., 1983-86; bd. dirs. Change All Souls Housing Corp., 1975—. Recipient Disting. Service citation All Souls Unitarian Ch., 1983, citation Human Rights Day, AAUW, Washington, 1976, 1985. Mem. AAUW (past v.p. program and mem. com. Washington br.) (pres.'s award, 1985), Nat. Women's Democratic Club, Vassar Coll. Assn. of Washington, Columbia Univ. of Washington (past pres.). Club: Garden of Montrose (Pa.), Montrose. Avocations: bridge; landscape painting; swimming; golf; tennis. Home: 2853 Ontario Rd NW Washington DC 20009

JESTER, JANICE MAY, nurse; b. Muncie, Kans., Jan. 4, 1941; d. Jessie Theodore and Gusta Fern (Bilyeu) J. Diploma Nursing, Bethany Hosp. Sch. Nursing, Kansas City, Kans., 1962. R.N. Staff nurse Bethany Med. Ctr., Kansas City, Kans., 1962-65, head nurse, 1965-70, rehab. coordinator, 1970-74, rehab. and enterostomal therapy nurse specialist, 1974—. Bd. dirs. Cancer Action, Inc., Kansas City, Kans., 1974-86, pres. bd., 1981-83; bd. dirs. Hospice Care Mid-Am., Kansas City, Mo., 1980-86; United Cancer Council, Inc., 1984; mem. nat. bd. Make Today Count, since 1986—; dir. children's dept. Faith Temple Family Worship Ctr., singer gospel music group. Mem. United Ostomy Assn. (nat. bd. dirs. 1984-87, advisor Greater Kansas City chpt. 1974-86, Sam Dubin award 1985), World Council for Enterostomal Therapy, Internat. Assn. for Enterostomal Therapy (bd. dirs. 1977-84, treas. 1980-84. Named Woman of Yr., Bus. and Profl. Women, Kansas City, Kans., 1984. Home: 3144 S 53d St Kansas City KS 66106 Office: Bethany Med Ctr 51 N 12th St Kansas City KS 66102

JETER, CHRYSTAL CARR, librarian, storyteller; b. Los Angeles, June 30, 1948; d. King and Naomi Ruth (Shackles) Carr; m. Abraham Jeter, Jr., Dec. 29, 1979. B.A., Calif. State U.-Los Angeles, 1970; M.L.S., U. So. Calif., 1972; postgrad. UCLA, 1976-77, U. Alaska, Anchorage, 1977-78, U. Wash., 1983. Library staff asst. Occidental Coll., Eagle Rock, Calif., 1971-72; librarian trainee Los Angeles Pub. Library, 1972; children's and adult librarian Inglewood (Calif.) Pub. Library, 1972-77; instr. speech dept. Los Angeles S.W. Coll., 1976-77; br. librarian Anchorage Mcpl. Libraries, 1977-84, asst. mcpl. librarian for spl. services, 1984-85, asst. librarian for community services, 1985—; bd. dirs. Alaska Pub. TV, 1978—. Bd. dirs. Alaska chpt. March of Dimes, 1982-83, Alaska Double Dutch League, 1982-83; storyteller Anchorage Sch. Dist., 1978—; active Alaska Black Caucus, 1982—; pianist Anchorage Ch. of God. Mem. ALA, Alaska Library Assn. (chmn. publicity 1979-80; local v.p. 1983), NAACP, Delta Sigma Theta. Democrat. Home: 740 Bounty Dr Anchorage AK 99515 Office: Anchorage Municipal Libraries 524 W 6th Ave Anchorage AK 99501

JETER, KATHERINE LESLIE BRASH (MRS. ROBERT MCLEAN JETER, JR.), lawyer; b. Gulfport, Miss., July 24, 1921; d. Ralph Edward and Rosa Meta (Jacobs) Brash; B.A., Tulane U., 1943, J.D., 1945; m. Robert McLean Jeter, Jr., May 11, 1946. Admitted to La. bar, 1945; assoc. mem. Montgomery, Fenner & Brown, New Orleans, 1945-46, Tucker, Jeter & Jackson, and predecessor firms, Shreveport, La., 1947-79, mem., 1980—judge pro-tem Dist. Ct., Caddo Parish, 1982; hon consul of France, Shreveport, 1982—. Pres., Little Threatre Shreveport, 1966-67, YWCA, 1963, LWV, 1950-51; treas. Am. Nat. Theatre and Acad., Shreveport, 1963; pres. Shreveport Art Guild, 1974-75; mem. council La. State Law Inst., 1980—; adv. com. La. Civil Code Revision, 1973; trustee Pub. Affairs Research Council, 1976-81, exec. com., 1981—. Recipient Disting. Grad. award Tulane Law Sch., 1983. Mem. ABA, La. Bar Assn., Shreveport Bar Assn. (pres. 1986), Nat. Assn. Women Lawyers, Shreveport Assn. Women Attys., La. Law Inst., Jr. League Shreveport, Order of Coif, Phi Beta Kappa. Editor: Tulane Law Rev., 1945. Home: 3959 Maryland Ave Shreveport LA 71106 Office: 905 Louisiana Tower 401 Edwards St Shreveport LA 71101

JETT, MILDRED SUNDAY, nurse, administrator; b. Bessmer, Ala., July 1, 1947; d. Jimmie and Inez (Norwood) Sunday; B.S.N. magna cum laude, U. Mich., 1975; L.P.N. diploma No. Mich. U., 1967; m. Arthur Robert Jett, Aug. 15, 1970; children—Nataki Elissar, Kanye Kamau. Lic. practical nurse Providence Hosp., Southfield, Mich., 1968-70; nurse St. Luke's Hosp., Marquette, Mich., 1970-72; lic. practical nurse Univ. Hosp., Ann Arbor, Mich., 1972-74, staff nurse, 1976-77; inservice instr. Kirwood Gen. Hosp., Detroit, 1976-77, dept. head, ednl. dir. hosp. staff devel., 1977—; tchr. CPR to sr. citizens. Capt., Nurses Corps, USAR. Mem. Detroit Black Nurses Assn. (2d v.p. 1978-80, 80-82), Am. Nurses Assn., Nat. Black Nurses Assn., Met. Detroit Health Edn. Council, Met. Detroit Coalition for Blood Pressure Control, Mich. Soc. Instructional Tech., Cable Health Coalition, Delta Sigma Theta, Sigma Theta Tau (membership com. 1975-76). Mem. Christian Ch. Office: 4059 W Davison Detroit MI 48238

JEWELL, DOROTHY LOUISE BEATTY, mortician; b. Newark, June 21, 1932; d. Edward and Muezetta (Grubbs) Jewell; m. Marvin Ernest Beatty, Jr., Sept. 15, 1956. Cert. Atlantic County Vocat. Sch., 1957; diploma Eckels Coll. Mortuary Sci., Pa., 1954. Apprentice mortician Donaways Mortuary, Atlantic City, 1950-55; mortician Woody Funeral Home, Newark, 1955-56; trade embalmer Williams Funeral Home, Phila., 1956, Greenidge Funeral Home, Atlantic City, 1962-72, DeBaptist Funeral Home, Atlantic City, 1972-78, Wesley Funeral Home, Bridgeton, N.J., 1972-80; mortician Jewell Funeral Home, Inc., Atlantic City, 1980—, also pres., owner; eye enucleator Eye Inst. N.J., 1979—, Eye Found. Delaware Valley, Phila., 1981—. Mem. N.J. Funeral Dirs. Assn., West Jersey Funeral Dirs. Assn., Nat. Funeral Dirs. Assn., Morticians Assn., NAACP (life), United Sons and Daus. of Islands. Club: Soroptimist (dir. 1983-85). Lodge: Order Eastern Star. Office: Jewell Funeral Home Inc 705 Arctic Ave Atlantic City NJ 08401

JILEK, ANITA GAIL, marketing and sales promotion executive; b. Oak Park, Ill., Sept. 20, 1951; d. Robert and Elsie Ruth (Rosenfeld) J.; B.S., U. Ill., Urbana-Champaign, 1973, M.A., 1974. Product sales mgr. Zenith Radio Corp., Chgo., 1975-77; div. dir. House of Vision Inc., Chgo., 1977-80; area mgr. Twentieth Century Fox Video, Detroit, 1980-81; gen. mgr. Feldman Assocs., Chgo., 1981-83, asst. v.p., 1983-85, v.p., 1985—; v.p. Incentive Travel Corp., Fulfillment Awards Ltd., 1983—; dir. Advt. & Design Services, Ltd.; mem. career day com. Northwestern U.; tchr. French cuisine Lyons Twp. (Ill.) High Sch. Adult Edn., 1977-78. Mem. blood assurance program Hinsdale (Ill.) Hosp., 1977—; mem. Oak Brook (Ill.) Park Dist. Com., 1980—. Mem. Nat. Assn. Female Execs., Nat. Premium Sales Execs., U. Ill. Alumni Assn. (life), Alpha Xi Delta Alumna Assn. Home: 1417 W Cuyler Chicago IL 60613 Office: 213 W Institute #703 Chicago IL 60610

JILES, SANDRA DIXON, construction company executive; b. Chgo., Sept. 18, 1949; d. James O. and Mary M. Dixon; m. Leroy Jiles, Jr., Aug. 5, 1978; children—Nathaniel, David. B.S. in Bus. Adminstrn., Roosevelt U., Chgo., 1971, M.B.A., 1977. Asst. dir. United Builders Assn., Chgo., 1971-75; adminstrv. exec. UBM, Inc., Chgo., 1975—; asst. buyer Sears, Roebuck & Co., Chgo., 1977-80. Recipient Young Blacks Doing Their Thing award Sta. WBEE, 1970; Filene fellow Roosevelt U., 1972-73. Mem. Am. Mgmt. Assn., Nat. Assn. Market Developers (treas. 1974-76), Phi Gamma Nu. Pentecostal. Avocations: music; theater; church's; young women's group; church's tape program. Office: UBM Inc 330 S Wells Chicago IL 60606

JIMENEZ, CARLA BARBARA, legal assistant; b. Santa Clara, Las Villas, Cuba, May 17, 1952; came to U.S., 1979; d. Amado Enrique and Nilda (Martinez) J.; m. Danilo Monzon, Sept. 4, 1971 (div. Dec. 1980); 1 son, Danilo Enrique. B.A., Universidad Nacional, Managua, Nicaragua, 1975; B.S., Fla. Internat. U., 1983; postgrad St. Thomas U. Sch. Law, 1984—. Exec. bilingual sec. Citibank N.A., Managua, 1972-75; ins. exec. Am. Internat. Underwriters, Tequcigalpa, Honduras and Managua, 1975-79; exec. bilingual sec. CBS Records Internat., Coral Gables, Fla., 1979-81; legal asst. G. David O'Leary, Esquire, Miami, 1981—, sec., exec. sec. Dominican Am. C. of C., Miami, 1980—. Mem. Nat. Assn. Female Execs., ABA. Office: Law Offices 2260 SW 8th St Miami FL 33134

JINKS, PAMELA FERN, meat processing quality control inspector; b. Wichita, Kans., May 5, 1953; d. Emmanuel Henry and Maxine (Wilt) J. Student Wichita State U., 1979-82. Quality control insp. Safeway Meat Processing, Wichita, Kans., 1978—, supr. trainee. Mem. Nat. Assn. Female Execs. Democrat. Home: 220 N Young Wichita KS 67212 Office: Safeway Meat Processing 2323 S Sheridan Wichita KS 67213

JNAH, EDWIGE CLAUDIA, designer; b. Paris, Sept. 26, 1946; came to U.S., 1965, naturalized, 1974; d. Marian and Christine Janina (Piekarski) Babeluck; B.A., Art Inst. Chgo., 1971; divorced; 1 son, N. Eric. Designer, Rydertypes, Chgo., 1966-67; freelance designer, 1967-72; art dir. Ladd/Wells/Presba, Chgo., 1972-75; graphic art coordinator U.S. League Savs. Assns., Chgo., 1975-78; Pres. Claudia Jnah Design, Inc., Chgo., 1978—. Vol., N.W. Neighborhood Fedn. Mem. Nat. Assn. Women Bus. Owners, Women in Mgmt. Democrat. Roman Catholic. Home: 5215 W Newport Ave Chicago IL 60641 Office: 300 W Grand Ave Suite 207 Chicago IL 60610

JOBE, ALICE, transportation company executive; b. Little Rock, Nov. 24, 1935; grad. high sch., Sheridan, Ark.; student industry spl. transp. Long Beach City Coll., 1960-61; m. K.L. Jobe, Mar. 12, 1957; 1 child, Cathy. With Nat. Equity Life Ins. Co., Little Rock, 1954-55, Cash Wholesale Co., Little Rock, 1956-57; with Bekins Internat., subs. Bekins Co., Wilmington, Calif., 1959-77, v.p., 1971-77; v.p. Imperial Internat., Inc., Torrance, Calif., 1977-78, exec. v.p., 1978-80, dir., 1977-81, pres. Imperial Van Lines Internat., Inc., 1980-81; industry cons., 1981-82; founder, pres. Caddo Internat., Los Alamitos, Calif., 1982—. Mem. Household Goods Forwarders Assn. (exec. com. 1977-78), Nat. Def. Transp. Assn. (life). Republican. Office: PO Box 739 Los Alamitos CA 90720

JOBE, MARTHA C., nurse; b. Sulphur Spring, Tex., July 8, 1919; d. Mark and Lonia Angeline (Portwood) Stribling; children—Gloria, Marcella. Student Jarvis Christian Coll., Hawkins, Tex., 1939; R.N., Hitchcock Hosp., Gladewater, Tex., 1953; student Bush Math Instn., Longview, Tex., 1969. Supr. nursing Edwards Hosp., Hawkins, 1953-60; charge nurse Good Shepherd Hosp., Longview, 1960-71; pvt. duty nurse Baylor Hosp., Dallas, 1972—. Den mother Boy Scouts Am., 1967, recipient plaque, 1969. Mem. Div. 4 Nursing Assn. Baptist. Lodge: Herion Jerico. Home: 934 Oxbow Ln Dallas TX 75241

JOE, GLENDA KAY, public relations executive, writer, Asian Am. community specialist, consultant; b. Houston, Apr. 7, 1952; d. Tong Bing and Barnette (Berry) J. Student U. Houston. Pres., Great Wall Enterprises, Houston, 1978—; exec. dir. Asian Am. Festival Assn., Houston, 1980—, dir. Asian Community Support Services Ctr., Inc., Houston, 1981—; mem. Task Force for Ednl. Excellence, Houston, 1982—; cons. Asian Am. Adv. Com. to Mayor, Houston, 1983—. Writer, S.W. Chinese Jour., 1981-82; producer video documentary Asian Am. Festival, 1982; producer weekly radio programming Amerasian Network, 1983; author screenplays, 1983. Community liaison U.S. Justice Dept. and Seabrook Police, Galveston Bay Area, Tex., 1981-82; cons. Houston Police Dept. Community Liaison Office, 1983, Houston Police Dept. Cadet Acad., 1983, Tex. Edn. Agy., Houston, 1983; bd. dirs. Houston Ctr., for Humanities, 1983—; bd. dirs. Cambodian Gardens Farming Project, 1984—; participant Tex. Leadership, 1986. Recipient cert. of appreciation, Houston Ind. Sch. Dist., 1983; Cultural Arts Council Houston grantee, 1983-86. Mem. Nat. Assn. Chinese Ams. (dir. 1981-82), Council Asian Am. Orgns. (coordinator 1982—), Orgn. Chinese Ams. (sec. 1981-82). Office: Asian Community Support Services Ctr 1714 Tannehill Dr Houston TX 77008

JOE, ROSE ANTONIA, engineering and construction accountant; b. Pascagoula, Miss., Sept. 7, 1951; d. Louis Lee and Lillian (Anderson) Joe. B.S. in Bus. Adminstrn., Alcorn State U., 1974. Cost. acct. Ingalls, Shippbuilding, Pascagoula, Miss., 1973-75, fin. analyst, 1975-78; budget analyst Northrop

DSD, Rolling Meadows, Ill., 1978-80; cost analyst Fluor Engrs, Inc., Houston, 1980-83, acct., 1983—. Mem., sec. Greater Hope Choir, Houston, 1983; mem. Mission Soc. II, Houston, 1983; program dir. Bapt. Tng. Union, Houston, 1983; mem. Pub. Issues Com., Houston, 1984. Democrat. Club: Fluor Supr. Address: 10555 Fondern #107 Houston TX 77096

JOFFE, GRACE, educator; b. N.Y.C., Feb. 22, 1937; d. Benjamin and Lena (Salander) Garfinkle, m. Jeffery E. Joffe, July 10, 1960. B.Edn., U. Miami, 1958, Ed.M., 1968. Tchr. phys. edn. Battin High Sch., Elizabeth, N.J., 1958-60; tchr. phys. edn., dance and English instr. Rahway, N.J., 1960-62; tchr. phys. edn. West Orange High Sch., N.J., 1962-63; tchr. phys. edn., English, speech and drama Dade County Pub. Schs., Miami, Fla., 1963—; chmn. lang. arts dept. North Dade Jr. High Sch., Miami, 1984—, chmn. phys. edn. dept., 1972-74, instr. English as 2d lang., 1967-69. Contbr. articles to profl. dog jours. Mem. United Tchrs. of Dade, Miami Obedience Club (pres. 1970-74, tng. dir.), Doberman Pinscher Club Fla. (pres., bd. dirs.), Doberman Pinscher Club Am. (bd. dirs.), Phi Lambda Pi, Phi Delta Pi, Iota Alpha Pi. Avocation: breeding, showing, training Doberman Pinschers. Home: 6920 SW 182 Way Fort Lauderdale FL 33331

JOFFE, ZERLINE CHARLOTTE HESS, designer; b. N.J., July 25, 1936; d. Richard Hess and Dorothy Kaye (Newman) Hess; student Hunter Coll., 1954-57; cert. Parsons Sch. Design, N.Y. Sch. Interior Design, 1972; m. Martin Lee Joffe, Oct. 8, 1958; children—Paul, Simeon. With Robert Caigan Assos., 1974-77; prin. firm Zerline Joffe Interiors, 1977-86; cons. archtl. firms. Mem. Allied Bd., Am. Soc. Interior Designers (assoc. mem.). Home and office: 145 W Broadway New York NY 10013

JOHANNES, ENID ERIKA RADO, architect; b. Budapest, Hungary, Mar. 3, 1933; came to U.S., 1957, naturalized 1964; d. Elemer and Elizabeth (Kohegyi) R.; m. Sandor Johannes, Mar. 17, 1961; 1 child, Erik Johannes. B.Arch., Tech. U. Hungary, 1956. Registered architect. Archtl. draftsman Fisher, David and Sudler Assoc., Denver, 1959-61, Earl C. Morris Archtl. Assocs., Denver, 1961-64, Norman Hodge Archtl. Assocs., Denver, 1965, Murray & Co. Gen. Contractors, Denver, 1965; architect U.S. Bur. Reclamation, Denver, 1965-79; chief archtl. sect. U.S. Bonneville Power Adminstrn., Portland, 1979—. Mem. archtl. com. Home Owners Assn., West Linn, 1985. Recipient 1st prize in design competition for graphic art emblem for the city of West Linn, 1984. Avocations: reading; music; hiking. Home: 2189 Hidden Springs Ct West Linn OR 97068

JOHANNSON, FRANCIA FAUST, utility company executive; b. London, Ont., Can., Mar. 17, 1937; d. Frank H. and Mildred (Corke) Faust; m. Thomas D. Johannson, Feb. 20, 1960 (div. Feb. 1985); children—Thomas Derek, Leslie Mariellen. B.A., Concordia U., Montreal, 1958; B.A., Coll. Notre Dame, 1982, postgrad., 1984—. On camera and editor PBS Consumer Survival Kit, Owings Mills, Md., 1972-78; program circulation mgr. Md. Pub. TV, Owings Mills, 1978-80; spl. projects mgr. McCormick & Co., Hunt Valley, Md., 1980-82; communications mgr. Balt. Gas & Electric, 1982—; mem. faculty Goucher Coll., 1985—. Bd. dirs. Metro Crime Stoppers, Balt., 1982—, chmn. bd. dirs. 1986—; pres. parish council Cathedral of Mary Our Queen, Balt., 1983-84; co chmn. gourmet gala March of Dimes, Balt., 1983. Mem. Pub. Relations Soc. Am. (v.p. and pres.-elect 1985-86, bd. dirs 1982—). Office: 1100 Baltimore Gas & Electric PO Box 1475 Baltimore MD 21203

JOHANSEN, CYNTHIA GLOVER, pharmacist; b. Aberdeen, S.D., Oct. 21, 1933; d. Roy Samuel and Sena (Williams) Glover; m. Richard Johansen, Dec. 23, 1953; children—Jay William, James Richard, Jess Douglas. B.S., S.D. State U., 1954; M.S., U. San Francisco, 1984. Pharmacist asst. mgr. Palace Drug Store, Manhattan, Kans., 1954-58; owner, mgr. Dakota Drug, Newell, S.C. 1961-69; asst. dir. pharmacy St. John's Hosp., Rapid City, S.D., 1970-74; dir. pharmacy, chief clin. pharmacy Kings View Corp., Reedley, Calif., 1974—; clin. pharmacist cons., 1974—. Author: Guidelines for Safe and Effective Use of Medication, 1977; Patient Drug Information/Consent, 1979, (chpt.) Drug Monitoring in Chronic Mentally Ill, 1981. Bd. dirs. Family Planning Tulare County, 1976-70. Mem. Calif. Soc. Hosp. Pharmacists (sec. 1979-82, sec. council clin. pharmacy and therapeutics 1977-78, sec. council organizing affairs 1985, membership com. 1986), Am. Soc. Hosp. Pharmacists (council clin. affairs 1982), Am. Pharm. Assn., Calif. Pharmacists Assn., Tulare Kings Pharm. Assn. (pres. 1976, 77, bd. dirs. 1978—), Sierra Soc. Hosp. Pharmacists (pres. 1986). Home: 6050 W Caldwell St Visalia CA 93277 Office: 42675 Rd 44 Reedly CA 93654

JOHE, SHARON DOYLE, lawyer; b. Mpls., July 28, 1939; d. Walter Anthony and Margaret Mary (Murphy) Doyle; m. Justin M. Spring, Apr. 23, 1960 (div. 1972); children—Margaret Faith, Justin Doyle, Arthur John III; m. Richard Edwin Johe, Aug. 18, 1984. Student Barnard Coll., 1957-60; J.D. cum laude, N.Y. Law Sch., 1972. Bar: N.Y. 1973, U.S. Dist. Ct. (so. and ea. dist.) N.Y. 1974. Assoc., Poletti, Freidin, Prashker, Feldman & Gartner, N.Y.C., 1971-76; gen. atty. corp. affairs Sea-Land Service, Inc., Edison, N.J., 1976-78, gen. atty. personnel and labor, 1978-79, counsel to Atlantic div. Sea-Land Service, Inc./Sea-Land Industries, Inc., 1979; Counsel-litigation R.J. Reynolds Tobacco Co., Winston-Salem, N.C., 1984—. Dist. leader Democratic Party, Upper Manhattan, 1967-71, state committeewoman for Upper Manhattan, 1969-71; mem. N.Y.C. Community Planning Bd. 12, 1967-72, chmn. parks com., 1968-71. Recipient Am. Jurisprudence award Lawyers Coop. Pub. Co., 1971. Mem. ABA, Maritime Law Assn., Assn. Bar City of N.Y. (com. on civil ct. City N.Y. 1976-78, admiralty com. 1982-84), Barnard Coll. Alumni Assn. (class pres. 1981-86), Order Barristers. Office: Law Dept RJ Reynolds Tobacco Co Reynolds Bldg Winston-Salem NC 27102

JOHN, ANITA JEAN, municipal administrator; b. Berks County, Pa., Nov. 29, 1935; d. George Sigman and Elizabeth Irene (Moore) Boyer; m. Glenn Webster John, Nov. 24, 1962; children—Glenn George, Elizabeth Ann. A.A., Pottstown Bus. Coll., 1958; student Montgomery County Community Coll. Engring. sec. Doehler-Jarvis, Pottstown, Pa., 1960-67; twp. clk. New Hanover Twp., Pa., 1969-75, twp. mgr., 1975—, twp. treas., 1979-85, twp. sec., 1979-85; bd. dirs. New Hanover Twp. Planning Commn., 1969-85, New Hanover Twp. Recreation Com., 1979-85. Co-organizer Swamp Creek Woman's Club, Gilbertsville, Pa., 1971; co-organizer New Hanover Twp. Fire Co., Ladies Aux., 1972; active Episcopal Ch. Women, Pottstown, Pa. Mem. Montgomery County Assn. Twp. Ofcls., Southeastern Pa. Mcpl. Mgrs., Assn. Pa. Mcpl. Mgrs. Office: New Hanover Twp 2943 N Charlotte St Gilbertsville PA 19525

JOHN, CAROLINE CARLTON, newspaper executive; b. Winston-Salem, N.C., Dec. 22, 1944; d. Romulus Lancaster and Caroline (Cheney) Carlton; B.A., Duke U., 1967; postgrad. Radcliffe Coll., 1967; m. David Vaughn John, Aug. 31, 1968 (div. 1984); children—Matthew Ian, Caroline Elizabeth. Dir. info. services and publs. Guilford Coll., Greensboro, N.C., 1967-68; asst. editor alumni publs. Duke U., 1968-70; account exec., creative dir. Farnan Advt., Atlanta, 1970-74; with Atlanta Jour.-Constn., 1974—, mktg. dir., 1981-83, circulation sales and mktg. dir., 1983—, circulation dir., 1984, v.p., 1986. Mem. Am. Mktg. Assn. (dir. 1980-82), Internat. Newspaper Promotion Assn. (dir. 1980, treas. 1983-84, v.p. 1984-85, pres. 1986-87), Atlanta Advt. Club, Newspaper Research Council, Internat. Circulation Mgrs. Assn. Democrat. Home: 2350 Bohler Rd Atlanta GA 30327 Office: 72 Marietta St NW Atlanta GA 30303

JOHN, DEBORAH ROEDDER, educator; b. St. Louis, Aug. 24, 1952; d. Charles George and Ruth Helen (Buchanan) R.; B.S.B.A. summa cum laude, St. Louis U., 1974; M.B.A., Kent State U., 1976; Ph.D., Northwestern U., 1980. Teaching fellow Kent (Ohio) State U., 1975-76; instr. Northwestern U., Evanston, Ill., 1979-80; asst. prof. Grad. Sch. Mgmt. UCLA, 1980-82, asst. prof. Grad. Sch. Bus., U. Wis., Madison, 1982—; cons. in field. Recipient doctoral dissertation award, Am. Psychol. Assn., 1981; Am. Mktg. Assn. doctoral dissertation grantee, 1978; Kent State U. grad. fellow, 1974-75; Northwestern U. grad. fellow, 1976-79. Mem. Am. Mktg. Assn., Am. Psychol. Assn., Assn. for Consumer Research, Alpha Sigma Nu, Beta Gamma Sigma. Contbr. articles to profl. jours. Home: 3516 Valley Ridge Rd Middleton WI 53562 Office: 1155 Observatory Dr Madison WI 53706

JOHN, MARTHA TYLER, teacher educator; b. Saranac Lake, N.Y., Apr. 22, 1930; d. Albert C. and Helen E. (Moss) Tyler; A.B., Eastern Nazarene Coll., 1951; M.S., Purdue U., 1958; Ed.D., Stanford U., 1966; m. Floyd John, Aug. 8, 1952; children—Floyd, Bruce, David. Asst. prof., assoc. prof. Boston U., 1967-74; assoc. prof. Bowie State Coll., Bowie, Md., 1974-77; research assoc. U. Dar-es-Salaam, Tanzania, 1978—; prof., chmn. div. edn. and psychology, phys. edn. Mid-Am. Nazarene Coll., Olathe, Kans., 1977-85; dean Sch. Edn. and Human Services, Marymount U., Arlington, Va., 1986—; Fulbright prof. U. Botswana, 1979; prof., head Ednl. Found., U. Swaziland, 1983-84; chmn. Swaziland Ednl. Research Assn., 1984. Active Youth Diversion Group, 1982-84. Mem. Internat. Reading Assn., Nat. Council for Social Studies, Kans. Assn. for Aging in Higher Edn., Assn. Supervision and Curriculum Devel. Internat. Assn. Cross Cultural Psychology, Pi Lambda Theta, Kappa Delta Pi, Phi Delta Kappa. Author: A Guide for Elementary Social Studies Teacher, 1972, 78; Using Media in the Elementary Classroom, 1979; Teaching and Learning: Philosophical, Psychological and Curricular Applications, 1975; Practice in Research and Study Skills, 1980; The Research Project, 1981; Teaching and Loving the Elderly, 1983; Geragogy: A Theory for Teaching the Elderly, 1986; editor Swaziland Inst. Edn. Research Bull., 1984; contbr. articles to profl. jours. Home: 3685 Childress Terr Laurel MD 20707 Office: Marymount U 2807 N Glebe Rd Arlington VA 22207

JOHNS, BEVERLY ANNE HOLDEN, special education administrator; b. New Albany, Ind., Nov. 6, 1946; d. James Edward and Martha Edna (Scharf) Holden; m. Lonnie J. Johns, July 28, 1973. B.S., Catherine Spalding Coll., Ky., 1968; M.S., So. Ill. U., 1970; postgrad. Western Ill. U., 1973-74, 79-80, 82, U. Ill., 1984-85. Cert. adminstr., tchr. Ill. Demonstration tchr. So. Ill. U., Carbondale, 1970-73; instr. MacMurray Coll., Jacksonville, Ill., 1977-79; intern Ill. State Bd. Edn., Springfield, 1981; program supr. Four Rivers Spl. Edn. Dist., Jacksonville, Ill., 1972—; chmn. Spl. Edn. Legis. Assn., Jacksonville, 1982—; conf. coordinator Ill. Alliance, Champaign, 1982—; cons. in field. Author: Report on Behavior Analysis in Edn., 1972; editor: Position Papers of Ill. Council for Exceptional Children, 1981. Contbr. articles to profl. jours., lectr. to profl. confs. Govt. relations chmn. Ill. Council Exceptional Children, 1982—; govt. relations chmn. Internat. Council Exceptional Children, 1984—; fed. liason Ill. Adminstrs. Spl. Edn., 1985-86. So. Ill. U. fellow, 1968; Resolution honoring Beverley H. Johns 60th Ann. Internat. Council for Exceptional Children Conv., 1982; Presdl. award Ill. Council Exceptional Children, 1983; Cert. of Recognition, Ill. Atty. Gen., 1985. Mem. Assn. Retarded Citizens (com. 1982—), Assn. Supervision and Curriculum Devel., Ill. Council for Children With Behavioral Disorders (founder, past pres., presdl. award 1985), Ill. Alliance for Exceptional Children (v.p 1982—), Ill. Council Exceptional Children (past pres., governing bd. 1984—), West Central Assn. for Citizens with Learning Disabilities (founder, com. chair 1976—), Delta Kappa Gamma. Roman Catholic. Avocation: world travel. Home: PO Box 340 Jacksonville IL 62651 Office: Four Rivers Spl Edn Dist 936 W Michigan Jacksonville IL 62651

JOHNS, CAROL JOHNSON, physician, educator; b. Balt., June 18, 1923; d. Ashmore Clark and Elsie Greacen (Carstens) Johnson; B.A., Wellesley Coll., 1944; M.D., Johns Hopkins U., 1950; D.H.L. (hon.), Coll. Notre Dame of Md., 1981; m. Richard James Johns, June 27, 1953; children—James Ashmore, Richard Clark, Robert Shanard. Intern, Johns Hopkins Hosp., 1950-51, asst. resident in medicine, 1951-53, fellow, 1953-54, physician outpatient dept., 1953-64, dir. Sarcoid Clinic, 1962—, active staff, 1964—, dir. med. clinic, 1967-76, dir. hosp. quality assurance, 1974-79, mem. hosp. med. bd., 1971-79; asst. in medicine Johns Hopkins U., 1951-58, instr., 1958-67, asst. prof., 1967-71, assoc. prof., 1971—, adv. bd. Applied Physics Lab., 1974-78; acting pres. Wellesley Coll., 1979-81, asst. dean, dir. continuing edn., 1981—; chmn. bd. Balt. City PSRO, 1975-79; pres. Internat. Sarcoid Conf., 1984; mem. pulmonary allergy adv. com. FDA, 1973-75; faculty adv. editorial bd. Johns Hopkins U. Press, 1981-84. Mem. vestry Ch. of Redeemer, 1967-70, sr. warden, 1976-79, layreader; bd. trustees Calvert Sch., 1968-72; bd. trustees Wellesley Coll., 1971—, exec. com., 1971-80, 84— chmn. nat. devel. fund, 1975-80, trustee fin. com., 1979—, chmn. trustee faculty relations com., 1984—; trustee St. Paul's Sch. for Girls, 1973-75; bd. dirs. Stetler Research Fund for Women, 1971-79, 84—; mem. Armed Forces Epidemiol. Bd., 1985—. Named Med. Woman of Yr. Med. Coll. Pa., 1984. Mem. Am. Clin. Climatol. Assn., Am. Thoracic Soc., Balt. City Med. Soc., Johns Hopkins Med. Surg. Assn. (sec.-treas. 1981—), Johns Hopkins Women's Med. Alumni Assn. (pres. 1957-59, dir.), Md. Med. Chirurg. Faculty (council 1978-79), Soc. Med. Coll. Dirs. Continuing Edn., Alliance for Continuing Med. Edn., Phi Beta Kappa, Sigma Xi, Alpha Omega Alpha (bd. dirs. 1978—, v.p. 1985—). Episcopalian. Clubs: Johns Hopkins, Wellesley Coll., Mt. Vernon. Contbr. articles med. jours., chpts. in textbooks. Home: 203 E Highfield Rd Baltimore MD 21218 Office: 17 Turner 720 Rutland Ave Baltimore MD 21205

JOHNSEN, VINA LEE, motivational training company executive; b. Shawnee, Okla., Sept. 7, 1941; d. James Ray and June Pearl (Meyers) Foster; m. William Carl Johnsen, Apr. 11, 1976 (div. 1980); children—Carl Day Johnsen Reavis, Kande Paulette. Student Am. Inst. Banking, 1960-68, Okla. Baptist U., 1961-64, Newspaper Inst. Am., 1964-66, Famous Writer's Sch., 1964-66, Famous Artist's Schs., 1964-66, Children's Inst. Lit., 1984-85; B.A. (hon.), Spurgeon Coll., London, 1964; B.S. in Bus. and English, Oklahoma City U., 1968; postgrad. East Central U., Ada, Okla., 1978-80. Teller 1st Nat. Bank, Oklahoma City, 1964-68; co-owner, mgr. Big-T, Sulphur, Okla., 1975-80; exec. asst. Databank, Shawnee, Okla., 1980-84; salesperson, trainer, instr. A Gathering of Eagles, Inc., Oviedo, Fla., 1982-86, coordinator programs, 1984-86; pres. New Beginnings, 1986—; designer, model Okla. Assn. Young Fashion Artists, Oklahoma City, 1964-69; interior, exterior decorator, designer for spl. occasions, 1965-86; substitute tchr., 1979-85. Recipient Miss Okla. Young Republican award Republic, 1967. Mem. Nat. Assn. Female Execs. (cert. 1985-86), Nat. Fedn. Bus. and Profl. Women, Nat. Office Products Assn. Democrat. Cover girl Okla. Today mag., 1967. Avocations: dance; drama and theater; creative design and decoration; floral design. Home: 1111 Laurel Oaks Ct Oviedo FL 32765

JOHNSON, ALATHEA HOWARD, writer, artist, educator; b. Seattle, July 1, 1925; d. Charles Ellis and Idamai Howard (Brown) Smith; m. Charles H. Simpson, Aug. 2, 1947 (div. 1954); m. Harold R. Johnson, Aug. 22, 1960 (dec. Sept. 1967); m. Gordon J. Mansley, Sept. 5, 1974 (dec. Oct. 1981); 1 dau., Aleta Elsa Howard Simpson Coop. A.A., Clatsop Coll., Astoria, Oreg., 1966; cert. Hollywood Screen Writers Guild Workshop Sch., Los Angeles, 1944. With Congress Hotel, Portland, 1954-56; feature writer Seaside Signal (Oreg.), 1965-75; columnist Cannon Beach Gazette (Oreg.), 1976-82; freelance writer various Oreg. newspapers. Charter mem. Holladay Park Hosp. Aux., Portland, 1950-56; co-founder North Coast Animal Haven Soc., Seaside, Oreg., 1973—; dir. pub. relations Sou'wester Garden Club, Seaside, 1978-82; contbg. mem. Oreg. Pub. Broadcasting, Portland, 1982—. Mem. Women in Communications, Oreg. Press Women (N.W. regional v.p. 1971-76, recipient various awards), Internat. Platform Assn., The Cat Fanciers Assn., Inc. Lodge: Am. Legion.

JOHNSON, ANDREA LYNN, lawyer; b. Cleve., Aug. 7, 1956; d. Henderson Andrew and Gwendolyn Cassie (Gregory) Johnson. Student Williams Coll., 1974-76; B.A., Howard U., 1978; J.D., Harvard U., 1981. Bar: D.C. 1982. Newscaster Sta. WGTB, Washington, 1977; copy editor, legal intern, ads clk. Washington Post, 1976-78, 79; legal asst. Sta. WGBH-TV, Boston, 1980-81; assoc. White & Case, Washington, 1981-84; pres. ACT Profl. Mgmt., Washington; asst. corp. counsel land use sect. City of Washington. Author book rev. in law jour., also articles. Trustee Legal Aid Soc. of D.C. Mem. ABA, Nat. Bar Assn., D.C. Bar Assn. (instr. D.C. street law project 1983-84), Nat. Conf. Black Lawyers (mem. communications task force), Phi Beta Kappa. Democrat. Home and Office: 1350 Franklin St NE Washington DC 20017

JOHNSON, ANNE STUCKLY, lawyer; b. Axtell, Tex., Jan. 8, 1921; d. Arnold Joseph and Angeline (Morris) Stuckly; m. Edward James Johnson, Oct. 9, 1943 (dec. 1967); children—Edward M., Ronald J., Dennis L., Shawn T., Rozlynn Jan, Anne J'lynn, Kevin J., Karal I., Donna Lynn. B.A., Baylor U., 1940; M.A., St. Mary's U., 1974, J.D., 1980. Bar: Tex. 1980. Claims clk. Social Security Adminstrn., Amarillo, Tex., 1940-42; asst. chief div. personnel Pantex Ordnance Plant, Amarillo, 1942-43; chief div. personnel Cactus Ord. Works, Dumas, Tex., 1943-44; citations unit supr. Gen. Hdqrs., Far East Command, Tokyo, 1950-51; v.p., treas. Drive-Safe Corp., San Antonio, 1967-69; counseling psychologist ARC, San Antonio, 1968-69, Div. Personnel Office, Ft. Sam Houston, 1969, personnel mgmt. specialist, 1969-77; mem. firm Oliver B. Chamberlin, San Antonio, 1981—. Active Am. Heart Assn., 1983—. Recipient Cert. Achievement, Gen. Hdqrs., Far East Command, 1951. Mem. San Antonio Bar Assn., Tex. Bar Assn., ABA, Am. Trial Lawyers Assn., Assn. Social Econs., Tex. Trial Lawyers Assn., Phi Alpha Delta, Pi Gamma Mu, Omicron Delta Epsilon. Democrat. Christian. Home: 115 Meadowood Ln San Antonio TX 78216 Office: Law Offices Oliver B Chamberlin 6019 Callaghan Rd San Antonio TX 78228

JOHNSON, ANNETTE MADELEINE, health educator; b. Windsor, Ont., Can., Nov. 17, 1950; d. Walter E.A. and Madeleine St. George (Wilson) J. B.S., Mich. State U., 1972; cert. Tuskegee Inst., 1973; M.S. in Health Edn., Columbia U. Tchrs. Coll., 1977; postgrad. Hunter Coll., 1980-81. Registered dietitian. Staff dietitian Bronx Mcpl. Hosp. Ctr., 1973, Bklyn. Hosp., 1974-77; clin. nutritionist, health educator Whitney M. Young Health Ctr., Albany, N.Y., 1977-80; nutritional cons. N.Y. State Office of Aging, 1980-81; nutritional edn. cons. N.Y. State Health Dept., 1981-84, dir. edn., 1984—; nat. cons. Assn. Retarded Citizens, Albany, N.Y., 1979-80, N.Y.C. Council Chs., 1985—, others. Mem. steering com. Black Women's Health Project, N.Y.C., 1985-86; co-chmn. Coalition of Blacks in the Nutrition Profession, N.Y.C., 1983-84. Mem. Am. Dietetic Assn. (chpt. sec. 1979), Am. Home Econs. Assn., Phi Delta Kappa, Pi Lambda Theta (chpt. sec. 1977), Nat. Assn. Female Execs., Bus. and Profl. Women USA (dist. chmn. 1986). Democrat. Avocations: travel; reading; collecting ceramics and glass; dance; theatre. Home: 91 Cambridge Pl Brooklyn NY 11238 Office: NY State Dept Health 10 E 40th St New York NY 10016

JOHNSON, ANNETTE TYREE, nursing educator; b. Phila., Oct. 26, 1957; d. Karl Gilbert and Shirley (Franklin) Tyree; m. Curtis H. Johnson, Jr., May 15, 1982. B.S., Syracuse U., 1979; M.S., 1983. Staff nurse, therapist Presbyn. Univ. Pa. Med. Center, Phila., 1979-82; staff nurse Le Moyne Coll. Infirmary, Syracuse, N.Y., 1982-83; nurse IV therapist Community Gen. Hosp., Syracuse, 1983—; asst. prof. nursing Syracuse U. Coll. Nursing, 1983—; faculty advisor Minority Student Nurses Orgn. Syracuse U., 1983—. Mem. N.Y. State Nurses' Assn., Am. Nurses' Assn., Sigma Theta Tau, Alpha Kappa Alpha. Democrat. Methodist. Office: Syracuse Univ Coll of Nursing 426 Ostrom Ave Syracuse NY 13210

JOHNSON, ASHLEY ALEXIS, personnel executive; b. Dallas, Dec. 6, 1949; d. Joseph Alex Bagley and Dora (Sharp) Spence; m. Jean Mark Johnson, Dec. 15, 1971; div. Sept. 15, 1977. B.A. in Psychology, cum laude, U. So. Fla., 1980. Employee relations mgr. Lawson & Assocs., Inc., Largo, Fla., 1972-79; human resources mgr. Affiliated Health Services, St. Petersburg, Fla., 1979-82; indusl. relations mgr. Speedling, Inc., Ruskin, Fla., 1982-83; corporate dir. personnel Arrowhead Jewelry, Inc., San Rafael, Calif., 1984—. Author: The Dancer (In Prospice), 1969; Alone (In Prospice), 1969. Mem. Am. Soc. for Personnel Adminstrn. Office: Arrowhead PO Box 3823 San Rafael CA 94912

JOHNSON, BARBARA BEE, investments cons.; b. Larned, Kans., Dec. 15, 1921; d. Thomas Kilburn and Hattie Leara (Fisher) Balman; student schs., Neosho, Mo.; m. Eddie Jack Johnson, Jan. 28, 1942 (dec.); children—Judith Ann, Jackie Carolee (dec.). Farm mgmt., Brawley, Calif., 1942—; mgr., owner riding stable, Descanso, Calif., 1960-65; office sec., Imperial Valley, Calif., 1965-75; owner, mgr. rental complex, Brawley, 1965-73; owner, operator real properties, money mgmt. Barbara Bee Johnson Investments Co., Palm Desert, Calif., 1973—. Democrat. Office: PO Box 2406 Palm Desert CA 92261

JOHNSON, BARBARA C., manufacturing company executive; b. Denver, Aug. 21, 1949; d. Jack Robert and Jeanette Maxine (Cizek) Cook; m. Lorin D. Hanson, June 28, 1986; 1 son, Darin Richard. A.A., Arapahoe Community Coll., 1980; B.S.B.A., Regis Coll., 1982. B.A., 1982. Trainer data processing Wright-McGill, Aurora, Colo., 1969-70; ind. contractor various firms, Denver, 1971-76; sec.-treas. Wilsa, Inc. dba Optikem Internat., Denver, 1976—. Bd. dirs. Animal Rescue and Adoption Soc. del. Small Bus. United, Denver, 1983, 84, 85. Named Small Bus. Person of Yr. in Colo., SBA, 1983, 84, Nat. Region VIII, 1984. Mem. Denver C. of C. (steering com. 1983, 84, 85). Republican. Home: 11452 W Hampden Pl Denver CO 80227 Office: Wilsa Inc dba Optikem Internat 2172 S Jason St Denver CO 80223

JOHNSON, BARBARA CORINNE, school principal; b. Detroit, Mar. 26, 1939; d. Gerald Simon Lucier and Helen Ann (Roche) Lucier Campbell; m. Carl L. Johnson, Aug. 11, 1979. B.A., Duchesne Coll., 1968; M.Ed., Xavier U., 1972; doctoral candidate in ednl. leadership and adminstrn. Western Mich U., 1984—. Tchr. parochial sch. system, Omaha, 1958-74; reading specialist Oscoda Area Schs., Mich., 1975-82; elem. prin. Effingham Community Schs., Ill., 1982-83; prin., interim supt. Galien Twp. Schs., Mich., 1983-84; elem. prin. Ionia Pub. Schs., Mich., 1984—; lectr. Central Mich. U., Mt. Pleasant, 1975-81. Active aux. guild Ionia County Meml. Hosp., 1985—. Named Outstanding Prin., Citizens for Ednl. Excellence, Effingham, 1983. Mem. Mich. Elem. and Middle Sch. Prins. Assn., Assn. for Supervision and Curriculum Devel., Delta Kappa Gamma. Republican. Roman Catholic. Avocation: traveling.

JOHNSON, BARBARA DENCIE, lawyer; b. Walla Walla, Wash., Mar. 3, 1949; d. Carl Leonard and Margaret E. (Hardin) Johnson. B.A. in English Lit., U. Wash., Seattle, 1971, J.D., 1975. Bar: Wash. 1975, Oreg. 1981, U.S. Supreme Ct. 1980. Dep. pros. atty. King County (Wash.), Seattle, 1976-79; pvt. practice, Vancouver, Wash., 1980—; mem. Wolfe, Mullins, Hannah & Mercer, Vancouver, 1983—. Bd. dirs. Clark County Child Abuse Project, Vancouver, 1980—, pres., 1985—; mem. Clark County Boundary Rev. Bd., 1986—, Columbian Newspaper Adv. Council, 1986—. Mem. Wash. Women Lawyers (pres. state bd. dirs. 1983, sec. 1982), Wash. Bar Assn. (spl. dist. council 1984—), Clark County Bar Assn. (v.p. 1986, trustee 1985), Oreg. Bar Assn., Phi Beta Kappa. Home: 13108-A NW 8th Way Vancouver WA 98685 Office: Wolfe Mullins Hannah & Mercer 604 W Evergreen Blvd Vancouver WA 98660

JOHNSON, BARBARA JANE, sales representative; b. Chgo., Aug. 19, 1946; d. Sidney and Norma Mona Shaffer; B.A. in Sociology and Psychology, U. Ill., 1968; postgrad. M.B.A. program, Roosevelt U., 1971-72; m. Gary Johnson, Aug. 25, 1968; 1 son, Eric Michael. Asst. personnel dir. Assoc. Mills, Chgo., 1967-69, Scholl Mfg. Co. Inc., Chgo., 1969-71; nurse recruiter Cook County Hosp. Governing Com., Chgo., 1971-73; recruiter Mt. Sinai Hosp., Chgo., 1973-76; sales rep. Stryker Corp., Kalamazoo, 1976-81, area trainer; sales rep. Physio Control Corp., Schaumberg, Ill., 1982—; founder Chgo. Area Nurse Recruiters; cons. positions as nurse recruiter. Vice pres. Budlong Community Action Group, 1979—; advisor Jr. Achievement, 1969-72; auction com. Ednl. TV; bd. dirs., trustee Mt. Sinai Hosp. Schwab Rehab. Ctr., 1983—. Recipient Lee Stryker sales award, 1979. Mem. Assn. of Operating Room Nurses (sponsor). Recipient first place Recruitment Brochure for Chgo. Area Bus. Communicators, 1975; salesman of year, 1979; first woman to achieve nat. award, 1979.

JOHNSON, BARBARA JEAN, judge; b. Detroit, Apr. 9, 1932; d. Clifford Clarence and Orma Cecile (Boring Barnhouse) m. Ronald Mayo Johson, June 24, 1965; 1 child, Belinda Sue. B.S., U. So. Calif., 1953; J.D., 1970. Bar: Calif. 1971. Ptnr., Anglea, Burford, Johnson & Tookey, Pasadena, Calif., 1971-77; judge Mcpl. Ct. Los Angeles, 1977-81, Los Angeles Superior Ct., 1981—; adj. prof. law Southwestern U., Los Angeles, 1975-77; instr. marital litigation U. So. Calif. Law Ctr., 1976-77. Contbg. author: Representing Clients in Spousal and Child Support Processes, 1975. Co-editor: Municipal Court Bench Guide. Bd. dirs. Legion Lex support group for Law Sch., U. So. Calif., 1974-77. Recipient Ernestine Stahlhot award, 1981. Mem. Nat. Assn. Women Lawyers, Calif. Women Lawyers (bd. dirs. 1975-77, pres. 1977), Women Lawyers Assn. Los Angeles (pres. 1975-76), Law in a Free Soc. (bd. dirs. 1977-78). Office: Los Angeles Superior Ct 111 N Hill St Los Angeles CA 90012

JOHNSON, BETTY JEAN, publishing company executive; b. Tulsa, Oct. 20, 1927; d. Walter L. and Izona (Broyles) Hicks; m. Charles Herbert Johnson, June 5, 1949; children—Cheryl D. Lee, Ronald C. Johnson, Walter Frederick Johnson. B.S., Hampton Inst., 1949; M.Ed., Tex. So. U., Houston, 1974. Cert. tchr., Tex. Sec., Johnson Funeral Home, Houston, 1949-59; tchr. Houston Ind. Sch. Dist., 1959-68, supr., 1968-73; cons. McGraw-Hill Pubs., N.Y.C., 1973-82; now cons. for workbooks, tchrs. guide; regional dir. ARISTA Corp., N.Y.C., 1982—; cons. Triple T Project, Indpls., 1970-72; media specialist Rice U., 1974-76. Treas., Citizens for Good Schools, Houston, 1973—; pres. Jack and Jill of Am. Found., Houston, 1978—; mem. rehab. com. United Way-Gulf Coast, 1980—. Mem. Internat. Reading Assn., Nat. Council Tchrs. Assn., Bay Area Reading Assn., Tex. Computer Assn. Democrat. Episcopalian.

JOHNSON, BETTY LOU GUGE, dietitian; b. St. Louis, May 19, 1924; d. Lee Brown and Louise Susanna (Reitz) Guge; B.S. in Home Econs., U. Mo., 1945; m. Harold Arthur Johnson, Oct. 1, 1954; children—Christopher Arthur, Stephen Paul. Dietetic intern Michael Reese Hosp., Chgo., 1945; dietitian VA Hosp., Van Nuys, Calif., 1945-49, Portland, Oreg., 1949-51; relief cons. dietitian Md. Dept. Health and Mental Hygiene, 1972, 76; dept. head, dir. dietary services Pineview Gardens Nursing Home, Clinton, Md., 1967-70; instr. U. Md. Adult Edn. Center, College Park, 1977; cons. dietitian to 5 health care facilities Washington area, 1977—; mem. dietetic curriculum adv. com. No. Va.

Community Coll.; mem. food mgmt. programs adv. com. Montgomery County Community Coll. (Md.); preceptor Hood Coll., Frederick, Md., U.S. Air Force dietetic interns Malcolm Grow Med. Ctr., Washington, Health Facilities Assn. Md. Edn. Com. Active PTA; den mother Cub Scouts, 1963-70; mem. Republican Nat. Com. Served with USAF, 1951-55; Korea. Mem. Am. Dietetic Assn. (registered; chmn. Cons. Dietitians-Health Care Facilities 1980-81, treas. 1978-79), Md. Found. Health Care, Md. Dietetic Assn. (chmn. div. consultation and pvt. practice 1985-86), Nutrition Today Soc. Lutheran. Club: Officers' Wives Andrews AFB. Editor cookbooks for service orgns.; cons. editor Today's Nursing Home, 1980-83 (editorial adv. bd. 1983—); editorial adv. bd. Aging Network News, 1985—. Home and Office: 9303 Gwynndale Dr Clinton MD 20735

JOHNSON, BRENDA FAYE, army officer; b. Fort Leavenworth, Kans., Jan. 13, 1953; d. Hugh Dorsey and Marguerite Elizabeth (Achilles) Johnson; m. Joseph Marion Babbitt, Aug. 19, 1978 (div. 1980); children—Beth Stella, Barbara Kaye. Cert. in lang. and humanities Scripps Coll., Claremont, Calif., 1970; cert. in fine arts U.S. Internat. U., San Diego, 1972; A.A. in Liberal Arts, Fresno City Coll., Calif., 1973; B.A. in Psychology/Sociology, Calif. State U.-Fresno, 1975; M.A. in German, Antioch Internat. U., Yellow Springs, Ohio, 1986; postgrad. in linguistics Union Coll., Cin., 1986—. Cert. educator, counselor, instr. U.S. Army. Commd. lt. U.S. Army, 1976; adjutant/test officer U.S. Army Armed Forces Entrance and Examining Sta., Mpls., 1978-80, asst. area club mgr., U.S. Army Command, Grafenwoehr, Fed. Republic Germany, 1982-83, contbg. editor U.S. Army-Trojan, Fort Leavenworth, 1983, spl. edn. instr. U.S. Army-Acad. div., 1983-84, ops., quality control supr. U.S. Army-Vocat. Tng., 1984-85, behavioral sci. research analyst U.S. Army-Dept. Mental Health, 1985—, lang. instr., cons. German-Am. relations, 1983-86. Author: Men in Power, 1986; co-author: The Trial, 1986; co-editor: (mag.) Stray Shots-Book of Poems, 1983. Cultural arts dir., phys. edn. dir. Mormon Ch., Mpls., 1978-79; campaign coordinator elections Fresno City Council, 1985. Decorated Army Commendation medal; Calif. Gov.'s scholar, 1969-75. Mem. Assn. U.S. Army, Nat. Assn. Female Execs., NOW, Jr. C. of C. (speech cons. 1983), Calif. Scholarship Fedn., Central Calif. Psychol. Assn., Alpha Gamma Sigma, Phi Theta Kappa. Republican. Avocations: swimming; sailing; skating; dance; tennis.

JOHNSON, CAROL LYNNE, lawyer; b. Salt Lake City, Oct. 6, 1957; d. S. Mark and Ellen (Rampton) Johnson. A.B., Bryn Mawr Coll., 1979; J.D., Duke U., 1982. Bar: Tex. 1982. Assoc., Strasburger & Price, Dallas, 1982-86; assoc. Pettit & Martin, San Francisco, 1986—. Mem. State Bar Tex., Dallas Bar Assn., Phi Delta Phi. Republican. Mormon. Office: Pettit & Martin 101 California St San Francisco CA 94111

JOHNSON, CATHERINE AUGUSTA, youth service worker; b. Mobile, Ala., Dec. 31, 1937; d. Claude H. and Mabel L. (Miller) Lewis; m. Charlie Johnson, Jr., Apr. 22, 1967; children—Roderick Earl, Cyrus Aleric, Traci Elizabeth. Student Bishop State Coll., 1958, U. Colo., 1971, 72, Westminster Community Coll., 1985. With Ridge Regional Ctr. for Mental Retardation, Wheat Ridge, Colo., 1964-81; youth service worker A, Adams County Detention Ctr., Brighton, Colo., 1981-85, youth service worker B, 1985—. Recipient profl. awards Mem. ASCAP (assoc.), Colo. Songwriters Assn., Nashville Songwriters Assn., Rocky Mountain Writers Guild, Am. Cablevision Littleton-Community Producers' Network. Seventh-day Adventist. Avocations: songwriting; singing; tennis; swimming; wildflowers. Home: 11751 Orleans Circle Commerce City CO 80022

JOHNSON, CATHERINE COMMON, newspaper executive; b. Watertown, N.Y., Feb. 12, 1914; d. James Allison and Minna (Anthony) Common; B.A., St. Lawrence U., 1935; M.S. in Journalism, Columbia U., 1937; m. John Brayton Johnson, June 21, 1941; children—John Brayton, Ann Catherine, Deborah Jane, Harold Bowtell. Reporter, editor Watertown (N.Y.) Daily Times, 1937-41, editorial and spl. features writer, 1950—; v.p., sec. Johnson Newspaper Corp., owners Watertown Daily Times, Batavia Daily News; dir. Creg Systems Corp., Watertown. Vice chmn. Thousand Islands State Park Commn. Recipient Alumni citation St. Lawrence U., 1972. Mem. Nat. League Am. Pen Women, North Country Artists Guild, AAUW (pres. Jefferson br. 1981-82). Republican. Presbyterian. Club: Coll. Women of Jefferson County (pres. 1954-56). Home: 221 Flower Ave Watertown NY 13601 Office: 260 Washington St Watertown NY 13601

JOHNSON, CATHY, college administrator; b. Abilene, Tex., Oct. 1, 1952; d. Raymond Lee and Mary Nell (Hopper) J. B.A., Southwestern Coll., 1975; M.A., Assemblies of God Theol. Sem., Springfield, Mo., 1980. Sec., Mobilization & Placement Service, Springfield, Mo., 1978-83; office coordinator Operation Sunrise, Springfield, 1979-84; exec. sec. Assemblies of God Hdqrs., Springfield, 1983; coordinator pub. relations Southwestern Coll., Waxahachie, Tex., 1983—. Mng. editor: Southwestern Outreach, 1983-85. Republican. Avocations: sewing; cooking. Home: 517 Virginia St Waxahachie TX 75165 Office: Southwestern Coll 1200 Sycamore St Waxahachie TX 75165

JOHNSON, CATHY ANNE, relocation firm executive; b. Passaic, N.J., Sept. 10, 1952; d. John Charles and Rose (DiGrazia) Stuckey; m. Mark Edward Johnson, Jan. 19, 1974; children—Jennifer Rose, Matthew Edward. B.A., Union Coll., 1974. Cert. real estate broker, N.J. Real estate salesperson Red Coach Realty, Rochester, N.Y., 1974-75; relocation counselor Homerica, N.Y.C., 1976; relocation dir. Weichert Realtors, Chatham, N.J., 1976-78; v.p. N.J. ops. Home Buyers Assistance Corp., Florham Park, N.J., 1978-82; pres. City Relocation Services Inc., Bridgewater, N.J., 1982-85; regional v.p. Relocation Resources, Inc., Bridgewater, 1985—. Treas. Festival of Trees com. Jr. League of Oranges and Short Hills, N.J., 1984—. Mem. Union Coll. Alumni (fundraiser ann. fund 1974-84). Republican. Episcopalian. Avocations: tennis; swimming; sailing. Office: Relocation Resources Inc Garden State Exec Plaza 77 Brant Ave Clark NJ 07066

JOHNSON, CECILE RYDEN (MRS. PHILIP JOHNSON), artist; b. Jamestown, N.Y.; d. Ernest Edwin and Agnes E. (Johnson) Ryden; A.B., Augustana Coll.; postgrad. Am. Acad. Fine Arts, Art Inst. Chgo., U. Wis., U. Colo., Pa. Acad. Fine Art, Scripps Coll.; m. Philip Arthur Johnson; children—Pamela Cecile, Stevan Philip. One-woman shows Grand Central Gallery, N.Y.C., 1965, 67, 69, 71, 73, 75, TWA Paris, 1973, Greenville Mus. Art, Remington Mus., 1980; exhibited with Am. Watercolor Soc., Washington Watercolor Soc., Artist Guild of Chgo., Art Dirs. Annual, Nat. Acad., N.Y.C., Soc. of Illustrators; designed and executed stained glass windows for Nursery Chapel, Augustana, Chgo., 12 paintings on Bermuda for collection Bank of Bermuda, 1964, mural for Bermuda Airport, 1966, 32 paintings for U.S. Naval Art Collection on women in naval service, ofcl. lithographs, nat. fine art com. Lake Placid Olympic Organizing Com., 1980; traveling solo exhibit, Am. Univs., 1964, 65, 66; designed covers Ford Times, Chgo. Tribune Sunday Mag., others; designed Am. UNICEF Christmas card for 1968; illustration in Motor Boating, Ford Times, Lincoln Mercury Times; designed and executed Memorable Mountains series for skiing mag., 1965-74, folios of ski prints for Aspen, Vail, Snowbird, Lake Tahoe, series of 16 prints for TWA on Paris, London, Rome, 1973, series of paintings and folio prints for Napa Valley Vinters, 1975, Broadmoor Hotel, Colorado Springs, 10 originals and 450 signed prints for Broadmoor West, 1976, mural for 1st Fed. Savings and Loan, St. Paul, Bicentennial painting of St. Paul's Fed. Courts Bldg., silk screen for U.S. Hockey Team, 1976 Olympics; represented in permanent collections Augustana Coll., Gen. Mills, Minn. Mining, Ford Motor Co., Nat. Safety Council, Henderson Coll., Wagner Coll., Skiing mag., Davenport Municipal Art Gallery, others; affiliation Grand Central Galleries, N.Y.C., others. Recipient awards All Ill. Watercolor, 1953, Ill. Fedn. Music Clubs, 1955; Outstanding Achievement award Alumni Assn. Augustana Coll., 1962; Woman of Achievement award in Art Nat. League Pen Women, 1962, named 1st Woman Artist by USN and NACAL com. Salmagundi Club; Catherine Lorillard Wolffe gold medal for watercolor, 1965; Disting. Citizen citation Macalester Coll., 1979. Mem. Am. Watercolor Soc., Soc. Illustrators. Lutheran. Featured in film Creating in Watercolor, on ABC Wide World of Sports, 1977, 79, in Am. Artists Mag., Jan. 1983. Studio: One W 67th St New York NY 10023

JOHNSON, CECILIA ANN, educator, researcher; b. Panama City, Fla., Nov. 22, 1940; d. Lott Warren and Cecilia Ann (Kuhlman) Middlemas; m. Joseph Asberry Johnson, Mar. 21, 1970. B.A., Agnes Scott Coll., 1962; M.A., Emory U., 1964, Ph.D., 1976. Golf profl. 1963; instr. Ga. State Coll., Atlanta, 1964-66; instr. world history Northwestern State U., Natchitoches, La., 1970-74, 85—. Pres. Natchitoches Humane Soc., 1972—; bd. dirs. La. Humane Soc., 1983—. Mem. Inst. Hist. Research (London), South Central Renaissance Conf., Met. Opera Guild, Audubon Soc. Democrat. Roman Catholic. Fla. State Women's Golf Assn. champion, 1956, 59. Avocations: reading; humane work; music. Home: 305 Poete St Natchitoches LA 71457

JOHNSON, CHARLENE ELIZABETH, language arts consultant; b. Aurora, Ill., June 7, 1933; d. Floyd Clark and Marion Priscilla Smith; B.S.E., Butler U., 1960, M.S.E., 1968, Ed.S., 1982; m. Bennett F. Johnson, July 25, 1955 (div. 1961): children—Roderick Julian, Marshall Floyd. Classroom tchr. Indpls. Public Schs., 1960-68, reading tchr., 1968-71, lang. arts cons., 1971—; condr. parent workshops in reading Flanner House, 1980. Instrumentalist, Butler U. Orch., C 2d Christian Ch. String Ensemble; trainer reading tutors Public Housing Authority. Pres. Christian Women's Fellowship. Mem. Internat. Reading Assn., Indpls. Reading Assn., Ind. Reading Assn., Nat. Council Negro Women, Indpls. Assn. Adminstrs., Suprs. and Consultants, NEA, Indpls. Edn. Assn., Ind. State Tchrs. Assn., NAACP, Delta Sigma Theta, Sigma Alpha Iota. Mem. Christian Ch. Author: Parent Primer, 1979. Research on Unifon, 1972.

JOHNSON, CHRISTINE MELSTER, business executive; b. Superior, Wis., Mar. 27, 1939; d. Lars Otto and Evelyn Margaret (Melster) Larson; m. Elert Marlin Johnson, June 20, 1959; children—Beverly Melster, Janet Halls, Eric Marlin. Ed. pub. schs. Pres., Identification Services, Inc., Mpls., 1976—. Mem. Twin West C. of C. (exec. com. and sec. 1984-85, bd. dirs. 1980—), Nat. Assn. Women Bus. Owners, Mpls. C. of C., Minn. Direct Mktg. Assn. (treas. 1978-80). Republican. Presbyterian. Avocation: bridge. Home: 3218 Flag N Minneapolis MN 55427 Office: Identification Services Inc 3410 Winnetka N Minneapolis MN 55427

JOHNSON, CORNELIA, computer programmer analyst, consultant; b. Bklyn., Nov. 9, 1955; d. Nathaniel and Lavinia (Moore) J. A.A.S. in Data Processing, LaGuardia Coll., 1976; cert. computer programming NYU, 1982; B.B.A. in Computer and Info. System Analysis, Bernard M. Baruch Coll., 1986. Programmer, Union Labor Life Ins. Co., N.Y.C., 1979-81; programmer analyst Barclays Bank, N.Y.C., 1981-82, Columbia-Presbyn. Med. Ctr., N.Y.C., 1982—. Author short stories, poems and articles. Mem. Nat. Assn. Female Execs., Women's Ctr., NAACP, Am. Mgmt. Assn. Office: Columbia-Presbyn Med Ctr 161 Ft Washington Ave New York NY 10032

JOHNSON, CYNTHIA ANNE, marketing company executive; b. Washington, Aug. 18, 1954; d. James D. and Doris (Russell) Johnson; m. Charles Milsop, May 25, 1974 (div. 1982). A.A., Burlington County Coll., 1974; B.S., Trenton State Coll., 1980; M.B.A., LaSalle U., 1982. Retail clk. Sears Roebuck & Co., Willingboro, N.J., 1971-75; sec. Gen. Energy Resources, Inc., Willingboro, 1974-78; personal asst. Comml. Plastics Ltd., Haddonfield, N.J., 1978-80; product mgr. trainee Nairn Am., Ltd., Cherry Hill, N.J., 1980-82, product mgr., 1982—. Vol. pharmacy Meml. Hosp. Burlington County, Mt. Holly, N.J., 1983-84; active United Way, Big Sisters, 1984—. Mem. Am. Mktg. Assn. Republican. Methodist. Office: T-97 Executive Mews 1930 E Marlton Pike Cherry Hill NJ 08034

JOHNSON, CYNTHIA SHAW, nurse; b. Lubmerton, N.C., Feb. 13, 1952; d. Ewen A. and Alfreda I. (Shaw) J. B.S.N., East Carolina U., 1976. R.N., N.C. Coronary care nurse New Hanover Meml. Hosp., Wilmington, N.C., 1976-78, Lake Waccamaw Convalescent Ctr., N.C., 1984; pub. health nurse, New Hanover County Health Dept., Wilmington, 1978—, nurse children's spl. health services, 1978—; dir./mgr. Home Maker Home Health Aide Program, Wilmington, 1983—. Bd. dirs. New Hanover County Heart Assn., 1981—; counselor Open House/Crisis Line, 1978; mem. Lower Cape Fear Hospice, Wilmington, 1979; mem. health adv. bd. Head Start, Wilmington, 1981-84. Mem. Am. Nurses Assn., N.C. Nurses Assn., Am. Pub. Health Assn., N.C. Pub. Health Assn. (mem. ad hoc com. resolutions 1985), Eastern Dist. Pub. Health Assn. (sect. vice-chair 1984—). Democrat. Baptist. Avocations: jogging; water sports; guitar. Home: 180 Pecan Ln Lake Waccamaw NC 28450 Office: 2029 S 17th St Wilmington NC 28403

JOHNSON, DEANNA K., educator, court reporter; b. Aug. 12, 1942, Paragould, Ark.; m. Howard and Agnes (Christian) Nichols; 1 child, Terri-Anne. Student Oakland City Coll., 1961-62, Acad. Steno Arts, 1973-76, Bay Area Inst. Ct. Reporting, 1976-78, Gadsden State Jr. Coll., 1983-84. Registered profl. reporter; cert. shorthand reporter, Calif. Exec. sec. various, Calif., 1960-75; ct. reporter Hendersheid & Assocs, San Francisco, 1976-78, DeSouza & Assocs., San Mateo, Calif., 1978-79; agy. owner, ct. reporter Johnson & Assocs., San Leandro, Calif., 1979-80; part-time ct. reporter freelance, Gadsden, Ala., 1980—; dir. Sch. Ct. Reporting, Gadsden State Jr. Coll., 1982—; hon. mem. faculty Ala. Supreme Ct./Jud. Coll., 1984. Author: Deposition Manual, 1985. Editor Under the Bench, 1983-85. Reviewer occupational brief Ct. Reporters No. 202, 1982. Ct. reporters Pres.'s Council on Mental Health, San Francisco, 1978; guest speaker in field. Mem. Nat. Assn. Female Execs., Ala. Shorthand Reporters Assn. (Ala. del. to nat. conv. 1984, 85, various coms. 1983—), Nat. Shorthand Reporters Assn. (chief examiner 1983—, various coms. 1983—), Nat. Notary Assn., Calif. Ct. Reporters Assn., Ala. Edn. Assn., NEA, U.S. Coast Guard Aux. Republican. Lodge: Internat. Order Job's Daus. (honored queen 1959, sec. 1973-77). Avocations: antiques; boating; reading; knitting; flying. Home: Buck Island Guntersville AL 35976 Office: Gadsden State Jr Coll George Wallace Dr Gadsden AL 35999

JOHNSON, DEBORAH, physician; b. N.Y.C., 1951; d. Almert Wright. A.B., Vassar Coll., 1973; M.D., Downstate Med. Coll. N.Y., 1978. Diplomate Am. Bd. Family Practice. Summer fellow dept. social medicine Montefiore Hosp., 1976; intern, Martin Luther King Jr. Hosp., Los Angeles, 1978-79; resident U. So. Calif., Los Angeles, 1979-81; part time physician Health Dept., Berkeley, Calif., 1981-82, Kaiser Permanente, Oakland, Calif., 1981-82; clin. instr. family and community medicine U. Calif.-San Francisco, 1982; family practitioner Southeast Health Ctr., San Francisco, 1982, The Council's Ambulatory Health Care Ctr., N.Y.C., 1983; asst. dir. clin. research Lederle Labs., Pearl River, N.Y., 1984—.

JOHNSON, DEBORAH ANN, healthcare company official, lawyer; b. New Orleans, Sept. 2, 1952; d. Leslie Martin and Odette Marie (Lacoste) J.; m. Hiram Ely, III, Oct. 22, 1977. B.A. (Outstanding Grad. in Polit. Sci.), U. Ala., 1974; J.D., Washington and Lee U., 1977. Bar: Ky. 1977. Atty. Humana, Inc., Louisville, 1978-82, mgr. bus. planning, 1982-83; dir. strategic planning, 1983—. Bd. dirs. Ky. Easter Seal Soc., Louisville, 1984; mem. Leadership Louisville, 1984; mem. budget com. Greater Louisville Fund for Arts, 1982-84; co-chmn. bd. dirs. Leadership Edn., Louisville, 1985; bd. dirs. Louisville Theatrical Assn., 1985-86. Burks scholar, 1976; recipient Chmn.'s award Humana, Inc., 1979. Mem. ABA, Ky. Bar Assn., Louisville Bar Assn., Phi Kappa Phi, Phi Alpha Theta. Club: Young Lawyers (Louisville). Home: 579 Sunnyside Dr Louisville KY 40206 Office: Humana Inc PO Box 1438 Humana Tower Louisville KY 40201

JOHNSON, DEBORAH TAYLOR, marketing executive; b. Oklahoma City, Jan. 11, 1949; d. James Byron and Emily (Mengerhausen) Taylor; m. Richard Kent Johnson, Aug. 22, 1970; children—Emily Mae, Richard Kent. B.S., Wis. State U.-Whitewater, 1970. Tchr. English, Brook Park, LaGrange, Ill., 1970-71; pres. Taylor-Johnson, Inc., Hinsdale, Ill., 1977—. Author: A Blooming Success, 1976; The Builder's Publicity Manual, 1983. Recipient Sammy award Home Builders Assn. Greater Chgo., 1979, 80, 81, 82, 83. Mem. Pub. Relations Soc. Am., Home Builders Assn. (bd. govs.), C. of C. (dir.), DAR, Nat. Assn. Real Estate Editors, Nat. Assn. Homebuilders, Inst. Residential Mktg., Sales and Mktg. Council. Republican. Presbyterian. Columnist Chgo. Suburban Tribune, 1976-82. Home: 819 S Lincoln St Hinsdale IL 60521 Office: Taylor-Johnson Marketing Communications 244 E Ogden Ave Hinsdale IL 60521

JOHNSON, D'ELAINE A HERARD, artist; b. Puyallup, Wash., Mar. 19, 1932; d. Thomas N. and R. Edna (Berry) Herard; m. John Laffette Johnson, Dec. 22, 1956. Diploma, Burnley Sch. Design, Seattle, 1950; B.A., Central Wash. U., 1954; M.F.A., U. Wash., 1957, postgrad., 1968-72. Tchr. art Seattle Pub. Schs., 1954-78; numerous one-woman shows including: Wash. State Mus., 1975, Vancouver Maritime Mus., B.C., 1982, Oreg. State U., Corvallis, 1982; exhibited in group shows: Seattle Art Mus., 1959, 65, 73-75, Fry Art Mus., 1964, 78; Whatcom Mus. Art and History, Bellingham, 1975-82, Shoreline Hist. Mus., 1978. 79, 80, Internat. Grand Prix XV, France, 1986, Centre International d'Art Contemporain, France, 1986, Oreg. State Chautauqua Art Festival, 1986, Nat. Art Gallery, Seattle, 1960-87, also galleries in N.C., Vancouver, B.C., Hawaii, Calif., 1954-75; commd. by U.S. Navy, 1980; executed series World Sea Mythological, 1960-86; represented in permanent collection: N.S. Mus. Can., Newport Mus., Oreg. Vancouver Maritime Mus., B.C., Whatcom Mus., Bellingham; art dir. Arts Inc., 1960-78; art cons. Exhibitors Inc., 1954-78. Recipient Two Dimensional Artists award Wash. State, 1981, Edmonds Art Commn. award, 1984; scholarships in art and music, 1950-54. Pres., Art Nature Preserve, Mt. Olympus, 1970-86, Edmonds Round Table, 1978—; bd. dirs. Student Art Exhibits, Seattle, 1954—. Mem. Internat. Soc. Artists, Kappa Pi, Internat. Platform Soc., Kappa Pi, Kappa Delta Pi., Nat. Artists Equity. Office: Pisces Studio 16122 72d Ave W Edmonds WA 98020

JOHNSON, DENA NANCEAN, real estate company executive; b. Des Moines, May 31, 1944; d. William W. and Genevieve Garland (Myrick) den Hartog; student Central Coll., Pella, Iowa, 1962-65, Coe Coll., summer 1965; B.A., Central Mo. State U., 1968; student Dijon (France) U., summer 1967; postgrad. Fla. State U., 1969; interior design cert. Griffith Opportunity Sch., 1975; m. Richard K. Johnson, Jan. 9, 1965; children—Scot Richard, Kurt William. Tchr., Gadsden County Sch. System, Quincy, Fla., 1969; with Junction Realty, Evergreen, Colo., 1977-79; salesman Pine Ridge Realty, Evergreen, 1979-80; v.p. Tamarac Ltd., Evergreen, 1978-82, Tamarac II, Ltd., 1982—; salesman, treas. Tamarac Homes, Ltd., Evergreen, 1974-82. Pres. Bear Mountain Homeowners' Assn., 1980-82. Lic. real estate salesman, Colo. Mem. Nat. Assn. Realtors, Colo. Assn. Realtors, Jefferson County Bd. Realtors, Evergreen Bd. Realtors, AAUW (charter mem. Lakewood), PEO. Mem. Unity Ch. Office: 2785 W Hampden Ave Englewood CO 80110

JOHNSON, DIANE SEELYE, wholesale distributor executive, accountant; b. Pueblo, Colo., Aug. 25, 1933; d. John Clarence and Vula Vona (Ward) Seelye; m. Leonard L. Johnson, Dec. 26, 1952; children—Michael Owen, Lori Lynn, Charles Leonard. B.S. with distinction in Bus. Adminstrn., U. So. Colo., 1974. X-ray technician, Pueblo, Colo., 1952, 56; treas., dir. Central Pipe and Supply Co., Houston, 1976-79, exec. v.p., dir., 1979—; sec., dir. Central Threading, Inc., Channelview, Tex., 1981—. Recipient Merit award Am. Soc. Women Accts., Denver, 1974. Mem. Now, Women's Equity Action League, Nat. Women's Polit. Caucus, Com. of 200. Office: Central Pipe and Supply Co 13025 Champions Dr Houston TX 77069

JOHNSON, DIANNE JEAN, human resources executive; b. Harvey, Ill., Sept. 12, 1948; d. Virgil Albert and Jean (Armstrong) J. B.B.A. in Mktg., U. Tex., 1970. Mktg. research asst. Belden Assocs., Dallas, 1970-72; personnel staff Meisel Photochrome Co., Dallas, 1972-75; personnel staff Geosource, Inc., Houston, 1975-77, corp. compensation specialist, 1977-78; personnel officer, compensation and benefits mgr. Capital Bank, Houston, 1978-79; compensation specialist Anderson Clayton & Co., Houston, 1979-81, dir. human resources Ranger Ins. subs., 1981-84, corp. compensation dir., 1984—. Mem. assoc. vestry Saint John the Divine Ch., Houston, 1983; bd. dirs. Meadowbriar Home for Girls, Houston, 1978-79. Mem. Houston Compensation Assn. (dir. 1983-84, pres. 1985-86), Houston Personnel Assn. (com. 1982-84), Am. Soc. Personnel Adminstrs., Am. Compensation Assn. (com. 1983, 85). Club: River Oaks Breakfast (Houston). Office: Anderson Clayton & Co 1100 Louisiana 38th Floor Houston TX 77002

JOHNSON, DOROTHY BERTRAM, lawyer; b. Chgo., Mar. 15, 1947; d. Frederick Jacob and Pauline (Otte) Bertram. B.A., Miami U., 1968; J.D., Ill. Inst. Tech., Chgo. Kent Coll. Law, 1973; student S. P. Chase Law Sch., Cin., 1968-70. Bar: Ill. 1973. Ptnr. Bertram & Johnson, Chgo., 1973; asst. states atty., Chgo., 1973-75; sole practice law, Chgo., 1975-76; ptnr. Johnson & Assocs. Chgo., 1976—; chmn. bd. dirs., sec., Chgo. Dance Medium, 1983—; instr. Walton div. Indsl. Coll. Engring., Chgo., 1981-85. Mem. Christian Indsl. League-Grainger Hall Steering com., 1983—. Mem. ABA, Chgo. Bar Assn. (mem. matrimonial law com. 1981—, co-chairperson tax subcom. 1984), Ill. State Bar Assn., Chgo. Kent Alumni Assn. Presbyterian. Club: University. Home: 100 E Walton St Chicago IL 60611 Office: Johnson & Assocs 77 W Washington St Chicago IL 60602

JOHNSON, DOROTHY PHYLLIS, counselor, art therapist; b. Kansas City, Mo., Sept. 13, 1925; d. Chris C. and Mabel T. (Gillum) Green; B.A. in Art, Ft. Hays State U., 1975, M.S. in Guidance and Counseling, 1976, M.A. in Art, 1979; m. Herbert E. Johnson, May 11, 1945; children—Michael E., Gregory K. Art therapist High Plains Comprehensive Mental Health Assn., Hays, Kans., 1975-76; art therapist, mental health counselor Sunflower Mental Health Assn., Concordia, Kans., 1976—, co-dir. Project Togetherness, 1976-77, coordinator partial hospitalization, 1978—; dir. Swedish Am. State Bank, Courtland, Kans., 1960—, sec., 1973-77. Mem. Kans., Am. art therapy assns., Am. Mental Health Counselors Assn., Kans. Mental Health Counselors Assn. (treas. 1986—), Am. Personnel and Guidance Assn., Kans. Assn. for Counseling and Devel., Assn. Specialists in Group Work, Phi Delta Kappa, Phi Kappa Phi. Contbr. articles to profl. jours. Home: Box 183 Courtland KS 66939 Office: 520 B Washington St Concordia KS 66901

JOHNSON, ELIZABETH DIANE LONG, lawyer; b. Pasadena, Calif., Nov. 16, 1945; d. Volney Earl and Sylvia Irene (Drury) Long; m. Lynn Douglas, Oct. 22, 1966; 1 dau., Barbara Annette. B.A., U. Houston, 1967; J.D., Rutgers U.-Camden, N.J., 1980. Bar: N.J. 1980, Pa. 1984, U.S. Supreme Ct. 1986. Sole practice, Delran/Riverside, N.J., 1980—. Mem. Tenby Chase Civic Assn., Delran, N.J., 1972—, v.p., 1976, treas., 1974. Mem. Assn. Trial Lawyers Am., ABA, N.J. State Bar Assn., Tri County Women Lawyers, Burlington County Bar Assn., Phi Alpha Delta, Mensa. Methodist. Office: 23 Scott St Suite C Riverside NJ 08075 also PO Box 274 Riverside NJ 08075

JOHNSON, ELVIRA LOUISE, real estate broker; b. Severy, Kans., July 2, 1932; d. Sylvan Leslie and Martha (Kessinger) McIntyre; m. Charles Joseph Johnson, Feb. 10, 1957; children—Tonya Sue, Charles Eugene. Student pub. schs. Sec. to logistics officer U.S. Air Force and U.S. Army, Ent AFB, Colorado Springs, Colo., Ft. Carson, Colo., Ft. Leonard Wood, Mo., 1956-65; owner, technician Johnson TV, Rolla, Mo., 1968-79; owner, broker Johnson Realty, Rolla, 1980—. Served with USMC, 1950-54. Home: Route 1 Box 238 Rolla MO 65401 Office: Johnson Realty 1104 N Rolla St Rolla MO 65401

JOHNSON, EMILY HIGH, financial company executive, consultant; b. Campti, La., Jan. 26, 1942; d. Webb and Hazel (Gillon) Jenkins; m. John Ulyssess Clark II, Nov. 19, 1961 (div.); children—Cedric Wendell, John Ulyssess III, Kenneth Lambert, Katrina Lynetta; m. Eddie George High, May 12, 1972 (dec.); m. Cleve Aaron Johnson, Nov. 24, 1981. Student So. U., 1959-61, U. Houston, 1979—. Clk. U.S. Post Office, Houston, 1962-66; tchr. elem. sch. Natchitoches Parish Schs., Clarence, La., 1966-67; flight data aide FAA, Houston, 1968-70; enumerator of data U.S. Dept. Commerce, Houston, 1970-73; tech. assembly worker Tex. Instruments, Houston, 1973-75; records technician The Coastal Corp., Houston, 1975—; co-owner, v.p. C. Johnson Enterprises, Houston, 1981—; fin. seminar dir., 1983—. Sec., religious workshop coordinator Bible Study Holy Ch., Houston, 1982—. Named Outstanding Hostess, Bellaire Desk and Derrick Club, Houston, 1981. Mem. Associated Loan Bankers America (charter, newsletter editor 1981—), Nat. Assn. Female Execs., Nat. Soc. Notaries, Today's Woman (pres. 1983-84, cert. appreciation for outstanding service 1983), Nat. Council Negro Women (Mary McLeod Bethune Impact award 1983) People Caring and Sharing (v.p. Houston, 1984—). Democrat. Home: 8201 Homewood Houston TX 77026 Office: C Johnson Enterprises PO Box 111248 Houston TX 77293

JOHNSON, EVANGELINE CAROLYN, accountant; b. Carteret, N.J., Feb. 16, 1925; d. William Douglas and Fannie Page (Howard) Dewberry; A.A.S. in Bus. Adminstrn., Camden County Coll., 1974; B.S. in Bus. Adminstrn. summa cum laude, Glassboro State Coll., 1982; m. Lonnie E. Johnson, Oct. 11, 1947; children—Lonnie, Anita, Enoch, Marcelia. Asst. underwriter Ins. Co. N.Am., Phila., 1966-68; faculty sec. English dept. Camden County Coll., Blackwood, N.J., 1968-74, purchasing agt., 1975-81; acct. Ins. Co. N.Am., Phila., 1981-82; auditor Navy Audit Service, Washington, 1983—; lectr. in field. Troop leader Girl Scouts U.S.A., Lawnside, N.J.; mem. scholarship com. Kaighn Ave. Baptist Ch. Mem. Am. Mgmt. Assn., Minister Wives Assn. So. N.J., NAACP, Colored Women's Civic Assn., Nat. Acctg. Assn., AAUW, Lawnside Master Choral Soc. Club: Lawnside Scholarship. Home: 46 E Oak Ave Lawnside NJ 08045

JOHNSON, EVELYN BRYAN, flying service executive; b. Corbin, Ky., Nov. 4, 1909; d. Edward William and Mayme Estelle (Fox) Stone; grad. Tenn. Wesleyan Jr. Coll., 1929; student U. Tenn., 1930-32; m. Wyatt J. Bryan, Mar. 21, 1931 (dec. 1963); m. 2d, Morgan N. Johnson, Feb. 25, 1965 (dec. 1977). With Morristown (Tenn.) Flying Service, Inc., 1947—, chief flight instr., 1949—, sec.-treas., 1949-62, pres., 1962-82; mgr. Moore Murrell Airport, 1962—. Gov.'s appointee Tenn. Aero. Commn., 1983-86. Recipient Carnegie Hero medal, 1958, Service to Mankind award Morristown Sertoma Club, 1981; named Flight Instr. of Yr., Nashville dist., 1973, 79, So. region, 1979, Nat., 1979 (all FAA); Outstanding Alumnus, Tenn. Wesleyan Coll., 1981. Mem. Morristown Area C. of C., Nat. Assn. Flight Instrs. (dir.), Ninety-Nines, Whirly Girls, Aircraft Owners and Pilots Assn., CAP, Univ. Aviation Assn., Silver Wings (Woman of Yr. 1981). Republican. Baptist. Home: Route 1 Osage Hills Jefferson City TN 37760 Office: PO Box 1013 Morristown TN 37814

JOHNSON, EVELYNE CLAIRE LEVOW, artist, author; b. N.Y.C., Jan. 20, 1922; d. David William and Rose (Geiger) Levow; student NAD, 1936-39; cert. in mktg. and advt. N.Y. U., 1941, postgrad., 1947; postgrad. CCNY, 1951; m. Frank A. Johnson, Jr., Oct. 10, 1942; 1 son, Barry Ellis. Pres., Evelyne Johnson Assocs., N.Y.C., 1964—; works include: The Elephants Ball, 1977, The Cookie Cookbook, 1979, I Am A Baby, 1979, Beddybye Baby, 1979, Fun in the Tub, 1979, Baby's Farm, 1979, Peek-A-Boo, 1979, My Animal Friends, 1979, My Favorite Toys, 1979, The Coloring Cookbook, 1982, The Cow in the Kitchen, 1983. Mem. Nat. Arts Club, Soc. Illustrators, Soc. Photographers and Artists Reps., Graphic Artists Guild, Met. Mus. Art. Democrat. Home and Office: 201 E 28th St New York NY 10016

JOHNSON, FAYRENE, librarian; b. Chgo., Mar. 19, 1957; d. Jimmie Lee and Queen Victoria (Williamson) J. B.A., Lewis U., 1979, postgrad., 1981—. Library supr. Bur Oak Library System, Shorewood, Ill., 1980-81, asst. librarian, 1981, chief librarian, 1981-85; chief librarian Corn Belt Library System, Normal, Ill., 1985—. Co-chmn. Nat. Alliance Against Racist and Polit. Repression, Chgo., 1986—. Recipient Outstanding Achievement award W.I.N.E. Social Service Orgn., Chgo., 1979. Mem. Am. Correctional Assn., Ill. Library Assn., Nat. Assn. Female Execs. Avocations: reading; singing. Home: 500 Dellwood St Lockport IL 60441 Office: 753 E 79th St Room 209 Chicago IL 60619

JOHNSON, FLORA, tax accountant; B.B.A., Bernard Baruch Coll., 1972; M.B.A., L.I. U., 1976. Tax acct., Price Waterhouse, N.Y.C., 1977-80; pvt. practice acctg.; instr. taxation Malcolm-King Coll., 1980. Recipient Dirs. award Manhattan Dist. IRS, Dept. Treasury; Outstanding Profl. Achievement award Bernard M. Baruch Coll. Mem. Nat. Assn. Black Accts. (v.p. N.Y. chpt. 1979-80), Bernard M. Baruch Coll. Alumni Assn. Contbr. articles to profl. jours.; pub. How to Save on your Income Taxes Now! Home: PO Box 1034 Stuyvesant Station New York NY 10009

JOHNSON, FLORIS, personnel administrator; b. Melbourne, Fla., Aug. 12, 1949; d. Henry and Floris (Aldridge) Gantt. B.S. in Bus. Edn., Fla. A&M U., 1971. Tchr., Brevard County Schs., Titusville, Fla., 1971-74; mktg. rep. Xerox Corp., Jacksonville, Fla., 1974-76; with CNA Ins. Co., 1976—, supr., Orlando, Fla., 1976-77, div. supr., Nashville, 1977-78, employee relations cons., Chgo., 1978-79, personnel mgr., Chgo., 1979-83, personnel mgr. subs. Claims Adminstrn. Corp., Rockville, Md., 1983—. Recipient Career Achievement award Young Women's Club Am., 1979. Mem. Human Resources Assn., Am. Soc. Personnel Adminstrs., Nat. Urban League, Washington Personnel Assn. (affiliate). Home: 11415 Ledbury Way Germantown MD

JOHNSON, FRANCES DELL, nurse, nursing administrator; b. Bolivar, Tenn., Jan. 4, 1941; d. Ernest R. and Estelle Frances (Granger) McLain; A.D. in Nursing, Barton County Community Jr. Coll., 1971; student Kans. State U. Extension, 1966-70; children by previous marriage—Mary Deborah, Linda Dell. Psychiat. technician Western Mental Health Inst., Bolivar, Tenn., 1961-62, Tenn. Psychiat. Inst., Memphis, 1962-64, Larned State Hosp., Larned, Kans., 1964-71; R.N. supr. Western Mental Health Inst., Bolivar, 1972—, now dir. nursing; staff nurse Meth. Hosp., Memphis, 1973-82. Mem. Tenn. State Employees Assn., Am. Heart Assn. Republican. Baptist. Home: PO Box 356 Bolivar TN 38008 Office: Western Mental Health Inst Bolivar TN 38074

JOHNSON, HAZEL ALICE, librarian; b. Wausau, Wis., Apr. 20, 1902; d. Albert and Wilhelmina F. (Liljequist) J. B.A., U. Oreg., 1925; B.L.S., Columbia U., 1929; postgrad. U. Chgo., 1933, 34-35, 40. Asst. circulation dept. U. Oreg. Library, Eugene, 1925-28; head reference dept. Hoyt Pub. Library, Saginaw, Mich., 1929-30; asst. librarian Scripps Coll. Library, Claremont, Calif., 1930-32, acting librarian, 1932-35, librarian, 1935-37; librarian Reed Coll. Library, Portland, 1937-43; prof. Conn. Coll., New London, 1946-68, librarian, 1943-68; vol. librarian Willamette View Manor, Portland, 1979—, Lyman Allyn Mus., New London, 1951-70. Editor: Checklist of New London Connecticut Imprints, 1709-1800, 1978. Mem. ALA, Conn. Library Assn. Democrat. Presbyterian. Home: 12705 SE River Rd Apt 202-E Portland OR 97222

JOHNSON, HAZEL WINIFRED, nurse, retired army officer; b. West Chester, Pa., Oct. 10, 1927; d. Clarence Lemont and Garnett (Henley) J.; R.N. diploma Harlem Hosp., N.Y.C., 1950; B.S.N., Villanova U., 1959; M.S.N., Tchr.'s Coll., Columbia U., 1963; Ph.D. in Nursing Edn., Catholic U. Am., 1978. Commd. 1st lt. U.S. Army Nurse Corps, 1955, advanced through grades to brig. gen., 1979; mem. staff U.S. Army Med. Research and Devel. Command, Washington, 1967-73; dir. Walter Reed Army Inst. Nursing, Washington, 1976-78; asst. for nursing Office of Surgeon, Med. Command, Korea, 1978-79; chief Army Nurse Corps, Office Surgeon Gen., Dept of the Army, Washington, 1979-83; cons. edn. com. Operating Room Nurses Assn. Decorated Legion of Merit, Meritorious Service medal, Army Commendation medal, Disting. Service Medal. recipient Evangeline G. Bovard Army Nurse of Yr. award Letterman Army Med. Center, San Francisco, 1964, Dr. Anita Newcomb McGee award DAR, Washington, 1971. Mem. Assn. Mil. Surgeons U.S., Am. Nurses Assn., Chester County (Pa.) Nurses Assn., Nat. League Nursing.

JOHNSON, JANET A., law school dean; b. Bridgewater, Iowa, Mar. 10, 1940; d. Leland Russell and Viola Lydia (Pfundheller) Taylor; m. Kenneth L. Johnson, Jan. 8, 1960 (div. 1981); children—Rodger (dec.), Sheri; m. Burton M. Leiser, Aug. 12, 1984; stepchildren—Shoshana, Illana, Phillip. A.B., U. Ill.-Chgo., 1968; J.D., Drake U., 1972; LL.M., U. Va., 1984. Bar: Iowa 1972. Cts. specialist Iowa Crime Commn., 1972-73; asst. prof. Law Sch., Drake U., Des Moines, 1973-75, assoc. prof., 1975-77, prof., 1977-78; assoc. judge Iowa Ct. Appeals, Des Moines, 1978-83; dean Sch. Law, Pace U., White Plains, N.Y., 1983—; mem. Iowa Bd. of Parole, 1975-78; bd. dirs. Fund for Modern Cts., N.Y.C., 1983—, Fortune Soc., 1983—, Burke Rehab. Ctr., 1985—; mem. Supreme Ct. Adv. Commn. Des Moines, 1980-81, 75. Contbr. articles to legal publs. Pres., bd. mem. Our Primary Purpose, Des Moines, 1981-83; vice chmn. adv. com. State Corrections Master Plan, 1977-78; bd. mem. Iowa Civil Liberties Union, 1974-76. Mem. ABA, Iowa Bar Assn., Westchester Women's Bar Assn., Westchester County Bar Assn. Office: Pace Univ Sch Law 78 N Broadway White Plains NY 10603

JOHNSON, JANET H., Egyptologist; b. Everett, Wash., Dec. 24, 1944; d. Robert A. and Jane N. (Osborn) J.; B.A., U. Chgo., 1967, Ph.D., 1972; m. Donald Whitcomb, Sept. 2, 1978. Instr., U. Chgo., 1971-72, asst. prof., 1972-79, assoc. prof., 1979-81, prof. Egyptology, Oriental Inst., 1981—, dir. Oriental Inst., 1983—. Grantee Nat. Endowment Humanities, 1978-81; 81-85, Smithsonian Instn., 1977-82, and Nat. Geographic, 1978, 80, 82. Mem. Egypt Exploration Soc., Am. Research Center Egypt (bd. govs. 1979—, exec. com. 1984—), Internat. Assn. Egyptologists (Am. rep. 1984—). Author: The Demotic Verbal System; (with Donald Whitcomb) Quseir al-Qadim: Preliminary Report, 1978, 1980. Office: 1155 E 58th St Chicago IL 60637

JOHNSON, JANET LOU, real estate executive; b. Boston, Aug. 22, 1939; d. Donald Murdoch and Helen Margaret (Slauenwhite) Campbell; m. Walter R. Johnson, Mar. 31, 1962; children—Meryl Ann, Leah Kathryn, Christa Helen. Student Boston U., 1959, Gordon Coll., Hamilton, Mass., 1962-64. Adminstr., account exec. Fuller/Smith & Ross, Boston, 1958-63; adminstr. Walter R. Johnson, P.E., Gloucester, 1970-76; broker Realty World, Gloucester, 1976-77, Hunneman & Co., Gloucester, 1977-79; pres., owner Janet L. Johnson Real Estate, Gloucester, 1979—. Mem. Mass. Assn. Realtors, Nat. Assn. Realtors, Cape Ann C. of C., Cape Ann Bd. Realtors (pres. 1984-85, state dir. 1985-86), Greater Salem Bd. Realtors. Home: 35 Norseman Ave Gloucester MA 01930 Office: Janet L Johnson Real Estate 79 Rocky Neck Ave Gloucester MA 01930

JOHNSON, JANET THERRIEN, banker; b. Montreal, Que., Can., Oct. 20, 1939; d. Achille and Lucille (Remillard) Therrien; came to U.S., 1960; B.B.A. summa cum laude, Western New Eng. Coll., 1969; M.B.A. in Fin., Northeastern U., 1978; 1 dau., Alexandra Tiffany. Chartered fin. analyst. Asst. trust investment officer Third Nat. Bank Hampden County, Springfield, Mass., 1963-73; sr. trust officer Bank of New Eng., 1973-84; v.p. investments Citizens Bank, Providence, 1984—; dir. Bullard Assos., Inc.; lectr. Grad. Sch. Bus. Adminstrn., Northeastern U., 1978—, U. Mass., 1978—, Brown U., 1986—. Author: Principles of Investment Management, 1980; Personal Financial Planning, 1984. Mem. Nat. Assn. Bank Women, Mass. Bankers Assn. (mem. edn. com. 1973-74), Boston Soc. Security Analysts. (dir., edn. com.), Providence Soc. Fin. Analysts, Fin. Analysts Fedn. (edn. com.). Roman Catholic. Home: 131 Coolidge Ave #215 Watertown MA 02172 Office: Citizens Bank Providence RI 02903

JOHNSON, JANICE FILIPOWSKI, grocery products company executive; b. Munhall, Pa., July 9, 1954; d. John Joseph and Marian (Tutera) Filipowski. Minor Art Therapy (Mental Health), St. Vincent's Med. Health Ctr., Erie, Pa., 1975; B.S. in Art Edn., Edinboro U., Pa., 1976. Substitute art tchr. West Mifflin Schs. and Steel Valley Schs., Munhall, Pa., 1977-78; sales rep. Ralston Purian Co., Cin., 1978; art. tchr. Newport News City Pub. Sch., Va., 1979-80; sales rep. Am. Home Products Corp., Am. Home Foods div., Newport News, 1980-82, mkt. mgr., Richmond Beach, Va., 1982-84, sales planning and devel. mgr., N.Y.C., 1984-85, product mgr., 1985—. Mem. Tidewater Food Dealers Assn. Democrat. Roman Catholic. Avocations: drawing, painting, tennis, jogging. Home: 908 Wellington Pl Aberdeen NJ 07747

JOHNSON, JANICE LOVELAND, musical director and conductor, vocal coach, soprano; b. Wichita, Kans., Apr. 9, 1947; d. James Edward and Virginia (Randle) Loveland. B.M.E. summa cum laude, U. Kans., 1969, M.M.E. with honors, 1980. Mem. voice and music theory faculty U. Kans., Lawrence, 1974-76; lectr. voice Wichita State U., Kans., 1976—, vocal coach, 1976—, also asst. condr. opera, 1978-80, also music dir. and condr. for theatre, 1979-83; music dir. Crown-Uptown Dinner Theatre, Wichita, 1984—; concert singer for various civic, social orgns., Wichita, 1978—; radio and TV commls. backup singer, 1982—; producer dir. various sacred concerts, Wichita, 1980—; dir. music Hillside Christian Ch., Wichita, 1985—; clinician/adjudicator Kans. High Schs. Activity Assn., Topeka, 1976—. Author: A Teaching Guide for Class Voice, 1980; also univ. course and degree design. Mem. Nat. Assn. Tchrs. Singing, Am. Choral Dirs. Assn., P.E.O., Mu Phi Epsilon, Pi Kappa Lambda, Pi Lambda Theta. Republican. Mem. Chirstian Ch. (Disciples of Christ). Home: 252 N Glendale Wichita KS 67208 Office: Crown-Uptown Dinner Theatre 3207 E Douglas Wichita KS 67218

JOHNSON, JEAN ELAINE, nurse, psychologist; b. Wilsey, Kans., Mar. 11, 1925; d. William H. and Rosa L. (Welty) Irwin; B.S., Kans. State U., 1948; M.S. in Nursing, Yale U., 1965; M.S., U. Wis., 1969, Ph.D., 1971. Instr. nursing, Iowa, Kans. and Colo., 1948-58; staff nurse Swedish Hosp., Englewood, Colo., 1958-60; in-service edn. coordinator Gen. Rose Hosp., Denver, 1960-63; research asst. Yale, New Haven, 1965-67; asso. prof. nursing Wayne State U., Detroit, 1971-74, prof., 1974-79, dir. Center for Health Research, 1974-79; prof. nursing, assoc. dir. oncology nursing Cancer Center, U. Rochester, 1979—. Recipient Bd. Govs. Faculty Recognition award Wayne State U., 1975; Disting. Contbrs. to Nursing Sci. award Am. Nurses Found.-Am. Nurses Assn., 1983; grantee NIH, 1972—. Fellow AAAS; mem. Inst. Medicine, Nat. Acad. Sci. (com. on patient injury compensation 1976-77, membership com. 1981-86), Am. Nurses Assn. (chmn. council for nurse researchers 1976-78, mem. commn. for research 1978-82), Acad. for Behavioral Medicine Research, Sigma Xi, Am. Psychol. Assn., Omicron Nu, Phi Kappa Phi. Contbg. author: Stress and Anxiety, vol. 2, 1975; Annual Review of Nursing Research, Vol. 2, 1984; contbr. articles to profl. jours. Home: 1412 East Ave Rochester NY 14610 Office: Cancer Center U Rochester Rochester NY 14642

JOHNSON, JEAN SUE, marketing executive; b. Racine, Wis., Apr. 4, 1944; d. John Bert and Loretta Laura (Richards) J.; 1 son, Eric David Spradling. B.A., U. Wis., 1966; postgrad. U. Oslo, Norway, 1965. Project coordinator U. Wis. Extension, Madison, 1966-67, Ctr. System, 1966-68; office mgr. Spradling Photography and Senrac Enterprises, Madison, 1969-71; prodn. mgr. jours. U. Wis. Press, Madison, 1971-72, asst. jours. mgr., 1972-77, asst. mktg. mgr., 1977-80; mktg. mgr. U. Ga. Press, Athens, 1980-84; mktg. mgr. U. Pa. Press, Phila., 1984—; lectr. in field; cons. in field. Recipient Western Pub. scholarship, 1962-66; Outstanding Jr. Women Journalism award, 1965; Cert. Appreciation, Marine Corps, 1966; After Sch. Day Care Assn. award, 1976-77. Mem. Women in Communications, Inc. (profl. chpt. pres. 1971, head community service 1972, 78, nat. com. to change the name 1972, speaker nat. meeting 1972), Women in Scholarly Pub. (nat. newsletter editor 1980-82), NOW, AAUW, Jeanette Rankin Found. Unitarian. Club: Madison Press (sec. 1977, 79). Home: 209 N 4th St Apt E-3 Philadelphia PA 19106 Office: U Pa Press Blockley Hall 418 Service Dr Philadelphia PA 19104

JOHNSON, JEANNE LOUISE, management consultant; b. Kenosha, Wis., Nov. 14, 1928; d. Byron Simpson and Amanda (Zeitler) Knight; B.S. cum laude, U. Dubuque, 1949. Head editing dept. Film Prodn. unit Ia. State U., 1954-56; head Continuity dept. WICS-NBC TV, Springfield, Ill., 1958-59; home service adv. Central Ill. Light Co., Springfield, 1959-61; instr. home economics Centralia (Ill.) City Schs., 1962-66; v.p. Tallman Robbins & Co., Springfield, 1967-77; v.p. Delta Business Forms, Cairo, Ill., 1971-77; mgmt. cons., 1977—; v.p. Adminstrv. Techs. Inc., Springfield, Ill., 1980-82; exec. v.p. Skill-Builders, Inc., San Antonio, 1982—; v.p. Computer Security Engring., Ltd., San Antonio, 1982—; cons., mktg. rep. ComputerLand of San Antonio, 1982—. Treas. Marion County Humane Soc. (Ill.), 1961-66. Mem. Data Entry Mgmt. Assn., Am. Soc. Tng. Dirs., Women in Bus., Profl. Secs. Assn., Greater San Antonio C. of C., Data Processing Mgmt. Assn., Internat. Orgn. Women Execs., Assn. Info. Systems Profls., Zeta Phi. Address: 7667 Callaghan Rd #701 San Antonio TX 78229

JOHNSON, JORENE KATHRYN, community organization administrator; b. Rockville Centre, N.Y., Jan. 6, 1931; d. Adam and Kathryn Lillian (Schoen) Freitag; B.F.A., Pratt Inst., 1952; M.P.A., U. Cin., 1975; student Mt. St. Joseph Coll., 1977-78; m. Roland E. Johnson, Oct. 10, 1954; children—Lorin, Melissa. Furniture designer Jacques Bodart, Inc., N.Y.C., 1952-54; interior decorator Albert Parvin Co., Los Angeles, 1955-57, Maria Bergson Assos., N.Y.C., 1957-61; office mgr., research asst. The Cin. Inst., 1973-74, research mgr., 1974-75; exec. dir. Friends of Cin. Parks Inc., 1975-77; community coordinator College Hill Forum, Cin., 1977-84; sec., insp. Green Twp. Zoning Bd., 1982-84; dir. Program for Cin., 1984—. Mem. Cin. Mayor's Energy Policy Com., 1982-83; mem. chmn. policy com. Mayor's Citizens Adv. Budget Task Force, 1984-85; v.p. Monfort Heights Civic Assn., 1977, pres., 1978; mem. Leadership Cin. Class III, 1979-80; mem. planning com. Community Chest, 1982—; mem. Program for Cin., The Cities We Build, 1982-83; bd. dirs. Hamilton County Assn. Retarded Citizens, 1983—; recorder endowment trustees 1st Unitarian Ch., 1983—. Mem. Hamilton County Statis. Census Com., Cincinnatus Assn. Home: 5200 Race Rd Cincinnati OH 45247 Office: 2306 E 9th St Cincinnati OH 45202

JOHNSON, JOSEPHINE POWELL, power and light company manager; b. Goldsboro, N.C., Apr. 23, 1941; d. William Howard and Vennie Ann (Johnson) Powell; m. William Gene Stephenson, Dec. 24, 1959 (dec. Feb. 1979); 1 child, Teresa Lynn; m. 2d, Amos James Johnson Jr., Aug. 15, 1981; stepchildren—Amos James III, Edward Spencer, Brian Keith. Student Fayetteville Tech. Inst., 1975-79, Mt. Olive Coll., N.C., 1980-83. With Carolina Power & Light Co., 1961—, adminstrv. asst. to dist. mgr., Goldsboro, N.C., 1979-80, area mgr., Mt. Olive, 1980-86, area bus. mgr., Goldsboro, 1986—. Bd. dirs. United Way, Wayne County, N.C., 1983—; pres. Mt. Olive Bus. Devel. Corp., 1983-86; bd. dirs., pres. Mt. Olive Indsl. Com. of 100, 1984; precinct vice chmn. Cumberland County, Manchester Twp., N.C., Mem. Am. Bus. Womens Assn. (v.p. 1983), N.C. Bus. and Profl. Women U.S.A. (v.p. 1982), C. of C. (v.p., bd. dirs. 1980—). Democrat. Home: 117 Club Knolls Mount Olive NC 28365 Office: S Center St Goldsboro NC

JOHNSON, JOY FAWN, stock broker; b. Tulsa, Nov. 20, 1960; d. William Calvin and Charlotte Louise (Taylor) Johnson. Grad. high sch., Dallas. Lock box clk. First Nat. Bank, Dallas, 1977-78; legal sec. Office Paul Brauchle, Atty. at Law, Dallas, 1978-79; vault cashier Homer's Hardware, Dallas, 1979-80; with option and over-the-counter trading depts. Rauscher Pierce Refsnes, Dallas, 1980-82; mcpl. bond trader Bear Stearns & Co., Dallas, 1982—. Mem. Dallas Women's Mcpl. Bond Club, Mcpl. Bond Club Dallas. Republican. Methodist. Home: 10850 Sandalwood Dallas TX 75228 Office: Bear Stearns & Co 1601 Elm St 40th Floor Dallas TX 75201

JOHNSON, JOYCE MARIE BETTS, stockbroker, columnist; b. East Chicago, Ind., Jan. 18, 1938; d. Hobart and Mattie (Upshaw) Betts; B.S., U. Md., Magna Cum Laude, 1976; m. Emmitt Johnson, July 6, 1959; children—Roderick, Terence. Tchr. shorthand Universal lang. Center, Taipei, Taiwan, 1963; adminstrv. asst., exec. sec. U.S. Army Intelligence, Munich, Germany, 1969-73; tchr. McArthur Jr. High Sch., Ft. Meade, Md., 1974-75; bus. mgr. The Reading Center, Gary, Ind., 1976-77; stockbroker A.G. Edwards Co., Merrillville, Ind., 1977—; columnist Dollars and Sense mag., Chgo., 1979—, Info Newspaper, Gary, 1979—, Post Tribune, Gary, 1981—, Chgo. Defender, 1981—. Bd. dirs. Women's Assn. NW Ind. Symphony Soc., 1978, NW Ind. Opera Theatre, Friends Lake County Library, 1978; adv. bd. CEDCO Businesswomen's Ednl. Forum; mem. Northwest Ind. chpt. Nat. Kidney Found. Mem. Nat. Council Negro Women, (dir. Gary-Merrillville br. 1977—), Am. Soc. Women Accts., League of Black Women, YWCA, Nat. Soc. Registered Reps., Bus. and Profl. Women's Club, NAACP, PUSH, Civitan Internat., Am. Symphony Orch. League (vol. council),Group. Phi Kappa Phi, Alpha Sigma Lambda, Delta Sigma Theta. Office: care Dollars and Sense Magazine 7853 S Stony Island Ave Chicago IL 60649

JOHNSON, JUANITA AVIS, civic worker, former life sciences educator, microbiologist; b. Spokane, Wash., July 7, 1909; d. Avery Clarence and Addie Mae (Steele) Rickel; m. James Johnson, Dec. 29, 1938 (div. Dec. 1946); children—Linda Lee, Judith Ann. B.S., U. Wash., 1934; M.S., Ft. Wright Coll., 1971. Microbiologist, Kitsap County Dairy, Bremerton, Wash., 1933-38; lab. technician for Dr. E.B. White, Spokane, 1945-47; microbiologist Early Dawn Dairy, Spokane, 1947-56; tchr. life sci. East Valley High Sch., Spokane, 1956-74, Fort Wright Coll., Spokane, 1974. Mem. Spokane County Democratic Precinct Com., 1952—; trustee Spokane County Library Dist., 1978-85; pres. Am. Bapt. Women for East Wash., North Idaho and West Mont., 1983-86; officer Am. Bapt. Women Pacific N.W., Seattle, 1974-86; 1st v.p. Am. Bapt. Chs. Pacific N.W., 1984—. Named Woman of Yr., Bus. and Profl. Women, 1961; Outstanding Biology Tchr., Nat. Assn. Biology Tchrs., 1972; recipient award of merit Wash. Sci. Tchrs., 1972; NSF grantee, 1969-71. Mem. NEA. Democrat. Baptist. Home: E 10901 9th Ave Spokane WA 99206

JOHNSON, JUANITA JERNICE, educator; b. Lake Harbor, Fla., Mar. 28, 1938; d. Ellis Johnson and Louise (Franklin) Francis; m. Nathaniel Malone Jr., July 28, 1980. B.S., Fla. A&M U., 1960; M.A., U. South Fla., 1975; Ed.S., Nova U., 1985. Cert. elem. tchr., Fla. Tchr. Rosenwald Elem., South Bay, Fla., 1971-80; primary resource tchr., 1980—. Chmn. Community Devel. Citizen Planning Adv. Com., Belle Glade, Fla., 1980—; vice chmn. Community Devel. Adv. Community, Palm Beach County, Fla., 1984—; organizer Jessie Jackson for Pres. Campaign. Recipient Outstanding Achievement award L.A. Lee Br. YMCA, 1978; Vol. of Yr. award Planned Parenthood, 1981. Mem. Classroom Tchr. Assn. (area rep. 1977-80, 83—), Internat. Reading Assn., NEA, Fla. United Teaching Profession, Fla. Reading Council, Phi Delta Kappa (historian 1985), Delta Sigma Theta (chpt. pres. 1976-79), Club: United Women (pres. 1971-75). Home: 637 S W 4th St Belle Glade FL 33430 Office: Rosenwald Elem Sch 1321 Palm Beach Rd W South Bay FL 33493

JOHNSON, JUDITH ANN, manufacturing company executive; b. Providence, Mar. 3, 1943; d. Lyman A. and Virginia (Briggs) Draper; student Valencia Community Coll., 1972-73; m. Donald R. Johnson, Oct. 8, 1976; children—Denise Ann, Tina Ann, Donald R. Sec. to dept. mgr. Pershing subcontracts Martin Marietta Corp., Orlando, Fla., 1961-64; sec. Lawrence Condict, Realtor/Appraiser, Orlando, Fla., 1973-74; legal sec. Nichols & Tatich, Orlando, 1974-76; exec. sec., office mgr., corp. sec., v.p. and partner Forms Mfrs. Equipment, Inc., Orlando, 1976—, now pres., chmn. bd., dir., 1977—. Mem. Nat. Assn. Female Execs., Internat. Bus. Forms Industries. Republican. Office: 1423 W Long St Orlando FL 32805

JOHNSON, JUDITH LAWSON, commodity broker; b. Memphis, Jan. 12, 1943; d. David Voss and Julia (Larkey) J.; B.A., Smith Coll., 1965; M.A.T., Duke U., 1966. Sales asst. Howard, Weil, Labouisse, Friedrichs, Inc., New Orleans, 1969-72, analyst, Chgo., 1975-77, 1st v.p., commodity sales mgr., New Orleans, 1977—. Mem. Chgo. Mercantile Exchange, N.Y. Futures Exchange, Futures Industry Assn. Presbyterian. Home: 3009 Constance St New Orleans LA 70115 Office: Howard Weil Labouisse Friedrichs Inc Energy Centre Suite 900 1100 Poydras St New Orleans LA 70163

JOHNSON, JUDY SHERRILL, business educator, educational consultant; b. McComb, Miss., Aug. 27, 1944; d. Samuel Benton and Eunice (Ikard) Sherrill; m. Bill Johnson, Dec. 27, 1985; stepchildren—Christie, Karen, Laurie, Leslie. B.S.C., U. Miss., 1966; postgrad. U. Fla., 1967, Fla. Atlantic U., 1971, 73, 76, U. Central Fla., 1984, Ark. State U., 1981. Lic. tchr. Tenn., Ala., Fla., Miss. Mem. faculty Santa Fe Jr. Coll., Gainesville, Fla., 1966-68, Broward County Bd. Pub. Instrn., Ft. Lauderdale, Fla., 1968-76; tchr. Huntsville City Sch., Ala., 1976-81; ednl. cons., sales rep. McGraw-Hill Book Co., N.Y.C., 1981-85; cons. Hillsborough County Bus. Edn. Tchrs., Tampa, Fla., 1982; mem. adv. bd. Pinellas County Indsl. Arts Dept., Clearwater, Fla., 1982-84; mem. adv. bd. bus. edn. Pinellas County, Clearwater, 1984-85, Hillsborough High Sch., Tampa, 1982-85, Gaither High Sch., Tampa, 1984-85, chmn. adv. bd. adult night sch., 1985; judge state contests Miss., 1977, Fla., 1982-85. Active Republican Party of Fla., 1982-85; mem. Symphony Guild, Ft. Lauderdale. Runner-up Advisor of Yr., Fla. Future Bus. Leaders Am., 1974. Mem. Delta Pi Epsilon, Alpha Delta Kappa (treas. 1980-81), Phi Mu Alumnae (pres. 1969-71, collegiate dir. State of Fla. 1968-69, state day coordinator 1970), Beta Sigma Phi, Phi Beta Lambda Alumnae. Methodist. Avocations: Cross stitch; sewing; fishing; gardening. Home: 1409 Governors Dr Huntsville AL 35801

JOHNSON, KARAL I., restaurant executive; b. Eng., June 3, 1957; d. Edward James and Anne (Stuckly) Johnson (parents Am. citizens). B.A. cum laude, North Tex. State U., 1979. Dir. community relations North Tex. State U., Denton, 1978-79; editor Victor Equipment, Denton, 1979; mktg. publicist Sarnoff Internat., Hollywood, Calif., 1979; promotion dir. Sta. WIGS-TV, Springfield, Ill., 1980-81; mktg. mgr. Jerrico/Long John Silver, St. Louis, 1981-83; dir. mktg. Mr. Gatti's Pizza, Austin, Tex., 1983—; mktg. cons. Pvt.

Industry Council, 1980-81. Mem. auction publicity com. Sta. KLRU, pub. broadcasting sta. Recipient Golden Addy awards for commls. and easel card. Mem. Women in Communications, San Antonio Mus. Assn., Ad Club. Home: 1120 Hollow Creek Apt D Austin TX 78704 Office: Mr Gatti's Inc 220 Foremost Austin TX 78747

JOHNSON, KARLA JEAN, costume designer; b. Amarillo, Tex., Nov. 18, 1959; d. James Robert and Joyce Ann (Dittberner) Johnson. B.F.A., So. Meth. U., 1981. Costume designer Stage 1, Dallas, 1981—, New Arts Theatre, Dallas, 1982, Theatre Three, Dallas, 1984—; costume shop mgr. Shakespeare Festival Dallas, 1982; wardrobe designer Pub. TV series The Write Way, 1982-83; exec. sec. to treas. Metro Hotels, Inc., Dallas, 1982—. Mem. Zeta Phi Eta, Alpha Delta Pi, Alpha Lambda Delta, Phi Eta Sigma. Presbyterian. Office: Metro Hotels Inc 6060 N Central Expressway Suite 122 Dallas TX 75206

JOHNSON, KATHARYN PRICE (MRS. EDWARD F. JOHNSON), civic worker; b. Smyrna, Del., Mar. 24, 1897; d. Lewis M. and Jennie Cairl (Smithers) Price; grad. Centenary Coll., 1915; student Goucher Coll., 1915-18; m. Edward F. Johnson, Nov. 16, 1920; children—Edward A., Jane Cairl Johnson Kent. With Liberty Loan Com. for Md. and Liberty Loan Assn. of Balt., 1918-20; pres. Women's Guild Hitchcock Meml. Ch., 1930-32; dir. Scarsdale Woman's Club, 1933-36; dir. White Plains Thrift Shop, 1930-43, pres, 1936-43; mem. exec. com. Scarsdale Community Fund, 1934-38; active Scarsdale council Girl Scouts, 1937-53, commr., 1939-41, now hon. mem. Scarsdale-Hartsdale council, 1953-69; mem. region 2 com. Girl Scouts U.S.A., 1942-56, mem. nat. bd., exec. com., 1947-55, chmn. orgn. and mgmt. dept., 1952-55, mem. nat. field com., 1943-55, mem. equipment service com. 1956-69, mem. internat. com., 1956-60, mem. meml. gifts com., 1974-81; mem. Bd. Edn., Scarsdale, N.Y., 1943-46; disaster chmn. Scarsdale chpt. ARC, 1942-45; mem. Commn. Human Rights, 1958-69, Commn. Status of Women, 1957-69; rep. World Assn. Girl Guides and Girl Scouts to UN, 1957-71, mem. NGO com. on UNICEF, 1965-72, sec., 1968-70; participant World Confs., World Assn. Girl Guides and Girl Scouts, Greece, 1960, Denmark, 1963, Japan, 1966, Finland, 1969, Can., 1972, Eng., 1975, Iran, 1978. Recipient Juliette Lowe World Friendship medal Girl Scouts. U.S.A., 1984. Mem. Nat. Council Women U.S., Scarsdale Hist. Soc., Olave-Baden-Powell Soc. (founder), Pi Beta Phi. Republican. Presbyterian. Clubs: Scarsdale Woman's (life), Village of Scarsdale; Nat. Women's Republican. Home: 165 Brewster Rd Scarsdale NY 10583

JOHNSON, KATHERINE, medical technologist; b. Fillmore, Utah, Mar. 27, 1955; d. Earl Teeples and Mary Katherine (McBride) J.; A.A.S. in Med. Tech., Weber State Coll., 1975; B.S. in Geology, U. Utah, Salt Lake City, 1983. Med. lab. technician Physicians Clin. Lab., Salt Lake City, 1975-76, Primary Children's Med. Center, Salt Lake City, 1976-77, 78—, Uinta County Meml. Hosp., Evanston, Wyo., 1977-78. Mem. Am. Soc. Clin. Pathologists, Geol. Soc. Am., Am. Assn. Petroleum Geologists, Utah Geol. Assn., Am. Soc. Med. Tech. Mormon. Home: 2240 Foothill Dr Salt Lake City UT 84109 Office: 320 12th Ave Salt Lake City UT 84103

JOHNSON, KATHERINE M. KING (MRS. NORMAN F. JOHNSON), art gallery director, artist, real estate broker; b. Lincoln, Nebr., 1906; d. John Ray and Clara (Plamondon) King; student U. Nebr. Coll. Fine Arts, 1923-24, U. Vt. Extension, 1941-42, Coll. of Desert, 1965-66; m. Norman F. Johnson, Sept. 4, 1925 (dec.); children—Raymond E., Lyman W., Carlene King (dec.). Land devel. designer, contractor Eastridge Acres, Piedmont Devels., Rutland, Vt., 1957—; corporator Marble Savs. Bank, Rutland; one man show Chester (Vt.) Art Guild, 1970; participant in three man art show, Shadow Mountain Club, Palm Desert, Calif., 1964; exhibited with So. Vt. Artists in major U.S. cities, 1950, N.Y. World's Fair with Mid Vt. Artists, 1964; exhibited one man show Chaffee Art Gallery, Rutland, 1967, 74, 83, retrospective, 1980; represented in permanent collections; displayed painting 1967 Nat. Christmas Tree from Vt. in Washington, 1967, painting now in permanent collection Lyndon B. Johnson Meml. Library, Austin, Tex. Co-chmn. Vt. Com. for Nat. Art Week, 1940; dir. bicentennial exhibit Rutland (Vt.) Mus. Arts, 1961; founder Chaffee Art Gallery, Rutland, trustee, 1961—, mem. Vt. Council on Arts 1963—, trustee art com. Manchester (Vt.) Art Center, 1984—, exhibiting mem., 1940—. Bd. dirs. Desert Art Center, Palm Springs, Calif., 1963. Recipient award merit Vt. Council Arts, 1977, recognition award AAUW, 1977, Katherine King Johnson Room dedicated in her honor Chaffee Art Gallery, 1983. Mem. Mid Vt. Artists (pres. 1941-49), Rutland Area Art Assn. (pres. 1962-74, chmn. bd. 1977-80, dir., chmn. bd. trustees 1980-82, sr. trustee 1983-86), Nat. League Am. Pen Women (pres. So. Vt. br., state art chmn. 1964-65, 74-75, 86-87, state pres. 1972-73, exhibitor nat. show 1974, Vt. State awards 1973, 75, 85), Shadow Mountain Palette Club, Sigma Kappa. Congregationalist. Home: 40 Piedmont Pkwy Rutland VT 05701 Office: Chaffee Art Center 16 S Main St Rutland VT 05701 also PO Box 403 Rutland VT 05701

JOHNSON, KATHLEEN SUZANNE, funeral director, embalmer, nurse; b. Tilden, Nebr., Oct. 14, 1958; d. Roger Everitt and Marian Agnes (Kent) Johnson. Student U. Nebr.-Lincoln, 1976-77, 79-80; diploma in nursing Bryan Meml. Hosp. Sch. Nursing, 1979; A.Funeral Service Edn., Mt. Hood Community Coll., 1981. Registered nurse; lic. funeral dir.; lic. embalmer. Staff nurse Our Lady of Lourdes, Norfolk, Nebr., 1981-82; apprentice Johnson-Stonacek Funeral Home, Norfolk, 1981-83; embalmer Butherus, Maser & Love, Lincoln, 1983; staff nurse Scribner Med. Clinic, Nebr., 1983-85; pres. Spear-Johnson Funeral Home, Scribner, 1983—. Tchr. 11th grade religion class St. Lawrence Ch., Scribner, 1984-85. Mem. Nebr. Funeral Dirs. Assn. (edn. com.), Nat. Funeral Dirs. Assn., Nat. Assn. Female Execs., Scribner C. of C. (pres. 1986), Scribner Jaycees. Roman Catholic. Avocations: golf; swimming; traveling; pool. Home: PO Box 530 Scribner NE 68057 Office: Spear-Johnson Funeral Home 509 Main St Scribner NE 68057

JOHNSON, LADY BIRD (CLAUDIA ALTA) (MRS. LYNDON BAINES JOHNSON), wife former pres. U.S.; b. Karnack, Tex., Dec. 22, 1912; d. Thomas Jefferson Taylor; B.A., U. Tex., 1933, B.Journalism, 1934, D.Letters, 1964; LL.D., Tex. Woman's U., 1964; D.Letters, Middlebury Coll., 1967; L.H.D., Williams Coll., 1967, U. Ala., 1975; H.H.D., Southwestern U., 1967; m. Lyndon Baines Johnson (36th Pres. U.S.), Nov. 17, 1934 (died Jan. 22, 1973); children—Lynda Bird Johnson Robb, Luci Baines. Mgr. husband's congl. office, Washington, 1941-42; owner, operator radio-TV sta. KTBC, Austin, Tex., 1942-63, cattle ranches, Tex., 1943—. Hon. chmn. Nat. Headstart Program, 1963-68, Town Lake Beautification Project. also cotton and timberlands, Ala. Mem. Advisory council Nat. Parks, Historic Sites, Bldgs. and Monuments; bd. regents U. Tex., 1971-77, mem. internat. conf. steering com., 1969; trustee Jackson Hole Preserve, Am. Conservation Assn., Nat. Geog. Soc.; founder Nat. Wild flower Research Ctr., Austin, 1982. Recipient Togetherness award Marge Champion, 1958; Humanitarian award B'nai B'rith, 1961; Businesswoman's award Bus. and Profl. Women's Club, 1961; Theta Sigma Phi citation, 1962; Disting. Achievement award Washington Heart Assn., 1962; Industry citation Am. Women in Radio and Television, 1963; Humanitarian citation Vols. of Am., 1963; Peabody award for White House TV visit, 1966; Eleanor Roosevelt Golden Candlestick award Women's Nat. Press Club; Damon Woods Meml. award Indsl. Designers Soc. Am., 1972; Conservation Service award Dept. Interior, 1974; Disting. award Am. Legion, 1975; Woman of Year award Ladies Home Jour., 1975; Medal of Freedom, 1977; Nat. Achievement award Am. Hort. Soc., 1984 . Life mem. U. Tex. Ex-Students Assn. Episcopalian. Author: A White House Diary, 1970. Address: LBJ Library 2313 Red River Austin TX 78705*

JOHNSON, LAURA WEST, art consultant firm executive; b. Bklyn., June 12, 1956; d. Harold and Irene (Zaren) W. B.S., U. Fla., 1980. Coordinating dir. Art League of Houston, 1980-81; corp. art cons. Art Collections, Inc., Houston, 1982-83; showroom mgr. Fidelity Arts, Houston, 1983; pres., owner LLW Fine Art, Houston, 1983—. Republican. Home: 7900 Westheimer #225 Houston TX 77063 Office: LLW Fine Art 5821 Southwest Freeway Suite 400 Houston TX 77057

JOHNSON, LAURICE JANINA (LARI), public relations and marketing specialist, consultant; b. Goldsboro, N.C., Nov. 12, 1946; d. Eugene F. and Laurice Agnes (Reyes) Sikorski; m. Charles Michael Johnson, Aug. 30, 1968; B.S. in Journalism, U. Fla., 1968, B.S. in Pub. Relations, 1968. Customs insp. U.S. Customs Service, Honolulu, 1970-75; editor-in-chief Classmate mag., Monterey, Calif., 1975-77; pub. relations dir. Assoc. Grocers, Seattle, 1978-80; pub. relations cons. Holiday Foods, Inc., Seattle, 1980-81; pub. affairs dir. Navy Exchange, Pearl Harbor, Hawaii, 1981-83, San Diego, 1983-85; pub. affairs specialist Naval Sta., San Diego, 1985; pub. affairs and mktg. dir. Base Spl. Services, Camp Pendleton, Calif., 1985—; mgr. Fed. Women's Program, Honolulu, 1981-83. Editor Assoc. Grocers, 1978, 79; The Scoop, Holiday, 1978-81; Nexus, 1981-83, Signal Bridge, 1985; contbr. articles to profl. jours. Recipient Heathcote scholar award St. Petersburg Times, 1965, 66; Mortar Bd. award U. Fla., 1968, Outstanding Grad. Coll. Journalism, 1968; Navy Info. award Dept. Navy, 1976-77. Mem. Women in Communications (pres. 1968), Pub. Relations Soc. Am. (charter mem., pres. 1968), Internat. Assn. Bus. Communicators, Phi Rho Pi. Democrat. Roman Catholic. Club: Toastmasters. Home: 3130 Poe St San Diego CA 92106 Office: Base Spl Services Bldg 1339 Camp Pendleton CA 92055-5018

JOHNSON, LAVERNE BOSTON, financial planner, personnel specialist; b. New Rochelle, N.Y., Aug. 19, 1943; d. Leroy Bernard and Geneva Theresa (Bracey) Boston; 1 child, Dawn Marie Williams. Cert., New Sch. Social Research, N.Y.C., 1973; A.A.S., Seton Coll., 1979; postgrad. Iona Coll., 1980-81, IBM Mgmt. Sch., Fairfield, Conn., 1980, 81, 82. Acctg. clk., N.Y. Telephone Co., White Plains, N.Y., 1961-68, sec. IBM Corp., Armonk, N.Y., 1968-80, adminstrv. mgr., White Plains, 1980-82, sr. data analyst, 1982-85, fin. planner, Valhalla, N.Y., 1985—; chmn. Stress Anonymous Internat., Jamaica, N.Y., 1986—; cons. Stress Tng. Inst., Jamaica, 1985—; dir. Technology Literacy Corp., Jamaica, 1984—. Tutor, supr. Literacy Vols. Am., Mt. Vernon, N.Y., 1973; insp. elections Westchester County Bd. Elections, New Rochelle, N.Y., 1984. Recipient Dirs. award IBM Corp., 1981, 83, 84, 85; Excellence award IBM Corp., 1986. Mem. Nat. Assn. Female Execs. Democrat. Roman Catholic. Avocations: chess; backgammon; reading; sewing; furniture refinishing. Home: 125 Union Ave New Rochelle NY 10801 Office: IBM Corp 400 Columbus Ave Valhalla NY 10595

JOHNSON, LEE, educator, publisher; b. Richmond, Va., May 11, 1931; d. Mildred Simms Wible; B.A., Pa. State U., 1950; postgrad. Trinity Coll., Hartford, Conn., Columbia U., New Sch., N.Y.C.; m. J. Jay Johnson, June 3, 1950. Pub., editor Kids' Stuff mag., 1960—; tchr. Malverne (N.Y.) Jr. High Sch., 1971-74, Jr. Acad., Bklyn., 1973; book critic Richmond Times-Dispatch, 1965-71; tchr. Roger Ludlow High Sch., Fairfield, Conn., 1962-65, Central High Sch., Bridgeport, Conn., 1963; founder, asso. librarian Calvary Jr. Library, Bridgeport, 1965-68; mgr. Treasure-trove, rare books and records, Avondale, Ga.; psychol. counselor Alpha Psi Omega. Sec., Fed. Grand Jury Assn., 1965-75. Mem. AAUW (ways and means chmn. 1963), Nat. League Am. Pen Women, DeKalb Hist. Soc., Avondale Hist. Soc. Episcopalian. Clubs: N.Y. Classical, Avondale Estates Woman's (archivist 1978-80, publicity chmn. 1978—), Stone Mountain Woman's, Avondale Estates Garden (student judge). Home: 7 Exeter Rd Avondale Estates GA 30002

JOHNSON, LESLIE GAINER, circuit judge; b. Florence, Ala., Dec. 9, 1944; d. William Warren and Jessie Elizabeth (Gainer) Johnson; m. J.B. Johnson, Aug. 26, 1967; children—Leslie Gainer, Rustin Bendall, Warren Franklin. B.S., Vanderbilt U., 1967; J.D., Samford U., 1969; M.S. U. Ala., 1984; LL.M., U. Miss., 1979. Bar: Ala. 1969. Sole practice, Florence, Ala., 1969-70; dep. dist. atty., Florence, 1970-76; cir. judge State of Ala., Florence, 1977—; mem. faculty Ala. Bar Inst.; instr. U. North Ala., Florence, N.W. Ala. St. Junior Coll., Phil Campbell, Ala.; lectr. State pres. United Cerebral Palsy, Inc., Florence, 1984-85; bd. dirs. Ret. Sr. Vol. Program, Florence, 1977—. Recipient Nat. Cert. of Jud. Skills Am. Acad. Jud. Edn., Washington, 1981. Mem. Ala. Assn. Circuit Judges, ABA, Ala. Bar Assn., Lauderdale County Bar, Am. Judge's Assn. Democrat. Home: Route 3 Box 329A-1 Killen AL 35645 Office: Circuit Judge State of Ala 503 Courthouse Florence AL 35630

JOHNSON, LETITIA ELAINE ROSE, home health agency executive, dietitian; b. Dayton, Mar. 9, 1924; d. Bert Andrew and Letitia Elaine (Downing) Rose; m. Isaac Ellis Johnson, III B.S., U. Dayton, 1946; M.A., Columbia U., 1948. Registered dietitian. Dietetic intern, Montefiore Hosp., N.Y.C., 1946-47; dietitian Hunter Coll., N.Y.C., 1949-50; therapeutic dietitian Hosp. for Spl. Surgery, N.Y.C., 1950-52; dietitian Pa. Hosp., Phila., 1953-56; food service dir. Phila. Gen. Hosp., 1956-59, patient food service coordinator, 1959-79; exec. dir. Vis. Homemakers, Gloucester County, N.J., 1979—; nutrition cons. Profl. Adv. Bd. State of N.Y., 1975—, Office on Aging of Gloucester County, Woodbury, N.J., 1979—; dir. Chest & Health Assocs., Hammondton, N.J., 1984—; mem. Gov.'s Task Force on Nutrition, Tenton, N.J., 1980. Bd. dirs. Holly Shores council Girl Scouts U.S.A., Woodstown, N.J., 1986—. Recipient Disting. Service award Food Service Suprs. Alumnae Assn., 1977; Disting. Service award City of Phila., 1978; installed in Legion of Honor, Chapel of Four Chaplains, Phila., 1979. Mem. Am. Dietetic Assn., Pa. Dietetic Assn. (pres. 1978-79), Phila. Dietetic Assn. (pres. 1975-76), Am. Home Econs. Assn., Nat. Assn. Female Execs., Delta Sigma Theta. Democrat. Club: The Link's (pres. 1982-83). Avocations. photography; gardening; collecting cookbooks. Home: 309 Deptford Ave Woodbury NJ 08096 Office: Vis Homemaker-Home Health Aide Service PO Box 73 Woodbury Heights NJ 08097

JOHNSON, LILLIAN BEATRICE, sociologist, educator; b. Wilmington, N.C., Nov. 8, 1922; d. James Archie and Mary Gaston (Atkins) J. A.A., Peace Coll., 1940; B.R.E., Presbyterian Sch. Christian Edn., 1942; M.S., N.C. State U., 1965, Ph.D., 1972. Dir. Christian edn. First Presbyn. Ch., Pensacola, Fla., 1945-47, Greenwood, S.C., 1947-48, Durham, N.C., 1948-51; club dir. Army Spl. Services, No. Command, Japan, 1951-53; teenage dir. YWCA, Washington, 1953-56, assoc. exec. Honolulu, 1956-59, exec. dir. Tulsa, 1959-62; instr. N.C. State U., 1962-72; asst. prof. Greensboro Coll., 1972-75; mem. faculty sociology dept. Livingston U., 1975—, now prof. Election law commr. State of Ala. Mem. Am. Sociol. Assn., So. Sociol. Soc., Ala.-Miss. Sociol. Assn. (treas.), Nat. Council Family Relations, Ala. Council on Family Relations (v.p. 1981-83), Alpha Kappa Delta (treas. 1984-86). Home: Meadowbrook Dr Livingston AL 35470 Office: Livingston U Livingston AL 35470

JOHNSON, LINDA JOYCE, electric components company sales manager; b. Lowell, Mass., Nov. 6, 1956; d. Emil and Esther Muriel (Ayer) Zabierek; m. James M. Johnson, Sept. 5, 1975 (div. Nov. 1979). Sec., M/A-Com, Inc., Burlington, Mass., 1978-79, mfg. adminstr., 1979, sales administr., 1979-81, sales specialist, 1981-84; regional sales mgr. Hyletronics, Littleton, Mass., 1984; regional sales mgr. Frequency Sources, Chelmsford, Mass., 1984—. Mem. Assn. Old Crows, Nat. Contract Mgmt. Assn., Nat. Assn. Female Execs. Avocations: golf; tennis; reading. Office: Frequency Sources Inc 16 Maple Rd Chelmsford MA 01824

JOHNSON, LINDA LOU, radio sales executive; b. Smith Center, Kans., Dec. 2, 1954; d. Forrest Jack Bock and Laneta Fern (Gilbert) Bock Karsting; m. Richard Lynn Johnson, Aug. 5, 1973 (div. July 1980); 1 child, Cody Ryan. Degree in fashion merchandising Patricia Stevens Sch., Wichita, Kans., 1973—. Asst. mgr. J. M. McDonald Co., Concordia, Kans. and Holdredge, Nebr., 1979-81; store mgr. Salking & Linoff Inc., Concordia and Sioux City, Iowa, 1982-83; account exec. Sentry Sta. KSEZ, Sioux City, 1983-84; sales mgr. Sta. KGLI, Cardinal Communications, Sioux City, 1984-85, gen. sales mgr. Stas. KGLI/KWSL, 1985—. Mem. Ad Club Sioux City, Nat. Assn. Female Execs. Home: 3728 Jones Sioux City IA 51104 Office: Cardinal Communications 113 Nebraska Sioux City IA 51105

JOHNSON, LOU AVAH PEVLOR, writer; b. Springfield, Ky.; d. C.L. and Edith (Long) Pevlor; B.A., U. Ky., 1947, postgrad., 1948-49; postgrad. U. Calif., Berkeley, 1968; m. John Riley Johnson Jr., Sept. 22, 1945; children—Jenefer, Cindy, John Riley III. Mem. The Writer's Center, Glen Echo, Md., 1976—. Mem. Women's Com. for Nat. Symphony Orch., Washington Met. Area, 1976—. Mem. Internat. Poetry Soc., Internat. Platform Assn., Nat. League Am. Pen Women, Songwriters Assn. Washington, No. Va. Literacy Council, AAUW, MLA, Poetry Soc. Va., Washington Ind. Writers, Washington Ed press, World Affairs Council Washington, Gen. Fedn. Women's Clubs. Contbr. articles and poetry to various newspapers, poetry mags. and anthologies. Home: 2009 Kirby Rd McLean VA 22101

JOHNSON, LUAN, educational editor, researcher; b. Provo, Utah, Apr. 27, 1956; d. Jack R. and Colleen (Kesler) J. B.A., Brigham Young U., 1981, M.A., 1984. Dir. Teaching Resource Ctr., Provo, 1980-84; teaching asst. communications dept. Brigham Young U., Provo, 1982-83; counselor Master Acad., Salt Lake City, 1985; staff asst. Teaching Resource Ctr., DeAnza Coll., Cupertino, Calif., 1986—; free-lance editor, 1984-85; tutor, 1984-85. Pres. Youth Assn. Retarded Children, Brigham City, 1976-77. Mem. Phi Kappa Phi. Republican. Mormon. Avocation: collecting and flying kites. Home: 4147 Briarwood Way Palo Alto CA 94306 Office: Teaching Resource Ctr 21250 Stevens Creek Blvd Cupertino CA 94014

JOHNSON, LUANNE ELIZABETH, financial planner, seminar moderator; b. Litchfield, Ill., Jan. 28, 1949; d. A. Edward and Margaret Elizabeth (Viner) J. B.A., MacMurray Coll., 1971; lang. arts specialist So. Ill. U.-Edwardsville, 1980. Cert. fin. planner. Elem. sch. tchr. Jacksonville Sch. Dist., Ill., 1971-74, Southwestern Sch. Dist., Piasa, Ill., 1974-83; adminstrv. dir. Computer Learning Source, Inc., St. Louis, 1983—; pres. LJ Resources, Alton, Ill., 1983—; seminar moderator Nat. Inst. Fin., South Plainfield, N.J., 1985—, Personal Fin. Seminars, Inc., St. Louis, 1985—; bd. dirs. Computer Learning Source, Inc., 1983—; chmn. St. Louis Fin. Planner of Yr., 1985—. Vestry woman St. Paul's Episcopal Parish, Alton, 1982-85, Sunday Sch. tchr., 1981—. Named Outstanding Tchr. of Yr., PTA Shipman, Ill., 1977; recipient Grand Cross of Color, Internat. Order Rainbow for Girls, 1968. Mem. Internat. Assn. Fin. Planning (bd. dirs. St. Louis chpt. 1985—), Inst. Cert. Fin. Planners, Nat. Assn. Female Execs., DAR (state treas. Ill. 1986—, named Outstanding Jr. Ill. Orgn. 1984), Jr. League Greater Alton (fin. com. 1984—). Lodge: Order Eastern Star. Avocations: antiquing; home renovation; aerobics. Home: 1426 Henry St Alton IL 62002 Office: 3383 N Hwy 67 Saint Louis MO 63033

JOHNSON, LUCILLE PATRICIA, hair care products company executive; b. Ponca City, Okla., Dec. 9, 1936; d. Charles Isreal and Nellie O. (Gillman) Sober; m. Clifford J. Johnson, Mar. 14, 1953 (div. Aug. 1971); children—Donna M. Johnson Rudisill, Johnnie D., Jimmie W. Student Shasta Jr. Coll., 1963-64. Shipping clk. Douglas Aircraft Co., El Segundo, Calif., 1956-60; constrn. supt. J.F. Shea Co., Redding, Calif., 1964-80; pres. Nicole Research Inc., Redding, 1981—; ptnr., acct. Rowan & Johnson, Redding, 1973—, R.D.J. Investments, Redding, 1976—, R.D.J.S., Redding 1978—; sec.-treas. Buzz McMillin Inc., Redding, 1984—. Mem. Beauty and Barber Supply Inst., Nat. Assn. Women in Constrn., Nat. Fedn. Ind. Bus., Redding C. of C., Ladies Profl. Golf Assn. Democrat. Avocations: golf; swimming; silk flower arranging. Home: PO Box 3094 Redding CA 96049 Office: Nicole Research Inc PO Box 3358 Redding CA 96049

JOHNSON, LYNNE ARDELL, lawyer; b. Spokane, Wash., Oct. 25, 1951; d. Gaylar Winton and Donna Lucille (Tolford) J. A.B. in Econs. with departmental honors and distinction, Vassar Coll., 1973; J.D., Yale U., 1976. Bar: Ga. 1977, N.Y. 1981. Asst. to gen. counsel Systems and Technics, S.A., Gland, Switzerland, 1976-77; assoc. firm Powell, Goldstein, Frazer & Murphy, Atlanta, 1977-79, firm Fried, Frank, Harris, Shriver & Jacobson, N.Y.C., 1979—. Hon. grad. fellow for legal studies, 1973-74. Mem. ABA (sects. corp., banking and bus. law, internat. law, and sci. and tech.), Am. Soc. Internat. Law, Internat. Bar Assn., Inter-Am. Bar Assn., Assn. Immigration and Nationality Lawyers, N.Y. County Lawyers' Assn., Atlanta Bar Assn. (sects. corp., banking and bus. law, internat. law), State Bar Ga. (sects. corp. and internat. law), Soc. Univ. Patent Adminstrs. Contbg. author: Exit Age: Reconsidering Compulsory Education for Adolescents—Studies in Law, Education and Social Science, 1981. Office: One New York Plaza New York NY 10004

JOHNSON, MADGE RICHARDS, sales manager; b. Washington, Oct. 4, 1952; d. Benjamin Ellsworth and Virginia (Oliver) Richards; m. Jeffrey Leonard Johnson, June 25, 1977; 1 son, Jared Benjamin. B.S. in Bus. Mgmt., Strayer Coll., 1973; postgrad. in Bus. Adminstrn., Am. U., 1975-77. Nat. govt. sales rep. G.F.C. Mfg. Co., Bklyn., 1972-75; ter. sales rep. John H. Breck, Am. Cyanamid, Wayne, N.J., 1975-77; ter. sales mgr. Drackett Products Co., Cin., 1977-81, E.J. Brach & Sons., Chgo., Annapolis, Md., 1981—. Mem. Nat. Assn. Female Execs., Grocery Mfrs. Reps., Women in Consumer Product Sales. Seventh-day Adventist. Home and Office: 625 Rolling Dale Rd Annapolis MD 21401

JOHNSON, MARCELITE ELAINE, computer management executive, consultant; b. Savannah, Ga., Mar. 19, 1949; d. Leon and Jane (Mohr) Dingle, m. Melvin Norman Johnson, Dec. 22, 1968; children—DeAndra Chanet, Monet Nichelle, Melvin Roschaun. B.A. in Math., U. Colo.-Boulder, 1972; M.S. in Edn., Ind. U.-Bloomington, 1979; postgrad. U. So. Calif., Stuttgart, W.Ger., 1984-85. Programmer analyst Hewlitt-Packard, Colorado Springs, 1979-81; sr. systems analyst Penrose Hosp., Colorado Springs, 1982-83; systems mgr. Penrose Cancer Hosp., Colorado Springs, 1981-82; systems mgr. Civilian Personnel Office U.S. Army, Stuttgart, W.Ga., 1983-85; br. support mgr. Wang Deutschland GmbH Fed. Systems Dist., Stuttgart, 1985—; lectr. U. Colo., 1980, City Colls. Chgo., Stuttgart, 1983-85. Mem. Nat. Assn. Female Execs., Alpha Kappa Alpha. Episcopalian. Avocations: tennis; bridge. Office: Wang Deutschland GmbH Vor dem Lauch 25 7000 Stuttgart 80 West Germany

JOHNSON, MARGARET ANN KIEFT, marquetry company executive; b. Chgo., Nov. 25, 1939; d. Charles Samuel and Betty Marie (Fridrich) Kieft; B.S. in Edn., No. Ill. U., 1961, postgrad., 1963-67, 86—; postgrad. Western Ill. U., 1962-63, (NDEA grantee) Northeastern U., 1967; m. Dale L. Johnson, Aug. 19, 1961; 1 child, Jeffrey Kieft. Tchr., Frew Elem. Sch., Aledo, Ill., 1961-62; tchr. English, Aledo High Sch., 1962-63; tchr. English, head dept. Hiawatha High Sch., Kirkland, Ill., 1963-72; sec.-treas., office mgr., dir. Inlaid Woodcraft Co., Kirkland, 1973—. Mem. adv. bd. Kirkland Parent-Tchr. Orgn., 1977-78; mem. steering com. Sycamore Parent-Tchr. Orgn., Sycamore, Ill., 1980-81; mem. membership com. DeKalb County (Ill.); mem. membership com. Ben Gordon Mental Health Center, 1980-81, supporting mem., 1982-85, benefactor, 1986; den leader Sycamore Pack #118, Three Rivers council Cub Scouts, Boy Scouts Am., 1981-82; mem. Sycamore Hosp. Aux., 1983-86. Mem. Marquetry Soc. Am., Nat. Fedn. Ind. Bus., Nat. Small Bus. Assn., Beta Sigma Phi (Order of Rose 1980, pres. exec. council 1982-83). Club: Order Eastern Star. Home: Ellen Dr PO Box 497 Genoa IL 60135 Office: 525 Brickville Rd Sycamore IL 60178

JOHNSON, MARGARET HELEN, welding executive; b. Chgo., June 3, 1933; d. Harold W. and Clara J. (Pape) Glavin; m. Odean Jack Johnson, Nov. 18, 1950; children—Karen Ann, Dean Harold. Student Moody Bible Inst., 1976-78. Vice-pres., treas. Seamline Welding, Inc., Chgo., 1956—, also dir.; trustee SWCEPS Trust, Chgo., 1963—. Author: Living Faith, 1973, 80; God's Rainbow, 1982; also articles. Mem. Republican Presdl. Task Force, 1982-86, Lake View Neighborhood Group, Chgo. Mem. ASCAP, Fedn. Ind. Small Bus. Sunday sch. tchr., 1985; mem. Mary Seat Wisdom Catholic Women's Club, 1970—. Republican. Roman Catholic. Home: 1200 S Chester St Park Ridge IL 60068

JOHNSON, MARGARET HILL, educational administrator; b. Dundee, Scotland, June 26, 1923; d. John Barnet and Isabella Rae (Watson) Hill; came to U.S., 1946, naturalized, 1957; student Inverness (Scotland) Royal Acad., 1940, Edinburgh (Scotland) Royal Coll. Art, 1940-43; doctoral candidate U. Mass., Amherst, 1980—; children—Ann Hill Doughty, James Appleton Doughty (dec.), Joanna Elizabeth Johnson. Latin and remedial English tutor Harvey Sch., N.Y.C., 1947-52; tchr. athletics Pingree Sch. for Girls, Hamilton, Mass., 1959-61; tchr. Shore Country Day Sch., Beverly, Mass., 1952-59; asso. dir. Theodore S. Jones & Co., design mgmt. cons., Milton, Mass., 1961-72; dir. career planning and placement Mass. Coll. Art, 1972—, coordinator human services; design cons. Theodore S. Jones & Co.; speaker Lesley Coll., 1977, Cambridge (Mass.) Community Schs., 1977—, MIT, Harvard U., R.I. Sch. Design, Hofstra U. Served with Brit. Women's Royal Naval Service, 1943-46. Mem. Coll. Placement Council, Mass. Assn. Women Deans and Counselors, Nat. Assn. Women Deans, Adminstrs. and Counselors, Am. Assn. Higher Edn., Coll. Art Assn. Am., Eastern Coll. Placement Officers, Arts Dirs. Club Boston, Graphic Artists Guild. Author: (with others) Your Future in Art and

Design, 1977. Home: Box 75 Off Summer St Marshfield MA 02051 Office: 621 Huntington Ave Boston MA 02115

JOHNSON, MARGARET KATHLEEN, educator; b. Baylor County, Tex., Oct. 30, 1920; d. George W. and Julia Rivers (Turner) Higgins; B.S., Hardin-Simmons U., 1940; M.Bus. Edn., N.Tex. State U., 1957, Ed.D., 1962; m. Herman Clyde Johnson, Jr., July 27, 1949 (dec.); 1 dau., Carolyn Kay. Clk., Farmers Nat. Bank, Seymour, Tex., 1940-41; adminstrv. sec. U.S. Navy, Corpus Christi, Tex., 1941-46; adminstrv. asst. Hdqrs. 8th Army, Yokohama, Japan, 1946-49; instr. Coll. Bus. Adminstrn., U. Ark., 1957-60; teaching fellow Sch. Bus. Adminstrn., N.Tex. State U., 1960-62, instr., 1962-63; asst. prof. bus. tchr. edn. and secondary edn. Tchrs. Coll., U. Nebr., Lincoln, 1963-65, asso. prof., 1966-70, prof., 1970—; guest lectr. U. N.Mex., 1967, Curriculum Devel. in Bus. Edn., N.S. Dept. Edn., 1969, N.Tex. State U., 1970, E.Tex. State U., 1972. Recipient United Bus. Edn. Assn. award as outstanding grad. student in bus. edn. N.Tex. State U., 1957; award for outstanding service Nebr. Future Bus. Leaders Am., 1968; Mountain-Plains Bus. Edn. Leadership award 1977. Mem. Nat. (exec. bd. 1975, 76-79, policies commn. for bus. and econ. edn. 1979—), Mountain-Plains (exec. sec. 1970-73, pres. 1975), Nebr. (pres. 1966-67, Service award 1979) bus. edn. assns., Nebr. Council on Occupational Tchr. Edn., Delta Pi Epsilon. Author: Standardized Production Typewriting Tests series, 1964-65; National Structure for Research in Vocational Education, 1966; Introduction to Word Processing, 1980; Introduction to Word/Information Processing, 1985. Editor: the Changing Office Environment, 1980; Introduction to Business Communication, 1981. Home: 7300 South St Lincoln NE 68506 Office: 303 Tchrs Coll U Nebr Lincoln NE 68588

JOHNSON, MARIE C. BELLAMY, lawyer; b. Boley, Okla., Nov. 25, 1911; d. Louis Cecil and Bertha (Watson) Taylor; LL.B., John Marshall Law Sch., 1947, J.D., 1970; grad. Nat. Jud. Coll., U. Nev.-Reno, 1983; m. Wesley Maurice Johnson, Aug. 17, 1944 (div. 1974); children—Harold Bellamy, Viola Cecile, Marie Christine. Admitted to Ill. bar, 1948; practice law, Chgo., 1948-58, 75—; atty. IRS U.S. Treasury, Chgo., 1958-62; hearings supr. appeals sub-div. Ill. Dept. Employment Security Benefits, 1963-86. Mem. Ill. State Bar Assn., Am. Bar Assn., Chgo. Bar Assn., Nat. Assn. Women Lawyers, Women's Bar Assn. of Ill., Chgo. Urban League. Club: Executive (Chgo.). Home: 300 N State St Chicago IL 60610 Office: 910 S Michigan Ave Room 706 Chicago IL 60605

JOHNSON, SISTER MARIE INEZ, retired librarian; b. Mitchell, S.D., June 2, 1909; d. Charles and Inez L. (Williams) Johnson; B.A. in English, Coll. St. Catherine, 1929, B.S. in L.S., 1939; M.S. in L.S., Columbia U., 1940; postgrad. U. Denver, 1951-52, U. So. Calif., 1953-54. Joined Sisters St. Joseph Carondolet, 1926; tchr. elementary schs. St. Paul, 1930-38; librarian Coll. St. Catherine, St. Paul, 1940-42, head librarian, 1942-74. Mem. steering com. U. Minn. Workshop for Librarians, 1956; library cons. survey Mt. Mercy Coll., Cedar Rapids, Iowa, 1963-64; bldg. cons. Fontbonne Coll., St. Louis, 1964—. Mem. Conf. Am. Folklore for Youth, St. Paul Speakers Bur., com. standard catalog for high sch. Cath. Support, Children's Lit. TV Series. Butler Fgn. Study fellow Coll. St. Catherine, 1958. Named Minn. Librarian of Year, 1967. Mem. Am. (various coms.), Cath. (various coms.) library assns. Editor column Cath. Library World, 1954—. Contbr. articles to profl. jours. Address: Coll St Catherine St Paul MN 55105

JOHNSON, MARILYN THERESE CURRAN, sales techniques company executive; b. N.Y.C., Oct. 22, 1936; d. Cark Frederick and Bridget (O'Brien) Bachmann; m. Harold Joseph Curran, Nov. 28, 1959 (div. 1972); 1 child, Jeffrey Francis; m. Ronald Hans Johnson Aug. 8, 1981; stepchildren—Ronald, Kristina. Student, Katherine Gibbs Sch., 1954-55, U. Conn., 1955-57; B.A. in Psychology, Rutgers U., 1969. Asst. to asst. sec. state State Dept., Washington, 1957-59; broker Merrill Lynch, N.Y.C., 1971-73; asst. mgr. sales Xerox, Princeton, N.J., 1973-80; nat. acctg. rep. Gen. Dynamics Co., Montvale, N.J., 1980-82; sales exec. No. Telecom, N.Y.C., 1982-85; pres., owner Selling Scis., Somerset, N.J., 1985—; cons. Barbizon Modelling Schs., Highland Park, N.J., 1964-69. Mem. Bus. and Profl. Women (chmn. young careerist 1984, chmn. foundation com. 1985). Avocations: French studies; skiing; tennis; travel; reading. Home: 144 Drake Rd Somerset NJ 08873

JOHNSON, MARJORIE JEAN TAYLOR, educator; b. Upper Darby, Pa., Feb. 4, 1951; d. Samuel Craig and Edna Jean (Cramer) Taylor; m. Gene Larry Johnson, Aug. 4, 1973; one child, Samuel Taylor. B.A. in Edn., Kearney State Coll., 1973, postgrad., 1977-84. Cert. tchr., Nebr. Elem. tchr. Bertrand Sch., Nebr., 1973-76; elem. tchr. Holdrege Pub. Schs., Nebr., 1976—, asst. problem-solving coach, gifted program, 1978-79. Block chmn. Am. Heart. Assn., Holdrege, 1984. Offut AFB Officer's Wives Club scholar Kearney State Coll., 1969; Kearney Found. scholar Kearney State Coll., 1969-73; State of Nebr. scholar Kearney State Coll., 1971-73; NSF grantee Kearney State Coll., 1977-78. Mem. Holdrege Edn. Assn. (rec. sec. 1978-79, bldg. rep. 1979-80), Nebr. State Edn. Assn., NEA, Bus. and Profl. Women, Alpha Phi (guard 1970-71, rec. sec. 1971-72). Republican. Episcopalian. Home: 3495 Scenic Dr Winston GA 30187 Office: Bill Arp Sch Douglasville GA 30135

JOHNSON, MARLENE, lieutenant governor; b. Braham, Minn., Jan. 11, 1946; d. Helen M. Nelson; B.A., Macalester Coll., 1968. Community organizer Ramsey Action Program, St. Paul, 1968-70; program dir. YMCA, St. Paul, 1970-71; pres., founder Split Infinitive Inc., St. Paul, 1971-82; lt. gov. State of Minn.; chair Minn. Project Innovation, Gov.'s Open Appointments Commn., Commn. on Minnesotans Outdoors, Women's Hist. Ctr. Task Force, Capitol Area Archtl. and Planning Bd., Mississippi River Pkwy. Commn. Minn., also coordinator Minn. tourism and small bus. programs. Vice-chmn. Minn. Task Force on Small Bus., 1978; mem. small bus. adv. com. U.S. Treasury Dept., 1978-80; co-chmn. Minn. del. White Ho. Conf. on Small Bus., 1980; mem. adv. bd. Sch. Mgmt., U. Minn.; bd. dirs. Spring Hill Ctr., Landmark Ctr., Minn. Public Programming Corp.; founder, past chmn. Nat. Conf. Women Execs. in State Govt.; bd. dirs. Minn. Wellspring, Minn. High Tech. Council, Midwest Tech. Devel. Inst.; mem. Democratic Policy Commn., 1985-86. Mem. Nat. Assn. Lt. Govs. (exec. com.), Nat. Assn. Women Bus. Owners (pres.), Nat. Women's Polit. Caucus, Minn. Women's Polit. Caucus (chmn. 1974-77), Com. of 200 (charter 1982). Democrat. Clubs: Minnesota, St. Paul Athletic. Office: 122 State Capitol Saint Paul MN 55155

JOHNSON, MARLENE CAROLE, banker; b. Somerville N.J., Apr. 10, 1950; d. Herbert E. and Thelma E. (Westerfield) J. B.A., Glassboro State Coll., 1972; M. Banking, Rutgers U., 1982. Cert. tchr., N.J. Asst. bookkeeper Franklin State Bank, Somerset, N.J., 1972-73; adminstr. North Plainfield (N.J.) State Bank, 1973-76, asst. sec., 1976-78, asst. v.p., 1978—. Mem. Voluntary Action Com., New Brunswick, N.J. Recipient Tribute to Women and Industry, YWCA, Westfield, N.J. Mem. Am. Inst. Banking (v.p. edn. Middlesex, Somerset, Union chpt. 1974-84, pres. chpt. 1984-85), Nat. Assn. Bank Women, Nat. Assn. Female Execs., Central N.J. C. of C. (vice chairperson). Club: Saint Luke's Singles. Contbr. articles to profl. jours. Home: 137 Bayberry Dr Somerset NJ 08873 Office: North Plainfield State Bank Route 22 and Rock Ave Box 1027 North Plainfield NJ 07060

JOHNSON, MARY ANN, management consultant; b. Memphis, Oct. 11, 1948; d. William Edward and Mary Ann (White) J. Bank teller cert. Cashier Tng. Inst., Memphis, 1966; secretarial diploma Griggs Bus. Coll., Memphis, 1968. Research asst. to A.A. Latting, Atty., Memphis, 1967-68; office mgr. Jerry Butler Prodns., Chgo., 1968-74; spl. asst. nat. dir. artist relations A&M Records, Los Angeles, 1975-79; pres. MJB Mgmt. Cons., Los Angeles, 1980—. Active neighborhood youth work; sec. council on ministries Wilshire United Methodist Ch., Los Angeles, 1983-86, mem. adminstrv. bd., 1986; active United Meth. Women, Los Angeles, 1985-86. Recipient Gold Album award A&M Records and Styx, 1975, 76, 77, 78, Platinum Album award A&M Records and Styx, 1977, Gold Single award A&M Records and Record Industry Assn. Am., 1977, Gold Album award A&M Records and Record Industry Assn. Am., 1977, 78, Platinum Album award A&M Records and Record Industry Assn. Am., 1978, various certs., awards Wilshire United Methodist Ch., 1982-85. Mem. Nat. Acad. Rec. Arts and Scis. (assoc.), Nat. Assn. Female Execs. Democrat. Avocation: writing mystery and science fiction books. Home: 7320 Hawthorn Apt 214 West Hollywood CA 90046 Office: MJB Mgmt Cons 2012 Thurman Ave Los Angeles CA 90016

JOHNSON, MARY CARTER, business risk analyst; b. Meriden, Conn., Feb. 9, 1947; d. Frederick Miles and Barbara (Wainwright) Carter; m. Paul Lee Johnson, June 20, 1970. B.A., Hobart and William Smith Colls., 1969; M.B.A., Pace U., 1979. Data analyst, statis. researcher Hobart and William Smith Colls., Geneva, N.Y., 1969-70; occupational therapist Sampson State Sch., Willard, N.Y., 1970-71; personnel asst. Graybar Electric Co., N.Y.C., 1971-72; youth services specialist City of N.Y., 1972-76, staff analyst, 1978-81; bus. risk analyst Citibank, N.Y.C., 1981—. Bd. dirs. St. Matthew and St. Timothy's Neighborhood Ctr., N.Y.C., 1975-80; alumnae career advisor Hobart and William Smith Colls., 1984—. Andrew Mellon Found. fellow Pace U., N.Y.C., 1976-79. Mem. Nat. Assn. Female Execs. Episcopalian. Home: 158 W 81st St Apt 62 New York NY 10024 Office: Citibank 575 Lexington Ave New York NY 10043

JOHNSON, MARY ELIZABETH, music educator, pianist; b. Tyler, Tex., Mar. 29, 1933; d. Robert Edward and Mamie Oberia (Walters) Spaulding; B.F.A., So. Methodist U., 1955; pvt. study with Bomar Cramer, Dallas, 1964-69; m. George Devereaux Johnson, Mar. 31, 1955; children—Bradford D., Robin Elizabeth. Music tchr. Dallas Country Day Sch., 1955; tchr. Dayton (Ohio) pub. schs., 1956-57; pvt. tchr. piano Dallas, 1962—; profl. accompanist, Dallas, 1965—; duo-pianist, Dallas, 1965—; sponsor-tchr. creative and performing arts program Dallas Ind. Sch. Dist., 1981-82, 83, 84; sponsor Jr. Melodie and Jr. Harmonie. Named to honor roll Nat. Guild Piano Tchrs., 1971, Hall of Fame, Am. Coll. Musicians, 1981. Mem. Nat. Guild Piano Tchrs. (cert.), Tex. Fedn. Music Clubs (historian 1974-76, state chmn. music service in the community 1971-73, dist. jr. counselor 1971-78, dist. chmn. music service in the community 1971-78; rec. sec. 5th dist. 1975-76, 1st v.p. 1977-78, jr. festival chmn. 1977-80, dist. chmn. Jr. Gold Cup awards 1980, 84, 85, asst. chmn. North Dallas div. 5th dist. jr. festival 1981-82), Music Tchrs. Nat. Assn., Jr. Pianists Guild of Dallas (chmn. jr. recitals 1983, chmn. sr. recitals 1984), Tex., Dallas music tchrs. assns., Music Study Club Dallas (chmn. piano program 1981-82), Piano Study Club, Dallas Fedn. Music Clubs (del. 1969-78, 1st v.p. 1977), Daus. Republic Tex. (1st v.p. Bonham chpt. 1975-76), Alpha Delta Pi. Clubs: Melodie (pres. 1969-71, 3d v.p. 1977—, choral accompanist, counselor jr. club, historian, press sec. 1981-82), Kalista (yearbook chmn. 1983-84, v.p. 1984-85). Home: 3848 Cedarbrush Dr Dallas TX 75229

JOHNSON, MARY LEA, film and theatrical producer; m. Martin Richards. Founder with Martin Richards The Producer Circle Co., 1976—, producer Broadway plays including: The Norman Conquests, On the Twentieth Century, 1978, Sweeney Todd (Tony award), 1979, Crimes of the Heart, 1981, Foxfire, 1982; co-producer off-Broadway musical March of the Falsettos; co-producer films including: The Boys from Brazil, The Shining, Fort Apache, The Bronx. Address: The Producer Circle Co 1350 Ave of the Americas New York NY 10019*

JOHNSON, MARY LEE, institute for restorative technology executive, group homes executive; b. Vancouver, Wash., June 20, 1921; d. George Fitch and Anne (Falk) Watson; m. Roy Arthur Johnson (dec. Dec. 1982); children—Karine Anne Johnson Guard, Candise Elaine Johnson Elmer, Barbara Jo Johnson Walla. Lic. nursing home adminstrn. Portland State Coll. 1970; A.S. in Nursing, Clark Coll., 1973; B.S. in Health Care Adminstrn., City Coll., Vancouver, Wash., 1979, B.S. in Nursing Adminstrn., 1979. R.N., lic. nursing home adminstr., Wash. Bus. mgr. Watson's Nursing Home, Battle Ground, Wash., 1950-54; owner, adminstr. Battle Ground Convalescent Home, 1954-74, Clark Inst. Restorative Tech., Battle Ground, 1975—, Alvador Residential Ctr., Vancouver, 1982—, Hewitt House Instn. for Mentally Retarded, Vancouver, 1980—. Developer tng. program on human sexuality for handicapped. Pres. field services Am. Cancer Soc., Vancouver, 1970-75. Mem. Wash. Health Facilities (sec. 1968-78), Am. Bus. Women's Club, Am. Nurses Assn., Am. Coll. Health Care Adminstrs., Wash. Health Facilities (pres. dist. 1965-67), Assn. Retarded Citizens (bd. dirs. 1978-80, Profl. of Yr. 1978, Outstanding Dedication award 1984), Battle Ground C. of C. (bd. dirs. 1978), Ladies Study Club (pres.). Democrat. Home: 512 N 5th Ave Battle Ground WA 98604 Office: Clark Inst Restorative Tech PO Box 218 Battle Ground WA 98604

JOHNSON, MARY LEONA, city official; b. Greenville, N.C., Sept. 21; d. Lewis and Leona (Anderson) Blow; B.A. in Sociology, Wayne State U., 1974; M.A., Antioch Sch. Law, 1982; 1 son, Reginald B. Johnson. With U.S. Treasury Dept., Washington, 1944-46; receptionist U.S. Army Tank Automotive Center, 1952-56; supr. Tb Registry, Detroit Dept. Health, 1956-71; Affirmative Action adminstr. Detroit Human Rights Dept., 1977—, cons. women's issues, 1975-77. Mem. Mich. State adv. council vocat. edn., 1980-83; mem. appeal bd. Selective Service System, Eastern Jud. Dist. Mich.; vice chmn. 1st Congl. Dist. Dem. Party Orgn. Recipient Christian Service award. Mem. Nat. Assn. Human Rights Workers of Mich. (pres. Mich. chpt.), Mich. Coalition for Human Rights, Nat. Assn. Exec. Women, Detroit Round Table of Christian and Jews Detroit Women's Forum, Women's Econ. Club. Democrat. Mem. Ch. of Christ. Office: Detroit Human Rights Dept 150 Michigan Ave 4th Floor Detroit MI 48226

JOHNSON, MARY TERESA, city official; b. Washington, Aug. 31, 1940; d. George Joseph and Mary Teresa (McQuillan) O'Hare; m. Robert Thomas Johnson, Oct. 1, 1960; children—Robert, Jr., Mary Lou, Bridget. Student U. Md., 1958-60. Profl. registration on parks and recreation, Md. Tchr., Holy Redeemer, College Park, Md., 1960-67; clk. Prince George Bar Assn., Hyattsville, Md., 1970-74; dir. parks and recreation City of Hyattsville, 1974—. Mem. Dem. State Central Com., Prince Georges County, Md., 1982—. Mem. Md. Recreation and Park Assn. (pres. 1985—; Quarterly award 1980), Park and Resource Conservation Found. (sec. 1983—), Md. Municipal League (pres. 1983—). Roman Catholic. Club: Prince George County Soropomist. Avocations: stamps, reading, cooking. Home: 4021 Ingraham St Hyattsville MD 20781

JOHNSON, MARYANN ELAINE, educational administrator; b. Franklin Twp., Pa., Nov. 1, 1943; d. Mary I. Sollick; B.S. in Elementary Edn., Mansfield State Coll., Pa., 1964; M.S. in Elementary Edn., U. Alaska, College 1973; Ed.D., Wash. State U., Pullman, 1981; married. Tchr. Nayatt Sch., Barrington, R.I., 1964-66, North Sch., North Chicago, Ill., 1966-67, Kodiak (Alaska) On-Base Sch., 1967-71; reading coordinator Eastmont Sch. Dist., East Wenatchee, Wash., 1971-77, now asst. supt. Sec. Parent Advisory Com., 1974-76. Mem. Assn. Supervision and Curriculum Devel., Wash. State Assn. Supervision and Curriculum Devel. (bd. dirs. 1986—, Educator of Yr. 1981), NEA, Wash. Assn. Sch. Adminstrs. (bd. dirs., chmn. curriculum and instrn. Job-Alike, profl. devel. com., Project Leadership), Am. Assn. Sch. Adminstrs., Delta Kappa Gamma (pres. 1982-84), Phi Delta Kappa, Phi Kappa Phi. Named Eastmont Tchr. of the Yr., 1973-74. Office: 460 N E 9th St East Wenatchee WA 98801

JOHNSON, MIRIAM P., travel and tourism company executive; b. N.Y.C., Nov. 23, 1929; d. William and Miriam Coombs (Barrus) Young; m. Theodore R. Johnson, Nov. 13, 1949 (dec. 1979); 1 child, Ronald. B.A., Queens Coll., 1947; M.A., Post Coll., 1952. Pres. Travel Profls., Ltd., N.Y.C., 1984—, Travel Round the World, Huntington, N.Y., 1976-84, St. Maarten Assistance Service, N.A., 1976-84, Villa Vacations, Ltd., Anguilla, W.I., 1976—; mktg. dir. Kelly Girls, N.Y.C., 1974-76; with sales promotion M.G.A. Assocs., Great Neck, N.Y., 1966-74; with MONY Ins., Huntington, 1961-66. Contbr. articles to profl. jours. Mem. Assn. Female Execs., Sales Promotion Execs., Caribbean Tourism Assn., Assoc. Soc. Travel Agts. Avocations: theatre; opera; ballet; philharmonic; skiing. Home: PO Box 188 Cold Spring Harbor NY 11724 Office: Travel Profls Ltd 141 E 55th St Suite 1A New York NY 11724

JOHNSON, MURIEL LEMON, association administrator, minister of education; b. Phila., Aug. 29, 1925; d. Robert and Louise Taylor; m. Emory L. Johnson, July 20, 1969. Receptionist Optometric Assn., 1942-52; tchr., 1958-64; real estate jr. exec. in charge of conveyancing, 1964-66; realtor Mt. Life Ins. Co., 1966-68; minister of edn.; pres. Internat. Assn. Minister's Wives. Author of articles, tracts and book; editor of Business and Profl. Women's official publ. Recipient 40 awards for civic and religious service to community. Fellow Internat. Acad. Poets; mem. NAACP, Girl Scouts (life). Office: 206-14 100th Ave Queens Village NY 11428

JOHNSON, NAN H., county legislator, political science educator; b. Pitts., Jan. 12, 1930; d. Vernon Eugene and Kathryn Jennings (Reed) Heffelfinger; m. James William Johnson, Oct. 5, 1957; children—Miranda Stuart, Reed Vann. B.A., Barnard Coll., 1952; M.A., U. Rochester, 1960; postgrad. Cornell U., 1952-53. Mem. Monroe County Legislature, Rochester, 1975—; adj. prof. U. Rochester. Trustee SUNY, 1976—, Landmark Soc. Western N.Y., 1971—; del. Democratic Nat. Conv., 1984. Home: 64 Oliver St Rochester NY 14607 Office: Monroe County Legislature 3/9 W Main St Rochester NY 14607

JOHNSON, NANCY LEE, congresswoman, former state senator; b. Chgo., Jan. 5, 1935; d. Noble Wishard and Gertrude Reid (Smith) Lee; B.A., Radcliffe Coll., 1957; postgrad. U. London, 1957-58; m. Theodore H. Johnson, July 16, 1958; children—Lindsey Lee, Althea Anne, Caroline Reid. Vice chmn. Charter Commn. New Britain, 1976-77; mem. Conn. Senate from 6th Dist., 1977-82; mem. 98th, 99th Congresses. Bd. dirs. United Way New Britain, 1976-79, New Britain Symphony Soc., 1975-77, Plainville Group Home, 1975-76; pres. Friends of Library, New Britain Pub. Library, 1973-76; lectr. Am. art New Britain Mus. Am. Art, 1968-71; pres. Radcliffe Club No. Conn., 1973-75; bd. dirs., pres. Sheldon Community Guidance Clinic, 1974-75; pres. Unitarian Universalist Soc. New Britain, 1973-75, dir. religious edn., 1967-72. Grantee English Speaking Union, 1958-59; recipient Outstanding Vol. award United Way, 1976. Republican. Office: Office of House Members care The Postmaster Washington DC 20515

JOHNSON, NANCY RUTH, nursing administrator; b. Lakewood, N.J., Sept. 5, 1949; d. Thomas Arthur and Ruth Estella (McFadden) Richards; m. Norman Gene Johnson, Dec. 2, 1972. B.S.Nursing, Wagner Coll., 1971; M.Nursing Adminstrn., UCLA, 1985. Mobile intensive care nurse Presbyn. Intercommunity Hosp., Whittier, Calif., 1976-78; home health nurse Staff Builders, Covina, Calif., 1979-81; head nurse New Hope Pain Ctr., Alhambra, Calif., 1981-84; nursing dir. City of Hope, Duarte, Calif., 1985—. Served as lt. USNR, 1971-76, comdr. Res., 1976—. Mem. Am. Assn. Neurosci. Nurses, Oncology Nurses Soc., Naval Res. Assn., Am. Mil. Surgeons in U.S., Women in Health Adminstrn. Home: 2017 Berkshire Ave South Pasadena CA 91030 Office: City of Hope Nat Med Ctr 1500 E Duarte Rd Duarte CA 91010

JOHNSON, NORINE GOODE, psychologist; b. Indpls., Dec. 3, 1935; d. Frank and Marie (Collins) Goode; B.A., DePauw U., 1957; Ph.D., Wayne State U., 1972; postgrad. Harvard Med. Sch., 1975-77; m. Charles W. Johnson, Aug. 23, 1958; children—Cammarie, Kathryn Carroll, Margaret Ellen. Psychology cons. to pediatrics Univ. Hosps. Cleve., 1968-69; asst. clin. prof. dept. neurology Boston U. Med. Sch., 1976—; adj. prof. psychology Boston Coll., 1978—; dir. psychology Kennedy Meml. Hosp., Brighton, Mass., 1970—. Pres. area bd. Mental Health and Retardation, 1973, regional bd., 1974; mem. Gov.'s Adv. Council Mental Health and Mental Retardation, 1974-76, chairperson children's subcom., 1976. NIMH scholar, trainee. Fellow Mass. Psychol. Assn. (pres. elect 1980, pres. 1981-83, dir., bd. profl. affairs 1977—, chairperson 1977-78, liaison to Mass. Psychiat. Soc. 1978); mem. Am. Psychol. Assn. (council of reps. 1985-88), Psi Chi. Club: Boston Athletic. Home: 1 Devonshire Pl #3209 Boston MA 02109 Office: 50 Warren St Brighton MA 02135

JOHNSON, NORMA HOLLOWAY, fed. judge; b. Lake Charles, La.; d. H. Lee and Beatrice M. (Williams) Holloway; B.S., D.C. Tchrs. Coll., 1955; J.D., Georgetown U., 1962; m. Julius A. Johnson. Admitted to D.C. bar, 1962; trial atty. U.S. Dept. Justice, Washington, 1963-67; asst. corp. counsel Office of Corp. Counsel D.C., 1967-70; judge Superior Ct. D.C., 1970-80; judge U.S. Dist. Ct., Washington, 1980—. Bd. dirs. Nat. Children's Center, Council for Ct. Excellence; past chmn. adv. com. Nat. St. Law Inst. Mem. Am. Judicature Soc. (dir.), Nat. Assn. Women Judges, Nat. Assn. Black Women Attys., Women's Bar, Nat. Bar Assn., Am. Bar Assn., D.C. Bar. Office: US Courthouse 3d and Constitution Ave NW Washington DC 20001

JOHNSON, NORMA J., specialty wool grower; b. Dover, Ohio, Aug. 30, 1925; d. Jasper Crile and Mildred Catherine (Russell) J.; student Heidelberg Coll., 1943; cert. drafting techniques Case Sch. Applied Sci., 1944; student Western Res. U., 1945-47, Ohio State U., 1951, Muskingum Coll., 1965; A.A., Kent State U., 1979; m. Robert Blake Covey, Oct. 7, 1951 (div. 1960); 1 dau., Susan Kay. Instr. arts and crafts Univ. Settlement House, Cleve., 1944; mech. drafstwoman Nat. Assn. Civil Aeros., Cleve., 1944-46; mfrs. rep. nat. spice house, 1947-49; tchr. econs., English, math, history, home econs., high sch., Tuscarawas County Sch. System, New Philadelphia, Ohio, 1962-69; owner, mgr. Sunny Slopes Farm, producer of splty. spinning wools, Dover, Ohio, 1969—; designed and built interior facilities for 96 animals, farm machinery storage, residence. Tchr., Meth. Sunday Sch., 1956-61; chaplain Winfield PTA, 1960; program dir. Brandywine Grange, 1960-62; troop leader Girl Scouts, U.S.A., 1961-70; mem. Tuscarawas County Jail Com., 1981. Recipient Ohio Wildlife Conservation award Tuscarawas County, 1972; 1st and 3d premiums for handspinning fleece Ohio State Fair, 1984, 8th and 9th premiums Mich. State Fair, 1985. Mem. Mid States Wool Growers, Am. Angus Assn. Club: Nat. Grange. Home and Office: Route 1 Box 398 Dover OH 44622

JOHNSON, NOTA, art educator, artist; b. Maryville, Mo., Nov. 20, 1923; d. Sam and Eva (Papathanasopoulos) J.; divorced; children—Sharon Ann Johnson, Vicki Lyn Johnson Groom. B.A., Okla. State U., 1945; M.A., U. Tulsa, 1973; secondary art edn. degree, 1969. Tchr. art Meml. High Sch., Tulsa, 1968-70; instr. art Tulsa Jr. Coll., 1970—. Recipient Graphics award Mus. Okla., 1979; 1st Place award Bartlesville Art. Assn., 1976. Mem. Nat. Assn. Women Artists (Print award 1980, 82, 84, mem. com. 1978—), So. Graphics Council (bd. dirs. 1980-82, v.p. 1980-82), Arts Humanities Council Tulsa (bd. dirs. 1978-81), Audubon Artists. Republican. Greek Orthodox. Club: Philoptohos (bd. dirs. 1984—). Lodge: Daus. of Penelope. Avocations: designing clothes; sports. Home: 1500 S Frisco Tulsa OK 74119

JOHNSON, PATRICIA ANN, advertising and public relations executive; b. Springfield, Mo., Dec. 2, 1952; d. Elvis Eugene and Jean Alice (Cain) J.; B.S., U. Mo., Columbia, 1975. With Am. Nat. Ins. Co., Galveston, Tex., 1975-81, pub. asst., 1975-77, editor The Tower, 1977-80, editor The Tower and Star Bull. mag., 1980-81; assoc. Amelia Bullock Realtors, Inc., Austin, Tex., 1983-85; nat. dir. advt. and pub. relations Fin. Ptnrs. Internat., Inc., 1985—. Bd. govs. Upper Deck Theatre, Galveston, 1976, 80, chmn. governing bd., 1977-78, sec., 1978-80; bd. dirs. Galveston County unit Am. Cancer Soc., 1977-79, sec., 1978-79; bd. dirs. Paramount Theatre for Performing Arts, Austin, 1983-85, Pebble Project, Austin, 1983-85; mem. Mayor's Task Force on Child Care, Austin, 1985; mem. Jr. League of Austin, Inc. Presbyterian. Home: 10711 B Newmont Austin TX 78758 Office: 6850 Austin Center Blvd Suite 200 Austin TX 78731

JOHNSON, PATRICIA ANNE, realtor; b. Montreal, Que., Apr. 13, 1928; came to U.S., 1946, naturalized 1950; d. George Alexander and Helen Lorraine (Haynes) Davidson; m. Kenneth F. Abbiss, July 13, 1947 (div. 1961); children—Craig, Stephen, Patricia; m. 2nd Lando H. Johnson, June 25, 1963. Student Sch. of Mgmt. Century 21 Internat., 1985; student U. N.H., 1984. Cert. realtor. Beautician, Boston, 1947-49; bookkeeper Derry Bank & Trust, N.H., 1970-73; realtor Century 21-Dumont, Manchester, N.H., 1980-84; pres., owner Century 21 Abbiss, Manchester, 1984—; securities dealer Nat. Assn. Security Dealers, N.H., national, 1985—; salesman Real Estate Commn., Fla., 1984—. Sustaining mem. Republican Nat. Com., 1985—. Named to One Million Dollar Club, Century 21 New Eng., 1983, Two Million Dollar Club, 1984, N.H. Top Salesmen Assn., Century 21 New Eng., 1983; recipient Pace Setter awards Century 21 New Eng., 1983, 84. Fellow Greater Manchester Bd. Realtors, Nat. Assn. Realtors; mem. Century 21 Investment Soc. Avocations: swimming, skiing, jogging, oil painting. Home: 30 Hills Rd Auburn NH 03022 Office: Century 21 ABBISS 225 Eddy Rd Manchester NH 03102

JOHNSON, PATRICIA CAREY, insurance company executive, real estate investment executive; b. Berlin, Md., Mar. 30, 1942; d. James Raymond and Ardis (Brannock) Carey; m. Charles P. Johnson, Aug. 10, 1968 (div.). B.S., U. Del., 1964. Cert. tchr., Del. Supr. New Castle County, Wilmington, Del., 1976-78, exec. asst., 1978-79, dir., 1979-81, supt., 1981; ops. mgr. CIGNA Corp., Phila., 1981-83, asst. to asst. v.p., Wilmington, 1983—; adj. prof. U. Del., 1978; dir. Am. Parks and Recreation Soc., Del. Recreation and Park Soc., Mid-Atlantic Regional Park and Recreation Council, Del. Assn. Health Phys Edn. and Recreation; project mgr. promotional campaign Leisure Creator, 1980; chairperson INFO Statewide Edn. Clearinghouse, Wilmington, 1977-81; vice-pres., sec., treas. New Castle County Continuing and Community Edn. Council, 1977-78; lay mem. New Castle County Sr. Ctrs. Project adv. bd., 1977-81. Named Dir. of Yr., Local 459 AFL/CIO, New Castle County, Del., 1980, Chairperson of Yr., Am. Parks and Recreation Soc., 1980. Mem. NOW, Am. Assn. Females Execs., Del. State Adv. Council, Nat. Recreation and Park Assn., AAHPER, Am. Assn. Leisure and Recreation. Republican. Methodist. Club: Rodney Square (Wilmington). Home: 712 N Franklin St Capitol Hill Wilmington DE 19805 Office: CIGNA Corp Executive Suite 4 East 1 Beaver Valley Rd Wilmington DE 19850

JOHNSON, PATRICIA MARY, publisher; b. Evanston, Ill., Mar. 14, 1937; d. Harold W. and Florence M. (Miller) J.; Interior Design degree LaSalle U.,

Chgo., 1972; student Art Inst., Chgo., 1970-73; m. Dirk G. Swart, Feb. 13, 1980; children—William, Nancy, Richard. Various office mgmt. positions, Chgo., 1957-72; owner Decor Interior Design, Chgo., 1972-76; interior design communicator, producer/host weekly syndicated cable TV program on interior design, 1980—; owner Design Communications, Rosenhayn, N.J., 1976-85; pub. PMJ Publs., Inc., 1985—. A Positive Approach mag. Recipient award N.J. Gov., 1985. Mem. Nat. Home Fashions League (Image Maker 1979), Nat. Writers Club, Am. Soc. Interior Designers, Nat. Fedn. Press Women, N.J. Press Women, Assoc. Photographers Internat., N.J. Assn. Women Bus. Owners, C. of C. Author: Eliminating Barriers from Your Lifestyle, 1985; columnist, Jersey Woman, 1979-86. Contbr. articles to profl. jours. and consumer mags.; also radio broadcaster. Home: PO Box 381 Rosenhayn NJ 08352 Office: PO Box 2179 South Vineland NJ 08360

JOHNSON, PAULA LEAH, marketing consultant, direct mail entrepreneur; b. Bay City, Mich., Sept. 23, 1957; d. Curtis Harry and Mary (Stanchak) J. B.A. in Journalism, Calif. State U., 1980. Account exec. Alfred Stern Co., Sherman Oaks, Calif., 1979-81; corp. communications dir. Gravity Guidance, Inc., Duarte, Calif., 1981-84; pres. The Johnson Group, Pasadena, Calif., 1984—; mem. Mademoiselle mag. Career Mktg. Bd., N.Y.C., 1980—; tchr. Calif. State U.-Northridge, 1981. Bd. dirs. Escalon, Inc., Altadena, Calif., 1985. Recipient award for product packaging Art Direction Mag., 1984. Mem. Internat. Assn. Bus. Communicators (Bronze Quill award 1983), Advt. Club Los Angeles, Pub. Relations Soc. Am., Am. Mktg. Assn. Democrat. Avocations: bodybuilding; clothing design.

JOHNSON, PHYLLIS AUDREY, banker; b. Darwin, Minn., July 25, 1923; d. John Emmanuel and Emma Elizabeth (Schneidegger) Nelson; m. Ellsworth Orr Johnson, Apr. 6, 1943; children —Elwood Oren (dec.), Christine Marie Johnson Wilbur, Elizabeth Ann Johnson Milne, Eric Christian. B.A., Met. State U., St. Paul, 1973; B. Applied Sci., U. Minn., 1974; diploma U. Wis. Grad. Sch. Banking. 1973; cert. Am. Inst. Banking, 1975. Asst. cashier Farmers State Bank, Darwin, 1941-42; mem. loan dept. office Nat. Bank Commerce, Longview, Minn., 1942-44; asst. cashier State Bank Anoka, Minn., 1944; staff booking office Am. Nat. Bank, Berkeley, Calif., 1944-46; cost acct. Red Wing Boast Works, Minn., 1956-57; banking generalist First Bank Southdale, Edina, Minn., 1960-70; asst. v.p. ops., personnel and purchasing S.W. Fidelity State Bank, Edina, 1970-71; auditor First Nat. Bank Glenwood City, Wis., 1973—, Hiawatha Nat. Bank, Hagen City, Wis., 1973—; employment mgr., personnel officer Bank Shares, Inc., Mpls., 1973-77; mortgage loan officer St. Anthony Park State Bank, St. Paul, 1978-79; mem. adv. com. bus. mgmt. program Mpls. Tech. Inst., 1975—, instr. bus. mgmt., 1979—; pres. DAAV Banking Services, Inc., Edina, 1984—; adv. com. banking program Suburban Hennepin Tech. Inst., White Bear Lake, Minn., 1972-77; speaker in field, 1974—. Precinct chmn. Edina Ind. Republicans, 1970-74; chmn. service unit, mem. coms., leader Edina and Red Wing councils Girl Scouts U.S.A., 1958-68; sec. Edina United Fund, 1963-64; pres. St. Paul's Lutheran Ch. Women, Mankato, Minn., 1965-67, St. Paul's Luth. Ch., Red Wing, 1950-58, Bethlehem Luth. Ch., Mpls., 1959—. Mem. Am. Banking Assn., Nat. Assn. Women Bus. Owners, Am. Bus. Women's Assn., Nat. Bus. Edn. Assn. Am. Vocat. Assn., Minn. Bus. Edn. Assn., Minn. Vocat. Assn. Clubs: Normandale Tennis, Winterset Dance, Interlachen Country. Home: 5301 Ayrshire Blvd Edina MN 55436 Office: 1415 Hennepin Ave S Minneapolis MN 55403

JOHNSON, POLLY A., association executive; b. Nelsonville, Ohio, July 16, 1923; d. Donald Ray and Ella Catherine (Gilbert) Johnson. B.A., Ohio U., 1945; M.S.W., Tulane U., 1950. Exec. dir. Girl Scouts U.S.A., Hammond, Ind., 1945-49, asst. exec. dir. Cleve., 1950-62, exec. dir. Western Res., Akron, Ohio, 1962-66, field exec., Burlingame, Calif., 1967-74, asst. regional dir., 1974-79, orgn. devel. cons., Dallas, 1979—. Mem. Assn. Girl Scouts Execs., Nat. Assn. Female Execs., AAUW. Republican. Office: Girl Scouts USA 2710 Stemmons Freeway Dallas TX 75207

JOHNSON, REBECCA MCGEORGE, home economist; b. Roanoke, Va., Aug. 10, 1948; d. Gilbert Wesley and Pauline (Brooks) McGeorge; A.A., Lees McRae Coll., 1968; B.S. in Home Econs. Edn., Mars Hill Coll., 1971; m. James Edin Johnson, Apr. 3, 1971. Home Economist Va. Poly. Inst. & State U. Extension div., Appomattox, 1971-73, home economist, Hanover, 1974-83; tchr. Campbell County (Va.) Schs., 1973-74; cons. in field. Mem. Criminal Justice Adv. Com., Lynchburg, Va., 1971-73, mem. consumer health adv. com., 1971-73; sec. Hanover Cannery Adv. Com., 1979-83. Mem. Nat. Assn. Extension Home Economists, Va. Assn. Extension Home Economists (state public relations chmn. 1980-82), AAUW, Embroiders Guild Am., Epsilon Sigma Phi, Va. Guild Needlewomen. Presbyterian. Contbr. in field. Home and Office: 3 Mill Creek Rd Denton MD 21629

JOHNSON, REGENA FIX, musician, educator; b. Shenandoah, Va., Apr. 2, 1911; d. Henry Arthur and Beatrice (Mills) Fix.; B. Music, Cin. Conservatory Music, 1932, postgrad. U. Cin., Madison Coll., summer 1937, U. Va. extension, 1965-67; m. Albert Dunston Johnson, June 15, 1940. Pvt. tchr. music, 1933—; tchr. music Shenandoah, 1936-37, Nansemond County (Va.) Pub. Sch., 1937-40; substitute tchr. Windsor (Va.) High Sch., 1941; music dir. Windsor Bapt. Ch., 1940—. Vice pres. Tidewater Music Tchrs. Forum, 1977-79; sr. adviser Windsor Jr. Women's Club, 1959—. Mem. Music Tchr. Nat. Assn. (cert. tchr.), Va. Music Tchrs. Assn. (cert. tchr., bylaws chmn. 1980-82, 2d v.p. 1983—, former parliamentarian, chmn. Eastern Dist. Levels, I, II auditions 1974-83), Nat. Guild Piano Tchrs., Southside Dist. Va. Fedn. Women's Clubs (pres. 1952-54), Delta Kappa Gamma, Phi Beta. Democrat. Baptist. Clubs: Windsor Women's (pres. 1941-42), Order of Eastern Star (worthy matron Sinai chpt. 18 1951-52). Home: PO Box 325 Windsor VA 23487

JOHNSON, RUTH EILEEN, dietitian, researcher, home economics educator; b. Hot Springs, S.D., July 23, 1927; d. George Ernest and Eva Mae Lebo; m. James H. Johnson Jr., Aug. 7, 1948; children—Kenneth L., Gary S. B.S., U. Nebr., 1947, postgrad., 1950-51; M.A., Calif. State U., 1971. Research asst. food and nutrition research dept. U. Nebr., Lincoln, 1947-51; research technician Scripps Coll., Claremont, Calif., 1969; instr., collaborating investigator men's phys. edn. Calif. State U.-Long Beach, 1970-71, instr. home econs., 1970-72; asst. prof. home econs. Calif. State U.-Los Angeles, 1971-75; chief nutritionist Mr. Fit Ctr., 1974-79; sr. nutritionist, clin. coordinator atherosclerosis research U. So. Calif. Sch. Medicine, 1979—; cons. in field. Author, co-author numerous text and reference materials. Editor Calif. Home Economist, 1964-75. Founding com. mem. Meals on Wheels, Whittier, Calif., 1969; Calif. Congress Parents and Tchrs., 1961-72; pres. Lowell High Sch., 1968-69; Dental health chmn. Macy and Starbuck Schs., 1962-68. Mem. Am. Heart Assn. (fellow council of epidemiology; Vol. of Yr. 1981), Am. Home Econs. Assn., Calif. Home Econs. Assn. (Outstanding Home Economist 1979, 83), Am. Dietetics Assn., Calif. Dietetics Assn., Nutrition Today Soc. Am. Soc. Testing and Materials, Greater Los Angeles Nutrition Council, Calif. Nutrition Council, Orange County Nutrition Council, AAUW (Las Distinguidas award 1985), Iota Sigma Pi, Phi Delta Gamma, Omicron Nu. Avocations: needlepoint; piano; bridge. Home: 10110 Pounds Ave Whittier CA 90603 Office: USC Sch Medicine KAM B-32 2025 Zonal Ave Los Angeles CA 90033

JOHNSON, SAMMYE LARUE, communications educator; b. Dallas, Oct. 8, 1946; d. Sam S. and Poppy (Hammond) Malosky; B.S. in Journalism with distinction, Northwestern U. Medill Sch. Journalism, 1968, M.S. in Journalism, with highest distinction, 1969. Asst. editor Where Mag., Chgo., 1969; feature writer Chicago Today newspaper, Chgo., 1969-71, Sunday mag. editor, 1971-73; asst. dir., public relations mgr. W. O. Darby Library, Nurnberg, W.Ger., 1974-75; editor San Antonio Mag., 1976-79; communications dir. VIA Met. Transit System, San Antonio, 1979; asst. prof. journalism William Allen White Sch. Journalism, U. Kans., Lawrence, 1979-80; assoc. prof. communication Trinity U., San Antonio, 1980—; cons. public relations Community Guidance Ctr., San Antonio, 1985—, Funding Info. Ctr., San Antonio, 1983—, Bexar County Women's Ctr., San Antonio, 1984—. Named Today's Woman of Achievement, San Antonio Light Newspaper, 1981, Pub. Relations Educator of Yr., Tex. Pub. Relations Assn., 1984-85. Mem. Women in Communications (dir. 1978-80, pres. chpt. 1983-84, Proliner award 1981, 82, 83, 86, Communications Headliner of Yr. 1984), Internat. Assn. Bus. Communicators (bd. dirs. 1979, Gold Quill award 1979, named Communicator of Yr. 1981, numerous other awards 1976-79), Assn. for Edn. in Journalism and Mass Communications (sec. mag. div. 1985—), Kappa Tau Alpha. Home: 2906 Spring Bend San Antonio TX 78209 Office: Dept Communication Trinity Univ 715 Stadium Dr San Antonio TX 78284

JOHNSON, SARAH LURLINE (CHERYL), sales recruiting agency executive; b. Little Rock, Jan. 21, 1940; d. Foster David and Lurline Fay (Rice) J.; m. James B. Williams (div. 1961); 1 son, Bradley Foster. Student U. Ark., 1957-59. Med. sales recruiter Dunhill of Houston, 1967-76; owner Johnson Cons., Houston, 1976—. Baptist. Office: Johnson Cons Inc 5850 San Felipe Suite 120 Houston TX 77057*

JOHNSON, SHARON SLITER, writer, producer; b. Midland, Tex., July 22, 1950; d. Warren Greenlee and Barbara Jean (Hayslip) Sliter; B.A., DePaul U., 1976; m. Stephan Glenn Johnson, Nov. 7, 1981; 1 son, Luke Daniel. Sec., adminstrv. asst. to chmn. bd. Ency. Brit. Ednl. Corp., Chgo., 1972-77, writer, producer, 1977—; freelance script cons., researcher, writer, 1978—; juror U.S. Indsl. Film Festival, 1981, 82, 83, jury chmn., 1982-83. Democrat. Methodist. Author: I Want to be a Clown, 1985. Home and office: 5124 W Dakin St Chicago IL 60641

JOHNSON, SUSAN BROOKS, gemology educator, gemology consultant; b. Oregon City, Oreg., July 29, 1952; d. Theodore Reed and Doreen Edith (Gillett) Merrell; m. James-Burr July 21, 1979. Grad. gemologist Gemol. Inst. Am., 1975; diploma, St. Olaf Coll., 1972. Asst. mgr. Bubar's Jewelers, Santa Monica, Calif., 1977-79; mgr. extension div. Gemological Inst. Am., Santa Monica, Calif., 1974-77, 1979—. Author: Lab Manual, Properties of —B—Gemstones, 1977. Mem. Am. Gem Soc. (cert.), Accredited Gemologists' Assn. (v.p. 1980-82), Meeting Planners Internat. Club: Golden State Rottweiler (sec., mem. bd. 1982—) (Los Angeles). Office: Gemological Inst of Am 1660 Stewart St Santa Monica CA 90404

JOHNSON, VERONICA ANN WILKERSON, government librarian; b. Detroit, Aug. 5, 1952; d. James Henry and Alberta (Dixon) Wilkerson; B.A., Wayne State U., 1975; M.A., U. Mich., 1977; m. Melvin Lee Johnson, Nov. 3, 1973; children—Dichondra Rosalyn, Christopher Lee. Lab. technician Wayne County Health Dept., Project Prescad, 1978-79; children's librarian Inkster (Mich.) br. Wayne Oakland Library Fedn., 1979, head community librarian, 1979-85; government services specialist State Library of Mich., 1985—. Newspaper columnist Library Lines. City of Inkster adviser Vol. Tng. for Youth Leadership Devel., Sister Cities Internat. Mem. City of Inkster Cable TV Task Force, 1981—; chmn. workshop com. Inkster Internat. Friendship Force Exchange, 1981—; sec. Inkster Community Project Pride, 1979-80. U. Mich. Sch. Library Sci. fellow, 1976-77. Recipient State of Mich. Young Librarian of Yr. award, 1982. Mem. NAACP, ALA, Med. Library Assn., Mich. Library Assn., Gamma Phi Delta. Mem. Ch. of Christ. Home: 22732 Cambridge St Detroit MI 48219 Office: Library of Michigan 735 E Michigan Ave PO Box 30007 Lansing MI 48909

JOHNSON, VICKI R., insurance company executive; b. Glens Falls, N.Y., June 19, 1952; d. Leonard H. and Rose (Petrosky) J. A.B., Franklin and Marshall Coll., 1974; postgrad. U. Portland, 1979-80; M.B.A., UCLA, 1986. Dir. Prudential Ins. Co. Am., Woodland Hills, Calif., 1974—; mem. Oreg. Accident and Health Claim Assn., 1976-81. Pres., Ridgeview Condominium Assn., 1978-81; mem. Los Angeles Olympic Organizing Com., 1984. Mem. Los Angeles Accident and Health Claim Assn., The Woods Homeowners Assn. Home and Office: Woodland Hills CA 91367 Office: 111 Lakeview Canyon Rd Westlake Village CA

JOHNSON, WENDY ROSALIND, dancer, owner dance studios; b. Hamilton, N.Z., July 14, 1946; came to U.S., 1974, naturalized, 1976; d. Rodney Prosser and Freda Elizabeth (Hunter) Thomas; m. Peter Spencer Smith, Nov. 26, 1967 (div. May 1974); m. Patrick George Johnson, Sept. 20, 1975; children—Marcus Patrick, Misty Ciara. Ed. Auckland Girls Grammar Sch., N.Z. Profl. dancer, 1974—; South Pacific ballroom and Latin Am. champion, 1970, N.Z. amateur ballroom and Latin Am. dance champion, 1970; dancer on TV, Auckland, 1967-68, numerous appearances on Merv Griffin shows, U.S., 1978-83, TV spl. Grease Day U.S.A., 1978; owner Arthur Murray Dance Studios, San Anselmo, Calif., 1974—, Santa Rosa, 1981—, Sacramento, 1982—, Portland, Oreg., 1983—, Santa Barbara, 1981—, San Francisco, 1985—; co-chmn. internat. dance bd. Arthur Murray Internat., Miami, Fla., 1982-85; dancer TV video Let's Dance, 1982. Recipient Profl. Dance awards Arthur Murray Internat., 1983. Home: 50 Rica Vista Novato CA 94947 Office: Arthur Murray Dance Studio 3401 Cleveland Ave Santa Rosa CA 94947

JOHNSON-CHAMP, DEBRA SUE, legal librarian, educator; b. Emporia, Kans., Nov. 8, 1955; d. Bert John and S. Christine (Brigman) Johnson; m. Michael W. Champ, Nov. 23, 1979; children—Natalie, John. B.A., U. Denver, 1977; J.D., Pepperdine U., 1980; postgrad. in library sci. U. So. Calif., 1983—. Bar: Calif. 1981. Sole practice, Long Beach, Calif., 1981-82, Los Angeles, 1981—; legal reference librarian, instr. Southwestern U. Sch. Law, Los Angeles, 1982—. Editor-in-chief: Southern Calif. Assn. Law Libraries Newsletter, 1984-85. Contbr. articles to profl. journs. Mem. law rev. Pepperdine U., 1978-80. West Pub. Co. scholar, 1983; trustee United Meth. Ch., Tujunga, Calif., 1986—. Recipient H. Wayne Gillis Moot Ct. award, 1980, Vincent S. Dalsimer Best Brief award, 1979. Mem. ABA, So. Calif. Assn. Law Libraries, Am. Assn. Law Libraries, Calif. Bar Assn., Southwestern Affiliates, Friends of the Library Los Angeles. Democrat. Home: 8258 Wentworth St Sunland CA 91040 Office: Southwestern U Sch Law 675 S Westmoreland Ave Los Angeles CA 90005

JOHNSON-JENSEN, KAREN SUE, computer systems analyst; b. Springfield, Mo., Mar. 7, 1955; d. E.E. Johnson and Jean Alice Cain. B.A., U. Tex. at Austin, 1977; postgrad. So. Meth. U., 1979—; m. John C. Jensen, Mar. 24, 1979. Lab. research asst. II Applied Research Labs., 1976-77; software design engr. Tex. Instruments Inc., 1977—. Campaign vol. Austin City Council, 1980-81, 82-83; blood fund co. coordinator Central Tex. Regional Blood Center, 1978—. Recipient Lifegiver award Central Tex. Regional Blood Center, 1979. Mem. Assn. Computing Machinery, IEEE, Mortar Bd., Alpha Chi Sigma, Pi Mu Epsilon. Presbyterian. Office: Tex Instrument PO Box 2909 Austin TX 78769

JOHNSON-MASTERS, VIRGINIA E., psychologist, sex therapist, institute administrator; b. Springfield, Mo., Feb. 11, 1925; d. Harry H. and Edna (Evans) Eshelman; ed. U., Mo. Columbia, Washington U., St. Louis; D.Sc. (hon.) U. Louisville, 1978; m. William H. Masters, Jan., 1971; children by previous marriage—Scott F. Johnson, Lisa E. Johnson. Editorial writer, adminstrv. sec. St. Louis Daily Record, 1947-50; mem. advt. dept. CBS, St. Louis, 1950-51; mem. research staff div. reproductive biology dept. ob-gyn Washington U., St. Louis, 1957-64, research asst., 1960-62, research instr., 1962-64, lectr. in human sexuality dept. psychiatry Sch. Medicine, 1981—; research assoc. Reproductive Biology Research Found. (now Masters & Johnson Inst.), St. Louis, 1964-69, asst. dir., 1969-73, co-dir., pres., 1973-80, dir., 1981—; pres. MVM Enterprises, Inc. Recipient Paul H. Hoch award Am. Psychopath. Assn., 1971; Biomed. Research award World Assn. Sexology, 1979; Rotary Internat. Paul Harris fellow, 1976. Edward Henderson Lecture award Am. Geriatrics Soc., 1981; Mem. AAAS, Am. Assn. Sex Educators, Counselors and Therapists, Author's Guild, Inc., Colombian Sexological Soc., Eastern Assn. Sex Therapy, Eastern Assn. Sex Therapy, Eastern Mo. Psychiat. Soc., Internat. Acad. Sex Research (treas. 1975-76), Internat. Platform Assn., Soc. Sci. Study Sex. Episcopalian. Author: (with William H. Masters), Human Sexual Response, 1966, Human Sexual Inadequacy, 1970, The Pleasure Bond, 1975; Homosexuality in Perspective, 1979; Ethical Issues in Sex Therapy and Research, 1977, Volume 2, 1980; (with others) Textbook on Sexual Medicine, 1979, 2d edit., 1985; Textbook of Human Sexuality for Nurses, 1979; Human Sexuality, 1982; mem. editorial bd. Science Digest, 1982—; contbr. numerous articles in field.

JOHNSTON, ANITA FAYE, lawyer; b. Wichita Falls, Tex., Apr. 16, 1949; d. Allan and Dorothy Faye (Eastus) Winham; m. Mike Johnston, May 20, 1971 (div. 1978); m. James Sanders, Mar. 27, 1984. B.S. in Elem. Edn., Okla. State U., 1971, M.A. in Edn. Media and Jr. Coll. Curriculum, 1972; Ed.D. in Adminstrn., Okla. U., 1977; J.D., Okla. City U., 1982. Cert. tchr. coll., library sci., media dir., elem. edn. Pub. relations dir., photographer Stillwater Pub. Schs. (Okla.), 1971; photographer, artist Okla. State U. TV Services, Stillwater, 1971-72; elem. tchr., St. Louis, 1972-73; media dir. Mustang Pub. Schs. (Okla.), 1973-76; asst. prof. edn., scholarship program dir. Oklahoma City U., 1977-82; assoc. Bloodworth & Assocs., Oklahoma City, 1982—; condr. creative teaching workshop Kirkwood Pub. Schs. (Mss.), 1973; del. region 7, mem. nomination com., treas.-sec. Okla. Assn. Edn. Communications and Tech.; mem. Nat. Library Week com., legis. com., gov.'s mansion library com. Okla. Library Assn.; mem. affirmative action com., program evaluator Assn. Ednl. Communications and Tech. Producer cassette tape Your Library Wants to Talk to You, 1976, other ednl. TV programs. Mem. AAUW, Okla. Assn. Tchr. Educators, Nat. Council Adminstrv. Women in Edn., ABA, Okla. Bar Assn., Assn. Trial Lawyers Am., Iota Tau Tau. Democrat. Mem. Ch. of Christ. Home: 2605 Tropicana St Bethany OK 73008 Office: 420 Hightower St Oklahoma City OK 73102

JOHNSTON, CARLA BROOKS, public policy and management consultant; b. Rochester, N.Y., Apr. 2, 1940; d. James Ovid Brooks and Helen (Porschet) Brooks Casety; m. Frederick L. Johnston, Jr., Dec. 30, 1961 (div. Dec. 1983); children—Frederick L., III, J. Elise. B.A., Coll. of Wooster, Ohio, 1961; M.A., Andover Newton Theol. Sch., Mass., 1966. Funding and devel. coordinator Mayor Ralph's Office, Somerville, Mass., 1970-73; exec. dir., budget analyst MBTA Adv. Bd., Boston, 1973-76; exec. dir. Met. Area Planning Council, Boston, 1977-79; dep. exec. dir. Union of Concerned Scis., Cambridge, Mass., 1979-81; founder, dir. New Century Policies, cons. firm, 1981—. Author: Reversing the Nuclear Arms Race, 1985. Editor: Under the Interstate, 1975. Dir. film City Roots, 1975. Elected mem. Dem. State Com., Mass., 1984-88, Dem. Nat. Platform com., San Francisco, 1984; selected Dem. Drafting com., Washington, 1984; founding mem. Nat. Freeze Voter, Fort Worth, 1983; candidate for U.S. Ho. of Reps. from 8th dist. Mass., 1986. Scholarships to India, 1961, to Germany, 1956; first peace fellow Radcliffe, Bunting Inst., 1983-84, Loeb fellow Harvard, 1973-74. Recipient NCCJ Community Service award, 1973. Mem. Nuclear Weapons Freeze Campaign (nat. strategy com. 1982-83), Women's Action for Nuclear Disarmament (nat. adv. bd. 1983), Cambridge Ctr. Adult Edn. (pres. 1983-85). Avocations: travel; walking; camping; cooking. Home: 86 Wendell St Cambridge MA 02138 Office: New Century Policies PO Box 963 Boston MA 02103

JOHNSTON, CHRISTINA JANE, real estate executive, mortgage broker, educator; b. Toronto, Ont., Can., June 3, 1952; d. George Elmer and Mary Selina (Northey) J. B.A. with honors, U. Western Ont., London, 1975. Researcher, writer House of Commons, Ottawa, Ont., 1975-77; adminstrv. mgr. sales Marco Beach Realty, Marco Island, Fla., 1977-79; pres., owner Marco Summit Realty, Marco Island, 1979-82; v.p., mortgage broker Windjammer of Marco, Marco Island, 1979—; instr. Realty World Acad., St. Petersburg, Fla., 1979—; pres., mgr. Fla. Sun Realty Co., Sarasota, 1982-86; v.p., mgr. Fla. Home Properties & Comml. Realty, Inc., 1986—; bd. dirs., chmn. edn. com. Sarasota Bd. Realtors, 1985—, also mem. realtors polit. action com. 1985—; pres. So. Gulf Council Realty World, 1980-82; bd. dirs. First Fla. region Broker's Council, Realty World, 1982-84; pres. Women's Council of Realtors, Sarasota, 1986—. Contbr. articles to profl. jours. Pres. Young Progressive Conservatives, Cambridge, Ont., 1968-70; Recipient Office of Yr. award Realty World, 1980, Top Listing Office award, 1981, Spl. award for Prodn., 1981, Million Dollar Sales Awards Marco Beach and Realty World, 1979-81. Mem. Sarasota C. of C., Marco Island C. of C. (chmn. Expo '82). Home: 4816 Village Gardens Dr Sarasota FL 33580 Office: Fla Home Properties & Comml Realty Inc 5647 Beneva Rd Sarasota FL 33583

JOHNSTON, CYNTHIA COCHRAN, physician, educator; b. Kansas City, Mo., Oct. 2, 1952; d. John A. and Mary L. (Leffler) Cochran; B.S. in Zoology with high honors, Ariz. State U., 1974; M.D., U. Ariz., 1976; m. Bruce G. Johnston, Dec. 29, 1973; children—Lauren Elizabeth, Stephen Shepherd. Diplomate Am. Bd. Family Practice. Resident in family practice U. Ariz., Tucson, 1976-79, chief resident in family practice, 1978-79; med. officer San Xavier Indian Health Center, Tucson, 1979, dir., 1979-82; assoc. faculty dept. family and community medicine U. Ariz., Tucson, 1979-81, adj. asst. prof., 1981—; staff physician Tucson Clinic, 1982—; physician ambulatory care dept. Tucson VA Med. Ctr., 1983—; Ariz.'s rep. to Nat. Conf. Family Practice Residents, 1978, 79. Served with USPHS, 1979—. Recipient John Grobe award for outstanding family practice resident in Ariz., 1979. Mem. Am. Acad. Family Physicians (resident rep. com. Indian health, rep. com. minority health affairs 1980-82, Warner-Chilcot award for outstanding tchr. 1979), Ariz. Acad. Family Physicians, (dir. 1981—), Soc. Tchrs. in Family Medicine, Phi Beta Kappa. Contbr. articles to profl. jours. Home: 6307 E Paseo Otono Tucson AZ 85715 Office: Tucson VA Med Ctr S 6th Ave Tucson AZ 85726

JOHNSTON, DEE SHELY, manufacturing company executive; b. Anderson County, Ky., Feb. 6, 1937; d. Tyler Gilbert and Sarah Eliza (Crooke) Shely; student George Peabody Coll., 1956-58; grad. Campbellsville Coll., 1956; student Jackson State U., 1974, Lord Fairfax Community Coll., 1981; D.D.A., Shenandoah Coll., 1986; m. Ronald E. Johnston, Aug. 13, 1957; children—Steven Christopher, Michael David, Kevin Eugene, Russell Desha. Dir. music and edn. First Bapt. Ch., Front Royal, Va., 1965; announcer, advt. copywriter Sta. WFTR, Front Royal, 1965-66; sec. Berryville (Va.) Primary Sch., 1967-70; fund raising staff United Way of Louisville, 1970-72; dir. music St. Andrew's Episcopal Ch., Kokomo, Ind., 1973; sec. ITT, Milan, Tenn., 1973-74; with O'Sullivan Corp., Winchester, Va., 1976—, dir. purchasing, 1984—. Mem. Nat. Assn. Female Execs., Nat. Assn. Purchasing Mgrs. (Pub. Relations Chmn. of Yr. award dist. V, 1983), Purchasing Mgrs. Assn. of the Old Dominion (editor newsletter 1980-83, dir. 1982-83, 2d v.p. 1984-85, 1st v.p. 1985-86 pres. 1986-87). Episcopalian. Home: Route 2 Box 4750 Berryville VA 22611 Office: PO Box 3510 Winchester VA 22601

JOHNSTON, DOROTHY G., occupational health nurse; b. Geneva, N.Y., Jan. 3, 1932; d. Edward Ward and Alice Florence (Pickard) Gaylord; m. Donald Kenneth Johnston, Mar. 6, 1954; children—Jeffrey Scott, Diane Marie and Dawn Eileen (twins). B.N., U. Rochester, 1953. Staff nurse Ob/Gyn Strong Meml. Hosp., Rochester, N.Y., 1953-54; staff nurse operating room Ventura Gen. Hosp. (Calif.), 1954-55; office nurse Dr. W. Achilles, Jr., Geneva, N.Y., 1956-60; spl. duty nurse various hosps., N.Y., 1956-66; night nurse supr. Lyons Community Hosp. (N.Y.), 1966-71; sr. occupational health nurse III Mobil Chem. Co., Macedon, N.Y., 1971—. Mem. utilization rev. com., Lyons, 1970-71; sec. Inservice Edn., Lyons, N.Y., 1971; mem. Regional Nursing Continuing Edn. Project, Rochester, N.Y., 1980-82. Mem. Am. Assn. Occupational Health Nurses, N.Y. State Assn. Occupational Health Nurses, Greater Rochester Assn. Occupational Health Nurses. Republican. Episcopalian. Home: 6250 Spiegel Pkwy North Rose NY 14516 Office: Mobil Chem Co Route 31 Macedon NY 14502

JOHNSTON, EMILY HIGHTOWER, lawyer; b. Jefferson, N.C., Mar. 8, 1954; d. Deward Earl and Jennie Clyde (Worth) Hightower; m. David Graham Johnston, May 22, 1982; 1 child, Peter Worth. B.A., U. N.C., 1976; J.D., U. Ga., 1979. Bar: Ga. 1979, N.C. 1980. Legal editor The Harrison Co., Norcross, Ga., 1979-82; staff atty. Preferred Research, Inc., Greensboro, N.C., 1982-84. Author: North Carolina Law of Damages, 1981; (with B. Finberg) Products Liability—The Law in North Carolina, 1980. Mem. N.C. State Bar, State Bar Ga. Methodist. Home: 209 S Tremont Dr Greensboro NC 27403

JOHNSTON, JOANN (JODY), realtor; b. Kansas City, Mo., Oct. 26, 1928; d. Cedric E. and Marie (O'Hare) Tucker; m. Darrel W. Johnston, June 17, 1951 (div. 1983); children—Dirk W., John S., Jan. B.S. in Sociology, Baker U., Baldwin City, Kans., 1950. Cert. tchr. Tchr. elem. schs., Prairie Village, Kans., 1950-54; realtor, sales assoc. Ebby Halliday Real Estate, Inc., Dallas, 1972—. Mem. Dallas Symphony League, 1970-72, Dallas Mus. Fine Arts. Recipient Top Co. Producer salesmanship award Ebby Halliday Real Estate Inc., 1978, 82, 83, 85, Diamond Circle recognition, 1977-85; Disting. Sales award Sales and Mktg. Execs. Dallas, 1979, 83-84. Mem. Nat. Assn. Realtors, Tex. Assn. Realtors, Women's Council Realtors (speaker), North Dallas C. of C., Delta Delta Delta (alumnae adviser 1958-60, 62-64). Republican. Presbyterian. Clubs: Lambda Chi Alpha Mothers, Pi Beta Phi Mothers. Home: 7243 Baxtershire Dr Dallas TX 75230 Office: Ebby Halliday Real Estate Inc 5999 W Northwest Hwy Dallas TX 75225

JOHNSTON, JOANNE SPITZNAGEL, lawyer, writing consultant; b. Peoria, Ill., Mar. 11, 1930; d. Elmer Florian and Anna E. (Kolb) Spitznagel; m. Charles Helm Bennett, June 12, 1951 (div. 1978); children—Mary Jaquelin Bennett Graub, Ariana Holliday, Caroline Helm, Joanne Mary; m. Donald Robert Johnston, Nov. 25, 1981. A.B., Vassar Coll., 1951; M.A., Ind. U., 1970, Ph.D., 1974; J.D., Ind. U.-Indpls., 1980. Bar: Ind. 1980, Minn. 1985. Lectr., Ind. U., Indpls., 1968-81, Ind. Central U., Indpls., 1970-76; writing cons. U. Minn., Mpls., 1982—; sole practice, Indpls., 1980-86, Mpls., 1986—. Vice-pres. Jr. League Indpls.; pres. Sch. 70 Parent Tchr. Orgn., Indpls. Mem. ABA, Am. Bus. Communication Assn., Ind. State Bar Assn. Methodist. Clubs: Indpls. Womans, Garden Club Am. (Indpls.); Woman's (Mpls.). Home: 5808 View Ln Edina MN 55436

JOHNSTON, JOSEPHINE R., chemist; b. Cranston, R.I., Aug. 9, 1926; d. Robert and Rose (Varca) Forte; student Carnegie Inst., 1945-47; B.S., Mich. State U., 1972, M.A., 1973; postgrad. Mass. Inst. Tech., 1973— m. Howard Robert Johnston, Mar. 7, 1949; 1 son, Kevin Howard. Med. technologist South Nassau Community Hosp., Rockville Centre, N.Y., 1947-50, Mich. State U., East Lansing, 1950-53, dept. pathology Albany (N.Y.) Med. Center, 1953-54; med. lab. supr. Bulova Watch Co., Jackson Heights, N.Y., 1954-57; sr. chemistry technologist Mid Island Hosp., Bethpage, N.Y., 1958-66; faculty specialist Mich. State U., East Lansing, 1966-76; sr. research asso. Uniformed Services Univ., Bethesda, Md., 1976-78, asst. to chmn. dept. physiology, 1978-82, asso. to chmn., 1982—. Mem. Analytical Chem. Soc., Data and Electronic Soc., Internat. Platform Assn. Lutheran. Contbr. articles in field to profl. jours. Office: 4301 Jones Bridge Rd Bethesda MD 20014

JOHNSTON, KAREN LANG, public relations executive; b. St. Petersburg, Fla., Nov. 10, 1949; d. James Talley and Dorothy Louise (Gustafson) Lang; m. Walter Eugene Johnston III, Apr. 13, 1983. B.A., U. Md., 1971. Aide to Congressman C.W. Young, 1972-73; aide Consultation and Guidance Center, 1973-76; legis. rep. Nat. Assn. Small Bus. Investment Cos., 1976-78; asso. dir. regulatory affairs Nat. Assn. Mfrs., 1978-79; congressional liaison U.S. Regulatory Council, 1979-81; spl. asst. to adminstr. for info. and regulatory affairs Office of Mgmt. and Budget, Washington, 1981; dep. dir. Office Congressional Relations, FTC, Washington, 1981-83, dir., 1985—; press sec. N.C. Reagan-Bush '84, 1984. Active Washington Internat. Ctr., 1972, Washington Ear, 1973, Rockville Free Clinic, Planned Parenthood, 1974-76; mem. 1st families steering com. Am. Children's Home, Lexington, N.C.; mem. membership com. Eastern Music Festival, Greensboro Civic Ballet Guild. Mem. Women in Govt. Relations, Nat. Fedn. Republican Women, Greater Greensboro Rep. Women, Greensboro Symphony Guild, Alpha Delta Pi. Methodist. Club: Jr. League (Washington). Office: 338 N Elm St Greensboro NC 27408

JOHNSTON, PATRICIA HAINES, medical technologist; b. Kansas City, Mo., Oct. 2, 1934; d. Robert Ashley and Grace Emoline (Sayer) Haines; children—Carol Ann Nicholas, Robert Bruce. B.S., U. Mo.-Kansas City, 1957. Spl. chemist Menorah Med. Ctr., Kansas City, Mo., 1958-61; chemist Bapt. Meml. Hosp., Kansas City, Mo., 1961-62; lab. supr. Richardson Gen. Hosp. (Tex.), 1963-70, Med. Lab. Services, Dallas, 1971-76; lab. chemist Ob-Gyn Lab., Dallas, 1978-82; lab. supr. Mary Shiels Hosp., Dallas, 1983—. Bd. dirs. Corps Devel. Council, chairperson pub. relations and devel. com. Tex. A&M U., 1984—. Mem. Am. Soc. Clin. Pathologists, Dallas A&M Mothers' Club (pres. 1979-80), Fedn. Tex. A&M U. Mothers' Clubs (pres. 1982-83). Republican. Presbyterian. Office: Mary Shiels Hospital 3515 Howell St Dallas TX 75204

JOHNSTON, RUBY CHARLOTTE, nurse; b. Freedom, Nebr., Oct. 6, 1918; d. William Murray and Delia Isabel (Morgan) Phillips; student Nebr. Sch. Agr., Curtis, 1932-36, U. Colo., Boulder, summer 1938; R.N., Denver Gen. Hosp., 1945; m. Gerald William Johnston, Sept. 19, 1943; 1 son, Leo F. Rural sch. tchr., 1936-41; sec. supt.'s office Nebr. Sch. Agr., 1941-42; staff nurse Denver Gen. Hosp., 1945-46; office nurse, Cambridge, Nebr., 1946-47; staff nurse St. Catherine's Hosp., McCook, Nebr., 1947-56, LaGrange County Hosp., LaGrange, Ind., 1956-58; obstet. supr. LaGrange County Hosp., 1958-68, dir. nurses, 1968-70; dir. nurses Miller's Merry Manor, LaGrange, 1970-76; county health nurse LaGrange County Health Dept., LaGrange, 1976-80, part-time staff nurse, 1980—; chmn. exec. com. Ind. Nurses Assn. Geriatric Conf., 1975-77. Bd. dirs. Mental Health Assn. LaGrange County, 1979-85, N.E. Ind. chpt. Am. Lung Assn., 1981—; Co-coordinator Focus on Health, LaGrange, 1982-85. Registered Mem. Ind. Nurses Assn., Nurses Assn. Am. Coll. Obstetricians and Gynecologists, Am. Legion Aux. Republican. Presbyterian. Clubs: Bus. and Profl. Women's, Eastern Star, River Oaks Extension. Home: Rural Route 2 Box 107A Howe IN 46746 Office: Cour House Annex LaGrange IN 46761

JOHNSTON, RUTH LE ROY, nosologist, med. record adminstr.; b. Elizabeth, N.J., June 19, 1915; d. James Archibald and Frances Ione Davis (Austin) Le Roy; B.A., Bob Jones U., Greenville, S.C., 1945; postgrad. in medicine Emory U.; m. Earl Benton Johnston, Aug. 19, 1944 (dec.); 1 son, Jonathan Bruce (dec.). Various hosp. positions Atlanta, Asheville, N.C., 1948-55; chief med. record librarian VA Hosp., Richmond, Va., 1955-60, Wood, Wis., 1960, Hines, Ill., 1960-62; supervisory med. classification specialist, nosologist research and stats. Social Security Adminstrn., HEW, Balt., 1962-68; med. record cons. health data service Md. Blue Cross-Blue Shield, Balt., 1970-71; chief med. record adminstr. Good Samaritan Hosp., West Palm Beach, Fla., 1971-74; med. record adminstr. Gorgas Hosp., U.S. C.Z., Panama, 1974-77; library asst. North Palm Beach Public Library, 1978-80; lectr. in field, cons. Mem. Save the Panama Canal Club; 1st vice-chmn. bd. dirs. Paradise Harbour Condominium, 1973; charter mem. Republican Presdl. Task Force. Registered med. record adminstr., nosologist, Fla. Recipient VA and civil service awards, 1960-68. Mem. Va. (treas. 1957-58, pres. 1960), Md. (v.p. 1963), Fla., Am. med. record assns., Internat. Platform Assn., Audubon Soc., Nat. Assn. Fed. Ret. Employees, Am. Assn. Ret. Persons. Baptist. Home: 100 Paradise Harbor Blvd North Palm Beach FL 33408

JOHNSTON, VIRGINIA EVELYN, editor; b. Spokane, Wash., Apr. 26, 1933; d. Edwin and Emma Lucile (Munroe) Rowe; student Portland Community Coll., 1964, Portland State U., 1966, 78-79; m. Alan Paul Beckley, Dec. 26, 1974; children—Chris, Denise, Rex. Proofreader, The Oregonian, Portland, 1960-62, teletypesetter operator, 1962-66, operator Photon 200, 1966-68, copy editor, asst. women's editor, 1968-80, spl. sects. editor (UPDATE), 1981-83; editor (FOODday/UPDATE), 1982-83, editor FOODday, 1982—; pres. Matrix Assos., Inc., Portland, 1975—, chmn. bd., 1979—; cons. Democratic party Oreg., 1969, Portland Sch. Dist. No. 1, 1978. Mem. Women in Communications, Inc., Inst. Profl. and Managerial Women, Nat. Assn. Female Execs. Democrat. Editor Principles of Computer Systems for Newspaper Mgmt., 1975-76. Home: 4140 NE 137th Ave Portland OR 97230 Office: 1320 SW Broadway Portland OR 97201

JOHNSTONE, JUDITH ANN, banker; b. Oklahoma City, Oct. 9, 1950; d. Thomas Patrick and Florence Marvin (Hutchinson) Harley; m. Albert E. Pitzer, Feb. 17, 1970 (div. 1976); children—Clint M., Alisha Ann, Jason Patrick; m. William O. Johnstone, Apr. 3, 1982. Student Okla. State U., 1977; B.S. in Acctg., Oklahoma City U., 1981. With ops. dept. Union Bank and Trust Co., Oklahoma City, 1973, asst. cashier, 1974-75, asst. v.p., 1975-77; v.p. United Check Processing, Inc., Oklahoma City, 1977-78, exec. v.p., 1978-79, pres., 1980—, also dir.; chmn., dir. United tulsa Check Processing, Tulsa; dir. United Data Services, Inc., Oklahoma City, United Tulsa Data Services. Vol., Am. Cancer Soc., Oklahoma City, 1985. Mem. Bank Adminstrn. Inst. (ops. and tech. commn. 1981-83, check processing conf. planning com. 1981, 83), Women's Econ. Club. Republican. Methodist. Avocations: reading; travel. Home: 12912 River Oaks Dr Oklahoma City OK 73142 Office: United Check Processing Inc 211 Greenfield Center Dr Oklahoma City OK 73127

JOHNSTONE, PAULA SUE, medical technologist; b. Springfield, Mo., July 5, 1947; d. Nathan Paul and Ina Louise (Glenn) Johnstone. B.S., S.W. Mo. State U., 1969. Cert. med. technologist Am. Soc. Clin. Pathologists. Vol., Cox Med. Ctr., Springfield, 1964-68; lab., office aid Springfield Med. Lab., 1964-68; chief technologist Springfield Gen. Osteo. Hosp., 1969-73; staff technologist St. John's Regional Health Ctr., Springfield, 1973-75, evening supr., 1975-76, asst. adminstrv. dir., 1976—. Dir., Glidewell Baptist Ch. Tng., Springfield, 1984-85. Mem. Am. Soc. Med. Technologists, Nat. Cert. Agy. Med. Lab. Personnel, Mo. Soc. Med. Technologists (pres. 1976-77, columnist newsletter 1976-77), Nat. Assn. Female Execs. Baptist. Clubs: Nat. Travel, $25-A-Day-Travel. Avocations: European travel; reading; knitting; house plants. Home: Route 5 Box 495C Springfield MO 65803 Office: St John's Regional Health Ctr 1235 E Cherokee Springfield MO 65804

JOHNSTON-THOMAS, PAMELLA DELORES, physician; b. Westmoreland, Jamaica, W.I., May 11, 1947; came to U.S., 1976; d. Wellesley and Hyacinth Ida (Muir) Johnston; m. Earl Alfonso Thomas, Apr. 9, 1977; children—Ramogi Odhiambo, Monifa Jamila. M.D., U. W.I., 1974. Intern, Brookdale Hosp., Bklyn., 1976-77; resident in Surgery Cath. Med. Centre, Queens, N.Y., 1978-79; attending physician N.Y.C. Transit, N.Y.C., 1983—, Brookdale Hosp., Bklyn., 1979-83. Mem. Am. Occupational Med. Assn., N.Y. Occupational Med. Assn., Am. Pub. Health Assn., N.Y. Pub. Health Assn.

JOINER, MARY ANN, engineer, manufacturing company executive; b. Hazlehurst, Miss., Dec. 12, 1947; d. Johnie L. and Jannie Ernestine (Brandon) J.; children—Vincent Edward, Valinda Claudette. Student Jackson County Jr. Coll., Gautier, Miss. Machine operator E.R. Moore/Swingster, Ocean Springs, Miss., 1968-73, supr., 1973-78, engr., 1978—; tax preparer H & R Block, Biloxi, Miss., 1977—; owner JAR, Ocean Springs, 1985—; cons. in field. Tchr. Macedonia Baptist Ch., Ocean Springs. NSF fellow, 1964. Mem. Nat. Assn. Female Execs. Lodge: Order Eastern Star. Avocations: cake decorating; sewing; crocheting; soft scupter dolls. Home: 431 Whispering Pines Dr Ocean Springs MS 39564

JONAS, HILDA, harpsichordist, pianist; b. Duesseldorf, Ger., Jan. 21, 1913; came to U.S., 1938, naturalized, 1943; d. Moritz and Ann (Lilienfeld) Klestadt; student Hochschule Musik, Cologne, 1932-33; diploma Gumpert Conservatory, Duesseldorf, 1934; pupil of Rudolf Serkin, Wanda Landowska; m. Gerald Jonas, Jan. 30, 1938; children—Susanne Leilani, Linda Irene. Owner pvt. piano studio, Honolulu, 1938-42, Cin., 1942-75; soloist maj. orchs. throughout world, 1932—; solo recitalist throughout world, 1932—; founder Put-in-Bay Harpsichord Festival, 1965, dir., 1965-75; rec. artist Educo, Sanjo Music, 1982—; harpsichordist for rec. Johann Kuhnau: Six Biblical Sonatas, 1982. Life mem. Brandeis, Hadassah. Jewish. Author articles in field. Address: 50 Chumasero Dr San Francisco CA 94132

JONES, ANN RUTLEDGE, motel exec.; b. Richmond, Va., Sept. 12, 1925; d. William and Roselyn Elmira (Hardy) Rutledge; student La. State U., 1942-43, Centenary Coll., 1943-44; m. Richard Lefavour Jones, Oct. 18, 1948; children—Richard R., Ann L., Sharon O., William W. Stewardess, C&O R.R., 1946-48; partner Salem (Mass.) Gallery, 1966-70; bookkeeper, Ramada Inn West, Jacksonville, Fla., 1970-73; asst. to comptroller Jacksonville Hilton (Fla.), 1973-74; dir. sales and public relations Ramada Inn West, Jacksonville, 1974—; mem. adv. com. mid-mgmt., hospitality and lodging, home econs., lectr. Fla. Jr. Coll.; mem. Tourist Devel. Council Duval County; chmn. pub. relations com. Tourist Devel. Council, Jacksonville; chmn. hospitality group Gator Bowl Assn., 1978-83, Bold City Classic, 1979-83. Mem. Fla. Public Relations Assn., Sales and Mktg. Execs. Jacksonville (scholarship com. 1980-82), Hotel Sales Mgmt. Assn., Jacksonville Hotel Motel Assn. (pres.), Fla. Hotel Motel Assn. (dir., public relations chmn.), Am. Bus. Women's Assn. (past chmn. scholarship Jacksonville), Fla. Soc. Assn. Execs., Women for Responsible Legislation. Democrat. Episcopalian. Clubs: Continental (Orange Park, Fla., North Fla. Cruising; Corinthian Yacht (Marblehead, Mass.). Office: 510 Lane Ave S Suite 280 Jacksonville FL 32205

JONES, ANNE ELIZABETH, motor license agent, insurance executive; b. Chgo., Nov. 26, 1945; d. George Edward and Betty Jane (Wise) Sybrant; m. Brenton Elvis Jones, Aug. 15, 1965 (div. June 1980); children—James Devon, Douglas Edward, Robert Derrick. Student Ark. City Jr. Coll., Kans., 1962-64, Okla. State U., 1964-65. Credit mgr. Koppel's, Bartlesville, Okla., 1966-67; collector Am. Collection Agy., Bartlesville, 1967-72; office mgr. Paul Stumpff & Assocs., Bartlesville, 1972-82; owner A.J. Leasing, Inc., Tulsa, 1982—, Sooner Assocs., Inc., Tulsa, 1982—; motor license agt. Central Tag Agy., Tulsa, 1982—. Mem. Motor Lic. Agts. Assn. (exec. v.p. 1984-85, polit. liaison 1984, tchr. ins. and lic. law 1984), Ins. Women Tulsa (legis. chmn. 1984, pub. relations chmn. 1985, tchr. ins. classes 1979-85, cert. profl. ins. woman), Nat. Assn. Ins. Women (state orgn. chmn. 1985, Rookie of Yr. 1981, regional winner Lace Speak-Off 1985, Tulsa C. of C., Okla. Soc. Chartered Ins. Counselors (charter), Profl. Ins. Agts. Okla. (seminar instr. 1979), Ind. Ins. Agts. Okla. (seminar instr. 1979-83). Club: Phoenix Toastmasters (adminstrv. v.p. 1985) (Tulsa). Avocations: public speaking; motivational seminars; antique dealing; oil painting; photography. Office: Central Tag Agency 2702 E 15th St Tulsa OK 74104

JONES, AUDREY HOWARD, utility executive; b. Bklyn., May 13, 1928; d. Edward Richard and Venie Ednora (Jacobs) Howard; B.A., Hunter Coll., 1949; M.S. in Marine Sci., L.I.U., 1969; m. Farrell Jones, June 16, 1951; children—Joanne Kathryn and Jacqueline Elinor (twins). Research biochemist Manhattan Eye, Ear and Throat Hosp., 1949-51, Downstate Med. Coll., SUNY, Bklyn., 1952-58; instr. biology Nassau Community Coll., Garden City, N.Y., also cons. Environ. Assocs. and Urban Edn., Inc., 1970-73; environ. scientist, then EEO mgr. L.I. Lighting Co., Hicksville, N.Y., 1972-79, personnel policies and services mgr., 1979—; adj. asst. prof. N.Y. Inst. Tech., 1979-80; field faculty adv. Goddard grad. program Norwich U., 1981-83; lectr. SUNY, Farmingdale; mem. career services adv. bd. Adelphi U., 1981—. Mem. citizens adv. com. N.Y. State Coastal Zone Mgmt. Program; mem. L.I. regional adv. com. N.Y. State External High Sch. Diploma Program; assoc. trustee L.I. Jewish Med. Ctr. Recipient various service awards, certs. appreciation. Mem. Am. Gas Assn. (urban affairs com.), Edison Electric Inst. (tng. and mgmt. devel. com.), L.I. Assn. (chmn. personnel dirs. council 1980-81), LWV, NAACP, L.I. Center for Bus. and Profl. Women (pres. 1982-84), Delta Sigma Theta. Democrat. Unitarian-Universalist. Clubs: Zonta, 100 Black Women of L.I. Home: 22 Driftwood Dr Port Washington NY 11050 Office: LILCO 175 E Old Country Rd Hicksville NY 11801

JONES, BARBARA CHRISTINE, educator, creative arts designer; b. Augsburg, Swabia, Bavaria, Germany, Nov. 14, 1942; came to U.S., 1964, naturalized, 1971; d. Martin Richard and Margarete Katharina (Roth) Schulz; m. Robert Edward Dickey, 1967 (div. 1980); m. Raymond Lee Jones, 1981. Student Philomatique de Bordeaux, France, 1962, U. Munich, 1961; B.A. in German, French, Speech, Calif. State U.-Chico, 1969, M.A. in Comparative Internat. Edn., 1974. Cert. secondary tchr., community coll. instr., Calif. Fgn. lang. tchr. Gridley Union High Sch., Calif., 1970-80, home econs., decorative arts instr., cons., 1970-80, English study skills instr., 1974-80, English as a second language coordinator, instr. Punjabi, Mex. Ams., 1970-72, curriculum com. chmn., 1970-80; program devel. adviser Program Devel. Ctr. Supt. Schs. Butte County, Oroville, Calif., 1975-77; opportunity tchr. Esperanza High Sch., Gridley, 1980-81, Liberty High Sch., Lodi, Calif., 1981-82, resource specialist coordinator, 1981-82; Title I coordinator Bear Creek Ranch Sch., Lodi, 1981-82, instr., counselor, 1981-82; free lance decorative arts and textiles designer; internat. heritage and foods adv. AAUW, Chico, 1973-75; workshop dir. Creative Arts Ctr., Chico, 1972-73; workshop dir., adv. Bus. Profl. Women's Club of Gridley, 1972-74; v.p. Golden State Mobile Home League, Sacramento, Calif., 1980-82. Designer weavings-wallhangings (1st place 10 categories 1970); winner youth swimming championships Swim Club Augsburg, 1955-57. Mem. United European Am. Club, Am. Assn. German Tchrs., U.S. Army Res. Non-Commd. Officer's Assn. (ednl. adv. 1984—), Kappa Delta Pi. Avocations: weaving; fiber designs; swimming; skiing; internat. travel and culture. Home: 8723 Cabra Ct Elk Grove CA 95624

JONES, BARBARA J., nurse; b. Lewistown, Pa., Aug. 27, 1960; d. Samuel Short and Arletta Jean (Kennedy) J.; m. Francis Mozea, Jr., Feb. 22, 1985. R.N., Geisinger Med. Ctr. Sch. Nursing, Danville, Pa., 1980; B.S.N., Indiana U. of Pa., 1983. Staff nurse Lewistown Hosp., 1980-81, Indiana Hosp., Pa., 1982-83; sr. staff nurse/nurse preceptor W.Va. U. Hosp., Morgantown, 1983—. Vol., In Touch and Concerned, Morgantown, 1984—. Mem. Am. Nurses Assn., W.Va. Nurses Assn., Nat. Multiple Sclerosis Soc. Republican. Methodist. Home: 372 Gilmore St Morgantown WV 26505 Office: WVa Univ Hosp Station 52 Morgantown WV 26505

JONES, BETTY DIXON, financial planner, manager; b. Severy, Kans., Sept. 24, 1927; d. Gernie G. and Gertrude (Blevins) Dixon; m. Harold Jones, Oct. 22, 1945; children—Linda, Ronald, Rodney. Sec., IRS, Hutchinson and Wichita, Kans., 1945-52; security sales rep. Waddell & Reed Inc., Salina and Wichita, 1964-78; br. mgr. E.F. Hutton & Co., Mulvane, Kans., 1978—. Mem. Inst. Cert. Fin. Planners (bd. dirs. 1976-78, sec. 1978-80, pres. 1980-81, chmn. bd. 1981-82), Bus. and Profl. Women. Democrat. Home: 408 Martha St Mulvane KS 67110 Office: E F Hutton & Co Inc 200 W Douglas Wichita KS 67202

JONES, BETTY HARRIS, educator; b. St. Louis, May 25, 1937; d. Homer and Pearl (Fulgham) Harris; A.B., Rutgers U., 1967; M.A., Bryn Mawr Coll., 1968, Ph.D., 1972; m. Calvin Walter Jones, Dec. 2, 1954; children—Christopher Walter, Nicholas Alexander. Instr. in English, Rutgers U., Camden, N.J., 1969-72, asst. prof., 1972—; mem. Nat. Faculty for Humanities, Arts, and Scis., 1983—; bd. dirs. Burlington County Opportunities Industrialization Ctrs.; cons. Phila. Sch. Dist. Grad. collector in English, Bryn Mawr Coll., mem. bd. cons., 1974-76. Danforth Found. fellow, 1967-68; Danforth Found. assoc., 1972; Rutgers U. summer fellow, 1975, faculty fellow, 1977; nominee Lindback award for excellence in coll. teaching, 1970, 77. Mem. MLA, AAUP, N.J. Coll. English Assn., Nat. Council Tchrs. English, Alumnae Assn. Bryn Mawr Coll. (3d v.p., exec. bd.). Contbr. articles to profl. jours. Home: 42 Norman Ln Willingboro NJ 08046 Office: Rutgers U Camden NJ 08102

JONES, BEVERLY ANN MILLER, nursing executive; b. Bklyn., July 14, 1927; d. Hayman Edward and Eleanor Virginia (Doyle) Miller. B.S.N., Adelphi U., 1949; m. Kenneth Lonzo Jones, Sept. 5, 1953; children—Steven Kenneth, Lonnie Cord. Chief nurse regional blood program ARC, N.Y.C., 1951-54; asst. dir., acting dir. nursing M.D. Anderson Hosp. and Tumor Inst., Houston, 1954-55; asst. dir. nursing Sibley Meml. Hosp., Washington, 1959-61; assoc. dir. nursing service Anne Arundel Gen. Hosp., Annapolis, Md., 1966-70; asst. adminstr. nursing Alexandria (Va.) Hosp., 1972-73; asst. adminstr. nursing service Longmont (Colo.) United Hosp., 1977—; instr. ARC, 1953-57; mem. adv. bd. Boulder Valley Vo.-Tech Health Occupations Program, 1977-80; chmn. nurse enrollment com. D.C. chpt. ARC, 1959-61; del. nursing adminstrs. good will trip to Poland, Hungary, Sweden and Eng., 1980. Bd. dirs. Meals on Wheels, Longmont, Colo., 1978-80; bd. dirs. Longmont Coalition for Women in Crisis; mem. Colo. Hosp. Assn. Task Force on Nat. Commn. on Nursing, 1982; mem. utilization com. Boulder (Colo.) Hospice, 1979-83; mem. council labor relations Colo. Hopsp. Assn., 1982-87; mem.-at-large exec. com. nursing service adminstrs. Sect. Md. Nurses' Assn., 1966-69. Mem. Am. Soc. Nursing Service Adminstrs. (chmn. com. membership services and promotions), Colo. Soc. Nurse Execs. (dir. 1978-80, 84-86, pres. 1980-81, chmn. com. on nominations). Home: 8902 Quail Rd Longmont CO 80501 Office: PO Box 1659 Longmont CO 80501

JONES, BRENDA ANN, financial company executive; b. Mobile, Ala., Nov. 7, 1943; d. Carl Hubert and Willie (Cathey) Jones; m. Virgil Dean King, Dec. 11, 1963 (div. 1967); children—Jenny Louise, Diana Maria. A.A., Stephens Coll., 1963; B.S., U. West Fla., 1970, M.B.A., 1972. Cert. info. systems auditor; cert. data processor. Instr. Pensacola Jr. Coll. (Fla.), 1970-73; system analyst Dept. Social Service, Columbia, S.C., 1973-74; asst. EDP auditor Bankers Trust, Columbia, 1974-76; vis. asst. prof. Lander Coll., Greenwood, S.C., 1976-78; internal auditor South New Eng. Telephone Co., New Haven, 1978-79; asst. v.p. Citytrust, Bridgeport, Conn., 1978—; mem. seminar teaching staff Inst. Internal Auditors, Altamonte Springs, Fla., 1979—, mem. internat. com. info. systems, 1983-84; seminar leader Ctrs. Network, N.Y., Boston, New Haven, 1981-85; coordinator coach Herment, San Francisco, 1984—. Mem. Electronic Data Processing Auditors Assn. (bd. dirs. 1981-82), Inst. Internal Auditors. Democrat. Unitarian. Home: 675 Townsend Ave #103 New Haven CT 06512 Office: Citytrust 961 Main St Bridgeport CT 06601

JONES, CAROL POWELL, retired school administrator; b. East Orange, N.J., Aug. 9, 1917; d. Manassau James and Hettie (White) Powell; student St. Paul's Coll., 1937-39; B.S., Va. State Coll., 1947, M.S., 1962; postgrad. Hampton Inst., 1948, Columbia U., 1965; m. Willie Edwin Jones, Aug. 30, 1963 (dec. Dec. 1972). Tchr. elem. grades Buckingham County (Va.) Sch. Bd., 1939-60, elem. supr., 1960-79, supr. Title I Summer Program, 1966-72, coordinator Supplemental Skill Devel. Program, from 1974; ednl. television coordinator Buckingham County. Sec. bd dirs. Buckingham Community Action Program, 1965-69; pres. Womans Missionary and Ednl. Conv. Aux., Slate River Baptist Assn. Central Va.; bd. dirs. Bapt. Gen. Conv., 1982—; 4-H leader; active Va. Lung Assn., Buckingham County Bicentennial Commn; life mem. Hist. Buckingham Inc.; life mem. women's div. Bapt. Gen. Conv., 1983—. Recipient cert. of merit award Alpha Phi Alpha, 1975, numerous other achievement, appreciation and merit awards. Mem. NEA, Am., Va. assns. for supervision and curriculum devel., Va. Assn. Sch. Execs., St. Pauls, Va. State Coll. alumni assns., Fedn. Colored Womans Club (dist. pres. 1978-82, dir. 1979, fin. sec. 1980-84), NAACP (life), Buckingham Friends of Library. Home: Route 1 Box 88 Dillwyn VA 23936

JONES, CAROL PYLE, artist; b. Concord Twp., Pa., June 15, 1911; d. Irwin W. and Gertrude (Martin) Pyle; m. Russell B. Jones, Oct. 1, 1932; children—Russell B., Richard I.G. One person exhbn. Newman & Saunders Galleries, Wayne, Pa., 1983; exhibited Smithsonian Instn., Phila. Art Alliance, Wilmington Art Center, Chester County Art Center, Am. Watercolor Soc.; represented in permanent collections Wilmington Soc. Fine Arts, U. Del., also pvt. collections. Recipient Gold medal Am. Penwomen Regional Show, 1957, 59; Best in Show, Smithsonian Instn., 1960; 1st prize Chester County Art Assn., 1962; Phila. Regional Council Art Centers, 1962. Assoc. Nat. Acad. Design. Address: care Newman & Saunders Galleries 120 Bloomingdale Ave Wayne PA 19087*

JONES, CAROLYN ELLIS, employment agency and business service company executive; b. Marigold, Miss., Feb. 21, 1928; d. Joseph Lawrence and Willie Decelle (Forrest) Peeples; m. David Wright Ellis, May 30, 1945 (div. 1966); children—David, Lyn, Debbie, Dawn; m. Frank Willis Jones, Jan. 1, 1980. Student La. State U., 1949. Owner, mgr. Personnel and Bus. Service, Inc., Greenwood, Miss., 1962—. Author: The Lottie Moon Storybook, 1985; Editor: An Old Soldier's Career, 1974. Contbr. articles to religious and gen. interest publs. Mem. adv. bd. career edn. Greenwood Pub. Schs., 1975-76, mem. adv. bd. vocat.-tech. dept., 1975—; conf. leader Miss. Bapt. Convention Singles Retreat, 1980; Mission Service Corps del. Home Mission Bd., So. Bapt. Conv., Hawaii, 1979. Mem. Greenwood C. of C. (edn. com. 1980—), Mothers Against Drunk Drivers, Altrusa Internat., Nat. Fedn. Ind. Bus., Miss Delta Rose Soc., Gideon Aux. Avocations: writing, rose exhibitions. Office: Personnel & Bus Service Inc Box 932 Greenwood MS 38930

JONES, CAROLYN JANE, clergywoman; b. Grove City, Pa., Jan. 28, 1937; d. Hester Clark and Winifred Eleanor (Hoag) J.; m. Thomas Woodward Golightly. B.A., Westminster Coll., 1958; M.A. in Edn., Syracuse U., 1963; M. Div., Pitts. Theol. Sem., 1977. Tchr. Am. Coll. for Girls, Cairo, 1958-61, Bethel Park High Sch., Pa., 1963-68; asst. dean women Syracuse U., N.Y., 1968-71, dir., asst. dir. activities and orgns. Office Student Affairs, 1971-74; assoc. in Christian edn. Pebble Hill Presbyterian Ch., DeWitt, N.Y., 1971-74; dir. Christian edn. Newlonsburg United Presbyn. Ch., Murrysville, Pa., 1975-77; assoc. pastor Glenshaw Presbyn. Ch., Pa., 1977-84; interim minister-at-large Pitts. Presbytery, 1984—; bd. dirs. Pitts. Theol. Sem.; bd. mgrs. New Wilmington Missionary Conf. Recipient Thomas Jamison scholar, 1977; Sylvester S. Marvin Meml. fellow, 1977. Mem. Cleric of Pitts., Assn. Presbyn. Ch. Educators. Home: 1524 King Charles Dr Pittsburgh PA 15237 Office: 801 Union Ave Pittsburgh PA 15212

JONES, CHERYL BEATRICE, medical technologist; b. N.Y.C., July 31, 1948; d. Frederick Douglas and Mary Magdalene (Reid) Campbell; m. Leroy Jones, Aug. 4, 1973; 1 child, Kaleah Marie. A.A.S., N.Y.C. Community Coll., 1969; B.S., Richmond Coll., 1973. Lab. technician, Met. Diagnostic Labs., Bklyn., 1969-72; lab. technician in chemistry Bklyn. Hosp., 1972-73; technologist in hematology, coagulation and clin. microscopy Lenox Hill Hosp., N.Y.C., 1973-77; tchr. biology Tehran Am. Sch., Iran, 1978; technologist in serology and immunohematology Path Lab, Inc., Nashville 1979-80; tech. services instr. ARC, Nashville, 1981—; mem. adv. com. Nashville State Tech. Inst., 1985—. Author abstract. Mem. Am. Assn. Blood Banks, Tenn. Assn. Blood Banks, Am. Soc. Clin. Pathologists, Nat. Assn. Female Execs. Democrat. Roman Catholic. Avocations: photography; coin collecting; traveling. Home: 819 Bellevue Rd Nashville TN 37221 Office: Am Red Cross 2201 Charlotte Ave Nashville TN 37203

JONES, CLARA PADILLA, state official, real estate broker; b. Albuquerque, Oct. 2, 1942; d. Julian and Suzanna (Padilla) Padilla; m. Ronald A. Jones, Apr. 28, 1960; children—Mary Clara Davis, Suzanna. Student El Camino Jr. Coll., Inglewood, Calif., 1966-68, Albuquerque Career Inst., 1975-76. Buyer, merchandising mgr. Bullock's, Los Angeles, 1959-68; cosmetics buyer, dept. mgr. Dillards, Albuquerque, 1968-78; assoc. Julian Padilla & Assocs., Albuquerque, 1978—; sec. of state State N.Mex., Santa Fe, 1983—; com. mem. Southwest Voter Registration Edn. Project, San Antonio, 1983—. Past vice-chmn. Bernalillo County Democratic party, Albuquerque; founder, past pres. Bernalillo County Valley Dem. Women, Albuquerque; founder, pres. Las Amigas de Nuevo Mejico; bd. dirs. Am. G.I. Forum, Albuquerque. Recipient Service-Above Self award Espanola Rotary Club, 1983; State Bus. award N.Mex. Highlands U., Las Vegas, 1983; Cert. of Merit, Am. G.I. Forum, 1984; Named Disting. Past Pres., Bernalillo County Valley Democratic Women, 1983; Pub. Service award Nat. Kidney Found. N.Mex., 1984. Mem. Fedn. Bus. and Profl. Women, Nat. Assn. Secs. of State (exec. bd., com. on voter edn. S.W. Bankers Assn. Democrat. Roman Catholic. Club: Zonta Office: Office of Sec of State Exec Legislative Bldg Santa Fe NM 87503

JONES, CLARICE RHODES, educator; b. Houston, Dec. 31, 1925; d. Charles Benton and Fannie Lillian (Bailey) Rhodes; B.A., Tex. State U., 1949; M.S. in Edn., U. So. Calif., 1969; 1 dau., Iverne Clarice. Profl. dancer with Carmen Jones, 1943-44, with Katherine Dunham, 1945-46; tchr. phys. edn., public schs., Houston, 1951-54; recreation dir., dance specialist City of Los Angeles, 1955-62; tchr. spl. edn., public schs., Duarte, Calif., 1963-69; tchr. 4th grade, public schs., Inglewood, Calif., 1970—; chairperson parent participation Sch. Adv. Council, Clyde Woodworth Sch., Inglewood; mem. consold. application adv. com. Project Invest. Mem. Calif. Tchrs. Assn., NEA, NAACP, Nat. Council Negro Women, YWCA, Los Angeles Urban League, Inst. Religious Sci., Delta Sigma Theta, Chi Kappa Rho. Democrat. Home: 7818 S Harvard Blvd Los Angeles CA 90047 Office: 3200 w 104th Inglewood CA 90303

JONES, DEBORAH ROGERS, nursing administrator; b. North Platte, Nebr., July 12, 1951; d. James Wesley and Corinne Margaret (Smith) Rogers; m. Mark Foulkes Jones, III, Jan. 8, 1977 (div. June 1981); children—Mark Foulkes IV, Tamara Corinne. Student U. Nebr., 1970-72; A.A., Santa Monica Coll., 1972; B.S. in Nursing, Calif. State U.-Los Angeles, 1975. Charge nurse UCLA Hosp., 1975-77; nurse supr. Home Health & Counseling, Sacramento, 1978-81; dir. nurses Med. Personnel Pool, Sacramento, 1981-84; exec. dir. Physician Resources Network, Inc., Fresno, Calif., 1985—. Mem. Community Services and Planning Council, 1983-84; co-chmn. Sr. Coalition Tng. Supervisory Task Force, Sacramento, 1983-84. Mem. Am. Assn. Continuity of Care, Gray Panthers Health Com. (chmn. 1983-84), Nat. Assn. Home Care, Calif. Assn. Health Services at Home (bd. dirs. 1983-85, chmn. long term care com.). Republican. Home: 1659 E Magill Fresno CA 93710

JONES, DEBRA LYNN, sales executive, lecturer; b. Shawnee, Okla., Sept. 6, 1954; d. Clifton Harold and Betty Jo (Carpenter) Branscum; m. Douglas Francis Jones, June 11, 1983. B.A., Okla. State U.-Stillwater, 1975, M.S., 1976. Tchr., Whitesboro pub. schs., Tex., 1976-77; sales rep., sales mgr. Lanier Bus. Products, Dallas, Denver, 1977-82; pres. Hark & Assocs., 1980—; nat. mktg. dir. MDG, Inc., Boulder, Colo., 1982; sales cons., trainer Denver, 1983—; account mgr. Secure Communications, Denver, 1983; bus. cons.; newsletter editing staff Exec. Women Internat., Denver, 1982; lectr. in field; Author: Peeking Out of the Rut. Performer, Young Oklahomans, Ada, 1973; campaign worker Young Republicans, Stillwater, 1974-76; fund raiser United Way, Stillwater, 1974, Pub. TV, Dallas, 1981. Mem. Nat. Assn. Female Execs., Salesman with a Purpose, Nat. Speakers Assn., Sigma Alpha Iota. Republican.

JONES, DELORES ELDER, administrative social worker, model; b. Memphis, Jan. 21, 1940; d. Otis Augustus II, and Mary Odessa (Jones) Elder; m. Walter Lewis Spinks, Oct. 26, 1957 (dec. 1966); children—Sedrick Duane Jones, Tedra Shaun Spinks-Hicks; m. Richard Henry Jones, Mar. 10, 1968. B.Social Welfare, Memphis State U., 1982, postgrad. in city planning, 1986—. Master barber. Men's hairstylist Jim's Barber Shop, Memphis, 1962-77; personal aide Isaac Hayes Movement, Memphis, 1970-77; pre-occupancy counselor Memphis Housing, 1977-83; adminstr., community and devel. social worker Diocese of Memphis Housing Corp., 1983—. Mem. housing com. Shelby County Kitchen Kabinet, Memphis; co-chmn. Tenn. Statewide Fair Housing Conf., 1986. Named Ms. Inspiration, Big Beautiful Women Mag., 1984, Role Model of Yr. 1985, Fed. Express and Booker T. Washington High Sch., Memphis, 1985; recipient cert. of recognition HUD, 1986. Mem. Nat. Assn. Social Workers, Memphis Community Housing Resource Bd., Memphis Assn. Dirs. of Vols., Nat. Assn. Housing and Redevel. Ofcls. Democrat. Baptist. Clubs: In Good Company, Young Sophisticates (advisor Memphis 1966-84). Avocations: reading; bowling; inspiring big women and women over 40. Home: 4605 White Pine Memphis TN 38109 Office: Diocese of Memphis Housing Corp 1130 Breedlove Memphis TN 38107

JONES, DENISE DEE, advertising agency executive; b. Lancaster, Pa., Sept. 16, 1958; d. Neil Helm and Dolores (Wesley) J. B.A., Franklin and Marshall Coll., 1979. Account exec. Kelly/Michener Advt., Lancaster, 1981-83; ptnr. Snyder & Snyder, Lancaster, 1983-85; account exec. Caravetta Allen Kimbrough/BBDO Inc., Miami, Fla., 1985—. Mem. Big Bros./Big Sisters, 1983-85. Mem. Phila. Club Advt. Women, Nat. Assn. Female Execs., Nat. Trust for Historic Preservation. Republican. Methodist. Avocations: piano; writing; theater. Home: 2930 Day Ave Apt N103 Coconut Grove FL 33133 Office: Caravetta Allen Kimbrough/BBDO 7200 Corp Center Dr Miami FL 33126

JONES, DIANNE ROBINSON, law educator; b. Moscow, Idaho, Aug. 14, 1946; d. Elmer Lloyd Ide and Patricia (Kidwell) Weninger; m. David L. Jones. B.A. with honors in English, UCLA, 1969; J.D. with honors, U. So. Calif.-Los Angeles, 1973; M. Philosophy, Cambridge U., 1982. Bar: Calif. 1973. Law clk. U.S. Ct. Appeals (9th cir.), 1973-74; dep. fed. pub. defender, Los Angeles, 1974-77; assoc. prof. law Gonzaga U., Spokane, 1977-78; assoc. O'Melveny & Myers, Los Angeles, 1978-80; assoc. prof. Sch. Law U. S.D., Vermillion, 1982—; assoc. clin. prof. psychiatry U. So. Calif. Inst. Behavioral Psychiatry, Los Angeles, 1976-80; panelist Southwestern Conf. on Women and the Law, 1975. Contbr. articles to legal jours. Bd. dirs. Calif. Prisoners Legal Services, Los Angeles, 1979-80; mem. legis. com. Women's Lawyers Assn., 1975-76. Briedenback Fund scholar, 1971-73. Mem Brit. Soc. Criminology, Fed. Bar Assn., ABA (chmn. civil detoxification program 1976), Calif. Bar Assn. (alt. state bar conv. 1976), Los Angeles County Bar Assn. (co-chmn. civil detoxification program 1976, fed. practice and procedure com. 1975-76, individual and human rights exec. com. 1975-76), Legion Lex (bd. dirs. 1975-78), Alpha Chi Omega, Order of Coif.

JONES, DOLORIS DOROTHEA, marine equipment company executive; b. Salem, Mass., Mar. 26, 1937; d. Rene George and Cecilia C. (Pasquinelli) Duchesne; m. Harry Elmer Jones, Feb. 16, 1957; children—Leslie Carlin, Ross Owen. Student U. Maine, 1966-67, St. Petersburg Jr. Coll., 1968-71, Houston Community Coll., 1978-83, Rice U., 1984-85. Diagnostician, Aldine Sch. Dist., Houston, 1972-75; owner, pres. Dee Paula Fashions, Houston, 1973-76; dept. asst. mgr. Nissho-Iwai Trading Co., Houston, 1976-79; gen. mgr. Hamanaka Internat., Inc., Houston, 1979—; project mgr. floating product platform Placid Oil Co., Dallas, 1984—; owner Alexandria of Houston. Patentee in field. Mem. LWV, Nat. Assn. Female Execs. Republican. Lutheran. Avocations: music; art; woodworking. Office: Hamanaka Internat Inc 1980 Post Oak Blvd Suite 1000 Houston TX 77056

JONES, DORIS MAE, court reporting company executive; b. Allentown, Pa., Nov. 24, 1938; d. Michael C. and Ann (Fedor) Hardony; m. Lewis M. Horwitz, Mar. 14, 1964 (div. 1984); children—Monica B., Pamela L. B.S., Mich. State U., 1960; postgrad. Cleve. Marshall Law Sch., 1962; cert. Emery Sch., 1975. Ct. reporter Doris O. Wong Assocs., Boston, 1975-79; ofcl. reporter U.S. Dist. Cts., Boston, 1979-81; pres. Doris M. Jones & Assocs., Boston, 1980—. Bd. dirs., sec. Lawrence Extended Day Program, Brookline, Mass., 1977-81; steering com. hospitality program, Episcopal Diocese, Boston, 1984—. mem. Nat. Shorthand Reporters Assn., Mass. Shorthand Reporters Assn. (sec. 1977-79, bd. dirs. 1977-80), Phi Gamma Nu, Delta Zeta. Avocations: reading; traveling; cooking; public speaking. Address: Doris M Jones & Assocs Inc 59 Temple Pl Boston MA 02111

JONES, DORIS W., ballet company director. Dir. Capitol Ballet Co., Washington. Office: Capitol Ballet Co 1200 Delafield Pl NW Washington DC 20011*

JONES, DOROTHY CAMERON, English language educator; b. Detroit, Feb. 5, 1922; d. Vinton Ernest and Beatrice Olive (Cameron) J.; B.A., Wayne State U., 1943, M.A., 1944; Ph.D., U. Colo., 1965. Attendance officer Detroit Bd. Edn., 1943-44; English tchr. Denby High Sch., Detroit, 1946-56, 57-58; exchange tchr., Honolulu, 1956-57; instr., asst. prof. English, Colo. Women's Coll., Denver, 1962-66; faculty U. No. Colo., Greeley, 1966—, prof. English, 1974—, Faculty research grantee, 1970, 76. Served with WAVES, USNR, 1944-46. Mem. Internat. Shakespeare Assn., Central States Renaissance Soc., Rocky Mountain Medieval and Renaissance Soc., Rocky Mountain MLA, Patrististic, Medieval, and Renaissance Conf., Delta Kappa Gamma, Pi Lambda Theta. Contbr. papers to profl. lit. Home: Apt 312 1009 13th Ave Greeley CO 80631 Office: Dept English 40 Michener Library U No Colo Greeley CO 80639

JONES, EDNA RUTH, business educator; b. Greene County, N.C., Jan. 31, 1932; d. Ralph H. and Letha (Whitley) J. B.S., E. Carolina U., 1954, M.A.Ed., 1982. Bus. tchr. Corinth-Holders Sch., Zebulon, N.C., 1954-56, Harnet County Schs., Angier, N.C., 1956-60, Wake County Schs., Wake Forest and Millbrook, N.C., 1960-68, No. Nash Sch., Rocky Mount, N.C., 1968-85; asst. prof. bus. Louisburg Coll., N.C., 1985—; advisor Future Bus. Leaders Am. Mem. Nat. Bus. Edn. Assn., N.C. Bus. Edn. Assn. (chmn. audit com. 1983-84, sec. 1984-85), Kappa Delta Pi. Democrat. Methodist. Club: Altrusa (sec. 1983-84, v.p. 1984-85, dir. 1985-86, v.p. 1986-87) (Rocky Mount). Home: PO Box 7602 Rocky Mount NC 27804 Office: Louisburg College 501 N Main St Louisburg NC 27549

JONES, EILEEN MARGARET, computer programmer; b. Quincy, Mass., Nov. 28, 1956; d. James Michael and Mary Virginia (Keating) Conley; m. Donald Patrick McCall, Aug. 19, 1979 (div. 1982); 1 child, Jaclyn Melissa McCall Jones; m. Gregory Tapply Jones, July 27, 1985. B.A. in French, Assumption Coll., 1978; student U. Nice, France, 1976-77. Cert. programmer. Flight attendant Capitol Airways, Jamaica, N.Y., 1978-80; interpreter Mass. Gen. Hosp., Boston, 1981-82; programmer Honeywell Info., Waltham, Mass., 1982-83; programmer/analyst Dynamics Research Corp., Wilmington, Mass., 1984, Digital Equipment Corp., Maynard, Mass., 1984-85; project leader Gen. Electric, Fort Wayne, Ind., 1986—. Mem. Mass. Businessman's Assn., Nat. Assn. Female Execs., AAUW. Episcopalian. Avocations: Sewing; skiing; boating. Home: 917 Flat Hill Rd Lunenburg MA 01462

JONES, ELIZABETH BROWN, writer; b. Kansas City, Mo., Sept. 27, 1907, d. James Riley and Agnes Julia (Gammage) Brown; student U. Mo., Kansas City, 1946, Mid-Am. Nazarene Coll., 1981; m. Clare Hartley Jones, June 4, 1929; children—Elizabeth Ann, Sara Denise, David Hartley, Phyllis Elaine. Free-lance writer, 1940-62, 78—; author numerous books, including: Teaching Primaries Today, 1974; Because God Made Me, 1975; Stories of Jesus, 1977; When We Share the Bible with Children, 1977; Let the Children Come, 1978; contbr. numerous stories, poems to children's publs.; author song lyrics; editor, curriculum planner, writer Nazarene Pub. House, Kansas City, Mo., 1962-78; workshop leader; speaker at writers' confs.; mem. nat. com. for planning Sunday sch. curriculum; book reviewer; speaker at parent's groups. Mem. Ch. of the Nazarene.

JONES, ELIZABETH RIEKE (MRS. WAYNE VAN LEER JONES), civic worker; b. Chgo., Oct. 15, 1903; d. Henry Edward and Vina Genevieve (Coulter) Rieke; A.B., Northwestern U., 1925; m. Wayne Van Leer Jones, Jan. 14, 1926; 1 son, Wayne Van Leer II. Dir. Houston Grand Opera Assn., 1956-77, mem. pres.'s council, 1977—. Charter mem. Assistance Guild Houston, 1966-68, Assistance League, 1968—, nat. fin. com., 1970. Donor The Wayne V. and Elizabeth R. Jones Fine and Performing Arts Resdl. Coll., Northwestern U., 1980. Mem. Houston U. Women's Alliance (pres. 1951-53, scholarship chmn. 1963-65, meml. scholarship chmn. 1965-83), Houston Geol. Aux. (parliamentarian, 1950-51, 60-61, 63-64), Kappa Kappa Gamma, Theta Sigma Phi. Republican. Presbyterian. Home: 5672 Longmont Dr Houston TX 77056

JONES, ETHEL LEAN, social worker; b. Marshall, Tex; July 15, 1953; d. Anderson and Arjera (Fitzpatrick) Jones; m. Fred Johnson, July 20, 1981 (dec. Nov. 11, 1981), 1 dau., Ariana Lynn; m. Sidney Earl Jones, July 31, 1982, 1 son, Anthony Clayton. B.Sc., E. Tex. State U. (Commerce), 1974; M.S.W., U. Houston, 1979. Lic. cert. social worker, Tex. Social worker Tex. Dept. Human Resources, Henderson, 1975-77, Houston, 1977—. Active Julis C. Hester House, Houston, 1970-71, Mayor's Summer Food Program, 1978; mem. exec. bd. La Rochelle Acad., Houston, 1977-81. Mem. Assn. Black Social Workers, Nat. Assn. Social Workers, Am. Pub. Welfare Assn. Democrat. Baptist. Home: 8031 Misty Vale Houston TX 77075 Office: Tex Dept Human Resources 2913 Louisiana Houston TX 77000

JONES, FRANCES SYLVIA, medical technology educator; b. Mangham, La., July 30, 1934; d. Harvel Traylor and Eva Dee (Weems) Jones; B.S., N.E. La. U., 1956; M.S., La. Tech. U., 1970. Chief technologist E.A. Conway Hosp., Monroe, La., 1956-62; staff technologist to supr. VA Med. Center, Shreveport, La., 1962-72; edn. coordinator Sch. Med. Tech., VA Med. Center, Shreveport, 1972-82; program dir. Sch. Med. Tech., clin. prof. Cantenary Coll., Shreveport, 1983—; clin. assoc. prof. La. Tech. U., Ruston; clin. asst. prof. Northwestern State U., Natchitoches, La.; clin. asst. prof. Allied Health Scis., Notheast La. U., Monroe; clin. instr. dept. pathology La. State U. Sch. Medicine, Shreveport; faculty mem. So. Regional Med. Edn. Ctr., 1977, 83; site surveyor Nat. Accreditation Agy. for Clin. Lab. Scis. Chmn., VA Fed. Employees Credit Union credit com., 1972-79, dir., 1978—, pres./bd. dirs., 1983—. Recipient Superior Performance award, VA Med. Center, 1971, 79, 83, 85; La. Heart Assn. grantee, 1953-54. Mem. Am. Soc. Clin. Pathologists, Am. Bus. Women's Assn., La. Soc. Med. Tech., Am. Soc. Med. Tech., Clin. Lab. Mgmt. Assn., Phi Mu (charter mem. 1956). Democrat. Baptist. Home: 1823 Pluto Dr Bossier City LA 71112 Office: 510 E Stoner Ave Shreveport LA 71130

JONES, GAIL KATHLEEN, educational administrator; b. Oklahoma City, June 28, 1935; d. Lloyd Clifton Jones and Cleo Kathleen (Shackelford) Ahlstedt; m. Jerry Lynn Jones, Aug. 8, 1954; children—Kathleen, Jerry Clifton, Gregory. B.A. in English, Central Wash. U., 1971. Coordinator outreach program Ellensburg City Library, Wash., 1971-77; dir. alumni affairs Central Wash. U., Ellensburg, 1977—; Publisher newsletter Central Today, 1977—. Mem. Wash. Gov.'s com. for Handicapped, 1978-83; officer United Way Bd., Ellensburg, 1982—; mem. Beautification Commn., Ellensburg, 1980-83, Distributive Edn. Adv. Council, Ellensburg, 1978-82. Mem. Council Advancement and Support Edn., AAUW, LWV, Ellensburg C. of C. Presbyterian. Home: 405 N Anderson Ellensburg WA 98926 Office: C W U Alumni Office Barge 310 Ellensburg WA 98926

JONES, GRETA JANE, marina executive; b. Kansas City, Mo., Mar. 31, 1932; d. Joseph Eugene and Greta Louise (Harbison) Houston; m. Charles Edward Jones, Dec. 30, 1955; 1 child, Emily Susan. Student, St. Mary's Coll. Sec., Am. Ins. Co., Kansas City, Mo., 1951-52, Potts-Woodbury Advt., Kansas City, Mo., 1952-54; exec. sec. Home Fed. Ins. Co., Kansas City, Mo., 1954-55; from gen. mgr. to owner, chief exec. officer, Blue Anchor Marina, Gravois Mills, Mo., 1969—. Republican. Methodist. Clubs: Kansas City Young Matrons, Lake of Ozarks Yachting Assn. Home: Route 1 Box 594 Gravois Mills MO 65037 Office: Blue Anchor Marina Inc Route 1 Box 594 Gravois Mills MO 65037

JONES, HELEN COOK, author; b. Los Angeles, Jan. 17, 1917; d. Clyde W. and Carrie May (Morrish) Cook; m. Hardin Blair Jones, Mar. 17, 1940 (dec. Feb. 1978); children—Carolyn, Hardin, Nancy, Mark. B.A., UCLA, 1938; postgrad. U. Calif.-Berkeley, 1938-39. Tchr., Hollywood High Sch. (Calif.), 1939-42, Pleasant Hill Intermediate Sch. Dist. (Calif.), 1953-54. Author: (with Beth Bond, Virginia Dobbin, Helen Gofman and Lenore Lyon) The Low-Fat, Low-Cholesterol Diet Book, 1951, rev. edits., 1971, 84; (with Hardin B. Jones) Sensual Drugs: Deprivation and Rehabilitation of the Mind, 1977; (with P. W. Lovinger) The Marijuana Question and Science's Search for an Answer, 1984. Mem. U. Calif. Faculty Wives Fgn. Student Com., Berkeley, Calif., 1970-80; bd. dirs. Am. Council on Drug Abuse, N.Y.C., 1978—; mem. adv. bd. Parents Who Care, Palo Alto, Calif., 1981—; contbg. editor Coms. of Corr., N.Y.C., 1982—. Mem. Nat. Fedn. Parents for a Drug Free Youth, Parent Resources and Info. on Drug Edn., Californians for Drug-free Youth. Club: Berkeley City (bd. dirs. 1981, 84—), Claremont Book (Berkeley, Calif.). Home: 1519 Oxford St Apt L Berkeley CA 94709

JONES, HESTER SINGLEY, design services company executive; b. Chatom, Ala., Sept. 4, 1934; d. Grafton G. and Loraine (Williams) Singley; m. Edwin L. Jones, Jr., July 2, 1953 (div. Dec. 1970); children—Mark Allan, Patricia Lynn. B.F.A., U. Houston, 1969; M.B.A., Pepperdine U., 1980. Designer, Suniland Furniture Co., Houston, 1969-73; project designer Marshall Clegg Assocs., San Antonio, 1973-75; pres. Clegg-Houston, Inc., 1975-80; facilities planning coordinator Pennzoil, Houston, 1980-83; v.p. Wilson's Bus. Products Services and Systems, Houston, 1983—. Telephone vol. Crisis Intervention of Houston, 1975-81, vol. of yr., 1979, bd. mem., 1980-85, bd. pres., 1982-84. Grad. fellow Rockwell Internat., 1980. Mem. Am. Soc. Interior Designers (nat. dir. 1980-81, chmn. bus. design com. 1980-81, pres. Tex. Gulf Coast chpt. 1979), Internat. Facility Mgrs. Assn. (membership chmn. 1982, program chmn. 1983), AIA (profl. affiliate). Episcopalian (vestry 1986—). Clubs: Houstonian (assoc. adv. com. 1983—), Houston West (pres. 1981, 1st v.p. 1985) (Houston).

JONES, IDA MAE, lawyer, educator; b. Omaha, Aug. 18, 1953; d. Jonathan and Mary (Cooper) J.; m. Harry Edward Williams, Aug. 16, 1977 (div.); children—Kenneth Elliott, Kamali Allen, Jamilla Marie, John Eugene. B.A. in Sociology, Creighton U., 1974; J.D., NYU, 1977. Bar: N.Y. 1978, Nebr. 1980, U.S. Dist. Ct. (so. dist.) N.Y. 1978, U.S. Dist. Ct. Nebr. 1980. Law clk. HEW, N.Y.C., 1976-77; assoc. appellate counsel Legal Aid-Criminal Appeals, N.Y.C., 1977-79; staff atty. Legal Aid Soc., Omaha, 1979-81; sole practice, Omaha, 1981—; asst. prof. U. Nebr., Omaha, 1981-85, assoc. prof., 1986—; bd. dirs. PILCO, Omaha, 1981-84. Mem. adv. bd. Child Saving Inst., Omaha, 1981—; bd. dirs. Gt. Plains Black Mus., 1984-85. Contbr. articles to profl. jours. Fellow ABA, Nebr. Bar Assn., Midlands Bar Assn. Democrat. Home: 3211 N 18th St Omaha NE 68110 Office: U Nebr Omaha Coll Bus 60th & Dodge Omaha NE 68182

JONES, IRMA JEWEL, social worker; b. Alton, Ill., Apr. 6, 1934; d. Damon and Willie Ann Jones; student So. Ill. U., Carbondale, 1952-54, San Francisco-Columbia Sch. Broadcasting, St. Louis, 1969-72. With Madison County (Ill.) Dept. Public Aid, 1956-72, 76—, social worker, caseworker, 1976—; adminstrv. sec., clk. III, So. Ill. U., Edwardsville, 1973-76; religious music radio announcer, producer, coordinator Sta. WOKZ, Alton, 1974—. Mem. Nat. Assn. Colored Women's Clubs (past 2d and 3d v.p.), Fedn. Methodist Women, Nat. Gospel Announcers Guild, Gospel Music Workshop Am. Mem. A.M.E. Ch. Author: Irma's Kreative Book of Religious and Kontemporary Works of Art, 1975—. Office: 2745 E Broadway Alton IL 62002

JONES, JANICE ARLENE, financial services executive; b. Long Beach, Calif., July 13, 1948; d. Don C. and Dorothy (Hilliard) J.; m. K.T. Mao, Dec. 27, 1984; 1 child, Justin Mao-Jones. B.A., Hunter Coll., 1973; Ph.D., Yeshiva U., 180. Fin. pub. relations counsel Haber Instruments, N.J., 1973-76; fin. v.p. Cameron Assocs., N.Y.C., 1976-80; pres., founder Chartwell Group Inc., Los Angeles, 1980—; fin. adviser, founding investor Cyanotech Corp., Woodinville, Wash., 1984—; pres., founder Chartwell Pub. Co., Inc. Recipient Hunter Coll. Hall of Fame award, 1986. Mem. NOW, Nat. Women's Polit. Caucus, Com. of 200. Baptist. Avocation: jazz and tap dancing. Office: Chartwell & Co 900 Wilshire Blvd Suite 714 Los Angeles CA 90036

JONES, JANICE MCCOY, lawyer, consultant; b. Berkeley, Calif., Jan. 17, 1948; d. Frederick and Emily Katherine (Wilson) McCoy; m. George Henry Jones, Aug. 1 (div.); 1 dau., Melanie Adrienne; m. 2d Calvin William Sharpe, Apr. 13, 1978. B.S., U. Calif.-Hayward, 1968; M.S., U. Calif.-Berkeley, 1969; J.D., U. Mich., 1973. Bar: Mich. 1974. Asst. regional atty. Ford Motor Co., Dearborn, Mich., 1973-75; with Wayne County Prosector's Office, Detroit, 1975; sr. atty. Montgomery Ward, Chgo., 1976-78; v.p., gen. counsel Booke & Co., Winston-Salem, N.C., 1978-83; v.p. Gottlieb Pension Services, Cleve., 1983—; adj. prof. U. Va., 1981-82, Wake Forest U., 1982-83; sec.; treas., dir. BRIC, Inc., Winston-Salem, 1982-83. Contbr. articles on tax and employee benefits to various publs. Bd. dirs. Winston-Salem Arts Council, 1982-83, Karanmu Women's Com., Cleve., 1984. Mem. ABA, Mich. Bar Assn., Cleve. Bar Assn., Forsyth County Women Attys. (sec.-treas.). Democrat. Home: 2350 Ardleigh Dr Cleveland Heights OH 44106

JONES, JO BOOT, psychologist; b. Visalia, Calif., Nov. 10, 1914; d. Edgar S. and Josephine A. (Westlake) Boot; B.A. in Art and French, U. Calif., Berkeley, 1939; M.A., San Francisco State U., 1951, postgrad., 1952, 55, 56, 57; postgrad. Claremont Grad. Sch., 1952-53, U. San Francisco, Mallorca, Spain, 1970, Centro des Artes y Lenguas Espanoles, Mex., 1971; m. William Sammons, June, 1939 (div. 1972); children—Toni, Sheri Sammons Schulster; m. 2d, Mark Wade Jones, July, 1976. Cons. psychology Norwalk City Schs., 1953-56; psychotherapist Deveraux Found., Santa Barbara, Calif., 1956-62, clin. adminstr., 1956-62, chmn. dept. psychotherapy, 1958-62; cons. psychologist Warner Child Guidance Center, Palm Springs, Calif., 1962, dir. 1963-64; dist. psychologist Palm Springs Unified Sch. Dist., 1963-64, supervising psychologist psychol. services, 1964-68; cons. psychologist Human Devel. Tng. Inst., San Diego, 1967-70; dist. psychologist Sequoia (Calif.) Union Sch. Dist., 1968-79; supr. doctoral and masters candidates clin. psychology State U. Hayward, Calif., also Calif. Sch. Profl. Psychology, San Francisco, 1968-80; pvt. practice clin. psychology, 1950—; guest panelist spl. edn. Calif. Dept. Edn., 1967; cons. El Dorado County Schs., 1980—; one woman shows of paintings include: U. Calif., Berkeley, 1935, 38, Mills Coll., Oakland, Calif., 1941, 44, San Francisco Adult Schs., 1950; group shows include: Oakland Art Mus., 1941, Los Angeles County Art Mus., 1954, Calif. Assn. Sch. Psychologists and Psychometrists, Los Angeles and San Francisco, 1970, 72, 73, 74, Placerville Art Club (Merit award oil), 1981; represented in pvt. collections. Recipient Outstanding Service award Sequoia Union High Sch. Dist., 1979. Mem. Am. Psychol. Assn., Calif. Psychol. Assn., Assn. Calif. Sch. Adminstrs., Placerville Art Club, Marin Art Guild, Delta Kappa Gamma. Democrat. Contbr. articles to psychology jours.; art editor Calif. Sch. Psychology, 1972-74. Home: PO Box 117 River Cliff Coloma CA 95613

JONES, JOAN ELIZABETH, asphalt contractor; b. Winchester, Mass., May 27, 1941; d. John Adolph McDowell and Eleanor Nellie (Cole) McDowell Rewis; m. Kenneth Wendell Jones, July 6, 1962; children—Wendy, David, Eric, Katherine. Jennifer. Grad. high sch., Ft. Lauderdale, Fla. Cert. contractor, Utah. Distbr., Ariz. Refining Co., Phoenix, 1984—; owner Bidwell Maintainance Engring., Salt Lake City, Utah, 1981—. Contbr. articles to publs. Mem. Utah Supplier Devel. Council. Avocations: horse training; photography. Office: Bidwell Maintenance Engring PO Box 342 Salt Lake City UT 84065

JONES, JOYCE FLORENCE, social worker; b. Lake Charles, La., Apr. 25, 1927; d. Joseph and Edna (Geyen) Wilson; B.A. cum laude, U. San Francisco, 1972; M.S.W., U. Calif., Berkeley, 1974; cert. Ethel Percy Andrus Sch. Gerontology, U. So. Calif., 1975; m. Alton Joseph Jones, Nov. 16, 1946 (dec.); children—Ronald, Stephen (dec.), Michele, Brian, Kenneth. Part-time substitute tchr., tchr.'s aide All Hallows Sch., San Francisco, 1965-67; social worker Bayview Hunter's Point Health Service, San Francisco, 1967-72; dir. info. and referral services, asst. to exec. dir. San Francisco Commn. on Aging, 1974-84, program analyst, monitor programs for the elderly, 1984—; speaker in field; coordinator workshops on elderly. Lic. social worker, Calif. Mem. Acad. Cert. Social Workers, Nat. Assn. Social Workers. Democrat. Roman Catholic. Home: 1775 Palou Ave San Francisco CA 94124 Office: 1360 Mission St 4th Floor San Francisco CA 94103

JONES, JUDITH DENISE, property management merchandising coordinator; b. Cherry Point, N.C., Apr. 4, 1960; d. Dennis Matthew and Judith Ann (Pearce) J. B.S. in Bus. Adminstrn., Lindenwood Coll., 1982. Dir. consumer relations Jones Med. Industry, St. Louis, 1979-82, also dir.; promotion dir. Dome Prodn., Inc., St. Louis, 1982-83; sales rep. Cambridge Plan Internat., Monterey, Calif., 1983-84; merchandising coordinator Northill Devel. Corp., Ft. Wayne, Ind., 1984—. Mem. Apt. Assn. of Ft. Wayne (co-chmn. guide com. 1985). Republican. Methodist. Avocations: travel; music; golf. Office: Northill Devel Corp 609 E Cook Rd Fort Wayne IN 46825

JONES, KATE LESTER, magazine editor; b. Oklahoma City, Jan. 25, 1948; d. Robert R. and Alice Loreta (Kuntz) Lester; m. Thomas M. Jones, Jan. 5, 1980. B.A., Grinnell Coll., Iowa, 1970; M.A., U. Mo.-Columbia, 1984. Asst. editor U. Mo. Press, Columbia, 1978-79; assoc. editor Mo. Life mag., Jefferson City, 1980-81; asst. editor Oklahoma Today mag., Oklahoma City, 1981-83, mng. editor, 1983-86; mng. editor Colo. Homes & Lifestyles mag., Denver, 1986—. Frank Luther Mott fellow, 1980. Mem. Regional Publishers Assn., Phi Beta Kappa. Democrat. Office: Colo Homes & Lifestyles Mag 2551 31st St Suite 154 Denver CO

JONES, LAURIE LYNN, editor; b. Kerrville, Tex., Sept. 2, 1947; d. Charles Clinton and Jean Laurie (Davidson) Jones; B.A., U. Tex., Austin, 1969; m. C. Frederick Childs, June 26, 1976; children—Charles Newell, Cyrus Trevor. Asst. to dir. coll. admissions Columbia U., N.Y.C., 1969-70, asst. to dir. Office Alumni, 1970-71; asst. advt. mgr. Book World, Washington Post/Chgo. Tribune, 1971-72; editorial asst. N.Y. Mag., N.Y.C., 1972-74, asst. editor, 1974, sr. editor, 1974-76, mng. editor, 1976—. Mem. Am. Soc. Mag. Editors, Women in Communication, Advt. Women N.Y. Republican. Methodist. Office: New York Mag 755 2d Ave New York NY 10017

JONES, LINDA NELL, real estate broker; b. Bonham, Tex., Sept. 17, 1939; d. Lowell Curn and Elta Agnes (Ridings) Shuler; student U. Mich., 1969; m. John David Jones, Sept. 6, 1957 (div. 1980); children—Angela Kay, Randal David. Salesperson, Arbor Oaks Realtors, Ann Arbor, Mich., 1969; salesperson Larson & Gillies, Ann Arbor, 1970-72; partner/broker Gillies Co., Ann Arbor, 1972-75; owner, broker Century 21-Arbor Homes, Inc., Ann Arbor, 1975—; sec., bd. dirs. met. council Century 21 of Mich., 1977-83. Cert.

residential specialist. Mem. Am. Soc. Profl. and Exec. Women, Nat. Assn. Female Execs., Ann Arbor Bd. Realtors (pres. women's council 1976, chmn. profl. standards com. 1982, grievance com. 1984), Century 21 of Mich. Investment Soc. (state pres. 1982-84), Mich. Assn. Realtors, Nat. Assn. Realtors. Baptist. Club: U. Mich. Faculty Womens (dir. 1970). Home: 1832 Vinewood Ann Arbor MI 48103 Office: 120 E Washington Ann Arbor MI 48104

JONES, LOIS MAILOU (MRS. VERGNIAUD PIERRE-NOEL), artist, educator; b. Boston; d. Thomas Vreeland and Carolyn (Adams) J.; m. Vergniaud Pierre-Noel, Aug. 18, 1953. Diploma Boston Mus. Sch., 1927; cert. Boston Normal Art Sch., 1928, Designers Art Sch., 1928, Academie Julian, Paris, 1938, Academie de la Grande Chaumière, 1962; A.B. magna cum laude, Howard U., 1945; student Harvard U., 1927, Columbia U., 1934-36; Ph.D., Suffolk U., 1981, H.L.D., 1981; Ph.D. (hon.), Colo. State Christian Coll.; Ph.D. in Fine Arts (hon.), Mass. Coll. Art, 1986. Exhibited in one man shows Vose Galleries, Boston, Barnett Aden Gallery, Washington, Howard U. Gallery Art, Washington, Los Angeles County Mus. Art, High Mus. Art, Atlanta, Pan Am. Union, Centre d'Art, Port au-Prince, Haiti, Galerie Internationale, N.Y.C., Mus. Fine Arts, Dallas, Lincoln U., Pa., Hampton Inst., Va., Cornell U., Ithaca, N.Y., W.Va. State Coll., Galerie Soulanges, Paris, Mus. Nat. Ctr. Afro-Am. Artists, Boston, Reynolds House Mus. Am. Art, Winston Salem, N.C., Harbor Art Gallery, U. Mass., Boston, Bethune Mus. Archives, Inc., Washington, Le Musee d'Art Haitien, Port au Prince; retrospective exhbn. Howard U. Gallery Art, 1972, Boston Mus. Fine Arts, 1973, Acts of Art Gallery, N.Y.C., 1973, Phillips Collection, Washington, 1979, Cooper Union, N.Y.C., 1986; exhibited group shows Salon des Artistes Français, 1938, 39, 66, Biennial exhbn. Corcoran Gallery Art, NAD, N.Y.C., Nat. Mus., Pa. Acad., Balt. Mus., Oakland Art Mus. (Calif.), Seattle Mus., Wash. State, A.C.A. Galleries, N.Y.C., Grand Central Art Galleries, San Francisco Mus. Art, Princeton U., Mus. Modern Art, N.Y.C., Fisk U., San Jose Mus. Art, Smith Coll., Carnegie Inst., Ill. State U., FESTAC, Nigeria, Galerie Jean Charpentier, Paris, Galerie de Paris, Salon des Independents, Paris, Rhodes Nat. Gallery, So. Rhodesia, King George VI Gallery, Port Elizabeth, Republic South Africa, Smith Coll., Harmon Found., Pa. U. Mus., Am. Embassy, Tanzania, Mus. of Nat. Ctr. of Afro-Am. Artists, Boston, 1983, Hofstra U., 1983-84, African-Am. Mus. Art, Los Angeles, 1984, Nat. Collection Fine Art and Nat. Potrait Gallery, Center Gallery, Bucknell U., Pa., Studio Mus. in Harlem, N.Y.C., Nat. Urban League, N.Y.C., Cooper Union, N.Y.C., Bellevue Art Mus., Wash.; represented permanent collections Phillips Collection, IBM Corp. Palais Nationale, Haiti, Howard U. Gallery Art, Atlanta U., Barnett Aden Gallery, Bklyn. Mus., 135th St. Public Library, Rosenwald Found., Retreat for Fgn. Missionaries, Washington, U. Panjab, Pakistan, Internat. Fair Gallery, Izmir, Turkey, Walker Art Mus., Am. Embassy, Luxembourg, Ebony hdqrs., Chgo., Boston Mus. Fine Arts, Met. Mus. Art, N.Y.C., Hirshhorn Mus. and Sculpture Garden, Nat. Portrait Gallery; designed stained glass window Andrew Rankin Meml. Chapel, Howard U. Prof. design and watercolor painting Coll. Fine Arts Howard U., Washington, now prof. emerita; lectr. Afro-Am. Artists, Contemporary Haitian Artists. Conducted 5 week Around the World Tour, summers 1966, 67; Howard U. Research grantee study tour 17 African countries, 1970, 71. Recipient many awards and prizes, including Robert Woods Bliss award, 1st Luban Watercolor award, 1958; Franz Bader award, 1962; 1st hon. mention for oil painting Societe des Artistes Francais, Paris, 1966; Howard U. Alumni award, 1978; diplome and decoration de l'Ordre Nat. D'Honneur et Merite Haitian Govt., 1954; Candace award Met. Mus., 1982; citation Mass. Ho. of Reps., 1982; D.C. Mayor's 3d Ann. Art award; honor award Women's Caucus for Art, 1986. Fellow Royal Soc. Arts; mem. Nat. Art Dirs. Club, Washington Soc. Artists, Am. Watercolor Assn. (asso.), Washington Watercolor Assn., Alumni Assn. Boston Mus. Sch., Artists Equity, Nat. Conf. of Artists (1st v.p.), Blenfalteur, Foyer Montparnasse, Paris, Alpha Kappa Alpha. Author: Peintures, Lois Mailou Jones, 1937-51, 1952; Caribbean and Afro-American Women Artists. Home: 4706 17th St NW Washington DC 20011

JONES, LORA LEE SIMS, nurse; b. Burbank, Calif., Aug. 24, 1942; d. Marion Dodd and Lora Beatrice (Clark) Sims; Asso. in Nursing, Grayson County Coll., Sherman, Tex., 1972; student Ardmore (Okla.) Higher Edn. Center; m. David Duke Jones, June 18, 1960; children—Gregory David, Kimberly Ann, Amy Lee. Sec.-treas. Jones Meat Packing Co., Inc., Old Fashioned Meat Market; dir. nurses Brookside Manor Nursing Home, Madill, Okal., 1972-73; supr., charge nurse Love County Health Center, Marietta, Okla., 1973-74; supr. Marshall Meml. Hosp., Madill, 1974-76; nurse Marshall County Pub. Health Dept., 1976-77; cons. nurse Texoma Health Care Facility, 1977-80; sch. nurse Kingston (Okla.) Public Schs., 1977-80; indsl. nurse UniRoyal Tire Co., Ardmore, Okla., 1981; public health nurse, Carter County Public Health Dept., 1981-82; sr. nurse Love County Public Health Dept., Marietta, 1982—. Mem. adminstrv. bd. First United Methodist Ch., 1975-76; co-founder Wildcat Teen Town, Inc., pres., 1977-78; bd. dirs. Madill Day Care Center, 1974-76. Mem. Okla. Pub. Health Assn., PTA, Am. Sch. Health Assn., Am. Nurses Assn. Century Club, Okla. Nurses Assn., Okla. Public Employees Assn. Democrat. Clubs: Eastern Star, Madill All Sports Booster (sec.-treas. 1977-78), Madill Round-Up, Madill T.M. (sec. treas. 1977-78). Home: 410 S 11th Ave Madill OK 73446 Office: 200 Medical Dr West Route B Box 5 Marietta OK 73448

JONES, MABEL MILLER, college administrator; b. Salisbury, N.C., Nov. 6, 1924; d. Will and Etta Jane (McHenry) Miller; m. Raymond Luther Jones, Dec. 14, 1956 (dec. May 1972); 1 child, Millicent Luthia. B.A., Livingstone Coll., 1945. Sec., Salisbury City Schs., 1945-47, tchr., 1947-56; missionary supr., dean missionary conf. African Methodist Episcopal Zion Ch., nat. and internat., 1956-72; ednl. coordinator Salisbury/Rowan Head Start, 1974-77; dir. alumni affairs Livingstone Coll., Salisbury, 1977—. Mem. Salisbury City Planning Bd., 1976-83; Rowan County Planning Bd., 1979-82, Agrl. Extension Adv. Bd., Salisbury, 1981—. Recipient plaques Western N.C. conf. A.M.E. Zion Ch., 1972, Moore's Chapel A.M.E. Zion Ch., Salisbury, 1981, City of Salisbury, 1982, Goler Met. A.M.E. Zion Ch., Winston Salem, N.C., 1982. Mem. Ch. Women United, AAUW (former treas., sec., historian). Lodges: Order Eastern Star, Calanthe. Avocations: cooking, reading, flower gardening, visiting elderly and sick. Office: Livingstone Coll 701 W Monroe St Salisbury NC 28144

JONES, MALINDA THIESSEN, telecommunications company executive; b. Perryton, Tex., Jan. 23, 1947; d. Chester Francis Thiessen and Bobbye Pearson (Wallis) Schwalm; m. Hollis Bass Jones, Mar. 21, 1969 (div. 1972); 1 child, Rashad. B.A. in Psychology, U. Mo.-Kansas City, 1975. Research asst. U. Kans. Med. Ctr., Kansas City, 1975-77; owner, mgr. Metro Shampoo Co., Kansas City, Mo., 1977-79; regional mgr. U.S. Telecom, Dallas, 1981-82, staff asst. to pres., Dallas, 1983-84, sr. planner, 1984-85; dir. mktg. Telinq Systems Inc., Richardson, Tex., 1985—; cons. in field. Editor conf. presentations, bus. plans. Vol. tchr. Sch. for Learning Disability, Operation Discovery, Kansas City, 1973-75; corp. liaison exec. assistance program Dallas C. of C./Dallas Ind. Sch. Dist., 1984; chmn. com. Therapeutic Riding Tex., Dallas, 1985. Recipient Outstanding Contbr. award Dallas Ind. Sch. Dist., 1984. Mem. Nat. Assn. Female Execs., Assn. Women Entrepreneurs Dallas. Home: 1122 Overlake Dr Richardson TX 75080 Office: Telinq Systems Inc 1651 N Glenville Dr Richardson TX 75081

JONES, MARGARET DORIS, small business owner; b. Mechanicsville, Md., June 15, 1942; d. George Henry and Cora Madeline (Goldsmith) Murphy; m. Joseph Paul Jones, Jr., Sept. 3, 1960; children—Joseph Paul Jones III, Margaret Dedie. Student, U. Md., 1972-74, George Washington U., 1969, Mgmt. Devel. Ctr. Md., 1978. Telephone operator C&P Telephone Co., Md., Leonardtown, 1960-62; tchr., tchr's aid Leonardtown Bd. Edn., 1967-70; with trial magistrate's system, 1970-71; dist. ct. clk. St. Mary County Dist. Ct., Leonardtown, 1971-86, mem. grievance com., 1976-77; owner Jones Countryside Antiques, Crafts and Collectibles. Sec., v.p. Hollywood Ladies Aux. Fire Dept., Md., 1965-70; sec. Oakville Elem. Sch. PTA, Mechanicsville, 1968; mem., chmn. Father Andrew White PTA, Leonardtown, 1972-80; worker St. Mary Ryken PTA, Leonardtown, 1976-84; coordinator Dist. Ct. United Way campaign, 1984. Democrat. Roman Catholic. Avocations: sewing; art; family history. Office: St Mary County Dist Courthouse PO Box 339 Leonardtown MD 20650

JONES, MARGO ROSCH, public relations, advertising agency executive; b. Balt., Oct. 9, 1944; d. Randolph Wilson, Sr. and Margaret (Rosch) Jones; m. Jack Saul Katzman, Mar. 14, 1982; 1 child, Linda Joy. B.A. in English, Mt. St. Agnes Coll., Balt., 1966. Prodn. asst. Am. Chem. Soc., Washington, 1972-73; with FPC Advt., Rock Hill, N.Y., 1974-79, v.p., 1978-79; mktg. dir. Cablevision Industries, Liberty, N.Y., 1979-80; pub. relations, tourism dir. Sullivan County Catskills, Monticello, N.Y., 1980—; pres., owner Advt. by Margo Jones, Monticello, 1984—; pres. Catskill Assn. Tourism Services, N.Y., 1983—; dir. adv. council Sullivan County Community Coll. Radio announcer Sta. WSUL Good News show, Monticello, 1982—. Treas. Sullivan County Forum, Monticello, 1984—; pub. relations dir., treas. Goshen Jaycees, N.Y., 1978-79; pub. relations vol. bd. Am. Heart Assn., Syracuse, N.Y., 1981-83; vol. Peace Corps, Bolu, Turkey, 1966-67. Mem. N.Y. State Travel and Vacation Assn. (2d v.p. 1984—), Travel Industry Assn. Am., Assn. Travel Mktg. Execs. Democrat. Roman Catholic. Avocations: yoga, swimming. Home: PO Box 804 Monticello NY 12701 Office: Sullivan County Catskills County Govt Ctr Monticello NY 12701

JONES, MARJORIE BERTHA, finance and loan broker; b. Mpls., Feb. 5, 1924; d. Vincent L. and Kathryn C. (McIntosh) J.; B.S. in Polit. Sci., UCLA, 1950; student U. Minn., 1942-43. Mgmt. trainee Coast Fed. Savs. & Loan Assn., Los Angeles, 1950-56; treas., controller Lytton Savs. & Loan Assn., Los Angeles, 1956-65; sr. v.p. Hemet Fed. Savs. & Loan (Calif.), 1965-75; pres., dir. Adobe Mortgage, Inc., Escondido, Calif., 1975-83; cons. in fin. Bd. dirs. Riverside-San Bernardino Better Bus. Bur., 1978-80. Served with USAAF, 1944-46; PTO. Decorated Army Commendation Medal. Mem. Am. Soc. Women Accts. Republican. Episcopalian. Clubs: Zonta Internat., Eastern Star. Home: 3298-C Via Carrizo Laguna Hills CA 92653

JONES, MARTHA ELLEN, public relations firm executive; b. Detroit, Nov. 3, 1948; d. Robert Everett and Bess Alice (Johnson) J.; student Williams Coll., 1969; B.A., Vassar Coll., 1970. With radio/TV news dept. Burson Marsteller, N.Y.C., 1974; account exec. Hill & Knowlton, N.Y.C., 1975-78; dir. public relations and environ. affairs Fla. Phosphate Council, Lakeland, 1978-81; pres. Jones & Assos., Public Relations, Lakeland, 1981—. Commr. Edn. apointee Fla. Adv. Council on Sci. Edn., 1979, vice chmn., 1980-81, chmn., 1981-82; mem. Gov.'s Task Force on Phosphate-Related Radiation, 1979-80; trustee Learning Resource Center, Lakeland, 1979-82; bd. dirs. Campfire Inc., Lakeland, 1982-85; mem. Lakeland Young Life Council, 1985; del. Diocesan Conv., St. Stephen's Episcopal Ch., 1982—, lay reader, 1983—, mem. vestry, 1984-86; mem. adv. council Fla. Defenders of Environ., 1980, United Way, 1980, Hist. Lakeland, 1979-80, Fla. Assn. Sci. Tchrs., 1981; active Leadership Lakeland, 1985-86. Recipient nat. 1st place Addy award Am. Advt. Fedn., 1978. Mem. Public Relations Soc. Am., Fla. Public Relations Assn. (bd. dirs. Polk chpt. 1983-84, Golden Image awards 1979, 80, 82, Grand All Fla. award 1982), Leadership Lakeland, Lakeland C. of C. Episcopalian. Club: Jr. League Greater Lakeland. Office: Jones & Assocs 4315 Highland Park Blvd PO Box 6555 Lakeland FL 33803

JONES, MARY DAILEY (MRS. HARVEY BRADLEY JONES), clubwoman; b. Billings, Mont.; d. Leroy Nathaniel and Janet (Currie) Dailey; student Carleton Coll., 1943-44, U. Mont., 1944-46, UCLA, 1959; m. Harvey Bradley Jones, Nov. 15, 1952; children—Dailey, Janet Currie, Ellis Bradley. Owner Mary Jones Interiors. Founder Jr. Art Council, Los Angeles County Mus., treas., 1953-55, v.p., 1955-56, mem. Pasadena (Calif.) Philharmon. com., Costume Council, co-founder Art Rental Gallery, 1953, chmn. art and architecture tour, 1955; founder mem. Art Alliance, Pasadena Art Mus., sec., 1955-56; benefit chmn. Pasadena Girls Club, 1959, bd. dirs., 1958-60; chmn. Los Angeles Tennis Patron's Assn. Benefit, 1965; sustaining Jr. League Pasadena; mem. docent council Los Angeles County Mus.; mem. costume council Los Angeles County Mus. Art., program chmn. 20th Century Greatest Designers; mem. blue ribbon com. Los Angeles Music Center; benefit chmn. Venice com. Internat. Fund for Monuments, 1971; co-chmn. benefit Harvard Coll. Scholarship Fund, 1974, Otis Art Inst., 1975; mem. Harvard-Radcliffe scholarship dinner com., 1985; mem. adv. bd. Estelle Doheny Eye Found., 1976, chmn. benefit, 1980; bd. dirs. Founders Music Center, Los Angeles, 1977-81; mem. nat. adv. council Sch. Am. Ballet, N.Y.C., nat. co-chmn. gala, 1980; adv. council on fine arts Loyola-Marymount U.; mem. Los Angeles Olympic Com. for 1984; founder mem. Mus. Contemporary Art, 1986. Mem. Kappa Alpha Theta. Clubs: Valley Hunt (Pasadena); California (Los Angeles). Home: 1270 Tower Grove Dr Beverly Hills CA 90210

JONES, MARY ELLEN, biochemist; b. La Grange, Ill., Dec. 25, 1922; d. Elmer E. and Laura A. (Klein) J.; B.S., U. Chgo., 1944; Ph.D., Yale U., 1951; children—Ethan Vincent Munson, Catherine Laura Munson. AEC fellow, Am. Cancer Soc. fellow, assoc. biochemist Mass. Gen. Hosp., Boston, 1951-57; asst. prof. grad. dept. biochemistry Brandeis U., Waltham, Mass., 1957-60, assoc. prof., 1960-66; assoc. prof. dept. biochemistry Sch. Medicine, U. N.C., Chapel Hill, 1966-68, prof. depts. biochemistry and zoology, 1968-71; prof. dept. biochemistry Sch. Medicine, U. So. Calif., 1971-78; prof., chmn. dept. biochemistry Sch. Medicine, U. N.C., Chapel Hill, 1978—, Kenan prof. biochemistry, 1980—; mem. study sect. Am. Cancer Soc., 1971-73, NIH, 1971-75; mem. sci. adv. bd. Nat. Heart, Lung and Blood Inst., 1980—; mem. metabolic biology study sect. NSF, 1978-81; mem. Merit rev. bd. VA, 1975-78; mem. life sci. com. NASA, 1976-78; pres. Chairs of Assn. Med. Sch. Depts. Biochemistry, 1985. Am. Cancer Soc. scholar, 1957-62; NIH grantee, 1957—; NSF grantee, 1957—. Mem. Am. Chem. Soc. (councilor 1975-79, mem. nominating com. 1971-72, chair 1973-74), Am. Soc. Biol. Chemists (councilor 1975-78, 81-84, pres. 1986), Nat. Acad. Scis., Inst. Medicine of Nat. Acad. Scis., Assn. Women in Sci., AAAS, N.Y. Acad. Sci., Sierra Club, Sigma Xi. Democrat. Unitarian. Club: Appalachian Mountain. Contbr. numerous articles on biochem. research to sci. publs.; editorial bd. Jour. Biol. Chemistry, 1975-80, 82-87, Cancer Research, 1982-86; assoc. editor Can. Jour. Biochemistry, 1969-74. Office: Dept Biochemistry Sch Medicine U NC Chapel Hill NC 27514

JONES, MARY FRANCES, management research analyst; b. Prairie Grove, Ark., Nov. 17, 1946; d. Virgil Dero and Mary Fredrika (Matthews) Jones; m. Raymond Vincent Terry, Aug. 10, 1974 (div. Oct. 1975). B.S. in Bus. Adminstrn., U. Ark., 1968; postgrad. in bus. adminstrn. Middle Tenn. State U. Asst. buyer M.M. Cohn Co., Little Rock, 1968-69; market analyst AMF Tuboscope Inc., Houston, 1970-73; field supr. Higginbotham Assocs., Houston, 1974-76; research asst. Baptist Sunday Sch. Bd., Nashville, 1977-80, research analyst, 1980-85, supr. statis. sect., 1985—. Contbr. articles to Bapt. Sunday Sch. Bd. Quar. Rev. Vol. counselor Peace of Mind phone answering service, Houston, 1973-74; officer in local Bapt. chs., 1973-76, 80-83; big sister Buddies of Nashville, 1979-81; bd. dirs. Huntington Ridge Homeowners Assn., Nashville, 1980-81. Mem. Am. Mktg. Assn., So. Baptist Research Fellowship. Home: 354 Huntington Ridge Dr Nashville TN 37211 Office: Baptist Sunday School Bd 127 9th Ave N Nashville TN 37234

JONES, MARY GARDINER, lawyer, educator, consumer interest organization executive; b. N.Y.C., Dec. 10, 1920; d. Charles Herbert and Anna Livingston (Short) Jones; B.A., Wellesley Coll., 1943; J.D., Yale U., 1948. Intern tchr. George Sch., Newtown, Pa., 1943-44; research analyst, research and analysis br. Internat. Law sect. OSS, Washington, 1944-46; admitted to N.Y. bar, 1949; asso. firms Donovan, Leisure, Newton and Irvine, 1948-53, Webster, Sheffield, Fleischmann, Hitchcock & Chrystie, 1961-64 (both N.Y.C.); trial atty. antitrust div. Dept. Justice, N.Y.C., 1953-61; commr. FTC, Washington, 1974; prof. Coll. Commerce and Bus. Adminstrn. and Coll. Law, U. Ill., Urbana, 1973-75; v.p. for consumer affairs Western Union Telegraph Co., Washington, 1975-82; pres. Consumer Interest Research Inst., Washington, 1983—; mem. Consumer Research Found. dir. MCA, Inc., Universal City, Calif., Safeway Stores, Oakland, Calif. Mem. com. on sci. and tech. Fed. Council Sci. and Tech.; non-trustee mem. research and policy com.; chmn. bd. Council Econ. Priorities, 1976-84, Inst. Future, 1977—; dir. Council Better Bus. Burs., 1982—; mem. Pres.' Panel on Antitrust Laws, 1977-78. Trustee Wellesley Coll., 1971—; nat. adv. council Hampshire Coll.; Mem. Fed. Bar Assn. Internat. Law Assn., Assn. Bar City N.Y., Am. Arbitration Assn., Yale Law Sch. Assn. (v.p. D.C. 1969-70, exec. com. 1971-76), AAUW (2d v.p. Washington br. 1968-69, adv. council). Bd. editors Jour. Consumer Affairs; editorial rev. bd. Jour. Consumer Interest; contbr. articles law jours. Home: 1631 Suter's Ln NW Washington DC 20007 Office: Suite 800 1819 H St NW Washington DC 20006

JONES, MARY JANE, business educator; b. Terre Haute, Ind., Apr. 1, 1934; d. Robert F. and Lillian H. (Shook) Scherer; student MacMurray Coll. Women, 1951-53, Ind. State U., 1955-57; diploma N.Y. Sch. Interior Design, 1974; student U. Tex., Arlington, 1978-79; m. Marvin D. Jones, Sept. 1, 1962; children—Valerie, Don, Mike, Karen. Exec. sec. dir. research Comml. Solvents Corp., 1956-57; exec. sec. to program mgr. Honeywell Corp., Mpls., 1960-61; tchr. bus. Met. Bus. Coll., Galveston, Tex., 1958-59, Ft. Worth Sch. Bus., 1980—; owner, mgr. M.J. Jones Interior Design, Ft. Worth, Tex., 1977-82; bus. instr. Draughon's Coll. Bus., Ft. Worth, 1983-86; guest speaker U. Tex. Grad Sch., Arlington. Contbr. articles to profl. jours. Active Circle T council Girl Scouts U.S.A., Ft. Worth, 1972-82. Mem. Nat. Assn. Women in Constrn., Ft. Worth C. of C., Nat. Assn. Historic Trust, Exec. Women Internat. Republican. Methodist. Home: 5617 Wonder Dr Fort Worth TX 76133 Office: 4232 McCart St Fort Worth TX 76115

JONES, MARY VIRGINIA, mechanical engineer; b. Roanoke, Va., Sept. 19, 1940; d. James Bernard and Evangeline (Jamison) Jones; B.S. in M.E. with honors, Va. Poly. Inst. and State U., 1962; M.S. in M.E., George Washington U., 1972, postgrad. 1972. Design engr. Atlantic Research Corp., Alexandria, Va., 1962—, head design engring. sect., Gainesville, Va., 1981, chief mech. design group, 1982—; research scholar asst. George Washington U., Washington, 1972. Mem. Va. State Bd. Architects, Land Surveyors, Profl. Engrs. and Landscape Architects, 1983—, chmn. engrs. sect., 1984, pres., 1986. Mem. bd. visitors Va. Poly. Inst. and State U., 1984—, Nat. Council Engring. Examiners, 1983—. Recipient Tau Beta Pi Woman's Badge, 1961; registered profl. engr., Commonwealth of Va. Mem. ASME, Soc. Women Engrs. (Balt./Washington v.p. 1981, pres. 83-84, sect. rPlastics Engrs., Fedn. Orgns. Profl. Women, Tau Beta Pi, Pi Tau Sigma, Phi Kappa Phi, Omicron Delta Kappa. Methodist. Home: 3137 Stratford Ct Oakton VA 22124 Office: 7511 Wellington Rd Gainesville VA 22065

JONES, MARY VIRGINIA WALTERS, newspaper editor; b. Dothan, Ala., Apr. 10, 1923; d. Thomas Jackson and Rachel Irell (Etheridge) Walters; B.A., in Journalism, U. Bridgeport, 1973; postgrad. in pub. communications Fordham U., 1975, U. Bridgeport, 1976-77; m. Raymond C. Jones, Dec. 3, 1943; children—Virginia Ann, Thomas Christopher, Edward William. Airways radio operator CAA, 1942-44; reporter, bur. chief Bridgeport Post-Telegram, 1960-73; editor Fairfield (Conn.) Citizen News, 1973-76, Westchester-Rockland Newspapers, White Plains, N.Y., 1976-77, Fairfield County Morning News, Trumbull, Conn., 1977—, Pensacola (Fla.) News Jour., 1978—. instr. journalism U. Bridgeport, 1974-78. Rep. Trumbull Town Council, 1955-59; vice chmn. Trumbull Democratic Town Com., 1959-61. Recipient editorial award New Eng. Press Assn., 1976. Mem. Women in Communications, Inc., Deadline Club N.Y.C., Soc. Profl. Journalists. Episcopalian. Club: Nat. Press (Washington).

JONES, MEADE BARNER, association executive; b. Richmond, Va., July 26, 1925; d. David Meade and Nelle (McClendon) Barner; student Coll. William and Mary, 1944-45; m. L. Davis Jones, Jan. 19, 1946; children—Davis Meade, Jonathan Brinton, Carter. Dir., Valley Forge (Pa.) Hist. Soc., 1967, v.p., 1971, pres., 1975—. Recipient Cert. of Merit, Pa. Hort. Soc., 1975. Mem. DAR. Republican. Episcopalian. Club: Twin Valleys Garden (pres. 1970-72). Home: Yellow Springs Rd Paoli PA 19301

JONES, MONICA CLAUDIETTE, university placement officer, career consultant; b. Norfolk, Va., July 5, 1952; d. Matthew Walter and Thelma Lenora (Whitehurst) J. B.S., Hampton Inst., 1974; M.Ed., Ga. State U., 1983. Speech clinician Va. Sch. for the Deaf, Staunton, 1974-76; clk. Atlanta Hilton Hotel, 1978-79; tng. specialist Atlanta Urban League, 1979-80; program dir. Young Women's Christian Assn., Atlanta, 1980; pvt. practice career cons., Atlanta, 1980—; placement officer Ga. State U., Atlanta, 1981—; cons. Project Discovery, Atlanta. Contbr. articles to profl. jours. Sec. Mayor's Task Force on Disabled Persons, Atlanta, 1985, Economic Opportunity Atlanta Bd. Dirs., 1985; pres. Atlanta Touch of the Visually Impaired Bd., 1985. Mem. Atlanta Assn. Black Journalists. Democrat. Methodist. Avocations: music, composition, creative writing. Home: 300 W Peachtree St 12-B Atlanta GA 30308 Office: Ga State Univ Placement 217 Alumni Hall Atlanta GA 30303

JONES, NANCY GEX, broadcast association executive; b. Cin., Feb. 1, 1952; d. Richard Stanley and Mary Kathryn (Brady) Gex; m. Jesse Holman Jones II, Oct. 1, 1983; 1 child, Malia Louise. B.S., Eastern Mich. U., 1976. Account exec. KTRH/KLOL Radio, Houston, 1981-83, sales mgr., 1983; broadcast cons. various radio stas., Tex., 1983-84; pres., owner Broadcast Resources, Inc., Houston, 1984—; exec. dir. Houston Assn. Radio Broadcasters, 1985—. Publicity chmn. guild bd. Am. Heart Assn., Houston, 1985—, also mem. communications com. Gulf Coast Council; mem. Houston Ballet Guild, 1984—; bd. dirs. Houston Zool. Soc., 1985—. Avocations: scuba diving; skiing; bicycling. Home: 2406 Locke Ln Houston TX 77019 Office: Houston Assn Radio Broadcasters PO Box 56021 Houston TX 77256

JONES, NORMA DELL, association executive; b. Lovelady, Tex., June 10, 1934; d. Louis Herbert and Eslie (Barron) Monzingo; m. Jerry Don Jones, Oct. 9, 1981. A.A., Stephens Coll., 1954; B.S., Sam Houston State U., 1962, M.Ed., 1972. Tchr., Crockett Ind. Sch., Tex., 1959-77; exec. dir. Sam Houston State U. Alumni Assn., Huntsville, Tex., 1977—. Recipient Merit award Sam Houston State U. Golf Team, 1983. Mem. Tex. State Tchrs. Assn. (dist. pres. 1967-68, state legis. chmn. 1971-73, state rights and responsibilities chmn. 1975-77, Outstanding Service award 1975, life mem.), Huntsville C. of C., Coll. Alumni Dirs. Tex. (pres. elect 1986), Daus. Republic Tex., DAR. Baptist. Avocations: raising Texas longhorn cattle; needlepoint; crewel; singing; snorkeling. Home: PO Box 385 Huntsville TX 77340 Office: Sam Houston Alumni Office PO Box 2022 Huntsville TX 77341

JONES, NORMA LOUISE, library science educator; b. Poplar, Wis.; d. George Elmer and Hilma June (Wiberg) J. B.E, U. Wis.; M.A., U. Minn., 1952; postgrad. U. Ill., 1957; Ph.D., U. Mich., 1965; archives tng. NARS, 1978, 79, 80, Newberry Library, 1978, Chgo. Hist. Soc., 1978; postgrad. Nova U., 1983—. Librarian, Grand Rapids Pub. Schs. (Mich.), 1947-62, Grand Rapids Pub. Library, 1948-49; instr. Central Mich. U., Mt. Pleasant, 1954, 55; librarian Benton Harbor Pub. Schs. (Mich.), 1962-63; lectr. U. Mich., Ann Arbor, 1954, 55, 61, 63-65, asst. prof., 1966-68; asst. prof. U. Wis.-Oshkosh, 1968-70, assoc. prof., 1970-75, prof., 1975—, chmn. dept. library sci., 1980—; mem. adv. com. Wis. Extention Program, 1981—, Wis. State Cert. Com. for Sch. Librarians, 1972-83. Recipient Disting. Tchr. award U. Wis., 1977. Mem. ALA (reference planning com. 1975, pub. relations com. young adult services div. 1982—, ALA, Library Adminstrn. and Mgmt. Assn. stats. com. 1982—), Am. Assn. Sch. Librarians, Assn. Library and Info. Sci. Educators, Spl. Library Assn., Soc. Am. Archivists, Wis. Library Assn., Phi Beta Kappa, Phi Kappa Phi, Pi Lambda Theta, Beta Phi Mu, Sigma Pi Epsilon. Contbr. to Wis. Library Bull. Home: 1220 Maricopa Dr Oshkosh WI 54901

JONES, PAMELA SUSAN, nurse; b. Chattanooga, Nov. 21, 1950; d. William Kenneth Jones and Helen Katie (Garner) Jones Allison; m. Larry Wayne Thomas, July 6, 1968 (div. Mar. 31, 1981; 1 child, William Forrest; m. Michael Sean O'Flaherty, Oct. 1, 1983. Assoc. Nursing, Baptist Coll. at Charleston, 1978. R.N., S.C. Cardiothoracic clinician surg. ICU, Med. U. S.C., Charleston, 1978-82; nurse intensive care and cardiac care Trident Regional Med. Ctr., Charleston, 1982-85; instr. advanced cardiac life support Am. Heart Assn., Charleston, 1983—; cons. Area Health Edn. Consortium, Walterboro, S.C., 1983—. Mem. Am. Assn. Critical Care Nurses. Home: 2430 Pristine View Charleston SC 29407 Office: Trident Regional Med Ctr Medical Plaza Dr Charleston SC 29418

JONES, PATRICIA CAROLINE, arts administrator; b. N.Y.C., Feb. 4, 1943; d. Robert Sackett and Mildred (Stadholz) J.; B.A. cum laude, Radcliffe Coll., 1964; M.S. Urban Planning, Columbia U., 1977. Reporter, editor Newsweek, Nature mags., N.Y.C., London, 1966-70; researcher, assoc. producer WNET, WGBH, BBC, ABC-UK, N.Y.C., Boston, London, 1965-72; assoc. editor, corp. pub. relations Mobil Oil Corp., N.Y.C., 1972-74; assoc. dir. Mcpl. Art Soc., N.Y.C., 1972-77; exec. v.p. Alliance for the Arts (Cultural Assistance Ctr.), N.Y.C., 1977—. Editor: Partners: Guide to Corp. Support and the Arts, 1982; author: Public and Private Support for Arts in N.Y.C., 1980. Treas., Archlt. League, N.Y.C., 1985—; bd. dirs. Non Profit Coordinating Com. N.Y.C., 1985—, Artist Mut. Housing Assn., 1984—; mem. Gov.'s Adv. Comm. for Westway Park, N.Y.C., 1981—. N.Y. region del. Metropolis 84 Conf., Paris, 1984. Mem. Ptnrs. for Liveable Places. Democrat. Home: 235 E 11th St New York NY 10003 Office: Alliance for the Arts 330 W 42d St New York NY 10036

JONES, PATRICIA EGAN, state executive; b. New Haven, Conn., Oct. 5, 1940; d. John Patrick and Julia (DiLorenzo) Egan; m. George W. Jones, Oct. 20, 1962; children—George W. III, Megan Elizabeth. A.A., Mount Aloysius Coll., 1960; B.S. in Polit. Sci., Rutgers U. Dir., co-founder Barrington Pre Sch., 1971-73; legis. aide Assemblyman E.F. Schuck, N.J., 1973-75, 5th Dist. Legis. Offices, 1975-79; dir., 1979-81; adminstrv. asst. senator Walter Rand, Camden, N.J., 1981—; planning commn. Tri County Water Quality Bd.; bd. dirs.

Camden County Environ. Agy.; planning com. Nat. Conf. State Legislators Nat. Legis. Security and Services Assn. Com. woman Camden County Dem. Com., 1982—; fund raising com. St. Francis De Sales; trustee Haddon Glen Swim Club Ops. Recipient Membership award N.J. State Fedn. Womans Clubs 1985; named Young Woman of Year 1970-72. Mem. Barrington Jr. Womans Club (past pres., hon.), Roman Catholic. Home: 527 DuBois Ave Barrington NJ 08007 Office: Senator Walter Rand 514 Cooper St Camden NJ 08102

JONES, PAULA DENISE, geophysicist; b. Standford, Tex., Oct. 19, 1949; d. Hubert Paul and Vivian Inaz (Glover) Powers; 1 dau., Jennifer Jelene. Student West Tex. State U., 1966-71, U. St. Thomas, 1983-84. Geophys. technician Western Geophys. Co., Houston, 1974-76; geophys., geol. asst. Shell Oil Co., Houston, 1976-80; seismic analyst, interim lease mgr. Seismograph Service Corp., Houston, 1980-82; sr. processing geophysicist Geo-Quest Internat., Inc., Houston, 1982-83; processing geophysicist Superior Oil Co., Houston, 1983—. Co-founder Women's Group, First Unitarion Ch., Houston, 1974, auctioneer service auction, 1982-83. Mem. Soc. Exploration Geophysicists, Geophys. Soc. Houston, Nat. Assn. Female Execs. Home: 3027 Purdue Apt 3 Houston TX 77005 Office: Superior Oil Geosci Lab 12401 Westheimer Houston TX 77005

JONES, PEGGY LAVERNE, health educator, administrator; b. Tampa, Fla., Dec. 25, 1939; d. James Andrew and Hazel Angelina (Wyrick) Menghini; children—Matthew, Erin, Todd. Student U. Tampa, 1959-61, Orange Coast Coll., Costa Mesa, Calif., 1963-64, Cerritos (Calif.) Jr. Coll., 1967-69. Free lance pub. relations specialist, 1964-74; clinic coordinator Planned Parenthood of No. Nev., Reno, 1975-76; exec. dir. Multiple Sclerosis Soc. Nev., Reno, 1976-79; supr. Washoe County Med Soc., Reno, 1979-80; head dept. St. Mary's Hosp., Reno, 1980-82, program dir. Heart Inst. No. Nev., 1982—, mem. cardiac task force 1982—. Bd. dirs. Homemaker Upjohn Home Health Corp., 1979-81; mem. adv. bd. Ret. Sr. Vol. Persons, 1980-82; mem. adv. bd. Com. to Aid Abused Women and Children, 1981-82. Mem. Am. Hosp. Assn., Health Adminstrs. No. Nev., Reno Women in Advt., Am. Bus. Women's Assn., Am. Mgmt. Assn., Am. Soc. Dirs. Vol. Dirs. of Vol. in Agys., Nat. Assn Women Execs., Nat. C. of C. for Women. Democrat. Baptist. Office: 667 N Arlington Ave Reno NV 89503

JONES, PHYLLIS GENE, judge; b. Fargo, N.D., May 29, 1923; d. Joseph C. and Rosina Belle (Pinkham) Bambusch; m. Dwight Bangs Jones, May 29, 1945 (dec.); children—Stephanie, Jacqueline, Kent Carroll; m. David D. Norman, Oct. 9, 1970 (dec.). B.A., Macalester Coll., 1944; J.D., William Mitchell Coll. Law, 1960. Bar: Minn. 60. Wirephoto operator AP, St. Paul, 1943-45; reporter St. Paul Pioneer Press, 1945-46; asst. county atty. Ramsey County (Minn.), St. Paul, 1960-71; gen. counsel Minn. Urban County Attys. Bd.-Minn. County Attys. Council, St. Paul, 1971-75; pvt. practice, St. Paul and Cottage Grove, Minn., 1975-84; judge Minn. Dist. Ct. 10th Jud. Dist., Anoka, 1984—; mem. Minn. Adv. Council to State Investment Bd., 1983-84; mem. Washington County Personnel Com., Stillwater, Minn., 1982—. Supr., Grey Cloud Town Bd. (Minn.), 1971-75. Mem. ABA, Minn. Bar Assn., State Bar Minn. (chmn. victimless crimes com. 1974-75), Ramsey County Bar Assn. Office: 10th Jud Dist 325 E Main St Anoka MN 55303

JONES, ROXANNE HARPER, state legislator; b. N.C., May 3, 1928; d. Gilford and Mary (Bruton) Harper; m. James H. Jones, 1957 (dec.); children—Patricia Hill, Wanda Crews. Student pub. schs. Bd. mem. Pa. State Transp. Adv. Com., Pa. Legis. Black Caucus, 1985—; minority chmn. game and fisheries com., mem. pub. health and welfare, urban affairs and housing and aging and youth, Democratic policy coms. Pa. State Senate, 1985—. Recipient Nat. Welfare Rights Orgn. Leadership award Nat. Welfare Rights Orgn., 1972, Woman of Yr. award Zeta Phi Beta, 1985, Achievement cert. Nat. Council Negro Women, 1985. Bd. dirs. Ams. for Democratic Action; co-chmn. Coalition Concerned Citizens; exec. dir. Phila. Citizens in Action; trustee Lincoln U., 1985—; mem. adv. council African-Am. studies Temple U. Mem. Apolstolic Ch. Office: Pa State Capitol Bldg Harrisburg PA 17120

JONES, RUBY DARLENE, home health care consultant; b. Tahoka, Tex., Nov. 19, 1940; d. Arthur Benjamin and Renda Clementine (Mullings) Jones; student Lamar U., 1965, U. Tex., Austin, 1974; 3 children. Nurse, Orange, Tex., 1966-69, charge nurse Jones Rest Home, Inc., Orange, 1969-74; partner England (Ark.) Flying Service, Inc., 1970-74, Delmar's Aerial Service, Kans. and Okla., 1970-74; Del Mar, Inc., Little Rock, 1975-76; charge nurse Bayshore Nursing Home, Inc., La Porte, Tex., 1976-80; regional adminstr. Home Health-Home Care, Inc., San Antonio, Tex., 1976-80, community relations dir., Orange, 1980-82, dir. community relations and devel. Tex. region, 1982-84; cons. R. Jones & Assocs., 1984—. Mem. Tex. Home Health Agys. Assn., Nat. Home Health Agys. Assn., Tex. Nursing Home Assn., LWV, Nat. Assn. Female Execs., San Antonio Women's Credit Union. Home: 1001 28th St Orange TX 77630

JONES, RUBY WILBORN, county board of elections supervisor; b. Clover, Va., Mar. 4, 1938; d. William H. and Mary (Coleman) Wilborn; m. Jamer M. Jones, June 12, 1963; 1 child, Jacqueline M. Cert. bus. adminstrn., Va. Union U., 1960; cert. banking, Pace Coll., 1970. Check processor Chase Manhattan Bank, N.Y.C., 1965-68, reconcilement savings bonds clk., 1968-72, fed. reserve money transfer clk., 1973-78; supr. Bd. Elections, Warrentown, N.C., 1982—. Pres. Community Watch, Norlina, N.C., 1982—; v.p. County Community Watch, Warrenton, 1984—; 2d v.p. PTA, Warrenton, 1983—; sec. Dem. Club, Bronx, 1963-65. Clubs: Homemakers (Norlina) (sec. 1980-84); Dem. Women (Warrenton). Avocations: crafts; bike riding; sewing; travel; cooking. Office: Warren County Bd Elections Front St PO Box 567 Warrenton NC 27589

JONES, RUTH GWENDOLYN, microscopic anatomy educator; b. Mobile, Ala., June 15, 1949; d. Rollo G. and Lora Dee (McPherson) J. B.S., Mobile Coll., 1970; M.S. (fellow), U. So. Miss., 1972; Ph.D. (fellow), Tex. A&M U., 1979. Research assoc. dept. micros. anatomy Baylor Coll. Dentistry, Dallas, 1974-77, instr., 1977-80, dir. electron microscopy, 1977—. Mem. N.Y. Acad. Scis., Am. Assn. Anatomists, So. Soc. Anatomists, Electron Microscopy Soc. Am., Tex. Soc. Electron Microscopists, Entomol. Soc. Am., Myo-Bio Club Dallas, Alpha Epsilon Delta, Sigma Xi. Baptist. Office: 3302 Gaston Ave Dallas TX 75236

JONES, SALLY DAVIESS PICKRELL, author; b. St. Louis, June 4, 1923; d. Claude Dildine and Marie Daviess (Pittman) Pickrell; student Mills Coll., Oakland, Calif., 1941-43, U. Calif.-Berkeley, 1944, Columbia, 1955-58; m. Charles William Jones, Sept. 2, 1943; 1 son, Matthew Charles. Author: (novel) The Lights Burn Blue, 1947. Mem. UN Women's Guild, Fgn. Policy Assn., Nat. Council Women, Asia Soc., English-Speaking Union, Met. Mus. Art. Episcopalian. Address: 311 E 58th St New York NY 10022

JONES, SHARON YVONNE, jewelry company executive; b. Endicott, N.Y., Sept. 7, 1954; d. Thomas R. and Marilyn J. (Card) J. B.A., SUNY-Oswego, 1976. Corp. v.p. Piercing Pagoda, Inc., Bethlehem, Pa., 1976—. Democrat. Office: Piercing Pagoda Inc 65 E Elizabeth Ave Bethlehem PA 18018

JONES, SHIRLEY GLYNN, association executive; b. Greenville, Tex., Dec. 3, 1938; d. Frank Allen Glasscock and Ira Eunice (Johnson) Glasscock Turner; m. Jerry Wayne Arnold, Oct. 5, 1959 (div. Mar. 1974); children—Jerry Wayne, Scott Allen; m. Bruce Jones, June 19, 1982. B.B.A. in Acctg., East Tex. State U., 1962. Controller Automatic Data Processing, Dallas, 1972-77; fin. and credit mgr. Tepco, Inc., Garland, Tex., 1977-82; account exec. Merchants Discount Service Assn., Houston, 1983; owner, pres. Retail Mchts. Discount Assn., Inc., Dallas, 1984—. Office: Retail Mchts Discount Assn 5307 E Mockingbird St Room 401 Dallas TX 75206

JONES, SHIRLEY WEED, college administrator; b. Arlington, Va., Sept. 2, 1935; d. Harold Lawrence and Susie Mae (Martz) Weed; m. Wayne C. Fortney, Nov. 1951 (div. Nov. 1963); children—Teresa, Sherrie, Edwin, Bruce; m. Burlen Jones, Oct. 29, 1974 (dec. Jan. 1981); 1 child, Dawn Christina. A.A., Strayer Coll., 1983. Vice pres. Bill Jones Enterprises, Inc., Lanham, Md., 1975-85; coordinator ct. and conf./secretarial sci. depts. Strayer Coll., Washington, 1984—. Mem. Md. Shorthand Reporters Assn., Nat. Shorthand Reporters Assn., Nat. Bus. Educators Assn., Nat. Assn. Female Execs., Beta Sigma Phi. Democrat. Baptist. Avocations: ceramics. Office: Strayer Coll 1100 Vermont Ave NW Washington DC 20005

JONES, SONIA JOSEPHINE, advertising agency executive; b. Belize, Brit. Honduras, Nov. 9, 1945; came to U.S., 1962, naturalized, 1986; d. Frederick Francis and Elsie Adelia (Gomez) Alcoser; m. John Marvin Jones, Mar. 21, 1970; children—Christopher William Edward, Joshua Joseph Paul. Student Lamar U., 1964-66. With Foley's Federated Dept. Store, Houston, 1965-67; media buyer Vance Advt., Houston, 1967-68; media buyer, planner O'Neill & Assocs., Houston, 1968-75; media supr. Ketchum Houston, 1975-76; v.p., media dir. Rives Smith Bladwin Carlberg/Y & R, Houston, 1976-85, exec. v.p., assoc. gen. mgr., 1985—; lectr. U. Houston, 1983—, mem. journalism adv. bd., 1983—. Vol., Women in Yellow, Houston, 1966. Mem. Houston Advt. Fedn., Houston Area Media Council. Republican. Roman Catholic Office: Rives Smith Baldwin Carlberg/Y&R 5444 Westheimer St Houston TX 77056

JONES, STELLA PINKNEY, obstetrician, gynecologist; b. Hasston, La., Jan. 16, 1946; d. Isaac and Mamie (Wormsley) Pinkney; m. Harry Wade Jones, Dec. 26, 1965; children—Brigette, Kali, Shaunna, Harry. B.S. in Pharmacy, Tex. Southern U., 1965; M.P.H., U. Tex., 1972; M.D., Tex. Tech. U., 1976. Staff pharmacist Grady Meml. Hosp., Atlanta, 1965-67, Harris City Hosp., Houston, 1967-71; resident ob.-gyn. Charity Hosp., New Orleans, 1976-80; practice medicine specializing in ob.-gyn., New Orleans, 1980—; clin. staff Tulane Med. Sch., New Orleans, 1981—. Active local political elections; bd. dirs. Southeast La. council Girl Scouts U.S.A. Named Woman of the Yr. Links, 1984. Fellow Am. Coll. Ob.-Gyn., Am. Med. Women's Assn., La. Med. Soc., Delta Sigma Theta (golden life). Roman Catholic. Clubs: Jack/Jill; Links Inc. (sec. 1981-86) (Cresent City). Avocations: reading; golf; interior decoration; collecting African art. Home: 6941 Lake Willow Dr New Orleans LA 70126 Office: 2538 Tulane Ave New Orleans LA 70119

JONES, STELLA SHENG, pharmaceutical company official; b. Nanking, China, Apr. 7, 1948; came to U.S., 1970; d. Wen and Whei Yuan (Lee) Sheng; m. Charles Andrew Jones, June 19, 1973. B.S., Nat. Taiwan U., 1970; Ph.D. (Gilman fellow), Johns Hopkins U., 1976. Assoc. sr. investigator preclin. research devel. Smith, Kline and French Labs., Phila., 1976-79, sr. investigator, 1979-81, sr. project adminstr. clin. R&D, 1981-82, project mgr. strategic planning and ops., 1982-83, mgr. internat. med. and sci. affairs, 1983—; research assoc. Johns Hopkins U., Balt., 1973-76. Mem. Am. Chem. Soc., Am. Mgmt. Assn., Project Mgmt. Inst., Sigma Xi. Republican. Baptist. Home: 24 Clearbrook Rd Newtown Square PA 19073 Office: 1500 Spring Garden St Philadelphia PA 19101

JONES, SUE CAROLE, employee relations executive; b. Calhoun, Ga., Apr. 15, 1940; d. James Norris and Eunice Alleene (West) Holcomb; m. Cornelius Jones, Sept. 19, 1959; children—Vicki Elizabeth, Velvet Leigh; 1 son by previous marriage, Michael Keith Burnett. B.S., Breanu Coll., 1983. With Dow Chem. U.S.A., Dalton, Ga., 1966—, sr. adminstrv. asst., 1974-75, adminstrv. service supr., 19-, employee relations supr., 1977-83, employee relations mgr., 1983—. Trustee, Dalton Jr. Coll. Found., 1983 ; sec. indsl. relations council Carpet and Rug Inst., Dalton, 1979-84; gen. campaign chmn. United Way of Northwest Ga., Dalton, 1983, vice chmn., 1982, bd. dirs., 1981; bd. dirs. Cheerhaven Schs., Dalton, 1983—. Mem. Am. Soc. Personnel Adminstrn. (bd. dirs., pres. 1982-83). Republican. Baptist. Club: Personnel. Home: 322 Cherry Hill Dr Calhoun GA 30701 Office: Dow Chem USA 1468 Prosser Dr SE Dalton GA 30720

JONES, SUSAN DORFMAN, corporate executive, writer; b. N.Y.C., Oct. 4, 1939; d. Joseph and Sarah (Sorrin) Dorfman; m. William Harry Jones, Sept. 18, 1960; children—Jeffrey Scott, Eric David, Timothy Mark. B.A., Syracuse U., 1961. Pres., owner Antiques Corp. Am., 1972-77; communications officer Riggs Bank, Washington, 1978-81; mgr. publs. Potomac Electric Power Co., Washington, 1981-82; sr. mgr. corp. communications MCI Corp., Washington, 1982-83, dir. corp. communications Sears World Trade, Washington, 1983-85; dir. corp. communications and govt. relations Oxford Devel. Corp., Bethesda, Md., 1985—; free-lance writer, cons., Washington, 1985—; radio personality Sta 4KQ, Brisbane, Australia, 1962. Author, mgr.: Capability booklet Riggs Bank, 1979 (Internat. Assn. Bus. Communicators prize 1980); author-editor-project mgr. corp. ann. reports. Playground treas. D.C. Recreation Dept., 1973-79; bd. dirs. March Elem. Sch., Washington, 1969; writer sch. bd. candidates and home rule campaign, Washington, 1970-76. Recipient 1st place award for columns N.Y. Press Assn., 1961. Mem. Internat. Assn. Bus. Communicators (treas. 1981), Nat. Assn. Bank Women, Women in Telecommunications, Nat. Press Club, Pub. Relations Soc. Am. Democrat. Jewish. Home: 7300 Burdette Ct Bethesda MD 20817 Office: 7316 Wisconsin Ave Bethesda MD 20814

JONES, SUSAN GAIL, lawyer; b. Hope, Ark., July 4, 1950; d. William Reid and Frances Charlene (Orr) Clark; m. Jimmy Lynn Jones, Dec. 1, 1973. B.A., Henderson Coll., 1972; J.D., U. Ark.-Little Rock, 1980. Bar: Ark. 1981. Service specialist Ark. Social Services, Hope, 1972-77, investigator, 1977-78, atty., Little Rock, 1981-84, asst. legal adviser, Magnolia, 1984—. Bd. dirs. Springhill Fire Dept., Benton, Ark., 1981-83. Mem. ABA, Ark. Women Lawyers, Phi Alpha Delta. Baptist. Club: Bus. and Profl. Women (young careerist award 1978-79). Home: Route 4 Box 152 Hope AR 71801 Office: Ark Social Services 811 Calhoun Rd Magnolia AR 71753

JONES, SUSAN LANGFORD, consumer economist; b. Richmond, Va., Dec. 29, 1945; d. E. Langford and Mildred Turnley (Howerton) J.; cert. U. d'Aix-Marseille (France), 1965; B.A., Vanderbilt U., 1967; M.B.A., N.Y.U., 1979; m. James Robert Scala, Feb. 28, 1981. Cons., ISIS Systems Inc., N.Y.C., 1976-79; fin. analyst CBS TV Network, N.Y.C., 1979-80, mgr. sales analysis devel., 1980-84, network economist, 1984—; guest lectr. NYU, 1979—. Mem. Nat. Assn. Bus. Economists, N.Y. Assn. Bus. Economists, Am. Statis. Assn., Am. Econ. Assn., Eastern Econ. Assn., Met. Econ. Assn., Econs. Club Conn., Madison Ave Sports Car Driving and Chowder Soc. (v.p.), Beta Gamma Sigma. Republican. Episcopalian. Guest on MoneyLine show, Cable News Network, 1981. Home: 1641 3d Ave New York NY 10128 Office: 51 W 52d St New York NY 10019

JONES, SUSAN SUTTON, educational administrator; b. Nanticoke, Md.; d. Douglas Judson and Emma Jerona (Evans) Sutton; B.S., Fisk U., 1946; M.Edn., Johns Hopkins U., 1965; Ed.D., Temple U., 1983; m. Clifton Ralph Jones, Apr. 2, 1978; 1 son, George Henry Miles, Jr. Caseworker Dept. Pub. Assistance, Phila., 1946-49; tchr. Balt. City Pub. Schs., 1949-63, counselor, 1963-67, adminstr., 1967—; prin. Edmonson Sr. High Sch., Balt., 1975—. NSF grantee, 1967-68. Mem. NAACP, Nat. Assn. Secondary Sch. Prins., Pub. Sch. Adminstrs. and Suprs. Assn. Balt., Continental Soc. Disadvantaged Youth, Delta Sigma Theta, Pub. Service Sorority. Democrat. Episcopalian. Home: 1190 W Northern Pkwy Baltimore MD 21210 Office: 501 Athol Ave Baltimore MD 21229

JONES, TERRI LYNN, advertising agency executive; b. Wagoner, Okla., Feb. 18, 1950; d. George R. and Dorothy Louise (Burress) J.; B.S. with honors in Communications, Phillips U., 1972; postgrad. Richland Coll., 1974-75, Brookhaven Coll., 1977-78. Media buyer Greene-Webb Assocs., Dallas, 1972-73; writer, public relations exec. McCrary-Powell, Inc., Dallas, 1973-74; account service and research adminstr. Crume & Assoc., Dallas, 1975; account supr. and stockholder KCBN, Inc., 1975-79; v.p. Preston Square, Inc., 1978-79; pres. Jones Communications Group, Inc., Dallas, 1979—; exec. v.p., dir. Fun Corp. Am., 1979-82; guest instr. U. Dallas, Arlington, Tex., 1977-78. Vol., Am. Cancer Soc., 1976-77, Am. Heart Assn., 1977-78; bd. dirs. Big Bros. and Sisters Met. Dallas, 1979, Campfire, Inc. Recipient Spl. Judges award Southwest VTR and TV Festival, 1975; Golden Pyramid award Internat. Assn. Splty. Advt., 1977; 1st pl. advt. award (2) Savs. Instns. Mktg. Soc. Am., 1978, 8 Gold medals, 1981; Golden Radio award Olney Savs., 1979; 3 Gold medals, 2 certs. of merit Wichita Falls Ad Club, 1981; named Saleswoman of Year, Big Bros. and Sisters of Met. Dallas, 1979. Mem. Am. Women in Radio and TV (pres. 1978-79, dir. 1979-80), Tex. Public Relations Assn. (Best of Tex. award, Cert. of Merit 1980, 2 Gold medals 1981) Assn. Broadcasting Execs. of Tex., Dallas Communications Council, Nat. Assn. Female Execs., Dallas Ad League (recipient 2 Gold medals, Cert. of Merit 1980, bd. dirs. 1982-83). Republican. Mem. Disciples of Christ Ch. Home: 7219 Colgate St Dallas TX 75225 Office: 4340 N Central St Dallas TX 75206

JONES, THELMA, physician; b. N.Y.C., Nov. 8, 1937; d. Jack and Etta Jones; m. Josua Sack, Nov 19, 1967; children—Amy, Michelle. B.A. cum laude, Barnard Coll., 1959; M.D. cum laude, SUNY-Downstate Med. Ctr., 1963. Intern, Jewish Hosp., Bklyn., 1963-64; resident in internal medicine, hematology Montefiore Med. Ctr., Bronx, N.Y., 1964-67; chief sect. hematology White Plains (N.Y.) Hosp., 1982—, attending physician medicine and hematology; assoc. attending physician Montefiore Hosp., N.Y.C.; asst. attending internal medicine St. Agnes Hosp., White Plains, N.Y.; pres. Central Westchester div. Am. Cancer Soc., 1981-83. Fellow ACP; mem. AMA, Am. Med. Women's Assn., Am. Soc. Internal Medicine, N.Y. State Soc. Internal Medicine, N.Y. State Med. Soc., N.Y. Acad. Medicine, Westchester County Med. Soc. Office: 105 Garth Rd Scarsdale NY 10583

JONES, VIRGINIA A., information management consulting company executive; b. Trumbull, Conn., Jan. 3, 1947; d. Raymond C. and Mary (Walters) J.; student Marywood Coll., 1977—. With Sikorsky Aircraft, Stratford, Conn., 1966-70; with Micro-Tech, Inc., New Orleans, 1970-71, Dikewood Corp., Albuquerque, 1971-76; micrographic specialist State Records Center, Santa Fe, 1976-80, chief records mgmt. div., 1980-81, chief micrographics services div., 1981-83; pres. info. mgmt. cons. co., 1983—. Author: Handbook of Microfilm Technology and Procedures. Mem. Nat. Assn. Female Execs., Am. Bus. Women's Assn., Assn. Record Mgrs. and Adminstrs., Internat. Micrographics Congress, Assn. for Info. and Image Mgmt. Democrat. Episcopalian. Home: 707 Agua Fria Santa Fe NM 87501 Office: 707 Agua Fria Santa Fe NM 87501

JONES, WILMA LOUISE, retired county official, researcher; b. Glasgow, Ky., May 2, 1920; d. William Goodnight and Dora Anna (Taylor) Eaton; m. Wilburn Hall Harrison, Aug. 1, 1942 (div. June 1961); 1 child, Wilburn Hall, Jr.; m. Bedford Jones, Oct. 23, 1963 (dec. Aug. 1982). Grad. High sch., Glasgow. Dispatcher Sheriff's Office, Gallatin, Tenn., 1957-62; clk. Register of Deeds, Gallatin, 1962-64, County Ct. Clk., Gallatin, 1964-67; registrar at large Sumner County Election Commn., Gallatin, 1967-82. Contbr. articles to profl. publs. Rec. sec. County Ct. Minutes, Gallatin, 1964-67; fin. bd. mem. vol. aux. Sumner Meml. Hosp., 1983—. Recipient cert. of Appreciation, U.S. Air Force, 1960, Gov. Lamar Alexander, 1982, Sumner County Legis. Body, 1982; Recipient Dedicated Service award Sumner County Election Commn., 1982. Mem. West End Ladies Soc. Democrat. Baptist. Avocation: humanitarian. Home: 800 Boles St PO Box 694 Gallatin TN 37066

JONES, WINONA NIGELS, library media specialist; b. St. Petersburg, Fla., Feb. 24, 1928; d. Eugene Arthur and Bertha Lillian (Dixon) Nigels; m. Charles Albert Jones, Nov. 26, 1944; children—Charles Eugene, Sharon Ann Jones Allworth, Caroline Winona Jones Pandorf. A.A., St. Petersburg Jr. Coll., 1965; B.S., U. South Fla., 1967, M.S., 1968; Advanced M.S., Fla. State U., 1980. Library media specialist Dunedin (Fla.) Comprehensive High Sch., 1967-76; library media specialist, chmn. dept. Fitzgerald Middle Sch., Largo, Fla., 1976—. Active Palm Harbor and Pinellas County Hist. Soc. Named Educator of Year, Pinellas County Sch. Bd. and Suncoast C. of C., 1983. Mem. Fla. Assn. Media in Edn. (pres.), ALA (com.), U. So. Fla. Alumni Assn., Assn. Ednl. Communication and Tech. (div. sch. media specialist, coms.), Am. Assn. Sch. Libraries (com.), Southeastern Library Assn., Fla. Library Assn., Assn. Supervision and Curriculum Devel., NEA, Fla. State Library Sci. Alumni, U. South Fla. Library Sci. Alumni Assn. (dir.), AAUW, Phi Theta Kappa, Phi Ro Pi, Beta Phi Mu, Kappa Delta Pi, Delta Kappa Gamma. Democrat. Club: Inner Wheel (Palm Harbor, Fla.) Pilot (Palm Harbor), Civic (Palm Harbor). Lodge: Order of Eastern Star (Palm Harbor) (past worthy matron). Home: 911 Manning Rd Palm Harbor FL 33563 Office: 5410 118th Ave North Largo FL 33543

JONES, YVONNE JOHNSON, educational administrator; b. Phila., Aug. 23, 1947; d. James and Dorothy Watson; B.S. in Secondary Social Sci. Edn., Cheyney State Coll., 1969; M.A., Norfolk State Coll., 1978; M.Ed. in Urban Edn., Antoich U., 1977; postgrad. Temple U., 1981—; m. Eric E. Jones, Oct. 3, 1970; 1 child, Jeffrey B. Instr., Opportunities Industrialization Center, Phila., 1969-70; tchr. Simon Gratz High Sch., Phila., 1970-75; tchr. trainer Affective Edn. Program, Phila., 1975-79; vis. prof. childcare/social adminstrn. Temple U., Phila., 1978-84; curriculum supr. Phila. Sch. Dist., 1979-85, supr. affective edn. programs, 1985—; adminstrv. asst. Dist. Two Supt., Phila. Sch. Dist., 1985—; cons. in field. Vol., Mercy Community Center for Aged, Phila., 1979-80, E. Luther Cunningham Community Center, Phila., 1979. Richard Humphries scholar, 1966-68; NSF fellow, 1971. Mem. Educator's Roundtable, Assn. Supervisors and Curriculum Devel., Nat. Assn. Female Execs. Baptist. Co-author: Parent's Guide to Coping Skills Book, 1978, Educator's Manual on Discipline K-12, 1980. Home: 529 Parnell Pl Philadelphia PA 19144 Office: Dist Two Office 6th and Carpenter Philadelphia PA 19147

JONES-BENNS, PATRICYA, customer service engineer; b. El Paso, Tex., Apr. 14, 1952; d. Charlie Anthony and Eunice Beatrice (Wright) Jones; m. Sylvester Joel Leslie, Mar. 10, 1970 (div. 1974); children—Anthony Todd, Columbus Earl; m. Joseph Oliver Benns, Jr., Apr. 22, 1983. Electro mechanic Halicrafters/Wilcox, El Paso, 1970-74; service rep. Sears Roebuck, Dallas, 1975-78; installer Southwestern Bell, Dallas, 1978-79; customer service engr. Xerox Corp., Dallas, 1979—. Tri-chmn. Nat. Polit. Congress of Black Women, Dallas chpt., 1985-86; pres. Minorities United in the So. Region, Dallas, 1983. Pres. Club, Xerox Corp., 1983. Mem. Nat. Assn. Female Execs. Baptist. Avocation: physical fitness. Home: 411 Dawn Dr Duncanville TX 75137 Office: Xerox Corp 222 Las Colinas Irving TX 75039

JONES-LUKÁCS, ELIZABETH LUCILLE, physician, former air force officer; b. Norfolk, Va.; d. Oliver C. and Gertrude (Layden) Jones; B.S., Oglethorpe U., 1955; m. Michel J. Lukacs (dec.); children—Amanda, Laurel, Angelique, Klara. Intern Beth Israel Hosp., N.Y.C., 1964-65; gen. practice medicine, Goshen, N.Y., 1965-73, Buckingham, Va., 1973-78; commd. maj. U.S. Air Force, 1978; flight surgeon, Andrews AFB, Md., 1978-85; ret., 1985; unit charge physician Student Health Ctr., U. Md., College Park, 1985—. Lt. col. USAFR. Diplomate Am. Bd. Family Practice. Mem. Am. Med. Womens Assn., Assn. Aerospace Physicians, Aerospace Med. Assn., Md. Thoroughbred Breeders. Episcopalian. Author: The Curies Radium & Radioactivity, 1962; The Golden Stamp Book of Flying Animals, 1963. Home: Star Route Box 56 Rattle N Snap Farm Buckingham VA 23921 Office: Student Health Office U Md College Park MD

JONES-WILSON, FAUSTINE CLARISSE, educator; b. Little Rock, Dec. 3, 1927; d. James Edward and Perrine Marie (Childress) Thomas; A.B., Ark. A.M.&N. Coll., 1948; A.M., U. Ill., Urbana, 1951, Ed.D., 1967; m. James T. Jones, June 20, 1948 (div. June 1977); children—Yvonne Dianne, Brian Vincent; m. 2d, Edwin L. Wilson, July 10, 1981. Tchr., sch. librarian, Gary (Ind.) Public Schs., 1955-62, 1964-67; asst. prof. Coll. Edn., U. Ill., Chgo., 1967-69; assoc. prof. adult edn. Fed. City Coll., Washington, 1970-71; prof. edn., grad. prof. Howard U., Washington, 1969-70, 1971—. Recipient Frederick Douglass award, Nat. Assn. Black Journalists, 1979; Disting. Scholar-Tchr. award Howard U., 1985. Mem. Am. Ednl. Studies Assn. (pres. 1984-85), John Dewey Soc., Soc. of Profs. of Edn., Adult Edn. Assn. of Met. Washington, Washington Women's Forum, NAACP. Democrat. Methodist. Editor Jour. Negro Edn., 1978—; author: The Changing Mood in America: Eroding Commitment, 1977; A Traditional Model of Educational Excellence: Dunbar High School of Little Rock, Arkansas, 1981. Home: 908 Dryden Ct. Silver Spring MD 20901 Office: Sch Edn Howard U 2400 Sixth St NW Washington DC 20059

JONES-WRIGHT, CAROL ANN, nurse, consultant, real estate salesperson; b. Balt., May 10, 1939; d. Leon Levi and Zylpha M. (Lewis) Jones; m. Lynford Earl Wright, June 11, 1967; children—Shellie Nicole, Angela Lynn, Laurie Carol. R.N., Bklyn. Hosp., 1960; B.S., Coll. of White Plains-Pace U., 1976; M.B.A., Ala. A&M U., 1982. Dir. nursing Tafferi Makonnen Hosp., Dessie, Ethiopia, 1962-66; chief evening supr. Bklyn. Hosp., 1966-71; dir. nursing Victory Lake Nursing Ctr., Hyde Park, N.Y., 1971-77; adminstrv. supr. Humana Hosp., Huntsville, Ala., 1977—; chief occupational health nurse Teledyne Brown Engring. Co., Huntsville, 1978—; v.p., sec.-treas., owner Mgmt. Enterprises Inc. cons. Dutchess Community Coll. Sch. Nursing, Poughkeepsie, N.Y., 1973-77; nursing service cons. Rheinbeck (N.Y.) Nursing Home 1976, North Huntsville Health Service, 1977-82, East Los Angeles Hosp., 1980; pres. bd. dirs. Central No. Ala. Health Services, Inc., Madison, 1982—. Sec. bd. dirs. Neighborhood Service Orgn., Poughkeepsie, 1973-76; vice chmn. Family Health and Day Care Ctr., Poughkeepsie, 1973-76; pres. Huntsville Area Sch. PTA, 1982-84. Recipient civic activity cert. Rotary Club, Hyde Park, 1975, service cert. Dutchess Community Coll., 1977; bd. dirs. Adventist Sr. Apts. Mem. Am. Mgmt. Assn., Assn. Adventist Nurses, Nat. Assn. Female Execs., Rocket City Assn. Bus. and Profl. Women Am. (1st v.p. 1984, pres. 1985, Woman of Distinction 1985-86). Democrat. Adventist. Office: Humana Hosp of Huntsville 911 Big Cove Huntsville AL 35801 also Teledyne Brown Engring Co 300 Sparkman Dr Huntsville AL 35807 also Fairway Real Estate Co 4035 Bonnell Dr Huntsville AL 35805

JONG, ERICA MANN, author, poet; b. N.Y.C., Mar. 26, 1942; d. Seymour and Eda (Mirsky) Mann; B.A., Barnard Coll., 1963; M.A., Columbia U., 1965. Faculty, English dept. CUNY, 1964-65, 69-70, overseas div. U. Md., 1967-69; m. Allan Jong (div. Sept. 1975); m. Jonathan Fast, 1977 (div. 1982); 1 dau., Molly. Mem. lit. panel N.Y. State Council on Arts, 1972-74. Recipient Bess Hokin prize Poetry mag., 1971, Alice Faye di Castagnola award Poetry Soc. Am., 1972; Nat. Endowment for Arts grantee, 1973. Mem. Authors Guild (dir. 1975), Writers Guild Am.-West, PEN, Phi Beta Kappa. Author: Fruits & Vegetables (poems), 1971; Half-Lives (poems), 1973; Fear of Flying (novel), 1973; Loveroot (poems), 1975; How to Save Your Own Life (novel), 1977; At the Edge of the Body (poems), 1979; Fanny, Being the true History of the Adventures of Fanny Hackabout-Jones (novel), 1980; Witches (art, fiction, poetry), 1981; Ordinary Miracles (poems), 1983; Parachutes & Kisses (novel), 1984. Office: care Morton L Janklow Assocs Inc 598 Madison Ave New York NY 10022 also care New American Library 1633 Broadway New York NY 10019

JORDAN, ALICE MACDONALD, lawyer, educator; b. N.Y.C., Oct. 17, 1943; d. Martin E. and Ruth (Rhoads) Macdonald; m. Carl Richard Jordan, Aug. 3, 1962; children—Richard Kent, Jason Kyle. B.S., Murray State U., 1964; student U. Mo.-St. Louis, 1966; J.D., So. Ill. U., 1980. Bar: Ill. 1980. Tchr., St. Louis City Schs., 1964-65, Ritenour Sch. System, St. Louis County, Mo., 1965-67, Harrisburg Schs. (Ill.), 1967-68, Eldorado Schs. (Ill.), 1968-69; mgr., purchasing agt. Jordan Pharm., Eldorado, Ill., 1969-77; law clk. Robert Wilson Law Office, Harrisburg, 1978-80; ptnr. law firm Richard C. Cochran, Fairfield, Ill., 1980—; bus. law instr. Frontier Community Coll., Fairfield, Ill. Bd. dirs. Central Bapt. Family Services, Olney, Ill., 1983-84, Wayne County Vols. for Youth, 1984—. Mem. ABA, Ill. Bar Assn., Am. Trial Lawyers Assn., Ill. Trial Lawyers Assn., Fairfield C. of C., Phi Alpha Delta, Kappa Delta Phi. Clubs: Fairfield Woman's, Bus. and Profl. Women's Assn. Home: 301 W Center St Fairfield IL 62837 Office: 302 E Main St Fairfield IL 62837

JORDAN, ANNIE RUTH, nursing administrator; b. Laurens, S.C., Jan. 2, 1932; d. Alfred T. and Alma (Thompson) Phillips; m. Chester L. Jordan, Aug. 27, 1952; children—Janneice Jordan Williams, Jocelyn Jordan Diener, Jonathan, James. Diploma Bapt. Meml. Hosp. Sch. Nursing, 1969; B.S.N., Union Coll., 1976; M.S.N., U. Colo., 1981. Staff nurse Bapt. Meml. Hosp., San Antonio, 1969; supr. San Antonio Osteo. Hosp., 1970-71; staff/charge nurse Parkview Episcopal Hosp., Pueblo, Colo., 1971-72; staff/charge nurse, adminstrv. supr. Porter Meml. Hosp., Denver, 1972-81; dir. nursing South Big Horn County Hosp., Greybull, Wyo., 1981—, Bonnie Bluejacket Meml. Nursing Home, Greybull, 1981—. Contbr. articles to profl. jours. Bd. dirs. 7th Day Adventist Ch., Greybull, 1981-85. Recipient 2d Place Scholastic award Bapt. Meml. Hosp., 1969. Mem. Assn. 7th Day Adventist Nurses (pres. Denver-Metro chpt., pres.-elect 1971-74, 76-78), Wyo. Orgn. Nursing Execs. (pres. 1983-85), Am. Assn. Critical Care Nurses (ad hoc com. 1975), Wyo. State Bd. Nursing (pres. 1985—), Sigma Theta Tau. Avocations: music; photography; wildflowers; handwork; poetry. Office: S Big Horn County Hosp River Route Greybull WY 82426

JORDAN, BARBARA C., former congresswoman, educator; b. Houston, Feb. 21, 1936; d. Ben and Arlyne Jordan; B.A. magna cum laude, Tex. So. U., 1956; LL.B., Boston U., 1959; Admitted to Tex. bar; adminstrv. asst. to county judge, Harris County; mem. Tex. Senate, 1966-72, pres. pro tem, 1972, chmn. labor and Mgmt. Relations Com. and Urban Affairs Study Com.; mem. 93d-95th Congresses from 18th Dist. Tex., mem. Com. on Judiciary, Com. Govt. Ops., Spl. Task Force on 94th Congress, mem. steering and policy com. House Democratic Caucus; Lyndon B. Johnson Public Service prof. L.B.J. Sch. Public Affairs, U. Tex., Austin, 1979-82, Lyndon B. Johnson Centennial prof. nat. policy, 1982—; mem. panel on multinat. corps. in South Africa and Namibia, UN, 1985. Named One of 10 Most Influential Women in Tex., One of 100 Women in Touch With Our Time, Harpers Bazaar mag.; A Woman of Year, Time Mag., 1975; recipient Eleanor Roosevelt humanities award, 1984. Barbara Jordan fund for gifted students established in her honor at Lyndon B. Johnson Sch. Pub. Affairs. Mem. AMA, Houston, Mass. bar assns., State Bar Tex., NAACP. Baptist. Office: Lyndon B Johnson Sch Public Affairs U Tex Austin TX 78712*

JORDAN, BARBARA SCHWINN, painter; b. Glen Ridge, N.J.; d. Carl Wilhelm Ludwig and Helen Louise (Jordan) Schwinn; grad. N.Y. Sch. Fine and Applied Art (Parsons), N.Y. and Paris; student Grand Central Art Sch., Art Students League, Grand Chaumiere, Academie Julien-Paris, Columbia U., NAD; m. Frank Bertram Jordan, Jr.; children—Janine Jordan Newlin, Frank Bertram III. Illustrator mags. including Vogue, 1930's, Ladies Home Jour., Saturday Evening Post, Colliers, Good Housekeeping, Cosmopolitan, McCall's, American, Town and Country, 1940's-50's. Women's Jour., Eng., Hors Zu, Germany, Marie Claire, France, other fgn. publs., 1950's-60's; portrait painter, including Queen Sirikit, Princess Margaret, Princess Grace; free lance painter, 1970—; one-man shows include Soc. of Illustrators, 1940, 50, Barry Stephens Gallery, 1950, Bodley Gallery, N.Y.C., 1971, 80, Community Coll., West Mifflin, Pa., 1973, Duquesne U., 1973; exhibited in group shows including NAD, 1955, Royal Acad., London, Guild Hall, N.Y., 1981, Summit N.J. Art Ctr., 1981, Meredith Long Gallery, Houston, 1983, Mus. Soc. Illustrators, N.Y., 1985, The Marcus Gallery, Sante Fe, 1985, 86, The Gerald Peters Gallery, Santa Fe, 1985, 86, Brandywine Mus., Pa., 1985, 86, New Britain Mus. Am. Art, 1986, works represented Holbrook Collection, Ga. Mus. Art, Eureka Coll., Ill., various pvt. and gallery collections; lectr., instr. illustration Parsons Sch., 1952-54; founder adv. council Art Instrn. Sch., 1956-70. Chmn. art com. UNICEF greeting cards, 1950-61 mem. com. Spence Chapin Sch., Philharm. Soc., 1950's-60's. Winner prizes Art Dirs. Club, 1950, Guild Hall, 1969. Asso. mem. Guggenheim Mus. Episcopalian. Club: Cosmopolitan N.Y. Author: Technique of Barbara Schwinn, 1956; World of Fashion Art, 1968. Home and Studio: Mecox Rd Rural Route 1 Box 882 Water Mill NY 11976

JORDAN, BETTIE ELLA NICHOLSON, savs. and loan exec.; b. Brenham, Tex., May 4, 1913; d. William Henry and Bettie Holcomb Nicholson; student Massey Bus. Coll., 1932, U. Houston extension, 1972-75, U. Tex., summers 1963, 64; m. William Henry Jordan, Sept. 13, 1936; children—Henry Carl, William John, Anna Elizabeth Jordan Khalili. Clerical and secretarial positions Houston Assn. of Credit Men, 1932-33, Gen. Electric Supply Corp., Houston, 1933-38, War Chest, 1944-45, United Fund, intermittently, 1955-57, Depelchin Faith Home, Houston, 1957-59; with Heights Savs. Assn., Houston, 1959—, loan officer, 1961-65, sec.-treas., 1965-75, sr. v.p., sec., 1975—; sec. to bd. dirs., 1965—. Mem. Presdl. Task Force, Heritage Found. Recipient Outstanding Woman award YWCA, 1978. Mem. Nat. Forum for Exec. Women of Nat. Savs. and Loan League, Fin. Officers Soc. of U.S. Savs. and Loan League, Washington Legal Found. Republican. Lutheran. Club: Senatorial. Office: Heights Savs Assn 204 W 19th St Houston TX 77008

JORDAN, BETTY SUE, retired educator; b. Lafayette, Tenn., Sept. 4, 1920; d. Aubrey Lee and Geneva (Freeman) West; m. Bill Jordan, Oct. 22, 1950; 1 child, L. Nicha. Student David Lipscomb Coll., 1939-41; B.S., U. Tenn., 1943; registered dietitian Duke U. Hosp., 1945; M.Ed., Clemson U., 1973. Dietitian, U. Ala., Tuscaloosa, 1945-46, Duke U., Durham, N.C., 1946-48, Stetson U., DeLand, Fla., 1948-50, Furman U., Greenville, S.C., 1950-52; elem. tchr. Greenville County Schs., S.C., 1952-66, tchr. orthopedically handicapped, 1966-85. Mem. NEA, Assn. Childhood Edn. (treas. 1980-85), United Daus. Confederacy (pres. Greenville chpt. 1978-85), Greenville Woman's Club, Lake Forest Garden Club (pres. 1980-81, historian 1981-85), Greater Greenville Rose Soc. (pres. 1983-84), Delta Kappa Gamma (pres. Tau chpt. 1972-74, state chmn. communications 1981—, state chmn. research 1983-85), Kappa Kappa Iota (state pres. 1972-73, conclave pres. 1983-85), Democrat. Methodist. Avocations: collecting antiques; growing roses; flower arranging. Home: 21 Lisa Dr Greenville SC 29615

JORDAN, JACQUELYN, health agency executive, rancher; b. Hamilton, Ohio, Feb. 11, 1935; d. Harry Adolph and Kathryn Marie (Baird) Herman; m. Nov. 21, 1953 (div. Feb. 1977); children—Steve, Diana, Jeff. Student Miami U., 1953-54, U. Ill., 1955-56, Tarrant County Jr. Coll., 1973-76. Sec., Bookkeeper North Central Tex. Home Health Agy., Inc., Fort Worth, 1970-73, asst. bus. mgr., 1973-75, bus. mgr., 1975-80, pres., 1980—; rancher registered Santa Gertrudis cattle. Mem. Tarrant County Health Planning Council; charter mem. Ft. Worth Boot Brigade, 1985. Mem. Tex. Assn. Home Health Agys. Inc. (Named Tex. Chairperson of Yr. 1985), Nat. Assn. Home Care Inc., Bus. and Profl. Women's Orgn., Nat. Assn. Women Bus. Owners, Ft. Worth C. of C., Women Entrepreneur, Inc., Santa Gertrudis Breeders Internat. Democrat. Mem. Ch. of Christ. Avocations: outside activities; handicrafts. Home: PO Box 985 Azle TX 76020 Office: North Central Tex Home Health Agy Inc 603 S Adams St Fort Worth TX 76104

JORDAN, JANITH MARY, college administrator; b. Detroit, Oct. 11, 1942; d. Joseph Walter and Wanda (Bonk) J. B.A., Wayne State U., 1965; postgrad. Summer Inst., U. London, 1967, Harvard U., 1977; M.S., U. Mich., 1968. Curriculum specialist Coll. Human Services, N.Y.C., 1968-70, acad. dir., 1971, ednl. planner, 1972-76, faculty, 1977, dir. inter-instl. devel., 1978-81, v.p., 1981—. Co-author: Taking Constructive Action, 1980. Roman Catholic. Home: 200 E 84th St New York NY 10028 Office: College for Human Services 345 Hudson St New York NY 10014

JORDAN, JESSIE MAE, educator; b. Leadwood, Mo., May 25, 1921; d. Thomas and Dora J.; B.S. in Elem. Edn., U. Mo., Columbia, 1948, M.Ed. in Spl. Edn. and Reading, 1956; postgrad. in learning disabilities Fontbonne Coll., St. Louis. Tchr. grade 3 Leadwood (Mo.) Sch. R-IV, 1944-52; tchr. spl. edn. Leadwood Sch., 1952-71; reading specialist West County RIV Public Schs., 1971—; speaker prof. confs. Active, East Side Ch. of God. Mem. St. Francois County, Mo. State tchrs. assn., Council Exceptional Children (nat., local-mem. chmn.), Internat. Reading Assn. (past pres. Mineral area chpt., mem. research com., treas. 1983-86). Specialist in spl. edn., educable mentally retarded, home-bound cerebral palsy, emotionally disturbed, reading specialist. Home: 205 E 9th St Leadwood MO 63653 Office: West County RIV Public Schs 1124 Main St Leadwood MO 63653

JORDAN, JOYCE MAE, podiatrist; b. Alton, Ill., Oct. 21, 1949; d. Edward Thomas and Catherine Lutichie (Yates) J.; 1 child, Paul Thomas. B.A., So. Ill. U., 1972; D.P.M., Ohio Coll. Podiatric Medicine, 1983. Recreation supr. Alton Park Recreation Dept., 1968-69; tutor, physics library clk. So. Ill. U., Edwardsville, 1968-72; circulation clk. Alton Telegraph, 1972-73; program dir. MCCADD, Alton, 1973-75; youth program dir. Coordinated Youth Services, Granite City, Ill., 1977-78; intern VA Hosp., Leavenworth, Kans., 1982; resident Mobile Foot Health Ctr., Ala., 1983-84; practice medicine specializing in podiatry Am. Podiatry Clinic, New Orleans, 1984—; podiatry cons. Lafon Nursing Home, New Orleans, 1985—, Prayer Tower Nursing Home, New Orleans, 1985—. Mem. La. Podiatry Assn., New Orleans Med. Assn., Nat. Assn. Female Execs., Alpha Kappa Alpha, Kappa Tau Epsilon. Democrat. Baptist. Avocations: singing; painting; collecting foreign artifacts. Home: 6896 Parc Brittany Blvd New Orleans LA 70126 Office: Americare Podiatry Clinic 3024 Gentilly Blvd New Orleans LA 70122

JORDAN, LUCILLE GALLOWAY, educational administrator; b. Transylvania County, N.C.; d. Thomas Pleasant and Mary Sue (Fisher) Galloway; m. Frederick L. S. Jordan, Dec. 24, 1945; 1 child, Noelle Thomasina. B.S., U. Tenn., Knoxville, 1948; M.Ed., U. Ga., 1964, Ed.D., 1966; postdoctoral study U Calif.-Santa Barbara, 1970, U. Colo., 1973, U. Keele, Staffordshire, Eng., 1974. Cert. tchr., adminstr., supr., Ga. Tchr. pub. schs. N.C., Tenn., Ga.; assoc. state supt. schs. State of Ga. Dept. Edn., Atlanta, 1978—. Author: The Five Senses, 1967; Learning Opportunities Surround Us, 1968; Does Individualization Make a Difference?, 1973. Co-author: Humanities Programs Today, 1970; Collaboration for Teacher Education, 1978; Educational Manpower, 1969. Bd. trustees, mem. exec. com. Ga. Econs. Council, 1980—. NSF fellow, 1974. Mem. AAUW (trustee edn. info. and referral system 1983—), Assn. Supervision and Curriculum Devel. (nat. pres. 1981-82; leadership award 1984), Phi Delta Kappa. Baptist. Clubs: Atlanta Athletic, Nat. Assistance League. Avocations: travel; sewing; collecting historical plates. Home: 2310 N Peachtree Way Dunwoody GA 30338 Office: Office Instructional Services Ga Dept Edn 1966 Twin Towers East Atlanta GA 30334

JORDAN, RUTH ANN, physician; b. Richmond, Ind., Oct. 12, 1928; d. Willard and Esther (Fouts) J.; children—Diane M., Linda J. A.B., Ind. U., 1950; M.D., Columbia U., 1957. Intern, St. Luke's Hosp., N.Y.C., 1957-58, asst. resident in medicine, 1958-59; physician clinic Met. Life Ins. Co., N.Y.C., 1960-62; physician med. clinic Standard Oil Col. of N.J., N.Y.C., 1962; physician in med. dept. MIT, Cambridge, 1963-72; asst. med. dir. New Eng. Mut. Life Ins. Co., Boston, 1972-74; fellow internal medicine Mass. Gen. Hosp., Boston, 1974-75; physician Simmons Coll., Boston, 1975-78, Northeastern U., Boston, 1976-78; physician Med. Clinic, New Eng. Mut. Life Ins. Co., Boston, 1963-66; therapeutic dietitian Meth. Hosp., Indpls., 1951-53, Presbyn. Hosp., N.Y.C., part-time 1954-57; assoc. med. dir. New Eng. Telephone Co., 1978, med. dir. clin. services, 1978—. Active Brownies. Fellow Am. Occupational Med. Assn. (membership com. 1985—, health edn. com. 1984—, bd. dirs. 1986—); mem. Ind. Dietitic Assn. (past pub. relations chmn.), AMA, DAR, Norfolk County Med. Soc., New Eng. Occupational Med. Assn. (bd. dirs. 1980—; pres. 1981-84), Mass. Med. Soc. (chmn. environ. and occupational health com. 1985—), Alpha Chi Omega. Clubs: Columbia U. of New Eng. (v.p. 1981-84), Roxbury Clin. Records, Wianno Yacht. Home: 105 Rockwood St Brookline MA 02146

JORDAN, SHARON ANN, clinical social worker; b. Detroit, July 22, 1953; d. Benneal and Myrtice Marie J., A.B. in Journalism, U. Mich., 1975, M.Urban Planning, 1977, M.S.W., 1979. Intern, research asst. City of Ann Arbor (Mich.), 1976-77; caseworker asst. Ann Arbor Community Center, 1977-78; caseworker aide ARC, 1978-79; parent orientation coordinator U. Mich., 1978, resident dir. housing, 1975-79; adminstrv. intern City of Ann Arbor, 1979; social worker, counselor, staff devel. coordinator U. Mich. opportunity program, 1979-84; child-family psychotherapist U. Mich. Children's Psychiat. Hosp., 1984—; program counselor Employee Assistance Assocs., Inc., 1984—. U. Mich. fellow, 1976-77. Mem. Nat. Assn. Social Workers, Acad. Cert. Social Workers, Huron Valley Unit (pres.), Phi Beta Kappa. Home: 3845 Greenbrier Blvd #338 C Ann Arbor MI 48105 Office: 300 N Ingalls #50 Ann Arbor MI 48109

JORDAN, WILMA ELIZABETH HACKER, publishing executive; b. Knoxville, Tenn., Sept. 19, 1948; d. Reo H. and Gertrude (Porter) Hacker; m. Ray C. Jordan, Dec. 19, 1970 (div.). B.S., U. Tenn., 1970. Vice pres., treas. 13-30 Corp., Knoxville, 1970-81, also dir. gen. mgr. Esquire Assocs., N.Y.C., 1981—, also dir.; dir. Assoc. Investments Harmsworth Ltd., London, First Women's Bank, N.Y./C., 1986—. Mem. Tenn. Reps., Nashville, 1978—; bd. advisors Audit Bur. Circulation; cons. Knoxville Women's Ctr., 1980—. Mem. Advt. Women N.Y., Exec. Women of Knoxville. Clubs: Old City (bd. dirs.), Club le Conte (Knoxville). Home: 1431 Cherokee Trail #132 Knoxville TN 37920

JORDAN, ZEMA LOUISE, educational administrator; b. Huntsville, Ala.; d. Willie Davey and Hattie (Jobe) Jordan; B.A., Tenn. A&I State U., 1953; M.Ed., Wayne State U., 1963, now doctoral candidate. Instr. English, Liberty (Miss.) High Sch., 1953-54; instr. English, part-time guidance counselor Wilson Jr. High Sch., Florence, S.C., 1954-64; instr. English, Hutchins Jr. High and Southwestern High Sch., Detroit, 1964-68; head English dept. Farwell Jr. High Sch., Detroit, 1968-75; instr. English, Wayne County Community Coll., Detroit, part-time, 1969—; adminstrv. unit head Richard Middle Sch., Detroit, 1976-77, Von Steuben Middle Sch., Detroit, 1977—; curriculum cons.; speaker profl. seminars and confs. Profl. Growth Center, Detroit Pub. Schs., Wayne State Univ., 1980—. Active Adult Gt. Books Discussion Group, Detroit, 1965—; leader Jr. Gt. Books, Detroit Pub. Library. Mem. Orgn. Sch. Adminstrs. and Suprs., Assn. Supervision and Curriculum Devel., Mich. Assn. Supervision and Curriculum Devel., Met. Detroit Alliance Black Sch. Educators, Nat. Alliance Black Sch. Educators, Tchrs. English to Speakers Other Langs., Nat. Council Tchrs. English, Mich. Council Tchrs. English, Internat. Reading Assn., Met. Detroit Reading Council, Internat. Platform Assn. NAACP, Delta Sigma Theta, Pi Lambda Theta. Methodist. Contbr. articles to profl. jours. Office: Von Steuben Middle Sch 12300 Linnhurst St Detroit MI 48205

JORDAN-TOPP, PAMELA, pest control company executive; b. Indpls., Dec. 18, 1953; d. Herman B. Jordan and Joyce Elaine (Dingman) Carr; m. Jaime Jordan-Topp, Sept. 12, 1981; 1 son, Nicholas. B.S. in Fin. and Mgmt., Ball State U., cum laude, 1977; cert. Cash Flow Vanderbilt U., 1980; cert. Union Free Mgmt., PTI Mgmt. Inst., 1983. Cert. pest control operator, Fla. With payroll dept. Arab Termite & Pest Control of Fla., Inc., Tampa, 1977-78, with field support and tng. dept., 1977-79, acctg. dept. mgr., 1979-81, fin. dir., 1981—, also sec./treas., dir.; pres., chmn. bd. Alternative Processing Systems, Tampa. Contbr. articles to profl. jours. Active mem. Tampa Com. of 100, First Family Tampa Childrens Home, 1983, 84, 85. Mem. Tampa C. of C., Nat. Pest Control Assn. (bd. dirs. 1984-85), Fla. Pest Control Assn. (sec., treas., chmn. of yr. 1983), Fla. Fla. C. of C. Republican. Presbyterian. Club: Clearwater Yacht. Avocations: sailing; snow skiing; reading; cooking and entertaining. Office: Arab Termite & Pest Control of Fla Inc 3105 W Waters Ave Ste 300 Tampa FL 33614

JORDE, JO ELLEN, cultural exchange programs director; b. Dallas, Jan. 17, 1932; d. Foster Friou and Zana Ell (Guthrie) Johnson; m. Keith Eugene Jorde, Dec. 29, 1952 (div. Mar. 1976); children—James, John, Ellen, Marta, Paul, Andrea. R.N., St. Barnabas Sch. Nursing, Mpls., 1953. Charge nurse surg. recovery room Dallas Children's Hosp., 1955; ptnr. Jorde Farms and Jorde Potato Co., Inc., Hereford, Tex., 1955-75; dir. Bi-centennial Project in State of Tex., Youth for Understanding, 1975-76; internat. dir. Americas Studies Confs., Tex. Cultural Alliance, Dallas, 1979—; pres. Vista Nueva, Inc., Dallas, 1976—; co-dir., founder Sch. Vol. Program, Hereford, Tex., 1976-80; founder program Reading is Fundamental, Hereford, 1977; coordinator Peace to the World, Tex. Cultural Alliance, 1979, founder Corazones Sin Fronteras Program, Tex., Puerto Vallarta, Guadalajara, Mexico, 1979—. Mem. ad hoc com. to obtain legislation for sch. volunteerism, State Tex., 1979-80; mem. Forum Humanity and Culture, Dallas, 1982-84; mem. com. Dallas Salutes the World, 1983-84; del. World Cultural Alliance, Tex. Cultural Alliance to Mainland China Exhibition Agy., 1983; coordinator Empathy, 1983; UNICEF good-will ambassador, 1984. Named Internat. Ambassador of Goodwill, Gov. Clements Tex., Dallas, 1980; recipient medal City of Guadalajara, Dept. of Patrimony, 1980; Plaque of City, Mayor of Puerto Vallarta, 1981; Jorde Internat. Artist Competition honor Tex. Cultural Alliance, Dallas, 1982. Mem. World Cultural Alliance (founder, pres. 1983—), Tex. Cultural Alliance (exec. bd. 1979—). Home: 3131 Maple Ave Apt 6G Dallas TX 75201 Office: PO Box 190248 3200 Maple Suite 509 Dallas TX 75219

JORDON, PEARL, psychotherapist, educator; b. N.Y.C., July 24, 1926; d. Max and Clara (Pineus) J.; B.A., Bklyn. Coll., 1959; M.S., Yeshiva U., 1960; M.S.W., Hunter Coll., 1963. Sr. social worker Manhattan State Hosp., Wards Island, N.Y., 1959-66, psychiat. cons. social service dept., 1967-68; psychiat. cons. Kings County Psychiat. Social Service Dept., Bklyn., 1969-71; asso. dir. dept. social services Montefiore Hosp. & Med. Center, Bronx, N.Y., 1971-77; asst. prof. N.Y.U., N.Y.C., 1966-71; lectr. Hunter Coll., N.Y.C., 1975-77, adj. clin. asso. prof., 1976—; clin. asso. prof. SUNY, Stony Brook, 1979-84, chmn. integrated practice concentration, 1980-83; adj. assoc. prof., coordinator individual treatment program Postmasters Clin. Program, Hunter Sch. Social Work, CCNY, 1984—; pvt. practice psychotherapy, N.Y.C., 1968—. Mem. social service adv. com. March of Dimes, Jericho, N.Y., 1980-81; guest speaker Nassau and Suffolk Health Systems Assn., Melville, N.Y., 1980; mem. com. Suffolk/Nassau Health Systems Agy., 1980-81. Fellow Soc. Clin. Social Work Psychotherapists, Am. Orthopsychiat. Assn., Council Social Work Edn.; mem. Nat. Assn. Social Workers, Soc. Hosp. Social Service Dirs., State Assn. Gerontology Educators, Council on Social Work Edn. Contbr. articles in field to profl. publs. Office: 160 E 88th St New York NY 10128

JORGENSEN, DIANE LEE, police officer; b. San Jose, Calif., Apr. 20, 1952; d. Clifford Carl and Joanna (Shubunka) J. A.A., Ohlone Coll., Calif., 1973; B.A. in Bus. Mgmt., St. Mary's Coll., Noraga, Calif., 1986. Cert. in police adminstrn. Calif. Police dispatcher Bay Area Rapid Transit Dist., Oakland, Calif., 1973-80, police officer, 1974-80, police sgt., 1980—, asst. supr. bus. ops., 1985—. Contbr. articles to profl. jours.; editor profl. newspaper, 1984-85. Recipient Rod Hendricks Law Enforcement award Ohlone Coll., Fremont, Calif., 1971. Mem. Women's Police Officer Assn. of Calif. (fund raising chair 1986—), Police Officers Research Assn. of Calif. Republican. Club: Sierra. Presbyterian. Avocations: Snow skiing; reading; aerobics; crocheting; cooking. Office: Bay Area Rapid Transit Dist Police Dept 800 Madison St Oakland CA 94607

JORGENSEN, JUDITH ANN, psychiatrist; b. Parris Island, S.C., Aug. 31, 1941; d. George Emil and Margaret Georgia Jorgensen; B.A., Stanford U., 1963; M.D., U. Calif., 1968; m. Ronald Francis Crown, July 11, 1970. Intern, Meml. Hosp., Long Beach, 1969-70; resident County Mental Health Services, San Diego, 1970-73; staff psychiatrist Children and Adolescent Services, San Diego, 1973-78; practice medicine specializing in psychiatry, La Jolla, Calif., 1973—; staff psychiatrist County Mental Health Services of San Diego, 1973-78; psychiat. cons. San Diego City Coll., 1973-78; asst. prof. dept. psychiatry U. Calif., 1978—; chmn. med. quality rev. com. Dist. XIV, State of Calif., 1982-83. Mem. Am. Psychiat. Assn., San Diego Psychiat. Soc. (chmn. membership 1976-78, v.p. 1978-80, fed. legis. rep. 1985-87), Am. Soc. Adolescent Psychiatry, San Diego Soc. Adolescent Psychiatry (pres. 1981-82), Soc. Sci. Study of Sex, San Diego Soc. Sex Therapy and Edn., San Diego County Med. Soc. (credentials com. 1982-84). Club: Rowing. Office: 470 Nautilus St Suite 211 La Jolla CA 92037

JORGENSEN, VIRGINIA TRIEST, psychiatrist; b. New Orleans, Mar. 22, 1923; d. Kenneth G. and Luise (Schiele) Triest; B.A. cum laude, Hofstra U., 1951; M.D., U. Copenhagen, 1957; postgrad. N.Y. Sch. Psychiatry, 1963; m. Eric Jorgensen, Aug. 5, 1951; children—Ellen Verena, Nina. Intern, Flushing (N.Y.) Hosp., 1957-58; resident in psychiatry Creedmore State Hosp., Queens, N.Y., 1959-62, sr. psychiatrist, 1962-64; practice medicine specializing in psychiatry, Garden City, N.Y., 1963—; psychiat. cons. Sch. for Emotionally Disturbed Children, Nassau County, N.Y., 1962-71, Children's Village, Dobbs Ferry, N.Y., 1964-65; asst. attending physican North Shore Univ. Hosp., Manhasset, N.Y., 1980-86, sr. asst. attending, 1986—; clin. instr. psychiatry Cornell U. Coll. Medicine, 1981. Mem. med. adv. bd. Planned Parenthood of Nassau County, 1966—; bd. dirs. Family Life Center, Garden City, 1981. Diplomate Am. Bd. Psychiatry. Mem. Am. Psychiat. Assn., Am. Med. Women's Assn., Nassau Psychiat. Soc. (dir. 1983—). Club: Garden City Ski. Office: 520 Franklin Ave Garden City NY 11530

JOSE, PHYLLIS ANN, librarian; b. Detroit, Mar. 15, 1949; d. William Henry and Isobel Eleanor (Mundle) J.; B.A., Mich. State U., 1971, M.A., 1972; M.A. in Library Sci., U. Mich., 1975. Library aide audio-visual div. Dearborn (Mich.) Dept. Libraries, 1973-76, librarian gen. info. div., 1976-77; reference library dir. Oakland County (Mich.) Library, 1977—. Officer Southfield Economic Devel. Corp., 1980—; mem. Southfield Tax Increment Fin. Authority, 1981—; bd. dirs. Southfield Arts Council, 1983—; coordinator Southfield Arts Festival, 1984, 85. Mem. ALA, Mich. Library Assn., LWV Southfield, Lathrup Village and Oak Park. Presbyterian. Office: 1200 N Telegraph Rd Pontiac MI 48053

JOSEFF, JOAN CASTLE, jewelry rental company executive, manufacturing executive; b. Alta., Can., Aug. 12, 1922; naturalized U.S. citizen, 1945; d. Edgar W. and Lottie (Coates) Castle; B.A. in Psychology, UCLA; widow; 1 son, Jeffrey Rene. With Joseff-Hollywood, jewelry rental, Burbank, Calif., 1939—, chmn. bd., pres., sec.-treas., 1948—; exec., aircraft components mfg. co. Mem. Burbank Salary Task Force, 1979—, Los Angeles County Earthquake Fact-Finding Commn., 1981—; bd. dirs. San Fernando Valley area chpt. Am. Cancer Soc.; mem. Republican Central Com.; del. Rep. Nat. Conv., 1980, 84. Hon. life mem. Women of Motion Picture Industry. Mem. Nat. Fedn. Republican Women (dir.), Calif. Rep. Women (dir.), N. Hollywood Rep. Women (pres. 1981-82). Home: 10060 Toluca Lake Ave Toluca Lake CA 91602 Office: 129 E Providencia Ave Burbank CA 91502

JOSELYN, JO ANN, space scientist; b. St. Francis, Kans., Oct. 5, 1943; d. James Jacob and Josephine Felzien (Firkins) Cram; B.S. in Applied Math., U. Colo. 1965, M.S. in Astrogeophysics, 1967, Ph.D. in Astrogeophysics, 1978. Research asst. astrogeophysics U. Colo., 1964-67; research asst. NASA/Manned Space Center, Houston, 1966; physicist NOAA/Space Environ. Lab., 1967-78, space scientist 1978—; U.S. del. study group 6 Consultative Com. Ionospheric Radio, 1981, 83. Recipient NOAA unit citation 1971, 80, 85. Mem. Am. Geophys. Union, Union Radio Sci. Internat., Internat. Union Geodesy and Geophysics, Assn. Geomagnetism and Aeronomy, AIAA, AAAS, AAUW, Boulder Council Internat. Visitors, High Noon Investment Club, Sigma Xi, Tau Beta Pi, Sigma Tau. Republican. Methodist. Club: PEO. Office: 325 Broadway St Boulder CO 80303

JOSEPH, EDNA WHITEHEAD (MRS. LAWRENCE J. JOSEPH), tax financial consultant, former banker; b. Everett, Mass., Feb. 4, 1924; d. Alfred Edward and Mary Kathleen (Butler) Whitehead; attended Boston U., Am. Inst. Banking; m. Lawrence James Joseph, May 30, 1958. With Nat. Shawmut Bank (name now Shawmut Bank of Boston, N.A.), 1941-55, 57-84, asst. tax officer, 1965-69, tax officer, 1969-79, sr. trust officer, 1979-84; owner The Old Looking Glass, antiques; income tax mgr. Sam C. Charlson, Manhattan, Kans., 1955-57. Bd. dirs. Found. of Hope, Boston; mem. Republican Nat. Com., Women's Rep. Club Essex County, Nat. Fedn. Rep. Women. Mem. Fiduciary Tax Assos.,

Mass. Bankers Assn. (vice chmn. taxation com. 1971-72, chmn. 1972-73, tax cons. com. 1975-84), Nat. Assn. Bank Women, Am. Inst. Banking, Nat. Early Am. Glass Club, North Shore Antique Assn., Soc. Preservation New Eng. Antiquities, Friends of Sandwich Mus., Woman 76 (Boston organizing com.), Soc. Jesus in New Eng. (liaison com. 1974-75, exec. com. 1975-76), Mus. Fine Arts, Bostonian Soc., Victorian Soc., Essex Inst., Peabody Mus., Jones Gallery Glass and Ceramics. Home: 8 Laurel Rd Lynnfield MA 01940

JOSEPH, GERI MACK, journalist, former ambassador to The Netherlands, institute administrator; b. St. Paul, June 19, 1923; d. Samuel S. and Edith E. Mack; B.A. magna cum laude, U. Minn., 1946; m. Burton M. Joseph, Apr. 2, 1953; children—Shelley Joseph Kordell, I. Scott, Jonathan. LL.D. (hon.), Bates Coll., 1982. Staff writer for health, edn. and welfare Mpls. Tribune, 1946-53, contbg. editor and columnist, 1972-78; ambassador to Netherlands, The Hague, 1978-81; sr. fellow Hubert H. Humphrey Inst. Pub. Affairs, U. Minn., 1984—; dir. Honeywell, George A. Hormel Co.; mem. adv. council NIMH, 1962-67; mem. adv. bd. Rutgers U. Center Am. Women and Politics, 1970-75; mem. vis. com. dept. govt. Harvard U., 1973-78; mem. adv. com. Women's Equity Action League, 1975-80; mem. Pres. Kennedy's Com. on Youth Employment, 1962-63; mem. Pres. Johnson's Commn. on Income Maintenance Programs, 1967-69; mem. task panel on public attitudes of media Pres.'s Commn. on Mental Health, 1977-78. State chairwoman Minn. Democratic-Farmer-Labor Party, 1958-60, nat. committeewoman, 1960-72; del. Dem. Nat. Conv., 1960, 64, 68, mem. exec. com. Dem. Nat. Com., 1960-71; vice-chmn. United Democrats for Humphrey, 1968; vice chmn., dir. women's activities Dem. Nat. Com., 1968-70; mem. Dem. Policy Council, 1969-71; Pres. Nat. Assn. Mental Health, 1968-69; bd. dirs. U. Minn. Found., 1973-78, Carleton Coll., 1975—, Freedom House, 1985—. Recipient Disting. Service award Minn. Jr. C. of C., 1952, Sigma Delta Chi award, 1952, award for writing Am. Newspaper Guild, 1947, 48, 49, 50, 51, Outstanding Achievement award U. Minn., 1974; award for excellence Journalism Alumni Soc. U. Minn., 1985. Mem. U. Minn. Alumni Assn. (dir. 1971-75).

JOSEPH, JUDITH ROSE, editor; b. Newark, Sept. 18, 1948; d. Siegmund and Yolanda (Klein) J.; B.A. with honors, N.Y.U., 1970; M.A., U. Va., 1973; m. Alan M. de Vries, June 1982; 1 child, Elizabeth Martha. Sales rep. Prentice-Hall Pub., Inc., 1973-75; pub. social sci. and humanities texts D. Van Nostrand Co., Inc., N.Y.C., 1975-79, v.p., publs. dir., 1979-81; sr. editor vocat. and tech. texts John Wiley & Sons, Inc., N.Y.C., 1981—. Recipient Cert. of Honor, Offender Aid and Restoration Charlottesville, Va., 1973. Mem. Am. Assn. Pub., Nat. Assn. Female Execs., NOW. Office: 605 3d Ave New York NY 10158

JOSEPH, MARGARET FONES, broadcast journalist, editor, educator; b. Des Moines, Oct. 20, 1945; d. Welzie Harte and Myrtilla (Daniels) Fones; m. Hyman Joseph, July 28, 1967 (div. 1976); 1 child, Daniel Harte; m. Barrie Zimmerman, Aug. 13, 1978. B.A., U. Iowa, 1966. Editorial asst. Am. Coll. Testing, Iowa City, Iowa, 1967-68; pub. affairs dir. KRNA Radio Sta., Iowa City, 1974-75, newscaster, reporter WTTS/WGTC Radio Sta., Bloomington, Ind., 1975-76; news dir., pub. affairs producer WFIU Radio Sta. Ind. U., Bloomington, 1976—; lectr. journalism Ind. U., 1981, lectr. telecommunications, 1983; producer and instr. Gifted Talented Workshop, 1982. Producer, writer, narrator, copy editor of various radio documentaries. Chpt. v.p. Hadassah, Iowa City, 1974-75; publicity chmn. UN Assn., Iowa City, 1972, Community Theater, Iowa City, 1968. Recipient Best News Documentary Ind. AP Broadcasters Assn., 1985. Mem. Bloomington Press Club (v.p. 1984-86, bd. dirs. 1983-84, sec. 1981-82). Mem. Christian Ch. Avocations: counseling journalism students; cooking; reading. Home: 331 W Sample Rd Bloomington IN 47401 Office: WFIU Radio Ind U Radio-TV Bldg Bloomington IN 47405

JOSEPH, MARY TERRELL, lawyer; b. Seymour, Ind., Sept. 30, 1944; d. John Searcy and Alexandrine (Querbes) Terrell; m. Cheney Cleveland Joseph, Jr., Dec. 21, 1967; children—John Terrell, Allen Fort. B.A., Hollins Coll., 1966; J.D., La. State U., 1970. Bar: La. 1970. Ptnr. firm Joseph & Joseph, Baton Rouge, 1970-78; assoc. firm Sanders, Downing, Kean & Cazedessus, Baton Rouge, 1978-83; ptnr. firm Rubin, Curry, Colvin & Joseph, P.L.C., Baton Rouge, 1983—; dir. Baton Rouge Gallery, Inc., La. State U. Union Art Gallery. Bd. dirs. dePaul Dyslexia Assn., 1980-82, United Way Services Agy., 1986—; mem. orgn. com. Stop Rape Crisis Ctr., Baton Rouge, 1977-79. Mem. ABA, Baton Rouge Bar Assn., Baton Rouge Assn. Women Attys., La. Bar Assn. Democrat. Episcopalian. Club: Baton Rouge Jr. League (past dir.). Home: 4859 Tulane Dr Baton Rouge LA 70808 Office: Rubin Curry Colvin & Joseph One American Pl Suite 1400 Baton Rouge LA 70825

JOSHI, SMITA KEDARNATH, physician, pathologist; b. Ahmedabad, India, Mar. 11, 1945, came to U.S., 1969, naturalized, 1978; d. Ramanlal Narotamdas and Bhanumati Ramanlal (Mahadevia) Magiawala; M.B., B.S., B.J. Med. Coll., 1975. Resident in pathology Mt. Carmel Mercy Hosp., Detroit, 1971-75; assoc. pathologist Samaritan Health Ctr., Detroit, 1976—. Diplomate Am. Bd. Pathology. Mem. Coll. Am. Pathologists, Am. Soc. Clin. Pathologists, Mich. Soc. Pathologists, Mich. Soc. Cytology, South Central Soc. Microbiology, Am. Soc. Cytology, Internat. Soc. Pathologists. Office: 3151 Walnut Lake Rd West Bloomfield MI 48033

JOSLIN, JEANNE EMILY, registered nurse; b. Rockville Centre, N.Y., Dec. 26, 1953; d. George John and Doris Edythe (Stearns) Lavelle; m. Wayne Leo Joslin, Sept. 16, 1978. A.A. in Nursing, Suffolk County Community Coll., 1975; B.S. in Nursing, Plattsburgh State U. Coll., 1977. R.N. Home health care nurse Homemakers Upjohn, Hauppauge, N.Y., 1976-77; staff nurse critical care St. Charles Hosp., Port Jefferson, N.Y., 1977; staff nurse evening charge nurse Wilford Hall USAF Med. Ctr., San Antonio, Tex., 1977-81; USAFR flight nurse 32d Aero Med. Evacuation Group, San Antonio, 1981-82; staff nurse Riverside Community Hosp. Med. Ctr., Calif., 1982—; USAFR flight nurse, charge nurse 68th Aero Med. Evacuation Squadron Norton AFB, San Bernardino, Calif., 1982—; cardio pulmonary resuscitation instr. Am. Heart Assn., San Antonio, 1979-82; guest lectr. 9th Aero Med. Evacuation Squadron, Philippines, 1985. Co-author patient edn. pamphlet on leukemia, 1978. Community fundraiser Am. Heart Assn., Moreno Valley, Calif., 1983, 84, Arthritis Found., Moreno Valley, 1983, 84; health asst. nurse Community Health Fair Riverside Community Hosp., 1985; co-chmn. Vicariate Adv. Bd. Deacons and Wives, Diocese of San Bernardino, 1985. Served to capt. USAF, 1977-81. Named Outstanding Flight Nurse of Quarter 68th Aero Med. Evacuation Squadron, 1983. Pres. Catholic Women of the Chapel March AFB Chapel, Riverside, 1982-83, sec. 1983-84. Mem. Aerospace Med. Assn., Res. Officers Assn., Am. Surgeons of U.S. Roman Catholic. Avocations: reading; skiing; watersports; music. Home: 11142 Fernview Pl Sunnymead CA 92388

JOY, CARLA MARIE, educator; b. Denver, Sept. 5, 1945; d. Carl P. and Theresa M. (Lotito) J. A.B. cum laude, Loretto Heights Coll., 1967; M.A. (Ford Found. fellow), U. Denver, 1969, postgrad., 1984—. Instr. history Community Coll. Denver; prof. history Red Rocks Community Coll., Golden, Colo., 1970—; adj. prof. Loretto Heights Coll.; mem. adv. panel Colo. Endowment Humanities; resource person Jefferson County Sch. System; cons. for innovative ednl. programs; reviewer fed. grants. Contbr. articles to profl. publs. Instr. vocat. edn. Mile High United Way, Jefferson County, 1975. Cert. in vocat. edn. Colo. State Bd. Community Colls. and Occupational Edn. Recipient cert. of appreciation Kiwanis Club, 1981; Master Tchr. award U. Tex. at Austin, 1982. Mem. NEA, Am. Hist. Assn., Nat. Council for Social Studies, Nat. Geog. Soc., Inst. Early Am. History and Culture, Colo. Council for Social Studies, Community Coll. Humanities Assn., Orgn. Am. Historians, Colo. Hist. Soc., Colo. Edn. Assn., Loretto Heights Coll. Alumni Assn. (pres's club), U. Denver Alumni Assn., Phi Alpha Theta. Designer individualized instructional programs for world civilization, 1972—. Home: 1849 S Lee St Apt D Lakewood CO 80226 Office: 12600 W 6th Ave Golden CO 80401

JOY, LA VERNE GOUGH, club woman; b. Campbell County, Va., Jan. 27, 1908; d. Glover Lafayette and Nancy Catharine (Bowling) Gough; m. Russell Samuel Joy, Oct. 27, 1929 (dec. Feb. 1971); 1 child, Betty Ann Cajigas. Tchrs. cert. Lynchburg Coll., 1929; student U. Va., summer 1928, Strayer Bus. Coll., 1941. Prin., tchr. Campbell County pub. schs., 1929-31, substitute tchr., 1931-41; various statis. and adminstrv. positions CIA, Washington, 1941-69. Recipient Outstanding Service award CIA, 1969; Pioneer Club plaque Lynchburg Coll., 1981; Bible Lands and Jerusalem study and tour awards Mayor of Jerusalem and W.F. Wagner, Bapt. minister, 1978-79. Mem. DAR (chpt. regent 1973-77, state treas. Va. 1979-82, Outstanding Achievement award 1983), Daus. Colonial Wars (state treas. Va. 1980—), Daus. Am. Colonists (state treas. D.C. 1982-85), Daus. Colonial Dames XVII Centruy (chpt. treas. 1983-85). Republican. Episcopalian. Home: 3886 Tusico Pl Fairfax VA 22030

JOYCE, BERNITA ANNE, U.S. Dept. Interior adminstr.; b. Omaha, Aug. 11, 1927; d. Albert A. and Margaret C. Joyce; B.A., Duchesne Coll.; M.B.A., U. Santa Clara, 1968, Ph.D., 1974; m. Kenneth B. Lucas, Aug. 2, 1975. Adminstr., Soc. of Sacred Heart, Menlo Park, Calif. and Seattle, 1957-71, regional adminstr., San Francisco, 1969-71; with Wolfe & Co., C.P.A.s, Washington, 1971-72; fin. dir. Nat. Forest Products Assn., Washington, 1972-74; budget fiscal officer ICC, Washington, 1974-77, Office Mgmt. and Budget, 1977-80; asst. dir. mgmt. services Bur. Mines, Dept. Interior, 1980-85, asst. dir. Office Policy Analysis, 1985—. Mem. Am. Inst. C.P.A.s, Sr. Execs. Assn., AAUW, Beta Gamma Sigma. Home: 6001 Bradley Blvd Bethesda MD 20817

JOYCE, FLORENCE V. MIENERT (MRS. GEORGE T. JOYCE), civic worker; b. Fosston, Minn., Feb. 13, 1923; d. William P. A. and Clara (Lindfors) Mienert; R.N., Ancker Hosp. Sch. Nursing, St. Paul, 1944; student U. Minn., 1944-45; m. George T. Joyce, Aug. 8, 1946; children—Roberta Eileen, Elizabeth Anne. Bd. dirs. N. Central Iowa chpt. ARC, 1960-66, 67-73, nursing services chmn., 1967-75; pres. Vols. Service League, St. Joseph Mercy Hosp., Mason City, Iowa, 1959-61; leader Girl Scouts U.S.A., 1948-66; bd. dirs. YWCA, 1963-66, Community Achievement award, 1979; precinct chmn. Cerro Gordo County Republican Central Com., 1971-82, co-chmn., 1984—, mem. fund raising com. Hospice of Cerro Gordo, Mason City, Iowa, 1982—. Mem. Am. Nurses Assn., Iowa Nurses Assn., Iowa Dist. 10 Nurses Assn. (dir. 1981-84), Nat. Trust for Historic Preservation, Cerro Gordo County Med. Aux., Ancker (Hosp.) Alumni Assn., Charles H. MacNider Art Guild (pres. 1972-73, mems. council 1973-80). Club: Mason City Womans (dir. 1965-75, pres. 1969-70). Roman Catholic. Home: 259 N Crescent Dr Mason City IA 50401

JOYCE, JOAN MARIE, nursing educator; b. Scranton, Pa., Aug. 17, 1929; d. William G. and Ann Rita (FLaherty) O'Malley; m. Edward R. Joyce, Dec. 30, 1950; children—Patricia, Edward, Matthew, Michael. Student Marywood Coll., 1968-69; R.N., Mercy Hosp. Sch. Nursing, Scranton, Pa., 1950; B.S. magna cum laude, U. Rochester, 1972; M.A. with distinction, U. South Fla., 1973, M.S.N. with distinction, 1986; Ed.D., Nova U., 1978. Head nurse Good Samaritan Hosp., Lebanon, Pa., 1950-53; charge nurse Mercy Hosp., Scranton, Pa., 1953-67; faculty instr., hosp. supr. St. Mary's Hosp., Rochester, N.Y., 1968-69, staff devel. coordinator/asst. dir. nursing, 1969-72; dept. chmn. nursing edn. Hillsborough Community Coll., Tampa, Fla., 1974-81, prof. nursing, 1982—; chmn. Inter-Agy. Inservice Group, Rochester, N.Y., 1970-71; vice-chmn. Inservice Program Planning Com., 1968-71; chmn. Hosp. Policy and Procedure Com., 1970; mem. Nursing Research and Devel. Com., 1971; mem. Deans and Dirs. Nursing Programs in State Fla., 1974-82; mem. So. Regional Edn. Bd., Council Collegial Nursing, 1974—; mem. ad hoc nurse edn. subcom. State Fla. Dept. Edn., 1975-82; chmn. equal access/equal opportunity com., Plant City campus Hillsborough Community Coll., 1977-79. Trustee to presdl. search com. Hillsborough Community Coll., 1983; vol. ARC. Author: Critical Care Nursing Handbook, 1983. Recipient Plaque, Nursing Educator's Assn. Tampa, 1978; Kellogg fellow, 1986. Mem. Am. Nurses Assn., Nat. League Nursing, Fla. Nurses Assn. (conv. del. 1983, mem. continuing edn. com. state level 1983-84, chmn. legis. com. 1984-85), Fla. League Nursing, Nursing Edn. Assn. Tampa, Hillsborough Vocat. Assn., Phi Kappa Phi, Sigma Theta Tau. Democrat. Roman Catholic. Club: Apollo Beach (Fla.) Woman's. Home: 6305 Balboa Ln Apollo Beach FL 33570 Office: Hillsborough Community Coll PO Box 30030 Tampa FL 33622

JOYCE, MARILYN SCHMIDT, training company executive; b. Covington, Ky., Sept. 3, 1942; d. Robert Andrew and Rita Marie (Stadtmiller) S.; m. Clayton Robert Joyce, Nov. 29, 1975; stepchildren—David Joyce, Kathryn Joyce Keehn, Robert Joyce. B.A., Thomas More Coll., 1964; M.Ed., Xavier U., 1968. Tchr., Colerain High Sch., Cin., 1964-68; tchr. N.E. High Sch., Ft. Lauderdale, Fla., 1968-69; chmn. dept. curriculum devel. Henderson High Sch., Atlanta, 1969-75; trainer, mgr. URS Corp., Seattle, 1977-80; founder, pres. Joyce Inst., Seattle, 1981—; Dataspan cons. GTE, 1983—, Boeing Co., Seattle, 1981—, Aetna Life & Casualty, 1983—, speaker Human Factors Soc., 1984. Editor tng. course: Dataspan, 1981. Co-author tng. manual: Pro-Read, 1972. Mem. Human Factors Soc., Am. Soc. Tng. and Devel., NEA, C. of C. Republican. Mem. Christian Ch. Clubs: Rainier, Columbia Tower. Home: 2220 40th Ave E Seattle WA 98112

JOYCE, PAMELA ANN, rehabilitation consulting firm executive; b. Dallas, May 21, 1949; d. Ernest LeRoy and Mary Rebecca (Niccolls) Fritchman; m. John Patrick Joyce, Apr. 5, 1970 (div. Oct. 1984). A.A., Mt. San Antonio Coll., Walnut, Calif., 1969; B.A., Calif. State Poly. U., 1972. Adminstrv. asst. Hazel Pearson Handicrafts, Temple City, Calif., 1972-73; benefits counselor State Compensation Ins. Fund, Arcadia, Calif., 1973-75, vocat. rehab. counselor, 1975-76; rehab. cons. State of Calif. Div. Indsl. Accidents, Pomona, Calif., 1976-78; rehab. cons., v.p. D.S. Assocs. Rehab. Cons., Burbank, Calif., 1978—. Mem. Calif. Assn. Rehab. Profls. (treas. 1983-84), Nat. Rehab. Assn. (bd. dirs. So. Calif. chpt. 1977-82), So. Counties Rehab. Exchange, Nat. Assn. Rehab. Profls. in Pvt. Sector (legis. com. Calif. chpt. 1986), City of Burbank C. of C. Avocations: travel; cruising; Americana collecting; penquin collecting; organist. Home: 212 W San Luis Rey Dr San Dimas CA 91773 Office: D S Assocs Rehab Cons 175 E Olive Ave Suite 212 Burbank CA 91502

JOYCE, SUE, corporate executive; b. Carthage, Mo., Sept. 4, 1946; d. Joseph J. Sloniker and Norma J. (Greiner) Sloniker Depue; m. John Joyce, Sept. 2, 1975 (div.). B.A., Ottawa U. Data processing mgr. City of Kansas City (Mo.), 1965-69; data processing mgr. Rupert Mfg. Co., Blue Springs, Mo., 1968-74, controller, 1974-78; account mgr. McMullen & Co., C.P.A.s, Kansas City, Mo., 1978-81; pres. Collet Ventures, Inc., Kansas City, 1981—; pres., chmn. of bd. Joyce & Assocs., Inc., Kansas City, 1981—; dir. Westport Bank, Kansas City, Omnipure, Inc., Houston, Gereatric Resources Ctr., Kansas City. Pres. Central Exchange, Kansas City, 1984; bd. dirs. Coro Found., Kansas City, 1983-84, Westport Tomorrow, Kansas City, 1984. Recipient Woman of Yr. award Savvy mag., 1984, Central Exchange, 1984. Mem. Com. of 200, Young Pres. Orgn., Nat. Alliance (dir. 1983-85). Republican. Club: Leawood. Office: Collet Ventures Inc 4141 Pennsylvania Kansas City MO 64111

JOYNER, ELIZABETH PRICE, public health administrator; b. Norfolk, Va., Dec. 22, 1946; d. James Gilbert and Ruth Hamilton (Green) P.; m. David Charles Joyner, June 7, 1969; children—Elisabeth, Stephanie, David. B.S. in Instl. Mgmt., James Madison U., 1968; M.P.H., U. N.C., 1980. Exec. dir. Dairy Council of Shenandoah Valley, Staunton, Va., 1968-70; nutritionist Roanoke-Chowan Hosp., Ahoskie, N.C., 1974-80; health dir. Dept. Health Bertie County, Windsor, N.C., 1980—; adj. assoc. prof. East Carolina U., Greenville, N.C., 1983—. Charter pres. Am. Diabetes Assn., Ahoskie, 1978-79; bd. dirs. Roanoke-Chowan Hospice, Inc., 1981—, pres., 1984—. Named Outstanding Health Dir. in N.C., N.C. Assn. County Commrs., 1985. Mem. N.C. Assn. Local Health Dirs. (pres. 1986), N.C. Pub. Health Assn. (chmn. awards 1982—), Eastern Carolina Health Systems Agy. (vice chmn. 1984, sec., 1983, 85), N.C. Assn. Home Care, James Madison U. Alumni Assn. (pres. 1970-71). Episcopalian. Office: Bertie County Health Dept Barringer St PO Box 586 Windsor NC 27983

JOYNER, SHERYL DIANNE, management consultant, social worker; b. Indpls., Dec. 17, 1956; d. John Erwin and Joyce Nadine (Sterling) Joyner. B.A., St. Mary's Coll., Notre Dame, Ind., 1977; M.S.W., Howard U., 1980. Tech. info. specialist HHS, Washington, 1979; mgmt. cons. Walter Reed Army Med. Ctr., Washington, 1979-80; asst. mgr. River Park Mut. Homes, Inc., Washington, 1980-81; project mgr. Triton Corp., Washington, 1981-83, dir., 1983; mgr. Maxima Corp., Bethesda, Md., 1983-85, asst. dir., 1985—; lectr. U. D.C., 1980; speaker Howard U., Washington, 1982; tech. adviser Nat. Med. Assn., Washington, 1982—, Family of the Future, Cairo, Egypt, 1983, Nat. Hwy. Traffic Safety Adminstrn., 1983. Author (with others) handbook Pre- and Post-Marital Chaplain Ministry, 1983. Tutor Neighborhood Study, South Bend, Ind., 1977; coordinator Southeast Group Ministry, Washington, 1979; campaign vol. John Glenn for Pres., Washington, 1983. Corp. rep. Am. Def. Preparedness Assn. Mem. Assn. Black Social Workers (2d v.p. Howard U. chpt. 1978-79), Am. Mgmt. Assn., Am. Soc. Tng. and Devel., Nat. Assn. Female Execs., Howard U. Alumni Assn., St. Mary's Alumni Club. Democrat. Roman Catholic. Office: Maxima Corp 2101 E Jefferson St at Exec Blvd Rockville MD 20852

JOYNER, SUZANNE DIMASCIO, pharmaceutical company executive, marketing consultant; b. Phila., Dec. 2, 1942; d. Placido L. and Lillian G. (Smith) Mosca; m. Richard DiMascio, Dec. 26, 1963 (div. Nov. 1976); children—Christopher, Jeffrey; m. James H. Joyner III, Jan. 1, 1980; children—James, Gordon, Christopher, Richard, Jeffrey. R.N. diploma, Chestnut Hill Hosp., Phila., 1963; nurse specialist in gerontology, Am. Nurses Assn., 1978. Dir. nursing North Pa. Convalescent Home, Lansdale, Pa., 1976-78; clin. research assoc. Pharmacia, Piscataway, N.J., 1978-80, product mgr., 1980-85, sr. product mgr., 1985-86, group product dir., 1986—; cons. nursing, 1977-79; cons. Thane Assocs., 1983-86. Author man.: Debrisan for Wound Care, 1977. Republican. Roman Catholic. Avocations: walking; swimming; aerobics. Home: 26 Solebury Mountain Rd New Hope PA 18938 Office: Pharmacia Piscataway NJ 08854

JOYNER, SYLVIA PETTIS, fundraiser; b. Galveston, Tex., Sept. 12, 1946; d. Louis James Pettis and Florence Gloria Lawton Cody; B.A., Tuskegee Inst., 1968; 1 son, Michael Pettis. Social service advisor Prichard (Ala.) Housing Authority, 1973-74; community rep. McDonald's of Mobile (Ala.), 1974-76; nat. VISTA worker, VISTA Spl. Project, Fedn. So. Coops., Epes, Ala., 1978; area devel. dir. United Negro Coll. Fund, Inc., Birmingham, Ala., 1978—. Bd. dirs. Vol. and Info. Center, 1980—, Birmingham Creative Dance Co., YWCA, Birmingham Festival of Arts; mem. Leadership Birmingham. Mem. Ala. Soc. Fund Raising Execs. (exec. com. 1980—, Outstanding Fundraiser award 1981), Urban League, NAACP, Nat. Assn. Young Children, Nat. Soc. Fundraisers, Alpha Kappa Alpha (Omicron Omega chpt.). Office: 1728 3rd Ave N Birmingham AL 35203

JUANPERE, NIEVES PAZO, legislative assistant; b. Havana, Cuba, Aug. 5, 1955; came to U.S., 1963, naturalized, 1973; d. Raul Heriberto and Evangelina (Rodriguez) Pazo; m. Pedro A. Juanpere, June 27, 1981; 1 child, Peter Andrew. Grad. Washington Sch. Secs., 1975. Sec., Am. Pharm. Soc., Washington, 1975; sec. to Congressman Rosenthal, Washington, 1976; leg. asst. to Congressman Tom Foley, Washington, 1976—; ptnr. Design Assocs., 1982-85; treas. Intec Group, Inc., Burke, Va., 1984—. Roman Catholic. Club: Concord (N. VA.) (pres. 1974). Avocations: Photography; gardening. Home: 10137 Walnut Wood Ct Burke VA 22015 Office: Congressman Thomas S Foley Room 1201 LHOB Washington DC 20515

JUBINSKY, LINDA LEE, hospital administrator; b. Scranton, Pa., July 22, 1957; d. George and Rosemary Ann (Guerrerri) J. B.S. in Health Planning and Adminstrn., Pa. State U., 1979; M.B.A. candidate U. Houston. Mgmt. trainee Advanced Health Systems, Irvine, Calif., 1979-80; mgr. Med. Adminstrn. Co., Denver, 1980-81; asst. adminstr. Raleigh Hills Hosp., Houston, 1981-82, Dallas, 1982, adminstr., Las Vegas, Nev., 1982-83, Houston, 1983—. Active Women's Resource Ctr., State College, Pa., 1976-79. Ike Gilbert scholar, 1979. Mem. Greater Houston Hosp. Council, Young Hosp. Adminstrs. Assn., Am. Coll. Hosp. Adminstrs., Am. Hosp. Assn., Tex. Hosp. Assn., Psychiat. Hosp. Adminstrs., Forum. Club: Health Planning and Adminstrn. (Pa. State). Office: Raleigh Hills Hosp 6160 S Loop E Houston TX 77087

JUDAY, CYNTHIA ELAINE, veterinarian, microbiologist; b. New Castle, Ind., Sept. 18, 1946; d. Robert Leon and Ora Isabelle (Southwood) Cable; m. Larry Eldon Juday, June 2, 1968. B.S. in Biology with highest distinction, Purdue U., West Lafayette, Ind., 1968; B.S., D.V.M. summa cum laude Tex. A&M U., College Station, 1980; postgrad. in immunology, U. Tex.-San Antonio, 1975-76. Lic. veterinarian, Tex., Oreg. Asst. microbiologist Mesa Luth. Hosp. (Ariz.), 1968-69; quality control dir. Jimenez Foods, Inc., San Antonio, 1975; research technician U. Tex. Med. Sch., San Antonio, 1975-76; veterinarian Travis Country Vet. Hosp., Austin, Tex., 1980-81, Lake Rd. Vet. Clinic, Killeen, Tex., 1981-83; veterinarian, owner Rose City Vet. Hosp., Portland, 1983—, also dir.; speaker in field. Mem. Am. Bus. Womens Assn., North Central Tex. Vet. Med. Assn. (project dir. 1981-82), AVMA, Tex. Vet. Med. Assn., Oreg. Vet. Med. Assn., Am. Assn. Feline Practioners (recipient Feline award 1980), Am. Animal Hosp. Assn. Clubs: Officers Wives; Book (Valdosta, Ga.); Humane Soc. (Killeen). Home: 4353 SW Stephenson St Portland OR 97219 Office: Rose City Vet Hosp 809 SE Powell Blvd Portland OR 97202

JUDD, DOROTHY HEIPLE, educator; b. Oakwood, Ill., May 27, 1922; d. Eldridge Winfield and Mary Luciel (Oliphant) Heiple; B.A., Ind. U., 1944; M.Ed., U. Toledo, 1971; Ed.S., Troy State U., 1976; Ed.D., No. Ill. U., 1981; m. Robert Carpenter Judd, Sept. 19, 1964; children by previous marriage—Patricia Ann Konkoly, Catherine Rafferty, Deborah Brown, Nancy Lee Arrington; stepchildren—Dianna Kay Judd Carlisi, Nancy Carol Judd Wilber, Linda Judd Marinaccio Pucci. Head lang. arts dept. Eisenhower Jr. High Sch., Darien, Ill., 1961-70; instr. devel. edn. Owens Tech. Coll., Perrysburg, Ohio, 1971-73; instr. edn. Troy State U., Montgomery, Ala., also right-to-read coordinator State of Ala., 1975-76; core dept. chmn. Community Consol. Sch. Dist. 15, Palatine, Ill., 1977-79; instr. curriculum and instrn. No. Ill. U., 1979-84; pres. R.C. Judd & Assocs., Bloomingdale, Ill., 1980—; asst. prof. edn. Southeastern La. U., Hammond, 1984—. Mem. Assn. Ednl. Data Systems, Assn. Supervision and Curriculum Devel., Assn. Tchr. Edn., Internat. Council Computers in Edn., Internat. Reading Assn., Nat. Council Social Studies, Nat. Council Tchrs. of English, Phi Delta Kappa, Pi Lambda Theta. Author: Mastering the Micro, 1984; contbg. editor Electronic Edn. mag.; mem. editorial bd. Computers, Reading and Lang. Arts jour.; contbr. articles to profl. jours. Home: 111 Bellewood Dr Hammond LA 70401 Office: 218 Teacher Edn Ctr Southeastern La Univ Hammond LA 70402

JUDD, PATRICIA HOFFMAN, social worker; b. Pitts., June 22, 1946; d. Joseph Andrew and Irene Patricia (Bednar) Hoffman; m. Lewis Lund Judd, Jan. 26, 1974. B.A., Marquette U., 1968; M.S.W., San Diego State U., 1970; doctoral candidate Calif. Sch. Profl. Psychology, 1983—. Dir. treatment services DEFY, Health Care Agy. of San Diego County, San Diego, 1973-75; coordinator emergency psychiat. services U. Calif. Med. Ctr., San Diego, 1975-77, mem. attending staff, 1975—; clin. coordinator crisis and brief treatment service Gifford Mental Health Clinic, U. Calif.-San Diego, 1975-79, coordinator clin. services, 1979-82, asst. dir., 1983—; clin. instr. dept. psychiatry U. Calif.-San Diego Sch. Medicine, 1976—; field instr. Sch. Social Work, San Diego State U., 1970—, lectr., 1978-80; pvt. practice psychotherapy, San Diego, 1979—. Mem. Nat. Assn. Social Workers, Acad. Cert. Social Workers, Soc. Clin. Social Workers. Office: 3427 4th Ave San Diego CA 92103

JUDELL, CYNTHIA N., craft company executive; b. N.Y.C., Mar. 23, 1924; d. Luma L. and Stella E. (Robins) Kolburne; m. Samuel Judell, Oct. 30, 1949; children—Joy C., Neil H.K. B.S.E.E., Antioch Coll., Yellow Springs, Ohio, 1945; M.A., Columbia U., 1948. Cert. secondary tchr. Engr., Jet Propulsion Lab., Pasadena, Calif., 1946-47; tchr. math., sci. Leonard Sch. for Girls, N.Y.C., 1948-49; substitute tchr. Bd. Edn., Ridgefield, Conn., 1964-67; part-time tchr. Bd. Edn., Brookfield, Conn., 1967-73; ptnr. T W M Enterprises, Wilton, Conn., 1976—. Dep. registrar of voters Town of Wilton, 1977—; budget chair, treas., League of Women Voters of Conn., Hamden, 1978—; elected mem. Bd. of Tax Review, Wilton, 1980—; treas. Town Assn., Inc., Wilton, 1980-84. Recipient Intergroup scholar Columbia U., 1948. Mem. Conn. Soc. Women Engrs. (treas. 1971-72). Office: T W M Enterprises PO Box 266 Wilton CT 06897

JUDGE, CAROLYN ELIZABETH, pharmacist; b. Houston, Oct. 30, 1953; d. Charlie Lee and Mary Louise (Sewell) Davis; m. John Allen Judge, June 27, 1981; 1 son, Jonathan Jarrell. B.S., U. Houston, 1979. Lic. pharmacist, Tex. Extern/intern VA Hosp., Houston, 1979; intern Prescription Lab., Houston, 1979; pharmacist/asst. mgr. Sommers Drugs, Houston, 1979-80; pharmacist/mgr. Eckerd Drugs, Houston, 1980—. Campaigner Democratic Party, Houston, 1973; model Ben Shaw Modeling Studio, Houston, 1973-74. Mem. Am. Pharm. Assn., Tex. Pharm. Assn., Harris County Pharm. Assn., Kappa Epsilon, Delta Sigma Theta. Democrat. Roman Catholic. Address: 3213 Binz St Houston TX 77004

JUDGE, JEAN FRANCES, journalist; b. Fall River, Mass., Mar. 18, 1930; d. James Edward and Dolores Veronica (Dunn) J.; B.A. magna cum laude in English Lit., Salve Regina Coll., Newport, R.I., 1951. Mem. staff Fall River Herald News, 1951—, editor woman's page, 1972-80, lifestyle editor, 1980—. Named Woman of Achievement Greater Fall River Bus. and Profl. Women's Club, 1982. Home: 716 Broadway Fall River MA 02724 Office: 207 Pocasset St Fall River MA 02722

JUDGE, MARGARET ANN, nurse, administrator; b. Simpson, Pa., Sept. 3, 1933; d. Grant Edward and Mary E. (Newcombe) Bishop; m. Joseph M. Judge, June 29, 1957; children—Ann E., Joseph, Thomas A., II, Carolyn M., Mary Catherine. Diploma in Nursing St. Joseph Hosp., 1954; B.S. in Pub. Sch. Nursing, Millersville State Coll., 1975; M.S. in Edn., Temple U., 1977; M.S. in Nursing, U. Del., 1984. Registered nurse, Pa., Del. Operating nurse Phila., Gen. Hosp., 1954-55, head nurse operating room, 1955-56; head nurse operating room Bryn Mawr Hosp., Pa., 1956-57; dir. inservice edn. Lancaster Gen. Hosp., Pa., 1974-77, dir. nursing sch., 1977—, v.p. nursing, 1983—. HEW grant, scholar, 1982. Mem. Am. Nursing Soc., Am. Orgn. Nurse Execs., Assembly Hosp. Schs. Nursing, Pa. Soc. Nurse Adminstrs., Operating Room Nurses Assn. (pres. Southeast Pa. 1973-74), Pa. Nurses Assn. (sec. dist. 16 1978-79), MidAtlantic Nurses Assn. (dir. 1982-84), Pa. Hosp. Assn. (governing councilor 1984—). Roman Catholic. Home: 436 Manor View Dr Millersville PA 17551 Office: Lancaster Gen Hosp PO Box 355 Lancaster PA 17551

JUDKINS, DOLORES ZEGAR, librarian; b. Portland, Oreg., Mar. 1, 1948; d. Frank John and Adeline Angela (Konieczny) Zegar; m. David Carl Judkins, Nov. 19, 1977; 1 child, Stephen Daniel. B.A., Portland State U., 1970; M.L.S., U. Oreg., 1973. Librarian, Peace Corps, San Pedro Sula, Honduras, 1973-74, Library Assn. Portland, 1974-77, Suffolk Coop. Library System, Bellport, N.Y., 1978-79, Good Samaritan Hosp., Portland, 1979-80; dental librarian Oreg. Health Scis. U., Portland, 1980—. Contbr. articles to profl. publs. Community organizer VISTA, Scottsbluff, Nebr., 1970-72. Community Coll. Library fellow U. Oreg., 1972. Mem. Med. Library Assn., Oreg. Health Scis. Libraries Assn. (pres. 1982), Oreg. Library Assn. Avocations: reading; sewing; hiking. Office: Oreg Health Scis U Dental Library 611 SW Campus Dr Portland OR 97201

JUDY, NANCY ELIZABETH, county commissioner; b. East Orange, N.J., Dec. 19, 1931; d. Ellsworth Rodman and Mary Ethel (Luppert) Bailey; m. Robert Walter Judy, Nov. 13, 1954; children—Robin Ann, Matthew Rodman. B.A., Pa. State U. Mem. sch. bd. Dallas Ind. Sch. Dist., 1972-76; exec. dir. Dallas County Rep. Party, 1977; county commr. Dallas County Commrs. Ct., 1979—. Chmn. Regional Transp. Council, 1983—, Dallas County Civil Service Commn., 1983—; bd. dirs. Dispute Mediation Service of Dallas County, 1980-85, Dallas Alliance; bd. dirs. Rep. Men's Club of Dallas County; precinct chmn. Dallas County Rep. Party, 1964-76; others. Mem. Dallas Assembly, Women's Council of Dallas Arboretum and Bot. Garden, Dallas Mus. Fine Arts. Roman Catholic. Address: 3346 Mayhew Dr Dallas TX 75228

JUE, BARBARA, government official; b. San Francisco, 1942; d. William and Diana Jue; m. William Bryan Davis. A.A., Peralta Coll., 1964. Periphel computer operator Dept. Def., Oakland, Calif., 1966, computer operator, 1966-74; computer programmer Exec. Br. Govt., analyst, San Francisco, 1974-79, agy. services coordinator, 1979-81, agy. assistance officer, 1981-84; dir. info. systems devel. Mil. Sealift Command, Oakland Calif., 1984—; sec. Intergovtl. Council on Tech. of Info. Processing, 1983-84, v.p., 1985. Avocations: writing; photography; music. Office: Mil Sealift Command Bldg 310-5 Code P81 NSCO Oakland CA 94625-5010

JUKOSKI, MARY ELLEN, educator; b. Massena, N.Y., May 17, 1949; d. Joseph and Helen (Oroszi) Jukoski. A.A., Mater Dei Coll., 1970; B.A. in English and Secondary Edn., Coll. of St. Rose, 1973, M.A. in English, 1979; M.S. in Curriculum Planning and Devel., SUNY, Albany, 1974 Ed.D., Memphis State U., 1983. Tchr. 6th grade Holy Family Sch., Watertown, N.Y., 1970-71; English tutor Albany (N.Y.) City Schs., Teenage Mothers Program, 1972-74; chemistry lab. receptionist Albany Med. Center Hosp., 1973-74; secondary English tchr. Acad. of Holy Names, Albany, 1974-77; asst. dean Center for Statewide Programs, Empire State Coll., Saratoga Springs, N.Y., 1977-80; asst. exec. dean World U., Miami, Fla., 1979-80; grad. asst. Center for Study of Higher Edn., Memphis State U., 1980, program asst. Inst. for Acad. Improvement and Higher Edn. for Adult Mental Health Project, NIMH, 1980-81, assoc. dir., 1981-83; dir. Univ. Without Walls, Loretto Heights Coll., Denver, 1983-85; dean continuing edn. Sacred Heart U., Bridgeport, Conn., 1985—. Mem. Am. Assn. for Higher Edn., AAUW, Denver Art Mus., Denver Botanic Gardens, Denver Mus. Natural History, Kappa Delta Pi, Omicron Delta Kappa, Kappa Gamma Pi. Author: A Study of Selected Accredited Nontraditional Institutions and Programs, 1981-82. Home: 63 Eaton St Bridgeport CT 06604 Office: Sacred Heart U Continuing Edn Office Bridgeport Ct 06604

JULIAN, MICHELE DENISE, research company executive; b. Wilmington, Del., Jan. 23, 1954; d. Stanford and Ida Margaret (Lea) Simpson; m. Raymond Charles Julian, May 27, 1979. B.A., Boston Coll., 1976; M.S. in Mgmt., Lesley Coll., 1984. Personnel asst. Star Market, Cambridge, Mass., 1976-78; personnel adminstr. Charles T. Main Co., Boston, 1978-80; sr. personnel rep. Orion Research Co., Cambridge, 1980-85, personnel mgr., 1985—. Contact person for student alumni relations Boston Coll., Chestnut Hill, Mass., 1983-84. Mem. Internat. Assn. Personnel Women, Am. Soc. Personnel Mgmt., Am. Bus. Women Assn. Democrat. Episcopalian. Office: Orion Research Inc 840 Memorial Dr Cambridge MA 02139

JULIANO, PATRICIA, city official; b. E. Orange, N.J., Dec. 8, 1930; d. John and Mildred (Petoia) Tricoli; A.S., Essex County Coll., 1975; B.A., Rutgers U., 1980; m. Carmen Juliano, May 10, 1952; children—John, Frank, Carmen, Angelo, Kathy, Michael, Joseph. Tchrs. aide Oakwood Ave. Sch., Orange, N.J., 1973-75; mem. Orange City Council, 1976—. Pres., PTA, Orange, 1960-61; v.p. Essex County Council PTA, 1963-65; vol. N.J. Assn. Retarded Children, 1965—; sec. to Parents of Orange PAL, 1962; co-founder Parents' Groups for Exceptional Children, 1975—, Orange Parents of Exceptional Children, 1978; mem. Community Service Council, United Way, 1976-84; lobbyist for better edn. for exceptional children; bd. dirs. Orange Child Devel. Corp., 1976—; mem. Essex County Community Action Bd., 1980—, Orange Planning Bd., 1984—; mem. governing bd. Community Mental Health Center, Region II, 1982—; mem. adv. bd. Women in Support of Essex; County Coll.; mem. Nat. Park Found.; co-ordinator Central Jersey Telephone Bank, Floria for Gov., N.J. Dem. Com., 1981; Orange chmn. Mother's March, March of Dimes Found., 1982. Recipient Outstanding Vol. award Community Services Council of United Way, 1977; Achievement award Essex council N.J. State Civil Service Assn., 1982, Outstanding Alumni award Essex County Coll., 1983. Mem. N.J. League of Municipalities (legis. com. 1980—), N.J. Assn. Elected Women Ofcls. (co-founder 1981, treas. 1982-84), Orange LWV, Am. Mus. Natural History, N.J. Fedn. Dem. Women, Rutgers U. Alumni Assn. Roman Catholic. Home: 390 Tremont Pl Orange NJ 07050 Office: 29 N Day St Orange NJ 07050

JUNG, DORANNE, educator, public relations counsel; b. Los Angeles, June 11, 1948; d. Harry Gordon and Frances (Wong) J.; B.A., Mills Coll., 1970; postgrad. U. Calif.-Berkeley, 1969, Fla. Presbyn. Coll., London, 1970; M.S., Boston U., 1972. Media asst. Young & Rubicam Internat., N.Y.C., 1970; communications coordinator New Eng. Spl. Edn. Instrnl. Materials Center, Boston, 1972-73; media dir./account exec. Harcomm Assocs., Cambridge, Mass., 1973-76; promotion, advt. and public relations mgr. Westinghouse Broadcasting, WBZ Radio, Boston, 1976-79; pres. Corcoran & Doranne, Inc., Cambridge, 1979—; asst. prof. Boston U. Sch. Public Communication, 1980—; producer/dir. video TV and radio shows; cons. Mem. public affairs com. Boston chpt. ARC, 1979—; mem. public relations com. Am. Heart Assn., 1978; mem. corp. com. United Way Mass. Bay, 1979-81; mem. Hale House/Back Bay Aging Concerns Benefit Com., 1981-83; mem. public relations com. Family Service Assn. Greater Boston, 1983—. Recipient award Ohio State Inst. Edn. by Radio/TV award, 1978, Broadcast Promotion Assn., 1978; Clarion award Women in Communications, 1978. Mem. Press Club Boston, Broadcast Promotion Assn., New Eng. Broadcasters Assn., Nat. Assn. TV Program Execs. Presbyterian. Contbg. author: Teaching About Funerals, 1980; author/dir. radio series Fishing and Our Law, 1979-80. Office: 640 Commonwealth Ave Boston MA 02215

JUNG, DORIS, opera singer, voice tchr.; b. Centralia, Ill., Jan. 5, 1924; d. John Jay and May (Middleton) Crittenden; student U. Ill., 1945-46, Manne Coll. Music, 1950, Vienna Acad. Performing Arts, 1954; pvt. voice studies with Julius Cohen, Emma Zador, Luise Helletsgruber, Winifred Cecil; m. Felix Popper, Nov. 3, 1951; 1 son, Richard Dorian. Debut as Vitellia in Mozart's Clemenza di Tito, Zurich Opera, 1955; appeared with Hamburg State Opera, Munich State Opera, Vienna State Opera, Royal Opera Copenhagen, Royal Opera Stockholm; appeared in Marseille, Strasbourg, France, Naples and Catania, Italy, with N.Y.C. Opera, Met. Opera, Washington, Portland, Oreg. and Aspen, Colo; soloist Wagner concert conducted by Leopold Stokowski, 1971; soloist with Syracuse Symphony, 1981; voice tchr.; condr. opera workshop.

JUNGELS, ELEANOR ELIZABETH, county official; b. Aurora, Ill., Jan. 29, 1922; d. Peter William and Marie Anna (Koerfer) J. Grad. high sch., Aurora. Chief clk. bd. of rev. Kane County, Ill., 1938-39, clk.-typist, recorder, 1940-43, supr. tract index, 1943-72, chief dep. recorder, 1952-72, elected recorder, 1972—. Mem. St. Anne's Soc. St. Nicholas Roman Catholic Ch.; bd. dirs. Aurora Hist. Soc., 1972—; rec. sec. Kane County Republican Central Com., 1982-84. Named Woman of Yr. in Professions YWCA, 1984. Mem. Aurora Bus. and Profl. Women (pres. 1985—), Ill. Assn. County Ofcls., Ill. Assn. County Clks. and Recorders (legis. com. 1981—), Clks. and Recorders of No. Ill. (pres. 1979-80, Pres. Plaque), Internat. Assn. County Ofcls., Nat. Assn. County Recorders and Clks., St. Cecilia Evening Music Club (pres. 1954-55). Office: Kane County PO Box 71 Geneva IL 60134

JUNGERS, MARY BLANCHE, educational administrator; b. Grayson, Ky., May 27, 1927; d. Arthur R. and Phebe Edith (Horton) Huff; B.A., Ky. Christian Coll., 1948; B.S. in Edn., Washington U., St. Louis, 1959; M.S. in Edn., So. Ill. U., 1968; Ph.D., St. Louis U., 1972; m. Jack R. Jungers, Jan. 1, 1978; children—Arthur Jordan, Carla Jordan, John Jordan, Jim Jordan. Mem. staff Alton (Ill.) Community Unit Sch. Dist. 11, 1959—, supt., 1964—, prin. Central Jr. High Sch., 1974-75, asst. supt. pupil personnel services, 1976-80, asst. supt. for elementary edn. services, 1980-84, condr. workshops. NEXTEP fellow, 1967-68; Ford Found. grantee, 1978. Mem. Am. Assn. Sch. Adminstrs., Ill. Assn. Sch. Adminstrs., LWV, Lovejoy Meml. Assn., Hon. Order Ky. Cols., Phi Delta Kappa, Pi Lambda Theta, Delta Kappa Gamma. Mem. Christian Ch. Author articles, short stories. Home: 4321 Wedgewood St Alton IL 62002 Office: 1854 E Broadway Alton IL 62002

JUNI, SUSANNAH ROSALYN, video company financial executive, consultant; b. Urbana, Ill., Jan. 18, 1956; d. Elliot and Rachel (Geitheim) J. Student Bennington Coll., 1973-76; B.B.A., Eastern Mich. U., 1980. C.P.A., Mich. Realtor assoc. Realty World, Ann Arbor, Mich., 1977-79; staff auditor Peat, Marwick, Mitchell, Detroit, 1979-82; dir. royalty acctg. CBS/Fox Video, Livonia, Mich., 1982—. Mem. Am. Inst. C.P.A.s, Nat. Assn. Female Execs., Acctg. Aid Soc. Met. Detroit (cons. 1979—), Beta Alpha Psi. Avocations: modern dance; jazz music. Home: 1825 Waltham Dr Ann Arbor MI 48103 Office: CBS/Fox Video 39000 Seven Mile Rd Livonia MI 48152

JUNK, SHALON JEAN, personnel adminstr.; b. Fort Wayne, Ind., Sept. 27, 1945; d. Edwin C. and Jean Opal Ezzelle; m. Richard Ellis Junk, Aug. 22, 1964; children—Richard Edwin, Scott Michael. Sec., Gen. Telephone Co., 1966-72; with Super Market Service, Fort Wayne, Ind., 1974—, personnel mgr., 1975-76, human resource mgr., 1976—. Mem. Am. Soc. Personnel Adminstrn., Am. Bus. Woman's Assn., Ind. Personnel Assn., Ft. Wayne Personnel Assn. (v.p.), Delta Sigma Kappa. Baptist. Home: 2109 Kentucky Ave Fort Wayne IN 46805

JUNKMAN, JACALYN MARIE, physicial education educator; b. Ft. Dodge, Iowa, Nov. 23, 1953; d. Earl Willis and Rose Marie (Krebs) J. B.A., Tarkio Coll. (Mo.), 1977; M.S. in Edn., Baylor U., 1979. Recreation counselor Devereux Found., Victoria, Tex., 1975-78; asst. volleyball and basketball coach Baylor U., Waco, Tex., 1978-79; head women's basketball coach, instr. San Jacinto Coll. N., Houston, 1979—; sponsor Gator Assn., Houston, 1983—. Mem. Tex. Assn. Health, Phys. Edn., Recreation and Dance, Tex. Jr. Coll. Tchrs. Assn., Tex. Assn. Basketball Coaches, Phi Beta Kappa. Democrat. Lutheran. Home: 3700 Watonga #2306 Houston TX 77092 Office: San Jacinto Coll N 5800 Uvalde Houston TX 77049

JURZYKOWSKI, MILENA CHRISTINE, film producer; b. N.Y.C., Sept. 25, 1949; d. Alfred and Milena J.; B.A., Boston U., 1968. Prodn. mgr., editor Nat. Assn. Broadcast Employees and Technicians, N.Y.C., 1973-76, editor, 1976-80; pres., exec. producer Cinetudes Film Prodns., Ltd., N.Y.C., 1976—; founder Atelier Cinema Video Stages and Cinetudes Cable Programming Assocs. Producer feature film No Big Deal, 1983. Mem. N.Y. Women in Communications, Nat. Assn. Broadcast Employees and Technicians, Internat. Indsl. TV Assn., Assn. Ind. Film and Video Makers, Info. Film Producers Am., Soc. Motion Picture and TV Engrs., N.Y. Women in Film. Office: 295 W 4th St New York NY 10014

JUSINO, PATRICIA SULLIVAN, jewelry consultant; b. Cambridge, Mass., Aug. 23, 1949; d. Peter Richard and Carolyn (Eaton) Sullivan; m. Sixto E. Jusino, Jr., July 8, 1972; 1 child, Jessica LaReina. A.S. in Mktg., Bryant & Stratton Jr. Coll., 1969. Buyer, merchandising exec. Markson Bros. Inc., Boston, 1972-83; pres. Gold Cons. Inc., East Braintree, Mass., 1984—, Weymouth Landing Jewelers. Mem. Gemological Inst. Am. Roman Catholic. Club: Braintree Rifle and Pistol. Avocations: theater; travel. Office: Gold Cons Inc 24 Commercial St East Braintree MA 02184

JUST, FAYE JORDAN, antique restoration co. exec.; b. Carthage, Miss., June 6, 1925; d. Neadham Guice and Ethel (Doude) Jordan; student UCLA, 1943-62, U. So. Calif., 1950-52; A.A. in M.E., Pierce Coll., 1965; B.S. in B.A. and Math., U. Calif., Northridge, 1969; m. Virgil Louis Just, May 2, 1970; children—Babetta, Sandra, Audrey. Loftswoman/flying wing Northrope Aircraft, Hawthorne, Calif., 1943-45; with Rockwell Internat., Los Angeles and Canoga Park, Calif., 1947-70, sr. research engr. rocket engines, to 1970; Co-owner Just Marine Engring., 1972-77, Just Enterprises, Ventura, Calif., 1977—. Office: Just Enterprises 2790 Sherwin Ave #10 Ventura CA 93003

JUST, GEMMA R., advt. agy. exec.; b. N.Y.C., Nov. 29, 1921; d. Philip and Brigida (Consolo) Rivoli; B.A., Hunter Coll., N.Y.C., 1943; m. Victor Just, Jan. 29, 1955. Copy group head McCann Erickson, N.Y.C., 1958-62; copy. supr. Morse Internat., N.Y.C., 1962-67; v.p., dir. creative services Deltakos div. J. Walter Thompson, N.Y.C., 1967-75; v.p., copy dir. Sudler & Hennessey, div. Young & Rubicam, N.Y.C., 1975—. Mem. Women of St. Bartholomew's Episcopal Ch., also ch. altar guild. Named Best Writer, Art Dirs. Club N.Y., 1979, Modern Medicine mag., 1980, Young & Rubicam, 1981. Mem. Council Communications Socs., Pharm. Advt. Council, Am. Med. Writers Assn. (exec. com. 1973). Home: 155 E 38th St New York NY 10016 Office: 1633 Broadway New York NY 10019

JUST-COTE, JEANINE, human resource development consultant; b. Wild Rose, Wis., Jan. 16, 1950; d. David Carl and Verona (Bohn) Kneip; m. Bayne Gerald Just, May 5, 1979 (div. Aug. 8, 1983); 1 child, Renee Adelle; m. John Cote, Nov. 7, 1985. Student pub. schs., Medinah, Ill. With customer service dept. Countryside News Agy., Bloomingdale, Ill., 1965-69; distbn. ctr. mgr. White-Houston Mfg. Co., Houston, 1969-74; salesperson Polk Bros., Schaumburg, Ill., 1974-79; regional mgr. sales Sasco Products, Dallas, 1979-83; pres., dir. J. Just & Assocs., Laguna Beach, Calif., 1983—; guest speaker in field. Contbr. articles to profl. jours. Mem. Nat. Assn. Female Execs., Saddleback C. of C. Mem. Ch. of Religious Sci. Avocations: reading; writing; snow skiing; decorating. Home: 384 Pine Crest Laguna Beach CA 92651 Office: J Just & Assocs PO Box 4649 Laguna Beach CA 92651

JUSTICE, DOROTHY DOBBS, food equipment manufacturing company executive; b. Woodstock, Ga., Apr. 13, 1932; d. Eugene Tiller and Bertha (Roe) Dobbs; m. Lester Joseph Justice, June 10, 1950. Student Marsh Bus. Coll., Atlanta, 1948-49. Office mgr. Norris Candy Co., Atlanta, 1964-68; exec. asst. Cornelius Co., Atlanta, 1968-70; v.p. adminstrn. Remarco, Atlanta, 1970-73; v.p. Refresco Internat., Atlanta, 1973-82, pres., chief exec. officer, 1982—; dir. Modular Engring. Corp., Atlanta. Pres. Mountain Park Homeowners Assn., Stone Mountain, Ga., 1984—. Mem. Nat. Assn. Food Equipment Mfrs. Democrat. Baptist. Clubs: Big Canoe Golf and Tennis (Ga.); Stone Mountain Garden, Stone Mountain Women's. Avocations: interior decorating; flower arranging. Home: 1524 Carlton Ave Stone Mountain GA 30087 Office: Refresco Internat Corp PO Box 1748 Stone Mountain GA 30086

JUSTICE, GLORIA JANE SMITH, public relations executive; b. Detroit, Mar. 14, 1951; d. H. James and Irene Margaret (Lulenski) Smith; m. Bruce Lloyd Justice, June 11, 1982; 1 child, Edith Irene. B.A. in Journalism, U. Mich., 1973. Mem. info. task force, Charter Revision, Commn., City of Detroit, 1972; editor Commn. on Profl. and Hosp. Activities, Ann Arbor, Mich., 1973-77; pub. relations dir. Port Huron Hosp. (Mich.), 1977-84; communications dir. Nat. Renal Adminstrs. Assn., 1985—; communication WeDezyn, 1985—. Bd. dirs. Vis. Nurse Assn. of St. Clair County, 1982, Mich. Waterways council Girl Scouts U.S., 1985—; mem. regional council Lung Assn. Mich., 1978-79. Mem. Am. Soc. Hosp. Pub. Relations (cert.), Mich. Assn. Hosp. Pub. Relations (dir. 1981—), Southeastern Mich. Hosp. Pub. Relations Assn. (dir. 1982-83), Women in Communications. Club: Quotz Internat. Editor: Your Magazine, 1975. Office: 1115 Rawlins St PO Box 129 Port Huron MI 48061

JUSTICE, SUSANNE DOROTHY, medical administrator; b. Flushing, N.Y., Aug. 28, 1942; d. Edward H. and Dorothy E. (Scholl) Lane; children—Edward P., Jennifer L. Diploma Jackson Meml. Hosp. Sch. Nursing, 1963. R.N., Fla. Group nurse Mt. Saini Hosp., Miami Beach, Fla., 1963-66; part-time group nurse, 1967-72; head nurse Jackson Meml. Hosp., Miami, 1966-67; hosp. coordinator, head coordinator Fla. Home Health Services, Miami, 1972-73; hosp. coordinator, assoc. dir. nursing Unicare, Inc., Miami, 1973-75; pres., adminstr. Medi-Health of Fla., Inc., Ft. Lauderdale, 1975—; cons. in field. Author: Problem Oriented Records for Home Health Agencies; mem. editorial adv. bd. Caring mag., 1983-84; contbg. author: Quality Assurance Workbook, 1978, 83. Mem. Nat. Assn. Women Bus. Owners, Fla. Assn. Home Health Agys. (v.p. 1981-83, pres. 1983-85, M.T. Terry Justice Meml. award 1980), So. Fla. In Home Services Consortium (pres. 1981-83), Am. Acad. Med. Adminstrs. (sec.-treas. Fla. chpt. 1983-84, pres. 1985-86), Nat. Assn. Home Care (dir. 1982), Nat. Assn. Home Health Agys. (dir. 1980-82). Lutheran. Home: 465 NE 157th Terr North Miami Beach FL 33162 Office: Medi-Health of Fla Inc 3500 N State Rd 7 Fort Lauderdale FL 33319

JUSTIS, JANICE CALIENDO, nurse; b. Washington, Jan. 25, 1946; d. Raymond James and Madeline Fay (Peer) Caliendo; m. Lloyd Edward Justis, May 26, 1973. R.N., Pitts. Hosp., 1967; B.S. in Nursing, Calif. State U., 1979, M.S.N., 1983. Staff nurse Pitts. Hosp., 1967-68; clin. nurse Meml. Hosp., Long Beach, Calif., 1968-79, supr. orthopedics, wound care, 1982-83, edn. coordinator orthopaedics and urology, 1984—; infection control nurse VA, Long Beach, 1979-82. Mem. Nat. Assn. Orthopedic Nurses, Assn. Practitioners Infection Control. Democrat. Roman Catholic Home: 20342 Camfield Ln Huntington Beach CA 92646 Office: Meml Hosp 2801 Atlantic Long Beach CA 90802

JUVELIS, PRISCILLA CATHERINE, antiquarian bookseller; b. Newark, Sept. 2, 1945; d. Steven and Odelite (Canning) Juvelis. B.A., Boston U., 1967. Dir. internat. dept. Harcourt Brace Jovanovich Internat. Corp., N.Y.C., 1971-76; rights dir. The Franklin Library, N.Y.C., 1976-78; owner, pres. Priscilla Juvelis, Inc., Boston, 1980—. Editor, pub.: The Book Beautiful and The Binding as Art, 1983, vols. 1 and 2. Mem. Antiquarian Bookseller's Assn. Am., Mass. and R.I. Bookseller's Assn. (sec. 1983-84, v.p. 1984—, pres. 1986—). Office: Priscilla Juvelis Inc 150 Huntington Ave Boston MA 02115

JUVIK, PATRICIA ANN, risk manager; b. Waukon, Iowa, July 2, 1949; d. Bertin Valdemar and Winifred Ann (Staack) Juvik. B.A. in Sociology and Psychology, Luther Coll., 1971; M.A. in Criminal Justice and Corrections, U. Iowa, 1976. Correctional counselor Iowa Dept. Social Services, Des Moines, 1971-73, parole officer, 1976-78, exec. asst. to dir. corrections, 1978-79, dist. mgr., Marshalltown, Iowa, 1979-80; risk mgr. Impell Corp., San Francisco, 1980—. Mem. Commonwealth Club Calif., Nat. Assn. Female Execs., Risk and Ins. Mgmt. Soc. Republican. Lutheran. Office: Impell Corp 220 Montgomery St San Francisco CA 94104

KABACK, ELAINE, career counselor-consultant; b. Phila., Feb. 22, 1939; d. Sol and Evelyn Zitman; student Pa. State U., 1956-58; B.A., Temple U., 1960; M.S., Calif. State U., 1977; children—Douglas, Stephen, Michelle. Tchr. English, Sayre Jr. High Sch., Phila. Public Schs., 1960-62; tchr. English and history Beth Tfiloh Pvt. Day Sch., Balt., 1968-72; mgmt. cons., trainer Sandra Winston Assos., Palos Verdes, Calif., 1975—; counselor Career Planning Center and Mid-Life Center, Long Beach City Coll., 1977-78, instr. in assertion tng. coll. extension; dir. program devel. Univance Career Centers, Inc., Los Angeles, 1978-80; pvt. practice career counseling, 1980—; coordinator career planning program, trainer/presenter UCLA Extension. Pres. Palos Verdes chpt. NOW, 1974-76, chairperson, lectr. Speaker's Bur., 1977—; treas. S.W. chpt. Nat. Women's Polit. Caucus, 1973, 78; bd. dirs. STEP Adult Edn. Programs, Palos Verdes, 1974—, cert. community coll. life counselor, Calif.; cert. tchr., Pa. Mem. Calif. Personnel and Guidance Assn., Calif. Career Guidance Assn., Am. Soc. Tng. and Devel., Am. Assn. Counseling and Devel., Women in Bus. Phi Kappa Phi. Office: 24222 Hawthorne Blvd Suite B Torrance CA 90505 also 924 Westwood Blvd Suite 850 Westwood CA 90024

KABRIEL, MARCIA GAIL, psychotherapist; b. El Reno, Okla., Jan. 8, 1938; d. Gail Frederick and Katherine (Marsh) Slaughter; B.A., U. Okla., 1965, M.S.W., 1968, also postgrad. Am. U.; m. J. Ronald Kabriel, May 25, 1957 (div. Sept. 1985); children—Joseph Charles, Jeffrey Gail, Jae B. Psychiat. social worker Dept. Mental Hygiene, N.Y.C., 1968-69; psychiat. social worker Washington Hosp. Center, 1970-72, asso. mem. dept. psychiatry, 1972-75, sr. psychotherapist Counseling Center, 1972-75; psychotherapist Md. Inst. Pastoral Counseling, Annapolis, Md., 1972—; chief dept. social services Washington Hosp. Center, 1979-82, cons. spl. projects, 1974-82; supr. continuing protective services State Md., 1983—; exec. v.p. Kent Island Transport, Inc., 1985—; field instr. Cath. U., Washington, 1973-75, U. Md., 1976-78. Mem. Nat. Assn. Social Workers, Acad. Cert. Social Workers. Democrat. Presbyterian. Home: 1416 Regent St Annapolis MD 21403 Office: 104 Forbes St Suite F Annapolis MD 21404

KACHMAR, LILLIAN SANDRA, lawyer, author; b. Phila., Jan. 13, 1954; d. Michael and Lillian (Corwonski) Kachmarchik; m. John F. Steele, Mar. 10, 1979; 1 dau., Barbara Courtney. B.A. in History maxima cum laude, LaSalle Coll., 1975; J.D., U. Villanova, 1978. Bar: Pa. 1978, Fla. 1979, U.S. Dist. Ct. (so. dist.) Fla. 1979, U.S. Ct. Appeals (5th cir.) 1979, Assoc. firm Ruden, Barnett, McClosky, Schuster & Russell, Ft. Lauderdale, Fla., 1978-80; counsel spl. project Control Fluidics, Inc., F/K/A I.W.S.S. Corp., N.Y.C., 1980; asst. counsel Reliance Ins. Co., Phila., 1980-81; sole practice law, Villanova, Pa., 1981—. Author: (novel) Zeus: The Cronus File, 1983. Mem. ABA, Fla. Bar Assn., Pa. Bar Assn. Republican. Roman Catholic.

KACIR, BARBARA BRATTIN, lawyer; b. Buffalo, July 19, 1941; d. William James and Jean (Harrington) Brattin; B.A., Wellesley Coll., 1963; J.D., U. Mich., 1967. Bar Ohio 1967, D.C. 1980; practiced in Cleve., 1967-79, 84—, Washington, 1980-83; assoc. firm Arter & Hadden, Cleve., 1967-74, ptnr., 1974-79; ptnr., firm Jones Day Reavis & Pogue, Washington, 1980-83, Cleve., 1983—; assoc. prof. law Case Western Res. U., 1974-78. Mem. nat. fund raising com. U. Mich. Law Sch., 1973-79, mem. nat. com. visitors, 1980-83. Mem. Am., Ohio (counsel dels. 1972-79, 84—), Cleve. (continuing legal edn. com. 1969-74, vice chmn. 1973-74, trustee 1974-77, mem. young lawyers com. 1968-72, arbitration com. 1971-74; mem. budget com. 1974-79, chmn. 1978-79, treas. 1978-79), D.C. bar assns., Am. Law Inst., Am. Arbitration Assn. (Cleve. regional council 1972-79). Home: 13705 Shaker Blvd Cleveland OH 44120 Office: Jones Day Reavis & Pogue 1700 Huntington Bldg Cleveland OH 44115

KACZANOWSKA, WIESLAWA, psychiatrist; b. Poland, Sept. 27, 1925; came to U.S., 1968, naturalized, 1977; d. Alfred and Janina (Chmielinska) Kozaczewski; M.D., Warsaw Sch. Medicine, 1952; Ph.D. in Psychiatry, Warsaw U., 1964; m. Mieczyslaw Kaczanowski, Dec. 6, 1951; 1 son, Peter. Staff psychiatrist, chief in-patient services, adj. prof. in psychiatry Neuropsychiat. Inst., Poland, 1952-66; registrar in psychiatry, Eng., 1966-68; resident Beth Israel Hosp., N.Y.C., 1969-72, staff psychiatrist, Brookdale Med. Center, Coney Island Hosp., Brooklyn, N.Y., 1972-74; faculty mem. U. Pa., Phila., 1974-77; psychiatrist Community Mental Health, Phila.; part time supervising psychiatrist N.E. Mental Health Ctr., 1983—; faculty mem. Jefferson Med. Coll., 1977—; cons. psychiatrist, social-vocat. programs Horizon House. Polish Govt. fellow, 1965. Mem. Am. Psychiat. Assn., Am. Med. Women's Assn., Pa. Psychiat. Soc. Research on psychiat. patients' response to antipsychotic medicine. Home: 728 Lombard St Philadelphia PA 19147

KACZMAREK, INGRID BERNICE, computer software consulting firm executive; b. Mannheim, Ger., Sept. 1, 1943; came to U.S., 1962; d. Albert and Lilli (Haller) Lang; m. Joseph W. Kaczmarek, Dec. 9, 1961; children—Lili, Steven. Keypunch operator N.Y. Central Mut. Ins. Co., Cleve., 1962-67; computer operator Penn Central Mut. Ins. Co., 1967-71; computer programmer R.R. Employees Mut. Ins. Co., 1971-77; pres. Datapro Cons., Cleve., 1977-82, Datapro Systems, Inc., Cleve., 1982—. Mem. Women Bus. Owners Assn. (Export award 1984, 85), Sales and Mktg. Execs., Council Smaller Enterprises, Greater Cleve. Growth Assn. Republican. Roman Catholic. Avocations: tennis; swimming; photography. Office: Datapro Systems Inc 815 Superior Ave Cleveland OH 44114

KADEC, SARAH THOMAS, information management consultant, retired government official; b. Winchester, Va., Dec. 15, 1932; d. Lemuel and Mary (Switzer) Thomas; m. Mark Mania Kadec, July 27, 1975. B.A., Madison Coll., 1952; M.L.S., Carnegie Library Sch., 1961. Acquisitions librarian Engr. Research and Devel. Labs., Fort Belvoir, Va., 1952-53; librarian Jeter Jr. High Sch., Covington, Va., 1953-55, J.H. Russell Elem. Sch., Quantico, Va., 1955-57; ref. librarian Def. Atomic Support Agy., Washington, 1975-60; ref. asst. Carnegie Library, Pitts., 1960-61; chief librarian Fairchild Library, Fairchild Stratos Corp., Hagerstown, Md., 1961-63; librarian Booz Allen Applied Research, Bethesda, Md., 1963-66; head reader's services Applied Physics Lab., Johns Hopkins U., Silver Spring Md., 1966-67; lectr., dir. continuing edn. U. Md., College Park, 1967-69; cons. in library and info. sci. Ctr. Sci. and Tech. Info., Tel Aviv, 1969-70; vis. lectr. Hebrew U. Sch. Library Sci., Jerusalem, 1970; librarian Commn. on Govt. Procurement, Washington, 1970-71; lectr. Cath. U. Am., Washington, 1971-75; chief library systems br. EPA, Washington, 1971-78; adj. lectr. U. Md. Sch. Library and Info. Services, College Park, 1972-74; dir. info. mgmt. and services div. Office Adminstrn., Exec. Office of Pres., Washington, 1978-79; dep. dir. Office of Adminstrn., 1979-81; mem. sci. and edn. mgmt. staff U.S. Dept. Agr., Washington, from 1982; dir. library program service Supt. U.S. Govt. Printing Office, 1982; dir. info. mgmt. and services div. EPA, Washington, 1983-84, dep. dir. Office Info. Resources Mgmt., 1984-85; info. mgmt. cons., 1985—; lectr. in field. Contbr. articles to profl. jours. Mem. numerous adv. bds., com. memberships including Environ. Scis. Adv. Com., Washington Tech. Inst., Library of Congress. Div. Blind and Physically Handicapped, Fed. Library Com., Fed. Energy Adminstrn. Library Bd., Fed. Library Networking; bd. dirs. Soc. Library and Info. Technicians, 1973-74. Mem. Spl. Libraries Assn. (assoc. editor documentation div. 1967-68), Am. Soc. Info. Sci., Assoc. Info. Mgrs. Presbyterian. Home: 2833 Gunarette Way Silver Spring MD 20906 Office: PO Box Silver Spring MD 20906

KADISH, ROSALYN SUNA, lawyer; b. N.Y.C., July 3, 1942; d. Harry and Helen Mae (Buchsbaum) Suna; m. Mark J. Kadish, Mar. 23, 1974; children—Ellen Grace Schlossberg, Richard Mark Schlossberg. A.B., Clark U., 1963; J.D. magna cum laude, Woodrow Wilson Coll. Law, 1980. Bar: Ga. 1980, U.S. Ct. Appeals (11th cir.) 1984. Assoc., Kadish, Davis & Brofman, Atlanta, 1980-83; ptnr. Kadish & Kadish, P.C., Atlanta, 1983-85; legal asst. Ct. Appeals for State of Ga., 1986—; asst. to editor Klower Law Book Pubs., Inc., 1985—. Contbr. articles, chpts. to profl. publs.; co-author: The Successful Defense of Narcotics Cases, 2 vols., 1985. Recipient Am. Jurisprudence awards, 1980. Mem. ABA, Ga. Bar Assn., Assn. Trial Lawyers Am., Nat. Assn. Criminal Def. Lawyers, Ga. Trial Lawyers Assn., Ga. Assn. Criminal Def. Lawyers, Atlanta Bar Assn. Democrat. Jewish. Club: Confrerie de la Chaine des Rotisseurs (charge de press 1983—). 955 W Wesley Rd NW Atlanta GA 30327

KAEDER, EILEEN MARIE, writer, TV news producer; b. Phoenix, Oct. 22, 1954; d. Kenneth Sanborn and Dona Kristine (Ring) Craft; m. Kennan Edward Kaeder, Nov. 24, 1984. B.S. in Journalism, Ariz. State U., 1976. News reporter Sentinel newspaper, San Diego, 1977-79, North Coast Pubs., Encinitas, Calif., 1980-81; writer, news producer Sta. KFMB-TV CBS, San Diego, 1981-84; freelance writer, 1984—. Recipient San Diego Emmy award for Best Mid-day News Cast, Nat. Assn. TV Arts and Scis., 1983. Democrat. Episcopalian.

KAEL, PAULINE, movie critic, author; b. Petaluma, Calif., June 19, 1919; d. Isaac Paul and Judith (Friedman) Kael; student U. Calif., Berkeley, 1936-40; LL.D., (hon.), Georgetown U., 1972; Litt.D. (hon.), Smith Coll., 1973, Allegheny Coll., 1979; L.H.D. (hon.), Kalamazoo Coll., 1973, Reed Coll., 1975, Haverford Coll., 1975; D.F.A. (hon.), Sch. Visual Arts, N.Y.C., 1980; 1 dau., Gina James. Movie critic New Republic mag., 1966-67, New Yorker mag., 1968—. Author: I Lost it at the Movies, 1965; Kiss Kiss Bang Bang, 1968; Going Steady, 1970; Deeper into Movies, 1973; Reeling, 1976; When the Lights Go Down, 1980; 5001 Nights at the Movies, 1982; Taking It All In, 1984; State of the Art, 1985; contbg. author: The Citizen Kane Book. Recipient Polk award in criticism, 1970; Nat. Book award, 1974; Front Page award Newswomen's Club N.Y., 1974, 83; Guggenheim fellow, 1964. Address: care The New Yorker 25 W 43d St New York NY 10036

KAGAN, JULIA LEE, magazine editor; b. Nuremberg, Germany, Nov. 25, 1948 (parents U.S. citizens); d. Saul and Elizabeth Johanna (Koblenzer) K. A.B., Bryn Mawr Coll., 1970. Researcher, Look Mag., N.Y.C., 1970-71; editorial asst., asst. editor McCall's Mag., N.Y.C., 1971-74, assoc. editor, 1974-78, sr. editor, 1978-79; articles editor Working Woman mag., N.Y.C., 1979-85, exec. editor, 1985—. Co-author: Manworks: A Guide to Style, 1980. Contbr. to books: The Working Woman Success Book, 1981; The Working Woman Report, 1984. Pres., Appleby Found., Rebecca Kelly Dance Co., N.Y.C., 1982-84; bd. dirs. Rebecca Kelly Dance Co., N.Y.C., 1979—, Woman's Counseling Project, N.Y.C., 1983—. Recipient 2d Ann. Advt. Journalism award Compton Advt., 1983. Mem. Am. Soc. Mag. Editors, Am. Soc. Pub. Opinion Researchers. Club: Princeton of N.Y. (N.Y.C.). Office: Working Woman Mag 342 Madison Ave New York NY 10173

KAGAN, MARCIA PESSIN, social worker; b. Hartford, Conn., Jan. 4, 1922; d. Israel George and Gussie Elizabeth (Marcus) Pessin; A.A., Hillyer Coll., 1943; B.A., U. Miami, 1947; M.S.W., U. Conn., 1969; m. Nathaniel D. Kagan, May 9, 1948; children—Larry H., Jeffrey M. With Dept. Children and Youth, Conn. State Dept. Welfare, Hartford and Torrington, 1947-74, program supr., 1969-74; sr. staff social worker Hartford Rehab. Center, 1974-80; pvt. practice social work, West Hartford, Conn., 1980-85; social work cons. Vis. Nurse and Home Care, East Hartford, Conn., 1985—. Bd. dirs. CAC 18, North Central Regional Mental Health Bd., 1979-82, Capital Region chpt. Mental Health Assn., 1980-82, Sunshine Group, Inc., 1980-82; trustee sisterhood Temple Beth Israel, 1982-83, mem. social action com., 1985—; mem. consumer adv. bd. Div. Vocat. Rehab., 1982-83; mediation counselor Better Bus. Bur., 1985—. Mem. Nat. Assn. Social Workers, Acad. Cert. Social Workers, Conn. Assn. Human Services. Democrat. Jewish. Club: B'nai B'rith (v.p. 1964-65). Home: 43 Whitehill Dr West Hartford CT 06117

KAGEY, F(LORENCE) EILEEN, educator; b. Lima, Ohio, July 29, 1925; d. Joseph Leonard and Florence Elizabeth (Niles) K.; B.S. in Edn., Ball State U., 1952; M.S. in Edn., Ind. U., 1955. Sec., Gen. Electric Co., Ft. Wayne, Ind., 1943-45, 48-49, Farnsworth Telephone and Radio Corp., Ft. Wayne, 1945-49; H.A. Jeep prof. Ball State U., 1949-52; elem. tchr. Harmar Sch., Ft. Wayne, 1952-54, Emerson Sch., Gary, Ind., 1954-58, Sch. 52, Indpls., 1959-61, George Kuny Sch., Gary, 1961—; sec. to v.p. Research and Rev. Service of Am., Indpls., 1958-59. Chmn. public relations Calumet Corner chpt. Sweet Adelines, Inc., Munster, Ind., 1980-82, mem., 1977—, bd. dirs., 1981-82. Mem. NEA (life), Am. Fedn. Tchrs. (bldg. rep. Local 4 1979—), Ind. State Tchrs. Assn., Assn. Supervision and Curriculum Devel., Ind. Assn. Supervision and Curriculum Devel., AAUW (v.p. charge program chpt.), Kappa Delta Pi. Democrat. Roman Catholic. Author: (juvenile) Jeremy: the People-Dog, 1974. Home: 3040 W 39th Pl Gary IN 46408 Office: 5050 Vermont St Gary IN 46409

KAHAN, HAZEL ELEANOR, marketing executive; b. Lahore, India, Jan. 2, 1939; came to U.S., 1973; d. Hermann Marcus and Kate (Neumann) Selzer; m. Michael James Kahan, Sept. 11, 1973; children—Daniel Gregory, Miranda. B.A., U. London, 1963; Ph.D., Australian Nat. U., 1970. Pres., Market Behavior Inc., N.Y.C., 1980-82; v.p. research and planning Warner Amex Cable Communication Inc, N.Y.C., 1982-84, Satellite TV Corp., Washington, 1984-85; pres. Hazel Kahan Research, N.Y.C., 1985—. Contbr. articles to profl. jours. Mem. Am. Mktg. Assn. (bd. dirs. 1983-85). Office: Hazel Kahan Research 122 E 25th St New York NY 10010

KAHLE, CATHY BENNING, librarian; b. Huntingburg, Ind., June 21, 1956; d. Leonard Henry and Anna Mae (Johnson) B.; m. Wayne Kahle, June 29, 1985; 1 child, Jesse. B.S., Elmhurst Coll. (Ill.), 1979; M.L.S., Ind. U., 1981. Instructional media asst. A.C. Buehler Library Elmhurst Coll., 1976-79; readers asst. Lilly Library Ind. U., Bloomington, 1980; asst. librarian Jasper Pub. Library-Dubois County Contractual Library, Jasper, Ind., 1981-84, dir., 1984—; bd. dirs. Ind. Coop. Library Services Authority, Indpls., 1981—. Bd. dirs. St. Paul United Ch. of Christ, Holland, Ind., 1983—. Mem. ALA, Ind. Library Assn. (chairperson Dist. VII 1982-83). Office: Jasper Pub Library-Dubois County Contractual Library 1116 Main St Jasper IN 47546

KAHN, ADA PASKIND, journalist, author, health care communications consultant; b. Chgo., Dec. 14, 1934; d. Ben and Ethel Paskind; m. Edward J. Kahn, Apr. 20, 1958 (div. Oct. 1966); 1 dau., Ruth Debra. B.S. in Journalism, Northwestern U., 1956, M.P.H., 1982. Pub. relations cons., 1957—; cons. AMA, 1967-70; editorial supr. New Home Med. Ency., Quadrangle Books, 1973; mgr. profl. communications Am. Acad. Dermatology, 1977-78; pub. info. and mktg. dir. Michael Reese Health Plan, 1973-80; owner Wordscope Assocs., Skokie, Ill., 1980—; mem. faculty dept. journalism Columbia Coll., Chgo., 1982, U. Health Scis./Chgo. Med. Sch., North Chicago, Ill., 1974-79; cons. Office Health Maintenance Orgns., Region V, HHS, Chgo., 1979. Author: Help Yourself to Health Series, 1983; Midlife Health: A Woman's Guide to Feeling Good, 1987; editor The Matrix, 1964-67; mem. Skokie Bd. Health, 1976—. contbr. articles to profl. jours. Fellow Am. Med. Writers Assn. (disting. service award Chgo. chpt. 1979, pres. 1976-77); mem. Women in Communications (pres. Chgo. chpt. 1968-69), Am. Soc. Journalists and Authors.

KAHN, ARLENE JUDY MILLER, nurse, educator; b. Chgo., Dec. 16, 1940; d. Fred and Sophie (Schelbe) Miller; R.N., A.B., U. Ill., Chgo., 1963, M.S. in Nursing, 1970; Ed.D., U. San Francisco, 1986; m. Roy M. Kahn, Oct. 25, 1968; 1 child, Jennifer M. Head nurse psychiat. unit Grant Hosp., Chgo., 1966; supervising nurse Ill. Psychiat. Inst., Chgo., 1967; instr. psychiat. nursing Calif. State U., San Francisco, 1968-70; mem. faculty Calif. State U., Hayward, 1974—, asso. prof. nursing, 1980—; cons. in field. Research grantee Calif. State U., Hayward, 1980-81. Fellow Am. Assn. Psychiat. Nursing; mem. United Profs. Calif., Calif. Nursing Assn., Sigma Theta Tau. Author articles in field. Home: 95 Sonia St Oakland CA 94618 Office: Hayward State U Sch Sci Hayward CA 94542

KAHN, BLOSSOM, motion picture exec.; b. N.Y.C., Aug. 16, 1936; d. Jules Franklin and Anita Beatrice (Arkin) K.; B.A. in English, Hofstra Coll., Hempstead, N.Y., 1958; postgrad. Columbia U. Sch. Journalism, N.Y.C. Exec., story dept. Universal Pictures Corp., N.Y.C., 1963-64; head motion picture, TV and play depts. Curtis Brown Lit. Agy., N.Y.C., 1964-68; pres. Kahn-Penney Lit. Agy., Los Angeles, 1968-77; dir. creative affairs First Artists Prodns., Los Angeles, 1977-78; exec. in charge creative projects Avco-Embassy Pictures, Los Angeles, 1978-82; v.p. prodn. Zupnick Curtis Enterprises, Inc., Los Angeles, 1982-83; West Coast creative cons. Polymuse, Inc., 1983—; lectr. Sherwood Oaks Coll., Marymount Coll., Los Angeles. Mem. Women in Film, Women in Communication. Office: 208 S Beverly Dr Beverly Hills CA 90212

KAHN, DEBORAH JEAN, broadcasting advertising executive; b. Pitts., Oct. 21, 1957; d. Robert Warren and Dorothy Jean (Kohn) Kahn. B.A., Grove City Coll., 1979. With Thompson, Matelan & Hawbaker, Inc., Pitts., 1979-82, asst. account exec., 1979-82, account exec., 1981-82; mgr. media and prodn. account exec. Tandem Inc., Pitts., 1982-83; mgr. advt., promotion, mktg. and merchandising Total Communication Systems, Pitts., 1984—. Mem. alumni council Grove City Coll., Pitts., 1979—. Mem. Pitts. Radio and TV Club. Mem. career bd. Mademoiselle Mag., 1979—. Republican. Presbyterian. Club: University. Office: Total Communication Systems 890 Constitution Blvd New Kensington PA 15068

KAHN, DONA SEEMAN, lawyer; b. Elizabeth, N.J., Oct. 7, 1932; d. David George and Lillian (Lazarus) Seeman; m. Arthur H. Kahn, Sept. 18, 1956; children—Robert, Walter, Andrew. A.B., Brandeis U., 1954; J.D., Rutgers U., 1957. Bar: D.C. 1959, Pa. 1976. Trial atty. U.S. Dept. Agr., Washington, 1960-72; chief legal br. region III, EPA, Phila., 1972-73; assoc. gen. counsel EEOC, Phila., 1973-76; ptnr. Harris and Kahn, Phila., 1976—; lectr. women's health issues and fed. civil litigation, discrimination in employment. Trustee, Brandeis U., 1979-84. Mem. Forum Exec. Women, D.C. Bar Assn., Phila. Bar Assn. (chmn. civil rights com. 1983, chmn. fee dispute com. 1977, mem. long-range planning com. 1982-86, mem. nominating com. 1983), ABA. Office: Harris and Kahn 14th Floor 1600 Market St Philadelphia PA 19103

KAHN, FAITH-HOPE, nurse, adminstr., writer; b. N.Y.C., Apr. 25, 1921; d. Leon and Hazel (Cook) Green; R.N., Beth Israel Med. Center, N.Y.C., 1942; student N.Y. U., 1943; m. Edward Kahn, May 29, 1942; children—Ellen Leora, Faith Hope II, Paula Amy. First scrub operating room Beth Israel Hosp., N.Y.C., 1942; supr., operating room Hunts Point Gen. Hosp., 1942; gynecol. reconstrn. procedures researcher Phoenixville (Pa.) Gen. Hosp., 1943, Sydenham Hosp., N.Y.C., 1945; supr. ARC Disaster Field Hosp., Queens, N.Y., 1950-51; adminstr., mgr. team coordinator Dr. Edward Kahn, FACOG, Queens Village, N.Y., 1945—; inventor; Publicity chmn. Girl Scouts U.S.A., 1953, exec. dir. publicity Woodhull Schs., 1936-60, pres., 1961-62; exec. dir. publicity N.Y. Dept. Parks Figure Skating, 1956-70; exec. dir. publicity and applied arts St. John's Hosp., Smithtown, N.Y., 1965-66; state advisor N.Y., U.S. Congressional Adv. Bd., Washington, 1981—; nat. adv. bd. Am. Security Council, 1978—; founder Am. Security Found. Recipient citation A.R.C., 1951, Am. Law Enforcement Officers Assn.; Bronze medal Am. Security Council Ednl. Found., 1978; cert. of appreciation Am. Police Acad., 1979; spl. recognition award Center Internat. Security Studies, 1979; Meml. Plate, Patriots of Am. Bicentennial, 1976; Great Seal of U.S.A. Plate. Mem. Am. Acad. Ambulatory Nursing Adminstrn., Nurses Assn., Nat. League Nursing, Am. Coll. Obstetricians and Gynecologists, Nat. Assn. Physicians' Nurses, Nat. Critical Care Inst., Assn. Operating Room Nurses, AAAS, N.Y. Acad. Scis., Am. Police Acad., Internat. Platform Assn., Security and Intelligence Fund, Nat. Rifle Assn. Clubs: Tiyospaye, Paul Revere, Sterlingshire Woman's. Author, editor: The Easy Driving Way for Automatic and the Standard Shift, 1954; (with Edward Kahn) The Pelvic Examination, Outline and Guide for Residents, Internes and Students, 1954; (with Edward Kahn) Traction Hysterosalpingography for Uterine Lesions, 1949; contbr. articles profl. and lay jours. Home: 213 16 85th Ave Hollis Hills NY 11427 Office: 213 16 85th Ave Queens Village NY 11427

KAHN, HANNAH, poet; b. N.Y.C., June 30, 1911; d. David and Sarah (Siegelbaum) Abrahams; widowed; children—Melvin A., Daniel L., Vivian Dale. B.A., Fla. Atlantic U., 1973. Poetry rev. editor Miami Herald, Fla., 1959-74; tchr. creative writing classes Miami Dade New World Campus, Miami, Broward Community Coll., Ft. Lauderdale, Fla. Author vols. of poetry; Eve's Daughter, 1962; Time, Wait, 1983. Contbr. poems to various publs. including: American Scholar, Harper's, N.Y. Times. Charter mem., past pres. Dade Assn. for Retarded Citizens, Miami. Recipient awards from various orgns. including: Poetry Soc. Am., Peltry Soc. Va.; winner Internat. Sonnet Competition, Poetry Soc. Gt. Britain and Am. Mem. Women in Communications, Poetry Soc. Am., Acad. Am. Poets, Poetry Soc. Ga. Home: 3301 NE 5th Ave Apt 318 Miami FL 33137

KAHN, JULIANNA B., financial analyst; b. Chgo., Aug. 17, 1953; d. Leroy Hirschfield and Esther (Levine) Blumenthal; B.S. in Acctg., U. Ill., Urbana, 1975; m. Frederick J. Kahn, Sept. 6, 1981; 1 child, Matthew Alexander. Auditor, B. L. Rosenberg & Co., Chgo., 1975-76; acct. Bankers Life & Casualty Co., Chgo., 1977-78, fin. analyst, 1978-81; prin. fin. analyst Chgo. Bd. Edn., 1981—. C.P.A., Ill. Home: 5354 Suffield Ct Skokie IL 60077

KAHN, KATHY, writer; b. Seattle, Apr. 2, 1945; d. Robert Arthur Moody and Donna (Green) Kelly; m. Simon Kahn, 1969 (div. 1974); children—Simon Peter, Jesse MacDougall. Author: Hillbilly Women, 1973 (Mademoiselle Woman of the Yr. 1974); Fruits of Our Labor (Nat. Endowment for the Humanities grant 1981), 1982. Playwright: The Contest, 1983. Contbr. articles to internat. mags. Avocation: international travel. Home: 151 1st Ave #4R New York NY 10003

KAHN, LINDA MCCLURE, actuary, executive; b. Jacksonville, Fla.; d. George Calvin and Myrtice Louise (Boggs) McClure; student Jacksonville U.; B.S. with high honors, U. Fla.; M.S., U. Mich., 1964; m. Paul Markham Kahn, May 20, 1968. Actuarial trainee N.Y. Life Ins. Co., N.Y.C., 1964-66, actuarial asst., 1966-69, asst. actuary, 1969-71; v.p., actuary USLIFE Ins./Calif., Pasadena, 1972-74; mgr. Coopers & Lybrand, Los Angeles, 1974-76, sr. cons., San Francisco, 1976-82; dir. program mgmt. Pacific Maritime Assn., 1982—. Bd. dirs. Heights Residents Assn., 1979—, sec.-treas., 1981; trustee ILWU-PMA Welfare Plan, Seafarers Med. Ctr., others. Enrolled actuary. Fellow Soc. Actuaries, Conf. Actuaries in Public Practice; mem. Internat. Actuarial Assn., Internat. Assn. Cons. Actuaries, Actuarial Studies in Non-Life Ins., Am. Acad. Actuaries, Western Pension Conf. (newsletter editor 1983-85, sec. 1985—), Actuarial Club Pacific States, San Francisco Actuarial Club (pres. 1981). Clubs: Met., Soroptimist (v.p. 1973-74), Commonwealth. Home: 2430 Pacific Ave San Francisco CA 94115 Office: 635 Sacramento St San Francisco CA 94111

KAHN, MERYL DENISE, financial planning company executive; b. Columbia, S.C., Dec. 25, 1950; d. H. Bernard Kahn and Revera Charlotte (Tolochko) Wayburn; m. Daniel McLean, Nov. 15, 1980. B.S., Met. State Coll., Denver, 1975; M.B.A., U. Chgo., 1977. Mgmt. cons. Kearney Mgmt. Cons., Chgo., 1975-76; market analyst Xerox Corp., Rochester, N.Y., 1977-78; ops. analyst Eastern Gas & Fuel, Boston, 1978-80; mktg. mgr. Data Gen. Service, Westboro, Mass., 1980-82; pres. MoneyworkS, Inc., Boston, 1982—. Treas. Boston Ctr. for Blind Children, 1982-84. Mem. Nat. Assn. Personal Fin. Advisors, Internat. Assn. Fin. Planners. Office: Moneywork$ Inc 20 Park Plaza Suite 537 Boston MA 02116

KAHN, SANDRA S., psychotherapist; b. Chgo., June 24, 1942; d. Chester and Ruth (Goldblatt) Sutker; m. Jack Murry Kahn, June 1, 1965; children—Erick, Jennifer. B.A., U. Miami, 1964; M.A., Roosevelt U., 1976. Tchr. Chgo. Pub. Schs., 1965-67; pvt. practice psychotherapy, Northbrook, Ill., 1976—; host Shared Feelings, Sta. WEEF, Highland Park, Ill., 1983—. Author: The Kahn Report on Sexual Preferences, 1981. Mem. Ill. Psychol. Assn., Chgo. Psychol. Assn. Jewish. Office: 2970 Maria Ave Northbrook IL 60062

KAHN, SUSAN BETH (MRS. JOSEPH KAHN), artist; b. N.Y.C., Aug. 26, 1924; d. Jesse B. and Jenny Carol (Peshkin) Cohen; student Parsons Sch. Design, 1945; pupil Moses Soyer, 1950-57; m. Joseph Kahn, Sept. 15, 1946 (dec. 1979); m. 2d, Richard I. Rosenkranz, Feb. 1, 1981. One-man shows at Sagittarius Gallery, 1960, A.C.A., Galleries, 1964, 68, 71, 76, 80, Charles B. Goddard Art Center, Ardmore, Okla., 1973, Albrecht Gallery Mus. Art, St. Joseph, Mo., 1974, N.Y. Cultural Center, N.Y.C., 1974, St. Peter's Coll., Jersey City, 1978; exhibited in group shows at Audubon Artists, N.Y.C., Nat. Acad., N.Y.C., Springfield (Mass.) Mus., City Center, N.Y.C., A.C.A. Galleries, N.Y.C., Nat. Arts Club, N.Y.C., Purdure U., Ind.; represented in permanent collections at Tyler (Tex.) Mus., St. Lawrence U. Mus., Canton, N.Y., Fairleigh Dickinson U. Mus., Rutherford, N.J., Syracuse U. Mus., Sheldon Swope Gallery, Terre Haute, Ind., Montclair (N.J.) Mus. Fine Arts, Butler Inst. Am. Art, Youngstown, Ohio, Reading (Pa.) Mus., Albrecht Gallery Mus. Art, St. Joseph, Cedar Rapids (Iowa) Art Center, U. Wyo., Laramie, Joslyn Mus., Omaha, S.A.I.S., Washington, Edwin A. Ulrich Mus., Wichita, Kans., Wichita State U. Recipient Knickerbocker prize for best religious painting, 1956, Edith Lehman award Nat. Assn. Women Artists, 1958, Knickerbocker Artists award, 1961, Simmons award Nat. Assn. Women Artists, 1961, Nat. Arts Club award, 1967, Knickerbocker medal of Honor, 1964, Famous Artists Sch. award, 1967. Mem. Nat. Assn. Women Artists (Anne Barnett Meml. prize 1981), Artists Equity, Knickerbocker Artists (Knickerbocker award 1985), Met. Mus., Mus. Modern Art. Home: 870 United Nations Plaza New York NY 10017

KAIGHIN, BARBARA ANN, police officer; b. St. Louis, Dec. 29, 1946; d. William Wesley and Kathleen Majorie (Vadner) Fisher; m. Donald Charles Kaighin, Nov. 4, 1975 (dec. Jan. 1982); children—Charles Jay, Angela Kay. Grad. Greater St. Louis Police Acad., 1973; B.S. in Criminal Justice, Northeast Mo. State Univ., 1978; M.A. in Mgmt., Webster Univ., 1983; postgrad. in counseling St. Louis U. Police officer St. Louis County Police, St. Louis, 1973-80; security police officer McDonnel Douglas Security, St. Charles, Mo., 1980-81; police officer City of Ballwin, Mo., 1982-85; trainere/advisor Police Reserves/Scouts, Ballwin, 1982-85; police officer, juvenile officer police community relations City of Maryland Heights, Mo., 1985—. Named Disting. Expert (Firearms) St. Louis Police Acad., 1973; Am. Business Women's Assn. scholar, 1983. Mem. Internat. Order Women Police, Mo. Assn. Women Police, Am. Soc. Tng. and Devel., Am. Assn. Counseling and Devel., Mo. Juvenile Officers Assn., St. Louis County Juvenile Justice Assn. Republican. Roman Catholic. Avocations: coach teen girls softball team; travel. Home: 4 Kilkenny Hills Pacific MO 63069 Office: Ballwin Police Dept 300 City Hall Dr Ballwin MO 63011

KAILEY, DEBORAH ANN, technical writer, programmer; b. McCook, Nebr., May 22, 1947; d. Robert Charles and Pauline Victoria (Urbom) K.; B.A. U. Nebr., 1969; M.S.W., Va. Commonwealth U., 1973, B.S.C.S., Coleman Coll., 1983. Caseworker, Lincoln (Nebr.) Regional Center, 1969-70; social worker, dept. social service Children and Youth Services, Denver, 1973-76, prin. social worker, 1977-80; clin. social worker Va. Commonwealth U., 1976-77; prin. social worker Adams County Dept. Social Services, 1980-82; software installer, technical writer Nat. Med. Computer Services, Inc., San Diego, 1983-84; tech. publs. specialist NCR Corp., 1984—. Office: NCR 16550 W Bernardo Dr San Diego CA 92127

KAISER, ELAINE JULIANN, communications executive; b. Miami, Feb. 12, 1949; d. Edward Joseph and Mary Jeannette (Foote) K. B.A., U. Ga., 1971. Adminstrv. asst. City of Miami Dept. Publicity and Tourism, 1968-69; assoc. dir. United Meth. Communications, Atlanta, 1971-73; pub. relations asst. Calhoun-Carroll Communications, Atlanta, 1973; sr. writer, press relations coordinator Blue Cross/Blue Shield, Atlanta, 1973-79, dir. pub. relations ARC, Atlanta, 1979-83; communications dir. Provident Life & Accident Ins. Co., Chattanooga, 1983—. Mem. campaign mktg. task force, mem. communications ops. com. United Way Met. Atlanta, 1979-83; mem. adv. council WXIA-TV, Atlanta, 1981-83. Recipient Good Guy award Ga. Bus. and Industry Assn., 1981. Mem. Am. Mktg. Assn., Internat. Assn. Bus. Communicators, Assn. Multi-Image, Pub. Relations Soc. Am. (pres. Ga. chpt. 1984, assebly del. 1986-88), Women in Communications, Inc. (Bernice McCullar leadership award Ga. chpt. 1982, pres. Ga. chpt. 1981-82, regional v.p. 1981-83, nat. v.p. programs 1983-85, nat. pres. 1986-87), Women's C. of C. of Atlanta (govt. affairs com. 1981, publicity com. 1980). Democrat. Roman Catholic. Home: 3131 Mountain Creek Rd Apt 14A-3 Chattanooga TN 37415 Office: Provident Life & Accident Ins Co Fountain Square Chattanooga TN 37402

KAISER, JOYCE ANN, government official; b. Jersey City, Aug. 30, 1939; d. Frederick and Louise (Feary) Neebling; m. Gordon Allen Biddle, Sept. 21, 1963 (div. 1974); 1 dau., Adrienne Louise; m. 2d, Dennis Lee Kaiser, June 5, 1975 (div. Dec. 1983). A.A., Coll. San Mateo, 1959; B.A., Calif. State U.-San Francisco, 1961. With Employment Devel. Dept., Sacramento, Calif., 1965-80; owner Adrienne's Furniture, Davis, Calif., 1975-80; personnel dir. Reagan Transition Team, Washington, 1980-81; exec. asst. to asst. sec. Employment and Tng., Washington, 1981-82, adminstr. policy and research, 1981-82; assoc. asst. sec. of labor Employment and Tng. Adminstrn., Washington, 1982-85; asst. dir. Office Internat. Tng., AID, Washington, 1985—; rep. Nat. Commn. on Employment Policy, Washington, 1981-83. Republican. Presbyterian. Office: AID SA-18 Suite 201 Washington DC 20523

KAISER, MARIA CHARLOTTE, nurse, counselor; b. Utica, N.Y., Nov. 28, 1938; d. Vito Charles and Minnie Elizabeth (Waters) Nicotera; m. Richard Eugene Kaiser, Oct. 6, 1959; children—Richard Phillip, Michael Vito. Nursing diploma Utica State Hosp. Sch. Nursing (N.Y.), 1959; B.S. in Behavioral Sci., St. Leo's Coll., 1984. R.N., Fla., N.Y., Ill., Mass., Alaska; cert. advanced cardiac life support. Head nurse psychiatry Utica State Hosp. (N.Y.), 1960-62; staff nurse med.-surg. Sisters Charity Hosp., Holyoke, Mass., 1962-66; ARC vol. R.N. Clark AFB Hosp., Philippines, 1967-68; staff nurse pulmonary disease U.S. Air Force Med. Ctr., Scott AFB, Ill., 1969-72; staff nurse med.-surg. U.S. Air force Regional Hosp., Elmendorf AFB, Alaska, 1972-75; asst. head nurse emergency room Highland Gen. Hosp., Sebring, Fla., 1976-81; night head nurse emergency room Walker Meml. Hosp., Avon Park, Fla., 1981—, also crisis intervention team, 1983—; R.N. coordinator Project Hope (services over 60), Sebring, Fla., 1975-76. Sec. St. James Parish Council, Lake Placid, Fla., 1978. Named to Dean's List, So. Fla. Jr. Coll., 1983. Mem. Emergency Dept. Nurses Assn., Am. Nurses Assn., Dist. 27 Nurses, Fla. Nurses Assn. Democrat. Roman Catholic. Club: St. James Women's of Lake Placid (chmn. family affairs commn. 1977-78). Home: 615 Loquat Rd NW Lake Placid FL 33852 Office: Walker Meml Hosp US 27 N Avon Park FL 33825

KALAYJIAN, ANIE, educator, psychoanalytic psychotherapist; b. Aleppo, Syria; came to U.S., 1971; d. Kevork and Zabelle (Mardikian) K.; m. Shahé Navasart Sanentz, Dec. 16, 1984. B.S. L.I. U., 1979; M.Ed., Columbia U., 1981, Ed.D., 1985; cert. photography, Pratt Inst., 1979. R.N., N.Y. Psychiat. nurse Met. Hosp., N.Y.C., 1979-84; staff nurse Manhattan Bowery Project, N.Y.C., 1978-86; instr. Hunter Coll., N.Y.C., 1980-82; prof. Bloomfield Coll., N.J., 1984-85; lectr. Jersey City Coll., 1985; prof. Seton Hall U., South Orange, N.J., 1985—. Recipient Clark Found. scholarship award, 1985; Endowed Nursing Edn., Columbia U., scholar, 1984; Armenian Relief Soc. scholar, 1976-77, Armenian Students Assn. Am. scholar, 1976-78. Fellow Council on Continuing Edn.; mem. Am. Orthopsychiat. Assn., Psychiat. and Mental Health Nursing (council), Inst. for Psychodynamics and Origins of Mind, Armenian Students Assn. (pres. 1981-83, scholarship chairperson 1983-85), Kappa Delta Pi, Sigma Theta Tau. Avocations: aerobics; photography; acting. Office: 127 W 79th St New York NY 10024

KALB, ESTHER LEBSACK, hospital administrator; b. Loveland, Colo., Apr. 4, 1933; d. Jacob and Marie Barbara (Lebsack) Lebsack; m. Kenneth Gene Kalb, Aug. 26, 1956 (div. 1977); children—Erin Wayne, Jerry Laurence. Nursing diploma, Presbyn. Hosp., 1955; B.S.N., U. Denver, 1956; M.A. in Nursing Adminstrn., U. Iowa, 1977. Part-time staff nurse Presbyn. Hosp., Denver, 1956; staff nurse obstetrics Pineview Gen. Hosp., Valdosta, Ga., 1956-57; staff nurse surg. unit U. Mo. Med. Ctr., Columbia, 1957; dir. nursing Boone County Hosp., Columbia, 1957-59; asst. dir. nursing Menorah Med. Ctr., Kansas City, Mo., 1959-61; in-service edn. coordinator St. Mary's Hosp., Madison, Wis., 1963-65; nursing coordinator Toronto Gen. Hosp. (Ont., Can.), 1970-73; clin. nursing specialist III, U. Iowa Hosps., Iowa City, 1973-80; asst. adminstr. patient services Ottumwa Hosp. (Iowa), 1980—. Founder, 1st pres. Families for Future, Inc., Schenectady, 1969; bd. dirs. Southeast Iowa Mental Health Ctr., Ottumwa, 1980—; bd. dirs. adv. com. Ottumwa Pub. Health Nursing Service, 1983—. Mem. Can. Nurses Assn., Am. Nurses Assn., Iowa Nurses Assn. (v.p. 5th dist. 1974, chmn. nursing mgrs. conf. group 1980), Orthopedic Nurses Assn., Am. Soc. Nursing Service Adminstrs. (nat. adv. com.), Am. Coll. Hosp. Adminstrs., Ottumwa Area C. of C., AAUW (chmn. ednl. founds.). Club: Soroptimist (sec. 1981-83, corr. sec. 1983—). Republican. Presbyterian. Office: Ottumwa Hosp 1001 E Pennsylvania Ave Ottumwa IA 52501

KALB, MARY LOUISE, county official; b. Cin., Oct. 9, 1932; d. Clyde Haley and Ilene (Coleman) McKibben; m. Wilbur Adam Kalb, June 29, 1952; children—Christopher Adam, Mary Elaine. Grad. high sch., Brooksville, Ky. Sec. Wald's Mfg., Maysville, Ky., 1950-52; dep. county clk. Bracken County Clk., Brooksville, 1952-54; adminstrv. sec. Bracken County Health Dept., Brooksville, 1954—, registrar vital stats., 1954—, acting adminstr., 1954-82. Exec. sec. Bracken County Red Cross, Brooksville, 1976—; sec. Bracken County Salvation Army, Brooksville, 1978—. Recipient 30 Yr. award Buffalo Trace Dist. Health Dept., Maysville, 1984. Mem. Ky. Pub. Health Support Personnel (pres. 1958-59), Ky. Pub. Health Assn. (bd. dirs. 1958-60). Democrat. Lutheran. Avocations: reading; cooking; music. Home: Route 2 Box 177 Brooksville KY 41004 Office: Bracken County Health Dept Box 117 Frankfort St Brooksville KY 41004

KALDOR, NANCY ELIZABETH, school administrator; b. Rochester, Minn., Feb. 10, 1942; d. Robert Benjamin and Helen Laura (Priebe) Kuhle; m. Richard H. Kaldor, June 15, 1963; children—Katheryn Rae and Kristin Rose (twins), Kori Lynn. B.S., Mayville State U., 1963; postgrad. U. Minn.-St. Paul, 1966-67; M.S., Kans. State U., 1979, Ph.D., 1983. Tchr. Fisher High Sch., Minn., 1963-64; tech. sec. ADCOM, Inc., Boston, 1964-66; reading specialist Cleveland Jr. High Sch., St. Paul, 1966-68, City Jr. High Sch., Junction City, Kans., 1973-80; prin. United Sch. Dist. 481, Hope, Kans., 1983-85; asst. prin. instructional services Austin High Sch., Minn., 1985—. Mem. statewide child abuse com., 1984—; mem. county wide child abuse prevention team, 1985—; mem. Community Services Adv. Council. Mem. Nat. Assn. Secondary Sch. Prins., Minn. Assn. Secondary Sch. Prins., S.E. Minn. Assn. Secondary Sch. Prins., United Sch. Adminstrs., Am. Assn. Curriculum Devel., AAUW, Zonta, Luth. Women's League. Avocations: downhill skiing; swimming; bridge; golf; backgammon. Home: 706 8th Ave NW Austin MN 55912

KALEDO, GRACE LUCILLE, public relations executive; b. Adrian, Mich., Dec. 17, 1928; d. Everett Ray and Ethel (Moore) Deken; student Adrian schs.; m. Charles Gordon Kaledo, June 22, 1946; children—Mary Lou Kaledo Mitchell, Kathryn Sue Kaledo DeMeritt, Larry Michael. Editor, publisher Lenawee Tribune, Adrian, 1968-74; pub. relations with community services dept. City of Adrian, 1975-79; adminstrv. dir. Croswell Opera House, Adrian, 1975-79, bd. dirs., 1978—; ptnr. Catalyst Promotions. Past mem. continuing edn. com. Adrian Coll.; bd. dirs. Southeast Travel & Tourism Commn.; co-chmn. Lenawee Heritage Festival; Croswell Players; past pres. Greater Adrian Inter Club Council; mem. operational support and outreach com. Mich. Council Arts; active Trenton Hills United Brethren Ch. Recipient Outstanding Community Service award Adrian Kiwanis, 1971, Service to Youth award, 1973. Mem. Nat. Fedn. Press Women, Nat. Assn. Female Execs., League Historic Am. Theatres, Nat. Writers Club, Lenawee C. of C. (travel and tourism com.), Mich. Press Women. Clubs: Lenawee Civitan, Adrian Zonta. Home: 124 W Hunt St Adrian MI 49221 Office: PO Box 306 Adrian MI 49221

KALENIK, SANDRA LEE, marketing consultant; b. Fairfield, Conn., Oct. 6, 1945; d. Leo Peter and Julia Mary (Magdon) Kalenik. B.A., Ohio State U., 1968; M.S., Am. U., 1972. Writer IBM, Bethesda, Md., 1972-74; writer, ptnr. Schultz & Conover, Washington, 1974-80; writer, cons., Washington, 1980—. Author: How to Get a Divorce, 1976; contbr. articles to mags. and newspapers including Washington Post Mag., Readers Digest, Mortgage Banking, N.Y. Times, Washington Star. Del. Republican party, Page County, Va., 1985; trustee Washington Area Iconoclastic Found., 1985. Sam S. Shubert Found. fellow, 1970. Avocation: squash. Home: RFD 3 Box 93 Luray VA 22835 Office: 1200 N Nash St Arlington VA 22209

KALFUS-GORDON, ELISE RUTH, management consultant; b. Norfolk, Va., Sept. 14, 1947; d. Seymour H. and Irene C. (Chernitzer) Chapel; m. Ira F. Kalfus, Dec. 22, 1972 (div. 1977); 1 son, Brian Eric; m. Marshall Gordon, Dec. 12, 1981; stepchildren—Howard David, Michael Kenneth, Jack Jay, Sheryl Patricia. Student, Norfolk pub. schs. Acctg. clk. Life Ins. Co. Ga., Atlanta, 1970-72; ind. contractor Atlanta Advertiser, Decatur, Ga., 1973-74; bookkeeper William Harvey Rowland & Co., Mableton, Ga., 1974-77; comptroller Sofas & Chairs, Inc., Atlanta, 1977-79; dir. security and distbn. Simon Mktg. Inc., Atlanta, 1979-80, dir. logistics, 1980-85; mgmt., transp. and Logistics, freight rate audit cons., 1979-85; pres. Traffic Mgmt. Cons., Inc., 1985—; computer newsletter editor. Mem. Women's Traffic Club Atlanta, Delta Nu Alpha, Atlanta Computer Users Group (founder; sec.-treas. 1982-85). Home: 2665 Moss Ln Marietta GA 30067 Office: Traffic Mgmt Cons Inc 1480 Terrell Mill Rd Suite 236 Marietta GA 30067

KALIK, BARBARA FAITH, state legislator; b. Bronx, N.Y., Nov. 8, 1936; d. Albert and Lydia (Cohen) Benowitz; student CCNY, 1953-55; children—Darcie Lynn, Andrew Jay, Lance Jon. Owner, operator Jolie Travel Center, Inc., Willingboro, N.J., 1968—; mem. N.J. Gen. Assembly, 1978—, dep. minority leader, 1986, chmn. revenue, fin. and appropriations com. 1984-85, vice chmn. joint appropriations com., 1984-85, mem. higher edn. and regulated professions com. Council mem. Willingboro, 1971-75; mayor, Willingboro, 1974, 77; pres. Willingboro Democratic Club, 1967; Dem. committeewoman Willingboro 16th Dist., 1965-85; vice chmn. Burlington County Dem. Com., 1970-77; mem. Nat. Dem. Policy Commn.; bd. dirs. Spl. Services Sch.; mem. N.J. Job Tng. Coordinating Council, 1984. Mem. Burlington County C. of C. (pres. 1984). Jewish. Office: Country Club Plaza Beverly-Rancocas Rd Willingboro NJ 08046

KALIN, LENORE GROSS, management consultant; b. Ventura, Calif., Nov. 26, 1946; d. Kenneth Oliver and Marie (Grenade) Gross; m. Neil Barry Kalin, Dec. 18, 1977 (div. Aug. 1981). A.A., Averett Coll., 1966; B.A. in Bus. Adminstrn., Colby Coll., 1968. Sr. group pre-sale underwriter New Eng. Mut. Life Ins. Co., Boston, 1968-73; pension staff asst. Towers, Perrin, Forster, & Crosby, Atlanta, 1973-75, assoc. pension cons., 1976-78, pension and compensation cons., 1979—. Mem. Freedoms Found. at Valley Forge. Mem. Am. Compensation Assn., Am. Soc. Personnel Adminstrs., Sigma Kappa. Republican. Club: Atlanta Polo. Office: Towers Perrin et al 3475 Lenox Rd NE Atlanta GA 30326

KALIN, MARCIA FAY, physician; b. N.Y.C., Sept. 12, 1954; d. Milton and Marilyn (Kravetz) Kalin; B.A. cum laude, Brandeis U., 1976; M.D., Mt. Sinai Sch. Medicine, 1980; m. Edward C. Houser, Oct. 12, 1980. Resident in internal medicine Overlook Hosp., Summit, N.J., 1980-81; editor Sci. Am., N.Y.C., 1981-83; resident in internal medicine Beth Israel Med. Ctr., N.Y.C., 1983-85, fellow in endocrinology, 1985—. Home: 16 E 98th St 2C New York NY 10029 Office: Beth Israel Med Ctr 10 Nathan D Perlman Pl York NY 10003

KALINS, DOROTHY, magazine editor; b. Westport, Conn., Oct. 9, 1942; d. Joseph M. and Gil G. Kalins. Student Skidmore Coll., 1960-62, Sorbonne U., Paris, 1962-63; B.A., Columbia U., 1965. Design writer Home Furnishings Daily, N.Y.C., 1965-68; freelance writer, 1969-74; exec. editor Apartment Life mag. (now Met. Home mag.), N.Y.C., 1974-78, editor-in-chief Met. Home mag., 1978—. Mem. Am. Soc. Mag. Editors (exec. bd.). Author: Researching Design in New York, 1968; Cutting Loose, 1972; The Apartment Book, 1979; The New American Cuisine, 1981; Renovation Style, 1986; contbg. editor N.Y. mag. Contbr. articles to various mags. including Cosmopolitan, N.Y. Mag. Office: Metropolitan Home Magazine 750 3d Ave New York NY 10022

KALLER, MARLENE, lawyer, businesswoman; b. Hartford, Conn., Sept. 5, 1945; d. Harold Milton and Marsha (Luchnick) K.; m. Philip Peter Apter, Dec. 26, 1976; 1 dau., Marsha Kaller-Apter. B.A. with honors and distinction, U. Conn., 1967; J.D., Cath. U. Am., 1972. Bar: Conn. 1972, U.S. Dist. Ct. Conn. 1975. Legis. legal advisor Conn. Gen. Assembly, Hartford, 1972-74; dir. legal and legis. services Conn. Assn. Bd. Edn., Hartford, 1974-76; sole practice, East Hartford, 1976-77; ptnr. Apter & Kaller, East Hartford, 1977—; v.p., dir. 721 Corp., East Hartford, 1983—; pres., dir. 723 Corp., East Hartford, 1983—; ptnr. OAK Mgmt. Co., East Hartford, 1981—. Mem. State of Conn. Bd. Edn. Adv. Panel Racial Imbalance, 1977; mem. com. guardianship and commitment procedures Dept. Mental Retardation, 1977-78; chair Felson for Council Com., West Hartford, 1983; active Greater Hartford Jewish Fedn. Young Leadership div., 1982—, Norfeldt Parent Tchr. Orgn., 1982—; mem. family activities com. Congregation Beth Israel, 1983—; mem. council West Hartford Parent Tchr. Orgn., 1983—; fin. chairperson Brick for Bd. Edn., 1981; chair West Hartford Task Force on Spl. Edn., 1982-83; mem. West Hartford Community Planning Adv. Com., 1984—, Democratic Town Com., 1981—; chair Roisman for State Senate Com., 1982; bd. dirs. Jewish Assn. Community Living, West Hartford, 1982—; v.p. Greater Hartford Jaycees, 1979-80, sec., 1979-80. Recipient Dir. of Yr. award Greater Hartford Jaycees, 1979; cert. of merit U.S. Jaycees, 1979; Govt. Civic Leadership award Conn. Jaycees, 1975, 78. Mem. Conn. Bar Assn., ABA, Hartford County Bar Assn., Pi Sigma Phi, Phi Alpha Theta. Democrat. Jewish. Office: Apter & Kaller PO Box 8764 531 Main St East Hartford CT 06108

KALUZNIACKI, SOPHIA BARBARA, veterinarian; b. Warsaw, Poland, May 11, 1942; came to U.S., 1952; d. Roman Julius and Stena (Zubrzycki) Kaluzniacki; m. George G. Kulesza, Dec. 27, 1971; 1 child, Christina. Student, U. Ariz., 1960-63, Ariz. State U., 1963-64; D.V.M., Wash. State U., 1968. Asst. prof. U. Ariz., Tucson, 1968-70; staff veterinarian Humane Soc. Ariz., Phoenix, 1970-71; pvt. practice vet. medicine, Green Valley, Ariz., 1971—. Contbr. articles to profl. jours. Adv. bd., sec. Pima County Animal Control, Tucson, 1978—; mem., sec. Ariz. State Bd. Vet. Examiners, Phoenix, 1980—; bd. dirs. Soc. Prevention Cruelty to Animals of Ariz., Inc., Tucson, 1972—. Mem. AVMA, Ariz. Vet. Med. Assn., So. Ariz. Vet. Med. Assn. Roman Catholic. Address: Green Valley Animal Hosp 220 E Duval Rd PO Box D Green Valley AZ 85622

KAM, LYDIA BEATRIZ, insurance company executive; b. Panama, July 31, 1952; d. Augustus Raymond and Beatriz Kam; m. Peter A. Lyew, May 27, 1976. B.A., Barat Coll., 1974; M.B.A., La. Tech. U., 1976. Underwriter Am. Internat. Group, N.Y.C., 1976-77, sr. underwriter, fin. analyst, 1977-78; facultative underwriter Gen. Reins. Corp., Dallas, 1978-80, asst. sec., 1980-82, asst. v.p., Greenwich, Conn., 1982—. Barat Coll. scholar, 1971-74, trustee grantee, 1971-74. Mem. Women in Mgmt., Soc. Ins. Research (com. chmn. 1982—), Nat. Assn. Female Execs., Beta Gamma Sigma, Phi Kappa Phi, Kappa Gamma Pi. Roman Catholic. Office: Gen Reins Corp 600 Steamboat Rd Greenwich CT 06830

KAMALI, NORMA, designer; b. N.Y.C., June 27, 1945; d. Sam and Estelle (Grub) Mariategui; grad. Fashion Inst., 1965. With Kamali Ltd., 1967-78; owner, designer O.M.O. Norma Kamali. N.Y.C., 1978—. Recipient Coty Winnie award, 1981, Return award, 1982, Hall of Fame award, 1983; Women's Fashion Designer of Yr. award Council Fashion Designers Am., 1983. Office: 11 W 56th St New York NY 10019*

KAMAN, CAROL KATZEN, county official; b. Phila., Feb. 23, 1929; d. William Wolf and Sylvia G. Katzen; m. Jack A. Kaman, Aug. 6, 1950; children—Cathy K., Karen J., John B. B.A., U. Pa., 1950; postgrad. U. Rochester, 1966-68. Research asst. Rochester Inst. Tech., N.Y., 1970-74, Rochester Area Colls., 1974; assessment specialist Empire State Coll., Rochester, 1974-80; town councilwoman Town of Pittsford, N.Y., 1972-80; clk. of Monroe County Legislature, Rochester, 1980-85; asst. dir. Monroe County Office for the Aging, 1986—; mem. br. adv. com. Community Savs. Bank, Pittsford, 1975-79. Committeewoman Pittsford Republican. Com., 1965-79, 1983—; del. Nat. Women's Polit. Conf., Aspen, Colo., 1978. Mem. Monroe County Bar Assn. (legis. com. 1981—), Friends of Library (program chmn.). Jewish. Club: U. Rochester Faculty. Home: 65 Alpine Dr Rochester NY 14618 Office: County of Monroe 39 W Main St Rochester NY 14614

KAMENITZER, DIANA HELOWICZ, accountant; b. Balt., Dec. 22, 1952; d. Frank P. and Madeline (Zientak) Helowicz; m. Eric Kamenitzer, Nov. 23, 1974 (div. Dec. 1980). B.S., U. Balt., 1974. Acct. Barry L. Dahne, Balt., 1970-74; auditor Ernst & Whinney, Balt., 1974-75; supr. U.S. Army, Camp Zama, Japan, 1975-77; sr. acct. Henry E. Pear, Laurel, Md., 1978-82; ptnr. Hoffman, Kamenitzer & Assocs., Chartered, Balt., 1982—. Mem. Am. Inst. C.P.A.s, Md. Assn. C.P.A.s. Avocation: golf. Home: 19 Ferndale Ave Glen Burnie MD 21061 Office: Hoffman Kamenitzer & Assocs Chartered 306 W Franklin St Baltimore MD 21201

KAMINE, DARLENE MARIS, lawyer; b. Cin., July 20, 1952; d. Jonas and Rose (Jupiter) Greenbaum; m. Charles Stephen Kamine, Aug. 12, 1973; 1 child, Elida Beth. B.A., Brandeis U., 1973; J.D., U. Denver, 1975. Bar: Ohio 1976. Staff atty. Pub. Defender Div., Cin., 1976-79; adj. asst. prof. Law Chase Coll. Law, Covington, Ky., 1979; sole practice, Cin., 1979-82; asst. atty. gen. State of Ohio, 1979-82; referee Hamilton County Juvenile Ct., Cin., 1982—; chmn. Nat. Legal Resource Ctr. for Child Advocacy and Protection, Washington, 1984-85; dir. Guardian Ad Litem Program, Cin., 1978-79; exec. com. mem. Hamilton County Regional Planning Unit for Juvenile Justice, Cin., 1980-83; bd. dirs. Inst. for Child Advocacy, Cleve., 1981-83; trustee Cin. Bar Found., 1980—. Bd. dirs. Parent's Anonymous, Cin., 1981—; bd. dirs., vice chmn. ProKids, Inc., Cin., 1981-85; mem. Jr. League, Cin., 1982—; mem. Community Chest Evaluation Task Force and Children's Services Planning Com., Cin., 1981-83. Mem. Cin. Bar Assn. (chmn. Day Care Com. 1981—), Ohio State Bar Assn. (pres. Young Lawyer's Sect. 1980-81, del. Council of Dels. 1983—), Member, American Bar Association House of Delegates 1980-84 Nat. Conf. of Bar Pres. (liaison 1980-82). Author: Child Abuse, Neglect and Dependency in Ohio, 1982. Office: 309 Gwynne Bldg 602 Main St Cincinnati OH 45202

KAMINSKY, ALICE R., educator; b. N.Y.C.; d. Morris and Ida (Spivak) Richkin; B.A., N.Y.U., 1946, M.A., 1947, Ph.D., 1952; m. Jack Kaminsky. Mem. faculty dept. English, N.Y.U., 1947-49, Hunter Coll., 1952-53, Cornell U., 1954-57, 59-63, Broome Community Coll., 1958-59; mem. faculty dept. English, SUNY, Cortland, 1963—, prof., 1968—; faculty exchange scholar SUNY, 1980. Mem. MLA, New Eng. MLA, Chaucer Soc., Am. Soc. Aesthetics. Author: George Henry Lewes as Critic, 1968; Logic: A Philosophical Introduction, 1974. Editor: Literary Criticism of George Henry Lewes, 1964; Chaucer's Troilus and Criseyde and the Critics, 1980; The Victim's Song, 1985; contbr. articles to profl. jours. Office: Dept English SUNY Cortland NY 13045

KAMINSKY, PHYLLIS, international organization official; b. Montreal, Que., Can., Dec. 1, 1936; came to U.S., 1945, naturalized, 1958; d. Julius and Betty (Shapiro) Levitt; B.A. in Polit. Sci., U. Mich., 1957; postgrad. Columbia U., 1957-58; m. I. Samuel Kaminsky, June 24, 1971; children—David, Glenn. Sec. speakers bur. Fgn. Policy Assn., N.Y.C., 1957-58; editor disarmament procs. UN, Geneva, 1958; secretarial supr. McKinsey and Co., Geneva, 1963-64; adminstrv. asst. Chrysler Internat. S.A., also Internat. Research Cons. S.A., Geneva, 1959-63, Grey Advt. Internat., N.Y.C., 1965-67; exec. asst. Lee Burdick Advt., Inc., N.Y.C., 1967-68; bi-lingual press attache S.B.M. Resort Complex, Monte Carlo, 1968-69; public relations asst. Mayor's Com. for 25th Anniversary of UN, N.Y.C., 1970-71; consular corps liaison officer N.Y.C. Dept. Public Events, 1967-68; media cons., public relations adv. United Jewish Appeal, N.Y.C., 1971-80; media cons. Bush for Pres. Campaign, Pa. and Ill., 1980; dep. dir. communications Coalition for Reagan-Bush, 1980; press sec. to sr. fgn. policy adv. Office of President-Elect, 1980-81; press liaison White House, Nat. Security Council, 1981; dir. Office of Public Liaison, USIA, 1981-83; dir. UN Info. Center, Washington, 1983—; mem. U.S. ofcl. del. 29th session UN Commn. on Status of Women, 1982. Co-founder Jerusalem Women's Seminar, 1979—. Recipient Gold Key award PR News, 1984. Mem. Public Relations Soc. Am., Internat. Pub. Relations Soc., AAUW, Women in Communications; (chmn. pub. affairs adv. bd. 1984-85), Exec. Women in Govt., Nat. Women's Forum. Club: Nat. Press (co-chmn. internat. women's media conf. 1986). Office: 1889 F St NW Washington DC 20006

KAMIYA, LURA ANN, insurance company executive; b. Gonzales, La., Sept. 26, 1952; d. Pershing James and Lee Ella (Lanoux) Mire; m. Shingo Kamiya, Dec. 28, 1973; children—Cheryl, Charlotte. B.A. magna cum laude, N. Tex. State U., 1975. Mgr. human resources Presbyn. Ministers Fund, Phila., 1976—. Fellow Life Mgmt. Inst.; mem. Am. Soc. Personnel Adminstrs., Nat. Assn. for Female Execs., Am. Mgmt. Soc., Delaware Valley Ins. Personnel Group, Internat. Assn. Personnel Women. Republican. Roman Catholic. Office: Presbyn Ministers Fund 1809 Walnut St Philadelphia PA 19103

KAMP, DAWN LEIGH, sales and marketing, importing company executive, retail manager; b. Conneaut, Ohio, June 29, 1951; d. Herbert H. Sandler and Muriel (Fink) Sandler Covner; m. Barry Saal, (div. June 1975); children—Diane, Andrea, Stacy and Julie (triplets); m. Julius Haskell Kamp, Mar. 22, 1981; 1 child, Roslyn. Grad. high sch., Cleve. Owner, operator Sacred Mushroom Sportswear, Cleve., 1968-71; chief exec. officer Dandeleau Ltd., Ignacio, Calif., 1975—; sales coordinator Contemporary Lighting of Calif., Ignacio, 1984—; ptnr., mgr. Raffles, San Rafael, Calif., 1984—. Advocate, establisher Countywide Paramedics, Marin, Calif., 1974-75; Sunday sch. tchr. Rodef Shalom, San Rafael, 1977-79. Named Mother of Yr., C.G. Pub., 1975. Mem. Am. Mgmt. Assn. Jewish. Club: Mother of Twins (pres. 1974-75). Avocations: swimming, ichthiology, local theater. Office: Dandeleau Ltd 6 Commercial Blvd Ignacio CA 94947

KAMPMEIER, FLORA LUISE, clerk of courts; b. Marietta, Ohio, Sept. 29, 1934; d. Oscar W. and Luise (Ruhe) K. Student pub. sch., Marietta. Dep. clk. of cts. Washington County, Marietta, 1952-75, clk. of cts., 1975—. Mem. Ohio Clk. of Cts. Assn. Republican. Nazarene. Home: 614 8th St Marietta OH 45750 Office: Clk of Cts Washington County 205 Putnam St Marietta OH 45750

KANAVY, MARGARITA GUADALUPE, educator; b. El Paso, Tex., Feb. 22, 1939; d. Jose Cruz and Maria G. (Fernandez) Burciaga; B.A. in English, Tex. Western Coll., 1963; M.A., U. Tex., 1969; m. Cletus C. Kanavy, Nov. 28, 1963; children—Patricia, Catherine. Librarian, U. Tex., El Paso, 1972-73; tchr. English, El Paso public schs., 1963-64, 73-79; lectr. English, U. Tex., El Paso, part-time, 1978—; communicative arts instr. U.S. Army Air Def. Arty. Sch., Ft. Bliss, Tex., 1979—; lectr. El Paso Community Coll. Bd. dirs. Mujeres de El Paso, 1980-84, exec. dir., 1984—; EEO counselor, Ft. Bliss, Tex., 1980—. Named Woman of Yr., Mujeres de El Paso, 1981. Mem. Pan Am. Roundtable, Nat. Council Coll. Tchrs. English, Loretto Acad. Alumnae Assn. Democrat. Roman Catholic. Office: DOTD USAADASCH Fort Bliss TX 79916

KANE, AMALIA ESTHER, healthcare agency executive, nurse; b. Balt., Jan. 9, 1938; d. Paul Sardo and Amalie (Hafer) Frank; m. Richard Sean Kane, Sept. 19, 1959; children—Julie Marie, Sean Edward, Paul Francis, Cynthia Louise. R.N. diploma Bon Secours Hosp., Balt., 1959; B.S. in Profl. Arts, St. Joseph's Coll., North Windham, Maine, 1983. Exec. dir. Vis. Nurse Assn., Montgomery County, Tex., 1973-75, dir., Broward County, Fla., 1976-81; pub. health nurse VA, Miami, Fla., 1981-82; dir. hosp. programs Med. Found. South Fla., Coconut Grove, 1983-84; area mgr. Profl. Found. Health Care, Tampa, Fla., 1984; exec. v.p., program dir. Med. Care Devel. Corp., Coral Gables, Fla., 1985; provider rep. for Dade County, Amicare, Miami, Fla., 1985—; guest lectr. Broward Community Coll., Miami, 1982. Sec. Mental Health Assn. Broward County, 1976-81. Mem. Am. Nurses Assn., Am. Pub. Health Assn. Avocations: bowling; writing; travel. Home: 9440 NW 23 St Pembroke Pines FL 33024

KANE, CAROL, actress, b. Cleve., June 18, 1952. Appeared with: touring co. of play The Prime of Miss Jean Brodie, 1966; with, Joseph Papp's Pub. Theatre, Charles St. Playhouse, Boston; film appearances include: Carnal Knowledge, 1971, The Last Detail, 1974, Dog Day Afternoon, 1975, Hester Street, 1975 (Acad. award nomination for Best Actress), Harry and Walter Go to New York, 1976, Annie Hall, 1977, Valentino, 1977, The World's Greatest Lover, 1977, The Mafu Cage, 1977, When a Stranger Calls, 1979, The Muppet Movie, 1979, La Sabina, 1979, Les Jeux, 1980, Strong Medicine, 1981, Norman Loves Rose, 1982, Over the Brooklyn Bridge, 1984; stage appearances include: The Effect of Gamma Rays on Man in the Moon Marigolds, 1978, Tales from the Vienna Woods, 1979, Benefit of a Doubt, 1979, The Tempest and Macbeth at Lincoln Center, Sunday Runners in the Rain, 1980, A Midsummer Night's Dream, The Fairy Garden, The Second Stage, 1984; appeared in TV films Many Mansions, An Invasion of Privacy, 1983; appeared in TV series Taxi. Recipient Emmy award for best supporting actress in a comedy series for Taxi, 1983. Office: care Creative Artists Agy Inc 1888 Century Park E Suite 1400 Los Angeles CA 90067

KANE, CARROLL O'BRIEN, educator; b. Hartford, Conn., d. Richard and Catherine (Normile) O'Brien; m. Theodore Gibbs Kane, July 13, 1946; children—T. Gibbs, Richard Sperry, Katherine Kane Nichols. B.A., Smith Coll., 1946. Tchr. Miss Fines Sch., Princeton, N.J., 1946-59, Princeton Day Sch., 1959-71, Sewickley Acad., Pa., 1972-77; dir. Sewickley Care and Devel. Ctr., 1980—, Union Aid Soc., Sewickley, 1984—. Trustee Princeton Pub. Library, 1968-72; bd. dirs. Sewickley Friends of Library, 1976. Republican. Roman Catholic. Clubs: Woman's Club of Sewickley Valley (pres. 1981-83), Query (pres. 1976-78), Village Garden. Home: 963 Beaver Rd Sewickley PA 15143

KANE, JACQUELINE ANNE, educational administrator; b. N.Y.C., Aug. 27, 1946; d. Philip and Jacqueline (Jones) K.; A.B., Morgan State Coll., 1968; M.S., SUNY Coll., Oneonta, 1974; postgrad. in sociology SUNY, Albany, 1980—. Caseworker, Dept. Social Services N.Y.C., 1968-70; counselor SUNY Coll., Oneonta, 1970-71, coordinator counseling and acad. advisement, 1971-75; asso. in higher edn. opportunity N.Y. State Edn. Dept., Albany, 1975—. Bd. dirs. Albany County Big Brothers/Big Sisters, 1977-80, Albany Area chpt. ARC, 1984—. Mem. Am. Council Edn. (nat. identification project, N.Y. state planning com.), Black Profl. Women's Network (dir. 1978-82), N.Y. State Assn. Non-White Concerns in Personnel and Guidance (pres.), Assn. Black Women in Higher Edn. (pres. 1978-81, conf. chmn. 1978—, dir. 1981—), Delta Sigma Theta (chmn. program and fin. coms. alumnae chpt. Albany, 1979-81, rec. sec. 1981-83, pres. 1983-85). Lutheran. Office: CEC 5A55 Empire State Plaza Albany NY 12230

KANE, JANET EMPIE, interior design firm executive, educator; b. Scotia, N.Y., Oct. 16, 1936; d. Kenneth Alfred and Helen Elizabeth Empie; m. Roger Carl Kane, Dec. 28, 1957 (div. May 1979); children—Peter Carl, Kenneth Chapple. B.F.A., Pratt Inst., 1958. Staff designer Bloomingdales, N.Y.C., 1958-60; project mgr. Van Dyck Corp., Westport, Conn., 1960-62, Thalhimers Bus. Interiors, Richmond, Va., 1968-71; mgr., design dir. Litton Office Products, Richmond, 1971-72; v.p., design dir. Interior Design Assocs., Richmond, 1972-74; pres. Janet Kane Interiors, Inc., Richmond, 1974—; bd. dirs. Futures Council, Va. Tech. State U., Blacksburg, 1984—; asst. prof. dept. interior design Va. Commonwealth U., Richmond, 1979-80. Treas., Republican Senatorial Campaign, Richmond, 1969. Named Interior of Yr., 3-M Co., Inc., Richmond, 1980; recipient Air Tycom-Quality of Life award Dept. Navy, Virginia Beach, Va., 1983. Mem. Am. Soc. Interior Designers (nat. regional v.p. 1981-82, mem. nat. industry found. 1981-85, pres. Va. chpt. 1986; outstanding contract interior 1978, presdl. citation 1982, nat. presdl. citation 1982-83), Retail Mchts. Assn. (membership com. 1979), Richmond C. of C. (membership com. 1986), Richmond Met. C. of C. (newcomers com. 1985). Republican. Presbyterian. Club: Insider's (Richmond) (pres. 1985-86). Avocations: bicycling; bowling; golf. Home: 14309 Winter Ridge Ln Richmond VA 23230 Office: Janet Kane Interiors Inc 1301 N Hamilton St Suite 105 Richmond VA 23230

KANE, JEAN CAROLINE, interior design fabricator; b. N.Y.C., May 2, 1941; d. James Alfred and Theresa Miriam (Schulz) Amoroso; A.S., Endicott Coll., 1961; m. John Francis Kane, May 2, 1964; 1 dau., Cathleen Theresa. Free-lance model with Candy Jones Modeling Agy., N.Y.C., 1950-8; asst. dept. mgr. Lord & Taylor, Scarsdale, N.Y., 1959, multi-br. mdse. mgr., N.Y.C., 1961-62; asst. advt. mgr. Van Raalte, Inc., N.Y.C., 1962-64; free-lance promotion coordinator for Van Raalte, Inc., 1965-68; free-lance interior design fabricator Mamaroneck, N.Y., 1969—; cons. Eye of the Needle, Larchmont, N.Y., 1965-85; Prentice-Hall tng. video on reupholstery, 1982-83; tchr. upholstery Bd. Coop. Ednl. Services, Yorktown, N.Y., 1979. Sec., Rye Neck Sch. Bd.; trustee Selection Com., Mamaroneck, 1976-77, pres., 1977-78; chairwoman club activities F.E. Bellos Sch. Parent Tchr. Student Assn., Mamaroneck, 1977-79, co-chairwoman book and art show, 1980; active Girl Scouts U.S.A., Mamaroneck community dir., 1978-83, del. ann. meeting Sackerah Path council, 1978-79, Westchester/Putnam council, 1979-82; active campaign for mayor of Mamaroneck, 1979. Roman Catholic. Designs include: 2 rooms of Larchmont Shore Club; fabric design for Bloomingdale Mansion, YWCA house tour; 3 rooms of 16th century replica French castle; members' needlpoint for doors of Temple Israel, Scarsdale. Home and Office: 116 Lawn Terr Mamaroneck NY 10543

KANE, MARCIA A., public relations executive; b. Pitts., May 9, 1932; d. Samuel and Annette (Braverman) Frankel; m. Sidney G. Kane, Sept. 12, 1959 (div. 1973); children—Michael Adam, Jonathan David. B.S., Carnegie Inst. Tech., 1955. Mgmt., promotion exec. Shopping Malls, Lancaster, Pa., 1974-77; account exec. Kelly Advt., 1977-79; dir. pub. relations Lancaster Osteo. Hosp., 1979-85. Mem. Internat. Assn. Bus. Communicators, Women in Communications, Lancaster Advt. Club, Acad. Hosp. Pub. Relations, Am. Soc. Hosp. Pub. Relations. Home: 1004 Olde Hickory Rd Lancaster PA 17601 Office: Lancaster Osteo Hosp 1175 Clark St Lancaster PA 17604

KANE, MARGARET BRASSLER, sculptor; b. East Orange, N.J., May 25, 1909; d. Hans and Mathilde (Trumpler) Brassler; student Packer Collegiate Inst., 1920-26, Syracuse U., 1927, Art Students League, 1927-29, N.Y. Coll. Music, 1928-29, John Hovannes Studio, 1932-34; Ph.D., Colo. State Christian Coll., 1973; m. Arthur Ferris Kane, June 11, 1930; children—Jay Brassler, Gregory Ferris. Work has appeared at Jacques Seligmann Gallery, N.Y., Whitney Ann. Exhbns., All Sculptors Guild Mus. and Outdoor Shows, 1900, Nat. Sculpture Soc. Ann. Bas-Relief Exhbn., 1938, Whitney Mus. Sculpture Festival, 1940, Bklyn. Mus. Sculptors Guild, 1938, Bklyn. Soc. Artists, 1942, Lawrence (Mass.) Art Mus., 1938, N.Y. World's Fair, 1939, Sculptors Guild World's Fair Exhbn., 1940, Robinson Gallery, N.Y., 1939, Traveling Mus. and Instns., 1938, Lyman Allyn Mus., 1939, Met. Mus., Internat. Exhbns., 1940, 1949, Roosevelt Field Art Center, N.Y.C., 1957, Phila. Mus., N.Y. Archtl. League, Nat. Acad., Pa. Acad., Chgo. Art Inst., Am. Fedn. Arts, Riverside Mus., Montclair Mus., Grand Central Art Galleries, Lever House, N.Y.C., 1959-82, Rye (N.Y.) Library, 1962, Lever House Sculptors Guild Ann. Exhbn., 1977—, and exhbns. of nat. scope, 1938—; executed plaque for Burro Monument, Fairplay, Colo.; solo sculpture exhibit Friends of Greenwich Library, 1962; exhibited N.Y. Bank for Savs., 1968, Mattatuck Mus., 1967, Lamont Gallery, N.H., 1967. Head craftsman for sculpture, arts and skills unit ARC, Halloran Gen. Hosp., N.Y., 1942-43. Jury mem. Brooklyn Mus., 1948, Am. Machine & Foundry Co. Art Exhibit, Greenwich, Conn., 1957; com. mem. Am. Group, Inc. Slide lectr. and sculpture demonstrator for art socs. and orgns. Recipient Ann Hyatt Huntington award, 1942; awards Am. Artists Profl. League, Montclair Art Assn., 1943; 1st Henry O. Avery prize, 1944; sculpture prize Bklyn. Soc. Artists, Bklyn. Mus., 1946, John Rogers award, 1951; Lawrence Hyder prize, 1952, 54; David Zell Meml. award, 1954-63; hon. mention U.S. Maritime Commn., 1941; A.C.A. Gallery Competition, 1944; medal of honor for sculpture, 1951, Nat. Assn. Women Artists, Nat. Acad. Galleries, N.Y.; prize for carved sculpture, 1955, animal sculpture, 1956, Ann. New Eng. Exhbns., Silvermine, Conn.; 1st award for sculpture Greenwich Art Soc., 1958, 60; award for creative work in sculpture Am. Biog. Inst., 1982. Fellow Internat. Inst. Arts and Letters; mem. Nat. Trust Hist. Preservation, Internat. Sculpture Ctr., 1983-86, Sculptors Guild (sec. to exec. bd. 1942-45, chmn. exhbn. com. 1942, 44), Nat. Assn. Women Artists (2d v.p. 1943-45), Artists Council, U.S.A., Bklyn. Soc. Artists, Greenwich Soc. Artists (council mem.), Pen and Brush, Silvermine Guild Artists. Contbr. articles to mags.; sculpture reproduced in books Contemporary Stone Sculpture, Contemporary American Sculpture; featured in Am. Artist mag., Jan. 1970, Dictionary of American Sculptors-Apollo Book, 1984. Home and Studio: 30 Strickland Rd Cos Cob CT 06807

KANE, NANCY ELLEN, college administrator; b. Taunton, Mass., July 10, 1947; d. Julius J. and Dorothy (Moscoff) K. B.A., NYU, 1969; M.A., Mich. State U., 1971; Ph.D., Fla. State U., 1982. Residence hall dir, intr. edn. Ill. State U.-Normal, 1971-72; residential area coordinator Cornell U., Ithaca, N.Y., 1972-74; dir. residence life U. So. Maine, Gorham, 1974-77; asst. dir. student activities Va. Commonwealth U., Richmond, 1977-80; research asst. Fla. State U., Tallahassee, 1980-83; dean of students Mary Baldwin Coll., Staunton, 1983—. Author: (with others) Creating Community in Residence Halls: A Workbook for Definition, Design, Delivery, 1980. Troop leader Girl Scouts Am., Portland, 1978-80. Recipient Alumnae award NYU, 1969; W. Hugh Stickler Meml. Fund award Fla. State U., 1982. Mem. Am. Coll. Personnel Assn. (exec. council 1980-85), Nat. Assn. Student Personnel Adminstrs., Am. Assn. Higher Edn., So. Coll. Personnel Assn. (dissertation of Yr. award 1983). Office: Mary Baldwin Coll New and Frederick Sts Staunton VA 24401

KANELY, EDNA AGATHA, former library administrator; b. Balt., Sept. 24, 1910; d. Charles Henry and Mary Agatha (Sudbrook) K. B.S. magna cum laude in Bus. Mgmt., U. Balt., 1958; M.S. in Library Sci., Cath. U., 1975. Asst. supr., statis. clk. and instr. Montgomery Ward & Co., Balt., 1929-41; with GPO, Washington, 1941-73, typist, stenographer, supr., asst. chief sect., 1951-65, chief customers service sect., 1965-69, with library sect., 1969, library adminstr., 1970-73; trainer personnel Carrollton Press, Inc., Inverness, Scotland, 1973, 74-75. Author, compiler: Baltimore and Ohio Railroad Employees, 1842-1857, 1982; Author, compiler, indexer: Cumulative Subject Index to Monthly Catalog of U.S. Government Publications 1895-1899, 2 vols., 1977; Cumulative Index to Hickcox's Monthly Catalog of U.S. Government Publications 1885-1894, 3 vols., 1981; compiler: Cumulative Subject Guide to U.S. Government Bibliographies 1924-1973, 7 vols., 1976, 77; co-compiler: Cumulative Subject Index to the Monthly Catalog of U.S. Government Publications 1900-1971, 15 vols.; contbr. articles to profl. jours. Recipient Outstanding vol. award Enoch Pratt Library, 1977; award for Superior Service, GPO, 1964; award CD Balt., 1956; others. Mem. Md. Hist. Soc. (com. genealogy 1981—, library com. 1981—, publs. com. 1983—), Geneal. Council Md. (chmn. ch. records com. 1983—), Md. Geneal. Soc. (librarian 1981—, award of merit 1982), Balt. County Geneal. Soc. (v.p. 1983-84), Del Geneal. Soc., Nat. Geog. Soc., Smithsonian Assocs., Archives Assocs., ALA (ad hoc subcom. fed. depository legis. 1976-77), Md. Library Assn., D.C. Library Assn., Spl. Libraries Assn. Democrat. Lutheran. Home: 3210 Chesterfield Ave Baltimore MD 21213

KANG, BANN, physician; b. Kyungnam, Korea, Mar. 4, 1939; d. Daeryong and Buni (Chung) K.; came to U.S., 1964, naturalized, 1976; A.B., Kyungpook Nat. U., 1959, M.D., 1963; m. U. Yun Ryo, Mar. 30, 1963. Intern, L.I. Jewish Hosp.-Queens Hosp. Center, Jamaica, N.Y., 1964-65, resident in medicine, 1965-67; teaching asso. Kyungpook U. Hosp., Taegu, Korea, 1967-70; fellow in allergy and chest Creighton U., Omaha, 1970-71; fellow in allergy Henry Ford Hosp., Detroit, 1971-72; clin. instr. medicine U. Mich. Hosp., Ann Arbor, 1972-73; asst. prof. Chgo. Med. Sch., 1973-74; chief allergy-immunology Mt. Sinai Hosp., Chgo., 1975—; asst. prof. Rush Med. Sch., Chgo. 1975-84, assoc. prof., 1984—; cons. allergy-immunology Edgewater Hosp., Chgo., 1976—, St. Anthony's Hosp., Chgo., 1976—. Recipient NIH award U. Mich., 1972-73. Diplomate Am. Bd. Internal Medicine, Am. Bd. Allergy-Immunology. Fellow ACP, Am. Acad. Allergy; mem. Am. Fedn. Clin. Research, AMA, Inter-Asthma Assn. Contbr. over 40 articles to profl. jours. Home: 1555 N Astor St Chicago IL 60610 Office: Mount Sinai Hosp Chicago IL 60608

KANIG, LAVINIA LUDLOW, former state legislator, educator, librarian; b. Spanish Fork, Utah, Jan. 8, 1916; d. Fred and Serena Lavena (Andrus) Ludlow; m. Charles William Kanig, July 8, 1941 (div. 1957); children—Frank Ludlow, Serena. B.S., Brigham Young U., 1939; postgrad. U. Utah, Boston U., Brigham Young U., Fresno State U.; student Taft Inst. Politics, Trinity U., 1975. Cert. librarian, Utah; cert. secondary tchr., Utah. Tchr. Kane County Schs., Kanab, Utah, 1948-59; librarian, researcher Nebo Sch. Dist., Spanish Fork, 1959-78; field coordinator Republican Nat. Com., Washington, 1971; messenger-communications Utah Ho. of Reps., 1973-82; mem. Utah Ho. of Reps., 1983-84, mem. joint appropriations community and econs. devel. com. 1983-84; area adminstrv. chmn. Utah County Republicans, Spanish Fork, 1965-80; mem. adv. com. Senator Hatch, 1980—. Field coordinator Rep. Nat. Com., 1971-72. Recipient Community Service award Spanish Fork City, 1981; Library Adminstrn. grantee Boston U., 1966. Mem. Order Women Legislators, Utah Federated Womens' Club (edn. chmn. 1984—), Utah Assn. Women (edn. chmn. Maple Mountain Chpt. 1984—), Aglaian Literary Club, Phi Chi Theta, Phi Delta Pi. Avocations: travel; camping; gardening. Home: 81 W 100 South Spanish Fork UT 84660

KANNRY, SYBIL, psychotherapist, consultant, b. Tulsa, Okla., Oct. 1, 1931; d. Julius and Celia Bertha (Triger) Zeligson; m. Daniel Kannry, June 12, 1977; children by previous marriage—Jeffrey Alan Shames, Erica Leslie Shames, Jonathan Adam Shames. Student U. Colo., 1949-51; B.A., U. Okla., 1953; M.S.W., NYU, 1974. Tchr. piano, Tulsa, 1956-61; psychiatric social worker Essex County Hosp., Cedar Grove, N.J., 1974-75, Rockland Psychiat. Ctr., Spring Valley, N.Y., 1975, adult team supr., 1975-78, adult team supr., Haverstraw, N.Y., 1978, clinic supr., Orangeburg, N.Y., 1978-83, clinic dir., Yonkers, N.Y., 1983-84; founder, dir. Indsl. Counseling Assocs., South Nyack, N.Y., 1982-84, ctr. for Corp. and Community Counseling, South Nyack, 1984—; founder, pres. Tulsa Assn. for Childbirth Edn., 1957-59. Fellow Soc. Clin. Social Work Psychotherapists; mem. Am. Assn. Marriage and Family Therapy (clin. mem.), N.Y. Milton H. Erickson Soc. for Psychotherapy and Hypnosis, Nat. Assn. Social Workers, Am. Orthopsychiat. Assn., Acad. Cert. Social Workers, Assn. Labor-Mgmt. Adminstrs. and Cons. on Alcholism, Soc. Clin. and Exptl. Hypnosis. Home and Office: 2 Clinton Ave South Nyack NY 10960

KANOVA, MARIA GRACE, sculptor, painter; b. Frenstatpod Radhostem, Moravia, Czechoslovakia, July 1, 1939; came to U.S., 1968; d. Frantisek Grygar Kana and Marie Srubar Kanova. Student Tech. Inst. Sch. Architecture, Brno, Czechoslovakia, 1957, 58; B.F.A., U. Applied Arts, Prague, Czechoslovakia, 1962, M.F.A., 1964. Cert. tchr. Acad. sculptor Czech. Inst. Fine Arts, Prague, 1964-68; pres. Kanova Fine Arts Studio, Gallery, Houston, 1968—; exec. tchr. Berlitz Sch. Langs., Houston, 1974-75. Author: New Art Style-Potentialism, 1980. One-woman show Festival USA on Strand, 1974 (Bicentennial Show award). Chmn. Czech. Sts. Cyril and Methodius Heritage Soc., Houston, 1983—. Recipient 1st prize internat. competition for Nat. Shrine, Washington, 1981, award Nat. Mus. Bozena Nemcova, Czechoslovakia, 1968, Internat. Telecommunication Union, Geneva, 1965. Mem. Nat. Sculpture Soc., Tex. Arts Alliance, Nat. Assn. Female Execs., UNESCO Internat. Assn. of Artists, Czechoslovakian Inst. Fine Arts. Roman Catholic. Office: Kanova Fine Arts Studio-Gallery 1747 Campbell Rd Houston TX 77080

KANOVSKY, HELEN RENEE, lawyer; b. Warren, Pa., Mar. 4, 1951; d. Hershel and Rose (Gernstat) K.; A.B. cum laude, Cornell U., 1973; J.D. cum laude, Harvard U., 1976; m. Marc Bernard Dorfman, Aug. 8, 1976. Dir. vols. Biden for Senate, Wilmington, Del., 1972; legis. aide to U.S. Senator Joseph R. Biden, Washington, 1973; admitted to D.C. Ct. Appeals bar, 1976, U.S. Dist. Ct. bar for D.C., 1977, U.S. Ct. Appeals bar for D.C., 1977; assoc. firm Dickstein, Shapiro and Morin, Washington, 1976-79; spl. asst. to sec. HUD, Washington, 1979; spl. asst. to sec. HEW, Washington, 1979-80, spl. asst. to the sec., assoc. exec. sec. to HHS and exec. asst. to undersec., Dept. Health and Human Services, 1980-81; assoc., then ptnr. Dickstein, Shapiro & Morin, Washington, 1981-84; ptnr. Leff & Mason, Washington, 1984—. Bd. dirs. Women's Legal Def. Fund, 1981-83. Recipient cert. spl. achievement Sec. HUD, 1979. Mem. Am. Bar Assn., D.C. Bar, Bar Assn. D.C. (chairperson ethics com. sect. young lawyers 1978-79), Phi Beta Kappa. Democrat. Jewish. Editor Harvard Civil Rights—Civil Liberties Law Rev., 1975-76. Home: 7004 Winslow St Bethesda MD 20817 Office: 1700 Pennsylvania Ave NW Suite 450 Washington DC 20006

KANTROWITZ, SUSAN LEE, lawyer; b. Queens, N.Y., Jan. 15, 1955; d. Theodore and Dinah (Kotick) Kantrowitz; m. Alexander Sirotkin, Aug. 30, 1981. B.S. summa cum laude, Boston U., 1977; J.D., Boston Coll., 1980. Bar: Mass. 1982. Assoc. producer Sta. KOCE-TV, Huntington Beach, Calif., 1980-81; account exec. Bozell & Jacobs, Newport Beach, Calif., 1981; atty. WGBH Ednl. Found., Boston, 1981-84, dir. legal affairs, 1984-86, gen. counsel, dir. legal affairs, 1986—. Co-Author: Legal and Business Aspects of the Entertainment, Publishing and Sports Industries, 1984. Mem. ABA, Mass. Bar Assn.

KANY, JUDY CASPERSON, state senator; d. Helmer C. and Florence P. Casperson; B.B.A., U. Mich., 1959; M.P.A., U. Maine; m. Robert H. Kany, 1958; children—Kristin, Geoffrey, Dan. Mem. Maine Ho. of Reps., del. 1975-82; mem. Maine Senate, 1982—, chair Joint Com. Energy and Natural Resources. Democratic Nat. Conv., 1976. Mem. Commn. Maine's Future. Office: Maine Senate State Capitol Augusta ME 04333*

KAO, YASUKO WATANABE, librarian; b. Tokyo, Mar. 30, 1930; came to U.S., 1957; d. Kichiji and Sato (Tanaka) Watanabe; m. Shih-Kung Kao, Apr. 1, 1959; children—John Sterling, Stephanie Margaret. B.A., Tsuda Coll., 1950; B.A. in Lit., Waseda U., 1953; M.S.L.S., U. So. Calif., 1960. Instr., Takinogawa High Sch., Tokyo, 1950-57; catalog librarian U. Utah Library, 1960-67, Marriott Library, 1975-77, head catalog div., 1978—. Contbr. articles to profl. jours. Vol., Utah Chinese Am. Community Sch., 1974-80, Asian Assn. Utah, 1981—. Waseda U. fellow, 1958-59. Mem. ALA, Assn. Coll. and Research Libraries, ALA Library and Info. Tech. Assn., Utah Acad. Sci. Utah Library Assn., Utah Coll. Library Council, Beta Phi Mu. Democrat. Address: 2681 Comanche Dr Salt Lake City UT 84108

KAPILOFF, HELEN BELL, social worker; b. Houston, Oct. 13, 1915; d. Wolf B. and Lena (Robinowitz) Bell; B.A., Rice Inst., 1935; M.A., U. Chgo., 1937; m. Gerald Kapiloff, Nov. 2, 1943 (div., dec.); 1 son, David. Med. social worker Johns Hopkins Hosp., 1937-38; social worker Com. for Care Jewish Tb, 1938-41; Caseworker ARC, 1941-43; supr. Harris County chpt., 1943-46; chief social worker VA Regional Office, Houston, 1946-49, VA Med. Center, Houston, 1949—; mem. adv. com. adj. faculty, lectr. U. Houston Grad. Sch. Social Work; social work adminstr. trainer VA, 1972-77. Mem. Nat. Assn. Social Workers (bd. dirs. 1974-77, past pres. Tex. council, pres. Houston unit 1980-82), Am. Soc. Hosp. Social Work Dirs., Tex. Soc. Hosp. Social Work Dirs. (past pres.). Office: VA Med Center 2002 Holcombe Blvd Houston TX 77211

KAPILOFF, LYNN GERSTENFELD, insurance consultant; b. Apr. 18, 1938; d. Norman and Louise (Mundheim) Gerstenfeld; m. Bernard Kapiloff, Jan. 29, 1961; children—Miriam, Mark, Michael. B.A., Sarah Lawrence Coll., 1959; postgrad. Johns Hopkins U., 1962. Assoc. buyer Lansburgh's, Washington, 1959-60; placement officer Patricia Stevens Inst. Fashion, Washington, 1960-61; ind. ins. cons., Balt., 1963—; mgr. Office Dr. Bernard Kapiloff, Balt., 1970—. Vol. ward clk. Sinai Hosp., Balt., 1961; tchr. Liberty Coop. Nursery, Balt., 1964-67; fundraiser Associated Jewish Charities, Israel Bonds, Balt., 1965-84; bd. dirs. Jewish Nat. Fund, 1974—, v.p., pres. women's aux., Balt., 1974-80; mem., chmn., co-editor newsletter Md. Bd. Social Services, 1971-83; bd. dirs. Marylanders for Right to Choose, 1978—, Women's Div. Israel Bonds, 1965—; hon. bd. mem. Balt. City Commn., 1973—. Recipient Disting. Citizenship award State Md., 1972; Scroll Honor, State Israel Bonds, 1972; N'Div Lev award Talmudical Acad., Balt., 1973; Israel Solidarity award State Israel, 1976. Mem. Friends of Artists Equity (dir.), Johns Hopkins Assocs., Friends Am. U., Jewish Community Ctr. Garden Club (exhibitor). Home: 5307 N Charles St Baltimore MD 21210 Office: 200 W Coldspring Ln Baltimore MD 21210

KAPLAN, ANNE KARP, marketing executive; b. N.Y.C., Mar. 26, 1938; d. Harold I. and Helen P. (Spiegel) Halperin; B.A., Vassar Coll., 1959; m. Richard Kaplan, May 20, 1984; 1 son, Clifford Karp. Advt. supr. Montgomery Ward, N.Y.C., 1963-69; publs. officer Community Coll. of Balt., 1978-79; asst. v.p. Mass Mktg. Systems Internat., N.Y.C., 1982-84; v.p. Assoc. Direct Mktg. Services, N.Y.C., 1984—; v.p. Md. Pub. Relations Affiliates, 1979. Bd. dirs. Md. New Directions for Women, 1977; mem. fed. funds grant com. Md. Displaced Homemakers, 1977. Recipient Wards Outstanding Performance award, 1967; Mead Award of Merit, 1979. Mem. Direct Mktg. Assn., Direct Mktg. Club N.Y., Women's Direct Response Group. Home: 219 E 69th St New York NY 10021 Office: 475 Park Ave S New York NY 10016

KAPLAN, ARLENE LAVENDER, banker; b. N.Y.C., Mar. 4, 1928; d. Michael and Leah Lavender; B.A. in Math. cum laude, SUNY, Albany, 1948; M.A. in Math., Columbia U., 1966; m. Bernard Kaplan, Aug. 23, 1952; children—Lee Michael, Jonathan Harris. Actuarial asst. G.B. Buck, Cons. Actuary, 1948-54; programmer Bankers Trust Co., N.Y.C., 1966-68, mgmt. scientist, 1968-72, asst. treas., asst. v.p. retail planning, 1972-79, v.p., head mgmt. info. systems in strategic planning dept., 1979—. Home: 27 Pryer Manor Rd Larchmont NY 10538 Office: 280 Park Ave New York NY 10015

KAPLAN, DOROTHY ANNE, clinical psychologist; b. N.Y.C., May 7, 1954; d. Milton and Madeleine (Hundert) Kaplan; B.A. with highest honors in Psychology, SUNY-Stony Brook, 1975; Ph.D. in Clin. Psychology (NIMH fellow), U. Vt., 1979. Asst. prof. psychology SUNY Coll. at Brockport, 1979-83; dir. psychol. services Children's Hosp. and Rehab. Ctr., Utica, N.Y., 1983-85; sr. clin. psychologist Nat. Rehab. Hosp., Washington, 1986—; cons. clin. psychologist Orleans County Mental Health, Job Corps., Office Vocat. Rehab., Bur. Disability Determination; lectr. U. Vt., 1978-79. Lic. psychologist, N.Y. Mem. Assn. for Advancement of Behavior Therapy, Am. Psychol. Assn., N.Y. State Psychol. Assn., Gennesee Valley Psychol. Assn. (v.p.), Soc. for Study of Social Issues, Phi Beta Kappa. Contbr. articles to profl. jours. Home: 1515 Casino Circle Silver Spring MD 20906 Office: Psychol Services Nat Rehab Hosp 102 Irving St Washington DC 20010

KAPLAN, ERICA LYNN, typing/word processing service company executive, pianist, vocal coach; b. Jamaica, N.Y., Aug. 6, 1955; d. George William and Raylia (Eagle) Kaplan; m. James Laurence Kellermann, Feb. 26, 1982. B.Mus., Manhattan Sch. Music, N.Y.C., 1976, M.Mus., 1979. Clk. dept. edn. 92d Street Y, N.Y.C., 1972-76, assoc. dept. pub. relations, 1977-78, catalogue coordinator, sec. to exec. dir., 1978, assoc. dept. performing arts, 1978-79, assoc. dir. dept. publications, 1979-80; pres. Erica Kaplan Typing/Word Processing/Music Services, N.Y.C., 1980—; resident pianist Am. Renaissance Theater, N.Y.C., 1981—; typist, cons. Horowitz, 1982-83. Translator: L'Anacrouse dans la Musique Moderne, 1978. Composer: Four by Feiffer, 1978, Hey Boys, 1984. Mem. New Eng. Anti-Vivisection Soc., Boston, 1982—, Common Cause, Washington, 1983—. Mem. Am. Fedn. Musicians, Nat. Assn. Female Execs., Union Concerned Scientists. Democrat. Jewish. Avocations: theater, traveling. Home: Box 102 141 E 89th St New York NY 10128

KAPLAN, HELENE L., lawyer; b. N.Y.C., June 19, 1933; d. Jack and Shirley (Jacobs) Finkelstein; A.B. cum laude, Barnard Coll., 1953; J.D., N.Y. U., 1967; m. Mark N. Kaplan, Sept. 7, 1952; children—Marjorie Ellen, Sue Anne. Admitted to N.Y. bar, 1967; individual practice law, N.Y.C., 1967-78; mem. firm Webster & Sheffield, 1978—; dir. Mitre Corp., May Dept. Stores Co., N.Y.C. Partnership. Trustee N.Y. Council for Humanities, 1976-81, chmn., 1978-81; trustee N.Y. Found., 1976-86; trustee Barnard Coll., 1973—, vice chmn., 1975-83, chmn., 1983—; trustee Columbia U. Press., 1977-80, John Simon Guggenheim Found., 1981—; trustee Carnegie Corp. N.Y., 1979—, vice-chmn., 1981-84, chmn., 1984—; trustee Mt. Sinai Med. Center, Hosp. and Sch., 1977—; trustee N.Y.C. Public Devel. Corp., 1978-83, vice chmn., 1979-81; mem. Women's Forum, 1982—; trustee Olive (N.Y.) Free Library, 1983—; mem. Gov. Cuomo's Task Force on Life and Law, 1985—; mem. U.S. State Dept. Adv. Commn. on South Africa. Mem. Assn. Bar City N.Y. (com. philanthropic orgn. 1978-81, com. profl. responsibility, com. problems concerning recruitment of new lawyers), Am., N.Y. State bar assns., Am. Arbitration Assn. (dir. 1980-83). Clubs: Cosmopolitan, Coffee House. Home: 146 Central Park W New York NY 10023 Office: One Rockefeller Plaza New York NY 10020

KAPLAN, JOAN ELLEN, art advisor, curator; b. N.Y.C., Dec. 30, 1943; d. Henry and Frieda (Peck) Goldman; B.A. with honors, Conn. Coll., New London, 1964; m. Stephen L. Kaplan, Aug. 14, 1966 (div.); 1 son, Craig Robert. Dir. Adria Art Gallery, N.Y.C., 1966-68; pres. Joan Kaplan Fine Art, N.Y.C., 1968—; advisor curator numerous corps, including Am. Express Co.; mem. organizing com. fine arts program XIV Olympic Games, Sarajevo, 1984. Mem. Assn. Profl. Art Advisors. Office: 525 E 86th St New York NY 10028

KAPLAN, JOCELYN RAE, financial planning firm executive; b. Lynbrook, N.Y., Apr. 23, 1952; d. Eugene S. and Adeline (Dembo) K. B.S., Northwestern U., 1975. Cert. fin. planner. Ins. agt. Fidelity Union Life Ins. Co., College Park, Md., 1976-77, Bankers Life Ins. Co., Rockville, Md., 1977-80; fin. planner Reutemann & Wagner, McLean, Va., 1980-82; fin. planning casewriter McLean Fin. Group, 1982-83; dir. fin. planning DeSanto Naftal Co., Vienna, Va., 1983-85; pres. Advisors Fin., Inc., Vienna, 1985—. Founding mem., treas. Congregation Bet Mishpachah, Washington, 1981, v.p., 1982, pres., 1983. Recipient Nat. Quality award Nat. Assn. Life Underwriters, 1978; Agt. of Yr. award Gen. Agt. and Mgrs. Assn., 1978. Mem. Internat. Assn. Fin. Planners, Inst. Cert. Fin. Planners. Home: 2224 N Pollard St Arlington VA 22207 Office: Advisors Fin Inc Suite 250 8321 Old Courthouse Rd Vienna VA 22180

KAPLAN, JUDITH HELENE, business executive; b. N.Y.C., July 20, 1938; d. Abraham and Ruth (Kiffel) Letich; B.A., Hunter Coll., 1960; postgrad. New Sch. Social Research, 1960-61; m. Warren Kaplan, Dec. 31, 1958; children—Ronald Scott, Elissa Ann. Registered rep. Herzfeld & Stern, N.Y.C., 1963-64; agt. N.Y. Life Ins. Co., N.Y.C., 1964-69; registered rep. Scheinman, Hochstin & Trotta, 1969-70; v.p. Alpha Capital Corp., N.Y.C., 1970-78; pres. Tipex, Inc., N.Y.C., 1966-83; v.p. Alpha Public Relations, N.Y.C., 1970-73; pres. Utopia Recreations Corp., 1971-73, Howard Beach Recreation Corp., 1972-73, Action Packers Inc., 1978—; chmn. bd. Alpha Exec. Planning Corp., 1970-72; life Underwriter N.Y. Life, 1974-75. Author: Space Patches from Mercury to the Space Shuttle, 1986. Co-chmn. Congressman Lester Wolff's Equal Rights Com.; cons. woman suffrage State of Wyo., 1979; co-convenor Central Fla. People of Faith for ERA; co-chairperson Ocala ERA Countdown Campaign. Mem. NOW (v.p. N.Y.; co-founder Ocala/Marion County chpt. 1982; creator, cachet dir. NOW-N.Y. Women's History Series of First Day Covers 1976-88), Women's Equity Action League, Women Leaders Round Table, Nat. Assn. Life Underwriters, Bus. and Profl. Women, Assn. Feminist Cons., Nat. Women's Polit. Caucus, Manhattan Women's Polit. Caucus, Am., L.I. (dir.) stamp dealers assns., Am. Philatelic Soc., Am. Topical Assn., Bus. and Profl. Women, AAUW, Internat. Assn. Philatelic Journalists, Am. First Day Cover Soc. Author: Woman Suffrage, 1977; contbg. editor Stamp Show News. Home: 577 Silver Course Circle Ocala FL 32672 Office: 344 Cypress Rd SSS Industrial Park Ocala FL 32672

KAPLAN, KAREN SUE, newspaper writer, editor, freelance writer; b. Mullens, W.Va., Feb. 3, 1954; d. William Clifford and Stella Mae (Ellis) Blevins; m. Maurice Malitz Kaplan, Apr. 21, 1973 (div. 1979); 1 dau., Nicholette Estelle. Student W.Va. Career Coll., 1973; secretarial degree Marshall U., 1972; student journalism Bluefield State Coll., 1978-80. Writer Beckley (W.Va.) Post-Herald, 1976-77; news reporter Sta. WCIR, Beckley, 1977-78; writer, editor Bluefield (W.Va.) Daily Telegraph, 1978—; dir. Communicator's Roundtable The Virginias, Bluefield, 1978—; coordinator Communicator's Roundtable Media Workshop, 1984. All W.Va. com. publicity coordinator Summit City Marathon and Festival, 1984. Author, editor 12th Ann. Coal Edit., 1981, 13th ann., 1982, 14th ann., 1984. Recipient 2nd place award for news reporting W.Va. Press Assn., 1981, 2nd place for pub. service, 1982, 1st place for editorial writing, 1982, 2nd place for mag. writing, 1982; service award Bluefield State Coll., 1984. Mem. W.Va. Press Women (various awards), Greater Bluefield C. of C. Republican. Mem. Christian Ch. Clubs: Kiwanis (hon.), Rotary (hon.), Summit Players. Home: 2602 Grossy Branch Bluefield WV 24701 Office: PO Box 208 412 Bland St Bluefield WV 24701

KAPLAN, MURIEL SHEERR, sculptor; b. Phila., Aug. 15, 1924; d. Maurice J. and Lillian J. (Jamison) Sheerr; B.A., Cornell U., 1946; postgrad. Sarah Lawrence Coll., 1958-60, U. Calif. at Oxford (Eng.), summer 1971, U. Florence (Italy), summer 1973, Art Students League, N.Y.C., summers 1975-85, New Sch., N.Y.C., 1974-78, m. Murray S. Kaplan, June 3, 1946; children—Janet Belsky, James S., Jerrold, Amy Sheerr Eckman. Exhbns. at Women's Clubs in Westchester, 1954-60, Allied Artists Am., 1958-73, Nat. Assn. Women Artists, 1966-78, Bklyn. Museum, 1968, Sculptors Guild, 1972, Bergen County (N.J.) Mus., 1974; 2-person shows: Camino Real Gallery, Boca Raton, Fla., 1980, Norton Art Gallery, Palm Beach, Fla., 1980; represented in permanent collections Jerusalem, Columbia U., Brandeis U., U. Tex.; executed twin 30 foot cor-ten steel sculptures, Tarrytown, N.Y., 1972, 2 large rotating steel sculptures Art Park, Trans-Lux Corp., 1978; art cons., interior designer, 1971-80; sec. commn. to establish art mus. in Westchester, 1956; chmn. Westchester Creative Arts Festival, 1956. Bd. dirs. Fedn. Jewish Philanthropies, 1956; chmn. 1st WNET, Channel 13 Art Auction; mem. com. art in pub. places, Palm Beach County, Fla., 1984; mem. Com. for the Arts, Palm Beach County, 1985—. Recipient prizes Nat. Assn. Women Artists, 1966, Westchester Women's Club, 1955, 56, Allied Artists Am., 1969. Mem. Art students League N.Y. Nat. Assn. Women Artists. Democrat. Address: 339 Garden Rd Palm Beach FL 33480

KAPLAN, SYLVIA YALOWITZ KAPLAN (MRS. MILTON I. KAPLAN), librarian, educator; b. Chgo., May 23, 1921; d. Max and Gertrude (Yalowitz) K.; Ph.B., Northwestern U., 1956; M.A. in L.S., Rosary Coll., 1961, postgrad., 1962; postgrad. U. Ill., 1965-69, HEA Inst. on Reclassification, Rosary Coll., 1969, DePaul U., 1970; doctoral candidate (scholar, grad. asst.) U. Pitts., 1980-86; m. Milton I. Kaplan, Apr. 5, 1959. Asst. librarian Argonne Nat. Lab., U. Chgo., 1943-50; chief med. librarian Mcpl. Tb Sanitarium, Chgo., 1953-57; sch. librarian, Gary, Ind., 1957-59; librarian Inst. Applied Research, U. Chgo., 1961-62; chief librarian, instr. med. bibliography Chgo. Med. Sch., 1960-64; librarian Michael Reese Hosp. Sch. Nursing, Chgo., 1964-66; chief librarian Ill. Dept. Mental Health, 1967-70; instr. library sci. Northeastern Ill. State Coll.,

1970—; asst. prof. library sci. Eastern Ill. U., Charleston, 1970—. Mem. AAUW, AAUP (officer), Med. Library Assn. (cert.), Am. Assn. Library Schs., Spl. Libraries Assn., Assn. Acad. Librarians, Internat. Assn. Semantics, Hadassah, Internat. Platform Assn. (hon.), Delta Kappa Gamma (hon.; scholar 1979). Democrat. Jewish. Contbr. revs. to profl. jours. Office: Eastern Ill U Dept Library Sci Charleston IL 61920

KAPLAN, VIOLA MARGUERITE, university official; b. Chgo., July 26, 1919; d. Charles J. and Rae Vesta (Pike) Epstein; A.A. in Math., UCLA, 1949; B.S. in Bus. Adminstrn., Rutgers U., 1973; m. Herbert G. Kaplan, Aug. 24, 1947; children—Ronna, Debra, Michael, Clifford. Research mathematician Forrestal Helicopter Lab., Princeton, N.J., 1954-55; tchr. math. and German, State Coll. (Pa.) Area High Sch., 1966-68; research asst. Pa. State U., University Park, 1967; bus. mgr. Ceramic Finishing Co., State College, Pa., 1968-69; asst. controller Atmos Tech. Corp., Edison, N.J., 1969-71; auditor Div. Mental Health and Hosps., State of N.J., Trenton, 1972-73; acct. and budget supr. Northwestern U., Chgo., 1973-75, asst. dir. adminstrv. and fin. services Med. Sch., 1975-78; adminstrv. analyst N.J. Commn. for Blind, Newark, 1978-84; bus. mgr. Hudson County Community Coll., Jersey City, N.J., 1984—; Vice pres. Samuel Everitt Sch. PTA, 1959-60; bd. dirs. Solomon Schechter Day Sch. of Somerset County, Temple Shalom, Plainfield, N.J., exec. bd. dirs., treas. Zimmerli Art Mus., New Brunswick, N.J. Mem. Am. Assn. Med. Colls., Nat. Assn. Accts., Hosp. Fin. Mgmt. Assn., Bus. and Profl. Women of North Shore, Hadassah (founder 1974, pres. 1974-76, pres. Somerset chpt. 1980-82). Club: Penn Valley Women's (pres. 1956-57), Toastmasters. Office: 168 Sip Ave Jersey City NJ 07036

KAPLAN, VIVIAN KLINE, construction company executive; b. Pitts., June 2, 1936; d. Lowry Adam and Esther Mary (Wamsley) Kline; student U. Pitts., 1964-69; grad. Mo. Auction Sch., 1985; m. Fred L. Kaplan, Dec. 4, 1972; children—Linda, Todd, Teri, Judy. Saleswoman, West Real Estate Agy., Gibsonia, Pa., 1966-71; with Tectonics Inc. Miami, Fla., 1972-82, San Antonio, 1982—, v.p., owner, mgr.; pres. Vikap, Inc., 1983—; partner, project mgr. fed. contracts Fortec Constructors, San Antonio, 1973-83. Mem. San Antonio Home Builders Assn., San Antonio Builders Exchange. Office: 10427 Perrin-Beitel Suite 113 San Antonio 78217

KAPP, NANCY GLADYS, savings and loan executive; b. Oak Park, Ill., Jan. 23, 1945; d. Andrew John and Gladys Abigail (Johnson) McClintock; m. Ted Martin Kapp, Sept. 28, 1973; children—Adam, Natalie, Pamela. B.S.Ed., No. Ill. U., DeKalb, 1968; postgrad. Nat. Coll. Edn., Evanston, Ill., 1969-70. Tchr. elementary/jr. high sch. Dist. 96, Riverside, Ill., 1968-71, high sch. substitute tchr., 1971-72; personnel dept. sec. St. Paul Fed. Bank for Savs., Chgo., 1971-73, sr. exec. sec. to pres., 1973-80, adminstv. asst. legal dept., 1980—. Dir., chmn. Community Sch. of Galewood, Chgo., 1983-84; mem. Republican Nat. Com., 1979—; sponsor GOP Victory Fund, Rep. Party, Washington, 1982—; mem. Rep. Presdl. Task force, 1984—. Mem. Nat. Assn. Female Execs., AAUW, Nat. Assn. Exec. Secs., Nat. Paralegal Assn. Republican. Episcopalian. Office: St Paul Fed Bank for Savs 6700 W North Ave Chicago IL 60635

KAPPA, MARGARET MCCAFFREY, resort hotel consultant; b. Wabasha, Minn., May 14, 1921; d. Joseph Hugh and Verna Mae (Anderson) McCaffrey; B.S. in Hotel Mgmt., Cornell U., 1944; grad. Dale Carnegie course, 1978; cert. hospitality housekeeping exec.; m. Nicholas Francis Kappa, Sept. 15, 1956; children—Nicholas Joseph, Christopher Francis. Asst. exec. housekeeper Kahler Hotel, Rochester, Minn., 1944; exec. housekeeper St. Paul Hotel, 1944-47, Plaza Hotel, N.Y.C., 1947-51; exec. housekeeper, personnel dir. Athearn Hotel, Oshkosh, Wis., 1952-58; dir. housekeeping The Greenbrier, White Sulphur Springs, W.Va., 1958-84; cons., 1984—; tchr. housekeeping U.S. and fgn. countries; cons.; vis. lectr. Cornell U. Pres. St. Charles Borromeo Parish Assn., White Sulphur Springs, 1962, v.p., 1980, 82; tech. adv., host 2 ednl. videos Am. Hotel and Motel Assn., 1986. Recipient diploma of honor Société Culinaire Philanthropique, 1961. Mem. Cornell Soc. Hotelmen (pres. 1980-81, exec. com. 1981-82), Nat. Exec. Housekeepers Assn. (pres. N.Y. chpt. 1950), N.Y.U. Hotel and Restaurant Soc. (hon. life). Republican. Roman Catholic. Clubs: Nat. Woman's; Quota (charter mem. Greenbrier County). Home and Office: 207 Azalea Trail White Sulphur Springs WV 24986

KAPPMEYER, BETTE JEANE, entertainment agency executive, producer; b. Chgo., Dec. 9, 1922; d. Emanuel Donald and Sophia Lee (Rowitz) Weiser; m. Charles Frank Kappmeyer, Feb. 23, 1946; children—Robert Joseph, Marcia Diane, Phyllis Darlene, Michelle Charlene. B.A., Md. U., 1960. Pres. Bette Kaye Prodns., 1946-69, treas., Sacramento, 1969—; founder, pres. Rete Inc., 1979-82, chmn. bd. dirs., 1982—; producer Mid State Fair, Paso Robles, Calif., 1968—, Stanislaus County Fair, Calif., 1969—. Organizer Wiesbaden PTA, Germany, 1948, YES Youth Employment Services, Travis AFB, 1954, choral clubs at various bases, 1950-61. Served with U.S. Army, 1944-45. Commended by resolution Calif. State Assembly, 1974, Calif. Senate Rules Com., 1973. Mem. Country Music Assn. (dir. 1981-84), Acad. Country Music (dir. 1984-85). Republican. Lutheran. Avocations: clown collector; travel; thoroughbred horses. Office: 2701 Cottage Way #14 Sacramento CA 95825

KAPTUR, MARCIA CAROLYN, congresswoman; b. Toledo, Ohio, June 17, 1946. B.A., U. Wis., 1968; M.Urban Planning, U. Mich., 1974; postgrad. U. Manchester (Eng.), 1974. Urban planner, asst. dir. for urban affairs, domestic policy staff White House, 1977-79; mem. 98th, 99th Congresses from 9th Ohio Dist. Bd. dirs. Gund Found. Mem. Am. Planning Assn., Am. Inst. Certified Planners (bd. dirs.), Nat. Ctr. for Urban Ethnic Affairs (adv. com.), U. Mich. Urban Planning Alumni Assn., NAACP, Urban League, Polish Mus., Polish Am. Hist. Assn., Democratic Women's Campaign Assn., Lucas County Dem. Bus. and Profl. Women's Club. Address: 1630 Longworth Bldg Washington DC 20510*

KAPUS, KERI LYNN, management training executive; b. Burbank, Calif., Aug. 23, 1963; d. Theodore Edmond and Theresa Marie (Budd) Kapus. B.S. in Bus. Adminstrn., U. Pacific, 1985. Sr. employee Dialyn Corp., Simi Valley, Calif., 1979-85; intern Senator John Garamendi, Stockton, Calif., 1985; mgr. Gallo Winery, South San Francisco, 1985—. Contbr. articles to profl. arbitration publs. Mem. AAUW, Nat. Assn. Female Execs., U. Pacific Alumni Assn., Delta Sigma Pi, Lambda Kappa Sigma. Avocations: sports; music; travel. Office: Gallo Sales Co 440 Forbes Blvd South San Francisco CA 94080

KARABASZ, JOELLEN FELICIA, data systems manager, consultant; b. Phila., Feb. 16, 1954; d. James Thomas and Mildred Mary (Lyons) Karabasz; m. Laurence Arthur Brown, Apr. 23, 1983. B.S.E., Wharton Sch. U. Pa., 1976; postgrad. in Indsl. Engring., Lehigh U., 1979. With installation dept. Sonco, Inc., Bala Cynwyd, Pa., 1976-78; account rep. Computer Scis. Corp., El Segundo, Calif., 1979-81; pres. Software Techniques, Allentown, Pa., 1982—; corp. treas. Surf Vibrations, inc., Allentown, Pa. instr. Allentown Coll., 1978—; lectr. Assn. Dental Assts., Pa., 1983—. Mem. youth ministry Roman Catholic Diocese of Allentown, 1978-82. Mem. Nat. Assn. Female Execs., Earthwatch Planetary Soc. (Boston). Republican. Club: Ocean City Yacht (N.J.). Home: R D 1 PO Box 258-1 Upper Black Eddy PA 18972 Office: Surf Vibrations 1922 Allen St Allentown PA 18104

KARAN, DONNA FASKE, fashion designer; b. Forest Hills, N.Y., Oct. 2, 1948; ed. Parsons Sch. of Design; m. Mark Karan (div.); 1 dau., Gabrielle; m. Stephan Weiss, 1983. With Addenda Co., to 1968; with Anne Klein & Co., N.Y.C., 1968-84, co-designer, 1971-74, designer, 1974-84; chief exec. officer Donna Karan Co., N.Y.C., 1984—. Winner Coty award, 1977, 81, Coty Hall of Fame award, 1982, citation, 1984. Showed first complete collection for Anne Klein & Co. in 1974; collaborated on Anne Klein collections with Louis dell'Olio. Office: Anne Klein & Co 205 W 39th St New York NY 10018*

KARASIK, GITA, concert pianist; b. San Francisco, Dec. 14, 1949; d. Monia and Bereni Karasik; pupil of Lev Shorr, Rosina Lhevinne, Karl Ulrich Schnabel. Debut as soloist, San Francisco Symphony, 1958; debut on nat. TV, Bell Telephone Hour, 1964; N.Y.C. debut Carnegie Hall, 1972; solo recitalist, pianist with major orchs. throughout world, 1955—; tchr. master classes, 1970—; 1st Am. pianist to make ofcl. concert tour of China, 1980; mem. music adv. panel solo artists Nat. Endowment Arts, 1980; interdisciplinary panel 1st D.C. Arts Commn., 1981; mem. Artists for Nuclear Disarmament, Artists to End Hunger. Recipient Solo Artists award Nat. Endowment Arts, 1981-82, Artists award and commd. concerto Ford Found., 1976, Musicians award Rockefeller Found., 1982, 1st prize Xerox/Affiliated Artists Internat. Piano Competition, 1982; winner Young Concert Artists Internat. Auditions, 1969; Solo artist sponsorship Pro Musicis Found., 1978—, Bösendorfer Piano Co., 1976—. Address: care Lee Caplin Prodns 8274 Grand View Los Angeles CA 90046

KARASOV, PHYLLIS, lawyer; b. St. Paul, Oct. 3, 1951; d. Elliott Karasov and Doris Unger; m. Alan David Olstein, Sept. 2, 1979; 2 children. B.A., U. Rochester, 1973; J.D., Emory U., 1976. Bar: Minn. 1976, Ga. 1976. Atty., NLRB, Mpls., 1976-81, Moore, Costello & Hart, St. Paul, 1981—; bd. dirs. U. Minn. Student Legal Services, Mpls., 1982—. Pres. bd. dirs. Talmud Torah of St. Paul, 1983-85; trustee Minn. Women Lawyers Polit. Action Com., Twin Cities, 1982-84; bd. dirs. Resources for Child Caring, 1985—. Recipient acad. scholarships Emory U. Sch. Law, Atlanta, 1973-76, U. Rochester, 1969-73. Mem. ABA, Minn. Bar Assn. (editor labor law sect. newsletter 1982-83), Minn. Women Lawyers (pres. 1979-80). Jewish. Home: 527 Laurel Ave Saint Paul MN 55102 Office: Moore Costello & Hart 1400 Norwest Ctr Saint Paul MN 55101

KARCH, KAREN BROOKE, school administrator; b. Greensburg, Pa., Feb. 17, 1944; d. John Daniel and Louise Fluke (Reinfried) Karle; m. Robert Charles Karch, Apr. 2, 1966; children—Kara Brooke, Krista Kimberly. B.A., Ohio Wesleyan U., 1965; M.Ed., Am. U., 1973, Ed.D., 1981. Tchr., Prince George County schs., Md., 1965-70; instr. English, Montgomery Coll., Rockville, Md., 1976-79, No. Va. Community Coll., Alexandria, 1977-79, reading specialist Frederick County Bd. Edn., Frederick, Md., 1979-81, media specialist, 1981-82, vice prin., 1982-83, prin. Middle sch., Walkersville, Md., 1983—. Leader Capital council Girl Scouts U.S.A., 1977-80. Mem. Md. Middle Sch. Assn., Nat. Middle Sch. Assn., Assn. Supervision and Curriculum Devel., Phi Kappa Phi, Phi Delta Kappa, Delta Kappa Gamma, Republican. Methodist. Avocations: running; skiing; sailing; tennis. Home: 13001 Glen Rd Gaithersburg MD 20878 Office: Walkersville Middle Sch 55 Frederick St Walkersville MD 21793

KARDASHIAN, JANE FLORA, dermatologist; b. Paterson, N.J., May 24, 1951; d. John Charles and Florence (Tashjian) Kardashian; m. Vatche Soghomonian, Aug. 8, 1981. Student Mich. State U., 1969-71; B.S. in Pharmacy, Rutgers U., 1974; M.D., U. Medicine and Dentistry of N.J., 1979. Diplomate Am. Bd. Dermatology. Resident in internal medicine U. Medicine and Dentistry of N.J., 1979-80, in dermatology, U. Calif.-San Francisco, 1980-83; practice medicine specializing in dermatology, Fresno, 1983—; mem. dermatology faculty Valley Med. Ctr. (div. U. Calif.), Fresno; cons. staff Valley Children's Hosp., Fresno Community Hosp., St. Agnes Hosp. Recipient Cert. of Recognition, Am. Med. Women's Assn., 1979. Fellow Am. Acad. Dermatology; mem. AMA, Am. Med. Women's Assn., Calif. Med. Assn., Am. Soc. Dermatologic Surgery, Armenian Women's League, Alpha Omega Alpha, Rho Chi, Alpha Lambda Delta. Club: Fresno Women's Trade. Home: PO Box 3825 Pinedale CA 93650 Office: 728 E Bullard Ave Fresno CA 93710

KARDON, JANET, museum administrator, curator; b. Phila. B.S. in Edn., Temple U.; M.A. in Art History, U. Pa. Lectr. Am. art and 20th century art Phila. Coll. of Art, 1968—, dir. exhbns., 1976-78; dir. Inst. Contemporary Art, U. Pa., Phila., 1979—; U.S. commr. Venice Bienale, 1980. Nat. Endowment Arts Research grantee, 1978. Mem. Coll. Art Assn., Pa. Council Arts, Assn. Art Mus. Dirs. Address: Inst of Contemporary Art U Pa 34th and Walnut Philadelphia PA 19104

KARELITZ-LESHAY, MAXINE HOFFMAN, social service agency executive, educator, psychotherapist, hypnotherapist; b. Bklyn., May 29, 1942; d. Jacob and Jean Lorraine (Fierstein) Hoffman; m. Julian Robert Karelitz, Oct. 2, 1960 (div. Dec. 1963); 1 child, Gavin Alexander Karelitz; m. Steven Vedder LeShay, Apr. 17, 1982. B.A., Bklyn. Coll., 1976; M.S.W., Barry Coll. Sch. Social Work, Miami Shores, Fla., 1978. Cert. social worker, N.Y. Social worker Seminole Indian Reservation, Hollywood, Fla., 1976-78, Children's Home Soc., Fort Lauderdale, Fla., 1977-78, United Cerebral Palsy, N.Y.C., 1978-80; pvt. practice psychotherapy and hypnotherapy, Williamstown, N.J., 1978—; instr. sociology and social work Glassboro State Coll., N.J., 1980—; dir. and cons. social services N.J. Meml. Home, Vineland, N.J., 1980—; exec. dir., founder Women On Their Own, Inc., Malaga, N.J., 1982—. Mem. Guideposts Women's Consortium, Glassboro State Coll., 1984—, mem. adv. bd. career direction for single parents and homemakers, 1985—; adv. citizen advocacy Assn. Retarded Citizens, Gloucester County, N.J., 1986—; active People Against Spouse Abuse, Woodbury, N.J., 1986—. Named hon. capt. U.S. Naval Res., 1980; child welfare trainee Barry Coll. Sch. Social Work, 1977-78; fellow L.I. Inst. Mental Health, Queens, N.Y., 1979-80; trained in hypnotherapy Morton Prince Ctr., N.Y.C., 1980. Mem. Nat. Assn. Social Workers, N.J. Assn. Displaced Homemakers, Nat. Assn. Female Execs. Jewish. Office: Women On Their Own Inc PO Box O Malaga NJ 08328

KAREN, RUTH, publishing, research and consulting firm executive; b. Germany, Feb. 18, 1922; came to U.S., 1940, naturalized, 1947; d. David and Paula (Freudenthal) Karpf; B.Sc., London Sch. Econs.; M.A., New Sch. Social Research, 1944; m. S. A. Hagai, Apr. 1962. Fgn., UN, and war corr., 1947-60, Reporter mag., Toronto (Ont., Can.) Star, 1947-60; columnist World Wide Press corr. Latin Am. Times, Bus. Abroad, 1960-66; with Bus. Internat. Corp., N.Y.C., 1966-85, editor, 1973, v.p. corp. public policy div., 1976-85; pres. Hagai Assocs., Inc., N.Y.C.; dir. Multinat. Stategies, Inc.; cons. in field. Recipient Mitchell prize, 1982. Club: Town Tennis. Author: The Land and People of Central America, 1965; Hello Guatemala, 1967; The Seven Worlds of Peru, 1968; Song of the Quail, 1969; Brazil Today: A Case History of Economic Development, 1972; Kingdom of the Sun, 1975; Feathered Serpent 1979; Questionable Practices, 1980; Toward an Unlimited Future, 1983; Terrorism: The Corporate Implications, 1984; Agribusiness and the Small Scale Farmer, 1985; Toward the Year 2000, 1985; mem. editorial bd. Nat. Dirs. Monthly. Home: 360 E 55th St New York NY 10022

KARGER, JUNE ELAINE, speakers bur. exec.; b. Lexington, Mass., June 24, 1931; d. Irving and Lillian (Friedman) Wermont; student Northeastern U., Boston Coll.; children—Janet, Richard, Nancy. Dir. adminstrn., regional sales mgr. Holidair Ltd., Boston, 1972-76; v.p., gen. mgr. Am. Program Bur., Inc., Chestnut Hill, Mass., 1976—; founder Sch. for Speakers, Boston. Mem. Internat. Platform Assn., Nat. Speakers Assn., Meeting Planners Internat., Nat. Assn. Female Execs., Exec. Club Boston C. of C., Women's Network Boston, Publicity Club Boston, Am. Soc. Assn. Execs., Nat. Acad. TV Arts and Scis. Home: 22 Chestnut Pl Brookline MA 02146 Office: 850 Boylston St Chestnut Hill MA 02167

KARKLIS, BARBARA LEE PARIS, nurse, director of nursing; b. Oak Park, Ill., June 21, 1942; d. James Archie and Doloris Muriel (Chaput) Paris; m. Zigurds Karklis, Jan. 28, 1966 (div. Aug. 1981); children—Elizabeth Ann, Edward Andrew. A.A.S., Bklyn. Coll., 1965; student Troy State U. Registered nurse, N.Y., Ga., ALa. R.N., staff nurse, unit coordinator Cobb Hosp., Phenix City, Ala., 1981-84; dir. nursing Chattahoochee Valley Nursing Services, Inc., Columbus, Ga., 1984—. Contbr. poetry and articles to various publs. Instr., Army Community Services, W. Ger., Va., Wash.; vol., instr. A.R.C., Nurnberg; trainer Pacific Peaks council Girl Scout U.S. Mem. Am. Nurses Assn., Ga. Nurses Assn. Roman Catholic. Clubs: Officers Wives, Non-Commissioned Officers Wives. Avocations: skin diving, macrame, water skiing, snow skiing, hiking, backpacking, sketching, sewing, interior decorating. Home: 3300 Primrose Rd Columbus GA 31907 Office: Chattahoochee Valley Nursing Services Inc 3318 Gentian Blvd Columbus GA 31907

KARKUT, ANN LOUISE, editor; b. Bellwood, Ill., June 30, 1924; d. Walter and Anna (Jacobs) Knippenberg; m. Edward Karkut, Mar. 20, 1943; children—Patricia, Edward, Stanley, Susan, Christopher. Ed. LaSalle U. Asst. editor Lockport Herald, Ill., 1960-63, editor, 1963-69; asst. editor Naperville Sun, Ill., 1969-70; editor Joliet Circle, Ill., 1970; editor Pointer Publs., Riverdale, Ill., 1970-72; asst. editor Lisle Sun, Ill., 1972-74; asst. editor Big Farmer mag., Frankfort, Ill., 1974-81. Sec., Homer Fire Dept. Aux., 1962, Dist. 92 Band Parents, 1967; mem. Homer Republican Precinct Com., 1976-86; charter mem. Homer Rep. Women, 1982—; Homer Twp. clk., 1981—. Mem. Lockport Bus. and Profl. Women's Club (charter mem., past pres., named Woman of Yr. 1979), Homer Twp. Bus. and Profl. Women (charter mem.; pres. elect 1986), Ill. Bus. and Profl. Women's Club (editor Ill. Bull.), Ill. Fedn. Bus. and Profl. Women's Clubs Found. (chmn., dir. dist. V 1984), Ill. Press Women's Assn., Women's Network Will County, Will County Hist. Soc. (pres., past bd. dirs.). Roman Catholic. Club: Waa-Shee Riders (pres.). Home: Route 2 Box 26 Gougar Lockport IL 60441 Office: 143d St Lockport IL 60441

KARKUT, IVY VERONICA, business executive; b. Chgo., Oct. 16, 1953; d. Edward and Aurelia (Presz) K.; m. Donald J. Smiley. Cert., MacCormac Jr. Coll., 1973. Regional sales mgr. Hukapoo Ligistxs, N.Y.C., 1980-83; v.p. sales Girbaud Co., N.Y.C., 1983-85, Yves St. Laurent, N.Y.C., 1985-86; v.p. sales and mktg. Amex, N.Y.C., 1986—. Home: 137 E 36th St Apt 7G New York NY 10016 Office: Amex 485 7th Ave New York NY 10018

KARLESKINT, THERESA MARIE, real estate broker; b. Fort Scott, Kans., May 15, 1937; d. L. Ben. and Marie E. Trendle Rei; m. Joseph C. Karleskint, Feb. 9, 1957; children—Erica, Terri, Brian, Julie, Elisa. Broker, owner Karleskint Real Estate, Parsons, Kans., 1976—; commnr. Kans. Real Estate, Topeka, 1980—. Pres. Youth Crisis Shelter, Parson, 1979-83, v.p., 1983—; dir. Kans. Children Service League, Topeka, 1981-84. Mem. Kans. Assn. Realtors (chmn. equal opportunity com. 1985—), Labette County Bd. of Realtors (sec., treas. 1979-81, pres. 1986, dir. 1980-83, realtor of the yr. 1982. Democrat. Roman Catholic. Club: Soroptimist Internat. (chmn. found.). Home: 1430 Morgan Parsons KS 67357 Office: Karleskint Real Estate 2310 Main Parsons KS 67357

KARLSON, KAREN LOUISE, radiologist; b. N.Y.C., May 6, 1950; d. Lloyd Alfred and Antoinette Sofia (Petersen) Bolling; B.A., CCNY, 1971; M.D., Columbia U., 1975; m. Thomas J. Karlson, May 19, 1971; children—Aurora, Alexandra. Intern, St. Vincent's Hosp., N.Y.C., 1975-76; resident Columbia Presbyn. Med. Center, 1976-79; fellow, 1979-80, asst. prof., 1980-81; attending radiologist St. Barnabas Med. Center, Livingston, N.J.; asst. prof. Cornell U. Med. Center-N.Y. Hosp. Mem. Columbia U. Coll. Physicians and Surgeons, Black and Latin Students Orgn., Am. Coll. Radiology, Radiol. Soc. N.Am. Lutheran. Contbr. articles to profl. jours. Home: 6 Orchard Ln Livingston NJ 07039 Office: Dept Radiology St Barnabas Med Center Livingston NJ 07039

KARLSON, MARGARET VERCELLOTTI, health care administrator; b. Joliet, Ill., Dec. 15, 1941; d. Joseph Francis and Mary Therese (Walowski) Vercellotti; B.S., Joliet Jr. Coll., 1962; B.S. in Adminstrn., U. Ill., 1973; grad. in asso. long-term care adminstrn., George Washington U., 1979; m. Bud Carter, July 26, 1981; children—Greg, Cyndie, Todd, Teri. Asst. dir. public relations St. Joseph Hosp., Joliet, 1975-76; asst. adminstr. Americana Healthcare Center, Joliet, 1976-79, v.p., adminstr., Decatur, Ga., 1981-82; adminstr. Beverly Enterprises, Glenwood Manor, Decatur, Ga., 1982-84; region mgr. DRIpride div. Weyerhaeuser Co., Alpharetta, Ga., 1984—; v.p., adminstr. Family Tree Care Center, Peoria, Ill., 1979-81; seminar condr.; TV panelist. Mem. Quad County Task Force on Aging, 1978; ednl. adv. com. Ill. Dept. Public Health; ednl. adv. com. Ill. Central Coll.; bd. dirs. Ill. Valley Health Systems Agy., 1979-81. Lic. nursing home adminstr., Ga., Fla., Ill. Fellow Am. Coll. Nursing Home Adminstrs.; mem. Ga. Healthcare Assn. (chair edn. com.), Am. Healthcare Assn., Continuity of Care Assn., Ga. Gerontology Soc., Ga. Exec. Women's Network, Atlanta Bus. and Profl. Women's Club, DeKalb C. of C. Club: Atlanta Bus. and Profl. Women's. Editor: The Growing Concern, 1980-81; The Voice of Experience, 1981-82; Milestones and Memories, 1982-84. Home and Office: 445 N Eagles Bluff Alpharetta GA 30201

KARMALI, RASHIDA ALIMAHOMED, biochemist, research scientist; b. Mitalamaria, Uganda, May 12, 1948; d. Alimahomed and Sakina (Walji) Karmali. B.S., Makerere U. (Uganda), 1971; M.S. in Nutrition Aberdeen U. (Scotland), 1973; M.S. in Anatomy, McGill U., 1977; Ph.D. in Biochemistry, Newcastle U., 1976. Postdoctoral fellow Clin. Research Inst., Montreal, Que., Can., 1976-78; research assoc. East Carolina U., Greenville, N.C., 1978-80; research staff Sloan-Kettering Inst. for Cancer Research, N.Y.C., 1980—; cons. Cappel Labs., Malvern, Pa., 1982, United Scis. of Am. 1985. Contbr. numerous articles to sci. jours. Mem. Cell Biology Soc., Leukemia Soc. Am., Sigma Xi. Club: Health and Raquet (N.Y.C.). Office: Sloan-Kettering Inst for Cancer Research 1275 York Ave New York NY 10021

KARNES, SUSAN MCKEAGUE, symphony society executive; b. Harvey, Ill., Mar. 31, 1954; d. Gordon Clark and Louise Marea (Jones) McKeague; student Tulsa U., 1971-77; m. Sam Bryant Karnes, Dec. 30, 1978; 1 son, Bryant. Tng. dir. Renberg's Inc., Tulsa 1977, personnel dir., 1978-79; v.p., dir. personnel Republic Bancorp, Inc., Tulsa, 1979-81; dir. fund raising, bd. dirs., mem. exec. com. N. Ark. Symphony, Fayetteville, 1982-83. Bd. dirs. Mgmt. Devel. Center U. Tulsa, 1980-81. Home: 6006 Abilene Trail Austin TX 78749

KARNIOL, HILDA HUTTERER, artist, educator; b. Vienna, Austria, Apr. 28, 1910; d. Simon and Josephine (Weisman) Hutterer; student Acad. for Women, Vienna, 1926-30, Mrs. Olga Konetzny-Maly and A. F. Seligman, Vienna, 1925-28; m. Frank Karniol, June 25, 1933; 1 son, William George. Over 100 one-man shows, including Susquehanna U., 1952-73, Pa. State Mus., Harrisburg, 1954, Neville Mus., Green Bay, Wis., 1958, Addha Artzt Gallery, N.Y.C., 1960, Cornell Library Gallery, Ithaca, N.Y., 1960, Drexel Inst. Tech., Phila., 1960, Farnsworth Mus., Rockland, Maine, 1960, Mary Buie Mus., Oxford, Miss., 1960, Columbus (Ga.) Mus., 1962, Rutgers U., 1965-66, Laurel (Miss.) Rogers Mus., 1962; La Salle Coll., Phila., 1964; Hallmark Art Gallery, Kansas City, Mo., 1967, U. Ill., Urbana, 1968, U. Minn., St. Paul, 1969, U. Mich., 1969, U. Ky., Elizabethtown, 1970, La. State U., New Orleans, 1971, Kans. State Coll., Pittsburg, 1972, Purdue U., 1973, Invitational Art Exhbn., Painters of Central Pa., State Coll., 1982, 83; represented in permanent collections at St. Vincent Arch Abbey, Latrobe, Pa., Susquehanna U., Selinsgrove, Pa., Lincoln Sch., Honesdale, Pa., Del. Art Center, Wilmington, HEW, Lycoming Coll., Williamsport, Pa., Bloomsburg (Pa.) State Coll., Lewisburg (Pa.) Art Council; instr. fine arts Susquehanna U., 1959-75; lectr., artist-in-residence Fed. Govt. Cultural Enrichment Program for Clearfield, Clinton, Centre and Lycoming counties, Pa., 1967; art adviser Sunbury Bicentennial Com., 1972; demonstrator, exhibitor Laurel State Festival, Wellsboro, Pa., 1975. Recipient 1st prize in portraiture Berwick (Pa.) Arts Center, 1965; purchase prize Lewisburg Arts Festival, 1975, 1st prize, 1978. Mem. Susquehanna Art Soc., Société d'Honneur Française, Pi Delta Phi, Sigma Alpha Iota. Home: 960 Race St Sunbury PA 17801

KARNS, GERI ANN, business services company personnel executive, consultant; b. Altoona, Pa., Jan. 9, 1947; d. William Lester and Frances Shirley (Clapper) K.; m. Stephen Adair Zubrod, Apr. 30, 1966 (div. Feb. 1979); children—Matthew Stephen, Danielle Kristine. Student Pa. State U., 1964-67, Boston U., 1976-77, Boston Coll., 1976-77. Pvt. tchr. piano, Newton and Roxbury, Mass., 1969-72; cons. Community Services & Info., Boston, 1972-75; staff mgr. Ketchum, Inc., Boston, 1975-77; mgr. career services Office of Mayor of Boston, 1977-80; corp. personnel dir. Diversified Bus. Services, Wakefield, Mass., 1980—; cons. career devel.; mem. bus. adv. bd. Hubert H. Humphrey Occupational Resource Ctr., Boston, 1981—; mem. adv. bd. Mass. Assn. 766 Approved Pvt. schs., Danvers, 1983—. Pres. bd. dirs. Newton-Wellesley Multi Service Ctrs. (Mass.), 1971; mem. exec. bd. Mass. Orgn. to Repeal Abortion Laws, Boston, 1972. Senate of Pa. scholar, 1965. Mem. Boston Women in Outside Sales, Am. Soc. Personnel Adminstrn., Nat. Assn. Female Execs. Episcopalian. Club: Auburndale Women's (music dir. 1969-70) (Newton). Home: 77 Maple St Newton MA 02166 Office: Diversified Bus Services Corp Pl 128 Audubon Rd Wakefield MA 01880

KARP, JUDITH ESTHER, oncologist; b. San Diego, July 15, 1946; d. Louis Moses and Bella Sarah (Perlman) K.; B.A. in Chemistry, Mills Coll., Oakland, Calif., 1966; M.D., Stanford U., 1971; m. Stanley Howard Freedman, Sept. 21, 1975. Intern medicine, jr. resident in medicine Stanford Hosps., 1971-72; asst. resident in medicine Johns Hopkins Hosp., 1972-73; clin. and research fellow oncology Johns Hopkins Med. Sch., 1973-75, instr. oncology and medicine, 1975-78, asst. prof., 1978-85, assoc. prof., 1985—; speaker Internat. Congress Chemotherapy, Vienna, Austria, 1983. Recipient Aurelia Henry Reinhardt prize Mills Coll., 1966, Cancer Research award Washington chpt. Awards for Research Coll. Scientists, 1975; San Diego Heart Assn. grantee, 1965-67; Am. Cancer Soc. Jr. clin. faculty fellow, 1976-79. Diplomate Am. Bd. Internal Medicine; recipient Resolution of Commendation, State of Md., 1982; Recognition award City of Balt., 1984. Mem. Am. Soc. Hematology, Am. Soc. Clin. Oncology, Cell Kinetics Soc. (clin. counsellor governing council 1985-87), Am. Soc. Microbiology, Internat. Soc. Exptl. Hematology, Nat. Bd. Med. Examiners, Phi Beta Kappa. Democrat. Jewish. Home: 15 Farmhouse Ct Baltimore MD 21208 Office: Oncology Center Johns Hopkins Hosp 601 N Broadway Baltimore MD 21205

KARPEN, MARIAN JOAN, financial executive; b. Detroit, June 16, 1944; d. Cass John and Mary Jay Karpen. A.B., Vassar Coll., 1966; postgrad. Sorbonne, Paris, NYU Grad. Sch. Bus., 1974-77. Registered rep. N.Y. Stock Exchange, Nat. Assn. Securities Dealers. New Eng. corr. Women's Wear Daily Fairchild

Publs.-Capital Cities Communications, 1966-68, Paris fashion editor, TV and radio commentator Capital Cities Network, 1968-69; fashion editor Boston Herald Traveler, 1969-71; nat. syndicated newspaper columnist and photojournalist Queen Features Syndicate, N.Y.C., 1971-73; account exec. Blyth Eastman Dillon, N.Y.C., 1973-75, Oppenheimer, N.Y.C., 1975-76; v.p., mcpl. bond coordinator Faulkner Dawkins & Sullivan (merged Shearson Hayden Stone), N.Y.C., 1976-77; mgr. retail mcpl. bond dept. A.G. Becker (Warburg, Paribas, Becker Group), N.Y.C., 1977-79, prin., v.p., 1979-83, sr. v.p., prin., 1983-84; ltd. ptnr., sr. v.p. Bear Stearns & Co., Inc., N.Y.C., 1985—. Mem. benefit com. March of Dimes, 1983, Am. Lung Assn.; vol. Whitney Mus. Am. Art. Recipient superior Prodn. award Becker Paribas, 1983. Mem. Nat. Assn. Securities Dealers, N.Y. Stock Exchange, English Speaking Union, Women's Econ. Roundtable, Am. Soc. Profl. and Exec. Women, AAUW, U.S. Figure Skating Assn. Clubs: Vassar, Skating (N.Y.C. and Boston). Mem. editorial bd. Retirement Planning Strategist, Newsletter Mgmt. Corp.; contbr. numerous articles and photographs to newspapers and mags., 1966—. Home: 233 E 69th St New York NY 10021 Office: Bear Stearns & Co Inc 55 Water St New York NY 10041

KARPIEL, DORIS CATHERINE, state legislator; b. Chgo., Sept. 21, 1935; d. Nicholas and Mary (McStravick) Feinen; m. Harvey Karpiel, 1955 (div.); children—Sharon, Lynn, Laura, Barry. A.A., Morton Jr. Coll., 1955; B.A., No. Ill. U., 1976. Real estate sales assoc. Bundy-Morgan BHG; coordinator Bloomingdale Twp. Republican Presdl. Hdqrs., Ill., 1960, 64, 68; former pres. Bloomingdale Twp. Rep. Orgn.; mem. Twp. Ofcls. of Ill.; trustee Bloomingdale Twp., 1974-75, supr., 1975-80; precinct committeewoman Bloomingdale Twp. Rep. Central Com., 1972, chmn., 1978-80; mem. Ill. Ho. of Reps., 1979-82, Ill. State Senate from 25th Dist., 1984—. Mem. Am. Legislators Exchange Council, Rep. Orgn. Schaumberg Twp.; former sec. Dupage County Suprs. Assn.; former sec. Dupage County Twp. Ofcls.; mem. Dupage County Women's Rep. Orgn., Meml. Hosp. Guild, Am. Cancer Soc. Mem. LWV, DuPage Bd. Realtors, Pi Sigma Alpha. Clubs: Bloomingdale Roselle and Streamwood Country, University Women's, St. Walters Women's. Office: Ill State Capitol Bldg Springfield IL 62706

KARPMAN, LAURA, composer. B. in Music Composition magna cum laude U. Mich., 1980; B. in Music Composition, 1982, M.Music, 1983; postgrad. Aspen Music Sch., 1980; additional studies Nat. Music Camp, Mich., 1970-74, U. So. Calif., 1977, Ecole d'Art Americaines, France, 1978. Original compositions: most recent Tow Songs on Texts by Keats, Music on Santorini Festival, 1983, numerous others; other compositions: Sigh no More Ladies, 1980; Suite for Solo Celloe, 1982; Six Etudes for Piano, 1983; commissions: Helene A. Mirich Studio; Dou Vivo; Detroit Civic Orchestra Brass Quintet; pianist: U. Mich. Jazz Band; pianist, vocalist Impressions, Take Five Jazz Quintets. Recipient Commendation, City of Beverly Hills, 1975; Music Faculty award Phillips Acad., 1977; Best Pianist and Vocalist award Conn. Jazz Festival, 1977; ASCAP grantee, 1981, 1983; Charles Ives scholar Am. Acad. and Inst. Arts and Letters, 1984. Mem. Am. Music Ctr., BMI, Phi Kappa Lambda. Address: 313 W 48th St Apt 4-B New York NY 10024

KARR, ELIZABETH MCRAE, hospital administrator; b. Birmingham, Ala., July 9, 1953; d. James Neal and Donna Mae (Paige) McRae; divorced; children—Kristopher Ryan, Brian Heath. A. in Nursing, Jefferson State Jr. Coll., 1974; Cert. in Health Services Adminstrv. Devel., U. Ala.-Birmingham, 1985. Lic. R.N., Ala. Staff nurse Cooper Green Hosp., Birmingham, 1974-81, operating room supr., 1981-83; clin. dir. Druid City Hosp., Tuscalousa, Ala., 1983; dir. surg. services Brookwood Hosp., Birmingham, 1983—; cons. Tuscalousa Surg. Ctr. Vol. local March of Dimes, 1980, ARC, 1981. Grantee March of Dimes, 1971, Davis & Geck, 1982. Mem. Assn. Operating Room Nurses (bd. dirs. 1982-84). Republican. Methodist. Avocations: camping; canoeing; reading. Home: 3420 Coventry Dr Birmingham AL 35243 Office: Brookwood Med Ctr 2010 Med Center Dr Birmingham AL 35209

KARRAS, DONNA CIRIPOMPA, dental hygienist, educator; b. Wheeling, W.Va., Aug. 1, 1951; d. George Henry and Eleanor Jane (Nyles) Ciripompa; A.S./B.S., W. Liberty State Coll., 1973; M.A. in Community Health, W.Va. U., 1978; m. Donald George Karras, Mar. 6, 1982; 1 child, Dane Anthony. Dental hygienist, Morgantown, W.Va., 1973-78; asst. prof. dental hygiene U. S.D., Vermillion, 1979-80, asst. prof., 1980-82, assoc. chmn. dept. dental hygiene, 1980-82; dental hygienist in pvt. practice, Aurora, Colo., 1982-84; clin. asst. prof dept. dental hygiene and periodontics U. Colo., research asst. dept. applied dentistry; instr. CPR various schools, univs. and orgns. Vol., Clay County (S.D.) Ambulance Dept., 1979-82. Named Outstanding Clin. Instr., U. Colo., 1986; Volunteerism award Nat. Council on Aging, 1986. Cert. CPR instr., dental hygienist. Mem. Nat. Dental Hygienist Assn., Am. Dental Hygiene Assn. (rep. dist. X), Colo. Dental Hygienist Assn. (v.p.), Colo. Assn. Dental Research (charter mem.), Metro Denver Dental Hygienists Assn. (regional conv. del.), Colo. Hygienists Polit. Action Com., Delta Zeta. Home: 28505 Little Big Horn Dr Evergreen CO 80439

KARRE, KATHLEEN MARY, laywer; b. Lafayette, La., Mar. 21, 1957; d. Albert Michael and Inez (Boustany) K. B.A., U. Southwestern La., 1978; J.D., La. State U., 1981. Bar: La. 1982, U.S. Ct. Appeals (5th cir.) 1984. Law clk. U.S. Dist. Ct. Western Dist. La., Lafayette, 1982-83, U.S. Ct. Appeals 5th Circuit, Lafayette, 1984; assoc. Broadhurst Brook Mangham Hardy & Reed, Lafayette, 1984—. Mem. ABA, La. Bar Assn., Lafayette Bar Assn., Acadiana Assn. Women Attys., Order of Coif, Phi Kappa Phi, Phi Delta Theta. Democrat. Roman Catholic. Home: 111 Twin Oaks Blvd Lafayette LA 70503 Office: Broadhurst Brook et al 666 Jefferson St PO Drawer 2879 Lafayette LA 70502

KARRENBAUER, BEVERLY WOLFORD, elementary school administrator, consultant; b. Marion Center, Pa., Aug. 5, 1938; d. Clarence Frederick and Thelma Pearl (MacArthur) Wolford; B.S. in Edn., Indiana U. of Pa., 1959; M.Ed., U. Pitts., 1963; m. Raymond Joseph Karrenbauer, Jr., Aug. 20, 1960; 1 son, Raymond Joseph, III. Supr. perceptual devel. Keystone Oaks Sch. Dist., Pitts., 1967-69; supr. early childhood edn. Dade County (Fla.) public schs., 1969-80; adminstr. Miami Gardens Elem. Sch., Opa-Locka, Fla., 1980-82; adminstr. Treasure Island Elem. Sch., Miami Beach, Fla., 1982—; ednl. cons. children's programming WTVJ-TV, 1981-82; sr. cons. early childhood program Scholastic Mag. Inc. Recipient Internat. Year of Child award, 1979, Kiwanis Appreciation award, 1963; Frick Found. scholar 1962. Mem. Assn. Children Learning Disabilities, Elementary Prins. Assn., Assn. Supervision and Curriculum Devel., Dade County Adminstrs. Assn., PTA, N.E. Improvement Assn., Delta Kappa Gamma. Democrat. Author: Perpetual Development, 1968. Home: 1040 NE 82d St Miami FL 33138 Office: 7540 E Treasure Dr Miami Beach FL 33141

KARSEN, SONJA PETRA, educator; b. Berlin, Germany, Apr. 11, 1919; d. Fritz and Erna (Heidermann) K.; came to U.S., 1938, naturalized, 1945; Título de Bachiller, Colombia, 1937; student Nat. U., Bogotá, Colombia, 1937-38; B.A., Carleton Coll., 1939; M.A. (scholar in French 1939-41), Bryn Mawr Coll., 1941; Ph.D., Columbia U., 1950. Instr. Spanish, Lake Erie Coll., Painesville, Ohio, 1943-45; instr. modern langs. U. P.R., 1945-46; instr Spanish, Syracuse U., 1947-50, Bklyn. Coll., 1950-51; asst. to dep. dir. gen. UNESCO, 1951-52, Latin Am. desk, tech. asst. dept., 1952-53, mem. tech. assistance mission Costa Rica, 1954; asst. prof. Spanish, Sweet Briar Coll., 1955-57; asso. prof., chmn. dept. Romance langs. Skidmore Coll., Saratoga Springs, N.Y., 1957-61, prof. Spanish and chmn. dept. Romance langs., 1961-65, prof. Spanish, 1961—, faculty research lectr., 1963, chmn. dept. modern langs. and lits., 1965-79; Fulbright lectr. Free U. Berlin, 1968. Decorated chevalier Ordre des Palmes Academiques, 1964; recipient Leadership award N.Y. State Assn. Fgn. Lang. Tchrs., 1973, 79, Nat. Disting. Fgn. Lang. Leadership award, 1979, Disting. Service award, 1983, service award, 1984; Spanish Heritage award, 1981; Alumni Achievement Award Carleton Coll., 1982; exchange student auspices Inst. Internat. Edn. at Carleton Coll., 1938-39; Buenos Aires Conv. grantee for research in Colombia, 1946-47; faculty research grantee Skidmore Coll., summer 1959, 61, 63, 65, 67, 69, 70, 73. Mem. AAUP, MLA (mem. del. assembly 1976-78, Mildenberger medal selection com. 1983-85), Am. Assn. Tchrs. Spanish and Portuguese, AAUW, Nat. Geog. Soc., Instituto Internacional de Literatura Iberoamericana, Asociación Internacional de Hispanistas, Nat. Assn. Self-Instructional Lang. Programs (treas. 1973-77, dir. 1978-81, v.p. 1981-82, pres. 1982-83), Ateneo Dr. Jaime Torres Bodet, UN Assn. of U.S.A., Phi Sigma Iota (chmn. nat. scholarship com. 1980-81, mem. 1983-84). Author: Guillermo Valencia, Colombian Poet, 1951; Educational Development in Costa Rica with Unesco's Technical Assistance, 1951-54, 1954; Jaime Torres Bodet: A Poet in a Changing World, 1963; Selected Poems of Jaime Torres Bodet, 1964; Versos y prosas de Jaime Torres Bodet, 1966; Jaime Torres Bodet, 1971; advisory bd. Modern Lang. studies, 1977—; editor: Lang. Assn. Bull., 1980-83; contbr. articles to profl. jours. Office: Skidmore Coll Saratoga Springs NY 12866

KARTJE, JEAN VAN LANDUYT, college dean; b. Great Lakes, Ill., Aug. 14, 1953; d. John Emil and Alice Louise (Graikowski) Van L.; m. John Karl Kartje, Mar. 10, 1979. B.A. in Psychology and English, Barat Coll., 1975; postgrad. U. Chgo., 1975-76, So. Ill. U., 1976-77; M.A. in Mgmt., Webster U., 1985. Dir. residence Barat Coll., Lake Forest, Ill., 1977-80, dean students, 1981—, also psychology instr.; employee Hotel Therme, Bad Vals, Switzerland, 1980-81. Mem. steering com. ann. awards YWCA Lake County, 1983; mem. Lake County Council on Women's Programs, 1982—. Mem. Assn. Campus Activities Adminstrs., Alumnae Assn. Barat Coll. (dir. at large 1984-85), Chicagoland Deans' Assn. Democrat. Roman Catholic. Avocations: reading; gardening; traveling. Home: W210 West Shore Dr Mundelein IL 60060 Office: Barat Coll 700 E Westleigh Rd Lake Forest IL 60045

KARTON, CAROL KAUFMAN, editor, writer; b. Buffalo, Nov. 10, 1941; d. William and Rhea (Olodort) Kaufman; m. Robert M. Karton, Aug. 1, 1964 (div. Feb. 1984); children—Deborah Lynn, Gary Stuart, Jeffrey Alan. B.A., U. Mich., 1963; M.A., Northwestern U., 1964. Cert. tchr., Ill. Tchr., writer Sch. Dist. 72, Skokie, Ill., 1964-67; project assoc. Northwestern U., Evanston, Ill., 1976-79; freelance writer, editor, Glencoe, Ill., 1975—; co-owner Ragtime, Ltd., Glencoe, 1979-81; asst. editor Scott, Foresman & Co., Glenview, Ill., 1981-83, assoc. editor, 1983-85, editor, 1985—. Mem. Glencoe Sch. Bd. Nominating Caucus, 1983-85. Mem. Women in Communication. Jewish. Home: 1182 Carol Ln Glencoe IL 60022 Office: Scott Foresman & Co 1900 E Lake St Glenview IL 60025

KARVIA, DONNA MARIE, civic administrator; b. Eckley, Colo., June 18, 1938; d. Leroy Ralph and Edna Stella (Cox) McEwen; m. John William Karvia, Sept. 1, 1956; children—Michael, Jack, Patrick. Student, Centralia Coll. Mem. staff agrl. extension service Wash. State U., Pullman, 1957-63; dep. clk. Lewis County Dist. Ct., Chehalis, Wash., 1969-76, dep. county clk., 1976-79, chief dep. county clk., 1979-84, county clk., 1984—. Mem., Wash. State Heart Assn., 1965—, Lewis County Child Abuse Council, Chehalis, 1985—. Women Judges Hist. Project, Olympia, 1985—; 1st vice chmn. Lewis County Dem. Central Com., 1985—; mem. Gov.'s adv. bd. on Wash. State Hist. Records, 1985—; mem. Devel. Disabled Planning Council. Mem. Wash. State Assn. County Clks., Wash. State Assn. Elected Officials, Wash. Elected Women, Legal Secs. Assn. Lutheran. Clubs: Soroptimist Internat. (Chehalis), Bus. and Profl. Women (Chehalis). Avocations: genealogy; reading. Office: Lewis County Clk Courthouse Chehalis WA 98532

KASAKOVE, SUSAN, interior designer; b. Newark, N.J., Nov. 11, 1938. B.F.A., U. Buffalo, 1958, Hunter Coll., 1960; postgrad. N.Y. Sch. of Interior Design, 1960-64, Pratt Inst., 1968-69, New Sch. for Social Research, 1967-68. Asst. interior designer Rodgers Assocs., N.Y.C., 1964-66; interior designer Walter Dorwin Teague Assocs., N.Y.C., 1966-70; sr. interior designer N.Y. State Facilities Devel. Corp., N.Y.C., 1970—. Interior designs include projects for Eli Lilly & Co., Bank of Bermuda, Quaker Oats Corp., N.Y. State Office of Mental Health, N.Y. State Office of Mental Retardation, Cattaraugus County, Warren County. Reading tutor Vols. for Childrens Services, N.Y.C., 1976-82; chmn. Friends of White Plains Symphony, N.Y., 1981-83; vol. guide ednl. dept. Met. Mus. of Art, N.Y.C., 1978—; treas. 11th Ward Republican Club, Yonkers, N.Y., 1979-81. Recipient Outstanding Service to Sch. award Lions Club, Rockland County, N.Y., 1955. Avocations: photography; history of art and architecture; golfing; swimming. Home: 793 Palmer Rd Apt 3-F Bronxville NY 10708 Office: NY State Facilities Devel Corp 909 3d Ave New York NY 10022

KASEL, JANE MARIE, publishing co. exec.; b. Bay City, Mich., June 19, 1947; d. Vincent A. and Jenotte Marie Curtis (Lipan) Emeott; B.A., U. Calif., Santa Barbara, 1970; postgrad. Calif. State U., Fullerton, 1972-73; m. Richard S. Kasel, Jr., Dec. 12, 1981. Salesperson, bookkeeper Heth Hardware, Baldwin Park, Calif., 1962-66; mgrs. asst. univ. approved housing U. Calif., Santa Barbara, 1968-70; exec. sec. contracts div. Aerojet Gen., Azusa, Calif., 1966-71; tchr. English, yearbook adv., adv. council Walnut (Calif.) High Sch., 1971-77; yearbook specialist Taylor Pub. Co., Covina, Calif., 1977—, mem. pres. adv. council, 1980-82, mem. sales adv. council, 1981-82. Mem., guide for communication seminars House of White Shell Woman; mem. Eastside Christian Ch., 1978—. Named Woman of Yr., Bank Am., 1967; recipient Mktg. awards Taylor Pub. Co., 1979, Pacesetter award, 1979, Half Million Dollar Club awards, 1981, 82, 83. also named Rookie of Yr. Mem. Journalism Educators Assn., So. Calif. Journalism Educators Assn., Nat. Assn. Female Execs., Alpha Gamma Sigma. Office: 562 Laguna Canyon Way Brea CA 92621

KASE-POLISINI, JUDITH BAKER, teacher, educator; b. Wilmington, Del., Dec. 13, 1932; d. Charles Robert and Elizabeth Edna (Baker) Kase; B.A., U. Del., 1955; M.A., Case Western Res. U., 1956; m. James F. Polisini; stepchildren—James, Elizabeth, John, Katherine, Ann. Tchr., dir. children's theatre Agnes Scott Coll., 1956, U. Tenn., 1957, U. Md., Germany, 1958-60, Denver Civic Theatre, Denver U., Kent Sch. for Girls, 1960-61; dir. children's theatre U. N.H., Durham, 1962-69; dir. theatre resources for youth, Somersworth, N.H., 1966-69; assoc. prof. theatre U. South Fla., Tampa, 1969-74, assoc. prof. edn., 1969-84, prof., 1984—, artistic dir. ednl. theatre, 1976—; project dir. Hillsborough County Artists-in-Schs. Evaluation and Inservice Project, 1980-82. Bd. dirs. Fla. Alliance for Arts Edn., sec., 1976-77, vice-chmn., 1979-82, chmn. 1982-84; mem. theatre adv. panel Arts Council Tampa-Hillsborough County; chmn. Wingspread Conf. on Theatre Edn., 1977; drama adjudicator Nat. Arts Festival, Ministry of Edn., Bahamas, 1975, 76, 79, 80; regional chmn. Alliance for Arts Edn., J.F. Kennedy Center for Performing Arts, 1983—; cons. theatre edn. and prodn. Mem. Children's Theatre Assn. Am. (pres.-elect 1975-77, pres. 1977-79, chmn. symposia 1981—), Am. Theatre Assn. (chief div. pres.'s coordinating council 1977-78 commn. on theatre edn. 1982—), Speech Communication Assn., Southeastern, Fla. theatre confs., Internat. Assn. Theatres for Children and Youth, Fla. Assn. for Theater Edn., Fla. Conf. Tchrs. English, United Faculty Fla., Tampa Mus. Democrat. Episcopalian. Club: Carrollwood Village. Author books on creative drama in a developmental context; editor: Creative Drama in a Developmental Context; Children's Theatre, Creative Drama and Learning; contbr. articles to profl. jours.; pub. playwright; dir. plays. Home: 5311 Taylor Rd Lutz FL 33549 Office: Dept Curriculum and Instrn U South Fla Tampa FL 33620

KASH, FRANCYS KAYGEY, civic worker, service organization executive; b. Sioux City, Iowa, Feb. 25, 1921; d. Jacob David and Ida (Schwab) Maron; student pub. schs., Sioux City; m. Louis Kash, Dec. 17, 1939; 1 dau., Leslie Jo Kash Brodie. Dir., Columbia Savs. and Loan Assn., Beverly Hills, Calif., 1976-81; v.p. 1st Pacific Bank, 1981-83; public affairs/cultural cons. Los Angeles County, 1983—. Vice pres. B'nai B'rith Women, Washington, 1965-76, mem. exec. bd., 1958, treas., 1963-65, internat. pres., 1976-78, chmn. constitution-policy com., 1982-86, former chmn. Anti-Defamation League planning com., life mem. exec. com., hon. life mem. Commn.; former commr. Hillel, B'nai B'rith Youth Orgn.; guest lectr. U. Calif. Extension, Los Angeles, 1977; mem. exec. com. western region, U.S. Com. for UNICEF, 1966; mem. Los Angeles City Human Relations Commn. Adv. Com., 1963—; mem. Calif. Atty. Gen. Constl. Rights Adv. Com., 1962-64; bd. govs. Jewish Fedn. Council Greater Los Angeles, 1984—; bd. govs., life mem., exec. com. B'nai B'rith Women. Named Woman of Achievement, N.Y. Women's Div. of Anti-defamation League, 1976; recipient Outstanding Service award State of Israel, 1973, Los Angeles Mayor award, 1976-77. Mem. Jewish Fedn. Council (bd. dirs. 1958-76, pres. women's conf. 1960-61, bd. govs. 1984—), Sisterhood Congregation Mogen David (life). Home: 9311 Alcott St Los Angeles CA 90035

KASHDIN, GLADYS SHAFRAN, painter, educator; b. Pitts., Dec. 15, 1921; d. Edward M. and Miriam P. Shafran; B.A. magna cum laude, U. Miami, 1960, M.A., 1962; Ph.D., Fla. State U., 1965; m. Manville E. Kashdin, Oct. 11, 1942 (dec.). Photographer, N.Y.C. and Fla., 1938-60; tchr. art, Fla. and Ga., 1956-63; asst. prof. humanities U. South Fla., Tampa, 1965-70, assoc. prof., 1970-74, prof., 1974—; works exhibited in 33 one-woman shows, 38 group exhbns.; maj. touring exhibits include: The Everglades, 1972-75; Aspects of the River, 1975-80; Processes of Time, 1981—; represented in permanent collections: Taiwan, Peoples Republic of China, Columbus Mus. Arts and Sci., LeMoyne Art Found., Tampa Internat. Airport, Tampa Mus. Art, Council of 100; lectr.; adv. bd. Hillsborough County Mus., 1975-83. Mem. U. S. Fla. Status of Women Com., 1971-76, chmn., 1975-76. Recipient Women Helping Women in Art award Soroptimist Internat., 1979; Motar Bd. award for teaching excellence, 1986. Mem. NOW, AAUW (1st v.p. Tampa br. 1971-72), Phi Kappa Phi (chpt.-pres. 1981-83). Home: 441 Biltmore Ave Temple Terrace FL 33617 Office: U South Fla Tampa FL 33620

KASINDORF, BLANCHE ROBINS, educational administrator; b. N.Y.C., May 18, 1925; d. Samuel David and Anna (Block) Robins; B.A., Hunter Coll., 1944; M.A., N.Y.U., 1948; postgrad. Cornell U., 1946-50; m. David Kasindorf, July 1, 1960. Tchr. pub. schs., Bklyn., 1945-56; instr. Bklyn. Coll., 1956-57; asst. in research for Puerto Rican study Ford Found. and N.Y.C. Bd. Edn., 1956-57; asst. prin. N.Y.C. Pub. Schs., 1957-59; research asso. ednl. programming and stats. N.Y.C. Bd. Edn., 1959-63, coordinator spl. edn. liaison div. child welfare for Bur. Curriculum Research, 1963-64; jr. prin., integration coordinator Bklyn. Sch. Dist. 44, 1964-65; prin. Pub. Sch. 8, Bklyn., 1965—; cons. to numerous social agys. Mem. NEA, Council Exceptional Children, N.Y.C. Elementary Sch. Prins., Council Supervisory Assns. Contbr. to profl. publs.; also editor instructional materials. Home: 1655 Flatbush Ave Brooklyn NY 11210 Office: PS 8 37 Hicks St Brooklyn NY 11201

KASPER, ANN MARIE, retail company executive; b. Spokane, Wash., Oct. 12, 1958; d. Harry Irving and Mary Elizabeth (McHarness) K. B.A., Mills Coll., Calif., 1981. Account exec. Morgan Stanley & Co., San Francisco and N.Y.C., 1981-83; nat. sales mgr. William Kasper & Co., The Cashmere People, Los Angeles and N.Y.C., 1984—. Mem. Calif. Literacy (bd. dirs. 1986—), NOW, Nat. Assn. Exec. Females, World Affairs Council, Mills Coll. Alumnae Assn. Democrat. Club: Marina City (Marina Del Rey, Calif.) Avocations: tennis; sculpture; painting; photography. Office: William Kasper & Co Inc 110 E 9th St Suite C251 Los Angeles CA 90079

KASPER, MYRA MERRELL, corporation executive; b. Cleve., Apr. 2, 1943; d. Roswell P. and Madeline E. (Bliley) Merrell, Jr.; m. Ronald C. Kasper, Oct. 22, 1966; 1 dau., Victoria. Assoc. in Comml. Sci., Dyke Coll., 1963. Personnel sec. Nat. City Bank, Cleve., 1963-68; sec. Glidden-Durkee, Cleve., 1968-70; office mgr. Booz, Allen & Hamilton, Cleve., 1970-73; adminstrv. asst. Soc. Corp., Cleve., 1973-83, asst. treas., dir. corp. devel., 1983—. Republican. Roman Catholic. Office: Soc Corp 127 Public Sq Cleveland OH 44114

KASPERSON, JEANNE XANTHAKOS, librarian, editor; b. Southbridge, Mass., Feb. 3, 1938; d. James and Mary (Mitsakos) Xanthakos; m. Roger Eugene Kasperson, Sept. 6, 1959; children—Demetri Alexander, Kyra Eleni. B.A. with honors in English, Clark U., 1959; postgrad. in L.S., U. Chgo., 1959-60, M.A. in English, 1962; M.S. in L.S., Simmons Coll., 1967. Asst. librarian circulation and reference Edn. Library, U. Chgo., 1959-60; asst. acquisitions librarian Wilbur Cross Library, U. Conn., Storrs, 1964-66, asst. to chief bibliographer Mich. State U. Library, East Lansing, 1966-67; research librarian Hazard Assessment Group, Clark U., Worcester, Mass., 1977-78, Center Tech., Environ., and Devel., 1979-86, World Hunger Program, Brown U., 1986—; editor Aquarius Project, 1972-73; dir. publs. CENTED, 1983—. Co-editor: Water Re-use and the Cities (best sci. book award 1977), 1977; Risk in the Technological Society, 1982; co-author, co-editor: Natural Hazards Observer, 1984; Perilous Progress: Managing the Hazards of Technology, 1985; Risk Analysis in Comparative Perspective, forthcoming, 1986; contbr. articles to profl. jours. Exec. bd. Woodstock Library Assn., 1974-75, v.p., 1975-77, pres., 1978-80, book selection com., 1980-85; pres. N. Woodstock Library Assn., 1977-82. Mem. ALA, N.Y. Acad. Sci., Soc. Risk Analysis, Research Com. Disasters, Internat. Disaster Inst., Internat. Assn. Impact Analysis. Democrat. Greek Orthodox. Office: World Hunger Program Box 1831 Brown Univ Providence RI 02912

KASPRZAK, JOYCE ANN, weight loss company executive; b. Greensburg, Pa., Sept. 28, 1946; d. Benjamin Steven and Palma Christine (Policastro) De Rosa; m. Richard E. Reid, Nov. 1, 1966 (div. Nov. 1977); 1 child, Brian Scott; m. 2d, Alan Lee Kasprzak, June 25, 1978. B.A. in Communication Arts, U. Dayton, 1967, postgrad., 1969-70; A.M.A., Wright State U., 1985. Social worker Welfare Dept., Dayton, Ohio, 1967-68; tchr. St. James Elem. Sch., Dayton, 1968-71, St. Helen Elem. Sch., Dayton, 1972-73; pres., dir. Diet Workshop, Dayton, 1973—, mem. nat. adv. bd., 1980—; chmn. creative cuisine Am. Heart Assn., 1979-80. Contbr. Diet Corner column several newspapers, 1974-79. Recipient numerous awards for outstanding performance Nat. Diet Workshop, 1974—; awards for fund-raising activities Nat. CARE Assn., 1976, St. Jude's Hosp., Memphis, 1977, 78, ARC, Dayton, 1979, 80; award Salute ot Women Entrepreneurs, Lazarus of Dayton, 1986. Mem. Women in Communications, Dayton C. of C., U. Dayton Pres.'s Club. Roman Catholic. Office: Diet Workshop PO Box 311 3220 N Main St Dayton OH 45405

KASS, BABETTE, advertising and marketing researcher; b. N.Y.C.; d. David and Sadie Gertrude (Fischel) Kass; m. Jacob M. Miller, Jan. 15, 1967. B.A., Hunter Coll., 1940; M.A., Columbia U., 1945. Dir. advt. and mktg. div., sr. research assoc. Bur. Applied Social Research, Columbia U., N.Y.C., 1948-55; tech. dir. research Young & Rubicam Advt. Agy., N.Y.C., 1955-60; owner Babette Kass Creative Research, Sun City, Ariz., 1960—. Fellow Am. Sociol. Assn.; mem. Am. Assn. Pub. Opinion Research (past mem. exec. council), Am. Mktg. Assn. Author: Economic Strength of Business and Professional Women, 1954, also articles. Jewish. Office: Babette Kass Creative Research 16838 103d Dr Sun City AZ 85351

KASSEBAUM, NANCY LANDON, U.S. Senator; b. Topeka, July 29, 1932; d. Alfred M. and Theo Landon; B.A., U. Kans., 1952; M.S. in Diplomatic History, U. Mich., 1956; m. Philip Kassebaum, 1955 (div. 1979); children—John Philip, Linda Josephine, Richard Landon, William Alfred. Vice pres. Stas. KFH-KBRA-FM, Wichita, Kans.; staff asst. Sen. James B. Pearson, Washington, 1975-76; mem. U.S. Senate from Kans., 1978—, mem. fgn. relations com., commerce, sci. and transp. com., budget com. Recipient Matrix award Women in Communications. Republican. Episcopalian. Office: US Senate 302 Senate Russell Office Bldg Washington DC 20510

KASSEWITZ, RUTH EILEEN BLOWER, hospital executive; b. Columbus, Ohio, May 15, 1928; d. E. Wallett and Helen (Daub) Blower; B.S. in Journalism-Mgmt., Ohio State U., Columbus, 1951; m. Jack Kassewitz, July 28, 1962 (dec.); 1 step son, Jack. Copywriter, Ohio Fuel Gas Co., Columbus, 1951-55, Merritt Owens Advt. Agy., Kansas City, Kans., 1955-56; account exec. Grant Advt., Inc., Miami, Fla., 1956-59; account supr. Venn/Cole & Assocs., Miami, 1959-67; dir. communications Ferendino/Grafton/Candela/Spillis Architects & Engrs., Miami, 1967-69; dir. communications Dade County Dept. Housing and Urban Devel., Miami, 1969-72; dir. communications Met. Dade County Govt., 1972-78; adminstr. community relations and mktg. U. Miami/Jackson Meml. Med. Center, 1978—. Pres., U. Miami Women's Guild, 1973-74; bd. dirs. Girls Scouts Tropical Fla., 1974-76, 81-83, Lung Assn. Dade-Monroe Counties, 1976—; mem. exec. com. Miami-Dade Community Coll. Found.; pres. Mental Health Assn. Dade County, 1982; mem. Miami Ecol. and Beautification Com., 1978—; bd. govs. Barry U., Miami, 1981-83; trustee Nat. Humanities Faculty, 1981-83; trustee United Protestant Appeal, 1984—; mem. Greater Miami Urban Coalition; treas., past chmn. Health, Edn., Promotion Council, Inc.; mem. Coral Gables Cable TV Bd., 1983-86; ch. moderator Plymouth Congl. Ch., 1986-88. Recipient Disting. Service award Plymouth Congl. Ch., Miami, 1979; Ann Stover award, 1983. Mem. Public Relations Soc. Am. (pres. South Fla. chpt. 1969-70, nat. chmn. govt. sect. 1973-74, nat. dir. 1974-78; continuing edn. council 1981-83; Silver Anvil award 1973, Assembly del. 1986-89), Internat. Platform Assn., Women in Communications (pres. Greater Miami chpt. 1962-63; Clarion award 1973, Community Headliner 1985), Fla. Hosp. Assn., South Fla. Hosp. Public Relations Assn., Miami Forum, Greater Miami C. of C. (gov. 1983-86), Fla. Women's Network. Conglist. Home: 1136 Aduana Ave Coral Gables FL 33146 Office: Jackson Meml Hosp 1611 NW 12th Ave Rm 0118 Miami FL 33136

KASTAMA, KATHLEEN SUSAN, pharmacist; b. Munich, Fed. Republic Germany, Sept. 27, 1957; d. Marvin Gust and Patricia Lee (McDowell) K. A.A. with honors, Cecil Community Coll., 1975; B.S. in Pharmacy, U. Md., 1981. Registered pharmacist, Md., N.H., Vt. Asst. pharmacy mgr. Klein's Pharmacy, Forest Hill, Md., 1981; pharmacy mgr. Rite Aid Discount Pharmacies, Aberdeen, Md., 1981-83, pharmacist, Tilton, N.H., 1983-85; pharmacist Farley's Pharmacy, Plymouth, N.H., 1985; pharmacy mgr. Brooks Drug, Meredith, N.H., 1985—; vol. VA Med. Ctr. Pharmacy, Perry Point, Md., 1975-79; cons. Roy Williams Pub. Sch., Havre de Grace, Md., 1977-84; clinician faculty mem. Inst. Medication Awareness, 1986—. Mem. dir. N.H. Pub. TV, 1985. Mem. N.H. Pharm. Assn., Am. Pharm. Assn., Nat. Assn.

Female Execs., Acad. Pharmacy Practice, U. Md. Sch. Pharmacy Alumni Assn. (life), Phi Theta Kappa/Alpha Alpha Theta (scholar 1977, past pres.). Lodge: Job's Daus. Avocations: country music; cats; dogs; pharmacy-related antiques; travel. Home: PO Box 133 Plymouth NH 03264 Office: Brooks No 683 Route 25 Meredith NH 03253

KASTROW, VIRGINIA WARRENE, insurance broker; b. Pocatello, Idaho, Nov. 21, 1956; d. Wayne M. and Evelyn V. (Phinney) Townsend; m. Robert Joseph Kastrow, Aug. 21, 1982. Student Portland State U., 1979, 80. Ins. clk. Columbia Dist. Hosp., St. Helens, Oreg., 1974-75; stock transfer clk. U.S. Nat. Bank, Portland, Oreg., 1975-77; purchasing supr. Grantree Corp., Portland, 1977-79; account rep. Rollins Burdick Hunter, Portland, 1979-85, account exec., Phoenix, 1985—. St. Helens Bus. and Profl. Women's Club scholar, 1975. Mem. Nat. Assn. Female Execs., Group Ins. Assn. Phoenix, Ins. Women of Phoenix, Western Pension Conf., Phoenix Young Democrats. Avocations: hiking; reading; calligraphy; painting. Office: Rollins Burdick Hunter 100 W Clarendon Suite 1100 Phoenix AZ 85013

KATH, LAURA ELIZABETH, sales director; b. Pontiac, Mich., July 26, 1960; d. Charles Mahlon and Anna Irene (Hubble) K. B.A. in Hotel, Restaurant Mgmt., Mich. State U., 1982. Sales trainee Seelbach Hotel, Louisville, 1982; sales mgr. Radisson Hotel Muehlebach, Kansas City, Mo., 1982-85, Canyon Resort, Palm Springs, Calif., 1985; dir. sales Santa Barbara Conf./Visitors Bur., Calif., 1985—. Mem. Sisters Cities Com. Santa Barbara/Puerto Vallarta, 1986; bd. dirs. Arthritis Found. Santa Barbara. Mem. Soc. Incentive Travel Execs., Meeting Planners Internat., Hotel Sales and Mktg. Assn. Avocations: swimming; bicycling; reading; travel. Office: Santa Barbara Conf and Visitors Bur PO Box 299 1330 State St Santa Barbara CA 93101

KATHIE, CAROLE AYN, business executive, writer, public relations consultant; b. Jersey City, N.J., July 1, 1949; d. John and Emily (Bures) Kasenchak. B.A. in History, Pace U., N.Y.C., 1971; postgrad. U. Houston, 1972-73; M.A. in Sociology, Hunter Coll., N.Y.C., 1976. With custody dept. Morgan Guaranty, N.Y.C., 1968-72; adminstrv. asst. U. Houston, 1971-72, Citizens Com. for Children, 1973-74, N.Y. State Conf. for Childrens Rights, N.Y.C., 1973-74, N.Y. State Assn. for Human Services, Albany, 1974-75, Girl Scouts U.S.A., N.Y.C., 1976-77; employment counselor Dept. Labor State N.J., Trenton, 1977-81; personnel mgr. Union Photo Co., Clifton, N.J., 1981-84; exec. recruiter Mgmt. Recruiters, Internat., N.Y.C., 1985—. Contbr. newspaper The Palisadian, 1980-85. Bd. dirs. N.Y. Coalition for Juvenile Justice, N.Y.C., 1973-74; pres. Bergen County Women's Polit. Caucus (N.J.), 1978-80; commr. Bergen County Commn. on Status of Women, 1979-82; mem. state adv. com. N.J. Commn. on Women, 1980-81; mem. help line Contact Teleministries, N.Y.C., 1981-82; state chmn. pub. relations N.J. Women's Bus. Owners Conf., 1984. Mem. Am. Soc. Personnel Adminstrs. (sec. 1983-84, v.p. 1984-86), Internat. Assn. Personnel in Employment Security (sec. 1980-81), N.J. Network of Bus. & Profl. Women, Nat. Assn. Female Execs., AAUW. Democrat. Dutch Reformed. Club: Fleet (v.p. pub. relations 1983) (Ft. Lee, N.J.). Home: 334 Coolidge Ave Fort Lee NJ 07024 Office: Mgmt Recruiters Internat 305 Madison Ave New York NY 10165

KATHMAN, MARY JO SUSAN, nursing educator; b. Cin., Mar. 8, 1953; d. Joseph Frank and Yvonne Beverly (Passmore) Ramundo; m. Richard Joseph Kathman, May 24, 1975; 1 son, Michael James. B.S. in Nursing, Coll. Mt. St. Joseph (Ohio), 1975, M.A. in Edn., 1983. R.N., Diabetic tchr., nurse St. George Hosp., Cin., 1975-76; nurse surg. intensive care unit Christ Hosp., Cin., 1977-81; nurse emergency treatment Health Care Ctr., Cin., part-time 1983—; nursing educator Good Samaritan Hosp. Sch. Nursing, Cin., 1981—, area chmn. Level II, 1986—. Vol. ARC, Cin., 1982. Recipient Cert. Merit La Societa Fuscaldese Femminile, Cin., 1975, 84. Mem. Am. Assn. Critical Care Nurses, Sigma Theta Tau. Democrat. Roman Catholic. Office: The Good Samaritan Hosp Sch Nursing Victoria Hall Clifton and Dixmyth Aves Cincinnati OH 45220

KATHURIA, NIRMAL BHATIA, physician; b. New Delhi, India, May 23, 1948; came to U.S., 1973, naturalized, 1980; d. Banarsi Das and Chander (Kanta) Bhatia; M.D., Lady Hardinge Med. Coll., New Delhi, 1969; m. Mineshwar Kathuria, Jan. 14, 1973. Intern, Lady Hardinge Med. Coll. and Hosp., 1970-72; resident in psychiatry Fairfield Hills Hosp., Newtown, Conn., 1974-77, staff psychiatrist, 1977-88; resident in psychiatry Yale-New Haven Hosp., Stamford (Conn.) Hosp., 1974-77; dir. outpatient clinic Charlotte Hungerford Hosp., Torrington, Conn., 1978-80, dir., chmn. psychiat. services, 1980—; cons. Country Place, Litchfield, Conn., 1979-82, bd. govs., 1979—; mem. adv. bd. Regional Health Services, Winsted, Conn., 1979-81; program chmn., mem. exec. com. Assn. Psychiat. Clinics Conn., 1981-82. Diplomate Am. Bd. Psychiatry and Neurology. Mem. Am. Psychiat. Assn., Conn. Psychiat. Soc. Home: Beach St Goshen CT 06756 Office: 778 E Main St Torrington CT 06790

KATSON, ROBERTA MARINA, economist; b. Albuquerque, Oct. 5, 1947; d. Robert V. and Penelope (Papafrangos) Katson; student Emory U., 1966-67, Ga. State U., 1967-69; B.A., U. N.Mex., 1974, M.A., 1977; m. Cyrus Butner, 1980; children—Justin Cyrus, Renee Alexis. Gen. mgr. Window Rock (Ariz.) Motor Inn, Navajo Reservation, 1972-73; research asst. dept. econs. U. N.Mex., Albuquerque, 1974-75, research asso. Resource Econ. Group, 1975-77; economist program analysis Econ. Devel. Adminstrn., Dept. Commerce, Washington, 1977-79; economist Dept. Energy, Washington, 1979-84. Mem. Phi Kappa Phi, Omicron Delta Epsilon. Democrat. Contbr. articles to profl. jours. Home: 11901 St Johnsbury Ct Reston VA 22091

KATTER, MARGARET ANN, school principal; b. Zeigler, Ill., July 4, 1939; d. Donald Anderson and Margaret A. (Gibbs) Bean; m. Donald Ray Katter, Aug. 19, 1961; children—Edward A., Daniel R., Gregory A. B.S., Purdue U., 1961, M.S., 1970; Adminstrn. cert. Ind. U., Ft. Wayne, 1980. Tchr., Middle Sch., Monticello, Ind., 1961-64, Ft. Wayne, 1974-77; tchr. High Sch., Jefferson-Lafayette, Ind., 1964-66, Adult Edn., Lafayette, 1964-70; instr. Purdue U., West Lafayette, Ind., 1970-73; prin. Blackhawk Middle Sch., Ft. Wayne, 1977—. Fund raiser United Way, Ft. Wayne, 1983—, Fine Arts Found., Ft. Wayne, 1983—, Snider High Sch. Marching Band, Ft. Wayne, 1981-85; v.p. Snider Music Boosters, 1983—. Mem. Ind. Middle Sch. Assn., Nat. Assn. Secondary Sch. Adminstrs., Ind. Assn. Secondary Sch. Adminstrs., Ft. Wayne Assn. Sch. Adminstrs., Nat. Middle Sch. Assn., Omicron Nu, Delta Kappa Gamma, Phi Delta Kappa. Republican. Baptist. Lodge: Order Eastern Star. Avocations: mothering, reading, flower arranging. Office: Blackhawk Middle Sch 7200 S State Blvd Fort Wayne IN 46815

KATTER, MARGARET ANN CASTRO, health maintenance organization executive; b. San Francisco, Mar. 30, 1940; d. Clarence Charles and Elaine Ruth (Bullock) Castro; B.A. magna cum laude, U. Colo., 1960; M.B.A., Harvard U., 1983; m. Lincoln Katter, Aug. 26, 1979; children by previous marriage—Richard Todd Radakovich, Michael Keith Radakovich, Gary Douglas Radakovich. Mgr. med. office, Ketchikan, Alaska, 1965-69; public relations asst. to U.S. Senator from Alaska, 1969-71; cons., instr. office staff Seattle Gen. Hosp., 1971-72; editor reports, asst. to dir. Rocket Research Corp., Redmond, Wash., 1972-74; exec. asst. to bd. of trustees Group Health Coop. of Puget Sound, Seattle, from 1974, now dir. bd. trustees, asst. sec., corp. officer; corporate officer subs. bds. Group Health of Wash., Group Health Enterprises; pres. Hospice of Snohomish County. Co-chmn. gubernatorial campaign of Wally J. Hickel, 1968-69; Alaska del. to Republican Women's Conf., 1970; vol. bd. trainer United Way of King County. Mem. Am. Mgmt. Assn., Group Health Assn. Am., Aircraft Owners and Pilots Assn. Republican. Lutheran. Club: Redmond Flying. Office: Group Health Coop Puget Sound 300 Elliott Ave W Seattle WA 98119

KATZ, ANNETTE SARA, editor, journalist; b. Miami, Fla., Jan. 25, 1948; d. Harold Orville and Jean (Bulafkin) Van Dam; B.S. in Journalism, U. Fla., 1970; m. Stephen K. Katz, Feb. 26, 1978; children—Matthew R, Jessica I. Reporter, Coral Gables (Fla.) Times, also The Guide, Coral Gables, 1970-71, women's editor, 1971-72, edn. editor, 1972-74; dir. communications United Tchrs. Dade County (Fla.), 1974—, media coordinator, 1980—, editor UTD Today (named best union newspaper in Fla. 1981-82). Mem. Fla. Women's Polit. Caucus, 1970-71. Recipient Sch. Bell award Fla. Edn. Assn., 1973, 74; Number Two Suburban Journalist in U.S. award Suburban Newspapers Am., 1973; resolution City of Coral Gables, 1973; 1st place feature writing Union Press, 1975; State Union Press award, 1976, 77; award for disting. journalism Fla. Tchr. Press Assn., 1980; 1st place award Ednl. Press Assn., 1983, Internat. Labor Press Assn.; 1st place award Fla. Med. Assn. for excellence in med. journalism, 1983; 1st place award for feature story Ednl. Press Assn. Am., 1984; 1st place for feature story, Internat. Labor Communications Assn., 1984, 3d place, 1985; excellence in journalism award Fla. Edn. Assn., 1984, 1st place award, 1985; others. Mem. Women in Communications (corr. sec. 1972-73, rec. sec. 1973-74), Nat. Union Tchrs. Press Assn. (1st place, gen. excellence 1985), Fla. Press Club. Democrat. Jewish. Office: 2929 SW 3d Ave Miami FL 33129

KATZ, BETSY LYNN, moving company executive; b. Atlanta, Mar. 19, 1942; d. Russell William and Goldie Elizabeth (Kelleher) Hart; m. Bruce Alexander Brast (div.); 1 child, Eric Alexander; m. Edward Richard Katz, Sept. 19, 1980. Grad. high sch., San Mateo, Calif. Exec. sec. Blue Cross of Atlanta, 1973-75; legal sec. U.S. Dept. Interior, Atlanta, 1975-82; pres. Tiffany Enterprises, Atlanta, 1982—, Peachtree Movers, Inc., Atlanta, 1983—. Mem. In Touch Ministries, Atlanta, 1985. Mem. Bldg. Owners and Mgrs. Assn. Republican. Baptist. Home: 4847 Cambridge Dr Dunwoody GA 30338 Office: Peachtree Movers Inc 1048 Northside Dr NW Atlanta GA 30318

KATZ, CAROLINE, lawyer, social work agency executive; b. Bklyn., Nov. 11, 1943; d. Abraham and Gertrude (Bernstein) K. B.A. cum laude, NYU, 1964; postgrad. Syracuse U., 1966-67; J.D., Fordham U., 1978. Bar: N.Y. 1979. Asst. coordinator com. devel. N.Y.C. Council Against Poverty, 1965-66; assoc. dir. and gen. counsel N.Y. Inst. for Human Devel., Inc., N.Y.C., 1967—; pres. and dir. Southwest Harlem Community Services, Inc., N.Y.C., 1979—; cons. Outreach Workshop, Nat. Inst. Drug Abuse, Dec. 1974. Recipient Am. Jurisprudence award, 1976. Mem. N.Y. State Bar Assn., N.Y. State Women's Bar Assn., Phi Beta Kappa. Democrat. Jewish. Home: 136 E 55th St New York NY 10022 Office: NY Inst Human Devel Inc 845 3d Ave New York NY 10022

KATZ, ESTHER, historian, editor, administrator; b. Brussels, Aug. 14, 1948; came to U.S., 1951; d. Harry and Rose (Katz) K. A.B., Hunter Coll., 1969; M.A., NYU, 1973, Ph.D., 1980. Instr. SUNY Coll.-Brockport, 1976, NYU, 1976, Coll. New Rochelle, N.Y.C., 1981; asst. prof. NYU, 1983-84, adj. prof. history, 1983-85; dep. dir. Inst. for Research in History, N.Y.C., 1983—; dir. Margaret Sanger Papers Project, 1984—; mem. planning com. N.Y.C. Commn. on Status of Women, 1982-84; mem. task force Women's Thesaurus Project of Nat. Council for Research on Women, N.Y.C., 1982-84; mem. nat. council advisors for exhibit censorship: 500 Yrs. of Conflict, N.Y. Pub. Library, 1983-84. Assoc. editor: Jour. Trends in History, 1983—; editor: Women's History: East and West, 1985; co-editor: Woman's Experience in America, 1980; Procs. of Conf. on Women Surviving Holocaust, 1983. Contbg. author, editor: Everywoman's Guide to Colleges and Universities, 1982. Moses Coit Taylor fellow, NYU, 1976. Mem. Am. Hist. Assn., Orgn. Am. Historians, Berkshire Conf. Women Historians, Assn. for Documentary Editing. Office: Inst for Research in History 1133 Broadway Room 923-924 New York NY 10010

KATZ, FRANCES R., school social worker; b. N.Y.C., Jan. 8, 1936; d. Arthur and Bertha (Klempner) Schechter; m. George A. Katz, Nov. 3, 1957; children—Deborah, Jodi, Amy. B.A., Adelphi U., 1978, M.S.W., 1980. Cert. social worker. Social worker Margaret Tietz Ctr. Nursing Care, Jamaica, N.Y., 1982-83; psychiat. social worker Pride of Judea Mental Health Ctr., Douglaston, N.Y., 1982-85; sch. social worker N.Y.C. Bd. Edn., 1984—. Mem. Soc. Psychoanalytic Psychotherapy, Nat. Assn. Social Workers, N.Y. State Soc. Clin. Social Workers. Democrat. Jewish. Avocations: tennis; bridge; reading; travel; theatre. Home: 1010 Fifth Ave New York NY 10028 Office: JH 67 Marathon Pkwy Little Neck NY

KATZ, HILDA (HULDA WEBER), artist, poet; b. N.Y.C.; d. Max and Lina (Schwartz) Katz; student N.A.D. (New Sch. Social Research scholar), 1940-41. One-woman shows: Bowdoin Coll. Art Mus., 1951, Calif. State Library, 1953, Print Club of Albany (N.Y.) Inst., 1955, U. Maine, 1955, 58, Jewish Mus. N.Y., 1956, Pa. State Tchrs. Coll., 1956, Masillon (Ohio) Mus., 1957, Ball State Tchrs. Coll., 1957, Springfield Art Mus., 1957, U. Maine, 1958, Miami Beach (Fla.) Art Center, 1958, Art Assn. Richmond (Ind.), 1959, Old State Capitol Mus. La., La. Art Commn., others; group shows include: Corcoran Bienniale Library Congress, Am. in the War (26 museums) Pa. Acad. Fine Arts, Soc. Am. Graphic Artists, Phila. Water Color Club, Audubon Artists, Print Club Albany, Albany Inst., Bklyn. Mus., Delgado Mus. Art-U.S.A., 1959, Jewish Mus., Boston Printmakers, Massillon Mus., Springfield Art Mus., NAD, Met. Mus. Art, Italian Fedn. Women in Art, Italy, Venice Biennial, Italy, Conn. Acad. Fine Arts, Congress Jewish Culture, Calif. State Library, Bowdoin U., State Tchrs. Coll. Pa., Art Assn. Richmond, Boston, N.Y. public libraries, Miami Beach Art Center, Children's Mus., Hartford, Conn., Washington Printmakers, Miniature Painters, Engravers and Sculptors Soc., Peoria Art Center, Engrs. Club. Phila., La. Art Commn., also numerous others in U.S., Eng., France, Italy, Israel, S.Am., S.E. Asia, Middle East; represented in permanent group collections Library of Congress, Balt. Mus. Art, Fogg Mus., Franklin D. Roosevelt Collection, Santa Barbara Art Mus., Colo. Springs Fine Arts Center, Soc. Am. Graphic Artists, U.S. Nat. Mus., Met. Mus. Art, Bezalel Nat. Mus., Jerusalem, Addison Gallery Am. Art, Springfield (Mo.) Art Mus., Newark Public Library, N.Y. Public Library, Calif. State Library, Pa. State Library, U. Minn., Print Club Albany, Safed Mus., Bat Yam Museum (both Israel), Peoria (Ill.) Art Center, St. Margaret Mary Sch. Art, State Mus. Albany, Jewish Mus. N.Y., Archives Am. Art, Smithsonian Instn., numerous others, including several colls. and univs.; pictures represented in spl. collections U.S. Nat. Mus., 1965-72 U. Maine, 1965, Library Congress, 1965, 71, Met. Mus. Art, 1965, 80, Nat. Gallery Art, 1965, Nat. Collection Fine Arts, 1966, 71, 78, Nat. Air and Space Mus., 1970, N.Y. Public Library, 1971, 78, New Britain Mus. Am. Art, 1978, Mus. City N.Y., 1979, Jewish Mus., N.Y.C., 1979, A. Hyatt Mayor Collection Met. Mus. Art, 1980, Ft. Lewis (Colo.) Coll., 1980, Israel Mus., Jerusalem, 1980, Boston Public Library, 1980, others. Recipient award graphic Nat. Assn. Women Artists, 1945, water color, 1947, Am. artists group prize Soc. Am. Graphic Artists, 1950; best painting in landscape Soc. Miniature Painters, Sculptors, Gravers, 1959, print award Peoria Art Center, 1960, Library of Congress Purchase Prizes; Purchase award Print Club of Albany, 1964, Peoria (Ill.) Art Center, 1964, U. Minn., Calif. State Library, Met. Mus. Art, State Tchrs. Coll. Pa., Art Assn. Richmond, N.Y. Public Library, Newark Public Library, St. Margaret Mary Sch. Art Coll., plaque of honor Hall of Fame, 1966, also life mem.; poetry awards, including James Joyce Poetry award Poetry Soc. Am. life fellow Met. Mus.; named Dau. of Mark Twain. Fellow-founder Internat. Acad. Poets; mem. Nat. Assn. Women Artists, Soc. Washington Print-makers, Am. Color Print Soc., Audubon Artists, Soc. Am. Graphic Artists, Internat. Platform Assn., Hunterdon Art Center, Conn. Acad. Fine Arts, Phila. Watercolor Club, Boston Print-makers (award 1955), Hunterdon County Art Center, Print Club Albany, Print Council Am., Poetry Soc. Am., Accademia di Scienze, Lettere, Arti (hon. consigliere), Classe Storia Letteratura Americana (Milan, Italy). Author (under pen name Hulda Weber) poems included in numerous anthologies. Contbr. numerous poems and short stories to mags., newspapers, internat. anthologies; all arts works in permanent collections 19 nat. and internat. art colls. and mus.; manuscripts in N.Y. State Mus./Archives, Albany. Address: 915 West End Ave Apt 5D New York NY 10025

KATZ, JANE, educator; b. Sharon, Pa., Apr. 16, 1943; d. Leon and Dorothea (Oberkewitz) Katz; B.S. in Edn., CCNY, 1963; M.A., NYU, 1966; M.Ed., Columbia Tchrs. Coll., 1972, Ed.D., 1978. Mem. faculty Bronx Community Coll., CUNY, 1964—, prof. phys. edn., 1972—; mem. U.S. Round-the-World Synchronized Swim Team, 1964; synchronized swimming solo tour of Eng., 1969; founding co-organizer, coach 1st Internat. Israeli Youth Festival Games, 1970; mem. winning U.S. Maccabiah Swim Team, 1957; vice chmn. Metro Master AAU Swim Team, 1974—; mem. AAU Nat. Masters All-Am. Swimming Team, 1974—, synchronized swimming solo champion, 1975; speaker, judge in field. Trainee Fed. Adminstrn. Aging, 1971-72; mem. Internat. Hall. of Fame, Ft. Lauderdale, Fla. Mem. U.S. Com. Sports for Israel (dir., co-chmn. women's swimming com. 1970—), AAHPER, Nat. Jewish Welfare Bd., Internat. Aquatics. Author: Swimming for Total Fitness, A Progressive Aerobic Program, 1981; Swimming Through Your Pregnancy, 1983; W.E.T. Workouts: Water Exercises and Techniques to Help You and Tone Up Aerobically, 1985; papers in field. Address: 400 2d Ave Suite 23B New York NY 10010

KATZ, JANICE ANN, lawyer; b. N.Y.C., Oct. 2, 1955; d. Henry and Roslyn (Levine) Katz. B.S. cum laude, U. Albany, 1976; J.D., Syracuse U., 1981. Bar: N.Y. 1982, U.S. Dist. Ct. (so. and ea. dists.) N.Y. 1982; cert. tchr. N.Y. Research asst. Skadden Arps, Slate, Meagher & Flom, N.Y.C., summer 1979; summer assoc. Finley, Kumble, Wagner, Heine, Underberg, Manley & Casey, N.Y.C., 1980, assoc., 1981-84; atty. Mfrs. Hanover Trust Co., N.Y.C., 1984—. Mem. editorial staff Syracuse U. Law Review, 1979-80, editor, 1980-81. Mem. ABA (litigation sect.), Pi Omega Pi. Home: 435 E 65th St New York NY 10021 Office: Mfrs Hanover Trust Co 270 Park Ave New York NY 10017

KATZ, JUDITH TERRY, food marketing specialist; b. N.Y.C., Apr. 17, 1946; d. Morris and Beatrice (Miller) K.; m. Arthur J. Schwartz, Nov. 14, 1984. B.A., Bklyn. Coll., 1966, M.A., 1968; grad. chef's cert. Le Cordon Bleu, 1977. Public relations dir., catering mgr. TWTF Restaurant Group, N.Y.C., 1972-76; exec. chef Ashleys, N.Y.C., 1977, LaGriglia, N.Y.C., 1977-78; dir. food service prodn. Macy's, N.Y.C., 1977-78; mgr. Marine Midland Food Service, Service Systems Corp., N.Y.C., 1978-79, Veggies Park Restaurants, N.Y.C., 1979; dir. mktg. and food standards Corp. Food Services Inc., N.Y.C., 1980-82; asst. to corp. dir. food services Allied Stores Corp., 1982-86, corp. mgr. food services, 1986—; free-lance restaurant cons., guest lectr. Restaurant Sch., Nassau Community Coll.; guest lectr. New Sch. Culinary Arts. Fund raiser Kennedy Found. Spl. Olympics, 1981—, Reader In-Touch Networks, 1983—. Mem. Am. Soc. Profl. and Exec. Women, Nat. Assn. Female Execs., Food and Beverage Mgrs. Assn., Mensa. Clubs: Scuba Sport Rites, Bottom Dwellers, N.Y. Roadrunners. Home and Office: 222 E 93d St New York NY 10128

KATZ, MARTHA LESSMAN, lawyer; b. Chgo., Oct. 28, 1952; d. Julius Abraham and Ida (Oiring) Lessman; m. Richard Maynard Katz, June 27, 1976. B.A., Washington U., St. Louis, 1973; J.D., Loyola U., 1977. Bar: Ill. 1977, Calif. 1981, U.S. Dist. Ct. (no. and so. dists.) Calif. 1981, 82, U.S. Dist. Ct. (no. dist.) Ill. 1977. Assoc., Fein & Hanfling, Chgo., 1977-80, Rudick, Platt & Victor, San Diego, 1981-82, 84—; asst. sec. and counsel Itel Corp., San Francisco, 1982-84. Mem. ABA (sect. corp. banking and bus. law, taxation), Calif. State Bar Assn., Ill. State Bar Assn., San Diego Bar Assn., Lawyers Club of San Diego, Phi Beta Kappa. Office: Rudick Platt & Victor 1770 4th Ave San Diego CA 92101

KATZ, MAXINE L(EVIN), insurance advisor, consultant, author; b. Bronx, N.Y., May 4, 1940; d. Morris Harvey and Ruth Hilda (Graber) Levin; m. Lewis W. Katz, Sept. 3, 1960; children—Susan R., Robert A., Michele D. Registered health underwriter. Ins. agt., Personal Prodn., Deerfield, Ill., 1971—; ins. coordinator Fiat-Allis, Inc., Deerfield, 1978-80; pres. L & M Ins. Services, Deerfield, 1980—, Womens Ins. Planning Service, Deerfield, 1982—. Author textbook: What Women Must Know About Insurance, 1984; contbr. indsl. articles to jours. Mem. Nat. Assn. Health Underwriters (pres. chpt.; nat. merit award 1983), Chgo. Assn. Health Underwriters (legis. chmn. 1982, membership chmn. 1982-83), Leading Producers Round Table (pres.'s council 1985, 86), Nat. Assn. Female Execs., Phi Theta Kappa. Office: Womens Ins Planning Service PO Box 439 Deerfield IL 60015

KATZ, PAMELA MAE, accountant; b. Cin., Aug. 19, 1952; d. Jerome and Lois Gail (Solomon) Pearson; 1 child, Kylila Jana Katz. B.S. in Acctg., Case Western Res. U., 1974. C.P.A., Ohio. Sr. acct. Peat, Marwick & Mitchell, Cleve., 1974-75, 77-79; various positions in industry, Cleve., 1975-77; ptnr. Katz & Jacobson, Cin., 1984—. Mem. Am. Inst. C.P.A.'s, Ohio Soc. C.P.A.'s, Am. Women's Soc. C.P.A.s. Office: Katz & Jacobson 8050 Hosbrook Rd 404 Cincinnati OH 45236

KATZ, PHYLLIS POLLAK, magazine publisher; b. N.Y.C., Dec. 29, 1939; s. Henry Abraham and Rose (Chaiken) P.; m. Edward Katz, Sept. 12, 1971; children—Charles Daniel, Jacob Evan. B.A., Cornell U., 1961; postgrad., U. Pa., 1961-68, Am. Sch. Classical Studies, Athens, 1964-66. Dept. asst. Univ. Mus., U. Pa.; lectr. N.Y. U., 1970-71; asst. editor Archaeology mag., N.Y.C., 1968-72, editor, 1972—, pub., 1978—. Archaeol. excavations, Gordion, Turkey, 1965, Porto Cheli, Greece, Samothrace, Greece, 1966, Torre del Mordillo, Italy, 1967. Heinemann fellow, 1964-66. Mem. Archaeol. Inst. Am., Soc. Am. Archaeology, Soc. Hist. Archaeology, Am. Anthrop. Assn., Asia Soc. Jewish. Office: 15 Park Row New York NY 10038

KATZEL, JEANINE ALMA, journalist; b. Chgo., Feb. 20, 1948; d. LeRoy Paul and Lia Mary (Arcuri) Katzel; B.A. in Journalism, U. Wis., 1970; M.S. in Journalism, Northwestern U., 1974. Publs. editor U. Wis. Sea Grant Program, Madison, 1969-72; editor research div. agrl. sch. U. Wis., Madison, 1972; research editor Prism mag. AMA, Chgo., 1972-73; free-lance writer, 1974-75; lit. editor Plant Engring. mag. Tech. Pub. Co., Barrington, Ill., 1975-76, news editor, 1976-77, asso. editor, 1977-79, sr. editor, 1979—. Eucharistic minister Saints Peter and Paul Roman Cath. Ch.; mem. Circle Ch. Spirit Singers. Recipient Elsie Bullard Morrison prize in Journalism, U. Wis., 1969; Peter Lisagor award Chgo. Headline Club, 1983. Mem. Women in Communications, Soc. Profl. Journalists, Am. Soc. Bus. Press Editors (pres. Chgo. chpt. 1977-78), Am. Inst. Plant Engrs., Assn. Energy Engrs., Nat. Fire Protection Assn. (tech. com. on fire pumps), Am. Soc. Safety Engrs., Soc. Fire Protection Engrs., AAUW, Internat. Soc. Fire Service Instrs., Phi Kappa Phi. Club: Chgo. Headline. Home: 16 Boxwood Ln Cary IL 60013 Office: 1301 S Grove Ave Barrington IL 60010

KATZEN, SALLY, lawyer, former government official; b. Pitts., Nov. 22, 1942; d. Nathan and Hilda (Schwartz) K.; m. Timothy B. Dyk, Oct. 31, 1981; 1 son, Abraham Benjamin. B.A. magna cum laude, Smith Coll., 1964; J.D. magna cum laude, U. Mich., 1967. Congressional intern Senate Subcom. on Constl. Rights, Washington, summer, 1963; legal research asst. civil rights div. Dept. Justice, Washington, summer 1965; law clk. to Judge J. Skelly Wright, D.C. circuit U.S. Ct. Appeals, 1967-68; admitted to D.C. bar, 1968, U.S. Supreme Ct. bar, 1971; asso. firm Wilmer, Cutler & Pickering, Washington, 1968-74, partner, 1975-79; gen. counsel Council on Wage and Price Stability, 1979-80; dep. dir. Council Wage and Price Stability, 1980-81; partner firm Wilmer Cutler and Pickering, 1981—; Mem. com. visitors U. Mich. Law Sch., 1972-85; mem. Jud. Conf. for D.C. Circuit, 1972-81, 83-86. Mem. Am. Bar Assn. (house of dels. 1978-80, council adminstrv. law sect. 1979-82; governing com. forum com. communications law 1979-82), D.C. Bar Assn., FCC Bar Assn. (exec. com. 1984—), Women's Legal Def. Fund (pres. 1977, v.p. 1978), Order of Coif. Editor-in-chief U. Mich. Law Rev., 1966-67. Home: 4638 30th St NW Washington DC Office: 2445 M St NW Washington DC 20037

KATZMAN, KAREN E., lawyer; b. Bklyn., May 21, 1949; d. Bernard and Selma (Slavin) Katzman. B.A. summa cum laude with high honors in Polit. Sci., Yale, U., 1971; J.D. cum laude, Harvard U., 1974. Bar: N.Y. 1975, U.S. Ct. Appeals (2d cir.) 1975, U.S. Dist. Ct. (so. and ea. dists.) N.Y. 1975, U.S. Supreme Ct. 1980, U.S. Ct. Appeals (3d cir.) 1985. Summer assoc. Davis, Polk & Wardwell, N.Y.C., 1973; assoc, Kaye, Scholer, Fierman, Hays & Handler, N.Y.C., 1974-83, ptnr., 1983—; asst. counsel Gov.'s Jud. Nominating Com., N.Y., 1982. Coll. chmn. Yale Alumni Fund, 1970-74; mem. Yale Alumni Schs. Com., N.Y.C., 1975—; mem. leadership devel. div. United Jewish Appeals, 1979—. Morse Coll. fellow Yale U., 1971. Mem. ABA (adhoc subcom. fed. cts. 1982, com. fed. procedure 1983—), N.Y. State Bar Assn., Bar Assn. City N.Y. Phi Beta Kappa. Democrat. Jewish. Club: Yale (N.Y.C.). Office: Kaye Scholer Fierman Hays & Handler 425 Park Ave New York NY 10022

KATZOWITZ, LAUREN, public affairs executive. B.S. in comparative Lit. with honors, Brandeis U., 1970; M.S. with honors, Columbia U., 1971. With, Newsweek mag., then Phila. Bull.; free-lance writer, editor, cons., until 1975; cons. Ford Found., 1972-75; mgr. PBS programs Exxon Corp., 1978-81, Great Performances, Live From Lincoln Center, Dance in America, NOVA, The MacNeil/Lehrer Report, communications mgr. Exxon Research and Engring. Co., 1981-84; regional liaison Europe and Africa, Exxon Corp., 1984-86; Director Foundation Service, Federation of Jewish Philanthropies, 1986—. Trustee Jennifer Muller and The Works, Bronx Ednl. Services, Community Family Planning Council of N.Y.C., Am. Friends of Institut Internat. d'Etudes Musicales, St. Maximin, France, B'nai B'rith Hillel/Jewish Association for College Youth. friend N.Y.C. Commn. on Status of Women. Named one of 12 Women to Watch in the Eighties, Ladies' Home Jour., 1979. Regional Finalist President's Commission on White House Fellowships 1984. Office: Foundation Service 130 E. 59th St New York NY 10022

KAUFFMAN, DONNA MAY, nursing educator; b. Rochester, Ind., July 6, 1947; s. Charles Edward and Donnabelle (Newell) K. Diploma Marion County Gen. Hosp. Sch. Nursing, Indpls., 1968; B.S.N., Ind. U., Indpls., 1974; M.S., Ball State U., 1979. Head nurse CICU, Meml. Hosp., Logansport, Ind., 1968-73; staff nurse Howard Community Hosp., Kokomo, Ind., 1973-74; staff nurse Gen. Hosp., Ft. Walton Beach, Fla., 1974-75; vis. lectr. nursing Ind. U., Kokomo, 1976-79; asst. prof. nursing Purdue U., West Lafayette, Ind., 1979—, asst. head student affairs, 1982—. Judge, Regional Sci. Fair, Lafayette, 1983, 84, counselor Area IV Council Aging, 1982; bd. dirs. Tippecanoe County Heart

Assn., 1979-81. Mem. Ind. Nurses Assn. (dist. 8 bd. dirs. 1982-83), Sigma Theta Tau. Methodist. Office: Purdue U Sch Nursing Northwestern Ave West Lafayette IN 47907

KAUFFMAN, ELAINE MARY, marketing executive; b. Rochester, N.Y., Oct. 13, 1952; d. James Marcus and Mildred Magdalen (Statt) K. B.S. in Bus. Adminstrn., Ariz. State U., 1974; student Houston Baptist U., 1981-86. Mfg. mgr. Tex. Instruments, Lubbock, Tex., 1978-79, internat. support mgr., 1979-81, product mktg. mgr., 1981-82, distbn. mgr., 1982-83, sales promotion mgr., 1983-84, mktg. strategy mgr., Dallas, 1984—; Tex. Instrument spokesperson for media interviews, 1984—. Mem. Am. Mktg. Assn. Avocations: travel; photography; aerobics. Home: 18040 Midway Rd #162 Dallas TX 75252 Office: Texas Instrument PO Box 225621 MS3660 Dallas TX 75265

KAUFFMAN, MARGARET A., advertising executive; b. Erie, Pa., Apr. 19, 1944; d. Eric Alfred and Agnes Mary (Logue) Jonsson; m. Walter L. Kauffman, July 15, 1966; children—Walter L., Eric Barton, Leslie Ann, Andrew John. Student parochial schs., Erie. Advt. account rep. The Greensheet, Erie, 1983-85, Lake Shore Visitor, Erie, 1985—. Editor Erie Philharm. Newsletter, 1977-78. Bd. dirs. YWCA, Erie, 1979-80; corr. sec. Hamot Aid Soc., Erie, 1980-81; v.p. Erie Philharm. Women's Assn., 1980-81. Mem. Nat. Assn. Female Execs. Democrat. Roman Catholic. Avocations: needlepoint; hot air ballooning; walking. Home: 1135 W 10th St Erie PA 16502 Office: Lake Shore Visitor 515 State St Erie PA 16512

KAUFFMAN, MARGARET ANNE, public relations executive, photojournalist; b. St. Louis, Sept. 9, 1945; d. Tom Harry and Margaret Ruth (Siebert) Goddard; m. William Francis Kauffman, June 29, 1968; children—Kathryn Ruth, Juliet Lynn. B.Journalism, U. Mo., 1968, postgrad., 1983, 84; postgrad. Jefferson Coll., 1984, 85. Writer, Am. Nat. Stores, St. Louis, 1968-69, J.C. Penny Co., St. Louis, 1969; dir. pub. info. St. Louis Dept. Health and Hosps., 1969-71, Jefferson Coll., Hillsboro, Mo., 1979—. Editor, Jefferson Coll. News, 1979—. Founding mem., sec.-treas. Friends Jefferson Coll., 1980—; mem. adminstrv. bd. Union United Methodist Ch., St. Louis, 1976—; chmn. blood dr. ARC, St. Louis, 1976-77. Recipient MacEachern award Am. Hosp. Assn., 1970. Mem. Mo. Assn. Community Jr. Colls., Council Advancement and Support of Edn.; Am Assn. Women in Community Jr. Colls., United Methodist Women. Home: 6601 Bancroft Saint Louis MO 63109 Office: Jefferson Coll PO Box 1000 Hillsboro MO 63050

KAUFFMAN, MARY KATHERINE, civic worker; b. Slusher, Ky, May 22, 1919; d. Charles and Lucinda (Sizemore) Slusher; m. Harry D. Kauffman, June 24, 1943 (div. 1963); children—Karl D., Karen K. Lambert. Dental asst. Dr. Korn, Ky., 1939-43; lab. tech. Kodak, Oak Ridge, Tenn., 1943-46; bd. pres. Southwicke Square (fed. housing), Trenton, Mich., 1972—. Democrat. Avocations: Reading; poetry; ceramic and china painting. Home: 1911-B Marian Dr Trenton MI 48183

KAUFFMANN, CAROL BROWN, paper converting company executive; b. Atlanta, Sept. 22, 1943; d. Matt Briggs and Carol Crystal (Beery) Brown; m. Norman Jacques, Oct. 31, 1970. Student Sophie Newcomb Coll., Tulane U., 1961-63; B.A. in Psychology and English, Ga. State U., 1965, postgrad., 1965-66. With pub. relations dept. Delta Air Lines, Inc., Atlanta, 1966-70; v.p., treas., owner, dir. NORCOM, Inc., Springfield, Mass., 1978-80, exec. v.p., treas., owner, dir., Atlanta, 1980—; career counselor Ga. State U., Atlanta; asst. editor Peachtree Papers mag., 1986, editor, 1987. Trustee Mary Brown Trust Fund. of Atlanta; mem. Republican Senatorial Club, Rep. Presdl. Task Force; pres. Women's Symphony League of Springfield, 1978. Mem. Jr. League Atlanta (bd. dirs. 1984—), Hist. Oakland Cemetery (bd. dirs. 1986-87), Ga. Mental Health Assn. (bd. dirs. 1984-85), Atlanta Zool. Soc. Republican. Presbyterian. Clubs: Georgian, Ashford. Home: 2565 Habersham Rd NW Atlanta GA 30305 Office: 6866 Jimmy Carter Blvd Norcross GA 30071

KAUFMAN, BEL, author, educator; b. Berlin; d. Michael J. and Lala (Rabinowitz) Kaufman; B.A. magna cum laude, Hunter Coll.; M.A. with highest honors, Columbia U.; LL.D., Nasson Coll., Maine; div.; children—Jonathan Goldstine, Thea Goldstine. Asst. prof. English, City U. N.Y.; lectr. New Sch. for Social Research; tchr. English, N.Y.C. high Schs.; lectr. throughout country, also appearances on TV and radio. Mem. Commn. Performing Arts; bd. dirs. Shalom Aleichem Found.; mem. adv. council Town Hall Found. Recipient plaque Anti-Defamation League; award and plaque United Jewish Appeal, Paperback of Yr. award, Bell Movie award, Nat. Human Resource award; awards for best articles on edn. Ednl. Assn. Am.; named to Hall of Fame Hunter Coll. Mem. Author's Guild (council), Dramatists Guild, PEN (exec. bd., membership com.), English Grad. Union, Phi Beta Kappa (editorial bd. Phi Delta Kappan). Author: Up the Down Staircase, 1965; Love, Etc., 1979; also short stories, articles, TV play, translations of Russian, lyrics for musicals.

KAUFMAN, BONNIE LOU WATSON, mfg. co. exec.; b. Winchester, Ind., July 29, 1930; d. Reece Lorris and Lulu Willette (Shouse) Watson; student Ind. Bus. Coll., 1965-67, Ball State U., 1970-72; children—Bonita Lee Streetman, Stephen Wayne, Dane Constantine. With Westinghouse Electric, Inc., Union City, Ind., 1958-64, J. Cody Longnecker, C.P.A., Winchester, 1965-66; with Overmyer Mould Co., Winchester, 1966—, sales and prodn. scheduling coordinator, traffic mgr., now inventory and material controller. Republican. Office: Overmyer Mould Co One Omco Sq Winchester IN 47394

KAUFMAN, CHARLOTTE KING, ednl. adminstr.; b. Balt., Dec. 5, 1920; d. Ben and Belle (Turow) King; A.B., Goucher Coll., 1969; M.P.H., Johns Hopkins U., 1972, M.Ed., 1976; m. Albert Kaufman, July 22, 1945; children—Matthew King, Ezra King. Dir. public relations Balt. Jewish Community Center, 1962-67; research and editor Johns Hopkins U. Sch. Hygiene and Public Health, Balt., 1969-72, admissions officer, 1972-74, dir. admissions and registrar, 1974—. Mem. Am. Pub. Health Assn., Am. Assn. for Higher Edn., Am. Assn. Collegiate Registrars and Admissions Officers. Democrat. Jewish. Home: 1 E University Pkwy Baltimore MD 21218 Office: 615 N Wolfe St Baltimore MD 21205

KAUFMAN, JOAN, real estate/investor executive; b. Bklyn., Nov. 22, 1935; d. Murray Lewis and Clare (Shaw) Kaplan; children—Eric, Patricia. B.A. in Women's Studies, SUNY-Old Westbury, 1979; postgrad. Sarah Lawrence Coll., 1980-81. Mgr., owner Jo-Me Car Washes, Inc., Huntington, N.Y., 1969-71; employment cons. Command Placement, Hicksville, N.Y., 1970-72, Sabre Personnel Agy., Plainview, N.Y., 1972-75; adminstr. Project: Turning Points, Old Westbury, N.Y., 1978-79; founder placement office SUNY, Old Westbury, 1979-80; pres., chief operating officer Creative Capital Cons., Ltd., N.Y.C., 1982—; dir. CCM Brokerage, Inc., CREA Real Estate Group, Inc., Creative Capital Devel. Corp. Career counselor Nassau County Office of Women's Services, 1977-78; cons. for suburban women N.Y. U. Placement Office, 1977; facilitator women's workshop series SUNY, 1977. Recipient cert. for acad. accomplishment SUNY, Old Westbury, 1977-78. Mem. Internat. Assn. Fin. Planners, Women Bus. Owners N.Y., Nat. Assn. Female Execs., Huntington C. of C. Office: Creative Capital Consultants Ltd 27 E 38th St New York NY 10016

KAUFMAN, JOYCE JACOBSON, chemist, educator; b. N.Y.C., June 21, 1929; d. Abraham and Sarah (Seldin) Deutch; m. Stanley Kaufman, Dec. 26, 1948; 1 child, Jan Caryl. B.S. with honors, Johns Hopkins U., 1949, M.A., 1959, Ph.D. in Chemistry, 1960; D.E.S. with honors in Theoretical Physics, Sorbonne, Paris, 1963. Analytical research chemist Army Chem. Ctr., Md., 1949-52; mem. chemistry research staff Johns Hopkins U., Balt., 1952-60; mem. quantum chemistry group Research Inst. Advanced Studies, Balt., 1960-69, staff scientist, 1965-69, head, 1963-69; prin. research scientist dept. chemistry Johns Hopkins U., Balt., assoc. prof. dept. anesthesiology Sch. Medicine, 1969—, assoc. prof. dept. surgery div. plastic surgery, 1977—; mem. sci. adv. com. Dept. Def., 1977; mem. rev. panel for undergrad. chemistry edn. NSF, 1977; Fogarty Internat. Exchange specialist NIH-USSR Ministry of Health, 1978. Mem. editorial adv. bd.: John Wiley and Intersci. Pubs., 1965—; Molecular Pharmacology, 1970—; Internat. Jour. Quantum Chemistry, 1967—; Jour. Computational Chemistry, 1980—; editor Benchmark Book Series in phys. chemistry-chem. physics, 1975—, overall chemistry editor, 1977—. Contbr. articles to profl. jours. Recipient Garvan medal as outstanding woman chemist Am. Chem. Soc., 1974; Md. Chemist award Am. Chem. Soc. Md. sect. 1974. Fellow Am. Phys. Soc., Am. Inst. Chemists; mem. Am. Chem. Soc. (chmn. Md. sect. 1972, councilor phys. chemistry div. 1971—, budget and fin. com. 1981—), Am. Soc. Pharmacology and Exptl. Therapeutics, European Acad. Scis., Arts and Letters (corr. mem.), Internat. Soc. Quantum Biology, Am. Soc. Anesthesiology, AAUP, Phi Beta Kappa, Sigma Xi. Office: Dept Chemistry Johns Hopkins U Baltimore MD 21218

KAUFMAN, KAREN LYNN, construction company executive; b. Akron, Ohio, Mar. 19, 1948; d. William B. and Edith (Gruber) Rogovy; div.; children—Amanda, Jonathan. Student U. Akron, 1966-68, Tex. Tech U., 1968-69, U. Calif.-Riverside, 1977-80; B.S., U. San Francisco, 1981. Lic. contractor, Calif. Project mgr. Bilsan Corp., Riverside, 1977-79; housing specialist County of Riverside, 1979-80; project mgr. Lewis Homes of Calif., 1980-81; cons. Williams & Burrows, Belmont, Calif., 1982-83; scheduling cons. LAX Terminal 1, Sheraton Grandé Hotel, Los Angeles; project mgr. Hyperion Energy Recovery System Site Utilities, Los Angeles, Morley Constrn. Co., 1983-86; owner, mgr. Amajon, Upland, Calif., 1982—. Mem. Bldg. Industry Assn., Nat. Assn. Home Builders, Community Assns. Inst., Comml. Indsl. Council. Democrat. Jewish. Club: Aero Club of So. Calif.

KAUFMAN, LISA NADINE, lawyer; b. Jacksonville, Fla., Sept. 7, 1953; d. Fred Robert and Faye Leah (Morgenstern) Kaufman. B.A. with distinction, Ind. U., 1975; J.D., U. Fla., 1978. Bar: Fla. 1978, D.C. 1981, Mo. 1985. Trademark atty. Patent and Trademark Office, U.S. Dept. Commerce, Washington, 1979-84, acting mng. atty., 1982-83; trademark atty. Ralston Purina Co., St. Louis, 1984—. Mem. ABA, Fla. Bar, D.C. Bar (mem. trademark com. 1983—), Bar Assn. Met. St. Louis, Nat. Council Jewish Women (program com. bus. and profl. sect.), Phi Beta Kappa, Alpha Lambda Delta. Lodge: Hadassah (fin. sec. 1982-83). Home: 9116 Eager Rd Saint Louis MO 63144 Office: Checkerboard Sq 9T Saint Louis MO 63164

KAUFMAN, LOUISE SUSAN, pharmaceutical company executive; b. Staten Island, N.Y., Dec. 4, 1952; d. Santo Michael and Selma Mary (Sidoti) Repage; B.S., Wagner Coll., 1975, M.S., 1978; M.B.A., St. John's U., 1983; m. Peter Joseph Kaufman, Sept. 18, 1976. Vet. technician Hylan Animal Hosp., Staten Island, N.Y., 1972-75; vet. abstractor Merck & Co., Inc., Rahway, N.J., 1975-78, regulatory affairs asst., 1978-79, sr. regulatory coordinator, 1979-82, mgr. registration, 1982-85; dir. regulatory affairs internat. Warner-Lambert Co., 1985—. Mem. Drug Info. Assn. (publicity dir. 1980-82, treas. 1982-86, gen. chmn. 1st internat. meeting, Rome), Nat. Soc. Microbiology, Am. Vet. Med. Assn. Aux., N.Y.C. Soc. Microbiology. Home: 165 Dutchess Ave Staten Island NY 10304 Office: Warner-Lambert Co Tabor Rd Morris Plains NJ 07905

KAUFMAN, PHYLLIS CYNTHIA, lawyer, author, theatrical producer; b. Phila., Nov. 4, 1945; d. Harry and Gertrude (Friend) K. B.A. cum laude, Brandeis U., 1967; J.D., Temple U., 1974. Bar: Pa. 1974, U.S. Dist. Ct. (ea. dist.) Pa. 1974. Sole practice entertainment law, Phila., 1977—; exec. producer Playhouse in the Park, Phila., 1979; dir. entertainment Caesar's Hotel-Casino, Atlantic City, N.J., 1980-81; v.p. entertainment Sands Hotel-Casino, Atlantic City, 1981-83; v.p. Kanadus Entertainment Inc., Toronto, 1982—. Co-author: No-Nonsense Financial and Real Estate Guides, 1985-86. Bd. dirs. Phila. Coll. Performing Arts, 1977-85, Creative Artists Network, 1986—. Ford Found. grantee, 1965-67. Mem. Phila. Bar Assn. Democrat. Jewish. Office: 1500 Locust St Suite 3805 Philadelphia PA 19102

KAUFMAN, RUTH HARTMANN, human relations educator; b. Passau, Germany, Sept. 7, 1930; came to U.S., 1938, naturalized, 1943; d. Max and Irma (Blattner) Hartmann; m. Arthur Leon Kaufman, June 28, 1952; children—Kenneth, Ronald, Douglas, Edward, Catherine. B.S., Cornell U., 1952; M.A., NYU, 1970. Cert. tchr., Conn. Tchr. human relations Staples High Sch., Westport, Conn., 1969—; cons. on sexuality to sch. systems and ch. groups, N.Y. State and Conn., 1971—; co-facilitator Sexuality Workshop, Syracuse U., N.Y., 1983-85. Mem. Am. Assn. Sex Educators, Counselors and Therapists (cert.), Assn. for Humanistic Psychology, Sex Info. Edn. Council of Conn., Cornell Club Conn. Democrat. Jewish. Avocations: jogging; skiing; hiking; theater. Home: 19 Covelee Dr Westport CT 06880 Office: Staples High Sch North Ave Westport CT 06880

KAUFMAN, SHIRLEY A. BEHNKE, educational consultant; b. Clawson, Mich., Aug. 18, 1931; d. Oren Leroy and Delta Mae (Rohrer) Adams; m. William Frederick Behnke, Apr. 18, 1954 (dec. 1982); children—Douglas, Curtis, Pamela; m. John M. Kaufman, Dec. 1, 1985. B.A., Ohio State U., 1953, M.A., 1971, E.A.S. (specialist), 1981, Ph.D., 1983. Cert. in secondary edn. and ednl. adminstrn. Reporter Wellington (Ohio) Enterprise, 1948-49; editor Ohio Council Chs., Columbus, 1953-55; tchr. Upper Arlington Schs., Columbus, 1971-83, adminstrv. asst. to supt., 1983-85; lectr. Ohio State U. Sch. Journalism, 1986; mem. State Adv. Com. for Community Edn., 1979-82; dir. Journalism Assn. of Ohio Schs., 1980-82. Contbr. articles to profl. jours. Mem. Promote Upper Arlington Com., 1983-84. Recipient Journalism Achievement award Newspaper Fund, 1977; Jennings scholar, 1981-82; Presdl. scholar, 1983. Mem. Women in Communications (pres. 1963-64), Soc. Profl. Journalists Sigma Delta Chi, Mensa, Phi Delta Kappa. Democrat. Home: 2566 Chester Rd Columbus OH 43221

KAUFMAN, SUSAN GAIL, executive search company executive; b. Bklyn., Feb. 28, 1943; d. William and Emma (Pollack) Zipkis; m. Michael David Kaufman, June 30, 1962; children—Robert, Craig. B.A. cum laude, Western Conn. State Coll., 1977; M.S.W., NYU, 1979. Cert. social worker, N.Y., Mass. Sr. clin. social worker No. Westchester Guidance Clinic, Mt. Kisco, N.Y., 1975-80; pres. Kaufman Assocs., Stamford, Conn., 1981-85; v.p. Staub, Warmbold & Assoc., Stamford, 1985—. Mem. Nat. Assn. Social Workers. Office: 1600 Summer St Stamford CT 06905

KAUFMAN, SUSAN JANE, banker; b. Denver, Nov. 13, 1942; d. William Douglas and Catherine Sue (Orrison) Morrison; m. Jerry Allen Kaufman, Mar. 10, 1962; children—Eric Douglas, Carrie Annette. B.A., U. Colo., 1968; M.A., U. Denver, 1972; M.B.A., John F. Kennedy U., Orinda, Calif., 1981. Librarian, Littleton (Colo.) Pub. Library, 1972-74, Kent Denver Country Day Sch., 1974-76; exec. dir. Colo. Library Assn., Denver, 1974-76; customer service rep. bus. office Pacific Telephone Co., Berkeley, Calif., 1977-80; br. mgr., asst. v.p. Citicorp Savs., Orinda, 1981—. Mem. Contra Costa County M-11 Commn. (Calif.), 1983—, Contra Costa Devel. Assn. 1984—. Mem. Jr. League Oakland/East Bay, Orinda C. of C. (pres.), Am. Mgmt. Assn., Orinda Hist. Soc., Am. Heart Assn., Delta Gamma. Republican. Club: Soroptimists. Home: 6 Lavenida Orinda CA 94563 Office: 77 Moraga Way Orinda CA 94563

KAUFMAN, VICTORIA BOYT, sales consultant; b. New Brunswick, N.J., July 20, 1944; d. Arnold Arpad and Mildred Louise (Mortenson) Boyt; m. Jeffrey Ian Kaufman, Jan. 29, 1966; children—Michael Boyt, Meredith Lara. B.A., Temple U., 1966; postgrad. Columbia U., 1974-77. Biology tchr. Germantown Acad., Ft. Washington, Pa., 1966-68; research assoc. Med. Coll. Ga., Augusta, 1968-69; sales rep. Boehringer Ingelheim, Ridgefield, Conn., 1978-81; nat. sales mgr. PlayCable Co., N.Y.C., 1981-83; pres. V. Kaufman Enterprises, River Vale, N.J., 1983—; sales cons. Hosp. Support, Bayonne, N.J., 1980-81. Mktg. vol. Bill Bradley for U.S. Senate campaign, Union, N.J., since 1984—. Mem. Nat. Assn. Homebased Bus., Women in Cable (mem. bd. 1983-84), N.Y. Women's Network, Am. Women Entrepreneurs. Democrat. Jewish. Club: Women's City of N.Y. (mem. program com. 1985-86). Avocation: collecting works of American women artists. Office: 373 Walnut St Englewood NJ 07631

KAUFMANN, PATRICIA ANNE, philatelic auctioneer; b. Richmond, Va., Dec. 11, 1947; d. William Woodrow and Helen Elizabeth (Davis) Cozad; m. Brian Michael Green, Apr. 23, 1966 (div. June 1973); m. John William Kaufmann, Sr., Feb. 14, 1975; stepchildren—Patricia, John Jr., Judith, Sharon, Deborah, Gail. Student Am. Coll., Paris, 1965. Vice pres. John W. Kaufmann, Inc., Washington, 1973—. Editor Confederate Philatelist mag., 1970—; sect. editor: Confederate State of America Stampless Cover Catalog, 1980. Contbr. articles to philatelic and other publs. Mem. Confederate Stamp Alliance (Haydn Myer award 1974, 80, Pres.'s award 1970, trophy 1971, promoted to gen. 1985), Am. Philatelic Research Library (trustee 1984—), Am. Philatelic Soc., Am. Stamp Dealers Assn., Internat. Fedn. of Stamp Dealers' Assns., Collectors Club N.Y., Soc. Philatelic Ams. (bd. dirs. 1972-76), Va. Postal History Soc. (bd. dirs. 1971-72), U.S. Philatelic Classics Soc. (life). Republican. Episcopalian. Avocations: blue water sailing; collecting antique valentines; needlework; horseback riding. Office: John W Kaufmann Inc 1522 K St NW Washington DC 20005

KAUNITZ, RITA DAVIDSON, religious organization official; b. N.Y.C., Apr. 18, 1922; d. David and Bessie (Golden) Davidson; B.A. magna cum laude, N.Y. U., 1942; M.A., Columbia U., 1946; Ph.D., Radcliffe Coll., 1951; m. Paul E. Kaunitz, Aug. 10, 1947; children—Victoria Moss, Jonathan Davidson, Andrew Moss. Adminstrv. asst. OPA, Washington, 1943-44; columnist planning and housing Progressive Architecture mag., N.Y.C., 1944-46; editor Plan for Rezoning, 1st year's studies, N.Y.C., 1948-49; asso. editor bull. housing and town and country planning UN Secretariat, 1950-52; cons. Center Housing, Bldg. and Planning, UN Secretariat, 1960-66; research asso. grad. program in city planning Yale U., 1955-57; policy and program specialist Model Cities Program, Bridgeport, Conn., 1969; project dir. Conn. Issues and Answers, Regional Plan Assn., N.Y.C., 1976-78; sci. adv. L.I. Sound Regional Study, New Eng. River Basin Commn., New Haven, 1972-75; asst. to dir. N.Y. chpt. Am. Jewish Com., N.Y.C., 1980—; adv. bd. adminstrv. council Jacob Blaustein Inst. for Advancement Human Rights, Am. Jewish Com., 1980—; vis. lectr. U. R.I., 1967-69; cons. in field, condr. seminars, planning cons., 1965—. Mem. Conn. Clean Air Commn., 1969-71; chmn. reorgn. task force Conn. Public Utilities Control Authority, 1976-77; chmn. com. housing and urban affairs Nat. Council of Women, N.Y.C., 1968-70; bd. dirs. Woman's Place, Darien, 1976-80. Recipient service citation Fulbright-Hayes Fellowships, 1975. Mem. Am. Soc. Planning Ofcls. (dir. 1973-76). Democrat. Club: Lower Fairfield County Radcliffe. Author articles. Address: 9 Marine Ave Westport CT 06880

KAUTZ, LISA VIRGINIA, sales executive; b. Lynn, Mass., Oct. 15, 1961; d. William Leonard and Virginia Ann (Grace) Kautz. B.S., U. Mass., 1983. Cert. tchr., Mass. Transp. coordinator handicapped affairs U. Mass., Amherst, 1980-82; personal care asst. Middlesex Falls Nursing Home, Melrose, Mass., 1981-83; youth care worker ctr. for Children and Families, Northampton, Mass., 1982-85; sales rep. Charles Holden Assocs., Melrose, 1983—; sales rep., buyer CAP WORLD div. Charles Holden Assocs., Saugus, Mass., 1985—; sales mgr. Charles Holden Assocs., Melrose, 1985—. Named Salesperson of Yr., Chateau Recreational Vehicles, 1985. Mem. Nat. Assn. Female Execs. Roman Catholic. Avocations: reading; music; running. Home: 606 Summer St Lynnfield MA 01940 Office: Charles Holden Assocs 15 W Emerson St Melrose MA 01276

KAUTZ, SANDRA ANN, organization executive; b. Farmersville, Tex., Nov. 11, 1933; d. Harold Martin and Leata (Farrar) K.; B.A., North Tex. State U., 1955. Dist. adviser Rio Grande council Girl Scouts U.S.A., El Paso, Tex., 1955-68, program services dir., 1968-75, dir. resident camp, 1967-74, exec. dir., 1975-79, exec. dir. Circle-T council, Ft. Worth, 1980—. Bd. dirs. Tex. United Community Services, 1973-77; chmn. council agy. execs. United Way of Met. Tarrant County, 1984-86. Mem. AAUW, Bus. and Profl. Women U.S., Assn. Girl Scout Exec. Staff (dir.), North Tex. State U. Alumni Assn. Home: 3113 Woodlark Fort Worth TX 76123 Office: 4901 Briarhaven Fort Worth TX 76109

KAUZOR, NANCY YOUNG, public relations executive; b. Evanston, Ill., July 3, 1947; d. Gustave August and Betty Jane (Bennett) Kauzor. B.A., U. Wis., 1969. Assignment editor, producer CBS, Inc., Chgo., 1973-77; mgr. info. services AM Internat., Chgo., 1977-79; mgr. advt. and pub. relations, Cheshire, a Xerox Co., Mundelein, Ill., 1979-81; dir. pub. relations Refco, Inc., Chgo., 1981-84; v.p., dir. communications and pub. relations Citicorp Services Inc., Chgo., 1984—; pres. Kauzor Co. communications consultants, Chgo., 1983—. Author movie script: Is the Pope Catholic, 1976; contbr. book reviews to newspapers, radio. Mem. Children's Home and Aid Soc., Chgo., 1982-84. Emmy award nominee, 1976; recipient Award of Excellence, Communication Arts, Calif., 1983, 3 advt. awards Chgo. Fin. Advertisers, 1983. Mem. Chgo. Area Pub. Affairs Group, Chgo. Women in Communications (organized Chgo. chpt., honored 1976), Lyric Opera of Chgo. Guild, Pi Beta Phi. Roman Catholic. Home: 4170 N Marine Dr Chicago IL 60613 Office: Citicorp Services Inc 8430 W Bryn Mawr Chicago IL 60631

KAVALER, SUSAN ADLER, clinical psychologist; b. N.Y.C., Jan. 31, 1950; d. Solomon and Alice (Zelikow) Weiss; m. Thomas Kavaler, July 12, 1970 (div. 1975); m. Saul Michael Adler, Aug. 14, 1982. Ph.D., Adelphi U. Inst. Avanced Psychol. Studies, 1974. Cert. psychotherapist Nat. Inst. Psychotherapies. Psychologist, Beth Israel Hosp., N.Y.C., 1974-76, Manhattan Psychiat. Children's Ctr., N.Y.C., 1977-81; pvt. practice psychotherapy-psychoanalysis, N.Y.C., 1976-81, 81—; mem. faculty Postgrad. Ctr. Mental Health, N.Y.C., 1984-86; faculty supr. Nat. Inst. Psychotherapies, N.Y.C., 1983—, sr. supr., tng. analyst Internat. Sch. Mental Health Practitioners, 1985—; bd. dirs. and faculty Bklyn. Inst. Psychotherapy, 1985—; adj. prof. Union of Experimenting. Contbr. chpts. to books, articles to profl. jours. Recipient Post-grad. Ctr. Hon. award, 1984-85. Mem. Am. Psychol. Assn., Nat. Inst. for Psychotherapies Profl. Assn. (chair writings group 1981—), Nat. Orgn. Female Execs., Women's Psychotherapy Referral Service. Jewish. Club: Montawk (Bklyn.). Office: 115 E 9th St New York NY 10003

KAWAGOE, HELEN, city clerk; b. Pasadena, Calif., 1927; m. Tak Kawagoe, 1947. Cert. completion U. Calif.-Santa Cruz, 1977; LL.D. (hon.), South Bay U. Coll. Law, 1977. Cert. mcpl. clk. Co-owner Carson Nursery, Torrance, Calif., 1962-71; account exec., v.p. mktg. and pub. relations Merit Savs. and Loan Assn., Los Angeles, 1971-74, city clk. City of Carson, Calif., 1974—; dir. Merit Savs. and Loan Assn. Mem. Carson Rose Float Assn., Carson Sister City Com., Carson High Sch. Boosters, United Way Regional Planning, Long Beach, Calif., Los Angeles County Consumer Affairs Commn. Recipient award Japanese Am. Citizens League, 1972; named Disting. Citizen of Carson, 1974. Mem. Internat. Inst. Mcpl. Clks. (1st v.p. 1985—), League of Calif. Cities/Clks. Dept. (pres. 1978-79, dir. 1979-81), Assn. Records Mgrs. and Adminstrs. Avocation: reading. Office: City of Carson 701 E Carson St Carson CA 90745

KAWAGUCHI, MEREDITH FERGUSON, lawyer; b. Dallas, Feb. 5, 1940; d. Hugh William Ferguson and Ruth Virginia (Perdue) Drewery; m. Harry Harumitsu Kawaguchi, Apr. 22, 1977. B.A., U. Tex., 1962, M.A., 1968; J.D., So. Meth. U., 1977. Bar: Tex. 1977. Translator, liaison Pan Am. Airways, Houston, 1963-64; researcher Ford Found., Austin, Tex., 1965-67; tchr. Lockhart High Sch. (Tex.), 1968-69; legal examiner oil and gas utilities R.R. Commn. Tex., Austin, 1977—; participant various seminars; mem. adv. com. Tex. Energy and Natural Resources Adv. Council, Austin, 1982. Recipient cert. recognition R.R. Commn. Tex., 1982. Mem. ABA, State Bar Tex., Travis County Women Lawyers Assn., Japanese Am. Citizens League, Kappa Kappa Gamma. Democrat. Episcopalian. Home: 5009 Westview Dr Austin TX 78731 Office: R R Commn Tex Capitol Sta PO Drawer 12967 Austin TX 78711

KAWALERSKI, SUSAN MARY, television news producer; b. Buffalo, Nov. 9, 1952; d. Thaddeus Daniel and Adele Stella (Widomski) K. B.S. in Broadcast Journalism, Syracuse U. Promotion mgr. Sta. WUTV-TV, Buffalo, 1974-75; owner Image, Buffalo, 1975-76; news producer Sta. WGR-TV, NBC, Buffalo, 1976-78, asst. news dir., 1980-81; sr. producer Sta. WCKT-TV, NBC, Miami, 1978-80; news exec. producer Sta. KDFW-TV, CBS, Dallas, 1981-86, asst. news dir., 1986—. Recipient Best Newscast award N.Y. State AP, 1977. Mem. Soc. Profl. Journalists (dir. 1981—). Roman Catholic. Club: Dallas Press. Office: KDFW-TV 400 N Griffin St Dallas TX 75202

KAY, HERMA HILL, law educator; b. Orangeburg, S.C., Aug. 18, 1934; d. Charles Esdorn and Herma Lee (Crawford) Hill; B.A., So. Meth. U., 1956; J.D., U. Chgo., 1959. Admitted to Calif. bar, 1960; law clk. to Justice Roger Traynor, Calif. Supreme Ct., 1959-60; asst. prof. law U. Calif.-Berkeley, 1960-62, asso. prof., 1962, prof., 1963—, dir. family law project, 1964-67, chairperson acad. senate, 1973-74; co-reporter uniform marriage and divorce law Nat. Conf. Commrs. on Uniform State Laws, 1968-70; vis. prof. U. Manchester (Eng.), 1972, Harvard U., 1976; mem. Gov.'s Commn. on Family, 1966. Trustee Russell Sage Found., chmn. bd. trustees, 1980-84; chmn. bd. dirs. Equal Rights Advs., Inc., 1977-83. Fellow Center for Advanced Study in Behavioral Scis., Palo Alto, 1963-64. Mem. Calif. State Bar Assn. (mem. family law com. 1964-67), Calif. Women Lawyers (bd. govs. 1975-77), Order of Coif (nat. v.p. 1980, nat. pres. 1983-85). Democrat. Contbg. author: Law in Culture and Society, 1969; co-author Text, Cases and Materials on Sex-Based Discrimination, 1974, author 2d edit., 1981, supplement, 1986; Conflict of Laws: Cases, Comments, Questions, 2d edit., 1975, 3d edit., 1981; contbr. articles to profl. jours. Office: Sch Law U Calif Berkeley CA 94720

KAY, M. JANE, utility executive; b. Detroit, Aug. 31, 1925; d. Albert A. and Celia (Betzing) Kay; B.S., U. Detroit, 1948; M.A., Wayne State U., 1952; M.B.A., U. Mich., 1963. Sr. personnel interviewer employment Detroit Edison

Co., 1948-60, personnel coordinator for women, 1960-65, office employment adminstr., 1965-70, gen. employment adminstr., 1970-71, dir. personnel services, 1971-72, mgr. employee relations, 1972-77, asst. v.p. employee relations, 1977-78, v.p. employee relations, 1978-82, v.p. adminstrn., 1982—; dir. First Am. Bank-Detroit; tchr. U. Detroit Evening Coll. Bus. and Adminstrn., 1963-75; seminar leader div. mgmt. edn. U. Mich., 1968-74, Waterloo Mgmt. Edn. Centre, 1972-77. Mem. Mich. Employment Security Adv. Council, 1967-81; chmn. bd. dirs. Detroit Inst. Commerce, 1976-79; exec. bd. NCCJ, 1980—, nat. trustee, 1984—. Recipient Alumni Tower award U. Detroit, 1967; Headliner award Women Wayne State U., 1970, Wayne State U. Alumni Achievement award, 1974, Career Achievement award Profl. Panhellenic Assn., 1973; named one of Top Ten Working Women of Detroit, 1970; Alumnus of Yr., U. Detroit, 1981; cert. Adminstrv. Mgmt. Soc., Am. Soc. Personnel Adminstrn. Mem. Internat. Assn. Personnel Women (pres. 1969-70), Women's Econ. Club (v.p. 1971-72, pres. 1972-73), Personnel Women Detroit (pres. 1960-61), U. Detroit Alumni Assn. (pres. 1964-66), Phi Gamma Nu (nat. v.p. 1955-57). Office: 2000 2d Ave Detroit MI 48226

KAY, MARY ELLEN, financial adviser; b. Sewickley, Pa., June 21, 1947; d. Edmond and Virginia (Stueber) Kay; student Point Park Jr. Coll., 1964-65, Carnegie-Mellon U., 1965-69, N.Y. Inst. Fin., 1970-73; m. Randolph Rudisill Croxton, Apr. 19, 1969. Stockbroker, Dupont-Walston, N.Y.C., 1971-73, Shearson-Am. Express, N.Y.C., 1973-75; sr. v.p. A.G. Becker, N.Y.C. 1975—; pres. K & W Music, N.Y.C., 1980—, Easy Street Music Prodns., N.Y.C., 1979—; mus. performer, writer 1978-81; cons. in field. Adv. bd. First Women's Bank, N.Y.C., 1974-75; chmn.'s adviser U.S. Congl. Adv. Bd., 1983—; mem. Senatorial Inner Council. Recipient Lyric Competition award Internat. Am. Song Festival, 1981. Mem. Am. Soc. Composers Authors and Publs. Author: A Time to Remember, 1980. Home: 16 E 84th St Apt 3-B New York NY 10028 Office: 55 Water St New York NY 10041

KAY, PATRICIA M., educator; b. Bklyn., June 22, 1934; d. Lawrence Peter and Helena Frieda (Seifert) McGoldrick; B.S., Cornell U., 1956; Ed.D., Rutgers U., 1969; m. Morris I. Kay; children—Mary Katherine, Andrew Stephen. Asst. prof., coordinator research and evaluation, div. tchr. edn. CUNY, 1970-73; asst. prof., assoc. prof., prof. edn. and ednl. psychology Baruch Coll. and Grad. Center, 1973—; cons. in field; mem. N.Y. State Tchr. Edn., Cert. and Practices Bd., 1980—. Mem. Metuchen (N.J.) Bd. Edn., 1971-77; trustee Chamber Symphony N.J., 1976-78, N.J. Youth Symphony, 1980—. Mem. Am. Ednl. Research Assn., Nat. Council on Measurement in Edn., Am. Psychol. Assn., Kappa Delta Pi. Cons. editor Jour. Exptl. Edn., guest editor Jour. Tchr. Edn.; contbr. articles to profl. jours. Home: 51 Linden Ave Metuchen NJ 08840 Office: 17 Lexington Ave New York NY 10010

KAY, SUSAN BARCUS, plastic surgeon; b. Stockton, Calif., Sept. 28, 1948; d. Robert Kirkpatrick and Betty Jane (Sullivan) B.; m. Gregory Louis Kay, Sept. 26, 1981; children—Brittany Paige, Morgan Allison. A.B. with distinction, Cornell U., 1970; M.D., U. Rochester, 1975. Diplomate Am. Bd. Plastic Surgery. Intern Johns Hopkins Hosp., Balt., 1975-76, resident, 1976-77; resident U. Louisville, 1977-78, Barnes Hosp.-Washington U., St. Louis, 1978-81; instr. plastic surgery Washington U. Sch. Medicine, St. Louis, 1981-83; asst. prof. plastic surgery Baylor Coll. Medicine, Houston, 1983-85; asst. prof. plastic surgery UCLA, 1985—. Chmn. ad hoc com. on black studies Cornell U., Ithaca, N.Y., 1969; coordinator voter registration drive, Rochester, N.Y., 1972. NSF research grantee Cornell U., 1969; Teaching asst. grantee Cornell U., 1969-70; recipient Faculty Letters of Commendation, U. Rochester Sch. Medicine and Dentistry, 1972, 73. Mem. Am. Soc. Plastic and Reconstructive Surgeons, Am. Med. Women's Assn., Phi Beta Kappa. Office: Dept Plastic Surgery UCLA Med Ctr Los Angeles CA 90024

KAYE, JUDITH S., state supreme court judge; b. Monticello, N.Y., Aug. 4, 1938; m. Stephen Rackow Kaye; children—Luisa, Jonathan, Gordon. Grad. Barnard Coll.; LL.B., NYU, 1962. Former atty. Sullivan & Cromwell, Olwine, Connelly, Chase, O'Donnel & Weyher, N.Y.C.; assoc. judge N.Y. State Ct. Appeals, 1983—. Trustee, NYU Sch. of Law-Law Ctr. Found. Fellow, Am. Bar Found.; mem. ABA, Assn. of Bar City of N.Y., Am. Judicature Soc. Office: Court of Appeals Hall Eagle St Albany NY 12207*

KAYE, LORI, travel academy executive; b. N.Y.C.; d. Eldin Bert and Katherine Angeline Onsgard; student Detroit Inst. Art, 1951, 56, U. N.Mex., 1960. Actress, radio and TV commls., 1951-82; actress Warner Brothers, 1960-64; dir., v.p. John Robert Powers Schs., Los Angeles, 1961-71; v.p. Electron Industries, Torrance, Calif., 1963-65; owner, v.p., Lawrence Leon Photography Studio, Los Angeles, 1964-68; pres. Lori Kaye Cosmetics, Hollywood, Calif., 1964-70; co-owner, v.p. K and S Employment, Calif. Fashion Mart, 1965-67; dir., internat. cons. Airline Schs. Pacific, Van Nuys, Calif., 1972-74; dir. Caroline Leonetti Ltd. Sch., Hollywood, 1976-79; internat. cons. Internat. Career Acad., Van Nuys, 1978—, Glendale Coll. Bus. and Paramed. (Calif.), 1980—, Acad. Pacific, Hollywood, 1981—; pres. Molori Publs., Studio City, Calif., 1981—, Internat. Travel Acad., Inc., 1984—; owner, dir. Acad. Travel Internat., North Hollywood, 1983—; cons. A&T Inst. Travel and Tourism, 1982; lectr., 1969—. Dir. project Camarillo State Hosp., 1963-69; cons. Job Corps. Recipient Mental Health Achievement award, 1967. Mem. Nat. Assn. Female Execs., AAU, Screen Actors Guild, AFTRA, Internat. Platform Assn., Better Bus. Bur., C. of C., Assn. Promotion Tourism to Africa, Calif. Assn. Pvt. Secondary Schs., U.S. Masters-Internat. Swim Club, Nat. Geog. Soc. Paintings included in UNICEF collection, 1957; hostess TV talk show The New You, KTTV, Hollywood, 1964-65. Office: Molori Publs 11684 Ventura Blvd Suite 134 Studio City CA 91604 also Internat Travel Acad 12123 Magnolia North Hollywood CA 91607

KAYE, LORI-NAN POSKANZER, corporation executive, lawyer; b. Albany, N.Y., Feb. 23, 1956; d. Jesse J. and Shirley Mae (Poskanzer) K.; m. John Andrew Myer, Sept. 5, 1983; 1 child, David Emmanual. B.A., Skidmore Coll., 1976; J.D., Georgetown U., 1979. Bar: D.C. 1979, Fla. 1982, Mass. 1982. Law clk. ITA, U.S. Dept. Commerce, Washington, 1977-78; asst. dir. admissions Georgetown U. Law Ctr., Washington, 1979-80; assoc. Kirby & Gillick, Washington, 1980-82; corp. sec. and gen. counsel Elscint, Inc., Boston, 1982—; lectr. Georgetown U. Law Ctr., summers 1977-81. Contbg. author: Abeunt Studia in Mores, 1983. Periclean scholar, Skidmore Coll., 1976. Mem. ABA, D.C. Bar Assn., Fla. Bar Assn., Mass. Bar Assn., Phi Delta Phi (grad. of yr Province II 1979, magister 1978-79), Phi Beta Kappa. Jewish. Home: 117 Glezen Ln Wayland MA 01778 Office: Elscint Inc 930 Commonwealth Ave Boston MA 02215

KAY-MIRICH, ELEANOR, medical facility administrator; b. East Chicago, Ind.; d. Joseph Eugene and Josephine Veronica Kay; m. Ernest Carl Mirich; 5 children. R.N., St. Elizabeth Sch. Nursing, Lafayette, Ind., 1958; B.S., Coll. St. Francis, Joliet, Ill., 1978, M.S. in Health Service Adminstrn., 1986. Profl. model Patricia Stevens, Chgo., 1959-60; surg. nurse St. Margaret's Hosp., Hammond, Ind., 1959; oncology research nurse Henry Ford Hosp., Detroit, 1960; chief exec. officer, chief fin. officer, health adminstr. Mirich Med. Corp., Merrillville, Ind., 1973—, also dir. rehab. Prevention and Cardio Ctr., 1983—. Community coordinator Cardiography Lab., Merrillville, 1985—; bd. dirs. Hospice N.W. Ind., Munster, 1985—. Recipient cert. recognition Nat. Republican Congl. Com., 1985. Fellow Menninger Found.; mem. Am. Coll. Hosp. Adminstrs., Soc. for Hosp. Planning of Am. Hosp. Assn., Assn. Univ. Programs in Health Adminstrn., Soc. Prospective Medicine, Nat. Health Lawyers Assn., Am. Health Lawyers Assn., Am. Health Planning Assn., Am. Assn. Med. Systems and Informatics, Am. Mktg. Assn. (exec. mem.), Spinal Cord Soc., Nat. Spinal Cord Injury Assn., Am. Med. Care and Rev. Assn., Ind. State Nurses Assn., Nat. Forum Women Health Care Leaders, Assn. Med. Rehab. Dirs. and Coordinators, Am. Pub. Health Assn., Rehab. Internat. U.S.A., World Future Soc. (profl.), Nat. Handicapped Sprots and Recreation Assn., Nat. Rehab. Adminstrn. Assn., Internat. Hosp. Fedn., Nat. Rehab. Assn., Apostolate for Handicapped Diocese Gary, Ind. Juvenile Officers Assn., Acad. for Health Services Mktg. of Am. Mgmt. Assn., Am. Camping Assn. (life), Nat. Geog. Soc., Smithsonian Assocs., Missionary Assn. of Mary Immaculata, others. Home: 1000W 127th Pl Crown Point IN 46307 Office: Mirich Med Corp 9001 Broadway Merrillville IN 46307

KAYTE, LILLIAN, writer, marketing print media specialist; b. Phila., Dec. 10, 1937; d. Philip and Sophie (Olessker) K.; m. Roy George Julow, Apr. 23, 1967 (div. Jan. 1977); children—Alexis, David, Eric, Heidi. Student U. Vt., 1960-64. Contbr. editor Creative Loafing, Atlanta, 1977-83; mng. editor Sr. Tribune, Atlanta, 1979-80; chief writer Profl. Writing Service, Atlanta, 1983-85; pres. Profl. Writers Group-Atlanta, Marietta, Ga., 1986—; feature story and bus. writer for various newspapers and mags.; mktg./advt. cons.; contbr. stories and articles to numerous publs. Office: Profl Writers Group-Atlanta 2470 Windy Hill Rd Suite 158 Marietta GA 30067

KAZANJIAN, WENDY COFFELT, educator, association executive; b. Hollywood, Calif., Aug. 21, 1946; d. R. Wendell andd Dolores (Storm) Coffelt; B.A., U. So. Calif., 1968, M.S. in Edn., 1970; J.D., Whittier Coll., 1984; m. Phillip Kazanjian, Feb. 5, 1972. Tchr., Los Angeles Unified Sch. Dist., 1970—; dir. Project Cold, ESEA Title IV-C Fed. Grant, Los Angeles, 1980-81; master/demonstration tchr. U. So. Calif., Los Angeles and Calif. State U., Los Angeles, 1972—; exec. dir. Polar Regions Soc., Inc., 1982—. Dir. youth programs United Fedn. Republican Women, 1980—; mem. exec. council law student sect. Los Angeles County Bar Assn., 1980—; active Am. Heart Assn., 1975—. Recipient Nat. Tchrs. medal Freedoms Found. Valley Forge, 1976; U.S. Congl. Record Tribute, 1977; Freedoms Found. scholar, 1978; Robert A. Taft scholar, 1979. Mem. U. So. Calif. Educare, Alpha Phi Alumni Assn. Republican. Office: 225 W Broadway Suite 500 Glendale CA 91204

KAZOLIAS, HELEN HANCOCK, nursing educator; b. Mt. Kisco, N.Y., Sept. 30, 1931; s. C. LeRoy and Helen C. (Rodgers) Hancock; m. Frederick Spiegelberg, Aug. 13, 1979; children by previous marriage—George S., Michael A., A. Peter. B.S., Russell Sage Coll., 1968; M.Ed., Tchrs. Coll., Columbia U., 1971, Ed.D., 1979. Instr., Columbia Meml. Hosp., Hudson, N.Y., 1964-71; asst. prof. nursing Pace U., N.Y.C., 1971-74, SUNY-Downstate Med. Ctr., 1974-79; assoc. prof. U. Tulsa, 1979-81; cons. nursing edn., Tulsa, 1981-83; asst. dean, assoc. prof. Coll. Nursing, U. Southwestern La., Lafayette, 1983-85; pvt. practice nursing, 1986—; cons. sex edn. N.Y.C. Bd. Edn., 1974-79; cons. nursing edn. Margaret Sanger Inst., N.Y.C., 1978; cons. elderly health care Heights Hills Community Council, Bklyn., 1974-79; asst. project coordinator HEW Pilot Program on Migrant Worker Health Care, Columbia County (N.Y.), 1969-70. Researcher: (audio-visual program and booklet) The Nursing Process, 1983; contbr. articles to profl. jours. Instructional programs chmn. ARC, Tulsa, 1982-83; bd. dirs. Margaret Hudson Program, Tulsa, 1980-83, Nursing Service, Inc., Tulsa, 1980-83, Children's Service adv. bd. Dept. Human Services, Tulsa, 1980-83. Recipient Hon. Recognition for Disting. Service, Dist. 13 N.Y. State Nurses Assn., 1979; Mead Johnson fellow, 1968; Am. Nurses Assn. fellow, 1968. Mem. Am. Nurses Assn., Nat. League Nursing, AAUP, Childbirth and Family Life, Sigma Theta Tau. Home: 1512 Myrtle Pl Lafayette LA 70506

KEALIINOHOMOKU, JOANN WHEELER, anthropologist, educator; b. Kansas City, Mo.; B.S.S., Northwestern U., 1955; M.A., 1965; Ph.D., Ind. U., 1976; 1 child, Halla K. Mem. faculty No. Ariz. U., Flagstaff, 1970-72, 75—, asso. prof. anthropology, 1980—; mem. faculty World Campus Afloat, fall 1972, 73; resident scholar Sch. Am. Research, Santa Fe, 1974-75; vis. faculty U. Hawaii, Hilo, spring 1973, summer 1973, 74, U. Hawaii-Manoa, fall 1981, NYU, summer 1980, 84. Bd. dirs. Native Americans for Community Action, Flagstaff Indian Center, 1977-82, sec., 1980-82. Grantee, Am. Philos. Soc. Wenner Gren Found.; Weatherhead fellow Sch. Am. Research, 1974-75; research fellow East-West Center, 1981; NEH grantee, 1986. Fellow Current Anthropology; mem. Soc. Ethnomusicology (councilor; co founder Southwestern chpt.), Dance Research Center (charter), Cross Cultural Dance Resources (founder 1981). Contbr. articles to profl. jours. Home: 518 S Agassiz St Flagstaff AZ 86001 Office: CU Box 15200 No Ariz U Flagstaff AZ 86011

KEAN, KATHERINE ANN, visual effects designer, artist; b. Huntington, W. Va., Aug. 9, 1956; d. Victor Alden and Betty L. (Berisford) Kean; m. John T. Van Vliet, May 5, 1984. B.F.A., R.I. Sch. Design, 1978. Prodn. art ednl. filmstrips Carr and Assocs./Meta-4, Los Angeles, 1979; animator: Dragonslayer, Conan, Star Trek II, etc., Visual Concept Engring., Hollywood, Calif., 1980-82, The Day After, etc., Praxis Filmworks, North Hollywood, Calif., 1982-83; animation designer Available Light Ltd., North Hollywood, 1983—; supr. 1st ann. student/alumni art show R.I. Sch. Design, Providence, 1976; animation cons. Allamaze, Providence, 1978; asst. to animation tchr. R.I. Sch. Design, 1977. Vol. art tchr. Ctr. for Arts., Boston, 1975. Recipient Globe Scholastic Portfolio award, Boston, 1974; Cert. of Acknowledgement, Acad. TV Arts and Scis. Home: 8724 1/4 Wyngate St Sunland CA 91040 Office: Available Light Ltd 3110 W Burbank Blvd Burbank CA 91505

KEAN, OPAL NORRIS MELLOWAY, social worker; b. Columbia, Mo., Nov. 19, 1906; d. John Franklin and Dottie May (Maupin) Melloway; A.B., U. Mo., 1932; M.S.W., Washington U., 1948; m. Robert E. Kean, June 14, 1933. Caseworker, Family Service, Kansas City, Mo., 1932-45; med. social worker Jewish Family and Children Service, Kansas City, 1947-55; dir. social service dept., psychiat. social worker Menorah Med. Center, Kansas City, 1955-66; pvt. practice as psychiat. social worker, Kansas City, 1966—. Mem. Nat. Assn. Social Workers, Acad. Cert. Social Workers (field work instr. 1950-54), Phi Beta Kappa, Alpha Kappa Delta. Methodist. Home and Office: 631 E 74th St Kansas City MO 64131

KEANE, CHRISTINE MARIE, advertising executive; b. Manhattan, N.Y., July 11, 1957; d. Edward Michael and Ann Theresa (Casserly) Keane. B.A., Pa. State U., 1979. Mktg. analyst, West Milford, N.J., 1975-79; asst. account exec. DKG Advt., N.Y.C., 1979-81; account coordinator Thomas G. Ferguson Advt., Parsippany, N.J., 1981; media dir. Lohmeyer Simpson Communications Inc., Morristown, N.J., 1981-83, dir. client services, 1983—. Mem. Advt. Women Am., Pa. State Alumni Assn. Republican. Roman Catholic. Home: Skytop Gardens 26-8 Parlin NJ 08859

KEANE, MICHELLE ANNE, investment, real estate executive; b. Pitts., Sept. 10, 1955; d. John Edgar and Janet Marie (Mackall) K.; B.A. in Urban Affairs, U. Pitts., 1977, M.B.A., 1982. TV account exec. Sta. KDKA-TV2, Pitts., 1977-84; brokerage rep. Oliver Realty, 1984—. Bd. dirs. Western Pa. chpt. Nat. Hemophilia Found.; mem. assocs. council U. Pitts. Grad. Sch. Bus. Anna R.D. Gillespie scholar, 1976-77; Pa. Senatorial scholar, 1976-77. Mem. Greater Pitts. Bd. Realtors, Omicron Delta Kappa, Chi Omega, Rho Lambda. Home: 2247 Manor Ave Pittsburgh PA 15218 Office: 2800 Two Oliver Plaza Pittsburgh PA 15222

KEARNEY, CAROL ANN, school library administrator; b. Buffalo, May 6, 1939; d. Robert and Inez (Lenore) Lacey Schubring; m. John Edward Kearney, Jr., July 4, 1959; children—Yvonne Carol, John Edward III, B.S., Geneseo State Tchrs. Coll., 1960; M.S., SUNY-Buffalo, 1970, Specialist Edn. Adminstrn., 1977. Library media specialist West Seneca (N.Y.) Central Schs., 1964-67, elem. library media specialist, 1967-69, jr. high library media specialist, 1969-71, sr. library media specialist, 1971-73, coordinator library services, 1969-73; dir. sch. library Buffalo Pub. Schs., 1973—; vis. lectr. Sch. Info. and Library Sci., Buffalo, 1978-82; chmn. Regents Adv. Council, N.Y. State Edn. Dept., 1981-85. Named Librarian of Yr., Sch. Info. and Library Sci., SUNY-Buffalo, 1975; Boss of Yr., Am. Bus. Women's Assn., 1975. Mem. ALA, N.Y. Library Assn. (pres. 1983-84), Sch. Library Media Sect. (pres. 1980-81), Sch. Media Suprs. N.Y. State (pres. 1976-78), Sch. Libraries Assn. Western N.Y. (pres. 1973-74). Christian Scientist. Home: 54 Suburban Ct West Seneca NY 14224 Office: Buffalo Pub Schs Room 418 City Hall Buffalo NY 14202

KEARNEY, ELIZABETH IRENE, consulting firm executive, writer; b. New Burnside, Ill., Dec. 7, 1934; d. E. William Edmondson and Verna P. (Greer) Eppley; m. M.L. Kearney, Feb. 7, 1953 (div.); children—Michael, Kim. B.A., UCLA, 1954; M.A., U. Pa., 1959; doctoral candidate. Tchr., program dir. Pasadena Unified Sch. Dist., Calif., 1959-84; v.p. J.P. Cleaver Co., Houston, 1984, Cole/Kearney Co., South Pasadena, 1984; pres. Kearney Enterprises, Los Angeles, 1979—. Author: How to Increase Your Vocabulary, 1964; How To Write A Term Paper, 1965; The American Novel: A Study Guide to 36 Great Books, 1966; The Continental Novel: A Bibliography of Criticism, Vol. I, 1967, Vol. II, 1982; Sales Magic, 1985; Management Magic, 1985; Sales Magic for Real Estate, 1985. Contbr. articles to profl. jours. Past editor CAG Communicator, Pipelines Newsletter, Previews newspaper. Pres. Terr. Park Assn., 1984—; bd. dirs. Pasadena Edn. Found.; vol. Nat. Trust Hist. Preservation, 1980—; adv. gifted children Calif. Advs. Gifted Edn., 1967—. Recipient Best Reference Book award ALA, 1967; fellow NDEA, 1968, Johns Hopkins U., 1971. Mem. Golden Voice, Nat. Speakers Assn., Leads Club, Women's Referral Services, Pasadena C. of C. (chmn. com. 1983-85). Republican. Episcopalian. Avocations: travel; writing; reading; historical preservation.

KEARNEY, SADIE MCPARLAND, civic worker; b. Masonville, Iowa, Mar. 10, 1901; d. Charles Francis and Cathryn Elizabeth (Holland) McParland; children—John A., Thomas Edward, James F. Student Loras Coll., 1919-21, Wright Coll., 1950-60, Triton Coll., 1981. Tchr., Buchanan County Schs., Independence, Iowa, 1919-22, Chgo. Pub. Schs., 1922-25; shipping clk. Sloan Valve Co., Chgo., 1941-69. Creator toys. Tutor reading and math. to elem. students, 1978—. Active with Cub Scouts and Boys Scouts, 1941-48, Oak Park/River Forest Citizen's Com. on Human Rights, 1980. Democrat. Roman Catholic. Club: Toastmistress (treas.). Avocations: reading; bridge. Home: 912 Home Ave Oak Park IL 60304

KEARNS, MERLE GRACE, county official; b. Bellefonte, Pa., May 19, 1938; d. Robert John and Mary Catharine (Fitzgerald) Grace; m. Thomas Raymond Kearns, June 27, 1959; children—Thomas, Michael, Timothy, Matthew. B.S., Ohio State U., 1960. Tchr. St. Raphael Elem. Sch., Springfield, Ohio, 1960-62; substitute tchr. Mad River Green dist., Springfield, 1972-78; instr. Clark Tech. Coll., Springfield, 1978-80; commr. Clark County, Ohio, 1981—; pres. bd. county commrs., 1982, 83, 86, v.p., 1985. Bd. dirs. Springfield Symphony, 1980—, Arts Council, 1980-85; mem. exec. com. Springfield Republicans, 1984—. Ohio State U., scholar, 1957-59; named Woman of Yr. Springfield Pilot Club, 1981. Mem. Abilities Unltd. Network, County Commrs. Assn. of Ohio (bd. dirs. 1985—, welfare adv. com. 1984—), Southwest Commrs. of Ohio (pres. 1985, sec., v.p. 1983-84), LWV (bd. dirs. 1964—, pres. 1975-78), Omicron Nu. Roman Catholic. Avocations: reading; golf. Home: 2664 Brookdale Dr Springfield OH 45502 Office: Bd Clark County Commrs 31 N Limestone St Springfield OH 45502

KEATING, NANCY CATHERINE, advertising copywriter; b. Bay Shore, N.Y., July 14, 1953; d. Patrick Christopher and Marie Faith (Donahue) K. B.A., Bucknell U., 1975; M.A., U. Minn., 1984. Editor Frogtown Forum, St. Paul, 1977-78; assoc. editor Highland Villager, St. Paul, 1978-80; copywriter Coleman & Christison, St. Paul, 1980-81; ad sales rep. Downtowner, St. Paul, 1981-82; free-lance writer, St. Paul, 1982-83; assoc. creative dir. Beissel, Inc., St. Paul, 1983-84; copywriter Cohen Okerlund Smith, Mpls., 1984-85, Campbell-Mithun, Mpls., 1985—. Del. 4th Dist. Democratic-Farmer-Labor Party, St. Paul, 1982-84, alt., 1980-82. Recipient Andy award of merit, 1983; Issue Coverage award Neighborhood Press Assn., Mpls., 1980. Mem. Art Dirs. and Copywriters' Club Twin Cities. Roman Catholic.

KEATING, RITA ANN, state government computer information consultant, Bed and Breakfast owner; b. Kansas City, Mo., Jan. 18, 1939; d. Bernard Anthony McAnarney and Beatrice Juanita (Brown) McAnarney Harvey; m. Harold Edward Keating, July 16, 1960; children—Erin, Jeffery, Michaela, Kara, Stephen. B.A. in Arts Adminstrn., The Evergreen State Coll., Olympia, Wash., 1979. Statis. analysis clk. AT&T, Kansas City, 1958-60; early childhood edn. adv. Contra Costa County, Concord, Calif., 1974-75; project coordinator Capital Area Assn. Performing Arts, Olympia, 1978-79; research analyst Dept. of Social and Health Services, Olympia, 1979-84, mgmt. analyst, 1984—. Cons., bus. mgr. Olympia Symphony Orch., 1985—; bd. dir., sec., 1980-84; com. mem. Wash. Ctr. for Performing Arts Presentation com., Olympia, 1984. Evergreen Found. scholar Evergreen State Coll., 1978-79. Mem. Olympia C. of C. Roman Catholic. Lodge: Soroptimists (alt. del. 1985). Office: Unicorn's Rest Bed & Breakfast 316 E 10th St Olympia WA 98501

KECLIK, JANICE LYNN, engineering and construction company executive; b. Chgo., Apr. 23, 1952; d. John and Lillian Lorraine (McCarty) Keclik; B.S., U. San Francisco, 1983. With Continental Ill. Bank & Trust Co., Chgo., 1970-72, Bruhnke & Silver, Cary, Ill., 1972-73, Libby, McNeill & Libby, Chgo., 1973, Sargent & Lundy, Chgo., 1973-81; dir. personnel Ultrasystems, Inc., Irvine, Calif., 1981—; cons. to several small firms, Calif., 1983—. Mem. Personnel and Indsl. Relations Assn., Nat. Assn. Female Execs. Office: Ultrasystems Inc 16845 Von Karman St Irvine CA 92714

KEDDERIS, PAMELA JEAN, insurance company executive; b. Waterbury, Conn., May 15, 1956; d. Leo Goerge and Evelyn Helen (Fenske) K. Student, U. Nice, 1976-77; B.A., Assumption Coll., 1978; M.B.A., U. New Haven, 1981. Credit analyst, Citytrust Bank, Bridgeport, Conn., 1980-81, sr. credit analyst, 1981-82, fin. analyst, 1982-83, seminar leader, 1981-83; planning analyst Continental Ins. Co., N.Y.C., 1983-84, sr. planning analyst, 1984-85, dir. planning, 1985—. Active YMCA, Union, N.J., 1985—. Mem. Nat. Assn. Female Execs. Democrat. Lutheran. Avocations: music, traveling. Home: Apt 67-B 230 W Summer Ave Roselle Park NJ 07204-1238

KEECH, ELOWYN ANN, interior designer; b. Berrien County, Mich., Oct. 5, 1937; d. Earl Docker and Elizabeth Hall (Paullin) Stephenson; 1 son, Robert Earl. Print designer, copywriter newspaper accounts, dept. stores, resorts, service orgns., industry, 1957-75; freelance interior designer, photoset and video set designer, St. Joseph, Mich., 1975—; owner Fog Horn Records & Tapes. Bd. dirs. Blossomland United Way, 1981—; bd. dirs., mem. steering and long-range planning coms. United Way Mich., 1980—. Designer interiors 1st Fed. Savs. & Loan Assn., Three Oaks, Mich., 1975, Holland (Mich.) Central Trade Credit Union, 1978. 1st. Fed. Savs. & Loan Assn., Holland, 1978, Yonker Realty, Co., Holland, 1979, People's Bank of Holland, 1979, exec. offices Whirlpool Corp., 1980—, human resources St. Joe div., 1985, Claeys Residence, 1984, Calley Dental Office, 1985, Sarett Nature Ctr., 1985, Imperial Printing, 1986, Complete Sink Residence, 1986, Miller Residence, 1986, Schraders Super Market, 1986, also others. Mem. AIA (profl. affiliate Western Mich. chpt.), Sarrett Nature Ctr., Nat. Trust Historic Preservation, St. Joseph Art Assn., Chgo. Art. Inst., St. Joseph Today. Club: South Shore Racquet. Home and Office: 375 Ridgeway Saint Joseph MI 49085

KEEFAUVER, BARBARA ATKINS, arts adminstr.; b. N.Y.C., June 13, 1928; d. Henry John and Emma (Fayen) Atkins; B.A. in Bus. Adminstrn., Pa. State U., 1949; postgrad. Rutgers U., 1968-69; m. William Lloyd Keefauver, July 9, 1949; children—Bruce Lloyd, Elizabeth Ann. With Equitable Life Assurance Co., N.Y.C., 1949-52; bd. dirs. Colonial Symphony, 1962-72; tchr. dramatics George Washington Sch., Morristown, N.J., 1971-72; with Arts' Council Morris Area, Drew U., Madison, N.J., 1972—, dir., 1973-82, exec. dir., 1982—. Dir. childrens plays, 1962—; bd. dirs. Jr. League Morristown, 1962-66; chmn. Arts Council N.J. Jr. Leagues, 1967-69, chmn. exec. council, 1969-71. Recipient Vol. of Yr. Award Jr. League Morristown, 1966. Mem. Nat. Assembly Community Art Agys., Am. Council for Arts, Jr. League Morristown, Delta Gamma. Republican. Episcopalian. Office: Arts Council Morris Area Drew Univ Madison NJ 07940

KEEFE, MARY MARGUERITE, molecular biologist, administrator; b. Old Town, Maine, Oct. 29, 1946; d. George Ernest and Winifred Mary (Olson) Fortier; m. Timothy Daniel Keefe, June 29, 1969 (div. 1983); children—Brendan Matthew, Daniel Jeffery. B.S. cum laude, U. N.H., 1968. Lic. med. technologist. Research asst. virology VA Hosp. Yale Lab, West Haven, Conn., 1968-70; med. technologist Middlesex Meml. Hosp., Middletown, Conn., 1970-73; tech. specialist quality control Internat. Biotechnology Inc., New Haven, 1982-84, asst. mgr., 1984-85, asst. dir. lab. ops., 1985-86, dir. quality control and custom services, 1986—; organizer Keefe Co. Realtors, Madison, Conn., 1977. Bd. dirs. No. Madison Congregational Ch., Conn., 1973-76. Mem. Nat. Assn. Female Execs., AAUW, Phi Mu Alumni Assn. Republican. Club: Newcomers (ways and means com. 1977-78) (Madison). Avocations: crafts, sewing, tennis, classical music. Home: 13 A Stonegate Briarwood Ln Branford CT 06405 Office: Internat Biotechnology Inc 275 Winchester Ave New Haven CT 06535

KEEFE, NANCY QUIRK, editor; b. Pittsfield, Mass., Nov. 20, 1934; d. John Gorman and Ann (O'Laughlin) Quirk; m. Kevin Brian Keefe, Oct. 3, 1959; children—Brendan, Clare, Maura. B.A., Coll. New Rochelle, 1956; M.S., Columbia U., 1958. Asst. telegraph editor Berkshire Eagle, Pittsfield Mass., 1958-59; copy editor World Telegram & Sun, N.Y.C., 1959-60; mng. editor, columnist Gannett Westchester Newspapers, White Plains, N.Y., 1981-84, editorial page editor, columnist, 1984—; columnist Berkshire Eagle, 1969—. Recipient Angela Merici medal Coll. New Rochelle, 1981. Roman Catholic.

Home: 79 Harmon Dr Larchmont NY 10538 Office: Gannett Westchester Newspapers 1 Gannett Dr White Plains NY 10604

KEEFREY, PATRICIA GAIL, landscape architect, fashion designer; b. Madison, Wis., Feb. 22, 1955; d. James Joseph Keefrey and Charlotte Leone (Svendsen) Keefrey-Shaw. B.S. in Landscape Architecture, U. Wis., 1977. Mem. team U. Wis.-Madison Environ. Awareness Ctr., 1977, student profl. asst., 1986—; teaching asst. N.C. State U., Raleigh, 1978; engring. asst. Glen Ward and Assocs., Raleigh, 1979; free-lance designer, landscape architect, Madison, 1980-84; designer, landscape architect Eklof-Farwell, Madison, 1985—. Contbg. author Am. Poetry Anthology: A Willow Now Tall, 1981. Designer: Keep It Together, 1985. Recipient spl. talents award N.C. State U., 1977-78. Mem. Am. Soc. Landscape Architects, Nat. Assn. Profl. Women. Mem. Baha'i Faith. Avocations: skiing; writing; sewing; bicycling; sailing. Office: Environ Awareness Ctr U Wis B120 Steenbock Library Madison WI 53706

KEEGAN, JANE ANN, insurance broker, consultant; b. Watertown, N.Y., Sept. 1, 1950; d. Richard Isidor and Kathleen (McKinley) K. B.A. cum laude, SUNY-Potsdam, 1972; M.B.A. in Risk Mgmt., Golden Gate U., 1986. C.P.C.U. Comml. lines mgr. Lithgow & Rayhill, San Francisco, 1977-80; risk mgmt. account coordinator Dinner Levison Co., San Francisco, 1980-83; ins. cons., San Francisco, 1983-84; account mgr. Rollins Burudick Hunter, San Francisco, 1984-85; account exec. Jardine Ins. Brokers, San Francisco, 1985—. Vol. San Francisco Ballet vol. orgn., 1981—; mem. Nob Hill Neighbors Assn., 1982—. Mem. Soc. Chartered Property Casualty Underwriters (spl. events chairperson 1982-84; continuing profl. devel. program award 1985). Democrat. Roman Catholic. Home: 1635 Clay St Apt 1 San Francisco CA 94109

KEELAND, DELPHA FLORINE, librarian; b. Glendive, Mont., June 3, 1925; d. Fred Peter and Anna (Buller) Deckert; m. Charles William Keeland, July 25, 1943; children—Charles, Richard James, Norma Lynn, Princess Ann, Ramona Joy, Dixie Lee, Dana Scott. Student pub. schs., Richey, Mont. Nurses aide McCone County Hosp., Circle, Mont., 1962-66, 74-76; owner Trail's End Cafe, Olympia, Wash., 1967-71; librarian Richey Pub. Library, Mont., 1980—. Mem. V.F.W. Aux., Am. Legion Aux. Methodist. Office: Richey Pub Library Richey MT 59259

KEELE, REBA LOU, health center consultant, educator; b. Emery, Utah, Oct. 28, 1941; d. Frederick Manning and Pearl Valentine (Peterson) K.; B.S., Brigham Young U., 1963, M.A., 1966; Ph.D., Purdue U., 1974. Asst. prof. communications, debate coach Brigham Young U., 1967-68, coordinator ednl. psychology, 1969-74, asso. dir. honors program, 1974-77, dir. honors program, 1977-78, assoc. prof. orgnl. behavior, 1979—; dir. Center for Women's Health, Cottonwood Hosp., Murray, Utah, 1984-85, cons., 1985—; founding ptnr. Health Care Innovations, Inc., 1985—; dir. Title III project; cons. numerous sch. dists.; vis. scholar Purdue U., 1978-79. Pres., Stake Relief Soc., Mormon Ch., Provo, Utah, 1975-77; speaker community, ch. groups; mem. advisory bd. women's history archives Harold B. Lee Library, 1976-81; exec. dir. Consortium for Utah Women in Higher Edn., 1977-78, 79-82; state facilitator Higher Edn. Resource Service W., 1979-82; bd. regents Utah System Higher Edn., 1981—; mem. Democratic Central Com., 1977-78; del.-at-large Internat. Women's Yr., 1977. Named Honors Prof. of Yr., Brigham Young U., 1983, recipient Maeser Disting. Teaching award, 1984; past Brigham Young U. fellow, Purdue U. fellow. Mem. Acad. Mgmt., Utah Women in History Assn. (adv. bd. 1977-78), Am. Mgmt. Assn., Phi Eta Sigma (nat. exec. com. 1983—), Phi Kappa Phi. Clubs: Alice Louise Reynolds, Fonta. Author: Let's Talk: Adults and Children Sharing Feelings, 1977; contbr. articles to profl. publs.; writer, instr. TV programs: Helping Your Child to Read, 1974. Home: 459 E 800 North Orem UT 84057 Office: 786 TNRB Brigham Young U Provo UT 84602

KEELER, VIRGINIA MARY, univ. ofcl.; b. San Antonio, Aug. 24, 1932; d. Thomas Love and Margaret Therese (Conway) K.; A.B., Chestnut Hill Coll., Phila., 1953. Sec. to Office of Pres., Georgetown U., 1953-54, sec. to pres., 1954-74, asst. sec. of univ., 1968-74, sec. of univ., 1974—. Recipient Vicennial medal Georgetown U., 1973, Patrick J. Healy medal Georgetown U. Alumni Assn., 1984. Mem. Am. Assn. Higher Edn., Assn. Governing Bds. Roman Catholic. Home: 2712 Wisconsin Ave NW 811 Washington DC 20007 Office: Georgetown University Washington DC 20057

KEEN, CHARLOTTE ELIZABETH, geophysicist; b. Halifax, N.S., Can., June 22, 1943; d. Murray Alexander and Elizabeth Randall (Cobb) Davidson; B.Sc. in physics with honors, Dalhousie U., 1964, M.Sc., 1966; Ph.D. in Geophysics, Cambridge U., 1970. Research scientist Atlantic Oceanographic Lab. Bedford Inst. Oceanography, Dartmouth, N.S., Can., 1970-73, Atlantic Geoscience Centre, 1973—; chmn. Canadian Com. on the Lithosphere. Fellow Royal Soc. Can., Geol. Assn. Can.; mem. Am. Geophys. Union, Commn. Marine Geology. Editor: Crustal Properties Across Passive Margins, 1979; contbr. numerous articles in field. Office: Atlantic Geoscience Centre Bedford Institute of Oceanography Dartmouth NS B24 4A2 Canada

KEEN, MARY FRANCES, nurse, educator; b. Lancaster, Pa., June 8, 1949; d. Robert Hess and Mary Carolyn (Greider) K.; diploma in nursing Johns Hopkins Hosp. Sch. Nursing, Balt., 1970; B.S.N., U. Md., 1973, M.S., 1976; D.N.Sc. (HEW profl. nurse trainee), Catholic U. Am., 1981; Instr. Johns Hopkins U. Sch. Health Services, 1976-79, nursing curriculum researcher Sch. Hygiene and Pub. Health, 1979-80; asst. prof. nursing U. Md., 1979-81; assoc. prof. U. Miami, Coral Gables, Fla., 1981—; cons. Pan Am. Health Orgn.; health fair vol. HEW research grantee, 1977-80; NIH grantee, 1981-83. Mem. AAUP, Am. Assn. Critical Care Nurses (nat. com. mem. 1984—), Am. Nurses' Assn., Nat. League Nursing (test item writer in med. nursing), Nat. Council Internat. Health Johns Hopkins Nurses Alumni Assn. (treas. 1977-79, pres. 1980-81), Am. Field Service, Phi Kappa Phi, Sigma Theta Tau (treas. 1984—. Research, publs. in field. Home: 14601 N Kendall Dr #K-403 Miami FL 33186 Office: PO Box 248106 Coral Gables FL 33124

KEENAN, CATHERINE CHARLOTTE, nursing instructor; b. Wilmington, Del., Aug. 3, 1947; d. Charles Edward and Catherine Ann (Murphy) Jackson; m. Joseph J. Keenan, Jr., June 20, 1970; 1 son, John Patrick. B.S. in Nursing, U. Del., 1969. Lic. nurse, Del. Head nurse Del. State Hosp., New Castle, 1969-70; asst. head nurse Norwich State Hosp (Conn.), 1970-71; asst. charge nurse Montgomery Gen. Hosp., Olney, Md., 1971-74; nurse therapist St. Francis Hosp., Wilmington, 1978-81; instr. nursing Del. Tech. and Community Coll., Newark, 1979—. Mus. guide Fort Del. Soc., Wilmington, 1982—; v.p. St. Peter's Parish Council, New Castle, 1982-84; chmn. long-range planning com. St. Peter's Sch. Mem. Nat. League for Nursing, Beta Beta Beta, Sigma Theta Tau. Democrat. Roman Catholic. Home: 111 Baldt Ave New Castle DE 19720 Office: Del Tech and Community College 400 Christiana Stanton Rd Newark DE 19702

KEENAN, MARY ANN, orthopaedic surgeon, researcher; b. Phila., Aug. 14, 1950; d. William Joseph and Irene Agnes (Obara) K. A.B., U. Pa., 1971; M.D., Med. Coll. Pa., 1976. Diplomate Am. Bd. Med. Examiners, Am. Bd. Orthopedic Surgery. Orthopaedic resident Albert Einstein Med. Ctr., Phila., 1976-81; fellow rehab. Rancho Los Amigos Hosp., Downey, Calif., 1981-82, cons. specialist, 1982—; attending surgeon Kaiser Found. Hosp., Bellflower, Calif., 1982—; asst. prof. orthopaedics U. So. Calif. Med. Sch., Los Angeles, 1982—. Contbr. articles in field to profl. jours. Recipient Annual Radiology prize Albert Einstein Med. Ctr., 1977, 78, 79, First Prize in research competition, 1980. Mem. AMA, Am. Acad. Orthopedic Surgeons, Am. Med. Women's Assn., Ruth Jackson Orthopaedic Soc., Am. Assn. Physicians for Human Rights, Profl. Staff Assn. Rancho Los Amigos Hosp., Alumnae Assn. Med. Coll. Pa. Democrat. Office: Dept Orthopaedic Surgery 9400 E Rosecrans Ave Bellflower CA 90706

KEENAN, RETHA VORNHOLT, nurse; b. Solon, Iowa, Aug. 15, 1934; d. Charles Elias and Helen Maurine (Konicek) V.; B.S.N., State U. Iowa, 1955; M.S.N., Calif. State U., Long Beach, 1978; m. Roy Vincent Keenan, Jan. 5, 1980; children from previous marriage—Scott Iverson, Craig Iverson. Public health nurse City of Long Beach, 1970-73, Hosp. Home Care, Torrance, Calif., 1973-75; patient care coordinator Hillhaven, Los Angeles, 1975-76; mental health cons. InterCityHome Health, Los Angeles, 1978-79; instr. Community Coll. Dist., Los Angeles, 1979-86; instr. nursing El Camino Coll., Torrance, 1981-86, NIMH grantee, 1977-78; instr. nursing Chapman Coll., Orange, Calif., 1982. Contbg. author: American Journal of Nursing Question and Answer Book for Nursing Boards Review, 1984, Nursing Care Planning Guides for Psychiatric and Mental Health Care, student edit., 1985. Cert. nurse practitioner adult and mental health, 1979. Mem. Am. Nurses Assn., Calif. Nurses Assn., AAUW, Calif. State U.-Long Beach Dept. Nursing Honor Soc., Phi Delta Gamma, Sigma Theta Tau, Phi Kappa Phi, Delta Zeta. Lutheran. Home: 27849 Longhill Dr Rancho Palos Verdes CA 90274 Office: Dept Nursing West Los Angeles Coll Culver City CA 90230

KEENAN, ROBERTA MONROE, insurance company executive; b. Webberville, Mich., May 6, 1934; d. Cecil Francis and Edna Almeda (Gowing) Monroe; m. Earl J. Gibson Jr., May 1, 1954 (div. 1972); children—Paula Steele, Christopher; m. 2d, James W. Keenan, Dec. 17, 1983. Student Lansing Community Coll., 1975-77. Cert. Ins. Inst. Am. Mgr. Citizens Credit Union, Howell, Mich., 1961-73; personnel adminstr. Citizens Ins. Co., 1973-77, personnel mgr., 1977-81, asst. v.p., 1981—. Mem. Am. Soc. for Personnel Adminstrn. Home: 239 Cornell Dr Howell MI 48843 Office: Citizens Ins Co Am 645 W Grand River Howell MI 48843

KEENE-BURGESS, RUTH FRANCES, army official; b. South Bend, Ind., Oct. 7, 1948; d. Seymour and Sally (Morris) K.; m. Leslie U. Burgess, Jr., Oct. 1, 1983. B.S., Ariz. State U., 1970; M.S., Fairleigh Dickinson U., 1978. Inventory mgmt. specialist U.S. Army Electronics Command, Phila., 1970-74, U.S. Army Communications-Electronics Materiel Readiness Command, Fort Monmouth, N.J., 1974-79; chief inventory mgmt. div. Crane (Ind.) Army Ammunition Activity, 1979-80; supply systems analyst Hdqrs. 60th Ordnance Group, Zweibruecken, Fed. Republic Germany, 1980-83; chief inventory mgmt. div. Crane (Ind.) Army Ammunition Activity, 1983-85, chief control div., 1985; inventory mgmt. specialist 200th Theater Army Material Mgmt. Ctr., Zweibruecken, 1985—. Mem. Federally Employed Women (chpt. pres. 1979-80), Nat. Assn. Female Execs., Soc. Logistics Engrs., Assn. Computing Machinery, Am. Soc. Public Adminstrn., Soc. Profl. and Exec. Women, Assn. Info. Systems Profls., AAAS, NOW. Democrat. Jewish. Home: 4916 W Pinchot Ave Phoenix AZ 85031 Office: 200th TAMMC Attention AEAGD-MMC-VS APO NY 09052

KEEP, JUDITH N., federal court judge; b. 1944. B.A., Scripps Coll., 1966; J.D., U. San Diego, 1970. Tchr. English, 1966; law clk. Westgate-Calif. Corp., 1970; individual practice law, 1973-76; legal staff Defenders, Inc., 1971-73; asst. U.S. atty., 1976; mcpl. ct. judge San Diego, 1976-80; fed. judge So. Dist. Calif., San Diego, 1980—. Office: Courtroom 6 US Courthouse 940 Front St San Diego CA 92189*

KEER, JANET S., financial executive; b. N.Y.C., June 8, 1936; d. Martin and Ada (Karnig) Katz; B.B.A., Baruch Sch. Bus. and Public Adminstrn., CUNY, 1956; children—Jennifer, Elizabeth. Asst. to advt. dir. WNEW-TV, N.Y.C., 1959-62; comptroller/ins. sales Joel Katz & Assos., Inc., Roslyn, N.Y., 1969-75; comptroller Am. Bus. & Profl. Program, Inc., Manhasset, N.Y., 1975—; sec.-treas. Arrandale Mgmt. Co., N. Shore Mgmt. Co., Roslyn Cons. Ltd., Melville Equities, Ltd., 1975—; mng. gen. partner Pueblo Sq. Assos., Manhasset, 1978—. Office: 1205 Northern Blvd Manhasset NY 11030

KEESEE, HELEN LEE, retail drug store chain executive; b. Beaumont, Tex., June 26, 1963; d. Raymond E. and Billie Ruth (Williams) K. Student pub. schs. Courtesy clk. Frey's Thriftway, Salem, Oreg., 1978-80; cashier, clk. Skillerns-Revco, Round Rock, Tex., 1980-81; mgr. Revco D.S., Inc., Round Rock, 1981-83, regional trainer, Austin, Tex., 1983—. Mem. Nat. Assn. Female Execs. Democrat. Methodist. Home: Apt 506 512 Eberhart Ln Austin TX 78745 Office: Revco D S Inc 5232 Burnet Rd Austin TX 78745

KEGGEREIS, NORMA JEAN, educator, musician, composer, arranger; b. Dallas, July 20, 1942; d. Marvin Ray and Rhonda Ruth (Mayo) Taylor; m. Everett Paul Keggereis; children—David Gene Mitchell, Merle Wayne Mitchell. Cert. in piano pedagogy Mus. Arts Conservatory, Amarillo, Tex., 1972. Pvt. educator piano, organ, Dallas, 1969—; accompanist Weekly Gospel TV Program, Dallas, 1968-71; co-owner, dir. pre-schs. kindergarten, elem. and secondary Schs., Dallas, 1977—. Composer: This The Way, 1971, One Day At A Time, 1973, My Best Friend, 1974, I Don't Mind...So It Don't Matter, 1975 and others. Music counselor, instl. rep. Dist. Circle 10 council Boy Scouts Am., 1973-77; tchr. adult Theory Classes; dir. Childrens' Choirs; ch. organist Lochwood Baptist Ch., Dallas, 1980-81, Orchard Hills Bapt. Ch., Garland, Tex. 1967-79; evangelistic pianist, organist, Profl. Ch., Dallas, 1952—. Mem. Dallas Dunning Piano Tchrs. Assn. (pres. 1973-78), Nat. Dunning Piano Tchrs Assn. Nat. Coll. Musicians (honor roll tchr.), Nat. Guild Piano Tchrs., Organ and Piano Tchrs. Assn., Tex. Fedn. Music Clubs (Tex. composers guild), Tex. Bapt. Evangelist Assn., Nat. Bapt. Evangelist Assn. Home: 6802 La Costa Rowlett TX 75088 Office: 9889 Ferguson Rd Dallas TX 75228

KEHOE, ALICE BECK, anthropologist, educator; b. N.Y.C., Sept. 18, 1934; d. Roman and Lena (Rosenstock) Beck; m. Thomas Francis Kehoe, Sept. 18, 1956; children—Daniel Miles, Thomas David, Cormac Joel. B.A., Barnard Coll., 1956; Ph.D., Harvard U., 1964. Asst. curator Mus. Plains Indian, Browning, Mont., 1956-58; lectr. U. Sask., Regina, 1964-65; asst. prof. U. Nebr., Lincoln, 1965-68; prof. anthropology Marquette U., Milw., 1968—. Author: North American Indians, 1981. Contbr. articles to profl. jours. Wenner-Gren Found. fellow, 1984. Fellow Am. Anthropol. Assn. (exec. bd. 1979-82); mem. Soc. Am. Archaeology (pub. relations com. 1985—), Archaeol. Inst. Am. (chpt. pres. 1985-86), Am. Ethnological Soc., Nat. Ctr. Sci. Edn. (co-chair Wis. com. corr. 1984—). Jewish. Avocations: bicycling; hiking. Home: 3014 N Shepard Ave Milwaukee WI 53211 Office: Marquette U Milwaukee WI 53233

KEHOE, PAMELA ANNE, association administrator; b. Niagara Falls, N.Y., Nov. 27, 1952; d. Richard Henry Kehoe and Betta Jane (Harrington) Kehoe Gelfand. Assoc. Liberal Arts, Niagara County Community Coll., 1972; B.A., U. Dayton, 1974; postgrad. U. Buffalo, 1975-76, Niagara U., 1982-83. Tech. asst., tng. coordinator Niagara County Employment and Tng., Lockport, N.Y., 1974-78; planning mgr. Niagara County Employment and Tng., Lockport, 1978-79, dep. dir., 1979-81; asst. exec. dir. Health Assn. Niagara County, Inc., Niagara Falls, N.Y., 1981—; mem. adv. council Human Resources Inst., U. Buffalo, 1978-81; advisor Performance Standards Task Force, U.S. Dept. Labor, Washington, 1980-81; trainer, advisor U.S. Dept. Labor, N.Y.C., 1978-80; adv. Jr. Achievement Buffalo, 1983-86. Vol., ARC, Niagara Falls, N.Y., 1977-80; bd. dirs., mem. personnel com. Niagara County council Girl Scouts; vol. Skating Assn. for Blind and Handicapped. Mem. Am. Soc. Personnel Adminstrn., Employee Benefits Conf., U. Dayton Alumni (support com. Buffalo 1981—). Democrat. Roman Catholic. Home: 367 Linwood Ave No 2 Buffalo NY 14209 Office: Health Assn Niagara County Inc 1302 Main St Niagara Falls NY 14301

KEIDEL, HELEN MARGARET (PEGGY), home health agency executive; b. N.Y.C., Oct. 1, 1926; d. Sidney Graham and Helen (Mar-Nale) Kelvington; student NYU, 1944, Mt. San Antonio Coll., 1961-62; m. Norman William Keidel, Oct. 20, 1951; 1 child, Leslie Ann Keidel-Young. Editor, Gt. Neck (N.Y.) Record, 1945-47, Flushing Sunday Times and Bayside Times, 1947-48, Kirby Publs. and Manga Pub. Co., 1949-51; producer Big Joe's Happiness Exchange, radio and TV, 1951-52; bus. mgr. Vis. Nurses Assn. East San Gabriel Valley, Covina, Calif., 1966-70, asst. adminstr., 1970-75, exec. dir., 1975-86; cons. on fiscal mgmt. to home health industry, 1976—. Pres., Aux. Inter-Community Hosp., 1962-63; trustee Inter-Community Hosp., Covina, 1972-81, mem. exec. com., 1979-81; bd. dirs. Inter-Community Hosp. Found., 1970-76; founder Hospice of the East San Gabriel Valley. Mem. Nat. Assn. Home Care, Nat. Hospice Orgn., Calif. Assn. Health Services at Home (dir. 1971-79, treas. 1973-75, v.p. 1977-79), Coalition of Visiting Nurse Assns./Services of So. Calif. (founding pres. 1983-84, pres. 1984-85), Am. Affliation of Visting Nurse Assns./Services (bd. dirs. 1984-85; treas. 1985), Covina C. of C., West Covina C. of C. Episcopalian. Office: 420 S Grand Covina CA 91724

KEIFER, MARY CARTER, law educator; b. Charlottsville, Va., Sept. 21, 1946; d. Carter Lewis and Anne Harrison (Crathorne) Loth; m. John Louis Keifer, Aug. 29, 1970; children—Marcy, Lisa, Kate, Kristin. A.B. in Math., Converse Coll., 1968; J.D., U. Va., 1971. Bar: Ohio 1971, U.S. Dist. Ct. 1974. Staff atty. Toledo Legal Aid Soc., 1971-74; asst. prof. bus. law Ohio U., Athens, 1974—. Contbr. papers to legal procs. Mem. Athens City Recreation Bd., 1978-83, pres., 1980; mem. Athens City Bd. Edn., 1978—, pres., 1984; officer Athens Coop. Nursery Bd., 1975-77; bd. dirs. Athens Swim Club. Mem. Ohio State Bar Assn., Tri-State Bus. Law Assn. (treas. 1986-87), Athens City Bar Assn. Presbyterian. Club: Athens Jr. Women's. Avocations: reading; lap swimming. Home: 201 Longview Heights Athens OH 45701 Office: Ohio U 216 Copeland Hall Athens OH 45701

KEISER, KAREN LYNNE, association executive; b. Dayton, June 29, 1960; d. Charles William and Doris Eloise (Preston) Keiser. B.A., Oglethorpe U., Atlanta, 1983. Asst. mgr. Proving Ground, Atlanta, 1981-83; program coordinator Muscular Dystrophy Assn., Atlanta, 1983-85, dist. dir., Palm Beach, Fla., 1985—. Author, editor: MDA Monthly News, 1985-86. Recipient Oglethorpe award Student Govt. Assn., 1982. Mem. Am. Mktg. Assn., Nat. Bus. Assn. Female Execs., Jr. C. of C. Republican. Roman Catholic. Club: Palm Beach Runners. Avocations: running; outdoor sports; horseback riding. Home: 641 Exec Ctr Dr 108 West Palm Beach FL 33401

KEISS, SISTER ISABELLE, college president; b. N.Y.C., Dec. 11, 1931; d. Walter and Sara (Boyle) K.; B.A., Villanova U., 1960; M.A., Cath. U., 1966; Ph.D., Notre Dame U., 1972; postgrad. Harvard U. Grad. Sch. Edn., 1972. Joined Religious Sisters of Mercy, 1952; tchr. English, Bishop Egan High Sch., Levittown, Pa., 1960-63; chmn. English dept. Walsingham Acad., Williamsburg, Va., 1963-65; teaching asst. U. Notre Dame (Ind.), 1967-71; pres. Gwynedd-Mercy Coll., Gwynedd Valley, Pa., 1971—; mem. com. on personnel affairs Pa. Assn. Colls. and Univs., 1975—, chmn., 1978; mem. instl. survey com. Commn. Ind. Colls. and Univs., 1976-79, chmn., 1977, mem. exec. com., 1977-80, mem. adv. bd. Nat. Cons. Network, Council Advancement Small Colls., 1976-80; mem. exec. com. Found. Ind. Colls. Pa., 1978-81; mem. exec. com. Conf. Small Pvt. Colls., 1978—; bd. dirs. Compact for Lifelong Ednl. Opportunities, 1982—. Bd. dirs. Mercy Cath. Med. Center, 1975—, Coll. Misericordia, 1979—. Recipient award Rotary Club, 1980. Home and Office: Gwynedd-Mercy Coll Gwynedd Valley PA 19437

KEITH, CAMILLE TIGERT, airlines public relations executive; b. Ft. Worth, Feb. 27, 1945; d. Marvin and Catherine (Tuscany) K. B.A., Tex. Christian U., 1967. Asst. promotion mgr. Sta. WFAA-TV, Dallas, 1967-71; dir. publicity Read-Poland, Inc., Dallas, 1971-72; pub. relations promotion dir. SW Airlines, Dallas, 1972—, asst. v.p., 1976-78, v.p. pub. relations, 1978—, now v.p. splty. mktg. Recipient excellence in pub. relations award Women in Communications, 1973; Most Valuable Mem., Dallas Advt. League, 1983; one of 10 "Rising Stars of Texas", Tex. Bus. Mag., 1984. Mem. DAR, children Am. Revolution (state officer 1960-67, sr. state officer 1967—), Freedom Found., 500 Inc., Exec. Women Dallas (bd. dirs.), Women in Communications, Dallas Advt. League (past pres.), Dallas Press Club. Mem. Christian Ch. (Sunday Sch. tchr. 1967—). Home: 3257 Lancelot Dallas TX 75229 Office: 8008 Aviation Pl Dallas TX 75235

KEITH, ELIZABETH MILLER, civic worker; b. Wayne, Pa., July 23, 1911; d. Edgar T. and Norah (Schweyer) Miller; grad. Baldwin Sch., 1930; B.A., Vassar Coll., 1934; postgrad. Maria Ouspenskaya Sch. Acting, 1934-36; cert. N.Y. Sch. Design, 1972; m. George R. Vila, Oct. 4, 1941 (div. Feb. 1970); children—John Desmond, Richard Lawrence; m. 2d, Percival Cleveland Keith, Jan. 17, 1976 (dec. July 1976). Actress, Essex (N.Y.) Summer Theatre, 1937, Barter Theatre, Abingdon, N.Y., 1938-39, Drove Players, Greenwich Village, N.Y.C., 1939-41, Canton Workshop (Conn.), 1941, Woonsocket (R.I.) Theatre, 1940. Nurse's aide ARC, Waterbury Hosp., 1942-48; chmn. Planned Parenthood; pres. Woodbury (Conn.) PTA, 1951-53; mem. Citizens Com. to Evaluate Pub. Sch. and Tchr. Tng., 1954; mem. restoration com. Wallace House, Somerville, N.J., 1966-68; chmn. decorating, seminar coms. Wykeham Rise Sch. Festival, 1972-73, mem. public relations com.; edn. chmn. N.Y. Bryant Park Flower Show, 1976-77, 77-78; bd. dirs. Vis. Nurse Assn., Somerset Hills, N.J., 1962-68, Washington, Conn., 1972-74; trustee Gunnery Sch., Washington, Conn., 1973-76, Wykeham Rise Sch., 1982—. Episcopalian (vestry 1973-76). Clubs: Garden of Am. (hort. zone rep. 1974-76, flower show zone rep. 1978-80, nat. flower show chmn. 1980-82, dir. 1982-84), Somerset Hills Garden (historian 1967-69); Vassar, Cosmopolitan (N.Y.C.); Washington (Conn.) Garden (hort. chmn. 1971-73, program chmn. 1973-75, vis. garden chmn. 1978-79, v.p. 1982-83); Washington (Washington). Home: Meadow Wind Washington Depot CT 06794

KEITH, GINNI, orchestra manager; b. Seattle, Oct. 1, 1949; d. George Dunlap and Elizabeth Emma (Patz) Paynton; B.A., U. Wash., 1973, B.Mus. cum laude, 1973; m. David Keith, July 5, 1972. Mgr., dir. devel. Los Angeles Mozart Orch., Los Angeles, 1975—; mem. London Symphony Orch. Chorus, 1973-74, Roger Wagner Chorale, 1975-77, Los Angeles Master Chorale, 1975-77. Mem. Phi Beta Kappa. Clubs: Am. Fedn. Aviculture, Nat. Wildlife Fedn.

KEKICH, BARBARA, lawyer; b. Pitts., Jan. 2, 1948; d. Marcus Stephen and Marie Eunice (Blank) Kekich; m. Joseph Forman, Nov. 12, 1978. B.A., Carlow Coll., 1969; J.D., Southwestern U., 1978. Bar: Calif. 1978, U.S. Dist. Ct. (cen. dist.) Calif. 1979. Atty., ptnr. King & Williams, Los Angeles, 1978—; judge protem small claims div. Los Angeles Mcpl. Ct. Bd. dirs. San Fernando Valley Ednl. Center, Canoga Park, Calif., 1979-83. Mem. ABA, Calif. Women Lawyers, Assn. So. Calif. Def. Counsel. Home: 10340 Calvin Ave Los Angeles CA 90025 Office: King and Williams 1875 Century Park East 8th Floor Los Angeles CA 90067

KELEHEAR, CAROLE MARCHBANKS SPANN, legal assistant; b. Morehead City, N.C., Oct. 2, 1945; d. William Blythe and Gladys Ophelia (Wilson) Marchbanks; m. Henry M. Spann June 5, 1966 (div. 1978); children—Lisa Carole, Elaine Mabry; m. Zachariah L. Kelehear, Sept. 15, 1985. Ed. Winthrop Coll., 1964, Draughon's Bus. Coll., 1965; cert. med. terminology, Greenville Tech. Coll., 1972. Office mgr. S.C. Appalachian Advt., Com., Greenville, 1964-68; office mgr. Wood-Bergheer & Co., Newport Beach, Calif., 1970-72; exec. sec. Lathem & McCoy, Greenville, 1972-75; legal asst. McNair Firm, Columbia, S.C., 1975-77; office mgr. Dr. James B. Knowles, Greenville, 1977-78, Constangy, Brooks & Smith, Columbia, 1978-83; legal asst. Bethea, Jordan & Griffin, Hilton Head Island, S.C., 1983—. Mem. Am. Bus. Women's Assn., Profl. Women of Hilton Head Island, Nat. Assn. Female Execs., Am. Soc. Notaries, Beta Sigma Phi. Democrat. Presbyterian. Club: Hilton Head Hosp. Aux. Avocations: reading; puzzle-working; cooking; horticulture. Home: PO Box 1174 Hilton Head Island SC 29925 Office: Bethea Jordan & Griffin PA PO Box 5666 Hilton Head Island SC 29938

KELL, CARLA SUE, publishing consultant; b. Highland Park, Mich., Sept. 15, 1952; d. Carl William and Margie May (Cannon) Bodner; m. Joseph Mark Kell, Oct. 10, 1971 (div. Dec. 1980). Student, Anderson Coll., 1970-71, Glendale Coll., 1976-77, Ariz. State U., 1978-79, Mesa Coll., 1979-80. Private tutor English, Federal Republic of Germany, 1971-74; office mgr. Bell & Schore, Rochester, Mich., 1974-75, COL Press, Phoenix, 1978-80; publicity mgr. O'Sullivan Woodside & Col, Phoenix, 1980-81, gen. mgr., 1982-84; pub. relations/promotion cons. GP1 Publs., Cupertino, Calif., 1985; pub. cons., 1985—; account coordinator Bernard Hodes Advt., Tempe, Ariz., 1981; cons. freelance mktg., Phoenix, 1983. Vol., Fiesta Bowl Parade Com., Phoenix, 1983. Home: 3155 Frontera Way #100 Burlingame CA 94010

KELL, CHRISTA BARBARA, educator, nurse; b. New Haven, June 26, 1949; d. Elmer E. and Hannelore (Bareis) Hallinger; m. John Z. Kell, Apr. 1, 1983; 1 child, John Z. 3d. B.S. in Nursing, U. Calif., San Francisco, 1972, M.S., 1973; counseling credential Calif. State U., 1975. Nursing supr., inservice edn. coordinator dept. psychiatry Highland Hosp., Oakland, Calif., 1973-75; health educator, sch. nurse Miramonte High Sch., Orinda, Calif., 1975-78; mental health cons. Center for Human Devel., Lafayette, Calif., 1978-79; instr. psychiatric nursing Samuel Merritt Coll. Nursing, Merritt Hosp., Oakland, 1979-81, coordinator acad. advisement, community relations, 1981-85, assoc. dean student services, 1986—. NIMH grantee, 1972-73. Mem. Nat. League Nursing, Psychiat.-Mental Health Nursing Interest Group, Sigma Theta Tau. Contbr. author: Tribes 1979. Office: Samuel Merritt Coll of Nursing Hawthorne and Webster Sts Oakland CA 94609

KELLAM, SANDRA, occupational therapist; b. Saginaw, Mich., May 14, 1940; d. I. Lee and Charlotte (O'Neall) Kellam; children—Scott, Richard, Piet. A.A., Stephens Coll., 1960; B.S., Coll. of William and Mary, 1962. Occupational therapist Met. Hosp., N.Y.C., 1963-65, Gen. Hosp. of Monterey County, Salinas, Calif., 1965-66; supr. occupational therapy Grant-Cuesta Hosp., Mountain View, Calif., 1968-71; dir. occupational therapy services Kennebec County Regional Health Agy., Waterville, Maine, 1976-82; occupational therapist Eastern Shore Regional Ednl. Continuum, Accomac, Va., 1982—; cons. in field. Chmn. For a Safe Park, Rangeley, Maine, 1973, Citizens for Longley for Gov., Rangeley, 1974; field worker Cohen for Senate, Maine, 1978; organizer Citizens for Responsible Govt., Dresden, 1980. Recipient cert. Merit

Occupational Therapy Club. Mem. Am. Occupational Therapy Assn., World Fedn. Occupational Therapists, Orthotics Unltd. (v.p. 1979-80). Republican. Presbyterian. Clubs: Subron Officers Wives (pres. 1967-68) (Rota, Spain); Skiers Anonymous (v.p. 1973-74) (Rangeley).

KELLEHER, DIANA LEE, vitamin company executive; b. Phila., July 9, 1947; LeeRoy and Margaret (Hopkins Hey) McKean; m. Gregory Kelleher, Feb. 9, 1968 (div. 1978). B.S., Drexel U., 1969; M.B.A., U. Chgo., 1975. With McKinsey & Co., Chgo., 1970-75; mgr. mdse. group forcasts and tech. service Sears Roebuck, Chgo., 1975-77; assoc. div. mktg. planning and mktg. mgr. Kitchens of Sara Lee div. Consol. Foods, Chgo., 1977-80; mktg. mgr. E&J Gallo Winery, Modesto, Calif., 1980-82; dir. mktg. Pharmavite Corp., Arleta, Calif., 1982, v.p. mktg., 1982—. Tchr., Jr. Achievement, 1983. Mem. AAUW. Office: Pharmavite Corp 12801 Wentworth St Arleta CA 91331

KELLEHER, ELIZABETH LUCY, human resources executive; b. N.Y.C., Apr. 25, 1933; d. John Thomas and Lucy Veronica (Maguire) Kelleher. B.S. magna cum laude, NYU, 1954, M.B.A., 1966; Indsl. Gerontology cert. The New Sch. Social Research, N.Y.C., 1983. Personnel asst. S.H. Kress & Co., N.Y.C., 1954-60, Carter-Wallace, Inc., N.Y.C., 1960-66; compensation analyst Cresap, McCormick & Paget, N.Y.C., 1966-70; with internat. div. Mobil Oil Corp., N.Y.C., 1971—, compensation and benefits coordinator, 1971-72, mgr. policy devel., 1972-74, mgr. personnel services, 1974-75, employee relations field cons. stationed in S.E. Asia, Nigeria, U.K., 1975-77, mgr. employee relations planning and research, 1977-78, dep. mgr. human resource devel., 1978-84, mgr. human resources, 1984—; adj. faculty NYU, 1982-86; lectr. in field. Bd. dirs. Any Place Theatre, Inc., 1984-85. Mem. Am. Soc. Personnel Adminstrn., Am. Soc. Personnel Adminstrn. Internat. (bd. dirs., chairperson publicity com. 1981), Beta Gamma Sigma. Home: 345 E 73d St New York NY 10021 Office: Mobil Oil Corp 19W904 150 E 42d St New York NY 10017

KELLEHER, KATHLEEN, ins. mktg. specialist; b. Suffern, N.Y., May 3, 1951; d. John James and Carol (Re) K.; B.A., Fairleigh Dickinson U., 1973. C.L.U. Ins. sales adminstr. Blyth Eastman Dillon & Co., 1977-79; product mktg. asso. Dean Witter Reynolds, N.Y.C., 1980-82; mgr. product mktg. annuities and ins. dept. Kidder, Peabody & Co., 1982-85; v.p. ins. sales Paine Webber, N.Y.C., 1985—. Mem. Am. Mgmt. Assn., Am. Soc. C.L.U.s. Internat. Platform Assn. Republican. Club: Coll. of Ridgewood. Home: 321 Mill Rd Saddle River NJ 07458 Office: Paine Webber 1285 Ave of Americas New York NY 10019

KELLER, FRANCES RICHARDSON, history educator; b. Lowville, N.Y., Aug. 14, 1914; d. Stephen Brown and Sarah Eliza (Bell) Richardson; m. Chauncey A.R. Keller, June 20, 1936 (div. 1964); children—Reynolds, Stephen, Julia, William; m. William P. Rhetta, May 10, 1969. B.A., Sarah Lawrence Coll.; M.A., U. Toledo; Ph.D., U. Chgo., 1973. Lectr., U. Ind.-Gary, 1966-67, U. Ill.-Chgo., 1967-68, Chgo. City Coll., 1968-70, Centre Inter. Universitaire, Paris, 1970-71, U. Calif.-Berkeley Extension, 1972-74, San Jose (Calif.) State U., 1974-78; adj. prof. history San Francisco State U., 1978—; panelist, reader NEH, 1978, 79, 81. Author: An American Crusade: The Life of Charles Waddell Chesnutt, 1978; editor, contbr.: The Struggles of Eve; translator, editor: Slavery and the French Revolutionists (Anna Julia Cooper), Mem. Nat. Women's Studies Assn. (chair publicity and pub. relations, founding conv. 1976, ofcl. historian 1978), Western Assn. Women Historians (program chair 1979, pres. 1981-83), Am. Hist. Assn. (nominating com. 1983—), Orgn. Am. Historians, Coordinating Council of Women in Hist. Profession, Western Soc. French History. Home: 835 Junipero Serra Blvd San Francisco CA 94127 Office: San Francisco State U Dept History San Francisco CA 94132

KELLER, GLENDA KAY, corporation executive; b. Harrisonville, Mo., Feb. 27, 1951; d. Glyndon Ritner and Shirley Ann (Wills) Divelbiss; div. 1982; children—Anne Elizabeth, Bryan Robert. B.A. in Polit. Sci., U. Mo., 1973, M.A. in Edn., 1976. Instr. U.S. Army/Tex. Coll., Kaiserslautern, Germany, 1977-79; mktg. com. specialist Honeywell Inc., Los Angeles, 1980-81, mgr. mktg. services, 1981-83, mgr. venture programs, 1983; mgr. market analysis and research, strategic planning computervision, Bedford, Mass., 1984-85, cons. Bain and Co., Boston. Dir. County Up with People (Music), Harrisonville, Mo., 1970-71; recruiter of instrs. Glenkirk Reaching Out to Women, Glendora, Calif., 1979-80; researcher Durenberger for U.S. Senate Campaign, Bloomington, Minn., 1982; bd. dirs. Sylmar Chamber Orch., Mpls., 1983—. Recipient Leadership award Mpls. YWCA, 1981; Individual Recognition award Honeywell, 1980, 81; U. Mo. Regents scholar, 1968; U. Mo. oboe performance scholar, 1968; named Outstanding Young Woman of Am., 1981. Mem. N.Am. Corporate Planning Soc., Assn. Devel. Computer Based Instructional Systems, Nat. Honor Soc.

KELLER, JOYCE GARVER, association executive, author; b. Cleve. Sept. 28, 1947; d. John H. and Zelda (Gershowitz) Garver; m. Steven Ray Keller, 1967; 1 child, Stuart Alan. Assoc. dir. ACLU of Ohio, 1972-78; polit. campaign cons., Columbus, Ohio, 1978-80; ops. supr. U.S. Census Bur., Columbus, 1980; exec. dir. Ohio Women, Inc., Columbus, 1980-82, People for the Am. Way, Columbus, 1982-85; dir. ops. Health Power of Columbus, Inc., 1986—; cons. various univs. Contbr. articles to profl. jours. and mags. Creative cons. TV documentary "Focus:Censorship", 1983 (Ohio State Bar Assn. Media award 1985). Bd. dirs. Alliance for Coop. Justice, Columbus, 1977-80, Ohio Hunger Task Force, Columbus, 1981-84, Columbus Area Women's Polit. Caucus, 1978-82; selection com. Ohio Women's Hall of Fame, Columbus, 1983; adv. Ohio Tchr. Edn. and Cert., Ohio Dept. Edn., 1984. Recipient Community Service award Ohio Ho. of Reps., 1982, City of Columbus and Franklin County, 1978, Civil Liberties award ACLU of Ohio Found., 1983. Mem. Nat. Assn. Female Execs., Nat. Women's Polit. Caucus (nat. site selection com.), Columbus Bus. and Profl. Women's Club. Democrat. Jewish. Office: Health Power of Coumbus Inc 1320 Parsons Ave Columbus OH 43206

KELLER, KAREN MARIE, army officer, nurse, educator; b. Bloomington, Ind., Oct. 15, 1952; d. Robert R. and Theresa (Hessig) McEllhiney; 1 dau., Stephanie Patricia; m. 2d, Lucien Fairfax Keller, Jr., Oct. 23, 1982. B.S. in Nursing, U. Evansville, 1975. Commd. 1st lt. U.S. Army Nursing Corps, 1975, advanced through grades to maj. 1977; staff nurse Fort Sill, Okla., 1975-76, 121st Evac. Hosp., Seoul, Korea, 1976-78; nurse instr. Acad. Health Scis., San Antonio, 1978-81, dep. dir. satellite TV program, 1981-83; practical nurse instr. Madigan Army Med. Ctr., Tacoma, Wash., 1983-85; exec. officer Med. Mobile Tng. Team, U.S. Mil. Mission, Liberia, West Africa, 1985; head nurse surg. ward Madigan Army Med. Ctr., 1985—. Author, editor instrnl. video tapes for U.S. Army, 1981-83. Decorated Army Commendation medals, 1978, 82, 85. Mem. Emergency Dept. Nurses Assn., Assn. Fed. Nurses (pres.), Am. Nurses Assn., Nat. League Nursing, 38th Parallel Nurses Assn. Republican. Baptist. Lodge: Order of the Eastern Star (Masons). Home: 8702 45 St West Tacoma WA 98466 Office: Madigan Army Medical Ctr Tacoma WA 98431

KELLER, MARGARET GILMER (MRS. GEORGE HENRY KELLER III), English language educator; b. Harrisburg, Pa., July 11, 1911; d. Charles Greenwalt Gilmer and Mary Ellen (Sullivan) Gilmer; A.B., Trinity Coll., 1933; A.M., Columbia U., 1934, cert., 1942; cert. State Tchrs. Coll., Bloomsburg, Pa., 1934; m. George Henry Keller, III, July 13, 1940; children—Mary Ellen, Margaret Marie, George Henry, IV. Acting chmn. dept. history Trinity Coll., Washington, 1935-36; chmn. classical dept. Convent Sacred Heart, 1936-37, Steelton (Pa.) High Sch., 1937-41; adj. prof. English dept. Univ. Coll., Rutgers U., 1946—, mem. dean's adv. com. Univ. Coll., 1968—, also advisor to women's clubs Univ. Coll.; chmn. classical dept. Glen Rock (N.J.) High Sch., 1956-59, chmn. fgn. lang. dept., 1959—; curriculum cons. Glen Rock Sch. Dist., 1980—. Mem. Sch.-Community Adv. Com. to Ridgewood (N.J.) Public Sch., 1956—, TV adv. bd., 1955—; active Am. Cancer Soc., United Fund, ARC, Girl Scouts U.S.A.; mem. nominating bd. Ridgewood Nursing Service, 1959-60; chmn. Trinity Coll. Devel. Fund Drive N.J.; trustee Trinity Coll., 1963-67, 74—81, life trustee, 1981, nat. chmn. 75th anniversary fund, 1975-76; committeewoman Republican County Com. Cited by Rutgers U., 1953, 61, 64, 65, 66, 71, 82, for disting. service to student activities, 1978, named to coll. honor soc., 1982; cited by Newman Province of N.J., 1963; recipient Robert Ax award for disting. teaching, 1971; Outstanding Educator award Jr. C. of C., 1973; Alumnae Service award Trinity Coll., 1977; citation Middle States Assn. Colls., 1979; U.S. Presdl. Achievement award, 1982; Pres.'s medal Trinity Coll., 1982; Henry Browne award Univ. Coll., Rutgers U., 1982, Faculty Adviser award, 1985; others. Mem. NEA, N.J. Edn. Assn., Am. Classical Soc., AAUW (past dir.), MLA, Chaplain's Aid Assn., Trinity Coll., Alumnae Assn. (nat. pres. 1963-67), Phi Chi Theta. Clubs: Newman (adv. Rutgers U.), Univ. Coll. Women (hon. Rutgers U.). Home: 200 Phelps Rd Ridgewood NJ 07450 Office: Rutgers U New Brunswick NJ 08903

KELLER, VESTA CHARLOTTE DERICKSON, nurse, family counselor, Reiki healer; b. Elam, Pa., June 1, 1930; d. Joseph Springer and Viola (Webster) Derickson; m. Lindberg Grant Keller, Feb. 14, 1958 (dec. Feb. 1977); children—Athena Dawn, David Grant. R.N., Wilmington Gen. Sch. Sch. Nursing, 1953; B.S. in Nursing, U. Pa., 1957; M.S. in Counseling, U. Del., 1979; Reiki healing I and II degree, 1983. Cert. in Silva Mind Control, 1982, therapeutic hypnosis, 1982; cert. to practice Mari-El Healing of complete body, mind and spirit, 1983. Operating room instr. Wilmington Gen. Hosp., 1953-55; instr. nursing arts and scis. Wilmington Gen. Hosp. Sch. Nursing, 1956-58; operating room asst. supr. Kent Gen. Hosp., Dover, Del., 1958-65; pvt. duty nurse, 1966-74; family counselor, counselor cons., Wilmington, 1977—; founder Pathways into Light ctr., Ashland, Ky., 1985—; Reiki healer, 1983—. Illustrator book: Purple Sammy, 1972. Contbr. to mags., Clover Collection of Verse, Vol. VII, 1974. Mem. Am. Personnel and Guidance Assn., Am. Assn. Sex Educators Counselors and Therapists, Edgar Caycey's Assn. Research & Enlightenment, Am. Mental Health Counseling Assn., Am. Holistic Nurses Assn., Am. Nurses Assn., Nat. League Nursing, Mayan Order, Rosicrucian Order. Methodist. Address: 5533 Don Dr Summit Ashland KY 41101

KELLERMAN, SALLY CLAIRE, actress; b. Long Beach, Calif., June 2, 1937; d. John Helm and Edith Baine (Vaughn) K.; student Los Angeles City Coll., Actor's Studio, N.Y.C.; m. Richard Edelstein, Dec. 19, 1970; 4 step-daus.; m. 2d, Jonathan Krane, 1980. Stage appearances include Breakfast at Tiffany's, Singular Man, N.Y.C.; films include MASH, Brewster McCloud, Last of the Red Hot Lovers, Reflection of Fear, Slither, Lost Horizon, Rafferty and the Gold Dust Twins, The Big Bus, The Boston Strangler, The April Fools, Welcome to L.A., A Little Romance, 1979, Foxes, Head On, Loving Couples, Serial; also TV roles Mannix, It Takes a Thief, Crysler Theatre; TV film Verna; USO Girl, 1978. Nominee Acad. and Golden Globe awards for MASH. Mem. Actor's Equity, AFTRA. Office: care Creative Artists Agy 1888 Century Park E Suite 1400 Los Angeles CA 90067*

KELLERS, KATHLEEN MARIE, federal government postal administrator; b. Jersey City, Jan. 19, 1956; d. Edward Vincent and Maria Joyce (Mehok) Keegan; m. Timothy Robert Kellers, Sr., Oct. 3, 1981; 1 child, Timothy Robert, Jr. B.A., Rutgers Coll., 1978. Letter carrier U.S. Postal Service, Toms River, N.J., 1978-83; supt. postal ops., Brielle, N.J., 1983—, dist. safety instr., Cherry Hill, N.J., 1985, officer in charge, Sea Girt, N.J., 1985. Recipient cert. appreciation Delaware Valley Dist. U.S. Postal Service, 1985. Mem. Nat. Assn. Letter Carriers, Nat. Assn. Postal Suprs. Roman Catholic. Avocations: reading; needlework; gardening. Home: PO Box 391 Brielle NJ 08730 Office: US Postal Service 412 Higgins Ave Brielle NJ 08730

KELLEY, DELORES GOODWIN, college dean; b. Norfolk, Va., May 1, 1936; d. Stephen Cornelius and Helen (Jefferson) Goodwin; B.A., Va. State U., 1956; M.A., N.Y.U., 1958, Purdue U., 1972; Ph.D., U. Md., 1977; m. Russell Victor Kelley, Dec. 26, 1956; children—Norma Delores, Russell Victor, III, Brian Todd. Instr. English, Morgan State Coll., Balt., 1966-70; grad. teaching fellow Purdue U., 1970-72; chmn. dept. lang., lit. and philosophy Coppin State Coll., Balt., 1976-79, dean lower div., 1979—; panelist, reviewer NEH; mem. Md. Dept. Edn. evaluation com. for Hood Coll., 1978—, Md. Commn. Values Edn., 1980—; dir. Harbor Bank Md., Balt., 1980—; chmn. Adv. Council Gifted and Talented Edn. Balt. City Schs., 1980—. Mem. Mayor Balt. Adv. Council Mental Health, 1981-84; elected to Dem. Central Com. from 42d legis. dist. Md., 1982-86; v.p. Cross Country Improvement Assn., 1980-82. Grantee Md. Com. Humanities and Public Policy, 1977; fellow Am. Coll. on Edn., 1982-83. Mem. Nat. Assn. Women Deans, Adminstrs. and Counselors, Nat. Council Tchrs. English, Md. Collegiate Honors Council (sec.-treas. 1981-82), Md. Assn. Higher Edn., Alpha Kappa Mu, Alpha Kappa Alpha. Lutheran. Home: 3400 Olympia Ave Baltimore MD 21215 Office: 2500 W North Ave Baltimore MD 21216

KELLEY, KATHRYN, psychologist, educator; b. Tulsa; d. Lawrence J. and Johnnie A. Kelley; married; 1 child, Lindsey. B.A. in Psychology, U. Okla.; M.S. in Social-Personality Psychology, Purdue U., Ph.D. in Psychology. Asst. prof. psychology Marquette U., Milw., 1977-78, U. Wis.-Milw., 1978-79; asst. prof. psychology SUNY-Albany, 1979-85, assoc. prof., 1985—. Author: Females, Males, and Sexuality, 1986; Alternative Approaches to the Study of Sexual Behavior, 1986. Bur. Indian Affairs higher edn. fellow, 1974-77. Mem. Am. Psychol. Assn., Eastern Psychol. Assn., Soc. Sci. Study of Sex. Office: Social Sci Dept Psychology SUNY Albany NY 12222

KELLEY, KAY FRANCES, navy officer, nurse; b. Portland, Maine, Oct. 20, 1945; d. John Wesley and Marie E. (Spaulding) Gearhart; children—Erin Michele, Eric Michael. A.A., U. Nev.-Las Vegas, 1973, B.S., 1976. Joined Nurse Corps, U.S. Navy, 1965, commd., 1976, advanced through grades to lt., 1981; staff nurse Sunrise Hosp., Las Vegas, 1970-74, Valley Hosp., Las Vegas, 1974-79, Naval Air Sta., Corpus Christi, Tex., 1979-82, Naval Air Sta. Jacksonville, Fla., 1982-86, Naval Hosp., Bethesda, Md., 1986—. Co-author: Intravenous Manual, 1982. Pres., organizer Am. Assn. IV Therapy, 1975. Lutheran. Avocations: cross stitch; gardening; collecting nurse dolls. Home: 9702 Mount Pisgah Rd #202 Silver Springs MD 20903 Office: Naval Med Command Nat Capital Region Bethesda MD 20814

KELLEY, MARIE ELAINE, educational administrator; b. St. Johns, Mich., Feb. 6, 1941; d. Berl Louis and Doris Louise (Tait) Foerch; B.A. (Mich. Bd. Edn. scholar), Central Mich. U., 1963; M.A., Mich. State U., 1965, Ph.D. (Grad. Faculty scholar), 1973; Ed.S., U. Nebr., Lincoln, 1976; m. Edgar Alan Kelley, Aug. 10, 1963; 1 son, Wesley Lynn. Tchr., Ovid Elsie (Mich.) Area Schs., 1963-67, Colon (Mich.) Community Schs., 1967-68, Lincoln (Nebr.) Public Schs., 1970-78; asst. prin. instrn. Lincoln East-Jr. Sr. High Sch., 1978-85 ; prin. Caledonia J. High Sch., Mich., 1985—; vis. prof. U. Nebr., Lincoln, 1976, 77, 80, 81; originator, 1st dir. Lincoln Writing Lab., 1975-78. Mem. Nat. Assn. Secondary Sch. Prins., Assn. Supervision and Curriculum Devel., Mortar Board, Phi Delta Kappa, Delta Kappa Gamma, Alpha Lambda Delta. Contbr. articles to profl. jours. Home: 6875 Glen Creek SE Caledonia MI 49316 Office: 330 Johnson St Caledonia MI 49316

KELLEY, MARILYN V., bookkeeping service owner; b. Tucson, Jan. 13, 1937; d. Marion and Lovetta (Merchant) Adkins; children—Russell D., Wanda L. (dec.), James H. Student Heald Bus. Sch., 1977, Regional Occupational Ctr., 1981. Bookkeeper Barbary Coast, San Jose, Calif., 1980-82, Argon Steel, San Jose, 1982-83, Indsl. Chimney, Hayward, Calif., 1984-85; owner Marilyn's Bookkeeping Service, Union City, Calif., 1985—; corp. sec.-treas. Rod's Trucking, Inc., Newark, Calif., 1985—. Fellow Nat. Assn. Female Execs. Republican. Episcopalian. Lodge: Order of Demolay (pres. mothers club 1979-80). Avocations: fishing; camping. Address: 118 Madrone Way Union City CA 94587

KELLEY, NANCY JOANNA, computer specialist, engineer; b. Concho, W.Va., Aug. 18, 1937; d. John S. and Freda A. (Montgomery) K. B.S., W.Va. Inst. Tech., 1960; cert. Bus. Tech. Inst., Pitts., 1970, Ind. Security Inst., Va., 1974; postgrad. U. Md., 1961-62. Programmer/analyst Planning Research Corp. McLean, Va., 1974-79; systems analyst Calspan Corp., Rosslyn, Va., 1979-81; systems cons. Calculon Corp., Germantown, Md., 1981-83; conf. mgmt. specialist Contel Info. Systems, Fairfax, Va., 1983-84; project engr. Lockheed Missile & Space Co., Austin, Tex., 1984—; sr. staff engr. Contel Info. Systems, Fairfax, 1984—, also tng. mgr. Mem. Nat. Assn. Female Execs., Spl. Interest Group for Mgmt. of Data, Library Computer and Info. Scis., Wilderness Soc., Smithsonian Assocs., Am. Mus. Natural History (assoc.), Nat. Trust Hist. Preservation. Democrat. Avocations: classical guitar; piano; theatre; history; archeology. Home: 2601 Park Center Dr C-611 Alexandria VA 22302 Office: Contel 12015 Lee-Jackson Hwy Fairfax VA 22033

KELLEY, ROSA LEE, federal government personnel security specialist; b. nr. Barnwell, S.C.; d. Leon and Eleanor (Dunbar) Bartley; m. Arthur Turner Jr., June 20, 1953 (div. 1959); 1 dau., Marlene Marie; m. William Junior Kelley, Oct. 29, 1960; children—Senora Faye Kelley Smallwood, Eleanor Lynn Kelley. B.S., Federal City Coll., 1976; M.S., U. D.C., 1979; student U. Md., 1980—. Clk.-typist Office of Quartermaster, Washington,, 1952-54, HEW, Balt., 1955-58, Dept. Treasury, Washington, 1958-59; sec., stenographer USIA, Washington, 1959-77, personnel security specialist trainee, 1977-78, personnel security specialist, 1978—. Mem., Four Corners/Forest Knoll Civic Orgn., Silver Spring, Md., 1983—. Mem. Am. Soc. Pub. Adminstrn., D.C. Bus. Edn. Assn., Am. Mgmt. Assn., U.D.C. Alumni Assn., Delta Pi Epsilon (historian 1980—). Baptist (soprano concert choir 1981—).

KELLEY, VICKY LYNN MONTGOMERY, nursing supervisor; b. Radford, Va., Apr. 14, 1955; d. Robert William and Albertine Faye (Akers) Montgomery; m. Stephen Ray Kelley, Mar. 10, 1978; 1 dau., Stephanie Autumn. Profl. Nursing Diploma, Roanoke Meml. Hosp., 1975; student Roanoke Coll., 1981—. Nurse neurol. intensive care unit Roanoke (Va.) Meml. Hosp., 1975-77; nurse oral surgery Dr. John E. Gardner, Jr., Roanoke, 1977-78; staff nurse Roanoke Valley Artificial Kidney Ctr., 1978—, supr. nursing, 1980—; acute hemodialysis nurse Valley Nephrology Assocs., Roanoke, 1981—. Lodge: Order Eastern Star. Home: 5540 Deer Park Dr NW Roanoke VA 24019 Office: Roanoke Valley Artificial Kidney Ctr 4330 Brambleton Ave Roanoke VA 24018

KELLISON, SYLVIA EILEEN, lawyer; b. Norfolk, Va., Apr. 22, 1952; d. Raymond Guy and Patricia Ann (Pedrotty) K.; student U. Calif., 1970-71; B.S., San Diego State U., 1975; student in Acctg., Loyola Law Sch., 1980-84, J.D., 1985. Bar: Calif. 1985. Internal revenue agt. IRS, Los Angeles, 1973—; chief steward, chmn. local negotiating com. Nat. Treasury Employees Union, 1976-85, mem. nat. bargaining team, 1978-80, 84-85 pres. chpt. 015, 1979-84, nat. v.p. 1984-85, mem. nat. resolutions com. nat. conv., 1981, chairwoman Los Angeles Joint Council, 1981-82; labor atty. firm Silver, Kreisler, Goldwasser & Shaeffer, Santa Monica, Calif., 1985—; cons. Fed. Sector Labor Relations. Active gen. com. Combined Fedn. Campaign Los Angeles County. Mem. Am. Soc. Women Accts., IRS C.P.A.s and Public Accts., Am. Bar Assn., Calif. Bar Assn., Calif. Women Lawyers, Women Lawyers of Los Angeles, Nat. Assn. Female Execs., Am. Arbitration Assn., Phi Alpha Delta. Democrat. Office: 1428 2d St Suite 200 Santa Monica CA90401

KELLNER-COLLINS, CYNTHIA ANN, credit union exec.; b. Milw., Nov. 4, 1948; d. Robert Q. and Alice (Barcz) K.; student U. Wis., Milw., 1970-72, Mt. Mary Coll., 1979—. Sec., Marquette U. Sch. Dentistry, 1966-68; sec., receptionist Edwards Advt. Agy., Inc., Milw., 1969-70, name changed to Edwards Commo-Net, Inc., sec. to pres., 1970-71, asst. to pres., 1971-73, v.p. charge ops., dir., 1973-80; mktg. dir. State Central Credit Union, Milw., 1980-81, sr. v.p. mktg., 1982—; speaker. Mem. Nat. Assn. Female Execs., Nat. Assn. Exec. Secs., Am. Mktg. Assn., Am. Soc. Profl. and Exec. Women. Home: 4120 N Ardmore Ave Milwaukee WI 53211 Office: 10015 W Greenfield Ave Milwaukee WI 53214

KELLOGG, MARY ALICE, writer, editor, lecturer; b. Tucson, June 6, 1948; d. Bertram Cecil Kellogg and Katherine (Sawyer) Kellogg Ringenbach; B.A., U. Ariz., 1970. Corr., Newsweek, Chgo. and San Francisco, 1970-76; assoc. editor, N.Y.C., 1976-77; corr. Sta. WCBS-TV, N.Y.C., 1977-78; sr. editor Parade Publs., N.Y.C., 1978-80; freelance writer/editor, N.Y.C., 1980—; profl. freelance chmn. Women in Communications, N.Y.C., 1983—; adj. prof. journalism NYU, N.Y.C., 1979—. Author: (nonfiction) Fast Track, 1978; contbr. articles to TV Guide, Glamour, Harper's Bazaar, GQ, Signature, Seventeen, New York, Adweek, The Dial, Travel & Leisure, N.Y. Times Mag., others. Founder, Dialogue, N.Y.C., 1977—. Named Outstanding Career Woman, Glamour mag., 1976; recipient Nat. Communications award Nat. Easter Seal Soc., 1978; Woman of Achievement, Cin. YMCA, 1980; Outstanding Alumna, U. Ariz., 1979. Mem. Women in Communications, Am. Soc. Journalists and Authors, Soc. Am. Travel Writers, Authors Guild, Sigma Delta Chi. Club: Overseas Press. Home and office: 287 W 4th St Suite 6 New York NY 10014

KELLY, ANNE C., retired city official; b. Buffalo, Mar. 6, 1916; d. John Patrick and Elizabeth Marie (Edwards) Donohue; m. Thomas Edward Kelly, Apr. 19, 1941; children—Maureen Anne, Michael Thomas, Edward John, Kevin Joseph, Theresa Elizabeth. Student SUNY-Buffalo. Tchr., St. Teresa Sch., Buffalo, 1956-64; clk. City of Buffalo, 1964, sec. to comptroller, 1967-70, council clk., 1970-76, sr. council clk., 1976-81. Mem. exec. bd. N.Y. Democratic Com., 1970—; vice chmn. Erie County Dem. Com., 1985—; past pres. Mercy League of Buffalo Mercy Hosp., Nash Ladies Guild, South Side Dem. Club. Roman Catholic. Clubs: Daus. of Erin, Nash Ladies. Home: 47 Marine Dr Apt 6-D Buffalo NY 14202

KELLY, AUDREY WELTMAN, travel agency executive; b. Stevens Point, Wis., July 6, 1943; d. Henry and Jean Charlotte (Woitczak) Weltman; m. Russell Henry Moody, Dec. 29, 1962 (div. 1980); children—Todd William, Traci Jo; m. Bruce Patrick Kelly, Oct. 19 1981. Student U. Wis., 1961-62, U. Alaska-Juneau, 1969-71, U. Alaska-Anchorage, 1973-76, 84-86. Cert. travel cons. Travel cons. Wright Travel Service, Palmer, 1973-76; owner, gen. mgr. Of All Places Travel Service, Wasilla, Alaska, 1976—. Travel columnist for newspaper, 1984-85. Mem. Am. Soc. Travel Agts., Nat. Fedn. Ind. Bus. Avocations: travel, geography. Office: Of All Places Travel Service 500 Main St PO Box 871781 Wasilla AK 99687

KELLY, CECILIA MARY, artistic director, choreographer; b. Beckenham, England, Mar. 22, 1922; d. James Robert and Emily Monica (Hewitt) Ellis; came to U.S., 1946, naturalized, 1949; student Ballet Sch., LaScala Theatre, Milan, Italy, 1931-36; m. Eugene Joseph Kelly, May 22, 1945; children—Eugene James, Chinta Monica (Mrs. Alvin Tucker). Mem. LaScala Co., Milan, 1936-38; concerts in Far East, Bombay, Cape Town, Penang, Singapore, 1938-41; mem. Sadler's Wells Ballet, England, 1941-46; guest chr., lectr. N.H., 1946-54; master classes, Taiwan, 1955-59; founder, dir. ballet, Ark. Arts Center, Little Rock, 1960-63; founder, dir. Shreveport (La.) Symphony Ballet, 1966-72, El Dorado Civic Ballet (Ark.), 1967-70, Twin City Civic Ballet, Monroe, La., 1970-83, artistic dir. emeritus, 1983—; guest artist So. Methodist U., Dallas, 1968; artist in residence Shreveport Symphony Ballet, 1974-75. Chmn., Save the Whale Com. La.; benefit performances March of Dimes, 1954, 70. Recipient award Gov. Faubus. Mem. Nat. Soc. Arts and Letters (nat. dance chmn. 1970-72, 74-76, 84—, nat. career award chmn. 1976-83). Roman Catholic. Home: PO Box 171 Greenwood LA 71033

KELLY, DARLENE OKAMOTO, administrative manager; b. Denver, Dec. 6, 1944; d. Ricky Rikio and Minnie Misao (Okada) Yamamura; m. Steven T. Okamoto, Jan. 11, 1964 (div. May 1974); 1 son, Jeffrey; m. 2d, Ronald William Kelly, Oct. 29, 1983; 1 stepson, Sean. Cert. Ins. Inst. Am., 1977; B.A. in Mgmt., St. Mary's Coll., 1983. Tax cons. H. & R. Block, Oakland, Calif., 1971-72; office mgr. Multi-Fin., Oakland, 1972-75; v.p. Dealey, Renton & Assocs., Oakland, 1975-84; assoc. Levine Fin. Group, San Francisco, 1984-85; adminstrv. mgr. Storek & Storek/Old Oakland, Oakland, 1985—. Trustee, Ind. Ins. Agts. & Brokers Found. for Edn. and Research, 1982-84. Mem. Ind. Ins. Agts. and Brokers Calif. (chmn. edn. com. 1982-84), Oakland Assn. Ins. Agts. (dir. 1983—), East Bay Assn. Ins. Women, A Central Place (dir. 1985—), Bus. Women's Expo. (dir. 1986—). Democrat. Buddhist. Club: Last Monday. Home: 4001 Midvale Ave Oakland CA 94602 Office: Storek & Storek/Old Oakland 484 9th St Oakland CA 94607

KELLY, DOROTHY ANN, college president; b. Bronx, N.Y., July 26, 1929; d. Walter David and Sarah (McCauley) Kelly; B.A., Coll. New Rochelle, 1951; M.A., Catholic U., Washington, 1958; Ph.D., U. Notre Dame, 1970; Litt.D. (hon.), Mercy Coll., Dobbs Ferry, N.Y., 1976; LL.D. (hon.), Nazareth Coll. of Rochester (N.Y.), 1979; D.H.L., Coll. St. Rose, 1981, Manhattan Coll., 1979. Joined O.S.U.; mem. faculty Coll. New Rochelle (N.Y.), 1957—, chmn. dept. history, 1965-67, acad. dean, 1967-72, acting pres., 1970-71, pres., 1972—. Trustee, vice chmn. Commn. Ind. Colls. and Univs. of State of N.Y., 1977-78, chmn. bd. trustees, 1978-80, mem. govt. relations com., 1980—; chmn. Com. Higher Edn. Opportunity, 1977; mem. commr. edn. Adv. Council on Higher Edn. for N.Y. State, 1975-77, subcom. on postsecondary occupational edn., 1975-77; exec. com. Empire State Found. Ind. Liberal Arts Colls., 1975—, vice chmn., 1977-81, chmn., 1981—; trustee, mem. exec. com. Assn. Colls. and Univs. of State of N.Y., 1976—; mem. exec. com. Assn. Colls. Mid-Hudson Area, 1976—, pres., 1979-81; mem. com. on purpose and identity Assn. Cath. Colls. and Univs., 1975-80, mem. Neylon Conf. steering com., 1978—, mem. bishops and presidents com., 1979-82; mem. adv. council on fin. aid to students Office Edn., HEW, 1978—; chmn. Women's Coll. Coalition, 1981-83; trustee United Student Aid Funds, 1980—; chmn. govt. relations adv. com. Nat. Assn. Ind. Colls. and Univs., 1981—; bd. dirs. Westchester County Assn., 1977-80, 81—. Mem. AAUP, Am. Hist. Assn., AAUW, Nat. Fedn. Bus. and Profl. Women, Am. Assn. Higher Edn., Nat. Assembly Women Religious. Address: Coll New Rochelle New Rochelle NY 10801

KELLY, DOROTHY MARGARET, management consultant; b. Jamaica, N.Y., Apr. 29, 1925; d. Charles Frank and Mary (Emken) Lehner; A.Bus., Kaupert Jr. Coll., 1945; student Katherine Gibbs Mgmt. for Women, 1974-75; m. George M. Kelly, June 25, 1944; children—Karen P. Kelly Dehncke, Kathleen M. Kelly Devlin, Richard C., Virginia D. Staff asst. to pres. Maxson Electronics, Great River, N.Y., 1962-66; exec. asst. to chmn. Eltra Corp., N.Y.C., 1966-74, Studebaker Worthington, Inc., N.Y.C., 1974-75; exec. asst. to pres. United Mchts., N.Y.C., 1975-77; exec. asst./adminstrn. group v.p., mem. pres.'s panel Equitable Life Assurance Soc. U.S., N.Y.C., 1977-79; asso. mgmt. cons. G L Staff Cons., N.Y.C., 1979—; lectr., cons. Mem. Nat. Assn. Female Execs. Roman Catholic. Clubs: Indian Hills Country, Brightwaters Yacht. Home: 415 Ackerson Blvd Brightwaters NY 11718 Office: Suite 16F 30 W 61st St New York NY 10023

KELLY, GRACE DENTINO, educational administrator; b. Peoria, Ill., Mar. 30, 1934; d. Michael and Arnita Balagna (Barto) Dentino; cert. med. technology, St. Francis Sch. Med. Tech., 1955; B.S., Bradley U., 1971, M.S., 1973; m. Robert N. Kelly, Aug. 31, 1957; children—Susan, James, Stephen, Patrick. Tchr. sci. St. Mark Sch., Peoria, asst. prin., 1980-83, chmn. jr. high sch. curriculum com. for drug edn.; prin. St. Thomas Sch., Peoria Heights, Ill., 1983—. Mem. ednl. adv. bd. Peoria Jour. Star Newspaper, 1973—. Recipient Econs. Educator award Joint Council on Econ. Edn., N.Y.C., 1982—, Esmark Found. award Ill. Council Econ. Edn., 1984. Mem. Nat. Sci. Tchrs. Assn., Am. Soc. Clin. Pathologists, Ill. Sci. Tchrs. Assn. (dir. region III, presenter papers), Ill. Jr. Acad. Sci. (dir. region I), AAUW. Roman Catholic. Home: 1815 W High St Peoria IL 61606 Office: 4229 N Monroe St Peoria Heights IL 61614

KELLY, JEAN M(C CORMICK), advertising agency executive; b. Norwalk, Conn., June 13, 1938; d. John M. and Dorothy (Bennett) McCormick; m. Kevin E. Kelly, Sept. 18, 1982; children—Gregory, Geoffrey, Stefanie. B.S., U. R.I., 1960. Copywriter Montgomery Ward, N.Y.C., 1960-62; asst. advt. dir. Advertiser Democrat newspaper, Norway, Maine, 1963-65; copy chief/women's editor Sta.-WMTW-TV, Poland Spring, Maine, 1965-67; continuity dir. Sta.-WEAT-TV-AM-FM, West Palm Beach, Fla., 1967-70; v.p., creative dir. William F. Haselmire Advt., West Palm Beach, 1970-85; ptnr. The Kodi Group, Palm Beach, 1985—. Republican. Club: Advt. (pres. 1976-77) (Palm Beach, Fla.). Home: 314 Minnesota St Lantana FL 33462 Office: The Kodi Group 230 S County Rd #3 Palm Beach FL 33480

KELLY, JOAN MARIE, psychologist; b. Plymouth, Mass., Dec. 31, 1940; d. Martin Edward and Margaret Mary (Roche) K.; B.A. in English and Edn., Boston Coll., 1968; M.A. in Sch. Psychology (NIMH fellow 1968-72), Columbia U., 1970, Ph.D., 1972; divorced; 1 son, Jon. Elem. sch. tchr. Mass. and Conn., 1961-66; sch. psychologist N.J. and N.Y., 1970-74; sch. psychologist, chmn. com. handicapped Greenwood Lake (N.Y.) Sch., 1974—; workshop presenter, cons. in field. Mem. Am. Psychol. Assn., Nat. Assn. Sch. Psychologists, Assn. Children with Learning Disabilities, Commn. Gifted Edn., ABC Reading Council, Mensa. Club: Middletown Scrabble (co-dir.). Author articles in field. Home: 53 Sarah Ln Middletown NY 10940 Office: Greenwood Lake Sch Waterstone Rd Greenwood Lake NY 10925

KELLY, JUDITH MARY, window shutter company executive; b. Lansing, Mich., Aug. 4, 1934; d. Sanford DeWitt and Mary Elizabeth (Atkison) Rathbun; m. James Marshall Kelly, Mar. 3, 1962; children—Robert Gordon, Thomas James. Pres. Roll-A-Shield, Inc., Phoenix, 1982—. Pres. Valley Big Sisters Aux., Phoenix, 1978-79; trustee Wasatch Acad., Mt. Pleasant, Utah, 1985. Republican. Presbyterian. Avocations: reading; travel; bowling; golf. Home: 3311 N Valencia Ln Phoenix AZ 85018 Office: Roll-A-Shield Inc 2919 E McDowell Rd Phoenix AZ 85008

KELLY, KATHLEEN ANNE, scientist; b. Providence, Feb. 5, 1955; d. Richard Thomas and Elizabeth Millie (Boudreau) K. Student Art Inst. Boston, 1975-77, Boston U., 1978-80, Cornell U., 1980-81, U.R.I., 1982-84. Research asst. oceanography Grad. Sch. Ocean U. R.I., Narragansett, 1982-84; scientist ocean sci. and tech. div. Sci. Applications Internat. Corp., Newport, R.I., 1984—. Avocations: quilting; swimming; photography; scuba diving. Home: 52 Narragansett Ave Narragansett RI 02882 Office: Sci Applications Internat Corp 221 3d St Admiral's Gate Newport RI 02840

KELLY, LEONTINE T.C., bishop; b. Washington; d. David D. and Ila M. Turpeau; m. Gloster Current (div.); children—Angela, Gloster Jr.; m. James David Kelly (dec.); children—John David, Pamela. Student W.Va. State Coll.; grad. Va. Union U., 1960; M.Div., Union Theol. Sem., Richmond, Va., 1969. Formerly sch. tchr.; former pastor Galilee United Methodist Ch., Edwardsville, Va.; later mem. staff Va. Conf. Council on Ministries; pastor Asbury United Meth. Ch., Richmond, 1976-83; mem. nat. staff United Meth. Ch., Nashville, 1983-84; bishop Calif.-Nev. Conf., San Francisco, 1984—. Office: United Meth Ch PO Box 467 San Francisco CA 94101*

KELLY, LESLIE ANN, training and development consultant; b. Hammond, Ind., June 13, 1945; d. Philip C. and Esther A. (Lardie) K.; B.S., Northwestern U., 1967; M.S. summa cum laude, Ind. U., 1973; m. Raymond S. Battey, Aug. 10, 1968; children—Christine Anna, Raymond Sutton. Assoc. faculty dept. speech, theatre and communications Ind. U.-Purdue U., Indpls., 1973—; pres. Kelly & Assos., tng. and devel. cons., Indpls., 1979—; mem. Ind. Bus. Adv. Council, SBA. Nnamed Ind. Women's Bus. Advocate of Yr., SBA, 1983 Mem. Am. Soc. for Tng. and Devel. (Nat. award for disting. contbn. to community and nation 1984), Am. Soc. for Personnel Adminstrs., Central States Speech Assn. (Outstanding Young Tchr. award 1971), Network of Women in Bus. (Bus. Woman of Yr. 1980), Nat. Assn. Women Bus. Owners (bd. dirs. 1985), Ind. State C. of C. (small bus. council). Quaker. Author: Packaging Yourself for Real Estate Success, 1979; Childbirth Education Manual, 1979; Negotiating Notebook, 1983; Successful Supervision, 1984; Productive Management, 1984; Sales Negotiating, 1985; editor: The Best of Sales and Marketing, 1986; contbg. author various manuals and handbooks on tech. report writing. Home: 6125 Graham Rd Indianapolis IN 46220 Office: 2625 N Meridian Suite 22 Indianapolis IN 46208

KELLY, MARGARET BRIDGET (PEG), radio station sales executive; b. N.Y.C., July 28, 1942; d. Patrick Joseph and Phyllis (Gannon) K. B.A., St. Johns U., Jamaica, N.Y., 1966. Broadcast supr. Foote Cone Belding, N.Y.C., 1972-77; sales account exec. nat./sales CBS/FM, N.Y.C., 1977-79, Sta.-WCBS-FM, N.Y.C., 1979-81; sales account exec. Sta.-WNBC, N.Y.C., 1981-82, local sales mgr., 1982-84, gen. sales mgr., 1984—. Home: 102-38 88 Ave Richmond Hill NY 11418 Office: WNBC Radio 30 Rockefeller Plaza New York NY 10020

KELLY, MARGARET RICAUD (MRS. THOMAS W. KELLY), educator; b. Dillon, S.C., Mar. 22, 1910; d. Robert Barry and Lulu Mowry (Crosland) Ricaud; A.B., Winthrop Coll., 1931; postgrad. Duke U., 1931, U. Miami, 1937, U. Fla., 1938, U. N.C., 1950, 52, 53, U. S.C., 1954, Coker Coll., 1954-55; m. John Quinton Maynard, Jan. 1, 1936; m. Thomas W. Kelly, Sept. 12, 1950. Prin. Ebenezer Sch., Marlboro County, S.C., 1932-35; tchr. public schs., Homestead, Fla., 1937-39; tchr. Fletcher Meml. Sch., McColl, S.C., 1940-46, 67-69, prin., 1942-45; attendance tchr. Marlboro County Schs., Bennettsville, 1946-50; tchr. elem. sch., Tabor City, N.C., 1950-51; tchr. pub. schs., Cordova, N.C., 1951-56, Society Hill, S.C., 1956-67; tchr. spl. edn. Blenheim (S.C.) primary schs., 1970-73; individual tutor, Bennettsville, 1973—. Mem. Marlboro Arts Council. Registered genealogist. Mem. Nat., S.C. edn. assns., Nat. Assn. Women Deans, Adminstrs. and Counselors, Marlboro County Tchrs. (chmn. public relations 1940-45), Colonial Dames 17th Century (registrar 1979-81), Magna Charta Dames, Soc. Decs. Most Noble Order of Garter, Geneal. Soc. London, French Huguenot Soc., Colonial Order of Crown, DAR, UDC (pres. 1983-85), Nat. Geneal. Soc., S.C., Marlborough hist. socs., Nat. Poetry Soc., Marlborough Arts Council. Author: Jack and the Flying Saucer, 1973; Poems by Margaret Ricaud Kelly, 1974; The Ricaud Family, 1976; A Short History of Marlboro County, S.C., 1600-1979, 1979; contbr. poetry to anthologies, articles to various local newspapers. Home: 402 Fayetteville Ave Bennettsville SC 29512

KELLY, MARY ELIZABETH, nurse, lawyer; b. Chgo., Jan. 27, 1953; d. Edward Joseph and Laurette Kathleen (Howe) K.; m. Thomas R. Garrick, May 30, 1981. B.S.N. with honors, U. Ill.-Chgo., 1976; J.D. with honors, DePaul U., 1979. Bar: Ill. 1979. Calif. 1983; R.N., Ill. Psychiat. nurse, Billings Hosp.-U. Chgo., 1976-78; law clk. to Kevin F. Forde, Chgo., 1978-79; jud. clk. to David Linn, Ill. Appellate Ct., 1979-81; law clk. to Arthur L. Alarcon, 9th cir. Ct. Appeals, Los Angeles, 1981-83; mem. firm Abzug & Kelly, Los Angeles, 1983—; adj. prof. law Southwestern U. Sch. Law, 1983—. Editor: (with Cynthia Northrop) Legal Issues in Nursing, 1984. Contbr. article to publ. Law Student's Civil Rights Commn. research grantee, 1978. Mem. Am. Assn. Nurse Attys. (dir. 1983, chmn. amicus com. and pub. relations), Assn. Trial Lawyers Am., Los Angeles County Bar Assn. (com. on bioethics), Los Trial Lawyers Assn., Los Angeles Women Lawyers Assn., Am. Nurses Assn., ABA (health law com.), Health Lawyers Assn., Am. Soc. Law and Medicine, Sigma Theta Tau. Office: Abzug & Kelly 1900 Ave of Stars Suite 2512 Los Angeles CA 90067

KELLY, MATTIE CAROLINE MAY, business woman; b. Vernon, Fla., Mar. 12, 1912; d. William W. and Mary Alice (Russ) May; student Rollins Coll., 1944-46, 48-49; A.B., Fla. State U., 1952, postgrad., 1970-71; m. Coleman Lee Kelly, Mar. 26, 1932 (div. June 1971); children—Carnera Lee, Lila Bernarr, Imogene (Mrs. H.J. Toole), Carol Kelly Adams, Cecelia Kelly Sims; m. 2d, Paul Sims, July 13, 1973 (div. May 1979). Tchr. public schs., Fla., 1928-33, 37; pres. Kelly Boat Service, Inc., 1980—, Kelly Homes, Inc., Destin, Fla., to 1978; co-owner, trustee Coleman L. Kelly Trust; co-organizer, owner, pres. Radio Sta. WMMK-FM, Destin. Mem. Okaloosa County Democratic Com., 1958—, exec. adv. bd., 1956-72; mem. State Dem. Exec. Com., mem. adv. bd., 1966-70, del. nat. conv., 1968, 72. Bd. dirs. Destin Library, 1956—, Fla. League Arts, 1980-81; bd. dirs. Okaloosa County chpt. ARC, 1954-60, chmn., 1957-58; adv. bd. diversified coop. tng. Choctawhatchee High Sch., 1960—; camp counsellor Senior Hi, Camp Weed, 1964; patron Stagecrafters, Okaloosa Community Concert Assn.; Benefactor Ft. Walton Beach Ballet Assn., Symphony Assn.; sponsor Playground Mut. Concert Assn.; founder, promoter, supporter Mattie M. Kelly Fine Arts Center, Destin. Mem. coordinating council for arts Okaloosa-Walton Jr. Coll., 1965—, rep. to Fla. Arts Council, 1966—; patron Okaloosa County Symphony, Ft. Walton Beach Ballet Assn.; adv. bd. Okaloosa County Mental Health Assn., 1978—, Women's Theatre Workshop Okaloosa-Walton Jr. Coll., 1978—; chmn. Historic Sites Commn., Okaloosa-Walton. Recipient award ARC, 1960; award for arts for Northwest Fla., Gov. Fla., 1982; Gov.'s citation, 1983; Harmony award SPEBSQSA, 1983. Mem. Am. Camellia Soc., Nat. Writers Club, Geneal. Soc. Okaloosa County, N.Y. Bot. Gardens Club, Okaloosa County Concert Assn., Nat. Hist. Soc., Playground Poets Assn. (coordinator 1977—), Ft. Walton Beach C. of C. (edn. com., mem. host com.; Ross and Nell Marler Citizenship award 1982). Fla. Boatsmen's Assn. (sec. 1972—), Hist. Soc. Okaloosa and Walton Counties, Ft. Walton Beach Woman's Club (chmn. fine arts com. 1957-58), Woman's Club (v.p. 1958-59), Gulf Coast Dem. Women's Club, AAUW (charter, legis. com. 1971—), Assoc. Council Arts, Choctaw Bay Music Club. Mem. Protestant Episcopal Ch. (adminstr., supt. ch. sch. 1953-60, br. chmn. Christian edn. 1955-60, dist. chmn. Christian edn. 1958-61, asst. organist, tchr., del. adult conf. 1957, 59, del. religious TV programming workshop 1955-56; dist. v.p. 1961-64; pres. church-women Diocese Fla. 1965-68). Author: Songs and Sonnets From the Sea (poetry), 1964; donor land and funds for Mattie M. Kelly Fine Arts Center. Address: PO Box 425 Indian Bayou Destin FL 32541

KELLY, MAXINE, manufacturing company executive; b. Noxpater, Miss., Apr. 25, 1939; d. L.W. and Lora May (Reed) Onstead; div. 1978; 1 dau., Debra Elizabeth. Grad. high sch., Corning, Ark. Model, Neiman Marcus, Dallas, 1956-57; asst. to pres. Alfred Werber, Inc., St. Louis, 1958-68; buyer, store mgr. Underwood Splty., Salisbury, N.C., 1968-69; buyer, div. mdse. mgr., gen. mdse. mgr. Robins Splty., Salisbury, 1970-71; buyer, div. mdse. mgr. Foley's Dept. Store, Houston, 1972-75; v.p. Monet div. Gen. Mills, N.Y.C., 1976-79; v.p., gen. mdse. mgr. Foley's Dept. Store, Houston, 1980-83; pres., chief exec. officer White Stag Mfg., Inc., Portland, Oreg., 1984—. Active United Way, Houston, 1982-83; exec. com. Jerry Lewis Telethon, Houston, 1982. Contbr. articles, interviews to newspapers, fashion and retailing jours. Recipient Effie award, 1982; Design awards for jewelry and display fixtures, 1976-79; named Woman of Yr., YMCA, Houston, 1981. Republican. Unitarian. Home: 600 SE Marion St Apt 307 Portland OR 97202 Office: White Stag Mfg Inc 5100 SE Harney Dr Portland OR 97206

KELLY, MAXINE ANN, developer, general contractor; b. Fort Wayne, Ind., Aug. 14, 1931; d. Victor J. and Marguerite Elizabeth (Biebesheimer) Cramer; m. James Herbert Kelly, Oct. 4, 1968 (dec. Apr. 1974). Cert. Internat. Coll., 1953, B.A., Northwestern U., 1956. Legal sec. Parry and Barns, Fort Wayne, Ind., 1951-52; trust sec. Lincoln Nat. Bank & Trust Co., Fort Wayne, 1956-58; sr. clerk steno Div. Mental Health, Anchorage, 1958-60; office mgr. Langdon Psychiatric Clinic, Anchorage, 1960-71; owner, operator A-1 Bookkeeping Service, Anchorage, 1972-76; ptnr. Gonder-Kelly Enterprises, A-is-A Constrn., Anchorage, 1975—. Treas. Libertarian Party, Anchorage, 1967, chmn., 1968; treas. Alaska Libertarian Party, Anchorage, 1974, chmn., 1975. Recipient Recognition for Exceptional Service award Anchorage Conv. & Visitors Bur., 1984. Mem. Am. Assn. Univ. Women (life), Whittier Boat Owners Assn. (treas. 1980-84), Greater Anchorage C. of C. Avocations: pets; boating; handiwork. Home and Office: 2300 D St #302 Anchorage AK 99503

KELLY, PATRICIA SUE HAGGERTY, chemical company executive; b. Pitts., June 12, 1950; d. Bernard Anthony and Helen Rita (Pellegrini) Haggerty; student Duquesne U., 1968-69; B.S. with highest honors, W. Liberty State Coll., 1972; M.B.A. magna cum laude, U. Pitts., 1974; m. Robert E. Kelly, Apr. 21, 1979 (div. June 1983). Sales clk. Gimbels Dept. Store, Pitts., 1969-70; supr. Mktg. Services Center, Pitts., 1973; market research analyst Koppers Co., Pitts., 1974-78; planning assoc. Mobil Chem. Co., Pitts., 1978-83, sr. mktg. analyst, 1983-84; sr. mktg. analyst Valspar Corp., Pitts., 1984-85, sr. mktg. analyst, mgr. acctg., customer service and order entry Office Adminstrv. Depts., 1985—; tchr. indsl. mktg. research Carnegie-Mellon Grad. Bus. U., 1977-78; cons. A. O. Smith Co., Pitts. Nat. Bank, Darlington Clay Products div. Gen. Dynamics. Bd. dirs., pub. notary Animal Care and Welfare, Inc., Soc. Prevention Cruelty to Animals, 1974—; adv. Explorers Program, 1974-78. Recipient Phi Chi Theta award U. Pitts. Grad. Sch. Bus., 1974. Mem. Assn. Time Share Users (sec.-treas.), Nat. Assn. Female Execs., Am. Mktg. Assn. (v.p. intercollegiate chpt.), Beta Gamma Sigma, Delta Mu Delta (sec.-treas.). Republican. Roman Catholic. Home: 1321 Great Oak Dr Pittsburgh PA 15220 Office: 2000 Westhall St Pittsburgh PA 15233

KELLY, SARAH FRANCES, insurance broker; b. Waynesburg, Pa., Sept. 13, 1941; d. Fred A. and V. Ruth (Sappington) Strope; m. Oren Leon Kelly, Apr. 15, 1961. Student Leuzinger High Sch., Lawndale, Calif. Cert. profl. ins. agt. File clk., typist Laven Ins., Hawthorne, Calif., 1957-62; ins. underwriter Harbor Ins., San Pedro, Calif., 1962-63; ins. underwriter Don Lock Ins., Hawthorne, 1963-65; ins. underwriter T.W. Newman & Assoc., Inglewood, Calif., 1965-69; v.p. Nickerson Ins. Services, Lomita, Calif., 1969—. Mem. Creative Services Network, San Pedro, Calif., 1983-84; pres. Westmont Homeowners Assn. (Calif.), 1980-81. Mem. Lomita C. of C., South Coast Chpt. Chartered Property Casualty Underwriter Assn. (pres. 1981-82), Nat. Assn. Ins. Women (dir. 1983-84), Profl. Ins. Agts. Assn., Ind. Ins. Agts. Brokers of South Bay, Nat. Assn. Female Execs. (pres. South Bay chpt. 1968-69). Republican. Methodist.

KELLY, SHANNON LYNN, stockbroker; b. Monterey, Calif., Sept. 10, 1956; d. Leonard Howard and Joni Dorothy (Twitchell) Higginbotham; m. Brian Andrew Kelly, Sept. 12, 1982. A.A., U. South Fla., 1974-76; B.A., U. Hawaii, 1979. Outer islands mgr. Gatliff Corp., Honolulu, 1979-81; stockbroker Paine Webber Jackson & Curtis, Honolulu, 1981—, also dir.; freelance writer, 1984—. Mem. Honolulu Bd. Realtors, Investment Soc. Hawaii. Republican. Office: Paine Webber Jackson & Curtis Inc 733 Bishop St Suite 1500 Honolulu HI 96813

KELLY, SHARON DELL TULLY, messenger company executive; b. Hartford, Conn., Sept. 14, 1943; d. James William and Doris Virginia (Craven) Tully; m. Robert John Blinn, Oct. 20, 1962 (div. 1965); 1 child, Tully Lee; m. John Michael Kelly, Nov. 19, 1977. Student pub. schs., East Hartford, Conn. Legal sec. Shipman & Goodwin, Hartford, 1962-64; office mgr., legal sec. Rosenthal, Wolfe, Clayman, 1964-67; adminstrv. asst. D.J. Edelman Pub. Relations, 1967-69; owner, pres. The Singing Messenger Co. Inc., West Hartford, 1980—; owner, v.p. Time Saver Services, Inc., 1985—. Mem. Assn. Entrepreneurial Woman, Conn. Hotel-Motel Assn. Democrat. Roman Catholic. Home: 45 Bloomfield Ave Hartford CT 06105 Office: The Singing Messenger Co Inc and Time Saver Services Inc 1007 Farmington Ave Suite 15 West Hartford CT 06107

KELLY, SHIRLEY LOUISE, therapeutic recreation executive; b. Harrisburg, Pa., Jan. 23, 1929; d. Alfred Peters and Anna Elizabeth (Shutt) Lego; m. Robert Leonard Kelly, Mar. 28, 1948; children—Donna, Robert E., Rick, Mark, Debra. Student pub. schs., Harrisburg. Nurses aide Bethany Village Retirement Ctr., 1967-72; dir. activities Bethany Village, 1972—. Mem. Pa. Therapeutic Recreation Soc., Nat. Remotivation Technique Orgn. (cert. instr., cons. Keystone chpt. 1978—). Methodist. Office: Bethany Village Retirement Ctr 325 Wesley Dr Mechanicsburg PA 17019

KELMAN, JUDITH ANN, writer; b. N.Y.C., Oct. 21, 1945; d. George Joseph and Flora (Underberg) Edelstein; B.S., Cornell U., 1967; M.A. (Fed. fellow), NYU, 1968; M.S., So. Conn. State Coll., 1977; m. Edward Michael Kelman, June 28, 1970; children—Matthew Steven, Joshua Kenneth. Tchr. educable mentally handicapped Valley Stream (N.Y.) Public Schs., 1968-71; recreation supr. Camp A.N.C.H.O.R., extracurricular activities for handicapped children, Town of Hempstead, (N.Y.), 1968-71; speech pathologist Greenwich (Conn.) public schs.; spl. edn. cons. Area Cons., Inc., N.Y.C.; freelance writer, 1981—; author: (novel) Prime Evil, 1986; work pub. in N.Y. Times, McCall's Working Mother, Redbook, Seventeen, Glamour, Good Housekeeping, Brides mags. Bd. dirs. Stamford (Conn.) Aid for Retarded, 1973-74; founder Touch, Inc., orgn. for parents of handicapped, Stamford, 1975, pres., 1975-76; assoc. Am. Acad. Cerebral Palsy; bd. dirs. Peyasus Therapeutic Riding, Inc. Mem. Council Exceptional Children., Am. Soc. Journalists and Authors. Democrat. Jewish. Club: Cornell of Fairfield County (Conn.) (sec. 1979—). Home: 60 Thornwood Rd Stamford CT 06903

KELMENSON, LITA, art educator, sculptor; b. Buffalo, June 30, 1932; d. Albert and Helene (Schniedt) Barback; m. Emanuel Kelmenson, Feb. 19, 1955; children—Gary, Steven. B.A. cum laude, SUNY-Buffalo, 1954; student Albright Art Sch., Buffalo, 1953; postgrad. Columbia, 1958; M.A., CUNY, Queens Coll., 1964. N.Y. State Tchrs. Certification, 1964. Tchr. art Robert Williams Sch., Jericho, N.Y., 1964-68, Jr. High Sch., West Islip, N.Y., 1968-70, East Islip High Sch., N.Y., 1970—; tchr. sculpture Adephia U., Garden City, N.Y., 1974, Hofstra U., Hempstead, N.Y., 1975-76; mem. adv. bd. Islip Art Mus., 1975-80, guest curator exhibit, 1975-80, dir. high sch. exhibit program, 1975-80. Contbr. articles to various publs; one-woman shows Mari Galleries Westchester, Ltd., Mamaroneck, N.Y., 1978, B. J. Spoke Gallery, Port Washington, N.Y., 1981, 85, Mari Galleries Westchester, Ltd., Mamaroneck, N.Y. 1981; group shows include Firehouse Gallery, Nassau Community Coll., Garden City, N.Y., 1973, DeAndreis Gallery, St. John's U., N.Y., 1974, Islip Town Art Gallery, East Islip, N.Y., 1976, Hansen Galleries, SoHo, N.Y., 1977, Hudson River Mus., Yonkers, N.Y., 1977, Elaine Benson Gallery, Bridgehampton, N.Y., 1978, Sculpture Garden, Union-Carbide Bldg., N.Y.C., 1978, Artists Craftsmen of N.Y., 1978, Sun Yat Sen Hall Gallery, St. John's U., Jamaica, N.Y., 1979, Gallery Odin, Port Washington, N.Y., 1980, Fed. Bldg. N.Y., 1980, Heckscher Mus., Huntington, N.Y., 1982, Nassau Mus. Fine Art, Roslyn, N.Y., 1982, Shadow Box Gallery, Glen Cove, N.Y., 1982, B.J. Spoke Gallery, Port Washington, 1983, Fed. Bldg. N.Y., Nat. Assn. Women Artists, 1984, Pleiades Gallery, SoHo, N.Y., 1985, Mussavi Art Ctr., NoHo, N.Y.C., 1985; represented in permanent collections Mari Galleries of Westchester Ltd.; pvt. collections including Mrs. Epstein, Wilmington, Del., Howard Rosengarten, Esq., Gwen Karnes, Al and Nonny Rosenman, L.I., N.Y. Recipient awards including Long Island Craftsmen's Guild award of excellence, Firehouse Gallery, Nassau Community Coll., Garden City, N.Y., 1973; First award Sculpture, Bay Shore Art Exhibit-Nat. N.Y., Islip Town Art Gallery, 1976; Jeffrey Childs Willis Meml. prize Nat. Assn. Women Artists, 1980. Mem. Nat. Art Edn. Assn., Nat. Assn. Women Artists. Advocations: music; philosophy. Office: East Islip High Sch Redman St Islip Terrace NY 11752

KELSEY, FRANCES OLDHAM (MRS. FREMONT ELLIS KELSEY), pharmacologist; b. Cobble Hill, Vancouver Island, B.C., Can., July 24, 1914; d. Frank Trevor and Katherine (Stuart) Oldham; B.Sc., McGill U., 1934; M.Sc., 1935; Ph.D., U. Chgo., 1938. M.D., 1950; m. Fremont Ellis Kelsey, Dec. 6, 1943; children—Susan Elizabeth, Christine Ann. Came to U.S., 1936, naturalized, 1956. Instr., asst. prof. pharmacology U. Chgo., 1938-50; editorial asso. AMA, Chgo., 1950-52; asso. prof. pharmacology U. S.D., 1954-57; med. officer FDA, Washington, 1960—, dir. div. sci investigations, 1967—. Recipient Pres.'s award for Disting. Fed. Civilian Service (refusal to approve coml. distbn. thalidomide in U.S.), 1962. Mem. Am. Soc. Pharmacology and Exptl. Therapeutics, Soc. Exptl. Biology and Medicine, Am. Med. Writers Assn., N.Y. Acad. Scis., Teratology Soc., Sigma Xi. Author: (with F.E. Kelsey, E.M.K. Geiling) Essentials of Pharmacology, 1960. Home: 5811 Brookside Dr Chevy Chase MD 20015 Office: FDA 5600 Fishers Ln Rockville MD 20857*

KELSOE, LYNDA CAROL, computer scientist; b. Birmingham, Ala., Apr. 5, 1943; d. Johnny Willard and Marjorie Nanette (Wallace) Simmons; B.S., U. Montevallo, 1966; student U. Ala., 1968; B.S., Stevens Inst. Tech., 1971; M.A., U. Houston, 1977, M.A., 1979; m. Neal Marshall Kelsoe, July 18, 1981. Tchr. English, Birmingham (Ala.) Public Schs., 1966-70; programmer Bell Telephone Labs., Whippany, N.J., 1971-74; sci. programmer Lockheed Electronics, Houston, 1973-74; programmer analyst IBM, Houston, 1974-76, Lockheed Electronics, Houston, 1977-78; sr. analyst Computer Scis. Corp., Houston, 1978-82; corp. staff Jefferson Assocs., Inc., Houston, 1982; mgr. Simulation and Computer Technology Intermetrics, Inc., Houston, 1982—. Mem. El Lago (Tex.) City Council, 1983—. Lic. pvt. pilot. Mem. Assn. Computing Machinery, Nat. Mgmt. Assn., Nat. Assn. Female Execs., Graphics Exchange. Home: 206 Yacht Club Ln Seabrook TX 77586 Office: 17625 El Camino Real Houston TX 77058

KELTNER, VICKI FLOYD, business executive; b. Aug. 8, 1948; married. Student in spl. studies Lit. Inst., London, 1968; B.F.A., So. Meth. U., 1970. Writer, interviewer, prodn. asst. BBC, London, 1968-69; nat. rep. Alpha Delta Pi, Atlanta, 1970-71; pres. Lynn Advt. & Pub. Relations Co., subs. Fairfield Co., Houston, 1971-72; mgmt. assistance officer, pub. relations officer Houston dist. office SBA, 1972-75; assoc. Mktg. Services Mgmt., Houston, 1975-78; pres. Small Bus. Publs., Houston, 1978-82, Success, Houston, 1981-84, Marine Enterprises, Houston, 1983—; cons. Sakowitz, Inc., 1982-84; del., co-chmn. Tex. del. White House Conf. on Small Bus., 1980; mem. Tex. Gov.'s Adv. Bd. on Small Bus., 1980-82; chmn. adv. bd. Houston dist. office SBA, 1980-82; lectr., seminar leader on small bus. and bus. success for women. Co-author: The Success Image, 1982; co-producer videotape series: The Success Image, 1983; pub.: Record Keeping for Small Businesses, 1980.; featured on numerous radio, TV interview programs and in newspapers, 1971—. Mem. distributive edn. adv. bd. Houston Ind. Sch. Dist., 1971-72; bd. dirs. Options Career Devel. Ctr., Houston, 1981—; mem. adv. bd. Teen Relationships Tng., Houston, 1982-83; chmn. Forum Adv. Council, The Houstonian, 1983. Recipient commendation Office of Pres. U.S., Office Emergency Preparedness, 1972; named Women in Bus. Advocate of Yr., Houston dist. SBA, 1981; recipient award of excellence Exec. Women's Adv. Council, 1983. Mem. So. Meth. U. Alumni Assn. (v.p., bd. dirs. 1970-71). Club: Magic Circle Republican Women's. Address: 5050 Woodway #2F Houston TX 77056

KEMP, BETTY RUTH, librarian; b. Tishomingo, Okla., May 5, 1930; d. Raymond Herrell and Mamie Melvina (Hughes) K.; B.A.L.S., U. Okla., 1952; M.S., Fla. State U., 1965. Extramural loan librarian U. Tex., Austin, 1952-55; librarian lit. and history dept. Dallas Public Library, 1955-56, head Oaklawn Br., 1956-60, head Walnut Hill Br., 1960-64; dir. Cherokee Regional Library, LaFayette, Ga., 1965-74; dir. Lee County Library, hdqrs. Lee-Itawamba Library System, Tupelo, Miss., 1975—; bd. library commrs. State of Miss., 1979-83, chmn., 1979-80. Active LWV, United Meth. Women. Mem. ALA, Southeastern Library Assn., Miss. Library Assn., Beta Phi Mu. Democrat. Club: AAUW. Home: 2112 President Tupelo MS 38801 Office: 219 Madison Tupelo MS 38801

KEMP, JUNE, employment specialist, educator; b. Homestead, Pa., Dec. 16, 1933; d. Patrick H. and Gladys Naomi (Pifer) Cloherty; m. Raymond Vargay, Apr. 21, 1953 (div. 1965); 1 child, Rose Marie. B.A. in Sociology, Fla. Internat. U., 1976, B.A. in Religion, 1978, M.P.A., 1980. Sec. U.S. Air Force, various bases, 1959-84; adj. prof. Miami-Dade Community Coll., Fla., 1980-82; equal employment opportunity staffing specialist U.S. Air Force, Homestead AFB, Fla., 1984—. Leader, cons. Girl Scouts U.S.A., 1952-83; Sunday sch. tchr. St. Peter's Lutheran Ch., Miami, 1974-85; bd. dirs. Dade Hire the Handicapped Com., 1985-86. Recipient Outstanding Employee of Yr. award Homestead AFB, 1980, 84; Fed. Employee of Yr. award Fed. Exec. Bd., 1984. Mem. Am. Soc. Pub. Adminstrn., Am. Bus. Women's Assn. (community service award 1982), AAUW, Air Force Assn., Nat. Assn. Female Execs., Phi Lambda Pi. Republican. Lutheran. Club: Toastmasters.

KEMP, LINDA JOYCE, sales executive; b. Rochester, N.H., June 24, 1952; d. Robert Carl and Lillian Frances (Goldthwait) Hersom; m. Robert W. Kemp,

Aug. 28, 1981 (div. 1983). B.S., Plymouth State Coll., 1974; postgrad. U. N.H., 1974-78. Tchr. phys. edn., coach Union Sch. Dist. 21, Seabrook, N.H., 1974-78, Dover High Sch., N.H., 1978-81; dist. sales mgr. Avon Products, Inc., 1981—, field trainer, 1982-83. Republican. Avocations: skiing; tennis; swimming. Home: 4 Sprucewood Dr Rochester NH 03867

KEMP, PEGGY SLOAN, educator, lawyer; b. Shepherdsville, Ky., June 5, 1948; d. Samuel Robert Sloan and Ernestine Masden; m. Kenneth Alfred Kemp, July 29, 1976; children—Kenneth N., Alfred C., Paul L. B.A., Berea Coll., 1969; postgrad. U. Mass. 1971-72; J.D., Harvard U., 1980. Bar: Mass. 1982. Tchr., Lewenberg Middle Sch., Boston, 1971-80; pvt. practice law, Cambridge, Mass., 1982—; head dept. history Boston Latin Sch., 1983—. Boston Edison scholar, 1986. Mem. ABA, Mass. Bar Assn., Mass. Black Women's Attys. Address: 386 Franklin St Cambridge MA 02139

KEMP, SUZANNE LEPPART, educator, clubwoman; b. N.Y.C., Dec. 28, 1929; d. Johm Culver and Eleanor (Buxton) Leppart; grad. Ogontz Jr. Coll., 1949; B.S., U. Md., 1952; m. Ralph Clinton Kemp, Apr. 4, 1953; children—Valerie Gale, Sandra Lynn, John Maynard, Renee Alison. Elem. sch. tchr. Mem. Nat. Soc. Women Descs. of Ancient and Hon. Arty. Co., Nat. Soc. Daus. of Founders and Patriots of Am. (corr. sec.), Nat. Soc. Dames of Court of Honor, Nat. Soc. Sons and Daus. of Pilgrims, Nat. Soc. U.S. Daus. of 1812 (chpt. organizing pres. 1977-79; state 2d v.p., chpt. v.p., 1979—), Nat. Soc. New Eng. Women (colony pres. 1978-80), Nat. Soc. Coloniel Dames XVII Century (state chmn. heraldry and coats of arms 1977-79), Nat. Soc. DAR (chpt. regent 1970-73, chpt. v.p.; Md. soc. chmn. transp. 1976-79), Md. State Officers Club, Md. Hist. Soc., Walters Art Gallery, Balt. Mus. Art, Friends of Animals, Defenders of Animal Rights, Inc., U. Md. Alumni, English Speaking Union, Star Spangled Banner Flag House Assn., Kappa Delta Alumni. Christian Scientist. Clubs: Baltimore Country; Lago Mar Country; Woman's of Roland Park. Editor: The Spinning Wheel, 1973-76. Home: 1206 Doves Cove Rd Towson MD 21204

KEMPE, BALLERIE LEE, banker, realtor; b. Kileen, Tex. Oct. 23, 1959; d. Eldon Lee and Roberta Jean (Faulder) Beavers; m. Mark Charles Kempe, June 23, 1984. Student, Stephen F. Austin State U., 1978-80; B.B.A. in Fin., U. Houston, 1982; postgrad. Am. Inst. Banking, Houston, 1982-85. Tax assessor, coll. rep. Assessments of the Southwest, Houston, 1977-78; realtor Space City Realtors, Clear Lake City, Tex. and Houston, 1981—; credit analyst, credit mgr. Comml. State Bank, Houston, 1982—, asst. cashier, 1984—, asst. v.p., 1986—. Mem. Am. Inst. Banking, Robert Morris Assocs., Houston Assn. Credit Mgmt., Nat. Bd. Realtors, Houston Bd. Realtors, Soc. Women Mgrs., Credit Reps. Assn. Club: Financial. Republican. Methodist. Avocations: tennis; aerobics; decorating; cooking; personal computing. Home: 9100 Fondren St Apt 206 Houston TX 77074 Office: Comml State Bank 9111 Eastex Freeway PO Box 11627 Houston TX 77293

KEMPER, DORLA DEAN (EATON), real estate broker; b. Calhoun, Mo., Sept. 10, 1929; d. Paul McVey and Jesse Lee (McCombs) Eaton; student William Woods Coll., 1947-48; B.S. in Edn., Central Mo. State U., 1952; m. Charles K. Kemper, Mar. 1, 1951; children—Kevin Keil, Kara Lee. Tchr. pub. schs., Twin Falls, Idaho, 1950-51, Mission, Kans., 1952-53, Burbank, Calif., 1953-57; real estate saleswoman Minn., 1967-68, Calif., 1971-73; Deanie Kemper, Realtor (name changed to Deanie Kemper, Inc. Real Estate Brokerage 1976), Loomis, Calif., 1974-76, pres., 1976—, also dir. Pres. Battle Creek Park Elem. Sch. PTA, St. Paul, 1966-67; mem. Placer County (Calif.) Bicentennial Commn., 1976; mem. real estate adv. com. Sierra Coll., 1981—. Named to Masters Club (lifetime) Sacramento and Placer County bds. Realtors, 1978; cert. resdl. specialist Realtors Nat. Mktg. Inst. Mem. Nat., Calif. assns. Realtors, Placer County Bds. Realtors, Grad. Realtors Inst., Auburn Travel Study Club (pres. 1978-79), DAR (chpt. regent 1971-73, organizing chpt. regent 1977—, dist. dir. Calif. 1978-80, vice-chmn. nat. def. com., registrar Calif. 1980-82, Calif. state regent 1984-86, nat. chmn. units overseas, mem. nab. resolutions com., nat. officer, rec. sec. gen. 1986—). Republican. Mem. Christian Ch. Clubs: Auburn Travel Study (pres.), Hidden Valley Women's (pres. Loomis club 1970-71). Republican Mem. Christian Ch. Home: 8165 Morningside Dr Loomis CA 95650

KEMPER, MARLYN J., librarian, historian; b. Balt., Mar. 26, 1943; d. Louis and Augusta Louise (Jacobs) Janofsky; m. Bennett I. Kemper, Aug. 1, 1965; children—Alex Randall, Gari Hament, Jason Myles. B.A., Finch Coll., 1964; M.A. in Anthropology, Temple U., Phila., 1970; M.A. in Library Sci., U. S. Fla., 1983. Dir., Hist. Broward County Preservation Bd., Hollywood, Fla., 1979—; automated systems librarian Broward County Main Library, Ft. Lauderdale, Fla., 1983—. Pub. info. officer Broward County Hist. Commn., 1975-79. Recipient Judge L. Clayton Nance award, 1977; Broward County Hist. Commn. award, 1979. Mem. ALA, Am. Soc. for Info. Sci., Spl. Libraries Assn., Orgn. Am. Historians, Associated Info. Mgrs., Beta Phi Mu, Phi Kappa Phi. Democrat. Jewish. Author: A Comprehensive Documented History of the City of Pompano Beach, 1982 A Comprehensive History of Dania 1983, Hallandale, 1984, Deerfield Beach, 1985, Plantation, 1986; author weekly columns Ft. Lauderdale News, 1975-76, 77-79; contbr. articles to profl. jours. Home: 2845 NE 35th St Fort Lauderdale FL 33306 Office: Broward County Main Library 100 S Andrews Ave Fort Lauderdale FL 33301

KEMPFERT, AMY ELLEN, lawyer; b. Beloit, Wis., Mar. 22, 1950; d. William Charles and Marianna Cadman (Moss) Vreeland; m. Peter James Kempfert, Apr. 3, 1970; 1 child, Stephan Chesbrough. B.S., U. Wis.-Stevens Point, 1972; J.D., U. Tulsa, 1981. Bar: Wis. 1981, Okla. 1982; cert. respiratory therapist, 1974. Therapeutic supr. respiratory therapy St. Michaels Hosp., Stevens Point, Wis., 1972-78; asst. dist. atty. Wood County, Wisconsin Rapids, Wis., 1981-82; assoc. Works, Lentz & Pottorf, Inc., Tulsa, 1982—. Editor Tulsa Law Jour., 1980-81. Mem. Young Republicans, Wis., 1966-74. Recipient Am. Jurisprudence awards, 1979, 80. Mem. Wis. Bar, Okla. Trial Lawyers, Oklahoma Bar Assn., Assn. Trial Lawyers Am., Tulsa County Bar Assn. Office: Works Lentz & Pottorf Inc Boston Place Bldg 50 E 15th St Tulsa OK

KEMPNER, RUTH LYDIA (BENEDICTA MARIA) (MRS. ROBERT M.W. KEMPNER), author, social worker; b. Geislingen, Germany; d. Hermann and Marie-Luise (Spring) Hahn; diploma social work Sch. Social Work, Berlin, 1930; postgrad. Pa. Sch. Social Work, Phila., 1940-41; m. Robert M. W. Kempner; children—Lucian K., Andre K. Social worker City of Berlin, 1929-33; dean women Fiorenza Coll., Florence, Italy and Nice, France, 1936-39; social-work agys. in Phila., 1941-45; M-project, Pres. F. D. Roosevelt, 1944-45; research analyst U.S. Army, Nuremberg War Crimes Trials, 1947-48; work on claims for health damage Catholic and Jewish Nazi victims, 1953-63; researcher martyr priests, 1963—, TV, radio documentations, Rome, Germany, U.S. Docorated Pro Ecclesia et Pontifice, Pope Paul VI; Cross of Merit, Govt. German Fed. Republic; recipient Golden Honor award Austrian Govt. Mem. Am. Assn. Social Workers, Am. Acad. Social Work, Internat. Pen Club Am. Author: (under pen name Benedicta Maria) Women in Nazi Germany, 1944; Priester before Hitler's Tribunals, 1966; Nuns under the Swastika, 1979; contbr. to Catholic mags. Home: 112 Lansdowne Court Lansdowne PA 19050

KEMPTON, GRACE FICKLING ARRINGTON (MRS. WILLETT MAIN KEMPTON), realtor, journalist; b. Rome, Ga., June 26; d. Homer Newell and Grace (Fickling) Arrington; A.B., Shorter Coll.; B.A. in Journalism, U. Ga., 1940; m. Willett Main Kempton, Aug. 5, 1939 (dec. Nov. 1962); children—Willett Main, Grace Arrington (dec. May 1973), John Houston. Soc. columnist Athens (Ga.) Banner Herald, 1940-41; with Clark County Draft Bd., Athens, 1941; spl. writer Atlanta Constn., 1942; reporter Army Public Relations, Atlanta, 1942-43; owner, mgr. Embassy Service Bur., Washington, 1946-47; adminstrv. asst. Congressmen Henderson Lanham, Ga., 1947-48; Washington soc. columnist Palm Beach (Fla.) Life, 1947; social news columnist Providence Jour., McLean, Va., 1952-53; columnist Courier of George Washington U. Med. Sch., 1952-57; owner, realtor Grace A. Kempton Realty Co., McLean, 1955—. Mem. women's bd. George Washington U. Hosp., Washington, 1953—; life mem. Athens Jr. Assembly; dir. McLean Horse Show Assn., 1950-70. Served from 2d lt. to capt., WAC, 1943-45. Mem. Nat., No. Va. bds. Realtors, Va. Real Estate Assn., Am. News Women's Club, Nat. Trust Historic Preservation, Ga. State Soc. (pres. 1975), Women in Communications, Chi Omega. Methodist. Clubs: Capitol Speakers, The Washington. Home: 1313 Rockland Terr McLean VA 22101 Office: 8112 Old Dominion Dr McLean VA 22102

KEMPTON, GRETA M., artist; b. Vienna, Austria; d. H.K. and Josephine K.; student Art Students League, N.Y.C., 1930; 1 dau., Daisy Dickson. One woman shows include: Corcoran Gallery Art, Washington, 1949, Canton (Ohio) Art Inst., 1964, Coll. of Wooster, 1963, Akron Art League, 1962, Circle Gallery, Cleve., 1963; group shows: NAD, N.Y.C., Dowling Coll., Oakdale, N.Y., Human Resources Center, Albertson, N.Y., L.I. U.; represented in permanent collections White House, Dept. Treasury, Washington, Truman Mus., Independence, Mo., U.S. Supreme Ct., Washington, Dept. Interior, Smithsonian Inst. Portrait Gallery, Lyndon Johnson Library, Austin, Tex., Georgetown U., also many other museums, pvt. collections. Fellow Royal Soc. Arts (London); mem. Soc. Arts and Letters (life), European Acad. Arts, Scis. and Humanities (corr.), Nat. Arts Club, Corcoran Gallery (life). Address: 14 E 75th St New York NY 10021

KEMP-WILLIAMS, MARGARET ESTELEAN, lawyer; b. Akron, Ohio, Dec. 1, 1948; d. Howard Albert and Louise (Talkington) Shreve; m. John Charles Kemp, Aug. 30, 1968 (div.); children—Kara Theresa, Lori Anne; m. 2d, Michael W. Williams, Dec. 19, 1979. B.A., Chapman Coll., 1970; M.S. in Teaching, U. Portland, 1971; J.D.S., U. Wis., 1983. Bar: Wis. 1983. Tchr. pub. schs., Ft. Knox, Ky., 1971-74; instr. Fox Valley Tech. Inst., Appleton, Wis., 1976-80; intern NLRB, Milw., 1982; summer assoc. Cades, Schutte, Fleming & Wright, Honolulu, 1982; law clk., Madison, Wis., 1981-83; assoc. firm Grutzner, Byron, Holland & Vollmer, Beloit, Wis., 1983-85, Jory, Peterson & Sagaser, Fresno, Calif., 1985-86, Richtel & Smith, Fresno, 1986—. Author: Political Parties, 1977; The Power of the Media, 1977; editor: Social Issues, 1976; Labor Relations, 1976; The Federal Government, 1976. Campaign worker Appleton Democratic Com., 1976; bd. dirs. Planned Parenthood, Appleton, 1978; fundraiser United Way, Beloit, 1983. Mem. ABA, Wis. Bar Assn., Calif. Bar Assn., Fresno County Bar Assn., Am. Trial Lawyers Assn. Methodist. Club: Altrusa (Beloit). Home: 1606 W Browning Fresno CA 93711 Office: Richtel & Smith 1111 Fulton Mall Suite 400 Fresno CA 93721

KENDALL, CHARLOTTE KALIKOHOU, contract adminstr.; b. Honolulu, Jan. 25, 1940; d. Charles Russel and Mililani Rose (Lucas) Kendall; student Colo. State Coll., 1959-60; children—Rhonda McKeague, Alex McKeague, Charles McKeague. Bookkeeper, So. Md. Oil, LaPlata, 1972-73; accounts payable, shipping-receiving mgr. Mammoth Mart Inc., Waldorf, Md., 1974-77; purchasing agt., contract adminstr. Plessey Micro Sci., Mountain View, Calif., 1977-81; subcontract adminstr. FMC Corp., San Jose, Calif., 1981—. Recipient outstanding achievement award Girls Club of Mid-Peninsula, 1978. Mem. Am. Electronics Assn., Am. Prodn. and Inventory Control Soc., Nat. Contract Mgmt. Assn., Purchasing Mgmt. Assn. No. Calif. Office: FMC Corp 1105 Coleman Ave Box 1201 San Jose CA 95108

KENDALL, DOLORES DIANE, artist, author, direct mail marketing executive; b. Newark, June 1, 1946; d. Dominick Pisapia and Ann Fanfone Pisapia Kendall; student Berkeley Bus. Coll., N.J., 1964-65, Middlesex County Coll., N.J., 1966-67, Rutgers U., 1967-69, Art Inst. Boston, 1976, Sch. Visual Arts, N.Y.C., 1978, NYU, 1977, Graham Art Studio, Boston, 1975-77, others. Proofreader, supr. N.J. State Diagnostic Center, 1965-74; apprentice instr. Graham Art Studio, Boston, 1975-77; dir. direct mktg. Boardroom Reports, Inc., N.Y.C., 1977-82; pres., chief operating officer Roman Managed Lists, Inc., N.Y.C., 1982; dir. direct mktg. Mal Dunn Assocs., N.Y.C., 1983; dir. list mgmt. Warren, Gorham & Lamont, Inc., N.Y.C., 1984-86; direct mktg. cons., 1986. Exhibited in group shows including city and county shows in N.Y.C., Boston, Middlesex and Somerset Counties (N.J.), 1965-74, Greenwich Village Art Show, N.Y.C., 1972, Graham Art Studio, Boston, 1975-77; represented in pvt. collections. Author: (poems) My Eyes are Windows, 1972, Feelings & Thoughts, 1979. Contbr. articles to profl. jours. Recipient Desi award for promotion package, 1980; awards for poetry. Mem. Direct Mail Mktg. Assn., Dir. Mktg. Creative Guild, Inc., NOW, Nat. Assn. Female Execs, Copley Soc., Nat. Mail Order Assn. (adv. bd. 1979-80), Internat. Platform Assn., Graham Art Studio. Home: 530 2d Ave New York NY 10016

KENDEL, DORLA DEAN (MRS. ROBERT LEWIS KENDEL), former mfrs. rep. co. exec., artist; b. Los Angeles, Apr. 16, 1930; d. Thomas Weston and Lois May (Oliver) Hall; grad. high sch.; m. Robert Lewis Kendel, Aug. 13, 1949; children—Robert L., Michael L., Richard L. Tchr. oil painting, LaCrescenta, Calif., 1960-62; with Air Conditioning Spltys. Co., Inc., mfrs. rep., LaCrescenta, 1962-79, corp. sec.-treas., 1970-79; artist, 1979—. Active Scouting, sch. and sport activities, 1956-70. Mem. ASHRAE. Address: 46-058 Verba Santa Palm Desert CA 92260

KENDRA, ARLENE MARIE, antique dealer and show promoter, financial planner, consultant; b. Sutersville, Pa., Nov. 7, 1934; d. Adolph and Florence M. (Ferretti) Panizzi; m. Robert T. Kendra, Aug. 8, 1959. Student St. Vincent Coll., 1984-86, Coll. Fin. Planning, 1984-87. Clk., Tully-Shipley Real Estate, McKeesport, Pa., 1952-56; sec., clk. bus. planning dept. U.S. Steel Corp., McKeesport, Pa., 1956-84; pvt. practice fin. planning, 1986—; mgr. Antique Shows, Greensburg, Pa., 1974—; promoter Alle-Kiski Hist. Soc., Tarentum, Pa., 1982—. Contbr. articles to antique publs. Promoter, mgr. Hanna's Town outdoor antique activities and festival, Greensburg, 1974—, Westmoreland Mus. Art, Women's Com., 1978-82. Mem. Westmoreland County Hist. Soc. (bd. dirs. 1974-79, charter mem., pres. Elizabeth Hanna Guild 1975), Rolling Hills Garden Club, Early Am. Industries Assn., Am. Orchid Soc., Western Pa. Orchid Soc. Avocations: gardening; antiques; growing orchids. Home and Office: 39 S Rolling Hills Irwin PA 15642

KENDRICK, PAMELA DALEY, lawyer, educator; b. Springfield, Mass., Oct. 1, 1952; d. Edward Murray and Elizabeth (Bloom) Daley; m. Calvert Tomlin Kendrick, Sept. 20, 1975. A.B., Princeton U., 1974; J.D., U. Pa., 1979. Bar: Pa. 1979. Tax atty. Morgan, Lewis & Bockius, Phila., 1979—, also prof. tax law U. Pa., 1982—. Recipient Carrye G. Barenkopf award U. Pa., 1978; McCall prize, 1979; Reeves award, 1979. Mem. ABA, Pa. Bar Assn., Phila. Bar Assn. Clubs: Princeton (N.Y.C.). Office: Morgan Lewis & Bockius 2000 One Logan Sq Philadelphia PA 19103

KENDRICK, RAE HANSEN, musician, singer, real estate sales executive; b. Evanston, Ill., Apr. 26, 1933; d. Arthur Stedry Hansen and Alice Charlotte (Hanson) Hansen Pettengill; m. Dale Alan Kendrick, Aug. 15, 1960 (div. Aug. 1978); children—Wendy Ann, Dean Arthur. Student Eastman Sch. Music, 1951-52, Am. Conservatory Music, 1952-53; Mus.B., Northwestern U., 1955; postgrad. in fine arts mgmt., Columbia Coll., Chgo., 1983—. Recitalist, guest soloist, Chgo., 1952-60, 77—; sec. De-Wen, Inc., Des Plaines, Ill., 1969-78; real estate mgr. Lake Forest, Ill., 1982—; dir., asst. treas. William Ferris Chorale, Chicago, 1980-81. Solo performer world premieres musical works by Hamilton Forrest, 1953, William Ferris, 1980, Daniel Tucker, 1982, Barry Rifkin, 1983, Wendy Kendrick, 1983. Mem. Delta Omicron. Home: 232 E Walton Pl Chicago IL 60611

KENDRICKS, VIVIAN DAVIS, education educator; b. Thomasville, Ga., May 24, 1928; d. Aurelius Darius and Eula Mae (Davis) Davis; m. Henry A. Hunt, June 4, 1974 (div. 1975); m. James W. Kendricks, Dec. 28, 1978. B.S., Clark Coll., Atlanta, 1948; M.S., S.C. State Coll., Orangeburg, 1966; M.A., Fisk U., Nashville, 1970; Ph.D., Fla. State U., 1976. Chairperson sci. Ctr. High Sch., Way Cross, Ga., 1968-70; chairperson dept. home econs. Fort Valley Coll., Ga., 1972-73; asst. prof. home econs., Fla. A&M U., 1973-76; assoc. prof. edn. Fort Valley State Coll., Ga., 1979-84, supr. student teaching, 1979-84; tchr. sci. Plant City High Sch., Fla., 1984-85; vis. sci. practitioner Hillsborough Community Coll., Tampa, Fla., 1985; vis. prof. allied scis. Fla. A&M U., Tallahassee, 1973-76. Named Tchr. of Yr., Way Cross C. of C., 1969. Mem. AAUW (chair internat. women 1984-85), LWV, Toastmistress Internat., Clark Coll. Alumnae Assn. (nat. sec. 1976-79), Sigma Xi, Delta Sigma Theta, Phi Delta Kappa, Democrat. Congregationalist. Avocations: bass guitar; piano; voice. Home: 1313 W State St Tampa FL 33606

KENIMER, KATHLEEN CULLEY, financial analyst, consultant, planner; b. Lexington, Ky., Sept. 19, 1953; d. Robert Lewis and Betty Jean (Dunn) Culley; m. William Curtis Kenimer, Dec. 6, 1975; children—Richard Cameron, Keenan Joel. B.A. in Edn., U. Ky., 1974; M.A. in Edn., Georgetown U., 1984. Tchr. Fayette County Schs., Ky., 1975-80; dist. mktg. dir. Lady Love Cosmetics, Dallas and Lexington, 1980-85; fin. analyst Waddell and Reed, Lexington, 1985—, also seminar instr., 1985—; tchr. fin. planning Bourbon County Schs., Ky., 1986. Adviser Christian Women's Club, Paris, Ky., 1984—. Named Boss of Yr., Am. Bus. Women's Assn., 1984; Scholar Ky. Baptists, 1971, Eta Sigma Phi, 1971. Mem. Phi Mu. Avocations: smocking; horticulture. Home: 311 Redmon Rd Paris KY 40361 Office: Waddell and Reed Inc 870 Corporate Dr Lexington KY 40503

KENNAN, ELIZABETH TOPHAM, college president; b. Phila., Feb. 25, 1938; d. Frank and Henrietta (Jackson) Topham; widow; 1 son, Frank Alexander. B.A. summa cum laude, Mt. Holyoke Coll., 1960; M.A. (Hon. Woodrow Wilson fellow, Marshall scholar), St. Hilda's Coll., Oxford (Eng.) U., 1962; Ph.D., U. Wash., 1966; L.H.D. (hon.), Trinity Coll., Washington, 1978, Amherst Coll., 1980, Oberlin Coll., 1983, St. Mary's Coll., 1982; Litt.D., Cath. U. Am., 1985; LL.D., Smith Coll., 1984. Asst. prof. history Catholic U. Am., 1966-70, asso. prof., 1970-78, dir. medieval and Byzantine studies program, 1970-78, dir. program in early Christian humanism, 1974-78, mem. pres.'s emergency adv. bd. on univ. fin., 1976-77; mem. bd. cons. Nat. Endowment for Humanities, 1975—; pres. Mt. Holyoke Coll., 1978—; dir. Bank of New Eng., Springfield, Mass., N.E. Utilities, Hartford, Conn., Berkshire Life Ins. Co., Pittsfield, Mass., NYNEX Corp., N.Y.C.; mem. Consortium on Financing Higher Edn., 1980—, chmn., 1982-83; chmn. com. on govt. relations Am. Council Edn., 1979-82. Bd. dirs. Miss Porter's Sch., 1981-85, Council on Library Resources, 1982—; mem. Council Fgn. Relations. Named Tchr. of Year, Cath. U. Am., 1977. Mem. Mediaeval Acad. Am. (councillor 1984-85), Phi Beta Kappa. Translator, author introduction and notes: (with John D. Anderson) On Consideration (St. Bernard of Clairvaux), 1976; contbr. articles to profl. pubis. Office: Pres's Office Mt Holyoke Coll South Hadley MA 01075

KENNARD, PAMELA DELENA, nurse; b. Mobile, Ala., Oct. 11, 1951; d. Ernest Lucier and Delores Wilhelmina (Gray) Freeman; m. John Henry Kennard, July 31, 1976; children—Cedric Alonzo, Benjamin Terrell, Alfred Lamar. B.S. Nursing, Tuskegee Inst., 1975. Staff nurse Crawford, W. Long Meml. Hosp., Atlanta, 1975-76, Greene County Hosp., Eutaw, Ala., 1976-77; nursing supr. West Ala. Health Services, Eutaw, 1977—. Mem. Am. Nurses Assn., Ala. State Nurses Assn., Tuskegee Inst. Alumni Assn. Baptist. Club: Alabama Gee Cee (Forkland, Ala.). Lodge: Order Eastern Star. Home: PO Box 483 426 Roebuck Ave Eutaw AL 35462 Office: West Alabama Health Services Inc PO Box 711 607 Wilson Ave Eutaw AL 35462

KENNEDY, CELISE CHICOLA, nurse; b. Alexandria, La., May 25, 1960; d. Vincent Francis and Esther (Cancienne) Chicola; m. Randall Wayne Kennedy, July 23, 1982. B.S. in Nursing, U. St. Thomas, Houston, 1982. R.N. Tex. Staff nurse St. Joseph Hosp., Houston, 1982-83; office nurse, research asst. Stehlin Found. for Cancer Research, Houston, 1983—. Author pamphlet: The New You, 1982. Nurse ARC, Houston. Democrat. Roman Catholic. Home: 7510 Brompton #512 Houston TX 77025 Office: 1315 Calhoun #1800 Med Place I Houston TX 77002

KENNEDY, DEBRA JOYCE, hospital marketing administrator; b. Covina, Calif., July 9, 1955; d. John Nathan and Drea Hannah (Lancaster) Ward; m. John William Kennedy, Sept. 3, 1977 (div.). B.S. in Communications, Calif. State Poly. U., 1977. Pub. relations coordinator Whittier (Calif.) Hosp., 1978-79, pub. relations mgr., 1980; pub. relations dir. San Clemente (Calif.) Hosp., 1979-80; dir. pub. relations Garfield Med. Ctr., Monterey Park, Calif., 1980-82; dir. mktg. and community relations Charter Oak Hosp., Covina, 1983-85; mktg. coordinator CPC Horizon Hosp., Pomona, Calif., 1985—. Mem. Am. Soc. Hosp. Pub. Relations, So. Calif. Soc. Hosp. Pub. Relations, Covina and Covina West C. of C., West Covina Jaycees. Republican. Methodist. Club: Soroptimists. Contbr. articles to profl. jours.

KENNEDY, EDNA W., public relations executive; b. Oak Park, Ill., Oct. 2, 1956; d. Clarence W. and Gloria Louise (Bennington) Clark; m. Samuel Edward Kennedy, Sept. 11, 1981; 1 child, Ellen Marie. B.S. in Bus. Adminstrn., Roosevelt U., 1978, postgrad. in bus., 1978-80. With pub. relations dept. Comstock Assocs., Chgo., 1980-83; pres. Kennedy Pub. Relations Assocs., Chgo., 1983—. Mem. Pub. Relations Assn. Am., Nat. Assn. Female Execs., Chgo. Pub. Relations Assn. Democrat. Episcopalian. Address: Werik Towers 24 N Wabash Ave Suite 823 Chicago IL 60602

KENNEDY, EVELYN SIEFERT, foundation executive; b. Pitts., Nov. 11, 1927; d. Carmine and Assunta (Iacobucci) Rocci; B.S. magna cum laude, U. R.I., 1969, M.S. in Textiles and Clothing, 1970; m. George J. Siefert, May 30, 1953 (div. 1974); children—Paul Kenneth, Carl Joseph, Ann Marie; m. Lyle H. Kennedy, II, Oct. 12, 1974. With Pitts. Public Schs., 1945-50; with Goodyear Aircraft Corp., Akron, Ohio, 1950-54; clothing instr. Groton (Conn.) Dept. Adult Edn., 1958-68; pres. Sewtique, Groton, 1970, Sewtique II, New London, Conn., 1986; v.p. Kennedy Capital Advisors, Groton, 1973-85, Kennedy Mgmt. Corp., Groton, 1974-85, Kennedy InterVest, Inc., Groton, 1975-85; pres., exec. dir. P.R.I.D.E. Found., Inc., Groton, 1978—; clothing cons. Coop. Extension Service, Dept. Agr.; internat. lectr. on clothing for disabled and elderly; adj. faculty U. Conn., Eastern Conn. State Coll., St. Joseph Coll.; fed. expert witness Care Label Law, FTC, 1976; mem. Major Appliance Consumer Action Panel, 1983. Regional adv. council SBA active corps Execs., Hartford; bd. dirs. Easter Seal Rehab. Center Southeastern Conn.; bus. adv. council U. R.I., 1979—, trustee, 1985—; active LWV; mem. Groton Vocat. Edn. Adv. Council. Recipient award of distinction U. R.I., 1969; Small Bus. Adminstrn. Adv. of Year, 1984. Mem. Better Sleep Council (consumer affairs rep.), Nat. Assn. Bedding Mfrs., Conn. Home Economists in Bus. (founder 1977), Nat. Home Economists in Bus. (chmn. internat. relations, nat. fin. chmn. 1986), Am. Home Econs. Assn., Coll. and Univ. Bus. Instrs. of Conn., Fashion Group, Omicron Nu, Phi Kappa Phi. Democrat. Roman Catholic. Clubs: New London Zonta, Bus. and Profl. Women's (Outstanding Women of Year 1977). Author: Dressing With Pride, 1980; Clothing Accessibility: A Lesson Plan to Aid the Disabled and Elderly, 1983. Office: 71 Plaza Ct Groton CT 06340

KENNEDY, GAY LOUISE, social services administrator; b. Hollister, Calif., May 23, 1931; d. Howard Ross and Harriet Elizabeth (Douglass) K.; m. Andrew Milos Gall, Aug. 30, 1952 (div.); children—Steven H., Kenneth J. (dec.). B.S. in Acctg., Calif. State U.-Fresno, 1981. Ptnr. Sergel Bus. Service, 1956-58; owner, mgr. Cardland, 1965-75, Anytime Bookkeeping, 1965-75; dir. Displaced Homemakers, 1979-81, Sr. Aides, Fresno, 1981-83; exec. dir. Older Ams. Orgns., 1983-85, Soc. Older Ams., 1985—. Mem. Human Rights Commn.; mem. Human Services Coalition; mem. citizens adv. com. City of Fresno; v.p. Displaced Homemakers Network; mem. state steering com. Nat. Women's Polit. Caucus. Mem. Western Gerontol. Soc., Nat. Council Sr. Citizens, Older Women's League, Fresno Career Women, Nat. Assn. Female Execs., NOW, Internat. Platform Assn., LWV. Democrat. Roman Catholic. Club: Soroptomists. Office: One Manchester Blvd Inglewood CA 90301

KENNEDY, HELEN MARIE, hospital administrator, consultant; b. Jersey City, May 3, 1942; d. Paul Joseph and Helen Mary (Murray) K. Registered Nurse, St. Mary's Hosp., Hoboken, N.J., 1962; B.S. in Nursing, Fairleigh Dickinson U., 1971; M.A. in Nursing Adminstrn., Columbia U., 1974; M.B.A., Fairleigh Dickinson U., 1987. Staff nurse St. Mary's Hosp., Hoboken, 1962-63, asst. head nurse, 1963, head nurse, 1963-65; adminstr. Central Med. Group, Union City, N.J., 1965-75; dir. nursing service Riverside Gen. Hosp., Secaucus, N.J., 1975-78, asst. adminstr., 1978-84, assoc. adminstr., 1984, exec. v.p., adminstr., 1984—; cons. Central Med. Group, Union City, 1975-85, Central Ob and Gyn Affiliates, Union City, 1981-86, Stafford Assocs., North Bergen, N.J., 1984—; preceptor adminstrn.-health services Ithaca Coll., N.Y., 1985—. Sponsor Heal the Children, N.J. div., Spokane, Wash., 1983-86, Met. Turner Syndrome Assocs., Convent Station, N.J., 1984-86. Mem. Am. Coll. Healthcare Execs., Am. Hosp. Assn., Soc. Law and Medicine, Am. Soc. Hosp. Nursing Service Adminstrs., Am. Nurses Assn., N.J. State Nurses Assn., Hudson Hosp. Council, Hudson Health Systems Agy. (bd. dirs. 1976-82), Meadowlands C. of C., St. Mary's Hosp. Nurses Alumnae, Fairleigh Dickinson U. Alumnae, Tchrs. Coll. Alumnae. Roman Catholic. Avocations: travel; reading; dancing. Office: Riverside Gen Hosp Meadowland Pkwy Secaucus NJ 07094

KENNEDY, JEAN THRASHER, writer, poet, educator; b. Atlanta, Aug. 5, 1932; d. Barton Edmonds and Winnie H. (Ham) Thrasher; A.B., Wesleyan Coll., Macon, Ga., 1954; M.A., Northwestern U., 1956; m. Victor N., June 30, 1956 (div. 1985); children—Philip, Elaine, Laura. Staff writer Atlanta Constn., 1952-54; tech. manuscript editor Jour. AMA, Chgo., 1956-57, Jour. ADA, Chgo., 1957-58; asst. to editorial page editor Waterloo (Iowa) Courier, 1972-76; writing tchr. Waterloo Recreation Commn., Iowa Arts Council and Waterloo YWCA, 1980—; instr. in English lang. and lit. U. No. Iowa, 1981—; contbr. fiction, non-fiction, poetry to various publs. Bd. dirs. Waterloo-Cedar Falls Jr. League, 1967-68; pres. Waterloo Reciprocity, PEO Sisterhood, 1981-82; mem. adult program com. YWCA, Waterloo, sec. bd. dirs., 1985-86, chmn. nominating com., 1986. Recipient prizes for poetry and fiction. Mem. Nat. League Am. Pen Women (v.p. Waterloo-Cedar Rapids br. 1980-82; bd. dirs.

1984—), AAUW, Iowa Council Tchrs. English, Nat. Council Tchrs. English. Presbyterian. Contbr. fiction to mags. Home: 857 Sunrise Blvd Waterloo IA 50701 Office: Dept English Lang and Lit U No Iowa Cedar Falls IA 50614

KENNEDY, JEWEL P., Human resources administrator; b. Princeton, N.J.; d. Theodore H. and Alice (Wilson) Kennedy. A.A., Green Mountain Coll., 1963; B.A., Bernard Baruch Coll., 1971; M.Human Resource, New Sch. Social Research, 1980—. Dir. fin. and adminstrn. Pvt. Concerns, Inc., N.Y.C., 1973-76; dir. adminstrn. Regional Plan Assn., N.Y.C., 1976-79; dir. personnel and mgmt. services Tri-State Regional Planning Commn., N.Y.C., 1979-81; dir. human resources Girl Scouts U.S.A., N.Y.C., 1981—; asst. exec. dir. Northwest Ga. Girl Scout Council, Atlanta; adult tng. cons. Rutgers U., 1982—; career counselor, 1979—. Bd. dirs. Atlanta YMCA. Author/editor Personnel Policies Manuals; contbr. articles to profl. jours. Active West Side Republican Club, 1981—. Mem. Council of Concerned Black Execs., N.Y. Personnel Mgmt. Assn., Schomburg Ctr. for Research in Black Culture (dir.), Delta U. Republican. Club: 100 Black Women. Office: Northwest Ga Girl Scout Council 100 Edgewood Ave Atlanta GA 30335

KENNEDY, KAY J., researcher-writer; b. S.D.; d. Edward James and Marie Amelia (Bowman) K.; B.A. in Geology, U. Wyo., 1931. Reporter, Gt. Falls (Mont.) Leader, 1944-45, Denver Post, 1945, Alaska Daily Empire, Juneau, 1950-51, Fairbanks (Alaska) Daily News-Miner, 1952-56; chief news bur. Alaska Visitors Assn., Seattle, 1957-60; news bur. chief Alaska Travel Promotion Assn., 1961-62; pub. relations Wien Alaska Airlines, Fairbanks and Anchorage, 1966-70; freelance research-writer, 1936—; producer 1st 2 Alaska Travel manuals, 1957-58; 68; author original copy Alaska Sunset Discovery Book, 1963, Wien Brothers Story, 1967. Recipient Lulu award Los Angeles Advt. Women, 1958; named Wash. Woman of Achievement, Wash. Press Women, 1978. Mem. Outdoor Writers Assn. Am., Alaska Press Women (founder, pres. 1961; awards 1969, 71), Wash. Press Women (award 1959), Soc. Am. Travel Writers. Clubs: Alaska Press (award 1959). Address: 330 3d Ave #407 Fairbanks AK 99701

KENNEDY, LORI DIANE ODELL, court reporting agency executive; b. Sacramento, Sept. 8, 1956; d. Gerald Wray and Karen Margaret (Lilleland) Odell; m. Patrick Champ Kennedy, Aug. 11, 1979; children—Lindsey Kristina, Matthew Garrett. A.A. in English and Court Reporting, Green River Coll., 1975; grad. Calif. Sch. Court Reporting, 1976; student CMR Inst., U. Ala. Registered profl. reporter; lic. cert. shorthand reporter, Calif. Staff reporter Sarnoff Court Reporters, Santa Ana, Calif., 1976; pres., owner Kennedy Court Reporters, Inc., Santa Ana, 1977—; dir., cons. Calif. Sch. Court Reporting, 1985—. Contbr. articles to profl. jours. Pres. Save Our Soil, Inc., Carmichael, Calif., 1972. Recipient Calif. Conservation award Calif. Conservation Soc., 1973, Gov.'s Conservation honor State Calif., 1972; citations and commendations. Mem. Nat. Shorthand Reporters Assn. (legis. rep.), Orange County Ct. Reporters Assn. (pres. 1978-79), Nat. Notary Assn., Polit. Action Com. of Calif. Court Reporters Assn. (legis. rep. Orange County 1982-84, polit. action com.), Santa Ana C. of C., Nat. Assn. Women-Owned Businesses. Democrat. Mem. Christian Ch. Avocations: jazz; flute; singing with musical group; contemporary Christian music; teaching children music. Home: Yorba Linda CA 92686 Office: Kennedy Court Reporters Inc 920 W 17th St Suite F Santa Ana CA 92706

KENNEDY, MARGARET ANN, music store executive, radio show host, educator; b. Terre Haute, Ind., Oct. 31, 1946; d. Billy Carter and Virginia Belle (Zerweck) Riley; m. John Leslie Kennedy; children—Kathleen, Rebecca. B.S., Ind. State U., 1969, M.S., 1973. Cert. tchr., Ind. English tchr. Mooresville Consol. Sch. Corp., Ind., 1969-75; substitute tchr. Brownsburg Community Sch. Corp., Ind., 1976, 82-83; writer, editor, co-owner Community Mag., Brownsburg, 1984; bus. mgr., co-owner Edn. Arts Ctr., Brownsburg, 1983-85, Main St. Music Store, Brownsburg, 1984—; bus. mgr., tchr. After Sch. Program, Brownsburg, 1984—; host local radio show. Precinct committeeman Democratic Party, Lincoln Twp., Hendricks County, 1975-82, state conv. del., 1978, 80; bd. dirs. Youth Variety Festival, Brownsburg, 1979-81; pub. relations dir. Brownsburg Halloween House, 1979—, Indpls. Zoo Guild, 1980-83; bus. mgr. Brownsburg Players, 1982-83. Recipient Best Marching Unit award Brownsburg Lion's Club, 1979, Outstanding Performance award Pittsboro July 4 Com., 1980, Best Performance award Plainfield Merchant's Assn., 1980. Mem. Brownsburg C. of C., AAUW. Lutheran. Avocations: piano; violin; mandolin; theatre; needlecraft. Home: 27 Southridge Dr Brownsburg IN 46112 Office: Main St Music Store 24 W Main St Brownsburg IN 46112

KENNEDY, MARGARET SWIERZ, magazine editor; b. Milford, Mass., Oct. 19, 1941; d. Mitchell Martin and Jennie (Novack) Swierz; m. Eugene Martin Kenndedy Jr., Nov. 7, 1964; 1 son, Eugene Martin. A.B., Clark U., 1963. Sec. Conde Nast. Publs., N.Y.C., 1963—; also asst. editor House and Garden Mag., N.Y.C., editor furniture and design projects; exec. editor House Beautiful Mag., N.Y.C., 1981—; guest editor Mademoiselle Mag., 1962. Mem. N.Y. Home Fashions League, Decorators Club, Decorative Arts Trust, Phi Beta Kappa. Roman Catholic. Home: 46 E 91st St New York NY 10128 Office: House Beautiful 1700 Broadway New York NY 10019

KENNEDY, MARY ELIZABETH, missionary sister, educational administrator; b. New Castle, Pa., Aug. 14, 1926; d. Thomas G. and Mary Ann (Holloway) Lee; m. Charles Cunningham Kennedy, June 25, 1949; children—Charles Cunningham, Mary Ann, Elizabeth Rose, Grace Lorraine. B.A., Temple U., 1948; M.Bible Theology, Internat. Bible Inst., Fla., 1981. Lic. tchr., adminstr., clergywoman; lic. midwife. Missionary sister Ch. of God in Christ, Memphis, 1949—; co-founder, prin. Community Country Day Sch., Erie, Pa., 1968—; co-founder, exec. dir. Community Drop-In Ctr., Erie, 1973-78; co-founder, dir. Community of Caring, Erie, 1982—; founder, dir. Project Hunger, 1984—; assoc. mem. Benedictine Sisters, Erie, 1982—; mem. internat. mission bd. Ch. of God in Christ, 1980—. Author: Love Therapy in Classroom Management, 1982; Teach Me, Lord, 1983. Bd. corporators Gannon U., Erie, 1980—; mem. adv. bd. Sta. WQLN, 1983—; mem. Nat. Polit. Congress Black Women, 1985—. Recipient Outstanding Educator award Mercyhurst Coll., Erie, 1973, Humanitarian award, 1980; Outstanding Educator award Gannon U., 1977; Kennedy Day proclaimed in her and spouse's honor Erie City and County, 1983. Mem. Internat. Assn. Psycho-Social Rehab. Services, Pi Gamma Mu. Democrat. Club: Zonta (Erie). Avocations: writing; singing; sports. Home: 2108 German St Erie PA 16503 Office: 5800 Zuck Rd Erie PA 16506

KENNEDY, MARY ELLEN, librarian; b. Pitts., Feb. 28, 1939; d. Joseph Michael and Stella Marie (Kane) K.; B.A., Villa Maria Coll., 1961; M.L.S., U. Pitts., 1970, Ph.D., 1980. Tchr., Pitts. Catholic Schs., 1962-65; tchr., Anne Arundel County Schs., Annapolis, 1965-67; legal sec., firm Joseph M. Kennedy, Pitts., 1967-70; cataloger Newport News (Va.) Library System, 1970-71; reference librarian Glenville (W.Va.) State Coll., 1971-80; asst. prof. library sci. Ball State U., Muncie, Ind., 1980-83, Purdue U., West Lafayette, Ind., 1983—. Sec. women Glenville Presbyn. Ch., 1973-74, pres., 1974-76, bd. deacons, 1979-80; chmn. library com. Presbyn. Ch. Muncie, 1981—; mem. belle com. W.Va. Folk Festival, 1973-80. Recipient Title III advanced study grant, 1977-78. Mem. ALA, Ind. Library Assn., Assn. Ind. Media Educators, Assn. Am. Library Schs., AAUW (corr. sec. 1981-82), Delta Kappa Gamma, Sigma Sigma Sigma. Democrat. Office: HSSE Library Purdue U West Lafayette IN 47907

KENNEDY, ROSE FITZGERALD (MRS. JOSEPH P. KENNEDY), mother of former Pres. of U.S.; b. Boston, July 22, 1890; d. John Francis and Josephine Mary (Hannon) Fitzgerald; ed. New Eng. Conservatory, Blumenthal Acad., Netherlands; LL.D. (hon.), Manhattanville Coll., Georgetown U., 1977. m. Joseph P. Kennedy, 1914 (dec.); children—Joseph (dec.), John Fitzgerald (Pres. of U.S. 1961-63, dec.), Rosemary, Kathleen (dec.), Eunice (Mrs. Robert Sargent Shriver), Patricia, Robert Francis (dec.), Jean (Mrs. Stephen Smith), Edward M. Named Papal Countess, Pope Pius XII. Roman Catholic. Author: Times to Remember, 1974. *

KENNEDY, SHEILA SUESS, lawyer; b. Indpls., Oct. 20, 1941; d. Joseph S. and Annette (Marcus) Simkin; A.A., Stephens Coll. Women, 1960; B.S., Ind. U., 1964, J.D., 1975; m. Robert N. Kennedy, Mar. 2, 1980; children—Michael Suess, Stephen Suess, David Suess. Bar: Ind. 1975. Assoc. firm Baker & Daniels, Indpls., 1975-77; corp. counsel City of Indpls., 1977-80; ptnr. firm Treacy Cohen Mears & Crawford, Indpls., 1980-82; ptnr. Mears Crawford Kennedy & Eichholtz, 1983—; instr. bus. law Ind. Central U., 1978. Republican candidate U. S. Ho. Reps., Ind. 11th Dist., 1980; mem. nat. bd. govs. Am. Jewish Com., 1977-83; chmn. Cable Franchise Bd., City of Indpls., 1982-84; mem. environ. mgmt. bd. State of Ind., 1982-83. Mem. Indpls. Bar Assn., Ind. Bar Assn., ABA. Republican. Jewish. Club: Columbia. Mng. editor Ind. U. Law Rev., 1974-75. Home: 628 Lockerbie St Indianapolis IN 46202 Office: 120 Monument Circle Suite 301 Indianapolis IN 46204

KENNEDY, SISTER ANNE, college president. Pres. Silver Lake Coll., Manitowoc, Wis. Office: Silver Lake Coll 2406 S Alverno Rd Manitowoc WI 54220*

KENNEDY, SUSAN JOANNE, volunteer/public education coordinator; b. Coatesville, Pa., Mar. 5, 1943; d. Lloyd F. and Alice Mae (Jackson) K.; A.A., Brevard Community Coll., 1977, A.S. in Human Service Tech., 1977; B.S. in Social Sci., Rollins Coll., 1979; postgrad. Stetson U., 1980-81; M.S. in Counseling Psychology, Nova U., 1983. Various positions with hotels and restaurants, Ill., Miss., Fla., 1965-74; social worker Brevard Achievement Center, Rockledge, Fla., 1977, vocat. placement specialist, 1978-84, vol./pub. edn. coordinator, 1984—; mem. Brevard Equal Opportunity Com., 1980-84; mem. Brevard Community Coll. Equal Access/Equal Opportunity Adv. Com., 1979-84; mem. Brevard County Job Developers Com., 1981; mem. Forum on Info., Community Schs. and Agts. Com., 1979-83; mem. Community Agts. and Schs. South Brevard, 1979-83, chmn. 1980-81; mem. human service tech. adv. bd. Brevard Community Coll., 1980-83. Sec. exec. com. Family Service Bur., 1976-77; scouting coordinator Boy Scouts Am., 1981-81; loaned exec. United Way, 1980, 81; mem. Brevard County Pvt. Industry Council, 1982-85. Recipient Community Service award Brevard Community Coll., 1977. Mem. Nat. Rehab. Assn., Fla. Vocat. Evaluation and Work Adjustment Assn., Brevard Vocat. Assn., Brevard Assn. Human Service Agys., Brevard Personnel Assn. (treas. 1984), Nat. Assn. Human Service Technologists, Am. Rehab. Counseling Assn., Fla. Personnel and Guidance Assn., Nat. Assn. Female Execs., VFW Aux. Democrat. Episcopalian. Home: 915 Dove Ave Rockledge FL 32955 Office: 1845 Cogswell St Rockledge FL 32955

KENNEDY, VARINA KUEHNERT, interior designer, color consultant; b. Newark, Ark., Dec. 4, 1940; d. Estel Charles and Valerie (Murphy) Kuehnert; m. Joseph Kennedy, Nov. 7, 1959. Cert. in interior design Clover Park Tech. Sch., Tacoma, 1972; student Solano Coll., Calif., 1972-73, San Bernardino Valley Coll., Calif., 1980. Designer trainee Breuner's Home Furnishings, Pleasant Hill, Calif., 1972-73; decorator cons. J.C. Penney Co., Concord, Calif. and North Little Rock, Ark., 1973-76; interior designer Walls Galore & More, Inc., North Little Rock, 1976-78, Nickell Flooring, San Bernardino, Calif., 1978-79; freelance designer, San Bernardino, 1980-83; owner Comprehensive Design Services, Tacoma, 1984—; instr., seminar speaker on color and design. Columnist Decorating Styles, North Beach Beacon, 1984. Mem. Am. Soc. Interior Designers (assoc.), Color Mktg. Group, Nat. Trust for Historic Preservation, Pacific N.W. Writers Conf., Nat. Assn. Female Execs. Office: Comprehensive Design Services PO Box 98119 Tacoma WA 98498

KENNELLY, BARBARA BAILEY, Congresswoman; b. Hartford, Conn., July 10, 1936; d. John Moran and Barbara (Leary) Bailey; B.A. in Econs., Trinity Coll., Washington, 1958; grad. Harvard-Radcliffe Sch. Bus. Adminstrn., 1959; M.A. in Govt., Trinity Coll., Hartford, 1971; hon. doctorate Sacred Heart U., Bridgeport, Conn., 1981, Mt. Holyoke Coll., 1984, U. Hartford, 1985; m. James J. Kennelly, Sept. 26, 1959; children—Eleanor Bride, Barbara Leary, Louise Moran, John Bailey. Mem. Hartford Ct. of Common Council, 1975-79; sec. of State of Conn., Hartford, 1979-82; mem. 98th and 99th Congresses from 1st Dist. Conn., mem. house ways and means com., steering and policy com.; mem. steering com. Northeast-Midwest Congl. Coalition; mem. exec. com. Congl. Caucus for Women's Issues; mem. exec. bd. Congl. Arts Caucus; Hartford rep., sec. exec. com. Capitol Region Council of Govts., 1975-79; Conn rep. Nat. Adv.'s Com. on Fine Arts, Washington; mem. Conn. Commn. Human Services, 1972-73. Bd. dirs. Hartford Architecture Conservancy, Hartford Riverfront Recapture, Inc.; chair Conn. Elected ofcls. for Soviet Jewry; mem. alumnae bd. dirs. Trinity Coll., Washington; mem. Conn. bd. dirs. Catholic Family Services, Inc.; trustee Trinity Coll., Hartford, Hartford Coll. for Women. Mem. Internat. Inst. Mcpl. Clks. Democrat. Roman Catholic. Office: 450 Main St Hartford CT 06103 also 1230 Longworth House Office Bldg Washington DC 20515

KENNEY, ESTELLE KOVAL, artist; b. Chgo., Feb. 15, 1928; d. Hyman English and Florence (Browman) Koval; B.F.A., Art Inst. Chgo., 1976, M.F.A., 1978; postgrad. Yale U., 1980; m. Herbert Kenney, Feb. 6, 1948; children—Carla, Robert. Art therapist Grove Sch., Lake Forest, Ill., 1973-78, New Trier High Sch. and Central High Sch., Winnetka, Ill., 1978-79, Mosely Sch., Chgo., 1979, Cove Sch., Evanston, Ill., 1979-82; dir. art therapy and art edn., instr. painting and drawing Loyola U., Chgo., 1981—; one woman shows: Evanston (Ill.) Library, 1971, Zaks Gallery, Chgo., 1977, 79, 82, Renaissance Soc.-Bergman Gallery, U. Chgo., 1980; group shows include: Ill. State Mus., 1975, Women Artists, Here and Now, 1976, Chgo. Connections travelling exhbn., 1976-77, Nat. Women's Caucus for Art, 1977, Nancy Lurie Gallery, 1978, Marycrest Coll. Gallery, Davenport, Iowa, 1982, Chgo. Internat. Art Expo, 1981, 82, 83, 84, Notre Dame U. Gallery, South Bend, Ind., 1982; represented in permanent collections: Ill. State Mus., Springfield, Union League Club of Chgo. Mem. Am. Art Therapy Assn., Ill. Art Therapy Assn. (pres. 1979—), Coll. Art Assn. Home: 3830 N Clark St Chicago IL 60613 Office: Loyola University of Chicago Dept Fine Arts 6525 N Sheridan Rd Chicago IL 60626

KENOE, LISA BROIDO, lawyer; b. Norwalk, Conn., June 22, 1957; d. Henry Williard and Lois (Richards) Broido; m. Andrew Scott Kenoe, Dec. 27, 1980. B.S., Northwestern U., 1979; J.D., Columbia U., 1982. Bar: Ill. 1982. Assoc. editor ABA, Chgo., 1978-79; assoc. Friedman & Koven, Chgo., 1982—. Assoc. editor Update on Law-Related Education, 1982. Contbr. numerous articles to legal jours. Harlan Fiske Stone scholar Columbia U., 1982. Mem. ABA, Chgo. Bar Assn., Ill. Bar Assn., Women's Bar Assn., Am. Judicature Soc. Office: Friedman & Koven 208 S LaSalle St Suite 900 Chicago IL 60604

KENT, DEBORAH LYNN, banker; b. Tampa, Fla., Mar. 3, 1955; d. Shirley Jewell and Vera Juanita (Anderson) Kent. B.A. magna cum laude in Psychology, St. Leo Coll., 1977; postgrad. Mercer Law Sch., 1978-79, 80-81; M.B.A., Barry U., 1986; security diploma Am. Inst. Banking, 1983, also cert. completion, 1983; cert. completion Fla. Suprs. Acad., 1982. Clk. 1st Nat. Bank, Homestead, Fla., 1972-73, teller, then head teller, 1973-78; head teller Dadeland Bank, Miami, Fla., 1979-80, Great Am. Bank, Homestead, 1981-82; asst. cashier, teller adminstr. Sunset Comml. Bank, Miami, 1982-83, asst. cashier, ops. officer, asst. v.p., 1984—, also trainer, instr., 1982-83, data processing coordinator, 1983, compliance officer, 1983. Author teller manual and editor policy manual for Sunset Comml. Bank, 1983. Campaign vol. Dan Lewis for Senator, Homestead, 1982. Mem. Nat. Assn. Bank Women (group membership chmn. 1986—, co-chmn. state conf. publicity com. 1986—), South Dade Bankers Assn., Am. Inst. Banking. Democrat. Baptist. Clubs: French (pres. 1971-73), Modern Music Masters (treas. 1972-73). Lodges: Homestead Assembly (worthy advisor 1972), Ad Astra. Home: 444 NW 21st St Homestead FL 33030 Office: Sunset Comml Bank 10899 Sunset Dr Miami FL 33173

KENT, ELIZABETH NOEL, editor; b. Greensboro, N.C., Dec. 6, 1940; d. William Alfred and Rosa Elouise (Baughn) K. B.S., Ga. So. Coll., 1962; M.A., Ball State U., 1983. Tchr. English, Bd. Edn. Savannah, Ga., 1962-67; tchr. English, Stenography Div., Fort Harrison, Ind., 1974-77; edn. specialist Directorate of Tng. and Doctrine, Dept. Army, Fort Harrison, Ind., 1977-79, editor, 1979-83, chief editor, 1983—; instr. English Vincennes U., 1979—; realtor Sargent and Assocs., 1986—. Served to capt. U.S. Army, 1967-74. Recipient Sustained Superior Performance award U.S. Army, 1976, Spl. Act award for superior editing, 1985. Mem. Fed. Women's Program, Federally Employed Women, Nat. Assn. Female Execs., Am. Legion, DAV. Anglican Catholic. Avocation: reading. Home: 11430 Wolf Ln Indianapolis IN 46229 Office: Publications Div DOTD USASSI USASSC Bldg One Fort Harrison Indianapolis IN 46216

KENT, JILL ELSBETH, government official; b. Detroit, June 1, 1948; d. Seymour and Grace (Edelman) K.; m. Mark Elliott Solomons, Aug. 20, 1978. B.A., U. Mich., 1970; J.D., George Washington U., 1975, LL.M., 1979. Bar: D.C. 1975. Mgmt. intern U.S. Dept. Transp., Washington, 1971-73; staff analyst Office Mgmt. and Budget, Exec. Office of Pres., Washington, 1974-76; legis. counsel U.S. Treasury Dept., Washington, 1976-78; dir. legis. reference div. Health Care Financing Adminstrn., Washington, 1978-80; sr. policy analyst Office Mgmt. and Budget, Exec. Office Pres., Washington, 1980-84; chief Treasury, Gen. Services, OMB, 1984-85; dep. asst. sec. for departmental fin. and planning U.S. Dept. Treasury, 1985—; pres. S&K Properties Investment Partnership, Washington, 1979—; lectr. D.C. Pub. Schs., 1976-78. Mem. U.S. Task Force on Electronic Funds Transfer, Washington, 1982—; mem. strategic planning group IRS, 1983—. Recipient Outstanding Service award Exec. Office of Pres., 1982, Adminstrs. award Health Care Financing Adminstrn., 1980. Mem. ABA, D.C. Bar Assn. Republican. Jewish. Home: 5300 27th St NW Washington DC 20015 Office: US Dept Treasury Washington DC 20220

KENT, JOAN GAY, business executive, writer; b. Mineola, L.I., N.Y.; d. William Lewis and Helen (Remsen) Gay; m. Stephen R. Kent, Dec. 12, 1959. B.A., Colby Coll. Vice-pres., mng. editor Missiles and Space, NATO Jour., Manhasset, N.Y., 1956-63; editor The Manhasset Mail, The Port Mail, Manhasset, 1964-66; editor United Tech. Publs., Garden City, N.Y., 1967, writer, advt. cons., 1968-78; prin. Kent Creative Services, Sands Point, N.Y., 1978—. Trustee, pres. Port Washington Library; bd. dirs. Sands Point Civic Assn.; v.p. Cow Neck Hist. Soc. Mem. Pi Gamma Mu. Club: N.Y. Colby Coll. Alumni. Home and Office: Sycamore Dr Sands Point NY 11050

KENT, JOAN SWAFFORD, real estate broker; b. Los Angeles, Aug. 14, 1927; d. Henry Watson and Lillian (Stanton) Swafford; m. William Kent III, Sept. 3, 1955; children—Lucinda, Nicholas, Augustus. Student Bennington Coll., 1947-48, U. Calif.-Berkeley, 1945-1947; B.A., UCLA, 1950. Cert. real estate broker. Sales assoc. Frank Howard Allen, Stinson Beach, Calif., 1970-75, Seadrift Co. Realtors, Stinson Beach, 1975-76, Cushman and Wakefield, San Francisco, 1976-80; broker assoc. Hill and Co., San Francisco, 1981—. Bd. dirs. San Francisco Symphony, 1981—; active in Modern Art Council, San Francisco, 1957—; Edgewood Aux., San Francisco, 1956—; assoc. dir. San Francisco Opera Guild, 1958—; mem. Childrens Theatre Assn., San Francisco, 1958—; charter mem. art mus. council Los Angeles County Mus. Art. Mem. Marin County Bd. Realtors, San Francisco Bd. Realtors. Republican. Episcopalian. Clubs: Town & Country, San Francisco Golf. Avocations: golf; reading; music; swimming; hiking. Home: 3196 Pacific Ave San Francisco CA 94115 Office: Hill & Co 2107 Union St San Francisco CA 94123

KENT, PAULA (MRS. STANLEY J. LLOYD), lecturer, public relations executive, management and marketing consultant; b. N.Y.; d. John and Estelle (Frye) Smith; B.S., State Tchrs. Coll., Worcester, Mass., 1939; Master's degree, Grad. Sch., Coll. Bus. Adminstrn., Boston U., 1941; m. Stanley J. Lloyd, Jan. 23, 1943; children—Diane Adrienne Noel, Robin Michele Cheri, Kevin Christopher Kent, Gisele Nicolette Jolie. Methods engr. IBM, 1941-42; personnel dir. Daily Jour., San Diego, also Sta. KSDJ, 1946-48; fashion editor San Diego Union, 1949; promotion dir. San Diego Union and Evening Tribune, 1950-70; v.p. La Jolla Clin. Labs., Inc., 1960—; speaker, master of ceremonies numerous bus., profl. and acad. meetings, convs. and confs., seminar speaker, Paris, Brussels, Madrid, 1960-71. Formerly active ARC, Am. Cancer Soc., Gray Ladies, Med. Aux., San Diego, Fiesta Del Pacifico, U. San Diego Aux.; dir. San Diego's Ann. Giant Sales Rally, 1953, 56, 63; chmn. Advt. Recognition Week Campaign, San Diego, 1953-54; dir. San Diego Ann. Soap Box Derby, 1951-59, Bowl Down Cancer, 1963, San Diego Ann. Golden Gloves Boxing Tournament, 1961-68, San Diego Ann. Metro Tennis Championships, 1952-70, San Diego Ann. Model Yacht Regatta, 1952-70, San Diego Ann. Power Boat Regatta, 1950-62, San Diego Ann. Hole-in-One Tournament, 1951-70; producer San Diego Ann. Investment Clinic, 1962-70; public relations cons. Mrs. Am. Pageant, San Diego, 1966, Unlimited Hydroplane Races, San Diego, 1964; producer Ann. Gentleman of Distinction awards, 1967, 68, 69, San Diego Advt. SalesRama, 1971, Woman of Year awards, 1967, 68, 69 (both San Diego), others. Commd. ensign, Women's Res., USNR, 1942, transferred USCG, served from ensign to lt., 1943-46. Recipient 158 awards 1950—, including 39 nat., 18 western states and Hawaii, 100 Calif. state awards, 1 local resulting from ann. competitions sponsored by Los Angeles Advt. Women's Club, Nat. Newspaper Assn. Mgrs., Calif. Newspaper Pubs. Assn., Calif. Press Women, Nat. Fedn. Press Women; named one of San Diego's Women of Achievement, 1958, 59, 64, One San Diego's Women of Valour, 1958, one of San Diego's Advt. Men of Distinction, 1972; recipient San Diego Outstanding Citizen award, 1961; Outstanding Service plaque Sales and Mktg. Execs. Club, 1963, 66, 67, 68, 71; San Diego Woman of Yr. award, Council Women's Service and Bus. Clubs, 1965; Los Angeles Man of Year award Sales Promotion Execs. Assn., 1965; Golden Spear award Twin Cities Sales Promotion Execs. Assn., Mpls., 1965; Woman of Achievement award Nat. Fedn. Bus and Profl. Women, 1966; Jeanne Hoffman Unique Coverage award, 1968, Don award Legion of Portola, 1960, Disting. Service award Investment Edn. Inst., Detroit, 1969, many others. Mem. Sales Promotion Execs. Assn. Los Angeles, Advt. and Sales Club San Diego (dir., former editor monthly bull). Sales and Marketing Execs. Club San Diego (dir., bull. editor, pres. 1970-71), Internat. Newspaper Promotion Assn. (pres. western region 1965, Disting. Service award 1971) Calif. Press Women, Nat. Fedn. Press Women (del. Russia 1973), Sales and Mktg. Execs. Internat. (internat. dir.-at-large 1971-73), Am. Mgmt. Assn., Soc. Advancement Mgmt. Am. Advt. Fedn. (western states edn. chmn. 1970-71). Roman Catholic. Home: 515 Bon Air St La Jolla CA 92037 Office: PO Box 2243 La Jolla CA 92038

KENT, ROSALIE HELEN, transportation executive, columnist, educator; b. Detroit, July 10, 1939; d. Harold J. and Anna Bernadine (McGlone) K. Cert. instr. internat. trade. Rate analyst USAC Transport Co., Detroit, 1960-64; asst. mgr. marine ins. dept. Security Storage Co., Washington, 1964-70; export co-ordinator Wilkerson Corp., Denver, 1970-73; ops. mgr. Samaras Internat., Denver, 1973-76; ptnr. World Cargo Ltd., Denver, 1976-79; dist. mgr. Schenkers Internat. Forwarders, Inc., Denver, 1979—; instr. internat. trade Community Coll. Denver; instr. internat. transp. and cargo movement Rocky Mountain Inst. Fgn. Trade and Fin., 1984—. Mem. Internat. Trade Assn. Colo. (dir. 1980-82, newsletter editor 1978-80), Traffic Club Denver (monthly publ. columnist), Delta Nu Alpha. Republican. Roman Catholic. Home: 10520 W 102d Pl Broomfield CO 80020 Office: Schenkers Internat Forwarders Inc PO Box 38457 Denver CO 80238

KENT, RUTH KIMBALL, lexicographer; b. Auburn, N.Y., Aug. 30, 1920; d. Charles Arthur and Nellie Corrinne (Gove) Kimball; m. Harold Thomas Kent, 1936 (div. 1960); children—Harold Thomas, David Arthur, Grace Ann Kent Richardson. B.A., Syracuse U., 1962, M.A., 1968. Copy editor Kent State U. Press (Ohio), 1964-68; assoc. editor Webster's New World Dictionary (now Simon & Schuster), Cleve., 1964—; columnist The Plain Dealer, Cleve., 1979-84. Author: Language of Journalism, 1970; editor: Collins Gem Dictionary of Synonyms, 1979. Mem. Women in Communications, Soc. Profl. Journalists. Republican. Methodist. Home: 14219D Triskett Rd 304 Cleveland OH 44111 Office: Simon & Schuster 850 Euclid Ave Suite 306 Cleveland OH 44114

KENVIN, HELENE SCHWARTZ, lawyer; author; b. N.Y.C., Oct. 25, 1941; d. Melvin C. and Ethel (Wiesenthal) Schwartz; m. Howard Kenvin, Sept. 24, 1981. Bar: N.Y. 1965, U.S. Ct. Appeals (2d cir.) 1967, U.S. Ct. Appeals (7th cir.) 1971, U.S. Supreme Ct. 1971. Pvt. practice, N.Y.C., 1965—; mem. faculty Law Sch., Rutgers U., Camden, N.J., 1972-83. Author: Lawyering; Justice By the Book: Aspects of Jewish and American Criminal Law, 1976; This Land of Liberty: A History of America's Jews, 1986. Editor Dorot, Jour. of Jewish Geneal. Soc., 1985. Contbr. articles to profl. jours. Mem. Jewish Geneal. Soc. (exec. council 1979-85), Phi Beta Kappa. Office: 5 Riverside Dr New York NY 10023

KENWORTHY, KATHERINE WINN, technical writer; b. Dover, Del., June 21, 1944; d. Harry Rudy and Mildred Winn (Varden) Ziegler; m. James Everett Kenworthy, Apr. 30, 1969; 1 dau., Judith Harriet; m. James Robert Singer, Oct. 14, 1964 (div. Aug. 1969); 1 child, Stacy James. B.A., Tex. A&M U., 1966. Tech. writer geology U. P.R., Mayaguez, 1981-82; market researcher Brittian Assocs., Atlanta, 1982-83; researcher, tech. writer Peak WPM, Roswell, Ga., 1983-85; procedures analyst Contel Services Corp., Atlanta, 1985—; cons Lakestone Assocs., Roswell, Vol. Tech. Services, Atlanta, 1985-86. Republican. Episcopalian. Home: 765 Lakestone Ct Roswell GA 300076 Office: Contel Services Corp 245 Perimeter Center Pkwy Atlanta GA

KENYON, JULIA CAROLINE, educator; b. Harvard, Nebr., Jan. 3, 1919; d. Peter J. and Anna Marie (Bartholoma) Pauley; m. Meril T. Kenyon, May 10, 1949. B.S., U. Nebr., 1941; M.Ed., Colo. State U., 1968; postgrad. (Colo. scholar), U. No. Colo., 1970, Utah State U., 1979, Colo. State U., 1980, others. Tchr. home econs., Philips, Nebr., 1941-43, Grand Island, Nebr., 1943-44; home supr. Farmers Home Adminstrn., Sherman, Howard, Hall and Adams Counties, Nebr., 1945-46; home extension agt. Perkins County, Nebr., 1947—;

tchr. home econs. Perkins County High Sch., Grant, Nebr., 1957-58, Holyoke High Sch., Nebr., 1959—. Served with Waves, 1944-46. Recipient Outstanding Home Econs. Humanitarian award State of Colo., 1977. Mem. NEA, Colo. Edn. Assn., Holyoke Edn. Assn., Am. Vocat. Assn., Colo. Vocat. Assn., Am. Home Econs. Assn., Colo. Home Econs. Assn., Colo. Vocat. Home. Home Econs. Assn. (adv. com.), Colo. Edn. Assn. (profl. affairs com.), Gen. Fedn. Women's Clubs (dist. treas. 1954-55, pres. 1954-55), Sigma Kappa, Alpha Kappa, Delta Kappa Gamma. Methodist. Clubs: Venango Fairy Dell (pres.), Mary Jane Extension, Order of Eastern Star (matron). Lodge: Am. Legion. Home: 205 S Belford St Holyoke CO 80734 Office: PO Box 193 Holyoke CO 80734

KEOHANE, NANNERL OVERHOLSER, college president, political science educator; b. Blytheville, Ark., Sept. 18, 1940; d. James Arthur and Grace (McSpadden) Overholser; m. Patrick Henry III, Sept. 16, 1962 (div. May 1969); 1 son, Stephan; m. 2d Robert Owen Keohane, Dec. 18, 1970; children—Sarah, Jonathan, Nathaniel. B.A., Wellesley Coll., 1961, Oxford U., Eng., 1963; Ph.D., Yale U., 1967. Lectr. Swarthmore Coll., Pa., 1967-69, asst. prof., 1969-73, Stanford U., Calif., 1973-78, assoc. prof., 1978-81; fellow Ctr. for Advanced Study in the Behavioral Scis.-Stanford U., 1978-79; pres., prof. polit. sci. Wellesley Coll., Mass., 1981—; corp. mem. State St. Boston Corp. Author: Philosophy and the State in France: The Renaissance to the Englightenment, 1980; co-editor: Feminist Theory: A Critique of Ideology, 1982. Trustee WGBH Ednl. TV Found., 1981—; corp. mem. Woods Hole Oceanographic Instn. Marshall scholar, 1961-63; Sterling fellow, 1966-67; AAUW dissertation fellow. Mem. Council on Fgn. Relations. Phi Beta Kappa. Democrat. Presbyterian. Clubs: Cosmopolitan (N.Y.C.); Saturday, Commercial, Algonquin (Boston). Office: Wellesley Coll Office of the Pres Wellesley MA 02181

KEON, PEGGY LUMPKIN, career management consultant; b. Chgo., Sept. 10, 1931; d. Richard Adamson and Mary Hart (Green) Lumpkin; B.A., Wellesley Coll., 1952; children—Pamela Ryan, Lisa Anne, Susan Tamara, Margaret Lynley, Joseph John, Katherine Stoddert. Career counselor, San Francisco, 1978-80; owner Careers for Women, San Francisco, 1980-83; owner Keon Assocs., Career Mgmt. Cons., Mill Valley, Calif., 1983—; dir. Utility Bond & Share Co. Mem. Nat. Assn. Profl. Saleswomen, Northbay Women's Network, AAUW Network Marin, Diocesan Commn. Peace. Republican. Episcopalian. Clubs: Wellesley Coll. of No. Calif. Home: 21 Windward Rd Belvedere CA 94920

KEOPPEL, DENEESE MONTGOMERY, medical technologist; b. Ogden, Utah, May 6, 1932; d. Lorenzo Vermont and Melba Eleanor (Montgomery) Colvin; B.S. cum laude in Med. Tech., Weber State Coll., 1972; m. Russell Joel Keoppel, June 23, 1950; children—Paul Joel, Jean, Dale Russell (dec.), Kent Ren. Blood bank supr. St. Benedict's Hosp., Ogden, Utah, 1972-76, supr., ednl. coordinator, 1979-82, lab. asst. dir., 1982-86, lab. adminstr. dir., 1986—, blood bank asst. supr. Latter Day Saints Hosp. Salt Lake City, 1976-79; mem. clin. faculty Weber State Coll. Allied Health, 1973—. Mem. Am. Assn. Blood Banks, Am. Soc. for Med. Tech. (rep.; recipient outstanding service award 1981), Utah Soc. for Med. Tech. (pres. no. chpt. 1983-84; Mem. of Yr. award 1983), Am. Soc. for Clin. Pathologists (affiliate mem., cert. med. technologist, specialist blood bank), Clin. Lab. Mgmt. Assn., Utah Soc. Med. Tech. (treas. 1985-87), Utah Immunohematology Soc. (pres. 1978-79), Phi Kappa Phi, Omicron Sigma. Mormon. Home: 4511 S 1975 W Roy UT 84067 Office: 5475 S 500 E Ogden UT 84403

KEPHART, LUCY COMPTON, retired corporate accountant; b. Warren County, Va., Mar. 11, 1916; d. Aylette Newton and Anna Belle (Sheetz) Compton; m. Luther Clayton Kephart, Feb. 4, 1939 (dec. 1968); chilren—Lorraine Kephart Dovell, Barbara Kephart Trettel, Linda Kephart Jordan. Student Warren County Coll. Office mgr. Skyline Frosted Lockers, Inc., Front Royal, Va., 1945-60; budget acct. FMC Corp. and Avtex Fibers, Inc., Front Royal, 1961-80. Active Salvation Army, Front Royal, 1959—, chmn. adv. bd., 1965-75; exec. dir. United Way, Front Royal, 1979-84. Mem. DAR (regent local chpt. 1984—). Democrat. Baptist. Avocations: sewing; reading; walking. Home: 802 Virginia Ave Front Royal VA 22630

KEPNER, RITA MARIE, sculptor, writer, editor; b. Binghamton, N.Y., Nov. 15, 1944; d. Peter Walter and Helena Theresa (Piotrowski) Kramnicz; student Elmira Coll., 1962-63; B.A., Harpur Coll., SUNY, 1966; m. John C. Matthiesen; 1 son, Stewart John, Matthiesen. One-woman shows include: Willoughby Wallace Meml. Gallery, Branford, Conn., 1967, Penryn Gallery, Seattle, 1970, 73, 76, Haines Gallery, Seattle, 1975, Zoliborz Gallery, Warsaw, Poland, 1981; group shows include: SUNY, Binghamton, 1966, Manawata Art Gallery, Palmerston North, N.Z., Modern Art Mus., Seattle, 1976, Portland (Oreg.) Art Mus., 1976; major works include: Peace Pipe, Zalalgerszeg, Hungary, Human Forms in Balance, City of Seattle, 1975, Unity, City of Znin, Poland, 1976, Rough to Smooth, Seattle Pub. Library, 1978; informal visual arts ambassador between U.S. and Poland, 1976-81; pres. fed. women's program council Seattle dist.; artist-in-residence City of Seattle, 1975, 77-78; del. Internat. Sculptors Conf., Toronto, Ont., Can., 1978; VISTA vol., 1982-84 Paramedic, bd. dirs. Aradia Med. Clinic, Seattle, 1972-74; writer, editor, pub. affairs specialist Seattle dist. U.S. Army C.E. Co-founder Bainbridge Island Arts Council. Recipient merit award for superior journalistic achievement U.S. Army C.E., 1984, 85, 2d place news category competition award, 1985; suggestion award Dept. Army, 1984, ofcl. commendation, 1985, 86; Kosciuszko Found. grantee, 1975, 76, 79, 81. Mem. Internat. Artists Assn. of UNESCO, Paris Artists Equity Assn., Internat. Artists Cooperation (Edewecht, W. Ger.), N.W. Multihull Assn. (commodore 1974). Contbr. articles to Northwest Arts, Seattle Post Intelligencer, Leonardo mag., Polska Panorama, Poland mag. Home: 6681 Flagler Rd Nordland WA 98358-9629 Office: Public Affairs Seattle Dist US Army Corps Engrs PO Box C-3755 Seattle WA 98124

KER, (ALICE) ANN STEELE, composer, educator, church musician; b. Warsaw, Ind., Nov. 10, 1937; d. George Arthur and Winifred Pauline (Foster) Steele; m. Charles Arthur Ker, Sept. 8, 1957 (div. 1980); children—Kelly Lynne, Karen Elizabeth, Kristin Ann. Student DePauw U., 1955-57, Butler U., 1958; B.Mus., Ind. U., 1973; postgrad Notre Dame U., 1974—. Pvt. instr. piano, organ, 1967—; organist First Presbyterian Ch., Warsaw, 1968-78; choirmaster Central Christian Ch., Huntington, Ind., 1980; instr. music Huntington Coll., 1974—; dir. music, asst. organist Redeemer Lutheran Ch., Warsaw, 1980—; tchr. music Redeemer Luth. Sch.; festival choir dir. Luth. Circuit of South Bend, Ind.; composer: Hear This, 1973; Three Men on Camelback, 1981; One Glorious God, 1982; Ways to Praise, 1984; Triptych, 1980; Softly, 1983; The House of the Lord, 1984. Bd. dirs. No. Ind. Opera Assn.; concert critic, bd. dirs. Lakeland Community Concert Assn.; vol. Kosciusko Community Hosp.; vol. Mobile Meals; vol. Christamore Aid Soc. Mem. Am. Guild Organists (dir. Ft. Wayne chpt. 1977-80), Internat. League Women Composers, Women in Music, Am. Musicol. Soc., Nat. Guild Piano Tchrs., Am. Choral Dirs. Assn., Music Tchrs. Nat. Assn., Pi Beta Phi, Kappa Kappa Kappa. Republican. Lutheran. Office: Huntington Coll Huntington IN 46750 also 1720 E Center St Warsaw IN 46580

KERAMIDA, VASILIKI, environmental pollution control executive, engineering educator, researcher; b. Athens, Greece, May 25, 1947; came to U.S., 1969, naturalized, 1981; d. Alcibiades and Ula (Boukos) Keramidas; m. Dan Lee Strahl, July 17, 1984. B.S., Purdue U., 1973, M.S., 1976, Ph.D., 1979. Pvt. cons. to major industries, 1979-81; water pollution engr. Ind. State Bd. Health, Indpls., 1981-82; mgr. indsl. pollution Dept. Pub. Works, Indpls., 1982-84, asst. adminstr., 1984—; vis. asst. prof. Purdue U., West Lafayette, Ind., 1980-82; adj. prof. Ind. U., Indpls., 1984-85; apptd. mem. Ind. Environ. Mgmt. Bd., 1984—; mem. Ind. Corp. Sci. and Tech., 1985—; lectr. in field. Author tech. papers; patentee: Treatment of metal plating wastes with vermiculite column, 1980. Recipient Indsl. Waste award Ind. Water Pollution Control Assn., 1985. Mem. Water Pollution Control Fedn., Ind. Water Pollution Control Assn., Am. Pub. Works Assn., Assn. Met. Sewerage Agys. Office: Dept Pub Works 2700 S Belmont Ave Indianapolis IN 46221

KERBER, LINDA KAUFMAN, historian; b. N.Y.C., Jan. 23, 1940; d. Harry Hagman and Dorothy (Haber) Kaufman; m. Richard Kerber, June 5, 1960; children—Ross Jeremy, Justin Seth. A.B., Barnard Coll., 1960; M.A., NYU, 1961; Ph.D., Columbia U., 1968. Asst. prof. Stern Coll., Yeshiva U., N.Y.C., 1963-68; asst. prof. San Jose (Calif.) State Coll., 1969-70; vis. asst. prof. Stanford (Calif.) U., 1970-71; assoc. prof. history U. Iowa, Iowa City, 1971-75, prof., 1975-85, May Brodbeck prof. liberal arts, 1985—. Author: Federalists in Dissent, 1970; Women of the Republic, 1980; (with Jane D. Mathews) Women's America, 1982; mem. editorial bd. Signs: A Jour. of Women in Culture and Soc., 1975—, Revs. in Am. History, 1984—. Kent fellow Danforth Found., 1966-68; Am. Bar Found. grantee, 1975; NEH fellow, 1976, 83-84. Fellow Soc. Am. Historians; mem. Orgn. Am. Historians (chmn. program com. 1980), Am. Antiquarian Soc., Am. Hist. Assn., Am. Studies Assn., Berkshire Conf. Women Historians. Jewish. Office: Dept History U Iowa Iowa City IA 52242

KERBIS, GERTRUDE LEMPP, architect; m. Walter Peterhans (dec.); m. Donald Kerbis (div. 1972); children—Julian, Lisa, Kim. B.S., U. Ill.; M.A., Ill. Inst. Tech.; postgrad., Grad. Sch. Design, Harvard, 1949-50. Archtl. designer Skidmore, Owings & Merrill, Chgo., 1954-59, C.F. Murphy Assocs., 1959-62, 65-67; pvt. practice architecture, Chgo., 1967—; lectr. U. Ill., 1969; prof. William Rainey Harper Coll., 1970—, Washington U., St. Louis, 1977, 82; archtl. cons. Dept. Urban Renewal, City of Chgo.; mem. Northeastern Ill. Planning Commn., Open Land Project, Mid-North Community Orgn., Chgo. Met. Housing and Planning Council, Chgo. Mayor's Commn. for Preservation Chgo.'s Hist. Architecture; bd. dirs. Chgo. Sch. Architecture Found., 1972-76; trustee Glessner House Found.; bd. dirs. Inland Architect Mag.; lectr. Art Inst. Chgo., U. N.Mex., Ill. Inst. Tech., Washington U., St. Louis, Ball State U., Muncie, Ind., U. Utah, Salt Lake City. Prin. archtl. works include, U.S. Air Force Acad. dining hall, Colo., 1957, Skokie (Ill.) Pub. Library, 1959, Meadows Club, Lake Meadows, Chgo., 1959, O'Hare Internat. Airport 7 Continents Bldg, 1963; prin. developer and architect: Tennis Club, Highland Park, Ill., 1968, Watervliet, Mich. Tennis Ranch, 1970, Greenhouse Condominium, Chgo., 1976, Webster Clark Townhouses, Chgo., 1985; exhibited in shows at Chgo. Hist. Soc., 1984, Chgo. Mus. Sci. and Industry, 1985, also in Paris, 1984. represented in: permanent archtl. drawings collection, Art Inst. Chgo. Recipient Outstanding Profl. Achievement award YWCA of Chgo., 1984. Fellow AIA (dir. Chgo. chpt. 1971-75, chpt. pres. 1980, mem. nat. com. architecture arts and recreation 1972-75, com. on design 1975—, head subcom. inst. honors nomination); mem. AAUP, ACLU, U. Ill., Ill. Inst. Tech. alumni assns., Art Inst. Chgo., Chgo. Council Fgn. Relations, Chgo. Women in Architecture (founder), Planned Parenthood Assn., Chgo. Network, Lincoln Park Zool. Soc., Chgo. Arts Club., Lambda Alpha. Club: Cliff Dwellers. Office: 172 W Burton Pl Chicago IL 60610

KERCHNER, ROCHELLE, home care agency executive, consultant; b. Boston, Apr. 18, 1943; d. Irving and (Gootkin) Ginsberg; divorced; children—Chad, Shelby. B.A., U. Mass., 1965; M.A., State U. Coll. of N.Y. Buffalo, 1968. Speech therapist Buffalo Pub. Schs., 1965-68, Three Village Sch., Stony Brook, N.Y., 1968-70, Riverhead Sch., N.Y., 1970-71; dir., treas. Comprehensive Home Care, Smithtown, N.Y., 1977—; cons. mgmt. in home care industry. Pres. Women's Am. Orgn. for Rehab. and Tng., Commack, N.Y., 1974-76. Jewish. Office: Comprehensive Home Care 414 Route 111 Smithtown NY 11787

KEREW-SHAW, DIANA, producer; b. Hackensack, N.J., Oct. 3, 1942; d. Samuel William and Esther (Freed) Kerew; student State U. Iowa, 1960; B.F.A. magna cum laude, Boston U., 1964; m. Steven Shaw, Aug. 5, 1973. Mem. prodn. staff N.Y. Shakespeare Festival and Public Theater, 1965-70; asst. to dir. creative affairs Paramount Pictures, N.Y.C., 1970-72; v.p. creative affairs, exec. producer Talent Assos./Time-Life Films, N.Y.C., 1972-80; exec. producer, sr. v.p. TV Highgate Pictures, N.Y.C., 1980-82; ind. producer, 1982—. Recipient Christopher awards, 1978, 81; Emmy award for Outstanding Children's Entertainment Spl., 1982, for children's series, 1983; Ohio State award, Peabody award, 1983. Mem. N.Y. Women in Film (dir. 1980-81, v.p. 1981-82). Democrat. Jewish. Producer 25 TV shows including: Breaking Up, 1977, Lovey, 1978, The Bunker, 1981, The Wall, 1982; Cougar!, 1983; Moms on Strike, 1984; I Want To Go Home, 1984; Don't Touch, 1985. Home: 520 E 90th St New York NY 10128

KERMEEN, BARBARA CORBETT, biophysicist; b. Mpls., Mar. 20, 1943; d. Everett Allen and Gayle Barbara (Jansen) Corbett; m. Byron Leonard Kermeen, June 8, 1979; children—Courtney Jansen, Claudia Corbett, Alexandra Chamberland. B.A., U. Minn., 1964, postgrad. 1966-69. Tchr. sci., dept. chmn. St. Margaret's Acad., Mpls., 1964-67; chief technician biophysics U. Ill., Urbana, 1968; founder, pres., chief exec. officer AVM Instrument Co., Ltd., Livermore, Calif., 1967—. Author: Radiotelemetry Equipment and Techniques Manual, 1979. Mem. Internat. Soc. Biotelemetry, Biol. Engring. Soc., Soc. Women Engrs., Am. Soc. Mammologists. Republican. Episcopalian. Avocations: flying; stained glass. Home: 482 El Rio Rd Danville CA 94526 Office: AVM Instrument Co Ltd 2368 Research Dr Livermore CA 94550

KERMOND, CAROLYN CONWAY, author; b. Boston, Oct. 2, 1927; d. John Edward and Evelyn L. (Canty) Conway; A.B., Trinity Coll., Washington, 1949; m. William L. Kermond, Jan. 23, 1954; children—Ellen, Peter, Richard, Justin, Louise. Author: Little Ways, 1962; More Little Ways, 1963; Little Ways to Heaven, 1983. Mem. CCD bd. St. Mary's Ch., Winchester, Mass.; bd. dirs. Middlesex East Dist. Med. Assn. Aux., Mass. Med. Assn. Aux. Roman Catholic. Home: 7 Sheffield W Winchester MA 01890

KERN, FRANCES MARIE, college administrator, nun; b. St. Louis, Dec. 27, 1950; d. John J. and Helen L. (Obremski) K. B.S., Quincy Coll., 1976; M. Adminstrn., Notre Dame U., 1984. Joined Sisters of Most Precious Blood, 1970. Athletic dir., tchr. St. Elizabeth's Acad., St. Louis, 1976-80; tchr. St. Brendan's Sch., Mexico, Mo., 1980-81; asst. dir. devel. Saint Mary's Coll., O'Fallon, Mo., 1981-82, dir. devel., 1982— Recipient Young Woman of Year award St. Peter's (Mo.) Jaycee Women, 1982. Mem. Bus. Profl. Women, Nat. Fund Raising Inst., Case Currents, St. Charles C. of C. O'Fallon C. of C. Roman Catholic. Home and Office: Saint Mary's College 200 N Main St O'Fallon MO 63366

KERN, JANE RUSSELL, educational adminstrator, reading consultant; b. Birmingham, Ala., Feb. 29, 1932; d. Robert Russell and Zada (Gonce) Deal; m. Kent Garfield Alm, May 3, 1952 (div.); children—Mary Jane, Steven, Kevin; m. Jack Davidson Kern, Jan. 27, 1978. Student Auburn U., 1950-52; B.S., U. N.D., 1963; M.S., Mankato State U., 1971; postgrad. U. Miami, 1976-77, U. S. Fla., 1977-78, 86. Elementary tchr. Grand Forks Pub. Sch., N.D., 1962-65, Mankato Pub. Sch., Minn., 1968-76; head tchr. high sch. Collier County Pub. Sch., Naples, Fla., 1976, supr. lang. arts, 1976-82; dir. Seacrest Sch., Naples, 1983—; speaker, workshop leader Delta Kappa Gamma, Collier County Pub. Sch., regional, state edn. confs., Naples, 1978-86. Bd. dirs. Seacrest Sch., Naples, 1983—; mem. Community Concert Assn., Naples, 1976—, Conservancy, Naples, 1983—. Mem. Collier Reading Council (pres. 1976-77), Collier County Early Childhood Assn., Phi Delta Kappa, Delta Kappa Gamma (chmn. personal growth 1984—), Alpha Chi Omega. Republican. Mem. Unity Ch. Avocations: music; reading; swimming; boating; gardening. Home: 2001 Unity Way Naples FL 33962 Office: Seacrest Sch 1986 Unity Way Naples FL 33962

KERN, LINDA KAY, metallographer; b. Columbus, Ohio, Mar. 20, 1952; d. Ralph William and Mary Evelyn (Robison) Pettet; m. Wilhelm David Kern, Aug. 2, 1975. Student Denison U., 1971-72, Central Ohio Tech. Coll., 1975-81, Am. Soc. Metals, 1981-84. Clk. typist Johns-Manville Products Corp., Newark, Ohio, 1973; sec., receptionist Kaiser Aluminum and Chem. Corp., Newark, 1974-77, cert. adminstr., 1977-82, phys. testing lab. supr., 1982—, metallographer, 1982—. Author short stories; photographer info. articles. candidate Pres.'s Conv. Am. Youth, Washington, 1970; supr., organizer crisis intervention Suicide Prevention/Drug Info. Ctr., Newark, 1971-74; vol. social worker Planned Parenthood, 1972, Leads Neighborhood Action Agy., 1972; asst. organizer Granville Youth Ctr., Ohio, 1976-77; vol. Am. Cancer Soc., Newark, 1976—; vol. solicitor Licking County Food Pantry Network, 1984-85. Mem. Internat. Metall. Soc., Central Ohio Metall. Soc. Democrat. Episcopalian. Clubs: Buckeye Z-28 Car (treas. 1977-79). Avocations: dancing; theatricals; photography; writing; musical instruments. Office: Kaiser Aluminum & Chem Corp PO Box 671 State Rd 79S Newark OH 43055

KERNER, FRANCINE JUDY, lawyer; b. Bronx, N.Y., Jan. 5, 1950; d. Seymour L. and Ruth T. (Glick) K.; m. Michael Klein; 1 child, Elizabeth B. B.A., Queens Coll., 1971; J.D., N.Y.U., 1974. Admitted to N.Y. bar, 1975; asst. dist. atty. Kings County (N.Y.) Dist. Atty.'s Office, 1974-79; counsel to insp. gen. Dept. Commerce, Washington, 1979—. Office: Insp Gen Dept Commerce Washington DC 20230

KERNEY-BURNS, EVELYN L., comunications company administrator; b. Tuscaloosa, Ala., Jan. 28, 1945; d. Robert Lee and Arnetta (Greene) Palmer; m. Robert Lee Kerney, Jr., May 17, 1985. B.A., Canisius Coll., 1983, M.S., 1985; postgrad. SUNY-Buffalo, 1985—. Lic. in real estate. With N.Y. Telephone, Buffalo, 1965, order typist, 1965-70, supr./acting., 1970—, exec. advisor for Jr. Achievement, 1977; salesperson Mil-Hil Realty, Buffalo, 1985—. Named to Black Achievers in Industry, Harlem YMCA, 1984, 85. Mem. Women in Communication, Nat. Assn. Female Execs., AAUW, Buffalo Urban League Guild, Assessors Assn. Western N.Y., Alpha Sigma Lambda. Republican. Avocations: racquetball; cross country skiing. Address: 362 Northland Ave Buffalo NY 14208

KERNS, AGATHA JOANNE, retirement home administrator, nurse; b. Richmond, Va., Dec. 27, 1954; d. Joseph Andrew and Bette Jean (Moore) K. Student in bus. mgmt. J. Sargeant Reynolds Community Coll., Richmond. Lic. practical nurse, cert. nursing home adminstr., cert. home for adults adminstr., Va. Charge nurse Westbrook Hosp., Richmond, 1972-75, Westport Manor, Richmond, 1975-76, Camelot Hall, Salem, Va., 1976-80; day charge nurse Dooley Madison Retirement Home, Richmond, 1981, dir. nursing, 1981-82, adminstr., 1982—. Mem. adv. com. Homes for Adults, VA Dept. Social Services. Mem. Va. Health Care Assn., Va. Assn. Homes for Adults (sec. 1984-85), Nat. Assn. Female Execs., Am. Legion Post 125 Women's Aux., Suburbanite Bowling League Richmond (v.p. 1981-82, pres. 1983-84). Republican. Methodist. Office: Dooley Madison Retirement Home 212 W Franklin St Richmond VA 23220

KERNS, FRANCES GIBBS, moving and storage company executive; b. Bassett, Va., Feb. 21, 1931; d. Ollis and Lottie Estelle (Young) Gibbs; m. Keever Creed Mullins, (div. May 1962); children—Stephen Wayne, Sandra Gibbs, Pamela Jayne; m. Robert Jack Kerns, Jan. 15, 1963. With Stanley Furniture Co., Stanleytown, Va., 1949-63, acctg. clk., 1959-63; bookkeeper, sec. Coble Dairy Co., Inc., Jacksonville, N.C., 1963-74, Kerns & Sons Moving & Storage, Jacksonville, 1974-80; pres., owner, operator Sentry Transfer & Storage, Jacksonville, 1980—. Mem. Jacksonville Movers Assn. (pres. 1980-81, sec.-treas. 1985—), Am. Bus. Women's Assn. (sec.-treas. 1968-69, v.p. 1969-70). Republican. Avocations: playing piano; dancing; hiking. Office: Sentry Transfer & Storage Inc PO Box 726 Jacksonville NC 28541

KERNS, GERTRUDE YVONNE, psychologist; b. Flint, Mich., July 25, 1931; d. Lloyd D. and Mildred (Ter Achter) Brewer; B.A., Olivet Coll., 1953; M.A., Wayne State U., 1958; Ph.D., U. Mich., 1979. Psychologist, Roseville (Mich.) public schs., 1958-68, also instr. psychology Macomb Community Coll., part time; psychologist Grosse Pointe (Mich.) public schs., 1968-86; pvt. practice psychology, Grosse Pointe, 1980—. Mem. Mich. Psychol. Assn., Am. Psychol. Assn., Mich. Edn. Assn., NEA, Psi Chi. Home: 28820 Grant St St Clair Shores MI 48081 Office: 63 Kercheval Grosse Pointe MI 48236

KERPER, MEIKE, family violence and addictions educator, consultant; b. Powell, Wyo., Aug. 13, 1929; d. Wesley George and Hazel (Bowman) K.; m. R.R. Milodragovich, Dec. 25, 1963 (div. 1973); children—Danny, Johnny, Teren, Tina, Stana. B.S., U. Mont., 1973; M.S., U. Ariz., 1975; postgrad. Ariz. State U., 1976-78. Cert. domestic violence counselor, alcoholism and drug abuse counselor Family therapist Cottonwood Hill, Arvada, Colo., 1981; family program developer Turquoise Lodge, Albuquerque, 1982; co-developer abusers program Albuquerque Shelter Domestic Violence, 1984; family therapist Citizens Council Alcoholism and Drug Abuse, Albuquerque, 1984-86; pvt. practice cons. and trainer family violence and treatment, Albuquerque, 1986—; mem. adv. bd. Charter Med., Albuquerque; advisor program devel. All Faiths Receiving home, Albuquerque. Co-author: Court Diversion Program, 1985; author Family Treatment, 1982. Lobbyist CCOPE, Santa Fe, 1983-86; mem. LWV, Albuquerque. Recipient commendation Albuquerque Shelter Domestic Violence, 1984. Mem. Nat. Assn. Prevention of Child Abuse, Nat. Assn. Alcoholism Counselors, N.Mex. Assn. Alcoholism Counselors, Families in Action, Delta Delta Delta. Republican. Episcopalian. Club: PEO. Avocations: Art history; reading; Indian culture; swimming; public speaking. Home: 621 Valverde SE Albuquerque NM 87108

KERR, CATHERINE EARL BAILEY, artist, music educator; b. Montgomery, W.Va., July 4, 1928; d. Alonzo K. and Lyn (Wilson) Bailey; degree in teaching of art, Mason Coll. Music and Fine Arts, Charleston, W.Va., 1953; postgrad. in art Art Student League (N.Y.C.); m. J. Kenneth Kerr, May 26, 1962; stepchildren—David, Terry. Owner, Kerr Internat. Sch. Art and Music for handicapped, Roswell, N.Mex., 1977—; internat. artist; piano and organ tchr.; designer architect; exhibited works at Ligoa Duncan Gallery, N.Y.C., Raymond Duncan Galleries, Paris, David's Gallery, Roswell, numerous others; represented in permanent collections in U.S. and fgn. countries including White House. Recipient awards Assn. Belgo-Hispanica, 1973, 74, Raymond Duncan Gallery, 1975, 76, Luxembourg Mus., 1979; named Dist. Handicapped Woman of Year, 1983, numerous others. Mem. Roswell Fine Arts League (corr. sec., dir., historian, 1st place award). Republican. Presbyterian. Address: 1412 W Hendricks St Roswell NM 88201

KERR, DEBORAH MACPHAIL, human resource executive; b. Gettysburg, Pa., June 14, 1951; d. John Arch and Jeanne Alma (Spangler) MacPhail; m. Robert Stair Kerr, Jr., May 25, 1974. B.S. in Music Edn., Gettysburg Coll., 1973. Selection/tng. coordinator Commonwealth Nat. Bank, Harrisburg, Pa., 1978-79; safety tng. mgr. Ralston Purina Co., Mechanicsburg, Pa., 1979-81; data processing edn. coordinator Hamilton Bank, Lancaster, Pa., 1981-82, dir. mgmt. devel., 1982-83; asst. v.p., dir. manpower devel. Hamilton Bank, subs. CoreStates, Lancaster, 1982-85; asst. v.p., dir. corp. devel. CoreStates Fin. Corp., Phila., 1985—; mem. corp. adv. bd. Lebanon Valley Coll., Annville, Pa., 1985—; instr. Am. Inst. Banking, Lebanon, 1983-84; mem. tng. degree adv. com. Pa. State U., Middletown, Pa., 1983-84; mem. state edn. exec. adv. com. Pa. Am. Inst. Banking, Harrisburg, 1982; lectr. in field. Mem. Am. Soc. Tng. and Devel. (chpt. pres. 1981; Leigh Woehling Meml. award 1985). Avocations: reading; gardening; hiking; camping.

KERR, ELAINE KAY, executive development company executive; b. Fort Worth, Oct. 21, 1939; d. G. Arthur and Lucy Mae (Williams) Henderson. Student U. Tex.-Arlington, 1957-58. Buyer, Leonard's Dept. Store, Fort Worth, 1958-63; restauranteur The Palms Restaurant, Anaheim, Calif., 1964-65; nat. sales dir. Aquq-Trail, Anaheim, 1967-69; pres. J-Kel Mfg. Co., Anaheim, 1970-73; owner, operator Old Rock Store, Junction, Tex., 1973-75, Springs Hotel, Rock Springs, Tex., 1977-78; dir. Conv. and Visitors Bur., Kerrville, Tex., 1978-79; west coast v.p. Exec. Devel. Systems, Anaheim, 1980—; dir. Fin. Services, Unlimited, Anaheim, 1982—. Author: The Synergist, 1984; Dreaming and Winning in America, 1984. Mem. Nat. Speakers Assn., Sales and Mktg. Execs., Women in Bus., Women's Econ. Career Advancement Network, Fullerton C. of C. Republican. Presbyterian. Clubs: Dadedalion (v.p. 1978-79), La Junta (pres. 1978-79) (Junction). Home: 3733 N Harbor Blvd #22 Fullerton CA 92635 Office: Exec Devel Systems 9778 Katella Suite 111 Anaheim CA 92804

KERR, ELIZABETH MARGARET, educator, author; b. Sault Ste Marie, Mich., Jan. 25, 1905; d. John Arthur and Katherine Dorothy (Hirth) Kerr; B.A., U. Minn., 1926, M.A., 1927, Ph.D., 1941. Instr. English, Tabor Coll., Hillsboro, Kans., 1929-30, U. Minn., Mpls., 1930-37, 38-43, Coll. of St. Catherine, St. Paul, 1937-38; asst. prof. Rockford (Ill.) Coll., 1943-45; instr. Milw. State Coll., 1945-55; asso. prof. U. Wis., Milw., 1956-59, prof., 1959-70, prof. emeritus English, 1970—. MLA research grantee, 1942; Summer Salary Support grantee U. Wis., Milw., 1959, 1961. Mem. MLA, Dickens Studies, Soc. for Study So. Lit. Democrat. Congregationalist. Author: Bibliography of the Sequence Novel, 1950; Yoknapatawpha: Faulkner's Little Postage Stamp of Native Soil, 1969; William Faulkner's Gothic Domain, 1979; William Faulkner's Yoknapatawpha: "A Kind of Keystone in the Universe," 1984, rev. edit., 1985. Home: 4259 N Sercombe Rd Milwaukee WI 53216

KERR, ESTA RAE, construction executive; b. Nashville, Aug. 25, 1945; d. Harry Raymond and Elizabeth Fern (Turner) Cantwell; m. Phillip D. Kerr, July 11, 1969 (div. 1977); 1 dau., Jeanine Elizabeth Kerr Kocurak. Girl Friday Neil Carlson veterinarian, Atlanta, 1963-69; office mgr. Roundtree Corp., Atlanta, 1969-74; supr. constrn. Gardner Blue Havel Pools, Houston, 1974-82; pres. Kerr-Curiel Gunite Corp., Houston, 1982—. Mem. Nat. Spa and Pool Inst. Office: Kerr-Curiel Gunite Corp 1545 Oak Tree Houston TX 77080

KERR, FRANCES MILLS, psychology educator; b. Atlanta, Oct. 21, 1919; d. William Morton and Nina (Walker) Mills; m. Oliver Wendell Kerr, Aug. 12, 1946; children—Judith Nina, Oliver Wendell. A.B., Livingstone Coll., 1939; M.A., State U. Iowa, 1943. Instr. child devel. Tuskegee Inst. (Ala.), 1943-46; dir./coordinator early childhood programs USAF, Tokyo, 1953-56; dir. early childhood program Episcopal Ch., Washington, Yellow Springs, Ohio, 1956-59; prof. psychology Mount Holyoke Coll., South Hadley, Mass., 1960—; cons. Headstart, Holyoke, Mass., 1966-69; Danforth assoc. Danforth Assocs. Program, 1971—. Trustee, Concord (Mass.) Acad., 1975-77, hon. trustee, 1977—; trustee Holyoke (Mass.) Hosp., 1978—; ARC, Holyoke, 1979—, Holyoke Chicopee Mental Health Assn., 1966—; bd. dirs. Vanguard Savs. Bank, Holyoke, 1972—; bd. dirs. Western Mass. Council Girl Scouts U.S.A., 1982—. Mem. Nat. Assn. Edn. Young Children, Western Mass. Assn. Edn. Young Children, Alpha Kappa Alpha. Democrat. Episcopalian. Office: Mount Holyoke Coll South Hadley MA 01075

KERR, KATHLEEN WALLACE, landscape architect, publisher; b. Mpls., Dec. 27, 1954; d. Francis Kenneth and Mary Louise (Niss) K.; m. Clyde G. Hanson, Oct. 21, 1978. B.L.A., U. Minn.-St. Paul, 1978. Registered landscape architect, Minn., Ky. Landscape architect Stanley Cons., Inc., Muscatine, Iowa, 1978-81; editor-in-chief, pres. Kerr Assocs., Inc., Mpls., 1979—; prin. Kathleen W. Kerr, L.A., Louisville, 1981-83; ptnr. Kerr-Thorson & Co., Mpls., 1983—. Editor, contbg. author: Cost Data for Landscape Construction, annually, 1980-85 (Ky. chpt. Am. Soc. Landscape Architects Honor award in communications 1982). Mem. Am. Soc. Landscape Architects (editor LA file 1981-83), Am. Soc. Cost Engrs., Minn. Women's Network. Avocations: sailing; cross-country skiing. Home: 1942 Irving Ave S Minneapolis MN 55403 Office: Kerr-Thorson & Co 1409 Willow Minneapolis MN 55403

KERR, MABEL DOROTHEA, physician, educator; b. Toronto, Ont., Can. (parents Am. citizens); d. George Houston and Mabel (Wark) Kerr; B.S., Ohio State U., 1944; M.D., Columbia, 1950. Intern dept. medicine St. Luke's Hosp., N.Y.C., 1950-51, resident, 1951-52; psychiat. resident Payne Whitney Clinic, N.Y. Hosp., 1952-57; practice medicine, specializing in psychiatry, N.Y.C., 1954—; assoc. attending psychiatrist N.Y. Hosp., 1979—; clin. asst. prof. psychiatry Cornell U. Med. Coll., 1968-79, clin. assoc. prof., 1979—; asst. med. examiner, officer chief med. examiner City of N.Y., 1957-66. Pres., Elmora Found. Fellow N.Y. Acad. Medicine; mem. AMA, Am. Psychiat. Assn., Nat. Assn. Med. Examiners, Women's Med. Soc. N.Y. State, Am. Med. Women's Assn. Address: 20 E 68th St New York NY 10021

KERR, NANCY KAROLYN, pastor, mental health consultant; b. Ottumwa, Iowa, July 10, 1934; d. Owen W. and Iris Irene (Israel) Kerr; student Boston U., 1953; A.A., U. Bridgeport, 1966; B.A., Hofstra U., 1967; postgrad. in clin. psychology Adelphi U. Inst. Advanced Psychol. Studies, 1968-73; m. Richard Clayton Williams, June 28, 1953 (div.); children—Richard Charles, Donna Louise. Pastoral counselor Nat. Council Chs., Jackson, Miss., 1964; dir. teen program Waterbury (Conn.) YWCA, 1966-67; intern in psychology N.Y. Med. Coll., 1971-72; research cons., 1972-73; coordinator home services, psychologist City and County of Denver, 1972-75; cons. Mennonite Mental Health Services, Denver, 1975-78; asst. prof. psychology Messiah Coll., 1978-79; mental health cons., 1979-81; called to ministry Mennonite Ch., 1981, pastor Cin. Mennonite Fellowship, 1981-83, coordinator campus evangelism, adv. ch. curriculum, 1981—; mem. Tri-County Counseling Clinic, Memphis, Mo., 1980-81. Mem. Waterbury Planned Parenthood, 1964-67; mem. MW Children's Home Bd., 1974-75; mem. Boulder (Colo.) ARC, 1977-78. Mem. Am. Psychol. Assn., Am. Assn. Mental Deficiency, Soc. Psychologists for Study of Social Issues, Am. Acad. Polit. and Social Scientists. Address: Associated Mennonite Biblical Seminaries 3003 Benham Ave Elkhart IN 46517

KERR, VALERIE ANN, nursing educator; b. Alma, Mich., Jan. 10, 1940; d. Floyd Arther and Martha Ella (Wells) Tomlin; m. Larry Lee Kerr, June 15, 1961; children—Kerry, Kristin, Karmen. Nursing diploma Saginaw Gen. Hosp. Sch. Nursing, 1961; B.S., Central Mich. U., 1983. Charge nurse Gratiot Community Hosp., Alma, 1961-66, 67-74; clin. nursing instr. Mid-Mich. Community Coll., Harrison, Mich., 1978-82, instr., 1982-86; supr. Mich. Masonic Home, Alma, 1986—; migrant program sch. nurse Montcalm Intermediate Sch. Dist., Stanton, Mich., 1981. Club leader, exchange student hostess Mich. 4-H, Gratiot County, 1975-77; fair dept. supt. Gratiot County Agrl. Soc., 1981-83; mem. Mich. Farm Bur./Gratiot Women's Orgn., 1978. Mem. Saginaw Gen. Hosp. Sch. Nursing Alumni Assn., Phi Kappa Phi. Home: 10838 Pingree Rd Elwell MI 48832

KERRAN, JANIS LOUISE, lubricants manufacturing executive; b. Oklahoma City, Mar. 11, 1949; d. Cameron L. and Joanne P. Kerran; B.A. in Math. Edn., Okla. State U., Stillwater, 1972. With Double Eagle Lubricants, Inc., Oklahoma City, 1971—, office mgr., comptroller, sec.-treas., 1972—; sec.-treas. Double Eagle Refining Co., Waste Oil Service Co., CAM-ML Enterprises, Inc. Republican. Home: 3243 Raintree Rd Oklahoma City OK 73120 Office: PO Box 11257 Oklahoma City OK 73136

KERR-GAGNON, BONNIE ETHEL, retail buyer; b. San Diego, Sept. 15, 1949; d. Stanton and Annabel Shirley (Briggs) Kerr; m. Daniel Lee Gagnon, July 10, 1982; Student San Diego State U., 1967-68. Asst. mgr. cosmetics dept. Montgomery Wards, La Mesa, Calif., 1968-72; sales, store mgr. Judy's, San Diego, 1972-76; ops. mgr. Ziba, San Diego, 1976-83; assoc. buyer, merchandiser Fashion Conspiracy, San Diego, 1979-83; chief buyer Nat. Theme Productions, San Diego, 1983—. Avocations: beading gowns and wedding dresses; craftwork; target shooting; boating; interior design. Home: 7821 Orien La Mesa CA 92041 Office: Nat Theme Productions 1843 Hotel Circle S #300 San Diego CA 92108

KERSCHEN, PATRICIA ANN, physician assistant; b. Wichita, Kans., Oct. 23, 1943; d. Russell Julius and Anne Elizabeth (Oeding) Wright; m. Daniel Alphons Kerschen, June 18, 1960; children—Danny, Jr., Timothy, Randall, Julianne, Kimberly, William. A.A., North Lake Jr. Coll., 1981; B.S., U. Tex., 1984. Cert. physician asst., Tex. Biology lab. asst. North Lake Jr. Coll., Irving, Tex., 1980-84; physician asst. Vets. Hosp., Dallas, 1985—. Fellow Am. Acad. Physician Assts., Tex. Acad. Physician Assts.; mem. Beta Sigma Phi. Roman Catholic. Avocations: golf; reading; fishing; crocheting; puzzles. Home: 4013 Golden Rd Irving TX 75038 Office: VA Hosp 4500 Lancaster St Dallas TX

KERSCHNER, VELMA LINOLA, health careers educator; b. Gonzales County, Tex., June 27, 1923; d. Daniel Madison and Clara Olive (Lincecum) Handley; R.N. diploma Brackenridge Hosp. Sch. Nursing, Austin, Tex., 1944; student U. Tex., 1943-45; B.S.N., Incarnate Word Coll., 1961; postgrad. in edn. Trinity U., 1970—; m. Harrison F. Kerschner, Sept. 14, 1947; children—Harrison Frederick III, Olivia Ann. Asst. nursing arts instr. Brackenridge Hosp. Sch. Nursing 1944-45; supr. operating room San Antonio State Chest Hosp., 1956-58; dir. nurses Southton Convalescent Hosp., San Antonio, 1958-60; dir. nurses Santa Rosa Med. Center, San Antonio, 1960-61; instr. San Antonio Sch. Vocat. Nursing, 1962-66, San Antonio Coll. asso. nursing program, 1969-72; assoc. prof. health careers St. Philips Coll., San Antonio, 1972—; Served with Nurses Corps, U.S. Army, 1945-46, 46-48. Mem. Am. Nurses Assn., Tex. Jr. Coll. Tchrs. Assn., Nat. Assn. Health Unit Clks-Coordinators (pres.), Nat. Assn. Female Execs. Author: Nutrition for Practical Nurses, 1969, 3d edit., 1982. Home: Route 1 Box 211 Lavernia TX 78121 Office: 2111 Nevada San Antonio TX 78203

KERSHAW, LANA JO, mfg. co. mktg. exec.; b. Minot, N.D., May 18, 1950; d. Martin Oscar and Josephine Constance (Boklep) Blestrud; student Mesa Community Coll., 1970-71; m. Ronald A. Kershaw, May 21, 1978; children—Lawrence C. Forsythe, Lariana Jo Marchelle Forsythe. Hostess, S.W. Restaurant Systems, Phoenix, 1972, supr., 1972, asst. mgr., 1973; sales rep., asst. food and beverage mgr. Camelback Sahara, Phoenix, 1974-75; supr. Windjammer Restaurant, Phoenix, 1975; sales sec. United Mobile Homes, Inc., Phoenix, 1975; mktg. dir. Roker, Inc., Phoenix, 1975-80; pres. Taries Assocs., Inc., Tempe, Ariz., 1976-77; adminstrv. asst. MS & Co., Sarasota, Fla., 1981—; pres. Taries Assos., Inc., 1976-77. Mem. Sarasota Bd. Realtors. Democrat. Lutheran.

KERSHNER, JILL FARREN, management consultant; b. Texarkana, Tex., Apr. 17, 1945; d. Paul Lester and June (Dunlop) Farren; m. Thomas Walter Kershner, Aug. 29, 1966; children—Andrew Scot, Gregory Alan, David Todd, Jeffrey Thomas. B.A., Vanderbilt U., 1966. Sec. Farren Cons. Service, Houston, 1956-65, mgmt. cons., 1979—, also dir.; advt. staff Record Service Ctr., Houston, 1965-68, owner, dir.; cons. Geodata Service, Inc., Houston, 1979—, author co. brochure, 1984. Tchr., adv. Meml. Drive Presbyn. Ch., Houston; pres., v.p., com. chmn., historian PTA Bds. of Spring Branch Schs. and Council, Houston, 1974—; com. chmn. Booster Club Meml. High Sch., Houston, 1985—; life mem. Tex. PTA, 1982. Mem. Geophysical Aux. of Houston, Am. Mgmt. Assn. Republican. Clubs: Green Valley Women's (Houston) (pres., v.p., parliamentarian, historian), River Oaks Luncheon. Lodge: Women of Rotary (bd. dirs., program chmn., parliamentarian 1981—). Office: Geodata Service Inc 5603 S Rice Ave Houston TX 77081

KERSHNER, MARY BETH, state official; b. Charleston, W.Va., Feb. 3, 1953; d. John Alvin and Pearl Jean (Hutchinson) K. B.S.W., W.Va. U., 1976; J.D., 1981. Bar: W.Va., 1981. Law clk. U.S. Dist. Ct., Charleston, W.Va., 1981-82; asst. atty. gen. W.Va. Atty. Gen., Charleston, 1982—. Mem. Families and Children Together, Charleston, 1983. Mem. Am. Pub. Welfare Assn., Assn. Am. Pub. Welfare Attys., Internat. Platform Assn. Democrat. Episcopalian. Office: Office Atty Gen. 6E-26 State Capitol Charleston WV 25305

KERSTEIN, PHYLLIS, pest control company executive; b. Chgo., Feb. 6, d. Harry and Yetta (Fishbein) K.; m. Milton S. Nusbaum, Nov. 26, 1952; children—Howard C., Susan Lee, Andrea Lynn. B.A., Roosevelt U., 1948. Pres., operator Advanced Exterminating Service, Inc., Chgo., 1948—; dir. Purdue Pest Control, West Layfayette, Ind., 1966, Am. Entomologic Assn., 1964-67. Mem. Ill. Pest Control Assn. (sec. 1961-66, bd. dirs. 1968-70), Nat. Pest Control Assn. (bd. dirs. 1968-70), Chgo. Real Estate Bd., South Central Real Estate Bd. Home: 4950 Chicago Beach Dr Chicago IL 60615 Office: Advanced Exterminating Service Inc 1356 S Michigan Ave Chicago IL 60605

KERYAN, MAUREEN FRANCIS WHELAN, educational psychology educator, researcher; b. Akron, Ohio, June 1, 1947; d. Geroge Raymond Whelan, Jr. and Grace Frances (Riordan) Caporale; m. David George Keryan, July 27, 1968 (div. June 1979). Student Kent State U., Denison U.; B.S., Ariz. State U., 1981, M.Ed., 1983. Data rev. technician Social Security Adminstrn., HEW, Akron and Alexandra, Va., 1974-76, claims rep., Newark, Ohio and Phoenix, 1976-78; research asst. in ednl. psychology Ariz. State U., Tempe, 1981-82, teaching asst., 1982-83, research asst. Coll. Nursing, 1986—; pvt. cons. in research design and data analysis, Phoenix, 1984—; cons. Codama, Phoenix, 1979-82; counseling intern Maverick House, Phoenix, summer 1981. Group facilitator Glendale Sch. Dist. Integration Project, Ariz., 1982. Mem. Exec. Female, Phi Kappa Phi. Roman Catholic. Avocations: singing; reading; creative writing; physical fitness, philosophy. Office: Dept Ednl Psychology Ariz State U Tempe AZ 85281

KESLER, MARY ELIZABETH, educational administrator; b. Gettysburg, Pa., Oct. 12, 1943; d. A. Dean, Sr., and Virginia (Peters) K. A.B., Randolph-Macon Woman's Coll., 1965; Mus. M., Northwestern U., 1966. Music tchr. Foxcroft Sch., Middleburg, Va., 1966-70, dir. admissions, asst. dean, 1969-71; dir. coll. counseling Hockaday Sch., Dallas, 1971-81, asst. headmistress, 1981—; trustee Coll. Bd., 1982—. Mem. Nat. Assn. Coll. Admissions Counselors (coms.), Tex. Assn. Coll. Admissions Counselors (pres. 1980-81), Nat. Assn. Prins. Schs. for Girls. Democrat. Methodist. Office: Hockaday School 11600 Welch Rd Dallas TX 75229

KESSEL, ELSIE IRENE, former municipal financial executive; b. Finland, Mar. 5, 1910; came to U.S., 1916, naturalized, 1926; d. Matt Leander and Marie Sophia Anderson; student public schs.; m. June 22, 1929 (dec.); children—David, Joy, Rosalind, Dianne, Barbara. In farming, Lake County, Irons, Mich., 1938-71; twp. treas. Eden Twp., Lake County (Mich.), 1935-38, 40-84. Address: Route 1 Irons MI 49644

KESSEN, ANTOINETTE IRION, sales executive; b. Dayton, Ohio, Oct. 2, 1945; d. Paul Oldham and Helene Florence (Irion) Miller; m. Lee William Kessen, Nov. 23, 1963 (div. Dec. 1985). B.S. in Bus. Mgmt., U. Dayton, 1978, M.B.A. magna cum laude, 1980. Adminstr., Frigidaire div. GMC, Dayton, 1965-71, distbn. specialist, 1971-75, office mgr., 1975-77, distbn. analyst, 1977-79; advt. mgr. Frigidaire Parts & Service Co., Dayton, 1979-81; account mgr. NCR Corp., Dayton, 1981-84; mktg. communications mgr. Reynolds & Reynolds, 1984-85; sales mgr. L.M. Berry & Co., 1985—. Editor quar. newspaper The Performer, Dayton Performing Arts Fund, 1982, vice chmn. fund, 1983; sustaining mem. Republican Nat. Com. Recipient Scholastic Achievement award U. Dayton, 1980; Hero award Dayton Performing Arts Fund, 1983. Mem. Dayton Advt. Club. Lutheran. Club: Toastmasters (com. chmn. 1983). Home: 8649 Sea Pines Ln Dayton OH 45459 Office: LM Berry & Co 3170 Kettering Blvd Dayton OH 45401-6000

KESSLER, ANN ELIZABETH, social science educator, nun; b. Aberdeen, S.D., Jan. 28, 1928; d. George William and Elizabeth Marcella (Sahli) K.; B.A., Mt. Marty Coll., 1953; M.A., Creighton U., 1957; Ph.D. (grad. fellow 1960), Notre Dame U., 1963. Joined Order St. Benedict, Roman Catholic Ch., 1945, tchr. parochial schs., S.D. and Nebr., 1949-56; vis. prof. Marquette U., Milw., 1969-70; acad. dean Mt. Marty Coll., Yankton, S.D., 1963-65, prof. social sci., 1962—. Mem. S.D. State Criminal Justice Commn., Pierre, 1977-82, S.D. Council of Humanists, Sioux Falls, 1980-82; mem. nat. screening com. Fulbright Scholarships, 1980-84; chmn. bd. dirs. Sojourn House for Troubled Youth, Yankton, S.D., 1981-84; mem. S.D. State Com. on Humanities, 1985—; chmn. (S.D.) Gov.'s Council on Aging., 1980-81. N.W. Area Found. grantee, 1969-72. Mem. Acad. Polit. and Social Sci., Am. Hist. Assn., LWV, S.D. Social Sci. Assn. (pres. 1976-77). Contbr. articles to profl. publs. Home: 1105 W 8th St Yankton SD 57078 Office: Mount Marty Coll Yankton SD 57078

KESSLER, BARBARA ANNE, lawyer; b. Dover, Del., Apr. 4, 1955; d. Myron Allison and Lillian Arlene (Osborne) Boorafti m. David Allen Kessler, Apr. 3, 1976; 1 dau., Amy Kathryn. B.A., Mercer U., 1977; J.D., 1981. Bar: Ga. 1981. Assoc. atty. Law Office of Luther Strickland, Macon, Ga., 1981-82; asst. dist. atty. Dist. Attys. Office, Southwestern Jud. Circuit, Americus, Ga., 1982—. Rep. bd. govs. Mercer Law Sch., Macon, Ga., 1980-81. Recipient Outstanding Service award Ga. Dept. Corrections and Offender Rehab., 1976, Young Careerist Program award Americus and Sumter County and Southwestern Dist. Ga. chpts. Bus. and Profl. Women, 1984. Mem. ABA, Southwestern Circuit Bar Assn., Ga. Bar Assn., Ga. Assn. Asst. Dist. Attys., Bus. and Profl. Women. Home: 605 Hnacock Dr Americus GA 31709 Office: Dist Attys Office Courthouse Annex PO Box 1328 Americus GA 31709

KESSLER, CAROLE STEVENS, construction company executive; b. Salt Lake City, July 10, 1937; d. Walter and Vera P. (Hopkinson) S.; m. Frederick Michael Kessler, Aug. 29, 1961; children—Kathryn Elizabeth, Kristen Jane. B.S., Brigham Young U., 1959. Tchr. Los Angeles Unified Sch. Dist., 1959-66; co-founder, officer Kessler Inc., Los Angeles, 1976—. Officer PTA, Los Angeles, 1974-78; leader San Fernando Valley Council Girl Scouts U.S.A., Los Angeles, 1971-81; mem. Sherman Oaks Girl Scout council, Los Angeles, 1978-81. Mem. Nat. Assn. Women in Constrn. Republican. Mormon. Avocations: classical music; knitting; reading. Home: 12946 Hesby St Sherman Oaks CA 91423 Office: Kessler Inc 5658 Colfax Ave North Hollywood CA 91601

KESSLER, DORIS HENRIETTA, army officer; b. New Kensington, Pa., Sept. 19, 1935; d. Francis Arthur and Dora Mary Molinari; B.S., Pa. State U., 1957; m. Otto F. Kessler, June 1958 (div.). Tchr., Duquesne (Pa.) High Sch., 1958-68; commd. 1st lt. U.S. Army, 1968, advanced through grades to lt. col. Adj. Gen.'s Corps, 1984; instr., Ft. McClellan, Ala., 1969-69; recruiting officer, N.Y.C., 1971-73; chief tng. mgmt. div., Ft. Belvoir, Va., 1973; co. comdr., Ft. Jackson, S.C., 1973-75, bn. exec. officer, 1975; ADP officer Computer Systems Command, Ft. Belvoir, 1975-79; project officer women in army study Dept. Army, 1977-78; chief systems software Comdr.-in-Chief Pacific Staff, 1979-82; chief adminstrv. team Readiness Group, Ft. Sheridan, Ill., 1983-84, automation mgmt. systems officer Army Planning Group, 1984; dir. Adminstrn. and Logistical Services Directorate, Res. Component Personnel and Adminstrn. Ctr., St. Louis, 1984—. Committeewoman, Allgheny County, Pitts., 1963-67. Decorated Meritorious Service medal, Army Commendation medal (2). Featured in Women in Combat, Army Mag., 1980. Mem. Nat. Assn. Female Execs., Assn. U.S. Army. Club: Mil. Dist. Washington Officers, Assn. of Met. Mus. of Art, Internat. Platform Assn., Met. Opera Guild, St. Louis Symphony Assn. Office: 1502 Mississippi Avenue St Louis MO 63104

KESSLER, JEAN S., executive secretary; b. New Brunswick, N.J., Oct. 20, 1954; d. John S. and Henrietta Marguerite (Pasquier de Lumeau) Kessler; m. Michael P. Gutzan, Sept. 16, 1984; A.A.S. with highest honors, Middlesex County Coll., 1981; postgrad. Edison State Coll., 1984—. Sec. to dir. Carter-Wallace, Inc., Cranbury, N.J., 1977-78, exec. sec. to corp. v.p., 1978-80; exec. sec. to v.p. Continental Ins. Co., Piscataway, N.J., 1981, exec. sec. to sr. v.p., 1981-84, exec. sec. to exec. v.p., 1984—. Recipient Sec. of Yr. award Profl. Secs. Internat., 1981-82. Cert. profl. sec. Mem. Profl. Secs. Internat. (chmn. civic com. New Brunswick chpt. 1980-81, sec. of yr. com. 1981-82; mem. nominating com. 1981, audit com. 1982, ways and means com. 1981-82), Nat. Assn. Female Execs., Nat. Assn. Ins. Women, Mensa, Nu Tau Sigma. Office: Two Corporate Pl S Piscataway NJ 08854

KESSLER, LEONA HANOVER, interior designer; b. Phila., Sept. 15, 1925; d. Herman and Ida (Gleaner) Hanover; B.S. in Textile Engring. (Sara Tyler Wister scholar), Phila. Coll. Textiles and Sci., 1948; m. Sydney Kessler, Aug. 28, 1948; children—Andrew Louis, Todd Hanover. Pvt. practice interior design and cons. Lee Kessler Interiors, Phila., 1957—; textile designer, stylist, color cons.; mem. faculty Moore Coll. Art, 1970-72, Art Inst. Phila., 1973-78, Phila. Coll. Textiles and Sci., 1972-81; juror textile design and interior design; works exhibited designer showcases, local house tours, faculty shows. Named Alumnus of Month, Textile Engr., 1971. Mem. Am. Soc. Interior Designers (dir. Pa. East chpt. 1967-78, chpt. recognition awards 1974, 80). Author: That Which Was Once a Warp, 1971; contbr. articles and photographs to mags. and newspapers. Address: 3421 Warden Dr Philadelphia PA 19129

KESSLER, PATRICIA ELLEN, advertising, marketing and public relations specialist; b. Mt. Pleasant, Pa., Mar. 30, 1937; d. Benjamin E. and Donna Natalie (Jones) Paladino; m. John Anthony Kessler, Aug. 25, 1962; children—Lisa, Tracy, Jon. B.A., Pa. State U.; M.A., Ohio State U. Pub. relations asst. Riverside Methodist Hosp., Columbus, Ohio, 1977-78; dir. coll. relations Ohio Dominican Coll., Columbus, 1978-81; dir. pub. relations North Central Mental Health Services, Columbus, 1981-83; account exec. Hameroff/Milenthal, 1984-85; dir. coll. relations Otterbein Coll., 1985—; pub. relations cons., Columbus, 1983—. Mem. pub. relations adv. com. YWCA, Columbus, 1982-83; mem. membership, pub. relations coms. Met. Women's Center, Columbus, 1981-82; mem. exec. bd. Players Theatre, Columbus, 1982—. Mem. Pub. Relations Soc. Am. (chpt. citations com. 1982-83), Internat. Assn. Bus. Communicators (chpt. dir. 1982-83), Kappa Tau Alpha, Phi Kappa Phi.

KESSLER-BERDY, ALICE CECELIA, computer software marketing executive; b. Teaneck, N.J., Feb. 15, 1952; d. Charles Emil and Fay (Galasso) Kessler; m. Jack M. Berdy, Sept. 5, 1983. B.A. in Lit., Ramapo State Coll., Mahwah, N.J., 1975; postgrad. Fairleigh Dickinson U. Clk., city desk The Record, Hackensack, N.J., 1975-76; v.p. mktg. communications On-Line Software Internat., Fort Lee, N.J., 1976—. Mem. Bus. Profl. Advt. Assn. (bd. dirs.). Office: On-Line Software Two Executive Dr Fort Lee NJ 07024

KESTER, PATRICIA ANNETTE, clinical psychologist, educator; b. Colorado Springs, Colo., Aug. 9, 1945; d. James Douglas and Lucille Erma (Townley) K.; B.A., U. Tex., Austin, 1967; M.Ed., U. Houston, 1973; Ph.D., U.S. Internat. U., 1978. Social worker Okla. Dept. Public Welfare, Oklahoma City, 1967-68, Tex. Dept. Public Welfare, Houston, 1968-69, Harris County Child Welfare, Houston, 1969-71; tchr. Houston Ind. Sch. Dist., 1971-72; counselor Tex. Research Inst. for Mental Sci., Houston, 1973-74; research assoc. dept. psychiatry SUNY, Stony Brook, 1974-76; psychol. intern Mercy Hosp., San Diego, 1977-78, lectr. dept. psychology U. Calif., San Diego, 1979; postdoctoral fellow Garrard Center for Psychology, La Mesa, Calif., 1979-80; pvt. practice clin. psychology, La Mesa, Calif., 1980-82, Orange, Calif., 1980—, La Jolla, Calif., 1982—; adj. asst. prof. Chapman Coll., Orange, 1979-84. Bd. dirs. Who Cares, community mental health center, Houston, 1973-74. NIH fellow, 1974-76; NIMH grantee, 1975-76. Mem. Am. Psychol. Assn., Calif. Psychol. Assn., Nat. Assn. Social Workers, Calif. Assn. Marriage and Family Therapists, Am. Assn. Sex Educators and Therapists, Acad. San Diego Psychologists, San Diego Soc. Sex Therapy and Edn. (pres. 1986—), Soc. Scientific Study Sex (local chpt. chair 1985-86, Western Region conf. chair 1986), Soc. for Personality Assessment. Contbr. articles to profl. publs. Home: PO Box 278 La Jolla CA 92038 Office: 8950 Villa La Jolla Dr Suite 2200 La Jolla CA 92037 also 1485 N Tustin St Suite 230 Orange CA 92667

KETZ, CHRISTINE MARY, transportation planning and marketing consultant; b. Scranton, Pa., Jan. 10, 1948; d. Edward George and Margaret (Surmaitis) Gruss; m. Gerald Charles Ketz, Oct. 4, 1969; 1 child, Erika, Kristen. B.S., Bloomsburg U., 1969; M.S., U. Louisville, 1973; M.B.A., Tenn. State U., 1981. Dir. current planning Louisville and Jefferson County Planning Commn., Louisville, 1971-79, pres. CK Cons., Nashville, 1979-81; market analyst Kaiser Permanente, Los Angeles, 1981-82; product specialist Computer Sci. Corp., Huntington Beach, Calif., 1982; mgr. cons. services div. Cordoba Corp., Los Angeles, 1984—. Recipient Spl. award County Judge/City Mayor Louisville, 1974. Mem. Am. Mktg. Assn., Am. Planning Assn. Republican. Roman Catholic. Avocations: Skiing; tennis. Home: 21303 Jaffrey Ave Torrance CA 90502 Office: Cordoba Corp 617 S Olive St Suite 810 Los Angeles CA 90014

KEULER, ASTRID LINNEA, resort hotel executive; b. N.Y.C., Oct. 24, 1929; d. Tage Ragnwald and Viktoria Hulda (Gustafson) Flyborg; student East Stroudsburg U., 1966-68; m. Jacob H. Keuler, Nov. 14, 1947; children—Daniel, Marc. Estimator, prodn. liaison Ind. Offset-Lithographers, N.Y.C., 1953-56; dir., owner The Art Gallery, Strathmore, N.J., 1960-63; treas., tchr. The Sch. at Kirkridge, Bangor, Pa., 1968-69; pres., Jacob-Clark Constrn. Co., Inc., Buck Hill Falls, Pa., 1971—; partner The Hamlet, residential community, Canadensis, Pa., 1972—; owner, v.p. Buck Hill Inn, Buck Hill Falls, Pa., 1981—; v.p. Classic Resorts, Ltd., 1981—, pres. Interiors by Astrid; tchr. interior design Monroe County Vocat. Tech. Sch., Bartonsville, Pa., 1975-77. Treas., Monroe County Indsl. Devel. Authority, Stroudsburg, Pa., 1975-84; founder, pres. Phoenix Players, 1965—; bd. dirs. Pocono Mountains Ctr. for Arts. Mem. Nat. Assn. Home Builders (nat. dir. 1977-82), Barrett Bus. Assn. (dir. 1979-81), Pocono Builders Assn. (dir. 1974-82), Pocono Mountains C. of C. (pres. 1980-81, Dir. of Yr. award 1978), Alpha Psi Omega. Democrat. Home: Box 15 Buck Hill Falls PA 18323 Office: Buck Hill Inn Resort and Conf Ctr Buck Hill Falls PA 18323

KEVESON, FLORENCE, artist, painter; b. N.Y.C., Oct. 14, 1926; d. Barnett and Ray (Price) Shillman; m. Peter Keveson, Oct. 15, 1949; 1 child. Degree in Art, Cooper Union Sch. Art, 1943; student Art Students League, 1944-49. Fashion illustrator Vogue Mag., N.Y.C., 1949-52; free lance illustrator, N.Y.C., 1952-62; free lance painter, artist, N.Y.C., 1962—. One-woman shows include Silvermine Guild of Artists, Soc., New Canan, Conn., 1969, Marist Coll., Poughkeepsie, N.Y., 1972; exhibited in group shows at Berkshire Mus., Mass., 1966-68, 72, Acad. Arts and Letters, N.Y., 1968, Butler Inst. Am. Art, Ohio, 1970, Wadsworth Atheneum, Conn., 1971-73, Audubon Artists, N.Y., 1966-85, Salmagundi Club, 1983 represented in permanent collections Silvermine Guild of Artists, Conn., Hist. Soc., Woodstock, N.Y. Recipient awards Acad. Arts and Letters Childe Hassam Purchase Fund, N.Y.C., 1968, Williamstown Bd. Trade-Berkshire Mus., Pittsfield, Mass., 1969, Doris Klein award for Contemporary Figure Painting, N.Y.C., 1976, First Prize in Oils Painters and Sculptors Soc., N.Y.C., 1985. Mem. Nat. Assn. Women Artists, Artists Equity Assn., Audubon Artists, Painters and Sculptors Soc., Am. Soc. Contemporary Artists. Home: 314 E 201 St Bronx NY 10458

KEVIL, TERESA JEAN, nursing educator; b. St. Louis, July 4, 1950; d. Gene A. and Rita Myrtle (Stroup) Thoma; m. Gregg Bruce Kevil, Aug. 12, 1969; children—Christopher Gene, Jennifer Todd. B.S.N., Northwestern State U., Natchitoches, La., 1974; M.N.Sc., U. Ark., 1980. Staff nurse VA Hosp., Shreveport, 1974-75; critical care nurse, 1976-77; critical care nurse La. State U. Hosp., Shreveport, 1978, clin. specialist, 1980; asst. prof. nursing Northwestern State U., Natchitoches, 1977—. Critical care expert witness 9th Jud. Ct. Sabine Parish, La., 1981—. Mem. Am. Assn. Critical Care Nurses, Nat. League Nursing, Am. Nurses Assn., Am. Heart Assn., Phi Mu, Sigma Theta Tau. Democrat. Roman Catholic. Home: 324 Peach Dr Shreveport LA 71106 Office: Northwestern State Coll Nursing 1800 Warrington Pl Shreveport LA 71101

KEWIN, NANCY ANN, sales/mktg. executive; b. Wyandotte, Mich., June 26, 1953; d. Arthur L. and Virginia M. (Lapham) Kewin; B.Music, U. Ariz., 1975; M.B.A., Pepperdine U., 1984. Keyboard dept. mgr. West Los Angeles Music, 1976-78; electronic merchandising specialist Norlin Corp., Lincolnwood, Ill., 1978-79; Western region sales/mktg. mgr. Moog Music/Norlin Corp., Los Angeles, 1979-84; dir. communications and edn. Roland Corp. U.S., Los Angeles, 1984—. Gen. Music scholar, 1971-72; Albert A. Haldeman Fine Arts scholar, 1972-75; recipient Moog Music Sales Achievement awards, 1980-82. Mem. Nat. Assn. Female Execs., Nat. Assn. Profl. Saleswomen. Republican. Home: 22040 Gault St Apt 47 Canoga Park CA 91303 Office: 2500 Walden Ave Buffalo NY 14225

KEY, DOROTHY LAUSBERG, financial planner; b. Arnold, Pa., Oct. 28, 1947; d. Robert Joseph and Alice Mae (Smith) Lausberg; m. Robert Joseph Key, May 10, 1976 (div. 1982). B.A. in Rehab. Edn., Pa. State U., 1969. C.L.U. Social caseworker Harmarville Rehab. Ctr., Pitts., 1969-75; sales rep. Key Bellevilles, Inc., Leechburg, Pa., 1975-82; agt. Prudential Ins. Co., Pitts., 1982-84; assoc. SMA Fin. Services, Pitts., 1984—. Mem. Life Underwriters Polit. Action Com., Pitts., 1985-86; sponsor Pa. Women's Campaign Fund, 1986. Mem. Am. Soc. C.L.U., Nat. Assn. Life Underwriters, Pitts. Assn. Life Underwriters, Nat. Assn. Health Underwriters, Pitts. Assn. Health Underwriters, State Mut. Agts. Assn., North Hills C. of C., North Hills Bus. and Profl. Women. Democrat. Roman Catholic. Club: Zonta. Avocations: reading; cultural events; continuing education. Office: SMA Financial Services 2000 Gateway Center Three Pittsburgh PA 15222

KEY, HELEN ELAINE, accounting, consulting company executive; b. Cleve., Jan. 16, 1946; d. Maud and Helen (Key) Vance. B.S., W.Va. State Coll., 1968; M.Ed., Cleve. State U., 1977. Tchr. Cleve. Bd. Edn., 1968—; instr. Cuyahoga Community Coll., Cleve., part-time, 1969-78, Dyke Coll., Cleve., part-time, 1979—; pres. H.E. Key & Assos., Cleve., 1983—; treas. BK4W Inc., Cleve., 1981. Mem. Am. Assn. Notary Pubs., Women Bus. Owners Assn., AAUW, NAACP, Cleve. Area Bus. Tchrs., NEA, Pi Lambda Theta, Alpha Kappa Alpha. Democrat. Baptist. Club: Toastmistress (sec. 1978) (Cleve.). Home: 23951 Lakeshore Blvd Apt 608B Euclid OH 44123

KEY, MARY RITCHIE, linguist, author, educator; b. San Diego, Mar. 19, 1924; d. George Lawrence and Iris (Lyons) Ritchie; student U. Chgo., summer 1954, U. Mich., 1959; M.A., U. Tex., 1960, Ph.D., 1963; postgrad. UCLA, 1966; children—Mary Helen Key Ellis, Harold Hayden Key (dec.), Thomas George Key. Asst. prof. linguistics Chapman Coll., Orange, Calif., 1963-66; asst. prof. linguistics U. Calif., Irvine, 1966-71, assoc. prof., 1971-78, prof., 1978—, chmn. program linguistics, 1969-71, 75-77; cons. Am. Indian langs., Spanish, in Mexico, 1946-55, S.Am., 1955-62, Easter Island, 1975, English dialects, 1968-74, U.S. Office Edn., 1969-72, Calif. State Dept. Edn., 1966-75; cons. Center Applied Linguistics, Washington, 1967, 69; lectr. in field. Fulbright-Hays grantee, 1975; U. Calif. Regents acad. grantee, 1974-75; recipient Friends of Library Book award, 1976. Mem. Linguistic Soc. Am., Am. Dialect Soc. (exec. council; regional sec. 1974-84), Internat. Reading Assn. (dir. 1968-72), Delta Kappa Gamma (local pres. 1974-76). Author numerous books, including: Male/Female Language, 1975; Paralanguage and Kinesics, 1975; Nonverbal Communication: A Research Guide and Bibliography, 1977; The Grouping of South American Indian Languages, 1979; Catherine the Great's Linguistic Contribution, 1980; Polynesian and American Linguistic Connections, 1984; founder, editor newsletter Nonverbal Components of Communication, 1972-76; editorial bd. Forum Linguisticum, 1976—, Language Sciences, 1978—, La Linguistique, 1979—; editor (with others) Organization of Behavior in Face-to-Face Interaction, 1975; contbr. articles to profl. jours. in field. Office: Program in Linguistics U Calif Irvine CA 92717

KEY, REBECCA, landscape lighting sales representative, fashion consultant; b. Cleburne, Tex., Oct. 14, 1954; d. Milford Marion, Jr., and Roma Dee (Fletcher) K. B.B.A., So. Meth. U., 1977. Bank examiner Tex. Dept. Banking, Dallas, 1977-78; bank auditor Lakewood Bank, Dallas, 1978-80; realtor Helena Underwood, Dallas, 1980-82; recruitment adminstr. Viai Hamilton, Dallas, 1982-83; sales rep. John Watson Co., Dallas, 1983—; mem. Dallas Law Recruiters, 1982-83. Mem. Dallas Jr. League, Dallas Mus. Fine Arts. Republican. Baptist. Clubs: Park Cities Christian Women's of Dallas (dir.), Slipper, Cotillion (Dallas). Home: 4507 Holland St Apt 106 Dallas TX 75219 Office: John Watson Co 1933 Regal Row Dallas TX 75235

KEY, ZADIE BOWLING, educational administrator; b. Murfreesboro, Tenn., Oct. 20, 1921; d. John William and Nancy Beatrice (Kelton) Bowling; B.S., Middle Tenn. State U., 1941; postgrad. U. Houston, 1955-56; m. Edward Key, Jan. 10, 1948; children—John Matthew, Edward Huey, James Bowling. Sec. to pres. W.S. Bellows Constrn. Co., Houston, 1953-61, Tenn. Aircraft, Inc., Nashville, 1961-66; asst. to dean Sch. Basic and Applied Scis., Middle Tenn. State U., Murfreesboro, 1971—. Chmn. Rutherford County (Tenn.) Democratic Com., 1978—, treas., 1974-78; bd. dirs. United Way, Murfreesboro, 1980—, now also v.p. Mem. Tenn. Fedn. Dem. Women (v.p. 1978, corp. sec. 1976-77), Murfreesboro-Rutherford County C. of C. (v.p. 1980, dir. 1978-80, ambassador), Tenn. Assn. Ednl. Secs., Profl. Secs. Internat. Mem. Ch. of Christ. Home: 304 4th Ave Murfreesboro TN 37130 Office: Peck Hall 101 Middle Tenn State Univ Box 83 Murfreesboro TN 37132

KEYS, DESLEY KAY, oil company executive, software exporter; b. Brisbane, Queensland, Australia, Oct. 25, 1951; came to U.S., 1977; d. Colin and Beverley Ellen (Darnell) Hoy; m. Robert Henry Keys, Sept. 16, 1978. B.A., Queensland U., Brisbane, 1971. Ind. tchr. English lang., Nagoya, Japan, 1970-71; adminstr. Dept. of Prime Minister, Australian Govt., Sydney, 1971-77; controller Western Natural Gas Co., La Jolla, Calif., 1981—, treas., 1984—; co-founder, v.p. MicroWorld Internat., Inc., La Jolla, 1983—. Mem. World Trade Assn. Avocations: reading; handcrafts; racquetball; swimming. Home: 5225 Marigot Place San Diego CA 92037 Office: Western Natural Gas Co 7755 Fay Ave Suite H La Jolla CA 92037

KEYS, GAIL DARLENE, nursing administrator, consultant; b. Amarillo, Tex., Feb. 14, 1939; d. Carlyle Francis and Lila Edith (Field) Moore; m. Gerald Wilburn Keys, July 19, 1957 (div. Sept. 1979); children; David W., Robert D., Kenneth G., Linda Keys Vice, Edward J. B.S., E. Central Okla. State U., 1978. Dir. nursing Drumright Meml. Hosp., Okla., 1980-81, Amarillo Home Health, 1982-83, Cimarron Meml. Hosp., Boise City, Okla., 1984-85, Choctaw Nation Health Services Authority, Talihina, Okla., 1985-86; dir. nursing service Anadarko Mcpl. Hosp., Okla., 1986—; advisor adv. council Kiamichi Area Vo-Tech, Talihina, 1985—. Mem. Okla. Nurses Assn., Am. Nurses Assn., Alpha Chi. Republican. Roman Catholic. Avocations: fishing; crocheting; camping. Home: 911 1/2 SW 5th St Anadarko OK 73005

KEYS, MARTHA ELIZABETH, congresswoman; b. Hutchinson, Kans., Aug. 10, 1930; d. S.T. and Clara (Krey) Ludwig; student Olivet Coll., Kankakee, Ill., 1946-48; A.B., U. Mo.-Kansas City, 1952; children—Carol, Bryan, Dana, Scott. Co-chairperson Manhattan (Kans.) Riley County United Way Dr., 1973; mem. spl. commn. for Manhattan recreational needs, 1973; mem. 94th-95th Congresses from 2d Kans. Dist.; exec. dir. Ctr. for a New Democracy, 1985—; dir. ednl. programs Assn. Former Mems. Congress, Washington, 1983-85; spl. adviser to sec. HEW, 1979; asst. sec. of edn., 1980; exec. dir. Friends of the Family, 1981; vis. prof. Am. U., SUNY-Oswego, Sangamon State U., Chatham Coll., U. Oreg., Mt. Vernon Coll., Salem Coll., No. Ky. U., Albion Coll., St. Norbert's Coll.; politician-in-residence Wells Coll., 1982. Kans. coordinator McGovern for Pres. campaign, 1972; del. dist. and state Dem. conv., 1972, alt. del. nat. conv., 1972; chmn. Riley County Dem. Club, 1973; co-chmn. Manhattan Arts Council, 1973; bd. dirs. Am. Council on Ger., Common Cause, Pan-Pacific Community Council, Nat. Council on Aging; mem. Nat. Commn. on Social Security Reform, 1982-83. Mem. AAUW, Nat. Women's Polit. Caucus, Civic Music Club, Sigma Alpha Iota. Contbg. author: Everywoman's Legal Guide. Office: 222 I St NE Washington DC 20002

KEYSTON, STEPHANI ANN, businesswoman; b. Baytown, Tex., Aug. 6, 1955; d. Herbert Howard and Janice Faye (Stowe) C.; m. George Keyston III, Oct. 8, 1983. A.A. with honors, Merced Coll., Merced, Calif., 1975; B.A. in Journalism with distinction, San Jose State U., 1976. Reporter, Fresno (Calif.) Bee, 1974-75; reporter, photographer Merced (Calif.) Sun-Star, 1974-77; pub. info. officer Fresno City Coll. (Calif.), 1977-80; dir. communications Aerojet Tactical Systems Co., Sacramento, 1980-83; co-owner, v.p. Keyco Landscape Contractor, Inc., Redwood City, Calif., 1984—. Co.-coordinator United Way Campaign, 1981; Aerojet Tactical Systems Co. coordinator West Coast Nat. Derby Rallies, 1981-83. Mem. Internat. Assn. Bus. Communicators (dir. Sacramento chpt. 1983), Citrus Heights C. of C. (v.p. 1983). Republican. Home: Redwood City CA Office: PO Box 3461 Redwood City CA 94064

KEZER, PAULINE RYDER, state legislator; b. Boston, Feb. 4, 1942; d. Paul Washington and Madeline (Farmer) Ryder; m. Kenneth Ronald Kezer, Sept. 23, 1962; children—Anne Elizabeth, Pamela Lynne, Cynthia Karen. B.Psychology, Colby Coll., 1963; postgrad. Central Conn. State Coll., 1978, 83. Tutor sci. and humanities New Britain Schs. Teenage Parent Program, New Britain Conn., 1964-78; mem. Conn. Ho. of Reps., Hartford, 1979—, asst. minority leader, 1981-84, asst. majority leader, 1985-86; dir. New Eng. Caucus Women Legislators, 1983-84, chmn., 1985-86; pres. Conn. Order Women Legislators, Hartford, 1981-82; mem. adv. com. Central Conn. State U. Polit. Inst., New Britain, 1983-84; mem. adv. bd. Colonial Bank, Plainville, Conn., 1980-85. Camp dir. Girl Scout Council, 1972-81, assoc. chair, 1975-78, v.p., 1979-85, nat. bd. dirs., 1984—; pres., v.p., treas., bd. dirs. YWCA, New Britain, 1971-79; chmn., sec. Inland Wetlands Com., 1972-79; mem. Republican Town Com., Plainville, 1977-84; exec bd. Eastern region Council State Govts.; vol. New Britain Cancer Soc., 1980-85; bd. dirs. Collaboration for Conn.'s Children, 1985—; mem. adv. bd. Tunxis Community Coll., 1984—; mem. nat. rev. team Project Hometown Am., 1986. Recipient Thanks Badge and Conn. Yankee award Conn. Yankee Girl Scout council, Farmington, 1982, 79; named Outstanding Citizen, Jaycees, Plainville, Conn., 1980; Outstanding Vol., New Britain YWCA, 1978; Legislator of Yr., Conn. Valley Girl Scout council, Hartford, 1984; recipient Women Helping Women award Soroptomists, Hartford, 1984—. Mem. Nat. Order Women Legislators (legis. chair 1986), Alpha Delta Pi. Republican. Episcopalian. Club: Newcomers (pres. 1965-67) (New Britain). Office: State Capitol Room 111 Hartford CT 06106

KHEEL, ANN SUNSTEIN, civic worker; b. Pitts., Nov. 5, 1915; A.B. with honors, Cornell U., 1936; m. Theodore Woodrow Kheel, July 1, 1937; children—Ellen Margaret (Mrs. Arnold S. Jacobs), Robert Jeffrey, Constance Elizabeth, Martha Louise, Jane Meredith, Katherine Emily. Columnist, Ithaca (N.Y.) Jour., assoc. editor Cornell Alumni News, 1936-37; asst. editor Tide Mag., N.Y.C., 1937-39; info. specialist Dept. Agr., Washington, 1939-43, editor Land Policy Rev.; bd. dirs. Play Schs. Assn., 1944-55; bd. dirs. Riverdale Neighborhood Assn., Riverdale/Bronx, N.Y., 1953-65, v.p., 1958-60; del. to President's Com. on Equal Employment Opportunity, Washington, 1963, 64; spl. corr. N.Y. Herald Tribune, 1957; sec., bd. dirs. N.Y. Urban League, 1965—, founder, chmn. ann. Frederick Douglass Awards Dinners, 1966—; corp. mem., trustee Schomburg Center for Research in Black Culture, 1971-86; mem. Mayor's Screening Panel for Bd. of Higher Edn. of N.Y.C., 1964-66; trustee Rand Inst. of N.Y.C., 1973-76; mem. Coop. Edn. Commn., N.Y.C. Bd. Edn., 1968—; appointee Regents Regional Coordinating Council for Post-secondary Edn., N.Y.C., 1974-76; chmn. State Parks and Recreation Commn. for N.Y.C., 1977-86. Home: 407 W 246th St Bronx NY 10471

KIBLER, CYNTHIA ANN, banker; b. Altoona, Pa., Feb. 5, 1957; d. Earl Anthony and Mary Lucy (Riner) K. B.S., Shippensburg U., 1979. State bank examiner intern Pa. Dept. Banking, Harrisburg, 1978; assoc. nat. bank examiner U.S. Treasury Dept., Washington, 1979-85; treas. Commerce Bank Harrisburg, Camp Hill, Pa., 1985—. Bd. dirs., treas. Family and Children Service, Harrisburg, 1986—. Kiwanis scholar, 1975. Mem. West Shore C. of C., Nat. Assn. Bank Women, Nat. Assn. Female Execs., Am. Bankers Assn., Bank Adminstrn. Inst., Nat. Assn. Accts. Republican. Roman Catholic. Club: Harrisburg Area Volleyball. Avocations: reading; volleyball; health club; cross country skiing; cooking. Home: 529 Lopax Rd Apt Q-20 Harrisburg PA 17112 Office: Commerce Bank/Harrisburg Senate Ave and Erford Rd Camp Hill PA 17011

KIBLER, RHODA SMITH, lawyer; b. Gainesville, Fla., Mar. 10, 1947; d. Chesterfield and Vivian Lee (Parker) Smith; m. David Burke Kibler IV, Sept. 16, 1971; children—John Vincent Cannon, Parker Smith Cannon. B.A., Skidmore Coll., 1972; J.D. cum laude, Fla. State Univ., 1982. Bar: Fla. 1982. Research asst. to U.S. Senator, Washington, 1967-68; lobbyist Colo. Civil Rights Commn., Denver, 1974-75; intern Fla. Commn. on Human Relations, Tallahassee, 1981-82; atty. Office of Gen. Counsel Dept. Ins., Tallahassee, 1982-84, hosp. cost containment spl. counsel, 1984—; ptnr. Kibler & Renard, Tallahassee, 1984—; legis. counsel Fla. Assn. HMOs, 1986—; mem. Ins. Commr's. Task Force on Discrimination in Ins., Tallahassee, 1983—; mem. Task Force on Elimination of Discrimination in Statutes, Tallahassee, 1984—. Bd. dirs. Capital Women's Network, Tallahassee, 1983—; mem. exec. com. Statute of Liberty-Ellis Island Centennial Commn., Fla., 1983—; bd. dirs. Anti-Recidivism Ctr., Denver, 1973-75; mem. LeMoyne art Found., Tallahassee, 1984—; state chmn. Overseas Edn. Fund Women, Law, and Devel., 1984-85; mem. S.E. Regional Conf. on Constl. System; Mem. Am. Judicature Soc., Fla. Bar Assn. (chair com. individual rights and responsibilities com. 1986, chair ins. com. 1986, legis. com. Young Lawyers), ABA (mem. sect. administrv. law, individual rights and responsibilities), Fla. Assn. Hosp. Attys., Fla. Hosp. Assn., LWV, Tallahassee Bar Assn., Tallahassee Assn. Women Lawyers, Tallahassee C. of C. (trustee's com. of 100), Fla. Women's Network (chair jud. appts. com. 1984—). Clubs: Capital Tiger, Bay (Tallahassee). Contbr. articles to profl. jours. Office: Kibler and Renard PO Box 1737 Tallahassee FL 32302

KIBRICK, ANNE, nursing educator; b. Palmer, Mass., June 1, 1919; d. Martin and Christine (Grigas) Karlon; R.N., Worcester (Mass.) Hahnemann Hosp., 1941; B.S., Boston U., 1945; M.A., Columbia Tchrs. Coll., 1948; Ed.D., Harvard, 1958; L.H.D. (hon.), St. Joseph's Coll., Windham, Maine, 1973; m. Sidney Kibrick, June 16, 1949; children—Joan, John. Asst. edn. dir. Cushing VA Hosp., Framingham, Mass., 1948-49; asst. prof. nursing Simmons Coll., Boston, 1949-55; dir. grad. div. Boston U. Sch. Nursing, 1958-63, dean, 1963-68, prof., 1968-70; chmn. dept. nursing Boston Coll. Grad. Sch. Arts and Sci., 1970-74; chmn. sch. nursing Boston State Coll., 1974-82; dir. Sch. Nursing, U. Mass.-Boston, 1982-85, dean, 1985—; cons. div. nursing USPHS, 1964-68; nat. adv. council nurse tng. USPHS, NIH, 1968-73; cons. Hebrew U.-Hadassah Med. Orgn., Jerusalem, 1971—; cons. Cumberland Coll., New South Wales, Australia, 1986; mem. Inst. Medicine of Nat. Acad. Scis., 1972—, mem. steering com. costs of edn. of health professions, 1972-74; mem. Nat. Med. Audiovisual Tng. Center, 1972-76; mem. Gov.'s Com. and Area Bd. Mental Health and Mental Retardation, Nat. Commn. for Study Nursing and Nursing Edn., 1970-73; mem. faculty com., regent's external degree program in nursing State U. N.Y., 1974-82; mem. hosp. mgmt. bd. U. Hosp., U. Mass., 1976-80; mem. Mass. Gov.'s Commn. to Study Nursing in Commonwealth, 1983—. Dir., Am. Jour. Nursing Co., Medic Alert. Bd. dirs. Brookline Mental Health Assn., Met. chpt. ARC, Mass. Med. Soc. Postgrad. Med. Inst., 1983—; v.p. Mass. Nurses' Found., 1983—; founding mem. AIDS Internat. Info. Found., 1985. Fellow Am. Acad. Nursing; mem. Nat. League Nursing (pres. 1971-73), Mass. League Nursing, Am. Nurses Assn., Mass. Nurses Assn. (dir. 1982—), Nat. Acad. Nursing Practice of Nat. Acads. Practice (charter), Sigma Theta Tau, Pi Lambda Theta. Mem. editorial bd. Mass. Jour. Community Health. Home: 381 Clinton Rd Brookline MA 02146

KICKLIGHTER, ALMA LOUISE, nurse, county administrator; b. Live Oak, Fla., Jan. 12, 1933; d. Eugene and Mary Bell (Ashley) Young; B.S. in Nursing, Fla. A&M U., 1958; m. Samuel Kicklighter; children—Carletta Ophelia, Harrell Alonzo, Samuel, June Renee. Tchr., Columbia County (Fla.) Schs., 1955; charge nurse, med., surg. and obstet. ward Mercy Hosp., St. Petersburg, Fla., 1958-62; public health nurse, sch. cons. Pinellas County (Fla.) Health Dept., 1959-63, public health nurse supr., 1964—, supr. epidemiology, 1979—; cons. on health careers for high sch. students. Chairperson equal employment com. HRS Dist. 5, St. Petersburg; bd. dirs. Latchkey, St. Petersburg; past 2d v.p. St. Petersburg Citizen's Council on Crime; past pres. PTA of Boca Ciega High Sch., St. Petersburg; organizer Open Door Bible study, 1980. Recipient plaque Equal Employment Com., 1979. Mem. Am. Nurses Assn., Fla. Nurses Assn., Fla. Pub. Health Assn., Am. Bus. Women's Assn. (Woman of Yr. 1978-79), Staff Assn. Community Nursing Service, Chi Eta Phi, Delta Sigma Theta. Democrat. Club: Registered Nurses. Home: 2137 19th St S Saint Petersburg FL 33712 Office: 500 7th Ave S Saint Petersburg FL 33701

KIDD, CATHY A., controller; b. Lexington, Ky., Oct. 24, 1957; d. Chester Allen and Lois Catherine (Horn) K.; m. Michael W. Stratton, July 8, 1978 (div. 1985). B.A. in Acctg., Georgetown Coll., Ky., 1978; postgrad. in mgmt. U. Phoenix, Tucson. Staff auditor Commonwealth of Ky., Frankfort, 1978-79; acct. Dept. Local Govt., Frankfort, 1979-80; controller Stouder Meml. Hosp., Troy, Ohio, 1980-82, Woodford Meml. Hosp., Versailles, Ky., 1982-84, Health Am. Corp., Tucson, 1984-86, St. Mary's Hosp., Tucson, 1986—. Mem. Healthcare Fin. Mgmt. Assn., Phi Mu, Phi Beta Lambda. Democrat. Mem. Disciples of Christ Ch. Avocations: needlepoint; macrame; swimming; bicycling; reading. Office: St Mary's Rd Tucson AZ 85745

KIDD, DEBRA JEAN, communications consultant; b. Chgo., May 13, 1956; d. Fred A. and Jean (Pezzopane) Winchar; m. Kim Joseph Kidd, July 22, 1978. A.A. in Bus. with high honors, Wright Jr. Coll., 1977. Legal sec. Sidley & Austin, Chgo., 1977-80; investment adminstr. Golder, Thoma & Co., Chgo., 1980-81, exec. asst., 1981-84; sales rep. Dataspeed, Inc., Chgo., 1984, midwestern regional mgr. Dataspeed, Inc., Chgo., 1985; communications cons. Chgo. Communications, Inc., Chgo., 1986—; owner, founder Captain Kidd's Video, Niles, 1981-84. Vol. Am. Lung Assn., Chgo., 1979, Our Lady Mother of Ch., Norridge, Ill., 1981-83. Mem. Nat. Assn. Female Execs., Nat. Assn. Bus. Women, Nat. Assn. Profl. Saleswomen, Nat. Network of Women in Sales, Bus. and Profl. Women's Club, Phi Theta Kappa. Roman Catholic. Avocations: camping; snow and water skiing; horseback riding; sailing; reading; needlepoint. Office: Chicago Communication Service Inc 9490 Franklin Ave Franklin Park IL 60131

KIDD, LINDA M., retail company official; b. Sedalia, Mo., Nov. 29, 1942; d. William H. and Loretta (Koenig) Bunn; 1 dau., Meridyth Marie. A.A., Stephens Coll., 1962; B.S., U. Mo.-Columbia, 1965; postgrad. U. S.W. La., 1969. Mgr. Mdse. Lord & Taylor, Houston, 1974-77; dir. John Robert Powers, Houston, 1978-80; mgr. tng. services Gen. Homes Co., Houston, 1980-81; dir. exec. devel. and tng. Joske's of Houston, 1981—; mem. faculty U. Houston, 1982—. Mem. curriculum adv. bd. Houston Community Coll. Mem. Houston Personnel Assn., Forum Club Houston, Fashion Group, Am. Soc. Tng. and Devel.

KIDD, NANCY VAN TRIES, psychologist, mediator; b. Huntingdon, Pa., June 5, 1933; d. Samuel Musser and Jesse Pauline (Haupt) Van Tries; m. Joseph Jerome Rowley, Jr., Aug. 4, 1956 (div. 1967); children—Linda Rowley Tawfik, Joseph J. III, Bruce; m. 2d Jerome Thomas Kidd, May 23, 1970. B.A. in Journalism and Fine Arts, Pa. State U., 1955, D.Ed. in Counseling and Psychology, 1977; M.Ed. in Elem. Edn. and Ednl. Psychology, Temple U., 1969. Assoc. prof. psychology and counseling Community Coll. R.I., 1973-82; psychologist Child, Adult and Family Psychol. Ctr., State College, Pa., 1981-83; family mediator, counselor Ariz. Counseling Ctr., Phoenix, 1983; psychologist, dir. Psychol. and Counseling Resources, Richmond, 1985—; mediator Greater Richmond Mediation Network, 1984—. Contbr. articles to profl. jours. Trustee Pa. State U., 1984. Mem. Am. Psychol. Assn., Va. Psychol. Assn., Va. Counseling Psychol. Assn. (legis. officer 1984), Acad. Family Mediators, R.I. Personnel and Guidance Assn. (exec. bd. 1978-79), Pa State Alumni Club, Phi Delta Kappa, Pi Lambda Theta, Kappa Kappa Gamma. Presbyterian. Office: Psychol and Counseling Resources 122 Granite Ave Richmond VA 23226

KIDD, REBECCA (LOUISE) MONTGOMERY, artist; b. Muncie, Ind., Nov. 29, 1942; d. Joe Bucklyn and Mary Marguerite (Mark) Montgomery; corr. student comml. art, Famous Artists Schs.; cert. of completion corr. course U. Sci. and Philosophy, Waynesboro, Va., 1976; m. Ben Roy Kidd, Apr. 10, 1964; children—Daniel Ben, Diana Piper. Character painter, 1966—; portrait painter and drawer, 1962-81, 83—; painter in oils, pastels; outdoor scene, still life, floral painter, 1969—; children's story illustrator, 1972-74; restorer old houses, 1972-81; adaptor of master's paintings, 1974-82; miniature painter, 1974-82; film illustrator, 1975; Am. Indian painter, 1975-81; trading pin designer, 1977, 78; lithograph printmaker, 1977; monotype printmaker, 1978—; one woman show: Roadside Gallery, Melfa, Va., 1982; group shows include: Roadside Gallery, 1977—, The Gallery, Ct. Plaza, Salisbury, Md., 1977—, Queens Coll., Cambridge U., 1982. Mem. Quality Edn. Accomack County (Va.), Exec. Com., 1979-80. Mem. Eastern Shore Art League (constn. and bylaws chmn. 1979, dir. 1982), Visual Artists and Galleries Assn., Nat. Mus. Women in Arts (charter), Nat. Trust Historic Preservation (assoc.), Internat. Platform Assn. (merit award and popular choice award 1984 conv.). Subject of articles in several news publs. Address: 9 Lake St Onancock VA 23417

KIDD, VIVIAN GRAVELY, non-profit organization administrator, consultant; b. Cool Ridge, W.Va., Oct. 4, 1947; d. Franklin S. and Zenobia Vivian (Peters) Gravely; m. Victor V. Kidd, Jan. 10, 1970. B.A., W.Va. Inst. Tech., 1969; M.S., W.Va. Coll. Grad. Studies, 1981. Tchr., Staunton (Va.) Pub. Sch., 1970-71; dir. pub. info. Goodwill Industries Kanawha Valley, Charleston, W.Va., 1971-73; dir. pub. info. Black Diamond council Girl Scout U.S.A., Charleston, 1973-76; communications dir. United Way of Kanawha Valley, Charleston, 1976-78; dep. commr. W.Va. Dept. Labor, Charleston, 1978-83; exec. dir. W.Va. Edn. Fund, Inc., Charleston, 1983—; mem. Gov.'s Honors Acad., Charleston, 1984. Bd. dirs. Literacy Vols. W.Va. Mem. W.Va. Indsl. Relations Research Assn. (v.p.). Democrat. Methodist. Office: WVa Edn Fund Inc 1126 Kanawha Valley Bldg Charleston WV 25301

KIDDER, MARGOT, actress; b. Yellow Knife, Can., Oct. 17, 1948; m. Tom McGuane (div.); 1 dau., Maggie; m. John Heard (div.); m. Philippe de Broca (div.). Attended U. B.C. Began career in Can. theater and TV; film debut in Gaily, Gaily, 1969; other films include: Quackser Fortune Has a Cousin in the Bronx, 1970, Sisters, 1972, Gravy Train, 1974, The Great Waldo Pepper, 1975, The Reincarnation of Peter Proud, 1975, 92 in the Shade, 1977, Superman, 1978, The Amityville Horror, 1979, Superman II, 1981, Some Kind of Hero, 1981, Heartaches, 1982, Trenchcoat, 1983, Superman III, 1983, Glitter Dome, 1983, Little Treasure, 1985; starred in TV series Nichols, 1972; appeared in TV series Mod Squad; appeared in TV movies Honky Tonk, 1974, Picking Up the Pieces, 1985, Vanishing Act, 1986. Office: care Creative Artists Agy Inc 1888 Century Park East Suite 1400 Los Angeles CA 90067

KIDDER, VICKI GORHAM, financial planning company executive; b. Rocky Mountain, N.C., Aug. 29, 1948; d. William Theodore and Mittie Morse (Jordan) Gorham; m. Lealon Phillip Strickland, Aug. 15, 1970 (div. 1978); children—Tondra Dawn, Teshia Leigh; m. Ronald Delbert Kidder, Oct. 21, 1978. Degree in practical nursing Holding Tech. Inst., 1969; B.S., U. Hawaii, 1981; M.B.A., Oklahoma City U., 1982. Critical care nurse Straub Hosp., Honolulu, 1977-81; nurse supr./inservice edn. Mission Hill Meml. Hosp., Shawnee, Okla., 1981-82; critical care supr. Okla. Children's Meml. Hosp., Oklahoma City, 1982-84; registered rep. IDS/Am. Express, Oklahoma City, 1984—. Mem. Bus. and Profl. Women's Club, Nat. Assn. Female Execs., Am. Assn. Critical Care Nurses, Okla. Nurses Assn., Shawnee C. of C. (small bus. council 1985—). Republican. Avocations: swimming; golf. Home: 3 Limousin Ln Shawnee OK 74801 Office: IDS/Am Express 101 N Broadway Suite 302 Shawnee OK 74801

KIEL, CAROLYN BEA, marketing services company executive; b. Salem, N.J., Aug. 30, 1959; d. Ronald Dean and Mary Grace (Bozorth) Prestis; m. Clyde Justin Kiel, Dec. 29, 1984. B.S., U. Ariz., 1983. Mktg. research asst. Fontana Mgmt. Cons., Tucson, 1981-82; mktg. research assoc. Mktg. Cons., Houston, 1982-83; various mktg. positions, Eugene, Oreg., 1983-84 Cin., 1985-86; dir. Consumer Pulse of Phila., 1986—. Co-chmn. corp. donations Easter Seals Nat. Telethon, Eugene, 1984. Recipient Photographic Soc. Vineland award, 1977; State Achievement grantee State of N.J., 1977. Mem. Am. Mktg. Assn., Mktg. Research Assn., Houston C. of C. (mem. shopping ctr. dir. com. 1982-83), Mythopoeic Soc. Methodist. Avocations: travel; mythopoeic literature; dancing; fashion. Home: 188 W Arbor Ave Vineland NJ 08360 Office: Consumer Pulse of Phila 2203 Plymouth Meeting Mall Plymouth Meeting PA 19462

KIEL-LIGHTLE, PATRICIA HALL, medical manufacturing manager; b. Drexel Hill, Pa., June 14, 1942; d. Robert Coleman Hall and Dorothy Helen (MacMaster) Hall Bidelman; m. Alan L. Kiel, Feb. 1, 1964 (div.); children—Susannah Christine, Jennifer Michelle; m. 2d, Kenneth E. Lightle, July 7, 1979; 1 son, Brian Scott. A.A., Centenary Coll., 1960; student Calif. State U.-Fullerton, 1978—. Med. sec. Phila. Gas Works, 1962-64; customer service rep. South New Eng. Telephone, New Haven, 1964-66; exec. sec. Air-Shields, Hatboro, Pa., 1974-78, sales rep., Mission Viejo, Calif., 1978-79, ter. mgr., 1980-81, area sales mgr., Laguna Hills, Calif., 1981-84, regional trainer, 1983, nat. accounts mgr. Western region, 1984—. Recipient Pres.'s Round Table award Air-Shields, 1981, 82, Sales Person of Yr. award, 1982, 100% Club award, 1978, 80, 81, 82, 83. Mem. Nat. Assn. Female Execs. Republican. Episcopalian. Home: 25502 Earhart Laguna Hills CA 92653 Office: Air-Shields 330 Jacksonville Rd Hatboro PA 19040

KIELSMEIER, CATHERINE JANE, school adminstr.; b. San Jose, Calif; d. Frank Delos and Catherine Doris (Sellar) MacGowan; M.S., U. So. Calif., 1964, Ph.D., 1971; m. Milton Kielsmeier; children—Catherine Louise, Barry Delos. Tchr., Pub. Schs. Maricopa (Calif.); sch. psychologist Campbell (Calif.) Union Sch Dist., 1961-66; asst. prof. edn. and psychology Western Oreg. State Coll., Monmouth, 1966-67, 70; asst. research prof. Oreg. System Higher Edn., Monmouth, 1967-70; dir. spl. services Santa Rosa (Calif.) Pub. Schs., 1972—. Mem. Sonoma County Council Community Services, 1976—, Sonoma County Orgn. for Retarded. Mem. Council Exceptional Children. Club: Commonwealth of Calif. Home: 7495 Poplar Dr Forestville CA 95436 Office: 211 Ridgeway Ave Santa Rosa CA 95402

KIELY, LAREE SUE, human communication consultant; b. Ft. Collins, Colo., Feb. 27, 1948; s. William R. and L. Maxine (Ross) K.; m. Daniel R.

Crary, Nov. 19, 1982; stepchildren—Jennifer, Julie. B.A., U. Colo., 1973, M.A., 1978; postgrad. U. So. Calif. Educator, Air Acad. Schs. USAFA, Colo., 1973-79, Jefferson County Schs., Lakewood, Colo., 1979-80; instr. U. Colo., Boulder, 1980-82, U. So. Calif., Los Angeles, 1982-86; pres. Possibilities, Inc., Denver, 1979-82; human communication cons. K/C Assocs., Fullerton, Calif., 1982—; cons., trainer Dispute Mediation Ctr., Dallas, 1982-84; career cons. Women's Sch. Network, Lakewood, Colo., 1979-81; ednl. cons. Giles Inst. Ednl. Research, Colorado Springs, Colo., 1977-79. Del., Colo. Democratic Conv. Polit. Action Com. for Edn., Colorado Springs, 1974-75; commr. Community Services Commn., Fullerton, 1985—. Mem. Acad. Family Mediators, Internat. Communication Assn., Speech Communication Assn., Western Speech Communication Assn., Internat. Soc. for Intercultural Ednl. Tng. and Research, Assn. for Tng. and Devel., Fullerton C. of C. (mem. legis. com.). Office: K/C Assoc PO Box 6426 Fullerton CA 92631

KIELY, MARGARET CLARE, clinical psychologist, educator; b. Tacoma; d. John Roach and Isabella (MacLean) K.; B.A., Central Coll. Edn., Wash., 1956; B.Sc. (hon.), U. Montreal, 1961, M.A. (hon.), 1963, Ph.D. (hon.), 1970. Prof. psychology Marianopolis Coll., Montreal, Que., Can., 1967-72; clin. psychologist Centre d'Orientation, Montreal, 1970-77; research psychologist Mental Hygiene Inst., Montreal, 1967-77; prof. clin. and community psychology U. Montreal, 1972—; cons. Montreal Diocesan Theol. Coll., 1972-75, Centre des Services Sociaux-Gaspe, 1976-79. Health and Welfare of Can. grantee, 1979—. Mem. Am. Psychol. Assn., Que. Corp. Psychologists, Internat. Council Psychologist, Internat. Assn. Applied Psychology, Nat. Register of Health Providers in Psychology of U.S., Can. Register Health Service Providers in Psychology, Orthopsychiat. Assn. Roman Catholic. Editorial bd. Essence, 1976—, Can. Jour. Community Mental Health; contbr. articles to profl. jours. Office: Psychology Dept Univ Montreal Case Postale 6128 Montreal PQ H3C 3J7 Canada

KIENHOLZ, LYN SHEARER, arts projects coordinator; b. Chgo.; d. Mitchell W. and Lucille M. (Hock) Shearer; student Sullins Coll., Md. Coll. Women. Assoc. producer Kurt Simon Prodns., Beverly Hills, Calif., 1963-65; owner, mgr. Vuokko Boutique, Beverly Hills, 1969-75; bd. dirs. Los Angeles Inst. Contemporary Art, 1976-79, Fellows of Contemporary Art, 1977-79, Internat. Network for Arts, 1979—, Los Angeles Contemporary Exhbns., 1980-82; exec. sec., bd. dirs. Beaubourg Found. (now George Pompidou Art and Culture Found.), 1977-81; visual arts adv. Performing Arts Council, Los Angeles Music Center, 1980—; bd. govs. Calif. Inst. Tech. Baxter Art Gallery, 1980-85; mem. adv. bd. dirs. Fine Arts Communications, pub. Images & Issues mag., 1981-85; founder, pres. bd. dirs. Calif./Internat. Arts Found., 1981—; bd. dirs., western chmn. ArtTable 1983—; exec. bd. Sovereign Fund, 1981—; exec. bd. dirs. Scandinavia Today, 1982-83; mem. adv. bd. Otis/Parsons Sch. Design, 1983-85, U. So. Calif. dept. fine arts, 1983-85; mem. Comité International pour les Museés d'Art Moderne, 1985—. Contbg. editor Calif. mag., 1984—. Address: 2737 Outpost Dr Los Angeles CA 90068

KIESOW, LINDA MCELROY, data processing administrator; b. Rock Island, Ill., July 5, 1953; d. Oscar R. and Helen F. (Junk) McElroy; m. James Thomas Kiesow, May 26, 1973. B.B.A., Western Ill. U., 1979; M.B.A., U. Iowa, 1985. Cert. data processor. Produce mgr. Carthage Supr Valu, (Ill.), 1974-75; aggregate sample analyst Valley Quarry, St. Augustine, Ill., 1975-76; data processing mgr. Moline Consumers Co., (Ill.), 1979—. Knoblaugh scholar Western Ill. U., 1977, Coll. of Bus. scholar, 1978, Acctg. Dept. scholar, 1978. Mem. Acctg. Soc. (v.p. 1977-78, banquet com. chmn.), Nat. Assn. Female Execs., Data Processing Mgmt. Assn., Am. Inst. Cert. Computer Programmers, Alpha Lambda Delta, Phi Kappa Phi. Republican. Baptist. Home: 4907 48th Ave Moline IL 61265 Office: Moline Consumers Co 313 16th St Moline IL 61265

KIEVMAN, BEVERLY STEIN, marketing, public relations and sales training executive; b. Atlanta, Nov. 21, 1937; d. Jack Clarence and Bess (Segal) Stein; student Rollins Coll., 1954-56; A.B. in Journalism, U. Ga., Athens, 1958; m. Michael Kievman, Apr. 30, 1977; children—Mark, Steve; stepchildren—Chris, Carson, Michele, Corin. Founder, pres. Atlanta Models & Talent, Inc., 1960-71; pres. Beverly Anderson & Assos., Atlanta, 1972-74; dist. mgr. Research Inst. Am., Atlanta, 1975-76, dir. mgmt. services, 1976-77, regional dir., 1977-78; founder, pres. Mktg. Innovations Corp., Atlanta, 1979—; dir. Nat. Bank of Ga., 1981—, Delta Queen Steamboat Co., 1984—. Pres. Ga. chpt. Leukemia Soc. Am., 1981-82; mem. Martin Luther King Jr. State Holiday Commn., 1985-86. Mem. Women's Forum, Inc. (nat. bd. dir. 1980-82), Women's Commerce Club Am. (dir. 1981—), Com. of 200, Sales and Mktg. Execs. (dir. 1980-81), Atlanta Advt. Club (dir. 1971-74), Women in Film (dir. 1974-76), Women Bus. Owners (dir. 1980-81), Nat. Speakers Assn. Author: The Complete Success Workbook for Today's Saleswoman, 1982. Home: 573 Tara Tr NW Atlanta GA 30327 Office: 6145 Barfield Rd NE Suite 135 Atlanta GA 30328

KIFUTHU, SUSAN MILLS, lawyer; b. Berkeley, Calif., May 20, 1948; d. Robert Gail and Mary Addie (Steer) Mills; m. James Mucungi Kifuthu, Apr. 15, 1972; 1 son, Christopher. B.A., U. Colo., 1969; M.A., UCLA, 1970; J.D., Rutgers U., 1982. Bar: N.J. 1983. Teaching asst. Makerere U., Kampala, Uganda, 1971-72; tchr. Kenya Tchrs. Service, 1972-74; library researcher Sibson & Co., Inc., Princeton, N.J., 1975-76; personnel analyst, staff atty. Div. EEO/Affirmative Action, N.J. Dept. Civil Service, Trenton, 1976—; vol. staff atty. Mercer County Legal Aid Soc., Trenton, 1983-85. Mem. ABA., N.J. State Bar Assn., Mercer County Bar. Democrat. Home: Butterfoss Ave Box 125 Rural Route 2 Titusville NJ 08560 Office: NJ Dept Civil Service 125 E State St Trenton NJ 08625

KIGGINS, MILDRED L., telemarketing firm executive; b. Hemstead, N.Y., Sept. 14, 1927; d. Wolfgang and Hannah Ingeborg (Olsson) Weissmann; m. Andrew Edward Kiggins, Jan. 8, 1962 (div. 1982); children—Daniel Mark, David Bruce. Student Donovan Bus. Coll., Hackensack, N.J., 1945, Luther Coll. Acad., 1947. Exec. sec. Am. Machine & Foundry Inc., Stamford, Conn., 1954-61; telemktg. rep. Adult Ind. Devel. Ctr., San Jose, Calif., 1977—, Harry Schoenfeld Ins. Services & Design, Los Gatos, Calif., 1985—, Am. Caging Inc., Sunnyvale, Calif., 1985—. Tchr. Sunday sch. St. John's Lutheran Ch., Stamford, 1948-50. Mem. Nat. Assn. Female Execs. Republican. Avocations: gardening; music; sports; church activities. Home: 4644 Pinto River Ct San Jose CA 95136

KIJANKA, DOROTHY M., library administrator; b. Mt. Olive, Ill.; d. Michael and Catherine (Zupsich) Kaganich; m. Stanley J. Kijanka, Jr., Nov. 20, 1970 (dec. 1981). A.B. in History with honors, U. Ill.; M.L.S., Rutgers U. Reference librarian Greenwich Pub. Library, Conn., 1966-68; reference librarian Fairfield U., Conn., 1968-74, assoc. librarian, 1974-84; dir. Sacred Heart U. Library, Fairfield, 1984—. Contbr. articles to profl. jours. Mem. Library Group of Southwestern Conn. (pres. 1977-78), Southwestern Conn. Library Council (trustee 1977-78), Fairfield County Library Adminstrs. Group (vice chmn. 1985—), ALA, New Eng. Library Assn., Conn. Library Assn. (chmn. reference sect. 1975), Assn. Coll. and Research Libraries. Office: Sacred Heart Univ Library PO Box 6460 Bridgeport CT 06606

KILDE, SANDRA JEAN, nurse anesthetist, nurse, educator, consultant; b. Eau Claire, Wis., June 25, 1938; d. Harry Meylan and Beverly June (Johnson) K. Diploma Luther Hosp. Sch. Nursing, Eau Claire, 1959; grad. anesthesia course Mpls. Sch. Anesthesia, 1967; B.A., Met. State U., St. Paul, 1976; M.A., Coll. St. Thomas, 1981; postgrad. in leadership in adult edn. Nova U., 1983—. R.N., Wis., Minn. Operating room nurse Luther Hosp., Eau Claire, 1959-61, head nurse operating room, 1961-63; supr. operating room Midway Hosp., St. Paul, 1963-66; staff anesthetist North Meml. Med. Ctr., Robbinsdale, Minn., 1967-68; program dir. Mpls. Sch. Anesthia, St. Louis Park, Minn., 1968—; adj. asst. prof. St. Mary's Coll., Winona, Minn., 1982—, program dir. Masters Degree Program, 1984—; ednl. cons. accreditation visitor Council on Accreditation of Nurse Anesthesia Ednl. Programs/Schs., Park Ridge, Ill., 1983—; presentations in field. Recipient Good Neighbor award Sta.-WCCO, Mpls., 1980. Mem. Am. Assn. Nurse Anesthetists (pres. 1981-82, pres. and bd. dirs. Edn. and Research Found. 1981-83, cert. profl. excellence 1976), Minn. Assn. Nurse Anesthetists (pres. 1975-76). Lutheran. Home: 11784 Madison St Blaine MN 55434 Office: Mpls Sch Anesthesia 6715 Minnetonka Blvd Saint Louis Park MN 55426

KILEY, JAN, broadcasting research executive; b. Urbana, Ill., Jan. 31, 1952; d. George Lowell and Jeanne Adaline (Grismer) K. B.A. cum laude with distinction, U. Ill., 1974. Research asst. Midwest TV, Inc., Stas. WCIA-TV, Champaign, Ill., WMBD-AM-TV and WKZW-FM, Peoria, Ill., KFMB-AM-FM TV, San Diego, 1969-74, researcher, 1974-75, dir. research, 1975—. Counselor, Illini Girls State, 1971, staff advisor, asst. to dir., sec. corp., 1972-76; bd. dirs. Livia Ball Meml. Presbyn. House, U. Ill.; bd. dirs. Exec. Club of Champaign County. Mem. Am. Assn. Pub. Opinion Research, Midwest Assn. Pub. Opinion Research, Am. Mktg. Assn. (past pres. Central Ill.), Ill. News Broadcasters Assn., Am. Women in Radio and TV (past pres. River City chpt. past nat. v.p. 1983-85), AAUW (bd. dirs.), Friends of Champaign Pub. Library, Carle Found. Hosp. Aux., Am. Legion Aux. (pres. club 1976-77), Alpha Lambda Delta, Kappa Delta Pi, Phi Alpha Theta, Phi Kappa Phi. Methodist. Lodges: Order Eastern Star, P.E.O. Home: 715 S Lynn Champaign IL 61820 Office: 509 S Neil Champaign IL 61820

KILEY, MARY LOUISE, psychiatric social worker; b. Newton, Mass., Apr. 10, 1952; d. Edward Joseph and Louise Agnes (Daly) K.; m. Norman Eric Swanberg, Dec. 30, 1978. B.A., Smith Coll., 1974; M.S.W., Boston Coll., 1977. Lic. clin. social worker. Calif. Social worker Newton & Wellesley Nursing Home, Wellesley, Mass., 1975-76; adoption, foster care social worker Cath. Charities, Brockton, Mass., 1977-78; social worker Cath. Social Service, Los Angeles, 1978-79; psychiat. social worker Family Health Program, Long Beach, Calif., 1979-81; Kaiser Permanente, La Mesa, Calif., 1982—; cons. Poway Pregnancy Counseling Ctr., Calif., 1985—. Bd. dirs. High Valley Assn., 1984—. Mem. Nat. Assn. Social Workers, World Trade Assoc., Acad. Cert. Social Workers. Democrat. Roman Catholic. Club: Smith Coll. (pres.) (San Diego). Avocations: racquetball; aerobics; camping. Home: 14815 High Valley Rd Poway CA 92064 Office: Kaiser Permanente 8010 Parkway Dr La Mesa CA 92041

KILGORE, CATHERINE C., economic geologist, researcher; b. Los Angeles, Dec. 25, 1956; d. Donald Evan and Elsie Ellen (Walden) Cook; m. Thomas Jefferson Kilgore, III, Aug. 5, 1978. B.S. in Geology, Fort Lewis Coll., 1978; postgrad. in mineral econs. Colo. Sch. Mines, 1981-82. Geologist, U.S. Geol. Survey, Denver, 1979, Colo. Dept. Health, Denver, 1979-80, U.S. Bur. Mines, Denver, 1980—. Author info. circulars, articles. Recipient spl. achievement award U.S. Bur. Mines, 1983. Mem. Soc. Mining Engrs. (session chmn. 1986). Avocations: stained glass art; gourmet cooking. Office: US Bur Mines MAFD Bldg 20 Denver Federal Center Denver CO 80225

KILGORE, ELAYNE STATTON, trade assn. exec.; b. Chgo., Mar. 7, 1921; d. Harry William and Harriet Margaret (Gordon) Statton; grad. Thornton Twp. (Ill.) Jr. Coll., 1938-40; postgrad. U. Ill., Northwestern U.; m. Charles A. Kilgore, Sept. 29, 1956. Mem. staff Bldg. Mgrs. Assn. Chgo., 1953—, asst. sec., 1961-72, exec. sec., 1972—; exec. sec. Bldg. Owners and Mgrs. Assn. Suburban Chgo., 1971-82; sec.-treas. N. Central Regional Conf. Bldg. Owners and Mgrs., 1967-77; pres. asso. execs. Bldg. Owners and Mgrs. Assn. Internat., 1973-75. Mem. Chgo. Bldg. Mgrs. Club, Chgo. Assn. Commerce and Industry, Execs. Club Chgo., Chgo. Soc. Assn. Execs., Am. Soc. Assn. Execs., Chgo. Real Estate Bd., Chgo. Bldg. Supts. Assn. (hon.). Club: Monroe. Home: 175 E Delaware Pl Chicago IL 60611 Office: 135 S LaSalle St Chicago IL 60603

KILGORE, KATHERINE GAYLE, contract specialist, specifications writer; b. Pound, Va., Nov. 26, 1945; d. Woodrow W. and Florence Elizabeth (Sturgill) Adams; m. James D. Kilgore, Oct. 19, 1968; children—Christopher D., Sean Patrick. B.S., East Tenn. State U., 1968. Tchr. Wise County Schs., Va., 1968-69; prodn. typist Thompson & Litton, Inc., Wise, 1970-76, word processing supr., 1976-78, contract specialist, specifications writer, 1978—. Mem. Constrn. Specifications Inst. Baptist. Avocations: reading, roller skating, walking, embroidery. Home: PO Box 1284 219 Spring Ave Wise VA 24293 Office: Thompson & Litton Inc PO Box 1307 102 Main St Wise VA 24293

KILKEARY, NAN M., communications specialist; b. Evergreen Park, Ill., Sept. 17, 1943; d. Robert M. and Barbara E. (Bailey) Lundberg; m. William P. Kilkeary, Dec. 17, 1966 (div. Aug. 1978); children—Timothy T., Christopher K. B.S., U. Ill., 1965; postgrad. U. Chgo., 1974-75. Editor, UPI Broadcast, Chgo., 1966-67, 69; asst. mgr. press relations CNA, Chgo., 1971-74; account supr. Harshe-Rotman & Druck, Chgo., 1974-76; dir. communications Allstate, Northbrook, Ill., 1976-81; v.p. communications Investors Diversified Services, Mpls., 1981-82, dir. communications Montgomery Ward, Chgo., 1982-85, pres. Kilkeary Communications, 1985—; owner, mgr. O'Rourke's Pub., Chgo., 1966-75. Contbr. articles to profl. jours. Founder, Ill. Housewives for ERA, Evanston, Ill., 1972. Recipient Golden Trumpet, Publicity Club Chgo., 1975, 79, 80, Shaunessy award, 1979, 80, Pres. award Internat. Assn. Bus. Communicators, 1979. Mem. Pub. Relations Soc. Am. (silver anvil 1977, 79), Nat. Investor Relations Inst. (chpt. dir. 1975-80), Women in Communications. Club. Democrat. Unitarian. Club: Carleton.

KILLEA, LUCY LYTLE, state official; b. San Antonio, July 31, 1922; d. Nelson and Zelime (Pettus) Lytle; B.A., Incarnate Word Coll., San Antonio, 1943; M.A. in History, U. San Diego, 1966; Ph.D. in History, U. Calif., San Diego, 1975; m. John F. Killea, May 11, 1946; children—Paul, Jay. Research analyst for Western Europe, Army Intelligence, Spl. Br., Washington, 1944-48; adminstrv. asst. Dept. State, London, 1946; econ. officer Econ. Coop. Adminstrn., The Hague, Netherlands, 1949; research analyst CIA, Washington, 1948-56; part time book reviewer USIS, 1956-60; teaching and research asst. U. Calif., San Diego, 1967-72; exec. dir., exec. v.p. Fronteras de las Californias, San Diego, 1974-78; mem. City Council, San Diego, 1978-82, dep. mayor, 1982, mem. planning commn., 1978-82; mem. Calif. State Assembly, 1982—; lectr. socioeconomics of Baja, Calif. and Mex., Southwestern Coll., Chula-Vista, 1976; lectr. dept. history San Diego State U., 1976-77; participant, organizer, panelist, moderator confs. in field, U.S., Mex.; mem. Palm City Sanitation Dist., 1978-82, Met. Transit Devel. Bd., 1978—. Regional Employment and Tng. Consortium Bd., 1978-80, City-County Reinvestment Task Force, 1978-80. Bd. trustees San Diego Zool. Soc., 1976-78; mem. San Diego County Cultural Heritage Com., 1971-78, vice chmn., 1973-75; mem. Hist. Site Bd., City San Diego, 1968-75, vice chmn., 1971-75; bd. dirs. San Diego Hist. Soc., 1971-77; chmn. Internat. Com. Conv. and Visitors Bur., 1978, host com., 1976-77; adv. bd. Sharp Hosp.; bd. dirs., com. mem. Friends of Library, U. Calif., San Diego; founding mem. Caridad Internacional; mem. James S. Copley Library Adv. Council, U. San Diego, 1981—; active community orgns. including LWV, Fine Arts Soc. San Diego, YWCA, San Diego Mus. Art, San Diego Chpt. ARC, Dimensions, Aardvarks Ltd., Pacific Beach Hist. Soc., San Diego Symphonic Assn. Research grantee, Justice Found., 1965, U. Calif., San Diego, 1971; recipient awards, Conf. Calif. Hist. Socs., 1966, Inst. for Protection of Children, City of Tijuana and Tijuana Com., 1966, Alice Paul Award, Nat. Women's Polit. Caucus, 1982; named one of 12 Women of Valor, Beth Israel Sisterhood of Temple Beth Israel, San Diego, 1966, Woman of Accomplishment, Bus. and Profl. Clubs. San Diego, 1979, Woman of Yr., San Diego Irish Congress, 1981; honored Leukemia Soc., 1980; named alumna of distinction Incarnate Word Coll., San Antonio, 1981. Mem. Nat. Women's Polit. Caucus, Calif., Women in Bus., Mus. Photog. Arts, San Diego Arts Center, Women in Mgmt., Nat. Trust Historic Preservation, San Diego Hist. Soc. (life), San Diego County Congress of History, Travelers Aid Soc., Navy League, Vietnam Vets. Assn. Mid City C. of C., San Diego C. of C., Nat. Assn. State Legislatures, NCCJ, World Affairs Council, Am. Fgn. Service Assn., Incarnate Word Alumnae Assn., U. San Diego Alumni Assn., U. Calif. San Diego Alumni and Friends, Calif. Elected Women's Assn. for Edn. and Research (bd. 1980—, sec., treas., 1980-81, v.p. 1982-85). Democrat. Roman Catholic. Clubs: Catfish, Army-Navy (Arlington, Va.). Contbr. writings to publs. in field. Office: Calif State Capitol Room 5128 Sacramento CA 95814

KILLEBREW, ELLEN JANE (MRS. EDWARD S. GRAVES), cardiologist; b. Tiffin, Ohio, Oct. 8, 1937; d. Joseph Arthur and Stephanie (Beriont) K.; B.S. in Biology, Bucknell U., 1959; M.D., N.J. Coll. Medicine, 1965; m. Edward S. Graves, Sept. 12, 1970. Intern, U. Colo., 1965-66, resident 1966-68; cardiology fellow Pacific Med. Center, San Francisco, 1968-70; dir. coronary care, Permanent Med. Group, Richmond, Calif., 1970-83; asst. prof. U. Calif. Med. Center, San Francisco, 1970-83, assoc. prof., 1983—. Robert C. Kirkwood Meml. scholar in cardiology, 1970; recipient Physician's Recognition award continuing med. edn. Diplomate in cardiovascular disease Am. Bd. Internal Medicine. Fellow ACP, Am. Coll. Cardiology: mem. Fedn. Clin. Research, Am. Heart Assn. (research chmn. Contra Costa chpt. 1975—, v.p. 1980, pres. chpt. 1981-82, chm. CPR com. Alameda chpt. 1984). Home: 30 Redding Ct Tiburon CA 94920 Office: 280 W MacArthur Blvd Oakland CA 94611

KILLEBREW, JOYCE, English educator; motivation business executive; b. N.Y.C., Apr. 20, 1945; d. Archie and Gertrude (Brown) Thomas Spriggs; m. Mack Lawrence Killebrew, June 27, 1963; 1 child, Richard Augustus. B.A., Federal City Coll., 1972; M.A.T., Trinity Coll., Washington, 1979. Tchr. English, Washington Public Schs., 1972—. Vice pres. Killebrew & Assocs., Washington, 1979—. Treas., Com. to Elect Bob King Ward 5 Councilman, 1982. Mem. Nat. Assn. Exec. Females. Baptist. Avocations: Sewing. Home: 909 K St NE Washington DC 20002 Office: 1017 U St NW Washington DC 20002

KILLEBREW, MIRIAM CLAIRE (SHARPE), sales company executive; b. Indpls., Oct. 25, 1920; d. Randle Percy and Lucille (Horton) Sharpe. A.A., Placer Coll. (name now Sierra Coll.), 1940; m. James Artell Killebrew, Sept. 14, 1940; children—Dorothy Jean, Deborah Jean. Vice pres. K & H Sales, Inc., San Leandro, Calif., 1946-76, pres., 1976—. Mem. altar guild, former treas. All Saints Episcopal Ch., San Leandro; mem. Nat. Right to Work Com., 1974—; mem. Better Bus. Bur. Eastbay, 1965—. Mem. Nat. Fedn. Ind. Bus., San Leandro C. of C., Oakland Mus. Assn. Club: Alta Mira (San Leandro). Lodge: Order Eastern Star. Home: 18397 Magee Way Castro Valley CA 94546 Office: K & H Sales Inc 1800 Williams St San Leandro CA 94577

KILLEBREW, RACHEL ELKINS, data processing cons.; b. McMinnville, Tenn., Aug. 9, 1942; d. Joseph E. and Emma (Henderson) Elkins; B.S., Tenn. Technol. U., 1964; M.B.A., Rockhurst Coll., 1980; div.; 1 son, Winston G. Denton. Analyst, IBM Corp., Kennedy Space Center, Fla., 1966-69; data processing specialist Mgmt. Sci. Am., Atlanta, 1969-71; cons. Stockholders System, Inc., Atlanta, 1971-73; mgr. data systems devel. TWA, Kansas City, Mo., 1973-85; v.p. RS Computing Assos., Inc., Kansas City, Mo., 1981—. Data processing seminar leader Career Crossroads for Women, 1980-81. Mem. Data Processing Mgmt. Assn. (dir. 1980-84), Trans World Airlines Mgmt. Club, Rockhurst Exec. Fellows Soc., Kappa Mu Epsilon. Clubs: Kansas City Ski, Assn. Research and Enlightenment, Friends of Art, Silva Mind Control, Erhardt Seminar Tng., Audubon Club. Home: PO Box 8062 Mc Minnville TN 37110 Office: TWA PO Box 21026 1-310 MCI Kansas City MO 64195

KILLENS, THÉRÈSE ROLANDE, member canadian Parliament; b. Trois-Rivieres, Que., Can., June 29, 1927; d. Omer Joseph and Cecile Marie (Thelland) Gauthier; student St. Agele de Laval Convent Boarding Sch.; m. Raymond Lowes Killens, Sept. 3, 1945; children—Francena, Doreen, Joanne, Daniel, Louise. Commnr., mem. exec. com. Montreal Catholic Sch. Commn., 1973-79; bd. dirs. Vanier CEGEP Coll., 1975, mem. exec. com. 1978, vice-pres. 1977-79; M.P., Saint-Michel, 1979—, parliamentary sec. to Hon. Judy Erola, Minister of State and Minister Responsible for Status of Women. Mem. Canadian Catholic Sch. Trustees Assn. (bd. govs. 1973-78), Spera Found. for Drug Addicts. Liberal. Roman Catholic. Office: Ho of Commons Confederation Bldg 417 Ottawa K1A 0A6 Canada

KILLIAN, JUDY ANNE, psychotherapist; b. New Holland, Pa., Dec. 21, 1940; d. Allen B. and Pauline K.; B.A., Millersville State Coll., 1972; M.S.W. cum laude, U. Pitts., 1976. Sec., Armstrong Cork Co., Lancaster, Pa., 1963-67; mgr. income maintenance Dept. Public Assistance, Lancaster, 1967-74; psychiat. social worker Crisis Intervention, Lancaster Guidance Center, 1976-86; pvt. practice psychotherapy, Lancaster. Steinman scholar, 1975. Mem. Acad. Cert. Social Workers, Nat. Assn. Social Workers, Crisis Intervention Assn. Methodist. Club: Soroptimists. Home: 17 N Mary St Lancaster PA 17603 Office: 18 S Duke St Lancaster PA 17602

KILLICK, KATHLEEN ANN, biochemist; b. Chgo., Jan. 22, 1942; d. Orson Smyth and Maori Madeline (Maloney) K.; B.S. in Biology (NSF undergrad. fellow, Pullman scholar), Ill. Inst. Tech., 1964, M.S. in Microbiology, 1966, Ph.D. in Biochemistry, 1969; cert., U. Uppsala, 1977; postgrad. Argonne (Ill.) Nat. Lab., U. Chgo., 1969-70. Postdoctoral fellow Boston Biomed. Research Inst., 1970-76, staff scientist dept. devel. biology, 1976-82; asst., prof., dept. of biol. scis., St. John's Univ., N.Y., 1982—; lectr. dept. microbiology and molecular genetics Harvard U. NSF trainee, 1968-69, spl. fellow, 1972-74, grantee, 1978—; AEC postdoctoral fellow, 1969-70; Selznick fellow Hereditary Disease Found., 1978. Mem. N.Y. Acad. Scis., AAAS, Am. Soc. Microbiology, Northeastern Soc. Microbiology, Am. Chem. Soc., Am. Soc. Biol. Chemistry, Gerontology Soc., Electrophorosis Soc., Carbohydrate Soc., Sigma Xi. Democrat. Roman Catholic. Office: Grand Central Utopia Parkways New York NY 11439

KILLINGBECK, JANICE LYNELLE (MRS. VICTOR LEE KILLINGBECK), journalist; b. Flint, Mich., Nov. 11, 1948; d. Leonard Paul and Ina Marie (Harris) Johnson; B.A., Mich. State U., 1970; postgrad. Delta Coll., 1971-72; m. Victor Lee Killingbeck, Sept. 26, 1970; children—Deeanna Dawn, Victor Scott. Tourist counselor Mich. Dept. State Hwys., Clare, 1969; copy editor Mich. State News, East Lansing, 1969-70; gen. reporter Midland (Mich.) Daily News, 1970; tchr. Saginaw (Mich.) Public Schs., 1971; public relations teller 1st State Bank of Saginaw, 1971-75; crew leader spl. census in Buena Vista Twp., Detroit Regional Office, U.S. Bur. Census, 1976, interviewer ann. housing survey-standard met. statis. areas, 1977-78, interviewer on-going health surveys, 1979—, Nat. Crime Survey, 1985—; editor AMEN newsletter United Meth. Women, Saginaw, 1984-85. Mem. Women in Communications, Sigma Delta Chi. Methodist. Home and Office: 4946 Hess Rd Saginaw MI 48601

KILLORAN, ELIZABETH MARY, librarian; b. Worcester, Mass., Mar. 10, 1953; d. Thomas Richard and Malvina Margaret (Gervais) Killoran. B.A. cum laude in English, Worcester State Coll., 1976; M.L.S., Simmons Coll., 1980. Vol. Worcester Art Mus. Library, 1978-80; reference, serials asst. Robert H. Goddard Library, Clark U., Worcester, 1978-80; dir. med. library Milford-Whitinsville Regional Hosp. (Mass.), 1980—. Mem. Grafton Hist. Soc. (Mass.), 1983; mem. Mass. Audubon Soc., Lincoln, Mass., 1983; foster parent Foster Parents Plan, Inc., Warwick, R.I., 1983; sponsor Maryknoll Fathers and Brothers (N.Y.), 1983. Mem. Worcester County Poetry Assn. (bd. dirs. 1972, poetry award 1972), Central Mass. Consortium of Health Related Libraries (chairperson 1985—), Mass. Health Scis. Library Network, Med. Library Assn., Soc. Preservation New Eng. Antiquities, Lambda Iota Tau. Roman Catholic. Office: Med Library Milford-Whitinsville Regional Hosp 14 Prospect St Milford MA 01757

KILLPACK, LORRAINE, police officer; b. Las Vegas, Dec. 7, 1954; d. Larry Movell and Joann (Alston) K. B.A. in Univ. Women Studies, U. Utah, 1975, M.B.A., 1979. Dispatcher U. Utah dept. parking services, Salt Lake City, 1973-77; patrol officer Salt Lake City Police Dept., 1977-80, field tng. officer, 1980-81, motorcycle officer, 1981-84, sgt., 1984—; self defense instr. Phoenix Inst., Salt Lake City, 1981-83; motorcycle rider course instr. Motorcycle Safety Foud., Salt Lake City, 1982-83. Founder Salt Lake Rape Crisis Ctr., 1975. Named Outstanding Police Recruit Utah Police Officer Standards and Tng., 1977, Top Acad. Recruit Salt Lake City Policy Acad., 1978. Mem. NOW (pres. Salt Lake chpt. 1973), Phi Beta Kappa, Phi Kappa Phi, Beta Gamma Sigma. Avocations: camping, sports, travel. Office: Salt Lake City Police Dept 450 S 300 E Salt Lake City UT 84111

KILPATRICK, RUBY NAPPIER, nursing educator; b. Deweyville, Tex., July 25, 1925; d. Emery Ellis and Annie Ethel (Oxley) Nappier; m. Rufus Underwood Kilpatrick, Mar. 23, 1946; children—Rufus Underwood, Emery Dale, William Gerard, Ruby Dianne, Bradford Lee. Diploma in nursing St. Mary's Sch. Nursing, 1945; B.S.N., Lamar U., 1979, postgrad., 1980—. Pub. health nurse City of Galveston, Tex., 1945; pvt. duty nurse Ofcl. Nursing Bur., Beaumont, Tex., 1946-47; regular relief nurse Bapt. Hosp., Beaumont, 1949-51; emergency room nurse, head nurse med. floor, charge nurse on coronary care St. Elizabeth Hosp., Beaumont, Tex., 1968-74; clin. instr. Lamar U., Beaumont, 1974—; sec.-treas. Kilpatrick's Bonded Warehouse, Beaumont, 1960—. Sec.-treas. Cub Scouts, Boy Scouts Am., Beaumont, 1983; mem. Legis. Wives, Austin, 1957—. Mem. Tex. Congress Parents and Tchrs., Lamar U. Alumni Assn., Dist. Nurses Assn. Dist. 12 (dir. 1982-84, legis. chmn. 1982-84), Mental Health Assn. Beaumont (adv. com.), Tex. Nurses Assn., Tex. Assn. Coll. Tchrs. Democrat. Mem. Ch. of Christ. Club: Woman's (sec. 1973-74) (Beaumont). Home: 785 Randolph Cir Beaumont TX 77706 Office: Lamar Univ Dept Nursing PO Box 10081 Beaumont TX 77710

KIM, BESS LEE, diversified sales and retail marketing company executive, sales consultant; b. Balt., Sept. 13, 1940; d. Robert Irvin and Mary Eunice (Winslow) Bailey; m. Harold Schriver, Dec. 24, 1961 (div. June 1971); children—Lynn Winslow Schriver, Collin Harold Schriver; m. 2d Derwin F. Kim, Apr. 7, 1972 (div. 1984); 1 dau., Lara Lee. B.A., U. Md., 1963. Tchr. Prince George County Bd. Edn. (Md.), 1962-64; sales mgr. Armor Bronze & Silver, Taunton, Mass., 1965-69; regional sales mgr. Dart Industries, Los

Angeles, 1969-74, area sales mgr., 1975-80, East coast sales mgr., corp. direct selling cons. Dart & Kraft, Northbrook, Ill., 1980-81; exec. dir. Castlebleu Inc., Taunton, 1981-82; pres. Bess Kim Industries, Bowie, Md., 1983-84, Lillymar Ltd., St.Louis, 1984—; cons. direct selling; motivational speaker Bailey-Kim Corp., Brandywine, Md., 1979-83. Author pamphlets, 1979, 80. Mem. Pres.'s Com. for Employment Handicapped, 1980-83. Mem. Am. Soc. Profl. and Exec. Women, AAUW, Md. Univ. Alumni Assn., NOW, Nat. Assn. Female Execs., Charles County C. of C. Republican. Episcopalian. Club: Over 35 Dance (Clinton, Md.). Office: Panache Creations Ltd PO Box 313 Brandywine MD 20613

KIMBALL, MARY LEE EVANS (MRS. CHASE KIMBALL), educator; b. St. Louis, Jan. 27, 1911; d. Dwight Durkee and Elmira (Lee) Evans; A.B. cum laude, Smith Coll., 1933; M.A., Radcliffe Coll., 1935; diplome d'etudes Univ. (Am. fellow Inst. Internat. Edn., 1936-37) Universite de Paris (France), 1937; diplome Ecole du Louvre, Paris, 1962; postgrad. (predoctoral fellow) U. Conn., 1967-68; M.A., Trinity Coll., 1971, U. Conn., 1971; m. Chase Kimball, June 27, 1942; children—Elmira Lee (Mrs. H. Thomas Byron, Jr.), Helen Chase, Mary Eliza. (Mrs. Guy D.D. Stanley). Tchr. French, Cambridge Sch., Kendall Green, Mass., 1937-38, Wheaton Coll., 1938-41, Greenwood Sch., Ruxton, Md., 1941-42, Montessori Sch., Calgary, Alta., Can., 1945, Milton Acad., Mass., 1948-52; instr. French, Tufts U., 1952-58; asst. prof. French, Newton Coll. Sacred Heart, 1958-59; asst. prof. French, Stonehill Coll., 1959-64; asso. prof. French, Salem (Mass.) State Coll., 1965; asst. prof. French, U. Mass., Boston, 1965-81. Bd. dirs. Heart Fund, Boston, to 1970; mem. womans bd. Day-Kimball Hosp., Conn.; Milton chmn. Boston Arts Festival, 1957-60. Pres., Milton Womens Republican Club, 1958-60; sec. Milton Rep. Town Com. Bd. dirs. French Library Boston, 1972—, Home for Aged Women, 1981—; chmn. UN Council of South Shore, 1983—; mem. corp. Milton Hosp., 1981—. Instr. French, U.S. Army, Whitehorse, Yukon, 1944. Decorated chevalier de l'ordre des Palmes Académiques (France). Mem. League Women Voters (voters' service chmn., internat. relations chmn. Milton 1948-52), Am. Assn. Tchrs. French, Modern Lang. Assn., Alliance Francaise, Am. Hist. Assn., UN Assn. Greater Boston (pres. 1981-84), UN Council South Shore (dir. 1975—), Fragment Soc. Boston, Colonial Dames Am. Clubs: Chromatic (pres. 1977—), Smith College (dir. 1955-61, 70-75, pres. Class of 1933, 1973-78), Women's City (Boston); Milton Women's (internat. relations chmn. 1958-60, 62-64 garden and conservation chmn. 1960-61). Home: Pomfret Centre CT 06259 also 434 Brush Hill Rd Milton MA 02186

KIMBALL, VERA F., editor, writer; b. Seward, Alaska, Feb. 8, 1903; d. Irving L. and Della (Carpenter) Kimball; A.B., Columbia U., 1929; m. William T. Castles, Jr., Dec. 2, 1942. On clerical staff Legislature of Ty. of Alaska, 1923; with Alaska R.R., Anchorage, 1923-24, N.A. Newspaper Alliance, Met. Mus. Art, Gen. Foods Corp., Todd-Robertson & Todd (all N.Y.C.), part time 1924-29; asst. to sec. Am. Inst. Chemists, 1929-35; editor Chemist, N.Y.C., 1935-68, asso. editor, 1968-70; sec. S.C. Inst. Chemists, 1970—. Mem. N.Y. Acad. Scis., Am. Inst. Chemists (hon. life), AAAS, Cook Inlet Hist. Soc., Alaska (charter), Chester County Hist. Soc. Club: Barnard College (N.Y.C.). Author: (with W. T. Castles) Firearms and Use, 1942; (with M. R. Bhagwat) Your Future in Chemistry, 1943. Contbr. to Am. Chemists and Chem. Engrs., World Scope Ency. Ency. of Chemistry, Herbert Ives Papers, 1979, year books, profl. and popular mags. Office: Route 2 Box 491 Chester SC 29706

KIMBELL, ANNIE MAE, retired educator; b. Lyerly, Ga., Nov. 3, 1911; d. Edward L. and Lena (Grogan) Bishop; B.A. in Elementary Edn., shorter Coll., Rome Ga., 1957; M. in Elementary Edn., U. Chattanooga, 1966; postgrad. in Learning Disabilities, W. Ga. Coll., Carrolton, 1975; m. Robert F. Kimbell; 1 son, Joe Frank. Tchr. Chattooga County (Ga.) Bd. Edn., Summerville, 1957-71, tchr. reading, 1971-74, resource tchr. learning disabilities, 1975-78. Mem. NEA, Chattooga Edn. Assn., Ga. Assn. Educators, Council Exceptional Children, Chattanooga chpt. Ret. Tchrs. Assn. (sec.), Kappa Kappa Iota (state nominating com., past local pres.). Certified in specific learning disabilities, Ga. Home: PO Box 206 Alpine St Lyerly GA 30730

KIMBLE, BARBARA ANN, government official; b. Toledo, Mar. 21, 1945; d. George Leroy and Elvera Betty (Rose) Kimble. B.A., U. Toledo, 1967. Modeling instr. Patricia Stevens Modeling and Career Coll., Toledo, 1966, Barbizon Sch. Modeling, Dallas, 1972; with Nat. Crime Info. Ctr., FBI, Dallas, 1983—, coordinator, 1986—. Named Miss Amity, Miss Tex. Universe Pageant, 1971; recipient Performance award, FBI, 1981-85. Mem. Nat. Baton Twirling Assn., Nat. Baton Twirling Judges Bur., Nat. Baton Twirling Tchrs. Assn., Tex. Criminal Justice Info. Users Group. Avocations: sewing; dancing; crocheting.

KIMBLE, GLADYS AUGUSTA LEE, nurse, civic worker; b. Niagara Falls, Can., June 28, 1906; d. William and Florence Augusta Baker (Buckton) Lee; R.N., Christ Hosp., Jersey City, 1929; B.S., Columbia U. Tchrs. Coll., 1938, M.A., 1948; m. George Edmond Kimble, Jan. 5, 1952. Nurse, Willard Parker Hosp., N.Y.C., 1931; asst. and supervisory relief nurse Margaret Hague Maternity Hosp., Jersey City, 1931-37; staff nurse, relief supr. Manhattan Eye, Ear and Throat Hosp., 1937-38; sr. staff, asst. nurse supr. Vis. Nurse Service, N.Y.C., 1938-41; sr. public health nurse USPHS, Little Rock, 1941-43; public health supr. Providence Dist. Nursing Assn., 1943-46; edn. dir. Jersey City Public Health Nursing Service, 1946-49, also instr. Seton Hall U., 1947-48; public health nurse cons. U.S. Inst. Inter-Am. Affairs, Brazil, 1949-51; dir. public health dept. Englewood (N.J.) Hosp., 1951-53; nurse coordinator exchange visitor nurse program Overlook Hosp., Summit, N.J., 1964-71. Recipient Appreciation award for service rendered Providence Hosp., 1944; Woman of Yr. award Essex County Bus. and Profl. Women, 1968. Fellow Am. Public Health Assn. (life), mem. Sarasota Geneal. Soc. (charter), AAUW. Episcopalian. Clubs: Daus. of the Nile (charter), Ladies Oriental Shrine of N. Am. (SAR-I Ct. 79), Royal Order of Jesterettes. Home: 4540 Bee Ridge Rd Villa 12 Sarasota FL 33583

KIMBRO, GINGER FAYE, interior designer; b. Houston, Sept. 27, 1949; d. William Troyce Chance and Margaret (Gill) Chance Webb; m. J. Michael Kimbro, Aug. 5, 1967; children—Kimberley Renee, Jennifer Michel. Student N. Harris County Community Coll., 1976-77. Free lance interior designer, Houston, 1977-81; designer Corner Collection, Tomball, Tex., 1981—. Chairperson numerous beauty pageants. Mem. Bus. and Profl. Women's Club. Democrat. Mem. Ch. of Christ. Home: 11402 Squiredale St Houston TX 77070 Office: Corner Collection 605 Mason Tomball TX 77375

KIMBROUGH, EMILY (EMILY KIMBROUGH WRENCH), writer; b. Muncie, Ind., Oct. 23, 1899; d. Hal Curry and Charlotte Emily (Wiles) Kimbrough; B.A., Bryn Mawr Coll., 1921; student The Sorbonne, Paris, 1922; m. John Wrench, Dec. 31, 1926; children—Margaret Achsah and Alis Emily (twins). Editor Fashions of the Hour, Marshall Field & Co., Chgo., 1922-27; fashion editor Ladies' Home Jour., 1927, mng. editor, 1927-29; writer, 1932—. Author: (with Cornelia Otis Skinner) Our Hearts Were Young and Gay, 1942; We Followed Our Hearts to Hollywood, 1943; How Dear to My Heart, 1944; It Gives Me Great Pleasure, 1948; The Innocents from Indiana, 1950; Through Charley's Door, 1952; Forty Plus and Fancy Free, 1954; So Near and Yet So Far, 1955; Water, Water Everywhere, 1956; And a Right Good Crew, 1958; Pleasure by the Busload, 1961; Forever Old, Forever New, 1964; Floating Island, 1968; Now and Then, 1972; Time Enough, 1974; Better Than Oceans, 1976. Home: 11 E 73d St New York NY 10021

KIMBROUGH, EVELYN SUE, environ. engr.; b. Nashville, Aug. 30, 1954; d. George Robert and Irene K.; A.A., Martin Coll., 1974; B.S., Vanderbilt U., 1976. Environ. scientist U.S. EPA, Research Triangle Park, N.C., 1977—. Methodist. Club: Order of Eastern Star. Home: 32 Justin Ct Durham NC 27705 Office: MD-14 Research Triangle Park NC 27711

KIMBROUGH, JUANITA CLAYTON, nurse; b. Marietta, Ga., Apr. 28, 1949; d. Ernest Lafayette and Clyde Mae (Barnett) Clayton; m. Bryant Fuller, Dec. 19, 1971 (div. Mar. 1978); m. Terry Earl Kimbrough, June 5, 1982. B.S.N., Ga. State U., 1976, M.S.N., 1983. Staff nurse Kennestone Hosp., Marietta, Ga., 1970-71, Grady Hosp., Atlanta, 1971-72; instr. Grady Hosp. Sch. Nursing, Atlanta, 1976-82; head nurse ICU, Clayton Gen. Hosp., Riverdale, Ga., 1982-83; clin. nurse specialist Grady Meml. Hosp., Atlanta, 1983—; pres. J. T. Kimbrough Constrn. Co.; instr. Ga. Bapt. Med. Ctrs. Sch. Nursing, 1986—. Served to lt. (j.g.) USN, 1972-74. Mem. Am. Nurses Assn., Am. Found. Nurses, Am. Assn. Critical Care Nurses, Am. Nephrology Nurses Assn., Ga. Nurses Assn. Democrat. Baptist. Home: 2344 Cherokee Valley Dr Lithonia GA 30058 Office: Grady Meml Hosp 80 Butler St Atlanta GA 30335

KIMBROUGH, SHARON MARLENE, advertising agency executive; b. Chgo., Mar. 23, 1944; d. Andrew and Grace (Walker) Jacobs; m. Walter William Kimbrough, Jr. Feb. 15, 1964 (div.); 1 dau., Crystal Yna. Creative sec. Burrell Advt. Inc., Chgo., 1974-75, traffic coordinator, 1976-77, broadcast bus. mgr., 1978-81, producer, 1982—. Mem. NAACP (life; exec. bd. 1983). Democrat. Office: 625 N Michigan Ave Chicago IL 60611

KIMES, BEVERLY RAE, editor, writer; b. Aurora, Ill., Aug. 17, 1939; d. Raymond Lionel and Grace Florence (Perrin) K.; m. James H. Cox, July 6, 1984. B.S., U. Ill., 1961; M.A. in Journalism, Pa. State U., 1963. Dir. publicity Mateer Playhouse, Neff's Mills, Pa., 1962, Pavillion Theatre, University Park, Pa., 1963; asst. editor Automobile Quar. Publs., N.Y.C., Princeton, N.J., 1963-64, assoc. editor, 1965-66, mng. editor, 1967-74, editor, 1975-81; editor The Classic Car, 1981—. Recipient Cugnot award Soc. Automotive Historians, 1978, 79; Thomas McKean trophy, 1984, 86. Mem. Internat. Motor Press Assn., Soc. Automotive Historians. Author: The Classic Tradition of the Lincoln Motor Car, 1968; (with R.M. Langworth) Oldsmobile: The First Seventy-Five Years, 1972; The Cars That Henry Ford Built, 1978; (with Rene Dreyfus) My Two Lives, 1983; (with Robert C. Ackerson) Chevrolet: A History from 1911, 1984; The Standard Catalog of American Cars 1805-1942, 1985; The Star and the Laurel: The Centennial History of Daimler, Mercedes and Benz, 1986; editor: Great Cars and Grand Marques, 1976; Packard: History of the Motor Car and the Company, 1979; Automobile Quarterly's Handbook of Automotive Hobbies, 1981.

KIMMEL, BARBARA LYNN, nurse; b. Dayton, Ohio, May 27, 1942; d. Robert Daniel and Jane Phyllis (Easterday) Overly; m. Kent Nevin Kimmel, June 27, 1964; 1 child, Heather Lynn. B.A., Miami U., Oxford, Ohio, 1964; R.N., Peninsula Gen. Hosp. Sch. Nursing, Salisbury, Md., 1973; M.A., Salisbury State Coll., 1981. R.N., Md. Microbiologist FDA, Washington, 1966-69; relief charge nurse Peninsula Gen. Hosp., Salisbury, 1973-78, 79-82, radiology nurse, 1982—; documentation and tng. cons. Holly Ctr., Salisbury, 1978-79. Mem. Am. Radiology Nurses Assn., Phi Sigma. Avocations: needlework; ballet; reading; biking. Home: 1410 Emerson Ave Salisbury MD 21801 Office: Peninsula Gen Hosp Med Ctr 100 E Carroll St Salisbury MD 21801

KIMMEL, ELLEN BISHOP, psychologist, educator; b. Knoxville, Tenn., Sept. 16, 1939; d. Archer W. and Mary Ellen (Baker) Bishop; B.A., U. Tenn., 1961; M.A., U. Fla., 1962, Ph.D., 1965; div.; children—Elinor, Ann, Jean, Tracy. Asst. prof., research asso. Ohio U., 1965-68; research asso. U. South Fla., 1971-72, asst. prof., 1971-72, assoc. prof., dir. Univ. Studies Coll., 1972-73, prof. psychology and ednl. psychology, 1975—; disting. vis. prof. psychology Simon Fraser U., Vancouver, B.C., Can., 1980-81; cons. numerous sch. systems, bus. and govt. Mem. Fla. Blue Ribbon Task Force on Juvenile Delinquency, 1976-77; mem. Fla. Gov.'s Commn. on Women, 1979—; mem. adv. bd. Stop Rape, Good Govt., Inc. Recipient Outstanding Teaching award U. South Fla., 1978; Woman of Achievement award U. Tenn., 1983. Fellow Am. Psychol. Assn. (governing council 1982—); mem. Am. Ednl. Research Assn., Am.Assn. Counseling and Devel., Assn. Women in Psychology, Women in Edn., Psychonomic Soc., Southeastern Psychol. Assn. (pres. 1978-79), So. Soc. Philosophy and Psychology, Athena Soc., Sigma Xi, Delta Kappa Gamma, Omicron Delta Kappa. Democrat. Contbr. articles to jours., chpts. to books. Office: FAO 268 U South Fla Tampa FL 33620

KIMMEL, MARJORIE ANNE, health care executive; b. Ft. Wayne, Ind., July 11, 1936; d. Edward Henry and Marie Virginia (Woodworth) Ernst; student Ind. State U., Ohio U.; B.S., Park Coll., Kansas City, Mo.; m. Kenneth Robert Kimmel, Nov. 24, 1955; children—Kathleen Marie Opdyke, Cynthia Louise Sniff. Sec. bd. trustees, then acting dir. Recovery Ctr., Inc. (formerly Washington County Council Alcoholism), Marietta, Ohio, 1978-79, exec. dir. 1979—. Mem. adv. bd. Washington County Dept. Human Services; v.p. Employee Assistance Resource Network; treas., trustee Eve, Inc., shelter battered women. Cert. alcoholism counselor. Mem. Assn. Labor, Mgmt., Adminstrs. and Cons. Alcoholism, Ohio Task Force Women and Alcohol, Nat. Council on Alcoholism/Ohio, Nat. Assn. Alcoholism and Drug Abuse Counselors, Ohio Assn. Alcoholism and Drug Abuse Counselors, Nat. Assn. Female Execs. Office: 427 2d St Marietta OH 45750

KIMMER, AMANDA JEAN, journalist; b. Aliquippa, Pa., June 21, 1961; d. William Cephus and Joan Elizabeth (Phillips) K. B.A., Fla. So. Coll., 1983, postgrad., 1986—. Asst. dir. Central Fla. Health Fair, Orlando, 1983-84; jours. prodn. editor Harcourt Brace Jovanovich Pub. Co., Orlando, 1984-86, book prodn. editor, 1986—; writer Ind. Newspapers, Winter Haven, Fla., 1986—. Founder, coordinator Renee Turbeville Meml. Scholarship in Acctg., Fla. So. Coll., Lakeland, 1984—; co-founder, dir. Images of Fla. Beauty Pageant, 1986. Mem. Nat. Assn. Female Execs., Fla. Pub. Relations Execs., Phi Chi Theta, Omicron Delta Kappa, Sigma Delta Chi. Democrat. Presbyterian. Avocations: photography, music, tennis, reading, poetry. Home: Apt 15 1103 Cypress Blvd Winter Haven FL 33880 Office: Ind Newspapers 124 W Central Ave Winter Haven FL 33880

KIMURA, FELICIA SOY KEE, state government health official; b. Honolulu, Dec. 11, 1955; d. Alfred Dai Cheong and Wai Quen (Chang) Goo; m. Brian Takao Kimura, July 1, 1978; children—Sharmaine L.M.T., Evan K.M.T. Student Creighton U., 1973-76, U. Nebr.-Omaha, 1977-78; B.A. in Psychology, Chaminade U., 1982. Audiometric technician Dept. Health, State Hawaii Sch. Health Support Services Br., Kona, Hawaii, 1982-84, casework mgr. Dept. Health-Mental Health, Kealakekua, 1986—; sales, mgr. H. Kimura, Inc., Kealakekua, 1978—; silk screener Felicia's Tees, Kealakekua, 1982—; sales cons. Liberty House of Hawaii, Kailua-Kona, 1985—. Mem. Nat. Assn. Female Execs., Kainaliu Bus. and Profl. Assn. Roman Catholic. Home: PO Box 557 Kealakekua HI 96750 Office: Dept Mental Health PO Box 228 Kealakekua HI 96750

KIMURA, LILLIAN CHIYEKO, human service agency executive; b. Glendale, Calif., Apr. 7, 1929; d. Homer and Hisa (Muraki) Kimura; B.A., U. Ill., 1951, M.S.W., 1954; postgrad. Inst. for Nonprofit Mgmt., Columbia U., 1985. Program dir. Olivet Community Center, Chgo., 1954-68; dir. Olivet Service Area, Chgo. Commons Assn., 1968-71; program cons. Nat. Bd. YWCA of U.S.A., 1971-78; dir. mid-states region, 1978-80, exec. field services, 1980-83, asst. exec. dir., 1984—. Pres., Japanese Am. Service Com., 1973-79; bd. dirs. Nat. Japanese Am. Citizens League, 1972-79; gov., 1974-79, pres. N.Y. chpt., 1986. Mem. Acad. Cert. Social Workers, Assn. Social Workers, orgn. Pan Asian Women, Nat. Women's Polit. Caucus, Nonprofit Mgmt. Assn. (bd. dirs.), Soc. Nonprofit Orgns. (bd. dirs.). Office: 726 Broadway New York NY 10003

KINCAID, TAMARA DUNCAN, customer service representative; b. Gastonia, N.C., May 2, 1959; d. Herman Junior and Barbara Sunshine (Duncan) K. B.A., Auburn U., 1981. Communications specialist Audichron Co., Atlanta, 1981-85, editor Audichronicle, 1983-84, com. mem., 1984; customer service rep. Audichron Co., Atlanta, 1985—. Mem. Women in Communications (v.p. fin. 1984-86), Soc. Profl. Journalists, Phi Mu (2d v.p. Atlanta alumnae chpt. 1983-84). Republican. Baptist. Home: 2452 Maclaren Circle Atlanta GA 30360 Office: Audichron Co 3620 Clearview Pkwy Atlanta GA 30340

KINCHELOE, MAXINE CAROL, state legislator; b. Austin, Tex., Aug. 14, 1929; d. Walter and Blanche (Pegram) Miller; student U. Phillipines, 1963; grad. Am. Inst. Banking, 1966-69; m. Lawrence Reed Kincheloe, Jan. 3, 1949; children—Cheryl, Teresa, Lawrence Reed. With Bank of Am., 1965-71; cons. taxes, Choctaw, Okla.; now mem. Okla. Ho. of Reps. Bd. dirs. Mental Health Assn. Oklahoma County. Mem. Nicoma Park Bus. and Profl. Women's Club, Choctaw C. of C. Am. Legis. Exchange Council. Republican. Baptist. Office: State Capitol Bldg Room 544 Oklahoma City OK 73105

KINCZEWSKI, KATHRYN, language educator; b. LaSalle, Ill., Nov. 9, 1951; d. Joseph C. and Dorothy M. (Urban) K. B.A. in Lang., U. Ill., 1973; M.A. in French, Yale U., 1974, M.Phil., 1977, Ph.D., 1981. Teaching fellow Yale U., New Haven, 1976-79; vis. asst. prof. Miami U., Oxford, Ohio, 1979-80; asst. prof. St. John's U., Collegeville, Minn., 1981; asst. prof. La. State U., Shreveport, 1981-82; asst. prof. French, U. Denver, 1982—; cons. and lectr. in field. Contbr. chpts. to books, articles to profl. jours. NEH fellow Princeton U., 1981; La. State U. Faculty fellow, 1982. Mem. MLA, Internat. Assn. for Philosophy and Lit., Soc. Critical Exchange, Rocky Mountain Lang. Assn., Pacific N.W. Council on Fgn. Langs., Phi Beta Kappa. Club: Le Club Sevigne (Denver). Home: 2708 Stout St Apt A Denver CO 80205 Office: U Denver Dept Fgn Langs and Lit Denver CO 80208

KINDER, GERRI GERALDINE, communications company executive; b. Pikeville, Ky., July 13, 1947; d. J. Ulius Thacker and Juanita (Coleman) Lowe; m. Kenneth Hobart Kinder, Aug. 18, 1967; 1 child, Kenneth Hobart, II. B.S., Pikeville Coll., 1968; postgrad. U. Ariz., 1971; M.A. in Edn., Morehead U., 1975, postgrad., 1975-79. Tchr., Intermountain Indian Sch., Brigham City, Ky., 1968-70, Pike County Bd. Edn., Pikeville, Ky., 1970-73; program asst., 1973-74, dir. IGE program, 1974-77; co-owner Thacker Cable Div., Inc., Pikeville, 1977—. Cleanup chmn. Pike County Fiscal Ct., 1980. Mem. Ky. Cable TV Assn. (conv. chmn. 1985). Avocations: reading, various sports. Home: Route 6 Box 666-A Pikeville KY 41501 Office: Thacker Cable Div Inc Rural Route C4 Box 600 Pikeville KY 41501

KINDER, SHARON MARIE, real estate division education manager; b. Spokane, Wash., May 13, 1939; d. Merle L. and Anna Marie (Petersen) Kinder. B.S. in Phys. Edn. and Edn., Wash. State U., 1961; postgrad. Eastern Wash. State Coll., 1962, Wash. State U., 1963, 64, U. Idaho, 1964. Cert. tchr., Wash. Phys. edn. instr. Sch. Dist. 140, Walla Walla, Wash., 1961-64; dir. vols. State Hosp. N., Orofino, Idaho, 1964-67, coordinator activity therapy, 1967-70; coordinator and pub. info. specialist State Hosp. S., Blackfoot, Idaho, 1970-74; ind. contractor real estate assoc. broker, Spokane, Wash., 1974-80; edn. mgr. Real Estate Div., Olympia, Wash., 1981—; bd. dirs. Northwest Danish Home, Seattle, 1976—. Editor Interagy. Council Service Directory, 1968, Wash. Real Estate News, 1981—. Mem. Interagy. Council, Orofino, 1968; pres. Clearwater County Comprehensive Health Plan Agy., Orofino, 1968; precinct worker Spokane Election Bd., 1976; sec. Health Systems Agy., Spokane, 1976. Mem. AAUW, Real Estate Educators Assn. (pres. Northwest chpt. 1985), Orofino C. of C. (v.p. 1970). Democrat. Lutheran (ch. council, v.p.). Club: Internat. Toastmistress (regional supr. 1974, internat. chmn. speech contest 1975). Lodges: Danish Brotherhood (v.p. 1983), Pacific NW Dist. Danish Brotherhood (pres. 1986—). Home: 1206 D Boone St SE Olympia WA 98503 Office: Real Estate Div Dept Licensing PO Box 247 Olympia WA 98503

KINDLE, MARY ETHEL SMYERS (MRS. CECIL HALDANE KINDLE), librarian; b. Aplin, Ark., Sept. 24, 1913; d. Dan Taylor and Ruby Robb (Neale) Smyers; B.S., U. Ark., 1936; M.S. in L.S., Columbia U., 1941, postgrad. Tchrs. Coll., 1941, 54-57, 69-74; postgrad. Fordham U., 1962-63; m. Cecil Haldane Kindle, Jan. 26, 1941; children—Mary Anne (Mrs. Roger Alan Stafford) (dec.), Elizabeth Lee (Mrs. Burke Baker III), Cecil Haldane, Millicent Robb. Asst. children's and adult depts. Little Rock Public Library, 1930-34; librarian elem. schs., Fort Smith, Ark., 1936-39, Liberty St. Elem. Sch., Nyack, N.Y., 1940-41; librarian young people's dept. Bloomingdale br. N.Y. Public Library, 1954, Nyack High Sch., 1954-57, Hilltop Jr. High Sch., Nyack, N.Y., 1957-68, Valley Cottage Elem. Sch., 1968-75. Cons. Bethlehem (Conn.) Public Library, 1958; sec. bd. dirs. Rockland Fed. Credit Union, Nyack, 1976-77. Mem. Vols. for Internat. Tech. Assistance, 1965-68; mem. search com. for supt. Nyack Public Schs., 1977-78, mem. citizens budget adv. com., 1978-79, mem. facilities com., 1979-80; pres. guild First Reformed Ch., Nyack, 1981—; pres. Rockland/Westchester Classical Union of Ref. Ch. Women, 1981—. Recipient Martha Washington medal SAR, 1971. Mem. NEA (co-chmn. membership Rockland County, N.Y. 1967-69), ALA, N.Y. Library Assn., Rockland County Sch. Librarians Assn. (rec. sec. 1963), N.Y. State, Rockland County (rec. sec. 1968-72), Nyack (v.p. 1974-75) tchrs. assns., Am. Security Council, Little Rock Jr. Fedn. Women's Clubs (charter), Kappa Delta Pi, Delta Kappa Gamma (charter mem. Ft. Smith, Ark. chpt. 1940, co-installer Epsilon chpt. N.Y.C. 1944, chmn. publicity and publs. com. Alpha Eta chpt. 1972—). Editor: Authors of Rockland County, 1960. Home: 332 N Midland Ave Upper Nyack NY 10960

KINDRED, JOAN HOVER, actress, civic worker, home economist; b. Poughkeepsie, Nov. 28, 1930; d. Ernest William and Florence (Christiansen) Hover; B.S., U. Md., 1953; m. John Joseph Kindred, III, Aug. 25, 1956 (div. Aug. 1980); 1 dau., Drewry Ann. Promotion and speech writer Sta. WTOP, Washington, 1953-54; producer, star daily TV women's culinary arts show Sta. WRC, Washington, 1955-56; home economist Potomac Electric Power Co., 1956; producer, star indsl. and comml. film for TV, 1956-59; pres. Snark, Ltd., repertory group, N.Y.C., 1969-72. Vice pres., bd. dirs. Twilight Park Assn., 1971-75; bd. dirs. Sheltering Arms Children's Service, 1974—, treas. aux., 1975-77. Republican. Presbyterian. Address: 1070 Park Ave New York NY 10128

KINDSCHI, ELIZABETH JANE NEECE, nurse; b. Cleve., Apr. 1, 1955; d. Robert H. and Marilyn Joy (Ploetz) Neece; m. Paul S. Kindschi, June 26, 1976; 1 child, Matthew Paul. Student Valparaiso U., 1973-75; B.S.N., U. Md., 1977. Staff nurse VA Med Ctr., Milw., 1981-82, head nurse, 1982—. Instr. CPR, Fort Knox, Ky., 1978-81, Milw., 1981—. Served to capt. AUS, 1973—. Democrat. Lutheran. Home: 5426 Middleton Dr Greendale WI 53129 Office: Zablocki VA Med Ctr 5000 W National Ave Milwaukee WI 53193

KINER, SUSAN LOUISE, advertising executive; b. Blue Island, Ill., Feb. 9, 1954; d. Donald Raymond and Billie Sue (Adams) Kiner; B.S. in Communications, U. Ill., 1976; M.M., Northwestern U., 1986; m. Jack Modzelewski, May 19, 1978. With Benton & Bowles, Inc., N.Y.C., 1976-78, Chgo., 1978-79, Tatham-Laird & Kudner, Chgo., 1979-80; account supr. D'Arcy-MacManus & Masius, Chgo., 1981-85; pres. Kiner Communications, 1985—. cons. for Chgo. comedian, Tim Cavanagh, 1980-81. State fundraiser John Anderson Presdl. campaign, 1980; exec. com. Nat. Unity Party, Ill., 1981; bd. dirs. Towers Condominium Assn. Recipient Chgo. YWCA Leadership award, 1981. Mem. Am. Advt. Fedn. (6th dist. conf. chmn. 1982-84). Club: Chgo. Advt. (co-chmn. seminars 1981, social chmn. 1981-82, bd. dirs. 1984, 85, roster chmn. 1984, seminar chmn. 1985), Women's Ad Club (bd. dirs., program chmn. 1984, edn. dir. 1985). Home and Office: 1221 N Dearborn Pkwy 610 S Chicago IL 60610

KINES, JOAN ELAINE, health care administrator, consultant; b. Rome, Ga., Jan. 12, 1949; d. James Benjamen Satterfield and Janie Lee (Potts) Smith. Student Floyd Jr. Coll., Rome, 1974-76. Reimbursement specialist Grady Hosp., Atlanta, 1968-73; quality assurance coordinator Redmond Park Hosp., Rome, 1974-77; mktg. dir. Zachiarias & Assocs., Columbus, Ga., 1977-79; office mgr. Interstate Health Mgmt., Atlanta, 1980-81; adminstr. InterCommunity Cancer Ctr., Rome, 1982—; cons. in field.; mem. health adv. bd. Coosa Valley Tech. High Sch., Rome, 1982—. Bd. dirs. Coosa Valley Home Health, Rome, 1981-83, mem. adv. bd., 1983—; vol. Am. Cancer Soc., Rome, 1982—. Mem. Soc. Radiation Oncology Adminstrs., Med. Assn. Group Adminstrs., Am. Coll. Med. Group Adminstrs, Ambulatory Care Adminstrs., Nat. Assn. Female Execs., Rome C. of C. Avocations: fishing; swimming; reading; traveling; hiking. Office: InterCommunity Cancer Ctr 321 W 5th St Rome GA 30161

KING, ANITA LUGO, construction company executive; b. Los Angeles, Mar. 23, 1926; d. William Dolphus and Anita (Lugo) Givens; m. Celestus A. King, III, May 2, 1942; children—Celestus A., Toni, Teri, Tobi. B.B.A., City U. Los Angeles, 1975. Ptnr., King Bail Bond Agy., Los Angeles, 1951—; v.p. K/G Constrn., Inc., Los Angeles, 1975—. Mem. Los Angeles Commn. on Status of Women, 1983; mem. State of Calif. Colorado River Bd., 1983; mem. Calif. Republican Central Com., 1983; mem. Rep. Presdl. Task Force; pres. Westside Rep. Women Federated, Los Angeles, 1982-84; founder Young Profl. Reps. Calif., 1983. Recipient awards Los Angeles County Rep. Women, others. Mem. Profl. Bondsmen U.S. Women's Aux. (pres. 1982—), Women in Constrn., NAACP, Nat. Assn. Female Execs., Wilshire C. of C., Smithsonian Assocs. Office: PO Box 19701 Los Angeles CA 90019

KING, BARBARA JEAN, nurse; b. Cape Girardeau, Mo., June 28, 1941; d. Otto Samuel and Goldie Elizabeth (Clover) Fowler; student Weatherford Jr. Coll., 1965; R.N., John Peter Smith Hosp. Sch. Profl. Nursing, 1969; m. Charles Basil King, Jr., Sept. 4, 1972; children—Otto Samuel, Christopher Lee. Head nurse pediatrics and isolation County Hosp., also intensive care and coronary care units Small Gen. Hosp., Ft. Worth, 1969-75; dir. nursing service Jarvis Heights Nursing Center, Ft. Worth, 1976-77; dir. nursing services Ft. Worth Rehab. Farm, 1978-83; staff nurse, asst. supr. shift Decatur Community Hosp. (Tex.), 1983—; instr. vocat. nursing Cooke County Coll., Gainesville, Tex., 1981; cons. convalescent centers and hosps. Chmn. child care com. Women of Moose, 1977—; ch. organist Zion Valley Cumberland Presbyterian Ch.; asso. organist St. Matthew Cumberland Presbyn. Ch. Served with M.C., USN, 1962-65. Mem. Dirs. Nursing Homes Assn. Tarrant County (v.p.). Democrat. Home: Route 1 Box 198 Alvord TX 76225

KING, BARBARA VIARENGO, beauty salon owner, consultant; b. Torrington, Conn., Mar. 27, 1942; d. Ceasar James and Elizabeth (DeMichael) Viarengo; m. John W. King, Sept. 1, 1962; children—David John, Dana Elizabeth. Student Shearpower, Redding, Pa., 1978, Jingles Acad., N.Y.C., 1979. Licensed stylist, Conn. Clk., Signa Ins. Group, Hartford, Conn., 1960-66, 69-70; stylist Gino's of Palm Beach, Torrington, Conn., 1976-77; owner, mgr. Hair Plus of Torrington, Inc., 1978—; stylist, cons., owner, mgr. Hair Plus Internat., Guilford, Conn., 1984—; advt. and mgmt. cons. Hair Plus Danbury, Conn., 1984—; advt. cons. Savvy Hair Design, Hartford, Conn., 1985—. Mem. Nat. Hairdresser Assn., Nat. Assn. Hairdressers and Cosmetologists (officer 1980—). Democrat. Roman Catholic. Avocations: reading; swimming; tennis. Home: 3 Simmons St Torrington CT 06790 Office: Barbara King's Hair Plus 7 S Main St Torrington CT 06790

KING, BILLIE JEAN MOFFITT, profl. tennis player; b. Long Beach, Calif., Nov. 22, 1943; d. Willard J. Moffitt; student Calif. State U., Los Angeles, 1961-64; m. Larry King, Sept. 17, 1965. Amateur tennis player, 1958-67, profl. 1968—; singles champion tournaments Wimbledon, 1966-68, 72, 73, 75, U.S. Open, Forest Hills, N.Y., 1967, 71, 72, 74, U.S. Hardcourt, 1966, Italian Open, 1970, West German Open, 1971, Australian Open, 1968, South African Open, 1966-67, 69, U.S. Indoor, 1966-68, 71, U.S. Clay Court, 1971, French Open, 1972; doubles champion at Wimbledon, 1961, 62, 65, 67, 68, 70-73, 79, U.S. Open, 1965, 67, 74, 78, 80, French, 1972, Italian, 1970, South African, 1967-70, Bridgestone, 1976, 78, 80, Va. Slims, 1974; mixed double champion at Wimbledon, 1967, 71, 73, 74, U.S. Open, 1967, 71, 73, 76, French, 1967, 70, South African, 1967, 70, Australian, 1968; winner 29 Va. Slims singles titles, 1970-77, 4 Colgate titles, 1977. Fedn. Cup, 1963-67, 76-79, Wightman cup, 1961-67; 70, 77, 78; World Tennis Team All-Star, 3 times; mem. Tennis Challenge Series, 1977, 78; host Colgate women's sports TV spl. The Lady is a Champ, 1975; co-founder, dir. Kingdom, Inc., San Mateo, Calif.; sports commentator ABC-TV, 1975-78; mem. U.S. Team which won Fedn. Cup, 1976; co-founder WomenSports mag., 1974. Named Sportsperson of Yr., Sports Illus., 1972, Woman Athlete of Yr., A.P., 1967, 73; Top Woman Athlete of Year, 1972, Woman of Yr., Time mag., 1976, One of 10 Most Powerful Women in Am. Harper's Bazaar, 1977, One of 25 Most Influential Women in Am., World Alumanac, 1977. Author: Tennis to Win, 1970; (with Kim Chapin) Billie Jean, 1974. Address: care US Tennis Assn 51 E 42d St New York NY 10017*

KING, CAROL LOUISE, city official; b. Detroit, Dec. 10, 1948; d. William Albert and Mary Theresa (Simon) K.; B.A. in English and Speech, Western Mich. U., 1971. Sales rep. Am. Can Co., Detroit, 1973-76; employment counselor, account exec. New Options, In., Detroit, 1976-78; congressional aide, 1978-79; pres. Mich. conf. NOW, 1979-80; placement coordinator Displaced Homemaker Project, Warren, Mich., 1980-82; adminstrv. asst. to Detroit City Councilwoman Maryann Mahaffey, 1982—; legis. liaison, cons. in field. Vice pres. Mich. conf. NOW, 1978-79, pres. Macomb County (Mich.) chpt., 1976-78, nat. chairperson reproductive rights com. 1978-79, nat. bd. dirs., 1980—; bd. dirs. Mich. Welfare Reform Coalition, S.E. Mich. Anti-Rape Network, Sojourner Found.; regional dir. NOW; bd. dirs. Planned Parenthood Detroit, 1980—; founding mem., mem. steering com. Democratic Citizens Caucus, 1980; chmn. Detroit Welfare Reform Coalitions; Mem. ACLU, Nat. Abortion Rights Action League, Voice of Reason, Older Women's League, Women's Econs. Club Detroit, Detroit Women's Forum. Democrat.

KING, CAROLYN MAE, educator, b. Fond du Lac, Wis., Oct. 23, 1946; d. John Francis and Adina Elnora (Bahr) K.; B.S., Wis. State U., Oshkosh, 1970; M.S., Niagara U., 1974. Tchr. phys. edn. Public Schs. Niagara Falls (N.Y.), 1970-83; women's swim coach Niagara (N.Y.) U., 1975-76; substitute tchr., Niagara Falls, 1983-84, tchr. phys. edn., 1984—. Water safety instr. ARC; mem. Nat. Ski Patrol. Recipient award Joseph P. Kennedy Jr. Found., 1972. Mem. Niagara Falls Tchrs., N.Y. State United Tchrs., Am. Fedn. Tchrs., Alpha Kappa Delta. Democrat. Lutheran. Club: College. Home: 459 Chicora Rd Lewiston NY 14092

KING, CORETTA SCOTT (MRS. MARTIN LUTHER KING JR.), lectr., writer, concert singer; b. Marion, Ala., Apr. 27, 1927; d. Obidiah and Bernice McMurray) Scott; A.B., Antioch Coll., 1951; Mus.B., New Eng. Conservatory Music, 1954, Mus. D., 1971; L.H.D., Boston U., 1969, Marymount Manhattan Coll., 1969, Morehouse Coll., 1970; H.H.D., Brandeis U., 1969, Wilberforce U., 1970, Bethune-Cookman Coll., 1970, Princeton, 1970; LL.D., Bates Coll., 1971; m. Martin Luther King, Jr., June 18, 1953 (dec. Apr. 1968); children—Yolanda Denise, Martin Luther III, Dexter Scott, Bernice Albertine. Concert debut, Springfield, Ohio, 1948, numerous concerts throughout U.S.; concerts India, 1959; performances Freedom Concert; voice instr. Morris Brown Coll., Atlanta, 1962; lectr., writer. Del. to White House Conf. on Children and Youth, 1960; sponsor Sane Nuclear Policy, Com. on Responsibility, Inc., Moblzn. to End War in Viet Nam, 1966, 67, Margaret Sanger Meml. Found.; pres. Martin Luther King Jr. Meml. Center for Social Change, 1968—, comentator Cable News Network, 1980—, Martin Luther King Found., co-chairperson Nat. Com. for Full Employment; mem. exec. bd. Nat. Health Ins. Com.; mem. So. Rural Action, Inc.; bd. dirs. So. Christian Leadership Conf., Martin Luther King Jr. Found. Gt. Britain; trustee Robert F. Kennedy Meml. Center, Ebenezeer Baptist Ch. Recipient Outstanding Citizenship award Montgomery (Ala.) Improvement Assn., 1959, Merit award St. Louis Argus, 1960, Woman of Year award Utility Club N.Y.C., 1962, Distinguished Achievement award Nat. Orgn. Colored Women's Clubs, 1962, 73, Louise Waterman Wise award Am. Jewish Congress Women's Aux., 1963, Myrtle Wreath award Cleve. Hadassah, 1965, Wateler Peace prize, 1968, Martin Luther King Meml. medal City Coll. N.Y., numerous others; named Woman of Year, Nat. Assn. Radio and TV Announcers, 1968. Mem. Nat. Council Negro Women (ann. Brotherhood award 1957), Women Strike for Peace (del. disarmament conf. Geneva, Switzerland 1962, citation for work in peace and freedom 1963), Women's Internat. League for Peace and Freedom, United Ch. Women (bd. mgrs.), Links, Inc. (Human Dignity and Human Rights award Norfolk chpt. 1964), Alpha Kappa Alpha (hon). Baptist (mem. choir, guild adviser). Author: My Life With Martin Luther King, Jr., 1969. Contbr. articles to mags. Address: care Press Relations Cable News Network 1050 Techwood Dr NW Atlanta GA 30318*

KING, DENISE MARIE, township official; b. Johnstown, Pa., Aug. 3, 1952; d. Francis Xavior and Elizabeth (Roscoe) K. B.S., Pa. State U., 1974; postgrad. Syracuse U., 1980, Rutgers U., 1983—. Swimming instr., counselor Pa. State U., State Coll., 1971-73; lifeguard, naturalist Pa. State Parks, Milroy, 1972-74; recreation supr., Princeton Twp. and Borough, Princeton, N.J., 1974-81; recreation dir. South Brunswick Twp., Monmouth Junction, N.J., 1981—; pres. Damian Inc., Princeton, N.J., 1980-83. Contbr. articles to profl. jours. Sec. Princeton Commn. on Aging, 1983-84, sec. treas., 1985. Recipient Harvey Inman Meml. award Central East Jersey Basketball Official, 1985. Mem. N.J. Recreation and Parks Assn. (exec. mem., sec. 1974-75), Women's Opportunities Com. (chmn. 1973-75), Princeton Women's Network, Princeton Jaycees (v.p. 1978-79), Middlesex C. of C. Roman Catholic. Club: Princeton Ski (sailing chmn. 1985—). Home: 364 Franklin Ave Princeton NJ 08540 Office: South Brunswick Recreation Dept Mcpl Bldg Monmouth Junction NJ 08852

KING, EMMA LOVICK, home economics administrator, educator, counselor, consultant; b. Pantego, N.C.; d. Granver Reginald and Sara (Clark) Lovick; m. Eddie Hubert King, June 9, 1958. B.S., N.C. Central U., Durham, 1948; M.S., Howard U., 1970; M.S., Catholic U., 1970, postgrad., 1978. Dietitian, N.Y.C. Hosp., N.Y.C., 1948-50; Tchr. Beaufort County Sch., Pantego, N.C., 1950-68, Sr. High Sch., Washington, 1969-78; asst. dir. D.C. Schs., Washington, 1978-80, supervising dir., 1980—. Named Outstanding Tchr. Beaufort County Bd. Edn., 1967, D.C. Home Econs. Assn., 1977. Mem. Am. Home Econs. Assn., Am. Vocat. Assn., Home Econs. Edn. Assn., Nat. Assn. Minority Polit. Women, Internat. Fedn. Home Economists, Alpha Kappa Alpha. Club: Nat. Council Negro Women, Woman's Nat. Democratic. Home: 2933 W St SE Washington DC 20020

KING, GEORGIANA, government official; b. Chgo., Oct. 22, 1948; d. Della Alberta (King) O'Shogay; m. Samson Keahna, Apr. 21, 1967 (div. July 1982); children—Sean Eric, Albert Dixon, Shannon Derek; m. Gustavus Dalton; 1 child, Gustavus. B.S. in Edn., Nat. Am. Ednl. Services, Chgo., 1978. Adminstrv. asst. Am. Indian Bus. Assn., Dept. Labor, Chgo., 1978-80, manpower counselor, 1980-81, asst. dir., 1981—, exec. dir., 1983—; mem. pvt. Industry Council, Chgo., 1983—; chmn. Region V grantees Dept. Labor 1983—; vice chmn. Native Am. Outpost, Chgo., 1983—; vice chmn. Am. Indian Econ. Devel., Chgo., 1984—. Democrat. Episcopalian. Avocations: volleyball; bowling; art and crafts. Office: Am Indian Bus Assn 4753 N Broadway Suite 700 Chicago IL 60640

KING, JANET FAYE, nurse; b. Bellefontaine, Ohio, Aug. 11, 1947; d. Robert Lee and Wanda Beatrice (Shields) Swartz; diploma Community Hosp. Sch. Nursing, Springfield, Ohio, 1968; student Southwestern Okla. State U., 1979; m. Dwayne King, Jan. 11, 1969; children—Michael Dwayne, Valerie Lynn, Michelle Renee. Staff nurse Doctors Hosp., Columbus, Ohio, 1968; head nurse Southwestern Meml. Hosp., Weatherford, Okla., 1970-73; substitute clin. instr. Western Okla. Area Vocat. Tech. Sch., Burns Flat, Okla., 1973-77; asst. dir. nursing, inservice dir. Cordell Christian Home (Okla.), 1977-83; vis. nurse Am. Home Health, Cordell, 1983—, dir. patient care, 1984—. Chmn. med. personnel ARC blood drive, Burns Flat, 1977—, instr., 1979—; chmn. Am. Cancer Soc., Burns Flat; tchr. Sunday Sch., Bapt. Ch., also mem. nursery com. Mem. Young Homemakers (treas. 1975-77). Clubs: New Direction Extension (treas. 1980-81). Home: 203 Potomac St Burns Flat OK 73624 Office: Am Home Health 206 S Market St Cordell OK 73632

KING, JEAN DOSTER, advertising and public relations company executive; b. Monroe, Ga., Nov. 1, 1937; d. Jake Monroe and Flora Jean (Keith) Doster; m. David Lloyd King, Mar. 5, 1959 (div. Sept. 1962); children—Jean Christiana Whatley, Donna Carole. Student, U. Ala., 1955-58. Writer, reporter Mobile Press Register, Ala., 1963-69; dir. pub. affairs Delchamps Inc., Mobile, 1969-77; pres. Jean King & Assocs., Mobile, 1977—. Bd. dirs. Med. Clinic Bd. City Mobile, 1985—, City Mobile Pub. Parks and Recreation Bd., 1977-79, sec., 1977-79; chmn. publicity Am. Cancer Soc., South Ala., 1984; del. Nat. Vol. Leadership Conf., Ala., 1967, 69; bd. dirs., sec., treas. Nat. Found. March Dimes, Mobile, 1963-69; bd. dirs. Sr. Citizen Services Mobile County, 1977-80; active in curriculum study com. Mobile County Pub. Schs., 1978-79, Leadership Mobile, 1974; bd. dirs. Mobile Bicentennial Community Com., 1975-76. Named Pub. Relations Practitioner of Year, Pub. Relations Council Ala. 1974; Disting. Young Woman, Mobile Mobile Area Jaycettes, 1974; Outstanding Career Woman, Mobile Gayfers 1980. Mem. Pub. Relations Soc. Am., Pub. Relations Council Ala. (pres., v.p. program and arrangements, v.p. membership, sec., treas.), So. Pub. Relations Fedn. (bd. dirs.), Pub. Relations Council Mobile (pres.), Press Club Mobile, Am. Advt. Fedn., Women's Bus. Ownership Council Small Bus. Adminstrn., Am. Mktg. Assn., Sales and Mktg. Execs., Mobile Area C. of C., Nat. Assn. Press Women. Republican. Baptist. Home: 2316 E High Point Dr Mobile AL 36609 Office: Jean King and Assocs Advt 716 Oak Circle Dr Mobile AL 36609

KING, JEANNE SNODGRASS, mus. registrar; b. Muskogee, Okla., Sept. 12, 1927; d. Chester Alba and Mabel Ethel (Etheridge) Owens; student Northeastern State Coll., 1944-46, U. Okla., 1947-49; m. Morris Eugene King, Apr. 16, 1977. Curator, asst. dir. Philbrook Art Center, Tulsa, 1955-68; mng. editor Ednl. Dimensions, Inc., Shaker Heights, Ohio, 1969-71; registrar Thomas Gilcrease Inst. Am. History and Art, Tulsa, 1973—; researcher, lectr. in field; art cons.; juror art competitions. Recipient award Indian Arts and Crafts Bd., Dept. Interior, Washington, 1966. Mem. Am. Assn. Mus., Native Am. Art History Assn. Author: American Indian Painters, A Biographical Directory, 1968; (catalogs) Native American Painting, 1981, Fred Beaver & Solomon McCombs/Meml. Exhibn., 1981; coordinator, author Oscar Howe Retrospective Exhbn. Catalog, 1982; contbr. articles to mags. Home: 3931 S Madison Tulsa OK 74105 Office: 1400 Gilcrease Museum Rd Tulsa OK 74127

KING, JOAN CARNAHAN, account executive, publisher, communications consultant; b. Pitts.; d. J. Lloyd and Eva Ferne (Riddle) Carnahan; B.A., Westminster Coll.; children by previous marriage—Peter John Koenig, Christina Joan Koenig. Researcher, Ketchum, McLeod & Grove Advt., Pitts.; copywriter Joseph Horne Co., Pitts., 1954-59; community relations ofcl. Coll. of DuPage, Glen Ellyn, Ill., 1973-76; assoc. dir. devel., public relations Meml. Hosp. of DuPage County, Elmhurst, Ill., 1976-79; pub. Memo, Women in Mgmt. mag.; account exec. AGA. Mem. Women in Mgmt. (nat. pres.-elect, dir.), Fashion Group, Chgo. Assn. Direct Mktg. Address: 1030 N State St 40-H Chicago IL 60610

KING, JOAN HONE, writer, art dealer, book researcher, editor; b. N.Y.C., Nov. 27, 1929; d. John Hone and Frederica (Stevens) Auerbach; cert. of studies Inst. Polit. Scis., Paris, 1950; B.A. cum laude, Bryn Mawr Coll., 1951; m. Nicholas LeRoy King, Feb. 19, 1955; children—Sarah, Bayard, Ledyard. Ledyard; m. Cass Canfield, Aug. 30, 1984. Cons. J. Walter Thompson, Paris, 1951-52; researcher, librarian Time-Life Inc., Paris, 1952-54; mgr. Ohrbach Dept. Store, N.Y.C., 1956-57, housing locator Am. embassy, Paris, 1963-69; spl. asst. for book and art research to Cass Canfield, Harper & Row, N.Y.C., 1971—; art dealer, N.Y.C., 1973—; cons. in field. Active fund raising Bryn Mawr Coll., 1970-72, Sr. Citizens' Center, Newport, R.I., 1975. Mem. Colonial Dames Am. Club: Byrn Mawr Club (N.Y.C.). Republican. Episcopalian. Illustrator: The Incredible Pierpont Morgan (Cass Canfield), 1974; researcher, illustrator: Sam Adam's Revolution, 1976; Outrageous Fortunes, 1980; author: Passages: The Iron Will of Jefferson Davis, 1978; Noni and Other Stories, 1983; author hist. and fictional works. Home and Office: 960 Park Ave New York NY 10028

KING, JOY LA SHRYELL, music educator; b. Pittsburg, Tex., June 19, 1954; d. Leroy and Mary Jo (Chappell) Jenkins; m. Robert Irvin King, Dec. 16, 1978. B.S. in Music, Bishop Coll., 1978; M.Ed., Prairie View U., 1982. Tchr. music Dallas Ind. Sch. Dist., 1978—; dir. choir Winneka Sch. Dist., Dallas, 1983—. Mem. Gamma Sigma Sigma. Baptist. Home: 2703 Garapan Dr Dallas TX 75224

KING, JOYCE CALISTRI, columnist; b. Charleroi, Pa., May 26, 1927; d. Jeremiah James and Vera Colette (Hurley) Calistri; m. William Louis King, II, Dec. 22, 1951; children—Mari Joyce, William Louis, III, Donald II. B.A., U. Pa. Coll. for Women, 1949. Tchr. Romper Room TV, WTPA-TV, Harrisburg, Pa., 1954-55, WGAL-TV, Lancaster, Pa., 1956-57; hostess, producer Joyce King Show, WHP-TV, Harrisburg, Pa., 1959-60; sta. mgr. WSUB-TV Cable, Shillington, Pa., 1969-70; publicity dir. Bavarian Festival, Barnesville, Pa., 1974-76; wine columnist Reading Eagle, Reading, Pa., 1978—; feature writer Reading Eagle, 1978—; freelance columnist newspapers, mags., 1972—; student activities dir. Reading Hosp. Sch. Nursing, Reading, Pa., 1965-69; newsletter editor Young Republicans, Harrisburg, Pa., 1949-50, AAUW, 1955-56; dir. publicity Green Hills Theatre, Reading, Pa., 1963-67. Scholar, Am. Legion, U. Pa., 1945. Mem. Am. Women Radio and TV (pres. 1960), AAUW (v.p. 1955). Republican. Roman Catholic. Home: 2624 Whittier Ave Sinking Spring PA 19608 Office: Reading Eagle 345 Penn St PO Box 582 Reading PA 19603

KING, JUDITH MARY, insurance executive; b. Seattle, May 22, 1934; d. Herbert Twinam and Theresa Rose (Parsons) King; m. David E. King, May 29, 1959; children—Thomas Herbert, Theresa Ann, Julia Louise. B.A. in Communications, U. Wash., 1956. Cert. ins. counselor; cert. profl. ins. agent. Reporter Seattle Times, 1956-57; dir. women's news Longacres, Inc., Seattle, 1957-58; from agent to pres. King Ins., Inc., Seattle, 1958—. Contbr. features to Seattle Times. Rep. precinct committeeman, Bellevue, Wash., 1980—. Named Gold Miner, Safeco Ins. Co., 1966-67; Mem. Ins. Agents and Brokers, Profl. Ins. Agents (ednl. com. State of Wash. 1984—), Women's Entrepreneurs Network (bd. dirs. 1984-85, Achievement award 1985), Women Bus. Owners (bd. dirs. 1984-85), Am. Bus. Womens Assn. (pres. 1982-83). Firemark Soc. Profl. Ins. Agents (life mem.), Chi Omega Sorority. Presbyterian. Clubs: Seattle Tennis (flight capt. 1985); Bellevue Athletic (ladies day com. 1982-83). Avocations: skiing; swimming; travel. Home: 1718 W Lake Sammamish Rd SE Bellevue WA 98008 Office: King Ins Inc 845 103d St NE Bellevue WA 98004

KING, JUDY REBECCA, public relations executive, sales consultant; b. Birmingham, Ala., Sept. 20, 1941; d. Rolfe Kermet Sr. and Gertrue Phedorah (Fuller) Levens; m. Robert Eugene King, July 19, 1963 (dec.); 1 dau., Trudy Pauline. A.A. in Psychology, S. Tex. Jr. Coll., 1972; B.A. in Polit. Sci., History, Houston Bapt. U., 1976. Sales cons. Mary Kay Cosmetics, Houston, 1978-79; mktg. rep. Enhance Corp., Houston, 1979-80; pres. J & J Distbrs., Houston, 1980-82; pub. relations rep., sales cons. Dranguet-Helmer, Inc., Houston, 1982—. Vol. Nat. Cancer Soc., Houston, 1977, March of Dimes, Houston, 1975; chmn. library, pub. schs. Houston, 1973, chmn. sci. dept., 1981. Served with USN, 1960-63. Recipient Pioneer award Bloodonor Programs, Inc., Houston, 1979; sales and leadership awards, Mary Kay Cosmetics, 1978, Pacesetter Achievement award, 1979; Gunnell Leadership award Enhance Corp., 1980. Mem. Nat. Assn. Female Execs. Republican. Methodist. Office: Dranguet Helmer Inc 9701 Forum Park Dr Houston TX 77036

KING, KATHLEEN, chamber of commerce executive; b. Endicott, N.Y., Sept. 21, 1956; d. Richard Francis and Maureen (Beale) K. Student NYU, 1976-78, Drexel U., 1974-76, George Mason U., 1985—. Data processing adminstr. Amstar Corp., N.Y.C., 1975-78; tech. writer Parsons, Brinckerhoff, Quade & Douglas, N.Y.C., 1978-79; tech. rep. Compuer Usage Co., Sunnyvale, Calif., 1979-81; systems engr. Computer Network Co., Washington, 1981-82; staff systems analyst Satellite Bus. Systems, McLean, Va., 1982-84; mgr. tech. support services C. of C. of U.S., Kensington, Md., 1984—. Mem. Nat. Assn. Female Execs., Nat. Office Adv. Panel. Democrat. Roman Catholic. Avocations: needlepoint; horseback riding; French language. Office: Chamber of Commerce of US 4940 Nicholson Ct Kensington MD 20895

KING, KATHY ANN, accountant, banker; b. Jellico, Tenn., Aug. 3, 1954; d. James Curtis and Martha Kathleen (Slaven) K.; m. Thomas J. Nelis, Sept. 3, 1983. B.S., U. Ky., 1975. C.P.A., Ga. Sr. auditor Coopers & Lybrand, Atlanta, 1975-78; sr. acct. Sangamo Weston, Atlanta, 1978-79; asst. v.p., group mgr. Citizens & So. Ga. Crp., Atlanta, 1979-82; asst. v.p., dir. internal audit Fed. Home Loan Bank Atlanta, 1982—; vol. instr. seminars Inst. Internal Auditors, Altamonte Springs, Fla., 1982—; v.p., dir. Care & Share, Atlanta, 1982. Bd. dirs. Ga. chpt. Epilepsy Found. Am., Atlanta, 1984—. U. Ky. scholar, 1971-75. Mem. Ga. Exec. Womens Network (dir. 1983—, treas. 1984-85), Ga. Soc. C.P.A.s (exec. com. chpt. 1983—, chmn. membership com. 1983—), Am. Inst. C.P.A.s, Inst. Internal Auditors, Fin. Mgrs. Soc. Democrat. Roman Catholic. Clubs: Atlanta Ski, Atlanta Ballet Soc., High Mus. Art. Office: Fed Home Loan Bank Atlanta 260 Peachtree St Atlanta GA 30303

KING, LAURA JANE, librarian, genealogist; b. Pemberville, Ohio, Jan. 19, 1947; d. Richard D. and Jessie Florence (Brown) Zepernick; B.A., Bowling Green (Ohio) State U., 1969, M.Ed., 1976; m. Bruce William King, June 17, 1972; 1 son, Christian Andrew. County extension agt. home econs. Ohio Coop. Extension Service, Paulding County, 1970-77; librarian Pemberville Pub. Library; mem. PRIDE com., vocat. home econs. dept. Paulding Exempted Village, 1975—; instr. genealogy Office Continuing Edn., Bowling Green State U. Mem. Paulding County Bicentennial Commn., 1975-77; organist 1st Presbyn. Ch., Pemberville, ruling elder, ch. historian. Recipient Tenure award Coop. Extension Service, 1975; cert. geneal. record searcher. Mem. Wood County Hist. Soc., Ohio Geneal. Soc. (pres. Wood County chpt. 1978-80, chmn. public relations chmn. 1982-83, chmn. First Families of Wood County com.), Berks County Geneal. Soc., Va.-N.C. Piedmont Geneal. Soc., Palatines to Am., Pa. German Soc., DAR (vice regent chpt. 1975-77, regent 1979-83; state vice chmn. pages 1978-80, state chmn. lineage research 1980—, state and div. outstanding jr. mem. 1980, state chmn. membership commn., state chmn. membership commn. 1983—), U.S. Daus. of 1812, First Families Ohio, Daus. Union Vets., Nat. Soc. Magna Charta Dames, Colonial Dames 17th Century, Daus. Am. Colonists (chpt. regent 1986—), Bus. and Profl. Women's Club (pres. Paulding 1975-76, v.p. 1974-75), Colonial Order Crown of Charlemagne, Phi Upsilon Omicron. Club: Order Eastern Star. Corr. docent DAR Mus., Washington. Home: 14553 N River Rd Pemberville OH 43450

KING, LAVONNA MAE, bank executive; b. Bowling Green, Ky., Aug. 14, 1953; d. Euthon Christy and Helen Marie (Cardwell) Watts; m. Cecil Walton King, June 30, 1972; children—Robert Brian, Emily Marie. Student, Western Ky. U., 1972-75. Mem. staff Am. Nat. Bank, Bowling Green, Ky., 1972-78, asst. cashier and asst. mgr. customer service, 1978—. Mem. bd. dirs. United Cerbral Palsy, South Central Ky., 1978-84, pres., 1979; chmn. Commn. Handicapped Children, Ky., 1985—. Democrat. Baptist. Avocations: cross stitch; crochet; knitting; racquetball. Home: 5974 Richpond Rd Bowling Green KY 42101 Office: Am Nat Bank PO Box 718C Bowling Green KY 42101

KING, LEATHA VANCE, designer; b. Los Angeles; d. Quinn Marion and Mable Krien (McBride) Vance; A.A. in Fashion Design, Los Angeles Trade Tech. Coll., 1961, cert. in photography, 1963; B.S. in Psychology, Calif. State U., 1972; children—Ruby Carol, Adrian, William, Ronald, Katriena, Katauna. Vocat. nurse White Meml. Hosp., Los Angeles, 1951-53; jewelry appraiser Watts Jewelry and Loan, Los Angeles, 1958-63; tchr., dir. playground Gompers Jr. High Sch., Los Angeles, 1963-69; tchr. Saugus (Calif.) Sch. Dist., 1976-81; designer Laur's, Semi Valley, Calif., 1981—; tchr. Calif. State U., Northridge, 1986—; ptnr. Corner Boys TV, Los Angeles, 1976-81. Vice pres. West Valley Democratic Coalition, 1979-81, mem. exec. bd. Nat. Women's Polit. Caucus, 1979-81; mem. Los Angelinos, 1974-81; mem. 1984 Olympic Com. active Cancer Soc., Sickle Cell Anemia, Arthritis Found., others; vol. ARC, Emergency Hosp. Mem. NAACP (exec. bd.), Nat. Assn. Female Execs., Canoga Park Urban League. Club: West Valley Christian Woman's. Home: 21913 Gresham St Canoga Park CA 91304 Office: 7331 Owensmouth St Suite A-6 Canoga Park CA 91303

KING, LIS SONDER, public relations executive; b. Roskilde, Denmark; came to U.S., 1956, naturalized, 1961; d. Carl Otto and Gerda Vohnsen (Soender) Petersen; grad. Roskilde Katedralskole; m. T.A. Pace; 1 dau., Dorte King. Feature writer Berlingske Tidende, Copenhagen, 1956-58, reporter, editor Moreau Pub. Co., Bloomfield, N.J., 1957-59; reporter, editor St. Thomas (V.I.) Daily News, Island Times, San Juan, P.R., 1962-63, Advance, Dover, N.J., 1963-64; v.p. pub. relations Keyes, Martin & Co., Springfield, N.J., 1964-69; pres. Lis King Pub. Relations, Mahwah, N.J., 1969—. Mem. Internat. Platform Assn., Nat. Home Fashions League. Author: St. Thomas Directory, 1961; Furniture: Make-Do, Make-over, Make Your Own, 1977; contbr. articles to various publs. Address: 30 Dundee Ct Box 725 Mahwah NJ 07430

KING, LYNDA ANNE WHITLOW, psychologist, educator; b. Danville, Va., Aug. 7, 1947; d. Detlef F. and Doris F. (Van Hook) Whitlow; student Coll. of William and Mary, 1965-67; B.S., U. Md., 1969; M.A., U. Washington, 1975, Ph.D., 1979; m. Daniel Walter King, Nov. 29, 1969. Research asst. Bur. of Sch. Service and Research, U. Washington, Seattle, 1975-76, research asso., 1976-77; instr. City Coll., Seattle, 1976-78; asst. prof. psychology Central Mich. U., Mt. Pleasant, 1979-83, assoc. prof., 1983—. Vol., ARC, 1981—. Served with Nurse Corps, U.S. Army, 1969-72. R.N., Wash. Mem. Am. Ednl. Research Assn., Midwestern Psychol. Assn., Common Cause, Phi Delta Kappa, Sigma Theta Tau, Phi Kappa Phi. Contbr. articles on psychology to profl. jours. Home: 500 Cedar Dr Mount Pleasant MI 48858 Office: Sloan Hall Central Mich Univ Mount Pleasant MI 48859

KING, MARCIA, librarian; b. Lewiston, Maine, Aug. 4, 1940; d. Daniel Alden and Clarice Evelyn (Curtis) Barrell; B.S., U. Maine, 1965; M.S.L.S., Simmons Coll., 1967; m. Howard P. Lowell, Feb. 15, 1969 (div. 1980); m. 2d, Richard G. King, Jr., Aug. 1980. Reference, field advisory and bookmobile librarian Maine State Library, Augusta, 1965-69; dir. Lithgow Public Library, Augusta, 1969-72; exec. sec. Maine Library Adv. Com., Maine State Library, 1972-73; dir. Wayland (Mass.) Free Public Library, 1973-76; state librarian State of Oreg., Salem, 1976-82; dir. Tucson Public Library, 1982—. Bd. dirs., sec. Tucson United Way; mem. KUAT adv. bd. com. PBS-TV and Radio. Mem. ALA, Pub. Library Assn., Ariz. State Library Assn., Assn. Specialized and Coop. Library Agys., Exec. Women's Council So. Ariz., Tucson C. of C. Unitarian. Address: Tucson Public Library 110 E Pennington PO Box 27470 Tucson AZ 85726

KING, MARJORIE SOMMERLYN, medical photographer; b. Conway, S.C., June 22, 1925; s. Bernard St. Lawrence and Mary Essie (Lupo) Sommerlyn; student Coker Coll., 1943-45; m. John L. King, Jan. 11, 1945; children—John Bernard, William Lawrence, Mary Elizabeth. Photopprinter for editor bus. pages Miami Daily News, 1954; owner, operator King's Portrait Studio, Conway, S.C., 1956-58; clk. bacteriol. lab. Jackson Meml. Hosp., Miami, 1963-65; photo lab. technician biomed. communications dept. U. Miami Med. Sch., 1965-67, photo lab. technician II, 1967-70, photographer III trainee, 1970-72, photographer III, 1973-76, photographer III supr., 1977-80; ret., 1985; owner M.S. King Enterprises, 1985—. Den mother Boy Scouts Am. Recipient Golden Key award Boy Scouts Am., 1957. Mem. Biol. Photog. Assn., DAR, UDC. Democrat. Episcopalian. Clubs: Miami Yacht, Coconut Grove Sailing (C gull pres.), West End Pool Aquatic (pres.). Home: 8035 SW 17th St Miami FL 33155 Office: PO Box 520875 Miami FL 33152

KING, MARY FRANCES GOOCH, nursing executive; b. Fredericksburg, Va., Dec. 28, 1925; d. Mercer Ray and Agnes Moncure (Brooks) Gooch; m. Robert Patrick King, Mar. 29, 1945; 1 child, Agnes Ann King Norris. Diploma in nursing, Sibley Meml. Hosp., 1945; B.S. in Psychology, Old Dominion Coll., 1965; M. Ed., Va. Poly. Inst., 1970; Ed.D., Va. Poly. Inst. and State U., 1976. Cert. R.N. Vol. sch. nurse Navy Dependents Sch., Naples, Italy, 1961-64; nursing instr. Norfolk City Schs., Va., 1965-69; nursing coordinator Kapiolani

Community Coll., Honolulu, 1970-72; vocat. edn. supr. State Dept. Edn., Richmond, Va., 1972-74; health occupations coordinator Richmond Pub. Schs., 1975-77; dir. nursing Bremerton Kitsap Health Dept., Wash., 1978—; 2d v.p. Hawaii League Nursing, Honolulu, 1971-72; cons. Maui Community Coll., Hawaii, 1971; co.-dir. health edn. curriculum project Va. Poly. Inst. and State U., Blacksburg, 1974-76; bd. dirs. Wash. Assn. Home Health Agencies, 1979. Author: (with others) On the Health Scene, 1976. V.p. Kitsap Community Action Program, Bremerton, 1985; bd. dirs. Kitsap Council Aging, Bremerton, 1979, Human Resources, Bremerton, 1980; adv. council Foster Grandparents, Bremerton, 1980. Dept. Edn. fellow 1974. Mem. Va. Assn. Vocat. Indsl. Clubs Am. (hon. life), Am. Nurses Assn., Wash. State Nurses Assn., Am. Pub. Health Assn., Wash. State Pub. Health Assn. Episcopalian. Avocations: sewing; spinning; tole painting. Home: 4829 NW Eldorado Blvd Bremerton WA 98312 Office: Bremerton Kitsap County Health Dept 109 Austin Dr Bremerton WA 98312

KING, MICHALENE ANN, nursing educator; b. Wheeling, W.Va., Sept. 28, 1951; d. Michael James and Elizabeth Dorothy (Kovalan) Matuska; m. George Thomas King, Oct. 26, 1974; 1 dau., Lisa. Diploma in nursing, Ohio Valley Hosp., 1972; B.S.N., West Liberty State Coll., 1980; M.S. in Edn., U. Dayton (Ohio), 1983; postgrad. in nursing, W.Va. U. Staff nurse Ohio Valley Hosp., Steubenville, 1971-82, mem. nursing faculty, 1982—. Mem. Am. Nurses Assn., Ohio Nurses Assn. Democrat. Roman Catholic. Home: 142 Susan Dr Wintersville OH 43952 Office: Ohio Valley Hosp Sch Nursing 380 Summit Ave Steubenville OH 43952

KING, PATRICIA, training consultant; b. Paterson, N.J., Mar. 17, 1941; d. Salvatore Francesco and Anna Marie (Pisacane) Puglise; A.B., Coll. St. Elizabeth, 1963; m. David Jay Clark, Sept. 7, 1974; 1 child, Kerry Ann King. With Equitable Life Assurance Soc., N.Y.C., 1963-65; personnel officer Bankers Trust Co., N.Y.C., 1965-72; founder, pres. Patricia King Assocs., N.Y.C., 1972—. Mem. Nat. Orgn. Italian-Am. Women (nat. bd. dirs.). Author: Perform-Planning and Appraisal; Mind to Disk to Paper: Business Writing on a Word Processor; (with others) The New Secretary: How to Get Respect, Rewards, Recognition; contbg. author: Affirmative Action for Women. Office: 243 Waverly Pl New York NY 10014

KING, PATRICIA MILLER, librarian; b. July 26, 1937, N.Y.C. A.B. in History, Radcliffe Coll., 1959, M.A., 1961; Ph.D. in History, Harvard U., 1970. Teaching fellow Harvard Coll., 1965-67, 68-70; asst. prof. Wellesley Coll., 1970-71; dir. research Haney Assocs., Inc., 1971-73; dir. Arthur and Elizabeth Schlesinger Library on History of Women in Am., Radcliffe Coll., Cambridge, Mass., 1973—. Mem. ALA, Am. Antiquarian Soc., New Eng. Archivists, Nat. Council Research on Women (bd. dirs.), Am. Hist. Assn., Berkshire Conf. Women Historians, Mass. Hist. Soc., Orgn. Am. Historians, Phi Beta Kappa. Address: Schlesinger Library Radcliffe Coll 10 Garden St Cambridge MA 02138*

KING, PEGGY SUE, banking officer; b. Marengo, Iowa, Dec. 25, 1950; d. Marvin Clark and Eunice Mildred (Jordan) Morse; B.A. magna cum laude in History, Trinity Coll., Deerfield, Ill., 1973; M.A. in European History, U. Iowa, Iowa City, 1974; M.B.A., Drake U., 1983; m. Merrill Jack King, June 26, 1976. Asst. head teller Iowa-Des Moines Nat. Bank, 1975-77; head teller Bankers Trust Co., Des Moines, 1979, consumer banker, 1980, asst. mng. officer, 1981—, mng. officer, 1982-83; comml. loan officer United Fed. Savs. Bank, Des Moines, 1983—. Mem. Nat. Assn. Bank Women, C. of C. Greater Des Moines, Nat. Assn. Profl. Saleswomen. Home: 1070 35th St Des Moines IA 50311 Office: Locus at 4th St Des Moines IA 50309

KING, RACHEL HADLEY, educator; b. Leavenworth, Kans., Apr. 27, 1904; d. Frank Campbell and Georgianna May (Brackett) King; B.A., Smith Coll., 1926; M.A., U. Chgo., 1927, U. Colo., 1931; Ph.D., Yale, 1937. Bible tchr., then head dept. Northfield (Mass.) Sch. Girls, 1928-31, 35-66; tchr. English, Kobe Coll., Japan, 1937-38; adj. prof. Bibl. studies Barrington (R.I.) Coll., 1972-85; vol. tchr. underprivileged children N.Y.C. Pub. Schs., summers 1969-71. Mem. Kobe Coll. Corp., 1960—; alumni council Yale Div. Sch., 1968-75. Recipient citation Council Religion in Ind. Schs., 1967. Mem. Am. Acad. Religion, Nat. Assn. Bible Instrs. (chmn. curriculum com. 1946-64), Am. Sch. Oriental Research, So. Bibl. Lit. Presbyterian. Author: George Fox and The Light Within 1650-1660, 1940; God's Boycott of Sin, 1946; Theology You Can Understand, 1956; The Omission of the Holy Spirit from Reinhold Neibuhr's Theology, 1964; The Creation of Death and Life, 1970. Home: The 60 Broadway Providence RI 02903

KING, REGINA ROBINSON, special education teacher; b. Crawfordsville, Ind., Dec. 11, 1947; d. Andrew Joseph and Jasmine (Ernest) Robinson; m. Tommy Sherwin King, June 25, 1983. B.A.E., Roosevelt U., 1977; postgrad. San Francisco State U., 1984—. Cert. spl. edn. tchr., Ill., Calif. Tchr. spl. edn. Chgo. Bd. Edn., 1977-83, San Francisco Unified Sch. Dist., 1983—. Mem. San Francisco Com. to Elect Jessie Jackson, 1984. Mem. Calif. Assn. Exceptional Children, Calif. Assn. Neurologically Handicapped Children, Nat. Assn. Female Execs., Cernitin Am. Tng. Leadership Council (sec.-treas. 1985—). Democrat. Baptist. Avocations: reading; roller skating; swimming; jogging; weight lifting. Office: Golden Gate Elem Sch 1601 Turk St San Francisco CA 94115

KING, ROSALIE ALICE, city official; b. Hurley, Wis., Mar. 1, 1936; d. John and Velia Thersa (Piazza) Grandelis; m. Kenton James King, Aug. 26, 1967; children—Thomas, David, Patricia, Rebecca. Grad. high sch., Hurley. Laborer Ottowa Wood Products, Caspian, Mich., 1975-76; clk., mgr. Caspian IGA, 1976-78; city clk. City of Caspian, 1978-79, city mgr., 1979—. Named Woman of Yr. County Bd., 1980. Mem. Caspian Ch. Choir, Northland Chorus. Roman Catholic. Home: 6 Berkshire Ave Box 273 Caspian MI 49915 Office: City Hall Caspian MI 49915

KING, ROSALIE ROSSO, educator; b. Tacoma, May 22, 1938; d. Stanley and Gertrude Emma (Conrad) Rosso; B.S., U. Wash., 1960, Ph.D., 1975; M.Ed., Mass. State Coll., Framingham, 1965; m. Indle Gifford King, Sept. 10, 1960; children—Indle Gifford, Paige Phyllis. Product devel. Lyndens (Wash.) State Coop., 1960; home economist Seattle Times, 1961; acad. adv. U. Wash., Seattle, 1965-67, asso. and lectr., 1967-75, chmn. div. textile sci. and costume studies, 1975-83; chmn. dept. home econs. Western Wash. State Coll., Bellingham, 1983—; mem. flammable fabrics adv. com. Consumer Product Safety Commn., 1977-79; cons. textile flammability litigation. Pres., Mercer Island Sch. PTA, 1972-73; active Cub Scouts, Girl Scouts. Denney fellow, 1973-74. Mem. Am. Assn. Textile Chemists and Colorists, ASTM, Am. Chem. Soc., Nat. Assn. Coll. Profs. Textiles and Clothing, Fashion Group, Pi Beta Phi, Omicron Nu (nat. v.p. 1978-80, nat. pres. 1981-83), Clubs: Women's Univ., U. Wash. Faculty (dir.). Contbr. articles to profl. jours.; participant fiber art exhbns. Home: 5075 W Mercer Way Mercer Island WA 98040 Office: 560 Old Main Western Wash U Bellingham WA 98225

KING, RUBY THOMPSON, educator, club woman; b. nr. Wrightsville, Ga.; d. Charles D. and Maude (Douglas) Thompson; student S. Ga. Coll.; B.A., Scarritt Coll., M.A.; postgrad. George Peabody Coll. Tchrs., U. Ga., Fla. State U., U. Edinburgh (Scotland); m. Seabron Larry King. Tchr. English, Brunswick, Ga.; tchr. Lowndes County Ga.; tchr. English, Coffee County (Ga.) high schs., 1966—. Conf. sec. missionary personnel Woman's Soc. Christian Service; active numerous local fund drives; coordinator Wesleyan Service Guild; 8th Dist. Sci. Fair committeewoman; sponsor Young Teens; charter mem. Tri-Hi-Y Internat., chmn. convocation; field rep. World Field Research, Inc.; editor Ga. Bull. Dir. Thompson-King Found.; trustee Florence Crittendon Home, Savannah, Ga.; mem. Pub. Library Bd.; White House appointment Nat. Traffic Safety Council, Washington; staff Am. Research Bur., Inc. state news reporter Atlanta Jour.; mem. Macon Music Chorus. Named Star Tchr., Ga. C. of C.; Douglas Citizen of Year for distinguished community service; Albert Schweitzer fellow. Mem. Home Demonstration Council So. Ga., Conf. Hist. Soc., Ga. Edn. Assn. (county chmn. pub. relations), NEA, Am. Soc. Psychical Research, Ga. Assn. Edn., Nat. Assn. English Tchrs., UDC, Internat. Platform Assn., Internat., Am. assns. univ. women, D.A.R., Philharmonic Club, Nat. Heritage Commn. Preservation Hist. Shrines, Nat. Council Tchrs. English, Am. Security Council, Canterbury Cathedral Assn., Nat. Shrine/Hist. Trust Preservation, Thespian Soc., Scarritt Alumni Club. Methodist. Clubs: Order Eastern Star, Garden Study; Fine Arts, Woman's Garden Guild. Author: History of Historic Ebenézer Methodist Church, 1800-1984; author poetry pub. in Am. Anthology of Verse, Nat. Anthology Poetry, Quaderni di Poesia, Anthology of Internat. Poetry; contbr. to poetry jours. in U.S., Scotland, Eng. and Italy. Address: 111 N Gaskin Ave Douglas GA 31533

KING, RUTH ALLEN, management consultant; b. Providence, Oct. 8, 1910; d. Arthur S. and Wilhelmina H. (Harmon) Allen; grad. Tefft Bus. Inst., Providence, 1929; 1 dau., Phyllis King Dunham. Sec. to atty., Providence, 1929; stenographer N.Y. Urban League, N.Y.C., 1929; with Nat. Urban League, 1929-75, asst. dir. placement services New Nat. Skills Bank, to 1975; cons. to chmn. EEOC, Washington, 1976; minority relations cons. Hazeltine Corp., Greenlawn, L.I., N.Y., 1976—; cons. to sr. v.p. Sony Corp. Am., 1980—; mgmt. cons., Bklyn., 1976—. Founder, sec. THE EDGES GROUP, INC., 1969—. Named Affirmative Action Pioneer, Met. N.Y. Project Equality, 1975; Ruth Allen King Scholarship Fund established, 1970; EDGES Ruth Allen King Ann. Excalibur award established, 1978; recipient Ann Tanneyhill award for commitment to Urban League Movement, 1975; Recognition award NCCJ, 1982; spl. citation Gov. of R.I. and Providence Plantations, 1981, citation Medgar Evers Coll., 1983; Ruth Allen King Appreciation Day proclaimed in her honor, N.Y.C., Sept. 18, 1975, Providence, Mar. 9, 1981; citation R.I. Ho. of Reps., 1981; plaque Urban League R.I., 1981; Woman of Yr. award Suffolk (N.Y.) chpt. Jack and Jill of Am., 1982; named one of top 100 black bus. and profl. women Dollars & Sense mag., 1986. Mem. N.Y. Personnel Mgmt. Assn., Council Concerned Black Execs., Julius A. Thomas Soc. (charter), NAACP (life). Home: Willoughby Walk Apts Apt 1715 185 Hall St Brooklyn NY 11205

KING, SHIRLEY ANN MIELKE, editor; b. Paulding, Ohio, June 5, 1935; d. Edward Michael John and Vanda Steiner (Schultz) Mielke; m. Lowell King, June 6, 1953 (div. Jan. 1977); children—Michael David, David Matthew. Student Ball State U., St. Francis Coll., Fort Wayne Sch. Fine Arts. Bookkeeper, Napoleon Egg Co., Albion, Ind., 1954-56, Noble County REMC, Albion, 1956-61; editor Avilla News (Ind.), 1971—. Recipient awards Avilla Jaycees, 1982, 83. Mem. Avilla C. of C. (chmn. festival 1982). Democrat. Lutheran. Home: 208 N Main Avilla IN 46710 Office: Tri-County Pub Co 209 S Main Churubusco IN 46723

KING, STEPHANIE ANN, social worker, music therapist; b. Kingsville, Tex., Mar. 12, 1950; d. Jesse and Althea Guinevere (Reese) Smith; m. Ronnie Carl King, Oct. 20, 1984; children—Nedric Harold and Norell Howard. Student in Music Therapy, Lincoln U., 1970, St. Philips Coll., 1972; B.S. in Music Therapy Tex. Woman's U., 1974; M.Ed. in Counseling, Prairie View A&M U., 1978. Supr. music therapy Timberlawn Hosp., Dallas, 1974-84; social worker Mental Health Ctr., Jacksonville, N.C., 1985—; cons. careers Middle High Sch., Dallas, 1977-84. Choir dir. St. Anthony Ch., Dallas, 1973-75; minister of music Holy Cross Ch., Dallas, 1974-77. Mem. Nat. Assn. for Music Therapy (alt. del. 1983-84), Alpha Kappa Alpha. Democrat. Roman Catholic. Avocations: piano playing; guitar; reading; hatha yoga; collecting turtles. Office: Brynn Marr Hosp 192 Village Dr Jacksonville NC 28540

KING, SUSAN M. ROBINSON, lawyer; b. Detroit, July 5, 1948; d. James Hathaway and Rose (Elliott) Robinson; m. Clinton Allen King, Aug. 16, 1969; children—Roscet Elizabeth, Marjon Robinson. B.A., Fisk U., 1970; J.D., U. Houston, 1978. Bar: Tex. 1978. Tchr., Met. Nashville pub. schs., 1970-73, Corpus Christi Ind. Schs., Tex., 1973-75; atty. Robert Hohenberger, Esq., Houston, 1980; atty./examiner Stewart Title Co., Galveston, Tex., 1980-83; title atty., examiner Susan R. King, El Paso, Tex., 1984—; tchr. Jones Coll. Real Estate, Houston, 1979-80. Coordinator Miss Black Corpus Christi Beauty Pageant, 1975; mem. nomination com., bd. dirs. YWCA, Corpus Christi, 1974-75; vol. Intervention Ctr. for Girls, 1974-75. Mem. ABA, Fisk U. Alumni Assn., El Paso County Women's Bar, Houston Lawyers Assn., Galveston County Women Attys., Delta Theta Phi, Alpha Kappa Alpha. Club: Jack and Jill of Am. Office: 1533 N Lee Trevino Suite 202 El Paso TX 79935

KING, SUZANNE SCHLITT, educational administrator; b. Berwyn, Ill., Feb. 22, 1950; d. George J. and Marian A. (Krinker) Schlitt; m. David Dewitt King, June 19, 1976. B.A., Mich. State U., 1971; M.Ed., U. N.C., 1978. Cert. tchr., adminstr. Tchr., Lansing, Mich., 1971-72, Wake County, N.C., 1972-77; chief cons. N.C. Dept. Pub. Instrn., Raleigh, 1977-79; prin. Wake County Sch. System, Raleigh, 1979-81, dir. curriculum devel., 1981-84, asst. supt.-curriculum, 1984-85, prin., 1985—. Mem. Assn. Supervsion and Curriculum Devel., N.C. Assn. Sch. Adminstrs., Phi Delta Kappa. Democrat. Methodist. Avocations: reading; tennis; swimming. Home: 1601 Beechgrove Rd Raleigh NC 27612 Office: 1018 E Davie St Raleigh NC 27601

KING, VERNA ST. CLAIR, school counselor; b. Berwick, La.; d. John Westley and Florence Ellen (Calvin) St. C.; A.B., Wiley Coll., 1937; M.A., San Diego State U., 1977; m. Alonzo Le Roy King, Aug. 27, 1939; children—Alonzo Le Roy (dec.), Joyce Laraine, Verna Lee Eugenia King Bickerstaff, St. Clair A., Reginald Calvin (dec.). Tchr., Morgan City, La., 1939-40; tchr. San Diego Unified Sch. Dist., 1955-67, parent counselor, 1967-78, counselor grades 1-9, 1978—; cons. Tucson Sch. Dist., 1977—, dir. compensatory edn., 1983—. Mem. Calif. Democratic State Central Com., 1950—, Dem. County Central Com., 1974—, del. nat. conv., 1976, 84, mem. exec. bd. Dem. State Central Com., 1982—; mem. San Diego County Sander Adv. Commn., 1982; hon. life mem. PTA; bd. dirs. YWCA, 1983—. Recipient Key to City, Mayor C. Dail, 1955, cert. United Negro Coll. Fund dr., 1980, Urban League Pvt. Sector award, 1982, 4th Ann. Conf. on Issues in Ethnicity and Mental Health Participants award, 1982; named Woman of Dedication, Salvation Army, 1985; Citizen of Yr., City Club and Jaycees, 1985; numerous other honors. Mem. NEA (women's council 1980-82), AAUW, Calif. Tchrs. Assn. (state council 1979—), San Diego Tchrs. Assn. (dir. 1958, 64, sec. 1964-67), Nat. Council Negro Women, Pres. Women, Inc., Alpha Kappa Alpha (pres. 1978-80), Delta Kappa Gamma. Methodist. Clubs: Women's Inc., Order Eastern Star. Home: 5721 Churchward St San Diego CA 92114 Office: San Diego Unified Sch Dist 2850 Logan Ave San Diego CA 92113

KING, VICTORIA VAN BEUREN, otolaryngologist; b. St. Louis, Jan. 16, 1953; d. Willard Van Beuren and Frances Howell (Lewis) K.; B.A. in Human Biology with honors, Stanford U., 1975; M.D., U. Mo., Columbia, 1979. Diplomate Am. Bd. Otolaryngology. Resident in otolaryngology Stanford U. Hosp., 1980-83, chief resident; practice medicine specializing in head and neck surgery, Palo Alto, Calif. Mem. U.S. Olympic Swimming Team, 1968, U.S. Swimming Teams to Australia, Tahiti, Can. and Eng., 1969-72. U.S. Nat. Swimming Champion, 1969; recipient award for scholastic achievement Am. Med. Women's Assn., Mem. AMA, Am. Acad. Facial Plastic and Reconstructive Surgery, Am. Acad. Otolaryngology/Head and Neck Surgery, Alpha Omega Alpha. Office: 770 Welch Rd Suite 370 Palo Alto CA 94304

KING, VIRGINIA, librarian; b. Akron, Ohio, May 12, 1917; d. Wilson Reed and Eunice Mina (White) King. B.S. in Music Edn., Greenville Coll. (Ill.), 1939, B.A., 1941; M.Music, U. So. Calif., 1954, M.S.L.S., 1967. Music tchr. Los Angeles Pacific Coll., 1943-45, 46-65, Greenville Coll. (Ill.), 1945-46; music prof. and librarian Azusa Pacific U. (Calif.), 1965-82, music and periodicals librarian, 1982—. Named Outstanding Tchr., 1975. Mem. ALA, Christian Librarians Assn., Coll. Music Soc., Choral Condrs. Guild, Music Educators Nat. Conf., Calif. Music Educators Assn., NEA, Calif. Tchrs. Assn. Office: Azusa Pacific Univ Citrus and Alosta Sts Azusa CA 91702

KING, YVONNE LEVELLE, insurance company executive; b. N.Y.C., Dec. 18, 1942; d. Granville Oliver and Mayme (Flemming) LeVell; m. Richard Alfred Kier, Sept. 8, 1962 (div. 1978); children—Richard, Roland; m. 2d Emmett Alonzo King, Oct. 19, 1980; stepchildren—Andre, Jackie. B.A. in Lang. Arts, Calif. State U.-Hayward, 1969; M.A., U. Calif.-Berkeley, 1972. Registered rep. Nat. Securities Dealers Assn. Instr., U. Calif.-Berkeley, 1970-72; edn. specialist-writer, producer Eastman Kodak, Rochester, N.Y., 1974-76; writer, cons. Hewitt Assocs., Stanford, Conn., 1977-78; planner, product mgr. Avon Products, N.Y.C., 1978-81; dir. investment products, product mgr. in pension ops. Equitable Life Assurance Soc. U.S., N.Y.C., 1982—. Awards chmn. Westport (Conn.) council Boy Scouts Am., 1981; bd. dirs., v.p. pub. affairs Tri-W-Black Families, Westport, 1981; bd. dirs., co-sec. Unity Ch. of Christ, Teaneck, N.J., 1984, v.p., 1985. Democrat. Office: Equitable Life Pension Ops 200 Plaza Dr Secaucus NJ 07094

KINGDON, LORRAINE BRADY, educational administrator; b. Minot, N.D., Feb. 11, 1927; d. Leo Frances and Margaret Amanda Brady; B.S., N.D. State U., 1948; M.S., U. Del., 1974; m. Frederick W. Kingdon, June 22, 1948 (div., 1970); children—Frederic W., Alice Marie Kingdon Labay, Susan Ellen Kingdon Lovelace, Leo F. Columnist, Newark (Del.) Weekly, 1965; public relations cons. Webb Assos., Newark, 1967; asst. agrl. editor U. Del., Newark, 1965-72; consumer info. specialist Wash. State U., Pullman, 1972-79; head dept. agrl. communications U. Ariz., Tucson, 1980—, communications instr. Farm Press Inst., Winter Sch.; communications cons. Mem. Agrl. Communicators in Edn. (regional dir. 1976-78, nat. pres. 1981, head ACTion Com. on communications tech., nat. communicators award 1971, nat. profl. award 1976), Women in Communications, Ariz. Agri-Press Club, Phi Kappa Phi. Author: Urban Opinions of Agriculture: Farm Press Institute Survey, 1970; Manual for Extension Radio Broadcasting, 1973, editor; New Directions: Proceedings National Extension Home Economics Communications Workshop, 1975; DBS-Revolution or Gamble?Office: 5 Nugent Univ Ariz Tucson AZ 85721

KING-ETTEMA, ELIZABETH DOROTHY, video and film editor, writer, photographer; b. Morristown, N.J., Sept. 29, 1953; d. James Claude and Martha Helene (Dawson) King; m. Dale Frederic Ettema, Feb. 13, 1982; children—Taylor Braam, Claire Elizabeth. B.A. in Art History, UCLA, 1975; postgrad. U. N.M., 1977-78. Writer, Bettis & Parks Advt., Albuquerque, 1975-76; bus. mgr. N.M. Ballet Co., Albuquerque, 1976-78; asst. editor Dury Assocs., Los Angeles, 1978, Another Editing Pl., Los Angeles, 1978-79, Bullywood Prodn., Los Angeles, 1979, Alan Landsburg Prodn., Los Angeles, 1980-81, Columbia TV, Los Angeles, 1982-83; video editor Am. Film Inst., Los Angeles, 1983-85. Video editor Scenario, 1984, U.S. 49/Calif. 1, 1985. Recipient scholarship UCLA Extension, 1979. Mem. Motion Picture and Videotape Editors Guild, Soc. Children's Book Writers, Internat. Documentary Assn. Democrat. Episcopalian. Club: Embroiderer's Guild of Am. (historian chpt. 1984-85). Avocations: photography, embroidery. Home and Office: 7235 Forbes Ave Van Nuys CA 91406

KING-JEFFERS, SHARON WINDSOR, lawyer; b. Chelsea, Mass., Mar. 17, 1940; d. Edward Windsor King and Mildred Bowman (Bannar) Moldenhauer; m. Leland Roland Jeffers, Apr. 20, 1968; children—Sean Edward, Lance Thomas. B.S.L., Western State U., Fullerton, Calif., 1974, J.D., 1975. Bar: Calif. 1978. Legal research supr. 1st Am. Title Ins. Co., Santa Ana, Calif., 1978-79; sole practice, Norco, Calif., 1979-80, Riverside, Calif., 1982—. Editorial staff Western State U. Law Rev., 1973-75. Trustee Chaffey Community Coll., Alta Loma, Calif., 1977-82, sec. 1977-79, v.p., 1979-80, pres., 1980-82; trustee Charter Grove Psychiat. Hosp., Corona, Calif., 1982—, pres., 1984-86; adv. bd. Charter Med. Network, 1983—; past pres. Corona Music Theater Assn.; former bd. dirs., pres., charter mem. vol. Aux. Kellogg Psychiat. Hosp., others; mem. Inland Empire Cultural Arts Found., Riverside, San Bernardino, 1983—; mem. Child Care Action Task Force, Riverside. Recipient Am. Jurisprudence award in criminal law Bancroft-Whitney Co., 1972; Calif. Legal Secs. scholar, 1973. Mem. State Bar Assn. Calif., Riverside County Bar Assn. (estate planning, probate, trust sect., fee arbitration, juvenile law coms. family law sect.), Nu Beta Epsilon. Republican. Roman Catholic. Club: Toastmasters Internat. Lodge: Soroptomists (co-chmn. intercommunity com. 1983-84, del. 1984-86). Office: 4255 Main St Suite 3 Riverside CA 92501

KINGMAN, ELIZABETH YELM, anthropology librarian; b. Lafayette, Ind., Oct. 15, 1911; d. Charles Walter and Mary Irene (Weakley) Yelm; B.A., U. Denver, 1933, M.A., 1935; m. Eugene Kingman, June 10, 1939; children—Mixie Kingman Eddy, Elizabeth Anne. Asst. in anthropology U. Denver, 1932-34; mus. asst. Ranger Naturalist Force, Mesa Verde Nat. Park, Colo., 1934-38; asst. to husband in curatorial work, Indian art exhibits Philbrook Art Center, Tulsa, 1939-42, Joslyn Art Mus., Omaha, 1947-69; tutor humanities dept. U. Omaha, 1947-50; asst. to husband in exhibit design mus. of Tex. Tech. U., 1970-75, bibliographer Internat. Center Arid and Semi-Arid Land Studies, 1974-75; librarian Sch. Am. Research, Santa Fe, 1978—; v.p. Santa Fe Corral of the Westerners, 1985-86. Mem. Archeol. Inst. Am. (v.p. Santa Fe chpt. 1981-83), N.Mex. Library Assn., LWV, Santa Fe Hist. Soc. (sec. 1981-83), Council Internat. Relations. Presbyterian. Home: 604 Sunset St Santa Fe NM 87501 Office: 660 Garcia St Santa Fe NM 87501

KING-REED, MYRTLE ELAINE, nurse; b. Hico, Tex., July 1, 1952; d. Joseph Henry and Bessie Sophia (McAnelly) King; m. George Cecil Reed, June 18, 1983. L.V.N., Stephenville Hosp., 1973; R.N., Central Tex. Coll., 1977; E.M.T., Ranger Jr. Coll., 1982. Staff nurse intensive care Hamilton Hosp. (Tex.), 1973-77, charge nurse, 1981—; nurse respiratory therapy S.W. Respiratory Care, Comanche, Tex., 1980-81; shift supr. Comanche (Tex.) Hosp., 1977-83; nurse intensive-coronary care DeLeon (Tex.) Hosp., 1983—; dir. ambulance emergency service Comanche Hosp., 1979-81, quality assurance chmn., 1981-82, dir. disaster planning, 1979-81. Fund raising mem. Comanche Ambulance Service, 1981-82, vol. ambulance attendent, 1978-83. Democrat. Baptist. Club: DeLeon Hosp. Aux.

KINGREY, CARMEN MONTEBON, educator, trucking company executive; b. Albuera, Leyte, Philippines, Nov. 15, 1948; came to U.S., 1970; d. Joe Iway and Connie (Espina) Montebon; m. Charles M. Kingrey, Aug. 3, 1970; children—Valorie, Charles, Derk, Anthony, Arabelle, Charen, Marigold, Chaene. B.S. cum laude in Edn., St. Peter's Coll., 1969; M.S. in Adminstrn. and Supervision, U. Dayton, 1980. Cert. tchr., Ohio. Tchr., Versailles Elem. Sch., Ohio, 1972—; owner C.M. Kingrey Trucking, Versailles, 1978—, Carmen's & Hers. Mem. NEA, Ohio Edn. Assn., Versailles Edn. Assn., Minority Edn. Assn. Republican. Roman Catholic. Avocations: tennis, traveling. Home: 763 E Water St Versailles OH 45380 Office: 130 W Ward St Versailles OH 45380

KINGSLEY, ELLEN, TV news reporter; b. N.Y.C., Oct. 1, 1951; d. Theodore Kingsley and Judith Kingsley Fitting; m. Robert M.A. Hirschfeld, Jan. 21, 1984. B.A., Sarah Lawrence Coll., 1973; M.A., N.Y.U., 1977. Speech writer for Elinor Guggenheimer, N.Y.C. Commr. Consumer Affairs, 1974-76, for John Sawhill, Pres. of N.Y.U., 1976-77; consumer affairs reporter, anchor WJZ-TV, Balt., 1977-80; consumer affairs reporter WDVM-TV, Washington, 1980—. Recipient World Hunger media award, 1983; Best Documentary award UPI, 1984; Consumer Journalism award Nat. Press Club, 1984; Media award Consumer Fedn. Am., 1985, others. Mem. AFTRA. Contbr. articles to newspapers, mags. Office: WDVM-TV 4001 Brandywine St NW Washington DC 20016

KING-SMITH, PAMELA DIANE, accountant; b. Washington, Nov. 21, 1958; d. Benjamin Louis and Gloria (Wood) K. B.S., Va. State U., 1980; M.S., U. Balt., 1985. Acct., King & Miller C.P.A.s, Balt., 1980-83; ptnr. King, Miller & King, C.P.A.s, Balt., 1983—. Treas. Chesapeake council Camp Fire Inc., Balt., 1984—. Am. Inst. C.P.A.s scholar, 1977-79. Mem. Nat. Assn. Black Accts., Md. State Bd. Pub. Accts., Alpha Kappa Alpha (treas. 1977-79). Democrat. Episcopalian. Home: 126 Hammershire Rd Reisterstown MD 21136 Office: King Miller & King CPAs 1509 Pennsylvania Ave Baltimore MD 21217

KINGSTON, MAXINE HONG, author; b. Stockton, Calif., Oct. 27, 1940; d. Tom and Ying Lan (Chew) Hong; B.A., U. Calif., Berkeley, 1962; m. Earll Kingston, Nov. 23, 1963; 1 son, Joseph Lawrence. Author: The Woman Warrior: Memoirs of a Girlhood Among Ghosts (Nat. Book Critics Circle award for non-fiction, 1976; cited by Time mag., N.Y. Times Book Rev. and Asian Mail as one of best books of year); China Men (Am. Book award, 1981; cited by Time mag., N.Y. Times Book Rev. and Asian Mail as one of best books of 1980); contbr. short stories, articles and poems to mags. and jours., including N.Y. Times Mag., New West, New Dawn, Hawaii Review, Viva, English Jour., Am. Girl, Ms., Am. Heritage, New Yorker, Iowa Rev.; tchr. English, Sunset

High Sch., Hayward, Calif., 1965-66, Kahuku (Hawaii) High Sch., 1967, Kahaluu (Hawaii) Drop-In Sch., 1968, Kailua (Hawaii) High Sch., 1969, Honolulu Bus. Coll., 1969, Mid-Pacific Inst., Honolulu, 1970-77; asst. prof. English, vis. writer U. Hawaii, Honolulu, 1977-80. Recipient Mademoiselle Mag. award, 1977, Anisfield-Wolf book award in race relations, 1978; Stockton (Calif.) Arts Commn. award, 1981; Calif. Council for Humanities award, 1985; NEA writing fellow, 1980; Guggenheim fellow, 1981. Living Treasure of Hawaii, 1980. Address: care Alfred A Knopf Inc 201 E 50th St New York NY 10022

KINLEIN, M(ARY) LUCILLE, nurse; b. Ellicott City, Md., Dec. 17, 1921; d. Julius Augustus and Mary Teresa (Plantholt) K.; B.A., Coll. Notre Dame, Balt., 1943; B.S. in Nursing Edn., Catholic U. Am., 1947, M.S., 1953. Asst. prof. nursing Cath. U. Am., 1947-69, dir. masters program in cardiovascular disease nursing, 1962-69; mem. faculty Georgetown U. Sch. Nursing, 1970-74; pres. D.C. Profl. Nurses Exam. Bd., 1955-61, D.C. Practical Nurses Exam. Bd., 1961-67; cons. HEW, 1964-74; ind. general nurse, 1971-79; ptnr. Détente Manor, McLean, Va., 1978-81; vis. prof. U. So. Miss., Hattiesburg, 1975-78, also coordinator Center Nursing Edn., Practice and Research; vis. lectr. univs. Wis., Va., Alaska Pacific U.; mem. Washington Nursing Devel. Conf. Group; founder Nat. Center of Kinlein, 1979, Inst. of Kinlein, 1983. Recipient Alumni Achievement award Coll. Notre Dame, 1973, Cath. U. Am., 1974; Linda Richards award Nat. League Nursing, 1977. Mem. Am. Nurses Assn., Nat. League Nursing, Am. Heart Assn., Sigma Theta Tau, Kappa Gamma Pi. Roman Catholic. Author: Independent Nursing Practice with Clients, 1977; Moving That Power Within, 1983, expanded edit., 1985; co-author: Concept Formalization in Nursing, 1973; founder Jour. of Kinlein, 1981. Home: 7015 Highview Terr W Hyattsville MD 20782 Office: 6525 Belcrest Rd Hyattsville MD 20782

KINNALLY, MARGARET THERESE, lawyer; b. Chgo., Aug. 21, 1949; d. James Sheridan and Anna Laura (Woods) Kinnally. B.F.A., Quincy (Ill.) Coll., 1972; postgrad. Ind. State U., 1972-74; J.D., John Marshall Law Sch., Chgo., 1981. Bar: Ill. 1981, U.S. Ct. Appeals (7th cir.), U.S. Dist. Ct. Ill. Nursing service clk. Ravenswood Hosp., Chgo., 1974-81; assoc. Schneider & Morrison Ltd., Chgo., 1981—. Recipient Promethian award Quincy Coll. Theatre, 1972. Mem. Chgo. Bar Assn., Ill. Bar Assn., ABA, Ill. Trial Lawyers Assn., Women's Law Group (dir. 1982-84). Roman Catholic. Office: Schneider & Morrison Ltd 1633 N North Park Chicago IL 60614

KINNAN, JOEN PRITCHARD, freelance writer, editor, consultant; b. Canton, Ohio, May 21; d. William Davis and Thelma (Gibbs) Pritchard; m. Donald Henry Kinnan, Mar. 8 (div.); children—Glynis Joen, Jason Pritchard. B.A., Denison U.; postgrad. Kent State U., Ohio State U. Cert. elem. and secondary tchr., Ohio, Mich. English, history, geography and social studies tchr. Upper Arlington Schs., Ohio, later John Norup Jr. High Sch., Berkley, Mich.; sketchwriter, editor Marquis Who's Who, Chgo., 1964-74, asst. dept. head, 1966-68, head sketchwriting dept., 1968-74, freelance writer, editor, 1974-86; sr. assoc., writer, workshop facilitator William M. Young & Assocs., Oak Park, Ill., 1978-83; freelance writer, editor, cons., River Forest, Ill., 1983—; freelance newsletter editor Talmis, Inc., Chgo., 1984; intermittantly pvt. adult tutor. Ghostwriter mag. articles in health care and ednl. field. Democratic precinct worker; past publicity chmn. Oak Park-Proviso-Riverside Ind. Dems.; active McCarthy and McGovern presdl. campaigns, Walker gubernatorial campaign, Stevenson and Simon senatorial campaigns; past mgr. River Forest Boys' Little League. Mem. Ind. Writers of Chgo., Chgo. Women in Pub., Greenpeace, Citizens for Better Environment, Smithsonian Instn., Delta Gamma. Avocations: cats; nouvelle and ethnic cooking; travel. Office: Mighty Pen 241 Thatcher Ave River Forest IL 60305

KINNE, KATHARINE (MRS. CHARLES E. SIGETY), home economist; b. Herkimer, N.Y., Nov. 23, 1921; d. Cornelius Harry and Katharine (Kinne) Snell; B.S., Cornell U., 1944; m. Charles Edward Sigety, July 17, 1948; children—Charles Birge, Katharine Kinne, Robert Griswold, Cornelius, Elizabeth. Tng. squad J.L. Hudson Co., Detroit, 1944; overseas recreation work ARC, 1945-46, nat. fund campaign speaker, 1947; publicity work Union Carbide and Carbon Corp., 1947-48; dist. sales mgr. Berger Bros., New Haven, 1948-50; European tour condr. Olson Travel Orgn., 1950; TV home economist Sally Smart's Kitchen, WOR-TV, 1951-53; on camera food editor Home Show, NBC-TV, 1953-56; owner, dir., gen. mgr. Video Vittles, Inc. N.Y.C., 1953—; food service cons. Florence Nightingale Health Center, N.Y.C., 1967—; sec. Piper Hill Operating Co., Inc. (Pa.); mgr. Cucumber's Restaurants, Pipersville, Pa.; dir. Profl. Med. Products, Inc., Greenwood, S.C. Co-chmn. nat. parents com. Bates Coll., Lewiston, Maine; bd. dirs. Parents League N.Y., Trinity Sch. Mothers Orgn., Grace Ch. Sch. Parents Orgn., 1966-67. Recipient scholarships N.Y. State Fedn. Women's Clubs, D.A.R. Home Econ., Women in Bus., Mortar Bd., Delta Delta Delta. Mem. Am. Home Econs. Assn., Am. Women in Radio and TV, AFTRA, Screen Actors Guild. Presbyterian. Address: 175 E 96th St New York NY 10128

KINNEAR, ALICE TAYLOR, telephone company executive; b. Buffalo, June 16, 1949; d. Floyd Davison and Marie Alice (Thomas) Taylor; B.S. cum laude, U. Bridgeport, 1971. Account rep. N.Y. Telephone, Manhattan, 1971-73; communications cons. So. New Eng. Telephone Co., New Haven, 1973-75, staff asst., 1975-76, staff mgr., 1976-77, account exec. II, 1977-79, staff mgr., 1979—. Mem. Am. Mgmt. Assn., DAR. Democrat. Methodist. Office: 367 Orange St New Haven CT 06511

KINNERSLEY, SUSAN VIOLA, health care administrator, nurse; b. Columbus, Wis., May 23, 1951; d. Lester Otto and Lois Viola (Rath) Henning; m. Ronald Lloyd Kinnersley, Aug. 15, 1970; children—Rebecca Sue, Kenneth Ryan. B.S. in Nursing, Olivet Nazarene Coll., Kankakee, Ill., 1973; M.S., Govs. State U., Park Forest South, Ill., 1977. R.N., Ill., Wis., Ind. Nurse Aide Columbus Community Hosp., Wis., 1967-69; nurse aide Riverside Hosp., Kankakee, 1971-73, R.N., 1973; R.N. Palos Community Hosp., Ill., 1973-74; instr. St. Joseph Hosp. Sch. of Nursing, Joliet, Ill., 1974-76; project coordinator Our Lady of Mercy Hosp., Dyer, Ind., 1976-78, asst. dir. nursing, 1978-80, dir. of spl. services, 1980-81; dir. of nursing services Culver Union Hosp., Crawfordsville, Ind., 1981-84, dir. of patient services, 1984, asst. adminstr., 1984—. Adv. bd. Am. Med. Home Care, Crawfordsville, 1984-85, Ivy Tech Assoc. Degree Program, Lafayette, Ind., 1985—. Mem. Am. Orgn. Nurse Execs., Ind. Soc. Hosp. Nurse Adminstrs., Am. Assn. Critical Care Nurses, Sigma Theta Tau (Delta Omicron chpt.). Republican. Nazarene. Club: Zonta (bd. dirs. 1985-87). Avocations: softball, reading. Office: Culver Union Hosp 1710 Lafayette Rd Crawfordsville IN 47933

KINNEY, JILL MCCLEAVE, psychologist, author; b. Seattle, Mar. 27, 1944; d. James Kreuger and Lillian Anna (Nesheim) McCleave; m. David Andrew Haapala, July 26, 1976; 1 child, Scott McCleave. B.S. with honors, U. Wash., 1965; M.S., Stanford U., 1969, Ph.D., 1969. Psychologist, evaluator Tacoma Schs., Wash., 1970-71; dir. child services Tacoma Comprehensive Mental Health Ctr., 1971-74; dir. homebuilders Cath. Community Services, Tacoma, 1974-82; co-dir. Behavioral Schs. Inst., Federal Way, Wash., 1981—; Author: Homebuilders: Keeping Families Together, 1985; (with others) Increasing Hypnotic Susceptibility, 1974, Training of In-Home Therapists, 1979, Assessment of Families in Crisis, 1981. Precinct chair Dem. Party, Pierce County, Wash., 1980-82; chair, mem. Gov.'s Juvenile Justice Adv. Com., 1979-83; mem. Wash. Juvenile Standards Disposition Commn., 1981—, Child Welfare League Permanent Families for Children Adv. Bd., 1984—, Child Welfare League Family Preservation Network, 1983—. Recipient numerous state and fed. grants. Mem. Phi Beta Kappa, Sigma Xi. Home: 1901 Markham Ave Tacoma WA 98422 Office: Behavioral Scis Inst 1717 S 341st Pl Federal Way WA 98003

KINNEY, LISA FRANCES, state senator; b. Laramie, Wyo., Mar. 13, 1951; d. Irvin Wayne and Phyllis (Poe) K.; m. Rodney Philip Lang, Feb. 5, 1971. B.A., U. Wyo., 1973, student Law Sch., 1983—; M.L.S., U. Oreg., 1975. Reference librarian U. Wyo. Sci. Library, Laramie, 1975-76; outreach dir. Albany County Library, Laramie, 1975-76, dir., 1977-83; mem. Wyo. State Senate, Laramie, 1985—. Contbr. articles to profl. jours. Editor, compiler pub. relations directory for ALA, 1982. Bd. dirs. Big Bros./Big Sisters, Laramie, 1980-83. Recipient Beginning Young Profl. award Mt. Plains Library Assn., 1980; named Outstanding Wyo. Librarian Wyo. Library Assn., 1977, Outstanding Young Woman State of Wyo., 1980. Mem. ABA (law student div.), Nat. Confs. of State Legislatures (fiscal affairs and budget com.), LWV, Am. Bus. Women's Assn. Democrat. Club: Snowy Range Internat. Folk Dance (pres. 1980—). Lodges: Zonta Internat., Gem City Lioness. Avocations: photography; dance; reading; travel; languages. Home: 603 Spring Creek Laramie WY 82070

KINNISON, JOYCE FORD, government official, consultant; b. Glasgow, Ky., May 27, 1933; d. Edd Lewis and Benora (Kinslow) Ford; children—Carole Sue, Mary Jane, Kelly Lynne. B.A. magna cum laude, Georgetown Coll., 1959; postgrad. Eastern Ky. U., 1967-69; Cert. advanced study U.N.C.-Chapel Hill Govt. Execs. Inst., 1980. Tchr., Bethel-Tate Schs., Bethel, Ohio, 1957-61, Jefferson County Schs., Louisville, 1962-63, 64-68; dir. developmental studies Lees Jr. Coll., Jackson, Ky., 1968-72; dir. coop. edn. Montreat-Anderson Coll., Montreat, N.C., 1972-76; ednl. cons./researcher, 1975-77; exec. dir. N.C. State Occupational Info. Coordinating Com., Raleigh, 1977—; mem. N.C. Employment and Tng. Council, Raleigh, 1978-83; mem. Gov.'s LMI Com., Raleigh, 1982—; cons., reader U.S. Office Edn., Washington, 1973-77. Author: Education for the Self-Built Self, 1976; mem. editorial bd. Jour. Coop. Edn., 1974-81; contbr. articles to profl. jours. Mem. Carter Task Force/Edn., 1976; mem. Democratic Nat. Com. Named Outstanding North Carolinian, Gov. N.C., 1983; U.S. Office Edn. research grantee, 1974-76. Mem. Am. Vocat. Assn., Coop. Edn. Assn., Assn. Computer-Based Systems, N.C. Coop. Edn. Assn. (exec. com., sec. 1974-76), N.C. Vocat. Guidance Assn. Democrat. Baptist.

KINSEY-CALORI, JOANNE, broadcasting firm exec.; b. McKeesport, Pa., Sept. 3; d. George Morris and Pauline Vivian (Anderson) Kinsey; B.A., M.A. Ohio State U., 1976; Ph.D., Harvard U., 1982; children—Paula Christine, Kevin Kinsey. Reporter, Sta. WOSU, Ohio State U., Columbus, 1969-70; communications asst. dept. continuing edn. Ohio State U., 1970-72, pub. relations dir. Coll. Adminstrv. Sci., 1974-75, acting asst. prof. communications, psychology, 1971-76; editor Columbus region Internat. Harvester Corp., 1973-77; pres., co-owner Profl. Broadcasting Services, Redondo Beach, Calif., 1976—. Pres. PTA, Marburn, Ridgeview, Whetstone schs., Columbus, 1965-70; campaign mgr. Republican party, Franklin County, 1965-68. Recipient spl. award for outstanding community service Columbus Pub. Schs. Mem. Nat. Acad. TV Arts and Scis., Women in Communications (Los Angeles chpt.), Pacific Pioneer Broadcasters, So. Calif. Wine Writers (charter mem.), Archaeology Soc. Columbus, Jr. League, Mirrors and Chimes, Phi Beta Kappa, Phi Kappa Phi. Presbyterian. Clubs: Worthington Music, Clintonville Women's, Columbus Players. Office: Suite 10 625 Esplanade Redondo Beach CA 90277

KINZIE, JEANNIE JONES, radiologist, educator; b. Gt. Falls, Mont., Mar. 14, 1940; d. James Wayne and Lillian Alice (Young) Jones; B.S., Mont. State U., 1961; M.D., Washington U., St. Louis, 1965; m. Joseph Kinzie, Mar. 25, 1965; 1 son, Daniel Joseph. Intern in surgery U. N.C., Chapel Hill, 1965-66; resident in radiology (radiation therapy) Washington U. Sch. Medicine, St. Louis, 1968-71, instr. radiology, 1971-73; Am. Cancer Soc. advanced clin. fellow, 1971-74; asst. radiologist Barnes Hosp., St. Louis, 1971-73; cons. radiology Homer G. Phillips Hosp., St. Louis, 1971-73; mem. med. records com., asst. prof. radiology Med. Coll. Wis., 1973-74; assoc. attending staff Milw. County Gen. Hosp., 1973-74; head radiation therapy dept. Wood (Wis.) VA Hosp., 1973-74; cons. in radiology Community Meml. Hosp., Menomonee Falls, Wis., 1974; radiology staff West Allis (Wis.) Meml. Hosp., 1973-74; asst. prof. radiology U. Chgo., 1975-78, assoc. prof., 1978-80; assoc. prof. radiation oncology Wayne State U., Detroit, 1980-85; prof. radiology U. Colo., Denver, 1985—, dir. radiation oncology, 1985—; mem. radiation studies sect. NIH, 1981—. NIH grantee, 1974-76. Diplomate Am. Bd. Radiology. Fellow Am. Coll. Radiology; mem. AMA, Am. Coll. Radiology (com. on edn.), Denver Med. Soc., Am. Soc. Therapeutic Radiologists, AAAS, AAUP, Am. Soc. Clin. Oncology, Soc. Head and Neck Surgeons, N.Y. Acad. Scis., Alpha Lambda Delta, Phi Kappa Phi, Mortar Bd., Sigma Xi. Republican. Lutheran. Home: 3221 Interlocken Dr Evergreen CO 80439 Office: Box A031 U Colo 4200 E 9th Ave Denver CO 80262

KINZLER, CAROL ANN MARIE, cosmetics company consultant; b. Pitts., Feb. 23, 1957; d. Edward L. and Stephanie A. (Kloiber) Kinzler. B.A., Indiana U. of Pa., 1979, M.A., 1980. Asst. dir. Community Univ. Studies, Indiana, 1976-80; regional product specialist Internote USA, Inc., Rahway, N.J., 1980-82; sr. store mgr. Gen. Nutrition Corp., Pitts., 1982-83, sales mgr., regional telxon coordinator, 1983-85, area sales mgr., L.I., 1983-85; cons. Mary Kay Cosmetics, Carnegie, Pa., 1985—. Vol., Rehab. Inst., Shallyside, Pa.; mem. Divine Providence Hosp. Aux. Author: Senior Citizens and Their Involvement with the Arts, 1980. Mem. Nat. Assn. Female Execs., Nat. Assn. for Tng. and Devel., Smaller Mfrs. Council Pitts., Bus. and Profl. Woman's Orgn. Republican. Roman Catholic. Home: 317 Ewing Rd Carnegie PA 15106 Office: Mary Kay Cosmetics Inc 317 Ewing Rd Carnegie PA 15106

KIPNIS-WILSON, NORMA, civic worker; b. Bklyn., July 4; d. Joseph Melvin and Ruth (Streifler) Carlin; ed. U. Miami (Fla.), Penland (N.C.) Sch. Crafts, N.Y. Inst. Fin.; m. Jerome Leon Kipnis; children—Daniel, David (dec.), Douglas, Donald, Diane; m. Allan Philip Wilson, 1985. Trustee, U. Miami; chmn. Dade County Sch. Vol. Adv. Bd.; pres. Friends of Dade County Sch. Vol. Program; bd. dirs. Nat. Children's Cardiac Hosp.; past sec.-treas., bd. dirs., exec. bd. Greater Miami Jewish Fedn.; bd. dirs. women's div. United Jewish Appeal, Council Fedns. and Welfare Fund, Joint Distbn. Com.; del. White House Conf. Nat. Sch. Vol. Program; on assignment to New World Festival of Arts, until 1982; mem. Dade County Commn. on Status of Women, 1986; mgmt. cons. Norwil, Inc. Recipient numerous awards, certs. of appreciation. Address: 3 Grove Isle Dr 609 Coconut Grove FL 33133

KIRBY, CHARLENE LOUISE, nurse; b. Madawaska, Maine, Oct. 7; d. Richard Paige and Arline Blanche (Wright) Slayton; m. John Francis Kirby, Oct. 18, 1958; children—Kathlene L., John F. III, Richard C., Kelly P. Diploma in Nursing, Winthrop Community Hosp., 1958; A.S., Massasoit Community Coll., 1983. Staff nurse Winthrop Community Hosp., Mass., 1958-62, Beverly Hosp., Mass., 1962-66; office nurse North Shore Pediatrics, Denvers, Mass., 1966-71; charge nurse Jordan Hosp., Plymouth, Mass., 1983—. Friend, helper Pine St. Inn for Women, Boston, 1981—. Mem. Mass. Nurses Assn. (sec./treas. 1985-87), Am. Nurses Assn. Democrat. Roman Catholic. Avocations: camping; knitting; counted cross stitch. Home: 28 Tavern Path Plymouth MA 02360 Office: Jordan Hosp Sandwich St Plymouth MA 02360

KIRBY, DEBORAH MACDONALD, rehabilitation psychologist; b. Washington, May 19, 1948; d. Robert Angus and Margarett Mary (Harrison) MacDonald; B.A., George Washington U., 1970; M.Ed., Am. U., 1972; m. Stephen Edward Kirby, Sept. 6, 1980; 1 dau., Jessica Lynn. Psychiat. asst. Chestnut Lodge Psychiat. Hosp., Rockville, Md., 1969-70; research psychologist Dept. Army, 1970; clin. intern Am. U. Counseling Center, 1972; clin. psychologist Bay County Guidance Clinic, Panama City, Fla., 1972-73; rehab. counselor State of Fla., Panama City, 1974; rehab. psychologist Woodrow Wilson Rehab. Center, Fisherville, Va., 1975-84; dir. Shenandoah Counseling Assos., 1978—. Mem. Am. Psychol. Assn., Va. Psychol. Assn., Va. Counselors Assn., Va. Mental Health Counselors Assn., Kappa Alpha Theta. Democrat. Club: Charlottesville-Albemarle Kennel (past dir.). Author papers in field. Office: Shenandoah Counseling Assos PO Box 500 Churchville VA 24421

KIRBY, DIANA CHERNE, nurse, army officer; b. Guttenberg, Iowa, Jan. 22, 1951; d. Albert Edward and Bernadette Lucretia (Berns) Cherne; B.S. in Nursing, U. Iowa, 1973; M.S. in Edn., U. So. Calif., 1977; postgrad. U. Md., 1985—; m. Fred W. Kirby, Nov. 24, 1981. Mem. nursing staff Mercy Med. Center, Dubuque, Iowa, 1973-74; commd. 1st lt. Nurse Corps, U.S. Army, 1974, advanced through grades to capt., 1976; service in W. Ger.; community health nurse William Beaumont Army Med. Center, 1978-80, Ft. Leonard Wood, Mo., 1980-82, 24th Med. Detachment, Schweinfurt, W.Ger., 1982-85. Mem. Am. Nurses Assn., Am. Nurses Found., Am. Pub. Health Assn., Nat. League Nursing, Assn. Mil. Surgeons U.S., Am. Philatelic Soc., Goebel Collectors Club, Sigma Theta Tau. Roman Catholic. Address: 3 Lincoln Woods Way 2B Perry Hall MD 21128

KIRBY, LINDA JEAN, marketing executive; b. Indpls., Aug. 23, 1946; d. Richard Gordon and Maxine (Tartar) Skaggs; children—Jeffery Barnett, Julie Barnett, Jason Barnett. Student pub. schs., Indpls. Receptionist Drs. Berger & Berger, D.D.S., Beech Grove, Ind., 1974-76; purchasing asst. Shambaugh & Son, Indpls., 1976-78; gen. mgr. Lane Restoration, Indpls., 1978-81; account exec. Exhibit House, Indpls., 1981-82; pres. Kirby & Assocs., Indpls., 1982-85; inhouse design mgr. for showrooms and trade show exhibits Delta Faucet Co., Indpls., 1985—; cons. White River State Games, Indpls., 1983-84, Indpls. Circle Fest, 1984; judge Marion County Health Dept. Day Symposium, Indpls., 1985. Mem. Advt. Club Indpls., Indpls. C. of C., Indpls. Conv. Bur. Republican. Avocations: racquetball; dancing; theater; music. Address: Delta Faucet Co 55 E 111th St Indianapolis IN 46280

KIRBY, MARY WEEKS, educator, reading specialist; b. Cheverly, Md., Nov. 23, 1947; d. Isaac Ralph and Dorothea (Huppert) Weeks; m. William Charlie Kirby, Feb. 14, 1976; children—Joie, Fatimah, Tariq. B.A. in Music Edn., James Madison U., 1969; M.Ed., Va. Commonwealth U., 1976. Cert. tchr. of music, reading and elem., Va. Music instr. Charles City County Schs., Providence Forge, Va., 1969-70, Hanover Learning Ctr., Va., 1970-72; sales cons. Boykins's Music Shop, Richmond, Va., 1972-74; elem. tchr. New Kent Pub. Schs., Va., 1974—, writing cons., 1980—; presentor ednl. and reading workshops, 1980-82. Sponsor Young Authors' Workshop, New Kent, 1985—; co-chmn., presentor Parents Anonymous of Va., 1984—; trustee Islamic Ctr. of Va., 1985—, sec., 1981-85; active Boy Scouts Am., Girl Scouts U.S. Mem. New Kent Edn. Assn. (officer 1977-81), Va. Edn. Assn., NEA, Richmond Area Reading Council (sec. 1982-83), Sigma Alpha Iota (life). Avocations: needlework; reading; swimming. Home: 1309 Bull Run Dr Richmond VA 23231 Office: New Kent Pub Schs Quinton VA 23141

KIRBY, REBECCA, veterinarian; b. Saint Louis, Oct. 10, 1951; d. William R. and Charity I. (Wattles) K. B.S. in Chemistry, Mo Valley Coll., 1973; D.V.M., U. Mo., 1977. Small animal internship Purdue U., West LaFayetteville, Ind., 1977-78, resident internal medicine U. Fla., Gainesville, 1978-80; internist vet. San Carlos Vet. Hosp., San Diego, 1980-81; clinician Emergency Animal Clinic, San Diego, 1981-82; dir. emergency, asst. prof. U. Pa. Vet. Hosp., Phila., 1982—. Youth Counselor Gainesville (Fla.) United Med. Ch., 1978-80. Mem. Am. Coll. Vet. Medicine (diplomate), AVMA, Calif. Vet. Med. Assn. Contbr. articles to profl. jours.

KIRBY, RITA MAYE KNOWLES (MRS. CARLTON BEDFORD WATTS), real estate management company executive; b. Dalhart, Tex., Sept. 10, 1941; cert. apt. mgr.; d. Luby F. and Jonnie Reta Knowles; student Frank Phillips Jr. Coll., Borger, Tex.; m. Jerry W. Kirby, May 6, 1961 (div. 1976); children—Michael, Daniel; m. Carlton Bedford Watts, Aug. 12, 1983. Property mgr. Villa France Apts., Irving, Tex., 1971-72; mgmt. v.p. First Property Mgmt. Corp., Chgo. and Dallas, 1972-80; v.p. ops. S&S Properties, Inc., Dallas, 1980—; exec. v.p., partner Capital Concept Mgmt. Corp., Dallas, 1980-84, pres., mng. ptnr., 1984—. Named Cert. Apt. Mgr. of Yr., 1984. Mem. Dallas Apt. Assn. (dir. 1979-85, sec.-treas. 1981-82, 1st v.p. 1982-83, pres. 1983-84), Tex. Apt. Assn. (dir. 1979—, chmn. edn. com. 1981), Nat. Apt. Assn. (dir. 1978-85, chmn. edn. com. 1980-81, chmn. Nat. Apt. Mgmt. Accreditation Bd. 1980, 85-86, regional v.p. 1983), Inst. Real Estate Mgmt. (cert. property mgr.). Baptist. Author: Community Directors Guide, 1975; co-author: Property Evaluation and Takeover, 1982. Home: 1606 W Shady Grove Irving TX 75060 Office: 4825 LBJ Freeway Suite 14C Dallas TX 75244

KIRCHNER, THERESA MARIE, radio network executive; b. St. Paul, Sept. 3, 1957; d. Eugene Joseph and Ellen Mae (Sobottka) K. Student St. Cloud State Coll., 1976-77, Control Data Inst., Mpls., 1983. Owner, operator Oliver's Tavern, Coralville, Iowa, 1978-80, TreeHouse Lounge, Coralville, 1979-81; computer programmer Lakeland Engrng., Mpls., 1983-84; acctg. bookkeeper Marriott-Service Systems, Mpls., 1984-85; sales supr. G.M.S.C., Mpls., 1985-86; exec. mktg. dir. Minn. FM Radio Network, Mpls., 1984—; sales cons. Success Edn. Tng. Co., Phoenix, 1984-85. Mem. Nat. Assn. Female Execs. Avocation: fitness. Office: Minn FM Radio Network 324 S Lake St Long Prairie MN 56347

KIRIAS, SUSAN HERNEY, public relations executive; b. San Diego, Aug. 27, 1942; d. Albert F. and Dorothy Ann (Charleson) Herney; B.A., U. Calif., Berkeley, 1964; m. Christopher H. Kirias, July 20, 1979; 1 son, Ross Royer Veal. Staff asst. U.S. Senator Thomas Kuchel, Washington, 1964; communications officer spl. projects Loyola U. New Orleans, 1965-68; planning coordinator community relations New Orleans Public Schs., 1968-70; conf. coordinator U. Utah, Salt Lake City, 1970-71; freelance communications cons., 1972-75; sr. cons. Osoro & Assocs., Denver, Phila., 1975-81; public relations dir. United Gilsonite Labs., Scranton, Pa., 1981—; lectr. U. Denver Grad. Sch. Social Work, 1979, U. Scranton, 1984. Chmn. human resources task force, citizens adv. com. Denver Regional Council Govts., 1974-77; bd. dirs. Big Sisters Colo., 1976-77, Planned Parenthood of Lackawanna County, 1982—; mem. Gov.'s Commn. Utah Environ. Conf., 1971; mem. Scranton Women's Coalition, 1980-82; mem. community relations com. United Way of Lackawanna County 1984. Mem. Women in Communications, Am. Soc. Tng. and Devel., Internat. Assn. Bus. Communicators, Advt. Club N.E. Pa., NOW, Pub. Relations Soc. Am., Alpha Xi Delta. Editor: Service Directory for Veterans in Colorado, 1977. Office: UGL PO Box 70 Scranton PA 18501

KIRK, COLLEEN JEAN, educator, conductor; b. Champaign, Ill., Sept. 7, 1918; d. Bonum Lee and Anna Catherine (Hoffert) K.; B.S. with high honors, U. Ill., 1940, M.S., 1945; Ed.D., Columbia U., 1953. Tchr. music Public Schs. Danvers (Ill.), 1940-44, Watseka (Ill.), 1944-45; instr. Univ. High Sch., Urbana, Ill., 1945-49; asst. prof. edn. and music U. Ill., 1949-58, asso. prof., 1958-64, prof., 1964-70; prof. Fla. State U., Tallahassee, 1970—, condr. choral union, 1970—; dir. music Wesley United Methodist Ch., Urbana, 1947-70; dir. jr. chorus Ill. Summer Youth Music, Urbana, 1963-71; choral clinician, condr. adjudicator. Recipient Fla. State U. Pres.'s award, 1979. Mem. Am. Choral Dirs. Assn. (pres. So. div. 1971-75, nat. pres.-elect 1979-81, nat. pres. 1981-83, nat. v.p. 1983—), Internat. Fedn. Choral Music (dir. 1981—), Assn. Profl. Vocal Ensembles, Am. Choral Found., Music Educators Nat. Conf., Fla. Music Educators Assn., AAUP, Coll. Music Soc., Fla. Vocal Assn., Fla. Coll. Music Educators Assn., Pi Kappa Lambda, Kappa Delta Pi, Sigma Alpha Iota. Author: (with others) Modern Methods in Elementary Education, 1959; contbr. Choral Jour., 1978—. Home: 2028 Wildridge Dr Tallahassee FL 32303 Office: Sch Music Fla State U Tallahassee FL 32306

KIRK, HELEN WHITE (MRS. KENNETH BURSON KIRK), club woman; b. Detroit; d. William John and Grace (Ramsay) White; B.A., U. Mich.; m. Kenneth Burson Kirk; children—Cynthia Grace, Helen Victoria. Sec.-treas., dir. Kirk Dial Corp., Beverly Hills, Calif.; bd. dirs. Beverly Hills Women's Club, 1936-37, Palm Springs (Calif.) Women's Club, 1953-54; pres. Lifelighters, 1955-56, 71-72, Palm Springs chpt. W.A.I.F., 1958-59; chmn. Bookworms of Assistance League So. Calif., 1967-68; mem. adv. bd. Los Angeles Women's chpt. Freedom's Found., 1972-84; mem. women's com. Los Angeles Philharmonic Orch., Opera Guild Soc. Calif.; gen. chmn. ladies div. Rotary Internat. Conv., 1962; pres. Palm Springs chpt. Nat. Charity League, 1965; v.p. women's aux. Desert Hosp., 1965; mem. adv. council Los Angeles County women's chpt. Freedoms Found. at Valley Forge; bd. dirs. Bel-Air Guild of Children's Hosp., 1981-82. Mem. Navy League U.S., Beverly Hills Council, Internat. Platform Assn. Clubs: Beverly Hills Garden (pres. 1978-80), Ebell, Beverly Hills Women's. Home: 702 N Bedford Dr Beverly Hills CA 90210 also 155 S Belardo Rd Palm Springs CA 92262

KIRK, MARILYN KAY FOSTER, fund-raising executive; b. Great Bend, Kans., Apr. 29, 1946; d. Harry Charles and Helen Kathryn (Radenberg) F. B.A., Kans. Wesleyan U., 1968; M.Ed., U. Okla., 1970; postgrad. U. Kans., 1982-84. Asst. dean of students Westmar Coll., LeMars, Iowa, 1970-72, dean of students, 1972-77; assoc. dir. devel. Carroll Coll., Waukesha, Wis., 1977-78; dir. devel. Kans. Wesleyan U., Salina, 1978-79; corp. dir. devel. Kans. State Hist. Soc., Topeka, 1979-84; dir. devel. Garrett-Evang. Theol. Sem., Evanston, Ill., 1984—; adviser in higher edn. Congressman Berkley Bedell of Iowa, 1976-77; cons. fund raising, 1980—. Mem. mktg. team Kaw Valley council Girl Scouts U.S.A., 1982-84; bd. dirs. Topeka YWCA, 1982-84, Kans. Com. for Humanities, Topeka, 1983-84; bd. mgrs. Kans. Expocentre, Topeka, 1983-84. Named Outstanding Young Alumna, Kans. Wesleyan U., 1977. Mem. Pub. Relations Soc. Topeka (dir. 1983-84), Nat. Assn. Fund Raising Execs., Topeka Fund Raisers, Nat. Assn. Women Deans, Adminstrs. and Counselors (coll. sect. dir. 1977-82). Democrat. Presbyterian. Club: PEO (treas. 1982-84, v.p. 1984—Topeka). Office: 2121 Sheridan Rd Evanston IL 60201

KIRK, SUSAN SHAW, lawyer; b. San Jose, Calif., Nov. 4, 1940; d. Wallace Garland and Dorothy (Kirk) Shaw; children—Jenifer Kirk Swaringen, Michael Penton Swaringen. A.B. in Communications and Pub. Policy, U. Calif.-Berkeley, 1962; postgrad. Stanford U., 1979, U. Mich., 1981; J.D., U. Santa Clara, 1981. Bar: Mich. 1981. Research asst. Council for Social Planning, Oakland, Calif., 1963; fellow Coro Found. Internship in Pub. Affairs, 1963; office mgr. AFL-CIO Com. on Polit. Edn., Oakland, 1963-64; legal asst. Moran, Lawlor & Rhea, Oakland, 1964-65; spl. asst. to dean of student affairs, planner/analyst Stanford U., 1965-79; extern to William A. Ingram, U.S. Dist. Ct., San Francisco, 1979; law clk. Ruffo, Ferrari & McNeil, San Jose, 1980; atty. Consumers Power Co., Jackson, Mich., 1981—. Mem. ABA, State Bar Mich., Am. Arbitration Assn. (panel of arbitrators). Episcopalian. Home: 715 W Michigan Ave Jackson MI 49202 Office: Consumers Power Co 212 W Michigan Ave Jackson MI 49201

KIRK, SUSANNE SMITH, editor; b. Washington; d. Harold Clair and Theodora (Varner) Smith; m. Donald Kirk, May 31, 1965 (div. 1985). Student Kaiserin-Theophanu Sch., Cologne, W.Ger., 1958; A.B., Smith Coll., 1963; cert. Goethe Inst., Berlin, 1963; M.S., Columbia U., 1965. Reporter, South China Morning Post, Hong Kong, 1965-67; corr. German News Agy., Saigon, Vietnam, 1968-69; editor Charles Tuttle Pubs., Tokyo, 1972-74; freelance journalist, 1965-74; asst. editor Charles Scribner's Sons, N.Y.C., 1975, editor, 1976-80, asst. v.p., 1977—, fgn. rights dir., 1978-82, sr. editor, 1980-85, exec. editor, 1985—. Contbr. articles to newspapers. Mem. Women's Nat. Book Assn. Clubs: Snarks Ltd. (v.p. 1983-84, pres. 1985-86), Smith Coll. (N.Y.C.). Home: 33 E End Ave New York NY 10028 Office: Charles Scribners Sons 115 Fifth Ave New York NY 10003

KIRKHART, KAREN EILEEN, educator; b. Pomona, Calif., Jan. 6, 1948; d. Harry Burdell and Mabel Eileen (Reinhardt) K.; B.A., Pomona Coll., 1970; M.S.W., U. Mich., 1972, Ph.D., 1979; m. Nick L. Smith, July 21, 1984. Community service worker Community Action Center, Adrian, Mich., 1970-71; therapist Family Service Agy. of Genessee County, Flint, Mich., 1971; therapist Family and Sch. Consultation Project, Ann Arbor, Mich., 1971-72; teaching asst. Psychology Dept., Sch. Social Work, U. Mich., 1974-77; asso. dir. evaluation curriculum devel. project Inst. Labor and Indsl. Relations, U. Mich.-Wayne State U., 1976-78; asst. prof. ednl. psychology U. Tex., Austin, 1979-85; assoc. prof. social work Syracuse U., 1986—; mem. epidemiologic and services research com. NIMH, 1981-84; research product evaluator NSF, 1980—. Mem. adv. bd. Office of Research and Evaluation, Austin (Tex.) Ind. Sch. Dist., 1980-84. Mem. Am. Psychol. Assn., Assn. for Advancement of Behavior Therapy, Evaluation Network (pres. 1981), Evaluation Research Soc. (council 1983-85), Am. Evaluation Assn. (bd. dirs. 1986), Eastern Evaluation Research Soc., Nat. Council Community Mental Health Centers, S.W. Psychol. Assn., Tex. Psychol. Assn., Am. Ednl. Research Assn., Soc. Psychol. Study of Social Issues, Nat. Orgn. Women. Home: 329 Germania Ave Syracuse NY 13219 Office: Sch Social Work Brockway Hall Syracuse U Syracuse NY 13210

KIRKLAND, ALICE MARIE SANFORD, educator, educational administrator; b. Sequim, Wash., Apr. 13, 1940; d. Hilton Horace and Edith Louise (Chism) Sanford; m. Billy J. Kirkland, June 30, 1958; children—Kenneth Wayne, David Michael, Alyson Renee. A.A., U. S.C.-Aiken, 1969; B.A., Augusta Coll., 1971; M. Ed., U. S.C., 1975. Sec./cashier Family Fin. Corp., Wilmington, Del., 1958-62; sec. Graniteville Co., S.C., 1963-65; tchr. Aiken County Schs., S.C., 1971-80, asst. prin., 1980-83, prin., 1983—. Mem. Greater Aiken C. of C., S.C. Elem. and Middle Sch. Assn., S.C. Assn. Sch. Adminstrs., Nat. Assn. Secondary Sch. Prins., Assn. Supervision and Curriculum Devel., Aiken County Adminstrs. Assn. Club: Ladies Ministries. Avocations: piano and organ accompanist. Home: RT 1 Box 88BZ Graniteville SC 29829 Office: Jackson Middle Sch Dual Ln Hwy Jackson SC 29831

KIRKLAND, BERTHA THERESA (MRS. THORNTON CROWNS KIRKLAND, JR.), engineer; b. San Francisco, May 16, 1916; d. Lawrence and Theresa (Kanzler) Schmelzer; m. Thornton Crowns Kirkland, Jr., Dec. 27, 1937; (dec. July 1971); children—Kathryn Elizabeth, Francis Charles. Supr. hosp. ops. Am. Potash & Chem. Corp., Trona, Calif., 1953-54; office mgr. T.C. Kirkland, elec. contractor, 1954-56; sec.-treas., dir. T.C. Kirkland, Inc., San Bernardino, Calif., 1958-74; design and build estimator Add-M Electric, Inc., San Bernardino, 1972-82, v.p., 1974-82; estimator, engr. Corona Indsl. Electric, Inc., 1982-83; asst. project engr. Fischbach and Moore, Inc., 1984—. Episcopalian. Club: Arrowhead Country. Home: 526 E Sonora St San Bernardino CA 92404

KIRKLAND, IRIS MCWHERTER, social worker, govt. personnel ofcl.; b. East St. Louis, Ill., June 29, 1946; d. James Washington and Artie Irene McWherter; B.A., Central State U., Wilberforce, Ohio, 1966; M.S.W., St. Louis U., 1969; m. Jack A. Kirkland, Jan. 5, 1979. Sch. social worker Sch. Dist. 189, East St. Louis, Ill., 1969-70; instr. social work Grambling (La.) Coll., 1971; dir. Air Force Alcohol Rehab. Program, Scott AFB, Ill., 1975-78; position classification specialist Dept. Army, St. Louis, 1978—, currently program analyst DOD; ptnr. Kirkland and Assocs.; cons. social work and personnel mgmt. Baptist. Contbr. articles to profl. publs. Home: 10806 Charlton Way Saint Louis MO 63141 Office: 4300 Goodfellow Saint Louis MO 63120

KIRKPATRICK, ANNE HELENE, educator; b. Herkimer, N.Y., June 21, 1936; d. John Philip and Helene Rosalie (Reilly) K.; B.A., Syracuse U., 1959, M.S., 1966. Tchr. math. jr. high sch., W. Canada Valley Central Sch., Middleville, N.Y., 1959-60; remedial reading tchr. Herkimer Central Sch., 1966-71, visually handicapped tchr., 1974-76, substitute tchr., 1978—; reading cons. Herkimer County Assn. for Retarded Children; guest speaker Herkimer County Community Coll. Cert. tchr., N.Y. State. Mem. Assn. Tchr. Educators, Assn. Supervision and Curriculum Devel., N.Y. State Ret. Tchrs. Assn. Inc., AAUW (edn. chmn., sec. Herkimer County br.), Alumni Assn. Utica Coll. of Syracuse U., Lit. Vols. Am., Orton Dyslexia Soc. Republican. Roman Catholic. Home: 300 N Bellinger St Herkimer NY 13350

KIRKPATRICK, ELEANOR BLAKE, civic worker; b. Mangum, Okla., Mar. 10, 1909; d. Mack Barkley and Kathryn (Talbott) Blake; m. John Elson Kirkpatrick, June 20, 1932; 1 child, Joan Elson. B.A. in French, Smith Coll., 1931; D.Humanities (hon.), Oklahoma City U., 1968. Ptnr. Kirkpatrick Oil Co., Oklahoma City, Kirkpatrick Oil & Gas, Oklahoma City. Bd. dirs. Kirkpatrick Ctr., Oklahoma City; treas. Kirkpatrick Found., Oklahoma City. Named to Okla. Hall of Fame, Okla. Heritage Assn., Oklahoma City, 1975; recipient Evergreen Disting. Service award Nat. Assn. Mature People, Okla., 1982, Bd. Trustees award Omniplex Sci. Mus., Oklahoma City, 1984. Mem. World Lit. Today (bd. dirs.), Oklahoma City U. Library Soc., Oklahoma City C. of C. (com. for internat. visitors). Avocations: bridge, cooking. Office: Kirkpatrick Oil Co 1300 N Broadway Dr Oklahoma City OK 73103

KIRKPATRICK, JEAN, sociologist; b. Quakertown, Pa., Mar. 2, 1923; d. Peter and Helen (Roberta) Spangler Romig. B.A., Moravian Coll., 1950; M.A., Lehigh U., 1954, postgrad., 1965-67; Ph.D., U. Pa., 1971. Dir. programming Ednl. Computer Corp., King of Prussia, Pa., 1967-73; founder, exec. dir. Women for Sobriety, Inc., Quakertown, Pa., 1974—; lectr., cons. women and alcoholism. Recipient Humanitarian award Moravian Coll., Bethlehem, Pa., 1980; named Woman of Yr. Bus. and Profl. Women's Assn., Quakertown, 1982. Mem. Internat. Commn. on Alcoholism. Republican. Lutheran. Author: Turnabout: Help for Life, 1978; A Fresh Start, 1981; Reflections, 1980; Goodbye Hangovers; Hello Life, 1986.

KIRKPATRICK, JEANE DUANE JORDAN, political scientist; b. Duncan, Okla., Nov. 19, 1926; d. Welcher F. and Leona (Kile) Jordan; A.A., Stephens Coll., 1946; A.B., Barnard Coll., 1948; M.A., Columbia U., 1950, Ph.D., 1968; postgrad. (French govt. fellow) U. Paris Inst. de Sci. Politique, 1952-53; hon. degrees, Mt. Vernon Coll., Georgetown U., U. Pitts., St. Anselms Coll., Franklin and Marshall Coll., St. John's U., Hebrew U., Jerusalem, Bethany Coll.; m. Evron M. Kirkpatrick, Feb. 20, 1955; children—Douglas Jordan, John Evron, Stuart Alan. Research analyst Dept. State, 1951-52; research assoc. Govt. Affairs Inst., 1953-54, George Washington U., 1954-56, Fund for Republic, 1956-57; asst. prof. polit. sci. Trinity Coll., 1962-67; assoc. prof. polit. sci. Georgetown U., Washington, 1967-73, prof., 1973—, Leavey prof. in founds. Am. freedom, 1978—; resident scholar Am. Enterprise Inst. for Pub. Policy Research, 1977—(on leave); mem. cabinet, U.S. permanent rep. to UN, 1981-85; co-chmn. task force presdl. election process 20th Century Fund; cons. Am. Council Learned Socs., Dept. State, HEW, Dept. Def., intermittently 1955-72; mem. nat. Commn. on Space, 1985—, Fed. Intelligence Adv. Bd., 1985—. Vice chmn. com. on v.p. selection Democratic Party, 1972-74, mem. nat. commn. party structure and presdl. nomination, 1975; mem. credentials com. Dem. Nat. Conv., 1976; mem. internat. research council Center for Strategic and Internat. Studies, Georgetown U.; trustee Helen Dwight Reid Ednl. Found., 1972—, Robert A. Taft Inst. Govt., 1978—; mem. bd. curators Stephens Coll. Recipient Disting. Alumna award Stephens Coll., 1978; Presdl. Medal of Freedom, 1985; Jabotinsky prize/Defender of Jerusalem award, 1985; Raymond and Miriam Klein Found. award, 1986; Earhart fellow, 1956-57. Mem. Internat. Polit. Sci. Assn. (exec. council), Am. Polit. Sci. Assn., So. Polit. Sci. Assn., Midwest Polit. Sci. Assn. Republican. Author: Foreign Students in the United States; A National Survey, 1966; Mass Behavior in Battle and Captivity, 1968; Leader and Vanguard in Mass Society: A Study of Peronist Argentina, 1971; Political Woman, 1974; The New Presidential Elite, 1976; Dismantling the Parties: Reflections on Party Reform and Party Decomposition, 1978; Dictatorships and Double Standards, 1981; The Reagan Phenomenon, 1983; editor, contbr.: Elections USA, 1956; Strategy of Deception, 1963; The New Class, 1978; The New American Political System, 1978; contbr. articles to Commentary, New Republic, Brit. Jour. Polit. Sci., Commonsense, Washington Quar., Publius, others. Office: Georgetown U Dept Govt 37th and O St NW Washington DC 20057*

KIRKPATRICK, NANCY FOSTER, museum administrator; b. Aurora, Ill., Aug. 21, 1933; d. Richard Joseph and Helen Irene (McGall) Foster; m. David Allen Kirkpatrick, Nov. 18, 1967 (dec. May 1977). Student Am. U., George Washington U. Budget analyst Smithsonian Instn., Washington, 1962-73, budget officer, 1973-77, exec. officer Hirshhorn Mus. and Sculpture Garden, 1977—. Mem. Am. Assn. Mus. Democrat. Presbyterian. Office: Hirshhorn Mus and Sculpture Garden Smithsonian Instn 8th at Independence Ave Washington DC 20560

KIRKPATRICK, SALLY ANN, lobbyist; b. Coshocton, Ohio, Apr. 6, 1950; d. William Arthur and Martha Sue (Williams) Kirkpatrick; m. David Flavous Lambert, III, Apr. 30, 1983. B.A., Denison U., 1972; J.D., Ohio No. U., 1975; student Purdue U., 1970-71. Legis. asst. Joe Skubitz, U.S. Ho. of Reps., Washington, 1976; govt. affairs rep. Am. Ins. Assn., Washington, 1977-80; sr. legis. counsel Alliance Am. Insurers, Washington, 1980-85; spl. asst. to asst. sec. for legislation HHS, Washington, 1985—; chmn. task force on FCIC, Grace Commn., Washington, 1982; mem. Women in Govt. Relations, Washington, 1980—, Washington's Women's Network, 1980—. Mem. Alpha Phi. Republican. Club: Women's Nat. Republican Avocations: travel; gourmet cooking; politics. Home: 1014 N Terrill St Alexandria VA 22304 Office: Asst Sec for Legislation Dept Health and Human Services 200 Independence SW Washington DC 20201

KIRSCH, DOROTHY ANN, publisher; b. Rochester, N.Y., Oct. 1, 1936; d. Edward and Sylvia E. (Moskin) Tejw; m. Donald Kirsch, June 6, 1959; children—Mark Adam, Karen Rebecca, Jonathan Bradford. A.B., U. Rochester, 1956. Treas., dir. Wall St. Group, Inc., N.Y.C., 1959—; pub., editor N.Y. Visitor's Reporter, Inc., N.Y.C., 1975—; treas., dir. Wall St. Group/Calif., Los Angeles, 1979—. Mem. N.Y. State Commn. Human Rights, 1972-75. Mem. Women's Orgn. of Brandeis U. (life), Phi Beta Kappa. Clubs: Wall Street, NYU, Citicorp (N.Y.C.). Office: NY Visitor's Reporter 63 Wall St New York NY 10005

KIRSCH, DOROTHY ITALIE, reading specialist, adult education educator; b. Phila., Feb. 21, 1915; d. Jacques Edouard and Bertha (Weis) Italie; m. Elmer A. Kirsch, Aug. 20, 1944; children—Michael, Martin. B.S. in Journalism, Temple U., 1936; M.S. in Elem. Edn., SUNY-New Paltz, 1959; Ed.D. in Reading, Hofstra U., 1973. Cert. reading specialist, elem. tchr. Glen Cove Elem. Schs., N.Y., 1956-72; clinician in reading Hofstra U., Hempstead, N.Y., 1970; tchr. adult basic edn., Glen Cove Schs., 1981-85, reading specialist, 1972-85; adj. prof. C.W. Post Coll., Greenvale, N.Y., 1985—, SUNY-Empire State Coll., Old Westbury, N.Y., 1985—; ednl. cons., 1985—; presenter Internat. Reading Assn., Hong Kong, 1984, Singapore, 1976, Vienna, Austria, 1974, New Orleans, 1974, Denver, 1973. Author: Bookbird, 1976; Elementary English, 1975; Research in Education, 1974. Reviewer of books and programs, 1974-85. Mem. Internat. Reading Assn., Nassau Reading Council, N.Y. State Reading Assn., Tchrs. English as a Second Language (presenter 1984). Jewish. Avocation: travel.

KIRSCHSTEIN, RUTH LILLIAN, physician; b. Bklyn., Oct. 12, 1926; d. Julius and Elizabeth (Berm) K.; A.B. magna cum laude, L.I.U., 1947; M.D., Tulane U., 1951; D.Sc. (hon.), Mt. Sinai Sch. Medicine, CUNY, 1984; LL.D. (hon.), Atlanta U., 1985; D.Sc. (hon.), Med. Coll. Ohio, 1986; m. Alan S. Rabson, June 11, 1950; 1 son, Arnold B. Intern, Kings County Hosp., Bklyn., 1951-52; resident in pathology VA Hosp., Atlanta, 1952, Providence Hosp., Detroit, 1952-54; Nat. Heart Inst. fellow, instr. Tulane U. Sch. Medicine, New Orleans, 1954-55; resident Clin. Center NIH, 1956, physician, 1960-72, 74—, chmn. grants peer rev. study team, 1975-76, dir. Nat. Inst. Gen. Med. Scis., 1974—; dep. assoc. commnr. sci. FDA, 1973-74; mem. expert group internat. requirements for biol. substances WHO; cons. in field. Recipient Superior Service award HEW, 1971, USPHS, 1978; Presdl. Meritorious Exec. Rank award, 1980. Mem. Am. Assn. Immunologists, Am. Assn. Pathologists, Am. Soc. Microbiology, Inst. Medicine, Nat. Acad. Scis. Author papers in field. Office: Bldg 31 Room 4A 52 NIH Bethesda MD 20205

KIRSHNER, JANET BERGER, public relations exec.; b. N.Y.C., Mar. 24, 1933; d. Elmer Steil and Elsie (Feinberg) Berger; student U. Calif.-Berkeley, 1951-53; B.S., UCLA, 1956; m. Lester Kirshner, Sept. 8, 1957; children: Elizabeth, Jonathan. Partner, H/K Communications, N.Y.C., 1974-78, pres., owner, 1981—; dir. public relations Branielle Assos., N.Y.C., 1978-79, Delphi Commodities, N.Y.C., 1979-80; v.p. public relations and adminstrn. Fahy Internat. Trading Corp., N.Y.C., 1980-81. Mem. Public Relations Soc. Am. Office: 500 Fifth Ave New York NY 10110

KIRZ, STEPHANIE AGER, public relations executive; b. Seattle, Apr. 28, 1946; d. Robert Lee and Jean (Purrington) Ager; B.A. in Art, U. Wash., 1969; m. Howard Lutz Kirz, Mar. 9, 1978. Pres., gen. mgr. Cole & Weber Pub. Relations subs. Ogilvy & Mather; pres. Ager & Assocs., advt. agy. Pres., Wash. Panhellenic, 1967-68. Mem. Women in Communications (v.p. fin. 1981), Pub. Relations Soc. Am. (Totem award 1980, 86), Kappa Kappa Gamma. Club: Seattle Tennis, Columbia Tower. Home: 705 McGilvra Blvd E Seattle WA 98112 Office: 1205 1st Ave S Seattle WA 98134

KISCHEL, BEATRICE, beautician educator, administrator; b. New London, Conn., Oct. 6, 1920; d. William and Fannie Ida (Lubchansky) Bronitsky; m. Jack Kischel, Mar. 26, 1944; children—Marc, Faye-Elaine Forman, Ilene. Cert. hairdresser, cometician instr. Instr., New London Acad. (Conn.), 1962-69; dean, instr. Albert-Beatrice Sch., New London, 1970—. Former pres. New London Hebrew Ladies Aid, Ednl. Soc. Yeshiva U. Women's Orgn.; dist. dir. Conn. PTA; neighborhood chmn. Girl Scouts U.S.A., New London. Mem. Conn. Hairdressers and Cosmeticians Assn. (sec. 1963-65, dir. 1973-75), Tchrs. Ednl. Council. Home: 962 Bank St New London CT 06320

KISER, MARIE VIVA JEAN BOSLEY, educator; b. Balt., Feb. 18, 1929; married, 3 children. B.S. in Elem. and Spl. Edn., Millersville (Pa.) U., 1965, M.Ed. in Spl. Edn., 1968; Ph.D. in Spl. Edn., U. Md., College Park, 1981; m. Norman Kiser; children—Dennis, Linda, David. Substitute tchr. So. York County Sch. Dist., Glen Rock, Pa., 1953-63, classroom tchr., 1963-68; instr. dept. spl. edn. Millersville U., 1968-71, asst. prof., 1971-79, asso. prof., 1979—. Mem. Council Exceptional Children, Assn. Tchr. Educators, Council Children with Learning Disabilities, Council Adminstrs. in Spl. Edn., Assn. Children with Learning Disabilities, Council Children with Mental Retardation, Assn. Severely Handicapped, Pa. Fedn. Council Exceptional Children (pres. tchr. edn. div. 1984-85, advisor student chpt. 1968-70, 81-84), Am. Assn. Mental Deficiency, AAUP, Pi Lambda Theta. Cert. elem. tchr., tchr. mentally retarded, emotionally handicapped, Pa. Home: 1057 Church St Landisville PA 17538 Office: Gerhart Bldg Millersville U Millersville PA 17551

KISER, NAGIKO SATO, librarian, media specialist, art historian; b. Taipei, Taiwan, Aug. 7, 1923; came to U.S., 1950, naturalized, 1965; d. Takeichi and Kinue (Soma) Sato; m. Virgil Kiser, Dec. 4, 1979 (dec. Mar. 1981). Secondary teaching credential Tsuda Coll., Tokyo, 1945; B.A., Trinity U., San Antonio, 1953; B.F.A., Ohio State U., 1956, M.A., 1959; M.L.S., cert. library media specialist SUNY-Albany, 1974. Reporter, with pub. relations dept. The Mainichi Newspapers, Osaka, Japan, 1945-50; contract interpreter U.S. Dept. State, Washington, 1956-58, 66-67; resource specialist Richmond (Calif.) Unified Sch. Dist., 1968-69; editing supr. CTB/McGraw-Hill, Monterey, Calif., 1969-71; multi-media specialist Monterey Peninsula Unified Sch. Dist., 1975-77; librarian Nishimachi Internat. Sch., Tokyo, 1979-80; librarian Sacramento City Unified Sch. Dist., 1977-79, 81-85; sr. librarian profl. library Camarillo State Hosp., Calif., 1985—. Editor: Tests of Basic Experience, 1970; Short Form Test of Academic Aptitude, 1970; Prescriptive Mathematics Inventory, 1970; producer video tape rec. prodn. Introduction to Origami, Part I and Part II, 1977. Mem. Matsuyama-Sacramento Sister City Corp., 1981—. Title II-B, Higher Edn. Act, U.S. Office Edn. scholar, 1974. Mem. ALA, NEA, AAUW, Calif. Library Assn., Calif. Tchrs. Assn., Calif. Media and Library Educators Assn., Calif. State Supts. Regional Council on Asian Pacific Affairs, Sacramento Area Librarians Orgn., Sacramento City Tchrs. Assn., Japanese Am. Citizens League, UN Assn. U.S.A., Ikenobo Ikebana Soc. No. Calif., Ikenobo Ikebana Soc. Am., Internat. House of Japan, Mus. Soc. Christian Scientist. Office: Profl Library Camarillo State Hosp Box A 1878 S Lewis Rd Camarillo CA 93011

KISER-BROWN, GAIL ANNETTE, nurse educator; b. Charlotte, N.C., Aug. 31, 1945; d. Walter Webb and Lottie Jane (Bumgarner) Kiser. A.D.N., Central Piedmont Community Coll., Charlotte, 1968; B.S. in Nursing with high honors, U. N.C.-Charlotte, 1973; M.S. in Nursing, U. N.C.-Chapel Hill, 1976. Staff nurse Charlotte Meml. Hosp., 1968-73, nursing coordinator, 1973-74, research asst., 1975; instr. nursing Clemson U., (S.C.), 1976-81, asst. prof., 1981—, chmn. fine arts com. Coll. Nursing, 1977-82, chmn. scholarship and awards, 1983—, coordinator emergency nursing course continuing edn., 1982-83; nursing extern coordinator Greenville Hosp. System (S.C.), summers 1977-81; clin. instr. Med. U. S.C., summer 1982; researcher in pain relief. CPR instr. S.C. Heart Assn., Pickens County, 1978—. Mem. Am. Nurses Assn., Sigma Theta Tau (pres. chpt. 1983-84, counselor 1984-86). Republican. Methodist. Home: Route 8 Nottingham Ln Easley SC 29640 Office: Coll Nursing Clemson Univ Clemson SC 29631

KISH, CARLA E., organization executive; b. Ann Arbor, Mich.; d. Leslie and Rhea (Kuleske) Kish; B.A., U. Mich., 1970, M.Sc., 1972; M.A., London Sch. Econs., Eng., 1974. Cons., Subcom. on Energy and Environment, Ho. Com. on Interior and Insular Affairs, 1976-80; Western rep. Western Orgn. Resource Councils, 1980; legis. asst. to Sen. Levin of Mich., 1980-84; dep. conservation dir. The Wilderness Soc., 1984—. Office: The Wilderness Soc 1400 Eye St NW Washington DC 20005

KISHEL, PATRICIA GUNTER, management consultant; b. Los Angeles, Sept. 4, 1948; d. John Exum and Pauline Beatrice (Smith) Gunter; B.A., UCLA, 1970, M.F.A., 1972; M.B.A., Calif. State U., Long Beach, 1978; m. Gregory Francis Kishel, July 1, 1977. Script writer Salenger Ednl. Media, Santa Monica, Calif., 1972-79; traffic/pub. service coordinator Theta Cable TV, Santa Monica, 1973-74; adminstr. C.B.S., Inc., Los Angeles, 1974-78; partner Kishel Cons. Group, Laguna Hills, Calif., 1978—; instr. Calif. State U., Long Beach, 1978-81, Long Beach City Coll., 1979—, Brooks Coll., 1978—. Mem. Authors Guild, Womens Nat. Book Assn., Book Publicists Assn. So. Calif., Network Group, AAUW. Author: Student Survival Guide, 1979; (with G.F. Kishel) How to Start, Run and Stay in Business, 1981; Your Business is a Success: Now What?, 1983; Dollars on Your Doorstep: The Complete Guide to Homebased Businesses, 1984; Cashing In On the Consulting Boom, 1985. Address: 22311 Caminito Tecate Laguna Hills CA 92653

KISHKON, ELIZABETH, mayor, broadcaster; b. Oshana, Ont., Can., Jan. 7, 1931; d. Alfred and Vi Irene (Jeffrey) Reeve; m. Nicholas Kishkon, Feb. 17, 1951 (div. 1977); children—Jan Elizabeth, Kim Victoria, Lisa Kay, Lynne (dec.), John (dec.). City councillor City of Windsor, Ont., 1970-72, 80-82, mayor, 1983—; radio broadcaster CBC, 1972-80. Author CBC radio documentary Alex Zonjic Jazz, 1979, Point Pelee and Its People, 1978. Mem. Windsor Planning Bd., 1978-80, Beautification Com., 1978-80, John Howard Soc., 1970-73. Mem. Womens Econ. Forum. Avocations: reading; political study; nature study; music. Home: 8888 Riverside Dr E Apt 2102 Windsor ON N9A 6S1 Canada Office: Mayors Office City Hall Square Windsor ON N9A 6S1 Canada

KISIEL, YVONNE MARIE, lawyer; b. Washington, Feb. 27, 1954; d. Joseph Francis and Marie Claire (Lavigne) Cassidy; m. Kenneth Walton Kisiel, Mar. 31, 1973. B.A. with honors, Fla. Atlantic U., 1977; J.D. with honors, George Washington U., 1981. Bar: Md. 1981. Legal intern U.S. Dept. Justice, Washington, 1979-81; assoc. firm Whiteford, Taylor & Preston, Balt., 1981—. Assoc. editor Jour. Internat. Law and Econs., 1980-81. Served with USAF, 1972-75. Mem. ABA, Md. State Bar Assn., Phi Kappa Phi. Democrat. Office: Whiteford Taylor & Preston Seven St Paul St Suite 1400 Baltimore MD 21202

KISKOWSKI, ANNA MARIE, school nursing administrator; b. South Bend, Ind., Aug. 7, 1928; d. Barnhard D. and Verna K. (Wilkeson) Johnson; m. Robert G. Kiskowski, May 21, 1983 (dec. Sept. 1984). B.S. in Nursing Edn., Ind. U., 1955, M.S. in Health and Safety, 1957. Cert. sch. nurse. Staff nurse Meth. Hosp., Indpls., 1949-51; pediatric supr. Meml. Hosp., South Bend, 1951-53; sch. nurse South Bend Community Sch. Corp., 1955-74, coordinator health services, 1974—; chmn. Ind. Sch. Nurse Consortium, Indpls., 1977-81; adv. com. Ind. U. Sch. Nursing, South Bend, 1981-84. Adv. com. Project Head Start, South Bend, 1980-86; bd. dirs. Child Abuse and Neglect Orgn., 1982-86, Diabetes Assn. St. Joseph County (Ind.), 1984-86, Meml. Continuing Edn. Inst., 1985-86; mem. Sexual Abuse Consortium, 1981-84. Recipient cert. of appreciation Ind. U. Sch. Nursing, 1982. Mem. Am. Sch. Health Assn., AAUW, Nursing Research Consortium North Central Ind., Delta Kappa Gamma. Lutheran. Home: 51742 Portage Rd South Bend IN 46628 Office: South Bend Community School Corp 635 S Main St South Bend IN 46601

KISLAK, JEAN HART, art director; b. Mineola, N.Y.; d. Frank Ernest and Isabelle Tayor (Ellis) Hart; student Peace Jr. Coll., Raleigh, N.C., Queens Coll., Charlotte, N.C.; m. William I. Herendeen, Aug. 22; m. 2d, Louis G. Johnson, Jan. 31; 1 dau., Jennifer Taylor; m. Jay Kislak, Apr. 7, 1985. With Storer Broadcasting Co., Miami, Fla.; with Southeast Banks N.A., Miami, Fla., 1974—, art dir., 1981-84; mem. Gov. Fla. Panel Visual Arts, 1980, Dade County Art in Public Places, 1979-81; art cons., 1974—. Bd. dirs. Viscaya Museum, Miami, 1963, Beaux Arts, U. Miami, 1968, Theatre Art Patrons, Miami, 1965; mem. Bacardi Imports Art Bd., 1983—, Kislak Art Found., 1986—. Recipient Gov. Fla. award art, 1976, 79, Miami Dade Public Library award, 1978, Bus. Com. for Arts award, 1975-79, WPBT Public TV award, 1976, 77, 80, Lowe Gallery, U. Miami cert. recognition, 1980, Dade County Art in Public Places cert. recognition, 1981. Address: 2 Palm Bay Ct Apt 21W Miami FL 33138

KISNER, SARAH L., management analyst; b. Aug. 18, 1948; d. Ernest Lee and Laura E. (Milton) Beck; m. Gerald D. Kisner, June 14, 1969 (div. Nov. 1983); children—Kimberly Christen, Samuel Edward. Student Cleve. State U. Personal sec. Congressman Louis Stokes, Cleve., 1969-72; exec. sec. Boston Police Commr., 1973-75; staff asst. Senator Edward Brooke, Boston, 1975; adminstrv. asst. Boston Police Commr., 1975-77; asst. personnel adminstr. Police Prosecutor of Cleve., 1977-79; mgmt. analyst Cleve. Dept. Human Services, 1981—; dir. Nat. City Bank, Cleve. Talk show host Sta. WJMO-AM, 1984—. Mem. pub. relations com. Harvard Community Service Ctr., Cleve., 1986; truste Glenville Devel. Corp., 1986—, Upward Bound, 1984—. Mem. NAACP (br. sec. 1984; award 1985). Baptist. Clubs: Cleve. City; Karamu Women's. Avocations: reading; sewing; racquetball; tennis; antiques. Home: 11219 Wade Park Ave Cleveland OH 44106

KISTIAKOWSKY, VERA, physics researcher and educator; b. Princeton, N.J., Sept. 9, 1928; d. George Bogdan and Hildegard (Moebius) K.; m. Gerhard Emil Fischer, June 16, 1951 (div. 1975); children—Marc Laurenz Fischer, Karen Marie Fischer. A.B., Mt. Holyoke Coll., 1948, Sc.D. (hon.), 1978; Ph.D., U. Calif.-Berkeley, 1952. Staff scientist U.S. Naval Research Def. Lab., San Francisco, 1952-53; fellow U. Calif.-Berkeley, 1953-54; research assoc. Columbia U., N.Y.C., 1954-57, instr., 1957-59; asst. prof. Brandeis U., Waltham, Mass., 1959-62, adj. assoc. prof., 1962-63; staff mem. MIT, Cambridge, 1963-69, sr. research scientist, 1969-72; prof. physics, 1972—; Phi Beta Kappa lectr., Washington, 1983-84. Author: Atomic Energy, 1959; One Way Is Down, 1967; contbr. articles on nuclear and elem. particle physics to profl. jours. Dir. Council for a Liveable World, Boston, 1983—. Recipient Centennial award Mt. Holyoke Coll., 1972. Fellow Am. Phys. Soc. (councilor 1974-77); mem. Assn.

for Women in Sci. (pres. 1982-83). Office: 24-522 MIT 77 Massachusetts Ave Cambridge MA 02139

KISZELY, JOY MILLER, educator, pianist; b. Cleve., May 16, 1941; d. Robert Karl and Betty (Andrews) Miller; student Mozarteum, Salzburg, Austria, 1961-62; B.M., Oberlin Coll., 1963; postgrad. Ind. U., 1966-67; m. Andor Kiszely, Sept. 2, 1967. Co-founder, co-dir. Main Line Conservatory of Music, Ardmore, Pa., 1967—; musical dir., condr. string orch., Wayne, Pa., 1972-78; lectr. on hist. keyboard instruments. Chmn. music com. Lower Merion Vol. Resource Program, 1972-78. Mem. Nat. Music Tchrs. Assn. (adjudicator), Pa. Music Tchrs. Assn. (v.p. 1973-75, Disting. Tchr. of Yr. award 1982), Phila. Music Tchrs. Assn. (dir. 1980—, pres. 1984), Am. Liszt Soc., Nat. Guild Piano Tchrs. (Hall of Fame 1982), Am. Music Scholarship Assn. (Eastern regional chmn. auditions Curtis Inst. 1984). Home: 925 Coopertown Rd Bryn Mawr PA 19010 Office: 27 W Lancaster Ave Ardmore PA 19003

KITAGAWA, AUDREY EMIKO, lawyer; b. Honolulu, Mar. 31, 1951; s. Yonoichi and Yoshiko (Nagaishi) K. B.A. cum laude, U. So. Calif., 1973; J.D., Boston Coll., 1976. Bar: Hawaii, 1977, U.S. Dist. Ct. Hawaii, 1977. Assoc., Rice, Lee & Wong, Honolulu, 1977-80; sole practice, Honolulu, 1980—. Exec. editor Internat. Law Jour., 1976. Mem. Historic Hawaii Found., 1984. Mem. Hawaii Bar Assn. (v.p. internat. law sect. 1985—, mem. family law com. 1980—), ABA, Assn. Trial Lawyers Am., Japan Hawaii Lawyers Assn. (v.p. 1982—), Law Office Mgmt. Discussion Group, Hawaii Lawyers Care, Phi Alpha Delta. Republican. Club: Honolulu. Office: 820 Mililani St Apt 615 Honolulu HI 96813

KITCH, DIANA LEBOSQUET, therapist; b. Wichita, Kans., July 1, 1941; d. John Rude and Florence Edith (Bergstresser) LeBosquet; B.A. in Philosophy and Religion, Southwestern Coll., 1963; M.A. in Psychology, Wichita State U., 1979; m. Paul Richard Kitch, Apr. 1, 1974; children—Mary Suzanne, William Russell Parlette. Staff counselor Wichita State U. Counseling Center, 1976—; cons. to chaplain VA Hosp., Wichita, 1980-81, psychology technician, 1979-80; cons. Developmental Vision Clinic, Wichita; vol. Suicide and Crisis Center, Honolulu, 1971-72. Acting chairperson Wichita Hospice, Inc., 1981-82. Mem. Am. Psychol. Assn., N. Am. Soc. Adlerian Psychology. Clubs: Wichita Country, Wichita. Contbr. articles to profl. jours. and books. Home: 8316 E Central Ave Wichita KS 67206 Office: PO Box 91 Wichita State U Counseling Center Wichita KS 67208

KITCHEN, MARY SUE, educator, consultant; b. Charleston, W.Va., May 1, 1943; d. Doy Edward and Lillian Catherine (Armstrong) Nangle; m. Jess Woodrow Kitchen, June 6, 1964; 1 child, Lisa Lynn. B.A. in Vocat. Home Econs., Glenville State Coll., 1964; M.A. in Home Econs. and Edn., Marshall U., 1967, specialization cert. in prevocat. exploration, 1983, M.S. in Vocat. Tech. Edn., 1984. Secondary tchr. Jefferson County Pub. Schs., W.Va., spring 1964; secondary tchr. Kanawha County Pub. Schs., W.Va., 1964-68, also adult educator, 1964-70; tchr. home econs. Sissonville Jr. High Sch., W.Va., 1970—, chmn. dept. applied arts, 1983—, dir. career open house, 1982—; adj. prof. W.Va. State Coll., Institute, 1975, Marshall U., Huntington, W.Va., 1985—; chmn. bd. dirs. Career Exploration Clubs W.Va., Charleston, 1983-86, co-planner officers tng. sch., Cedar Lakes, 1984-85. Co-author: Career Exploration Clubs of West Virginia Handbook, 1983; also ednl. guides. Mem. Tri-County Home Econs. Assn. (sec. 1984-85, pres. 1985—), Am. Home Econs. Assn., Horace-Mann-John Dewey Soc., Am. Vocat. Assn., W.Va. Edn. Assn., Nat. Assn. Female Execs., Kappa Omicron Phi, Phi Delta Kappa. Democrat. Methodist. Lodge: Shriners (dance unit). Home: 1713 Bristol Dr Charleston WV 25320 Office: Sissonville Jr High 8316 Old Mill Rd Sissonville WV 25320

KITTO, KATHLEEN LEONE, metallurgical engineer; b. Butte, Mont., Oct. 7, 1956; d. Howard Stanley and Elizabeth Mary (Murphy) K.; A.S., Mont. Coll. Mineral Sci. and Tech., 1976, B.S. with high honors, 1978, M.S., 1981. Student engr. Hanna Mining Co., 1977; research engr. Mont. Coll. Mineral Sci. and Tech., Butte, 1978-81; cons. metall. engr. Mineral Research Center, Butte, 1981—; pres. Mont. Micromet, Inc., 1983—; instr. dept. metallurgy Mont. Coll. Mineral Sci. and Tech., Butte, 1981—, also mem. human resources student experience com. Vol. judge high sch. sci. fair, Westinghouse Talent Search, 1974. Newmont scholar, 1974-78, Anaconda Sci. Fair scholar, 1972-74. Mem. Am. Soc. Metals, Am. Ceramic Soc., AIME, Soc. Women Engrs., Assn. Women in Computing, Alpha Sigma Mu, Mu Beta Pi. Republican. Roman Catholic. Contbr. articles to profl. jours. Home: 643 S Main St Butte MT 59701 Office: Mont Coll Mineral Sci and Tech 106 Metallurgy Bldg West Park St Butte MT 59701

KITTRELL, LAURA FRANCES, former employment counselor; b. Dallas, Jan. 12, 1918; d. William Henry and Frances Louise (Wasson) K. B.A. in Sociology, Tex. Women's U., 1939; M.Liberal Arts, So. Meth. U., 1973. Youth counselor Nat. Youth Adminstrn., Dallas, 1939-41; interviewer Tex. Employment Commn., Dallas, 1942-45, interviewer, counselor, 1950-76; mem. nat. staff ARC, Washington, 1945-46. Vol. Dallas County Democratic Com., 1976. Lutheran. Home: 5623 W Hanover Dallas TX 75209

KIZER, CAROLYN ASHLEY, poet, educator; b. Spokane, Wash., Dec. 10, 1925; d. Benjamin Hamilton and M. (Ashley) K.; m. Stimson Bullitt, Jan. 1948 (div.); children—Ashley Ann, Scott, Jill Hamilton; m. John Marshall Woodbridge, Apr. 11, 1975. B.A., Sarah Lawrence Coll., 1945; postgrad. Columbia U., 1946-47; studied poetry with Theodore Roethke, U. Wash., 1953-54. Specialist in lit. U.S. Dept. State, Pakistan, 1964-65; 1st dir. lit. programs Nat. Endowment for Arts, 1966-70; poet-in-residence U. N.C., Chapel Hill, 1970-74; Hurst prof. lit. Washington U., St. Louis, 1971; lectr. Spring Lecture Series, Barnard Coll., 1972; acting dir. grad. writing program Columbia U., 1972, prof. Sch. Arts, 1982; McGuffey lectr., poet-in-residence Ohio U., 1974; vis. poet Iowa Writer's Workshop, 1975, SUNY-Albany, 1982; prof. dept. English, U. Md., College Park, 1976-77; disting. vis. poet Centre Coll., Ky., 1979, Eastern Wash. U., 1980, Bucknell U., 1982; Elliston prof. poetry U. Cin., 1981; Bingham disting. prof. U. Louisville, 1982; prof. Stanford U., 1986; participant Internat. Poetry Festival, London, 1960-70, Yugoslavia, 1969, 70, Pakistan, 1969, Rotterdam, Netherlands, 1970, Knokke-le-Zut, Belgium. Author: The Ungrateful Garden, 1961; Knock upon Silence, 1965; Midnight Was My Cry, 1971; YIN: New Poems, 1984 (Pulitzer prize 1985); Mermaids in the Basement: Poems for Women, 1984; The Nearness of You, 1986; Carrying Over (transl.), 1986. Founder, editor Poetry N.W., 1959-65. Contbr. poems and articles to profl. jours. Recipient Gov.'s award, State of Wash., 1965, 85; 6 Borestone awards; 3 Pushcart awards; award Am. Acad. and Inst. Arts and Letters, 1985; award in lit. San Francisco Arts Commn., 1986. Mem. Poetry Soc. Am. (Masefield award), Acad. Am. Poets, PEN, ACLU, Amnesty Internat. Address: 1401 Leroy Ave Berkeley CA 94708

KIZMAN, SUSAN LEE, food company executive; b. Chgo., Apr. 27, 1947; d. William Fred and Violet Ann (Brandenburg) Herod; m. Joseph J. Kizman, Jr., Dec. 28, 1968 (div. July 1973); children—Michael, Wendy. Student Wright Coll., 1965-66, Triton Coll., 1980, 82, Roosevelt U., 1983-86. Coordinator exec. edn. IBM Corp., Chgo., 1968-69; sec., v.p. mktg. Bresler's 33 Flavors, Inc., Chgo., 1973-75, adminstrv. asst., 1975-77, dir. adminstrv. services, 1977-85, v.p., 1979-85; exec. v.p. Mama Tish's Enterprises, Ltd., 1985—. Mem. Women in Mgmt., Nat. Assn. Female Execs., Roundtable for Women in Food Service. Lutheran. Home: 8507 W Gregory St Chicago IL 60656 Office: 5345 N Rose St Rosemont IL 60018

KIZZEE, MARGARET LEIGH, finance editor, investment representative; b. Huntsville, Tex.; d. Amos Ulishes and Minnie Faye (Watkins) Leigh; m. Matthew Kizzee, June 3, 1978. B.S. with honors, Sam Houston State U.; postgrad. Houston Baptist U. Registered investment rep., Tex. Page editor Sam Houston State U., Huntsville, 1975-76, assoc. editor, 1976, editor, 1976-77; copy editing intern Roanoke Times & World-News, Va., 1977; fin. writer Bus. & Energy Internat., Inc., Houston, 1978-79; fin. editor Am. Capital Fin. Services, Inc., Houston, 1980—. Sam Houston State U. Alumni Assn. scholar, 1974; Jesse H. Jones Found. scholar, 1976; recipient Bill Hay Meml. award Bill Hay Found., 1977. Mem. Nat. Assn. Female Execs., Internat. Assn. Bus. Communicators, Sigma Delta Chi. Baptist. Avocations: restoring antiques; collecting rare books, coins and stamps; horticulture. Office: Am Capital Fin Services Inc 2800 Post Oak Blvd Houston TX 77056

KLAGSBRUNN, ELIZABETH RAMSEY, physician, placentologist; b. N.Y.C., Feb. 17, 1906; d. Charles Cyrus and Grace (Keys) Ramsey; grad. Bishop's Sch., LaJolla, Calif.; B.A., Mills Coll., 1928; fellow Inst. Internat. Edn., Hamburg, Germany, 1928-29; M.D., Yale U., 1932; D.Sc., Med. Coll. Pa., 1965; m. Hans Alexander Klagsbrunn, Jan. 27, 1934. Intern, asst. resident New Haven Hosp., 1932-34; asst. pathology Yale U., 1933-34; asso. pathology George Washington U., 1934-41, professorial lectr., 1941-55; asst. chief Office Med. Info., NRC, 1942-45; guest investigator dept. embryology Carnegie Inst., Washington, 1934-51, research asso. and pathologist, 1951-63, staff mem. placentalogy and pathology, 1963-71, research asso., 1976—; Mamie A. Jessup vis. prof. ob-gyn. U. Va. Sch. Medicine, 1972-76; Bartholomew Mosse Meml. lectr. Rotunda Hosp., Dublin, Ireland, 1970; professorial lectr. ob-gyn. Georgetown U. Sch. Medicine, 1981—. Bd. dirs. Nat. Symphony Orch., 1949—, 2d v.p., 1952-55, mem. exec. com., 1955-64, 67-68, 73-79, chmn., 1955-61, pres. women's com., 1950-52; trustee Cathedral Choral Soc., 1967-81, 83—. Recipient Alumna of Year citation Bishop's Sch., 1960, Lewis prize Am. Philos. Soc., 1970, diplome d'Honneur, Federation Internationale de Gynecologie Infantile et Juvenile, 1972. Hon. fellow Chgo. Gynec. Soc.; mem. Audubon Naturalist Soc. Central Atlantic States (dir. 1961-64), Am. Assn. Anatomists (exec. com. 1963-66, v.p. 1974-76), Am. Coll. Obstetricians and Gynecologists (hon. asso., recipient disting. service award 1976, named to Hall of Fame 1985), Am. Gynecol. Soc. (hon.), Perinatal Research Soc. (charter), Soc. Gynecologic Investigation (hon.), AAAS, Acad. Med. Scis. (Cordoba, Argentina) (acad. fgn. corr.), Soc. Perinatal Obstetricians, Phi Beta Kappa, Sigma Xi. Episcopalian. Club: City Tavern. Author: The Placenta of Laboratory Animals and Man, 1975; (with Martin W. Donner) Placental Vasculature and Circulation, 1980; The Placenta, Human and Animal, 1982; mem. editorial bd. Placenta. contbr. to profl. jours. Home: 3420 Q St NW Washington DC 20007 also Salem Farm Route 1 Box 600 Purcellville VA 22132

KLAJBOR, DOROTHEA M., lawyer, former state agency administrator; b. Dunkirk, N.Y., Dec. 2, 1915; d. Joseph M., Sr., and Susan R. (Schrantz) K.; student George Washington U., 1949-52; J.D., Am. U., Washington, 1956. Bar: D.C. 1957. Successively legal asst., legis. atty., atty., 2d asst. to chief U.S. marshal, civil rights compliance officer Dept. of Justice, Washington, 1938-70; supr. Town of Dunkirk, N.Y., 1973-76; mem. N.Y. State Liquor Authority, Buffalo, 1976-82; legal consultant, 1982—. Bd. dirs. Center for Women Govt., Albany, N.Y., 1978-82; mem. Chautauqua County Task Force on Aging, 1972-73, Town of Dunkirk Indsl. Devel. Agy., 1972-76, Chautauqua County Planning Bd., 1973-76, No. Chautauqua County Intermcpl. Planning Bd., 1974-76, Chautauqua County Overall Econ. Devel. Planning Bd., 1974-76, Literacy Vols., 1972-76, Dunkirk Vol. Fire Dept., 1973—; adv. bd. Dunkirk Sr. Citizens, 1974-76, bd. dirs., 1983; mem. women's div. N.Y. State Democratic Com. Recipient Industry Person of Yr. award, 1980; Calista Jones award for advancement rights of women, 1984. Mem. Am. Bar Assn., Fed. Bar Assn., Women's Bar Assn. D.C., AAUW, Nat. Lawyers Club, Cath. Daus. Am., Kappa Beta Pi. Democrat. Roman Catholic. Clubs: Chautauqua County Dem. Women's (treas. 1974-76), Town of Dunkirk Dem., Zonta (status of women com.). Home: 91 Forest Pl Fredonia NY 14063

KLAMERUS, KAREN JEAN, pharmacist, educator; b. Chgo., Aug. 10, 1957; d. Robert Edward and Jane Mary (Nawoj) K.; m. Frederick P. Zeller. B.S. in Pharmacy, U. Ill., 1980; Pharm. D., U. Ky., 1981. Registered pharmacist Ky., Ill. Staff pharmacist Haggin Meml. Hosp., Harrodsburg, Ky., 1980-81, Regional Med. Ctr., Madisonville, Ky., 1982; critical care liasion, 1982; clin. pharmacist resident U. Nebr., Omaha, 1983; clin. pharmacist cardiothoracic surgery U. Ill., Chgo., 1983—, clin. asst. prof. dept. pharmacy practice, 1983-86, asst. prof. dept., 1986—, affiliate dept. pharmaceutics, 1986—; cons. Dimensional Mktg. Inst., Chgo., 1983—, Channing, Weinbergs' Co., Inc., N.Y.C., 1983—; mem. rev. bd. Am. Jour. Hosp. Pharmacy, Clin. Pharmacy, Drug Intelligence and Clin. Pharmacy. Bd. dirs. Heart Assn. Du Page County, 1986—. Mem. Am. Assn. Colls. Pharmacy, Am. Coll. Clin. Pharmacy, Am. Heart Assn., Am. Soc. Hosp. Pharmacists, No. Ill. Soc. Hosp. Pharmacists, Rho Chi. Avocations: computers, sports, gardening, sewing. Office: U Ill Chgo 833 S Wood St Room 244 Chicago IL 60612

KLANS, VALERIE MARIE, medical center administrator, respiratory therapist; b. Chgo., Aug. 20, 1950; s. Robert Edward and Mary Ann (Zidarich) K. A.S., Triton Coll., 1976. Registered respiratory therapist. Staff therapist MacNeal Meml. Hosp., Berwyn, Ill., 1976, supr. respiratory therapy, 1976-81; critical care coordinator Mt. Sinai Med. Ctr., Miami Beach, Fla., 1981-86, dir. cardiopulmonary services Humana Hosp. Bennett, Plantation, Fla., 1986—; clin. instr. Triton Coll., 1981; clin. coordinator Med. Careers Inst., Chgo., 1980; clin. tutor Met. Group Hosp., Chgo., 1976-80. Contbr. articles to profl. jours. Bd. dirs. Sea Camp for Children Cystic Fibrosis, Key Largo, Fla., 1983, coordinating therapist, 1983; instr. CPR, Jewish Community Ctrs., North Miami, 1981. Mem. Internat. Assn. Quality Circles (v.p. Miami Dade chpt. 1983, bd. dirs. 1982-83), Fla. Com. Respiratory Therapy Edn. (sec. 1983-84), Fla. Soc. Respiratory Therapy (dir. chpt. affairs 1983-84, pres.-elect 1986-87). Roman Catholic. Office: Humana Hosp Bennett 8201 W Broward Blvd Plantation FL 33324

KLASSEN, ORETTA SUE, banker, bookkeeper; b. Avon Park, Fla., June 20, 1944; d. Richard Carl and Ethel Caroline (Mailten) Majors; m. Jan. 7, 1961; children—Max Jay, Mike Roy. Part-time bookkeeper Alfalfa County Bank, Cherokee, Okla., 1977-79, full-time bookkeeper, 1979-80, supr. of bookkeeper, 1980-82, asst. cashier, 1982, asst. v.p., 1982—. Mem. Nat. Assn. Bank Women. Home: PO Box 123 Burlington OK 73722 Office: Alfalfa County Bank 200 S Grand Cherokee OK 73728

KLEBANOW, BARBARA ELAINE, educator; b. N.Y.C., Dec. 6, 1936; d. Joseph Herman and Helen (Feldstein) Klebanow. B.A., U. Conn., 1958; M.S., Yeshiva U., 1960; profl. diploma U. Conn., 1965; M.S., Lehman Coll., 1977. Cert. sch. dist. adminstr., N.Y.; cert. reading specialist, N.Y.; cert. spl. edn. tchr., N.Y. Elem. classroom tchr. North Rockland Central Sch. Dist., Stony Point, N.Y., 1960-64, reading specialist elem. level, 1964-69, adminstv. internship in reading, reading specialist secondary level, 1977—; Internat. Reading Assn. state coordinator for N.Y., 1985-88. Fellow Assn. Women Adminstrs. in Westchester, Rockland Reading Council; mem. N.Y. State Reading Assn. (pres. 1983-84), Phi Delta Kappa. Avocations: travelling; reading; handicrafts. Office: North Rockland Central Sch 117 Main St Stony Point NY 10980

KLEE, MARGARET ANN, software engineer; b. Boston, Feb. 18, 1961; d. James Butt and Lucille Janet (Holljes) Klee. B.A., Simon's Rock Coll., 1981. Programmer, Goodyear Atomic Corp., Piketon, Ohio, 1982-84, software engr., 1984-85; software engr. Gen. Dynamics Corp., Fort Worth, 1985—. Mem. IEEE, Assn. for Computing Machinery, Soc. for Computer Simulation, Tex. Gould Users Group (chmn. Fort Worth 1985—), Ada Spl. Interest Group-Gould Users Group (chmn. 1985—), Nat. Assn. Female Execs. Episcopalian. Avocations: sailing; singing. Home: 209 Covington Dr Benbrook TX 76126

KLEFMAN, JUDITH ASHLEY JOHNSON, education and training consultant; b. Portland, Oreg., Nov. 19, 1941; d. Donald Christian and Jean Elizabeth (Rawson) Johnson; m. Melvyn Paul Klefman, Oct. 4, 1962 (dec.); 1 child, Ronald Paul. B.A. in English, U. Oreg., 1963; Tchr. schs. in Oreg., 1965-67; instl. social worker Multnomah County Sheriff's Dept., Portland, 1967-68; caseworker children's services div. Oreg. Dept. Human Resources, 1968-79; propr. Satori Assocs., Portland, 1979—; N.W. regional dir., internat. bd. dirs. Inst. Reality Therapy, practicum supr. level I and II, intensive week instr. level I, 1983—. Chmn. edn. and tng. subcom. Minority Bus. Opportunity Council, 1981—. Recipient various certs. of appreciation, letters commendation; cert. reality therapist. Mem. Nat. Assn. Female Execs. (network dir. 1979-80), NEA, Oreg. Corrections Assn., Oreg. Edn. Assn., Inst. Reality Therapy, Parents without Partners (chpt. pres. 1971-72, zone conf. chmn. 1975, assoc. zone adminstr. 1975-76), U. Oreg. Alumni Assn. (past pres. 1983-84, bd. dirs. 1983—). Republican. Episcopalian. Office: PO Box 8287 Portland OR 97207

KLEIMAN, MELODIE YVONNE, chief assistant county counsel; b. La Porte, Ind., Oct. 12, 1945; d. John and Edna Mae (Printup) McLennan; m. Theodore William Kleiman, Oct. 22, 1972; children—Marjorie, T'Anne, Sarah Margaret, Alexis Leah. A.B., U. So. Calif., 1968; J.D., Stanford U., 1971. Bar: Calif. 1972. In-house counsel Atlantic Richfield Co., Los Angeles, 1971-74; sole practice, Ventura, Calif., 1974-83; asst. county counsel County Ventura, Calif., 1983-85, chief asst. county counsel, 1985—; pres. Calif. Women Lawyers, 1978-79. Mem. Calif. State Bar. Democrat. Jewish. Office: Office of County Counsel 800 S Victoria Ave Ventura CA 93009

KLEIN, BETTY LUCILLE, educator; b. Big Springs, Nebr., Feb. 22, 1927; d. James Ray and Ella Nora (Lindauer) Barnica; m. Emanuel Leo Klein, Jan. 30, 1952; children—Joseph Stanley, John Lee. B.A., U. Ariz., 1962, M.Ed., 1967. Tchr., Day Sch., Big Springs, Nebr., 1944-46, Ogallala Pub. Schs., Nebr., 1947-52; tchr. Tucson Unified Sch. Dist., 1962-80, counselor, 1980-82; owner, dir. Spanish Trail Sch., Tucson, 1980—; tchr. Ariz. Dept. Spl. Edn., Phoenix, 1975-77. Mem. NEA, Nat. Assn. Edn. Young Children, Ariz. Assn. Child Devel. and Edn., U.S. C. of C., Delta Kappa Gamma. Democrat. Methodist. Avocations: Oil Painting; crafts; baking; reading. Home: 3740 Calle Guaymas Tucson AZ 85716 Office: Spanish Trail Sch 9395 E Old Spanish Trail Tucson AZ 85710

KLEIN, CHARLOTTE, owner dance studio; b. Worcester, Mass., Mar. 4, 1934; d. Herbert and Anna (Zack) Zitowitz; m. Benjamin Zalman Klein, June 12, 1955; children—Laura, Elisa (dec.). B.A. in Sociology, Worcester State Coll., 1975. Teaching cert. Dance Masters of Am. Owner, dir., dance tchr. Charlotte Klein Dance Ctrs., Inc., Worcester, 1952—; artistic dir. dance concert, 1983, 84. Mem. Dance Masters New Eng. (pres. 1978-80), Dance Tchrs. Club Boston, Worcester Ballet Soc. (trustee 1982—). Democrat. Jewish. Home: 9 Barr St Worcester MA 01602 Office: Charlotte Klein Dance Centers Inc 1122 Pleasant St Worcester MA 01602

KLEIN, ESTHER MOYERMAN (MRS. PHILIP KLEIN), publisher; b. Phila., Nov. 3, 1907; d. Louis and Rebecca (Feldman) Moyerman; B.S., Temple U., 1929; student U. London, 1954; m. Philip Klein, Apr. 26, 1930; children—Arthur, Karen Louise Klein Mannes. Reporter, Phila. Jewish Times, 1925, Atlantic City Times, 1927; feature writer Pub. Ledger Syndicate, 1928-29, Pub. Ledger, Evening Bull., Phila. Record, 1929-32; pub. relations counsellor, editor Art Alliance Bull., 1945-49; commentator Sta. WPEN, 1949-53; pub. Phila. Jewish Times, 1953-74; author, hist. researcher, 1974—; lectr. women's clubs, 1951—. Del. Internat. Conf. Residential Adult Edn., Holland, 1957, Germany, 1959; participant in first workshop Residential Adult Edn. for Adult Edn. Assn. U.S., 1954. Mem. Gov.'s Commn. on Charitable Orgns., 1969—; chmn. Rittenhouse Sq. Women's com. for Phila. Orch., 1957; organizer bicentennial women's com. Walnut St. Theatre; adv. com. Friends Nat. Independence Hist. Park; chmn. bicentennial program Beth Zion - Beth Israel Congregation; bd. dirs. Rittenhouse Found., Phila. Jewish Times Inst., also dir. ann. cooking festivals; exec. com. Long Beach Island Found. Arts and Scis., N.J. Named Distinguished Dau. Pa.; recipient Gimbel Phila. award, 1975; awards Alumnae Girls High Sch., Phila. Art Alliance, Temple U., City Council Phila., Colonial Hist. Soc.; Klein Recital Hall at Temple U. named in her honor. Mem. Pa. Newspaper Pubs. Assn., Temple U. Alumni (honored at 80th anniversary, 1964), Phila. High Sch. for Girls Alumnae, Hannah Penn House, Emergency Aid of Pa., Chgo. Art Mus., Mus. Modern Art N.Y., Pan Am. Assn. Club: Print. Author: A Guidebook to Jewish Philadelphia, 1965; International House Celebrity Cookbook, 1965; History and Guidebook of Fairmount Park, 1974. Address: 135 S 18th St Philadelphia PA 19103

KLEIN, FRANCES ANN WANG (MRS. ELVIN B. KLEIN), toy co. exec.; b. Bklyn., June 18, 1923; d. Philip and Sarah (Eckstein) Wang; B.S. with high honors, U. Ill., 1945; m. Elvin B. Klein, June 23, 1943 (div.); children—Michael, Bari Klein Freiden, Philip. Pre-sch. tchr. Kansas City (Mo.) Co-op. Pre-Sch., 1952-59; co-founder U.S. Toy Co., Inc., Kansas City, Mo., 1952, exec. v.p., 1952—, founder Constructive Playthings div., 1954; guest lectr. at tchr.-tng. instns., 1959—; mem. adv. council, spl. edn. dept. Shawnee-Mission Sch. Dist., 1972. Mem. Mo. (state sec. 1967-68), Kansas City (v.p. 1956-57) assns. for edn. young children, Johnson County Assn. Children with Learning Disabilities (v.p. 1970-71), Council Jewish Women, Phi Sigma Sigma. Jewish. Clubs: Hadassah, Altrusa (dir.) (Kansas City, Mo.). Home: 8301 Briar Ln Prairie Village KS 66207 Office: 1227 E 119th St Grandview MO 64036

KLEIN, HARRIET FARBER, lawyer; b. Elizabeth, N.J., Apr. 30, 1948; d. Melvin Julius and Frances Mildred (Novit) Farber; m. Paul Martin Klein, Sept. 9, 1973; children—Andrew, Zachary. B.A. with honors, Douglass Coll., New Brunswick, N.J., 1970; J.D., Rutgers U., 1973. Bar: N.J. 1973, U.S. Dist. Ct. N.J. 1973. Jud. clk. chancery div. Superior Ct. N.J., 1973-74; assoc. Budd, Larner, Kent, Gross, Picillo & Rosenbaum, Newark, 1974-78; ptnr. Greenbaum, Rowe, Smith, Ravin, Davis & Bergstein (and predecessor), Woodbridge, N.J., 1979—; reader N.J. State Bd. Bar Examiners, 1977—, mem. Essex-Newark Legal Services Vol. Project, 1983-84. Lt., Fourth of July Com., Maplewood, N.J., 1980—; pres. Sisterhood of Congregation B'nai Israel, Millburn, N.J., 1985—. Mem. Essex County Bar Assn., N.J. Bar Assn., ABA, Order of Barristers, Phi Alpha Theta. Home: 45 Ridgewood Terr Maplewood NJ 07040 Office: Greenbaum Rowe et al PO Box 5600 Woodbridge NJ 07095

KLEIN, IRMA FRANCES, career development educator, consultant; b. New Orleans, Jan. 5, 1936; d. Harry Joseph and Gesina Frances (Bauer) Molligan; m. John Vincent Chelena (dec. 1963); 1 child, Joseph William; m. Chris George Klein, Aug. 14, 1965; 1 stepchild, Arnold Conrad. Student pub. schs., New Orleans. Mgr. Stan Weber & Assocs., Metairie, La., 1971-75; tng. dir., 1975-81; cons. Coldwell Banker Comml. Co., New Orleans, 1981; dir. career devel. Coldwell Banker Residential Co., New Orleans, 1982—. Author: Career Development, 1982; Training Manual, 1978. Mem. La. Realtors Assn. (bd. dirs. 1973-74, grad. Realtors Inst. 1976), Jefferson Bd. Realtors (v.p. 1984), Research Club of New Orleans (pres. 1984-85), Realtors Nat. Mktg. Inst. (ambassador Tex. and La. 1985—, Outstanding Achievement award 1985, cert. broker 1980, residential specialist 1977), CRB (La. chpt.; pres. 1982-83, chmn. edn.). Republican. Roman Catholic. Clubs: Antique Study Group of New Orleans, Confederate Lit. (New Orleans). Avocation: antiques.

KLEIN, JO ANN MARTUCCI, office systems methods analyst; b. Mt. Vernon, N.Y., Mar. 4, 1947; d. Joseph Anthony and Ann Gloria Isabell (Paparatto) Martucci; m. Henry Alexander Klein, Oct. 22, 1972. Student in Math., Columbia U., 1965-67; A.A., Fairleigh Dickinson U., 1984, B.S., 1986. Cert. tchr., spl. edn., N.Y. Exec. asst. Gordon W. White Inc., N.Y.C., 1965-66; asst. editor Columbia U., N.Y.C., 1966-69, mgr. classified documentation/data processing, 1969-72; asst. security officer Riverside Research Inst., N.Y.C., 1972-75; internal cons. Consolidated Edison, N.Y.C., 1975—; cons. and lectr. in field. Contbr. articles to profl. jours. Chairperson major gifts program Juvenile Diabetes Found., N.J. and N.Y. chpt., 1972-86; chairperson publicity and fund raising Am. Diabetes Assn., N.J., 1985-86. Mem. Office Products Exchange Network (founder, pres. 1984-86, dir.-editor OPEN newsletter 1984-85), Am. Mgmt. Assn., Assn. Info. Systems Profls., Assn. Women in Computing, Nat. Assn. Female Execs., Cons. Interface, Am. Soc. Indsl. Security. Avocations: golf; swimming; interior decorating; photography; handicrafts.

KLEIN, KAREN, pension analyst; b. Detroit, Feb. 3, 1959; d. Henry Morton and Eleanore (Tand) Klein. B.A., Vanderbilt U., 1980. Benefits adminstr. Commerce Union Bank, Nashville, 1980-81; benefits coordinator InterFirst Corp., Dallas, 1981-83, pension analyst, 1984—. Active Washington Workshops, 1976; sponsor 500, Inc., arts support group, 1986—; mem. Dallas Summer Musicals Guild. Named hon Ky. col., 1979. Mem. Vanderbilt U. Alumni Assn., Alpha Delta Pi. Republican. Home: 9821 Summerwood Circle Apt 2403 Dallas TX 75243 Office: InterFirst Corp PO Box 83000 Dallas TX 75283

KLEIN, KIMBERLY, fundraising executive; b. Durango, Colo., Nov. 17, 1953; d. Charles Frederick and Phyllis (Hum) Klein. B.A., Beloit Coll., 1976. Devel. assoc. Pacific Sch. Religion, Berkeley, Calif., 1977-78; fundraising coordinator Coalition for Med. Rights of Women, San Francisco, 1978-81; fundraising trainer, self-employed, Inverness, Calif., 1981—; faculty Fund Raising Sch., San Rafael, Calif., 1982—. Co-publisher, editor mag. Grassroots Fundraising Jour., 1982; author: Fundraising for Social Change, 1984; contbr. articles to profl. jours. Bd. dirs. DES Action Nat., San Francisco, 1982—, Coalition for Med. Rights of Women, 1981-83, Environ. Forum, San Rafael, Calif., 1984; co-founder A Safe Place-Shelter for Battered Women, Oakland, Calif., 1977-80. Mem. Nat. Soc. Fund Raising Execs., Devel. Execs. Roundtable, Mortar Bd., Omicron Delta Kappa. Home: 105 Vision Rd Inverness CA 94937 Office: Kim Klein PO Box 640 Inverness CA 94937

KLEIN, SISTER M. ROSALIE, educational administrator; b. Milw.; B.S. in Nursing, Marquette U., 1952, M.S. in Nursing, 1960; M.Med. Sci., Tulane U., 1968, D.Sc., 1970. Nursing supr. St. Francis Hosp., Cape Girardeau, Mo., 1952-54; nursing supr. St. Michael Hosp., Milw., 1954-56, dir. nursing service, 1956-59; instr. Marquette-U. Milw., 1959-62, asst. prof. 1962-67, coordinator, basic program in nursing, 1965-67, dean Coll. Nursing, 1970—. Bd. dirs. St.

Joseph's Hosp., St. Michael's Hosp., Marian Catholic Home for Aged. Mem. Nat. League Nursing, Am. Assn. Colls. Nursing, Wis. Assn. Collegiate Schs. Nursing, Am. Nurses Assn., Am. Pub. Health Assn., Am. Assn. Higher Edn., Western Soc. Research in Nursing, Milw. Dist. Nurses Assn. Home: 3066 N 49th St Milwaukee WI 53210 Office: Marquette U Coll Nursing 510 N 16th St Milwaukee WI 53233

KLEIN, MARGRETE SIEBERT, physicist, research administrator; b. Cleve., Feb. 28, 1938; d. Arthur Aloysius and Martha Margrete (Siebert) K.; B.S., Baldwin-Wallace Coll., 1960; M.S., U. Mich., 1964; Ph.D., Northwestern U., 1978; m. Jacques Paul Klein, Aug. 24, 1968; children—Christian Andre-Albert, Maia Margrete-Odile. Asst. prof. physics Chgo. City Colls., 1964-71; researcher, writer, cons. Bremen, Berlin, Bonn, Germany, Washington, 1974-80; staff assoc. NSF, Directorate Sci. and Engring. Edn., Washington, 1980, program mgr. info. dissemination sci. edn., 1980-82, staff assoc. div. physics, 1982-83, dir. vis. professorships for women program, research opportunities for women program, 1983—; chmn. Citizens Adv. Com. Gifted and Talented Edn., Falls Church (Va.) City Schs., 1981-83. Internat. Research and Exchanges Bd. grantee, 1982. Mem. exec. com. Citizens for a Better City, Falls Church, Va., 1980-82. Mem. LWV, AAAS, AAUP, Nat. Sci. Tchrs. Assn., Nat. Soc. Study Edn., Comparative and Internat. Edn. Soc. Author: The Challenge of Communist Education: A Look at the German Democratic Republic, 1980; sr. editor: Science Education in Global Perspective: Lessons from Five Countries, 1984. Office: NSF Div Research Initiation and Improvement Washington DC 20550

KLEIN, PAULA SCHWARTZ, development officer; b. Chgo., Oct. 16, 1941; d. Arthur A. and Rosalyn (Davidson) Schwartz; student Mich. State U., 1959-60; B.A., Governors State U., 1974, M.A., 1975; m. Sanford David Klein, Dec. 18, 1960 (div. 1981); children—Gregory Scott, Julie Ann. Mem. editorial staff Okinawa Morning Star. Machinato, 1960-63; exec. dir. Bloom Twp. Com. on Youth, Chicago Heights, Ill., 1975-81; dir. dept. fund devel. and public relations South Chgo. Community Hosp., 1981-85, also v.p. South Chgo. Health Care Found.; dir. devel. and pub. relations Chgo. Crime Commn., 1985—. Mem. Calumet Indsl. Commn. Mem. Nat. Soc. Fund Raising Execs., Nat. Assn. Prevention Profls., So. Suburban Youth Service Alliance, Criminal Def. Consortium, Nat. Assn. Hosp. Devel., Twp. Ofcls. Ill., Youth Network Council, Sierra Club. Jewish. Home: 2100 Lincoln Park W Chicago IL 60614 Office: Chgo Crime Commn 79 W Monroe St Chicago IL 60603

KLEIN, PHYLLIS KATZ, public relations executive; b. Trenton, N.J., Aug. 14, 1945; d. Milton and Frieda (Green) Katz; m. Neil Kleinhandler, 1970 (div. 1978). B.S., Boston U. Sch. Communication, 1967. Adminstrv. asst. Am. Petroleum Inst., N.Y.C., 1967-69; account exec. Irving Straus Assocs., N.Y.C., 1969-70; account exec., supr. Daniel J. Edelman Inc., N.Y.C., 1971-72; dir. publicity-pub. relations Clairol, N.Y.C., 1972—; corporate spokesperson various TV talk shows, 1980—. Mem. Am. Women in Radio and TV (chairwoman publicity N.Y. chpt. 1983-84), Women in Communications, Fashion Group. Democrat. Jewish. Office: Clairol 345 Park Ave New York NY 10154

KLEIN, RUTH B., civic worker, packaging co. exec., poet, author; b. Cin., Jan. 31, 1908; d. Samuel and Minnie (Schunke) Becker; student U. Calif. at Los Angeles, 1926-28, San Jose State Coll., 1928-29; m. Charles Henle Klein, Sept. 23, 1938; children—Betsy Klein Schwartz, Charles Henle, Carla Klein Fee III. Sec., Novelart Mfg. Co., Cin., 1960—, dir., 1960—. Vol. Aid to Visually Handicapped program Cin. sect. Nat. Council of Jewish Women, 1951-82, sec., 1954-56, 63-64, bd. dirs., 1952-70; bd. dirs. Civic Garden Center of Greater Cin., 1956-63, chmn. spl. services for aid to visually handicapped, 1952-82. Mem. Nat. Braille Assn., Greater Cin. Writers League, Verse Writers' Guild Ohio. Club: Contemporary Literary. Author: Latitude of Love; Longitude of Lust, 1979; contbr. poems to various anthologies. Home: 6754 Fair Oaks Dr Cincinnati OH 45237

KLEIN-GILLIGAN, BONNEE, advertising executive; b. Pitts., May 27, 1954; d. James J. and Patricia R. (Redrick) Klein; m. James Vincent Gilligan, July 4, 1981. Diploma in graphic arts, York Acad. Arts, 1975. Art. dir. Imaging Systems Corp., Derry, Pa., 1978-81; advt. mgr. Pelikan, Inc., Franklin, Tenn., 1981-84; pres., owner Personal Expressions Advt., 1983—. Freelance designer, 1975-85; Recipient plaque Office Mag., 1978, Office World News Mag., 1981; Best Read Ad award Geyers' Dealer Topics Mag., 1982. Mem. Am. Advt. Fedn., Nashville C. of C. Office; 164 8th Ave N Nashville TN 37203

KLEINLEIN, KATHY LYNN, career counseling executive; b. S.I., N.Y., May 2, 1950; d. Thomas and Helen Mary (O'Reilly) Perricone; m. Kenneth Robert Kleinlein, Oct. 30, 1983. B.A., Wagner Coll., 1971, M.A., 1974; M.B.A., Rutgers U., 1984. Cert. secondary tchr., N.Y., N.J., Fla. Tchr. English, N.Y.C. Bd. Edn., S.I., 1971-74, Matawan (N.J.) Bd. Edn., 1974-79; instr. English, Middlesex County Coll., Edison, N.J., 1978-81; med. sales rep. Pfizer/Roerig, Bklyn., 1979-81, mgr. tng. ops., N.Y.C., from 1981; pres. Women in Transition, career counseling firm; personnel mgmt. officer U.S. Army Res., N.J., 1981—; cons. Concepts & Producers, N.Y.C., 1981-85. Trainer United Way, 1982-83, mem. polit. action com., 1982—; mem. Republican Presdl. Task Force, Washington, 1983—. Served to Capt., U.S. Army, 1974-78. First woman in N.Y. Army N.G., 1974; first woman instr. Empire State Mil. Acad., Peekskill, N.Y., 1976. Mem. Nat. Soc. Pharm. Sales Trainers, Sales and Mktg. Execs., Am. Soc. Tng. and Devel., N.J. Assn. Women Bus. Owners, LWV, Matawan C. of C., Alpha Omicron Pi. Republican. Roman Catholic. Club: Atlantis Divers (N.Y.C.). Home: 93 Idolstone Ln Matawan NJ 07747 Office: Women in Transition 93 Idolstone Ln Matawan NJ 07747

KLESPIES, LINDA SUE, company administrator; b. Akron, Ohio, May 12, 1952; d. Nicholas Joseph and Willie Ruth (Bryan) K. Mus.B., Mt. Union Coll., 1974; Mus.M., Wichita State U., 1976; B.Mus. Edn., Ohio State U., 1979; postgrad. in Musicology, Ind. U., 1977. Tchr. music Bd. Edn. Findlay (Ohio), 1979-80; mgr. trainee Friendly Restaurant, Canton, Ohio, 1980; asst. mgr. Ponderosa Inc., Kent, Ohio, 1980-82, dist. tng. instr., Kansas City, Kans., 1982, designer, Dayton, 1982-83, orgn. devel. specialist, Dayton, 1983-85; personnel adminstr. Frito-Lay, Inc., 1985-86; human resource systems mgr. Stone Container Corp., 1986—. Dir. children's choir Ch. of Master, Akron, 1972-73; dir. choir Salem United Meth. Ch., Wichita, 1974-76; mem. bd. advisors hospitality mgmt. program Ohio State U., 1984-85, home study div. Cornell U., 1984-85. Mem. Internat. Assn. Quality Circles, Am. Soc. Tng. and Devel., Nat. Assn. Female Execs., Smithsonian Assocs., Mortar Bd., Mu Phi Epsilon, Pi Lambda Theta, Alpha Lambda Delta. Democrat. Methodist. Office: Stone Container Corp PO Box 105 Cantonment FL

KLIEBHAN, MARY CAMILLE, university president; b. Milw., Apr. 4, 1923; d. Alfred Sebastian and Mae Eileen (McNamara) K.; B.A., Cath. Sisters Coll., Washington, 1949; M.A., Cath. U. Am., 1951, Ph.D., 1955. Joined Order of St. Francis of Assisi, Roman Cath. Ch., 1945; legal sec. Spence and Hanley, Milw., 1941-45; instr. edn. dept. Cardinal Stritch Coll., Milw., 1955-62, asso. prof., 1962-68, prof., 1968—, head dept. of edn., 1962-67, dean of students, 1962-64, chmn. grad. div., 1964-69, v.p. acad. and student affairs, 1969-74, pres., 1974—, bd. dirs., 1974—; treas. Wis. Found. of Ind. Colls., 1974-79, v.p., 1979-81, pres., 1981-83. Bd. dirs. De Paul Rehab. Hosp., Sacred Heart Sch. Theology, Holy Redeemer Coll., Waterford, Wis., 1984-85, Mental Health Assn. in Milw. County, 1983—, Internat. Inst. Milwaukee County, 1985—, Wis. Sch. Profl. Psychology, 1985—. Mem. Am. Psychol. Assn., Wis. Assn. for Tchr. Educators, TEMPO, Phi Delta Kappa, Delta Epsilon Sigma, Psi Chi, Delta Kappa Gamma. Contbr. monograph to profl. publs.

KLIEWER, PAULINE ANNETTE, nursing educator; b. Tofield, Alta., Can., Jan. 1, 1939; d. Franz Abram and Helena (Konrad) Peters; came to U.S., 1967; m. Henry Kliewer, Aug. 24, 1968; children—John Richard, Laura Jean. B.S. in Nursing, U. B.C., 1961; B.R.E., Mennonite Brethren Bible Coll., Winnipeg, Man., 1963; M.A., U. Wash., 1969, Ph.C. in Speech Communication, 1985. Nursing diplomate. Staff nurse Vancouver Gen. Hosp., 1960-61; vis. nurse Victorian Order of Nurses, Winnipeg, 1962-63; prof. English, Osaka Women's U. (Japan), 1964-67; nursing supr. Snohomish County Health Dept., Everett, Wash., 1970-71; instr. nursing Everett Community Coll., 1974-86, dir. curriculum project nursing div., 1983-86; asst. prof. Pacific Luth. U., 1986—; cons. nursing curriculum Fresno Pacific Coll. (Calif.), 1980-81. Workshop leader Free Methodist Conf., 1983, Mennonite Bibl. Sem., 1982. Crown Zellerbach Corp. research grantee, 1960; U. Wash. scholar, 1985. Mem. Am. Nurses Assn., Internat. Speech Communication Assn., Western Speech Communication Assn., Nat. League Nursing, Orton Soc. (Seattle). Office: Everett Community Coll 801 Wetmore Ave Everett WA 98201

KLIMAN, SYLVIA MAY STERN, filmmaker, writer, editor, realtor; b. Boston, July 16, 1934; d. Edward I. and Bernice Stern; A.B., Vassar Coll., 1956; m. Allan Kliman, June 24, 1956; children—Gilbert Harrow, Douglas Hartley. Editorial asst. Harvard Law Sch. profs., Cambridge, Mass., 1956-58; editor Vassar Miscellany News, Poughkeepsie, N.Y., 1953-56; editor founder Park Parent, Brookline, Mass., 1968-73; pres. Sylvia S. Kliman Real Estate Brokerage, 1971—; pres. Dunewind Films, 1979—. Vol. Mass. ARC Blood program, 1970-73; polit. speechwriter, 1960—. Trustee Park Sch., Brookline, 1970-73; bd. friends Peter Bent Brigham Hosp., 1970-75; bd. dirs. Spl. Com. to Restore Ogunquit Dunes, 1975—. Mem. Park Sch. Parents Assn. (pres. 1968-70), Norfolk Dist. Med. Soc. Womens Aux., Boston Museum Fine Arts. Unitarian. Club: Vassar (dir.) (Boston). Home: 40 Newton St Brookline MA 02146 also Dunewind Ogunquit ME 03907

KLIMECZKO, CHRISTINE ROSE, computer company executive; b. Buffalo, July 2, 1951; d. Joseph Anthony and Helen Barbara (Klawitter) K.; B.A., Elmira Coll., 1973; postgrad. Cornell U., 1973. Programmer, analyst, mgr. Dalrymple Constrn. Co., Elmira, N.Y., 1972-75; computer operator, programmer trainee, programmer Ingersoll Rand Co., Painted Post, N.Y., 1975-79; systems engr. Four-Phase Systems Motorola, Syracuse, N.Y., 1979-81, sr. systems engr., 1981-82, sr. sales support analyst, Dallas, 1982-83, sr. mktg. instr., 1983—. Contbr. article to profl. jour. Mem. Data Processing Mgrs. Assn. (v.p.), Jacques Cousteau Soc., Smithsonian Instn. Democrat. Roman Catholic. Office: 12720 Hillcrest Suite 300 Dallas TX 75006

KLIMKIEWICZ, BERNADETTE MARIE, banker; b. Jersey City; d. William L. and Elizabeth V. (Flynn) Hoy; student Am. Inst. Banking, 1950-51, N.Y. U., 1967; m. Wallace L. Klimkiewicz, June 28, 1952; children—Karen Dunne, Wallace (dec.). With Bankers Trust Co., N.Y.C., 1945-47, Chem. Bank & Trust Co., N.Y.C., 1947-54; v.p. mut. fund and corp. services First Jersey Nat. Bank, Jersey City, 1961, now sr. v.p. Fidelity Union Banks/First Nat. State Bank. Office: First National State Bank of New Jersey Jersey City NJ 07303*

KLINCK, PATRICIA EWASCO, state librarian Vt.; b. Albany, N.Y., May 13, 1940; d. Albert C. and Mary Ann (Sopko) Ewasco; B.A. in History, Smith Coll., 1961; M.S. in Library Sci., Simmons Coll., Boston, 1963; postgrad. in edn. SUNY, Albany, 1964-67; m. C. Hoagland Klinck, Jr., Sept. 12, 1970; 1 dau., Natalie Childs. Young adult worker Boston Public Library, 1961-63; library dir. Colonie Central High Sch., Albany, 1963-67; librarian Library/U.S.A., U.S. Pavilion, N.Y. World's Fair, summer 1965; library dir. Simon's Rock Coll., Gt. Barrington, Mass., 1967-70; regional dir. NW Regional Library, Vt. Dept. Libraries, Montpelier, 1970-72, dir. extension services div., 1972-73, 73-74, acting asst. state librarian, 1973, asst. state librarian, 1974-77, state librarian, 1977—; chmn. New Eng. Library Bd., 1979-81. Mem. Am., New Eng., Vt. library assns., Am. Soc. Public Adminstrs., Chief Officers of State Library Agys. (dir. 1978-80, vice chmn. 1980-81, chmn. 1981-82). Home: 47 Brewer Pkwy South Burlington VT 05401 Office: 111 State St Montpelier VT 05602

KLINE, COLLEEN MORGAN, broadcast executive: b. Amarillo, Tex., June 9, 1936; d. George Franklin and Mildred (Adams) Gathright; m. Robert Conrad Morgan, Nov. 20, 1958 (div. 1964); 1 child, Michael Conrad; m. Donald E. Kline, Apr. 21, 1970 (div. 1977). Student U. Hawaii, 1955-58; B.S., West Tex. State Coll., 1959. Asst. to v.p. of on-the-air promotion ABC-TV Network, N.Y.C., 1960-63; asst. to local, nat. sales mgr. McLendon Broadcasting, Dallas, 1964-69; owner, cons. Polyhedron, Buffalo, N.Y., 1969-72; city clk. City of Vail, Colo., 1972-83; gen. mgr., part-owner Sta. KRVV, Vail, 1983—; cons. Eris County Dept. Mental Health, Buffalo, 1969-72; cons., trainer jobs to program U.S. Dept. Labor, Buffalo, 1970-71; cons. Taft Broadcasting Co., Sta. WGR-TV, Buffalo, 1971. Developer mktg. course N.Y. State Dept. Continuing Edn., 1969. Mem. Vail City Council, Colo., 1983—; exec. com. Eagle County Democratic Com., Vail, 1983—; county chmn. Dems. for Hart Campaign, Vail, 1984—; chmn. bd. dirs. Eagle County Airport Commn., Vail, 1982—. Mem. Vail Resort Chamber Assn., Vail Bus. and Profl. Women. Methodist. Office: Sta KRVV 1000 S Frontage Rd W Suite 100 Vail CO 81657

KLINE, KRISTINE JO, city official; b. Havre, Mont., Oct. 22, 1957; d. Edwin John and Donna Louise (Purdy) Haugen; m. Donald Ralph Kline, June 24, 1978; children—Cole Edwin, Cortney Dawn. A.S. in Water, Waste Water Tech., No. Mont. Coll., 1979; B.S. in Microbiology, Mont. State U., 1981. Part-time instr. No. Mont. Coll., Havre, 1981-82, 84-85; supt. waste water treatment plant City of Havre, 1980—. Mem. City and County Health Bd., Havre, 1984—. Mem. Water Pollution Control Assn. (chmn. edn. com. 1985-87, pres.-elect 1985-86), AAUW. Methodist. Home: 1129 Cleveland Ave Havre MT 59501 Office: City of Havre Box 231 Havre MT 59501

KLINE, LINDA, human resources consultant; b. Boston, Aug. 8, 1940; d. George and Eva (Weiner) Kline; B.A. in Biology, Boston U., 1962. Personnel dir. Block Engring. Inc., Cambridge, Mass., 1964-66; brokerage mgr. Eastern Life Ins. Co. N.Y., Boston, 1966-68; mgr. direct placement Lendman Assos., N.Y.C., 1968-72; dir. women-in-mgmt. div. Roberts-Lund, Ltd., N.Y.C., 1972-77; pres. Kline-McKay, Inc., Exec. Search and Outplacement Cons., Maximus Cons., Inc., N.Y.C., 1978—; exec. dir. Majority Money, women's network, 1976-79; tchr. fin. planning for women Marymount-Manhattan Coll., 1977; lectr. and/or cons. women's programs at several colls. and univs. and corps. Bd. dirs. Women Bus. Owners Edn. Fund, 1982—, Mom's Amazing, 1985—; community bd. dirs. Mt. Sinai Med. Ctr., 1984—. Mem. Women Bus. Owners N.Y. (dir. 1978-82). Co-author: Career Changing: The Worry-Free Guide, 1982. Address: 3 E 48th St #6 New York NY 10017

KLINE, MABLE CORNELIA PAGE, educator; b. Memphis, Aug. 20, 1928; d. George M. and Lillie (Davidson) Brown; 1 dau., Gail Angela Page. Student LeMoyne Coll.; B.S.Ed., Wayne State U., 1948, postgrad. Tchr., Flint, Mich., 1950-51, Pontiac, Mich., 1953-62; tchr. 12th grade English, Cass Tech High Sch., Detroit, 1962—, coordinator Summer Sch. High Sch. Proficiency Program. Life mem. YWCA, NAACP. Mem. NEA (life), Assn. Supervision and Curriculum Devl., Am. Fedn. Tchrs., Nat. Council Tchrs. English, Internat. Platform Assn., Wayne State U. Alumni Assn., Delta Sigma Theta. Episcopalian. Home: 1101 Lafayette Towers W Detroit MI 48207 Office: 2421 2d Ave Detroit MI 48207

KLINE, MIRIAM MARIE, educational administrator, township official; b. Hamburg, Pa., Sept. 28, 1934; d. Emanuel James and Mabel Elsie (Heimbach) Wagner; m. Richard Daniel Kline, Mar. 31, 1956; children—Eugene Richard, Ann Marie Kline Womack. Student pub. schs., Hamburg. Supr. Am. Casualty, Reading, Pa., 1952-55; sec. Hamburg Area Sch. Dist., 1961-85, sec., dir. dist. support services, 1985—; sec.-treas. Twp. of Perry, Shoemakersville, Pa., 1973—. Author: (booklet) Effective Educational Secretary, 1983. Mem. Berks County Assn. Ednl. Secs. (v.p. 1985—), State Assn. Ednl. Secs. State Assn. Twp. Suprs., State Assn. Mcpl. Secs., Pa. Sch. Bds. Assn., Nat. Assn. Ednl. Office Personnel, Bus. and Profl. Womens Club. Republican. Lodge: Women of Moose. Avocations: quilting; reading; travel. Home: 681 Ridge Rd Shoemakersville PA 19555 Office: Hamburg Area Sch Dist Windsor St Hamburg PA 19526

KLINE, THERESE RUTLEDGE, commercial real estate leasing executive; b. Houston, Oct. 28, 1960; d. Wayne Rutledge and Mary (Taylor) Rutledge Fouts; m. David Forrest Kline, Aug. 14, 1982; 1 child, Kyle; stepchildren—Steve; Kim. Comml. leasing mgr. McLester Grisham Gardner Investors, Inc., Austin, Tex., 1984-86; v.p. Kline Properties, Inc., Austin, 1984—; v.p., comml. leasing specialist James F. Parker Interests, Austin, 1986—. Mem. Nat. Assn. Female Execs., Austin Bd. Realtors, Bldg. Owners and Mgrs. Assn., Office Leasing Brokers Assn., Network, Austin Jr. Forum. Republican. Clubs: Capitol, Great Hills Country, Tex. Exposition and Heritage Ctr. (founder). Avocations: golfing; scuba diving. Home: 10402 Holme Lacey Ln Austin TX 78750 Office: James F Parker Interests 9420 Research St Austin TX 78759

KLING, CANDACE, architectural lighting design consultant; b. Phila., Oct. 30, 1945; d. Harry C. and Rosemary Roberta (McLaughlin) Wilson. Broadway lighting designer Jean Rosenthal, N.Y.C., 1963-68, Howard Brandston Lighting Design, 1968-70; assoc. Jules Horton Lighting Design, N.Y.C., 1970-72; with Marriott Hotel Corp., Washington, 1972-80; owner C.M. Kling & Assocs., Inc., Falls Church, Va., 1980—; guest lectr. Mt. Vernon Coll., Cath. U. Am., U. Md. Design Schs. Recipient award of Merit, Chgo. Marriott Hotel Lighting Design. Mem. Illuminating Engrs. Soc., Internat. Assn. Lighting Designers, NOW. Office: Suite 100 113 Park Ave Falls Church VA 22046

KLING, SARAH ELIZABETH, advertising executive; b. Bradford, Pa., Dec. 7, 1939; d. John Allen and Theresabell Ann (Luke) Cassick; m. James Anthony Vesneski, Sept. 16, 1961 (div. Aug. 1966); 1 dau., Jody Ann Vesneski Loder; m. 2d, Ivan Roy Kling, May 14, 1971 (div. Sept. 1976). Student York Coll., 1976-77, 84, Syracuse U., 1981, 82; cert. advt. specialist Distributor Mgmt. Sch., U. Houston, 1983. Sec., Beckwith Machinery Co., Bradford, Pa., 1957-61; inventory control supr., inside sales corr., exec. sec. Corning Glass Works, Bradford, 1961-63; exec. sec., bookkeeper Duro-Lite Co., Bradford, part-time, 1964-66; exec. sec., office mgr. Plexwood, Inc., Bradford, 1966-71; exec. sec., adminstrv. asst. to pres. Ordnance Products Co., North East, Md., 1971-72; pres. Kling Assocs., mfrs. sales reps., Balt., 1972-83; owner, operator Klings Antique Ctr., New Oxford, Pa., 1975-76; sales rep. Mehl Ad-Assocs., York, Pa., part-time 1977, Martin Meyers Co., Glenside, Pa., 1977-79; dist. sales mgr. Shedd Brown Inc., Mpls., 1979-80; pres. Dynamic Achievements Unltd., York, 1983—; div. mgr. splty. advt., premiums and incentives Quaker City Paper & Chem. Co., York, 1980—. Bd. dirs. Jr. Achievement, York; mem. U.S. Congl. Adv. Bd.; mem. Republican Presdl. Task Force, Washington. Mem. Am. Bus. Women's Assn., Am. Mktg. Assn. (1st v.p. 1983-84, dir.), C. of C. York Area (President's award), Lancaster Advt. Club, Sales and Mktg. Execs. (pres. York chpt. 1982-83, Order of Bell award, bronze and silver awards), Women's Network of York, Young Businessmen's Assn. York, Nat. Assn. Profl. Saleswomen, Nat. Assn. Female Execs., Splty. Advt. Counselors Delaware Valley (Norman Constantine scholarship award 1982), Nat. Rifle Assn., U.S. Coast Guard Aux. (mem.-at-large), Beta Sigma Phi. Clubs: Economics, York Ski, Sawmill Racquetball, Indsl. Mgmt. (York); Soroptomist. Office: Quaker City Paper & Chemical Co PO Box 3451 York PA 17402

KLINGENSMITH, THELMA HYDE (MRS. DON J. KLINGENSMITH), retired educational administrator; b. Rauville, S.D., May 23, 1904; d. Eber Watson and Ida (Lebert) Hyde; B.A. magna cum laude, John Fletcher Coll., 1928; M.S. in Ed., U. N.D., 1962; m. Don Joseph Klingensmith, Sept. 11, 1930; children—Merle Joseph, Eunice Victoria Klingensmith Evans. Tchr. rural schs., Almont, N.D., 1922-24; exec. sec. Young People's Gospel League, Chgo., 1928-30; asst. supt. Ponca Meth. Indian Mission, Ponca City, Okla., 1936-43; tchr. English, Almont High Sch., 1951-54; supt. schs. Morton County, Mandan, N.D., 1959-73; mem. Am. Assn. Sch. Adminstrs. seminar to Russia, 1969. Bd. dirs. N.D. div. Am. Cancer Soc., 1958-72, chmn. pub. edn. com., 1958-60, sec., 1960-66; sr. v.p. N.D. Young Citizens League, 1959-63, sr. pres., 1963-65; legis. rep. N.D. Council County Supts. Assn., 1963-66; adviser Morton County Library Bd., 1960—, trustee, 1977-83, 84—; sec.-treas. Heart River Gospel Assn., 1950-66, dir., 1950—; dir., treas. N.D. Action Com. for Environ. Edn., 1968-75; bd. dirs. Dickinson Coll. Found.; v.p. West Wis. Conf., Women's Soc. Christian Service, Methodist Ch., 1945-46; legis. rep. N.D. Woman's Christian Temperance Union, 1978—; Western dist. coordinator Christian Social involvement N.D. Conf., United Meth. Women, 1979-83; Western dist. coordinator Christian Personhood, 1983-85; Dakota area del. Internat. Conf. Christian Heritage in Govt., United Meth. Ch., London, 1981; co-chmn. nat. Conv. Prohibition Party, 1983; treas. N.D. Council on Gambling Problems, 1985—. Named N.D. Mother of the Yr., 1965; recipient citation for conservation edn. Nat. and N.D. wildlife fedns., 1974, Pres.' citation Vennard Coll., 1984, tribute and statuette N.D. Eagle Forum, 1985. Mem. Mandan Hosp. Aux., Mandan Friends of the Library, N.D. Assn. Sch. Adminstrs., Am. Bible Soc., N.D. Library Assn. (trustee citation award 1980, cert. of appreciation 1982), N.D. Library Trustees Assn. (v.p. 1967-68, 74-76, sec. 1971-73, dir. 1976-82, pres. 1979-81), N.D. Wildlife Fedn. (chmn. essay contest 1973-78), Marquis Library Soc. (adv. mem.). Clubs: Golden Grad of Vennard Coll. (pres. 1981-84) (University Park, Iowa); Zonta (dist. VII chmn. pub. affairs com. 1968-70; del. internat. convs. 1968, 70, 72). Editor: Almont Jubilee History Book, 1956; Morton County Elementary Tchrs. Bull., 1959-73. Home: 206 Collins Ave PO Box 613 Mandan ND 58554

KLINGER, MARILYN SYDNEY, lawyer; b. N.Y.C., Aug. 14, 1953; d. Victor and Lillyan Janet (Hollinger) K. B.S., U. Santa Clara, 1975; J.D., Hastings Coll. Law, 1978. Bar: Calif. 1978. Assoc. Chickering & Gregory, San Francisco, 1978-81, Steefel, Levitt & Weiss, San Francisco, 1981-82, Sedgwick, Detert, Moran & Arnold, San Francisco, 1982—; lectr. Surety Forum, San Francisco; officer Hastings Democrats, San Francisco, 1975-78; vol. atty. Lawyers Com. Urban Affairs, San Francisco, 1978-80, Sta. KQED Call-A-Lawyer, San Francisco, 1978—. Recipient Thurston Soc. award Hastings Coll. Law, 1977. Mem. ABA (surety and fidelity com.), Queens Bench, San Francisco Bar Assn., No. Calif. Surety Claims Assn. (lectr.), Order of Coif. Democrat. Club: Tiburon Yacht (Calif.). Home: 213 Jamaica St Tiburon CA 94920 Office: Sedgwick Detert Moran & Arnold 1 Embarcadero Ctr San Francisco CA 94111

KLINK, SHARON MAY, sales executive; b. Whittier, Calif., Feb. 8, 1946; d. Hubert Miller and Garnet May (Prater) Jones; m. Gary Lee Klink, June 18, 1966; children—Robert Douglas, Jeffrey Loren. Student Pasadena Coll. (scholar), 1963-65; A.A., Rio Hondo Coll., 1978; student Calif. State U.-Fullerton, 1978; B.S.B.A., U. Redlands, 1982. Sec. Armorlite Lens Co., Pasadena, 1963-64, James, Pond & Clark, Pasadena, 1964-65; sales sec. Fiberboard Paper, Commerce, Calif., 1965-67; instr. aide East Whittier Sch. Dist., Calif., 1974-78; sales rep. Gen. Can Co., Montebello, Calif., 1978-86, Brouse-Whited Creative Packaging, Marina del Rey, Calif., 1986—. Sec. ch. bd. Ch. of the Nazarene, 1973-76, children's dir., 1965-69; youth dir. Women's Christian Temperance Union, 1965-69; treas. P.T.A., 1977-79. Democrat. Mem. Nat. Assn. Female Execs. Avocations: writing; golfing; snorkling; cooking. Office: Brouse-Whited Creative Packaging 4551 Glencoe Ave Marina del Rey CA 90292

KLINMAN, JUDITH POLLOCK, biochemist, educator; b. Phila., Apr. 17, 1941; d. Edward and Sylvia (Fitterman) Pollock; m. Norman R. Klinman, July 3, 1963 (div. 1978); children—Andrew, Douglas. A.B., U. Pa., 1962, Ph.D., 1966. Postdoctoral fellow Weizmann Inst. Sci., Rehovoth, Israel, 1966-67; faculty dept. chemistry Univ. Coll., London, 1967-68; postdoctoral assoc. Inst. for Cancer Research, Phila., 1968-70, research assoc., 1970-72, asst. mem., 1972-77, assoc. mem., 1977-78; asst. prof. biophysics U. Pa., Phila., 1974-78; assoc. prof. chemistry U. Calif.-Berkeley, 1978-82, prof., 1982—; mem. ad hoc biochemistry and phys. biochemistry study sects. NIH, 1977-84, phys. biochemistry study sect., 1984—. Mem. editorial bd. Jour. Biol. Chemistry, 1979-84; contbr. numerous articles to profl. jours. Fellow NSF, 1964, NIH, 1964-66. Mem. Am. Chem. Soc. (exec. council biol. div. 1982-85), Am. Soc. Biol. Chemists (membership com. 1984-86, nominating com. 1985—), Sigma Xi. Office: Univ Calif Dept Chemistry Berkeley CA 94720

KLIPSCH, LEONA KATHERINE, former newspaper publisher-editor; b. Vancouver, Wash., Feb. 24, 1914; d. Louis John and Marie Rosetta (Debitt) Hinkel; A.B., Smith Coll., 1935; student Sorbonne, Paris, 1934, Columbia U. Grad. Sch. Library Service, summers 1942-44; m. Robert Darius Klipsch, Nov. 25, 1937; children—Phyllis Marie Klipsch Smith, Katharine Klipsch Abbott, Marjorie Klipsch McCracken. Tchr. French and library sci. Marshall U., Huntington, W.Va., 1949-54; br. librarian Albuquerque Public Library, 1955-56; high sch. librarian, Gallup, N.Mex., 1963-65; co-owner, editor Defensor Chieftain, Socorro, N.Mex., 1965-82, pub., 1980-82. Bd. dirs. Socorro Gen. Hosp. Republican. Presbyterian. Author: Treasure Your Love (Librarian prize for jr. novel 1958); (as Jean Kirby) A Very Special Girl, 1963. Home: 1304 Kitt Pl PO Box V Socorro NM 87801

KLOBASA, LINDA, executive recruiter, personnel agency executive; b. St. Louis, May 27, 1947; d. Louis William and Marie (Urban) Guckes; m. E. Alan Klobasa, Aug. 16, 1970 (div. 1981). Cert. U. Besancon, France, 1968; B.A., Knox Coll., 1969; postgrad. U. Mo., 1969-70. Tchr. Van Buren Pub. Sch., Belleville, Mich., 1970-72; personnel asst. Will Ross, Inc., Milw., 1972-74, sales personnel adminstr., 1974-75; nat. specialist mktg. Dunhill of Milw., 1976-79; pres. MarketSearch, Inc., Thiensville, Wis., 1979—. Com. mem. North Suburban YMCA, Wis., 1984—. Mem. Am. Mktg. Assn., Bus. and Profl. Advt. Assn., Ind. Businessmen's Assn., Milw. Ad Club, Milw. World Trade Assn., Sales and Mktg. Execs. Internat., TEMPO. Office: MarketSearch Inc 216 N Green Bay Rd Suite 111 Thiensville WI 53092

KLOCEK, KATHLEEN ANNE, parent educator; b. Pitts., Nov. 5, 1948; d. Alexander and Frances Florence (Tropeck) Kravec; m. Daniel Leonard Klocek, Dec. 26, 1970; children—Joseph, Timothy, Kara, Matthew. B.S., Duquesne U.,

1970. Exec. officer mgr. Kaufmann's, Pitts., 1970-71; nat. parenting trainer Am. Soc. Psychoprophylaxis in Obstets./Lamaze, Washington, 1977-81; exec. dir. Parenting Assocs., Verona, Pa., 1980—; cons. Mom's House, Inc., Pitts., 1986—. Contbr. articles to Childbirth Educator mag., 1982—. Mem. Family Resource Coalition, Am. Soc. Psychoprophylaxis in Obstetrics (bd. dirs. 1975-81), Mothers Are People Too Program. Republican. Byzantine Catholic. Avocations: genealogy; ice skating; swimming; reading; photography. Office: Parenting Assocs 8243 Lincoln Rd Verona PA 15147

KLOCEK, SHIRLEY JEAN, lawyer; b. Marietta, Ohio, Jan. 28, 1956; d. Henry Samuel and Bernice Eileen (Oliver) Schwartz; m. Robert Andrew Klocek, June 25, 1983; 1 child, Catherine Elizabeth. B.A. summa cum laude, Mt. Union Coll., 1977; J.D., Ohio State U., 1980. Bar: Ohio 1981. Law clk. Ohio Dept. Rehab. and Correction, Columbus, 1979-80; atty. F. & R. Lazarus Co., Columbus, 1981-83; research assoc. Walker, McClure, Bohnen & Brehmer, Monterey, Calif., 1983-85. Mem. ABA, Ohio Bar Assn., Mt. Union Coll. Alumni Assn., Ohio State U. Alumni Assn. (life), Alpha Delta Pi (Panhellenic rep. 1976, Panhellenic pres. 1977), Alpha Lambda Delta, Alpha Mu Gamma. Republican. Roman Catholic. Home: 2615 Crystal Cove Ct Jacksonville FL 32224

KLOCK, SALLY JEAN, social service executive; b. Gloversville, N.Y., Dec. 13, 1948; d. Ward Carl and Florence (Pedrick) K.; B.A. magna cum laude in Psychology and Sociology, SUNY-Buffalo, 1971; M.Social Adminstrn., Case Western Res. U., 1974; M.B.A., Cleve. State U., 1981; student Cleve. Marshall Coll. Law, 1983—; m. Michael M. Kleiman, Sept. 3, 1977. Bldg. mgr. Marc Equity Corp., Buffalo, 1971-72; community safety organizer Western Res. Area Agy. on Aging, Cleve., 1974-75, coordinator monitoring and evaluation, 1975-76; exec. dir. Lake County Council on Aging, Painesville, Ohio, 1976—; adv. bd. Ret. Sr. Vol. Program, 1976—; mem. Cleve. State U. Gerontol. Research Adv. Bd., 1984—. Mem. Ohio Citizens Council, 1977-78. N.Y. State Regents scholar, 1967; Ohio Manpower grantee, 1972; Social and Rehab. Services grantee, 1973. Mem. Am. Mktg. Assn. (chair health care services com. 1983—), Am. Mgmt. Assn., Nat. Council on Aging, Phi Beta Kappa, Beta Gamma Sigma. Home: 6193 Pepperwood Ct Mentor OH 44060 Office: 105 Main St Painesville OH 44077

KLODOWSKI, AMY MARTHA AUSLANDER, lawyer; b. N.Y.C., Oct. 13, 1952; d. Oscar and Beatrice (Feinberg) Auslander; m. Harry F. Klodowski, Jr., Nov. 12, 1983; 1 child, Deborah Bea. B.A., Kent State U., 1974; J.D., U. Pitts., 1978. Bar: Pa. 1978. Atty., Equitable Resources, Inc., Pitts., 1978—. Mem. ABA, Pa. Bar Assn., Allegheny County Bar Assn. Club: Rivers (Pitts.). Office: Equitable Resources Inc 420 Blvd of the Allies Pittsburgh PA 15219

KLOPFLEISCH, STEPHANIE SQUANCE, social services agency administrator; b. Rupert, Idaho, Dec. 21, 1940; d. William Jaynes and Elizabeth (Cunningham) Squance; B.A., Pomona Coll., 1962; M.S.W., UCLA, 1966; m. Randall Klopfleisch, June 27, 1970; children—Elizabeth, Jennifer, Matthew. Social worker, Los Angeles County, 1963-67; program dir. day care, vol. services Los Angeles County, 1968-71; div. chief children's services Dept. Public Social Services, Los Angeles County, 1971-73, dir. bur. of social services, 1973-79; chief dep. dir. Dept. Community Services, Los Angeles County, 1979—; with Area 10 Devel. Disabilities, 1981-82; bd. dirs. Los Angeles Fed. Emergency Mgmt. Act, 1985—. Mem. Calif. Commn. on Family Planning, 1976-79; mem. Los Angeles Commn. Children's Instns., 1977-78; bd. dirs. United Way Info., 1978-79; chmn. Los Angeles County Internat. Yr. of Child Commn., 1978-79; bd. govs. Sch. Social Welfare, UCLA, 1981-84. Mem. Nat. Assn. Social Workers, Am. Public Welfare Assn., Am. Soc. Pub. Adminstrn.

KLOSTER, CAROL GOOD, video cassette distribution company executive; b. Richmond, Va., Aug. 18, 1948; d. David William and Lucy (McDowell) Good; m. John Kenneth Kloster III, Feb. 15, 1975; children—John Kenneth IV, Amanda Eileen. A.B., Coll. William and Mary, 1970. Personnel supr. Charles Levy Circulating Co., Chgo., 1974-75, warehouse supr., 1976-77, warehouse mgr., 1978-80, dir. sales, 1980-83, asst. v.p., dir. mktg., 1984; v.p., gen. mgr. Video Trend of Chgo., 1985—. Recipient Algernon Sidney Sullivan award Coll. William and Mary, 1970. Presbyterian. Home: 322 Bonnie Brae Hinsdale IL 60521 Office: Video Trend 5490 Milton Pkwy Rosemont IL 60018

KLOTE, LUANNA MAE, accountant; b. Carrollton, Mo., Feb. 1, 1951; d. Earl Edwin and Ethel Louise (Lungren) Bell; m. Paul Joseph Klote, Feb. 27, 1982. B.S., Central Mo. State U., 1973; M.B.A., U. Mo.-Kansas City, 1978; postgrad Johnson County Community Coll., 1983—. C.P.A., Mo., Kans.; cert. mgmt. acct. Jr. acct. Panhandle Eastern Pipe Line Co., Kansas City, Mo., 1973-75, acct., 1975-77, sr. acct., 1977—. Mem. Nat. Assn. Accts. (assoc. dir. 1979-82, assoc. dir. spl. activities 1983-84, dir. IMA programs 1984-85, assoc. dir. tech. programs 1984-85), Central Mo. State U. Alumni Assn., U. Mo.-Kansas City Alumni Assn., Inst. Mgmt. Acctg., Mo. Soc. C.P.A.s, Acctg. Assn., Acctg. Club, Beta Alpha Psi, Alpha Phi Delta. Home: 6852 Mastin Dr Merriam KS 66203 Office: Panhandle Eastern Pipe Line Co 3444 Broadway Kansas City MO 64111

KLOTZ, NANCY SLOSBERG, gallery owner; b. Norwich, Conn., Apr. 4, 1940; d. Harold J. and Rose (Pasnik) Slosberg; m. Paul N. Klotz, Feb. 5, 1961; children—Julie, Meredyth A., Abbey S., Hilary B. B.A., Tufts U., 1961; M.A., Conn. Coll., 1974. Art dir. Westerly Pub. Library, R.I., 1973-75; ptnr. Ocean House Artisans, Charlestown, R.I., 1974-76; owner Sun-Up Pottery, Misquamicut Hills, Westerly, 1975—; pres. Sun-Up Gallery, Inc., Westerly, 1977—; officer Butler Bros. Oil, Westerly, 1975—; dir. Am. Propane Corp., Waterford, Conn., Downs Patterson Corp., Westerly, Pawaget Devel. Corp., Westerly; cons. Conn. Scholastic Art Awards, 1985. Mem. R.I. Network, Ctr. for the Arts. Home: Misquamicut Hills Westerly RI 02891 Office: Sun-Up Gallery 55 Beach St Westerly RI 02891

KLOTZMAN, DOROTHY ANN, conductor, composer, music educator; b. Seattle, Mar. 24, 1937; d. Henry and Irva (Graham) Hill; B.S., Juilliard Sch., 1958, M.S., 1960. Prof., chmn. music Bklyn. Coll., 1971-81, dir. Conservatory of Music, 1981—; condr. Bklyn. Coll. Symphonic Band, 1970-81, Symphony Orch., 1980—; 1st woman condr. Goldman Band, 1973, guest condr., 1973, 75, 78, bd. dirs., 1979; guest condr. Guggenheim Concerts Band, 1980, 81, 82, 83, Goldman Meml. Band, 1984, 85. Mem. citizens adv. bd. WNCN, 1976-81; bd. dirs. Guggenheim Concerts, 1980-84, Goldman Meml. Band, 1984—, Bklyn. Ctr. for Performing Arts at Bklyn. Coll., 1983—; trustee Bklyn. Coll. Found., 1981-83. Recipient N.Y. Philharm. Young Composers' Contest 1st prize, 1953-54; Benjamin award in composition, 1955, 58; Fromm prize composition Aspen Music Sch., 1960; Danforth Found. E. Harris Harbison award, 1972. Mem. Am. Music Center, Am. Musicol. Soc., Coll. Music Soc., Music Library Assn., ASCAP. Composer: Three Songs from Chamber Music; Sonatine for Piano; Poetical Sketches; Sonata for Trumpet and Two Trombones; Exulta filia Sion; Nothing Heavy and Nothing at Rest (symphonic band); Cantata; Good Day Sir Christmas (soprano solo, chorus and instrumental ensemble); Divertimento (chamber orch.); Concerto (saxophone and orch.); Chimera (ballet); Variations (orch.); Overture for a Dedication; arranger: Grand Centennial March (Zeuner); President Garfield's Inauguration March (Sousa); Slavonic Dance No. 12 (Dvorak); editor Richard Franko Goldman: Selected Essays and Reviews, 1948-1968. Home: 543 E 24th St Brooklyn NY 11210

KLOZE, IDA IRIS, lawyer; d. Max and Bertha (Samet) K. A.A., George Washington U., 1944, A.B., 1947; LL.B., U. Md., 1926. Bar: Md. 1927, U.S. Supreme Ct. 1949. Sole practice, Balt., 1927-34; dep. collector IRS, Balt., 1934-39; with GAO, 1943-45, War Assets Adminstrn., 1945-49, Labor Dept., 1950-53, FTC, 1956-71; vol. atty. Pro Bono Law Litigation Div. Pub. Citizen, Washington, 1972—. Mem. Mrs. Rosalyn Carter's Com. Mental Health; exec. sec. Commn. for Prevention Infantile Paralysis, Balt., 1940-42; lobbyist Md. Legislature for Widows and Old Age Pensions, Balt., 1938-40; sec. Citizen's Commn. Md., Balt., 1935-39. Mem. ABA, Women's Bar Assn. (v.p. Balt. 1928-32), Profl. Women's Councils (pres. 1928-33), Nat. Women's Party (lobbyist, legal asst. life mem. 1951—), Fed. Bar Assn. (rec. sec., mem. nat. council, sec. com. gen. counsels 1951-52).

KLUCKMAN, KRISTINE ANN, oil company accountant; b. Raymondville, Tex., Aug. 10, 1959; d. Ralph Lawrence and Joan Theresa (Turbak) K. B.B.A., Southwest Tex. State U., 1981. C.P.A., Tex. Asst. bookkeeper, Raymondville Lumber Co. (Tex.), summers 1977-80; tchrs. asst. Raymondville Ind. Sch. Dist., summers, 1978-80; officer worker, keypunch operator Delta Coop. Compress & Warehouse, Raymondville, summers 1979-80; staff acct. Arthur Andersen & Co., Houston, 1981-83; partnership acct. Kirby Exploration Co., Houston, 1983—. Vol. Rob Mosbacher for U.S. Senate, 1983; mem. steering com. Young Profls. to re-elect Bill Clements for gov., 1986. Mem. Nat. Assn. Accts., Am. Women's Soc. C.P.A.s, Tex. Soc. C.P.A.s, Arts Symposium Houston, Women's Cotillion of Houston, Houston Jaycees (internat. relations and ann. consular ball coms.), Alpha Lambda Delta, Alpha Kappa Psi (scholar 1980-81). Roman Catholic. Home: 2153 Winrock St #1 Houston TX 77057 Office: Kirby Exploration Co 1717 Saint James Pl Houston TX 77056

KLUK, NADA, insurance company executive; b. Munich, Germany, Oct. 22, 1946; d. Marko and Zorka (Medic) Borkovich; m. Ronald Andrew Kluk, June 1, 1968. Student ins. Life Office Mgmt. Assn. and Health Ins. Assn. Am. Asst. supr. Washington Nat. Ins. Co., Evanston, Ill., 1969-72, supr., 1972-74, gen. supr., 1974-75, asst. mgr., 1975-77, mgr., 1977—, mem. mgmt. adv. council, 1979-81. Vol. Am. Cancer Soc., Chgo., 1980-85; capt. vols. bus. div. United Way, Evanston, 1981-84; nominee YWCA Leader Luncheon, 1979. Mem. Soc. Group Contract Analysts (host meeting 1985). Democrat. Roman Catholic. Avocations: reading; walking; working out. Office: Washington Nat Ins Co 1630 Chicago Ave Evanston IL 60201

KLUSKA, B. HARRIET, human resources administrator; b. Florence, S.C., Oct. 28, 1947; d. Harry Presley and Margaret Ernestine (Jones) McMillar; B.S. in Bus. Adminstrn., Oral Roberts U., 1970; postgrad. in psychology U. Tulsa, 1971-73; m. Dale Francis Kluska, June 16, 1973. Personnel mgr. Lit Bros., Reading Pa., 1974-75, Belk Simpson Co., Greenville, S.C., 1976-77; group tng. and communications mgr. Belk Hudson Co., Spartanburg, S.C., 1977-78, sales, basic inventory control mgr., 1978-79, group personnel dir. and ops. mgr., 1979-85; personnel dir. Rich's, 1985—; chmn. Belk Personnel Workshop, 1982; speaker in field Tri-County Jr. Coll., 1976; mem. Merchant Assn., 1975, Greenville Area Personnel Assn., 1977. Adv. com. on community services Spartanburg Tech. Coll.; pres. bd. dirs. Westgate Mall, 1980; mem. retail adv. com. Spartanburg Methodist Coll., 1980. Recipient Belk award of excellence, 1980. Mem. Am. Mgmt. Assn., YWCA. Republican. Contbr. article to orgn. publ. Home: 1212 Farragut Dr Spartanburg SC 29302 Office: Rich's Haywood Mall Greenville SC

KLYCE, ELLEN COOPER, college administrator; b. Memphis, Sept. 12, 1953; d. Robert Maxwell and Polly Jane (Cohen) C.; m. Walter Brigham Klyce, Jr., Jan. 23, 1982; 1 child, Pauline Whittinghill. A.B., Radcliffe Coll., 1975. T.V. producer KDKA-TV, Pitts., 1975-78; devel. officer Harvard U., Cambridge, Mass., 1979-82; dir. for devel. Memphis Coll. Art, 1982—; mem. community bd. WKNO-TV, Memphis, 1983—; mem. long range planning com. Le Bohneur, Memphis, 1985. Mem. Nat. Soc. Fundraising Execs., Council for Advancement and Support of Edn. Unitarian. Avocations: singing; swimming; travel. Home: 2189 Monroe St Memphis TN 38104 Office: Memphis Coll Art Overton Park Memphis TN 38112

KNAACK, SUSAN FRANCIS, radio station manager; b. Appleton, Wisc., Dec. 5, 1942; d. Marion Frances and Katherine T. (Theder) Hoover; m. Richard I. Knaack, May 12, 1973; children—Andrea, Katy. B.A., U. Wis. Oshkosh, 1972, M.A., 1974. Copy writer Sta. WMKC, Oshkosh, Wis., 1974-77, Sta. WHBY, Appleton, 1977-78; creative service dir. WHBY/WAPL-AM-FM, Appleton, 1978-80, acct. exec., 1980-82, gen. sales mgr., 1982-84, gen. mgr., 1984—. Mem. small bus. adv. bd. Fox Valley Tech. Inst., Appleton, 1982—. Mem. Sales Mktg. Execs., Fox Valley Advt. Assn. (dir. 1984—), Fox Valley Broadcasters Assn. (v.p. 1984—), Fox Cities C. of C. (bd. dirs. 1985—). Republican. Roman Catholic. Club: Midday Bus. Profl. Women (pres. 1982-84). Avocation: presenting motivational seminars. Home: W 3980 Hwy 10 Menasha WI 54952 Office: WHBY/WAPL PO Box 1519 Appleton WI 54913

KNACKERT, PAMELA MARGARET, marketing research analyst; b. Milw., Dec. 3, 1953; d. Richard Julian and Doris Florence (Kleinmann) K. B.B.A., U. Wis.-Milw., 1977, M.B.A., 1980. Mktg. research analyst Rexnord, Inc., Milw., 1977-80; sales forecasting analyst Miller Brewing Co., Milw., 1980-84, mktg. research analyst, 1984—. Mem. Am. Mktg. Assn. Roman Catholic. Avocations: tennis; jogging. Home: 4612 W Norwich St Milwaukee WI 53220 Office: Miller Brewing Co 3939 W Highland Blvd Milwaukee WI 53208

KNAP, NANCY ELLEN, mall management company executive; b. Milw., Apr. 7, 1957; d. Florian Joseph and Delphine Anna (Kosmider) K. B.S., U. Wis., 1979. Area sales mgr. Woodward & Lothrop, Washington, 1979-80; instr. Madison Area Tech. Coll., Wis., 1982; asst. mgr., promotion dir. Jacobs, Visconsi & Jacobs, Charleston, S.C., 1982-83, Beaumont, Tex., 1983-84, mall mgr., promotion dir., Manalapan, N.J., 1984-85, Jackson, Tenn., 1985 . Mem. Nat. Assn. Female Execs., Omicron Nu, Chi Omega. Avocations: antique restoration; photography; needlework.

KNAPP, BARBARA CURTIS, marketing and public relations executive, editor; b. Perryopolis, Pa., Nov. 1, 1933; d. Earle Edwin and Elizabeth Boyd (Knox) Curtis; m. Peter Osborn Knapp, June 11, 1957; children—Curtis Merriam, Elizabeth Evelyn. B.S., Kent State U., 1955. Asst. dir. co. history project McGraw-Hill Pub. Co., N.Y.C., 1955-57; sec., dir. law sch. devel. U. Pa., Phila., 1957-59; docent coordinator Cin. Art Mus., 1974-75; dir. pub. relations and mkgt. Dayton Philharmonic Orch. (Ohio), 1979—; dir. Dayton Philharmonic Women's Assn., 1976—. Editor, writer Rhythm and News, 1980—; book reviewer Dayton Daily News. Assoc. bd. dirs. Dayton Art Inst., 1983-88; bd. dirs. Jr. League Cin., 1972-74; council mem. Jr. League Phila., 1969-71; bd. dirs. New Neighbors League Dayton, 1976. Mem. Am. Women in Radio and TV Women in Communications, Inc., Cardinal Key, Laurels, Alpha Psi Omega. Episcopalian. Home: 1321 Tall Timber Trail Dayton OH 45409 Office: Dayton Philharmonic Orch Assn 125 E 1st St Dayton OH 45402

KNAPP, MILDRED FLORENCE, social worker; b. Detroit, Apr. 15, 1932; d. Edwin Frederick and Florence Josephine (Antaya) K.; B.B.A., U. Mich., Ann Arbor, 1954, M.A. in Community and Adult Edn. (Mott Found. fellow 1964), 1964, M.S.W. (HEW grantee 1966), 1967. Dist. dir. Girl Scouts Met. Detroit, 1954-63; planning asst. Council Social Agencies Flint and Genessee County, 1965; sch. social worker Detroit Public Schs., 1967—; field instr. grad. social workers. Mem. alumnae bd. govs. U. Mich., 1972-75, scholarship chmn., 1969-70, 76-80, chmn. spl. com. women's athletics, 1972-75, class agt. fund raising Sch. Bus. Adminstrn., 1978-79; mem. Founders Soc. Detroit Inst. Art, 1969—, Friends Children's Museum Detroit, 1978—, Women's Assn. Detroit Symphony Orch., 1982—; trustee Children's Mus., 1984—. Recipient various certs. appreciation. Mem. Nat. Assn. Social Workers, Acad. Cert. Social Workers, Nat. Community Edn. Assn. (charter), Outdoor and Edn. Camping Council (charter), Mich. Sch. Social Workers Assn. (pres. 1980-81), Detroit Sch. Social Workers Assn. (past pres.), Detroit Assn. U. Mich. Women (pres. 1980-82), Detroit Fedn. Tchrs. Methodist. Clubs: Detroit Boat, Detroit Women's City. Home: 702 Lakepointe Grosse Pointe Park MI 48230 Office: 4300 Marseilles Detroit MI 48224

KNAPP, ROSALIND ANN, lawyer; b. Washington, Aug. 15, 1945; d. Joseph Burke and Hilary (Eaves) K.; B.A., Stanford U., 1967, J.D., 1973. Admitted to Calif. bar, 1973, D.C. bar, 1980; with Dept. Transp., Washington, 1973—, asst. gen. counsel legislation, 1979-81, dep. gen. counsel, 1981—. Mem. D.C. Bar Assn., Calif. Bar Assn. Office: 400 7th St SW Washington DC 20590

KNAPP, VIRGINIA ESTELLA, retired educator; b. Washington, May 11, 1919; d. Bradford and Stella (White) Knapp; B.A., Tex. Tech. U., 1940; M.A., U. Tex. 1948; postgrad. Sul Ross Coll., 1950, Stephen F. Austin U., 1964-68. Tchr. journalism, high schs., Silverton, Tex., 1940-41, Electra, Tex., 1941-42, Joinerville, Tex., 1942-60, Carthage, Tex., 1961-69; tchr. history and journalism Longview (Tex.) High Sch., 1969-80; instr. Trinity U., San Antonio, summer 1972; fellowship tchr. Wall St. Jour., Tex. A&M U., College Station, summers 1964-67. Chmn., Rusk County (Tex.) Hist. Commn., 1980—. Recipient Wall St. Jour. award Outstanding Journalism Tchrs. of Yr., 1965-66; Trail Blazer award Tex. High Sch. Press Assn., 1980; Woman of Yr. award, 1983. Mem. Tex. State Tchrs. Assn., Classroom Tchrs. Assn., Tex. Assn. Jour. Dirs., Rusk County Heritage Assn., Rusk County Hist. Commn., Women in Communications (pres. Longview chpt. 1972-74, Service award 1975), Tex. Press Women, DAR. Episcopalian. Contbr. hist. writing to Ala. Rev., Progressive Farmer, Rusk County C. of C. Brochure, Rusk County Heritage, numerous others. Home: 321 College Ave Henderson TX 75652 Office: 514 N High Henderson TX 75652

KNAUER, VELMA STANFORD, savs. and loan assn. exec.; b. Pottstown, Pa., July 4, 1918; d. Chester Miller and Pearl Fretz (Miller) Stanford; student public schs.; m. Joseph Daniel Knauer, Feb. 17, 1940; children—Joseph Daniel, Susan Velma Knauer Metz. With U.S. Axle Co., Inc., Pottstown, 1936-45; with First Fed. Savs. & Loan Assn., Pottstown, 1953—, controller, 1953—, asst. treas., 1953-62, asst. sec., 1962-75, treas., 1976—. Mem. Am. Soc. Profl. and Exec. Women. Home: 970 Feist Ave Pottstown PA 19464 Office: Box 1 High and Hanover Sts Pottstown PA 19464

KNAUER, VIRGINIA HARRINGTON WRIGHT (MRS. WILHELM F. KNAUER), government official; b. Phila., Mar. 28, 1915; d. Herman Winfield and Helen (Harrington) Wright; B.F.A., U. Pa., 1937, LL.D. (hon.); postgrad. Pa. Acad. Fine Arts, Royal Acad. Fine Arts, Florence, Italy, 1938-39; LL.D., U. Pa., Phila. Coll. Textiles and Sci., Allentown Coll. St. Francis de Sales, Widener Coll., Chester, Pa., Tufts U.; Litt.D., Drexel U.; L.H.D., Jacksonville U., Russell Sage Coll., Pa. Coll. Podiatric Medicine; m. Wilhelm F. Knauer, Jan. 27, 1940; children—Wilhelm F., Valerie H. Knauer Burden. Dir., Pa. Bur. Consumer Protection, 1968-69; spl. asst. consumer affairs to Pres., White House, 1969-77, 81—, spl. adv. to Pres. for consumer affairs and dir. U.S. Office Consumer Affairs, 1971-77, 81—; pres. Virginia Knauer & Assos., Inc., Washington, 1977-81; chmn. Council for Advancement of Consumer Policy, 1979-81; U.S. rep., vice chmn. consumer policy com. OECD, 1970-77; mem. Council Wage and Price Stability, 1974-77. Councilman-at-large, Phila., 1960-68; vice-chmn. Philadelphia County Rep. Com., 1958-77; pres. Phila. Congress Rep. Women's Councils, 1958-77; dir. Pa. Council Rep. Women, 1963-80; founder N.E. Council Rep. Women, pres., 1956-64. Bd. dirs. Hannah Penn House, 1956—, v.p., 1971; former trustee Pa Coll. Podiatric Medicine; co-founder Knauer Found. Historic Preservation. Recipient Gimbel-Phila. award; named Disting. Dau. Pa. 1969. Mem. Nat. Trust Historic Preservation, Zeta Tau Alpha, Kappa Delta Epsilon (hon.) Episcopalian. Office: US Office Consumer Affairs Washington DC 20201

KNAUF, JANINE BERNICE, educator; b. Rochester, N.Y., Apr. 10, 1945; d. William Charles and Ila May (Hauss) Knauf; S.B., M.I.T., 1967; M.B.A., Rutgers U., 1971; M.Ph., Columbia U., 1979, Ph.D., 1981; 1 son, Christopher Robert Burgess. Research engr. Northrop/Norair, Hawthorne, Calif., 1965-66; sci. research engr. Rockwell Internat., Los Angeles, 1967-68; acct. Knauf and Knauf, Rochester, 1968-69, 76, 78; lectr. mgmt. dept. Poly. Inst. N.Y., 1972-73; asst. prof. info. systems Rutgers U., Newark, N.J., 1973-80; computer cons. Keefe, Bruyette & Woods, Inc., N.Y.C., 1978—; asst. prof. acctg. Fla. State U., Tallahassee, 1980—. C.P.A., Fla., N.Y. Mem. Soc. Women Engrs., Internat. Platform Assn., AIAA, Am. Woman's, Am. Inst. C.P.A.s, N.Y. State socs. C.P.A.s, Fla. Inst. C.P.A.s, Am. Acctg. Assn., Aircraft Owners and Pilots Assn., Beta Gamma Sigma, Sigma Gamma Tau.

KNECHT, DENISE JEAN, lawyer; b. Akron, Ohio, Nov. 14, 1948; d. William H. and Rita (Poydock) Knecht; B.A., U. Akron, 1970; postgrad. U. Wis., 1976, Cleve. State U., 1975, J.D., Cleve. Marshall Coll. Law, 1981. Fashion coordinator O'Neils Co., Akron, 1970-72; freelance pub. relations and promotional mktg. N.Y., Fort Lauderdale, Miami, Cleve., 1972-74; program dir. Am. Cancer Soc., Cleve., 1974-76, exec. dir. Lorain and surrounding counties, 1977; dir. pub. relations Marcus Advt., Cleve., 1977-79; public relations cons., Cleve., 1979-81; practice law, 1981—; v.p., Women's Law Fund, Inc., 1984—; producer, moderator radio program Women's Connection, Stas. WBBG and WWWM-FM, 1978-84; radio commentator Legal Pad, Cuyahoge Community Coll., 1983-85. Cons. pub. relations, senatorial and mayoral campaigns Ohio. Mem. Cleveland Women Lawyers Assn., Cuyahoga County Bar Assn., Women in Communications, NOW, Alpha Delta Pi. Club: Women's City of Cleve. (pres. 1985—). Author, pub.: The Pocket Guide to Cleveland. Home: 1721 Fulton Rd Cleveland OH 44113 Office: 922 Leader Bldg 140 Public Sq Cleveland OH 44114

KNEE, RUTH IRELAN (MRS. JUNIOR K. KNEE), social worker, health care consultant; b. Sapulpa, Okla., Mar. 21, 1920; d. Oren M. and Daisy (Daubin) Irelan; B.A., U. Okla., 1941, cert. social work, 1942; M.A., U. Chgo., 1945; m. Junior K. Knee, May 29, 1943 (dec. Oct. 21, 1981). Psychiat. social worker, asst. supr. Ill. Psychiat. Inst., U. Ill. at Chgo., 1943-44; psychiat. social worker USPHS Employee Health Unit, Washington, 1944-46, chief psychiat. social worker, 1946-49; psychiat. social work asso. Army Med. Center, Walter Reed Army Hosp., Washington, 1949-54; psychiat. social work cons. HEW, Region III, Washington, 1955-56; with NIMH, Chevy Chase, Md., 1956-72; chief mental health care adminstrn. br. USPHS, 1967-72, assoc. dep. adminstr. Health Services and Mental Health Adminstrn., 1972-73, dep. dir. Office of Nursing Home Affairs, 1973-74; long-term mental health care cons.; mem. com. on mental health and illness of elderly HEW, 1976-77; mem. panel on legal and ethical issues Pres.'s Commn. on Mental Health, 1977-78; liaison mem. Nat. Adv. Mental Health Council, 1977-81. Bd. dirs. Hillhaven Found., 1975—. Fellow Am. Public Health Assn. (sec. mental health sect. 1968-70, chmn. 1971-72), Am. Orthopsychiat. Assn. (life), Gerontol. Soc.; mem. Am. Assn. Psychiat. Social Workers (pres. 1951-53), Nat. Conf. Social Welfare (nat. bd. 1968-71, 2d v.p. 1973-74), Inst. Medicine/Nat. Acad. Sci. (com. study future of pub. health), Council on Social Work Edn., Nat. Assn. Social Workers (sec. 1955-56, nat. dir. 1956-57, 84-86, chmn. competence study com., practice and knowledge com. 1963-71), Am. Public Welfare Assn., DAR, Phi Beta Kappa, Psi Chi. Club: Women's Nat. Democratic. Editorial bd. Health & Social Work, 1979-81. Address: 8809 Arlington Blvd Fairfax VA 22031

KNEIPP, MARIANNE HAGAR, medical writer; b. Davenport, Iowa, Feb. 14, 1948; d. Norman Bramblett and Mary Jane (Hilkemeyer) Hagar; 1 child, Lindsay Sharyn Kneipp. B.A. in English, U. Iowa, 1970. Cert. tchr. Tchr. tech. writing Houston Ind. Sch. Dist., 1970-76; med. writer Tex. Heart Inst., Houston, 1976—; editorial cons. Tex. Heart Inst. Jour., 1977—. Editor: (with Denton A. Cooley) Surgical Treatment of Aortic Aneurysms, 1985; Reflections and Observations, Essays of Denton A. Cooley, M.D., 1985; Techniques in Cardiac Surgery, 1984. Mem. Am. Med. Writers Assn. (editor, writer core curriculum 1985), Council of Biology Editors, Women in Communications, Pi Beta Phi. Republican. Presbyterian. Home: 3725 Murworth Houston TX 77025 Office: Tex Heart Inst PO Box 20345 Houston TX 77025

KNEZEVIC, ELLEN MARIE, nursing adminstrator; b. Humbolt, S.D., Apr. 11, 1940; d. Martin Max and Florence Evelyn (Stageberg) Fiegen; m. Tomislav Miki Knezevic, Sept. 7, 1975. Diploma Nursing Program, St. Mary's Sch. Nursing, Rochester, Minn., 1961; student U. Ill., 1985—. Head nurse St. Mary's Hosp., Rochester, 1961-63; staff nurse Variety Club Heart Hosp., U. Minn., Mpls., 1963-65; nurse charge ICCU Ravenswood Hosp., Chgo., 1965-69; asst. dir. nursing Bethany Methodist Hosp., Chgo., 1969—; advanced cardiac life support instr. Am. Heart Assn., Chgo., 1983—. Recipient Most Outstanding Nurse award Bethany Meth. Hosp., Chgo., 1985. Mem. Am. Nurses Assn., Ill. Nurses Assn., St. Mary's Sch. of Nursing Alumni Assn. Democrat. Serbian Orthodox. Avocations: bowling; sewing; cooking. Home: 4917 N Paulina Ave Chicago IL 60640 Office: Bethany Meth Hosp 5025 N Paulina Ave Chicago IL 60640

KNEZO, GENEVIEVE JOHANNA, science and technology policy researcher; b. Elizabeth, N.J., Aug. 8, 1942; d. John and Genevieve (Sadowski) K.; 1 child, Alexandra M. A.B. in Polit. Sci., Douglass Coll., Rutgers U., 1964; M.A. in Sci., Tech. and Pub. Policy, George Washington U., 1981. With Congl. Research Service, Library of Congress, Washington, 1967—, specialist in sci. and tech., 1979—. Author profl. publs. Mem. AAAS, Washington Women's Network, NOW, Toastmasters Internat., Sierra Club, Phi Beta Kappa, Pi Sigma Alpha. Avocations: white-water canoeing; hiking; gymnastics; classical music. Home: 606 Oakley Pl Alexandria VA 22302 Office: Sci Policy Research Div Congl Research Service Library of Congress Washington DC 20540

KNIGHT, ALICE D. TIRRELL, state legislator; b. Manchester, N.H., July 14, 1903; d. Nathan Arthur and Clara (Stiles) Tirrell; B.A., U. N.H., 1925, postgrad., 1933; postgrad. Boston U., 1941-42; m. Norman Knight, Nov. 15, 1952. Tchr., Newton Falls (N.Y.) High Sch., 1925-26; prin. Oswegatchie (N.Y.) Union Sch., 1926-27, Bartlett Sch., Goffstown, N.H., 1932-35; home lighting specialist Public Service Co. N.H., Manchester, 1935-39; tchr. merchandising Mt. Ida Jr. Coll., Newton Centre, Mass., 1939-45; home service dir. Boyd Corp., Portland, Maine, 1945-47; dist. home economist Frigidaire Sales Corp., Boston, 1948-64; mem. N.H. Ho. of Reps., 1967-74, 76-78, 80—; rep to N.H. Gen. Ct., 1967—; mem. joint legis. com. on elderly affairs, 1983—. Mem. budget com. Town of Goffstown, 1966-72; mem. Gov.'s Adv. Com. Alcoholism, 1972-73, 74-78, Statewide Health Coordinating Council, 1977-78; past pres. bd. dirs. Hillsborough County North Cancer Soc.; bd. dirs. N.H. Cancer

Soc. Recipient award N.H. Program on Alcohol and Drug Abuse, 1971, 75. Mem. Am. Home Econs. Assn., Nat. Home Fashions League (pres. 1957-58), Nat. Order State Legislators, Am. Women in Radio and TV, LWV, N.H. Council World Affairs, Nat. Grange, DAR (regent 1974-76), Nat. Order Women Legislators (treas. 1968-71), Manchester Bus. and Profl. Women (pres. 1972-74). Clubs: Republican. Mem. Unity Ch. Clubs: Order Eastern Star (life), Soroptomist (life) (Boston); Goffstown Unity, Goffstown Garden (pres. 1976-78), Goffstown Shirley (pres. 1977-78).

KNIGHT, CHARLOTTE ANNE, lawyer; b. Memphis, May 28, 1952; d. John Jake and Helen Charlotte (Watson) K. B.A., Central Mich. U., 1974; J.D., U. Tenn., 1976; postgrad. Memphis State U., 1977. Bar: Tenn. 1977, U.S. Dist. Ct. (we. dist.) Tenn. 1978, U.S. Supreme Ct. 1981. Sole practice, Memphis, 1977-78; asst. staff atty. Memphis Light, Gas and Water Div., 1978—. Founding mem. Brooks Meml. Art Gallery, Memphis, 1982-84; mem. Commitment Memphis, Friends of Dixon Gallery and Gardens, Network, NCCJ. Mem. ABA (litigation sect. corp. counsel com. 1980—, asst. editor affiliate newsletter Young Lawyers Div.), Tenn. Bar Assn. (Young Lawyers Conf. sec. 1985-86, litigation sec.-treas. 1985-86), Memphis and Shelby County Bar Assn. (young lawyers sect. coms.), Alpha Xi Delta, DAR, Capleville Community Club (pres. 1983-85). Home: 4754 Lamar Ave Memphis TN 38118 Office: Memphis Light Gas & Water Div 220 S Main St Memphis TN 38103

KNIGHT, GEORGIA MARY, emergency medicine consulting firm executive; b. Mt. Clemens, Mich., Dec. 6, 1939; d. Melvin James and Charlotte Martha (Miller) Lucksted; m. James Thomas Knight, Jan. 7, 1961 (dec. May 1975); children—Damon Allan, Darrin Adam. Student Flint Community Jr. Coll., 1959-61. With Grayling State Bank, Mich., 1958-59, First Nat. Bank, Mansfield, Ohio, 1961; underwriters asst. Lumbermen's Mut. Ins. Co., Mansfield, 1961-63; comml. underwriter Kemper Ins. Co., Mansfield, 1963-65; owner, operator Georgia's Lingerie, Grayling, 1970-71; v.p., dir. mktg. Emergency Cons., Traverse City, Mich., 1975—; speaker Am. Coll. Emergency Medicine, 1982-83. Mem. Grayling City Council, 1976. Mem. Med. Group Mgmt. Assn. Club: Flint Antique (v.p. 1965-66). Roman Catholic. Avocations: reading; skiing; lingerie creation; hiking; woods lore. Home: 4316 Deerfield Ln Traverse City MI 49684 Office: Emergency Cons Inc 2240 S Airport Rd Traverse City MI 49684

KNIGHT, GEORGINE MARIE, medical technologist; b. Hazleton, Pa., Feb. 22, 1954; d. George and Eleanor Marie (Subally) K.; B.S. in Med. Tech., Wilkes Coll., 1977. Med. technologist, asst. crew chief chemistry Nesbitt Meml. Hosp., Kingston, Pa., 1977—. Winner Northeastern Pa. Philharm. Talent Competition, 1971. Mem. Am. Soc. Clin. Pathologists (affiliate, registered med. technologist). Home: 458 Monument Ave Wyoming PA 18644 Office: 562 Wyoming Ave Kingston PA 18704

KNIGHT, LILA CUCKSEE, sales executive; b. Chattanooga, Apr. 11, 1931; d. William Henry and Anna Leona (Bonine) Cucksee; children—David Earl, Jonathan Ray, Paul Ervin, Sheryl Gaye Knight Carlock, Joel Reece. Diploma in Sectl. Sci., Edmondson Jr. Coll., 1983; life ins. lic. Modern Woodmen Sch., 1983. Lic. ins. agt., Ga. Pre-need sales woman Lakewood Memory Gardens, Rossville, Ga., 1983, Tenn./Ga. Meml. Park, Rossville, 1983; dist. rep. Modern Woodmen of Am., Rossville, 1983-84; ins. agt. United Ins. Co. of Am., Chattanooga, 1984-86; sales mgr. World Book/Child Craft, Chattanooga, 1986—. Mem. Lakeview Home-Sch. Orgn., Fort Oglethorpe, Ga., 1955—. Mem. Nat. Assn. Female Execs., Sunbelt Resorts, Buckhorn Landing. Republican. Baptist. Club: Lakeview Happy Healthy Homemakers. Avocations: poetry; hiking; swimming; singing. Home: PO Box 611 Rossville GA 30741 Office: World Book-Childcraft 3629 Dayton Plaza Chattanooga TN 37415

KNIGHT, MARCIA, clinical psychologist; b. N.Y.C., July 1, 1946; d. Murray M. and Ruth (Lynn) Knight; B.A., Brown U., 1968; M.A., Yeshiva U., 1975; Ph.D. (NIMH fellow), 1979. Adj. lectr. Bklyn. Coll., 1971-74; staff psychologist Met. Hosp., N.Y.C., 1974-80; pvt. practice psychology, forensic psychology, N.Y.C., 1980—; cons. psychologist Gracie Sq. Hosp., N.Y.C., Sage Garden Acad., Bronx, N.Y.; supervising psychologist Child Devel. Center affiliated with Flower and Misericordia Hosps., Bronx; assoc. Dr. Karen Blaker Psychotherapy Center, N.Y.C. Mem. Am. Psychol. Assn., N.Y. Soc. Clin. Psychologists, N.Y. State Psychol. Assn., NOW (psychology com.), Internat. Assn. for Human Relations Lab. Tng. (bd. advisors, editor Newsletter). Home: 224 E 18th St New York NY 10003 Office: 224 E 18th St New York NY 10003

KNIGHT, MARGARETT LEE, lawyer, editor; b. Newtown, Ind., Jan. 3, 1923; d. Charles Oscar and Edna (Pace) Smith; m. Robert Cook Knight, June 20, 1961. LL.B., Ind. U., 1945, J.D., 1965; A.B., Mills Coll., 1953; LL.M., Yale U., 1955. Bar: Ind. 1945. Dep. atty. gen. Ind. Home: 1318 Hoover Ln Indianapolis IN 46260 Office: Atty Gen 219 State House Indianapolis IN 46204

KNIGHT, MARY LUCILLE, convalescent center adminstr.; b. Enid, Okla., Dec. 5, 1938; d. Otis Stanley and Mary Ellen (Record) Kile; m. E. Harmon Knight, Apr. 30, 1962; children—Sherri, Fran, Cathy. Med. asst. Dr. Fred Thomas, Dallas, 1963-67; x-ray asst., physicians' asst. Prevost Meml. Hosp., Donaldsonville, La., 1967-72; asst. adminstr. Archusa Convalescent Center, Quitman, Miss., 1976—, sec. bd. dirs., 1976-78. Lic. adminstr. Mem. Miss. Nursing Home Assn. Republican. Baptist. Home: 10 Betty Circle Quitman MS 39355 Office: Hwy 511 E Quitman MS 39355

KNIGHT, NAOMA BEERS, retired librarian; b. Hilo, Hawaii, July 9, 1910; d. William Henry and Maude Olive (Hansen) Beers; m. Wiley Wheeler Knight, July 8, 1939 (dec. Jan. 1981); children—Philip, Ione, Wiley. B.S. in L.S., U. Wash., 1932; postgrad. U. Hawaii, 1936, San Jose State Coll., 1968, Okla. State U., 1970. Librarian elem. and intermediate schs., Hilo and Honokaa, Hawaii, 1932-33, 37-40; vol. librarian Hilo Meml. Hosp., 1940-41; librarian Benicia Pub. Library (Calif.), 1944, Hawaii County Library, Hilo, 1945-46; sch. and circulation librarian, asst. county librarian, Redwood City, Calif., 1947-56; dist. librarian Menlo Park City Sch. Dist. (Calif.), 1956-75; substitute librarian Hawaii Dept. Edn., Hilo, 1975—; librarian Lyman Meml. Mus., Hilo, 1976-82. Mem. Nat. Ret. Tchrs. Assn., Am. Assn. Ret. Persons, ALA, Hawaii Library Assn., Volcano Art Ctr. Republican. Episcopalian. Club: Hilo Womens. Lodge: Order Eastern Star. Home: 2084 Kalanianaole Ave Hilo HI 96720

KNIGHT, SHIRLEY, actress; b. Goessel, Kans., July 5, 1936; d. Noel J. and Virginia (Webster) K.; D.F.A. (hon.), Lake Forest Coll., 1979; m. John Hopkins; children—Kate, Sophie. Address: Hazelnut Farm RFD 1 Fairfield CT 06430

KNIGHT, SUSAN BAILEY, food company executive; b. Nasha, N.H., May 6, 1958; d. Burton Stanley and Wilene (Cowles) K. B.A., Duke U., 1980. Sales rep. Procter and Gamble, Tampa, Fla., 1980; retail merchandiser Sunshine Biscuits, Inc., Natick, Mass., 1981, sales supr., 1981, sales mgr., Wellesley Hills, Mass., 1982—. Vol., McKernan for Congress, Portland, Maine, 1982. Recipient Leadership award Albany Sales Team, 1982. Mem. Nat. Assn. for Female Execs., Am. Camping Assn., Maine Youth Camping Assn. Republican. Avocation: competitive swimming; sailing; skiing; canoeing; hiking. Office: Susan B Knight PO Box 262 Cape Elizabeth ME 04107

KNIPP, MYNDA ANN, air force official, editor; b. Hugo, Okla., Oct. 21, 1934; d. John Dudley and Mozelle (Wall) Holman; m. Earl W. McGuire, Oct. 11, 1952 (div. 1980); 1 son, Michael John; m. F. Carl Knipp, June 9, 1984. B.A., U. Okla., 1978, M.A., 1980, postgrad., 1981; postgrad. Ohio State U., 1982-83. Continuity dir. Sta. WROB, West Point, Miss., 1960-62; writer U.S. Air Force, Tinker AFB, Okla., 1964-72, editor Tinker Take Off, 1973-81; pub. affairs officer Air Force Logistics Command, Wright-Patterson AFB, Ohio, 1981-83; chief family affairs Air Force Service and Info. News Ctr., Kelly AFB, Tex., 1983—; columnist Airman mag., 1983—; editor monthly news clip-sheet Family News, 1983—. Co-author (with James R. Estes) Prairie Flowers, 1980. Mem. exec. com. Coll. Liberal Studies, U. Okla., 1977; mem. Oklahoma City Mayor's Complete Count Census '80 Com., 1980. Recipient outstanding newspaper award U.S. Air Force, 1973, 74, Thomas Jefferson award Dept. Def., 1974. Mem. Internat. Communication Assn., Speech Communication Assn., AAUW (legis. liaison 1982), Women in Communication, Armed Forces Pub. Affairs Council San Antonio. Lutheran. Home: 1906 Encino Bluff San Antonio TX 78259 Office: Family Affairs Air Force Service and Info News Ctr Kelly AFB TX 78241

KNIPPSCHILD, ERNESTINE, psychic consultant; b. Sfintu Gheorghe, Transylvania, Romania, July 13, 1932; came to U.S., 1949; d. Adalbert Julius and Elizabeth Emilia (Lichtfuss) Ott; m. William Knippschild, Aug. 29, 1951; children—Clara Elizabeth, William Albert, Robert Bryan. E.S.P. devel. tchr., coordinator Ridley High Sch., Ridley Twp., Pa., 1972—; lectr. Parastudy, Inc., Chester Heights, Pa., 1969-80; lectr., cons. Kiwanis, DeWitt Club, Liverpool, N.Y., 1978-84; pres., owner Rainbow Parasensory Sci. Assn., Edgemont, Pa., 1980—; psychic cons. Rainbow Parasensory Sci., Edgemont, 1980—; psychic cons. Nat. Assn. Rev. Appraisers and Mortgage Underwriters, Scottsdale, Ariz., 1985—; stress cons. Field Service Assocs., Newtown Square, Pa., 1981—. Mem. Spiritual Frontiers Fellowship, Nat. Assn. Female Execs. Avocations: writing; traveling; helping people. Home: 1300 Stackhouse Mill Rd Newtown Square PA 19073 Office: Rainbow Parasensory Sci Assocs PO Box 495 Edgemont Township PA 19028

KNISELY, SALLY, psychotherapist; b. Baraga, Mich., Mar. 17, 1917; d. Henry Samuel and Flora (Hagerman) Knisely; A.B., U. Mich., 1944; M.A., U. Chgo., 1946; Ed.D., Columbia U., 1964. Day nursery caseworker Bur. Family Service, Orange, N.J., 1946-49; caseworker to mentally ill vets. VA, N.Y.C., 1949-53; child psychotherapist Inter-Agy. Guidance Center, Yonkers, N.Y., 1953-58; child psychotherapist Monsey (N.Y.) Mental Health Clinic, 1957-58; child psychotherapist New Rochelle (N.Y.) Guidance Center, 1958-59; pvt. practice psychotherapy, Stamford, Conn., 1954—; cons. numerous nursery sch. and presch. programs. Fellow Conn. Soc. Clin. Social Workers; mem. Am. Orthopsychiat. Assn., Council Psychoanalytic Psychotherapists, Nat. Assn. Edn. Young Children, Soc. Health and Human Values, Nat. Assn. Social Workers, Nat. Assn. of Deaf, Am. Deafness and Rehab. Assn., AAUW. Home and office: 69 Jordan Ln Stamford CT 06903

KNIZESKI, JUSTINE ESTELLE, insurance company executive; b. Glen Cove, N.Y., June 4, 1954; d. John Martin and Elsie Beatrice (Gozelski) Knizeski. B.A., Conn. Coll., 1976; M. Mgmt., Northwestern U., 1981. Customer service supr. Brunswick Savs., Freeport, Maine, 1977-79; investment analyst Bankers Life and Casualty Co., Chgo., 1980-83, dir. corp. planning and analysis, 1983—. Chmn. bd. dirs. Alternatives, Inc., Chgo., 1984-85, bd. dirs., 1983-84; mem. Chgo. Council Fgn. Relations, 1984-85. Mem. Planning Execs. Inst., Midwest Planning Assn., Nat. Assn. Female Execs. Avocations: sailing; bicycling; traveling; painting.

KNOBBE, MARY LOUISE SIEFER, library consultant; b. Cherryvale, Kans., Aug. 26, 1918; d. Clarence E. and Lula (Funkhouser) Siefer; A.B., Washburn U. 1940; postgrad. Sch. Library Sci. and Information U. Md., 1965-67; m. Ray H. Knobbe, Jan. 23, 1946; children—Ann, Jane. Library asst. Washburn U., Topeka, 1941-42; librarian Dept. Research, Kansas City, Mo., 1944-46; reference librarian Carnegie Library, Steubenville, Ohio, 1950-51; planning librarian Md. Nat. Capital Park and Planning Commn., Silver Spring, 1961-67; librarian Met. Washington Council Govts., 1967-79; library cons., 1979—; dir. Inter Library Users Assn., 1972-79. Mem. women's guild Episcopal Ch. Home, Washington, 1983—. Mem. Council Planning Librarians, Spl. Libraries Assn. (chmn. social sci. div. D.C. chpt. 1967-68, chpt. dir. 1968-70; mem. govt. info. services com. 1971-75, chmn. urban affairs sect. 1975-76, chmn. govt. info. services com. 1975-77), Kans. Soc. Washington, Pi Gamma Mu. Episcopalian. Editor: Planning and Urban Affairs Library Manual, 3d edit., 1975; Planning, Building and Housing Libraries, 1969. Home and Office: 2300 Eccleston St Silver Spring MD 20902

KNOEBEL, BETTY LOU MARGARET, food service executive; b. Hobart, Ind., July 12, 1931; d. Frank Orville and Louise Caroline (Sohn) Burnett; radiol. technician Meth. Hosp. Sch. Radiology, 1950; student Ind. U., 1952-54, St. Joseph's Hosp. Sch. Nursing, 1950-51, Calif. Western Res. U., 1976—; m. F. C. Knoebel, Apr. 27, 1974. Bookkeeper, Nash Agy., Gary, Ind., 1948-49; x-ray technician Gilfillan Clinic, Bloomfield, Ia., 1950-51; med. sec., x-ray technician Meth. Hosp., Gary, Ind., 1951-52; chem. lab. and indsl. x-ray technician Cast Armor Div., Am. Steel Foundry, East Chgo., Ind., 1952-53; med. sec., surg. asst., med. asst., R. G. Nilges, M.D., neurosurgeon, 1953-60; ins. sec., sales and claims sec. Farm Bur. Ins., Crown Point, Ind., 1960-63; med. sec., surg. and med. asst. M.R. Bernard, M.D., neurosurgeon, 1963-65; exec. sec. to v.p. mktg. and sales The Anderson Co., Gary, 1965-71; x-ray technician Melissa Meml. Hosp., Holyoke, Colo., 1971; corp. sec., adminstrv. asst. Nobel, Inc., Denver, 1971—; stockholder, pres. B&K Motor Sports, Inc., Englewood, Colo. Sec., Tolleston Ch. of Christ, Gary, 1940-48; pianist, tchr. Glen Park Assembly of God, Gary, 1948-71. Am. Cancer Soc. radiology grantee, 1949. Mem. Colo.-Wyo. Restaurant Assn. (chmn. 1978-79), Ind. Soc. Radiologic Technicians, Profl. Businesswomen's Assn., Nat. Secs. Assn., AAUW. Republican. Assemblies of God. Home: 5 Village Rd Englewood CO 80110 Office: 1101 W 48 Ave Denver CO 80217 also B&K Motor Sports Inc 5030 S Broadway Englewood CO 80110

KNOEBEL, SUZANNE BUCKNER, physician, educator; b. Fort Wayne, Ind., Dec. 13, 1916; d. Doster and Marie (Lewis) Buckner. A.B., Goucher Coll., 1948, D.Sc., 1984; M.D., Ind. U., 1960. Diplomate Am. Bd. Internal Medicine. Intern, Ind. U. Med. Ctr., Indpls., 1960-61, resident, 1961-62; asst. prof. Ind. U., Indpls., 1966-69, assoc. prof., 1969-72, prof. medicine, 1972-77, Krannert prof. medicine, 1977—, asst. dean research, 1975—; acting chief cardiology Roudebush VA Med. Ctr., Indpls., 1983—; assoc. dir. Krannert Inst. Cardiology, Indpls., 1974—; attending physician Ind. U. Hosps., Indpls., 1964—. Contbr. articles to profl. jours. Recipient Matrix award Ind. Women in Communication, 1983. Fellow Am. Coll. Cardiology (chmn. govt. relations com. 1982—), Am. Heart Assn. (council on clin. cardiology); mem. Assn. Univ. Cardiologists, Am. Fedn. Clin. Research, Central Soc. Clin. Investigation. Office: Ind U Sch Medicine 1100 W Michigan St Indianapolis IN 46223

KNOEBER, MARGARET MARY, college administrator, chemistry educator; b. Spearville, Kans., Feb. 13, 1931; d. John Clement and Olivia Clothilde (Habiger) K. B.S., Sacred Heart Coll., Wichita, Kans., 1961; postgrad. Boston U., 1971; postgrad. U. Notre Dame, 1967-68, Ph.D., 1967. Joined Sisters Adorers of Blood of Christ Religious Community, 1950. Tchr. elem. schs. Diocese of Wichita, 1955-60; tchr. Sacred Heart Acad., Wichita, 1960-61; teaching and research asst. U. Notre Dame, 1963-67; prof. chemistry Kans. Newman Coll., 1967-78, dir. alumni relations, 1983—. Recipient Recognition award Kans. Newman Coll., 1977. Mem. Council for Advancement and Support Edn., Am. Chem. Soc., Kans. Acad. Scis., Sigma Zeta. Democrat. Avocations: music; gardening. Home: 1165 Southwest Blvd Wichita KS 67213 Office: Kans Newman Coll 3100 McCormick Ave Wichita KS 67213

KNOERLE, SISTER JEANNE, college chancellor; b. Cleve., Feb. 24, 1928; d. Harold and Bernedine (Seufert) Knoerle; B.A., St. Mary-of-the-Woods Coll., 1949; M.A., Ind. U., 1961, Ph.D., 1966, LL.D., 1975, M.B.A., 1987; LL.D., Rose Hulman Inst. Tech., 1971; LL.D., Ind. State U., 1972; D.D., Ind. Central U., 1978. Tchr. high schs., 1952-54; chmn. dept. journalism St. Mary-of-the-Woods Coll. (Ind.), 1954-63, asst. to pres., assoc. prof. Asian studies, 1967-68, pres., prof., 1968-83, chancellor, dir. endowment program, 1984—; pres. Woods Assocs., mgmt. and mktg. cons. to non-profit orgns.; vis. prof. Providence Coll., Taichung, Taiwan, 1966-67. Mem. Gov.'s Commn. Status of Women, 1973-75; pres. Ind. Conf. Higher Edn., 1973-74; dir. Fed. Home Loan Bank, Indpls.; mem. adv. council div. research resources NIH, 1975-79; mem. exec. com. Women's Coll. Coalition-Assn. Am. Colls.; mem. adv. council Ind. Acad. in Pub. Service; bd. dirs. Fund for Improvement Postsecondary Edn., 1982-85, Council Independent Colls., 1980-82, Ctr. for Constl. Studies, Mercer U., 1980. Bd. dirs. Union Hosp., Terre Haute, Ind., United Way of the Wabash Valley, 1971-75, Mental Health Assn. Vigo County, 1971-78, Wabash Valley Goodwill Industries, 1970-78, Terre Haute Med. Edn. Found., 1974-79; pres. Alliance for Growth and Progress Econ. Devel. Group, Terre Haute, Ind., 1983-85; mem. Ind. Gov.'s Com. for Ind.'s Utility Future. Mem. Assn. Cath. Colls. and Univs. (chmn. 1978-80), Am. Council Edn. (dir. 1978-80, mem. com. on women in higher edn. 1976-79), Nat. Cath. Ednl. Assn. (dir.), Assn. Am. Colls. (dir. 1976-80), Internat. Assn. Univ. Presidents (adv. council N.Am. council 1977-79), Asso. Colls. Ind. (sec. 1970-72, v.p. 1978—), Council Advancement Small Colls. (dir. 1980-83), Ind. Conf. Higher Edn. (exec. com. 1972-73, pres. 1982-84), Delta Kappa Gamma. Author: The Dream of the Red Chamber, a Critical Study, 1972. Contbr. articles to profl. jours. Address: St Mary-of-the-Woods Coll St Mary-of-the-Woods IN 47876

KNOLLE, MARY ANNE ERICSON, human resources company official; b. Kilgore, Tex., Jan. 7, 1941; d. Evert Eric and Frances Leone (Scott) Ericson; m. John W. Knolle, Mar. 14, 1980; children—by previous marriage—Clay Claflin, Sunny Claflin; Sara Anne Knolle, Evelyn Knolle. B.A., North Tex. State U., 1962; M.A., U. Tex.-Austin, 1968; postgrad. UCLA, 1964-66, U. Houston, 1974-76. Editor co. publs. Gt. S.W. Life Ins. Co., 1962; prof. U. Balt., 1968, Miami (Fla.) Dade Coll., 1968, Savannah (Ga.) State Coll., 1969, U. Houston, 1972-76; dir. pub. relations Alvin (Tex.) Coll., 1970-72; founder, pres. Panorama Programs, Houston, 1972-76; mgmt. devel. tng. coordinator Brown & Root, Inc., Houston, 1970-79; div. founder, mgr. mgmt. and orgnl. devel. systems Diversified Human Resources Group, Inc., Houston, 1979—; founder, pres. Panorama Mgmt. Inst., Houston, 1979—; cons. moot ct. U. Tex. Law Sch., 1965—. Regional speech contest judge Houston Jaycees, Recipient Blockbuster award United Way, 1979. Mem. Am. Soc. Tng. and Devel., Houston C. of C. (chmn. edn. com.), Alpha Delta Pi (pres. alumnae). Presbyterian. Club: Houston Indoor Tennis. Office: 12307 Broken Arrow Houston TX 77024

KNOL-TART, JANA BETH, association executive; b. Edmond, Okla., July 19, 1954; d. John J. and Norma Jeanne (Dunlap) Knol; m. John Anthony Tart, Oct. 4, 1985. B.S., U. Houston, 1977; M.Allied Health Edn., Central State U., Edmond, Okla., 1978; postgrad. Baylor Coll. Medicine/U. Houston, 1982-84. Radiologic technologist Meml. Hosp. System, Houston, 1975-77; examinations coordinator Am. Urol. Assn., Houston, 1980-84; dir. Am. Soc. Radiologic Technologists Ednl. Found., Albuquerque, 1985—. Mem. ednl. planning com. Am. Cancer Soc., 1984-85. John Duren Meml. scholar, 1971-73. Mem. Am. Soc. Assn. Execs., Nat. Assn. Female Execs., Am. Soc. Radiologic Technologists, Kappa Delta Pi. Republican. Avocations: piano; skiing; shelling; stamp collecting; writing poetry. Office: ASRT Ednl Found Inc 15000 Central Ave SE Albuquerque NM 87123

KNORR, ANTOINETTE FRAZIER, hotel executive; b. Phila., Sept. 24, 1951; d. William Knorr and Florence (Rowe) Genser. B.A., Pa. State U., 1973; M.P.S. in Hotel Adminstrn., Cornell U., 1977; Diplome-Intermed. La Varenne Ecole de Cuisine, 1982. Catering mgr. Hyatt Regency Hotel, Chgo., 1977-79, dir. catering, Cambridge, Mass., 1979-81, Dallas, 1982—; lectr. Cornell U., Ithaca N.Y., 1978-81. Active March of Dimes, Dallas, 1978-81. Recipient Donald N. Pritzker award, Chgo., 1983. Mem. Nat. Assn. Catering Execs. Republican. Episcopalian. Home: 4800 Northway Dr Apt 4D Dallas TX 75206 Office: Hyatt Regency Dallas 300 Reunion Blvd Dallas TX 75207

KNORR, LINDA CAROL, nurse; b. Wilkes-Barre, Pa., Aug. 22, 1958; d. Joseph John and Nancy Jane (Thomas) K. B.S., Wilkes Coll., 1980. R.N., Wilkes-Barre Gen. Hosp., 1980-81; operating room nurse intern Med. Coll. Va., Richmond, 1981, operating room nurse, 1981-83, orthopedic nurse, 1983-84, R.N. clinician-A orthopedics, 1984—. Mem. Nat. Assn. Orthopedic Nurses, Sigma Theta Tau. Avocations: sewing; reading; needlework; bicycling. Home: 523 Rossmore Rd Richmond VA 23225

KNOTT, MEREDITH LEE, computer scientist; b. Chgo., July 20, 1941; d. John Otis and Florence Margene (Lee) K.; B.A., Maryville (Tenn.) Coll., 1963; divorced; children—Shawn Charles, Laurel Lee. Instr., Colo. Mountain Coll., Glenwood Springs, 1970-71; IBM programmer, analyst Petro-Systems, Lakewood, Colo., 1980; tech. lead, computer graphics software engr. Martin Marietta Denver Aerospace, 1980—; tchr. computer sci. Founder, organizer, race sec., coach Buddy Werner Ski League, Glenwood Springs, 1973-74. Mem. Assn. Computing Machinery, Nat. Assn. Computer Graphics, Colo. Assn. Gifted and Talented. Republican. Home: 10695 Devils Head Mountain Littleton CO 80127

KNOTT, TARA DAVIS, evaluation consultant; b. Alexandria, La., Dec. 5, 1943; d. Raoul Lynwood and Ruby Montez (Luneau) Brister; B.A. in Psychology, Memphis State U., 1971, M.A. in Speech Pathology, 1975; B.A. in Speech and Music, La. State U., 1961; Ph.D. in Evaluation Research, Clayton U., 1978; m. David Howard Knott, Aug. 6, 1978. Evaluator family practice dept. U. Tenn. Center for Health Scis., 1976-78; research cons. Deafness Found., 1978, Nat. Hearing Assn., 1978; evaluation cons. Covington Mental Health Center, 1978-79; head data collection Project WOMAN, 1978-79; evaluation cons. Mid South Hosp., 1979—, Jackson Splty. Hosp., 1980—; United Inns, 1981—, Memphis Mental Health Inst., U. Tenn. Center Health Scis., 1979—, Rivendell Corp. Am., 1984—, Hosp. Corp. Am., 1983—; pres. Evaluation Resources, Inc., 1983—; cons., tchr. hosps., colls. and univs. Grantee in alcoholism and drug abuse. Mem. Evaluation Network, Evaluation Research Soc., Soc. Neurosci., Employee Assistance Soc. N.Am., Am. Fitness in Industry, Tenn. Evaluation Network. Democrat. Methodist. Contbr. articles to profl. jours. Home and Office: 4646 Poplar Suite 305 Memphis TN 38117

KNOWLES, BRENDA ERNESTYNE, business law educator, lawyer; b. Evansville, Ind., Aug. 5, 1946; d. Ernest Emmett and Madge Laverne (Farrar) Knowles; m. Paul Stanislaus Kochanowski, Jan. 12, 1980; children—Laura, David, Erica, Michael. B.A. magna cum laude, U. Evansville, 1968; M.A., Miami U., 1971; J.D., Ind. U., 1977. Bar: Ind. 1977, U.S. Dist. Ct. (so. dist.) Ind. 1977, U.S. Dist. Ct. (no. dist.) Ind. 1981. Grad. research asst. dept. English, Miami U., Oxford, Ohio, 1968-69, grad. teaching asst., 1969-70; instr. English Concord Coll., Athens, W.Va., 1971-74; grader, grad. teaching asst. Ind. U. Sch. Bus., Bloomington, 1975-77; assoc. prof. bus. law Ind. U., South Bend, 1977—. Bd. dirs. A.C.T.I.O.N., Inc., South Bend, 1980-82; mem. central planning com. pub. policy choices task force, South Bend, 1980. Recipient All-Univ. Disting. Teaching award Amoco Found. Ind. U., Bloomington, 1982; Ind. U.-South Bend summer faculty fellow, 1979-83; Danforth Found. assoc., St. Louis, 1981. Mem. Am. Bus. Law Assn., ABA, Ind. Bar Assn., St. Joseph County Bar Assn., Phi Alpha Delta, Beta Gamma Sigma, Phi Kappa Phi, Alpha Lambda Delta, Phi Mu. (sec. Evansville 1966-68). Co-author: Business Law Principles and Cases, 1984; contbr. articles to profl. jours. Office: Ind Univ Div Bus Econs PO Box 7111 1700 Mishawaka Ave South Bend IN 46616

KNOWLES, CONNIE FISHER, banker; b. Delaware, Ohio, Dec. 22, 1916; d. Robert Morgan and Dora L. (Albright) Fisher; m. Jack O. Knowles, Nov. 28, 1939 (div. 1977); children—Donna L. Knowles Born, Jane Ann Knowles Wise. Student Ohio State U., 1933-35; A.B., Depauw U., 1937; B.E., Capital U., 1938. Sec., Miami YWCA, Fla., 1938-39; asst. v.p. Coconut Grove Bank, Miami, 1984—. Founder Guild Mus. and Sci., Miami, 1952, Guilded Lillies for Crippled Children, Miami, 1974; bd. dirs. Miami YWCA. Mem. So. Fla. Hist. Assn., Am. Inst. Banking, Miami Women's Panhellenic Assn. (pres. 1960-61), AAUW (pres. 1940-41); Alpha Chi Omega (pres. 1947-48). Club: Riviera Country. Home: 6810 Tordera St Coral Gables FL 33146 Office: Coconut Grove Bank 2701 S Bayshore Dr Miami FL 33133

KNOWLES, GLORIA BALL, personnel administrator; b. Magna, Utah, Mar. 14, 1937; d. Alfred Thomas and Virginia (Hatton) Ball; student public schs., San Francisco; m. Sanderson Llewellyn, Apr. 2, 1955; children—Douglas Llyn, Thomas Ross. Bookkeeper, Wells Fargo Bank, San Francisco, 1954-56; with Bank of Am., Richmond and Oakland, Calif., 1956-59, 60; credit/loan clk. Central Bank, Concord, Calif., 1972-73; sr. acctg. clk. produce div. Safeway Stores, Inc., Oakland, 1973-75, affirmative action rep., 1975-76, HRD Supply Divs., Walnut Creek, Calif., 1977-81, employee relations supr., 1981-83, human resources supr., 1984—. Contra Costa County regional occupation program adv. com., 1978—; mem. sci. adv. com., sec. Diablo Valley Coll., 1979-80, 80-81; United Way coordinator Safeway Stores, Inc., 1979-80; bd. dirs. Shadelands Children's Center, Walnut Creek. Recipient United Way Pacesetter Coordinator cert., 1980. Mem. Am. Mgmt. Assn., Diablo Employers Assn., Nat. Assn. Female Execs. Republican. Mem. Ch. Jesus Christ of Latter-day Saints. Office: 2800 Ygnacio Valley Rd Walnut Creek CA 94598

KNOWLES, PATRICIA KAIRALLA, dancer, choreographer; b. W. Palm Beach, Fla., May 14, 1942; d. George E. and Mireille Sylvia (Cowan) Kairalla; B.A. in English, Fla. State U., Tallahassee, 1964, M.A. in Dance, 1966; m. Frank L. Knowles, June 26, 1966. Instr., choreographer, dancer U. Ga., Athens, 1966-70, Eastern Mich. U., Ypsilanti, 1970-73; dir. dance, choreographer, performer Brevard (N.C.) Music Center, summers 1968-70; head dept. dance U. Ill., Champaign-Urbana, 1973—; dancer, cons. in field.; mem. panel dance Ill. Arts Council, 1979-80; choreographer Ill. Dance Theatre, univ. and regional dance cos., others. Grantee Mich. Arts Council, Ill. Arts Council, Australian Council; 3 works commd. by Harbinger Dance Co. Mem. Council Dance Adminstrs., Am. Coll. Dance Festival Assn. (bd. dirs.), Nat. Assn. Schs. Dance (treas. 1982-86). Democrat. Roman Catholic. Home: 401 W Indiana St Urbana IL 61801 Office: 4-501 Krannert Center Krannert Center 500 S Goodwin St Urbana IL 61801

KNOX, CAROL RUTH, writer; b. Somerville, Mass., Dec. 16, 1938; d. Harold Lester and Gladys Ann (Laye) K. B.A., Tufts U., 1960; M.A., Brown U., 1964;

Ph.D., Calif. Inst. Integral Studies, 1983. Ordained to ministry Unity Ch., 1970; tchr. Norton High Sch. (Mass.), 1960-62; dir. Mass. Assn. Adult Blind, Scituate, Mass., summers 1962-64; dir. music Ledyard High Sch., (Conn.), 1963-68; exec. dir., minister Unity Ctr., Walnut Creek, Calif., 1970—; speaker before civic groups; lectr. Diablo Valley Coll., John F. Kennedy U., 1971-84. Author: You've Got A Friend, 1974, Manna from Stones, 1978; Prayer of the Heart, 1983; Incredible Journey, 1984; also articles. Pres. bd. dirs. Synergy Sch., Martínez, Calif., 1978-79 (recipient award 1978); bd. dirs. Contra Costa County Mental Health Assn., 1979-81, Calif. Inst. Integral Studies, San Francisco, 1983—; mem. staff, bd. dirs. Rosebridge Inst., Walnut Creek, 1981—. Mem. Assn. Unity Chs. (v.p., dir. 1970—), Spiritual Realization Fellowship, Am. Bus. Women's Assn., AAUW. Republican. Home: 214 W 9th St Antioch CA 94509 Office: Unity Ctr Walnut Creek 1871 Geary Rd Walnut Creek CA 94596

KNOX, ELISABETH ANN, nurse, educator; b. Princeton, Ind., Dec. 31, 1936; d. Harry Dorsey and Mary Duncan (Fitzsimmons) Keneipp; B.S.N., Ind. U., 1958, M.S. Health Ed., 1968; M.S.N., U. Evansville, 1982; m. Lawrence J. Knox, Feb. 21, 1976; children—David L. Furr (dec.), Byron D. Furr (dec.). Staff nurse Riley Hosp., Indpls., 1958-59, VA Hosp., Indpls., 1959, Deaconess Hosp., Evansville, Ind., 1961; sch. nurse North Gibson Sch. Corp., Princeton, 1962-68; dir. assoc. degree program Olney (Ill.) Central Coll., 1968-72, assoc. dean allied health, 1985—; dir. assoc. degree nursing program U. Evansville, 1972-76, vis. asst. prof., 1982-85. Bd. dirs. Richland Meml. Hosp. Aux., 1977—, Olney Central Coll. Found., 1979—; mem. council ministries 1st United Meth. Ch., 1978—. bd. dirs. Fellow Am. Sch. Health Assn.; mem. Am. Nurses Assn., Ill. Nurses Assn. (awards com.), Dist. 12 Nurses Assn. (pres. 1978-80, dir. 1976-78, 80—), Nat. League Nursing (visitor for assoc. degree nursing programs 1973-76), Phi Kappa Phi, Sigma Theta Tau. Club: Richland Country. Address: 1200 N East St Olney IL 62450

KNOX, KAREN ATWELL, computer company executive; b. Cleve., Oct. 16, 1957; d. William L. and Nancy A. (Johnson) Atwell; m. Jeffrey Charles Knox, Sept. 5, 1981. Student Ohio U., 1975-77. Owner mgr., Mainely Books Shop, Deer Isle, Maine, 1975-77; adtv. saleswoman Telegraph newspaper, Painesville, Ohio, 1977-79; ins. saleswoman Lincoln Nat. Life Ins. Co., Fort Wayne, Ind., 1979-80; dist. mgr. ADP Corp Cleve., 1980-81; account rep. Computer Language Research Corp. Cleve., 1981—. Mem. Nat. Assn. Female Execs. (network dir. 1983—), Northcoast Exec. Women's Network (founder, exec. dir. 1983—). Republican. Methodist. Office: Computer Language Research Corp 4807 Rockside Rd Independence OH 44131

KNOX, KATHERINE ELIZABETH, lawyer; b. Erie, Pa., Dec. 7, 1953; d. William Wallace and Agnes (Graham) K. B.S., U. Mich., 1976; J.D., U. Pitts., 1980. Law clk. U.S. Dist. Ct. (ea. dist.) Pa., Phila., 1980-81; assoc. Schnader, Harrison, Segal & Lewis, Phila., 1981-84; sr. atty. IU Internat. Corp., Phila., 1984—. Recipient Coll. All-Am. Swimming award Assn. Intercollegiate Athletics Women, 1974, 75, 76. Mem. ABA, Pa. State Bar Assn., Phila. Bar Assn. Home: 1018 Spruce St Philadelphia PA 19107 Office: IU Internat Corp 1500 Walnut St Philadelphia PA 19102

KNOX, MARGARET ELLIOTT, newspaper editor; b. Norfolk, Va., Aug. 16, 1919; d. Roy and Mary (Upshur) Elliott; A.B. cum laude, U. Ala., 1941; m. Robert Bost Knox, Jr., Apr. 26, 1944 (dec.). With Raleigh (N.C.) Times, 1941, Raleigh News and Observer, 1942, Richmond (Va.) Times Dispatch, 1942-44, New Orleans States-Item, 1944-46, N.Y. World Telegram & Sun, N.Y.C., 1946-59, Norfolk Virginian-Pilot, 1962-63; founder, editor Leader, Research Triangle Park, N.C., 1966-81, editor emeritus, 1981—; editorial bd. adv. Capitol Broadcasting Co., Raleigh, 1981—. Life mem. bd. dirs. Friends of Library, N.C. State U., 1984—. Recipient Best Series award N.Y.C. Newspaper Women's Club, 1951; Headliner award N.C. Women in Communications, 1981. Mem. N.C. Press Assn. Episcopalian. Home: 2922 Wycliff Rd Raleigh NC 27607 Office: 10 Park Plaza Research Triangle Park NC 27709

KNOX, REBECCA HOWLAND, occupational therapy consultant; b. Wilmington, Del., May 5, 1943; d. F. Stratton, Jr. and Elizabeth Hussey (Brown) K.; m. Gerald W. McCollum, June 6, 1964 (div. Apr. 1975). B.A., Brown U., 1965; cert. Tufts U., 1968; M.A., St. Mary's Coll., Winona, Minn., 1983. Registered occupational therapist; lic. in Mass. Occupational therapist Robert Breck Brigham Hosp., Boston, 1968; research asst. Inst. for Family and Youth, Cambridge, Mass., 1968-73; occupational therapy cons. Wellmet Project, Inc., Cambridge, 1973, Boston Area Nursing Homes, 1973—, Center House, South Boston, Mass., 1976—, Wellsprings, Cambridge, 1985—; cons. Liberty Sch., Cambridge, 1974—; researcher Tigerlily Research, Cambridge, 1985—. Sponsor 2 children Holy Land Christian Mission Internat., 1983—; mem. Harbor Area Mental Health Human Rights Com., Boston, 1985—. Mem. Am. Occupational Therapy Assn., Mass. Occupational Therapy Assn., Internat. Transactional Analysis Assn., Boston Orthomolecular Soc., Assn. for Psychol. Type, Nat. Assn. for Female Execs., Mass. Fair Share, Mensa. Democrat. Buddhist. Avocations: observing cats; drawing psychological maps. Office: Wellsprings PO Box 175 Cambridge MA 02141

KNUDSEN, BETTY ANN, public and governmental relations consultant; b. Kingsport, Tenn., Oct. 10, 1926; d. Lester Bolton and Nelle Virginia (Lloyd) Leonard; m. John Peter Knudsen, Aug. 27, 1949; children—John Erik, Karl Edward, Karen Louise. A.B. in Psychology, U. Ga., 1948. Kindergarten tchr. St. Timothy's Day Sch., Raleigh, N.C., 1963-65; dir. religious edn. Ch. of the Good Shepherd, Raleigh, 1967-70; community coordinator Goals for Raleigh, 1972-75; county commr. Wake County, N.C., 1976-84, chmn. bd. commrs., 1979-80; cons. pub. and govtl. relations, Raleigh, 1985—; extension edn. tchr. Meredith Coll., Raleigh, 1981-82; mem. N.C. Gov.'s Sci. and Tech. Bd., 1978—; bd. dirs. N.C. Ctr. Pub. Policy Research, Raleigh, 1978—; del. White House Conf. on Small Bus., 1986. Author successful application for Raleigh to be All-Am. City, 1975. Editor booklets on civic issues. Pres. LWV, Wake County, 1973-75; founder, active Women's Polit. Caucus Wake County, 1975—; pres.-elect Women's Forum N.C., Raleigh, 1985—; candidate for sec. of state N.C., 1984; mem. N.C. Democratic Exec. Com. Named Tarheel of Week, Raleigh News and Observer, 1975, Vol. of Yr., City of Raleigh, 1975; recipient Civic award Wake County Opportunities, 1978. Mem. Raleigh C. of C., Nat. Bus. Women Owners, Triangle Internat. Trade Assn., AAUW, Bus. and Profl. Women, NOW, Phi Beta Kappa, Psi Chi, Alpha Lambda Delta, Phi Kappa Phi. Episcopalian. Avocations: American Indian archeology; lepidoptery; lapidary work. Home and Office: 617 Macon Pl Raleigh NC 27609

KNUDSEN, SHIREE S., office system specialist; b. South Bend, Ind., Jan. 15, 1951; d. Rolland and Helen (Hutchinson) Thorpe; children—Keith J., Kirk R. Student Ivy Tech., 1980, Ind. U., 1981-82. Sec., NROTC, U. Notre Dame, Ind., 1979-83; computer support rep. Bus. Communication Ctr., South Bend, 1983-84; office systems specialist U. Notre Dame, Ind., 1985—; cons. U. Notre Dame, 1985-86, ops. rep. Apple Univ. Consortium. Author/editor: Beginning Computing Training Material, 1985, Introduction to Word Perfect, 1985, others. Served with USNR, 1973-85. Mem. Assn. Info. Systems Profls. Republican. Presbyterian. Avocations: sailing. Office: Dept Info Systems Rm 400 Adminstrv Bldg Notre Dame IN 46556

KNUDSON, KATHRYN HELEN MALLOY, psychologist, army officer; b. St. Louis, Mar. 19, 1949; d. Albert Joseph and Julia (Kozar) Malloy; B.A. magna cum laude, U. Mo., St. Louis, 1971; M.A., U. Calif., Riverside, 1974, Ph.D. (NIMH fellow), 1978; m. Gregory Blair Knudson, Oct. 21, 1972; children—Todd Christopher, Kimberley Christina. Commd. 2d lt. U.S. Army, 1971, advanced through grades to capt., 1979; research psychologist Walter Reed Army Hosp. Research Inst., Washington, 1979-84; staff officer/research psychologist U.S. Army Med. Research and Devel. Command, Ft. Detrick, Md., 1984—. Mem. Am. Psychol. Assn., Assn. Women in Psychology. Home: 8123 Old Hagerstown Rd Middletown MD 21769 Office: USAMRDC SGRD-PLC Fort Detrick MD 21701

KNUTH, JOANN KEROLA, computer services company executive; b. Youngstown, Ohio, Dec. 1, 1931; d. Joseph J. and Mary (George) Kerola; m. Richard L. Knuth, July 4, 1957; children—Richard L., Mary Jo. Student U. Notre Dame Coll., 1949-50; B.A., Youngstown State U., 1952, postgrad., 1970-72; postgrad. Kent State U., 1966-67. High sch. tchr., Hubbard, Ohio, 1952-54, 56-57; editorial asst. Catholic Exponent, 1955-56; computer programmer IBM, Kingstown, N.Y., and Lexington, Mass., 1956-57; mathematician Boeing Airplane Co., Seattle, 1957-58; instr. Youngstown State U., 1966-80; pres. Knuth Computer Services, Inc., Hubbard, 1978—; corp. sec./treas. PI&I Motor Express, Inc., 1966—, Grandview Realty and Devel. Co., Inc., 1967—. Pres. Hubbard High Sch. PTA, 1976, 77. Office: 4 Walnut Pl Hubbard OH 44425

KOART, NELLIE HART, real estate investor and company executive; b. San Luis Obispo, Calif., Jan. 3, 1930; d. Will Carleton and Nellie Malchen (Cash) Hart; m. William Harold Koart, Jr., June 16, 1951 (dec. 1976); children—Kristen Marie Kittle, Matthew William. Student Whittier Coll., 1947-49; B.A., U. Calif.-Santa Barbara, 1952; M.A., Los Angeles State Coll., 1957. Life diploma elem. edn., Calif. Farm worker Hart Farms, Montebello, Calif., 1940-48; play leader Los Angeles County Parks and Recreation, East Los Angeles, Rosemead, Calif., 1948-51; elem. tchr. Potrero Heights Sch. Dist., South San Gabriel, Calif., 1951-55, vice prin., 1955-57; real estate salesman William Koart Real Estate, Goleta, Calif., 1963-76, real estate investor KO-ART Enterprises, Goleta, 1976—, pres. Wm. Koart Constrn. Co., Inc., Goleta, 1975—; real estate sales person Joseph McGeever Realty Co., Goleta, 1976—; adv. bd. Bank of Montecito, Santa Barbara, Calif., 1983—. Editor: Reflections, 1972. Treas. Santa Barbara County Fedn. Republican Women, Alamar-Hope Ranch, 1981-82, treas. County Bd., 1983-84; treas. Com. to Recall Hone, Maschke and Shewczyk, Goleta, 1984, 1983—; assoc. mem. state central com. Calif. Republican Party, 1985—. Mem. Santa Barbara Apartment Assn., Antique Automobile Club of Am. (sec. treas. Santa Barbara 1980-84). Club: Cardinal and Gold (Los Angeles). Avocations: swimming; numismatics; college and professional football. Office: KO ART Enterprises Post Office Box 310 Goleta CA 93116

KOBAYASHI, ANN H., state legislator; b. Honolulu, Apr. 10, 1937; m.; 3 children. Student Pembroke Coll., Northwestern U. Officer family corp.; former legis. aide, adminstrv. asst. Hawaii Senate, now mem. Senate from 14th Dist. Republican. Office: Hawaii State Senate State Capitol Bldg Honolulu HI 96813*

KOBAYASHI, CHARLOTTE CHIYO, import food company executive; b. Olaa, Hawaii, Sept. 2, 1942; d. Ginzo and Yukie (Horike) K.; B.A., U. Hawaii; M. Early Childhood Edn., Loyola U., Chgo., 1970; 1 dau., Marissa Rikka. Vice pres., mgr. Soken Trading Inc., Mill Valley, Calif., also. dir.; pres., mgr. Bon Parti, Mill Valley, Calif. Contbr. articles to jours., mags. Mem. Nat. Assn. Edn. of Young, Internat. Platform Assn. Office: 591 Redwood Hwy Suite 2125 Mill Valley CA 94941

KOBAYASHI, HESTER ATSUKO, environmental scientist; b. Honolulu, Oct. 4, 1938; d. Teruo and Kinuyo (Shinkawa) K. B.A., U. Hawaii, 1960, M.S., 1963; M.S. in Pub. Health, UCLA, 1976, D.P.H., 1981. Mgr. Arctic research U. So. Calif., Los Angeles, 1968-72, research assoc., 1973; marine environmentalist Port of Los Angeles, 1972-73; researcher in environ. sci. UCLA, 1976-81; research assoc. in environ. sci. U. Ill., Urbana, 1980-82; environ. researcher Standard Oil Research Ctr., Cleve., 1982—; cons. EPA, 1984—. Contbr. articles to profl. jours.; patentee in field. Mem. Am. Soc. Microbiology, Am. Chem. Soc., Soc. Environ. Toxicology and Chemistry, Water Pollution Control Fedn., Sigma Xi. Office: Standard Oil Co 4440 Warrensville Center Rd Cleveland OH 44128

KOBE, LAN HWA, medical physicist; b. Semarang, Indonesia; naturalized; d. O.G. and L.N. (The) Kobe. B.S. in Physics, IKIP U. Bandung, Indonesia, 1964, M.S. in Physics, 1967; M.S. in Med. Physics and Biophysics, U. Calif.-Berkeley, 1975. Physics instr. Sch. Engring., Tarumanegara U., Jakarta, Indonesia, 1968-72; research fellow dept. radiation oncology U. Calif.-San Francisco, 1975-77; clin. physicist in residence dept. radiation oncology UCLA, 1977-78, asst. hosp. radiation physicist, 1978-80, hosp. radiation physicist, 1980—; instr. radiation oncology to resident physicians. Contbr. sci. papers to profl. publs. Newhouse grantee U. Calif.-Berkeley, 1974-75, grantee dean grad. div. U. Calif.-Berkeley, 1975; recipient Pres. Work Study award U. Calif., Berkeley, 1974-75, Employee of Month award UCLA, 1983. Mem. Am. Assn. Physicists in Medicine (nat. and So. Calif. chpts.). Lodge: Rosicrucion Order. Office: UCLA Hosp and Clinics Dept Radiation Oncology Los Angeles CA 90024

KOBEL, ROSE ANNE, library executive; b. Saginaw, Mich., Jan. 20, 1950; d. Philip Raymond and Angeline Alice (Brink) Grybowski; m. Thomas Howard Kobel, July 25, 1980. A.A., Delta Coll., 1969; B.A., Mich. State U., 1971; M.A., U. S. Fla., 1977. Cert. permanent profl. librarian, Mich. Library aide, librarian Orlando Pub. Library, Fla., 1973-78; sales rep. Baker & Taylor, Momence, Ill., 1978-81; pub. relations officer Saginaw Pub. Library, 1981-83; librarian Delta Coll., University Center, Mich., 1983-85; supr. user services Grace Dow Library, Midland, Mich., 1985—; chmn. Video Cassettes in Pub. Libraries Conf., 1986. Chmn. networking YWCA, Bay City, Mich., 1985; trustee Carollton pub. schs., Mich., 1985—. Mem. ALA, Mich. Library Assn. (pub. relations com. 1981-84, chmn. intellectual freedom com. 1985-86, presenter Best of Show awards 1984, panel mem. conf. 1984), AAUW (newsletter editor 1983-84). Mormon. Clubs: Saginaw Networking; Bay City Networking (chmn. 1985). Avocations: classical music, theater, travel, swimming, reading.

KOBER, ARLETTA REFSHAUGE, civic worker; b. Cedar Falls, Iowa, Oct. 31, 1919; d. Edward and Mary (Jensen) Refshauge; B.A., U. No. Iowa, 1940, M.A., 1970; m. Kay Leonard Kober, Feb. 14, 1944; children—Kay Mary, Karilyn. Tchr. high schs., Soldier, Iowa, 1940-41, Montezuma, Iowa, 1941-43, Waterloo, Iowa, 1943-50; tchr. East High Sch., Waterloo, 1966—; head dept. coop. career edn. West High Sch., Waterloo Community Schs., 1966—. Mem. Waterloo Sch. Health Council; nominating com. YWCA, Waterloo; Black Hawk County chmn. Tb Christmas Seals; ward chmn. ARC, Waterloo; co-chmn. Citizen's Com. for Sch. Bond Issue; pres. Waterloo PTA Council, Waterloo Vis. Nursing Assn., 1956-57, Kingsley Sch. PTA, 1959-60; pres. Waterloo Women's Club, 1963-64, trustee bd. clubhouse dirs., 1957—; mem. Gen. Fedn. Women's Clubs, Nat. Congress Parents and Tchrs.; Presbyterial world service chmn. Presbyn. Women's Assn.; bd. dirs. Black Hawk County Republican Women, 1952-53, United Services of Black Hawk County; bd. dirs. Broadway Theatre League, v.p., 1963-65. Mem. AAUW (v.p. 1964-47), NEA, League Women Voters (dir. Waterloo 1951-52), Delta Pi Epsilon (charter mem. Alpha Delta chpt.), Delta Kappa Gamma. Clubs: Town (dir.) (Waterloo), P.E.O. Home: 1046 Prospect Blvd Waterloo IA 50701 Office: 503 W 4th St Waterloo IA 50701

KOBERSTEIN, ABBIE POREE, researcher, manufacturing supervisor; b. Schenectady, Dec. 12, 1953; d. O'Neil Alphonse and Eileen Bernice Poree; m. Terry Gene Koberstein, Sept. 10, 1983; 1 child, Stafany Kara. B.S., Eastern Mich. U., 1976; postgrad. in Profl. Mgmt., Ind. No. Grad. Sch., 1980-82. Internal auditor Gen. Motors, Westland, Mich., 1974; retail mgmt. Frank's Nursery, Ann Arbor, Mich., 1977; mfr. supr. Ford Motor Co., Livonia, Mich., 1977-79, John Deere Plow & Planter, Moline, Ill., 1979-82, Hobart Corp., Chicago Heights, Ill., 1982-83; pvt. practice as researcher, Preemption, Ill., 1983-86; dist. supr. Southland Corp., Davenport, Iowa, 1986—. Recipient Harvard Bus. Rev. award Ind. No. Grad. Sch., 1981. Mem. Nat. Assn. Female Execs., Career Women's Network. Democrat. Lutheran. Avocations: reading; bicycling; jazz dancing; white water rafting; hiking. Home: PO Box 486 Preemption IL 61276 Office: 2010 E 30th St Davenport IA 52807

KOCH, CAREL EVELYNN, designer; b. Lincoln, Nebr., Mar. 23, 1960; d. Robert Carl and Gertrude Evelyn (Kornmuller) K. B.S., Drexel U., 1982. Design asst. Sydney Carvin Milliken, N.Y.C., 1981, 82-83, Jones New York, N.Y.C., 1983-84; sales rep., designer Asymmetry, N.Y.C., 1984-85; designer Rayman/Ridless, N.Y.C., 1985—; designer, producer, sales rep. Carel Koch Indsl. Design, N.Y.C., 1983. Mem. Nat. Assn. Female Execs., Phi Eta Sigma, Phi Kappa Phi, Omicron Nu. Avocations: dance, film, art, making jewelry, travel. Home: 151 Dekalb Ave Apt 1 Brooklyn NY 11217 Office: Rayman Ridless Products Group 10 W 32d St New York NY 10001

KOCH, ELAINE L., success planning company executive; b. Milw., May 18, 1938; d. Martin and Priscilla (Kalscheuer) K. B.S., Marian Coll., Wis., 1961; M.S., U. Wis., 1972. Psychotherapist, Cudahy Mental Health Ctr., Mil-, 1970-72, Mercy Hosp., Chgo., 1972-79; trainer Rust-Oleum, Vernon Hills, Ill., 1979-80, mgr., 1980-84; pres., owner Success Planning Assocs., Chgo., 1984—. Contbr. articles to profl. jours. Mem. Network Women Entrepreneurs (bd. dirs.), Nat. Network Women in Sales, Chgo. C. of C. (small bus. devel. com.). Avocations: skiing; theatre. Home: 837 W Barry #3A Chicago IL 60657 Office: Success Planning Assocs 990 W Fullerton Chicago IL

KOCH, FRANCES ANN, nurse; b. Spur, Tex., Apr. 13, 1939; d. T.J. and Mary Frances (Van Meter) Taylor; R.N., B.S., Tex. Christian U., 1961; postgrad. Tex. Tech. U., summer 1958, nights 1967-68; M.S. in Nursing (USPHS grantee), U. Ariz., 1971; m. Stuart Alan Koch, Mar. 20, 1970; children—Lesleigh, Brett, Todd. Operating room supr. W.Tex. Hosp., Lubbock, 1961-69; operating room supr., instr. nursing Coll. Medicine, U. Ariz., Tucson, 1970-73; sch. nurse Torrejon AFB, Madrid, Spain, 1974-75; dir. operating room Seton Med. Center, Austin, Tex., 1975-79; dir. surg. services Scott & White Meml. Hosp., Temple, Tex., 1979-85; dir. operating room services Spohn Hosp., Corpus Christi, Tex., 1985—; clin. instr. U. Mary Hardin Baylor Coll. Nursing, 1981; adv. com. operating room tech. program Pima County Jr. Coll., Austin Community Coll. Nursing cons. Am. Cancer Soc., Lubbock, 1968, profl. edn. com., Ariz., 1972. Cert. nurse operating room. Mem. Assn. Operating Room Nurses (pres. Central Tex. 1981-82, pub. chpt. newsletter 1979-82, nat. subcom. recommended practice 1981), Tex. Assn. Operating Room Nurses (pres.-elect 1981-82, pres. 1982-83, 85-86, dir. 1979-81), Assn. Advancement of Med. Instrumentation (pres. regional council 1983, nominating com. 1983), Am. Nurses Assn., Sigma Theta Tau. Republican. Methodist. Instr. continuing edn. for operating room nurses, U. Ariz., 1972, speaker on subject nat. congress Assn. Operating Room Nurses, 1974. Home: 14105 White Cap Corpus Christi TX 78418 Office: 600 Elizabeth Corpus Christi TX 78404

KOCH, JUNE QUINT, government official; b. Bklyn., Jan. 18, 1933; d. Eli and Minnie Quint; B.A., Bklyn. Coll., 1954; M.A., Temple U., 1957; Ph.D., Columbia U., 1965; m. Noel Clinton Koch, Sept. 10, 1967; children—Justin, Monica, Jennie, Gabriel, Elias. Instr., Temple U. 1958-65; asst. prof. Widener Coll. 1965-68; asst. prof. Bryn Mawr Coll. 1968-73; dir. Fed. Liaison Phila. '76 Inc. 1973-75; v.p. Koch Assocs., Inc. 1976-80; dep. undersec. HUD, Washington from 1981, now asst. sec. for policy devel. and research. Dir. intergovernmental relations Reagan-HUD Transition Team, 1980-81. Nat. Endowment Humanities grantee, 1972-73. Mem. Republican Women's Forum, RNC Women's Network, Phi Beta Kappa. Jewish. Contbr. articles in field to profl. jours. Office: HUD 451 7th St SW Washington DC 20410*

KOCH, PATRICIA ELLEN, lawyer; b. Hackensack, N.J., Apr. 2, 1947; d. George Frederick and Jane Elizabeth (Kinsella) Koch. B.A., Georgian Ct. Coll., 1969; J.D., Seton Hall U., 1972. Bar: N.J. 1972. Law sec. to judge Morris County Superior Ct. (N.J.), 1972-73; dep. pub. defender State of N.J., Newton-Morristown, 1973-79; atty. N.J. Bell Telephone Co., Newark, 1979—. Counsel Morris County unit Am. Cancer Soc., 1975—; mem. Morristown Town Council, 1982-85, pres. council, 1984; mem. Morris County Democratic Com., 1982, 84, Morristown Planning Bd., 1983, ALFRE, 1981 ; mem. N.J. Bd. Architects, 1980—, pres., 1983; trustee St. Thomas Aquinas Coll., Sparkill, N.Y., 1974—; v.p., trustee Morris County Legal Aid Soc., 1979—. Mem. ABA, N.J. Bar Assn., Morris County Bar Assn., Assn. Corp. Counsel, Zonta Internat. (pres. 1980-81 Morristown). Roman Catholic. Home: Two Rona Rd Morristown NJ 07960 Office: NJ Bell Telephone Co 540 Broad St Newark NJ 07101

KOCH, RITA ELIZABETH, computer specialist; b. Middletown, Conn., Mar. 22, 1948; d. Francis Xavier Joseph and Margaret (Whalen) K.; m. Salvatore Sclafani, Dec. 29, 1984. B.A., U. Conn., 1971; postgrad. Calif. State U.-Hayward, 1972, New Sch. for Social Research, 1982-83, Baruch Coll., 1983, NYU, 1980. Computer programmer U.S. Dept. HUD, Washington, 1977-79, computer specialist, N.Y.C., 1979-84; computer specialist IRS, Washington, 1984—; mem. Fed. Women's Program, N.Y.C., 1982. Mem. Concord Village Assn.-Communications, Bklyn., 1982-83, Consumer Council Health Ins. Plan, N.Y.C.-Bklyn., 1983-84. Mem. Assn. Computing Machinery, Nat. Assn. Female Execs., Nat. Trust for Hist. Preservation, Capitol Hill Restoration Soc., Poetry Ctr. Avocations: historic preservation; Victorian era; poetry. Home: 535 Second St SE Washington DC 20003

KOCHANOWSKI, VIVIAN FRENCH, nurse; b. Blue Mound, Kans., Mar. 1, 1939; d. Carlton Clyde and Vivian Electa (Squires) French; B.S.N., U. Kans., 1961; M.S. in Adult and Occupational Edn., Kans. State U., 1975; m. Glen Frederick Kochanowski, Nov. 30, 1963; children—Glenda Lynn, Patrick Eugene, Sean Andrew. Staff nurse Hempstead (N.Y.) Gen. Hosp., 1963-66; instr. nursing Asbury Hosp., Salina, Kans., 1966-79, dir. Sch. Nursing, 1979—, chmn. Kans. Assn. Hosp. Schs. of Nursing, 1980—. Served to lt. (j.g.), USNR, 1961-63. Mem. Am. Nurses Assn., Kans. League Nursing (v.p. 1985), Nat. League Nursing. Office: 400 S 7th St Salina KS 67401

KOCHER, CYNTHIA, clown, nurse; b. Columbiana, Ohio, Oct. 9, 1916; d. Arthur Chester and Elma Jane (Vaughan) Tidd; m. William R. Thrasher, Feb. 14, 1940 (div. 1947); m. Robert Wilson Kocher, Mar. 27, 1951 (div.); children—Diana Jean, Dorothy Jane. Student Wooster Coll., 1935-38; B.A. in Chemistry and History, Youngstown Coll., 1941; grad. Youngstown Hosp. Assn. Sch. Nursing, 1951. R.N., Ohio. Analytical chemist Atlas Powder Co., Ravanna, Ohio, 1941-42; riveter, insp. Goodyear Tire & Rubber Co., Akron, Ohio, 1942-43; trouble-shooter Continental Aircraft, Denver, 1943-47; psychiat. nurse Youngstown Receiving Hosp., Ohio, 1951-53; pvt. duty nurse, Sarasota, Fla., 1953-55; clown, named Mum-The Majik Clown, Glendale, Ariz., 1959—; mem. various clown groups, 1964-79. Mem. Phoenix Clown Club, Links Republican. Mem. Ch. of Jesus Christ of Latter-day Saints. Avocations: designing clown costumes; costumes for Society for Creative Anachronism. Address: 5519 W State Ave Glendale AZ 85301

KOCHER, CYNTHIA, real estate developer and agent; b. Lompoc, Calif., May 6, 1954; d. John Wayland and Marjorie (Bartle) K. B.A. in Asian Studies, U. Oreg., 1976; M.Internat. Mgmt., Am. Grad. Sch. Internat. Mgmt., 1978. Comml. asst., mgr. Far East imports Barber S.S. Lines, N.Y.C., 1978-80; asst. sec. internat. cash mgmt. Mfr.'s Hanover Trust Co., N.Y.C., 1980-84; sales staff Century 21-Gordon Agy., 1984—; pres. Restorations Unltd., 1985—. Recipient 5th pl. award Internat. Speech Contest in Japanese, Asahi Shimbun, 1975. Mem. Japan Soc., Asian Mgmt. Bus. Assn., Assn. M.B.A. Execs., Nat. Assn. Female Execs., DAR (geneal. records chmn. 1985-86, schs. chmn. 1985-86, yearbook co-chmn. 1983-84). Home: Box 3408 Jersey City NJ 07303 Office: 250 Newark Ave Jersey City NJ 07302

KODA-CALLAN, ELIZABETH, illustrator; b. Stamford, Conn., Sept. 26, 1944; d. Alexander John and Helen (Wojciehowski) Koda; m. J. Michael Callan, Aug. 14, 1971 (div. 1978); 1 dau., Jennifer Kristen. B.A. in Art, U. Dayton, 1966; postgrad Sch. Visual Arts, 1969-70, 72-75. Designer Glamour mag. Condé Nast Publs., N.Y.C., 1967-69; designer, art dir. CBS, N.Y.C., 1969-70; designer, illustrator Mademoiselle mag., N.Y.C., 1970-71; asst. to illustrator Visible Studio, N.Y.C., 1973-75; designer, art editor, assoc. art dir. Scholastic Inc., N.Y.C., 1975-81; illustrator Pushpin Lubalin Peckolick, N.Y.C., 1982—; designer, assoc. art dir. Scholastic's Early Childhood Program Teaching Guides, 1981 (Am. Inst. Graphic Arts book design show award 1982); illustrator 200 Years of American Illustration, 1976. Recipient illustration awards, Soc. Illustrators, 1975; Art Dirs. Show, Art Dirs. Club, 1980, Print Mag. N.Y. Regional Show, 1982; Graphis Annual, Zurich, Switzerland, 1983-84. Mem. Graphic Artists Guild. Democrat. Home and Office: 792 Columbus Ave New York NY 10025

KODIS, MARY CAROLINE, retail and restaurant consultant; b. Chgo., Dec. 17, 1927; d. Anthony John and Callis Ferebee (Old) K.; student San Diego State Coll., 1945-47, Latin Am. Inst., 1948. Controller, div. adminstrv. mgr. Fed. Mart Stores, 1957-65; controller, adminstrv. mgr. Gulf Mart Stores, 1965-67; budget dir., adminstrv. mgr. Diana Stores, 1967-68; founder, treas., controller Handy Dan Stores, 1968-72; founder, v.p., treas. Handy City Stores, 1972-76; sr. v.p., treas. Handy City div. W.R. Grace & Co., Atlanta, 1976-79; founder, pres. Hal's Hardware and Lumber Stores, 1982-84; retail and restaurant cons., 1979—. Treas., bd. dirs. YWCA Watsonville, 1981-84, 85—; mem. Santa Cruz County Grand Jury, 1984-85. Recipient 1st Tribute to Women in Internat. Industry, 1978. Republican. Home and Office: 302 Wheelock Rd Watsonville CA 95076

KODMAN, PHYLLIS ANN, auto painting company executive; b. Bakersfield, Calif., Mar. 27, 1947; d. Lee Frank and Louise (Rice) Willis; m. Robert Anthony Kodman, June 5, 1964; children—Kimberlee Louise, Cynthia Lee. Student Cuesta Coll., 1973-74. Co-owner Color Glow West, San Luis Obispo, Calif., 1976—; sec. Kodman Enterprises, Inc., Fresno, Calif., 1982—; realtor assoc. Vista Assocs., Inc., 1986—. Chmn. fund raising ARC, 1985-86; pub. chmn. Central Coast Womens League, 1985—. Mem. San Luis C. of C. Avocations: skiing; racquetball; snorkeling. Home: 1752 Royal Ct San Luis

Obispo CA 93401 Office: Color Glow West 750 Francis St San Luis Obispo CA 93401 Also Vista Assocs Inc 1034 Mill St San Luis Obispo CA 93401

KODNER, PHYLLIS B., interior designer; b. St. Louis, Feb. 7, 1932; d. Norman and Mania (Gillerman) Mathless; student Washington U., 1949-50; m. Mike Kodner, Feb. 14, 1953; children—Karen, Susan, Jacqueline, Robert, Thomas. Pres., Phyllis Kodner Interior Designs, Inc., Creve Coeur, Mo., 1970—. Mem. Am. Soc. Interior Designers (assoc.), Mariam Found., Jewish Fedn., Nat. Council Jewish Women. Jewish. Mem. Hadassah. Home: 44 S Spoede Rd Creve Coeur MO 63141

KOE, LINDA MASSOCK, banker; b. Bloomington, Ill., Apr. 29, 1943; d. William Paul and Lucille (Snow) Massock; m. Bruce Gary Koe, Aug. 21, 1965; children—Tracy Ann, David Andrew. B.A., U. Ill., 1965; grad. Nat. Comml. Lending Sch., Norman, Okla., 1981. Stock broker Prescott, Wright, Snider, Kansas City, Mo., 1975-76, A.G. Edwards, Kansas City, 1976-78; asst. v.p. First Nat. Bank, Kansas City, 1978-82; product mktg. mgr. United Info. Services, Overland Park, Kans., 1982-83; v.p. non-credit services Boatmen's Bank & Trust Co., Kansas City, 1983-85; v.p. corp. banking services Boatmen's First Nat. Bank, Kansas City, 1985—; instr. Ottawa U., Kansas City, 1977. Sec. Human Relations Bd., Manhattan, Kans., 1966-68; pres. adminstrv. bd. Suburban Jackson County YWCA, Raytown, Mo., 1969-73; area chmn. Channel 19 TV Auction, Kansas City, 1972-76; leader Girl Scouts U.S.A., Independence, Mo., 1973-75; bd. dirs. Dimensions Unltd., Kansas City, 1977-79; mem. bd. William Southern PTA, Independence, 1975-76; bd. dirs., treas., 2d v.p. YWCA, Kansas City, 1979-83; bd. dirs. Response, Inc., Kansas City, 1981-82; mem. council United Community Services, Kansas City, 1982; bd. dirs., treas., chmn. audit com., chmn. fin. com. Comprehensive Mental Health Services, Independence, 1982-85; bd. dirs., sec. Inst. for Independent Living, Independence, 1983-84; bd. dirs. Independence Indsl. Devel. Authority, 1980-83. Mem. Nat. Corp. Cash Mgmt. Assn., Nat. Assn. Bank Women, Am. Inst. Banking, AAUW (bd. dirs. Independence 1975-76), Women Brokers Greater Kansas City (founder 1978), Chi Omega Alumnae Assn. (bd. dirs. 1968-82). Republican. Mem. Unity Ch. Clubs: Kansas City, Central Exchange (Kansas City, Mo.). Home: 14601 E 44th St Independence MO 64055 Office: Boatmen's First Nat Bank 10th and Baltimore St PO Box 38 Kansas City MO 64183

KOEHLER, CHARLENE, hearing aid specialist; b. Tyler, Tex., Dec. 13, 1938; d. Charles Potter Brodie and Helen Ruth (Browning) Bassett; m. William Albert Koehler, Feb. 8, 1958 (div. Aug. 1981); children—Nancy M. Koehler Hamilton, Patrick W., Jeannette Lee, Charles M.; m. 2d, LaVerne Samuel Jensen, Sept. 11, 1981. Student pub. schs., Pleasanton, Tex. Lic. hearing aid specialist, Tex. Sec. hearing aid dept. Sears, Dallas, 1974-79, hearing aid sales, 1979-83; owner, operator Charlene Koehler & Assocs., Dallas, 1983—. Pres. Self-Help for Hard of Hearing, Dallas, 1985—. Mem. Dallas Assn. Hearing Aid Specialists (sec. 1981-83), Tex. Hearing Aid Assn., Nat. Hearing Aid Soc. Democrat. Roman Catholic. Club: Quota Internat. Home: 2622 Langdon Ave Dallas TX 75235 Office: Charlene Koehler & Assocs 10143 Shoreview Dallas TX 75238

KOEHLER, ISABEL WINIFRED, poet, artist; b. Boston, Feb. 5, 1903; d. George Wallace and Mary Elizabeth (Strout) Goodwin; student art courses Harvard U., M.I.T., others; m. Frederick Mills Koehler, Apr. 16, 1925; 1 son, Alden Goodwin. Contbr. articles to Boston Daily Post, Boston Herald-Traveler, poetry to Boston Daily Globe, Melrose Free Press, Everett Leader Herald, others; exhibited numerous galleries, festivals, ann. exhbns. Recipient first place for watercolor book illustrations Everett Bicentennial Arts Exhibit, 1976, 1st and 3d place awards in landscape oil, 1981; Diploma of Merit Università delle Arti (Italy) for cultural and profl. achievement, 1982; book Bouquets of Poems selected for permanent archives Am. Biog. Inst., N.C., other awards, prizes. Mem. Mass. Poetry Soc., New Eng. Women's Press Assn., Agnes Carr Writers Club (pres., exec. bd.), Internat. Poetry Soc., N.Y. Poetry Forum, Everett Art Assn., Old Boston Soc. Ind. Artists, Am. Biog. Inst. Research Assn. (assoc.), Centro Studi e Scambi Internazionali (Silver medal 1975, Gold medal in poetry 1976, diploma of recognition 1983, Star of Contemporary Poetry award 1984), Leonardo de Vinci Accademia (hon. rep., commemorative medal for art achievement 1973, Gold medal 1976, Poet of Month award 1980, Poet Laureate award 1980 Diploma of Honor for outstanding achievement in contemporary art 1982, v.p. 1982—). Author: Bouquets of Poems, 1974; Versified Variety, 1978; contbr. poetry to Bay State Echo, Mass. State Poetry Anthologies. Address: 30 Fremont Ave Everett MA 02149

KOEHLER-KENNEDY, SUSAN, utility company executive; b. Methuen, Mass., May 15, 1950; d. Richard and Dorothy Donovan (Fenton) Koehler. Cert. Katharine Gibbs Secretarial Sch., Boston, 1968; student Boston U., 1969; B.B.A. in Econs., Boise State U., 1975, M.B.A., 1977. Resource analyst Idaho Dept. Water Resources, Boise, 1977-80; fin. analyst Intermountain Gas Co., Boise, 1980-81, mgr. planning services, 1981-85, mgr. treasury services, 1985—. Bd. dirs. Alzheimer's Disease and Related Disorders Assn., Boise, 1985. Mem. Am. Gas Assn., Am. Mgmt. Assn., Boise C. of C. Avocations: jogging; skiing; racquetball; reading. Office: Intermountain Gas Co PO Box 7608 Boise ID 83707

KOEHLER-SAPP, JANICE MANCINELLI, proposal manager, consultant; b. Colorado Springs, Colo., Jan. 2, 1948; d. Albert Daniel and Yolanda (Conte) Mancinelli; m. Edward Frank Koehler, Nov. 23, 1968 (div. 1981); 1 dau., Jordan Conte; m. 2d, David Brewer Sapp, May 7, 1983; stepchildren—Lara Elizabeth, Catherine Leigh. B.A., U. Md., 1971; M.A., George Mason U., 1982; student Wesley Theol. Sem., Am. U., Washington, 1985—. Tchr. Pub. Sch. Bds., Montgomery County, Md., 1971-76, Stafford County, Va., 1976-78; instr. Quantico Marine Base (Va.), 1978-79; editor CACI, Arlington, Va., 1979-81; proposal mgr. ORI, Arlington, 1982-83; pres., owner Janus Communications, Burke, Va., 1980—; proposal mgr. No. Va. Office Magnavox, Falls Church, 1983—; asst. pastor Mt. Vernon United Meth. Ch., Alexandria, Va., 1985—. Author, coordinator promotional mats, 1982; contbr. articles to children's publs. (award Va. Edn. Assn. 1978). Founder, Offspring, Washington, 1980—; cons. Potency Restored, Silver Spring, Md., 1981—, Women's Kaleidoscope, Alexandria, Va., 1982—; ch. educator United Meth. Ch., Fairfax, Va., 1983-84, researcher women's issues, 1983. Recipient letter of commendation. PRI, Inc., Alexandria, 1979-80. Democrat. Clubs: Andrews Aero (student pilot 1983-84). Washington Calligrapher's Guild. Home: 10325 Mockingbird Pond Ct Burke VA 22015 Office: Mt Vernon United Meth Ch 2006 Belleview Rd Alexandria VA 22306

KOEHN, BEVERLY DIANNE, management consultant; b. Temple, Tex., June 30, 1953; d. James E. and Patsy Jean (Williams) Anderson; m. Ray E. Koehn, Sept. 17, 1977. B.B.A., U. Tex., 1978; A.A.S., Temple Jr. Coll., 1975. Lic. Realtor, Tex. Staffing adminstr. Tex. Instruments, Inc., Temple, 1978-81; Realtor assoc. Century 21 Norris, New Braunfels, Tex., 1982-83; v.p. Todays American Builder, New Braunfels, 1983-86; Realtor, RDS Devel. Corp., New Braunfels, 1985—; mgmt. cons. Robert L. Siegel & Assocs., 1986—; ind. real estate cons., 1984—. Temple Jr. Coll. music scholar, 1971. Mem. Nat. Sales and Mktg. Council, Tex. Assn. Builders, Nat. Homebuilders Assn. Republican. Baptist. Avocations: running; scuba diving; skiing. Home: PO Box 692 New Braunfels TX 78131 Office: 413 Marsh Oval New Braunfels TX 78130

KOELLER, SHIRLEY ANN, educator; b. Cin.; d. Maurice Lipian; A.B., U. Calif., 1959; M.A., U. Colo., 1971, Ph.D., 1975; 1 son, Kevin. Tchr., San Francisco Public Schs., 1966-67, Jefferson County Public Schs., 1967-69; teaching asso. U. Colo., 1971-74; coordinator elem. Tech. Center Sheridan (Colo.) Public Schs., 1974-75; lectr. Calif. State Coll., San Bernardino, 1975-78; asst. prof. Tex. Tech. U., Lubbock, 1978-83, assoc. prof., 1983—; dir. Caprock Area Writing Project, 1985. Editor Tex. Reading Report, 1983—. Mem. Am. Ednl. Research Assn., Assn. Childhood Edn., Assn. Supervision and Curriculum Devel., Internat. Reading Assn., Nat. Council Social Studies, Nat. Council Tchrs. English, S.W. Ednl. Research Assn., Kappa Delta Pi, Phi Delta Kappa. Contbr. articles in field to profl. jours. Office: PO Box 4560 Texas Tech U Lubbock TX 79409

KOENIG, JOAN FOSTER, real estate broker; b. Harrisburg, Ill., Feb. 15, 1930; d. William Jennings and Adria May Foster; B.S., Miami U., 1951; M.A., Ariz. State U., 1967; m. Alan Eastman Disbrow, June 26, 1978; children—William R., Theodore J. Airline stewardess Am. Airlines, Inc., 1951-52; research investigator Procter & Gamble Co., Cin., 1952-53; co-owner, v.p. Koenig Aviation, Inc., Casa Grande, Ariz., 1953-69; real estate sales assoc. Ed Post Realty, Scottsdale, Ariz., 1978-79; real estate broker Koenig Real Estate, Casa Grande, 1980—. Bd. govs. Casa Grande Town Hall, 1972-75; bd. dirs. Hoemako Hosp. Aux.; vice-chmn. Pinal County Democratic Com., 1972-76, dist. 6 chmn., 1972-76, mem. state exec. com., 1972-76; pres. West Pinal County Dem. Women's Club, 1975, 84. Recipient Women's Flight Achievement award Internat. Flying Farmers, 1964. Mem. AAUW (pres. Casa Grande br.), Women's Council Realtors, Ariz. Fedn. Democratic Women's Clubs (3d v.p.), Casa Grande Valley Cotton Wives, Casa Grande Panhellenic (pres. 1970), Mortar Board, Kappa Kappa Gamma. Democrat. Episcopalian. Club: Woman's of Casa Grande (bd. dirs. 1985-86), Desert Woman's. Home: Route 1 Box 469 Casa Grande AZ 85222 Office: PO Box 432 Casa Grande AZ 85222

KOENIG, KATHRIN ANN, lawyer; b. Chgo., Dec. 28, 1952; d. Rudolph Hugo Koenig and Arlene Carol (Lukes) Koenig Smith. B.A., U. Ill., 1975; J.D., Northwestern U., 1978. Bar: Ill. 1979. Assoc. DeJong, Poltrock & Giampietro, Chgo., 1978—. Mem. ABA, Ill. Bar Assn., Chgo. Bar Assn., Nat. Trial Lawyers Assn., Phi Beta Kappa. Democrat. Office: DeJong Poltrock & Giampietro 221 N LaSalle St Suite 2600 Chicago IL 60601

KOENIG, NANCY MARION, lawyer; b. San Antonio, July 24, 1951; d. Oliver and Sue Ellen (Mansfield) McClellan; m. Richard Alan Koenig, Aug. 31, 1974. B.A., U. Tex; Austin, 1972, M.A., 1975; J.D., Tex. Tech U., 1982. Bar: Tex. 1982. Pub. info. officer Mental Health/Mental Retardation Regional Ctr. East Tex., Tyler, 1975; communications dir. Alcoholism Council Tex., Inc., Austin, 1976-78; asst. dir. communications Tex. Automobile Dealers. Assn., Austin, 1978-79; law clk. to Chief Judge Halbert O. Woodward, No. Dist. Tex., Lubbock, 1982-83; asst. gen. counsel State Bar Tex., Austin, 1983-84; asst. U.S. atty., Lubbock, 1984—. Mem. ABA, Lubbock County Bar Assn., Young Lawyers Assn., Women in Communications, AAUW, Phi Alpha Delta. Home: 2310 59th St Lubbock TX 79412 Office: US Atty's Office 1205 Texas Ave Suite C-201 Lubbock TX 79401

KOEPPEL, MARY SUE, communications educator; b. Phlox, Wis., Dec. 12, 1939; d. Alphonse and Emma Petronella (Marx) K.; B.A., Alverno Coll., 1962; M.A., Loyola U., Chgo., 1968; postgrad. U. Wis., St. Louis U., U. N.H., U. Calif., U. Fla. Tchr., St. Joseph High Sch, Milw., 1962-68, Pius XI High Sch., Milw., 1968-72; instr., head dept. communications, dir. learning center Waukesha County Tech. Inst., Pewaukee, Wis., 1972-80; pres., exec. bd. West Suburban Council Teaching Profession, 1976-80; adv. Waukesha chpt. Parents Without Partners, 1975-80; cons. Learning Centers, 1976—, also coll. and univ. faculties; instr. communications Fla. Jr. Coll., Jacksonville, 1980—; instr. Inst. for Tchrs. of Writing, Westbrook Coll., Portland, Maine, summers 1980-84, instr. nat. master tchr. seminar, summers 1982—; mem. Sherman Park Community Center, 1975-80; co-founder, bd. dirs. Instructional Network for Coll. Faculty, 1981-85. NDEA grantee, 1968. Mem. Fla. Edn. Assn., Adult Vocat. Assn., Am. Adult Edn. Assn., Nat. Council Tchrs. of English, Nat. Assn. Female Execs Editor Instructional Network Notes, 1982-85. Contbr. articles to profl. jours. Home: 3879 Oldfield Trail Jacksonville FL 32223

KOERING, MARILYN JEAN, educator, researcher; b. Brainerd, Minn., Jan. 7, 1938; d. Clement J. and Vi K. (Holtkamp) K.; B.A., Coll. St. Scholastica, Duluth, 1960; M.S., U. Wis., Madison, 1963, Ph.D., 1967, postgrad., 1968. Instr. dept. anatomy U. Wis., 1963-64; asst. prof. George Washington U., 1969-73, assoc. prof., 1973-79, prof., 1979—; vis. assoc. div. biology Calif. Inst. Tech., 1976; affiliate scientist Wis. Primate Research Center, Madison, 1975-78; guest worker Pregnancy Research br. NICHD, 1977-84; vis. scientist Jones Inst. Reproductive Medicine, Eastern Va. Med. Sch., 1985—. NIH fellow, 1967-68, NIH grantee, 1969—. Mem. Am. Assn. Anatomists, Soc. Study Reproduction, AAAS, Washington Assn. Electron Microscopists, Sigma Xi. Mem. editorial bd. Biology of Reproduction, 1974-78; contbr. in field. Office: Department of Anatomy George Washington University Medical Center 2300 I St NW Washington DC 20037

KOERTGE, NORETTA, philosophy of science educator, novelist; b. Olney, Ill., Oct. 7, 1935. B.S. with honors in Chemistry, U. Ill., 1955, M.S., 1956; Ph.D. in Philosophy of Sci., London U., 1969; postgrad. NSF Summer Inst. U. Iowa, 1961, U. Mich., 1962. Instr. chemistry Elmhurst Coll. (Ill.), 1960-63; head chemistry sect. Am. Coll. for Girls, Istanbul, Turkey, 1963-64; asst. prof. philosophy of sci. Ont. Inst. for Studies in Edn., Toronto, Can., 1969-70; asst. prof. dept. history and philosophy of sci. Ind. U., Bloomington, 1970-73, assoc. prof., 1973-81, prof., 1981—; vis. lectr. Sir John Cass Coll., London, 1967, Borough Poly., London, 1968, Harvard U., Cambridge, 1973; symposium leader Osterreichisches Coll., Alpbach, Austria, 1975, 81. John Dewey Sr. Research fellow Ctr. for Dewey Studies, Carbondale, Ill., 1983-84. Editor: Nature and Causes of Homosexuality: A Philosophic and Scientific Inquiry, 1981. Author: Who Was That Masked Woman?, 1981; Valley of the Amazons, 1984; contbr. numerous articles to profl. jours.

KOEWERS, MARY LYNN, lawyer; b. Grand Rapids, Mich., Jan. 1, 1945; d. Charles Henry and Agnes Margaret (Illg) Brudi; m. John Edward Koewers, June 28, 1963 (div. 1970); children—Deanna Lynn, Kimberly Sue, John Edward; m. 2d David H. Cossin, Dec. 10, 1983. B.A. in Polit. Sci., U. Mich., 1978, B.A. in Journalism, 1978; J.D., Thomas M. Cooley Law Sch., 1981. Bar: Mich. 1981. Assembler, Lescoa, Inc., Kentwood, Mich., 1970-72; legal sec. Wheeler, Upham, Bryant & Uhl, Grand Rapids, Mich., 1972-75, Cholette Perkins & Buchanan, Grand Rapids, 1977-78; law clk. firm Dilley & Dilley, Grand Rapids, 1981; sole practice law, Grand Rapids, 1981—. Mem. ABA, State Bar Mich., Women Lawyers Assn. Mich. Republican. Lutheran. Home: 6777 Rix SE Ada MI 49301 Office: 1017 Parchment St SE Grand Rapids MI 49506

KOFF, GAIL JOANNE, lawyer; b. N.Y.C., May 15, 1945; d. Murray and Sylvia Joan (Winer) Koff; B.A., U. Calif., Berkeley, 1967; J.D., George Washington U., 1970; m. Ralph Brill, Oct. 8, 1978; 1 son, 1 dau. Asst. to dir. Tng. and Demonstration program, Legal Services Program, Washington, 1969-71; admitted to N.Y. Bar, 1972, D.C. bar 1972; asso. firm Gasperini & Savage, N.Y.C., 1972-76, Skadden, Arps, Slate, Meagher & Flom, N.Y.C., 1976-78; founder, partner firm Jacoby & Meyers, N.Y.C., 1978—; lectr. in field. Chmn. Community Action for Legal Services, N.Y.C., 1979-81; mem. Com. of 200. Mem. Assn. Bar City N.Y. (chmn. com. on legal assistance 1976-79, exec. com. 1979—), N.Y. Bar Assn. Jewish. Author: Jacoby & Meyers Practical Guide to Everyday Law, 1985. Editor: Legal Delivery Systems, 1977. Office: 1457 Broadway New York NY 10036

KOFFORD, KAREN JEAN, glassblower, glass sculptor; b. Orem, Utah, May 25, 1946; d. Weston Meiling and Lenore (Pyne) K.; student Coll. So. Utah, 1967-68, Steven Henegars Bus. Coll., Salt Lake City, 1966-67, Brigham Young U., Provo, 1965-67. Owner, pres. Krystal Kreations Glassblowing, Orem, 1967—, Jackson, Wyo., 1969—; developer swirled kneading process. Republican. Mormon. Home: 15 West 300 North Orem UT 84057 Office: K-133 University Mall Orem UT 84057 also PO Box 2077 Jackson WY 83001

KOGA, RUTH KAMURI, retailing executive; b. Honolulu, July 19, 1929; d. Nenichi and Mino (Ozama) Kamuri; B.A., Smith Coll., 1951; m. George Koga, Nov. 22, 1958; 1 dau., Suzanne. With Ritz Dept. Stores, Honolulu, 1951-84, pres., 1975-84; pres. Suzanne at the Royal, 1984-86. Bd. dirs. Am. Cancer Soc., 1972-80, Hawaii Visitors Bur., 1984-86. trustee St. Louis High Sch., 1980—, Hawaii News Agy., Found., 1980—; fund raiser Kuakini Hosp. Aux., 1956-65; active fund raising for charity and scholarships. Recipient award Am. Cancer Soc., 1976. Mem. Nat. Retail Mchts. Assn., Honolulu C. of C., Honolulu Art Acad. Democrat. Clubs: Smith Alumni, Waialae Country. Home: 1254 Center St Honolulu HI 96816

KOGELSCHATZ, JOAN LEE, psychotherapist, psychologist; b. Detroit, Nov. 26, 1940; d. Edgar Rolfe and Helen Josephine (York) K.; B.A., U. Fla., 1963; postgrad. Wayne State U., 1964-65; M.S.W., Fla. State U., 1967, Ph.D., 1975. Intern, VA Hosp., Bay Pines, Fla., 1966, div. child and adolescent psychiatry, dept. psychiatry U. Fla. Med. Center, Gainesville, 1966; instr. psychiatry div. child Adolescent psychiatry U. Fla. Med. Center, Shands Teaching Hosp. & Clinics, Gainesville, 1967-72; field supr., instr. Fla. State U., 1973, field supr., instr. Sch. Social Work, 1973-74; pvt. practice psychology, Dothan, Ala., 1975—; guest lectr. Shands Teaching Hosp. & Clinics, 1975; cons. Lyster Army Hosp., Ft. Rucker, Ala., 1975-78; guest lectr. Dept. Mental Health, Ft. Rucker, 1975; lectr. in field; asst. prof. U. Ala., 1976-77; cons. Bd. dirs. Ala. Soc. Crippled Children and Adults, 1981—, cons., 1981—, fin. chmn., 1983—; apptd. mem. adv. bd. Law Enforcement Planning Agy. Ala., 1980—; chmn. Children's Trust Fund Council, Ala. 2d Congl. Dist., 1984. Lic. profl. counselor, Ala.; lic. psychologist, Ala.; lic. clin. psychiat. social worker, Ala. Named Woman of Yr., Nat. Fedn. Bus. and Profl. Women, 1984. Mem. Am. Psychol. Assn., Acad. Psychosomatic Medicine, Am. Orthopsychiat. Assn., Am. Assn. Psychiat. Services for Children (chmn. pub. edn. com. 1984), Internat. Soc. Clin. Hypnosis, Am. Soc. Clin. Hypnosis, Am. Assn. Marriage and Family Therapists, Nat. Assn. Social Workers, Acad. Cert. Social Workers, Nat. Council Family Relations, Southeastern Council on Relations, Am. Assn. Sex Educators, Counselors and Therapists, Gulf Coast Assn. Marriage and Family Therapy, Alpha Kappa Delta. Contbr. articles to profl. jours. Office: 1015 Honeysuckle Rd Dothan AL 36301

KOGUT, KATHLEEN MARIE, surgeon, medical educator; b. Phila., July 31, 1954; d. John and Anna Marie (Breslin) K.; m. Robert C. Garrett, June 24, 1978. B.S., Pa. State U., 1975; M.D., Jefferson Med. Coll., 1977. Diplomate Am. Bd. Surgery. Resident, St. Vincent's Hosp., N.Y.C., 1977-82; attending surgeon Met. Hosp., N.Y.C., 1982—; asst. prof. surgery N.Y. Med. Coll., Valhalla, 1983—. Contbr. articles to publs. Recipient commendation, Mayor of N.Y.C., 1981. Mem. N.Y. State Med. Soc., ACS. Democrat. Mem. Bulgarian Eastern Orthodox Ch. Home: 437 E 87th St Apt 2 New York NY 10128 Office: Met Hosp Dept Surgery 1901 1st Ave New York NY 10029

KOHAN, JULIANNE, chemical company executive; b. Wichita, Kans., Sept. 14, 1950; d. George Bernard and Ruth Josephine (Alexander) Johnson; m. Dennis Lynn Kohan, Feb. 16, 1979; children—Bart Quincy, Elyse Renee. Grad. high sch., Greeley, Colo. Share draft coordinator Welco Credit Union, Greeley, 1981-82; group ins. mgr. United Agri Products subs. Con Agra, Greeley, 1983—. Key person Greeley Independence Stampede, 1979—; sec.-treas. Wranglers, Inc., Greeley, 1984-85; vol. chmn. Greeley unit ARC, 1982; leader local Girl Scouts U.S., 1983-84; pvt. counselor cancer patients, Greeley, 1980—. Recipient cert. of merit Nat. Assn. Home Builders, 1983. Mem. Women's Network, Weld County Republican Women. Avocations: travel; swimming; racquetball. Office: United Agri Products 419 18th St PO Box 2557 Greeley CO 80631

KOHL, CATHERINE E., computer consultant; b. N.Y.C., May 26, 1955; d. Gustave Albert and Shirley (Seifert) Kohl. B.A. in Econs., CUNY, 1977, postgrad., 1986—; M.A. in Sociology, Fordham U., 1985. Actuary N.Y. Life Ins., N.Y.C., 1977-78; with Les Copains, Bologna, Italy, 1978-79; actuary D. Kalish-F.S.P.A., N.Y.C., 1979-80; retail sales rep., N.Y.C., 1980-83; researcher Fordham U., N.Y.C., 1983-85; cons. computers Automatic Data Processing, N.Y.C., 1985—; cons. in field. NIMH grad. researcher, 1983-84. Avocations: skiing; tennis; horseback riding; swimming. Home: 45 Adrian Ave #5A New York NY 10463

KOHL, DORA DIERKS (MRS. CHARLES WILLIAM KOHL JR.), savings and loan executive; b. Sugar Land, Tex., Aug. 7, 1922; d. Hans Fritz and Elizabeth Amelia (Pilz) Dierks; student pub. schs.; m. Charles William Kohl, Jr., Feb. 27, 1944; 1 son, Charles Johann. With Marshall Canning Co., Sugar Land, 1939-45, Montgomery Ward, Denver, 1945-46; with Liberty County Fed. Savs. & Loan Assn., Liberty, Tex., 1951-85, treas., controller, 1972-77, v.p. personnel, 1977-79, v.p., adminstrv. asst., 1979-85; bookkeeper Black Gold Press, 1985—. Sec., Liberty chpt. Am. Cancer Soc. Mem. Am. Savs. and Loan Inst. (pres. Beaumont chpt.), Nat. Soc. Controllers and Financial Officers. Home: 2001 Magnolia St Liberty TX 77575 Office: 1406 Browning Liberty TX 77575

KOHLER, JUDITH ANN, association administrator; b. Cleve., Feb. 12, 1943; d. Joseph John and Victoria R. (Maycheck) Konecsni; m. Fred Eric Kohler, Mar. 20, 1965; 1 dau., Erika. B.Sc., Ohio State U., 1964. Med. social worker Cuyahoga County Welfare, Cleve., 1964-65; social worker Operation Head-start, Columbus, Ohio, 1965-67; exec. sec. Ill. Commn. on Status of Women, 1974-80, exec. dir., 1980-85; assoc. dir. Women Employed, 1985—. Bd. dirs. McDonough County Youth Services Bur., Macomb, Ill., 1978-80; bur. rep. Macomb Youth Guidance Council, Macomb, 1978-80; campaign mgr. for local sch. bd. candidate, 1975, 78, 81; campaign mgr. for legis. candidate, 1980; mem. adult adv. bd. Ill. Dept. Corrections. Mem. NOW, Ill. Citizens Council on Women, Nat. Women's Polit. Caucus (Ill. bd. dirs. 1975), Ill. Women's Lobby Corp. Home: 3130 N Lake Shore Dr Apt 305 Chicago IL 60657 Office: Women Employed 5 S Wabash Ave Suite 415 Chicago IL 60603

KOHLER, RUTH DEYOUNG, arts center exec.; b. Chgo., Oct. 24, 1941; d. Herbert Vollrath and Ruth Miriam (DeYoung) Kohler; ed. Smith Coll., U. Hamburg (Ger.), Kunsthochschule, Hamburg, U. Wis. Instr. in fine arts U. Alta. (Can.), Calgary, 1964-66; asst. dir. John Michael Kohler Arts Center, Sheboygan, Wis., 1968-71, dir., 1972—; chmn. Wis. Arts Bd.; mem. mus. adv. panel, crafts panel Nat. Endowment for Arts; dir., mem. Kohler Found., Inc.; mem. Wis. Am. Revolution Bicentennial Commn.; mem. Nat. Crafts Planning Bd., trustee Beloit Coll. Office: 608 New York Ave Sheboygan WI 53081

KOHN, JULIEANNE, corporate executive; b. Detroit, Apr. 15, 1946; d. Ralph Merwin and Jane Tacke (Meyers) K.; B.A., Heidelberg Coll., Tiffin, Ohio, 1968; postgrad. Eastern Mich. U., 1969-70; diploma Inst. Cert. Travel Agts., 1979. Travel agt. Am. Express Co., Detroit, 1970-73, Thomas Cook Inc., Detroit, 1973-75; mgr. Island Traveller, Grosse Ile, Mich., 1975-76; pres., owner Flying Suitcase, Inc., Grosse Ile, 1976—; pres., owner Kohn Engring. Corp., Taylor, Mich., pres. Taylor Grinding Co.; ptnr. Tri-Kohn Investments. Cert. travel. cons. Mem. Am. Soc. Travel Agts. Episcopalian. Club: Grosse Ile Golf and Country. Home: 27081 E River Rd Grosse Ile MI 48138 Office: 8117 Macomb St Grosse Ile MI 48138 also 8830 S Telegraph Rd Taylor MI 48180 also 8830 S Telegraph Rd Taylor MI 48180

KOHN, KAREN JOSEPHINE, graphic designer, exhibition designer; b. Muskegon, Mich., Jan. 8, 1951; d. Herbert George and Catherine Elizabeth (Johnson) K.; m. Robert Joseph Duffy, Jr., July 10, 1982. B.F.A., cum laude, U. Mich., 1973; M.F.A., Sch. Art Inst. Chgo., 1975. Free lance designer, Chgo., 1976-77; designer Stevens Exhibits, Chgo., 1977-78; artist-in-residence Chgo. Council on Fine Arts, 1978-79; dir. design Chgo. Hist. Soc., 1979-84; prin. Karen Kohn & Assocs., Chgo., 1985—. Designer Chicago History quar. mag., 1979-84 (3 awards of merit Am. Assn. Mus. 1982, 83), poster for Holabird & Root Exhbn., 1980 (award Am. Assn. Mus. 1982), invitation Ill. Toys Exhbn., 1982 (award Am. Assn. Mus. 1983), poster Chgo. Furniture Exhbn., 1984, exhbn. catalog Byrne/Wright Exhbn., 1982, ann. report, co. history Baird & Warner, 1981. Mem. Nat. Assn. Mus. Exhibitors (Midwest regional rep. 1983-84), Soc. Typog. Arts, Chgo. Mus. Communicators. Office: 952 N Hoyne Chicago IL 60622

KOHN, MARY LOUISE BEATRICE, nurse; b. Yellow Springs, Ohio, Jan. 13, 1920; d. Theophilus John and Mary Katharine (Schmitkons) Gaehr; A.B., Coll. Wooster, 1940; M.Nursing, Case Western Res. U., 1943; m. Howard D. Kohn, 1944; 1 child, Marcia R. Nurse, Univ. Hosps., Cleve., 1943-44, Atlantic City Hosp., 1944, Thomas M. England Gen. Hosp., U.S. Army, Atlantic City, 1945-46, Peter Bent Brigham Hosp., Boston, 1947, Univ. Hosps., Cleve., 1946-48; mem. faculty Frances Payne Bolton Sch. Nursing Case Western Res. U., 1948-52; vol. nurse Blood Service, ARC, 1952-55; office nurse, Cleve., part time 1955—; free-lance writer. Bd. dirs. Aux. Acad. Medicine Cleve., 1962-70, officer, 1976; mem. Cleve. Health Mus. Aux.; mem. women's com. Cleve. Orch., 1970; women's council WVIZ-TV. Mem. Am., Ohio nurses assns., alumni assns. Wooster Coll., Frances P. Bolton Sch. Nursing (pres. 1974-75), Assn. Operating Rm. Nurses, Antique Automobile Assn. Am., Western Res. Hist. Soc., Am. Heart Assn., Cleve. Playhouse Aux., U.S. Humane Soc., Friends of Cleve. Ballet, Smithsonian Instn., Council World Affairs, Orange Community Arts Council. Clubs: Cleve. Racquet, Women's City, Women's of Case-Western Res. U. Sch. Medicine. Author: (with Atkinson) Berry and Kohn's Introduction to Operating Room Technique, 6th edit., 1986; asst. editor Cleve. Physician, Acad. Medicine Cleve., 1966-71. Home: 28099 Belcourt Rd Cleveland OH 44124

KOHNERT-NICHOLSON, JILL ILENE, official; title and abstract company; b. Mpls., June 18, 1950; d. Carl Creighton and June Ilene K.; student So. Methodist U., 1968-69; student U. Tex., 1970; m. George A. Nicholson, Jr., Apr. 14, 1984. B.A., U. Houston, 1972. Exec. sec. real estate and archtl. firms, Houston, Dallas, Austin, Tex., 1972-75; exec. asst. to exec. dir. State Bar Tex., Austin, 1975-77; exec. dir. Tex. Lawyers Ins. Exchange, Austin, 1978-81; exec. asst. Tex. Commerce Bank, Austin, 1981-83; adminstrv. asst. GSD&M, Inc., Austin, 1983-85; exec. asst. to pres. Lawyers Title & Abstract Co., 1985—. Mem. Zachary Scott Theatre Guild, Austin, 1979-85, Laguna Gloria Art Mus. Guild, 1981; mem. Austin Bus. Forum, 1981, Friends of Gov.'s Mansion,

Austin, 1984—. Lic. securities dealer, Tex. Mem. Exec. Women Internat., Nat. Assn. Female Execs., Am. Inst. Banking, PEO. Club: Pilot. Home: 6908 Moonmont St Austin TX 78745 Office: Lawyers Title & Abstract Co 1250 Capital of Tex Hwy S Bldg One Suite 260 Austin TX 78746

KOHNKE, ELAINE ESTHER, jewelry store owner; b. Chgo., July 7, 1924; d. Barnard Albert and Grace Agnes (Olson) K. Sec., Nat. Union Fire Ins. Co., Chgo., 1942-45; mgr. jewelry mfg. Marcasite Mono Co., Chgo., 1945-68; owner Elaine's Marcasite Monogram Co.-Warren Jewelers, Chgo., 1968—. Republican. Roman Catholic. Office: Elaine's Marcasite Monogram Co Warren Jewelers 7 W Madison St Chicago IL 60602

KOHR, E(DITH) VALERIE, nurse; b. Sioux City, Iowa; d. Hilding Gerald and Myrtle Marie (Morey) Anderbery; m. Ronald E. Kohr, Oct. 15, 1977 (div. Apr. 1984); 1 child, Danielle Marie. Diploma in Nursing, Harrisburg Hosp. Sch. Nursing, 1971. Staff nurse Vets. Med. Ctr., Lebanon, Pa., 1971—; mem. nursing services, instr. ARC, Lebanon, Pa., 1978—. Active Girl Scouts U.S. Democrat. Lutheran. Avocations: sewing; reading. Home: 118 N Cornwall Rd E Lebanon PA 17042 Office: Vets Med Ctr Lebanon PA 17042

KOHRS, CHARLOTTE ANN, librarian; b. Talco, Tex., Nov. 7, 1938; d. Houston Pink and Juanita E. (Smith) Kelley; m. Richard H. Kohrs, Jan. 2, 1981; children—Carla E. Curtis, Peggy L. Curtis. A.A., Ventura Coll., 1968, U. Houston, 1980. Librarian, tech. standards rep. Raytheon Co., Goleta, Calif., 1970-76; supr. info. Peat, Marwick, Mitchell & Co., Houston, 1977—. Sec., Republican County Central Com., Santa Barbara, 1973-76; bd. dirs. Santa Barbara Young Reps., 1972-76. Mem. Spl. Library Assn. (editor Bus. and Fin. div. newsletter 1982-84, chair bus. and fin. div. 1985-86), Am. Soc. Info. Sci., S.W. Assn. Law Librarians. Home: 2301 Lakenheath Dr Dickinson TX 77539 Office: 3000 RepublicBank Ctr Houston TX 77002

KOHUT, A. LORENE, artist; b. La Port, Tex., Nov. 16, 1929; d. Patrick E. and Alma Severance; m. Mike Kohut, Jan. 6, 1950; children—Michael D., Karen M., Michelle A. Exhibited one-woman shows: Gallery 252, Phila., 1965, Carspecken-Scott Gallery, Wilmington, Del., 1975, Kalon Gallery, McLean, Va., 1974, Ogunouit (Maine) Art Center, 1969, McBride Gallery, Annapolis, Md., 1982, Touch of Glass Gallery, Alexandria, Va., 1982; exhibited group shows: Nat. Artclub, N.Y.C., 1969, NAD, 1969, Acad. Artists Assn., Springfield, Mass., 1970, 71, 72, 73, Am. Artist Profl. League, N.Y.C., 1981. Served with WAC, 1948-51. Mem. Artist Equity, Phila. Art Alliance, Am. Artist Profl. League. Address: 440 N Jefferson LaGrange TX 78945

KOHUT, MARYBETH, healthcare administrator, registered nurse; b. Bridgeport, Conn., Aug. 16, 1944; d. William Stoneman and Genevieve (Keating) Lyhne; m. Andrew Kohut, Dec. 19, 1964; children—Matthew P., Amy L. A.S.N., Rutgers U. Coll. Nursing, 1964; B.A., Douglass Coll., 1977. R.N. Tchr. intern early childhood Eden Inst. for Autistic Children, Princeton, N.J., 1977-81; nurse Med. Ctr. Princeton, 1981-82, Princeton Brain Bio Ctr., Skillman, N.J., 1982-83; program dir. immunization edn. N.J. Hosp. Assn., Princeton, 1983-85, program dir. health promotion, 1985—. Mem. task force on pub. info. Gov.'s Council on Prevention on mental retardation, New Brunswick, N.J., 1984-85; mem. working group on Sudden Deaths Survivor Guidlines, Trenton, N.J., 1985—; adult advisor Safe Rides Program, Princeton, 1983—; sec., trustee Eyescreening Coordinating Council N.J., 1986—; mem. N.J. Task Force on Fetal Alcohol Syndrome. Mem. N.J. Soc. Pub. Health Educators, N.J. Soc. for Healthcare Edn. and Tng., Nat. Wellness Assn. Avocation: tennis. Office: N J Hospital Assn 760 Alexander Rd CN-1 Princeton NJ 08543

KOHUT, ROSEMARY DER HAGOPIAN, dental hygiene educator; b. Providence, Mar. 28, 1952; d. Jacob John and Mary (Kachadorian) Der Hagopian; m. Ronald Kohut, July 15, 1978. A.S., U. R.I., 1973, B.S., 1974; M.Ed., Pa. State U., 1978. Dental hygienist Dr. J. Shapiro's Office, Providence, 1973-75; clin. instr. Ind. U. South Bend, 1975-78; program coordinator Ind. U.-Northwest, Gary, 1978-81; clin. coordinator U. Bridgeport, Conn., 1981—. Mem. Conn. Dental Hygienists Assn. (sec. 1983-84, v.p. 1984-85, pres.-elect 1985—), New Haven Dental Hygienists Assn. (legis. chmn. 1983—), Am. Dental Hygienists Assn. Home: 4 N Forest Circle West Haven CT 06513

KOHUTEK, NANCY CAROL, freight transportation company executive; b. Wichita Falls, Tex., Oct. 2, 1949; d. J.E. and Marguerite Kohutek; m. Edwin G. Halperin; 3 stepchildren. B.S.E., Midwestern U., 1972; M.A., U. Tex.-El Paso, 1974; postgrad. U. N.Mex., 1976. Co-owner, Burnham & Kohutek, El Paso, 1978-81; ptnr., adminstr. Sch. for Edn. Enrichment, El Paso, 1979-81; dir. mktg./adminstrn. SunCity Service Corp., El Paso, 1982—. Author: (with Edwin Halperin and Joshua Halperin) Symbol-Simons, 1979, Symbol-Simons Too!, 1981. Founder, Transitional Living Ctr., Inc., El Paso, 1976-81, bd. dirs., 1981-82; chmn. El Paso Women's Polit. Caucus, 1981-82; mem. fin. com. Re-elect Ron Coleman for Congress, El Paso, 1983; mem. El Paso County Restitution Adv. Council, 1983. Named Outstanding Young Women Am., U.S. Jaycees, 1979; named Rising Star in Bus., Tex. Bus. mag., 1980; mem. Leadership El Paso, El Paso Alumni Bd. Dirs., 1981. Mem. Am. Soc. Personnel Adminstrs., Am. Mgmt. Assn., Leadership El Paso Alumni Assn. Office: SunCity Service Corp 9 Zane Grey El Paso TX 79906

KOLANSKY, ELSA HARWITZ, journalist; b. Scranton, Pa., May 17, 1927; d. Isaac Harold and Hilda (Heller) Harwitz; B.A. in Journalism, Pa. State U., 1948; postgrad. New Sch. Social Research, 1975, Phila. Writers Sch., 1977, Temple U. Grad. Seminars, 1978-80, Pa. State U. Real Estate Inst., 1978; m. Harold Kolansky, June 8, 1948; children—Jeffrey M., Betta, Daniel M. Lic. real estate, Ill. Freelance writer, editor, 1948—; reporter Phila. weeklies, 1950-54, Beth Sholom Congregation Newsletter, 1970-72, Jenkintown Times Chronicle Bi-Centennial Edition, 1975; feature editor Am. Acad. of Child. Psychiatry Newsletter, 1978—; editor Aux. News-The Phila. Geriatric Ctr., 1985—. contbg. author chpt. Montgomery County-Second Hundred Years, 1983. Active Pa. State U. fund raising; mem. Beth Sholom Congregation and Sisterhood Bd., co-chmn. Sisterhood Adult Edn., 1982-83; mem. Hadassah, Faculty Wives Jefferson Med. Coll. and Hosp. Mem. Women's Com. Phila. Assn. Psychoanalysis (treas. 1970), AAUW, Phila. Geriatrics Center (bd. dirs.), Phila. Writers Conf. (2d prize interview div. 1981), LWV. Republican. Club: Cheltenham Racquet.

KOLBE, KATHRYN WONDERLIC, author, publisher; b. Evanston, Ill., Dec. 5, 1939; d. Eldon F. and Winifred E. Wonderlic; B.S. in Journalism, Northwestern U., 1961; children—Karen, David. Vice pres. E.F. Wonderlic & Assos., Inc., Northfield, Ill., 1962—; editor, pub. Think Inc., ednl. materials, Phoenix, 1976—; pres. Resources for Gifted Inc., Phoenix, 1974—; chmn. Problem Solving Systems, 1980—; pres. Kathy Kolbe Concept, 1983—; spl. edn. instr. Ariz. State U.; cons. in field, 1973—; pres. Kolbe Concepts, Inc., 1985—. Bd. dirs. Samaritan Health Found.; vice chmn. Citizens Task Force on Future Financing; nat. bd. advisors Coll. Bus. and Pub. Adminstrn., U. Ariz.; mem. exec. com. Small Bus. Council Ariz., 1983; mem. Phoenix Local Devel. Corp.; mem. exec. bd. Ariz. Law in Edn., 1984, Charter 100, 1984. Named Small Bus. Person of Yr. in Ariz., SBA, 1982. Mem. Nat Assn. Gifted Children, Nat. Council Critical and Creative Thinking, Nat. Direct Mail Assn., Am. Assn. Pubs., Am. Mgmt. Assn., Phoenix C. of C. (exec. com. 1983). Author: Nonsense and Common Sense About the Gifted, 1978; Joy of Learning, 1982; Risk Taking, 1983; Tip of the Iceberg, 1984; others; designer ednl. games Mind's Eyes, 1980, Logi-Sticks, 1980, Something Search, 1983, Why There, 1983, Hide and Seek It, 1984. Office: 3421 N 44th Pl Phoenix AZ 85018

KOLBE, MARGARET ANN, data processing training consultant; b. Chgo., Sept. 19, 1948; d. Walter A. and Catherine M. (Herda) Lisowski; m. Michael Joseph Kolbe, Dec. 8, 1973. B.S. in Psychology magna cum laude, Loyola U., Chgo., 1970; cert. Honeywell Inst. Info. Sci., 1970. Data processing cons. COMSI, Inc., Oak Brook, Ill., 1970-75; v.p. product devel. Deltak, Inc., Naperville, Ill., 1975-84; v.p., ptnr. The Info. Engrs., St. Charles, Ill., 1984—. Author tng. series, also poetry. Ill. Acad. Sci. scholar, 1966. Mem. Ind. Writers Chgo., Soc. Tech. Communication, Assn. Devel. of Computer-based Instructional Systems, Ind. Computer Cons. Assn., Nat. Soc. Performance and Instrn., Nat. Writers Club. Roman Catholic. Avocation: creative writing. Office: Info Engrs 36W290 Crane Rd Saint Charles IL 60174

KOLBEN, CAROLYN KURTZACK, lawyer; b. Sept. 18, 1957; d. Irwin Joseph and Pauline (Oppenheim) Kurtzack. B.A. cum laude, Duke U., 1979; student Mt. Holyoke Coll., 1975-76; J.D., Walter F. George Sch. Law, 1982. Bar: Fla. 1982. Intern congressman U.S. Ho. of Reps., Washington, summer 1978; intern presiding justice Dade County Circuit Ct., Miami, summer 1979; intern presiding justice U.S. Dist. Ct. (so. dist.) Fla., Miami, summer 1980; law clk. Fowler, White, Hurley, Banick & Strickroot, Miami, summer 1981; asst. state atty. Dade County, Miami, 1982-86; litigation assoc. Shutts and Bowen, Miami, 1986—. Mem. ABA, Dade County Bar Assn., Assn. Trial Lawyers Am., Phi Delta Phi. Home: 4530 Prairie Ave Miami Beach FL 33140

KOLBESON, MARILYN HOPF, advertising executive; b. Cin., June 9, 1934; d. Henry Dilg and Carolyn Josephine (Brown) Hopf; children—Michael Llen, Kenneth Ray, Patrick James, Pamela Sue Kolbeson Lang, James Allan. Student U. Cin., 1947, 48, 50. Sales and mktg. mgr. Xoc Patrick United Van Lines, 1977-80; sales mktg. mgr. Creative Incentives, Houston, 1980-81; pres. Ad Sense, Inc., Houston, 1981—; lectr., cons. in field. Mem. adv. bd. Alief Ind. Sch. Dist., 1981—, pres., 1983-84; bd. dirs. Santa Maria Hostel, 1983, v.p., 1983-84; founder, pres. Mind Force, Houston, 1978—. Mem. Greater Houston Conv. and Visitors Council, loaned exec., 1986—; mem. adv. bd. Am. Inst. Achievement, 1986—. Mem. Houston Advt. Splty. Assn. (bd. dirs. 1984, treas. 1985, v.p. 1986), Galleria Area C. of C. (bd. dirs. 1986—). Republican. Episcopalian. Clubs: Toastmasters (area gov. 1978), Grand (v.p. 1986), Regency. Office: Ad Sense Inc 800 Post Oak St Houston TX 77056

KOLE, JANET STEPHANIE, lawyer, writer, photographer; b. Washington, Dec. 20, 1946; d. Martin J. and Ruth G. (Goldberg) K. A.B., Bryn Mawr Coll., 1968; M.A., NYU, 1970; J.D., Temple U., 1980. Bar: Pa. 1980. Assoc. editor trade books Simon & Schuster, N.Y.C., 1968-70; publicity dir. Am. Arbitration Assn., N.Y.C., 1970-73; freelance photojournalist, N.Y.C., 1973-76; paralegal Morgan Lewis & Bockius, Phila., 1977-80; assoc. Schnader, Harrison, Segal & Lewis, Phila., 1980-85, Cohen, Shapiro, Polisher, Shiekman & Cohen, Phila., 1985—; author books including: Post Mortem, 1974; contbr. numerous articles to gen. interest publs., profl. jours.; bd. editors New Am. Rev. Mem. Mayor's Task Force on Rape, N.Y.C., 1972-77; adv. Support Ctr. Child Advs., Phila., 1980—; mem. Phila. Vol. Lawyers for the Arts; steering com. Lawyers' Com. Reproductive Rights. Mem. Assn. Trial Lawyers Am., ABA (editor Litigation News, chmn. com. on monographs and unpublished papers, com. spl. pubs.). Democrat. Office: Cohen Shapiro Polisher Shiekman & Cohen 12 S 12th St Philadelphia PA 19107

KOLKO, NAOMI GREENWOOD, clinical social worker; b. Phila., Feb. 12, 1941; d. David Nisan and Emma (Morgenstern) Greenwood; B.A. in Sociology with honors, U. Pa., 1962; M.S.W., Smith Coll., 1964; m. Burton S. Kolko, June 17, 1962; children—David Joseph, Joshua Howard. Clin. social worker St. Elizabeths Hosp., Washington, 1964-69; social worker children's unit Psychiat. Inst., Washington, 1972-76, assoc. dir. social work, 1976-79, acting dir., summer 1979; pvt. practice clin. social work, Bethesda, Md., 1979-84; co-founder, ptnr. North Bethesda Assocs., 1984—; cons. Community Psychiat. Clinic, Wheaton, Md., 1980-83, Gaithersburg, Md., 1983-85; provisional vice chmn. Precinct 7-14, Montgomery County, Md., 1982-84. Lic. clin. social worker. Fellow Am. Orthopsychiat. Assn.; mem. Nat. Assn. Social Workers, Greater Wash. Soc. Clin. Social Workers, Am. Assn. Sex Educators, Counselors and Therapists, Wash. Women's Network. Democrat. Jewish. Clubs: Plowman and Fisherman, Hadassah. Home: 8313 Beech Tree Rd Bethesda MD 20817 Office: Wyngate Med Park 5654 Shields Dr Bethesda MD 20817

KOLLER, KAREN ANDERSON, b. Brockton, Mass., Jan. 16, 1954; d. Lawrence Wellman and Emmaline Davis (Gillock) Anderson; B.S., Medaille Coll., 1981; postgrad. in bus. Fitchburg State Coll. Asst. mgr., personnel dir. Gurney Bros. Jewelers, Inc., Brockton, Mass., 1970-75; adminstrv. asst./asst. sports info. dir. Stonehill Coll., North Easton, Mass., 1975-77; substitute tchr. public schs., Hodgdon, Maine, 1977-78; supr. Magrams, Glens Falls, N.Y., 1978-79; supr., unit head Exchange Mut. Ins. Co., Buffalo, 1979-82; asst. personnel dir., asst. coordinator pub. relations Community Health and Counseling Services, Bangor, Maine, 1983; workshop coordinator Montachusett Employment and Tng. Program, Inc., Gardner, Mass., 1984; mem. adv. bd., 1984—; employment supr. Nypro Inc., Clinton, Mass., 1984—. Bus. mgr. Brockton Community Sch. Playhouse, 1976-77; chmn. vols., bd. dirs. Summerfest '75, Brockton Community Sch. Program; mem. adv. bd. employment unit Div. for Youth, 1981-82; active Govt. Services Fair, Maine Dept. Labor, 1983. Recipient cert. of commendation N.Y. Regional Data Ednl. Systems, 1981. Mem. Personnel Mgmt. Assn., Clinton C. of C., Nat. Orgn. for Female Execs. Lutheran. Clubs: Internat. Order Rainbow Girls (worthy adviser 1972). Home: 668 Merriam Ave Leominster MA 01453 Office: Nypro Inc Clinton MA

KOLLSTEDT, PAULA LUBKE, communication specialist; b. Cin., Aug. 27, 1946; d. Elmer George and Mary Margaret (Kelly) Lubke; m. Stephen Leonard Kollstedt, Jan. 21, 1968; children—Kelly, Lance, Stacey, Jonathan. B.A., Xavier U., 1968, M.Ed., 1982. Cert. secondary tchr., Ohio. Editor, writer Shillito's Dept. Store, Cin., 1966-69; freelance writer, Cin., 1969-74; writer, instr. Prince William County Parks and Recreation Com. (Va.), 1974-75; communications coordinator City of Cin. Recreation Com., 1975-78; cons. Warner Amex Cable Television, Cin., 1982-84, Moellers Assocs., Cin., 1982-84; exec. Communication Specialist Gen. Electric Aircraft Engine Bus. Group; speaker Cin. Preschool Coops., 1981, Cin. Women's Conf., 1984, lectr., presenter workshops on self-esteem for parents, 1975—. Author: Surviving the Crisis of Motherhood, 1982; contbr. articles to newspapers; writer, producer multi-media presentation Communication Cincinnati, (Unique Program award Ohio Parks and Recreation), 1978. Mem. Women in Communications (v.p. programs 1981-82; Gt. Lakes regional 1st pl. award 1984, 86), chmn., Communicator of Yr. 1983 Cin. Editors Assn. Roman Catholic. Home: 5391 Haft Rd Cincinnati OH 45247 Office: GE Aircraft Engine Bus Group 1 Neumann Way MD-C12 Evendale OH 45215

KOLMAR, VIRGINIA (GINNY), theatrical agency executive, publisher; b. Chgo., Nov. 28, 1932; d. Norman W. and Carol Dorothy (Reinganum) Slott; m. Alan Harvey, July 24, 1953 (div. Nov. 1956); 1 child, Karin Hoefeld Stern; m. Hanns H. Kolmar, Dec. 28, 1960. Student U. Calif.-Santa Barbara, 1950-52. Exec. asst., William Morris Agy., Beverly Hills, Calif., 1956-58; media dir. Farnell & Polk Advt. Agy., Los Angeles, 1959-60; press agt. Kolmar Assoc. and Kolmar Raush Assoc., San Francisco, 1961—; pub. Share the Wealth newsletter, San Francisco, 1971—. Guest theatre critic San Francisco Chronicle, 1968, 70, 76, San Mateo Times, 1968, 70, 76. Co-founder Fifth Bus., San Francisco, 1980; pub. relations counselor Am. Cancer Soc., San Francisco, 1975-78. Mem. Assn. Theatrical Press Agts. and Mgrs. Avocations: reading; travel; classical music; drama. Office: Share the Wealth 3216 Geary Blvd San Francisco CA 94118

KOLOSEUS, KAREN BERNADETTE, health care service accountant; b. Rock Island, Ill., Dec. 18, 1953; d. Bernard Thomas and Margaret Theresa (Tollenaer) K.; B.A. in Bus. Adminstrn., St. Ambrose Coll., Davenport, Iowa, 1975; M.B.A., Drake U., 1977. Collection mgr., asst. patient account mgr. Franciscan Med. Center, Rock Island, Ill., 1976-79; bus. office mgr. trainee Eastern region Am. Med. Internat., Atlanta, 1979; bus. office mgr., budget coordinator Parkway Gen. Hosp., North Miami Beach, Fla., 1979-82; fin. cons. Profl. Hosp. Services div. Am. Med. Internat., Los Angeles, 1982—; cons. in accounts receivables mgmt., 1982—. Cert. patient accounts mgr. Mem. Hosp. Fin. Mgmt. Assn., Am. Guild Patient Accounts Mgrs., Am. Mktg. Assn., Receivables Mgmt. Task Force, Gold Coast Exec. Women's Network, Nat. Assn. Female Execs., M.B.A. Execs. Assn. Office: Profl Hosp Services Div Am Med Internat 12960 Coral Tree Pl Los Angeles CA 90066

KOMECHAK, MARILYN GILBERT, psychologist; b. Wabash, Ind., Aug. 28, 1936; d. Russell and Evelyn Georgianna (Snyder) Gilbert; B.S., Purdue U., 1954; B.S., Tex. Christian U., 1966, M.Ed., 1968; Ph.D., North Tex. State U., 1975; m. George J. Komechak, Aug. 23, 1958; children—Kimberly Ann, Gilbert Matthew. Tchr. elem. sch., Huntsville, Ala., 1959-60; counselor clin. staff Child Study Center, Ft. Worth, 1968-74; assoc. dir. behavioral Sch. for Community Service, North Tex. State U., Denton, 1974-77; pvt. practice psychology, Ft. Worth, 1977—; adj. prof. Tex. Christian U., U. Tex., Arlington; dir. Jon Pierce, Inc.; cons. to schs. and mgmt.; mem. adv. bd. Trinity Valley Mental Health/Mental Retardation, Mental Health Assn. Tarrant County, 1980; presenter to profl. groups, 1974—. Mem. Sanger-Harris adv. bd. for Dallas/Ft. Worth, 1983—; hon. trustee World Olympiads of Knowledge. Mem. Am. Psychol. Assn., Tex. Psychol. Assn., Tarrant County Psychol. Assn. (officer 1977), Am. Soc. Clin. Hypnosis, Psi Chi, Delta Gamma. Episcopalian. Author: Getting Yourself Together, 1982; contbr. articles on counseling and psychology to profl. jours., poetry to anthologies. Office: 5280 Trail Lake Dr Fort Worth TX 76133

KOMODA, ELAINE, printing company executive; b. Paia, Maui, Hawaii, Oct. 20, 1930; d. Toichi and Umeno (Kawaguchi) Miyata; m. Roy Shoichi Komoda, Apr. 8, 1950 (dec.); children—Blake Shigeo, Lloyd Sakae, Noel Jay. Grad. Maui High Sch., Hamakuapoko, Hawaii. Office clk. Puunene Hosp., 1948-53; sec. Mehl Mfg. Co., Cin., 1953-54; office clk. Cin. Gen., 1954-55; owner, pres. Ace Printing Co., Ltd., Wailuku, Hawaii, 1960—. Democrat. Home: 267A Alu Rd Wailuku Maui HI 96793 Office: Ace Printing Co 1748 A Mill St Wailuku HI 96793

KOMP, BARBARA ANN, technical writer; b. La Porte, Ind., Nov. 3, 1954; d. Gerald Lee and Betty Mae (Schelin) K. B.A. in Elem. Edn., Ball State U., 1977; student mech. engring. tech. Purdue U., 1984—, Elec. Engring. Tech., 1984—. Quality control insp. Foreman Mfg. Co., Rolling Prairie, Ind., 1978-80; quality control insp. Weil-McLain Co., Michigan City, Ind., 1980-81, jr. quality control engr., 1981-84, tech. writer, 1984—. Adviser Jr. Achievement, Michigan City, 1982-83; fund raiser Statue Liberty Save the Lady drive, 1985; tchr. Vacation Bible Sch., 1986. Mem. Am. Soc. Quality Control (cert., membership chmn. 1981-83, treas. 1984-85), Weil-McLain Employees Club (nominating com. 1983—, chmn. by laws com. 1986), Delta Gamma (chpt. sec. 1976-77). Avocations: Local theatre, photography, writing children's stories. Office: Weil-McLain-A Marley Co Blaine St Michigan City IN 46360

KONEZNY, LORETTE M. S., publisher, manufacturing company executive; b. N.Y.C., Sept. 5, 1948; d. Jack and Florence (Silver) Sobol; m. Gerald Walter Konezny, June 4, 1972; 1 child, Scott David. B.S., U. Bridgeport, 1971; postgrad. Adelphi U., 1972-73, Parsons Sch. Design, 1977. Instr. Middle Sch., Malverne, N.Y., 1971-72; pvt. art instr. Long Island, 1972-76; instr. adult art edn. Rockville Centre, Oceanside and Lawrence, N.Y., 1976-79; pres. Pen Notes Inc., Freeport, N.Y., 1979—; founding pres. Long Island Networking Entrepreneurs, 1984-85, bd. dirs., 1985-86; cons. in field. Group exhibits: Adelphi U., 1973, Hewlett East Rockaway Temple, 1976; permanent collections: Yeshiva U., Los Angeles. Author, pub.: Learning to Print, 1980, Writing Script, 1981, Learning How to Tell Time, 1982; subject Cable TV show Working Mother, 1984; profiled in Working Women (guide), 1984; patentee: Calligraphy Guide. Mem. Soc. Scribes, Baldwin C. of C. Address: 134 Westside Ave Freeport NY 11520

KONHEIM, CAROLYN S(ALMINEN), environmental consultant; b. Flushing, N.Y., Jan. 20, 1938; d. Carl H. and Irene (Ahti) Salminen; m. Brian T. Ketcham, July 27, 1984; children—Eric, Alexander. B.A., Skidmore Coll., 1959; postgrad. Grad. Sch. History, Columbia U., 1960. Asst. commr. Dept. Air Resources N.Y.C., 1967-71; exec. dir. Scientists' Com. for Pub. Info., 1973-76; regional dir. N.Y. State Dept. Environ. Conservation, 1976-77; project mgr. Combustion Equipment Assocs., N.Y.C., 1978-81; pres. Konheim & Ketcham, Inc., Bklyn., 1981—; v.p. Environ. Action Coalition, Inc., 1986; vice chmn. permanent citizens adv. com. to Met. Transp. Authority, 1981-83; chmn. N.Y.C. Transit Authority Adv. Com., 1983-85; founder, 2d pres. Citizens for Clean Air, Inc., 1964-67. Dep. dir. N.Y. state campaign McGovern for Pres., 1972; co-mgr. Bella Abzug for Mayor. Recipient first merit award for citizen leadership U.S. EPA, 1975. Mem. Women's Transp. Seminar, Nat. Resource Recovery Assn., Am. Soc. Mech. Engrs. Home and Office: 175 Pacific St Brooklyn NY 11201

KONIOR, LYNNE BARTLETT, public relations executive; b. Paoli, Pa., Feb. 21, 1953; d. John B. and Dorothy F. (Lemon) Willey. B.S. cum laude, U. Mass., Amherst, 1979. Coordinator devel. and spl. projects Nat. Recreation and Parks Assn., Arlington, Va., 1979-81; dir. pub. relations Weight Watchers Eastern Mass. and R.I., Boston, 1981-82; dir. devel. and pub. relations Nat. Kidney Found. Mass., Boston, 1982-84; v.p. pub. relations Arnold & Co., Boston, 1984-85; ptnr. King Konior & Co., Boston, 1985—. Mem. adv. com. Boston for the World, 1985—; devel. cons. Summer Solstice Art Festival, 1984; publicity chair Advt. Club Boston Christmas Gala, 1985. Mem. Publicity Club Boston (Bell Ringer award 1985, Spl. Merit award 1985), Nat. Assn. Female Execs., Advt. Club Greater Boston. Avocations: ceramics; racquetball; jazz and classical ballet. Office: King Konior & Co 10 Thacher St #106 Boston MA 02113

KONJOLKA, TANYA KAYE, lawyer; b. Monessen, Pa., Sept. 11, 1941; d. John and Helen (Macosta) Karpiak; m. Walter J. Konjolka, Dec. 26, 1968; children—Tara, Ena. B.A., California (Pa.) State Coll., 1962; J.D., Boston Coll., 1975. Bar: Mass. 1975, U.S. Dist. Ct. 1976. Asst. editor Ladies' Home Jour., N.Y.C., 1965-68; freelance writer, N.Y.C., 1968-74; reporter Sta. WNAC-TV, Boston, 1974-80, WNEV-TV, Boston, 1982-83; columnist Boston Globe, 1982—; assoc. Murphy, Lamere and Murphy, Braintree, Mass., 1980—; dir. Consumer Credit Counseling Service, Boston, 1975—, Mass. Assn. Consumers, 1981-82. Mem. Gov.'s Commn. on Status of Women, 1977. Recipient Headliner award, Mall Dodson Meml. award, 1976. Mem. Mass. Bar Assn. Assn. Trial Lawyers Am., Boston Bar Assn. Contbr. numerous articles to popular mags. Home: 35 Kelveden Rd Waban MA 02168 Office: Murphy Lamere and Murphy PO Box 456 250 Granite St Braintree MA 02184

KONTZ, MARY MARGARET, nurse, educator; b. St. Paul, Dec. 13, 1955; d. Milo James and Loretta Margaret (Winkler) K. B.S. in Nursing, U. Miami, Coral Gables, Fla., 1978, M.S. in Nursing, 1984, postgrad., 1986—. R.N., Fla. Mem. surg. staff Mercy Hosp., Miami, 1978-79; mem. emergency staff Parkway Hosp., Miami, 1979-80; mem. faculty Jackson Meml. Hosp., Miami, 1980-86, dir. nursing edn., 1986—; cons. community hosps., Miami, 1982—. Mem. N.Am. Nursing Diagnosis Assn., Am. Nurses Assn., Fla. Nurses Assn., So. Region Nursing Diagnosis Group (program com., State rep. 1985), Sigma Theta Tau. Home: 9301 SW 92 Ave Apt 315-B Miami FL 33176 Office: Jackson Meml Hosp 1611 NW 12 Ave Miami FL 33136

KOOP, ANITA LOUISE, resort company executive, utility company owner; b. Edna, Tex., Apr. 28, 1942; d. Arnold Fred and Anita (Wiede) K.; m. Darrell Joe Burditt, Aug. 31, 1963 (div. Dec. 1977). A.A., Del Mar Coll., 1963, cert. performance, 1964; B.Mus., U. Corpus Christi, 1968. Ins. clk. H.E. Butt Grocery Co., Corpus Christi, 1964-66; tchr. music Odem Ind. Sch. Dist., Tex., 1968-71; pvt. tchr. piano and music theory, Refugio, Tex., 1971-77; sec. Koop, Inc., Edna, Tex., 1977-83; mng. ptnr. Carancahua Beach Properties, Port Alto, Tex., 1977-80; pres. Anita's Resort Properties, Inc., Port Alto, 1980—; pres. Sunilandings Utilities, Inc., Port Lavaca, Tex., 1981—, Sunilandings Property Owners Assn., Port Lavaca, 1982—; Sunilandings Marina, Port Lavaca, 1984—; co-owner Sunilandings Investments and Real Estate Mgmt., Port Lavaca, 1984—. Co-author: All Levels Music Theory, 1971. Judge Miss Am. Preliminary Pageant, South Tex. area, 1978—. Jackson County fair queen Jackson County Fair Assn., 1959, Miss. Tex. Farm Bur., 1961. Mem. Nat. Builders Assn., Marina Assn. Tex., Builders Assn. Victoria, Builders Assn. Tex., Boating Trades Assn. Tex., Calhoun County Bd. Realtors, Calhoun County C. of C. (tourism com. 1982—), Jackson County Hist. Soc., Am. Bus. Women's Assn. Democrat. Lutheran. Avocations: fishing; water and snow skiing; reading; land design and planning; entertaining. Home: 6/II Marshall Johnson Ave Port Alto TX 77979 Office: Anita's Resort Properties Inc Route 3 Box 98 Port Lavaca TX 77979

KOPACK, LAURA REYES, lawyer, consultant; b. Laredo, Tex., June 23, 1953; d. Jose Lino and Dora Guillermina (Moreno) Reyes; m. Alan Joseph Kopack, Aug. 11, 1973; 1 child, Samantha Terese. B.A. in Philosophy, Wayne State U., 1975; J.D., U. Detroit, 1980. Bar: Mich. 1981. Community service worker City of Detroit, 1974-75; program coordinator New Detroit Inc., 1975-77; legal intern U.S. Magistrates Office, Detroit, 1979-80, U.S. Attys. Office, Detroit, 1980, City of Detroit Legal Dept., 1979-82; staff atty. Detroit

Edison Co., 1982—. Editor Mich. Bar Assn. Tax Jour., 1980; contbr. articles to profl. jours. Cons. Mich. Republican State Com., Lansing, Mich., 1981-82, Nat. Alliance Bus., Detroit, 1981-82, League United Latin Am. Citizens, Detroit, 1982-83, Service Employment Redevel., Detroit, 1983—; bd. dirs. Southwest Detroit Hosp./Westland Med. Ctr. Inner City Bus. Improvement Forum, Detroit, 1983, Internat. Inst., Detroit, 1983—, Mich. Women's Campaign Fund, Detroit, 1984; bd. dirs., vice chmn. Service Employment Redevel., 1983; treas. Republican Nat. Hispanic Assembly, Mich., 1982; active United Found., Detroit, 1982; mem. Detroit Pvt. Industry Council, New Detroit Inc., Minority Econ. Devel. Com., others. Recipient Most Polit. award Hispanic Leadership Program, Detroit, 1982. Mem. ABA, Mich. Bar Assn., Detroit Bar Assn., Women Lawyers Assn., Latin Bar Assn. Roman Catholic. Clubs: Edison Power, Women's Econ., Edison Athletic (Detroit), Meridian. Office: Detroit Edison Co 688 WCB 2000 2d Ave Detroit MI 48226

KOPACK, PAMELA LEE (MACMINN), business services executive; b. Portland, Maine, July 25, 1951; d. Everett John Foye and Lois Florence (Loveland) MacMinn; student Sears, Roebuck Extension Inst., 1969-73, Newspaper Inst. Am., 1979-85; m. Charles Thomas Kopack, Apr. 2, 1971. Sales staff Sears Roebuck & Co., Cleve., 1966-69, credit collector, 1972-75; positions with various cos., 1969-72; exec. sec., asst., Cole Nat. Corp., Cleve., 1976-79; various positions as employment counselor, travel cons., bridal cons., model, photographer, advt. aide; pres. Kopack Service Bur., Cleve., 1979—; distbr. Shaklee, 1984—; cons. credit dept. Meritech, Inc., 1984—; author poetry pub. in Poetry-People, 1975, other publs., 1974—, lyrics for songs recorded on single records and albums, 1974-79; author greeting cards, articles, short stories. Mem. Career Guild (New Feature award 1982), Secs. Workshop, P.S. for Profl. Secs. (Bur. Bus. Practice, article award 1979), Internat. Platform Assn., Nat. Assn. Female Execs. Clubs: Homeowners Assn., Women's Opportunity Workshop, Nat. Assn. Notaries, George Washington Exec. Recipient poetry award for Facets of a Housewife, pub. in Beyond Verse, 1977. Compiler Royal Doulton Manual for Collectors. Office: PO Box 38171 Olmsted Falls OH 44138

KOPENHAVER, JOSEPHINE YOUNG, painter, educator; b. Seattle, June 9, 1908; d. George Samuel and Blanche Cecilia (Castle) Young; A.B., U. Calif., 1928; M.F.A. (scholar 1936-37), U. So. Calif., 1937; spl. student Claremont Grad. Sch., 1951, 67, Chouinard Art Inst., 1946-47, Otis Art Inst., 1954-55; m. Ralph Witmer Kopenhaver, Apr. 11, 1931. Prof. art Chaffee Jr. Coll., Ontario, Calif., 1946-47, Los Angeles City Coll., 1948-73, Woodbury U., Los Angeles, 1973-76, summer sessions Calif. State U., Los Angeles, 1950, Pasadena City Coll., 1949, Otis Art Inst., Los Angeles, 1959, Pasadena Art Inst., 1948; profl. painter, exhibiting artist, 1933—; work included in exhibits mus. and pvt. galleries U.S. and Mex., 1933—, including Hatfield Galleries, Los Angeles; art juror. Winner first award in oil Los Angeles Art Festival, 1936, various art awards. Mem. Los Angeles Art Assn. (trustee), Nat. Watercolor Soc. (sec.), Audubon Artists, Artists for Econ. Action, Calif. Tchrs. Assn. Clubs: Los Angeles Athletic, Zeta Tau Alpha. Office: PO Box 10666 Glendale CA 91209 Office: PO Box 10666 Glendale CA 91209

KOPENHAVER, PATRICIA ELLSWORTH, podiatrist; b. N.Y.C., Aug. 18; d. J. Emerson and Rose Ellsworth; A.B., George Washington U., 1954; M.A., Columbia U., 1956; Dr. Podiatric Medicine, SUNY, 1963. Practice podiatric surgery and sports medicine, Greenwich, Conn., 1964—; mem. staff Laurelton Convalescent Hosp., Greenwich. Mem. Greenwich Women's Club; v.p. Monmouth Opera Festival, 1964, trustee, 1966; mem. Greenwich Woman's Gardeners Club; mem. Philharmonia, Met. Opera Co., YWCA; chmn. dist. 7, Greenwich Women's Republican Club, 1977; bd. dirs. Monmouth Opera Guild, 1965; mem. Greenwich Art Council, Greenwich Exchange for Woman's Work. Recipient Hosp. Fund award for med. research translations ARC. Diplomate Nat. Bd. Podiatric Medicine Examiners. Mem. Am. (pres. 1970, com. library and archives 1982-83), Conn., Fairfield, podiatry assns., Am. Assn. Women Podiatrists (charter pres. 1969-78), Acad. Podiatry, Am. Podiatric Circulatory Soc., Am. Podiatry Council, Columbia U. Alumni Assn., UN Assn. U.S.A., George Washington U. Alumni Assn., Nat. Assn. Professions, AAUW (1st v.p. 1982, chmn. fundraising 1984, chmn. woman's worth-woman's work 1985), NOW. Clubs: Soroptomist, Greenwich Woman's (scholarship chmn. 1985, pres. gardeners 1985), Republican, Woman's (internat. com. 1980-83, program com. 1981; v.p. dist. 1984—, 4th congl. dist. rep. 1984), Wings, Toastmasters. Home: 2 Sutton Pl S New York NY 10022 also 8 Dearfield Dr Greenwich CT 06830

KOPLEY, MARY KATHERINE, legislative consultant/lobbyist; b. Cortland, N.Y., May 13, 1956; d. Andrew Michael and Barbara Ann (Stoker) K.; m. Richard Z. Steinhaus, Sept. 25, 1982. B.A. in Polit. Sci. with honors, Russell Sage Coll., 1978. Mem. research staff N.Y. State Assembly Banks Com., 1975; legis. analyst Steinhaus & Hochauser, N.Y.C., 1976; legis. cons. Richard Z. Steinhause Esquire, Tarrytown, N.Y., 1977-80; ptnr. Richard Z. Steinhaus Assocs., Albany, N.Y., 1981—; guest lectr., mem. career network Russell Sage Coll. Office: 90 S Swan St Albany NY 12210

KOPMEIER, ANNE, family therapist; b. Phoenix, June 21, 1943; d. John Henry and Pauline (O'Brien) K. A.B., Trinity Coll., Washington, 1965, M.B.A., 1979; M.Ed., Am. U., 1969; M.S.W., Cath. U. Am., 1983. Lic. clin. social worker, Va., Md., D.C. Economist, U.S. Dept. Commerce, Washington, 1966-67; sch. counselor D.C. Pub. Schs., 1970-83; practice family therapy, Washington, 1983—; pres. Clin. Cons., Annandale, Va., 1984—. Mem. Nat. Assn. Social Workers, Am. Assn. Counseling and Devel., Am. Soc. Tng. and Devel., NOW, AAUW, Nat. Assn. Female Execs. Democrat. Avocations: copper enameling; swimming; tennis; gardening. Home: Annandale VA 22003 Office: Clin Cons 7361 McWhorter Pl Suite 300 Annandale VA 22003

KOPP, JENNIFER LEE, technical illustrator; b. Phoenix, May 30, 1949; d. Leonard Owen and Gloria Belle (Shaffer) Kelly; student Los Angeles Pierce Coll., 1976-78, Moorpark Coll., 1981-83; m. Glenn Robert Kopp, Sept. 7, 1969; children—M. Scott, G. Douglas (dec.). Supr., Volt Tech. Corp., Van Nuys, Calif., 1977-78, project coordinator, El Segundo, Calif., 1979-80; checker in drafting Mainstream Engring., Sherman Oaks, Calif., 1978-79; sr. tech. illustrator Dynaction Resources, Chatsworth, Calif., 1979; sr. tech. illustrator Litton Data Command Systems, Agoura Hills, Calif., 1980—. Alt. com. mem. North Shore chpt. Gt. Salton Sea Experience, 1986; sec.-treas. North Shore Vol. Fire Co., 1985-86. Recipient Presdl. Sports award Pres.' Council on Phys. Fitness, 1973, 4 awards of Merit for sports L.A. Pierce Coll., 1977; Sportsmanship award Women's Internat. Motorcycle Assn., 1976, Citizenship award, 1978. Mem. Nat. Abortion Rights Action League, Nat. Women's Polit. Caucus, NOW, Calif. Abortion Rights Action League, Nat. Rifle Assn., Nat. Assn. Female Execs. Club: Litton Data Command Systems Rod and Gun (pres. 1982-83, v.p. 1984-85). Home: 101760 Sea Breeze Dr North Shore CA 92254 Office: PO Box 5000 Agoura Hills CA 91301

KOPP, NANCY KORNBLITH, state legislator; b. Coral Gables, Fla., Dec. 7, 1943; d. Lester and Barbara M. (Levy) Kornblith; B.A. with honors, Wellesley Coll., 1965; M.A., U. Chgo., 1968; m. Robert E. Kopp, May 3, 1969; children—Emily, Robert E. III. Instr. polit. sci. U. Ill. at Chgo., 1968-69; mem. profl. staff, spl. subcom. on edn. U.S. Ho. of Reps., Washington, 1970-71; legis. staff Md. Gen. Assembly, Annapolis, 1971-74; mem. Md. Ho. of Dels., 1975—, chmn. appropriations Subcom. on edn. and human resources, 1981—; rep. to Nat. Conf. State Legislators. Mem. Am. Polit. Sci. Assn., LWV, AAUW, Common Cause. Democrat. Jewish. Office: Lowe House Office Bldg Room 223 Annapolis MD 21401

KOPPEL, AUDREY FEILER, electrologist, educator; b. N.Y.C., Sept. 25, 1944; d. Jules Eugene and Lee (Gibel) Feiler; m. Mark Alyn Koppel, May 28, 1967; children—Jason, Seth. B.A., Bklyn. Coll., 1972; diploma in electrolysis Hoffman Inst., 1975; postgrad. George Washington U., 1984, Essex Community Coll., 1984, Kree Inst., 1980. Electrologist, Bklyn., 1976, Glemby Internat., N.Y.C., 1976-78, Island Electrolysis, Manhasset, N.Y., 1982-84; registrar, supervising instr. Kree Inst., N.Y.C., 1978-82; pres. North Shore Electrolysis, Manhasset, 1982-84; dir., electrologist Bklyn. Studio, 1982—. Editor, author pamphlet Glossary for Electrolysis, 1985. Active Greater N.Y. council Boy Scouts Am., 1977-84. Mem. Am. Electrolysis Assn. (v.p. 1984—, edn. chmn. 1984—, continuing edn. coordinator 1985), N.Y. Electrolysis Assn. (corr. sec. 1983-85, pres. 1985—), Internat. Guild of Electrologists (merit award 1978). Democrat. Jewish. Clubs: U.S. Power Squadron, Bklyn. Yacht. Avocations: boating; swimming; music. Office: Bklyn Studio of Electrolysis 2376 E 16th St Suite 1 Brooklyn NY 11229

KOPRIVICA, DOROTHY MARY, management consultant, real estate and insurance broker; b. St. Louis, May 27, 1921; d. Mitar and Fema (Guzina) K. B.S., Washington U., St. Louis, 1962; cert. in def. inventory mgmt. Dept. Def., 1968. Mgmt. analyst Transp. Supply and Maintenance Command, St. Louis, 1954-57, Dept. Army Transp. Materiel Command, St. Louis, 1957-62; program analyst Dept. Army Aviation System Command, St. Louis, 1962-74, spl. asst. to comdr., 1974-78; ins. broker D. Koprivica, Ins., St. Louis, 1978—; real estate broker Century 21 KARE Realty, St. Louis, 1978—, also dir. Mem. Bus. and Profl. Women (pres. 1974-75). Eastern Orthodox. Lodge: Order Eastern Star.

KORDICK, MARY FRANCES, hospital administrator, consultant; b. Pitts., Sept. 29, 1949; d. Rudolph Joseph and Sophia (Labinsky) K. R.N., Pitts. Hosp., 1970; B.S., St. Mary's Coll., 1980; M.B.A., Rosary Coll., 1986. R.N., Western Pa. Inst. and Clinic, Pitts., 1971-74, Chgo. Lakeshore Hosp., 1978-79; program mgr. Joint Commn. Accreditation of Hosps., Chgo., 1979-80, quality assurance cons., 1980-85, cons. faculty, 1980—; quality assurance mgr. Westlake Community Hosp., Melrose Park, Ill., 1981-86. Author: Quality Assurance Psychiatric and Mental Health, 1980. Author tng. manual, 1982, 84. Mem. Nat. Assn. Quality Assurance Profls., Am. Nurses Assn., Ill. Nurses Assn. Avocations: equestrian activities; jogging. Office: Westlake Community Hosp 1225 Superior St Melrose Park IL 60160

KOREY, LOIS BALK, advt. co. exec.; b. N.Y.C., May 19, 1933; d. Samuel and Lillian (Rosenblatt) Balk; student N.Y. U., 1951-52; m. Stanton Korey, Jan. 12, 1958 (div.); children—Susan, Christopher. Writer TV shows including Steve Allen Tonight, Ernie Kovacs, Wide Wide World, Andy Griffith, Sunday Night Comedy Hour; jr. partner Jack Tinker & Partners Advt. Co., N.Y.C., 1964-66; jr. partner, copywriter McCann Erickson Advt. Co., N.Y.C., 1967-69; creative dir. Revlon, N.Y.C., 1972; exec. v.p., creative dir. Needham, Harper & Steers Advt., Inc. N.Y.C., 1973-82; pres. Korey, Kay & Partners, N.Y.C., 1982—. Recipient 18 Clios, Am. TV Comml. Festivals: 8 Andys, Advt. Club N.Y., Cannes Film Festival TV Comml. award, 1973; 10 Hollywood Film Festival awards. Mem. Writers Guild Am., Dramatists Guild. Contbr. articles to mags. and profl. jours. Home: 130 Fifth Ave New York NY 10011

KORIAN, ANN DODAKIAN, travel agency executive; b. N.Y.C., Dec. 25, 1945; d. Steven and Mary (Vajibian) Dodakian; m. Paul P. Korian, July 13, 1969; children—Peter Paul, Steven John, Karen Anoush. B.S., Fisher Coll. Legal sec. Ropes & Gray, Boston, 1967-68, Goodwin, Proctor & Hoar, Boston, 1968-70; sec. to pres. Star Market Co., Cambridge, Mass., 1970-72; pres. Uniglobe Bay State Travel Inc., Cambridge, 1982—. Chmn. Sahag Mesrob Sch., Watertown, Mass., 1975-80. Democrat. Armenian Apostolic. Club: Belmont Woman's (Mass.). Avocations: travel; reading; music. Home: Belmont MA 02178 Office: Uniglobe Bay State Travel Inc 91 Blanchard Rd Cambridge MA 02138

KORN, JUDITH ANN, human relations consultant; b. N.Y.C., Mar. 23, 1947; d. Eugene and Bertha (Magaram) Kron; B.A. cum laude, SUNY, Buffalo, 1968; M.A., Columbia Univ. Tchrs. Coll., 1969; m. Barry Paul Korn, Aug. 2, 1969; children—Lisa Michele, Suzanne Leslie, Amy Beth. Speech, hearing pathologist Long Island Jewish Hillside Med. Center, New Hyde Park, N.Y., 1969-71; dir. Human Relations Inst., White Plains, N.Y., 1979—; adj. prof. Coll. New Rochelle, 1981—. Mem. Am. Soc. Tng. and Devel., Am. Personnel and Guidance Assn., Assn. Humanistic Edn. and Devel., Phi Beta Kappa. Office: 7 Pine Brook Dr White Plains NY 10605

KORNBLEET, LYNDA MAE, insulation contractor; b. Kansas City, Kans., June 15, 1951; d. Seymore Gerald Kornbleet and Jacqueline F. (Hurst) Kornbleet Malka. B.A., U. St. Thomas, Houston, 1979. Lic. real estate salesperson. Temporary counselor Lyman's Personnel, Houston, 1974-75; real estate salesperson Coldwell Banker, Houston, 1975-77; sales, office mgr. Acme Insulation, Dallas, also Houston, 1977-79; pres., owner Payless Insulation, Houston, 1979—. Mem. Nat. Assn. Remodeling Industry (bd. dirs. Houston 1982-84), Houston Air Conditioning Council (bd. dirs. 1982-83), Cellulose Insulation Contractors (chmn. Houston 1981-82). Democrat Jewish. Avocations: bridge; golf; baseball; basketball; other sports. Office: Payless Insulation 207 Reinerman St Houston TX 77007

KORNER, HILDA, personnel executive; b. N.Y.C., June 2, 1931; d. Manuel and Sadie (Brookman) Troob; m. Herbert Korner, Aug. 1, 1953 (div. Feb. 1971); children—David, Peter. B.S. in Personnel Adminstrn, SUNY-Rochester, 1974. Owner, operator Gallery III, Marin County, Calif., 1964-69; supr. personnel services SUNY-Buffalo, 1970-72, dir. recruitment and promotion of women, 1972-75, coordinator human research devel., 1975-77; mgr. employment Stanford Linear Accelerator Ctr., Calif., 1977-83, asst. personnel dir., 1983—; instr. D'Youville Coll., Buffalo, 1973-74, Ohlone Coll., Fremont, Calif., 1982-83; co-owner, ptnr. Korn Kompany, Palo Alto, Calif., 1985—. Workshop leader Resource Ctr. for Women, Palo Alto, 1981-83. Avocations: theater; symphony; chamber music; travel; reading. Home: PO Box 7414 Menlo Park CA 94026 Office: Stanford Linear Accelerator Ctr PO Box 4349 Stanford CA 94305

KORNEY, RITA LOIS, financial printing company executive; b. Phila., Mar. 24, 1934; d. Bernard and Bea (Cohen) Kauffman; m. Jordan F. Miller, July 31, 1955 (div. Jan. 1964); children—Gary, Scott, Lori; m. Michael Stanley Korney, May 24, 1964. B.S., UCLA, 1956. Vice pres. Sales mktg. Bowne of L.A., Los Angeles, 1972-82; pres. Merrill Calif., 1982—. Mem. Women in Bus. (chmn. downtown group 1983—). Democrat. Jewish. Avocations: gourmet cooking; baking; dining. Office: Merrill California 1926 E 14th St Los Angeles CA 90021

KORNFELD, PHYLLIS LORRAINE SCHAUM, educator; b. Bklyn.; d. Max and Gussie (Goldberg) Schaum; B.A., Bklyn. Coll., M.S.; postgrad. CCNY; Ed.D., Columbia U., 1972; children—Keith D., Elise J. Tchr. public sch., Bklyn.; reading clinician Bklyn. Community Counsel Center, N.Y. Infirmary; sr. lang. disabilities therapist Coney Island (N.Y.) Hosp.; remedial edn. tchr. Children's Aid Soc.; lectr. grad. div. Bklyn. Coll.; asst. prof. lang. arts and reading Paterson Coll., Wayne, N.J., Bklyn. Coll., CUNY; asst. prof., co-dir. Reading Center Ferkauf Grad. Sch. Yeshiva U., N.Y.C.; asst. prof. Coll. New Rochelle; adj. asso. prof. C.W. Post Coll. Fellow Am. Orthopsychiat. Assn.; mem. Manhattan Council Internat. Reading Assn. (pres. 1969-70), Mensa, AAUP, Internat. Reading Assn., Phi Delta Kappa. Office: 16 W 16th St New York NY 10011

KORP, PATRICIA ANNE, communications/public info. specialist; b. Lincoln, Nebr., Nov. 15, 1942; d. Theodore R. and Elizabeth Anne (Olson) Munn; B.S. in Journalism, U. Wyo., 1967, M.A., 1974; m. Vince L. Korp, Jan. 15, 1965; children—Kathleen Anne, Karen Lee. Women's editor Sheridan (Wyo.) Press, 1964-66; public info. and research asst. Wyo. Dept. Edn., 1967-69; dir. public relations and communications Wyo. Edn. Assn., 1969-71; coordinator info. services Mountain Plains Program, Glasgow, Mont., 1972-73; freelance public relations, Laramie, Wyo., 1973-74; public info. specialist Bur. Land Mgmt., Rawlins, Wyo., 1975-76, Cheyenne, Wyo., 1976-81, chief Office Pub. Affairs, 1981-85, Washington hdqts. office, 1985—; communications specialist Wyo. Spl. Olympics, 1978-79. Mem. Wyo. Council Children and Youth, 1976-77. Recipient All-Am. award Ednl. Press Assn. Am., 1st place award Nat. Fedn. Press Women, 1980. Mem. Nat. Fedn. Press Women, Federally Employed Women, Wyo. Press Women (sec.), Seton Cath. High Sch. Athletic Assn. (sec. 1981-83, pres. 1984), Sigma Delta Chi. Democrat. Roman Catholic. Editor: Wyo. Edn. News, 1969-71; asst. editor Wyo. Horizons, 1976-80, editor, 1980-85. Home: 409 Maple Ct Herndon VA 22070 Office: 18th and C Sts NW Washington DC 20240

KORRICK, GAIL HELENE, social work therapist, educator, consultant; b. Boston, Jan. 26, 1937; d. Louis Abraham and Molly (London) Goldman; m. Ira Korrick, Aug. 3, 1975. A.A., Boston U., 1956; B.S., U. Buffalo, 1958; M.S.S.W., Boston U., 1960. Jr. caseworker Mass. Meml. Hosp., Boston, 1960-63; field work instr. Boston U. Sch. Social Work, 1962-63; clin. social worker dept. social work-medicine and surgery Yale New Haven Hosp., 1963-82; field work instr. U. Conn. Sch. Social Work, Storrs, Conn., 1966-76; clin. instr. social work-medicine Yale U. Sch. Medicine, New Haven, 1965—; social work cons. New Haven Ostomy Assn., 1968-81; field work instr. So. Conn. U., New Haven, 1974-80; social work cons. in-service teaching program Yale New Haven Hosp. Nursing Dept., 1975-82; clin. social work cons. Gastrointestinal Tumor Study Group Project sect. gastroenterology Yale U. Sch. Medicine, New Haven, 1975-86; social work cons. Gen. Oncology Clinic, Yale/New Haven Hosp., 1979-81; mem. recruitment com. undergrad. divs. Boston U., 1978—; co-chmn. Com. to Develop a Social Work Oncology Group in Conn., 1978-79; mem. planning com. Social Work Oncology Group, 1980—; pvt. practice clin. social work, New Haven, 1980—; mem. speakers bur., metro unit Am. Cancer Soc., New Haven, 1980-82; Bd. mem. Nat. Found. Ileitis and Colitis, 1983. Recipient Plaque, So. Conn. State Coll., 1976. Mem. Nat. Assn. Social Workers, Nat. Council Social Welfare, Acad. Cert. Social Workers, Acad. Clin. Social Workers, Conn. Social Work Oncology Group, Mass. Social Work Oncology Group, Conn. Oncology Assn. Democrat. Jewish. Office: 2 Church St S Suite B1 New Haven CT 06519

KORSMEYER, MARY DRAKE, lawyer, court officer; b. Portsmouth, Ohio, Oct. 27, 1937; d. James Clinton Drake and Eliza Abigail (Bradford) Mitchell; m. Jerome Daniel Korsmeyer, June 25, 1960; children—Carol, David, Keith. B.A., Cornell U., 1959; J.D., U. Pitts., 1978. Bar: Pa. 1978, U.S. Supreme Ct. 1983. Securities analyst Irving Trust Co., N.Y.C., 1960; sewing instr. Joseph Horne Co., Pitts., 1972-75; law clk. Commonwealth Ct. of Pa., Washington, 1979-80; sole practice law, McMurray, Pa., 1980-81; assoc. firm Peacock, Keller, Yohe, Day & Ecker, Washington, Pa., 1981—; standing master in divorce, child custody officer Washington County Ct. Common Pleas, 1983-84. Mem. Pa. Trial Lawyers Assn., Washington County Bar Assn. (exec. com. 1984—, treas. law library com. 1981-83, chmn. 1983-84), Allegheny County Bar Assn., Delta Delta Delta (sec. South Suburban Alumnae chpt. 1981-83, treas. 1983-85). Democrat. Roman Catholic. Home: 132 Highland Dr McMurray PA 15317 Office: Peacock Keller Yohe Day & Ecker 70 E Beau St Washington PA 15301

KORTE, VIRGINIA LOU, automobile dealer official; b. Phoenix, July 27, 1953; d. Raymond Erni and Marianna (Daines) K. A.A., Glendale Community Coll., 1974; B.S., No. Ariz. U., 1979, M.S., 1983. Mktg. dir. pub. relations Ray Korte Chevrolet, Scottsdale, Ariz., 1981-84, customer relations mgr., 1984-85, dir. fixed ops., co-owner, dir. service dept., 1985—; mem. adv. bd. Scottsdale Vocat. Tech. Career Ctr., 1985—. Co-author articles in profl. jours. Adv. bd. Reach, Touch, Teach Found., Phoenix, 1984—. Recipient Achievement awards, Bot. Soc. Am., 1979, Biology Dept. No. Ariz. U., 1979. Mem. Profl. Womens Network (sec. 1984-85), Camelback Bus. Profl. Assn. Republican. Avocations: Photography; hiking; backpacking. Office: Ray Korte Chevrolet 7224 E McDowell Scottsdale AZ 85257

KORTH, CHARLOTTE BROOKS, furniture and interior design firm exec.; b. Milw., Nov. 16, 1920; d. Lewis C. and Marguerite Peil Brooks; student U. Wis., 1941; m. Robert Lee Williams, Jr., Oct. 25, 1944 (dec.); children—Patricia, Melissa Williams O'Rourke, R. Brooks; m. Fred Korth, Aug. 23, 1980. Vice pres., co-owner Charlotte's Inc., El Paso, Tex., 1951-76; pres. Paso del Norte Design, Inc., El Paso, 1978—; chmn. bd., chief exec. officer Charlotte's, Inc., El Paso, 1979—; mem. adv. bd. Mountain Bell Telephone Co., 1976-79; First City Nat. Bank, El Paso, 1981—. Mem. women's com. El Paso Symphony Orch.; charter mem. Com. of 200, 1982—. Recipient Silver plaque Gifts and Decorative Accessories mag., 1978; named Woman of Year, Women's Polit. Caucus, 1979, Outstanding Woman Entrepreneur El Paso, Am. Bus. Women's Assn., 1979. Mem. Am. Soc. Interior Designers (dir. Tex. 1977—), El Paso C. of C. (dir. 1976—), El Paso Women's C. of C., Delta Gamma. Roman Catholic. Clubs: Coronado Country, El Paso, Internat. (El Paso). Home: 1054 Torrey Pines El Paso TX 79912 Office: Charlotte's Fine Furniture Pepper Tree Square 5411 N Mesa St El Paso TX 79912

KORTH, CONSTANCE MARIE, nurse; b. Painesville, Ohio, Oct. 28, 1956; d. Russell Lloyd and June (Shirley Melcher) Korth. R.N., Trumbull Meml. Sch. Nursing, Warren, Ohio, 1977. Staff nurse Univ. Hosps., Cleve., 1977-82, asst. head nurse, clin. nurse, 1982—. Mem. Am. Nurses Assn., Ohio Nurses Assn., Greater Cleve. Nurses Assn. Republican. Methodist. Avocations: gardening; refinishing furniture.

KORTMAN, JOYCE ELAINE, graphic arts company executive, civic worker; b. Holland, Mich., Dec. 24, 1935; d. Henry John and Jeanette (Van Kampen) De Ridder; ed. Davenport Coll., Hope Coll., Western Theol. Sem.; m. Harris Jay Kortman, May 15, 1956; children—David, Calvin, Lafon, Renee, Mark. Mem. advisory council Nat. Inst. Arthritis, Metabolism, Digestive Disease, NIH, 1973-75; mem. West unit Health Systems' Agy. Bd., HEW, 1972-83; active Mich. affiliate Am. Diabetes Assn., 1970—, vice chmn. nat. coordinating com. for pub. activities, mem. com. on pub. affairs and Mich. del. co-chmn. work group on nat. resources Nat. Commn. on Diabetes, 1975; cons., speaker, and consumer adv. in health; propr. DaCal Printing Co., Heritage Printing Service, Holland. Mem. adv. bd. Mich. Dept. Pub. Health, 1974—; mem. Commn. on Handicapped Concerns, Mich. Dept. Labor. Recipient certificate of appreciation Am. Diabetes Assn., 1970, citation for outstanding contbn., 1973, Vol. of Yr. award, 1976, Meritorious award, 1976. Mem. Holland C. of C. (1st vice chmn. bd.), Holland Christian Schs. Parent-Tchr. Assn. (mother club), Calvinette Internat. (counselor, co-chmn. com. on curriculum revision). Office: 16935 Riley St Holland MI 49423

KOSAKOWSKI, JUDITH ANNE, business executive; b. Rochester, N.Y., Apr. 18, 1957; d. Frank Joseph and Mary Anne (Zeller) K. B.S., Fla. State U., 1979; postgrad. Corpus Christi State U., 1981-82. Purchasing assoc. Gen. Telephone Co., Durham, N.C., 1979-81; buyer 1, Celanese Chem. Co., Bishop, Tex., 1981-82; buyer 11, Kimberly Clark Corp., Beech Island, S.C., 1983-84; sr. buyer Pellerin Milnor Corp., Kenner, La., 1984-85; sr. buyer NEC Am., Richardson, Tex., 1985—. Mem. Nat. Assn. Purchasing Mgmt., Am. Prodn. and Inventory Control Soc. Avocations: travel; photography; soccer; running; designing and making clothes. Home: 5426 Meadowcreek Rd Apt 1049 Dallas TX 75248 Office: NEC Am 383 Omni Dr Richardson TX 75080

KOSECHER, PATRICIA ANN, manufacturing company executive; b. Susquehanna, Pa., Mar. 11, 1937; d. Charles Albert and Sadie Lafrazia (McNulty) Welch; children—Susan, Lori Ann, Kathleen, Margaret. B.S., SUNY-Binghamton, 1981. With Gen. Electric Co., Binghamton, 1956-63, program acct., 1964-75, mgr. cost estimating, 1975-80, mgr. F18 program account, 1980-81, subsect. mgr., 1981-83, with mil. programs acctg. dept., 1983—; office mgr. Sullivan Bros., Binghamton, 1963-64. Bd. dirs. S.O.S. Shelter for Battered Women, Endicott, N.Y., 1982-83, treas., 1983-84; solicitor United Way Capital Campaign, Binghamton, 1982; leader Tioga Council Girl Scouts U.S.A., 1972. Mem. Nat. Contract Mgmt. Assn., Nat. Assn. Female Execs., AAUW, Gen. Electric Exec. Assn. (vice chmn. 1983-84, treas. 1982-83). Republican. Methodist. Home: 202 Marshland Rd Apalachin NY 13732 Office: General Electric Co PO Box 5000 Room 118 Binghamton NY 13902

KOSHLAND, MARIAN ELLIOTT, immunologist; b. New Haven, Oct. 25, 1921; d. Waller Watkins and Margaret Ann (Smith) Elliott; B.A., Vassar Coll., 1942, M.S., 1943; Ph.D., U. Chgo., 1949; m. Daniel Edward Koshland, Jr., May 25, 1945; children—Ellen R., Phyllis A., James M., Gail F., Douglas E. Research asst. Manhattan Dist. Atomic Bomb Project, 1945-46; fellow dept. bacteriology Harvard Med. Sch., 1949-51; assoc. bacteriologist biology dept. Brookhaven Nat. Lab., 1952-62, bacteriologist, 1963-65; asso. research immunologist virus lab. U. Calif., Berkeley, 1965-69, lectr. dept. molecular biology, 1966-70, prof. dept. microbiology and immunology, 1970—, chmn., 1982—; mem. Nat. Sci. Bd., 1976-82; mem. adv. com. to dir. NIH, 1972-75. Mem. Nat. Acad. Scis., Am. Acad. Microbiology, Am. Assn. Immunologists (council 1977-83, pres. 1982-83), Am. Soc. Biol. Chemists, Phi Beta Kappa, Sigma Xi. Contbr. articles to profl. jours. Office: Dept Microbiology and Immunology U Calif Berkeley CA 94720

KOSIBA, PATRICIA ANN, high technology equipment manufacturing company executive; b. Flushing, N.Y., Nov. 8, 1949; d. Edward Albert and Mary Josephine (Pikor) Kosiba. Student Bryant Coll., 1967-68, Sacred Heart U., Fairfield, Conn. With Perkin-Elmer Corp., Norwalk, Conn., 1969-79, Wilton, Conn., 1979—, supr. data services, 1977-79, supr. human resources, 1979-83, mgr. human resources, plasma systems div., 1983-85, compensation and benefits for semiconductor equipment group, 1985—. Mem. Am. Soc. Personnel Administrs., Internat. Assn. for Personnel Women, Assn. Human Resources Systems Profls. Roman Catholic. Home: 159 Tahmore Dr Fairfield CT 06430 Office:The Perkin-Elmer Corp Semiconductor Equipment Group 50Danbury Rd Wilton CT 06897

KOSKI-PONTON, ELLEN IRENE, sales executive, management consultant; b. Louisville, June 10, 1947; d. Edward Zacharias and Doris Jean (Speer) Koski; m. George Evan Ponton, Oct. 12, 1985; children by previous marriage—Monica Linette Arnold, Matthew David Arnold, Marcus Aaron Arnold; stepchildren—Yvonne Larae Ponton, Colleen Ruth Ponton. A.S. in Bus. Adminstrn., Tidewater Community Coll., 1983; B.A. in Interdisciplinary

Studies, U. S.C.-Lancaster, 1985, postgrad., 1985—. Adminstrv. asst. Northwestern Mut. Life, Norfolk, Va., 1981-83, asst. dir. mktg., Charlotte, N.C., 1983-84; ind. distbr. Herbalife, Monroe, N.C., 1983—; eligibility specialist Union County Dept. Social Services, 1985—; mgmt. cons. Dorey Electric, Norfolk, Va., Advanced Marine Enterprises, Virginia Beach, Va., 1982-83. Foster parent Ohio Youth Commn., Delaware, 1976-79, Cath. Family Services, Virginia Beach, 1980-81; pres. Tidewater Assn. Talented and Gifted, Virginia Beach, 1982; vol. Rape Crisis Companion, Monroe, N.C., 1985—. Clubs: Nat. Rifle Assn. (Washington); Amateur Trapshooting Assn. (Vandalia, Ohio). Avocations: trapshooting; reading; swimming. Home: 4610 Nesbit Rd Monroe NC 28110

KOSLAN-SCHWARTZ, JOAN HELEN, artist, architectural interior designer; b. N.Y.C., Aug. 30, 1934; d. Barnett and Mille (Spitz) Koslan; m. Benjamin L. Schwartz, Sept. 9, 1956; children—Justin, Beryl, Mila. Student Pratt Inst., 1953-55; B.S., Ohio State U., 1957; M.A., Embroiderers' Guild, London, 1964. Free-lance artist, Monterey, Calif., 1960-64; owner, dir. The Needle's Point Studio, Washington, 1965—; instr. Smithsonian Instn., Washington, 1967-77; artist-in-residence Temple Rodef Shalom, Falls Church, Va., 1981-86. Work in fiber arts. Group shows include: Craftsmans Br. Nat. Invitational Show, Pitts., 1968 (Best-In-Show award), Carmel Art Festival, Calif. (Best-in-Show), 1962, Embroiderers' Guild, London, 1975, Touchstone Retrospective Invitational, Washington, 1985 86; work represented in churches, synagogues, museums and pvt. collections throughout U.S. and abroad; guest artist radio and television programs. Recipient Nat. award AIA, 1981, 83. Mem. Embroiderers' Guild London, Embroiderers' Guild (founding mem. Congl. chpt., Washington), Nat. Standards Council Am. Embroiderers (founding mem., dir. 1968-70). Jewish. Home: 216 Apple Blossom Ct Vienna VA 22180 Office: Needle's Point Studio 216 Apple Blossom Ct Vienna VA 22180

KOSS, HELEN L., state legislator; b. N.Y.C., June 3, 1922; A.B., Bennington Coll., 1942; married. Mem. Md. Ho. of Dels., 1971—, chmn. constl. and adminstrv. law com., 1979—, mem. legis. policy com., 1979—, co-chmn. task force on election laws, 1979—; mem. ethics and elections com. Nat. Conf. State Legislatures, 1975—; mem. human resources com. Met. Council Govts., 1975-79; del. Constl. Conv. of Md., 1967-68; chmn. Com. on Suffrage and Elections; bd. visitors Bowie State Coll.; mem. Gov.'s Commn. on Reapportionment, Gov.'s Commn. on Crime and Delinquency; mem., Montgomery County Task Force on Community Edn., 1977, Gov.'s Commn. to Study Pub. Service Commn., Md. Hwy. Safety Coordinating Com. Recipient Ann London Scott award for legis. excellence NOW, 1978, NAACP cert. of merit, 1978, Hendrick Ibsen award Md. Conf. Social Concern, 1976, Common Cause award, 1979, Leadership award Md. Assn. Counties, 1983, numerous others. Mem. LWV (pres. Md. 1963-67), AAUW (outstanding mem. award Md. 1978), Nat. Order Women Legislators. Nat. Women's Dem. Club. Address: 3416 Highview Ct Silver Spring MD 20902

KOSSAN, NANCY E., real estate executive; b. Chgo., Aug. 9, 1952; d. Joseph E. and Madelyn E. (Cowan) K. B.A., Yale U., 1974; Ph.D., Stanford U., 1978. Asst. prof. U. Rochester, N.Y., 1978-81; benefits acctg. mgr. Harvard U., Cambridge, Mass., 1981-84, sec. to adv. com. on shareholder responsibility, 1982-84; v.p. Harvard Real Estate, Inc., Cambridge, 1984—. Contbr. articles to profl. jours. Mem. Nat. Assn. Corp. Real Estate Execs., Assn. Univ. Real Estate Ofcls., Bldg. Owners and Mgrs. Assn. (bd. dirs. 1984—), Rental Housing Assn. (bd. dirs. 1984—), Phi Beta Kappa. Office: Harvard Real Estate Inc 1350 Massachusetts Ave Cambridge MA 02138

KOSSIN, SUSAN FRANCES, government official, consultant; b. N.Y.C., May 3, 1949; d. Benjamin and Evelyn Peace (Flaks) K. B.A., George Washington U., 1970; M.S., Boston U., 1973. Adminstrv. asst. Rockefeller Found., N.Y.C., 1970-71; writer, reporter, editor WBUR-FM and other radio stas., Boston, N.Y.C., 1971-74; asst. to regional adminstr. U.S. Gen. Services, N.Y.C., 1974-75; mgmt. intern, 1975; exec. dir. N.Y. Fed. Exec. Bd., N.Y.C., 1975—. Vol., Planned Parenthood, N.Y.C., 1983. Named Outstanding Greek Woman, Panhellenic Council, George Washington U., 1970; recipient Spl. Achievement awards U.S. FAA, N.Y.C., 1976, 80; Appreciation award U.S. Dept. Labor, N.Y.C., 1984. Mem. Federally Employed Women N.Y. (dir. 1974—, legis. chmn. 1983—). Office: NY Fed Exec Bd care OPM 26 Federal Plaza New York NY 10278

KOSSOW, SUELLEN ELIZABETH, bank executive; b. Milw., July 23, 1953; d. John Frederick and Patricia Jean (Mulvaney) K. B.S., Barry U., 1981; M.B.A. in Internat. Bus., U. Miami, 1983. Writer, reporter The Oracle, Tampa, Fla., 1971-72; tech. writer Southeast Banks, Miami, Fla., 1974-75; tech. writer Bank of Miami, 1975-76, dir. personnel, 1976-79, dir. tng. and tech. writing, systems analyst, 1979-80, dir. mircocomputers, 2d v.p., 1980-84, corp. exec. offices dir. pub. relations and community involvement program, 2d v.p., 1984—; sec., dir. Popular Computers, Inc., Miami, 1983—; adj. lectr. Barry U., Miami, 1984—; pres. Holly Morgan Assocs., Inc., 1985—. Docent, Ctr. for Fine Arts, Miami, 1985—; chmn. com. Miami's for Me, 1986; mem. South Fla. Hist. Soc., Mus. Natural History, N.Y.C., Smithsonian Soc. Mem. Nat. Assn. Bank Women. Office: Bank of Miami 100 E Flagler St Miami FL 33131

KOTCHER, SHIRLEY J. W., lawyer; b. Bklyn., June 6, 1924; d. Irving and Violet (Miller) Weinberg; m. Harry A. Kotcher, Mar. 22, 1948; children—Leslie Susan, Dana Anne. B.A., NYU, 1944; J.D., Columbia U., 1947. Bar: N.Y. 1948. In-house counsel Booth Meml. Med. Ctr., Flushing, N.Y., 1975-83, gen. counsel, 1983—; advisor health care Borough Pres. Queens, N.Y., 1978. Author: Hidden Gold and Pitfalls in New Tax Law, 1970. Mem. Nassau County Bar Assn., Am. Soc. Hosp. Attys., Am. Soc. Law and Medicine, Am. Soc. Risk Mgrs., Greater N.Y. Hosp. Assn. (legal adv. com. 1976—). Home: 9 Chestnut Rd Manhasset NY 11030 Office: Booth Meml Med Center Main St Flushing NY 11335

KOTCHIAN, SARAH BRUFF, environmental health government official; d. John and Winifred (Rennebohm) Kotchian; m. Robert Nellums, 1977; 1 child, Laura Bruff. B.A. cum laude, Middlebury Coll., 1975; M.Ed., Harvard U., 1977; M.P.H., U. Wash., 1985. English tchr. Cushing Acad., Ashburnham, Mass., 1975-76; staff assoc. Chrysalis, Inc., Cambridge, Mass., 1977; instr. Harvard U., Cambridge, 1977; career counselor Roxbury/Harvard Sch. Program, Roxbury, Mass., 1977-78; health educator Planned Parenthood, Albuquerque, 1978-79; health edn. and tng. coordinator New Mex. Family Planning Council, Albuquerque, 1979-82; adminstrv. asst. Environ. Health and Energy Dept., Albuquerque, 1982-83, dep. dir., 1983—; mem. FDA Ob/Gyn Devices Com.; intern archaeology/geography field trip Middlebury Coll., winter 1975; co-leader month-long camping trip of teenagers through Appalachian South, summer 1976; co-leader Crossroads Interlocken, Hillsboro, N.H., summer 1977; presenter numerous workshops and media presentations. Recipient YWCA award for contbns. to pub. health, 1985; Gov.'s award as Outstanding N.Mex. Woman, 1986; named to Glamour mag. list of Top Ten Working Women, 1986. Mem. Am. Pub. Health Assn. (joint policy com., membership com., environ. sect. council), N.Mex. Pub. Health Assn. (legis. chmn. 1985), Nat. Women's Health Network, Nat. Women's Health Network of N.Mex. (co-founder and chmn. 1982, publicist 1983—), Nat. Conf. Local Environ. Health Adminstrs., N.Mex. Environ. Health Assn., Nat. Family Planning and Reproductive Health Assn., N.Mex. Com. on Fetal Alcohol Syndrome Prevention (chmn. edn. com. 1980), N.Mex. Com. on Improved Pregnancy Outcome, Phi Delta Kappa.

KOTLARZ, SHIRLEY ANN, nursing services executive; b. Aliquippa, Pa., Sept. 6, 1938; d. Michael Andrew and Anne (Casp) K. Diploma in Nursing, Mercy Hosp., 1959; B.S.N., Med. Coll. Ga., 1968; M.S. in Nursing, Emory U., 1970. Staff nurse Aliquippa Hosp. (Pa.), 1959-61, Holy Cross Hosp., Ft. Lauderdale, Fla., 1961-62; head nurse Charlotte Meml. Hosp. and Med. Ctr. (N.C.), 1962-63, dir. staff, 1963-65, assoc. dir. nursing, 1973-76, v.p., 1976—; parttime staff nurse Piedmont Hosp., Atlanta, 1965-69; clin. coordinator Northside Hosp., Atlanta, 1970-71, asst. dir. nursing, 1971-72, dir. patient care, 1972-73; adj. prof. U. N.C.-Charlotte, 1975—. Bd. dirs. Hospice, Charlotte, 1979-81; active tech. advance com. Dept. Human Resources State of N.C., Raleigh, 1980, Charlotte AHEC Resource Group, 1981-82; chairperson nursing adv. com. Central Piedmont Community Coll., Charlotte, 1976-83, Deans and Dirs. Nursing, Charlotte AHEC, 1982-85. Recipient Women's Club scholarship Aliquippa Women's Club, 1956. Mem. Nat. League Nursing, Am. Nurses Assn., Am. Soc. Hosp. Nursing Service Adminstrs., N.C. Soc. Nursing Services Adminstrs., Student Nurse Assn., Sigma Theta Tau, Alpha Lambda Delta. Club: Women's Exec. Office: Charlotte Meml Hosp and Med Ctr PO Box 32861 Charlotte NC 28232

KOTLER, NANCY KELLUM, lawyer; b. Boston, Mar. 27, 1936; s. Ralph and Ethel (Sandler) Kellum; m. Philip Kotler, Jan. 30, 1955; children—Amy, Melissa, Jessica. Student, Radcliffe Coll., 1953-55; B.A., U. Chgo., 1958; M.A., Northwestern U., Evanston, Ill., 1959; J.D., Loyola U.-Chgo., 1977. Bar: Ill. 1977. Instr. English, U. Ill.-Chgo., 1961-62; instr. English and linguistics Northwestern U., Chgo., 1962-68; instr. English, Nat. Coll. Edn., Evanston, Ill., 1970-71; instr. legal writing Kent Coll. Law, Chgo., 1979-80; assoc. Lurie, Sklar & Simon Ltd., Chgo., 1982—. Woodrow Wilson Fellow, 1958. Mem. Chgo. Bar Assn., ABA.

KOTOWSKI, CHRISTINE ANNE, registered nurse; b. Buffalo, Feb. 8, 1947; d. Leonard Michael and Irene (Jedrzejewski) Zmozynski; m. David M. Kotowski, Oct. 26, 1968; children—Jeffrey, Jennifer, Kenneth, Gregory. B.S. in Nursing Cum Laude, Daemen Coll., N.Y., 1983. Registered profl. nurse N.Y. Nurse's asst. St. Joseph Inter-Community Hosp., Cheektowaga, N.Y., 1978-80; camp nurse Jewish Ctr., Greater Buffalo, Amherst, 1981; charge nurse Williamsville Suburban Nursing Home, N.Y., 1981, day supr., 1982, asst. dir. nursing, 1982-84; nurse cons. Brown, Kelly, Turner, Hassett & Leach, Buffalo, 1984—; cons. and lectr. in field. Pre-Cana sponsor Our Lady of Blessed Sacrament Ch., Depew, N.Y., 1985-86. Mem. Nat. Assn. Female Execs., Profl. Nurses Assn. Western N.Y., Western N.Y. Paralegal Assn., Delta Epsilon Sigma. Republican. Roman Catholic. Club: St. Mary's High Sch. Athletic (Lancaster). Avocations: Choir; church projects; tennis; little league baseball; reading. Office: Brown Kelly Turner Hassett & Leach 290 Main St Buffalo NY 14202

KOTUK, ANDREA MIKOTAJUK, public relations firm executive; b. New Brunswick, N.J., Oct. 19, 1948; d. Michael and Julia Dorothy (Muka) Mikotajuk. B.A., Douglass Coll., Rutgers U., 1970. Pub. relations asst. Wall St. Jour. Newspaper Fund, Princeton, N.J., 1970; editorial asst. Redbook mag., N.Y.C., 1970-71; asst. pub. relations dir. Children's Aid Soc., N.Y.C., 1971-75; assoc. pub. relations dir. Planned Parenthood, N.Y.C., 1975-80; pres. Andrea & Assocs., N.Y.C., 1980—. Writer, publicist ads, newsmags., healthcare corps., for non-profit agys.; contbg. editor Arts Mag., 1970-75. Mem. Healthcare Businesswomen's Assn. (writer 1982—), Nat. Assn. Female Execs. Office: Andrea & Assocs 396 Broadway New York NY 10013

KOUBA, LISA MARCO, lawyer; b. Chgo., July 1, 1957; d. Edward Samuel and Phyllis LaVergne (Pincus) Marco; m. Kenneth Edward Kouba, Sept. 24, 1983. B.A. with honors, U. Ill., 1978; J.D. cum laude, Loyola U., Chgo., 1981. Bar: Ill. 1981, U.S. Ct. Appeals (7th cir.) 1981, U.S. Ct. Appeals (6th, 8th and 10th cirs.) 1982, U.S. Supreme Ct. 1984. Assoc. Clausen, Miller, Gorman, Caffrey & Witous, P.C., Chgo., 1981—. Editor Loyola Law Jour., 1981. Mem. Ct. Jesters improvisational group, Chgo., 1982—. Judge John C. Hayes scholar Loyola U., 1981. Mem. ABA, Chgo. Bar Assn. (co-chmn. young lawyers sect. 1982-83, 86-87), Phi Kappa Phi, Alpha Lambda Delta. Office: Clausen Miller Gorman Caffrey & Witous PC 5400 Sears Tower Chicago IL 60606

KOUKOL, SUSAN MARIE, dietitian, marketing executive; b. Chgo., Dec. 26, 1953; d. Earl James and Helen Lillian (Beckstrom) K. B.S., Bradley U., 1975; M.S., No. Ill. U., 1976; M.B.A., Loyola U., Chgo., 1986. Diet therapist Kishwaukee Hosp., De Kalb Ill., 1976; clin. dietitian Palos Hosp., Palos Heights, Ill., 1977-79; mini course instr. DePaul U., Chgo., 1980-82; nutrition cons. Carsten's Health Systems, Chgo., 1983-85; chief dietitian St. Joseph Hosp., Chgo., 1979-86; mktg. mgr. Ekco Products, Wheeling, Ill., 1986—. Editor: Eat Well Guide to Good Dining in Chicago, 1983. Bike-A-Thon chmn. Am. Diabetes Assn., Evanston Route, 1981. Mem. Am. Dietetic Assn. (young dietitian of yr. award 1981), Ill. Dietetic Assn., Chgo. Heart Assn. (Eat Well Tag chmn. 1983-84), Chgo. Dietetic Assn. (pres. 1982-83, historian 1984, legis. chmn. 1983-84), Dietitians in Bus. and Industry (pres.-elect Ill. chpt.), Kappa Omicron Phi, Sigma Kappa. Office: St Joseph Hosp 2900 N Lake Shore Dr Chicago IL 60657

KOVACEVICH, SHIRLEY LAVERNA, drilling company executive; b. Monahans, Tex., Feb. 9, 1939; d. Chester Arthur and Flossie Irene (Collum) Redman; m. Thomas Dale Kovacevich, Nov. 3, 1978; m. David Randal Best, Feb. 1, 1959 (div. June 1972); children—Sherrie Lynn, Jane Leslie. A.A., Ventura Jr. Coll., 1970; B.A., Calif. State Coll.-Fresno, 1974. Co-owner Pyramid Drilling Co., Inc., Manchester, Ky., 1980—; owner Spas & More, Cottonwood, Ariz., 1984—; owner, pub. The View newspaper, Cottonwood, 1985—. Recipient hon. service award YMCA, 1970, Ventura Sch. Dist., 1971. Mem. PTA (hon. life mem.). Republican. Methodist. Lodge: Women of the Moose. Avocation: Single engine pilot; artist.

KOVACHEVICH, ELIZABETH ANNE, federal court judge; b. Dec. 14, 1936; d. Daniel and Emilie Mary K. B.B.A., U. Miami, 1958; J.D., Stetson U., 1961. Assoc. firm DiVito & Speer, 1961-62; individual practice law, St. Petersburg, Fla., 1962-73; circuit judge 6th Fla. Jud. Circuit, 1973-82; judge Middle Fla. dist. U.S. Dist. Ct., Orlando, 1982—. Recipient Woman of Yr. award Fla. Fedn. Bus. and Profl. Women, 1981. Mem. ABA, Fla. Bar Assn., St. Petersburg Bar Assn., Pinellas County Bar Assn., Am. Judicature Soc., Assn. Trial Lawyers Am. Office: 635 US Courthouse 80 N Hughey Ave Orlando FL 32801*

KOVACS, HANNA NAGY, chemist; b. Szeged, Hungary, Oct. 31, 1919; came to U.S., 1957, naturalized, 1963; d. Antal and Ilona (Hodi) Nagy; Ph.D. in Chemistry, U. Szeged, 1945; m. Joseph Kovacs, July 1, 1950; children—Andrea Kovacs-Loomis, Joseph Antal. Instr. chemistry U. Szeged, 1944-46, research chemist Inst. Physiology, 1946-50; instr. Inst. Organic Chemistry, U. Budapest (Hungary), 1950-56; research asso. Inst. Bacteriology, U. Basel (Switzerland), 1957, Wayne State U., 1958, Detroit Inst. Cancer Research, 1958-59, St. John's U., Jamaica, N.Y., 1959-63; research chemist Naval Applied Sci. Lab., 1963-70; clin. chemist Mt. Sinai Hosp., N.Y.C., 1970—. NIH grantee, 1961-63. Mem. N.Y. Acad. Scis., Am. Assn. Clin. Chemistry, Am. Chem. Soc., Sigma Xi. Research, 27 publs. on peptides, polymers, heterocylic and clin. chemistry. Office: Mt Sinai Hosp 5th Ave and 100th St New York NY 10029

KOVALIC, JOAN MARIE, lawyer; b. Pitts., Dec. 27, 1948; d. Francis Bernard and Margaret Dolores (Poyma) Kovalic; B.A., Carnegie Mellon U., 1970, M.S., 1972; J.D., George Washington U., 1979; m. Keith Earl Bernard, May 22, 1982. Bar: Pa. 1979, D.C. 1980. Water resources analyst Com. Environment and Public Works, U.S. Senate, Washington, 1971; manpower policy analyst Office Asst. Sec. for Policy and Evaluation, U.S. Dept. of Labor, 1972-73; profl. staff mem. for water resources Com. Public Works and Transp., U.S. Ho. of Reps., 1973-78, asst. counsel for water and environ., 1979-80; dep. dir. Office Water Program Ops., U.S. EPA, 1980-82; asso. firm Taft, Steffinius and Hollister, Washington, 1982-85; gen. counsel, v.p. Weston, Inc., Washington, 1985—; exec. dir., gen. counsel Interstate Conf. Water Problems, 1982—; gen. counsel, sec. Nat. Water Alliance, 1983—. Mem. Am. Bar Assn., Pa. Bar Assn., D.C. Bar Assn., Women's Bar Assn., Water Pollution Control Fedn., Am. Public Works Assn., Phi Kappa Phi, Phi Alpha Delta. Office: 2300 M St NW Suite 800 Washington DC 20037

KOVALSKY, MARY ELLEN, lawyer; b. S.I., N.Y., Dec. 20, 1952; d. Michael and Jenny Ellen (Van Reyen) K.; m. Reid George Kennedy, Oct. 10, 1981; 1 dau., Alexandra Kovalsky Kennedy. B.A. in Polit. Sci., Pa. State U., 1974, B.A. in History, 1974; J.D., Woodrow Wilson Sch. Law, 1979. Bar: Ga. 1981. Paralegal, Law Offices of Edwin Marger, Atlanta, 1975-76, Garcia & Kennedy, Atlanta, 1976-78; paralegal Kennedy & Kennedy, Marietta, Ga., 1978-81, assoc., 1981—. Vol. Legal Aid Assn., Marietta, 1982; counsel Homeowners' Assn., Marietta, 1983—; active local polit. campaign, Cobb County, Ga., 1978. Mem. ABA, State Bar Ga., Assn. Trial Lawyers Am. Republican. Episcopalian. Office: Kennedy & Kennedy 1495 Powers Ferry Rd Marietta GA 30067

KOVELESKI, KATHRYN DELANE, educator; b. Detroit, Aug. 12, 1925; d. Edward Albert Vogt and Delane (Bender) Vogt; B.A., Olivet (Mich.) Coll., 1947; M.A., Wayne State U., Detroit, 1955; m. Casper Koveleski, July 18, 1952; children—Martha, Ann. Tchr. schs. in Mich., 1947—; tchr. Garden City Schs., 1955-56, 59—, resource and learning disabilities tchr., 1970—. Mem. PTA, NEA, Mich. Edn. Assn., Garden City Edn. Assn., Bus. and Profl. Women (2d v.p. Garden City 1979-80, 1st v.p. 1981-82, pres. 1982-83). Congregationalist. Clubs: Wayne Lit. (past pres., past parliamentarian, v.p. 1984-86), Sch. Masters Bowling League (v.p. 1984-85, 85-86), Odd Couples Bowling League (pres. 1982-83). Office: 33411 Marquette St Garden City MI 48135

KOVEN, JOAN FOLLIN HUGHES, designer, special events administrator; b. Washington, Nov. 9, 1937; d. John Rodgers and Viola Brockett (Pugh) Hughes; B.S., W.Va. U., 1959; postgrad. Scarritt Coll., 1959, U. Salisbury (Zimbabwe), 1961, Sorbonne, 1962, 63, Am. U., 1973, George Washington U., 1979; m. Ronald Pierre E. Koven, Mar. 29, 1965 (div. 1977); children—Michele Elise Josette, Martine Sarah Aimee. Tchr., dir. home econs. dept., art dept., library Old Umtali Schs., Zimbabwe, 1960-62; adolescent counselor, Dreux High Sch., France, 1962-65; freelance market researcher, Paris, 1965-66; dir. student recreation center, Dreux, 1966; v.p. Koven Freres jewelry, N.Y.C., 1971-75; designer, fabricator jewelry, Washington, 1977—; exec. asst. in spl. events, adminstrv. mgmt. to M.B. Patterson, Washington, 1976—. Mem. zoning comm. Palisades Citizens Assn., 1974; mem. commn. on missions Met. Meml. Methodist Ch., 1984; mem. adv. council Calvert Marine Mus., 1983-84; bd. dirs. Friends of Patterson Park; tech. planning com., mem. adv. council J. Patterson Hist. Park and Mus.; bd. dirs. MARPAT Found.; mem. Earthwatch Research Team, Fiji, 1984, U. Calif. research project, Fiji, 1986. Kroger scholar, 1955; cert. scuba diver. Mem. Am. Malacological Union, Conchologists Am., Hawaiian Shell Club, Omicron Nu, Phi Upsilon Omicron. Club: Nat. Capital Shell. Home: 4812 V St Washington DC 20007

KOWALCZEWSKI, DOREEN MARY THURLOW, communications company executive; b. London, May 5, 1926; came to U.S., 1957, naturalized, 1974; d. George Henry and Jessie Alice (Gray) Thurlow; B.A., Clarke Coll., 1947; postgrad. Wayne State U., 1959-62, Roosevelt U., 1968; m. Witold Dionizy Kowalczewski, July 26, 1946; children—Christina Julianna, Janet Alice, Stephen Robin. Agy. supr. MONY, N.Y.C., 1963-67; office mgr. J.B. Carroll Co., Chgo., 1967-68; mng. editor Sawyer Coll. Bus., Evanston, Ill., 1968-71; mgr. policyholder service CNA, Chgo., 1971-73; EDP coordinator Canteen Corp., Chgo., 1973-75; mgr. documentation and standards LRSP, Chgo., 1975-77; data network mgr. Computerized Agy. Mgmt. Info. Services, Chgo., 1977—; founder, chmn. Tekman Assos., 1982—. Pres., Univ. Park Assn., 1980-85. Mem. Nat. Assn. Female Execs., Network Users Assn. (dir. 1985-87), Chgo. Orgn. Data Processing Educators, Women in Mgmt., Mensa. Home: 3712 Madison Ave Brookfield IL 60513

KOZA, JOAN LORRAINE, fabric mfg. co. exec.; b. Berwyn, Ill., Apr. 28, 1941; d. Frank Louis and Lorraine Frances (Thomas) K.; B.S. in Communications, U. Ill., 1963. Office mgr. Dwan Med. Center, Summit, Ill., 1959-64; law office mgr. firm Gordon, Reicin & West, Chgo., 1964-73; sales mgr. Ambassador Hotels, Chgo., 1973-76; v.p. sales and mktg. M. Putterman & Co., Inc., indsl. and recreational fabrics, Chgo., 1976—; owner, mgr. JK Advt., 1977—; pres. Chgo. Legal Secs. Assn., 1970-72; v.p. Ill. Assn. Legal Secs., 1970-73. Pres., chmn. bd. Children's Research Found., 1963-66. Named Chgo. Legal Sec. of Yr., 1972, Ill. Legal Sec. of Yr., 1972. Mem. Alpha Lambda Delta, Theta Sigma Pi. Roman Catholic. Home: 546 Banyon Ln LaGrange IL 60525 Office: 4834 S Oakley Pl Chicago IL 60609

KOZAC, KAREN, lawyer; b. N.Y.C., Apr. 12, 1950; d. Harry Arthur and Jeanne (Fox) K.; m. Allen Gary Reiter, Sept. 16, 1979. B.A., U. Pa., 1971; J.D., Bklyn. Law Sch., 1978. Bar: N.Y. 1979, U.S. Dist. Ct. (so. and ea. dists.) N.Y. 1979, U.S. Supreme Ct. 1982. Asst. dist. atty. New York County, 1978-81; assoc. Halperin Shivitz Eisenberg Schneider & Greenawalt, N.Y.C., 1981-83; staff atty. State Commn. Jud. Conduct, N.Y.C., 1984—. Mem. ABA, N.Y. State Bar Assn., Assn. Bar City N.Y., N.Y. Women's Bar Assn. Home: 1641 3d Ave New York NY 10128 Office: State Commn Jud Conduct 801 2d Ave New York NY 10017

KOZAR, ERIKA MARIE, insurance company official; b. Great Lakes, Ill., Apr. 28, 1951; d. Walter Elmer and Erika Elizabeth (Krebs) Schroeder; m. Thomas Joseph Kozar, May 9, 1970; 1 son, Thomas Joseph. Cert. ins. counselor, profl. ins. woman. With Liberty Mut., Red Bank, N.J., 1969-70; rep. account service Silberman-Braun, Oakhurst, N.J., 1970-72; mgr. personal lines H. Wm. Mullaney, Oakhurst, N.J., 1974-78; account exec. Meeker-Sharkey-Moffatt, Sea Girt, N.J., 1978—, br. mgr., 1979-81. Mem. Ins. Women Monmouth County (past sec., v.p., pres.), Ind. Ins. Agts. Republican. Roman Catholic. Home: 418 Crestview Terr Brick Town NJ 08723 Office: Meeker-Sharkey-Moffatt 21 Commerce Dr Cranford NJ 07716

KOZAR, JENNIFER LEA, osteopathic physician; b. Mexia, Tex., Mar. 10, 1948; d. James Marlin and Betty Jo (Long) Wrenn; m. Raymond Davis Brendle, Nov. 8, 1968 (div. 1980); m. Bradley Kenneth Kozar, June 19, 1982. B.A., Austin Coll., 1975, D.O., Kirksville Coll. Osteo. Medicine, Mo., 1980. Intern Okla. Osteo. Hosp., Tulsa, 1980-81; gen. practice osteo. medicine, Westside Clinic, Mount Pleasant, Mich., 1981—; chmn. family practice dept., chief staff, trustee Central Mich. Community Hosp. Bd. dirs. Sexual Assault Task Force, Mount Pleasant, 1983-85; physician advisor Hospice Central Mich., Mount Pleasant, 1984-85. Mem. Am. Osteo. Assn., Mich. Assn. Osteo. Physicians and Surgeons, Mich. State Med. Soc., Mount Pleasant C. of C., Delta Omega. Republican. Episcopalian. Lodge: Zonta. Avocations: travel; swimming. Home: 11705 Gillette St Mount Pleasant MI 48858

KOZLOFF, JUDITH BONNIE, lawyer; b. St. Louis, Mar. 4, 1926; d. Isador and Ruth (Gould) Friedman; B.S., Northwestern U., 1947; J.D., U. Denver, 1968; m. Lloyd M. Kozloff, June 16, 1947; children—James S., Daniel I., Joseph H., Sarah R. Law clk. Mr. Justice Day, Colo. Supreme Ct., Denver, 1969-70; admitted to Colo. bar, 1969, Calif. bar, 1981; asso. Holland & Hart, Denver, 1970-73; sec., gen. counsel Affiliated Bankshares Colo., Boulder, 1973-78; atty. Mountain States Tel.&Tel. Co., Denver, 1979-80, Pacific Bell, San Francisco, 1981—. Recipient award Pacific Telephone Employees for Women's Affirmative Action, 1981. Mem. Colo. Bar, Calif. Bar Assn., San Francisco Bar Assn. Office: 1 Montgomery St San Francisco CA 94104

KOZMINSKY, ELLEN CLARE, lawyer; b. Bklyn., Nov. 19, 1951; d. Milton and Gertrude (Schnipper) K. B.A. magna cum laude, SUNY-Stony Brook, 1973; J.D. cum laude, New Eng. Sch. Law, 1976. Bar: Mass. 1977, N.Y. 1977; assoc. Erdheim, Shalleck & Frank, N.Y.C., 1977-78, Stephen Gassman, Garden City, N.Y., 1978-79, Mitchell Salem Fisher & Kemper, N.Y.C., 1979-81, Lans, Feinberg & Cohen, 1981-82; house counsel McMahan, Brafman, Morgan & Co., 1982—. Author and mem. editorial bd.: Family Law Practice, A Systems Manual, 1982. Chmn. spl. events, mem. planning bd. Havurah affiliates Sutton Place Synagogue, 1983—; mem. exec. com., chmn. legal com. 24035 Tenant's Assn., 1982—; bd. dirs., 1st v.p. 24035 Owners Corp., 1984—. Lic. real estate broker, N.Y. Mem. ABA, N.Y. State Bar Assn., Assn. Bar City of N.Y., Nassau County Bar Assn. Office: McMahan Brafman Morgan & Co 40 Wall St New York NY 10005

KRA, PAULINE SKORNICKI, French educator; b. Lodz, Poland, July 30, 1934; came to U.S., 1950, naturalized, 1955; d. Edward and Nathalie Skornicki; student Radcliffe Coll., 1951-53; B.A., Barnard Coll., 1955; M.A., Columbia U., 1963, Ph.D., 1968; m. Leo Dietrich Kra, Mar. 10, 1955; children—David Theodore, Andrew Jason. Lectr., Queens Coll., City U. N.Y., 1964-65; asst. prof. French, Yeshiva U., N.Y.C., 1968-74, assoc. prof. French, 1974-82, prof., 1982—. Mem. MLA, Am. Assn. Tchrs. French, Am. Soc. 18th Century Studies, Société française d'étude du XVIII siècle, Assn. for Computers and Humanities, Assn. for Literary and Linguistic Computing, Phi Beta Kappa. Club: Radcliffe. Author: Religion in Montesquieu's Lettres persanes, 1970; contbr. articles to profl. jours. Home: 109-14 Ascan Ave Forest Hills NY 11375 Office: 500 W 185 St New York NY 10033

KRACH, MARILYN JEAN, airline executive; b. Howell, Mich., Nov. 7, 1943; d. Ervan Robert and Virginia (Harter) Donahoe; married; children—Heidi Virginia, Frederick William Morton, Hansel Clarence. B.A., Spring Arbor Coll., Mich., 1965; M.S., Ind. U., 1971. Elem. sch. tchr. Winfield Twp., Lake County, Ind., 1965-68, Lake Ridge Schs., Lake County, Ind., 1968-69; elem. asst. prin. Lake Ridge Schs., Lake County, 1969-71; pres. ACE Air Cargo Express, Cleve., 1976—. Pres., Montessori Assn., Berea, Ohio, 1978-80; v.p. Middleburg Heights PTA, Ohio, 1981-82. Republican. Lutheran. Avocations: boating, singing, cooking. Home: 15093 Pine Valley Trail Middleburg Heights OH 44130 Office: ACE Air Cargo Express Inc 6200 Riverside Dr Cleveland OH 44135

KRACOFF, ELLEN KAREN, lawyer; b. N.Y.C., May 22, 1950; d. Beatrice (Kaplan) Newman; m. Gordon H. Kracoff, Mar 28, 1969; 1 child, Mark A. B.S. magna cum laude, Barry Coll., 1973; M.S., Fla. Internat. U., 1977; J.D., Nova U., 1980. Bar: Fla. 1981, U.S. Dist. Ct. (so. dist.) Fla. 1981, U.S. Ct. Appeals (5th and 11th dists.) 1982. Registered securities rep., mortgage broker. Tchr. Madonna Acad., Hollywood, Fla., 1974-78; legal clk., 1978-81; assoc. firm

Lawrence Bunin, P.A., Hollywood, 1981-84; ptnr. firm Berman, Kracoff and Sherman, 1985—, Pioneer Diversified Investments, Inc., 1985-86. Staff Law Jour., Nova U., 1978-80; contbr. article. Recipient John F. Kennedy Community Service award Miami-Dade Community Coll., 1971. Mem. ABA, Fla. Bar Assn., Am. Home Econs. Assn. (adv. bd. 1972-73), Attys. Title Ins. Fla., Kappa Omicron Phi, Delta Epsilon Sigma. Republican. Jewish. Home: 5318 SW 86th Way Cooper City FL 33328 Office: 2000 W Commercial Blvd Suite 133 Fort Lauderdale FL 33309

KRADAS, MELISSA ANN, management development consultant; b. Newark, Dec. 20, 1953; d. William Daniel and Gloria (Russomanno) Bonser; m. Michael Joseph Kradas, June 21, 1975; 1 dau., Erica Autumn. B.A., Conn. Coll., 1975. Substitute tchr. Bds. Edn., Nutley and Wayne, N.J., 1975; group claims examiner Mutual Benefit Life Ins. Co., Newark, 1976-77; tng. and procedures asst., 1977, tng. and procedures specialist, 1977-78; sr. instr. Union Trust Co., Stamford, Conn., 1978-82; tng. coordinator Hewitt Meml. Hosp., Shelton, Conn., 1982-85; career devel. speaker Kelly Services, Inc., New Haven, 1980, Conn. Coll. placement dept., New London, 1982; mem. computer based tng. panel Talmis, Inc., Oak Park, Ill., 1983—. Mem. Am. Soc. Tng. and Devel. (co-treas. So. Conn. chpt. 1980, mem. authorization com. 1983—, sr. trainer caucus, 1983—), Conn. Hosp. Assn. (mem. educator's group 1982—), Lakewood Research Tng. Group. Democrat. Home: 269 Sherwood Pl Stratford CT 06497

KRADITOR, AILEEN S., historian; b. Bklyn., Apr. 12, 1928; d. Abraham and Henrietta K.; B.A., Bklyn. Coll., 1950; M.A., Columbia U., 1951, Ph.D., 1962. Instr., R.I. Coll., Providence, 1962-63, asst. prof., 1963-67; vis. prof. history Sir George Williams U., Montreal, Que., Can., 1968-69; prof. history Boston U., 1973-80, prof. emerita, 1980—. Recipient Ansley award Columbia U., 1963; Nat. Endowment Humanities fellow, 1975-76; Guggenheim fellow, 1976-77; Radcliffe Inst. fellow, 1975-76. Mem. Orgn. Am. Historians, Soc. Am. Historians. Republican. Jewish. Author: The Ideas of the Woman Suffrage Movement, 1890-1917, 1965; Up from the Pedestal, 1968; Means and Ends in American Abolitionism, 1834-1850, 1969; The Radical Persuasion, 1890-1917, 1981. Home: 117 Brook St Wellesley MA 02181

KRAEMER, JEAN ANN, legislative agent; b. Elizabeth, N.J., Oct. 23, 1940; d. Benson and Edith Carolyn (Krouse) Rosenberg; m. Waldron Kraemer, June 17, 1962; children—Adam, Elise. B.A., Wellesley Coll., Mass., 1962. Research chemist Merck & Co., Rahway, N.J., 1962-65; dir. govtl. affairs Home Health Agy. Assembly of N.J., Princeton, 1978—. Co-chmn. Columbia High Sch. Fgn. Exchange Com., Maplewood, N.J., 1982—; bd. dirs. LWV, Maplewood, 1982-83; mem. nat. domestic affairs com. Am. Jewish Com., N.Y.C., 1974-84, co-chmn. annual dinner, 1975-77; bd. dirs. family advocacy com. Jewish Counseling and Service Agy., 1979—; alumna rep. Wellesley Coll., 1980—; organizer Maplewood Anti-Vandalism Campaign, 1975; v.p. South Orange-Maplewood Pub. Edn. Com., 1975-76; pres. Jefferson Sch. PTA, 1974-75; coordinator events Del Tufo for Gov. Campaign, 1984, Degnan for Gov. Campaign, 1981; Maplewood chmn. Shapiro for County Exec., 1978; dir. of speakers Bureau Essex County Byrne for Gov., 1977; fund raising coordinator state staff, Jordon for Gov., 1977; Democratic candidate for Maplewood Township Com., 1976. Jewish. Avocations: travel; sailing; swimming. Home and Office: 5 Euclid Ave Maplewood NJ 07040

KRAEMER, PHYLLIS FERSTER, software company executive; b. Newark, Apr. 15, 1933; d. Charles and Blanche (Tropp) Ferster; m. Paul William Kraemer, Dec. 25, 1952; children—David, Beth, Samuel. B.A., Barnard Coll., 1954; postgrad. Newark State Tchrs. Coll., 1962-64. Exec. tng. Bambergers, Newark, 1954-55; tchr. Normandy Park Sch., Morris Township, N.J., 1964-72; exec. AO2 Med., Dania, Fla., 1972-79; pres. AMBI Med. Mgmt. Systems, Los Angeles, 1979—; lectr. in field. Democrat. Jewish. Avocations: Music; art; interior design; philanthropy; travel. Office: AMBI 1202 Olympic Blvd Santa Monica CA 90404

KRAETZER, MARY C., sociologist, educator, author, consultant; b. N.Y.C., Sept. 12, 1943; d. Kenneth G. and Adele L. Kraetzer. A.B., Coll. New Rochelle, 1965; M.A., Fordham U., 1967, Ph.D., 1975. Instr. Mercy Coll., Dobbs Ferry, N.Y., 1969-70, asst. prof., 1970-75, assoc. prof., 1975-79, prof., 1979—; research asst. Fordham U., Bronx, N.Y., 1965-67, teaching asst., 1967-68, teaching fellow, 1968-69, adj. instr., 1971-75, adj. asst. prof., 1975-76; adj. assoc. prof. L.I. U. Grad. Br. Campus Mercy Coll., 1976-79, adj. prof., 1979-81, coordinator M.S. in Community Health Program, 1976-81; research cons. elem. schoolbooks Nat. Council of Chs./Church Women United Task Force on Global Consciousness, N.Y.C., 1971; mem. adv. com. edn. and society div. Nat. Council Chs., 1975-78; mem. evaluation team Middle States Assn. Colls. and Secondary Schs. Commn. on Higher Edn., Monmouth, N.J., 1976. Contbr. chpts. to books, articles to profl. jours. Recipient citation Am. Men and Women of Sci., 1978; Bd. Regents scholar, 1961-65, Fordham U. scholar, 1965-68; Fordham U. fellow, 1968-69; grantee Mercy Coll., 1984, 85; NSF summer intern, 1967. Mem. Am. Sociol. Assn., Am. Pub. Health Assn. Office: Mercy Coll 555 Broadway Dobbs Ferry NY 10522

KRAFT, ELAINE JOY, corp. communications ofcl.; b. Seattle, Sept. 1, 1951; d. Harry J. and Leatrice M. (Hanan) K.; B.A., U. Wash., 1973; M.P.A., U. Puget Sound, 1979; m. Lee Somerstein, Aug. 2, 1980; children—Paul Kraft, Leslie Jo. Reporter, Jour. Am. Newspaper, Bellevue, Wash., 1972-76; editor Jour./Enterprise Newspapers, Wash. State, 1976; mem. staff Wash. Senate, 1976-78; mem. staff Wash. Ho. of Reps., 1978-82, public info. officer, 1976-80, mem. leadership staff, asst. to caucus chmn., 1980—; ptnr., pres. Media Kraft Communications; mgr. corp. info., advt. and mktg. communications Weyerhaeuser Co., 1982-85; dir. communications Weyerhaeuser Paper Co., 1985—. Publicity chmn. Am. Diabetes Assn. S.W. Wash., 1978—. Recipient state and nat. journalism design and advt. awards. Mem. Nat. Fedn. Press Women, Women in Communications, Wash. Press Assn. Home: 14329 SE 63d Bellevue WA 98006 Office: Weyerhauser Co Tacoma WA 98477

KRAFT, ELLEN J., public radio station executive; b. Queens, N.Y., Jan. 4, 1956; m. Gary Richard Caldwell, May 4, 1979. B.S., Va. Commonwealth U., 1977. News anchor Sta. WHPN-AM, Hyde Park, N.Y., 1977-78; news reporter Conn. Pub. Radio, Hartford, 1978-79, ops. dir., 1979-82; program mgr. Sta. WGBH, Boston, 1982-84, asst. radio mgr. programming, 1984—; adj. faculty U. Hartford, 1981-82. Producer radio programs Music from the Paradise Ghetto, 1978, Forum—Speaking Properly (Corp. Pub. Broadcasting Awards hon. mention 1979), Forum, 1979 (Conn. Edn. Assn. award 1979); assoc. producer radio program A Concert of Musicke, 1981 (Ohio State award 1981). Va. Assn. Broadcasters scholar Va. Commonwealth U., Richmond, 1973. Avocations: gardening; cooking. Home: 14 Salem St Cambridge MA 02118 Office: Sta WGBH 125 Western Ave Boston MA 02134

KRAFT-ALLEN, ADRIENNE DIANNE, social services administrator, psychotherapist; b. Denver, Dec. 28, 1946; d. Joseph Raymond and Mary Catherine (Bellm) Kraft; m. Dennis Allen, Nov., 1985 (civil ceremony), April, 1986 (blessing). B.A., San Francisco Coll. for Women, 1967; M.A., U. Chgo., 1970; cert. in theory and practice of psychotherapy of children Inst. Psychoanalysis, Chgo., 1978. Certified social worker. Psychiat. social worker Psychiat. Inst. of Cir. Ct. Cook County, Chgo., 1970-72; casework therapist, adoption coordinator supr., exec. dir. St. Mary's Services, Chgo., 1972—; pvt. practice psychotherapy, Chgo., 1974-83; workshop speaker Washington, Chgo., Los Angeles. Contbr. articles to profl. jours. Network coordinator Women in Charge Conf., Chgo., 1985; bd. dirs. Nat. Com. for Adoption, 1980—. Mem. Assn. Child Psychotherapists, Child Care Assn. Ill., Ill. Soc. Clin. Social Work., Female Execs. Am. Club: Executive (Chgo.).

KRAGULAC, OLGA GOLUBOVICH, interior designer; b. St. Louis, Nov. 27, 1937; d. Jovica Todor and Milka (Slijepcevich) Golubovich; A.A., U. Mo., 1958; cert. interior design UCLA, 1979. Interior designer William L. Pereira Assocs., Los Angeles, 1977-80; assoc. Reel/Grobman Assocs., Los Angeles, 1980-81; project mgr. Kaneko/Laff Assocs., Los Angeles, 1982; project mgr. Stuart Laff Assocs., Los Angeles, 1983-85; restaurateur The Edge, St. Louis, 1983-84; pvt. practice comml. interior design, Los Angeles, 1981—. Mem. invitation and ticket com. Calif. Chamber Symphony Soc., 1980-81; vol. Westside Rep. Council, Proposition 1, 1971; asst. inaugural presentation Mus. of Childhood, Los Angeles, 1985. Recipient Carole Eichen design award U. Calif., 1979. Mem. Am. Soc. Interior Designers, Inst. Bus. Designers, Phi Chi Theta, Beta Sigma Phi. Republican. Serbian Orthodox. Office and Home: 700 Levering No 4 Los Angeles CA 90024

KRAJICEK, MICHELE STEPHENS, interior designer; b. San Angelo, Tex., Oct. 1, 1944; d. Morris Glen and Martha Mai (Gill) Stephens; m. Wesley Dale Nelson, June 25, 1967 (div. 1976); m. Richard William Krajicek, Sept. 17, 1978. B.A. in Interior Design, Tex. Tech. U., 1966. Interior designer Evans Monical Inc., Houston, 1970-73, Ufer Nimmons Barbaria, Houston, 1974-77; space planner, designer Marathon Oil Co., Houston, 1977-78; owner, designer Michele Nelson Interiors, Houston, 1978-83; prin. owner, ptnr. Nelson Frey Assocs., Houston, 1983—. Mem. Republican Party Harris County, Houston, New Age Hospice, Houston, 1983, Planned Parenthood, 1983. Mem. AIA (Interior Architects), Delta Delta Delta. Episcopalian. Home: Nine Woods Edge Houston TX 77024 Office: Nelon Frey Assocs 1101 Post Oak Blvd Houston TX 77056

KRAKOWSKY-DAVIDSON, ZINA, restaurant executive; b. San Pedro, Calif., July 7, 1944; d. Henry Hyman and Frances (Kurtzman) Krakowsky; m. Mar. 18, 1984. A.A., Vallejo Jr. Coll., 1964; student U. Mo., Columbia, 1963, (scholar) San Francisco Acad. Art, 1964, Calif. Coll. Arts and Crafts, 1966. Grocery checker Safeway and Lucky Stores, Vallejo, Concord, Calif., 1964-66; owner feather flower bus., Tahoe, 1966-70; cashier, waitress, cook, cocktail waitress, mgr. various restaurants, Tahoe-Squaw Valley area, 1966-70; developer, owner, operator O'B's Board Restaurant, Truckee, Calif., 1970-80, C. B. White's Restaurant, Catering & Antiques, Truckee, 1979—. Chmn. Nevada County Historic Preservation Adv. Council. Mem. Truckee Downtown Mchts. Assn., Truckee Hist. Soc., Truckee-Donner C. of C. Democrat. Jewish. Home: 13059 Donner Pass Rd Donner Lake CA 95734 Office: PO Box 396 10292 Donner Pass Rd Truckee CA 95734

KRALJEVIC, SUSAN CURRY, editor, marketing consultant; b. Covington, Va., Oct. 6, 1946; d. Robert Wilton and Virginia Colaw Curry; student Concord Coll., 1964-67; B.S. in Clothing, Textiles, and Related Art (home econs. scholar), Va. Poly. Inst. and State U., 1969; m. Vladimir Kraljevic, Oct. 27, 1970; children—Vladimir Brando, Kristian Marko, Virginia Susanna. Merchandising/mktg. asst. Glamour mag., N.Y.C., 1969-71, mktg. editor, 1972, press editor 1973-76, pub. relations dir., 1976-78; publicity supr. Info. Center of Internat. Gold Corp., Ltd., N.Y.C., 1978-84; mktg. cons. precious jewelry, 1984—; assoc. editor Fashion Galleria mag., 1986—. Sec./treas. N.Y. Upbeat, 1974-76. Named Outstanding Alumna, Merchandising and Design Soc. of Va. Poly. Inst. and State U., 1982. Mem. Kappa Omicron Phi. Republican. Presbyterian. Contbg. editor Fodor's Mid-Atlantic, 1974, Aurum, 1981, 84. Home: 220 Highbrook Ave Pelham NY 10803 Office: 110 W 40th St Suite 1405 New York NY 10018

KRAM, SHIRLEY WOHL, federal court judge; b. N.Y.C., 1922. Student Hunter Coll., CCNY; LL.B., Bklyn. Law Sch., 1950. Staff atty. Legal Aid Soc., 1951-53, 62-71; legal staff Simons & Hardy, 1954-55; individual practice, 1955-60; judge Family Ct., 1971-83; judge So. dist. N.Y., U.S. Dist. Ct., N.Y.C., 1983—; adj. prof. Baruch Coll., 1979-80. Author: (with Neil A. Frank) The Law of Child Custody - Development of the Substantive Law. Office: US Courthouse Foley Sq New York NY 10007*

KRAMER, BARBARA SUE, mfg. co. exec.; b. N.Y.C., June 15, 1941; d. Sidney I. and Belle Rose Kramer; B.A. in English Lit., Barnard Coll., 1963. Mem. advt. promotion staff McCall's Mag., N.Y.C., 1963-66; account exec. Peter Rothholz Assos., N.Y.C., 1969-72; pres. Bobbie Kramer Assos., N.Y.C., 1972-73; dir. public relations Stiefel/Raymond Advt., N.Y.C., 1974-81, Art Carved div. Lenox China Inc., N.Y.C., 1981—. Mem. LWV (chmn. Ga. chpt. 1967-68), Women in Communications. Club: Publicity (N.Y.). Home: 315 E 56th St New York NY 10022 Office: 450 W 33d St New York NY 10001

KRAMER, CECILE EDITH, librarian; b. N.Y.C., Jan. 6, 1927; d. Marcus and Henrietta (Marks) K.; B.S., CCNY, 1956, M.S. in Library Sci., Columbia U. 1960. Reference asst. Health Scis. Library, Columbia U. 1957-60, sr. reference asst., 1960-61, asst. librarian 1961-75; dir. Med. Library Northwestern U., Chgo., 1975—; instr. continuing edn. Med. Library Assn., 1966-75; instr. Grad. Sch. Library Sci., Rosary Coll., 1981—; lectr. in field. Mem. Med. Library Assn. (chmn. med. sch. libraries group 1975-76, editor News 1974-77), Assn. Acad. Health Scis. Library Dirs. Office: Northwestern N Med Library 303 E Chicago Ave Chicago IL 60611

KRAMER, JANE, author; b. Providence, Aug. 7, 1938; d. Louis Irving and Jessie (Shore) K.; m. Vincent Crapanzano, Apr. 30, 1967; 1 dau., Aleksandra. B.A., Vassar Coll., 1959; M.A., Columbia U., 1961. Cons. German Marshall Fund. Writer: The Morningsider, 1962, The Village Voice, 1963, New Yorker Mag. 1963—; books include Off Washington Square, 1963, Allen Ginsberg in America, 1969, Honor to the Bride, 1970, The Last Cowboy, 1978, Unsettling Europe, 1980. Recipient Am. Book award for nonfiction, 1981; Overseas Press Club Am. award, 1979; Front Page award, 1977; named Woman of Yr. Mademoiselle, 1968. Mem. Council Fng. Relations, Com. to Protect Journalists (dir.), PEN, Environ. Def. Fund, Authors Guild and League, Writers Guild, Nat. Book Critics Circle. Office: New Yorker 25 W 43d St New York NY 10036

KRAMER, JOAN LOUISE, photo agt.; b. Phila., Oct. 21, 1937; d. Samuel and Ida (Perchick) Shuster; student New Sch. Social Research; m. Erwin Kramer, Dec. 24, 1956; children—Ilene, Lee Mitchell. Corr. sec. Sterling Warner Co., N.Y.C., 1957-60; pres. Joan Kramer & Assocs. Inc., N.Y.C., 1971—. Mem. Soc. Photographer and Artist Reps., Am. Soc. Mag. Photographers, Am. Soc. Picture Profls. Office: 720 Fifth Ave New York NY 10019

KRAMER, JUDY CHARLENE, brake manufacturing company executive; b. Parsons, Kans., May 10, 1951; d. John William and Lela Mae (Cox) Tipping; m. David Lee Kramer, Jan. 13, 1973; children—Michael Scott, John Ross. Student Neosho County Jr. Coll. (Kans.), 1969-70; B.S. in Bus. Administrn., Kans. State U., 1972. Acct., Kretzmeier & McCammon, Iola, Kans., 1973-75; acct. Midland Brake, Inc. div. Echlin, Inc., Iola, 1975-81, acctg. mgr., 1981-82, controller, 1982—. Mem. AAUW (br. treas. 1978-81), St. Martin's Altar Soc. Roman Catholic. Home: Rural Route 1 Iola KS 66749 Office: Midland Brake Inc 2702 N State St Iola KS 66749

KRAMER, LYNNE ADAIR, lawyer; b. Oceanside, N.Y., June 25, 1952; d. Pau and Ruth (Kleiner) K.; m. Frederick Eisenbud, Aug. 29, 1976; children—Joshua Kramer-Eisenbud, Benjamin Kramer-Eisenbud. B.A., Smith Coll., 1973; J.D., Hofstra U., 1976. Bar: D.C. 1976, N.Y. 1977, Va. 1977; assoc. firm Thomas Stanton, Alexandria, Va., 1976-77, firm Dominic A. Barbara, Carle Place, N.Y., 1977-78; sole practice, Commack, N.Y., 1979—; lectr. Suffolk Acad. Law (N.Y.), 1981—; guest lectr. Hofstra U. Law, 1983-84, Toro Sch. Law, 1982-83. Trustee, Temple Beth David, 1981; legal adviser Human Rights Commn. and Women's Equal Rights Congress Com., 1982-84. Mem. Nassau/Suffolk Women's Bar Assn. (bd. dirs., chmn. judiciary 1982-83, sec. 1983-84, pres. 1984-85), Matrimonial Bar Assn. Suffolk (bd. dirs., treas. 1983-84), Assn. Trial Lawyers Am., ABA, N.Y. State Bar Assn., Suffolk County Bar Assn. (lawyers referral com. 1982-84, cts. com. 1983-84, fee disputes com. and judiciary com. 1985—), Nassau County Bar Assn., Womens's Bar Assn. State of N.Y. (bd. dirs. 1984-85, judiciary appeals panel 1984-85), Smith Coll. Club Suffolk County (pres. 1982-83). Republican. Jewish. Home: 7 Bradshaw Ln Fort Salonga NY 11768 Office: Lynne Adair Kramer 6165 Jericho Turnpike Commack NY 11725

KRAMER, MARCIA GAIL, journalist; b. Greenfield, Mass., Dec. 30, 1948; d. Louis Aaron and Blanche Shirley (Weiner) K.; m. Richard N. Runes. B.A. in Polit. Sci., Boston U., 1970. Reporter, Greenfield Recorder Gazette, 1969, N.Y. Daily News, 1970—; guest appearances various radio and TV programs; lectr. various colls. and univs., N.Y.C.; adj. prof. journalism Columbia U., 1980, N.Y.U., 1982-84. Mem. Gov.'s Adv. Com. on Drug Abuse, 1978. Recipient Public Service award Kings County Borough, 1974; Gold Typewriter award and Bobby Spellman Heart of N.Y. award N.Y. Press Club, 1979; Legis. Reform award Patrolman's Benevolent Assn., 1981; Ret. Detectives Ardee award, 1981, award Boy Scouts Am., 1983, By-Line award for deadline writing, 1984. Mem. N.Y. Press Women (v.p. 1977-78), N.Y. Press Club (fin. sec. 1979-80, 1st v.p. 1980-81, 84-85, 2d v.p. 1981-83, pres. 1985—). Office: NY Daily News 220 E 42d St New York NY 10017

KRAMER, MARGUERITE MOREAU, insurance company executive; b. Jeanerette, La., Aug. 22, 1916; d. Paul Edmund and Susan Mary (Walker) Moreau; m. Frank Lloyd Kramer; children—Suzanne Kramer Perret, Frank L., Karl Joseph. Student Tulane U., 1968. Mgr., Franklin C. of C., La., 1960-63; agt. N.Y. Life Ins., Franklin, 1963—. Govt. appted. mem. Tourist Promotion La., 1975-79; sec. Women's Leaders Round Table, N.Y.C., 1969; pres. St. Mary Parish Landmark Assn., La., 1963-65. Mem. Bus. and Profl. Women Franklin (Woman of Yr. 1959). Republican. Roman Catholic. Avocation: house restoration. Home: 221 Morris St PO Box 221 Franklin LA 70538

KRAMER, MARY LOU, graphics company executive; b. Dayton, Ohio, Dec. 14, 1929; d. Harry Clifford and Mildred Juanita (Hayes) Heider; m. John R. Kramer, Feb. 14, 1953; children—Kristine Marie, Karen Lee, Kathryn Louise, John R., Kelley Anne, Karol Lynn. Artist Stanley Greeting Card Co., Dayton, 1947-49; fashion artist The Home Store, Dayton, 1949-51; TV and film artist Swank Films, Dayton, 1951-54; free-lance comml. artist, Dayton, 1954-75; pres. Kramer Graphics, Dayton, 1975—. Recipient Library of Congress award, 1980; Quill award Internat. Assn. Bus. Communicators, 1984. Mem. Women in Communications (treas. Dayton 1984—), Exec. Women Internat. (charter mem.; publs. dir. Dayton chpt. 1985—), Art Ctr. Dayton, Dayton Advt. Club (Hermes award 1984), Assn. Female Execs. Roman Catholic. Club: Weaveweave (Dayton). Avocation: watercolorist. Office: Kramer Graphics Inc 3975 Rockfield Dr Dayton OH 45430

KRAMER, NORA, author, sculptor, book consultant; b. Pendleton, Eng.; d. Harris and Rachel (Wolf) Atkins; student Beaux Arts Inst., N.Y., 1920-21, Sch. Mus. Fine Arts, Boston, 1929-30, City Coll. N.Y., 1939-43, sculpture and fine arts workshops New Sch. for Social Research, 1970—; m. Sidney David Kramer, Oct. 27, 1917 (dec. June 1955); children—Karl Robert, Virginia Kramer Stein, Joan Kramer Stoliar. Cons. (under name of Eleanor Brent) The Little Bookshop, Macy's, N.Y., 1943-53; originator Little Bookshop Art Show Teas, 1947-53; creator The Bookplan, 1944, dir., 1944—; editorial cons. Scholastic's Arrow Book Club, 1958-75; leader juvenile writing workshop Colo. U., 1955; mem. Child Study Children's Book Commn., Bank Street Coll. Edn., 1934—, NCCJ, 1947—, English-Speaking Union Books-Across-the-Sea, 1953—; judge for Herald Tribune spring book festival, 1947, 53, Thomas Edison Awards Com., 1950, Boys Clubs Am., 1952, 54, 57, Scholastic Ann. Jr. Article Writing Awards, 1958—; sculpted works include portrait busts of children and adults, figures in round; exhibited in shows including Catharine Lorillard Wolfe Art Club Show, N.Y.C., 1974, 75, 76, 78, 79, 80, 81; represented in pvt. collections. Recipient award for Young Dreamer, 1975, award for After the Ball, 1979, award for Friendship, 1980. Mem. Woman's Nat. Book Assn. (past 1st v.p. and mem. bd.), Author's League Am., English-Speaking Union, Child Study Assn. Am. (children's book com. 1934—), Catharine Lorillard Wolfe Art Club. Author: Nora Kramer's Storybook for Threes and Fours, 1955; Nora Kramer's Storybook for Fives and Sixes, 1956; The Cozy Hour Storybook, 1960; The Arrow Book of Ghost Stories, 1960; The Grandma Moses Storybook, 1961; Princess Tales, 1971; Tricky Tales, 1970; The Ghostly Hand and Other Haunting Stories, 1972; co-author: (with Karl Robert Kramer) Coppercraft and Silver Made at Home, 1958, paperback edit., 1972. Editor-in-chief The Bookwoman, 1954-56. Editor: Grimms' Fairy Tales, 1962; (abridged editions) Swiss Family Robinson, 1960, Hans Brinker, 1967, Dracula, 1971, Ramona, 1972, Journey To The Center of The Earth, 1973. Address: 46 Jane St New York NY 10014

KRAMER, RUTH, accountant; b. N.Y.C., June 20, 1925; d. Isidore and Sarah (Heller) Kleiner; B.A., Bklyn. Coll., 1946; m. Paul Kramer, Oct. 27, 1946; children—Stephen David, Lynne Adair. Tchr. elem. sch. N.Y.C. Bd. Edn., 1946-50; acct. Lichtenstein & Kramer, N.Y.C., Lynbrook, N.Y., 1954; jr. partner Paul Kramer & Co., Lynbrook, 1954-56, partner, 1956-65, mng. partner, 1965—; cons. Nassau County (N.Y.) Dist. Attys. Office, 1956-65; expert witness acctg. matters Nassau County Grand Juries, 1956-65; mem. IRS liaison com. Bklyn. Dist., 1965-76; mem. N.Y. State Bd. for Pub. Accountancy, 1982—; dir. Flinch & Bruns Funeral Home, Inc. Troop leader Girl Scouts U.S.A., 1947-48; chmn. Tri-Town sect. Anti Defamation League, 1952-53; active Heart Fund; pres. Lynbrook Women's Republican Club, 1956-58; treas. Assembly Candidates Campaign Com., 1964; mem. Nassau County Fedn. Rep. Women, Syosset Woodbury Rep. Club. Named Woman in Acctg., local TV channel, 1974. Registered public acct., N.Y. Mem. Nat. Soc. Public Accts. (del.), Empire State Assn. Public Accts. (Meritorious Service award, 2d v.p., 1975-76, 1st v.p. 1977-78, pres. 1978-79, Pres.'s award, 2d past pres. exec. bd. 1979-80, 1st past pres. exec. bd. 1981-82, pres. Nassau County chpt. 1962, 63, 75, 76, state dir. 1980—, Woman of Year award 1982), Tax Inst. C.W. Post Coll., Acctg. Inst. C.W. Post Coll. Jewish. Clubs: Sisterhood North Shore Synagogue; Am. Jewish Congress, Lynbrook Pythian Sisters. (past chief). Home: 23 Hilltop Dr Syosset NY 11791 Office: 23 Hilltop Dr Syosset NY 11791

KRAMER, URSULA ANN, dialysis facility administrator; b. Aachen, W.Ger., May 12, 1932; came to U.S., 1949; d. Max and Elli Lowenstein Cohn; m. David Joseph Kramer, Mar. 1, 1953; children—Kathryn Kramer Wilson, Craig. Student Am. Inst., La Paz, Bolivia, 1949, Los Angeles City Coll., 1950-53. Office mgr., Warner Hirsch, 1949-51; with Bernard G. Ramos-Import/Export Firm, 1951-56; office mgr. Victor A. Valente Ins., 1958-63; medicare-med. specialist Continental Assurance Co., Los Angeles, 1966-72; with Mildred Silver-Renal Hygienics, Inc., Tarzana, Calif., 1972-81; adminstr. San Fernando-West Kidney Ctr., G & S Dialysis Assocs., Canoga Park, Calif., 1981—. Instrumental in passing resolution in Calif. Senate. Mem. Kidney Found. CNNT Calif., Calif. Dialysis Council (v.p.), Renal Adminstrs. Assn., Women in Mgmt., Exec. Women's Assn. Club: Soroptimist Internat. Avocations: music; reading; knitting. Home: 5559 Ostin Ave Woodland Hills CA 91367 Office: San Fernando West Kidney Ctr 7230 Medical Ctr Dr #101 Canoga Park CA 91307

KRAMER-HARVEY, SHARON, computer company manager, accountant; b. Los Angeles, Mar. 4, 1955; d. Jerold and Aida (Lewin) Kramer; m. Donald Aaron Harvey, June 26, 1981; 1 stepdau., Lisa N; 1 child, Aaron Turner. A.A. in Bus., Santa Monica Coll., 1974; B.S. in Acctg. and Mktg., Calif. State U.-Northridge, 1979; postgrad. Pepperdine U. Fin. analyst McCulloch Corp., Los Angeles, 1977-79; internat. fin. analyst Addressograph/Multigraph, Internat., Los Angeles, 1979-80; internat. fin. supr. Max Factor & Co., Los Angeles, 1980-81; regional fin. mgr. Computervision, Culver City, Calif., 1981—. Mem. Culver City C. of C. Democrat. Jewish. Office: Computervision Corp 300 Corp Pointe Culver City CA 90230

KRAMM, DEBORAH ANN, auditor; b. Pasadena, June 24, 1949; d. Donald F. and Mary (Roach) Coonan; m. Kenneth R. Kramm, Dec. 20, 1969; children—Deidre Lyn, Jonathan Russel. B.A., U. Calif.-Irvine, 1971; M.S., Mich. Tech. U., 1981. Math. asst. NASA-Jet Propulsion Lab., Pasadena, 1967-70; library asst. U. Calif. Irvine Library, 1967-71; research assoc. Mich. Tech. U. Animal Behavior Lab., Houghton, 1971-80; programmer/analyst Shell Oil Co., Houston, 1981-85, corp. auditor EDP, 1985—; chmn. bd. MMARK, Houston, 1983-85. Contbr. articles to profl. jours.; design/program application software: Shell Point-of-Sale Terminal, 1983-84 Co-leader Boy Scouts Am., Houston, 1981-83. AAUW scholar, 1980; Calif. State scholar, 1967-71. Mem. Nat. Assn. Female Execs., AAUW (pres. br. 1975-81). Club: Shell Data Processors. Home: 5814 Pinewilde Houston TX 77066 Office: Shell Oil Info Ctr 1500 Old Spanish Trail Houston TX 77225

KRAMPITZ, NORMA CYNTHIA, painter, weaver; b. Big Lake, Minn., June 8, 1911; s. August and Hilda Christina (Gunderson) Peterson; student Macalaster Coll., 1929-31, Western Res. U., 1952-56; m. Lester O. Krampitz, Feb. 21, 1932; 1 dau., Joyce R. Krampitz Hansen. One-man shows: Theatre Cleveland Inc., 1960, Western Res. Sch. Medicine, 1966; group shows include: Jewish Community Center, Cleve., 1963, 64, 66, 67, Cleve. Mus. Art, 1966, Masillon (O.) Mus. 1965, 68, Textile Arts Show, Cleve., 1968, 70. Pres. Western Reserve U. Med. Wives, Cleve., 1950-52; active Hearing and Speech Center, Cleve., 1958. Recipient William C. Grawer Artist award Western Res. U., 1965, Baldwin Purchase award for weaving Massilion Mus., 1968, painting and weaving awards Ohio Art Contest. Mem. Nat. League Am. Pen Women, Cleve. Mus. Art, Textile Arts Club, Am. Craft, Western Res. Hist. Soc., Nova, Orgn. Visual Arts. Democrat. Presbyterian. Home: 2476 Taylor Rd Cleveland Heights OH 44118

KRANITZKY, MARY LISA, auditor; b. Schenectady, N.Y., July 20, 1955; d. Charles William Kranitzky, and Shirley Ann (Thomas) Ballou. B.S. in Fin., U. Ala., 1982. Fin. specialist Gen. Elec. Co., Birmingham, Ala., 1981-83, supv. acctg. adminstrn., Atlanta, 1984-85, corp. auditor, Schenectady, 1985—. Bd. dirs. Southern Regional Opera, Birmingham, 1980—. Recipient Acad. Excellence medal Fin. Execs. Inst., 1982. Mem. Beta Gamma Sigma, Phi Kappa Phi, Omicron Delta Epsilon. Episcopalian. Avocations: music; water skiing;

reading. Home: 103 N College St #3E Schenectady NY 12305 Office: Gen Elec Co One River Rd Building 5-5E Schenectady NY 12345

KRANZ, CHERYL ELAINE, motivation company executive; b. Rochester, Minn., Nov. 2, 1945; d. Theodore Ludwig and Bernice Irene (Bishop) K. A.A., Rochester Jr. Coll., Minn., 1965; B.A., U. Minn., 1967. Dir. coordination Bus. Incentives, Edina, Minn., 1973-76; mgr. client services McRand Inc., Lake Forest, Ill., 1977-78; regional mgr. E.F. MacDonald, Plymouth, Minn., 1978-79, dir. travel ops., 1979-83, dir. sales adminstrn., 1983-84, v.p. ops. Carlson Mktg. Group, 1984—. Mem. Meeting Planners Internat., Soc. Incentive Travel Execs., Nat. Assn. Female Execs. Mem. Christian Ch. (Disciples of Christ). Avocations: catering; gourmet cooking. Office: Carlson Mktg Group Meetings Div 12755 Hwy 55 Plymouth MN 55441

KRASNOW, E. JUDITH LEVINE, mental health official; b. Stamford, Conn.; d. Harry Hirsh and Adele Rae (Steinhauer) Levine; A.B., Boston U., 1958; M.S., Sch. Social Work Simmons Coll., 1960; D.S.W., Cath. U. Am., 1969; m. Erwin G. Krasnow, Sept. 4, 1960; children—Michael Andrew, Catherine Beth. Caseworker Boston Children's Services Assn., 1960-61; psychiat. social worker, dep. dir. treatment unit Alexandria (Va.) Community Mental Health Center, 1962-69, dir. preventive services and tng., 1969-77, dir., 1978—; field instr. Cath. U., Howard U., George Washington U.; cons. various social agys. and schs.; examiner Va. Bd. Social Workers. Bd. dirs. Nat. Child Research Center, 1974-76; rep. Parents Assn. steering com. Sidwell Friends Sch., 1981-82, sec., 1984-86; mem. Social Welfare Adv. Com., U.S. Employment Service, 1966-68. NIMH tng. grantee in mental health, 1959-60. Mem. Nat. Assn. Social Workers (clin. register bd.), Acad. Cert. Social Workers, Am. Orthopsychiat. Assn., Mental Health Assn., Fedn. Clin. Social Workers, Nat. Council Community Mental Health Centers, Va. Assn. Mental Health Center Dirs., Mental Health Adminstrs. Assn. Editorial bd. Social Work Met. Washington, 1976-77; contbr. research articles to profl. publs. Home: 5604 Surrey St Chevy Chase MD 20815 Office: 206 N Washington St Alexandria VA 22314

KRAUK, ELSIE ALEXANDRIA, educator; b. N.Y.C., Oct. 28, 1919; d. Harry and Katherine Huczko Harasym; B.A., Hunter Coll., 1941; M.A., Tchrs. Coll., Columbia U., 1942; postgrad. Johns Hopkins U., 1949-56, Towson State U., 1949-50, U. Md., 1956-59; m. Pembroke Mitchell Krauk, July 18, 1943; 1 son, James Mitchell. Tchr. phys. edn. Thomas Johnson Elem. Sch., Balt., 1942-43; social caseworker Dept. Public Welfare, Balt., 1948-49; tchr. grade 4 and 5 Guilford Ave. Elem. Sch., Balt., 1949-52, Glenmount Elem. Sch., 1952-77, ret., 1977; tutor, vol. work, 1977—. Tchr. rep. exec. bd. PTA, 1956-58, 63-65, area tchr. representing Balt., 1961-63. Mem. Ret. Public Sch. Tchrs. Assn., Md. Ret. Tchrs. Assn., NEA. Home: 6216 Walther Ave Baltimore MD 21206

KRAUS, JOY ELAINE, respiratory therapist; b. Giddings, Tex., Mar. 11, 1957; d. Elvis William and Idell Amelia (Schoenberg) Kraus. A.A.S. in Respiratory Therapy, S.W. Tex. State U., 1980, B.S. in Health Professions, 1980. Registered respiratory therapist, cert. respiratory therapist, Tex. Staff respiratory therapist Brackenridge Hosp., Austin, 1980-81; supr. respiratory therapy Hermann Hosp., Houston, 1981-83; staff respiratory therapist St. Luke's Episcopal Hosp., Houston, 1983—. Mem. Am. Assn. for Respiratory Therapy, Tex. Soc. for Respiratory Therapy (sec.-treas. S. Tex. region 1983-84). Lutheran. Home: 7825 Corporate Dr Apt 907 Houston TX 77036 Office: St Lukes Episcopal Hosp Respiratory Therapy Tex Med Center Houston TX 77030

KRAUS, LILI, pianist, educator; b. Budapest, Mar. 4, 1908; d. Victor and Irene (Bak) Kraus; student of Zoltan Kodaly, Bela Bartok; student Royal Acad. Music, Budapest, 1915-22, tchrs. diploma, 1925; student of Steuermann, New Acad., Vienna, Austria, 1925-27, M.A., 1927; student Artur Schnabel, Berlin, 1930-34; Mus.D. (hon.), Chgo. Mus. Coll., Roosevelt U., 1969, Williams Coll., 1975; D.H.L. (hon.), Tex. Christian U., 1980; m. Otto Mandl, Oct. 31, 1930 (dec. Aug. 1956); children—Ruth Maria (Mrs. Fergus Pope), Michael Otto Patrick. Pianist with orchs. in Europe, 1926—, Dutch East Indies, 1940; formed Kraus-Goldberg duo with violinist Szymon Goldberg, 1930's; Japanese prisoner of war, 1941-45; pianist in Australia and N.Z., 1945—, Europe, N. and S. Am., Asia, 1949—; world tours, appearances with major orchs. and all major European music festivals, 1925—; gave concert in Eng.'s Canterbury Cathedral, 1st concert ever performed in Brasilia (Brazil); appeared with Salzburg Chamber Orch., Royal Moroccan Mozart Festival, orchestral concert honoring Bertrand Russell's 90th birthday, Royal Festival Hall, London; first to play all 25 Mozart piano concerti in N.Y., 1966-67; premiered newly-discovered Schubert Grazer Fantasy, CBS-TV, 1969; recorded all 25 Mozart piano concerti and complete Mozart piano sonatas for CBS; now recording complete Schubert piano repertoire; lectr. various univs., U.S. and Europe; head piano dept. Cape Town U., South Africa, 1949-50; artist-in-residence Tex. Christian U., 1967-83; adjudicator Van Cliburn Internat. Piano Competition, Tex. Named hon. citizen N.Z., late 1940's; decorated Cross of Honor for Sci. and Art (Austria). Hon. mem. Music Tchrs. Assn. Calif., Sigma Alpha Iota. Author: The Complete Original Cadenzas by W.A. Mozart for His Solo Piano Concertos. Office: care Alix Williamson 1860 Broadway New York NY 10023

KRAUS, MARGERY, consultant; b. Franklin, N.J., May 20, 1946; d. Soland Lily (Cvern) Rosen; B.A. in Polit. Sci., Am. U., 1967, M.A. in govt., 1970; m. Stephen Kraus, Sept. 4, 1966; children—Lisa, Evan, Mara. With Close Up Found., Arlington, Va., 1971-84, v.p., 1976-84; with APCO Assocs., cons., Washington, 1984—; dir., v.p. Intervest, Inc.; cons., speaker in field. Bd. dirs. Small World, 1979-80; fund raising chmn. Green Hedges Sch.; active local Girl Scout. Mem. Am. Assn. Female Execs., Am. Polit. Sci. Assn. Jewish. Editor Civic mag., 1975-77. Home: 9609 Whitecedar Ct Vienna VA 22180 Office: 1200 New Hampshire Ave NW Washington DC 20036

KRAUS, MOZELLE DEWITTE BIGELOW (MRS. RUSSELL WARREN KRAUS), psychologist, educator; b. Vicksburg, Miss., Sept. 29, 1929; d. Raymond Demar and Henrietta (DeWitte) Bigelow; B.S., D.C. Tchr's. Coll., 1952; M.A., George Washington U., 1954; Ed.D., Am. U., 1965; m. Russell Warren Kraus, Sept. 30, 1961. Instr., Dept. Def., Washington, 1952-54; tchr. Wheaton (Md.) High Sch., 1954-55; grad. asst. Am. U., 1955-56; research asst., then asso. to Dr. Leonard Carmichael, former sec. Smithsonian Instn., Washington, v.p. Nat. Geog. Mag., 1956-72; pvt. practice, Washington, 1972—; asso. prof. psychology George Washington U., 1965—; instr. psychology USDA Grad. Sch., 1964—; vis. prof. U.S. Naval Sch. Hosp. Adminstrn., 1968-69; group therapy Social Service Agy., Washington, 1980—. Fellow Am. Orthopsychiat. Assn.; mem. AAAS, Am. Psychol. Assn., Va. Psychol. Assn., Nat. Register Health Providers, Internat. Council Psychologists, D.C. Psychol. Assn., Psychiat. Outpatient Clinics Am., DAR, Salvation Army Aux., Phi Delta Gamma, Sigma Xi, Psi Chi, Sigma Kappa, Kappa Delta Epsilon. Episcopalian. Contbr. articles to profl. jours.; author newspaper column Person to Person. Home: 5500 Friendship Blvd 925 N Chevy Chase MD 20815

KRAUS, NORMA JEAN, personnel executive; b. Pitts., Feb. 11, 1931; d. Edward Karl and Alli Alexandra (Hermanson) K. B.A., U. Pitts., 1954; postgrad. NYU Grad. Sch. Bus. Adminstrn., 1959-61, Cornell U. Grad. Sch. Labor Relations, 1969-70. Personnel mgr. for several cos., 1957-70; corp. dir. personnel TelePrompter Corp., N.Y.C., 1970-73; exec. asst. to lt. gov. N.Y. State, Office Lt. Gov., Albany, 1974-79; corp. dir. personnel, indsl. relations and stockholder relations Volt Info. Scis., Inc., N.Y.C., 1979—. Co-founder, Manhattan Women's Polit. Caucus, 1971, N.Y. State Women's Polit. Caucus, 1972, vice chmn. N.Y. State Women's Polit. Caucus, 1978. Served to lt. (s.g.) USNR, 1954-57. Pa. State Senatorial scholar, 1950-54. Mem. Women's Econ. Roundtable, Indsl. Relations Research Assn. Democrat. Avocations: politics, women's rights. Office: Volt Info Scis Inc 101 Park Ave New York NY 10178

KRAUS, PANSY DAEGLING, gem consultant; b. Santa Paula, Calif., Sept. 21, 1916; d. Arthur David and Elsie (Pardee) Daegling; A.A., San Bernardino Valley Jr. Coll., 1938; student Longmeyer's Bus. Coll., 1940; grad. gemologist diploma Gemological Inst. Am., 1966, Gemmological Assn. Gt. Britain, 1960; m. Charles Frederick Kraus, Mar. 1, 1941 (div. Nov. 1961). Clk., Convair, San Diego, 1943-48; clk. San Diego County Schs. Publs., 1948-57; mgr. Rogers and Boblet-Art Craft, San Diego, 1958-64; part-time editorial asst. Lapidary Jour., San Diego, 1963-64, assoc. editor, 1964-69, editor, 1970-84, sr. editor, 1984-85; gem cons., 1985—; lectr. gems, gemology local gem and mineral groups; gem and mineral club bull. editor groups. Mem. San Diego Mineral and Gem Soc., Gemmol. Soc. San Diego, Gemmol. Assn. Great Britain, Mineral. Soc. Am., Epsilon Sigma Alpha. Editor, layout dir.: Gem Cutting Shop Helps, 1964; The Fundamentals of Gemstone Carving, 1967; Appalachian Mineral and Gem Trails, 1968; Practical Gem Knowlege for the Amateur, 1969; Southwest Mineral and Gem Trails, 1972; revision editor Gemcraft, 1977. Home: 6127 Mohler St San Diego CA 92120

KRAUSE, DOROTHY ELAINE, nurse; b. Salt Lake City, Nov. 9, 1923; d. Herbert Henry William and Bessie Clare (Hobbs) Stones; m. Edward C. Krause, July 9, 1948 (dec. Jan. 1985); children—Paul Henry, Timothy Neal, Rosemary Clare, Kenneth Charles. Nurse, VA, Wadsworth, West Los Angeles, 1947-49, Howrd Meml. Hosp., Willits, Calif., 1949-52, Orange County Gen. Hosp., Orange, Calif., 1957-58, Garden Park Hosp., Anaheim, Calif., 1958-79; nurse, diabetes educator Martin Luther Hosp. Med. Ctr., Anaheim, 1979—. Mem. Am. Diabetes Assn., Diabetes Teaching Nurses So. Calif.

KRAUSE, KRISTINE MARY, civil engineer; b. Milw., Sept. 8, 1954; d. James Louis and Monica Helen K.; B.S. in Civil Engring., Mich. Tech. U., 1976; M.S., Marquette U., 1983. Insp., coop. student Wis. Dept. Transp., Milw. and Green Bay, 1973-75; design engr. Allegany Power Service Corp., Greensburg, Pa., 1976-78; project adminstr. power plant Wis. Electric Power Co., Milw., 1979-80, constrn. supr., 1980—. Mem. Nat. Ski Patrol, 1980—, sec.-treas., 1982—; mem. sci./engring./math. adv. com. Alverno Coll., 1983—. Registered profl. engr., Wis. Mem. ASCE (S.W. br. Wis. newsletter editor 1980-82, dir. 1983—), Exptl. Aircraft Assn., Aircraft Owners and Pilots Assn. Republican. Roman Catholic. Home: 10880 W Donna Dr Milwaukee WI 53224 Office: 231 W Michigan St Milwaukee WI 53201

KRAUSE, MARY ELIZABETH, insurance company executive; b. Pearsall, Tex., Sept. 22, 1934; d. Richard Marvin and Mary Lee (Coffee) Dillahunty; children—Lorinda Lee, Brenda Marie. B.S., Pan.Am. U., 1954; M.B.A. cand. Amber U., 1979—. With GAO, C.Z., 1955-56; auditor to C.P.A., McAllen, Tex., 1957-59; spl. audit staff Price Waterhouse, Dallas, 1960-63; mem. mgmt. staff Allstate Ins. Co., Dallas, 1969-83, sales staff, Nurst, Tex., 1983—. Mem. Dallas Career Women's Network, Arlington Bus. Women's Network. Office: Allstate Ins Co 7000 Northeast Mall Hurst TX 76053

KRAUSE, MARY FAITH, computer consulting company executive; b. Mt. Clemens, Mich., July 28, 1953; d. Richard Louis and Alyce Jean Boden; m. William Heinrich Krause, Mar. 15, 1980. B.S., Ariz. State U., 1979; M.B.A., City U., Seattle. Recruiter, Search Northwest, Bellevue, Wash., 1979-80; pres. MFK Internat., Kirkland, Wash., 1980—; pres. Cottage Industries Internat., 1983-84; cons. Custom Clothing Guild, 1983-84. Co-author: China Brief Experience, 1985. Contbr. articles to various sales, mktg. jours. Bd. dirs. Seattle-Chongqing Sister City Assn., 1985. Mem. Kirkland C. of C. (membership com. 1983), Seattle C. of C., Electronic Businesswomen's Assn. (chmn. 1983-84), Forum East (chmn., dir. 1982-83), Am. Mgmt. Assn., Pacific Northwest Personnel Mgmt. Assn., Northwest Consultants Assn. (pub. relations com. 1984-85), Am. Soc. Personnel Adminstrn. Republican. Roman Catholic. Office: MFK Internat 805 16th Ave W Kirkland WA 98033

KRAUSKOPF, JOAN MIDAY, lawyer, educator; b. Canton, Ohio, Apr. 24, 1932; d. Clement I. and Elizabeth (Bellinger) Miday; m. Charles Joseph Krauskopf, July 4, 1954; children—Timothy Karl, David Andrew. A.B., Ohio U., 1954; J.D., Ohio State U., Columbus, 1957. Bar: Ohio 1958, Colo. 1961, Mo. 1969. Instr. law Ohio State U., Columbus, 1957-59, asst. prof., 1959-60; sole practice, Boulder, Colo., 1961-62; adj. prof. U. Mo., Columbia, 1963-74, prof., 1974—; William Maier, Jr. chair law, W.Va., 1986-87. Author: Advocacy for the Aging, 1983; Law for the Elderly, 3d edit., 1984. Mem. Mo. Human Rights Commn., 1976-83; bd. dirs. NOW Legal Def. and Edn. Fund, 1980—, Mo. Gerontology Inst., Columbia, 1980—; mem. policy bd. Ctr. Aging Studies, Columbia, 1980—. Recipient Teaching award U. Mo. Alumnae, 1977; U. Mo.-Columbia Faculty Alumni award, 1985; Medal of Merit, Ohio U., 1979; Research award Sch. Law, 1981. Mem. ABA, Mo. Bar Assn. (chmn. family law), Am. Trial Lawyers Assn., Am. Law Inst. Democrat. Unitarian. Office: U Mo Sch Law Tate Hall Columbia MO 65211

KRAUSS, VIRGINIA MILLER, real estate management executive, management consultant; b. Athens, Ga., Nov. 16, 1922; d. Frank Oliver and Margaret Upton(Cave) Miller; m. W. Ransom Krauss, June 13, 1945; children—W. Ransom, Jr., Miller P., Paul B., Ethel M. Krauss Moore. Student Grace Martin Secretarial Sch., Pitts., 1939-40, Louise Salinger Sch. Design, Pitts., 1942-43. Chief clk. Selective Service System, Newport, N.H., 1963-71; head bookkeeper Pine Tree Castings, Newport, 1972-74, Hanslin Assocs.-Eastman, Grantham, N.H., 1975-79; mgr. Maple Manor Apts., Newport, 1979—; co-owner, bookkeeper Krauss Mgmt., Newport, 1961—; advisor to owner Montgomery Ward Agy., Claremont, N.H., 1982-85; dir. County Coach Transit, Claremont; mgmt. cons. Brands, etc., Claremont, 1985—. Chmn. Water and Sewer Study Com., Newport, 1970-73; trustee Newport Hosp., 1968-83; mem. Newport Budget Com., 1965-80, Newport Bd. Adjustment, 1965-68. Recipient Plaque of Appreciation, Newport Housing for Elderly and Handicapped, 1980. Republican. Club: Newport Hosp. Aid (pres. 1959-61). Avocations: sewing; cooking; music. Office: Maple Manor Apts 44 Maple Manor Newport NH 03773

KRAUT, JOANNE LENORA, computer programmer, analyst; b. Watertown, Wis., Oct. 29, 1949; d. Gilbert Arthur and Dorothy Ann (Gebel) K.; B.A. in Russian, U. Wis., Madison, 1971, M.S. in Computer Sci., 1973. Computer programmer U. Wis. Sch. Bus., Madison, 1969-72, Milw. Ins. Co., 1973-74; tech. coordinator Wis. Dept. Justice, Madison, 1974-83; sr. systems programmer/analyst Benchmark Criminal Justice Systems, Waukesha, Wis., 1983—. Mem. Lakewood Gardens Assn. (dir. 1981-83), Phi Beta Kappa. Home: 609 Dundee Ln Hartland WI 53029 Office: 600 Larry Ct Waukesha WI 53187

KRAUTH, DOROTHY COLETTE, real estate broker; b. Boston, Oct. 26, 1938; d. Edward Vincent and Ethel May (Sanford) Walsh; B.S., Harvard U., 1960; m. Gerald C. McDonald, May 23, 1959 (dec.); children—Gerald C., Deborah L. McDonald, Hermanson, Gregory Christopher; m. 2d, Carl H. Krauth, Jr., Dec. 15, 1980; 1 stepson, Carl H. III. Various secretarial positions, 1958-59. model, 1958-75; model, personal shopper Filene's, Chestnut Hill, Mass., 1974-78; designer program covers Boston Red Sox, 1974-76; TV facts girl for TV comml. T.V. Facts mag., 1974-75; real estate broker Channing Assos., Inc., Wellesley, Mass., 1976-81, N.B. Taylor & Co., Inc., Sudbury, Mass., 1986—; broker Boca Blossom Realty Co., Boca Raton, Fla., 1979-81. Roman Catholic. Home: 230 N Federal Hwy Deerfield Beach FL 33441 also 25 Brimstone Ln Sudbury MA 01776 Office: NB Taylor & Co Inc 356 Boston Post Rd Sudbury MA 01776

KRAVITCH, PHYLLIS A., fed. judge; b. Savannah, Ga., Aug. 23, 1920; d. Aaron and Ella (Wiseman) K.; B.A., Goucher Coll., 1941, LL.D., 1981; LL.B., U. Pa., 1943. Admitted to Ga. bar, 1943, U.S. Supreme Ct., 1948; gen. practice law, Savannah, 1944-76; judge Superior Ct. Eastern Jud. Circuit Ga., 1977-79; judge 5th Circuit U.S. Ct. Appeals, Atlanta, 1979-81, 11th Circuit, 1981—. Trustee, Inst. Continuing Legal Edn. in Ga., 1979-82; mem. Bd. Edn. Chatham County (Ga.), 1949-55. Recipient Hannah G. Solomon award Nat. Council Jewish Women, 1978. Fellow Am. Bar Found.; mem. ABA, State Bar Ga., Savannah Bar Assn. (pres. 1976), Am. Law Inst., Am. Judicature Soc. Jewish. Office: PO Box 8085 Savannah GA 31412

KRAWIEC, STELLA STANISLAWA, economist; b. Sloboda, Poland, May 7, 1942; came to U.S., 1972, naturalized, 1979; d. Jan and Janina (Miszuk) Byczko; M.S. in Indsl. Econs., Sch. Econs., Wroclaw, Poland, 1965; Ph.D., Sch. Planning and Stats., Warsaw, Poland, 1971; m. Frank Krawiec, Aug. 15, 1965; children—Marzena, Peter, Margaret. Asst. prof. dept. indsl. econs. Sch. Planning and Stats., Warsaw, 1966-71; economist Public Utility Commn., Harrisburg, Pa., 1973-74, corp. planning dept. Am. Natural Resources Co., Detroit, 1974-76; sr. research economist dept. labor and industry Office Econ. Research, Trenton, N.J., 1976-78; sr. planner, economist Solar Energy Research Inst., Golden, Colo., 1978-82; sr. research analyst dept. econs. and forecasting Pub. Service Co. Colo., Denver, 1982—; cons. Mem. People to People Citizen Ambassador Program. Mem. Eastern Econ. Assn., Internat. Assn. Energy Economists, Am. Statis. Assn., AIAA. Contbr. numerous articles to profl. jours. Home: 11900 W 22d Pl Lakewood CO 80215 Office: Public Service Co Colo 550 15th St Denver CO 80202

KRCMAR, JANET A. DIXON (MRS. LUDWIG LEOPOLD KRCMAR IV), librarian; b. Morehead, Minn., June 9, 1936; d. Minet Lafayne and Anabel (Lee) Dixon; B.A., Los Angeles State Coll., 1955; D.Litt. (hon.), Hamilton State U., 1973; m. James Columbus Adams, Aug. 16, 1954 (div. Sept. 1961); children—Kirk, Corey, Kimberleigh, Nancie; m. 2d, Ludwig Leopold Krcmar IV, Dec. 27, 1964. Dir. Tanglewood Sch. for Girls, Canoga Park, Calif., 1956-58; librarian Riker Labs., Northridge, Calif., 1958-62; head librarian Thompson-Ramo-Wooldridge, Canoga Park, 1962-64, Bunker-Ramo Corp., Canoga Park, 1964—. Mem. Los Angeles City Schs. Career Guidance Bd., 1965-68; project chmn. Calif. Industry-Edn. Bd., 1966-68; pres. San Fernando Council Industry-Edn., 1970; sec.-treas. Los Angeles County Industry-Edn. Council, 1971-73, Calif. State exec. bd., 1976-79. Master adv. com. Los Angeles Trade Tech. Coll., 1966-77, Los Angeles Valley Coll., 1973-78. Mem. Am. Soc. for Info. Sci. (publs. chmn. 1966-72, pres. 1973, nat. awards chmn. 1976-77, nat. councilor-at-large 1978-80), Spl. Libraries Assn. (sci. tech. chmn. 1967-69, pres. 1977), Am., Calif. library assns., Assn. of Computing Machinery, Simi Valley Art Assn. (pres. 1976), Am. Fedn. of Minerologists, Phi Delta Phi, Alpha Psi Omega, Mu Phi Epsilon. Club: Sierra. Editor Library Mgmt. Bull., 1982-83, Simi Valley Art Assn. Newsletter, 1981—. Home: 1529 Kane Ave Simi CA 93065 Office: Arete Assocs 5445 Balboa Blvd Encino CA 91316

KREAGER, EILEEN DAVIS, school administrator; b. Caldwell, Ohio, Mar. 2, 1924; d. Fred Raymond and Esther (Farson) Davis; m. James Scott Kreager, Sept. 26, 1953 (div. 1956). B.S.B.A., Ohio State U., 1945. Proofreader, Ohio State U., Columbus, 1942-43, research calculator, 1944; mem. acctg. staff M & R Dietetic Labs. Inc., Columbus, 1945-50; bookkeeper Magic Seal Paper Products, Columbus, 1950-53, A. Walt Runglin Co., Los Angeles, 1953-54; office mgr. Roy C. Haddox & Son, Columbus, 1954-60; bursar Methodist Theol. Sch. in Ohio, Delaware, 1961—; contbr. numerous profl. seminars. Fellow Am. Biog. Inst.; mem. Internat. Platform Assn., AAUW, Am. Inst. Mgmt. (exec. council 1979), Ohio State U. Alumni Assn. (reunion com.), Kappa Delta. Club: Faculty (Ohio State U.). Avocations: Behavior psychology; handwriting; diet; property and antiques.

KREBS, MARGARET ELOISE, publishing company executive; b. Clearfield, Pa., Apr. 20, 1927; d. Henry Louis and Delia Louise (Beahan) K.; grad. high sch. With Progressive Pub. Co., Inc., Clearfield, 1945—, bus. office mgr., 1956-60, bus. mgr., 1960-63, asst. to pub., 1963-69, asso. pub., 1981—, dir., exec. v.p., 1969-77, pres., 1977—; sec., dir. Indiana Broadcasters, Inc. (Pa.), Stas. WDAD-AM and WQMU-FM, 1967—; sec. Clearfield Broadcasters, Inc., Stas. WCPA-AM and WQYX-FM, 1965—, dir., 1971—; sec. Centre Broadcasters, Inc., State College, Pa., 1977—. Mem. Pa. Newspaper Women's Assn., Clearfield Bus. and Profl. Women's Club (pres. 1952-53, dist. membership chmn. 1952-53), Sigma Delta Chi. Democrat. Roman Catholic. Club: Lake Glendale Sailing (sec. 1966—). Home: 526 Ogden Ave Clearfield PA 16830 Office: 206 E Locust St Clearfield PA 16830

KRECEK, VICTORIA JEAN, association executive; b. Seattle, Dec. 23, 1942; d. John Stewart and Jean Wanita (Morris) Elliott; B.A., U. Nebr., 1965; m. David Arthur Krecek, June 13, 1965; children—John Stewart, Mark Morris. Mgr. agr. and transp. Omaha C. of C., 1983—; freelance writer, Omaha, 1968-74, North Platte, Nebr., 1974-76; mgr. community devel. City of Omaha Dept. Housing and Community Devel., 1976-79; mgr. communications Greater Omaha C. of C., 1979-83. Bd. dirs. Omaha Symphony Guild Bd., 1969-72; mem. Omaha Zoning Bd. Appeals, 1973-74; mem. Nebr. adv. com. U.S. Commn. on Civil Rights, 1976-85; bd. dirs. Coll. World Series, 1980-83, Operation Bridge, Urban League of Nebr.; membership drive chmn. YWCA, 1981-83. Mem. Public Relations Soc. Am. (accredited), Nat. Assn. Housing and Redevel. Ofcls., Omaha Press Club, Nebr. News Women, Omaha Women's Network, Am. C. of C. Execs., Nebr. Press Women, Delta Gamma. Democrat. Home: 12839 Jones St Omaha NE 68154 Office: 1302 Harney St Omaha NE 68102

KREEGER, JEAN ANN, insurance company executive; b. York, Pa., July 16, 1950; d. Frank G. and Ardene (Livingstone) Kopp; 1 child, Michelle L. B.S., York Coll. of Pa., 1972; M.Ed., Millersville U., 1973. Lic. ins. agt., Pa. Juvenile probation officer County of York, Pa., 1974-79; agt. State Farm Ins. Co., Dallastown, Pa., 1979-83, agy. mgr., York, 1983—. Named to Millionaire Club State Farm, 1980, 81, 82, 83, 85, Legion of Honor, 1982, 83. Mem. Nat. Assn. Life Underwriters. Methodist. Home: RD 3 Box 439 Dallastown PA 17313 Office: State Farm Ins 2709 S Queen St York PA 17403

KREEGER, ROMA, children's center administrator; b. Logan, Utah, May 23, 1929; s. Leonard Clarence and Vivian John Mathews; m. Lawrence Eugene Kreeger, Nov. 15, 1947; children—Stephen Eugene, Michael Lawrence, Carolyn Suzette. A.A., Long Beach City Coll., 1964; student U. Long Beach, 1965-67, Calif. State U.-Los Angeles, 1968. Instr. Pioneer Sch., Bellflower, Calif., 1959-60; tchr. music Exceptional Children's Found., Long Beach, 1960-62; dir. head start program Lakewood, Calif., 1968-69; devel. cons. Orange Glen High Sch., Escondido, Calif., 1971-72; counsel. Wonderday Sch., Escondido, 1969—. Tchr. adult and children Ch. Jesus Christ Latter-day Saints, 1958-69; mem. Voting Bd. Mcpl. Elections, Lakewood, Calif., 1961. Mem. Pre-School Assn. (treas. 1972-75), Escondido C. of C. (exec.). Republican.

KREEK, MARY JEANNE, physician; b. Washington; d. Louis Francis and Esperance (Agee) Kreek; B.A., Wellesley Coll., 1958; M.D., Columbia, 1962; m. Dr. Robert A. Schaefer, Jan. 24, 1970; children—Robert A., Esperance Anne. Med. research NIH, Bethesda, Md., 1957-62; intern, resident Cornell N.Y. Hosp. Med. Center, N.Y.C., 1962-65, fellow, 1965-67; instr. medicine Cornell Med. Coll., 1966-67; acad. medicine specializing in internal medicine, endocrinology, gastroenterology, clin. pharmacology, N.Y.C., 1966—; mem. staff N.Y. Hosp.-Cornell U., 1968-77, clin. asst. prof., asst. attending physician, now asso. attending physician, adj. asso. prof.; asst. prof. Rockefeller U., 1967-72, sr. research assoc., physician, 1972-83, assoc. prof., physician, 1983—. mem. gen. medicine study sect. NIH, 1973-77; co-chmn. John E. Fogarty (NIH) Internat. Conf. Hepatotoxicity Due to Drugs and Chems., 1977; vis. prof. Pahlavi U., Shiraz, Iran, summer 1977; spl. adv. Nat. Inst. Drug Abuse, 1976—; mem. gastroenterology adv. com. FDA, 1975-79, NIH Gen. Clin. Recipient Borden Research award, 1962; Career Scientist award Health Research Council City N.Y., 1974—; Research Scientist award HEW, 1978-88. Research Center Study Sect., 1979-83, chmn., 1982-83; mem. exec. com. Com. Problems Drug Dependence, 1982—, chmn. exec. com., 1985-87. Mem. Am. Fedn. for Clin. Research, Shakespeare Soc. of Wellesley, Am. Gastroent. Assn., Endocrine Soc., Am. Assn. Study Liver Diseases, Internat. Assn. Study Liver, Internat. Narcotic Research Conf. Group, Research Soc. on Alcoholism, Am. Coll. Neuropsychopharmacology, Phi Beta Kappa, Sigma Xi. Home: 1161 York Ave New York NY 10021 Office: Rockefeller U New York NY 10021

KREIMENDAHL, SHERLYN JEAN, wallpapering group executive; b. Kansas City, Kans., Mar. 5, 1950; d. Robert and Gwyanetha June (Stockton) Norton Hicks; m. Robert John Kreimendahl, Sept. 22, 1978; children—Chad Josef, Tara Jonet, Brittany Lynn. B.S., Drury Coll., 1972. Lic. realtor; lic. social worker; approved foster care mother. Real estate saleswoman Gaslight Realtors, Gladstone, Mo., 1974-77; social worker Vis. Nurse Assn., Kansas Ciy, Mo., 1979-82; owner Touch of Class Wallpapering Group, Olathe, Kans., 1982—. Baptist. Avocations: softball; soccer; swimming; arts and crafts. Home: 1001 E Elizabeth St Olathe KS 66061

KREIPE, LAURINE RIEDEL, paralegal educator; b. Tipton, Kans., July 27, 1930; d. Michael Xavier and Anna Mary (Kohn) Riedel; m. Paul G. Kreipe, Sept. 1, 1956; children—Lisa, Eric, Karl. B.A., Washburn U., 1979, J.D., 1981. Bar: Kans. 1982. Gen. atty. Office State Treas., Topeka, 1981-82; program dir., assoc. prof. paralegal dept. Washburn U., 1982—. Mem. ABA, Kans. Bar Assn., Kans. Trial Lawyers Assn. Democrat. Roman Catholic. Home: 8129 SE 2nd St Tecumseh KS 66542 Office: Washburn U Topeka KS 66621

KREISER, PEGGY LEE, personnel analyst; b. Harrisburg, Pa., July 4, 1952; d. Robert Lee and Janet Marie (Pugh) Kreiser. B.S. in Elem. Edn., E. Stroudsburg State Coll., 1974; postgrad in computer programming, Pa. State U., 1982-85. Cert. elem. tchr., Pa. Playground instr. Susquehanna Twp. Recreation Assn., Harrisburg, 1972-74; salesperson Young Jrs., Harrisburg, 1974; subs. tchr. Harrisburg, 1974; clk. typist Harrisburg State Hosp., 1974-81, adminstrv. asst., 1981-84, personnel analyst, 1984—, bd. dirs. blood bank, 1983—. Editor HSH Happenings, 1981-84. Vol. Civil Def., Harrisburg, 1972. Mem. Nat. Assn. Female Execs., Nat. Edn. Tchrs. Assn. Republican. Presbyterian. Avocations: tennis; reading; writing; stitchery; sports.

KREITZBURG, MARILYN JUNE, librarian; b. Rockford, Ill.; d. A.E. and Margaret Louise (Harvey) K.; student Rockford Coll. for Women, 1948-50; A.B. magna cum laude, Knox Coll., 1954; M.A., U. Va., 1956; cert. philosophy U. Edinburgh (Scotland), 1960. Copywriter radio and TV, Black Hawk Broadcasting Co., Waterloo, Iowa, 1956-57; freelance promotion, N.Y.C., 1957; lectr. on Asia, women and fgn. affairs, Ill., Iowa, 1959-60; order librarian, asst. to coll. librarian Knox Coll., Ill., 1960-72; librarian, asst. prof. U. Pitts. at Johnstown, 1972—, reference librarian and head library instructional services, 1977—. Bd. dirs. Prairie Players Civic Theater, 1962-64; rescue vol. Richland Twp. Vol. Fire Dept., 1977, ARC Disaster Inquiry Service; mem. Inter-Service Club Council, 1976-80. Recipient medal DAR, 1948; Helen Lee Wessels fellow, 1954-55; Fulbright fellow at large, 1957-59. Mem. Women's Assn. U. Pitts. at Johnstown (pres. 1978-79, exec. bd.), Assn. Coll. and Research Libraries, ALA, Johnstown Art League, Inter Nos, Phi Beta Kappa, Delta Kappa Gamma, Pi Sigma Alpha, Sigma Alpha Iota, Pi Beta Phi. Clubs: Soroptimists (pres. 1978-80, exec. bd.), Sr. Citizens Hobby Show (publicity and hospitality com. 1977-78). Founder, editor: Ivory Tower Chronicle, 1961-64. Office: Library Univ Pittsburgh Johnstown PA 15904

KREJCSI, CYNTHIA ANN, textbook editor; b. Chgo., Dec. 28, 1948; d. Charles and Dorothea Bertha (Hahn) K.; m. Daniel Neil Ehlebracht, May 16, 1986. B.A., North Park Coll., 1970; student Nat. Coll. Edn. Evanston, Ill., 1983—. Prodn. editor Ency., Brit. Chgo., 1970-71, style editor, 1971—; asst. editor Scott, Foresman & Co., Glenview, Ill., 1972-77, assoc. editor, 1977, editor, 1978-84, sr. editor, 1984—; sr. editor Benefic Press, Westchester, Ill., 1977-78. Mem. Nat. Assn. Female Execs., Chgo. Council on Fgn. Relations, Field Mus. Natural History, Chgo. Women in Pub., Internat. Reading Assn. Democrat. Lutheran. Office: Scott Foresman & Co 1900 E Lake Ave Glenview IL 60025

KREMENITZER, JANET PICKARD, educator, child development researcher; b. Bklyn., Sept. 12, 1949; d. Leonard and Francine (Saltzman) Pickard; B.A., Queens Coll., City U. N.Y., 1971; M.A., Tchrs. Coll. Columbia U., 1972, Ed.M., 1974, Ed.D., 1977; m. Martin William Kremenitzer, Dec. 21, 1974; children—Rebecca Jolie, David Aaron. Instr., Barnard Coll. Columbia U., N.Y.C., 1971-73; tchr. Dalton Sch., N.Y.C., 1972-73; lectr. CCNY, 1973-75; asst. prof. Western Conn. State Coll., Danbury, 1977-79; mem. adj. faculty, 1982; ednl. cons., Newtown, Conn., 1979—; research cons. Associated Neurologists Danbury, 1982—; research asst. Rose F. Kennedy Center for Research in Mental Retardation and Human Devel., Albert Einstein Coll. Medicine, 1973-74; v.p., founding dir. edn. Maimonides Acad. Western Conn., Inc., 1978-80, bd. dirs., 1978—, coordinator early childhood program, 1983—. Mem. Am. Psychol. Assn., Soc. Research in Child Devel., Internat. Soc. Devel. Psychobiology, AAPHER, Pi Lambda Theta. Club: Hadassah. Address: Brookwood Dr Newtown CT 06470

KREMENTZ, JILL, photographer, author; b. N.Y.C., Feb. 19, 1940; d. Walter and Virginia (Hyde) K.; student Drew U., 1958-59, Art Students League, Columbia; m. Kurt Vonnegut, Jr., Nov., 1979; 1 dau., Lily. With Harper's Bazaar, 1959-60, Glamour mag., 1960-61; pub. relations staff Indian Industries Fair, New Delhi, 1961; reporter Show mag., 1962-64; staff photographer N.Y. Herald Tribune, 1964-65, Vietnam, 1965-66; asso. editor Status-Diplomat mag., 1966-67; contbg. editor N.Y. mag., 1967-68; corr. Time-Life Inc., 1969-70; contbg. photographer People mag., 1974—; contbg. editor Savvy mag., 1985—; one-woman photography shows Madison (Wis.) Art Center, 1973, U. Mass., Boston, 1974, Nikon Gallery, N.Y.C., 1974, Del. Art Mus., Wilmington, 1975; represented in permanent collections Mus. Modern Art, Library of Congress. Photographer: The Face of South Vietnam (text by Dean Brelis), 1968; Words and Their Masters (text by Israel Shenker), 1974; photographer, author: Sweet Pea—A Black Girl Growing Up in the Rural South (foreword by Margaret Mead), 1969; A Very Young Dancer, 1976; A Very Young Rider, 1977; A Very Young Gymnast, 1978; A Very Young Circus Flyer, 1979, A Very Young Skater, 1979; The Writer's Image, 1980; How It Feels When A Parent Dies, 1981; How It Feels To Be Adopted, 1982; How It Feels When Parents Divorce, 1984; The Fun of Cooking, 1985; Lily Goes to the Playground, 1985; Jack Goes to the Beach, 1985. Mem. P.E.N., Women's Forum. Contbr. numerous U.S. and fgn. periodicals. Recipient Washington Post/Children's Book Guild award, 1984. Address: care Alfred A Knopf Pubs 201 E 50th St New York NY 10017

KREMER, HONOR (NOREEN) FRANCES, business executive; b. Ireland, Aug. 9, 1939; came to U.S., 1961; d. Patrick Joseph and Mary (Malone) Queally; B.S., City U. N.Y., M.S., Baruch Coll.; m. Manny Kremer, May 17, 1963; 1 son, Patrick David. Group sec. Bentalls, Ltd., Kingston-On-Thames, Surrey, Eng., 1954-58, Central Secondary Sch., Hamilton, Ont., Can., 1959-61; office mgr. Aschner Assocs., N.Y.C., 1961-63; public relations asst. McMaster U., Hamilton, 1963-64; office mgr. Packaging Components, N.Y.C., 1965-67; head acctg. Shaller Rubin Assos., N.Y.C., 1967-72, v.p. fin. and adminstrn., 1972-79, sr. v.p., 1979-82, sr. v.p., mem. exec. com., 1982—, sec.-treas. multi-media div., 1972—, dir., 1975—. Mem. Nat. Fedn. Bus. and Profl. Women (dir., v.p.), Advt. Fin. Mgmt. Group. Roman Catholic. Office: 122 E 25th St New York NY 10010

KRENEK, GERALDINE ANN, real estate broker; b. Cleve., Apr. 24, 1943; d. John and Mildred Helen (Pleta) Ulicky; m. Richard Frank Krenek, July 6, 1963; children—Richard Frank, Robert John. Student Ohio Cosmetology Coll., Cleve., 1961-62. Sales assoc. Don Cies Co., Norman, Okla., 1973-75, broker assoc., 1975-81; broker, owner Classic Realty & Investment, Inc., Norman, 1981—; dir. Norman Multi-List, 1976-77; mem. Profl. Standards Com., Norman, 1980-81. Pres. Welcome to Norman Club, 1972-73, Norman Jr. Women's Club, 1975-76, Rotary Ann's, Norman, 1978-79, U. Okla. Engring. Faculty Wives, 1979-80. Mem. Norman Bd. Realtors (edn. com. 1981-83, v.p. 1983-84, pres. 1984—), Grad. Realtors Inst., Women's Council Realtors, C. of C., Assistance League Norman, Zeta Tau Alpha. Home: 4209 Oxford Way Norman OK 73069 Office: Classic Realty and Investments Inc 3625 W Main St Norman OK 73069

KREPPS, ETHEL CONSTANCE, lawyer; b. Mountain View, Okla., Oct. 31, 1937; d. Howard Haswell and Pearl (Moore) Goomda; R.N., St. John's Med. Center, 1971; B.S., U. Tulsa, 1974, J.D., 1979; m. George Randolph Krepps, Apr. 10, 1954; children—George Randolph, Edward Howard Moore. Nurse, St. John's Med. Center, Tulsa, 1971-75; admitted to Okla. bar, 1979; individual practice law, Tulsa, 1979—; atty., dir. Indian Child Welfare Program, 1981—; atty. Native Am. Coalition, Inc., Kiowa Tribe Okla., Tulsa Indian Youth Council. Chmn., Okla. Indian Child Welfare Orgn., 1981—; tribal sec. Kiowa Tribe Okla., 1979-81. Mem. Fed. Bar Assn., Am. Bar Assn., Okla. Bar Assn., Tulsa County Bar Assn., Am. Indian Nurses Assn. (v.p.), Am. Trial Lawyers, Native Am. C. of C. (nat. sec.). Democrat. Baptist. Author: A Strong Medicine Wind, 1979; Oklahoma Memories, 1981. Home: 3326 S 93d East Ave Tulsa OK 74145 Office: 1740 W 41st St Tulsa OK 74107

KREPS, JUANITA MORRIS, economist; Lynch, Ky., Jan. 11, 1921; A.B., Berea Coll., 1942; M.A. (fellow), Duke U., 1944, Ph.D., 1948; m. Clifton H. Kreps, Jr., 1944; children—Sarah Blair, Laura Ann, Clifton H., III. Instr. econs. Denison U., Granville, Ohio, 1945-46, asst. prof., 1947-50; lectr. Hofstra U., Hempstead, N.Y., 1952-54, Queens Coll., N.Y., 1954-55; vis. asst. prof., Duke U., Durham, N.C., asst. prof., 1958-61, assoc. prof., 1962-67, prof., 1967-77, dean Women's Coll., asst. provost, 1969-72, James B. Duke prof., 1972-77, v.p., 1973-77; U.S. sec. of commerce, Washington, 1977-79; dir. N.Y. Stock Exchange, 1972-77, AT&T, Armco, Inc., Citicorp., UAL, Inc., United Air Lines, RJR Nabisco, Eastman Kodak Co., J.C. Penney Co., Zurn Industries, Inc., Deere & Co., Chrysler Corp.; trustee Duke Endowment, Tchrs. Ins. and Annuity Assn.; mem. Coll. Retirement Equities Fund. Bd. dirs. Ednl. Testing Service, 1971-77, Nat. Merit Scholarship Bd., 1972-77, Am. Assn. Higher Edn., 1974-77. Trustee, Berea Coll. Ford faculty fellow, 1963-64. Co-author: Principles of Economics; Contemporary Labor Economics, 1974; Sex, Age and Work, 1975; Women in the American Economy, 1975; author: Lifetime Allocation of Work and Income, 1971; Sex in the Marketplace: American Women at Work, 1971. Editor: Employment, Income and Retirement Problems of the Aged, 1963; Technology, Manpower and Retirement Policy, 1966. Office: 115 East Duke Bldg Duke U Durham NC 27708

KRESCH-HAGLER, SANDRA DARYL, communications executive; b. N.Y.C., Sept. 13, 1945; d. Howard and Jean (Goldsmith) Gleich; B.S., U. Pa., 1966; m. Samuel H. Hagler, Jan. 6, 1973. Research assoc. Simat, Helliesen & Eichner, Inc., N.Y.C., 1966-67; study dir. Nat. Analysts, Inc., Phila., 1968-69; pres. Sandra D. Kresch Cons. Services, Calif., 1969-70; v.p., mgr. market research Nat. Analysts, Inc., Chgo., 1970-75; v.p. Booz, Allen Venture Mgmt., N.Y.C., 1976-78; v.p. corp. devel. Booz Allen Hamilton, Inc., N.Y.C., 1978-80, v.p. mgmt. cons., 1980-83; v.p. mktg. Time Video Info. Services, Inc., 1983-84; dir. strategic planning Mag. Group, Time Inc., 1984-86; dir. internat. devel. Time Mag., 1986—. Bd. dirs. Vol. Urban Cons. Group; chmn. bd. Candidate Service Adv. Council; bd. dirs. Spence-Chapin Services to Families, also chmn. personnel and pension com., exec. com., policy rev. com.; pres. bd. dirs. Jose Limon Dance Found., Inc. Recipient Tribute to Women in Internat. Industry award, 1978. mem. Am. Mktg. Assn., Women in Cable, Fin. Woman's Assn., Advt. Women N.Y. Democrat. Jewish. Club: Hemisphere. Home: 14 E 75th St New York NY 10021 Office: 1271 Ave of the Americas New York NY 10020

KRESS, JERRILY HANNAH RODDEN, architect; b. St. Louis, Mar. 2, 1945; d. Jeremiah William and Alraine (Winters) Rodden; B.Arch. (Dean's scholar 1966-68), Mont. State U., 1970; 1 dau., Kiersten. Project architect/designer Saunders, Cheng & Appleton, Alexandria, Va., 1971-72; assoc. architecture Chatelain, Samperton & Carcaterra, Washington, 1973-78; prin., dir. architecture E/A Design Group, Washington, 1978-80; pres. KressCox Assocs., Washington, 1980—; guest lectr. Agr. Grad. Sch., 1978; mem. D.C. Bd. Occupational Health and Safety Adminstrn., 1983—; vice chmn. D.C. Bldg. Codes Adv. Com., 1983—; work exhibited Inter-Am. Devel. Bank, 1976. Past pres. D.C. United Way, dir. social planning; 1984—; dir. summer jobs for youth program Greater Washington Bd. Trade, 1980, bd. dirs., 1982—, exec. com., 1986—; bd. dirs. Heroes Inc. Mem. AIA (scholastic award 1969, merit award 1971 historic preservation award 1982, merit design award 1983), Constrn. Specifications Inst., Washington Bldg. Congress, Nat. Trust Historic Preservation, Women in Bus. (bd. dirs. adv. com. 1985—), Women's Forum, Mortar Board, Delta Phi Delta. Featured architect on NBC-TV program A Woman Is. Home: 1615 Q St NW Apt 907 Washington DC 20009

KRESSE, SUZANNE, editor, publisher; b. Milw., Sept. 27, 1945; d. Ralph Steven and Laverne (Czerwinski) Otto; children—Michael, Paul, Lynn, Laura. B.A., Alverno Coll., 1967. Art tchr. Milw. Catholic Schs., 1967-75; art dir. Kustom Kutouts, Chgo., 1975-78; communications dir. Century 21/Midwest regional office, Milw., 1978-81; editor Glad Tidings Inc., Milw., 1981—. Patentee in field. Mem. Mag. Pubs. Assn., Council Periodical Distributors Assn. Republican. Roman Catholic. Avocations: needlecraft; golf; reading. Office: Glad Tidings Inc 5225 N Ironwood Rd Milwaukee WI 53217

KRESSIN, EILEEN KAY, real estate sales agent; b. Port Washington, Wis., July 1, 1950; d. Harold Frederick and Emma Helen (Nierode) K. B.S., Central Mo. State U., 1974. Directory rep. Southwestern Bell Tel. Co., Kansas City, Mo., 1975-76, directory sales supr., Houston, 1976-78, staff mgr. directory tng., St. Louis, 1978-80, dist. mgr., directory tel. sales, clerical, Kansas City, Mo., 1980-81, div. sales mgr. yellowpages, Oklahoma City, 1981-85; sales assoc. Apple Realty, Inc., Oklahoma City, 1985—. Organist, Holy Cross Lutheran Ch., Oklahoma City, 1982—. Mem. Am. Mktg. Assn. (v.p. 1980), Sales Mgmt. Exec. Assn., Central Mo. State U. Alumni Assn. Republican. Lutheran. Club: Oklahoma City Ski. Office: Apple Realty Inc 11317 Western Suite 100 Oklahoma City OK 73170

KRESSMAN, ANNABELLE CARNEY, fund raising executive and consultant; b. Pennsville, N.J., Dec. 6, 1932; d. Robert McKinley and Anna S. Carney; B.A. in Psychology, Glassboro State Coll., 1979; student Goldey Bus. Coll., 1950-51; children by previous marriage—Jay D. II, Pamela, Robert, Daphne. Exec. sec. E.I. du Pont de Nemours & Co., Newark, Del., 1951-55; substitute high sch. tchr. Salem (N.J.) City Schs., 1966-73; field adv. Holly Shores council Girl Scouts U.S.A., 1973-75, adult edn. dir., 1975-77, public relations and fin. devel. dir., 1977-79; exec. dir. Chesapeake Bay council, 1980-85; v.p. Kressman Cons., Newcastle, Del., 1985—; workshop leader in communications skills, 1975—; cons. to Salem, Gloucester and Cumberland community colls. women's programs, Women's Center U. Del., 1976-81; team trainer Girl Scouts U.S.A., 1977. Bd. dirs. Appel Farm, Cultural Arts Center, Elmer, N.J., 1978-81, Internat. Women's Year, Assn. for Preservation of New Castle, 1984-86; mem. Del. Commn. for Women, 1981—; mem. Del. Gov.'s Commn. on Status of Women, 1980—. Cert. trainer Parent Effectiveness Tng., Youth Effectiveness Tng. Mem. Women in Communications, Assn. Girl Scout Exec. Staff (dir. 1967—, 1st v.p. 1982-84), Assn. Humanistic Soc. Am., AAUW, LWV, Nat. Soc. Fund Raising Execs., Wilmington Women in Bus. (dir., 1981-83), Zonta. Presbyterian. Author: Resource Manual for Finance Development, 1978. Home and Office: 17 The Strand New Castle DE 19720

KRETCHMER, JOY DARLENE, government official, realtor; b. Great Falls, Mont., Nov. 5, 1929; d. Robert John and Jessie May (Connolly) Doran; student Am. Open U./N.Y. Inst. Tech.; cert. assoc. contracts mgr.; divorced; children—Linda May, Jo Ann. With U.S. Govt., 1960—, contract adminstr./contracting officer Washington Area Contracting Center, Andrews AFB, 1979-80, procurement analyst Def. Logistics Agy., Alexandria, Va., 1980-83, Air Force Ctr. for Studies and Analyses, Pentagon, 1983—; with Met. Home, Realtors and Better Home and Gardens, Alexandria, 1985—; cons., speaker on govt. careers. Chmn. Housing Hygiene Bd., City of Alexandria, 1981—. Recipient various govt. and NCMA awards. Mem. Nat. Assn. Realtors, Va. Assn. Realtors, No. Va. Bd. Realtors, Women's Council Realtors, Nat. Contract Mgmt. Assn., Nat. Assn. Female Execs. (network dir.), Nat. Council Career Women, Washington Women's Network, Am. Bus. Women Assn. (exec. bd.). Democrat. Roman Catholic. Clubs: Mont. State Soc.; Washington Ski, Emmett J. Kelly Collectors Soc. Home: 2623 N Van Dorn St Apt 202 Alexandria VA 22302 Office: Met Home Realtors 3690 B King St Alexandria VA 23202 also AF Ctr for Studies and Analyses (SAMQ) Pentagon Washington DC 20330

KREVOY, SUSAN BARBARA, clin. psychologist; b. Los Angeles, Dec. 6, 1944; d. Melvin Sigal and Minerva Harriet (Knell) K.; student U. Calif., Berkeley, 1962-63; B.A., UCLA, 1966, M.A., 1972, Ph.D., 1978; m. Sam Kahn, Aug. 5, 1979; children—Jennifer, Heather. Fellow, Wright Inst., Los Angeles, 1977-79, cons., 1981—; pvt. practice psychology, Beverly Hills, Calif., 1980—; cons. Beverly Hills Schs., 1982—, Help Anorexia, 1982—. Leader, Girl Scouts U.S.A., 1976—. Mem. Am. Psychol. Assn., Calif. Psychol. Assn., Women In Bus. (chmn. health profls.), Los Angeles Inst. Psychoanalytic Studies (pres. students assn. 1983—), UCLA Alumni Assn. Home: 1947 Prosser Ave Los Angeles CA 90025 Office: 360 N Bedford Dr Beverly Hills CA 90210

KRICKA, HANNA HALYNA, pharmaceutical company official; b. Czestochowa, Poland, Jan. 1, 1939; d. Leonid and Helena (Sachnofska) Kryckyj. B.S. in Basic Scis., Drexel Inst. Tech., 1962; M.S. in Info. Scis., Drexel U., 1971; M.Bus. Policy, Columbia U., 1981. Lit. scientist Merck Sharp & Dohme Research Labs., West Point, Pa., 1963-64; sr. lit. scientist Merrell-Nat., Phila., 1964-69; assoc. dir. clin. info. and sr. info. scientist, Hoechst Pharm. Inc., N.J., 1970-73; dir. sci. info. internat. div. Bristol Myers Co., N.Y.C., 1973—. Mem. Am. Chem. Soc., N.Y. Acad. Scis., Am. Soc. Info. Sci., Assn. Computing Machinery, Drug Info. Assn., Am. Mgmt. Assn., Assn. Info. Mgrs., Ukrainian Engrs. Soc. Republican. Byzantine Catholic. Club: Columbia (N.Y.C.). Home: 215 E 80th St PH-J New York NY 10022 Office: 345 Park Ave New York NY 10152

KRIEG, REBECCA JANE, editor; b. Bloomington, Ill., Oct. 7, 1953; d. Russell Edward and Betty Ilena (Clesson) Krieg. B.A. summa cum laude in Christian Edn., Lincoln Christian Coll., 1977; student U. Ky. Trainer self-help skills for retarded Lincoln Devel Center (Ill.) 1975-76; women's editor Lincoln Courier, 1977-84; campus ministry intern Christian Student Fellowship, U. Ky., Lexington, 1984; copy editor Lexington Herald-Leader, Ky., 1985—. Vol. rep. Central Ill. chpt. Cystic Fibrosis Found.; a founder Logan County Com. Against Domestic Violence and Sexual Assault, 1983, v.p., bd. dirs., 1983-84; vol. Rape Info. and Counseling Service, Springfield, Ill., 1982-83. Mem. Delta Epsilon Chi. Mem. Christian Ch. Office: Lexington Herald-Leader Main at Midland Lexington KY 40507

KRIENKE, CAROL BELLE MANIKOWSKE (MRS. OLIVER KENNETH KRIENKE), realtor; b. Oakland, Calif., June 19, 1917; d. George and Ethel (Purdon) Manikowske; student U. Mo., 1937; B.S., U. Minn., 1940; postgrad. UCLA, 1949; m. Oliver Kenneth Krienke, June 4, 1941; children—Diane (Mrs. Robert Denny), Judith (Mrs. Kenneth A. Giss), Debra Louise (Mrs. Ed Paul Davalos). Demonstrator, Gen. Foods Corp., Mpls., 1940; youth leadership State of Minn. Congl. Conf., U. Minn., Mpls. 1940-41; war prodn. worker Airesearch Mfg. Co., Los Angeles, 1944; tchr. Los Angeles City Schs., 1945-49; realtor DBA Ethel Purdon, Manhattan Beach, Calif., 1949; buyer Purdon Furniture & Appliances, Manhattan Beach, 1950-58; realtor O.K. Krienke Realty, Manhattan Beach, 1958—. Manhattan Beach bd. rep. Community Chest for Girl Scouts U.S.A., 1957; bd. dirs. South Bay council Girl Scouts U.S.A., 1957-62, mem. Manhattan Beach Coordinating Council, 1956-68; mem. Long Beach Area Childrens Home Soc. (v.p., 1967-68, pres. 1979; charter mem. Beach Pixies, 1957—, pres. 1967; chmn. United Way, 1967); sponsor Beach Cities Symphony, 1953—. Recipient Rose and Scroll award for outstanding community service Manhattan Beach C. of C., 1985. Mem. DAR (citizenship chmn. 1972-73, v.p. 1979, 83—), Colonial Dames XVII Century (charter mem. Jared Eliot chpt. 1977, v.p., pres. 1979-81, 83—), Friends of Library, Torrance Lomita Bd. of Realtors, South Bay Bd. Realtors, Nat. Soc. New England Women (Calif. Poppy Colony), Internat. Platform Assn., Soc. Descs. of Founders of Hartford, Friends of Banning Mus. Republican. Mem. Community Ch. (pres. Women's Fellowship 1970-71). Home: 1716 Manhattan Beach Blvd Manhattan Beach CA 90266 Office: 1716 Manhattan Beach Blvd Manhattan Beach CA 90266

KRIER, CYNTHIA TAYLOR, state legislator, lawyer; b. Beeville, Tex., July 12, 1950; m. Joseph Krier. B.J., U. Tex., 1971, J.D., 1975. Bar: Tex. 1975. Assoc. Lang, Cross, Ladon, Boldrick & Green, San Antonio; mem. Tex. State Senate from 26th dist., 1985—. Mem. ABA, Tex. Bar Assn., San Antonio Bar Assn., Omicron Delta Kappa, Phi Kappa Phi, Phi Delta Phi. Republican. Office: Tex State Senate State Capitol Austin TX 78711*

KRIESE, FRANCES ANNE, medical technologist; b. Syracuse, N.Y., June 18, 1950; d. William Francis and Mathilda (Ineich) K.; B.S. in Biology, LeMoyne Coll., 1972; B.S. in Med. Tech. SUNY Health Sci. Center, 1974. Biology lab. asst. LeMoyne Coll., Syracuse, N.Y., 1971-72; lab. technician clin. pathology Upstate Med. Center, Syracuse, 1973-74, med. technologist, research asst. dept. anesthesiology, 1975—; med. technologist Syracuse Clin. and Ref. Lab., 1974-75. Mem. Am. Soc. Microbiology, Am. Soc. Clin. Pathologists (asso. mem., cert. med. technologist), Am. Heart Assn., Nat. Mus. Women in Arts (charter), Smithsonian Assocs., AAAS. Republican. Roman Catholic. Home: 110 Male Ave Syracuse NY 13219 Office: 750 E Adams St Syracuse NY 13210

KRIGSMAN, NAOMI, psychologist, consultant; b. Haifa, Israel, Apr. 30; came to U.S., 1953, naturalized, 1961; d. Bezalel and Regina (Yacobi) Goussinsky; m. Ruben Krigsman, July 29, 1956; children—Michael W., Richard G., Jonathan H. Lic. psychologist, N.Y. State. M.S., CCNY, 1955; Ph.D., Hofstra U., 1983. Psychologist Mental Retardation Clinic, Flower-Fifth Avenue Hosp., N.Y.C., 1954-56, Children's Ctr., N.Y.C. Dept. Welfare, 1954-56, Rehab. Clinic, St. Barnabas Hosp., Newark, 1956-57, United Cerebral Palsy Ctr., Roosevelt, N.Y., 1957-58, 63-65, Burke Rehab. Ctr., White Plains, N.Y., 1967-70, New Rochelle City Sch. Dist., N.Y., 1970—; cons. on employment selection, career devel., quality circles, U.S. and Israel; feature writer N.Y. Womensweek, 1978-79. Co-author tng. materials for quality circles; also author articles. Chmn. parent edn. com. Eastview Jr. High Sch. PTA, White Plains, 1971-74; mem. human relations com. White Plains High Sch. PTA, 1973-74. Fellow N.Y. State Mental Health Dept., 1958-59. Mem. Am. Psychol. Assn., Westchester County Psychol. Assn. (chmn. profl. edn. com. sch. psychology div. 1976-78 now establishing divl indsl./orgnl. psychology). Home: 13 Dupont Ave White Plains NY 10605

KRIM, KARAN LEE, telecommunication company executive; b. N.Y.C., Feb. 13, 1949; d. Norman and Renee (Dobrozensky) K.; m. Eliot C. Nasoff, Nov. 14, 1970 (div. Dec. 1978); m. Herbert Marvin, 1986. Regional account mgr. NYNEX, N.Y.C., 1983—. County committeewoman Morris County, N.J., 1986—. Office: NYNEX Service Co 441 Ninth Ave New York NY 10001

KRINER, PHYLLIS ANNE, nurse, educator, adminstr.; d. Ernie V. and Theresa J. (Stella) Kriner; B.S. in Nursing, St. Ambrose Coll., Iowa, 1959; postgrad. Iowa State U., 1961, U. Ill., 1965. Clin. psychiat. nurse Mercy Hosp., Davenport, Iowa, 1958-60; tchr., counselor of student practical nurses Davenport Pub. Schs., 1960-64; tchr. practical nursing edn. Health Occupational Careers Program, Chgo. Pub. Schs., 1965-73, asst. coordinator practical nurses, lab. assts. and nurses aides sects. and faculty, 1966-68, head curriculum com., 1969-71; mem. nursing staff Columbus Hosp., Chgo., 1973-75, head nurse of med.-surg. and infectious unit, 1975-79, nurse epidemiologist, 1979-80; faculty human resource devel. Sch. Nursing, Cabrini Hosp., 1980-82; profl. nursing staff Columbus Hosp., Chgo., 1982—; tchr. nat. tchr. edn. inst. for new health occupations tchrs. U. Iowa 1968. Certified tchr. Chgo. Bd. of Edn. Mem. Am., Ill. nurses assns. Co-developer practical nursing course Davenport Pub. Schs. Home: 3100 N Lake Shore Dr Chicago IL 60657 Office: Columbus Hospital Chicago IL

KRINER, SALLY GLADYS PEARL, artist; b. Bradford, Ohio, Jan. 29, 1911; d. Henry Walter and Pearl Rebecca (Brubaker) Brant; m. Leo Louis Kriner, Feb. 28, 1933; children—Patricia Staab, Jane Palombo. Grad. Arsenal Tech. sch. Indpls.; student Ind. U.-Indpls., 1954, Herron Sch. Art, Indpls., 1958. Exhibited in one woman shows Hoosier Salon, Indpls., 1960, Village Art Gallery, Southport, Ind., 1967, 70, 73, Brown County Art Guild, Nashville, Ind., 1970, 74, 77, 80, 83; group shows include South Side Art League, Indpls., 1959-74, Indpls. Art League, 1959-64, Brown County Art Guild, 1974—; represented in permanent collections Riley Hosp., Indpls., others. Founder Southside Women's Symphony Com., Indpls., 1958; treas. Perry Twp. Republican Club, Ind., 1960-65; pres. State Assembly Women's Club, 1965-67; bd. dirs. ARC, Indpls., 1942-45, Southside Civic Orgn., Indpls., 1954, Clowes Hall Women's Com., Indpls., 1963. Recipient citation ARC, 1946; citation Marion County Meritorious Service Award, 1959; citation Greater Southside Civic Orgn., 1961; Art award Kappa Kappa Kappa, 1967, 68, 70, 71. Fellow Indpls. Art League Found. (numerous awards 1960-66); mem. Southside Art League, Inc. (pres. 1964-65, numerous awards 1964-75, founder), Ind. Artists Club, Inc. (Purchases award 1978), Ind. Heritage Arts, Inc., Rutland Art Assn., Brown County Art Guild (pres. 1980-83, v.p. 1983—), Ind. fedn. Arts Clubs (bd. dirs. 1963-73), Ind. Artist (chmn. prize fund 1974-75), Hoosier Salon, Indpls. Mus. Arts, Nat. Soc. Arts and Letters, Nat. Mus. Women in Arts, Hoosier Group Women in Arts. Presbyterian. Avocation: growing flowers. Home and Studio: Rural Route 3 Box 208 Nashville IN 47448

KRINSKY, SUSAN FAYE, property management company executive, hotel executive; b. St. Johnsbury, Vt., Mar. 27, 1949; d. George Bernard and Harriett Winifred (Conley) Benoit; children—Lori S.W., Glen L.B. A. in Mktg., Burdett Coll., Boston, 1969; B.B.A., Boston U., 1971. Food and beverage mgr. Continental 93 Inn, Littleton, N.H., 1977-80; sales and mktg. dir. Dean Foster Signs, Amesbury, Mass., 1980-83; gen. mgr. Shawmut Inn, Kennebunkport, Maine, 1983-85; gen. mgr. Eastern Inns, Kittery, Maine, 1984—; ops. dir. Creative Bus. Mgmt., Wells, Maine, 1985—; v.p. devel. Creative Tour and Travel, Kennebunk, Maine; mem. restaurant adv. panel Restaurant Bus., Des Plaines, Ill., 1985. Mem. Seacoast Council on Tourism, Portsmouth C. of C., Nat. Assn. Female Execs., Bus. Women's Network of Maine (bd. dirs. 1985-86). Avocations: racquetball; tennis; sailing; skiing; theatre; nautilus; classical music. Office: Creative Bus Mgmt 38 Main St Kennebunk ME 04043

KRINTZMAN, B. J., real estate broker, TV show host; b. Worcester, Mass., Dec. 30, 1946; d. Sumner B. and Shirley R. (Sigel) Cotzin; m. Steven Krintzman, Aug. 9, 1969 (div. Jan. 1978); children—Douglas Andrew, Joshua Barrett. A.B., Vassar Coll., 1968; M.B.A., Harvard U., 1970. Lic. real estate broker, Mass. Mng. dir. Boston Shakespeare Co., 1979-82; dir. planning Boston Symphony Orch., 1982-84; talk/game show hostess Newton Continental Cablevision, Mass., 1984—; real estate broker Hughes Assocs., Newton, 1984—. Mem. adv. bd. WBZ-TV Fund for the Arts, 1982—; mem. adv. bd. Boston Shakespeare Co., 1982-84, bd. dirs., 1979-82; bd. govs. Harvard Bus. Sch. Alumni Assn., 1983—; trustee Mass. Cultural Alliance, 1980-84; mem. scholarship com. Worcester County Vassar Club, 1976-82, chairperson, 1982; commr. Human Rights Adv. Bd., Worcester, 1977-78. Named 1 of 10 Outstanding Young Leaders of Greater Boston, Boston Jaycees, 1980. Mem. Greater Boston Real Estate Bd., Harvard Bus. Sch. Assn. (bd. govs. 1983—). Jewish. Club: New Eng. Backgammon (Boston). Avocations: crossword puzzles; antiques; theatre; tennis. Home: 30 Avalon Rd Waban MA 02168 Office: Hughes Assocs 1631 Beacon St Waban MA 02168

KRIPALANI, LAKSHMI ASSUDOMAL, educator; b. Hydersbad Sindh, Pakistan, Aug. 24, 1920; came to U.S., 1962, naturalized, 1972; d. Assudomal Shewakram and Hari Assudomal (Advani) K.; diploma Montessori Internat., 1946; B.A. with honors, U. Bombay, 1962; M.A., Iowa U. and Seton Hall U., 1966, cert. supr. and prin., 1976. Founder, headmistress New India Sch., 1943-47; founder Pawai Refugee Camp Sch. for Refugees, Bombay, India, 1947;

head mistress Garrison Sch., Bombay, 1948-62; dir. Montessori Sch., Iowa City, 1962-64; founder Montessori Sch., Newark, 1964-65; founder. Montessori Center of N.J., 1966, now gen. dir.; internat. examiner Montessori Tchr. Tng. Centers; cons. in field. Mem. Assn. Supervision and Curriculum Devel., N.J. Edn. Assn., Nat. Assn. North Am. Montessori Tchr. Assn., Assn. Montessori Internat., Nat. Council Montessori Tchr. Trainers. Republican. Hindu-Unitarian. Contbr. in field. Home and Office: 340 N Fullerton Ave Upper Montclair NJ 07043

KRISTOF, FAITH MARILYN, banker; b. Tigerton, Wis., Mar. 22, 1951; d. Ralph O. and Violet V. Hermann; B.S. (scholar), U. Wis., Stevens Point, 1973; m. James D. Kristof, May 25, 1974; children—Jill Renee, Paul James. With Citizens State Bank of Wittenberg, Wis., 1973—, asst. v.p., br. mgr., Eland, Wis., 1975—. Pres., Maple Hills Golf Course Women's League, 1977-78. Mem. Am. Women Bankers Assn. Lutheran. Club: Maple Hills Golf. Home: Rt 2 Box 94A Wittenberg WI 54499 Office: Box A Eland WI 54427

KRISTOFEK, DAISY REA, dietitian; b. Valley Falls, Kans., Jan. 20, 1925; d. Harry Benton and Edith May (Mallory) Martin; B.A., U. Kans., 1951; M.S., State U. Iowa, 1953; m. Andrew Kristofek, June 16, 1953; children—Jo Andrea, Jacqueline Kay, Andrew, Margaret Fae. Elem. sch. tchr., Kans., 1942-43, jr. high sch. tchr., 1946-47; chief dietitian King's Mountain Hosp., Bristol, Va., 1952-53; therapeutic dietitian, tchr. R.N. program Meml. Hosp., Johnson City, Tenn., 1954-56, cons., 1956-76, clin. and adminstrv. dietitian, 1976-78; dir. dietetic services Johnson City Med. Center Hosp., 1980—; mem. Sullins Coll., Bristol, 1956-76, trustee, 1968-76; guest lectr., cons. in field; bd. advisers Sch. Applied Sci. and Tech., East Tenn. State U., 1982-84, also mem. spl. adv. com. dept. econs. Recipient Victor B. Cook award Sullins Coll., 1976. Mem. Am. Dietetic Assn., Am. Soc. Parenteral and Enteral Nutrition, Nutrition Today Soc., TriCities Dietetic Assn. (dir.), Va. Dietetic Assn., Am. Soc. Hosp. Food Service Adminstrs. (pres. Appalachian chpt.), Bus. and Profl. Women's Club. Democrat. Methodist. Home: 600 Garden Ln Bristol VA 24201 Office: 400 State of Franklin Rd Johnson City TN 37601

KRIZINOFSKI, MARIAN THERESA, educator, mental health specialist; b. Johnson City, N.Y., Nov. 28, 1938; d. Andrew Louis and Mary Josephine (Pekar) Lesko; m. Ronald Joseph Krizinofski, Sept. 2, 1961 (dec.). Dip., Binghamton State Hosp. Sch. Nursing, 1958; postgrad. Columbia U., 1959; B.A., State U. N.Y., 1962, M.S., 1970; Ph.D., Syracuse U., 1984. Staff nurse, head nurse, acting supr. Binghamton Psychiat. Center, N.Y., 1958-63, Ideal Hosp., Endicott, N.Y., 1958; dormitory nurse Columbia U., and Barnard Coll., N.Y.C., 1959; infirmary nurse SUNY-Binghamton, 1959-60; staff nurse Lourdes Hosp., Binghamton, 1960-62; instr. sch. nursing Binghamton Psychiat. Center, 1963-70, clin. specialist, psychiat. mental health nursing and inservice educator, 1970-72; lectr. State U. N.Y., Binghamton, 1972-75; clin. specialist psychiat. mental health nursing in pvt. practice, Binghamton, 1972-80, clin. co-dir. Crisis Call and Suicide Prevention Service, Binghamton, 1971-74; asst. prof. SUNY-Binghamton, 1975-78, assoc. prof., 1978—, adj. faculty Med. Sch., 1979-80, asst. prof., 1986—; cons. in field; condr. numerous workshops. Pres., Broome County Mental Health Assn., 1973-75, bd. dirs., 1967-76; trainer of volunteers Crisis Call and Suicide Prevention Service, 1971-74, Women's Center Hotline and Rape Counseling Center, 1974-76, Men's Identity Crisis and Gay Hotline, 1976-80, others; mem. mental health com. N.Y. Pa. Health Planning Council, 1972-73; bd. dirs. Alcoholism Center of Broome County, 1977-78; mem. Nurses Polit. Action Group, 1977-78; mem. Broome County mental health adv. bd. N.Y. State Legislature, 1978, chmn., 1984. Zonta Club scholar, 1955-58; N.Y. State Dept. Mental Hygiene scholar, 1959, 1959-67; USPHS grantee, 1968-70; certified psychiat. mental health nursing clin. specialist, 1975; HEW fellow, 1977, 79, 80. Diplomate Am. Coll. Nursing Practice. Mem. Am., N.Y. State (chmn. psychiat. mental health conf. group 1976-78, chmn. certification credentials com., mem. council on certification 1976-78) nurses assns., Council Advanced Practitioners in Psychiat. Mental Health Nursing. Republican. Unitarian Universalist. Contbr. articles to profl. jours. Home: 4149 Cheryl Dr Binghamton NY 13903 Office: State U of NY Binghamton NY 13901 also 46 Riverside Dr Binghamton NY 13905

KROCIL, CARLA TERESA, temporary employment service company executive; b. Bklyn., Oct. 23, 1936; d. Charles Carl and Renee T. (DeMarco) K.; B.A., Hofstra U., 1959. Vice-pres. pres. Tempositions, Inc., N.Y.C., 1962-71; gen. mgr. TAD, Inc., N.Y.C., 1971-72; gen. mgr. City Wide Temporary Service, N.Y.C., 1972-74; news corr. Bergen Even Record, Va. Cablevision, Pompton Lakes, N.J., 1974—; pres. Status Temporary Help Co., 1981-82; now ops. mgr. Scandinavian Girl Temporary Office Services of N.Y.; nat. field service rep. Career/Temp Force, Inc., 1980-81; account exec./personnel mgr. Western Temporary Services, Inc.; placement counselor Drake Bus. Sch. Mem. Nat. Assn. Female Execs., Am. Mgmt. Assn., Profl. and Bus. Women, Assn. Temporary Contractors, Internat. Assn. Personnel Women.

KROHA, ANITA PEGGY, chamber of commerce executive; b. Pensacola, Fla., Sept. 17, 1942; d. Curt Willy and Lisbet Hilda (Richter) K. Student Okaloosa-Walton Jr. Coll., 1970-73. File clk. to underwriter Am. Fire and Casualty Ins. Co., Orlando, Fla., 1960-64; agy. mgr. Rogers-Atkins Ins. Agy., Tallahassee, Fla., 1964; ins. sec. Waldorff Ins. and Bonding Co., Ft. Walton Beach, Fla., 1964-68; loan officer Gulf Fed. Savs. and Loan Assn., Ft. Walton Beach, 1968-70; exec. mgr. Destin C. of C., Fla., 1975—; adv. bd. 1st Nat. Bank of Okaloosa County, Destin, 1983; bd. dirs. Destin Fishing Rodeo, 1984—; chmn. rules com. Shark Fishing Tournament, Destin, 1983—; coordinator Destin Seafood Festival, 1980—. Editor: Destin Guidebook, 1977—; Destin Fishing Rodeo Book, 1982-84. Charter mem, bd. dirs. Preservation of Destin, 1981; charter mem. Animal Protection League, Ft. Walton Beach, 1981, Destin Alliance, 1977—. Mem. NOW, Pensacola Bus. and Profl. Women's Club, Ft. Walton Bus. and Profl. Women's Club (dist. sec. 1967), Fla. C. of C. Democrat. Episcopalian. Club: Destin Women's. Avocations: reading; fishing; treasure hunting; local history; preservation. Home: 109 Brooks St SE Fort Walton Beach FL 32548 Office: Destin C of C 209 U S Hwy 98 East Destin FL 32541

KROL, SUSAN AGNES, real estate broker; b. Lawrenceville, N.J., Dec. 11, 1948; d. Stephen Joseph and Rose Marie Krol; degree Rider Coll., Trenton, 1966, Trenton State U., 1973. Engaged in real estate bus., 1961—; broker, owner Krol Realtors, Princeton, N.J., 1971—; real estate broker, Fla. Recipient various sales awards. Mem. Nat. Assn. Female Execs., N.J. Assn. Comml. Realtors, N.E. Region Comml. Realtors, Somerset County Bd. Realtors, Mercer County Bd. Realtors, Hunterdon County Bd. Realtors, Middlesex County Bd. Realtors, Princeton Real Estate Group (exec. dir. 1978-80). Unitarian. Club: Princeton Women's Athletic Assn. Address: 3912 S Ocean Blvd PH-12 Highland Beach FL 33431

KROLL, BEVERLEY JANE, market research executive; b. Chgo., Jan. 2, 1929; d. Ralph and Agnes Jane (Patton) Layman; m. Harold Kroll, Oct. 26, 1957; children—Jeffrey Joseph, Daniel Ralph. B.A., Nat. Coll., Evanston, Ill., 1970, M.S., 1983. Chief sensory lab. Quartermaster Food & Container Inst., Chgo., 1952-61; pres. Peryam & Kroll Research Corp., Chgo., 1961—. Contbr. articles on sensory methodology to profl. jours. Mem. Am. Mktg. Assn., Mktg. Research Assn. Republican. Club: Lincolnwood (Ill.) Afternoon. Home: 3300 W North Shore Ave Lincolnwood IL 60645 Office: Peryam & Kroll Research Corp 4300 W Peterson Ave Chicago IL 60646

KROLL, EVELYN BRENNAN, sporting goods manufacturing executive; b. Staten Island, N.Y., Oct. 5, 1927; d. John Cornelius and Evelyn May (Sanford) Maher; m. John L. Kroll, Dec. 29, 1966; children by previous marriage—John and James Brennan; 1 stepdau., Sharon. Student Hunter Coll., 1949-57. Tchr. pub. schs., N.J., 1952-53; advt. rep. N.Y. Times, 1954-60, asst. dir. sch. and camp advt. dept., 1960-65; prin. Sanmarev Advt. Agy., Stamford, Conn., 1965-67; dir. advt. and pub. relations Jayfro Corp., Waterford, Conn., 1968-72, v.p. mktg. and pub. relations, 1972-79, pres., dir., 1979—; co-founder, dir. Nat. Catalog Distbn. Corp., Harbor City, Calif., 1973; co-founder, mng. editor Nat. Trade Newsletter, 1973—; founder Kroll Press, Waterford, 1978. Author: (with John L. Kroll and Frank Smith) It Doesn't Pay to Work Too Hard, 1977; pub., editor: Blueprint for Safety in Sports and Recreation, 1978; regular mktg. and salesmanship columnist The Sporting Goods Dealer mag., 1974-79; contbr. articles other publs. in field. Trustee Eugene O'Neill Theater Ctr., Waterford and N.Y.C., 1974-79; corporator Southeastern Conn. YMCA, 1982—; dir. East Conn. Symphony Orch.; mem. Friends of Mitchell Coll., New London, Conn. Mem. Nat. Sporting Goods Mfrs. Assn., Nat. Sch. Supply and Equipment Assn. (dir.), Am. Sports Edn. Inst., S.E. Conn. C. of C. (dir.). Clubs: La Coquille (Palm Beach, Fla.); Delray Beach (Fla.); N.Y.U. (N.Y.C.); 2001 (Dallas). Home: 535 Pequot Ave New London CT 06320 also 4201 S Ocean Blvd Highland Beach FL 33431 Office: Jayfro Corp PO Box 400 Hartford Turnpike Waterford CT 06385

KROLL, LAUREN, pharmaceutical company official; b. Camp Kilmer, N.J., July 27, 1952; d. Robert Allen Kroll and Alma Hope (Peebles) Knappenberger. Student Boston U., 1970-71; B.A. magna cum laude, Glassboro (N.J.) State Coll., 1975. Cert. tchr. in early childhood and elem. edn. Head tchr. A Child's Place, Lincroft, N.J., 1976-77; legal asst. Chamlin Esq., West Long Branch, N.J., 1979-81; adminstrv. asst. MSK Assocs., Middletown, N.J., 1981-82; purchasing agt. Sidmak Labs., Inc., East Hanover, N.J., 1982-83, purchasing mgr., 1983-84, ops. mgr. Amera Chemie, Ltd., Garden City, N.Y., 1984-85; acct. mgr. Staff Builders Health Care Services, Inc., N.Y.C., 1986—. Mem. Nat. Assn. Pharm. Mfrs., Drug, Chem. and Allied Trades Assn., Sales Assn. of Chem. Industry, Proprietary Assn., Nat. Assn. Female Execs. Republican. Home: 51 Hillside Ave Cresskill NJ 07626 Office: Staff Builders Inc 122 E 42d St New York NY 10017

KROM, ANN MARIE, nurse; b. Montpelier, Vt., July 10, 1958; d. Walter Lawrence and Shirley Ann (Skirry) Champine; m. Stephen Charles Krom, Sept. 19, 1981; 1 child, Nicholas Andrew. R.N., Albany Med. Ctr. Sch. Nursing, N.Y., 1979. R.N., N.Y. Staff nurse Albany Med. Ctr., 1979-81, Horton Hosp., Middletown, N.Y., 1981-82, Benedictine Hosp., Kingston, N.Y., 1982—. Mem. Rhinebeck Legion Band. Roman Catholic. Avocations: reading; bowling. Home: 19 Lindsley Ave Kingston NY 12401 Office: Benedictine Hosp 105 Mary's Ave Kingston NY 12401

KROMHOUT, ORA MORLIER, instructional systems designer; b. New Orleans, Nov. 26, 1925; d. Dudley Hypolite and Wilhelmine Louise (Cooper) Morlier; B.A., Newcomb Coll., Tulane U., 1945; M.S., U. Ill., 1951; Ph.D., Fla. State U., 1975; m. Robert Andrew Kromhout, Dec. 21, 1950; children—Sharon, Brian, Ethan. Physicist U.S. Dept. Agr., New Orleans, 1945-50; research physicist Zenith Radio Corp., Chgo., 1952-56; ednl. research asso. Computer Assisted Instrn. Center, Tallahassee, Fla., 1966-72; project mgr. Center for Instructional Devel. and Services, Tallahassee, 1974—. Mem. Tallahassee Mcpl. Code Enforcement Bd., 1981—; sec. LeMoyne Art Found., 1967-69. Mem. LWV Fla. (v.p., state legis. chmn. 1971-75), LWV Tallahassee (mem. bd. 1958-63, 1980-85), IEEE (exec. bd. 1980—), Am. Ednl. Research Assn., Phi Kappa Phi, Phi Delta Kappa, Pi Mu Epsilon, Sigma Delta Epsilon. Home: 206 Westminster Dr Tallahassee FL 32304 Office: College of Edn Fla State Univ Tallahassee FL 32306

KROMINGA, LYNN, cosmetic and health care company executive, lawyer; b. Los Angeles, May 16, 1950; d. Dale E. and Phyllis M. Krominga; B.A. in German, U. Minn., 1972, J.D., 1974; m. Barry Fox, Feb. 26, 1981. Bar: Minn. 1974, N.Y. 1976. Assoc. firms in Mpls. and N.Y.C., 1974-77; assoc. counsel Am. Express Co., N.Y.C., 1977-80; sr. internat. counsel Revlon, Inc., N.Y.C., 1981—, v.p., 1984—. Mem. ABA, Internat. Bar Assn., Phi Beta Kappa. Home: 565 West End Ave New York NY 10024 Office: 767 Fifth Ave New York NY 10153

KRONEBUSCH, PATRICIA LOUISE, state senator; b. Mpls., Mar. 17, 1927; d. James Raymond and Luella Louise (Anez) Keller; B.A., Coll. of St. Teresa, Winona, Minn., 1948; M.S., Winona State U., 1969; m. Paul J. Kronebusch, May 30, 1949; children—Paula, Anne, Carol, Mary, Barbara, James, Stephanie, Kathleen. Tchr., Rollingstone, Minn., 1971-80; mem. Minn. Senate, 1980—. Active LWV; mem. Winona Sch. Bd. Dist. 861, 1973-80. mem. Nat. Order of Women Legislators, Minn. Women Elected Ofcls. (bd. dirs.). Ind. Republican. Roman Catholic. Office: Room 153 State Office Bldg Saint Paul MN 55155

KRONIN, BERNADETTE SMITH, editor, publisher, advertising executive, public relations consultant; b. N.Y.C., Feb. 23, 1943; d. Stanley Allen and Toby (Percak) Smith; children—Amy Bernadette Rose, Karen Edna Wendy. B.A. in History and English, Bucknell U., 1964; M.A. in Liberal Studies, SUNY-Stony Brook, 1971; Ed.M., Columbia U., 1982. Tchr. history N.Y., 1964-69; innovator pre-sch. programs, Shoreham, N.Y., 1975-79; editor, pub. Community Jour., Wading River, N.Y., 1978—, advt. mgr., 1978—, editor Shoreham-Wading River Newsletter, 1978—; profl. breeder, shower A.K.C. golden retriever dogs; cons., workshop leader, 1979—. Editor: C. of C. Directory, Shoreham, 1983, 84. Advisor Teen Recreation Adv. Com., Rocky Point, N.Y., 1979-82; mem. Nuclear Emergency Evacuation Com., 1979-82, pres. PTA, Wading River, 1980-83; v.p. Spl. Edn. PTA, Wading River, 1979-80; active Com. Gifted and Talented Children, Wading River, 1979-80, Occupational Edn. Commn., 1979-80; mem. Suffolk County Human Rights Commn. Recipient Disting. Service award Am. Cancer Soc., 1982-83; award of merit N.Y. State Pub. Relations Assn., 1982-83; award of honor Nat. Sch. Pub. Relations Assn., 1981. Mem. Wading River C. of C. (bd. dirs. 1979-80), Suffolk County Bus. and Profl. Women's Assn., Women's Equal Rights Congress, East End Women's Network, Rocky Point C. of C., Sigma Delta Chi, Kappa Kappa Gamma. Roman Catholic. Club: L.I. Press. Home: PO Box 619 Wading River NY 11792 Office: Community Jour PO Box 619 Wading River NY 11792

KRONMAN, CAROL JANE, lawyer; b. Passaic, N.J., Mar. 25, 1944; d. Robert M. and Helen (Harris) K.; m. William D. Lipkind, Aug. 15, 1965 (div. 1975); children—Audrey Jayne, Heather Sue. A.B., Cornell U., 1965; M.A., Columbia U., 1966; J.D., Yeshiva U., 1980. Bar: N.Y. 1981, N.J. 1981, Fla. 1981. Asst. prof. William Paterson Coll., Wayne, N.J., 1967-69; treas. Capital Theatre Inc., N.J. Corp., 1977-83; coordinator paralegal studies Montclair State Coll. (N.J.), 1982-83, prof., 1982—; ptnr. Kronman & Kronman P.A., Totowa, N.J., 1981-85; ptnr. Max E. Greenberg, Cantor & Reiss, 1986—; pvt. investment adviser, N.J., 1977—. Recipient Certs. of Appreciation, Rotary Club, Caldwell and Parsippany, N.J., 1983. Mem. ABA, N.J. Bar Assn., N.Y. Bar Assn., Fla. Bar Assn., Passaic County Bar Assn, Bergen County Bar Assn. Home: 26 Spruce Rd North Caldwell NJ 07006 Office: 3 Empire Blvd South Hackensack NJ 07606

KROPP, MARCELYN MARIE, corporate communicator; b. Lawrence, Kans., Nov. 11, 1956; d. David Lee Baldwin and Carolyn Marie Mathews; m. Phillip Lee Kropp, Aug. 16, 1980 (div. May 1986). B.A. in Communications, Calif. State U.-Fullerton, 1985. Cert. in corp. communications U. So. Calif. Asst. editor United Indian Planners Assn. News, Washington, 1976-77; sales mgr. Southwestern Co., Nashville, 1978-79; asst. mgr. Wilderness Adventure, Stillwater, Okla., 1979-80; info. specialist Hunt-Wesson Foods, Inc., Fullerton, Calif., 1980-81; v.p. ops. Western Walkie Talkie, Inc., Anaheim, Calif., 1981-83; pub. affairs dir. Indian Ctrs., Inc., Los Angeles, 1984; publs. anaylst Rockwell Internat., Seal Beach, Calif., 1984—; pub. relations cons. to rock bands, Orange County, Calif., 1980-85; media relations cons. Los Angeles Indian Ctrs., 1985; mktg. cons. Turning Point, Irvine, Calif., 1985; guest lectr. Calif. State U., Fullerton, 1985—. Contbr. articles to newspapers and jours. Ednl. Expdns. internat. scholar, Iceland, 1974; HEW scholar Nat. Outdoor Leadership Sch., 1973; DAR scholar, 1975, Cornell U. scholar, 1975; scholar Am. Assn. Bus. Women, 1984; Coors pub. relations scholar, 1985. Communications asst. Am. Indian Women on the Move, Los Angeles, 1984-85. Mem. Native Am. Press Assn., Women in Communications (Woman of Achievement award 1984, chpt. pres. 1985, Nat. Outstanding chpt. award 1985), Women in Mgmt. (newsletter dir. 1985—, scholar 1984, 85), Internat. Assn. Bus. Communicators (Helios award 1985, 86). Democrat. Episcopalian. Avocations: tennis; plays; reading. Office: Rockwell Internat 2600 Westminster Blvd Seal Beach CA 90740

KROSKA, RITA CAROLINE ANN, nurse, educator; b. Duelm, Minn., July 6, 1921; d. Anthony (Tony) John and Alma Mary (Herbst) Kroska; B.S. in Nursing, Cath. U. Am., 1945; M.S. in Nursing Edn., 1956; cert. nurse-midwife Cath. Maternity Inst., 1948; M.P.H., U. Minn., 1961, Ph.D. in Anthropology, 1965. Instr. in nurse-midwifery Cath. Maternity Inst., Santa Fe, 1948-57; asst. prof. Sch. Public Health U. Minn., Mpls., 1965-71; prof. nursing U. N.Mex., Albuquerque, 1971-72, Marquette U., Milw., 1972-74, Mankato State U., Minn., 1974-76, Coll. of St. Teresa, Winona, Minn., 1976-78; assoc. prof. U. Tex., El Paso, 1978-84; Disting. Vis. Sorrel prof., holder Anise J. Sorrell chair in nursing Troy (Ala.) State U., 1982-83. Mem. Am. Coll. Nurse-Midwives (founding mem.), Am. Anthrop. Assn., Am. Nurses Assn., Nurses Assn. Roman Catholic. Contbr. articles in field to profl. jours. Home: 735 Calle del Ensalmo Green Valley AZ 85614

KROSSNER, RHONDA PARRELLA, psychologist; b. Mt. Vernon, N.Y., Dec. 29, 1951; d. Joseph and Ida (Cornacchia) Parrella; B.S. summa cum laude, Fordham U., 1973, M.A. (NIMH fellow), 1975, Ph.D., 1983; m. William J. Krossner, Jr., Sept. 4, 1977; 1 son, Steven. Vice pres. Psy Minn. Corp., Duluth, 1977-84; head neuropsychology div. Neurosci. Inst., Duluth, 1984—. Mem. Nat. Acad. Neuropsychologists, Am. Psychol. Assn., Phi Beta Kappa. Home: PO Box 3047 Duluth MN 55803 Office: 205 W 2d St Duluth MN 55802

KROUSE, SUSAN APPLEGATE, museum curator; b. Detroit, July 1, 1955; d. John D. and Carol Edith (Summers) Applegate; m. Ned Allen Krouse, Aug. 19, 1978. A.B., Ind. U., 1976, M.A., 1981. Acting curator I.U. Museum, Bloomington, Ind., 1978-79; curator New Hanover County Mus., Wilmington, N.C., 1981—. Mem. Am. Assn. for State and Local History, Council for Mus. Anthropology. Office: New Hanover County Mus 814 Market St Wilmington NC 28401

KRUCKEBERG, VICKY LEE, home economist; b. Alton, Ill., Nov. 13, 1951; d. Kenneth and Hertha May (Brewer) K.; B.S., So. Ill. U., Carbondale, 1974, M.S., 1975. Grad. teaching asst. So. Ill. U., 1974-75; saleswoman Paul Harris Stores, St. Louis, 1975; textile conservator U.S. Cav. Mus., Ft. Riley, Kans., 1979, N.Y. State Parks, Recreation and Historic Preservation Dept., 1980-85; costume conservator Kent State U. Mus., Ohio 1985—; project dir. Intermus. Services Conservation Project, 1984, conservation project Inst. Mus. Services, 1984; project dir. 1985; instr. clothing and textiles Kans. State U., Manhattan, 1975-80. Recipient Home Econs. Faculty Research award Kans. State U., 1977, Grad. Sch. Faculty Research award, 1978. Mem. Am. Assn. Mus., Am. Assn. State and Local History, Am. Inst. Conservation, Costume Soc. Am., Assn. Coll. Profs. Textile and Clothing, Am. Home Econs. Assn., Internat. Com. Museums, Embroiderers Guild Am. Republican. Presbyterian. Author papers in field.

KRUEGER, BETTY JANE, telecommunication company executive; b. Indpls., Oct. 4, 1923; d. Forrest Glen and Hazel Luellen (Taylor) Burns; student Butler U., 1948-49; m. Alan Douglas Krueger, Apr. 4, 1975; 1 son by previous marriage—Michael J. Vornehm. Supr., instr. Ind. Bell Telephone Co., Indpls., 1941-54; supr. communications Jones & Laughlin Steel Co., Indpls., 1954-56, Ford Motor Co., Indpls., 1956-64, U.S. Govt., Camp Atterbury, Ind., 1964-66; dir. communications Meth. Hosp. of Ind., Indpls., 1966-79; pres. owner Rent-A-Radio, Inc. of Ind., Indpls., after 1979; sec.-treas. Communications Unltd., Inc. Former pres. Am. Legion Aux.; chmn. for Ind., Girls State U.S.A., 1972-77; probation officer vol., 1973-74; suicide prevention counselor, 1972-73. Recipient award for outstanding community service Ford Motor Co., 1961. Mem. Am. Soc. Hosp. Engring., Am. Hosp. Assn., Nat. Assn. Bus. and Ednl. Radio, Inc., Internat. Teletypewriters for the Deaf, Asso. Public Safety Communications Officers, Inc., Am. Bus. Women. Methodist. Home: Rural Route 2 Box 119 Franklin IN 46131 Office: 4032 Southeastern Ave Indianapolis IN 46203

KRUEGER, BONNIE LEE, editor, writer; b. Chgo., Feb. 3, 1950; d. Harry Bernard and Lillian (Soyak) Krueger; m. James Lawrence Spurlock, Mar. 8, 1972. Student Morraine Valley Coll., 1970. Adminstrv. asst. Carson Pirie Scott & Co., Chgo., 1969-72; traffic coordinator Tatham Laird & Kudner, Chgo., 1973-74; traffic coordinator J. Walter Thompson, Chgo., 1974-76; prodn. coordinator, 1976-78; editor-in-chief Assoc. Pubs., Chgo., 1978—; editor-in-chief Sophisticate's Hairstyle Guide, 1978—, Sophisticates Beauty Guide, 1978—, Complete Woman, 1981—; pub., editorial services dir. Sophisticate's Black Hair Guide, 1983—. Mem. Statue of Liberty Restoration Com., N.Y.C., 1983; campaign worker Cook County State's Atty., Chgo., 1982; poll watcher Cook County Dem. Orgn., 1983. Mem. Soc. Profl. Journalists, Nat. Assn. Female Execs., Sigma Delta Chi. Lutheran. Clubs: Sierra, Cousteau Soc. Office: Associated Publications Inc 1165 N Clark St Chicago IL 60610

KRUEGER, DEBORAH JOAN, management consultant; b. Jamestown, N.D., Mar. 11, 1956; d. Lester James and Phyllis Jean (Koenig) K.; B.A. in Biology, U. Calif.-Santa Barbara, 1978; M.H.A., Duke U., 1980. Cardiopulmonary clk. Cottage Hosp., Santa Barbara, 1978; patient account rep. Durham (N.C.) County Hosp., 1979-80; health adminstrn. fellow Duke U. Hosp., Durham, 1980-81; cons. Amherst Assocs., Atlanta, 1981-84, Tampa, 1984—. Vol. Imola State Hosp., Napa, Calif., 1973-74; big sister St. Vincents Sch. for Mentally Handicapped, Santa Barbara, 1974-78; fund raiser Duke U. Health Adminstrn. Dept., 1980—; assoc. coordinator Catholic Young Adults, Durham, 1980-81; bd. dirs. Hospice of Pinellas County, St. Petersburg, Fla., 1984. Calif. State Scholar, 1974; scholar. Am. Bus. Women's Assn., Loyal Order of Moose, Napa, Calif. Mem. Am. Coll. Hosp. Adminstrn., Healthcare Fin. Mgmt. Assn., Nat. Assn. Female Execs., Alpha Delta Pi (v.p., pres. 1977; Violet award 1978), Phi Sigma Kappa (little sister). Roman Catholic. Office: Amherst Associates 4830 W Kennedy Blvd Suite 450 Tampa FL 33624

KRUEGER, DONNA MARIE, travel agency owner; b. The Dalles, Oreg., July 5, 1927; d. Francis Henry and Gerda Marie (Gasman) Pashek; m. Rollin Joseph Kennard, June 5, 1948 (div. July 1964); m. David Harry Krueger, Aug. 26, 1966 (dec. June 1974); children—Karen L. Newton, B. Jeffrey, Curtis J., Brent W. Student U. Wash., 1945-47; B.A., U. Calif.-Irvine, 1977. Cert. travel cons. Adminstrv. asst. U. Calif.-Irvine, 1966-77; travel cons. Newport Hills Travel, Newport Beach, Calif., 1978-80, Balboa Travel, Calif., 1980-81; owner, mgr. Back Bay Travel, Costa Mesa, Calif., 1981—. Mem. Am. Soc. Travel Agts., Inst. Cert. Travel Agts., Pacific Area Travel Assn., Caribbean Travel Assn., Orange County Travellarvans (v.p. programs 1983-85). Home: 2400 Elden Ave #24 Costa Mesa CA 92627 Office: Back Bay Travel 2675 Irvine Ave Costa Mesa CA 92627

KRUEGER, KATHERINE KAMP, lawyer; b. Chgo., Apr. 7, 1944; d. Rudolph Pollay and Josephine Yvette (Marland) Kamp. Student U. Paris, Sorbonne, 1963-64; B.S. magna cum laude, Tulane U., 1965, M.S., 1968; J.D., Northwestern U., 1980. Bar: Tex. 1980. Micropaleontologist, Gulf Oil Corp., New Orleans, 1967-68; custodian collections geology Field Mus., Chgo., 1968-76, lectr., 1975-76; lectr. earth sci. Northeastern Ill. U., Chgo., 1977; atty. oil and gas Gulf Oil Corp., Houston, 1980-81, Amoco Prodn. Co., Houston, 1981—; bd. dirs. The Eureka Soc., Escondido, Calif., 1974—; vol. lectr. Desk and Derrick, Houston, 1983. Contbr. articles to profl. jours. Campaign vol., poll watcher Ind. Democratic candidate for Ill. Constl. Conv., Chgo., 1968; poll watcher Ind. Democratic candidate for Ill. Rep., Chgo., 1978; del. Dem. Senatorial Dist. 7 Conv., Tex., 1984. NSF Student grantee microbiol. dept. U. Miami Marine Lab., 1960-64; grantee La. Heart Found., Sophie Newcomb Coll. Botany Dept., 1962-63, Grad. Sch. Tulane U. Scholars and Fellows Orgn., 1965-66; named Steinmayer Best Geol. Student, Tulane U., 1965; Houston Bar Found. fellow, 1982—. Mem. ABA, State Bar Tex., Houston Bar Assn., Phi Beta Kappa, Sigma Gamma Epsilon, Eta Sigma Phi. Home: 10426 Knoboak Dr Houston TX 77043 Office: Amoco Prodn Co PO Box 3092 Houston TX 77253

KRUG, ADELE JENSEN (MRS. WALTER JOHN KRUG), library science educator; b. Thief River Falls, Minn., Mar. 30, 1908; d. Anton Martin Hulbert and Tillie Manspand (Johnson) Jensen; B.A., Gallaudet Coll., 1930; M.S., Cath. U. Am., 1961; m. Walter John Krug, June 18, 1932 (dec. May 1962); children—Janice Krug Riley, Diana Krug Armstrong, Walter F., Warren J. Instr., R.I. Sch. for Deaf, 1930-32; instr. library sci. Gallaudet Coll., Washington, 1955-63, asst. prof., 1963-67, assoc. prof., 1967-75. Pres., Stuart Jr. High Sch. PTA, Washington, 1954-56, McKinley High Sch. PTA, 1956-57. Mem. Conv. Am. Instrs. Deaf, Nat. Assn. of Deaf, D.C. Women's Aux., Nat. Luth. Home, Phi Kappa Zeta (nat. alumnae pres. 1954-60). Contbr. to Am. Anns. of Deaf. Home: Crystal Sq W 511 1515 S Jefferson Davis Hwy Arlington VA 22202

KRUKOWSKI, MARILYN DENMARK, biology educator, biology researcher; b. N.Y.C., May 3, 1932; d. Henry and Julia Marian (Lipshitz) Denmark; m. Lucian Krukowski, Jan. 14, 1955; 1 child, Samantha Henriette. B.A., Bklyn. Coll., 1954; M.S., NYU, 1962, Ph.D., 1965. Instr. N.Y. Med. Coll., N.Y.C., 1964-66, asst. prof., 1966-69; asst. prof. Washington U., St. Louis, 1969-75, assoc. prof. biology, 1975—. Contbr. sci. articles to profl. jours. Recipient Founders Day award NYU, 1965. Mem. AAAS, Am. Soc. Bone and Mineral Research, Am. Soc. Cell Biology, Sigma Xi. Democrat. Home: 24 Washington Terr Saint Louis MO 63112 Office: Dept Biology Washington U Saint Louis MO 63130

KRULEWICH, HELEN D., lawyer; b. Paterson, N.J., Apr. 6, 1948; d. George and Kathrine P. (Vanderheide) Dworetzky; m. Leonard M. Krulewich, Sept. 2, 1972; children—Sara Heide. B.S., Syracuse U., 1970; J.D., Suffolk U., 1974. Bar: Mass. 1974, N.J., U.S. Supreme Ct. Assoc. Rackemann, Sawyer & Brewster, Boston, 1974-75; sole practice, Boston, 1975-78, assoc. regional counsel real estate ops. Prudential Ins. Co. Am., Boston, 1978-85; counsel

Kargert Krulewich & Arnowitz, Boston, 1985—. Bd. dirs., chmn. edn. com. Govt. Ctr. Childcare Corp.; mem. Hist. Neighborhoods Found.; mem. auction com. Big Sisters. Mem. Mus. Fine Arts, Condominium Assn., Beacon Hill Civic Assn., Opera Assn., Inst. Contemporary Art, Mus. Modern Art New Eng. Women in Real Estate, ABA, Mass. Bar Assn., Boston Bar Assn., Mass. Conveyancers Assn., Urban Land Inst., Mass. Assn. Women Lawyers (scholarship found.), Women's Bar Assn., LWV, Friends Pub. Garden. Office: Karger Krulewich & Arnowitz 18 Tremont St Boston MA 02108

KRULFELD, RUTH MARILYN, anthropologist, educator; b. N.Y.C., Apr. 15, 1931; d. Leon and Frances (Rosenberg) Pulwers; B.A. cum laude, Brandeis U., 1956; Ph.D., Yale U., 1974; m. Jacob Mendel Krulfeld, Aug. 28, 1964; 1 son, Michael David. Field researcher micro-geographic research farms in Singapore, Malaya, 1951-53; anthrop. research in Jamaica, 1957, Costa Rica, Nicaragua, Panama, 1958, Lombok Indonesia, 1960-62; asst. prof. anthropology, dir. grad. students George Washington U., Washington, 1964-72, assoc. prof., 1973-76, prof., 1976—, now chmn. dept. anthropology, also dir. spl. grad. research degree program. Currier scholar Yale U., 1958; Found. for Study of Man grantee, 1957; Ford fellow, 1960-62; Am. Council Learned Socs. and Social Sci. Research Council grantee, 1963. Mem. Anthrop. Assn. of Washington, Am. Anthrop. Assn., Anthrop. Soc. Washington. Jewish. Contbr. articles in field to profl. jours. Home: 4012 N Woodstock St Arlington VA 22207 Office: Dept Anthropology George Washington U Washington 20052

KRUPA, ANNA GRAZYNA, nurse; b. Podwoloczyska, Poland, Jan. 21, 1935; came to U.S., 1974; d. Zbigniew and Janina (Kubrakowska) Szczurkiewicz; m. Roman Krupa, June 2, 1979; 1 son, Tomasz Modrzejowski. Degree Nat. Inst. for Spl. Edn., Poland; B.S., Coll. for Human Services, 1979; B.S. in Nursing, U. So. Miss., 1984, postgrad., 1986—. Spl. edn. tchr., Poland, 1960-74; exec. dir. Community Service Orgn., Bklyn., 1976-79; project dir. Youth Ctr., Bklyn., 1977-79; practical nurse Gulfport Meml. Hosp. (Miss.), 1981-82, R.N., 1984—. Mem. Nat. Student Nurses Assn. Sigma Theta Tau. Democrat. Roman Catholic. Office: VA Med Ctr Biloxi MS 39531

KRUPNIK, VEE M., business executive; b. Chgo.; d. Phillip and Jane (Glickman) K.; m. Melvin Drury, Sept. 24, 1978. B.S., Northwestern U., C.P.A., real estate broker, ins. broker, Ill. Assoc. dir. corp. fin. Weis, Voisin, Cannon, Chgo., 1967-68; pres. PEC Industries Inc., Ft. Lauderdale, Fla., 1969-71; acct., real estate and ins. broker Vee M. Krupnik & Co., Chgo., 1971-73; sales cons. Baird & Warner Inc., Chgo., 1973-81, asst. v.p. comml.-investment div., 1981-85, v.p. corp. group, 1985—. Mem. Internat. Assn. Fin. Planning (bd. dirs. 1985—), Internat. Council Shopping Ctrs., Nat. Assn. Corp. Real Estate Execs., Nat. Assn. Securities Dealers, Women's Exec. Network, Nat. Assn. Realtors (bd. dirs. 1983-84, comml. investment council), Cert. Comml. Investors (pres. Ill. chpt. 1983-84), Ill. Assn. Realtors (bd. dirs. 1983-84), Chgo. Bd. Realtors (bd. dirs. 1982-85, comml. investment pres. 1982-84), Chgo. Assn. Commerce and Industry. Club: Comml. Real Estate Orgn. Home: 5757 N Sheridan Rd Chicago IL 60660 Office: Baird & Warner Inc 200 W Madison St #2500 Chicago IL 60606

KRUPSAK, MARY ANNE, lawyer, former lieutenant governor N.Y.; b. Schenectady, Mar. 26, 1932; d. Ambrose Michael and Mamie (Wytrwal) K.; B.A. in History, U. Rochester, 1953; M.S. in Pub. Communications, U. Boston, 1954, LL.D. (hon.), 1975; LL.D., U. Chgo., 1962; H.H.D. (hon.), Russell Sage Coll., 1973; Litt.D. (hon.), Clarkson Coll., 1975; L.H.D., Mt. Mary Coll., 1977, Alliance Coll., 1977, Keaka Coll., 1977; m. Edwin Margolis, June 30, 1969. Program asso. Gov. Averell Harriman, 1954-58; adminstrv. asst. to Congressman Samuel Stratton, 1958-59; admitted to N.Y. State bar, 1962; pvt. practice; asst. counsel Office of Temp. Pres., N.Y. State Senate; mem. staff Speaker N.Y. Assembly, until 1968; mem. N.Y. State Assembly, 1968-72, N.Y. Senate, 1972-74; lt. gov. N.Y., 1975-79; pvt. practice law, 1979—; dir. Coleco Industries, Hartford, Conn. Co-chairperson N.Y. del. Democratic Nat. Conv., 1972; bd. dirs. Cornell U., Coll. Environ. Scis. and Forestry, Syracuse U. Mem. N.Y. State, Montgomery County bar assns., AAUW, Bus. and Profl. Women, Zonta, Soroptomists, Women's Polit. Caucus, NOW, Nat. Council Women U.S., Kosciusko Found., Assn. Bar City N.Y., Rosary Soc. Roman Catholic. Office: One Commerce Plaza 99 Washington Ave Suite 1134 Albany NY 12260

KRUSE, ANN GRAY, computer programmer; b. Oklahoma City, Jan. 4, 1941; d. Floyd and Bernice Florence (Follansbee) Gray; A.B., Randolph Macon Woman's Coll., 1963; M.B.A., U. Chgo., 1973; m. Roy Edwin Kruse, Mar. 20, 1971 (dec.). Programming mgr. Ind. Info. Controls, Valparaiso, Ind., 1966-67; systems programmer Nat. Bus. Lists, Inc., Chgo., 1968-69, Am. Steel Foundries, Hammond, Ind., 1970-73; engr. applications programming Bell Helicopter Textron, Fort Worth, 1974-76; lead systems programmer Harris Data Communications, Dallas, 1976-81; sr. systems programmer Lone Star Gas Co., Dallas, 1981-82; sr. software specialist E-Systems, Dallas, 1982—. Republican. Episcopalian. Home: 6128 Blackberry Ln Dallas TX 75248 Office: PO Box 660023 Dallas TX 75266

KRUSE, CHRISTINE G., nurse, author, poet; b. Denver, May 21, 1952; d. Dean Elwood and Charlotte Grace (Lake) Oglevie; children—Pamela Rouchelle, Gregory Peter. R.N., B.S.N., Olivet Nazarene Coll., 1974. R.N., Mo. Charge nurse Trinity Luth. Hosp., Kansas City, Mo., 1974-75, staff nurse surgery, 1975-77; nursing audit coordinator Bethany Med. Ctr., Kansas City, Kans., 1977-79, spl. projects asst., 1978-80, adminstrv. coordinator, 1980-83, PRN nurse, 1983-84, primary nurse, 1984—; audit cons. Olathe Community Hosp. (Kans.), 1979. Author: Patient-Centered Audit, 1984. Pres., Dist. 512 Kans. Parents Assn. for Hearing-Impaired Children, Shawnee Mission, 1983-84, 79-80; exec. Parent Adv. Council to Sch. Bd., Shawnee Mission, 1983-84. Mem. Mid Am. Romance Authors, Romance Writers Am. Democrat. Home: W 6927 Prairie Post Falls ID 83854

KRUSE, JOANN, corporation executive; b. Ada, Okla., June 17, 1946; d. Elmer M. Powell and Laura H. (Brewer) Cooper; m. Donald E. Kruse, June 1, 1963; children—Bill, Donny, Laurie. A.A., Ventura Jr. Coll., 1966; B.A., Calif. State U.-Northridge, 1968; M.A., Calif. Luth. Coll., 1969, also teaching cert. Tchr. various elem. schs., Calif., 1969-78; prin. Mesa Union Sch., Camarillo, Calif., 1978-80; instr. adult edn. Ventura Coll., 1980-82; corp. exec. sec.-treas. Channel Electric, Inc., Ventura, 1981—, also personnel and acctg. mgr., 1981—, bookkeeper, computer programmer, 1980-81; cons. Diversified Electronics, Los Angeles, 1982—. Mem. Nat. Assn. Women in Constrn., Nat. Assn. Women in Edn. Club: Los Posas Country (Camarillo). Home: 1748 Hedon Circle Camarillo CA 93010 Office: Channel Electric Inc 1982 E Thompson Blvd Ventura CA 93001

KRYNICKI, MARGARET, employee relations manager; b. Long Beach, Calif., Nov. 8, 1953; d. Thaddeus S. and Winifred (Kirwan) Krynicki. B.A., Calif. State U.-Long Beach, 1976, M.A., 1982; postgrad. U. So. Calif. Human resources asst. TRW ISD, Long Beach, 1976-78; personnel adminstr. Mattel, Inc., Hawthorne, Calif., 1978-79, TRW Elec. & Def., Redondo Beach, Calif., 1979-82; employee relations specialist, employee relations mgr. Rockwell Internat./NAAO, El Segundo, Calif., 1982—; human resources cons. TRW Electronics, 1982. Mem. Nat. Mgmt. Assn., Internat. Communications Assn. Office: Rockwell N Am Aircraft Ops PO Box 92098 Los Angeles CA 90009

KRYSIAK, MARGARET ANNE, librarian; b. Cleve., Jan. 4, 1933; d. Edward A. and Anna (Molinski) Krysiak; m. Stanley Goscinski, Oct. 2, 1954; children—Laurence, Michael, Mary Elisabeth. B.A., U. Fla., Gainesville, 1976, postgrad., 1977-80; M.S., Fla. State U., Tallahassee, 1981. Library aide Riley Ave. Sch., Calverton, N.Y., 1966-68; tech. asst. U. Fla. Library, 1982-83, asst. librarian., 1983—. Mem. Cleve. Orch. Chorus, 1956-58. Mem. ALA, Med. Library Assn., Assn. Coll. and Research Libraries, Phi Beta Kappa, Beta Phi Mu, Sigma Tau Sigma. Club: Polish Singers Alliance (sec. 1951-55). Home: 1519 NE 12th St Gainesville FL 32601 Office: 131 Library W U Fla Gainesville FL 32611

KU, CECILIA CHOU YUAN, analytical chemist, researcher; b. Peking, China, Jan. 9, 1942; came to U.S., 1966; naturalized, 1974; d. Hsiao-Hsing and Chin-Chung (Shih) Yuan; m. James Chen Ku, June 3, 1967; children—Grace, Philip. B.S., Nat. Taiwan Normal U., Taiwan, 1966; M.S., Carnegie-Mellon U., 1968. Cert. tchr., Pa. Chemist U. Pitts., 1969-71, Research Triangle Inst., N.C., 1974-75; chemist, scientist Carnegie-Mellon U., Pitts., 1971-73; analytical chemist, quality control chemist OSHA, US Dept. Labor, Salt Lake City, 1976—, cons., 1982—. Mem. Am. Indsl. Hygiene Assn. Mem. Evangelical Free Ch. Avocations: computers; statistical process control; cooking; piano. Office: US Dept Labor OSHA Analytical Lab 1781 S 300 W PO Box 15200 Salt Lake City UT 84115

KUBAITIS, DIANE MARIE, communications director; b. Evergreen Park, Ill., Feb. 1, 1958; d. Andrew George and Pauline Josephine (Bumber) K. B.A. in Mktg., Bradley U., Peoria, Ill., 1980. Mktg. trainee Continental Group, Chgo., 1977-80; mktg. asst. Hayes Hill Inc., Chgo., 1980-81, office services mgr., Dallas, 1981-85; dir. communications Price Waterhouse, Dallas, 1985—. Mem. Am. Mktg. Assn., Internat. Assn. Bus. Communicators, Dallas Bus. Vol. Council, Am. Legion Aux., Dallas Dialogue, Female Exec. Club, Press Club Dallas. Democrat. Roman Catholic. Office: Price Waterhouse 1400 First City Ctr Dallas TX 75201

KUBISTAL, PATRICIA BERNICE, elementary school principal; b. Chgo., Jan. 19, 1938; d. Edward John and Bernice Mildred (Lenz) Kubistal; A.B. cum laude, Loyola U. of Chgo., 1959, A.M., 1964, A.M., 1965, Ph.D., 1968; postgrad. Chgo. State Coll., 1962, Ill. Inst. Tech., 1963, State U. Iowa, 1963, Nat. Coll. Edn., 1974-75. With Chgo. Bd. Edn., 1959—, tchr., 1959-63, counselor, 1963-65, adminstrv. intern, 1965-66, asst. to dist. supt., 1968-69, prin. spl. edn. sch., 1969-75, prin. Simpson Sch., 1975-76, Brentano Sch., 1976—; supr. Lake View Evening High Sch., 1982—; lectr. Loyola U. Sch. Edn., Nat. Coll. Edn. Grad. Sch., Mundelein Coll.; coordinator Upper Bound Program of U. Ill. Circle Campus, 1966-68. Active Crusade of Mercy; mem. com. Ill. Constl. Conv., 1967-69; mem. Citizens Sch. Com., 1969-71; mem. edn. com. Field Mus., 1971; edn. adv. North Side Chgo. PTA Region, 1975; chmn. Pathfinder dist. Boy Scouts Am., 1978-80; bd. govs. Loyola U., 1961—, chmn. alumni scholarship com., 1982. NDEA grantee, 1963, NSF grantee, 1965, HEW Region 5 grantee for drug edn., 1974; U. Chgo. adminstrv. fellow, 1984; recipient Outstanding Intern award Nat. Assn. Secondary Sch. Prins., 1966; named Outstanding History Tchr., Chgo. Public Schs., 1963, Outstanding Ill. Educator, 1970, Outstanding Women of Ill., 1970; St. Luke's-Logan Sq. Community Person of Yr., 1977. Mem. Ill. Personnel and Guidance Assn., NEA, Ill., Chgo. edn. assns., Am. Acad. Polit. and Social Sci., Aux. Chgo. Prins. Assn. (pres.), Chgo. Prins. Club, Nat. Council Adminstrv. Women, Chgo. Council Exceptional Children, Chgo. Council Fgn. Relations, Chgo. Urban League, Loyal Christian Benevolent Assn., Kappa Gamma Pi (pres. Chgo. chpt. 1979-80), Pi Gamma Mu, Phi Delta Kappa, Delta Kappa Gamma (editor-in-chief Lambda State Newscaster), Delta Sigma Rho, Phi Sigma Tau. Book rev. editor of Chgo. Prins. Jour., 1970-76; editor-in-chief Chgo. Prins. Reporter, 1981—. Home: 5111 N Oakley Ave Chicago IL 60625 Office: 2723 N Fairfield St Chicago IL 60647

KUCERAK, MARION LEE, county official; b. N.Y.C., Sept. 24, 1946; d. Henry and Erica (Rosenbaum) Michael; m. Steven Edward Kucerak, Jan. 4, 1981; 1 child, Stephanie Elizabeth. B.A. cum laude, SUNY-Buffalo, 1968; M.P.A. with distinction, Pace U., 1982. Social caseworker Westchester County Dept. Social Services, White Plains, N.Y., 1968-74, unit mgr., 1974-80, program specialist, 1980-83, adminstr. personnel/human resource office, 1983—, 85, on-call dir. emergency services, 1983, dir. Westchester County Social Services, Mt. Kisco Dist. Office, 1985—; lectr. in field; curriculum task force mem. Pace U., 1981. Exec. com. 61/41 Dorchester Tenants Assn., New Rochelle, N.Y., 1982-83; active Big Bros./Big Sisters, White Plains, 1974-79; nat. student coordinator SUNY-Buffalo, 1965-66. Recipient hon. plaque Big Bros./Big Sisters, 1978. Mem. Cap and Gown, Pi Alpha Alpha. Jewish. Home: 94 Park Dr Mount Kisco NY 10549 Office: Westchester County Dept Social Services 25 Moore Ave Mount Kisco NY 10549

KUCHENBECKER, RUTH HELEN, constrn., carpet co. exec.; b. Neenah, Wis., Mar. 4, 1937; d. August Herman and Rose E. (Buss) Peapenburg; student public schs., Neenah; m. Alfred Paul Kuchenbecker, Nov. 16, 1957; children—Ann Marie, Mary Kay, Amy Lynn. Sec., bookkeeper Wis. Paper Group, Menasha, 1955-65, Towne, Inc., Mech. Contractors, Appleton, Wis., 1967-69; partner, sec.-treas. Kuchenbecker Builders, Neenah, 1968—; sec.-treas. Wholesale Builders Supply, Inc., 1970—; owner, pres. Kuchenbecker Carpets Inc., Neenah, 1975—; partner D&K Leasing, Neenah, 1979—, Kuchenbecker Custom Woodworking, 1981—. Mem. Nat. Right to Work Com. Mem. Nat. Assn. Women in Constrn. (past pres., bd. dirs. Fox Valley chpt.), Nat. Assn. Home Builders Women's Aux. Republican. Lutheran. Office: 1573 N Deerwood Neenah WI 54956

KUCHNIR, FRANCA TAGLIABUE, physicist, educator; b. Russe, Bulgaria, July 18, 1935; came to U.S., 1960, naturalized, 1973; d. Luigi and Matilde (Perez) Tagliabue; B.S., U. San Paulo, 1958; M.S., U. Ill., 1962, Ph.D., 1965; m. Moyses Kuchnir, Aug. 6, 1960; children—Louis, Deborah. Research asst. U. Ill., 1960-65, asst. prof., 1969-70; fellow nuclear physics Argonne Nat. Lab., 1966-68, asst. physicist, 1970-71; fellow med. physics U. Chgo., 1971-73, asst. prof., 1973-74, assoc. prof., 1974—, dir. med. physics, 1980-84. Mem. Am. Phys. Soc., Am. Assn. Physicists in Medicine, Radiol. Soc. North Am. Contbr. articles in field to profl. jours. Office: 5841 S Maryland Ave Chicago IL 60637

KUCHULIS, VALERIE ELAYNE, beverage company executive; b. Sacramento, Feb. 28, 1959; d. Constantine William and Dena (Kouretas) K. B.S. in bus. and mktg., Calif. State U.-Long Beach, 1981. Sales rep. Procter & Gamble, San Mateo, Calif., 1981-83; dist. mgr. sales and mktg. Coca-Cola USA, Wichita, Kans., 1983—. Mem. choir, steward Holy Trinity Greek Orthodox Ch., Wichita, 1984—. Mem. Wichita C. of C. Avocations: racquetball; tennis; snow skiing; golf. Home: 1450 S Webb Rd #223 Wichita KS 67207

KUCK, MARIE ELIZABETH BUKOVSKY, ret. pharmacist; b. Milw., Aug. 3, 1910; d. Frank Joseph and Marie (Nozina) Bukovsky; Ph.C., U. Ill., 1933; m. John A. Kuck, Sept. 20, 1945 (div. Nov. 1954). Pharmacist, tchr. Am. Hosp., Chgo., 1936-38, St. Joseph Hosp., Chgo., 1938-40, Ill. Masonic Hosp., Chgo., 1940-45; chief pharmacist St. Vincent Hosp., Los Angeles, 1946-48, St. Joseph Hosp., Santa Fe, 1949-51; dir. pharm. services St. Luke's Hosp., San Francisco, 1951-76; pharmacist Mission Neighborhood Health Center, San Francisco, 1968-72; mem. peer rev. com. Drug Utilization Com., Blue Shield Calif. and Pharm. Soc. San Francisco. Recipient Bowl of Hygeia award Calif. Pharm. Assn., 1966. Mem. No., Calif. (legis. chmn. aux. 1967-69, chmn. fund raising luncheon 1953-71, pres. San Francisco aux. 1974), Nat., Am., No. Calif. (pres. 1955-56, pres. San Francisco aux. 1965-66, editor ofcl. publ. 1967-70), San Francisco (sec. 1977-79, treas. 1979-80, pres. 1982-83; Pharmacist of Yr. award 1978) pharm. socs., Am. Pharm. Assn. (pres. No. Calif. br. 1956-57, nat. sec. women's aux. 1970-72, hon. pres. aux. 1975—), Calif. Council Hosp. Pharmacists (organizer 1962, sec.-treas. 1962-66), Am. Soc. Hosp. Pharmacists, Assn. Western Hosps. (gen. chmn. hosp. pharmacy sect. conv. San Francisco 1958), Internat. Pharmacy Congress (U.S. del. Brussels 1958, Copenhagen 1960), Fedn. Internationale Pharmaceutique, Lambda Kappa Sigma. Home: 2261 33d Ave San Francisco CA 94116

KUEHN, KAREN JEANNE, recreation facility administrator, bookkeeper, developer; b. Waterloo, Iowa, Apr. 1, 1948; d. Dale Joseph and Inez (Evans) Clark; m. James A. Kuehn, Oct. 6, 1972; children—Lora Jeanne, Brian James. Student U. No. Iowa, 1966. Bookkeeper Plastic Ingenuity, Cross Plains, Wis., 1977—; land developer Melody Acres III, Cross Plains, 1982—; owner, mgr. Hampton Office Bldg., Iowa, 1981—, Cross Plains Lanes, 1984—. Coach Cross Plains Jr. Bowling League, 1984—; chmn. Parks, Playgrounds and Recreation Com., Cross Plains, 1978-83; mem. St. Francis Catholic Women. Named Woman of Yr., Cross Plains Jaycees, 1980. Club: Lunch Bunch. Avocations: piloting pvt. plane; softball; bowling; fishing. Home: 2221 Spring St Cross Plains WI 53528 Office: Cross Plains Lanes Inc 1017 Main St Cross Plains WI 53528

KUEKER, VIOLET LOUISE, educator; b. East St. Louis, Ill., June 27, 1929; d. Marcellus C. and Mildred M. (Meyer) Hartman; student MacMurray Coll., 1947-49; B.S. in Edn., So. Ill. U., Carbondale, 1951; M.Ed., U. Ill., 1957; m. Edmund E. Kueker, Mar. 31, 1951. Home econs. tchr. Zeigler (Ill.) High Sch., 1951-52, Waterloo (Ill.) Public High Schs., 1952—. Past mem. North Central Evaluation Team; mem. Ill. Vocat. Evaluation Team, 1981—. Recipient Outstanding Tchr. award Waterloo High Sch., 1982. Mem. NEA (life), Am. Home Econs. Assn., Nat. Assn. Vocat. Home Econs. Tchrs., Am. Vocat. Assn., Am. Council Consumer Interests, Ill. Coop. Vocat. Edn. Coordinators Assn., Ill. Edn. Assn., Ill. Home Econs. Assn., (pres. dist. V 1981-82), Ill. Vocat. Home Econs. Tchrs. Assn. (steering and publ. com. 1961-64, chair region V, 1983-85), Ill. Vocational Assn., Monroe County Homemakers Extension Assn., Monroe County Fair Assn., Monroe County Hist. Soc., Waterloo Classroom Tchrs. Assn., Delta Kappa Gamma. Mem. United Ch. of Christ. Clubs: Evening Women's Guild; Peterstown Heritage Soc. Waterloo IL 62298 Office: Bellefontaine Dr Waterloo IL 62298

KUELZOW, ANN LISA, chemical engineer; b. Baia Mare, Roumania, Jan. 1, 1956, came to U.S., 1963; d. Nicholas and Lea Lilly (Levy) Klein; m. Chris Kuelzow, Aug. 12, 1978. B.S. in Chem. Engring., Clarkson Coll. Tech., Potsdam, N.Y., 1978. Engring. supr. Colgate-Palmolive, Jersey City, 1978-79; asst. plant engr. Sterling Drug, Inc., Trenton, N.J., 1979—Mem. Am. Inst. Plant Engrs., Am. Inst. Chem. Engrs., Instrument Soc. Am. Author tech. papers. Office: Sterling Drug Inc 2144 E State St Trenton NJ 08619

KUESTER, MARY-BETH, management consulting executive; b. New London, Wis., Nov. 15, 1938; d. Joseph Nathaniel and Rosetta Louise (Wotruba) Kuester. B.S. in Home Econs., U. Wis.-Madison, 1969, M.S. in Family and Consumer Econs., 1974. Home services dir. Wis.-Mich. Power Co., Appleton, Wis., 1961-73; teaching asst., lectr. U. Wis.-Madison, 1974-79; pres. Consumer Communications Resources, Inc., Madison, 1978—; consumer program coordinator Wis. Bankers Assn., Madison, 1977—; faculty Mt. Mary Coll., Milw., 1978-80. Chmn. bus. edn. adv. com. Stritch Coll., Milw., 1982—; v.p. Wis. Inflation Survival Council, 1982—; vice chmn. Dane County Pvt. Industry Council, Madison, 1983—; mem. steering com. Dane County Pub. Affairs Council. Named Woman of Yr., Madison Bus. and Profl. Women's Club, 1982; one of 80 leaders for Wis. in the 80s, Milw. Jour., 1980. Mem. Am. Council on Consumers Interest, Am. Mktg. Assn., Am. Mgmt. Assn., Nat. Assn. Bank Women, Am. Home Econs. Assn. (Inst. Life Ins. fellow 1978), AAUW, Wis. Consumer League, Wis. Home Econs. Assn. (exec. sec. 1974-82), Elec. Women's Roundtable (exec. sec. 1980-82, Julia Kiene fellow 1979), Tempo-Madison, Tempo-Milw., Omicron Nu (nat. pres. 1980-81). Clubs: Madison, Maple Bluff Country. Mailing Address: PO Box 232 Madison WI 53705 Home: 3650 Lake Mendota Dr Madison WI 53705

KUGLER, IDA CAROLYN, museum director; b. Bancroft, Nebr., Dec. 22, 1905; d. Herman and Petrine (Pedersen) Grunke; cert. Montevideo (Minn.) Tchr. Tng. Dept., 1925; A.A. with honors, St. Cloud (Minn.) State U., 1931; B.S. with distinction, U. Minn., 1941, M.A., 1956; Ph.D., Walden U., Naples, Fla., 1972; m. William John Kugler, Nov. 8, 1940. Tchr., Chippewa County, Minn., 1925-30, Rushford, Minn., 1930-31, Lakefield, Minn., 1931-35, St. Paul Public Schs., 1935-61; pioneering prin. Aiyepe High Sch., Ogun State, Nigeria, 1961-65; tchr. St. Paul Public Schs., 1965-74; v.p. Kugler Musical Instrument Mus., St. Paul, 1974—, also edn. dir., registrar. Chmn. Chippewa County Field Day, 1929; tchr. English to Chinese immigrants from Hong Kong, 1965—; nat. adv. bd. Am. Security Council; mem. Republican Nat. Com., U.S. Senatorial Club. Mem. St. Paul Ret. Tchrs. Assn., Nat. Ret. Tchrs. Assn., Am. Assn. Museums, OAS, Cath. Golden Age. Roman Catholic. Office: 1133 W California Ave Saint Paul MN 55108

KUHAR, JUNE CAROLYNN, retired fiberglass manufacturing company executive; b. Chgo., Sept. 20, 1935; d. Kurt Ludwig and Dorothy Julia (Lewand) Stier; student William Rainey Harper Coll., Chgo., Ins. Inst. Am.; m. G. James Kuhar, Feb. 5, 1953; children—Kathleen Lee, Debra Suzanne. Engaged in fiberglass mfg., 1970—; sec.-treas. Q-R Fiber Glass Industries Inc., Elgin, 1970—. Lic. realtor assoc. Mem. Bus. and Profl. Woman's Orgn. Northwest. Home: 2303 Meadow Dr Rolling Meadows IL 60008 Office: 701 N State St Elgin IL 60120

KUHL, KATHY, data processing consultant; b. Olney, Ill., Oct. 26, 1956. B.S., Eastern Ill. U., 1977. Programmer, analyst John Alden Ins. Co., Coral Gables, Fla., 1979-80, Group Health Inc., 1980; programmer analyst Western Ill. U., Macomb, 1980-83, systems analyst, 1983, systems programmer, 1983-85; data processing cons., Mattoon, Ill., 1985—. Mem. Nat. Assn. Female Execs. Office: 927 Marshall Ave Mattoon IL 61938

KUHL, MARGARET HELEN CLAYTON (MRS. ALEXIUS M. KUHL), banker; b. Louisville; d. Joseph Leonard and Maude (Mitzler) Clayton; student Loyola U. Home Study Div., Chgo., 1955—, Buena Vista Coll., Storm Lake, Iowa, summer 1964-65, 66; m. Alexius M. Kuhl, Apr. 21, 1936; children—Carol Lynn Ford Wassmuth, James Michael (adopted). Sales lady, buyer Silverberg, Akron, Iowa, 1924-34; owner dress shop, Fonda, Iowa, 1934-40; librarian, Fonda, 1940-43; bookkeeper, teller First Nat. Bank, Fonda, 1943-44; tchr. speech and drama, librarian asst. Our Lady Good Counsel Sch., Fonda, 1963-69; pres., chmn. bd. Pomeroy State Bank, 1975-83, also dir. Recipient Adult Leadership award Catholic Youth Orgn., 1967, Pro Deo Juventute award, 1969. Mem. Cath. Daus. Am. (dist. dep. 1964-70, state chmn. ecumenism 1970-72, state treas. 1970-72), Diocesan Council Cath. Women (chmn. orgn. and devel. 1964-65), Nat. Council Cath. Women (diocesan pres. 1968-70, diocesan sec. 1966-67; chmn. Women in Community Service Sioux City Diocesan Bd. 1971-72), Internat. Platform Assn., Women in Community Service (pres. Iowa bd. 1972-73), Legion of Mary (pres. curia 1964-66, 67-70). Clubs: Sun City Country (Ariz.), Fonda Country, Lakes (Sun City, Ariz.). Home: 5th and Queen Sts Fonda IA 50540

KUHLE, SHIRLEY JEAN, law enforcement administrator, victimology specialist, crime commissioner; b. Sioux Falls, S.D., Jan. 14, 1936; d. Earl John and Palma Ruth (Knutson) Albertus; m. Donald Eugene Kuhle, June 4, 1954; children—Kim Jean, Kathy Joan, Kenneth John, Kris June. Grad. Realtors Inst., 1969-77; cert. in mgmt. devel. U. Nebr., 1984. Cert. residential specialist; ARC home nursing instr. Co-owner, asst. mgr. Beltline Tractor Sales, Inc., Lincoln, Nebr., 1960-84; appraiser Nebr. Real Estate Commn., 1974—, broker, 1964—; mem. Nebr. Crime Commn., Lincoln, 1980—; adminstr. Victim/Witness Unit, Lincoln Police Dept., 1981—. Author articles and tng. manuals on victim assistance. Mem. Lincoln/Lancaster County Justice Council, 1981; v.p. Willard Community Ctr., 1982-83; cons. Nebr. Parents Anonymous, 1981, Region VII Rural Domestic Violence Ctr., 1981; pres. Nebr. Task Force Domestic Violence, 1979, 80, 81; pres. Capitol Beach Community Assn., 1979; v.p. Nebr. Coalition Victims of Crime, 1985. Program grantee, Fed. Govt., 1980, 81; recipient admiralship State of Nebr., 1975; Meritorious Service citation City of Lincoln, 1978. Mem. Nat. Orgn. Victims Assistance (life, exec., bd., 1979-84, conf. del.), Police Officers Nebr., Nebr. Sheriffs and Peace Officers Assn., Combined Orgn. of Police Services, Nat. Criminal Justice Assn. (charter). Democrat. Roman Catholic. Home: 930 Manchester Dr Lincoln NE 68528 Office: Victim/Witness Unit Lincoln Dept 233 S 10th St Lincoln NE 68508

KUHLMANN, HELEN JUANITA, counselor; b. Vicksburg, Miss., July 22, 1926; d. Clarence Baron and Mary Anne (Cunningham) Huff; m. Arthur Henry Kuhlmann, Oct. 11, 1945 (div. Dec. 1973); children—Jeff David, Lynn Carol, Jack D'Owen, Casey Richard, Susan Anne, Barbee, Kris. Student La. State U., 1942-44. Owner, mgr. h.k. farm, Leoti, Kans., 1973-76; outpatient dir. Baton Rouge Chem. Dependency Unit, 1977-81; inpatient dir. Cyprus Hosp. alcohol program, Lafayette, La., 1981; pres., counselor Recovery Resources, Baton Rouge, 1982—; owner, counselor The Recovery Group, Baton Rouge, 1983—; cons. The Turning Point, Baton Rouge, 1985—, Love Life Workshops, Baton Rouge, 1985—; lectr. Baton Rouge Chem. Dependency unit, 1983-85. Chmn. bd. dirs. Chem. Dependency Funding Found., 1985—. Mem. La. Assn. Substance Abuse Counselors, Nat. Assn. Alcoholism, and Drug Abuse Counselors. Republican. Mem. Unity Ch. Avocations: Yoga; stitchery. Office: Recovery Group 9040 Florida Blvd Baton Rouge LA 70815

KUHLTHAU, CAROL COLLIER, librarian, educator; b. New Brunswick, N.J., Dec. 2, 1937; d. Fred Robert and Lillian Lucille (Houghton) Collier; m. John Suydam Kuhlthau, June 21, 1958; children—Eleanor, Ann, Leslie. B.S., Kean Coll., 1959; M.L.S., Rutgers U., 1974, Ed.D., 1983. Cert. ednl. media specialist N.J. Tchr. Florham Park Pub Schs. (N.J.), 1959-62, New Brunswick Pub. Schs. (N.J.), 1962-63; ednl. media specialist North Brunswick High Sch., 1974-78, East Brunswick Pub. Schs. (N.J.), 1978-80; head librarian East Brunswick High Sch., 1980—; asst. prof. Sch. Communication, Info. and Library Studies, Rutgers U., New Brunswick, N.J., also head ednl. media program; nat. adviser Miss. Instructional TV, Jackson, 1982—. Author: School Librarian's Grade-by-Grade Activities Program, 1981. Author: Teaching the Library Research Process, 1985. Reviewer CARE div. Prentice-Hall, N.Y.C. Mem. N.J. Ednl. Media Assn. (pres., chmn. profl. devel.), Am. Assn. Sch. Librarians (research com., chmn. library skills instrn. com.), Am. Library Assn., Rutgers Grad. Sch. Alumni Assn. (exec. bd. 1981-83). Home: 402 Franklin Rd North Brunswick NJ 08902 Office: Sch Communication Info and Library Studies Rutgers U 4 Huntington St New Brunswick NJ 08903

KUHN, ANNE NAOMI WICKER (MRS. HAROLD B. KUHN), educator; b. Lynchburg, Va.; d. George Barney and Annie (Hicks) Wicker; m. Harold B. Kuhn. Diploma Malone Coll., 1933, Trinity Coll. Music, London, 1937; A.B., John Fletcher Coll., 1939; M.A., Boston U., 1942, postgrad., 1965-70; postgrad. (fellow) Harvard U., 1942-44, 66-68: Boston U.; hon. grad. Asbury Coll., 1978. Instr., Emmanuel Bible Coll., Birkenhead, Eng., 1936-37; asst. in history John Fletcher Coll., University Park, Iowa, 1938-39; librarian Harvard U., 1939-40; tchr. adult edn. program U.S. Armed Forces, Fuerstenfeldbruck Air Base, Germany, 1951-52; prof. Union Bibl. Sem., Yeotmal, India, 1957-58; lectr. Armenian Bible Inst., Beirut, Lebanon, 1958; prof. German, Asbury Coll., Wilmore, Ky., 1962—, co-dir. coll. study tour to E. Ger. and W. Ger., 1976, 77, 78, co-dir. acad. tours, 1979, 80; dir. acad. tour, Russia, 1981, 85, Scandanavia, 1982, Indonesia, Singapore, 1983, Hong Kong and Thailand, 1983, 85, E.Ger., W.Ger., France and Austria, 1983, Russia and Finland, 1984, 85, Peoples Republic China, 1984, 85, Estonia, Latvia, 1985; tchr. Seoul Theol. Sem., fall 1978. Author: (pamphlet) The Impact of the Transition to Modern Education Upon Religious Education, 1950; The Influence of Paul Gerhardt upon Wesleyan Humnody, 1960. Transl. German ch. records, poems, letters. Contbr. articles to profl. jours. Del. Youth for Christ World Conf., 1948, 50, London Yearly Meeting of Friends, Edinburgh, Scotland, 1948, World Council Chs., Amsterdam, 1948, World Friends Conf., Oxford, Eng., 1952, World Methodist Conf., Oslo, Norway, 1961, Deutscher Kirchentag, Dortmund, Germany, 1963, German Lang. Congress, Bonn, W. Ger., 1974, Internat. Conf. Religion, Amsterdam, Netherlands, Poland, West Berlin, Fed. Republic Germany, 1986; participant Internat. Congress World Evangelization, Lausanne, Switzerland, 1974. Recipient German Consular award, Boston, 1965, Thomas Mann award Boston U., 1967; named Ky. Col., 1978. Fellow Goethe-Institut für Germanisten, Munich, 1966-68, 70-71. Mem. AAUW, Am. Assn. Tchrs. German, NEA, Ky. Ednl. Assn., Lincoln Lit. Soc., Protestant Women of Chapel, Delta Phi Alpha (award 1963, 65). Quaker. Club: Harvard Faculty. Home: 406 Kenyon Ave Wilmore KY 40390

KUHN, KATHLEEN JO, accountant; b. Springfield, Ill., Aug. 9, 1947; d. Henry Elmer and Norma Florene (Niehaus) Burge; B.S. in Bus., Bradley U., 1969; m. Gerald L. Kuhn, June 22, 1968; children—Gerald Lynn, Brett Anthony. Controller, Byerly Music Co., Peoria, Ill., 1969-70; staff acct. Clifton Gunderson & Co., Columbus, Ind., 1970-71; acct. Dept. ot Transp., State of Ill., Springfield, 1972-76; acct. Gerald L. Kuhn & Assos., C.P.A.'s, Springfield, 1976-78, partner, 1979—. Recipient attendance award Continuing Profl. Edn. for Accts., 1977, 78, 79, 82, 83, 84, 85; notary public, Ill.; C.P.A., Ill. Mem. Am. Inst. C.P.A.s, Ill. Soc. C.P.A.s, Am. Woman's Soc. C.P.A.s. Lutheran. Clubs: Olympic Swim, Metro. Federated Jr. Women's. Writer, editor Policy Guideline of Gerald L. Kuhn & Assocs., 1979-80. Home: 2511 Westchester St Springfield IL 62704 Office: 323 S Grand Ave W Springfield IL 62704

KUHN, LUCILLE ROSS, retired naval officer; b. Washington, July 19, 1927; d. Lilburn Joseph and Flora Lee (Perry) K.; A.A. with distinction, George Washington U., 1959, B.A., 1960. Ins. clk. Southwestern Life Ins. Co., Richmond, Va., 1945-48; joined U.S. Navy, 1949, advanced through grades to capt., 1975; woman officer rep. 2d Navy Recruiting Area, Washington, 1963-65; U.S. Naval Security Group, Washington, 1965-68; dir. mil. personnel 12th Naval Dist., San Francisco, 1968-70; mem. staff Office Asst. Sec. Def. for Legis. Affairs, Washington, 1971-74; dir. Officer Candidate Sch., Newport, 1975-77; dir. pay/personnel adminstrv. support system Bur. Naval Personnel, Washington, 1977-79; comdg. officer Recruit Tng. Command, Orlando, Fla., 1979-81; dep. comdr. Navy Recruiting Command, Washington, 1981-84. Aide de camp to Va. govs., 1960—. Decorated Legion of Merit with gold star, Meritorious Service medal with gold star, Nat. Def. Service medal with bronze star. Mem. Am. Sailing Assn., Naval Hist. Found., Naval Inst., Psi Chi. Home: 2302 Kenmore Rd Richmond VA 23228

KUHN, MARGARET (MAGGIE), political activist; b. Buffalo, 1905; d. Samuel Frederick and Minnie Louise (Kooman) K.; B.A., Case-Western Res. U., 1926. Formerly with YWCA, Cleve., Phila.; Gen. Alliance Unitarian Women, Boston, later with United Presbn. Ch. U.S.A., N.Y.C., editor, writer for ch. mag. Social Progress; alt. observer for Presbyns. at UN; ret., 1970; a founder Gray Panthers, 1970, now nat. convener; cons. nat. task force on women United Presbyn. Ch., 3d v.p. health, edn. and welfare assn.; lectr.; mem. nat. adv. bd. Hospice, Inc.; adv. TV series Over Easy; former mem. Fed. Jud. Nominating Com. Pa. Recipient 1st ann. award for justice and human devel. Witherspoon Soc., 1974, Disting. Service award in consumer advocacy Am. Speech and Hearing Assn., 1975, Freedom award Women's Scholarship Assn. Roosevelt U., 1976, ann. award Phila. Soc. Clin. Psychologists, 1976, Peaceseeker award United Presbyn. Peace Fellowship, 1977, Humanist of Yr. award Am. Humanist Assn., 1978. Author: Get Out There and Do Something about Injustice, 1972; Maggie Kuhn on Aging, 1977. Office: Gray Panthers 311 S Juniper St Philadelphia PA 19104

KUHN, MARGARET NELSON, veterinarian; b. Petersburg, Va., Feb. 8, 1953; d. Elmer Lionel and Sarah Elizabeth (Rogers) Nelson; m. Thomas Bovard Kuhn, May 27, 1978; children—Emmeline Rogers, Peter Bovard. B.S.A. in Biochemistry magna cum laude, U. Ga., 1975, D.V.M., 1978. Lic. D.V.M., Va., N.C., Ga., Fla. Assoc. veterinarian Clearwater Animal Clinic (Fla.), 1978-80, Hughey Dickson Animal Clinic, Gastonia, N.C., 1980-82, Gaston Animal Hosp., Gastonia, 1980-82; owner, veterinarian Animal Hosp. East, Asheville, N.C., 1981—; conv. pet therapy Appalachian Hall Hosp. and VA Hosp., Asheville, 1983; cons. Girl Scouts, Fairview, N.C., 1983, Boy Scouts, Asheville, 1983. Adminstrv. bd. Warren Wilson Coll. Child Care, Asheville, 1983-84; mem. presch. bd. Grace United Methodist Child Care, Asheville, 1984, chmn., 1985—, mem. ch. adminstrv. bd., 1985, council ministries, 1985; bd. dirs. YWCA, Advocates for Nuclear Arms Freeze, 1982. Mem. AVMA, Am. Animal Hosp. Assn., N.C. Vet. Med. Assn., Western N.C. Vet. Med. Assn. Democrat. Club: Am. Orchid Soc. Home: 550 Warren Wilson College Rd Swannanoa NC 28778 Office: 1275 Tunnel Rd Asheville NC 28805

KUHNERT, HELEN LAVON, nurse clinical specialist; b. Wichita Falls, Tex., Sept. 25, 1940; d. Cecil Vaughn and Helen Maurine (Castlebury) Graves; m. Robert Waldon Harmon, June 9, 1962 (div. Feb. 1975); children—Alison, Amy, Laurie, Warren; m. 2d, Robert Morris Kuhnert, July 23, 1976. Diploma in nursing, Meml. Hosp. Sch. Nursing, Houston, 1961; B.S.N., Tex. Women's U., 1974. R.N., Tex. Asst. head nurse Meml. Bapt. Hosp., Houston, 1961-62; staff nurse Highland Gen. Hosp., Pampa, Tex., 1964-69, Presbyn. Hosp., Dallas, 1969-70, 74-75; supr. stresslab Cardiology Assocs., Dallas, 1975-77; research nurse U. Tex. Health Sci. Ctr. at Dallas, 1977-79, clin. specialist, 1979—; mem. task force Am. Heart Assn., Dallas, 1977-82, hypertension screening capt., 1978-80. Contbr. articles to med. jours. Mem. Sanctuary Choir, Richardson Heights Baptist Ch. (Tex.), 1979—; mem. Richardson High Sch. Band Club. Mem. Am. Nurses Assn., Tex. Nurses Assn., Nat. Assn. Research Nurses and Dietitians, Assoc. of Clin. Pharmacology, Sigma Theta Tau. Republican. Club: Theta Moms (Richardson). Home: 7131 Townbluff Dallas TX 75248 Office: U Tex Health Sci Center 5323 Harry Hines Dallas TX 75235

KUIK, LAUREN, software vendor company executive; b. Trenton, N.J., Jan. 4, 1947; d. Willard Leslie and M. Evelyn (Mabey) Culver; m. Joseph Paul Kuik, Nov. 29, 1969; children—Jennifer Evelyn, Leslie Rebecca. Assoc. Liberal Arts, Trenton Jr. Coll., 1966. Sec., bookkeeper Kuik Hauling, Titusville, N.J., 1974—; with Applied Data Research, Inc., Princeton, N.J., 1983—, mgr. order and revenue processing, 1986—. Pres., Welcome Wagon of Hopewell, N.J., 1979. Mem. Internat. Tng. in Communication Council (pres. 1984), Nat. Assn. Female Execs. Lutheran. Office: Applied Data Research Inc Route 206 and Orchard Rd CN-8 Princeton NJ 08540

KUKEC, ANNA MARIE, journalist; b. Chgo., Feb. 3, 1958; d. Ernest P. and Angeline (Malpede) K. A.A. with honors, Moraine Valley Community Coll., Palos Hills, Ill., 1978; B.A. in Mass Communications and Journalism, St. Xavier Coll., Chgo., 1983. Columnist, TV editor Economist Newspapers, Chgo., 1977—; guest lectr. various schs. and radio. Contest judge TV Chgo. Internat. Film Festival, 1982-83; telethon vol. March of Dimes, Chgo., 1983; bd. dirs. Mademoiselle Mag., 1979. Recipient Student Achievement award Continental Bank of Chgo., 1977, Paderewski Meml. award, 1978; Nat. Piano Playing Auditions winner Nat. Guild Piano Tchrs., 1968-78. Mem. Women in Communications, Nat. Fedn. Press Women, Ill. Women's Press Assn., Chgo. Headline Club (bd. dirs.), Sigma Delta Chi. Club: Suburban Press (various awards). Home: 2844 W 98th St Evergreen Park IL 60642 Office: Daily Southtown Economist 5959 S Harlem Ave Chicago IL 60638

KUKLIN, REBA MAGID, publisher, author; b. Nashville, Aug. 25, 1914; d. Victor and Becky (Frankel) Magid; B.S. with distinction in Edn., U. Nebr., 1955, M.Ed., 1962; m. Harry H. Kuklin, Dec. 25, 1939; children—Bailey Howard, Bonnie Irene, Victor Alan. Tchr. elem. schs., Lincoln, Nebr., 1955-57; tchr. jr. high sch. English and social studies, Lincoln, 1957-77; founder, pres. Mercantine Press, Lincoln, 1979—; author: Learn to Invest and Trade on Wall Street, 1979. Mem. NEA, Assn. Women Entrepreneurs, Nebr. Edn. Assn., Lincoln Edn. Assn., Hadassah. Address: 4351 Washington St Lincoln NE 68506

KUKLINSKI, JOAN LINDSEY, librarian; b. Lynn, Mass., Nov. 28, 1950; d. Richard Jay and M. Claire (Murphy) Card; B.A. cum laude, Mass. State Coll., Salem, 1972; M.L.S., U. R.I., 1976; m. Walter S. Kuklinski, June 17, 1972. Classified librarian U. R.I. Extension Div. Library, Providence, 1974-75, U. R.I. Cataloging Dept., Kingston, 1975-79; original cataloger Tex. A&M U. Library, College Station, 1979-82; cataloger Goldfarb Library, Brandeis U., Waltham, Mass., 1982-83; automation coordinator, 1983-85; network coordinator Minuteman Library Network, Framingham, Mass., 1985—. Mem. Town of South Kingstown (R.I.) Women's Adv. Commn., 1977-79. Mem. ALA (mem. resources and tech. services div. 1980—), Library Info. Tech. Assn. (reference and adult services div. 1984—),Assn. Coll. and Research Libraries, On-Line Audiovisual Catalogers, Library and Info. Tech. Assn., Am. Contract Bridge League, Delta Tau Kappa. Office: Minuteman Library Network 49 Lexington St Framingham MA 01701

KUKURIN, KAREN ANN, public relations executive; b. Pitts., July 21, 1953; d. George William and Dolores Ann K. B.S., Pa. State U., 1975. Staff reporter Standard Observer, Pitts., 1975-78; asst. pub. relations dir. Tournament of Roses, Pasadena, Calif., 1980-81; editor corp. communications Equitable Gas Co., Pitts., 1978-80; sr. account exec. Cerrell Assocs. Inc., Los Angeles, 1981-83; v.p. Englander Group, Newport Beach, Calif., 1984-85; ptnr. Mercier/Kukurin, Beverly Hills, Calif., 1985—. Media cons. United Way, Los Angeles, 1981-83; lobbyist Tobacco Inst., 1983-84. Bd. dirs. Response Ctr. Cedars Sinai Med. Ctr.; prodn. asst. Nat. Broadcast Hollywood Christmas Parade, Hollywood C. of C., 1981-85; Named Intern of Yr. Womens Press Club Pitts., 1976. Mem. Women in Pub. Affairs, Los Angeles Pub. Affairs Officers Assn., Los Angeles West C. of C., Pub. Relations Soc. Am., Calif. Women Bus. Owners Assn. Avocations: English riding. Office: Mercier Kukurin 9701 Wilshire St Suite 805 Beverly Hills CA 90212

KULESH, CARRIE JOHNSON, lawyer, bank executive; b. Wichita, Kans., Aug. 30, 1957; d. Harlan Glenwood and Sara Ann (Shepherd) Johnson; m. William Jay Kulesh, Sept. 5, 1982. B.A. in Psychology, U. Nebr., 1979; J.D., Creighton U., 1982. Bar: Nebr. 1982, Ariz. 1983. Legal clk. Met. Utilities Dist., Omaha, 1981-82; personal trust adminstr. First Interstate Bank Ariz., Phoenix, 1983—. Mem. Ariz. Humane Soc., Phoenix, 1983—. Mem. ABA, Nebr. State Bar Assn., Ariz. State Bar Assn., Phi Mu (exec. bd. Lincoln 1977-79). Republican. Lutheran. Home: 1074 E Pueblo Rd Phoenix AZ 85020 Office: First Interstate Bank Ariz 100 W Washington Phoenix AZ 85002

KULLMANN, JEANNETTE MARGHERIO, field construction executive; b. Santa Monica, Calif., Dec. 2, 1936; d. Bart and Jessie (Baker) Margherio; m. Charles Dean Kullmann, Aug. 26, 1956 (div. 1973); children—Jeffrey Brian, Janice Lynn, Jason Bradley. B.B.A., Woodbury Coll., 1956. Adminstrn. asst. Bechtel Constrn., Inc., San Onofre, Calif. and Handford, Wash., 1977-83, engr. asst., 1984—, chmn. edn. com. for Women, 1977-80; engr. Pullmann Power Products, Avila Beach, Calif., 1983-84. Leader Camp Fire Girls, Carlsbad, Calif., 1966. Mem. Beta Sigma Phi (pres. 1974). Republican. Presbyterian. Avocations: swimming; tennis; camping.

KUMIN, LIBBY BARBARA, speech pathologist, college administrator; b. Bklyn., Nov. 11, 1945; d. Herbert H. and Berniece (Shuch) K.; m. Martin J. Lazar, Jan. 18, 1969; 1 child, Jonathan Kumin. B.A. summa cum laude, LIU, 1965; M.A., NYU, 1966, Ph.D., 1969. Lic. speech pathologist, Md. Asst. prof. speech pathology U. Md., College Park, 1972-76; cons., 1976-80; adj. prof. Loyola Coll., Balt., 1976-80, assoc. prof., 1980—, chmn. dept. speech, 1983—, dir. Speech and Lang. Ctr. Mem. Speech/Lang./Hearing Commn., Howard City Bd. Edn., Columbia, Md., 1982—; Author: Aphasia, 1978. Vol. cons. Howard County Office on Aging, 1977—. Contbr. articles to profl. jours. Recipient Outstanding Individual of Year award Howard County Assn. Retarded Citizens, Aaron and Lillian Straus Found. grantee, 1983; Columbia Found. grantee; recipient summer research award Loyola Coll., 1983. Mem. Am. Speech/Lang./Hearing Assn. (cert.), Md. Speech and Hearing Assn., Nat. Downs Syndrome Congress, ARC, Sigma Tau Delta, Pi Lambda Theta. Office: Loyola Coll Dept Speech Pathology 4501 N Charles St Baltimore MD 21210

KUMIN, MAXINE WINOKUR, writer; b. Phila., June 6, 1925; d. Peter and Doll (Simon) Winokur; A.B., Radcliffe Coll., 1946, M.A., 1948; m. Victor Montwid Kumin, June 29, 1946; children—Jane Simon, Judith Montwid, Daniel David. Free-lance writer, 1953—; mem. Poetry Soc. Am. Author: (poems) Halfway, 1961, The Privilege, 1965; (novel) Through Dooms of Love, 1965; (novel) The Passions of Uxport, 1968; (poems) The Nightmare Factory, 1970; Up Country, 1972 (Pulitzer prize for poetry 1973); (novel) The Designated Heir, 1974; (poems) House, Bridge, Fountain, Gate, 1975, The Retrieval System, 1978; (essays) To Make a Prairie, 1980; (poems) Our Ground Time Here Will Be Brief, 1982, The Long Approach, 1985; (short stories) Why Can't We Live Together Like Civilized Human Beings, 1982; poetry cons. Library of Congress, 1981-82; contbr. poems to nat. mags. Woodrow Wilson vis. fellow, 1979-80; recipient award Am. Acad. and Inst. Arts and Letters, 1980. Fellow Acad. Am. Poets. Address: care Curtis Brown Ltd 575 Madison Ave New York NY 10022

KUMKE, SHERRIE ANN, government official; b. Dallas, Feb. 22, 1943; d. Truett Borden and Lillie (Hicks) Minton; m. John Bernard Kumke, Oct. 8, 1939; children by previous marriage—G. Todd Harrell, Sean Reed Harrell. Student Mountain Lake Community Coll., 1977, U. Tex.-Arlington, 1978. Stenographer, U.S. Postal Services, Dallas, 1974, personnel asst., 1974-80, mgr. women's program, 1980-82, dir. employee relations, Texarkana, Tex., 1981, officer-in-charge, Brady, 1981-82, sr. assoc. consumer affairs, Washington, 1982—, chmn. women's adv. council, Dallas, 1975-79; chmn. Combined Fed. Camp, Dallas, 1979—. Exec. com. YMCA, Dallas, 1970. Recipient 4 awards of commendation U.S. Postal Service. Mem. Washington Women's Network, Soc. Consumer Affairs Profls., Quill and Scroll.

KUMM, DORIS JEAN, state legislator; b. Watertown, S.D., Oct. 27, 1929; d. Earl Edward Lebert and Minnie Augusta (Schwanke) Lebert Richardson; grad. Cosmetology Sch., Watertown, S.D.; m. Vincent Jerald Kumm, May 29, 1949; children—Deborah, Kelly, Roxanne, Marty, Todd, Kathy. Mem. S.D. Ho. of Reps., 1978—, mem. natural resources, transp. and bonding coms. Mem. S.D. Republican Com., del. state conv., 1978; del. Rep. Nat. Conv., 1980; mem. exec. com. Codington County (S.D.) Rep. Com. Mem. BPW, Women In Mgmt., Roundtable Extension, Rep. Women, Nat. Order Women Legislators (regional dir.). Home: 521 6th St SE Watertown SD 57201 Office: State Capitol Pierre SD 57501

KUMMER, RUTH MARY ANN, chaplain; b. Wyandotte, Mich., July 27, 1930; d. Archibald Jacob and Anna Lucille (Copp) Lambrix; m. Joseph Talbot Kummer, May 17, 1974; children—Frederic Joseph, Mariane, David T., Joseph T. B.S., Siena Heights Coll., 1960, M.A., 1969; student (NFS grantee) Wayne State U., 1965. Tchr., Roman Catholic Diocese Chgo., 1948-52, Toledo, 1953-59, Detroit, 1959-67, tchr. jr. high sch. Diocese Lansing, Mich., 1967-68; prin. elem. sch. Archdiocese Detroit, Chelsea, Mich., 1968-69, dir. religious edn., 1970-74; clinic supr. edn. Breast Cancer Detection Ctr., U. Mich., Ann Arbor, 1975-79; chaplain, coordinator lay ministers St. Joseph Hosp., Ann Arbor, 1980—; pres. Roman Cath. Dominican Laity, Chgo., 1980—, presentor, Buffalo, 1983, del., Bologna, Italy, 1983. Contbr. articles to profl. jours. Vol., Meals on Wheels, Ann Arbor, 1979. Roman Catholic. Home: 3904 Golfside Rd Ypsilanti MI 48197

KUND, LAUREN SUE, educator; b. Los Angeles, Jan. 24, 1948; d. Seymour and Esther Mildred (Nadler) Elowe; m. William Kund, Aug. 26, 1970 (div. 1978). B.A. in Spanish, Valley State Coll., 1969; M.A. in Polit. Sci., Calif. State U.-Los Angeles, 1983. Cert. secondary tchr., Calif. Tchr. Lindero Cyn Middle Sch., Agoura, Calif., 1970-72, Am. Internat. Sch. of Rotterdam (Netherlands), 1972-76, Washington Prep. High Sch., Los Angeles, 1976—; sponsor Marthonians Club, 1976-83; coordinator Inter Club Council, 1978-83; advisor Model UN, 1980-83; coordinator English Second Lang., 1981-82. Leader, Girl Scouts, Netherlands, 1974-76; asst. chmn. Global Edn. Com., Calif. State U.-Los Angeles, 1980-83; high sch. coordinator End Hunger Network, Los Angeles, 1983. Mem. United Tchrs. Los Angeles, Fgn. Lang Tchrs. Los Angeles. Democrat. Jewish. Home: 739 Rose Ave Long Beach CA 90814 Office: Washington Prep High Sch 10860 S Denker Ave Los Angeles CA 90047

KUNDE, LYNN ELLEN, real estate broker; b. Chgo., Jan. 21, 1952; d. Richard Earl and Shirley Mae (Lietz) K.; married. student U. Ill., 1969-71; B.C.S. in Acctg. with high honor, DePaul U., 1977. Adminstr., Centre Properties Ltd., Chgo., 1973-75, Arthur Rubloff & Co., Chgo., 1975-79; sec.-treas. Joseph Dillon & Co., Bensenville, Ill., 1979-82; with Bennett & Kahnweiler Assocs., Rosemont, Ill., 1982—. Recipient Citation, City of Chgo., 1977, CPA, Ill. Mem. Greater O'Hare Assn. Commerce and Industry, Suburban Assn. of Commerce and Industry, Ill. CPA Soc., Chgo. Soc. of Women CPAs, Assn. Indsl. Real Estate Brokers (membership chmn.), Ledger & Quill. Office: Bennett & Kahnweiler 9700 W Bryn Mawr Rosemont IL 60018

KUNDERT, ALICE E., state official; b. Java, S.D., July 23, 1920; d. Otto J. and Maria (Rieger) Kundert; elementary tchr.'s certificate No. State Coll., Aberdeen, S.D., state tchr. certificate; L.H.D. (hon.), Black Hills State Coll., 1985. Tchr. elementary grades, 1939-43, 48-54; clk., mgr., buyer Gates Dept. Store, Beverly Hills, Calif., Clifton Dress Shop, Hollywood, Calif., 1943-48; dep. supt. schs. Campbell County, S.D., 1954; county ct. clk., 1955-60; register deeds, 1955-69; town treas. Mound City, 1965-69; auditor State of S.D., Pierre, 1969-79, sec. state, 1979—. Leader, 4-H Club, 1949-53, county project leader in citizenship, 1963-64; sec. Greater Campbell County Assn., 1955-?; organizer, leader Mound City Craft and Recreation Club, 1955-60; chmn. Heart Fund, March Dimes, Red Cross, Mental Health drives; mem. Gov.'s Study Commn., 1968—; mem. State and local adv. com. region VIII Office Econ. Opportunity; bd. mem., cmn. Black Hills Recreation Lab., 1956-61; exec. sec. Internat. Leaders Lab. Ireland, 1963. Polit. county vice chmn. Republican Com., 1964-69, sec.-treas. fin. chmn., 1968; mem. State Rep. Adv. Com., 1966-68; state and nat. counselor Tenn Age Rep. Club Campbell County, 1964—; Rep. candidate for gov. S.D., 1986; hon. chmn. for S.D., Easter Seals Soc., 1982—. Named Outstanding Teenage Rep. advisor in nation, 1970, 71, 76; recipient Distinguished Alumni award No. State Coll., 1975. Home: 407 N Van Buren St Pierre SD 57501 Office: State Capitol Bldg Office of Sec State Pierre SD 57501

KUNDL, JUDITH, lawyer; b. Bryn Mawr, Pa., Sept. 17, 1951; d. Martin John and Elizabeth Theresa (Sharkey) K. B.A., Mt. Holyoke Coll., 1973; J.D. cum laude, Suffolk U., 1980. Bar: Mass. 1980. Criminal list mgr. Dist. Atty.'s Office, Northampton, Mass., 1973-75; paralegal Bergson, Borkland, Margolis & Adler, Washington, 1976-77; law clk. EPA, Boston, 1979-80; jud. clk. Supreme Ct. N.H., Concord, 1980-81; assoc. Growhoski, Callahan, Howard & Miles, Northampton, 1981—. Recipient Am. Jurisprudence award Lawyers Coop. Pub. Co., 1979. Mem. ABA, Mass. Bar Assn., LWV (chmn. natural resources 1983). Office: Growhoski Callahan Howard & Miles 60 State St Northampton MA 01060

KUNDRAT, MARY ANN, nursing administrator; b. Jefferson, Iowa, Apr. 30, 1951; d. George and Mary Elizabeth (Dowling) K.; m. Patrick John McNulty, Mar. 26, 1982; children—Kathleen, Elizabeth. Student Iowa State U., 1969-71. B.S. in Nursing, Mt. Mercy Coll., Cedar Rapids, Iowa, 1971-73; M.A. in Nursing, U. Iowa, 1976. R.N., Iowa. Staff nurse U. Iowa Hosps., Iowa City, 1973-74, nurse clinician, 1974; head nurse CCU, VA Med. Ctr., Iowa City, 1976-80; asst. chief nursing VA Med. Ctr., Knoxville, Iowa, 1980-85; head nurse Des Moines VA Med. Ctr., 1985—; adj. asst. prof. U. Iowa Coll. Nursing, 1981—; adj. instr. Grandview Coll., Des Moines, 1981-84; cons. VA Med. Ctr., Seattle, 1983. Contbg. author: Continuity of Care, 1985. Chmn. EEO com. VA. Med. Ctr., 1984-85, chmn. research com., 1984-85, fed. women's coordinator, 1981-85, mem. human studies research com., 1985—. Recipient Outstanding award Cedar Rapids Jaycees, 1973, Dir.'s commendation VA Med. Ctr., 1982; named one of Outstanding Young Women of Am., 1984. Mem. Am. Assn. Critical Care Nurses (chpt. pres. 197-75, 77-78), Am. Nurses Assn., Iowa Nurses Assn. (chmn. mental health com. 1981-83), Nursing Service Administration. Assn. (research com. 1984-85), Am. Nurses Found. (charter), NOW, Iowa Civil Liberties Union, Sigma Theta Tau, AAUW, Women's Polit. Caucus. Avocations: reading; cooking. Home: 1814 69th St Des Moines IA 50322 Office: VA Med Ctr 30th & Euclid Des Moines IA 50310

KUNIN, MADELEINE MAY, gov. Vt.; b. Zurich, Switzerland, Sept. 28, 1933; came to U.S., 1940, naturalized, 1947; d. Ferdinand and Renée (Bloch) May; B.A., U. Mass., 1956; M.S., Columbia U., 1957; M.A., U. Vt., 1967; L.H.D. (hon.), Norwich U., 1979; m. Arthur S. Kunin, June 21, 1959; children—Julia, Peter, Adam, Daniel. Newspaper reporter Burlington (Vt.) Free Press, 1957-58; guide Brussels Worlds Fair, 1958; TV asst., producer Sta. WCAX-TV, Burlington, 1960-61; freelance writer, instr. English, Trinity Coll., Burlington, 1969-70; mem. Vt. Ho. of Reps., 1973-78; lt. gov. State of Vt., Montpelier, 1978-82; gov. State of Vt., 1984—; fellow Inst. Politics, Kennedy Sch. Govt., Harvard U., 1983; lectr. Middlebury Coll., St. Michael's Coll., 1984; mem. Vt. Gov.'s Commn. on Children and Youth, 1973-77, Vt. Commn. on Adminstrn. of Justice, 1976-77; mem. exec. com. Nat. Conf. Lt. Govs., 1979-80; mem. exec. com. Democratic Policy Commn. Named Outstanding State Legislator, Eagleton Inst. Politics, Rutgers U., 1975, Nat. Gov.'s Assn. (exec. com.), New Eng. Gov.'s Assn. (vice chair). Democrat. Author: (with Marilyn Stout) The Big Green Book, 1976. Contbr. articles to various mags. and newspapers. Office: Pavilion Montpelier VT 05602

KUNISHI, MARILYN MITSUE, nurse; b. Honolulu, July 24, 1946; d. Arthur Yoshito and Hanayo (Saiki) K. B.S., U. Hawaii, 1968; M.S., U. Calif.-San Francisco, 1969. Clin. nurse specialist St. Francis Hosp., Honolulu, 1979-80, VA Out-Patient Clinic, Honolulu, 1980—. Author: Cancer Care Protocols for Hospital and Home Care Use, 1981. Mem. Internat. Assn. Enterostomal Therapy, Am. Assn. Diabetic Educators, Am. Bus. Women's Assn. (rec. sec. 1983-84). Home: 2806 Kahaloa Dr Honolulu HI 96822 Office: VA Outpatient Clinic 300 Ala Moana Blvd PO Box 50188 Honolulu HI 96850

KUNKEL, GEORGIE MYRTIA, former school counselor; b. Seattle; d. George Riley and Myrtia (McLaughlin) Bright; m. Norman C. Kunkel, June 25, 1946; children—N. Joseph D.C., Stephen Gregory, Susan Ann, Kimberly Jane. B.A. in Edn., Western Wash. U., 1945; M.Ednl. Psychology, U. Wash., 1968. Typist, clk. FHA, Seattle, 1940; tchr. pub. schs. Vadar, Centralia, Wash., Seattle, 1941-67; pvt. cons., Seattle, 1970-85; counselor Highline Pub. Schs., Seattle, 1967-82; sch. counselor rep. State of Art Conf., Balt., 1980; cons. Project Equality, Highline Sch. Dist., Seattle, 1975-76. Editor Women and Girls in Edn., 1972-75. Contbr. articles to profl. jours. Organizer Women and Girls in Edn., Wash. state, 1971; pres. Wash. State NOW, 1973; mem. West Seattle Community Council, 1980. Grantee Women Adminstrs. Wash. State, 1971, Edn. Service Dist., Seattle, 1980. Mem. NEA (sec. pub. relations), Am. Assn. Counseling and Devel. (pres. state br. 1982-83), Am. Sch. Counseling Assn. (pres. state div. 1980-81), Seattle Assn. Counseling and Devel. (organizer), Holmes Harbor Homeowners Assn. Democrat. Unitarian Universalist. Club: Past Presidents (Seattle). Avocations: writing; singing. Home and Office: 3409 SW Trenton St Seattle WA 98126

KUNSTADTER, GERALDINE S., foundation executive; b. Boston, Jan. 6, 1928; d. Harry Herman and Nettie Sapolsky; m. John W. Kunstadter, Apr. 23, 1949; children—John W., Lisa, Christopher, Elizabeth. Student MIT, 1945-48. Draftsman, U. Chgo. Cyclotron Project, 1948; engring. asst. Gen. Electric Corp., Lynn, Mass., 1948-49; v.p., dir. A. Kunstadter Family Found., N.Y.C., 1966—; host family program dir. N.Y.C. Commn. for UN, 1971—; pres. Nat. Inst. Social Scis., 1979-81. Bd. dirs. Ptnrs. of Ams. Found., Washington, Menninger Found., Topeka, Yale-China Assn., Inst. Current World Affairs, English-Speaking Union, Eliot Feld Ballet, N.Y.C., Ctr. U.S.-China Arts Exchange, N.Y. Regional Assn. Grantmakers, East Side Internat. Community Ctr.; mem. resource council Partners of Ams., Washington; mem. com. on internat. grantmaking Council on Founds., mem. nat. com. U.S.-China relations; mem. Peace Links Leadership Network, Overseas Devel. Council; past mem. coms. MIT; trustee, chmn. bd. Windham Coll., Putney, Vt. Club: Am. Women's, Hurlingham, Lansdowne (London).

KUNTZ, MARION LUCILE LEATHERS, classics educator; b. Atlanta, Sept. 6, 1924; d. Otto Asa and Lucile (Parks) Leathers; B.A., Agnes Scott Coll., 1945; M.A., Emory U., 1964, Ph.D., 1969; children—Charles, Otto Alan (Daniels); m. 2d, Paul G. Kuntz, Nov. 26, 1970. Lectr. Latin, Lovett Sch., Atlanta, 1963-66; faculty Ga. State U., Atlanta, 1966—, assoc. prof., 1969-73, prof. Latin and Greek, 1973—, chmn. fgn. lang. dept., 1975-84, Regents' prof. classics, 1975—, research prof., 1984—, Fuller E. Callaway disting. prof., 1985—. Named Latin Tchr. of Yr., State Ga., 1965; Semple scholar, 1965; Am. Classical League scholar, 1966; Am. Council Learned Socs. grantee, 1970, 73, 78, 81. Mem. Am. Philol. Assn., Renaissance Soc. Am., Archaeol. Inst. Am., Classical Assn. Midwest and South (Semple award 1965), Medieval Acad., Soc. Medieval-Renaissance Philosophy, Am. Cath. Philos. Assn., Société Française des Seiziémistes, Venetian Seminar, Am. Philos. Assn., Ch. History Soc., Am. Acad. Rome (sec., treas. 1970-72), Internat. Soc. Neo-Latin Studies, Am. Soc. Aesthetics, Internat. Soc. Neo-Platonic Studies, Am. Soc. for Study of European Ideas, Center for Reformation Research, Italian Cultural Soc., Phi Beta Kappa. Roman Catholic. Club: Hellenic Study (pres. Atlanta 1974). Author: Colloquium of the Seven About Secrets of the Sublime of Jean Bodin, 1975; Guillaume Postel, Prophet of the Restitution of all Things: His Life and Thoughts, 1981; Jacob's Ladder and the Tree of Life: Concepts of the Great Chain of Being, 1986. Mem. editorial bd. Library Renaissance Humanism. Home: Atlanta GA 30307

KUNTZ, VESTA MCCLAIN, stockbroker; b. Oklahoma City, Aug. 8, 1952; d. Vester and Pat (Reeves) McClain; m. Terry Dewey, Jan. 3, 1971 (div. 1975); m. Hal Goggan Kuntz, Oct. 7, 1983. B.A., Southwestern U., 1974; M.B.A., U. Houston, 1980. Auditor, tax analyst Okla. Pub. Co., Oklahoma City, 1974-76; auditor Seidman & Seidman C.P.A.s, Houston, 1976-77; auditor, tax analyst Tenneco, Inc., Houston, 1977-80; stockbroker Underwood, Neuhaus, Houston, 1980-84, Kidder, Peabody & Co., Houston, 1984—. Fundraiser Houston Republican Party, 1982, Houston Opera Ball, 1985, Houston Multiple Sclerosis Soc., 1985. Mem. Houston Securities Assn., Houston Women's Assn. Methodist. Office: Kidder Peabody & Co 1000 Louisiana St Suite 5800 Houston TX 77001

KUNZ, LINDA MARIA, health care and scientific products company manager; b. Chgo., Mar. 20, 1949; d. Daniel James and Anna Marie (Manzo) K. B.A. in Biology, Northeastern Ill. U., 1972; Ph.D. in Biochemistry, Johns Hopkins U., 1979; M.S. in Mktg., Am. U., 1983; postgrad. in mktg. and strategic planning Rutgers U., 1983. Tchr. gifted students Balt. County Bd. Edn., 1971-72; sr. scientist, product mgr. Meloy Labs., Springfield, Va., 1979-82; mktg. and sales mgr. Biochem. Products div. Cooper Biomed./Worthington, Freehold, N.J. and Malvern, Pa., 1982-84; cancer bus. product mgr. Abbott Labs., North Chicago, Ill., 1984—. Contbr. articles to profl. jours. Lectr. Freehold Parents Orgn., 1983; counselor Johns Hopkins U. Office Residential Life, Balt., 1975; advisor Indsl. Biol. Safety Com., Springfield, Va., 1979-81. NIH fellow, 1972-76; Johns Hopkins U. grantee, 1976-79; recipient Northeastern Ill. U. Sci. Talent award, 1970-71. Mem. Am. Mktg. Assn., Sci. Equipment Makers Assn., Am. Mgmt. Assn., Biomed. Mktg. Assn. Club: Princeton Profls. Office: Abbott Labs North Chicago IL 60064

KUO, MAVIS MAI-HUA, jewelry corporation executive; b. Taipei, Taiwan, Dec. 11, 1950; came to U.S., 1971, naturalized, 1983; d. Richard Wu-Chiao and Cheng Hua (Chan) Kuo; m. Wey Chaung Kuo, Apr. 12, 1975; children—Anne, Andrew. A.A., San Francisco Community Coll., 1975. Waitress January restaurant, San Francisco, 1971-73; bookkeeper, sec. George Oshima, C.P.A., San Francisco, 1973-75; pres. Kuo W.M. Co., Troy, Mich., 1975—. Office: Kuo W M Co 2959 Crooks Rd Troy MI 48084

KUPCINET, ESSEE SOLOMON, events producer; b. Chgo., Dec. 7; d. Joseph David and Doris (Schoke) Solomon; Ph.B., Northwestern U., 1937; m. Irv Kupcinet, Feb. 12, 1939; children—Karyn (dec.), Jerry S. Asst. to dir. psychology dept. Michael Reese Hosp., Chgo., 1939-41; exec. producer eight Jefferson Award Shows; producer 1st Literary Arts Ball, Cultural Center, Chgo., 1979; talent coordinator Kup's Show, Chgo., 1964-84; producer for spl. events, 1978—. Mem. adv. bd. Wisdom Bridge Theatre; prodn. chmn. Acad. Honors, 1984—; chmn. bd. trustees Acad. Sch. Performing Arts, 1984—; prodn. chmn. Variety Club Telethon, 1984, 85; bd. dirs. Mus. Broadcasting Commn.; exec. com. Chgo. Tourism Council, 1984—; exec. bd. Internat. Theatre Festival, 1985-86; mem. sponsors com. Chgo. Pub. Library, 1985—. Decorated Knight of Orange Nassau (Netherlands); recipient Spl. award Jefferson Com., 1976; Cliff Dwellers award, 1975; Emmy award CBS, 1977, 79; Artisan award Acad. Theatre Arts and Friends, 1977; Prime Minister's medal for service to Israel, 1974; Woman of Yr. award Facets Multimedia, 1982, others. Mem. Nat. Acad. TV Arts and Scis. (governing bd., program chmn. 1982—). Jewish. Club: Arts.

KUPER, BARBARA ROZALIA, chemist, sculptress; b. Czestochowa, Poland; d. Stanislaw and Franciszka (Lewenhoff) Meryn; M.S., Cracow, Poland, 1948; postgrad. McGill U., 1961-63, Sir George Williams U. Mus. Fine Arts, 1961-70, Saidye Bronfman Centre, Montreal, 1967-70; m. Anthony Kuper, 1947; 1 dau., Eva. Analyst Warnock Hersey, Montreal, Que., Can., 1950-55; with quality control and forumulating depts. Internat. Paints Co., Montreal, 1955-61; chief lab. Globe Fur Blending, Montreal, 1961—; also owner sculptor studio, Montreal. One-woman shows: Dominion Gallery, Montreal, 1975, 78, 80, Stuart Hall, Point Claire, Que., 82, Confrontration 1982, Montreal, Man and His World, Que. Pavillion, 1982, Arnot Art Mus., Elmira, N.Y., 1982, Fredericton, N.B., Can., 1982, Sarnia, Ont., Can., 1982; group shows include: Saidye Bronfman Centre ann. exhbns., 1968-73, Dominion Gallery, 1976, Artist Showcase, Montreal, Herman Abramowitz chpt. Hadassah, 1979, Confrontation 83, Montreal, 1983, Salon National des Galeries d'Art, 1983, Salon des Femmes, Montreal, 1985; represented in permanent collections: Sculptors Soc. Can., Met. Mus., Coral Gables, Fla., Confedn. Center, Charlottetown, P.E.I., DuPont Coll., Brenink-Meyer Coll., Baron Art Gallery of Ben-Gurion U. of Negev, Israel, also pvt. collections. Mem. Assn. des Sculpteurs du Que., Sociétéd'Etudes et de Conferences de Montreal, Chem. Inst. Can., Order Chemists Que., Can. Soc. Chem. Engring., Sculptors Soc. Can. Internat. Sculpture Ctr. Washington. Home: 852 Berwick Crescent Montreal PQ H3R 2K9 Canada

KUPER, DANIELA F., advertising executive; b. Chgo., June 18, 1950; d. Harry W. and Anne F. (Fisher) K.; children—Judah E., Sahra J. B.A., So. Ill. U., 1972. Account exec., copywriter, creative dir. Griff Advt., Boulder, Colo., 1978-82; pres. Kuper Advt., Boulder, 1982—; speaker in field. Vol. creative writing with children Foothill Sch., Boulder, 1985. Recipient Alfie award Denver Ad Fedn., 1983, 85; award Art Dir. Club Denver, 1985; Addie award, 1985. Mem. Denver Ad Fedn., Boulder C. of C., Art Dirs. Club Denver. Office: Kuper Advt Inc 2903 Broadway Boulder CO 80302

KUPPERMAN, HELEN SLOTNICK, lawyer; b. Boston; d. Morris Louis and Minnie (Kaplan) Slotnick; B.A., Smith Coll.; postgrad. Royal Acad. Dramatic Art, London; J.D., Boston Coll., 1966; m. Robert H. Kupperman, Dec. 23, 1967; 1 dau., Tamara. Bar: Mass. 1966, D.C. 1986. Atty., advisor NASA, Washington, 1966-73, sr. atty., 1973-77, asst. gen. counsel for gen. law, 1977-86, assoc. gen. counsel, 1986—, chairperson contract adjustment bd., 1974—, rep. on U.S. delegation to legal subcomittee of UN Com. on Peaceful Uses of Outer Space, 1977—. Recipient NASA Sustained Superior Performance award, 1977, Exceptional Service medal, 1983, NASA Ses Bonus, 1980, 85, Space Station Task Force Group Achivement award NASA, 1984. Mem. U.S. Assn. of Internat. Inst. Space Law (sec. 1981), ABA, Fed., Mass., D.C., Boston bar assns., Internat. Women Lawyers Assn., Internat. Inst. Space Law, Am. astronautical Assn. (gen. counsel 1986). Jewish. Bus. editor Boston Coll. Indsl. and Comml. Law Rev., 1965-66. Home: 2832 Ellicott St NW Washington DC 20008 Office: 400 Maryland Ave SW Washington DC 20546

KUR, CAROL OLIVER, editor; b. New Haven, Mar. 24, 1939; d. Stewart S. Oliver and Sylvia (Ledewitz) Oliver Rosen; m. Mitchell Cowan Kur, June 22, 1958; children—Alison Laurel, Susan Oliver, Dana Beth. B.S., Boston U., 1960. Reporter, Ft. Wayne News Sentinel (Ind.), 1960-61; owner Gallery III, Sudbury, Mass., 1967-71; writer, editor The Paper, Framingham, Mass., 1971-74; mng. editor Moment mag., Boston, 1975—. Trustee, mem. exec. com. Bur. Jewish Edn., Boston, 1981—; v.p. Temple Beth Am, Framingham, Mass.; life mem. Hadassah, pres. Utica chpt. 1964-65; mem. nat. leadership devel. com. Council Jewish Fedns., 1975-76; speaker various nat., regional and local Jewish orgns. and synagogues. Mem. Sigma Delta Chi. Home: 108 Willard Rd Brookline MA 02146 Office: Moment 462 Boylston St Suite 301 Boston MA 02116

KURCZ, SYLVIA MARIE, human resources administrator; b. Chgo., Sept. 8, 1947; d. Joseph John and Helen Rose (Fitz) Kurcz. M.S., DePaul U., 1982; B.A., Roosevelt U., 1969, M.A., 1973. Tchr. Chgo. Sch. System, 1969-73; adminstrv. asst. personnel Goldblatt Bros., Chgo., 1973-74; adminstrv. personnel supr. Goldblatt Bros., 1974-78; personnel interviewer/recruiter St. Mary of Nazareth Hosp., Chgo., 1978-79; human resources supr. Gen. Instrument Lamp Div., Chgo., 1979-81, human resources adminstr., 1981—; lectr. in field; instr. DePaul U., Chgo., 1982-83; seminar instr. DePaul U., 1983. Editor-in-chief Lamplighter, 1982—; contbr. articles to profl. jours.; contbg. editor Soc. Personnel Adminstrs. Newsletter, 1984—. Mem. Am. Soc. Personnel Adminstrs., Midwest Personnel Mgmt. Assn. Democrat. Roman Catholic. Clubs: Mayer Kaplan Jewish Community Ctr., Leaning Tower YMCA. Office: General Instrument Lamp Div 4433 N Ravenswood Ave Chicago IL 60640

KURDLE, FLORENCE BECK, planning administrator; b. Battleboro, Vt., May 7, 1939; d. William Henry and Eva Dorothy (Lenz) Beck; m. Albert Ellison Kurdle, Apr. 20, 1963; children—Kyle David, Christopher Beck. A.B., Goucher Coll., 1961; postgrad. Cath. U., 1965, U. No. Colo., 1969. Caseworker, Dept. Welfare, Balt., 1961-62; planner Planning & Zoning, Anne Arundel County, Md., 1962-66, planner, 1968-75, dir., 1975—; assoc. F.E. von Schwerdtner & Assocs., Annapolis, Md., 1966-68; instr. Johns Hopkins U., Balt., 1982-85. Bd. dirs. YWCA, Annapolis and Anne Arundel County, 1981-83, v.p., 1984-85; bd. dirs. YMCA Anne Arundel County, 1983-84, v.p., 1985; vice chmn. Chesapeake Bay Critical Areas Commn., Md., 1984-85. Recipient Janet L. Hoffman award Sec. Pub. Adminstrs., Md., 1983. Mem. Am. Planning Assn. (pres. 1980-82), Md. Assn. County Planning Ofcls. (pres. 1981). Republican. Episcopalian. Avocations: reading; walking; biking. Office: Office of Planning and Zoning 44 Calvert St Annapolis MD 21404

KURETSKY, SUSAN DONAHUE, art historian; b. Charleston, S.C., Oct. 11, 1941; d. James Kenneth and Esther (Lawshe) Donahue; A.B., Vassar Coll., 1963; M.A. (Woodrow Wilson fellow), Harvard U., 1964, Ph.D. (Bernice Cronkhite fellow), 1971; m. Robert L. Kuretsky, July 17, 1969. Teaching fellow Harvard U., 1965-67; asst. prof. art Boston U., 1969-74; asso. prof. art Vassar Coll., 1975—; cons. pub. programs Nat. Endowment Humanities. Smith fellow in Dutch and Flemish art Nat. Gallery, Washington, 1974-75. Mem. Coll. Art Assn. Am. Author: The Paintings of Jacob Ochtervelt, 1979; (with others) Gods, Saints and Heroes: Dutch Painting in the Age of Rembrandt, 1980-81; contbr. articles and revs. to profl. jours. Office: Box 114 Vassar College Poughkeepsie NY 12601

KURKE, KATHY ANN, lawyer; b. Buffalo, Va., Feb. 19, 1954; d. Martin Ira and Joy Barbara (Edinger) Joseph. A.B., Ripon Coll., 1975; J.D., George Washington U., 1978, postgrad., 1981-82. Bar: Va. 1978, U.S. Claims Ct. 1980, U.S. Ct. Apls. (fed. cir.) 1983. Law clk. Statland & Zaslav, Washington, 1975-77, Rhyne & Rhyne (Nat. Inst. Mcpl. Law Officers), Washington, 1977-78; asst. counsel for procurement Office Chief Counsel U.S. Army C.E., Washington, 1978-82, counsel Humphreys Engr. Center, Fort Belvoir, Va., 1982—. Appted. mem. Arlington County Fair Housing Bd., 1979-81; chmn. legal and covenants com. Marina Towers Condominium, Alexandria, 1982-84; mem. steering com. Women's ORT, 1986. Recipient Ofcl. commendation U.S. Army, 1981, 82. Mem. Laurel Soc., Fed. Bar. Assn., Va. Bar Assn., ABA, Va. Women Attys. Assn. Democrat. Jewish. Home: 501 Slaters Ln #1016 Alexandria VA 22314 Office: Humphreys Engr Center US Army Corps Engrs Suite 1A01 Kingman Bldg Fort Belvoir VA

KURRAS, DOROTHY ANN, accountant; b. Patchogue, N.Y., July 5, 1937; d. Charles A. and Anna Elizabeth (Reuther) K. A.A. summa cum laude, Lake-Sumter Community Coll., 1964; B.B.A. summa cum laude, U. Central Fla., 1971. Gen. officer worker, bookkeeper DeBono, Inc., Patchogue, N.Y., 1955-57; office mgr. Swift Boats, Inc., Tangerine, Fla., 1957-62; staff acct. Greenlee, Paul & Furnas, Eustis, Fla., 1964-72; ptnr. Greenlee, Kurras, Rice & Brown, Mount Dora, Fla., 1972—, chmn. council ptnrs., 1985; sec., dir. PSI, Inc., Eustis, Fla., DARA, Inc., Mount Dora. Mem. bus. adv. com. Lake-Sumter Community Coll., Leesburg, Fla., 1980—; treas. Ice House Players Inc.-Civic Theatre, Mount Dora, 1978-81; treas. Pasco Vol. Fire Dept. Aux., Mount Dora, 1974-82; treas. Faith Luth. Ch. and Sch., Eustis, 1957—. Recipient Outstanding Acctg. Student award Osburn Henning & Co., C.P.A.s, Orlando, Fla., 1971. Mem. Am. Inst. C.P.A.s, Fla. Inst. C.P.A.s, Nat. Fedn. Ind. Businesses, Mount Dora C. of C., Bus. and Profl. Women (treas. 1973-75). Republican. Lutheran. Avocations: music; ceramics; golf; travel. Home: 260 Branch Ave Mount Dora FL 32757 Office: Greenlee Kurras Rice and Brown 627 N Donnelly St PO Box 8 Mount Dora FL 32757

KURRASCH, TERRIE LEE, hospital administrator, consultant; b. Oakland, Calif., Nov. 16, 1946; d. Chester Harold and Kathryn Verna (Mansfield) Ensign; m. Arthur Allen Kurrasch, June 15, 1969. B.S., Calif. State U.-Hayward, 1969; M.P.H., U. Calif.-Berkeley, 1980. Dir. child life Children's Hosp. Med. Ctr. No. Calif., Oakland, 1970-78; health planner H.O.M. Group, Inc., San Francisco, 1981-83; dir. planning Providence Hosp., Oakland, 1983—; lectr. Calif. State U.-Hayward, 1978-80. Bd. dirs. Alameda Family Service Agy. (Calif.), 1980-83; mem. adv. bd. Alameda council Boy Scouts Am., 1982—. Mem. Am. Hosp. Assn., Soc. Hosp. Planners, Am. Pub. Health Assn., Health Care Execs. No. Calif., Am. Coll. Hosp. Adminstrs. (nominee), AAUW. Clubs: Encinal Yacht (Alameda); Sierra. Lodge: Job's Daughters.

KURTTS, MARY ALTA, hospital nursing administrator; b. Birmingham, Ala., Aug. 20, 1936; d. William Hugh and Alta Mae (Mewbourne) Walker; m. Raymond Edward Kurtts, June 8, 1957; children—Karen Leigh Kurtts Alley, Laura Kathleen. Diploma, St. Vincent's Hosp. Sch. Nursing, Birmingham, 1957; student U. Ala.-Birmingham. R.N., Ala. Staff nurse VA Hosp., Birmingham, 1961-63, head nurse surg. service, 1963-65; head nurse surg. intensive care unit U. Ala. Hosps., Birmingham, 1966-67, dir. cardiovascular surg. nursing, 1967-70, dir. profl. standards rev. orgn./quality assurance, 1974—; dir. nursing service Medictrs. Am., Inc., Birmingham, 1971-74. Mem. exec. com. Birmingham Regional Health Systems Agy., 1976-82, sec. bd. dirs., chmn. nominating com., 1979-80, chmn. appropriateness rev. com., 1980-82; mem. Ala. Statewide Health Coordinating Council, 1976-81, vice chmn., 1979-80, chmn., 1980-81; bd. dirs. Family Med. Services, 1982—, vice chmn., 1985, chmn.-elect, 1986; bd. dirs. Ala. Health Plan, 1985-86. Mem. Am. Nurses Assn., Ala. State Nurses Assn. (dist. 3 pres. 1975-76, Nurse of Year in Dist. 1973), Nat. Assn. Quality Assurance Profls., Nat. League for Nursing. Republican. Roman Catholic. Home: 448 Indian Crest Dr Helena AL 35080 Office: Dept Med Care Review U Ala Hosps 619 S 19th St Birmingham AL 35233

KURTYKA, JULIA CAROLYN, musician, educator; b. Detroit, Sept. 14, 1943; d. Joseph and Mary (Krainiak) K.; B.Mus., U. Mich., 1965, M.Mus., 1967. Tchr. music Toledo Bd. Edn., 1962-78; prin. violinist Toledo Symphony, 1965-78, music librarian, 1970-75; 1st violinist Toledo String Quartet, 1971-78; founder, dir. Parochial Sch. String Program and Orch., 1969-71; tchr. music Frankfort Area Schs., 1978-81; instr. music Northwestern Mich. Coll., 1978-85; tchr. violin, Traverse City, Mich., 1978-85; dir., condr. Benzie Area Symphonette, 1979-85; concertmistress Northwestern Mich. Symphony, 1979-85, Midland (Mich.) Symphony orchs., 1979-82; soloist N.W. Symphony, 1981; tchr. Suzuki violin class, Cadillac, Mich., 1982-85, Manistee, Mich., 1984-85; violinist Northwood Orch., 1979—, also librarian, personnel mgr., 1981—, gen. mgr., 1986—; violinist Cass City Bach Festival Orch., 1978—, librarian, 1981—; violinist Boulder Bach Festival, 1986—, Inland Empire Symphony, 1985, Redlands Symphony, 1985—, Riverside Symphony, 1985—; ops. mgr. Inland Empire Symphony, Calif., 1985—; tchr. Community Music Sch., Redlands U., Calif., 1985—. Mem. Am. String Tchrs., Am. Suzuki Tchrs. Assn., Sigma Beta. Russian Orthodox. Address: 28 North Ctr Redlands CA 92373

KURTZ, BARBARA BRANDON, educational administrator; b. Hillsdale, Mich., Jan. 17, 1941; d. Robert Dale and Dortha May (Bird) Brandon; m. Robert Roger Kurtz, June 20, 1964; children—Kevin, Christopher, Kathryn. B.S. in Music Edn., Western Mich. U., 1963; M.A. in Edn., Mich. State U., 1969; postgrad. John Carroll U., 1979-80; Ph.D. in Early Childhood Edn., Clayton U., 1983. Pres. adminstrn. U. Iowa Coop. Preschool, Iowa City, 1972-75; dir. Coral Nursery, Iowa City, 1975-77; head tchr. Covenant Early Childhood Programs, Cleve., 1977-79, dir., 1979—; supr. practicum Case Western Res. U., Cleve., 1977—; adj. faculty Lakeland Community Coll., Kirtland, Ohio, 1981—; project coordinator Child Day Care Planning Project of Cuyahoga County, Cleve., 1985—. Author: Center-Sponsored Family Day Care Homes, 1984. Editor: (with Brenda Boyd) Student Aide Training Packet, 1978. Contbr. articles to profl. jours. Mem. adv. panel Beginnings jour., 1984—; mem. day care adv. council Ohio Dept. Human Services. Recipient Gov.'s Spl. Recognition award State of Ohio, 1985. Mem. Nat. Assn. for Edn. of Young Children, Nat. Coalition for Campus Child Care, Ohio Assn. for Edn. of Young Children, Cleve. Assn. for Edn. of Young Children (Early Childhood award 1984). Democrat. Roman Catholic. Avocations: cross-country skiing; snowshoeing; hiking; travel; reading. Home: 8856 Kirtland-Chardon Rd Kirtland OH 44060 Office: Covenant Early Childhood Programs 11205 Euclid Ave University Circle Cleveland OH 44060

KURTZ, CAROLE JANE, publishing company personnel executive; b. Columbus, Ohio, Feb. 10, 1938; d. Gaylord Charles and Mary Jane (Wickliffe) Chatfield; m. Martin E. Kurtz, Sept. 26, 1959; children—Gregory, Douglas, Andrew. Student Ohio State U., 1956-57. Account rep. Ohio Bell Tel. Co., Columbus, 1955-60; personnel rep. Pollock Paper Co., Columbus, 1960-64; employment mgr. Pendleton Tool Industries, Columbus, 1967-69; dir. personnel Merrill Publ. Co., Columbus, 1975—. Mem. Westerville Area C. of C. (trustee 1984—), personnel Soc. Columbus, Am. Soc. Personnel Adminstrs., Am. Mgmt. Assn., Nat. Assn. Female Execs. Office: Charles E Merrill Publ Div 1300 Alum Creek Dr Columbus OH 43216

KURTZ, JUDITH MIRIAM, rehabilitation services director; b. N.Y.C., Mar. 13, 1933; d. Louis and Mae (Salzberg) Kurtz. B.A., Bklyn. Coll., 1954; cert. phys. therapy Med. Coll. Va., 1955; M.B.A., Adelphi U., 1979. Staff phys. therapist Med. Coll. Va., Richmond, 1956; asst. chief phys. therapy St. Vincent's Hosp., N.Y.C., 1956-63; chief phys. therapist Hosp. for Spl. Surgery, N.Y.C., 1963-71, dir. rehab. services, 1971—; rehab. cons., mem. profl. adv. bd. Vis. Nurse Service, N.Y.C., also mem. utilization rev., 1985—. Author rehab. therapy manuals. Mem. Am. Phys. Therapy Assn., Assn. Allied Health Profls., Am. Congress Rehab. Medicine, Arthritis Found. Allied Health Profls., Assn. Med. Rehab. Dirs. and Coordinators (cert.), Delta Mu Delta. Democrat. Jewish. Office: Hospital for Special Surgery 535 E 70th St New York NY 10021

KURTZ, MAXINE, personnel research officer, lawyer; b. Mpls., Oct. 17, 1921; d. Jack Isadore and Beatrice (Cohen) K. B.A., U. Minn., 1942; B.S. in Govt. Mgmt., U. Denver, 1945, J.D., 1962; postdoctoral student U. Calif.-San Diego, 1978. Bar: Colo. Planning analyst Tri-County Regional Planning, Denver, 1945-47; chief, research and spl. projects, Planning Office, City and County of Denver, 1947-66, tech. dir., evaluation dir. Model Cities Program, 1966-71; personnel research officer, Denver Career Service Authority, 1972—; expert witness, nat. com. on urban problems U.S. Ho. of Reps., U.S. Senate. Author: Law of Planning and Land Use Regulations in Colorado, 1966; co-author; Care and Feeding of Witnesses, Expert and Otherwise, 1974; bd. editors: Pub. Adminstrn. Rev., Washington, 1980-83; prin. investigator book: Employment: An American Enigma, 1979. Active Women's Forum of Colo., LWV, Denver, Democratic Party, Denver. Sloan fellow, U. Denver, 1944-45; recipient Outstanding Achievement award U. Minn., 1971. Mem. Am. Inst. Planners (sec. treas. 1968-70, bd. govs. 1972-75), Am. Soc. Pub. Adminstrn. (nat. council 1978-81; Donald Stone award), ABA, Colo. Bar Assn., Denver Bar Assn., Order St. Ives, Pi Alpha Alpha. Jewish. Home: 2361 Monaco Pkwy Denver CO 80207 Office: Denver Career Service Authority 414 14th St Denver CO 80202

KURTZ, PATRICIA ANN, lawyer; b. N.Y.C., Sept. 2, 1953; d. Harry Aaron and Lillian Madeline (Welti) K. B.A., Bucknell U., 1975; J.D., St. John's Sch. Law, 1978. Bar: N.Y. 1979, U.S. Dist. Ct. (so. dist.) N.Y. 1979, U.S. Dist. Ct. (ea. dist.) N.Y. 1979. Assoc., Willkie Farr & Gallagher, N.Y.C., 1978—. Articles editor St. John's Law Rev., 1977. Mem. ABA, N.Y. State Bar Assn. Office: Willkie Farr & Gallagher 153 E 53d St New York NY 10022

KURTZ, PATRICIA ROSE, educator; b. Detroit, Jan. 13, 1944; d. Albert G. and Rose (Jasinski) Kurtz. B.A., Madonna Coll., 1963; postgrad. U. Mich., 1966-67. Cert. elem. tchr. Tchr., Livonia Pub. Schs. (Mich.), 1963—; observer elem. classes in Russia, 1967, China, 1971. Vol., Beaumont Hosp., Royal Oak, Mich., 1980—(Silver Pin award for 500 hrs. service 1984); vol. Rep. Conv., Detroit, 1980. Mem. NEA, Mich. Edn. Assn., Livonia Edn. Assn., PTA. Roman Catholic. Club: Cranbrook Acad. Art (Bloomfield Hills, Mich.). Home: 3835 Quarton Rd Bloomfield Hills MI 48013

KURTZIG, SANDRA L., computer software company executive. B.S., UCLA, 1967; M.S., Stanford U., 1968. Former math analyst TRW Systems; salesperson Gen. Electric Co., 1969-72; chmn. bd. dirs. chief exec. officer ASK Computer Systems, Los Altos, Calif., 1972-85. Address: Ask Computer Systems Inc 730 Distel Dr Los Altos CA 94022

KURTZMAN, CHERYL DIANE, advertising executive; b. Los Angeles, Aug. 25, 1951; d. Myron and Selma L. (Roth) K. B.A., U. Calif.-Berkeley, 1973. Mem. staff Daily News, Los Angeles, 1973-74; pub. relations dir. March of Dimes, Los Angeles, 1974-75; media buyer McCann, Erickson, Inc., San Francisco, 1975-77; media planner Foote, Cone & Belding, Inc., San Francisco, 1977-79; media dir. Commart Advt. Inc., Santa Clara, Calif., 1979-82, v.p., 1982—. Mem. Sierra Club (Calif. newsletter editor 1979-82; Disting. Service award 1983), Bus. and Profl. Advt. Assn., Med. Mktg. Assn., Peninsula Women in Advt., Bay Area Media Profls. Office: Commart Advt Inc 4701 Patrick Henry Dr Santa Clara CA 95050

KURZ, JEANNE ANNE WALSH, chiropractor, career advisor; b. Richmond Hill, N.Y., Nov. 19, 1935; d. George Valentine and Catherine Frances (McCann) Walsh; m. E.R.H. Kurz, Sept. 20, 1963; children—Scott George, Laurie Jeanne. A.A.S. in Nursing, Queensborough Community Coll., Bayside, N.Y., 1968-70; B.S., C.W. Post Coll., 1973, postgrad., 1974-76; D.C., Life Chiropractic Coll., Marietta, Ga., 1982. Nurse, Wyckoff Heights Hosp., Bklyn., 1964-66, Southampton Hosp., N.Y., 1968-73; pvt. practice chiropractic, Southampton, N.Y., 1982—; career advisor C.W. Post Coll., Greenvale, N.Y., 1984—. Mem. Internat. Chiropractic Assn., Am. Chiropractic Assn., N.Y. Chiropractic Assn., Pub. Health Assn., Sigma Phi Chi, Phi Theta Kappa, Phi Beta Kappa. Club: Topping Riding (Bridehampton, N.Y.). Avocations: art; archery; aviation; equestrian skills; writing; fencing. Home and Office: Wickapogue Rd Southampton NY 11968

KURZENBERGER, ANNE ELIZABETH, communications executive, publishing specialist; b. Morristown, N.J., July 16, 1958; d. Walter Philip and Ruth Eleanor (Robinson) K. B.A. in History, Georgetown U., 1980. Asst. editor Officer mag., Washington, 1981; editor, art prodn. mgr. Rutgers U., New Brunswick, N.J., 1981-84; supr. corp. info. AT&T Bell Labs., Short Hills, N.J., 1984; systems analyst, 1985—. Mem. NOW, Phi Alpha Theta. Avocations: graphic arts; architecture; gourmet cooking; interior design; gardening. Office: AT&T Bell Labs 101 J F Kennedy Pkwy Short Hills NJ 07078

KUSE-WARREN, KRISTIN KAY, marketing executive; b. Marshfield, Wis., Sept. 8, 1955; d. Warren Franklin and Grace Louise (Hurd) Kuse; m. Danny Dean Warren, Jan. 8, 1983; 1 child, Christoffer Daniel. B.S. in Bus. Adminstrn., U. Wis.-Eau Claire, 1977. Exchange dir. AIESEC-U.S., N.Y.C., 1978-79, exchange coordinator AIESEC-Internat., Brussels, 1979-80; sales specialist Snelling and Snelling, Mpls., 1980-81; market research analyst Weigh-Tronix Inc., Fairmont, Minn., 1981—; cons. and researcher in mktg. Mem. AAUW (internat. relations 1984-85), Bus. and Profl. Women Orgn. (named Young Career Woman 1984). Republican. Roman Catholic. Avocations: Sewing; aerobics; travel.

KUSHNER, EVA, educator, author; b. Prague, Czechoslovakia, June 18, 1929; d. Josef and Anna (Kafkova) Dubsky; m. Donn Jean Kushner, Sept. 15, 1949; children—Daniel Peter, Roland Joseph, Paul Joel. B.Ph., Coll. Marie de France, Montreal, 1946; B.A., McGill U., 1948, M.A. in Philosophy, 1950, Ph.D. in French Lit., 1956. Lectr. French, McGill U., Montreal, 1952-55, instr. French, summers 1956, 58, 61-62, 67-69, prof. French lang. and lit., 1976—; sessional lectr. philosophy Sir George Williams U., 1952-53; lectr. Univ. Coll., London, 1958-59; lectr. Carleton U., 1961, asst. prof. French and comparative lit., 1963, assoc. prof., 1965, prof., 1969-76, chmn. comparative lit., 1965-69, 70-72, 75-76, adj. prof. lit., 1976-79; mem. exec. com. Can. Council, mem., 1975-81; v.p. Social Scis. and Humanities Research Council Can., 1983-86; mem. adv. bd. Nat. Library Can.; pres. Humanities Research Council Can., 1970-72. Author: Patrice de La Tour de Pin, 1961; Le mythe d'Orphee dans la litterature francaise contemporaine, 1961; Chants de Boheme, 1963; Rina Lasnier collections Ecrivains canadiens d'aujourd'hui, 1964; Poetes d'aujourd'hui, 1969; Saint-Denys Garneau, 1967; Francois Mauriac, 1972, Japanese transl., 1976; co-author anthology Que. poetry, transl. into Hungarian, 1978, Polish, 1985; co-editor Proc. VII Congress Internat. Comparative Lit. Assn., also Vol. IV, Evolution of the Novel, IX Congress; editor Renewals in the Theory of Literary History; co-dir research Renaissance vols. Histoire comparee des litteratures de langues européennes; mem. editorial com. Can. Comparative Lit. Rev., Dalhousie French Studies; mem. internat. adv. bd. Comparative lit. Studies. Contbr. articles to profl. publs. Fellow Royal Soc. Can. (v.p. 1980-82); mem. Academie Européenne des lettres, des sciences et des arts, Am. Comparative Lit. Assn. (adv. bd.), Internat. Comparative Lit. Assn. (pres. 1979-82), MLA (del. assembly, chmn. 16th century French lit. div., mem. exec. council 1983-86), Assn. internat. des etudes francaises, Assn. des profs. de francais des univs. canadiennes, Assn. canadienne de litterature comparee (v.p. 1969-71), Internat. Assn. Neo-Latin Studies, Soc. canadienne d'etudes de la Renaissance, Assn. des litteratures canadienne et quebocoise, Can. Soc. Semiotic Research. Mem. United Ch. Canada. Office: 3460 McTavish St Montreal PQ H3A 1X9 Canada

KUSHNER, LAURYN BONNIE, plastic manufacturer company official; b. Chgo., July 23, 1955; d. Herman and Rae (Bittenfeld) K. Asst. office mgr. Law Firm of Jenner & Block, Chgo., 1974-78; Midwest distbn. mgr. Supreme Equipment & Systems Corp., Chgo., 1980-85; chief operating officer Thermoform Plastics, Inc., 1986—; pres. Women Artist's Gallery, 1981. Chmn. bd. E.P.I.C., Inc., Chgo., 1982. Mem. Nat. Assn. Female Execs., Am. Film Inst., Smithsonian Assocs. Jewish.

KUSKO, MARY ANN, newspaper editor; b. Allentown, Pa., Jan. 7, 1956; d. Joseph and Mary (Hreshko) Kusko. Student Lafayette Coll., 1973-75; B.A., Pa. State U., 1979. Tennis profl. Vantage Point Club, Allentown, Pa., 1979; newspaper reporter The Free Press, Emmaus, Pa., 1980-81, editor-in-chief, 1981—; feature writer Daily Collegian, University Park, Pa., 1978. Confraternity of Christian doctrine tchr. St. Catherine's Allentown, Pa., 1977—; editor-in-chief Allentown Diocese Cath. Soc. Agy., Allentown, Pa., 1981-82. Acad. scholar Lafayette Coll., 1973-75. Mem. Internat. Assn. Bus. Communicators, AAUW (speaker), Pa. Newspaper Press Assn. Republican. Roman Catholic. Clubs: Racquetball (Allentown), Stonecrest Swim and Tennis. Home: 1045 N Main St Allentown PA 18104 Office: Free Press 408 Chestnut St Emmaus PA 18049

KUSMA, KYLLIKKI, lawyer; b. Tartu, Estonia, Dec. 8, 1943; came to U.S., 1951, naturalized, 1958; d. August and Helju (Traat) K.; B.F.A., Ohio U., 1966; M.A. (Vets. Rehab. Adminstrn. fellow), Ohio State U., 1967; J.D., Ohio No. U., 1976; M.L.T., Georgetown U., 1980. Bar: Ohio 1977, D.C. 1978. Speech and hearing therapist Lima (Ohio) Meml. Hosp., 1967-70, Tipp City (Ohio) Schs., 1970-74; atty.-adv. Office Chief Counsel, IRS, Washington, 1977-81; v.p., asso. tax counsel Security Pacific Nat. Bank, Los Angeles, 1981-83; atty. Brownstein Zeidman & Schomer, Washington, 1983—; instr. Wright State U., 1972-76. Vol. local civic, polit. activities. Mem. ABA, D.C. Bar Assn., Ohio Bar Assn., D.C. Women's Bar Assn., Phi Kappa Phi. Democrat. Home: 5114 Fairglen Ln Chevy Chase MD 20815 Office: 1401 New York Ave NW Washington DC 20005

KUTCHINSKY, LEIGH ELENA, public health epidemiologist, educator; b. N.Y.C., Aug. 4, 1947; B.S., U. Calif., Berkeley, 1976, M.P.H., 1977, Ph.D., M.D., 1978; children—Buddy, Tad, Scott, Yaakov. Epidemiologist, Contra Costa (Calif.) VD Program, 1973-75; lectr. U. Calif., Berkeley, 1976-77; epidemiologist Colo. Dept. Health, Denver, 1977-78; asst. prof. U. Colo. Med. Center, 1977-80; pres. Medi-Search, Inc., 1980—; co-founder West Contra Costa Clinic; childbirth and Lamaze instr. Brighton Hosp. Chairperson, Contra Costa Childcare Adv. Bd., 1973-75; mem. Joint Strategy Action Com. on Medi-Cal Reform, 1975-77, Com. on Access to Health Care, 1975-78, Med. Com. for Human Rights, 1968—, U. Calif. Acad. Affairs Council, 1975-77. Chmn. issues com. Adams County Democratic Women's Caucus; mem. exec. bd. Adams County. Calif. State fellow, 1976-78, Regents fellow, 1976-78; A-CC/AMA scholar, 1975-76; HEW trainee, 1976-78. Mem. Am. Public Health Assn., Am. Med. Women's Assn., Colo. Public Health Assn., Am. Trauma Soc., Colo. Holistic Health Network, Am. Acad. Polit. Sci., EST, Mensa, Phi Beta Kappa, Alpha Gamma Sigma (Gold Pin award). Democrat. Jewish. Club: Am. Kennel. Research on herpes virus. Home and office: 2490 Channing Way Apt 503 Berkeley CA 94704

KUTTICHIRA, RACHEL JOSEPH, pediatrician; b. Bombay, India, June 25, 1945; came to U.S., 1973, naturalized, 1980; d. C. Joseph and Annamma (Easow) Easow. M.B. B.S., G.S. Med. Coll. Bombay, India, 1970; Diploma Child Health, Coll. Physicians and Surgeons, Bombay, 1972. Med. officer Pub. Health Dept., Bombay, India, 1972-73, Youville Hosp., Cambridge, Mass., 1974-76; resident in pediatrics Flushing Hosp. (N.Y.), 1976-79; fellow in ambulatory pediatrics, Nassau County Med. Centre, East Meadow, N.Y., 1979-80; practice medicine specializing in pediatrics, Hempstead, N.Y., 1980—. Recipient Dr. Shirvalkar Silver Medal in Surgery, G.S. Med. Coll., 1965. Jr. fellow Am. Acad. Pediatrics; mem. N.Y. Med. Soc., Nassau Pediatric Soc. Democrat. Syrian Christian. Home: 384 Demott Ave Rockville Centre NY 11570 Office: 312 Greenwich St Hempstead NY 11550

KUYKENDALL, JANICE HAVILAND, marine supply company executive; b. Houston, June 17, 1944; d. John Thompson and Doris Evelyn (Brock) Rector; m. Dean Kings Haviland, May 12, 1962 (div. Feb. 1981); children—Carol, Shelby; m. 2d, Herbert Brent Kuykendall, Jan. 1, 1984. Student U. Tex., 1962-64, Tex. A&M U., 1964-65. Far East regional mgr. Grolier Internat. Corp., Tokyo, 1967-72; dir. Tech. Ctr., Inc., Houston, 1972-74; sr. sales counselor Snelling & Snelling, Houston, 1974-78; v.p. Blue Water Marine Supply, Houston, 1978-84; pres. AIMS, marine supply co., Houston, 1984—. Mem. Marine Services Assn. Tex. (dir.), Tex. Safety Assn., Nat. Assn. Female Execs., Propeller Club Houston. Republican. Home: 1121 Robert St Pearland TX 77581 Office: AIMS 9805 Monroe Houston TX 77075

KUYKENDALL, PATRICIA ANNE, hospital executive; b. Kewanee, Ill., Mar. 27, 1935; d. Samuel Burton and Theresa Mary (McEnroe) Ensley; diploma nursing St. Anthony Hosp., Rock Island, Ill., 1960; B.S. in Nursing, Incarnate Word Coll., San Antonio, 1961; M.S., St. Louis U., 1965; m. James K. Kuykendall, Jan. 17, 1973. Dir. staff devel. Barnes Hosp., St. Louis, 1969-74; program dir. oncology nursing project U. Tex., Houston, 1974-77; mem. nursing staff U. Tex. Med. Br., Galveston, 1977—, dir. nursing surg. operating suite, ICU and sterile processing dept., 1980-81, exec. dir., dir. nursing surg. operating and acute care support services, 1981—; mgmt. cons. in field. Mem. lay adv. bd. Forest Park Community Coll., St. Louis, 1972-74; participant Leadership Tex., 1984. Johnson & Johnson-Wharton nurse fellow, 1983. Mem. Am. Nurses Assn., Am. Hosp. Assn., Am. Bus. Women's Assn. (treas. Elan chpt. 1984), Sigma Theta Tau (chpt. treas. 1977-79). Roman Catholic. Office: U Tex Med Br University and Mechanic Sts Galveston TX 77550

KUYKENDALL, RUTH JANE, real estate company executive; b. Jackson, Mich., Aug. 22, 1908; d. James Elwood and Nellie Bethune (Allen) Bartlett; student Mich. State U., 1927-28, Fla. State Coll. for Women, 1930-31; m. Hubert Paul Kuykendall, June 12, 1945. Mgr., Myakka Hotel, Venice, Fla., 1931-41; corp. sec. J.E. Bartlett & Sons, Inc., 1931-54, pres., 1955-56; owner, mgr. Kuykendall Real Estate Co., 1951-85. Mem. Internat. Platform Assn., Am. Inst. Parliamentarians, Gulf Coast Parliamentarians (past v.p.), DAR, (parlimentarian 1980—), Am. Legion Aux., Daus. Am. Colonists, (state chmn. historic landmarks and memls. 1982—), V.F.W. Colonial Dames XVII Century, Descs. Mayflower, Magna Charta Dames, Plantagenets Soc., La Boutique des Huit Chapeaux et Quarante Femmes. Republican. Methodist. Home: 261 Ponce de Leon Ave Venice FL 33595

KUYPER, FRANCES IRENE, cake decorator, educator; b. Harvey, Ill., June 26, 1918; d. John August William and Lovie DeVal (Smith) Schultz; m. Frank Kuyper, Aug. 17, 1947; 1 child, Carol Jean. Student Afleck Art Studio Sch. of Design, Cin., 1947; diploma Aaron Bros., Buena Park, Calif., 1969; master cake decorator Wilton Sch., 1974. Entertainer show bus. Sister Team, E. of Miss. River, 1935-46; home bus. of personalized cakes, Compton, Calif., 1950-55; head decorator bakeries, Los Angeles, 1955-74; tchr. coordinator Wilton Enterprises, Chgo., 1974-79; owner Cake Lady Services, Anaheim, Calif., 1979—, Pasadena, 1979—; cons. in field; cons. Baskin Robbins, 1980—; condr. classes in Australia, Indonesia; lectr., Kuala Lumpur, Malaysia, Osaka and Japan, 1986. Author Plaid Enterprises; Norcross, Ga., 1983-85; demonstrator Parrish's Cake Supplies, Los Angeles, 1956-86; instr. Cake Lady Services, Pasadena, 1979-86. Author: How to Air Brush on Cake, 1979; Craft Book-Stencil-A-Cake, 1983, Star Spangled speakers, 1982, others; also video tapes. Goodwill ambassador Internat. Cake Exploration Société World, 1977, bd. dirs., 1982, v.p., 1983, internat. liaison, 1984. Inducted in Internat. Cake Decorators Hall of Fame, 1985; recipient Key to cities of Sulphur and Lafayette, La., 1983; hon. citizen City of Houston. Mem. Calif. Cake Club (hon. advisor), Soc. Craft Designers, Demonstrators, Golden Voice chpt. Nat. Speakers Assn. Republican. Methodist. Clubs: Assn. of Ret. Persons, Nat. Assn. Letter Carriers, Calif. Cake Club (organizer). Avocations: crafts; music; arts. Home: 432 N Lola Ave Pasadena CA 91107 Office: The Cake Lady Services 432 N Lola Ave Pasadena CA 91107

KWAN-CHOW, RHODA, electronics company executive; b. Canton, China, Oct. 27, 1932; came to U.S., 1969, naturalized, 1974; d. Bye Yen and Sok Hing (Tang) Wong; m. Chan Wan Kwan, Oct. 21, 1951 (div. 1981); children—Helen, Edgar, Rebecca, Edmund; m. Tom Chow, May 24, 1982. B.S. in Math., Canton U., 1953; cert. in Bus. Acctg., Heald Bus. Coll., 1973. Pres., Rhoda Devel. Corp., Hong Kong, 1962-69; founder, pres. Monitron Corp., San Jose, Calif., 1979—. Mem. Canton Alumni Assn. (pres. 1950-64), Assn. Pub. Relations Canton (chmn. 1954-56). Avocation: music. Office: Monitron Corp 1450 Seareel Ln San Jose CA 95131

KWOLEK, STEPHANIE LOUISE, chemist; b. New Kensington, Pa., July 31, 1923; d. John and Nellie (Zajdel) K. B.S., Carnegie-Mellon U., 1946; D.Sc. (hon.), Worcester Poly. Inst., 1981. Chemist, E.I. duPont de Nemours & Co. Inc., Wilmington, Del., 1946-59, research chemist, 1959-67, sr. research chemist, 1967-74, research assoc., 1974—. Contbr. articles to profl. jours.; patentee in field. Recipient award for contbns. to Kevlar, Am. Soc. Metals, 1978, engring./tech. award Soc. Plastics Engrs., 1985; inducted into U. Akron Polymer Processing Hall of Fame, 1985 . Mem. Am. Chem. Soc. (award for creative invention 1980), Am. Inst. Chemists (Chem. Pioneer award 1980), Franklin Inst. Phila. (Howard N. Potts medal 1976), Carnegie Mellon U. Alumni Assn. (merit award 1983), Sigma Xi, Phi Kappa Phi. Club: DuPont Country (Wilmington). Office: EI duPont de Nemours & Co Inc Experimental Sta Pioneering Research Lab Wilmington DE 19898

KYDD-DECATUR, SUZANNE NOEL, veterinarian; b. Lowell, Mass., Feb. 28, 1948; d. William Arthur Perrins and Renee Maria (Fellner) Kydd; m. William Ted Brackett (div.); m. Thurston Rensselaer Decatur, III, Oct. 18, 1982; 1 son, Jakob Fellner. Student U. Pitts., Ohio State U., N.C. State U., D.V.M., U. Ga., 1975. Assoc. veterinarian Hendersonville Animal Hosp. (N.C.), 1975-76; small animal practice vet. medicine North State Vet. Clinic, Hendersonville, 1976—; part-time instr. Blue Ridge Tech. Coll., Hendersonville, 1980-81. Contbr. articles on animal health to newspapers. Bd. dirs. YMCA, Hendersonville, 1979-82. Recipient Merck Vet. Small Animal award 1975. Mem. AVMA, Am. Animal Hosp. Assn., Western N.C. Vet. Med. Assn. (pres. 1976-78). Democrat. Episcopalian. Home: 1103 4th Ave W Hendersonville NC 28739

KYES, HELEN G. (MRS. ROGERS M. KYES), civic leader; b. Marion, Ohio; d. Benjamin and Bess (Gilmore) Jacoby; B.A., Oberlin Coll., 1926; Ph.D. (hon.), Oakland U., 1980; m. Roger M. Kyes, June 5, 1931; children—Carolyn Kyes Eggert, Frances (dec.), Katharine Kyes Leab, Anne Kyes Smith. Sec., pres. Federated Women's Club, Marion, Ohio, 1927-31; bd. dirs. Cleve. Coll. Club, 1936-41, Cleve. YWCA, 1938-41; mem. bd. Woman's Nat. Farm and Garden, 1943-56, 60—, sec., 1943-45, 54-55; dir. Children's Aid and Home Friendless, 1949—, v.p., 1961—; bd. dirs. Brookside Sch., Cranbrook, 1952-58, sec., 1957-58; bd. dirs. Kingswood Sch., Cranbrook, 1968—; charter mem. bd. trustees Oakland U. Found., 1958, v.p. exec. bd., 1960—; trustee Oakland U., 1970—; mem. Woman's Assn. Detroit Symphony; com. 100 Detroit Met. Opera; capt. spl. gifts Detroit United Fund, 1959-61; mem. Detroit Mus. Art Founders Soc.; mem. com. Detroit Foster Home Edn. and Recruitment Program, 1960—. Mem. DAR, AAUW (past treas., v.p. Marion). Presbyterian (vice moderator deacons). Clubs: Bloomfield Hills Country, Detroit, Village Woman's, Ocean (Delray Beach, Fla.); Gulfstream Bath and Tennis. Home: 945 Cranbrook Rd Bloomfield Hills MI 48013 also 6861 N Ocean Blvd Ocean Ridge FL 33435

KYLE, CORINNE SILVERMAN, research executive; b. N.Y.C., Jan. 4, 1930; d. Nathan and Janno (Harra) Silverman; B.A., Bennington Coll., 1950; M.A., Harvard U., 1953; m. Alec Kyle, Aug. 29, 1959 (div. Feb. 1969); children—Joshua, Perry (dec.), Julia. Assoc. editor Inter-Univ. Case Program, N.Y.C., 1956-60; co-founder, chief editor Financial Index, N.Y.C., 1960-63; research analyst McKinsey & Co., N.Y.C., 1963-64; sr. research assoc. Mktg. Sci. Inst., Phila., 1964-67; founding partner Phila. Group, 1967-70; sr. assoc. Govt. Studies and Systems, Phila., 1970-72, cons. program planning and control, Phila., 1972-80, sr. assoc. Periodical Studies Service, 1978-80; v.p., dir. research Total Research Corp., 1978-80; mgr. social sci. research group Gallup Orgn., Inc., Princeton, N.J., 1982-85; v.p. Response Analysis Corp., Princeton, 1985—; dir. Verbena Corp., N.Y.C.; lectr. Temple U., 1981. Mem. adv. council to 8th Dist. city councilman, Phila., 1971-78; mem. 22d Ward Democratic Exec. Com., 1971-78, State Dem. Com., 1974-76, Princeton Ward committeeman, 1981-82; trustee Princeton Regional Scholarship Found., 1982-85, pres., 1985; mem. Pa. Gov.'s Council on Nutrition, 1974-76; v.p. Miquon Upper Sch. Bd., Phila., 1977-79, mem. Princeton Regional Sch. Bd., 1984—. Mem. Am. Polit. Sci. Assn., Am. Assn. Pub. Opinion Research. Contbr. numerous articles to profl. publs. Home: 141 Spruce St Princeton NJ 08542

KYLE, JANET HINKLE, modeling school administrator, irrigation company executive; b. Portland, Oreg., Aug. 14, 1918; d. Walter Berkeley and Minnie (Naylor) Hinkle; m. David M. Kyle, May 4, 1940 (dec. 1980); children—Michaele Kyle Leitch, Kris Kyle Ross, David M. III. B.S.S., Oreg. State U., 1939. Lic. irrigation contractor; lic. psychologist, Fla. Founder, owner, operator Turnabout Modeling Sch., and Agy. Stuart, Fla., 1970—, Vero Beach, Fla., 1973-85, franchisor Vero Beach ops., 1985—; owner, operator St. Lucie Pump and Water Supply, Stuart, 1980—; owner, mgr. Kyle Ctr., Stuart, 1980—; Columnist, Mil. Press, Hawaii, 1962-65. Fashion editor Indian River Life, 1979-81. Author, editor: Save Your Blushes, 1938. Mem. Ctr. for Arts, Vero Beach, 1980—, Arts Found. Martin County, Stuart, 1982—. Mem. Stuart C. of C., Vero Beach C. of C., Internat. Talent/Modeling Schs. Assn. (sec. 1983-84, v.p. 1984-85, bd. dirs. 1978-85), Internat. Modeling Assn. (adv. bd.), Nat. League Am. Pen Women, Alpha Chi Omega. Republican. Avocations: reading; travel; writing. Office: Turnabout Modeling Sch 584 SE Monterey Rd Stuart FL 33497

KYLE, NANCY R., financial executive; b. Hazleton, Pa., June 4, 1952; d. Robert H. and Frances M. (Dvorshock) Krensavage; B.S., Pa. State U., 1973; M.B.A., LaSalle U., 1979; m. Joseph B. Ritvalsky, Nov. 29, 1975. Chief evaluator United Cerebral Palsy Assn., Phila., 1973-76; controller United Way of S.E. Delaware County, Chester, Pa., 1976-79; corp. fin. analyst Alco Standard Corp., Valley Forge, Pa., 1979-81, asst. to pres. in charge corp. planning, 1981-84, mergers and acquisitions, 1984—; fin. cons. Bd. dirs. ARC, 1980-82, instr. CPR, advanced first aid, 1975—; mem. Republican Nat. Com., 1978—; mem. bus. adv. council LaSalle U.; mem. fund raising com. Dressage at Devon. Recipient citation ARC, 1981. Mem. Fin. Mgmt. Assn., Eastern Fin. Assn., Planning Forum (bd. dirs.), Phila. Fin. Assn., Pa. State U. Alumni Assn., LaSalle U. Alumni Assn., LaSalle U. Council of Pres.'s Assocs. Republican. Roman Catholic. Contbr. articles to profl. jours. Office: PO Box 834 Valley Forge PA 19482

KYLE-RENO, SHELIA ANN, lawyer; b. Owensboro, Ky., Sept. 13, 1951; d. Herman William and Evelyn Maxine (Johnson) Kyle; m. Charles Edward Reno, Feb. 7, 1974; 1 child, La Mer Kyle-Reno. B.A., Wright State U., 1978; J.D., U. Dayton, 1983. Bar: Ohio 1983. Computer operator Owensboro Mcpl. Utilities, 1971-73; community organizer City Mgrs. Office, Owensboro, 1972-73; hotline coordinator Ky. Wesleyan U., Owensboro, 1971-73; law extern U.S. Magistrates, Dayton, 1981-82; law clk. Henley Vaugh Becker, Wald, Dayton, Ohio, 1982-83; atty. Legal Aid Soc. of Dayton, 1983—, EEO officer, 1983—, coordinator Contract Atty. Program, 1985—, mng. atty. family law unit, 1985—, coordinator client services, 1985—, acting exec. dir., 1986—. Pres. Womens Polit. Caucus, Dayton, 1980; mem. People for Am. Way, 1982. Key to City, City of Owensboro, 1971. Mem. ABA, Ohio Bar Assn., Dayton Bar Assn., Am. Acad. Trial Lawyers, Ohio Acad. Trial Lawyers, Miami Valley Assn. Women Attys., ACLU, NOW, Phi Alpha Delta. Democrat. Home: 5565 Hummock Rd Dayton OH 45426 Office: Legal Aid Soc Dayton 117 S Main St Suite 515 Dayton OH 45402

KYRA, artist, educator; b. Harbin, China (parents Am. citizens); B.F.A., Ariz. State U., 1973; M.F.A., Fla. State U., 1975. Mem. faculty Broward Community Coll., Pembroke Pines, Fla., 1975—, dept. chmn. humanities, 1981-83, gallery dir., 1981—; mem. faculty Miami-Dade Community Coll., 1975, Barry U., Miami, Fla., 1981-82; lectr. and cons. in field; one-woman shows Artful Dodger Gallery, Tallahassee, 1975, Bainbridge Jr. Coll., 1975, The Gallery, Fla. State U., 1975, William D. Pawley Creative Arts Ctr., 1976, Womanart Gallery, N.Y.C., 1977, 78, An Alternative Gallery, Miami, 1979, A.I.R. Gallery, N.Y.C., 1979, Art and Culture Ctr. Hollywood, 1980, Fla. Atlantic U. Library, Boca Raton, 1981, Broward Community Coll., 1982, Fine Arts Gallery, Broward Community Coll., 1977, 1982, 84, 85, 86, The Gallery, Bailey Hall, 1983, Met. Mus. and Art Ctr., 1985; exhibited in group shows Gallery 741, 1975, Burdines Gallery, 1975, Boca Raton Ctr. for Arts, 1976, Grove House, 1976, 81, Lowe Art Mus., 1976, U. Miami, 1977, Avery Fisher Hall, Lincoln Ctr., 1977, Soho 20 Gallery, 1977, Womanart Gallery, 1977, An Alternative Gallery, 1978, Grove House South Gallery, 1978, Jeanne Taylor Gallery, 1978, Long Galleries, 1978, Womanart Galleries, 1978, Broward Art Guild, 1979, Hanson Galleries, 1980, Aventura Libary, 1980, Lowe-Levinson Gallery, 1980, Alain Bilhaud Gallery, 1981, Barry U., 1981, Nova U., 1982, Mus. Art, Ft. Lauderdale, 1982, Continuum Gallery, 1982, Broward Community Coll., 1983, Art and Culture Ctr. of Hollywood, 1983, Union Art Gallery, U. Wis., Madison, 1984, numerous others. Fla. Art Council fellow 1982-83; Broward Art in Pub. Places Comm. for So. Regional Courthouse, Hollywood, 1981; named Outstanding Artist of S.E., Am. Art/S.E., 1978; Gene Segal award Sta. WPBT-TV, 1981, Ltd. Edit. award, 1980, 1st Nationwide Savs. award, 1982, numerous juried arts awards. Mem. Women's Caucus for Art (dir. Fla. chpt., nat. dir.), Coalition Women's Art Orgns. (nat. dir., v.p.), Fla. Assn. Community Colls., AAUP (dir. Fla. chpt.), Coll. Art Assn. Am., Democrat. Contbr. articles to profl. jours., books. Home: PO Box 6735 Hollywood FL 33021 Office: Broward Community Coll 7200 Hollywood Blvd Pembroke Pines FL 33024

KYRIAKOU, LINDA GRACE, chemical company executive; b. N.Y.C., Dec. 5, 1943; d. Frank Thomas and Dolores Helen (Coscia) LaGamma; B.A., Hunter Coll., 1965; m. Konstantinos Kyriakou, May 7, 1967; 1 dau., Christina Elena. Info. editor Nat. Bur. Econ. Research, N.Y.C., 1967-69; dir. research/account officer Booke & Co., N.Y.C., 1969-75; mgr. communications services C.I.T. Fin. Corp., N.Y.C., 1975-79; dir. corp. communications Sun Chem. Corp., N.Y.C., 1979—. Mem. Public Relations Soc. Am., Nat. Investor Relations Inst. (dir. N.Y. chpt. 1981-82), Women's Bond Club N.Y. (bd. govs. 1978-80). Home: 300 E 59th St New York NY 10022 Office: 200 Park Ave New York NY 10166

LABAND, KAREN ELIZABETH, leasing and management company executive; b. Seattle, Oct. 23, 1942; d. Thomas Hume and Eileen Burness (Markle) Grove; m. Manfred Laband, Nov. 28, 1968; 1 dau., Amy Elizabeth. Student bus. U. Wash., 1960-63, B.A. in Fine Arts, 1971. Paralegal sec. Culp, Dwyer, Guterson & Grader, Seattle, 1963-68; freelance profl. artist, Mercer Island, Wash., 1971—; sec., dir. Perinco, Inc., Mercer Island, 1980, v.p., dir., 1981, pres., 1981—; art cons. Doctors Hosp. Seattle, 1971-73, Renton Family Practice Clinic (Wash.), 1980. Exhibited oil paintings in one-woman shows Doctors Hosp., 1973, The Good Yrs. Gallery, 1975, Erica Williams Gallery, 1978; exhibited group shows including Frye Art Mus., 1976, Am. Painters in Paris, 1975. Pres., Mercer Island Presch. Assn., 1974; treas., dir. Mercer Island Children's Choir, 1983-84. Mem. Am. Mgmt. Assn., Seattle Art Mus., Cornish Art Inst., Brandeis Women's Assn. Clubs: Mercer Island Country; Bellevue Athletic (Wash.). Home: 3735 81st SE Mercer Island WA 98040 Office: Perinco Inc 3735 81st SE Mercer Island WA 98040

LABARBERA, ELLEN, editor; b. Passaic, N.J., Oct. 17, 1948; d. Jack Howells and Mary (Singer) Samson; B.A., Antioch Coll., 1971, m. Michael J. LaBarbera, May 20, 1973; children—Jessica Mary, Julia Anne, Cara Jane. Editor, Marcel Dekker, Inc., N.Y.C., 1971-73, Thomas Bouregy & Co., Inc., N.Y.C., 1973-76; sr. editing supr. McGraw-Hill Book Co., N.Y.C., 1976-78, sponsoring editor, 1978-83; free-lance editorial cons., 1983—.

LA BARGE, MARY JANE, retired business executive; b. Ticonderoga, N.Y., Nov. 30, 1930; d. Albert J. and Marguerite D. LaB.; student Katharine Gibbs Sch., N.Y.C. Corp. sec. Martin Marietta Corp., Bethesda, Md., 1977-86, Martin Marietta Aluminum Inc., Bethesda, 1977-84. Mem. Am. Soc. Corp. Secs Inc. Office: 6801 Rockledge Dr Bethesda MD 20817

LABEDZ, BERNICE R., state legislator; b. Omaha, Sept. 19, 1919; m. Stanley J. Labedz, May 9, 1942; children—Terry, Jan, Toni, Frank. Student pub. schs. Former businesswoman, mem. Nebr. State Dept. Revenue, then mayoral, senatorial asst., pub. relations dir.; mem. Nebr. State Legislature, 1976—. Recipient community service awards. Office: Nebr State Capitol Bldg Lincoln NE 68509*

LABELLA, ARLEEN ELDA, educator, author, lecturer; b. Rome, N.Y., Mar. 26, 1945; d. Paul Anthony and Elda Marie (Guaspari) LaBella; m. Dennis James O'Brien, Sept. 1, 1979; 1 child, Colin LaBella O'Brien. B.A., SUNY-Oswego, 1967; M.Edn., North Adams State Coll., 1971, U. Buffalo, 1975; Ed.D., U. Mass., 1985. Cert. elem. tchr., N.Y. Pub. sch. tchr. various pub. schs., Vt., N.Y., 1967-74; adj. prof. U. Buffalo, N.Y., 1975-79; psychol. counselor Bennington Coll., 1975-82; co-founder, co-dir. Profl. Resources, Inc., Reston, Va., 1982—; cons./trainer numerous U.S. corps., govt. agys. and orgns., 1975—; nat. seminar leader Rutherford Training Workshops, Boulder, Colo., 1980-82, CareerTrack Seminars, Boulder, 1982-84; chairperson steering com. Women's Resource Ctr., Bennington, Vt., 1977; cons. Women in State Employment, Mpls., 1984-85. Co-author: Personal Power, 1983, Managing Assertively (trainer's manual), 1978, Personal Effectiveness (audio-cassette series). Contbr. numerous articles to profl. jours. Task force mem. Gov.'s Commn. on Status of Women, Burlington, 1975-76. Mem. Am. Soc. Tng. and Devel. Avocations: aerobics, traveling. Office: Profl Resources Inc 1954 Winterport Cluster Reston VA 22091

LABELLE, SARAH JEAN, transportation systems engineer, researcher; b. Evanston, Ill., July 19, 1950; d. James Cullen and M. Vivian (Lukanitsch) LaB. B.S. in Systems Engring., U. Ill.-Chgo., 1972; M.S. in Civil Engring., Northwestern U., Evanston, Ill., 1978. Registered profl. engr., Ill.; certified planner. Jr. planner DuPage County Regional Planning Commn., Wheaton, Ill., 1973; bus driver Village of Wilmette, Ill., 1974; research assoc. Argonne Nat. Lab., Ill., 1974-77, asst. environ. systems engr., 1977-81, transp. engr., 1981—; transport/energy specialist Regional Urban Design Assistance Team, Kansas City, Mo., 1979. Chmn. Transp. Com., Village of Oak Park, 1981; mem. Parking and Traffic Commn. Village of Oak Park, 1984. Mem. Am. Planning Assn. (treas. transp. div. 1984-86), Transp. Research Bd., Nat. Assn. Environ. Profls. (assoc.). Avocations: backpacking; home rehabilitation and remodeling. Home: 537 S Ridgeland Ave Oak Park IL 60304 Office: Argonne Nat Lab EES Bldg 362-2B Argonne IL 60439

LABEN, JOYCE KEMP, nursing educator; b. Elgin, Ill., Mar. 2, 1936; d. Berton John and Lois Elizabeth (Heath) Kemp; B.S.N., U. Mich., 1957; M.S.N., U. Calif., San Francisco, 1963; J.D., Suffolk U., 1969; m. Robert J. Laben, Feb. 27, 1971. Nurse, U. Calif. San Francisco Med. Center, 1957-59, 61-62; surg./office nurse, San Francisco, 1960-61; instr. Boston State Hosp., 1964-65; asst. prof. Sch. Nursing, Boston U., 1965-70; assoc. prof. Sch. Nursing, Vanderbilt U., Nashville, 1970-78, prof., 1978—, chmn. behavioral scis. as applied to nursing, 1975-81, acting assoc. dean undergrad. studies, 1981-82, assoc. dean undergrad. studies, 1982-84, coordinator grad. program in psychol./mental health nursing, 1985—, pres. women's faculty orgn., 1980-81. Dir. forensic services sect. Tenn. Dept. Mental Health, Nashville, 1972-74; cons. Tenn. Dept. Mental Health/Mental Retardation, 1974—, others; mem. task force panel Pres.'s Commn. on Mental Health, 1977. Bd. dirs., v.p. Opportunity House, Nashville, 1973-80; bd. dirs. Nat. Commn. on Confidentiality of Health Records, 1976-79. Recipient Cert. of Spl. Recognition, Tenn. Dept. Mental Health, 1974; Mem. Am. Nurses Assn. (spl. recognition award 1980, mem. council advanced practitioners in psychiat./mental health nursing), AAUP, Am. Soc. Law and Medicine, Am. Assn. Nurse Attys., Am. Orthopsychiat. Assn. Contbr. articles to profl. jours. Office: Godchaux Hall Vanderbilt U Nashville TN 37240

LABER, MARIAN ROBERTA OPPENHEIM, real estate broker; b. Hanford, Calif., Jan. 18, 1918; d. Leon and Isabelle (Estrada) Oppenheim; student San Francisco City Coll., 1966, Golden Gate Coll., 1969; m. Lawrence E. Laber, Feb. 22, 1941 (dec. 1980); children—Lawrence E., Pamela, Deborah Laber McDermott, James Harrison. Telephone operator Pacific Tel.&Tel. Co., 1936-39, instr., 1940-42; mgr. office Press Wireless, Washington, 1942-43; owner Marian Lawrence, children's shop, San Francisco, 1945-48; owner, mgr. San Bruno 5-10, San Francisco, 1947-50; girl Friday, Lampley Realty, San Francisco, 1968-72, owner, real estate broker Century 21 Lampley Realty, 1972-84; 1972-83, Marian Laber Real Estate, 1983—. Active Boy Scouts Am., Girl Scouts U.S.A., Camp fire Girls, ARC; pres. local PTA, 1954-55; trustee Drew Coll. Prep. Sch., chmn. bd., 1975-76, 81-83. Mem. Am. Cancer Soc., San Francisco Real Estate Bd., Calif. Real Estate Assn. Roman Catholic (pres. ch. group 1950-51). Home: 2235 Laguna St Apt 405 San Francisco CA 94115 Office: 1070 Howard St San Francisco CA 94103

LABNO, LAURA ANN, marketing executive; b. Evergreen Park, Ill., Sept. 26, 1956; d. Albin and Florence (Ladovich) L. B.A., U. Ill., 1978, M.A., 1980; M.B.A., Ohio State U., 1981. Tchr., research asst. U. Ill., Urbana, 1979-80; research asst. Ohio State U., Columbus, 1981; statis. systems mgr. Zale Corp., Dallas, 1982-83; project mgr. J.C. Penney Co., Dallas, 1983-84; project mgr. NFO Research, Inc., Chgo., 1984-85; research mgr. The Signature Group, Schaumburg, Ill., 1985—. Mem. Am. Mktg. Assn., Direct Mktg. Assn. Home: 88 Kimbark Rd Riverside IL 60546 Office: The Signature Group Montgomery Ward Ins Tower 200 N Martingale Rd Schaumburg IL 60194

LABONTE, DOROTHY HAZEL, hospital nursing executive; b. Springfield, Mass., Oct. 13, 1925; d. Albert Edward Ernest and Merle Evelyne (Richings) Ellett; diploma Waltham Hosp. Sch. Nursing, 1947; B.A., Simmons Coll. Sch. Nursing, 1970; M.A., Framingham State Coll., 1982; m. Edward W. LaBonte, Sr., Sept. 28, 1947; children—Michele Shea, Edward W. Staff nurse, head nurse Waltham (Mass.) Hosp., 1947-50; staff nurse, supr. Leonard Morse Hosp., Natick, Mass., 1950-56, asst. dir. nursing, 1956-63, dir. nursing, 1963-76, dir. patient care services, 1976-81, asst. to exec. v.p., 1981-82; dir. nursing Fairlawn Hosp., Worcester, Mass., 1982—. Corporator Framingham (Mass.) Union Hosp.; mem. Hospice at Home, Wayland, Mass.; mem. Worcester Art Mus. Cert. nursing adminstr. Am. Nurses Assn. Mem. Am. Orgn. Nurse Execs., Small Hosps. Nurse Execs. of Mass., Nat. League Nursing, Am. Heart Assn., Mass. Orgn. Nurse Execs., Mass./R.I. League Nursing, Central Mass. Nursing Adminstrs. Unitarian. Home: Box 325 Brookfield MA 01506 Office: 189 May St Worcester MA 01602

LABORDE, MARY PURCELL (MRS. JOSEPH GASTON LABORDE), club woman, ret. educator; b. Pelican, La., May 19, 1905; d. George Dowell and Ela Lee (Browne) Purcell; Christian culture diploma M.E. Ch. S., 1922; Lic. instr. Mansfield (L.I.) Female Coll., 1923; postgrad. La. State U., 1924, 45, Centenary Coll., 1925-26; cert. N.Y. Sch. Interior Decorating, 1931; B.A., Nicholls State Coll.; m. Joseph Gaston LaBorde, Apr. 24, 1926 (dec. 1978); 1 son, Joseph Newton. Tchr., Caldwell Parish, La., 1923-25, S. Highlands Sch., Shreveport, La., 1925-26, Lady of Mercy Sch., Baton Rouge, 1958-60, St. Theresa's Sch., Shreveport, 1960-61, Trinity Elem. Sch., Baton Rouge, 1969-70; active in glee club, ch. and club music; 2d v.p. UDC, Henry W. Allen chpt., Baton Rouge, 1960-61, 3d v.p. Martha Ried chpt., 1954-57; bd. dirs. Emma Gayle McFadden chpt. Children of Confederacy, Jacksonville, Fla., 1955-57, dir. John McGrath chpt., Baton Rouge, 1958-60, organizing dir. G.B. Saucier chpt., 1974-76; mem. and del. Katherine Livingston chpt. DAR, Jacksonville, 1949-52, del. nat. congress, 1950-63, treas. Kan Yuk Sa, 1955-57, del. state conf., 1964; chmn. music La. 6th dist. La. Fedn. Women's Clubs, 1974-76; organized Jr. Nat. Soc. Sons and Daus. of Pilgrims; active Gray Ladies ARC; mem. Confederate Mus., Richmond, Va., 1971-72; hostess Found. for Hist. La., 1965-71; mem. Pres. Reagan's Task Force, 1982, 84. Recipient awards (2) Nat. Soc. So. Dames Am., 1966; Medal of Merit, Presidential Task Force, 1982. Mem. Descs. Knights of Garter, Plantagenet Soc., Ams. Royal Descent, Nat. Trust Hist. Preservation, Magna Charta Dames (v.p. La. Soc. 1967-69, rec. sec. 1974—), Nat. Soc. Sons and Daus. of Pilgrims (gov. La. br. 1962-64, nat. rec. sec. 1965-66, del. nat. congress 1963, del. Gen. Ct., state registrar 1968-70), Nat. Soc. So. Dames (award 1966, charter; La. eye bank chmn. 1964-65, v.p. La. 1964-65, award of merit 1967), UDC (nat. com. preservation hist. sites and records 1967-68, nat. and state geneal. records 1967-69, rec. sec. H.W. Allen chpt. 1966-67, chmn. music 1967-68), W.S.C.S., Tchrs. Assn., La. Parliamentarians, Nat. Assn. Parliamentarians, First Families of Am., 1974-75, Huguenot Soc. La. (compiled handbook; state registrar 1975-77), Marquis Biog. Library Soc. (adv.), Washington Family Descs., Tex. Geneal. Soc., Epsilon Sigma Omicron (chpt. book reviewer 1974-77). Methodist (youth dir.). Clubs: Music, Baton Rouge Women's, Baton Rouge Music, Order of Crown, High Heritage, Woman's, 700. Home: 11645 Archery Dr Baton Rouge LA 70815

LACAFF, REGINA MAE KIRKLAND, mathematics educator; b. Twin Falls, Idaho, Oct. 4, 1946; d. Troy Leonard and Rose (Spreier) K.; B.A., Ariz. State U., 1968; M.A., U. Central Fla., 1980; m. William King Lacaff, Nov. 23, 1968. Tchr. Carver Elem. Sch., Little Rock, 1970-73, Montessori Sch., Calabasas, Calif., 1973-75, Dawson Sch., Columbus, Ga., 1975-77; math. remediation tchr. Stonewall Jackson Jr. High Sch., Orlando, Fla., 1978, tchr. math., from 1978, chmn. faculty-staff relations, 1978-80, guidance com. chmn., 1980-81, tennis coach, 1980-82; now chmn. math. dept. Howard Jr. High Sch., Orlando; owner La Math Tutoring Service. Mem. Nat. Council Tchrs. Math., Fla. Council Tchrs. Math., Orange County Council Tchrs. Math., Fla. League Middle Schs., Council Elem., Math. Specialists, Okla. State Alumni Assn., Fla. Teaching Profession, NEA, Assn. Supervision and Curriculum Devel., Central Fla. Assn. Life Underwriters, Kappa Delta Pi, Delta Kappa Gamma, Kappa Delta. Home: 113 Woodmill Rd Longwood FL 32779 Office: Howard Jr High Sch Orlando FL

LACEY, CASSANDRA OVERFELT, performing arts administrator, musician; b. Norfolk, Va., Sept. 7, 1943; d. Daniel Elmo and Maude Dudley (Mason) Overfelt; m. Dennis Buren Lacey, June 15, 1964; children—Denise, Cathleen, Lorraine. B.A. in Piano Performance, Old Dominion U., 1965. Music dir. Fairmount Park Ch., Norfolk, 1964; asst. Nat. Bank of Washington, 1965-66; service rep. C & P Telephone Co., Arlington, Va., 1967-68; owner, tchr. Lacey Music Studio, Woodbridge, Va., 1975-77, Midlothian, Va., 1977-81; owner, dir. Swift Creek Acad. Performing Arts, Midlothian, 1981—; chmn. jr. festival Dist. III Va. Fedn. Music Clubs, 1983—. Ways and means chmn. Lake Ridge Garden Club, 1974-75; mem. youth adv. council Brandermill Ch., Midlothian, 1983—. Named Outstanding Music Student, Sigma Alpha Iota, 1962. Mem. Nat. Fedn. Music Clubs, Music Tchrs. Nat. Assn., Nat. Guild Piano Tchrs., U.S. C. of C., Am. Coll. Musicians, Delta Phi Omega. Avocation: sailing. Office: Swift Creek Acad Performing Arts 2808 Fox Chase Ln Midlothian VA 23113

LACEY, JUNE ARMSTRONG, retired educator; b. Windfall, Ind., Dec. 28, 1912; d. Ray and Pearl (Shawhan) Armstrong; m. Dudley Howarth Lacey, Feb. 15, 1936; children—Michael Lacey, Patricia Lacey Woods. Student Central Normal U., 1932; B.S. in Edn., Ball State Tchrs. Coll., 1960; M.A. in Edn., Ball State U., 1966. Cert. elem. tchr., Ind. Tchr. Windfall Elem. Sch., Ind., 1932-35, 44-57, Whitewater Elem. Sch., Richmond, Ind., 1935-36, Jefferson Sch., Tipton, Ind., 1957-60, Kokomo Ctr. Twp. Schs., 1960-77; mem. Govs. Council Children and Youth, Indpls., 1940-50; instr. math lab. Ind. U., Kokomo, 1977. Pres. Windfall PTA, 1940-49; mem. Howard County Hist. Soc., 1975-77; v.p. Methodist Women, 1980—; pres. Tipton br. Am. Cancer Soc., 1985, co-chmn. Daffodil Days, 1984-85; dep. assessor Wildcat Twp., Tipton County, Ind., 1984—; dep. Windfall Trustees Office, 1984—. Mem. Ind. Retired Tchrs. Assn. Democrat. Methodist. Club: Homemakers. Lodge: Eastern Star. Avocations: Writing poetry; antiques; home decorating. Home: 312 W Sherman Box 265 Windfall IN 46076

LACEY, MARY LOU, college administrator, nun; b. Holyoke, Mass., Apr. 28, 1929; d. Edward Aloysius and Grace Catherine (Finn) L. Joined Congregation of Sisters of St. Joseph, 1946; B.A., Coll. Our Lady of Elms, 1958; M.A., Boston Coll., 1967. Tchr. Ou Lady of Hope Sch., Springfield, Mass., 1949-54, Holy Family Sch., Springfield, 1954-59, Holy Name Sch., Springfield, 1959-61, Cathedral High Sch., Springfield, 1961-80; dir. pub. relations Our Lady of Elms Coll., Chicopee, Mass., 1980—. Editor: Women in a Changing Church, 1979, The Elms Today, 1980—. Contbr. articles to profl. jours. Mem. Network (Catholic Social Justice Lobby), Washington, 1982—; bd. dirs. Ctr. for Spiritual Direction, Springfield, 1984—. Mem. Pioneer Valley Press Assn. Roman Catholic. Avocations: genealogy; needlework; choral singing. Home: 311 Springfield St Chicopee MA 01013 Office: Our Lady of Elms Coll Pub Relations Office 291 Springfield St Chicopee MA 01013

LACH, ALMA ELIZABETH, home economics writer; b. Petersburg, Ill.; d. John H. and Clara E. (Boeker) Satorius; diplome de Cordon Bleu, Paris, 1956; m. Donald F. Lach, Mar. 18, 1939; 1 dau., Sandra Judith. Feature writer Children's Activities mag., 1954-55; creator, performer TV show Let's Cook, children's cooking show, 1955; performer TV show Over Easy, PBS, 1977-78; food editor Chgo. Daily Sun-Times, 1957-65; pres. Alma Lach Kitchens Inc., Chgo., 1966—; dir. Alma Lach Cooking Sch., Chgo.; lectr. U. Chgo. Downtown Coll., Gourmet Inst., U. Md., 1963, Modesto (Calif.) Coll., 1978, U. Chgo., 1981; resident master Shoreland Hall, U. Chgo., 1978-81; food cons. Food Bus. Mag., 1964-66, Chgo.'s New Pump Room, Lettuce Entertain You, Bitter End Resort, Brit. V.I., The Berghoff Restaurant, Flying Food Fare (Midway Airlines), Carlyn Berghoff Catering; columnist Modern Packaging, 1967-68, Travel & Camera, 1969, Venture, 1970, Chicago mag., 1978, Bon Appetit, 1980, Tribune Syndicate, 1982. Recipient Pillsbury award, 1958; Grocery Mfrs. Am. Trophy award, 1959, certificate of Honor, 1961; Chevalier du Tastevin, 1962; Commanderie de l'Ordre des Anysetiers du Roy, 1963; Confrerie de la Chaine des Rotisseurs, 1964; Les Dames D'Escoffier, 1982. Mem. U. Chgo. Settlement League, Am. Assn. Food Editors (chmn. 1959). Clubs: Tavern, Quadrangle (Chgo.). Author: A Child's First Cookbook, 1950; The Campbell Kids Have a Party, 1953; The Campbell Kids at Home, 1953; Let's Cook, 1956; Candlelight Cookbook, 1959; Weekly TV food show CBS, 1962-66; Cooking a la Cordon Bleu, 1970; Alma's Almanac, 1972; Hows and Whys of French Cooking, 1974. Contbr. to World Book Yearbook, 1961-75, Grolier Soc. Yearbook, 1962. Home and Office: 5750 Kenwood Ave Chicago IL 60637

LACH, EILEEN MARIE, lawyer; b. Mpls., June 27, 1950; d. Andrew Anthony and Adeline Florence (Smuda) L. Student Osmania U., Hyderabad, India, 1971-72; B.A. in Internat. Relations magna cum laude, U. Minn., 1973; M.P.A. in Internat. Affairs, Princeton U., 1976; J.D., NYU, 1977. Bar: N.Y. 1978, U.S. Dist. Ct. (so. dist.) N.Y. 1982, U.S. Dist. Ct. (ea. dist.) N.Y. 1982. Assoc. Lord, Day & Lord, N.Y.C., 1977-79; corp. atty. Wender, Murase & White, N.Y.C., 1979-82; assoc. Boulanger, Finley & Hicks, P.C., N.Y.C., 1982-83, ptnr., 1984—; gen. counsel Amnesty Internat. Minn. chmn. Young Democrats., 1968-69. McConnell fellow, 1973-76. Mem. Assn. Bar City N.Y., ABA, Internat. Law Assn., Phi Beta Kappa. Office: Boulanger Finley & Hicks PC 405 Park Ave New York NY 10022

LACHENBRUCH, TERESA COX, banker; b. Wichita, Kans., Jan. 16, 1956; d. Loren Eugene and Virginia Lee (Hayman) Cox; m. Roger Bennett Lachenbruch, Feb. 11, 1978. B.S. magna cum laude, U. Colo.-Denver, 1981; M.B.A., U. San Francisco. Research analyst Ind. Bankshares Corp., San Rafael, Calif., 1981-83; product mgr., asst. v.p. Westamerica Bank, San Rafael, 1983—. Mem. Am. Mktg. Assn. (Outstanding Mktg. Student 1981), Phi Chi Theta, Beta Gamma Sigma. Office: Westamerica Bank 1108 5th Ave San Rafael CA 94901

LACHMAN, ELEANOR, dance studio executive; b. Guyana, May 6, 1951; came to U.S., 1965, naturalized, 1972; d. Edward Lachman and Elaine Besessar L. B.Sc. in Nursing, U. Cin., 1975—. Dance instr., counselor, supr. Arthur Murray Dance Studio, Cin., 1972-79, mgr., 1979-80; pres. Cin. Dance Ctr. Inc., doing bus. as Arthur Murray Dance Studio, Cin., 1980—; treas. Dance Cin. Inc., 1984-85. Office: Cincinnati Dance Ctr Inc 700 Walnut St Cincinnati OH 45202

LACKAS, SANDRA LEE, pharmaceutical company official; b. Hartford, Wis., Aug. 19, 1942; d. Alfred Michael and Maxine J. (Cook) L. B.S., Mt. Mary Coll., Milw., 1964. Cert. in med. tech., in nuclear med. tech. Research asst. Internal Medicine Clinic, U. Heidelberg (W.Ger.), 1968-73; supr. radioimmunoassay lab., edn. coordinator Sch. Nuclear Med. Tech., St. Mary's Hosp., Milw., 1973-76; tech. mktg. rep. Nuclear Med. Lab., Dallas, 1976-79, mgr. quality control labs., 1979-81, tech. mktg. rep., Santurce, P.R., 1982-83; with Warner-Lambert Co., Morris Plains, N.J., 1976-83, product mgr., 1981-82, mktg. mgr. Key Pharms., Inc., Miami, Fla., 1983—. Developer control serum, 1981; researcher articles on gastrointestinal research, 1969-72; contbr. article to jour. Mem. Am. Soc. Med. Technologists. Roman Catholic. Home: 2333 Brickell 2814 Miami FL 33129 Office: 4400 Biscayne Blvd Miami FL 33137

LACKS, PATRICIA EVERETT, clinical psychologist, educator; b. Ontario, Oreg., Feb. 22, 1941; d. Franklin A. and Viola L. (Chamberlain) Everett; B.A., Washington U., St. Louis, 1961, M.A., 1962, Ph.D. (USPHS trainee 1961-66), 1966; m. Paul Gawronik, Apr. 4, 1981; children by previous marriage—Jeffrey, Amy. Staff psychologist Malcolm Bliss Mental Health Center, St. Louis, 1966-70; dir. research Jewish Employment and Vocat. Service, St. Louis, 1970-72; asso. prof. clin. psychology Washington U., 1972—. NIH grantee, 1981-85. Fellow Mo. Psychol. Assn. (pres. 1976); asso. fellow Inst. Rational Emotive Therapy; Mem. Am. Psychol. Assn., AAUP, Assn. Advancement Behavior Therapy. Author papers in field, 1 book. Office: Psychology Dept Washington U Saint Louis MO 63130

LACOGNATA, ESTHER GONCY, state official; b. Budapest, Hungary, July 25, 1937; came to U.S., 1949; d. Laszlo and Mary Lenard (Goncy) Gonczi; m. Angelo A. Lacognata, June 11, 1957 (div. Dec. 1980); children—Stuart, Suzanne. B.A., Mich. State U., 1961. Research assoc. U. Rochester (N.Y.), 1957-59; pres. LWV, Portland, Maine, 1971-73; research cons. Land Use Regulation Commn., Augusta, Maine, 1973-74, commr., 1974-75; citizen participation coordinator Council of Govt., Portland, Maine, 1975-77; coastal zone mgr. Maine State Planning Office, Augusta, 1977-80; bur. dir. Maine Dept. Agr., Augusta, 1980—. Mem. state bd. League of Women Voters, Portland, 1971-73, pres., dir., 1971-73, v.p., 1972; bd. mem. Natural Resource Council Maine, Augusta, 1976-77. Mem. Am. Soc. Pub. Adminstrn. (dir.), Maine Assn. and Planner (dir. 1975-77).

LACOMIS-COTE, KAREN ELIZABETH, communications software engineer, consultant; b. Buffalo, June 20, 1962; d. Joseph Edward and Mary Ann (Jalowiec) Lacomis; m. Marc Francis Cote, Aug. 18, 1984. B.S. in Computer Sci., Rochester Inst. Tech., 1984. Cons. Rochester Inst. Tech., N.Y., 1981-84; programmer, analyst Hartman Engring., Victor, N.Y., 1982-83; communications software engr. Harris Corp.-GISD, Melbourne, Fla., 1984—. Mem. alumni admissions bd. Rochester Inst. Tech. Mem. Mensa. Republican. Roman Catholic. Club: Harris Toastmasters (grammarian 1986). Avocations: equitation; skiing; golf. Home: 2700 Croton Rd Apt 2-23 Melbourne FL 32935 Office: Harris Corp-GISD Wickham Rd W2/7732 Melbourne FL 32935

LACOUNT, LOUISE WINTER, savings and loan executive; b. Salt Lake City, Feb. 9, 1921; d. Stephen Henry and Gladys (Robison) Winter; m. Sherwood Keith LaCount, Oct. 10, 1953 (dec. Feb. 1972). B.A., San Francisco State Coll., 1948. Radio producer Compton Advt., N.Y.C., 1951-53; actress, bus. mgr. Boothbay & Deertrees Theatres, Maine, 1953-56; exec. asst. sta. KDAY, Los Angeles, 1958-60; pres. Brittin Agy., talent agy. for entertainment industry, Hollywood, Calif., 1960-67; dir. pub. relations promotion Laurel Plaza Shopping Ctr., North Hollywood, Calif., 1968-70; v.p. human resources USLIFE Savs & Loan, Los Angeles, 1970-81; v.p. human resources and adminstrv. services Santa Paula Savs. & Loan, Ventura, Calif., 1981—. Mem. exec. com. nat. adv. council Grad. Sch. Mgmt. Brigham Young U., Provo, Utah, 1977—, Mgr. Ventura Geneal. Library, Ch. Jesus Christ of Latter-day Saints, 1983—. Mem. Am. Soc. Personnel Adminstrs., Am. Mgmt. Assn., Calif. League Savs. Insts. (chmn. affirmative action com. 1978—). Republican. Office: Santa Paula Savs & Loan 801 S Victoria St Ventura CA 93003

LACOUR, MURIEL DREW, educator; b. Providence, Jan. 29, 1924; d. Louis Robert and Isabella (Drew) L. B.A., Tuller Coll., 1946; M.S., Southampton Coll., 1981. Entered Episcopal Order of Tchrs. of Children of God, 1942. Tchr. The Tuller Schs., Fairfield Conn. and Sag Harbor, N.Y., 1946—, prin. All Saints Tuller Sch., Ft. Worth, 1952-54, St. Philips in the Hills Tuller Sch., Tucson, Tuller Sch., Tucson, 1956-64, Tuller Sch., Maycroft, Sag Harbor, 1964—. Mem. L.I. Episcopal Schs. Assn. (pres.). Address: Tuller Sch at Maycroft Sag Harbor NY 11963

LACROIX, CARLENE, realtor; b. Muskogee, Okla., Sept. 21, 1933; d. Carl William and Clarice Denton (Cantrell) Stoddard; m. Stephen R. LaCroix, May 16, 1952; children—Marc Stephen, Curt Alan. Student William Woods Coll., U. Okla. Sales assoc. Coldwell-Banker Ed Post, Scottsdale, Ariz., 1972-82; sales mgr. City Property Mgmt., Scottsdale, 1982-83; owner, broker LaCroix Realty, Scottsdale, 1983—. Mem. Nat. Assn. Realtors, Ariz. Regional Multiple Listing Service, Scottsdale Bd. Realtors, Scottsdale C. of C., Phoenix Conv. Visitors Bur., Scottsdale Racquet Club. Republican. Avocations: tennis; traveling. Office: LaCroix Realty 4419 N Scottsdale Rd Suite 122 Scottsdale AZ 85251

LACROIX, PEGGY MARIE, graphic artist; b. Jefferson, Mo., July 30, 1954; d. Harry Jefferson and Betty-Jean Juanita (Weihe) Carpenter; m. Ronald Alan LaCroix, Jan. 15, 1977; 1 child, Jolie Marie. A.A., Citrus Coll., 1974; B.A., Calif. State U., Fullerton, 1976. Artist, Avery Label, 1973-77, resale art dir., 1977-79; graphic arts supr. Interstate Elec. Corp., Anaheim, 1979-85, graphic arts br. mgr., 1985—. Art dir. (video) On Track, 1984. Recipient Acknowledgement award IEC Commitment to Excellence Program, 1985. Mem. Nat. Computer Graphics Assn., Interstate Mgmt. Club (bd. dirs. 1981-82), Advt. Club Los Angeles. Republican. Home: 1230 Vina Del Mar Placentia CA 92670 Office: Interstate Electronics Corp 1001 E Ball Rd Anaheim CA 92803

LACY, ADA LEE, educator, camp counselor; b. Houston, Sept. 23, 1931; d. David R. and Leotha (Jean Baptiste) Beasley; m. Isaac Lee, Nov. 8, 1954 (div. Oct. 1961); 1 son, David Charles; m. 2d, L.C. Lacy, Nov. 27, 1961; children—Cecil, Malcolm, Leotha. B.S., Tex. So. U., 1959; M.S. in Edn., 1984. Cert. elem. and secondary tchr., Tex. Elem. tchr., Houston Ind. Sch. Dist., 1962-80, chmn. dept., 1981—; tchr. jr. high sch. sci. Attucks Jr. High Sch., 1981—. Leader, counselor Camp Fire, Inc., 1975—; mem. com. adminstrn. Blue Triangle br. Houston YWCA, 1979—; corr. sec. Central City Civic Club, 1980-81; fund raiser Houston United Fund, 1976-80, United Negro Coll. Fund, 1976-80. Recipient Human Relations award B'nai B'rith, 1979, Houston Ind. Sch. Dist., 1976, 80, Disting. Service award Houston Met. YWCA, 1981; named Neophyte of Yr., Eta Phi Beta, 1978, Tchr. of Yr. Montgomery Elem. Sch., 1978, 80; named Outstanding Woman, Houston YWCA, 1981, Vol. award disting. service, 1984; Fipes fellow Baylor Coll. Medicine, 1983-84. Mem. Houston Tchrs. Assn., Tex. Tchrs. Assn., Tex. Assn. Environ. Edn. (charter), YWCA (life), Nat. Council Negro Women (Community Service award, 1979, 83), Eta Phi Beta. Democrat. Roman Catholic. Home: 2948 Payson St Houston TX 77021 Office: Attucks Middle School 4330 Belfort St Houston TX 77051

LACY, CARLENE HAMILTON, convenience store specialist; b. Clovis, N.Mex., July 13, 1942; d. Stephen Montgomery and Annie Iona (Bullock) Hamilton; m. Buck Cowart, July 24, 1960 (div. 1972); children—Suzan Annette, Joseph Buck, Jacquelyn Maurie; m. 2d Billy P. Lacy, Apr. 17, 1976. Student civil engring. N.Mex. State U., 1966-67. Draftsman, Bridgers & Paxton, Albuquerque, 1967-68; mech. draftsman, jr. designer Environ. Environ. Engring., Dallas, 1968-71; mech. designer Gaynor & Sirmen Cons. Engring., Dallas, 1971-73; stores planning mgr. Southland Corp., Dallas, 1973-80, 7-Eleven stores equipment devel. mgr., 1980-84; dir. sales devel. projects IMI Cornelius Co., Anoka, Minn., 1984—. Del., Tex. Democratic Conv., 1980, 82. Recipient Max award Southland Corp., Dallas, 1983. Mem. Nat. Restaurant Assn., Am. Soc. Plumbing Engrs. (treas. 1978-79, pres. 1981), LWV. Club: The 500 (Dallas). Home: 1170 Benton Way Arden Hills MI 55112

LACY, CAROL ANGELA, insurance executive; b. Watford, Eng., July 15, 1943; came to U.S., 1967, naturalized, 1976; d. Thomas and Winifred Joan (Stromberg) Carney; m. Floyd Raymond Lacy, May 25, 1968; children—Susan, Timothy. Claims adjuster Central Mut. Ins. Co., Toronto, Can., 1964-68; exec. sec. TransFresh Corp., Salinas, Calif., 1968-70; claims examiner Monterey Bay Found., Salinas, 1972-78; pres., account mgr. ABC Med. Claims Services, Salinas, 1978—; chmn. bd. dirs. Monterey County Spl. Health Care Authority, Salinas, 1982-85. Chmn. adv. bd. Natividad Hosp., Salinas, 1979-82, North Monterey County Bd. Edn., Salinas, 1977-83; treas. Monterey County Bds. Assn., Salinas, 1981-83; mem. Monterey County Grand Jury, Salinas, 1984-85; pres. Prunedale PTA, Salinas, 1976. Recipient Honorary Service award Prunedale PTA, 1982. Mem. Monterey Bay Life Underwriters Assn. Republican. Baptist. Avocations: stamp collecting; fishing; gardening.

LACY, HELEN B., university, television administrator; b. Burbank, Calif., Feb. 17, 1945; d. Hal Arnold and Margaret Mary (Samuels) L.; m. Donald E. Smith, June 10, 1978. B.S., U. Utah, 1972. Producer/dir. instrnl. TV, U. Utah, Salt Lake City, 1973-80, TV prodn. mgr. Inst. Media Services, 1980-81, mgr. prodn. services, 1981—; cons. Producer A Peoples' History of Utah, 1980-83. Mem. Women in Communications (pres. 1974-75), Assn. Ednl. Communications and Tech., Am. Women Radio and TV. Office: Instructional Media Services 207 MBH U Utah Salt Lake City UT 84112

LACY, JULIA RICE, learning disabilities consultant, business owner; b. Tyler, Tex., Aug. 25, 1917; d. Lester Holcomb and Nina Marie (Rice) Lacy; m. Floye Stanley Funk, May 5, 1944 (div.); children—Stephen, Karen Funk Van Zandt. B.A. in Journalism, U. Tex.-Austin; M.Ed., North Tex. U., 1976. Asst. dir. Office War Info., Dallas, 1942-44; editor Fed. Res. Bank, Dallas, 1946-48; adminstr. learning disabilities program Schreiner Coll., Kerrville, Tex., 1979-82; owner, mgr. Bibliobuffs, Kerrville, 1978—. Editor state newsletter for Tex. Assn. Children with Learning Disabilities, Austin, 1976-78; freelance writer; real estate broker. Mem. Women in Communications, Mensa. Presbyterian. Home: 106 Wild Timber Kerrville TX 78028

LACY, LILLIE MAE, teacher; b. Monroe, La., Aug. 16, 1939; d. Willie and Velma (Jackson) Love; m. Sammy Ray Lacy, June 15, 1962; children—Alicia Michelle, Rhonda LaJune, Sammy Ray. B.S., So. U., 1961; M.Ed., Tex. So. U., 1971; M.L.S., Sam Houston State U., 1973. Librarian, Washington High Sch., Lake Charles, La., 1961-64, Yates Sr. High Sch., Houston, 1965-68, Ryan Jr. High Sch., Houston, 1968-70; media specialist Long Jr. High Sch., Houston, 1970-71, Johnston Jr. High Sch., Houston, 1971-79; reading coordinator, tchr. Dowling Sch., Houston, 1979—, reading specialist Houston Ind. Sch. Dist. Tutorial Program, 1983-84, speech and drama coach, 1979-84. Active Girl Scouts Am. Mem. ALA, Internat. Reading Assn., Tex. So. Reading Council, NEA, Tex. State Tchrs. Assn., Houston Tchrs. Assn., Iota Phi Lambda. Democrat. Baptist. Home: 6318 Heatherbloom Dr Houston TX 77085 Office: Dowling Middle Sch 14000 Stancliff St Houston TX 77045

LACY, M(ILDRED) PAULINE JONES, fashion executive, consultant; b. Kilgore, Tex., Apr. 12, 1936; d. Paul Burleson Jones and Irma Nola (DeRamus) Doggett; m. Eugene Shirley Lacy, Dec. 28, 1954; children—Sheri Lacy Dews, I. Lance. Student home study courses Harvard U., 1961-62, Kilgore Library, 1964-65, Hume Fin. Edn. Service, 1982-83, Commodore Discs, 1984, Hume Pub., 1985. Legal sec. Neal & Girand, Hobbs, N.Mex., 1953-54; bookkeeper Randall & Hebbard Gen. Ins. Agts., Jacksonville, Fla., 1955-58; exec. sec. to personnel mgr., notary pub. Home Savs., Houston, 1959-60; co-owner (with husband) The Toggery Shoe Salon, Kilgore, 1963-68, The Toggery Inc., ladies splty. store, Kilgore, 1968, exec. v.p., 1971—; style show producer, dir. Civic Garden Club, Kilgore, 1975, Tex. Liquor Cov., Dallas, 1980, others; fashion cons., advisor Fashion Mdse. Mktg. Sch., Kilgore Coll.; designer Kilgore city flag. Leader local Girl Scouts U.S.A. and Cub Scouts, 1962-69; tchr. Methodist Ch., 1963; chmn. edn. and family living com. PTA; 1st v.p. City Council PTA, 1965-67; active various benefit style shows; producer, dir. Tex. Sesquicentennial, East Tex. Area, 1986. Recipient City Merit award, 1982, Yr. Book award PTA of Tex., 1966, Promotion and Pub. Relations award Helene Sidel (couture designer), 1979; gold belt named Pauline in her honor by accessory designer Alexis Kirk, 1981, silk pump named Pauline's Pet by shoe designer Stewart Weitzman, 1986. Mem. Tex. Retailers Assn., Nat. Assn. Female Execs., Smithsonian Assocs., Community Concert Assn., Tex. C. of C., Kilgore C. of C., Beta Sigma Phi. Methodist. Clubs: Roy H. Laird Country (Kilgore); Summit (Longview, Tex.). Avocations: investments; reading; home computer; flower gardening; swimming. Office: The Toggery Inc 104 N Kilgore St Kilgore TX 75662

LADD-KIDDER, LISA KATHERINE, clinical psychologist; b. Boston, July 13, 1944; d. Alexander Hackett and Eleanor Mary (Murphy) Ladd; B.A., U. South Fla., 1966; M.Ed. (Office Edn. fellow), U. Ga., 1970; M.S., Hahnemann Med. Coll., 1973; m. James Kidder, 1977. Geog. analyst C.I.A., Washington, 1967-69; dormitory dir., counselor Swarthmore Coll., 1971-72; counselor counseling and psychol. services Kutztown U., 1972-85, dir. acad. advisement dept. acad. services, 1985—, also assoc. prof.; pvt. practice psychology, 1978—; workshop presenter. Recipient 1st prize Fla. Poetry Contest, 1966; lic. tchr. spl.

edn., emotionally disturbed, Pa.; lic. for pvt. practice, Pa. Mem. Am. Psychol. Assn., Assn. Pa. State Coll. and Univ. Faculties, Internat. Transactional Analysis Assn. (cert.) Democrat. Author: Cartographic Analysis of Southeast Asia, 1966. Home: 239 Pennsylvania Ave Kutztown PA 19530 Office: 307 Administration Bldg Kutztown U Kutztown PA 19530

LADLEY, JOANNE BURNLEY, food company executive; b. Lancaster, Pa., Aug. 31, 1952; d. Robert Clarence and Patricia (Kling) Burnley; m. Thomas William Ladley, Dec. 28, 1974; children—Allyson Patricia, Scott William. B.A. in German, Washington and Jefferson Coll., 1974. With Kitchen Kettle Foods, Inc., Intercourse, Pa., 1974—, v.p., adminstrv. mgr., 1977—. Trustee Washington and Jefferson Coll., Washington, Pa., 1981-84; bd. dirs. Pa. Dutch Visitors Bur., Lancaster, 1984-87, mem. mktg. com., 1985-87; trustee Highland Presbyn. Ch., Lancaster, 1983-86. Mem. Inst. Mgmt. (bd. dirs. 1984—). Republican. Club: Lancaster Opera Workshop (v.p. 1981-82). Office: PO Box 380 Intercourse PA 17534

LADNER, JUDITH SLEPPY, educational administrator; b. Salt Lake City, Apr. 9, 1940; d. George S. and Bertha Annetta (Garrett) Sleppy; B.A., U. No. Colo., 1962; M.A., San Jose State U., 1976; Ed.D., U. Pacific, 1979. Primary and intermediate tchr. Union Sch. Dist., San Jose, Calif., 1962-67, intermediate and jr. high sch. tchr., 1968-76, coordinator media services, 1976-77; intermediate tchr. Colegion Nueva Granda, Bogota, Colombia, 1967-68; prin. Alta Vista Sch., Los Gatos, Calif., 1977-80; asst. supt. Mountain View (Calif.) Sch. Dist., 1980-85; asst. supt. Oak Grove Sch. Dist., San Jose, 1985—. Mem. exec. bd. Mountain View United Way; mem. planning and allocations council United Way of Santa Clara County; chmn. exec. bd. YMCA of Mountain View-Los Altos. Mem. Assn. Calif. Sch. Adminstrs. (pres. Santa Clara County), AAUW, Delta Kappa Gamma (chpt. pres. 1978-80), Phi Delta Kappa, Home: 1210 Blackberry Terr Sunnyvale CA 94087 Office: Oak Grove Sch Dist 6578 Santa Teresa Blvd San Jose CA 95119

LADNER, MILDRED DIEFENDERFER, journalist; b. Allentown, Pa., June 24, 1918; d. Orlando and Mary Susan (Fahler) Diefenderfer; m. John Ladner, Aug. 19, 1950 (dec.); children—Mary Patricia Robertson, Edward Ladner, Helen Ladner; m. Thomas Kirkland Thompson, June 1, 1985. B.A., Moravian Coll., 1939; M.A., U. Wis., 1942. Reporter, Allentown Chronicle, 1941-43, AP Bur., Phila., 1943-45, Wall St. Jour., Washington, 1945-50; book editor Tulsa World, 1977-85, now travel writer. Author: O.C. Seltzer: Painter of the Old West, 1979; William de la M. Cary: Painter on the Missouri, 1984; also articles in art mags. Recipient Aviation Writers award Trans-World Airlines, Washington, 1948; Comenius award Moravian Coll., 1962. Mem. Women in Communications (Outstanding Profl. award Tulsa chpt. 1972). Presbyterian. Club: Tulsa Press. Home: 2116 S Detroit Ave Tulsa OK 74114 Office: Tulsa World PO Box 1770 Tulsa OK 74102

LADRILLONO, NIEVA EVANGELISTA, medical technologist; b. Manila, Philippines, Aug. 15, 1943; d. Lucrecio Sahagun and Dolores (Magsaysay) Evangelista; came to U.S., 1965, naturalized 1973; B.S., U. Santo Tomas, 1963, A.B., 1964; postgrad. Golden Date U., 1985; m. Conrado Pascual Ladrillono, Nov. 23, 1968; children—Jennifer Jo, James Paul, Joshua Steven. Sr. technologist Harford Meml. Hosp., Havre De Grace, Md., 1971-74; supr. blood bank Gulf Coast Community Hosp., Biloxi, Miss., 1976-78; chief technologist Children's Hosp. of King's Daus., Norfolk, Va., 1979, lab. adminstr., 1979—. Mem. Va. Soc. Med. Tech. (mem. of yr. 1982; dir., 1980-81), Clin. Lab. Mgmt. Assn. (pres. Tidewater chpt. 1983), Am. Soc. Med. Technology Am. Soc. Clin. Pathologists, Am. Asso. Blood Banks, Am. Assn. Clin. Chemists, Nat. Assn. Female Execs. Roman Catholic. Home: 1625 Kingsway Rd Norfolk VA 23518 Office: 800 W Olney Rd Norfolk VA 23507

LA FARGE, PHYLLIS, editor; b. N.Y.C., June 10, 1933; d. Thomas Sergeant and Marie (Iselin) La F.; student Radcliffe Coll., 1955; m. Chester H. Johnson, Sept. 13, 1958 (div. 1980); children—Clare, Thomas. Contbg. editor Parents mag., N.Y.C. Mem. PEN, Am. Soc. Mag. Editors. Author: Keeping Going; (with Joan Costello) Dr. Strangelove's Kids: Growing Up American. Office: 685 3d Ave New York NY 10017

LAFAYE, CARY DUPRE, librarian; b. Horry County, S.C., June 22, 1945; d. Moffatt Barmore and Helen Elizabeth (Cappelmann) DuPre; m. Angus Bird Lafaye, Mar. 21, 1970; 1 dau., Helen Cary. B.A. cum laude, U.S.C., 1967, M. Librarianship, 1973. Reading, history tchr. Moultrie Jr. High Sch., Mount Pleasant, S.C., 1967-69; tchr. French, history Irmo High Sch. (S.C.), 1969-71; library asst. U.S.C., Columbia, 1971-72; librarian Richland County Pub. Library-Cooper Br., Columbia, S.C., 1973-74; reference librarian Midlands Tech. Coll., Beltline Library, Columbia, 1975—. Mem. Ala, S.C. Library Assn., Southeastern Library Assn., Phi Beta Kappa, Beta Phi Mu (chpt. pres. 1983-84), Kappa Delta. Home: 1412 Haynsworth Rd Columbia SC 29205 Office: Midlands Tech Coll Beltline Library PO Drawer 2408 Columbia SC 29202

LAFFAL, FLORENCE, artist; b. N.J., Jan. 3, 1921; d. Jacob and Sarah (Berman) Schultz; B.S. in Fine Arts Edn., So. Conn. Coll., 1957; M.A. in Fine Arts and Fine Arts Edn., Columbia, 1958; m. Julius Laffal, Aug. 24, 1943; children—Paul David, Kenneth. Tchr. art North Haven Sch. System, 1958-66; free-lance artist 1966-80; owner gallery, 1969-80; editor, pub. Folk Art Finder. Mem. Silvermine Guild Artists, Soc. Conn. Craftsmen (pres., dir. 1968-74). Author: Artist-Craftsmen of Connecticut Datebook, 1971; Breads of Many Lands, 1975. Office: Gallery Press Inc 117 N Main Essex CT 06426

LA FLEUR, HELENE, electronic company executive; b. Paris, France, Apr. 17, 1926; came to U.S., 1950; m. James K. La Fleur, May 4, 1964. Certificat Secondaire Coll. de Jeunes Filles, Pau, France. Lang. prof., translator, 1950-57; internat. pub. relations interpreter Douglas Aircraft Co., Santa Monica, Calif., 1957-58, J. Walter Thompson Indsl. Div., Los Angeles, 1958-60; pres., owner Kaylane Co., Los Angeles, 1959-66; v.p. Indsl. Cryogenics, Toluca Lake, Calif., 1966—. Kaylane Advt., Toluca Lake, 1980—; sec. Am. Graves Registration Services, U.S. Army, Paris, 1944-46, Radiodiffusion Francaise, Paris, France, 1948-50, Office Fgn. Liquidation in Europe, Paris, 1946-48. Republican. Clubs: University, Duquesnes (Pitts.); New York Yacht (N.Y.C.); Royal Cork Yacht (Crosshaven, Ireland); Lakeside Golf (Toluca Lake); Assocs. Caltech (Pasadena, Calif.). Home: 4337 Talofa Ave Toluca Lake CA 91602

LAFLEUR, MYRNA WEBER, educator, author; b. Arcola, Sask., Can., Oct. 17, 1941; d. Francis John and Christina May (Kramer) Weber; m. Lawrence Harrison LaFleur; 1 child, Danielle Simone. R.N., Regina Grey Nuns Hosp., 1962; Ed.B. in Vocat. Edn., No. Ariz. U., 1977. Nurse, St. Joseph's Hosp., Comox, B.C., 1962-63, Children's Hosp., San Francisco, 1963; dir. staff devel. Doctors Hosp., Phoenix, 1964-70; program dir., instr. Maricopa Tech. Community Coll., Phoenix, 1970, div. chair health sci. dept., 1984—; founder Nursing Unit Mgmt. Systems; health care cons. Mem. Am. Vocat. Assn., Nat. Assn. Health Occupation Tchrs., Health Occupations Edn. Assn. (Creativity award 1981), Nat. Assn. Health Unit Clks.-Coordinators (founder, adv., exec. bd.), Ariz. Health Unit Clks.-Coordinators Assn. (founder, pres. 1980), Maricopa County Community Coll. Dist. Faculty Assn., Women in Higher Edn. Ariz., Nat. Council Staff, Program and Orgn. Devel. Co-author: Unit Clerking in Health Care Facilities, 1979; Medical Service Coordinator Clinical Evaluation Handbook, 1980; Exploring the Language of Medicine, 1984; contbr. articles to profl. jours. Home: 709 W Seldon Ln Phoenix AZ 85021 Office: 108 N 40th St Phoenix AZ 85034

LA FOLLETTE, ELLEN UNWIN MCHUGH, professional fundraiser; b. Lawrence, Mass., Mar. 15, 1933; d. Francis Paul and Mary Dorothea (Herlihy) McHugh; m. Charles Sanborn La Follette, Apr. 24, 1954; children—Laetitia Amelia, Lizellen, Anne Unwin, Charles McHugh. A.B., Radcliffe Coll., 1954. Instr. Am. lit. Corning Community Coll., N.Y., 1962-64; English tutor Lycée Montaigne, Paris, 1968-71; v.p. Compass Assocs., San Francisco, 1980—; fin. coordinator UN 40th Commemoration, San Francisco, 1984-85. Bd. dirs. Achievement Rewards for Coll. Scientist, San Francisco, 1971-80, Russian Hill Improvement Assn., San Francisco, 1972—; trustee Radcliffe Coll., Cambridge, Mass., 1979-83; fin. chmn. election campaign, San Francisco, 1980; mem. adv. com. San Francisco Day Sch., 1984—. Mem. Harvard Alumni Assn. (bd. dirs. 1984—), Cercle Interalliée Paris. Republican. Clubs: Radcliffe (San Francisco) (pres. 1974-78); Harvard (San Francisco, Boston, N.Y.C.). Home: 2620 Larkin St San Francisco CA 94109 Office: Compass Assocs 3074 Pacific Ave San Francisco CA 94115

LAFONTANT, JEWEL STRADFORD, lawyer; b. Chgo., Apr. 28, 1922; d. Cornelius Francis and Aida Arabella (Carter) Stradford; A.B., Oberlin Coll., 1943; J.D., U. Chgo., 1946; LL.D. (hon.), Chgo. Med. Sch. U. of Health Scis., 1982; 13 other hon. degrees; 1 son, John W. Rogers III. Admitted to Ill. bar, 1947; asst. U.S. atty., 1955-58; sr. partner firm Vedder, Price, Kaufman & Kammholz, P.C., Chgo.; dep. solicitor gen. U.S., Washington, 1972-75; dir. Trans World Airlines, Mobil Oil Corp., Continental Bank, Foote, Cone & Belding, Bendix Corp., Equitable Life Assurance Soc. U.S., Harte-Hanks Communications, Inc., Pantry Pride, Inc. Mem. U.S. Adv. Commn. Internat. Edn. and Cultural Affairs, Nat. Council Minority Bus. Enterprises, Nat. Council on Ednl. Research; mem. Pres. Regan's Transition Team, 1980, Pres. Commn. on Exec. Exchange, 1982; mem. exec. com. Pres.'s Pvt. Sector Survey on Cost Control, 1982; chmn. adv. bd. Civil Rights Commn. Trustee Lake Forest (Ill.) Coll., Oberlin Coll., Howard U., Tuskegee Inst.; bd. dirs. U.S. C. of C. Fellow Internat. Acad. Trial Lawyers, Am. Bar Found.; mem. Chgo. Bar Assn. (bd. govs.), Internat. Acad. Trial Lawyers. Former bd. editors Am. Bar Assn. Jour. Office: Veddor Price Kaofman & Kammholz 115 S La Salle St Chicago IL

LAFORET, ADELINE ANNE, nurse, health care administrator; b. Thunder Bay, Ont., Can., Mar. 7, 1937; d. Joseph Anton and Helen (Heisler) Harrison; m. Albert Joseph Laforet, Nov. 21, 1959; children—Mary, Albert, John, Michelle. Diploma in Nursing, St. Joseph Sch. Nursing, Thunder Bay, 1957. R.N., Mich. Dir. nursing Med. Personnel Pool, Southfield, Mich., 1972-74, Temporary Health Care Service, Detroit, 1974-75; pres. Health Care Profls., Ltd., Southfield, 1975—. Mem. bus. adv. council Central Mich. U., Mount Pleasant, 1983—; bd. dirs. Small Bus. Assn. Mich., Lansing, 1984—. Named. Nat. Women in Bus. Advocate, SBA, 1983. Mem. Am. Nursing Assn., Nat. League Nursing, Mich. League Nursing, Mich. Assn. Women Bus. Owners (Bus. Woman of Yr. award 1982), Nat. Assn. Women Bus. Owners, Nat. Head Injury Alliance, Mich. Head Injury Alliance, Nat. Assn. Home Care, Mich. Home Health Alliance, Women's Econ. Club, Greater Detroit C. of C., Mich. State C. of C., Southfield C. of C. Roman Catholic. Club: Farmington Hills Country. Avocations: running, cross-country skiing, downhill skiing, golf, reading. Home: 3553 Port Cove Dr Apt 31 Cass Lake Pontiac MI 48054 Office: Health Care Profls Ltd Suite 350 17000 W Eight Mile Rd Southfield MI 48075

LAFORGE, MARY CECILE, marketing educator; b. Mobile, Ala., Dec. 31, 1945; d. Siegfried Cecil and Nona Francis (Cardwell) Brutkiewicz; m. Robert Lawrence LaForge, June 10, 1972; children—Ryan Christopher, Scott Lawrence. B.B.A., Samford U., 1965, M.B.A., 1968; Ph.D. in Mktg., U. Ga., 1980. Asst. mktg. research mgr. Progressive Farmer/So. Living Mags., Birmingham, Ala., 1965-67, asst. prof. mktg. James Madison U., Harrisonburg, Va., 1977-81; asst. prof. mktg. Clemson U. (S.C.), 1981—. Fellow Acad. Mktg. Sci.; mem. Am. Mktg. Assn., So. Mktg. Assn., Assn. Consumer Research, Beta Gamma Sigma. Baptist. Home: 108 Knight Circle Clemson SC 29631 Office: Dept Mktg Clemson U Sirrine Hall Clemson SC 29631

LAFOUREST, JUDITH ELLEN, editor, publisher, writer, educator; b. Indpls., Jan. 10; d. Edward Elston and Dorothy Jeanette (Parker) LaFourest; B.A., Ind. U.-Purdue U., Indpls., 1972; M.A.T., Ind. U., 1980; m. William E. Lugar; 1 dau., Beth Anne Gruner; 1 son, Paul Christopher Stewart Pitts Lugar LaFourest. Lead pre-vocat. instr., ednl. adminstr. Opportunities Industrialization Center, Indpls., 1972-76; part-time English and human relations instr. Profl. Careers Inst., Indpls., 1975-78; editor, pub. Womankind, Indpls., 1977-83; co-dir. Womankind Center, 1981-82; editor, creative writer, photographer Bio-Feed-Back Bio Dynamics/BMC, Indpls., 1977-80; mem. assoc. faculty, creative writing inst. Ind.U.-Purdue U., Indpls., 1979—, supr. student tchrs. of English, 1983—; adj. faculty dept. English, Butler U., 1984—; also lectr., free-lance editor. Ind. sec. NOW, 1978-80. Recipient Disting. Alumni award Ind. U.-Indpls., 1980. Mem. Nat. League Am. Pen Women, Nat. Women's Studies Assn., Ind. U.-Indpls. Liberal Arts Alumni Assn. (pres. 1982), Sigma Tau Delta. Office: Butler U Dept English 4600 Sunset Ave Indianapolis IN 46208

LAFREE, BONNIE SUE, excavating company executive; b. Bremen, Ind., Jan. 14, 1955; d. Richard C. and Ann (Gilbert) LaFree. A.A., Ball State U., 1975; B.A., St. Mary's Coll., 1978. Salesperson, Miller & Co., Chgo., 1978-79, Dodge Mfg. div. Exxon, Mishawaka, Ind., 1979-80; with Castcel Constrn. Co., South Bend, Ind., 1981-82; v.p. LaFree Excavating Co., Osceola, Ind., 1982—. Dir., Builders Exchange St. Joe County, South Bend, 1982—. Mem. Nat. Orgn. Women in Constrn., Home Builders Assn. Office: LaFree Excavating Ino 11252 W 3d St Osceola IN 46561 Home: 11252 W 3d St Osceola IN 46561

LAGANGA, DONNA BRANDEIS, publishing company sales executive; b. Bklyn., June 27, 1949; d. Sidney L. and Sylvia (Herman) Brandeis; B.S. in Bus. Edn., Central Conn. State Coll., New Britain, 1972, M.S., 1975; m. Thomas LaGanga, Aug. 11, 1974. Various secretarial positions, 1969-72; tchr. bus. Lewis S. Mills Regional High Sch., Burlington, Conn., 1972-78; cons. Southwestern Pub. Co., Pelham Manor, N.Y., 1978-84, dist. sales mgr., 1984—; co-owner Colonial Welding Service; seminar condr., 1980—. Adv. bd. secretarial sci. dept. LaGuardia Community Coll., Long Island City, N.Y., 1982—; adv. bd. Kriessler Bus. Inst. EDPA grantee, 1973; cert. profl. sec. Mem. Nat. Assn. Female Execs., Assn. Info./Systems Profls., Am. Mgmt. Assn., Nat. Bus. Edn. Assn., Profl. Secs. Internat., Eastern Bus. Edn. Assn., Conn. Bus. Edn. Assn., New Eng. Bus. Edn. Assn., Profl. Secs. Assn. N.Y., Nat. Assn. Cert. Profl. Secs., Delta Pi Epsilon. Home: 612 S Main St Torrington CT 06790 Office: 925 Spring Rd Pelham Manor NY 10803

LAGIUSA, BETTY JEAN, accountant; b. Eureka, Calif., Oct. 12, 1927; d. Earl Chancel and Ruby Jewel (Cox) Lackey; student Foothill Coll., 1967, San Jose State U., 1972, Golden Gate U. Taxation, 1976; children—Jere, Marla, Mario. Pvt. practice bus. and tax acctg. Campbell, Calif., 1975—. Am. Bus. Women's Assn., 1971-72, 1978-79. Mem. Am. Bus. Womens Assn. (chpt. pres., Women of Yr. award 1972, 79), Assn. Enrolled Agts. (chpt. pres.), Calif. Soc. Enrolled Agts. (sec. 1983-84), Nat. Soc. Pub. Accts., Am. Bus. Women's Assn. Democrat. Roman Catholic. Office: 595 N Millich Dr Campbell CA 95008

LAGO, MARY MCCLELLAND, English educator, editor; b. Pitts., Nov. 4, 1919; d. Clark Russell and Olive Arabella (Malone) McC.; m. Gladwyn Vaile Lago, Mar. 4, 1944; children—Jane Hazel, Donald Russell. B.A. in English, Bucknell U., 1940, D.Litt. (hon.), 1981; M.A. in English, U. Mo., 1965, Ph.D. in English, 1969. Pub. relations staff Friendship Press, N.Y.C., 1941-44; asst. editor Nat. Hdqrs. Congregational Chs., N.Y.C., 1945-47; lectr. U. Mo., Columbia, 1971-77, assoc. prof., 1977-79, prof. English, 1979—; organizer Mo. Symposium I, II, 1979, 81; guest lectr. Asian Studies. Mem. editorial bd. Twentieth Century Lit., Hofstra U., Hempstead, N.Y., 1980—; hon. vis. prof. U. Manchester, 1985-86. Editor: Imperfect Encounter, 1972; Max and Will, 1975, Men and Memories, 1979; Burne-Jones Talking, 1981; Calendar of the Letters of E.M. Forster, 1985; Co-editor: Selected Letters of E.M. Forster, 1983, 85. Author: Rabindranath Tagore, 1976; co-translator; Tagore, The Housewarming and Other Selected Writings, The Broken Nest; contbr. articles to profl. jours. Mem. community adv. bd. Sta. KBIA-FM, 1975—; organizer Columbia Bach Singers, 1949-51. Fellow Cambridge U., 1982-83; grantee Am. Philos. Soc., 1966, Am. Council Learned Socs., 1972, NEH, 1981-83; recipient Faculty-Alumni award U. Mo., 1979, Disting. Faculty award U. Mo., 1985. Mem. MLA, Soc. of Authors (London), Virginia Woolf Soc., Phi Beta Kappa. Democrat. Club: Univ. Women's Club (London). Avocations: choral singing; sewing; travel. Home: 834 Greenwood Ct Columbia MO 65203 Office: Dept English U Mo Columbia MO 65211

LAGRONE, LAVENIA WHIDDON, chemist, real estate broker; b. Conroe, Tex., Feb. 27, 1940; d. James Lewis and Cora Lee (DeLuish) Whiddon; A.A., Kilgore Coll., 1960; B.S., North Tex. State U., 1962; grad. med. technology Baylor U. Med. Center, 1962; m. Doyle W. LaGrone, June 26, 1959 (div. Sept. 1965); 1 child, Russell Randal. Sr. technologist in spl. chemistry Baylor U. Med. Center, Dallas, 1962-63; research chemist, supr. labs., cardiovascular surgery Southwestern Med. Sch., Dallas, 1964-69, Upstate Med. Center, SUNY, Syracuse, 1969-70; research assoc., supr. lab., dept. surgery U. Tex. Med. Br., Galveston, 1970-74, research assoc., supr. labs., pediatric nephrology, 1974—, mem. chem. safety com., 1984-85; real estate broker DeLanney & Assocs., realtors, 1979-83; owner La Grone & Assocs., Realtors, 1983—. Chmn. student activities PTA Galveston, Tex., 1976-77. Recipient Top Real Estate Sales award, Top Real Estate Producer award, DeLanney & Assocs., 1979, also Broker's Excellence award and Top Real Estate Commn. award, 1980, also Million Dollar Producer award, 1980-83, Multi-million Dollar producer, 1984-85. Mem. Am. Soc. Clin. Pathologists (registered med. technologist), Nat. Assn. Realtors, Tex. Assn. Realtors, Galveston Bd. Realtors, Phi Theta Kappa. Club: Bus. and Profl. Women's (pub. relations officer 1985-86). Contbr. articles to chemistry and med. jours. Home: 142 San Fernando St Galveston TX 77550 Office: U Tex Med Br 301 University Blvd Galveston TX 77550

LAGUNA, ASELA RODRÍGUEZ, Spanish educator; b. San German, P.R., Dec. 6, 1946; came to U.S., 1968; d. Ramon Rodríguez and Eugenia Seda; B.A. in Humanities, U. P.R., Mayaguéz, 1968; M.A. in Comparative Lit., U. Ill., Champaign-Urbana, 1970, Ph.D., 1973; m. Elpidio Laguna-Diáz, June 21, 1975; children—Asela, Maria E., Alexandra. Teaching asst. U. Ill., 1969-73; mem. faculty Rutgers U., Newark, 1973—, assoc. prof. Spanish, 1979—; organizer, dir. 1st nat. pub. conf. on images and identities: The Puerto Rican in Literature, 1983. Research grantee Rutgers U., 1977-78, merit award, 1983; N.J. Dept. Higher Edn. grantee, 1985. Mem. Internat. Comparative Lit. Assn., Am. Comparative Lit. Assn., Assn. Tchrs. Spanish and Portuguese, Assn. Latin Am. Studies. Roman Catholic. Author: Shaw in the Hispanic World, 1981; editor: Imagénese identidades: el puertorigueño en la literatura, 1985; Images and Identities: The Puerto Rican in Two World Contexts, 1986; Puerto Rican Literature: An Introduction, 1986; also articles in field. Home: 207 39th St Union City NJ 07087 Office: Dept Modern and Classical Langs and Lits Rutgers U Conklin Hall Newark NJ 07102

LAHAISE, SHARON KAY, nurse, infection control practitioner; b. San Bernardino, Calif., Jan. 22, 1941; d. Raymond Theodore and Arabell Margaret (Greer) Manning; m. Eugene Ernst LaHaise, Feb. 17, 1962 (div. Aug. 1975); children—Curtis Michael, Craig Thomas. A.S., San Bernardino Valley Coll., 1961, 73; B.S. in Nursing, Calif. State U.-Fullerton, 1978; M., cert. in edn., U. Calif.-Riverside, 1980-82; Ph.D./M.A. in Edn. and Health Services Adminstrn., Columbia Pacific U., Mill Valley, Calif., 1985. R.N.; cert. in pub. health nursing, adult edn., community coll. teaching, mgmt. and supervisory devel., Calif. Microbiology lab. asst. San Bernardino Valley Coll., 1971-73; nursing coordinator critical care Kaiser Hosp., Fontana, Calif., 1973-78; Western region hosp. specialist Merck & Co., Inc., Rahway, N.J., 1978-81; asst. dir. nursing United Health Careers Inst., San Bernardino, 1981-82; patient care supr. Home Health Care Assn., Colton, Calif., 1981-82; dir. infection control, infection surveillance officer Hemet Valley Hosp. Dist., Hemet, Calif., 1982—; cons. math. and sci. Hdqrs. U.S. Army Armor and Desert Tng. Ctr., Dept. Def., Fort Irwin, Calif., 1963-71; mem. AIDs task force Inland Counties Health Systems Agy.; v.p. exec. bd. Inland AIDs Project; cons. in infection control; lectr. Contbr. poetry to Calif. Anthology (winner 1st place award), 1958; inventor anoxia and model of decompression chamber, winner 1st place in aerospace medicine, 1959; author: Model for Sexuality Counseling, 1978. Precinct clk. Democratic party, Colton, 1958; dir. wildflower festival Barstow (Calif.) C. of C., 1962; art dir. Colton Recreational Dept., 1962; So. Calif. educator coordinator Student Vocat. Nurses Assn., 1981-82, named Outstanding Nursing Educator, 1982. Recipient 1st place award in sci. talent search Westinghouse Corp., 1958; Alpha Gamma Sigma Soc. scholar, 1959, 70-71; named Outstanding Nursing Grad., dept. nursing San Bernardino Valley Coll., 1973. Mem. Am. Assn. Critical Care Nurses, Assn. Practitioners in Infection Control, Nat. Critical Care Inst. Edn., Nurse Cons. Assn., Am. Nurses Found. (charter mem. Century Club), Calif. Vocat. Nurse Educators, Nat. Assn. Female Execs. Roman Catholic. Home: 715 Canary Dr Colton CA 92324 Office: Hemet Valley Hospital District 1116 E Latham Ave Hemet CA 92343

LAHIFF, ROSEMARY THERESA, nurse; b. Cambridge, Mass., Aug. 5, 1958; d. Michael Austin and Catherine Theresa (Shea) L. B.S. in Nursing, Boston Coll., 1980. R.N., Mass. Staff nurse New Eng. Med. Ctr., Boston, 1980-83, asst. head nurse, 1983, head nurse, 1983—. Mem. Council Middle Mgmt., Sigma Theta Tau. Avocations: running; travel; reading. Home: 15 Boston St Somerville MA 02143 Office: New Eng Med Ctr 185 Harrison Ave Boston MA

LAHOOD, MARY ANNE, real estate investor; b. Grosse Pointe Farms, Mich., Aug. 23, 1947; d. Tom and Melania (Simon) LaHood. B.A., Wayne State U., 1972. Ptnr. LaHood Lanes, Inc., St. Clair Shores, Mich., 1972—, LaHood Properties, Grosse Pointe Shores, Mich., 1974—. Founder, Founders Soc. Detroit Inst. Arts, 1985. Clubs: Scarab (Detroit); Grosse Pointe Yacht. Home: 20 Stillmeadow Ln Grosse Pointe Shores MI 48236 Office: LaHood Properties 771 Lakeshore Dr Grosse Pointe Shores MI 48236

LAHRMAN, DOLORES MARIE, archivist; b. Indpls., June 11, 1920; d. Walter M. and Helen M. (Kahl) L. B.S. in Edn., St. Francis Coll., Ind., 1941; student Loyola U., Chgo., 1944, 46, 47; M.A. in Library Sci., Ind. U., 1964. Tchr., St. Andrew's Sch., Ft. Wayne, Ind., 1941-44, St. Mary of the Angels Sch., New Orleans, 1944-45, St. John Baptist Sch., Earl Park, Ind., 1945-46, St. Francis High Sch., Lafayette, Ind., 1946-48; asst. archivist Ind. U., Bloomington, 1962-77, archivist, 1977—. Poet. Hist. preservation advocate Monroe County Hist. Soc., 1970-78; archivist/curator Andrew Wylie Hist. House, 1977—. Mem. Sisters of St. Francis, Ind., 1935-48, Discalced Carmelites, La., 1948-62. Mem. Soc. Ind. Archivists (charter), Midwest Archives Conf., Soc. Am. Archivists, Nat. Assn. Female Execs., Ind. German Heritage Soc., AAUW, Clover Internat. Poetry Assn., Ind. U. Alumni Assn., Beta Phi Mu. Roman Catholic. Avocations: reading; writing; Imperial Russian history; music; opera. Home: 5470 W Beach Ln Bloomington IN 47401 Office: Ind U Archives Bryan Hall 201 Bloomington IN 47405

LAINE, DOLORES MAE (DEL), city official; b. Vallejo, Calif., Mar. 20, 1930; d. Leslie Merritt and Mabel Ysabel (Paulson) Wright; A.A., City Coll. San Francisco, 1950; B.A., Calif. State U., Berkeley, 1953; M.Sc., Calif. State U., San Francisco, 1960; m. Ed Laine, Mar. 30, 1962; children—Paul, Brooke, Alison, Paige. Dir. Lake Tahoe (Calif.) Recreation Div., 1961-62; co-owner Laine Assocs. Advt. and Pub. Relations, South Lake Tahoe, Calif., 1961-72, Laine Assocs. Photography, South Lake Tahoe, 1962—; pres. Del Laine and Daus., 1985—; owner Laine Assocs. Cons., 1983—; chmn. South Lake Tahoe Parks and Recreation Commn., 1974-76; councilwoman City of South Lake Tahoe, 1976-80, 84—, mem. affirmative action task force, 1978-80, mayor pro-tem, 1976-77, 86-87, mayor, 1977-78. Co-founder, producer Lake Tahoe Children's Theatre, 1962-72; chmn. Tahoe Regional Planning Agy. Urban Design Com., 1973-76; chmn. Tahoe Basin Transp. Authority, 1979—; chmn. Tahoe Regional Transp. Dist., 1981—; mem. adv. com. to Calif. Dept. Transp., 1983—. Mem. Nat. Women's Polit. Caucus, South Tahoe Women's Center (pres. 1980—, dir.), Lake Tahoe Hist. Soc. (pres. 1970-74). Presbyterian. Club: Soroptimist Internat. (regional gov. 1976-78). Office: Box 7322 South Lake Tahoe CA 95731

LAING, KAREL ANN, magazine publisher; b. Mpls., July 5, 1939; d. Edward Francis and Elizabeth Jane Karel (Templeton) Hannon; m. G. R. Cheesebrough, Dec. 19, 1959 (div. 1969); 1 child, Jennifer Read; m. Ronald Harris Laing, Jan. 6, 1973; 1 child, Christopher Harris. Student U. Minn., 1957-60. Sales mgr., pub. Guthrie Symphony Opera Program, Mpls., 1969-71; account supr. Colle & McVoy Advt. Agy., Richfield, Minn., 1971-74; owner, The Cottage, Edina, Minn., 1974-75; sales promotion rep. Robert Meyers & Assocs., St. Louis Park, Minn., 1975-76; cons. Webb Co., St. Paul, 1976-77, account mgr., pub., 1977—. Contbr. articles to profl. jours. Community vol. Am. Heart Assn., Am. Cancer Soc., Edina PTA; charter sponsor Walk Around Am., St. Paul, 1985. Mem. Bank Mktg. Assn., Fin. Instn. Mktg. Assn., Advt. Fedn. Am., Am. Bankers Assn., St. Andrews Soc. Republican. Presbyterian. Avocations: painting; gardening; reading; travel. Office: The Webb Co 1999 Shepard Rd Saint Paul MN 55116

LAING, MAI, financial planning company executive; b. Greenwood, S.C., Aug. 4, 1933; d. Cleveland and Bessie (Terry) Moon; m. Amos J. Laing. Student, Edward Waters Coll., 1945-47; B.S., Temple U., 1953. Procurement specialist U.S. Army, N.Y.C., 1961-64, U.S. Navy, N.Y.C., 1964-67; claims rep. Social Security Adminstrn., N.Y.C., 1967-78; pres. Laing & Assocs., Atlanta, 1978—. Mem. Am. Bus. Women Assn., Nat. Council Negro Women, Female Execs. Assn. (dir. 1983—). Office: Laing & Assocs Fin Planning PO Box 42689 Atlanta GA 30311

LAINO, JANE FERN, telecommunications consulting executive; b. Jersey City, June 8, 1947; d. William Alfred and Fern (Overlees) Coe; m. Richard Laino, July 5, 1968. B.A., CUNY, 1973. Rep., N.Y. Telephone, Rego Park, 1969-73, Southwestern Bell, Clayton, Mo., 1973-75, Northwestern Meml. Hosp., Chgo., 1975-76; v.p. Nat. Com, Inc., N.Y.C., 1976-79; pres., owner Corp. Communications Cons. Inc., N.Y.C., 1979—. Editor: Lines, 1983-84. Designer tradersoft telecommunications mgmt. software. Mem. Empire Women in Telecommunications, Soc. Telecommunications Cons. (bd. dirs. 1983-85, v.p., treas. 1985-86). Avocations: running; writing. Office: Corporate Communications Cons Inc 370 Lexington Ave New York NY 10017

LAIR, HELEN MAY, poet; b. New Castle, Ind., Jan. 3, 1918; d. Harry and Loma D. (Delon) Humphrey; student Anderson Coll., U. Wis., John Herron Sch. Art; m. Marvin E. Lair, July 2, 1966; children—Michael Lucas, Joan Lucas Krueckegerg, Nancy Lucas (dec.). Author book of poetry; Lair Of The Four Winds, 1978, Earth Pilgrim, 1981; contbr. numerous poems to anthologies and publs. including Poetry Rev., Our Western World's Greatest Poems, Today's Best Poems, Best Loved Contemporary Poems, Adventures in Poetry; author column New Castle Courier Times, 1982—. Pres. Henry County (Ind.) Art Guild. Recipient Farnell award, N.Y. Poetry Forum, Richard Miller award, Muncie (Ind.) Star 1st place award, Ind. State Fedn. Poetry 1st place award. Mem. Women in Communication, Acad. Women Poets, Nat. Fedn. Poets, Internat. Poets Achievement, N.Y. Poetry Forum, Accademia Leonardo da Vinci, Epsilon Sigma Alpha. Roman Catholic. Office: 1202 Mourer St New Castle IN 47362

LAIRD, DORIS ANNE MARLEY, humanities educator, musician; b. Charlotte, N.C., Jan. 15, 1931; d. Eugene Harris and Coleen (Bethea) Marley; m. William Everette Laird, Jr., Mar. 13, 1964; children—William Everette, III, Andrew Marley, Glen Howard. B.Mus., Converse Coll., Spartanburg, S.C., 1951; spl. student New Eng. Conservatory, Boston, 1953-56; M.M., Boston U., 1956; Ph.D., Fla. State U., 1980. Leading soprano roles S.C. Opera Co., Columbia, 1951-53, Plymouth Rock Ctr., Duxbury, Mass., 1953-56; instr. Stratford Coll., Danville, Va., 1956-58, Sch. Music, Fla. State U., Tallahassee, 1958-60, dept. humanities, 1960-68; asst. prof. Fla. A&M U., Tallahassee, 1979—; soprano Pro Musica, Boston, 1956, New Eng. Opera, Boston, 1956. Contbr. articles to profl. jours. Soprano Trinity United Meth. Ch., Tallahassee, 1983—; mem. St. Andrews Soc., Tallahassee, 1985; judge Brain Bowl, Tallahassee, 1981-84. Phi Sigma Tau scholar, 1960. Mem. AAUP, AAUW, Nat. Art Educators Assn., Tallahassee Music Tchrs. Assn., Tallahassee Music Guild, DAR (mus. rep. 1984-85), Colonial Dames of 17th Century (music dir. 1984-85). Democrat. Club: University Women's. Avocations: traveling; performing in musical productions. Home: 1125 Mercer Dr Tallahassee FL 32312 Office: Fla A&M U Humanities Dept Tallahassee FL 32307

LAIRD, JEAN ELOUISE RYDESKI (MRS. JACK E. LAIRD), author, educator; b. Wakefield, Mich., Jan. 18, 1930; d. Chester A. and Agnes A. (Petranek) Rydeski; Bus. Edn. degree Duluth (Minn.) Bus. U., 1948; postgrad. U. Minn., 1949-50; m. Jack E. Laird, June 9, 1951; children—John E., Jane E., JoanAnn P., Jerilyn S., Jacquelyn T. Tchr., Oak Lawn (Ill.) High Sch. Adult Evening Sch., 1964-72, St. Xavier Coll., Chgo., 1974—. Writer newspaper column Around The House With Jean, A Woman's Work, 1965-70, Chicagotown News column The World As I See It, 1969, hobby column Modern Maturity mag., travel column Travel/Leisure mag., beauty column Ladycom mag., Time and Money Savers column Lady's Circle mag., consumerism column Ladies' Home Jour. Mem. Canterbury Writers Club Chgo. (past. pres.), Oak Lawn Bus. and Profl. Women's Club, St. Linus Guild, Mt. Assisi Acad., Marist, Queen of Peace parents clubs. Roman Catholic. Author: Lost in the Department Store, 1964; Around The House Like Magic, 1968; Around The Kitchen Like Magic, 1969; How To Get the Most From Your Appliances, 1967; Hundreds of Hints for Harrassed Homemakers, 1971; The Alphabet Zoo, 1972; The Plump Ballerina, 1971; The Porcupine Story Book, 1974; Fried Marbles and Other Fun Things To Do, 1975; Hundreds of Hints for Harassed Homemakers; The Homemaker's Book of Time and Money Savers, 1979; Homemaker's Book of Energy Savers, 1981; also 260 paperback booklets. Contbr. numerous articles to mags. Home: 10540 S Lockwood Ave Oak Lawn IL 60453 also Whitewood Ave Grand Beach MI 49118 also Lake Geneva WI 53147

LAKAH, JACQUELINE RABBAT, political scientist, educator; b. Cairo, Apr. 14, 1933; came to U.S., 1969, naturalized, 1975; d. Victor Boutros and Alice (Mounayer) Rabbat; B.A., Am. U. Beirut, 1968; M.Ph. (Rockefeller Found. scholar, Columbia Faculty fellow, NDEA Title IV fellow), Columbia U., 1974, cert. Middle East Inst. (fellow), 1975, Ph.D., 1978; m. Antoine K. Lakah, Apr. 8, 1951; children—Micheline, Mireille, Caroline. Adj. asst. prof. polit. sci. and world affairs Fashion Inst. Tech., N.Y.C., 1978—; asst. prof. grad. faculty polit. sci. Columbia U., N.Y.C., summer 1979, vis. scholar, 1982-83, also mem. seminar on Middle East; guest faculty Sarah Lawrence Co., 1981-82; cons. on Middle East; faculty research fellow SUNY, summer 1982. Mem. Am. Polit. Sci. Assn., Acad. Polit. Sci., Internat. Polit. Sci. Assn. Roman Catholic. Home: 41-15 94th St Queens NY 11373 Office: 227 W 27th St New York NY 10001

LAKE, ANN WINSLOW, lawyer; b. Lowell, Mass., May 14, 1919; d. Frank and Helen Jablonski; B.S., Lowell State Coll., 1940; J.D., U. Detroit, 1946; M.A., Boston State Coll., 1964, Boston U., 1967; m. Thomas E. Lake, Sept. 5, 1942; children—Beverly Wilkes, Douglas, Warren. Tchr. schs. in Maine, Ga. and Detroit, 1940-43; admitted to Mass. bar, 1946; ind. practice, Dedham, Mass., 1946—; prof. law Salem (Mass.) State Coll., 1970—; mem. Mass. Commn. Study Labor Laws, 1972-74, Mass. Mental Health Legal Advisers Com., 1974-79. Mem. Mass. Adv. Commn. Acad. Talented Pupils, 1960-64, Mass. State Coll. Bldg. Authority, 1964-67, Mass. Com. to Recruit and Screen Candidates for Office Atty. Gen., 1974-78, U. Lowell Found., 1977-82. Recipient award Mass. State Coll. Alumni Assn., 1963, 64, 72, Mass. Assn. Mental Health, 1969, 72. Fellow Am. Bar Found., Mass. Bar Found.; mem. Nat. Assn. Women Lawyers (pres. 1980-81), Polish Bus. and Profl. Women's Club Greater Boston (pres. 1977-79), Norfolk Mental Health Assn. (pres. 1972-73), Mass. Assn. Women Lawyers (pres. 1971-72), Assn. Mass. State Colls. Alumni (pres. 1961-64), Riverdale Improvement Assn. (pres. 1959). Republican. Address: 40 Sawyer Dr Dedham MA 02026

LAKE, BLAIR MOODY, nursing educator; b. Nashville, June 14, 1932; d. Marlin Sheridan and Sara Alice (Blair) Moody; m. Richard Harrington Lake, July 17, 1954; children—Richard Moody, Mary Anne (dec.), William Moody, Sara Blair. Cert., U. Neuchatel, Switzerland, 1950; Diploma, U. Paris (Sorbonne), 1951; B.A., U. Tenn., 1952; A.A.S., No. Va. Community Coll., 1971; M.S.N., Cath. U. Am., 1978; cert. oncology nursing edn. Georgetown U. Sch. Nursing, 1978. Personnel adminstr. U.S. Civil Service, Fort Sheridan, Ill., 1952-53; office mgr. U.S. Navy Exchange, Bangkok, Thailand, 1955-56; staff and charge nurse, Fairfax Hosp., Va., 1971-72; econs. cons. R.H. Lake Asscos., 1970—, Thailand, 1972; primary nurse oncology Arlington Hosp., Va., 1979-80; oncology clin. practitioner Georgetown U. Hosp., Washington, 1980-82; assoc. prof. nursing Brevard Community Coll., Cocoa, Fla., 1982-85. Vol. sch. nurse Fairfax County Public Schs., 1974-76; crisis intervention counselor Haven of No. Va., Annandale, 1977-78; vol., pub. and profl. edn. Am. Cancer Soc., Fairfax County, Va., Brevard County, Fla., 1978—. Mem. Am. Nurses Assn., Oncology Nursing Soc., Sigma Theta Tau, Alpha Delta Pi. Episcopalian. Clubs: Daus. of U.S. Army; Washington Bangkok Women's Club. Avocations: equitation; swimming; historical research; current affairs. Office: RH Lake Assocs Box 385 Annandale VA 22003

LAKE-SMITH, NANCY JOYCE, publishing company executive; b. Chgo., Aug. 25, 1951; d. Donald Kent and Elaine Joyce (Newman) Gedman; m. C.J. Lake-Smith, Nov. 8, 1985. B.A. in Journalism, U. Minn., 1973, J.D., 1977. Asst. dir. U. Minn. Alumni Assn., St. Paul, 1973-74; admitted to Minn. bar, 1977; partner firm Margoles & Gedman, St. Paul, 1978-80; mgr. acquisitions and mktg. Mason Pub. Co., St. Paul, 1980-81; pres. Butterworth Legal Pubs. div. Butterworth (London-established 1818)-Reed Internat. P.L.C., Stoneham, Mass., 1981-85; pres. Butterworth Legal Pubs., St. Paul, 1985—. Office: Butterworth Legal Pubs 289 E 5th St Saint Paul MN 55101

LAKICH, LILIANA DIANE (LILI), neon artist, museum director; b. Washington, June 4, 1944; d. Ognjan Ivan and Dorothy (Trbovic) L. B.F.A., Pratt Inst., 1967; cert. London Sch. Film Technique, 1965. Asst. art dir. Internat. Food Service, Beverly Hills, Calif., 1972-74; art dir. Seiniger Advt., Los Angeles, 1974-81; ptnr. Calko and Lakich, Los Angeles, 1981—; founder, dir. Mus. of Neon Art, Los Angeles, 1981—. Author: Neon Lovers Glow in the Dark, 1986. Artist (poster) Mona, 1981 (award of Distinction Am. Assn. Mus. 1984). Recipient Mayor's Cert., Los Angeles, 1984. Mem. The Woman's Bldg. (Vesta award 1984), Mus. Contemporary Art. Democrat. Serbian Orthodox. Office: Mus Neon Art 704 Traction Ave Los Angeles CA 90013

LAKOS, MARCILLE HARRIS, clin. psychologist; b. Ontario, Oreg., Dec. 10, 1917; d. Marvin and Una Leota (Smith) Hurst; B.S. in Psychology, U. Oreg., 1947, M.S. in Psychology, 1949; m. Eugene A. Lakos, Mar. 3, 1957; 1 son, John Stuart. Co-therapist, Nathan W. Ackerman, Family Inst., N.Y.C., 1955-60, 62-72; pvt. practice clin. psychology, N.Y.C., 1972—. Mem. Am. Psychol. Assn., Fedn. Am. Scientists, AAAS, N.Y. State Psychol. Assn., N.Y. Acad. Scis., Nat. Register Health Service Providers in Psychology (cert., council), Sigma Xi. Home and Office: 201 E 66th St New York NY 10021

LAKOSKY, IRENE MARYAN, nursing administrator; b. Chgo., Oct. 12, 1932; d. Adolf and Agnes Christine (Dorau) Heigl; R.N., Triton Jr. Coll., 1970; B.S. in Profl. Arts, St. Francis Coll., 1975; M.S. in Nursing Adminstrn., Columbia Pacific U., 1980, D.Sc. in Wholistic Health, 1981; children—Michael, Linda, Steven, James. Adminstrv. asst. Mich. Mut. Liability Co., Chgo., 1955-60; charge nurse Loyola Hosp., Maywood, Ill., 1970-72, 1972, Rush-Presbn.-St. Luke's Hosp., Chgo., 1972; staff nurse Cook County Hosp., Chgo., 1972-73; charge nurse Loretto Hosp., Chgo., 1973-75; night nursing adminstr. West Suburban Hosp., Oak Park, Ill., 1975—; dir. nursing Home Med-Care Found., Oak Park, 1977-83; holistic health practitioner, cons. doing bus. as Wellness for Life; also sexual dysfunction therapist. Mem. bd. Head Start Program, 1966-68. Mem. Ill. Nurses Assn., Am. Nurses Assn. (cert. nursing adminstr.; council on nursing adminstrn.), Am. Nurses Found. Century Club, Am. Holistic Nurses Assn. (founding mem.), Women's Connection of Oak Park, Al Anon. Republican. Roman Catholic. Contbr. articles to profl. jours.

LAL, INDU MOHAN, physician, consultant; b. Lucknow, India, May 29, 1949; came to U.S., 1976; d. Nityanand Mohan and Susheela M. L. B.S., U. Allahabad (India), 1967, M.B., B.S., 1972; postgrad. U. Conn., 1977-80. Intern, resident Waterbury Hosp., St. Mary's Hosp., Farmington Health Ctr.; established med. help in village of India, 1973-74; med. officer Lady Dufferin's Hosp., Allahabad, 1974-76; practice medicine specializing in pediatrics, Hopewell Junction, N.Y., 1980—; mem. staff Vasser Bros. Hosp., Poughkeepsie, N.Y., 1980—, Highland Hosp., Beacon, N.Y., 1981—; cons. for adolescent medicine. Fellow Am. Acad. Pediatrics; mem. AMA, Dutchess County Med. Soc., N.Y. Med. Soc. Office: PO Box 574 Route 82 Hopewell Junction NY 12533

LALIME, ANDREA JEAN, lighting studio executive; b. Lynn, Mass., Jan. 14, 1953; d. Ronald Francois and Elaine Marie (Vadaboncoeur) L.; m. Gregory Andrews, Jan. 31, 1975 (div.). B.S., U. Orono, 1977. Technician, Lalime's Drug Store, Waterville, Maine, 1967-77; history tchr. Foxcroft Acad., Dover Foxcroft, Maine, 1977-78; sci. tchr. Dexter Regional High Sch. (Maine), 1978-80; gen. mgr. Bay Comml. Lighting, San Francisco, 1981-86. Mem. Illuminating Engrng. Soc. (sustaining), Designer Lighting Forum (dir.), Nat. Assn. Female Execs., Chi Omega. Clubs: Karate-Do (San Francisco); Sub-Aqua (instr.). Office: Lighting Studio 1808 Fourth St Berkeley CA 94708

LALLATIN, CARLA SUE, business executive; b. Casper, Wyo., Apr. 27, 1946; d. Carl Dabney and Dorothy May (Stuart) Moulden; student U. Mo., 1971-72; A.A., Met. Jr. Coll., 1971; 1 dau., Natalie. Typesetting mgr. Allen Typesetting Co., Kansas City, Mo., 1967-69; publs. dir. United Computing Systems, Kansas City, Mo., 1969-74; purchasing state adminstr. State Wyo., Cheyenne, 1974-79; dep. commr. mcpl. supplies City of N.Y., 1979-85; v.p. network services Bid Net, 1985—; guest lectr. World Trade Inst., Mich. State U., Nat. Inst. Govtl. Purchasing, 1975—. Fin. adviser Girl Scouts U.S., 1977-79. Recipient Award of Merit and Award of Excellence, Internat. Assn. Bus. Communicators, 1974. Mem. Nat. Inst. Govt. Purchasing (bd. dirs., cert. of appreciation), Nat. Assn. State Purchasing Ofcls. (cert. of merit Cronin Club), Nat. Contract Mgmt. Assn., Am. Pub. Works Assn., Am. Bus. Women's Assn. (pres. 1978-79, Top Ten Bus Women of Year). Home: 61-15 97th St Apt 7A Rego Park NY 11374 Office: 5 Choke Cherry Rd Rockville MD 20850

LALLY, ANN MARIE, former educational administrator; b. Chgo., Sept. 23, 1914; d. Martin J. and Della (McDonnell) Lally; A.B., Mundelein Coll., 1935; A.M., Northwestern U., 1939, Ph.D., 1950; postgrad. Chgo. Tchrs. Coll., Chgo. Art Inst., 1935-36. Tchr., Amundsen High Sch., 1935, Lindblom and Von Steuben high schs., Chgo., 1936-38; chmn. art dept. Schurz High Sch., 1938-40; supr. art Chgo. Pub. Elementary Schs., 1940-48, dir. art Chgo. Public Schs., 1948-57; prin. John Marshall High Sch., 1957-63; supt. Dist. 16, Chgo. Pub. Schs., 1963-64, Dist. 5, 1964-80; lectr. Wright Jr. Coll., 1948; instr. creative drawing Chgo. Acad. Fine Art, 1941; instr. interior design Internat. Harvester Co., 1946-48; lectr. in edn. DePaul U., 1952-74; lectr. in edn. and art U. Chgo., 1956-59; lectr. edn. Chgo. Tchrs. Coll., 1960-62. Trustee Pub. Sch. Tchrs. Pension and Retirement Fund Chgo., 1957-71, sec.-treas., 1960-65, pres., 1965-70. charter mem. women's bd. Loyola U.; charter mem. women's bd. Art Inst., Chgo. Mem. Am., Ill. assns. sch. adminstrs., N.E.A. (life), Ill. Edn. Assn., Dist. Supts. Assn. (pres. 1973-75), Ill. Women Adminstrs. Assn. (award 1979), Nat. Council Adminstrv. Women in Edn. (profl. relations chmn. 1958-62), Assn. Supervision and Curriculum Devel., Chgo. Area Women Adminstrs. in Edn. (award for outstanding adminstrn. 1981), Nat. Art Edn. Assn. (mem. council 1956-60), Western Arts Assn. (pres. 1956-58), Internat. Soc. Edn. in Art, Ill. Art Edn. Assn. (pres. 1955), LWV of Chgo., Chgo. Art Educators Assn. (a founder; past v.p., sec. and treas), Ill. Club Cath. Women (dir., 1981—, rec. sec. 1982-86), Chgo. Pub. Sch. Art Soc., Chgo. Hist. Soc., AAUW (Chgo. chmn. elem. and secondary edn., dir.-at-large 1962-66, 78-80), Chgo. Area Reading Assn. (dir. 1963-69), Nat., Ill. assns. secondary sch. prins., Artists Equity Assn., Chgo., Council on Fgn. Relations, Mundelein Coll. Alumnae Assn. (past pres., chmn. bd., Magnificat medal 1964), Pi Lambda Theta, Delta Kappa Gamma. Club: Chgo. Woman's. Contbr. articles to art and ednl. jours. Home: 1130 S Michigan Ave Chicago IL 60605

LALONDE, GEORGIA JEAN, lawyer; b. Dallas, July 23, 1950; d. George Bernard and Bettye Jean (McCoy) LaLonde. B.A., North Tex. State U., Denton, 1972; J.D., So. Methodist U., 1981. Bar: Tex. 1982. Tchr. Dallas Ind. Sch., 1972-73, Terrell (Tex.) Ind. Sch., 1973-77; legal aide Neiman-Marcus Co., Dallas, 1978-80; compliance specialist InterFirst Bank, Dallas, 1980-82; assoc. firm Hart & Krohn P.C., Houston, 1982-83, McLain & Niehaus P.C., Houston, 1983—; dir. Sepilian Corp., Houston, SF Internat., Inc., Warren Internat., Inc. Bd. dirs. Sharma Found., Houston, 1983—. Mosbacher Found. scholar, Houston, 1977. Mem. ABA (internat. law com.), Houston Bar Assn., Tex. Bar Assn. (internat. law com.), Houston C. of C. (internat. bus. com.). Chi Omega. Office: McLain Cage, Hill & Niehaus 6363 Woodway Suite 800 Houston TX 77057

LAM, AMY YUEN-HAR, financial executive; b. Hong Kong, June 23, 1954; came to U.S., 1973; d. Yin and Fung (Chan) Kwok; B.A. cum laude in Econs. (departmental honors), Yale U., 1977; M.S. in Mgmt., Purdue U., 1979; m. Michael Lam, Aug. 12, 1978. Actuarial analyst Aetna Ins. Co., Hartford, Conn., 1977-78; fin. analyst Internat. Harvester, Chgo., 1980; mfg. support analyst Xerox Corp., El Segundo, Calif., 1980-81, fin. analyst, 1981—. Group coordinator Internat. Assn. Students in Econs. and Bus., 1975; vol. Yale-New Haven Hosp., 1976. Mem. Nat. Assn. Female Execs., Beta Gamma Sigma. Home: 27642 Warrior Dr Rancho Palos Verdes CA 90274 Office: 101 Continental Blvd El Segundo CA 90245

LA MACCHIA, SUSAN THERESA, marketing executive; b. Jefferson City, Mo., Oct. 21, 1949; d. Raphael H. and Angeline (Hentges) F.; m. John B. LaMacchia, Jr., July 7, 1973. B.A., Stephens Coll., 1972. Student loan officer Frontier Ins. Co., Jefferson City, Mo., 1972; v.p. mktg. Standard Analytical, St. Louis, 1973—, dir., 1978—. Vicinities chmn. St. Louis Symphony Soc., jr. div., 1983. Recipient Internat. Farm Youth exchange award State Mo., France, 1972. Mem. Nat. Fraternal Congress, Mo. Real Estate Brokers, Stephen Coll. Alumni. Club: Creve Coeur Racquet (St. Louis). Office: Standard Analytical Service Inc 12 N Central Ave Saint Louis MO 63105

LAMAR, CLARICE JORDAN, educator; b. Dallas, Aug. 31, 1938; d. James Henry and Arzee Olis (Ferguson) Jordan; m. Julius Lamar, Jr., Dec. 27, 1958 (div. 1972); 1 son, Julius Lamar III. B.S., Bishop Coll., 1960; M.E., Prairie View U., 1972. Tchr., Mansfield (Tex.) Ind. Sch. Dist., 1960-62, Dallas Ind. Sch. Dist., 1962-69, Los Angeles Ind. Sch. Dist., 1969-70, Dallas Ind. Sch. Dist., 1971—; dir. music Alex Sanger Sch., Dallas, 1972—. Named Tchr. of Yr., Alex Sanger Faculty, Dallas, 1976. Mem. NEA, Tex. State Tchrs. Assn., Dallas Music Educators Assn., Classroom Tchrs. Dallas. Democrat. Methodist Episcopal. Home: 5718 Rich St Dallas TX 75227 Office: Alex Sanger Sch 8410 San Leandro Dr Dallas TX 75228

LA MARRE, MILDRED HOLTZ, business executive; b. Phila., May 10, 1917; d. Philip and Dora H.; student George Washington U., 1939-40; B.A., U. Md., 1966; m. Jack Understein, Dec. 25, 1938 (dec.); children—Robert, Norma, Lisa, Norman, Gary; m. 2d, John La Marre, Feb. 14, 1981. With Jack Understein Co., Washington, 1960-71; exec. asst. Muskie for Pres., Washington, 1971-72; researcher Carnegie Endowment Internat. Peace, Washington, 1973-76; personal asst., adminstrv. asst. to Under Sec. Lucy Wilson Benson, U.S. Dept. of State, 1977-78; exec. asst. Mike Barnes for Congress, 1978; pres. Internat. Personal Shopping Service, Ltd., N.Y.C., 1980-84; exec. asst. John La Marre Appraisers, 1982—. Bd. dirs. Hebrew Home Greater Washington, 1970-83, Internat. Sickle Cell Anemia Research Inst., Washington, 1976-83. Democrat. Address: 880 5th Ave Apt 7A New York NY 10021

LAMB, ELIZABETH ANNE, lawyer; b. Kingston, N.Y., Nov. 8, 1946; d. John Patrick and Marie Winifred (Delaney) L. B.A., Coll. Mt. St. Vincent, Riverdale, N.Y., 1968; J.D., St. John's U., Jamaica, N.Y., 1975. Bar: N.Y. 1976. Asst. press sec. to Commr. Bess Myerson, N.Y.C., 1969-70; press sec. Congressman Hugh L. Carey, N.Y.C. and Washington, 1970-74; legis. asst. to Gov. Hugh L. Carey, N.Y.C., 1974-75; assoc. gen. counsel N.Y., State Criminal Justice Service, N.Y.C., 1975-80; sr. EEO counsel St. Regis Paper Co., N.Y.C., 1980-82; exec. v.p. Marcon Mgmt. Services, Inc., N.Y.C., 1982—. Mem. Assn. Bar City N.Y., N.Y. State Bar Assn., ABA, Met. Mus. Art. Democrat. Roman Catholic. Home: 12 E 86th St New York NY 10028 Office: Marcon Mgmt System Inc 1 Penn Plaza Suite 100 New York NY 10119

LAMB, JOAN EUGENIA, government official; b. Phila., July 27, 1939; d. Joseph N. and Eugenia A. Juliano; B.A., George Mason U., 1973; postgrad. Am. U., 1974-75; m. James Patrick Lamb, Dec. 29, 1958; children—Joseph Julian, James Gerard. Public affairs officer Navy Office Info., The Pentagon, Washington, 1973-79, Naval Ordnance Sta., 1979-80; pub. affairs dir. SSS, Washington, 1980-84, asst. dir., 1984-86; exec. asst. to adminstr. VA, Washington, 1986—. Recipient Selective Service Silver medal for superior achievement, 1981. Mem. League Women Voters, Women in Communications, Pub. Relations Soc. Am., AAUW. Roman Catholic. Home: 4709 Newcomb Pl Alexandria VA 22304

LAMB, MAUREEN, county official; b. Casper, Wyo., Jan. 17, 1922; d. Irving Goff and Fannie LeRoy (Sands) McCann; m. William E. Lamb, Jan. 10, 1941 (div. 1980); children—Carol, William E., Peter, Maureen; m. Stoddard Knowles, Dec. 22, 1981. Student Pa. State U. Assoc., Giddings & Assocs., Real Estate, 1978-82; elected mem. Anne Arundel County Council, Annapolis, Md., 1982—. Recipient numerous awards for profl. and community service. Mem. Zonta Internat., Md. Assn. Counties (treas.), Md. Assn. Elected Women (treas.). Home: 3 Goodrich Rd Annapolis MD 21401 Office: Anne Arundel County Council Calvert & Northwest St Annapolis MD 21401

LAMB, URSULA SCHAEFER, historian, educator; b. Essen, Germany, Jan. 15, 1914; came to U.S., 1935, naturalized, 1949; d. Waldemar Joachim and Maria Katharina (Hoffmann-Fallersleben) Schaefer; student U. Berlin, 1932-34, Smith Coll., 1935-36; M.A., U. Calif.-Berkeley, 1937, Ph.D., 1949; m. Willis E. Lamb, Jr., June 5, 1939. Lectr. history Barnard Coll., asso., 1949-51; tutor Brasenose Coll., lectr. Oxford, Eng., 1958, 60; lectr., research asso. Yale U., New Haven, 1962-74; prof. history U. Ariz., Tucson, 1974-85, prof. emerita, 1985—. Am. Learned Socs. grantee, 1943, Soc. Sci. Research grantee Columbia U., 1947, Guggenheim fellow, 1968-69, NEH fellow, 1972-73, Am. Philos. Soc. grantee, 1975, NSF grantee, 1978-79; Jeannette Black fellow John Carter Brown Library, Spring 1985. Mem. Soc. History Discoveries (pres. 1976-79), Am. Hist. Assn. (council mem. Pacific br. 1977-79), Conf. Latin Am. History, Pan Am. Inst. Geography and History (mem. bibliography com.), Internat. Reunion Nautical Sci. (U.S. rep.), Colloque Internat. de l'Histoire Maritime (U.S. rep. 1979, 80), Soc. Spanish and Portuguese Hist. Studies. Author: Frey Nicolás de Ovando, Gobernador de las Indias, 1501-1509, 1956; A Navigator's Universe: The Libro de Cosmographía of 1538 (Pedro de Medina), 1972; The E. G. R. Taylor Lecture, 1981; assoc. editor Hispanic Am. Hist. Rev., 1976-81. Office: 215 Social Sci Campus U Ariz Tucson AZ 85721

LAMBERT, BIRTHALE, nurse, educator, health care facility administrator; b. Houston, Miss., Jan. 6, 1947; d. Moses Beatty and Josephine (Hill) Gordon; m. Dennis Ray Moore, 1963 (div. 1977); 1 son, Jerry Allyn; m. Kelly G. Lambert, Jr., May 13, 1978. A.D.N., Grand Rapids Jr. Coll., 1970; B.S., Aquinas Coll., Grand Rapids, Mich., 1978; postgrad. Wayne State U., 1983-84; R.N., Mich. Charge nurse in med./surg. nursing, intensive care unit, emergency room Osteo. Hosp., Grand Rapids, 1970-74; instr. sci. Med. Asst. Program, Grand Rapids, 1973-74; instr. nursing Mercy Central Sch. Nursing, Grand Rapids, 1974-82; adminstr. Faith Nursing Home, Grand Rapids, 1983; prof. nursing Grand Valley State Coll., Allendale, Mich., 1983—; mem. bd. grand Rapids Jr. Coll. Adv. Bd. Instr., vol. ARC, Grand Rapids, 1970—; pres. St. Andrew's Parochial Sch. Booster Club, Grand Rapids, 1975-77; dir. nurses guild First Community A.M.E. Ch., Grand Rapids, 1978—, exec. dir. nursery program, 1979—, steward, 1979—; vote recruiter for senate com., Grand Rapids, 1982-83; mem. Kent County council for Prevention Child Abuse and Neglect, 1983—; mem. Grand Rapids Bd. Edn., 1984; Recipient Helen Barnes award Kent County chpt., ARC, 1975; Urban League Scholar, 1967-70. Fellow Mich. Black Nurses Assn. (v.p. 1977-79, chmn. programs 1977-79); mem. NAACP. Club: Grand Valley Faculty (Allendale). Designed Adopt-A-Grandparent program. Home: 3860 E Norwalk SE Kentwood MI 49508 Office: Grand Valley State Coll Allendale MI 49401

LAMBERT, JEAN MARJORIE, health care executive; b. Bay City, Mich., Mar. 19, 1943; d. Richard William and Fidelis Renee (LeVasseur) L. B.A., Madonna Coll., Livonia, Mich., 1967; M.A., Eastern Mich. U., 1975. Dir. religious edn. Archdiocese of Detroit, 1970-75, dir. of evaluation, 1975-77; assoc. dir. programming Intermedia Found., Santa Monica, Calif., 1977-78; acad. dean St. John Provincial Sem., Plymouth, Mich., 1978-84; asst. dir. quality mgmt. Sisters of Mercy Health Corp., Farmington Hills, Mich., 1984—; asst. prof. homiletics St. John Sem., Plymouth, Mich., 1978-85, St. Mary of the Woods Coll., Terre Haute, Ind., summer 1985, St. Meinrad Sem., Ind., summer 1984. Editor Religious Edn., 1975-77. Nat. Cath. Edn. Assn.-Assn. Theol. Schs. for U.S. and Can. grantee, 1983. Mem. Internat. Teleconferencing Assn., Nat. Assn. Female Execs., Am. Hosp. Assn. Roman Catholic. Avocations: woodcarving; photography; school. Office: Sisters of Mercy Health Corp 28550 Eleven Mile Rd Farmington Hills MI 48018

LAMBERT, MARIE CHRISTINE, computer software company executive; b. Paris, Nov. 23, 1949; came to U.S., 1979; d. Arthur Jacques Charbonnier and Lysyinne Charbonnier Coutansais; m. Rene Henri Lambert, Oct. 18, 1972 (div. 1981); 1 child, Frederique. B.S. in Math., Lycee Pilote, 1968; M.B.A., U. V CNAM, Paris, 1975, M.S., 1976, Ph.D. in Computer Sci., 1978. Vice pres., mgr. SNCI Constrn. Co., Yerres, France, 1976-79; pres., chief exec. officer TGCI Service Bur., El Toro, Calif., 1979-82; regional mgr. S.D.&G. Software Co., San Jose, Calif., 1982-84, C.R.I. Software Co., San Jose, 1984—; chief fin. officer C.G.S., Inc., San Francisco, 1979-80, Vector Corp., Irvine, Calif., 1980-84, Schinus Corp., Irvine, 1982—. Charter mem. Write Your Congressman Club, Newport, 1980-85, Republican Senatorial Com., Washington, 1981—, Presdl. Task Force, Washington, 1981—; tchr. Catholic Sch. of Religion, Laguna Falls, Calif., 1981-84. Avocations: writing; travel; photography. Home: 12550 Lake Ave Lakewood OH 44107

LAMBERT, MARIE M., judge; b. Cirella Reggio Calabria, Italy; d. Nicola and Lucia (Bellasai) Macri; ed. Bklyn. Coll., N.Y.U.; m. Grady Lee Lambert, Aug. 18, 1946 (dec.); 1 son, Gregory L. Admitted to bar; mem. firm Chadbourne, Hunt, Jaeckle & Brown, 1944-46, Carroad & Carroad, 1946-49; individual practice, N.Y.C., 1949-74; partner Katz, Shandell, Katz Erasmous & Lambert, 1974-77; judge Surrogate's Ct. N.Y. County, 1978—; lectr. in field. Pres., Jr. Women's League; bd. dirs. Nyopia Research Found. Recipient awards Italian orgns.; Law Day award. Mem. Italian Execs. Am. (charter mem. dir.), St. Citizens Assn. (dir.), N.Y.C. Fedn. Women's Clubs, Women's Equity Action League, Women's Political Caucus, ABA, Nat. Coll. Probate Judges, Nat. Assn. Women Judges, N.Y. State Trial Lawyers Assn (past pres.), Met. Women's Bar, N.Y. Assn. Women Judges (v.p.), Am. Justinian Soc. Jurists, Nat. Probate Council, Am. Judges Assn., N.Y. Women's Bar Assn., Bklyn-Columbian Lawyers Assn., Internat. Fedn. Women Lawyers. Co-author: You May be Losing Your Inheritance. Home: 737 Park Ave New York NY 10021

LAMBERT, REBECCA FOTOUHI, broadcasting executive; b. Binghamton, N.Y., Jan. 31, 1947; d. Abol Hassan and Eleanor Margaret (Page) Fotouhi; student Williams Coll., 1968-69; B.A., Simmons Coll., 1969; Harvard U. Bus. Sch. Advanced Mgmt. Program, 1982. Vice pres., treas. Champlain Properties, Inc., Burlington, Vt., 1971-75; pres. Chardick Property, Inc., Southampton,

L.I., 1973-74, Chatelian, Ltd., 1973-74; staff asst. U.S. Rep. James Jeffords, 1975; adminstrv. aide Nat. Republic Senatorial Com., Washington, 1975-76; cons. Wallop for Senate campaign, 1976-77; chief of staff Senator Malcolm Wallop, Washington, 1977-80; with Reagan Transition Team, 1980; dep. asst. sec. Dept. Energy, Washington, 1981-82; assoc. dep. sec. Dept. Commerce, Washington, 1982-83; dir. corp. info. CBS, N.Y.C., 1983-84; pres. Lambert Assocs., Inc., govt. relations cons., 1984-85, Lambert Broadcasting, Inc., 1985—. Mem. Governor's Commn. on Status of Women, 1970-75, statewide chmn. presdl. campaign, 1972; pres. Bellevue Hosp. Assn., Inc.; trustee St. Stephens Sch., Rome; mem. Am. Council Young Polit. Leaders; treas. Am. PAC, 1979-80. Van Lear fellow, 1978. Presbyterian. Home: 410 E 57th St Apt 8F New York NY 10022

LAMBERT, SHEILA SONABEND, business information company executive; b. N.Y.C., Feb. 13, 1947; d. David Howard and Roslyn G. Sonabend; B.A. magna cum laude, Miami U., Oxford, Ohio, 1968; M.A. with honors, U. Mich., 1969; postgrad. N.Y. U., 1974; m. July 26, 1970; 1 son. Personnel asst. Dun & Bradstreet, Inc., N.Y.C., 1971-72, personnel mgr., 1972-74, dir. employee relations, 1974-75, dir. personnel, 1976-77, v.p. personnel, 1977-79; v.p. human resources Moody's Investors Service, N.Y.C., 1980-81, sr. v.p., pub., 1981—. Mem. Am. Soc. Personnel Adminstrs., N.Y. Credit Mgmt. Assn., Phi Beta Kappa. Office: Moody's Investors Service 99 Church St New York NY 10007

LAMBERT-KELLY, PIERRETTE EDNA, group personnel manager; b. Woonsocket, R.I., Sept. 20, 1950; d. Jean-Aime and Noella (Cote) L.; m. James J. Kelly, Oct. 12, 1975 (dec. Mar. 1979). B.A., R.I. Coll., 1972; M.A., Am. Internat. Coll., 1975. Cons., A Proudfoot Co., Chgo., 1973-75; trainer Raytheon Co., Andover, Mass., 1975; tng. mgr. Lechmere Sales, Cambridge, Mass., 1976; personnel mgr. Digital Equipment Corp., Maynard, Mass., Augusta, Maine, 1976—; mem. Assoc. Industries Maine Personnel Network, Augusta, 1983-86. Mem. planning com. Colby Coll., Waterville, Maine, 1981-83. Named Outstanding Woman in Bus., Augusta Bus. and Profl. Women, 1983. Mem. Am. Soc. Personnel Adminstrs., Am. Soc. Tng. and Devel., Kennebec Valley C. of C. (dir. 1983-86, chair personnel com. 1983-86, Dir. of Yr. award 1986). Roman Catholic. Home: 114 Potter Rd Lexington MA 02173 Office: Digital Equipment Corp 146 Main St Maynard MA 01754

LAMBERTSEN, JANET LOUISE, travel agency executive; b. Iowa Falls, Iowa, Mar. 6, 1942; d. Hillis Keith and Alice Minnie Elsie (Ott) Rodgers; m. Roland D. Lyman, Mar. 27, 1979 (div. 1983); children—Theresa, Curt. Grad. high sch., Alden, Iowa. Pvt. sec. Dial Fin., Des Moines, 1960-61; supr. State of Okla., Lawton, 1961; bookkeeper Citizen State Bank, Iowa Falls, 1961-63, travel cons. Allen Travel, Iowa Falls, 1969-80; owner, operator All Around Travel, Iowa Falls, 1980—. Mem. Iowa Falls C. of C. (bd. dirs. 1983—), Bus. and Profl. Women. Lutheran. Avocations: traveling; skiing; photography; sewing. Office: All Around Travel 617 Washington Ave Box 88 Iowa Falls IA 50126

LAMBERT-WALRAVEN, TERESA ANN, rental car company executive; b. Lafayette, Ala., Feb. 17, 1959; s. Terry Alan and Mary Ann (Combs) Lambert; m. Stephen Leslie Walraven, July 31, 1982. B.S. in Bus. Adminstrn., No. Ariz. U., 1981. Rental agt. Hertz Rent a Car, Phoenix, 1981-82, San Jose, 1982-83, sta. mgr., San Jose, 1983, ops. mgr., 1983-84, sr. sta. mgr., 1984-85, asst. city mgr., 1985, city mgr., 1985—. Mem. Nat. Assn. Female Execs. Republican. Avocations: reading; old movies; sight seeing; aerobics; weight lifting. Office: Hertz Corp 1617 Airport Blvd San Jose CA 95110

LAMBERTZ, ELIZABETH LOUISE, nursing educator; b. Wichita, Aug. 7, 1953; d. Laverne Nicholas and Mary Jane (Pracht) L. B.S.N., Creighton U., 1975; postgrad. U. Nebr. Med. Ctr., 1983—. Staff nurse, charge nurse St. Joseph's Hosp., Omaha, 1975-78; staff nurse Omaha Vis. Nurses, 1978-79; instr. nursing Meth. Hosp., Omaha, 1979-83, 84—. instr. nursing Coll. St. Mary, Omaha, 1983-84. Mem. steering com. Inst. Latin Am. Concern, Omaha, 1982-83, 84—, nursing profl. participant, 1982, 83, 84. Mem. Nat. Assn. Am. Coll. Ob-Gyn, Greater Omaha Childbirth Educators Assn., Transcultural Nursing Soc., Council on Nursing and Applied Anthropology, Smithsonian Inst., Joslyn Art Mus., Joslyn After Hours. Democrat. Roman Catholic. Office: Methodist Hosp 8301 W Dodge Rd Omaha NE 68114

LAMBIRD, MONA SALYER, lawyer; b. Oklahoma City, July 19, 1938; d. B.M., Jr., and Pauline A. Salyer; B.A., Wellesley Coll., 1960, LL.B., U. Md., 1963; m. Perry A. Lambird, July 30, 1960; children—Allison Thayer, Jennifer Salyer, Elizabeth Gard, Susannah Johnson. Admitted to Okla. bar, 1968, also admitted to practice before Ct. Appeals Md., Supreme Ct. Okla., U.S. Dist. Ct., U.S. Supreme Ct.; atty. civil div. Dept. Justice, Washington, 1963-65; individual practice law, Balt. and Oklahoma City, 1965-71; mem. firm Andrews, Davis, Legg & Bixler, Milsten & Murrah, Inc., Oklahoma City, 1971—; cons. World Orgn. of China Painters; adv. Oklahoma City Media Council. Profl. liaison com. City of Oklahoma City, 1974-79; mem. Okla. Election Bd., 1983—; mem. Hist. Preservation of Oklahoma City, Inc., 1970—; del. Oklahoma County and Okla. State Republican Party Conv., 1971—; women's com. Okla. Symphony Orch., legal adv., 1973—, bd. dirs., 1973—; bd. dirs. RSVP Oklahoma County, 1978—, pres., 1982-83; bd. dirs. Vis. Nurses Assn., 1983—. Mem. ABA, Md. Bar Assn., Okla. Bar Assn. (profl. responsibility tribunal 1984—), Okla. County Bar Assn., Jr. League Oklahoma City (dir. 1973-76, Okla. County and State Med. Assn. Aux. (fin. adv., dir.), Friends of Okla. County Libraries (dir. 1979—). Methodist (adminstrv. bd.). Club: Seven Colls. (pres. 1972-76). Editor, Briefcase of the Okla. County Bar Assn., 1976. Home: 419 NW 14th St Oklahoma City OK 73103 Office: 500 W Main Oklahoma City OK 73102

LAMBKIN, CLAIRE ALICE, librarian; b. Bklyn., Nov. 16, 1925; d. Clarence Vincent and Pauline Eliza (Rooney) L.; B.A., Bklyn. Coll., 1953; M.L.S., St. John's U., Jamaica, N.Y., 1957. Tchr. of library N.Y.C. Bd. Edn., 1953-57; adminstrv. librarian U.S. Army Europe-W.Ger., 1959-61; librarian Am. Mgmt. Assn., N.Y.C., 1961-69, chief librarian, 1969—. Mem. Spl. Libraries Assn. (chmn. info. tech. group N.Y. chpt. 1980-81), Am. Soc. Info. Sci., L.I. Hist. Soc. (counselor 1982-85), Bklyn. Coll. Alumni Assn. (dir.). Roman Catholic. Office: American Management Assn 135 W 50th St New York NY 10020

LAMBORN, JANICE BOND, nurse; b. San Francisco, Nov. 25, 1952; d. Willis L. and Betty J. (Anderson) Bond; m. Lee Reuel Lamborn, June 10, 1977; children—David Reuel, Katie Marie. B.S.N. magna cum laude, U. Utah, 1976. Staff nurse, pediatrics U. Utah Med. Ctr., Salt Lake City, 1976-77; community health nurse Bear River Health Dept, Logan, Utah, 1977; staff and charge nurse Logan Hosp., 1977-80; clin. instr. nursing Weber State Coll., Ogden, Utah, 1981-85; staff nurse Primary Children's Med. Ctr., Salt Lake City, 1985—. Mem. primary bd. West Jordan 30th Ward, Ch. Jesus Christ Latter-day Saints, 1985. Mem. Am. Nurses Assn., Utah Nurses Assn., Alpha Lambda Delta, Phi Kappa Phi. Home: 9291 S Brown Ave West Jordan UT 84084 Office: Infant Spl Care Unit Primary Children's Med Ctr 320 12th Ave Salt Lake City UT 84103

LAMBUTH, LUANN LYNN, public relations specialist, writer; b. Crawfordsville, Ind., June 3, 1959; d. Albert Edward Lambuth and Wilma Ann (Banta) Beauchamp. B.A. in Journalism and Forensic Studies, Ind. U., 1981. Reporting intern Rochester Democrat & Chronicla (N.Y.), summer 1980; pub. info. specialist Ind. State Police, Indpls., 1981-83; calendar editor Miami Today (Fla.), 1983—; pub. relations asst. Broward Gen. Med. Ctr., Ft. Lauderdale, Fla., 1983—. Research editor Indiana State Police History, 1983; contbr. article to mag. Ernie Pyle scholar, 1978. Mem. Women in Communications (chpt. pres. 1980-81, biography chmn. 1983-84), Gold Coast Hosp. Pub. Relations Soc. Democrat. Home: 3800 Van Buren St Hollywood FL 33021 Office: Broward Gen Med Ctr 1600 S Andrews Ave Fort Lauderdale FL 33316

LAMEL, LINDA HELEN, professional college administrator, lawyer; b. N.Y.C., Sept. 10, 1943; m. John E. Sands, July 31, 1977; 1 child, Diana Ruth. B.A. magna cum laude, Queens Coll., 1964; M.A., NYU, 1968; J.D., Bklyn. Law Sch., 1976. Bar: N.Y. 1977, U.S. Dist. Ct. (3d dist.) N.Y. 1977. Mgmt. analyst U.S. Navy, Bayonne, N.J., 1964-65; secondary sch. tchr. Farmingdale Pub. Sch., N.Y., 1965-73; curriculum specialist Yonkers Bd. Edn., N.Y., 1973-75; program dir. Office of Lt. Gov., Albany, N.Y., 1975-77; dep. supt. N.Y. State Ins. Dept., N.Y.C., 1977-83; pres., chief exec. officer Coll. of Ins., N.Y.C., 1983—; dir. First Women's Fin. Corp., Hollywood, Fla. Contbr. articles to profl. jours. Campaign mgr. lt. gov.'s primary race, N.Y. State, 1974. Mem. ABA (tort and ins. sect. com. chmn. 1985—), N.Y. State Bar Assn. (exec. com. ins. sect. 1984—), Phi Beta Kappa, Kappa Delta Pi, Phi Alpha Theta. Office: Coll of Ins 101 Murray St New York NY 10007

LAMM, CAROLYN BETH, lawyer; b. Buffalo, Aug. 22, 1948; d. Daniel John and Helen Barbara (Tatakis) L.; m. Peter Edward Halle, Aug. 12, 1972. B.S., SUNY Coll.-Buffalo, 1970; J.D., U. Miami (Fla.), 1973. Bar: Fla., 1973, D.C., 1976, N.Y. 1983. Trial atty. frauds sect. civil div. U.S. Dept. Justice, Washington, 1973-78, asst. chief comml. litigation sect. civil div., 1978, asst. dir., 1978-80; assoc. White & Case, Washington, 1980-84, ptnr., 1984—; mem. faculty Nat. Inst. Trial Advocacy. Fellow Am. Bar Found.; mem. Am. Law Inst., ABA (chmn. young lawyers div., sec. sect. of litigation, mem. nominating com.; del. from young lawyers div. to ho. of dels.), Fed. Bar Assn. (chmn. sect. on antitrust and trade regulation), Bar Assn. D.C. (bd. dirs., sec. 1985-86), D.C. Bar (steering comm. litigation div.), Women's Bar Assn. D.C., Womens Forum D.C. Democrat. Club: City Tavern (Washington). Contbr. articles to legal publs. Home: 2101 Connecticut Ave NW Washington DC 20008 Office: 1747 Pennsylvania Ave NW Suite 500 Washington DC 20006

LAMM, MARY ANN ELIZABETH, county official, adminstrator; b. East St. Louis, Ill., Dec. 21, 1938; d. Bernard Herman and Dorothy Ethel (Barton) Drummond; m. John Frederick Lamm, Jan. 25, 1958; children—Robert, Steven, Therese, Melissa. Clk., Village of Southern View, Springfield, Ill., 1961-72; town auditor Capital Twp., Springfield, 1972-76; recorder County of Sangamon, Ill., 1976—; mem. panel Ill. Farm Bur., Bloomington, 1980. Pres., sec. treas. Little Flower Sch.-Parish Law Council, Springfield, 1960-85; co-chmn. county govt. fund drive United Way, Springfield, 1977-81; bd. dirs. United Way, 1980-85, sec., 1984-85; precinct committeewoman Sangamon County Democratic Orgn., Springfield, 1968—. Named Boss of Yr., Am. Bus. Women's Assn., 1983, Woman of Yr., Am. Bus. Women's Assn., 1985. Mem. Ill. County Clks. and Recorders Assn. (legis chmn. 1985—), Ill. Assn. County Ofcls., Internat. Assn. Clks. and Recorders Elected Ofcls. and Treas., Assn. Records Mgrs. and Adminstrs. Clubs: Zonta, Women's. Avocations: volunteerism; sewing. Home: 21 Hyde Park Pl Springfield IL 62703 Office: Sangamon County Recorder 106 County Bldg Springfield IL 62701

LAMONICA, BAIBA, human resource executive; b. Peine, Germany, July 1, 1945; d. Eric Linne and Lucija (Stolcers) Pulins; m. James Brewer, Sept. 1964 (div. 1970); 1 child, Laura. Student Consol. Bus. Coll., Ind., 1968, U. Calif.-Berkeley, 1973-78. With United Vintners, Inc., San Francisco, 1973-77; dir. pension and benefits Falstaff Brewing Corp., San Francisco, 1977-78; corp. sr. compensation and benefits analyst Crowley Maritime Corps., 1978-80; mgr. corp. human resources Am. Forest Products Co., San Francisco, 1980-82; mgr. human resources Heublein Wines, San Francisco, 1983-84; project leader compensation Am. Savs. and Loan, Stockton, Calif., 1984—. Mem. Am. Latvian Assn., Balt., 1985-86. Mem. Am. Compensation Assn., Am. Soc. Personnel Adminstrs., Women's Assn. of Allied Beverage Industries. Republican. Lutheran/Presbyterian. Avocations: martial arts; stamps, snow skiing; swimming. Office: Am Savs & Loan 11 S San Joaquin Stockton CA 95207

LAMONT, ALICE, accountant, consultant; b. Houston, July 19; d. Harold and Bessie Bliss (Knight) L. B.Sc., Mont. State U.; M.B.A. in Taxation, Golden Gate U., 1982. Tchr. London Central High Sch., 1971-80; acct. Signetics, Sunnyvale, Calif., 1980-82, Metcalf, Frix & Co., Atlanta, 1983-84; propr. Alice Lamont Ltd., 1985—. Mem. AAUW (life), Ga. Soc. C.P.A.s. (assoc.), EDP Auditors, Inst. Internal Auditors, English Speaking Union. Episcopalian. Club: Atlanta Woman's.

LAMONT, BRIDGET LATER, librarian, consultant; b. Evanston, Ill., Nov. 13, 1948; d. George Phillip and Margaret (Behrens) Later; m. Thomas R. Lamont, Mar. 8, 1947; 1 child, Michael Thomas. B.A., Clarke Coll., 1970; M.S., U. Ill., 1972. Asst. dir. children's services Champaign Pub. Library (Ill.), 1971-72; cons. Ill. State Library, Springfield, 1972-78, assoc. dir. library devel., 1978-81, dep. dir., 1981-83, dir., 1983—. Contbr. chpts. to books. Mem. ALA, Ill. Library Assn., Beta Phi Mu. Roman Catholic. Office: Ill State Library Centennial Bldg Springfield IL 62756

LAMONT, FRANCES STILES, state legislator; b. Rapid City, S.D., June 10, 1914; d. Frederick Bailey and Frances (Kenney) Stiles; m. William Mather Lamont, 1937 (dec.); children—William Stiles, Nancy, Peggy, Frederick. B.A., U. Wis., 1935, M.A., 1936. Mem. staff McCalls mag., N.Y.C., 1936-37; vice-chmn. Gov.'s Commn. on Status of Women, 1964-73; chmn. Gov.'s Adv. Council on Aging, 1967-73; mem. S.D. State Senate from 3d Dist., 1975—. Named S.D. Mother of Yr., 1974. Mem. DAR, AAUW, LWV, Phi Beta Kappa, Kappa Alpha Theta. Republican. Episcopalian. Office: SD State Capitol Bldg Pierre SD 57501*

LAMONT, ROSETTE CLEMENTINE, foreign language and literature educator, writer, translator; b. Paris; came to U.S., 1941, naturalized, 1946; d. Alexandre and Loudmilla (Lamont) L.; m. Frederick Hyde Farmer, Aug. 9, 1969. B.A., Hunter Coll., 1947; M.A., Yale U., 1948, Ph.D., 1954. Tutor Romance langs. Queens Coll., CUNY, 1950-54, instr., 1954-61, asst. prof., 1961-64, assoc. prof., 1965-67, prof., 1967—; mem. doctoral faculty French and comparative lit. CUNY, 1968—; State Dept. envoy Scholar Exchange Program, USSR, 1974; research fellow, 1976; lectr. Alliance Francaise, Maison Francaise of NYU. Author: the Life and Works of Boris Pasternak, 1964; De Vive Voix, 1971; Ionesco, 1973; The Two Faces of Ionesco, 1978; contbr. to various books; mem. editorial bd. Centerpoint; contbg. editor Performing Arts Jour.; contbr. articles to profl. jours., Columbia Dictionary of Modern European Lit. Decorated chevalier, then officier des Palmes Academiques, officier Arts et Lettres (France); Guggenheim fellow, 1972-74; Rockefeller Found. humanities fellow, 1983-84. Mem. MLA, Am. Soc. Theatre Research, Internat. Brecht Soc., P.E.N., Phi Beta Kappa, Sigma Tau Delta, Pi Delta Phi. Club: Yale. Home: 260 W 72d St New York NY 10023 also 51 W Chester St Nantucket MA 02554 Office: Dept Romance Languages Queens Coll CUNY Flushing NY 11367 also Grad Center CUNY 33 W 42d St New York NY 10036

LAMONTAGNE, NANCY HARTSHORN, technology research and automotion specialist; b. Gardner, Mass., June 14, 1949; d. Charles and Pauline Flora (Blouin) Hartshorn; B.S. in Math. and Computer Sci., U. Mass., 1971; M.Mgmt., Simmons Coll., 1981; m. Stephen Paul Lamontagne, Mar. 1, 1980. Project evaluation satellite specialist M.I.T. Lincoln Lab., Bedford, Mass., 1972-74; mfg. systems analyst USM Corp., 1974-77; fin. and mfg. systems sr. programmer Digital Equipment Corp., 1977-80; mgmt. info. systems mgr. The Gillette Co., Andover, Mass., 1980-84; corp. mgr. tech. research and planning Sanders Assocs., Inc., Nashua, N.H., 1984—; cons. data processing and office mgmt.; lectr. Simmons Coll., Network for Exempt Women at Sanders. Commr. town dist., 1984-86; vol. N.H. Spl. Olympics, 1986; mem. computer adv. bd. St. Anselm's Coll. Recipient Disting. Woman Leader award Southern N.H., 1984. Mem. Am. Mgmt. Assn., Data Processing Mgmt. Assn. Home: 15 Viau Rd Windham NH 03087 Office: Sanders Assocs Daniel Webster Hwy S Nashua NH 03061

LAMONTAGNE, ROCHELLE ANNE, resort company executive; b. Detroit, May 10, 1958; d. Rock Joseph and Marjorie (Roddy) Lee. B.A. in Mktg. and Advt., Mich. State U., 1980. Sales mgr. Vail Resort Assocs., Colo., 1981-84; dir. sales The Lodge at Vail, 1984-85; sales mgr. Walt Disney World, Orlando, Fla., 1985—; cons., researcher, Vail, 1985. Author: (sales guide) How To Conduct a Familiarization Trip, 1985. Recipient Young Career Woman award Bus. and Profl. Women, 1982, named Career Woman for State of Colo., 1983. Mem. Meeting Planners Internat., Nat. Assn. Female Execs., Am. Advt. Fedn., Vail Hotel and Mktg. Mgmt. Republican. Roman Catholic. Avocations: golf; reading; skiing. Home: PO Box 22565 Lake Buena Vista FL 32820 Office: Walt Disney World Sales PO Box 40 Lake Buena Vista FL 32820

LAMPERT, ELEANOR VERNA, employment development specialist; b. Porterville, Calif., Mar. 23; d. Ernest Samuel and Violet Edna (Watkins) Wilson; student in bus., fin. Porterville Jr. Coll., 1977-78; grad. Anthony Real Estate Sch., 1971; student Laguna Sch. of Art, 1972, U. Calif.-Santa Cruz, 1981; m. Robert Mathew Lampert, Aug. 21, 1935; children—Sally Lu Winton, Lary Lampert, Carol R. John. Bookkeeper, Porterville (Calif.) Hosp., 1956-71; real estate sales staff Ray Realty, Porterville, 1973; sec. Employment Devel. Dept., State of Calif., Porterville, 1973-83, orientation and tng. specialist CETA employees, 1976-80. Author: Black Bloomers and Han-ga-ber, 1986. Sec., Employer Adv. Group, 1973-80; mem. U.S. Senatorial Bus. Adv. Bd., 1981-82, 83-84; charter mem. Presdl. Republican Task Force, 1981-86; mem. Rep. Congl. Com.; mem. Friends of Porterville Library; vol. Calif. Hosp. Recipient Merit Cert., Gov. Pat Brown, State of Calif., 1968. Mem. Lindsay Olive Growers, Sunkist Orange Growers, Am. Kennel Club, Internat. Assn. Personnel in Employment Security, Nat. Wildlife Fedn., Nat. Rifle Assn., Friends of Porterville Library. Clubs: Internat. Sporting and Leisure; Porterville Women's. Address: 1180 Putnam St Porterville CA 93257

LAMPKIN, BARBARA JO, medical laboratory systems computer analyst; b. Lynn, Mass., Nov. 24, 1947; d. George James and Ella Margaret (Lunsford) L. B.S. in Med. Tech., Woman's Coll. of Ga., 1969; postgrad. Boston U., 1978—. Registered med. technologist Am. Soc. Clin. Pathologists. Med. technologist Med. Ctr. of Central Ga., Macon, 1969-71; hematology head tech. Coliseum Park Hosp., Macon, 1971-74; hematology chief tech. Boston City Hosp., 1974-76; satellite lab. supr. Smith-Klein Labs., Waltham, Mass., 1976-77; blood bank technologist ARC, Boston, 1977-78; hematology chief tech. Bioran Med. Labs., Cambridge, Mass., 1978-84; computer analyst The Mumps Collaborative, Newton, Mass., 1984—. Campaign vol. Democratic Nat. Com., Mass., 1980—; bd. dirs. Mass. Choice, Boston, 1985—, vol., 1983—; mem. Nat. Abortion Rights Action League, Washington, 1974—. Mem. Am. Soc. Clin. Pathologists (affiliate), Nat. Assn. Exec. Women. Roman Catholic. Club: Boston Beanstalk Tall (bd. dirs. 1984—, pub. relations chmn. 1984—). Avocations: gourmet cuisine; skiing; travel. Office: The Mumps Collaborative 797 Washington St Newton MA 02160

LAMPROS, ANGELIQUE, educator; b. West Orange, N.J.; d. Nicholas and Vasiliki William (Kyriakarakos) Lampros; B.A., Montclair State Coll., 1958; M.A., George Washington U., 1973; postgrad. Seton Hall U., 1973-74, Fordham U., 1970-71, Kean Coll., 1960-63, Drakes Bus. Sch., 1955-56, Berlitz Sch. Lang., 1962-63. Tchr., Emerson High Sch., Union City, N.J., 1958-61; tchr. Jefferson Sch., Maplewood, N.J., 1961-83; acting prin., 1971-81, chmn. faculty adv. bd., 1971-72; basic skills improvement coordinator Seth Boyden Sch., 1983; congl. legis. aide to Congressman Nicholas Galifianakis, Washington, 1972-73; chemistry lab. asst. Montclair State Coll., N.J., 1954-55. Supt. Religious project, Greek Orthodox Archdiocese of N. and S. Am., 1964-65; bd. dirs. ARC, 1967-69; chmn. bd. dirs. Met. Greek Chorale, Inc., 1979—; chmn. community study com. Middle States Elem. Evaluation, Maplewood, 1983—. Mem. N.J. Edn. Assn., NEA, Nat. Assn. Female Execs., South Orange-Maplewood Edn. Assn. (dir. fund raising, scholarships 1970-73, chmn. profl. improvement 1981-82), Hellenic Heritage Found. Greek Orthodox. Clubs: Daus. of Penelope.

LAMSON, EVONNE VIOLA, computer software company executive, computer consultant; b. Ithaca, Mich., July 8, 1946; d. Donald and Mildred (Perdew) Guild; m. James E. Lamson, Nov. 2, 1968; 1 child, Lillie D. Assoc. in Math., Washtenaw Community Coll., Ypsilanti, Mich., 1977; student Eastern Mich. U., 1977—. Data base mgr. ERIM, Ann Arbor, Mich., 1978-81; mgr. product services Comshare, Ann Arbor, 1981—; founder, pres. G & L Consultants, Brighton, Mich., 1982—. Study leader Brighton Wesleyan Ch., 1981—; program dir. Wesleyan Womens Assn. of Brighton, 1983—. Mem. Am. Mgmt. Assn., Nat. Assn. Female Execs., Fairbanks Family of Am. Avocations: skiing; speaking; reading. Home: 7375 Cedardale St Brighton MI 48116 Office: Comshare 3001 S State St Ann Arbor MI 48104

LANCASTER, CINDY HALLMAN, collectables retailer; b. Aiken, S.C., Oct. 24, 1952; d. La-Verne Keller and Vivian Margarie (Johnson) Hallman; m. Glenn Wilmont Lancaster, July 1, 1972; children—Jason Travis, Tiffany Brooke. A.S., Orangeburg Jr. Coll., 1972. Sec. to mgr. Rogers, Gregory & Brigman, Barnwell, S.C., 1973-76; relief postmaster, Olar, S.C., 1980-83; owner, mgr. Palmetto Collectables, Norway, S.C., 1983—. Fund raiser Multiple Sclerosis, Govan, S.C., 1982-83, Muscular Dystrophy, 1980-82. Baptist. Clubs: Garden, Lions. Avocations: needlework; reading; walking. Home: Rt 1 Box 106 Olar SC 29843 Office: Rt 1 Box 87 C Norway SC 29113

LANCASTER, ELAINE LAKIN, banker; b. Hennessey, Okla., July 20, 1935; d. Linley R. Krebs and Violet Elma Krebs Benson; B.S., U. Md., 1963; m. William Duval Lancaster, Apr. 30, 1977; children from previous marriage—Cameron Lakin, Jeffrey Lakin. Loan officer Am. City Bank, 1970-72; consumer fin. officer 1st Western Bank, 1972-73; regional loan officer Calif. Fed. Savs. and Loan, Los Angeles, 1973-77; mgr. consumer loans Coast Fed. Savs. and Loan, Hawthorne, Calif., 1977-78; regional consumer loan officer Glendale Fed. Savs. & Loan, Downey, Calif., 1978-83, sr. loan officer, Riverside, Calif., 1983-86, mgr. student loan OFF. Mary Hardin Baylor Coll. scholar, 1955: Ford Found. fellow, 1965-66. Mem. Savs. and Loan League, Am. Inst. Banking, Nat. Notary Assn., AAUW, Coast Mgmt., YWCA, NOW. Democrat. Club: Toastmistresses. Office: Glendale Fed Savs & Loan 401 N Brand Ave Glendale CA

LANCASTER, MARGARET GUTIERREZ, mathematician; b. Chapel Hill, N.C., July 27, 1938; d. Andrew and Margaret (Nesbitt) Gutierrez; m. Leslie Eugene Lancaster, Feb. 12, 1966. Mathematician, ops. evaluation group MIT, Pentagon, Washington, 1957-59; mathematician Analytic Services Inc., Baileys Crossroads, Va., 1959-63, Roland F. Beers, Alexandria, Va., 1963-65, Environ. Research Corp., Alexandria, 1965—. Active local chpts. Cancer Soc., Heart Assn., Diabetes Assn. Mem. Sigma Alpha Iota. Methodist. Home: 5812 Lamont Dr New Carrollton MD 20784

LANCASTER, SALLY RHODUS, foundation executive; b. Gladewater, Tex., June 28, 1938; d. George Lee and Milly Maria (Meadows) Rhodus; B.A., So. Methodist U., 1960, M.A., 1979; Ph.D., East Tex. State U., 1983; m. Olin C. Lancaster, Jr., Dec. 23, 1960; children—Olin C. III, George Charles, Julie Meadows. Tchr. English, Tex. pub. schs., 1960-61, 78-79; exec. v.p., grants adminstr. Meadows Found., Inc., Dallas, 1979—, also trustee, dir. Trustee So. Meth. U., 1980—; bd. dirs. East Tex. State U. Found., Housing and Econ. Devel. Corp. of Dallas, Tex. Interscholastic League Found. Mem. Am. Personnel and Guidance Assn., Conf. S.W. Founds. (sec.), Council on Founds. (profl. devel. com.), Phi Beta Kappa (assoc. pres. 1980-82, nat com. on assns. 1983-85), Kappa Delta Pi. Presbyterian. Office: 2922 Swiss Ave Dallas TX 75204

LANCASTER, SHARON BOATWRIGHT, music educator, pianist; b. Valdosta, Ga., Feb. 24, 1942; d. Clifford Eugene and Margaret Louise (Shaw) B.; m. John E. Lancaster (div.); children—Laurie Lancaster Swift, John Kevin. A.B. in Music, Valdosta State Coll., 1963; M.A. in Edn., Eastern Ky. U., 1973; cert. Yamaha Music Schs. Am., 1976. Instr., Cumberland Coll., Williamsburg, Ky., 1971-75; music dir. First Baptist Ch., Williamsburg, 1973-75; owner, dir. Music Lab., Valdosta, Ga., 1976-85; instr. music Valdosta State Coll., 1977—; pianist Lee St. Bapt. Ch., Valdosta, 1984—; lit. meet adjudicator Southeastern Assn. Ind. Schs., 1982, 84. Named to Outstanding Young Women Am., U.S. Jaycees, 1974. Mem. Music Tchrs. Nat. Assn., Ga. Music Tchrs. Assn. (cert., v.p. publicity and editor newsletter 1981-82), South Ga. Music Tchrs. Assn. (pres. 1978-79), Sigma Alpha Chi, Alpha Chi. Democrat. Baptist. Avocations: sewing; gardening. Home: 1818 Northside Dr Valdosta GA 31602

LANCE, JEANNE LOUISE, editor, writer; b. Morristown, N.J., May 31, 1945; d. LeRoy Hildebrant and Helen Glenda (Hoffman) L.; m. Peter John Holland, Nov. 18, 1975. A.B., Bryn Mawr Coll., 1967; M.A., U. Toronto, 1971. Cert. tchr., Calif. Editorial asst. Worth Pubs., N.Y.C., 1968-73; editor Far West Lab. for Ednl. Research and Devel., San Francisco, 1974-80, Nat. Assn. Social Workers, N.Y.C., 1981—; assoc. Writers in Performance, Manhattan Theatre Club, N.Y.C., 1980-85. Author poems, short stories. Fellow Squaw Valley Community Writers; mem. Poets and Writers. Democrat. Home: 25 Carlin St Norwalk CT 06851 Office: Nat Assn Social Workers 257 Park Ave S New York NY 10010

LANCE, KAREN HUFFMAN, accountant; b. Poplar Bluff, Mo., Mar. 13, 1958; d. Amos J. and Audrey Maxine (Canady) Huffman; m. John Steward Lance, Sept. 2, 1982; children—John Tyler, Karen Kourtney. A.A., Three Rivers Community Coll., 1978; B.S. in Acctg., Ark. State U., 1980. Office asst. Kneibert Clinic, Poplar Bluff, 1972-80; internal auditor State of Mo., St. Louis, 1980-81; staff acct. James V. Stallings Co., Inc., Sikeston, Mo., 1981-82; asst. corp. controller Health Care Affiliates, Inc., Dexter, Mo., 1982-83; controller Huffman, Inc., Poplar Bluff, 1983—; ptnr. Lance Farms, Poplar Bluff, 1982—; acct. Davis Constrn. Co., Poplar Bluff, 1984—. Mem. Am. Soc. Women Accts., Nat. Assn. Female Execs., Bus. and Profl. Women's Club. Baptist. Home: Route 9 Box 108 Poplar Bluff MO 63901 Office: Huffman Inc 1550 Black River Industrial Park Rd Poplar Bluff MO 63901

LAND, GERALDINE MARIE, legal assistant; b. Tucson, Apr. 9, 1948; d. Jack B. and Pauline Elizabeth (Goebel) Pittman; 1 dau., Lindsay Marie. Owner;

Geri Land Assocs. Paralegal Services. Vice pres., sec., then pres. Casao Presidio Homeowners Assn., 1981-84. Mem. Nat. Assn. Legal Secs., Ariz. Assn. Legal Secs. (1st v.p. 1973-74, legal edn. chmn. 1977-78, editor AALS Abstract 1970-72, 73-74), Tucson Legal Secs. Assn. (sec. 1971-72, v.p. 1972-73, pres. 1973-74, Legal Sec. of Yr. 1973), Tucson Assn. Legal Assts. (pres. 1979-81; nat. liaison chmn. 1981-83), Nat. Assn. Legal Assts. (charter mem., nominations and elections chmn. 1975-76, regional dir. 1975-78, public relations chmn. 1978-79, chmn. law office mgmt. splty. sect. 1979-80, credentials chmn. 1979-80). Democrat. Baptist. Home: 3053 N Sparkman Tucson AZ 85716 Office: 3131 N Country Club Suite 206 Tucson AZ 85716

LAND, MARY ELIZABETH, author, composer; b. Benton, La., Sept. 28, 1908; d. Thomas T. and Elizabeth (Langford) Land; student Gulf Park Coll., Gulfport, Miss., 1924-25, Cheyney Trent Sch. Poetry, Calif., 1937, U. Chgo., 1938; m. Edward Timothy Kelly, 1925; 1 dau., Patricia Kelly Stevens; m. 2d, George T. Lock, 1931; 1 son, George T. Lock-Land. Mem. staff La. Conservation Rev., La. Dept. Conservation, New Orleans, 1940-41, Miss. Valley Sportsman, 1948, So. Outdoors Mag., Atlanta, 1959, 60, 61, West Bank Guide, New Orleans, 1962, Sportsman's News, Hot Springs, Ark., 1960; author (with Arthur Van Pelt) syndicated column, Outdoors South, for weekly newspapers Miss., La., 1947, 48; feature writer Fisherman Mag., 1954, R X Sports and Travel Mag., 1971, Down South Mag., 1964, Natchitoches Times, 1970. Named Co-Poet Laureate for Tenn., 1941; recipient Blue Ribbon award Gulf Coast br. Nat. League Am. Pen Women, Merit certificate Nash Motor Co., 1953, 1st Pl. award La. Press Assn., 1969-70, Merit certificate and 2 Keys to City Mayor New Orleans, 1954, Outstanding Contbn. certificate La. Soc. Colonial Dames, 1971, certificate Am. Bicentennial Research Inst., 1973. Mem. Nat. League Am. Pen Women (past br. pres.), Nat. Fedn. Am. Press Women, La. Press Women, Outdoor Writers Assn. Am., La. Outdoor Writers Assn. (charter), Fedn. Musicians. Author: Shadows of the Swamp (poetry), 1940, Mary Land's Louisiana Cookery, 1954 (So. Books award 1956), New Orleans Cuisine, 1968 (2d pl. award Fedn. Am. Press Women 1969), Abode (poetry), 1972, Dreams (poetry), 1977; contbr. conservation articles to mags., poetry to anthologies; composer: You Hang In My Heart, 1959, As Strange As You Are, 1959, Drink Deep, 1959, Piano Cho Cho Zarzosa, 1959, Voice-Allehandra Allegra, 1959. Address: 1314 Williams Ave Natchitoches LA 71457

LANDA, BETH KIM, psychologist; b. Manhattan, N.Y., Oct. 18, 1954; d. Jay Myron and Ruth (Kaplan) L.; m. Steven Goldstein, May 19, 1985. B.A. cum laude, Hofstra U., 1975, M.A. with distinction (Univ. fellow), 1977, Ph.D., 1980. Teaching asst. Hofstra U., 1975-76, research asst./assoc. 1977-78, mem. assoc. faculty, internship supr., 1980-83; biostatistician divs. psychiatry and medicine L.I. Jewish/Hillside Med. Center, Glen Oaks, N.Y., 1978-84; instr. child psychology, mem. adj. faculty C.W. Post Center, L.I. U., Greenvale, N.Y., 1982; estimating research analyst Avon Products Inc., N.Y.C., 1984—. Mem. Psi Chi (pres. chpt. 1974-75). Home: 235 Lawrence Ln Glen Cove NY 11542 Office: Avon Products Inc 9 W 57th St New York NY

LANDAU, DOROTHY RUTH, local government executive; b. Staten Island, N.Y., Oct. 5, 1957; d. Robert August and Dorothy Faith (Schaut) L. A.S. in Applied Sci., SUNY-Farmingdale, 1977; B.S. in Biology, Wagner Coll., 1979. Sci. tchr. Bais Yaakov, Staten Island, 1979-81; dental asst. Dr. Marvin Freeman, Staten Island, 1981-82; office mgr. Dr. Bennett C. Fidlow, Staten Island, 1982-85; polit. aide to S.I. Borough Pres., 1985—. Environ. chmn. S.I. League for Better Govt., 1984—; pres. Tottenville Improvement Council Inc., Staten Island, 1985—; founder, pres. environ. group S.I.L.E.N.T., Staten Island, 1985; 2d v.p. 123d Community Council, Staten Island, 1986; social chmn. S. Shore Democratic Club; founding mem. Friends of Clay Pit Pond Park; mem. Protectors of Pine Oak Woods Inc., Roserio Alliotta Dem. Club, Dem. Orgn. of Richmond. Mem. Nat. Assn. Female Execs., Nat. Fedn. Bus. and Profl. Women. Roman Catholic. Avocations: photography; sports; ceramics; youth programs. Home: 406 Sleight Ave Staten Island NY 10307 Office: Staten Island Borough Pres Office Borough Hall Staten Island NY 10301

LANDAU, EDYTHE, motion picture production executive; b. Wilkes-Barre, Pa., July 15, 1927; d. Harry and Rose (Zatcoff) Rudolph; B.A., Wilkes Coll., 1948; J.D., U. West Los Angeles, 1981; m. Ely A. Landau, Mar. 13, 1959; children—Jon, Tina, Kathy. Exec. v.p. Nat. Telefilm Assocs., Inc., 1953-60, Landau Prodns., 1960-70, Am. Film Theatre, 1970-75; producer, v.p. Edie & Ely Landau, Inc., Los Angeles, 1978—; producer films: Hopscotch, Beatlemania, The Chosen, The Holcroft Covenant; for TV, The Deadly Game, Separate Tables, Mr. Johnson and Mr. Halpern; admitted to Calif. bar, 1981;produced award-winning films including: Long Days Journey Into Night, 1962, The Pawnbroker, 1965, King - A Filmed Record, Montgomery to Memphis (Oscar nomination best documentary). 1970; Man in the Glass Booth 1975; The Chosen (best picture Montreal World Film Festival), 1981. Mem. Acad. Motion Pictures Arts and Scis., Women in Film, ABA, Calif. State Bar Assn., Beverly Hills Bar Assn.

LANDAZURI, COLLEEN ANN, public health nurse; b. Fond du Lac, Wis., Sept. 8, 1950; d. James Edward and Elizabeth Ann (Masloff) Flood; B.S. in Nursing, Marquette U., 1972, postgrad. (fed. nurse traineeship grant, 1976-77), 1976-77; m. Gabriel Landazuri, Oct. 26, 1974; children—Dario James, Patrick Xavier, Alexander Gabriel. Staff nurse Milw. Health Dept., 1972-76, dist. supr., 1976-80, program dir. prenatal edn. and assessment program, 1980—; coordinator-cons. interdisciplinary dental-nursing student assessment program Marquette U. Dental Sch., 1977. Mem. Milw. Public Sch. Critical Health Problems Curriculum Adv. Com., 1981-86, co-chmn., 1982-85; mem. Milw. Healthy Baby Coalition, Greater Milw. Com. Concerned with Unmarried Parents Services, 1985, co-chmn., 1986; mem. March of Dimes Adv. Com.; mem. Family Hosp. Teen Pregnancy Service Adv. Council, Milw. Pub. Sch.-Sch. Age Parent Health Adv. Comm. Mem. Orgn. Twin-Blessed Mothers (sec. 1984), Sigma Theta Tau. Roman Catholic. Club: North Shore Jr. Woman's. Office: 841 N Broadway Suite 228 Milwaukee WI 53202

LANDBERG, ANN LAUREL, psychotherapist; b. Chgo., June 20, 1926; d. Carl Ryno and Ebba Sadie Elvira (Engstrom) Granlund; m. Harry Morton Landberg, Apr. 1, 1953 (dec. Feb. 1967); stepchildren—Rosabel, Marcene. R.N., Swedish Hosp. Sch. Nursing, Seattle, 1948. Asst. head nurse Halcyon Hosp., Seattle, 1948; doctor's asst. Office of H.M. Landberg, M.D., Seattle, 1948-50, psychotherapist, 1950-67; pvt. practice psychotherapy, Seattle, 1967—; cons. Good Shepherd Sch. for Disturbed Girls, Seattle, 1954—, bd. dirs., 1954-60. Mem. Am. Psychotherapy Assn., King County Med. Aux., Stevens Hosp. Aux. (life), Swedish Hosp. Alumni (pres. 1952-53), Nat. Council Jewish Women, City of Hope, Edmonds Arts Assn. (life patron), Seattle Forensic Inst. (charter). Club: Swedish (Seattle). Home: 16900 Talbot Rd Edmonds WA 98020 Office: 1007 Spring St Seattle WA 98104

LANDER, KATHLEEN GELCHER, writer, editor; b. Los Angeles, Apr. 24, 1923; d. Joseph and Grayce Clara (McCormick) Gelcher; B.A., U. So. Calif., 1944; postgrad. U. Calif.-Irvine, 1972-73, N.Y.U., 1977; m. Robert Frank Lander, Sept. 6, 1947 (div. 1974); children—Jeffrey, Richard, Lisa, Marc. Reporter, editor, San Marino (Calif.) Tribune, Inglewood (Calif.) Daily News, Rodgers-McDonald Newspapers, Los Angeles, 1944-47; owner public relations co., Inglewood, 1947-49; west coast editor High Fidelity Trade News, 1972-74; editor Consumer Electronic Product News, N.Y.C., 1974-77; free-lance writer-editor consumer and trade publs., N.Y.C., 1977—; sr. editor Leisure Time Electronics; editor LTE Reports, 1980-85. Founding mem., pres. LWV, Santa Ana, Calif., 1961-63, chmn. Orange County Council, LWV, 1958; bd. dirs. Orange County Community Action Council, 1964-69. Mem. Women in Communications, Inc., Mortar Bd. Alumnae of So. Calif. (pres. 1945-46), LWV. Home: 144 E 36th St Apt 1-C New York NY 10016

LANDERHOLM, ELIZABETH JANE, educator; b. Oak Park, Ill., Jan. 13, 1941; d. Daniel R. and Dorothy Thomkins (Ellis) LaBar; B.A., DePauw U., 1963; M.S.T., U. Chgo., 1966; Ed.D., No. Ill. U., 1980; m. Wayne A. Landerholm, June 6, 1964; 1 son, Arthur Scott. Group worker Marcy Newberry Center, Chgo., 1963-64; youth counselor Ill. State Employment Service, Chgo., 1964-65; tchr. Chgo. Public Schs., 1966-69; co-founder, dir. Ednl. Service Pool, 1971-72; mem. faculty Nat. Coll. Edn., Chgo., 1972-80, dir. student teaching, 1974-80, ednl. coordinator early childhood field based program, 1975-80; asst. prof. early childhood edn. Roosevelt U., Chgo., 1980—; cons. Theraplay Inst., Chgo.; coordinator Project RHISE/Outreach, Rockford, Ill., 1984—. Mem. Ind. Precinct Orgn., Chgo. Roosevelt U. Dean's grantee, 1980-81, 81-82. Mem. Nat. Assn. Edn. Young Children, Council Exceptional Children, Pi Lambda Theta. Mem. Ch. of Christ. Author articles and monographs. Home: 325 N Humphrey Oak Park IL 60302 Office: 430 S Michigan Ave Chicago IL 60605

LANDERS, ANGELA MAY, real estate salesperson; b. Tampa, Fla., May 14, 1949; d. Michael Dominic and Anne Marie (Crescenzi) Testa; m. William Eugene Landers, Aug. 3, 1968; children—Anita Anne, Erik Michael. B.S., U. Tampa, 1970; bus. degree Patricia Stevens Sch., Tampa, 1971; student State of Fla. Mortgage Brokers, 1982-84; cert. real estate Hillsborough Coll., 1985. Mortgage broker Pioneer Savs., Tampa, 1976-85; real estate salesperson J. Matthews, Tampa, 1985-86; prin. Angela M. Landers, Tampa, 1986—; cons. Union Mortgage, Tampa, 1979-83; assoc. Fla. Real Estate Salesman's Rev. Outline, 1985. Mem. Real Estate, Inc. (sec. 1984-85), Mortgage Brokers, Inc. (v.p. 1976-85), Nat. Assn. Female Execs. (local bd. dirs. 1983-86), Tampa Bd. Realtors. Democrat. Roman Catholic. Avocations: swimming; tennis; baseball. Office: PO Box 15998 Tampa FL 33684

LANDERS, ANN (ESTHER P. LEDERER), columnist; b. Sioux City, Iowa, July 4, 1918; d. Abraham B. and Rebecca (Rushall) Friedman; student Morningside Coll., 1936-39, L.H.D., 1964; Hum.D., Wilberforce (Ohio) Coll., 1972; L.H.D., U. Cin., 1974; L.H.D., Am. Coll. Greece, Deree-Pierce Coll., 1975, LL.D., 1979; hon. degrees Meharry Med. Coll., 1981, Jacksonville U., 1983, St. Leo Coll., 1984, Fla. Internat. U., 1984, Med. Coll. Pa., 1984, New Eng. Coll., 1985, U. Wis.-Madison, 1985; m. Jules W. Lederer, July 2, 1939 (div. 1975); 1 dau., Margo (Mrs. Ken Howard). Syndicated columnist News Am. Syndicate, Chgo., 1955—; pres. Eppie Co., Inc., Chgo. Chmn. Eau Claire (Wis.) Gray-Lady Corps, A.R.C., 1947-53; chmn. Minn.-Wis. council Anti-Defamation League, 1945-49; asst. Wis. chmn. Nat. Found. Infantile Paralysis, 1951-53; hon. nat. chmn. 1963 Tb Christmas Seal Campaign; bd. sponsors Mayo Clinic, 1970; mem. sponsors com. Mayo Found., nat. adv. bd. Dialogue for the Blind, 1972; adv. com. on better health services AMA. County chmn. Democratic Party of Eau Claire. Bd. dirs. Rehab. Inst. Chgo.; nat. bd. dirs. Am. Cancer Soc.; vis. com. bd. overseers Harvard Med. Sch.; trustee Hereditary Disease Found., Menninger Found., Nat. Dermatology Found., Am. Coll. Greece, Deree-Pierce Coll., Athens, Meharry Med. Sch.; adv. bd. Nat. Cancer Inst. Recipient award Nat. Family Service Assn., 1965; Adolf Meyer award Assn. for Mental Health, N.Y., 1965; Pres.'s Citation and nat. award Nat. Council on Alcoholism, 1966, 2d nat. award, 1975; Golden Stethoscope award Ill. Med. Soc., 1967; Humanitarianism award Internat. Lions Club, 1967; plaque of honor Am. Friends of Hebrew U., 1968; Gold Plate award Acad. Achievement, 1969; Nat. Service award Am. Cancer Soc., 1971; Robert T. Morse award Am. Psychiat. Assn., 1972; plaque recognizing establishment of chair in chem. immunology Weizmann Inst., 1974; Jane Addams Public Service award Hull House, 1977; Health Achievement award Nat. Kidney Found., 1978; Nat. award Epilepsy Found. Am., 1978; James Ewing Layman's award Soc. Surg. Oncologists, 1979; citation for distinguished service AMA, 1979; Thomas More medal Thomas More Assn., 1979; NEA award, 1979; Margaret Sanger award, 1979; Stanley G. Kay medal Am. Cancer Soc., 1983; Albert Lasker pub. service award, 1985. Fellow Chgo. Gynecol. Soc. (citizen hon.); mem. LWV (pres. 1948), Brandeis U. Women (pres. 1960), Sigma Delta Chi. Author: Since You Asked Me, 1962; Teen-agers and Sex, 1964; Truth is Stranger..., 1968; Ann Landers Speaks Out, 1976; The Ann Landers Encyclopedia, 1978. Clubs: Chgo. Econs. (dir. 1975); Address: Chgo Sun-Times 401 N Wabash Ave Chicago IL 60611

LANDERS, MAUREEN SULLIVAN, lawyer; b. Bklyn., June 2, 1954; d. John Joseph and Mary Virginia (McCabe) Sullivan; m. John Quincy Landers, Jr., Sept. 8, 1979. B.A. summa cum laude (Durant scholar) Wellesley Coll., 1976; J.D., U. Pa., 1979. Bar: N.Y. 1979, Calif. 1980. Assoc. firm Milbank, Tweed, Hadley & McCloy, N.Y.C., 1979-80, Brobeck, Phleger & Harrison, San Francisco, 1980—. Mem. ABA, Calif. State Bar Assn., Phi Beta Kappa. Club: Meadow. Home: 2811 Adeline Dr Burlingame CA 94010 Office: Brobeck Phleger & Harrison Two Embarcadero Pl 2200 Geng Rd Palo Alto CA 94303

LANDERS, THELMA LEE, nursing home administrator; b. Mar. 20, 1923; d. Thad L. and Pearl B. (Landrum) Evans; m. Laddie Dee Landers, Dec. 25, 1944; children—Laddie Dee, Penny Annette, Jeri Saundra. A.S., Paris Jr. Coll., 1975; lic. vocat. nurse Mary Leigh Legg Sch. Nursing, Mt. Pleasant, Tex., 1955. Lic. vocat. nurse, Tex. Adminstr. Currey Nursing Home, Inc., Mt. Pleasant, 1952—. Mem. Tex. Nursing Home Assn. (longevity service awards 1972, 77), Bus. and Profl. Women's Club. Democrat. Mem. Ch. of Christ. Home: 1315 S Jefferson St Mount Pleasant TX 75455 Office: Currey Nursing Home Inc 901 N Jefferson St Mount Pleasant TX 75455

LANDERS, VERNETTE TROSPER, educator, author; b. Lawton, Okla., May 3, 1912; d. Fred Gilbert and LaVerne Hamilton (Stevens) Trosper; A.B. with honors, U. Calif. at Los Angeles, 1933, M.A., 1935, Ed.D., 1953; Cultural doctorate (hon.), Lit. World U., Tucson, 1985; m. Paul Albert Lum, Aug. 29, 1952 (dec. May 1955); 1 child, William Tappan; m. 2d, Newlin Landers, May 2, 1959; children—Lawrence, Marlin. Tchr. secondary schs., Montebello, Calif., 1935-45, 48-50, 51-59; prof. Long Beach City Coll., 1946-47; asst. prof. Los Angeles State Coll., 1950; dean girls Twenty Nine Palms (Calif.) High Sch., 1960-65; dist. counselor Morongo (Calif.) Unified Sch. Dist., 1965-72, coordinator adult edn., 1965-67, guidance project dir., 1967; clk.-in-charge Landers (Calif.) Post Office, 1962-82; ret., 1982 Vice-pres., sec. Landers Assn., 1965—; sec. Landers Vol. Fire Dept., 1972—; life mem. Hi-Desert Playhouse Guild, Hi-Desert Meml. Hosp. Guild. Bd. dirs., sec. Desert Emergency Radio Service. Recipient internat. diploma of honor for community service, 1973; Creativity award Internat. Personnel Research Assn., 1972; cert. of merit for disting. service to edn., 1973; Order of Rose, Alpha Xi Delta, 1978; named Soroptimist of Year, 29 Palms Soroptimist Club, 1969; poet laureate Center of Internat. Studies and Exchanges, 1981; diploma of merit in letters U. Arts, Parma, Italy, 1982; Golden Yr. Bruin UCLA, 1983; World Culture prize Nat. Ctr. for Studies and Research, Italian Acad., 1984; Golden Palm Diploma of Honor in poetry Leonardo Da Vinci Acad., 1984; Diploma of Merit and titular mem. internat. com. Internat. Ctr. Studies and Exchanges, Rome, 1984; Recognition award San Gorgonio council Girl Scouts U.S.A., 1985; Cert. of appreciation Morongo Unified Sch. Dist., 1984; plaquefor contribution to postal service and community U.S. Postal Service, 1984; Biographee of Yr. award for outstanding achievement in the field of edn. and service to community Hist. Preservations of Am.; named Princess of Poetry of Internat. Ctr. Cultural Studies and Exchange, Italy, 1985; community dinner held in her honor for achievement and service to Community, 1984; other awards and certs. Fellow Internat. Acad. Poets (life); mem. Am. Personnel and Guidance Assn., Internat. Platform Assn., Nat. Ret. Tchrs. Assn., Montebello Bus. and Profl. Women's Club (pres.), Nat. League Am. Pen Women (sec. 1985-86), Leonardo Da Vinci Acad. Internat. Winged Glory diploma of honor in letters 1982), Landers Area C. of C. (sec. 1985-86) (Presdl. award for outstanding service), Desert Nature Mus., Phi Beta Kappa. Clubs: Soroptimist (sec. Twenty Nine Palms 1962, life mem.); Whitter (Calif.) Toastmistress (pres. 1957); Homestead Valley Women's (Landers). Author: Impy, 1974, Talkie, 1975; Impy's Children, 1975; Nineteen O Four, 1976, Little Brown Bat, 1976; Slo-Go, 1977; Owls Who and Who Who, 1978; Sandy, The Coydog, 1979; The Kit Fox and the Walking Stick, 1980; contbr. articles to profl. jours., poems to anthologies. Home: 632 Landers Ln PO Box 3839 Landers CA 92285

LANDEY, FAYE HITE, consultant; b. Atlanta, May 12, 1943; d. Irving and Sophia (Held) Hite; m. Benjamin Landey, Aug. 30, 1964; children—Leah, Sharon. Student U. Ill., 1961, Hebrew U., Jerusalem, 1962; B.A., Emory U., 1964. Cert. housing mgr. Office mgr. Grolier Interstate, Atlanta, 1969-72; asst. adminstr. Campbell-Stone, Atlanta, 1972-78; owner Cupboard Gift Shop, Atlanta, 1974-78; adminstr. Campbell-Stone North, Atlanta, 1978-81; sales mgr. Apex Supply Co., Atlanta, 1981-83; owner Landey & Assocs., Atlanta, 1983—; advisor Fulton County Council on Housing, 1982. Treas., charter mem. Sandy Springs (Ga.) Arts and Heritage Soc., 1981; dir. Sandy Springs C. of C., 1982; founder Coalition Fulton County Civic Assns., 1983; mem. bd. com. Sandy Springs Benefit Ball, 1978-83; state del. Republican Party. Mem. Am. Assn. Homes for Aging (nat. house del. 1981), Ga. Assn. Homes for Aging (pres. elect 1982). Jewish. Club: Woman's Forum (Atlanta). Home and Office: 495 Tahoma Dr NE Atlanta GA 30338

LANDI, DIANE MARIE, designer; b. Paterson, N.J., Apr. 27, 1952; d. Mario Gustave and Josephine (Ryba) L.; student Sch. Visual Arts, N.Y.C., 1969-72. Chief designer Medallion Industries, 1971-76; designer, asst. art dir. Equitable Bag Co., Long Island City, 1977-83; owner, art dir. Landigraphics Co., advt. art services, Queens, N.Y., 1977—; design cons., partner R-Art, Inc., N.Y.C. Mem. Am. Inst. Graphic Arts, Mensa (asst. editor Chess-for-Fun), Beethoven Soc., Nat. Taxpayers Union, Amnesty Internat. Libertarian. Home: 75-12 35th Ave Jackson Heights NY 11372 Office: 50-18 70th St Woodside NY 11377

LANDI, JEANNIE PEAK, psychologist, business executive; b. Portsmouth, Va., Jan. 26, 1937; d. Charles Theodore, II, and Cuma Catherine (Thornton) Peak; B.A. in Psychology, Berea Coll., 1959; postgrad. New Sch. Social Research, 1960; U. Calif., Long Beach, 1967-69; M.A. in Psychology, SUNY, New Paltz, 1974; Ph.D. in Psychology, Union Grad. Sch., 1986; m. Anthony William Landi, Sept. 24, 1961; children—Michael, Carol. With IBM Computer Brokerage Systems, N.Y.C., 1959-60; IBM computer analyst, devel. first profl. football scouting computer system, Dallas, 1960-61, devel. tests for selection of USAF officers, Lackland, Tex., 1961-62; IBM cons., Los Angeles, 1965-68; with airborne computer design Litton Industries, Los Angeles, 1962-65; cons. behavior modification workshops SUNY-New Paltz, 1970-74; with IBM computer and info. sci. and math. models, Poughkeepsie, N.Y., 1974-76, computer design and micro programmer, 1976-80, implementation nat. alcohol and drug program for IBM, corp. hdqrs., Armonk, N.Y., 1980-82, mgr. advanced central processor, Poughkeepsie, 1982-84, mgr. employee assistance program, Armonk, 1984—; counsellor, lectr. alcohol and drug abuse. Active Dutchess County council Boy Scouts Am., 1980—, chief advisor, resource chmn. Computer Sci. Explorer Post 158, implementer, 1980, tchr. computer sci., coordinator staff advisors, 1980—. John Hay Whitney scholar, 1959, 61. Mem. Am. Psychol. Assn., Soc. Behaviorists, Assn. Computing Machinery, Phi Kappa Phi, Psi Chi. Methodist. Club: Poughkeepsie Tennis. Home: Route 2 Wetherill Rd Brewster NY 10509 Office: IBM Corporate Hdqrs 2000 Purchase St Purchase NY 10577

LANDIS, SALLY LOU, furniture manufacturers representative, restaurant executive; b. Youngstown, Ohio, Oct. 13, 1950; d. Eugene Louis and Mary Grace (Murphy) Dougherty. Interior designer Strouss Dept. Stores, Youngstown, 1973-74, dir. 3 design studios, 1975-77, upholstery, occasional buyer, 1978-81; furniture sales rep. Bruard's Inc., No. Ohio ter., 1982—, Furniture Imports Inc., State of Ohio, 1982—, Hickory Ridge Furniture Inc., No. Ohio, 1984—, Progressive Furniture Inc., State of Ohio, 1986—; owner Cornerburg Pizza franchise, 1984—. Mem. Cleve. Home Furnishings Reps. Assn., Nat. Assn. Female Execs. Democrat. Roman Catholic. Avocations: interior design, golf, gourmet cooking. Office: PO Box 3155 Youngstown OH 44512

LANDMAN, LIBBY GELLER LYNCH, librarian, educator; b. Springfield, Mass., Nov. 24, 1929; d. Isadore Loeb and Shirley (Bershatsky) Geller; student N.Y.U., 1958-68; B.A. in Russian Lit., Manhattanville Coll., 1973; M.A. in L.S., U. Wis., 1974; postgrad. Columbia U., 1974-77, Wright State U., 1977-78; Oxford U., 1981; M.Pub.Adminstrn., U. Okla., 1984; m. Jerome S. Lynch (dec.); children—Priscilla B. Lynch, Jonathan H. Lynch, Andrew S. Lynch; m. 2d, Nathan M. Landman, June 26, 1977. Public librarian Larchmont (N.Y.) Public Library, 1975-77; sch. librarian Scarsdale (N.Y.) and Mamaroneck Pub. Schs., 1975-77; info. cons. Netter Internat., N.Y.C., 1976-77; sch. librarian Fairborn (Ohio) Pub. Schs., 1978; European rep. NASCO Internat., Ft. Atkinson, Wis., 1979-81; public librarian Queens Borough Public Library, N.Y.C., 1981-82; public services librarian, instr. Coll. New Rochelle (N.Y.), 1982; lectr. in field. Mem. Bd. Edn., Larchmont Temple, N.Y., 1968-70; treas. Officers' Wives 401st Combat Support Group, Spain, 1979-80; mem. PTA, 1969-74, ways and means treas., 1970; head librarian Larchmont Temple Library, 1967-70; chmn. victory luncheon United Jewish Appeal, 1974; librarian detention facility Juvenile Ct., Montgomery County, Ohio, 1977-78. Recipient Humanitarian Fellowship award, 1967; citation for religious leadership Union Am. Hebrew Congregations, 1971; cert. of appreciation U.S. Air Force, 1981; cert. librarian, N.Y., Ohio. Mem. ALA, Am. Soc. Public Adminstrs., Freedom To Read Found., Wis. Alumni Assn., Phi Beta Mu. Republican. Jewish. Clubs: Officers' Wives, Am. Women's (Madrid). Contbr. articles to profl. publs. Home: 15 Lookout Circle Larchmont NY 10538 Office: Gill Library Coll of New Rochelle New Rochelle NY 10801

LANDRAM, CHRISTINA LOUELLA, librarian; b. Paragould, Ark., Dec. 10, 1922; d. James Ralph and Bertie Louella (Jordan) Oliver; m. Robert Ellis Landram, Aug. 7, 1948; 1 child, Mark Owen. B.A., Tex. Woman's U., 1945, B.L.S., 1946, M.L.S., 1951. Preliminary cataloger Library of Congress, Washington, 1946-48; cataloger U.S. Info. Ctr., Tokyo, Japan, 1948-50, U.S. Dept. Agr., Washington, 1953-54; librarian Yokota AFB, Yokota, Japan, 1954-55; librarian St. Mary's Hosp., West Palm Beach, Fla., 1957-59; librarian Jacksonville (Ark.) High Sch., 1959-61; coordinator Shelby County Libraries, Memphis, 1961-63; head catalog dept. Ga. State U. Library, 1963—. Contbr. articles to library jours. Mem. Ga. Library Assn. (chmn. resources and tech. services sect. 1969-71), Metro-Atlanta Library Assn. (pres. 1967-68), ALA (chmn. cataloging norms 1979-80, nominating com. 1977-78), Southeastern Library Assn. (mem. govtl. relations com. 1975-78, intellectual freedom com. 1984-86). Presbyterian. Home: 1478 Leafmore Ridge Decatur GA 30033 Office: Pullen Library Ga State U 100 Decatur St SE Atlanta GA 30303

LANDRENEAU, ELLEN RITA, educator, consultant; b. Ville Platte, La., Jan. 26, 1949; d. Joseph Otis and Clamie (Fusilier) L.; B.S., U. Southwestern La., 1971; M.S., U. So. Miss., 1978; m. A. Dale Thibodeaux, Feb. 21, 1981. Staff nurse Wuesthoff Meml. Hosp., Cocoa, Fla., 1971-72; pub. health nurse Brevard County Health Dept., Melbourne, Fla., 1972-74; day camp nurse Baton Rouge Assn. Retarded Citizens, 1974; staff nurse ICU, Earl K. Long Hosp., Baton Rouge, 1976; lab. asst. Southeastern La. U., 1974-77; instr. nursing Pearl River Jr. Coll., Poplarville, Miss., 1978; edn. cons. Acadiana Mental Health Center, Lafayette, La., 1979; asst. prof. U. Southwestern La., Lafayette, 1978-85; staff nurse Cypress Hosp., 1985—; nursing standards cons., 1984—. Mem. Maximum Health Potential and United Scis. Am., Am. Nurses Assn., La. Nurses Assn., AAUP, Am. Heart Assn., Sierra Club, Alpha Lambda Delta, Phi Kappa Phi, Sigma Theta Tau. Roman Catholic. Home: 100 Edgebrook Circle Lafayette LA 70508

LANDRUM, MARGO WADSWORTH, communications company executive; b. Washington, Dec. 14, 1940; d. Joseph Rodgers and Genevieve Frances (Folse) Wadsworth; B.A. in English, St. Mary's Dominican Coll., 1965; m. James F. Landrum, June 9, 1962; children—Courtney, Jay, Colin. Ptnr., Rent-A-Writer, San Jose, Calif., 1978—; pres. MS BS, Inc., San Jose, 1981—; cons. in field. Vice pres. League of Friends of Commn. Status of Women, 1985, 2d v.p., 1986; honey chmn. cookie dr. Girl Scouts, 1986; alt. del. White House Conf. Small Bus., 1986. Named Kiwanis Citizen of Month, 1986. Mem. San Jose C. of C. (publicity/historian chmn. 1980-81, program chair 1983), San Jose Women in Bus. (gen. chmn. 1985). Democrat. Roman Catholic. Club: Quota. Contbr. articles to profl. jours. Home: 6631 Mount Royal Dr San Jose CA 95120 Office: 1610 Blossom Hill Rd Suite 9 San Jose CA 95124

LANDRUM-BRUMMUND, FRANCES ANN, choreographer, dance instr.; b. N.Y.C., Apr. 5, 1918; d. Edmond Charles and Mary Elizabeth (Lannon) Lourie; student Vestoff-Serova Sch. of Dance, 1927-35, Tarasoff Sch. of Dance, 1929-31, Martha Graham Sch. Dance, 1935-36; m. Theodore Wayne Brummund, July 27, 1979; children by previous marriage—Elizabeth Ann Gwynn, Robert Bascom Landrum II. Ballet dancer Russian Opera Co., 1930, Lee Schubert Prodns., 1931; soloist Corps du Ballet, Radio City Music Hall, N.Y.C., 1933-42; founder, owner, dir. Landrum Sch. of Dance, N.Y.C., 1948—; founder Young People's Dance Group of L.I., 1964—; artistic dir. Ballet Repertory of L.I.; producer R.K.O. Keith's Flushing Theatre, 1960—, also Andre Eglevsky Ballet Co. Active, Concerned Citizens for the Arts. Recipient merit award N.Y. State Commn. on World's Fair, 1964. Mem. Am. Assn. Dance Cos., N.Y. Dance Alliance. Presbyterian. Office: 14 34 150th St Whitestone NY 11357

LANDRUS, VICTORIA MEECE, county administrator; b. Decatur, Ill., Sept. 13, 1952; d. William E. and Patricia M. Meece; m. Timothy A. Landrus, 1974. B.A., Calif. State U., 1974; M.P.A., U. So. Calif., 1981. Capital projects analyst County of Orange, Santa Ana, Calif., 1975-78; sr. analyst U. Calif. Coll. Medicine, Irvine, 1978-82; asst. adminstr. Occupational Health Care, Inc., Carson, Calif., 1982; adminstrv. aide City of Garden Grove (Calif.), 1983-84; adminstrv. analyst County of Orange, Santa Ana, 1984—. Mem. Nat. Women's Polit. Caucus, Irvine, Calif. Presidential Mgmt. intern, 1981. Mem. Am. Soc. Pub. Adminstrn., Calif. State Grange, Praetors (life), Western Govtl. Research Assn.

LANDRY, BRENDA LEE, securities analyst; b. Wolfboro, N.H., June 24, 1942; d. Christopher Lee and Barbara F. (Sullivan) Landry; m. Franklin Winfield McCann, June 28, 1980. B.A., Vassar Coll., 1964. Sales analyst Polaroid Co., Cambridge, Mass., 1966-70; 1st v.p. White Weld, N.Y.C.,

1970-78, Merrill Lynch, N.Y.C., 1978-80; v.p. Morgan Stanley & Co., Inc., N.Y.C., 1980—. Contbr. articles to profl. jours.; various TV appearances. Mem. N.Y. Soc. Security Analysts, Women's Fin. Assn., Photo Mfrs. Assn. Republican. Club: Vassar. Home: PO Box 10 Water Mill NY 11976 Office: Morgan Stanley 1251 Ave of Americas New York NY 10020

LANDRY, MARGARET AVET, medical technologist; b. Houma, La., Oct. 19, 1947; d. Philip Royce and Wilma (King) Avet; B.S., Nicholls State Coll., 1970, postgrad. 1977-78; M.S., La. State U., 1979; m. Jimmy John Landry, Sept 7, 1968. Med. technologist, Terrebonne Gen. Hosp., Houma, La., 1969, Bapt. Meml. Hosp., Memphis, 1970-71, Terrebonne Gen. Med. Ctr., Houma, 1972—; research asst. La. State U., 1978-79, teaching asst., 1979. Mem. Am. Soc. Clin. Pathologists (assoc.), Am. Soc. Microbiology, Planetary Soc., Jane Asten Soc. N. Am., Hist. and Cultural Soc. Terrebonne Parish, Friends of the Zoo. Office: Dept Pathology 936 E Main St Houma LA 70360

LANDSBERGER, BETTY HATCH, human development professional, gerontologist, educator; b. Tampa Aug. 9, 1918; d. Hugh Brenton and Margaret Lauder (Macdonell) Hatch; B.A. in Sociology, Fla. State U., 1939; M.A. Ed., U. Mich., 1940; Ph.D., Cornell U., 1951; m. Henry A. Landsberger, June 10, 1951; children—Margaret Ann Landsberger Thomas, Samuel Ernest, Ruth Elizabeth Landsberger Hazard. . Mem. faculty edn. dept. Fla. State U., Cornell U., Roosevelt U., Chgo., 1941-54; program asso. evaluation research Learning Inst. N.C., Durham, 1969-71; mem. faculty U. N.C. Sch. Nursing, Chapel Hill, 1976—, asst. prof. nursing, 1979-81, asso. prof., 1981—; cons. N.C. Div. Health Services, public schs. Chmn. Orange County Sr. Citizens Bd., 1981-84. Mem. N.C. Assn. Research in Edn. (pres. 1975-76), AAUP (chpt. pres. 1983), Phi Beta Kappa, Phi Kappa Phi, Pi Lambda Theta. Democrat. Author: Long Term Care for the Elderly; contbr. articles to profl. jours. and textbooks. Home: 807 Kings Mill Rd Chapel Hill NC 27514 Office: Sch Nursing U NC Chapel Hill NC 27514

LANDSEADEL, CHERYL BAKER, builder, developer, general contractor; b. Groton, Conn., Feb. 15, 1949; d. George Haywood and Violet Elizabeth (Gibson) Kendall; m. Jay Bradley Landseadel, May 21, 1983; m. Thomas Michael Baker, July 18, 1970 (dec. July 1979); 1 son, Thomas Michael. B.A., U. N.C., 1972. Claims supr. Mass. Gen. Life Ins. Co., Boston, 1972-73; asst. dir. govt. affairs Menswear Retailers Am., Washington, 1973-78; sec. T.M. Baker Co., Inc., McLean, Va., 1975-79, pres., owner, 1979—. Mem. parent council Country Day Sch., McLean, 1981-82, 84-85; chmn. social action bd. Rock Spring Congregational Ch., Arlington, 1982-83; mem. bd. property planning Rock Spring Ch., Arlington, 1984—. Mem. No. Va. Builders Assn., Nat. Assn. Home Builders. Republican. Avocations: Hiking; sailing. Office: TM Baker Co Inc PO Box 145 McLean VA 22101

LANDSKE, DOROTHY SUZANNE (SUE), state legislator; b. Evanston, Ill., Sept. 3, 1937; d. William Gerald and Dorothy (Drewes) Martin; m. William Steve Landske, 1957; children—Catherine Jeffery Hudson, Jacqueline Jeffery Basilotta, Pamela, Cheryl, Eric. Student St. Joseph's Coll., 1955, Ind. U., 1976, U. Chgo. Grad. Sch. Bus., 1979. Former sch. tchr., realtor; dep. clk.-treas. Cedar Lake, 1975; chief dep., twp. assessor Central Twp., Crown Point, 1976-78, twp. assessor, 1978-84; vice chmn. Lake County Republican Central Com., 1978—, 5th Congl. Dist. Reps., 1978—; mem. Ind. State Senate from 6th Dist., 1984—, mem. judiciary, civil law subcom., legis. apportionment and elections, natural resources and environ. affairs coms. Named Sagamore of the Wabash, Ind. Gov., 1980, 83, Outstanding Freshman Republican, Senator, Ind. Broadcasters Assn., 1985. Mem. Nat. Council State Govts., Bus. and Profl. Women's Club (v.p. 1983-84), VFW, Cedar Lake Hist. Assn., Nat. Order Women Legislators. Roman Catholic. Address: 7325 W 143d Ave Cedar Lake IN 46303

LANDSMANN, LEANNA, editor, publisher; b. Ithaca, N.Y., May 26, 1946; d. George and Katherine (Mehenbacher) Abraham; m. Guy Landsmann, July 14, 1968. B.A., St. Lawrence U., 1968. Tchr. public schs., Ivory Coast, West Africa, 1968-69, Prattsburg, N.Y., 1969-70; assoc. editor Instr. Publs. Inc., N.Y.C., 1971-76, editor-in-chief, 1976—, pub., 1978—, also pres. Instr. Publs. Inc.; v.p. Harcourt Brace Jovanovich Inc.; mem. faculty Stanford U. Pub. Course, 1980, 81. Vol. public schs., vol. public relations work in edn. Mem. EDPRESS, Nat. Assn. Edn. Young Children, Internat. Reading Assn., Assn. Childhood Edn. Internat., Mag. Pubs. Assn., Assn. Supervision and Curriculum Devel. Office: Instructor Publs Inc 545 Fifth Ave New York NY 10017

LANDWIRTH, TRUDY KOPF, medical librarian; b. Lexington, Nebr., May 9, 1946; d. Gerhardt Albert and Alice Lorraine (Schmidt) Kopf; m. Michael Allen Landwirth, Sept. 14, 1979. Student Cornell Coll., Mt. Vernon, Iowa, 1964-66; B.A., U. Iowa, 1968; M.S. in Library Sci., U. Ill., 1972. Dental hygienist, various pvt. offices, Glen Ellyn, Ill., Peoria, Ill., 1968-71; dir. med. library Meth. Med. Ctr. Ill., Peoria, 1972-85; br. librarian U. Ill. Coll. Medicine-Peoria, 1985—. Nat. Library Medicine fellow, 1971-72. Mem. Health Scis. Librarians Ill. (sec. 1979-81), Ill. OCLC Users Group (treas. 1984-86), Med. Library Assn., ALA, Phi Beta Kappa, Sigma Phi Alpha. Lutheran. Home: 6923 N Hunters Trace Peoria IL 61614 Office: Library Health Scis U Ill Coll Medicine PO Box 1649 Peoria IL 61656

LANE, CHERYL ANN GROSS, nursing consultant; b. Pitts., Sept. 24, 1948; d. Charles N. and Maryalda (Freund) Gross; Asso. Sci. with honors, Jr. Coll. of Broward County, 1968; B.S. in Nursing, N.C. A. and T. U., 1981; m. Timothy Gerald Lane, June 20, 1969; children—Tamala Ann, Wendelyn Joy, Justin Bradley. Staff nurse Broward Gen. Hosp., Fort Lauderdale, Fla., 1968, asst. head nurse, 1969; oncology nurse clinician Bowman Gray Sch. Medicine, Winston-Salem, N.C., 1969-71, dir. cancer center nursing Oncology Research Center, 1971-81; asst. instr. nursing S.E. Mo. State U., 1981-84; oncology nursing cons., 1981—; mem. tumor registry com. N.C. Bapt. Hosp., 1980-81. Mem. N.C. Adv. Council on Cause and Control of Cancer Task Force, 1978. Mem. Am. Cancer Soc. (bd. dirs. N.C. div. 1979-81),Oncology Nursing Soc. (chairperson membership com. 1979-84, v.p. 1984—), Piedmont Oncology Assn. (chairperson nursing com. 1979-81), Phi Theta Kappa. Roman Catholic. Author: (manual) Cancer Chemotherapy Guidelines, 1978; contbr. articles on nursing care to profl. jours. Home: 255 Madrid Ct Merritt Island FL 32953 Office: 1257 Florida Ave Rockledge FL 32955

LANE, CONSTANCE CARMICHAEL RENICK, retired school administrator; b. Rockford, Ill., Nov. 9, 1921; d. James Alexander and Nozella (Oda) Carmichael; B.S. magna cum laude in Edn., W.Va. State Coll., 1943; M.A., Northwestern U., 1962; m. Andrew J. Lane, June 20, 1964; children—Betty Anne Renick (Mrs. Flynn Jefferson), James Renick. Tchr., Rockford Public Schs., 1954-62, helping tchr. elem. math., 1962-63; prin. Henrietta Primary and Intermediate Schs., Rockford, 1963-66; prin. W. Ray McIntosh Sch., Rockford, 1966-79; Area IV coordinator Rockford Public Schs., 1971-79, asst. supt. for elem. edn., 1979-85; part-time instr. Rockford Coll., evenings 1964-79; pres. Family Consultation Service, 1983-84. Mem. Taus, Inc. (pres. 1960-63, 74-78, treas. 1972-74), Ill., Rockford edn. assns., NEA, AAUW, Nat. Council Tchrs. Math., Assn. Supervision and Curriculum Devel., Rockford Prins. Assn., Nat. Elementary Prins. Assn., Ill. Women Adminstrs. (pres. 1984), Winnebago-Boone Ret. Tchrs. (v.p. 1985—), Delta Kappa Gamma, Phi Delta Kappa. Episcopalian. Contbr. articles to profl. jours. Home: 2224 Clover Ave Rockford IL 61102

LANE, ELIZABETH ANN, educational administrator; b. New Orleans, Oct. 24, 1944; d. Jeremiah Lurry and Eunice Frances (O'Dwyer) L.; B.A., La. State U., New Orleans, 1966; M.Ed., Loyola U. of South, New Orleans, 1970; Ed.D. in ednl. adminstrn. U. So. Miss. Tchr., C. F. Rowley Elem. Sch., St. Bernard Parish (La.) Sch. Bd., Chalmette, 1966-75, prin., 1975—; cons. So. Assn. Schs. and Colls. Named Outstanding Young Educator, St. Bernard Parish Jaycees, 1972, La. State Tchr. of Yr., 1972; Delta Kappa Gamma Soc. Internat. Epsilon State scholar, 1981. Mem. St. Bernard Parish Prins. Assn. (v.p. 1977-79), Nat. Sci. Tchrs. Assn., Nat. Assn. Elem. Sch. Prins., Delta Kappa Gamma Soc. Internat., Phi Delta Kappa, Kappa Delta Pi. Democrat. Roman Catholic. Editor newsletter St. Bernard br. AAUW, 1966-76.

LANE, KATHLEEN MARGARET, optical company administrator; b. Mpls., Oct. 25, 1946; d. Bernard Melvin and Margaret (Beck) Aanerud; m. Kenneth LeRoy Lane, Sept. 1, 1979; 1 child, Dennis Leon. Cost acct. Honeywell, Mpls., 1964-66; bank bookkeeper Columbia Heights State Bank, Minn., 1966-71; inventory control mgr. Hodes Optical Inc., Torrance, Calif., 1972-75, office mgr., 1975-79; lens supr. Coburn Optical Industries, Inc., Carson, Calif., 1979-85, br. mgr., St. Paul, 1985; customer relations Opti Fair, Aneheim, Calif., 1978-83. Mem. Am. Inst. Banking, Nat. Assn. Female Execs. Avocations: restoring old furniture; camping; knitting. Office: Coburn Optical Industries Inc 1471 Brewster St Saint Paul MN 55108

LANE, MARGARET BEYNON TAYLOR, librarian; b. St. Louis, Feb. 6, 1919; d. Archer and Alice (Jones) Taylor; B.A., La. State U., 1939, J.D., 1942; B.S. in L.S., Columbia U., 1941; m. Horace C. Lane, Jan. 6, 1945; children—Margaret Elizabeth, Thomas Archer. Reference and circulation asst. Columbia Law Library, N.Y.C., 1942-44; law librarian, asst. prof. U. Conn. Sch. Law, Hartford, 1944-46; law librarian La. State U. Law Sch., Baton Rouge, 1946-48; recorder documents La. Sec. of State's Office, Baton Rouge, 1949-75; law librarian Lane Fertitta, Lane & Tullos, 1976—. Mem. depository library council to Pub. Printer, 1972-77; mem. plan devel. com. La. Fed. Depository Library, 1982-83. Treas. Delta Iota House Bd. of Kappa Kappa Gamma, 1965-68. Mem. ALA (interdivisional com. public documents 1967-74, chmn. 1967-70; govt. documents round table, state and local documents task force 1972—, coordinator 1980-82; James Bennett Childs award 1981), La. Library Assn. (Essae M. Culver Disting. Service award 1976; chmn. documents com. 1982-83, Lucy B. Foote award subject specialist sect. 1986), La., Baton Rouge bar assns., Mortar Bd., Phi Delta Delta, Kappa Kappa Gamma. Club: Baton Rouge Library. Author: State Publications and Depository Libraries, 1981. Home: 7545 Richards Dr Baton Rouge LA 70809 Office: POB 3335 Baton Rouge LA 70821

LANE, NANCY LEE, diagnostic systems personnel executive; b. Boston, Sept. 3, 1938; d. Samuel M. and Gladys (Pitkins) Lane. Student U. Oslo, 1961; B.S., Boston U., 1962; M.P.A., U. Pitts. Grad. Sch. Pub. and Internat. Affairs, 1967; cert. program for mgmt. devel. Harvard U. Grad. Sch. Bus. Adminstrn., 1975. Project mgr. Westinghouse Broadcasting Co., 1964-66; dep. dir. personnel Nat. Urban League, N.Y.C., 1967-72; 2d v.p. Chase Manhattan Bank, N.Y.C., 1972-73; v.p. personnel Off Track Betting Corp., N.Y.C., 1973-75; v.p. personnel and adminstrn., dir. Ortho-Diagnostic Systems, Inc., Raritan, N.J., 1976—. Home: 37 W 12th St New York NY 10011 Office: Ortho Diagnostic Systems Inc Route 202 Raritan NJ 08869

LANE, ROBIN R., lawyer; b. Kerrville, Tex., Nov. 28 1947; d. Rowland and Gloria (Benson) Richards; m. Stanley Lane, Aug. 22, 1971 (div. 1979); m. 2d, Anthony W. Cunningham, Nov. 12, 1980; children—Joshua Lane, Alexandra. B.A. with honors in Econs., U.Fla., 1969; qM.A., George Washington U., 1971; J.D., Stetson Coll. Law, 1978. Mgmt. trainee internat. banking Gulf Western Industries, N.Y.C.; internat. research specialist Ryder Systems, Inc., Miami, Fla., 1973, project mgr., 1974; assoc. Wagner, Cunningham, Vaughan & McLaughlin, Tampa, Fla., 1979-85; sole practice, 1985—; guest lectr. med. jurisprudence Stetson Coll. Law, 1982-83. Contbr. articles to various revs. Recipient Am. Jurisprudence award-torts, Lawyers Co-op. Fla., 1979; Scottish Rite fellow, 1968-69. Mem. Acad. Fla. Trial Lawyers (mem. com. 1983-84), Assn. Trial Lawyers Am., Fla. Bar Assn., ABA, Fla. Women's Network, Omicron Delta Epsilon, Delta Delta Delta. Clubs: Palma Ceia Tampa; Tower. Home: 3301 Bayshore Blvd Tampa FL 33609 Office: Robin Lane PA 1106 N Franklin St Tampa FL 33602

LANE, SHARI LEA, distribution company executive; b. Carmel, Calif., Oct. 20, 1950; d. Joseph Reynolds and Joan Martha (McBride) McElrath Lane. B.A., U. Va.-Fairfax, 1972. Notary pub.; real estate broker; grad. Realtors Inst. Asst. dir. personnel Mayflower Hotel, Washington, 1972-73; personnel adminstr. PRC Planning Research Corp., McLean, Va., 1973-75; dir. sales 1928 Jewelry Co., Burbank, Calif., 1975-78; dir. new home sales Sterpa Realty Register, Glendale, Calif., 1978-82; nat. accounts mgr. Bekins Moving & Storage, Glendale, Calif., 1982-83; mgr. customer service Applause div. Wallace Berrie, Woodland Hills, Calif., 1983—. Mem. Nat. Assn. Female Execs. (assoc.), Womens Assn. Realtors (sec. treas. 1980-82). Republican. Episcopalian. Avocations: swimming (Ala. state champion 1966 breastroke); gourmet cooking; travel. Home: 1516 S Adams St Glendale CA 91205

LANES, AVA MARIE, educator; b. Bowman, N.D., Mont., May 15, 1952; d. George Oscar and Kathryn Eloise (Davis) Odegaard; m. Paul Robert Lanes, Aug. 20, 1977. B.S. cum laude in Edn., U. N.D., 1974; M.A., Ball State U., 1977. Cert. spl. edn. Speech pathologist Dickinson Pub. Schs., 1974-76, preschool speech pathologist, 1977-78, speech, language, hearing coordinator, 1978-81, asst. dir. spl. edn., 1981-84, adminstrv. asst. for curriculum and instruction, 1984—; adj. prof., U.N.D., Dickinson, 1978; private therapist, Dickinson, 1978-81. Bd. dirs. Dickinson C. of C., 1979-80, Statewide Tchr. Ctr., Grand Forks, N.D., 1980-82, Dickinson Tchr. Ctr., 1979-83, Dickinson Consortium, 1979-80. Recipient Acad. Achievement award Ball State U., 1977. Mem. N.D. Council for Exceptional Children (rec. sec. 1983-84, pres.-elect 1984-85), Council for Exceptional Children (chpt. pres.-elect 1979-80, pres. 1980-81), AAUW (publicity chmn. 1975-76), Am. Speech/Language/Hearing Assn. (publicity chmn. 1977-78), N.D. Council of Sch. Adminstrs. Republican. Lutheran. Avocations: photography (People's choice award 1984-85), cross country skiing, gardening. Home: 1470 2nd Ave Dickinson ND 58601 Office: Dickinson Pub Schs 202 E Villard St Dickinson ND 58602-1057

LANES, DENISE DEE, international trading company executive; b. Bklyn., Feb. 14, 1951; d. Irving and Sylvia (Maltz) L.; B.A., SUNY, Stony Brook, 1972; M.B.A., St. Johns U., 1977. Sales asst. Mitsui & Co. (U.S.A.), Inc., N.Y.C., 1972-81, asst. gen. mgr., 1981-85; owner, mgr. World Traders (U.S.A.), Inc., Rego Park, N.Y., 1981—. Mem. N.Y. C. of C. and Industry, Sell Overseas Am., Nat. Assn. Women Bus. Owners, Defenders of Wildlife, Women Bus. Owners N.Y. Clubs: Lunch Impressions, Appalachian Mountain. Office: World Traders (USA) 98-05 67th Ave Rego Park NY 11374

LANES, SELMA GORDON, critic, author, editor; b. Boston, Mar. 13, 1929; d. Jacob and Lily (Whiteman) Gordon; B.A., Smith Coll., 1950; M.S. in Journalism, Columbia, 1954; m. Jerrold B. Lanes, Nov. 21, 1959 (div. Mar. 1970); children—Andrew Oliver, Matthew Gordon. Asst. to publicity dir. Little Brown & Co., Boston, 1950-51; asso. editor Focus Mag., N.Y.C., 1951-53; travel page editor Boston Globe, 1953; spl. editorial asst., researcher Look Mag., 1956-60; children's entertainment editor Show Mag., 1961-63; critic children's books for Book World (N.Y. Herald-Tribune, later World Jour. Tribune, Wash. Post and Chgo. Tribune), 1965-71, N.Y. Times Book Rev., 1966—; articles editor Parents Mag., 1971-74; editor-in-chief Parents Mag. Press, 1974-78; cons. to Penguin Books, 1967, Starstream Books, 1980-81; lectr. New Sch./Parsons Sch. Design, 1975-77, Del. Art Mus., 1979; dir. Schiller-Wapner Galleries, 1983-84; freelance writer, 1984—. Judge, Children's Spring Book Festival, 1970, dir., 1972; judge N.Y. Times Ten Best Illus. Children's Books, 1973, 79, 80. Trustee Fund for Art Investment, N.Y.C. Mem. Phi Beta Kappa. Author (juvenile) Amy Loves Good-byes, 1966; The Curiosity Book, 1968; Down the Rabbit Hole, A critical work for adults on children's literature, 1971, paperback, 1976; The Art of Maurice Sendak, 1980; selector-adapter: A Child's First Book of Nursery Tales, 1983. Office: 26 E 91st St New York NY 10028

LANESE, JILL RENEE, computer automation consultant; b. Neptune, N.J., June 3, 1952; d. William Herman and Blossom Roslyn (Feldman) Epstein; m. Louis Lanese, June 10, 1984. B.A., C.W. Post Coll., 1974. Word processing specialist Nat. Produce Co., Inc., Neptune, 1974-78; systems mgr. AT&T, Basking Ridge, N.J., 1978-81; sr. systems mgr. ITT, N.Y.C., 1981-84; info. systems mgr. Breed, Abbott & Morgan, N.Y.C., 1984-86; word processing/data processing dir., advisor Compu-group, N.Y.C., 1985—; computer automation cons. Jill Lanese Automation Cons., Bklyn., 1986—. Bd. dirs., pres. Am. Found. for Animals, West End, N.J., 1982—. Mem. Assn. Info. Systems Profls., Assn. for Women in Computing, Nat. Assn. Female Execs. Republican. Avocations: writing, reading, floral design, nutrition, dogs, travel. Address: 8874 24th Ave Brooklyn NY 11214

LANEY, ELIZABETH CARDWELL, freelance photojournalist; b. Bluefield, W.Va., Aug. 19, 1912; d. Alexander Drake Cardwell and Harriet Louise (Parker) Martin; m. Luther Hubbard Laney, Apr. 6, 1941; 1 son, Charles. Student St. Paul Normal Coll., 1930-31, Franklin U., Ohio State U., Bliss Bus. Sch., Columbus Bus. Coll., St. Mary of the Springs, Ill. Wesleyan Coll., Columbus Tech. Inst., Ohio Dominican Coll., Capital U.; cert. Poro Sch. Cosmetology, 1941. Stenographer, U.S. Govt., Dayton, Ohio, 1941-43; cosmetician, mgr., owner Laney Beauty Salon, Columbus, Ohio, 1945-50; sec., auditor City of Columbus, 1950-75; spl. feature contbg. writer The Ohio State Sentinel, 1960-62, Call and Post Newspaper (syndicated), 1967—, photojournalist, 1977—; editor Ohio Bapt. Jour. Ohio Bapt. Gen. Conv., 1984—. Author: (poetry) Poetry in Prayer, 1977. Editor Centennial Jour., 1969; 100 Years, Shiloh Baptist Church History, 1974. Composer numerous hymns. Ch. sch. tchr., dir. pub. relations Shiloh Bapt. Ch., 1970—, Sunday Sch. sec., treas., founder Gleaners class; dir. pub. relations Eastern Union Missionary Bapt. Assn., Eastern Union Assembly Ground, Eastern Union Bapt. Coll., Ohio Bapt. Gen. Conv., 1983; sec. bd. trustees Eastern Union Bapt. Coll.; mem. Eastern Union Assembly Ground; publicity chmn. Christian Women's Workshop; active mem. Urban League, Urban League Guild, Women's Service Bd. Grant Hosp. (life), Ch. Women United (life), Ohio Bapt. Women's Conv. (life); founder, organizer Triangle Civic Assn., 1945; sec. Eastgate Garden/Civic Assn., 1955-57. Named Woman of Yr., Shiloh Bapt. Ch., 1962, 71, 75; recipient Cert. of Honor, Mayor Tom Moody, 1975, Cert. of Honor, Columbus City Council, 1975; 1st, 2nd, 3rd prize certs. Columbus Writers Guild, 1965-70; 1st, 2nd, 3rd place ribbons Golden Hobby Show, 1979-81; numerous ribbons, prizes Ohio Dominican Coll., 1980-81; selected as guest photojournalist Israel Journalist, Jerusalem Post Newspaper; 1 of 5 selected for Equal Opportunity Day, Columbus Call and Post Newspaper, 1962; recipient Mayor's award for vol. service, 1984. Mem. Women in Communications, Nat. Assn. Colored Women's Clubs, Eta Phi Beta (named chpt. Black Woman of Yr. 1983). Republican. Lodge: Order Eastern Star. Avocations: music; arts; writing; photography; travel. Office: Laney's Public Relations 1941 Ardenrun Way Columbus OH 43219

LANEY, SUSAN FERGUSON, secretarial services company executive; b. Amarillo, Tex., Dec. 31, 1956; d. Douglas J. and Patricia Jean (Cantrell) Ferguson; m. Perry Dale Laney, Oct. 20, 1979; children—Eric, Diana. Student Ga. So. Coll., 1975-77. Asst. broker Gresham & Hartje, Atlanta, 1977-79; adminstrv. asst. Hopper Ins. Agy., Decatur, Ga., 1979-81; office mgr. Am. Wealthbuilders Assocs., Atlanta, 1981-83; corp. pres., owner Performance Now, Inc., Lawrenceville, Ga., 1983-84, Atlanta, 1984—; cons. Video Voyage, Atlanta, 1984—, Profl. Bus. & Tax Consultants, Lawrenceville, 1983—, Children's Ednl. Leasing, Raleigh, N.C., 1983—. Baptist. Mem. Chi Omega. Avocations: yard work, movies, family. Office: Performance Now Inc 4470 Chamblee-Dunwoody Suite 350 Atlanta GA 30338

LANEY-DIBELLA, JACQUELINE EILEEN, travel company executive; b. Utica, N.Y., Sept. 22, 1941; d. Joseph Anthony and Isabelle Jeanette (Scalise) Marasco; m. William Myron Laney, June 12, 1971 (div. 1981); 1 son, Robert William; m. 2d John C. DiBella, May 12, 1984. A.S., Rochester (N.Y.) Bus. Inst. 1961; student Nazareth Coll., Rochester, 1961-62. Sec. to gen. mgr. Farrel Co., Rochester, 1964-68; asst. personnel dept., 1968-71; v.p. East Avenue Travel Co., Rochester, 1972-77; owner, mgr. Faith Tours, Rochester, 1978-81; exec. v.p. Premier Travel Co., Rochester, 1981-84; pres. Primier Travel Service, 1984—. Mem. Am. Soc. Travel Agts. (Crest award 1982, 74), Am. Mgmt. Assn., Women in Communications. Democrat. Home: 42 Rand Pl Rochester NY 14534

LANG, ALICE MARIE, pharmacist; b. Mobile, Ala., Oct. 10, 1947; d. James Leslie and Sara Augusta (Pope) L.; B.S., Xavier U., New Orleans, 1970. Mgmt. trainee Osco Drugs, Chgo., 1970-72; chief pharmacist Williams Clinic, Chgo., 1972-73; pharmacy supr. Cook County Hosp., Chgo., 1973-76; chief pharmacist Truwick Pharmacy, Chgo., 1976-77; with Jackson Park Hosp., Chgo., 1977-84, asst. dir. pharmacy, 1978-80, dir. pharmacy, 1980-84; owner Lang's Prescription Pharmacy, Chgo., 1983—, AML's Profl. Pharmacy, Chgo., 1984—. Mem. Am. Pharm. Assn., Nat. Pharm. Assn., Ill. Pharm. Assn., Chgo. Pharm. Assn., Am. Soc. Parenteral and Enteral Nutrition. Home: 6700 S Oglesby Ave Apt 401 Chicago IL 60649 Office: 9004 S Stony Island Ave Chicago IL 60617

LANG, BARBARA BETNER, management consultant; b. Bryn Mawr, Pa., Apr. 21, 1947; d. Thomas Eugene and Harriet (DeMott) Betner; B.A., Finch Coll., 1969; postgrad. in banking and econs. N.Y. Inst. Fin., 1973-77; m. Richard W. Lang, Jr., May 1, 1980; children—Richard W. III, Morgan Betner. With research dept. Lehman Bros. Inc., N.Y.C., 1972-73; v.p., investment mgr. instl. clients Fischer, Francis, Trees & Watts subs. Charter Atlantic Corp., N.Y.C., 1973-84, mgmt. cons., 1984—. Mem. N.Y. Jr. League. Republican. Episcopalian. Club: Bay Head Yacht. Office: 717 Fifth Ave New York NY 10022

LANG, BARBARA BRYANT, image consultant; b. Jacksonville, Fla., Oct. 16, 1943; d. Chester A. and Margaret (Small) Bryant; m. Gerald B. Lang, Apr. 30, 1962; 1 child, Yalanda Maria. B.S. in Bus. Edn., Edward Waters Coll., Jacksonville, Fla., 1965; postgrad. Calif. Research Lab., Sacramento, 1982. Adminstrn. mgr. IBM, Atlanta, 1976-78, mgr. adminstrn. ops., 1978-80, mgr. secretarial services, 1980-84, sr. fin. mgr., 1984-85; pres. GYB Assocs., Atlanta, 1985—. Past chpt. pres. Jack and Jill Am., 1983; co-chair adv. com. Southside High Sch., Atlanta, 1985-86; mem. task force Just Us Theatre, Atlanta, 1986. Mem. Women Bus. Owners, Am. Soc. Tng. and Devel., Nat. Assn. Female Execs., Atlanta C. of C. (women's workshop com. 1985), The Profl. Woman (bd. dirs.). Democrat. Presbyterian. Avocation: interior decorating. Home: 8700 Mount Rushmore Dr Alpharetta GA 30201 Office: GYB Assocs PO Box 250131 Atlanta GA 30201

LANG, CAROLINE OLMSTEAD, county official; b. Amsterdam, N.Y., Jan. 4, 1925; d. William R. and Laura V. (Hanson) Olmstead; m. Edward Albert Lang, July 27, 1943; children—Edward W., Charleen F. Cert. bookkeeping and shorthand Amsterdam Bus. Sch., 1942. Payroll clk. Mohawk Carpet Mills, Amsterdam, 1941-43; dep. commr. jurors Montgomery County, Fonda, N.Y., 1956-73, commr. jurors, 1974—; sec., treas. 4th Dist. Commn. Jurors, N.Y.C., 1968-70, v.p., 1970-72, pres., 1972-74. Sec. Fonda Fair Assn., 1965-75; Sunday sch. tchr. Glen Reformed Ch., Glen, N.Y., 1964-79. Republican. Club: Deborah Glen Study (pres. 1980—). Lodge: Order of Eastern Star. Avocations: crocheting; crafts; baking; rug making; gardening. Home: R D 1 Lang Dr Amsterdam NY 12010 Office: Montgomery County Commr Jurors Park St Fonda NY 12068

LANG, DOE, communication specialist, author, actress, educator; b. N.Y.C.; d. Samuel Nathaniel and Florence Edith Caplow; B.A., Bennington Coll.; postgrad. (Fulbright fellow) U. Perugia (Italy), 1951, Acad. of St. Cecilia, Rome, 1951-52; postgrad. Julliard Sch. Music, 1961-63, New Sch. for Social Research, 1975-76; children—Andrea Ilona, Brian Simpson. Profl. actress in Broadway shows West Side Story, Mame, also numerous off-Broadway shows, numerous TV commls. and TV voice-overs; dubbed numerous fgn. films; appeared in day-time TV series: Edge of Night, Another World, appeared as Karen Adams in As The World Turns; pres. Charismedia, speaking services firm, N.Y.C., 1975—; dir. Charisma Found.; pub. New Choices Press, 1985—; author: The Charisma Book: What It Is and How To Get It, 1980, 2d edit., The Secret of Charisma, 1982; author books for Sears Roebuck: Voice, Image and Self-Confidence; contbr. articles to New Woman, Woman's Day, Good Housekeeping mags.; mem. faculty New Sch. for Social Research; lectr., cons. in field; TV, radio appearances. Founder, producer, dir. and mistress-of-ceremonies People Party to Save the N.Y. Public Library and the Performing Arts Library, N.Y.C., 1972; mem. Com. to Save Sta.-WNCN, N.Y.C., 1976; a founder, bd. dirs. Symphony Space Cultural Center, N.Y.C.; mem. music com. Cathedral St. John the Divine, N.Y.C. Mem. Assn. Humanist Psychology, Assn. Transpersonal Psychology, DeToqueville Soc., Am. Psychol. Assn., Am. Lang. Assn., Authors Guild, Actors Equity, AAUP, AFTRA, Assn. Women Bus. Owners (dir. 1978-79), Subject of numerous articles; author memo to Pres. Carter on TV debates; author cassettes on stress mgmt., 1979-81. Office: 610 West End Ave New York NY 10024

LANG, GLORIA HELEN, tool engineer; b. N.Y.C., Mar. 15, 1932; d. Michael and Elizebeth (Snyder) L.; student Kent State U., 1957-61, Youngstown State U., 1977; A.A., SUNY, 1982. Retail salesman, 1947-51; owner, operator tax service, Tampa, Fla., 1954-55; tool and die maker Gen. Motors Corp., Warren, Ohio, 1955—; tool and die apprentice Ohio State U., 1972-76; tooling engr., cutting tool cons., pres., chief exec. officer Lang Industries, Inc., Warren, 1977—; lectr. on females in modern machine trades. Served with U.S. Army, 1951-54. Mem. Nat. Assn. Female Execs., Nat. Tool, Die and Precision Machining Assn., Nat. Small Bus. Assn., NOW, Internat. Platform Assn., Am. Soc. Bus. and Profl. Women, Am. Legion (past comdr. post 748 Warren). Home: 4793 Ardmore Ave Youngstown OH 44505 Office: Lang Industries Inc 2026 McMyler St NW Warren OH 44485

LANG, JEAN MCKINNEY, editor, educator; b. Cherokee, Iowa, Nov. 6, 1921; d. Roy Clarence and Verna Harvey (Smith) McKinney; B.S., Iowa State U., 1945; M.A., Ohio State U., 1969; postgrad. U. South Fla., 1972; 1 dau., Barbara Jean (Mrs. Michael L. Wilcox). Merchandiser, jewelry buyer Rike-

Kumler Co., Dayton, Ohio, 1952-59, Met. Co., Dayton, 1959-64; tchr. DeVilbiss High Sch., Toledo, 1966-67; chmn. dept. retailing Webber Coll., Babson Park, Fla., 1967-72; asso. editor Wet Set Illustrated, 1972-75; sr. editor Pleasure Boating, Largo, Fla., 1975—; tchr. bus. adminstrn. St. Petersburg (Fla.) Jr. Coll., 1974—. Mem. U.S. Senatorial Bus. Adv. Bd.; mem. Nat. Boating Safety Adv. Council, 1979-81; Recipient recognition Nat. Retail Mchts. Assn., 1971, certs. of appreciation U.S. Power Squadron, 1976, Webber Coll., 1972. Mem. Fla. Women's Network, Greater Tampa C. of C., AAUW, Tampa Aux. Power Squadron, U.S. Coast Guard Aux., Sales and Mktg. Execs. of Tampa (pres.'s award 1973), Fla. Outdoor Writers Assn., Am. Mktg. Assn., Gulf Coast Symphony, Internat. Platform Assn., Fla. Council Yacht Clubs, Chi Omega. Republican. Presbyterian. Clubs: Toledo Yacht (hon.), Tampa Yacht and Country. First woman to cruise solo from Fla. to Lake Erie in single-engine inboard, 1969, to be accepted into Fla. Council Yacht Clubs; yachting accomplishments published in The Ensign, Lakeland Boating, Yachting, Boote mags. Office: PO Box 402 Largo FL 34294

LANG, JUNE ESTELLE, trucking company executive, sports club executive; b. Milw., Dec. 22, 1940; d. Ernest J. and Elfrieda (Natzke) Runnoe; m. John F. Lang, Aug. 29, 1959; children—Michael D., Scott M., Pamela A. Clk., Fanny Farmer, Milw., 1956-57; payroll clk. John Hennes Trucking Co., Milw., 1958-60, office mgr., 1974-75, corp. sec., 1975—; gen. office worker Hennes Trucking, Zanesville, Ohio, 1970-74; owner, mgr. Kettle Moraine Racquet Club, Germantown, Wis., 1978—. Mem. Heavy Specialized Carriers Conf. Women's Aux. Republican. Roman Catholic. Club: Beaver Lake Yacht. Home: N62 W30431 Beaumont Ln Hartland WI 53029 Office: John Hennes Trucking Co 320 S 19th St PO Drawer 10H Milwaukee WI 53201

LANG, KATHERINE ANNE, counseling psychologist; b. Benson, Minn., Jan. 22, 1947; d. Howard James and Barbara Anne (Bennett) L. B.A. in Art History, Smith Coll., Northampton, Mass., 1969; M.A., Bethel Theol. Sem., St. Paul, 1973; M.Ed., U. Mo.-Columbia, 1978, Ph.D., 1982. Lic. psychologist, Calif. Tchr., Am. Sch., Barcelona, Spain, 1970-71; campus ministry Univ. Reformed Ch., East Lansing, Mich., 1973-76; counselor Univ. Counseling Ctr., U. Mo., Rolla, 1978-79; coordinator Ctr. for Student Vols. Action, 1979-81; counseling psychologist U. Calif., Davis, 1982—; pvt. practice counseling psychologist, Sacramento, Calif., 1986—; cons. in field. Mem. Am. Psychol. Assn., Am. Assn. Counseling and Devel., Am. Coll. Personnel Assn., Christina Assn. Psychol. Studies. Avocations: workshops on prayer; skiing; tennis; racquetball; writing. Office: Counseling Ctr Univ Calif Davis CA 95864

LANG, MABEL LOUISE, educator; b. Utica, N.Y., Nov. 12, 1917; d. Louis Bernard and Katherine (Werdge) Lang; B.A., Cornell U., 1939; M.A., Bryn Mawr Coll., 1940, Ph.D., 1943; Litt.D., Coll. Holy Cross, 1975, Colgate U., 1978. Mem. faculty Bryn Mawr Coll., 1943—, successively instr., asst. prof., 1943-50, assoc. prof., 1950-59, prof. Greek, 1959—, chmn. dept., 1960—, acting dean coll. 2d semester 1958-59, 60-61; chmn. mng. com. Am. Sch. Classical Studies, Athens, 1975-80, chmn. admissions and fellowship com., 1966-72; Blegen disting. research prof. semester I, Vassar Coll., 1976-77. Guggenheim fellow, 1953-54; Fullbright fellow, Greece, 1959-60. Mem. Am. Philos. Soc., Am. Acad. Arts and Scis., German Archaeol. Inst., Am. Philol. Assn., Archaeol. Inst. Am., Soc. Promotion Hellenic Studies (Eng.), Classical Assn. (Eng.). Co-author: Athenian Agora Weights, Measures and Tokens; author: The Palace of Nestor, Vol. II; The Frescoes; Athenian Agora Graffiti and Dipinti, 1976; Herodotean Narrative and Discourse, 1984. Contbr. articles to profl. jours. Home: 905 New Gulph Rd Bryn Mawr PA 19010 Office: Department Greek Bryn Mawr College Bryn Mawr PA 19010

LANG, MARIE LOEWENTHAL, public relations, communications executive, editor; b. N.Y.C., Jan. 24, 1935; d. Frederick George and Janet (Rosenhain) Loewenthal; B.A., NYU, 1957. Writer/producer radio/TV, N.Y.C., 1959-65; dir. pub. relations All Saints Episcopal Hosp., Ft. Worth, 1965-74; dir. community relations Am. Med. Internat., Inc., Beverly Hills, Calif., 1974-75; cons. community relations, Ft. Worth, 1977-82; dir. communications, community relations, publs. editor Tarrant County Med. Soc., Ft. Worth, 1982—. Author/editor: Chiropractic Research Found., 1979, 80; editor Tarrant County Physician, 1982, 83, 84, 85; producer film series House Calls, 1983, 84, 85, Mem. adv. council YWCA-Ft. Worth, 1982, 83, 84, 85, Tarrant County Youth Collaboration, Ft. Worth, 1983, 84, Ft. Worth/Tarrant County Epilepsy Assn., 1983-85. Mem. Women in Communications, Tex. Pub. Relations Assn., Bus. and Profl. Women's Club. Democrat. Jewish. Office: Tarrant County Med Soc 3855 Tulsa Way Ft Worth TX 76107

LANG, MARY SUE, lawyer; b. East Liverpool, Ohio, Jan. 11, 1936; d. Francis Harover and Rachel Louise (Boyce) Lang. B.F.A., Ohio Wesleyan U., 1957; M.A., Western Res. U., 1959; J.D. cum laude, Cleve. State U., 1974. Bar: Ohio 1974, U.S. Dist. Ct. (no. dist.) Ohio, 1976, U.S. Supreme Ct. 1978. Chmn. art dept. Kirk Jr. High Sch., East Cleveland, Ohio, 1959-63; tchr. art East Cleveland Bd. Edn., 1959-63; coordinator, dept. chmn., tchr. Rocky River (Ohio) Bd. Edn., 1963-75; sole practice law, East Liverpool, Ohio, 1975—. Exhibited in group shows Ohio State Fair, 1958, local shows in Rocky River and East Liverpool; murals executed Ogilvies Dept. Store, 1977, Central Service Automobile Dealer, 1978, First Nat. Bank, 1979, Crooks Furniture Store. Mem. East Ohio Conf. Commn. Status and Roles Women, United Meth. Ch., 1976-81, v.p. bd. trustees East Ohio Conf., 1981-85, pres., 1985—; chmn. council ministries 1st United Meth. Ch., East Liverpool, 1981-83; pres., dir. East Liverpool Area United Way, 1979-81; mem. bd. Kinoka Council, East Liverpool, 1976-80. Recipient John Collier award in bus. and fin. Kinoka council Campfire, 1981. Mem. ABA, Columbiana County Bar Assn., Ohio Bar Assn., Nat. Assn. Women Lawyers, Helen Gould Lit. Soc., Beta Kappa Pi. Republican. Club: Quota (dir. 1979—; 2nd v.p. 1983-85, 1st v.p. 1985-86, pres. 1986—) (East Liverpool). Home: 9 Highland Pl Dr East Liverpool OH 43920 Office: Mary Sue Lang Atty at Law 517 Broadway PO Box 103 East Liverpool OH 43920

LANG, PATRICIA ANN, software firm executive, writer; b. Oak Park, Ill., Mar. 20, 1947; d. John Joseph and Frances Elizabeth (Kirke) L.; m. Douglas Allen Braun, Sept. 16, 1967 (div. Sept. 1976). B.A. cum laude, Beloit Coll., 1969; postgrad. Boston U., 1971-72. Tchr. First Baptist Presch., Oak Park, 1966, 67-68, St. Brigid Sch., Boston, 1969-72; regional adminstr. TRW Fin. Systems, Wellesley, Mass., 1972-76; customer support rep. Olivetti Corp., Boston, 1976; mgr. mktg. communications Computer Sharing Services, Denver, 1976-82; dir. corp. communications Corp. Mgmt. Systems, Denver, 1982-85; sr. copywriter On-Line Software Internat., Fort Lee, N.J., 1985-86; mgr. corp. communications Health Mgmt. Systems, N.Y.C., 1986—. Warden, vestry mem. Trinity Ch., Wrentham, Mass., 1974-76; mem. vestry St. Philip and St. James Episcopal Ch., Denver, 1983; vol. Hospice of Holy Spirit, Lakewood, Colo., 1980-83; dir. pub. relations Bus. Roundtable on Nat. Security, Colo., 1983-84. Mem. Denver Advt. Fedn. (bd. dirs. 1981-83, Alfie award 1984), Colo. Conf. Communicators (Denver Advt. Fedn. liasion 1981-84), Bus. Execs. for Nat. Security. Democrat. Home: Box 718 Long Beach NY 11561 Office: Health Mgmt Systems 401 Park Ave S New York NY 10016

LANGDON, MARY, educator, musician; b. Fall River, Mass., Apr. 9, 1919; d. Richard and Mabel Rebecca (Hanscom) Leather; student Hartt Coll. Music, 1952-54; m. Wilbur Spencer Langdon II, Aug. 27, 1938; children—Carol Langdon Kohankie, Wilbur Spencer III. Numerous concert, oratorio, orch. and opera performances, 1952—; pvt. voice tchr., Mystic, Conn., 1952—; faculty U.R.I., Kingston, 1974—, asst. prof. music, 1981-84, assoc. prof., 1984—; adj. instr. in voice Conn. Coll., 1980. Bd. dirs. Music Sch. of Westerly Center for the Arts, 1980—. Mem. Nat. Assn. Tchrs. Singing (gov. Conn. chpt.), Music Tchrs. Nat. Ass., Internat. Assn. Research in Singing. Republican. Congregationalist. Home: 27 Gravel St Mystic CT 06355 Office: University of Rhode Island Music Dept Kingston RI 02881

LANGE, BETHANY KNOLL, behavioral disorder educator; b. Coshocton, Ohio, Aug. 4, 1951; d. N. Jean (Marvin) Knoll; m. Bruce A. Lange; 1 child, Dustin Knoll. B.S. in Edn., Ohio State U., 1976; M.Edn. with honors, Ohio U., 1982. Tchr. spl. edn. Licking County Schs., Newark, Ohio, 1976-80; spl. edn. supr.., intern Ohio U., Athens, 1982; dir. edn. and pub. relations Gallipolis Bus. Coll., Chillicothe, Ohio, 1982-83; mgr. tng. and devel. Scioto-Point Valley Mental Health Ctr., Chillicothe, 1983; dir. resource and mgmt. Comml. Hosp., Inc., Hilton Head Island, S.C., 1984; behavioral disorder tchr. Savannah-Chatham County Pub. Schs., Ga., 1985—; creative design cons. Front Page Design, Savannah, Ga., 1985-86; workshop presenter. Author: Contracting for Success. Mem. Nat. Assn. Female Execs., Ohio State U. Assn., Profl. Assn. Ga. Educators, Council for Exceptional Children, Council for Children with Behavioral Disorders, Phi Delta Kappa, Kappa Delta Pi. Jewish. Office: Wilder Middle Sch 1300 E 66th St Savannah GA 31404

LANGE, CATHERINE L, photographer; b. Chgo., Oct. 18, 1949; d. Frank Michael and Irene Josephine (Kozak) L.; B.A. in Visual Arts, DePaul U., 1982; postgrad. Inst. Design, Chgo., 1982-84; 1 dau., Jennifer C. Schmidt. Circulation and mktg. mgr. Ragan Communications, Inc., Chgo., 1978-80, mng. editor The Ragan Report, 1978-81, editor The Reporter's Report, 1979-81, contbg. editor Speechwriter's Newsletter, 1980-82; dir. Ragan Books, 1980-82; freelance photographer, 1982—. Home: 5138 S Whipple St Chicago IL 60632

LANGE, JESSICA, actress; b. Minn., Apr. 20, 1949; d. Al and Dorothy L.; m. Paco Grande, 1970 (div. 1982); 1 dau., Hannah Jane. Student, U. Minn., with Etienne DeCroux, Paris. Dancer Opera Comique, Paris; model Wilhelmina Agy., N.Y.C. Films include King Kong, 1976, All That Jazz, 1979, How to Beat the High Cost of Living, 1980, The Postman Always Rings Twice, 1981, Frances, 1982 (Acad. award nominee for best actress 1982), Tootsie, 1982 (Acad. award for best supporting actress 1982); appeared in summer sotck prodn. Angel on My Shoulder, N.C., 1980. Office: care Creative Artists Agy Inc Suite 1400 Los Angeles CA 90067*

LANGE, MAUREEN SYLVIA, motel owner; b. Detroit, Feb. 5, 1937; d. Stanley Francis and Pauline Stella (Glinka) Staniec; m. Richard A. Lange, May 5, 1962; children—Lisa Lynn, Lance Larry. Ph.B., U. Detroit, 1959; postgrad. Wayne State U., 1961, Saginaw Valley State Coll., 1979. Sec., Gen. Motors Corp., Detroit, 1954-57; advt. aid Ross-Roy Advt. Agy., Detroit, 1961; Specialized Communications, Detroit, 1958-60; sec. R.L. Polk & Co., Detroit, 1959-60; mgr. Pinconning Trail House, Mich., 1968-75, In Town Inn, Standish, Mich., 1975—. Mem. Mich. Lodging Assn., E. Mich. Tourist Assn., Huron Shores Tourist Alliance, Bay County YWCA, Bay County Hist. Soc., Pinconning C. of C., Standish C. of C., Mid-Mich. Rose Soc., Friends of Polish Culture. Democrat. Roman Catholic. Clubs: Pinconning Women's Community (pres. 1980-84), Women's Guild of St. Juliana (v.p. 1965-68). Home: PO Box 718 222 E Pinconning Rd Pinconning MI 48650 Office: PO Box 118 304 N Main St Standish MI 48658

LANGENBACH, LISA GAYE, educator; b. Norfolk, Va., Aug. 10, 1958; d. Robert Warren and Gaye (Hilliard) L.; B.A., Mary Washington Coll., 1980; M.A., Purdue U., 1982, Ph.D. candidate, 1982—. Teaching asst. Purdue U., 1980-82, instr. polit. sci., 1982—. Mem. ACLU (chpt. pres.), NOW (treas. 1978), Women's Caucus for Polit. Sci., Am. Polit. Sci. Assn., Pi Sigma Alpha. Democrat. Unitarian. Office: Purdue U West Lafayette IN 47907

LANGENTHAL, SHARI JOY, lawyer, auctioneer; b. Brookline, Mass., June 18, 1955; d. Phoebe (Smith) L. Student Simmons Coll., 1972-73; A.B. magna cum laude, Brandeis U., 1976; diploma in edn. McGill U., 1977; J.D., Suffolk U., 1982. Bar: Mass. 1983, U.S. Dist. Ct. Mass. 1983; lic. auctioneer, Mass.; real estate broker, Mass. Auctioneer's asst. Mark E. Pearlmutter Co., Boston, 1973-83, cons. research and appraisal, part-time 1983—; intern Judge Santo J. Ruma, Boston, summer 1978; legal intern Suffolk County Dist. Atty.'s Office, Appellate Div., Boston, 1981; assoc. Karger, Krulewich & Arnowitz, Boston, 1983—; owner Auctions by Shari, Brookline, Mass., 1983—. Recipient award Brandeis U. Alumni Assn., 1976; Am. Jurisprudence award, 1979-80. Mem. ABA, Mass. Bar Assn., Boston Bar Assn., Assn. Trial Lawyers Am., Comml. Law League Am., Phi Delta Phi. Democrat. Jewish. Club: New Century. Home: 101 Saint Paul St Brookline MA 02146 Office: Karger Krulewich & Arnowitz 18 Tremont St Boston MA 02108

LANGER, DOROTHY, venture capitalist; b. Boston, Aug. 1, 1942; d. Harold Aaron and Goldie (Fineman) Potcherkoff; B.S. in Chemistry, Simmons Coll., 1964. Tech. librarian Shell Chem. Co., N.Y.C., 1964-65; research chemist Radiation Research Corp., Westbury, L.I., 1965-68; systems engr. IBM, 1968-71, mktg. rep., 1972-73, process industry rep., 1973-74, mktg. mgr., 1974-76, regional mktg. mgr., 1976-77, corp. mktg. cons., 1977-79, br. mgr., 1980-81; v.p. mktg. Gartner Group, Inc., Stamford, Conn. 1982-83; dir. N.E. ops. Businessland, Inc., Stamford, 1983-84; with 3i Ventures, Boston, 1985—; lectr. on women's issues. Trustee, Simmons Coll., 1977-82; bd. dirs. Capital Dist. Jr. Achievement, 1980-82; chmn. corp. giving Simmons Coll. Pride II, 1981-86. Mem. Boston Computer Soc., Beacon Hill Civic Assn., Mensa. Office: 3i Ventures 99 High St Boston MA 02110

LANGER, EVA MARIE, marketing executive; b. Oceanside, Calif., Sept. 23, 1958; d. William Frank and Clotilde (Gonzalo) Langer. B.S., San Diego State U., 1980. Audio engr. Peters Prodns., San Diego, 1980-83; news writer Sta. KSDO, San Diego, 1981-82; audio prodn. engr. Tuesday Prodns., San Diego, 1983-85; video technician Voice & Video, San Diego, 1983-84, ednl. sales staff, 1984-85, govt. and ednl. mktg. saleswoman, 1985-86, corp. and comml. mktg. saleswoman, 1986—; ind. radio producer, San Diego, 1984—, ind. music searcher, 1984-85. Camera operator Mothers Embracing Nuclear Disarmament, San Diego, 1985. Mem. Am. Women in Radio and TV (dir.-at-large 1985, editor newsletter 1985), Nat. Assn. Female Execs., Am. Film Inst., Internat. Interactive Communications Soc. Democrat. Home: 4826 Jean Dr San Diego CA 92115 Office: Voice & Video Inc 5038 Ruffner St San Diego CA 92111

LANGER, JUDITH, marketing researcher; b. N.Y.C., July 27, 1941; d. Albert Paul William and Augusta (Truell) Wollheim. A.B., Smith Coll., 1962; M.A., Columbia U., 1964. Mem. coding staff Louis Harris Assocs., N.Y.C., 1963-64; coding head Roger Assocs., N.Y.C., 1964-66; research asst. Brand Rating Index, N.Y.C., 1966; project dir. NBC, N.Y.C., 1966-70; v.p. qualitative research, MPI Mktg. Research, N.Y.C., 1970-76; v.p., Lieberman Research West, Los Angeles, 1969-79; dir. Langer Assocs., N.Y.C., 1979—; pres. Qualitative Research Cons. Assocs., N.Y.C., 1983—. Contbr. articles to profl. jours. Mem. Advt. Research Found., Qualitative Research Cons. Assn., Am. Mktg. Assn., Nat. Assn. Women Bus. Owners. Office: Langer Assocs Inc 133 E 58th St New York NY 10022

LANGEVIN, JUDITH BEVIS, lawyer; b. Tampa, Fla., Sept. 18, 1948; d. Harold Wayne and Colleen Beverly (Lunsford) Bevis; B.A., U. Calif., Berkeley, 1970; J.D., U. Minn., 1973; m. Steven Paul Lapinsky, June 1982; children—Jacob, Joshua. Bar: Minn. 1973. Social planner City of St. Paul, 1973, spl. asst. to mayor, 1973-74, asst. dir. dept. human rights, 1974-75; conciliator Minn. Dept. Human Rights, St. Paul, 1975-79, asst. commr., 1979-81; partner firm Horton and Langevin, Mpls., 1981-85, Robins, Zelle, Larson & Kaplan, 1985—; mem. Hennepin County Legal Advice Clinic; adj. faculty William Mitchell Coll. Law, St. Paul. lectr., cons. on employment law, civil rights. Author: Equal Employment Laws and How They Affect Your Business, 1984. Chmn., Mayor's Adv. Com. on Health, St. Paul, 1974. Mem. Am. Bar Assn., Minn. Bar Assn. (exec. council sect. labor and employment law 1983-86), Hennepin County Bar Assn. (co-chair com. labor and employment law 1985-86). Democrat. Office: 1800 Internat Centre 900 2d Ave S Minneapolis MN 55402

LANGFELD, MARILYN IRENE, creative art company director; b. St. Louis, Apr. 28, 1951; d. Norman Max and Celeste (Brown) L. Student, Vanderbilt U., 1968-70; B.A. cum laude, Sonoma State U., 1978-80. Printer, Sojourner Truth Press, Altanta, 1971-73; carpenter apprentice Housebuilders Union, Atlanta, 1973-74; self employed housebuilder, Perry, Me., 1974-75; graphic artist Cuthberts Printing, San Rafael, Calif., 1976-77; graphic Designer Community Type & Design, Fairfax, Calif., 1977-80; owner, creative dir. Langfeld Assocs., San Francisco, 1980—. Mem. People Speaking Adv. Bd., 1979-83. Sonoma State scholar, Bank of Sonoma County, 1979-80; Vanderbilt U. scholar, 1968-69, 69-70. Mem. Bookbuilders West, San Francisco C. of C., Am. Inst. Graphic Designers, San Francisco Art Dirs. Club, Internat. Assn. Bus. Communicators, Assn. Multi-Image, Western Art Dirs. Club. Art Dirs. and Artists of Sacramento, San Francisco C. of C. Democrat. Jewish. Office: 381 Clementina St San Francisco CA 94103

LANGFORD, MARY ANNE, geologist; b. Columbia, S.C., Dec. 8, 1956; d. John Monroe and Ramona Dare (Addy) Langford. B.Sc. (magna cum laude), U. S.C., 1979, M.Sc., 1981. Geol. lab. tech. U. S.C., Columbia, 1976-79, field mapping geologist Mediterranean region, 1979-80; geologist Exxon Co. USA, Houston, 1981-82, sr. petroleum geologist, 1983—. Amoco Scholar, 1978-79; La. State U. grantee, 1979-80. Mem. Am. Assn. Petroleum Geologists, Houston Geol. Soc., Phi Beta Kappa. Republican. Lutheran. Club: Houston Exxon. Home: 5603 Cactus Forest Dr Houston TX 77088 Office: Exxon Co USA PO Box 2180 4550 Dacoma-Gulf Coast Div Houston TX 77001

LANGHAM, NORMA, educator, author, composer; b. California, Pa.; d. Alfred Scrivener and Mary Edith (Carter) Langham; B.S., Ohio State U., 1942; B. Theatre Arts, Pasadena Playhouse Coll. Theatre Arts, 1944; M.A., Stanford, 1956, postgrad. Summer Radio-TV Inst., 1960; student Pasadena Inst. Radio, 1944-45. Tchr. sci. California High Sch., 1942-43; asst. office pub. info. Denison U., Granville, Ohio, 1955; instr. speech dept. Westminster Coll., New Wilmington, Pa., 1957-58; instr. theatre. California U. of Pa., 1959, asst. prof., 1960-62, assoc. prof., 1962-79, emeritus, 1979—, co-founder, sponsor, dir. Children's Theatre, 1962-79; founder, producer, dir. Food Bank Players, 1985, Patriot Players, 1986. Recipient award exceptional acad. service Pa. Dept. Edn., 1975; Appreciation award Bicentennial Commn. Pa., 1976. Henry C. Frick Ednl. Commn. grantee. Mem. Theatre Assn. Pa., Children's Theatre Assn., Internat. Platform Assn., California U. of Pa. Assn. Women Faculty (founder, pres. 1972-73), AAUW (co-founder California br., 1st v.p. 1971-72, pres. 1972-73; Outstanding Woman of Yr. 1986), Dramatists Guild, DAR, Alpha Psi Omega, Omicron Nu. Presbyn. (elder). Author: (play) Magic in the Sky, 1963; (text) Public Speaking; (play) John Dough (Freedoms Found. award 1968); (plays) Who Am I?, Hippocrates Oath, Gandhi; composer-lyricist (play) Why Me, Lord?; Music in Freedom, The Day the Moon Fell. Home: Box 455 California PA 15419

LANGHOUT-NIX, NELLEKE, artist; b. Utrecht, Netherlands, Mar. 27, 1939; came to U.S., 1968, naturalized, 1978; d. Louis Wilhelm Frederick and Geertruida (Smits) Nix; M.F.A., The Hague, 1958; m. Ernst Langhout, July 26, 1958; 1 son, Klaas-Jan Marnix. Head art dept. Bush Sch., Seattle, 1969-71; dir. creative projects Project Reach, Seattle, 1971-72; artist-in-residence Fairhaven Coll., Bellingham, Wash., 1974, Jefferson Community Center, Seattle, 1978-82, Lennox Sch., N.Y.C., 1982; dir. NN Gallery, Seattle, 1970—; guest curator Holland-U.S.A. Bicentennial show U. Wash., 1982, Birdshow, Chase Gallery, 1983; executed wall hanging for King County Courthouse, Seattle, 1974; one-woman shows: Nat. Art Center, N.Y.C., 1980, Gail Chase Gallery, Bellevue, Wash., 1979, 80, 83, 84, Original Graphics Gallery, Seattle, 1981, Bon Nat. Gallery, Seattle, 1981, Kathleen Ewing Gallery, Washington, 1986; 3-man show Exhbn. Space, N.Y.C., 1982; group shows include: Cheney Cowles Mus., Spokane, 1977, Bellevue Art Mus., 1978, Renwick Gallery, Washington, 1978, Kleinert Gallery, Woodstock, N.Y., 1979, Artcore Meltdown, Sydney, Australia, 1979, Tacoma Art Mus., 1979, 83, Ill. State Mus., Springfield, 1979, Plener Sandomierz, Poland, 1980, Plener Kielce, Poland, 1980, Western Assn. Art Museums traveling show, 1979-80, Madison Square Garden, N.Y.C., 1981; represented in permanent collections Plener Collection, Sandomierz, Poland; Bell Telephone Co. Collection, Seattle, Children's Orthopedic Hosp., Seattle, installations Tacoma Art Mus. Bd. dirs. Wing Luke Mus., Seattle, 1978-81; v.p. Denny Regrade Community Council, 1978-79; mem. Seattle Planning Commn., 1978-84. Recipient Wallhanging award City of Edmonds (Wash.), 1974; Renton 83 merit award, 1984; Merit award Internat. Platform Assn. Art Exhibit, 1984, silver medal 1st place, 1985. Mem. Denny Regrade Arts Council (co-founder). Allied Arts Seattle, Nat. Platform Assn., Wash. State Art Alliance, Nat. Mus. Women in Arts (a founder), Seattle-King County Community Arts Network (bd. dirs. 1983—, chmn. 1984—). Mailing address: PO Box 375 Mercer Island WA 98040

LANG-JETER, LULA L., federal government administrator; b. Carrollton, Ala., May 19; d. John W. Sr. and Annie Lee (Cole) Lang; m. James Jeter; B.S. in Acctg., Central State U., Wilberforce, Ohio, 1951. Acct. Central State U., Wilberforce, 1951-60, v.p. fiscal affairs, 1967-68; with IRS, 1960-67, 68—; br. chief, Washington, 1975-78, asst. dir., Indpls. and Washington, 1979—; mem. adv. bd. Fed. Employed Women, 1983-85. Co-chmn. minority task force Am. Cancer Soc., Arlington, Va., 1982-85; mem. Arlington Coalition Minority Affairs; bd. dirs. Coalition 100 Black Women, Washington; sec. Links, Inc., Arlington, 1984-85. Named to Top Ten Women of Miami Valley, Dayton Daily News, Ohio, 1969, Fed. Employee of Yr., Fed. Exec. Bd., Cin., 1971, Fed. Woman of Yr., IRS, 1972, Fed. Employee of Yr., IRS, 1983; recipient Outstanding Services award Ala. A&M Alumni Assn., Detroit, 1973. Mem. Am. Soc. Women Accts., Bus. and Profl. Women's Fin. Assn., Nat. Council Negro Women named in 100 Outstanding Black Women, Indpls. 1983), LWV, Alpha Kappa Alpha (nat. treas., nat. treas. Ednl. Advancement Found. 1982—). Methodist. Lodges: Eastern Star, Daughters of Isis. Avocation: bowling. Home: 1001 S Queen St Arlington VA 22204 Office: IRS 1111 Constitution Ave Washington DC 20224

LANGLEY, LYNNE SPENCER, newspaper editor, columnist; b. West Palm Beach, Fla., June 4, 1947; d. George Hosmer and Elwa June (Harries) Spencer; B.A. with honors, Coll. of Wooster, 1969; student Glasgow U., Scotland, 1967-68; m. William A. Langley, Oct. 10, 1970. Feature writer, asst. women's editor Palm Beach Times, West Palm Beach, Fla., 1969-70; asst. editor Brunswick (Maine) Times Record, 1971; investigative reporter Maine Times, Topsham, 1971-75; asst. mng. editor York County Coast Star, Kennebunk, Maine, 1976-78; gardening editor, nature columnist, reporter Charleston (S.C.) Post-Courier, 1979—; editor Maine Audubon Soc. News, 1975-76; stringer Newsweek mag., 1971-75; freelance writer; speaker. Active Charleston Natural History Soc., Nat. Audubon Soc. Recipient Communicator of Yr. award S.C. Wildlife Fedn., 1983; journalism awards S.C. Press Assn., S.C. Assn. Mentally Retarded, Charleston Natural History Soc., 1985, Charleston County Parks and Recreation Commn., 1985. Mem. Am. Hort. Soc., Garden Writers Assn. Am., PEO (sec. chpt. D Maine 1975-76, corr. sec. chpt. J S.C. 1986-87), Sigma Delta Chi. Home: PO Box 97 Adams Run SC 29426 Office: 134 Columbus St Charleston SC 29401

LANGLIE, RAGNHILD IRENE, state civil service executive; b. Niagara Falls, N.Y., Aug. 10, 1946; d. Olaf Martin and Lillian (Hayes) L. B.A. in Psychology, SUNY-Buffalo, 1972. Personnel examiner N.Y. State Civil Service, Albany, 1980-84, staffing services rep., 1984—, chairperson career devel. com., 1984—. Recipient cert. merit N.Y. State Civil Service Commn., 1983. Mem. Orgn. Mgmt. Confidential Employees, Internat. Personnel Mgmt. Assn. Republican. Club: Scandinavian Circle (Albany). Avocations: travel; collecting Viking and cat statues; reading. Office: New York State Dept Civil Service State Office Bldg Campus Albany NY 12239

LANGLOIS, CYNTHIA JEAN, software vendor executive, consultant; b. Norway, Mich., Oct. 11, 1947; d. Arthur Louis and Antoinette (Arvia) L. Site mgr. Applied Info. Devel., Oak Brook, Ill., 1977-82; tech. account mgr. Tritec Cons., Des Plaines, Ill., 1982; mgr. Bus. Systems Corp. Am., Chgo., 1982—; cons. in field, Hinsdale, Ill., 1982—. Tchr. Notre Dame Catholic Ch., Clarendon Hills, Ill., 1979-82. Mem. Nat. Assn. Female Execs. Republican. Avocations: decorative sewing; golf; fishing; word puzzles. Office: Bus Systems Corp Am 2 N Riverside Pl Chicago IL 60606

LANGLOIS, DONNA LEE, beauty trade school administrator; b. Harvey, Ill., Nov. 1, 1936; d. Leonard Clay and Mildred Anna (Seibert) Hampton; m. Robert Marvin Langlois, Oct. 15, 1974; children—Renee A. Holsen, Scott C. Farrand. Student U. Chgo., 1955-57, Art Inst. Chgo., 1956-58. Office mgr. Luth. Brotherhood Life Ins. Co., Chgo., 1959-72; sales dir. Mary Kay Cosmetics, Dallas, 1972-76; exec. sec. to pres. and chmn. bd. Talal Abu-Ghazaleh & Co., Kuwait, 1976-77; area mgr. Luzier Cosmetics Co., Kansas City, Kans., 1977-78; nat. dir. home mktg. div. Yves Roche Internat., Northbrook, Ill., 1979-81; mgr. Wilfred Am. Ednl. Corp., N.Y.C., 1981—. Recipient various sales awards. Mem. Chgo. Assn. Women Bus. Owners, Nat. Assn. Female Execs. Lutheran. Avocations: professional organist; reading; golfing. Home: 1230 N State Pkwy Chicago IL 60610 Office: Wilfred Am Ednl Corp 65 E South Water St Chicago IL 60601

LANGNER, WANDA LOU TRIPLETT, family marriage therapist, psychotherapist; b. Des Moines, Feb. 8, 1943; d. Charles Roy and Elizabeth Jean (Schockley) Triplett; m. K. Ronald Langner, May 25, 1968 (div. May 1984); children—Kathryn Grace, Jonathan Taylor. B.A., Simpson Coll., Indianola, Iowa, 1965; M.S.W., U. Iowa, 1973, Post Bachelorate, 1974; Family Therapy degree, Menninger Found., Topeka, 1982. Lic. social worker, Ark. Asst. prof. home econs., Simpson Coll., 1964-65; with mktg. div. Maytag, Newton, Iowa, 1965-68; dir. licensing Dept. Social Service State of Iowa, Polk County, 1968-70, protective services supr., Polk and Jasper County, Iowa, 1968-71; program dir., coordinator Child Devel. Labs. for Children's Edn., 1972-76; social work coordinator Heartland Area Edn. Agy., Ankeny, Iowa, 1976-80; dir. family counseling services Mid-West Clin. Assocs., Des Moines, 1981-84, Iowa Methodist Ch., Des Moines, 1981-84, Poweshiek County Mental Health Ctr., Grinnell, Iowa, 1981-84; out-patient therapist Ozark Guidance Ctr., Springdale, Ark., 1984—, cons. br. Corp. Growth Cons., 1984—. Mem., rep. Iowa Democratic Assn., Jasper County, 1978-83; deacon First United

Presbyterian Ch., Grinnell, 1982-84. Mem. Am. Assn. Marriage and Family Therapists, Lic. Cert. Social Workers Ark., Nat. Assn. Cert. Social Workers. Methodist. Club: Soroptimist Internat. (v.p.-pres. 1980-82). Avocations: swimming; horseback riding; volunteer services to nursing care facilities. Office: Ozark Guidance Ctr 219 S Thompson St Springdale AR 72764

LANGSTAFF, ELEANOR MARGUERITE, library science educator; b. Washinton, June 21, 1934; d. William Truman and Bernice Louise (Tharpe-Mecum) De Selms; m. David Knox Langstaff, June 19, 1970. B.A., Colo. State U.-Ft. Collins, 1958; M.A., Fordham U., 1961; M.S., Catholic U. Am., 1970; postgrad. CUNY, 1979—; cert. in tropical edn. U. London/Makerere Coll., Uganda. Mem. Tchrs. for East Africa program Columbia U., N.Y.C., 1961-64; fgn. service officer USIA, 1965-69, acting country pub. affairs officer, Bangui, Central African Republic, 1967-68, regional books officer, Lagos, Nigeria, 1968-69; librarian Sch. Library and Info. Sci., Pratt Inst., N.Y.C., 1970-72; assoc. prof. library sci. Bernard M. Baruch Coll., CUNY, 1973—; cons. on info. Langstaff-French Assocs., Manchester, Vt., 1982—. Author: Andrew Lang, 1978; (with Thomas V. Atkins) Access to Information: Library Research Methods, 1979; Panama, 1982. Vol., ARC, Bklyn., 1972—. Recipient excellence in French lit. award French Govt., 1958. Mem. ALA, Library Assn. CUNY (v.p. 1974-75, pres. 1975-76), Assn. Coll. and Research Libraries, Phi Beta Mu. Episcopalian. Home: 100 Remsen St Brooklyn NY 11201 Office: 317 Baruch Coll CUNY 156 E 25th St New York NY 10010

LANGSTON, LEE ANN, museum curator, preservationist; b. Takoma Park, Md., Feb. 28, 1957; d. William Greenwood and Joann Katherine (Hawkes) Langston. B.A., St. Mary's Coll., 1979; postgrad. U. Kent, Canterbury, Eng., 1979; M.A., U. Calif.-Riverside, 1981. Office asst. Bannockburn, U. Calif.-Riverside, 1978; intern dir. Palm Springs Hist. Soc., Calif., 1980, dir., curator, 1981-83; dir. Scottsboro-Jackson Heritage Ctr., Ala., 1984-86; curator James Monroe Law Office/Mus., Fredericksburg, Va., 1986—; intern Md. State Hall of Records, Annapolis, 1978, Smithsonian Inst. Mus. Am. History, 1976; vol./student intern St. Mary's City Commn., Md., 1977. Rep. El Mirador Tower Preservation Bd., Palm Springs, 1980-82; bd. dirs. League Women Voters, Palm Springs, 1982-83; bd. dirs. LWV Task Force on Children's Issues, 1981-83; bd. advisors Riverside County Arts Council, Palm Springs, 1983; mem. planning com. Calif. State Preservation Bd., Riverside and Palm Springs, 1981-82; dist. rep., bd. dirs. Ala. Mus. Assn., Scottsboro, 1985-86; rep. El Mirador Tower Preservation Bd., Palm Springs, 1982-83. Recipient Melba B. Bennet award Palm Springs Hist. Soc., 1981. Mem. Nat. Assn. Exec. Females, Am. Assn. Museums, Am. Assn. State and Local History, Smithsonian Assocs. (assoc.), Ala. Mus. Assn. (dist. rep. 1985-86), Va. Mus. Assn. Roman Catholic. Club: Newcomer's (Scottsboro, Ala.). Avocations: archaeology; reading; dancing; hiking. Home: 1403 Caroline St Fredericksburg VA 22401 Office: James Monroe Mus and Meml Library 908 Charles St Fredericksburg VA 22401

LANGSTON, MARY JANE, educator, daycare administrator; b. Huntsville, Ala., June 15, 1940; d. Walter Edmund and Charlotte Elizabeth (White) Daniels; m. Daniel Roger Langston, Dec. 21, 1963; children—Daniel Stuart, Roger Evin. B.S. in Home Econs. Edn., U. Ala.-Tuscaloosa, 1962; postgrad. Ala. A&M U., 1967. Asst. home demonstration agt., 4-H leader Auburn U. Ext. Service, Ft. Payne, Ala., 1962-63; tchr. Huntsville City Schs., 1963-66; counselor, tchr. Madison County Schs., Ala., 1966-72; owner, dir. Ann's Nursery Sch., Kindergarten and Day Care Ctr., Huntsville, 1972—. Mem. adv. com. for child devel. area Madison County Tech. Schs., 1975—; mem. planning com. Stop Child Abuse and Neglect, 1983-84; active 1st Bapt. Ch., Huntsville, 1983—. Mem. Nat. Assn. Edn. Young Children, Assn. Childhood Edn. Internat. (treas. 1983-85), Day Care Dirs. Assn. Of Huntsville (pres. 1972-74, v.p. 1975-76). Club: Huntsville Country. Avocations: gardening; sewing; costume design. Home: 2016 Big Cove Rd SE Huntsville AL 35801 Office: Ann's Nursery Sch 1837 Bankhead Pkwy Huntsville AL 35801

LANGSTON, SALLY J., librarian; b. Shreveport, La., May 13, 1947; d. Joseph Boles and Rebecca Anne (Taylor) L.; B.A., Tex. Woman's U., 1968, M.L.S., 1969. Reference librarian Bishop Coll., Dallas, 1969-71; cataloger U. Houston Law Ctr., 1971-73; tech. services librarian So. Meth. U. Law Sch., Dallas, 1973-78; law librarian Arnold, White & Durkee, Houston, 1978-79; pub. services librarian S. Tex. Coll. Law, Houston, 1979—; dir. library services Barrister Club, Houston, 1985—; archivist Southwest Film Archive, Dallas, 1976-78. Recipient Dept. Edn. scholarship, 1968-69. Mem. Am. Assn. Law Libraries, Houston Area Law Librarians (sec. 1983-84). Democrat. Avocations: reading; book and record collecting, breeding Arabian horses. Home: Route 2 Box 673 F Willis TX 77378-9401 Office: S Tex Coll Law 1303 San Jacinto Houston TX 77002

LANGWORTHY, AUDREY HANSEN, state senator; b. Grand Forks, N.D., Apr. 1, 1938; d. Edward and Arla (Kuhlman) Hansen; m. Asher C. Langworthy, Jr., Sept. 8, 1962; children—Kristin Hansen, Julia Hodges. Student, Colo. Coll., 1956-57; B.S., U. Kans., 1960, M.S., 1962. Tchr. jr. high Shawnee Mission Sch. Dist., Johnson County, Kans., 1963-65; councilman City of Prairie Village, Kans., 1981-85; mem. Kans. Senate, 1984—; del. Midwestern Conf. State Legislatures, 1985—; alt. del. Nat. Conf. State Legislatures, 1985—. Bd. dirs. Greater Kansas City ARC, 1975—, chmn., 1983-84; bd. dirs. Kansas City Eye Bank, 1979—, pres., 1981-84; bd. dirs., chmn. United Way PAR Bd., Kansas City, 1983—; city co-chmn. Kassebaum for Senate, 1978, Winn for Congress, 1980, 82. Recipient Bernie Hoffman Outstanding Vol. Community Services award, 1983; Confidence in Edn. award Kans. Friends of Edn. City Govt., 1984. Mem. LWV, Jr. League of Kansas City (pres. 1976-77), AAUW, English-Speaking Union, U. Kans. Alumni Assn., Nat. Republican Legislators Assn., Kappa Kappa Gamma. Republican. Lutheran. Avocations: hunting; running; family. Home: 6324 Ash Prairie Village KS 66208

LANHAM, BETTY BAILEY, anthropologist, educator; b. Statesville, N.C., Aug. 12, 1922; d. Clyde B. and Naomi (Bailey) L.; B.S., U. Va., 1944, M.A., 1947; Ph.D., Syracuse U., 1962. Faculty, River Falls State Tchrs. Coll., 1948-49, U. Md., 1949-50, Randolph Macon Womens Coll., 1954-55, Oswego State Tchrs. Coll., 1956-58, Hamilton Coll., 1961-62, Ind. U., 1962-65, Western Mich. U., 1965-67, Albany Med. Coll., 1967-70; prof. anthropology Indiana U. of Pa., 1970—; vis. prof. Wakayama (Japan) U., 1951-52, U. Guyana, 1969-70. Werner-Gren Found. for Anthrop. Research fellow, 1951-52, AAUW research fellow, 1959-60. Mem. Am. Anthrop. Assn., Assn. for Asian Studies. Democrat. Methodist. Contbr. articles to profl. jours. Home: 121 Dolores Circle Indiana PA 15701 Office: Dept Sociology-Anthropology Indiana U of Pa Indiana PA 15705

LANIER, ALISON RAYMOND, author, intercultural specialist; b. N.Y.C., Apr. 1, 1917; d. Edward Holman and Isabel (Ashwell) Raymond; B.A. cum laude, Bryn Mawr Coll., 1938; m. Albert G. Lanier, Sept. 9, 1967. Asst. dir. pub. relations Bryn Mawr (Pa.) Coll., 1941-42; co-dir. N.Y. Office Internat. Child Welfare Union Geneva, N.Y.C., 1946-47; pub. relations dir. World Affairs Council Phila., 1947-51, Eastern area Pa. CD, Phila., 1951-55; exec. dir. Com. of Corr., N.Y.C., 1955-61; editor monthly publ. for UN personnel under Carnegie Endowment for Internat. Peace, N.Y.C., 1961-65; dir. meetings and programs Fgn. Policy Assn., N.Y.C., 1965-66; founder, pres. Overseas Briefing Assocs., N.Y.C., 1967-81; pres. Resources Internat., Ex-Patriot Newsletter; intercultural cons. to numerous multinat. corps., 1981—; lectr. New Sch. Social Research, N.Y.C., U.S. Dept. State Fgn. Service Inst., Washington, World Trade Inst., N.Y.C., Am. Mgmt. Assn., N.Y.C. Served with USN, 1942-46; comdr. Res. (ret.). Mem. Internat. Cons. Found., Soc. Internat. Edn., Tng. and Research, Am. Soc. Tng. Dirs., Soc. Internat. Devel., U.S. Nat. China Relations Com., Nat. Writers Club, Fgn. Policy Assn., Res. Officers Assn. Club: Bryn Mawr (N.Y.C.). Author 23 books including China Today: The Family and the Nation, 1974; Living in the U.S.A., 1975; Living in Europe, 1975; series of updates on countries including Update: Saudi Arabia, 1981, Update: Indonesia, 1982; editor, co-pub. Living Abroad (now called The International American), 1982—; contbr. numerous articles to mags. Home: 66 Little Brook Rd Wilton CT 06897 Office: 201 E 36th St New York NY 10016

LANIEWSKI, SUSAN ANNE, government analyst, intelligence researcher in law enforcement and security; b. Pitts., Aug. 29, 1955; d. Stephen Michael and Mary Richiemer (Williams) L. Student Pa. State U., University Park, 1973-76; B.A. in Sociology and Criminal Justice magna cum laude, La Salle Coll., Phila., 1978; M.P.A. magna cum laude, Inst. Pub. Adminstr., Pa. State U.-Radnor, 1980. Vol. counselor Montgomery County Ct., Norristown, Pa., 1973; statistician Del. Crime Commn., Wilmington, 1976-78; adminstrv. asst. to chief Bristol Twp. Police, Levittown, Pa., 1978-80; analyst Office of Dir., U.S. Marshal's Service, McLean, Va., 1980-84; program analyst Office of Insp. Gen., Dept. Agr., Washington, 1984—; conclave chmn. Arnold Air Soc., Phila., 1975-76; presdl. mgmt. intern Dept. Justice, Washington, 1980-82, mem. violence prone group task force, 1983; tng. officer Fed. Law Enforcement Tng. Ctr., Glynco, Ga., 1982-84. Editorial bd. book: ABA Jury Standards, 1982; editorial bd. Policenet, 1984, also editorial adviser, 1983-84. Mem. exec. council Air Force ROTC, Pa. State U., University Park, 1975-76; co-writer community crime prevention legis. State of Del., Wilmington, 1977; tutor G.E.D. Learning Program, Fairfax County Schs., Va., 1983—, Vol. Learning Program, Fairfax County, 1983—. Recipient Service award Air Force Assn., State College chpt., Pa., 1975, Theodore C. Marrs award Air Force Assn., Phila., 1976, Outstanding Comdr. award LaSalle Coll. ROTC, 1977. Mem. Nat. Assn. Female Execs., Am. Assn. Criminology, Am. Polit. Sci. Assn., Internat. Assn. Law Enforcement Intelligence Analysts (cert. intelligence analyst), Soc. Criminal Justice Ethics, Am. Soc. Pub. Adminstrn., Alpha Epsilon. Republican. Roman Catholic. Lodge: Frat. Order Police. Avocations: stamp collecting; international travel; sewing and embroidery; computer programming; interior decorating. Home: 102 S Virginia Ave Falls Church VA 22046 Office: Dept Agr Office Insp Gen 14th and Independence SW Washington DC 20250

LANKAU, JUDITH LAMPMAN, utility company executive; b. Rochester, N.Y., Apr. 17, 1943; d. Elmer Franklin and Helen Alma (Schroth) Lampman; m. Paul Allan Lankau, July 14, 1962; children—Paul Allan, Kelly, Kristyn. B.S., Pa. State U., 1977. Paralegal MacCartney Law Offices, Nyack, N.Y., 1963-79; supr. Orange and Rockland Utilities, Spring Valley, N.Y., 1979-80, mgr. consumer affairs, 1980-85, mgr. community relations, Pearl River, N.Y., 1985-86, mgr. community relations and conservation services, 1986—. Bd. dirs. Rockland County United Way, N.Y., 1985, Jr. Achievement of Rockland County, 1985-86, Rockland Tchrs. Ctr., Stony Point, N.Y., 1985-86; mem. adv. bd. Impact II, Spring Valley, 1985-86. Recipient Chairman's award Orange and Rockland Utilities, 1984, 85, Tribute to Women in Industry award TWIN Forum, 1985. Mem. Women in Mgmt. (pres. 1986—, Achievement award 1985), Soc. Consumer Affairs Profls., Am. Gas Assn., Electric Edison Inst., Pub. Relations Council. Avocations: tennis; boating; swimming. Home: 46 Jerrys Ave Nanuet NY 10954 Office: Orange and Rockland Utilities Inc 75 West Route 59 Spring Valley NY 10977

LANKENAU, TAMARA LYNNE, marketing firm executive, horse trainer; b. Dearborn, Mich., Dec. 27, 1957; d. Jerry Julius and Sandra Hall (Chipley) L. B.S. in Bus. Adminstrn., William Woods Coll., 1980; postgrad. Webster U., 1984-85. Asst. trainer Irish Ln. Farm, Delavan, Ill., 1980; instr., horse trainer, St. Louis, 1980—; project coordinator Hanley Partnership, St. Louis, 1981-83; account exec. Cornerstone Mktg. Inc., St. Louis, 1984—. Mem. Am. Horse Show Assn., Am. Morgan Horse Assn., Gateway Morgan Horse Club (founder, sec./treas. 1985-86), Mississippi Valley Morgan Club (publicity sec. 1985-86). Republican. Presbyterian. Avocations: music, designing. Office: Cornerstone Mktg Inc 4435 W Pine Blvd Saint Louis MO 63108

LANKFORD (PURTLE), MARIE JO-ANN, insurance executive; b. Tampa, Fla., Aug. 18, 1938; d. Charles C. and Jennie (Boromei) Mirabella; m. William D. Lankford, Aug. 9, 1958 (div. 1973); children—William D., John Anthony, Billy Andrew; m. Glynn Ray Purtle, Dec. 3, 1983. B.S. summa cum laude, U. Tampa, 1958; cert. Educable Mentally Retarded Edn., U. Ky., 1969; M.S., E. Tex. State U., 1973, postgrad., 1972-73; postgrad. Midwestern State U., 1971-72. Lic. ins. agt.; cert. securities dealer. Tchr. Washington, Germany, Tampa, Lexington, Ky., 1958-70; tchr. spl. edn. Wichita Falls, Tex., 1970-77; tchr. adult basic edn., Wichita Falls, 1977-79; gen. agt. State Mut. Life Assurance Co. Am., Wichita Falls, 1981—; prin. Marie Lankford & Assocs., Wichita Falls, 1981—; assoc. Professional Ins., Wichita Falls, 1986—. Author articles, monograph on spl. edn. Dir. rehab. Beacon Lighthouse for the Blind, 1977-79, co-founder evaluation and tng. procedures. Mem. Million Dollar Round Table, 1979—, Tex. Leaders Roundtable, Lone Star Leaders; fed. govt. scholar, 1971-73; Wichita Falls City Council of PTAs scholar, 1973-74; named Outstanding Educator in Tex., 1974; recipient Pioneer award, State Mut. Life Assurance Co., 1982; mem. Inner Circle Club, 1983-85; recipient Nat. Quality award, 1985, Health Ins. Quality award, 1985, Nat. Sales Achievement award, 1985. Mem. Nat. Assn. Life Underwriters, Nat. Women's Life Underwriters, Am. Profl. Bus. Women, Wichita Falls Assn. Life Underwriters (pres. 1983-84). Methodist. Office: Professional Insurance 1401 Holliday Suite 204 Wichita Falls TX 76301

LANPHEAR, MARTHA JEAN, lawyer; b. Wichita Falls, Tex., Jan. 28, 1944; d. Clarence Ernest and Kathern Martha (Golden) Eldridge; m. Thomas Joseph Lanphear, Jan. 5, 1974; children—Kathern Eileen, Laura Patricia. A.B., U. Mich., 1965; J.D., George Washington U., 1977. Bar: Va. 1977. Personnel specialist CSC, Washington, 1966-72, appeals officer, 1972-79; appeals officer, atty. Merit Systems Protection Bd., 1979-80, acting regional dir., Washington, 1982, hearing officer, 1980-86, adminstv. judge, 1986—. Recipient Performance award Merit Systems Protection Bd., 1982, 84, 85. Office: Merit Systems Protection Bd 5203 Leesburg Pike Falls Church VA 22041

LANPHERE, BETTY JOANNE, ct. reporter; b. Indpls., Mar. 26, 1938; d. Paul Sheldon and Doris Mae (Mathis) Furry; student Browning Bus. Coll., Albuquerque, 1967-68; m. James A. Lanphere, June 2, 1962; children—Michael, Lisa, Kristine, Scott, Jamie, Kimberly, Susan, Kevin, Julie, Jill, Kelly. Sec., Sandia Corp., Albuquerque, 1955 62, legal firm Jones, Gallegos, Snead & Wertheim, Santa Fe, 1967-68, firm Stephenson, Campbell & Olmsted, Santa Fe, 1968-69; ct. reporter Nye Reporting Service, Santa Fe, 1969, Lanphere Reporting Service, Santa Fe, 1969—; ofcl. reporter U.S. Dist. Ct., Santa Fe; mem. N.Mex. Ct. Reporting Bd., 1975—; mem. Nat. Audio-Video Com. on Electronic Rec., 1974—. Roman Catholic. Office: PO Box 449 58 S Federal Pl Santa Fe NM 87501

LANS, DEBORAH EISNER, lawyer; b. N.Y.C., Oct. 26, 1949; d. Asher and Barbara (Eisner) Lans. A.B. magna cum laude, Smith Coll., 1971; J.D. cum laude, Boston U., 1974. Bar: N.Y. 1975. Assoc. firm Lans Feinberg & Cohen, N.Y.C., 1975-80, ptnr., 1980-84; ptnr. Morrison Cohen & Singer, N.Y.C., 1984—. Mem. Assn. Bar City of N.Y. (chmn. young lawyers com. 1981-82, sec., 1979-81, mem. spl. com. on membership 1983-85, mem. joint com. on fee conciliation 1982—, com. judiciary 1984-85, exec. com. 1985—), ABA, N.Y. State Bar Assn. (ho. of dels.). Office: Morrison Cohen & Singer 110 E 59th St New York NY 10022

LANSBURY, ANGELA BRIGID, actress; b. London, Oct. 16, 1925; U.S., 1940, naturalized, 1951; d. Edgar and Moyna (Macgill) L.; m. Peter Shaw, Aug. 12, 1949; children—Anthony P., Deirdre A. Student, Webber-Douglas Sch. Drama, London, 1939-40, Feagin Sch. Drama, N.Y.C., 1940-42. Actress, Metro-Goldwyn-Mayer, 1943-50; motion pictures include: Gaslight, 1944, National Velvet, 1944, The Picture of Dorian Gray, 1944, The Harvey Girls, 1946, Till the Clouds Roll By, 1946, If Winter Comes, 1947, State of the Union, 1948, Samson and Delilah, 1949, Kind Lady, 1951, The Court Jester, 1956, The Long Hot Summer, 1957, Reluctant Debutante, 1958, Summer of the 17th Doll, 1959, A Breath of Scandal, 1959, Dark at the Top of the Stairs, 1960, Blue Hawaii, 1961, All Fall Down, 1962, Manchurian Candidate, 1963, In the Cool of the Day, 1963, The World of Henry Orient, 1964, Out of Towners, 1964, Something for Everyone, 1969, Bedknobs and Broomsticks, 1970, Death on the Nile, 1978, The Lady Vanishes, 1979, The Mirror Crack'd, 1980, The Last Unicorn, 1982, The Pirates of Penzance, 1983; appeared in plays Hotel Paradiso, 1957, A Taste of Honey, 1960, Anyone Can Whistle, 1964, Mame (on Broadway), 1966, revival, 1983, Dear World, 1968, Gypsy, 1974, The King and I, 1978, Sweeney Todd, 1979, Hamlet, Nat. Theatre, London, 1976, Nat. Theatre, London, 1976, A Little Family Business (Broadway), 1982; star TV series Murder, She Wrote, 1984—; appeared in TV miniseries Little Gloria...-.Happy at Last, 1982, Lace, 1984, The First Olympics—Athens 1896, 1984. Recipient Woman of Yr. award Harvard Hasty Pudding Theatricals, 1968; Antoinette Perry award, 1966, 69, 74, 79, Sarah Siddons award, 1974, 80, 83; inducted Theatre Hall of Fame, 1982. Address: care William Morris Agency 151 El Camino Beverly Hills CA 90212

LANSDOWNE, KAREN MYRTLE, retired English language and literature educator; b. Twin Falls, Idaho, Aug. 11, 1926; d. George and Effie Myrtle (Ayotte) Martin; B.A. in English with honors, U. Oreg., 1948, M.Ed., 1958, M.A. with honors, 1960; m. Paul L. Lansdowne, Sept. 12, 1948; children—Michele Lynn, Larry Alan. Tchr., Newfield (N.Y.) High Sch., 1948-50, S. Eugene (Oreg.) High Sch., 1952; mem. faculty U. Oreg., Eugene, 1958-65; asst. prof. English, Lane Community Coll., Eugene, 1965-82, ret., 1982; cons. Oreg. Curriculum Study Center. Rep., Cal Young Neighborhood Assn., 1978—; mem. scholarship com. First Congl. Ch., 1950-70. Mem. MLA, Pacific N.W. Regional Conf. Community Colls., Nat. Council Tchrs. English, U. Oreg. Women, AAUW (sec.), Jaycettes, Pi Lambda Theta (pres.), Phi Beta Patronesses (pres.), Delta Kappa Gamma. Co-author: The Oregon Curriculum: Language/Rhetoric, I, II, III and IV, 1970. Home: 15757 Rim Rd LaPine OR 97739

LANSING, TATIANA CHRISTINA, construction company executive, consultant; b. Fairfax County, Va., July 8, 1956; d. Ralverdan Kaahanuii Wagner and Olga Mary (Gruenin) L.; m. John Russell Dovel, Feb. 11, 1984. Student U. Va., 1972-78; A.A.S. in Math. and Speech, No. Va. Community Coll., Annandale, 1979; B.S. in Econs., Am. U., 1981, B.S. in Communications, 1981. Notary pub., Va. Anchor, reporter Warner-Amex Cable TV, Reston, Va., 1979-81, also writer, researcher Sta. WRC-TV, NBC, Washington, 1979-81; v.p. Mgmt. Services, Fairfax, Va., 1981—, pres. Structural Concepts, Fairfax, 1981—, pres., dir. All Steel Constrn., Inc., Gaithersburg, Md., 1981—; dir. Structural Concepts, Mgmt. Services; speaker. Mem. Fairfax County Republican Com., 1976-80; vol. Martha's Table Soup Kitchen, 1983—, Calvary Shelter for Homeless, 1983—, various Republican campaigns; outreach com. All Saints Ch., Chevy Chase, Md. Mem. Nat. Assn. Female Execs. (network dir.), Am. Inst. Constructors (sec., exec. com. Met. Washington chpt.), Assoc. Builders and Contractors, Am. Inst. Steel Constrn., Am. Sub-Contractors Assn., Women in Communications. Episcopalian. Home: 3042 Cedar Ln Fairfax VA 22031 Office: All Steel Construction Inc 9 Meem Ave Gaithersburg MD 20877

LANSKY, JUDITH GUERTIN, career consultant; b. Boston, July 19, 1946; d. Merton Warren and Ida (Waitzkin) Lansky; B.A., Barnard Coll., 1968; M.A. (tuition scholar), U. Rochester, 1969; M.B.A. with distinction, DePaul U., 1979. Coordinator acad. programs Reid Hall, Paris, 1969-70; grants adminstr. Inst. Internat. Edn., Chgo., 1974-76; dir. student employment services Columbia Coll., Chgo., 1976-78; mktg. adminstr. W.B. Dolphin & Assos., Chgo., 1978-79; mktg. cons. Technomic Consultants, Chgo., 1980-81; adminstr. pediatric nursing Rush-Presbyn.-St. Luke's Med. Center, Chgo., 1981-82; founder Lansky Career Cons. Bd. dirs. Flexible Careers, Chgo., 1975-78, Chgo. Coalition on Women's Employment, 1976-78; steering com. mem. Ill. Women's Agenda, 1976-77. Mem. Women in Mgmt. (chair career devel. 1983-84), Met. Bus. Assn. (bd. dirs.). Editor: The Job Hunter's Notebook, 1975. Home: 535 W Addison Chicago IL 60613 Office: 676 N Saint Clair Ct Suite 1860 Chicago IL 60611

LANTERMAN, PATRICIA MARY, athletic coach, team owner; b. Seattle, Nov. 13, 1959; d. Alton Kirk and Mary Ann (Eveleigh) L. B.A. in Bus., U. Wash. Asst. coach Gymnastics, Inc., Seattle, 1978-79; owner, head coach Northwest Aerials, Kirkland, Wash., 1979—. Mem. U.S. Gymnastics Fedn. (state bd. dirs. 1984—), Mod III Assn. (pres. 1985—), Elite Coaches Assn., U.S. Assn. Ind. Gymnastics Clubs. Republican. Episcopalian. Office: Northwest Aerials 12815 NE 125th St Suite E Kirkland WA 98034

LANTRIP, KAY LYNN, civil engineer; b. Herrin, Ill., Aug. 25, 1953; d. Robert F. and Pauline K. Osowski; student So. Ill. U., 1971-73; B.S. in Civil Engring., U. Ill., 1975; m. Bruce M. Lantrip, Aug. 3, 1974; 1 child, Emily Katherine. Civil engr., Old Ben Coal Co., Benton, Ill., 1975-77, Bechtel Power Corp., Gaithersburg, Md., 1977; civil engr. Ralph M. Parsons Co., Balt. Regional Rapid Transit System, Balt., 1977-80; sr. project mgr. George Hyman Constrn. Co., 1980—. Registered profl. engr. Mem. Chi Epsilon. Home: 5452 Thunder Hill Rd Columbia MD 21045

LANZILLO, DEBRA ANNE, broadcasting company sales manager, corporate secretary; b. Shamokin, Pa., Aug. 3, 1951; d. James Allan and Anne Louise (Gee) Spotts; m. Vito Anthony Lanzillo, Feb. 19, 1972; 1 child, Alexis Anne. Sec., G.T.E., N.Y.C., 1969-70; sales rep. Emporium Broadcasting Co., Pa., 1970—, sales mgr., corp. sec., 1971—; sales cons. Sta. WBPZ, Lock Haven, Pa., 1982; expansion co-planner WLEM Radio, Emporium, 1976-83; co-founder Sta. WQKY-FM, Emporium, 1982-85. Author text and reference materials. Co-chmn. March of Dimes/Mothers March, Cameron County, Pa., 1974-76; bd. dirs. Mental Health/Mental Retardation, Elk-Cameron Counties, 1974-76. Mem. Nat. Assn. Broadcasters, Pa. Assn. Broadcasters, Radio Advt. Bur. Methodist. Avocations: photography; ballet; tap dancing; jazz dancing; clogging. Home: R D #2 Box 43A Emporium PA 15834 Office: WLEM-AM/WQKY-FM 145 E 4th St PO Box 310 Emporium PA 15834

LAPADOT, SONEE SPINNER, automobile manufacturing company official; b. Sidney, Ohio, Apr. 19, 1936; d. Kenneth Lee and Helyn Kathryn (Hobby) Spinner; m. Jan. 13, 1955 (div. Apr. 1970); 1 son, Douglas Cameron; m. Robert Stephen Lapadot, May 4, 1974. Student U. Cin., 1954-56, U. Akron, 1966. Mgr. engring. change implementation Terex div. Gen. Motors, Hudson, Ohio, 1975-77, mgr. prodn. scheduling, 1977-78, gen. adminstr. product purchasing, 1978-79; sr. staff asst. non-ferrous metals Gen. Motors, Detroit, 1979-80, mgr. tires and wheels, 1980-83, mgr. staff purchasing, 1983—. Active fund-raising Boy Scouts Am., Grosse Pointe, Mich., 1980-82, United Fund, Detroit, 1980-84, Jr. Achievement, Detroit, 1984. Mem. Soc. Automotive Engrs., Am. Soc. Profl. and Exec. Women, Am. Prodn. and Inventory Control Soc., Automotive Industry Action Group (schedule stabilization com.), Nat. Assn. Female Execs. Club: Women's Econ. Detroit. Home: 2700 Steamboat Springs Rochester MI 48063 Office: General Motors New Center One Bldg 3031 W Grand PO Box 33113 Detroit MI 48232

LAPAN, SYDNEY GARRET, computer programmer; b. Denver, Oct. 6, 1952; d. Charles H. and Ferne (Garon) L. A.S., El Paso Community Coll., 1975; B.S., Regis Coll., 1986. Programmer, Mgmt. Scis., Denver, 1977-78, Colo. Computer Ctr., Denver, 1978-80, Mountain Bell, Denver, 1980-82; programmer, analyst II Nat. Ctr. Atmospheric Research, Boulder, 1982—; cons. in field. Asst. engr. record album: Crossroads, 1979. Active Nat. Orgn. Women, 1984-86, Nat. Gay Task Force, 1983-86; treas., steering com. Lesbian Connection, 1985-86. Mem. Colo. Pick Users, Mensa (membership sec. chpt.). Democrat. Jewish. Avocations: reading; collecting books; bicycling; cooking; music. Home: 305 E Chester St Lafayette CO 80026

LAPHAM, DOROTHY MAY, accountant; b. Quidnick, R.I., May 21, 1921; d. Elbridge Jackson and Laura (Berard) L. B.S. in Acctg., Bryant Coll., 1945, B.B.A. in Bus. Adminstrn., 1947. Lic. real estate broker, Mich.; lic. contractor-builder, Mich. Acct. various firms, Muskegon, Mich., 1953-60; pres., developer D & L Constrn. Co., Muskegon, 1961-64; controller various nursing homes, Muskegon, 1964-66; owner, mgr., cons. D & L Acctg. Co., Muskegon, 1966—; pres. D & M Acctg. Co., 1978—. Served with U.S. Army, 1948-53. Mem. Ind. Accts. Assn. Mich. (sec. local chpt. 1973—, state bd. dirs. 1977-79), Am. Soc. Women Accts. (treas. local chpt. 1962-64), Nat. Soc. Pub. Accts. (ednl. com. 1979-80). Republican. Avocations: golf; boating; fishing; needlepoint; photography. Home: 120 2d Ave Muskegon MI 49444 Office: D & L Acctg Co PO Box 4324 Muskegon MI 49444

LAPIN, SHARON JOYCE VAUGHN, interior designer; b. Lagrange, Mo., July 28, 1938; d. John Nolan and Wilma Emma (Huebotter) Vaughn; B.A., U. Wash., Seattle, 1960; cert. in interior design, Maryville Coll., 1977; m. Byron Richard Lapin, Oct. 14, 1972. Appearing in various Broadway shows, TV commercials and TV shows, 1962-72; owner Sharon Lapin Designs St. Louis. Bd. dirs. St. Louis Conservatory and Schs. for Arts, 1977—, v.p., 1982—; chmn. bd. Studio Set, 1978-81, pres., 1975-78, bd. dirs., 1975-83; bd. dirs. Friends of Sci. Mus., 1980—, v.p., 1984-85; pres. Assocs. of Bd. Dirs., St. Louis Sci. Ctr., Inc., 1986-87; bd. dirs. Jr. Div., St. Louis Symphony Women's Assn., 1973—. Mem. AFTRA, Screen Actors Guild, Actors Equity Assn., Am. Soc. Interior Designers, Pi Beta Phi. Republican. Baptist.

LAPOINT, HOLLY JO, radio announcer; b. Springfield, Mo., Dec. 19, 1958; d. Joseph Richard Gaston and Annette Fae (Johnston) Zink; m. William Randal Lapoint, July 28, 1978. News anchor Sta. WKMX Inc., Enterprise, Ala., 1978-81; radio announcer Sta. WRJM, Troy, Ala., 1981—. Named Best Anchor, AP Ala., 1980. Methodist. Home: Route 2 Box 401A Ozark AL 36360 Office: Sta WRJM PO Box 708 Troy AL 36081

LAPONZINA, ANGELA, businesswoman; b. N.Y.C., Sept. 22, 1947; d. Thurston Joseph and Josephine (Genova) VanWickel; m. Michael R. LaPonzina, Jan. 28, 1967; children—Jennifer, Craig, Douglas. Exec. officer Minuteman Press, Smyrna, Ga. Chairperson Jr. Women Assn., Cheshire, Conn., 1978-79; pres. Homeowners Assn., Norcross, Ga., 1980-81; co-chmn. com. small bus. devel. Cobb County C. of C., Ga., 1984-84. Recipient Customer Service award Minuteman Press Internat., 1984; named Smyrna Businessperson of Yr., 1985. Roman Catholic. Avocations: Fine arts; history; tennis. Address: 2620 Cobb Pkwy Smyrna GA 30080

LAPOTAIRE, JANE ELIZABETH MARIE, actress; b. Ipswich, Suffolk, U.K., Dec. 26, 1944; d. Louise Elise Burgess; 1 child, Rowan Joffe. Student Grammer Sch., 1963. Leading actress Royal Shakespeare Co., Nat. Theatre of Gt. Brit., London, 1967—; free-lance television and film actress BBC-TV, ITV, Paramount Pictures, MGM and United Artists, Broadway, N.Y.C.; mem. com. Women's Playhouse Trust, 1981—; vis. fellow Brighton U., Sussex. Co-author film script Do Us Part, 1982. Pres. Southwark Globe Project Com. CARE; mem. appeals com. Marie Curie Cancer Found. Recipient London Critics award, 1979, S.W.E.T. award, 1980, Variety Club of Gt. Brit. award, 1980, "Tony" award, 1981. Avocations: walking; Cordon Bleu cookery; water colors.*

LAPP, JANET ELIZABETH, psychologist; b. Montreal, Que., Can., Nov. 1, 1943; came to U.S., 1981; d. Herman Clark Lapp and Helen Grace (Maguire) Turney; m. William Reid, Aug. 22, 1966 (div. 1977); children—Carolyn Reid, Susan Reid. R.N., St. Michaels Hosp., Toronto, Ont., Can.; B.A. with honors, Concordia U., Montreal, 1975; Ph.D. with honors, McGill U., Montreal, 1980. Lic. psychologist, Calif. Asst. prof. McGill U., Montreal, 1981; assoc. prof. Calif. State U.-Fresno, 1981—; prin. Janet E. Lapp, Ph.D., Inc., 1982—; pres. Stress Mgmt. Cons., Fresno, 1983—, Personnel Devel. Seminars; daily TV program Taking Care of You, CBS, PBS, Broadcasting, 1983—; Health Watch, Internat. News Network. Author: Behavior Disorders: A Programmed Guide, 1981. Contbr. articles to profl. jours. Bd. dirs. St. Agnes Med. Ctr., Fresno, 1983—, YMCA Med. Adv. Bd., Fresno, 1983—. J.H. McConnell fellow, 1976-80; Calif. State U.-Fresno research grantee, 1981—. Mem. Am. Psychol. Assn., San Joaquin Psychol. Assn. (legis. chmn. 1984—), AAAS, Assn. for Advancement Behavior Therapy, Soc. Behavioral Medicine, Nat. Register Health Service Providers in Psychology. Office: Dept Psychology Calif State U Cedar and Shaw Fresno CA 93740

LAPPANO-COLLETTA, ELEANOR RITA, management consultant; b. N.Y.C., Jan. 12, 1930; d. Ernest and Mary Carmella (Spicciato) Lappano; B.S. in Chemistry, Fordham U., 1951, M.S. (teaching fellow 1951-53), 1953, Ph.D. in Biology (Office Naval Research fellow, NSF fellow), 1955; m. Archangelo Colletta, Nov. 18, 1961; children—Mary Elizabeth, John Ernest, Gina Rose. Mem. faculty N.Y.U. Postgrad. Med. Sch., 1956-58; mem. faculty, research asso. devel. biology Rockefeller U., 1958-59; instr. pathology SUNY Downstate Med. Center, Bklyn., 1959-60; biochem. cytologist Hosp. for Spl. Surgery, N.Y.C., 1960-62; research asso. animal behavior Am. Mus. Natural History, N.Y.C., 1962-67; asst. prof. Manhattan Coll., Riverdale, N.Y., 1967-72; asso. Sloan-Kettering Inst., N.Y.C., 1973-74; asst. prof. pathology N.Y. Med. Coll., Valhalla, 1974-75; mgmt. analyst performance analysis Office Comptroller N.Y.C., 1977-78; mem. nat. adv. research resources council NIH, 1973-77; devel. scientist personal products div. Lever Bros., Edgewater, N.J., 1979-80; ind. mgmt. cons., Bronx, N.Y., 1980—. Pres. Public Sch. 122 Community Sch. Bd. 10 N.Y.C. Parents Assn., 1970-72, treas. parents and prins. forum, 1972-73; edn. chmn. Community Coalition for Scatter Site Housing, 1972-74, West Bronx Civic Improvement Assn., 1971-79; bd. dirs. United Owners Assn., Somers, N.Y., 1979-81. NIH grantee, 1957-58, fellow, summer 1958. Mem. AAAS, AAUW, Sigma Xi. Author papers, reports in field. Address: 3238 Tibbett Ave Riverdale NY 10463

LAPPE, FRANCES MOORE, writer, educator; b. Pendleton, Oreg., Feb. 10, 1944; d. John and Ina Moore; B.A. in History, Earlham Coll., 1966; postgrad. Martin Luther King Sch. for Social Change, 1966, U. Calif.-Berkeley, 1968-69; L.H.D. (hon.), Starr King Sch. Religious Leadership, Berkeley, 1979, Lewis and Clark Coll., Portland, Oreg., 1982, St. Mary's Coll., Notre Dame, Ind., 1982, Macalester Coll., St. Paul, 1986; children—Anthony, Anna. Author: Diet for a Small Planet, 1971, rev. edit., 1981; (with Joseph Collins) Food First: Beyond the Myth of Scarcity, 1977, World Hunger: Ten Myths, 1977; (with Bill Valentine) What Can We Do?, 1980; (with Adele Beccar-Varela) Mozambique and Tanzania: Asking the Big Questions, 1980; (with Joseph Collins, David Kinley) Aid As Obstacle, 1980; (with Peter Sketchley) Casting New Molds: First Steps to Worker Control in a Mozambique Steel Factory, 1980; (with Joseph Collins) Now We Can Speak: A Journey Through the New Nicaragua, 1982, World Hunger: Twelve Myths, 1986; What To Do After You Turn Off the TV, 1985; contbr. articles to mags.; co-founder Inst. Food and Devel. Policy, San Francisco, 1975; lectr. in field. Office: 1885 Mission St San Francisco CA 94103

LAPRE, KATHRYN MARY, computer scientist; b. Manchester, N.H., May 3, 1939; d. Clayton Gerald and Margaret May (Flood) Hobbs; B.A. magna cum laude, Providence Coll., 1972, M.B.A., 1976, C.D.P., 1977, C.S.P., 1985; m. Robert Henry Lapre, Sept. 30, 1959 (div.); children—Donna Marie, Robert James, Michael Jon. With Raytheon Co., 1961-69; programmer analyst Kay Windsor, New Bedford, Mass., 1969-70; programmer analyst Providence Pile Fabric, Fall River, Mass., 1970-72; systems analyst Citizens Bank, Providence, 1972-74; project leader, lead analyst R.I. Hosp. Trust Nat. Bank, Providence, 1974-77; instr. bus. and computer sci. Providence Coll., 1977-81; research and devel. systems coordinator, adj. instr. U. Fla. Gainesville, 1981-82; mgr computer services GMI Engring. and Mgmt. Inst., Flint, Mich., 1982-84; dir. computer ctr. Denison U., Granville, Ohio, 1984—; Bd. dirs. Camp Fire Girls, 1972-73; active Explorer Scouts, 1982-84, chmn. Post 407, 1983-84. Author: Getting Started in BASIC, 1980. Served with USAF, 1957-58. Mem. Assn. Systems Mgmt. (sec. 1979-80), Assn. Women in Computing. Home: 102 Chapin Pl Granville OH 43023 Office: Computer Ctr Fellows Hall Denison U Granville OH 43023

LAPSLEY, DIANE ELIZABETH, nurse; b. London, Sept. 30, 1953; came to U.S., 1953, naturalized, 1969; d. Ronald James and Ellen (Cashman) Panton; m. Paul Francis Lapsley, June 26, 1982; 1 child, Catherine. B.S. in Nursing magna cum laude, U. Mass., Amherst, 1975; M.S. in Nursing magna cum laude, Boston U., 1980. Staff nurse Brockton Hosp., Mass., 1975-78, S. Shore Hosp., South Wehmouth, Mass., 1978-79, Univ. Hosp., Boston, 1979-80; clin. specialist VA Med. Ctr., West Roxbury, Mass., 1980—; clin. preceptor Boston, U., 1981—. Prin. investigator research study of return to work vets., 1984. Mem. Am. Heart Assn. (lectr. 1980—), Am. Assn. Critical Care Nurses (lectr. 1983), Sigma Theta Tau. Roman Catholic. Avocations: reading; bicycling; swimming. Office: VA Med Ctr 1400 VFW Pkwy West Roxbury MA 02401

LARAMIE, KATHLEEN CUTLER, social worker; b. Plattsburgh, N.Y., Mar. 17, 1942; d. George McKinley and Grace (DeCarr) Cutler; m. Walter W. Laramie, June 26, 1966 (div. 1985); children—Melissa Lyn, Andrea Marie. B.S., St. Lawrence U., 1964; postgrad. SUNY-Plattsburgh, 1984-85. Caseworker Dept. Social Services, Plattsburgh, 1966-71, sr. caseworker, 1971-73; dir. Clinton County Office for Aging, Plattsburgh, 1979—. Columnist Sr. Sentinel, 1979—. Mem. choir St. Patricks Ch., 1984. Mem. Nat. Assn. on Aging, N.Y. State Assn. on Aging. Republican. Roman Catholic. Avocations: weaving; creative writing. Home: 14 Pratt St Rouses Point NY 12979 Office: Clinton County Office Aging 135 Margaret St Plattsburgh NY 12901

LAREDO, RUTH, concert pianist; b. Detroit, Nov. 20, 1937; d Ben and Miriam (Horowitz) Meckler; diploma Curtis Inst. Music, 1960; m. Jaime Laredo, June 1, 1960 (div. Nov. 1976); 1 dau., Jennifer. N.Y.C. debut with Leopold Stokowski and Am. Symphony, 1962; debut with Boulez and N.Y. Philharmonic, 1974; soloist with major Am. orchs., including those in N.Y.C., Cleve., Detroit, Phila., and Nat. and Am. symphonies; performed at Aspen, Marlboro, Spoleto, Israel and Caramoor festivals; recordings with Columbia Records include Ravel's La Valse, 1967, piano sonatas of Alexander Scriabin, 1970-71, complete solo piano works of Rachmaninoff; asst. prof. Yale U. Sch. Music, 1974; editor C.F. Peters Internat. Rachmaninoff Piano Music, 1980—. Address: care Shaw Concerts 1995 Broadway New York NY 10023

LARGE, DARLENE DINTINO, association executive, art educator; b. New Brunswick, N.J., Mar. 31, 1935; d. Albert William Dintino and Sophia (Terbovich) Terrill; m. Bruce Derr Large, June 16, 1956; children—Dirk, Letti, Todd, Rajakumari. B.S., Pa. State U., 1959; postgrad. Centro Venezuelano Americano, Caracas, Venezuela, 1956-57, Colinas des Bellos Artes, Caracas, 1957-58, Millersville State U., Pa., 1973-75. Cert. art tchr., Pa. Tchr. art Haven Jr. High Sch., Evanston, Ill., 1969-70; founder, pres. HOINA (Homes of the Indian Nation), South India, 1972—; tchr. art Ephrata Area Sch. Dist., Pa., 1973-78; lectr. Pa. State U.-Grove City Coll., 1979—; tchr. art Dist. of Manheim Twp., Lancaster, Pa., 1984-85. Den mother Boy Scouts Am., Evanston, 1967-69; chmn. programs PTO Clay Elem. Sch., Ephrata, Pa., 1977; coordinator vols. Spanish Ctr., Lancaster, Pa., 1972-73; chmn. Cancer Drive, West Earl Twp., Pa., 1973. Named Woman of the Yr., Soroptomists, Lancaster, Pa., 1979; recipient Disting. Alumna award Pa. State U., 1982. Democrat. Avocations: reading; stitchery; painting; ceramics; batik; writing; walking. Home: 41 N Hershey Ave Box 115 Leola PA 17540 Office: HOINA 41 N Hershey Ave Leola PA 17540

LARGEN, MARY ANN, policy analyst, consultant; b. Big Clifty, Ky., June 30, 1943; d. Justice E. and Ruth A. (Golladay) Hawks; m. David A. Largen (div.); 1 child, Stacia Alana. B.A., U. Md. Coordinator nat. rape task force NOW, 1973-76; program cons. NIMH, Rockville, Md., 1976-77; dir. New Responses, Inc., Arlington, Va., 1978-80; dir. legis. affairs Nat. Coalition Against Sexual Assault, 1980-84; policy analyst Ctr. for Women Policy Studies, Washington, 1984-85; program assoc. Stone Counseling Ctr., Wellesley Coll., Mass., 1985—; mem. sec.'s adv. com. on rape prevention and control HHS, 1976-79. Recipient cert. for community services Prince Georges County Govt., Md., 1973, award for leadership Nat. Coalition Against Sexual Assault, 1982. Mem. Nat. Assn. Female Execs. Avocations: reading; hiking; horseback riding. Home: 955 S Columbus St Arlington VA 22204

LARIMER, CECILY ANN, office supply company executive, construction executive; b. Louisville, Jan. 29, 1942; d. Julious Charles and Lavene Imogene (Deckard) Schaffer; m. Gene Arther Larimer, May 12, 1961 (div. July 1977); children—December Ann, Carmel Lynn Larimer Martin; m. William Robert Mosier. Mgr., Ind. Office Supply Co., Bloomington, 1961-81, owner, 1981—; ptnr. Mosier Excavating, Bloomington, 1979—, CB Enterprises, Bloomington, 1980—; reporter Hoosier Equestrian, 1955-58. Troop leader Tulip Trace council Girl Scouts U.S., 1973-74, counselor, 1975. Mem. Am. Contract Bridge League. Republican. Avocations: reading; riding; fishing. Home: 6769 E Gross Rd Bloomington IN 47401 Office: Ind Office Supply Co PO Box 1776 421 E Kirkwood Bloomington IN 47402

LARIVEY, ROBERTA MARIE, manufacturing company executive; b. Buffalo, June 29, 1950; d. Robert Edmund and Marie Ellen (McNiff) L.; m. Edward Colter Bumbalo, Dec. 27, 1980 (div. 1984). A.A.S. in Bus. Adminstrn., Erie Community Coll., 1970; B.S. in Bus. Adminstrn., SUNY-Buffalo, 1976; M.B.A., Pepperdine U., 1980. Lab. technician in cancer research Roswell Park Meml. Inst., Buffalo, 1968-77; pres., gen. mgr. Calif. Orthopaedic Lab., Lakewood, Calif., 1978—. Mem. Long Beach C. of C. Lodge: Soroptimists. Home: 1717 California St Huntington Beach CA 92648 Office: Calif Orthopaedic Lab Inc 3710 Industry Ave Suite 201 Lakewood CA 90712

LARKAM, BEVERLEY MCCOSHAM, clinical social worker; b. Vancouver, Can., Mar. 3, 1928; d. William Howard and Marjorie Isabel (Jerome) McCosham; came to U.S., 1951; assoc. Royal Conservatory of Mus. of Toronto, U. Toronto, 1948; B.A., U. B.C., 1949, B.S.W., 1950, M.S.W., 1951; children—Elizabeth, Charles, Daphne, Peter, John. Psychiat. social worker Brackenridge Hosp., 1952-54; chmn. dept. sr. high sch. Univ. Presbyn. Ch., Austin, Tex., 1952-55, mem. Christian edn. com., 1961-67, mem. community orgn. to establish classes for mentally retarded children, 1966-68, bd. dirs. developing and organizing nursery sch., 1967-70; social worker Counseling-Psychol. Services Center U. Tex., 1971-72; psychiat. social worker, chief supr. adult mental health, children's mental health Human Devel. Center-South, Austin, 1972-79; pvt. practice marriage and family therapy, sex therapy and individual and group psychotherapy, Austin, 1975—; field supr. Sch. Social Work U. Tex.; cons. in field. Mem. City of Austin Commn. for Women, 1978—, chmn., 1982—, emeritus, 1985—; organizer Austin Assn. for Marriage and Family Therapy, 1980-82; bd. dirs. Nat. Assn. Commns. for Women, 1985—. Lic. clin. social worker. Tex.; cert. social worker-advanced clin. practitioner, Tex.; mem. Register of Clin. Social Workers. Mem. Am. Assn. Marriage and Family Therapy (approved supr.), Am. Assn. Sex Educators, Counselors and Therapists (cert. sex therapist), Soc. for Sci. Study of Sex, Am., Southwestern group psychotherapy socs., Am. Orthopsychiat. Soc., Acad. Cert. Social Workers, Nat. Assn. Social Workers, Tex. Council on Family Relations, Nat. Registry Health Care Providers in Clin. Social Work, PEO. Presbyterian. Home and Office: 2102 Raleigh Ave Austin TX 78703

LARKIN, JACQUELINE LEE, sales manager; b. Framingham, Mass., Aug. 29, 1948; d. Livio Charles and Genevieve (Ward) Costa; m. Jay V. Larkin, Mar. 12, 1971 (div. Aug. 1974). Student Framingham State U., 1966-69, Sch. Practical Arts, Boston, 1969-71. Mgr. adminstrn. TEE, Inc., Boston, 1978-81; telemktg. mgr. Warren Gorham & Lamont, Boston, 1982-85; communications cons. Larkin Communications, Boston, 1985—; telemktg. mgr. R.S. Means, Inc., Kingston, Mass., 1985—. Author: Good Connections: Successful Telephone Selling, 1984; co-author: Telemarketing Operations Handbook, 1985. Mem. Nat. Assn. Female Execs., Nat. Assn. Women in Sales, Profl. Pubs. Mktg. Group (steering com. 1983-85), DMA Telephone Mktg. Council, Am. Telemktg. Assn. Democrat. Unitarian. Avocations: photography; writing. Home: 29 School St Wayland MA 01778 Office: Larkin Communications 284 Park St Dorchester MA 02124

LARKIN, JANE RITA, brokerage company executive; b. N.Y.C., May 14, 1917; d. Edward Francis and Catherine Veronica (Keenan) L. B.S. with highest honors, St. John's U., N.Y.C., 1938. Br. office ops. mgr. Merrill Lynch, Bklyn., 1942-59; allied mem. N.Y. Stock Exchange, Hirsch & Co., N.Y.C., 1959-70, mem. N.Y. Stock Exchange, 1970—; allied mem. N.Y. Stock Exchange DuPont Glore Forgan, N.Y.C.; dep. dir. compliance, v.p. Paine Webber, N.Y.C., 1974—; mem. arbitration panel N.Y. Stock Exchange. Republican. Roman Catholic. Office: Paine Webber 120 Broadway New York NY 10271

LARKIN, JOAN KUPERSMITH, lawyer; b. N.Y.C., Jan. 30, 1953; d. Seymour and Ruth (Schechner) K.; m. Christopher Craig Larkin. B.A., NYU, 1973; J.D., New Eng. Sch. Law, Boston, 1976. Bar: N.Y. 1977, D.C. 1978, Fla. 1978, Calif. 1980. Intern, Mass. Attys. Gen. Office, Boston, 1974-75; reporter, cons. Bur. Nat. Affairs, Washington, 1975-76; trademark atty. U.S. Patent and Trademark Office, Washington, 1976-79; assoc. firm Fulwider, Patton, Rieber, Lee & Utecht, Los Angeles, 1979-84; ptnr. firm Fulwider, Patton, Rieber, Lee & Utecht, Los Angeles, 1984—; mem. pub. adv. com. for trademark affairs U.S. Dept. Commerce, 1979—. Contbr. in field. Recipient spl. achievement awards U.S. Dept. Commerce, 1978. Mem. ABA, U.S. Trademark Assn. (co-chmn. Paralegal Forum 1986), Assn. Bus. Trial Lawyers, Women Lawyers Assn. Los Angeles, Trademark Soc. (pres. 1978-79), Los Angeles Patent Law Assn. (co-editor newsletter 1980), Phi Alpha Delta. Office: Fulwider, Patton Rieber Lee & Utecht 3435 Wilshire Blvd Los Angeles CA 90010

LARKIN, JUNE NOBLE, foundation executive; b. N.Y.C., June 17, 1922; d. Edward John and Ethel Louise (Tinkham) Noble; m. David Shiverick Smith, Dec. 8, 1945 (div. 1968); children—E.J. Noble, David Shiverick, Jeremy T., Bradford D.; m. Frank Yoakum Larkin, Mar. 4, 1968. B.A., Sarah Lawrence Coll., 1944; L.H.D. (hon.), St. Lawrence U., 1980; D.Mus. (hon.), Mannes Coll. Music, 1984. Chmn., pres. Edward John Noble Found., Inc., N.Y.C., 1972—; mem. N.Y.C. Cultural Council, 1971-74, Nat. Parks Centennial Com., 1972-73, Mayor's Com. on Cultural Policy, N.Y.C., 1974, Presdl. Task Force on Arts and Humanities, 1981. Bd. trustees, Sarah Lawrence Coll., Bronxville, N.Y., 1964-73, chmn. bd. trustees, 1971-73; bd. trustees Greenwich Hosp.; Conn., 1967-82, Mus. Collaborative, N.Y.C., 1973-76, Eaglebrook Sch., Deerfield, Mass., 1974-81, Mus. Broadcasting, N.Y.C., 1982—, Ptnrs. for Livable Places, Washington, 1982-85; bd. dirs. Repertory Theatre Lincoln Ctr., N.Y.C., 1969-72, Cultural Council Found., N.Y.C., 1976-79, Alliance for Arts, N.Y.C., 1978—, Philharmonic Symphony Soc. N.Y.C., 1979—; bd. trustees Mus. Modern Art, N.Y.C., 1969—, v.p., 1978—; bd. dirs. Lincoln Ctr. Performing Arts, 1985—, N.Y. Internat. Festival of Arts Inc.; trustee Juilliard Sch., N.Y.C., 1974—, chmn., 1985—. Mem. N.Y. Regional Assn. Grantmakers (bd. dirs. 1984—), Arts Coalition of Empire State (bd. dirs. 1984—). Clubs: Colony (N.Y.C.); Sulgrave (Washington). Office: Edward John Noble Found 32 E 57th St New York NY 10022

LARKIN, MARY PATRICIA, publicity specialist; b. Newark, July 4, 1957; d. Francis Xavier and Patricia Ann (Kenney) L. B.A., Providence Coll., 1979. Publicity asst. Dodd, Mead & Co., N.Y.C., 1979-81; publicity coordinator Pocket Books/Simon & Schuster, N.Y.C., 1981—. Mem. Pubs. Publicity Assn. Republican. Roman Catholic. Club: Providence Alumni. Home: 49 Cambridge Rd Montclair NJ 07042 Office: Pocket Books/Simon & Schuster 1230 Ave of Americas New York NY 10020

LARKIN, MOLLY CHRISTINE, nurse; b. Rochester, N.Y., May 4, 1953; d. Joseph W. and Jean A. (Judson) L.; diploma De Paul Sch. Nursing, 1975; B.S. in Nursing, Old Dominion U., 1980, postgrad., 1980—. Map evaluator State Hwy. Dept., Petersburg, Va., summer, 1972; WATS-line operator E.R. Carpenter Co., Richmond, Va., 1973; cashier Holiday Inn, Petersburg, Va., summer, 1974; staff nurse Norfolk (Va.) Gen. Hosp., 1975-79, asst. dir. nursing, 1979-86; vis. nurse Commonwealth Health Care, 1984—; cons. Mediscus Products, Richmond, Va. coordinator Skills Lab., Old Dominion U., Norfolk, 1982-83. Mem. Am. Nurses Assn., Va. Nurses Assn. Roman Catholic. Home: 4495 Sir John's Ln Virginia Beach VA 23455

LA ROCCA, ANGELA TERESA, city official; b. New Rochelle, Apr. 8, 1911; d. Joseph and Rose Marie (Ringa) Di Buono; m. Lucien J. La Rocca, Oct. 6, 1935 (dec. 1970); 1 child, Phyllis. Cert. mcpl. city clk. Sec., stenographer, 1933-47; bookkeeper New Rochelle Water Co., 1947-50; bookkeeper, bus. adminstr. R & M Combustion Co., N.Y.C., 1950-78; city clk./registrar vital stats. City of New Rochelle, 1978—; cons. New Rochelle Bd. Edn., 1983—. Dist. leader Westchester County (N.Y.), 7th election dist.; treas., sec. 4th ward New Rochelle city com.; trustee New Rochelle Police/Fire Pension Funds. Mem. Internat. Inst. Mcpl. Clks., N.Y. State Conf. Mcpl. Officers (scholarship com., 1980-81, co-chmn. membership com., 1982-83, edn. com. 1983-84. Roman Catholic. Avocations: gardening; music. Office: City Clk City Hall 515 North Ave New Rochelle NY 10801

LAROCHE, FAY HELEN NILSEN, shoe manufacturing company executive; b. Thomaston, Maine, Sept. 10, 1932; d. Leino Ilmari and Elssi Elisabet (Jarvi) Koskinen; m. Ronald E. Nilsen, May 18, 1952 (div. 1978); children—Barry D., Greta M. Chirco, Gregory C., Laurie F. Persuitte; m. Alvin A. LaRoche, Jr., Jan. 10, 1986. A.S., Mt. Wachusett Community Coll., 1977; B.S., Lesley Coll., 1982. Lic. real estate broker, Mass. Customer service mgr. Anwelt Corp./Am. Footwear, Fitchburg, Mass., 1974-76, adminstrv. asst. export dept., 1978-81, exec. asst. Am. Country div., 1982-84, communications dir., pub. relations/community relations, pres.'s asst., 1984—; treas., dir. Our Father's House, Inc., Fitchburg; dir. Our Father's Table, Fitchburg; freelance writer. Sec. Republican Com., Ashburnham, Mass. Mem. Nat. Writers Club. Episcopalian. Avocations: gardening, reading. Home: 421 S Ashburnham Rd Westminster MA 01473 Office: Anwelt Corp 1 Oak Hill Rd Fitchburg MA 01420

LAROCQUE, MARILYN ROSS ONDERDONK, corporate official; b. Weehawken, N.J., Oct. 14, 1934; d. Chester Douglas and Marion (Ross) Onderdonk; B.A. cum laude, Mt. Holyoke Coll., 1956; postgrad. N.Y.U., 1956-57; M.Journalism, U. Calif., Berkeley, 1965; m. Bernard Dean Benz, Oct. 5, 1957 (div. Sept. 1971); children—Mark Douglas, Dean Griffith; m. 2d, Rodney Clarence LaRocque, Feb. 10, 1973. Jr. exec. Bonwit Teller, N.Y.C., 1956; personnel asst. Warner-Lambert Pharm. Co., Morris Plains, N.J., 1957; editorial asst. Silver Burdett Co., Morristown, 1958; pub. relations cons., 1963-71, 73-77; pub. relations dir. Shaklee Corp., Hayward, Calif., 1971-73; dir. pub. relations Fidelity Savs. & Loan Assn., Oakland, Calif., 1977-78; exec. dir. No. Calif. chpt. Nat. Multiple Sclerosis Soc., 1978-80; v.p. public relations Cambridge Plan Internat., Monterey, Calif., 1980-81; sr. account exec. Hoefer-Amidei Public Relations, San Francisco, 1981-82; dir. spl. projects, asst. to chmn. Cambridge Plan Internat., Monterey, Calif., 1982-83, dir. corp. communications, 1983-84; dir. communications Buena Vista Winery, Sonoma, Calif., 1984-86, asst. v.p. communications and market support, 1986—; instr. U. Calif. Extension, San Francisco, 1977-79. Mem. exec. bd., rep-at-large Oakland (Calif.) Symphony Guild, 1968-69; cabinet mem. Lincoln Child Center, Oakland, 1967-71, cabinet pres., 1970-71, 2d v.p. bd. dirs., 1970-71; pub. relations chmn. Oakland Mus. Assn., 1974; mem. Calif. Republican Central Com., 1964-66; bd. dirs. Calif. Spring Garden and Home Show, 1970-77, First Agrl. Dist. Calif., 1970-77; v.p. Piedmont council Boy Scouts Am., 1977. Mem. Pub. Relations Soc. Am. (dir. San Francisco Bay Area chpt. 1980-82), Carneros Quality Alliance (sec., exec. com. 1985—), Wine Inst. Calif. (market devel. com. 1985—), Sonoma Valley Vintners Assn. (dir. 1984—), Women in Communications, Nat. Trust for Historic Preservation, U. Calif. Alumni Assn., Mus. Soc. San Francisco, Calif. Hist. Soc., Oakland Smithsonian Assos., AAUW, Clubs: Mt. Holyoke Coll. Alumnae, East Bay Press, Sonoma County Press, East Bay Women's Press, Contra Costa Press; Commonwealth of Calif. Author: Maestro Baton and His Musical Friends, 1968; Happiness is Breathing Better, 1976. Home: 99 Dominican Dr San Rafael CA 9490 Office: 27000 Ramal Rd Sonoma CA 95476

LAROE, DANNIE MARLENE, psychotherapist; b. Jasper, Tex., Jan. 14, 1931; d. charles Alton and Dovie Faye (DeShazo) LaR.; M.S.W., Smith Coll., 1953; m. DeWitt Shelton, Mar. 18, 1978; 1 son, Slater Vaugn Welte. Therapist in med. rehab. VA Hosp., Houston, 1953-55; asst. dir. social services Polio Found., Houston, 1955-57; with Family Service Bur., Houston, 1957-59; asso. prof. sociology Sam Houston State Coll., Huntsville, 1961-63; lectr. dept. sociology U. Houston, 1963-65, vis. lectr. Sch. Social Work, 1974-75; vis. lectr. U. Tex. Med. Sch., Houston, 1977-79; pvt. practice social psychotherapy, Houston, 1959—; lectr. in field; mem. State Bd. Examiners in Social Psychotherapy, Austin, 1980-81. Mem. Acad. Cert. Social Workers, Smith Coll. Alumni Assn., Authors Guild, Nat. Assn. Social Workers. Republican. Author: How Not to Ruin a Perfectly Good Marriage, 1979; contbr. articles to profl. jours. Office: 50 Briar Hollow Suite 250E Houston TX 77027

LAROSA, LINDA MARGARET, horticulturist, floral designer; b. Columbia, S.C., Apr. 21, 1952; d. Frank and Virginia (Wilkes) LaR. B.S., Midlands Coll., 1975. Tchr. R. Earl David Elem. Sch., Columbia, 1972-77; asst. horticulturist World Trade Ctr., N.Y.C., 1982; owner-operator Linda LaRosa Interior Plantscapes, N.Y.C., 1982—; designer, dir. theme convs. for various bus. firms, orgns. and cultural instns., 1984—; owner, operator Plant Care Mobile, N.Y.C., 1986—; Coordinator floral tng. program, tchr. interior plant design, floral design dir. floral guild Cathedral St. John the Divine, N.Y.C.; tchr. floral design St. Luke's Ch., N.Y.C. Mem. Nat. Trust Hist. Preservation, Am. Hort. Soc., N.Y. Hort. Soc. Home: 2850 Broadway New York NY 10025 Office: Linda LaRosa Interior Plantscapes 2731 Broadway New York NY 10025

LAROUNIS, MARY GEORGE, psychiatric social worker; b. Cefalonia, Greece, Dec. 21, 1934; came to U.S., 1953, naturalized, 1960; d. George P. and Stamatia O. (Razis) Efthymiatos; student Pierce Coll., Athens, Greece, 1951-53; B.A., Hunter Coll., 1955; M.S.W., Columbia U., 1957; AESA, U. Paris VII; m. George P. Larounis, Jan. 13, 1958; 1 dau., Daphne H. Case worker Community Service N.Y., 1957-60; caseworker Am. Aid Soc., Paris, 1964-66, asst. dir., 1966-79; asst. dir. Am. Student and Family Counselling Service, 1979—; pres. Internat. Counseling Service, Paris, 1979—. Mem. Nat. Assn. Social Workers, Acad. Cert. Social Workers. Clubs: Polo (Paris), Racing

(France). Home: 9 Blvd du Chateau Neuilly-sur-seine France 92200 Office: 65 Quai D'Orsay Paris France 75007

LARRABEE, VIRGINIA ANN STEWART, educator; b. Jacksonville, Fla., Nov. 21, 1923; d. Edwin Homer and Clara Victoria (Anderson) Stewart; student Pine Manor Jr. Coll., 1941-43; B.A., Wellesley Coll., 1945; M.Ed., U. Vt., 1961; Ed.D., Boston U., 1969; m. Wesley Campbell Larrabee, May 4, 1947; children—Susan Ann, Diane Elaine, Linda Jane, Judith Ann. Asst. buyer B. Altman & Co., N.Y.C., 1945-46; tchr. public schs., Forest Dale, Vt., 1955-59, Shoreham, Vt., 1959-62; audiovisual dir., Shoreham, 1959-62; elem. supr., Castleton, Vt., 1962-64; instr., master tchr. Harvard, summers 1963-65; elem. supr. public schs., Rutland, Vt., 1964-66; asst. prof. edn. Castleton State Coll., 1966-68, assoc. prof., 1969-74, prof., 1974—, chmn. dept. edn., 1972—, dir. grad. program in reading, 1974—, dir. Edn. Computer Ctr., 1984—; mem. adv. com. Right to Read, Vt., 1974—; mem. Vt. Edn. Commr.'s Forum, 1981—; owner, operator farm and orchard, 1953—. Sunday Sch. supt. Congregational Ch., Shoreham, 1948-60, choir dir., 1958-64. Mem. New Eng. (past dir.), Vt. (dir., pres. 1978—, editor newsletter 1980—) reading councils, Internat. Reading Assn., Nat., Vt. (past pres.), New Eng. (past dir.) assns. supervision and curriculum devel., Phi Delta Kappa, Delta Kappa Gamma, Pi Lambda Theta. Clubs: Vt. Wellesley, Shoreham Hist. Home: RFD Box 56 Shoreham VT 05770 Office: Castleton State Coll Castleton VT 05735

LARSEN, GRACE HUTCHISON, educator; b. Pomona, Calif., Dec. 4, 1920; d. Forest Glen and Pearl Carrie (Wolfe) Hutchison; B.A., U. Calif., Berkeley, 1942, M.A., 1945; Ph.D., Columbia U., 1955; m. Charles Edward Larsen, Nov. 27, 1943; children—Charles Eric, Douglas Edward. Instr., Rutgers U., Newark, 1947-49, 51-55; lectr. Bryn Mawr (Pa.) Coll., 1949-50; instr. Swarthmore (Pa.) Coll., 1949-51; asst. specialist in agrl. econs. U. Calif., Berkeley, 1955-62, asso. specialist, 1962-66; prof. history Holy Names Coll., Oakland, Calif., 1966—, acad. dean, 1970-80; mem. Accreditation Comm. for Sr. Colls. and Univs. and Community and Jr. Colls. Archbishop Riordan fellow in Am. History, 1942-43; Genevieve McEnerney fellow in history, 1945-46; Sigmund Martin Heller travelling fellow, 1946-47; Nat. Endowment for Humanities summer grantee, 1980. Mem. Am. Hist. Assn., West Coast Women Historians, Agrl. History Soc., Phi Beta Kappa. Contbr. articles to profl. jours.; author: (with H.E. Erdman) Revolving Finance in Agricultural Cooperatives, 1965. Home: 4649 Meldon Ave Oakland CA 94619 Office: 3500 Mountain Blvd Oakland CA 94619

LARSEN, JEAN MAYCOCK, educator; b. Provo, Utah, Feb. 23, 1931; d. Lawrence S. and Lorna (Booth) Maycock; B.S., Brigham Young U., Provo, 1953, M.S., 1960; Ph.D., U. Utah, 1972; m. A. Dean Larsen, Feb. 14, 1958; children—David Lawrence, Paul Joseph, Ann, Charlotte. Tchr. schs. in Oreg. and Utah, 1953-55, 57-58; mem. faculty Brigham Young U., 1960—, assoc. prof. family scis., 1976-85, prof., 1985—, coordinator early childhood edn. program, 1980—; past chmn. Utah Child Care Adv. Council. Mem. Nat. Assn. Edn. Young Children, Assn. Childhood Edn. Internat., Utah Assn. Edn. Young Children (past pres., chmn. adv. bd.), Am. Ednl. Research Assn., Soc. Research Child Devel. Republican. Mormon. Author curriculum materials in field; also research. Home: 2678 North 880 East Provo UT 84604 Office: 1319-A SFLC Brigham Young U Provo UT 84602

LARSEN, REBECCA YASUKO, educational administrator; b. Denver, Jan. 28, 1947; d. Henry Chikara and Clara Tokiko (Nakamura) Takahashi; m. Raymond James Imatani, June 17, 1967 (div. 1979); children—Wendy Jill, Stefanie Paige, Garrick Mathew; m. Robert Ray Larsen, Aug. 29, 1982. Student U. No. Colo., 1966-67; student Met. State Coll., 1967-69, B.A., 1979. Patient rep. Platte Valley Med. Ctr., Brighton, Colo., 1976-79, dir. vols., 1976-79; dir. alumni, found. Met. State Coll., Denver, 1979—, exec. dir. found., 1982—; cons. Northwestern Mich. Coll., Traverse City, 1983. Bd. dirs. Adams County Grievance Bd., Colo., 1985—. Recipient Cert. Appreciation, Platte Valley Med. Ctr. Aux., 1976-79, Girl Scouts U.S.A., 1974-76. Mem. Council for Advancement and Support Edn. (Excellence in Total Alumni Program award 1984), Colo. Assn. Fund Raisers, Higher Edn. Assn. Rockies (pres. 1984—), Am. Council on Edn. (nat. identification program), Women's Network, AAUW (scholarship chmn. Brighton chpt. 1984—). Democrat. Presbyterian. Avocations: cooking; singing; tennis; stained glass design, pottery. Home: 1770 San Candelo Fountain Valley CA 92708

LARSON, CAROLE HENNING, lawyer, educator; b. Crete, Nebr., Jan. 2, 1941; d. Alvin George and Effie Marie (Pottorff) Henning; m. Wayne Lee Evers, Nov. 5, 1965 (div.); children—Jennifer Marie, Jane Frances; m. 2d, Danny Ross Larson, Dec. 21, 1974; 1 son, Richard. B.A., Doane Coll., 1963; J.D., U. Nebr., 1980. Bar: Nebr. 1980, U.S. Dist. Ct. Nebr. 1980, U.S. Bankruptcy Ct. for Nebr. 1980. Tchr. English, Crete High Sch. (Nebr.), 1963-64, Campbell High Sch. (Nebr.), 1966-68, Seward High Sch. (Nebr.), 1968-74; atty. Haessler et al, Wahoo, Nebr., 1980-83; sole practice, Crete, Nebr., from 1983; now sr. ptnr. firm Larson, Buhrmann & Resz, P.C.; in-house counsel Pacesetter Corp., Omaha. Commr. 1st Dist. Nebr., Nebr. Commn. on Status of Women, 1984-86. Mem. Nat. Assn. Criminal Def. Lawyers, Assn. Trial Lawyers Am., ABA, AAUW, Bus. and Profl. Women, Nebr. Bar Assn., Saline County Bar Assn. Democrat. Episcopalian. Home: Route 2 Wahoo NE 68066 Office: The Pacesetter Corp 4343 S 96th Omaha NE 68127

LARSON, DENISE ANITA, advertising executive; b. N.Y.C., May 1, 1956; d. Walter William and Anita Helen (Strunk) L. A.A.S. in Mktg., Nassau Community Coll., 1976; B.S. in Mktg., C.W. Post Coll., 1978; M.B.A., Adelphi U., 1983. Account research supr. Young & Rubicam Inc., N.Y.C., 1976-85; assoc. research dir. J. Walter Thompson, N.Y.C., 1985—. Recipient John H. Crichton award Am. Assn. Advt. Agys., 1980. Mem. Am. Mktg. Assn. Avocations: tennis; skiing.

LARSON, E(LIZABETH) ANN, marketing company marketing executive, consultant; b. Brunswick, Maine, Nov. 10, 1943; d. Harvey and Mary Elizabeth (Robinson) L. Collector GECC, Washington, 1962; sales fin. adminstr. Servamatic Solar, San Ramon, Calif., 1983-86; sr. v.p., sec. Hydro-Magic of Long Beach Inc., Calif., 1986—; fin. cons. Mem. Nat. Assn. Female Execs., Nat. C of C., Lakewood C. of C. Republican. Lodges: Sitzmarkers, Tyrolians. Office: Hydro-Magic of Long Beach Inc 1984 Obispo Ave Suite 1B Long Beach CA 90804

LARSON, EMILIE G., retired educator; b. Northfield, Minn., Apr. 28, 1919; d. Melvin Cornelius and Frieda (Christiansen) Larson; A.B., St. Olaf Coll., 1940; M.A., Radcliffe Coll., 1946; student U. Chgo., 1951-52. Tchr. Hanska (Minn.) High Sch., 1940-42, Two Harbors (Minn.) High Sch., 1942-45; tchr. J. W. Weeks Jr. High Sch., Newton, Mass., 1946-56, guidance counselor, 1956-79; counselor Warren Jr. High Sch., Newton, 1979-81. Deacon, Univ. Luth. Ch., 1979; corp. rep. St. Olaf Coll.; mem. bd. Bus. History and Econ. Life Program, Inc., Northeastern U., Boston; v.p. Minn. UN Rally Bd. Mem. AAUW (state v.p. for program devel., topic chmn. Mass. div. 1975-76; past br. rep. for edn. Boston, bd. dirs. Minn. div. 1984-86, area rep. internat. relations Minn. div.), St. Olaf Coll. Alumni Assn. (dir. 1982-85), Virginia Gildersleeve Internat. Fund for Univ. Women Inc., PEO, Pi Lambda Theta. Lutheran. Contbr. articles to profl. jours. Address: 216 Ames St E Northfield MN 55057

LARSON, JACQUELYNNE BORST (PENNY), real estate auction company executive; b. Glens Falls, N.Y., Nov. 3, 1938; d. Jacque Becker and Madeline (Edmunds) Borst; m. Donald F. Larson, Apr. 4, 1957 (div. Feb. 1981); children—Daniel, David, Christy. Student U. Ill., 1956-57. Lic. real estate salesperson. Sole propr. Larson Enterprises, Glenview, Ill., 1960-72; controller Ada S. McKinley Community Services, Chgo., 1973-82; ptnr. Kaufman Lasman Assocs., Inc., Chgo., 1982—. Officer, bd. dirs. LWV, Glenview, 1973-74, North Shore Assn. for Retarded, Evanston, 1969-71; mem. East Maine Dist. 63 Sch. Bd., Des Plaines, Ill., 1974-79; deacon Presby. Ch. of Glenview, 1974. Recipient $25 Million Sales award Kaufman Lasman Assocs., 1985. Mem. Nat. Assn. Realtors, Chgo. Real Estate Bd. (Salesperson of Yr. 1985). Home: 303 W Eugenie St Chicago IL 60614 Office: Kaufman Lasman Assocs Inc 100 S Wacker Dr Chicago IL 60606

LARSON, JEANNE M., health services company executive, consultant, researcher; b. Mpls., May 1, 1949; d. Emlen Kermit and Mildred Evangeline (Gulsvig) L.; m. Arne Eugene Skaalure, May 13, 1972 (div. 1981); m. Dewey A. Johnson, Aug. 24, 1985. B.A., Gustavus Adolphus Coll., 1971; M.B.A., St. Thomas Coll., 1982. Sch. nurse Dept. Defense Overseas Dependents Sch., Okinawa, Japan, 1972-74; staff nurse U.S. Army Camp Kuwae Hosp., Okinawa, 1974-75; instr. diabetes and health edn. Metro. Med. Ctr., Mpls., 1976-79; dir. and mktg. mgr. Competent Nursing Services, Mpls., 1979-81; pres., v.p. Austin Larson Corp., Mpls., 1981-83; pres. Optional Care Systems, St. Paul, 1984—; research cons. U. Minn. Sch. Nursing Mpls., 1982—; cons. Honeywell Corp., Mpls., 1984. Author: Diabetes Manual, 1979; Healthcare Cost Management, 1985. Recipient U.S.A. award for Graphics Design, 1981, Nat. Creative Nurse award Minn. Nurses Assn., 1979, Allene Von Son Nat. award, 1978. Mem. Ind. Bus. Assn. Minn. (v.p., bd. dirs. 1982—, Small Bus. Woman of Yr. 1983), Nat. Assn. Home Care (info. resource com. 1984, nominating com. 1985). Office: Optional Care Systems Inc 1885 University Ave St Paul MN 55104

LARSON, JULIA LOUISE, land use planner; b. Bethesda, Md., July 11, 1950; d. James A. and Helen J. (Grubb) Fink; m. Louis C. Larson, May 27, 1978 (div. Dec. 1981). B.S., Radford Coll., 1972; M.S., Oreg. State U., 1975. Geography tchr. Rappahannock County High Sch., Washington, Va., 1972-73; research asst./sec. Oreg. Natural Area Preserves Adv. Com., 1974-75; energy conservation specialist Oreg. Dept. Energy, Salem, 1976-77; mem. Oreg. Fire Protection Master Planning Com., 1978-79, Oreg. State Environ. Edn. Adv. Com., 1977-80; growth mgmt. planner Salem Fire Dept., 1978-79; land use planner Salem Dept. Community Devel., 1979-83; field rep. Data Research & Applications, Inc., Atlanta, 1983-84; land use coordinator Ga. Mfd. Housing Assn., Atlanta, 1984—; cons. Contbg. editor: 1979 Sun Calendar; co-editor: 1976 Energy Calendar. Vice-pres. Liberty Jaycee Women, Salem, 1981; land use adv. Northside Neighbors, Salem, 1979. Recipient cert. of appreciation City of Salem, 1983. Mem. Am. Inst. Cert. Planners, Ga. Planning Assn. (editor Ga. Planner, 1986-87), Am. Mgmt. Assn., AAUW (group leader 1985-87), Ga. Assn. Zoning Adminstrs. and Bldg. Ofcls., High Mus. Art, Smithsonian Assocs., Ga. Conservancy. Avocations: backpacking; writing; wine tasting. Home: 4717 Roswell Rd K-11 Atlanta GA 30342

LARSON-EMISON, JANE BALE, interior design firm executive; b. Dickinson, N.D., Sept. 30, 1946; d. Stanley Walter and Hazel Eleanor (Bartow) Bale; B.S., N.D. State U., 1968. Home fashion coordinator Montgomery Wards, Mpls., 1968-69; staff interior designer McClain, Hedman & Schultz, St. Paul, 1969-72; sales, design mgr. Dayton's Contract Interiors, Mpls., 1972-73; v.p., contract mgr. Contemporary Designs, Inc., Mpls., 1973-79; pres., owner J.B. Larson Assocs., Inc., Mpls., 1979—, Jane Larson-Emison Designs, Deephaven, Minn., 1983-85. Mem. adv. bd. design dept. U. Minn. Coll. Home Econs., 1982-84. Recipient Merit award Minn. Soc. of AIA, 1979, Architecture Minn. Pubs. Design award, 1980, Architecture Minn. Advt. award excellence, 1981. Mem. Inst. Bus. Designers, Mpls. C. of C. (cultural activities com. 1980), Fashion Group. Club: Mpls. Woman's Boys and Girls (sec.), Women's Bd. Home and Office: 19255 Cedarhurst St Deephaven MN 55391

LARUE, LINDA CUMMINGS, child care center administrator; b. Sanford, N.C., May 22, 1948; d. Charles Lee and Betty Jo (Shinault) Cummings; m. Robert Russell LaRue, Apr. 1, 1966; children—Charles Channing, Rusty Lee, Katherine Cummings. Student public schs. Sanford, N.C. Dir., Mini-Skool Ltd., Winston Salem, N.C., 1973-79; owner, ptnr. Dandy Lion Ltd., Winston Salem, 1980-84, Kelly's Sta., Sanford, N.C., 1981-85; pres. LaRue, Inc., Kernersville, N.C., 1980—, Learning Ctr. Assocs., 1984—, A Brighter Child Learning Ctr., 1984—. Treas. Kernersville Childrens Little Theatre, 1983-84, pres., 1984-85. Republican. Presbyterian. Club: Kernersville Womans (2d v.p. 1985—). Avocations: sailing; painting; needlecrafts; biking; photography. Home: 222 Vandyke St Kernersville NC 27284 Office: A Brighter Child Learning Ctr 820 Salisbury St Kernersville NC 27284

LARWOOD, LAURIE, psychologist; b. N.Y., 1941; Ph.D., Tulane U., 1974. Pres., Davis Instruments Corp., San Leandro, Calif., 1966-71, cons., 1969—; asst. prof. organizational behavior State U. N.Y. at Binghamton, 1974-76; assoc. prof. psychology, chairperson dept., assoc. prof. bus. adminstrn. Claremont (Calif.) McKenna Coll., 1976-83, Claremont Grad. Sch., 1976-85; prof., head dept. mgmt. U. Ill.-Chgo., 1983—; mem. western regional advisory council SBA, 1976-81; dir. The Mgmt. Team; pres. Mystic Games, Inc. Mem. Acad. Mgmt. (editorial rev. bd. Rev. 1977-82, past chmn. women in mgmt. div.), Am. Psychol. Assn., Assn. Women in Psychology. Author: (with M.M. Wood) Women in Management, 1977, Organizational Behavior and Management, 1984, Women's Career Development, 1986, mem. editorial bd. Sex Roles, 1979—, Group and Orgn. Studies, 1982-84, editor, 1986—; founding editor Women and Work, 1983, Jour. Mgmt. Case Studies, 1983—; contbr. numerous articles, papers to profl. lit. Home: 6219 Grand Ave Downers Grove IL 60516 Office: Dept Mgmt U Ill Chgo Box 4348 Chicago IL 60680

LARY, MARILYN SEARSON, librarian; b. Walterboro, S.C., Sept. 3, 1943; d. Charles Baring and Julia Caroline (Rizer) Searson; A.B., Newberry Coll., 1964; M.S. in L.S., U. N.C., 1965; Ph.D., Fla. State U., 1975; m. Jahangir Lary, Oct. 27, 1975; children—Sara, Heidi. Young adult librarian Greenville County (S.C.) Library, 1965-66; library dir. U. S.C., Sumter, 1966-69; instr. Radford (Va.) Coll., 1969-70; asst. prof. East Carolina U., Greenville, 1970-72; reference librarian Clemson U., S.C., 1972-73; asst. prof. U. Mich., Ann Arbor, 1975-78, U. South Fla., Tampa, 1978-84; librarian Hillsborough Community Coll.-Brandon Ctr., Tampa, 1984—. Mem. ALA, Fla. Library Assn., Assn. Am. Library Schs., Fla. Assn. Community Colls. Methodist. Home: 1509 Warman Ct Tampa FL 33613 Office: Hillsborough Community Coll-Brandon 3010 S Kings Ave Brandon FL 33511

LASCALA, LUCY BRADFIELD EVANS, abrasive manufacturing company executive; b. Niagara Falls, Ont., Can., Feb. 22, 1927 (parents Am. citizens); d. John William and Sia Mona (Patience) Hudson; student public schs., Niagara Falls, N.Y.; m. Raymond W. Bradfield, July 23, 1949 (dec. Feb. 1963); children—William R., Robert L., Richard W.; m. 2d, William L. Evans, Aug. 7, 1971 (dec. Aug. 1972); children—Mary Beth Evans Finke, William L. III, JoAnn Evans Paris, Donald R.; m. 3d, Samuel S. LaScala, Sept. 10, 1976 (dec. Sept. 1984). Telephone/telegraph operator data processing and fin., 1966-69, scheduling sec., 1969-74, office mgr., flight ops. coordinator, 1974-83; adminstrv. asst. Advanced Refractory Techs., Inc., Buffalo, 1984—. Vice-pres. children's activities Parents Without Partners, 1964-65, 72-75; active Cub Scouts, Cancer Soc., PTA, Ch. Sch. Riverside Presbyn., Little League Baseball. Named Single Parent of Year, Parents Without Partners, Internat., 1976. Republican. Presbyterian. Clubs: Carborundum Management, Women of Moose. Home: 6887 Joanne Circle Niagara Falls NY 14304 Office: 699 Hertel Ave Buffalo NY 14207

LASCH, JUDITH, television producer, author; b. Hudson County, N.J., Feb. 3, 1939; m. (dec. 1962); children—Callie, Amy and Beth (twins). A.A., Brookdale Community Coll.; B.A., Thomas A. Edison Coll. Fashion dir. Talon, N.Y.C., 1972-78; cons. to DuPont Co., N.Y.C., 1978-80, Xerox, N.Y.C., 1980-83; exec. producer Focus on New York, N.Y.C., 1983—, China-Am. Exchange (video show airing in China); lectr. Fashion Inst. Tech., N.Y.C., other ednl. instns. Author: The Teen Model Book, 1986; (workbook) The Teen Guide to Beauty, 1982. Pres. N.J. State Fedn. Women's Clubs, 1964, civics and legis. dist. leader, 1966; leader Girl Scouts U.S.A.; group leader African Safari and student trips to France. Mem. Am. Women Entrepreneurs, Nat. Assn. Female Execs., Victorian Soc. Am. Avocations: travel; crafts; arts; reading; gardening; camping; cooking; nature. Home: 235 E 22d St New York NY 10010

LASCHER, WENDY JEAN COLE, lawyer; b. Palo Alto, Calif., July 14, 1950; d. John Louis and Peggy Ann (Stern) Cole; m. Roger Wilner, Jan. 5, 1969 (div. Aug. 1979); children—Joseph B., John J.; m. 2d, Edward Leonard Lascher, Feb. 7, 1980; 1 son, William C. B.A. with distinction in Polit. Sci., Stanford U., 1970; J.D., U. Mich., 1973. Bar: Calif. 1973, U.S. Ct. Appeals (9th cir.) 1974, U.S. Ct. Appeals (7th cir.) 1978, U.S. Supreme Ct. 1976. Assoc., Law Offices of Edward Lascher, Ventura, Calif., 1973-77; ptnr. Lascher & Lascher, Ventura, 1977—; mem. com. appellate cts. Calif. State Bar, 1976-80, chmn., 1979-80; lectr. Calif. Continuing Edn. of Bar, 1982-86, Hastings Coll. Advocacy, 1985. Instnl. rev. com. Ventura County Gen. Hosp., 1981—. Mem. Calif. Acad. Appellate Lawyers (pres. 1986), Los Angeles Bar Assn., Ventura County Bar Assn. (newsletter editor 1982-85), Calif. Women Lawyers, Ventura County Women Lawyers. Democrat. Home: 362 Agnus Dr Ventura CA 93003 Office: Lascher & Lascher 605 Poli St PO Box AJ Ventura CA 93002

LASHBROOK, VELMA JANET, consulting executive, researcher; b. Pipestone, Minn., May 26, 1948; d. August Jacob and Lorita Belle (Swift) Wenzlaff; m. William Bradshaw Lashbrook, Sept. 4, 1971; children—Nicole Maurine, Christopher Cromwell. B.S., Iowa State U., 1970; M.S., Ill. State U., 1971; Ed.D., W. Va. U., 1976. Communication tchr., debate coach Woodruff High Sch., Peoria, Ill., 1971-73; asst. prof. communication W.Va. U., Morgantown, 1976-77; asst. prof. mktg. Auburn U., Ala., 1977-79; v.p., research Wilson Learning Corp., Eden Prairie, Minn., 1979—. Author: Proana5, 1974. Contbr. articles to profl. jours. Mem. editorial bd. Human Communication Research, 1976-77, Communication Education, 1982-84, New Management, 1984-86. Mem. Western Speech Communication Assn., Internat. Communication Assn., Am. Ednl. Research Assn., Evaluation Research Soc., Am. Soc. Tng. and Devel., Nat. Soc. Performance and Instruction, Acad. Mgmt., Am. Mktg. Assn., Japanese Psychol. Assn., Internat. Assn. Applied Psychology. Avocations: swimming; camping; music. Home: 9566 Woodridge Dr Eden Prairie MN 55344 Office: Wilson Learning Corp 6950 Washington Ave So Eden Prairie MN 55344

LASHLEE, JOLYNNE VAN MARSDON, army officer, nurse, administrator; b. Asheville, N.C., May 22, 1948; d. William Reid and Frances (Furey) Van Marsdon; B.S. in Nursing, U. Fla., 1971; M. Health Care Adminstrn., Baylor U., 1982. Team leader surg. specialties Shand Teaching Hosp., Gainesville, Fla., 1971; commd. lt. U.S. Army Nurses Corps, 1971, advanced through grades to maj., 1981; asst. head nurse organ transplant service unit Walter Reed Hosp., Washington, 1972; staff nurse surg. ICU, head nurse multi-service nursing unit Nurnberg, W. Ger., 1972-75; head nurse recovery room William Beaumont Army Med. Center, Ft. Bliss, El Paso, Tex., 1975-76, dep. dir. patient care specialist course, 1976-78; ednl. coordinator, project officer U.S. Lyster Hosp., Ft. Rucker, Ala., 1978; adminstrv. resident Madigan Army Med. Center, Tacoma, 1981-82; chief nurse methods div. Walter Reed Hosp., 1982-85; mem. Army Surgeon Gen.'s Task Force on Health Care, 1985—. Active Boy Scouts Am. Mem. Am. Hosp. Assn., Am. Coll. Hosp. Adminstrs., Assn. Health Care Adminstrs. Nat. Capital Area, Am. Assn. Critical Care Nurses, Baylor U. Healthcare Adminstrs. Alumni. Home: 4500 S Four Mile Run Apt 1123 Arlington VA 22204 Office: DASG-ZC Pentagon Washington DC 20310

LASHLEY, REBECCA EYRE, speech pathologist; b. Lincoln, Ill., Apr. 29, 1924; d. Richard Daniel and Harriet S. (Hoopes) Robbins; m. Julian Jennings Edwards, Dec. 20, 1948 (div. 1975); children—Nancy Lee Maertens, Rebecca Eyre Moore; m. Forrest Elwyn Lashley, Jan. 2, 1976. B.S., No. Ill. U., 1945; M.A., George Peabody Coll. Tchrs., 1952. Various positions as tchr. and speech pathologists, Ill., Fla., Ga., 1945-70; speech pathologist Richmond City Schs., Va., 1970-73; Henry County Schs., Ga., 1973-77; tchr. hearing imparied Meridian Separate Schs., Miss., 1977-81, speech pathologist, 1981-85; speech pathologist Clayton County Schs., 1985—. Bd. dirs. Jr. League, Pekin, Ill., 1951-52; leader Gateway council Girl Scouts U.S., 1960-68. Mem. Am. Lang. Speech and Hearing Assn., Miss. Speech and Hearing Assn., East Miss. Speech and Hearing Assn. (pres. 1983-84), NEA, Miss. Assn. Educators, Assn. Meridian Educators. Republican. Baptist. Club: Thomaston Country (officer) (Ga.). Lodge: Eastern Star (various stations). Avocations: travel; entertaining guests; relaxing in nature; sewing; reading. Home: 221 Upper Riverdale Rd 18-B Jonesboro GA 30236

LASKO, GLORIA ELIZABETH, communications company executive; b. Jackson Heights, N.Y., Aug. 26, 1953; d. James Socrates and Agnes (Rado) L. B.A. cum laude, Adelphi U., 1975; paralegal cert., 1978. Salesperson, Lafayette Radio, Syosset, N.Y., 1970-76; client service rep. Reed, Roberts Assoc., Garden City, N.Y., 1976-80; acct. exec. Gates, McDonald, N.Y.C., 1980-85, Western Union, N.Y.C., 1986—. Mem. Small Bus. Council of L.I., Melville, N.Y., 1980-82, mem. Am. Cancer Soc., 1984—; mem. Statue of Liberty Ellis Island Found., Inc., N.Y.C., 1985. Mem. Nat. Assn. Female Execs. Avocations: tennis; racquetball; museums; theater; books. Home: 77 Lucille Ave Elmont NY 11003 Office: Western Union 600 3d Ave New York NY 10016

LASNIER, RINA, writer; b. St.-Gregoire d'Iberville, Que., Can., Aug. 6, 1910; d. Moise and Laura (Galipeau) Lasnier; Docteur Honoris Causa, U. Montreal (Que., Can.), 1977. Author 24 books of prose, poetry, and on theater; mem., v.p. Council of Arts Que. Recipient Prix Duvernay, 1957, Prix Molson, 1964, Smith prize U. Mich., 1974, Prix France-Can., 1974, Prix David, Province Que., 1974, Prix Edgar-Poe, France, 1979. Mem. Academie canadienne francaise, Societe royale du Canada, Institut Gracian, academie internationele. Roman Catholic.

LASS, LESLIE JANE, writer, public relations consultant; b. Bklyn., Sept. 17, 1951; 1 dau., Emily Arden. B.A., U. Calif.-Berkeley, 1974, M.A., 1978. Teaching asst. English dept. U. Calif.-Berkeley, 1975-78; assoc. editor mktg. publs. Bank of Am., San Francisco, 1978-80; owner LL Communications, Oakland, Calif., 1980—, pub. relations specialist Bechtel, San Francisco, 1986—. Contbr. articles to profl. and lit. jours.

LASSEN LORD, BARBARA JEAN, lawyer; b. Grosse Pointe, Mich., Apr. 11, 1948; d. Donald R. Shirk and Mary T. (Walsh) Kanaby; m. Gregory Fisher Lord, July 10, 1982. B.A., Wayne State U., 1977; J.D. cum laude, Detroit Coll. Law, 1982. Bar: Mich. 1982. Legal asst. Riley & Roumell, Detroit, 1979-80; jud. asst. Wayne County Cir. Ct., Detroit, 1980-82; ptnr. firm Lord & Lassen, P.C., Southfield, Mich., 1982—. Mem. Assn. Trial Lawyers Am. Office: Lord & Lassen PC 17117 W 9 Mile Rd Suite 1330 Southfield MI 48075

LASSER, FAITH, medical researcher executive, administrator, civic worker; b. N.Y.C., Mar. 4, 1924; d. Maurice Ernst and Carrie (Paul) L.; m. Robert Schwarz, Jr., June 4, 1944 (div. Dec. 1981); children—Hope S. Foster, David M., Jan Schwarz Miller. B.A., Wellesley Coll., Mass., 1945; postgrad. Columbia U., 1957. Exec. dir. Com. for Pub. Justice, N.Y.C., 1974-75, Irvington House Inst. for Med. Research, N.Y.C., 1981—; project dir. Sci. Inst. for Pub. Info., N.Y.C., 1975-76; dir. Calif. Mil. Audit Project, Los Angeles, 1976-79; cons. Urban Policy Research Inst., Los Angeles, 1973-81; cons. Nat. Com. on Resources for Youth, N.Y.C., 1974-76. Exec. com. Health and Welfare Council, Bergen County, N.Y., 1965-76, Urban League of Bergen County, 1965-76. Mem. N.Y. Acad. Scis., AAAS. Office: Irvington House Inst for Med Research 120 E 56 St New York NY 10022

LASSER, GAIL MARIA, psychologist, educator; b. Saddle River, N.J., Feb. 29, 1952; d. Dominick A. and Genevieve M. Sanzo; B.A., Seton Hall U., 1971; teaching cert. William Paterson Coll., 1973; M.A., Montclair State Coll., 1975; cert. staff psychologist, N.J., 1977; lic. real estate agt., N.J.; notary pub.; m. Lloyd M. Lasser, Aug. 31, 1978; children—Michael, Jason. Public relations rep. European Health Spa, 1970-71; med. asst. Sci. Prevention and Rehab. Assn., 1973; grad. teaching and research asst. Montclair State Coll., 1973-74; clin. asst. Dr. Brower, 1974; instr. psychology Essex County Coll., 1976-77; clin. psychologist intern Community Mental Health Center, Mt. Carmel Guild, Newark, 1976-77; lectr. St. Michaels Med. Center-N.J. Coll. Medicine, 1977-80; instr. psychology Bergen Community Coll., Paramus, N.J., 1977—; asst. to ct. adminstr. Bergen County Cts., 1977-78. Mem. Am. Psychol. Assn., Am. Soc. for Psychical Research, Pi Lambda Theta, Psi Chi. Home: 7 Westwind Ct Saddle River NJ 07458

LASTER, JENNY CATHERINE, management consultant; b. St. Louis, Feb. 6, 1940; d. Russell Vincent and Luvenia (Massey) Hayes Scott; m. Lawrence Philip Laster, Feb. 3, 1960 (div. Jan. 1983); 1 dau., Gina Marie. Tchr., St. Louis City Pub. Schs., 1965-74; tng. adminstr. Bi-State Devel. Agy., St. Louis, 1974-79; dir. human resources Am. Pub. Transit Assn., Washington, 1979-81; v.p. ATE Mgmt. & Service Co., Inc., Cin., 1981—. Mem. adv. bd. Wharton Sch., Phila., 1983—. Bd. dirs. Planned Parenthood Assn., Cin., 1983—, Community Adv. Bd., 1983—; chmn. bd. trustees Black Career Women's Resource Ctr., 1983-84. Recipient Sibling award Conf. Minority Transp. Ofcls. Chgo., 1981, Achievement Against the Odds award Black Career Women, 1982. Mem. Am. Soc. Tng. and Devel., Am. Soc. Personnel Adminstrs., Conf. Minority Transp. Ofcls. (exec. bd.). Democrat. Baptist. Home: 1004 B Celestial St Cincinnati OH 45202 Office: ATE Mgmt & Service Co Inc 617 Vine St Suite 800 Cincinnati OH 45202

LATHAM, ALICE FRANCES PATTERSON, public health nurse; b. Macon, Ga., Dec. 18, 1916; d. Frank Waters and Ruby (Dews) Patterson; R.N., Charity Hosp. Sch. Nursing, New Orleans, 1937; student George Peabody Coll. Tchrs., 1938-39; B.S. in Pub. Health Nursing, U. N.C., 1954; M.P.H., Johns Hopkins U., 1966; m. William Joseph Latham, July 21, 1940 (dec. Apr. 1981); children—Jo Alice (Mrs. James Ziegler), Marynette (Mrs. Charles Stephens), Lauruby Cathleen (Mrs. Kevin Gold); m. Sidney Dumas Herndon, Apr. 26, 1985. Staff pub. health nurse assigned spl. venereal disease study USPHS, Darien, Ga., 1939-40; county pub. health nurse Bacon County, Alma, Ga., 1940-41; USPHS spl. venereal disease project, Glynn County, Brunswick, 1943-47; county pub. health nurse Glynn County, 1949-51, Ware County,

Waycross, 1951-52; pub. health nurse supr. Wayne-Long-Brantley-Liberty Counties, Jesup, 1954-56 dist. dir. pub. health nursing Wayne-Long-Appling-Bacon-Pierce Counties, Jesup, 1956-70; dist. chief nursing S.E. Ga. Health Dist., 1970-79, organizer mobile health services, 1973—. Exec. dir. Wayne County Home Health Agy., 1968-80; exec. dir. Ware County Home Health Agy., 1970-79, mem. exec. com., 1978—; mem. governing bd. S.E. Ga. Health Systems Agy., 1975-82; mem. governing bd. Health Dept. Home Health Agy., 1978—, also author numerous grant proposals. Bd. dirs. Wayne County Mental Health Assn., 1959, 60, 61, 81, 82, Wayne County Tb Assn., 1958-62; a non-alcoholic organizer Jesup group Alcoholics Anonymous, 1962-63; mem. adv. council Ware Meml. Hosp. Sch. Practical Nursing, Waycross, Ga., 1958; mem. Altar Guild, St. Paul's Episcopal Ch., 1979—, vestrywoman, 1981-82. Recipient recognition Gen. Service Bd., Alcoholics Anonymous, Inc. Fellow Am. Pub. Health Assn.; mem. Am., 8th Dist. (pres. 1954-58, sec. 1958-60, dir. 1960-62, 1st v.p. 1962), Ga. (exec. bd. 1954-58, program rev. continuing edn. com. 1980—) nurses assns., Ga. Pub. Health Assn. (chmn. nursing sect. 1956-57), Ga. Assn. Dist. Chiefs Nursing (pres. 1976). Contbr. to state nursing manuals. Home: Route 6 Box 46 Brunswick GA 31520

LATHAM, CAROLINE JANET MACDONALD, retired state official, home economist; b. Raymond, Wash., Jan. 9, 1917; d. John Richard and Alice Alzina (Campbell) MacDonald; m. Charles A. Latham, Nov. 19, 1938 (div. June 1966); 1 son, Richard E. A.A., Grays Harbor Coll., 1937; student U. Wash., 1938-39; B.S. in Home Econs., U. Idaho, 1956; M.S. in Home Econs. Edn., 1965. Buyer, Fredrick & Nelson, 1938; tchr. Buhl (Idaho) High Sch., 1943-64; grad. asst., vis. prof. U. Idaho, 1964-65; asst. state supr. home econs. Idaho Bd. for Vocat. Edn., Boise, 1965-72, acting state supr., 1972-73, state supr. home econs. edn., 1973-83, ret., 1983; exec. sec. Idaho Vocat. Assn., 1983—. Bd. dirs. Future Homemakers Am., 1966-68, 76-78; circle pres. First Methodist Ch., 1974. Recipient hon. chpt. degree Idaho Assn., Future Homemakers Am., 1955, hon. state degree, 1956; disting. service award, Future Homemakers Am. 1985, Idaho Vocat. Assn., 1985; named Outstanding Buhl Bus. Women, 1958; Iowa State U. fellow, 1967; Mich. State U. fellow, 1969. Mem. Home Econs. Edn. Assn., Am. Vocat. Assn., Am. Home Econs. Assn., Nat. Assn. State Suprs. Home Econs. (pres. 1975), Idaho Home Econs. Assn. (pres. 1974-75), Boise C. of C. (sec. women's div. 1969), Bus. and Profl. Women, Idaho Pub. Employees Assn. (sec. River Run chpt. 1985—), Phi Omicron Upsilon, Delta Kappa Gamma. Methodist.

LATHAM, EMILEIGH MAXWELL, communications executive; b. Pink Hill, N.C., Oct. 26, 1923; d. Hugh Edgar and Emily (Turner) M.; student Woman's Coll., Univ. N.C., 1940-42; B.A. in Journalism, U. N.C., 1944; m. Herald Rowe Latham, May 26, 1951; children—Lynn Corbell, Diann, Herald Jeffrey. News dir. Sta WTAR-AM-FM-TV Norfolk, Va., 1947-51; public relations mgr., products div. Holiday Inns, Inc., Memphis, 1972-74; community relations dir. Sta. WKNO-TV-FM, Memphis, 1974-76; project coordinator Auction, Sta. WNET, N.Y.C., 1977; asst. dir. community relations L.I. Coll. Hosp., Bklyn., 1978; asst. dir. public affairs Fairfax Hosp. Assn., Springfield, Va., 1981-83; pub. relations dir. CompHealth: Comprehensive Home Health Service for No. Va., Inc., 1983—. Mem. Internat. Assn. Bus. Communicators, Am. Med. Writers Assn., Women in Communications, Inc., Methodist. Editor: Pacesetter, Holiday Inns, Inc., 1973; Healthline, L.I. Coll. Hosp., 1978. Home: 5303 Queensberry Ave Springfield VA 22151 Office: 5405 B Port Royal Rd Springfield VA 22151

LATHAM, MARY ELIZABETH, clergywoman; b. Cin.; d. Lawrence Lorenzo and Eugenia (Peters) Latham; B.A. cum laude, Asbury Coll., 1929. Tchr. math. and Latin, McAfee High Sch., Mercer County, Ky., 1929-32; entered ministry of evangelism Ch. of the Nazarene, 1933, ordained to ministry, 1937; traveled in work of evangelism and Christian edn., 1937-48; internat. dir. vacation Bible schs. Dept. Ch. Schs., Kansas City, Mo., 1948-67; dir. audiovisuals Ch. of the Nazarene, 1962-74; chmn. audiovisual com. Council of Chs. Greater Kansas City, 1955-58, chmn. com. on communications edn., 1966-67; chmn. Latham Communications, 1975—; also lectr. Recipient Albert F. Harper award Adult Ministries, Ch. of Nazarene, 1980. Author: Vacation Bible School, Why, What, and How, 1954, 9th rev. edit., 1968; Adventures with Jesus, 1948, rev. edits., 1951, 54, 57, 60, 63; Teacher, You Are an Evangelist, rev. edit., 1977; contbr. numerous covers and articles to periodicals; dir. prodn. films The Great Transition, motion picture of Nazarene Colls., 1964; Sing His Wonderful Name, 1965; Would You Believe It?, 1967; The Debtors and They Do Not Wait, 1968; The Way Out and God's Word for Today's World, 1969; Moving Ahead, 1970; Just for the Love of It, 1971; To Make a Miracle, 1972; To New Worlds, 1972; The Church of the Nazarene, 1974; The Alabaster Story, 1974; dir. filmstrips with cassettes How Young Is Our Welcome? and What Made the Orange Go Away?, 1976; producer videotape Roy T. Williams-the Man and the Leader, 1983. Address: 10268 Cedarbrooke Ln Kansas City MO 64131

LATHAM, PATRICIA HORAN, lawyer; b. Hoboken, N.J., Sept. 5, 1941; d. Patrick John and Rosemary (Moller) Horan; m. Peter Samuel Latham, June 12, 1965; children—John Horan, Kerry Patricia. B.A., Swathmore Coll., 1963; J.D., U. Chgo., 1966. Bar: D.C. 1967, U.S. Dist. Ct. D.C. 1967, U.S. Ct. Appeals 1967, U.S. Supreme Ct. 1970. Assoc. Fried Frank Harris Shriver & Kampelman, Washington, 1966-69; atty. Office of Gen. Counsel, SEC, Washington, 1969-71; assoc. Martin & Smith, Washington, 1971—, ptnr., 1974—; lectr. Columbus Sch. of Law, Cath. U. Am., Washington, 1978—; dir. IB Realty Corp., Washington. Mem., legal adviser League of Rep. Women of D.C., 1983—; mem. Rep. Women's Fed. Forum, Washington, 1983—; Mem. ABA, Fed. Bar Assn., Bar Assn. D.C., D.C. Bar (com. on corps., partnerships and other bus. orgns. 1979—, corp. counsel com. 1983—), Am. Arbitration Assn. (panel of arbitrators). Roman Catholic. Clubs: City Tavern, Nat. Lawyers (Washington). Home: 7000 Loch Edin Ct Potomac MD 20854

LATHAN, PAMELA ANNE, jewelry company executive; b. Ada, Okla., Nov. 3, 1944; d. Roy Clayton and Betty Anne (Glasby) Glasgow; m. Terry Roy Lane (div. Jan. 1973); m. Marvin Edward Lathan, June 9, 1973; children—Paul, Lisa, Leslie, Mike, Teri Lyn. Student public schs. Lawton, Okla. Nursing asst. St. Mary's Hosp., Canton, Ohio, 1971-73, Meml. Hosp., Lawton, Okla., 1973-75; tchr. preschool Ch. of God, Lawton, Okla., 1975-78; v.p. Classique Creation Co., Lawton, 1979—, also dir. Clubs: Altrusa, Womens Christian. Avocations: Boating; bowling; fishing; outdoors. Home: 232 Crystal Hills Dr SW Lawton OK 73505 Office: P&M Enterprises Classique Creations 1805 Cache Rd Lawton OK 73507

LATHEM, BETTY BROOKS, business executive; b. Griffin, Ga., Aug. 16, 1931; d. Raymond England and Annie Ezelle (Chappell) Brooks; student public schs., Griffin, Ga.; m. Charles Malcolm Lathem, July 18, 1950; children—Charles Thomas, Richard Lee, Betty Kathryn. With So. Bell Telephone Co., Griffin, Ga., 1949-50, J.D. Jewell, Inc., Gainesville, Ga., 1950-54; part-time sec., various cos., Gainesville, 1954-59; with Jacobs, Matthews & Parker, Architects, Gainesville, 1959-69; self-employed ind. sec., Gainesville, 1969-70; adminstrv. asst. Internat. Mgmt., Gainesville, 1970-84; ptnr. Sunstar Farm; owner Windfield Creations, 1984—; specialist in orgn., research and preparation of bus. and profl. books and articles for publ. Democrat. Baptist. Home and Office: 142-A Baker Circle PO Box 223 Clermont GA 30527

LATHROP, GERTRUDE ADAMS, chemist, consultant; b. Norwich, Conn., Apr. 28, 1921; d. William Barrows and Lena (Adams) Lathrop; B.S., U. Conn., 1944; M.A., Tex. Womans U., 1953, Ph.D., 1955. Devel. chemist textiles Alexander Smith & Sons Carpet Co., Yonkers, N.Y., 1944-52; research assoc. textiles Tex. Women's U., 1952-56; chief chemist Glasgo Finishing Plant div. United Mchts. & Mfrs., Inc. (Conn.), 1956-57, chief chemist Old Fort Finishing Plant div. (N.C.), 1957-63; research chemist United Mchts. Research Center, Langley, S.C., 1963-64; lab. mgr. automotive div. Collins & Aikman Corp., Albemarle, N.C., 1964-78; chief chemist, lab. mgr. Old Fort Finishing Plant div. United Mchts., 1979-82. Recipient Disting. Alumni award U. Conn. Sch. Home Econs. and Family Studies, 1980-81. Mem. Am. Chem. Soc., Am. Assn. Textile Chemists and Colorists (sect. research chmn., treas., vice chmn. 1962-64; chmn. edn. com. Piedmont sect. 1977-78), ASTM (chmn. transp. fabrics on flammability com. 1973-75), Bus. and Profl. Womens Club (pres. chpt. 1974-76, Woman of Yr. 1979, 80), Iota Sigma Pi. Home: 301 Mountain St Black Mountain NC 28711

LATHROP, JOYCE KEEN, civic worker; b. Los Angeles, Nov. 25, 1939; d. William Lavern Trewin and Therese (Wenig) Keen; student Russell Sage Coll., 1957-58, Goucher Coll., 1958-59; B.A., U. So. Calif., 1961; m. Mitchell Lee Lathrop, June 29, 1959 (div. 1977); children—Christin Lorraine, Alexander Mitchell, Timothy Trewin Mitchell. Dir. Assistance League Glendale, 1964-70, Pasadena (Calif.) Sr. Center, 1966-68; dir. jrs. Los Angeles Orphanage Guild, 1968-78, 83-87, pres., 1974-75, treas., 1972-73, v.p., 1973-74; mem. Symphonians Los Angeles Philharm. Orch., 1969-73, Opera Assocs. Music Center, 1965-77, Met. Opera Assos., 1967-78, 85—, Aux. Hosp. Good Samaritan, Los Angeles; mem. Nat. Council Met. Opera, N.Y.C., 1970-77; mem. Aux. Pasadena Sr. Center; bd. dirs. Los Angeles Music Center Opera Assn., 1973-74; bd. dirs. Calif. Mus. of Sci. and Industry Council, 1979—, pres., 1981-83, chmn. bd., 1983-85. Recipient vol. service award Huntington Meml. Hosp., Pasadena, 1967; vol. service award Calif. Mus. Sci. and Industry, 1984, 85, 86; decorated officer Mil. and Hospitaller Order St. Lazarus of Jerusalem. Episcopalian. Clubs: Goucher of So. Calif. (treas. 1966-67, sec. 1964-66) (Los Angeles); Valley Hunt (Pasadena). Home: 1375 Inverness Dr Pasadena CA 91103

LATIMER, HEATHER, writer, lecturer, photographer; b. Essex, Eng.; d. Robin and Jessie (Rose) Latimer; Pitman's Coll., London, Eng., 1943-45; m. Walther B. Neubauer, Aug. 24, 1957 (dec. Apr. 1976). Photographer's head and shoulders model, 1946-51; free lance writing and publicity projects, 1951-63; TV and radio publicity dir. Standard Reference Works Pub. Co., N.Y.C., 1963-65; asst. to pres. W. H. Schneider, Inc., advt., N.Y.C., 1965-67; patron relations to patrons Met. Opera, N.Y.C., 1968-70; asst. to dir. Bide-A-Wee Animal Protection Assn., N.Y.C., 1970-72; contbg. editor Dogs mag., N.Y.C., 1972-77; freelance writer, 1972—. Pres., Internat. League of N.Y., 1957-67. Recipient award for best nat. series Dog Writers' Assn. Am., 1972. Mem. Internat. Platform Assn., English Speaking Union. Club: Princeton of N.Y. Author: How to Make Money As A Professional Party Organizer in The Great New Leisure Time Market; Tidypet—How To Make Your Dog An Indoor Toilet and Teach Puppy or Grown Dog To Use It; One is Fun; Dogs: Everything You Need to Know to Care for Your Pet; Cats: Everything You Need to Know to Care For Your Pet; Louis Wain-King of the Cat Artists; Curse of the Painted Cats. Office: 155 Crary Ave Room 1E Mount Vernon NY 10550

LATIMER, SUZANNE LOUISE, hospital administrator; b. Albany, N.Y., Mar. 3, 1954; d. Olin Kenneth and Madeline Louise (Weeks) Latimer; R.N., Albany Med. Center Sch. Nursing, 1975; B.S.N., Russell Sage Coll., 1981, M.S. in Health Services Adminstrn., 1984. Gen. staff nurse labor and delivery Albany (N.Y.) Med. Center, 1975-81; physician's asst. Bellevue Maternity Hosp., Schenectady, 1979, interim dir. nursing, 1980, adminstrv. asst. to adminstr., 1980-82, quality assurance coordinator, 1980—, dir. patient support services, 1982—, risk mgr., 1983—. Vol., educator Am. Cancer Soc., 1975—; vol., instr., ARC, 1980—. Mem. Am. Soc. Hosp. Risk Mgrs., Nat. Commn. for Certification of Physician's Assts., N.Y. State Assn. Quality Assurance Profls., Nat. Assn. Quality Assurance Profls., Nat. Assn. Female Execs., Nat. Fire Protection Agy., Am. Pub. Health Assn., N.Y. State Pub. Health Assn. Democrat. Roman Catholic. Home: 1698 Crane St Schenectady NY Office: 2210 Troy Rd PO Box 1030 Schenectady NY 12301

LATINI, SUSAN CAROL, substance abuse and mental health administrator; b. N.Y.C., Nov. 27, 1949; d. Jules Polansky and Ruth Braverman (Polansky) Hatten; m. Francis Anthony Latini, Apr. 22, 1977; 1 child, Marissa Frances. B.A. in Psychology, U. Fla., 1976, M.Ed., 1984, Edn. Specialist, 1984. Social worker Health and Rehab. Services, Gainesville, Fla., 1977-79, social work supr., 1979-83; case mgr. Mental Health Services, Gainesville, 1983, clin. supr., 1983—; counselor instr. U. Fla., Gainesville, 1983-85; counselor career and personal Santa Fe Community Coll., 1981-83. Mem. Am. Assn. Counseling and Devel., Am. Mental Health Counselors Assn., Fla. Alcohol and Drug Abuse Assn., Phi Kappa Phi, Pi Lambda Theta. Avocations: dancing; aerobics; bicycling; gardening; holistic health care. Home: 1046 NE 14th Ave Gainesville FL 32601 Office: Mental Health Services Inc 516 SW 2d Terr Gainesville FL 32601

LATIOLAIS, MINNIE FITZGERALD, nurse, hosp. adminstr.; b. Vivian, La., Dec. 26, 1921; d. Thomas Ambrose and Mildred Surita (Nagle) Fitzgerald; R.N., Touro Infirmary, New Orleans, 1943; m. Joseph C. Latiolais, Jr., July 19, 1947; children—Felisa, Diana, Sylvia, Mary, Amelia, Joseph Clifton, III. Orthopedic surg. nurse Ochsner Clinic, New Orleans, 1943-47, asst. dir. nursing, 1947; supr. Lafayette (La.) Gen. Hosp., 1960-64; adminstrv. asst., supr. operating room Abbeville (La.) Gen. Hosp., 1964-68; gen. mgr., neurol. surg. nurse J. Robert Rivet, neurol. surgeon, Lafayette, 1968-78; hosp. cons. asso. B.J. Landry & Assos., hosps. cons., Lafayette, 1979—; dir. nursing Acadia St. Landry Hosp., Church Point, 1981-82; supr. supplies, processing and distbn. Univ. Med. Center, Lafayette, 1982—; bd. dirs. S.W. La. Rehab. Assn., 1975—, pres., 1979-80; mem. Mid-La. Health Systems Agy., 1977-82, project rev. chmn., 1978-80; bd. dirs. Acadica Regional Clearing House, vice chmn., 1984—; mem. crafts and practical nurse com. Lafayette Regional Vocat.-Tech. Inst., 1980-84, chmn. 1983-84. Mem. Am. Nurses Assn., La. State Nurses Assn., Lafayette Dist. Nurses Assn. (pres. 1967-69). Roman Catholic. Clubs: Lafayette Woman's, Lafayette Garden. Home: 1121 S Washington St Lafayette LA 70501

LATNER, SELMA, psychoanalyst; b. Bronx, N.Y., Aug. 11, 1920; d. Isidore and Jennie (Reisman) Levy; m. Harold Latner, Mar. 23, 1959 (dec. 1972); children—Gail, Karen, Irwin. B.B.A., CCNY, 1942; M.S.W., U. Pitts., 1945; Ph.D. in Psychoanalysis, Heed U., 1984. Lic. marriage and family therapist, N.J. Caseworker, Jewish Family Service, N.Y.C., 1949-53, Community Service Soc., Queens, N.Y., 1950's; sr. caseworker Jewish Family Services, Hackensack, N.J., 1965-68; sr. family and marriage therapist Bergen County Family Counseling Service, Hackensack, 1968-83; pvt. practice psychoanalyst, Teaneck, N.J., 1981—; Bd. dirs. Am. Anorexic and Bulimia Assn., Teaneck, 1984-88. Recipient plaque for Outstanding Profl. Human Services, Am. Acad. Human Services, 1974-75. Mem. Nat. Alliance Family Life, Nat. Assn. Social Workers, N.J. Soc. Clin. Social Work, Nat. Assn. Advancement Psychoanalysis, N.J. Inst. Tng. Psychoanalysis. Avocations: tennis; music; dance forms; art. Home: 416 Beatrice St Teaneck NJ 07666

LATTA, DIANA LENNOX, interior designer; b. Lahaina, Maui, Hawaii, Aug. 5, 1936; d. D. Stewart and Jean Marjorie (Anderson) Lennox; grad. the Bishop's Sch., La Jolla, Calif., 1954; student U. Wash., 1954-56; m. Arthur McKee Latta, Jan. 26, 1957 (dec.); children—Mary-Stewart, Marion Mckee (Mrs. Marshall V. Davidson). Dir., Vero Beach (Fla.) br. of Wellington Hall, Ltd., Thomasville, N.C., 1970-72; asst. to chief designer Rablen-West Interiors, Vero Beach, 1972-75; design and adminstrv. asst. to pres. Design Studio Archtl. & Interior Design Concepts, Inc., Vero Beach, 1975-82; owner, designer The Designery, Vero Beach, 1983—. Mem. Indian River Meml. Hosp. Women's Aux., Vero Beach, 1957-70, chmn. Charity Ball, 1960, v.p., 1962-64; leading actress in Vero Beach Theatre Guild prodns.: The Laughmaker, 1964, Oklahoma, 1966; model for Holly Fashion Show, Vero Beach, 1962-69; mem. adv. bd. Indian River County 4-H Horsemaster's Club, 1973-76; bd. dirs. Vero Beach Mut. Concert Assn., 1973-76, chmn. hospitality com. 1974; bd. dirs. Vero Beach Theatre Guild, 1964. Mem. Internat. Platform Assn., Republican Women Aware. Kappa Kappa Gamma. Republican. Episcopalian. Club: Riomar Bay Yacht (club tennis champion 1964, 66, chmn. tennis com. 1964-66). Home and Office: 555 Honeysuckle Ln Vero Beach FL 32963

LATTIMER, AGNES DOLORES (MRS. FRANK BETHEL, JR.), physician; b. Memphis, May 13, 1928; d. Arthur Oneal and Hortense (Lewis) Lattimer; A.B., Fisk U., 1949; M.D., Chgo. Med. Sch., 1954; m. Bernard Goss, Jan. 16, 1952 (div.); 1 son, Bernard C.; m. 2d, Frank Bethel Jr. Rotating intern Cook County Hosp., Chgo., 1954-55, resident pediatrics, 1955-56; resident pediatrics Michael Reese Hosp., Chgo., 1956-57, chief pediatric resident, 1957-58, dir. sect. ambulatory pediatrics, attending physician div. pediatrics; dir. div. ambulatory pediatrics Cook County Hosp., 1983-85, med. dir., 1986—; research fellow Chgo. Heart Assn., 1958-59, heart disease control program Chgo. Bd. Health, 1959-61; adj. physician Provident Hosp.; pediatric cons. Bethany Hosp.; mem. staff, chmn. dept. pediatrics Mary Thompson Hosp.; clin. instr. dept. preventive medicine U. Ill. Med. Sch.; asso. prof. dept. pediatrics Chgo. Med. Sch., 1970-85, prof. pediatrics, 1986. Vice pres. bd. dirs. Greater Lawndale Conservation Commn. Diplomate Am. Bd. Pediatrics, Nat. Bd. Med. Examiners. Recipient Elsie and Phillip Tsang award, 1968; Disting. Alumni award Chgo. Med. Sch., 1971. Fellow Am. Acad. Pediatrics (chpt. chmn. 1983-86), Internat. Coll. Applied Nutrition, Inst. Medicine, mem. Ambulatory Pediatric Assn., Chgo. Pediatric Soc., Am. Public Health Assn. Contbr. articles to profl. publs. Office: 1825 W Harrison St Chicago IL 60612

LAUBACH, M(ARTHA) JEAN, state government official, financial consultant; b. Fairfield, Iowa, Mar. 10, 1948; d. Freddie O'Neil and Martha Morrell (Nelson) Laubach. B. Applied Studies, U. Minn., 1977. Adminstrv. asst. Mchts. Nat. Bank, Cedar Rapids, Iowa, 1968-72; adminstrv. asst. 1st Nat. Bank of Mpls., 1972-75, fin. services rep., 1975-76, credit analyst, 1976-77, comml. banking officer, 1977-79; dir. grants and loans State of Minn., St. Paul, 1979-80, asst. commr. Bur. Capital Investments, 1980-81, dep. commr. Minn. Dept. Energy and Econ. Devel., St. Paul, 1981—; cons. fin. packaging; fin. com. small bus. adv. council SBA; creator Minn. Plan financing, 1981-82. Author: Guides to Profit Planning, 1978. Participant Thanksgiving Meals on Wheels, St. Paul/Mpls., 1982, 83; fundraising vol. Guthrie Theatre, 1977; loan reviewer State of Minn., 1977-79; mem. Horizon 100. Named Banker Adviser of Yr., SBA, St. Paul, 1983. Mem. Mpls. C. of C., Epsilon Sigma Alpha. Republican. Home: 5108 Abbott Ave S Minneapolis MN 55410 Office: Minnesota Dept of Energy and Economic Devel 480 Cedar St Saint Paul MN 55101

LAUBE, DIANA P., telephone co. exec.; b. Jersey City, June 29, 1934; d. Harold J. and Emily M. Pohl; grad. high sch.; m. Norman Laube, Oct. 3, 1952; children—Susan, Norma, Norman. With Vernon (N.Y.) Telephone Co., 1952—, treas., 1960-72, pres., treas., 1972—. Fin. chmn. United Methodist Ch. Named Bus. Woman of Yr. in Oneida and Madison Counties, 1983. Mem. N.Y. State Telephone Assn. (dir. 1978-79), U.S. Ind. Telephone Assn., U.S. C. of C. Republican. Office: PO Box A Vernon NY 13476

LAUBER, ANN LOUISE, college personnel director; b. Phila., Oct. 17, 1934; d. Graham and Ruth (Anderson) L. Student Pierce Jr. Coll., Phila., 1952-54. Asst. office mgr. H. G. Kuch & Co., Phila., 1954-62; personnel sec. Certainteed, Ardmore, Pa., 1962-63; sec. to dir. personnel The Am. Coll., Bryn Mawr, Pa., 1964—. Judge of Elections, Montgomery County, Wynnewood, Pa., 1974-80. Mem. Am. Soc. Personnel Adminstrs., Coll.-Univ. Personnel Assn., Nat. Assn. Female Execs., Cleve. Bay Horse Soc. Am., American Horse Show Assn., American Driving Soc. Republican. Advocation: breeding of half bred Cleve. Bays. Republican. Office: The American Coll 270 Bryn Mawr Ave Bryn Mawr PA 19010

LAUBER, MIGNON DIANE, food processing company executive; b. Detroit, Dec. 21; d. Charles Edmond and Maud Lillian (Foster) Donaker; student Kelsey Jenny U., 1958, Brigham Young U., 1959; m. Richard Brian Lauber, Sept. 13, 1963; 1 dau., Leslie Viane. Owner, operator Alaska World Travel, Ketchikan, 1964-67; founder, owner, pres. Oosick Soup Co., Juneau, Alaska, 1969—. Treas., Pioneer Alaska Lobbyists Soc., Juneau, 1977—. Mem. Bus. and Profl. Women, Alaska C. of C. Libertarian. Club: Washington Athletic. Author: Down at the Waterworks with Jesus; Failure Through Prayer. Home: 321 Highland Dr Juneau AK 99801 Office: PO Box 1625 Juneau AK 99802

LAUCKS, EULAH CROSON, educational foundation executive; b. Gold Hill, Nev., Oct. 23, 1909; d. George Edward and Nettie (Lagomarsino) Croson; m. Irving Fink Laucks, Nov. 9, 1942 (dec. Mar. 1981); 1 child, Mary Lisa. A.B. cum laude, U. Wash., 1938; Ph.D., U. Calif.-Santa Barbara, 1978. Promotional writer Laucks Lab., Inc., Seattle, 1938-42; pres. Laucks Found., Inc., Santa Barbara, 1978—. Author: The Meaning of Children, 1981; also articles in mags., chpt. in book. Bd. dirs. Ctr. for Study Democratic Instns., 1965-79, Channel City Women's Forum, 1975—.

LAUDENSLAGER, WANDA LEE, speech pathologist; b. San Jose, Calif., July 22, 1929; d. Victor Vierra and Florence Lorene (Houck) Silveira; A.A., Coll. San Mateo, 1960; B.A., San Jose State U., 1962, M.A., 1965; m. Leonard E. Laudenslager, Apr. 26, 1952; children—Leonard E. II, Dawn Marie. Speech pathologist Newark (Calif.) Unified Sch. Dist., 1962-65, dist. coordinator speech, hearing and lang. dept., 1965—; trainer student tchrs. Certified in supervision, teaching, speech, standard designated services, Calif.; lic. real estate broker, gen. bldg. contractor, audiometrist, speech pathologist, Calif.; lic. speech pathologist, Calif.; cert. clin. competence in speech pathology Am. Speech, Lang. and Hearing Assn. recipient Crown Zellerbach Found. award, 1961; hon. life mem. Calif. Congress Parents and Tchrs., Inc. Mem. Phi Kappa Phi, Alpha Gamma Sigma, Pi Lambda Theta, Kappa Delta Pi. Home: 37733 Logan Dr Fremont CA 94536 Office: 5715 Musick Ave Newark CA 94560

LAUDER, ESTEE, cosmetics company executive; b. N.Y.C.; m. Joseph Lauder (dec. 1983); children—Leonard, Ronald. Chmn., Estee Lauder Inc., N.Y.C., 1946—. Created Adventure Playgrounds through Estee and Joseph H. Lauder Found., N.Y.C. Mem. N.Y. State Women's Council. Author: Estée: A Success Story, 1985. Decorated chevalier Legion of Honor (France); recipient Neiman-Marcus Fashion award, 1962; Nat. Cancer Care Found. award, 1963; Spirit of Achievement award Albert Einstein Coll. Medicine, 1968; Kaufmann's Fashion Fortnight award, 1969; Bamberger's Designer's award, 1969; Gimbel's Fashion Forum award, 1969; Internat. Achievement award Frost Bros., 1971; Pogue's Ann. Fashion award, 1975; award Assn. Better N.Y., 1977; medaille de Vermeil de la Ville de Paris, 1979; 4th Ann. award for Humanitarian Service Girls Club N.Y., 1979; 25th Anniversary award Greater N.Y. council Boy Scouts Am., 1979; Ayres Look award, 1981; named one of top ten outstanding women in bus., 1970. Address: Estée Lauder Inc 767 Fifth Ave New York NY 10022

LAUDER, JANE, consulting architectural engineer; b. Camden, N.J., July 26, 1951; d. Frederic Ernest and Janet Perrigo (Hesse) L.; m. James Haworth Gray, Aug. 14, 1976; children—Russell B. Warren W., Frederic L. B.A., Case Western Res. U., 1972; M.S.C.E., Rensselaer Poly. Inst., 1976. Registered civil engr., Calif. Asst. to chief planner Guyahoga Met. Housing Authority, Cleve., 1971; prin. asst. G. A. Cruickshank Land Surveyor, Clifton Park, N.Y., 1973-76; engr. GS-7 Mare Island Naval Shipyard, Vallejo, Calif., 1977; sr. engr. Internat. Engring., San Francisco, 1978-79, 1982-83; pvt. practice cons., Vallejo, 1979—. Bd. dirs., past pres. Vallejo Archtl. Heritage Found., 1980-84; mem. Vallejo Archtl. Heritage and Landmarks Commn., 1985—; corp. mem. Vallejo Heighborhood Housing Service, 1980—; active Lincoln Sch. PTA, Vallejo, 1984—; rep. Central Core Restoration Com., Vallejo, 1980-82. Am. Soc. Pub. Adminstrs. intern, 1971. Mem. ASCE (assoc.). Mem. Religious Soc. of Friends. Avocations: gardening; camping; natural history; old house restoration. Home and Office: 731 Napa St Vallejo CA 94590

LAUDER, VALARIE ANNE, editor, educator; b. Detroit, Mar. 1, 1926; d. William J. and Murza Valerie (Mann) L.; A.A., Stephens Coll., Columbia, Mo., 1944; postgrad. Medill Sch. Journalism, Northwestern U. With Chgo. Daily News, 1944-52, columnist, 1946-52; lectr. Sch. Assembly Service, also Redpath lectr., 1952-55; freelance writer for mags. and newspapers including N.Y. Times, Yankee, Ford Times, Travel & Leisure, Am. Heritage, 1955—; editor-in-chief Scholasatic Roto, 1962; editor U. N.C., 1975-80, lectr. Sch. Journalism, 1980—; nat. chmn. student writing project Ford Times, 1981-86; pub. relations dir. Am. Dance Festival, Duke U., 1982-83, lectr., instr. continuing edn. program, 1984; contbg. editor So. Accents mag., 1982-86. Mem. nat. fund raising bd. Kennedy Center, 1962-63. Recipient 1st place award Nat. Fedn. Press Women, 1981; 1st place awards Ill. Women's Press Assn., 1950, 1951. Mem. Pub. Relations Soc. Am. (treas. N.C. chpt. 1982, v.p. 1984, pres. 1986), Women's Press Club N.C. (3d v.p. 1981-83; 1st pl. awards 1981, 82), Women in Communications (v.p. matrix N.C. Triangle chpt.), N.C. Press Women, DAR, Soc. Mayflower Desc. (dir. Ill. Soc. 1946-52), Chapel Hill Hist. Soc. (dir. 1981-85, chmn. publs. com. 1980-85), Chapel Hill Preservation Soc. Clubs: Chapel Hill Woman's, N.C. Press (2d v.p. 1983-85, pres. 1985, 1st pl. awards 1981, 82, 83, 84). Lodge: Order Eastern Star. Office: Howell Hall 021A U NC Chapel Hill NC 27514

LAUDONE, ANITA H., lawyer, business executive; b. 1948; B.A., Conn. Coll., 1970; J.D., Columbia U., 1973; married. Bar: N.Y. 1974. Practiced in N.Y.C., 1973-79; asst. sec. Phelps Dodge Corp., N.Y.C., 1979-80, sec., 1980-84, v.p., sec., 1984-85.

LAUFER, BEATRICE, composer; b. N.Y.C.; d. Samuel and Fanny (Silverman) L.; m. Theodore Lassoff, Oct. 2, 1940 (dec. 1955); 1 child, Samuel; m. Seymour H. Rinzler, Oct. 19, 1969 (dec. 1970). Student Julliard Sch. Music, 1944. Composer: Symphony No. 1 (performed by Eastman-Rochester Symphony Orch., 1945-46, performance Germany and Japan under auspices of State Dept., 1948, performed by Nat. Gallery Orch., Washington, 1982), Dance Festival (performed by Eastman-Rochester Symphony, 1946-47); choral compositions include: Under the Pines, Spring Thunder Performed Tanglewood, 1949, Song of the Fountain, Inter-racial Chorus, UN Freedom celebration, 1952; Small Concerto for Chamber Orch. performed McMillan Theatre, Columbia, 1949-50, Ile, opera, world premiere Royal Opera Co.,

Stockholm, Sweden, 1958, recorded by Yale U. Orch. 1978, Broadcast Nat. Pub. Radio, 1980; Second Symphony performed by Oklahoma City Orch., 1961; premiere concerto at Donnell Library Ctr., 1962; premiere performance Prelude and Fugue for Orch., Brevard Music Ctr., N.C., 1964, Cry! orchestral prelude, Orch. of Am., Town Hall, 1966, Lyric, string trio, Bowdoin Coll. Contemporary Music Festival, 1966; Cry! performed with Eastman-Rochester Symphony, 1968, Shreveport Symphony Orch., 1978, Berkshire Symphony Orch., 1981; In the Throes performed Shreveport Symphony, 1980, New Orleans Symphony Orch., 1982, Berkshire Symphony Orch., 1985; Conn. Found. of Arts grantee for performance And Thomas Jefferson Said, Norwalk Symphony Orch., 1976, 3 excerpts performed by USAF Chamber Players, Washington, 1985, premiere vbersion for concert band baritone solo performed by The Goldman Meml. Band, 1986; master ceremonies Young Am. Artists, radio sta. WNYC; hostess The Conductor peaks series sta. WNYC. Mem. ASCAP, Am. Symphony Orch. League, Am. Music Ctr. Address: PO Box 3 Lenox Hill Sta New York NY 10021

LAUGHLIN, JUDITH ANN, management development executive; b. Buffalo, Dec. 13, 1947; d. Eugene M. and Catherine L. (Ryan) Larouere; B.S. in Nursing, D'Youville Coll., 1969; M.S. in Community Health Nursing, SUNY, Buffalo, 1972, Ph.D. in Orgnl. Communication and Policy, 1980; m. Daniel E. Laughlin, July 29, 1967. Public health nurse Erie County Health Dept., 1969-70; gen. duty nurse psychiatry E.J. Meyer Hosp., Buffalo, 1971; coordinator lead detection and prevention program Erie County Health Dept., 1972-73; public health nurse cons. Erie County Dept. Mental Health, 1973-75; dir. Erie County Dept. Anti-Rape and Sexual Assault, 1975-77; asst. prof., area dir. health planning and mgmt., nursing SUNY, Buffalo, 1977-81, now clin. assoc. prof.; dir. human resources Am. Precision Industries, Inc., Buffalo, 1981-82; owner Mgmt. Devel. Group, Buffalo, 1982-85; dir. nursing services, dir. ednl. services Upstate N.Y. Mgmt. Cons. Practice, Ernst & Whinney, Buffalo, 1985—; mgmt. cons. Chmn. Erie County Victim/Witness Coordination Bd., 1978-85; bd. dirs. Buffalo chpt. ARC, 1978-83, chmn. tng. and devel. com., 1979-83; chmn. Erie County Sexual Assault Task Force, 1974; mem. Erie County Energy Com., 1973; chmn. Image of Nursing Speakers Bur., 1983—; mem. Am. Lung Assn., 1983—. Recipient awards for county programs, resolution for leadership in victim services Erie County Legislature, 1979. Mem. Am. Nurses Assn., Internat. Communications Assn., N.Y. State Public Health Assn., Nat. Orgn. Victim Assistance, Am. Soc. Tng. and Devel., Sigma Theta Tau, Pi Lambda Theta. Contbr. articles to profl. jours. Home: PO Box 211 Wales Center NY 14169 Office: 901 Western Bldg 15 Court St Buffalo NY 14202

LAUGHLIN, MARILYN JEAN, financial services company executive; b. Chgo., Mar. 27, 1936; d. Herman William and Alice (Donahue) Bendig; B.A., Lake Tahoe (Calif.) U., 1959; diploma in reins., Coll. Ins., N.Y.C., 1977; m. Terry Laughlin, May 14, 1966. From sec. to reins. adminstr. CNA Ins. Co., 1956-81; v.p. Laughlin Assos., Inc., Roselle, Ill., 1981—. Mem. Nat. Assn. Female Execs. Roman Catholic. Home: 56 N Salt Creek Rd Roselle IL 60172 Office: 100 E Irving Park Rd Roselle IL 60172

LAUGHTON, NAOMI CAROL, nurse, administrator; b. Sumter, S.C., June 11, 1931; d. Wendell and Louise (Johnson) McDuffy; m. Calvin Neil Laughton, Dec. 23, 1951; children—Karen Denise, Andrea Juliette. Student Bklyn. Coll., 1964-65; A.A.S. with honors, N.Y.C. Community Coll.; postgrad. Bklyn. Coll., 1975-76, L.I.U., 1976-77, Regents Coll. External Degree Program, 1985—. Cert. enterostomal therapist, R.N., N.Y. Staff nurse Brookdale Hosp. Med. Ctr., Bklyn., 1969-70, asst. head nurse, 1970-71, head nurse, 1972-77, supr., administr., enterostomal therapist, 1977—, enterostomal therapist, clin. nursing care coordinator, 1985—; lectr., adj. clin. ostomy specialist Bapt. Med. Ctr. and Surf Side Nursing Home, 1985; cons. and lectr. in field. Contbr. articles to profl. jours. Mem. Am. Nurses Assn., N.Y. State Nurses Assn., Internat. Urol. Soc., Internat. Assn. Enterostomal Therapists, United Ostomy Assn., Ostomy Assn. of Bklyn. (founder, v.p., med. advisor, program chairperson 1982), Am. Acad. Sci., Am. Nurse Research Fund, World Council of Enterostomal Therapist Ostomy Internat., Nat. Assn. Female Execs., Am. Cancer Soc., Brookdale Ileostomy Assn. (founder, pres. 1979). Fund raiser United Negro Coll. Fund; foster mother World Vision; mem. Democratic Club in Queens. Methodist. Home: 137-16 159 St Springfield Gardens NY 11434 Office: Brookdale Hosp Med Ctr Brooklyn NY 11434 also 9221 Ave L Brooklyn NY 11236

LAUMAN, KERRI JANET, lawyer; b. Seattle, May 27, 1941; d. Leon Levy and Kathryn Craig (Crowley) Wolfstone; m. William Verne Lauman Jr., June 20, 1963; children—Galen Marie, David William. A.B., Stanford U., 1963; teaching credential, U. Wash., 1964; J.D. magna cum laude, U. Puget Sound, 1982. Bar: Wash. 1982, U.S. Dist. Ct. 1982, U.S. Ct. of Appeals (9th cir.) 1983. Tchr. pub. schs., Bellevue, Wash., 1964-67; assoc. firm Perkins, Coie, Stone, Olsen & Williams, Seattle, 1982-85; prin. Law Offices of Kerri Wolfstone Lauman, Seattle, 1985—. Pres., Planned Parenthood Snohomish County, Washington, 1977-78, bd. dirs., 1974-79; mem. Children's Orthopedic Hosp. Guild, Seattle, 1964-74, pres., 1973-74. Recipient AmJur award Am. Jurisprudence Assn., 1980. Mem. ABA, Wash. State Bar Assn., Seattle-King Bar Assn. (trustee Young Lawyers div.), Wash. State Trial Lawyers Assn. Unitarian. Home: 1714 Evergreen Pl Seattle WA 98122 Office: Law Offices of Kerri Wolfstone Lauman 3000 Smith Tower Seattle WA 98104

LAUMAN, VONA KATHRYN (MRS. JAMES WESLEY LAUMAN), printing, publishing company executive; b. Strawberry Point, Iowa, Nov. 20, 1927; d. Otto Fred and Emma Katherine (Meinken) Weger; m. James Wesley Lauman, June 28, 1950; 1 child, Lori Ann. B.S.C., U. Iowa, 1950. Sec., Owens Ill. Glass Co., Chgo., 1950-51; sec. to treas. Pacific Coast Coca-Cola Bottling Co., Los Angeles, 1951-53; office mgr. Reynolds Aluminum Co., Indpls., 1953-56; office mgr. Central Pub. Co., Indpls., 1956-59, corp. sec., 1959-65, sales mgr., 1965-69, v.p., asst. gen. mgr., 1969-78, exec. v.p., chief operating officer, 1979—, also dir.; corp. sec. Weger Farms, Inc., Strawberry Point, Iowa, 1969—, also dir.; corp. sec., dir. Graphic Arts Data Systems, Indpls. Mem. Iowa U. Alumni Assn., Ind. Bus. Communicators, Ind. Soc. Assn. Execs. (bd. dirs.), Network of Women in Bus., Exec. Women Internat., Women in Communications, Inc., Indpls. C. of C. Republican. Lutheran. Clubs: Toastmasters, Columbia, Raquet Four. Home: 8029 Burn Ct Indianapolis IN 46217 Office: 401 N College Ave Box 1657 Indianapolis IN 46206

LAUNZEL-PENNES, MARGARET ANNE, advertising agency executive, fashion show consultant; b. Queens, N.Y., Jan. 24, 1955; d. Edward Anthony and Elaine Anne (Saracino) Launzel; m. David Michael Pennes, Sept. 6, 1980. Student Ithaca Coll., 1972-74, Fashion Inst. Tech., 1974-75. Stylist, Damon Creations, N.Y.C., 1975-76; fashion coordinator Carber Enterprises, N.Y.C., 1976-78; account supr. BJB Graphics, N.Y.C., 1978-79; pres. Northeast Advt., N.Y.C., 1980—; fashion show dir. F.I.C.E. Madrid, Spain, 1979, Cherokee Shoes, Gardena, Calif., 1982-83; exec. dir. N.Y.C. Salute to Fashion and Beauty Industries, N.Y.C., 1982-83. Copywriter, Tourette Syndrome Found., N.Y.C., 1982. Mem. Advt. Women N.Y. Republican. Roman Catholic. Home: 49 Beechwood Glen Head NY Office: Northeast Advt Group Inc 310 Madison Ave New York NY 10017

LAUREL, ALICIA BAY, author, illustrator, vocalist, songwriter; b. Los Angeles, May 14, 1949; d. Paul Alan and Verna (Lebow) Kaufman. Author, designer, illustrator: Living on the Earth, 1971, also Japanese; Being of the Sun, 1973, also Japanese; 3 books for children—The Family of Families, 1973, Sylvie Sunflower, 1973, The Rainbow Lady, 1973, (calendar) Earth Time, 1972; illustrator, designer: The Earth Mass, 1973; illustrator: Home Comfort, 1974; William Shakespeare's The Tempest, 1978. Named Woman of Yr., Mademoiselle mag., 1971; PTA art scholar, Otis Art Inst., 1965. Mem. Authors Guild, Soc. Children's Book Writers, Nat. Acad. Songwriters. Home and Office: PO Box 986 Kihei HI 96753

LAURENCE, MARGARET, author; b. Neepawa, Man., Can., July 18, 1926; d. Robert Harrison and Margaret Campbell (Simpson) Wemyss; m. John Fergus Laurence, 1947 (div. 1969); 1 child. B.A., United Coll. (now U. Man.), 1947; D.Litt., (hon.), McMaster U., 1971, Trent U., 1971, U. Toronto, 1971, Carleton Coll., 1974, Brandon, 1975, U. Western Ont., 1975, Mt. Allison, 1976, Simon Fraser U., 1977, York U., 1980; LL.D. (hon.), Dalhousie U., 1971, Queens U., 1975; D.Litt.S. (hon.), Victoria U., Toronto, 1982. Author: A Treee for Poverty (transl.), This Side Jordan, 1960, The Prophet's Camel Bell, 1963, The Tomorrow-Tamer, 1963, The Stone Angel, 1964, A Jest of God, 1966 (Gov. Gen.'s Fiction award 1966), Long Drums and Cannons (essays on Nigerian lit.), 1968, The Fire Dwellers, 1969, Jason's Quest (juvenile), 1969, A Bird in the House, 1970, The Diviners, 1974 (Gov. Gen.'s Lit. award 1974), Heart of a Stranger (essays), 1976, The Olden Days Coat (juvenile), 1979, Six Darn Cows (juvenile), 1979, The Christmas Birthday Story (juvenile), 1980. Contbr. articles and stories to publs. including Prism, Tamarack Rev., Saturday Evening Post, Ladies Home Jour., Chatelaine, Atlantic Monthly, Argosy, Holiday Mag.; writer-in-residence U. Toronto, 1969-70, U. Western Ont., 1973, Trent U., 1974. Recipient best 1st novel award Beta Sigma Phi, 1960; Pres.'s medal U. Western Ont., 1961, 62, 64; Molson award, 1975, Periodical Distbrs.' award, 1977, City of Toronto Merit award, 1978; decorated companion Order Can.; named Woman of Yr., Toronto Women's br. B'nai B'rith, 1976. Fellow Royal Soc. Can. Office: care Knopf 201 E 50th St New York NY 10022*

LAURISKI, SUSAN CATHERINE, banker; b. Detroit, Dec. 3, 1945; d. Charles Louis III and Eleanor Marie (Henchel) Roehm; A.S., Phoenix Coll., 1981; B.A. in Mgmt., U. Phoenix, 1986. Data processing specialist Detroit Bank & Trust Co., 1963-66; with First Nat. Bank of Ariz. (name changed to First Interstate Bank of Ariz. 1981), Phoenix, 1970—, br. mgr., 1980—, v.p., asst. div. v.p., 1982-85, v.p., br. loan adminstr., 1985, v.p., dept. head IRA dept., 1985—. Bd. dirs. Maricopa Camp Fire Council, Phoenix, 1981—; adv. Jr. Achievement, Phoenix, 1978-81; chmn. March of Dimes Walk-a-Thon, Phoenix, 1977-81. Nat. Assn. Bank Women Western Regional scholar, 1981-82. Mem. Nat. Assn. Bank Women (pres. state council 1984-85, mem. class VII Valley leadership program 1985-86). Republican. Roman Catholic. Home: 315 W Edgemont St Phoenix AZ 85003 Office: 114 W Adams St Phoenix AZ 85001

LAURO, KATHLEEN ANN, graphics and advertising executive; b. N.Y.C., Apr. 1, 1948; d. Francis Joseph and Eleanor Veronica (Lynch) Sisk; m. Frank James Lauro, June 17, 1967; children—Frank Andrew, Karen Elaine. Student pvt. schs. Exec. sec. Union Carbide, N.Y.C., 1965-67, Gen. Motors, N.Y.C., 1967-70; feature writer, columnist Beacon Newspaper, Romeoville, Ill., 1982; producer, host Romeoville Cable News, 1982; exec. dir. Romeoville C. of C., 1982-84; mgr. Romeo Constrn. Inc., 1984. Columnist Good News, Newsworthy Neighbors, 1982. Cons. The Better Party, Romeoville, 1982-83. Mem. Romeoville Jaycees, Ill. Assn. Chamber Execs., Ill. C. of C., U.S. C. of C. Roman Catholic. Home: 330 Hickory Ave Romeoville IL 60441

LAURO, SHIRLEY MEZVINSKY, playwright, educator; b. Des Moines, Nov. 18, 1933; d. Phillip and Helen Frances (Davidson) Shapiro; m. Norton Mezvinsky, July 22, 1956 (div. 1967); 1 child, Andrea Mezvinsky; m. Louis Paul Lauro, Aug. 18, 1973. B.S. cum laude, Northwestern U., Evanston, Ill., 1955; M.S., U. Wis., 1957; postgrad. Columbia U., 1970-73. Instr. speech and theater CCNY, N.Y.C., 1967-71; instr. speech, theater and playwriting Yeshiva U., N.Y.C., 1971-76; instr. creative writing Manhattan Marymount Coll., N.Y.C., 1978-79; instr. speech and drama Manhattan Community Coll., N.Y.C., 1978-79; lit. cons. Ensemble Studio Theater, N.Y.C., 1975-80, prodn. critic, 1975—, mem. council, 1975—. Author novel: The Edge, 1965; author play: The Contest (Nat. Found. for Jewish Culture playwright's award 1981), 1975; The Coal Diamond (Heidemann Prize Actors Theater of Louisville's Festival of New Am. Plays 1980, Best Short Plays of 1980), 1979; Open Admissions (N.Y. Dramatists Guild Hull-Warriner Playwrights award 1981, Samuel French Playwrights award 1979, Ten Best Plays of 1981 N.Y. Times), 1984; Nothing Immediate (Samuel French playwright's award 1979), 1979; Margargaret and Kit (Nomination for Susan Blackburn Prize 1980), 1980; I Don't Know Where You're Coming From at All, 1979; In the Garden of Eden, 1984; Open Admissions (Tony nominee, Drama Desk nominee, Theater World award), 1984. N.Y. Found. Arts Playwright's fellow, 1985; John Guggenheim Playwrights fellow, 1986; NEA Playwrights fellow, 1987. Mem. PEN, Ensemble Studio Theater, League Profl. Theater Women, Dramatists Guild, Authors League, Authors Guild. Democrat. Jewish. Office: Care Gilbert Parker 1350 Ave of Americas William Morris Agy New York NY 10019

LAUTEN, ELLEN NEW, librarian; b. Gastonia, N.C., May 17, 1921; d. William Williams and May (Tatlock) New; m. William Tatum Lauten, June 16, 1943; children—William Tatum III, Tatlock, David, Elizabeth Ellen, Janet. A.B., U.N.C., 1942, M.S., 1943. Childrens librarian Norfolk Pub. Library (Va.), 1943; librarian Nob Hosp., 1944-46, Newport News Shipbuilding and Drydock Co. (Va.), 1948-50, Dixie Hosp., Hampton, Va., 1959-60, learning resource specialist Houston Ind. Sch. Dist., 1965—. Mem. AAUW, ALA, Tex. Library Assn., Houston Assn. Sch. Librarians. Democrat. Episcopalian. Home: 6023 Rutherglenn Houston TX 77096 Office: Austin Sr High Library 1700 Dumble St Houston TX 77023

LAUTZENHEISER, BARBARA JEAN, insurance company executive; b. LaFeria, Tex., Nov. 15, 1938; d. Fred E. and Verna V. L. B.A. with high distinction, Nebr. Wesleyan U., 1960. Actuarial trainee Bankers Life Ins. Co. Nebr., Lincoln, 1960-64, programmer and systems analyst, 1964-65, asst. actuary, 1965-69, assoc. actuary, 1969-70, 2d v.p., actuary, 1970-72, v.p., actuary, 1972-80; sr. v.p. Phoenix Mut. Life Ins. Co., Hartford, Conn., from 1980; now pres. Montgomery Ward Ins. Group, Schaumburg, Ill. Contbr. articles to profl. jours. Bd. dirs. Nebr. Wesleyan U., 1977-82. Fellow Soc. Actuaries (pres. 1982-83, dir. 1975-80, 81-82, chmn. adminstrn. and fin. com. 1981-82); mem. Am. Acad. Actuaries (dir. 1974-77, chmn. com. on publs. 1980-81), Nebr. Actuaries Club (dir. 1969-70, 71-74, chmn. 1973-74, pres. 1972-73, sec., treas. 1971-72), Life Office Mgmt. Assn. (corp. fin. planning com. 1974-81, chmn. 1976-78), Am. Council Life Ins. (risk classification com. 1973-81). Office: Montgomery Ward Ins Group 200 N Martingale Rd Schaumburg IL 60194

LAUVER, PATRICIA ELLEN, engineer; b. Elizabeth, N.J., Oct. 22, 1951; d. Milton Renick and Edith Marie (Gedeon) L.; B.S. in Math. with honors, Mich. State U., 1973; M.B.A., Xavier U., 1978. Mem. tech. staff Rockwell Internat., Anaheim, Calif., 1974-75, Columbus, Ohio, 1975-78; dept. head design assurance Teledyne CAE, Toledo, 1978-85; mgr. life cycle cost GTE, Billerica, Mass., 1985-86; mgr. cost engring. dept. HAY Systems, Inc., 1986—; instr. U. Toledo Community and Tech. Coll., Owens Tech. Coll. Adviser Jr. Achievement, 1976-77, 78-79; sec. ch. council Luth. Ch. Recipient Twin award City of Toledo YWCA, 1982. Mem. Nat. Mgmt. Assn. (treas Buckeye Council 1980-81, v.p. youth activities Rockwell Internat. Columbus chpt. 1976-77, pres. Teledyne CAE chpt. 1981-82, chairperson bd. chpt. 1982-83, nat. dir. 1984-85), Soc. Women Engrs., Soc. Logistics Engrs., Am. Soc. Quality Control, Joint Tech. Coordinating Group/Aircraft Survivability, AAUW (study group leader 1983-84). Home: 8 Holbrook Dr Nashua NH 03062 Office: 5 Cross St Merrimack NH 03054

LAVALLE, EDITH, arbitrator, consultant; b. New Haven, Dec. 24, 1919; d. Joseph and Mary Ann (Rapuano) Zuccarelli; m. Francis LaValle, July 1, 1944; children—Fern LaValle Julianelle, Gary R. A.A. in Bus. Adminstrn., Larson Jr. Coll., 1939; B.A. in Human Services, Franconia Coll., 1977. Exec. dir. Conn. Laborers Health and Pension Funds, West Haven, 1961-83; arbitrator Am. Arbitration Assn., Hartford, Conn., 1983—; lectr. U. New Haven, 1980; cons. health and pension fund planning. Contbr. book revs. Bd. dirs. Youth Continuum, New Haven, 1976— (Community Service award 1985); fund raising program dir. Tng. Research Inst. Residential Youth Ctrs., New Haven, 1986—; counselor for aged St. John the Evanelist Ch., New Haven, 1981-84; vol. arbitrator Better Bus. Bur., New Haven, 1982—; pres. Baybrook Arms Housing Corp., West Haven, 1979—. Roman Catholic. Home: 41 Jones Hill Rd Apt 202 West Haven CT 06516

LAVALLEE, THERESA CORRERA, repair service company executive; b. Providence, Mar. 14, 1935; d. Louis John and Maria (DeFeo) Correra; m. Leo P. Lavallee, Jr., Oct. 13, 1958; children—Leo P., Jeannine M., Elizabeth A. B.Ed., R.I. Coll., 1957. Tchr., Warwick Sch. Dept., R.I., 1957-58, Shrewsbury Sch. Dept., Mass., 1958-59; v.p. Nutmeg Utility Products, Inc., Cheshire, Conn., 1977—; pres. Gemtun Service Co., Inc., Cheshire, 1983—, chmn. bd., 1983—; dir. Nutmeg Products, 1977—. Mem. Social Action Com., Cheshire, 1974-76; leader Girl Scouts U.S.A., Cheshire, 1974-75. Mem. U.S. Telephone Suppliers Assn., Cheshire C. of C. Roman Catholic. Club: Cheshire Jr. Women's. Avocations: gardening, gourmet cooking; reading; traveling.

LAVENDER, MARY ANN, voluntary action center administrator; b. Canton, Ohio, Sept. 21, 1925; d. Lyman Hathaway and Mary Marcella (McClelland) Clark; m. Clinton Frederick Lavender, Dec. 8, 1945; children—Jane Lavender Levi, Mary Lavender Fujii, Patricia Lavender Melby. B.A., Case Western Res. U., 1945. Exec. dir. Voluntary Action Ctr., Sandusky, Ohio, 1982—; cons. to social service and non profit orgns.; lectr. in field. Active Erie County Mental Health Assn., Ohio, 1951-85; bd. dirs., officer Erie Shores council Girl Scouts U.S.A., Lorain, Ohio, 1957-75; chmn., founder Youth Services Com., Erie County, 1971-85; bd. dirs. LWV, Erie County, 1979-82. Recipient Thanks Badge, Erie Shores Girl Scouts, 1975; Disting. Service award Sandusky Jayceetts, 1983; Woman of Yr. award Beta Sigma Phi, 1983. Mem. Assn. Vol. Adminstrn., Vol. Ohio. Republican. Episcopalian. Avocations: theatre; music; art; swimming; cross country skiing. Home: 1609 Willow Dr Sandusky OH 44870 Office: Voluntary Action Ctr 158 E Market St #610 Sandusky OH 44870

LAVENDER, WANDA KINZEL, nursing adminstr.; b. Wellsville, Ohio, Dec. 25, 1923; d. Leonard J. and Rebecca Cecile (Thomas) Kinzel; grad. Youngstown Hosp. Assn. Sch. Nursing, 1945; B.A. cum laude, Jersey City State Coll., 1970, M.A., 1974; postgrad. in obstetrics Margaret Hague Maternity Hosp., 1946; m. James Lavender, Aug. 30, 1946; children—Nancy, Mark, Scott, Amy. Head nurse Youngstown (Ohio) Hosp., 1945; supr. nursing Bayonne (N.J.) Hosp., 1946-47, Greenville Hosp., Jersey City, 1948; supr. Salvation Army, Door of Hope, Jersey City, 1949-52; head nurse Mary Hague Maternity Hosp., Jersey City, 1958-67, asst. instr., 1967-69, asst. dir. nursing, 1969-75; asst. dir. nursing inservice edn. Jersey City Med. Center, from 1976, now dir. edn. Mem. Am. Nurses Assn., Hudson County Council of Nursing Educators, Youngstown Hosp. Nurses Alumni Assn., Hudson County Perinatal Assn., Am. Cancer Soc. (nursing edn. com.), N.J. Civil Service Assn., Nat. League Nursing, Kappa Delta Pi. Mem. Ch. of Christ. Clubs: Order Eastern Star, DeMolay Mothers (pres.), 21 (past pres.). Home: 918 Avenue C Bayonne NJ 07002 Office: Jersey City Medical Center 50 Baldwin Ave Jersey City NJ 07304

LAVERGNE, MARY LOU, mfg. co. exec.; b. Detroit, Oct. 5, 1940; d. Bernard Clark and Lillian Bertha (Hackbart) Sherwood; student public schs.; divorced; 1 dau., Anita R. Secretary, 1958-60; office mgr. R.M. Richardson Co., Southfield, Mich., 1960-72; controller Seaman Mfg. Co., Pontiac, Mich., 1972-78; treas. Seamco Enterprises, Inc., steel rule die cutting, Kendallville, Ind., 1978—, v.p. fin. and adminstrn., 1984—, also dir. Sec., Mich. Jr. Miss. Pageant, Pontiac, 1969-70, bd. dirs., 1975-76; pres. Pontiac Jaycee Aux., 1968, 70; co-chmn. residential area Pontiac United Fund drive, 1971. Named Pontiac Jaycette of Yr., 1969. Mem. Am. Mgmt. Assn., Nat. Assn. Female Execs., Am. Inst. Corp. Controllers. Home: 215 S Riley St Kendallville IN 46755 Office: 2525 Progress Dr Kendallville IN 46755

LAVERTY, MARY LOUISE, college dean; b. Pitts, July 3, 1952; d. John P. and Mary (Bedont) L. B.S., St. Francis Coll., 1974; M.S., Shippensburg State Coll., 1976; Ed.D., Ind. U., 1984. Grad. counselor Shippensburg State Coll., Pa., 1974-76; residence hall dir. St. Mary's Coll., Notre Dame, Ind., 1976-77; dir. student activities St Mary's Coll., 1977-80; grad. asst. Ind. U., Bloomington, 1980-82; dean students Coll. Notre Dame of Md., Balt., 1983—; adv. bd. Washington Ctr., 1984-85. Contbr. articles to profl. jours. Vol., My Sisters Place for Battered and Displaced Women, Balt., 1984—. Mem. Nat. Assn. Student Personnel of Am. (adv. bd.), Nat. Assn. Campus Activities, Nat. Orientation Dirs. Assn., Am. Counseling and Personnel Assn. Roman Catholic. Avocations: travel, golf; music; reading. Address: Coll of Notre Dame of Md 4701 N Charles St Baltimore MD 21210

LAVERY, BEATRICE CANTERBURY, city official; b. Los Angeles, d. Charles Milton and Bernice Mae (Peacock) Canterbury; A.B., U. So. Calif., 1948; m. Frederic William Wile, Jr., 1952 (dec. 1960); 1 child, Geoffrey; m. Emmet G. Lavery, Sept. 27, 1963, (div.); 1 child, Tracy. Editor Whittier (Calif.) Reporter, 1944; reporter Wave Publs., Los Angeles, 1944-45; with Publicity Pfd., Los Angeles, 1946-48; press rep. NBC, Hollywood, 1949-52; fashion dir. Bullocks Dept. Store, Los Angeles, 1960-63; advt. dir. Rose Marie Reid Swimsuits, Los Angeles, 1963-65; merchandising dir. Compton Advt., Los Angeles, 1966-67; freelance advt. and public relations cons., 1967-70; adminstrv. coordinator to Mayor Tom Bradley of Los Angeles, 1973—, now chief of protocol. Publicity Mannequins of the Assistance League of So. Calif., 1954-56; worker public relations UN Assn., Los Angeles, 1953-54, Encino Property Owners Assn., 1968-72; campaign worker Janice Bernstein candidate for Sch. Bd., Los Angeles, 1970; mem. Speakers Bur. Alan Cranston for senator campaign, 1968; public relations worker Tom Bradley for mayor campaign, 1969, 73. Bd. govs. U. So. Calif., 1973—; mem. Nat. Com. U.S.-China Relations; adv. bd. Asia Soc.; bd. dirs. Youth Opportunities Found. Decorated Order of Orange Nassau (Netherlands), Order of Merit, Fed. Republic of Germany; recipient award Media Women Founder's, 1970, award Los Angeles City Human Relations Bur., 1970. Mem. Women in Communications (pres. 1949-51), Los Angeles Advt. Women (Lulu award 1965), Fashion Group (dir. 1958-63), Hollywood Women's Press Club, U. So. Calif. Journalism Alumni Assn. (pres. 1972-73), Am. Women for Internat. Understanding, Trusteeship for Betterment of Women. Home: The Penthouse Apt G-8 101 Ocean Ave Santa Monica CA 90402 Office: 200 N Spring St Los Angeles CA 90012

LAVINE, BEAU, chocolate factory executive; b. Willemstad, Curacao, Netherlands Antilles, Sept. 15, 1940; came to U.S., 1967; d. Leo S. and Sabina (Walfenzao) Berlinski; m. Thomas G. Lavine, May 20, 1970; children—Suzette Alyssa, Michelle Lee. B.S., U. Amsterdam, 1963, M.S., 1964; postgrad., 1965. Mng. dir. Berlinski's Aruba, Netherlands Antilles, 1966-67; account exec. Text Communications, N.Y.C., 1967-69, People to People, N.Y.C., 1969-70; mng. dir. World Trade Co., N.V., Los Angeles, 1971—. Chmn. Master Calendar, Los Angeles, 1985—; bd. dirs. Dolls Inc., Los Angeles, 1985—, Operation Children, Los Angeles, 1983—; mem. Dance Gallery Guild, League for Crippled Children. Mem. Nat. Assn. Female Execs., Retail Confectioners Internat., Nat. Assn. Splty. Food Trade. Lodge: Soroptimists (membership com. 1984—). Home: 2496 Angelo Dr Los Angeles CA 90077

LAVINE, FRANCES HOFFMAN (MRS. MAX H. LAVINE), newspaper exec.; b. Chgo., Jan. 7, 1906; d. Louis and Sophie (Tauber) Hoffman; student Northwestern U., 1924, Gloucester (Mass.) Theater, 1923, Goodman Theater Sch., Chgo., 1926; D.H.L. (hon.), Coll. St. Scholastica, 1978, Northland Coll. Ashland, Wis., 1981; m. Max H. Lavine, Dec. 26, 1935; 1 son, John Morgan. Dramatic dir. House Top Studio Theater Arts, Duluth, Minn., 1926-39; founder, dir. Children's Theater, Duluth, 1928-37; one woman show for various colls. and clubs, 1933—; narrator Nutcracker Ballet, Duluth Symphony, 1957, 59, Peter and the Wolf Symphony, 1961; drama artist in residence on number of coll. campuses, 1965—; pres. Daily Register, newspaper, Portage, Wis., 1964—, Herald Telegram Pub. Co., Chippewa Falls, Wis.; mem. adv. bd. KDAL Radio-TV Corp. Pub. relations worker Superior chpt. ARC (Wis.), 1941-48; active Easter Seal Soc., Community Chest, 1950's; mem. Wis. Gov.'s Com. on Employment of Handicapped, 1956; pilot tchr. Mom Program, 1965; resident volunteer tchr. Job Corps, 1968. Exec. bd. Duluth Superior Ednl. TV Corp., bd. dirs. U. Wis. Found., Superior; trustee St. Joseph's Hosp., 1965, Coll. of St. Scholastica, Duluth, Minn. Mem. Nat. Friends of Pub. Broadcasting. Home: 3800 London Rd Duluth MN 55804

LAVIOLETTE, DIANA JANE, lawyer; b. Sullivan, Ind., Aug. 29, 1945; d. Lozier C. and Elizabeth Bell (Fryback) Ziegler; m. John Leon LaViolette, May 17, 1975; children—Alan Paul, Jean Marie. B.A., Tex. Christian U., 1967; M.A., Duquesne U., 1973; J.D., Ind. U.-Indpls., 1981. Bar: Ind. 1981. Tchr., Kansas City (Mo.) Schs., 1967-69; vol. Peace Corps, Istanbul, Turkey, 1969-70; welfare caseworker Ind. Dept. Pub. Welfare, Danville, 1971; high sch. tchr. N. Putnam Schs., Bainbridge, Ind., 1973-74; adult basic edn. tchr. Dept. Corrections, Indpls., 1974-77; sole practice, Greencastle, Ind., 1981—; dep. prosecutor Putnam County; cons. atty. DePauw U. Winter-Term Mock Trial, 1982-84. Mem. Ind. State Bar Assn., ABA, Assn. Trial Lawyers Am., Bus. and Profl. Women, LWV. Republican. Disciples of Christ. Home: 707 E Franklin St Greencastle IN 46135 Office: Brewer & LaViolette 110 W Walnut St Greencastle IN 46135

LAVITT, WENDY ADLER, author; b. N.Y.C., Nov. 28, 1939; d. Ralph M. and Eve Evelyn (Sperling) Adler; B.A., Finch Coll., N.Y.C., 1961; m. Mel S. Lavitt, Sept. 10, 1959; children—Kathy, John, Meredith. Copy editor Holt, Rinehart & Winston, N.Y.C., 1961-63; docent Mus. Am. Folk Art, 1978-79, guest curator Am. Folk Dolls show, N.Y.C., 1983-84; freelance mag. writer, 1979-84; antique dealer, 1978-81; owner Made in America, antiques, N.Y.C., 1981-84; lectr. in field, 1980—. Author: American Folk Dolls, 1983; Dolls: Knopf Collector Guide, 1983; also articles. Home: 15 E 91st St New York NY 10028

LAVORGNA, DENISE APRIL, computer systems programmer; b. Phila., Apr. 26, 1952; d. Emanuel and Mafalda (Gentile) Lavorgna. B.S., Drexel U., 1973. Computer programmer Drexel U., Phila., 1972-73, Def. Personnel Support Ctr., Phila., 1973-79, computer systems analyst, 1979-85, computer systems programmer, 1985—. Mem. Nat. Assn. Female Execs., DPSC Mgmt. Club, Nat. Wildlife Found., Phila. Zool. Soc., Phi Kappa Phi, Beta Gamma Sigma. Baptist. Avocations: painting; sculpting; piano; ballet; sewing. Office: Defense Personnel Support Center 2800 S 20th St Philadelphia PA 19101

LA VOY, BARBARA ANAPOL, lawyer; b. Miami, Fla., Apr. 6, 1951; d. Jerome and Bernice (Graff) Anapol; m. Richard T. La Voy, Aug. 26, 1972 (div.). Student Jacksonville U., 1969-71; B.A. in Polit. Sci. and Pub. Adminstrn., U. No. Fla., 1975; J.D., U. Bridgeport, 1980. Bar: Conn. 1981, U.S. Dist. Ct. (2d dist.) Conn. 1981. Research asst. Barnett Banks Fla., Jacksonville, 1975; legal asst. Broad and Cassels, Bay Harbor Islands, Fla., 1975-76; law clk. Conn. Superior Ct., Stamford, 1980-82; adj. prof. Norwalk State Community Coll. (Conn.), 1983—; assoc. Saul A. Rothman, Stamford, 1982-84; v.p., gen. counsel Anchor Capital Corp., Stamford, Conn., 1984—. Mem. ABA, Conn. Bar Assn., Assn. Trial Lawyers Am., Westchester-Fairfield County Corp. Counsel Assn., Stamford/Darien Bar Assn. Republican. Home: 130 South Ave New Canaan CT 06840 Office: Plaza W 2001 W Main St Stamford CT 06902

LA VOY, DIANE EDWARDS, foundation executive; b. Caracas, Venezuela, Nov. 10, 1948; d. Edward Edwards and Margaret Lucille (Buchheit) Edwards Ross-Jones; B.A., Wellesley Coll., 1970; M.Pub. Affairs, Princeton U., 1977; m. David Wayne La Voy, Apr. 3, 1971; 1 dau., Sarah Edwards. Intern, Friends Com. on Nat. Legis., Washington, 1970-71; assoc. mgr. Quaker House, Washington, 1971-74, art dir., 1973-74; asst. editor Ams. mag. OAS, Washington, 1971-73; founder/dir. Washington Office on Latin Am., 1974; mem. profl. staff U.S. Senate Select Com. To Study Govtl. Activities with Respect to Intelligence, 1974-76; mem. profl. staff Subcom. Evaluation and Oversight of Ho. of Reps. Permanent Select Com. on Intelligence, 1977-83; staff Inter-Am. Found., 1983—, rep. for Chile, 1984—. Founder, 1st pres. E St. Friends, 1979-80; active Am. Friends Service Com., 1971-84; elder Presbyn. Ch., 1982—. Democrat. Author articles and reports in field. Home: 1614 E St SE Washington DC 20003 Office: 1515 Wilson Blvd Roslyn VA 22209

LAW, ARDITH ELAINE, pet shop owner; b. Spokane, Wash., Nov. 26, 1931; d. Charles Vernon and Mildred Maurene (Ricks) Steele; student Cascade Coll., Portland, Oreg., 1950-51, Wenatchee Bus. Coll., 1951-52; m. Noble Orin Law, Aug. 8, 1953; children—Stuart Dean, Keith DeWayne, Stanford William. Sec., Halstead & MacGregor, attys., Prosser, Wash., 1953-54, Prosser Jr. High Sch., 1954-55, Okanogan (Wash.) Elem. Sch., 1956-57, Hatcher & Son, Omak, Wash., 1957-60, James M. Greene Ins., Oroville, Wash., 1960-61, B.L. Schrader Co., 1964-65, D.A. Thorndike & Sons., Oroville, 1966-67; warehouse stamper, checker Stadelman Fruit Co., Oroville, 1967-71, Tonoro Fruit Co., Tonasket, Wash., 1971-78; owner, operator The Pet Net, Tonasket, 1979—. Pres., Presch. PTA, Oroville, 1964-65; pres. Kiwanis Ladies Aux., Oroville, 1965-66; organist United Methodist Ch., Oroville, 1961-69, Tonasket (Wash.) Community United Ch. of Christ, 1973-85. Mem. Wash. State Pet Industry Assn., (corr.). Mem. Ch. of Christ. Home: 31940 N Hwy 97 Tonasket WA 98855 Office: 619E Woodin Chelan WA 98816

LAW, CAROL JUDITH, psychotherapist; b. N.Y.C., May 1, 1940; d. Aldo and Jennie (Feldman) Settimo; m. Perry J. Koll, Dec. 26, 1967 (div. Nov. 1974); 1 son, Perry J.; m. 2d, Edwin B. Law, June 1, 1979. B.A., Upsala Coll., 1962; postgrad. Rutgers U., 1964-66; M.A., Columbia Pacific, 1982, Ph.D., 1984. Personnel dir. Hotel Manhattan, N.Y.C., 1961; supr. social work Essex County, Newark, 1962-67; exec. dir. USO, Vungtau, South Vietnam, 1967-68; dir. Dept. Health and Rehab. Services, Pensacola, Fla., 1968-79; therapist, tchr. Franciscan Renewal Ctr., Scottsdale, Ariz., 1982—; mem. state adv. bd. Parents Anonymous, Phoenix, 1982; chmn. Gov.'s Adv. Commn. Drugs and the Elderly, Tallahassee, 1978. Pres. Jaycettes, Pensacola, 1969; chmn. social com. United Way Fund, Pensacola, 1977; mem. adv. bd. USO, Pensacola, 1973. Fellow Am. Acad. Polit. and Social Sci.; mem. Am. Assn. Pub. Adminstrs. Republican. Roman Catholic. Club: Phoenix Country. Home: 8214 E Del Cadena St Scottsdale AZ 85258 Office: Family Counseling and Psychol Services 8300 N Hayden Rd Suite 112 Scottsdale AZ 85258

LAW, MARY C., county official; b. Manchester, Ky., June 27, 1931; d. Clyde and Pearl (Brown) Craft; m. Richard Carlisle Law, Nov. 24, 1950; children—Richard Scott, Gregory Alan. Grad. high sch., Hamilton, Ohio. Office adminstr. Prodential Ins. Co., Hamilton, 1950-81; County treas. Butler County, Ohio, 1981—. Deaconess First Baptist Ch., Hamilton, 1982-83; pub. service chmn. United Way, 1983-84, govt. chmn., 1985; auditor Butler County Women's Republican Party, 1985, Mental Health Assn., Hamilton, 1982—, O'Tucks Orgn., Hamilton, 1982—; mem. long range planning com. Fort Hamilton Hosp., 1984-85, Hosp. Support Services Task Force, 1985—; mem. rev. bd. Adv. Bd. Hamilton High Sch., 1984-85; Sunday sch. tchr. First Bapt. Ch., 1950-69. Recipient Outstanding Woman of Yr. award Hamilton/Fairfield Jaycees, 1983; named One of 25 Most Influential Persons in Butler County Hamilton Jour. News, 1983, 84. Mem. Ohio State Treas. Assn. (legis. com. 1983-84), Eighth Congl. Awards Council (treas. 1984—), Bus. and Profl. Women (v.p. 1984—), Am. Bus. Women's Assn. (com. chmn. 1982—). Lodge: Altrusa Internat. Home: 1300 Hamilton New London Rd Hamilton OH 45013 Office: Butler County Seat County Courthouse Hamilton OH 45011

LAWHON, TOMMIE COLLINS MONTGOMERY, home economics educator; b. Shelby County, Tex., Mar. 15; d. Marland Walker and Lillian (Linsley) Collins; m. David Baldwin Montgomery, Mar. 31, 1962 (dec. Aug. 1964); m. John Lawhon, Aug. 27, 1967; 1 child, David Collins. B.S., Baylor U., 1954; M.Ed., Tex. Woman's U., 1964, Ph.D., 1966. Cert. tchr., Tex. Tchr., Victoria Pub. Schs. (Tex.), 1954-55; stewardess, supr. Am. Airlines, Dallas/Fort Worth, 1955-62; prof. home econs. Eastern Ky. U., Richmond, 1966-67, North Tex. State U., Denton, 1968—; profl. presenter Profl. Devel. Inst., North Tex. State U., 1981—. Co-author: Children are Artists, 1971; Hidden Hazards for Children and Families, 1982; editor: What to do with Children, 1974; Field Trips for Children, 1984, contbr. articles to profl. jours. Chmn., United Way North Tex. State U., 1980-81; chmn. crusade Am. Cancer Soc., Denton County, 1982-83; chmn. nominating com. First Bapt. Ch., Denton, 1983-84, 84-85. Recipient Presdl. award Tex. Council on Family Relations, 1979; Fessor Graham award North Tex. State U., 1980; Service award Am. Cancer Soc., 1983; Outstanding Home Economists Alumni award Baylor U., 1985 named Honor Prof. North Tex. State U., 1975. Mem. Tex. Council on Family Relations (pres. 1977-79), Denton Assn. for Edn. of Young Children (pres. 1970-72, 84-85, 85-86), Tex. Home Econs. Assn. (nominating com. 1983-84), Nat. Council on Family Relations (com. 1982-83), North Tex. Home Econs. Inter-orgnl. Council (adviser 1983-85). Alpha Iota/Phi Upsilon Omicron (advisor 1970-82, chmn. nat. com. 1984-85). Democrat. Club: Tri D (v.p. Baylor U. 1953-54); Graduate (pres. Tex. Woman's U. 1965-66). Office: North Tex State U Sch Home Econs Denton TX 76203

LAWLER, JEAN MARIE, lawyer; b. San Francisco, Aug. 7, 1954; d. Jack Wofford and Evelyn Mary (Matkovich) Suggs; m. Timothy Lawler, May 20, 1978; children—Kathleen, Megan, Colleen. A.A., Riverside City Coll., 1974; student San Diego State U., 1974; B.B.A., Loyola Marymount U., Los Angeles, 1976; J.D., Loyola U. Law Sch.-Los Angeles, 1979. Bar: Calif. Supreme Ct. 1979, Oreg. Supreme Ct. 1981. Assoc. law firm David L. Rosner, Los Angeles, 1979-80; instr. Lane Community Coll., Eugene, Oreg., 1981-82; sole practice law, Eugene, 1981-82, Beaverton, Oreg., 1982—. Editor: Copyright Law, 1979-80; Business Associates Review, 1974; contbr. poetry to Coll. Poetry Rev., 1974, 76. Chmn. legal asst. adv. com. Lane Community Coll., 1981-82. Recipient Riverside County Bar Assn. scholarship, 1977; Loyola U. Jesuit Community scholarship, 1978. Mem. State Bar of Calif., Oreg. State Bar Assn., ABA, Washington County Bar Assn. Democrat. Roman Catholic. Club: Columbia-Edgewater Country. Office: Jean Lawler 8196 SW Hall Blvd Suite 310 Beaverton OR 97005

LAWLER, MARY DE KAY KENNEDY, educator; b. Washington, July 24, 1942; d. Maurice de Kay Thompson and Gertrude Marguerite (Mooney) Kennedy; m. James Joseph Lawler, Jr., Aug. 7, 1971; children—Craig, Diane, Jill and Erin (Twins). B.S. in Nursing, U. Mich., 1964; M.Nursing, U. Pitts., 1968; postgrad. in family relations and home econs, Okla. State U. R.N., Okla. Staff nurse Univ. Hosp., Ann Arbor, Mich., 1964-65, asst. head nurse, head nurse, 1965-67; instr. U. Pitts., 1969-71, No. Okla. Coll., Tonkawa, 1972; dir., coordinator Indian Meridian Area Vocat. Sch., Stillwater, Okla., 1974-75; asst. prof. nursing Langston (Okla.) U., 1981-82. Contbr. articles to profl. publs. Mem. Stillwater Bd. Edn., 1981—, pres., 1986; mem. task force Edn. Found., Stillwater Publ. Schs.; grad. Leadership Stillwater; pres. bd. dirs. Stillwater Domestic Violence and Parents Assistance Ctr.; den leader Cub Scouts Am. Mem. Am. Nurses Assn., Okla. Nurses Assn. (pres. dist. 12), Am. Vocat. Assn., Sigma Theta Tau. Home: 1109 N Skyline Stillwater OK 74075 Office: Dept FRCD Coll Home Econs Okla State U Stillwater OK 74078

LAWLER, PATRICIA CARMELLA, consultant; b. N.Y.C., Jan. 6, 1953; d. John Joseph and Rose A. (DeMarco) Lanigan; m. Michael D. Lawler, Aug. 21, 1982. A.A.S., Manhattan Community Coll., 1972; B.S., St. John's U., Jamaica, N.Y., 1975, M.B.A., 1978. Corporate planning analyst Eastern States Bankcard, Lake Success, N.Y., 1975-79; mgr. planning and devel. Nat. Data Corp., Fairfield, N.J., 1979-82; product mgr. Dun & Bradstreet, Norwalk, Conn., 1982-83; cons., owner Lawler Assocs., Stamford, Conn., 1983—. Bd. dirs. N.Y.C. NASCP, 1980-83. Mem. Info. Industry Assn., Am. Mktg. Assn., Pres.'s Soc. Alumni Assn. (bd. reps.). Office: 185 Ocean Dr E Stamford CT 06902

LAWLESS, CHRISTINE EUNICE, internist; b. Chgo., Dec. 21, 1952; d. John D. and Cecilia B. (Bibro) Lawless. B.S. in Biology summa cum laude, No. Ill. U., 1974, M.D., Loyola U., Maywood, Ill., 1977. Diplomate Am. Bd. Internal Medicine, Am. Bd. Cardiovascular Medicine. Resident in internal medicine Loyola U. Hosp., Maywood, Ill., 1977-80, cardiology fellow, 1981-83, assoc. chief fellow, 1982-83; research fellow, hon. registrar Royal Postgrad. Med. Sch., Hammersmith Hosp., London, 1980-81; asst. prof. medicine Loyola U., 1983—; staff cardiologist Hines VA Hosp. (Ill.), 1983—. Harvey Feyerherm scholar No. Ill. U., 1974; recipient CIBA-Geigy Co. award for community service Loyola U. Hosp., 1975. Mem. ACP, Am. Fedn. Clin. Research, Am. Coll. Cardiology (assoc.). Contbr. articles to profl. jours. Office: Loyola University Hospital 2160 1st Ave Maywood IL 60153

LAWLEY, JO RODGERS, retail executive; b. Reform, Ala., May 16, 1939; d. Lewis Manley and Lella Maude (Davidson) Rodgers; m. William Davis Lawley, Sr., Mar. 18, 1961; 1 son, William Davis. B.S., U. Ala.-Tuscaloosa, 1960. Buyer, Pizitz, Inc., Birmingham, Ala., 1961-66, mdse. mgr., 1966-70, v.p. sales promotion, 1970-74; v.p. sales promotion Halle's, Cleve., 1974-79; sr. v.p. mktg. M. O'Neil Co., Akron, Ohio, 1979-85, 86—; sr. v.p. Famous-Barr, St. Louis, 1986—; dir. Malone, Inc., Akron and Charlotte, N.C. Dir. Akron Jr. League, 1983—; adv. bd. U. Akron, 1983—; dir., officer Nat. Retail Mchts. Assn. Mktg. Div., 1974—; mem. parents council Hampden-Sydney Coll.; mem. Founders Club Hampden-Sydney Coll. Mem. U. Ala. Alumni Assn. (Outstanding Alumni award 1984), Alpha Chi Omega. Republican. Methodist. Office: Famous-Barr 601 Olive St Saint Louis MO 63101

LAWLIS, PATRICIA KITE, air force officer, computer consultant; b. Greensburg, Pa., May 5, 1945; d. Joseph Powell, Jr., and Dorothy Theresa (Allshouse) Kite; m. Mark Craig Lawlis, Sept. 17, 1976 (div. 1983); 1 child, Elizabeth Marie. B.S., East Carolina U., 1967; M.S. in Computer Sci., Air Force Inst. Tech., 1982. Cert. secondary math. tchr. Employment counselor Pa. State Employment Service, Washington, Pa., 1967-69; math. tchr. Fort Cherry Sch. Dist., McDonald, Pa., 1969-74; commd. 2d lt. U.S. Air Force, 1974, advanced through grades to maj., 1986, data base mgr. Air Force Space Command, Colorado Springs, Colo., 1974-77, computer systems analyst, USAF in Europe, Birkenfeld, Germany, 1977-80, prof. computer sci. Air Force Inst. Tech., Wright-Patterson AFB, Ohio, 1982—; computer cons. C.J. Kemp Systems, Inc., Huber Heights, Ohio, 1983-86; Ada cons., Ada Joint Program Office, Washington, 1984-86. State treas. NOW, Pa., 1973-74. Recipient Mervin E. Gross award Air Force Inst. Tech., 1982, Prof. Ezra Kotcher award, 1985. Mem. Assn. Computing Machinery, Computer Soc. of IEEE. Office: Air Force Institute of Technology School of Engineering Wright-Patterson AFB OH 45433

LAWRENCE, BONNIE MAE, lawyer, business consultant, publisher; b. N.Y.C., Oct. 5, 1951; d. Belle L. B.A. UCLA, 1973; J.D., Whittier Coll., 1980. Bar: Calif. 1980, U.S. Ct. Apls. (9th cir.) 1980. Fin. analyst Atlantic Richfield Co., Los Angeles, 1973-76; acct. C.P.A. firm, Los Angeles, 1976-77; sole practice, Los Angeles, 1980—; owner, pres. Am. Bus. Publs., Inc. Mem. ABA, Womens Referral Service. Office: 10850 Wilshire Blvd #800 Los Angeles CA 90024

LAWRENCE, DEAN GRAYSON, lawyer; b. Oakland, Calif.; d. Henry C. and Myrtle (Grayson) Schmidt; A.B., U. Calif., Berkeley, 1934, J.D., 1939. Bar: Calif. 1943, U.S. Tax Ct., 1944, U.S. Dist. Ct. 1944, U.S. Ct. Appeals 1944, U.S. Supreme Ct. 1967. With U.S. Treasury Dept., 1945; assoc. with Pillsbury, Madison & Sutro, San Francisco, 1944, 1945; gen. practice, Oakland, 1946-50, San Jose, 1952-60, Grass Valley, 1960-63, 66—; county counsel Nevada County, 1964, 65, bd. suprs. 2d dist., 1969-73, chmn., 1971; sec. Nevada County Humane Animal Shelter Bd., 1966—; pres. Nevada County Humane Soc., 1974—; state humane officer, 1966—; mem. Nevada County Health Planning Council, 1973-79, Golden Empire Areawide Health Planning Council, 1974-75; mem. Nevada County Democratic Central Com., 1980—, sec., 1982—. Mem. Humane Soc. U.S., Fund for Animals, AAUW, State Bar Calif., Bus. and Profl. Women's Club, Phi Beta Kappa, Sigma Xi, Kappa Beta Pi, Pi Mu Epsilon, Pi Lambda Theta. Episcopalian. Office: PO Box 66 Grass Valley CA 95945

LAWRENCE, DEBORAH ANNE, financial consultant; b. Maplewood, N.J., Dec. 2, 1948; d. Francis Edmund and Loretta Claire (Sheridan) L. B.A. in English, Seton Hall U., 1970, M.A., 1973; M.B.A. in Fin., Fordham U., 1986. Tchr. English, Vailsburg High Sch., Newark, 1972-73, Abraham Clark High Sch., Roselle, N.J., 1973-75; mortgage review officer Carteret Savs. and Loan Assn., Cranford, N.J., 1976-79; litigation paralegal Pitney Hardin & Kipp, Morristown, N.J., 1979-80; cons. Sweeney Assocs., Inc., N.Y.C., 1980—. Vol. Jr. League of N.Y., 1981—. Mem. The Exec. Female, Aircraft Owners and Pilots Assn., Smithsonian Assocs. Republican. Roman Catholic. Club: Porsche (Morristown, N.J.). Avocations: flying; tennis; skiing; horseback riding. Home: 43 Iroquois Ave Oceanport NJ 07757 Office: Sweeney Assocs Inc c/o Trustee John Muir & Co 11 Broadway Suite 1470 New York NY 10004

LAWRENCE, DORIS EDWINA, justice of the peace; b. Swanville, Minn., Jan. 9, 1911; d. Charles Deo and Jessie Irene (Willson) Barber; m. Louis Walter Lawrence, Aug. 11, 1932 (dec. 1970); children—Betty Lou Irene, Jeanne Ardyce. Seamtress, Montgomery Ward, St. Paul, 1932-33; co-owner Lawrence Printing Co., Saint Paul, 1942-47; co-owner, pub., editor The Mountaineer, Big Sandy, Mont., 1947-71; nurse's aide Heritage Home, Big Sandy, 1971-83; sec., treas., Chouteau County Council on Aging, Fort Benton, Mont., 1974-83; justice of the peace Chouteau County, Big Sandy, 1974—. Organizer, Big Sandy Sr. Citizen Ctr., 1974; active Centennial Lodge Sr. Citizen Housing, 1981; organizer PTA, Big Sandy, 1949-50. Named Sr. Citizen of Yr. Area 3 Council on Aging, 1981. Mem. Am. Legion Aux. Club: Am. Luth. Ch. Women (Big Sandy) (pres. 1948—). Lodge: Mystic Tie Rebekah #113 (noble grand 1974-75). Avocations: sewing; crocheting; knitting. Home and Office: PO Box 492 Big Sandy MT 59520

LAWRENCE, ESTELENE YVONNE, transit district executive, musician; b. Lynch, Ky., Aug. 10, 1933; d. Samuel Coleridge and Florence Estelle (Gardner) Taylor; m. Otto Lee Lawrence, Sept. 14, 1957; children—Stuart, Neil, Adelbert. Student Fenn Coll., 1953-60, Cleve. Inst. Music, 1955-56, John Carroll U., 1977-78, Northeastern U., 1979-80. Stenographer Cleve. Transit System/Regional Transit Authority, 1951-76, tng. asst., 1976-78, personnel devel. asst., 1978-82, dist. adminstr., 1983—; supr./mgmt. skills instr. RTA, 1976—; dir. music Friendly United Baptist Ch., 1947—; piano tchr., 1953-73; pianist/organist Nat. Bapt. Conv., 1971, 80. Publicity chmn. Moses Cleve. Sch. PTA, 1965-75; audit chmn. RTA Main Office Credit Union, 1980-83; dist. sec. Boy Scouts Am., 1982-83; chmn. adv. bd. Baldwin Wallace Coll., 1984—; mem. adv. bd. Cleve. Mgmt. Devel. Consortium, 1985—. Mem. Cleve. Mgmt. Seminars (treas. 1979-81, pres. 1981-83), Conf. Minority Transp. Ofcls., Phi Kappa Gamma (pres. 1966-69). Mem. A.M.E. Ch. Clubs: East 153d Street (v.p. 1980—), East Ky. Social. Home: 4066 East 153d St Cleveland OH 44128 Office: Greater Cleveland Regional Transit Authority 615 Superior St NW Cleveland OH 44113

LAWRENCE, GLORIA EDITH, non-profit organization executive; b. N.Y.C.; d. Victor R. and Mamie (Moss) L.; B.S., CCNY, 1956; postgrad. Columbia U., 1959, New Sch. Social Research, 1960-62. Dir. devel. So. Elections Fund, N.Y.C., 1969-70, Harlem Dowling Children's Center, N.Y.C., 1975-77; pub. relations exec. March of Dimes, N.Y.C., 1980—; with fin. devel. unit Nat. bd. YWCA, N.Y.C., 1982-85; pres. Gloria Lawrence Cons. Firm; dir. Third World Women's Bank. Bd. dirs. Ams. for Democratic Action, 1977—; apptd. mem. Archives and Reference Research for N.Y.C., 1978—; mem. N.Y. County Com., 1973-78; del. Dem. Nat. Conv.; spl. asst. to pres. N.Y.C. Council, 1977; mem. N.Y. State Econ. Devel. Task Force, N.Y.C. Urban Affairs Com. Mem. Nat. Women's Polit. Caucus. Episcopalian. Club: Women's City (bd. dirs.). Home: 165 West End Ave New York NY 10023

LAWRENCE, JACQUELINE BURNS, management company executive, consultant, builder; b. Washington, Dec. 22, 1945; d. Jack and Pauline (Hardie) Burns; m. Charles Edward Lawrence, II, Dec. 31, 1968 (dec. 1973); 1 child: Charles Edward, III. B.A., Emory U., 1967; Tchr. Cert., Ga. State U., 1968. Tchr., Willis High Sch., Marietta, Ga., 1967-69. Slater-Marietta Sch., Greenville, S.C., 1969-70; pres. Southeast Office Mgmt., Lilburn, Ga., 1979—; pres. JBL Investments Inc., 1985—; ptnr. Premier Builders; cons. Homeland Communities, Atlanta, 1979—, CLS Land Co., Atlanta, 1981—, Falling Water Investment, Inc., Atlanta, 1983—, DLC Enterprises, Atlanta, 1984—. Mem. Nat. Assn. Home Builders, Home Builders Assn. Metro Atlanta, Sales and Marketing Council. Republican. Methodist. Advocations: reading; tennis; boating; sports cars. Home: 382 Westminster Ln Lilburn GA 30247 Office: Southeast Office Mgmt Inc 5075 Roswell Rd Atlanta GA 30342

LAWRENCE, JEAN HOPE, writer, database marketing executive; b. Waukegan, Ill., Mar. 5, 1944; d. George Herbert and Hope Delinda (Warren) L.; m. Jonathan N. Hess, Sept. 15, 1981; 1 child, Kelsey Hope. B.A., George Washington U., 1966. Tech. editor, Am. Chem. Soc., Washington, 1966; proposal writer Krohn-Rhodes Inst., Washington, 1966-67; legislative counsel Aerospace Industries Assn., Washington, 1967-82; v.p., co-owner Data Specific, Washington, 1985—; editorial adviser Am. C. of C. Execs., Alexandria, Va., 1983—, lectr., 1984—. Contbg. editor: Communications Concepts, 1983—. Contbr. numerous articles to mags. Mem. Women in Govt. Relations, Washington Edn. Press Assn., Washington Ind. Writers. Democrat. Methodist. Avocation: essayist. Home: 1607 Corcoran St NW Washington DC 20009

LAWRENCE, JODI (JODI FERRARO), broadcast executive; b. Bristol, Pa., Sept. 7, 1938; d. Joseph and Beatrice (Crowfoot) Vattimo; m. Arthur Richard Ferraro, Sept. 25, 1972; 1 child, Ross McKean. A.B. magna cum laude, U. So. Calif., 1960, M.A., 1968; postgrad. U. Copenhagen, U. Calif.-Berkeley, Calif. State U.-Dominquez Hils, Enselhom Folk Sch., Denmark. Cert. tchr., Calif. Various writing and editorial positions with mags. and newspapers including: Today's Film Maker, Pro Film, N.Y. Times, Met. Digest, Intermission, Lens, Los Angeles Times; owner, program dir. Sta. KRRI-FM, Boulder City, Nev., 1982—. Author: Alpha Brain Waves, 1972; Off the Beaten Track in Hawaii, 1973; Search for the Perfect Orgasm, 1974. Contbr. articles to profl. jours., chpt. to book. Co-writer and producer HUD, Year of Action. Stage prodns. include: Sun Stroke, Sugar Tome is Dead, Once a Rebel. Lectr. in field. Recipient Lowell prize, commendations; Scandinavian Seminar for Cultural Studies fellow. Mem. Women in Communications, Soc. Mag. Writers, Authors Guild Am., Authors League Am., Actors Studio West (writers unit), AAUW, Bus. and Profl. Women, Press Club, Henderson C. of C., Boulder City C. of C. Avocations: sailing; shooting; painting; mineralogy; lepitoptery. Home: PO Box 97 Boulder City NV 89005 Office: KRRI-FM 1658 Nevada Hwy Boulder City NV 89005

LAWRENCE, KAREN, editor; b. Springfield, Mass., Oct. 5, 1950; d. Arthur Julius and Ruth Irene (Johnson) C.; m. Robert William Lawrence, Apr. 14, 1984; 1 child, Brian Gerald. B.A., Wheaton (Mass.) Coll. 1972; M.L.S., Columbia U., 1973. Cataloger, H.W. Wilson Co., Bronx, N.Y., 1973-79; asst. editor Wilson Library Bull., Bronx, 1979-85; freelance editor, 1985—. Editor: Senior High School Library Catalog, 1977. Davison-Forman grad. fellow. Mem. ALA, N.Y. Library Assn., Women's Nat. Book Assn. Lutheran. Clubs: N.Y. Library, Wheaton Club N.Y. Office: 50 Main St Montvale NJ 07645

LAWRENCE, KATHLEEN WILSON, government official; b. N.Y.C., Dec. 7, 1940; d. Jules William and Catherine (Kelly) Wilson; m. James J. Balsdon, Oct. 31, 1959 (div. 1968); children—Julia A. Balsdon Wise, Maryclaire; m. G. Andrew Lawrence, July 6, 1974; 1 child, Andrew W. Student, Queens Coll., 1959, U. Va., 1977, No. Va. Community Coll., 1976-80, Harvard U., 1985. Staff asst. to pres. White House, Washington, 1969-73; exec. dir. Nat. Fedn. Republican Women, Washington, 1974-75; dir. adminstrn. Citizens for Reagan, Washington, 1976; pres. Lawrence Co., Alexandria, Va., 1977-84; dep. undersec. U.S. Dept. Agr., Washington, 1984—; dir. Tri Cities Communication, Craig, Colo., Rural Telephone Bank, Washington. Mem. exec. com. Am. Cancer Soc., Alexandria, 1983-84, bd. dirs., 1980-85; mem. corp. bd. Alexandria Hosp., 1980—; bd. dirs. Va. Fedn. Republican Women, 1981-82, Olde Belhaven Towne Civic Assn., Alexandria, 1984-85. Mem. Exec. Women in Gov., Nat. Assn. Women Bus. Owners. Roman Catholic. Avocations: travel; reading; needlework. Office: US Dept Agr 14th and Independence SW Washington DC 20250

LAWRENCE, MARLINA THERESA, insurance and banking company executive; b. Bklyn., Jan. 21, 1953; d. Harry Coote Lawrence. B.A. summa cum laude, Marymount Manhattan Coll., 1975; casualty claims law assoc. Am. Ednl. Inst., 1980. Claims trainee, rep. Ins. Co. N.Am., N.Y.C., 1976-77, asst. claim supr. employers self ins. service unit Med. Malpractice Claims, N.Y.C., 1977-78, claims supr. gen. liability, automobile and malpractice claims, 1978-81; project controller group automobile project Equitable Life Assurance Soc. U.S., N.Y.C., 1981-82, project controller property and casualty reins. run-off project, 1982, dep. div. benefits mgr., 1982-83, Northeastern regional benefits project mgr., 1983, employee devel. services mgr., 1983-86; employee/strategic planning project, retail processing dept. head Irving Trust, N.Y.C., 1986—. Recipient scholarships Marymount Manhattan Coll., 1971-75, Dyson Found., 1971; Gerard scholar Marymount Manhattan Coll., 1975; recipient Gold medal Marymount Manhattan Coll., 1975; Outstanding Performer award Ins. Co. N.Am., 1980, 81. Mem. Nat. Assn. Female Execs., AAUW. Democrat. Roman Catholic. Home: 200 La Bonne Vie Dr Apt 6B East Patchogue NY 11772 Office: Irving Trust One Wall St New York NY 10015

LAWRENCE, PATRICIA ANNE, nurse; b. Worcester, Mass., Nov. 14, 1931; d. Ralph Seavey and Maude Irma (Hayward) L.; A.B., Bates Coll., Lewiston, Maine, 1954; M.A., Columbia U., 1960. Staff nurse Cornell U. Med. Center, 1954-57, Newton (Mass.)-Wellesley Hosp., 1957-58; instr. Cornell U.-N.Y. Hosp. Sch. Nursing, 1958-59, 60-61, Rutgers U. Coll. Nursing, 1961-64; asst. prof. Duke U. Sch. Nursing, 1964-70; ednl. dir. diabetes project N.C. Regional Med. Program, 1969-73; assoc. prof. U. N.C. Sch. Nursing, Chapel Hill, 1973—; site visitor, cons. diabetes research and tng. centers NIH, 1977-78, adv. bd. Nat. Diabetes Clearinghouse, 1978-80; bd. dirs. Am. Assn. Diabetes Educators, 1973-75. Mem. Am. Nurses Assn., N.C. Nurses Assn., Am. Diabetes Assn. (dir. 1974-79, sec. 1976-77, v.p. 1977-79, dir. N.C. affiliate 1973-79, 81-83), Internat. Diabetes Fedn., AAUP, Am. Kennel Club (tracking judge), Durham Kennel Club, Am. Belgian Tervuren Club, Co-author: Picture Pages for Diabetic Care, 1973; also numerous articles, chpts. in books. Co-editor: Educating Diabetic Patients, 1981; editorial bd. Diabetes care, 1977-83. Home: 4711 Easley St Durham NC 27705 Office: Carrington Hall 214H Chapel Hill NC 27514

LAWRENCE, RACHEL REGINA (GINA), computer retailer; b. Hattiesburg, Miss., Nov. 13, 1960; d. Wayne Byron and Rachel W. (Sullivan) Lott; m. John Roland Lawrence, Sept. 1, 1984. A.A., Pearl River Jr. Coll., 1980; B.S., U. So. Miss., 1982. Paralegal asst. Ingram, Matthews & Fowler, Hattiesburg, 1982-83; sales rep. ComputerKraft, Hattiesburg, 1983-84, ComputerWorld, Jackson, Miss., 1984-85; mgr. AC3 Computing Products, Jackson, 1985—. Named Top Sales Rep. of Yr., ComputerWorld, 1985. Mem. Am. Bus. Women's Assn., Nat. Assn. Female Execs. Republican. Methodist. Club: Stonegate Ladies. Avocations: tennis; sewing; skiing; swimming. Home: 222 Creekline Dr Madison MS 39110 Office: AC3 Computing Products 805 S Wheatly St Ridgeland MS 39157

LAWRENCE, RUTH BECKER, nurse; b. Bklyn., June 16, 1925; d. Edward F. and Lillian (Davis) Becker; B.S., nursing diploma Simmons Coll., 1947; m. W. Leland Lawrence, Feb. 8, 1948; children—Stoddard, Thomas, Jeffrey, Leland Davis, Leigh Anne, Richard. Instr. nursing, Simmons Coll., Boston, 1947; staff nurse Nassau Hosp., Mineola, N.Y., 1947-48; staff pediatric nurse Hartford (Conn.) Hosp., 1948-49; dir. nursing service Springfield (Vt.) Hosp., 1977-86; now nurse cons. Choir, tchr. Sunday Sch., Congl. Ch.; den mother Boy Scouts Am.; vol. ARC; bd. dirs. Springfield Sch. Bd., 1962-72. Mem. Am. Nurses Assn., Council Nursing Adminstrs., Vt. Hosp. Assn. Dirs. Nursing.

LAWRENCE, SALLY CLARK, art college administrator; b. San Francisco, Dec. 29, 1930; d. George Dickson and Martha Marie Alice (Smith) Clark; m.

Henry Clay Judd, July 1950; children—Rebecca Ann, David Clark, Nancy; m. John I. Lawrence, Aug. 12, 1976. Owner, dir. Sally Judd Gallery, Portland, Oreg., 1968-75; pvt. practice art consulting, appraising, Portland, 1975-80; interim dir. Pacific Northwest Coll. Art, Portland, 1981, asst. dir., 1981-82, acting dir., 1982-84, dir., 1984—; mem. Contemporary Crafts Gallery, Portland, 1983—, Portland Ctr. for the Visual Arts, 1981—; bd. dirs. Neskowin Coast Found., Oreg., 1981—. Mem. Oreg. Art Inst., Nat. Assn. Schs. of Art and Design (bd. dirs. 1984—), Art Coll. Exchange (pres. 1983-85, bd. dirs. 1983—). Democrat. Office: Pacific Northwest Coll Art 1219 SW Park Portland OR 97205

LAWRENCE, STELLA, elec. engr., educator; b. Montreal, Que., Can., Feb. 2, 1918; came to U.S., 1924, naturalized, 1945; d. M. and Fannie (Broide) Hertchikoff; B.A. magna cum laude, N.Y. U., 1938, M.S., 1941; B.E.E. summa cum laude, Poly. Inst. Bklyn., 1949, M.E.E., 1952. Devel. engr. Control Instrument Co., 1943-47; lectr. physics CCNY, 1958-70; mem. switching systems devel. dept. Bell Telephone Labs., 1947-60; asst. prof. Bronx Community Coll., 1960-65, asso. prof. elec. engring. tech., 1966-80, prof., 1980—; cons. advanced tech. dept. Ampex Corp., 1975—; cons. orbiting systems Aerospace Corp., summer 1978; cons. Jet Propulsion Lab., summer 1980; vis. scientist Lawrence Berkeley Lab., U. Calif., summer 1981, L.B. Johnson Space Center, summer 1982; cons. Air Force Wright Aero. Labs., Ohio, summer 1983. Mem. Community Planning Bd. 7, Bronx, N.Y.C., 1970—. Faculty research fellow Argonne (Ill.) Nat. Lab., 1974, NASA Langley Research Center, summer 1976, NASA Marshall Space Flight Center, summer 1977, NSF fellow, 1977-80. Fellow Bklyn. Engrs. Club; mem. IEEE (sr., exec. com. N.Y. sect. 1956—, regional exec. com. 1975), Soc. Women Engrs. (sr., charter), Am. Soc. for Engring. Edn., N.Y. Acad. Scis., Phi Beta Kappa, Sigma Xi, Pi Mu Epsilon, Sigma Pi Sigma. Home: 3288 Reservoir Oval E Bronx NY 10467 Office: 181st and University Ave Bronx NY 10453

LAWRENCE, TELETÉ ZORAYDA, speech and voice pathologist, educator; b. Worcester, Mass., Aug. 5, 1910; d. James Newton and Cora Valeria (Hester) Lester; A.B. cum laude, U. Calif., Berkeley, 1932; M.A., Tex. Christian U., 1963; pvt. study voice with Edgar Schofield, N.Y.C., 1936-41, drama with Enrica Clay Dillon, N.Y.C., 1937-40; m. Ernest Lawrence, Oct. 9, 1939; children—James Lester, Valerie Alma. Mem. Am. Lyric Opera Co., 1939—; instr. speech Sch. Fine Arts, Tex. Christian U., Fort Worth, 1959-66, asst. prof., 1966-71, asso. prof., 1971-75, prof., 1975-76, emeritus, 1976—, speech pathologist specializing voice disorders Speech and Hearing Clinic, 1959—, faculty research leave, Gt. Britain, Western Europe, Hungary, 1968; pvt. practice speech and voice pathology, 1960—. Mem. bd. Sunshine Haven, home for retarded children, 1957-59; gen. chmn. Ft. Worth and Tarrant County, Nat. Retarded Children's Week, 1954; mem. family and child welfare div. Community Council Ft. Worth and Tarrant County, 1955-57, mem. health and hosp. div., 1959-60, mem. women's com. Ft. Worth chpt. NCCJ, 1956-59; exec. v.p. Fine Arts Found. Guild of Tex. Christian U., 1955-56, past exec. sec., past fin. sec. Recipient Faculty Research grant Tex. Christian U., 1961. Fellow Internat. Soc. Phonetic Scis.; mem. Nat. Council Chs. (bd. joint com. missionary edn. Pacific Coast area, 1952-55), United Ch. Women of Ft. Worth (chmn. Christian world missions dept. 1955-57, pres. 1957-59). Ft. Worth Area Council Chs. (v.p. 1955-57, exec. com. 1957-59, bd. dirs. 1959-60), U. Calif. Alumni Assn. (life), Am. Speech-Lang.-Hearing Assn. (life; cert. clin. competence in speech pathology), Tex. Speech and Hearing Assn., Ft. Worth Council for Retarded Children, Speech Communication Assn. (sec. speech and hearing disorders interest group 1962-63, mem. com. 1961-64), Am. Dialect Soc., Internat. Assn. Logopedics and Phoniatrics, Phonetic Soc. Japan, AAUP (emeritus), Lambda Ma'ams of Lambda Chi Alpha (pres. Ft. Worth 1962-63), Phi Beta Kappa Assn., Ft. Worth, Phi Beta Kappa (Alpha of Calif. chpt.; charter mem., v.p. Delta of Tex. chpt. 1971-73, pres. 1973-74), Delta Zeta, Psi Chi, Sigma Alpha Eta. Republican. Mem. Christian Ch. Clubs: Woman's of Fort Worth, Women of Rotary. Participant, 13th Congress of Internat. Assn. Logopedics and Phoniatrics, Vienna, 1965, 14th Congress, Paris, 1968, 15th Congress, Buenos Aires, 1971, 16th Congress, Interlaken, Switzerland, 1974, 17th Congress, Copenhagen, 1977, 18th Congress, Washington, 1980, 19th Congress, Edinburgh, Scotland, 1983; participant 10th Internat. Congress of Linguists, Bucharest, 1967; participant 6th Internat. Congress of Phonetic Scis., Prague, 1967, 7th Internat. Congress, Montreal, 1971, 8th Internat. Congress, Leeds, Eng., 1975; participant 1st Congress Internat. Assn. Sci. Study Mental Deficiency, Montpellier, France, 1967, Semmelweis Ann. Week, Budapest Acad. Scis., 1968, 3d World Congress Phoneticians, Tokyo, 1976. Author: Handbook for Instructors of Voice and Diction, 1968; contbr. articles to profl. jours. Home: 3860 South Hills Circle Fort Worth TX 76109

LAWS, JUDITH A., human resources consultant; b. St Louis, July 3, 1937; d. James C. and H. Idell (McIntyre) L. B.A., Washington U., St. Louis, 1959; B.Metaphysics, Claregate Coll., London, 1980. Vol., Peace Corps, Cameroon, 1962-63; personnel generalist HEW, Washington, 1964-66, asst. to dir. 1970 White House Conf. Children and Youth, 1966-68; manpower devel. and tng. cons., Washington, 1969-73; alcohol edn. cons., Washington, 1974—; credential program devel. coordinator Assn. Labor-Mgmt. Adminstrs. and Cons. on Alcoholism, Arlington, Va., 1984—. Contbg. editor Quarante, 1985—; contbr. articles to The Beacon. Mem. adv. council Alcoholism Treatment Ctr. Washington, 1976-78; bd. dirs. Whitman-Walker Clinic, Washington, 1979. Mem. Washington Ind. Writers, Nat. Writers Club, Inst. Noetic Scis. Avocations: playwriting; acting; psychospiritual research. Home: 2800 Woodley Rd NW Washington DC 20008 Office: ALMACA 1800 N Kent Suite 907 Arlington VA 22209

LAWS, PHE, home economist; b. Kewanee, Ill., Jan. 2, 1925; d. Charles Eldon and Fern Izzetta (Green) Wyand; m. Albert Laws, Aug. 10, 1944 (dec. Nov. 1983); children—Richard T., Carmela. A.A., Canada Coll., 1969; B.A., San Jose State U., 1972. Coordinator Litton Microwaves, San Franciso, 1972-74; writer Hidden House Pubs., Palo Alto, Calif., 1973-79; tchr., lectr. San Francisco Bay area, 1972-83; tchr. Canada Coll., Redwood City, Calif., 1981—; writer food sect. Lambert Advt., Burlingame, Calif., 1982; pub. Laws Pub., Redwood City, 1983—; demonstrator, tchr. Whirlpool, Santa Clara, Calif., 1975-76; tchr. Ohlone Coll., Fremont, Calif., 1973-74. Author: International Gourmet Cooking with Microwave, 1975; Vegetable Magic with Microwave, 1978; Vegetable Cookery, 1979. Mem. Am. Home Econs. Assn., Internat. Microwave Power Inst., Home Economists in Bus. Republican. Clubs: Sequoia Yacht, Horse Mens Assn. (Redwood City, Calif.). Home and Office: 207 Mountain Vista Ln Santa Rosa CA 95405

LAWSON, ANN MARIE MCDONALD, librarian; b. Jersey City; d. William and Mary Agnes (Dolan) McDonald; student Columbia, 1947, N.Y. U., 1949, City Coll. N.Y., 1959, Pratt Inst., 1963; m. Philip James Lawson, Apr. 26, 1952. Methods analyst Rueben H. Donnelley Corp., N.Y.C., 1953-57; librarian chems. div. Union Carbide Corp., N.Y.C., 1957-65, Tatham Laird & Kudner, N.Y.C., 1965-67, Met. Transp. Authority, N.Y.C., 1967-80; cons., 1980—; active library tng. program Ballard Sch. (YWCA), 1949—; cons. WHO, Geneva, Switzerland, 1950; lectr. Pratt Inst. Grad. Library Sch., 1967. Mem. Assn. Records Mgrs. and Adminstrs. (pres. 1948-50); Spl. Libraries Assn. Republican. Contbr. articles to mags. Home and office: 119 Washington Pl New York NY 10014

LAWSON, BRENDA MICKLOW, financial planner; b. Birmingham, Ala., Feb. 19, 1954; d. Andrew William and Geraldine (Cooley) Micklow; B.S., Jacksonville State U., 1976, M.S., 1977; m. James Ronald Lawson, July 24, 1976; 1 dau., Lori. Pres. Investors Diversified Services, Birmingham, 1981—; adj. faculty U. Ala.-Birmingham. Named 1st runner up Miss Ala. U.S.A., 1974; cert. fin. planner. Mem. Internat. Assn. Fin. Planners (past pres., chmn. bd., now dir. Ala. chpt.), Inst. Cert. Fin. Planners, Phi Mu. Rupublican. Author: The Cashless Society, 1976; Value Issues in Counseling, 1978; composer: When, 1978. Home: 1313 Al Seier Ln Birmingham AL 35226 Office: 202 Park West Suite 310 Birmingham AL 35209

LAWSON, JOYCE FINCH, word processing service executive; b. Yoakum, Tex., Jan. 7, 1942; d. Douglas Gerald and Ethel Lea (O'Neill) Finch; m. Gordon B. Lawson, Sept. 10, 1960 (div. 1969); children—Gerald Ray, Jay Scott; m. 2d, R.J. Hrapsky, Apr. 26, 1983. Grad. high sch., Austin, Tex. Legal sec. Sneed & Vine, Austin, 1969-71; exec. sec. Hyde Park Baptist Ch., Austin, 1961-69; legal sec. B. Joe Thomson, Houston, 1971-73; adminstrv. asst. Travis County Bd. Commrs., Austin 1973-76; owner Joyco Word Processing Service, Houston, 1976—. Mem. Assn. Info. Processing Specialists, Nat. Assn. Profl. Secretarial Services, Nat. Assn. Women Bus. Owners. Baptist.

LAWSON, LAURIE LEE, human services director, free-lance writer; b. Crisfield, Md., Aug. 22, 1949; d. George Edgar and Marie Roselind (Favata) Lawson; m. John Worth Horner, Dec. 6, 1975 (div.). B.A. summa cum laude in Sociology, U. Md., 1976. Personnel dir. Shore Up! Inc., Salisbury, Md., 1970-78, Phoenix House Found., N.Y.C., 1978-82; personnel dir., exec. asst. Seamen's Ch. Inst., N.Y.C., 1982-83; dir. resources Phoenix House Found., N.Y.C., 1983-85; cons. Med. Referral System, N.Y.C., 1982-83; coordinator Project SSI Alert, Lower Eastern Shore Md., 1974-75, cons., coordinator nutrition project, 1973-74; bd. dirs. Not-for-Profit Personnel Dirs. Assn., N.Y.C., 1983—. Contbr. articles and essays to nat. mags. Shore Up! Inc. grantee, 1971. Mem. N.Y. Personnel Mgrs. Assn., Am. Soc. Personnel Adminstrn., Nat. Assn. Female Execs., AAUW, Md. Career Devel. Com. (v.p. 1971-73), Mensa. Democrat. Club: Wall St. Network. Home: 301 W 45th St Apt 8F New York NY 10036

LAWSON, LINDA MAE, construction company executive; b. Torrance, Calif., May 17, 1943; d. Jessie David and Doris Maxine (Lobach) K.; m. John D. Lawson, Oct. 26, 1959 (div. 1980); children—Pamela G., Matthew Todd. Grad. high sch. Lubbock, Tex.; student Am. Inst. Banking. Floral designer Allen's Floral, Lubbock, 1962-64; bank clk. First Nat. Bank, Lubbock, 1964-74; office mng. W.R. Batson Co., Inc., Lubbock, 1974-78; sec., treas. McLean Roof Deck Co., Inc., Lubbock, 1978—; owner SNO-CO Supply, 1985—. Republican. Baptist. Clubs: Bus. and Profl. Women (pres. 1976-77), state convention chmn. 1978). Avocations: floral designing; painting; piano; raising Dobermen Pinchers. Office: McLean Roof Deck Co Inc 313 Paris St PO Box 5705 Lubbock TX 79417

LAWSON, MELISSA ARCHILLA, bilingual educator; b. Ft. Worth, Oct. 22, 1950; d. Eliel and Foye (Jackson) Archilla; m. Billy Granville Lawson, Feb. 26, 1971 (div. 1975). 1 son, Mark Christopher. B.S. in Edn. cum laude, N. Tex. State U., 1978; M.Ed., So. Meth. U., 1981. Cert. elem. tchr., English elem. tchr., bilingual tchr., Tex. Bilingual tchr. Dallas Ind. Sch. Dist., 1978-82, Richardson, Tex., 1982—. Interpreter 1980 Census, Dallas, 1980. Scottish Rite Masons scholar, 1968; Masters Degree grantee, 1978. Mem. Dallas Assn. Bilingual Educators, Tex. Tchrs. ESL, Richardson Edn. Assn., Assn. Adult Educators, Tex. Ret. Tchrs. Assn. Republican. Baptist. Club: Alpha Delta Pi. Office: Richardson Ind Sch Dist 400 S Greenville Ave Richardson TX 75081

LAWSON, PATRICIA JANE, radio executive; b. Chgo., Nov. 18, 1950; d. Alden John and Sadie Elizabeth (Guyler) Lawson. B.A. in English, St. Joseph's Coll., 1972; M.A. in English, U. Denver, 1977. Asst. to v.p. Agy. for the Performing Arts, Inc., Chgo., 1972-73, 74; actress, dir. pub. relations Earth Theatre/Earth Prodns. Ltd., Chgo., 1974; asst. to dir. grad. studies U. Denver, 1974-77; adminstrv. asst. to v.p., gen. mgr. Sta. WKQX-FM, Chgo., 1978-83; adminstr. advt. and promotion Sta. WMAQ-AM, Chgo., 1984—. Editor comparative poetry book: Style and Prosody, 1976; contbr. articles to profl. jours. U. Denver grad. scholar, 1974-77; St. Joseph's Coll. grantee, 1968-72. Mem. U. Denver Grad. Student Assn. (dir. 1976-77). Roman Catholic. Home: 922 E 100th Pl Chicago IL 60628 Office: WMAQ AM Radio NBC Suite 1941 Merchandise Mart Plaza Chicago IL 60654

LAWSON, SANDRA SUE, personnel executive; b. Chester, Pa., Jan. 26, 1945; d. George William and Kathleen (Burnettee) Lawson; m. Frank Pratt Newton, Jr., Feb. 8, 1969 (div. June 1980). B.S., U. Tenn., 1966, postgrad., 1973-75; postgrad U. Va., 1967-68. Personnel asst. U. Tenn., Knoxville, 1973-75; benefits mgr. M.D. Anderson Hosp., Houston, 1975-76; asst. personnel dir. Jefferson Davis Hosp., Houston, 1976-77; co-owner, mgr. 3d St. Souvenir Mart, Las Vegas, 1977-80; owner mgr. T Shirts by Sandra, Las Vegas, 1980—; employment mgr. EG & G/EM, Las Vegas, 1984—. Bd. dirs. Family Planning, Las Vegas, 1985, Child Find/Nev. Assn. Missing Children, 1984-85; supporting mem. opportunity Village for Retarded Citizens. Mem. So. Nev. Personnel Assn. (sec. 1985-86), Rocky Mountain Personnel Assn. (dir. Las Vegas chpt.), So. Nev. Indsl. Employers, Nat. Asn. Exec. Females. Republican. Club: Soroptimists (pres. 1983-85, Blanch Edgar award 1985). Avocations: Travel; collect clowns and wind chimes; reading; golfing. Mailing Address: 116 N 3d St Las Vegas NV 89101 Home: 4634 Michillinda St Las Vegas NV 89121 Office: EG & G/cM Po Box 1912 Las Vegas NV 89125

LAWSON, VOLA THERRELL, city manager; b. Atlanta, Sept. 14, 1934; d. David Clowe and Josephine (O'Connor) Therrell; m. David H. O. Lawson, Dec. 21, 1959; children—David, Peter. Student Stetson U., George Washington U. Asst. editor The Pilot, nat. aviation mag., Bethesda, Md., 1961-61; contract mgr. with consulting firms for VISTA and Peace Corps, Washington, 1969-71; asst. dir. Alexandria Econs. Opportunities Commn. (Va.), 1971-75; coordinator City of Alexandria community devel. block grant and neighborhood improvements programs, 1975-80, asst. city mgr. for housing, 1981-85, city mgr., 1985—. Chmn., Alexandria Ad Hoc Com. on Status of Women, 1972-74; pres. Alexandria FISH, 1970-71; organizer, mem. bd. dirs. Parkfairfax Citizens Assn., 1969-71; founding charter mem. L'Enfant Montessori Sch., 1961-63; mem. Alexandria Central Democratic Com., 1969-70. Recipient George Washington leadership medal C. of C., 1982; Women's Comm. award, 1982. Mem. Nat. Assn. of Housing and Redevel. Ofcls., Am. Soc. for Pub. Adminstrn. (charter mem. No. Va. chpt). Contbg. editor 50 Yrs. of Am. Gen. Aviation, 1939-64, Places to Fly, 1965. Home: 1111 Bayliss Dr Alexandria VA 22302 Office: Alexandria City Hall Alexandria VA 22314

LAWTON, CHARLOTTE DENISE, business official; b. St. Louis, Feb. 27, 1952; d. Charles Allen and Vivian Geneva (Hayden) L. B.A. in Sociology, U. Mo., 1973. With Div. Family Service, St. Louis, 1971-75; sales coordinator 3M Co., St. Louis, 1975-76; sales rep. Xerox Corp., St. Louis, 1976-80, geog. mgr., 1980-81, ISD sales mgr., 1981-82, mem. region staff, 1982-83, product sales mgr., 1983—. Active NAACP, St. Louis, 1976—; coordinator United Way Campaign-Xerox, St. Louis, 1983. Recipient Yes I Can award Sentinal newspaper, 1983; Outstanding Contbns. award Inter-Regional Council Xerox, 1982. Mem. Women's Commerce Assn., Xerox Black Female Mgrs. Assn. (steering com. 1981—), Black Employees Xerox (exec. com. 1976—, chmn. 1982). Democrat. Roman Catholic. Home: 2223 Lovett Dr St Louis MO 63136 Office: Xerox 12115 Lackland St Louis MO 63146

LAWTON, HELEN B., lecture agency executive; b. Indian Orchard, Mass., Dec. 6, 1912; d. John A. and Clara E. (Moren) Buckley; student N.Y. U., 1930-31; m. C. Herbert Lawton, Mar. 20, 1941. Asst. editor Funk & Wagnalls, N.Y.C., 1928-39; with W. Colston Leigh, Inc., exec. lecture agy., N.Y.C., 1939—, asst. treas., 1957-62, treas., 1962-85. Mem. Nat. Council of Women of U.S. Roman Catholic. Home: 57 Broad St Matawan NJ 07747 Office: Colston Leigh Inc 49-51 State Road Princeton NJ 08540

LAWTON, JACQUELINE AGNES, communications company official; b. Bklyn., June 9, 1933; d. Thomas Joseph and Agnes Rose (McLaughlin) Maguire; grad. N.Y.C. public schs.; m. George W. Lawton, Feb. 14, 1954; children—George, Victoria, Thomas. With Bell System, 1954—, mktg. mgr. govt. edn. and med. midstate, N.Y. Telephone, 1978-81, mktg. mgr. health care, N.Y.C., 1981-82, AT&T dist. field market mgr. health care and lodging Northeast and Mid-Atlantic, N.Y.C., 1982-83, regional mgr. personnel mktg. and sales AT&T Info. Systems, Parsippany, N.J., 1983—; mgmt. cons., Cornish, N.H., 1986—; lectr. in field. Mem. Sales and Mktg. Execs. Internat., Am. Mgmt. Assn., Nat. Assn. Female Execs. Republican. Roman Catholic. Home and Office: PO Box 163 Cornish Flat NH 03746

LAWYER, VIVIAN JURY, lawyer; b. Farmington, Iowa, Jan. 7, 1932; d. Jewell Everett Jury and Ruby Mae (Schumaker) Brewer; m. Verne Lawyer, Oct. 25, 1959; children—Michael Jury, Steven Verne. Tchr.'s cert. U. No. Iowa, 1951; B.S. with honors, Iowa State U., 1953; J.D. with honors, Drake U., 1968. Bar: Iowa 1968. Home econs. tchr. Waukee High Sch. (Iowa), 1953-55; home econs. tchr. jr. high sch. and high sch., Des Moines Pub. Schs., 1955-61; sole practice law, Des Moines, 1972—; dir. Micah Corp.; chmn. juvenile code tng. sessions Iowa Crime Commn., Des Moines, 1978-79, coordinator workshops, 1980; assoc. Law Offices of Verne Lawyer, Des Moines, 1981—; co-founder, bd. dirs. Youth Law Center, Des Moines, 1977—; mem. com. rules of juvenile procedure Supreme Ct. Iowa, 1981—; trustee Polk County Legal Aid Services, Des Moines, 1980-82; mem. Iowa Dept. Human Services and Supreme Ct. Juvenile Justice County Base Joint Study Com., 1984—; mem. Iowa Task Force permanent families project Nat. Council Juvenile and Family Ct. Judges, 1984—. Editor: Iowa Juvenile Code Manual, 1979, Iowa Juvenile Code Workshop Manual, 1980; author booklet in field, 1981. Mem. Polk County Citizens Commn. on Corrections, 1977. Iowa Dept. Social Services grantee, 1980. Mem. ABA, Iowa Bar Assn., Polk County Bar Assn., Polk County Women Attys. Assn., Assn. Trial Lawyers Am., Assn. Family Counseling in Juvenile and Family Cts., LWV, Purple Arrow, Phi Kappa Phi, Omicron Nu. Republican. Home: 5831 N Waterbury Rd Des Moines IA 50312 Office: 427 Fleming Bldg Des Moines IA 50309

LAX, MARY JANE, beauty industry executive; b. Santa Paula, Calif., Oct. 31, 1947; d. James Virgil and Ethel Clara (Poltrock) Davidson; m. Allen Jay Gaer, Aug. 21, 1965 (div. Sept. 1975); children—Kimberly Dawn, Brian James; m. Milton Elliot Lax, Oct. 17, 1982. A.A., Cerritos Jr. Coll., Calif., 1975. Lic. manicurist, Calif. Asst. mgr. Vons Grocery, Sherman Oaks, Calif., 1973-78; credit mgr. Indsl. Freight, San Fernando, Calif., 1978-80; manicurist Nails Etc., Northridge, Calif., 1980-81; owner Hands Up Nail Salon, Northridge, 1981—; chmn. Salon Spltys., 1983—. Judge Long Beach Hairdressers Guild, Calif., 1984; judge R.N. Prodns., Buena Park, Calif., 1984, Scottsdale, Ariz., 1985; judge Finger & Toe Carnival, Las Vegas, Nev., 1985. Mem. Calif. Cosmetology Assn., Calif. Nat. Assn. Nail Artists (cons.). Republican. Office: Salon Specialties 9349 Melvin Ave Suite 9 Northridge CA 91324

LAY, NANCY (BARBARA), loan executive; b. Virginia, Minn., Oct. 14, 1960; d. Robert Edward Lay and Frances Gloria (Hailand) Lay Derr. Escrow officer asst. Safeco Title Co., San Francisco, 1979, Walnut Creek, Calif., 1979-80; asst. to v.p. Union Home Loans, West Los Angeles, Calif., 1980-84; v.p., mgr. loan dept. Marshal Plan, Inc., Santa Monica, Calif., 1984—. Mem. Nat. Assn. Female Execs., Nat. Notary Assn. Republican. Christian Scientist. Club: Jobs Daus. (Northridge, Calif.). Avocation: roller skating. Home: 1560 Saltair St Apt 201 Los Angeles CA 90025 Office: Marshal Plan Inc 3231 Ocean Park Blvd Suite 208 Santa Monica CA 90405

LAY, RUTH RYNER, tennis professional; b. Vienna, Ga., Dec. 26, 1925; d. James Buford and Ruth (Lewis) Ryner; m. Joseph Ewell Lay, Sept. 13, 1947; 1 dau., Ruth Lewis. B.A., Agnes Scott Coll. 1946. Profl., mgr. Cumberland Tennis Club, Atlanta, 1968-71; asst. mgr. Tennis Lady, Inc., Atlanta, 1972-76; profl. coach, 1976-84; profl. WCT/Peachtree World of Tennis, Norcross, Ga., 1985—. Recipient Touchstone trophy So. Tennis Assn., 1966; Nat. Service bowl U.S. Tennis Assn., 1971; Jacobs bowl So. Tennis Assn., 1978; named to So. Tennis Hall of Fame, 1982. Mem. U.S. Tennis Assn. (chmn. Jr. Wightman Fedn. Cup 1975-84), Atlanta Profl. Tennis Assn., So. Tennis Assn. (officer 1965-78). Democrat. Presbyterian. Avocations: fishing. Home: 3755 Grand Forest Dr Norcross GA 30092 Office: WCT/Peachtree World of Tennis 6200 Peachtree Corners W Norcross GA 30092

LAYCOCK, DEANE CLARK, banker; b. Lutherville, Md., Apr. 23, 1921; d. Robert Otto and Sadie (Robinson) Clark; student Balt. Coll. Commerce, 1937-38; m. Zane B. Laycock, Dec. 6, 1952. With Fiduciary Trust Co., Boston, 1962-68, 74—, trust officer, 1974—, v.p., 1981—; exec. asst. to pres. Yale U., 1969-74; asst. treas. Radcliffe Coll., 1975-83. First v.p., chmn. fin. com. Boston YWCA, 1976-79, bd. dirs., 1976-79; exec. com., chmn. planning and evaluation com., trustee United Community Planning Corp., Boston, 1977-83, asst. treas., 1981-82, dir., v.p fin., 1981-82; bd. dirs. Mass. chpt. Arthritis Found., 1981-83; bd. dirs., mem. council, chmn. research com. YMCA of U.S.A., 1981—, v.p. council, 1984—, vice chmn. bd. dirs., 1984—. Mem. Nat. Alliance Profl. and Exec. Women's Networks (founding mem., bd. dirs. 1980—, pres. 1980-83), Boston Luncheon Club Bus. and Profl. Women (founder, pres. 1975-80, exec. com. 1975—), Clubs: Harvard, Federal (Boston). Office: 175 Federal St Boston MA 02105

LAYMAN, LISA MILLER, lawyer; b. Jacksonville, Fla., Nov. 10, 1957; d. William Preston and Ann Elizabeth (Sessions) Miller; m. David Michael Layman, July 3, 1982. B.A. with high honors, U. Fla., Gainesville, 1979, J.D. with honors, 1981. Bar: Fla. 1982, U.S. Dist. Ct. (mid. and so. dists.) Fla., 1983. Assoc. Holland & Knight, Ft. Lauderdale, Fla., 1981-82, Barnett & Alagia, Palm Beach, Fla., 1982-83, Wien, Malkin & Bettex, Palm Beach, 1983—. Bd. dirs. Epilepsy Assn. of the Palm Beaches, 1984; asst. campaign coordinator Marcia Beach Campaign for County Commn., Broward County, 1982; hosp. lay visitor Bethesda-by-the Sea Episcopal Ch., Palm Beach, 1983; Alumni adv. com. Fla. Blue Key, U. Fla., 1983. Mem. Fla. Bar Assn. (Young Lawyers guest activities chmn. conf. 1983-84), Palm Beach County Young Lawyers (asst. chmn. law week 1983-84), Order of Coif, Phi Beta Kappa (v.p. U. Fla. 1979-80), Kappa Kappa Gamma (pres. U. Fla. chpt. 1978-79). Democrat. Episcopalian. Home: 9334 Long Meadow Circle Boynton Beach FL 33436 Office: Wien Malkin & Bettex 306 Royal Poinciana Plaza Palm Beach FL 33480

LAYMAN, MARY LUCIA, pharmaceutical company personnel executive, consultant; b. Flint, Mich., Nov. 10, 1937; d. Oscar Harold and Edith Lorraine (Smith) L. R.N. diploma Hurley Hosp. Sch. Nursing, Flint, 1958; B.S., Central Mich. U., 1961; cert. pub. health nursing U. Calif.-Berkeley, 1970; M.S., San Jose State U., 1972. Head nurse Project Hope, Guayaguil, Ecuador, 1962-63; instr. nursing San Jose Hosp. Sch. Nursing, Calif., 1964-68; pub. health nurse Santa Clara County Health Dept., Calif., 1968-71, supr. pub. health nursing, 1971-76; v.p., founding ptnr. Incentive Mgmt. Assocs., Palo Alto, Calif., 1976-81; mgr. human resources devel. Syntex Corp., Palo Alto, 1981—; cons. Am. Electronics Assn., Palo Alto, 1976-81. Asst. Werner Erhard Assocs., 1974-82; active Hunger Project, San Francisco, 1977—. Mem. LWV, NOW (Calif. rep. 1967-70). Democrat. Episcopalian. Avocation: travel. Office: Syntex Corp 3401 Hillview Ave Palo Alto CA 94304

LAYNE, LISA ANNE, accountant; b. Winston-Salem, N.C., Oct. 28, 1957; d. Allan Roy and Irene (Friedman) Coe; m. Douglas I. Layne, Dec. 26, 1981. B.S. in Bus. Adminstrn., U. Fla., 1979; M.Taxation, Fla. Internat. U., 1984. C.P.A., Fla. Supr. acctg. and auditing function splty.-rate regulated industries Rachlin & Cohen, C.P.A.s, Coral Gables, Fla., 1979—. Fund raiser, treas. Mary Beth Weiss Med. Clin. for Retarded, Miami. Mem. Am. Inst. C.P.A.s, Fla. Inst. C.P.A.s, Am. Legion Aux. Democrat. Jewish. Office: Rachlin & Cohen CPAs 1320 S Dixie Hwy PH Coral Gables FL 33146

LAYTON, BRENDA SMITH, medical laboratory technician; b. Spartanburg, S.C., June 1, 1941; d. Robert Paul and Agnes A. (White) Smith; M.T., Spartanburg Gen. Hosp., 1960; student U. S.C., 1973-74; cert. med. asst.; m. Eugene Layton, June 8, 1963; 1 son, Clarence Eugene. Med. lab. technician Spartanburg (S.C.) Gen. Hosp., 1960-64, Dr. Otis M. Hill, Enoree, S.C., 1964-65, Dr. Otis Hill, Dr. Thomas Jenkins, Dr. Samuel H. Rankin, Laurens, S.C., 1965—. Pres. Cross Anchor Grade Sch. PTA, 1973-75; bd. dirs. Laurens Christian Women's Club, 1980-81. Mem. Am. Soc. Clin. Pathologists, Am. Assn. Med. Assts. Democrat. Baptist. Club: Homemakers. Address: Route 2 Enoree SC 29335

LAYTON, KATHLEEN MARGARET, computer company marketing executive, consultant; b. St. Louis, Dec. 20, 1947; d. Paul Thomas and Margaret (Boultinghouse) Dunn; m. Jon J. Layton, July 26, 1968 (div. July 1979); children—J. Thomas, Jennifer M. B.S. in Math., S.E. Mo. U., 1971; M.B.A., Washington U., St. Louis, 1986. Pricing analyst Vico Corp., St. Louis, 1976-78; mgr. fin. analysis LLC Corp., Clayton, Mo., 1978-80; tech. cons. Control Data Corp., St. Louis, 1980-81, account mgr., 1981-82, region mgr., 1982-85, dir. mktg.-emerging markets, 1986—; speaker to women in bus., 1980-85. Com. chmn. Ethical Soc., Clayton, 1978—; v.p., treas. Francis Howell Sch. Dist., St. Charles, 1982-84; bd. dirs., publicity chmn. RIII Baseball Assn., St. Charles, 1983-84. Curator's scholar Southwest Mo. U., Cape Girardeau, 1967; Control Data Corp. scholar Washington U., 1984-86. Mem. Nat. Assn. Female Execs., NOW (polit. action com.), Am. Ethical Union (rep.). Avocations: racquetball; hiking; canoeing; reading. Home: 3 La Baron Ct Saint Charles MO 63303 Office: Control Data Corp 425 N New Ballas Rd Saint Louis MO 63141

LAYTON, MARION GRACE, nurse; b. Evergreen Park, Ill., Aug. 10, 1948; d. Walter Marion Joseph and Shirley Grace (Solberg) Zawislak; m. Warren Anthony Layton, Oct. 13, 1973; children—Eric Anthony, Joseph Patrick. R.N., Presbyn. St. Lukes, 1968; B.S.N., Fla. Internat. U., 1974. Staff nurse South Miami Hosp., Miami, Fla. 1979-80; team leader oncology Kuakini Med. ctr., Honolulu, 1980-83; nurse Med. Personnel Pool, Evergreen Park, Ill., 1983; staff nurse oncology Sparks Family Hosp., Nev., 1984; asst. dir. Peace Meml. Home, Evergreen Park, 1984—, also mem. home health care com. Mem. Nat. Assn. Female Execs., Nat. Assn. Registered Nurses, Regional Area Nursing Home reps. for Infection Control. Mem. United Ch. Christ. Avocations: Tennis; needlecrafts. Home: 9956 S Trumbull St Evergreen Park IL 60642 Office: Peace Meml Home 10124 S Kedzie Evergreen Park IL 60642

LAZANSKY, ELENORE MAY, psychologist; b. Manila, May 1, 1909 (parents Am. citizens); d. Milton William and Carrie May (Ward) L.; A.B., U. Calif., Berkeley, 1931, M.A., 1932; postgrad. in ednl. psychology. Tchr. math., counselor, testing chmn. Oakland (Calif.) Public Schs., 1935-74, organizer, evaluator gifted program, 1957-61; instr. Merritt City Coll., Oakland, 1956-57, 61-62; head dept. math. Castlemont High Sch., Oakland, 1968-69; tchr. U. Calif. summer demonstration secondary sch., 1943, 44, 51; pvt. practice ednl. psychology, Lafayette, Calif., 1975—; adviser, dir., treas. Calif. Scholarship Fedn., 1967-74; curriculum cons. NSF fellow, 1963-65. Fellow AAAS; mem. Nat. Council Tchrs. Math. (past dir.), Am. Ednl. Research Assn., Calif., Contra Costa (sec.-treas. 1976-77) psychol. assns., NEA, Calif. Tchrs. Assn., Phi Beta Kappa, Sigma Xi, Pi Lambda Theta, Pi Mu Epsilon, Mt. Diablo Iris Soc. Republican. Presbyterian. Club: San Francisco Bay West Highland White Terriers. Author articles, reports, curriculum materials.

LAZAR, LOIS ANN, publisher, advertising agency executive; b. Bklyn., July 16, 1929; d. Bertram R. and Lillian (Goodman) Levy; m. Jack J. Lazar, June 4, 1950 (div. 1978); children—Richard, William; m. Oscar Weissman, Nov. 27, 1982. B.A. in Psychology, Syracuse U., 1950; postgrad. CCNY, 1950. Lic. real estate broker. Tchr. North Merrick Elem. Sch., N.Y., 1950-51; v.p. sales L.I. Comml. Rev., Plainview, N.Y., 1963-69; pub. LL & IL Pub., Inc., Manhasset, N.Y., 1969—; officer LL & IL Advt., Manhasset, 1969—. Pub. The Real Estate Guide, The Real Estate Newsletter, other directories. Pres. Sisterhood Merrick Jewish Ctr., 1959; bd. dirs. Univ. Gardens Home Owners Assn., Great Neck, N.Y., 1985. Republican. Jewish. Avocations: tennis; swimming; bridge. Office: LL & IL Pub Co Inc 1615 Northern Blvd Manhasset NY 11030

LAZAR, MARDA GOLDFINE, cosmetics company executive; b. Chgo., Jan. 12, 1956; d. Judd Arnold and Audree (Lazarus) Goldfine; m. Andrew P. Lazar, Apr. 18, 1982; 1 child, Michael Goldfine. B.F.A., Ariz. State U., 1977; student U. Iowa, 1973-75, Hispanic Inst., Burgos, Spain, 1975. Lic., real estate, Ill. Cosmetic, indsl., corp. designer Frederick Vallarta & Assocs., Chgo., 1978; toy, indsl., package designer Playskool, Inc., Chgo., 1978-79; space utilization analyst Baxter Travenol Labs., Inc., Deerfield, Ill., 1979-82, exec. staff asst. to dir., 1982-83; pres. DermaLab Ltd., Bensenville, Ill., 1983—, also dir. chmn. publicity Crusade of Mercy, Baxter Travenol, 1982; womens bd. dirs. Lambs Farm, Libertyville, 1982—. Mem. Ind. Cosmetic Mfrs. Assn., Jewish. Club: Northmoor Country. Lodge: B'nai B'rith. Avocations: Running; travel; gourmet cooking; golf; art. Office: DermaLab Ltd 400 Country Club Dr Bensenville IL 60106

LAZAR, NANCY PADGETT, law librarian; b. Newberry, S.C., June 3, 1932; d. Price J. and Caroline (Weeks) P.; B.S., Northwestern U., 1953; M.L.S., U. Md., 1972; J.D., Georgetown U., 1977; m. David Lazar, Aug. 6, 1953. Bar: D.C. 1977. Asst. librarian U.S. Ct. Appeals for D.C. Circuit, Washington, 1972-74, supervisory librarian, 1974-81, circuit. librarian, 1981—. Mem. D.C. Bar Assn., Am. Assn. Law Libraries, D.C. Law Librarians Soc., Am. Library Assn., D.C. Library Assn., Spl. Library Assn. Home: 5301 Duvall Dr Bethesda MD 20816 Office: United States Court House Washington DC 20001

LAZAROVIC, KAREN, financial columnist; b. Bklyn., June 30, 1947; d. Alex and Lillian (Kurlanchik) Schwartzberg; children—Laura, Michael. B.A. cum laude, Bklyn. Coll., 1968. Proofreader Consumers Handbook, Great Neck, N.Y., 1975-77; sports dept. asst. N.Y. Post, N.Y.C., 1977-78, fin. dept. asst., 1978-79, reporter fin., 1979-84, columnist fin., 1984—; editor, pub. Wall St. Monitor newsletter, 1983—. Poetry pub. various jours. Avocations: tennis; photography.

LAZARUS, CAROL NUNES, clinical psychologist; b. Bethlehem, Pa., Oct. 27, 1929; d. Lee and Louise Adler (Comens) Nunes; A.B., U. Pitts., 1950, M.S., 1951; M.A., Adelphi U., 1975, Ph.D., 1978; postdoctoral diploma in psychotherapy and psychoanalysis; m. Harold Lazarus, June 22, 1952; children—Mark, Eric. Social work asst. L.I. Jewish-Hillside Med. Center, 1973; instr., lectr. Hofstra U., 1955-65; psychologist, program supr. S.E. Nassau Guidance Center, 1977—; adj. prof. psychology Fla. Inst. Tech., 1980-83. U. Pitts. scholar, 1950-51. Mem. Am. Psychol. Assn., Nassau County Psychol. Assn., ACLU, Adelphi Soc. Psychoanalysis and Psychotherapy, LWV (v.p. human resources Nassau County 1970-72; pres. Hempstead Central 1968-70). Home: 225 Wellington Rd Garden City NY 11530 Office: SE Nassau Guidance Counseling Center 3375 Park Ave Wantagh NY 11793

LAZO, JACQUI FISKE, lawyer; b. Balt., Apr. 4, 1951; d. Guy W. and E. Jacqueline (Strachan) Fiske; m. John Stephen Lazo, Oct. 12, 1974; 1 dau., Jacquelyn Kristina. Student Mills Coll., 1969-71; B.A. with honors, Goucher Coll., 1973; J.D. with honors, U. Conn., 1978. Bar: Conn. 1978. Assoc., Sohcot & Jacks, East Haven, Conn., 1978-81; ptnr. Gallant, Mednick & Gallant, New Haven, 1982-83, Tirola, Herring, Pober & Lazo, Westport, Conn., 1984—. Sec., dir. Guilford Nursing and Homemaker Services, 1980-85; vice chmn. Guilford Zoning Bd. Appeals, 1982-85. Mem. ABA, Conn. Bar Assn. (exec. com. real property sect.), Phi Beta Kappa. Home: 8 St Ronan Terr New Haven CT 06511 Office: Tirola Herring Pober & Lazo 1221 Post Rd E Westport CT 06880

LE, JACKIE HADO, nurse; b. Hanoi, North Vietnam, Aug. 7, 1953; came to U.S., 1975, naturalized, 1982; d. Hung Viet and An (Phung) Do; m. Hoan Vu Le, June 10, 1978. Student Dalat U., South Vietnam, 1972-75; B.S. in Nursing, U. Iowa, 1982. Mgr., Mini Thuongxa, Chgo., 1983-84; nurse Northwest Hosp., Chgo., 1982-83, Med. Relief Services, Chgo., 1984—, Children's Meml. Hosp., Chgo., 1985—; cons. Vietnamese Student Assn., Iowa City, 1982—. Vol., ARC, Guram, 1975, YMCA, Fort Chaffee, Ark., 1975. Asian Social Inst. scholar, 1985. Mem. U. Iowa Alumni Assn. Roman Catholic. Club: Women's Work Out. Avocations: music; exercise; reading; knitting; writing. Home: 2616 N 73d Ct Elmwood Park IL 60635

LEAB, KATHARINE KYES, publisher; b. Cleve., Mar. 17, 1941; d. Rogers Martin and Helen Gilmore (Jacoby) Kyes; m. Daniel J. Leab, Aug. 17, 1964; children—Abigail, Constance, Marcus. B.A., Smith Coll., 1962; postgrad. Columbia U., 1963-64. Sr. editor Columbia U. Press, 1966-72; editor/pub. Am. Book Prices Current, 1972—; creator, mgr. BAMBAM(Bookline Alert: Missing Books and Manuscripts), UTOPIA. Author: (with husband) The Auction Companion, 1981; contbr. articles to profl. jours., anthologies. Trustee Washington Montessori Sch., 1984—. Mem. ALA (security com. Rare Books and Manuscripts sect.). Club: Cosmopolitan. Office: Bancroft Parkman Inc Titus Rd PO Box 236 Washington CT 06793

LEACHMAN, CLORIS, actress; b. Des Moines, ed. Northwestern U.; m. George England, 1953 (div. 1979); 5 children. Motion picture appearances include Kiss Me Deadly, The Rack, Butch Cassidy and the Sundance Kid, The Last Picture Show, W.U.S.A., Dillinger, Daisy Miller, Young Frankenstein, 1974, Crazy Mama, High Anxiety, 1977, The North Avenue Irregulars, 1979, Scavenger Hunt, 1979, Herbie Goes Bananas, History of the World, Part I, 1981; plays include Sundown Beach, Story For a Sunday Evening, 1950, Come Back Little Sheba, As You Like It. TV appearances include Lassie, 1957, Route 66, Laramie, Trials of O'Brien, Mary Tyler Moore Show, Phyllis, 1975-77; appeared in TV movie Brand New Life, The Migrants, Death Scream, 1975, A Girl Named Sooner, 1975, Ladies of the Corridor 1975. The New Original Wonder Woman, 1975, The Love Boat 1976, The Woman Who Willed a Miracle, Am. Beauty, Love is Never Silent, 1985. Recipient Oscar award as best supporting actress in The Last Picture Show, Nat. Acad. Motion Picture Arts and Scis., 1971; 6 Emmy awards for Mary Tyler Moore Show and others. Address: care McCartt Oreck Barrett 9200 Sunset Blvd Suite 1009 Los Angeles CA 90069

LEAF, MARILYN GROSSMAN, clinical social worker; b. Detroit, Jan. 7, 1942; d. Sol C. and Pauline (Fried) Grossman; B.A., U. Mich., 1963; M.A., U. Chgo., 1965; div.; children—Matthew Aaron, Jeffrey Adam. Clin. social worker Psychiat. and Psychosomatic Inst., Michael Reese Hosp., Chgo., 1965-66, 67-68; clin. social worker, med. student preceptor Stanford U. Med. Center, Palo Alto, Calif., 1966-67; psychotherapist med. student supr. La Rabida Children's Hosp., Chgo., 1969-71; pvt. practice psychotherapy, Chgo., 1971-73; cons. Ancoma Montessori Sch., Chgo., 1971-72; asst. tchrs. profl. vol. Thalians Community Mental Health Center, Cheerful Helpers Nursery Sch.; Los Angeles, 1977-78; clin. social worker, program coordinator Northridge (Calif.) Hosp. Med. Clinic, 1978—; pvt. practice psychotherapy, Woodland Hills, Calif., 1978—; Mem. Community Relations Com., San Fernando Valley Region, Jewish Fedn. Council Greater Los Angeles, 1981-84. NIMH grantee, 1964-65. Fellow Nat. Assn. Social Workers; mem. Acad. Cert. Social Workers, Calif. Lic. Clin. Social Workers, Nat. Registry Health Care Providers, Soc. Clin. Social Work, Nat. Hospice Orgn., Hospice Orgn. of So. Calif.

LEAHY, JEANNETTE (JEANNETTE OLIVER LEAHY TINEN KAEHLER), actress; b. Eau Claire, Wis., Sept. 9, 1927; d. Kenneth A. and Berthe Hortence (Borie) Oliver; student various acting workshops; m. Thomas J. Leahy (dec.); children—Denyse Leahy Karsten Feeney, Thomas J.; m. William J. Tinen, June 15, 1969 (dec.); m. 3d, Wallace W. Kaehler, Jan. 13, 1980. TV personality Jeannette Lee, Sta. WFBM-TV, Indpls., 1950-53; actress Peninsular Players, summer stock theatre, Door County, Wis., 1960—, also radio, TV, stage, film, commls. Vice-pres., Evanston Drama Club, 1961-62; dir. Wilmette Children's Theatre, 1960-65; bd. dirs. Easter Seal Soc., 1970-75. Mem. Actors Equity Union, SAG, AFTRA, Chgo. Unlimited. Republican. Roman Catholic. Clubs: North Shore Country, Michigan Shores, Wilmette-Kenilworth (pres. 1956-57), North Shore Assos. (pres. 1982-83).

LEAHY, MARJORIE ANNE, communications firm executive; b. Jackson, Tenn., Aug. 31, 1938; d. John and Marjorie Elizabeth (Aylor) Solinsky; m. Edward James Leahy, July 2, 1960; children—James Peter, Laura Marjorie, John Edward. B.S., Syracuse U., 1960. Reporter, TV editor Rome Sentinel (N.Y.), 1961-62; free-lance writer, Croton, N.Y., 1967-78; editor Clearwater, Inc., Poughkeepsie, N.Y., 1974-76; reporter news, features Gannett Westchester, Tarrytown, N.Y., 1978-81; pres. Five String Prodns., Croton, 1981—; cons. publs. Revlon Health Care Group, Tuckahoe, N.Y., 1981—, Am. Brands, Inc., N.Y.C., 1986—. Mem. Croton Conservation Adv. Council, 1978-86; coordinator Clearwater Hudson River Festival, Croton, N.Y., 1978-86; bd. dirs. Clearwater Inc., 1984-86, exec. com., 1985-86. Mem. Women in Communications (chairperson publicity 1982-83, v.p. 1983-84). Home and Office: 62 Van Wyck St Croton-on-Hudson NY 10520

LEAHY, MARY SHEEHAN, rare book librarian, book collection administrator; b. Phila.; d. John J. and Mary Helena (Adams) Sheehan; m. John J. Leahy, June 7, 1958; 1 son, John Mark. B.A., Immaculata Coll., 1954; M.A. in Econ. Theory, Bryn Mawr Coll., 1955, M.A. in History of Art, 1983; postgrad. U. Pa. Wharton Sch., 1955, Villanova U Sch. Library Sci., 1972-73. Librarian Bryn Mawr Coll. (Pa.), head rare book collection, 1971—; dir. activities Friends of Bryn Mawr Coll. Library; speaker Nat. Pre-Conf., ALA, 1982. Participant in publ.: Bookbinding in America: 1680-1910, 1983; dir. rare book room exhbns. Bryn Mawr Coll., the most recent being: Signs, Symbols & Emblems, 1982; Bookbinding in America, 1983; author: Susan Macdowell Eakins and The Adelman Family, 1985. Bryn Mawr Coll. scholar, 1954. Mem. ALA. Clubs: Philobiblon, Hroswitha, Grolier. Home: 425 Caversham Rd Bryn Mawr PA 19010 Office: Mariam Coffin Canaday Library Bryn Mawr Coll Bryn Mawr PA 19010

LEAK, MARGARET ELIZABETH (PEGGY), personnel exec.; b. Atlanta, Sept. 9, 1946; d. William Whitehurst and Margaret Elizabeth (Whitsitt) L.; B.S. in Psychology, Okla. State U., 1968; postgrad. U. Okla., 1960-69, Cornell U., 1976-78; grad. Advanced Mgmt. Program, Harvard Bus. Sch., 1983. Editor, Communications, Eastern State Bankcard Assn., N.Y.C., 1969-71; sr. edn. specialist Citibank, N.Y.C., 1971-73; adminstr. orgn. devel. NBC, N.Y.C., 1973-74; mgr. tng. and devel. Atlantic Cos., N.Y.C., 1974-76, sec. human resources, 1976-78, v.p. human resources, 1978-84, v.p. human resources, corp. communications, 1984—. Mem. adv. bd., grad. mgmt. program for women Pace U., 1976-78. Mem. Am. Soc. Personnel Adminstrn., 1984—, Ins. Co. Edn. Dirs. Soc. (nat. v.p. 1978), Gamma Phi Beta. Presbyterian. Office: Atlantic Cos 45 Wall St New York NY 10005

LEAR, PAMELA KAYE, occupational health nurse practitioner; b. Greenville, Ky., Apr. 29, 1953; d. Hansen and Maedoll (Vincent) Knight; m. Ronnie Douglas Lear, Feb. 14, 1975. A.D. in Nursing, Madisonville Community Coll., 1973; B.S. in Nursing, U. Evansville, 1980; M.S. in Nursing, U. Ky., Lexington, 1983. Staff nurse Muhlenberg Community Hosp., Greenville, Ky., 1973-75; charge nurse intensive coronary care, 1977-79, nursing supr., 1975-77, emergency room charge nurse, 1980-82, nurse practitioner, unit coordinator, health assessment coordinator, 1984; preceptor Ky. Wesleyan Coll., 1984; occupational nurse practitioner TVA, 1984—. Contbr. articles to publs. Edn. scholar U. Ky., 1971-73; U. Evansville Alumni Assn. grantee, 1979-80; ednl. non-service trainee U. Ky., 1983. Mem. Bluegrass Advanced R.N. Practitioners, Am. Nurses Assn. (cert. family nurse practitioner), Ky. Nurses Assn. Democrat. Missionary Baptist. Home: Route 1 Greenville KY 42345 Office: TVA Paradise Health Sta #1 Drakesboro KY 42337

LEARMAN, JEANNE, nurse anesthetist; b. Detroit, July 9, 1944; d. James Claire and Mary Loretta (Ryan) Buckley; m. Joseph S. Learman, Apr. 20, 1968; children—Stan, Steve, Audrey. B.A., Ottawa U., Kansas City, 1978; diploma Mt. Carmel Mercy Hosp. Sch. Nurse Anesthesiology, Detroit, 1967, St. Marys Hosp. Sch. Nursing, Saginaw, 1965. R.N., Mich. Staff anesthetist Mt. Carmel Mercy Hosp., Detroit, 1967-69; pvt. contractor anesthesia services, Mich., 1971-76; coordinator anesthesiology services Saline Hosp., Mich., 1974—; prs. Saline Anesthesia Assocs., 1980—; assoc. dir. Northwest Anesthesia Seminars, Pasco, Wash., 1982—. Bd. dirs. United Way Saline, 1979-82, pres., 1980, campaign chmn., 1982. Mem. Mich. Assn. Nurse Anesthetists (bd. dirs. 1985—), Am. Assn. Nurse Anesthetists, Mich. Heart Assn. instr. CPR, ARC, 1980—. Avocations: Running; golf; tennis. Home: 4475 Waterworks St Saline MI 48176 Office: Saline Community Hosp 400 W Russell St Saline MI 48176

LEARY, EILEEN ANNE, marketing executive; b. Buffalo, Dec. 9, 1955; d. Albert Frederick and Gertrude Grace (Shreenan) L. A.A.S. in Radiologic Tech., Trocaire Coll., 1975; B.S. in Bus. Mgmt., SUNY-Buffalo, 1984. Chief radiologic technologist Buffalo Children's Hosp., 1981-85; mktg. exec. Elma Nuclear Corp., Buffalo, 1985—; instr., rep. aerobics Shiela's Aerobic Jazz, Williamsville, N.Y., 1983—; assoc. clin. instr. Trocaire Coll., Buffalo, 1983—. Mem. South Buffalo Democratic Assn., 1980—. Mem. Niagara Frontier Soc. Radiologic Technologists. Roman Catholic. Club: Checkers Athletic (capt. women's racing team 1984—, v.p. 1985—). Avocations: running; interior design; real estate. Home: 60 Shepard Kenmore NY 14217 Office: Elma Nuclear Corp Buffalo NY 14215

LEARY, KATHLEEN ANN, lawyer; b. New Bedford, Mass., July 6, 1954; d. Arthur Vincent and Louise Anita (Clark) L.; m. Urs Felix Nager, Jr., June 31, 1980. B.A. in Psychology summa cum laude, Boston Coll., 1976, J.D. cum laude, 1979. Admitted to Conn. bar, 1979, U.S. dist. ct. Conn., 1980. Investigator, State of Conn. Pub. Defenders Office, Bridgeport, summer 1977; summer assoc. firm Cummings & Lockwood, Stamford, Conn., 1978, assoc., Danbury, Conn., 1979—. Mem. rev. com. Mgmt. Assistance Program, Vol. Bur. of Danbury, 1984. Named One of 13 Leading Women in Danbury, Fairfield County Women Newspaper, 1983. Mem. ABA, Conn. Bar Assn. (workers compensation subcom., young lawyers labor and employment sect.), Danbury Bar Assn., Phi Beta Kappa. Democrat. Roman Catholic. Clubs: Quota Club Internat. (pres. Danbury 1983-84), Danbury Area Women's Network (chmn. Danbury 1983-84). Office: Cummings & Lockwood 30 Main St Danbury CT 06810

LEARY, MARY ELLEN, personnel executive; b. Mpls., Nov. 23, 1951; d. David Edmond and Gail Margaret (Walbom) Terry; B.A., Coll. of St. Catherine, 1973. Personnel dir. Marsh & McLennan, Mpls., 1977—, now asst. v.p.; personnel adminstr. Travelers Express Co., Inc., Mpls., 1973-77; workshop facilitator. Active, United Way of Mpls., 1980—. Accredited personnel mgr. Personnel Accreditation Inst., 1980. Mem. Am. Mgmt. Assn., Am. Soc. Personnel Adminstrn., Internat. Assn. Personnel Women (pres. 1981-82), Twin Cities Personnel Assn. (chmn. 1981-83, v.p. adminstrn. 1983, pres. 1984), Speakers Bur. Roman Catholic. Clubs: Blaisdell Women's, Greenway Athletic. Home: 420 Johnson Pkwy Saint Paul MN 55106 Office: 1500 Northstar Center Minneapolis MN 55402

LEASE, JANE ETTA, librarian; b. Kansas City, Kans., Apr. 10, 1924; d. Joy Alva and Emma (Jaggard) Omer; B.S. in Home Econs., U. Ariz., 1957; M.S. in Edn., Ind. U., 1962; M.S. in L.S., U. Denver, 1967; m. Richard J. Lease, Jan. 16, 1960; children—Janet (Mrs. Jacky B. Radifera), Joyce (Mrs. Robert J. Carson), Julia (Mrs. Earle D. Marvin), Cathy (Mrs. Edward F. Warren); stepchildren—Richard Jay II, William Harley. Newspaper reporter Ariz. Daily Star, Tucson, 1937-39; asst. home agt. Dept. Agr., 1957; homemaking tchr., Ft. Huachuca, Ariz., 1957-60; head tchr. Stonebelt Council Retarded Children, Bloomington, Ind., 1960-61; reference clk. Ariz. State U. Library, 1964-66; edn. and psychology librarian N.Mex. State U., 1967-71; Amway distbr., 1973—; cons. solid wastes, distressed land problems reference remedies, 1967; ecology lit. research and cons., 1966—. Ind. observer 1st World Conf. Human Environment, 1972; mem. Las Cruces Community Devel. Priorities Adv. Bd. Mem. ALA, Regional Environ. Edn. Research Info. Orgn., Nat. Assn. Female Execs., P.E.O., D.A.R., Internat. Platform Assn., Las Cruces Antique Car Club, Las Cruces Story League, N.Mex. Library Assn. Methodist (lay leader). Address: 2145 Boise Dr Las Cruces NM 88001

LEASURE, JUNE N. RUFF, educational administrator; b. Steubenville, Ohio, Dec. 25, 1951; d. Flavil Leon and Elizabeth Mary (Hopkins) Ruff; m. Charles William Leasure, June 19, 1976. B.S. in Elementary Edn., U. Steubenville, 1974; M.S. in Edn., U. Dayton, 1983. Tchr., East Liverpool Christian Sch., Ohio, 1974-77, adminstr., 1983—; adminstr., tchr. Jefferson County Christian Sch., Steubenville, Ohio, 1977-83, founder, developer, 1977. Choral dir. Tri-State Youth for Christ, Toronto, Ohio, 1973-74; counselor Christian Youth Ctr., Steubenville, 1973-76, bd. dirs., 1973-76. Recipient Service award Jefferson County Christian Sch., Steubenville, 1983. Mem. Nat. Fellowship Christian Sch. Adminstrs., Assn. Supervision and Curriculum Devel. Methodist. Avocations: singing gospel and contemporary Christian music; leading and teaching Bible study groups. Home: RD 1 Briar Hill Rd Steubenville OH 43952 Office: E Liverpool Christian Sch 46682 Florence St East Liverpool OH 43920

LEATHERWOOD, BETTY JEANE, newspaper executive; b. LeFlore, Okla., June 30, 1944; d. Thomas Fred and Opal W. (Wagner) Kitchens; m. Ronald Gray, Feb. 9, 1963 (div.); children—Lee, Karl; m. 2d, James Leatherwood, Feb. 12, 1981. Assoc. Real Estate, San Jacinto Jr. Coll., 1980. Dist. mgr. Ark. Democrat, Little Rock, 1976-78; mgr. Beaumont Enterprise (Tex.), 1978-83; circulation supr. USA Today, Houston, 1983-84, circulation mgr., 1984—. Named Mgr. of Yr., Beaumont Enterprise, 1978, Ark. Democrat, 1977. Mem. Am. Bus. Women's Assn. (membership, entertainment, fundraising coms. Beaumont 1978-81), Phi Theta Kappa. Office: USA Today 6001 South Loop E Houston TX 77033

LEAVELL, ALMA MALONE, emeritus dean; b. Clay County, Ala., Nov. 15, 1916; d. William Robert and Alice Swillie (Reagan) Ingram; B.S., Jacksonville State U., 1938; M.Ed., Hardin-Simmons U., 1950; Ed.D., George Peabody Coll., 1965; m. Clifton James Malone, May 7, 1941 (dec. 1959); m. 2d, James Berry Leavell, Dec. 22, 1972; children—Mary Carolyn Williams, Judith Anne Finch. Tchr. pub. schs., Clay County, Ala., 1934-41, Abilene, Tex., 1955-60; tchr. pub. edn. Hardin-Simmons U., Abilene, 1961-65; asst. prof. edn. Houston Baptist U., 1965-79, Disting. prof. edn., 1979-84, chmn. dept. edn., 1973-84, dean Coll. Edn. and Behavioral Studies, 1980-84, dean emeritus, 1984—; cons. lang. arts Houston Area Schs. Recipient Ted Booker Outstanding Tex. Educator award, 1983; Outstanding Educator award Religious Heritage of Am., 1983; endowed acad. scholarship established in her honor Houston Bapt. U., 1984. Mem. Am. Assn. Colls. Tchrs. Edn., Tex. Assn. Tchr. Educators, Tex. Assn. Coll. Tchrs. of Edn., Internat. Reading Assn., Delta Kappa Gamma, Kappa Delta Pi. Democrat. Baptist. Home: 8112 Fondren Houston TX 77074 Office: 7502 Fondren Houston TX 77074

LEAVITT, AUDREY FAYE COX, TV programming executive; b. Old Hickory, Tenn., June 1, 1932; d. James Aubrey and Bernice (Hudnall) Cox; student David Lipscomb Secondary Sch. and Coll., 1947, Tenn. Sch. Broadcasting, 1949-50, Vanderbilt U., 1948-50; children—Jack, Teresa. Woman commentator, continuity chief radio sta. WGNS, Murfreesboro, Tenn., 1949-50; announcer, continuity chief, traffic dir. Sta. KDWT, Stamford, Tex., 1950-51; sales account exec. Sta. KMAC, San Antonio, 1952; continuity chief, announcer Sta. KEYL-TV, San Antonio, 1952-54, also firm dir.; film buyer, mgr. Sta. WOAI-TV, San Antonio, 1954-68, ops. mgr. film, video-tape traffic, continuity, 1968-71; film and videotape operations mgr., film buyer Sta. KENS-TV, San Antonio, 1972-79; exec. v.p. Jim Thomas & Assos., San Antonio, 1979-80; owner Communique Internationalé, TV programming syndication, 1981—; co-owner P.R. Inc., public relations cons.; exec. producer TV series The Lone Star Sportsman Show; writer, exec. producer and dir. TV series Weather or Not; writer, producer gourmet cooking show For Men Only. Republican. Office: PO Box 6493 San Antonio TX 78209

LEAVITT, JOAN KAZANJIAN, state official; b. Boston, Jan. 14, 1926; d. Varaztad Hovannes and Marion V. (Hanford) Kazanjian; A.B., Radcliffe Coll., 1947; M.A., Smith Coll., 1949; M.D., Boston U., 1953; m. Don K. Leavitt. Intern in pediatrics Boston City Hosp., 1953-54, resident in pediatrics, 1954-55; resident in pediatrics Mass. Gen. Hosp., Boston, 1955-56, 57-58; pediatrician Comanche County (Okla.) Guidance Center, Lawton, 1959; pvt. practice medicine specializing in pediatrics, Altus, Okla., 1959-64; med. dir. Jackson County (Okla.) Health Dept., 1960-67, Kay County (Okla.) Health Dept., 1967-75, Kay County and Payne County Health Depts., 1975-76; chief maternal and child health service Okla. Health Dept., 1976, dep. commr. for personal health services, 1976-77, commr. health, 1977—; mem. numerous bds., commns., councils and coms. in field. Mem. AMA, Okla. State Med. Assn., Okla. Public Health Assn., Oklahoma County Med. Soc., Assn. State and Territorial Health Ofcls., Sigma Xi.

LEAVITT, JOYCE ELLEN SANFORD, nurse; b. Bangor, Maine, Dec. 13, 1959; d. George William and Hazel Inez (Moon) Sanford; m. Raymond Emil Leavitt, Aug. 20, 1983. Diploma in Nursing, Eastern Maine Med. Ctr. Sch. Nursing, 1982. Staff nurse Eastern Maine Med. Ctr., Bangor, 1982—. Mem. Nat. Assn. Orthopaedic Nurses, Maine State Nurses Assn. Avocations: embroidery; counted cross stitch; bicycling; cross country skiing. Home: 52 Eaton St Old Town ME 04468 Office: Eastern Maine Med Ctr 489 State St Bangor ME 04401

LEAVITT, JUDITH KLINE, nursing educator, consultant; b. Trenton, Feb. 28, 1942; d. Joseph Jay and Rose (Greenberg) Kline; m. Richard Marshall Leavitt, May 12, 1963; children—Noah, David. B.S. in Nursing, U. Pa., 1963; M.Ed., Columbia U., 1966. R.N., N.Y., N.J., Pa. Pediatric staff nurse Orange (N.J.) Meml. Hosp., 1964; staff nurse Operation Head Start, Newark, 1965; pub. health nurse, field instr. Children's Health Services, N.Y.C., 1966; asst. dir. admissions Community Coll., Phila., 1967, instr. nursing, 1967-68; prof. nursing Tomkins Cortland Community Coll., Dryden, N.Y., 1976—; mem. faculty Nursing Bds. Rev., N.Y.C., 1983—; reviewer manuscripts and books Wadsworth Press, Mosby, 1983. Organized and led interagency program for single mothers, 1970-73; organized 1st interdisciplinary course in women's health Tompkins Cortland Community Coll., 1979—; bd. dirs. Family Children's Service, Ithaca, N.Y., 1972-76, Planned Parenthood of Tompkins County, Ithaca, N.Y., 1975-77; coordinator Congl. Dist. 28 Nurses Coalition for Action in Politics, Am. Nurses Assn., Washington, 1982—; organizer, chmn. local polit. action com., N.Y. State Nurses Polit. Action Com., Ithaca, 1982—, sec., 1984. Invited to White House Conf. Outstanding Women, 1966; named Master Tchr. Nat. Conf. Teaching Excellence, 1984. Mem. Am. Nurses Assn. (congl. dist. coordinator), Nat. League Nursing, Kappa Delta Pi, Shinx and Key, Pi Lambda Theta. Home: 870 Highland Rd Ithaca NY 14850 Office: Tompkins Cortland Community Coll 170 North St Dryden NY 13053

LEAVITT, MARY JANICE DEIMEL, educator, civic worker; b. Washington, Aug. 21, 1924; d. Henry L. and Ruth (Grady) Deimel; B.A., Am. U., Washington, 1946; postgrad. U. Md., 1963-65, U. Va., 1965-67, 72-73, 78-79, George Washington U., 1966-67; m. Robert Walker Leavitt, Mar. 30, 1945; children—Michael Deimel, Robert Walker, Caroline Ann Leavitt Snyder. Tchr., Rothery Sch., Arlington, Va., 1947; dir. Sunnyside, Children's House, Washington, 1949; asst. dir. Coop. Sch. for Handicapped Children, Arlington, 1962, dir., Arlington, Springfield, Va., 1963-66; tchr. mentally retarded children Fairfax (Va.) County Pub. Schs., 1966-68; asst. dir. Burgundy Farm Country Day Sch., Alexandria, Va., 1968-69; tchr., substitute tchr. specific learning problem children Accotink Acad., Springfield, Va., 1970-80; substitute tchr. learning disabilities Children's Achievement Center, McLean, Va., 1973-82, Psychiat. Inst., Washington and Rockville, Md., 1976-82, Home-Bound and Substitute Program, Fairfax, Va., 1978-84; asst. info. specialist Ednl. Research Service, Inc., Rosslyn, Va., 1974-76; docent Sully Plantation, Fairfax County (Va.) Park Authority, 1981-86; sec. Widowed Persons Service, 1983-85, mem., 1985—. Mem. edn. subcom. Va. Commn. Children and Youth, 1973-74. Den mother Nat. Capital Area Cub Scouts, Boy Scouts Am., 1962; troop fund raising chmn. Nat. Capitol council Girl Scouts U.S.A., 1968-69; capt. amblyopia team No. Va. chpt. Delta Gamma Alumnae, 1969; vol. Prevention of Blindness, 1980—; fund raiser Martha Movement, 1977-78. Recipient award Nat. Assn. for Retarded Citizens, 1975. Mem. AAUW (co-chmn. met. area mass media com. D.C. chpt. 1973-75, v.p. Alexandria br. 1974-76, fellowship co-chmn. Springfield-Annandale br. 1979-80, name grantee ednl. found. 1980, historian 1980-82, cultural co-chmn. 1983-84), Assn. Part-Time Profls. (co-chmn. Va. local groups, job devel. and membership asst. 1981), Older Women's League, Smithsonian Resident Assoc. Program, Delta Gamma (treas. No. Va. alumnae chpt. 1973-75, pres. 1977-79, found. chmn. 1979-81). Roman Catholic. Club: Arlington Hall Officer's. Home: 7129 Rolling Forest Ave Springfield VA 22152

LEBEDA, KAY ELLEN, college administrator; b. Cedar Falls, Iowa, Nov. 15, 1945; d. Robert Earl and Katharine M. (Gallagher) Lamb; m. James William Lebeda, Jan. 11, 1969; children—Michael James, Sara Katherine. Student U. No. Iowa, 1963-65, U. Scranton, 1966, Kings Coll., 1967; B.S. in Bus. Adminstrn., Marywood Coll., Scranton, Pa., 1967. Bookkeeper, Standard Mfg. Co., Cedar Falls, Iowa, 1967-68; sec.-bookkeeper Real Estate, Inc., Ames, Iowa, 1970, Mgmt. Recruiters, Des Moines, 1971-73; asst. to dir. alumni affairs Simpson Coll., Indianola, Iowa, 1975-78, asst. dir. devel., 1978-79, dir. alumni affairs, 1979—. Editor Alumnus, 1979-85. Mem. Council for Advancement and Support of Edn. Roman Catholic. Clubs: Simpsonia (bd. dirs. 1982), Indianola Golf and Country Ladies Assn. (co-chmn. 1986). Avocations: golf; snow skiing; boating; gardening. Home: 807 N 8th St Indianola IA 50125 Office: Simpson Coll 701 North C St Indianola IA 50125

LEBEDA, MILDRED RUTH, hospital administrator; b. Sterling, Colo., Feb. 5, 1933; d. Frederick and Amalia Luft; student Northeastern Jr. Coll., U. No. Colo., St. Louis U., Colo. Women's Coll.; children—Valerie Jo Richards Hettinger, Renae Ruth Richards. Co-owner Fish's Profl. Pharmacy, Sterling, 1967-70: acct. Ceres Land & Cattle Co., Sterling, 1970-75; acct. Monfort of Colo., Greeley, 1975-77; adminstr. Meml. Hosp. of Greeley, 1977—, also bd. dirs. Trustee, No. Colo. Osteo. Hosp. Found.: active disaster com. City of Greeley. Mem. Am. Hosp. Assn., Am. Osteo. Hosp. Assn. (trustee 1981—, com. small and rural hosps. 1981—, pres. 1982, 83, 84), Colo. Hosp. Assn., Colo. Osteo. Hosp. Assn. (sec.-treas. 1980—), N. Central Colo. Hosp. Adminstrs. Council (pres. 1982), Larimer/Weld Counties Hosp. Planning Council, Colo. Small and Rural Hosp. Task Force, TONACK (Osteo.) Assn. (sec.-treas. 1982, v.p. 1983, pres. 1984), People to People Internat./AHA goodwill ambassador to Australia and N.Z. 1981), 157 Greeley C. of C. (city improvement com. 1984), Phi Sigma Alpha. Lutheran. Contbr. articles to profl. publs. Office: 928 12th St Greeley CO 80631

LEBEDEFF, DIANE ALEXIS, judge; b. Detroit, June 25, 1943; d. Alexis M. and Vera A. Lebedeff; B.A., U. Mich., 1965, J.D., 1968. Admitted to N.Y. bar, 1969, Mich. bar, 1969; asso. appellate counsel Legal Aid Soc., N.Y.C., 1968-71; atty. div. criminal justice services N.Y. State, 1971-73; atty. N.Y.C. Dept. Rent and Housing Maintenance, 1976-80, gen. counsel, 1976-80, also counsel N.Y.C. Rent Guidelines; housing judge N.Y. Civil Ct., 1980-82, judge, 1983—. Mem. Community Bd. 2, N.Y.C., 1979-80. Mem. Assn. Bar City N.Y., Am. Bar Assn., Nat. Assn. Women Judges, N.Y. State Assn. Women Judges (bd. dirs. 1984-86, sec. 1986—), N.Y. State Bar Assn., N.Y. Women's Bar Assn. Clubs: Women's City, City (N.Y.C.). Address: 111 Centre St New York NY 10013

LEBLANC, CAROLINE ANNE, nurse, psychotherapist; b. Worcester, Mass., Dec. 11, 1947; d. Leonard Eugene and Gertrude Rita (Plamondon) LeB.; B.S.N. cum laude, Boston Coll., 1969; M.S., U.Md., 1978; postgrad. Georgetown U., 1980-83; m. Jon Ralph Hager, May 24, 1969; children—Keith Erik Hager, Brant William Hager. Public health and psychiat. staff nurse, 1969-71; occupational health nurse Def. Supply Agy., Boston, 1971-72; sr. asst. nurse officer USPHS, 1972-74; asst. prof. psychiat. nursing Bloomsburg (Pa.) State Coll., 1978-81; pvt. practice contractural services rural nursing and mental health, clin., ednl. and consultative services, Williamsport, Pa., 1977-82; commd. capt. Nurse Corps, U.S. Army, 1982; nurse/psychotherapist Walson Army Hosp., Ft. Dix, N.J., 1982-86; asst. prof. dept. psychiat. nursing Sch. Nursing Med. Coll. Ga., Augusta, 1986—; faculty adv. Bloomsburg State Coll. Campus Child Care Center, 1980-81. Founding mem. Balt. Nurses NOW Task Force; founding mem. Wellspring (Md.) Center Human Potential, 1974-75. Served with USPHS, 1972-74. Cert. specialist in psychol. and mental health nursing. Mem. Am. Nurses Assn., Am. Orthopsychiat. Assn., Pa. Nurses Assn., Phi Kappa Phi, Sigma Theta Tau. Home: 191 Blackstone Camp Rd Martinez GA 30907

LEBLANC, KAREN MARIE, realtor; b. Waltham, Mass., May 29, 1945; d. Moise S. and Mary E. (Murphy) LeB.; student pvt. schs., also various banking courses. With Bank of Watertown, 1964—, asst. v.p. lending div., 1979-80, v.p. mortage and consumer lending, 1980-86; mgr. Century 21 West Realty, Waltham, 1986—. Mem. Savs. Bank Women Mass. (officer 1981-82), Watertown C. of C. (bd. dirs.), Nat. Assn. Bank Women, Savs. Bank Officers Club. Address: 14 Blackmer Rd Sudbury MA 01776

LEBLANC, MARGARET A(MY) PEGGY, lawyer; b. New Orleans, Mar. 24, 1950; d. Charles Stafford and Margaret Ellis (Dunn) LeB. B.A., La. State U., 1972, J.D., 1976. Bar: La. Sole practice law, New Orleans, 1976-82; ptnr. LeBlanc & Thompson, New Orleans, 1982-84, Tobias, LeBlanc, Thompson and Waldrup, 1984—. Vice chmn. Battered Women's Program Adv. Com. YWCA, New Orleans, 1983—. Mem. ABA, La. State Bar Assn., Assn. for Women Attys. (pres. 1982-84), La. Assn. for Women Attys. (pres. 1979-81), Nat. Conf. Women Bar Assn. (rec. sec. 1983-84, v.p. 1984—), La. State U. Law Alumni Assn. (sec. 1977-78), Democrat. Roman Catholic. Office: Tobias LeBlanc Thompson & Waldrup 610 Poydras St Suite 318 New Orleans LA 70130

LEBO, MARIE, mortgage broker; b. Newark, Jan. 22, 1941; d. Frank Joseph and Anna (Ferrara) Vumbaca; lic. in real estate Profl. Sch. Bus., Union, N.J., 1973; student NYU, 1974; m. Richard Lebo, Apr. 4, 1959; children—Corey Allen, Linda Marie. Sec. to pres. J.I. Kislak Mortgage Co., Newark, 1962-72, mortgage loan originator sales dept., 1972-77, asst. v.p., 1974-77; partner, owner Mortgage Brokerage Services Co., East Orange, N.J., 1977-81; v.p. Supreme Fin. Services, Inc., Somerville, N.J., 1982-83, J.I. Kislak Mortgage Corp., 1983-84, Premier Fin. Group, 1984-85; sr. v.p. GAF Fin., 1986—. Mem. Nat. Assn. Female Execs., Am. Soc. Profl. and Exec. Women, Nat. Assn. Rev. Appraisers and Mortgage Underwriters. Home: 320 Eileen Way Bridgewater NJ 08807 Office: 155 Prospect Ave West Orange NJ 07052

LEBOW, SUSAN M., lawyer; b. Bklyn.; d. Philip Jay and Anne (Benjamin) Weingard; B.A. magna cum laude, Bklyn. Coll., 1959; LL.B. cum laude, Bklyn. Law Sch., 1964; m. Marvin LeBow, Dec. 20, 1959; children—Adam, Douglas, Jacqueline, Philice. Admitted to N.Y. bar, 1964; staff atty. law dept. Port Authority N.Y.-N.J., 1964-70; editor Mathew Bender & Co. Legal Pubs., N.Y.C., 1970-73; partner Sarisohn, Sarisohn, Carner, Steindler, Creditor & LeBow, Esqs., Commack, N.Y., 1973—; former counsel Huntington chpt. NOW; former counsel to N.Y. State Assn. for Gifted and Talented. Trustee Suffolk County council Girl Scouts U.S.A., 1975-81; Suffolk County liaison officer N.Y. State Lt. Gov., 1974-78; mem. adv. bd. Women's Ednl. and Counseling Ctr., SUNY, Farmingdale. Recipient cert. of appreciation Suffolk County, 1977. Mem. Suffolk County Bar Assn., Nassau County Bar Assn., N.Y. State Bar Assn., Nassau-Suffolk Women's Bar Assn., Nat. Acad. TV Arts and Scis., Phi Beta Kappa. Office: 350 Veterans Memorial Hwy Commack NY 11725

LEBOWITZ, CATHARINE KOCH, state legislator; b. Winchester, Mass., June 30, 1915; d. William John and Carolyn Sophia (Kistinger) Koch; m. Murray Lebowitz, Sept. 21, 1971 (dec. Oct. 1978). Student Northeastern U., 1948-49, Boston Coll., 1949-52. Sec., ERA, Bangor, Augusta, Maine, 1935-38, WPA, Portland, Maine, 1938-42; personnel officer, exec. sec. USN, Portland, 1942-47; exec. sec. Clark Babbitt, Boston, 1947-48; adminstrv. asst. Moore Bus. Forms, Boston, 1948-52; pvt. sec. Alvin T. Portland Credit Bur., 1980-86; mem. Bangor City Council, 1985—; mem. Maine State Legislature. Sec., Symphony Women, Bangor, 1964-84; bd. dirs. Opera House Com., Bangor, 1978-80; mem. Bangor C. of C. Consumer Relations Council, 1981—; coordinator Bangor 150th Anniversary Prodn. Music Man, 1984; del. Rep. Nat. Conv., 1984; mem. Spl. Task Force to Study Child Abuse, 1985—; adv. com. Maine Devel. Found., 1984—. Recipient Civilian Meritorious Service award USN, Portland Maine, 1946; Named Hon. Alumnus Secretarial Sci., Husson Coll., 1980. Mem. Credit Women Internat. (treas. 1975-77, Credit Woman of Yr. 1969), Bangor Community Theater (treas. 1973—, award 1973), U. Maine Maine Masque Theater (judge 1983—), Maine N.G. Assn. (hon.), Credit Women Bangor (sec. 1965-67), Bangor Hist. Soc., Penobscot County Republicans, Penobscot County Rep. Women's Club (sec. 1979). Club: Zonta (pres. Bangor 1962-64, 80-82). Office: State Legislature State House Sta Augusta ME 04330

LEBOWITZ, CHARLOTTE MEYERSOHN, social worker; b. Germany, Dec. 22, 1924; d. Franz and Magda (Wellisch) Meyersohn; came to U.S., 1938, naturalized, 1943; B.A., Brown U., 1946; M.S.W., Simmons Coll., 1948; m. Marshall Lebowitz, Aug. 7, 1949; children—Wendy Lebowitz Nowak, Marian, Mark. Psychiat. social worker Jewish Family and Children's Service, Boston, 1948-49, ARC Home Service Dept., Boston, 1949-53, Youth Guidance Center, Framingham, Mass., 1962-69, Brandon Sch., Natick, 1969-74, Natick Pub. Schs., 1975—; adj. clin. instr. Boston Coll. Sch. Social Work, 1981-82; mem. exec. bd. Natick Service Council, 1982—; cons. YWCA, 1970-71. Exec. bd. mem. PTA, 1955-71, chmn. pre-sch. unit, 1955-56, mem. council, 1956-70; trustee council Leonard Morse Hosp., 1976—. Mem. Acad. Cert. Social Workers, Nat. Assn. Social Workers, Sch. Adjustment Counselors Assn., Social Workers Employed Less Than Full Time, Boston Inst. Devel. Infants and Parents, Simmons Coll. Sch. Social Work, Brown U. alumni assns., LWV, Nonesuch Pond Improvement Assn. Jewish. Clubs: Sisterhood of Temple Israel of Natick, Rivers Sch. Tennis. Home: 2 Abbott Rd Natick MA 01760 Office: Natick Sch Dept Natick MA 01760

LEBSACK, PHYLLIS JEAN, county clerk; b. McCook, Nebr., July 22, 1921; d. George and Katherine Elizabeth (Kechter) Gettman; m. Samuel Lebsack, Aug. 8, 1942 (dec. Mar. 1981); children—Julie Ann, Christy Jean, Todd Douglas. Court clerk Red Willow County Ct., McCook, 1944-45, 1947-48, deputy county clk. 1970-77, county clk., 1977—; clk. City of McCook, 1948-50; sec. Red Willow County Health Bd., 1977—, Red Willow County Commrs., 1977—; county registrar Bur. Vital Statistics, Red Willow County, 1977—; dir. Election Registration Bd., McCook, 1952-67; vice chmn. clerks W. Central Dist., Nebr., 1984—. Democrat. Avocations: crafts; bridge; golf. Home: 911 E 3d St McCook NE 69001 Office: Court House McCook NE 69001

LECHTMAN, PAMELA JOY, travel writer; b. St. Paul, Apr. 29, 1943; d. Ben L. and Leona Betty (Cell) Price; B.S., U. Minn., 1965; m. Allen Lee Lechtman, June 16, 1967; children—Arthur Thomas, Anthony Grant. Tchr. art St. Paul Ind. Sch. Dist., 1966-67; tchr. Alameda (Calif.) Unified Sch. Dist., 1967-68; with public relations dept. Fitness, Inc., 1976-79; travel writer, 1979—; travel editor Shape mag., Woodland Hills, Calif., 1982—; travel columnist News Chronicle, Thousand Oaks, Calif., 1980; instr. tourism Ventura (Calif.) Coll., 1978-80; producer radio program Update, Sta. KVEN-AM, Ventura, 1974-80; spa editor Total Health; segment reporter Sta. KCSN, Northridge, Calif.; contbg. West Coast editor Connections; author broadcasting guide You're On The Air, 1979; travel editor Ventura County Mag.; travel corr. Word on Travel, KFAC Radio, Los Angeles. Cert. travel counselor Inst. Cert. Travel Agts. Mem. Am. Assn. Travel Editors, AAUW (Grant fellow Ventura County br. 1976, individual grantee 1980). Home: 668 Camino Rojo Thousand Oaks CA 91360 Office: Shape Mag 21100 Erwin St Woodland Hills CA 91367

LECKIE, CAROL MAVIS, state government administrator; b. Watertown, Wis., Feb. 25, 1929; d. Arthur Walter Bessel and Effie Vada (Squires) Downs; m. Leonard John Leckie, Sept. 30, 1977; m. Ralph Junior Judd, Sept. 27, 1947 (div. Dec. 1952); children—Russell Howard, Barbara Rae. Grad. Madison East High Sch., 1946. Mgr. data processing Dept. Justice, State of Wis., Madison, 1971-79, mgr. Records Mgmt. Program, 1979-83, mgr. Typography Sect., 1983—. Mem. com. State of Employees Combined Campaign, Madison, 1986. Mem. Assn. Records Mgrs. and Adminstrs. (pres. 1983-84), Bus. Forms Mgmt. Assn., Internat. Assn. Printing House Craftsmen. Lutheran. Avocations: travel; aerobics. Home: 1213 Iowa Dr Madison WI 53704 Office: Wiscomp Sect B345 1 W Wilson St Madison WI 53702

LECLOUX, MARIA JACINTA, nurse; b. Green Bay, Wis., Feb. 28, 1957; d. Joseph Wallace and Patricia Ann (Koss) Mastalir; m. Darrell Edward LeCloux, June 12, 1982; 1 child, Jonathan. B.S. in Community Health Edn., U. Wis.-LaCrosse, 1979; Assoc. in Tech. Nursing, NE Wis. Tech. Inst., 1983. R.N., Wis. Coordinator adult program Kewaunee County Devel. Ctr., Algoma, Wis., 1979-81; staff nurse Door Co. Meml. Hosp., Sturgeon Bay, Wis., 1983—. Mem. Wis. Nurses' Assn., Door County Nurses' Assn. Avocations: sewing; needlework; piano; guitar. Home: 2378 Settlement Rd Sturgeon Bay WI 54235 Office: Door County Meml Hosp 330 S 16th Pl Sturgeon Bay WI 54235

LE COCQ, RHODA PRISCILLA, author, educator; b. Lynden, Wash.; d. Ralph B. and Nellie O. (Straks) Le C.; B.A., Wash. State U.; M.A. in Creative Writing, Stanford U.; M.A. in Philosophy, U. Calif.-Santa Barbara, 1967; Ph.D., Calif. Inst. Integral Studies, 1970. Radio writer and actress sta. KHQ, Spokane, sta. KOIN, Portland, Oreg., sta. KIRO, Seattle; owner Le Cocq Luray, N.Y.C.; lit. scout Farrar, Straus & Cudahy, N.Y.C.; public relations dir. art sch. Honolulu Acad. Arts, 1957-58; owner, propr. public relations counseling firm, Honolulu, 1958-61; info. officer Office CD City and County of Honolulu, 1961-63; info. and legis. officer Sacramento County (Calif.) Dept. Social Welfare, 1969-80; research cons. Integral Sci. Found., Inc., 1981-86; instr. U. Hawaii, 1960-61; asst. prof. philosophy extension dept. U. Calif., Davis, 1970-71; assoc. prof. Calif. Inst. Integral Studies, 1972-81; lectr. Bombay, India, 1973, Cultural Integration Fellowship, 1975-80, Regional Assn. Transpersonal Psychology, 1977. Served to lt. USNR, 1942-46, ret. Res., 1970. Recipient cert. for contbn. to East-West Understanding, Cultural Integration Fellowship, 1969, Author Aiding Internat. Understanding, Cambridge, Eng., 1973, photog. and publs. awards NACID, 1974. Mem. Public Relations Soc. Am., Internat. Platform Assn., Smithsonian Assocs., USNR Assn., Audubon Soc., Wash. State U. Alumni Assn., U. Calif. Santa Barbara Alumni Assn., Stanford Alumni Assn., Mensa, Armed Forces Writers League, Kappa Alpha Theta, Theta Sigma Phi. Clubs: San Francisco Press; Marines Meml. (life) (San Francisco). Author: Heidegger and Sri Aurobindo, 1972; Vision of Superhumanity, 1973; The Mother/Father Pair, 1977; short story Behold A Pale Horse included in several anthologies, dramatized TV, 1957. Mailing Address: Box 2009 Mill Valley CA 94942

LE COUNT, VIRGINIA G., communications company executive; b. Long Island City, N.Y., Nov. 22, 1917; d. Clifford R. and Luella (Meier) LeCount; B.A., Barnard Coll., 1937; M.A., Columbia, 1940. Tchr. pub. schs., P.R., 1937-38; supr. HOLC, N.Y.C., 1938-40; translator Guildhall Publs., 1940-41; office mgr. Sperry Gyroscope Co., Garden City, Lake Success, Bklyn. (all N.Y.), 1941-45; billing mgr. McCann Erickson, Inc., N.Y.C., 1945-56; v.p., bus. mgr., bd. dirs. Infoplan Internat, Inc., 1956-69; v.p., bus. mgr. Communications Affiliates Ltd., Communications Affiliates (Bahamas) Ltd., 1968-71; bus. mgr. Jack Tinker & Partners, Inc., 1969-70; mgr. office services Interpublic Group of Cos., Inc., N.Y.C., 1970-72, corp. records mgr., 1972-83, mktg. intelligence data mgr., 1978-83. Mem. Alumnae Barnard Coll. Mem. Marble Collegiate Ch. Club: Atrium. Home: 136 E 55th St Apt 10Q New York NY 10022

LECUYER, ELLEN DELPHINE, publishing company junior executive; b. Montreal, Que., Can., May 10, 1956; d. Lucien and Doris (Daly) L.; m. Michael S.L. Levesque, Dec. 30, 1983. B.Commerce, Concordia U., Montreal, 1977. Research analyst Reader's Digest, Montreal, 1977-79, asst. mgr. mktg. research, 1979-81, mgr. mktg. research, 1981—. Mem. Am. Mktg. Assn., Profl. Market Research Soc. Avocations: cross country skiing; curling. Home: 4554 Royal Ave Montreal PQ H4A 2M8 Canada Office: Reader's Digest Assn Can 215 Redfern Ave Westmount PQ H32 2V9 Canada

LECZNAR, ROMUALDA MARIE, nursing home administrator, nurse; b. Ciechocinek, Poland, Sept. 16, 1927; came to U.S., 1966; d. Henryk Antoni and Janina Jda (Wendlandt) Dominik; m. Thaddeus Witold Lecznar, Apr. 28, 1946; children—John Francis, Robert Henry, Richard Andrew, Elysia Christine. Grad. Nursing Sch., Salzkotten, Germany, 1947; cert. in Nursing Home Adminstrn., Mich. State U., 1973-74. R.N.; lic. nursing home adminstr., Mich., Fla. Nursing supr. Bloomfield Hills Nursing Center (Mich.), 1966-67, nursing home adminstr., 1976-79; inservice dir. Skill Care Nursing Centers, Bloomfield Hills, 1967-70, dir. nurses, 1970-74, nursing coordinator, 1974-76; nursing home adminstr. Georgian Bloomfield, Bloomfield Hills, 1980—. Vol. instr. ARC, 1970. Mem. Mich. Nurses Assn., Am. Nurses Assn., Am. Coll. Nursing Home Adminstrs., Detroit and Birmingham C. of C. Lutheran. Home: 4448 Squirrel Rd Bloomfield Hills MI 48013 Office: Georgian Bloomfield Inc 2975 Adams Rd Bloomfield Hills MI 48013

LEDANE, CARLA GAYLE, nurse, pageant executive; b. Huntington, W.Va., Apr. 5, 1945; d. Carl Oscar and Rayma June (Ray) Covey; m. Albert Lamarre, Oct. 11, 1965 (div. July 1984); children—Alan, Daniel, Shane, Angel; m. Robert E. LeDane, Aug. 10, 1984. Student Ohio State U., 1963-65; L.P.N., Sheridan Vocat. Sch., Hollywood, Fla., 1975. Pvt. practice nursing, 1975—; pres. Internat. Pageant Systems of Fla., Inc., North Miami Beach, Fla., 1984—; exec. v.p. United Charities Internat. Inc., North Miami Beach, 1984—. Mem. Nat. Assn. Female Execs. Democrat. Lutheran. Avocations: dancing, gymnastics. Home: 980 NE 170th St #106 North Miami Beach FL 33162

LEDBETTER, SANDRA GALE SHUMARD, political party administrator; b. Little Rock, Oct. 18, 1948; d. Frank Ney and Mildred Elizabeth (Oldham) Shumard; B.A., U. Ark., 1971; m. Joel Yowell Ledbetter, Jr., Dec. 16, 1971; children—Elizabeth Talbot, Ann Shay, Mildred Myonne Mitzi. Tchr., Pulaski County (Ark.) Spl. Sch. Dist., 1970-72, Miss Selma's Sch., Little Rock, 1972-74, Pulaski Acad., Little Rock, 1976-80; adminstrv. asst. to gov. of Ark., 1980-82; mem. advance team for Joan Mondale, Mondale for Pres. campaign, 1982; campaign coordinator Dem. Party of Ark., 1982. Mem. Pulaski County Democratic Com., 1976-82, Dem. State Com., 1976-82; del. Dem. Nat. Conv., 1980; co-chmn. Dem. State Adv. Com., 1981—; mem. president's roundtable U. Central Ark., also mem. advancement com.; trustee U. Ark., 1986—. Mem. Assn. Dem. Exec. Dirs. (bd. dirs.), Jr. League Little Rock (dir. 1981-82, 86-87, project chmn. 1982-83). Methodist. Home: 7 Foxhunt Trail Little Rock AR 72207

LEDBETTER, SHARON FAYE WELCH, school principal; b. Los Angeles, Jan. 14, 1941; d. James Herbert and Verdie V. (Mattox) Welch; m. Robert A. Ledbetter, Feb. 15, 1964; children—Kimberly Ann, Scott Allen. B.A., U. Tex.-Austin, 1963; learning disabilities cert. Southwestern U., Tex., 1974; M.Ed., Southwest Tex. State U., 1979, prin. and supt. cert., 1984. Speech pathologist Midland Ind. Sch. Dist., Tex., 1963, Austin Ind. Sch. Dist., Tex., 1964-71; speech pathologist, asst. prin. Round Rock Ind. Sch. Dist., Tex., 1971-84 also mem. coms.; prin. Hutto Ind. Sch. Dist., 1984—. Pres., Berkman PTA, 1983-84; sponsor Jr. Woman's Club, 1980-82. Recipient Appreciation awards Round Rock Sch. Dist., 1984, St. Judes Children's Research Hosp., 1985, Soc. Disting. Am. High Sch. Students, 1985. Mem. Nat. Assn. Secondary Sch. Prins., Tex. Assn. Secondary Sch. Prins., Tex. Elem. Suprs. and Prins. Assn., Nat. Assn. Female Execs., Tex. Assn. Community Schs., Gen. Fedn. Women's Club, Tex. Fedn. Women's Clubs (com. chair), Round Rock Women's Club (pres.), AAUW, Phi Delta Kappa, Delta Kappa Gamma. Avocations: horses; spectator sports. Home: Rt 1 Box 8A Hutto TX 78634 Office: 302 College St Hutto TX 78634

LEDBETTER-STRAIGHT, NORA KATHLEEN, insurance company executive; b. Gary, Ind., May 11, 1934; d. Jacob F. and Nora I. (Bollen) Moser; student U. Houston, 1954-58; m. Robert L. Straight, Aug. 9, 1975; 1 dau., Cindy Kathleen Ledbetter Baurax. Vice pres. Hindman Mortgage Co., Inc., Houston, 1960-70, also mng. partner Assocs. Ins. Agy.; corp. sec. N.Am. Mortgage Co., Houston, 1970—; mng. partner N.Am. Ins. Agy., 1970—, now also pres. and mng. officer; ins. counselor Houston Apt. Assn., 1978—, dir. product service council, 1981—; v.p., sec. Better Bodies of Tex., Inc. C.P.C.U.; cert. Ins. Inst. Am., Soc. Cert. Ins. Counselors. Mem. Ind. Ins. Agts. Am., Soc. Cert. Ins. Counselors, Soc. C.P.C.U.'s, Community Assos. Inst. (dir. 1976-80), Ind. Ins. Agts. Tex., Ind. Ins. Agts. Houston (dir. 1974-78). Republican. Methodist. Author curriculum materials in field. Office: 900 Threadneedle Houston TX 77224

LEDBURY, DIANA GRETCHEN, educator; b. Denver, Mar. 7, 1931; d. Francis Kenneth and Gretchen (Harry) Van Ausdall; m. Chander Parkash Lall, Dec. 26, 1953 (div. Aug. 1973); children—Anne, Neil, Chris; m. Eugene Augustus Ledbury, Sept. 13, 1976; stepchildren—Mark, Cindy, Rob. B.A. in Sociology, Colo. U., 19. Instr. Home, and family life Community Coll., Seattle, 1957-71; asst. tchr. Renton Sch. Dist., Wash., 1974-83; adult edn. tchr. Mental Health Network, Renton, 1984—; coordinator Inter-Study, Renton, 1985—. Mem. Renton Area Youth Services Bd., Sch. and Community Drug Prevention Program, Renton dist. council PTA, Renton Citizen's Com. on Recreation; vol. Griffin Home for Boys; coordinator Modern Dance Prodn., Carco Theater; mem. bd. Allied Arts of Renton; mem. Bicentennial Com. for a Cultural Arts, Edn. and Recreation Ctr.; PTA rep. Dimmit Jr. High Sch.; mem. Sch. and Community Recreation Com.; founder Handicapped Helping Themselves, Mental Health Network; precinct committeeperson 11th dist. Republican party, Wash., 1976-85. Recipient Golden Acorn award Wash. State Congress PTA, Renton, 1972. Mem. Assn. Social and Health Services (mem. com. 1984-83), AAUW (legis. chmn. 1983-85). Episcopalian. Club: Campfire Horizon (leader). Avocations: arts; culture, recreation, child and family advocate.

LEDERBERG, VICTORIA, state legislator, lawyer, psychology educator; b. Providence, July 7, 1937; d. Frank and Victoria (Marzilli) Santopietro; m. Seymour Lederberg, 1959; children—Tobias, Sarah. A.B., Pembroke Coll., 1959; A.M., Brown U., 1961, Ph.D., 1966; J.D., Suffolk U., 1976. Mem. R.I. Ho. of Reps., 1975-82, chmn. subcom. on edn., fin. coms., 1975-82, subcom. on mental health, retardation and hosps. and health, spl. legis. commns pub. sch. funding and funding handicapped edn. programs; mem. Democratic Nat. Exec. Com.; mem. R.I. State Senate, 1985—; prof. psychology R.I. Coll., 1978—; atty firm Levy, Goodman, Semonoff & Gorin, Providence. USPHS fellow physiol. psychology, 1964-66. Mem. New Eng. Psychol. Assn., R.I. Psychol. Assn., Women Educators, New Eng. Edn. Research Orgn., ABA, R.I. Bar Assn., Sigma Xi. Office: RI State Capitol Bldg Providence RI 02903*

LEDERER, DEBRA YUHAS, educator, educational administrator; b. Akron, Ohio, Aug. 23, 1950; d. John and Marjorie Mae (Stuart) Yuhas; B.A., U. Md., 1974, Ph.D., 1980; M.Ed., Towson State U., 1976; m. James Brian Lederer, Nov. 11, 1976; children—Jeremy Bryant, Jessica Lynne. English tchr. Howard County, Md., 1974-76, lang. arts tchr. for gifted and talented, 1976-78, program developer gifted and talented programs, 1976-78; grad. asst. Reading Center, U. Md., College Park, 1978-79, faculty lectr., asst. prof., 1979-80, research asst., clin. supr., supr. undergrad. students, 1979; asst. prin. River Dell Jr. High Sch., River Edge, N.J., 1980-82, Saddle River (N.J.) Schs., 1982—; adj. prof. Kean Coll., Union, N.J., 1980—; adj. grad. prof. Fairleigh Dickinson U., Teaneck, N.J., 1981—; cons. Manassas (Va.) City Park Sch. System, 1980, Md. State Dept. Edn., 1978-80, Howard County Bd. Edn., 1978. Mem. Nat. Assn. for Supervision and Curriculum Devel., Bergen County Assn. Elem. and Middle Sch. Prins., Coll. Reading Assn., Middle Sch. Assn., Internat. Reading Assn., Nat. Assn. Secondary Sch. Prins., Phi Kappa Phi. Home: 41 Beverly Rd Oradell NJ 07649 Office: 97 E Allendale Ave Saddle River NJ 07458

LEDERER, MARIE A., political campaign official; b. Phila., Oct. 24, 1927; d. Donato and Edith (Vitacolonna) Panosetti; ed. Phila. Public Relations Inst., 1966-67, Temple U., 1973-76; m. William J. Lederer, June 17, 1950; children—Doneda M. Lederer Guyon, William M., Regina M. Instr. polit. sci. Temple U., Phila., 1976-77; exec. dir. Jackson for Pres. Com., 1976; del. Dem. nat. conv., 1976, 84; voter registration chmn. Dem. exec. com., 1978-79; adminstrv. asst. to Congressman Joseph F. Smith, Pa., 1981-82; asst. to Dep. Auditor Gen. of Pa., 1985. Dir. Southeastern Pa. Heart Assn., 1968-71; mem. bd. dirs. Balch Inst., ARC, U.S.S. Cruiser Olympia Ship; mem. Phila. Art Alliance. Recipient Pa. Ho. of Reps., 1974, certs. of merit U.S. Ho. of Reps., 1982. Roman Catholic. Clubs: Am. Legion Ladies Aux., Hist. Ships Assn., Mexican Soc. Home: 1237 Shackamaxon St Philadelphia PA 19125

LEDERMAN, MARIE JEAN, university dean; b. Bklyn., Dec. 28, 1935; d. Samuel and Gladys Candel; B.S. magna cum laude, N.Y.U., 1957, Ph.D. (teaching fellow), 1966; M.A., Bklyn. Coll., 1963; 1 son. Tchr. English, N.Y.C. Bd. Edn., 1957-59; instr. N.Y.U., 1965-66; from lectr. to asst. prof. English, N.Y.C. Community Coll., City U. N.Y. Center, 1966-68, asst. prof. SEEK program, 1968-69; from asst. prof. to prof. Baruch Coll., 1969-79; univ. dean Office Acad. Affairs, City U. N.Y., 1979-85; dean Freshman skills La Guardia Community Coll., 1985—; v.p. N.Y.C. Assn. Tchrs. English, 1979—; mem. minority affairs com. Coll. Composition and Communication, 1982—; cons. in field. Recipient Faculty Research award City U. N.Y./PSC, 1976-78; grantee Fund for Improvement Postsecondary Edn, 1981-84, 84—. Mem. Nat. Council Tchrs. English, MLA, Am. Com. Irish Studies, Internat. Reading Assn., Community Coll. Gen. Edn. Assn. (dir.), Jean Cocteau Repertory Theater (dir.). Jewish. Club: Women's City (N.Y.C.). Author articles in field. Contbr. profl. procs. Office: 535 E 80th St New York NY 10021

LEE, ALISON ANN, medical technologist; b. Holyoke, Mass., June 30, 1950; d. Robert Keating and Audrey Ethel (Emery) L.; student Russell Sage Coll.; 1968-70; B.A., Mt. Holyoke Coll., 1973; M.A., Central Mich. U., 1985. Lab. technician Holyoke Hosp., 1969-72; research asst. U. Mass. Health Services, Amherst, 1972-73; med. technologist Wesson unit Baystate Med. Center, Springfield, Mass., 1973-78; cons. Tulsa City-County Health Dept., 1979-81, Moton Health Center, Tulsa, 1980-84; lead med. technologist St. Francis

Hosp., Tulsa, 1978—, vol. pediatric orientation program. Alumnae admissions rep. for Greater Tulsa, Mt. Holyoke Coll.; past public edn. chmn., mem. profl. edn. com., bd. dirs. Am. Cancer Soc.; vol. various community activities. Mem. Am. Soc. Clin. Pathologists, Am. Soc. Clin. Chemistry, Nat. Mgmt. Assn., Am. Soc. Med. Tech., Okla. Assn. Med. Tech., Alumnae Assn. Mt. Holyoke. Home: 6370 H South 80 East Ave Tulsa OK 74133

LEE, AMY HSUAN, mechanical engineer; b. Swatow, Kwangtung, China, Oct. 27, 1952; came to U.S. 1972; d. Paul Sewtuk and Sally Sharping (Lee) L. B.S. in Mech. Engring., Ill. Inst. Tech., 1979, M.S. in Mech. Engring., 1982. Sr. engr. corp. mfg. and devel. of engring. group Baxter Travenol Labs., Inc., Round Lake, Ill., 1982-83, prin. engr. for product devel. Fenwal div., 1983—. Mem. ASME, AAAS, Soc. Women Engrs., Sigma Xi, Pi Tau Sigma (life mem., v.p. 1979, treas. 1979), Tau Beta Pi (life mem., sec. and group leader 1979). Office: Baxter Travenol Labs Inc Route 120 and Wilson Rd Round Lake IL 60073

LEE, ANALYN ANDERSON, television writer and producer, model; b. Lufkin, Tex., Nov. 6, 1955; d. Doyle Shofner and Louvena (Estep) Anderson; m. Mark S. Lee, 1984. B.A. in Communication, Stephen F. Austin State U., Nacogdoches, Tex., 1977; postgrad. in French. L'institut Catholique, Paris, 1980. Reporter, TV Sta. KATC TV-3, Lafayette, La., 1977-80; writer-producer Gulf Oil Corp., Houston, 1981-82; freelance writer/producer, Houston, 1982—; appears on commls. and indsl. videos. Author mag. articles, 1983. Vol., Ch. Community Service Center, Houston, 1983—. Recipient Most Valuable Student Staffer award The Lufkin News, 1973. Mem. Internat. TV Assn., Motion Picture Council/Houston, Soc. Profl. Journalists, Sigma Kappa (rec. sec. alumnae chpt., social chmn.). Methodist (dir. TV broadcasts St. Luke's Ch., Houston). Home: 1026 Chantilly Ln Houston TX 77018

LEE, ANNE NATALIE, nurse; b. Bklyn.; d. Taras Pavlovich and Maria (Jukovskaya) Dubovick; B.A., Hunter Coll., 1940; M.A., N.Y.U., 1948; R.N., McLean Hosp. Sch. Nursing, Waverly, Mass., 1946; M.S., Boston U., 1958; m. Henry Lee, Feb. 20, 1945; adopted children—Alice, Jennifer, Philip. Pvt. duty nurse, N.Y.C., 1946-48; staff nurse Vis. Nurse Service, 1947-48; staff nurse health dept. Schoharie Co., N.Y., 1948-51; supervising nurse N.Y. Dept. Health, Syracuse, 1951-53, cons. hosp. nursing, Albany, 1958-63, cons. nurse in service edn., 1963-75, dir. Bur. of Hosp. Nursing Services, 1975-80; cons. nursing services and adminstrn., 1980—; dir., coordinator nursing service instr. program co-sponsored N.Y. State Dept. Health, N.Y. State Hosp. Assn., N.Y. State League Nursing, N.Y. State Nurses Assn., 1954-57; sometimes lectr. Mem. Am. Nurses Assn. (cert. advanced nursing adminstrn.), Sigma Theta Tau. Contbr. articles to profl. jours. Home and Office: 1149 Hillsboro Mile Hillsboro Beach FL 33062

LEE, ANTOINETTE JOSEPHINE, architectural historian, preservationist; b. Berwyn, Ill., July 5, 1948; d. Stephen K.F. and Katharine (Whitworth) Lee; m. Allan Leroy Olson, Aug. 11, 1978. B.A. in History, U. Pa., Phila., 1969; M.Ph. in Am. Civilization, George Washington U., Washington, 1973; Ph.D. in Am. Civilization, 1975. Cons. hist. preservation, Washington, 1972-77, coordinator edn. services Nat. Trust Historic Preservation, Washington, 1977-82; dir., supr. architect project Columbia Hist. Soc., Washington, 1982—; cons. hist. preservation Office of Planning D.C., Washington, 1982; cons. U.S. com. Internat. Council on Monuments and Sites, Washington, 1985-86, Victorian Soc. in Am., Phila., 1985; cons. historian Archtl. League, N.Y.C., 1985-86; cons. historian archtl. firms and neighborhood assns., 1985-86. Editor: Guide to Undergraduate and Graduate Education in Historic Preservation, 1981, A Biographical Dictionary of American Civil Engineers, 1972; contbr. numerous articles in field to publs. Winston-Churchill Meml. fellow Washington br. English-Speaking Union, 1976; material culture fellow George Washington U., 1970-71. Mem. Soc. Archtl. Historians (bd. dirs.), Am. Studies Assn., Assn. Preservation Tech., Am. Planning Assn., Arts Club of Washington. Home: 4851 N 28th St Arlington VA 22207 Office: Columbia Hist Soc 1307 New Hampshire Ave NW Washington DC 20036

LEE, BARBARA ANNE, educator, lawyer; b. Newton, N.J., Apr. 9, 1949; d. Robert Hanna and Keren (Dalrymple) L.; m. James Paul Begin, Aug. 14, 1982. B.A. (Corse fellow), U. Vt., 1971; M.A., Ohio State U., 1972; J.D., Georgetown U., 1982; Ph.D., Ohio State U., 1977. Bar: N.J. 1983. Instr., Franklin U., Columbus, Ohio, 1974-75; research asst. Ohio State U., Columbus, 1975-77; policy analyst U.S. Dept. Edn., Washington, 1978-80; dir. data trends Carnegie Found., Princeton, N.J., 1980-82; asst. prof. Grad. Sch. Edn., Rutgers U., 1982-84; asst. prof. Inst. Mgmt. and Labor Relations, Rutgers U., New Brunswick, N.J., 1984—; mem. Study Group on Excellence in Higher Edn., Nat. Inst. Edn., 1983-84; project dir. Carnegie Corp., N.Y.C., 1982-84. Recipient John F. Kennedy Labor Law award Georgetown U., 1982. Mem. ABA, Assn. Study of Higher Edn., Am. Ednl. Research Assn., Indsl. Relations Research Assn., N.J. Bar Assn. Office: Inst Mgmt Rutgers U Ryder's Ln New Brunswick NJ 08903

LEE, CAROL MON, trust company executive, lawyer; b. Brockton, Mass., July 20, 1947; d. Mong Q. and Elsie (Chang) Lee; m. William S. Miller, May 17, 1974 (div.). B.A., Barnard Coll., Columbia U., 1969, M.A., 1970; J.D., U. Calif.-San Francisco, 1974. Bar: Calif. 1974, Hawaii 1977; Assoc. Palmer & Bartenetti, Los Angeles, 1974-76; vis. asst. prof. U. Hawaii Sch. Law, Honolulu, 1976-78; staff atty. 1978 Hawaii Constl. Conv., Honolulu, 1978; v.p. Am. Trust Co. Hawaii, Inc., Honolulu, 1978—; adv. bd. U. Hawaii Law Sch. Law Rev., 1980—. Sec. Chamber Music Hawaii, 1981—; bd. trustees St. Andrew's Priory, 1984. Mem. So. Calif. Chinese Lawyers Assn. (v.p. 1975-76), Hawaii State Bar Assn. (v.p. corp. counsel sect. 1984), Hawaii Women Lawyers (pres. 1980; outstanding woman lawyer of yr. 1983), Hawaii Bar Found. (sec. 1984), Hawaii Estate Planning Council (dir. 1984). Clubs: Pacific, Honolulu. Home: 1221 Victoria St Apt 1402 Honolulu HI 96814 Office: Am Trust Co Hawaii Inc 841 Bishop St 12th Floor Honolulu HI 96813

LEE, CHERYL HESSER, learning center administrator; b. Stillwater, Okla., Dec. 16, 1946; d. Abe Lee and Pauline Earnestine (Mayfield) Hesser; B.S. in Edn., Okla. State U., 1969; M.A., Tex. Women's U., 1980; m. Jeffrey Gordon Lee, Aug. 5, 1972; children—Tracy Renee, Amanda Marie. Primary sch. tchr., Colo., Okla. and Tex., 1969-78; dir. Carrollton Ednl. Toy Co., 1981-82; dir. Creative Learning Ctr., Richmond, Va., 1983—. Bd. dirs. First Baptist Sch., Carrollton, Tex., 1978-81. Chmn. Carrollton March of Dimes, 1979; active Am. Cancer Soc., Am. Heart Assn.; vol. Childrens Miracle Network, 1983, 84, 85, 86. Mem. Assn. Achievement Human Potential, Assn. Supervision and Curriculum Devel., NEA, Tex. Assn. Gifted Children, Tex. Edn. Assn., Nat. Assn. Edn. Young Children, Va. Assn. Edn. Young Children, Richmond Assn. Edn. Young Children (Olympic of Mind coach; chmn. Week of Young Child 1983, 84), Juvenile Diabetes Assn., Kappa Delta. Home: 10509 S Falconbridge Ct Richmond VA 23233 Office: Second Baptist Ch River at Gaskins Rds Richmond VA 23233

LEE, CHRISTINE CHANCEY, lawyer; b. Ft. Lauderdale, Fla., Aug. 7, 1949; d. Gene Tyler and Betty Lynn (Chancey) Prominski L.; m. Donald George McAneny, Nov. 19, 1966 (div. Mar. 1968); 1 dau., Valerie Ann McAneny. A.A., Broward Community Coll., 1970; B.B.A., Fla. Atlantic U., 1972; M.P.S., Nova U., 1978; J.D. with highest honors, Fla. State U., Tallahassee, 1981. Personnel technician Fla. Atlantic U., Boca Raton, Fla., 1972-74; sales rep. Burroughs Corp., Ft. Lauderdale, Fla., 1974-75; systems analyst Community Service Council, Ft. Lauderdale, 1975-78; law clk. U.S. Ct. Appeals (11th cir.), Miami, 1981-82; assoc. atty. Ruden, Barnett, McClosky, Schuster & Russell, P.A., Ft. Lauderdale, 1982—. Exec. editor Fla. State U. Law Rev., Tallahassee, 1980-81. Mem. Leadership Broward-Broward County C. of C., Ft. Lauderdale, 1982—. Mem. Fla. Bar Assn., Broward Bar Assn. (mem. exec. com. young lawyers sect. 1983-84), Fla. Trial Assn., Order of Coif, Phi Alpha Delta (chpt. clk. 1979-80). Republican. Office: Ruden Barnett McClosky Schuster & Russell PA Penthouse B 110 E Broward Blvd Fort Lauderdale FL 33301

LEE, DEANNA JEAN, marketing executive; b. San Francisco, Apr. 13, 1948; d. Hall Sik and Pearl Jean (Yue) Lee. Student, San Francisco State U., 1966-68, U. Hawaii, 1982—. Freelance TV/film producer, Honolulu, 1971-74; advt. and promotion dir. Koko Marina Shopping Center, Honolulu, 1974-75; account exec. Milici/Valenti Advt., Honolulu, 1975-76; owner, dir. Bus. and Comml. English Centre, Turin, Italy, 1977-79; dir. mktg. Pentagram Corp., Honolulu, 1979-82; product mgr. Gasco, Inc., Honolulu, 1982—. Mem. Sales and Mktg. Execs. (chpt. treas. 1983-85), Am. Mktg. Assn. (chpt. dir. 1983—), Honolulu Advt. Fedn. (2d v.p. 1982-83), Pi Sigma Epsilon (Outstanding Contbn. award 1982). Office: Gasco Inc 733 Bishop St Honolulu HI 96813

LEE, DEENA, meeting planner; b. Hartford, Conn., Dec. 18, 1933; d. N. Edward and Lillian Farber; m. Arthur Lee; children—Kenneth, Bradley. B.A., U. Conn., 1953. Cert. meeting profl. Dir. meetings and confs. Anti-Defmation League, N.Y.C., 1977—. Mem. Meeting Planners Internat. (program com. mem. 1983—, co-chmn. luncheons program com. 1985-86), Nat. Assn. Female Execs. Avocations: piano; music arranging. Home: 240 E 27th St New York NY 10016 Office: Anti-Defamation League 823 United Nations Plaza New York NY 10017

LEE, DIANA BELINDA, banker; b. Florence, S.C., July 2, 1953; d. Henry Barker and J Jeannine (Berry) L. A.B., Coker Coll., 1973; A.A., Fashion Inst. Am., 1973; diploma retail banking Am. Inst. Banking, 1983; postgrad Coker Coll. Customer service rep. 1st Nat. Bank S.C., Columbia, 1974-79; with S.C. Nat. Bank, Florence and Columbia, 1979-82; with S.C. Fed., various locations, 1982—, br. mgr., Columbia, 1983-85, asst. sec., br. mgr., Hartsville, 1985—. Bd. dirs. Am. Cancer Soc., 1985—, chmn. regional edn. funds crusade, 1985—; chmn. Hartscapades parade, 1986. Mem. C. of C. Columbia, Forest Acres Area Council C. of C. (pres. 1985), Na. Assn. Bank Women, Am. Bus. Womens Assn. (chmn. fund raising 1984-85), Am. Inst. Banking. Republican. Presbyterian. Avocations: Reading; sewing; dance; crafts; designing. Home: 319 W Richardson Cir PO Box 424 Hartsville SC 29550 Office: SC Fed Savs Bank 208 W Home Ave PO Box 429 Hartsville SC 29550

LEE, DONNA MAE, practical nurse, educator; b. Long Beach, Calif., Oct. 7, 1949; d. Donald Curtis Staudinger and Wilma May (Barnett) Tinsman; m. Charles Deward Lee, Nov. 18, 1968; children—Ruth Carolyn, Sandra Mae, Sarah Ellen. A.S. in Practical Nursing, Coll. So. Idaho, Twin Falls, 1982; A.A. in Early Childhood Edn., Orange Coast Coll., Costa Mesa, Calif., 1978. L.P.N., Idaho; cert. tchr. in early childhood edn., Calif. Nurses aide Motion Picture and TV Hosp., Woodland Hills, Calif., 1967-68; pre-sch. tchr. Liberty Christian Schs., Huntington Beach, Calif., 1973-78, pre-sch. dir., 1978-80; emergency room registrar Magic Valley Regional Med. Ctr., Twin Falls, Idaho, 1981-82, L.P.N., 1982—. Recipient Irene E. Oliver award Magic Valley Regional Med. Ctr., 1982, cert. of appreciation Orange Coast Coll., 1979; named Student of Yr., Coll. So. Idaho, 1982. Mem. Assn. L.P.N.s. Republican. Baptist. Home: 873 Mountain View Dr Twin Falls ID 83301

LEE, ELEANOR, state senator; b. Elgin, Ill., July 17, 1931; d. Earl Herbert and Catherine (Goldback) Selle; student Wash. State U., 1949-51; B.A. in Polit. Sci., Evergreen State Coll., 1973; m. David Hammond Lee, June 23, 1951; children—Virginia, Phyllis, Marcia. With Cooperative Ext. Service, Wash. Dept. Agr., 1949, 50; with Wash. State U. Food Service, 1951; bus. mgr. Fairman Lee Co., Seattle, 1965—; mem. Wash. Ho. of Reps., 1975-77, Wash. State Senate, 1977—. Commnr., Fire Dist. Civil Service, 1976-80; commnr. Wash. State Land Commn., 1971-73; chmn. CAP Adv. Council, 1976—; chmn. Puget Sound Air Quality Coalition, 1968-70; pres. Lake Burien PTA, 1964-65; pres. Seahurst Jr. High Sch. PTA, 1966-67. Trustee, Highline Youth Found. Mem. Nat. Conf. State Legislators, Burien C. of C., Nat. Republican Legislators Assn., Am. Legislative Exchange Council, Wash. Women United, Wash. State Women's Polit. Caucus, Bus. and Profl. Women. Republican. Clubs: Soroptomist Internat., Elected Wash. Women (founder). Office: Wash State Senate State Capitol Olympia WA 98504*

LEE, FLORA LIN, food company executive; b. N.Y.C., Dec. 2, 1947; d. Kuo-Yung and Florence (Shen) Lin; m. James P. Lee, Apr. 4, 1970. B.S. with honors, Cornell U., 1968, M.S., 1972; postgrad. Yale U., 1968-69. Statistician Lederle Labs., Pearl River, N.Y., 1969-70, 71-72; cons. mgmt. scis. General Foods Corp., White Plains, N.Y., 1972-76, with product mgmt. dept., 1976-78, sr. product mgr., 1979-81, product group, mgr., 1981-83, mgr. strategic planning, 1984—. Home: 310 Valley Rd New Canaan CT 06840 Office: Gen Foods Corp 250 North St White Plains NY 10625

LEE, FRANCES HELEN, editor; b. N.Y.C., Jan. 6, 1936; d. Murray and Rose (Rothman) Lee; B.A., Queens Coll., 1957; M.A., NYU, 1962. Editorial asst. Christian Herald Family Bookshelf, N.Y.C., 1957-62; with Gordon and Breach Sci. Pubs., Inc., N.Y.C., 1964-66, Am. Electric Power Service Corp. AEP Operating Ideas, N.Y.C., 1966-69, Indsl. Water Engring. Mag., N.Y.C., 1969-71; directory editor Photographic div. United Bus. Publs., N.Y.C., 1971-80; editor Am. Druggist Blue Book, Hearst Books/Bus. Publs. Group, 1980-81, spl. projects coordinator motor manuals Hearst Book div., 1981-82, editor New Price Report, 1982-84; editor Am. Druggist Blue Book, 1982—. Supr. Bronx div. N.Y. State CD, 1953-59. Mem. com. on N.Y.C. charter revision Citizens Union, 1975, com. on city personnel practices, 1975-76, com. on city mgmt., 1977—, bd. dirs., 1978—, co-chmn. com. on N.Y.C. Cultural Concerns, 1979—. Recipient cert. of honor NYU Alumni Fedn., 1985, Meritorious Service award, 1986 . Mem. N.Y. Bus. Press Editors, Women's Equity Action League (chmn. research com.), NYU Alumnae Club (dir. 1976-78, rec. sec. 1978—, v.p. 1980-82, pres. 1982—, rep. to bd. dirs. fedn. 1984—). Home: 170 2d Ave New York NY 10003

LEE, HELEN MARJORIE, genealogist; b. Warrick County, Ind., Apr. 14, 1908; d. Dalton and Katheryn (Johnson) Wilson; B.Public Sch. Music, Ind. U., 1930; M.A., U. Miami, 1953; M.A., U. Boca Raton, Fla., 1963, M.A. in Edn., 1972; m. James K. Rice, Sept. 14, 1935; 1 dau., Katheryn Jean; m. 2d, Walter J. Lee, May 23, 1944. Tchr., Dade County (Fla.) public schs., 1954-75; ret., 1975. Mem. PACE Symphony, Opera Guild Miami; regent John McDonald chpt. DAR; chaplain Fleur de Lis chpt. Huguenot Soc. Fla.; pres. Lady Alice Needham br. Colonial Dames XVII Century; treas. Geneal. Children Am. Colonists; pres. Dames of Magna Carta, Col. William Carroll Lee chpt. Daus. 1812, Descs. of Colonial Clergy; sr. pres. Mockingbird chpt. Children Am. Revolution, also state v.p.; mem. Ancient and Hon. Arty. Recipient Outstanding Community Service award Phi Mu, 1971. Mem. Pi Lambda Phi. Republican. Episcopalian.

LEE, LILLIAN VANESSA, clinical microbiologist; b. N.Y.C., June 1, 1951; d. Wenceslao and Ada (Otero) Cancel; B.S. in Biology, St. Johns U., 1972; M.S. in Microbiology, Wagner Coll., 1974; m. Thomas Christopher Lee, June 11, 1972; children—Tovan, John-Peter, Phillip-Michael. Grad. lab. asst. in microbiology Wagner Coll., S.I., N.Y., 1972-74; clin. microbiology technologist Queens Hosp. Center, Jamaica, N.Y., 1974-81, clin. microbiology supr., 1981-84; sect. head microbiology Nyack Hosp. (N.Y.), 1984—. Cert. registered microbiologist and specialist in microbiology, clin. lab. specialist. Mem. Am. Soc. Clin. Pathologists, Am. Soc. Microbiology, Am. Acad. Microbiology, Med. Mycology Soc., N.Y., N.Y. Acad. Scis., Nat. Cert. Agy. Med. Lab. Personnel, Synergists Soc. Home: 14 Continental Dr West Nyack NY 10994 Office: Nyack Hosp N Midland Ave Nyack NY 10960

LEE, LILY KIANG, scientific research company executive; b. Shanghai, China, Nov. 23, 1946; came to U.S., 1967, naturalized, 1974; d. Chi-Wu and An-Teh (Shih) Kiang; B.S., Nat. Cheng-Chi U., 1967; M.B.A. (scholar), Golden Gate U., San Francisco, 1967; m. Robert Edward Lee; children—Jeffrey Anthony, Michelle Adrienne, Stephanie Amanda, Christina Alison. Acct., then acctg. supr. Am. Data Systems, Inc., Canoga Park, Calif., 1969-73; sr. acct. Pertec Peripheral Equipment div. Pertec Corp., Chatsworth, Calif., 1973-76; mgr. fin. planning and acctg., then mgr. fin. planning and program control Sci. Center div. Rockwell Internat. Corp., Thousand Oaks, Calif., 1976—. Mem. allocations com. United Way. Mem. Am. Mgmt. Assn., Nat. Mgmt. Assn., Nat. Property Mgrs. Assn., Nat. Assn. Female Execs. Republican. Baptist. Office: PO Box 1085 1049 Camino Dos Rios Thousand Oaks CA 91360

LEE, MARGARET MCDANIEL, marketing executive, management consultant; b. Parkersburg, W.Va., Jan. 6, 1955; d. John Milton Jr. and Janie (McDaniel) Lee; m. Richard K. Ault, Mar. 1, 1980 (div.). B.S., U. Del., 1977; postgrad. Fairleigh Dickinson U., 1978-79. Writer, editor, market researcher D.F. Healy & Assocs., Newark, Del., 1975-77; sales rep., product specialist Dow Corning, Parsippany, N.J., 1977-81; mktg. mgr. Essex Specialty Products, Inc., Clifton, N.J., 1981-84; mgmt. cons., Clifton, N.J., 1981-84; gen. mgr. spclty. products div. Jamak, Inc., Weatherford, Tex., 1984—; adj. lectr. U. Del., U. N.H., Wesley Coll., Newark High Sch., Caesar Rodney High Sch. Contbr. articles to profl. jours. Vol. aide Newark Manor Nursing Home, 1970-76; sponsor Save the Children Fedn., Westport, Conn., 1978—, WNET-TV Pub. Broadcasting, N.Y.C., 1982-83. Recipient Warner award, 1977, Mortar Board, 1976, U. Del. Mem. Clifton Bus. and Profl. Women's Assn. (chmn. bd. dirs. 1983—), Nat. Assn. Female Execs. (N.Y.C. network dir. 1983-84), Polyurethane Mfrs. Assn. (com. chair 1983), Nat. Truck Equipment Assn., Truck Body and Equipment Assn., Pi Delta Phi, Alpha Mu Alpha, Beta Gamma Sigma. Republican. Presbyterian. Home: 3824 Walton Ave Fort Worth TX 76133 Office: Jamak Inc 1401 N Bowie Dr Weatherford TX 76086

LEE, MARGARET NORMA, artist; b. Kansas City, Mo., July 7, 1928; d. James W. and Margaret W. (Farin) Lee; Ph.B., U. Chgo., 1948; M.A., Art Inst. Chgo., 1952. Lectr., U. Kansas City, 1957-61; cons. Kansas City Bd. Edn., Kansas City, Mo., 1968—; guest lectr. in portrait painting U. Mo.-Columbia, summer 1983, 85. One-man shows Univ. Women's Club, Kansas City, 1966, Friends of Art, Kansas City, 1969, Fine Arts Gallery U. Mo. at Columbia, 1972, All Souls Unitarian Ch., Kansas City, Mo., 1978; two-man show Rockhurst Coll., Kansas City, 1981; exhibited in group shows U. Kans., Lawrence, 1958, Chgo. Art Inst., 1963, Nelson Art Gallery, Kansas City, Mo., 1968, 74; represented in permanent collections Amarillo (Tex.) Art Center, Kansas City (Mo.) Pub. Library, Park Coll., Parkville, Mo. Mem. Coll. Art Assn. Roman Catholic. Contbr. art to profl. jours. Home and studio: 4109 Holmes St Kansas City MO 64110

LEE, MARVA JEAN, counselor, physical educator, family life education consultant; b. Cleveland, Miss., Feb. 16, 1938; d. Henry Davis and Willie Mae (Caver) Hardy. B.S., George Williams Coll., 1960, M.A., Northeastern Ill. U., Chgo., 1972; M.Edn., Loyola U., Chgo., 1978. Child care worker Inst. Juvenile Research, Chgo., 1960-61; phys. educator Chgo. Bd. Edn., 1961-69; instr. George Williams Coll., Downers Grove, Ill., 1969-73; phys. educator Chgo. Bd. Edn., 1973-86, counselor, 1986—, workshop leader family life edn., 1983—. Chmn. Chgo. Pub. Sch. campaign United Negro Coll. Fund, Chgo., 1981, 82, chmn. profl. women's aux., 1983—; bd. dirs. Chgo. com. NAACP Legal Defense and Edn. Fund, 1980—; sec. bd. dirs. Treshan Youth Found., Chgo., 1977—; mem. Com. to Elect/Re-elect Roland Burris State Comptroller, 1978—, Com. to Elect Harold Washington Mayor Chgo., 1982-83. Named Outstanding Vol., Mid-Am. chpt. ARC, Chgo., 1976, Outstanding Vol., United Negro Coll. Fund, N.Y.C., 1982; recipient Image award Fred Hampton Found., 1979. Mem. AAHPER and Dance, Ill. Assn. Health, Phys. Edn. and Recreation (mem. exec. com. Chgo. dist.), Ill. Council Family Relations, Alpha Kappa Alpha. Avocations: community vol.; community fundraiser; travel. Home: 8300 S Peoria St Chicago IL 60620 Office: Sol R Crown Community Acad 2128 S St Louis St Chicago IL 60623

LEE, MARY BENDELLA, educator; b. Vicksburg, Miss., Jan. 26; d. Robert Edward, Sr., and Artimease (Montgomery) L. B.A., U. Miss., 1970; M.Ed., Tex. So. U., 1974. Cert. tchr. sec. dept. sociology U. Miss., Oxford, 1968-70; community developer, tchr., Diabetic Youth Found., San Francisco, 1970; tchr. Peace Corps, Uganda, 1971-72, Sierra Leone, 1972-74; tchr. Houston Ind. Sch. Dist., 1975—, sec. faculty adv. council, 1976-77; instr. Houston Community Coll., 1975-78; sch. rep. Textbook Adoption Com., Houston, 1975-77; debate coach, dir. Ryan Jr. High Sch., Houston, 1976-77; presented workshop in English, 1977. Author: A Collection of Plays Performed by Junior High School Students, 1979; author: Religious Dramatic Plays, 1983-84. Sunday Sch. tchr. Mvara Secondary Sch., Uganda, 1972-73; scripture union dir. Kamakwie Secondary Sch., West Africa, 1972-74, youth supr., 1973; v.p. Mission Soc., Sunday Sch. tchr. Philadelphia Missionary Bapt. Ch., Houston, 1982—. Recipient cert. of recognition Gulf Coast Legal Found., 1976-77, Orgnl. Council, Ryan Jr. High Sch., 1978. Mem. NEA, Houston Tchrs. Assn., Tex. State Tchrs. Assn., Houston Council Tchrs. of English. Democrat. Baptist. Club: Cassette. Lodge: Order Eastern Star. Office: Houston Ind Sch Dist 3830 Richmond Ave Houston TX 77027

LEE, MARY EILEEN, retail manager, educator, consultant; b. Cin., Apr. 11, 1950; d. George H. and Virginia M. (Loechel) McManis; m. James L. Lee, Jan. 15, 1972; children—Sean, Mark. B.A., U. Cin., 1971. Asst. buyer H&S Pogue, Cin., 1970-71, assoc. buyer, 1971-72; mem. faculty, head dept. So. Ohio Coll., Cin., 1972-76; mem. faculty Nassau Community Coll., Garden City, N.Y., 1982—; service mgr. Macy's, Garden City, 1982-85, tng. mgr. Macy's, 1985—; prin. Lee Services, cons., Baldwin, N.Y., 1978-82. Pres., Baldwin Newcomers Club, 1982-83; adv. Nassau County Democratic party, 1984. Mem. La Leche League (leader 1978—). Home: 2321 Harrison Ave Baldwin NY 11510

LEE, MAY HONG-MAN, lawyer; b. Hong Kong, Nov. 8, 1952, came to U.S., 1980; d. Ming and Maria Chiu-Kwan (Tseng) L.; m. William Chen, Aug. 2, 1977 (div. Aug. 1981). Student Calif. Luth. Coll., 1969-71; B.S. in Communications, U. Ill., 1973; J.D., Loyola U., Los Angeles, 1982. Bar: Calif. 1983; notary pub., Calif. Creative dir. Ideamart Advt. (HK), Ltd., Kowloon, Hong Kong, 1974-76; media rep. Mediareps, Inc., Hong Kong and Philippines, 1976; group gen. mgr. Maria Lee's Enterprises, Ltd., Hong Kong, 1975-83; law clk. Singer & Akullian, Los Angeles, 1981, Steven Lewin Law Offices, Los Angeles, 1983; extern to Judge John L. Cole, Los Angeles Superior Ct., 1982; assoc. Daniel Y.L. Wu Law Offices, Los Angeles, 1983—; dir. Maria's Bakery Co., Ltd., Hong Kong, Maria Lee's Enterprises, Hong Kong, Ltd., Hong Kong. Mem. ABA, Calif. State Bar, Los Angeles County Bar Assn., ACLU, Soc. Profl. Journalists. Club: Royal Hong Kong Yacht. Home: 969 Hilgard Ave Apt 308 Los Angeles CA 90024 Office: Daniel YL Wu Law Offices Suite 2518 3435 Wilshire Blvd Los Angeles CA 90010

LEE, MAYA, psychologist; b. Chgo., Sept. 30, 1937; d. Philip B. and Renee A. (Roll) Dispensa; B.A., Governors State U., Park Forest, Ill., 1974, M.A., 1975; Ph.D., U.S. Internat. U., San Diego, 1977; children by previous marriage—Barbara P., Elizabeth R., Renee M. Foss, Kelly A. Profl. artist, 1969-73; intern San Bernardino County (Calif.) Mental Health, 1977-78, psychologist, 1978-80; pvt. practice psychotherapy, San Bernardino, 1980—; mem. faculty Crafton Hills Coll., Yucaipa, Calif., Calif. State Coll., San Bernardino; one-woman art exhibit Monroe Gallery, Chgo., 1973. Bd. dirs. S. Suburban Women's Liberation Coalition, 1972-75, Park Forest YWCA, 1974-75, Rape Crisis Center, San Bernardino, 1980-81. Mem. Am. Psychol. Assn., Inland Psychol. Assn., NOW. Democrat. Jewish. Address: 1797 N Arrowhead Ave San Bernardino CA 92405

LEE, MICHELE, actress; b. Los Angeles, June 24, 1942; d. Jack and Sylvia Helen (Silverstein) Dusick; m. James Farentino, Feb. 20, 1966 (div. 1983); 1 son, David Michael. Appeared in: Broadway play How To Succeed in Business Without Really Trying, 1962-64; Seesaw, 1973; appeared in movie How To Succeed in Business Without Really Trying, 1967, The Love Bug, 1969; TV series Knots Landing, 1979—; TV films include: Only With Married Men, 1974, Dark Victory, 1976, Having Babies, 1978, Bud and Lou, 1978; dir. Oliver!, Civic Light Opera, San Jose, Calif., 1979. Recipient Top Star of Tomorrow award Motion Picture Exhibitors of U.S. and Can., 1967, Drama Desk award Broadway Critics, 1973, Outer Critics Circle award, 1973; nominated for Antoinette Perry award, 1973-74, Emmy for Knots Landing, 1981-82. Office: care CBS Entertainment Press Info Knots Landing Set 51W 52d St New York NY 10019

LEE, MILDRED SCHIFF, art cons., art gallery exec.; b. Columbus, Ohio, Apr. 4, 1920; d. Robert W. and Rebecca (Lurie) Schiff; B.A., U. Wis., 1941; m. Herbert C. Lee, Oct. 21, 1941; children—Thomas H., Richard S., Jonathan. Owner, operator Lee Gallery, Belmont, Mass., 1970—; mem. art bd. overseers Brandeis U., 1963-72; mem. visitors com. Mus. Fine Arts, 1973-77; chmn. Com. to Rescue Italian Art, 1967; art history tchr. Belmont Hill Sch., 1965-68; modern art lectr. Adult Edn. Groups, 1960-68; co-chmn. art exhbns. and sales, bd. dirs. Friends of Art, Boston U., 1960-61; mem. council of friends, mem. acquisition com. Decordova and Dana Mus.; charge outdoor art exhbns. and music festivals Cape Cod Conservatory Music and Art, 1958-59. Pres., Friends of Rose Art Mus.; sec. bd. dirs. Assn. of Art of Music; bd. dirs. Boston U. Youth Symphony Orch., New Arts Orch., Young Audiences, Am. Jewish Com., Jewish Family and Childrens Service, League Women Voters of Brookline; trustee, adviser music com. Belmont Community Center; trustee womens com., Belmont area chmn. Combined Jewish Appeal; mem. womens com. Brandeis U., leader art study groups, mem. Extended Ednl. Program for Women; bd. overseers Met. Center. Clubs: Belmont Country, Belmont Hill. Home: 94 Juniper Rd Belmont MA 02178

LEE, MIRANDA, advertising agency executive; b. Hong Kong, July 12, 1952; came to U.S., 1959; d. Patrick and Vicky (King) L. B.A., Sarah Lawrence Coll., 1973. Acct. exec. BBDO, N.Y.C., 1973-77, Grey Advt., N.Y.C., 1977-79; mgmt. supr. Rosenfeld, Sirowitz & Lawson, N.Y.C., 1979-82; v.p., mgmt. rep. Needham Harper & Steers, N.Y.C., 1982-84; sr. v.p. J. Walter Thompson, N.Y.C., 1984—. Office: Brouillard Communications 420 Lexington Ave New York NY 10017

LEE, NANCY ELLEN, med. technologist; b. Southington, Conn., Apr. 30, 1954; d. Joseph and Martha (Luty) Pellecchia; B.S. in M.T., U. Conn., 1976; m. Robert E. Lee, June 27, 1981; 1 dau., Sarah Ann. Bench technologist William W. Backus Hosp., Norwich, Conn., 1976-81, chemistry/spl. chemistry supr., 1981—. Bd. dirs. Northeastern Conn. Home Health Care Assn., 1980-81. Mem. Am. Soc. Clin. Pathologists. Office: 326 Washington St Norwich CT 06360

LEE, NELDA S., art dealer, art appraiser, television producer; b. Gorman, Tex., July 3, 1941; d. Olan C. and Onis L.; A.S. (Franklin Lindsay Found. grantee), Tarleton State U., Tex., 1961; B.A. in Fine Arts, N. Tex. State U., 1963; postgrad. Tex. Tech. U., 1964, San Miguel de Allende Art Inst., Mexico, 1965; 1 dau., Jeanna Lea Pool. Head dept. art Ector High Sch., Odessa, Tex., 1963-68. Bd. dirs. Odessa YMCA, 1970, bd. dirs. Am. Heart Assn., Odessa, 1975; fund raiser Easter Seal Telethon, Odessa, 1978-79; bd. dirs. Ector County (Tex.) Cultural Center, 1979—, Tex. Bus. Hall of Fame, 1980-85; bd. dirs., mem. acquisition com. Permian Basin Presdl. Mus., Odessa, 1978; bd. dirs., chairperson acquisition com. Odessa Art Mus., 1979—; pres. Mega-Tex. Prodns., TV and movie producers; pres. Ector County Democratic Women's Club, 1975. Recipient Designer-Craftsman award El Paso Mus. Fine Arts, 1964. Mem. Am. Soc. Appraisers, Appraisers Assn. Am., Appraisers of Fine Arts Soc., Nat. Soc. Lit. and the Arts, Tex. Assn. Art Dealers (pres. 1978-79), Odessa C. of C. Mem. Ch. of Christ. Contbr. articles to profl. jours. Office: PO Box 6385 Odessa TX 79767

LEE, NORMA REBECCA, fundraiser; b. Oklahoma City, Jan. 10, 1942; d. James Norman and Ruth Rebecca (Stephens) Blalock; m. Gerald Hugh Graham, Dec. 28, 1960 (div. June 1972); children—Gerald Hugh Jr., Jay Courtland, Kelly Ryan. B.Gen. Studies, Wichita State U., 1976. Nat. sales rep. Sta. KAKE-TV, Wichita, 1976-77; fundraiser Muscular Dystrophy Assn., Wichita, 1977-78, Wichita State U. Endowment Assn., 1978—; lectr. seminars Southwestern Bell Telephone Co., Oklahoma City, also Kansas City, Kans., 1979—. Chairperson budget rev. sub-com. United Way, Wichita, 1980—; bd. dirs. YWCA, Wichita, 1979. Mem. AAUW, Women in Communications, Council for Advancement and Support Edn. (Excellence award 1979, Spl. Merit award 1980), Univ. Faculty Wives (dir. 1968-72). Republican. Methodist. Office: Wichita State U Endowment Assn 1845 Fairmount Wichita KS 67208

LEE, PAMELA ANNE, auditor; b. San Francisco, May 30, 1960; d. Larry D. and Alice Mary (Reece) L. B.A. in Bus., San Francisco State U., 1981. C.P.A. Typist, bookkeeper, tax acct. James G. Woo, C.P.A., San Francisco, 1979-85; tutor bus. math. and statistics San Francisco State U., 1979-80; teller to ops. officer Gibraltar Savs. and Loan, San Francisco, 1978-81; sr. acct. Price Waterhouse, San Francisco, 1981—; acctg. cons. New Performance Gallery, San Francisco, 1985, San Francisco Chamber Orch., 1986—. Mem. Am. Inst. C.P.A.s, Calif. Soc. C.P.A.s, Nat. Assn. Female Execs. Republican. Avocations: Reading; music; travel. Office: Price Waterhouse 555 California Suite 3600 San Francisco CA 94104

LEE, ROBERTA, health and behavioral sciences consultant, counselor, educator; b. Antioch, Calif., June 26, 1939; d. Earnest Maurice and Maxine Norene (Wilber) Nathan; m. Jerold Lee Eustace; children—Melissa Lorraine, Douglas Nathan. B-Grad. Bible Philosophy, Am. Bible Inst., Kansas City, Mo., 1981, D. Metaphysics, 1981, D.D., 1981; diploma in Dietetics, Brantridge Forest Sch., Sussex, Eng., 1983. Pvt. practice health and behavioral problems counselor, Newport Beach, Calif., 1963-72; owner, dir. Leeway Personal Devel. Inst., Montgomery, Ala., 1975—; pvt. practice health and behavioral problems counseling, Wilmington, N.C., 1982—; dir. Atlantean Way Health Resort, Antigua, Guatemala, 1987—; cons. and lectr. in field; numerous appearances in radio and TV. Author: Rainbow Disconnection, 1987; A Road Map to Life, 1979. Contbr. articles to profl. jours. Mem. Republican Presidential Task Force Com., 1980—, U.S. Senatorial Club, 1984—. Recipient Certificate of Appreciation, N.C. Chiropractic Assn., 1982; Honorary Recognition award N.C. Dept. Labor, 1985. Mem. Nat. Assn. Female Execs. Avocations: gourmet cooking; horseback riding; water sports; gardening. Office: PO Box 7155 Wilmington NC 28403

LEE, SHERYL LINETTE DUVONG, public health nutritionist; b. Oakland, Calif., Sept. 10, 1945; d. David Alvin and May Moytan (Hum) L.; A.A., Merritt Coll., 1965; B.S., U. Calif.-Berkeley, 1967, M.P.H., 1970, postgrad., 1971; postgrad. Ariz. State U., 1979—. Clin. dietitian, intern instr. Peter Bent Brigham Hosp., Boston, 1968-69; nutrition cons. maternal and child health Ariz. Dept. Health Services, Phoenix, 1971-76, regional nutrition coordinator, 1976-79; instr. dept. home econs. Ariz. State U., Tempe, 1981; chief Bur. Nutrition Services, Ariz. Dept. Health Services, Phoenix, 1979—; adj. faculty assoc. Ariz. State U., 1979—; asst. clin. prof. U. Hawaii, Manoa, 1986—; adj. faculty Central Ariz. Coll. nutrition cons. Devel. Assocs. Inc., Health Learning Systems, Gen. Foods Corp., Case Western Res. U., Ralston Purina Co., sta. KAET, Ariz. State U., 1984—. Editorial bd. Topics in Nutrition Jour. USPHS grantee, 1969-70. Mem. Soc. Nutrition Edn. (dir.), Am. Dietetic Assn., Ariz. Dietetic Assn., Central Ariz. Dist. Dietetic Assn., Am. Public Health Assn., Ariz. Public Health Assn., Nutrition Council Ariz., Assn. State and Territorial Public Health Nutrition Dirs., Chinese-Am. Profl. Assn. Ariz., Sigma Omicron Pi. Democrat. Presbyterian. Clubs. Phoenix Chinese Tennis Assn., Phoenix Young Chinese Americans. Office: 1740 W Adams St Phoenix AZ 85007

LEE, SHIRLEY RAE, court official; b. Ottawa, Ill., July 5, 1947; d. Roy Abner and Evelyn Elizabeth (Thompson) Johnson; m. Donald Ray Lee, June 21, 1969; children—Christopher Ray, Peggy Sue. Clerk Kendall County Treas., Yorkville, Ill., 1967-71, traffic clk., 1972-80, dep. circuit clk., 1974-80, circuit clk., 1980—; v.p. Zone 5 area Ill. Circuit Clks. Assn., 1983—. Twp. chmn. Cancer Soc., Big Grove, Ill., 1975-78; community rep. Kendall County 4-H Youth Council, 1982-86, mem. 4-H Teen Leadership Devel. Com., 1985-86. Mem. Newark Community Club, 1970-75; Kendall County Woman's Republican. Club. Mem. Ill. Assn. Ct. Clks., Ill. Assn. County Ofcls. Lutheran. Avocations: handcrafts; sewing; reading. Home: 104 Fayette St Box 293 Newark IL 60541 Office: Kendall County Circuit Clerk Box M Yorkville IL 60560

LEE, SHIU TAO, statistician; b. Taichung, Taiwan, Mar. 19, 1940; came to U.S. 1967, naturalized 1975; d. Su and Yei Nu (Liu) Hung; m. Chun-Cheng Lee, Jan. 8, 1967; children—Eming R., Cincy H. B.A., Taiwan Normal U., 1965; M.Stats., N.C. State U.-Raleigh, 1970, postgrad. 1971-72. Tchr., Taichung, 1958-61; tchr. high sch. English, Taipei, Taiwan, 1965-66; statis. analyst N.C. State Govt., Raleigh, 1973-74; programmer/analyst Power & Light Co., Raleigh, 1974-75; scientist N.C. Power & Light Co., Raleigh, 1975-76; statistician NIOSH, Cin., 1976—; cons. in field. Contbr. articles to profl. jours. Pres. Cin. Taiwanese Women's Club, 1984-85. Recipient NIOSH cash award, 1985. Mem. AAAS, Am. Statis. Assn. Home: 10285 Gentlewind Dr Cincinnati OH 45242 Office: Nat Inst Occupational Safety and Health 4676 Columbia Pkwy Cincinnati OH 45226

LEE, SUSANNA NESTER, educational administrator, speech therapist; b. Phila., June 24, 1952; d. Orville Brown and Mildred (Veit) Nester; m. Edward Johnson Lee, Aug. 20, 1977. B.S. magna cum laude, W.Va. U., 1973; M.A., Gallaudet Coll., 1975; Ed.D., U. Del., 1984. Tchr. deaf edn. Kendall Demonstration Sch., Washington, 1974-75; tchr. deaf and blind Statewide Deaf-Blind Program, Newark, Del., 1975-77; coordinator deaf and blind program State of Del., 1977-78; prin. deaf sch. Christina Sch. Dist., Newark, 1978—; pres. Del. Registry Interpreters for Deaf, 1978-80. Mem. Alexander Graham Bell Assn., Conv. Am. Instrs. Deaf, Assn. Secondary Sch. Adminstrs., Del. Assn. Sch. Adminstrs., Council Exceptional Children, Nat. Assn. Deaf. Methodist. Club: Del. Underwater Swim (treas. 1980-82) (Wilmington). Lodge: Order Eastern Star. Office: Margaret S Sterck Sch for Hearing Impaired 620 E Chestnut Hill Rd Newark DE 19713

LEE, VIVIAN INEZ, administrator; b. Teague, Tex., May 27, 1941; d. Sanford and Annie B. (Moseley) Burks; m. Wilford Chancey Lee, Dec. 24, 1961; children—Avery Bernard, Adedra, Nina. Student Merritt Coll., 1967-68, Vista Coll., 1980; B.A., St. Mary's Coll., 1978. Contract asst. Def. Logestic Agy., Alameda, Calif., 1966-68, contract specialist, Burlingham, Calif., 1968-73, contract adminstr., Sunnyvale, Calif., 1973-77, San Jose, Calif., 1977-79, adminstrv. contracting officer, San Bruno, Calif., 1979—. EEO counselor Def. Contract Adminstrn. Service, Peninsula Offices, San Jose, 1977-79; Black history chmn. Def. Contract Adminstrn. Service Mgmt. Area, San Bruno, Calif., 1981-82; sec. PTA, Berkeley Unified Sch. Dist., 1972, pres., 1973. Mem. Nat. Contract Mgmt. Assn., Mt. Zion Dist. Assn. (v.p. 1969-78), Nat. Bapt. Conv. of America (v.p. 1975-78).

LEECH, ELEANOR BERNICE, foreign service officer; b. Providence, d. Francis R. and Cecelia M. (Smith) L. Student Sophia U., Tokyo, 1961-63, Montgomery Coll., Md., 1981, 82, 83, Fgn. Service Inst., Arlington, Va., 1983-84. With Fgn. Service (Civil Service), U.S. State Dept., 1955—, chief ofcl. travel U.S. Passport Office, Washington, 1976-80, chief spl. services, 1981-83, Am. Consul Am. Embassy, Lima, Peru, 1984—, fed. women's program coordinator, 1984—. Nurses' aide Vols. of Am., Providence, 1950-55; cadet CAP, 1949-52. Mem. Consular Officers Corps Lima and Callao, Fgn. Service Assn. Club: Pilot (Lima). Avocations: painting; ceramics; photography; sailing; scuba diving. Office: US Embassy Lima APO Miami FL 34031

LEEDOM, BARBARA SUE, writer, producer; b. Bklyn., July 26, 1938; d. John H. and Helen P. (Treadwell) Dirlam; m. Guy H. Leedom, Aug. 26, 1961 (div. 1978); children—Dennis, Cheryl, Timothy. B.S. in English and Edn., SUNY-Cortland, 1960; postgrad. Harvard U. Tchr. pub. schs., Norwalk, Calif. and Wilmington, Del., 1961-63; news reporter Town Crier, Inc., Wayland, Mass., 1967-76; editor Jimmy Fund, Boston, 1978-78; communications specialist John Hancock Co., Boston, 1979—; writer, producer John Hancock Video Network. Contbr. articles to trade publs. Tutor English as 2d lang. Action for Boston Community Devel., 1972—, fundraiser Oxfam of Am., 1979—; pub. relations vol. for Democratic senatorial candidate, Mass., 1980—. Mem. Women in Communications, Publicity Club, Internat. TV Assn., Boston Assn. Bus. Communicators. Episcopalian. Home: 26 Wolcott Ave Andover MA 01810 Office: John Hancock Co PO Box 111 Boston MA 02117

LEEDS, CANDACE, public relations executive; b. N.Y.C., July 28, 1947; d. Lawrence and Phyllis (Friedman) L. B.S., Skidmore Coll., 1969; M.A., NYU, 1971. Assoc. dir. Town Hall, N.Y.C., 1972-76; account exec. Grey & Davis, N.Y.C., 1976-77, v.p., 1977-78, sr. v.p., 1978-80; sr. v.p. The Rowland Co., N.Y.C., 1980—. Nat. bd. dirs. Young Audiences, N.Y.C., 1982—, N.Y. Lyric Opera, N.Y.C., 1980—, Ronald McDonald House. Spl. scholar Juilliard Sch. Music, N.Y.C., 1959-65; recipient Cert. of Achievement, Fontainebleau Ecole d'Art Am., 1968. Mem. Women in Communication. Club: Liberty (N.Y.C.). Office: The Rowland Co 415 Madison Ave New York NY 10017

LEEDS, ELIZABETH LOUISE, miniature collectibles executive; b. Los Angeles, July 24, 1925; d. Charles Furnival and Etta Louise (Jackson) Mayes; m. Walter Albert Leeds, Jan. 20, 1973 (dec.); children—Pam Ravey Lewis, Linda Ravey McCallam, Diane Ravey Lathrop, Tom Ravey. Student pub. sch., Prescott, Ariz. Lic. real estate agt., Ariz., cert. motel mgr. Real estate agt., Prescott, Ariz., 1962-64; sec. to mgr. Kon Tiki Hotel, Phoenix, 1964-65; draftsman Goleta Water Dist., Calif., 1965-68; asst. to vp research and design House of Mosaics, Santa Barbara, Calif., 1968-69; exec. chmn. poster design, dept. music U. Calif.-Santa Barbara, 1969-74; v.p. Colorform West, Inc., Santa Barbara, 1974-75; pres. Leeds Miniatures, Inc., Lincoln City, Oreg., 1975—; lamp and silk screen designer Colorform West, Inc. Illustrator: Just A Story by Gustav Coenod, 1964. Mem. Hobby Industry Am., Miniatures Industry Assn. Am., Nat. Assn. Female Execs. Republican. Clubs: Assn. Huanistic Psychology, Internat. New Thought Alliance, Assn. Transpersonal Psychology. Home: PO Box 269 Lincoln City OR 97367 Office: PO Box 269 Lincoln City OR 97367

LEEDY, EMILY L. FOSTER (MRS. WILLIAM N. LEEDY), consultant; b. Jackson, Ohio, Sept. 24, 1921; d. Raymond S. and Grace (Garrett) Foster; B.S., Rio Grande Coll., 1949; M.Ed., Ohio U., 1957; postgrad. Ohio State U., 1956, Mich. State U., 1958-59, Case Western Res. U., 1963-65; m. William N. Leedy, Jan. 1, 1943; 1 son. Dwight A. Tchr., Frankfort (Ohio) schs., 1941-46, Ross County Schs., Chillicothe, Ohio, 1948-53; elementary and supervising tchr. Chillicothe City Schs., 1953-56; dean of girls, secondary tchr. Berea City Schs., 1956-57; vis. tchr. Parma City Schs., 1957-59; counselor Homewood-Flossmoor High Sch., Flossmoor, Ill., 1959-60; teaching fellow Ohio U., 1960-62; asst. prof. edn., 1962-64; assoc. prof., counselor Cuyahoga Community Coll., 1964-66; dean of women Cleve. State U., 1966-67, assoc. dean student affairs, 1967-69; guidance dir. Cathedral Latin Sch., 1969-71; dir. women's service div. Ohio Bur. Employment Services, 1971-83; cons. in edn. Mem. adv. com. S.W. Community Info. Service, 1959-60; youth com. S.W. YWCA, 1963-70, chmn., 1964-70, bd. mgmt., 1964-70; group services council Cleve. Welfare Fedn., 1964-66; chmn. Met. YWCA Youth Program study com., 1966, bd. dirs., 1966-72, v.p., 1967-68; chmn. adv. council Ohio State U. Sch. Home Econs., 1977-80. Named Cleve. area Woman of Achievement, 1969; named to Ohio Women's Hall of Fame, 1979. Mem. AAUW, Am., Northeastern Ohio (sec. 1958-59, exec. com. 1963-64, public relations chmn. 1962-64, newsletter chmn., editor 1963-64, del. nat. assembly 1959-63) personnel and guidance assns., Nat. Vocational Guidance Assn., Am., Ohio sch. counselors assns., Am. Rehab. Counseling Assn., Nat. (publs. com. 1967-69, profl. employment practices com. 1980-82, Meritorious Service award 1984), Ohio (program chmn. 1967, editor Newsletter 1968-71) assns. women deans and counselors, Cleve. Counselors Assn. (pres. 1966), Women's Equity Action League, Zonta Internat. (exec. bd. 1968-70, treas. 1970-72, chmn. dist. V Status of Women 1980-81), Nat. Assn. Commns. for Women (dir. 1980-81, sec. 1981-83), Rio Grande Coll. Alumni Assn. (Atwood Achievement award 1975), Bus. and Profl. Women's Club (Nike award 1973), Delta Kappa Gamma. Club. Women's City (Cleve.). Home: 580 Lindberg Blvd Berea OH 44017 Office: 699 Rocky Rd Chillicothe OH 45601

LEEK, SANDRA DONNETTE, lawyer; b. Durham, N.C., Oct. 8, 1954; d. James Donald Leek and Inez (Rempson) Leek Anderson. B.A., Tufts U., 1976; J.D., Ind. U., 1979. Bar: Ind. 1979. Asso. instr. Ind. U., Bloomington, 1977-78; with Legal Services Orgn. Ind., Indpls., 1978-81, staff atty., 1979-81; dir. Ind. Legal Services Support Center, Indpls., 1981-86. You and the Law, 1983-86, mgr. atty., 1986—. Bd. dirs. Nat. Low-Income Housing Coalition, Washington, 1983; chair pub. affairs and world mutual services cons. Indpls. YWCA, 1983-86. Bd. dirs. Ind. Black Expo, Inc., 1985—, Fall Creek YMCA, 1986—. Mem. Marion County Bar Assn. (v.p. 1985-86), Nat. Legal Aid and Defender Assn. (civil com. rep. 1983—), Ind. Bar Assn., Coalition 100 Black Women (polit. action com., chair 1985—), Delta Sigma Theta. Democrat. Office: Ind Legal Services Support Center 107 N Pennsylvania St Suite 1008 Indianapolis IN 46204

LEEMAN, LINDA BONNIE, electric utility executive; b. Milw., Nov. 30, 1949; d. Wilson Woodrow and Lois Jane (Becker) L.; m. Gary Wayne Davis, Aug. 9, 1968 (div. 1972); m. 2d, Stan Ryan Baker, June 22, 1974. Student U. Wis., 1972-74; B.A. in Bus. Adminstrn., U. South Fla., 1980. Clk. printing services Schlitz Brewing Co., Milw., 1972-74; office mgr. Fla. Printing Services, Ft. Myers, 1974-77; sec. engring. Lee County Elec. Coop., Ft. Myers, 1977-78, personnel asst., 1978-79, mgr. employment, 1979-80, mgr. human resources, 1980—. Chmn., Lee County Sch. Bd. Career Adv. Com., Ft. Myers, 1980—; mem. Lee Vo-Tech Bus. Adv. Com., 1981—; pres. Big Bros./Big Sisters, 1982—. Mem. Am. Soc. Personnel Adminstrs. (v.p. 1984, pres. 1985), Personnel Assn. Southwest Fla. Office: Lee County Electric Coop 197 Bayshore Rd North Fort Myers FL 33903

LEE-RIFFE, NANCY MCLAURINE, English educator; b. Danville, Ky., Jan. 16, 1933; d. Madison Johnson and Nan Danzler (Mayers) Lee; m. William Joseph Riffe, Aug. 25, 1955 (div. 1972); children—Christopher Joseph, Madison McLaurine, Daniel Lee, Sara Elizabeth, Susanna Jestine. B.A., Agnes-Scott Coll., 1954; A.M., Radcliffe-Harvard U., 1955; Ph.D., U. Ky., 1963. Instr. Temple U., Phila., 1960-64; profl. asst. Ednl. Testing Service, Princeton, N.J., 1964-65; asst. prof. Ursinus Coll., Collegeville, Pa., 1965-67; assoc. prof. LaSalle Coll., Phila., 1967-68; prof. English Eastern Ky. U., Richmond, 1968—; reader Ednl. Testing Service, Princeton, 1965—. Author: (manuel) Utilization of Library Resources, 1982. Contbr. articles to profl. publs. Fellow Woodrow Wilson Found., 1954-55, AAUW, 1959-60, Henry E. Huntington, 1977, 79, NEH, 1978. Mem. Phi Beta Kappa. Home: 110 Leimaur Dr Richmond KY 40475 Office: Eastern Ky U Wallace 217 English Richmond KY 40475

LEESON, JANET CAROLINE TOLLEFSON, cake specialties company executive; b. L'Anse, Mich., May 23, 1933; d. Harold Arnold and Sylvia Aino (Makikangas) Tollefson; student Prairie State Coll., 1970-76; master decorator degree Wilton Sch. Cake Decorating, 1974; m. Raymond Harry Leeson, May 20, 1961; 1 son, Barry Raymond; children by previous marriage—Warren Scott, Debra Delores. Mgr., Peak Service Cleaners, Chgo., 1959; co-owner Ra-Ja-Lee TV, Harvey, Ill., 1961-66; founder and head fgn. trade dept. Wilton Enterprises, Inc., Chgo., 1969-75; tchr. cake decorating J.C. Penney Co., Matteson, Ill., 1975; office mgr. Pat Carpenter Assocs., Highland, Ind., 1975; pres. Leeson's Party Cakes, Inc., cake supplies and cake sculpture, Tinley Park, Ill., 1976—; lectr. and demonstrator cake sculpture and decorating. Sec., Lutheran Ch. Women; active worker Boy Scouts Am. and Girl Scouts U.S.A., 1957-63; bd. dirs. Whittier PTA, 1962-70; mem. Bremen Twp. Republican Orgn.; councillor Calumet council Boy Scouts Am.; mem. Ingalls Meml. Hosp. Aux., 1963—. Recipient numerous awards for cake sculpture and decorating, 1970—, 1st place award at nat. level Retail Bakers Am., 1983. Mem. Am. Bus. Woman's Assn. (chpt. public relations dir.), Chgo. Area Retail Bakers Assn. (1st pl. in regional midwest wedding cake competition 1978, 80, 2d place 1983), Internat. Cake Exploration Soc. Lutheran. Home: 6713 W 163d Pl Tinley Park IL 60477 Office: Leeson's Party Cakes Inc 6713 W 163d Pl Tinley Park IL 60477

LEESS, LYNELLE S., advertising company executive, creative consultant; b. Kingston, N.Y., Sept. 26, 1954; d. Herbert Franklin and Sara Jane Schwartz; m. Jonathan Marc Leess, Apr. 26, 1980. B.A. in English, B.S. in Bus. Adminstrn., Skidmore Coll., Saratoga Springs, N.Y., 1976; postgrad. New Sch., N.Y.C. Creative asst. Revlon, N.Y.C., 1976-77; advt./promotion coordinator L'Oreal, N.Y.C., 1978; copywriter Ted Bates Advt., N.Y.C., 1979-81; creative group head, sr. v.p. Benton & Bowles Advt., N.Y.C., 1981—; adj. prof. advt.; cons. in field. Contbr. articles to profl. jour. Recipient Effie award. Club: Skidmore (Saratoga). Home: 515 E 79th St New York NY 10021 Office: Benton & Bowles 909 3d Ave New York NY 10022

LEET, BARBARA EVANS, former financial analyst, stockbroker; b. Allentown, Pa., July 28, 1951; d. Raymond Edward and Elsie Marie (Wagner) Evans; m. Douglas Charles Leet, June 20, 1981. Student, Wheaton (Ill.) Coll., 1969-71; B.S. in Nursing, Columbia U., 1973; M.S. In Nursing, U. N.C., 1978, M.B.A., 1981. R.N.; lic. real estate broker, N.C.; registered stockbroker. Nurse, N.C. Meml. Hosp., Chapel Hill, 1975-78; market research analyst Eli Lilly Co., Indpls., 1980; real estate broker Village LandMarks, Inc., Chapel Hill, N.C., 1978-81; mgr. mktg. Mallinckrodt, Inc., Raleigh, N.C., 1982-83; fin. analyst, stockbroker Am. Comml. Securities, Raleigh, N.C., 1983—. Com. mem. N.C. Mus. Natural History, 1983—, Wake County Med. Aux., 1981—; mem. Chapel Hill Service League, 1978-79. Recipient Johnson Scholarship award, 1976-78. Mem. Am. Mktg. Assn., M.B.A. Alumni Assn. (mem. orgn. com. 1983—), Jr. League Raleigh, Republican. Club: Brookhaven Garden (com. mem. 1981—). Home: 6004 Winthrop Dr Raleigh NC 27612

LEET, MILDRED ELOWSKY, consultant; b. N.Y.C., Aug. 9, 1922; d. Samuel Milton and Isabella (Zeitz) Elowsky; B.A., NYU, 1942; m. Louis J. Robbins, Feb. 23, 1941 (dec. 1970); children—Jane, Aileen; m. 2d, Glen Leet, Aug. 9, 1974. Partner, Leet & Leet, cons. on women in devel., N.Y.C., 1978—. Pres. women's div. United Cerebral Palsy, N.Y.C., 1951-52, bd. dirs., 1953—, chmn. bd., 1953-55; rep. Nat. Council Women U.S. at UN, 1957-64, 1st v.p., 1959-64, pres., 1964-68, hon. pres., 1968-70; sec., v.p. conf. group U.S. Nat. Orgns. at UN, 1961-64, 76-78, vice chmn., sec., 1962-64, mem. exec. com., 1961-65, 75-79, chmn. hospitality info. service, 1960-66; vice chmn. exec. com. NGO's with UN Office Pub. Info., 1976-78, chmn. ann. conf., 1977, chmn. com. on water, desertification, habitat and environment Conf. NGO's with consultative status with ECOSOC, 1976—, mem. exec. com. World Conf. of UN Decade for Women, 1980; mem. exec. com. Internat. Council Women, 1960-73, v.p., 1970-73; chmn. program planning com., women's com. OEO, 1967-72; cons. Club of Rome, UNITAR-CEESTEM, Joint Symposium on Regionalism and the NIEO, UN, 1980; chmn. com. on natural disasters N.Am. Com. on Environment, 1973-77; N.Y. State chmn. UN Day, 1976; co-chmn. Vols. for Stevenson, N.Y. State, 1956; vice chmn. task force Nat. Dem. Com., 1969-72; mem. N.Y. State Commn. on Power of Local Govt., 1970-73; chmn. Coll. for Human Services; bd. dirs. Save the Children Fedn., Trickle Up Program, N.Y.C., 1979—; v.p. Am. Council Human Services, 1981; mem. presdl. del. to Brazzaville (Congo) Centennial Celebration, 1980; sec. Inst. for Mediation and Conflict Resolution, Spirit of Stockholm, Hotline Internat.; rep. Internat. Peace Acad. at UN, 1974-77, Internat. Soc. Community Devel., 1977—; del. at large 1st Nat. Women's Conf., Houston, 1977; chmn. task force on internat. interdependence N.Y. State Women's Meeting, 1977; bd. dirs. New Directions, 1978-81; mem. Task Force on Poverty, 1977-81, chmn. Task Force on Women, Sci. and Tech. for Devel., 1978-80; U.S. del. UN Status of Women Commn., 1978; U.S. del. UN Conf. Sci. and Tech. for Devel., 1979, mem. global adv. bd. Internat. Expn. of Rural Devel.; trustee Internat. Inst. Haiti, 1981-85, Overseas Edn. Fund, 1983—; fellow council internat. fellows U. Bridgeport, 1982—; mem. Panel Experts on Sci., Tech. and Women, 1983—. Editor: UN Calendar and Digest, 1959-64; Measure of Mankind, 1963: bd. editors Peace & Change, 1980; contbr. articles to various publs. Home: 54 Riverside Dr New York NY 10024 also 2 Briar Oak Dr Weston CT 06883 Office: 790 Madison Ave New York NY 10021

LEETARU, ILSE, artist, printmaker; b. Tallinn, Estonia, Oct. 27, 1915; came to U.S., 1949; d. Aleksander and Pauline (Laas) Kopper; m. Edmund Edvard Leetaru, Dec. 19, 1936; children—Tonis, Hannes. Student Conservatorium of Music, Tallinn, 1936; diploma Sch. Visual Arts, N.Y.C., 1964; postgrad. New Sch., N.Y.C., 1970. Freelance fashion illustrator, N.Y.C., 1964-68. One woman shows: N.Y.C., 1978, 82, Toronto, Ont., Can., 1985; group shows include: Paris, 1976, 78, 81, Stockholm, 1980, Egypt, 1981, Yokohama, Japan, 1982, 83, 84, Tokyo Met. Art Mus., 1985. Recipient Prix de Paris award Academia R Duncan, Paris, 1976, 78; Medaille de Bronze Academia R Duncan, 1981. Mem. Nat. Assn. Women Artists (1st prize printmaking 1978). Lutheran.

LEFEVER, MARGARET BRIGGS, media specialist; b. Marathon, Iowa, Feb. 17; d. Edwin Arnold and M. Louise (Smith) Briggs; m. Ernest W. Lefever, June 24, 1951; children—David, Bryce. A.A., Stephens Coll., Columbia, Mo., 1946; B.S. in Edn., Northwestern U., 1948; M.S. in Library Sci., Cath. U. Am., 1971. Supr., UN Guides, N.Y.C., 1953-55; media specialist Montgomery County Pub. Schs., Rockville, Md., 1970-81, 84—, tchr. specialist, 1981-84; audio-visual editor Social Edn. mag., 1985—; book indexer. Mem. Chevy Chase (Md.) Town Council, 1964-68. Fulbright fellow, Israel, 1983. Mem. ALA, Am. Assn. Sch. Librarians, Soc. Sch. Librarians Internat. (founding bd. 1986—), Beta Phi Mu, Phi Delta Kappa. Republican. Episcopalian. Home: 7106 Beechwood Dr Chevy Chase MD 20815 Office: Montgomery County Pub Schs 850 Hungerford Dr Rockville MD 20815

LE FEVRE, CAROL BAUMANN, psychologist; b. Pierron, Ill., Nov. 26, 1924; d. Berhard Robert and Eunice Leone Hoyt (Heston) Baumann; A.A., Stephens Coll., 1944; M.A. in Sociology, U. Chgo., 1948, M.S. Teaching in Edn., 1965, Ph.D. in Human Devel., 1971; m. Perry Deyo Le Fevre, Sept. 14, 1946; children—Susan Le Fevre Hook, Judith Ann, Peter Gerret. Tchr., Chgo. Theol. Sem. Nursery Sch., 1962-63, U. Chgo., Lab. Sch., 1965-66; asst. prof. psychology St. Xavier Coll., Chgo., 1970-74, asso. prof., 1974-85, acting chmn. dept. psychology, 1970-71, chmn. dept. psychology, 1971-77, asst. dir. Inst. Family Studies, 1973-82, dir., 1982-85; intern in clin. psychology with Adlerian pvt. practitioner, Chgo., 1973-75; pvt. practice clin. psychology, Chgo., 1975—; mem. staff Logos Inst. Chgo. Theol. Sem., 1973-76; speaker in field. Pub. Health Service tng. grantee NIMH, 1969; registered psychologist, Ill. Mem. Am., Ill. psychol. assns., Gerontol. Soc., N.Am. Soc. Adlerian Psychology, Phi Beta Kappa. Mem. United Ch. of Christ. Research, publs. on subjects including returning women grad. students' changing self-conceptions, women's roles, inner city children's perceptions of sch., aging and religion. Home: 1376 E 58th St Chicago IL 60637 Office: 400 Ravinia Pl Orland Park IL 60462

LEFEVRE, GERALDINE, librarian; b. Seminole, Okla., Nov. 18, 1925; d. Herman Cecil and Mary Elizabeth (Hill) Sullivan; 1 dau., Kathleen. B.A. in Library Sci., U. Okla., 1947. Children's librarian San Antonio Pub. Library, 1950-55, librarian-in-charge br., 1955-61, children's coordinator, 1961-70, asst. library dir., 1970—. Mem. San Antonio Council Pres., 1978-80; bd. mem. Beautify San Antonio. Recipient Spl. Recognition award San Antonio Council Pres., 1979; awards of appreciation San Antonio Youth Orgn., 1979, San Antonio Ind. Tchrs. Council, 1979. Mem. Tex. Library Assn. (past chmn. dist. 10, past chmn. pub. library div., chmn. local arrangements 1982), Bexar Library Assn. (chmn. 1960-61, Julia Grothaus award 1982), San Antonio Coll. Library Technicians (adv. bd. 1983). Home: 15118 Circle Oak San Antonio TX 78232

LEFF, JULIETTE, painter, educator; b. Rockville Centre, N.Y., Mar. 20, 1939; d. Samuel and Marie (Rosenberg) Simon; B.A. with honors in Art, CCNY, 1962; M.A., Hunter Coll., 1976; student (Max Beckmann Painting fellow), Bklyn. Mus. Art Sch., 1962-64; Margaret Lowengrund scholar Pratt Graphic Ctr.; studied with Mark Rothko, Adolph Gottlieb, Tony Smith,

Eugene Goosen; children—Alexandra, Gabriela. Art edn. coordinator Bronx Mus., 1976-77; artist-in-residence teaching grantee, 1977-82; adj. faculty Kingsborough Community Coll., 1979, Goddard Coll. at Bank St. Coll., 1981; tchr. privately; N.Y.C. Bd. Edn. fine art tchr. at Mus. Natural History, 1984-85; selected exhbns.: N.Y. Found. for the Arts, 1977, Paul Kessler Gallery, 1968, Loeb Center, NYU, 1971, L.I. U., 1972, Purdue U., Occlectix, Columbia U., 1969, Butler Inst. Am. Art, Youngstown, Ohio, 1970, NYU, 1971, Yr. of the Woman Reprise, Bronx Mus. Arts, 1976, What is Feminist Art? Writings of 200 Woman Artists, La. World Expn., 1984, Studio in a Sch. Assn., 1984, Marymount Coll., W.C.A., Coll. Art Assn., 1983, Cathedral of St. John the Divine, 1977, Westbeth Gallery, 1985-86, La. World's Fair, 1984; represented in permanent collections: Chase Manhattan Bank Art Collection, U.S.I.A. Print Collection, Aubrey Cartwright Mus. Religious Art, Cathedral of St. John the Divine, Jewish Bd. Guardians, SUNY-Albany, others. Recipient Louis Comfort Tiffany Nat. award in painting, 1966-67; Change Artist's grantee, 1978; Dorland Found. grantee, 1983; Hambidge Found. grantee, 1983; Pollock/Krasner Found. grantee, 1986—. Mem. Coll. Art Assn., Women's Caucus for Art. Address: Westbeth 463 West St Apt H961 New York NY 10014

LEFFERTS, JACQUELINE MOORE, lawyer; b. Houston, Dec. 14, 1939; d. James Cecil and Ethel (Lentschke) Moore; m. Jacob Rapalyea Van Mater Lefferts, III, Aug. 5, 1969; children—Lizabeth Marisa, Anthony R.V.M., Jacob R.V.M., IV. B.S., Monmouth Coll., 1971; J.D., So. Tex. Coll. Law, 1979. Bar: N.J. 1982. Singer, Arthur Godfrey's Talent Scouts, 1957; pvt. practice law, Middletown, N.J., 1982—. Mem. Women's Resources and Survival Ctr., Keyport, N.J., 1983—, Republican Senatorial Inner Circle, Washington, 1982, Presdl. Task Force, Washington, 1984—, Women's Polit. Caucus, Washington, 1982. Mem. N.J. Assn. Women Bus. Owners, So. Tex. Coll. Law Alumni Assn., Middletown C. of C., N.J. Bar Assn., N.J. Women Lawyers Assn., Monmouth County Bar Assn., Women Lawyers in Monmouth County, ABA, Assn. of Fed. Bar, Assn. Trial Lawyers of Am., Assn. Trial Lawyers of N.J., Am. Judiciary Soc., Trial Attys. N.J. Republican. Roman Catholic. Office: 950 Hwy 35 PO Box 107 Middletown NJ 07848

LEFFLER, NELL FOUST, Realtor, retired librarian; b. Humboldt, Tenn., Dec. 25, 1922; d. Asa Burnette and Lucile (Sinclair) Foust; student Vanderbilt U., 1942-43; B.A., Lambuth Coll., 1944; M.A., Fla. State U., 1951; m. John Edward Leffler, Nov. 26, 1952. Asst. librarian Fla. State U. Library, 1952, 65-72, head serials cataloging, 1970-74, univ. librarian, head dept. cataloging, 1974-79, univ. cataloging librarian, 1979-84, reference librarian sci. div., 1984-85, ret., 1985; real estate salesman, 1986—; asst. librarian Colquitt-Thomas County Regional Library, Moultrie, Ga., 1952; reference librarian Fla. Legis. Reference Bur., Tallahassee, 1954-63; research librarian Fla. Bd. Regents, Tallahassee, 1963-65. Mem. ALA, Southeastern Library Assn., Audubon Club, Beta Phi Mu, Pi Beta Phi. Democrat. Methodist. Club: Apalachee Yacht. Home: 2413 Miranda Ave Tallahassee FL 32304 Office: 165 Library Fla State U Tallahassee FL 32306

LEFKOWITZ, JEANETTE CATHERINE, health educator; b. N.Y.C., Aug. 5, 1949; d. George and Ethel (Kraft) Unger; m. Martin Joel Lefkowitz, Mar. 14, 1979; 1 son, Donald Christopher. A.A., Queensboro Community Coll., 1977, A.A.S. in Nursing, 1980; B.S. in Human Services, St. John's U., 1983. Dental Claims examiner Blue Cross, Inc., N.Y.C., 1970-72; staff nurse Elmhurst (N.Y.) Gen. Hosp., 1980, Staff Builders, N.Y.C., 1981-83; patient advocate Queens Hosp. Ctr., Jamaica, N.Y., 1982-83; instr. nursing Upjohn Healthcare Services, Hicksville, N.Y., 1983—; admission nurse Vis. Nurse Service, N.Y.C., 1984-86. Mem. Am. Nurses Assn., Am. Pub. Health Assn., N.Y. Acad. Scis. Methodist. Home: 212-07 75th Ave Apt 6J Bayside NY 11364

LEFTWICH, GAIL MAUREEN, lawyer; b. Phila., Sept. 8, 1956; d. Charles William Leftwich and Joan (Whittle) McClane. B.A., Bryn Mawr Coll., 1977; J.D., U. Chgo., 1981. Bar: D.C. U.S. Dist Ct. 1982. Assoc. firm Arent, Fox, Kintner, Plotkin & Kahn, Washington, 1981—. Mem. World Affairs Council, Washington, Mem. ABA, Women's Econ. Round Table, Nat. Economist Club. Club: Banker's (Washington) Home: 2900 Connecticut Ave NW Apt 237 Washington DC 20008 Office: Arent Fox Kintner Plotkin & Kahn 1050 Connecticut Ave NW Washington DC 20036

LEFTWICH, MERRY ANN, medical technologist; b. Seattle, July 6, 1917; d. Peter Hill and Esther (Redfield) Ottosen; student Goucher Coll., 1935-38; hon. alumnus U. Calif., San Diego, 1964; m. James A. Leftwich, Mar. 12, 1963; children by previous marriage—Edward Redfield Lewis, Peter Hill Lewis. Histologic technician Renton (Wash.) Hosp., 1952-57, King County Hosp., Seattle, 1957-59, Scripps Meml. Hosp., La Jolla, Calif., 1959-64; dir. tech. services Oral Pathology Service, La Jolla, 1964-81; dir. tech. services pathology lab. oral medicine dept. Scripps Clinic and Research Found., La Jolla, 1982—; lectr. in field. Mem. Am. Soc. Clin. Pathologists. Nat. Assn. Histotechnology, Social Service League of La Jolla, Colonial Dames Am., Soc. Mayflower Descs. in State of Wash., Gamma Phi Beta. Republican. Episcopalian. Club: La Jolla Beach & Tennis. Contbr. articles to profl. jours.; author: Pathology Careers for Tissue Technicians, 1971; A Pathology Lab Can Be Attractive, 1975; Historic Microscope Replicas, 1981, others. Home: 2056 Torrey Pines Rd LaJolla CA 92038 Office: 10666 N Torrey Pines Rd Scripps Clinic and Research Found LaJolla CA 92038

LE GALLIENNE, EVA, actress; b. London, Jan. 11, 1899; d. Richard and Julie (Norregaard) Le G.; ed. Collège Sévigne, Paris; M.A. (hon.), Tufts Coll., 1927; D.H.L., Smith Coll., 1930, Ohio Wesleyan U., 1959, Goucher Coll., 1960, U. N.C., 1964, Bard Coll., 1965, Fairfield U., 1966; Litt.D., Russell Sage Coll., 1930, Brown U., 1933, Mt. Holyoke Coll., 1937. Debut in The Laughter of Fools, Prince of Wales Theatre, London, 1915; N.Y. debut in The Melody of Youth, 1916; appeared in N.Y. and on tour in Mr. Lazarus, 1916-17; with Ethel Barrymore in The Off Chance, 1917-18; Not So Long Ago, 1920-21; Liliom, 1921-22; The Swan, 1923; Hannele in The Assumption of Hanele, by Hauptmann, 1923; Jeanne d'Arc, by Mercedes de Acosta, 1925; The Call of Life, by Schnitzler, 1925; The Master Builder, by Ibsen, 1925-26; founder, dir. Civic Repertory Theatre, N.Y.C., opening October 25, 1926; presented over 30 plays in 7 years including Three Sisters, Cradle Song, Inheritors, Peter Pan, Romeo and Juliet, Camille, Allison's House (Pulitzer prize), Alice in Wonderland; starred in Therese Roquin, 1945; co-founder with Margaret Webster of Am. Repertory Theatre, which produced (1946, 47), Shakespeare's Henry the Eighth, Barrie's What Every Woman Knows, Ibsen's John Gabriel Borkman, Shaw's Androcles and the Lion, Howard's Yellow Jack, Lewis Carroll's Alice in Wonderland, 1948; toured in The Corn is Green, 1949-50; on Broadway in The Southwest Corner, 1955; as Queen Elizabeth in Schiller's Mary Stuart, N.Y.C., 1957, on tour, 1959-60; in Maxwell Anderson's Elizabeth the Queen, 1961-62; toured in Sea Gull, Nat. Repertory Theatre, 1963-64, in Madwoman of Chalilot and The Trojan Women; appeared with APA Repertory Theatre, N.Y.C. as Marguerite in Exit The King; also directed Chekov's The Cherry Orchard, 1967-68, Doll's House, Seattle Repertory, 1975; appeared as Countess in All's Well That Ends Well, Shakespeare Festival Theatre, Stratford, Conn., 1970, in The Dream Watcher, White Barn Theatre, 1975; The Royal Family, Helen Hayes Theatre, N.Y.C., 1976, nat. tour, 1976-77, To Grandmother's House We Go, Biltmore Theatre, N.Y.C., 1980-81; appeared in movie Resurrection, 1979; dir., role of White Queen, Alice in Wonderland revival Va. Theatre, 1982-83. Recipient Brandeis U. award for drama, 1966; winner of Pictorial Rev. Achievement award, 1926; gold medal Soc. Arts and Town Hall Club award, 1934; Am. Acad. Arts and Letters medal for good diction on the stage 1945; Outstanding Woman of Year award Women's Nat. Press Club, 1947; spl. award ANTA, 1964, award, 1977; Spl. Tony award Am. Theatre Wing, 1964; Handel medallion City N.Y., 1976; Emmy award, 1978; decorated cross Royal Order St. Olaf, 1961. Mem. Actors' Equity Assn., Dramatists Guild. Author: At 33 (autobiography), 1934; Flossie and Bossie, 1949 (London edit. 1950); With a Quiet Heart, 1953; The Mystic in the Theatre, a study of Eleonora Duse, 1966. Translator many works of Henrik Ibsen, Hans Christian Andersen.

LEGENDRE, MARGARET FRAHER, educational administrator; b. Boston, Nov. 30, 1949; d. John Patrick and Margaret Ann (Jenks) F.; m. Paul Nicholas LeGendre, Apr. 15, 1973. B.A., Emmanuel Coll., Boston, 1971; M.Ed., Boston State Coll., 1973; Ed.D., U. Mass., 1979. Tchr.-in-charge adolescent unit Boston State Hosp., 1971-74; chairperson dept. spl. edn. English High Sch., Boston, 1974-76, flexible campus coordinator, 1976-78, coordinator Tchr.'s Ctr., 1978-79, housemaster, 1979-80; asst. prin. Fundamental Sch., Cambridge Pub. Schs., Mass., 1980—; pres. Prime Cut, Inc., Boston, 1980—; adj. asst. prof. U. Mass., Amherst, 1983—; cons. in field. Bd. dirs. Downtown Crossing Assn., Boston, 1980-82. Recipient Disting. Achievement award Am. Assn. Colls. for Tchr. Edn., 1979. Mem. AAUW, Am. Edn. Research Assn., Cape Cod C. of C., Boston Computer Soc. (bd. dirs. 1985—), Phi Delta Kappa, Pi Lambda Theta. Republican. Roman Catholic. Club: Boston Osborne Group (pres. 1984-86). Avocations: computer programming; sailing; reading. Home: 9 Springvale Ave West Roxbury MA 02132 Office: Fundamental Sch 459 Broadway Cambridge MA 02138

LEGER, MARGARET ANN, brewery sales executive; b. Fitchburg, Mass., Oct. 25, 1953; d. Pierre Louis and Cecile (Leger) L.; m. Abner H. Donnan, Jr., June 29, 1984. B.A., Anna Maria Coll., 1975. Office mgr. Thermoplastics Co., Inc., Worcester, Mass., 1977-80; inventory systems coordinator Miller Brewing Co., Albany, Ga., 1980-82; plant buyer, 1982-84, mdse. rep., New Orleans, 1984-85, area mgr., Milw., 1985—. Mem. Purchase Mgmt. Assn. (v.p. 1983-84). Roman Catholic. Avocations: gardening; photography. Home: 1225 Galway Dr Billings MT 59105 Office: Miller Brewing Co 2851 S Parker Rd #950 Aurora CO 80014

LEGG, CHARLOTTE RUTH MILLION, public relations executive; b. Chgo., July 31, 1950; d. Elmer Garr and Ruth Aulick (Hatfield) Million; m. Mark Allen Legg, June 1, 1974 (div. Sept. 1983); 1 child, Laura Elizabeth. B.A. magna cum laude, U. Redlands, 1972; M.A., U. Mo., 1974. Dir. pub. info. St. Mary Coll., Leavenworth, Kans., 1975-78; sr. info. specialist U. Mo., Kansas City, 1978-80; dir. pub. relations William Jewell Coll., Liberty, Mo., 1980—; cons. Dean Wilder Singers, Liberty, Mo., 1985—, Mo. Bapt. Conv., Jefferson City, Mo., 1985—, Second Bapt. Ch., Liberty, 1983—, Econ. Devel. Com., Clay County, Mo., 1984—, Liberty Living Landmark Com., 1984—. Editor: Understanding and Interpreting the Bible, 1983. Communications specialist Liberty Sales Tax Campaign, 1984, Liberty City Hall Bond, 1982; Sunday Sch. dir. Second Bapt. Ch., Liberty, 1985—. Recipient Key to City, Liberty, Mo., 1982. Mem. Council for Advancement and Support of Edn. (Nat. silver award 1985, dist. newsletter editor), Internat. Assn. Bus. Communicators (pub. relations task force, chpt. award 1985), Bapt. Pub. Relations Assn. (Albert McClellan award 1985). Baptist. Avocations: music; creative writing; aerobic swimming; walking; racquetball. Home: 1213 Old Manor Rd Liberty MO 64068 Office: William Jewell Coll Liberty MO 64068

LE GOFF, ROSEMARIE VAZQUEZ, engineer; b. Bronx, N.Y., Jan. 27, 1958; d. Andrew and Lydia Vazquez; m. Patrick Le Goff, Aug. 30, 1980. B.M.E., Columbia U., 1980. Engr., nuclear cons. Stone & Webster Engring. Corp., N.Y.C., 1980-84; telecommunications engr. N.Y. Telephone, Bklyn., 1984—. Mem. Soc. Women Engrs., Nat. Assn. Female Execs. Roman Catholic. Club: Columbia U. Alumni. Office: New York Telephone Brooklyn NY 11201

LEGOY, SHIRLEY MCDONOUGH, accountant; b. Tonopah, Neb., Mar. 18, 1929; d. James Joseph and Marie McDonough; m. Leo Robert LeGoy, Feb. 18, 1950; children—Leo Robert, James Michael, Philip Richard. B.S., U. Nev., 1950, M.B.A., 1976. Cert. fin. planner; C.P.A. Staff acct., Elmer Fox & Co., Reno, 1967-75, Barnard & Hildahl, C.P.A.s, Reno, 1975-77; prin. Shirley M. LeGoy, C.P.A., Reno, 1977, 85—; ptnr. Samon, LeGoy & Co., C.P.A.s, Reno, 1978-84; chmn. continuing profl. edn. com. State Bd. Nev. Accountancy, 1977-79; mem. Nev. State Bd. Equalization, 1978. Treas. Mary Gojack for Senate campaign, 1980, Congress campaign, 1982. Mem. Am. Inst. C.P.A.'s, Nov. Soc. Pub. Accts., Inst. Cert. Fin. Planners, Internat. Assn. Fin. Planning. Republican. Lodge: Soroptimist Internat. Home: 1245 Washington St Reno NV 89503 Office: Samon LeGoy & Co 216 Mount Rose St Reno NV 89509

LE GUIN, URSULA KROEBER, author; b. Berkeley, Calif., Oct. 21, 1929; d. Alfred Louis and Theodora (Kracaw) Kroeber; B.A., Radcliffe Coll., 1951; M.A., Columbia, 1952; m. Charles A. Le Guin, Dec. 22, 1953; children—Elisabeth, Caroline, Theodore. Recipient Boston Globe-Hornbook award for excellence in juvenile fiction, 1968; Nebula award, 1969, 75; Hugo award for best novel, 1969, 75, best novella, 1973, best short story, 1974; Newbery honor medal, 1971; Nat. Book award, 1973; Gandalf award, 1979; Fulbright fellow, France, 1953-54. Mem. Authors League, Writers Guild, Sci. Fiction Research Assn., NOW, Planned Parenthood, PEN, Phi Beta Kappa. Author: Rocannon's World, 1966; Planet of Exile, 1967; City of Illusion, 1967; A Wizard of Earthsea, 1968; The Left Hand of Darkness, 1969; The Tombs of Atuan, 1971; The Lathe of Heaven, 1971; The Farthest Shore, 1972; The Dispossessed, 1974; Wild Angels, 1975; The Wind's Twelve Quarters, 1975; A Very Long Way from Anywhere Else, 1976; Orsinian Tales, 1976; The Language of the Night, 1979; Malafrena, 1979; Leese Webster, 1979; The Beginning Place, 1980; Hard Words, 1981; The Compass Rose, 1982; The Eye of the Heron, 1983; King Dog, 1985; Always Coming Home, 1985.

LEHMAN, CLARA MAY HILEMAN, physician; b. Sharon, Pa., Oct. 30, 1901; d. Mayberry and Clara May (Keasey) Hileman; B.S., Pa. State U., 1924; postgrad. Columbia, 1927-28, Marine Biol. Lab., 1930-31; M.D., Woman's Med. Coll., Pa., 1935; m. Robert N. Lehman, Apr. 24, 1938; 1 dau., Mary Dorcas. Intern Lancaster (Pa.) Hosp., 1935-36, resident, 1936-37; practice gen. medicine, Pa., 1936-47; practice staff geriatrics U.S. Army Hosp., Ft. Meyer, Va., 1948-51, VA Hosp., Aspinwall, Pa., 1955-57, Woodville State Hosp., Carnegie, Pa., 1957-68. Mem. AMA, Pa., Allegheny County med. socs., Royal Soc. Health, Alpha Omega Alpha, Alpha Epsilon Iota. Address: 801 Washington Ave Tyrone PA 16686

LEHMAN, EVELYN JEANNE, lawyer; b. Ann Arbor, Mich., June 13, 1930; d. Arthur Conrad and Mildred Georgianna (Pearce) L.; B.A., Mt. Holyoke Coll., 1951; LL.B., U. Mich., 1954; m. Apr. 4, 1959; 1 son, Arthur Scott Long. Admitted to N.Y. State bar; assoc., then partner firm Gifford, Woody, Palmer & Serles, N.Y.C., 1957-85, Townley & Updike, 1985—. Pres., YWCA of City of N.Y., 1982—. Mem. Am. Bar Assn. Office: 405 Lexington Ave New York NY 10147

LEHMAN, PRISCILLA LILLIAN, medical education programs distributing company executive, nurse; b. Cleve., July 17, 1945; d. Charles Louis and Jeannette Anne (Karda) L. Diploma Fairview Hosp. Sch. Nursing, Cleve., 1966; B.S. in Nursing, U. Va., 1972; M.S., Case Western Res. U., 1977. Nurse, supr. Parma Community Hosp., Ohio, 1966-69; charge nurse U. Mich. Hosp., Ann Arbor, 1969-70; staff devel. instr. Fairview Gen. Hosp., Cleve., 1972-73, dir. audio visual communications, 1973-82; pres. Lehman & Hall Assocs., Inc., Cleve., 1982—; distrb. Care Video Prodns., Cleve., 1982—. Writer and producer med. edn. videos. Recipient Golden Reel of Excellence award Internat. TV Assn., 1980, 81; Award of Merit Chgo. Internat. Film Festival, 1981. Mem. Nat. Assn. Female Execs., Greater Cleve. Growth Assn. Republican. Avocations: golf; cross country skiing; swimming; reading. Home and Office: 25730 Hilliard Blvd Westlake OH 44145

LEHMAN, SANDRA KAY, association executive; b. Johnstown, Pa., Dec. 29, 1940; d. William O. and Helen M. (Blough) L.; B.S., Pa. State U., 1962; postgrad. U. So. Calif., Rensselaer Poly. Inst., spl. corp. courses. Procurement agt. Def. Fuels Supply Center, Alexandria, Va., 1964-67; programmer, analyst Def. Supply Ag., Alexandria, 1967-69; mgr. OCR services and ops. SDA Corp., Cheverly, Md., 1969-73; chief program devel. unit Assn. State and Territorial Health Ofcls., Washington, 1973-74; dir. composition and OCR services Informatics, Inc., Riverdale, Md., 1974-77; assoc. dir. student services Assn. Am. Med. Colls., Washington, 1977-79, assoc. dir. computer services, 1979—; cons. Hewlett Packard laser printer, treas. Regional Users Group, 1981-83; mgmt. cons. Maine Dept. Health, 1979, MCI Corp., 1983—. Treas., fund raiser Alexandria Choral Soc., 1978-84, rep. to Alexandria Performing Arts Council, 1978-84. Mem. Mu Phi Epsilon, Gamma Phi Beta, Mensa. Home: 815 Church St Alexandria VA 22314 Office: 1 Dupont Circle NW Washington DC 20036

LEHMANN, BARBARA LOWIS, association executive; b. Taylorville, Ill., Sept. 20, 1934; d. Frank Ashton and Dorothy Jane (Beaty) Lowis; m. John Richard Lehmann, June 24, 1956; children—Nancy, Richard (dec.). B.S., U. Ill., 1955, M.S., 1958. Tchr., advisor Champaign High Sch., Ill., 1958-61; mgr. Walnut Lake Farms, Morrisonville Ill., 1964-81; pres., mgr. Walnut Lake Farms, Inc., Morrisonville, 1981—; bd. mem., program initiator Girl Scout Council of Nation's Capital, Washington, 1966—. Active PTA, Rockville, Md., 1966-75; docent chmn. Nat. Mus. of Am. History, Smithsonian Inst., Washington, 1978-79; docent, program initiator history Smithsonian Instn., 1970—. Recipient Thanks Badge, Girl Scouts U.S.A., 1975. Mem. AAUW. Methodist. Avocations: stained glass; gardening; reading.

LEHMANN-CARSSOW, NANCY BETH, educator, coach; b. Kingsville, Tex., Sept. 9, 1949; d. Valgene William and Ella Mae (Zajicek) Lehmann; m. William Benton Carssow, Aug. 1, 1981. B.S., U. Tex., 1971, M.A., 1979. Free-lance photographer, Austin, Tex., 1971—; tchr., tennis coach Austin Ind. Sch. Dist., Tex., 1971-78, 79—; salesperson, mgr. What's Going On-Clothing, Austin, 1972-78; area adminstr. Am. Inst. Fgn. Study, Austin, 1974-81; area rep. World Encounters, Austin, 1981—, tour guide, Egypt, Kenya, 1977, 79, 81. Author curriculum materials. Photographer for book: Bobwhites, 1984. Recipient Merit award Nat. Council Geog. Edn., 1975, Creative Teaching award Austin Assn. Tchrs., 1978; Fulbright scholar, Israel, 1983. Mem. Nat. Council Social Studies, NEA, Nat. Council Geog. Edn., East African Wildlife, Earthwatch (participant archaeol. dig. in Swaziland 1984), Delta Kappa Gamma, Phi Kappa Phi. Democrat. Roman Catholic. Avocations: stained glass; photography; tennis; gardening; needlepoint. Home: 1025 Quail Park Dr Austin TX 78758 Office: Lanier High Sch 1201 Peyton Gin Rd Austin TX 78758

LEHMER, ELLEN CURRENT, banker; b. Newton, N.J., May 25, 1950; d. Wilson Strader and Jennie (Miller) Current; m. Ronald Lee Lehmer, Nov. 9, 1966; children—Sherri Lee, Kristi Lee. Student Am. Inst. Banking, Sussex County, N.J., 1974-81, Morris County Community Coll., 1983. Proof operator, bookkeeper Midlantic Nat. Bank; head teller Sussex Mchts. Bank, Newton, 1970-74, N.J. Bank N.A., Sparta, N.J., 1974-76, Morris County Savs. Bank, Rockaway, N.J., 1977—, also sr. savs. clk. Coach, instr., v.p. Struttin Spartans, 1971-76; coach, organizer Sparta Wrestling Cheerleaders, 1970-76; instr. Sparta High Sch. Twirling, 1973-74; vol. Sparta Ambulance Corp., 1976-77; active various softball leagues. Democrat. Presbyterian. Avocations: softball; coaching; needleworking; kites; music. Home: 10 Carlson Ln Sparta NJ 07871 Office: Morris County Savs Bank 88 Pawnee Ave Rockaway NJ 07871

LEHNER, EDITH ANNE, bldgs. mfg. co. exec.; b. Raleigh N.D., May 5, 1932; d. Daniel D. and Scholastica (Volk) Dirk; student Minot (N.D.) State Coll., 1949-50, Mt. Marty Coll., 1950-51, St. John's U., Summer 1959; B.A., Coll. St. Benedict, 1960; postgrad. State U. N.D., 1965, Marquette U., 1967, U. Pa., 1976; m. George F. Lehner, Feb. 17, 1975. Tchr. Bismarck (N.D.) Parochial Schs., 1949-55, 56-64; tchr. drama, speech Minot (N.D.) Public Schs., 1964-66; tchr. English, speech Upper Merion Sr. High Sch., King of Prussia, Pa., 1966-70; tchr. pvt. voice, piano, Minot, N.D., 1960-66; v.p. in charge field constrn., office mgmt. and fin. Bldg. Concepts, Inc., Douglassville, Pa., 1975—. Mem. Internat. Platform Assn., Nat. Real Estate Assn., Pa. Real Estate Assn., Pa. Manufactured Housing Assn., Bldg. Industries Exchange. Democrat. Roman Catholic. Home: 140 N Wall St Spring City PA 19475 Office: 236 Benjamin Franklin Hwy Douglassville PA 19518

LEHR, ANDREA RENÉ, data services company executive; b. Pittsburg, Kans., Mar. 17, 1962; d. William George and Diane Jocelyn (Davis) L. B.S., Pittsburg State U., 1983. Accounts mgr. Twentieth Century Computer Maintenance Co., Kansas City, Mo., 1983, adminstrv. ops. mgr., 1983-85, v.p., 1985; 3d party adminstr. Decision Data Services, Inc., Horsham, Pa., 1985—; audit cons. Nat. Computer Maintenance Co., Atlanta, 1984; dir. Dynaphase Electric Inc., Bellingham, Wash. Mem. Nat. Assn. Female Execs., Am. Bus. Women's Assn. Republican. Roman Catholic. Avocations: water skiing, modeling, dancing, snow skiing. Office: Decision Data Services Inc 400 Horsham Rd Horsham PA 19044

LEHRER, SUSAN, sociology educator; b. N.Y.C., Apr. 8, 1938; d. Isidore Gibby and Edith N.; m. Robert Lehrer; children—Ruth, Peter, Judith. B.A., U. Chgo., 1959; M.A., New Sch., N.Y.C., 1971; Ph.D., SUNY-Binghamton, 1980. Mem. faculty Manhattan Community Coll., N.Y.C., 1971-72, CUNY-Bklyn., 1972-73; asst. prof. SUNY-New Paltz, 1973—. Mem. N.Y. Abortions Rights League, Poughkeepsie, N.Y., Women's Studies, SUNY-New Paltz. Mem. Conf. Critical Legal Studies, Eastern Sociol Soc. Avocation: hiking.

LEHTO, ARLENE IONE, educator, former state legislator; b. Duluth, Minn., Sept. 14, 1939; B.A. Speech, U. Minn.-Duluth; M.P.A., Harvard U., 1984. Beauty salon mgr., hairstylist 1961-67; pres. ops. Lehto's Printing, Inc. 1970-82; editor, Lake Superior News, 1969-74; mem. Minn. Ho. of Reps., St. Paul, 1976-82, vice chmn. local and urban affairs com., mem. criminal justice, environ. and natural resources, govtl. ops. coms. Bd. dirs. United Devel. Achievement Ctr. Duluth, 1974-82. Recipient Citizen award EPA Minn., 1974, Albert J. Chesley award Minn. Pub. Health Assn.; named among Women Who Made a Difference ABC-TV, 1981; Bush fellow, 1983. Mem. Save Lake Superior Assn. Editor: Ahoy, Charles River Power Squadron. Mem. adminstrv. council, chmn. Calvary United Methodist Ch., Arlington, Mass. Home: 35 Mott St Arlington MA 02174

LEIBENSPERGER, JOYCE IRENE, civic worker; b. Kutztown, Pa., Feb. 18, 1931; d. Homer Ambrose and Jennie Irene (Snyder) Moyer; m. Randolph Jacob Leibensperger, Feb. 12, 1951; children—Gregory Randolph, Weatherly Jenni Leibensperger Bergstrom. Student pub. schs., Kutztown. Chairperson Recreation Bd., Kutztown, 1962-75; Kutztown Republican committeewoman, 1965-75; mem., pres. Bd. Sch. Dirs., Kutztown, 1977—; bd. dirs. Berks County Intermediate Unit, Reading, Pa., 1982—. Mem. Women's Club, Hist. Soc. Kutztown. Republican. Lodge: Order Ea. Star. Home: Route 4 Box 363 Kutztown PA 19530 Office: Kutztown Area Sch Dist Constitutional and Trexler Kutztown PA 19530

LEIBOWITZ, SUZANNE RUTTENBERG, lawyer; b. N.Y.C., Jan. 16, 1938; d. Myer and Mary (Liebman) Ruttenberg; m. Martin Leibowitz (div. 1968). A.B., Smith Coll., 1959; M.A., Columbia U., 1961; J.D., U. West Los Angeles, 1979. Bar: Calif. 1979. Assoc., Mix & Hodges, Redondo Beach, Calif., 1981-83; sole practice, Encino, Calif., 1983—. Recipient Am. Jurisprudence award, 1976. Mem. Los Angeles County Bar Assn., State Bar Calif., Los Angeles Trial Lawyers Assn. Home and Office: 17348 Burbank Blvd Apt 6 Encino CA 91316

LEIFERMAN, SILVIA WEINER (MRS. IRWIN HAMILTON LEIFERMAN), artist, civic worker, bus. exec., philanthropist; b. Chgo.; d. Morris H. and Anna (Caplan) Weiner; student U. Chgo., 1960-61; studied design and painting Chgo., Mexico, Rome, Madrid, Provincetown, Mass.; m. Irwin Hamilton Leiferman, Apr. 20, 1947. One woman shows include: D'Arcy Galleries, N.Y.C., 1964, Stevens Annex Bldg., Chgo., 1965, Hollywood (Fla.) Mus. Art, Schram Galleries, Ft. Lauderdale, Fla., 1966, 67, Miami Mus. Modern Art, 1966, 72, Contemporary Gallery, Palm Beach, Fla., 1966, Westview Country Club, 1968, Gallery 99, Miami Beach, Fla., 1969, Hall Gallery, Miami Beach; group shows include: Bryn Mawr Country Club, 1961, 62, Riccardo Restaurant Gallery, Chgo., 1961, 62, Covenant Club, 1963, D'Arcy Galleries, N.Y.C., 1965, 66, 67, Miami Mus. Modern Art, 1967, Baccardi Gallery, Miami, 1967, Internat. Platform Assn., 1967, Barry Coll., 1968, Gallery 99, Miami Beach, 1968, Hollywood Mus. Art, 1968, Lowe Art Mus., Beau Art Gallery Lowe Mus. at U. Miami; work represented in numerous pvt. collections; chmn. bd. Leiferman Investment Co., 1969-78, chmn. bd., 1968—; pres. Active Accessories by Silvia; v.p., sec. Silvia and Irwin H. Leiferman Found. Founder, Mt. Sinai Hosp., Miami Beach, 1969, Greater Technion Inst. Tech., Israel, 1972, Silvia and Irwin H. Leiferman Found.; organizer, met. chmn., charter mem. womens div. Hebrew U., Chgo., 1947; originator, met. chmn. Ambassador's Ball, State of Israel, 1956, Presentation Ball, 1963, 64, 65; organizer women's div. Edgewater Hosp., 1954; chmn. salute to med. research met. campaign City of Hope, 1959; met. Chgo. chmn. Dior Israel Fashion Show, 1962; originator, chmn. presentation com. Ambassador's Ball, Bonds for Israel, 1963, 64, 65; originator, met. chmn. Paris in the Spring fashion show Nat. Council Jewish Women, also Alice in Fashion Land; originator met. chmn. Hawaii Holiday, Nathan Goldblatt Soc. Cancer Research; chmn. spl. sales and events Greater Chgo. Com. for State of Israel; met. chmn. opening gala luncheon, mem. bd. North Shore women's aux. Mary Lawrence Jewish Children's Bur.; internat. chmn. Bal Masque, Miami Ballet Soc., 1971, 72; patron Royal Ballet Soc. Miami, Lowe's Mus. Art, Greater Art Center Miami, Philharmonic Soc. Miami, Greater Miami Opera Guild; patron Greater Miami Cultural Arts Center, mem. hon. com. for gala, 1972; trustee, life mem. Nathan Goldblatt Soc. Cancer Research; trustee Jewish Fedn. Greater Miami; mem. bd. North Shore aux. Jewish Fedn. Chgo., Mary Lawrence chpt. Jewish Children's Bur., Nat. Council Jewish Women, Fox River Sanitorium, Temple Sholom, Edgewater Hosp., Orgn. Rehab. and Tng., women's guild Greater Miami Philharmonic Soc., numerous others; mem. nat. bd. govs. Bonds for Israel; hon. chmn. Miami Art Center. Named Woman of Valor, State of Israel, 1963; 73; recipient Achievement award State of Israel, 1963; keys of all 5 met. dists. Miami and surrounding counties, 1972; Pro Mundo Beneficio gold medal and diploma Brazilian Acad. Humanities, 1976;

Donor award Miami Heart Inst., 1976; numerous plaques and citations. Fellow Royal Soc. Arts and Scis. (life); mem. Internat. Platform Assn. (The Club), Internat. Council Museums, Am. Fedn. Arts, Miami Beach Opera Guild, Artists Equity Assn., Miami Art Center, Greater Miami Cultural Art Center, Sculptors of Fla., Inc., Lowe Art Mus. (life), Friends of Lowe's Mus., Am. Contract Bridge League, Am. Friends of Hebrew Univ., Ft. Lauderdale Mus. Arts, Miami Mus. Modern Art (life), Art Inst. Chgo. (life), numerous others. Clubs: Internat., Whitehall, Key, Covenant, Standard, Bryn Mawr Country (Chgo.); Westview Country, Brickell (Miami); Greenacres Country (Northbrook, Ill.); Runaway, Jockey (Miami Beach). Address: 10155 Collins Ave Bal Harbour FL 33154

LEIGH, RUTH S., realtor; b. N.Y.C., Feb. 19; d. A. Lawrence and Anne (Frieder) Sokolski; student Hunter Coll., 1934-36, Wharton Sch., U. Pa., 1942; m. Murray Stuart Leigh, June 13, 1943 (dec. Jan. 1983); 1 dau., Leslie Susan Leigh Griffith. Sales dept. mgr., buyer Saks 34th St., N.Y.C., 1935-37; radio commls. WMCA, N.Y.C., 1936-39; interior decorator Roxberg, Inc., N.Y.C., 1937-40; broker Harold N. Sloane Co., Ins. brokers, N.Y.C., 1940-43; br. mgr. Manpower Inc., N.Y.C., 1952-53; interior designer Storr & Co., N.Y.C., 1949—; builder-broker Ruth S. Leigh, N.Y.C., 1965—; mem. Real Estate Bd. N.Y., 1970—. Dist. dir. Girl Scouts U.S.A., 1952-54; fund raiser N.Y. Heart Assn., 1955—, Salvation Army, 1960—, bd. dirs. Interfaith Neighbors, 1964-66; dist. liaison officer Black & White Assos. supporting Oddyssey House Drug Addicts, 1969-70; trustee Bloomingdale Ho. of Music, N.Y.C., 1970-71; mem. U.S. Senatorial Bus. Adv. Bd., mem. chmn.'s com., 1980; mem. Republican Senatorial Inner Circle, 1983-85. Recipient civic awards. Mem. Unitarian-Universalist Womens Fedn. (dist. pres. 1966-72), Am. Unitarian Assn. (asst. non-govtl. orgn. rep. UN, nat. chmn. UN seminars 1958-62). Unitarian (v.p. bd. 1972, deacon 1974—).

LEIGH, SUSAN JANE, lobbyist; b. Winchester, Va., June 7, 1951; d. Louis Henry and Barbara Jane (Stephens) L.; m. Richard Neal Brunner, Apr. 8, 1972 (div. Apr. 1978); m. Joseph Allen Ross, Feb. 2, 1980; children—Erin Brunner, Kristin Brunner, Matthew Ross. B.A., Fla. State U., 1974; M.S., Okla. State U., 1978. Design cons. Higdon Furniture, Paducah, Ky., 1976; instr. Murray State U., Ky., 1976-77, Okla. State U., Stillwater, 1977-78; mgr. research and communications Homes and Land, Tallahassee, 1979-83; dir. legis. and tech. affairs Fla. Home Builders Assn., Tallahassee, 1983—; bd. mem. Fla. Weatherization Adv. Council, Tallahassee, Fla. Collaborative Elderly Housing Initiative, Tallahassee, Onsite Sewage Disposal Systems Research Adv. Council. Editor, dir.: Housing Reference Manual, 1985, Energy Update, 1986. Contbr. articles to Homebuilder mag., 1983 . Chmn. Tallahassee Housing Found., 1984-86; bd. mem. Fla. Low Income Housing Coalition, Tallahassee, 1986. Mem. Am. Assn. Housing Educators (govtl. affairs chmn. 1985-86), Nat. Assn. Women in Constrn., So. Bldg. Code Congress, Bldg. Ofcl. Assn. Fla., Nat. Assn. Housing and Redevel. Ofcls. Democrat. Methodist. Office: Fla Home Builders Assn 201 E Park Ave Tallahassee FL 32302

LEIGHTON, CLARE, artist, writer; b. London, Eng., Apr. 12, 1899; d. Robert L. and Marie (Connor) L.; came to U.S. 1939, naturalized, 1946; m. Henry Noel Brailsford. Student Slade Sch., U. London, 1921-23; D.F.A. (hon.), Colby Coll., 1940. One-person exhbns. Mary Ryan Gallery, N.Y.C., 1983; exhibited group shows Victoria and Albert Mus., London Nat. Gallery, Stockholm, Nat. Gallery Can., Met. Mus., N.Y.C., others; commd. 33 stained glass windows St. Paul's Cathedral, Worcester, Mass.; mosaic, Convent Holy Family of Nazareth, Monroe, Conn.; windows Luth. Ch. Waterbury, Conn.; windows Math. Ch., Wellfleet, Mass. Mem. Royal Soc. Painters, Etchers and Engravers (London), Nat. Acad. Design, Soc. Am. Graphic Artists, Soc. Wood Engravers (London), Nat. Inst. Arts and Letters. Author, illustrator: The Farmer's Year, Four Hedges, Country Matters, Southern Harvest, Where Land Meets Sea, others. Address: care Mary Ryan Gallery 452 Columbus Ave New York NY 10024

LEIGHTON, GERTRUDE CATHERINE KERR, lawyer, educator; b. Belfast, Ireland, Dec. 9, 1914; came to U.S., 1915, naturalized, 1918; d. Archibald O. and Gertrude (Hamilton) L. A.B., Bryn Mawr Coll., 1938; LL.B., J.D., Yale U., 1945, postgrad. fellow in law, 1947-48. Bar: N.Y. 1947. Lectr., Barnard Coll., N.Y.C., 1940-42; with Carter, Ledyard & Milburn, N.Y.C., 1945-47; asst. in research Yale U., 1947-48; vis. lectr. law Yale U., 1949-50; asst. prof. polit. sci. Bryn Mawr Coll. (Pa.), 1950-55, assoc. prof., 1955-64, prof., 1964-82, emeritus prof. 1982, vis. McBride prof., 1982—, sec. faculty, 1975-82, chmn. dept., 1963-65, 68-71; lectr. law U. Pa., Phila., 1959-61, vis. assoc. research prof. law and psychiatry, 1961-65. Contbr. articles to legal jours. Fund for Advancement Edn. fellow, 1953-54, Rockefeller Found. fellow, 1957-58. Mem. ABA, Am. Soc. Internat. Law.

LEIGHTON, MARGARET CARVER, author, lecturer; b. Oberlin, Ohio, Dec. 20, 1896; d. Thomas Nixon and Flora Frazee (Kirkendall) Carver; student pub. schs., Cambridge, Mass., Lycée Fenelon, Paris, France, Villa Rogivue, Switzerland; A.B., Radcliffe Coll.; m. James Herbert Leighton, May 5, 1921 (dec. Feb. 1935); children—James Herbert, Mary (Mrs. Carson F. Thomson), Thomas Carver, Sylvia (Mrs. Douglas Wikle). Former mem. bd. edn., Westfield, N.J.; past mem. Santa Monica Library Bd., Calif. Served in Army Sch. of Nursing, World War I. Named Honored Grad., Radcliffe Coll., 1968. Mem. Writers' Guild (Calif.), Authors League Am., PEN. Republican. Author: Junior High School Plays, 1938, The Secret of the Old House, 1941, Twelve Bright Trumpets (pub. in Eng. as The Conqueror), 1942; The Secret of the Closed Gate, 1944; The Singing Cave, 1945 (Jr. Lit. Guild selection, also received silver medal Commonwealth Club Calif.), 1946; Judith of France, 1948; Sword and the Compass, 1951; The Secret of Bucky Moran, 1952; The Story of Florence Nightingale, 1952; The Story of General Custer, 1954; Who Rides By, 1955; Comanche of the Seventh, 1957; The Secret of Smuggler's Cove, 1959; Journey for a Princess, 1960; Bride of Glory (Dorothy Canfield Fisher award, Dorothy C. McKenzie award), 1962; Voyage to Coromandel, 1965; The Canyon Castaways, 1966; A Hole in the Hedge, 1968; Cleopatra, 1969; The Other Island, 1971; Shelley's Mary, 1973. Contbr. to Child Life, American Girl, Portal, Target, Classmate, Girls Today, Boys Today, also anthologies and sch. readers. Address: 1053 20th St Santa Monica CA 90403

LEIGHTON, VERONICA VENUS, publishing company executive, fashion show producer; b. Navotas, Rizal, Philippines, May 31, 1940; came to U.S., 1966; d. Cipriano and Adoracion (Francisco) Bacatan; m. Robert A. Leighton, May 29, 1971; 1 son, Robert E. B.S. in Fgn. Service, U. Philippines, Diliman, 1962. Soc. columnist Philippine News, Chgo., 1976—, also asst. bur. chief; pres. Verrene, Inc., Chgo., 1978—, Veron Publishing Co., Chgo., 1981—; pub. Via Times, Chgo.; columnist Maynila Mag., Chgo., 1983. Producer: Chicago's Prettiest Filipinas, 1978. Chairperson Habagat Cotillion, 1979; mem. exec. bd. Friends of Channel 11, Chgo., 1981—; del. Filipino-Am. Council Chgo., 1982—; mem. Ninoy Aquino Movement, Chgo., 1983—. Mem. Nat. Assn. Female Execs., Philippine C. of C. (dir.). Roman Catholic. Clubs: U.P. of Am. (dir.), Chgo.-Philippine Press (treas. 1982—). Chgo. Philippine Lioness (dir.). Home: 5855 N Sheridan Rd Chicago IL 60660

LEIKEN, ERANA, corporate planner, marketing executive, writer; b. Chgo., May 23, 1943; d. Bernard and Beulah (Conkis) Weiss; m. Richard Wayne Leiken, July 3, 1965 (div. Jan. 1980); children—Brian, Dana. B.A., U. Ill., 1965; M.A., U. Richmond, 1970. TV news reporter NBC, Peoria, Ill., 1977-79; asst. editor PJS Publs., Peoria, 1979-80; database acquisition and design videotex, Peoria Jour. Star, 1980; mgr. product devel. Source Telecomputing, McLean, Va., 1981-82; dir. research and devel. Internat. Reporting Info. Systems, Arlington, Va., 1982-83; sr. mgr. planning ITT Dialcom, Inc., Silver Spring, Md., 1983-84; v.p. Mktg. Services Group L Corp., 1984-85; dir. mktg. Maxim Technologies, Inc., 1985—; mem. ITT Task Council ITT COINS, Secaucus, N.J., 1983-84. Recipient media citation of excellence Ill. Edn. Assn., 1978. Mem. Women in Communications, Nat. Soc. Corporate Planning, Am. Women in Advt. and Mktg., Washington Ind. Writers, Alexandria Commn. Arts, Sigma Delta Chi. Unitarian. Office: Maxim Technologies Inc 8618 Westwood Ctr Dr Vienna VA 22180

LEINER, MELISSA GAYLE, fin. planner and cons.; b. Salinas, Calif., Feb. 20, 1953; d. Fred B. and Helen G. (Gertner) L.; B.A., Skidmore Coll., 1975. Sales asst. Paine Webber Jackson & Curtis, N.Y.C., 1976, Kidder Peabody, Washington, 1977-78; v.p., fin. cons., fin. planner Shearson Lehman Bros., McLean, Va., 1978—. Active United Jewish Appeal, Nat. Council Jewish Women. Cert. fin. planner. Mem. Internat. Assn. Fin. Planners, Stockbrokers Soc., Skidmore Coll. Alumni Assn. Club: Skidmore Coll. Alumni (pres. Washington area). Home: 1021 Arlington Blvd Apt E-1213 Arlington VA 22209 Office: Shearson 8260 Greensboro Dr McLean VA 22102

LEINO, DEANNA ROSE, educator; b. Leadville, Colo., Dec. 15, 1937; d. Arvo Ensio Leino and Edith Mary (Bonan) Leino Malenck. B.S. cum laude in Bus. Adminstrn., U. Denver, 1959, M.S. in Bus. Adminstrn., 1967; postgrad. Community Coll. Denver, U. No. Colo., Colo. State U., U. Colo., Met. State Coll. Cert. tchr., vocat. tchr., Colo. Tchr. Jefferson County Adult Edn., Lakewood, Colo., 1963-67; tchr. bus., coordinator coop. office edn., Jefferson High Sch., Edgewater, Colo., 1959—; instr. Community Coll. Denver, Red Rocks, 1967-81, U. Colo. Denver, 1976-79, Parks Coll. Bus., 1983—; dist. adviser Future Bus. Leaders Am. Active City of Edgewater Sister City Project Student Exchange Com.; past pres. Career Women's Symphony Guild; treas. Phantoms of Opera, 1982—; active Opera Colo. Assocs., I Pagliacci; ex-officio trustee Denver Symphony Assn., 1980-82. Recipient disting. service award Jefferson County Sch. Bd. 1980; Jefferson High Sch. Wall of Fame 1981. Mem. NEA (life), Colo. Edn. Assn., Jefferson County Edn. Assn., Colo. Vocat. Assn., Am. Vocat. Assn., Colo. Educators for and about Bus., Profl. Secs. Internat., Career Women's Symphony Guild, Profl. Panhellenic Assn., Colo. Congress Fgn. Lang. Tchrs., Wheat Ridge C. of C. (edn. com.), Delta Pi Epsilon, Phi Chi Theta, Beta Gamma Sigma, Alpha Lambda Delta. Republican. Roman Catholic. Club: Tyrolean Soc. Denver.

LEIPZIG, LIBBY (MRS. FRED LEIPZIG), state official, automotive products company executive; b. Easton, Pa.; d. Benjamin and Mary (Bizar) Black; student Paterson Normal Sch., N.J., 1928, Rutgers U., 1943-44, Fairleigh Dickinson U., 1962; m. Fred Leipzig, Apr. 12, 1940; 1 dau., Marta Beth; 1 stepson, Howard A. Leipzig. With N.J. State Employment Service, Passaic, 1941—, supr. profl. comml. dept., Paterson, N.J., 1962-69, supr. indsl. services dept., Passaic, 1969-72; v.p. Major Automotive Products Co., Inc., Clifton, N.J. 1945-69, sec.-treas., 1969—. Home: The Promenade 5225 Pooks Hill Rd Bethesda MD 20814

LEIS, WINOGENE B. (MRS. HENRY PATRICK LEIS, JR.), nurse assn. exec.; b. Clay, W.Va., Feb. 27, 1919; d. Gruder L. and Daisy M. (Young) Barnette; R.N. cum laude, Kanawha Valley Hosp., 1939; m. Henry Patrick Leis, Jr., Jan. 8, 1944; children—Henry Patrick III, Thomas Federick. Nurse, Kanawha Valley Hosp., 1939-43. Decorated lady comdr. Equestrian Order Holy Sepulchre Jerusalem. Mem. Woman's Aux. Internat. Coll. Surgeons (corr. sec. N.Y. State surg. div. 1955-57, v.p. 1961-63, pres. 1963-67; pres. U.S. sect. 1970, dir. 1970—), Flower Fifth Avenue Hosp. Woman's Aux. (dir. 1956-59, 69—), Woman's Aux. N.Y. Acad. Scis., Woman's Aux. N.Y. State Med. Soc., Woman's Aux. Internat. Coll. Surgeons (corr. sec. 1972-74, pres. 1977-78, dir. 1978—), Woman's Aux. Cabrini Med. Ctr., Woman's Aux. Westchester County Med. Ctr., Woman's Aux. Lenox Hill Hosp. Republican. Roman Catholic. Home: 147-03 5th Ave Whitestone NY 11357 and 113 The Pines Eleventh Ave N N Myrtle Beach SC 29582

LEISER, BONNIE TERESA, corporate executive; b. Salt Lake City, Aug. 7, 1947; d. Robert A. and Elinore C. McGregor; m. Michael W. Leiser, Apr. 3, 1966; 1 son, Walker. B.S. with high honors (Xerox scholar), Portland State U., 1980. Acctg. mgr., cons. Component Resources, Inc., Portland, Oreg., 1978-80; fin. mgr. Far West Office Products, Inc., Portland, also pvt. practice fin. mgmt. cons., Portland, 1981; bus. devel. officer Barclays Am./Bus. Credit, Inc., Portland, 1982—. Recipient 1st Place in photography Lake Oswego Festival Arts, 1980. Mem. Inst. for Profl. and Managerial Women, Nat. Assn. Comml. Fin., Phi Kappa Phi, Beta Gamma Sigma. Home: 10592 SW 63d Dr Portland OR 97219 Office: Barclays Am Bus Credit Inc 1001 SW 5th Ave Suite 1000 Portland OR 97204

LEITCH, ALMA MAY, city official; b. Fredericksburg, Va., Nov. 24, 1924; d. Maurice Andrew Doggett and Nora May (Spicer) L.; grad. James Monroe High Sch., Fredericksburg; various specialized courses U. Va., Va. Poly. Inst. Dep. commnr. revenue City of Fredericksburg, 1946-69, commr. revenue, 1970—; mem. Va. Adv. Legis. Council, 1977-78; mem. subcom. Commonwealth Va. Revenue Resources and Econ. Commn., 1978. Bd. dirs. Fredericksburg chpt. ARC, 1960—, chmn., 1969; sec. Democratic Com. Fredericksburg, 1964; pres., bd. dirs. Rappahannock United Way for Fredericksburg, Spotsylvania, and Stafford counties, 1979. Recipient various service awards; Outstanding Citizenship award Fredericksburg Area C. of C., 1979. Mem. Commrs. Revenue Assn. Va. (pres. 1979-80), Va. Govtl. Employees Assn. (dir.-at-large 1979-80), League No. Va. Commrs. Revenue (pres. 1972), Va. Assn. Local Exec. Constl. Officers (exec. com.), Internat. Assn. Assessing Officers, Va. Assn. Assessing Officers, Hist. Fredericksburg Found., Bus. and Profl. Women's Club. Club: Ann Page Garden (pres. 1980-82, Mary B. Benoit award 1977), Altrusa. Home: 511 Hanover St Fredericksburg VA 22401 Office: City Hall Box 644 Fredericksburg VA 22401

LEITER, BEULAH G. (MRS. ROBERT PAUL LEITER), lawyer; b. Chgo.; d. Jehiel D. and Rose (Rossman) Liebling; J.D., John Marshall U., 1945, LL.M., 1946; student U. Chgo., U. Ga., Emory U.; m. Robert Paul Leiter, May 10, 1936; children—Darryl J., Paula S. Admitted to Ga. bar, 1945, U.S. Dist. Ct. (5th and 11th dists.) Ga., U.S. Ct. Appeals (5th cir.), U.S. Supreme Ct.; since practiced in Atlanta; mem. firm Leiter & Leiter, 1946—; dep. sheriff, 1958—. Mem. Iota Tau Tau, 1951—, So. chancellor, 1955-57, Internat. supreme chancellor, 1955-59, mem. supreme council, 1955-63, supreme asso. dean, 1959-61, internat. supreme dean, 1961-63. Mem. nat. women's com. Brandeis U., 1961—. Mem. Internat. Fedn. Women Lawyers (legal edn. com. 1958, penal law, outer space law, UN com. coms. 1959-60), Nat. Assn Women Lawyers (mental health com.), Am. Trial Lawyers Assn., Internat. Platform Assn., Am. Judicature Soc., Com. Women in Pub. Service, Ga. Assn. Women Lawyers (past v.p., rec. sec., exec. com.), U. Ga. Alumni Soc., Nat. Sheriffs Assn., Ga. Bar Assn., Fulton County Lawyers Assn. (charter, trustee 1952, rec. sec. 1956—), Nat. Assn. Claimant Attys., Am. Bus. Women's Assn., PTA, Atlanta Art Assn., Phi Kappa Delta. Clubs: Equity (publicity com. 1959-60, 62—), Old War Horse Lawyers, Nat. Travel, Smithsonian Assos. Am. Mus. Natural History. Home: 1265 Poplar Grove Dr NE Atlanta GA 30306 Office: PO Box 1492 Atlanta GA 30301

LEITH, PRISCILLA MARIE, consultant; b. Utica, N.Y., Jan. 17, 1935; d. John Schrader and Gertrude Marie (Walsh) Tremper; A.B., Vassar Coll., 1956; M.B.A., Babson Coll., 1982; m. John Douglas Leith, Aug. 4, 1957; children—Jennifer, Margery. Engring. asst. Atomic Power Equipment div. Gen. Electric Co., San Jose, Calif., 1956-57; engring. aide U.S. Geol. Survey Office, Honolulu, 1958; instr. U. Wis. Extension div., Madison, 1962-64; contbg. editor Newton (Mass.) Times, 1973-74; free-lance corr. Newton Graphic, 1976-77; pres. Leith Assocs., 1985—. State coordinator Mass. NOW, 1977-78; legis. coordinator, 1985—; mem. steering com. Mass. Women's Polit. Caucus, 1973-75; co-founder Newton Women's Polit. Caucus, 1973; 2d v.p. Newton League of Women Voters, 1972-73; pres. Oshkosh (Wis.) League of Women Voters, 1967-69; 2d vice chmn. Winnebago County (Wis.) Democratic Party, 1969-71. Mem. New Eng. Women's Press Assn., Women's Equity Action League, NOW. Club: Vassar (Boston). Contbg. author, editor: (booklet) Politics Is for Women, 1973; editor: Solid Waste in Newton, 1972. Contbr. numerous articles to newspapers. Office: 162 Islington Rd Newton MA 02166

LEIVISKA, NANCY LYNN, entertainment production company executive; b. Evanston, Ill., July 19, 1948; d. Laurie and Dorothy June (Sterner) Leiviska; student Wis. State U., La Crosse, 1966-68, UCLA, 1968-70; 1 child, Stefan Kendall Gordy. Sec. to Sammy Davis, Jr., 1968-70; with Motown Records, Hollywood, Calif., 1970-71, editor Motown Newsletter, 1972-75, asst. to chmn. bd., 1976-78, dir. video ops., 1979-82, exec. dir. video prodn. film div., 1982-83; pres. Stefanino Prodns., Hollywood, 1984—; owner Leiviska & Assocs., 1982—. Mem. Am. Film Inst., AFTRA, ASCAP, Archives Music Preservation (v.p. bd.), Orgn. Women in Music. Republican. Mem. Self-Realization Fellowship.

LEIWANT, JOAN DIAMOND, advertising agency executive; b. Newark, Aug. 20, 1945; d. Morris David and Sue Harriet (Kastner) Diamond; m. Bruce Harlan Leiwant, July 1, 1982. B.A., U. Miami, 1968. Advt. asst. Suburban Pub. Corp., Union, N.J., 1969; assoc. dir. recruitment advt. div Keyes, Martin & Co., Springfield, N.J., 1969-81; v.p., dir. recruitment advt. div. David H. Block Advt., Inc., Montclair, N.J., 1982—; classified advt. symposium speaker N.J. Press Assn., 1981; recruitment advt. speaker N.J. Employers Assn., 1982. Office: David H Block Advt Inc 33 S Fullerton Ave Montclair NJ 07042

LEJA, CAROLYN HEDWIG, lawyer; b. Chgo., Sept. 11, 1946; d. Casimir Edward and Helen Magdalena (Cebula) Leja. B.A. in Sociology, De Paul U., Chgo., 1977; J.D. with high honors, Ill. Inst. Tech.-Chgo. Kent Coll. Law, 1983. Bar: Ill. 1983, Fla. 1984. Escrow officer Chgo. Title and Trust Co., 1971-78; research atty. Ill. Criminal Justice Info. Authority, Chgo., 1982-84; atty. Adminstrv. Office of the Ill. Cts., Springfield, 1984—; sole practice, Lombard, Ill., 1983. Mem. Gov.'s Task Force Juvenile Records; reading tutor Northwest Community Orgn., Chgo., 1964-67. Ill. Inst. Tech.-Chgo. Kent Coll. Law scholar, 1980-83, Mem. Chgo. Bar Assn., Ill. State Bar Assn., Phi Alpha Delta. Republican. Religious Scientist. Club: Windy City Post Card (pres. 1967).

LEJEUNE, MARJORIE ANN, veterinarian; b. New Roads, La., Sept. 29, 1949; d. Julius A. and Marjorie J. (Fontenot) Cline; m. John R. LeJeune, July 5, 1967 (div. 1983). D.V.M., La. State U., 1979. Stenographer La. Dept. Hwys., Baton Rouge, 1967-68, dept. Welfare, 1968-69, sec. Dept. Pub. Works, 1969-73; vet., owner, Ridgefield Animal Hosp., Thibodaux, La., 1979—; dog show judge; editor, author The Cold Wet Nose, 1981-82. Active Thibodaux Vol. Fire Dept., dep. LaFourche Parish Sheriff's Office, Roman Cath. youth activities. Mem. AVMA, La. Vet. Med. Assn. Democrat. Office: Ridgefield Animal Hospital 1713 Ridgefield Rd Thibodaux LA 70301

LEMASTER, SHERRY RENEE, college administrator; b. Lexington, Ky., June 25, 1953; d. John William and Mary Charles (Thompson) LeM. B.S., U. Ky., 1975, M.S., 1984. Cert. fund raising exec. Lab. technician in virology, serology Central Ky. Animal Disease Diagnostic Lab., Lexington, 1976-77; grant, environ. specialist Commonwealth Ky. Dept. for Natural Resources and Environ. Protection, Frankfurt, 1977-78; coordinator student activities Murray State U., Ky., 1978-80; dean students Midway Coll., Ky., 1980-81, v.p. for devel., alumnae affairs, 1981—. Ambassador, U. Ky. Coll. Agr., 1977—; chmn. Midway chpt. Am. Heart Assn., 1981, co-chmn. Woodford County chpt., 1983; mem. adminstrv. bd. First United Meth. Ch., 1982-84; mem. Council for Advancement and Support Edn., 1981—, chmn. Ky. conf., 1982; planning com. Nat. Disciples Devel. Execs. Conf., 1984. Named Ky. col., hon. sec. state. Mem. Am. Council on Edn., Nat. Soc. Fund Raising Execs. (bd. dirs. Lexington chpt. 1985—), Nat. Assn. Female Execs., Greater Lexington Area C. of C., Advancement Women in Higher Edn. Adminstrn. (state planning com.), Ky. Assn. Women Deans Adminstrs. and Counselors (editor Newsletter 1981), U. Ky. Alumni Assn. (life), Gen. Fedn. Womens Clubs, P.E.O., Ninety-Nines (vice chmn. Ky. Bluegrass chpt. 1986-87), Pi Beta Phi Nat. Alumnae Assn. (alumnae province pres. 1980-81, sec. bd. dirs. Ky. Beta chpt. 1982-84), Alpha Kappa Psi Alumnae Assn. (charter Murray chpt.). Club: Lexington Zonta (bd. dirs., Amelia Earhart Fellowship awards dist. chmn. 1984—, Keeneland Day chmn. 1983, Amelia Earhart com. chmn. 1983). Avocations: needlecrafts; aerobics; piano; racquetball; private pilot. Home: 110 Highview Dr Midway KY 40347 Office: Midway Coll Stephens St Midway KY 40347

LEMASTER, SUSAN M., marketing executive, writer; b. Cody, Wyo., May 9, 1953; d. Floyd Morris and Virginia Kristena (Renner) LeM.; B.A., U. Wyo., Casper, 1979; A.A., Casper Coll., 1977. Reporter, night editor Casper Star Tribune, 1972-76; copy editor, editor In Wyo. mag., Casper, 1979; info. dir. Wyo. Rural Electric Assn., Casper, 1980-81; story editor Wyo. Horizons mag., Casper, 1981-82; asst., instr. English lab. Casper Coll., 1982-84; mktg. mgr. Chen & Assocs., Inc., 1984—; freelance writer, 1982—; night sch. instr. Casper Coll., 1983-84, summer sch. instr., 1984; editor Casper Jour., summers 1983-84. Recipient First Place News Story, Wyo. Press Assn., 1973; First Place Editing award Wyo. Press Women, 1980. Mem. Soc. for Mktg. Profl. Services (co-chair membership com. Denver chpt.), NOW. Democrat. Roman Catholic. Home: 382 S Logan Denver CO 80209 Office: 96 S Zuni Denver Co 80223

LEMASURIER, MARY LOUISE, shop proprietor, interior designer, lecturer; b. Crookston, Minn., Apr. 13, 1928; d. Henry Arthur and Eva Catherin (LePage) Buhn; m. Phillip Cameron LeMasurier, Oct. 28, 1948; children—Phyllis, Mary Catherine, Dann, David. Student Moorhead State Tchrs. Coll., N.D. U., Long Beach State Coll.; hon. A.A.I.D., 1980. Bookkeeper N.D. U., Grand Forks, 1947-48; buyer J.C. Penney, Crookston, Minn., 1948-52; co-propr. Keith's Pottery, Manhattan Beach, Calif., 1953—; lectr. Mayan culture Los Angeles Schs., 1963-72; color coordinator Tony Perierra, Los Angeles, 1965-80. Active Young Republicans, 1963—; sec. P.T.A., El Segundo, 1965, pres., 1966; organist St. Michael's Ch., El Segundo, 1953-73. Mem. Delphinian Soc., Profl. Bus. Women's Orgn., Archeol. Soc. Anglican. Lodge: Eastern Star (organist). Office: Keiths Pottery 240 S Sepulveda Blvd Manhattan Beach CA 90266

LEMBO, KAREN KLEPPE, lawyer; b. Hinesville, Ga., Sept. 28, 1956; d. Arthur Rudolph and Elsie Marie (Christensen) Kleppe; m. August Thomas Lembo, July 26, 1980; 1 dau., Marguerite Katherine. A.B. in Theology, Georgetown U., 1978; J.D., Seton Hall U., 1981. Bar: N.J. 1981. Jud. law clk., Elizabeth, N.J., 1981-82; assoc. Gern, Stieber, Dunetz, Davison & Weinstein, West Orange, N.J., 1982-83, Bartel & Bartel, Fair Lawn, N.J., 1984—; instr. family law, estates and trusts Am. Inst. for Paralegal Studies, Inc., Mahwah, N.J., 1984—; vol. panelist Union County Matrimonial Early Settlement Panel, Elizabeth, 1983—. Case and comments editor Seton Hall Law Rev., 1980-81. Mem. ABA, N.J. Bar Assn. (family law and young lawyers divs.), Essex County Bar Assn., Union County Bar Assn., Alpha Sigma Nu. Democrat. Roman Catholic. Home: 76 Gould Pl Caldwell NJ 07006 Office: Bartel & Bartel 169 Lincoln Ave Fair Lawn NJ 07410

LE MENAGER, LOIS MAE, incentive merchandise and travel company executive; b. Cleve., Apr. 25, 1934; d. Lawrence M. and Lillian C. (Simicek) Stanek; m. Charles J. Blabolil (dec. 1982); children—Sherry L., Richard A.; m. Spencer H. Le Menager, Mar. 23, 1984. Grad. high sch., Cleve. Bank teller, sec. to v.p., Peoples Savs. and Loan, Cleve., 1951-56; travel counselor Mktg. Innovators, Rosemont, Ill., 1978-80, mktg. dir., 1980-82, chmn., chief exec. officer, owner, 1982—; dir. Northwest Commerce Bank, Rosemont. Mem. Des Plaines C. of C., Soc. Incentive Travel Execs., Am. Soc. Travel Agents, Nat. Assn. Women Bus. Owners, Chgo. Assn. Commerce and Industry, Am. Mgmt. Assn., Nat. Assn. Female Execs., Czechoslovak Soc. Am. Republican. Congregationalist. Club: Executive (Chgo). Office: Mktg Innovators 9701 W Higgins Rd Rosemont IL 60018

LEMESSURIER, MARY J., Canadian government official; b. Montreal, Que., June 12, 1929; m. Ernest Dawes; children—Willa, Jill, Tim, Andrew. Student McGill U., Royal Victoria Hosp. Minister of Culture, Alta, 1979—. Vice pres., then pres. Miles for Millions, 1973-77; provincial chmn. Jr. Girls Golf in Alta.; nat. pres., past provincial pres. Can. Save the Children Fund; mem. Organizing Com. 1980 Lassie, Can. ladies curling championship. Mem. Alta. Ladies Golf Assn. (local and provincial officer). Conservative. Office: 402 Legislative Bldg Edmonton AB T5K 2B6 Canada

LEMIEUX, LUCILLE CHENETTE, sch. prin.; b. Worcester, Mass., Dec. 16, 1935; d. Lionel Joseph and Dorothy May Ellen Chenette; B.A., Anna Maria Coll., 1958; M.Ed., State Coll. Worcester, 1967; M.S., Pepperdine U., 1975; postgrad. UCLA, 1977—; m. Bertrand Jean LeMieux, Nov. 22, 1958; children—Marc Kevin, Celeste Marie. Med. technologist Meml. Hosp., 1956-58; research asst. Surprenant Mfg. Co., Clinton, Mass., 1958-59; instr. math. Langford Jr. High Sch., Augusta, Ga., 1959-61; tchr. Worcester City Hosp., 1963-64; lectr. Anna Maria Coll., Paxton, Mass., 1962-65; tchr. sci. Arlington Sch., Torrance, Calif., 1970-72, instructional TV specialist, tchr., 1972-75, adminstr., 1975—; prin. Calle Mayor Middle Sch., 1976—. Vice pres. Torrance Hist. Soc., 1974, Torrance Sister City Assn., 1975; bd. dirs. Los Cancioneros, 1971-74; den leader, coach, merit badge counselor Boy Scouts Am., 1969-71. Recipient Yr. of Educator medallion Los Angeles County Bd. Suprs., 1982; Pi Lambda Theta scholar UCLA, 1980-81. Mem. Assn. Torrance Sch. Adminstrs. (pres. 1982-83), Assn. Calif. Sch. Adminstrs., Assn. Supervision and Curriculum Devel., Nat. Assn. Female Execs., Dean's Council UCLA, Torrance Area Reading Council, Torrance Friends of Library. Writer, producer, All Over This Lands TV series, 1972-74, also Step by Step (award Assn. Ednl. Communications and Tech.), 1974. Office: 4800 Calle Mayor Torrance CA 90505

LEMKE, CORRINE LARUE, university employee; b. Sabin, Minn., May 25, 1934; d. Oswald Edward and Ida M. (Krabbenhoft) L. B.A. in Philosophy, Moorhead State U., 1972. Notary pub., Minn. With WDAY radio and TV sta., Fargo, N.D., 1953-67; fin. aid grant coordinator Moorhead State U., 1967—, mem. task force study of changing student mix, 1983-84. Vol. Comstock Hist. House, Moorhead. Recipient cert. Gov. Minn., 1976, 10 yr. service award

Moorhead State U., 1980, letter of commendation U.S. Dept. Edn., 1983. Mem. Minn. Hist. Soc., State Hist. Soc. Wis., Concordia Hist. Inst. of St. Louis, Phoenix Soc. of Moorhead, Concordia Coll. Alumni Assn., Moorhead State U. Alumni Assn. Lutheran. Author pvt. family history publs. Home: 128 Pierce Trailer Ct Moorhead MN 56560 Office: Moorhead State U Moorhead MN 56560

LEMLEY, PATRICIA RIOUX, educator; b. El Campo, Tex., Aug. 19, 1938; d. William E. and Arleene Anna (Wendel) Rioux; m. Richard Lemley, June 16, 1962. B.A., So. Meth. U., 1960; M.A., Tex. A&I, 1966. Tchr. pub. schs. Tex., 1960-66; mem. faculty N. Tex. State U., Denton, 1967-68; tchr. Carrollton Farmers Br. Ind. Sch. Dist., Carrollton, Tex., 1969-74, 82—; sec., treas. Am. Constrn. Systems, El Campo, 1974-79; dir. Rioux, Inc., El Campo, 1975—. Mem. Nat. Council Tchrs. English, Tex. Joint Council Tchrs. English, Assn. Supervision and Curriculum Devel. Avocations: reading; hand work. Office: Dewitt Perry Carrollton-Farmers Br ISD 1709 Beltline Carrollton TX 75006

LEMMONS, MIRIAM ELISE, nurse, social worker, rehabilitation counselor; b. New Orleans, Jan. 3, 1932; d. Walter Simpson and Ola Adele (Carruth) Weathersby; Asso. Nursing, Iowa Lakes Community Coll., 1977; B.A., Buena Vista Coll., 1978; M.S., Mankato State U., 1981; m. Ronald Lemmons, June 22, 1962; children—Robert, Linda, Mark, Kevin, Robin. R.N., Holy Family Hosp., Estherville, Iowa, 1977-82, dir. med. social services, 1981—, dir. home health dept., 1981—, dir. Hospice, 1982—. Named Citizen of Yr., Estherville City Councilwoman, Estherville C. of C. Mem. Nat. Hospice Assn., Am. Nurses Assn., Nat. League Nursing, Assn. Rehab. Nurses, Nat. Rehab. Assn., Iowa Hospice Orgn. (bd. dirs., officer), NOW, Social Workers in Health Facilities, Am. Soc. Profl. and Exec. Women, Nat. Assn. Rehab. Profls. Democrat. Methodist. Home: 33 Manor Circle Estherville IA 51334 Office: 826 N 8th St Estherville IA 51334

LEMMONS, PATRICIA KATHERINE, public relations executive; b. Decatur, Ill., Dec. 4, 1957; d. Lowell Maynard and Lou Ellen (Cox) L. B.A. (James Millikin scholar), Millikin U., 1980; M.S., Northwestern U., 1981. Promotions asst. Herald and Review, Decatur, 1977; asst. dir. pub. relations Nat. Coll. Edn., Evanston, Ill., 1981-85, dir. pub. relations, 1985—; publicity dir. Theatre 7, Decatur, 1980; pub. relations coordinator Trinity Theatre, Evanston, 1983-85. Recipient Dr. and Mrs. W. J. Darby prize Millikin U., 1980. Mem. Women in Communications Inc. bd. dirs. North Shore chpt. 1984-86, pres. North Shore chpt. 1986—), Ill. Theatre Assn., Sigma Delta Chi-Soc. Profl. Journalists, Phi Kappa Phi. Home: 1121 Church St Apt 406 Evanston IL 60201

LEMOINE, HELEN LOUISE, nurse; b. Millford, Tex., Feb. 20, 1929; d. Chester Randolph and Ina Louise (Dotson) Riddels; R.N., Parkland Hosp. Sch. Nursing, 1951; profl. tng. in gerontol. nursing U. Southwestern La., 1983; m. Louis M. Escude, Dec. 26, 1950; children—Annette, Escude, Michael Escude, Donna Escude McInnis; m. 2nd Albert L. Lemoine, Dec. 21, 1980. Staff nurse Wichita Falls Clinic Hosp., 1952, McConnell and Dupree Clinic and Hosp., Bunkie, La., 1955-65, Bayou Vista Manor Nursing Home, Bunkie, 1965; dir. nursing Avoyelles Manor Nursing Home, DuPont, La., 1966—. Mem. La. Health Care Associated Dirs. of Nursing in Action (region rep.), Parkland Nurses Alum Assn., Am. Legion Aux., Cath. Daus. Am. Democrat. Roman Catholic. Club: Nurses Book, Altar Soc. Home: Route 1 Box 597A Cottonport LA 71327 Office: Route 1 PO Box 215 Plaucheville LA 71362

LEMON, BERNICE THORSON, nurse; b. Houston, Minn., Mar. 6, 1926; d. Theodore O. and Bertha Olivia (Karlsbraten) Thorson; m. George Lawton Lemon, Dec. 31, 1950; children—Ted Charles, Bernice Krin, Susan Jo, Laura Thorson, Barbara Anne. R.N. diploma Mounds Midway Sch. Nursing, 1947. Head nurse operating room U. Minn., Mpls., 1947-50; nursery nurse Midway Hosp., St. Paul, 1947-48; office nurse Dr. Lemon, Lewisburg, W.Va., and self-employed pvt. duty nurse, intermittently, 1959-68; homemaker, nurse, 1968—; nurse vol. to World Conf. at Caux, Switzerland, 1974, 80, 81, 84. Founder, mem. Sing Out Roanoke Valley, 1973-78, Gymn-Sing Roanoke Valley Inc., 1978-81; participant cultural exchanges, including HEW and Kennedy Found. Arts Exchange to Poland, 1977, Am. Friendship Alumni to Mainland China and Romania, 1980; counselor Offender Aid Restoration, Inc., Roanoke, Va., 1979-81; initiated and promoted Drug Dependency Alert, Roanoke Valley, 1981; chaplain Roanoke Democratic Club, 1980-81; active Bible Study Fellowship. Served with USPHS, 1942-43. Recipient Roanoke Valley Outstanding Service award Roanoke Bicentennial Commn., 1976, recognition for artistic presentation on 2d Polish Am. Symposium of Music, Krakow Conservatory, Poland, 1977. Lutheran. Avocations: sports; reading; music appreciation; needlework; gardening. Home: 6924 River Ridge Dr Nashville TN 33722

LEMON, LINDA GLASSON, hospital security and safety official, healthcare consultant; b. Nassawadox, Va., July 2, 1947; d. William Robert and Doris (Savage) Glasson; m. Charles William Lemon, Sr., Mar. 21, 1969 (div. 1973). Student Eastern Shore Br. U. Va., 1965-67, J. Sargent Reynolds Community Coll., 1976-80, Old Dominion U., 1981, Va. Wesleyan Coll., 1985. Cert. ambulance emergency med. technician. Clk.-typist G.L. Webster Co., Inc., Cheriton, Va., 1962-70; tchrs. aide Cape Charles High Sch., Va., 1970-72; dir. recreation and infirmary asst. United Methodist Children's Home, Richmond, Va., 1972-73; stockroom mgr. Flair Clothing Store, Richmond, 1973-74; with med. record dept. Richmond Meml. Hosp., 1974-75, asst. utilization rev. coordinator, 1975-80, hosp. police sgt., 1977-80; dir. safety and security Maryview Hosp., Portsmouth, Va., 1980—, chmn. hosp. safety com., 1980—, mem. disaster com., 1980—. Contbg. author tng. manuals, articles in profl. publs. Instr. first aid and personal safety ARC, 1970-85, multimedia first aid instr., 1983—, first aid chmn. bd. dirs. Henrico chpt., 1979-80, vol. emergency med. technician ambulance state fair annually 1974—. Mem. Nat. Assn. Female Execs., Internat. Assn. Hosp. Security (sr., chmn. Region III 1985, v.p./sec., 1985), Am. Soc. Indsl. Security (mem. nat. standing com. healthcare security 1979-84, v.p. 1983-84). Baptist. Avocations: Golf; softball; swimming; reading; classical music; basketball. Office: Maryview Hospital 3636 High St Portsmouth VA 23707

LEMONDS, KATHRYN JOYCE, technical executive; b. Oroville, Calif., June 9, 1948; d. Homer Bertus Daily and Betty Louise (Owens) Daily Owens; m. Thomas Andrew Lemonds, Apr. 1, 1967 (div. Aug. 1972); 1 child, Laura Marie. Student Wash. State U., 1966-67; A.A., Diablo Valley Coll., 1985; student J.F. Kennedy U., 1985—. Engring. asst. Pacific Gas & Electric Co. Research Lab., San Ramon, Calif., 1972-82, sr. tech. specialist, 1982—; chief software designer LeMonde Designer Software, San Ramon, 1986—. Supr. host com. Democratic Nat. Conv., San Francisco, 1984. Mem. Software Entrepreneurs Forum, NOW. Club: Lafayette Orinda Presbyterian Ch. Singleship (Calif.). Avocations: studying ballet; tap and jazz dancing; skiing; traveling; reading. Home: 2604 Shadow Mountain Dr San Ramon CA 94583

LE MONE, EVELYN FRANCES, dance theatre administrator; b. Upland, Calif., Aug. 17, 1907; d. William Francis and Nina Evelyn (Webster) Crist; m. Wallace Albin Le Mone, June 25, 1931 (dec. 1971); children—Lawrence William, Sharon (dec.). Grad. high sch. Pasadena, Calif. Dance instr. YWCA, Pasadena, 1933-35, PTA, Pasadena, 1945-54; assoc. prof. dance Pasadena Playhouse, 1952-65; dir. studio Le Mone, Inc., Pasadena, 1935-78; artistic dir. Pasadena Dance Theatre, 1958—; lectr. in field. Contbr. articles, reviews to profl. jours. Named to Pantheon Hall of Honor Pasadena Playhouse Alumni Assn., 1985. Mem. Pasadena Arts Council (vol. 1983—, Performing Arts award 1971), Los Angeles Dance Assn., Pacific Regional Ballet Assn. (chmn. choreography 1980—, chmn. membership com. 1972-76), Republican. Roman Catholic. Office: Pasadena Dance Theatre South Pasadena CA 91030

LEMONGELLO, DEBORAH LYNN, sales supervisor, food broker; b. Findlay, Ohio, Jan. 11, 1956; d. James Arthur Horn and Joan Arlene (Beck) Hauman; m. Mark Lemongello, May 28, 1983. B.S., Ind. State U., 1978. Merchandiser, Colgate-Palmolive, N.Y.C., 1982-82, Bardell-Horn, Phoenix, 1982, sales rep., 1982-84; sales rep. Bromar Ariz., Phoenix, 1984, asst. sales supr., 1984-85; sales supr. Bromar Gouley Burcham, Phoenix, 1985—. Names Salesperson of Yr., Bardell-Horn, 1983. Mem. Nat. Assn. Female Execs. Republican. Roman Catholic. Avocations: Golf; skiing. Office: Bromar Gouley Burcham 77 E Thomas Phoenix AZ 85012

LEMOS, GLORIA ELLIOTT, soft drink company executive; b. Royston, Ga., Apr. 29, 1946; d. Richard F. and G. Maxine (Brown) Elliott; A.A., Emmanuel Jr. Coll., 1966; student Oglethorpe U., 1966-68; 1 son, Joseph David. With Coca-Cola Co., Atlanta, 1967-77, Washington, 1977—, v.p. internat. govt. affairs, 1979—. Bd. dirs. Community Found. Washington, 1980—, Inst. Study of Diplomacy, Georgetown U., 1981—, Am. Com. East-West Accord, 1982—; trustee Fed. City Council, 1978—, Meridian House Internat., 1981—, Am. U., 1983—, Nat. Multiple Sclerosis Soc., 1985—. Mem. Washington Internat. Bus. Council, UN Internat. Bus. Council, Internat. Mgmt. and Devel. Inst., So. Center Internat. Studies. Club: Internat. Office: Coca-Cola Co 1627 K St NW Suite 800 Washington DC 20006

LENAHAN, JULIE ELAINE, foundation executive; b. Lawrence, Kans., Nov. 21, 1956; d. James Richard and Helen Pauline (Laughlin) Lenahan. B.A., St. Mary Coll., 1977; postgrad. U. Kans., 1978. Writer, editor Holy Land Christian Mission, Kansas City, Mo., 1978-79; pub. info. specialist Wyandot Mental Health Ctr., Inc., Kansas City, Kans., 1979-83; dir. community services and ednl. programs Christian Found. for Children, Kansas City, Mo., 1983-84; regional office coordinator, nat. publicity dir. St. Vincent Pallotti Ctr. Apostolic Devel., St. Louis, 1984—. Mem. Nat. Assn. Mental Health Info. Officers (pres. 1983), Women in Communications, Bus. and Profl. Womens Club. Democrat. Roman Catholic. Home: 1611 E Elm St Olathe KS 66062 Office: 401 S Lindbergh Blvd Saint Louis MO 63131

LENEHAN, PAMELA FARRELL, investment banker; b. Stamford, Conn., May 19, 1952; d. John R. and Elsie M. (White) Farrell; m. Donald B. Lenehan, May 25, 1974; children—Sarah, Paul. B.A. in Math. Econs. magna cum laude, Brown U., 1974, M.A. in Econs. with honors, 1974. Vice pres. electronics div. corp. banking Chase Manhattan, N.Y.C., 1974-81; v.p. high tech. group corp. fin. First Boston Corp., N.Y.C., 1981—. Republican. Roman Catholic. Club: Field. Home: 90 Boulder Trail Bronxville NY 10708 Office: The First Boston Corp Park Ave Plaza New York NY 10055

L'ENGLE, MADELEINE (MRS. HUGH FRANKLIN), author; b. N.Y.C., Nov. 29, 1918; d. Charles Wadsworth and Madeleine (Barnett) Camp; A.B. with honors, Smith Coll., 1941; postgrad. Columbia U., 1960—; hon. degrees Gordon Coll., Indpls. Christian Theol. Sem., Miami U. (Ohio), Wheaton Coll., Wilson Coll., Yale Divinity Sch., Smith Coll., Berkeley Div. Sch. at Yale U., Alexandria Theol. Sem.; m. Hugh Franklin, Jan. 26, 1946; children—Josephine Morrison Franklin Jones, Maria Franklin, Bion Barnett. Appeared in Broadway plays Uncle Harry, 1944, The Cherry Orchard, 1945, The Joyous Season, 1946; appeared in summer stock, radio, TV, 1941—; tchr. St. Hilda's and St. Hugh's Sch., N.Y.C., 1960—; writer in residence Ohio State U., 1970; lectr. U. Minn., U. Mich., Ind. U., U. Rochester, Wheaton Coll., U. So. Mo., U. So. Miss., Kent State U., others; writer-in-residence Cathedral St. John the Divine; author: The Small Rain, 1945; Ilse, 1946; And Both Were Young, 1949; Camilla Dickinson, 1951; A Winter's Love, 1957; Meet the Austins, 1960; A Wrinkle in Time, 1962 (Newbery medal 1963; Sequoyah award 1965); The Moon by Night, 1963 (Austrian State Lit. award 1970); The Twenty-Four Days Before Christmas, 1964; The Arm of the Starfish, 1965; Camilla, 1965; The Love Letters, 1966; The Journey with Jonah, 1967; The Young Unicorns, 1968; Dance in The Desert, 1969; Lines Scribbled on an Envelope, 1970; The Other Side of the Sun, 1971; A Circle of Quiet, 1972; A Wind in the Door, 1973; The Summer of The Great-Grandmother, 1975; Dragons in the Waters, 1976; The Irrational Season, 1977; A Swiftly Tilting Planet, 1978; The Weather of the Heart, 1978; Ladder of Angels, 1979; A Ring of Endless Light, 1980; Walking on Water, 1980; The Sphinx at Dawn, 1981; The Anti-Muffins, 1982; A Severed Wasp, 1983; And It Was Good, 1983; A House Like a Lotus, 1984; A Stone for a Pillow, 1986; Many Waters, 1986; author poems, plays. Pres. Crosswicks Found.; bd. dirs. Author's Guild Found. Decorated Order of St. John of Jerusalem; recipient Lewis Carroll Shelf award, 1965; Hans Christian Anderson Internat. Runner-up award; Sequoiah award; Austrian State prize for lit., 1969; medal U. So. Miss., 1978; Smith medal, 1980; Regina medal, 1984; Smith Coll. Sophie award, 1984. Mem. Authors League (bd. dirs., children's book com., membership com., mem. council), Authors Guild (pres.), PEN, Internat. Platform Assn., Writers Guild Am. Mem. Anglican Ch. (choir dir. 1953-59).

LENHER, IRENE K. (MRS. SAMUEL LENHER), artist; b. Rye, N.Y., Oct. 4, 1907; d. John Wilkinson and Elena (Hellmann) Kirkland; student Slade Sch. Art, U. Coll. (London), 1925-26, Grande Chaumiere, Paris, 1927-28; M.A. (hon.), U. Del., 1968; m. Samuel Lenher, Dec. 14, 1929; children—John K., Ann B., George V. Exhibited one-woman shows: Warehouse Gallery Arden, Decoy Gallery, Kennett Square, Pa., Hunter Gallery, 1965, Books, Inc., Wilmington, 1966, Grand Gallery, Wilmington, 1978; exhibited two and three man shows, also group shows: Wilmington (Del.) Soc. Fine Arts, Rehoboth (Del.) Art League, Cottage Tour Art, West Chester, Pa.; staff artist Cokesbury Courier; work represented in collections: Wilmington Trust Co., Hotel Du Pont, Del. Hosp. Sustaining mem. Everyman's Gallery; represented permanent collections: Wilmington Soc. Fine Arts, Copeland Purchase Fund, U. Del. Asso. mem. bd. Del. Hosp. Recipient 2d prize, best of show awards Nat. League Am. Pen Women shows, award of merit, 1962. Mem. Nat. League Am. Pen Women (state pres.), Colonial Dames Am., Am. Watercolor Soc. (asso.), Soc. Mayflower Descs. (past gov.), Wilmington Studio Group, Phila. Art Alliance. Episcopalian. Clubs: Greenville Country, Wilmington Country. Home: Cokesbury Village Box 50 Hockessin DE 19707 Studio: 1616 Rodney St Wilmington DE 19806

LENIX-HOOKER, CATHERINE JEANETTE, library administrator; b. Camden, S.C., May 10, 1947; d. Frank and Annie Louise (Blyther) Lenix; m. Frank R. Hooker, Nov. 8, 1973 (div.); 1 son, Frank R. B.A., Howard U., 1968; M.L.S., U. Md., 1970. Chief black studies div. Martin Luther King Jr. Pub. Library, Washington, 1970-77, temporary chief librarian, 1977; dir. pub. services Anaheim (Calif.) Pub. Library, 1977-81; asst. chief Schomburg Ctr. for Research in Black Culture, N.Y. Pub. Library, N.Y.C., 1981-83, interim adminstr., 1983-84, asst. chief P.L. Schomburg Ctr. for Research in Black Culture, 1984—; cons. Corp. Pub. Broadcasting, Washington, 1975; freelance writer Crippled Children's Soc. Los Angeles, 1979-81. Founding mem. Internat. Harlem Renaissance Com., N.Y.C., 1982; mem. exec. bd. Harlem Hosp. Community Bd., 1982—, chairperson bd., 1985—; bd. dirs. North Gen. Home Attendant Corp., N.Y.C., 1982-84. Recipient Community Service award N.Y. club Nat Assn. Negro Bus. and Profl. Women's Clubs, 1985. Mem. NAACP, ALA (exec. bd. black caucus), Howard U. So. Calif. Alumni Assn. (scholarship chmn. 1980-81). Democrat. Baptist. Address: 940 St Nicholas Ave Apt 1I New York NY 10032

LENKE, JOANNE MARIE, testing materials publishing executive; b. Chgo., Aug. 27, 1938; d. August Julian and Dorothy Anna (Gold) L.; B.S., Purdue U., 1960; M.S., Syracuse U., 1964, Ph.D., 1968. Tchr. pub. schs., Evanston, Ill., 1960-63; editor Test Dept., Harcourt, Brace & World, Inc., N.Y.C., 1967-70; research psychologist Harcourt Brace Jovanovich, Inc., N.Y.C., 1970-73, exec. editor, 1973-75; asst. dir. ednl. measurement div. The Psychol. Corp., N.Y.C., 1975-83, dir. ednl. measurement and psychometrics, Cleve., 1983-85, San Antonio, 1986—; field reader U.S. Office Edn., 1972, NSF grantee, 1963-64. Mem. Nat. Council on Measurement in Edn., Am. Psychol. Assn., Internat. Reading Assn., Am. Ednl. Research Assn. Adv. editor Jour. of Ednl. Measurement, 1974-78. Home: 1311 Vista del Monte San Antonio TX 78216 Office: The Psychological Corp 555 Academic Ct San Antonio TX 78204

LENKER, MARLENE NAGLER, artist; b. Passaic, N.J., Mar. 7, 1932; d. Curt M. and Marianne (Dorch) Nagler; m. John N. Lenker, Sept. 11, 1954; children—Cynthia S., Brian R. A.A., Fairleigh Dickenson Coll., 1951; M.A., Montclair State Coll., 1976. Lectr., artist in residence Nat. Acad., N.Y.C., 1976-79. One women shows: Fairleigh Dickinson U., N.J., 1968, Found. of Arts and Scis., N.J., 1970, Lord & Taylor Gallery, N.J., 1972, Bloomfield Coll., N.J., 1973, Montclair State Coll., N.J., 1973, County Coll. of Morris, N.J., 1974, Unitarian Soc. of Plainfield, N.J., 1976, Caldwell Coll., N.J., 1977, Wolff Gallery, N.J., 1979, David Gary Ltd., N.J., 1980-81, Rauchbach Gallery, Fla., 1982, David Gary Ltd., N.J., 1983, Adelle M. Taylor Gallery, Dallas, 1986; exhibited in group shows: Edward Williams Coll., N.J., 1969, Korby Gallery, N.J., 1969, Discovery Gallery, N.J., 1973, Benedict Gallery, N.J., 1975, Doubletree Gallery, N.J., 1975, Gallery 52, 1975, 76, Unitarian Soc. of Morristown, N.J., 1976, Bergen Mus., N.J., 1977, 80, 82, Wolff Gallery, N.J., 1979, Hait Gallery, N.J., 1980, Nat. Assn. Jewish Women Exhbns., 1975-84, Adelle Mus. Fine Arts, Dallas, 1984, RauchbachSklar, Boca Raton, Fla., 1984, U.S. Senate, Washington, 1984, Montclair Mus., N.J., Jersey City Mus., Nat. Acad., N.Y.C., Penacola Art Ctr., Fla., Adelphi U., N.Y., Holyoke Mus., N.J., Newark Mus., Morristown Mus., N.J., Newark Pub. Library, Richmond Art Ctr., Ind., McAllen Internat. Mus., Tex., George Washington Carver Mus., Ala., U. Nebr., Springfield, Coll., Mass., Watkins Inst., Tenn., Washington Sumter Gallery of Art, Birger-Sanzen Meml. Gallery, Kans., U. Ga., Va. Mus., Mint Mus., N.C., Cayuga Mus., N.Y., Bergen Mus., Jesse Besser Mus., Mich., Rockhurst Coll., Md., Charles Frye Mus., Summit Art Ctr., N.J., Pelham Art Ctr., N.Y., Corcoran Galleries, Washington, Albrecht Mus., Mo., Greenville Mus., N.C., Charles B. Goddard Ctr., Okla., Lycoming Coll., Pa., Graphic Eye Gallery, N.Y., Sunset Cultural Ctr., represented in permanent collections. Mem. Nat. Assn. Women Artists (painting bd. 1984-86), Artists Equity. Lutheran. Avocations: tennis, music. Home and studio: 28 Northview Terr Cedar Grove NJ 07009 also 13 Crosstrees Hill Rd Essex CT 06426

LENNOX, SHIRLEY ANN, artist, educator, consultant; b. San Francisco, Nov. 8, 1931; d. James Joseph and Mildred Mae (Hall) Amos; m. Arthur James Lennox, Jan. 6, 1951; children—Sharron Kay, Kathleen Melanie, Bonnie Marie, Colleen Leta. Student pub. schs., South Glens Falls, N.Y. Window display artist Fowlers' Inc., Glens Falls, 1948-51; owner, operator Discovery House Gallery, Palo Alto, Calif., 1969-71; owner, operator, tchr. porcelain painting Lennox Art Sutdio, Santa Maria, Calif., 1972—; cons. art, Santa Maria, 1985—; owner, operator Gallerie 272, Morton, N.Y., 1979-81; resident artist, gallery mgr. Options Gallery, Shell Beach, Calif., 1985. Exhibited paintings in one-woman shows: Village Gallery, Hilton, N.Y., Lake George Inst. History and Art, N.Y., 1974, Swan Gallery, Albion, N.Y., 1979, Options Gallery, Shell Beach, Calif., 1984, Morro Bay Mus. Natural History, 1985; group shows include: The Calif. Scene (with Ansel Adams and others), Foothill Coll., Los Altos, Calif., 1970, Suburban Rochester Art Group shows, N.Y., 1976-80, Santa Inez Art Shows, Calif., 1983-84, Los Padres Artists Guild Shows, 1983-86, Faulkner Gallery, 1985; represented in permanent collections: Old Courthouse Mus., Lake George, N.Y., Shelter Cove Lodge, Pismo Beach, Calif. Bd. dirs. Santa Maria Arts Council, 1983-85. Mem. Internat. Porcelain Arts Tchrs., Internat. Soc. Marine Painters Inc. (juried profl. mem.), Nat. Soc. Painters in Casein and Acrylic (assoc.), Santa Maria Women's Network, Santa Barbara Art Assn. (juried), San Luis Obispo Art Assn., Porcelain Portrait Soc. Republican. Avocations: photography; camping. Studio: 4123 Mayfield St Santa Maria CA 93455

LENNOX (FISCH), CAROL JEANINE, advertising agency executive; b. Wichita Falls, Tex., Sept. 13, 1952; d. Johnny Melvin and Betty Joy (Chastain) Cole; m. Scott Michael Lennox, Mar. 25, 1972 (div. Oct. 1979); m. Elliot Ronald Fisch, Apr. 26, 1986; stepchildren—Julie Ellen, Kendra Elissa. B.S., Tex. Christian U., 1975; postgrad. Tex. Wesleyan Coll., 1979, 80. Teaching cert., Tex. Tchr. learning disabled Ft. Worth Ind. Sch. Dist., 1975-78; fundraiser, editor, coll. relations Tex. Wesleyan Coll., Ft. Worth, 1978-81; account exec., account supr. DBG & H, Inc., Ft. Worth, 1981-84, mgmt. supr., 1984-85; pres. The Lennox Group, Arlington, Tex., 1985—; v.p. Synergy Works, Arlington, 1984—, Diversified Media Reps., Arlington, 1985—; lectr. local univs. Contbr. articles to local mag. Mem., instr. Continuing Health Edn. Ctr., Ft. Worth, 1985-86; cons. Ft. Worth Opera, 1986, mem. mktg. com., 1986—. Recipient Council for Advancement and Support of Edn. award, 1981. Mem. Nat. Assn. Female Execs., Network of Exec. Women, Advt. Club Ft. Worth (bd. dirs. 1983-85). Democrat. Mem. Christian Ch. (Disciples of Christ). Avocations: reading; writing; dancing; windjammer cruises; metaphysics. Office: The Lennox Group 107 W Randol Mill Rd Arlington TX 76011

LENNSTROM, NANCY, librarian; b. Hood River, Oreg., June 15, 1931; d. George Minshall and Elsie Winnifred (McLucas) Knox; m. Charles Owen Lennstrom, Nov. 26, 1952; children—Kathleen Marie Mason, Diane Louise, Peter Charles, Heidi Annette. B.A. in English, U. Wash., 1974, M.L.S., 1975. Readers service librarian Highline Coll. Library, Midway, Wash., 1975—. Bd. dirs. Child Hearing League, Seattle, 1960-62; leader Camp Fire Girls, Seattle, 1961-64, elem. and jr. high schs., Seattle, 1958-65; advisor liberal religious youth Unitarian Universalist Ch., Seattle, 1969-74; mem. adv. com. Seattle Internat. U. Library. Mem. Assn. Coll. and Research Libraries (sec. 1982-84, nat. conf. 1984 com.), Community Coll. Librarians and Media Specialists. Democrat. Unitarian. Home: 1915 SW 170th St Seattle WA 98166 Office: Highline Community Coll Library Midway WA 98032

LENNY, MARY RUTH, college administrator, nursing educator; b. Potosi, Mo., Nov. 24, 1922; d. Joseph Lynn and Katherine (Kelsey) Thurman; m. Norman K. Lenny, Sept. 4, 1949; children—David, Douglas, Deborah, Noel, Alan, Catherine, Cynthia. Diploma, St. John's Hosp. Sch. Nursing, St. Louis, 1943, B.S. in Nursing, Washington U., St. Louis, 1949; M.S. in Psychiat. Nursing, 1963; Ph.D. in Higher Edn. Adminstrn., St. Louis U., 1980. Instr., course coordinator Mo. Baptist Hosp., St. Louis, 1958-62, 1965-67, Belleville Area Coll., Ill., 1967-80; div. chmn. McKendree Coll., Lebanon, Ill., 1980-81, MacMurray Coll., Jacksonville, Ill., 1981-85, Maryville Coll., 1985—; cons. St. Elizabeth Hosp., Granite City, Ill., 1973—, St. Mary's Hosp., East St. Louis, Ill., 1975-80, Belleville Meml. Hosp., 1968-70. Contbr. articles to profl. jours. Served to lt. (j.g.) USN, 1944-46. Recipient Alumnae Book award Washington U., 1963; Dr. Scholl grantee, 1982-84. Mem. Ill. Nurses Assn. (10th dist. pres., 9th dist. pres.-elect 1983-85), AAUP (pres. 1973-75, bd. dirs. 1968-73), Internat. Toastmistresses, Delta Kappa Gamma, Sigma Theta Tau. Roman Catholic. Avocations: Swimming; bicycling; dancing; doll collecting. Home: Route 5 Wheeler Rd Windy Lakes Apt 44 Louisville TX 37777 Office: Maryville Coll Maryville TN

LENOX, MARY FRANCES, university dean; b. Chgo., July 19, 1944; d. Eleazar and Truesillia (Bryson) L. B.S., Chgo. State U., 1966; M.A., Rosary Coll., 1968; Ed.D., U. Mass., 1975. Tchr., librarian Chgo. pub. schs., 1967-71; asst. reference librarian Ctr. for Inner City Studies, Northeastern Ill. U., Chgo., 1971-72; dir. ednl. materials ctr. Chgo. State U., 1971-72; mgr. circulation dept. learning resource ctr., faculty mem. Governors State U., Park Forest South, Ill., 1973-75; media specialist Chgo. Pub. Schs., 1975-78; mem. faculty Nat. Coll. Edn. Urban Campus, Chgo., 1977-78; assoc. prof. Sch. Library and Info. Sci., U. Mo.-Columbia, 1978-84, dean, 1984—; vis. prof. U. Denver, 1979, Stephens Coll., Columbia, 1980, 81; faculty-in-residence Chgo. Pub. Library, 1981; cons., speaker in field. Contbr. articles to profl. jours. Bd. dirs. Halfway House Com., Inc., Chgo., 1977, New Wave Corp., Columbia, 1981-85; mem. adv. bd. The Legal Inst., Burbank, Calif., 1977—; mem. bd. cons. The High-Low Report, N.Y.C., 1979-83; producer, moderator Black Women: African Past to Columbia Present Sta. KOPN-FM, Columbia, 1979; mem. editorial bd. Top of the News. Named Outstanding Educator, Dist. II Chgo. Pub. Schs., 1977; Kellogg Nat. fellow, 1982-85. Mem. ALA (Grolier awards com. 1980), Am. Assn. Sch. Librarians (sch. media program of yr. awards com. 1979-80), Mo. Library Assn. (chmn. library educators 1978—, outreach roundtable 1980-81), AAUW, Assn. Study Afro-Am. Life and History, Assn. Library and Info. Sci. Educators, Pi Lambda Theta, Delta Kappa Gamma, Kappa Delta Pi. Avocations: hiking, photography, floral designs, rock collecting, travel, environmental preservation. Office: U Mo-Columbia Sch Library and Info Sci 104 Stewart Hall Columbia MO 65211

LENSMITH, BETTY, business executive; b. Oconomowoc, Wis., Oct. 3, 1928; d. Alex F. and Vera (Zeiters) Henschel; m. Eugene A. Lensmith, Nov. 14, 1949; children—Lissa Kathleen, Larry Eugene. Receptionist, Schrader Studio, Milw., 1947; mgr. Tooley Myron Studios chain, 1948-49; owner, mgr. Country Studio, Oconomowoc, 1950—, Town and Country Studio, 1957—; founder, pres., treas. Photographers Specialized Services, Inc., Oconomowoc, 1968—; founder, pres. Ret. Persons Specialized Services, 1981—, Golden World Products, 1982—, Photo-Treasures, 1984—; instr. Winona Sch. Photography, 1975—, Miami and Traingle Inst. (Pa.), 1977, No. Ga. Sch. Photography, 1978. Recipient awards Kodak Co. Mem. Profl. Photographers Am. (cert. photographic craftsman, recipient various awards), Am. Soc. Photographers, Am. Mgmt. Assn., Studio Suppliers Assn., Female Execs., 700 Club, Presidents Club. Author: The Guide to Lighting, Posing and Composing, 1971, rev. edit., 1986; Selling, The Name of the Game, 1976; Profitable Promotions and Merchandising Techniques, 1977; The Basic Guide to Commercial Photography, 1979. Home: 423 N Lake Rd Oconomowoc WI 53066 Office: 650 Armour Rd Oconomowoc WI 53066

LENTI, JEAN MARIE, athletics educator; b. Chgo., July 25, 1956; d. Frank J. and Rose M. (Frangella) L. B.S., DePaul U., 1978. Asst. basketball coach DePaul U., 1978-82, asst. athletic dir., 1982-83, assoc. athletic dir., 1983—; chmn. basketball com. North Star Conf., 1983-84. Mem. Nat. Assn. Collegiate Dirs. Athletics, Collegiate Council Women Athletic Adminstrs. Democrat. Roman Catholic. Office: DePaul U 1011 West Belden St Chicago IL 60614

LENTINI, COLLEEN GAIL SHERWOOD, government official; b. Middleboro, Mass., Oct. 22, 1944; d. Robert Bridge and Jeanette Louise (Letendre) Sargent; A.A., Montgomery Coll., 1983; m. Joseph Charles Lentini, Dec. 5, 1983; children—Stephen, Suzanne, Richard. Personnel asst. Nat. Cancer Inst., Bethesda, Md., 1974-76, adminstrv. asst., 1976-79, adminstrv. officer, 1979-81;

spl. asst. program planning and evaluation Nat. Inst. Arthritis, Diabetes and Digestive and Kidney Diseases, Bethesda, Md., 1981-82, spl. asst. program analysis, 1982-83; adminstrv. officer Office of Insp. Gen., EPA, Washington, 1984—. Recipient Superior Performance awards Dept. Health and Human Services, 1970, 72, 77, 79. Mem. Nat. Assn. Female Execs., Phi Theta Kappa. Democrat. Roman Catholic. Home: 18420 Tranquil Ln Olney MD 20832 Office: Office of Insp Gen EPA 401 M St SW Washington DC 20460

LENTS, PEGGY IGLAUER, marketing executive; b. St. Louis, Apr. 14, 1950; d. Hank S. and Elizabeth Ruth (Metzger) Iglauer; B.A. magna cum laude (univ. fellow), Jackson Coll., Tufts U., 1971; M.P.A. (fellow), Kennedy Sch. Govt., Harvard U., 1974; m. Don G. Lents, Aug. 27, 1972; children—Stacie Lee, Kelsey Lynn. Legis. aide Congressman Symington, Washington, 1971; adminstrv. mgr. May Co., London (Eng.) Hdqrs., 1974, buyer Famous Barr (May Co.), St. Louis, 1976-78; gen. mdse. mgr. Roman Co., St. Louis, 1978-80, mktg. dir., 1981-82, v.p., 1982; mktg. cons., 1983-86; ptnr. The Write Stuff; cons. Human Resources Adminstrn., N.Y.C.; teaching fellow Tufts U., 1971-72. Bd. dirs. Lucky Lane Sch., 1980-81, Shaare Emath., 1986—; v.p. planning and devel. NCJW, 1986—; chmn. NDC Nat. Leadership Program, 1974; cons., Washington, 1972, polit. campaigns N.D., Iowa. Mem. Am. Mgmt. Assn., Fashion Group, Pioneers, Direct Mail Club St. Louis, Women in Bus., Directory Group (U.K.). Club: Westwood Country. Home: 1166 Hampton Park Dr Saint Louis MO 63117

LENTZ, ROBIN JO, credit union executive; b. Los Angeles, Oct. 27, 1947; d. Joseph Vincent and Nellie Nancy (Tennenblum) Incorvaia; m. Bob Monte Hannah, Feb. 1, 1969 (div. 1973); children—Kimberly, David; m. 2d, Robert George Lentz, Mar. 15, 1975. Student Nat. U., San Diego, 1983-85; grad. Western Regional Sch. Credit Union Execs., 1975, Advanced Mgmt. Inst., 1982. Mrg., chief exec. officer Whittier (Calif.) Gentelco Fed. Credit Union, 1966-75; account rep. Members Ins. Co., Irvine, Calif., 1975-78; chief exec. officer Van Camp Fed. Credit Union, San Diego, Calif., 1978-79; pres., chief exec. officer Cabrillo Fed. Credit Union, San Diego, 1979—; treas. San Diego Regional Ad Council, 1983. Mem. Credit Union Execs. Soc., San Diego Mgrs. Assn. (pres. 1984), Nat. Assn. Fed. Credit Unions, Calif. Credit Union League (pres. San Diego chpt. 1982-83), San Diego C. of C. Democrat. Roman Catholic. Home: 13802 Paseo Cardiel San Diego CA 92129 Office: Cabrillo Federal Credit Union 110 W C St 1711 San Diego CA 92101

LENYOUN, KAREN CHRISTIAN, insurance company executive; b. Los Angeles, Oct. 15, 1955; d. Raymond Benton and Joanne Helen (Mazziotti) Christian; m. Estean Hanson Lenyoun III, July 9, 1977; children—Estean Hanson IV, Xavier Christian. B.A. in Indsl. Psychology, San Diego State U., 1977. C.P.I.W. Research analyst Naval Electronics Lab. Ctr., 1974-77; comml. liability and umbrella underwriter Indsl. Indemnity Co., San Diego, 1977-80, comml. and personal lines mktg. rep., 1980-83; comml., personal lines and life mktg. rep., terr. mgr. Unigard Mut. Ins. Co. and Unigard Olympic Life Ins. Co., San Diego, 1983, sr. comml. lines underwriter United Pacific Reliance Ins. Co., San Diego, 1984; account exec. Tipton and Co., Park City, Utah, 1985—; underwriting supr. Ohio Casualty Ins. Co. Mem. Friends of Park City Library, 1984-85, Women's Info. Network, Park City, 1985; v.p. Shepherd of the Mts. Lutheran Ch. Council, Park City, 1985, pianist, 1985. Mem. Cert. Profl. Ins. Women, Ins. Fieldperson Assn. (treas. 1982-83), Ind. Ins. Agts. of Utah, San Diego Ins. Women, San Diego Ind. Ins. Agts. and Brokers Assn., Ind. Ins. Agts. of Am. Democrat. Avocations: piano; cooking; crafts; running; skiing; swimming; jetskiing; reading; travel. Home: 3025 Oakrim Ln Park City UT 84060 Office: PO Box 355 Park City UT 84060

LEÓN, CARMENCITA, librarian; b. Quebradillas, P.R.; d. Antonio Hernández and María Jiménez; m. José A. León, July 11, 1951; children—José, Edgardo, Ethel Viviane. B.Ed., U. P.R., Río Piedras, 1955, M.L.S., 1970. Cert. tchr., sch. prin., supt., librarian, library supr. Tchr., Dept. Edn. P.R., 1950-63, librarian, 1963-65, sch. library coordinator San Juan region, 1967-69, dir. sch. library system, Hato Rey, 1971-84; cons., 1984—; dir. spl. library Social Sci. Coll., U. P.R., 1965-67; active White House Conf. on Libraries; chair Citizens Com. for Internat. Yr. of Libraries, P.R., 1983. Author: Legislación Bibliotecaria en Puerto Rico, 1970; El niño y su expresión creadora, 1971. Mem. Union de Mujeres Americanas, 1967, Club Cívico de Damas, 1983— (both San Juan). Recipient plaque Pre-White House Conf. Library and Info. Services, P.R., 1979; others. Mem. P.R. Tchrs. Assn. (former del. gen. assembly), NEA, ALA (councilor 1980-84), Am. Assn. Sch. Librarians (liaison to P.R.), P.R. Soc. Librarians (pres. 1978-80, chair legis. com. 1982-84, 86, chair pub. relations com. 1982-84; awards 1978-80, 84, award Leccion Magistral Jose fina del Toro Fulludosa 1986), Nat. Assn. State Edn. Media Profls., Phi Delta Kappa, Caribbean Assn. Univ. Research Libraries, P.R. Pub. Relations Assn., P.R. Assn. Sch. Librarians (pres. 1986). Clubs: Exchangettes (Rio Piedras) (pres. 1969; service awards 1965-69); Hato Rey Bus. and Profl. Women. Home: Condominium Ponce de León Gardens Apt 702-Villa Caparra-Guaynabo PR 00657

LEON, CHERYL ANN, nurse; b. Woodward, Okla., Feb. 16, 1950; d. Edwin and Stella Verna (Knight) Watson; m. John Richard Leon, Mar. 16, 1974; children—Ashley Ann, Joseph Andrew, Magdalena Marie, John Daniel. B.S.N., U. Okla., 1974. Team leader adult psychiatry Bapt. Med. Ctr., Oklahoma City, 1974-78; charge nurse acute psychiat. unit Okla. Children's Meml. Hosp., Oklahoma City, 1978-81, head nurse, 1981—. Mem. Sudden Infant Death Syndrome Parents Group Nat. SIDS Found., Oklahoma City, 1979—; coordinator for series World Wide Marriage Encounter, Oklahoma City, 1981—. Mem. Orthopsychiat. Assn., Okla. U. Coll. Nursing Adolescent Weight Control Group (bd. dirs.), State of Okla. Teaching Hosps. Nursing Research Forum Bd. (sec. 1983-84), Am. Nurses Assn. (cert. psychiat. and mental health nurse 1981-86). Democrat. Roman Catholic. Clubs: Corpus Christi Parent Tchr. (chmn. membership com.), Corpus Christi Sch. Band Boosters (treas. 1982—). Home: 1015 NW 14th St Oklahoma City OK 73106 Office: Okla Childrens Meml Hosp Acute Psychiat Unit 930 NE 13th St Oklahoma City OK 73125

LEON, DOROTHY SILVER, public relations executive; b. Boston, Nov. 1, 1913; d. Louis and Sophia (Gerson) Silver; A.A., Los Angeles City Coll., 1950; m. Alfred Leon, Mar. 13, 1934; children—Boris, Leah, Marion, Richard, Dai. Public relations coordinator Los Angeles Unified Sch. Dist. Vol. Program, 1960-70; pub. relations coordinator Soc. Children's Book Writers, Hollywood, Calif., 1970—. Recipient Minor awards. Mem. P.E.N., Nat. Women's Book Assn., Soc. Children's Book Writers (dir.), So. Calif. Council Lit. for Children and Young People. Author: One Eye, Two Eyes, Three Eyes, Four, 1980; By These Names I Am Known, 1980; Anybody Can Be Somebody, 1980; The Secret World of Underground Animals, 1982; also articles and stories. Office: 7095 Hollywood Blvd Suite 718 Hollywood CA 90046

LEON, MARGARET ADELE, financial service marketing company executive; b. Boston, Mar. 19, 1948; d. Richard and Florence (Hattub) L. B.S., Boston State Coll., 1969; M.A. in Counseling, Salem State Coll., 1977. Tchr. Chelsea Schs., Mass., 1969-76, guidance counselor, 1977-82; group therapist Behavioral Assocs., Brookline, Mass., 1977-79; real estate agt. Gen. Devel., Peabody, Mass., 1979-81; ins. and securities agt. A.L. Williams, Lynn, Mass., 1981-83, regional v.p., 1983—. Roman Catholic. Avocations: photography, sewing, cooking, skiing. Office: A L Williams Corp 679 Western Ave Suite 2 Lynn MA 01905

LEON, PATRICIA EUBANK, sports association executive; b. Richmond, Va., Nov. 2, 1948; d. Thomas Franklin and Estelle Redford E; m. Joseph W. Leon, Jan. 31, 1983. A.A., U. Richmond, 1969. Legal sec., Hamel, Park, McCabe & Saunders, Washington, 1970-73; sec. Nat. Football League Players Assn., Washington, 1973-79, asst. dir. licensing and spl. events, 1979-85, dir. mktg. and spl. projects, 1984—. Bd. dirs. Nat. Capital Area march of Dimes, 1983. Democrat. Roman Catholic. Avocations: Physical fitness; art; music. Office: NFL Players Assn 1300 Connecticut Ave NW Washington DC 20036

LEONARD, DEBI LYNN, manufacturing company marketing executive; b. Dodge City, Kans., May 6, 1955; d. Harold Duane and Kynta Lov (Kennedy) L. Student, Marymount Coll., 1972-76, Vo-Tech. U., Salina, Kans. 1976-78. Comml. art sales rep. Shoppers Guide, Salina, 1977-81; sales rep. Sta. KYEZ-AM, Salina, 1981-82, Freedom News, Denver, 1982-83; designer Delyns Fashions, Denver, 1983-86; mktg. mgr. Lenko Enterprises, Cripple Creek, Colo., 1981—. Vol. Annual Bridal Show, Salina, 1985; active Am. Cancer Soc., membership drive YMCA. Mem. Life Underwriters Assn., Am. Bus. Womens Assn. Midwest Corvette Assn., Denver Advt. Assn. Avocations: windsurfing; skiing; swimming; hot air ballooning. Office: Lenko Enterprises 2026 Raymond Ave Salina KS 67401

LEONARD, EILEEN ANN, motion picture trust fund executive; b. N.Y.C., Oct. 4, 1941; d. Errol Thomas and Marjorie (Cleary) Connelly; m. Wayne Leonard, Jan. 28, 1967 (div. Mar. 1975); 1 dau., Kimberly Anne; m. 2d Kenneth Paul Vensel, Sept. 6, 1980. B.A., Fairleigh Dickinson U., 1963. French sec. French Railroads, N.Y.C., 1964-65; legal sec. W.R. Grace Co., N.Y.C., 1965-67; exec. sec. Internat. Industries, Los Angeles, 1968-70; adminstr. Contract Services Adminstr. Trust Fund, Los Angeles, 1974-76, dir., 1976—. Pub. relations chairperson Los Angeles Basin Equal Opportunity League, 1975—; bd. dirs. Internat. Inst., Los Angeles, 1983—. Mem. Dir. Guild Am., Women in Film. Roman Catholic. Home: 12431 Landale St Studio City CA 91604 Office: Contract Services Adminstr Trust Fund 14144 Ventura Blvd Sherman Oaks CA 91604

LEONARD, FLORENCE IRENE, educator; b. Trenton, Apr. 12, 1934; d. Esau and Alverine (Arnold) Courtney; B.A., Trenton State Coll., 1968, M.Ed., 1979, supr./prin. cert., m. Henry L. Leonard, Feb. 21, 1953; children—Guy Anthony, Carl Henry, Celeste Alverine, Troy Courtney. Librarian asst. dept. edn. N.J. State Library, 1960-64; tchr. Harrison Elem. Sch., Trenton, 1968—, supr., 1981—, also part-time acting prin. Deaconess local ch. Chs. of God in Christ, Trenton. Mem. NEA, N.J. Edn. Assn., Trenton Edn. Assn., Mercer County Edn. Assn. Author: The Xerox Intermediate Dictionary, 1973; designer mural of the Crucifixion, Holy Trinity Ch. of God in Christ. Trenton, 1954, girls' dormitory for Chs. of God in Christ, Monrovia, Liberia, 1959. Home: 9 James Cubberly Ct Trenton NJ 08610 Office: Harrison School Genesee St Trenton NJ 08611 also Trenton Bd Edn N Clinton Ave Trenton NJ 08609

LEONARD, FLORENCE JONES, teacher educator; b. Camden, N.J.; d. John Henry and Florence May (Johnson) Jones; A.B., Rutgers U., 1955; M.Ed., Towson State U., Balt., 1972; Ph.D., U. Md., 1984; m. Charles Brown Leonard, Jr., Aug. 26, 1955; children—Charles Brown, III, Bruce Joseph. Tchr., Moorestown pub. schs. (N.J.), 1955-56; dir. Mt. Hebron Presbyn. Presch. Center, Howard County, Md., 1964-72; dir. Student Day Care Center, Towson (Md.) State U., 1972-74, mem. faculty, 1974—, asst. prof. early childhood edn., 1979—, also faculty dir. Aliza Brandwine Center Parent-Infant Devel.; bd. dirs. Md. Com. Children; cons. in field. Recipient Aethenaeum award Rutgers U., 1954. Grantee, Towson State U., 1979, 80, 4-C, 1979. Mem. AAUP, Orgn. Mondial Edn. Prescholaire, Assn. Childhood Edn. Internat., Nat. Assn. Edn. Young Children, Phi Kappa Phi, Phi Delta Kappa. Mem. Ch. of Nazarene. Club: University at Towson. Home: 9202 Furrow Ave Ellicott City MD 21043 Office: Early Childhood Edn Dept Towson State U Baltimore MD 21204

LEONARD, KATHIE MERRILL, textile company executive; b. Benton Harbor, Mich., Feb. 14, 1952; d. Earl Merrill and Maria (Virgili) Phillips; m. John Haley Leonard, Jr., Oct. 13, 1973; 1 child, Colin Matthew. Dir. pub. relations Elan One Corp., Poland Spring, Maine, 1974-76; product mgr. W.S. Libbey Co., Lewiston, Maine, 1977-79; pres., co-founder Auburn Mfg. Inc., Mechanic Falls, Maine, 1979—. Broker, Maine Real Estate Commn., 1976—. Mem. adv. bd. Key Bank Central Maine, 1983—. Mem. Maine World Trade Assn., Mechanic Falls Bus. Assn. Avocations: Auto racing; youth hockey. Home: 25 Heritage Dr Auburn ME 04256 Office: Auburn Mfg Inc 5125 Walker Rd Mechanic Falls ME 04256

LEONARD, PATRICIA LYNN, university administrator; b. Rockville, Centre, N.Y., May 28, 1955; d. John Thomas and Grace Lillian (Foster) L.; B.A. in Social Work and Secondary Edn. in Social Studies, Coll. Misericordia, 1977; M.A. in Coll. Student Personnel Adminstrn., Mich. State U., 1979. Grad. resident adviser Mich. State U., 1977-79; residence coordinator U. N.C., Charlotte, 1979-80; area coordinator Miami U., Oxford, Ohio, 1980-83, instr. in personnel and guidance, 1980-83; assoc. dean students U. N.C.-Wilmington, 1983—; cons. to student affair staff Coll. Misericordia. Mem. Am. Assn. Counseling and Devel., Nat. Assn. Fgn. Student Advisors, So. Assn. Coll. Student Affairs, Am. Coll. Personnel Assn., Ohio Coll. Personnel Adminstrs., Phi Delta Kappa, Alpha Delta Mu. Office: U NC Wilmington NC 28403

LEONARD, RHONDA, charter fishing boat company executive, consultant; b. Kearny, N.J., May 18, 1950; d. Gilbert Richard and Margaret Cross (Anderson) Forsyth; m. Henry Paul Harper, Feb. 1, 1969 (div. Sept. 1972); m. Henry Louis Leonard, Oct. 25, 1975. Student pub. schs., Middletown, N.J. Sec. Lily-Tulip Cup Corp., Holmdel, N.J., 1968-69; underwriter SGS Agy., Matawan, N.J., 1969-74; pres., owner Nine-O-Six, Inc., Belmar, N.J., 1974—; personnel cons. for small bus. Mem. Belmar C. of C. (bd. dirs. 1984-85). Republican. Presbyterian. Avocations: travel; scuba diving; boating. Office: Ocean Beach Enterprises Inc PO Box 1064 Belmar NJ 07719

LEONARDO, ANN ADAMSON, marketing and sales executive, consultant; b. Hamilton, Lanark, Scotland, Jan. 4, 1944; d. James Walker and Margaret Patterson (Burnside) Adamson; m. John Constantine Leonardo, Jr., Mar. 29, 1975; 1 child, Elizabeth Margaret. B.S. in Mktg. and Bus., Ryerson Coll., 1970. Market research mgr. MacLaren Advt., Toronto, Can., 1965-70; group product mgr. Menley & James, Montreal, 1970-74; mktg. mgr. Maybelline Div.-Plough, Toronto, 1974-75; v.p. mktg. Van De Kamp's Bakery, Glendale, Calif., 1976-80; v.p. mktg. and sales Cal West Periodicals, Oakland, 1980-84; mktg. cons., Novato, Calif., 1984—; dir. Family House Inc., San Francisco. Mem. Am. Mktg. Assn. Home: 102 La Merida Ct Novato CA 94947

LEONE, GLORIA MARIE, city official; b. Boston, Mar. 11, 1930; d. Nicholas and Michelina (DeBenedictis) L. Student pub. schs., Medford, Mass. With H.E. Harris & Co., Boston, 1947-53; with City of Medford, Mass., 1953—, city purchasing agt., 1976—. Sec., pres. Jr. League, Women's Italian Club of Boston, 1948-65. Named Medford Citizen of the Year, Medford Concerned Taxpayers, 1981. Mem. New Eng. Pub. Purchasing Assn. (pres. 1982-84). Clubs: Zonta, Bass Rocks Beach (pres.). Home: 6 George St Medford MA 02155 Office: Medford City Hall 85 George P Hasset Dr Medford MA 02155

LEONE, PATRICIA BUDER, system engineer, meteorologist; b. St. Louis, Oct. 18, 1947; d. Evatt Edward and Mary Catherine (Solich) Buder; m. Vincent Fowler Simmon, July 26, 1975 (div. Mar. 1977), David Michael Leone, Sept. 19, 1981. Student Fairleigh Dickinson U., Rutherford, N.J., 1967-69; B.S., St. Louis U., Mo., 1971; S.M., MIT, 1973; postgrad. in Bus. Adminstrn., U. Santa Clara, 1982—. Summer trainee U.S. Weather Bur., St. Louis, summer 1969, 70; research asst. MIT, Cambridge, Mass., 1971-73; Atmospheric fellowship Univ. Corp. for Atmosphere Research, Boulder, Colo., summer 1971, 72; research meteorologist SRI Internat., Menlo Park, Calif., 1973-81; staff engr. Lockheed Missiles & Space Co., Sunnyvale, Calif., 1981—. Contbr. articles to profl. jours. Sloan fellow. Mem. Am. Meteorol. Soc. (program chmn. N. Calif. chpt. 1977-78, chmn. N. Calif. chpt. 1978-79), Nat. Mgmt. Assn., Sigma Xi, Pi Mu Epsilon, Phi Zeta Kappa. Avocations: interior design; snow and water skiing; racquetball.

LEONIDOW, NATASHA MATRINA, hospital administrator, nurse; b. Nyack, N.Y., June 12, 1958; d. Paul and Matrina (Butich) L. A.A. Sci., Rockland Community Coll., 1979; B.S. in Nursing cum laude, SUNY Coll. Technology, Utica, 1982; M.S. in Nursing magna cum laude, Syracuse U., 1985. R.N., N.Y. Staff nurse Englewood Hosp., N.J., 1979-80; charge nurse Mary Imogene Bassett Hosp., Cooperstown, N.Y., 1980-82, nursing service coordinator, 1983-86, asst. dir. systems devel., 1986—. Translator: Excellence in Russian Language, 1976 (Otrada award). Mem. Nat. League of Nursing. Sigma Theta Tau. Office: Mary Imogene Bassett Hosp Atwell Rd Cooperstown NY 13326

LEPERE, GENE HARRIET, home furnishings industry cons.; b. N.Y.C., Oct. 16, 1926; d. Joseph Herman and Jennie (Berman) Hirshhorn; A.B., U. So. Calif., 1949; M.B.A. with honors, Pace U., 1977; m. Edward M. Kelley, Sept. 11, 1955; m. 2d James E. LePere, Mar. 15, 1963. Mgr., Los Angeles County Probation Dept., 1955-63; v.p., gen. mgr. LePere, Inc., antiques and fine arts, N.Y.C., 1966-75; mgr. mktg. info. Furniture div. Sperry & Hutchinson Co., N.Y.C., 1976-79; owner, pres. Gene LePere Assos., Mt. Kisco, N.Y., 1979—. Mem. Nat. Home Furnishings League, Nat. Assn. Exec. Women, Jewish. Contbr. articles to profl. publs.

LEPIDI-CARINO, MADELINE JOANNE, clinical social worker, therapist; b. Greensburg, Pa., Sept. 23, 1944; d. Massimo and America Mary (Vittori) Lepidi; m. Fernando Jaico Carino, Spet. 11, 1971; children—Carla Celeste, Claudette Marie, Christopher Felipe. B. Elem. Edn., U. Pitts., 1967; M. Social Adminstrn., Case Western Res. U., 1970; post-masters certificate, Gestalt Inst. Cleve., 1986. Cert. social worker. Social worker, Catholic Service League, Akron, 1973-75; psychiat. social worker Akron Child Guidance, 1980-82; psychiat. social worker St. Joseph Hosp., Warren, Ohio, 1984-86; clin. social worker, Warren, 1986—. Mem. Nat. Assn. Female Execs., Nat. Assn. Social Workers. Roman Catholic. Avocations: horseback riding; exercise; reading. Home: 2843 Middleton Rd Hudson OH 44236

LEPOER, ANNA MARIE DIBLASI, nurse anesthetist, educational adminstrator; b. Amsterdam, N.Y., Oct. 29, 1940; d. Tony and Maria (Macario) DiBlasi; children—Tammy, Tina, Toni. Grad., Albany Med. Ctr. Sch. Nursing, 1962, Fairfax Hosp. Sch. Nurse Anesthetists, Va., 1972; B.S. in Anesthesia, George Washington U., 1979; M. in Bus. and Pub. Adminstrn., Southeastern U., Washington, 1982; Ph.D., Columbia Pacific U., 1983. Cert. registered nurse anesthetist. Staff nurse West Seattle Gen. Hosp., 1962-64; office nurse Filmore Buckner, M.D., Seattle, 1964-66; staff nurse anesthetist Fairfax Hosp., 1972-73; staff nurse anesthetist Potomac Hosp., Woodbridge, Va., 1973, chief nurse anesthetist, 1973-84; dir. Potomac Hosp. Sch. for Nurse Anesthetists and Sch. for Nurse Anesthesia; faculty mem. Columbia Pacific U., 1973—; guest lectr. No. Va. Community Coll., Inservice Potomac Hosp., George Washington U. Mem. Am. Assn. Nurse Anesthetists, Va. Nurse Anesthesia Assn. Home: 12300 Mulberry Ct Woodbridge VA 22192

LEPOME, PENELOPE MARIE, rehabilitation counselor, educator; b. Buffalo, Dec. 17, 1945; d. Raymond Arthur and Mildred Evelyn (Johnson) Kramer; m. Robert Charles LePome, May 26, 1966 (div. Jan. 1982); children—Lisa Anne, Kathryn Jane, Robert Charles II. B.A. in Biology, SUNY-Buffalo, 1967; M.S. in Vocat. Rehab., U. Nev.-Las Vegas, 1984. Cert. rehab. counselor; cert. tchr., Nev. Co-owner, salesman Flamingo Realty, Las Vegas, Nev., 1974-76; substitute tchr. Clark County Sch. Dist., Las Vegas, 1969-74, 1982-84; adj. faculty Clark County Community Coll., Las Vegas, 1984—, mem. Bus. and Industry Field Specialist Tng. Inst., 1985-86; probation officer on call Clark County Juvenile Services, Las Vegas, 1984; counselor Nike House, Las Vegas, 1984; mental health technician III, State of Nev., 1984—; pvt. practice rehab. counseling, 1984—. Active Nev. Womens Political Caucus, Las Vegas, 1983-84; carnival chmn. Rex Bell PTA, Las Vegas, 1974-75, treas., 1975-76; leader Frontier Area Girl Scouts, Las Vegas, 1975-76, cookie sale chmn., 1980; treas., bd. dirs. Young Audiences, Las Vegas, 1979-80. N.Y. State Regents scholar, 1963. Mem. Am. Assn. Counseling & Devel., AAUW (div. officer Nev. 1983-85, pres. 1982-83, v.p. programming 1981-82, v.p. membership 1980-81, life mem.), Assn. Part-time Profls. (bd. dirs., v.p. 1986), So. Nev. Personnel Assn. Republican. Office: BE Ltd 4550 W Oakey Las Vegas NV 89102

LEPSKY, HENRIETTA, nursing administrator; b. Cin., Sept. 27, 1938; d. Harry Oscar and Nellie (Molle) L.; R.N., B.S., U. Mich., 1956; M.S. in Community Health Planning, U. Cin., 1974; M.H.A., Xavier U., Cin., 1978; children—Stephanie, Steven. Mgmt. systems coordinator nursing dept. Cin. Gen. Hosp., 1971-74; dir. nursing Holmes Hosp., U. Cin., 1974-76; asst. adminstr., dir. nursing Holmes div. U. Cin. Med. Center, 1976-84; asst. v.p. nursing Huron Rd. Hosp., Cleve., 1984-84; v.p., dir. nursing White Plains Hosp. Med. Ctr., N.Y., 1986—; mem. faculty Edgecliff/Xavier U. Sch. Nursing, U. Cin. Coll. Nursing and Health; leader to People's Republic of China, China/U.S. Sci. Exchanges Inc., Sept. 1983, trustee Nurses Profl. Registry Cin. Kings Fund scholar, Eng., 1978. Cert. in advanced nursing adminstrn. Am. Nurses Assn. Mem. Am. Soc. Nursing Service Adminstrs. (bd. dirs. 1980-82), Am. Coll. Hosp. Adminstrs., Ohio Soc. Nursing Service Adminstrs. (pres. 1978-79), Greater Cin. Dirs. Nursing Service (pres. 1977-78). Jewish. Home: 37 Byramlake Rd Armonk NY 10504 Office: White Plains Hosp Med Ctr Davis at East Post Rd White Plains NY 10601

LERMAN, EILEEN R., lawyer; b. N.Y.C., May 6, 1947; d. Alex and Beatrice (Kline) L.; B.A., Syracuse U., 1969; J.D., Rutgers U., 1972; M.B.A., U. Denver, 1983. Admitted to N.Y. State bar, 1973, Colo. bar, 1976; atty. FTC, N.Y.C., 1972-74; corp. atty. RCA, N.Y.C., 1974-76; corp. atty. Samsonite Corp. and consumer products div. Beatrice Foods Co., Denver, 1976-78, assoc. gen. counsel, 1978-85, asst. sec., 1979-85; ptnr. Donnell, Davis & Lerman, Denver, 1985—; dir. Legal Aid Soc. of Met. Denver, 1979-80; guest lectr. Regis Coll., U. Denver, Colo. Women's Coll. Samsonite chmn. United Way, 1981; bd. dirs. Colo. Postsecondary Ednl. Facilities Authority, 1981—; mem. Leadership Denver, 1983; bd. dirs. Am. Jewish Com., 1984—. Mem. Colo. Women's Bar Assn. (dir. 1980-81), ABA, Colo. Bar Assn., Denver Bar Assn., Rutgers U. Alumni Assn. Club: Soroptimist. Home: 1018 Fillmore St Denver CO 80206 Office: 50 Steele St Suite 420 Denver CO 80209

LERMAN, JEANETTE PAULA, television producer, communications consultant; b. N.Y.C., Jan. 13, 1948; d. Miles and Rosalie C. (Laks) L. B.A., Brandeis U., 1969; M.A., Stanford U., 1971. Freelance film editor, 1969-71; editor, assoc. producer Internat. Cinemedia, Montreal, Que., Can., 1971-73; editor, dir. Nat. Film Bd. Can., Montreal, 1973-77; supr., producer CIL-TV, Montreal, 1977-78; mgr., exec. producer Merrill Lynch Video Network, N.Y.C., 1978—; cons. U.S. Holocaust Meml. Council, Washington, 1979—; lectr. NYU/New Sch., N.Y.C., 1978—; workshop leader Visual Communications Congress, N.Y.C., 1980—. Contbr. articles to mags. Dir., Ctr. for Holocaust Studies, N.Y.C., 1982—. Recipient awards Chgo., Internat. Film Festival, 1982, San Francisco Internat. Film Festival, 1983; Monitor award Video Producers Assn., 1983; Silver Screen award U.S. Indsl. Film Festival, 1984; Golden Reel award Internat. TV Assn., 1984. mem. Internat. TV Assn. (pres. Montreal chpt. 1977-78). Office: Merrill Lynch Video 165 Broadway 30th Floor New York NY 10080

LERNER, GERDA, history educator; b. Vienna, Austria; B.A., New Sch. Social Research, 1963; M.A., Columbia U., 1965, Ph.D., 1966; Litt.D., Colby-Sawyer Coll., 1981; D. Letters (h.c.),Bucknell U., 1982; D. Letters, New Sch. Social Relations, 1985. m. Carl Lerner (dec. 1973). Lectr., New Sch. then instr. Social Research 1963-65; assoc. prof. L.I. U., 1965-68; faculty Sarah Lawrence Coll. 1968-80; Robinson-Edwards prof. history U. Wis.-Madison, 1980—, Alumni Research Found. Sr. Disting. Research Prof., 1984. NEH fellow, Lilly fellow, Ford fellow, Guggenheim fellow; Orgn. Am. Historians grantee, 1980-83. Mem. Orgn. Am. Historians (pres. 1981-1982), AAUP, Authors League, PEN, Am. Hist. Assn. Author: The Grimké Sisters from South Carolina: Rebels Against Slavery 1967; The Woman in American History 1971; Black Women in White America: A Documentary History 1972; The Female Experience: An American Documentary 1976; A Death of One's Own, 1978; The Majority Finds Its Past 1979; Teaching Women's History 1981. Office: 5123 Humanities Bldg University of Wisconsin Madison WI 53706

LERNER, MILDRED SHERWOOD, clinical psychologist and psychoanalyst, counselor; b. N.Y.C., Mar. 29, 1929; d. Samuel Jerome and Rose (Malina) Sherwood; B.A. with honors, CCNY, 1951, M.A., 1952; Ph.D., N.Y.U. 1957; children—Andrew Roy, Julie Sue. Pvt. practice, N.Y.C., 1962—; supr. N.Y. Clinic Mental Health, N.Y.C.; instr. adult edn. CCNY, 1952-54; chief psychologist High Point Hosp., Port Chester, N.Y., 1954-61; dean student tng. Nat. Psychol. Assn. for Psychoanalysis, N.Y.C., 1968-73, pres. 1972-74; cons. Children's Aid Soc., N.Y.C., 1961-65; prof. Womanschool, N.Y.C., 1974-76; dir. grad. program in psychoanalysis Internat. Grad. U., Leysin, Switzerland, 1975-76. Bd. dirs. Chambers Ballet. Alvin Johnson scholar, 1951; Psychology fellow CCNY, 1952-54, Fellow Am. Psychol. Assn.; mem. N.Y. State Psychol. Assn., N.Y. Soc. Clin. Psychologists, Am. Assn. Psychotherapy, Psychotherapists in Pvt. Practice, Am. Humanistic Psychol. Assn., Am. Group Psychol. Assn., Mcpl. Art Soc., Humane Soc. N.Y., Psi Chi. Contbr. articles to profl. jours. Address: 2 Fifth Ave New York NY 10011 also 23 Old Mill Westport CT

LERNER, SUSAN A., psychologist; b. N.Y.C., Sept. 6, 1946; d. Harry and Annette (Ober) Herbst; B.A. cum laude, Queens Coll., CUNY, 1973; M.A., St. John's U., 1975; Ph.D., Howard U., 1980; m. Daniel J. Lerner, June 2, 1974; 1 son, Scott Paget. Prisoner liaison Queens House of Detention, Forest Hills, N.Y., 1972-73; grad. asst. dept. psychology Howard U., Washington, 1976-78; research asst. Human Resources Research Orgn., Alexandria, Va., 1978; staff psychologist, coordinator student tng. Gt. Oaks Center, Silver Spring, Md., 1978-82; staff psychologist Patuxent Instn., Jessup, Md., 1982-83; assoc. clin.

dir. for mental health services PSI Assocs., Inc., Washington, 1983-84; dir. clin. services PSI Services Inc., Landover, Md., 1984-85; clin. adminstr. div. forensic programs St. Elizabeth's Hosp., Washington, 1986—; cons. KHI Services Inc., Rockville; instr. dept. psychology Prince George's Community Coll., Largo, Md. NSF trainee, 1978-79. Mem. Am. Psychol. Assn., Md. Psychol. Assn., Eastern Psychol. Assn., Southeastern Psychol. Assn., D.C. Psychology Assn., Nat. Honor Soc. in Psychology. Contbr. to microfilms in field. Home: 12621 Red Pepper Ct Germantown MD 20874

LERSCH, DELYNDEN RIFE, electrical engineer; b. Grundy, Va., Mar. 22, 1949; d. Woodrow and Eunice Louise (Atwell) Rife; B.S. in E.E., Va. Poly. Inst. and State U., 1970; postgrad. Boston U., 1975—; m. John Robert Lersch, May 9, 1976; children—Desmond, Kristofer. With Stone & Webster Engring. Corp., 1970—, elec. engr., supr. computer applications, Boston, 1978-80, mgr. computer graphics, 1980-84, mgr. engring. systems and computer graphics, 1984—. Named Stone and Webster's Woman Engr. of Yr., 1976, 79; Mass. Solar Energy Research grantee, 1978; honored by Engring. News Record mag. for contbns. to constrn. industry, 1983. Mem. Assn. Women in Sci., Soc. Women Engrs. (sr.), IEEE (sr.), Women in Sci. and Engring., Energy Communicators, Nat. Computer Graphics Assn., Profl. Council New Eng., Nuclear Energy Women (dir. Mass. chpt. 1978, New Eng. region 1979), LWV. Congregationalist. Club: Boston Bus. and Profl. Women's. Author: Cable Schedule Information Systems As Used in Power Plant Construction, 1973, 2d edit., 1975; Information Systems Available for Use by Electrical Engineers, 1976; contbr. articles in field of computer aided design and engring. Home: 6 Blue Skye Dr Hingham MA 02043 Office: 245 Summer St Boston MA 02101

LESCH, ANN MOSELY, researcher; b. Washington, Feb. 1, 1944; d. Philip Edward and Ruth (Bissell) Mosely; B.A., Swarthmore Coll., 1962; Ph.D., Columbia U., 1973. Research asso. Fgn. Policy Research Inst., Phila., 1972-74; asso. Middl East rep. Am. Friends Service Com, Jerusalem, 1974-77; Middle East program officer Ford Found., N.Y.C., 1977-80, program officer, Cairo, 1980-84; assoc. Univs. Field Staff Internat., 1984—. Bd. dirs. Am. Near East Refugee Aid; mem. Quaker UN Com., 1979-80; mem. U.S. adv. com. Interns for Peace, 1978—. Fellow Catherwood Found., 1965; NDFL fellow, 1967-71. Mem. Middle East Studies Assn., Middle East Inst., Am. Polit. Sci. Assn. Unitarian. Author: Political Perceptions of the Palestinians on the West Bank and Gaza, 1980; Arab Politics in Palestine, 1979; The Politics of Palestinian Nationalism, 1973; contbr. articles to profl. jours. Office: Univs Field Staff Internat 620 Union Dr Indianapolis IN 46202

LESCHEN, CHRISTY ELIZABETH, retardation professional, consultant; b. St. Louis, Aug. 15, 1950; d. Harry John and Eleanor Lee (Patterson) L. B.A. in Psychology, Rollins Coll., 1973, M.Ed., 1976. Cert. tchr., Fla. Residential life unit supr. Sunland Tng. Ctr., Orlando, Fla., 1977-81; dir. St. Petersburg Cluster, Fla., 1981-83; adminstr. ARA DevCon Inc., Tallahassee, Fla., 1982-83, regional program cons., 1983—. Mem. Fla. Assn. Behavioral Analysis. Episcopalian. Home: 1563 B Willow Bend Way Tallahassee FL 32301 Office: ARA DevCon Inc 2639 N Monroe St Suite 152A Box 54 Tallahassee FL 32303

LESH, ANGELA DAWN, marketing executive; b. Altadena, Calif., Dec. 23, 1947; d. Olin Eugene and Betty Jean (Carroll) Lesh; m. Michael James Cussen, Nov. 20, 1974 (div. July 1981). B.A. in Rhetoric, U. Calif.-Davis, 1970; M.A. in Communications, Calif. State U.-Sacramento, 1971. Jr. research analyst Doremus, San Francisco, 1971-73; market research analyst Med. Care Found., Sacramento, 1973; dir. market research Wells Fargo Bank, San Francisco, 1973-78; sr. project mgr. Shaklee Corp., San Francisco, 1978-79; pres. A. Dawn Lesh & Assocs., Kensington, Calif., 1979-81; dir. market research Bank of Am., San Francisco, 1981-86; v.p. mktg. research N.Y. Stock Exchange, 1986—. Mem. Kensington Property Owners Assn. (Calif.), 1975—. Mem. Am. Mktg. Assn. (dir. 1983-84), Women in Communication Fields (founder), Advt. Research Found. Fin. Research Council (co-chmn. fin. workshop 1984—), Mktg. Sci. Inst., Bank Mktg. Assn., Fin. Women's Assn., Calif. Aggie Alumni Assn. Democrat. Home: 110 Bleecker St Apt 12 New York NY 10012 Office: NY Stock Exchange 11 Wall St New York NY 10005

LESH, NANCY LOU, librarian; b. Anchorage, May 25, 1944; d. Keith Myron and Enid Mabel (King) L. B.A. in English, Willamette U., Salem, Oreg., 1966; M.L.S., Simmons Coll., Boston, 1967. Librarian, Anchorage Community Coll., 1968-72; asst. dir. Library U. Alaska, Anchorage, 1972-80, assoc. dir., 1980—. Mem. Historic Landmarks Preservation Commn., Anchorage, 1983-84. Mem. ALA (chpt. councilor 1978-81), Pacific N.W. Library Assn. (Alaska rep. 1976-77), Alaska Library Assn. (pres. 1969-70; co-editor jour. Sourdough 1977-79), WLN Alaska Users Group (chmn. 1980-84, rep. GNOSIS governance council 1984—). Club: Pioneers of Alaska.

LESKO, STEPHANIE MARIE, advertising agency executive; b. Montebello, Calif., Dec. 16, 1955; d. Steve and Vincentia Beatrice (Ginevra) Lesko. A.A., Mt. San Antonio Coll., 1976; B.A. in Communications, Calif. State U.-Fullerton, 1981. Lead person Disneyland, Anaheim, Calif., 1974-79; mgr. RTM, Inc.-Arby's, Anaheim, 1979-80; creative mgr. B.P. Rice & Co., Inc., Cerritos, Calif., 1980-85; pres. Twenty Nineteen Advt. Inc., Long Beach, Calif., 1985—; career cons. Calif. State U., Fullerton, 1983-84, Gardena High Sch., 1984-85. Named Most Supportive Mem., Most Profl. Mem., Los Angeles Advt. Women, 1985, 1985. Mem. Los Angeles Advt. Women (dir. 1984-86), Nat. Assn. Female Execs., Am. Advt. Fedn. Democrat. Roman Catholic. Avocations: sports; designing clothes; art and antique collecting. Office: Twenty Nineteen Advt Inc 3645 Long Beach Blvd Long Beach CA 90807

LESSE, ETTA GORDON (MRS. S. MICHAEL LESSE), psychiatric social worker; b. Trenton, N.J.; d. H. Charles and Rose (Miers) Gordon; B.A., Beaver Coll.; M.Social Sci., Smith Coll.; postgrad. Bryn Mawr Coll. Sch. Social Economy; U. Pa. Sch. Social Work; m. S. Michael Lesse; children—Toni Gordon and Cathy Ross (twins). Exec. sec. Clinic for Child Psychiatry, Temple U. Med. Sch., Phila.; psychiat. social worker Bur. Family Service, Orange, N.J., Family Welfare Soc., Newport, R.I.; intake worker Bur. Family Service, Orange, N.J.; case supr., asst. to chief social worker VA, Phila.; consultant for social agys. and ct. Social and health counsellor to Draft Bd., Orange, N.J.; organizer steering com. for establishment case work sect. Council Social Agys., Newport, R.I.; chmn. Workshop for Profl. Social Workers Lehigh Valley; group chmn. regional conf. pub. edn. Gov.'s Commn. Pub. Edn., Pa. Gov.'s Commn. on Aging; cons. foster home devel. Northampton County Children's Aid Soc.; profl. participant in religion and psychiatry seminars, Easton, Pa.; interviewer Easton-Phillipsburg (Pa.) Commn. Human Relations; mem. adv. bd. Northeastern region Pa. Dept. Pub. Welfare. Lectr. to child study group PTA, Easton, Pa. Bd. dirs. Lehigh Valley Center Performing Arts Assn., v.p.; bd. dirs. Lehigh Valley Community Council, 1975—, Planned Parenthood of Northampton County; exec. bd. Am. Heart Assn., 1978—; mem. adv. bd. Jr. League of Lehigh Valley. Mem. Nat. Assn. Social Workers, Acad. Certified Social Workers, AAUW (past br. pres., dir. Eastern br., chmn. career advancement loan fund, named Outstanding Woman of Yr. 1981-82), Lehigh Valley Mental Health Assn. (dir., chmn. com. on personnel and nominating), Allentown Art Mus., Women's Com. Phila. Assn. Psychoanalysis, Northampton County Med. Soc. Aux., (dir. 1980—, v.p., pres., chmn. scholarships, chmn. med. and profl. nursing students loan fund), Phila. Orch. Assn., Met. Opera Assn., Smith Coll. Alumni Assn. Contbg. author Two Hundred Years of Life in Northampton County, Pa. Home: 2768 Stephens St Easton PA 18042

LESSENDEN, EDITH ANN FLEMING, writer; b. Garden City, Kans., Jan. 21, 1922; d. Arthur Milo and Edith Ann (Hambleton) Fleming; m. Chester Merral Lessenden, June 1, 1943; children—Sandra L. Denicke; Marged L. Amend, Eve L. Supica, Mark Charles. A.B., Kans. U., 1946, M.A., 1952. Editor-writer Med. Aux. News, Kans., 1958-60, Allegro, Topeka Symphony, 1970—; writer, dir. musical revues; contbr. articles to various publs. Organizer, chmn. Symphony League, Topeka, 1966-70, bd. dirs., 1966—; bd. dirs. Kans. Med. Aux., 1958—, pres., 1964-65; bd. dirs. AMA Aux., 1970-77, fund-raiser, 1973-75, regional v.p. 1975-77. Recipient Charles Marling award Topeka Symphony Soc., 1984. Mem. Nat. League Am. Pen Women (Roller award 1985), Kans. Authors Club, P.E.O. (chpt. pres. 1959-60, coop. bd. pres. 1961-62), Mortar Bd. Republican. Methodist. Clubs: Minerva (pres. 1963-64), Western sorosis (pres. 1980-81). Avocations: French conversation; sewing; needlepoint; reading.

LESSER, MIMI KORACH, painter, illustrator; b. N.Y.C., Apr. 25, 1922; d. Dean and Viola (Weinberg) Korach; m. Bert Lesser, Apr. 17, 1951; children—Steven Dean, Robin Deane. Student Sch. Art, Yale U., 1940-43. One woman shows: Barbizon Plaza Gallery, N.Y.C., 1948, Silvermine Guild, New Canaan, Conn., 1977, Pindar Gallery, N.Y.C., 1980, 83, 86; group shows include Am. Acad. Arts and Letters, N.Y.C., 1976, Silvermine Guild, 1976, 78, 81, Hudson River Mus., Yonkers, N.Y., 1976, 78, 81, Butler Inst. Am. Art, Youngstown, Ohio, 1979; freelance illustrator for books and mags., 1945-70; sketched over 1000 servicemen for USO in France, Belgium and Ger., 1945. Recipient numerous awards from art orgns. including Hudson River Mus., 1981. Jewish. Home: 24 Stonewall Ln Mamaroneck NY 10543

LESSTRANG, BARBARA HILLS, pub. co. exec.; b. Grand Rapids, Mich., Jan. 24, 1935; d. John Henry and Ouida Louise (Russell) Hills; student U. Mich., 1951-52; m. Jacques LesStrang, Nov. 17, 1969; children—Steven, Linda, Christian; stepchildren—Michelle, Diane, Paul, David. Dir. sales and pub. relations Charter Hotels, Ann Arbor, Mich., 1967-69; v.p. advt. and sales, dir. Gt. Lakes Press, Traverse City, Mich., 1970—; dir. Gt. Lakes Mktg. Corp.; dir., vice chmn. Harbor House Pubs., pres., 1979—. Republican. Christian Scientist.

LESTER, MICHELE MARIE, social worker; b. Odessa, Tex., Jan. 8, 1951; d. Robert D. and Colleen M. (Moore) Brown. B.A. in Social Scis., Mich. State U., 1972. Eligibility worker Dept. of Pub. Social Services, Nevada City, Calif., 1974-83; eligibility technician Div. Pub. Assistance, Bethel, Alaska, 1983—; eligibility systems info. resource person Div. Pub. Assistance, Bethel, 1984—, trainer of fee agts., 1985. Author short stories. Contbr. articles to profl. jours. Bd. dirs. Tundra Women's Coalition, Bethel, 1984—, trainer-crisis line intervention, 1983-84; bd. dirs. A Woman's Place, Nevada City, 1976; chmn. Regional Woman's Conf. of 1986-Task Force, Southwest Alaska, 1985. Mem. NOW, Alaska Pub. Employees Assn. Democrat. Avocations: computer programming; word processing; reading; needlecraft. Home: PO Box 441 BNC Townhouse 18 Bethel AK 99559 Office: Div Pub Assistance PO Box 365 BNC Bus Bethel AK 99559

LESTER, VIRGINIA LAUDANO, college president, consultant; b. Phila.; d. Edward M. and Emily Laudano; divorced; children—Pamela Lester Golde, Valerie Lester. B.A., Pa. State U., 1952; M.Ed., Temple U., 1955; Ph.D., Union Grad. Sch., 1972; student Stanford U. Law Sch., 1985—; Tchr. elem. schs., Pa. and N.Y., 1952-56; instr. edn. Skidmore Coll., Saratoga Springs, N.Y., 1962-64, dir. ednl. research, 1967-72, asst. to pres., 1968-72; asst. dir. Capitol dist. Regional Supplemental Ednl. Ctr., Albany, N.Y., 1966-67; assoc. dean, asst. prof. state-wide programs Empire State Coll., Saratoga Springs, 1973-75, sr. assoc. dean, asst. prof., 1975-76, acting dean, 1976; cons. core faculty Union Grad. Sch., Cin., 1975-82; vis. faculty fellow Harvard U., Cambridge, Mass., 1976; pres., prof. interdisciplinary studies Mary Baldwin Coll., Staunton, Va., 1976-85; mem. exec. com. Va. Found. Ind. Colls., 1983-85; dir. So. Bank, Richmond, Va. Author: Unit Coordinators Handbook, 1975; A Faculty Guide to the Award of Advanced Standing, 1975. Mem. Gov's. Commn. to Study Future of Va., 1982-84, Gov's. Adv. Com. Awards for Arts, 1979, Citizen's Adv. Com. Saratoga Springs Bd. Edn., 1964-70; bd. dirs. Nat. Urban League, N.Y.C., 1979—, Haverford Coll., Pa., 1981—; mem. Hanes Adv. Council Social Responsibility, Winston-Salem, N.C., 1983—, Am. Council on Edn., Washington, 1983-85, Pres's. Commn. of Nat. Collegiate Athletic Assn., 1984—, Mission Study Commn. Va. Mil. Inst., 1985. Mem. Nat. Collegiate Athletic Assn. (div. 3, vice chmn. 1984-85), Women's Coll. Coalition (exec. com. 1983-85), Council Ind. Colls. in Va., Assn. Ch.-Related Colls. and Univs. South (v.p. 1982, pres. 1983), Am. Acad. Polit. and Social Scis. Mem. Soc. Friends.

LETICA, HELEN, advertising executive; b. Belgrade, Yugoslavia, July 21, 1923; d. Charles and Renee Santich; came to U.S., 1941, naturalized, 1945; B.A. in Journalism, NYU, 1945; postgrad. Columbia U., 1946; m. Jack W. Fine, Aug. 4, 1967; children—Gregory, Nicholas. Pres., Zeller & Letica, Inc., N.Y.C. Mem. Direct Mktg. Assn., Mail Advt. Service Assn., Direct Mktg. Club N.Y. Democrat. Club: Mill River (Upper Brookville, N.Y.). Contbr. articles in field of direct mail advt. to profl. jours. Office: 15 E 26th St New York NY 10010

LETTS, MARY JANE CRAIG, educator; b. Cherokee, N.C., Nov. 20, 1936; d. Robert D. and Bertha A. (Bradley) Craig; m. Ray Don Letts, Aug. 2, 1959; 1 child, Bradley Brady. B.S. in Edn., Northeastern Okla. State U., 1959; postgrad. U. No. Colo., 1977-78. Tchr., Jefferson County Schs., Lakewood, Colo., 1959-78; mgr. Craig's Motel, Cherokee, 1978-82; adult devel. activity program coordinator Vocat. Opportunity of Cherokee Sheltered Workshop, 1982—. Bd. dirs. Hinton Ctr., Haynesvill, N.C., 1980—, Cherokee Children's Home, 1982—; mem. nomination com., core planning group United Methodist Women, SE region, 1980-84; co-chair Speak-out for Minority Women, 1984; mem. edn. com. Unto These Hills Scholarship Fund, Cherokee, 1983—. Mem. AAUW (chpt. treas. 1979-81), Smokey Mountain Sch. PTA (treas. 1979-80), Beta Sigma Phi (v.p. 1983-84), Sigma Sigma Sigma. Democrat. Office: PO Box 653 Cherokee NC 28719

LEUER, MARY MARGARET, educator; b. Long Beach, Calif., Dec. 7, 1929; d. Anthony Arnold and Mary Margaret (Amsden) Leuer. A.A., Long Beach City Coll., 1949; B.A., Long Beach State U., 1951, M.A., 1953; M.S.Ed., U. So. Calif., 1969. Part-time sec., credentials technician Long Beach State U. (Calif.), 1949-51, demonstration and master tchr., 1957-68; tchr. Paramount Unified Sch. Dist. (Calif.), 1951—; vol. tchr. Chgo.'s Head Start Program, summer 1965; part-time prof. Compton Community Coll. (Calif.), 1975-81; State of Calif. Nursery Sch. dir. for Lakewood Garden's Parent Coop. Nursery Sch., 1978-82; sch. psychologist, counselor Pepperdine U., 1981-82; del. NEA meeting N.Y.C., 1954; del. PTA meeting San Francisco, 1955; founder, head. Paramount Unified Sch. Dist. Emergency Fund for Employees, 1955-59. Mem. Paramount Coordinating Council, 1968-70; Co-founder Paramount Child Guidance Center 1969-70. Mem. Calif. State Trustee Assn. Neurol. Handicapped Children, Delta Zeta Co-founder, v.p. 1950-51), Phi Delta Gamma. Club: Long Beach Cath. Nat. Coll. Alumni (Calif. Co-founder, v.p. 1955). Office: Collins Sch 6125 Coke St Long Beach CA 90805

LEVACK, ANN MARIE, producer, talent consultant; b. N.Y.C., Sept. 11, 1940; d. Arthur Paul and Helen G. (O'Brien) L. B.A., Marymount Coll., 1962. Dir. spl. promotions Muscular Dystrophy Assn., N.Y.C., 1974-81, N.Y. assoc. producer Jerry Lewis Telethon, 1978-81; adminstrv. dir. Actors & Dirs. Lab., N.Y.C., 1982-83; producer Salute to Corp. Stars, Leukemia Soc., N.Y.C., 1984, 85, 86, Gospel According to Della, N.Y.C., 1985; talent cons. CBS-TV, N.Y.C., 1985—; bd. dirs. 42nd St. Theatre Row, N.Y.C., 1982-83. Alt. del. Democratic 1st Jud. Dist. Conv., N.Y.C., 1984; Mem. N.Y. County com. 63d Dem. Assembly, 1985; mem. exec. com. Mid-Manhattan-New Dem. Club, N.Y.C., 1985—. Roman Catholic. Club: Can. Women's of N.Y. (N.Y.C.). Home: 951 1st Ave New York NY 10022

LEVALLEY, JOAN CATHERINE, accountant; b. Decatur, Ill., Nov. 27, 1931; d. Clarence and Pearl Mae (McClure) Krall; m. Charles R. LeValley, Apr. 13, 1958; children—Curtis Ray, Cara Marie. B.A. in Bus., Manchester Coll., 1957. Acct. with various firms, 1960-76; pvt. practice acctg., Park Ridge, Ill., 1964-79; pres., dir. LeValley & Assocs., Inc., Park Ridge, 1979—, LeValley Data Systems, Inc., Park Ridge, 1982—; dir. DSS Investment Corp., Chgo. Mem. Nat. Assn. Pub. Accts., Ind. Acct. Assn. Ill. (state 2d v.p. 1985-86), Bus. and Profl. Women Park Ridge (pres. 1974-75, Bus. Woman of Yr. 1983), Park Ridge C. of C. (treas. 1985-86). Baptist. Avocations: baking; sewing; gardening. Home: 1215 Linden Ave Park Ridge IL 60068 Office: LeValley & Assocs Inc and LeValley Data Systems Inc 841 W Touhy Ave Park Ridge IL 60068

LEVAN, JOAN S., retail company executive; married. B.S., Seton Hall Coll., 1961. Vice pres. merchandising Woodward & Lothrop, 1976-78; mgr. market div. Assoc. Dry Goods Corp., 1978-80, div. v.p., exec. v.p. market div., 1980, now v.p. and pres. ADG Mktg. div. Address: Assoc Dry Goods Corp 417 Fifth Ave New York NY 10016*

LEVANDOWSKI, BARBARA SUE, educator; b. Chgo., Mar. 16, 1948; d. Earl F. and Ann (Klee) L.; B.A., North Park Coll., 1970; M.S., No. Ill. U., 1975, Ed.D., 1979; Tchr., Round Lake (Ill.) Sch. Dist., 1970-75; tchr., asst. prin. Schaumburg (Ill.) Sch. Dist., 1975—; curriculum cons. Spring Grove (Ill.) Sch. Dist., 1980—. Mem. staff Round Lake Park Dist., 1973—. Recipient numerous awards for excellence in teaching. Mem. Ill. Assn. Women Adminstrs., Ill. Assn. for Supervision and Curriculum Devel., Assn. Supervision and Curriculum Devel., Ill. Prins. Assn., Phi Delta Kappa. Mem. editorial bd. Ill. Sch. Research and Devel. Jour., 1981—; contbr. articles to profl. jours. Home: 508 Garfield St Ingleside IL 60041 Office: 1100 Laurie Ln Hanover Park IL 60103

LEVBARG, DIANE, fashion industry executive; b. Mar, 18, 1950; d. Morrison Levbarg and Ann-Louise Lewis; m. Martin I. Klein, May 23, 1974. Cert. in retail studies Coll. for Distributive Trades, London; student Vassar Coll., 1972. Exec. Trainee Harrods, London, 1970-71; exec. trainee, asst. dept. mgr., asst. buyer Saks Fifth Ave, N.Y.C., 1971-73; asst. buyer, buyer Bonwit Teller, N.Y.C., 1973-75; assoc. buyer, buyer, group mgr. Bloomingdale's, N.Y.C., 1975-82; pres., fashion cons. Diane Levbarg & Assocs. Inc., N.Y.C., 1982—; exec. v.p. Missoni U.S.A.; cons. Nina Ricci, Daniel Hechter, Christian Dior U.S.A., Bogner U.S.A. Named One of 100 Women of Promise, Good Housekeeping. Address: 200 E 72d St New York NY 10021

LE VECQUE, CHARLOTTE ROSE, psychiatric social worker, psychotherapist; b. Darby, Pa., Nov. 11, 1944; d. George Alfred and Charlotte Vivian (Bungart) Le V.; B.S., Western Mich. U., 1966; M.S.W., Adelphi U., 1968. Psychiat. social worker Patton State Hosp., Patton, Calif., 1968-71; sr. psychiat. social worker mental health unit San Bernardino (Calif.) County Hosp., 1971-74; licensed clin. social worker dept. psychiatry So. Calif. Permanente Med. Group, Fontana, Calif., 1974—. Lic. clin. social worker; cert. social worker, N.Y. Mem. Acad. Cert. Social Workers, Soc. Clin. Social Work, Nat. Assn. Social Workers, Nat. Registry Health Care Providers, Alpha Omicron Pi. Democrat. Clubs: American Fox Terrier, Western Fox Terrier Breeders Assn. (bd. govs. 1973, 78, 84, editor Kliptails 1984, 85), Orange Empire Terrier Group (v.p. 1984), San Bernardino Humane Soc., Santa Ana Valley Kennel, Kennel Club of Palm Springs (v.p. terrier group 1985, corr. sec. 1986). Office: 325 W Hospitality Ln Suite 312 San Bernardino CA 92408

LEVEEN, CORALIE KREINIK, interior designer, textile cons.; b. N.Y.C., Aug. 23, 1929; d. Harold Hyman and Jeanne Sophie Kreinik; grad. Ann-Reno Inst. N.Y., 1951; B.S. in Edn., Adelphi Coll., 1951; grad. N.Y. Sch. Interior Design, 1961; m. Irwin Arnold Leveen, Mar. 18, 1951; children—Judith May, Deborah Ann. Tchr., Les Coquelicots Nursery Sch., 1951-52; owner Coralie Leveen Interiors, Great Neck, N.Y., 1961—; v.p. E.F. Leveen Sales Corp; cons. textiles for interior decorating. Bd. dirs. various schs., 1957-75; pres. John F. Kennedy Sch., 1966-67; sec. United Parent Tchr. Council, 1965-67; bd. dirs. Gt. Neck (N.Y.) Edn. Assn., 1960-72, Citizens Sch. Com., 1965-73, Assn. Help of Retarded Children, 1972-78, Children's Med. Center of L.I. Jewish Hosp., 1975-78; mem. Sisterhood Temple Beth-El; membership chmn. North Shore chpt. Am. Technion; rec. sec. Lake chpt. Women's Am. ORT. Home: 97 Beach Rd Great Neck NY 11023 Office: 55 W 39th St New York NY 10018

LEVELL, ROSEMOND HULL, disability analyst; b. N.Y.C., Mar. 15, 1939; d. Roseman and Eva Adela (Wright) Hull; m. David S. Levell, June 20, 1959; 1 child, Marsha. B.A., Queens Coll., 1976; M.Profl. Studies in Disability Determination, NYU, 1984. Tchr. Bd. Edn., N.Y.C., 1977-79; social service disability analyst Office of Disability Determinations, N.Y.C., 1979—; social service disability analyst-liaison to Social Security Adminstrn. Dist. Office 120, Jamaica, N.Y., 1984—. Sec., Cambria Heights Sports Com., N.Y., 1978, 232 Block Assn., Cambria Heights, 1975-84. Seek-Ace scholar Queens Coll.; N.Y. State Dept. Social Services grantee NYU. Mem. N.Y. Assn. U. Women (chpt. sec. 1983—), Nat. Assn. Disability Examiners, Pub. Employees Fedn. (sec. black caucus Office Disability Determinations div. 1983-85). Episcopalian. Club: NYU (N.Y.C.). Home: 116-48 232d St Cambria Heights NY 11411 Office: 110 William St New York NY 10038 also 92-31 Union Hall St Jamaica NY 11433

LEVENDOGLU, HULYA, gastroenterologist; b. Sansun, Turkey, Nov. 20, 1948; came to U.S., 1973; d. Ali Riza and Hidayet (Acar) L.; m. Mustafa Orhan Kaymakcalan, June 21, 1974 (div. 1981). M.D., Hacettepe U., 1972. Diplomate Am. Bd. Internal Medicine; Intern and resident in internal medicine Cook County Hosp., Chgo., 1973-76, fellow, 1976-78, attending physician, 1978-80, chmn. div. gastroenterology, 1983—; attending physician, asst. prof., Downstate Med. Ctr., Bklyn., 1980-83; acting chief div. gastroenterology Bklyn. VA Hosp., 1981-83. Contbr. articles to profl. publs. Research grantee SUNY, 1981, Eli Lilly & co., 1984. Mem. ACP, Am. Gastroent. Assn., Am. Soc. for Gastrointestinal Endoscopy, Am. Soc. for Study of Liver Diseases. Moslem. Office: Div Gastroenterology Cook County Hosp 1835 W Harrison St Chicago IL 60612

LEVENE, PATRICIA JANIE GORICK, court reporter; b. Johnson City, N.Y., May 15, 1950; d. Alfred Frank and Stephanie (Petersen) Gorick; Applied Asso. Sci. Degree, Alfred State Coll., 1970; m. David Harry Levene, July 7, 1979; 1 child, Maxwell John. Ct. stenographer Jack W. Hunt & Assocs., Buffalo, 1970-71; hearing reporter N.Y. State Dept. Labor Workers' Compensation Bd., Binghamton, N.Y., 1971-81; freelance ct. reporter, 1981—. Sec. Broome County Republican Com., Binghamton, 1975—; bd. dirs. Broome County Young Rep. Club, 1973-77, v.p., 1978-79; mem. adv. com. ct. reporting dept. Alfred State Coll., 1975-79. Mem. Nat. Shorthand Reporters Assn. (registered profl. reporter), N.Y. State Shorthand Reporters Assn., Broome County Rep. Women's Club, Temple Israel Sisterhood, Hadassah. Home: 525 Midvale Rd Binghamton NY 13903

LEVENTHAL, A. LINDA, lawyer; b. Albany, N.Y., June 10, 1943; d. David Henry and Shirley R. (Asofsky) L. B.A., SUNY, Buffalo, 1965; J.D., Union U., 1968. Bar: N.Y. 1968, U.S. dist. ct. (no. dist.) N.Y. 1968. Ptnr. Rosenblum & Leventhal, Albany, 1968-78; sole practice, Albany, 1978-84, Schenectady, 1978-84; ptnr. Leventhal & Kirsch, Albany, 1984—; ptnr. Taub & Leventhal, 1982—. Lectr. continuing legal edn., family law sect. seminars N.Y. State Bar Assn., 1981—; bd. dirs. Legal Aid Soc. Northeastern N.Y., Inc. Bd. mgrs., pres. Commons of East Greenbush Condominium. Mem. ABA, N.Y. State Bar Assn., N.Y. State Women's Bar Assn., Nat. Assn. Women Lawyers, Nat. Assn. Female Execs., Nat. Fedn. Bus. and Profl. Women. Club: Zonta. Home: 247 S Manning Blvd Albany NY 12208 also 9707 E Mountain View Rd Scottsdale AZ 85258 Office: Pieter Schuyler Bldg 600 Broadway Albany NY 12208 also 115 Clinton St Schenectady NY 12305

LEVENTHAL, RUTH LEE (MRS. BERNARD SENNET), sculptor; b. N.Y.C., Oct. 5, 1923; d. Isador H. and Ethel (Karp) Lee; student N.Y.U., Nat. Acad., Art Students League; m. Bernard Sennet, Feb. 19, 1972; children by previous marriage—Ricki (Mrs. Ivan Delbyck), Peter Leventhal. Exhibited sculpture in one-man shows at Lynn Kottler Galleries, N.Y.C., Chapman Sculpture Galleries, N.Y.C., Mus. Modern Art, Israel; exhibited in group shows at Nat. Acad. Galleries, N.Y.C., Nat. Arts Club, N.Y.C., Parke Bernet Galleries, N.Y.C., Met. Mus. Art, N.Y.C., 1979; represented in permanent collections at Mus. Modern Art, Israel, Tel Aviv (Israel) U., Riverside Meml. Chapel, N.Y.C., Goldsmith's Hall, London, Secular Sch., Bet Shean, Israel. Recipient Nat. 3M award, 1969; gold medal for sculpture Catherine Lorrilard Wolfe Arts Club, 1970, 81; Gold medal Nat. Arts Club, 1973; award Nat. Acad., 1978; sculpture award Allied Artists Am., 1982. Fellow Royal Soc.; mem. Nat. Soc. for Arts and Letters (dir.) Allied Artists Am. (sculpture award 1975), ASCAP, Am. Guild Authors and Composers. Clubs: Catherine Lorrilard Wolfe (dir.), Salmagundi (award 1975, 76, 78, 79, 81) (N.Y.C.). Allied Artists Am. Patentee hosp. and home care equipment. Home: 425 E 58th St New York NY 10022

LEVENTHAL, SHEILA SMITH, educator; b. Raymondville, Tex., May 4, 1941; d. M. C. and Jessie Mae (Sansom) Smith; m. Ira Yale Leventhal, Aug. 5, 1966; 1 child, Adam Yale. B.S., N. Tex. State U., 1963, M.Ed., 1965; postgrad. Nova U., 1972, MIT, 1979. Elem. tchr. Grapevine Pub. Schs. (Tex.), 1963-65; tchr., team leader Lamplighter Sch., Dallas, 1965—, mem. steering com., computer staff, 1979-84. Staff mem. Episcopal Sch. of Spirituality, Dallas, 1983. Mem. NEA, Tex. Tchrs. Assn., Women of St. Francis (v.p. Dallas 1983), Phi Delta Kappa. Home: 2947 Talisman Dr Dallas TX 75229 Office: Lamplighter Sch 11611 Inwood Rd Dallas TX 75229

LEVERING, MARY BERGHAUS, lawyer, librarian, educator; b. West Palm Beach, Fla., June 1, 1940; d. Theodore Francis and Genevieve Valentine (Mahoney) Berghaus; B.A. maxima cum laude, U. Portland (Oreg.), 1965; M.L.S. with highest honors (Cath. Library Assn. nat. scholar), U. Wash., Seattle, 1966; J.D. (sr. editor law jour. 1975-77), Georgetown U., 1977; m. Robert John Levering, Oct. 16, 1976. Tchr. elem. and jr. high schs., Mass. and Wash., 1958-64; mgmt. intern Library of Congress, 1966-67, mem. staff, 1967—, chief network div. Nat. Library Service for Blind and Physically Handicapped, 1980—; adv. women career advisors program Georgetown U., 1981—; sec., pres. dir. Harbour Sq. Owners, Inc., 1981-83; admitted to D.C. bar, 1977. Bd. dirs. R.O.M.P. Sch., Wilmington, Del., (various offices and coms.), 1980—. Recipient Disting. Alumnus award U. Wash. Grad. Sch. Library and Info. Sci., 1986. Mem. ALA, Women's Nat. Book Assn. (chpt.

pres. 1984—), Fed. Bar Assn. D.C. Bar, Supreme ct. Bar, Women's Bar Assn. D.C., Nat. Assn. Women Lawyers, D.C. Library Assn., Washington Book Pubs., Library of Congress Philatelic Soc., Delta Epsilon Sigma; Beta Phi Mu. Club: Chevy Chase Swim and Tennis. Author articles in field. Home: 3508 Leland St Chevy Chase MD 20815 Office: NLS/BPH Library of Congress Washington DC 20542

LEVESQUE, THERESE ALICE, educational administrator; b. W. Warwick, R.I., May 8, 1917; d. J. Wilfred and Mathilda Phoebe (Smith) Levesque. B.A., Rivier Coll., 1938; M.A. in Classics, Fordham U., 1947, Ph.D., 1961. Tchr. pub. schs., Coventry, R.I., 1938-43, Chenango Forks, N.Y., 1947-50; tchr. Latin and French chmn. dept. fgn. langs. Tappan Zee High Sch., Orangeburg, N.Y., 1950-63, asst. prin., 1963-66; founding prin. South Orangetown Middle Sch., Blauvelt, N.Y., 1966-72; dir. fed. project South Orangetown Central Sch. Dist., Blauvelt, 1972-74, asst. to supt., 1974-75, asst. supt., 1975-78; Fulbright exchange tchr. to Montpelier, France, 1953-54; cons. Nat. Cath. Office for Motion Pictures. First chmn. sch. bd. Albertus Magnus High Sch., Bardonia, N.Y., 1981-84. Served as 1st lt., USMC, 1943-47. Recipient Outstanding Tchr. award, St. Thomas Aquinas Coll., 1965; Jenkins Meml. Fund award, PTA, 1972. Mem. Am. Assn. Sch. Adminstrs., Fordham Alumni Assn. (pres. Rockland County chpt. 1963-65), Delta Kappa Gamma (chpt. pres. 1967-69). Roman Catholic (lector St. Ann's Ch., Nyack). Author: Reinforcement Drills in Basic Reading Skills for Sixth Level and for Advanced Level, 1981. Address: 38 4th Ave Apt 2F Nyack NY 10960

LEVI, TAMARA, marketing executive; b. Belgrade, Yugoslavia, Feb. 7, 1947; came to U.S., 1953, naturalized, 1967; d. Jakov M. and Slava Hulda Ruth (Spitzer) Levi. A.B. in English, Clark U., 1968; tchr. cert. Hunter Coll., 1971; postgrad. Columbia Tchr.'s Coll., 1973-74, Bank St. Coll., 1975-78. Cert. tchr., N.Y. Tchr. East Harlem Block, N.Y.C., 1973-78; mem. adj. faculty Bank St. Coll., N.Y.C., 1976-78; exec. v.p. SBI Pubs., South Lee, Mass., 1978—; direct mkgt. services mgr. Flaghouse, Inc., N.Y.C., 1980—; pres. Clean Lists Assocs., N.Y.C., 1983—; prin. SBI Advt. and Mktg., 1984—; instr. direct mkgt. Marymount Manhattan Coll., 1985—; devel. cons. Conn. Women's Edn. and Legal Fund, Hartford, Conn., 1983—; In Touch Networks, N.Y.C., 1982—. Adaptor script for film, staging The Only Jealousy of Emer, 1968. Bd. dirs. Berkshire Pub. Theater, Pittsfield, Mass., 1979-81; active career resources com. Clark Alumni Assn., 1980—. Mem. Am. Women Entrepreneurs. Jewish. Home: 531 E 72d St New York NY 10021 Office: Flaghouse Inc 18 W 18th St New York NY 10011

LEVI, VIKTORYA, biochemist, researcher; b. Canakkale, Turkey; Jan. 15, 1950; came to U.S., 1972; d. Hinto and Ester (Zakuto) L.; m. Hector Juarez-Salinas, Oct. 2, 1981. B.S., Bogazici Univ., Istanbul, Turkey, 1972; postgrad. Bucknell Univ., 1972-74; Ph.D., N. Tex. State Univ., 1981. Teaching asst. Bogazici Univ., Istanbul, 1971-72; teaching research asst. Bucknell Univ., Lewisburg, Pa., 1972-74, N. Tex. State Univ., Denton, 1975-80; postdoctoral fellow Univ. Tex. Health Sci. Ctr., Dallas, 1981-83, Univ. Calif., San Francisco, 1984-85, vis. research biochemist; application chemist Rainin Instrument Co., Inc., Emeryville, Calif., 1986—. Author: ADP-Ribosylations of Regulatory Enzymes and Proteins, 1980; contbr. articles to profl. jours. Mem. Alpha Chi Sigma. Jewish. Home: 1700 Lincoln Village Circle #2306 Larkspur CA 94939 Office: 1715 64th St Emeryville CA 94608

LEVICK, MYRA FRIEDMAN, art psychotherapist, educator; b. Phila., Aug. 20, 1924; d. Louis and Ida (Segal) Friedman; B.F.A., Moore Coll. Art, 1963; M.Ed., Temple U., 1967; Ph.D., Bryn Mawr Coll., 1982; m. Leonard J. Levick, Dec. 26, 1943; children—Bonnie, Karen, Marsha. Art psychotherapist Albert Einstein Med. Center, Phila., 1963-67; dir. adjunctive therapies and dir. grad. tng. program in art therapy, Hahnemann Med. Coll. and Hosp., Phila., 1967-73, dir. masters creative arts in therapy tng. program, 1973-86, prof. mental health scis. dept. Hahnemann U., 1977—; cons. affiliated clinics and instns. Recipient Outstanding Alumni award Moore Coll. Art, 1975; Humanitarian award Ronald Bruce Nippon Assn., 1976; NIMH grantee, 1975-78. Mem. Am. Art Therapy Assn. (founder, 1st pres. hon. life mem.), Family Inst. Phila. (exec. bd. 1982-84), Am. Psychol. Assn., Pa. Psychol. Assn., Am. Ortho-Psychiat. Assn., Internat. Soc. Psychopathology of Expression, Am. Soc. Psychopathology of Expression. Author: They Could Not Talk and So They Drew, Children's Styles of Coping and Thinking, 1983; Mommy, Daddy, Look What I'm Saying: What Children Are Telling You Through Their Art, 1986; contbg. author: Current Psychotherapies, 1976; Handbook of Innovative Psychotherapies, 1981; sr. editor The Arts in Psychotherapy, 1975-81, editor-in-chief, 1982-86, emeritus, 1986—; contbr. articles to profl. lit. Home: 1901 Kennedy Blvd Apt 2623 Philadelphia PA 19103 Office: Hahnemann Med Coll and Hosp 230 N Broad St Philadelphia PA 19102

LEVIN, AMY BETH, magazine editor; b. Bklyn., Jan. 11, 1942; d. Herbert Daniel Suesholtz and Shirley (Burrows) Alter; m. Robert J. Levin, May 10, 1967 (dec. May 1976); m. 2d Arthur M. Cooper, June 9, 1979. B.A., Syracuse U., 1963. Asst. editor Redbook Mag., N.Y.C., 1964-65, assoc. editor, 1966-70, sr. editor, 1971-76, assoc. articles editor, 1976-78; articles editor Ladies Home Jour., N.Y.C., 1978-80; editor-in-chief Mademoiselle Mag., N.Y.C., 1978—. Recipient citation for gen. excellence Am. Soc. Journalists and Authors, 1982. Mem. Am. Soc. Mag. Editors, Media Women. Jewish. Office: Mademoiselle Magazine 350 Madison Ave New York NY 10017

LEVIN, BARBARA REUBEN, artist; b. Hartford, Conn., Aug. 27, 1932; d. David Neville and Sadye (Aaron) Reuben; m. Ira Alexander Levin, Aug. 30, 1953; children—Nancy, Susan, Jacqueline, Jane. B.A., Brown U., 1954; M.A.L.S., Wesleyan U., 1983. One woman shows include: Slater Mus., Norwich, Conn., 1973, Gallery on Green, Canton, Conn., 1974, John Slade Ely House, New Haven, 1975, U. Conn., Waterbury, 1976, Hartford Jewish Community Ctr. Galleries, Conn., 1979, Zilkha Gallery, Ctr. for the Arts, Wesleyan U., Middletown, Conn., 1982, Promenade Gallery, Bushnell Meml., Hartford, 1983, Wall Focus Art, Chester, Conn., 1985, Hartford Coll. Women, 1986; exhibited in group shows: Greater Hartford Civic & Arts Festival, Springfield Coll., U. Conn., Conn. Acad. of Fine Arts, Slater Mus. Art Show, Wadsworth Atheneum, George Walter Vincent Smith Art Mus., New Britain Mus. Art, Nat. Assn. of Women Artists, Nat. Acad. Design, 150th Ann. Exhbn.; represented in permanent collections. Group, Curator, Beth El Internat. Art Exhbn., Hartford, 1977-80; art dir., cons. Emanuel Synagogue, Hartford, 1981—; trustee Hartford Conservatory of Mus. and Dance, 1983—. Recipient Enfield Art Festival awards, 1965, 66; Granby Art Festival first prize watercolor award, 1966, Podorowsky award, 1975, 77, Ward Mfg. award 1980, Beth El Invitational. Mem. Nat. Assn. Women Artists (Doris Kreindler award 1976), Conn. Acad. of Fine Arts (Second Conn. Acad. Prize, 1964), Conn. Watercolor Soc. (Sage-Allen Prize 1972, William Hoppin Prize, 1978, Hartford Framing Co. award 1973, Gallery on The Green awards 1971, 76), Conn. Women Artists, Inc. (award 1963, patrons prize for Best Landscape 1965, painting prize 1971, Color Mart Prize 1972, Slater Meml. Mus. award 1973, Mechanics award 1981, Grumbacher Silver Medal 1983, Mechanics Savs. Bank award 1985), New Haven Paint and Clay Club, Inc. (1st prize 1979, Wintonbury Art League, Grumbacher Gold Medallion for Painting 1984). Avocation: distance swimming. Home: 28 Fox Chase Ln West Hartford CT 06107

LEVIN, BETSY, lawyer, educator, administrator; b. Balt., Dec. 25, 1935; d. M. Jastrow and Alexandra (Lee) L. A.B., Bryn Mawr Coll. (Pa.), 1956; LL.B., Yale U., 1966. Bar: D.C. 1967, Colo. 1982. Law clk., Judge Sobeloff U.S. Ct. Appeals (4th cir.), Balt., 1966-67; spl. asst. to Arthur J. Goldberg, U.S. ambassador to UN, N.Y.C., 1967-68; dir. edn. studies The Urban Inst., Washington, 1968-73; prof. law Duke U., 1973-80; gen. counsel U.S. Dept. Edn., Washington, 1980-81; prof. law U. Colo., Boulder, 1981—, dean, 1981—; disting. vis. prof. U. Western Australia, Perth, 1983. Editor: Future Directions for School Finance Reform, 1975; (with W. Hawley) The Courts, Social Science and School Desegregation, 1977; co-author: Educational Policy and the Law, 1982. Mem. Colo. State Banking Bd., 1982-85. White House Fellow, 1967-68. Fellow Colo. Bar Found., Am. Bar Found.; mem. Colo. Bar Assn. (bd. govs. 1981—), Soc. Am. Law Tchrs. (nat. bd. dirs. 1981—), Am. Law Inst. (mem. council 1983—), Assn. Am. Law Schs. (mem. exec. com. 1983-86). Club: Women's Forum Colo., Inc. Office: Univ Colo Law Sch Campus Box 401 Boulder CO 80309

LEVIN, DEBBE ANN, lawyer; b. Cin., Mar. 11, 1954; d. Abram Asher and Selma Ruth (Herlands) L. B.A., Washington U., St. Louis, 1976; J.D., U. Cin., 1979; LL.M., NYU, 1983. Bar: Ohio. Staff atty. U.S. Ct. Appeals 6th Circuit, Cin., 1979-82; assoc. Schwartz, Manes & Ruby Co., L.P.A., Cin., 1983—; lectr. Cin. Tax Conf., 1984, 85. Recipient Judge Alfred Mack prize U. Cin., 1979. Mem. ABA, Cin. Bar Assn., Ohio Bar Assn., Order of Coif. Office: Schwartz Manes & Ruby Co LPA 36 E 4th St Cincinnati OH 45202

LEVIN, GAIL, author, photographer, educator; b. Atlanta, Feb. 19, 1948; d. Barron and Shirley (Sunshine) Levin. B.A., Simmons Coll., 1969; M.A., Tufts U., 1970; Ph.D., Rutgers U., 1976. Instr. New Sch. for Social Research, N.Y.C., 1973-75, Bernard Baruch Coll., CUNY, 1974; asst. prof. art history Conn. Coll., New London, 1975-76; vis. prof. art history Grad. Center CUNY, 1979-80; curator Whitney Mus. Am. Art, N.Y.C., 1976-84; vis. prof. Nesbit Coll. Design, Drexel U., 1985-86; asst. prof. art histroy Baruch Coll., 1986—; producer, host Art at Issue, Manhattan Cable TV, 1985—. Author: Abstract Expressionism: The Formative Years 1978; Synchromism and American Color Abstraction, 1910-25, 1978; Edward Hopper: The Complete Prints, 1979; Edward Hopper as Illustrator, 1979; Edward Hopper: The Art and the Artist, 1980; Edward Hopper, 1984; author, photographer: Hoppers Places, 1985; contbr. articles to profl. jours.; one-person shows: Kingston Artists Group, Gallery Rondout, 1984; Kennedy Galleries, Inc., N.Y.C., 1985, Jane Voorhees Zimmerli Art Mus., 1985, Meml. Art Gallery, U. Rochester, 1985, Fay Gold Gallery, Atlanta, Barridoff Gallery, Portland, 1986, Cedar Rapids Art Mus., 1986; group shows Catskill Ctr. for Photography, Woodstock, N.Y., 1985, A.I.R. Gallery, N.Y.C., 1985. Recipient Alumnae Achievement award Simmons Coll., 1986. Mem. Coll. Art Assn., Pen Freedom to Write, Internat. Assn. Art Critics. Address: 125 E 84th St New York NY 10028

LEVIN, IRENE STAUB, librarian; b. Bklyn., Sept. 30, 1928; d. Harry and Regina (Klein) Staub; B.A., Hunter Coll., CUNY, 1949; M.L.S., L.I.U., 1969; m. Harold E. Levin, Nov. 19, 1950; children—Alan, Leslie, Kim, Paula. Reference librarian and young adults Henry Waldinger Library, Valley Stream, N.Y., 1969—, program coordinator public relations, 1976—; cons. on Jewish books and libraries. Trustee, Sisterhood Temple B'nai Israel of Elmont, 1969-71, Temple B'nai Israel of Elmont, 1982. Recipient Library Public Relations Council award, 1973. Mem. Nassau County Library Assn., Assn. Jewish Libraries (editor Bull., 1973-83, Newsletter, 1978—), Am. Mizrachi Women, Hadassah. Contbr. to Contemporary Literary Criticism, Vol. 13, 1979. Office: Henry Waldinger Library 60 Verona Pl Valley Stream NY 11580

LEVIN, JEANETTE BROOKS, market researcher, travel agt., property mgmt. co. exec.; b. Buffalo, Aug. 5, 1930; d. Morris Jacob and Anna Pearl (Orzech) Brooks; student U. Buffalo, 1950-58, SUNY, Buffalo, 1965-70; cert. Guided Observation Tchr. Program, Cheektowaga (N.Y.) Schs., 1968; m. Frank Levin, July 11, 1954; children—Arnold, Robert, David, Susan. Adult edn. tchr. Cleveland Hill Sch., Cheektowaga, 1965-68; founder, owner, prin. Buffalo Survey & Research, Inc., 1965—; property mgmt. agt. Jackson Sq. Assos., Buffalo, 1978—; pres., mgr. Buffalo Survey Travel Tours, 1978—; cons. politics, image-making for candidates, 1974—. Pres., Temple Shaarey Zedek Sisterhood, Buffalo, 1977-78, Past Pres.'s Council, 1981-83. Honoree Temple Shaarey Zedek Ann. Ball, 1977; recipient citation for ch. worker of week Amherst Bee, 1978, citations for high degree of accuracy in polling Buffalo Evening News, 1971, 81. Mem. Mktg. Research Assn., Am. Assn. Public Opinion Research, Am. Mktg. Assn., Am. Contract Bridge League. Columnist Buffalo. Jewish Rev., 1976-80; media pollster Buffalo newspaper and TV; survey on U.S. tourism, 1973. Home: 324 Crosby Blvd Buffalo NY 14226 Office: 1255 Eggert Rd Buffalo NY 14226

LEVIN, LUBBE, university administrator; b. Wels, Austria; came to U.S., 1949, naturalized, 1955; d. Charles S. and Sonia Levin; student U. Nantes (France), 1966; A.B. with gt. distinction, Stanford U., 1967; M.A., U. Calif., Berkeley, 1968, Ph.D. in French, 1973; m. David Medlinsky. Asst. prof. French, Washington U., St. Louis, 1973-75; mem. staff systemwide adminstrn. U. Calif., 1976—, dir. policy devel., spl. asst. to v.p., 1979—, dir. acad. and staff employee relations, 1982-83, asst. v.p. acad. and staff employee relations, 1983—; lectr. French, U. Calif., Berkeley, 1980—. Calif. State scholar, 1965-66; NDEA fellow, 1971-72; faculty Research grantee Washington U., 1974. Mem. Acad. Academic Personnel Adminstrn., Indsl. Relations Research Assn., NOW, MLA, Calif. Women in Govt., Phi Beta Kappa. Author articles in field. Office: 191 University Hall U Calif Systemwide Adminstrn Berkeley CA 94720

LEVIN, MARLENE, human resource consulting company executive, educator; b. Detroit, Oct. 7, 1934; d. Louis and Cele (Drapkin) Bertman; m. Jerome J. Goodman, Apr. 4, 1954 (dec. Mar. 1962); children—Bennett J., Marc R.; m. Herbert R. Levin, June 7, 1967. Student U. Miami, 1952-53; B.A., Coll. of New Rochelle, 1975; M.P.A., NYU, 1978. Cert. human resource mgr. Asst. adminstr. Richmond Children Ctr., Yonkers, N.Y., 1973-74; research assoc. Westchester Country Dept. Mental Health, N.Y., 1975-80, clinic adminstr., 1980-82; founder, pres. The Phoenix Group, Armonk, N.Y., 1982—; adj. prof. Iona Coll., New Rochelle, N.Y., 1978—; cons. Social Area Research, Scarsdale, N.Y., 1983-84; lectr./trainer Volvo of Am., Inc., Rockleigh, N.J., 1983-84, Lederle Labs., Spring Valley, N.Y., 1984—. Contbr. articles on sociol. subjects to profl. jours. Mem. Mental Health Council, Mount Kisco, N.Y., 1981-83, Council for Youth, Armonk, 1984-85; mem. legis. adv. com. N.Y. State 37th Dist., 1984. Mem. Nat. Staff Devel. Council, NOW (v.p. White Plains 1978-80). Democrat. Jewish. Avocation: stamp collecting. Home: 14 Day Rd Armonk NY 10504 Office: Phoenix Group Ltd 14 Day Rd Armonk NY 10504

LEVIN, SUSAN R. RAVITZ, interior designer; b. Phila., Feb. 7, 1949; d. Ben and Esther (Miller) Klein; m. Steven Jay Ravitz, May 10, 1970 (div.); children—Jason Allen, Shawn Darren, Brett Justin; m. Harvey Levin, Dec. 26, 1985. B.A. in Art Edn., Tyler Sch. Art, Temple U., 1971. Art tchr. Cherry Hill High Sch., N.J., 1971-72; profl. artist Designs by Susan, Cherry Hill, 1971-76; owner, instr. South Jersey Acad. of Art, Cherry Hill, 1974-76; interior designer Touch of Class Interior Designs, Cherry Hill, 1977-86, Phila., 1985—. Bd. trustees Jewish Community Ctr., Cherry Hill, 1980-81; co-chmn. First Annual Cultural Arts Program, Cherry Hill, 1981; com. officer Women's Inst. for Self Enrichment, Cherry Hill, 1976-81, chmn., 1979-80. Mem. Cherry Hill C. of C., N.J. Assn. Women Bus. Owners. Jewish. Avocations: Painting; reading. Home: 516 Gatewood Rd Cherry Hill NJ 08003 Office: Touch of Class Interior Designs 710 S 5th St Philadelphia PA 19147

LEVIN, TOBE JOYCE, educator; b. Long Branch, N.J., Feb. 16, 1948; d. M. William and Janice M. (Metz) Levin; B.A. summa cum laude, Ithaca Coll., 1970; M.A., N.Y. U. in Paris, 1973; maîtrise, U. Paris, 1974; M.A., Cornell U., 1977, Ph.D., 1979; m. Stephen Edward Richards, Aug. 7, 1979 (div. 1985); m. Christoph Alfred Baron von Gleichen-Russwurm, Dec. 17, 1985. Teaching asst. Cornell U., Ithaca, N.Y., 1973-75; reader, reviewer fgn. publs. Frauenoffensive Verlag, Munich, W. Ger., 1977—; tchr. French, Munich elem. schs., 1977-79; lectr. Cornell U., 1979; lectr. dept. English, Univ. Coll., European div. U. Md., Heidelberg, W. Ger., 1979—, Am. studies U. Frankfurt, 1986—. Active in W. Ger. women's movement. Recipient various scholarships and fellowships. Mem. MLA, Nat. Women's Studies Assn., African Studies Assn., West German Women's Studies Assn., ACLU, Fund for a Democratic Majority, Amnesty for Women, Terre des Femmes, Assn. for Women in Devel., Assn. Ams. Resident Overseas, NOW, Phi Kappa Phi. Democrat. Jewish. Co-editor: Materialien zur Unterstutzung von Aktionsgruppen gegen Klitorisbeschneidung, 1979; contbg. editor Women's Studies Quar.; contbr. articles to jours. Home: Martin-Luther Strasse 35 6000 Frankfurt 60 Federal Republic of Germany Office: U Md European Div Im Bosseldorn 30 69 Heidelberg Federal Republic of Germany

LEVINE, BARBARA ROSEN, acquisition/development manager; b. Rutland, Vt., Mar. 14, 1934; d. David Solomon and Pearl (Seff) Rosen; m. Robert I. Levine, June 12 1955; children—Marc, Gary. B.S. in Occupational Therapy, Columbia U., 1955. Registered occupational therapist, N.Y., NJ. Dir. pub. relations U.S. Navy Ship's Stores, Yokosuka, Japan, 1956-58; dir. occupational therapy Roosevelt Hosp., Edison, N.J., 1964-66; editor in chief Am. Jour. Occupational Therapy, N.Y.C., 1966-68; cons. N.Y. Occupational Therapy Assn., N.J. Occupational Therapy Assn., West Bergen Mental Health Assn., Hackensack Hosp. (N.J.), others, 1969-79; acquisition devel. mgr. Xerox Learning Systems, Stamford, Conn., 1980—; cons. Family Counseling, Jr. League/ARC, Infant Devel. Pilot Program, Ridgewood, N.J., 1975-78. Bd. dirs. LWV, Metuchen, N.J., Ridgewood, N.J.; bd. dirs. Family Counseling Service, Ridgewood, 1974-78. Mem. Am. Soc. Tng. Devel., Nat. Soc. Performance Instrn. Republican. Clubs: Upper Ridgewood Tennis, Innis Arden Country. Editor-in-chief: Am. Jour. of Occupational Therapy, 1966-68. Office: Xerox Learning Systems 1600 Summer St Stamford CT 06904

LEVINE, BETTE ANN, marketing executive; b. Cin., Oct. 7, 1945; d. Milton Judson and Janet Pearl (Pomerantz) Rappoport; m. Steven Myron Levine, Oct. 26, 1968; children—Scott Howard, Brad Charles. B.S.B.A., Washington U., 1967. Research asst. Grey Advt., N.Y.C., 1967-68; econs. advisor HUD/Model Cities, San Antonio, 1969-70; sr. research assoc. Dancer Fitzgerald Sample, N.Y.C., 1971-73; ptnr. Fine, Travis & Levine, N.Y.C., 1974-78; pres., chief exec. officer Mktg. Perceptions, Inc., Englewood Cliffs, N.J., 1979—. Mem. Mortar Bd., Beta Gamma Sigma. Avocations: tennis; fishing; biking. Home: 2100 Linwood Ave #19W Fort Lee NJ 07024 Office: Marketing Perceptions 15 Engle St Englewood NJ 07631

LEVINE, DIANE ENID, aviation market researcher, publisher; b. N.Y.C., Dec. 31, 1947; d. Coleman and Jeannette (Sheifer) Lustig; m. Bruce Levine, Apr. 14, 1966; children—Shari Robin, Dawn Michele. Student Bklyn. Coll., 1965-68, Queen's Coll., 1972-74. Researcher Vance A/C Brokers, Hawthorn, N.J., 1978-80; market research aide Exec. Air Fleet, Teterboro, N.J., 1980-82; founder, pres. Amstat Corp., Fair Haven, N.J., 1982—; founder, chief exec. officer Stratus, Inc., Red Bank, N.J., 1985—. Mem. Nat. Assn. Female Execs. Avocations: painting; gardening; tennis. Home: 6 Popomora Dr Rumson NJ 07760 Office: Stratus Inc 68 White St N Red Bank NJ 07760

LEVINE, ELLEN R., magazine executive; b. Feb. 19; d. Eugene and Jean Jacobson; ed. Wellesley Coll.; m. Richard V. Levine; children—Daniel, Peter. Reporter, The Record Newspaper, N.J. 1964-70; formerly food and decorating editor Cosmopolitan mag., N.Y.C; now v.p., editor-in-chief Woman's Day mag., N.Y.C.; dir. N.J. Bell Telephone Co. Trustee, Elisabeth Morrow Sch.; Englewood, N.J.; mem. U.S. Atty. Gen.'s Commn. on Pornography. Named to YWCA Acad. of Women Achievers, 1982; honor award Girl Scout Council Bergen County, N.J., 1984; Woman of Achievement award N.J. State Fedn. Women's Clubs and Douglass Coll. of Rutgers U. Office: 1515 Broadway St New York NY 10036

LEVINE, ESTHER MAE, ins. agy. exec.; b. Walker, Minn., 1936; d. Ervin P. and Marjorie E. Hansen; student in ins. Broward Community Coll., 1975-77. Am. Inst. Property and Liability Underwriters, 1975-80, Ga. State U., 1978-80; m. J.J. Levine, 1973. Underwriter, J. Kenneth King Ins., Davie, Fla., 1964-67, Fast & Co., Ft. Lauderdale, Fla., 1967-72; agt. RISE/Paige Ins., Pompano, Fla., 1972-78, regional sales dir., 1976-78; regional sales rep. RISE/Warren & Welsh, Atlanta, 1978-82, resident v.p., 1981—. C.P.C.U. Mem. Ins. Women Broward County, Cars and Trucks Rental and Leasing Assn., Am. Car Rental Assn., Nat. Assn. Female Execs. (network dir.), Ga. Soc. C.P.C.U.s, Nat. Women's Automotive Assos. Republican. Contbr. articles to profl. jours.; sign lang. interpreter. Office: 4501 Circle 75 Pkwy Suite 1260 Atlanta GA 30339

LEVINE, HELEN SAXON (MRS. NORMAN D. LEVINE), med. technologist; b. San Francisco; d. Ernest M. Saxon and Ann S. Dippel; A.B., U. Ill., 1939; m. Norman D. Levine, Mar. 2, 1935. Supr. lab. San Francisco Dept. Pub. Health Tb Sanatorium, 1944-46, U. Ill. Health Services, Urbana, 1952-65; research asso. in immunobiology, zoology dept. U. Ill., 1965—. Mem. AAUP, AAAS, Am. Heart Assn., Ill. Acad. Sci., Ill. Pub. Health Assn., Am. Soc. Med. Technologists, Am. Soc. Clin. Pathologists, Sigma Delta Epsilon. Research and publs. on devel. nematode antigens. Home: 702 LaSell Dr Champaign IL 61822 Office: Morrill Hall U Ill Urbana IL 61801

LEVINE, JANIS E., financial analyst; b. Akron, Ohio, Apr. 7, 1953; d. Paul and Sarah (Levin) L.; student U. Cin., 1971-73; B.S. in Acctg., U. Akron, 1975; M.B.A., Xavier U., 1978. Acctg. intern Price Waterhouse & Co., Cleve., 1974-75; systems acct. Mead Corp., Cin., 1975-77; internal auditor, sr. capital expenditures analyst Champion Internat. Corp., Stamford, Conn., 1977—. Vol., Headstart and ARC; adv. Jr. Achievement; mem. Young Republicans. Recipient Young Citizens Achievement award for Headstart, 1969. Mem. Women in Mgmt., Bus. and Profl. Women, Young Leadership Council, Nat. Assn. Female Execs., Stamford Forum for World Affairs, Westport-Weston Arts Council, Assn. M.B.A. Execs., Nat. Assn. Accts. (community programs dir.), AAUW, Am. Jewish Congress, B'nai B'rith Women Beta Alpha Psi (sec.). Office: Champion International Corp 1 Champion Plaza Stamford CT 06921

LEVINE, JOANN, civic organization executive; b. Cin., Apr. 3, 1943; d. Jerome and Molly (Lucas) Apseloff; m. Marc Samuel Levine, Jan. 29, 1965; children—Ami Jennifer, Shelley, Benjamin. Student, Ohio State U., 1963-66, U. Houston, 1981. Sec., Ohio State U., Columbus, 1966-67, sec., treas. United DC Inc., Houston, 1981—. Mem. Nat. Assn. Female Execs., Orgn. Rehab. and Tng. Jewish. Club: Hadassah (Houston). Avocations: reading; tennis. Home: 6235 Queensloch Houston TX 77096 Office: United DC Inc 8947 Market St Houston TX 77029

LEVINE, NATHALIE CHRISTIAN, ballet adminstr., educator; b. Las Animas, Colo., July 21, 1929; d. Fleming Vincent and Juanita Jeanne (Jobe) Christian; B.A. in Polit. Sci. magna cum laude, UCLA, 1958; ballet student Mia Slavenska, Vincenzo Celli, Rozelle Frey, Bronislava Nijinska, Valentina Pereyslavec, Michel Panaieff, Errol Addison and Pamela May (Royal Ballet Sch.), Nora Kiss (Paris); m. Victor T. LeVine, July 19, 1958; children—Theodore Vincent, Nicole Jeanette. Soloist profl. dance cos. including Ballets de Los Angeles, 1948-49, Ballet Concerto, 1947 51, Radio City Music Hall, 1952-53, musical summer stock, Calif. and N.J.; dancer TV and theater prodns. and films including Greatest Show on Earth, Samson and Delilah; tchr. Wilcoxon Sch. of Dance, Los Angeles, 1946-48, Sutro-Seyler Studio, Los Angeles, 1949-51, Brown Gables Conservatory of the Arts, Los Angeles, 1952-61, Ecole de Danse, Yaounde, Cameroun, 1961-62, with Michel Simms, St. Louis, 1963-67, Dawn Quist Sch. of Dance, Accra, Ghana, 1969-70, Washington U., St. Louis, 1968-69, 70-71, Nathalie Le Vine Acad. Ballet, St. Louis, 1964—; guest tchr. Calif., Hawaii, Ind., 1955—; choreographer for prodns. including Ballet Concerto, Los Angeles, 1950, classical ballet groups Los Angeles and St. Louis, 1948—, St. Louis Dance Theater, 1966-72, Met. Ballet of St. Louis; co-founder, co-artistic dir. St. Louis Dance Theater, 1966-72; founder, artistic dir. Met. Ballet of St. Louis, 1974—. Organizer dance programs Montessori Sch., Chesterfield, Mo., Step-by-Step Pre-Sch., University City, 1973-78; participant planning and prodns. St. Louis Bicentennial, summer 1976, Dance Concert Soc. Dance Week, St. Louis, 1978, 79; organizer Dance Camp of the Arts, Jewish Community Centers Assn., St. Louis, 1977; co-planner, organizer Dance Workshops, St. Louis, 1977, 78; cons. Phelps County Dance Assn. and Rolla (Mo.) Bd. of Parks and Recreation, 1978—. Mem. Nat. Soc. Arts and Letters, Phi Beta Kappa. Office: 11607 Olive Blvd Saint Louis MO 63141

LEVINE, REBECCA-SUE, lawyer; b. N.Y.C., July 1, 1946; d. Isaac and Jeanette (Katz) Kurash; m. Paul Edward Levine, Dec. 22, 1968 (dec.). B.S.J., Ohio U., 1967; J.D., Bklyn. Law Sch., 1982. Bar: N.Y. 1983. Editor-in-chief Fairchild Publs., N.Y.C., 1969-78; adj. instr. journalism Fashion Inst. Tech., N.Y.C., 1972—; editor Booke and Co., N.Y.C., 1983-85; sole practice law, N.Y.C. and Forest Hills, N.Y., 1985—. Pres. Quality-Ruskin Tenants Fedn., Forest Hills, N.Y., 1974, 75; fundraiser Mental Health Assn. Greater N.Y., 1976—; vol. Humane Soc. N.Y., 1978-79; active Bronx Zoo, Mus. Natural History. Mem. ABA, N.Y. State Bar Assn., Women in Communications; Networks Unltd., Mortar Bd., Chimes.

LEVINE, ROSALYN, investment banker; b. Bridgeport, Conn., July 13, 1952; d. Benjamin and Sally (Lifszyc) L.; m. Lazaro N. Pomeraniec, Aug. 26, 1978; children—Danielle Margot, Isaac Jonathan. B.A., Barnard Coll., 1975; M.B.A., Columbia U., 1977, M.P.H., 1980. Assoc. Loeb Rhoades & Co., N.Y.C., 1977-80; v.p. pub. fin. Wertheim & Co., Inc., N.Y.C., 1980—; vis. instr. Columbia U. Sch. Pub. Health, 1979; alumni cons. Barnard Coll., N.Y.C., 1975—, Columbia U. Grad. Sch. Bus., N.Y.C., 1977—. Bd. dirs. Coop. Housing Corp., 1983—. Mem. Nat. Assn. Securities Dealers. Jewish. Avocations: travel; cooking. Home: 65 E 76th St New York NY 10021 Office: Wertheim & Co Inc 200 Park Ave New York NY 10166

LEVINE, SANDRA MARY, advertising and marketing agency executive; b. Newark, May 30, 1935; d. Samuel P. and Josephine E. (Sinisgalli) Marzano; B.A., Rutgers U., 1957; m. Sidney I. Levine, Apr. 5, 1973; children—Joseph B. Martinez, Samuel A. Martinez. Exec. v.p. Staflex Co., N.Y.C., 1968-83; prin. SML Levine Enterprises, Inc., N.Y.C., 1983—. Mem. Internat. Assn. Clothing Designers (exec. dir.), Women's Bus. Club. N.Y. (founder, pres.), B'nai B'rith, Hadassah. Office: SML Levine Enterprises Inc 450 7th Ave Suite 808 New York NY 10123

LEVINE, SUZANNE BRAUN, magazine editor; b. N.Y.C., June 21, 1941; d. Imre and Esther (Bernson) Braun; m. Robert Franklin Levine, Apr. 2, 1967; 1 son, Joshua. Grad. with honors, Radcliffe Coll., 1963. Editor, writer, Seattle mag., 1963-65; with Time/Life Books, 1965-67, Mademoiselle mag., 1967-69, McCall's mag., 1969-71, Sexual Behavior mag., 1971-72; mng. editor Ms. mag., N.Y.C., 1972—; vis. lectr. Yale U., Poynter fellow, 1982; journalism instr. NYU; vis. Woodrow Wilson fellow, 1983; speaker Chautauqua Instn., 1984. Co-editor: The Decade of Women: A Ms. History of the Seventies in Words and Pictures, 1980; exec. producer TV spl.: She's Nobody's Baby: A History of American Women in the 20th Century (George Foster Peabody award for journalism); contbr. articles to publs. including Ladies Home Jour., Cosmopolitan, Today's Health; lectr. in field. Mem. Am. Soc. Mag. Editors (exec. com.), Women's Action Alliance (exec. com.), Women's Media Group (founding). Office: Ms Found for Edn and Communication 119 W 40th St New York NY 10018*

LEVINE, YARI, artist; jewelry designer; b. Minsk, Russia; came to U.S. 1927; d. Samuel and Lillian (Lapidus) Turboff; m. Samuel S. Levine, June 10, 1945; children—Steven Robert, Mark Eric. Cert. in Fine Arts, Pratt Inst., 1939; student Am. Artists Sch., 1941, New Sch. Social Research, 1942-43. One-woman shows at: Ward Egleston Galleries, 1964, Washington Hebrew Congregation, N.Y.C., 1959, Brandeis U., 1966, U. Wis., 1969, Union of Am. Hebrew Congregations, 1953, 66, Nassau Community Coll., 1970, Art and Design Atelier, 1980, Hebrew Tabernacle, 1981; exhibited in group shows at: Creative Gallery, John Myers Gallery, 1952, A.C.A. Gallery, 1954, 55, 56, Nat. Acad. Galleries, 1953-78, Internat. Jewish Conf. Exhibit, Los Angeles, 1955, Suffolk Mus., 1957, 300th Houston Commemorative Exhibit, 1957, Art League of L.I., 1957, Heckscher Mus., 1962, Lido Gallery, 1970, Harbor Gallery, 1974, Hudson Guild Gallery, 1980, Artists Equity of N.Y., 1980, Lever House, 1983, Jacob K. Javits Fed. Bldg., 1984, 85; works represented in permanent collections at House of Living Judaism of Union of Am. Hebrew Congregations, N.Y.C., Westchester Reform Temple, Temple Sinai of Washington, U. Wis., others. Named Artist of Jewish Yr., Union of Am. Hebrew Congregations, 1966. Fellow Internat. Inst. Arts and Letters; mem. Artists Equity of N.Y., Nat. Assn. Women Artists, Jewish Visual Artists Assn. of Nat. Council on Arts in Jewish Life, Internat. Platform Assn. Address: 63 Hamlet Rd Levittown NY 11756 Studio: 24 Fifth Ave Suite 214 New York NY 10011

LEVINE-SHNEIDMAN, CONALEE, psychologist; b. N.Y.C., Feb. 22, 1930; d. Robert and Lillian (Kurlander) Levine; m. J. Lee Shneidman, Sept. 3, 1961; children—Philip, Jack. Student Black Mountain Coll. (N.C.); Ph.D., NYU, 1959. Cert. in psychoanalysis and psychotherapy. Pvt. practice psychoanalysis and psychotherapy, N.Y.C., 1961—; assoc. prof. psychology NYU, 1965-70; adj. assoc. prof. Yeshiva U., 1970-73. USPHS grantee, 1958. Mem. Am. Psychol. Assn., Am. Orthopsychiat. Assn., N.Y. State Psychol. Assn., Psychoanalytic Soc. of Postdoctoral Program for Tng. and Research. Office: 27 W 86th St New York NY 10024

LEVINSON, ADA ROBERTA, health education consultant; b. Bklyn., Feb. 28, 1949. R.N., St. Johns Episcopal Sch. Nursing, 1968; B.S., St. Joseph's Coll., North Windham, Maine, 1984. Asst. head nurse emergency services St. John's Episcopal Hosp., Bklyn., 1968-69; psychiat nurse Interboro Gen. Hosp., Bklyn., 1969-70; team leader medicine/surgery/orthpedics and gynecology N.Y. Med. Coll., Flower Fifth Ave Hosp., N.Y.C., 1970-72; head nurse communications N.Y.C. Health and Hosp. Corp. Emergency Med. Services, 1972-73, supr. nurses emergency med. services tng. div., Maspeth, N.Y., 1973-80, dir. edn. program emergency med. services tng. div., Queens Hosp. Ctr., N.Y.C., 1980-81, exec. adminstr. Emergency Med. Services Acad., Queens Hosp. Ctr., 1981-86; co-founder, exec. dir. Wagler Assocs., health edn. cons., 1986—; cons. health services div. N.Y.C. Emergency Med. Service, Maspeth, 1983—; liaison from emergency med. service to Bur. Emergency Health Services, N.Y. State Dept. Health, Albany, 1981—. Mem. N.Y. State Nurses Assn., Nat. Assn. Emergency Med. Technicians, N.Y. Acad. Scis., N.Y.C. Regional Emergency Med. Services Council. Democrat.

LEVINSON, DOROTHY JANICE, jr. high sch. tchr.; b. Laurel, Miss., Feb. 1, 1918; s. Solomon Louis and Bessie Marian (Mindel) Wisenberg; B.A., Rice Inst., Houston, 1937; M.A., Northeastern Ill. U., Chgo., 1970, Northwestern U., 1974; m. Nathan Levinson, Jan. 11, 1945 (dec.); children—Irving Walter, Robert David. Tchr., Houston public schs., 1938-44, Edgewood Jr. High Sch., Highland Park, Ill., 1967—. Pres. Volta PTA, Chgo., 1959-61. Served with WAVES, 1944-45. Mem. Nat. Council Tchrs. English, NEA, Ill. Congress Parents and Tchrs. (dist. publs. chmn. 1961-62), Hadassah, Phi Beta Kappa. Jewish. Home: 8000 Foster Ln Niles IL 60648

LEVINSON, ROCHELLE FOX, cleaning company executive; b. Chattanooga, May 30, 1949; d. Isaac Israel and Bertha (Klempner) Fox; m. Morton Allen Levinson, July 12, 1970 (dec. 1982); children—Jason Franklyn, Lori Anne. Student Memphis State U., 1967-68, Draughon's Bus. Coll., 1968-69. Pres. Clean Team, Inc., Arlington, Tex, 1978—. Active Widowed Persons Services, Arlington Women's Shelter Aux., Mid-Cities Jewish Community Ctr., Congregation Beth Shalom Ladies Aux.; bd. dirs. Tarrant county Crime Stoppers, Jewish Singles Community of Tarrant County; mem. nat. panel consumer arbitrators Better Bus. Bur. Mem. Arlington C. of C. (ambassador's com., law, order and justice com.), Fort Worth C. of C., Nat. Assn. Female Execs., Women's Forum, Network for Exec. Women, Single Profl. Men Women. Club: Altrusa (info. chmn. 1985—, yearbook editor 1984-85). Lodge: B'nai Brith (past pres. Mid-Cities Couples). Avocations: dancing traveling; photography. Office: PO Box 3644 Arlington TX 76010

LEVINTON, PAULA HEICHLER, marketing executive; Washington, Oct. 30, 1952; d. Lucian and Muriel Ruth (Nordsiek) Heichler; m. Philip C. Levinton, Aug. 26, 1978; 1 son, Christopher. Student U. Chgo., 1970-72; cert. Institut Africain de Genève, Switzerland, 1973. Asst. dir. agy. and tour sales Hilton Hotels, Washington, 1974-75; mem. staff communications group Am. Bankers Assn., Washington, 1975-76; cons. health care practice Arthur Young & Co., Washington, 1976-78; mgr. health systems documentation Libra Tech., Rockville, Md., 1978-84; mktg. services mgr. Recognition Equipment, McLean, Va., 1984—; instr. public sector mktg., project planning. Mem. Assn. Computing Machinery. Lutheran. Research on computerized mental health info. systems, use of automated documentation aides for health care systems. Home: 14720 Turkey Foot Rd Darnestown MD 20878

LEVIT, SHERRY CHAMOVE, lawyer, city official; b. San Francisco, June 3, 1942; d. Arnold and Elyse (Shirek) Chamove; A.B., Stanford, 1964; postgrad. San Francisco State U., 1974-77; m. Victor B. Levit, Feb. 25, 1962; children—Carson, Victoria. Assoc. Nielsen, Hudgson, Parrinello & Mueller, 1985—. Mem. Belvedere (Calif.) City Council, 1974-83, mayor, 1977-78; mem. exec. com. Assn. Bay Area Govts., 1975-83; mem. San Francisco Bay Conservation and Devel. Commn., 1978-83; mem. Marin County Council of Mayors and Councilmen, 1974-83; chmn. Belvedere Parks and Recreation Commn., 1973-74; mem. Marin County Parks and Recreation Commn., 1977-79; dir. Tiburon Peninsula Adv. Com., 1976—; spl. asst. to San Francisco Mayor Joseph Alioto, 1968-70. Bd. dirs. Tiburon Peninsula Little League Baseball, 1974, coach, 1974-78; coach Tiburon Peninsula Soccer League, 1974-78; mem. women's pub. interest com. San Francisco Symphony Assn., 1966—. Mem. Florence Crittenton Home Women's Aux., San Francisco Lawyer's Wives, San Francisco Mental Health Assn., Calif. Acad. Sci., Tiburon-Belvedere Landmarks Soc., San Francisco Mus. Soc., San Francisco Mus. of Arts Soc. Clubs: Calif. Tennis, Metropolitan, Tiburon Peninsula. Address: 650 California St Suite 2660 San Francisco CA 94108

LEVITAS, MIRIAM C. STRICKMAN, educational center administrator; b. Phila., Aug. 3, 1936; d. Morris and Bella (Barsky) Cherrin; m. Bernard Strickman, June 3, 1956 (dec. 1975); children—Andrew, Brian, Craig, Deron; m. Theodore Clinton Levitas, Apr. 25, 1976; children—Steven, Leslie, Anthony. Student Temple U., 1953-56, LaSalle U., Chgo., 1968. Vice-pres. programming interior design Nat. Home Fashions League, Atlanta, 1974-75; salesman Ga. Bd. Realtors, 1971; adminstr. Stanley H. Kaplan Ednl. Center, Atlanta, 1974-84; owner, pres. Levitas Services, Inc. (Internat. Destinations), Atlanta, 1984—; owner, v.p. Nat. Travel Services and Internat. Destinations, Atlanta, 1984-85; realtor Sotheby's Internat. Realty, 1985—. Soloist piano Paul Whiteman TV, Phila. Youth Orchestra, Frankford Symphony Orch. Pres., Ahavath Achim Sisterhood, Atlanta, 1977-79; mem. Young Women of the Arts Atlanta, Atlanta Symphony, High Mus. Art, Nat. Mus. of Women in Arts (charter), Alliance Theater Atlanta. Phila. Bd. Edn. Scholarship awardee, 1952. Mem. Nat. Assn. Health Professions, Atlanta Bd. Realtors, Nat. Home Fashions League, Nat. Com. for Prevention of Child Abuse, Brandeis Nat. Women (life), Hadassah (life), Nat. Council Jewish Women (life), N'nai Brith (life). Democrat. Jewish.

LEVKOFF, LIZABETH H., real estate investor; b. Miami Beach, Fla., Nov. 13, 1948; d. Jack Irvine and Ruby (Fogel) L.; m. Martin Victor Herzog, Dec. 4, 1974; children—Jacob, Samuel, Luba. B.A., Tulane U., 1970; M.A. in French, NYU, 1971, M.B.A., 1977. Mgmt. trainee Filene's Boston, 1971-73; asst. buyer Bonwit Teller, N.Y.C., 1973-74; prin. Liz Levkoff, N.Y.C., 1977—. Mem. Am. Mizrachi Women. Mem. Council Owner Occupied Housing, Rent Stabilization Assn., Small Property Owners N.Y. Republican. Jewish. Home: 2 E 10th St New York NY 10003 Office: 335 Broadway Room 1100 New York NY 10013

LEVY, ALEXANDRA SUSAN, construction company executive; b. Rockville Centre, N.Y., Apr. 26, 1949; d. Alexander Stanley and Anna Charlotte (Galasieski) Jankoski; m. William Mack Levy, Aug. 12, 1977. Student Suffolk Community Coll., Brentwood, N.Y., 1976; cert. constrn. assoc., Nawic Edn. Found., Fort Worth, 1985. Cert. constrn. assoc., N.Y. Supr., N.Y. Telephone Co., Babylon, 1970-74; v.p. Aabbacco Equipment Leasing Corp., Lindenhurst, N.Y., 1974-81; pres., owner Femi-9 Contracting Corp., Lindenhurst, 1981—. Mem. N.Y. state affirmative action adv. council N.Y. State Dept. Transp., Albany, 1984—; mem. Presdl. Task Force, Washington, 1982—. Served with U.S. Army, 1967-69. Mem. Nat. Assn. Women in Constrn. (founder L.I. chpt., pres. 1983—), Nassau Suffolk Contractors Assn. (sec. 1984—, bd. dirs.), Women Constrn. Owners and Execs., Forum Internat. Exchange. Republican Roman Catholic. Avocations: reading; writing; golfing. Home: 183 Otis Ln West Bayshore NY 11706 Office: Femi-9 Contracting Corp 305 E Sunrise Hwy Lindenhurst NY 11757

LEVY, AUDREE JOAN, artist, gallery executive, art fair organizer; b. Detroit, Apr. 5, 1931; d. Ben and Sophia (Blumberg) Tolmich; m. Kenneth Levy, Mar. 14, 1953 (div. Sept. 1978); children—Sandra, Amy, Marc, David. Student fine arts Soc. Arts and Crafts, Detroit, 1950-52. Group exhbns. include: Ann Arbor (Mich.) Street Art Fair, 1967, Flint (Mich.) Art Fair, 1970-72, State Street Art Fair, Ann Arbor, 1968-73; commnd. portrait Cantor J. Sonenklar Congregation Sharrey Zedek, Southfield, Mich., 1972; interior designer Ruth Schwartz, Southfield, 1968-70; owner Arbor Art Mart, Ann Arbor, Mich., 1971-75; pres. Invitational Art Fairs, Inc., Dallas, 1973—; art fair dir. State St. Area Assn., Ann Arbor, 1968-72. Mem. Dallas 500, Inc., 1983, Nat. Council Jewish Women, 1983. Recipient 1st place Painting award Howell Arts Festival (Mich.), 1970, Flint Art Fair, 1971. Mem. Ann Arbor Art Assn., D-Art Visual Art Ctr., Ann Arbor Profl. Arts Council (show dir.). Jewish. Club: Temple Emanu-El Sisterhood (Dallas). Home: 10629 Park Preston Dallas TX 75230 Office: Invitational Art Fairs Inc 10629 Park Preston Dallas TX 75230

LEVY, BARBARA MINA WEXNER, writer/pub., editor; b. Hot Springs, Ark., Jan. 30, 1927; d. Henry David and Helen Ruth (Loeb) Wexner; A.A., Lindenwood Coll., 1945; student U. Houston, 1958-59; m. Herbert E. Levy, July 25, 1945; children—Barbara Dian, Richard H., Lauren. Feature writer Houston Town, 1957-58; regional editor Boot & Shoe Recorder, Houston, 1958-65; with customer service Scholastic Mag., Englewood Cliffs, N.J., 1966-67; fashion shoe editor Window Shopping World, N.Y.C., 1967-68; women's fashion editor Boot & Shoe Recorder, N.Y.C., 1968-74; pub., editor Barbara's Report/Shoes and. . . , Miami, Fla., 1974—; lectr. in field. Mem. alumnae bd. Lindenwood Coll., 1967-68, v.p., 1969. Mem. Footwear and Accessories Council N.Y.C. (pres. 1973, chmn. bd. 1974, honored for creative contbn. to industry 1982), Fashion Group, Women in Communications. Contbr. articles to profl. jours. Address: 1236 NE 92nd St Miami FL 33138

LEVY, BARBARA RIFKIN, theatre administrator; b. Schenectady, Apr. 25, 1941; d. Sam and Jane E. (Goodman) Rifkin B.S., U. Vt., 1962; postgrad. Ithaca (N.Y.) Coll. Music, Ohio U., U. Ariz.; m. Martin R. Levy, July 21, 1963; children—Douglas M., Mitchell B. Elem. sch. music tchr., Conn., Ohio, 1962-64; music therapist Athens (Ohio) State Hosp., 1964-66; dir. devel. Ariz. Opera, 1974-78; dir. devel. Ariz. Theatre Co., Tucson, 1978—; cons. Found. for Extension and Devel. of Am. Profl. Theatre, Ariz. Commn. on the Arts; mem. adv. com. for model solicitation law project Nat. Assn. Attys. Gen. Mem. Nat. Soc. Fund Raising Execs. (founding pres. Southern Ariz. chpt.), Fund Raising Inst., Nat. Soc. Fund Raising (nat. bd. dirs.). Jewish. Office: 56 W Congress Tucson AZ 85701

LEVY, CHARLOTTE LOIS, lawyer; b. Cin., Aug. 31, 1944; d. Samuel M. and Helen (Lowitz) L.; B.A., U. Ky., 1966; M.L.S., Columbia U., 1969; J.D., No. Ky. U., 1975; bar: Colo. 1979, N.Y. 1985, Ky. 1985; m. Herbert Regenstreif, Dec. 11, 1980; 1 dau., Cara Rachael. Law librarian No. Ky. U., 1971-75; law librarian, assoc. prof. law Pace U. Law Sch., 1975-77; mgr. Fred B. Rothman & Co., Littleton, Colo., 1977-79; law librarian, prof. Bklyn. Law Sch., 1979-85; atty. Cabinet for Human Resources, Commonwealth of Ky., 1985—; adj. prof. Pratt Inst. Grad. Sch. Library and Info. Sci.; cons. in field. Mem. Am. Bar Assn., Ky. Bar Assn., Am. Assn. Law Libraries, Law Library Assn. Greater N.Y. Democrat. Jewish. Author: The Human Body and The Law, 1975; Computer-Assisted Litigation Support, 1984; Library Automation, 1985; bd. editors No. Ky. U. Law Rev., 1974-75. Office: 275 E Main St 4 W Frankfort KY 40621

LEVY, HARRIETTE JOAN, psychotherapist; b. Indpls., Feb. 27, 1940; d. Joseph Mendel and Clara (Craft) Bassler; children—Sydney Michelle, Mark Edward. B.S., Ohio State U., 1961, M.A., 1973. Lic. profl. counselor, social psychotherapist, Tex. State Bd. Examiners. Staff therapist Riverside Meth. Hosp., Columbus, Ohio, 1973-75; part-time practice psychotherapy, Columbus, 1973-75; clin. dir. adolescent ctr. Houston Internat. Hosp., 1975-79; psychotherapist Drs. Ctr. Psychiatry Clinic, 1978-80, Med. Ctr. del Oro Psychiat. Clinic, 1979-81; cons. Drs. Ctr. Psychiatry Clinic, 1981—, Healthcare Services Am., Inc., Birmingham, Ala., 1984—; pvt. practice psychotherapy, Houston, 1981—; co-founder Profl. Devel. Seminars, 1982; psychotherapy cons. Heights Psychiat. Clinic, Houston, 1980—; med. dir. adolescent chem. abuse program Spring Shadow Hosp., 1983—. Contbr. articles to profl. jours. Bd. dirs. Mental Health Assn. Houston/Harris, 1979—, chmn. children's com., 1979-82; vice-chnn. children's adv. council Mental Health/Mental Retardation Authority Houston, 1983—. Named Vol. of Yr., Mental Health Assn. Houston/Harris County, 1982. Mem. Houston Group Psychotherapy Soc., Tex. Psychotherapy Assn. Democrat. Jewish. Office: Heights Psychiatric Clinic 427 W 20th St Houston TX 77008

LEVY, JUDITH AMDUR, lawyer; b. Cleve., Mar. 28, 1940; d. Max and Frances Amdur; B.S., Ind. U., 1962; postgrad. Purdue U., 1968-71; J.D., Valparaiso U., 1976; m. Joel C. Levy, June 4, 1961; children—Janice Ruth, Julie Ann. Bar: Ind. 1976. Mem. Singleton, Levy, Crist and Johnson, Highland, Ind., 1976—; home bound tutor Munster (Ind.) Sch. System. Sec. Munster Human Relations Council, 1968-70; mem. Greater Hammond Community Services, 1977-79; bd. dirs. Lake Area United Way, 1983—; trustuee N.W. Ind. Forum, 1985—; lectr., panelist Ind. Continuing Legal Edn., 1986; mem. Lake County Task Force Calumet Women United Against Rape. Mem. Am. Bar Assn., Fed. Bar Assn., Ind. Bar Assn., Hammond Bar Assn. Jewish. Home: 9124 Walnut Dr Munster IN 46321 Office: 9013 Indianapolis Blvd Highland IN 46322

LEVY, NORMA BERTA, lawyer; b. Denver, Sept. 1, 1943; d. Harry and Dora Ida (Troy) Levy. B.A. cum laude, Mills Coll., 1965; M.A., U. Wis., 1968; J.D., Yale U., 1974. Bar: N.Y. 1975. Evaluation supr. City of N.Y. Manpower Career and Devel. Agy., 1968-69; project mgr. AT&T, N.Y.C., 1969-71, atty., 1975-76; assoc. Skadden Arps, Slate, Meagher & Flom, N.Y.C., 1977-81; assoc. Kissam, Halpin & Genovese, N.Y.C., 1981-83, ptnr., 1984—; del. Spl. Task Force on Donnelly Act, N.Y.C., 1983. Contbr. articles to legal jours. Inst. Study of Poverty fellow, 1968-69. Mem. ABA, Assn. Bar City N.Y. (trade regulation com., chmn. vertical restraints subcom. 1983-86), N.Y. State Bar Assn. (chmn. anti-trust law com., exec. com. sect. 1985—), N.Y. Women's Bar Assn. Clubs. Yale, Dialogue II (N.Y.C.). Home: 142 West End Ave Apt 27L New York NY 10023 Office: Kissam Halpin & Genovese 101 Park Ave New York NY 10178

LEVY, PHYLLIS CHARLOTTE, interior designer, trade showroom executive, product designer; b. Bklyn., Aug. 14, 1929; d. Irving George and Norma Sarah (Tucker) Gross; m. Gilbert Levy, June 25, 1950; children—Jill Levy Brooks Esquire, Fran Enid Levy Katz. A.A., Wilsey Ints., Hempstead, N.Y., 1970. Underwriter Continental Ins. Co., N.Y.C., 1948; legal asst. Consol. Tax Payers, Bklyn., 1949-50; jewelry salesperson Fortunoff's, Westbury, N.Y., 1967-69; owner, designer Phyllis Levy Interiors, Dix Hills, N.Y., 1970-79, Fact & Fantasy Ltd., West Palm Beach, Fla., 1979—. Fund raiser City of Hope, East Meadow, N.Y., 1953-63, del. to pilot ctr., Duarte, Calif., 1965. Jewish. Avocations: collecting art and antiques; watercolor, oil and pastel painting. Office: Fact & Fantasy Ltd D & D Centre 401 Clematis St West Palm Beach FL 33401

LEVY, TIBBIE (MRS. ELI BENNETT LEVY), lawyer, painter; b. N.Y.C., Oct. 29, 1908; d. David and Minnie (Hoffman) Goldstein; A.B., Cornell U., 1929, postgrad., 1929-30; J.D., N.Y. U., 1931; studied with Arshile Gorky, Art Students League, Andre L'Hote, Academic de la Grande Chaumiere, Cornell U., also Vincenzo; m. Eli Bennett Levy, Nov. 19, 1931; children—Lynn (Mrs. Leland S. Zaubler), John Hoffman (dec.). Admitted to N.Y. bar, 1932; pvt. practice of law, N.Y.C., 1932—. Profl. painter under name of Lysan and Tibbie Levy; exhibited one-man shows in N.Y.C., Pa., Paris, Madrid, London, Tokyo; represented numerous permanent museum collections, Phoenix Mus. Art, Witte Mus., San Antonio, Jewish Mus. Hebrew Union Coll., Cin., Evansville (Ind.) Mus. Art and Sci., Boston U., Brandeis U., Cornell U., Ga. Mus., Jewish Mus., Cin., Mus. Modern Art, Miami, Witte Meml. Mus., Tex., George Peabody Mus., Tenn., Princeton, Palm Springs Mus., Barnard Coll., Fairleigh Dickinson U., N.J., Syracuse U., Colgate U., Rutgers U., N.Y. U., U. Notre Dame, Fashion Inst. Tech., Horace Mann Sch., Pace Coll., Drexel Mus., Pa., Passaic Community Coll.; also pvt. and indsl. collections. Pres. patrons council Barnard Sch. for Boys; mem. Speakers Bur., Anti-Defamation League; pres. Freedom chpt., mem. Speakers Bur., B'nai B'rith; pres. Parents Assn. Calhoun Sch.; bd. dirs. Hebrew Kindergarten and Infants Home, NCCJ. Home: 2 Sutton Pl S New York NY 10022

LEW, GINGER, lawyer; b. San Mateo, Calif., Nov. 3, 1948; d. Bing and Suey Bow (Ng) Lew; m. Carl Lennart Ehn, Feb. 2, 1984; children—Melissa, Jeremy. B.A., UCLA, 1970; J.D., U. Calif.-Berkeley, 1974. Bar: Calif. 1974, D.C. 1980. Dep. city atty. Los Angeles, 1974-75; asst. regional counsel U.S. Dept. Energy, San Francisco, 1975-77, dep. regional counsel, 1977-78, chief counsel, 1978-80; dep. asst. sec. for E. Asia, U.S. Dept. State, Washington, 1980-81, spl. advisor, Washington, 1981-82; atty. HUD, Washington, 1983; ptnr. Stovall, Spadlin, Armstrong and Israel, Washington, 1983—. Regional dir. Asian Democratic Caucus, Washington, 1983-84. Recipient Outstanding Achievement award U.S. Dept. State, 1980, 81. Mem. Asian Pacific Bar Assn. (dir. 1981-83), Women's Bar Assn., ABA, Orgn. Chinese Americans, Coalition for a Democratic Majority (dir.), Pi Sigma Alpha. Club: Commonwealth, San Francisco. Office: 1819 H St NW Suite 700 Washington DC 20006

LEW, KAREN LESLIE, writer; b. Washington, Feb. 19, 1942; d. Lyman Littlefield and Betsy Mae (Dekema) Woodman; student San Francisco State Coll., 1960-61, El Camino Jr. Coll., 1966, UCLA, 1967, U. Alaska, Anchorage, 1971, 75, 77, Sheldon Jackson Coll., 1979, Anchorage Community Coll., 1980, 81, 82, 83; m. Dan Wing Lew, Jan. 12, 1962 (div. 1970); children—Kent Charles, Danika Leslie, Mark Daren. Info. specialist ITT Arctic Services, Inc., Anchorage, Alaska, 1969-71; adminstrv. asst., Mike Ellis Advt., Anchorage, 1971; copywriter, continuity dir. sta. KYAK, Anchorage, 1971-72; copywriter, media buyer Graphix West, Anchorage, 1972-73; classified advt. mgr. Anchorage Daily News, 1973-74; media specialist Alaska Native Commn. on Alcoholism/Drug Abuse, 1974-75; copywriter, continuity dir. Sta. KYAK/KGOT, Anchorage, 1976-77; advt. mgr. Alaska Advocate, Anchorage, 1977-78; advt. rep., writer Alaskafest mag., Anchorage, 1979; info. officer Dept. Natural Resources, State of Alaska, Anchorage, 1979-83, Dept. Fish and Game, 1983-85; freelance writer, 1969—; adj. lectr. composition Anchorage Community Coll., 1982; speaker in field ednl. and community groups. First v.p. Anchorage Council on Alcoholism, 1976-77; vol. arts writer; adv. bd. Independence Mine State Historic Park. Recipient various state and nat. awards for writing, 1969-86. Mem. Nat. Fedn. Press Women, Alaska Press Women (v.p., 1973, 85, rec. sec. 1982), Public Relations Soc. Am., Fireweed Mountaineers Ltd. (pres. 1983-84). Unitarian-Universalist. Clubs: Anchorage Chess, U.S. Chess Fedn., Theatre Guild, Anchorage Community Theatre, Audubon Soc. Editor newsletter Alaska State Council on the Arts; arts columnist Alaskafest Mag. Home: PO Box 211470 Auke Bay AK 99821

LEWELLEN, WANDA PAULINE, hospital adminstrator; b. Chandler, Okla., Apr. 13; d. Newell A. and Montie F. (Kanady) Pittser; m. Wallace S. Dobbs, Oct. 2, 1948 (div. Aug. 1956); children—Pamela R. Dobbs Pettigrew, Dawna Kay Dobbs Graham; m. 2d, Bill Lewellen, May 2, 1958. Diploma bus. edn. Nat. Sch. Bus., Oklahoma City, 1950; student Tulsa U., 1964. Stenographer, Okla. State Dept. Health, Oklahoma City, 1950-53; office mgr. YMCA, Oklahoma City, 1953-55; office mgr., dir. personnel Hillcrest Hosp., Oklahoma City, 1955-82, acting adminstr., 1982, dir. human resources, 1982—. Trustee Hillcrest Osteo. Hosp., Oklahoma City, 1984—. Recipient Woman of Yr. award Capitol Hill Am. Bus. Women's Assn., 1977. Mem. Am. Hosp. Assn., Am. Personnel Assn., Okla. Pub. Relations Soc., Okla. Hosp. Assn. (sec. 1978), Okla. Hosp. Pub. Relations Soc., Oklahoma City Personnel Assn., Am. Bus. Women's Assn. (pres. 1963-64), Bus. and Profl. Women's Club. Democrat. Clubs: TIPS (Oklahoma City), Pilot. Home: 1331 Hill Cross Ct Oklahoma City OK 73159 Office: Hillcrest Osteo Hosp 2129 SW 59th St Oklahoma City OK 73119

LEWELLYN, SUZANNE ELLEN, dance educator; b. Bklyn., May 13, 1943; d. John D. and Verna Ellen (Swanson) Bono; div. Mar. 1978; 1 child, Hope Jennifer Schaffer; m. Carl Bryan Lewellyn, Aug. 20, 1983. Rockette, Radio City Music Hall, N.Y.C., 1959-61; dancer Little Me touring co., 1962; owner, operator, tchr. Rockland Sch. Performing Arts, New City, N.Y.; dir. off-ice body conditioning for competition figure skaters Low Tor Ice Ctr., Garnerville, N.Y., 1982—; dir. faculty fitness program Bluefield Sch., East Rampao Sch. Dist., N.Y., 1983; dir. fitness program Citicorp Corp., Rye, N.Y., 1982; owner, operator Aerotonic Fitness Ctr. Star cable TV show: Dance World, 1975. Dir. cassette tape: Aerotonic Fitness, 1985. Com. mem. Helen Hayes Hosp. Charity Ball, West Haverstraw, N.Y., 1984-85. Recipient Fitness award Pres.'s Council on Phys. Fitness, 1982. Mem. Exec. Female Assn., Rockette Alumnae Assn., Dance Educators Am., New City C. of C. Democrat. Roman Catholic. Creator Aerotonics fitness program. Office: Rockland Sch Performing Arts 385 S Main St New City NY 10956

LEWIN, CAROLINE TOEPFER, clinical psychologist; b. Newark, Feb. 17, 1944; d. Chester Leon Throckmorton and Caroline Amanda Lange; B.A. in Psychology (Cleve. Found. scholar), Kent State U., 1965, M.A., 1967, Ph.D. (NIMH fellow), 1969; m. William Lewin II, Sept. 10, 1979; 1 son, Neil Norval. Social worker Fallsview Mental Health Center, 1965, Sagamore Hills Children's Psychiat. Hosp., 1966; psychologist Portage County Welfare Dept., 1966-68; intern Univ. Hosps., Case Western Res. U., 1968; asst. prof., dir. student interns Slippery Rock State Coll., 1969-75; pvt. practice clin. psychology Youngstown, Ohio, 1974-80, Columbus, Ohio, 1980—; chief psychol. cons. Bur. Disability Determination, Bur. Vocat. Rehab.; med. adv. Office Hearings and Appeals, Social Security Adminstrn.; speaker, guest lectr.; condr. workshops; ptnr. Lewin & Rain Jury Selection Cons., 1984—. Mem. Selective Service Bd. 41. Lic. clin. psychologist, Ohio. Mem. Am. Psychol. Assn., Ohio Psychol. Assn., Psi Chi. Editor: Supplementary Readings in Applied Psychology and Human Behavior, 1970; (with Bicknell, Fox, Kirk and Sayre) Environmental Psychology, 1972. Home: 6473 Borr Ave Reynoldsburg OH 43068 Office: PO Box 2485 Columbus OH 43216

LEWIN, ELIZABETH SAMELSON, financial planner; b. Bridgeport, Conn., Feb. 26, 1938; d. Lester and Edith Hecht Samelson; B.A., N.Y. U., 1959; A.S., Sacred Heart U., 1977; cert. fin. planner, Adelphi U., 1980; children—Valerie, Eric. With Hirsch Travel, 1974-76; founder, dir. Budget Adv. Service, Westport, Conn., 1977-84; sr. v.p. Black & Nash Assocs., Wilton, Conn., Mineola, N.Y. and N.Y.C., 1984-86; fin. planning officer, Soc. for savs., Hartford, Conn., 1985—; lectr. on money mgmt., fin. planning. Mem. Internat. Assn. Fin. Planners (v.p. 1980-83, pres. 1983-84), Women's Place, Author's Guild, Nat. Assn. Female Execs. Author: Your Personal Financial Fitness Program, 1983; Financial Fitness for Newlyweds, 1984. Contbr. articles to money mgmt. publs.

LEWIS, ANN FRANK, politician; b. Jersey City, Dec. 19, 1937; d. Samuel and Elsie (Golush) Frank; student Radcliffe Coll., 1954-55; children—Patricia Fay, Beth Ellen, Susan Jane. Asst. to mayor of Boston, 1968-75; dep. campaign mgr. Bayh for President, 1975-76; congl. adminstrv. asst., 1976-81; polit. dir. Democratic Nat. Com., 1981-85; co-leader Mass. Women's Polit. Caucus, 1972-74; recorder Nat. Women's Polit. Caucus, 1972-75; mem. Newton (Mass.)

Dem. City Com., 1972-75; mem. nat. bd., exec. com. Americans for Dem. Action, from 1975, nat. dir., 1985—. Mem. Women's Equity Action League, NOW. Jewish. Office: Ams for Dem Action 1411 K St NW Washington DC 20005*

LEWIS, BARBARA ANN, writer, public relations consultant; b. Buffalo, July 8, 1945; d. Earl and Rose (Galante) Spellburg; m. Knoxie Henry Lewis, Sept. 6, 1975 (div. 1982). B.S., Daemen Coll., 1966; postgrad. SUNY, 1967-69. Exec. sec., sci. instr. Erie Community Coll., Buffalo, 1966-69; beauty and fashion dir., v.p. U.S. Universal, 1971-73; originator, pres. Magic of Venus Internat., Inc., Chgo., 1971-73; writer, producer, narrator The Beauty of It All radio show (nationwide), 1973-75; writer charm curriculum Erie Community Coll., 1968-69; author, producer charity benefit play: The City of Hope, 1972; pub. relations cons. Chgo., 1974-76, Houston, 1982—. Syndicated newspaper columnist The Beauty of It All, 1970-73; contbr. articles to profl. jours. Adoptive parent World Vision, Nairobi, Kenya, 1980—; campaigner Whale Protection Fund, 1978—; mem. Middlebrook Community Assn., Houston, 1978—; charter mem. Statue of Liberty-Ellis Island Commn. Named Student Tchr. of Yr., Nat. Bus. Edn. Assn., 1966; recipient Outstanding Achievement in Bus. Edn. award Nat. Assn. Bus. Tchr. Edn., 1966. Mem. Nat. Bus. Edn. Assn., AAUP, N.Y. Assn. Jr. Coll. Tchrs., Am. Fedn. Tchrs., Faculty Senate of Erie Community Coll., Tex. Mariners Cruising Assn., Alumni Assn. Daemen Coll. Roman Catholic. Office: 15815 Stonehaven Dr Houston TX 77059

LEWIS, BARBARA JIMMIE, artist; b. El Paso, Tex., Mar. 14, 1932; d. Frederick Howard and Mildred (Neilson) Cushing; m. Rollin C. Lewis, Oct. 27, 1951; children—Lynn, Bradley, David. Student, U. Tex.-El Paso, 1950-70, U. Nev., 1982—. Tchr., El Paso Pub. Schs., 1954-69; condr. various art classes, workshops; represented by Gallery "20", Farmington, N.Mex., Artistic License, Farmington. Exhibited in group shows in Salt Lake City, Las Vegas, Nev., Farmington, N.Mex.; nat. and regional shows in Calif., Utah, Tex., Nev., N.Mex. (first prize watercolor 1982) Mem. N.Mex. Watercolor Soc., Nev. Watercolor Soc., Am. Watercolor Assn. (assoc.), Nat. League Am. Penwomen, Watercolor West Assn. (assoc.).

LEWIS, BETTY ANN, writer, historian, researcher; b. Fresno, Calif., June 1, 1925; s. Roy William and Dorothy Fredricka (Porter) Bagby; student Hartnell Coll.; m. Monte Randall Lewis, Jan. 11, 1946; children—Christine, Marci, Mike, Kelly. Author: Victorian Homes of Watsonville, 1974; Walking and Driving Tour of Historic Watsonville, 1975; Highlights in the History of Watsonville, 1975; Watsonville Memories That Linger, 1976; Monterey Bay Yesterday, 1977; Watsonville Yesterday, 1978, Watsonville Memories That Linger, Vol. II, 1980; W.H. Weeks, Architect, 1985; speaker, cons. research radio programs. Mem. Watsonville Library Bd., 1982—; mem. Santa Cruz County Hist. Resource Commn., 1985—. Recipient SCOPE awards, 1977, 78; San Jose State U.-Sourisseau Acad. research grantee. Mem. Nat. League Am. Pen Women, Theatre Historians, Calif. Hist. Soc., Calif. Conf. Hist. Socs., (v.p. 1982), Pajaro Valley Hist. Assn. (pres. 1980-81, Hubert Wyckoff Meml. award 1979), Santa Cruz Soc. for Hist. Preservation (award for book on W.H. Weeks 1986). Republican. Presbyterian (elder). Office: Mansion House 420 Main St Suite 204 Watsonville CA 95076

LEWIS, BETTY JANE, real estate executive, restaurant executive; b. Grove City, Pa., May 22, 1920; d. George Franklin and Nancy Blanche (McGarvey) Weston; A.B.D., Grove City Coll., 1939; student Duquesne U., 1967-68, Carnegie Inst. Tech., 1965-68; m. Edward Denny, Feb. 7, 1942; children—Edward, Mark, William. Dist. supr. Comml. Labs., Newark, N.Y., 1960-65; owner Key Realty Co., Butler, Pa., 1971—; owner, operator Burger Huts(3), Butler, 1979—. Mem. Nat. Restaurant Assn., Butler County Bd. Realtors, Nat. Bd. Realtors, Mental Health Assn., Human Relations Assn. (pres.), Assoc. Artists (dir.). Republican. Methodist. Club: Women's, Quota (dir.). Home: 106 Randy Dr Butler PA 16001 Office: 1734 N Main St Extension Butler PA 16001

LEWIS, CAROLYN ANNE, real estate company executive; b. Austin, Tex., Oct. 25, 1954; d. R.B. and Margaret (Sibley) Lewis. B.A., Duke U., 1976; M.B.A., Harvard U., 1982. Account exec. So. Bell Telephone Co., Atlanta, 1976-80; v.p. corp. planning Distbn. Systems, Inc., Houston, 1982-84; pres. Houston Trailer, Inc., 1984-86, Peachtree Land Co., 1986—. Mem. Houston C. of C. (ambassador 1983, participant exec. on loan program 1983—, Pres.'s Circle award 1983). Office: Peachtree Land Co PO Box 10011 Atlanta GA 30319

LEWIS, CHARLENE, data processing executive; b. Manson, Ark.; d. Robert Leo and Dorothy Donibee (Kidd) Lewis; B.S. in Acctg., San Diego State U., 1971; M.B.A., Nat. U., 1980. Gen. acct. Datagraphix, Inc., San Diego, 1970-73, adminstrv. acct., 1973-76, acctg. group leader, 1976-77, supr. acctg., 1977-79, sr. fin. analyst, 1979-84, mgmt. info. systems specialist, 1984—. Mem. Mgmt. Club, Women in Data Processing. Clubs: San Diego Track; San Diego Marathon Clinic. Home: 12719 La Tortola San Diego CA 92129 Office: Datagraphix Inc PO Box 82449 San Diego CA 92138

LEWIS, CYNTHIA ANN, lawyer; b. Columbia, Mo., Oct. 11, 1953; d. Raymond Charles and Mary Jeanne (Payne) L.; m. Michael Lee Gassmann, Sept. 3, 1977. B.A. with high honors, Coll. William and Mary, 1975; J.D. cum laude, Harvard U., 1978. Bar: D.C. 1978, U.S. Dist. Ct. D.C. 1979, U.S. Ct. Appeals D.C. Circuit 1979, U.S. Supreme Ct. 1983. Prin. Beveridge & Diamond, P.C., Washington, 1978—. Mem. ABA, Fed. Bar Assn., D.C. Bar Assn., Phi Beta Kappa. Office: Beveridge & Diamond PC 1333 New Hampshire Ave NW Washington DC 20036

LEWIS, DOROTHY ROE, journalist; b. Alba, Mo., May 18, 1904; d. Daniel Perkins and Anna Florence (Tibbs) Roe; B.J., U. Mo., 1924; m. John Bettington Lewis, July 4, 1937 (dec.); children—Judith Jennifer Lewis White, Jo Anne Lewis Schreiber. Reporter, Eldorado Daily News, 1924-25; shopping news columnist Los Angeles Examiner, 1926; feature writer Chgo. Herald-Examiner, 1927, Universal Service, 1927-37; freelance feature writer N.Y. World, 1927-28; co-pub. Burlington (N.J.) Daily Enterprise, 1939-40; women's editor AP, N.Y.C., 1941-60; ghost writing assignments for celebrities in women's field Putnam, Lippincott, Prentice-Hall pub. cos., 1944-60; asst. women's editor King Features, 1940-41; columnist Chgo. Tribune-N.Y. News Syndicate, 1960-70; mem. journalism faculty U. Mo., Columbia, 1964-74; editor Mo. Republican, 1975-80; freelance writer for mags., newspapers, 1980—; judge Penney-Mo. Women's Page awards, 1962-74. Recipient Mo. medal for disting. service in journalism, 1958, Zonta Internat. Newswoman of Yr. award, 1958. Mem. Women in Communications. Republican. Mem. Christian Ch. (Disciples of Christ). Club: Fortnightly (U. Mo.). Author: (with Lilly Dache) Talking Through My Hats, 1946, Lilly Dache's Glamour Book, 1956; The Trouble with Women Is Men, 1962. Home: 2806 W Rollins Rd Columbia MO 65201

LEWIS, ELEANOR ROBERTS, lawyer; b. Detroit, Jan. 5, 1944; d. David Edward and Patricia Mary (Easterbrook) Roberts; m. Roger Kutnow Lewis, June 24, 1967; 1 child, Kevin Michael. B.A., Wellesley Coll., 1965; M.A.T., Harvard U., 1966; J.D., Georgetown U., 1974. Bar: D.C. 1975, U.S. Dist. Ct. D.C. 1975, U.S. Ct. Appeals (D.C. cir.) 1975, U.S. Ct. Appeals (10th cir.) 1976, U.S. Supreme Ct. 1980. cert. tchr. Tchr., Waltham (Mass.) High Sch., 1966-67, Holton-Arms Sch., Bethesda, Md., 1967-71; atty. HUD, Washington, 1974-76, asst. gen. counsel, 1979-82; assoc. firm Brownstein Zeidman & Schomer, Washington, 1976-79; asst. gen. counsel U.S. Dept. Commerce, Washington, 1982—. Author, editor (with others) Street Law, 1975. Contbr. chpts. to books, articles to legal and fin. jours. Bd. dirs. Dana Place Condominium, Washington. Wellesley Coll. scholar, 1963-65. Mem. ABA, Fed. Bar Assn., D.C. Bar Assn., Women's Bar Assn. D.C., Women in Housing and Fin., Women's Legal Def. Fund. Home: 5034 1/2 Dana Pl NW Washington DC 20016 Office: US Dept of Commerce 14th and Constitution Ave NW Washington DC 20230

LEWIS, ELIZABETH NANCY, hospital administrator; b. St. Paul, Aug. 23, 1945; d. Clyde E. and Elsie I. (Larson) Hegman; R.N., St. Barnabas Hosp. Sch. Nursing, 1968; B.A.S., U. Minn., 1976; M.S., Ph.D., Columbia Pacific U. Staff nurse Mpls. St. Paul area hosps., 1968-74; asst. coordinator staff devel. and inservice edn. Midway Hosp., St. Paul, 1974-77; adminstrv. asst., dir. nursing Northwest Gen. Hosp., Milw., 1977-78; dir. nursing adminstrn. San Dimas Community Hosp., Calif. 1978-79; asst. adminstr. Doctors Hosp., Pinole, Calif., 1979-84; cons. research and devel. Nat. Med. Enterprises, Los Angeles, 1984-85; assoc. adminstr. Ross Gen. Hosp., Republic Health Corp., Ross, Calif., 1985—. Co-author: Nurse Staffing and Patient Classification; Strategies for Success, 1984. Bd. govs. St. Paul div. Minn. affiliate Am. Heart Assn.; mem. senate and student bd. U. Minn. Mem. East Bay Nursing Adminstrs. Council, Am. Orgn. Nurse Execs., Flying Samaritans Internat., Calif. Soc. Nursing Service Adminstrs., Sigma Theta Tau. Home: 15 Mt. Burney Ct San Rafael CA 94903 Office: Ross Gen Hosp 1150 Sir Francis Drake Blvd Ross CA 94947

LEWIS, ERMA, account executive; b. N.Y.C., June 6, 1946; d. Leonard and Renee (Epstein) Lewis. B.A., Bklyn. Coll., 1968. Sec. Internat. Council Shopping Ctrs., N.Y.C., 1966-71, Ruder & Finn, Inc., N.Y.C., 1971-77; asst. pub. relations dir. Seatrain Lines, Weehawken, N.J., 1977-79; prodn. mgr. Weiss & Geller, N.Y.C., 1979-81; account exec. Ruder Finn & Rotman, N.Y.C., 1981-84, Spencer & Rubinow, Ltd., N.Y.C., 1985—. Democrat. Jewish.

LEWIS, EVELYN, communications and public relations executive; b. Goslar, Germany, Sept. 19, 1946; came to U.S. 1952, naturalized 1957; d. Gerson Emanuel and Sala (Mendlowicz) L. B.A., U. Ill.-Chgo., 1968; M.A., Ball State U., 1973, Ph.D., 1976. Research analyst Comptroller, State Ill., Chgo., 1977-78; lectr. polit. sci. dept. Loyola U., Chgo., 1977; asst. to commr. Dept. Human Services, Chgo., 1978-81; group mgr. communications Arthur Anderson & Co., Chgo., 1981-84; dir. communications and pub. relations Heidrick & Struggles, Inc., Chgo., 1984—. Mem. Children of the Holocaust, Chgo., 1982. Mem. Internat. Assn. Bus. Communicators, Publicity Club Chgo., Nat. Assn. Female Execs. Jewish. Club: Metropolitan (Chgo.). Avocations: writing, poetry, biking, hiking. Office: Heidrick & Struggles Inc 125 S Wacker Dr Chicago IL 60606

LEWIS, EVELYN LYNNETTE, physician; b. Wilmington, N.C., Aug. 4, 1956; d. Alfonso L. Lewis and Eloise Deloris (Welch) Welch. B.S., Spelman Coll., 1978; postgrad. Brown U., 1978-81; M.D. Chgo. Med. Sch., 1983. Diplomate Am. Bd. Family Medicine. Commd. ensign U.S. Navy, 1978, advanced through grades to lt., 1983; resident in family practice Naval Air Sta., Jacksonville, Fla., 1983-84; sr. med. officer U.S. Simon Lake, Kings Bay, Ga., 1984—, med. dept head, 1984—. Mem. AMA, Fla. Med. Assn., Nat. Naval Officers Assn., Nat. Med. Assn., Beta Kappa Chi. Democrat. Roman Catholic. Avocations: sketching; bike riding; photography; music and dance prodns. Home: 2413 1st Ave unit G-2 Fernandina Beach FL 32034

LEWIS, FLORA, journalist; b. Los Angeles; d. Benjamin and Pauline (Kallin) L.; B.A., UCLA, 1941; M.S., Columbia U., 1942; LL.D. (hon.), Princeton U., 1981; Litt.D. (hon.), Mt. Holyoke Coll., 1982; D.C.L. (hon.), Bucknell U., 1983; hon. doctorate Columbia U., 1984, U. Mass., 1984, Marymount Coll., 1984; m. Sydney Gruson, Aug. 17, 1945 (div.); children—Kerry, Sheila, Lindsey. Reporter, Los Angeles Times, 1941, AP, N.Y.C., Washington, London, 1942-46; freelance or contract for Observer, Economist, Financial Times, France-soir, Time mag., N.Y. Times mag., London, Warsaw, Berlin, Hague, Mexico City, Tel Aviv, 1946-54, Prague, Warsaw, 1956-58; editor McGraw-Hill, N.Y.C., 1955; bur. chief Washington Post, Bonn, London, N.Y.C., 1958-66; syndicated columnist Newsday, Paris, N.Y.C., 1967-72; bur. chief N.Y. Times, Paris, 1972-80, European diplomatic corr., 1976-80, fgn. affairs columnist, 1980—; Arthur D. Morse fellow in communications and society Aspen Inst. for Humanistic Studies, 1977. Bd. dirs. Internat. Inst. Strategic Studies, Inst. East-West Security Studies. Decorated chevalier Legion d'Honneur; recipient awards for best interpretation fgn. affairs, 1956, best reporting fgn. affairs 1960 Overseas Press Club, Columbia Journalism Sch. 50th Anniversary Honor award, 1963; award for disting. diplomatic reporting George Washington U. Sch. Fgn. Service, 1978; Acad. award UCLA, 1984. Mem. Phi Beta Kappa. Author: Case History of Hope, 1958; Red Pawn, 1964; One of Our H-Bombs is Missing, 1967; contbr. to anthologies, books, mags. Office: NY Times Foreign News Desk 229 W 43d St New York NY 10036 also NY Times 3 Rue Scribe Paris 9e France

LEWIS, GAYLE ROBIN, lawyer; b. N.Y.C., Oct. 7, 1947; d. Frank and Elinor (Scheinman) Lewis. B.A., Russell Sage Coll., 1968; M.A., NYU, 1969; J.D., Rutgers U., 1974. Bar: Pa. N.J. 1974, 1976. Environ. health cons. N.Y. State Health Dept., N.Y.C., 1969-71; asst. atty. gen. Commonwealth of Pa., Harrisburg, 1974-78; dep. adminstr. med. Arbitration Panels for Health Care., Phila., 1978-81; sole practice law, Phila., 1981—; med/legal cons., 1981—. Author/editor newsletter: Verdict: Phila. Trial Lawyers, 1982; contbr. articles to profl. jours. Melvin Belli Soc. Seminarian, 1983; Disting. Service in Edn. award, Phila. Trial Lawyers, 1983. Mem. ABA, Pa. Bar Assn., Phila. Bar Assn., Phila. Trial Lawyers (chmn. 1982—, program coordinator), Women and Law Nat. Coop. Democrat. Club: Lawyers. Home: 610 Broad Acres Rd Narberth PA 19072 Office: 5th Floor 2100 Arch St Philadelphia PA 19103

LEWIS, GLADYS SHERMAN, nurse, educator; b. Wynnewood, Okla., Mar. 20, 1933; d. Andrew and Minnie Elva (Halsey) Sherman; R.N., St. Anthony's Sch. Nursing, 1953; student Okla. Bapt. U., 1953-55; A.B., Tex. Christian U., 1956; postgrad. Southwestern Bapt. Theol. Sem., 1959-60, Escuela de Idiomas, San Jose, Costa Rica, 1960-61; M.A. in Creative Writing, Central (Okla.) State U., 1985; m. Wilbur Curtis Lewis, Jan. 28, 1955; children—Karen, David, Leanne, Cristen. Mem. nursing staff various facilities, Okla., 1953-57; instr. nursing, med. missionary Bapt. mission and hosp., Paraguay, 1961-70; vice-chmn. edn. commn. Paraguay Bapt. Conv., 1962-65; sec. bd. trustees Bapt. Hosp., Paraguay, 1962-65, chmn. personnel com., handbook and policy book officer Bapt. Mission in Paraguay, 1967-70; trustee Southwestern Bapt. Theol. Sem., 1974-84, chmn. student affairs com., 1976-78, vice chmn. bd. 1978-80; partner Las Amigas Tours; writer, conference leader, campus lectr., 1959—. Active Democratic party; leader Girl Scouts U.S.A., 1965-75; Okla. co-chmn. Nat. Religious Com. for Equal Rights Amendment, 1977-79; tour host Meier Internat. Study League. Mem. AAUW, Evang. Women's Caucus, Am. Nurses Assn., Internat., Am. colls. surgeons women's auxiliaries, Okla. State, Okla. County med. auxiliaries, Nat. Women's Polit. Caucus, Okla. Women's Polit. Caucus. Author: On Earth As It Is, 1983; Two Dreams and a Promise, 1984; also religious instructional texts in English and Spanish; editor Sooner Physician's Heartbeat, 1979-82; contbr. articles to So. Bapt. and secular periodicals. Home: 14501 N Western Ave Edmond OK 73013

LEWIS, GRACE GRAVES, nurse educator; b. Lynchburg, Va., Jan. 18, 1948; d. Duvall Sidney and Katherine Iola (Wood) Graves; m. Cecil Lewis, Aug. 21, 1971; children—Cecil, Courtney. B.S. in Nursing, Hampton Inst., 1970; M.S., Ga. State U., 1980. Cert. clin. nurse specialist med.-surg. nursing. Staff nurse intensive care Holy Family Hosp., Atlanta, 1971-72; staff nurse Doctor's Meml. Hosp., Atlanta, 1972-73; nurse supr. Med. Measurements, Atlanta, 1973-74; asst. chmn. med.-surg. nursing Ga. Bapt. Sch. Nursing, Atlanta, 1974-80; asst. prof. nursing Tuskegee Inst. Sch. Nursing, Atlanta, 1980-84, 3d level coordinator, 1983-84; instr. nursing Crawford Long Sch. Nursing, Atlanta, 1984—; nurse specialist cons. New Horizons Transitional Ctr., Atlanta, 1983—; nurse cons. Drew, Eckl and Farnham, Atlanta, 1984—; vol. participant ARC Health Fair, Atlanta, 1979—. Mem. exec. bd. Atlanta Area Sch. Deaf, Clarkston, Ga., 1983-85; v.p. Parent, Tchr., Deaf Adult Assn., Atlanta, 1983-85, chmn. program com., 1983-85. Ga. Bd. Regents scholar, 1979; State Ga. scholar, 1980; recipient Outstanding Faculty Performance award in Teaching, Tuskegee Inst., 1984; commendation New Horizons Transitional Ctr. Mem. Nat. League for Nursing, Nat. Honor Soc. Nursing. Club: LNO (treas. 1982—). Avocations: reading; attending theatrical performances; sewing. Home: 7200 Buck Creek Dr Fairburn GA 30213 Office: Crawford W Long Hosp Sch Nursing 543 W Peachtree St Atlanta GA 30308

LEWIS, HARRIET GERBERT, plumbing fixtures manufacturing company executive; b. Chgo., Nov. 30, 1919; d. Max and Lottie (Schiffman) Gerber; m. Maurice L. Lewis, Oct. 12, 1940; children—Ila J., Nancy G., Alan G. B.A., Northwestern U., 1941. With Gerber Plumbing Fixtures Corp., Chgo., 1953—, chmn. bd. dirs., pres., chief exec. officer, 1983—. Trustee Northshore Congregation Israel. Named Woman of Yr., Am.-Israel C. of C., 1983, Hon. Dir., Women's div. Jewish United Fund, 1985. Mem. Com. of 200. Office: Gerber Plumbing Fixture Corp 4656 W Touhy Ave Chicago IL 60646

LEWIS, HELEN PHELPS HOYT, assn. exec.; b. Lakewood, N.J., Dec. 27, 1902; d. John Sherman and Ethel Phelps (Stokes) Hoyt; A.B., Bryn Mawr, 1923; M.A., Columbia, 1925; m. Bryon Stookey, May 11, 1929 (dec. Oct. 1966); children—John Hoyt, Lyman Brumbaugh, Byron; m. 2d, Robert James Lewis, Aug. 5, 1971. Mem. bd. mgrs. Christodora House Settlement, N.Y.C., 1927-38, 1st v.p., 1929-38; mem. nat. bd. YWCA, 1927-30; mem. womens adv. council N.Y. Bot. Gardens, 1952—; mem. nursing com. Columbia-Presbyn. Med. Center, 1944-54; trustee Columbia-Presbyn. Med. Center, 1969—; mem. women's aux. Neurol. Inst., 1939—, chmn., 1949-54; mem. womens exec. comn. United Hosp. Fund, 1951-64; vice chmn. womens campaign com., 1961-62, vice chmn. womens exec. com., 1963-64; pres. gen. Colonial Dames Am., 1953-56; pres. Darien Garden Club, 1935-38; pres. Millbrook Garden Club; bd. dirs. Met. Opera Guild, 1971—. Mem. Daus. of the Cincinnati. Republican. Presbyterian. Club: Colony (gov. 1954-76, sec. 1956-59, 69-71, v.p. 1969-71, pres. 1972-76, chmn. membership com. 1956-71). Home: 580 Park Ave New York City NY 10021

LEWIS, JANE ELIZABETH, editor, employee information specialist; b. Montgomery, Ala., Sept. 24, 1957; d. Howard Jackson and Cecile Anne (Westmoreland) Lewis. B.S. in Journalism, U. Fla., 1980. Pub. affairs asst. Fed. Emergency Mgmt. Agy., Atlanta, 1980; editor, writer Equifax, Inc., Atlanta, 1980-81; art designer, typesetter Atlanta Printing Co., 1981-82; editor, employee info. specialist Atlanta Gas Light Co., 1982—. Mem. com. young careers group High Mus. Art, Atlanta, 1981—; officer Peachtree Presbyn. Ch., Scions Group, Atlanta. Mem. Internat. Assn. Bus. Communicators (mem. coms.), Women in Communications. Republican. Clubs: Ski, Track, Sierra (Atlanta). Office: Atlanta Gas Light Co PO Box 4569 Atlanta GA 30302

LEWIS, JENNIFER ROSE, utility company executive, lobbyist; b. Birmingham, Ala., Jan. 10, 1947; d. John Davis and Rose Louise (Twinn) Shacklett; B.A. in Bus. Adminstrn., Nat. U., 1979; m. Fred G. Lewis, Nov. 19, 1978; 1 stepdau., Lynn Ellyn. Mktg. rep. Pacific Telephone, San Diego, San Francisco, 1967-68; Master Charge rep. So. Calif. 1st Nat. Bank, San Diego, Orange, Los Angeles, 1968-71; customer service rep., teleprocessing design rep., customer info. supr., collections supr., customer service supr. San Diego Gas & Electric Co., 1971-80, sr. regulatory affairs rep., 1980-82, regulatory supr., 1982-85, mgr. investor relations, 1985—; sec., chief fin. officer Fred Lewis Prodns., Inc.; cons. in field. Pres. bd. govs. Arthritis Found., mem. nat. ops. com., exec. com., fed., state lobbyist, chmn. govt. affairs com., 1979-81, mem. speakers corps., 1978-81; mem. Mayor's Adv. Com., 1982; active United Way, 1979; bd. dirs. Nat. Friends of Arthritis Found. Mem. Nat. Alliance Businessmen (active jobs campaign 1975-76), Alpha Phi Alumnae. Clubs: Balboa Tennis, San Diego Tennis Patrons. Home: 6117 Caminito Pan San Diego CA 92120 Office: 101 Ash St San Diego CA 92101

LEWIS, JOAN MARIE, executive office leasing company executive; b. Galveston, Tex., June 20, 1944; d. Robert Walter and Fern Elizabeth (Rocket) Snipes; m. Austin Lester Lewis, Jr., Feb. 1, 1963 (div. Nov. 1973); children—Elizabeth, Carrie, Amy. Mgr. Preston Forest Exec. Suites, Dallas, 1973-75; sec. to pres. Mich. Gen. Corp., Dallas, 1975-76; sec. North Park Exec. Suites, Dallas, 1976-79; ptnr. P & L Exec. Suites, Dallas, 1979-82; owner, pres. Joan M. Lewis Co., Inc., also Town Center Exec. Suites, Inc., Dallas, 1982—. Mem. Nat. Assn. Secretarial Services, Dallas-Ft. Worth Exec. Women's Assn. (pres. 1984-85, Woman of Yr. 1984). Republican. Methodist. Office: Joan M Lewis Co Inc 8235 Douglas Ave Suite 1000 Dallas TX 75225

LEWIS, JOAN MENDENHALL, spice company executive, researcher; b. Aberdeen, Wash., Dec. 7, 1929; d. William Swartz and Verna Bernice (Rader) Mendenhall; m. Robert John Lewis, July 28, 1950 (div. 1971); children—James Radar, Michael Steven, Tamara Jean. B.A., U. Wash., 1950; M.S., Calif. State U.-Hayward, 1970. Cert. secondary tchr. and coll. instr., Calif. Mem. guided missile team Boeing Aircraft Co., Seattle, 1950-51; importer Custom Bldg. Products, Moraga, Calif., 1961-65; program coordinator Martinez Sch. Dist., Calif., 1965-68; research dir. Contra Costa Coll., San Pablo, Calif., 1968-69; dir. Experiential Research Assocs., Emeryville, Calif., 1969-79; founder, pres. Bayseng, Orinda, Calif., 1979—; cons. Nat. Alliance Businessmen, Washington, 1969; researcher Mananan Enterprises, Seattle, 1983—. Author: Counseling for Employment, 1969. Film producer: Complete and Unabridged Job Guide for Serious Dreamers, 1972. Inventor vacuum dehydration equipment, Participant Cannes Film Festival, France, 1982-84. Organizer Neighborhood Youth Corps, San Francisco, 1965-68; mem. No. Calif. Industry Edn. Council, 1964-75, San Francisco Symphony Assn., 1976-77, Mental Health Assn. Contra Costa, 1980-81. NDEA grantee, 1965; Calif. Dept. Vocat. Edn. grantee, 1966, 67, 68, 72, 73; Calif. Dept. Rehab. grantee, 1970; Calif. Community Colls. grantee, 1973. Mem. AAUW, Moraga C. of C., Delta Zeta. Republican. Mem. Christian Ch. Avocations: home and landscape design; travel; art. Home: 9 Archer Circle Moraga CA 94556

LEWIS, LINDA DONELLE, neurologist, educator; b. Columbus, Ohio, Nov 27, 1939; d. Donald Peter and Ann Elizabeth (Karn) Lewis, B.S., Bethany Coll., 1961, D.Sc. (hon.), 1981; M.D., W.Va. U., 1965; m. Gary Gambuti, Oct. 6, 1979. Practice medicine specializing in neurology, N.Y.C., 1971—; asst. prof. neurology Coll. Physicians and Surgeons, Columbia U., N.Y.C., from 1971, now assoc. clin. prof., assoc. dean student affairs, 1979—; cons. in field; mem. N.Y. State Bd. for Profl. Med. Conduct, 1979—. Recipient Outstanding Teaching award Columbia U., 1977. Mem. AMA (nat. com. on med. edn.), N.Y. State Med. Soc. (del.), New York County Med. Soc., Am. Assn. Med. Colls., Am. Acad. Neurology, AAAS. Contbr. articles to sci. jours. Home: 320 Central Park W New York NY 10025 Office: 710 W 168th St New York NY 10032

LEWIS, LONA LEE, association executive, educator; b. Topeka, Kans., Jan. 18, 1943; d. Walter Lee and Eunice Pearl (Hudson) Moeller; m. Terry Lynn Lewis, May 25, 1962; 1 child, Dawson Lee. B.S. in Biology, U. Nebr., 1965, M.S., 1970. Tchr. Omaha pub. schs., 1965-68, Parkway Schs., Chesterfield, Mo., 1970-81; instr. biology U. Nebr., Omaha, 1967-70; pres. Mo. NEA, Jefferson City, 1979-80, 1981-85; co-owner TDL, Inc.; cons. jr. high sci. program Rand McNally, Chgo., 1967-75. Pres.-elect. Nat. Council of State Edn. Assns., Washington, 1981-85, coordinating v.p., 1981-84, pres., 1985—; dept. leader biology curriculum ind. study project Title V U.S. Govt., 1975-77. Column writer Educationally Speaking, 1981-85. Del. Dem. Nat. Conv., San Francisco, 1984. Mem. Nat. Sci. Tchrs. Assn., NEA, Nat. Wildlife Fedn. Avocations: reading; stamp collecting, rehabing houses. Home: 768 Winding Bend Ln Manchester MO 63021 Office: Missouri NEA 612 Eastland Jefferson City MO 65101

LEWIS, LORRIE (LORRAINE), travel consultant; b. N.Y.C., May 8, 1926; d. Sol and Grace (Goldberg) Strauss; m. Philip L. Lewis, Mar. 1946; children—Donald, Hal. B.A., Hunter Coll., 1946. Social editor Springfield Leader, N.J., 1957-65; pres. Creative Travel Service Inc., Springfield. Active Springfield Democratic Com., 1958-68; chairperson Am. Cancer Soc., Springfield, 1959-60; del. Dem. Presdl. Conv., Chgo., 1968; pres. Springfield PTA, 1955-56; active Union County Mental Health Bd., Elizabeth, N.J., 1964-65. Mem. N.J. Soc. Travel Agts. (chairperson maritime com. 1983—, exec. bd. 1983—). Jewish. Club: Maplewood Country. Avocation: bridge. Office: Creative Travel Service Inc PO Box 613 Springfield NJ 07081

LEWIS, MARCIA ANN, business and asset management executive, real estate executive; b. Los Angeles, Nov. 6, 1940; d. Leroy Alan and Alma Verdie (Reddick) L.; children—James L. Vess, Patrick A. Vess, Christine M. Vess. Student Midwest Bus. Coll., Colorado Springs, Colo. Sec., receptionist Col-Terra Investments, Colorado Springs, 1972-76, gen. mgr., 1976-83; pres., owner Marcia L, Inc., Colorado Springs, 1983—; dir. First Am. Devel. Corp., Rocky Mountain Savs. & Loan. Republican. Methodist. Avocations: stamp collecting, skiing. Home: 360E W Rockrimmon Blvd Colorado Springs CO 80919 Office: Marcia L Inc 118 N Tejon 301 Colorado Springs CO 80903

LEWIS, MARGARET SHIVELY, librarian; b. Indpls., Sept. 27, 1925; d. William E. and Florence Ann (Knox) Shively; m. Phillip Fenton Lewis, Sept. 10, 1948; children—David William, Catharine Ann, Frederick Michael, Thomas Griffith. B.A., Oberlin Coll., 1947; M.L.S., St. John's U., 1971. Librarian, Optometric Ctr. of N.Y., 1971; SUNY Coll. of Optometry, N.Y.C., 1971—; mem. Met. Coop. Acquisition Program com., N.Y.C., 1980-83. Author: SUNY Library Handbook, 1979. St. John's U. fellow, 1969. Fellow Am. Acad. Optometry; mem. Assn. Vision Sci. Librarians (chmn. 1976-77), ALA, SUNY Council Head Librarians, Phi Beta Kappa. Episcopalian. Avocations: needlework; gardening. Office: Coll Optometry SUNY 100 E 24th St New York NY 10010-3677

LEWIS, MARIANNE ELIZABETH, systems analyst; b. Washington, June 6, 1939; d. Samuel and Margarette Ann (Simms) Jenifer; A.S.B.A., Southeastern U., Washington, 1975, B.S.B.A., 1976; M.B.A., City U., Seattle, 1981; children—Joe Jr., Darwin Randolph, Roderick Michael, Yolanda Anita. Keypunch operator, supr. Bank of Am., San Francisco, 1961-64, Boeing Co., Seattle, 1964-66; data processing supr. Group Hosp., Washington, 1966-70; keytape operator Dept. Commerce, 1971-73, adminstrv. asst., 1973-77; systems analyst Boeing Co., Seattle, 1978—; pres. MAR-I-Gold; software cons.; tchr. Tng. dir. Boy Scouts Am., 1970-77; v.p. Bd. Edn. Catholic Sector, Washington,

1975-77; dir. Youth Choir, 1979—. Served with USAF, 1957-60, Res., 1976—. Mem. Am. Mgmt. Assn., Mark IV Systems Group (sec. 1979-80), Nat. Office Black Caths., Inner-City Youth (dir.), Internat. Platform Assn. Roman Catholic. Club: Toastmistress (pres. 1975-76). Home: 1922 18th Ave S Seattle WA 98144 Office: Boeing Kent Benaroya Bldg 7-48-12 Kent WA 98031

LEWIS, MARY ELLEN, psychotherapist; b. Green Bay, Wis., Nov. 17, 1948; d. Lawrence Edward, Jr., and Irene Marie (Mumm) L.; B.A. in Sociology, U. Wis., Madison, 1970, M.S.S.W., 1972; m. Thomas Duncan Nagel, May 8, 1976. Psychotherapist Central Comprehensive Mental Health Center, Centralia, Ill., 1972-75, clin. dir., 1975-76; psychotherapist Family Counseling, Aurora, Ill., 1977-80, dir. individual and family counseling div., 1980-83 pvt. practice psychotherapy, counseling, 1983—. Program chmn. Kane County NOW; adv. bd. YWCA, Aurora. Cert. sch. social worker, parent effectiveness tng. instr., Ill. Mem. Women in Mgmt., Women in Networking (adv. bd.), Nat. Assn. Social Workers, Acad. Cert. Social Workers, Am. Assn. Ethical Hypnotists, Am. Assn. Sex Educators, Counselors and Therapists (cert. sex counselor). Home: 1791 Lily St Aurora IL 60505 Office: Office: 411 W Galena Blvd Aurora 60506

LEWIS, MARY THERESE, artist; b. Blue Island, Ill., June 21, 1951; d. Christian Henry and Marie Anne (Corcoran) Berns; B.S. in Math. with highest honors, U. Ill., 1974; M.S. in Physics, U. Chgo., 1978; m. Richard W. Lewis, Feb. 16, 1979. Lead engr. research and devel. robotics and artificial intelligence Boeing Mil. Airplane Co., Wichita, Kans., 1978-84; self-employed artificial intelligence engr., 1984-85; artist, 1985—. Mem. Am. Assn. Artificial Intelligence, Internat. Platform Assn., Phi Kappa Phi. Home and Office: 2221 Inwood Dr Wilmington DE 19810

LEWIS, MICHELLE MARIE, hotel corporation executive; b. Novata, Calif., June 8, 1953; d. Charles Orlando Hovey and Janet (Austin) Hardie; m. David Grant Lewis, Oct. 27, 1973 (div. 1978). A.S., Allan Hancock Extension Coll., 1977. Exec. sec. ITT/FEC Div., Vandenberg AFB, Calif., 1975-78; office mgr. Bratten & Evers Advt. Agy., San Diego, 1978-80; media dir. Teckemeyer & Shields Advt. Agy., San Diego, 1980-81; sales mgr. comml. accounts Atlas Hotels, Inc., San Diego, 1981-84, dir. comml. accounts, 1984, sales mgr., Scottsdale, Ariz., 1984—. Vol. Dem. Com. for Gary Hart, Santa Barbara, 1971, Aurora (Women's Polit. Inst.), San Diego, 1983-84. Mem. Travel and Transp. Council (sec. 1982-83, v.p. II 1983-84, exec. v.p. 1984-85), Hotel Sales and Mktg. Assn., Am. Mktg. Assn., Subscribers of Sabre Club. Democrat. Mem. Religious Sci. Ch. Office: Sunburst Resort Hotel and Conf Ctr 4925 N Scottsdale Rd Scottsdale AZ 85251

LEWIS, NANCY, publicist; b. Northampton, Mass., Aug. 29, 1948; d. Donald Alexander and Rena (Scogin) L.; student U. Mass., Amherst, 1966-69. Account exec. Osborne Assocs., N.Y.C., 1977-80, Drucilla Handy Co., N.Y.C., 1980-81; pres. Nancy Lewis Public Relations, Durham, N.C., 1981—. Mem. Women in Communications, Am. Soc. Interior Designers, Nat. Home Fashions League (chpt. v.p. Jour. Sales 1980, 81, 82, 83, 84). Episcopalian. Contbg. editor Budget Decorating and Remodeling, 1978-79; contbr. articles, photographs to nat. home furnishing and consumer mags. Home: 1102 N Gregson St Durham NC 27701 Office: 1102 N Gregson St Durham NC 27701

LEWIS, RITA HOFFMAN, plastic products manufacturing company executive; b. Phila., Aug. 6, 1947; d. Robert John and Helen Anna (Dugan) Hoffman; m. David J. Lewis, Oct. 4, 1981; 1 child, Stephanie Blake. Student Jefferson Med. Coll. Sch. Nursing, 1965-67; Gen. mgr. Sheets & Co., Inc. (now Flower World, Inc.), Woodbury, N.J., 1968-72; dir., exec. v.p., treas. Hoffman Precision Plastics, Inc., Blackwood, N.J., 1973—; ptnr. Timer Assocs.; guest speaker various civic groups, 1974—. Author: That Part of Me I Never Really Meant to Share, 1979; In Retrospect: Caught Between Running and Loving. Mem. Com. for Citizens of Glen Oaks (N.J.), 1979—, Gloucester Twp. Econ. Devel. Com., 1981—, Gloucester Twp. Day Scholarship Com., 1984—; chairperson Gloucester Twp. Day Scholarship Found., 1985—; bd. dirs. Diane Hull Dance Co. Recipient Winning Edge award, 1982. Mem. Sales Assn. Chem. Industry, Blackwood Businessmen's Assn. Roman Catholic.

LEWIS, RUBY PAULINE, educator; b. Enfield, Ill., Aug. 8, 1922; d. Luther Rudolph and Clemie Jessie (York) Foley; B.S. in Edn., So. Ill. U., 1963; M.S. in Edn., Ind. State U., 1969; postgrad. So Ill. U., U. Hawaii, 1977; m. Merle Porter (dec. 1944); children—Merle Ann (dec.), Sharon Kay; m. 2d, William Lewis, June 24, 1947; children—William II, Brian David. Elem. tchr. Springerton (Ill.) Sch., 1942-43, Nubbin Ridge Sch., Enfield, Ill., 1945-46, Jefferson Sch., Carmi, Ill., 1946-47, Centerville Sch., Carmi, 1960-62, Washington Sch., Carmi, 1962-74, Washington Middle Sch., Carmi, 1974—; coordinator for gifted. Mem. Bus. and Profl. Women, Ill. Edn. Assn., NEA, Ill. Vocat. Home Econs. Assn., Carmi Edn. Assn. (pres. 1973-74, 81-82, negotiator 1981-82). Club: Federated Women's Spirit of Progress (pres. 1976-77). Home: RR 1 Box 206 Enfield IL 62835 Office: 201 W Main St Carmi IL 62821

LEWIS, RUTH SUTHERLAND, real estate development and management company executive; b. Mathis, Tex., Aug. 1, 1926; d. John Wade and Margaret (Carr) Sutherland; m. John Armstrong Lewis, Feb. 25, 1965; stepchildren—Carolyn Lewis Drenzek, Elizabeth Lewis Iles. B.A., Our Lady of the Lake, San Antonio, 1947; Med. Technician, Bapt. Hosp., San Antonio, 1948. Med. technician Mathis Hosp., Tex., 1950-62; mgr. Doctors' Clinic, Rockport, Tex., 1963-64; dir., sec. Peninsula Devel. Co., Rockport, 1965-74, pres., 1974—. Bd. dirs., treas. Aransas County Med. Services, Rockport, 1979—. Roman Catholic. Avocations: painting; antiques; reading; gardening. Home: 606 Allegro St N Rockport TX 78382 Office: Peninsula Devel Co 100 Ivy Ln Rockport TX 78382

LEWIS, SHERI, organizational consultant, solar manufacturing company executive; b. San Jose, Calif., Nov. 17, 1937; d. Raymond Glen and Edith Coffin (Brookover) Robertson; m. Miles S. Tully, Aug. 10, 1958 (div. 1972); children—Stephen N., David W.; m. Donald F. Lewis, Aug. 13, 1974 (dec. 1978). B.A. in Edn., San Jose State U., 1959. Tchr. pub. schs., ptnr. Campbell Office Machines and Furniture, Campbell, Calif., 1968-72, Don Lewis Assoc., Amador City, Calif., 1974-78; owner Interiors by Sheri, Los Gatos, Calif., 1972-74; pres. Lewis & Assoc., Grass Valley, Calif., 1978—; exec. dir. Foothill Solar Exchange, Grass Valley, Calif., 1980—. Patentee in field. Chairperson Grass Valley Energy Commn., 1982-84; bd. dirs. Sierra Com., Grass Valley, 1979-85; founder Network for Community Effectiveness, Nevada County, 1984. Mem. Solar Energy Inds. Assn. (chmn. bus. liaison com. 1984—). Calif. Solar Energy Inds. Assn. (pres. Foothills/Sacramento, Calif. 1982-84), Energy Network (steering com. 1981—), Am. Solar Energy Soc. (bus. liaison com. chmn. 1984—), Assn. Calif. Energy Ofcls., Sacramento Soc. Assn. Execs., Solar Access Assn. (bd. dir. 1981—), Amador County C. of C. (tourism dir. 1975-78). Avocations: hiking; camping; sailing. Home: 105 Rockwood Dr Grass Valley CA 95945 Office: Lewis & Assocs 105 Rockwood Dr Grass Valley CA 95945

LEWIS, SUE BLASINGAME, real estate broker; b. Miami, Fla., Dec. 3, 1933; d. Earnest LeRoy and Clara Louise (Collins) Blasingame; student public schs.; grad. Realtors Inst., 1973; m. James C. Lewis, Apr. 5, 1952; children—Susan C., James C. III, Douglas C. Saleswoman Claytons' Realty, Winter Park, Fla., 1972-76; polit. aide, 1976, 78, 79, 80; pres. Sue Lewis Cons., Inc., Winter Park, 1980—; speaker in field. Chmn. Seminole County Planning and Zoning Commn., 1980—, Seminole County Land Planning Agy., 1981—; vice chmn. Met. Transp. Authority. Republican. Home: 2532 Long Iron Ct Longwood FL 32779 Office: 2251 Lucien Way Suite 130 Maitland FL 32751

LEWIS, VERNITA ANN WICKLIFFE, beauty culturist, fast food restaurant executive; b. Chgo., Apr. 6, 1955; d. Kernett Henry and Clara Lillian (Wells) Robinson; m. Lloyd Maurice Wickliffe, Sr., Jan. 31, 1976 (dec. 1982); children—Calvin Earl, Nicole Latrice, Lloyd Maurice Jr.; m. Kenneth Lewis, Feb. 17, 1985. Student William Jones Comml. Bus. Sch., 1971-72; degree Pivot Point Inst., 1982-83. Clerk Typist I & II State Dept. Pub. Aid., Chgo., 1972-74, caseworker I, 1975-77, med. caseworker II, 1978-79, med. caseworker III, 1979-83; cosmetology student instr. Lyndon Beauty Acad., Steger, Ill., 1985—; owner Kenney's for Ribs and Pizza, Chgo., 1985—; lectr., cons. Huth Jr. High Sch., Matteson, Ill., 1985—. Recipient 2d and 3rd place trophies Unique Beauty Sch. Competition, 1982, Morris Acad., 1982; 4th and 3rd place trophies Pivot Point Beauty Sch., 1983; Creative Service award Environ. Conservation Commn., 1984. Mem. Nat. Assn. Female Execs., Nat. Hair Dressers and Cosmetologists Assn., Nat. Assn. Nail Artists. Democrat. Club: Sno Goffers Ski. Avocations: music; bowling; gardening.

LEWIS, VIRGINIA ELNORA, museum director; b. Sault Ste. Marie, Ont., Can., Apr. 7, 1907; d. Dan and Katherine (Barres) L.; A.B., U. Pitts., 1931, M.A., 1935; postgrad. Carnegie Inst. Tech., 1932-33. Proofreader, Carnegie Inst. Tech. Press, 1931-33; mem. faculty U. Pitts., 1934—, prof. fine arts, 1957-67, prof. emeritus, 1967—, acting head dept., 1954, 57-58, summers, 1940-63, curator exhbns. Henry Clay Erick fine arts dept., 1946—, head librarian Henry Clay Frick fine arts library, 1963-65, asst. dir. Henry Clay Frick fine arts bldg., 1965-67; dir. Frick Art Mus., Pitts., 1969—; researcher Helen C. Frick Found., 1967-69; dir. Dennis (Mass.) Art Gallery, 1953; cons., dir. Westmoreland County Mus. Art, 1954-56; adv. group 1981 Disting. Performance Awards, Chatham Coll., Pitts. Served as ensign USNR, 1941. Recipient salute Kaufmann's Dept. Store, Pitts., 1974; named Woman of Year, Pitts. Post Gazette, 1956, Disting. Dau. of Pa., 1977. Fellow Morgan Library, The Frick Collection (hon.); mem. Soc. Archtl. Historians (dir., chmn. Pitts. chpt. 1956), Coll. Art Assn. Am., Am. Assn. Mus., Pa. Hist. Soc., 100 Friends Pitts. (exec. bd.), Nat. Trust Hist. Preservation (chmn. session 14th ann. meeting), Print council Am., Internat. Council Mus., Arts and Crafts Center Pitts., Pitts. Bibliophile Soc., Spl. Libraries Assn., Xylon. Clubs: Women's Press, Zonta, Monday Luncheon (pres. 1970—), Women's City (Pitts.), Author: Andrey Avinoff: The Man, 1953; Russell Smith: Romantic Realist, 1956; also articles, exhbn. catalogues, revs.; contbr. New Cath. Ency. Office: Frick Art Museum 7227 Reynolds St Pittsburgh PA 15208

LEWIS, WANDA ELLA, nurse; b Portsmouth, Ohio, June 12, 1927; d. George Frank and Emma Abigail (Rice) Jarrell; R.N., Christ Hosp. Sch. Nursing, 1951; m. Ramon Lamar Lewis, May 2, 1960; children—Kris, Gail Jean. Supr. nurses Clinton Meml. Hosp., Wilmington, Ohio, 1951-53; staff nurse Pima County Hosp., Tucson, 1953-55; field nurse Bur. Indian Affairs-Alaska Native Service, Bethel, 1955-58; stewardess Wien Airlines, Fairbanks, Alaska, 1958-61; admissions supr. Providence Hosp., Anchorage, 1972-75; staff nurse, charge nurse Spring View Center, Springfield, Ohio 1975-80; dir. nurses Good Shepherd Nursing Home, 1980-81; supr. St. John's Nursing Home, Springfield, 1981-82; staff nurse Community Hosp., 1982-85; gen. supr. Ohio Masonic Home, Springfield, Ohio, 1985—. Active with mentally retarded, 1975-80; vol. instr. English, Udornthani, Thailand and Vientiene, Laos, 1965-67. Republican. Home: 2650 E High St Springfield OH 45505

LEWIS CONGDON, REBECCA ANN, TV station traffic manager; b. Whiteville, N.C., Dec. 8, 1942; d. Benjamin Brinson and Marjory Johnson (Powell) Lewis; m. Frederick Voorhees Congdon, Dec. 31, 1978; children—Suanne, Christopher, Jon. A.B. in Polit. Sci., U. N.C., 1965. Traffic mgr. WGXI Radio, Atlanta, 1965-70, WAGA-TV, Atlanta, 1970-74; nat. sales coordinator WXIA-TV, Atlanta, 1974-80; traffic mgr. WGNX-TV, Atlanta, 1980—. Mem., ERA, Ga., 1978—, NOW, 1979—, Nat. Women's Polit. Caucus, 1983—, LWV, Atlanta, 1985. Recipient Golden Mike award Coll. Students in Broadcasting, U. Ga., 1978. Mem. Am. Women in Radio and TV (pres. Atlanta chpt. 1978-79, 84-85, S.E. conf. chair 1985), Nat. Acad. TV Arts and Scis., PTA. Democrat. Methodist. Club: Shamrock High Band Boosters (hospitality chmn. 1983-84, publicity chmn. 1986-87). Avocations: reading; crossword puzzles; bridge. Office: WGNX-TV 1810 Briarcliff Rd Atlanta GA 30329

LEWIS-FAVERMANN, BARBARA DALE, architecture and design company executive; b. Bklyn., Jan. 20, 1955; d. Henry and Joy (Goldfarb) Lewis; m. Mark L. Favermann. B.S. in Bus. Adminstrn., SUNY-Albany, 1976; M.B.A., Suffolk U., 1978. Ops. auditor Hit or Miss, Stoughton, Mass., 1978-79; v.p. Favermann Assocs., Boston, 1980—; pres. Flying Colors, Boston, 1980—; grad. asst. Suffolk U., Boston, 1978. Mem. Soc. Mktg. Profls. Office: Favermann Assocs/Flying Colors 127 South St Boston MA 02111

LEWTER, LINDA VERZONE, social work administrator; b. Mobile, Ala., May 24, 1944; d. Felix and Mary Lee (Hall) Verzone; m. Fred A. Lewter III, Dec. 19, 1981; children—William E. Goff, Michele Lewter. Student, William Carey Coll., Hattiesburg, Miss., 1966-69; B.A., Mobile Coll., Ala., 1972; M.S.W., U. So. Miss., 1983. Lic. social worker Ala. Clerical staff Investors Diversified Services Inc., Mobile, 1961-62; stenographer Fed. Aviation Agy., Dauphin Island, Ala., 1962-63; legal stenographer presiding Judge, Hattiesburg, Miss., 1964-69, Hand, Arendall Attys., Mobile, 1972-73; social worker Dept. Pensions & Securities, Mobile, 1973-79; exec. dir. Penelope House Inc., Mobile, 1979—; adj. faculty U. So. Miss., Hattiesburg, 1984—, U. South Ala., Mobile, 1985—, Springhill Coll., Mobile, 1986—. Neighborhood worker Am. Heart Assn., Am. Cancer Soc.; vol. Epilepsy Ctr., Friends of Exceptional Children, Mobile. Named Outstanding Career Woman, Gayfers Career Club, Mobile, 1982; Social Worker of Yr., Mobile unit Nat. Assn. Social Workers, 1984. Mem. Nat. Assn. Female Execs., Nat. Assn. Social Work (publicity chmn. 1986), Vols. of America (bd. sec. 1981-84 Mobile), Parents Anonymous (bd. sec., pres., founder Mobile 1983, adv. bd. Ala.), Nat. Coalition Against Domestic Violence (legis. rep. 1979-81), Residential Care Assn. (treas. Mobile 1986), United Way Agy. Dir. Orgn., Vol. Dirs. Assn., Am. Bus. Women Assn. (scholarship chmn. 1984), Exec. Women's Forum (program co-chmn. 1986), Ala. Conf. Social Work, Ala. Council Family Relations, Ala. State Coalition Against Domestic Violence (pres. 1980, bd. dirs.), S.E. Region Tech. Assistance Ctr. Against Family Violence (steering com. rep. 1979-82), Mobile Inter-Agy. Com. on Alcoholism, Mobile Community Com. Against Family Violence (workshop chmn. 1983-84), Alpha Delta Mu. Democrat. Presbyterian. Club: Aventrepreneur Investment (sec. 1986, Mobile). Lodge: Order Eastern Star (Mobile). Avocations: reading; swimming; travel. Home: Rt 16 Box 172 Mobile AL 36609 Office: Penelope House Inc PO Box 6871 Mobile AL 36660

LEY, SANDRA DAWN, veterinarian; b. Windsor, Can., Feb. 14, 1950; d. Edwin Byron and Doris Louisa (Hennessey) Ley; m. Charles Francis Risten, Oct. 28, 1978. B.Sc., C.W. Post Coll., 1970; D.V.M., Mich. State U., 1974. Veterinarian A&A Animal Hosp., Franklin Square, N.Y., 1975-76, Great Neck Animal Hosp., N.Y., 1976, Lawrence Animal Hosp., Elmhurst, N.Y., 1976-79, Kings Park Animal Hosp., Smithtown, N.Y., 1979; pvt. practice vet. medicine, Smithtown, 1979—; vet. supr. regional dog shows; speaker local high sch. career days. Mem. AVMA, N.Y. State Vet. Med. Assn., L.I. Regional Assn. Veterinarians, Am. Avian Vet. Assn., Smithtown Women's Network, Nat. Assn. Female Execs. Democrat. Episcopalian. Office: 1215 Route 25A Smithtown NY 11787

LEYDA, JEAN CRAVENS (MRS. VIRGIL WILLIAM LEYDA), author, retired editor, educator, club woman; b. Granby, Mo., Jan. 15, 1903; d. William A. and Lois (Harmon) Cravens; A.A., Stephens Coll., 1920; B.A., Mt. Holyoke Coll., 1923; M.A. in English Lit., U. Wis., 1930; m. Virgil William Leyda, Aug. 10, 1945; 1 foster son, Leonard Breckler. Tchr. English, Freeport (Ill.) High Sch., 1923-26, head English dept., 1926-27; head English dept. Mishawaka (Ind.) High Sch., 1929-45, dir. English, Mishawaka Jr. and Sr. High Schs., 1938-45; co-author lit. anthologies Scott, Foresman Co., Chgo., 1940-50, editorial staff, after 1945; now ret. Pres., Chandler (Ariz.) Woman's Club, 1954-55, chmn. community service com., 1961-63; edn. chmn. Ariz. Fedn. Women's Clubs, 1955-57. Mem. founding adv. bd. Chandler Pub. Library. Recipient alumnae achievement award Stephens Coll., 1956. Former mem., past pres. Ind. Council Tchrs. English. Mem. Ind. Ret. Tchrs. Assn., Nat. Ret. Tchrs. Assn., DAR, Colonial Dames 17th Century, PEO, Phi Theta Kappa. Democrat. Presbyn. (trustee 1951-53, life elder). Mem. Order Eastern Star, Daus. of Nile. Club: Desert (past pres.). Author: (with others) Enjoying Life through Literature, 1951; Exploring Life through Literature, 1951. Address: 400 N Hartford St Chandler AZ 85224

LEYPOLDT, RUTH SHULL, real estate executive; b. North Platte, Nebr., July 19, 1920; d. Harry White and Naomi Caroline (Pruden) Shull; m. Lowell Lowry Leypoldt, Sept. 24, 1944 (dec. 1983); 1 son, Timothy S. B.S., U. Nebr., 1941. Chief clk. to trainmaster Union Pacific R.R., Sidney, Nebr., 1941-48; office mgr. Flory's Shoe Co., also sec., treas. Flory's, Inc., Cheyenne, Wyo., 1952-78; sales assoc. Century 21 Bell Real Estate, 1979—, also mem. Million Dollar Club. Mem. AAUW, Am. Soc. Women Accts. (dir. 1975-76). Republican. Presbyterian. Home: 1409 1/2 Rollins Rd Cheyenne WY 82001 Office: Century 21 Bell Real Estate 2103 Warren Ave Cheyenne WY 82001

LEZAK, CHERYL COROL, business executive, consultant; b. Los Angeles, Oct. 12, 1950; d. Morris and Esther (Bass) Corol; m. Daniel Sherwin Lezak, Nov. 19, 1983. B.A., U. Ariz., 1972. Tchr. Los Angeles City Schs., 1972-74; paralegal law firms, Los Angeles, about 1974-82; corp. sec. Lezak Group, Inc., Calabasas, Calif., 1982—, also dir.; cons. Five Star Energy, Calabasas, 1984—; sec., dir. CD Mgmt., Inc., CD Mortgage Investors, Inc.; dir. Contempo Pub., Nev. Office: Lezak Group Inc 23501 Park Sorrento Suite 104 Calabasas CA 91302

LEZEAU, GLADYS DAVIS, educator, evangelist; b. N.Y.C., July 25, 1937; d. Robert and Pearl Gertrude (Vaughan) Davis; B.S., State U. N.Y., 1960; M.S., Pace U., 1977; m. Lesly Lezeau, Sept. 10, 1976; 1 son, Leonel. Tchr. adult edn. Yonkers (N.Y.) Bd. Edn., 1960—; nat. evangelist Ch. of God in Christ, 1961-77; founder Women for Christ-Worldwide, 1970; founder Prayer and Praise, 1978, exec. dir., 1978-80; radio evangelist St. Paul's Ch., Westchester, 1968-80; founder, dir. Sun's of God, Inc., 1980—. Recipient award for dedicated service Women for Christ-Worldwide, 1968; Am. Studies fellow Eastern Bapt. Coll., summer 1970. Mem. N.Y. State Home Econs. Assn., Yonkers Fedn. Tchrs. Club: 700. Home: 105 Bruce Ave Yonkers NY 10705 Office: 145 Palmer Rd Yonkers NY 10701

LHAMON, JUDITH ANN, university official; b. Quantico, Va., Sept. 2, 1945; d. George M. and Mary B. (Taylor) L. B.A. in English, Am. U., 1968; M.A.T. in History and Edn., Trinity Coll., 1970. Tchr. Washington pub. schs., 1970-73; orientation, internship coordinator Antioch Sch. Law, Washington, 1973-75, placement dir., 1975-77; recruitment specialist Legal Services Corp., Washington, 1977-81; dir. recruiting firm Steptoe & Johnson, Washington, 1981-84; dir. career planning and placement Yale U. Law Sch., 1984—. Pres. Fairfax Village III Condo, 1981-84; mediator Citizen's Complaint Ctr., 1979-83. Mem. Women's Legal Def. Fund, Nat. Assn. Law Placement (co-chmn. employment practices com. 1982-84). Democrat. Episcopalian. Author: Lawful and Effective Interviewing Practices, 1984; A Survey of Law Firms-A Success Story for Minorities?Office: Box 401A Yale Station New Haven CT 06520

LI, TU LEUNG, management executive; b. N.Y.C., Nov. 10, 1948; d. Gum Ming and Toa Moy (Wong) Lee; m. Ta M. Li, Dec. 31, 1969; 1 child, Ta Ming. B.S., U. Utah, 1977. Sr. cons. Aetna Ins. Co., Salt Lake City, 1977-78; advt. mgr. Assn. Surg. Technologist, Littleton, Colo., 1978-80; research mgr. MET-Research Co., Lakewood, Colo., 1980-82; pres., chief exec. officer Tatum & Assocs., Littleton, 1982—; acct. Martin Marietta Data Systems Inc., 1985—; dir. Asian X-M Ltd, Loveland, Colo. Contbr. articles on computer mgmt. techniques to publs. Sec., Friends of Littleton Library, 1984. Mem. AAUW (bd. dirs. 1983-84). Club: Argonauts Investment (pres. 1982-83) (Littleton).

LIAN, NANCY WINTSCH, association executive; b. Waterbury, Conn., Nov. 8, 1935; d. Harry and Enid Hildegard (Steig) Wintsch; m. Edvin B. Lian, Apr. 29, 1961; children—H. Tanja, Heidi E. B.A., Carleton Coll., 1957; postgrad. Tchrs. Coll. Columbia U., 1964. Cert. assn. exec. Tchr. ESL, Doshisha High Sch., Kyoto, Japan, 1957-59; pub. relations asst. Takashi-maya, Inc., N.Y.C., 1959-60; research MLA, N.Y.C., 1960-65; asst. sec.-treas. N.E. Conf. on Teaching Fgn. Langs., N.Y.C., 1965-76; dir. adminstrn. and meetings Nat. Home Improvement Council, N.Y.C., 1976-81; exec. dir. N.Y. Library Assn., N.Y.C., 1981—; bd. regents Inst. for Orgn. Mgmt. U.S. C. of C., Washington, 1983—, chmn. N.E. bd. regents, 1986; mem. N.Y. State Continuing Library Edn. Com., 1981-84. Co-author; Foreign Language Offerings and Enrollments in Secondary Schools, 1961-62, 1962. Dir. Carleton Coll. Alumni Bd., 1982-85; coordinator Carleton Alumni Admissions Met. N.Y., 1978-82; leader Experiment in Internat. Living, Ulm, Germany, 1960. Recipient Assn. Exec. of Yr. award N.Y. State Assn. Conv. Burs., 1984. Mem. Am. Soc. Assn. Execs. (nominating com. 1983). N.Y. Soc. Assn. Execs. (dir. 1982-85, chmn. coms., 1979-80, 82, 86), Internat. Assn. Library Execs. (1st v.p. 1983-84, pres. 1985). Congregationalist. Office: NY Library Assn 15 Park Row New York NY 10038

LIANG, VERA BEH-YUIN TSAI, psychiatrist; b. Shanghai, China, July 7, 1946; came to U.S., 1970, naturalized, 1978; d. Ming Sang and Mea Ling Chu Tsai; m. Hanson Liang, Nov. 6, 1971; children—Eric G., Jason G. M.B.B.S., U. Hong Kong, 1969. Diplomate Am. Bd. Psychiatry and Neurology. Intern, Cambridge Hosp. (Mass.), 1970-71; resident Hillside div. L.I. Jewish Med. Ctr., New Hyde Park, N.Y., 1971-73; fellow Albert Einstein Coll. Medicine, Bronx, N.Y., 1973-75; instr. SUNY-Downstate Med. Ctr., Bklyn., 1975-79; asst. prof. SUNY-Stony Brook, 1979—; med. dir. Hillside Eastern Queens Ctr., Queens Village, N.Y., 1978—; vis. lectr. Jamaica Hosp., Queens, N.Y., 1980; cons. in field. Mem. Am. Psychiat. Assn., Am. Acad. Child Psychiatry, N.Y. Council Child Psychiatry. Contbr. articles to profl. jours. Office: HEQ Center 96-09 Springfield Blvd Queens Village NY 11429

LIAPAKIS, PAMELA ANAGNOS, lawyer; b. Queens, N.Y., Jan. 26, 1947; d. Charles G. and Mary (Andriakos) Anagnos; m. John Liapakis, Nov. 9, 1969 (div. 1981). B.A., Bklyn. Coll., 1967; J.D., St. John's U. Sch. of Law, 1970. Bar: N.Y., U.S. Supreme Ct. Assoc., Harry H. Lipsig, P.C., N.Y.C., 1969-72, Berman & Frost, N.Y.C., 1972-75; pvt. practice law, Bklyn., 1975-76; sr. ptnr. Lipsig, Sullivan & Liapakis, P.C. N.Y.C., 1976—. Mem. N.Y. Women's Bar Assn. (rec. sec. 1974-75, 3rd v.p. 1976-77, treas. 1975-76), Am. Trial Lawyers Assn., N.Y. State Trial Lawyers Assn. (bd. dirs. 1985-86), Assn. Bar City N.Y. Greek Orthodox. Home: 515 E 79th St Apt 14D New York NY 10021 Office: Lipsig Sullivan & Liapakis PC 100 Church St New York NY 10007

LIBARLE, EMILY MARIE, retired nurse, civic worker; b. San Francisco, Jan. 4, 1915; d. George and Pia (Giusti) Benedetti; m. Lucien George Libarle, Apr. 29, 1939; children—Denise, Daniel, Marc, Jeffrey. Student Santa Rosa Jr. Coll.; R.N., St. Luke's Sch. Nursing, 1935. R.N., Calif. Nursing dir. Community Immunization Program, Well Baby Clinic, Sonoma County, Calif., 1945-60; surg. nurse open heart surgery team Meml. Hosp., Santa Rosa, Calif., 1965-70. Pres. Sonoma County Catholic Social Service, Santa Rosa, 1965—; founder, pres. St. Anthony Farm Aux., Petaluma, Calif., 1965—; mem. Community Guild, Sonoma County, 1940—; vice chmn. Sonoma County Grand Jury, 1980-81; founder, v.p. Family Info. Ctr., Sonoma County, 1976-83; bd. dirs. Sonoma-Marin Fair, 1975-79, Santa Rosa Symphony Assn., 1963—, Luther Burbank Performing Arts Ctr., 1984—. Recipient Woman of Yr. award We-Tip, 1981-82. Mem. P.E.O. Internat. Republican. Roman Catholic. Avocation: support of symphony. Home: 705 W Railroad Ave Cotati CA 94928

LIBASSI, PATRICIA CAMPBELL, writer; b. Mason City, Iowa, Sept. 29, 1929; d. David Lawrence and Mary Beatrice Campbell; R.N., St. Joseph Hosp. Sch. Nursing, South Bend, Ind., 1949; student Ind. U., U. Buffalo; m. Paul Joseph LiBassi, Aug. 12, 1950; children—Michael, Mark, David, J. Douglas, Patricia Ann, Suzanne Marie. Staff nurse, then night supr. William Coleman Hosp. for Women, 1952; staff nurse, pvt. duty nurse Ft. Leavenworth Army Hosp., 1954, Buffalo Gen. Hosp., Childrens' Hosp., St. Joseph Intercommunity Hosp., 1956, 57, 60; with Call for Action, Sta. WIVB-TV, Buffalo, 1976—, co-dir., 1979—, dir., 1980-83, regional dir., 1980; tchr. great books elem. sch., 1967, 68. Contbr. Buffalo Evening News, Youngstown Youth Club paper. Bd. dirs. Call for Action, Inc., 1980-83. Mem. Nat. Writers Club, Action Line Reporters Assn., Am. Film Inst., Notre Dame Alumni Wives, Nat. Geog. Soc. Clubs: Youngstown Yacht, Niagara on the Lake Sailing. Home and Office: 4990 Pine Ledge Dr W Clarence NY 14031

LIBBY, JUDITH LYNN, lawyer; b. Elgin, Ill., Oct. 20, 1948; d. Jules Leon and Virginia Marie (Marshall) L.; B.A. in English Lit., Roosevelt U., 1970; J.D. with highest distinction (Scholar), John Marshall Law Sch., 1977; m. Richard J. Coffee, II, Feb. 14, 1981; children—David Patrick, Brent William. Tchr. humanities Craigmore High Sch., Smithfield, South Australia, Australia, 1971-73; admitted to Ill. bar, 1977; assoc. firm Taussig, Wexler & Shaw, Ltd., Chgo., 1977-78; chief counsel Ill. Dept. Ins., Springfield, 1978-80; partner firm Libby & Coffee, Springfield, 1981-84; asst. defender Office of State Appelliate Defender. Mem. ABA, Ill. State Bar Assn., Chgo. Bar Assn. Central Ill. Women's Bar Assn. (pres. 1984-85). Office: 300 E Monore Suite 200 Springfield IL 32701

LIBERMAN, MERLE FRAN, data processing manager; b. Chgo., Apr. 20, 1950; d. Leo and Shirley (Young) Liberman. B.A., Northeastern Ill. U., 1972; M.B.A., U. Chgo., 1980. Tchr., Cass Elem. Sch., Dupage County, Ill., 1972-74; systems analyst Allstate Ins., Northbrook, Ill., 1974-78; programmer analyst Am. Mgmt. Systems, Chgo., 1978-79; project leader Tymshare, Chgo., 1979-80; pres. Merlin & Assocs., Detroit, 1980-84; product mgr. Info. Builders, N.Y.C., 1984—; cons. Affiliated Resources, Chgo., 1976—; tech. edn. advisor High Tech Learning Ctr., Warren, Mich., 1983-84; cons. Profl. Women, Troy, Mich., 1982-84; tech. cons. R.F. Nussbaum, Inc., Chgo., 1978—. Mem. Nat. Assn. Female Execs., Nat. Focus Users Group. Jewish. Club: Defuse (founding dir. 1983-84, Detroit). Avocations: tennis; scrabble; needlepoint; science fiction reading. Home: 207 Jefferson Ave River Edge NJ 07661

LIBET, ALICE QUANTE, clinical psychologist; b. Savannah, Ga., Feb. 7, 1949; d. Albert Herman and Anita (Mahany) Quante; B.A. cum laude with gen. honors, (Ga. Regents scholar, Ga. State Tchrs. scholar), U. Ga., 1971, M.S., 1974, Ph.D., 1977; m. Julian Mayer Libet, Nov. 27, 1976; children—Jared Quante, Ariel Quante. Instr. Ga. Retardation Center, Athens, 1974-75; research psychologist VA Med. Center, Charleston, S.C., 1978-81; clin. psychologist dept. pediatrics Med. U. S.C., Charleston, 1977-83; adminstr. community program S.C. Dept. Mental Retardation, 1983—. Mem. Am. Psychol. Assn., Charleston Area Psychol. Assn., Psi Chi. Contbr. articles to profl. jours. Home: 28 Hillcreek Blvd Charleston SC 29412 Office: Summerall Center Suite 907 19 Hagood Ave Charleston SC 29403

LIBONE, JOYCE MARIE, nurse; b. Bridgeport, Conn., Sept. 13, 1927; d. George Robert and Margaret M. (Gaffney) Roland; m. Donato D. Libone, Jan. 29, 1949; children—John J., Ralph D. Diploma St. Vincent's Hosp., 1948. Operating room supr. Mary Shiels Hosp., Dallas, 1949-51, Community Hosp., Dallas, 1970-73; pediatrics nurse Dr. Piranio, Dallas, 1951-54; orthopedic nurse, asst. supr. St. Paul's Hosp., Dallas, 1973-78; operating room nurse Morton Hosp., Dallas, 1978-81; med. reviewer Blue Cross Blue Shield Ins., Dallas, 1983-86; utilization coordinator and discharge planner Labouré Care Ctr., Dallas, 1986—. Vol. nurse Cath. Sch. System. Mem. Operating Room Nurses Assn. Roman Catholic. Clubs: Cath. Daughters Am. (1st vice regent), Alhambra (sec.-treas.). Home: 4031 Treeline Dr Dallas TX 75224 Office: 1950 Record Crossing Dallas TX 75235

LICARI, MARY CASTANIETO, social worker; b. Brawley, Calif., Oct. 7, 1948; d. Toribio Casogoc and Manuela (Plascencia) Castanieto; m. Gabriel Necochea, Feb. 20, 1969 (div. 1971); 1 son, Alexis Gabriel; m. Jack Salvatore Licari, Feb. 19, 1972; 1 son, Jason Anthony. A.A. in Social Sci. with great distinction, Imperial Valley Coll., 1970; B.A. in Social Work with distinction, San Jose State U., 1978, M.A. in Social Work with honors, 1980. Evening admissions clk. Imperial Valley Coll., Calif., 1967-70; affirmative action asst. Stanford Research Inst., Menlo Park, Calif., 1972-74; eligibility worker Santa Clara County Dept. Social Services, San Jose, Calif., 1974-77, social worker, 1977-83, mem. Speaker's Bur., 1981-83, select com. mem. child abuse, 1982-83; social service practitioner Riverside County Dept. Social Services, Calif., 1983—, mem. Speaker's Bur.; cons., trainer Family Edn. Ctr., San Jose, 1982-83. Mem. Santa Clara County Delinquency Prevention Commn., 1982-83, Santa Clara County Prevention of Child Abuse Commn., 1982-83, MECHA-Mexican American, 1970; vol. United Farm Workers Union, San Jose, 1970—, Woman's Alliance Shelter for Battered Women, San Jose, 1979-80; canvasser Democratic Party, 1974-80; active Milpitas council Boy Scouts Am., 1981-83. Scholar Women's Venture Club, 1967, Brawley Rotary Club, 1967, Am. GI Forum, 1967, Santa Clara County, 1979. Mem. Nat. Assn. Social Workers, Inland Empire Task Force Child Abuse, Queen's Hon. Soc. (life), Calif. Scholarship Fedn. (life), Quill and Scroll Lit. (life), Social Services Union (steward asst. Local 535, 1982), Alpha Gamma Sigma. Roman Catholic. Club: San Jose/Milpitas Womans. Avocations: tennis; writing poetry; clown collecting. Office: Riverside County Dept Pub Social Services 3950 Reynolds Rd Riverside CA 92503

LICHTENDORF, SUSAN SIEGEL, science writer, author; b. N.Y.C., Jan. 16, 1941; d. Harry B. and Mildred (Sharfstein) Siegel; B.A., Queens Coll., City U. N.Y., 1962; postgrad. N.Y. U. Inst. Fine Arts, 1963-64; m. Arthur E. Lichtendorf, Dec. 14, 1969; 1 dau., Victoria Jane. Women's news feature writer L.I. (N.Y.) Press, 1962-66, gen. assignment news reporter, 1966-68; sci. writer nat. office Am. Cancer Soc., N.Y.C., 1968-80; freelance writer books and articles, 1970—; speaker nat. maternal and child health confs., 1979-80; vol. speechwriter ERAmerica, 1976. Mem. Nat. Assn. Sci. Writers, Women in Communications, Authors Guild, Women's Ink, Internat. Childbirth Edn. Assn., Nat. Women's Health Network. Co-author: (with Phyllis Gillis) The New Pregnancy: The Active Woman's Guide, 1979; author: Eve's Journey: The Physical Experience of Being Female, 1982; editor Women's Occupational Health Resource Ctr., Columbia U. Sch. Pub. Health, 1984-85; contbr. numerous articles to various mags., newspapers. Home and Office: 141 E 89th St New York NY 10128

LICHTENFELD, ARLENE, data processing executive; b. Jersey City, Feb. 8, 1954; d. David and Betty (Golipsky) Tesser; m. Sam J. Lichtenfeld, July 4, 1976. B.A. in Math., Fairleigh Dickinson U., 1975. Programmer, Equitable Life Ins. Co., N.Y.C., 1975-76, programmer/analyst, 1976-78; cons. analyst Computer Horizons Corp., N.Y.C., 1978-80, cons. analyst Gen. Electric Info. Services Co., Piscataway, N.J., 1980-81, account mgr., 1981-83, tech. dir., 1983—; cons. AT&T, 1979-80, Exxon Corp., 1980-82, Volvo of Am. Corp., 1982-83, Johnson & Johnson, 1983. Mem. New Frontier Democratic Orgn., Bayonne, N.J., 1976—. Mem. Am. Mgmt. Assn., Nat. Assn. Female Execs. Democrat. Jewish. Club: Library Engring. and Computer Sci. Office: Gen Electric Cons Services Corp 45 Knightsbridge Rd Piscataway NJ 08054

LICHTENSTEIN, DORIS HARRIS, hospital executive; b. East St. Louis, Ill., July 10, 1928; d. Guy Webster and Mary Ester (Dettenbach) Waters; m. Howard Hamilton Harris, Jr., May 17, 1943 (dec. June 1955); children—Howard Hamilton III, Guy William (dec. Aug. 1973), Bruce Carlton; m. David Benjamin Lichtenstein, Jr., Apr. 13, 1974; stepchildren—David Benjamin III, Davida Beatrice, Matthew Aaron. A.B., Washington U., St. Louis, 1958, postgrad., 1958-61. Tchr., Belleville (Ill.) Jr. High Sch., 1958; asst. personnel dir. Boyd Richardson, St. Louis, 1958-61; personnel dir. Mo. Bapt. Hosp., St. Louis, 1961-83, asst. v.p., 1983—; instr. evening div. Forest Park Community Coll., St. Louis, 1980. Mem. dist. council community Family and Children's Service, Clayton, Mo., 1983—; bd. dirs., mem. exec. com. YWCA, St. Louis, 1974-78, also chmn. personnel com. Mem. Am. Soc. Hosp. Personnel Adminstrn. (regional dir. 1983—, exec. com.), Hosp. Personnel Mgmt. Assn. Mo. (pres. 1980-81), Hosp. Personnel Mgmt. Assn. Greater St. Louis (pres. 1979-81), Am. Soc. Personnel Adminstrn., Indsl. Relations Assn., Am. Hosp. Assn., Hosp. Assn. Met. St. Louis, Mo. Hosp. Assn., Phi Beta Kappa. Baptist. Office: Mo Bapt Hosp 3015 N Ballas Rd St Louis MO 63131

LICHTER-HEATH, LAURIE JEAN, lawyer; b. Bklyn., Mar. 13, 1951; d. Irving and Beatrice (Gelber) Lichter; m. Donald Wayne Heath, Feb. 28, 1981; 1 son: Michele Samuel. B.S. with honors, U. Tenn.-Knoxville, 1972; J.D., John Marshall Law Sch., 1975; postgrad. NYU, 1978; LL.M., Georgetown U., 1979. Bar: Ill. 1975, D.C. 1977, N.Y. 1980, Nev. 1981. Law clk. D.C. Ct. Appeals, Washington, 1975-77; atty. enforcement div. SEC, Washington, 1977-78; lectr. N.Y. U. Sch. Continuing Edn. in Law and Taxation, 1980-81; atty. govt. relations asst. Met. Life Ins. Co., N.Y.C., 1978-81; assoc. atty. Miller & Daar, Reno, Nev. 1981; legal cons. Stockton, Calif., 1981-84; asst. prof. U. Pacific, Stockton, 1984—. Instr., YMCA, Knoxville, 1969-72; leader Concerned Parents, Stockton, Calif., 1984. U. Ill. fellow, 1972. Mem. Nev. Bar Assn., N.Y. Bar Assn. D.C. Bar Assn., Ill. Bar Assn., ABA, AAUW, Sierra Club.

LICHTI, BARBARA JEAN, accountant; b. Corydon, Ind., Jan. 14, 1942; d. Lester and Evelyn Rose Ferguson; diploma acctg. Bryant and Stratton Bus. Coll., Louisville, 1962; enrolled to practice before IRS; m. Marvin Lichti, Dec. 20, 1963; 1 dau., Diana. Acct., Sta. WLKY, Louisville, 1962-64; head dept. grain storage Dept. Agr., Champaign, Ill., 1964-68; acct. Larry Buhrmester, Champaign, 1968-73, Armstrong & Acord, C.P.A.s, Champaign, 1973-75; self-employed acct., Champaign, 1976—. Mem. Twin Cities Bus. and Profl. Women's Club, Nat. Assn. Tax Practioners, Assn. Bus. Accts., Nat. Assn. Enrolled Agts., Nat. Soc. Pub. Accts., Ill. Ind. Accts. Assn. Address: 909 Devonshire St Champaign IL 61820

LICKEY, MARY KAYE MAUCK, educator; b. Martinsburg, W.Va., Feb. 20, 1948; d. Percy Martin and Rosemary (Shrader) Mauck; m. Sylvester Warren Lickey, Aug. 31, 1968; 1 child, Brian Martin. B.A. in Secondary Edn., Shepherd Coll., Shepherdstown, W.Va., 1970; M.A. in Secondary Edn. summa cum laude, W.Va. U., 1982. Cert. tchr. lang. arts and gifted edn., W.Va. Class room tchr. Bereley County Bd. of Edn., Martinsburg, 1970—; choreographer creative arts dept. Hedgesville High Sch., W.Va., 1975-79, band front instr., 1980-84; clinic instr. marching bands, W.Va., Va., Pa., 1985—; coordinator gifted practicum W.Va. U., Morgantown, 1985—. Author Berkeley County Gifted Program, 1984—. Com. chmn. Jr. Civic League, Martinsburg, 1976-79; treas. Little League, Martinsburg, 1985—. Nominee Nat. Tchr. of Yr., Council of Chief State Sch. Officers, 1984. Mem. Seekers of Ednl. Excellence, NEA, W.Va. Edn. Assn., Berkeley County Edn. Assn., Quill and Scroll Honor Soc. (adviser 1971). Republican. Methodist. Lodges: Ladies of the Elks (chmn. 1975-78), Order of Rainbow (worthy adviser, state rep. 1966). Avocation: doll collecting. Home: 801 Penn St Martinsburg WV 25401 Office: Hedgesville High Sch Route 1 Box 89 Hedgesville WV 25427

LIDDELL, CYNTHIA ANN, corporate administrator, psychologist; b. San Rafael, Calif., Nov. 11, 1951; d. James Nelson and Bettyjane (Hambridge) Liddell. B.S. cum laude, U. Calif.-Davis, 1973; M.A. summa cum laude, Calif. State U.-Sacramento, 1975. Cert. psychologist, community coll. tchr., Calif. Asst. prof. Calif. State U.-Sacramento, 1972-74; adminstr. State of Calif., Sacramento, 1974-79; mng. ptnr. Liddell & Assocs., 1979-81; owner, adminstr. The Seed Machine Co. Inc., Sacramento, 1981—; ptnr. Windmill Bldg. Inc., Sacramento, 1980—. Mem. Calif. Gov.'s Roundtable, Sacramento, 1975. Calif. State scholar 1969. Mem. AAUW, Psi Chi, Mu Alpha Theta, Calif. Women in State Service North Calif. (program mgr., pres. 1974-76), Democrat.

LIDDELL, JANE HAWLEY HAWKES, civic worker; b. Newark, Dec. 8, 1907; d. Edward Zeh and Mary Everett (Hawley) Hawkes; A.B., Smith Coll., 1931; postgrad. in art history, Harvard U., 1933-35; M.A., Columbia U., 1940; Carnegie fellow Sorbonne, Paris, 1937; m. Donald M. Liddell, Jr., Mar. 30, 1940; children—Jane Boyer, D. Roger Brooke. Pres., Planned Parenthood Essex County (N.J.), 1947-50; trustee Prospect Hill Sch. Girls, Newark, 1946-50; mem. adv. bd., publicity and public relations chmn. N.J. State Mus., Trenton, 1952-60; sec., then v.p. women's br. N.J. Hist. Soc.; women's aux. prodn. chmn. Englewood (N.J.) Hosp., 1959-61; pres. Dwight Sch. Girls Parents Assn., 1955-57; v.p. Englewood Sch. Boys Parents Assn., 1958-60; mem. Altar Guild, women's aux. bd., rector's adv. council St. Paul's Episcopal Ch., Englewood, 1954-59; bd. dir. N.Y. State Soc. of Nat. Soc. Colonial Dames, 1961-67, rep. conf. Patriotic and Hist. Socs., 1964—; bd. dirs. Huguenot Soc. Am., 1979-86, regional v.p., 1979-82, historian, 1983-84, co-chmn. Tercentennial Book, 1983-85; bd. dirs. Soc. Daus. Holland Dames, 1965-82; bd. dirs., mem. publs. com. Daus. Cin., 1966-72; bd. dirs. Ch. Women's League Patriotic Service, 1962—, pres., 1968-70, 72-74; bd. dirs., chmn. grants com. Youth Found., N.Y.C., 1974—; chmn. for Newark, Smith Coll. 75th Ann. Fund, 1948-50; pres. North N.J. Smith Club, 1956-58; pres. Smith Coll. Class 1931, 1946-51, 76-81, editor 50th anniversary book, 1980-81. Recipient various commendation awards. Republican. Mem. Colonial Dames Am. (N.Y.C. chpt.). Clubs: Colony, City Gardens, Church (N.Y.C.); Jr. League Bergen County; Needle and Bobbin, Nat. Farm and Garden; Englewood Woman's, Englewood Field; Hillsboro (Pompano Beach, Fla.). Editor: Maine Echoes, 1961.

LIDDELL, JEAN A. FISK, child development clinic administrator; b. Aberdeen, S.D., June 11, 1946; d. Darwin A. and Ardith (Severance) F.; m. Giles Banks Lidell, II, Dec. 28, 1985; 1 stepson, Giles Banks III. B.S., U. Wis., Oshkosh, 1972; M.S.Ed., U. Wis., Whitewater, 1974; postgrad. Nat. Coll. Edn., Evanston, Ill., 1975, No. Colo. U., 1979. Supr., N.W. Spl. Edn. Dist., Freeport, Ill., 1972-73; cons. Racine County Spl. Edn., Union Grove, Wis., 1973-74; instr. Nat. Coll. Edn., 1974-77; founder, exec. dir. Chgo. Clinic for Child Devel., 1976—; in-service dir., cons. to schs. Recipient Title VI-D fellowship award, 1972. Mem. Assn. for Children with Learning Disabilities, Exec. Female Assn., Council for Adminstrs. in Spl. Edn., Hyde Park Businessmen's Assn., Council for Exceptional Children. Christian. Club: Zonta. Author: EmH-SLD????, 1972; Handbook for Parents of Children with Learning Disabilities, 1973; Nonsense Syllables as an Aide to Teaching Reading, 1973. Office: 1525 E 53d St Chicago IL 60615

LIDDELL, MARLANE ADAIR, magazine editor; b. San Diego, Feb. 11, 1944; d. Robert Randall and Beatrice Sylvia (Waite) L.; m. C. Gregory Gay, Apr. 21, 1979; stepchildren—Merrill, Brian. B.A. in English Lit., San Diego State U., 1965. Pub. affairs writer EEOC, Washington, 1965-67; text editor Topic Mag., USIA, Washington, 1967-68, photo editor, 1968-70; asst. editor Smithsonian Mag., Washington, 1970-74, articles editor, 1974—; photo editor Acad. Press, Orlando, Fla., 1983. Editor: (textbook) Introduction to Criminal Justice. Mem. Chi Omega (bd. dirs. 1962-65). Democrat. Episcopalian. Clubs: Nat. Press, Washington Press (sec. 1982-83, v.p. 1983-84, pres. Found. 1984—). Avocations: swimming; tennis. Office: Smithsonian Mag 900 Jefferson Dr Washington DC 20002

LIDDY, MARIE THERESE, career cons. co. exec., b. Newark, July 27, 1932, d. Joseph A. and Veronica Cecelia (Beston) L.; B.A. in English and Music, Chestnut Hill Coll., Phila., 1967; M.A. in English and Drama, St. Bonaventure U., Olean, N.Y., 1972, M.A. in Theology and Psychology, 1977. Tchr., counselor John Carroll High Sch., Bel Air, Md., 1968-70; instr. English, asso. in counseling St. Bonaventure U., 1970-72; lectr., career adv. Temple U., Phila., 1972-76; co-dir. campus community, counselor, adminstr. LaSalle Coll., Phila., 1977-78; research and devel. staff Am. Inst. Property and Liability Underwriters, 1978-80; pres., exec. dir. Mainstream Access, Inc., Phila., 1980—; seminar leader, 1968—. Mem. Interreligious Task Force Soviet Jewry, 1976-81, Phila. Human Relations Commn., 1972-76; co-sponsor Women's Inter Faith Dialogue on Middle East, 1976-78. Mem. Nat. Assn. Female Execs., Am. Soc. Tng. and Devel., Phila. Women's Network. Contbr., Insurance (Job Finder series), 1981; contbr. articles to profl. jours. Home: 64 Southgate Rd Mount Laurel NJ 08054 Office: Ave of the Arts Bldg Philadelphia PA 19107

LIDE, NEOMA JEWELL LAWHON (MRS. MARTIN JAMES LIDE, JR.), poet; b. Levelland, Tex., Apr. 1, 1926; d. Charles Samuel and Juel (Yeager) Lawhon; Secretarial cert. Draughon's Bus. Coll., 1943; student U. Tex., 1944-46; R.N., Jefferson-Hillman Sch. Nursing, 1950; m. Martin James Lide, Jr., Nov. 12, 1950; children—Martin James, III, Brooks Nathaniel, Gardner Lawhon. Writer column Baldwin Times, Bay Minette, Ala., 1964-68, Shades Valley Sun newspapers, Birmingham, Ala., 1974-75; v.p., sec. Martin J. Lide Assocs., Inc., Birmingham, 1977-81; R.N. supr. St. Martin's in the Pines, 1984. Mem. def. adv. com. Women in Services, for Ala., 1961-63; coordinator women's activities Nat. Vets. Day, Birmingham, 1961-68; mem. exec. com., 1968-70; exec. bd. Women's Com. of 100 for Birmingham, 1964-65. Mem. Gorgas bd. U. Ala., Tuscaloosa, 1959. Recipient citation Merit, Muscular Dystrophy Assn. Am., 1961. Author: (poetry) Instead of Sunset, 1973; (fiction) Life of Service-These are My Jewels, 1979; Music in the Wind - The Story of Lady Arlington, 1980; Brother James Bryan-Hope Lives Eternal, 1981; Music of the Soul, 1982; The Past and Psyche of Arlington, 1983. Home: 3536 Brookwood Rd Mountain Brook Birmingham AL 35223

LIDSKY, ELLA, librarian; b. Wilno, Poland; came to U.S. 1962; d. Leib and Sheina (Izygzon) Cwik; m. Alexander Lidsky, Feb. 20, 1963; 1 son, David Abraham. B.A., Pedagogical Inst. Odessa, USSR; M.S., Columbia U., 1966; M.A., 1973. Cert. Russian and Hebrew lang. tchr. Tchr. high sch., USSR, 1944-46, Poland, 1948-1951, elem. sch. Israel, 1961-62; catalog librarian Tchrs. Coll., Columbia U., N.Y.C., 1966-68; cataloger librarian Fairleigh Dickenson U., Teaneck, N.J., 1968-69, asst. dir. tech. services, Madison, N.J., 1973-84; asst. librarian U.S. Ct. Internat. Trade Law Library, 1985—; cataloger librarian Ramapo Coll., Mahwah, N.J., 1971-73. Mem. ALA, N.Y. Tech. Services Librarians. Democrat. Jewish. Office: US Court Internat Trade One Federal Plaza New York NY 10007

LIEBELER, SUSAN WITTENBERG, lawyer, educator; b. New Castle, Pa., July 3, 1942; d. Sherman K. and Eleanor (Kilvans) Levine; B.A., U. Mich., 1963, postgrad. Law Sch., 1963-64; LL.B. (Stein scholar), UCLA, 1966; m. Wesley J. Liebeler, Oct. 21, 1971; 1 dau., Jennifer. Bar: Calif. 1967, Vt. 1972. Llaw clk. Hon. Gordon L. Files, Calif. Ct. of Appeals, 1966-67; asso. firm Gang, Tyre & Brown, 1967-68, firm Greenberg, Bernhard, Weiss & Karma, Los Angeles, 1968-70; asso. gen. counsel Republic Corp., Los Angeles, 1970-72; gen. counsel Verit Industries, Los Angeles, 1972-73; prof. of law Loyola Law Sch., Los Angeles, 1973—; spl. counsel, chmn. John S. R. Shad, SEC, Washington, 1981-82; vis. prof. U. Tex., summer 1982; Commr. U.S. Internat. Trade Commn. Washington, 1984—, now vice chmn.; cons. Office of Policy Coordination, office of Pres.-elect, 1981-82; cons. U.S. Ry. Assn., 1975, U.S. EPA, 1974, U.S. Price Commn., 1972. Mem. State Bar Calif., Los Angeles County Bar Assn. (bus. and corp. sect.), Women Lawyer's Assn. Los Angeles, Order of Coif. Independent. Jewish. Sr. editor UCLA Law Review, 1965-66; contbr. article to legal publ., 1978.

LIEBEL-WECKOWICZ, HELEN PAULINE GRIT, historian, educator; b. N.Y.C., June 17, 1930; d. Emil Frederick and Anna Wilhelmina Johanna (Bonk) Liebel; B.A. summa cum laude, Bklyn. Coll., 1952; M.A., Northwestern U., 1953, Ph.D., 1959; m. Thaddeus E. Weckowicz, July 11, 1966. Asso. editor Chgo. Consol. Ency., 1954-55; mem. Am. Hist. Assn. microfilming project of captured German war documents, 1958-59; Sessl lectr. Bklyn. Coll., 1959-62; mem. faculty U. Alta., Edmonton, Can., 1962—, prof. history, 1972—; mem. Can. nat. com. Internat. Hist. Congress, 1967-70, 77-80; research dir. Can. Council grants, 1969-71, 73-74; cons. in field; referee NEH. Fulbright grantee, W.Ger., 1955; scholar AAUW, 1956-57; grantee Carnegie Fund, 1957-58, U. Alta., 1962-82, Am. Com. Promotion of Habsburg Studies, 1984—. Mem. Am. Hist. Assn., Am. 18th Century Studies Assn., Can. 18th Century Studies Assn., Can. Hist. Soc., Conf. Group Central European History, Internat. Econ. Hist. Soc., Internat. Soc. 18th Century Studies, Internat. Com. History Rep. and Parliamentary Instns., German Studies Assn. Democrat. Club U. Alta. Faculty. Author books, articles in field; editorial bd. Can. Jour. History, Etudes Danubienners, Austrian Hist. Yearbook. Office: Dept History U Alta Edmonton T6G 2H4 Canada

LIEBEN, EILEEN BROOKS, univ. adminstr.; b N.Y.C., Jan. 23, 1916; d. Thomas and Margaret (Culkin) Brooks; B.A., Manhattanville Coll., 1937; M.A., Creighton U., 1962; m. Theodore J. Lieben, Dec. 13, 1941; children—Peter, John, Thomas Geoffrey. Asst. dean of women Creighton U., Omaha, 1962, instr. English, 1963-64, dean of women, assoc. dean students, 1963—, acting v.p. student personnel, 1982-84, assoc. v.p. Student services, 1984—, coordinator fall honors program, 1978—. Bd. dirs. Performing Artists Omaha, 1981—. Recipient Creighton Disting. Adminstr. Service award, 1973, Mary Lucretia Creighton award for Advancement of Women, 1981; Sperry Hutchinson, Nebr. Com. Humanities grantee; Nebr. Arts Council grantee; Musicians Union grantee. Mem. Joslyn Mus. Women's Assn. Am. Assn. Higher Edn., Nat. Assn. Women Deans, Adminstrs. and Counselors, Assn. Am. Colls., AAUW. Roman Catholic. Home: 514 S 57th St Omaha NE 68106 Office: 2500 California St Omaha NE 68178

LIEBER, ANNA, magazine production director, graphic designer, art director; b. Germany, Aug. 13, 1947; came to U.S., 1949; d. Sol and Miriam (Scher) L. B.A., Hunter Coll., 1969; postgrad. NYU, 1972-73; postgrad. in design Sch. Visual Arts, 1981-83. Lic. tchr., N.Y. Asst. art dir. Archie Comics, N.Y.C., 1969-70; asst. prodn. mgr. Appleton-Century-Crofts Pub., N.Y.C., 1970-71; tchr. art and Engligh, Beha Jr. High Sch., N.Y.C. 1971-76; coordinator After-Sch. Workshops, Bd. Edn. N.Y.C., 1971-76; prodn. dir. Nat. Rev. mag., N.Y.C., 1976—, art dir. 1986—; free-lance graphic designer Lieber Design, N.Y.C., 1983—. Designer Egglectric Light, 1983. Mem. Women in Prodn. (charter, bd. mem. 1982-83, newsletter editor 1982-83), Graphic Artists Guild (spl. projects coordinator, steering com. officer 1983—), Women in Design, Am. Inst. Graphic Arts.

LIEBER, MIMI, sociologist; b. Detroit, Mar. 22, 1928; d. Theodore and Rhoda (Katzin) Levin; B.A., U. Chgo., 1949, M.A., 1951; postgrad. Harvard U., 1959-60; m. Charles D. Lieber, July 17, 1960; children—John Nathan, James Edmund, George Theodore, Anne Gabrielle. With Columbia Bur. Applied Social Research, Internat. Research Assocs., N.Y.C., 1951-53; with Research Services Ltd., London, 1953-55; assoc. creative research dir. Tatham-Laird, Chgo., 1955-59; pres. Lieber Attitude Research, N.Y.C., 1960-83; mng. dir. LAR/Decision Research Corp., N.Y.C., 1986—. Trustee Jewish Bd. Guardians, 1968-75; mem. Community Planning Bd., N.Y.C., 1975-82; trustee Soc. Advancement Judaism, 1971-73; mem. N.Y. State Bd. Regents, 1981—. Mem. Am. Sociol. Assn., Am. Mktg. Assn. Club: Harvard. Office: 1841 Broadway New York NY 10023

LIEBERMAN, LINDA GAIL, bleach company executive; b. Phila., Jan. 12, 1959; d. Jules Howard and Myrna Caroline (Konikow) L. B.S., Pa. State U., 1979. Employment liaison A.P. Orleans, Phila., 1980-81; sales mgr. Lever Bros., Phila., 1981-84; terr. mgr. The Clorox Co., Boston, 1984, dist. mgr., Pitts., 1984—. Vol. counselor Eagleville Drug Rehab. Ctr., Pa., 1980-81. Recipient 4 in 3 award The Clorox Co., 1948, 85. Mem. Nat. Assn. Female Execs., Alpha Gamma Delta. Jewish. Avocations: skiing; running; squash; reading. Office: The Clorox Co 3 Militia Dr Lexington MA 02173

LIEBERMAN, NANCY ANN, lawyer; b. N.Y.C., Dec. 30, 1956; d. Elias and Elayne Hildegarde (Fox) L. B.A. summa cum laude, U. Rochester, 1977; J.D., U. Chgo., 1979; LL.M. in Taxation, NYU, 1981. Bar: N.Y. 1980. White House intern, 1975; law clk. to presiding justice U.S. Ct. Appeals 5th Cir., Shreveport, La., 1979-80; assoc. Skadden Arps Slate Meagher & Flom, N.Y.C., 1981—. Recipient McGill prize, 1977; N.Y. State Regents' scholar, 1973. Mem. ABA, Assn. Bar City N.Y., Phi Beta Kappa. Republican. Jewish. Club: Internat Forum (gen. counsel 1982-84) (N.Y.C.). Home: 145 E 84th St Apt 5D New York NY 10028 Office: Skadden Arps Slate Meagher & Flom 919 3d Ave New York NY 10022

LIEBERMAN, PEARL NAOMI, philatelist; b. Chgo., Aug. 24, 1918; d. Harry and Katherine (DeKoven) Feldman; m. Eugene Lieberman, Aug. 3, 1947; children—Mark Joel, Robert Frederic, Steven Terry. B.A., U. Ill., 1940. Tchr. bus. edn. Chgo. Pub. Schs., 1946-83, Roberto Clemente High Sch., 1975-83; philatelist, 1945—. Served with AUS, 1943-45: CBI, PTO. Recipient Silver medal Internat. Philatelic Exhbn., Taipei, 1981; Gold medal Compex Vatican Exhbn., 1978; Silver medal Can. Nat. Philatelic Exhbn., 1981; Silver medal Internat. Philatelic Exhbn., Korea, 1984, Australia, 1984. Mem. Chgo. Bus. Tchrs. Assn. Club: Ill. Athletic (Chgo.). Home: 801 LeClaire Ave Wilmette IL 60091

LIEBERMAN, ROCHELLE PHYLLIS, relocation company executive; b. Bklyn., June 27, 1940; d. Solomon and Freda (Shapiro) Beller; m. Melvyn Lieberman, June 10, 1961; children—Eric Neil, Marc Evan. B.A., Bklyn. Coll., 1961; M.Ed., Duke U., 1977. Tchr., Bklyn. pub. schs., 1961-64; instr. Carolina Friends, Durham, N.C., 1967-70; grad. intern Duke U., Durham, 1974-75, faculty adviser, 1975-76; sales assoc. Kelly Matherly, Durham, 1978-81; pres. Shelli, Inc., Durham, 1981—. Treas. Duke Forest Assn., Durham, 1980-85. Mem. LWV, Durham and Chapel Hill Bd. Realtors, Women's Council of Realtors (sec. 1980-81), Kappa Delta Pi. Republican. Jewish. Clubs: Duke Faculty, Duke Campus (Durham). Avocations: piano; walking; knitting; writing; reading. Office: Shelli Inc 1110 Woodburn Rd Durham NC 27705

LIEBL, CATHERINE JEAN, oil company executive; b. Portland, Oreg., Apr. 22, 1946; d. Charles and Iris Pauline (Mortimer) Liebig; B.B.A., CCNY, 1967; m. Hans Liebl, Feb. 19, 1967. With Arthur Young & Co., C.P.A.s, 1967-75, successive audit staff positions to audit mgr., N.Y.C., until 1975; mgr. fin. reports and consol. Mobil Corp., N.Y.C., 1975-77, mgr. fin. analysis, 1977-80, controller films div. Mobil Chem. Co., Pittsford, N.Y., 1981-83, asst. controller, 1983-85; mgr. info. systems U.S. mktg. and refining Mobil Oil, 1985-86; mgr. applications devel. Mobil Corp., 1986—. Mem. Am. Inst. C.P.A.s, Nat. Assn. Female Execs. Office: Mobil Corp 150 E 42d St New York NY 10017

LIEBLEIN, VIRGINIA LUCY, veterinarian; b. Ft. Monmouth, N.J., Apr. 1, 1943; d. Merrill Dewey and Virginia Concetta (Pace) Beam Peters; m. Edward Lieblein, June 7, 1964. B.A., Douglass Coll., 1965; R.N., Monmouth Med. Ctr., 1969; V.M.D. summa cum laude, U. Pa., 1978. Biologist, Hosp. of U. Pa., Phila., 1965-67; infection control nurse Monmouth Med. Ctr., Long Branch, N.J., 1969-70, head nurse in orthopedics, 1970-72; assoc. state veterinarian Freehold (N.J.) Raceway, 1978—; pvt. practice vet. medicine, Long Branch, 1978—. Recipient Pfizer award Pfizer Corp., 1978. Mem. Am. Assn. Equine Practitioners, AVMA, Am. Animal Hosp. Assn., N.J. Assn. Equine Practitioners, Jersey Shore Vet. Med. Assn., Monmouth Med. Ctr. Nurses Alumni Assn. Episcopalian. Home: 684 Westwood Ave West End NJ 07740

LIEBOW, JOANNE ELISABETH, college public information specialist; b. Cleve., May 15, 1926; d. Arnold S. and Rhea Eunice (Levy) King; m. Irving M. Liebow, June 30, 1947 (div. Jan. 1972); children—Katherine Ann Liebow Frank, Peter. Student (Sophia Smith scholar 1946), Smith Coll., 1944-47; B.A., Case Western Res. U., 1948. Cleve. reporter Fairchild Publs., N.Y.C., 1950-51; free-lance pub. relations, Cleve., 1972-78; pub. info. specialist Cuyahoga Community Coll., Cleve., 1979—. Founder, pres. Mt. Sinai Hosp. Jr. Women's Aux., Cleve., 1948-50; pres. PTA, Bryden Elem. Sch., Beachwood, Ohio, 1964; mem. bd., pres. Beachwood Bd. Edn., 1968-76. Recipient Exceptional Achievement award Council for Advance Edn., 1982, Citation award, 1982, Grand Prize, 1983. Mem. Women in Communications, Inc. (Cleve. Communicator's award 1982). Home: 23511 Chagrin Blvd Apt 211 Cleveland OH 44122 Office: Cuyahoga Community Coll Eastern Campus 4250 Richmond Rd Warrensville Twp OH 44122

LIEBSCHUTZ, SARAH FISHER, political scientist, educator; b. Honesdale, Pa., Nov. 24, 1934; d. J. Harold and Goldye (Kurlancheek) Fisher; m. Sanford

J. Liebschutz, Aug. 26, 1956; children—David Samuel, Jane Margaret. B.A., Mt. Holyoke Coll., 1956; Ph.D., U. Rochester, 1971. Asst. prof. polit. sci., SUNY-Brockport, 1970-75, assoc. prof., 1977-81, prof., 1981—; research assoc. The Brookings Instn., Washington, 1975-77, field assoc., 1973-77; field assoc. Princeton U., 1980-85. Chmn. Rehovot, Israel Sisters cities Com., Rochester, N.Y., 1977—; mem. Region II Nat. Archives Adv. Council, 1972-75; mem. SUNY Research Found. Joint Award Council, 1980-81. Mem. Am. Polit. Sci. Assn., Am. Soc. Pub. Adminstrn., Phi Beta Kappa. Jewish. Co-author Brookings reports on community devel. block grants (4), 1976-83; Author: Federal Aid to Rochester, 1984; contbr. articles to profl. jours. Home: 6 S Pittsford Hill Ln Pittsford NY 14534 Office: Dept Political Science SUNY Coll at Brockport Brockport NY 14534

LIEDER, MARY ANDREA, sales and marketing consulting company executive; b. Mpls., Sept. 6, 1938; d. William H. and Anne J. (Gamradt) Berney; m. James Edward Lieder; children—Timothy, Jon, William, Kristin. A. Liberal Arts, U. Minn., 1958; B.A., Met. State U., 1976. Lic. real estate broker, Minn. Property mgr. Sage Co., Madsen Constrn. Co., Mpls., 1967-69; cons. Coult Mortgage Co., St. Paul, 1969-77; social worker Courage Ctr., Mpls., 1977-78; dir. sales and mktg. Swanson Abbott Devel. Co., Mpls., 1978-81; dir. condominium and townhouse div. Edina Realty, Mpls., 1981-83; pres., owner Lieder Corp., Mpls., 1983—; mem. examining bd. Truth in Housing, City of Mpls., 1984—; bd. dirs. Project for Pride in Living, Mpls. Mem. Minn. Multi-Housing Assn. Republican. Roman Catholic. Avocation: painting in oils and mixed media. Home: 2501 Kyle Ave N Minneapolis MN 55422 Office: Lieder Corp 3100 W Lake St Minneapolis MN 55416

LIEF, INEZ, real estate executive; b. Newark, Sept. 19, 1926; d. Jacob and Sophie (Levin) Hyatt; student public schs.; grad. Grad. Realtors Inst., 1974; m. Teddy Lief, Oct. 20, 1946; children—Linda, Barry (dec.), Scott. Cert. residential specialist, real estate brokerage mgr., residential specialist, residential broker mgmt. Engaged in real estate, 1967—; mgr. Burgdorff Realtors, Morristown, N.J.; mgr. property mgmt. dept. Weichert Co., Realtors, Mendham, N.J., 1980—; partner Bernard Shub Real Estate; owner Century 21 Arbor House; mem. condemnation comm. Superior Ct. N.J., 1980—. Recipient Harry L. Schwarz award Morris County Bd. Realtors, 1975, named Realtor of Yr., 1983. Mem. Morris County Bd. Realtors (pres. 1981, 82), N.J. Assn. Realtors (3d dist. v.p. 1983-85), Nat. Assn. Realtors (cert. trainer in ethics and arbitration), Somerset County Bd. Realtors, Nat. Assn. Exec. Women, Nat. Mktg. Inst. Home: 15 Humphrey Rd Convent Station NJ 07961 Office: 4 E Main St Mendham NJ 07945

LIEMANDT, PEGGY LOUISE, candy company executive; b. Wichita, Kans., Aug. 7, 1944; d. Frank Wellington and Margaret Elizabeth (Salser) Wichser; m. Daniel George Liemandt, Feb. 23, 1967. B.A., U. Minn., 1964. Metro Group Fashion dir. J.C. Penney Co., Chgo., 1966-69; fashion, TV dir. Donaldson's, Mpls., St. Paul, 1969-72; pres. Liemandts Tour Conv. Services, Mpls., 1972-79, Godiva Chocolates, Mpls., 1979-85; pres., chmn. bd. Truffles Chocolatier, Mpls., 1980—; lectr., cons. in field. Benefit mem. Laura Baker Sch. for Retarded, 1985; vols. Minn. Soc. for Blind, 1978-79; com. mem. Minn. Sympony Orch., 1979—; benefit mem. Whitney Mus., N.Y.C., 1984; bd. dirs. Jr. Achievement, Minn., 1985—. Recipient Highest Achievement award Tobe-Coburn Sch., N.Y.C., 1984. Mem. Minn. Women's Network (exec. br.), Am. Women in Bus. Owners Assn., Sales and Mktg. Execs. of Mpls., Nat. Sales Mgmt. Assn. (dir.), Am. Fedn. Radio and TV Artists, Screen Actors Guild, Alpha Gamma Delta. Republican. Methodist. Avocations: scuba diving; snorkeling; swimming; windsurfing; water skiing. Home: 11616 Live Oak Dr Minnetonka MN 55343 Office: Truffles Group Inc 7116 Shady Oak Rd Eden Prairie MN 55344

LIENHARD, PATRICIA ANNE, college administrator; b. Platte, S.D., Jan. 17, 1931; d. Joseph Mervin and Kathryn (Boland) Hanson; m. Jerome Travers Lienhard, July 16, 1955; children—Jerome, James, John. B.A., Immaculate Heart Coll., 1957; M.S., Calif. State U., 1971; Ed.D., U. So. Calif., 1982. Elem. tchr. San Gabriel Sch. Dist., Calif., 1952-55, La Canada Sch. Dist., Calif., 1968-70; counselor, instr. Glendale Community Coll., Calif., 1971-75, dean student services, 1975-85, dean coll. services, 1985—. Volunteer Glendale Meml. Hosp., 1982-83. EPDA grantee 1970. Recipient Woman Helping Women award Soroptimists Internat. 1978. Mem. Glendale Bus. and Profl. Women (named Woman of Yr. 1984), Oakmont League, Delta Epsilon. Club: Oakmont Country. Lodge: Soroptomists (1st v.p. 1983-84). Avocations: tennis; travel; writing. Home: 2947 Hermosita Glendale CA 91208 Office: Glendale Community Coll 1500 N Verdugo Rd Glendale CA 91208

LIERMAN, EILEEN CLAIRE, health care administrator; b. Bklyn., Dec. 16, 1951; d. Stephen A. and Nancy (Cunningham) Myers; m. E. Paul Lierman, June 2, 1973. B.A., Fordham U., 1973; M.S., NYU, 1975; M.B.A., Fordham U., 1981; postgrad. Columbia U., 1984—. Supr. nuclear medicine Montefiore Hosp. Affiliation, Bronx, N.Y., 1978-85; dir. fin. St. Vincent-North Richmond, S.I., N.Y., 1985—; mem. adv. bd. nuclear medicine Manhattan Coll., Bronx, 1981-85. Recipient Dir.'s award Montefiore Hosp. Affiliation, 1984. Mem. Health Care Fin. Mgmt., Nat. Assn. Female Execs., Soc. Nuclear Medicine. Roman Catholic. Avocations: antiques, hiking, tennis. Home: PO Box 91 South St Putnam Valley NY 10579 Office: St Vincent-North Richmond CMHC 355 Bard Ave Staten Island NY 10310

LIESCHKE, MARY LOUISE, boarding kennel owner; b. Hays, Kans., Jan. 12, 1927; d. Frank Philip and Frances Ida (Rooney) Mandeville; m. John Patrick McCormack, Apr. 2, 1949 (div. 1967); children—Timothy, Michael, James, Erin; m. Allan Lindsay Lieschke, July 19, 1969 (dec. 1978). Student U. Iowa, 1943-44, Washburn U., 1944-45. Cert. kennel owner. Co-owner Kangaroo Maint, Leawood, Kans., 1974-76; owner, operator Calabasas Boarding Kennels, Calif., 1976-84. Mem. Calabasas C. of C. (dep. 1980, 2d v.p. 1983-84), Am. Boarding Kennel Assn. (area rep. 1981-84). Republican. Episcopalian.

LIESSE, DEBRA LOUISE READ, marketing executive; b. Houston, Feb. 7, 1953; d. Jack Woodrow and Val Dean (Werner) Read; m. Richard William Liesse, May 15, 1982; 1 son, Nicholas William. B.S. in Advt., U. Tex.-Austin, 1975; postgrad. in bus. U. Houston, 1978-79. Pub. relations coordinator Turner Collie & Braden, Houston, 1975-80; mktg. dir. Sharpstown Ctr., Houston, 1980—. Vol. March of Dimes, Austin and Houston, 1975—; active Cordettes U.S. Army Aux., Austin, 1973-75, Houston Zool. Soc., 1982—, Travis County Young Republicans, Austin, 1974-75; auction asst. Sta. KUHT-TV, Houston, 1979—. Mem. Pub. Relations Soc. Am., Internat. Council Shopping Ctrs. (MAXI award for mktg. excellence 1982, cert. mktg. dir.), Houston Advt. Fedn., Ex-Students Assn. U. Tex. (life mem.), Delta Delta Delta (newsletter chmn. 1974, auction com. 1983-84). Home: 10614 Olympia Houston TX 77042 Office: Sharpstown Ctr 7500 Bellaire Blvd Suite 201 Houston TX 77036

LIFGREN, SHERYLE KAYE, business systems consultant, writer; b. Delhi, N.Y., July 15, 1951; d. Derwood Keith and Hildegard Dorothy (Hubig) L. Fortran IV cert. NYU, 1971; instr. cert. N.Y.C. Police Acad., 1975; A.A., NYU, 1976, B.A., 1979. With computer sci. program NYU, N.Y.C., 1970-71, N.Y.C. Police Dept., 1971-76, Fed. Home Loan Bank N.Y., N.Y.C., 1976-79; ops. systems analyst Dean Witter Reynolds, Inc., N.Y.C., 1979-80; policy and procedures coordinator Teleprompter Corp., N.Y.C., 1980-82; sr. cons. SBS Systems and Bus. Solutions, Inc., Paoli, Pa., 1982—; pres. Associated Solutions Inc., 1985—; guest lectr. consumer econs. La Guardia Coll., Queens, N.Y., 1983; cons. Bakst Works, N.Y.C., 1981—, Arlene Hawkins Cosmetics, N.Y.C., 1981—, Morgan Guaranty Trust Co., N.Y.C., 1982—, N.Y. Clearing House, N.Y.C., 1982, Merrill Lynch and Co., Inc., N.Y.C., 1982, Am. Internat. Group, N.Y.C., 1982, AFIA Worldwide Ins., Wayne, N.J., 1982, othears. Mem. Inst. Indsl. Engrs., Assn. Female Execs., Steuben Soc. Office: 235 E 5th St New York NY 10003

LIFKA, MARY LAURANNE, history educator; b. Oak Park, Ill., Oct. 31, 1937; d. Aloysius William and Loretta Catherine (Juric) L. B.A., Mundelein Coll., 1960; M.A., Loyola U., Los Angeles, 1965; Ph.D., U. Mich., 1974; postdoctoral student London U., 1975. Life teaching cert. Prof. history Mundelein Coll., Chgo., 1976-84, coordinator acad. computer, 1983-84, prof. history Coll. St. Teresa, Winona, Minn., 1984—; chief reader in history Ednl. Testing Service, Princeton, N.J., 1980-84; cons. world history project Longman, Inc., 1983—; cons. in European history Coll. Bd., Evanston, Ill., 1983—; mem. Com. on History in the Classroom. Author: Instructor's Guide to European History, 1983; contbr. articles to publs. Speaker, Midwest Women's Bur., Chgo., 1977—. Mem. Orgn. Am. Historians, Am. Hist. Assn., Soc. for History Edn., Ednl. Testing Service Devel. Com. of History. Democrat. Roman Catholic. Home: 556 Kerry Dr Winona MN 55987

LIGENZA, ANDREA, nurse; b. Coaldale, Pa., Apr. 7, 1952; d. Stanley Walter and Mary (Porambo) L. Diploma in Nursing, Hosp. of U. Pa., 1973; R.N., B.S. in Nursing, U. Pa., 1976. Cert. nurse practitioner, Pa. Staff nurse Hosp. of U. Pa., Phila., 1973-79, nurse practitioner cardio-thoracic surgery sect., 1979—; preceptor nursing students U. Pa., 1985—; founder, group leader Self Esteem Workshops, 1986—. Vol. Gary Hart for Pres. campaign, Phila., 1984. Mem. People for Am. Way, Center City Running Club, Puccini Inst., Sigma Theta Tau. Democrat. Roman Catholic. Avocations: classical music, tennis, travel, writing poetry. Office: Hosp Pa 34th and Spruce St Philadelphia PA 19104

LIGEROS, M. SUE, transport refrigeration executive; b. Boulder, Colo., June 25, 1948; d. Michael George Ligeros and F. Evelyn (Summers) Leonard. Student Denver Woman's Coll. Mgr. Ohio Skate, Toledo, 1974-76; gen. mgr. M.G.L. Leasing Co., Denver, 1976-77, Thermo King Sales of Denver, 1977-81, pres., gen. mgr., 1982—. Recipient Pres.'s award Thermo King Corp., 1982. Mem. Thermo King Dealer Adv. Council (sec.-treas. 1984-86). Republican. Greek Orthodox. Avocations: hiking; camping; outdoor sports. Office: Thermo King of Denver Inc 5455 E 52d Ave Commerce City CO 80022

LIGGET, FRANCES HAMMOND, civic worker; b. Phila., Oct. 28, 1901; d. Levi John and Frances Purves (Bernard) Hammond; ed. Agnes Irwin Sch., Phila., Phila. Sch. Design for Women (scholar); m. Robert Charles Ligget, Oct. 28, 1922 (dec. 1976); children—Frances Bernard (dec.), Audrey Hammond (Mrs. Frederick Robert Snyder). Chmn. ARC Camp and Hosp. Council Service Southeastern Pa., 1945-46; vice chmn. radio Emergency Aid Pa., World War II; sec. Women's Aux. Pa. Hosp., Phila., 1947; sec. house com. Presbyn. Hosp., 1937-39; organizing chmn. Valley Forge Hist. Soc. Mus. Aux., 1951. Recipient White Ribbon award Garden Club Fedn. Pa., 1952, community recognition award Chapel of Four Chaplains, Phila., 1974, citation Pa. Ho. of Reps., 1974. Mem. DAR, Am. Legion Aux., Women Nat. Farm and Garden Assn. (pres. Valley Forge br. Keystone div. 1935), Daus. Am. Colonists (flag chmn. 1970-73), Daus. of Colonial Wars (state chaplain 1974-77), Swedish Colonial Soc. (historian 1960-70), Nat. Soc. Colonial Dames XVII Century (state chmn. of insignia 1975-77), Dames of Loyal Legion State of Pa. (councilor, former chmn. of insignia), Nat. Soc. Descs. Early Quakers (founding), Nat. Soc. Colonial Daus. 17th Century. Republican. Presbyterian. Clubs: Acorn (Phila.); Merion Cricket (Haverford); Waynesborough Country. Compiler local history. Home: Valley Forge PA 19481

LIGGETT, TWILA MARIE CHRISTENSEN, TV executive producer; b. Pipestone, Minn., Mar. 25, 1944; d. Donald L. and Irene E. (Zweigle) Christensen; B.S., Union Coll., Lincoln, Nebr., 1966; M.A., U. Nebr., 1971, Ph.D., 1977; m. Kenneth R. Liggett, June 2, 1966. Dir. vocal and instrumental music Sprague (Nebr.)-Martell Public Sch., 1966-67; tchr. vocal music public schs., Syracuse, Nebr., 1967-69; tchr. Norris Public Sch., Firth, Nebr., 1969-71; cons. fed. reading project public schs., Lincoln, 1971-72; curriculum coordinator Westside Community Schs., Omaha, 1972-74; dir. State program Right-to-Read, Nebr. Dept. Edn., 1974-76; asst. dir. Nebr. Commn. on Status of Women, 1976-80; asst. dir. devel. and acquisitions Great Plains Nat. Instructional TV Library, U. Nebr., Lincoln, 1980—; exec. producer Reading Rainbow, Pub. Broadcasting Service (Emmy nominated children's series); cons. U.S. Dept. Edn., 1981; Far West Regional Lab., San Francisco, 1978-79. Bd. dirs. Planned Parenthood, Lincoln, 1979-81. Mem. Assn. Supervision and Curriculum Devel., Phi Delta Kappa. Presbyterian. Home: 3001 Kipling St Lincoln NE 68516 Office: PO Box 80669 Lincoln NE 68501

LIGHT, DOROTHY KAPLAN, lawyer, insurance executive; b. Alden, Iowa, May 20, 1937; d. Edward T. and Bessie (Nachazel) Kaplan; m. Ernest Isaac Light, Dec. 28, 1959; children—Christina, William, Samuel, David (twins). B.A., U. Iowa, 1959, J.D., 1961. Bar: Iowa 1961, N.J. 1973; C.P.C.U. Sole practice, Marshalltown, Iowa, 1962-63, Iowa City, 1963-71; with U.S. Army, N.J., 1972-74; asst. gen. counsel Prudential Property & Casualty Ins. Co., Holmdel, N.J., 1974-75, assoc. gen. counsel, 1975-77, dir. corp. services, 1977-79, dir. pub. affairs mktg. dept., 1979-82, dir. pub. affairs, 1982-83, v.p. govt. affairs, 1982—; bd. dirs. N.J. Natural Gas Co. Vice-pres., legis. chmn. Monmouth Ocean Devel. Council N.J., 1980—; trustee Monmouth Conservation Found., 1982—; mem. Airport Adv. Study Com. Monmouth County, 1984; exec. adv. com. Family and Children's Services. Mem. Iowa Bar Assn., N.J. Bar Assn. Republican. Roman Catholic. Office: Prudential Property & Casualty Ins Co 23 Main St Holmdel NJ 07733

LIGHT, MARGARET COE, controller; b. Waterbury, Conn., July 16, 1947; d. John Allen and Margaret (Connick) Coe. Student U. Calif.-Davis, 1965-67; B.A., UCLA, 1969, M.B.A., 1975. C.P.A., Calif. Cert. mgmt. acct. Trust adminstr. Hong Kong and Shanghai Bank, Beverly Hills, Calif., 1969-71; jr. acct. George P. Madok, C.P.A., Los Angeles, 1972-75; sr. acct. Ernst & Whinney, Trenton, N.J., 1976-78; staff acct. Dart Industries, Inc., Los Angeles, 1978-82, audit mgr. Dart & Kraft, Inc., Atlanta, 1982-84; sr. fin. analyst Kraft, Inc., 1984-85, asst. controller fin. planning and analysis Food Service Group, 1985—; speaker Inst. Internal Auditors, N.Y.C., 1983. Mem. Calif. State Soc. C.P.A.s, N.J. State Soc. C.P.A.s, Nat. Assn. Accts. (dir. N.J. chpt. 1977, Los Angeles chpt. 1980), Am. Inst. C.P.A.s, Ill. Racquetball Assn. (bd. dirs.), Beta Gamma Sigma. Episcopalian. Office: Kraft Inc 3-W Kraft Ct Glenview IL 60025

LIGHT, PAMELA DELAMAIDE, interior designer; b. Pittsburg, Kans., Sept. 16, 1950; d. Jack Riley and Pearl Darlene (Nelson) Delamaide; m. Kenneth Layne L Light, July 25, 1970 (div. Apr. 1974). Student Ohio U., 1968-70; B.S. in Art, Ball State U., 1973. Office sec., acct. Anderson City Hall (Ind.), 1970-71; interior design apprentice Jon Wilding Studio, Anderson, 1970-71; interior designer Suniland Office Furniture, Houston, 1973-83; furniture rep. Reeves, Rice & Light, Houston, 1983—; cons. Front to Back, Houston, 1982—. Mem. Inst. Bus. Designers (v.p. programs Houston 1983), Citizens for Animal Protection, Houston Humane Soc. Republican. Methodist. Office: Suniland Office Furniture 2800 Fondren St Houston TX 77063

LIGHTBODY-LONG, DIANA LYNNE, cabinet company executive; b. Washington, Feb. 7, 1956; d. Fred Herman and Doris Jean (White) Chaffin; m. James Finley Lightbody, Jr., Apr. 29, 1975 (div. 1983); 1 stepson, James Anthony; m. Edgar Earl Long, June 29, 1984; stepchildren—Kristine, Michael. Salesman Scotty's, Inc., Winter Haven, Fla., 1972-82; salesman Keller Cabinets, Deland, Fla., 1982-83, sales mgr., 1983-84, nat. sales mgr., 1985—; regional sales mgr. Keller Industries, Miami, Fla., 1984-85. Democrat. Presbyterian. Avocations: skiing; beach. Home: PO Box 1711 Eaton Park FL 33840 Office: Keller Cabinets PO Box 1089 Deland FL 32721

LIGHTFORD, BRENDA MARIE, financial executive; b. Greensboro, N.C., Oct. 21, 1954; d. Wilton and Dorothy (Smith) L. B.S. in Commerce, N.C. Central U., 1976, M.B.A., 1979. Lic. real estate broker, N.C.; notary pub., N.C. Supervisory survey statistician U.S. Bur. Census, Charlotte, N.C., 1979-81, New Orleans, 1981; budget analyst U.S. EEO Commn., Charlotte, 1982—; sole propr. Scholarship Adv. Service, Charlotte, 1985—. Vol. Charlotte March of Dimes, 1980, 84, 85, Siegle Ave. Presbyn. Ch. Girls Club, 1986. Recipient Outstanding Performance award U.S. EEO Commn., 1984, 85. Mem. Nat. Assn. Female Execs., Am. Entrepreneurs Assn., AAUW, NAACP, Delta Sigma Theta. Democrat. Baptist. Avocations: travel, reading, tropical fish. Office: Scholarship Adv Service PO Box 31216 Charlotte NC 28231

LIGHTHIPE, AUDREY GAIL, construction company executive; b. Forrest Hills, N.Y., Feb. 27, 1946; d. Max I. and Elisa J. (Magni) Esses; m. Michael J. Lighthipe, Jan. 26, 1966; children—Lisa Anne, Jeffrey Marcus, Mark James. A.A., Long Beach City Coll., 1965. Purchasing clk. N.Am. Aviation, Downey, Calif., 1964-68; engring. sec. Genisco Tech., Compton, Calif., 1969-73; contracts adminstr. Rachelle Labs., Long Beach, Calif., 1973-76; asst. purchasing agt. Mayer Constrn. Co., Downey, 1976-78; purchasing dir. EPAC Devel., Long Beach, 1978-81; pres. Unique Devel. & Unique Mgmt. Services, Orange, Calif., 1981—; mem. purchasing-subcontractor com. Bldg. Industry So. Calif., 1985—. Fund-raiser Am. Field Service, Orange, 1983-85. Mem. Residential Purchasing Council So. Calif. (plaque 1979, 80, 82, 83, 84, pres. 1984, 85), Orange C. of C. Republican. Lutheran. Home: 209 S Violet Ln Orange CA 92669 Office: Unique Devel & Unique Mgmt Services 171 S Anita Dr Suite 101 Orange CA 92668

LIGHTNER, CANDY LYNNE, advocate, consultant; b. Pasadena, Calif., May 30, 1946; d. Dykes Charles and Katherine (Karrib) Doddridge; children—Serena, Travis. Student pub. schs., Fairfield, Calif.; hon. D.Humanities, St. Francis Coll., Johnstown, Pa., 1984. Dental asst., various pvt. offices, 1964-70; real estate salesperson, Calif., 1972-80; founder, pres., chmn. bd. Mothers Against Drunk Driving, Hurst, Tex., 1980-85, cons., Arlington, Tex., 1985-87. Contbr. articles to profl. jours. Mem. Sacramento County Task Force on Drunk Driving, Presdl. Commn. on Drunk and Drugged Driving; bd. dirs. Nat. Commn. on Drunk Driving, 1984—, Nat. Partnership for Drug Free Use, Nat. Hwy. Safety Adv. Com., others. Named to Good Housekeeping's Most Admired Woman's Poll, 1986; recipient YWCA Woman of Year award, 1986; Commonwealth award U. Del., 1986, Black and Blue award Thomas Jefferson U. Hosp. Emergency Medicine Soc.; Human Dignity award Kessler Inst. for Rehab.; Woman of Year award Mortar Bd Soc., Baylor U., 1985; selected by Johns Hopkins U. to participate in Anglo-Am. Successor Generation program, 1985; honored as one of Seven Who Succeeded, Time Mag., 1985, Testimonial award Civitan Internat., 1984, Epilepsy Found. award, 1984, Jefferson award Am. Inst. for Pub. Service, 1983; Pres.'s Vol. Action award, 1983; honored by Esquire mag. as mem. Am.'s New Leadership Class, 1985. others. Avocations: reading; swimming; traveling. Office: PO Box 121425 Arlington TX 76012

LIGON, HELEN HAILEY, educator; b. Lott, Tex., Feb. 7, 1921; d. Rolla W. and Bobbye A. (Ruble) Hailey; B.S. in Bus. Adminstrn., Tex. Women's U., 1942, M.A. in Accounting and Econs., 1945; Ph.D. in Bus. Analysis, Tex. A. and M. U., 1976; m. William Grady Ligon, July 26, 1941; 1 son, William Grady III. Tutor in bus. adminstrn. Tex. Women's U., Denton, 1942-44; tchr. pub. schs., Lott (Tex.), 1947-52, Marlin (Tex.), 1952-55; exec. sec. Gen. Tire & Rubber Co., Waco, Tex., 1956-58; asst. prof. quantitative analysis Hankamer Sch. Bus., Baylor U., Waco, 1958-62, prof., 1962—, also dir. Casey Computer Center, 1962—. Cert. data processor; cert. systems profl. Named Most Popular Bus. Prof., Baylor U., 1964, 69, 78, Outstanding Woman Faculty Member, 1967, Outstanding Baylor U. Tchr., 1979. Mem. Soc. Mgmt. Info. Systems, Data Processing Mgmt. Assn., Am. Statis. Assn., Assn. of Computing Machinery, Delta Kappa Gamma, Beta Gamma Sigma, Sigma Iota Epsilon. Democrat. Presbyterian. Author: Changing Concepts in Management Information Systems, 1978; Successful Management Systems, 1978, 2d edit., 1985. Home: PO Box 388 Lott TX 76656 Office: Baylor U Waco TX 76798

LIGON, LORA MICHELLE, lawyer, financial planner; b. Terre Haute, Ind., Oct. 20, 1953; d. Julius and Margaret Lorraine (Bell) L. B.A., Ind. U., 1974, J.D., 1977. Bar: Ind. 1977. Atty., Lincoln Nat. Life Ins. Co., Fort Wayne, Ind., 1977-79, Prudential Ins. Co., Los Angeles, 1979-82, CIGNA Corp., Los Angeles, 1982—. Battered wives vol. YWCA, Fort Wayne, 1977-78. Hoosier State Scholar, 1971, 72. Mem. ABA, Nat. Bar Assn., Ind. Bar Assn., Internat. Assn. Fin. Planners, Nat. Assn. Life Underwritters Chgo., Alpha Kappa Alpha.

LIGON, PATTI-LOU ELSIE, real estate investor; b. Riverside, Calif., Feb. 28, 1953; d. Munford Ernest and Patsy Hazel (Bynum) L. B.S., San Diego State U., 1976; B.B.A., Nat. U., San Diego, 1983, M.A. in Bus. Adminstrn., 1984. Cert. profl. counselor. Escrow asst. Cajon Valley Escrow, El Cajon, Calif., 1978-79; escrow asst. Summit Escrow, San Diego, 1979-81; escrow officer Fidelity Nat. Title, San Diego, 1982-84, Dawson Escrow, San Diego, 1984; owner, property mgr., investment adviser Ligon Enterprises., San Diego, 1980—, cons., 1982—. Chmn. com., alumnae and assocs. San Diego State U., 1983, 84, 85; com. chmn. San Diego Zool. soc., 1985; pres. Friends of Symphony, Riverside, Calif., 1978. Recipient commendation City and County of Honolulu, 1981. Mem. Nat. Notary Assn., Calif. Escrow Assn., Am. Home Econs. Assn., Nat. Assn. Female Execs, Sigma Kappa (pres. 1974, v.p. sorority corp. 1976—). Republican. Methodist. Club: Spinster (pres. 1981) (San Diego). Avocations: racquetball; clothing design; photography; travel. Home: 4545 Collwood Blvd Unit 12 San Diego CA 92115 Office: Ligon Enterprises 4545 Collwood Blvd San Diego CA 92115

LIKIS, LORI LIENHARD, educator; b. Oak Park, Ill., June 30, 1956; d. John Hugo and Elizabeth Jean (Atkinson) Lienhard; B.A., Bard Coll., 1977; M.A. in English, U. Chgo., 1978. Permissions editor Winthrop Pubs., Inc., Cambridge, Mass., 1978-80; circulation mgr. Datek of New Eng., Newtonville, Mass., 1981; instr. English Auburn (Ala.) U., 1981-83; tech. writer Bus. and Profl. Software, Inc., Cambridge, Mass., 1984-85, Harper & Shuman, Inc., Cambridge, 1985—. Democrat. Home: 103 Fayerweather St Cambridge MA 02138

LILES, FRANCES ROSE, marketing executive; b. Richmond, Va., Jan. 4, 1943; d. Milford Kenyon and Helen Frances (Boston) L.; student Coll. William and Mary, 1961-63: B.A., U. Toledo, 1965. Adminstr., AID, Dept. of State, Washington, 1965-67; analyst Def. Intelligence Agy., Lisbon, Portugal, Madrid and Washington, 1968-75; mgr. Spanish programs Jet Engine Group, Gen. Electric Co., Madrid, 1976; proposal mgr. Atlantic Research Corp., Alexandria, Va., 1977-82; sr. mem. adv. staff Computer Scis. Corp., Falls Church, Va., 1982-85; bus. devel. mgr. PSI Internat., Falls Church, 1985—. Chmn. youth com. Am. Embassy, Lisbon, 1968-70. Mem. Data Processing Mgrs. Assn., Internat. Platform Assn., Nat. Fedn. Bus. and Profl. Women (chmn.), Women in Info. Processing, Nat. Assn. Female Execs., Smithsonian Assocs., NOW, Mu Phi Epsilon, Sigma Delta Pi, Pi Beta Phi. Episcopalian. Home: 4638 N 23d St Arlington VA 22207 Office: 510 N Washington St Falls Church VA 22046

LILES, JANE HISAKO, chemical engineer; b. Fontana, Calif., Mar. 18, 1957; d. Hisashi James and Shinako Marilyn (Matsumoto) Matoi; m. Robert Charles Liles, Mar. 1, 1980. B.S. in Chem. Engring., U. Calif.-Davis, 1978. Chem. engring. cert., Calif. Research engr. Dow Chem. Co., Pittsburg, Calif., 1978-83, sr. prodn. engr., 1983—. Mem. Am. Inst. Chem. Engrs. Republican. Club: Antioch Delta Tennis (treas. 1982—), Deac Bowling League (Antioch)(sec.-treas. 1984—). Avocations: tennis; bowling; biking. Home: 5 W Lake Pl Antioch CA 94509 Office: Dow Chem Co Loveridge Rd Pittsburg CA 94565

LILJEDAHL, LINDA ANNE, lawyer; b. New Orleans, Jan. 26, 1951; d. Raymond Leroy and Violet Ann (Kennedy) L.; m. L. Kevin Coleman, Oct. 15, 1983. Student La. State U.-Baton Rouge, 1969-71; B.A. cum laude, U. New Orleans, 1974; J.D., Tulane U., 1979. Bar: La. 1979. Spl. instr. Readak, Inc., New Orleans, 1974-75; law clk. Dodge, Friend, et al, New Orleans, 1977-79, assoc., 1979-83; assoc. Windhorst, Pastorek & Gaudry, Gretna, La., 1983—. Block rep. Neighborhood Watch Assn., New Orleans, 1980—. La. State U. scholar, 1969-71; U. New Orleans scholar 1973-74; Tulane U. scholar, 1976-79. Mem. ABA (rep. 1983), La. Bar Assn., New Orleans Bar Assn., Fed. Bar Assn., Def. Research Inst., La. Assn. Def. Counsel. Home: 2835 Ponce de Leon St New Orleans LA 70119 Office: Windhorst Pastorek & Gaudey 72 West Bank Expressway Gretna LA 70053

LILLY, DIANE PALMER, business executive; b. Mpls.; d. Leroy Sheldon and Irene Palmer; m. David Lilly, Jr. Student Newton Coll. of Sacred Heart. Dir. research adminstrn. Fed. Res. Bank, Mpls., 1972-75, dir. research, 1975-77, spl. asst. to pres., 1977-78; fed. govt. relations officer Norwest Corp., Mpls., 1978-81, v.p. govt. relations, 1981—. Downtown area chairperson gen. bus. div. campaign United Way, Mpls., 1978; bd. dirs. Guthrie Theater, 1978-84, Hennepin Ctr. for Arts, YWCA, Minn. Citizens for Arts, 1983-85, Planned Parenthood of Minn.; active Minn. Women's Econ. Roundtable; participant Leadership Mpls.; active Minn. Bus. Partnership, Nat. Conf. Fin. Services, Washington. Mem. Am. Bankers Assn. (exec. com., chmn. legis. liaison adv. com. 1984-86). Club: Nat. Economists. Office: Norwest Corp 1200 Peavey Bldg Minneapolis MN 55479

LILORE, DOREEN MARY, librarian, labor union official; b. Newark; d. Alfred and Jane Elizabeth (Dodd) Lilore. B.A., Newark State Coll., 1971; M.L.S., Pratt Inst., 1972; D.L.S., Columbia U., 1982. Cert. profl. librarian, tchr., N.J. Reference librarian Paterson Pub. Library (N.J.), 1971-78; teaching asst. Columbia U., N.Y.C., 1979; staff rep. council 52 Am. Fedn. State, County and Mepl. Employees, AFL-CIO, Jersey City, 1979—. Author: Public Librarian Local Unions, 1984. Mem. ALA (sec. staff orgns. round table), Indsl. Relations Research Assn., Beta Phi Mu, Alpha Sigma Lambda. Roman Catholic. Home: 51 Menzel Ave Maplewood NJ 07040

LIN, ANGELA ELIZABETH, pediatric cardiologist; b. Phila., June 11, 1954; d. Paul Min and Sylvia (Spina) Lin. B.S., St. Joseph Coll. U., Phila., 1976, M.D., Thomas Jefferson U., Phila., 1980. Diplomate Nat. Bd. Med. Examiners, Am. Bd. Pediatrics. Resident in pediatrics Children's Hosp., Pitts., 1980-83;

cardiology fellow UCLA, 1983-85, Children's Hosp. Pitts./Phila., 1985-86. Mem. Physicians for Social Reponsibility. Home: 32-B Bethany Dr Pittsburgh PA 15215

LIN, MEI-YING, librarian; b. Fukien Province, China, Dec. 9, 1944; d. Chen-Liu and Shu-Yu (Wu) L.; B.A., Nat. Cheng-Chi U., 1966; M.S. in Library Sci., Wayne State U., 1969. Asso. librarian Asia Library, U. Mich., Ann Arbor, 1969—; cons. Am. Chinese edn. and culture Center, Detroit, Detroit Bd. Edn. Contbr. articles to profl. jours. Home: 2663 Prairie St Ann Arbor MI 48105

LIN, SHARON CHIEN, librarian; b. Nanking, China, Aug. 22, 1933; came to U.S., 1958; d. Bins C. and Yinlow (Fan) Chien; m. Duo-Liang, June 8, 1963; children—Jennifer, Kenneth. B.A., Nat. Taiwan U., 1956; M.A., U. Minn., 1960. Cataloger, sr. cataloger Yale U. Library, New Haven, 1960-64; head periodicals dept. State U. Coll., Buffalo, 1965-67; vis. librarian Stanford U. Library, Calif., summer 1966; vis. staff Oxford U. Library, Eng., fall 1970; vis. librarian Tsing Hwa U. Library, Peking, China, spring 1978; serials cataloger SUNY-Buffalo, 1978-79, 80—; librarian Buffalo Gen. Hosp. Library, fall 1980. Author: (with M. Leung) Chinese Libraries and Librarianship: an annotated bibliography, 1986. Contbr. articles to profl. jours. Grantee N.Y. State United Univ. Professions, 1985. Mem. ALA (officer resources and tech. services div., com. cataloging Asian and African materials 1983-85), Internat. Relations Round Table, Chinese-Am. Librarian's Assn., Assn. Coll. and Research Libraries (western N.Y. chpt.). Clubs: Chinese of Buffalo (sec. 1979-80), Greater Buffalo (treas 1984—). Home: 152 Northington Dr East Amherst NY 14051 Office: SUNY-Buffalo Maple Rd Buffalo NY 14260

LIN, SOPHIA SHOU FUN, occupational therapist, consultant; b. Taipei, Taiwan, Aug. 22, 1950; came to U.S., 1975; d. Sung-Chen and Chiu Hsia L. B.S. in Dentistry, Chung-Shan Med. Coll., Tai-Chung, Taiwan, 1975; M. Occupational Therapy, Tex. Woman's U., Denton, 1978. Registered occupational therapist, Tex. Occupational therapist S.W. Meml. Hosp., Houston, 1978-79; dir. occupational therapy Home Health-Home Care, Inc., Pasadena, Tex., 1979—; cons. S.A. Devel. Ctr., San Augustine, Tex., 1980—, Holiday Nursing Home, Center, Tex., 1980-82. Mem. Am. Occupational Therapy Assn., Tex. Occupational Therapy Assn. Roman Catholic. Home: 6218 Grandvale St Houston TX 77072 Office: Home Health-Home Care Inc 3009 Strawberry St Pasadena TX 77502

LINCOLN, ANN FRANDSEN, author, home economist; b. Story City, Iowa, July 27, 1917; d. Theodore Peter and Amy Amelia (Shogerboe) Frandsen; m. Russell Laverne Lincoln, June 20, 1941; children—Timothy, Nancy, Mark, Todd. B.S. in Home Econs., Iowa State U., 1939; diploma N.Y. Sch. Interior Design, 1944; postgrad. Oreg. State U., 1962-65. Tchr. high sch., Stanton, Iowa, 1939-41; clk. Macy's Dept. Store, N.Y.C., 1943-44; owner, mgr. House of Lincoln, Corvallis, Oreg., 1968—; cons. in field. Author: (pamphlet) Nutrition Power, 1978; (meal planning kit) Ann's Menu Minder, 1969, 78; (book) Food for Athletes, 1979; contbr. numerous articles to mags. Vol., YWCA, Logansport, Ind., 1941-43, PTA, Corvallis, Oreg., 1952-62; trustee, chmn. various coms. Methodist Ch., Corvallis, 1947-86; crusade chmn., various offices Am. Cancer Soc., Benton County, Oreg., 1954-80; v.p., precinct chmn. Benton County Republican Com., 1974-86; mem. consumer panel Downtown Mchts. Assn., 1981-86. Mem. Oreg. Nutrition Council, Oreg. Home Econs. Assn., Iowa State U. Home Econs. Alumni Assn. Home and Office: 7 NW Edgewood Dr Corvallis OR 97330

LINCOLN, CATHERINE RUTH, direct marketing company executive; b. Fulmer, Bucks, Eng., Apr. 29, 1941; came to U.S., 1975; d. Geoffrey Morris and Marjorie Elizabeth (Harrison) Allen; m. Robert Adams Lincoln, Feb. 19, 1968; children—Henry Allen, Thomas Adams. B.A. in Modern History with honors, Oxford U., 1962, M.A. in Modern History, 1972; cert. with distinction in contract and criminal law Coll. Law, London, 1975. Researcher, Brit. Diplomatic Service, London, 1962-64, jr. attaché Brit. High Commn., Delhi, Calcutta and Madras, India, 1964-67, 3d sec., Ankara, Turkey, 1967-68; dir. capital campaign St. Paul's Episcopal Coll., Lawrenceville, Va., 1977-79; account exec. The Viguerie Co., Falls Church, Va., 1979-82, supr., until 1982, v.p. creative div., 1982—. Del. county, dist., state convs. Va. Republican Party, 1977—; block capt., precinct rep., mem. Fairfax County Rep. Com. (Va.), 1979—; mem. nat. membership com., mem. devel. com. English Speaking Union U.S.A., 1980—; bd. dirs. Indo-Chinese Refugees Social Services, Inc., Washington, 1980-82; bd. dirs. St. Paul's Episcopal Coll. Bd. Assocs., 1981—; lay reader Holy Comforter Ch., Vienna, 1982—. Mem. Direct Mktg. Assn. Washington (dir. 1981—, pres. 1986), One Hundred Million Club (1980-82). Office: Viguerie Co 7777 Leesburg Pike Falls Church VA 22180

LINCOLN, LILLIAN NOVELLA HOBSON, building services contractor; b. Powhatan, Va., May 12, 1940; d. Willie David and Arnetha (Hobson) Hobson; m. Roy Lincoln, June 8, 1968; children—Darnetha LaRoi, Tasha Renee'. B.A., Howard U., 1966; M.B.A., Harvard U., 1969. Account exec. Ferris & Co., 1972-76; exec. v.p. Unified, 1973-76; pres. Centennial One, Crofton, Md., 1976—. Named Small Bus. Person of Yr., State of Md., 1981; Female Minority Contractor of Yr., Dept. of Commerce, 1984. Mem. Bldg. Service Contractors Assn., Capitol Assn. Bldg. Service Contractors (dir.), Prince George C. of C. (dir. 1984). Republican. Baptist. Avocations: reading; traveling. Home: 1305 Lavall Dr Gambrills MD 21054 Office: 2411 Crofton Ln Suite 14 Crofton MD 21114

LINCOLN, SHEILA VALREEN, interior architect, interior design consultant; b. Lubbock, Tex., July 17, 1959; d. Albert Wallace and Rose Marie (Davis) L. B.S., U. Tex., Austin, 1981. Interior designer 3D Internat., Houston, 1981-82, IPC, Dallas, 1982-83; interior architect Hellmuth, Obata, Kassabaum, Architects, Dallas, 1983—; adv. mem. Fider/Founder for Interior Design Edn./Research, 1980-81. Mem. Am. Soc. Interior Designers (lectr. 1980—, pres. U. Tex. chpt. 1979-80, nat. regional v.p. S.W. region 1980-81), Inst. Bus. Designers, Delta Sigma Theta. Office: Hellmuth Obata Kassabaum Architects 2501 Cedar Springs Dallas TX 75201

LIND, MARILYN MARLENE, artist, writer, genealogical researcher, consultant; b. New Ulm, Minn., Aug. 15, 1934; d. Fred S. and Emma L. (Steinke) Thiem; student pub. schs., Aitkin, Minn.; m. Charles R. Lind, Aug. 22, 1952; children—Michael, Bonnie, Vickie. Photographic asst., Aitkin, 1951-52; bookkeeper, office mgr. Rural Electric Assn., Aitkin, 1953-54; office mgr. N.E. Minn. Edn. Assn., Cloquet, 1970-77; pres. The Linden Tree, Cloquet, 1981-86; exhibited in one-woman show: Lake Superior Art Center, Duluth, 1972, Old Towne Gallery, Duluth, 1983. group shows include: Lutheran Brotherhood Ctr. Gallery, Mpls., 1977. Precinct chmn. Ind. Republicans Minn., 1976-77, co-chmn. Carlton County/Senate Dist. 14, 1977-80, vice chairwoman, 1984—, 8th Congl. Dist. Com., 1977-80, mem. Minn. state central com., 1977-82, county, dist. and state conv. del., 1976—. Recipient Gallery awards, Duluth, 1972, Mpls., 1977. Mem. Geneal. Soc. Carlton County (founder, bd. dirs. 1977—, v.p. 1980-81) Sec., 1982-83. Lutheran. Author: Christoph and August, A Dream and a Promise, 1981; Beginning Genealogy, 1983; Researching and Finding Your German Heritage, 1984; Using Maps and Aerial Photography in Your Genealogical Research, 1984, 2d edit., 1985; Immigration, Migration and Settlement in the United States; Continuing Your Genealogical Research in Minnesota, 1986. Home and Office: 1204 W Prospect Ave Cloquet MN 55720

LIND, PENELOPE DOUGALL, media and advertising agency executive; b. New Rochelle, N.Y., Sept. 21, 1941; d. Bernard W. and Alice (Shepard) Dougall; m. Douglass Theodore Lind, July 31, 1965. Student Wheelock Coll., Boston, 1959-61, Columbia U., 1961-62. Group tour dir. NBC, N.Y.C., 1963-69; asst. to pub. Simon & Schuster, N.Y.C., 1969-71; exec. producer Westchester Young Actors Theatre, New Rochelle, 1971-73; asst. to advt. dir. Brooks Newspapers, Westport, Conn., 1973-79; media buyer Strategic Advt., Darien, Conn., 1979-80; v.p., dir. media Davidoff & Ptnrs., Fairfield, Conn., 1980-86; research analyst Mkgt. Corp. of Am., Westport, Conn., 1986—. Chmn. community adv. bd. Conn. Pub. TV, 1981-83; mem. Rep. Town Meeting, Westport, 1981-86; deacon Presbyterian Ch., 1980-82. Mem. Fairfield County Ad Club. Democrat. Home: 17 Edgewater-Hillside Westport CT 06880 Office: Mkgt Corp Am Riverside Ave Westport CT 06880

LINDAUER, LOIS LYONS, weight control company executive; b. N.Y.C., Feb. 6, 1933; d. Ken and Rose (Schneidman) Lyons; A.B., Brandeis U., 1953; m. William Seltz, Nov. 12, 1972; children by previous marriage—Karen Lyons, Amy Hope. Copywriter, Herbert Frank Advt. Agy., Boston, 1956-57; pres. Paisley workshop, handmade plaques and wall decor, N.Y.C., 1962-65; nat. dir. Diet Workshop, Inc., Boston, diet cons. Alba Non-Fat Skim Milk, Sweet N Low sugar substitute, Ladies Home Jour. Author: It's In to Be Thin, 1971; The Diet Workshop Restaurant Manual, 1972; The Fast and Easy Teenage Diet, 1973; The Success Diet, 1978. Home: One Longfellow Pl Boston MA 02114 Office: 111 Washington St Brookline MA 02146

LINDBERG, ELAYNE VERNA, art appraiser; b. Browerville, Minn., Apr. 27; d. Leslie and Velma (Breighhaupt) Averill; M.Social Sci., U. Minn., 1967; m. Russell H. Lindberg; children—Gary, Bonnie Lindberg Carlson. With Dayton's Dept. Store, Mpls., 1965-71; pres., chief exec. officer Elayne Galleries, Inc., Mpls., 1971—; art restorer and appraiser, 1970—. Mem. Am. Soc. Appraisers (assoc.), Internat. Soc. Appraisers, Internat. Assn. Questioned Document Examiners (charter), Internat. Graphoanalysis Soc., New Eng. Appraiser Assn. Club: Calhoun Beach (Mpls.). Composer verse, sacred music. Home: 2950 Dean Pkwy Minneapolis MN 55416 Office: 6111 Excelsior Blvd Saint Louis Park MN 55416

LINDBERG, MARY KLINGER, methodologies analyst, data processing educator; b. Albany, N.Y.; d. Julius L. and Anna Friedman; m. Bertil C. Lindberg, Oct. 12, 1979; 1 son, Erik B.A. B.A. magna cum laude, Bklyn. Coll., 1965; M.A. in English, NYU, 1966, Ph.D., 1970. Asst. prof. English Baruch Coll., 1972; assoc. prof. Calif. State U., Northridge, 1972-77; adj. assoc. prof. NYU, 1978-81; asst. to chancellor L.I. U., 1981; cons. Con Edison, N.Y.C., 1981; mgr. devel. methodologies edn. Chem. Bank, N.Y.C., 1982-85; project mgmt. coordinator Merrill Lynch, N.Y.C., 1985—; pvt. practice communications cons., 1978—. Contbr. articles to profl. jours. poetry to jours. Calif. State U. Northridge grantee, 1974-77; Inst. Internat. Edn. fellow, 1966; Andrew Mellon fellow, 1977; Penfield fellow, 1969-70; Founders' Day award, 1971. Mem. ASTD, MLA, Soc. Theatre Research, Am. Soc. Theatre Research, Am. Soc. Aesthetics, Phi Beta Kappa, Alpha Sigma Lambda. Home: 3 Hanover Square Apt 10F New York NY 10004 Office: 2 Broadway New York NY 10004

LINDBLAD-GOLDBERG, MARION, psychologist; b. Akron, Ohio, Mar. 1, 1943; d. Alvar Willard and Marion Mitchell (MacLeod) Lindblad; B.A., Ohio Wesleyan U., 1965; M.A., U. Minn., 1967; Ph.D., Temple U., 1977; m. Martin Goldberg, May 26, 1978; 1 son, David; stepchildren, Meryl, Karen, Dara. Psychologist, Phila. Psychiat. Center, 1967-73, Phila. Child Guidance Clinic, 1973-75, dir. clin. services, 1975-79; assoc. prof. psychiatry, dir. Family Therapy Center, U. Cin. Med. Sch., 1979—. HEW grantee, 1978-81. Mem. Am. Psychol. Assn., Am. Orthopsychiat. Assn., Am. Assn. Marriage and Family Therapists, Nat. Register, Am. Family Therapy Assn. Home: 2343 Vista Pl Cincinnati OH 45208 Office: 231 Bethesda Ave Cincinnati OH 45267

LINDEMAN, ANNE ELIZABETH, state senator; b. East Orange, N.J., Sept. 10, 1932; d. Roy James Wensley and Elizabeth Mae (Antis) O'Leary; m. Robert W. Lindeman (dec.); children—Robert, Kurt, Kristofer. Grad., Meml. Hosp. Sch. Nursing, South Bend, Ind., 1954. Mem. Ariz. Ho. of Reps., 1972-76; mem. Ariz. Senate, 1976—, parliamentarian, 1979-84, majority whip, 1983—. Mem. Edn. Commn. of States, 1976—, mem. nat. child abuse adv. council, 1976-78, chmn. policy and priorities adv. council, 1982-83, vice chmn., 1983; Mem. State Vocat. Edn. Adv. Commn., 1977; mem. com. on edn. and social services Western Conf., Council State Govts., 1979-80; mem. Maricopa County Skill Adv. Com., 1980—; mem. Pres.'s Adv. Council on Federalism, 1982; bd. dirs. Nat. Ctr. for Higher Edn. Mgmt. Systems, 1983, Jobs for Am.'s Grads., 1983—, Jobs for Ariz. Grads., 1983—, Nat. Assessment of Ednl. Progress, 1984—; mem. Nat. Inst. Edn. Lab. Study Group, 1983-84; mem. United Student Aid Funds Adv. Council, 1983—; chmn. U.S. Aid Fund/Ariz. Ednl. Loan Program, 1983-84; mem. Ariz. Bar Found.'s Law Related Edn. Com., 1984; mem. Council of State Govts. Com. on Suggested Legislation, 1985; chmn. Intergovtl. Adv. Council on Edn., 1985—. Named Maryvale C. of C. Woman of Yr., 1975, 77; Nat. Republican Legislator of Yr., Nat. Republican Legislators Assn., 1982; Legislator of Yr., Ariz. Vocat. Edn. Assn., 1981, 82; recipient Program Service award Nat. Vocat. Agrl. Tchrs. Assn., 1981-82; Appreciation award Concerned Citizens for Good Govt., 1982; Disting. Service award Edn. Commn. of States, 1984, Hall of Fame award Ariz. Assn. Pvt. Agys. of Devel. Disabled, 1985; Disting. Citizen's award Phoenix Union High Sch. Dist., 1985, others. Mem. Nat. Conf. State Legislators (chmn. edn. com. 1980, chmn. state fed. assembly 1983-84, bd. govs. 1984). Home: 6542 W Earll Dr Phoenix AZ 85033 Office: Ariz State Senate 1700 W Washington St Phoenix AZ 85007

LINDEMAN, CAROL ANN, university dean; b. Racine, Wis., Jan. 16, 1935; d. Edgar Walter and Linda Irene (Wolff) Lehmann; m. George Lindeman, Apr. 12, 1958; children—Timothy, Steven, Michael, Daniel. B.S., U. Minn., 1957, M.Ed., 1958; Ph.D., U. Wis., 1964. Staff nurse Deaconess Hosp., Milw., 1955; pvt. duty nurse, Mpls., St. Paul, 1955-56; instr. Coll. St. Catherine, St. Paul, 1959-61; head nurse St. Joseph's Hosp., St. Paul, 1960; teaching asst. U. Wis., Madison, 1962-63, research asst., 1962-63; spl. lectr. extension div., 1964-65; asst. prof. Coll. St. Catherine, 1963-66; asst. prof. Wis. State U., Eau Claire, 1965-67, coordinator psychiat. and pub. health nursing, 1966-67, assoc. prof., coordinator psychiat. nursing, 1967-68; dir. nursing research Luther Hosp., Eau Claire, 1968-72; asst. program dir. Western Interstate Commn. for Higher Edn., Boulder, Colo., 1972-73, program dir. nursing research devel., 1973-76; dean Sch. Nursing, U. Oreg. Health Scis. Ctr., Portland, 1976—. Mem. Am. Nurses Found., 1970; vice-chmn. Eau Claire Youth Tapline, 1970-72; mem. profl. adv. com., home care program Boulder City-County Health Dept., 1973. Recipient Outstanding Achievement award Evang. Deaconess Hosp., 1969; Brookdale award for research. Fellow Am. Acad. Nurses; mem. Minn. League for Nursing, Wis. League for Nursing, Am. Nurses Assn. (vice chmn. council nurse researchers 1971-74), Minn. Nurses Assn., Wis. Nurses Assn., Colo. Nurses Assn., Sigma Theta Tau, Pi Lambda Theta. Contbr. numerous articles on clin. nursing research to profl. publs.; research columnist Jour. Nursing Adminstrn., 1974—. Office: Sch Nursing U Oreg Health Scis Ctr 3181 SW Sam Jackson Park Rd Portland OR 97201*

LINDEN, JANINE MAGER, public relations executive; b. N.Y.C., Oct. 2, 1946; d. Moses F. Mager. B.A., U. Pa., 1968. Fashion credits editor Harper's Bazaar, N.Y.C., 1969-71; assoc. pub. relations Cotton Inc., N.Y.C., 1971-73; press officer Harrods Ltd., London, 1973-74; project mgr. J.C. Penney Co., N.Y.C., 1974-75; pub. relations dir. Kenyon & Eckhardt, N.Y.C., 1975-77; sr. v.p. pub. relations Saatchi & Saatchi Compton, N.Y.C., 1977—. Contbr. articles to mags. Bd. dirs. Girl's Club N.Y., N.Y.C., 1980-85. Mem. Pub. Relations Soc. Am., Advt. Women of N.Y., Publicity Club London. Republican. Club: Cosmopolitan, Coffee House, Doubles, Mashomack Fish and Game. Office: Saatchi & Saatchi Compton Inc 625 Madison Ave New York NY 10022

LINDEN, JUDITH MARSHA, symphony director; b. Bklyn., Nov. 17, 1951; d. Morton and Selma Samilow; B.A. cum laude, Ithaca Coll., 1973; postgrad. Renssalear Poly. Inst., 1976-78; m. Jay Linden, Sept. 2, 1973; children—Jessica Nicole, Daniel Elliot. Placement dir. Mass. Med. Soc., 1973-74; public relations dir. Albany (N.Y.) Regional Med. Program, 1974-76; asso. dir. alumni relations Renssalear Poly. Inst., Troy, N.Y., 1976-78; exec. dir. Queens Symphony Orch., Rego Park, N.Y., 1978-83; fundraising cons. Carnegie Hall, New Community Cinema, N.Y.C., 1984—. Bd. dirs. Open Door Parenting Center. Mem. Am. Symphony Orch. League, Bus. and Profl. Women's Assn. Home: 170 Hillpark Ave Great Neck NY 11021 Office: 99-11 Queens Blvd Rego Park NY 11374

LINDGREN, LAVADA MAE, financial executive, consultant; b. Morris County, Kans., Sept. 20, 1941; d. C. Harold and Erma Adelle (Scott) L.; m. Ronald James Perry, Dec. 22, 1959 (div. Oct. 1974); children—Ronald James, Teri Lee, Lynn Marie. B.Acctg. cum laude, Johnson & Wales Coll., 1977; postgrad. Providence Coll., 1976-78. Sec. to purchasing agt. Claflin Co., Providence, 1963-64; sec. to v.p. Paramount Restaurant Supply, Providence, 1964-68; sec. to chief systems engr. BIF, Providence, 1968-71; acct. Amtel, Inc., Providence, 1971-78; controller South Central Oil Co., Houston, 1978-82; chief fin. officer Kell Internat. Inc., Houston, 1983—; cons. Bus. Staffing Centre, Houston, 1983—, Molly Brown Enterprises, St. Louis, 1983—. Leader Girl Scouts U.S.A., East Providence, R.I., 1970-74; tchr. United Meth. Ch., East Providence, 1968-75; mem. reelection com. East Providence Democratic Com., 1974; project leader Boy Scouts Am., East Providence, 1975; dancer Mothers' Dancing Club, East Providence, 1972-78. Recipient president's cert. IBM, Boca Raton, Fla., 1979; Matrix Mgmt. Achievement award Wharton Sch. Fin., 1980. Mem. Am. Mgmt. Assn. Republican. Methodist. Club: Emblem (organist 1973-75) (East Providence). Home: 11418 Green Glade Dr Houston TX 77099 Office: Kell Internat Inc 5637 Richmond Ave Houston TX 77057

LINDHOLM, KATHRYN JEANNE, research psychologist; b Chgo., Aug. 3, 1954; d. Carroll Raymond and Sally Ann (Elmore) Lindholm; B.A., U. Calif., Santa Barbara, 1976; M.A., UCLA, 1977, PH.D., 1981; m. Amado Manuel Padilla, Aug. 1, 1981; 1 child, Diego Amado Lindholm Padilla. Research asst. Spanish Speaking Mental Health Research Center, UCLA, 1976-77, research assoc., 1977-81, asst. research psychologist, 1981-85, adj. lectr., 1981—; research psychologist Ctr. for Lang. Edn. and Research UCLA, 1985—; cons. to Calif. State Dept. Edn., Sacramento, 1979-80, 85—. Calif. State scholar, 1972-76; NSF grantee, 1974; NIMH grantee, 1981. Mem. AAAS, Am. Psychol. Assn., Am. Sociol. Assn., Research Com. on Sociolinguistics, Western Psychol. Assn., Am. Scandinavian Found., Sigma Xi. Author: Proposal Writing Strategies, 1981; contbr. chpts. to books. Home: 16759 Rayen St Sepulveda CA 91343 Office: CLEAR UCLA 1100 Glendon Ave 1740 Los Angeles CA 90024

LINDHOLM, SUE CAREY, lawyer; b. Atlanta, Jan. 4, 1944; d. William Oscar and Sue Carey (Rooney) Lindholm; children—Gregory de Torony, Sue Carey de Torony. A.A., Gulf Park Coll., 1962; A.B.J., U. Ga., 1964, J.D., 1982. Bar: Ga. 1982. Asst. editor Briefings Dean Rusk Ctr., Athens, Ga., 1982-83; sole practice, Athens, 1983-84; law clk. for Justice George T. Smith, Ga. Supreme Ct., 1984—. Mem. ABA, Ga. Bar Assn. Address: 5400 Memorial Dr Apt H-6 Stone Mountain GA 30083

LINDLEY, JANE ANN, government official; b. Logansport, Ind., Oct. 2, 1942; d. Gerald Davis and Mary Jane (Beale) L.; B.A., Butler U., 1964; M.L.S., U. Md., 1973. With Library of Congress, Washington, 1964—, librarian, bibliographer, 1971-76, intern, 1975-76, congl. research adminstr. Congl. Research Service, 1976-82, pub. affairs specialist, 1982—; cons. Battelle Meml. Inst., 1970—. Grantee U.S. Internat. Communication Agy., 1981, USIA, 1982; Japan Econ. Found., 1984, Asia Fiund., 1985, 86. Mem. Nat. Assn. Female Execs., Spl. Libraries Assn., Women in Info. Processing, Internat. Fedn. Library Assns. and Instns., Beta Phi Mu, Kappa Kappa Gamma. Home: 2435 Mary Pl Fort Washington MD 20744 Office: Congressional Research Service Library of Congress Washington DC 20540

LINDLEY, MARALEE IRWIN, county official, consultant, speaker; b. Springfield, Ill., June 30, 1925; d. Oramel Blackstone and Rachel Virginia (Elliott) Irwin; M. Joseph Perry Lindley, Sept. 18, 1948; children—Joseph Perry, Richard Fleetwood. B.S., Northwestern U., 1947; M.A., Sangamon State U., 1973, 79. Cert. tchr., Ill. Bookkeeper, acct. Ill. State Bar Assn., Springfield, 1947-48; curriculum coordinator, tchr. Sch. Dist. 186, Springfield, 1966-80; auditor, trustee Woodside Twp., Springfield, 1977-81; county auditor Sangamon County, Ill., 1980-84, 84—. Co-author/developer Ill. Elem. Gifted Program, 1977-80 (exemplary citation 1978). Mem. Mayor's Commn. on Internat. Visitors, Springfield, 1964—; sec. Sangamon State U. Found., 1984-86, Symphony Guild, Springfield, 1983-86; treas. Springfield Women's Polit. Caucus, 1983-85; pres. Capitol City Republican Women's Club, Springfield, 1985-87. Recipient hon. Thanks award Land of Lincoln council Girl Scouts U.S., 1958, Appreciation award City of Springfield, 1964, Disting. Citizen award Sch. Dist. 186; named to Women of Achievement in Govt., Sangamon State U., 1985, One of 5 Rep. County Ofcls. of Yr., 1985. Mem. Ill. Assn. County Auditors (sec. 1982-84, treas. 1984-86, v.p. 1986), Assn. Govt. Accts. (pres. 1984-85), Am. Soc. Pub. Adminstrn., Nat. Assn. Govt. Accts. (regional v.p.-elect), Ill. Women in Govt. (treas.), Women in Mgmt. (Woman of Achievement award 1985), LWV. Lodge: Zonta. Avocations: dulcimer; folk singing; sports; reading; public speaking. Home: 2332 Noble Ave Springfield IL 62704 Office: Sangamon County Auditor's Office Sangamon County Bldg Springfield IL 62701

LINDLEY-DOMINGUEZ, PATRICIA J., lawyer; b. Sapulpa, Okla., Mar. 13, 1940; d. Allen L. and Cornelia Madelyn (Brown) Monroe; m. Clyde E. Lindley, June 8, 1958 (div. 1970); children—Kenton K., Rafaella D.; m. Oscar Dominguez, July 21, 1979. A.A., Kansas City Jr. Coll., 1961; B.A., Avila Coll., 1968; J.D., U. Mo., 1974. Bar: Mo. 1974, C.Z. 1974, U.S. Ct. Appeals (5th cir.) 1976, U.S. Ct. Claims 1979, U.S. Supreme Ct. 1979. Social worker, supr. Mo. Div. Welfare, 1961-69; asst. coordinator U. Mo.-Kansas City, 1969-70; social work dir. Project Headstart, Kansas City, 1970-71; intern pvt. law firm and Legal Aid, Kansas City, Mo., 1971-74; staff atty. Panama Canal Commn., 1974—, asst. gen. counsel, 1983—, mem. women's adv. council, 1975-84, legal advisor Panama Canal Coll. Charter Commn., 1978; adj. prof. Nova U., Panama Regional Ctr., 1978-79. Vol. legal advisor U.S.A. Girl Scouts-Panama, 1975—; vol. Balboa Youth Recreation Council, 1974-79, Joint Com. Infant and Child Protection, 1974-79, Foster Home Com., 1974-79. Mem. ABA, C.Z. Bar Assn. (sec., v.p., pres. 1977-79), Mo. Bar Assn., Am. Assn. Trial Lawyers, Fed. Bar Assn. (v.p. Panama chpt. 1980). Democrat. Home: 610 Calle Mindi Balboa Heights Panama Office: Office of Gen Counsel Panama Canal Commn APO Miami FL 34011

LINDNER, CHARLOTTE K., librarian; b. N.Y.C., Feb. 28, 1922; d. Louis B. and Ada (Kreitman) Fisch; B.A., N.Y.U., 1942; M.L.S., Columbia U., 1959; children—Carol, Gregory, Amy. Asst. cataloger D. Samuel Gottesman Library, Albert Einstein Coll. Medicine, Bronx, N.Y., 1958-63, cataloger, 1963-76, asst. librarian, 1974-76, acting dir. library, 1976-78, dir. library, 1978—. Mem. Med. Library Assn.

LINDNER, ERNA CAPLOW, educator, choreographer, movement therapist; b. N.Y.C., May 26, 1928; d. Abraham Murray and Mildred T. (Farb) Caplow; A.B., Bklyn Coll., 1948; M.S., Smith Coll., 1950; Ph.D., Columbia Pacific U., 1986; m. Norman Lindner, June 18, 1950 (dec. Sept. 1981); 1 dau., Amy Beth. Instr. dance Brown U., 1950-54, Rutgers U., 1954-55; dance specialist Samuel Field YM—YWHA, Queens, N.Y., 1962-68; dance specialist N.Y.C. Bd. Edn., 1963-69; asst. dance dir., choreographer Martin de Porres Center, Queens, 1967-70; dir. Saturday Cultural Program, Rochdale Village Nursery Sch., Queens, 1964-73; dir.-choreographer Danceabouts Co., N.Y.C., 1966-80; prof. health, phys. edn. and recreation Nassau Community Coll. SUNY, L.I., 1968—; adj. prof. phys. edn. and dance Adelphi U., 1979—; lectr. on dance for spl. populations. Active Dance Library in Israel; charter mem. Queens Council on Arts, exec. bd. dirs., 1970-74; sec., mem. exec. com. Nat. Ednl. Council Creative Therapies. Mem. Am. Dance Guild (charter mem., past nat. pres., nat. exec. bd.), N.E. 4 State Region Dance Guild (officer), Queens Dance Guild (founding), Am. Dance Therapy Assn., Am. Assn. Sex Educators, Counselors and Therapists (cert. sex educator, sex counselor). Contbr. chpts. on dance to Fun for Fitness; interviewer on dance Sta. WHPC-FM; (with others) selected music and wrote manual for Special Music for Special People, Ednl. Act Rec. Co., 1977; Special Dancing on Your Feet and in Your Seat, 1982. Author: (with others) Therapeutic Dance/Movement, 1979; (monograph) Use of Dance in Sex Education and Counseling, 1974; also articles on geriatric dance therapy. Home: PO Box 993 Woodside NY 11377 Office: Nassau Community Coll Stewart Ave Garden City NY 11530

LINDQUIST, EDITH LORRAINE, physical education educator; b. Duluth, Minn., Aug. 2, 1931; d. Andrew H. and Edith Margaret (Nordmark) Lindquist; B.S. (Calif. State scholar 1952), U. Calif., Santa Barbara, 1953; M.S., U. So. Calif., 1955; Ph.D. (teaching asst. 1962, 65), U. Mich., 1968. Instr. phys. edn. Los Angeles city schs., 1953-65; research grantee Horace R. Rackham Sch. Grad. Studies, U. Mich., 1968; prof. phys. edn. San Jose (Calif.) State U., 1966—, coordinator undergrad. maj. program; research chmn. Western Soc. Phys. Edn. Coll. Women, 1975-78, spl. projects chmn., 1975; cons. in field. Grantee HEW, 1971; spl. projects grantee Western Soc. for Phys. Edn. Coll. Women, 1977-78; Calif. State Dept. Edn. grantee, 1979-80. Mem. AAPHERD (fellow Research Consortium on Completed Research), Calif. Assn. Health, Phys. Edn. and Recreation, Calif. Tchrs. Assn., N.Am. Soc. Psychology of Sport and Phys. Activity, Can. Soc. Psychomotor Learning and Sport Psychology, Alpha Delta Pi. Democrat. Author papers in field. Asso. editor Motor Skills: Theory into Practice, 1976—. Home: 6035 Montgomery Corner San Jose CA 95135 Office: San Jose State Univ San Jose CA 95192

LINDQUIST, LINDA JANETTE, city official; b. Jonesboro, Ark., May 31, 1951; d. Davis Edward and Reba (Eades) Thomas; m. Harry A. Lindquist; children—Jeffrey, Julie, Michael. Market analyst Time-Life Inc., Chgo., 1969-71; account rep. Coca-Cola, Atlanta, 1974-77; acct. Deltaco (W.R. Grace), Atlanta, 1980-81; acct. Village of Romeoville, Ill., 1982-83, fin. dir., 1983—, treas. Police Pension Bd., 1983—. Vol. Romeoville Parade Assn., 1984-85, Romeoville Beautification Com., 1984; tabulator Miss Romeoville Pageant, 1984-85. Mem. Govt. Fin. Officers Assn., Exec. Women Nat. Assn., Ill. Treas. Assn. Avocations: water colors; ceramics; camping. Home: 214 Linden Romeoville IL 60441 Office: Village of Romeoville 13 Montrose Dr Romeoville IL 60441

LINDSAY, FREDA THERESA, church association executive, editor; b. Burstall, Sask., Can., Apr. 18, 1914; d. Gottfred and Kaity (Saklofsky) Schimpf; m. Gordon Lindsay, Nov. 14, 1937 (dec. 1973); children—Carole Ann Sorko-Ram, Gilbert Livingston, Dennis Gordon. B.A., L.I.F.E., 1938, D.D. (hon), 1977. Co-pastor Ch. of Foursquare Gospel, Oreg., 1950; pres., editor Christ for the Nations, Dallas, 1973-85, chmn. bd., 1985—. Author: My Diary Secrets, 1976; Freda, 1984. Editor books. Named Christian Woman of Yr. Acts Ministry Am. Christian Voice Found., 1983. Mem. Full Gospel Fellowship of Chs. and Ministers Internat. (v.p. 1977—, bd. dirs. 1976). Republican. Avocations: reading; swimming. Office: Christ for the Nations Inc 3404 Conway St Dallas TX 75224

LINDSAY, JUDY INDIRA, public relations executive; b. Bombay, India, Feb. 9, 1962; came to U.S., 1969; d. Robert Lewis and Sasamma Phoebee (Zachariah) L. B.S. in Communications, Southwestern Adventist Coll., 1984. New dir. Sta. KJCR, Keene, Tex., 1983-84, Sta. KZEE, Weatherford, Tex., 1984; advt. exec. Sta. KCLE, Cleburne, Tex., 1984—, advt. and promotions exec., 1984-85; devel. officer Southwestern Adventist Coll., Keene, Tex., 1985—. Pub. relations Am. Cancer Soc., Cleburne, 1985—; mem. Boy Scouts Dist. Bd., Cleburne. Mem. Am. Bus. Womens Assn., Radio TV News Dirs. Assn. Republican. Mem. Seventh Day Adventist Ch. Lodge: Zonta (mem. pub. relations com.). Avocations: music; fashion show presentations; reading; outdoor sports. Home: PO Box 426 Cleburne TX 76031 Office: Southwestern Adventist Coll Keene TX 76059

LINDSAY, JUDY LEE, air force officer; b. Erie, Pa., June 21, 1946; d. James Goodison, Jr. and Joan Carlton (Ward) Williams; m. Malcom Walling Lindsay, Sept. 14, 1973 (div. Sept. 1984). B.A., Mercyhurst Coll., Erie, Pa., 1968; M.A., Webster Coll., 1977. Tchr. Ft. LeBoeuf High Sch., Pa., 1968-69; substitute tchr. pub. schs., Miami, Fla., 1969-70; commd. USAF, 1970, advanced through grades to lt. col., 1986; various assignments, continental U.S., Korea, Hawaii, 1970—, transp. officer, squadron comdr. U.S. Air Force Acad., Colo., since 1983—. Mem. Nat. Assn. Female Execs., Air Force Assn., Soc. Logistics Engrs., Jr. League. Republican. Episcopalian. Avocations: running, golf, tennis, reading. Home: 5901 Mt Eagle Dr #316 Fairfax VA 22303

LINDSEY, BARBARA ANN, publishing executive, dress designer; b. Corry, Pa., Sept. 11, 1940; d. Melvin C. and Madge Jeanette (Peterson) Gable; ed. U. Palm Beach, Indian River Jr. Coll., USDA Grad. Sch., Washington; children—Melody Layne, Merry Lee, Lorrie Ann, Jewel Lynne, Mona Louise. Head librarian, dept. sec. RCA, Palm Beach Gardens, Fla., 1960-63; legal sec. Thurlow & Thurlow, Stuart, Fla., 1963-64; v.p. R. C. Lindsey Plumbing, Inc., 1962-82; Amway distbr., dress designer Candi Lin, 1958—; pres. Lindsey, Gable, Conroy & Assocs., Inc., Stuart, 1979-82; pres. Am. Advt. Agy.; editor, pub. Prominent People in Fla. Govt. Republican state committeewoman Martin County; mem. exec. bd. Rep. Party of Fla., 1976-80; Rep. nominee for commr. agr. and consumer affairs State of Fla., 1982; alt. vice chmn. 10th Congl. Dist.; mem. Rep. Nat. Com., Congl. Adv. Bd.; bd. advisors Am. Security Soc.; mem. Nat. Congl. Adv. Com. Named Sec. of Yr., Palm Beach Profl. Secs., 1968, Mem. of Yr., Treasure Coast Home Builders Aux., 1979. Mem. Profl. Secs. Internat., Nat. Home Builders Aux., Women for Responsible Legislation, Internat. Entrepreneurs Assn., Fla. Direct Markets Assn., Fla. Farm Bur., Stuart C. of C., Gold Coast Direct Mktg. Assn., Internat. Platform Assn. Baptist. Clubs: United Women's Rep. (pres.), Rep. of Fla., Women's Rep. of Martin, Fla. Fedn. Rep. Women., Fla. State Soc., Conservative Network, Citizens for Am., Forum, Delphi, Renissance Women. Office: Buchanan House Suite 1031 2301 S Jefferson Davis Hwy Arlington VA 22202

LINDSEY, DOTTYE JEAN, educator; b. Temple Hill, Ky., Nov. 4, 1929; d. Jesse D. and Ethel Ellen (Bailey) Nuckols; B.S., Western Ky. U., 1953, M.A., 1959; m. Willard W. Lindsey, June 14, 1952 (div.). Owner, Bonanza Restaurant, Charleston, W.Va., 1965; tchr. remedial reading Alice Waller Elem. Sch., Louisville, 1967-75, tchr., 1953-67, 1975—, contact person for remedial reading, 1968—; profl. model Cosmo/Casablancas Modeling Agy., Louisville, 1984—. Bn. sponsor ROTC Western Ky. U., 1950. Named Miss Ky., 1951. Mem. NEA, Ky. Edn. Assn., Jefferson County Tchrs. Assn., various polit. action coms., Internat. Reading Assn., Am. Childhood Edn. Assn., Met. Louisville Women's Polit. Caucus (treas. 1980—). Democrat. Baptist. Office: 7410 LaGrange Rd Suite 104 Louisville KY 40222

LINDSEY, MARCIA JEAN, psychologist; b. Kansas City, Mo., Nov. 12, 1944; d. Jay Gordon and Virginia Anne (Smith) Crawford; m. William Grimes Lindsey, Feb. 14, 1976. B.A., Benedictine Coll., 1966; M.S.W., U. Denver, 1970, Psy.D., 1980. Lic. psychologist, Tex. Psychotherapist, Profl. Psychiat. Clinic, Denver, 1973-76; pvt. practice, Denver, 1976-79, Houston, 1981—; cons. Kent-Denver Country Day, Englewood, Colo., 1977-79; postdoctoral fellow VA Med. Ctr., Houston, 1980-81; with psychology services West Oaks Hosp., Houston, 1981-82; cons. DePelchin Children's Ctr., Houston, 1982-85. Mem. Houston Psychol. Assn. (exec. com. 1982-86, pres. 1985-86), Tex. Psychol. Assn. (exec. com. 1986), Am. Psychol. Assn. Club: River Oaks Bus. Women's Exchange (Houston). Office: SW Psychol Services PC 4710 Bellaire Blvd Suite 160 Bellaire TX 77401

LINDSEY, MARY DONNAVE, art and craft gallery administrator, artist; b. Columbus, Ga., Nov. 23, 1919; d. Cyril Macauley and Mary Margaret (Stelzenmuller) Brennan; m. Clifford Forrest Taylor, June 30, 1947 (dec. Feb. 1975); m. John Richard Lindsey, May 6, 1978 (dec. Nov. 1984); 1 stepchild, Elizabeth Brooks Rice. B.A.A., Auburn U., 1941. Layout artist Fawcett Publs., N.Y.C., 1945-47, W.T. Grant Co., N.Y.C., 1952-74; layout artist, illustrater May Co. Dept. Stores, Los Angeles, 1948-52; mng. dir. Sac's Gallery, Montgomery, Ala., 1979—. Artist (watercolor) Fat Doll (2d place 1981), Ala. River (2d place 1982); (watercolor painting) The Fountain (Best in Show 1984); (oil painting) Mary Lynne (Best in Show 1985). Fellow Montgomery Art Guild; mem. Soc. Arts and Crafts (pres. 1978-80, corr. sec. 1985—). Democrat. Presbyterian. Club: Pinedale Women's (1st v.p.). Home: 3774 Audubon Rd Montgomery AL 36111 Office: Sac's Gallery 1033 S Hull St Montgomery AL 36111

LINDSKOG, MARJORIE OTILDA, educator; b. Rochester, Minn., Oct. 13, 1937; d. Miles Emery and Otilda Elvina (Hagre) L. B.A., Colo. Coll., 1959, M.A. in Teaching, 1972. Field advisor/camp dir. Columbine Girl Scout Council, Pueblo, Colo., 1959-65; staff mem. Wyo. Girl Scout Camp, Casper, 1966; camp dir. Wyo. Girl Scout Camp, 1967; asst. camp dir. Pacific Peaks Girl Scouts, Olympia, Wash., 1968; camp dir. Pacific Peaks Girl Scouts, 1969; tchr. Dist. 60, Pueblo, Colo., 1966—; campcraft instr. Am. Camping Assn., 1969—, dir. instrs., 1975—, camp standards visitor, 1976—; instr. Jr. Great Books Program, 1981—. Contbr. articles to profl. jours. Bd. dirs. Columbine Girl Scout Council, 1983-85; area co-chmn. Channel 8 Pub. TV Auction, Pueblo, 1984—; mem. Pueblo Nature Ctr., 1981—; mem. credit com. Pueblo Tchr.'s Credit Union. Mem. Intertel, Mensa, Alpha Phi, Phi Delta Kappa (v.p., newsletter editor). Lutheran. Club: Pueblo Country. Lodge: Sons of Norway. Home: 2810 7th Ave Pueblo CO 81003 Office: Sunset Park Sch 110 University Circle Pueblo CO 81005

LINDSKOG, MARY ELIZABETH, retired school administrator, consultant; b. Toungoo, Burma, Dec. 11, 1926; came to U.S., 1931; d. James Lee and Betty (Ryden) Lewis; m. Paul W. Lindskog, June 7, 1949; children—Eric Woodrow, Jon Lewis. B.A., Macalester Coll., 1949. Tchr. pub. schs., Pequot Lakes, Minn., 1949-50, Duluth, Minn., 1950-51; tchr. Robbinsdale Sch. Dist., Minn., 1958-63, dir. publs. and pub. relations, 1963-84; cons., lectr. in field. Contbr. articles to profl. jours.; editor various curriculum guides. Mem. Nat. Sch. Pub. Relations Assn. (chpt. pres., regional v.p. 1976-81). Home: 2485 Regent Ave N Minneapolis MN 55422

LINDSTEDT-SIVA, K. JUNE, petroleum company executive, environmental scientist; b. Mpls., Sept. 24, 1941; m. 1969. A.B., U. So. Calif., 1963, M.S., 1967, Ph.D., 1971. Asst. coordinator sea grant programs U. So. Calif., 1971; environ. specialist So. Calif. Edison Co., 1971-72, cons., 1972; asst. prof. biology Calif. Luth. U., 1972-73; sci. advisor Atlantic Richfield Co., Los Angeles, 1973-77, sr. sci. advisor, 1977-81, mgr. environ. sci., 1981—; cons. Jacques Cousteau, Metromedia Producers Co., 1970. Contbr. articles to profl. jours. Mem. Nat Sci. Bd., 1984—, mem. research subcom., 1986; bd. dirs. So. Calif. Acad. Scis., 1984-86; mem. biology adv. council Calif. State U.-Long Beach, 1980—; mem. adv. bd. Cabrillo Marine Mus., Los Angeles, 1986—; trustee Bermuda Biol. Sta. Research, 1979. Mem. Soc. Petroleum Industry Biologists (former pres.), Marine Technol. Soc., Am. Soc. Zoologists, AAAS, Sigma Xi. Office: Environ Sci Dept Atlantic Richfield Co PO Box 2679 Los Angeles CA 90051

LINDVIG, ELISE KAY, ednl. psychologist; b. Sidney, Mont., Feb. 10, 1952; d. William F. and Katheryn E. (Taylor) L.; student Carroll Coll. (Mont.), 1970-71; B.A. in Psychology with honors, U. Mont., 1974; M.S. in Clin. Psychology with high honors, U. Idaho, 1979. Assoc. coordinator Dept. Community Affairs, State of Mont., Glendive, 1974-75; teaching asst. U. Idaho, Moscow, 1975-79; sch. psychologist Hamilton, Mont., 1979-82, diagnostician, cons. in field; bookkeeper, musician, 1975-79. Mem. Am. Psychol. Assn. (assoc.), Mont. Assn. Sch. Psychologists (cons.), Idaho Mental Health Assn., Am. Quarter Horse Assn., Am. Kennel Club, Nat. Hot Rod Assn. Republican. Roman Catholic. Clubs: Eagles Aux., Moose Aux. Condr. research on malnutrition in primates; author: Nutrition and Mental Health, 1979; Grade Retention: Evolving Expectations and Individual Differences, 1982. Home: PO Box 5 Livingston CA 95334

LINEBACH, LAURA MARIE, nurse, writer; b. St. Louis, Aug. 3, 1949; d. Paul George and Ada Marie (Sullivan) Regna; m. Edward Grant Linebach, Nov. 19, 1971; children—Anastasia, Grant, Sean. A.D.N., Mercy Jr. Coll., 1970; B.S.N. magna cum laude, Avila Coll., 1977. R.N. Flight attendant T.W.A., Kansas City, Mo., 1970-78; staff nurse med./surg. dept. St. Luke's Hosp., Kansas City, Mo., 1970-77; staff nurse psychiat. dept. Kans. U. Med. Ctr., Kansas City, 1978-79; writer, mng. editor Greater Kansas City Nursing, Overland Park, Kans., 1982-83; founder, co-trustee, chmn. Nursing Heritage Found., Kansas City, 1980—; adv. com. mem. U. Mo.-Kansas City Sch. Nursing, 1980-81. Author: History of V.N.A. of Kansas City, 1985. Author, photographer of slide presentation Nurses for Nursing, 1982. Co-leader Brownies, Kansas City, 1984—. Recipient Award of Excellence T.W.A., 1973. Mem. Am. Nurses Assn., Am. Assn. History of Nursing, Mo. Nurses Assn. (editor newsletter dist. 2 1978—, editorial bd. 1982—), Sigma Teta Tau, Beta Lambda (counselor 1981-84). Club: Clipped Wings (Kansas City) (internat. reporter 1984—). Office: Nursing Heritage Found 222 W Gregory St Suite 203 Kansas City MO 64114.

LINEBACK, AUDREY CLARE, marketing executive; b. New Ringgold, Pa., June 3, 1940; d. Raymond William and Shirley Hill (Geiger) Gilbert; m. Robert Milton Lineback, June 10, 1960 (div. Mar. 1983); children—Robert, Teresa, Melissa. B.S., U. S. Fla., 1975. Cert. work evaluator, cert. fingerprint technician. Stewardess Eastern Airlines, Miami, Fla., 1958-60; fingerprint technician Fed. Bur. Investigation, Washington, 1960-61; vision and hearing specialist Highlands County Sch. Bd., Sebring, Fla., 1973-75, work evaluator, 1975-80; pres. A Lineback & Assocs., Lake Wales, Fla., 1980—; dir. mktg. Kimball Farms at Lenox, Mass., 1986—; cons. Am. Retirement Corp., Nashville, 1985-86, Gen. Health Mgmt., Bloomfield, Conn., 1985—, Alexian Village of Tenn., Chattanooga, 1983-85, Touko Haus, Tokyo, 1985-86, Lutheran Chs., St. Louis, 1975-80. Pres. Luth. Womans Missionary League, Sebring, Fla., 1980-82; treas. 99's- Internat. Women Pilots, Winter Haven, Fla., 1981-83. Mem. Am. Assn. Homes for Aging, Am. Mktg. Assn., Am. Assn. Female Execs., Chattanooga Bus. and Profl. Women. Lutheran. Avocations: private pilot. Home: 3801 Bruce Blvd Suite 4S Lake Wales FL 33853 Office: Kimball Farms at Lenox 4 Main St Lenox MA 01240

LINEBAUGH, VICTORIA JANE BUERCK, accountant; b. Perryville, Mo., Dec. 11, 1951; d. Earl William and Mary Norma (Hoffman) Buerck; m. Gary L. Ervin, Mar. 9, 1974 (div.); m. 2d, Gary L. Linebaugh, Sept. 25, 1981. A.A. in Computer Sci., S.E. Mo. State U., 1972. Acctg. supr. Charter Investment Co., Cape Girardeau, Mo., 1972-74, Plywood Paneling Co., Memphis, 1974-76, Music Factory Inc., Memphis, 1976-77; controller Soultastic Prodns., Memphis, 1977-78; dir. fin. SMR Enterprises, Memphis, 1978-80; v.p. L&R Leasing Co., Memphis, 1981—; mem. franchise relations com. Fantastic Sam's Haircare Ctrs. Franchise Owner's Adv. Council, Memphis, 1980—. Mem. Am. Bus. Women's Assn. Roman Catholic. Home: 4233 Lady Slipper Ln Memphis TN 38115 Office: L&R Leasing Co Inc 3180 Old Getwell Rd Memphis TN 38118

LINEBERGER, MARILYN HAZZARD, psychologist; b. Abbeville, S.C., Dec. 10, 1952; d. Sanders and Louise (Lomax) Hazzard; B.A., U. S.C., 1975; M.S., U. Ga., 1977, Ph.D., 1979; m. Frank James Lineberger, Jr., Sept. 1, 1979; 1 child, Winsheket Nicole. Lic. clin. psychologist, Ga. Counselor, Gleams Community Action Agy., Greenwood, S.C., summers 1973-75; asst. prof. psychology Kent (Ohio) State U., 1979-80; asst. prof. psychology and clin. psychologist Emory U., Atlanta, 1980-85, adj. asst.prof. psychology, 1985—; ind. clin. and cons. practice, Atlanta, 1985—. Vol. various polit. campaigns; active Big Bro. and Big Sister orgns. Mem. Am. Psychol. Assn., Assn. Advancement Behavior Therapy, Assn. Black Psychologists, Council on Children, AAAS, Midwestern Psychol. Assn., Mortar Bd., Nat. Honor Soc., Phi Beta Kappa, Psi Chi. Democrat. Methodist. Club: Pre-Profl. Psychology (adviser). Contbr. research articles to profl. lit. Home: 3668 Crossvale Rd Lithonia GA 30058 Office: Dept Psychology Emory U Atlanta GA 30322

LINEFSKY, RAE, educational and vocational services executive; b. Phila., May 1, 1944; d. Samuel and Celia (Berlman) L.; children—Jordan David Zielin, Sasha Linefsky Zielin. Student U. Wis.; B.A., Boston U., 1967, M.A., 1969. Instr. adult basic edn. U. Conn., Storrs, 1968; state supr. adult basic edn. Mass. Dept. Edn., Boston, 1967-69; manpower program specialist Nat. Alliance of Bus., Boston, 1969-70; unit leader Parkway Program, Phila. Bd. Edn., 1970-73; cons. Research for Better Schs., Phila., 1974-77; exec. dir. Court Employment Project, N.Y.C., 1977-81; sr. v.p. Fedn. Employment and Guidance Service, N.Y.C., 1981—. Contbr. articles to profl. jours. Press Block Assn., Ft. Greene, Bklyn., 1982. Mem. Nat. Youth Employment Coalition (vice chmn. bd. dirs. 1985—), Empire State Orgn. of Youth Employment Services (bd. dirs. 1984—). Avocations: cooking; travel; theatre. Office: Fedn Employment and Guidance Service 62 W 14th St 7th Floor New York NY 10011

LINEHAN, HELEN M., sales administrator; b. N.Y.C., Sept. 4, 1939; d. Timothy Finbar and Emma Louise (deLuis) O'Callaghan; m. William Linehan, Nov. 14, 1958 (div. 1979); children—M.E. Linehan, Sarah L. Linehan. Student, Fordham U., 1976-79. Asst. adminstr. Rudolf Steiner, N.Y.C., 1972-76; dir. sales adminstrn. Boris Kroll Fabrics Inc., N.Y.C., 1976—, asst. v.p., 1986—; edn. com. ACT, N.Y.C., 1986—. Democrat. Roman Catholic. Avocations: Marine life; communications with mammals; swimming; writing. Office: Boris Kroll Fabrics Inc 979 Third Ave New York NY 10022

LINEN, DIANE HEALEY, broadcasting company executive; b. Boston, May 17, 1947; d. Mike and Dorothy (Silverstein) Blumenthal; m. Peter F. Healey, Aug. 7, 1976 (div. Aug. 1983). B.A., U. Pa., 1969; M.A., U. Sussex, Brighton, Eng., 1971; M.B.A., Harvard U., 1975. Vice pres. affiliated corp. relations NBC, N.Y.C., 1975-85; sr. v.p. Communications Equity Assocs., Tampa, Fla., 1985—. Named YWCA Woman of Yr., 1983. Home: 212 Nottingham Rd Richmond VA

LINGENFELTER, SHARON MARIE, data processing company executive; b. Nyssa, Oreg., June 17, 1947; d. Floyd LeRoy and Ruth Irene (Bale) Martin; (div.); children—Brian James Lingenfelter, Kevin James Lingenfelter. Student George Fox Coll., 1966, Portland State U., 1968. Vice pres. adinstrn. Century Data, Inc., Portland, 1982—. Editing cons. Century Direct Mktg., Inc., 1983—; office systems analyst C.I. NorCal, San Francisco, 1985—. Mem. Nat. Assn. Female Execs. Republican. Avocations: skiing; writing; travel. Office: Century Data Inc 2355 NW Quimbly St Portland OR 97210

LINGHAM, MARCELLA ERMA, community health center administrator; b. Phila., Jan. 15, 1942; d. Harry Boyd and Gladys Marcella Lawson; student Temple U., 1960-62; B.S. in edn., Cheyney State Coll., 1965; M.Ed., Temple U, 1970; Ed.D., Rutgers U., 1980. Tchr., Sch. Dist. Phila., 1965-70; curriculum devel. specialist, reading specialist RCA Service Co., Cherry Hill, N.J., 1970-72; project dir., curriculum developer, ednl. cons. Research for Better Schs., Inc., Phila., 1972-79; asst. prof. Rutgers U. Newark Coll. Arts and Scis., 1980-83; exec. dir. Primary Community Health Ctr. of Mantua, Inc., 1983—. Vice chairperson bd. dirs. 2501 Health Care Corp., Phila., 1980—, bd. dirs. Black Family Services. Mem. Am. Ednl. Research Assn., Internat. Reading Assn., AAUW, Am. Pub. Health Assn., Assn. Supervision and Curriculum Devel. Democrat. Baptist. Home: 119 S Peach St Philadelphia PA 19139 Office: Primary Community Health Ctr of Mantua Inc 34th and Haverford Ave Philadelphia PA 19104

LINGLE, MARILYN FELKEL (LYN), radio station executive; b. Hillsboro, Ill., Aug. 16, 1932; d. Clarence Frederick and Anna Cecelia (Stank) Felkel; m. Ivan L. Lingle, Oct. 4, 1950; children—Ivan Dale, Aimee Lee Lingle Galligan, Clarence Craig. Sec. Ill. State Police, 1950; with welfare dept. Ill. Pub. Aid, Hillsboro, 1951-52; researcher Small Homes Council, Champaign, 1952-53; sec. Hillsboro Schs., 1954; office, payroll clk. Eagle Picher Zinc, Hillsboro, 1955-56; continuity dir. Sta. WSMI, Litchfield, Hillsboro, 1966—. Contbr. poetry to profl. jours. Fin. chmn. Hillsboro Hosp. Aux., 1972; pres., bd. dirs. Montgomery Players and Encore Play Theatre, 1954-70; active PTA, Girl Scouts, Cub Scouts, ch. youth activities. Democrat. Lutheran. Club: Hillsboro Country. Avocations: bridge; golf; gardening; travel; reading. Office: Sta WSMI Radio PO Box 10 Litchfield IL 62056

LINGO, CATHERINE MALLIA, real estate executive; b. Galveston, Tex., Aug. 10, 1947; d. Simon Aloysius Mallia, Jr. and Aleta Jo (Wooten) Mallia Benson; m. Kenneth Anthony Van Nostrand, Feb. 5, 1966 (div. Aug. 1979); 1 son, Scott Anthony; m. 2d Carl Wesley Lingo, Nov. 5, 1983; children—John Jason, Mitzi Leigh. Student Galveston Coll., 1971-73, Houston Community Coll., 1975-78. Office sec. Am. Nat. Ins. Co., Galveston, 1965-67, U.S. Army C.E., Galveston, 1967-69; legal sec. Royston, Rayzor, Cook & Vickery, Galveston, 1969-74; adminstrv. asst. Moody House, Inc., Galveston, 1974-75; real estate broker with various firms, Houston, 1975-81; mktg. dir. Spectrum Devel., Houston, 1981-84; owner CML Interests, 1984—. Pres., Tallowood Homeowners Assn., Houston, 1980; v.p. bd. dirs. Dad's Club, YMCA, Houston, 1979. Mem. Women in Comml. Real Estate and Leasing. Home: 10111 Jademont Ln Houston TX 77070 Office: CML Interests 4606 FM 1960 W Suite 250 Houston TX 77069

LINHART, FRANCINE, music industry executive, writer, educator; b. Chgo., Sept. 17, 1951; d. Raymond Richard and Elizabeth (Domelle) L. B. Mus. Edn., DePaul U., Chgo., 1974; student Nat. U., San Diego, 1982, Elgin Community Coll., 1984-85. Sales trainer, Wurlitzer, DeKalb, Ill., 1973-76, bus. and product mgr., 1984—; dist. mgr. Yamaha Internat. Corp., Buena Park, Calif., 1976-80, dir. mktg., 1980-83; asst. sales mgr. Hal Leonard Pub., Milw., 1983-84; tchr. jazz and beginning keyboard U. Wis., Milw., 1983-84. Author: Beginning Keyboard, 1983, Cats, 1984, The King & I, 1984. Contbr., cons. Keyboard Mag., 1982-84. Chmn. membership Orange County Performing Arts Ctr., Irvine, 1983; organist Unitarian Ch., Geneva, Ill., 1984—. Mem. Chgo. Sales Tng. Assn. (bd. dirs. 1985), Nat. Assn. Electronic Keyboard Mfrs. (sec. treas. 1984-85, v.p. 1985-86). Republican. Clubs: Mensa, Toastmasters. Avocations: reading; music; sewing; gardening. Home: 401 North Ave Saint Charles IL 60174 Office: Wurlitzer 403 E Gurler Rd DeKalb IL 60115

LINICH, JACQUELINE JEAN, personnel consultant, nurse; b. Joliet, Ill., Apr 3, 1950; d. Theodore Charles and Pauline Marie (Galle) L. Diploma, Good Samaritan Sch. Nursing, Phoenix, 1972. R.N. Staff nurse respiratory therapy John C. Lincoln Hosp., Phoenix, 1969-74; staff nurse Vis. Nurse Service, Phoenix, 1974-77; rehab. cons. Southwestern Rehab. Ctr., Phoenix, 1977-78; personnel cons. Dunhill of Pasadena (Calif.), 1978-79, Dunhill of Phoenix, 1979—; nursing supr. Huntington Meml. Hosp., Pasadena, 1978; lectr. Ariz. State U., Tempe, 1983-84. Chmn. pub. relations com. Young Reps. Phoenix, 1974-76, mem. Gerald Ford Re-Election Campaign, Phoenix, 1976, Big Sisters Phoenix, 1982. Recipient profl. awards. Mem. Ariz. Search Cons., Ariz. Small Bus. Assn., Am. Hosp. Assn., Dunhill Health Care Core Group, Phi Upsilon Omicron (lectr. 1984). Roman Catholic. Office: Dunhill of Phoenix 2712 N 7th St #3 Phoenix AZ 85006

LINK, IRENE MAY AMMONS, educator, poet; b. Pueblo, Colo., Apr. 18, 1939; d. Elbert A. and Jennie D. (Panepinto) Ammons; B.A., N.W. Nazarene Coll., 1964; postgrad. U. Hawaii, 1968; m. Peter M. Link, Dec. 19, 1965. Feature writer, photographer Times-News, Twin Falls, Idaho, 1975—; instr. bus. dept. Coll. So. Idaho, Twin Falls, 1972—; instr. speech and English Twin Falls High Sch., 1965-70; v.p. Link Land and Livestock Co.; cons. image making, advt. and public relations; lectr. bus. women's seminars Mem. Idaho Edn. Assn., Idaho Assn. Bus. Tchrs., AAUW, NEA, Am. Soc. Profl. and Exec. Women, Nat. Assn. for Female Execs. Office: Coll So Idaho PO Box 1238 Twin Falls ID 83301

LINK, LAURA JEAN, electrical engineer; b. Chgo., Feb. 10, 1955; d. Allen Bruce and Ethel Alberta (Meske) L. A.S.E.E., Cypress Coll., 1983; B.S.E.E., Calif. State U.-Fullerton, 1986. Mgr. Software design Computer Systems Approach, Fullerton, 1983-84; design engr. Hughes Aircraft, Fullerton, 1985—. Served with U.S. Army, 1976-79. Mem. Nat. Assn. Female Execs., Mensa, VFW, Phi Kappa Phi. Home: 133 N LaPlaza Anaheim CA 92805 Office: Hughes Aircraft 1901 W Malvern Mail Sta 682 B103 Fullerton CA 92634

LINK, MAE MILLS (MRS. S. GORDDEN LINK), aerospace medicine research consultant; b. Corbin, Ky., May 14, 1915; d. William Speed and Florence (Estes) Mills; B.S., George Peabody Coll. for Tchrs., 1936; M.A., Vanderbilt U., 1937; Ph.D., Am. U., 1951; grad. Air War Coll., 1965; m. S. Gordden Link, Jan. 11, 1936. Instr. social sci. Oglethorpe U., 1938-39; instr. English, Drury Coll., 1940-41; assoc. dir. edn. Ga. Warm Springs Found., 1941-42; mil. historian Hdqrs. Army Air Forces, 1943-45, Office Mil. History, Dept. of Army, 1945-51; spl. asst. to surgeon gen. and sr. med. historian U.S. Air Force, Washington, 1951-62; cons. in documentation and space medicine historian NASA, Washington, 1962-64, coordinator documentation and life scis. historian, 1964-70; research assoc. Ohio State U. Found., 1970-72; trustee, dir. fellows Koontz Meml. Center Advanced Studies, 1972—. Trustee, Univ. Press Fund, Amos R. Koontz Meml. Found. Recipient Meritorious Service award U.S. Air Force, 1955, Outstanding Performance awards, 1956-62; Friday Nighters cup, 1960; Outstanding Alumna award Sue Bennett Coll., 1977. Fellow Am. Med. Writers Assn. (past dir. Middle Atlantic region); mem. Aerospace Med. Assn. (standing com. on sci. communication in bioastronautics and space medicine), Am. Inst. Aeros. and Astronautics (hist. adv. com.), Air Force Hist. Found. (charter), Am. Assn. Med. History, Internat. Congress History Medicine, Soc. for History Tech., Societe International d'Histoire de la Medecine. Republican. Episcopalian. Clubs: Garden Va. Author: Medical Support of the Army Air Forces in World War II, 1955; Annual Reports of the U.S. Air Force Medical Service, 1949-62; Space Medicine in Project Mercury, 1965; (with others) Foundations of Space Biology and Medicine (U.S./USSR Joint Publ.), 1976. Editor: U.S. Air Force Med. Service Digest, 1957-62. Contbr. to Ency. Brit., Collier's Ency., Funk & Wagnall's New Ency.; contbr. articles to profl. jours. Home: Dellbrook Riverton VA 22651 Office: Hist Dir Koontz Center for Advanced Studies Riverton VA 22651

LINK, NINA BETH, publisher; b. Bklyn., Sept. 19, 1943; d. Robert R. and Helen (Cohen) Levine; B.A., Beaver Coll., 1965; m. Harry J. Link, July 1, 1966; children—David Jon, Gregory Adam. Sec., WCBS TV, N.Y.C., 1965-66; ednl. systems analyst edn. div. Xerox, N.Y.C., 1966-68; cons. The Link Group, Inc., N.Y.C., 1968-78; v.p., publisher Children's TV Workshop, N.Y.C., 1978—; cons. publishing, communications cos. Mem. Direct Mail Mktg. Assn., Writer's Guild, Dramatist's Guild, Internat. Reading Assn., Mag. Pubs. Assn., Acad. Women Achievers of YWCA. Home: 222 W 83d St New York NY 10024 Office: 1 Lincoln Plaza New York NY 10023

LINK, PHOEBE FORREST, educator, author; b. Palmerton, Pa., Feb. 20, 1926; d. John Nevins and Phoebe Eleanor (Lewis) Forrest; m. Robert H. Link, July 13, 1962; children—David Forrest, Anne Harris. B.A. in Psychology, Pa. State U., 1947, M.S. in Child Devel. and Family Relationships, 1952; postgrad. U. Rochester, 1957-59, Harvard U., 1958. Dir. teen age program YWCA, Lansing, Mich., 1947-50, Rochester, N.Y., 1952-56; research asst. Pa. State U., State College, 1950-52; tchr. Rochester, 1956-60, William Antheil Sch., Trenton, N.J., 1960-63; mem. faculty Trenton State Coll., 1960-63; tchr. State College area schs., 1971—; lectr. Am. Home Econs. Assn. Conv. cons. family studies, leader continuing edn. workshops Pa. State U., 1977; mem. staff dean women Harvard U., Cambridge, Mass., summer 1958. Author: Small? Tall? Not At All, 1973. Active Fair Housing, Inc.; trustee Sch. Pub. Library, State College, Pa., 1980-83; founder, first chmn. poetry com. Central Pa. Festival Arts. AAUW Simmons grantee, 1984. Mem. NEA, Pa. Edn. Assn., State Coll. Area Edn. Assn., AAUW, Mortar Board Alumni (founder, 1st pres.), Pa. State U. Coll. Human Devel. Alumni (bd. dirs.). Phi Delta Kappa, Omicron Nu Alumni (founder), Tau Phi Sigma. Contbr. articles to profl. jours. Home: 22 Cricklewood Circle State College PA 16803

LINKE, RUTH ANNA, home economist; b. N.Y.C., Aug. 26, 1926; d. George and Elsie (Schmidt) Renz; B.S., N.Y.U., 1946, Ph.D., 1957; M.A., Columbia U., 1947; m. William F. Linke, Apr. 14, 1949; children—William, Robert Christopher, Jennifer Ann. Instr. part time N.Y. U., Tchrs. Coll., Columbia U., Hunter Coll., Lehman Coll., 1950-64; asst. prof. dept. home econs. and nutrition N.Y. U., 1973-76, assoc. prof., 1976—, acting chmn. dept., 1974-75, dep. chmn., 1979—. Mem. Bd. Edn. Stamford (Conn.), 1962-71, pres., 1964-65,

68-69; mem. urban edn. com. Conn. Assn. Bds. of Edn., 1966-70; mem. Conn. State Advisory Com. for Ednl. Profl. Devel. Act, 1966-70. Mem. Am., N.Y. State (dir., v.p. 1982-84, treas. dist. 5 1977-79, dist. pres. 1980-81) home econs. assns., Coll. Tchrs. Household Equipment (membership com. 1979-80), Assn. Home Econs. Tchrs. N.Y.C., Elec. Women's Round Table, Am. Assn. Housing Educators, Am. Vocat. Assn., N.Y. State Home Econs. Tchrs. Assn., AAUW, Omicron Nu, Pi Lambda Theta. Contbr. articles to profl. jours. Home: 75 Ridgecrest Rd Stamford CT 06903 Office: Dept Home Econs and Nutrition NY U Washington Sq New York NY 10003

LINLEY, MARILYN WILLIAMS, TV producer; b. Waukesha, Wis., Oct. 26, 1922; d. Arthur Joseph and Vivian Jeanette Marie (LaHaie) Williams; B.A., Carroll Coll., 1944; M.A., Marquette U., 1969; m. Herbert Laflin Linley, 1945 (div. 1963); children—Marilyn Margaret, Elizabeth Anne, Jane Milton. Tchr., Fort Atkinson (Wis.) High Sch., 1944-45; substitute tchr. Accelerated High Sch., Balt., 1945-46; tchr. public schs. Rahway, Long Branch, Eatontown and Oceanport, N.J., 1946-60; columnist Long Branch (N.J.) Daily Record, 1960; tchr. Long Branch Schs., 1960-61; tchr. Mukwonago (Wis.) Union High Sch., 1962-70, team tchr., 1970-71; cons., tchr. English Houston High Sch. for Performing and Visual Arts, 1971-73; tchr. Tng. Center Human Resources Devel. and Edn. Renewal, 1973-74; media staff devel. tchr. Continuing Careers Devel. Center, MacGregor, 1973-74; instr. TV specialist Instructional Media Services, Houston, 1974; instructional TV producer, Houston, 1977—. Former bd. dirs. Episcopal Churchwomen Diocese N.J., Rahway Service League (N.J.), Jr. League, Monmouth, N.J., Welfare Council, Monmouth, Long Branch (N.J.) Public Health Nursing Assn., PTA, Long Branch, N.J., Waukesha, Wis., Waukesha Symphony Orch., 1969; pres. Waukesha Symphony Aux., 1970, Friends U. Wis., Waukesha, 1963-71; mem. devel. adv. council KUHF Pub. Radio. Named Girl of Year, Monmouth Jr. League, 1959; recipient award of achievement Gulf Region Ednl. TV Affiliates, 1980. Mem. Women in Communications, Inc. (Headliner award 1980), Internat. TV Assn. (chmn. bd. Houston), Am. Women in Radio and TV (chmn. bd. Houston), NEA (del. 1973), Cable TV Task Force (exec. bd. 1970-74), Tex. Assn. Ednl. Technologists, Tex. State Tchrs. Assn. (chmn. publicity 1973), Tex. Classroom Tchrs. Assn. (del. 1973, 74), Houston Tchrs. Assn. (faculty rep. 1972—), Tex. Ednl. TV Assn., Houston Area Sch. Librarians, Broadcast Pioneers. Home: 5206 Memorial Dr Houston TX 77007 Office: 3830 Richmond Ave Houston TX 77027

LINN, JOY, business executive; b. Monterey Park, Calif., Nov. 8, 1936; d. Herbert A. and Kathleen L. (Stilton) Shuttleworth; m. James Bouwkamp, May 6, 1985; children—Robin, Kim, Jackie, Joe. A.A. in Real Estate Law, Fullerton Coll., 1974. Cert. escrow officer, Calif. Escrow officer Best Escrow Corp. of Hollywood, Calif., 1961-69; personnel coordinator Camac Corp., Bristol, Va., 1970-72; escrow officer Walker & Lee Escrow Corp., 1972-74; adminstr. Christ Ch. Anaheim, Calif., 1974-76; br. mgr. Escrow div. F.M. Tarbell, Buena Park, Calif., 1976-77; mgr. Escrow dept. main br. The Chartered Bank of London, 1977-79; mgr. escrow and loan depts. Hawthorne Savs. and Loan Assn., N. San Diego, 1979-82; pres., chief exec. officer Pathways Assocs., Inc., 1982-85 pres., chief exec. officer Pillar Enterprises, Inc., Garden Grove, Calif., 1985—. Contbr. articles to profl. jours.; author stage plays. Served with USAF, 1950-52. Recipient Hon. Service award Calif. Christian Inst. Human Relations, 1982; Disting. Service award, Calif. Republican Party, 1982. Mem. Calif. Escrow Assn. (dir. 1979-81), Am. Soc. Composers, Authors and Pubrs., Pathways to Happiness, Abingdon Soc. Preservation Native Art Va. Christian Reform. Lodge: Job's Daus. Avocations: golf; swimming; writing.

LINN, TERE, advertising/marketing company executive; b. Columbus, Ohio, Sept. 27, 1956; d. William Dean Linn and Norma Ann (Vermillion) Linn Murphy; m. Daniel L. Hostetler, Oct. 17, 1981. B.F.A., Bowling Green State U., 1978. Jr. designer Bowling Green State U., Ohio, 1977-79, graphic design supr., 1979, asst. dir. pub. relations, 1980-81; art dir. Miller/Pelton/Bellone, Schenectady, 1982-84; sr. art dir., v.p. H. Linn Cushing, Inc., Albany, N.Y., 1984—. Mem. Ad Club Northea. N.Y. (bd. dirs. 1985—, Nori award 1985), Univ. and Coll. Designers Assn. (Silver award 1979), Am. Women in Radio and TV, Nat. Assn. Female Execs., Art Dirs. Club Greater Boston, Advt. Club Greater Boston. Democrat. Methodist. Avocations: bicycling; tennis; racquetball; sewing. Office: H Linn Cushing Inc 4 Corporate Plaza Washington Ave Extension Albany NY 12203

LINNANSALO, VERA, engineer; b. Helsinki, Finland, Oct. 9, 1950; came to U.S., 1960, naturalized, 1969; d. Boris and Vera (Schkurat-Schkuropatsky) L. B.S. in Computer and Info. Sci., Cleve. State U., 1974, B.M.E., 1974; M.B.A., U. Akron, 1983. Engring. assoc. B.F. Goodrich Co., Akron, Ohio, 1974-75, assoc. product engr., 1975-77, tire devel. engr., 1977-79, advanced tire devel. engr., 1979-84, quality devel. engr., 1984-85, sr. quality devel. engr., 1985—. Mem. Am. Soc. Quality Control, ASME. Home: 1262 Culpepper Dr Akron OH 44313 Office: BF Goodrich Co D/6007 B/24-E 500 S Main St Akron OH 44318

LINNELL, KAREN MAE, home health agency executive; b. St. Paul, Dec. 9, 1941; d. Daniel Nelson and Laura Mae (Miller) Rice; m. Richard Phillip Linnell, Dec. 21, 1963; children—Richard Daniel, Matthew Phillip. B.S., U. Minn., 1963; student U. Detroit, 1983-85. Tchr. Roseville Pub. Schs., Minn., 1963-64, Birmingham Pub. Schs., Mich., 1964-70; pres., adminstr. Renaissance Health Care, Detroit, 1976—; bd. dirs. Wayne State U. Med. Sch. Adv. Bd., Detroit, 1984—; founder Am. Fed. Home Health Agencies, Washington, 1980; del. Revion V Home Health Adv. Com., Chgo., 1981—. Recipient Tchr. of Yr. award Detroit Free Press, 1968. Mem. Am. Acad. Med. Adminstrs., Am. Fed. Home Health Agys., (pres. 1982-83, v.p. 1980-82), Am. Fed. Home Health Agys. (pres. 1982-83, regional dir. 1985—), Mich. Home Health Agy. (vice pres. 1983-85, bd. dirs. 1981-82, 85—). Democrat. Presbyterian. Office: Renaissance Health Care 20700 Greenfield Suite 320 Detroit MI 48237

LINSAO, RIADEL DURAN, nurse; b. Tarlac, Tarlac, Philippines, Dec. 8. 1960; came to U.S., 1970; d. Ricardo Manio and Adelina (Duran) L. B.Nursing, U. Wash., 1983. Nurses aide Bellevue Terrace Nursing Home, Wash., 1977-82; sr. student employee Swedish Hosp. Med. Ctr., Seattle, 1983-84, grad. nurse, 1984; nurse Children's Orthopedic Hosp. Med. Ctr., Seattle, 1984—. Mem. Tagalog Circle, Rosary Group. Democrat. Roman Catholic. Avocations: playing the piano; reading; sightseeing. Home: 10012 NE 28th Pl Bellevue WA 98004 Office: Children's Hosp and Med Ctr Seattle WA

LINSCOMBE, NEVA NELL, nursing home executive; b. Crowley, La., Mar. 21, 1945; d. Gurvis Joseph and Elvie Mary (Abshire) Leger; m. Bobby Ray Linscombe, May 18, 1963; children—Lisa, Robert. Student U. So. La., 1973, McNeese U., 1975-76; A.D. in Nursing, La. State U.-Eunice, 1978. Mgr. Love's Studio & Camera Shop, Crowley, La., 1963-65; office mgr. Linscombe's Constrn. Co., Crowley, 1965-67; asst. adminstr. Jennings Guest House, La., 1972-78, dir. nursing, 1979-81; regional mgr. U.S. Care Co., Jennings, 1981—; chmn. La. Nurses' Liaison Com., 1979-81; dir. Progressive Nat. Bank, Rayne, La. Mem. scholarship com. Bus. and Profl. Women's Club, Jennings, 1980; parish coordinator Election of James David Cain for Congress, Jefferson Davis Parish, La., 1985—; bd. dirs. Success in Missions, Mexico, 1985-86. Mem. La. Nursing Home Assn. (bd. dirs. 1982, sec.-treas. 1982-85), Am. Coll. Nursing Home Adminstrs., Nat. Assn. Female Execs., Phi Lambda Phi. Democrat. Mem. Assembly of God Ch. Avocations: travel; gardening; reading; cooking. Home: PO Box 507 Jennings LA 70546

LINTERMANS, GLORIA, columnist; b. Bklyn., May 11, 1947; d. Harold and Adele (Brooks) Aisley; m. Eric Lintermans, June 15, 1968 (div. 1981); children—Richard A., Evan D. Columnist, Inter-Continental Press, Glendale, Calif., 1978-82, Universal Press Syndicate, 1982—; internat. columnist Editors Press, N.Y.C., 1980—; radio host Square Wheel Prodns., Van Nuys, Calif., 1982—, TV host, 1983—; ptnr. Square Wheel Prodns./The Consultancy, 1984—; author Capistrano Press, Ltd., Long Beach, Calif., 1980—; lectr. Aimee Entertainment, Van Nuys, Calif., 1983—. Author: The Professional Babysitter's Guide, 1980; internationally syndicated column Looking Great, 1978—; star syndicated TV and radio shows: Looking Great with Gloria Lintermans; editor, contbg. author ency.: Looking Great: A Guide To Beauty, 1982; pub. editor The Gloria Lintermans' Looking Great Newsletter; lectr. Hamberger Home, Los Angeles, 1981—. Spokesperson, Foster Parents Plan, Los Angeles, 1982. Mem. The Fashion Group, Inc., Women in Communications, Inc., AFTRA, Greater Los Angeles Press Club, Sigma Delta Xi. Office: Square Wheel Prodns/The Consultancy PO Box 675 Van Nuys CA 91408-0675

LINTON, CYNTHIA CARPENTER, newspaper editor; b. Bronxville, N.Y., Aug. 17, 1938; d. Ralph Emerson and Cynthia (Ramsey) Carpenter; m. John Marshall Linton, June 8, 1963; children—Terrence M., Robert C. B.A., Boston U., 1968. Staff writer Lerner Newspapers, Highland Park, Ill., 1972-78, mng. editor, 1978-80, sr. editor, Chgo., 1980—. Recipient awards for writing excellence Suburban Press Club Chgo., 1980, 81, Ill. Press Assn., 1982, Suburban Newspapers Am., 1979, Nat. Newspaper Assn., 1976, Peter Lisagor award, 1983, 84. Mem. Chgo. Headline Club, Chgo. Press Club, Sigma Delta Chi. Office 7519 N Ashland Ave Chicago IL 60626

LINTON, KATHLEEN MARIE, sales executive; b. Akron, Ohio, Jan. 15, 1954; d. Charles Joseph Linton and Marilyn Jeanne (Wilson) French. B.S. in Bus. Adminstrn., U. Akron, 1978. Customer service rep. BF Goodrich, Akron, Ohio, 1978-80, product specialist, 1980-81; dist. sales mgr. Borden, Inc., Atlanta, 1981-84; dir. sales and mktg. Nat. Gypsum, Wakefield, Mass., 1984—. Mem. Women in Outside Sales, Sales and Mktg. Execs. of Greater Boston. Democrat. Lutheran. Avocation: music. Office: Nat Gypsum Decorative Products Corporate Place 128 Wakefield MA 01880

LINZALONE, MARY JANE, pianist, educator; b. Somerville, N.J., Feb. 6, 1928; d. Einar Christensen and Marie (Andersen) Börnick; m. Ceasar Anthony Linzalone, Jan. 15, 1955 (dec.); 1 son, Gary Brooks. Student Julliard Sch. Music, 1940-46, Reifling Conservatory, Oslo, Norway, 1948-49. Concert pianist, N.Y., N.J., 1949-51; pianist, entertainer, U.S.A. and Can., 1951-57; mgr., buyer Town and Tweed, Rutherford, N.J., 1957-60; owner, mgr., tchr. Baldwin Piano, Passaic, Rutherford, Ridgewood, N.J., 1961-76, exec. dir. Williams Ctr. Performing Arts, Rutherford, 1978-83, cons., tchr., 1983—, trustee. Dir. Williams Ctr. Artist's Adv. Bd., Rutherford, 1979-84; bd. dirs. Pinellas County chpt. Am. Diabetes Assn. Recipient Citizen of Yr. award Meadowlands C. of C. (N.J.), 1982. Republican. Presbyterian. Home: 316 Orangewood Ln Harbor Bluffs Largo FL 33540

LIONBERGER, ERLE TALBOT LUND, Republican committeewomen; b. St. Louis, Apr. 29, 1933; d. Joel Y. and Erle (Harsh) Lund; m. John S. Lionberger, Jr., June 23, 1956; children—Erle Talbot, Louise Shepley. Student Mary Inst., 1951; A.B., Vassar Coll., 1955. Republican committeewoman Hadley Twp., St. Louis County, 1965—; mem. St. Louis County Rep. Central Com., 1965—; mem. Rep. State Com., 1966-78, 84—; del. Rep. Nat. Conv., 1972, 76, 80, 84, alt. del., 1968; Mo. chmn. Women for Reagan-Bush, 1984. Bd. dirs. Landmarks Assn. St. Louis, Inc., 1973-76, counselor, 1982—, coordinator Historic Preservation Pilgrimage, 1974; bd. dirs. Friends of Winston Churchill Meml., 1975-76, Save Grant's White Haven, Inc., 1985—; mem. women's exec. bd. Mo. Bot. Garden, 1977-80; mem. St. Louis County Hist. Bldg. Commn., 1976—, Capitol Complex Commn. on Fine Arts, 1983—, Thomas Hart Benton Homestead Meml. Commn., 1983—; chmn. Mo. 7th Senatorial Dist. Com., 1978-84; chmn. Mo. Adv. Council on Hist. Preservation, 1982—; Mo. rep. Lewis and Clark Nat. Hist. Trail Adv. Council, 1984—; bd. dirs. Mo. Heritage Trust, 1982—, Mo. Parks Assn., 1982—. Mem. Jr. League St. Louis, Mo. Fedn. Republican Women (bd. dirs.), Nat. Soc. Colonial Dames Am. (Mo. bd. dirs. 1976-80, hist. properties chmn. 1975-81), St. Louis Christmas Carols Assn. (area co-chmn. 1979-85). Address: 21 Dartford St St Louis MO 63105

LIPFORD, AUDREY HELENE, business writer; b. Buffalo, Aug. 30, 1956; d. Benjamin M. and Audrey Pauline (Hankins) Lipford; B.S. in Newspaper Journalism, Syracuse U., 1978. Proofreader, typesetter, news, society 1959 (dec.); features reporter, features editor The Amherst (N.Y.) Bee, 1978-80; sportswriter Hornell (N.Y.) Tribune, 1980; sports writer high sch. girls' and coll. women's athletics Buffalo Courier Express, 1981-82; gen. news reporter Vineland Times Jour. (N.J.), 1983-84; bus. writer Metalworking News/Am. Metalmarket, 1984—. Recipient Page One First Pl. award for developing news Buffalo Newspaper Guild, 1982. Mem. Sigma Delta Chi. Office: Metalworking News/Am Metalmarket 7E 12th St New York NY 10003

LIPHAM, NANCY CHARLENE, financial consultant; b. Anniston, Ala., May 6, 1954; d. Luther Garfield and Edna (Daniel) L. B.A., Samford U., 1976, postgrad., 1977. Congl. intern, Washington, 1974; sr. fin. cons. Merrill, Lynch, Pierce, Fenner & Smith, Anniston 1979—, asst. v.p., 1986—. Mem. Talladega County Hist. Assn., Ala., Anniston Mus. Natural History. Samford U. scholar, 1976. Mem. Nat. Assn. Female Execs., Calhoun County C. of C., Nat. Assn. Miniature Enthusiasts, Samford U. Alumni Assn., Gamma Sigma Sigma. Republican. Methodist. Clubs: Altrusa (Anniston). Avocations: flying; collecting miniatures and antiques. Home: 3 Mark Woods Rd Anniston AL 36201 Office: Merrill Lynch Pierce Fenner & Smith 206 E 6th St Anniston Al 36201

LIPIN, JOAN CAROL, association executive; b. Denver, Aug. 25, 1947; d. Theodore and Kathe (Pardo) Lipin. B.A., NYU, 1969; postgrad. MIT, 1972-73; M.B.A., Boston U., 1977. Adminstrv. staff MIT, Boston, 1969-74; adminstr. Mass. Gen. Hosp., Boston, 1975-76, mgmt. cons., 1976; dept. head N.Y. Hosp., N.Y.C., 1977-80; exec. v.p. Gordon-Keeble, N.Y.C., 1980-83; v.p. mktg. Rocket USA, 1983; pres. Thor Scientific, N.Y.C., 1983-86; sr. mgr. ARC in Greater N.Y., 1986—; cons.; mem. rev. bd. Ind. Testing Lab., N.Y.C., 1981-85. Cons. and tng. coordinator Am. Women Econ. Devel.; mem. Forum Corporate Responsibility. Mem. Opinion Research Corp., Pharm. Mktg. Assn., Nat. Assn. Female Execs., Am. Soc. Zoologists, Am. Mgmt. Assn., Planning Forum, Audubon Soc., World Wildlife Fund. Home: 45 E 89th st Apt 14G New York NY 10128 Office: ARC in Greater NY 150 Amsterdam Ave New York NY 10023

LIPINSKI, JANE LYNN, medical-surgical equipment sales representative; b. Columbia City, Ind., Aug. 20, 1953; d. Wilbur Demoines and Ruth Lucille (Cordill) Bennett; m. James Martin Lipinski, Oct. 26, 1983. B.A. in Bus., Purdue U., 1976. Orthopedic sales rep. Zimmer Co., Mpls., 1978-81; asst. to orthopedic physician, Clearwater, Fla., 1981-82; asst. dir. materials mgmt., Mease Hosp., Dunedin, Fla., 1982-84, sterile processing supr., 1982-84; med./surg. sales rep., surg. instrument specialist Edward Weck & Co., Inc., Research Triangle Park, N.C., 1984—. Mem. Nat. Assn. Female Execs., Assn. Operating Room Nurses, Assn. Hosp. Central Supply Mgrs. Republican. Avocations: scuba diving; underwater photography; tennis. Home: 12525 56th Pl N Royal Palm Beach FL 33411 Office: Edward Weck & Co PO Box 110580 Royal Palm Beach FL 33411

LIPKA, RUTH PLANTE, educational administrator; b. Woonsocket, R.I., Dec. 30, 1937; d. Philias Leo Plante and Olida Mathilda (Riendeau) Plante Michaud; m. Stephen Lipka, Sept. 1, 1958; children—Craig Stephen, Deanne Ruth. A.A.S. in Secretarial Sci., Bergen Community Coll., 1972; B.A. in Bus. Edn., Montclair State Coll., 1974, M.A. in Bus. Edn., 1977. Tchr. Teaneck Bd. Edn. (N.J.), 1974-75; placement dir. Sawyer Sch., Clifton, N.J., 1976-77; dir., owner Berdan Inst., Totowa, N.J., 1977—. Mem. Pvt. Career Sch. Assn. N.J. (bd. dirs. 1982—, sec. 1984-86, v.p. 1986—), Nat. Bus. Edn. Assn., N.J. Bus. Edn. Assn., Nat. Assn. Fin. Aid Adminstrs., N.J. Assn. Fin. Aid Adminstrs., Word Processing Info. Assn., Delta Pi Epsilon. Roman Catholic. Home: 13 Jonquil Ct Paramus NJ 07652 Office: Berdan Inst 265 Route 46 W Totowa NJ 07512

LIPKIN, MARY CASTLEMAN DAVIS (MRS. ARTHUR BENNETT LIPKIN), former psychiatric social worker; b. Germantown, Pa., Mar. 4, 1907; d. Henry L. and Willie (Webb) Davis; student grad. sch. social work U. Wash., 1946-48; m. William F. Cavenaugh, Nov. 8, 1930 (div.); children—Molly C. (Mrs. Gary Oberbillig), William A.; m. 2d, Arthur Bennett Lipkin, Sept. 15, 1961 (dec. June 1974). Nursery sch. tchr. Miquon (Pa.) Sch., 1940-45; caseworker Family Soc. Seattle, 1948-49, Jewish Family and Child Service, Seattle, 1951-56; psychiat. social worker Stockton (Calif.) State Hosp., 1957-58; supr. social service Mental Health Research Inst., Fort Steilacoom, Wash., 1958-59; engaged in pvt. practice, Bellevue, Wash., 1959-61. Former mem. Phila. Com. on City Policy. Former diplomate and bd. mem. Conf. Advancement of Pvt. Practice in Social Work. Mem. Acad. Cert. Social Workers, Nat. Assn. Social Workers, Internat. Conf. Social Work, Menninger Found., Union Concerned Scientists, Physicians for Social Responsibility, Center for Sci. in Pub. Interest, Jr. League, Seattle Art Mus., Asian Art Council, Wing Lake Mus., Bellevue Art Mus., Pacific Sci. Center, Western Wash. Solar Energy Assn., Nature Conservancy, Wilderness Soc., Mcpl. League of Seattle-King County, Sierra Club, Common Cause, ACLU, Pa. Acad. Fine Arts. Clubs: Cosmopolitan, Cricket (Phila.); Women's University (Seattle). Home: 9102 N Mercer Way #101 Mercer Island WA 98040

LIPKINS, AUDREY, insurance underwriter; b. N.Y.C., Dec. 25, 1947; d. Charles and Marjorie (Cohen) L. B.A., Miami Dade Community Coll., 1970. Claims adjuster Bankers Standard Ins., Miami, Fla., 1974-77; personal lines underwriter Poe & Assocs., Miami, 1977-83; Sternbaum Ins., Miami, 1983—. Recipient cert. of appreciation Miami Dade Community Coll. Student Govt., 1968. Vice pres. ways and means Nat. Children's Cardiac Hosp., Dade/Broward chpt., 1982—, Woman of Yr. 1982, 83. Mem. Nat. Assn. Female Execs. (Fla. dir.), Ins. Women of Miami (corr. sec. 1979-81). Democrat. Jewish. Home: 20515 E Country Club Dr 648 North Miami Beach FL 33180 Office: Sternbaum Ins 909 Brickell Plaza Miami FL 33169

LIPKVICH, DENISE O'CONNELL, market research analyst; b. New Haven, July 18, 1952; d. John Patrick and Marietta (Lanthier) O'Connell; m. Richard Alan Lipkvich, July 29, 1978; children—Keith Alan, Erica Anne. Student U. Lancaster (U.K.), 1973-74; B.A., Russell Sage Coll., 1974; M.A., U. Denver, 1977. Database specialist AMF, Inc., Stamford, Conn., 1977-79; database analyst Gen. Electric Co., Bridgeport, Conn., 1979-80, info. specialist, 1980-82, adminstr. corp. mktg., 1982—; personal computer hobbyist Yale affiliated Computer Learning Ctr., Branford, Conn., 1983—; instr. online databases regional library, Branford, 1978—. Mem. mother's support group Vis. Nurses Assn., Branford, 1984—; membership chmn. Coop. Library Service Unit Rev. Bd., Hartford, Conn., 1979-81; chmn. fund raising United Way AMF, Inc., Stamford, 1979. Mem. Am. Mktg. Assn. (host. com.), On-Line Users Group, (instr.), Southwestern Conn. Library Council (trustee 1979-81), Spl. Libraries Assn. (edn. com. Conn. 1977, charter mem. U. Denver 1976), Branford Hist. Soc. (patron). Republican. Roman Catholic. Home: 31 Riverside Dr Branford CT 06405 Office: Gen Electric Co 1285 Boston Ave Bridgeport CT 06602

LIPMAN, WYNONA, state legislator; b. Ga.; children—Karen Anne, William (dec.). Student Talladega Coll., Atlanta U.; Ph.D., Columbia U.; LL.D. (hon.), Kean Coll., Bloomfield Coll. Former high sch. tchr., lectr. Seton Hall U., Assoc. prof. Essex Community Coll.; mem. N.J. State Senate, 1971—, chmn. state govt. com., mem. joint appropriations com., revenue, fin. and appropriations com. Chmn., Commn. on Sex Discrimination in the Statutes. Recipient Outstanding Woman award Assn. Women Bus Owners, 1983. Office: NJ State Capitol Bldg Trenton NJ 08625*

LIPP, NORMA, insurance company executive; b. Ottawa, Ont., Can., Dec. 7, 1938; d. Isadore and Mary (Magalnick) Klaman; m. Lawrence D. Meno, Feb. 1, 1964 (div. 1969); m. Jules Lipp, Apr. 10, 1975; children—Michael, Traci, A.J. B.A., Mansfield Finishing Sch., 1959; grad. Sch. Design, Miami, Fla., 1978. Asst., Dept. Nat. Revenue, Ottawa, Ont., 1956-58; supr. info. services Can. Broadcast Corp., Ottawa, 1961-63; mgr., comptroller Metr Petroleum Co., Miami, Fla., 1968-69; asst. to pres. Gabor & Co., Inc., Miami, 1969-82; treas., dir. Fin. Planning Assocs., Miami, 1982—; chmn., dir. Fin. Planning Realty, Miami, 1985—. Assoc. Com. to Elect the Pres., Miami, 1984; assoc. mem. Rep. Nat. Com., Miami, 1984. Clubs: Westview Country, Cricket (Miami). Home: 20251 NE 25th Ave North Miami Beach FL 33180 Office: Financial Planning Assocs 5300 NW 77 Ct Miami FL 33166

LIPPA, BARBARA JEAN, planning ofcl.; b. Rochester, N.Y., Sept. 3, 1952; d. Frank and Joan Patricia (Vitello) Lippa; B.S., SUNY, Brockport, 1974; M.A., George Washington U., 1977, M.S.A., 1982. Legis. intern Com. on Human Resources, U.S. Senate, Washington, 1974; edn. cons., 1974; cons. Nat. Adv. Council on Indian Edn., 1974; staff Nat. Adv. Council on Edn. of Disadvantaged Children, Washington, 1974-77; planning aide Fairfax County (Va.) Planning Commn., 1978-79; dep. exec. dir. Fairfax County Planning Commn., 1979—. Religious edn. tchr. Roman Cath. Ch., Alexandria, 1974-80, coordinator Bible sch., 1977. Recipient award for excellence HEW, 1975, unusual ability increment award, 1982. Mem. Am. Planning Assn., Nat. Assn. Exec. Women, Zonta Internat. Home: 14436 Manassas Gap Ct Centreville VA 22020 Office: 10th Floor 4100 Chain Bridge Rd Fairfax VA 22320

LIPPE, PAMELA TOWEN, creative director; b. N.Y.C., Mar. 28, 1952; d. Vincent Stuyvesant and Barbara (Crane) Lippe. B.A., Hampshire Coll., 1977. Legis. assoc. Friends of the Earth, Washington, 1976-79; found. dir. MUSE Found., N.Y.C., 1979-81; creative dir. Nat. Com. for an Effective Congress, N.Y.C., 1981—; cons. Environ. Def. Fund, N.Y.C., 1986—; sec., dir. Citizens Vote, Inc., N.Y.C., 1982-86. Celebrity liaison Mondale-Ferraro campaign, 1984. Democrat. Office: Nat Com for an Effective Congress 10 E 39th St 601 New York NY 10016

LIPPITT, ELIZABETH CHARLOTTE, writer; b. San Francisco; d. Sidney Grant and Stella Lippitt; student Mills Coll., U. Calif., Berkeley. Writer, performer own satirical monologues; contbr. articles to 85 newspapers including Chgo. Tribune, Phoenix Republic, N.Y. Post, Los Angeles Examiner, St. Louis Globe-Democrat, Union Leader, Utah Ind., Pasadena Star-News, Jackson News, South W.Va. Enterprise, others. Recipient 7 Congress of Freedom awards. Mem. Nat. Assn. R.R. Passengers, Nat. Trust for Historic Preservation, Am. Security Council, Internat. Platform Assn., Com. for Free China, Am. Conservative Union, Guide Dogs for Blind, Amvets, Childrens' Village (Los Angeles), Com. For Free Afghanistan, Am. Space Frontier Com., several humane socs. and antivivisection orgns. Clubs: Metropolitan, Olympic, Commonwealth. Pop singer, recorder song album Songs From the Heart. Home: 2414 Pacific Ave San Francisco CA 94115

LIPSCHUTZ, ILSE HEMPEL, educator; b. Boennigheim, W.Ger., Aug. 19, 1923; came to U.S., 1946, naturalized, 1952; d. Joseph Martin Paul and Fanny (Wurzburger) Hempel; lic. ès lettres, Sorbonne, Paris, 1943, Diplôme d'Etudes Sup., 1944, Diplome Institut des Professeurs de Française àl'Etranger, 1945; Diploma de Estudios Hispánicos, U. Madrid, 1945; M.A., Radcliffe Coll., Harvard U., 1949, Ph.D., (AAUW fellow, N.Y. State, 1950-51, Anne Radcliffe fellow, 1950-51), 1958; m. Lewis D. Lipschutz, Feb. 6, 1952; children—Elizabeth, Marion, Marc, Margaret. Teaching fellow Radcliffe Coll.-Harvard U., 1947-51; instr. to prof. French, Vassar Coll., Poughkeepsie, N.Y., 1951—, dept. chmn., from 1975, Andrew W. Mellon prof. humanities, 1981—; cons., collaborator Spanish Ministry Culture, Madrid, 1979-81; lectr. Prado Mus., Madrid, 1983; Vassar faculty fellow, 1960, 67; research fellow Treatise of Friendship U.S.-Spain, 1979-80, summer 1981; sr. research fellow Fulbright-Hays Commn., 1983-84. Mem. AAUW, AAUP, Soc. Theophile Gautier. Democrat. Author: Spanish Painting and the French Romantics, 1972, 2d edit., 1984; co-author: La Imagen Romántica de España, 1981; contbr. articles in field to publs. Office: Vassar College Poughkeepsie NY 12601*

LIPSCOMB, ANNA ROSE FEENY, hotel executive; b. Greensboro, N.C., Oct. 29, 1945; d. Nathan and Matilda (Carotenuto) L. B.A., Queens Coll., 1977. Reservations agt. Am. Airlines, St. Louis, 1968-69, ticket agt., 1969-71; coll. rep. CBS, Holt Rinehart Winston, Providence, 1977-79, sr. acquisitions editor Dryden Press, Chgo., 1979-81; owner, mgr. Taos Inn, N.Mex., 1981—; founder Spring Arts, N.Mex., 1986. Editor: Intermediate Accounting, 1980; Business Law, 1981. Contbr. articles to profl. jours. Bd. dirs., 1st v.p. Taos Arts Assn., 1982-85; founder, bd. dirs. Taos Spring Arts Celebration, 1983—; founder, dir. Meet-the-Artist Series, 1983—; founding mem. Assn. Hist. Hotels, Boulder, 1983—; organizer Internat. Symposium on Arts, 1985; bd. dirs. Arts in Taos, 1983, Taoschool, 1985. Recipient Outstanding English Student of Yr. award Queens Coll., 1977. Mem. Millicent Rogers Mus. Assn., Taos Lodgers and Restaurant Assn., Taos Art Assn., Taos County C. of C., Phi Beta Kappa. Democrat. Home: Talpa Route Taos NM 87571 Office: Taos Inn PO Drawer N Taos NM 87571

LIPSCOMB, PEGGY ELAINE, pharmacist, real estate broker; b. Quitman, Tex., July 27, 1924; student Tex. Women's U., 1941-43; B.B.A., So. Meth. U., 1945; M.S., East Tex. State U., 1951; postgrad. U. Colo., 1953-54; B.S. in Pharmacy, U. Tex., 1959. High sch. tchr., Dallas, 1951-55; pharmacist, Dallas, 1959-63; pharmacist, owner Lipscomb's Pharmacy, Quitman, 1964-80; asso. realtor Fletcher's Realtors, Dallas, 1963—; asso. Tex-Lands Realty and Investment Co., Dallas, 1980—. Past chmn. Wood County chpt. Easter Seal Soc. for Crippled Children; mem. nat. voter adv. bd. Am. Security Council, Wood County del. to Tex. Democratic Conv.; Wood County precinct chmn. Mem. Am. Pharm. Assn., Nat. Assn. Retail Druggists, Tex. Pharm. Assn., Tex. Real Estate Assn., Dallas Bd. Realtors, Learning Labs. Corp., Internat. Traders, Mellinger Import-Export Assn., Bus. and Profl. Women's Club, Kappa Epsilon (past v.p.), Beta Sigma Phi. Clubs: Dallas Gun, United European Am. Address: PO Box 578 Clear Lakes Village Quitman TX 75783

LIPSCOMB, REGINA DARLENE, army officer; b. Paris, Tex., Apr. 5, 1957; d. Kenneth Raymond and Minnie Mae (Beauford) L. Diploma Bishop Coll., 1979; certs., Adj. Gen. Officers Basic Course, 1979, Adj. Gen. Advanced Ctrs., 1983; diploma Combined Arms Service Staff, 1985. Cert. tchr. elem. edn.

Commd. 2d lt. U.S. Army, 1979, advanced through grades to capt., 1983; custodian postal effects 40th Adj. Gen. Detachment, Hanau, Fed. Republic Germany, 1979-81; asst. chief personnel actions div. V Corps, Frankfurt, Fed. Republican Germany, 1981-82; adj. gen. readiness coordinator Army Readiness Mob Region, Ft. Dix, N.J., 1983, company comdr. U.S. Army Tng. Ctr. (HHC), 1983-85, adj./S1 Basic Tng. Com. Group, 1985; sec., recorder DA Discharge Rev. Bd., Pentagon, Washington, 1985—. Mem. Nat. Assn. Female Execs., Assn. U.S. Army, Delta Sigma Theta (parliamentarian 1981-82). Avocations: racquetball; jogging. Office: DA Discharge Rev Bd Pentagon Washington DC 20310

LIPSKY, LINDA ETHEL, hospital administrator; b. Bklyn., June 2, 1939; d. Irving Julius and Florence (Stern) Ellman; m. Warren Lipsky, June 12, 1960 (div. Sept. 1968); 1 child, Phillip Bruce. B.A. in Psychology, Hofstra U., 1960; M.P.S. in Health Care Adminstrn., L.I. U., 1979. Child welfare social worker Nassau County Dept. Social Service, N.Y., 1960-64; adminstr. La Guardia Med. Group of Health Ins. Plan of Greater N.Y., Queens, 1969-72; cons. Neighborhood Service Ctr., Bronx, N.Y., 1973-78; dir. DDA Health Ctr., Bklyn., 1978-82; pres. Millin Assocs., Inc., Nassau, N.Y., 1982—. Mem. Health Care Fin. Mgmt. Assn., Nat. Assn. Community Health Ctrs., Hofstra U. Alumni Assn. (mem. senate 1984—, chairperson membership com. 1985—), Pi Alpha Alpha. Republican. Jewish. Avocations: cooking; writing; reading. Office: Millin Assocs Inc 521 Chestnut St Cedarhurst NY 11516

LIPSMAN, CLAIRE KAPLAN, government official, b. Malden, Mass., Oct. 16, 1925; d. Bernard and Minna (Bernstein) Kaplan; m. Alexander Lipsman, Sept. 20, 1945; children—Mark, Joshua, Benjamin. A.B., Radcliffe Coll., 1945; M.A., Catholic U. Am., 1965, Ph.D., 1967. Grad. asst., tchr. Cath. U. Am., 1964-66; vocat. guidance specialist VISTA, OEO, Washington, 1966-68; research assoc. Behavior Sci. Corp., McLean, Va., 1968-70; program analyst Employment and Tng. Adminstrn., U.S. Dept. Labor, Washington, 1970-79; dir. program accountability, div. family nutrition programs Food and Nutrition Service, U.S. Dept. Agr., Alexandria, Va., 1979—; sr. staff assoc. com. evaluation of employment and tng. Nat. Acad. Scis., 1976-77. Author: The Disadvantaged and Library Effectiveness, 1972; (with others) CETA, The Early Years, 1978; contbr. articles to profl. jours. Mem. Am. Pub. Welfare Assn., Aircraft Owners and Pilots Assn., Internat. Flying Farmers. Office: US Dept Agr Food & Nutrition Service 3101 Park Ctr Dr Room 615 Alexandria VA 22302

LIPSON, RENEE SUE, organization development consultant; b. Cleve., Dec. 10, 1930; d. Louis and Celia Switky) Rosenfield; m. Leon Lipson, June 24, 1952; (div. Oct. 1964); children—Sheri Ellen Lipson Bidwell, Jodi Faith. B.S., case Western Res. U., 1952; B.S., Youngstown U., 1963; M.A., John Carroll U., 1968; Ph.D., Mich. State U., 1976; postgrad. Kent State U., 1968-72. Mem. staff Am. Arbitration Assn., Cleve., 1951-52; hostess Welcome Wagon, Youngstown, Ohio, 1952-55; tchr. elem. grades Cleveland Heights, University Heights Bd. Edn., 1963-67; tchr. Hanna Pavilion, Univ. Hosps., Cleve., 1967-68; guidance counselor Warrensville Heights Bd. Edn., Ohio, 1968-70; dir. drug Edn. Ctr., Cleve. Helath Mus. and Edn. Ctr., 1970-72; pres. Living Dynamics, Cleve., 1972-73; cons. Mich. Dept. Edn. Sustance Abuse Prevention Edn. Program, Lansing, 1973-79; adminstr., Mich. Senate Edn. Com., Lansing, 1980; cons. prevention services Mich. Dept. Civil Rights, Lansing, 1979-80, 80-84; pres. Profl. Cons. Services, Lansing 1984—; adj. prof. Mich. State U., Lansing, 1979—; cons. Ohio Dept. Edn., 1971-73, Am. Social Health Assn., 1971-73, NSF, Wasington, 1971-73. Edn. Research Council Am., Cleve., 1965-70. Co-founder Cuyahoga County Health Coalition, Cleve., 1968-72; 1st chair Ingham County Democratic Womens Caucus, 1983-84; mem. East Lansing Fine Arts Commn., 1980-82; fundraiser Democratic activities, 1980—. Mem. Am. Soc. Tng. and Devel., Lansing Regional C. of C. (com. chmn.), Women Bus. Owners, Mich. Orgn. Devel. Network, Women in Mgmt. Network, ACLU, Common Cusee, Women in State Govt. (co founder 1979), Mich. Council for Women in Ednl. Adminstrn. (com. chair), Am. Humanist Assn., Captial Area Womens Network. Jewish. Avocations: Travel; theater; music; crafts. Office: Profl Cons Services Lansing Bus and Law Ctr 121 E Allegan St Lansing MI 48933

LIPSTATE, JO ANN, cemetery executive, public relations consultant; b. San Antonio, Aug. 4, 1930; d. Herbert and Beatrice (Adelman) Davis; m. Eugene J. Lipstate, Feb. 26, 1950; children—James Mitchell, Betsy Ann Lipstate Horner. Student in fine arts and English, U. Tex., 1947-49. Copywriter Sta.-KATC-TV, Lafayette, La., 1970-73; pres. Lipstate Creative Services, Lafayette, 1973-80; pub. relations cons. N.W. Oil Co., Lafayette, 1979—; v.p. Eugene J. Lipstate, Inc., 1979; pres. Eterna, Inc., doing bus. as Fountain Meml. Gardens and Mausoleum, Lafayette, 1983—; bd. dirs. Mid La. Health Systems Agy., Lafayette, 1980-83, chmn. project, 1982-83; found. mem. Women's Hosp. Acadiana, Lafayette, 1982—. Bd. dirs. Lafayette Juvenile and Young Adult Program, 1969, art therapist, 1970. Mem. Ad Club Acadiana (pres. 1978-79, 3 TV comml. awards 1972). Republican. Jewish. Clubs: City, Oakbourne Country (Lafayette). Avocations: golf; tennis; fishing; painting; gardening. Home: 401 Shelly Dr Lafayette LA 70503 Office: Bldg 12 Oil Center Dr at Heyman Blvd PO Box 52421 Lafayette LA 70505

LIPTAY, LYNNE MIRIAM, pediatrician; b. Panama, C.Z., Nov. 3, 1947; d. Thomas Emil and Lea Miriam (Maki) Oakland; m. John Stephen Liptay, Dec. 30, 1972; children—Thomas John, Steven Robert. B.A., Swarthmore Coll., 1969; M.D., Yale U., 1973. Diplomate Am. Bd. Pediatrics. Intern in pediatrics Montefiore Hosp. and Med. Ctr., N.Y.C., 1973-74, resident in pediatrics, 1974-76; practice medicine specializing in pediatrics, Hyde Park, N.Y., 1976—; mem. staff No. Dutchess Hosp., Rhinebeck, N.Y., 1976—. Co-author: Talk & Toddle, 1983. Fellow Am. Acad. Pediatrics. Office: 7 Pine Woods Rd Hyde Park NY 12538

LIPTON, JOAN ELAINE, advertising agency executive; b. N.Y.C., July 12; B.A. Barnard Coll.; 1 son, David Dean. With Young & Rubicam, Inc., advt. agy., N.Y.C., 1949-52, Robert W. Orr & Assocs., advt. agy., N.Y.C., 1952-57, Benton & Bowles, Inc., advt. agy., N.Y.C., 1957-64; asso. dir. Benton & Bowles, Ltd., London, 1964-68; with McCann-Erickson, Inc., advt. agy., N.Y.C., 1968-85, v.p., 1970-79, sr. v.p., creative dir., 1979-85; pres. Martin & Lipton Advt., Inc., N.Y.C., 1985—. Bd. dirs., past v.p. Advt. Women N.Y. Found.; trustee Film-Video Arts, Inc.; bd. dirs. Ph.D. program in bus. CUNY; mem. Bus. Council for the UN Decade for Women, 1977-78. Named Woman of Yr., Am. Advt. Fedn., 1974, Advt. Woman of Yr., 1984; recipient Honors award Ohio U. Sch. Journalism, 1976; Matrix award, 1979; YWCA award for women achievers, 1979. Mem. Advt. Women N.Y. (1st v.p. 1975-76, dir. 1984—), Women in Communications (pres. N.Y. chpt. 1974-76, named Nat. Headliner 1976). Office: 128 E 56th St New York NY 10022

LIPTON, SUSAN LYTLE, investment banker, lawyer; b. Ft. Warren, Wyo., Oct. 23, 1945; d. James and Bette Lytle; m. Martin Lipton, Feb. 17, 1982. A.B., U. Miami, 1967, J.D., 1970; LL.M., Harvard U., 1971. Bar: Fla. 1970, N.Y. 1984. Assoc., then ptnr. firm Greenberg Traurig Askew, Miami, Fla., 1970-77; assoc. then v.p. Goldman Sachs & Co., N.Y.C., 1977-81; v.p., then mng. dir. L.F. Rothschild, Unterberg, Towbin, N.Y.C., 1981—. Office: LF Rothschild Unterberg Towbin 55 Water St New York NY 10041

LIPTON, ZELDA, insurance company executive; b. N.Y.C., Mar. 11, 1923; d. Jacob and Sadie (Bell) Simon; m. Louis Lipton, Mar. 9, 1947; children—Judith Lipton Binstock, Jay. B.A., Hunter Coll., 1943; M.A., NYU, 1945. Tchr., N.Y.C. high schs., 1945-47; with Conn. Gen. Life, Hartford, 1964-79, dir. product devel., 1977-79; 2nd v.p. life/med. product Union Mut. Life Ins. Co., Portland, Maine, 1979-83, 2nd v.p. flexible compensation, 1983—. Contbg. author: Group Life and Health Insurance, A, B and C, 1974—; Handbook of Employee Benefits, 1983; co-author: Health Insurance Answer Book, 1986. Mem. Gov.'s Certificate of Need adv. com., Maine, 1983—. Fellow Life Mgmt. Inst.; mem. Health Ins. Assn. Am., Ins. Acctg. and Systems Assn. Democrat. Office: Union Mutual 2211 Congress St Portland ME 04122

LIRETTE, LINDA LOUISE, advertising/real estate broker-owner; b. New Orleans, June 30, 1951; d. Robert Raymond and Frances Isabel (Robertson) L.; 1 dau., Sharon Elizabeth. Student U. New Orleans, 1969-71; A.A., Houston Community Coll., 1984. Receptionist CMS, New Orleans, 1971-74; with personnel dept. Snelling & Snelling, New Orleans, 1974-76; sales mgr. for 3 states Amtico Flooring div. Am. Biltrite, New Orleans, 1976-77; exec. search for engrs. Mgmt. Search, Houston, 1977-79; mktg. supr. Mattco Property Mgmt., Houston, 1979-81; div. promotion mgr. Ency. Britannica, Houston, 1981-82; account exec. Goodwin, Dannenbaum, Littman & Wingfield, Houston, 1982; pres. Lirette Advt. and Pub. Relations, Houston, 1982—; v.p. Time Share Vacation Home, Inc., New Orleans, 1982; mktg. dir. Infocom Computer Systems, Inc., Houston, 1983; broker-owner The Realty Market, Houston, 1985—. Pub. relations chmn. Jaycees Christmas Extravaganza, 1983; pub. relations com. Bluebonnet Bowl, 1983-86. Mem. Houston Bd. Realtors, Nat. and Tex Assn. Realtors, Am. Women in Radio and TV (historian, program com.), Pub. Relations Soc. Am. Methodist. Club: University.

LIS, YVONNE, marketing executive; b. Amsterdam, N.Y., June 14, 1957; d. Charles John and Rose Emily Lis; B.S. cum laude, SUNY, Albany, 1978; M.B.A., San Francisco State U., 1979; m. William D. Greenroad, Oct. 6, 1979. Adminstrv. asst. Office Lt. Gov. N.Y. State, Albany, 1975-78; price adminstrn. supr. Intel Corp., Santa Clara, Calif., 1979-80, customer mktg. engr., 1981-82; product mktg. mgr. Shugart Assocs., Sunnyvale, Calif., 1982-84; product line mgr. Ampex Corp., Cupertino, Calif., 1984, Fujitson Am., Inc., 1984—. Mem. Am. Mktg. Assn., Assn. M.B.A. Execs. Roman Catholic. Home: 651 E McKinley Ave Sunnyvale CA 94086 Office: 3055 Orchard Dr San Jose CA 95134

LISBOA-FARROW, ELIZABETH OLIVER, public relations consultant; b. N.Y.C., Nov. 25, 1947; d. Eleuterio and Esperanza Oliver; student pvt. schs., N.Y.C.; m. Jeffrey Lloyd Farrow, Dec. 31, 1980; 1 son, Hamilton Oliver Farrow; 1 stepson, Maximillian Robbins. With Harold Rand & Co. and various other public relations firms, N.Y.C., 1966-75; dir. public relations N.Y. Playboy Club and Playboy Clubs Internat., 1975-79; pres. Lisboa Assocs., Inc., N.Y.C., 1979—; sec. Nat. Acad. Concert and Cabaret Arts; mem. nat. adv. council SBA, 1980-81. Mem. Nat. Assn. Female Execs., Bus. Execs. Nat. Security. Democrat. Clubs: Variety (dir.) (Washington), Woman's Nat. Dem., Doubles Internat. Office: 1317 F St NW Washington DC 20004

LISEK, NANCY ANN TARASEVICH, advertising and fundraising executive; b. Kingston, Pa., Sept. 28, 1941; d. Theodore and Mary M. (Muscavage) Tarasevich; m. Edward Martin Lisek, Nov. 10, 1962; children—Gregory Edward Paul, Damien Blair. Grad. Strayer's Bus. Sch., Balt., 1960, Barbizon, Towson, Md., 1983, Archdiocese Balt., 1976; student Essex Community Coll. Sec. Henry Rose, Balt., 1964-66, Lloyd's London, Balt., 1959-64; field mgr. Hamrah & Assocs., Glendale, Calif., 1984-85; pres., chief exec. officer, owner NATEL Enterprises, Balt., 1985—. Contbr. articles to profl. jours. Nat. legis. chmn. Md. P.T.A., Balt., 1978-80, sec., 1980-82, 1st v.p., 1982-84; mem. Washington legis. service com. Nat. P.T.A., 1979-85; chmn. Md. P.T.A. Convention, Hunt Valley, 1983; co-ordinator Nat. P.T.A. Legis. Conf., Washington, 1984, 85; chmn. Md. Coalition to Save Pub. Edn., Balt., 1979; mem. White House Conf. on Families, Washington, 1980; mem. White House Conf. on Small Bus., 1985. Recipient Appreciation award St. Urusla's Cub Pack, Parkville, Md., 1976. Mem. Nat. Assn. Female Execs., Balt. Attractions Assn., Balt. Conv. Bur., Am. Entrepreneurs Assn. Roman Catholic. Avocations: travel; sewing; knitting. Home: 3511 Hiss Ave Baltimore MD 21234 Office: NATELL Enterprises 3511 Hiss Ave Baltimore MD 21234

LISONI, GAIL MARIE LANDTBOM, lawyer; b. San Francisco, Mar. 11, 1949; d. William A. and Patricia Ann (Cruden) Landtbom; m. Joseph Louis Lisoni, Mar. 24, 1984. B.A., Dominican Coll., Calif., 1971; J.D., U. West Los Angeles, 1978, cert. paralegal, 1974. Bar: Calif. 1979. Campaign treas. Calif. for Lisoni, Arcadia, 1979-81; assoc. Joseph Lisoni, Esq., Los Angeles, 1981, Arnold S. Malter, Esq., Los Angeles, 1982; ptnr. Lisoni & Lisoni, Los Angeles, 1983—. Mem. Assn. Trial Lawyers Am., Calif. Trial Lawyers Assn., Los Angles Trial Lawyers Assn., ABA, Italian Am. Lawyers Assn. Democrat. Roman Catholic. Lodge: Sons of Italy. Office: 3701 Wilshire Blvd Suite 700 Los Angeles CA 90010

LITLE, MARIANNE MILLER, radiologic technologist, educator; b. Amarillo, Tex., Oct. 4, 1936; d. William Fredrick and Ethel Bowen (Thompson) Miller; m. William E. Litle, Nov. 16, 1963 (div.); children—Kruger E., Midge Smith, William B., Marc S. B.S., U. Tex.-Dallas, 1979; M.S., East Tex. State U., 1983. Cert. radiol. technologist; Radiol. technologist to Dr. Brooks, Dallas, 1961-62, nuclear medicine technologist Parkland Hosp., Dallas, 1962-64; clin. coordinator El Centro Coll., Dallas, 1979—. Contbr. chpt. in book. Mem. Dallas Soc. Crippled Children, 1972—, The Auction for Cultural Arts, 1973. Mem. Tex. Soc. Radiol. Technologists, Am. Soc. Radiol. Technologists, Tex. Soc. Allied Health Profls., Tex. Jr. Coll. Tchr. Assn., Phi Theta Kappa. Republican. Episcopalian. Office: El Centro College Main St and Lamar Dallas TX 75201

LITMAN, ROSLYN MARGOLIS, lawyer; b. N.Y.C., Sept. 30, 1928; d. Harry and Dorothy (Perlow) Margolis; children—Jessica, Hannah, Harry. B.A., U. Pitts., 1949, J.D., 1952. Bar: Pa. 1952, U.S. Dist. Ct. (we. dist.) Pa. 1952, U.S. Ct. Appeals (3d cir.) 1970. Adj. prof. U. Pitts. Sch. of Law, 1958—; ptnr. Litman, Litman, Harris, Watzman & Brown, P.A., Pitts., 1952—. Bd. dirs. Pitts. chpt. ACLU, mem. nat. bd., 1986—; chmn. Pitts. Parking Authority, 1970-75; mem. Exec. Women's Council, bd. dirs. Pitts. Pub. Theater, 1975-81; permanent del. Conf. of U.S. Ct. of Appeals 3d cir. Mem. Allegheny County Bar Assn. (pres. 1975), Pa. Bar Assn. (gov. 1976-79), ABA (ho. of dels. 1980-83, lectr. anti-trust health professions), Pa. Bar Inst. (course planner, faculty mem). Office: Litman Litman Harris Portnoy & Brown PA 1701 Grant Bldg Pittsburgh PA 15219

LITTELL, PATRICIA L., contracting corporation executive; b. Albuquerque, May 28, 1954; d. Birnie Glenn and Eleanor Marie (Maloney) Hammock; student U. N.Mex., 1972-73, Coll. Santa Fe, 1984—; m. E. Austin Littell, Nov. 19, 1979; 4 stepchildren. Exec. sec. to v.p. systems integration BDM Corp., Albuquerque, 1976-80; pres., treas., co-founder Littell and Assocs., Albuquerque, 1979—; cons. small bus. firms. Recipient Corp. safety award Associated Gen. Contractors Am., 1980. Mem. Nat. Assn. Female Execs. Rebuplican. Methodist. Home: 1605 Camino Rosario NW Albuquerque NM 87107 Office: PO Box 5596 Kirtland AFB Albuquerque NM 87185

LITTENBERG, JEWEL, ladies sportswear manufacturing company executive; b. Rochester, N.Y., Apr. 27, 1938; d. Haskell Charles and Ray (Miller) Goldstein; m. Edward Stephen Littenberg, Feb. 20, 1965; 1 child, Michael Richard. A.A.S., Rochester Inst. of Tech., 1958; cert. Traphagen Sch. Fashion, N.Y.C., 1960. Freelance fashion designer, N.Y.C., 1960-77; pres. Jewel of Palm Beach, West Palm Beach, Fla., 1977—. Jewish. Avocations: painting; piano; reading; cooking. Home: 437 Palo Alto Palm Springs FL 33461 Office: Jewel of Palm Beach Inc 1401 Allendale Rd West Palm Beach FL 33405

LITTLE, DOLORES MAE, hospital administrator; b. Omaha, Feb. 19, 1932; d. Charles J. and Marie A. (Stehno) Krajicek; m. John W. Little, Mar. 25, 1953 (dec. 1970); m. Walter E. Penk, Jan. 11, 1985; children—Judith M., John T., George W., Thomas C. B.A., Duchesne Coll., 1953; M.A., U. Ky., 1961; Ph.D., Tex. A&M U., 1973. Asst. prof. Sam Houston State U., 1973-74; allied health edn. coordinator VA Med. Ctr., Dallas, 1974-76, assoc. chief of staff, 1977-81; asst. dir. trainee VA Hosp., San Antonio, 1981-82; assoc. dir. VA Med. Ctr., Big Spring, Tex., 1982-84; assoc. dir. Edith Nourse Rogers Meml. Vets. Hosp., Bedford, Mass., 1984—; psychologist, cons. to various orgns. Contbr. articles to various publs. Mem. Am. Coll. Hosp. Adminstrs., Am. Psychol. Assn. Roman Catholic. Club: Texas A&M Alumni of New Eng. (sec. 1985-86). Office: Edith Nourse Rogers Vets Hosp 200 Springs Rd Bedford MA 01730

LITTLE, FLORENCE ELIZABETH HERBERT, educator; b. Streator, Ill., July 7, 1911; d. Charles Arthur and Bertha (Schlachter) Herbert; B.A., Mich. State U., 1932; M.S.E., Drake U., 1962; m. Alfred Lamond Little, July 26, 1933 (dec.); children—Alan Rush, Barbara Jean Little Bell. Accompanist, Mich. State U., 1930-32, 33-36, mem. faculty, 1930-32; tchr., pub. schs., Bridgeport, Ill., 1945, Holt, Mich., 1945-46, Hanover, Mich., 1949-50, Pittsford, Mich., 1950-53, Des Moines, 1953-73; now substitute tchr., tutor, public schs., La Place, La.; pvt. tchr. piano and voice, 1932-56. Active CD, Crime Watch, Am. Fedn. Police Nat. CB Posse; mem. Tri-Parish Republican Women's Club. NSF grantee, 1963-64. Mem. Am. Bus. Women's Assn., Smithsonian Instn., NEA, Iowa Edn. Assn., Des Moines Edn. Assn., Orchid Soc. Jefferson, Kappa Kappa Iota, Mu Phi Epsilon. Presbyterian. Club: CB. Instituted elem. music programs, various schs.; hon. mem. editorial adv. bd. Am. Biog. Inst., 1980-83. Home: 1093-A Belle Terre Dr La Place LA 70068

LITTLE, HAZEL JOYCE, county official, hair model; b. Memphis, Aug. 26, 1955; d. Roger Jr. and Annie (Simmons) L. B.B.A., Memphis State U., 1976, postgrad., 1978-79, real estate cert., 1984. Bank processing operator Union Planters Bank, Memphis, 1973-76; fire safety insp. Tenn. State Fire Marshalls, Memphis, Nashville, 1976-79; field operation supr. U.S. Dept. Commerce, Memphis, 1979-80; bus. mgr./supr. Peabody Hotel, Memphis, 1981-83; adminstrv. asst. Shelby County Clks.'s Office, Memphis, 1983—; cons. informant County Clk.'s Office, 1984—. Editor Shelby County Clks. procedures manual Personnel and Procedures (cert. appreciation 1984), 1984; movie extra. Chairperson Harold Ford for Congress, Memphis, 1975-76; big sister Big Sisters, Memphis, 1982—. Named Outstanding Woman of Yr., Jurisdiction of Chs., Memphis, 1983-84; recipient best regional report award Dept. Census, Memphis, 1980. Mem. Assn. Tenn. Clks., Dem. Women Assn., Alpha Kappa Alpha. Avocations: reading; traveling; tennis. Home: 3440 Winchest Park Ct Memphis TN 38118 Office: Shelby County Clks Office 160 N Mid-America Mall Memphis TN 38103

LITTLE, JANE WALLING, lawyer; b. Dallas, June 10, 1946; d. Robert Alvin and Virginia (Bullock) Walling. B.S., North Tex. State U., 1968, M.Ed., 1972, M.L.S., 1977; J.D., St. Mary's U., San Antonio, Tex., 1981. Bar: Tex. 1982, U.S. Dist. Ct. (no. dist.) Tex. 1982, U.S. Ct. Apls. (5th cir.) 1982, U.S. Supreme Ct. 1985. Tchr. English, Dallas Ind. Sch. Dist., 1968-76; apt. mgr. Robert A. McNiel, Dallas, 1977; legal sec., Dallas, 1977-78; assoc. Blassingame & Osburn, Dallas, 1981-83; asst. dist. atty. Dallas County Dist. Atty., 1983—. Lela Lee Williams scholar Delta Kappa Gamma, 1976. Mem. Bus. and Profl. Women Dallas (legis. chmn. 1983), State Bar Tex., Tex Assn. Dist. Attys., ABA, Assn. Trial Lawyers Am., Dallas Bar Assn., Delta Theta Phi. Episcopalian. Office: Dist Atty Dallas County 600 Commerce St Dallas TX 75201

LITTLE, JEANNETTE LEWIS, lawyer, judge; b. LaGrange, Ga., Oct. 20, 1954; d. Henry Frank and Martha Wessie (Norton) Lewis; m. Thomas Randy Little, July 24, 1974; children—Wesley Richard, Joshua Daniel. B.A., LaGrange Coll., 1976; J.D., Mercer Law Sch., 1979. Bar: Ga. 1979. Judge, Small Claims Ct., LaGrange, 1979-83; chief magistrate, LaGrange, 1983—; assoc. Zackery & Kirby, P.C., LaGrange, 1983-85; ptnr. Zackery, Kirby & Little, P.C., 1985—; bd. dirs., atty. Project L.O.V.E., LaGrange, 1983—. Mem. ABA, Troup County Bar Assn. Democrat. Baptist. Club: Pilot (bd. dirs., LaGrange). Home: Box 111 Route 4 LaGrange GA 30240 Office: 200 N Lewis St LaGrange GA 30240

LITTLE, SANDRA LYNN, recreation park and educator; b. Wenatchee, Wash., July 30, 1941; d. Chester Leon Kelso and Yvonne Evelyn (Brandenburg) Bergeman; B.A., U. La Verne (Calif.), 1963; M.S., Ind. U., 1964; Ph.D., Pa. State U., 1985; m. Larry J. Little, Dec. 21, 1968 (div. 1985); 1 dau., Caroline A. Asst. dir. recreation Oak Park (Ill.) Recreation Dept., 1966-70; supt. recreation Elk Grove (Ill.) Park Dist., 1970-71; recreation supr., pre-sch. dir. Johnson County Park and Recreation Dist., Shawnee Mission, Kans., 1972-73; recreation coordinator Park Dist. Park Ridge (Ill.), 1973-75; instr. Triton Coll., River Grove, Ill., 1974; instr. recreation and parks Pa. State U., University Park, 1975-85; asst. prof. recreation and parks Ill. State U., Normal, 1985—. Bd. dirs., sec. Civic Symphony of Oak Park-River Forest, 1964-71; bd. dirs. Oak Park Village Day Care Center, 1967-68; v.p. LWV, Kansas City, Kans., 1971-73; recreation and park commr. Borough of Shippensburg (Pa.), 1978-79. Mem. AAHPERD, Am. Assn. Leisure and Recreation, Nat. Recreation and Park Assn., Soc. Park and Recreation Educators, Ill. Recreation and Park Soc. Office: 101 McCormick Hall Normal IL 61761

LITTLE, SHERYL LYNN, financial management specialist; b. Lansing, Mich., Oct. 30, 1960; d. Robert Landgon and Patricia Ann (McGee) Little. B.S., Mich. State U., 1983. Office mgr. Corp. Colors, Lansing, 1983-84; staff analyst Jack Martin & Co., C.P.A., Birmingham, Mich., 1984, staff acct., 1984-85; fin. mgmt. analyst U.S. Dept. Labor, Washington., 1985—. Mem. Nat. Assn. Female Execs., Alpha Kappa Alpha (Delta Zeta chpt.). Avocations: reading; needlepoint; weightlifting; running.

LITTLEDALE, FREYA LOTA BROWN, writer, editor; b. N.Y.C., d. David Milton and Dorothy (Passloff) Brown; B.S., Ithaca Coll., 1951; postgrad. N.Y. U., 1952; 1 son, Glenn David. Tchr. English, Public Schs. Willsboro (N.Y.), 1952-53; editor South Shore Record, L.I., N.Y., 1953-55; asso. editor Maco Mag. Corp., N.Y.C., 1960-61, Rutledge Books and Ridge Press, N.Y.C., 1961-62; juvenile book editor Parents' Mag. Press, N.Y.C., 1962-65; free-lance writer-editor, 1965—; writer Silver Burdett div. Time-Life Corp., 1965; editor, anthologist Arrow Book Club div. Scholastic Book Services; adj. prof. Fairfield U., 1984, 86. Author: The Magic Fish, 1967; (with Harold Littledale) Timothy's Forest, 1969; King Fox and Other Old Tales, 1971; The Magic Tablecloth, The Magic Goat, and The Hitting Stick, 1972; The Boy Who Cried Wolf, 1975; The Elves and the Shoemaker, 1975; Seven at One Blow, 1976; The Snow Child, 1978; The Magic Plum Tree, 1981; editor: A Treasure Chest of Poetry, 1964; Fairy Tales by Hans Christian Andersen, 1964; Aesop's Fables, 1964; Grimm's Fairy Tales, 1964; 13 Ghostly Tales, 1966; Ghosts and Spirits of Many Lands, 1970; Ghosts, Witches, and Demons, 1971; Strange Tales from Many Lands, 1975; (poetry) I Was Thinking, 1979; (plays) The King and Queen Who Wouldn't Speak, 1975; Stop That Pancake, 1975; The Giant's Garden, 1975; The Magic Piper, 1978; adapter: Pinnochio, 1979; Snow White and the Seven Dwarfs, 1981; The Wizard of Oz, 1982; Frankenstein, 1983; The Sleeping Beauty, 1984; The Little Mermaid, 1986; contbr. to Scribner's Anthology for Young People, 1976; A New Treasury of Children's Poetry, 1984. Mem. Soc. Children's Book Writers, Authors Guild, PEN. Office: care Curtis Brown Ltd 10 Astor Pl New York NY 10003

LITTLEFIELD, SUZANNE ALICE, lawyer, banker; b. Neenah, Wis., Apr. 11, 1955; d. Charles A. and Alice (Van Housen) L.; m. Douglas M. Brooks, June 7, 1980. B.B.A., U. Wis.-Whitewater, 1977, M.B.A., 1980; J.D., U. Wis.-Madison, 1980. Bar: Wis. 1980; notary pub., Wis. Law clk. DeWitt, Sundby et al, Madison, 1978-80; assoc. firm Velte, Molzow & Littlefield, Neenah, 1980-84; tax adminstr. trust dept. Associated First Neenah Bank, 1984-85, tax officer trust dept., 1985—. Legis. chmn. Winnebago County Republican Women, 1982-85 bd. dirs. Best Friends of Neenah-Menasha, Inc., 1981—. Mem. ABA, Wis. Bar Assn., Winnebago County Bar Assn. Republican. Methodist. Home: 127 5th St Neenah WI 54956 Office: Assoc First Neenah Bank 100 W Wisconsin Ave Neenah WI 54956

LITTLETON, VERA PERRY, savings and loan officer, jewelry consultant; b. Eudora, Ark., Sept. 17, 1945; d. James and Leaoter (White) Perry; m. Nathaniel Littleton, July 16, 1966; 1 son, Tracey Omar. B.A., Northeastern U., Chgo., 1977. Tchrs. asst. pub. schs., Chgo., 1967-77, tchr., 1977-80; savs. officer Ill./Service Fed. Savs. and Loan, Chgo., 1980—; Mem. Operation PUSH. Recipient Cert. of Merit, Edn. Leadership Inst., Chgo., 1977. Mem. NAACP, Chgo. Tchrs. Union, Exec. Female, Inc., Phi Beta Lambda (sec. 1974-75). Club: Social Lite (pres. 1978—) (Chgo.). Lodge: Elks (capt. 1979-81, 83—, sec. conv. dept. Ill./Wis. states chpt., recipient several outstanding service awards).

LITTMAN, LYNNE, film director; b. N.Y.C., June 26, 1941; d. Carl and Yetta (Abler) L.; m. Taylor Hackford, May 7, 1977; 1 child, Alexander Littman; 1 stepson Rio Hackford. B.A., Sarah Lawrence Coll., 1962; student The Sorbonne, Paris, 1960-61. Researcher for CBS News, 1965; assoc. producer Nat. Ednl. TV, 1966-69; dir. NIMH film series on drug abuse UCLA Media Center, 1970; producer, dir. documentary films, news and pub. affairs series KCET Community TV So. Calif., 1971-77; dir. WNET Ind. Filmmakers Series, 1979; co-producer, dir. TV spl. Rick Nelson, It's All Right Now, 1978; films include: Till Death Do Us Part (CPB award), 1976, In The Matter of Kenneth (Los Angeles Emmy award), 1974, Wanted: Operadoras (Los Angeles Emmy award), 1974, Women in Waiting, 1975; dir. film Testament, 1983, short films, Number Our Days (1977 Academy award, best short documentary), Once a Daughter, 1979, Running My Way, (1982 Cine Golden Eagle award). Recipient numerous awards including Los Angeles Press Club award, 1977, San Francisco Internat. Film Festival award, 1977, Corp. for Public Broadcasting award, 1977, Los Angeles Emmy award, 1972, 73, 74, 77; Columbia/Dupont Journalism award, 1977; Ford Found. grantee, 1978. Mem. Dirs. Guild Am. Address: LDL Films 8489 W Third St Los Angeles CA 90048*

LITUS, TONYIA J., hearing specialist, psychotherapist; b. Parkersburg, W.Va., Jan. 13, 1944; d. John and Margaret (Sandy) Allevato; m. Lawrence M. Litus, May 3, 1966; 1 child, Sabrena. B.A., U. Tampa, 1965; M.S., U. S. Fla., 1972; M.S., Nova U., 1983. Hearing specialist Brevard County Schs., Melbourne, Fla., 1975—; psychotherapist Assocs. in Psychology, Melbourne, 1984—. Mem. cultural com. C. of C., Melbourne, 1985—; bd. dirs. Brevard Regional Assn. of Deaf, Cocoa, Fla., 1977—, Brevard County Detention Ctr., Titusville, 1977-78. Named Tchr. of Yr., Exceptional Edn. of Brevard County, 1981, 83. Mem. Fla. Speech and Hearing Assn., Brevard Mental Health Assn.,

Alexander Graham Bell Assn., Am. Group Psychotherapy Assn., Fla. Group Psychotherapy Assn., Fla. Biofeedback Soc., Fla. Educators of Hearing Impaired. Democrat. Clubs: Space Coast Runners, Space Coast Assn. Physically Handicapped. Avocations: jogging; traveling; cross country skiing. Home: 5281 Palomino Dr Melbourne FL 32935 Office: Associates in Psychology 1250 S Harbor City Blvd Melbourne FL 32901

LITWACK, ARLENE DEBRA, psychotherapist, psychoanalyst, consultant, educator; b. Brookline, Mass., July 18, 1945; d. Hyman and Bessie Litwack. B.A. cum laude, Boston U., 1967; M.S., Columbia U., 1969; postgrad. Ctr. for Mental Health, N.Y.C., 1981, Inst. for Psychoanalytic Tng. and Research, 1980—. Caseworker, Pride Treatment Ctr., Douglaston, N.Y., 1969-73, supr., 1973-78, sr. worker, 1978-80; pvt. practice psychotherapy and psychoanalyst, N.Y.C., 1980—; mem. faculty Inst. for Mental Health Edn., Englewood, N.J., 1983—; dir. child therapy dept. L.I. Consultation Ctr., Rego Park, N.Y., 1980-85; faculty workshop leader Human Services Workshops, N.Y.C.; adj. faculty Columbia U., 1977—. Contbr. articles to profl. jours. Mem. Psychoanalytic Study Ctr. Home: 14 Horatio St 10A New York NY 10014

LITWOK, EVELYN, psychologist, financial consultant; b. N.Y.C., July 30, 1951; d. Zygmunt and Genia (Kohn) L.; B.A. in Psychology, U. Buffalo, 1969; M.A. in Psychology (research fellow 1973-75), Temple U., 1975. Dir. Child Devel. Research Lab., Temple U., Phila., 1973-75; dir. evaluation and research W. Phila. Community Mental Health Center, 1975-78; co-dir. Women's Resources, Inc., Phila., 1978-84; exec. dir. Women's Resources Distbn. Co., 1981-84; corp. fin. cons. Merrill Lynch Pierce Fenner & Smith, Inc., 1984—; cons. in mgmt., fiscal planning, comprehensive fund-raising. Named one of the women to watch in '82, Phila. Mag. Mem. Am. Psychol. Assn., Assn. Women in Psychology. Jewish. Contbr. articles to profl. publs. Home: 690 Greenwich St Apt 5C New York NY 10014

LIU, MARGARET, real estate broker; b. Chungking, China, Jan. 31, 1941; came to U.S., 1968; d. Tien-Oung and Shin-Yin (Tung) Liu; m. Edward Bauman Collins, Jan. 29, 1982; children—Magdalene, Samuel. B.S., U. Calif.-Berkeley, 1965; postgrad. Montclair State U., 1971-72, Rutgers U., 1973. Pres. Liu Realty, Inc., San Francisco, 1979—, Liu Internat. Mgmt., Inc., San Francisco, 1984—; v.p. Liu Internat., Inc., Lebanon Oaks, Inc., Rosemead, Inc., F.M. 2281, Inc., Preston Oak, Inc., 1981-83; dir. Nat. Am. Bank, San Francisco, 1984, Integrated CMOS Systems, Inc., 1985. Vice pres., sec. Marin Wood, Inc., Dallas, 1981-83, Repulse Bay, Inc., 1981—; sec. Sandridge, Inc., Houston, 1981—; sec. Dover, Inc., Houston, 1981—; mem. Rep. Presdl. Task Force, 1982, Rep. Trustees, 1984. Mem. Nat. Assn. Realtors, Calif. Assn. Realtors, Clubs: St. Francis Yacht, Metropolitan (San Francisco). Office: 360 Pine St San Francisco CA 94104

LIVAS, SAN JUANITA (JANIE), ednl. adminstr.; b. Comales, Tamps, Mexico, Jan. 20, 1949; naturalized citizen, 1960; d. Domingo and Angelina (Villarreal) Flores, B.S., Pan Am. U., 1971, M.Ed., 1979; m. Arturo Livas, Dec. 18, 1971; children—Adrian Lee, Aliza Lynn, Annette Lorraine. Tchr., Edcouch-Elsa High Sch., Edcouch, Tex., then tchr. math. lab., coordinator reading/math. labs., sch. dist., now supr. Central Jr. High.; cons. Tex. Migrant Conf., 1980. Mem. Tex. State Tchrs. Assn. Classroom Tchrs. Assn., Assn. Supervision and Curriculum Devel., Assn. Compensatory Educators Tex., Rio Grande Valley Council Tchrs. Math., Tex. Assn. Bilingual Edn., Delta Kappa Gamma. Democrat, Roman Catholic. Home: 512 E 3d St Elsa TX 78543 Office: 501 E 2d St Elsa TX 78543

LIVELY, JENNIFER ELIZABETH, brokerage house executive; b. Miami, Fla., Jan. 19, 1954; d. Michael Eric and Elizabeth Doreen (Mears) Lively; m. Eric Winston Edmondson, June 5, 1982. B.A. summa cum laude, NYU, 1977; M.A. with high honors, Stanford U., 1978; postgrad. Northwestern U. Sch. Journalism, 1979. Asst. editor Self Mag., N.Y.C., 1978-80; arts and travel editor Avenue Mag., N.Y.C., 1980-83; freelance writer, Phila., 1978—; mgr. travel incentives dept Shearson Lehman Bros. Inc., from 1983, now v.p., dir. sales incentives. Mem. jr. com. Am. Cancer Soc., bd. dirs.; active Boys Club Am.; active Stanford U. fund drives as eastern rep. Recipient Service award Am. Cancer Soc. Episcopalian. Clubs: Yale; Seawanaka Corinthian Yacht; Stanford U. Home: 400 E 58th St New York NY 10022 Office: Shearson Lehman Bros Inc World Fin Ctr New York NY 10285

LIVERANCE, DIANE EDLUND, nurse; b. Mpls., Apr. 6, 1944; d. Wallace Reid and Veda Loretta (Deits) Edlund; R.N., Bronson Meth. Sch. Nursing, 1965; A.S., Purdue U., 1977, B.S., 1978; M.S., Ind. U., 1983; children—Joseph, Kristin, Kerrin. Instr., Ind. Vocat. Tech. Coll., Lafayette, 1970-72; health services dir. Centralab Electronics, Lafayette, 1973-74; occupational health nurse Rea Magnet Wire, Ft. Wayne, Ind., 1975-76; dir. nursing and health services ARC, Ft. Wayne, 1976—, asst. exec. dir., 1980-82; supr. employee and community health edn. Wellness Center Parkview Meml. Hosp., 1982—; dir. Community Health Cons., 1978—. Active No. Ind. Health Systems Agy., 1977—, Ft. Wayne Area Consortium for Health Promotion, 1979-83; chairperson, 1982-83; adminstrv. dir. Pain Mgmt. Ctr., Burns Clinic Med. Ctr., P.C., Petoskey, Mich., 1985—; host radio show Words of Wellness, Sta. WBNI, Ft. Wayne, 1984-85; prin. d.e. liverance & Assocs., lifestyle counseling, wellness cons., Ft. Wayne and Petoskey, 1984—; mem. Adolescent Pregnancy Awareness and Concern Task Force, 1979—, Ft. Wayne Women's Bur., 1978—, Purdue U. Alumni Bd., 1978—; adv. bd. Regional Vocat. Center, 1979—. Recipient Ft. Wayne Ednl. TV Found. public service award, 1982. Mem. Ind. Nurses Assn. (pres. elect), Am. Nurses Assn., Am. Soc. Tng. and Devel., Am. Pain Soc. Methodist. Clubs: Ft. Wayne Track; Zonta. Contbr. articles to profl. jours.; co-producer tv spl. Do You Know Where Your're Going to: A Journey into Wellness, 1982. Home: 301 Lafayette Apt D-304 Petoskey MI 49770 Office: Burns Clinic Med Ctr PC 560 W Mitchell St Petoskey MI 49770

LIVINGSTON, DENISE M., lawyer, accountant; b. Seattle, 1951. B.A., Evergreen State Coll., 1973; J.D., U. Puget Sound, 1979. Bar: Wash. 1980; C.P.A., Wash. Singer, songwriter The Co-Respondents theatre group, performing nationwide, 1972-75; session atty., legal intern Wash. State Senate and Ho. of Reps., Olympia, 1978-80; atty., acct., Olympia, 1980-83; acct. Evergreen State Coll., Olympia, 1983—; atty., acct. Bowen Hafey & Pennington, C.P.A.s, Olympia, 1984—. Mem. Wash. State Bar Assn., Wash. Women Lawyers (state treas. 1982-83), Wash. Soc. C.P.A.s, Am. Assn. Atty.-C.P.A.s, Am. Women's Soc. C.P.A.s, Women's Polit. Caucus, NOW. Address: PO Box 7143 Olympia WA 98507

LIVINGSTON, MARGARET MORROW GRESHAM, civic leader; b. Birmingham, Ala., Aug. 16, 1924; d. Owen Garside and Katherine Molton (Morrow) Gresham; grad. The Baldwin Sch., Phila., 1942; A.B., Vassar Coll., 1945; M.A., U. Ala., 1946; m. James Archibald Livingston, Jr., July 16, 1947; children—Mary Margaret, James Archibald, Katherine Wiley, Elizabeth Gresham. Tutor in math., 1949-55; substitute elem., secondary sch. tchr., 1953-60; judge arts and crafts shows, founder edn. program Birmingham Mus. Art, 1962, acting dir., 1978-79, 81, chmn. bd. dirs., 1978—, sec. bd. dirs. 1978—, co-editor bulletin, 1970-75, pres. bd. dirs., 1971—, chmn. bd. Birmingham Mus. Art Edn. Council, 1968—; bd. dirs., past pres. Children's Aid Soc., 1959-81, treas., 1950, v.p., 1951; mem. arts com. Birmingham Civic Center Authority, 1970—; bd. dirs. U. Ala. Art Gallery, Birmingham, 1978—, Altamont Sch., Birmingham, 1959—, Greater Birmingham Arts Alliance, 1979-81. Mem. Am. Assn. Mus. (trustees com., edn. com., public relations com.), Internat. Com. of Mus. (edn. com. 1981—), Am. Fedn. Arts, So. Assn. Mus. Episcopalian. Clubs: Jr. League, English Speaking Union, Colonial Dames of Commonwealth of Va., Linly Heflin Unit, Ala. State Tennis Assn. Co-editor Spain Rehabilitation Arts Catalog, 1976-77. Home: 12 Country Club Rd Birmingham AL 35213 Office: Birmingham Mus of Art 2000 8th Ave N Birmingham AL 35203

LIVINGSTON, MARION GASKILL, civic worker; b. Phila., June 28, 1924; d. Joseph Franklin and Marion Elizabeth (Cook) Gaskill; m. N.B. Livingston, Jr., Jan. 9, 1946; children—John M., Peter G., William C. Mem. Franklin County Bd. Elections, 1982—. Mem. Franklin County Republican Exec. Com.; del. Rep. Nat. Conv., 1984; committeeman Upper Arlington Ward 6; mem. women's bd. March of Dimes; mem. by-laws com. Aux. to Ohio State Med. Assn.; trustee Martha Kinney Cooper Ohioana Library; mem. County Bd. Visitors. Mem. Navy League U.S. (dir. Columbus council), Republican. Home: 4890 Shackleford Ct Upper Arlington Columbus OH 43220

LIVINGSTON, MOLLIE P., designer; b. N.Y.C.; d. Abraham and Sarah Parnis; m. Leon Jay Livingstone; 1 child, Robert Lewis. Sec.-treas. Parnis Livingston Inc.; pres. Mollie Parhis Co., Mollie Parnis Boutique, Mollie Parnis at Home. Designer cadet nurses uniforms. Founder, Dress Up Your Neighborhood awards, Jerusalem, 1967—, N.Y.C., 1972—; founder Livingston Awards for Young Journalists, 1980—; founder Mollie Parnis Sch. Program for Keeping Surroundings Clean, 1975—; overseer Parsons Sch. Design, 1983—. Named Woman of Yr., Einstein Coll. Medicine, 1985—. Home: 812 Park Ave New York NY 10021 Office: 135 Madison Ave New York NY 10016

LIVINGSTON, MYRA COHN, author; b. Omaha, Aug. 17, 1926; d. Mayer Louis and Gertrude (Marks) Cohn; B.A., Sarah Lawrence Coll., 1948; m. Richard Roland Livingston, Apr. 14, 1952; children—Joshua, Jonas, Jennie Marks. Profl. French horn player, 1941-48; book reviewer Los Angeles Daily News, Los Angeles Mirror and asst. editor Campus Mag., 1948-50; public relations staff, pvt. sec. to Hollywood personalities, 1950-52; tchr. creative writing Dallas Public Library, 1958-64; poet-in-residence Beverly Hills (Calif.) Unified Sch. Dist., 1966-84; sr. instr. UCLA extension, 1973—; lectr. in field; cons. in field. Bd. dirs. Poetry Therapy Inst., 1975—; officer, mem. Beverly Hills PTA Council, 1966-75; pres. Friends of the Beverly Hills Pub. Library, 1979-81; bd. dirs. Reading is Fundamental, 1980—. Recipient Honor award, N.Y. Herald Tribune Spring Book Festival, 1958; So. Calif. Council on Lit. for Children and Young People Comprehensive Contribution award, 1968, 72; Tex. Inst. Letters awards, 1961, 80, 84; Excellence in Poetry award, Nat. Council Tchrs. English, 1980; Silver medal Commonwealth Club, 1985. Mem. Authors Guild, PEN Internat., Tex. Inst. Letters, Internat. Reading Assn., Soc. Children's Book Writers, So. Calif. Council on Lit. for Children and Young People. Author: Poems of Christmas, 1980; No Way of Knowing, Dallas Poems, 1980; How Pleasant to Know Mr. Lear, 1982; A Circle of Seasons, 1982; Why Am I Grown so Cold?, 1982; Sky Songs, 1984, The Child as Poet, Myth or Reality?, 1984; Monkey Puzzle and Other Poems, 1984; A Song I Sang to You, 1984, Celebrations, 1985, Thanksgiving Poems, 1985, numerous others. Address: 9308 Readcrest Dr Beverly Hills CA 90210

LIVINGSTON, PAMELA ANNA, image consultant; b. Richmond Hill, N.Y., Nov. 21, 1930; d. Paul Yount and Anna Margaret (Altland) L.; B.A., Adelphi U., 1951; postgrad. N.Y.U., 1952, Columbia U., 1959, Am. Acad. Dramatic Art, 1954, IBM Systems and Mktg. Schs., 1967-70, Brandon Sch. Electronic Data Processing, 1973. Personnel and public relations depts. Am. Can Co., N.Y.C., 1951-60; exec. sec. to pres. York (Pa.) div. Borg-Warner Corp., 1962-65; freelance writer, 1965-67; mktg. ofcl. IBM, 1967-70; research analyst, dir. new EDP bus. Ins. Co. N.Am., 1971-74; asst. to v.p. corp. affairs IU Internat., Phila., 1974-75, communications and mktg. mgmt. cons., specializing in devel. corp. identity and image programs and corp. repositioning programs for execs., 1975—, image cons., 1984—, personal identity and image programs, 1986—. Recipient various journalism awards, award in mktg. and sales IBM, 1969-70, award for innovative product application, 1969. Mem. Sales/Mktg. Execs. Internat., Art Alliance, Public Relations Soc. Am., Econs. Club of York C. of C., Phila. Club Advt. Women, AAUW, Phila. Acad. Fine Arts, World Affairs Council, English-Speaking Union, Kappa Kappa Gamma. Contbr. articles to tech. jours. Home and Office: 108 S Rockburn St York PA 17402

LIVINGSTON, PATRICIA ANN (PAT MURPHY), manufacturing company executive; b. Manila, July 30, 1934; d. Marion Michelin and Phoebe (Nelson) Karolchuck; B.A., Reed Coll., 1955; m. Johnston R. Livingston, Sept. 4, 1965; adopted children—Henry, Ann, Jane, David. With George Washington U. Office Human Resources Research, 1955-58; asst. sec.-treas. Bus. Equipment Mfg. Assn., N.Y.C., 1958-60; fin. writer N.Y. Post, 1961-62, Chgo. Daily News, 1962-66; fin. columnist Dallas Morning News, 1966-71, also syndicated by Newsday, 1968-69; v.p. fin. Enmark Corp., Denver, 1971—; also dir. Trustee, Colo. Women's Coll., 1979—, U. Denver, 1982—; mem. exec. bd. U. Denver Theatre Assn., 1978—. Episcopalian. Club: Denver. Home: 869 Vine St Denver CO 80206 Office: 5070 Oakland St Denver CO 80239

LIVINGSTON-MCCABE, LINDA, cosmetics company executive; b. Rockaway N.Y., Mar. 5, 1945; d. Morton B. and Marian (Orgel) Livingston; divorced; 1 son, Ari Seth. Student, Bklyn Coll., 1961-64. Asst., UNIVAC div. Sperry Rand, 1964-68; adminstrv. mgr. REC Enterprises, N.Y.C., 1968-74; EEO mgr. Revlon, Inc., 1974—. Mem. Office of Fed. Contract Compliance Programs, Indsl. Liaison Group, Nat. Assn. Female Execs. Office: Revlon Inc 767 Fifth Ave New York NY 10153

LIVINGSTON-ROTH, MARY FRANCES, homemaking agency and home care nursing executive, b. Kansas City, Mo., Oct. 6, 1944, d. Carl Emanuel and Frances (Livingston) Roth; m. Kenneth Reeve Sly, Aug. 31, 1963 (div. 1970); children—Kenneth Reeve Jr., Cynthia Denise. Student Green Mountain Coll., 1962-63; nursing edn. Middlesex Meml. Hosp./Vinal Tech., Middletown, Conn., 1980-81. Lic. practical nurse, Conn. Staff nurse Middlesex Meml. Hosp., 1981-82, Talmadge Park Health, East Haven, Conn., 1982-86; founder, owner, pres. South Central Homemaker Agy., Inc., Guilford, Conn., 1983—; founder, co-owner, pres. Conn. Home Care, Inc., Waterford, Conn., 1985—; supporter competitive employment Marrakech, New Haven, 1985—; developer bedmaking program, marketer, instr. Easter Seal Rehab. Ctr., New Haven, 1985—; cons. Dept. Vocat. Rehab., New Haven, 1985—. Writer instructional manuals for nurse aid programs. Mem. Guilford C. of C., Nat. Assn. Female Execs., Ladies Aux. VFW, Am. Legion Aux. Republican. Roman Catholic. Avocations: walking, swimming, gardening, reading, traveling. Home: 137 Water St Guilford CT 06437 Office: South Central Homemaker Agy Inc 137 Water St Guilford CT 06437

LI-WALKER, PAMELA JOYCE MERRILL, tour, travel and bus companies executive; b. Darby, Pa., Nov. 17, 1944; d. Harvey Bertram and Sylvia Louise (Macdonald) Merrill; m. Jose Guillermo Li Chau, 1970 (div. Sept. 1974); children—Andrea Valerie Li, Jennifer Renata Li; m. Lawrence Eugene Walker, Oct. 3, 1981. B.F.A., Carnegie Mellon U., 1966. Dir. mktg. and sales Student Tours Internat., Atlanta, 1967-69; asst. dir. pub. relations Alliance Theatre, Atlanta, 1975-76; group mgr. Prestige Travel, Atlanta, 1976-78; v.p. Cobb Motorcoach & Tours, Atlanta, 1981—; pres. So. Directions Tours & Travel, Atlanta, 1978—; dir. Sci. Instruments & Sales Co., Atlanta. Mem. tourism com. Atlanta Conv. and Visitors Bur., 1978—; charter mem. South Eastern Tourism Soc., Atlanta, 1983—; social chmn. Cedar Cliffs Neighborhood Assn., Atlanta, 1984; mem. Leadership Cobb, Cobb County, Ga., 1984—. Mem. Travel Industry Assn. Am., Travel Industry Assn. Ga. (scholarship chmn. 1978—), Atlanta Assn. Interpreters and Translators (founder, pres. 1976), Am. Soc. Travel Agts., Am. Bus Assn., Southeastern Tourism Soc., Cobb C. of C. (tourism com. 1981—). Republican. Presbyterian. Avocations: photography; scuba diving; riding; tennis; reading. Office: So Directions Tours and Travel 6281 Oakdale Rd Atlanta GA 30059

LIZOTTE, SHIRLEY GUICE, insurance sales agent; b. Carpenter, Miss., Oct. 2, 1935; d. Malcolm Gilchrist and Emma Audrey (Linton) Guice; m. Charles Joel Lizotte, Oct. 8, 1961. Student U. Tex.-Arlington 1982-83. C.L.U. Sec. First Nat. Bank, Jackson, Miss., 1954-61; office mgr., trainee, supr. Mony, Dallas, Ft. Worth, Jackson, 1961-84; adminstrv. asst. Thomas M. Dunning Ins., Dallas, 1984-85; ins. salesman Gen. Am., Ft. Worth, 1986—. Sec. bd. edn. Most Blessed Sacrament Ch., Arlington, Tex., 1985. Mem. Am. Soc. C.L.U., Nat. Assn. Female Execs., Beta Sigma Phi, Life Ins. Co. Office Mgrs. Assn. (sec. 1982-84), Am. Bus. Women's Assn. (pres.), DAR, First Families of Miss. Roman Catholic. Home: 2015 Elmridge Dr Arlington TX 76012 Office: Gen Am Ins 1200 Summit St Suite 500 Fort Worth TX 76102

LIZUT, NONA MOORE PRICE, former state health official; b. Quay, N.Mex., Aug. 8, 1923; d. Charley W. and Alba Moore; student N.Mex. State U., 1941-42; m. Charles P. Price, Jr., 1944; 1 son, Charles P. III; m. 2d, William J. Lizut, May 27, 1970. Sec., N.Mex. Health Dept., Santa Fe, 1942-44: sec. environ. div., 1951-68; adminstrv. sec. environ. div. N.Mex. Health and Social Services Dept., Santa Fe, 1968-74, adminstrv. asst. to dep. dir., 1974-78; adminstrv. asst. to dep. sec. N.Mex. Health and Environ. Dept., Santa Fe, 1978-82, adminstr. health services div., 1982-84; owner, mgr. Secretarial Services, Santa Fe, 1984—. Mem. N.Mex. Water Pollution Control Assn. (life, adminstrv. officer 1956-71), N.Mex. Public Health Assn. (sec.-treas. 1962-68, pres. elect 1969), Nat. Secs. Assn. (v.p., program chmn. rec. sec., corr. sec.), Santa Fe C. of C. (women's div.), N.Mex. Round Dance Assn. (co-pres. 1981-82, newsletter editor 1979-82). Club: Capitol City Bus. and Profl. Women's (v.p., program chmn.). Home: 1408 Santa Rosa Dr Santa Fe NM 87501

LJUNG, GRETA MARIANNE, statistician, educator; b. Jakobstad, Finland; d. Paul Johannes and Ellen Alina L. M.S. in Psychology, Abo Acad., Turku, Finland, 1968; M.S. in Stats., U. Wis., 1972, Ph.D. in Stats., 1976. Instr. in stats. Abo Acad., 1967-69; research and teaching asst. U. Wis., Madison, 1970-74, research assoc. Math. Research Ctr., 1975-77; asst. prof. stats. U. Denver, 1977-79; asst. prof. quantitative methods Boston U. Sch. Mgmt., 1979-86; vis. assoc. prof. applied math. MIT, 1986—; cons. in field; presentations at nat. confs. Research, numerous articles, tech. revs. and reports in time series analysis and forecasting; assoc. editor Jour. Forecasting, Internat. Jour. Forecasting. Research grantee U. Uppsala (Sweden), 1968. Mem. Am. Statis. Assn., Inst. Math. Stats., Internat. Inst. Forecasters. Office: 704 Commonwealth Ave Boston MA 02215

LLEWELLYN, BETTY HALFF, archivist; b. Midland, Tex., June 12, 1911; d. Henry Mayer and Rose (Wechsler) Barnet; m. Martin Zinn, Jr., Nov. 12, 1935 (div. 1947); children—Martin III, Henry Harold, Mary Elizabeth Zinn Stewart; m. 2d, George W. Llewellyn, Nov. 9, 1948 (div. 1966). B.A., So. Meth. U., 1934; grad. Gemological Inst. Am., Santa Monica, Calif., 1968. Dir., New Theater, Dallas, 1936-40; exec. dir. McCord Theater Collection, Dallas, 1968—; ptnr. Halff Ineress, Dallas, 1934—; pub. Walnut Hill Pub., Dallas, 1983—; contbr. to numerous schs. and museums, 1978—. Author: (with A.C. Greene) I Can't Forget, 1984. Officer, Lake Charles (La.) LWV, 1946-47; bd. dirs. Lake Charles ARC, 1941-45. Recipient James Smithson Bronze medal Smithsonian Instn., 1978, James Smithson Silver medal, 1980. Mem. So. Meth. U. Alumni Assn., Circus Fans Am., Circus Hist. Assn., Clowns of Am., Mineral. Assn. Dallas, Lone Star Showmans Club, James Smithson Soc., Dallas Gem and Mineral Soc., B'nai B'rith Women, Zeta Phi Eta. Jewish.

LLEWELLYN, MARY FRANCES, librarian; b. Pitts., Sept. 16, 1959; d. William David and Margaret Mary (Chapman) L. B.A. in Polit. Sci., So. Conn. State Coll., 1981; M.L.S., U. Pitts., 1982. Cataloguer, Ansonia Library (Conn.), 1982-85; part-time librarian So. Conn. State Coll., New Haven, 1983-84; adult services librarian Watertown Library Assn., Conn., 1985—. Bd. dirs. Seymour Pub. Library, Conn., 1985—. Mem. ALA, Conn. Library Assn., So. Conn. Library Council (regional reference com. 1984—), Planetary Soc. Republican. Roman Catholic. Home: 71 Johnson Ave Seymour CT 06483 Office: Watertown Library Assn 470 Main St Watertown CT 06795

LLOYD, ARLEEN MARTIN, business educator, account executive, marketing consultant; b. N.Y.C., May 18, 1957; d. David Paul and Ligia (Zeledon-Masis) L. A.A., Miami Dade Community Coll., 1976; B.B.A., Fla. Internat. U., 1979, M.A. in Internat. Bus., 1983. Cert. tchr., Fla. Sales mgr. Jordan Marsh, Miami, Fla., 1979-80, asst. dir. selling services, 1980-81, asst. buyer, 1981-82; tchr. Miami Springs Sr. High Sch. (Fla.), 1981—; v.p. sales Expediter, Inc., Miami, 1983; bus. instr. Internat. Fine Arts Coll., Miami 1983—; pvt. practice mktg. cons., Miami, 1983-84; account exec. Avanti, Miami, 1984—. Recipient fund raising award United Way Dade County, 1979. Mem. Dade County Tchrs. Assn., Nat. Assn. Female Execs., Bus. and Profl. Womens Assn., Internat. Platform Assn., Delta Epsilon Chi (advisor 1983). Republican. Roman Catholic. Home and office: 73 Ludlum Dr Miami Springs FL 33166

LLOYD, DENISE DEE, magazine publisher; b. Ft. Mead, Md., Nov. 20, 1955; d. Wayne Gordon and Gloria Jean (Newcomer) Lloyd. B.A., Youngstown State U., 1978. Assoc. editor Babcox Publs., Akron, Ohio, 1979-80, mng. editor, 1980-81, editor, 1981-85, editor, assoc. pub., 1985-86, pub., 1986—. Bd. dirs. Am. Cancer Soc., Akron, 1984—, chmn. pub. info., 1985—; big sister Big Bros. and Sisters, Akron, 1982—. Recipient outstanding performance award Babcox Publs., 1983; cert. of appreciation Soc. Collision Repair Specialists, 1983; Service to Industry award Ind. Automotive Service Assn. Office: Babcox Publs 11 S Forge St Akron OH 44304

LLOYD, GLORIA LORETTA, insurance company executive; b. Bolton, Miss., Jan. 4, 1956; d. Willie and Alice Jeannette (Thompson) Lloyd. B.S., Jackson State U., 1977. Reporter TV news Sta. WAPT-TV, Jackson, Miss., 1977-81; mktg. rep. United Liberty Life, Houston, 1982—, asst. tng. mgr., family counseling, fin. planning, 1982—. Recipient awards Million Dollar Producers Club, United Liberty Life, 1982. Mem. Project Media, Nat. Assn. Exec. Women, Jackson State U. Alumni. Democrat.

LLOYD, JILL, public relations executive, photojournalist; b. Los Angeles, Oct. 11, 1956; d. A. Thomas and Gloria Irma (Striplin) L.; m. Timothy Steven Bowers, July 8, 1978 (Sept. 1984); 1 child, Steven. B.S. in Communication Arts, Calif. Poly. State U.-Pomona, 1978. Asst. pub. relations dir. Orange County Fair, Costa Mesa, Calif., 1975-84, media and pub. relations dir., 1984—; v.p. pub. relations Profl. Media Services, Del Mar, Calif., 1984—; mem. adv. com. awards Internat. Assn. Fairs and Expositions, 1984—. Vol. Hospice-Orange County; mem. adv. bd. Fullerton Sch. Dist. Vocat. Agr. Bd., Calif.; mem. Ken Johnson Scholarship Com., Costa Mesa, 1978-83; leader 4-H, Fullerton, 1975-80, 83-84. Mem. Women in Communications, Internat. Assn. Fairs and Expos (service mem., Best Pub. Relations program award 1979, 1st place awards 1984, 85), Western Fairs Assn. (Merrill award 1986), Nat. Assn. Female Execs. Avocations: photography; tennis; travel. Home: 165 Cornell Irvine CA 92715 Office: Profl Media Services PO Box 850 Del Mar CA 92014

LLOYD, JOYCE L. E. POLK, educator; b. Altair, Tex., Sept. 20, 1932; d. Willie, Jr., and Ethel (Allen) Polk; m. Maurice Earnest Lloyd, July 17, 1955; 1 son, Earnest Rheinold Rousseve. B.A., Huston-Tillotson Coll., Austin, Tex., 1952; M.Edn., Prairie View A&M U., 1962. Cert. elem. and secondary tchr., supr., Tex. Elem. tchr. Garwood (Tex.) Sch. Dist., 1953-55; secondary tchr. Columbus (Tex.) High Sch., 1955-57; elem. tchr. Dallas Ind. Sch. Dist., 1957—, resource person, 1979-82; instr. D.E. Johnson Bible Inst., Dallas, 1979—. Author: Inspirational Insights, 1980; Programs for Challenge, 1982; editor Reporter weekly newspaper, 1977—. Dir. tchr. tng. Carver Heights Baptist Ch., 1983-84. Named Woman of Yr., People's Bapt. Ch., Dallas, 1974; recipient award Carver Heights Bapt. Ch., 1982. Mem. NEA (life), Tex. Tchrs. Assn. (life), Phi Delta Kappa, Zeta Phi Beta. Democrat. Lodge: Daus. of Isis (high priest 1975-78). Home: 5418 Stoneboro Trail Dallas TX 75241

LLOYD, KATE RAND, editor, writer; b. Mpls.; d. Rufus Randall and Helen Starkweather (Chase) Rand; B.A. cum laude, Bryn Mawr Coll., 1945; m. John Davis Lloyd, Feb. 25, 1950; children—Kate Angeline, Ann Elizabeth, John Rand. Staff writer Vogue mag., N.Y.C., 1945-51, feature writer, 1951-54, sr. editor, 1963-67, feature editor, 1967-74, mng. editor, 1974-77; feature editor Glamour mag., 1954, mng. editor, 1954-63; with Working Woman mag., N.Y.C., 1977—, former editor-in-chief, now editor-at-large; adj. lectr. Columbia U. Sch. Journalism, from 1975. Mem. council Hunger Project, from 1977; mem. Nat. Commn. on Working Women; bd. dirs. Planned Parenthood Fedn. Am., 1978-84, Nat. Black Theatre, 1980-82, Council on Econ. Priorities, 1985—, Alan Gutlmacher Inst., 1984—, Women's Equity Action League, 1986—, Child Care Action Campaign, 1984—; mem. adv. bd. Inst. Women and Work, Cornell U., from 1980; trustee OEF Internat.; mem. N.Y.C. Commn. on Status of Women, 1982—, mem. N.Y. State Job-Tng. Partnership Council, 1985—. Recipient First prize Vogue Prix de Paris, 1945; named YWCA Woman of Achievement, 1978. Mem. Am. Soc. Mag. Editors, Women in Communications (Headliner award 1983), Women's Forum (bd. dirs.), Advt. Women of N.Y. (bd. dirs.), Fin. Women's Assn. Club: Colony (N.Y.C.). Editor: Glamour Mag. Party Book, 1965; Vogue Beauty and Health Guide, 1975, 76; editorial supr. Vogue's Book of Etiquette (rev. edit.), 1969; Vogue Real-Life Fashion Guide, 1976. Office: Working Woman Mag HAL Publs Inc 342 Madison Ave New York NY 10173*

LLOYD, LEONA LORETTA, lawyer; b. Detroit, Aug. 6, 1949; d. Leon Thomas and Naomi Mattie (Chisolm) L. B.S., Wayne State U., 1971, J.D., 1979. Bar: Mich. Speech, English tchr. Detroit Bd. Edn., 1971-75; instr. criminal justice Wayne State U., Detroit, 1981; sr. ptnr. Lloyd and Lloyd, Detroit, 1982—. Wayne State U. scholar, 1970, 75; recipient Kizzy Image award, 1985; named to Black Women Hall of Fame, Fred Hampton Image award, 1984; merit award Black Law Students U. Detroit, 1986; Minority Bus. of Yr. award Assn. Black Students Wayne State U., 1986; Community Service award Wayne County, 1986; award of outstanding community leadership Nat. Coalition 100 Black Women, 1986. Mem. ABA, Wolverine Bar Assn., Mary McLeod Bethune Assn. Office: Lloyd and Lloyd Law Firm 600 Renaissance Ctr Suite 1400 Detroit MI 48243

LLOYD, MARGARET ANN, psychologist, educator; b. Weiser, Idaho, Sept. 14, 1942; d. Laurance Henry and Margaret Jane (Patch) L.; B.A., U. Denver, 1964; M.S. in Edn., Ind. U., 1966; M.A., U. Ariz., 1972, Ph.D., 1973. Asst. dean of women Carroll (Wis.) Coll., 1966-68, instr. psychology, 1972-73; asst. prof. psychology Suffolk U., Boston, 1973-76, assoc. prof., 1976-79, prof.,

1979—, chairperson dept., 1981—. Author: Adolescence, 1985. Mem. AAUP, Am. Psychol. Assn. (commn. on undergrad. edn. 1985—), New Eng. Psychol. Assn. (steering com. 1984-86), Mass. Psychol. Assn. (sec. 1979-81, chairperson bd. acad. and sci. affairs 1981-82). Home: 39 Gannett Pasture Ln Scituate MA 02066 Office: Suffolk U Beacon Hill Boston MA 02114

LLOYD, MARILYN, congresswoman; b. Ft. Smith, Ark., Jan. 3; d. James Edgar and Iva Mae (Higginbotham) Laird; grad. Shorter Coll., 1963; m. Joseph P. Bouquard (div.); children—Nancy Lloyd Smithson, Mari, Mort II, Deborah Lloyd Riley. Mem. 94-99th Congresses from 3d Tenn. Dist.; past owner, operator radio sta. WTTI, Dalton, Ga. Democrat. Office: Room 2266 Rayburn House Office Bldg Washington DC 20515*

LLOYD, MARILYN ANN, personnel service agency executive; b. Frankfurt, Ind., Apr. 8, 1944; d. James Newton and Etta Jane (Hughes) Beaman; m. Michael James Lloyd, Sept. 16, 1972; children—Bridgena Ann, Terrina Leonne, Lisa Dawn. Owner Tex. Decorating, Dallas, 1962-78; co-owner, v.p., gen. mgr. Snelling Snelling, Dallas, 1979—. Mem. North Dallas C. of C., Am. Bus. Women's Assn. (Carrillon chpt.), Internat. Platform Assn., Republican Assembly. Home: 700 Pleasant View Hurst TX 76053 Office: Suite 544 12900 Preston St Dallas TX 75230

LLYWELYN, MORGAN, novelist; b. N.Y.C., Dec. 3, 1937; d. Joseph John and Henri Llywelyn (Price) Snyder; m. Charles Patrick Llywelyn, Jan. 1, 1957 (dec. 1985); 1 son, John Joseph. Horse trainer, participant competitive horse shows, 1960-75. Author: The Wind from Hastings, 1978; Lion of Ireland, 1980 (Cultural Achievement award Washington FEIS for Irish Am. Community 1981); The Horse Goddess, 1982 (Book of Month Club selection 1982, selected ALA one of best novels for young adults 1983, best novel Nat. Am. League Penwomen nat. contest 1984; Bard: The Odyssey of the Irish, 1984; Grania: She-King of the Irish Seas, 1986. Named Woman of Yr., Irish Heritage and Cultural Com., 1986. Mem. Nat. League Am. Penwomen, Authors Guild, Sci. Fiction Writers Am., Gaelic Arts Soc., Irish Soc. Pitts. Republican. Episcopalian. Home and Office: 29 Rockwell Ct Annapolis MD 21403

LOBALZO, SUSAN VIRGINIA, interior designer; b. Wheeling, W.Va., Sept. 28, 1952; d. Nick and Grace (Hadjis) Karnell; student Ohio State U., 1970-72; B.A., Kent State U., 1974, M.A., 1979; student Parsons Sch. Design, 1981, Harvard Grad. Sch. Design, 1983; m. Richard Lobalzo, July 21, 1973; children—Lisa, Dana. Successively mgr. custom drapery and bedspread dept., asst. buyer drapery dept., designer accessories, lamps and paintings Halle's Dept. Store, Cleve., 1975-78; grad. asst. Kent State U., 1978-79; freelance interior designer, Akron, Ohio, also instr. Kent State U., 1979-82; owner, prin. Lobalzo Design Assocs., 1984—; lectr. U. Akron, 1983-86; conv. speaker. Cleve. Found. grantee, 1979; recipient Scalamandre award for hist. preservation, 1978, Presdl. citation Am. Soc. Interior Designers, 1980, 81. Mem. Am. Soc. Interior Designers (sec. chpt. 1982-83, chpt. bd. dirs. 1984-85, pres. Ohio North chpt. 1985, 86, chpt. award as Designer of Yr. 1986), Nat. Trust Hist. Preservation, Nat. Center Barrier Free Environ., Akron Art Mus., Cleve. Art Mus., Stan Hywct Hall Found. Democrat. Presbyterian. Home: 1190 Meadow Spur Akron OH 44313

LOBL, MARYJANE, fin. planning exec.; b. Cleve., Jan. 19, 1939; d. Robert S. and Olive Belle (Weaver) Hall; student Western Res. U., 1957-59; m. Julian W. Lobl, May 17, 1980; children—D. Fletcher, Robert William, William, John. Adminstrv. asst. Allyne M. Gottlieb, Cleve., 1965-70; pvt. cons. on benefits, Cleve., 1970-75; asst. to pres. Empire Life Ins. Co., Cleve., 1975-77; v.p. N.E. Fin. Group, Inc., Cleve., 1977—. Cantorial soloist Brith Emeth Synagogue, Pepper Pike, Ohio, 1982. Mem. Am. Guild Organists. Dir. music Valley Luth. Ch., Chagrin Falls, Ohio, 1975—. Republican. Jewish. Office: NE Fin Group Inc 33 Public Sq Suite 250 Cleveland OH 44113

LOBOREC, PATRICIA ANN, bookstore manager; b. Weirton, W.Va., Aug. 23, 1955; d. Perry Ralston and Mary Elizabeth (Knowlton) Westlake; m. Anthony Jack Loborec, May 12, 1984. Cert. T.R.I. Bus. Sch., 1974, G.C. Murphy Mgr. Tng. Sch., 1978. Sales promoter G.C. Murphy Co., McKeesport, Pa., 1973-76, asst. mgr., 1976-80; asst. mgr. Brooks Fashions, St. Clairsville, Ohio, 1982-83; bookstore mgr. Wheeling Coll. Bookstore, W.Va., 1983—; mgr./designer sales promotion display Nat. Hosiery Week, 1977 (3rd place award); college ring cons. Josten's 1984. Recipient Walkamerica cert. March of Dimes, Wheeling, 1985. Republican. Roman Catholic. Avocations: reading, biking, running. Home: 3 Clay Ave Wheeling WV 26003 Office: Wheeling Coll Bookstore 316 Washington Ave Wheeling WV 26003

LOBRON, BARBARA L., writer, editor, photographer; b. Phila., Mar. 19, 1944; d. Martin Aaron and Elizabeth (Gots) L.; student Pa. State U., 1962-63; B.A. cum laude, Temple U., Phila., 1966; student photography Harold Feinstein, N.Y.C., 1970, 79-80. Reporter, writer Camden (N.J.) Courier-Post, 1966-68; editorial asst. Med. Insight mag., N.Y.C., 1970-71; mng. editor Camera 35 mag., N.Y.C., 1971-75, also asso. editor photog. anns. for U.S. Camera/Camera 35, 1972, 73; freelance editor as Word Woman, N.Y.C., 1975-77, 79—; copy editor Camera Arts mag., N.Y.C., 1981-83; editorial coordinator Center Mag., Nat. Ctr. Health Edn., 1985; contbg. editor Photograph; photographer, group exhbns. include: Photograph Gallery, N.Y.C., 1981, Rockefeller Center, N.Y.C., 1976, Internat. Women's Art Festival, N.Y.C., 1975; represented in collection Library of Calif. Inst. Arts, Valencia. Recipient 1st pl. honors Dist. 1, Internat. Assn. Bus. Communicators, 1977. Mem. Authors Guild, Editorial Freelancers Assn. Copy editor: Camera Arts, 1981-83, The Complete Guide to Cibachrome Printing, 1980; The Popular Photography Question and Answer Book, 1979; The Photography Catalog, 1976; Strand: Sixty Years of Photography, 1976; You and Your Lens, 1975; contbr. articles to comml. publs., chpts. to books. Home: 85 Hicks St Brooklyn NY 11201

LOCHAYA, ELLEN TEPER, retail marketing executive, public relations consultant; b. Albany, N.Y., Mar. 8, 1939; d. Eugene and Tilda Teper; 1 son, Ned. B.S., Syracuse U., 1960; cert. teaching English as 2d lang. U. Mich., Ann Arbor, 1962; student Inst. Fund Raising, N.Y.C., 1977. Copywriter, asst. to account exec. Grant Advt. Inc., Boston, 1960-61; publs. officer MIT, Cambridge, Mass., 1961-62; instr. English, Peace Corps, Thailand, 1962-64, Lang. Center, Bangkok, 1964-65; asst. to editor U.S. News & World Report, Bangkok, 1965-67; mng. editor, feature writer N.Y. State Dept. Health, Albany, 1969-70; sr. public info. specialist N.Y. State Dept. Commerce, Albany, 1970-72; public relations cons. N.Y. State Assembly, Albany, 1972-74; spl. projects asst. to indsl. commnr., N.Y. State Dept. Labor, Albany, 1974-76; upstate public relations dir. Group Health Inc., Albany and N.Y.C., 1976-77, public relations dir., 1977-78; owner Ellen Lochaya Public Relations, Albany, 1977—; pres. AsianAttic, Inc., 1981—. Mem. Albany C. of C. Home: 373 Manning Blvd Albany NY 12206 Office: AsianAttic Northway Mall Albany NY 12205

LOCKE, EDITH RAYMOND, editor; b. Vienna, Austria, Aug. 3, 1921; came to U.S., 1939, naturalized, 1944; d. Herman and Dora (Hochberg) Laub; student Bklyn. Coll., 1940-42, CCNY, 1942-45; m. A. Ralph Locke, Jr., May 29, 1963; 1 dau., Katherine Dee. Asst. to advt. dir. Harper's Bazaar, N.Y.C., 1945-46, asso. mdse. editor Jr. Bazaar, 1946-48; fashion dir. Abbott Kimball Advt. Agy., N.Y.C., 1948-49; asso. fashion editor Mademoiselle mag., N.Y.C., 1949-59, fashion editor, 1959-67, exec. editor, 1967-72, editor-in-chief, 1971-80; editor/producer/host weekly cable TV show for women You Magazine, 1981—; fashion and TV cons.; mem. Coty award jury Am. Fashion Critics, 1950—. Bd. dirs. Am. Women's Econ. Devel. Mem. Am. Soc. Mag. Editors, Fashion Group (pres. 1972-73). Author: The Red Door, 1965. Office: 308 E 73d St Apt 2A New York NY 10021

LOCKER, GLENDA KAY, nursing educator; b. Amarillo, Tex., Dec. 4, 1951; d. E.H. and Odessa (Talley) Dunham; m. Darrell Lynn Locker, Mar. 17, 1979. B.S.N., U. Tex.-Ft. Worth, 1974; A.D., Frank Phillips Coll., 1972. Staff nurse John Peter Smith Hosp., Ft. Worth, 1974; charge nurse Highland Gen. Hosp., Pampa, Tex., 1975-77, inservice dir. infection control, 1977; instr. nursing Odessa Coll. (Tex.), 1977-79; instr. nursing Odessa Coll. Extension Pecos, Tex., 1979—, dir. vocat. nursing, 1979—. Republican. Baptist. Home: 1512 Iowa St Pecos TX Office: Odessa Coll Vocational Nursing Program Pecos TX 79772

LOCKETT, ELIZABETH RUTH, educational administrator; b. Orange, N.J., Aug. 22, 1929; d. Waverly and Theresa Fernandez (Da Cruz) Lockett. B.S., Pratt Inst, 1954; M.S. in Nutrition, Hunter Coll., 1959; sch. adminstrn. cert. Pace U., 1972; cert. continuing edn. Notre Dame U. Dietitian St. Anthony's Hosp., Queens, N.Y., 1954-55; adminstrv. dietitian Meml.-Sloan Kettering Hosp., N.Y.C., 1955-57; secondary tchr. N.Y.C. Bd. Edn., 1957-68, sch. adminstr., 1968—. Vol. Vanguard Polit. Club, Bklyn., 1984—. Recipient John F. Kennedy Community Service award C Sch. Dist. 16-Jr. High Sch. 57, Bklyn., 1978. Mem. N.Y.C. Adminstrv. Women in Edn., Secondary Sch. Adminstrs., Assn. Curriculum Devel. and Supervision, Council Suprs. and Adminstrs. (rep. exec. bd. 1973—, Service award 1985), Assn. Asst. Prins. (v.p. 1977—), Lambda Kappa Mu (nat. Disting. Service Key award 1976, past nat. officer). Roman Catholic. Avocations: travel; reading; painting on glass; handicrafts. Office: NYC Bd Edn Jr High Sch 324 800 Gates Ave Brooklyn NY 11221

LOCKETT, SANDRA A. JOHNSON BOKAMBA, librarian; b. Hutchinson, Kans., Nov. 18, 1946; d. Herbert Wales and Dorothy Bernice (Harrison) Johnson; B.S., U. Kans., 1968; M.L.S., Ind. U., 1973; children—Eyenga Marthe Bérènice Bokamba, Madeline Bernice. Spl. assignments librarian Gary (Ind.) Public Library, 1973-74, Alcott br. librarian, 1974-76, asst. dir. public relations and programming, 1976-78, head extension services and public relations, 1978-79; head govt. documents dept. U. Iowa Law Library, Iowa City, 1979-84; librarian-in-charge Center Street Library, Milw. Pub. Library, 1984—. Pres., Iowa City Community Sch. Dist. Equity Com., 1980-81; mem. Iowa City Com. Community Needs, 1981-83; mem. Assn. Study Afro-Am. Life and History, 1976-78. Gary Public Library grantee, 1978, Community Devel. Block Grant Fund grantee. Mem. NAACP (sec. 1980-81), Am. Assn. Law Librarians, Mid-Am. Law Library Assn., Iowa Library Assn. (vice-chmn., chmn. elect govt. documents div. 1980-83), Am. Library Assn., Wis. Library Assn., Alpha Kappa Alpha. Democrat. Roman Catholic. Home: 4282 N 28th Street Milwaukee WI 53216 Office: Center Street Library 2620 W Center Street Milwaukee WI 53206

LOCKETT-EGAN, MARIAN W., advertising executive; b. Murray, Ky., May 5, 1931; d. Otis H. Workman and Myrtle A. (Jones) Workman-Jordan; m. Barker Lockett, Oct. 11, 1963 (div.); m. 2d, Douglas S. Egan Jr., Feb. 14, 1981; children—Reed Nasser, Jennifer Stephens, George M. Potts, Cynthia Klenk, Stephen R.W. Lockett. Student Murray State U., 1962. Asst. media dir. Noble-Dury & Assocs., Nashville, 1963; asst. research dir. Triangle Broadcast Div., Phila., 1964-68; assoc. Media dir. Lewis & Gilman, Phila., 1968-72; v.p. advt. media, Scott Paper Co., Phila., 1972-83; pres. DMS Communications Inc., Ardmore, Pa., 1983—; faculty adviser The Media Sch., N.Y.C., 1983-85, exec. dir. mktg. and media edn., 1985—; mem. TV com. Assn. Nat. Advertisers, N.Y.C., 1977-83; guest lectr. Wharton U., Phila., 1981-82; Gannet vis. prof. U. Fla. Sch. Journalism, Gainesville, 1982. Guest editor Media Decisions, 1981. Trustee Meth. Hosp. Found., Phila., 1974—; pres. Llanfair Homeowners Assn., Ardmore. Mem. TV and Radio Advt. Club (pres. 1974). Republican. Episcopalian. Home: 45 Llanfair Circle Ardmore PA 19033 Office: PO Box 110 Ardmore PA 19033

LOCKETT-POWELL, FRANKIE ANN, personnel executive; b. Feb. 27, 1942; d. Dave and Wealthie Lee (Scales) Lockett; student Coll. of DuPage, 1971-72; A.A.S., Florissant Valley Community Coll., 1980; B.S., St. Mary-of-the-Woods Coll., 1984; children—Andre Fernandez, Debra Yvette, Avery Cortez. Postal clk., U.S. Govt., E. St. Louis, Ill., 1965-68; clk. Sch. Dist. 189, E. St. Louis, 1969-70; personnel sec. Atlantic Cos., Chgo., 1970-72; sec. Honeywell Inc., St. Louis, 1972-73; sr. personnel clk. ACF Industries, St. Charles, Mo., 1973-76; personnel and tng. asst. Church's Fried Chicken, Inc., St. Louis, 1976; personnel specialist Prudential Savs. & Loan Assn., Clayton, Mo., 1977-80; personnel dir., office services adminstr. S.W. Truck Body Co., St. Louis, 1980-82; mgr. employee benefits ITT Comml. Fin. Corp., 1982—; adv. student placement State Community Coll., E. St. Louis, 1977—; mem. com. United Negro Coll. Fund., 1979—; sec. Parker Rd. Baptist Ch., 1978—, mem. long range planning com., 1979—; active Practical Edn. Now program, 1979-80. Recipient Urban League St. Louis Sentinel "Yes I Can" award, 1977; State Community Coll. Certificate of Appointment, 1977. Mem. Indsl. Relations Assn. Greater St. Louis. Am. Bus. Women's Assn. Home: 7274 N Hanley Rd Hazelwood MO 63042 Office: 8251 Maryland Ave Clayton MO 63105

LOCKHART, DEBORAH ANN, computer programmer; b. Mineral Wells, Tex., Feb. 20, 1945; d. Joe Royce and Billie Louise (Crow) Williams; B.S., Tex. Christian U., 1967; postgrad. U. Tex., Arlington, 1971; m. Scott Charles Lockhart, June 17, 1976 (div. 1983); children—Amy Louise, Adam Conan. Programmer aid Ling Temco Vought, Grand Prairie, Tex., 1966-67, 68-69; programmer analyst Trinity U., San Antonio, 1967-68; programmer analyst Info. Systems Tech., Dallas, 1969-71; systems engr. Optimum Systems Inc., Dallas, 1972-75; sr. programmer analyst Univ. Computing Co., Dallas, 1971-72, 75-81; mgr. CIF project Banking Systems, Inc., Dallas, 1981-83; project mgr. Shared Fin. Systems, Dallas, 1983—. Pres. Chapel Downs Community Ctr., 1986—. Mem. Mensa. Presbyterian. Office: 15301 Dallas Pkwy Dallas TX 75248

LOCKHART, MADGE CLEMENTS, educator; b. Soddy, Tenn., May 22, 1920; d. James Arlie and Ollie (Sparks) Clements; student East Tenn. U., 1938-39; B.S., U. Tenn., Chattanooga and Knoxville, 1955, M.Ed., 1962; m. Andre J. Lockhart, Apr. 24, 1942 (div. 1973); children—Jacqueline, Andrew, Janice, Jill. Elem. tchr. Tenn. and Ga., 1947-60, Brainerd High Sch., Chattanooga, 1960-64, Cleveland (Tenn.) City Schs., 1966-82; owner, operator Lockhart's Learning Center, Inc., Cleveland and Chattanooga, 1975—; co-founder Dawn Center, Hamilton County, Tenn., 1974, Hermes, residential, day care and workshops orgn., 1972. Pres., Cleveland Assn. Retarded Citizens, 1970, state v.p., 1976; pres. Cleveland Creative Arts Guild, 1980, Cherokee Easter Seal Soc., 1973-76; bd. dirs. Tenn. Easter Seal Soc., 1974-77, 80-83, recipient awards; chair Bradley County Internat. Yr. of Child; pres. Hermes, Inc., 1973-79. Recipient Service to Mankind award Sertoma, 1978. Gov.'s award for service to handicapped, 1979. Mem. NEA (life), Tenn. Edn. Assn., Am. Assn. Rehab. Therapy, Cleveland Edn. Assn., Council Exceptional Children, Tenn. Conf. Social Welfare, Bradley-Cleveland C. of C. Clubs: Byliners, Fantastiks. Mem. Ch. of Christ. Contbr. articles to prof. jours. and newspapers; writer poetry, short stories and fiction. Home: 3007 Oakland Dr Cleveland TN 37311

LOCKHART, NELL HENDERSON, association executive, consultant; b. Birmingham, Ala., Jan. 3, 1936; d. Homer DuBose and Myrtle Nell (Isbell) Henderson; m. James Edward Lockhart, Aug. 25, 1956; children—Jonathan Mark, Leigh Anne. B.A., Howard Coll. (now Samford U.), 1956; postgrad. Meramec Community Coll., 1976-77. Tchr. pub. schs., Birmingham, 1956-57, Louisville, 1957-60, Atlanta, 1960-61; research librarian Christian Civic Found. St. Louis, 1972-76; dir. communications, program and spl. events Religious Heritage of Am., St. Louis, 1978-81, chief adminstrv. officer, 1981-82, exec. v.p., 1982-85, editor Newsbriefs newsletter, 1982-85; account exec. St. Louis Scene, Inc., 1985—. State officer Mo. Hosp. Assn. Aux. and Vol. Services, Jefferson City, 1967-72; pres. Mo. Baptist Hosp. Aux., St. Louis, 1968—. Mem. Meeting Planners Internat. (pres. St. Louis chpt. 1983-84), Religious Pub. Relations Council (v.p. 1980), Nat. Assn. Female Execs., St. Louis Soc. Assn. Execs., Kirkwood Hist. Soc. Republican. Baptist. Club: Woodgate Women's (pres. 1965-66) St. Louis. Home: 1238 Woodgate Dr Kirkwood MO 63122 Office: St Louis Scene 8600 Delmar Penthouse Suite 1 Saint Louis MO 63124

LOCKHART, ROSALIE PERGANTIS, broadcasting official; b. Mobile, Ala., Mar. 16, 1938; d. George Demetri and Marie Amelia (Napolillo) Pergantis; A.B., Springhill Coll., 1960; postgrad. U. Ala., 1962; m. James M. Lockhart, Jr., Dec. 22, 1973. Promotion mgr. Mobile Press Register, 1954-68; producer WSMB Radio, New Orleans, 1968—, now v.p., gen. mgr. Vol. worker Mobile Infirmary Aux., 1961-68, Mobile Gen. Hosp., 1961-68; mem. La. Gov.'s Movie Industry Bd. active Young Democrats. Ala. Mem. Am. Women in Radio and TV, La. Assn. Broadcasters, New Orleans Assn. Broadcasters, Nat. Assn. Broadcasters, AAUW, Jefferson Bar Aux. Roman Catholic. Home: 5225 Zenith St Metairie LA 70001 Office: Maison Blanche Bldg New Orleans LA 70112

LOCKLEAR, AUDREY JEAN, steel company executive; b. Detroit, May 6, 1956; d. Marvin and Nina L.; children—Wahkuna Chenoa Jacobs, Tony Dean Jacobs Jr. Student Robeson Tech. Coll., 1974, Pembroke State U., 1975, Richmond Tech., 1980; Diploma Drafting & Design, Arundel Inst., 1981. Cert. contractor, N.C., cert. minority contractor, N.C., S.C. Drafter/tracer MRC Corp., Md., 1980-81, The Docu-Data Corp., Balt., 1981-82, Binswanger Glass Co., Fayetteville, N.C., 1982-83, Cumberland County Planning Dept., N.C., 1983-84, Robeson County Tax Mapping Dept., N.C., 1984; owner, pres. Performance Steel Erectors, Pembroke, N.C., 1984—. Democrat. Avocations: fishing; cooking; dancing; weight lifting. First woman in N.C. to subcontract reinforced steel; first Indian woman to enter the contracting construction business in N.C. Home and Office: PO Drawer 1209 Pembroke NC 28372

LOCKMAN, JOANN, tax auditor; b. Detroit, Feb. 22, 1942; d. James V. and Rose (Grasso) Franchione; children—Janine, Jennifer Ann, JoEllen. Student Wayne State U. A.A. in Bus., Scottsdale Community Coll. With County Hosp., Phoenix, 1981; now sales tax auditor City of Phoenix. Recipient VFW award, 1953. Mem. Cert. Fin. Planners. Republican. Avocations: painting; sewing; playing the flute. Home: 1149 N 92d St #158 Scottsdale AZ 85256 Office: City of Phoenix Irvine Plaza Suite 216 1724 E Indian School Rd Phoenix AZ 85016

LOCKMAN, MARCIA ANN, commercial real estate consultant; b. Louisville, July 26, 1951; d. George John and Jean Norman (Hamilton) Korfhage; m. James Richard Lockman, May 25, 1974. B.A., Miami U., Ohio, 1973; M.S., U. Wis.-Milw., 1974; M.B.A., U. Minn., 1984. Project dir. NFO Research, Toledo, 1974-76; sales assoc. Welles Bowen, Toledo, 1976-78; research analyst Green Giant, Mpls., 1978-79; market research mgr. Fingerhut, Mpls., 1979-83; self employed market research cons., Mpls., 1983-85; real estate assoc. Keewaydin, Mpls., 1985; instr. U. Toledo, 1977. Commr. Eden Prairie Human Rights and Services, 1978-84; chmn. Eden Prairie Human Service Needs Com., 1980-83; chmn. spl. projects 1983 U.S. Sr. Open Golf Tournament, Chaska, Minn., 1982-83; auctioneer KTCA Pub. TV, St. Paul, 1982. Mem. Pi Beta Phi (Service award 1973). Republican. Methodist. Clubs: Toledo Country, Flagship Athletic, Hazletine Nat. Golf. Avocations: golf; interior design. Address: 7952 S Bay Curve Eden Prairie MN 55344

LOCKRIDGE, KAREN SUE, restaurant executive; b. Goshen, Ind., Nov. 23, 1948; d. Leslie Eugene and Rhea Jean (Reed) L.; B.A., Purdue U., 1971. With Allen & O'Hara, Inc., mgrs. Holiday Inns, 1967-82, sales dir., asst. gen. mgr. Holiday Inn, Tampa, Fla., 1975-82; corp. dir. sales Midway Motor Lodges, Brookfield, Wis., 1982-84, v.p. sales and mktg., 1984-85; owner, operator Apricot Annie's Cafe and Bar and Daiquiri Shack. Recipient Human Relations award City of Tampa, 1980. Mem. Am. Soc. Assn. Execs., Sales and Mktg. Execs., Meeting Planners Internat., Wis. Soc. Assn. Execs., Milw. Conv. and Visitors Bur. (bd. dirs.), Religious Conv. Mgrs. Assn., Nat. Tour Brokers Assn., Am. Bus. Assn., Episcopalian. Home: 2025 E Greenwich Unit 04 Milwaukee WI 53211 Office: 275 W Wisconsin Ave Milwaukee WI 53203

LOCKWOOD, BARBARA JORDAN, nurse administrator; b. Landshut, W. Ger., Aug. 23, 1948; d. Ernest Bob and Christa Barbara (Tilgner) Jordan (father Am. citizen); B.S. in Nursing with honors, U. Colo., 1970, M.S. in Med.-Surg. Nursing, 1973. Staff nurse Denver Gen. Hosp., 1970-72, Med. Personnel Pool, Denver, 1973; flight nurse St. Anthony Hosp. Systems, Denver, 1973-75, flight nurse supr., 1975-76, mgr. critical care services, 1976-79, systems dir. nursing services, 1979-81, asst. exec. dir. nursing services, 1981-86, v.p. patient care services, 1986—; pres. St. Anthony Home Health Services, Inc., 1985—; sec. Alina Health Systems, 1985—; tchr. Am. Assn. Operating Room Nurses, 1976, Am. Assn. Critical Care Nurses, 1977, 78, Chautauqua confs. Colo. Assn. Nurses, 1977, 78, 79, 80, 81, Colo. Student Nurses Assn., 1979; vol. nurse Comitis Crisis Center, Aurora, Colo., 1970-73. Cert. critical care practitioner ACS. Mem. Am., Denver assns. critical care nurses, Nat. League for Nursing, Colo. League for Nursing (sec. 1982-86), Sigma Theta Tau. Democrat. Lutheran. Contbr. chpt. on flight nursing to Critical Care Nursing, 1977; also articles. Office: St Anthony Hosp Systems 16th & Raleigh Sts Denver CO 80204

LOCKWOOD, MOLLY ANN, communications company executive; b. London, Sept. 19, 1936; d. Warren Sewell and Ann Frances (Gleason) L.; B.S., Pa. State U., 1958. With exec. tng. program Lord & Taylor, N.Y.C., 1958-60; assoc. merchandising editor House & Garden Mag., N.Y.C., 1960-65; advt. dir. Status Mag., N.Y.C., 1965-70; merchandising dir. Holiday Mag., N.Y.C., 1970; account mgr. Ladies' Home Journal Mag., N.Y.C., 1970-72; adv. dir. Girl Talk Mag., N.Y.C., 1972-74; mktg. dir./assoc. pub. East/West Network Mag., N.Y.C., 1974-77; chief exec. officer, pres. treas., partner Catalyst Communications, Inc., N.Y.C., 1977—; mktg. and sales dir. Mus. mag., 1979-83, nat. advt. dir. Goodlife mag., 1983—. Mem. Advt. Women N.Y., Am. Soc. Travel Agts., Caribbean Travel Assn., Kappa Kappa Gamma Alumnae Assn. Club: Liberty. Home: 1133 Park Ave New York NY 10128 Office: Catalyst Communications Inc 244 Madison Ave New York NY 10128

LOCKWOOD, SANDRA BROWN, realtor; b. Youngstown, Ohio, Nov. 7, 1934; d. Joseph Daniel and Alice Edna (Koenig) Brown; m. Edward Whiting Lockwood, Mar. 6, 1954 (div. 1973); children—Linda Rae, Gale Elizabeth, Edward Whiting, Jr., Heather Anne, William Bruce, III. Student Miami U., 1952-54. Lic. real estate broker, Mich. Homemaker, Indpls., 1954-64, Traverse City, Mich., 1964-74; with real estate sales E.C. Marshall & Co., Suttons Bay, Mich., 1974-75, Dave Williams Real Estate, Traverse City, 1975-79; owner, pres. Properties North Inc., Traverse City, 1979—; Traverse City, 1984. Mem. Traverse City Bd. Realtors (dir. 1984-86, chmn. grievance com., 1980-83), Mich. Assn. Realtors, Nat. Assn. Realtors. Republican. Presbyterian. Clubs: Yacht, Zonta (dir. 1984-85). Avocations: sailing; downhill and cross-country skiing; gardening. Office: Properties North Inc 1040 E Front St Traverse City MI 49684

LODEN, KAREN CLARK, nurse; b. Perth Amboy, N.J., Aug. 23, 1946; d. Francis Anthony and Mary (Cupsie) Clark; B.S. in Nursing, Loretto Heights Coll., Denver, 1968; M.N. in Nursing, La. State U. Med. Ctr., New Orleans, 1983; m. Michael Loden, May 1, 1969; 1 son, Jonathan. Staff nurse St. Anthony Hosp., Denver, 1968; charge nurse prince William Hosp., Manassas, Va., 1969; staff nurse, charge nurse ICU-CCU Meml. Gen. Hosp., Las Cruces, N.Mex., 1970-71; staff nurse, charge nurse ICU-CCU Lee County Hosp., Opelika, Ala., 1972-73; charge nurse, acting head nurse pediatrics Jackson County Schneck Hosp., Seymour, Ind., 1974-75; mead nurse med.-surg. Drs. Meml. Hosp., Baton Rouge, 1975-77, inservice dir., 1977-79, asst. dir. nursing service, 1979-81; asst. unit dir. E. Jefferson Gen. Hosp., Metairie, La., 1981; staff nurse Lakeside Hosp., Metairie, La., 1982-83; asst. dir. nursing Hôtel Dieu Hosp., New Orleans, 1983—; clin. preceptor Children's Hosp., New Orleans, 1984-85; clin. instr. nursing Our Lady of Holy Cross Coll., New Orleans, 1986—; CPR instr., trainer Am. Heart Assn. Vol. ARC, Baton Rouge. Mem. Am. Assn. Critical Care Nurses, Am. Soc. Nursing Service Adminstrs., Council Assos., Am. Heart Assn., Baton Rouge Soc. Gifted and Talented, Sigma Theta Tau. Roman Catholic. Home: 917 Trudeau Dr Metaire LA 70003

LODESTRO, VALERIE CATHERINE, marketing services manager, travel agent, medical assistant; b. Bayshore, N.Y., Apr. 29, 1955; d. William and Marie Roseanne (Chiocco) Logios; m. Charles Vincent Lodestro, Oct. 2, 1982. A.A.S., Nassau Community Coll., 1975; B.B.A., Hofstra U., 1983. Med. unit asst. Lydia Hall Hosp., Freeport, N.Y., 1976-83; mktg. service mgr. Arrow Electronics, Melville, N.Y., 1983-84; mktg. com. mgr. Computerland, Syosset, N.Y., 1984-85; mktg. mgr. Prestige Univ., Deer Park, N.Y., 1985—; travel agt. Travel Partners, Bellmore, N.Y., part time, 1985—. Vol. ARC, Lynbrook, 1972, Head Start, Hempstead, N.Y., 1972; tchr. religious edn. Our Lady of Peace, Lynbrook, 1969-73. Scholar, Hofstra U., 1976-83, nominated spl. honors, Sch. Bus., 1982. Fellow Internat. Assn. Travel Agts., Nat. Assn. Female Execs. Republican. Roman Catholic. Avocations: writing poetry; dancing; reading; aerobics; skating. Home: 2411 Aberdeen St East Meadow NY 11554

LODOLCE, ANN CAMILLE, lawyer; b. N.Y.C., Oct. 7, 1943; s. Charles James and Santa (Stefania) LoDolce; m. Michael L. Washak, May 31, 1975; 1 son, Marc. B.S., Skidmore Coll., 1966; M.A., U. Conn.-Storrs, 1958; J.D., Suffolk U., 1974. Bar: Mass. 1974. Mem. firm LoDolce & Epstein, Brockton, Mass., 1975—; assoc. prof. music history and law Massasoit Community Coll., Brockton, 1968-75. Mem. Plymouth County Bar Assn. (exec. com. 1978-82), Mass. Bar Assn., ABA, NOW, Mass. Assn. Women Lawyers, Women's Bar Assn. Mass. Address: 63 Main St Suite 35 Brockton MA 02401

LODWICK, KATHLEEN LORRAINE, history educator; b. St. Louis, Feb. 7, 1944; d. Algha Claire and Kathryn Elizabeth (Worthington) L. B.S. with honors, Ohio U., 1964, M.A., 1965; Ph.D., U. Ariz., 1976. Instr. history Ohio U., Portsmouth, 1969-72; asst. prof. history U. No. Colo., Greeley, 1976-77; asst. prof. history Ind. State U., Terre Haute, 1977-78; research assoc. John King Fairbank Ctr. East Asian Research, Harvard U., Cambridge, Mass., 1978-79; asst. prof. history S.W. Mo. State U., Springfield, 1979-82, assoc. prof., 1982—, dir. Chinese Recorder Project, 1978-85. Author: The Chinese

Recorder Index: A Guide to Christian Missions in Asia, 1867-1941, 2 Vols., 1986. Contbr. articles to profl. publs. Pres., UN Assn., Springfield, 1982-83, bd. dirs., 1981—. Grantee East-West Ctr., Honolulu, 1966-68, NEH, 1978-81, 83-85, 86, Pacific Cultural Found., 1986, AAUW, 1978. Mem. Am. Hist. Assn., Assn. Asian Studies, Am. Soc. Ch. History, Phi Alpha Theta. Democrat. Mem. Soc. of Friends. Home: 2934 E Southeast Circle Springfield MO 65802 Office: History Dept SW Mo State U Springfield MO 65804

LOEB, BARBARA SHERMAN, preschool program administrator; b. New Orleans, May 21, 1937; d. Morris and Gertrude (Davis) Sherman; m. Charles Edward Loeb, June 8, 1958; children—David, Teri Ellen, Suzanne Beth. B.A., Newcomb Coll., 1959; M.Ed., Tulane U., 1968; postgrad. student Wheelock Coll., 1982, 84, Gesell Inst., 1983. Cert. tchr., La. Substitute tchr. Newman Sch., New Orleans, 1960-67; tchr. Head Start, New Orleans, 1968; kindergarten tchr. Orleans Parish, 1968-73; pre-kindergarten tchr. McGehee Sch., New Orleans, 1973-76; dir. Gates of Prayer Presch., Metairie, La., 1976-78, Children's Pl., Ltd., New Orleans, 1978—; instr. Delgado Jr. Coll., New Orleans, 1979-81; staff mem. U. New Orleans, 1980—; cons. Beginnings mag., 1983—. Mem. Com. for Concerned Citizens for Child Care, La., 1984; bd. dirs. Nat. Council Jewish Women, New Orleans, 1970's, Temple Siani Sisterhood, 1970's. Mem. La. Assn. for Edn. Young Children (pres. local chpt.), Nat. Assn. Edn. Young Children, Southern Assn. for Children Under Six, La. Assn. for Children Under Six, Kappa Delta Pi. Office: Children's Place Ltd 6317 Argonne Blvd New Orleans LA 70124

LOEB, DOROTHY PEARL, lawyer; b. N.Y.C., Mar. 2, 1935; d. Victor Joseph and Jean (Albert) Caesar; m. Frank D. Loeb, June 26, 1955 (dec. 1972); children—Matthew S., Eric V. Student Bates Coll., 1952-55; B.A., Boston U., 1956; J.D., Columbia U., 1971. Bar: N.Y. 1972, U.S. Supreme Ct. 1976. Asst. dist. atty. Rockland County (N.Y.), 1972-75; atty., counsel to commr. Dept. Social Services Rockland County, West Nyack, 1975-77; asst. counsel in charge litigation N.Y. State Dept. Social Services, Albany, 1977-78; asst. dir. N.Y. State Office of Child Support Enforcement, Albany, 1978-80; atty.-advisor Office of Gen. Counsel, Dept. Air Force, Washington, 1980—. Mem. select constn. com. Rockland County Legislature 1974; counsel First Unitarian Ch. Rockland County, Pomona, 1973-75; mem. adv. bd. Rockland County Assn. for Visually Impaired, Pomona, 1976-82; legal advisor, dir. Nyack Child Day Care Ctr., 1974-82; chmn. ad hoc com. on legal affairs Rotunda Condominium Assn. Mem. ABA, Fed. Bar Assn., Am. Judicature Soc., Assn. Trial Lawyers Am., Nat. Dist. Attys. Assn., LWV, AAUW (sec. McLean br.). Unitarian. Office: Office of Gen Counsel Dept Air Force The Pentagon Washington DC 20330

LOEB, FRANCES LEHMAN (MRS. JOHN L. LOEB), civic leader; b. N.Y.C., Sept. 25, 1906; d. Arthur and Adele (Lewisohn) Lehman; student Vassar Coll., 1924-26; L.H.D. (hon.), NYU, 1977; m. John L. Loeb, Nov. 18, 1926; children—Judith Loeb Chiara, John L., Ann Loeb Bronfman, Arthur Lehman, Deborah Loeb Brice. N.Y.C. commr. for UN and Consular Corps, 1966-78. Exec. com. Population Crisis Com., Washington; life mem. bd. Recreation Service for Children of Bellevue, 1974—; bd. dirs. Internat. Presch., Inc., N.Y. Landmarks Conservancy; chmn. bd. East Side Internat. Community Center, Inc.; mem. UN Devel. Corp., 1972—; mem. Women's Nat. Republican Club; life trustee Collegiate Sch. for Boys, N.Y.C.; trustee Cornell U., Inst. Internat. Edn.; bd. overseers Cornell U. Med. Coll., 1983—. Mem. UN Assn. (dir.). Clubs: Cosmopolitan, Vassar, Women's City (N.Y.C.). Home: 730 Park Ave New York NY 10021 also Anderson Hill Rd Purchase NY 10577

LOEB, JEANETTE WINTER, investment banker; b. N.Y.C., June 18, 1952; d. Leon and Fay (Rotenberg) Winter; m. Peter Kenneth Loeb, Nov. 1, 1980. B.A., Wellesley Coll., 1974; M.B.A., Harvard Bus. Sch., 1977. Assoc. Goldman, Sachs & Co., N.Y.C., 1977-81, v.p., 1981—. Wellesley Coll. Devel. Fund chmn. for N.Y. Mem. Phi Beta Kappa. Club: India House. Office: Goldman Sachs & Co 85 Broad St New York NY 10004

LOEB, JOYCE LICHTGARN, interior designer, civic worker; b. Portland, Oreg., May 20, 1936; d. Elias Lichtgarn and Sylvia Amy (Margulies) Freedman; m. Stanley Robinson Loeb, Aug. 14, 1960; children—Carl Eli, Eric Adam. Student U. Calif.-Berkeley, 1954-56; B.S., Lewis and Clark Coll., 1958; postgrad. art and architecture, Portland State U., 1976. Tchr. art David Douglas Sch. Dist., Portland, 1958-59, 61-64; tchr., chmn. art dept. Grant Union High Sch. Dist., Sacramento, 1959-60; designer, pres. Joyce Loeb Interior Design, Inc., Portland, 1976—; cons. designer to various developers of health care facilities. Chairperson fundraisers for civic orgns. and Jewish orgns., bd. dirs. Met. Family Services, Portland, 1968-71, Young Audiences, Inc., Portland, 1970-76, 78-80, Portland Opera Assn., 1978-84, Arts Celebration, Inc., Portland, 1984—, Congregation Beth Israel, 1986—; chmn. ArtQuake Festival, 1985; v.p. Beth Israel Sisterhood, 1981-83. Mem. Inst. Bus. Designers, Nat. Council Jewish Women. Democrat. Club: Multnomah Athletic. Home: 1546 SW Upland Dr Portland OR 97221

LOENING, SARAH ELIZABETH LARKIN, author; b. Nutley, N.J., Dec. 9, 1896; d. Adrian Hoffman and Katherine Bache (Saterthwaite) Larkin; student pvt. schs., N.Y.C., Paris; m. Albert Palmer Loening, Nov. 22, 1922; 1 son, Albert Palmer. Author: Three Rivers, 1934; The Trevals, a Tale of Quebec, 1936; Radisson, 1938; Dimo, French edit., 1940, 2d edit., 1978, English edit., 1979; Joan of Arc, 1950; The Old Master, 1958; Zulli, 1954; The Old Master and Other Tails, 1967; Mountain in the Field, 1972; The Gift of Life, 1978; Vignettes of a Life, 1983. Chmn. arts and skill corps ARC, Camp Upton, 1944, chmn. Hampton chpt. ARC, 1946; pres. Cathedral Guild St. John the Divine, 1961-64, 66-68, chmn. Bibl. Garden, 1972—, chmn. Gardeners of St. John, 1950-58. Mem. Huguenot Soc., Nat. Soc. Colonial Dames, Am. Order St. John of Jerusalem (dame), Order St. Luke the Physician. Episcopalian. Clubs: Colony, Hroswitha, Southampton Garden (past pres.). Home: PO Box 905 Harvest Lane Southampton NY 11968

LOESCHKE, NADIA, steel fabrication plant executive; b. St. Clair Shores, Mich., Jan. 28, 1954; d. Donald Raymond and Diane Helene (Scott) L.; m. Kim Fitzpatrick, June 1, 1974 (div. Oct. 1980); 1 child, Timin Raymond. Student Hillsdale Coll., 1967-70. Sec., Hercules Container, Montebello, Calif., 1970-74; v.p. Arpico Steel Corp., Montebello, 1980—; pres. Hercules Fabrication, Corona, S.D., 1980—; v.p. Metales Don Sadecu, Mexicali, Mexico, 1986—. Mem. Save the Seals, Laguna Beach, Calif., 1983—. Mem. San Bernardino Refuse Assn., Am. Metal Fabrication Assn. Lutheran. Club: Female Execs. (N.Y.C.). Home: 4421 N Ohio St Yorba Linda CA 92686 Office: Arpico Steel Corp 712 Roosevelt Ave Montebello CA 90640

LOEWALD, ELIZABETH LONGSHORE, psychiatrist; b. San Francisco, Dec. 23, 1923; d. Isaac Holcomb and Edna (O'Connor) Longshore; m. Hans Walter Loewald, Jan. 4, 1954; children—Katherine, Caroline. A.B., U. Calif.-Berkeley, 1944; M.D., Johns Hopkins Sch. Medicine, 1948. Intern Doctor's Hosp., Washington, 1950-51; resident in psychiatry Sheppard & Enoch Pratt Hosp., Towson, Md., 1951; physician Balt. Health Dept., 1953-55, New Haven Health Dept. (Conn.), 1955-61; resident in psychiatry Yale Sch. Medicine, New Haven, 1975-77, child psychiatry fellow Yale Child Study Ctr., 1977-79, asst. clin. prof. psychiatry Yale Med. Sch., 1979—; practice medicine specializing in child, adult psychiatry, 1979—. Mem. St. Elizabeth's Hosp. Med. Assn., Am. Psychiat. Assn., Conn. Council Child Psychiatrists, Phi Beta Kappa, Alpha Omega Alpha. Contbr. articles to profl. jours. Office: 63 Trumbull St New Haven CT 06510

LOEWY, BECKY WHITE, psychology educator; b. Fountain Inn, S.C., July 24, 1931; d. James Ernest and Agnes (Roberts) White; student Mary Washington Coll., U. Va., 1948-50; B.A., Vanderbilt U., 1952; M.A., Ohio State U., 1953; Ph.D., U. Calif., Berkeley, 1957; m. Frederick Arnold Loewy, Aug. 28, 1962; children—Julia Anne, Caroline Marie. Residence counselor Ohio State U., Columbus, 1953-55; asst. prof. edn. psychology, sr. counselor Duke U., 1957-59; asst. prof. San Francisco State U., 1959-63, assoc. prof., 1963-69, prof. psychology, 1969—, program dir. gerontology, 1977-82. Danforth assoc., 1979. Mem. Am. Psychol. Assn., Soc. Research in Child Devel., Am. Assn. for Counseling and Devel., Western Gerontol. Soc., Psi Chi, Pi Lambda Theta. Home: 1275 Tuolumne Rd Millbrae CA 94030 Office: Psychology Dept San Francisco State U 1600 Holloway San Francisco CA 94132

LOGAN, CATHERINE ROSE, music educator; b. Asheville, N.C., Apr. 2, 1939; d. Harry Rollins and Flora Virginia (McPhail) Logan; student Mars Hill Coll., 1957-59; B.A. in Music, Furman U., 1961; B.Ch. Music, So. Sem., 1964, M.Ch. Music, 1965; postgrad. Fla. State U., 1969-71. Instr., Union U., Jackson, Tenn., 1965-67, S.W. Bapt. Coll., Bolivar, Mo., 1967-69; prof. voice, music history, dir. choral activities Truett-McConnell Coll., Cleveland, Ga., 1971—; guest condr. Ga. 9th Dist. Honors Chorus, 1980; recitalist, adjudicator for profl., religious and civic orgns. in S.E., 1965—; choir dir. Bethlehem Bapt. Ch., Clarkesville, Ga., 1972—; guest soloist throughout South. Regional dir., v.p. music conf. Ga. Bapt. Conv., 1976—. Mem. Nat. Assn. Tchrs. Singing, Sigma Alpha Iota. Home: Route 5 Box 5545 Cleveland GA 30528 Office: Truett-McConnell College Cleveland GA 30528

LOGAN, GRACE ELEANOR MILLER (MRS. HENRY WHITTINGTON LOGAN), educator; b. Valencia, Pa., June 22, 1908; d. Alvah John and Lillian (Gibson) Miller; B.S., Temple U., 1930, M.S., 1931; postgrad., 1955-56; m. Henry Whittington Logan, Mar. 16, 1940; 1 son, Henry Whittington III. English instr. Temple U., 1930-33; asst. prof. to dept. head Moravian Coll., Bethlehem, Pa., 1933-42; asso. prof. edn. and philosophy Widener U., Chester, Pa., 1956-67, prof. English, 1967-85, prof. emeritus, 1985—; dir. Coll. Reading Services, 1958-85; dir. Fed. Office of Edn. Equal Opportunities Tng. Br. Insts., 1965—; cons., lectr. in biblical studies, 1985—; only woman on faculty any mil. coll. U.S. for 8 yrs. Elder, Presbyterian Ch.; mem. adv. bd. Pa. Inst. Tech. Mem. AAUP, Delaware County Hist. Soc. (dir.), Nat. Council Tchrs. English, Coll. English Assn., Coll. Reading Assn., Internat. Reading Assn., Pa. Council of Tchrs., Am. Acad. Religion, Kappa Delta Epsilon, Pi Delta Epsilon. Home: 201 Sykes Ln Wallingford PA 19086 Office: Widener Univ Chester PA 19013

LOGAN, KAYLEEN ANN, nurse; b. Rock Springs, Wyo., Jan. 18, 1954; d. Andrew Robert and Lois Ann (Lowe) Logan; B.S. cum laude, U. Utah, 1976; M.S. in Nursing, U. Colo. Health Scis. Ctr., 1984. ICU nurse U. Utah Med. Center, Salt Lake City, 1976-77; charge nurse ICU, Holy Cross Hosp., Salt Lake City, 1977-78; public health nurse Sweetwater County, Rock Springs, Wyo., 1978-80; nursing dir. Miner's Respiratory Clinic, Rock Springs, 1980-82; asst. prof. U. Wyo., 1984—. Vice pres. bd. dirs. Diabetic Assn.; bd. dirs. Wyo. Home Health Care; mem. Task Force on Eating Disorders. March of Dimes scholar, 1972-74. Mem. Am. Nurses Assn. Episcopalian. Home: 1116 Mc Cabe Rock Springs WY 82901

LOGAN, SANDRA ROGERS, funeral service company executive; b. Lansing, Mich., Apr. 25, 1955; d. Carol Edward and Ardis M. (West) Rogers; m. James A. Logan, Jr., Oct. 24, 1981 (dec. Sept. 1983). Student in social work, Eastern Mich. U., 1978—. Office supr. Bur. Vocational Rehab., Ann Arbor, Mich., 1978-79; adminstrv. asst. reception ctr. Jackson State Prison, Mich., 1979-81; co-owner Geer-Logan Funeral Home, Ypsilanti, Mich., 1981-83, pres., owner, 1983—. Exec. bd. Women Bus. Owners Com., Ypsilanti, 1983—; adv. bd. Salvation Army, 1983—. Mem. Ypsilanti C. of C., Nat. Funeral Dirs., Mich. Funeral Dirs. Assn., Women in Funeral Service Assn. Democrat. Baptist. Club: Zonta Internat. Home and Office: 320 N Washington St Ypsilanti MI 48197

LOGAN, SHARON BROOKS, lawyer; b. Easton, Md., Nov. 19, 1945; d. Blake Elmer and Esther N. (Statum) Brooks; children—John W., III, Troy Blake. B.S. in Econs., U. Md., 1967, M.B.A. in Mktg., 1969; J.D., U. Fla., 1979. Bar: Fla. 1979. Mem. firm Raymond Wilson, Esq., Ormond Beach, Fla., 1980, Landis, Graham & French, Daytona Beach, Fla., 1981, Watson & Assocs., Daytona Beach, 1982-84, Sharon B. Logan, Esq., Ormond Beach, Fla., 1984—; legal advisor to paralegal program Daytona Beach Community Coll., 1984—, Jon Hall Chevrolet, Daytona Beach, 1984—, Jon Hall Honda, Daytona Beach, 1984—, Holly Hill Heritage, Inc., Fla., 1984—; trustee Ocean Pointe Pro, Dayton Beach Shores, 1984—. Sponsor Nat. Pedal Sport Assn., Dayton Beach, 1981—, Eastern Surfing Assn., Daytona Beach, 1983—. Recipient Rotary Citizenship award Rotary Club, 1962-63; Woodrow Wilson fellow U. Md., 1967. Mem. Fla. Bar Assn. (real property and probate sect.), Volusia County Bar Assn., ABA, Fla. Assn. Women Lawyers, Volusia County Estate Planning Council, Daytona Beach Area Bd. Realtors, Ormond Beach C. of C., Beta Gamma Sigma, Alpha Lamba Delta, Phi Kappa Phi, Omicron Delta Epsilon, Delta Delta Delta (Scholarship award 1964), Sigma Alpha Epsilon. Democrat. Episcopalian. Clubs: Indigo Lakes, Gator. Avocations: cooking; sewing; golf; tennis; racquetball. Office: Sharon B Logan Esq 400 S Atlantic Suite 110 Ormond Beach FL 32074

LOGAN, VERYLE JEAN, retail executive; b. St. Louis, Oct. 24, 1946; d. Benjamin Bishop and Eddie Mae (Williams) Logan. B.S., Mo. U., 1968; postgrad. Wayne State U., 1974, 76, U. Mich.-Detroit, 1978, 80. With Hudson Dept Store, Detroit, 1968-84, Dayton Hudson, Mpls., 1984—, div. mdse. mgr., 1983-84, mgr. dresses, coats, 1984—. Named Woman of Yr., Am. Bus. Women, 1984. Mem. Am. Bus. Womens Assn. (v.p. 1983-84), Minn. Black Networking (exec. bd. 1985), Delta Sigma Theta, Mpls.-St. Paul Alumnae Assn. of U. Mich. (rec. sec. 1985-86). Democrat. Baptist. Club: M.L. King Tennis Buffs. Office: Dayton Hudson Dept Store Co 700 on the Mall Minneapolis MN 55407

LOGAN, VICKI DIANE, writer; b. Oakland, Calif., Aug. 3, 1954; d. Robert Lee and Freida Elizabeth (Luckett) L.; B.S. in Bus. Adminstrn. magna cum laude, Pepperdine U., 1976; M.Internat. Mgmt., with honors, Am. Grad. Sch. Internat. Mgmt., 1979. Asst. to dep. dir. HUD, Washington, 1978; account exec. Doyle Dane Bernbach Advt., Inc., N.Y.C., 1979-81; writer Jordan Case & McGrath Advt., N.Y.C., 1981—. Office: 445 Park Ave New York NY 10022

LOGEMANN, JERILYN ANN, speech pathologist; b. Berwyn, Ill., May 21, 1942; d. Warren F. and Natalie M. (Killmer) L.; B.S., Northwestern U., 1963; M.A., 1964, Ph.D., 1968. Grad. asst. dept. communicative disorders Northwestern U., 1963-68; instr. speech and audiology DePaul U., 1964-65; instr. dept. communicative disorders Mundelein Coll., 1967-71; research assoc. depts. neurology and otolaryngology and maxillofacial surgery Northwestern U. Med. Sch., Chgo., 1970-74, asst. prof., 1974-78, dir. clin. and research activities of speech and lang., 1975—, assoc. prof. dept. neurology, otolaryngology and maxillofacial disorders, communicative disorders, 1978-83, prof. dept. neurology, otolaryngology and maxiofacial disorders, communicative disorders, 1983—, chmn. dept. communicative disorders, 1982—; mem. assoc. staff Northwestern Meml. Hosp., 1976—; assoc. dir. cancer control. Ill. Comprehensive Cancer Council, Chgo., 1980-82. Mem. rehab. com. Ill. div. Am. Cancer Soc., 1975-79, chmn., 1979—. Nat. Inst. Neurologic Disease, Communicative Disorders and Stroke postdoctoral fellow Northwestern U., 1968-70; Inst. Medicine Chgo. fellow, 1981—, Nat. Cancer Inst. grantee, 1975-84, Am. Cancer Soc. grantee, 1981-82. Fellow Am. Speech, Lang. and Hearing Assn.; mem. Internat. Assn. Logopedics and Phoniatrics, AAUP, Acoustic Soc. Am. (program com. Chgo. regional chpt.), Linguistic Soc. Am., Speech Communication Assn., Am. Cleft Palate Assn., Ill. Speech and Hearing Assn., Chgo. Heart Assn., Chgo. Speech Therapy and Auditory Soc. Author: The Fisher-Logemann Test of Articulation Competence, 1971; Evaluation and Treatment of Swallowing Disorders, 1983; assoc. editor Jour. Speech and Hearing Disorders, 1978-82. Home: 1002 Greenleaf St Wilmette IL 60091 Office: Dept Otolaryngology Northwestern U Med Sch 303 E Chicago Ave Chicago IL 60611

LOGGANS, SUSAN VON BROCKHOEFT, nurse; b. New Orleans, June 29, 1955; d. George Emmett and Dorothy Claire (Castellano) Von Brockhoeft; m. Joseph Stewart Loggans, May 12, 1977. B.S. in Nursing La. State U., New Orleans, 1977. Staff nurse Oktibbeha County Gen. Hosp., Starkville, Miss., 1977-78; charge nurse Lowdnes County Gen. Hosp., Columbus, Miss., 1978-79, F.E. Hebert Hosp., New Orleans, 1979-81; asst. unit dir. East Jefferson Hosp., Metairie, La., 1981—. Mem. Ctr. for Environ. (Save the Whales) Edn., Washington, 1982—. Mem. Nat. Wildlife Fedn., Nat. Audubon Soc., Greenpeace. Republican. Roman Catholic. Home: 3805 Houma Blvd Apt B-303 Metairie LA 70002 Office: East Jefferson Hosp 4200 Houma Blvd Metairie LA 70002

LOGIUDICE, ROSEMARY JOANNE, veterinarian; b. Albany, N.Y., Feb. 5, 1955; d. Frank Joseph and Mafalda Rosalie (DeVirgilio) LoGiudice. B.S. with honors in Agr., U. Ill., 1977, B.S. in Vet. Medicine, 1979, D.V.M., 1981. Lic. veterinarian. Student vet. asst. Oak Knoll Animal Hosp., Ltd., Moline, Ill., 1974-81; vet. Plato Computer programmer Coll. Vet. Medicine, U. Ill., Urbana, 1978-81; student vet. asst. Quad City Downs and Friendship Farms, East Moline, Ill., 1974-79; staff veterinarian Ingmire Large Animal Clinic, Joliet, Ill., 1981-83, staff veterinarian, corp. ptnr., 1983—; Dept. Agr. meat inspector Illini Beef Packers, Inc., Geneseo, and Wilson Foods, Monmouth, Ill., 1979. Editor U. Ill. Coll. Vet. Medicine Yearbook, 1980. Choir dir. St. John's Cath. Chapel, Champaign, Ill., 1974-79; mem. Peoria Cath. Diocese Liturgical Music Commn., 1975-77; coach nat. champion team Ill. Arabian Horse Assn. Youth Horse Judging Team, 1978, also mem. nat. res. champion team, 1972; mem. U. Ill. Women's Glee Club, 1973-79, pres., 1975-76, tour mgr., 1973-74; mem. U. Ill. Horse Judging Team, 1975-77; coach youth horse judging team Will County 4-H Clubs, Joliet, Ill., 1981-82; alto soloist Joliet Community Chorale, 1982—. Recipient U. Ill. Mother's Assn. award, 1973. Mem. Am. Assn. Equine Practitioners, Ill. State Vet. Med. Assn. (equine practitioners com. 1981—), Kankakee Valley Vet. Med. Assn. (program chmn. 1983-84), AVMA (Outstanding Service award U. Ill. Student chpt.), Mortar Bd. (pres. 1977), Omega Tau Sigma (pres. 1980, Outstanding Sr. award 1981), Gamma Sigma Delta, Alpha Zeta, Atius, Alpha Lambda Delta. Roman Catholic. Club: Upper Midwest Competitive and Endurance Ride Assn. (ride veterinarian 1981—). Office: Ingmire Large Animal Clinic Ltd 1410 Mills Rd Joliet IL 60433

LOGSDON, JUDITH MARIE, nurse; b. Los Angeles, July 4, 1951; d. Charles George and Carolyn Winifred (Smock) L. A.S., Rio Hondo Coll., 1974. Registered nurse, Calif. Telephone receptionist R.V. Dorweiler Co., El Monte, Calif., 1970-71; apprentice animal groomer, Calif., 1971-72; nurse, White Meml. Med. Ctr., Los Angeles, 1974-76, Kaiser Found. Hosp., San Francisco, 1976—. Mem. Am. Nurses Assn., Calif. Nurses Assn., Golden Gate Nurses Assn., Nursing Mothers Counsel (San Francisco regional chpt.). Democrat. Lutheran. Club: Skiers Unlimited (Lake Tahoe).

LOGUE, LOIS JOAN, medical technologist, medical association executive; b. Mt. Pleasant, Mich., June 28, 1936; d. Daniel Edward and Thelma Margaret (Hanke) Hughes; student U. Tex., 1954-56; B.S., Incarnate World Coll., 1958; m. William J. Logue, Jr., Oct. 12, 1957; children—Kathleen Sue, William Joseph. Hematology supr. Meml. Hosp. of Chester County, West Chester, Pa., 1967-68; adminstrv. technologist Paoli (Pa.) Meml. Hosp., 1968-78; adminstrv. dir. Nat. Com. for Clin. Lab. Standards, Villanova, Pa., 1979-84; exec. dir. Clin. Lab. Mgmt. Assn., Paoli, Pa., 1984—; v.p. Health Systems Concepts Inc., 1985—; key man State of Pa. for Am. Soc. Med. Technologists, 1977-82. Recipient Chi Omega award for outstanding service to the Profession, Am. Soc. Med. Technologists, 1980, 81. Mem. Am. Soc. Clin. Pathologists, Am. Soc. Med. Technologists, Clin. Lab. Mgmt. Assn. (nat. pres. 1978-79, dir. 1977—, pres. Del. Valley chpt. 1977-80), Clin. Ligand Assay Soc., Chi Omega. Republican. Roman Catholic. Mem. editorial bd. Lab. World, 1978-82. Home: 601 Waynesfield Dr Newtown Square PA 19073 Office: 195 W Lancaster Ave Paoli PA 19301

LOGUE, PEGGY KING, accounting executive; b. Washington, Oct. 30, 1958; d. Lloyd Lee and Barbara (Allen) King; m. Stephen Andrew Logue, Aug. 28, 1982 (separated Dec. 1985); 1 child, Travis Stephen. B.S. in Acctg., Tenn. Tech. U., 1981; postgrad. in bus. adminstrn. Southeastern U., Washington, 1984—. Asst. fin. mgr. Associated Real Estate Mgmt., McLean, Va., 1981-84; collection adminstr. Rolm Corp., Vienna, 1984; jr. acct. Verdix Corp., Chantilly, Va., 1984-85, acctg. supr., 1985—. Mem. NOW, Nat. Assn. Female Execs. Avocations: running; bicycling; softball; swimming. Home: 713 Brethour Ct Sterling VA 22170 Office: Verdix Corp 14130-A Sullyfield Circle Chantilly VA 22021

LOHAN, DIANE LEGGE, architect; b. Englewood, N.J., Dec. 4, 1949; d. Richard C. and Patricia (Roney) Legge; student Wellesley Coll. 1967-69, B.A. in Architecture, Stanford U., 1972; M.Arch., Princeton U., 1975; m. Dirk Lohan, Dec. 1, 1978. Draftsman various firms, N.Y.C. and Calif., 1970-75; designer The Ehrenkrantz Group, N.Y.C., 1975-77; Successively assoc., assoc. partner, now partner Skidmore, Owings & Merrill, Chgo. Mem. Met. Housing and Planning Council. Mem. AIA, Nat. Council Archtl. Registration Bds. Clubs: Racquet of Chgo., Arts, Tavern, Chgo. Yacht. Designs include: Ritz Carlton Hotel Addition, Boston, 1980, Chgo. Tribune Printing Plant, 1981. Office: Skidmore Owings and Merrill 33 W Monroe St Chicago IL 60603*

LOHMAN, MARION BETH SIMPSON BECKER, educational administrator; b. Sheridan, Mont., Nov. 30, 1918; d. Thomas Alexander and Maude Murilla (Bullerdick) Simpson; m. Peter Wilson Becker, June 28, 1941 (dec.); children—Laura Lynn, Karen Lee, Joyce Lenore; m. 2d, Michael S. Lohman, July 12, 1976 (dec.). Teaching degree Mont. State Normal Coll., 1939; B.S., Gonzaga U., 1956, M.S., 1964. Cert. librarian, Calif. Tchr., Mont. State Orphans Home, Twin Bridges, 1939-41, Post Falls, Idaho, 1952-54; librarian Greenacres Jr. High Sch., Spokane, Wash., 1956-63; media coordinator Edison High Sch., Huntington Beach, Calif., 1963—; exec. rep. Crescent Cement Co., Costa Mesa, Calif., 1977-83. Sponsor Chess Club (nat. championship 1975), other sch. clubs. Served to chief yoeman USCG, 1942-45. Mem. Calif. Tchrs. Assn., Nat. Curriculum, Assn. Supervision and Curriculum Devel., Am. Bus. Profl. Women. Republican. Lodge: Order Eastern Star (life). Home: 3244 New York Ave Costa Mesa CA 92626 Office: Edison High Sch 21400 Magnolia St Huntington Beach CA 92646

LOHR, CATHERINE ODETTE, writer, consultant; b. Bronx, N.Y., Jan. 8, 1949; d. Lydia Fabienne (Sananès) L. B.A., U. Mass./Boston State Coll., 1981; cert. in electronics, Women's Tech. Inst., Boston, 1983. Telephone cons. Americall Answering Service, Brookline, Mass., 1966-82; dir. Women's Ctr. of Boston State Coll., 1979-81; researcher Mass. Research Corp., Boston, 1982; transp. cons. Bay State Taxi Assn., Brookline, 1983; writer Dynamics Research Corp., Wilmington, Mass., 1983—. Author poetry, pamphlets. Mem. Network Women in Trade and Tech. Jobs, Nat. Women's Mailing List, Daus. of Bilitis, Psi Chi. Jewish. Club: Randolph (Mass.) Country.

LOKMER, STEPHANIE ANN, pharmaceutical sales representative, consultant; b. Wheeling, W.Va., Nov. 14, 1957; d. Joseph Steven and Mary Ann (Mozney) L. B.A. in Communications, Bethany Coll., 1980. Vice-pres., Wheeling Coffee and Spice, W.Va., 1981-82; pharm. sales rep. Bristol Labs., Wheeling, 1982-84, pharm. hosp. rep., 1984-85; pharm. sales rep. Boehringer Ingelheim, Nashville, 1985—; exec. v.p. cons. Wheeling Coffee and Spice Co., Inc., 1981—. Recipient cert. of achievement Bristol Labs., 1982. Mem. Nat. Assn. Female Execs., Mid.-Tenn. Pharm. Assn., Zeta Tau Alpha. Republican. Roman Catholic. Avocations: flying; traveling; biking; reading. Home: 327 Lakebrink Dr Nashville TN 37214

LOMAN, DIANE LOUISE MOORE, nurse, sales representative; b. Connellsville, Pa., Feb. 22, 1948; d. Glenn and Dorothy May (Eager) Moore; m. Terry Eugene Loman, Apr. 4, 1970; children—Kimberly Joan, Kathy Lynn. Diploma in Nursing with honors, Mercy Hosp. Sch. Nursing, Johnstown, Pa., 1969; A.A. with high honors, U. S.C., 1978. Staff nurse Brunswick Hosp. and Clinic, Memphis, 1972, Ochsner Hosp. Stress Unit, New Orleans, 1981; nurse supr. New River Nursing Home, Jacksonville, N.C., 1973-77, Willowwood Home for Jewish Aged, New Orleans, 1979-80; dir. nursing Elderlodge (formerly New River Nursing Home), Jacksonville, N.C., 1981-84; sales rep. E.F. Hutton Life, N.Y. Life, Jacksonville, 1984-85; nurse specialist, mgr. Portamedic Health Care, Harrisburg, Pa., 1986. Mem. Johnstown Community Chorus, 1968-69. Served to lt. (j.g.) USNR, 1969-71. Recipient letter of appreciation USNR, 1971. Mem. N.C. Nurses Assn. (pres. dist. 1977), Life Underwriters Assn., Am. Bus. Women's Assn., Assn. Rehab. Nurses, Phi Theta Kappa, Gamma Beta Phi (coordinator tutoring). Republican. Roman Catholic. Home: 2300 Lincoln St Camp Hill PA 17011 Office: 875 Poplar Church Rd Camp Hill PA 17011

LOMAN, HELAINE BETH, securities company executive; b. Newark, May 7, 1960; d. Irwin Maurice and Myrna (Cooperman) L. B.A., Brown U., 1982. With accelerated ops. mgmt. dept. Merrill Lynch, N.Y.C., 1982-83, supr. regional ops., Phila., 1983-85, asst. ops. mgr., 1985-86; methods analyst Drexel Burnham Lambert, 1986—. Democrat. Jewish. Home: 440 E 81st St Apt LH New York NY 10028 Office: 60 Broad St New York NY 10004

LOMAX, DONNA LUCINDA, wholesale/retail giftware company executive; b. Washington, Aug. 15, 1945; d. George Weston and Evelyn Mae (Cawthorne) Jennings; m. LeRoy Alphonso Brannock, June 18, 1963 (div. 1967); children—Tracey Angela, Lisa Michelle; m. 2d, James Webster Lomax, May 19, 1968; children—Jasmine, Alexandria. Student D.C. Tchrs. Coll., 1960-62; Strayer Coll., 1976-78. Pres. Jimmys Light Experience, Washington, 1969-75; night supr. Cadwalder Wickersham & Taft, Washington, 1979-81; pres. Donna's Place, Washington, 1980—; mgr. Donna and Daughters, Washington, 1983—. Mem. Am. Assn. Black Women Entrepreneurs (nat. sec. 1982-83). Democrat. Episcopalian. Home: 2308 Park Pl SE Washington DC 20020

LOMAX, LOUISE LE DONYA, nurse; b. Atlanta, Sept. 1; d. Eddie, Sr., and Cluster Pearl (Slayton) Lomax. R.N., Lamar Sch. Nursing, Univ. Hosp., Augusta, Ga.; B.A., H.H. Lehman Coll., 1978, M.S., 1982; postgrad. Columbia

Pacific U. Staff nurse Bellevue Hosp., N.Y.C., 1947-54, N.Y. Hosp., N.Y.C., 1954-55; night supr. Hunts Point Hosp., Bronx, N.Y., 1955-56; psychiat. nurse Bronx Mcpl. Hosp. Center, 1956-60; pvt. duty nurse, 1960-71; psychiat. asst. head nurse Bronx VA Hosp. Med. Center, 1970—, nursing adminstrv. coordinator for nights, 1984—; health resource person Community Orgn., Bronx, 1980—. Contbr. articles to publs. Mem. Am. Nurses Assn., Am. Found. Nurses, N.Y. State Nurses Assn. Democrat.

LOMBARD, SUSAN, corp. exec.; b. Greenfield, Iowa, Oct. 4, 1942; d. Myron L. and Maudelln (Wallace) L.; B.A. in Polit. Sci., Grinnell Coll., 1964. Exec. sec. Coast Fed. Savs. & Loan Assn., Los Angeles, 1975-76; adminstrv. asst. to pres. Western Asset Mgmt., Los Angeles, 1977-78; adminstr. Baker Ancel & Hall, Los Angeles, 1979-80; corp. sec., adminstr. Dynasty Computer Corp., Dynasty Mfg. Co. and Dynasoft, Inc., Dallas, 1980—. Mem. Nat. Assn. Female Execs., Meeting Planners Internat. Republican. Home: 13354 Emily Rd Dallas TX 75240 Office: 14240 Midway Rd Dallas TX 75234

LOMBARDO, CATHLEEN J., engineer; b. Bridgeport, Conn., Jan. 2, 1961; d. Anthony and Josephine (Euzzine) L. B.S. in Mech. Engring., Northeastern U., 1984. Staff engr. Metcalf & Eddy, Inc., Silver Spring, Md., 1984-85; mech. engr. seal systems command Dept. of Navy, Washington, 1986—. Mem. Nat. Assn. Female Execs., Asme. Avocations: biking, swimming, photography. Home: 2817 38th St NW Washington DC 20007 Office: Dept of Navy Naval Sea Systems Command Crystal City Washington DC 20376

LOMEGA, DOLORES CORTE, importing company executive; b. Jersey City, June 16, 1934; d. Manuel and Encarnacao (Gomes) Corte; m. Michael Lomega, June 21, 1959 (dec. 1967); children—Susan, Michael Jr., Ellen, David. B.A., Montclair State U., 1955. Tchr. St. Mary's Sch., Rutherford, N.J., 1955-59; salesperson Corte & Co., Jersey City, 1967-71; chief exec. officer Cortco Internat., Newark, 1975—; v.p. Portuguese Continental Ins. Co., Newark, 1978-80, Portuguese Continental Fedn. Credit Union, Newark, 1980-81. Trustee Rutherford Bd. Edn., 1980-85, pres., 1985-86; bd. dirs. Garden State Theater Co., Rutherford, 1983-85; chairperson Selective Service System, Bergen City, N.J., 1983-85; dir. Portugal-U.S. C. of C., N.Y.C., 1984-86. Mem. Nat. Assn. Specialty Foods to Trade, Am. Mgmt. Assn. Democrat. Roman Catholic. Avocations: reading; writing; acting; singing. Office: Cortco Internat Corp 419 Hoboken Ave Jersey City NJ 07306

LOMONTE, LANECE POPE, educator; b. Trinity County, Tex., Sept. 4, 1934; d. Alton Lee and Bonnie Irene (Lawrence) Pope; B.S., Sam Houston State U., 1954, postgrad. 1961; M.Ed., U. Md., 1967; 1 dau., Emily Chandler. Asst. to dir. food services Dow Chem., Freeport, Tex., 1954-59; instr. Georgetown Visitation Coll., Washington, 1962-63; tchr. Anne Arundel County (Md.) public schs., 1963-70; asst. to dir. admissions St. John's Coll., Md., 1970-72; owner S:HE, Annapolis and Dallas, 1972-78; adminstrv. aide Hubbard & Assos., Dallas, 1977-80; contracts coordinator Community Health Computing, Houston, 1980-81; tchr. Spring Branch (Tex.) Public Schs., 1981—; cons. U. Md., 1964-70. Active, Nottingham W. Civic Assn., Houston, 1980—. Mem. AAUW, Am. Home Econs. Assn. Democrat. Episcopalian. Home: 14007 Myrtlea Houston TX 77079

LONDON, CHARLOTTE ISABELLA, reading specialist; b. Guyana, S.Am., June 11, 1946; came to U.S., 1966, naturalized, 1980; d. Samuel Alphonso and Diana Dallett (Daniels) Edwards; B.Sc., Fort Hays State U., 1971; M.S., Pa. State U., 1974, Ph.D., 1977; m. David Timothy London, May 26, 1968; children—David Tshombe, Douglas Tshaka. Elem. sch. tch., Guyana, 1962-66, secondary sch. tchr., 1971-72; instr. lang. arts Pa. State U., University Park, 1973-74; reading specialist/ednl. cons. N.Y.C. Community Coll., 1975; dir. skills acquisition and devel. center Stockton (N.J.) State Coll., 1975-77; reading specialist Pleasantville (N.J.) Public Schs., 1977—; v.p. Atlantic County P.T.A., 1980-82; del. N.J. Gov.'s Conf. Future Edn. N.J., 1981 Sec. Atlantic County Minority Polit. Women's Caucus. Mem. Internat. Reading Assn., Nat. Council Tchrs. English, Assn. Supervision and Curriculum Devel., NEA, N.J. Ednl. Assn., AAUW, Pi Lambda Theta, Phi Delta Kappa (sec.). Mem. African Methodist Episcopal Ch. Home: 1419 Cedar Dr Mays Landing NJ 08330 Office: Pleasantville Pub Schs West Decatur Ave Pleasantville NJ 08232

LONDON, FLORENCE AILEEN, realtor; b. N.Y.C., Nov. 9, 1932; d. Murray Abraham and Grace Sarah (Gold) Stern; m. Jerome Howard London, Sept. 30, 1956; children—Lisa, Mona, Lari, Mark. Student U. Miami (Fla.), 1950, UCLA, 1950-52. Lic. real estate broker, Calif. mgr. Golden Touch Realty Co., Palm Springs, 1975-78; owner London & Co. Realty, Palm Springs, 1978—; cons. Real Estate Appraisers, Palm Springs, 1975—. Co-chmn. Sister Cities Internat., 1968-80; mem. Desert Mus., Palm Springs, 1983. Recipient Sister City Best Single award Reader's Digest, 1973. Mem. Nat. Assn. Realtors, Palm Springs Bd. Realtors, Calif. Assn. Realtors. Club: Racquet (Palm Springs). Home: 566 Fern Canyon Dr Palm Springs CA 92262 Office: Flo London & Co Realtors 467 E Tahquitz St Palm Springs CA 92262

LONDON, MARY ELLEN LEWIS, ednl. cons. and coordinator; b. Hutchinson, Kans., Apr. 3, 1927; d. Chester Iaasic and Edna Louise (Anderson) Lewis; grad. in Fine Arts/Edn., Kans. U., 1949; M.A. in Early Childhood Edn., Goddard Coll., 1973; m. Jesse London, Sept. 30, 1967; 1 son by previous marriage, Richard Norman Batie. Design engr. Boeing, Wichita, Kans., 1952-59; supr., trainer Parent Child Guidance Center Head Start, Los Angeles, 1968-74, Fedn. Head Start trainer, supr., 1974-78; pvt. practice cons. early childhood edn., Los Angeles, 1971—; dir. Creative Environment Learning Center, Los Angeles, 1971-73; instr., asst. prof. Long Beach (Calif.) State U., 1975-77; asst. prof. early childhood edn. Pepperdine U., Los Angeles, 1975-78, Calif. State U. Los Angeles, 1980—, Pacific Oaks Coll., 1980—, LaVerne (Calif.) U., 1975—; field coordinator state program career incentive program Inst. for Profl. Devel., 1978-80; dir. Assistance League Day Nursery, 1981—; adv. bd. on follow through Graham Elem. Sch.; adv. bds. on early childhood edn. S.W. Coll., Valley City Coll., Compton Coll., Dominguez Hills U., Calif. State U. Long Beach; adv. bds. Harbor Coll., El Camino Coll.; cons. assessor Urban Inst., Region IX ACYF-HEW, 1979—. Recipient awards Kans. Regional Art Exhibit, 1944, Head Start, 1968, 75, efficiency economy award Lockheed, 1962; tchr. tng. cert. OEO, 1966; Supr. of Yr. trophy Head Start, 1974, 78. Mem. So. Calif. Assn. for Edn. Young Children (Los Angeles v.p., 1976-78), Calif. Assn. for Edn. Young Children (chmn. Internat. Yr. of Child, 1978-79), Nat. Assn. for Edn. Young Children (governing bd., public policy task group, Washington, 1977—, local coordinator conf., Anaheim, 1976), Child Devel. Consortium (field rep., Washington 1975), Alpha Kappa Alpha (Black Heritage chmn., 1977-79, 25 year medalion, 1979, community service award, 1979, exhibit award, 1979), Black Women's Forum Los Angeles, Exec. Female, Methodist. Artist, organist, dress designer; participant art exhibit, Oakland, Calif., 1965; author: Creative Environment Learning Center, 1973. Home: 1235 Stearns Dr Los Angeles CA 90035 Office: 1375 St Andrews Pl Los Angeles CA 90028

LONDON, MIMI, interior design company executive, furniture and accessory designer; b. San Francisco, Nov. 6, 1936; d. Dan E. and Claire (Chester) L. Student Conn. Coll. for Women, 1954-56. Fashion model Ford Agy., N.Y.C., 1959-64; news reporter Sta. KQED-TV, San Francisco, 1968-70; mineral and fossil art dealer London Assocs., San Francisco and La Jolla, Calif., 1969-71; pres. London Marquis Inc., Los Angeles, 1973-85; Mimi London, Inc., 1985—; guest speaker UCLA Sch. Design, 1976—. Episcopalian. Office: Mimi London Inc Suite 151 8687 Melrose St Los Angeles CA 90069

LONERGAN, JOYCE, state legislator; b. Benton County, Iowa, Mar. 5, 1934; d. Robert and Fannie Mary (Duda) Jacobi; student public schs.; m. Paul J. Lonergan (dec.); children—Patrick Joseph, Peter Thomas, Kathleen Ann, Staci Marie. Mem. Iowa Ho. of Reps. from 87th Dist., 1975—. Mem. Nat. Order Women Legislators, Am. Bus. Women's Assn. Democrat. Roman Catholic. Office: State House Des Moines IA 50319

LONETREE, GEORGIA L., rehabilitation counselor; b. Portage, Wis., Sept. 22, 1946; d. Edward and Minnie I. (Decorah) L.; children—Lucinda J., Aaron E. Yazzie. B.S. in Vocat. Rehab., U. Wis.-Stout, 1976, postgrad., 1976-77; M.S. in Vocat. Rehab. Counseling, U. Wis., 1981, postgrad., 1981-82. Team tchr. U. Wis.-Stout, 1976, Native Am. coordinator ednl. and cultural enrichment program, 1977-78; statewide specialist Indian edn. and community programs U. Wis. Extension, 1978-79; sec. to tribal atty. Wis. Winnebago Bus. Com., Madison, 1980; rehab. counselor intern Waisman Ctr. Mental Retardation and Human Devel., U. Wis., 1981, project evaluator Madison Indian parent com., 1981-82; vocat. evaluator, edn. coordinator Project Hogan Naa Nish, Navajo Vocat. Rehab. Program, Tuba City, Ariz., 1982-83; homeliving specialist guidance dept. Shonto (Ariz.) Boarding Sch., 1984—; instr. rehab. edn. Navajo Community Coll., Tsaile, Ariz. Vocat. adv. com. Tuba City High Sch., 1982; treas. Wisconsin Dells chpt. Native Am. Ch., 1979-80; sec.-treas. Ho-Chunk Housing Authority, Wis. Winnebago Bus. Com., Nekoosa, 1979-80; past officer, mem. Native Am. Awareness Club, U. Wis.-Stout, 1972-76. Continuing edn. scholar Dells Indian Club, Inc., 1982; Am. Indians into Grad. Edn. fellow, 1981-82; Advanced Opportunity fellow, 1980-81; recipient Am. Indian Scholarship award, 1976, Chancellor's award for high acad. achievement, 1975. Mem. Am. Rehab. Counseling Assn., Am. Personnel and Guidance Assn. Home: 752 Spruce St PO Box 364 Shonto AZ 86054

LONG, BARBARA, travel agent; b. Montclair N.J., Dec. 15, 1938; d. George H. and Marjorie (Beaumont) Richards; children—Kirsten Jacobsen, Keely Jacobsen. B.A., Finch Coll., 1960. Pres., Wabba Travel, Basking Ridge, N.J., 1973—, Barjac, 1980—. Author: Guide to Lagos, 1963; Guide to Melbourne, 1967. Mem. Nat. Soc. Arts and Letters (program chmn. 1984-85). Avocations: sailing; pottery; painting. Home: PO Box 267 Bernardsville NJ 07924 Office: Wabba Proprietory Ltd PO Box 436 Basking Ridge NJ 07920

LONG, BETTYE VIRGINIA, financial manager; b. Bernice, La., July 13, 1924; d. Luther C. and Bernice Elaine (Lowrey) Bolt; m. Henry Lawrence Long, Oct. 20, 1946; children—Larry T., Charles E., L. Allan, J. Steve. A.A., Kilgore Coll., 1943; B.A. in Gen. Studies, U. Tex.-Tyler, 1980. Mng. trustee The Long Trusts, Kilgore, Tex., 1954-78, joint mgr., 1978—; sec.-treas. Rusk County Well Service, Kilgore, 1970—, Cherokee Oil Traders, Kilgore, 1972-79, pres., 1979—. Mem. Tex. Hist. Commn., Austin, 1979—, vice chmn., 1983-84; treas. Kilgore Sesquicentennial Commn., 1983—; pres. Mental Health Assn., Gregg County (Tex.), 1984. Named First Lady of Kilgore, Beta Sigma Phi Sorority, 1985. Mem. East Tex. Independent Producers and Royalty Owners Assn., Tex. Independent Producers and Royalty Owners Assn., Evergreen Garden Club (pres. 1967-68). Baptist. Club: Cherokee (Longview, Tex.) (pres. 1985). Avocations: travel; reading; collecting antiques. Office: The Long Trusts 118 S Kilgore St Kilgore TX 75662

LONG, BEVERLY WHITAKER, speech communication educator; b. Memphis, July 16, 1936; d. Earl and Berniece (Sifford) Whitaker; B.A., Hendrix Coll., Conway, Ark., 1957; M.A., La. State U., 1962, Ph.D., 1967; m. William F. Long, Dec. 13, 1975. Dir. speech and drama Newport (Ark.) High Sch., 1957-60; teaching asst., instr. speech La. State U., 1966; instr. S.W. Tex. State U., 1962-65; mem. faculty U. Tex., Austin, 1967-76; adj. prof. DePauw U., Greencastle, Ind., 1976-77; chmn. dept. speech communication U. N.C., Chapel Hill, 1978-83, prof., 1978—. Recipient Communication Teaching Excellence award U. Tex., 1971; grantee U. Tex. Research Inst., 1975, Pogue Research Inst., 1982. Mem. Speech Communication Assn. (pres. 1985), Assn. Communication Adminstrs., So. Speech Communication Assn. (pres. 1975), Nat. Council Tchrs. English, Am. Theatre Assn., Am. Soc. Aesthetics, Brit. Soc. Aesthetics, MLA, Modern Poetry Assn., N.C. Speech and Drama Assn. Democrat. Methodist. Clubs: Chapel Hill Country; U. N.C. Faculty. Coauthor: Group Performance of Literature, 1977; Performing Literature, 1982. Editor Lit. in Performance, 1979-83; co-editor: Contemporary Speech, 1977. Contbr. articles, revs. to profl. jours. Home: 313 Country Club Rd Chapel Hill NC 27514 Office: 210 Bingham Hall 007A U NC Chapel Hill NC 27514

LONG, BONNIE SINE, company executive; b. New Market, Va., Sept. 28, 1950; d. James Lester Sine and Doris Try (Wilkinson) Grim; m. Louis Franklin Southerd, Sept. 12, 1969 (div. 1974); 1 child, Tiage A.D. A.S. magna cum laude, Piedmont Va. Coll., 1976; B.S. cum laude, U. Md., 1986. Asst. ednl. resource mgr. Assn. Trial Lawyers Am., Washington, 1977-79; sales mgr. Skyline Inn, Washington, 1979-80; membership services dir. Gen. Fedn. Women's Clubs, Washington, 1980-81; fin. program analyst Advance Technology, Inc., Crystal City, Va., 1981-83; pres. Body Connections, Inc., Gaithersburg, Md., 1983—; sec./treas., bd. dirs. Corp. Systems Technology, Indian Head, Md., 1982—. Editor, designer artwork for flyers and programs ATLA, 1977-79; designer logos for tee shirts, 1976-78; designer advt., 1983—. Researcher on pay discrimination U. Md., 1985; bd. dirs., sec. Methodist Ch., New Carrollton, Md., 1977-78. Mem. Nat. Assn. Female Execs., Gold Key Honor Soc., Mensa. Avocations: Reading and writing science fiction; art; piano; travel. Home: 4910 Hollywood Rd College Park MD 20740

LONG, CATHY (MRS. GILLIS LONG), mem. U.S. Congress; b. Dayton; m. Gillis W. Long; (dec.); children—George Harrison, Janis Catherine. B.A. in Sociology/Psychology, La. State U., 1948. Formerly staff asst. to U.S. Senator Wayne Morse, U.S. Congressman James Polk; mem. 99th Congress from 8th Dist., La., 1985—. Del., Democratic Nat. Conv., 1980, 84; mem. La. Democratic Fin. Council; dir. spl. events Spl. Olympics; research asst. Grocery Manufacturers of Am.; lectr. Washington Inc.; mem. Gillis W. Long Poverty Law Ctr. Com., Loyola U., New Orleans; mem. Nat. Council Sr. Citizens; fundraiser Nat. Inst. Neural Research; mem. Nat. Trust Historic Preservation, M.A.D.D. (Mothers Against Drunk Driving), AMVETS, La. State Med. Planning Bd., La. Arts Council, Rapides Parish Library Bd., Rapides Parish Symphony Guild. Served with USN. Mem. AAUW. Address: 1338 Longworth Washington DC 20515*

LONG, DANA LEE CHRISTENSON, court referee; b. East Chicago, Ind., Dec. 9, 1952; d. Milford Paul and Margaret Mary (Mosny) Christenson; m. Dennis Allan Long, Dec. 20, 1975. B.S. with distinction, Ind. U., 1975, M.S. with distinction, 1977, J.D., 1980. Bar: Ind. 1980, U.S. Dist. Ct. (so. dist.) Ind. 1980. Math. tchr. Highland Jr. and Sr. High Schs. (Ind.), 1974-75, East Chicago Roosevelt High Sch. (Ind.), 1975-76; apt. mgr. Long Real Estate Investments, Bloomington, Ind., 1976-80; instr. bus. law Ind. State U., Terre Haute, 1980; law clk. Mallor and Assocs., Bloomington, 1980; ct. referee, judge pro tem Brown Cir. Ct., Nashville, Ind., 1980—; dir. Tri-L Corp., Bloomington. Recipient Bausch and Lomb Sci. award, 1971. Mem. ABA, Ind. Bar Assn., Brown County Bar Assn., Lambda Alpha Delta. Home: 4409 Scenic Dr Bloomington IN 47401 Office: Brown Circuit Ct PO Box 85 Nashville IN 47448

LONG, ELIZABETH EHLERS, lawyer; b. Fresno, Calif., Oct. 2, 1936; d. Henry and Mary (Wilson) Ehlers; m. Clay C. Long, June 21, 1959; children—Mary Pender, Catherine Ehlers. A.B., U. Calif.-Berkeley, 1958; postgrad. London Sch. Econs., 1958-59; J.D., Emory U., 1975. Bar: Ga. 1975. Exec. sec. Harvard U., Cambridge, Mass., 1959-60, adminstrv. asst., 1960-61; law clk. Ga. Supreme Ct., Atlanta, 1975-77; assoc. firm King & Spalding, 1977-79; ptnr. firm Gordon & Long, 1979—. Bd. dirs., pres. Council on Battered Women, 1984—. Mem. ABA, Ga. Assn. Women Lawyers, Ga. Bar Assn., Atlanta Bar Assn., Found. Women Lawyers. Home: 997 Nawench Dr NW Atlanta GA 30327 Office: Gordon & Long 230 Peachtree St NW Suite 300 Atlanta GA 30303

LONG, ERNESTINE MARTHA JOULLIAN, educator; b. St. Louis, Nov. 14, 1906; d. Ernest Cameron and Alice (Joullian) Long; A.B., U. Wis., 1927; M.S., U. Chgo., 1932; Ph.D., St. Louis U., 1975; postgrad. Washington U., St. Louis, 1932-68, Eastman Sch. Music, 1956, (NSF fellow) So. Ill. U., 1969-70. Tchr. scis. pub. schs. Normandy dist., St. Louis, 1927-66, Red Bud, Ill., 1966-70, St. Louis, 1970-75; coordinator continuing edn. U. Mo., St. Louis, 1976-79; ednl. cons. Area IV, St. Louis Pub. Schs. Recipient Community Service award St. Louis Newspaper Guild, 1978-79. Mem. AAAS, Am. Inst. Physics, Am. Physics Tchrs. Assn., Am. Personnel and Guidance Assn. (treas. St. Louis br. 1954), Am. Chem. Soc., Central Assn. Sch. Sci. Math. Tchrs. (chmn. chemistry sect.), Am. Soc. for Microbiology, LWV, St. Louis Symphony Soc. (women's div., docent), Am. Guild Organists, NEA, Nat. Sci. Tchrs. Assn. Home: 245 N Price Rd Ladue MO 63124

LONG, IRENE DUHART, physician. Student Northwestern U.; M.D., St. Louis U. Diplomate in preventive medicine (aerospace medicine). Gen. surgery intern Cleve. Clinic; resident Mt. Sinai Hosp., Cleve., Wright State U. Sch. Medicine, Dayton, Ohio; now chief Med. and Environ. Health Office, NASA Kennedy Space Center, Fla. Address: NASA Kennedy Space Center Medical and Environmental Health Office MD-MED Kennedy Space Center FL 32899

LONG, JUDY LEE, brokerage executive; b. Washington, Nov. 5, 1944; d. Albert Leroy Krause and Dorothy Ida (McDaniel) Krause Hubscher; m. Robert P. Long, Sept. 7, 1973 (div. July 1982). Grad. high sch., South Whitley, Ind. Adminstrv. asst. Redwood Electric Co., Beltsville, Md., 1971-73; sr. sales asst., mgr.'s sec. Merrill Lynch, Hallandale, Fla., 1974-80, account exec., 1980—. Mem. Nat. Orgn. Women in Sales, Nat. Assn. Female Execs. Democrat. Methodist. Office: Merrill Lynch 1250 Hallandale Blvd Hallandale FL 33009

LONG, LINDA JEAN, speech educator, consultant; b. Dallas, Jan. 26, 1934; d. Clarence Tandy and Tommy (Hughes) Cadenhead; m. Gene Felton Giggleman, Aug. 11, 1950 (dec. Dec. 1979); children—Gene Felton, Karen, Craig Martin; m. 2d, Ralph Lamar Long, May 23, 1981. A.A., El Centro Coll., 1969; B.F.A., So. Meth. U., 1971; M.S., North Tex. State U., 1974; Ed.D., East Tex. State U., 1978. Sec. Reliance Ins. Co., Dallas, 1957-69; prof. Mountain View Coll., Dallas, 1971-78; prof. speech North Lake Coll., Irving, Tex., 1978—; cons. speech, Dallas, 1978—. Author workbook: Voice and Diction, 1975. Mem Tex. Speech Communication Assn., Speech Communication Assn. Am., So. Speech Assn., Shakespeare Festival and Guild, Tex. Women's Polit. Caucus (del. 1981—), Soc. Prevention of Cruelty to Animals, Tex. Congress Parents and Tchrs. (life), Phi Delta Kappa, Zeta Phi Eta, Phi Theta Kappa. Democrat. Baptist. Home: 6336 Highgate Ln Dallas TX 75214 Office: North Lake Coll 5001 N MacArthur Irving TX 75038

LONG, LORNA ERICKSON, human resources executive; b. Worcester, Mass., Nov. 18, 1944; d. Roland Axel and Roxie Sophie Erickson; A.B., Mt. Holyoke Coll., 1966; m. Bruce C. Long, Sept. 8, 1972; children—Christopher Carson, Jessica Erickson. Various positions in personnel and mgmt., 1966-69; systems analyst Paul Revere Life Ins. Co. subs. Avco Corp., Worcester, Mass., 1970-71, personnel asst., 1971-74, mgr. compensation and benefits, 1974-78, v.p., 1980-84; corp. dir. compensation, corp. hdqrs. Avco Corp., Greenwich, Conn., 1978-79, corp. dir. compensation and benefits, 1979-80, exec. dir. human resources AVCO Corp., Greenwich, 1984—. Bd. dirs., chmn. personnel com. Montachusett council Girl Scouts U.S.A., Worcester, 1976-78, mem. nominating com. Montachusett council, 1982-83; mem. council, vice chmn. subcom., manpower planing council CETA adminstrn. City of Worcester, 1977-78. Republican. Home: 242 Stanwich Rd Greenwich CT 06830 Office: AVCO Corp 1275 King St Greenwich CT 06830

LONG, LYNDA ANNE CAREY, government official; b. Kingston, Pa., Oct. 5, 1942; d. William Henry and Thelma Loretta (Tripp) Carey; A.B.A., Benjamin Franklin U., 1978; m. John Devlin Long, July 21, 1978; children by previous marriage—James Sinkavitch, Ned Sinkavitch; stepchildren—John Devlin, Douglas, Debra, Teri. Mgmt. analyst Def. Nuclear Agy., Washington, 1973-77; dep. comptroller Orgn. Joint Chiefs of Staff, Pentagon, Washington, 1983—; mem. Nuclear Reporting Mgmt. Group, 1978-83, Computer Measurement Group, 1981—. Pres., Our Savior Luth. Parent Tchrs. Assn., 1971; mgr. Fed. Women's Program, Def. Nuclear Agy., 1982-83. Recipient outstanding performance awards, 1980-81, 81-82; cert. of achievement Def. Nuclear Agy., 1975, Meritorious Civilian Service award, 1983. Mem. Am. Soc. Mil. Comptrollers. Republican. Lutheran. Club: Pine Ridge Womens.

LONG, MARIA-TERESA ELIZABETH, financial planner; b. St. Louis, July 10, 1947; d. Terry and Mary-Louise Katharyn (Madden) Butler; B.S., N.E. Mo. State U., 1972; M.A., Washington U., 1973; m. Ellery Long, Sept. 21, 1975; 1 child, Korttné. Dir. guidance Kinloch (Mo.) High Sch., 1973-74; vocat. counselor Ferguson-Florissant Sch. Dist., Ferguson, Mo., 1974-79; fin. planner Met. Life Ins. Co., St. Louis, 1979-82, Prudential Ins. Co., Houston, 1982-83, gen. agt., 1983—; v.p. CAP Enterprises. Bd. dirs. Urban League Met. St. Louis, 1976—. Washington U. grantee, 1973. Mem. Am. Personnel and Guidance Assn., NEA (del., sec. 1976-77), Florissant-Ferguson Community Tchrs. Assn. (sec. 1976-77), Am. Vocat. Assn., Nat. Assn. Life Underwriters, Assn. Profl. Negotiations Teams, Delta Sigma Theta. Roman Catholic. Office: 7001 Corporate Dr Houston TX 77036

LONG, MARILYN LEONA, computer sales company executive; b. Canton, Ill., Apr. 11, 1944; d. John Henry and Charlotte A. (Merrill) Bolender; B.S.B.A., U. Denver, 1968, M.B.A., 1974. Mgr. fin. ops. Info. Handling Services (Indianhead), Denver, 1976-78; fin. analyst Mountain Bell, Denver, 1978-80; mgr. cost and inventory control PAMCO (Research-Cottrell), Denver, 1980-81; field acctg. mgr. NL Baroid/NL Industries, Denver, 1981-85; pres. System Solutions for Business, Inc., 1985—. C.P.A., Colo. Mem. Am. Inst. C.P.A.s, Am. Woman's Soc. C.P.A.s, Colo. Soc. C.P.A.s. Home: 10879 E Powers Dr Englewood CO 80111 Office: 2320 S Race Denver CO 80210

LONG, MARY COLE, retired English language educator, author; b. Dallas, Oct. 1, 1922; d. Ernest E. and Sadie Flynn (Boone) Farrow; B.A., Baylor U., 1944; M.A., 1965; m. William Bowman Long, June 3, 1944; children—William Farrow, Daryl Elizabeth, Robert John, Linda Sue. Instr. English. Mary Hardin-Baylor U., Belton, Tex., 1965-72, asst. prof. English, 1972-83. Pres., Leon Heights PTA, 1956, City Council PTA, 1957. Mem. Central Tex. Poetry Soc. (pres. 1972-77), Poetry Soc. Tex. Home: 415 Downing St Belton TX 76513

LONG, MAXINE CAMPBELL, microbiologist; b. Tazewell, Tenn., Jan. 27, 1929; d. Arthur L. and Elizabeth Grey (Ball) Campbell; B.A., U. Tenn., 1950; postgrad. Northwestern U., eves.; m. Robert H. Long, Mar. 31, 1951 (dec.); children—Russell L., Mary E. With Oak Ridge Health Dept., 1950-51; research asst., tissue technologist U. Chgo. Clinics, 1951-58; microbiologist Ill. Dept. Pub. Health, Chgo., 1958-70; microbiologist Ill. EPA, Chgo., 1970—, on detail to U.S. EPA Region V, 1976-80, quality assurance coordinator div. labs., Chgo., 1980—; speaker on quality assurance and lab. cert. to profl. groups. Sec., Harvard-St. George Sch. PTA, Chgo., 1971-72. Mem. Lake Michigan Water Analysts (pres. 1980), ASTM (mem. coms.), Am., Ill. (editor newsletter 1973-74) socs. for microbiology, Water Pollution Control Fedn. Mem. United Ch. of Hyde Park. Office: 2121 W Taylor St Chicago IL 60612

LONG, PHYLLIS WILLETTS, lawyer; b. Whiteville, N.C., Feb. 15, 1951; d. Adrian Larnell and Lois Jane (Sasser) Willetts; m. Atwood Edward Long, III, June 19, 1976. B.A. in Edn., U. N.C.-Chapel Hill, 1973; J.D., Washington and Lee U., Lexington, Va., 1980. Bar: N.C. 1980. Tchr., Fairmont City Schs. (N.C.), 1973-74; adminstrv. asst. N.C. Dept. Transp., Raleigh, 1974-76; atty. Springs Industries, Inc., Ft. Mill, S.C., 1980—. Mem. ABA, N.C. Bar Assn. (EEOC liason com. 1983—), Mecklenburg County Bar Assn. Republican. Methodist. Office: Springs Industries Inc 205 N White St Fort Mill SC 29715

LONG, RUTH MARY, interior contracting corporation executive; b. Somers Point, N.J., May 10, 1932; d. Lynford Preston and Luella (Golden) Fowles; m. Donald Keith Long, June 30, 1967. B.A., U. Fla., 1953. Mgr. corr. study dept. U. Fla. Bookstore, Gainesville, 1953-54; statistician Jacobs Jewelers, Jacksonville, Fla., 1955-56; claims rep. Social Security Adminstrn., Gastonia, N.C., Washington, 1956-67; adminstrv. coordinator Duncan Long, Inc., Long Island City, N.Y., 1967—; acctg. advisor Great Outdoors Pub. Co., St. Petersburg, Fla., 1979-80. Recipient Hon. Membership Fla. Players, 1955; Fla. Ho. of Reps. scholar, 1949. Democrat. Avocations: reading; collecting cookery books and lit.; Caribbean and Jamaican studies. Home: 531 Main St Apt 122 Roosevelt Island New York NY 10044 Office: Duncan Long Inc 10-40 46th Ave Long Island City NY 11101

LONG, SANDRA KAY, recreation administrator; b. Highland, Ill., May 30, 1949; d. Raymond Adolph and Eloise Charlene (Erickson) Long. B.S., Western Ill. U., 1971, postgrad., 1981-82. Asst. supt. recreation Lombard (Ill.) Park Dist., 1971-84, asst. dir. recreation, 1984—; teaching asst. dept. recreation and park adminstrn. Western Ill. U., Macomb, 1981-82. Mem. Lombard Youth Council, 1972-74, sec., 1979-81; mem. adv. com. Nat. Coll. Edn., Lombard, 1982-83. Mem. Nat. Recreation and Park Assn., Ill. Park and Recreation Assn. (mem. bd. adminstrn. and fin. sect. 1980), Ill. Community Edn. Assn. (asst. to exec. dir. 1982), Suburban Park and Recreation Assn. Mem. United Ch. of Christ. Home: 420 N Mill Rd Apt 12 Addison IL 60101 Office: Lombard Park Dist 150 S Park Ave Lombard IL 60148

LONG, SHARON LEE, publisher, writer; b. Buckhannon, W.Va., July 15, 1938; d. Albert H. and Edna G. (Slaughter) Hicks; student W.Va. Bus. Coll., 1956, U. Ill., 1958, U. Pitts., 1964-65; m. C. Alvin Long, Nov. 1966 (dec. 1975); children—C. Alvin, Lori Ellen. Newspaper reporter The Clarksburg Telegram, Clarksburg, W.Va., 1956-58; continuity dir. Sta. WPDX, Clarksburg, 1960-61; adminstrv. asst. Fuller, Smith & Ross, Pitts., 1962-64; adminstrv. asst. to program mgr. Sta. WIIC-TV, Pitts., 1964-66; media buyer Campbell Ewald Advt. Co., San Francisco, 1966; media dir. Long Advt. Co., San Jose, Calif., 1966-67; pres. Lee Rothchild, Ltd. and subsidiaries, 1980—. Mem. Nat. Writers Club, Calif. Commonwealth Club, Internat. Platform Assn. Author: Love Has No Boundaries, 1982; Anyone Can Fall in Love, 1982.

LONG, SHARON WALTERS, personnel agency executive; b. Menominee, Mich., Aug. 5, 1950; d. Lester Bernard and Mary (Figas) Walters; 1 dau., Leslie Amber. Assoc. degree Hardbarger Jr. Coll., Raleigh, N.C., 1969. Personnel supr. Stackpole Components Co., Raleigh, 1969-82; employee relations supr. Baker Perkins, Inc., Raleigh, 1982-84; mgr. VIP Personnel and VIP Temporaries, Cary, N.C., 1984—. Mem. Am. Soc. Personnel Adminstrn., Raleigh-Wake Personnel Assn. (sec. 1982, treas. 1983-84), Epsilon Sigma Alpha (philanthropic chmn. N.C. Council 1981-82, treas. 1982-83, 1st v.p. 1985-86, pres. 1986-87; N.C. Woman of Yr. 1982), Alpha Sigma (pres. 1981-82, 1984-85). Office: VIP Personnel 104B Fountain Brook Circle Cary NC 27511

LONG, SHELLEY, actress; b. Ft. Wayne, Ind.; m. Bruce Tyson, Oct. 1981; 1 child, Juliana. Attended Northwestern U. Worked in TV in early 1970's, Chgo., also mem. Second City improvisational troupe; guest appearances various TV programs; TV series Cheers, 1982—; films: A Small Circle of Friends, 1980, Caveman, 1981, Night Shift, 1982, Losin' It, 1983, Irreconcilable Differences, 1984, The Money Pit, 1986. Recipient Emmy award for outstanding actress in comedy series, 1983. Address: Care William Morris Agency Inc 151 El Camino Beverly Hills CA 90212

LONG, SHIRLEY JEAN, paralegal, law office adminstrator; b. Alexandria, La., Aug. 5, 1951; d. Troy Leland and Marie (Laird) Tuneberg; m. Kenneth Woodrow Long, Jan. 30, 1971; children—Kayla Marie, Kenneth Blake. Assoc., B.A., La. State U., 1971; paralegal degree Northwestern State U., 1982-85. Legal sec. Gravel, Roy & Burnes, Alexandria, La., 1969-71, William E. Skye, Alexandria, 1972-74; paralegal Provosty, Sadler & deLaunay, Alexandria, 1975—, law office adminstr., 1983—; advisor Northwestern State U., Natchitoches, La., 1982-83. Mem. Nat. Assn. Female Execs., Nat. Assn. Legal Assts., Central La. Personnel Assn., Rapides Parish Legal Sec. Assn. Republican. Avocations: fresh and salt water fishing; reading. Home: 222 Brookwood Dr Woodworth LA 71485 Office: Provosty Sadler & deLaunay Law Firm PO Drawer 1791 934 3d St Suite 903 Alexandria LA 71309-1791

LONG, SUZANNE LYNN, silk screening company executive; b. Stockton, Calif., May 27, 1957; d. H. Donald and Nancy J. (Foosaner) L. B.A., Calif. State U.-Sacramento, 1980. Labor relations investigator State of Calif., Sacramento, 1980; ptnr. Pacific Silk Screening, Laguna Beach, Calif., 1980—. Mem. Friends of Sea Lions. Avocations: yachting; languages; scuba diving. Office: Pacific Silk Screening 2307 Laguna Canyon Rd Laguna Beach CA 92651

LONGARDNER, CAROLINE MAE, insurance agent, genealogical researcher; b. Paulding, Ohio, Feb. 24, 1943; d. Albert Francis and Kathryn Irene (Soule) Wells; m. John K. Longardner, Jr., Dec. 22, 1962; children—Melanie, John Nicholas, Julius. Assoc. Internat. Bus. Coll., 1963; grad. Life Underwriters Tng. Council, 1984. Exec. sec. Gen. Electric, Ft. Wayne, Ind., 1963-64; ins. adminstr. Paulding County Farm Bur., Paulding, 1966-72; ins. agt. Caroline Longardner Ins. Agy., Antwerp, Ohio, 1982—. Editor newspaper column Paulding County Pedigree, 1980—. Bd. dirs. Friends of St. Paul's Ch. Hist. Soc., Hicksville, Ohio, 1980—, John Paulding Hist. Soc., 1977—. Recipient Outstanding Jr. award Ohio Soc. DAR, 1979. Mem. Nat. Assn. Life Underwriters, John Paulding Soc. Children of American Revolution (organizing pres. 1977; sr. sec. 1982—), Soule Kindred Am., Colonial Dame, XVII Century, Daus. Union Vets., Ohio Geneal. Soc. (past pres. Defiance chpt.), Antwerp C. of C., Nat. Outstanding Jrs. Club of DAR. Democrat. Episcopalian. Home: Route 2 Box 187 Antwerp OH 45813 Office: Caroline Longardner Insurance Agy 101 W River St PO Box 668 Antwerp OH 45813

LONGINO, LOYCE WHITE, financial analyst; b. Texas City, Tex., Oct. 1, 1944; d. Delbert Loy and Emma Barr (Walker) W.; m. Charles F. Longino, Jr., July 11, 1964; children—Laura Elizabeth, Charles F. B.A., U. N.C.-Chapel Hill, 1966; postgrad. U. Miami. Asst. grant writer Office Devel., U. Miami and Inst. Aging, 1978, grants mgr. dept. psychology U. Miami, 1980, dir. research office devel., 1981; exec. dir. Miami Choral Soc., 1983-85; fin. analyst U. Miami, 1985—; bd. dirs. Cultural Execs. Council, 1983. Convener div. on adminstrn. Riviera Presbyn. Ch., 1982, elder, 1980. Mem. Am. Assn. Counseling and Devel. Presbyterian.

LONGLEY, BERNIQUE, painter, muralist, sculptor; b. Moline, Ill., Sept. 27, 1923; d. Eli James and Effie Marie (Coen) Wilderson; grad. Art Inst. Chgo., 1945; postgrad. Instituto de Allende, Mex., 1971, Santa Fe Sch. Arts and Crafts, 1975; m. James Alexander Orr, Apr. 15, 1968; 1 dau., Bernique Longley Glidden. One-woman shows Mus. N.Mex., 1947, 50, 52, 53, Little Shop, Santa Fe, 1952-58, Maurice Appleman Gallery, Denver, 1953-54, Van Dieman Lilienfield, N.Y.C., 1953, Rotunda-City Paris, San Francisco, 1955-56, Sanger-Harris Gallery, Dallas, 1968, Lars Laine, Palm Springs, Calif., 1963-69, Gallery A, Taos, 1966-69, Cushing Galleries, Dallas, 1977, Gov.'s Gallery, N.Mex. State Capitol, 1978, Santa Fe East, Austin, Tex., 1979, Woman's Bank of Denver, 1982; group shows include Art Inst. Chgo., 1946, 48, Denver Art Mus., 1948-49, Mus. N.Mex., 1952, 53, 68, also Summer Gallery, Santa Fe, Blair Gallery, Santa Fe, Santa Fe Festival Arts, 1977-81, St. John's Coll., Santa Fe, Santa Fe East Gallery, 1985, 86, Leslie Levy Gallery, Scottsdale, Ariz., 1985, also others; retrospective exhbn. Santa Fe East Gallery, 1982; executed murals La Fonda del Sol restaurant, N.Y.C., home Alexander Girard, Santa Fe, 1960; represented in permanent collections of Red Skelton, Greer Garson, Mark Harris, Tex. Instruments, Dallas, First Nat. Bank Denver, Santa Fe Hilton Hotel, Dome Oil Exploration Co., San Francisco, Coll. Santa Fe, Mus. N.Mex., Santa Fe, Coll. Santa Fe, Colorado Springs Fine Arts Center, others. Bryan Lathrop fgn. traveling fellow, 1945. Mem. Art Inst. Chgo. Alumni Assn. Home: 427 Camino Del Monte Sol Santa Fe NM 87501

LONGO, KATHRYN MILANI, pension consultant; b. Jersey City, N.J., July 22, 1946; d. Joseph John Baptiste and Kathryn (Sacco) Milani; B.A., Adelphi U., 1969; postgrad. N.Y. U., 1968-69, Hunter Coll., 1969-70; m. John Carmine Longo, Mar. 15, 1970 (div. June 1984). Pension cons. Laiken, Siegel & Co., N.Y.C., 1967-84, ptnr., 1977-84; mng. ptnr. Laventhol & Horwath Retirement and Employee Benefit Cons. Div., 1984—; pres., creative cons. Pinch-Hitters, Inc., North Bergen, N.J., 1978-82. Co-founder, co-chmn. Greater N.Y. Pension Cons. Workshop, 1974—; jazz dance tchr. Kay Marie Sch. Dance Arts, Hammonton, N.J., 1976-83; guest choreographer Regis Drama Soc., Regis High Sch., N.Y.C., 1978-79. Adelphi U. scholar, 1964-68. Mem. Am. Soc. Pension Actuaries (assoc.), N.J. Assn. Women Bus. Owners, Nat. Assn. Female Execs., Am. Soc. Profl. and Exec. Women. Roman Catholic. also 71 Union Ave Rutherford NJ 0766

LONGO-GURNEY, DIANE, university official; b. Bklyn., June 18, 1957; d. Ralph Francis and Teresa Marie (Scotto) Longo. Cert. grad. Katharine Gibbs Sch., 1976. Exec. sec. Allstate Ins. Co., Farmingville, N.Y., 1977-80, Torrance, Calif., 1980-81; adminstrv. asst. Pepperdine U. Sch. Law, Malibu, Calif., 1981-83, asst. to dean, 1984—; cons. Law Offices Ronald R. Helm, Oakland, Calif., 1986—. Mem. Meeting Planners Internat., Nat. Assn. Female Execs. Republican. Roman Catholic. Club: Jr. Women's (Woodland Hills, Calif.). Avocations: skiing; tennis; cooking. Office: Pepperdine U Sch Law 24255 Pacific Coast Hwy Malibu CA 92065

LONGTIN, MAMYE RUTH, school librarian; b. Bradshaw, Tex., Dec. 21, 1925; d. Thomas Alcon and Cora Mae (Cooke) Lewis; m. F. Thomas Longtin, June 8, 1946; children—Linda Longtin Payne, Tomi Longtin Spence. Student State Tchrs. Coll., Ala., 1942-43, Hardin Simmons U., 1956; B.S. in Elem. Edn., Tex. Tech U., 1966, M.Edn., 1972, Supervision Cert., 1980; Sch. Library Cert., Tex. Women's U., 1972. Tchr. pvt. kindergarten, Slaton, Tex., 1958-66; tchr. elem. sch. Slaton Ind. Sch. Dist., 1966-77, elem. librarian, 1978—; mem. Gen. Adv. Bd. Edn., Service Ctr. Region XVII, Lubbock, Tex., 1982—. Mem. Friends of Library, Slaton, 1983—; sponsor Tex. Classroom Tchrs.' Legis. Program, Austin, 1966—, Tex. Library Assn. Legis. Program, Austin, 1982-83; mem. Staton Library Bd., 1984—. Recipient Grand Cross of Color, Supreme Assembly Internat. Order Rainbow for Girls, McAlister, Okla., 1964; named Tex. Tchr. of Yr., VFW Aux., 1983; Freedom Found. Seminar scholar, summer 1984. Mem. Slaton Classroom Tchrs. (Outstanding Service award 1978-79, pres. 1978-79), Tex. Classroom Tchrs. (del. 1978-79, Outstanding Service award 1978-79) Tex. Library Assn., Tex. Assn. Sch. Librarians (dist. chmn. 1979-80), Tex. State Tchrs. Assn. (dist. rep. to county 1976), Lubbock Area Library Assn., West Tex. Assn. Supervision and Curriculum Devel., Ladies Aux. VFW. Mem. Disciples of Christ Ch. Lodge: Order of Eastern Star, Home: 725 W Division St Slaton TX 79364 Office: Slaton Ind Sch Dist 300 S 9th St Slaton TX 97364

LONIGRO, LENORE, lawyer; b. Chgo., Aug. 21, 1956; d. Jerry Francis and Antonet Joane (Zomparelli) L. B.A. magna cum laude, Tufts U., 1978; J.D. with honors, Marquette U., 1981. Bar: Ill. 1981, Wis. 1981, U.S. Ct. Appeals (7th cir.) 1982, U.S. Dist. Ct (ce. and so. dist.) Calif., U.S. Dist. Ct. (no. dist.) Ill. 1981, U.S. Dist. Ct. (ea. and we. dists.) Wis. 1981, Calif. 1985. Legal intern U.S. atty., Milw., 1979-81, antitrust div. U.S. Dept. Justice, Chgo., 1980; atty.-at-law Burke and Smith, Chgo., 1981-83, McDermott, Will & Emery, Chgo., 1983-85, O'Melvery & Myers, 1985-86, Chapman & Cutler, 1986—; chmn. law day Justinian Soc., Chgo., 1983; pres. Women and Law, Milw., 1979-81. Author: (with Ramon Klitzke) Patents and Antitrust, 1981. Benefactor Chgo. Council on Fgn. Relations, 1981—; chmn. alumni admissions council Tufts U., Chgo., 1981—; mem. Art Inst. Chgo., 1982—. Recipient Am. Jurisprudence awards Marquette Law Sch., Milw., 1981; Outstanding Young Am. award, 1984; Meserve scholar Tufts U., 1974-75; Portia scholar Marquette Law Sch., Milw., 1979-80. Mem. ABA, Ill. State Bar Assn. (mem. assembly 1983-86), Chgo. Bar Assn. (legis. com. 1982—), Chgo. Alumni Council (chmn. 1981—).

LONNEMAN, PHYLLIS KAY, lawyer, educator; b. Oneida, Ky., Mar. 19, 1948; d. John and Minnie (Minton) Byrley; m. George H. Lonneman, 1972 (div.); children—Dawn, Tara. B.S. with honors, Eastern Ky. U., 1969, M.S. with honors, 1974; J.D. with honors, No. Ky. U., 1981. Bar: Ky. 1981. Tchr., Cin. Tech. Coll., 1977-81, No. Ky. U., Highland Heights, 1980-82, Simon Kenton High Sch., Independence, Ky., 1969-82; sole practice, Covington, Ky., 1981-82; sole practice, 1982—; juvenile counselor Kenton County Juvenile System, Covington, 1978-81. Mem. Independence City Council, 1980-82; probation officer Juvenile Ct. Diversion Program, Covington, 1979-82; bd. dirs. Kenton County YMCA, 1979-82; foster parent Kenton County, 1979-82; adv. bd. Parents Anonymous. Named Tchr. of Yr. for Kenton County, Simon Kenton High Sch., 1978-81; Republican Women's Club scholar, 1980; Danforth fellow nominee, 1969. Mem. Ky. Edn. Assn., Ky. Bar Assn., Ky. Ornithol. Soc., Ky. Acad. Sci., Phi Delta Kappa. Baptist. Home: Route 1 Box 186 Boston KY 40107 Office: Phyllis K Lonneman 204 N MulberryElizabethtown KY 42701

LONSFORD, FLORENCE ELIZABETH HUTCHINSON, artist, designer, writer; b. Lebanon, Ind., Jan. 7, 1914; d. Frank Edwin and Jennie Cecelia (Pugh) Hutchinson; B.S. in Sci., Purdue U., 1936; student Nat. Acad. Fine Arts, 1956-58; M.A., Hunter Coll., 1963; student Art Students League, John Herron Art Inst., Barnard-NBC Inst. Radio-TV; m. Graydon Lee Lonsford, Dec. 18, 1938 (dec. Sept. 1958). Owner, operator greeting card design bus., 1966-69; tchr. fine arts N.Y. Public Schs., 1960-80; freelance artist and designer; freelance artist, copywriter Harper's Pub. House; illustrator Morningstar Prodns.; greeting card artist Curzart, Rust Craft Pubs., Dedham, Mass., Nat. Artcrafts, Detroit; paintings sold in decorating dept. Lord & Taylor; illustrator ch. publs.; art editor The Key of Kappa Kappa Gamma, 1947—; paintings shown nat. and regional shows, including: Hoosier Salon (Indpls.), Cooperstown, N.Y., Brockton, Mass., Mystic, Conn., Ind. State Fair, Jackson, Miss., N.Y., Ky., Ohio and Mich.; graphics rev. in Revue Moderne, Paris, 1967; writer Artists Equity; contbr. to Woman's Home Companion, Christian Sci. Monitor, Saturday Rev., N.Y. Times, Woman's Day, small verse and lit. mags. Recipient art prizes Ind. State Fair, Nat. Art League, Salmagundi, Hoosier Salon; named Outstanding Educator, Met. Mus. and N.Y. Center Arts and Humanities, 1977; recipient Prix de Honneur, Monaco, 1966; finalist Deauville and Cannes Grand Prix, 1973. Mem. Nat. Council Tchrs. of English, Women's Aux. N.Y. Acad. Scis., Am. Artists Profl. League, Nat. Art League, Cooperstown Art Assn., Artists Equity, Portrait Club N.Y., Am. Portrait Soc., Nat. Opera Club Am. (dir.), Oil Pastel Soc. Am., N.Y. Art Tchrs. Assn. (exec. bd.), Greensward Found., Wilderness Soc., Kappa Kappa Gamma (nat. officer), Mortar Bd., Alpha Lambda Delta. Republican. Presbyterian. Home and Office: 311 E 72d St New York NY 10021

LOO, CHARLENE, business executive; b. Foochow, Fukien, China, Oct. 21, 1935; d. Chin Chun and Jen Yu (Chen) Chow; m. Jack Loo; children—Christine, Jerry, Wayne, B.A., Coll. Law and Commerce, Taipei, Taiwan, 1960. Owner Ying's Restaurant, N.Y.C., 1967-85; pres. Ever Ready Blue Print Corp., N.Y.C., 1977—. Office: Ever Ready Blue Print Corp 200 Park Ave S Suite 1316 New York NY 10003

LOOK, JEANNE NEARY, music producer; b. N.Y.C., Dec. 16, 1944; d. William Joseph and Helen (Ferris) Neary; B.A., Manhattanville Coll., Purchase, N.Y., 1966; m. Richard Edwards Look, Dec. 14, 1974; children—Hannah Mariah, Heartie Helena. Stylist, rep. Roy Coggin Photography, N.Y.C., 1969-73; rep., producer Steckler Films, N.Y.C., 1973-74; rep., producer, founder Look & Chapin, N.Y.C., 1975—; ptnr. Look and Co., advt. music co., 1984—; lighting dir. Bob Greene's World of Jelly Roll Morton, Carnegie Hall, 1978; 1976-78; styled photographs for nat. publs; produced The Pride is Back Born in America, (theme song) Hands across America. bd. dirs. Gramercy Neighborhood Assos.; mem. Cultural Council Found. and Ballettore. Recipient Clio award for advt., 1978. Mem. Soc. Advt. Music Producers and Composers, Nat. Arts Club, Mcpl. Arts Soc., Nat. Trust Hist. Preservation. Office: 45 E 22d St 4th Floor New York NY 10010

LOOKABILL, MYRA LEE, advertising executive; b. Cleve., May 10, 1947; d. Richard Paul and Helen Virginia (Pratus) Cisan; m. Daniel L. Lookabill, Oct. 3, 1970. A.A., Fullerton Coll., 1967. Office mgr., corp. sec. Oddo & Reed Ins., Los Angeles, 1971-76; account mgr. Gerald J. Sullivan & Assocs., Los Angeles, 1976-79; asst. v.p. Frank B. Hall & Co., Inc. Calif., Los Angeles, 1979-81; dir. ins. mktg. Direct Mktg. Group, N.Y.C., 1981-83; owner Advt. Plus, Anaheim, Calif., 1983—. Fund raiser Hollenbeck Youth Ctr., St. Jude Found., Nat. Jewish Fund. Mem. Direct Mail Mktg. Assn., Direct Mail Assn. Orange County. Office: 2651 E Chapman Suite 105 Fullerton CA 92631

LOOKER, ELLEN JEAN, banker; b. Maribel, Wis., Apr. 30, 1925; d. Edward M. and Ellen M. (Oestreich) Benishek; m. Edward C. Looker, July 2, 1944; children—Tom, Mark, Gregg, Jon. Grad. high sch., Manitowoc, Wis. Payroll clk. Mirro Aluminum Co., Manitowoc, 1942-46; teller Maribel-Whitelaw Bank, Maribel, Wis., 1955-67, asst. cashier, 1967-72, v.p., 1972-74, pres., 1974—. Bd. dirs. Maribel Non-Profit Housing, 1976-85. Mem. Nat. Assn. Bank Women, Manitowoc County Bankers Assn. (bd. dirs. 1979-85). Republican. Presbyterian.

LOOMANS, KATHRYN ELIZABETH, classical music radio producer, host radio symphony broadcasts; b. Stevens Point, Wis., Nov. 5, 1953; d. Homer Clarence and Mary Louise (Sampson) L. B. in Gen. Studies with high distinction, U. Mich., 1977. Producer, announcer Sta. WCBN-FM, Ann Arbor, Mich., 1975-78; bus. editor Inst. Social Research, Ann Arbor, 1976-78; camera operator Ann Arbor Cablevision, 1977-78; floor dir. Sta. KQED-TV, San Francisco, 1979-81; ops. dir., announcer Sta. KQED-FM, San Francisco, 1981-83, exec. producer, 1984—. Mem. Women in Communications. Office: Sta KQED-FM 500 8th St San Francisco CA 94103

LOOMIS, JACQUELINE CHALMERS, photographer; b. Hong Kong, Mar. 9, 1930 (parents Am. citizens); d. Earl John and Jennie Bell (Sherwood) Chalmers; m. Charles Judson Williams III, Dec. 2, 1950 (div. Aug. 1973); children—Charles Judson IV, John C., David F., Robert W.; m. Henry Loomis, Jan. 19, 1974; stepchildren—Henry S., Mary Loomis Han Kinson, Lucy F., Gordon M. Student U. Oreg., 1948-50, Nat. Geog. Soc., 1978-79, Winona Sch. Profl. Photography, 1979, Sch. Photo Journalism, U. Mo., 1979. Pres. J. Sherwood Chalmers Photographer, Middleburg, Va., 1979—; pres. Windward Corp., Middleburg, 1984—. Contbr. photos to Nat. Geog. books and mag., Ducks Unltd., Living Bird Quar., Orvis News, Frontiers Internat., other publs., calendars. One-woman show Woodbury-Blair Mansion, Washington, 1980; rep. in pub. and pvt. collections. Trustee, Sta.-WJCT-TV, Jacksonville, Fla., 1965-73, mem. exec. com., chmn., 1965-66; co-chmn. Arts Festival, Jacksonville, 1970, chmn., 1971; bd. dirs., mem. exec. com. Nat. Friends Pub. Broadcasting, N.Y.C., 1970-73; bd. dirs. Washington Opera, 1976—, bd. dirs. Jacksonville Art Mus., 1968-70, treas., 1968; bd. dirs. Pub. Broadcasting Service, Washington, 1972-73; bd. dirs. Planned Parenthood N. Fla., 1968-70. Recipient Cultural Arts award Jacksonville Council Arts, 1971, award Easton Waterfowl Festival, 1982, 1st and 2d prizes, 1984. Mem. Profl. Photographers Am. (Merit award 1982), Photog. Soc. Am., Am. Soc. Picture Profls., Jr. League Jacksonville Inc. Republican. Presbyterian. Clubs: Fla. Yacht (Jacksonville); Amelia Island Plantation (Fla.); Ctr. Harbour Yacht (Brooklin, Maine). Avocations: travel; golf; sailing; shooting; skiing; riding. Home and Office: Route 1 Box 122 Middleburg VA 22117

LOONEY, KATHLEEN MITCHELL, nurse; b. Memphis, Aug. 4, 1943; d. David DeMint and Louise M. (McKinney) Mitchell; B.S.N., La. State U., 1976, M.Nursing, 1983; m. James Holland, Feb. 11, 1979; children by previous marriage—Mary Ann King, Margaret Ann King. Night supr. Audubon Health Care Center, New Orleans, 1976, house supr., 1976, dir. nursing, 1976-77; div. mgr. nursing Taylor House, New Orleans, 1977-83; gerontol. clin. nurse specialist So. Bapt. Hosp., New Orleans, 1983—. Mem. Am. Nurses Assn. (cert. gerontol. nurse, gerontol. nurse practitioner), Council of Nursing Home Nurses, S.W. Soc. Aging, Acad. Gerontol. Nurses, Assn. La. State Nurses, New Orleans Soc. Clin. Specialists. Mem. Christian Ch. Office: 2700 Napoleon Ave New Orleans LA 70115

LOONEY, MARY LOU, retail company executive; b. Carroll, Iowa, July 30, 1948; d. Vincent Patrick and Edna Margaret (Schultz) Rowan; m. Ralph Bernard Looney, Oct. 1, 1977; m. W.J. Pick, Jan. 7, 1967 (div. May 1975); children—Rebecca Ann, Brenda Louise. Student U. S.D., 1969-72, Met. Tech. Community Coll., Omaha, 1980. Sec., Wall Lake Community Sch. (Iowa), 1966-67; adminstrv. asst. U. S.D., Vermillion, 1969-73; mgr., buyer Rocking Horse, Vermillion, 1973-75; bookkeeper, Nebr. Builders Product, Omaha, 1975-76; office mgr. Restaurant Mgmt., Omaha, 1976-80; controller LaGrange Equipment Co., Omaha, 1980-82, pres., 1982—. Mem. Nat. Assn. Female Execs., Profl. Women's Assn., Greater Resources for Omaha Women. Republican. Methodist. Home: 11412 Queens Dr Omaha NE 68164

LOOPER, FELDA KATHRYN, boutique owner; b. Kansas City, Mo., Jan. 9, 1955; d. Omer Joe and Emma Maxine (Moody) L.; m. Brian Stockwell, Dec. 30, 1978. B.A. in Polit. Sci., U. Okla., 1977; M.A. in Spl. Studies, George Washington U., 1978. Counselor Internat. Counseling Service, Paris, 1980-82; owner, mgr. Felda's, A European Boutique, Washington, 1983—. First female page in U.S. Ho. of Reps., 1973. Democrat. Home: 4379 Westover Pl NW Washington DC 20016 Office: Felda's A European Boutique 3000 M St NW Washington DC

LOPATIN, FLORENCE, comptroller, financial management executive; b. Detroit, May 28, 1928; d. Leo and Edith (Atkins) Grossman; m. Lawrence Harold LoPatin, Dec. 3, 1950; children—Mark Bruce, Norman Stuart. B.A., U. Mich., 1949; postgrad. Wayne U., 1949-50; B.Acctg., Walsh Coll., Troy, Mich., 1978. Mng. ptnr., Trade Markets, catalogue bus., Southfield, Mich., 1976-78; comptroller Bagel Nosh of Mich., Southfield and Detroit, 1978-85; comptroller L.H. LoPatin & Co., Southfield, 1978—; gen. ptnr., chief operating officer Trees of Life Mgmt. Co., Southfield, Mich., 1978—; comptroller, v.p., treas. River Crest Properties, Inc.; comptroller Westpoint Manor Mobile Home Park, Westridge Mobile Home Park; comptroller, mgr. Willow Oak Profl. Bldg. Brichwood Profl. Bldg.; ptnr., cons. Westpoint Manor Devel. Co., Nottingham Estates, W.R. Southfield Assocs., Birchwood Med. Ctr., Willow Oak Med. Ctr. Chmn. United Fund, Southfield, 1970; bd. dirs. Nat. Council Jewish Women, 1974-78; mem. Women's Assn. Detroit Symphony, 1975—. Mem. Southfield C. of C., Walsh Coll. Alumni Assn. Office: 3000 Town Ctr Suite 1000 Southfield MI 48075

LOPER, JANET SWANSON, data processing executive; b. Dunkirk, N.Y., Sept. 17, 1934; d. Ralph Edwin and Isabel Spencer (Emerson) Swanson; B.S. in Sales Mgmt., Syracuse U., 1956; m. Lyle C. Loper, Oct. 15, 1971. Systems engr. IBM, Rochester, N.Y., 1956-58, tech. writer, product planner, Endicott, N.Y., 1959-66, planner instruction systems devel. dept., Los Gatos, Calif., 1966-70, mem. R.B. Johnson fellow program, 1970-72, communications analyst, gen. systems div., 1972-79, application devel. cons., 1975-79; v.p., dir. communications Citibank, N.Y.C., 1979-84; pres. Info. Integrators, Inc., 1984—; cons. U.S. Office Edn., 1970. Recipient Outstanding Contbn. award IBM, 1975. Mem. Am. Bus. Women's Assn. (pres. Binghamton chpt. 1964-66), Soc. Tech. Communications (past program dir.), Data Processing Mgmt. Assn. (past internat. dir.). Office: 4 Sutton Pl Wilmington DE 19810

LOPEZ, KATHRYN PHILLIPS, school librarian; b. Hale Center, Tex., July 7, 1922; d. Clyde C. and Ada Erma (Stutzman) Phillips; m. Theodore Lewis Lopez, June 27, 1948; children—Stephen William, Ralph Antonio. B.S., West Tex. State Coll., 1943; postgrad. U. Utah, part-time 1962-73, U. N.Mex., part-time 1978-80. Tchr. homemaking Lockney Pub. Schs. (Tex.), 1943, Hale Center Pub. Sch. (Tex.), 1943-44, Springer Pub. Sch. (N.Mex.), 1944-48, teller Bank of N.Mex., Albuquerque, 1948-56; head tchr. Casa Solano Kindergarten, Santa Fe, 1963-68; jr. high sch. librarian Santa Fe Pub. Schs., 1968—, chmn. secondary sch. librarians, 1980—. Trustee, St. John's Meth. Ch., Albuquerque, 1955-57; rec. sec. St. John's Meth. Ch., Santa Fe, 1984—. Mem. ALA, Am. Assn. Sch. Librarians, N.Mex. Library Assn., N.Mex. Media Assn., Delta Kappa Gamma. Democrat. Home: 210 Sereno Dr Santa Fe NM 87501

LOPEZ, LINDA SINGLETON, mortgage banking administrator; b. Paris, Tex., Sept. 11, 1946; d. Charles Bennett and Floy Evelyn (Ryan) Singleton; m. Phillip D. Lopez de Esquevar, Apr. 19, 1969 (dec. Aug. 1974); 1 child, Charles Robert Thomas. B.A., Brigham Young U., 1969; Cert. ct. reporter/paralegal Chapman Ct. Reporting Coll., 1973. Exec. asst. to chief exec. officer Am. Inst. Mortgage, Grand Prairie, Tex., 1974-76; office mgr., cons. The Exception, Dallas, 1976-79; office mgr., bookkeeper Heatilator, Inc., Carrollton, Tex., 1979-80; office mgr., title officer Wood Investments, Houston, 1980-83; escrow adminstr. Consol. Capital Co., Emeryville, Calif., 1983—; cons. L. Lopez Acctg. Service, Houston, 1980-83, Lopez Enterprises, Novato, Calif., 1985—. Author: Mortgage Banking Terms, 1985; also articles on title and land law. Sec. Daus. of Bilitis, Dallas, 1975-76; founder, pres. N. Dallas chpt. NOW, 1979-80, state del., 1980; social chmn. The Other Side, San Rafael, Calif., 1985-86; vol. acct. Westheimer Art Colony, Houston, 1980-83; vol. clown, entertaining at Spl. Olympics, other events, 1985—. Mem. Mensa. Democrat. Avocations: art; astrology; sewing; needlework; volunteer work with children's groups. Office: Consol Capital Co 2000 Powell St Emeryville CA 94608

LOPEZ, NANCY, professional golfer; b. Torrance, Calif., Jan. 6, 1957; d. Domingo and Marina (Griego) Lopez; m. Ray Knight, Oct. 25, 1982; children—Ashley Marey, Erinn Shea. Student U., Tulsa, 1976-78. Profl. golfer, 1978—, first victor at Bent Tree Classic, Sarasota, Fla., 1978; winner tournaments including World Championship of Women's Golf, 1984, LGPA championship, 1985, Hall of Fame Championship, 1985, Henredon Classic, 1985. Named AP Athlete for 1978; recipient Vare trophy, 1985. Mem. Ladies Profl. Golf Assn. (Player and Rookie of Yr. 1978). Republican. Baptist. Author: The Education of a Woman Golfer, 1979. Office: care LPGA Membership Dept 1250 Shoreline Dr Sugarland TX 77478*

LOPEZ, PRISCILLA, actress; b. Bronx, N.Y., Feb. 26, 1948; d. Francisco and Laura (Candelaria) L.; m. Vincent Fanuele, Jan. 16, 1972. Grad., Performing Arts High Sch., N.Y.C. Broadway appearances include What's A Nice Country Like You Doing in a State Like This; appeared in off-Broadway prodn. Key Exchange, 1982; other theater appearances include Buck, 1983, Non Pasquale, 1983; TV appearances in Dinah show; TV series In The Beginning, 1979; appearance as Harpo Marx in: A Day in Hollywood-A Night in the Ukraine; film appearance in: Cheaper to Keep Her. (Recipient Obie award for A Chorus Line, Tony award for A Day in Hollywood-A Night in the Ukraine. Address: William Morris Agy 1350 Ave Americas New York NY 10019*

LOPEZ, ROSALIE MERCEDES, personnel executive; b. Tucson, Sept. 6, 1954; d. Manuel Rodriguez and Geraldine (Bender) Lopez; m. Myron Paul Books, Feb. 1, 1975; 1 child, Seth Clayton Paul. A.S., No. Ariz. U., 1979; B.S. in Bus. Adminstrn., U. No. Colo., 1980; M.B.A., N. Tex. State U., 1982. Office mgr. Lockhart Exploration Co., Casper, Wyo., 1979-80; personnel rep. Continental Telephone, Dallas, 1980-83; field personnel mgr. Hewlett-Packard Co., San Antonio, 1983—; v.p., dir. Petroleum Cons. Services, Houston, 1984—. Contbr. articles to profl. jours. Co-chmn. Mayor's Commn. on Status Women-Women's Forum, San Antonio, 1984; mem. adv. com. Bexar County Ctr. for Women, San Antonio, 1984. William Olsten scholar N. Tex. State U., 1981. Mem. Am. Soc. for Personnel Adminstrn. (nat. EEO com. 1980—), Mex.-Am. Bus. and Profl. Women's Group. Republican. Roman Catholic. Home: 12314 Moorcreek Dr Houston TX 77070 Office: Hewlett-Packard Co 1020 Central Pkwy S San Antonio TX 78232

LOPEZ, SARA ISABEL, chemical and industrial engineer; b. Ocotal, Nicaragua, May 1, 1951; came to U.S., Dec. 4, 1978; d. Ricardo Andres and Emilia Mercedes (Barrios) Lopez; diploma chem. and indsl. engr. U. Centro Americana, 1975; M.B.A. in Fin. and Banking, U. San Francisco, 1984; m. John Kemink, Nov. 6, 1978 (div. 1982); 1 son, Ricardo; m. David Mata, Dec. 2, 1982. Plant engr. Polimeros Centroamericanos S.A., Managua, Nicaragua, 1975-76; mixing and baking supt. Nabisco Cristal S.A., Managua, 1976-77; prodn. and quality control mgr. Jaboneria Prego, S.A., Granada, Nicaragua, 1977-78; indsl. cons. tech. dept. Central Bank of Nicaragua, 1978; indsl. engr. Shaklee Corp., Hayward, Calif., 1979-80; chem. engr. system design Bechtel Petroleum, Inc., San Francisco, 1979-82, progress monitoring engr., indsl. engr. Def. Contract Adminstrn. Services, 1984—; mem. St. Stephen's Women's Guild. Mem. Indsl. Engrs. Assn., Calif. Alumni Assn., Assn. M.B.A. Execs., Am. Chem. Soc., Fgn. Affairs Council. Republican. Roman Catholic. Club: Bechtel Employees. Home: 819 Masson Ave San Bruno CA 94066 Office: 1250 Bayhill Dr San Bruno CA 94066

LOPEZ, VIVIAN GALLUCCI, lawyer, educator; b. Newark, July 14, 1949; d. Giuseppe Italo and Anna (Trucco) Gallucci; m. Jacinto Lopez, Apr. 7, 1967 (div. 1976); children—Jack, Andrew. B.S., Oneonta State Coll., 1973; M.A., Kean Coll., 1977; J.D., Rutgers U., 1982. Bar: N.J. Tchr., Newark Bd. Edn., 1973-79; sr. adjournments clk., Office Adminstrv. Law, Newark, 1979-80, chief jud. mgmt. ops., 1980-85, supervising research analyst, 1985—; instr. Inst. for Paralegal Studies, Linden, N.J., 1983—, Union County Coll., Rutgers U. Bd. dirs. Rahway Landmarks, Inc. Mem. ABA, N.J. Bar Assn., Women's Polit. Caucus. Roman Catholic. Home: 1264 Pierce St Rahway NJ 07065 Office: Div Youth and Family Services One S Montgomery St Trenton NJ 08625

LOPEZ-MUNOZ, MARIA ROSA P., land development company executive; b. Havana, Cuba, Jan. 28, 1938; came to U.S., 1960; d. Eleuterio Perfecto and Bertha (Carmenati Colon) Perez Rodriguez; m. Gustavo Lopez-Munoz, Sept. 9, 1973. Student, Candler Coll., Havana, 1951-53; Sch. Langs., U. Jose Marti, Havana, 1954-55. Vice pres. Fantasy World Acres, Inc., Coral Gables, Fla., 1970-84, pres., dir., 1984—; sec. Sandhills Corp., Coral Gables, Fla., 1978-85, dir., 1978—. Treas. Am. Cancer Soc., Miami, Fla., 1981; bd. dirs. Am. Heart Assn., Miami, 1985, also chmn. Hispanic div.; bd. dirs. Young Patronesses of Opera, Miami, 1985. Recipient Merit award Am. Cancer Soc., 1980, 81, 82, 83, 84; Woman with Heart Award, Am. Heart Assn., 1985, Merit awards, 1980-84. Mem. Real Estate Commn. Republican. Roman Catholic. Clubs: Ocean Reef (Key Largo, Fla.); Opera Guild (Miami); Key Biscayne Yacht; Regine's International (Paris). Avocations: yachting; snow skiing; scuba diving; guitar. Office: Fantasy World Acres Inc 147 Alhambra Circle Suites 220-21 Coral Gables FL 33134

LOPEZ-ROMANO, SYLVIA SILVA, educational program executive; b. Las Vegas, Nev., Dec. 11, 1937; d. Enrique A. Silva and Faustina Flores; B.A. in Social Welfare, Calif. State U., Chico, 1973, B.A. cum laude in Spanish, 1973, M.A. in Edn., 1981; postgrad. U. San Francisco; m. 2d, Aldo Romano, Apr. 30, 1977; children—Peter John, Marie, Henry, Vincent, Renee. Migrant edn. community aide, 1968-70; case aide counselor Mental Retardation Service, Chico, Calif., 1970-72; elem. sch. tchr., 1973-75; instr., lectr. Calif. State U., Chico, 1975-78, coordinator Upward Bound project, 1976-80, dir. ednl. equity services programs, dir. student affirmative action, 1980—; adminstrv. fellow Calif. State U.-Chico, 1982-83; lectr. cross cultural awareness for counseling program Laverne U., 1984—; distbr. Success Motivation programs, 1985—; mem. adv. bd. Western Assn. Ednl. Opportunity Programs. Chairperson Student Affirmative Action Adv. Bd.; co-founder Hispanic Profl. Group. Mem. AAUW, NAACP, Nat. Assn. Female Execs., Hispanic Assn. Community and Edn. (bd. dirs.), Greater Chico C. of C., Concilio Mejicano de Chico, Delta Phi Upsilon, Delta Kappa Gamma. Democrat. Roman Catholic. Home: 555 Vallombrosa #14 Chico CA 95926 Office: U Bldg 2d and Chestnut St Chico CA 95929

LORANGE, JOANNE, college administrator; b. Southbridge, Mass., Jan. 2, 1946; d. Albert Lucien and Lorraine Marguerite (Briere) Lorange; B.A., St. Elizabeth Coll., 1968; M.A., Columbia U., 1971, M.A. in Higher and Adult Edn., 1972; m. Ronald Davis Herron, May 18, 1974; 1 dau., Jocelyn Lorange-Herron. Dir. residential programming, adminstrv. asst. for housing Tchrs. Coll., Columbia U., 1969-72; dir. fin. aid Richmond Coll., CUNY, S.I., 1972-76; asso. dean students Barnard Coll., Columbia U., 1975-77; dir. admissions/external relations Antioch/New Eng. Grad. Sch., Keene, N.H., 1978—; ptnr. Marketplace Gourmet, Keene, 1985—; instr. New Eng. Coll., Henniker, N.H., 1977-78, Sch. for Lifelong Learning, N.H., 1982-84; cons. Upward Bound, Keene State Coll., N.H., 1982—. Advisor, Women's Center, Richmond Coll., S.I., 1972-75; judge N.H. Jr. Miss Contest, 1980; fund-raising trainer United Way; bd. dirs. Grand Monadnock Arts Council, Keene Summer Theatre, Family Planning Services Southwestern N.H.; asst. Campaign chmn. Monadnock United Way. Mem. N.H. C. of C., N.H. Women in Higher Edn. (pres.), Nat. Assn. Women Deans, Counselors and Adminstrs., Nat. Assn. Student Personnel Adminstrs. Club: Kiwanis. Jour. reviewer Nat. Assn. Student Personnel Adminstrs. Region I, 1980. Home: 105 Bradford Rd Keene NH 03431 Office: Antioch NE Roxbury St Keene NH 03431

L'ORANGE, MARGARET ELIZABETH HICKSON, retired nurse, artist; b. West Ringe, N.H., July 4, 1914; d. George Abraham and Blanche Leona (Lefever) Hickson; m. Finn Faye L'Orange, Nov. 25, 1937; children—Mundalea Worrell, Deborah Karen, Martha Jane Juniper, John O. Student Wesleyan U., Ohio, 1931-32, Cleve. Coll., 1940-41; Diploma St. Luke's Hosp., 1936. R.N., Ohio. Staff nurse St. Luke's Hosp., Cleve., 1936-39, 70-77; office mgr. F.F. L'Orange Dental Office, Cleve., 1939-42, 46-51. Vol. nurse ARC, Cleve.; vol. instr. ceramics Girl Scouts U.S.A. and mentally retarded adults; mem. United Methodist Women's Group. Mem. Women's Art Club of Cleve. (pres. 1984—), Nat. League Am. Pen Women in Art, Cleve. Gen. Nurses Alumni Assn. (bd. dirs.), St. Luke's Nurses Alumnae Assn. (bd. dirs.), Cleve. Dental Soc. Aux. (pres. 1970-71), Assn. Retarded Citizens, Heights Gem and Mineral Soc. Avocations: travel; painting; writing poetry; lapidary. Home: 2665 Endicott Rd Shaker Heights Cleveland OH 44120

LORANT, MARJORIE ANNE, lawyer; b. Long Beach, Calif., Feb. 10, 1947; d. Stanley Dale Jennings and Marjorie Frederica (Bahler) Hall; m. Charles Phillip Lorant, Sept. 11, 1970; 1 son, Weylin Jennings. B.A., Calif. State U.-Long Beach, 1969, M.A., 1972; J.D. with honors, Western State U.-Fullerton, 1980. Bar: Calif. 1981. Tchr., Long Beach Unified Sch. Dist. (Calif.), 1969-77; assoc. atty. Law Office of Matt Kurilich, Irvine, Calif., 1981-82; law clk. R.A. Bender, Huntington Beach, Calif., 1979-81; sole practice, Norwalk, Calif., 1982—. Contbr. articles to profl. jours. Chmn. sch. adv. Council ABC Unified Sch. Dist., 1982-84, com. mem. math.-sci. fair, 1983; bd. dirs. Family Guidance Ctr., Cerritos, Calif.; unit commr., tng. staff Long Beach Area council Boy Scouts Am. Recipient William H. Thomas Oral Advocacy award Delta Theta Phi, 1979, Scouter's Tng. award Boy Scouts Am., 1985. Mem. ABA, Women's Bus. Network of Calif., Calif. Women Lawyers, Orange County Bar Assn., S.E. Dist. Bar Assn., Calif. Bar Assn., Delta Theta Phi, AAUW (chmn. internat. relations com. 1983-84, pres. La Palma-Cerritos br. 1985-86). Democrat. Lutheran. Home: 19524 Georgina Circle Cerritos CA 90701 Office: 13031 San Antonio Dr Suite 208 Norwalk CA 90650

LORBEER, LILLIAN MAY, genealogist, educator; b. Stockton, Calif., June 16, 1903; d. Ira Edward and Lillian May (Crum) Smith; m. Howard Burwell Lorbeer, Oct. 18, 1930; 1 child, James Wendell. B.A., Mills Coll., 1925; postgrad. Calif. Coll. Arts and Crafts, 1926, Rudolph Schaeffer's Sch. Design, 1927. Tchr. art Convent and Coll. of Holy Names, Oakland, Calif., 1925; tchr. art and music Victor Valley Union High Sch., Victorville, Calif., 1926-27, Fairfax High Sch., Los Angeles, 1927-30, Chloe P. Canfield Meml. Home, Los Angeles, 1929-30; tchr. adult art Fillmore Union High Sch., Calif., 1937-41; tchr. art Oxnard Union High Sch., Calif., 1946-47. Author: The Laurel Wreath, 1966, 71. Den mother Cub scouts Boy Scouts Am., Fillmore, Calif., 1940-43; pres. Fillmore Rep. Women's Club, 1955-56; mem. Santa Paula Meml. Hosp. Aux., 1979—. Mem. Calif. Ret. Tchrs. Assn., Pomona Coll. Assocs., Alumnae Assn. Mills Coll. Clubs: Ventura County Garden (treas. 1971), Fillmore Ebell (pres. 1937-38). Lodge: Order Eastern Star (worthy matron 1961). Republican. Address: 558 Mountain View St Fillmore CA 93015

LORCH, BARBARA RUTH DAY, educator; b. Pendleton, Oreg., Sept. 30, 1924; d. George Washington and Ruth Irene (Spangler) Day; B.S., Wash. State U., 1946, M.A., 1947; Ph.D., U. Wash., 1956; m. Robert Stuart Lorch, Dec. 19, 1964; 1 son, John Day. Instr. sociology Ariz. State U., Tempe, 1947-48, Bowling Green (Ohio) State U., 1948-50; asst. prof. U. Ariz., Tucson, 1952-53; acting instr. U. Wash., Seattle, 1953-56; asst. prof. U. Mont., Missoula, 1956-57, assoc. prof., 1957-59; asst. prof. to prof. Calif. State U., Long Beach, 1959-69; prof. U. Colo., Colorado Springs, 1969—. Mem. Am. Sociol. Assn., Western Social Sci. Assn., Phi Beta Kappa, Delta Delta Delta, Phi Kappa Phi, Pi Lambda Theta, Alpha Kappa Delta, Psi Chi. Episcopalian. Contbr. articles to profl. jours. Office: U of Colo Austin Bluffs Pkwy Colorado Springs CO 80907

LORCH, LINDA BRYAN, lawyer; b. New Albany Ind., Mar. 13, 1952; d. Basil Harold and Maxine (McGovern) Lorch, Jr.; m. Joseph R. Hagedorn. A.B., Ind. U., 1974, J.D. cum laude, 1979. Bar: Ind. 1979. Ptnr., Lorch & Lorch, New Albany, 1979-82; juvenile referee Floyd County Circuit Ct., New Albany, 1979-80; ptnr. Lorch Moyer Gesenhues & Bitzegaio, New Albany, 1982—. Mem. adv. bd. Spouse Abuse Center So. Ind., 1982—, Floyd County Youth Shelter, New Albany, 1982-86; chairperson bd. dirs. Interfaith Community Council, New Albany, 1982-86; bd. dirs. Easter Seal Soc., 1982—. Mem. ABA, Ind. Bar Assn., Floyd County Bar Assn. (sec.-treas. 1981-83, v.p. 1985-86, pres. 1986-87). Home: 707 Brittany Ln New Albany IN 47150 Office: 506 State St PO Box 692 New Albany IN 47150

LORD, BARBARA JOANNI, public official, lawyer; b. Bay Shore, N.Y., Aug. 7, 1939; d. Theodore and Doris Aileen (Smith) Joanni; m. Robert Wilder Lord, June 24, 1967. B.A., U. Miami, 1961; LL.B., NYU, 1966. Bar: N.Y. 1967, Fla. 1978. Asst. editor A.M. Best Co., N.Y.C., 1961-64; contract analyst Guardian Life Ins. Co., N.Y.C., 1964-66; legal trainee N.Y. State Liquor Authority, 1966-67, atty., 1967-70, sr. atty., 1970-80, assoc. atty., 1980—, sec., 1979—. Mem. ABA, N.Y. State Bar Assn., Fla. Bar Assn. Office: New York State Liquor Authority 250 Broadway New York NY 10007

LORD, BETTE BAO, writer; b. Shanghai, China, Nov. 3, 1938; came to U.S., 1946, naturalized, 1964; d. Sandys and Dora (Fang) Bao; B.A., Tufts U., 1959, M.A., 1960, hon. doctorate, 1982; hon. doctorate, U. Notre Dame, 1985; m. Winston Lord, May 4, 1963; children—Elizabeth Pillsbury, Winston Bao. Asst. to dir. East-West Cultural Center, Honolulu, 1961-62; program officer Fulbright Exchange Program for Sr. Scholars, 1962-63; dancer, tchr. modern dance, Geneva and Washington, 1964-73; conf. dir. Assoc. Councils of the Arts, N.Y.C., 1970-71; writer, lectr. Leigh Bur., 1982—; author: (non-fiction) Eighth Moon (Readers' Digest Condensed Books; winner Nat. Graphic award for Photography), 1975; (novel) Spring Moon, a novel of China (Am. Book award nominee; Lit. Guild selection), 1982; In the Year of the Boar and Jackie Robinson (named one of best books for children AIH), 1984. Mem. selection bd. White House Fellows, 1979-81; bd. dirs. Nat. Com. U.S.-China Relations, Inc., N.Y.C., 1982. Named Woman of Yr., Chinatown Planning Council, 1982; recipient Disting. Ams. Fgn. Birth award, 1984. Mem. Asia Soc. (Pres.'s council). Address: 740 Park Ave New York NY 10021

LORD, JACQUELINE WARD, accountant, photographer, artist; b. Andalusia, Ala., May 16, 1936; d. Marron J. and Minnie V. (Owen) Ward; m. Curtis Gaynor, Nov. 23, 1968. Student U. Ala., 1966, Auburn U., 1977, Huntingdon Coll., 1980, Troy State U., 1980; B.S. in Bus. Adminstrn., Dallas Bapt. U., 1985. News photographer corr. Andalusia (Ala.) Star-News, 1954-59, Sta. WSFA-TV, Montgomery, Ala., 1954-60; acct., bus. mgr. Reihardt Motors, Inc., Montgomery, 1962-69; acct. Chambers Constrn. Co., Montgomery, 1972-75; pres. Foxy Lady Apparel, Inc., Montgomery, 1973-76; office mgr., acct. Central Ala. Supply, Montgomery, 1969-71; acct. Rushton, Stakely, Johnston & Garrett, attys., Montgomery, 1975-81; acctg. supr. Arthur Andersen & Co., Dallas, 1981-82; staff acct. Burgess Co., C.P.A.s, Dallas, 1983; owner Lord & Assocs. Acctg. Service, Dallas, 1983—; tax acct. John Hasse, C.P.A., Dallas, 1984—. Election law commr. Sec. of State of Ala. Don Siegelman, Montgomery, 1979-80. Recipient Outstanding Achievement Bus. Mgmt. award Am. Motors, 1968. Mem. Am. Soc. Women Accts. (pres. Montgomery chpt. 1976-77, area day chmn. 1978, del. ann. meeting 1975-78). Home: 11029 Watterson Dr Dallas TX 75228

LORD, JUNE HARRAH, sculptor, painter; b. Harrah, Wash., Dec. 9, 1910; d. Julius Theophilus and Constance (Raymond) Harrah; m. Jere Williams Lord, Jr., Dec. 6, 1941 (div. 1970); children—Harrah Lord Cohen Argentine, Jere Williams, III, Lonna Davis. Owner, June Harrah Gallery, N.Y.C., 1969-75, North Salem, N.Y., 1975—. Republican. Avocations: riding; swimming; tennis; jogging; ice skating. Office: June Harrah Gallery North Salem NY 10560

LORDI, KATHERINE M., lawyer; b. Jersey City, Mar. 24, 1949; d. Peter G. and Hilde E. (Illy) L. A.B., Trinity Coll., Washington, 1971; J.D., Fordham U., 1975. Bar: N.J. 1975, U.S. Supreme Ct. 1983. Law clk. Friedman & D'Alessandro, East Orange, N.J., 1974-75, assoc., 1975-76; sole practice, Bloomfield, N.J., 1976—; adj. instr. Coll. St. Elizabeth, Convent Station, N.J., 1978—; legal adviser Mcpl. Ct. Clks. Assn., 1977-84. Trustee, Cath. Family and Community Services, 1980—; adv. bd. Acad. St. Elizabeth, Convent Station, N.J., 1980-84; vice chmn. Essex County Adv. Bd. Status of Women, 1983-85, chmn., 1985-86. Mem. ABA, N.J. Bar Assn., Essex County Bar Assn., Bloomfield Lawyers Club (pres. 1983-84), Bloomfield C. of C. (bd. dirs.). Roman Catholic. Club: N.J. Profl. Women. Office: 54 Fremont St Bloomfield NJ 07003

LORE, DIANE CHRISTINE PALLADINO, journalist, educator; b. N.Y.C., Nov. 19, 1955; d. Dominick and Dolores Florence (Wilczak) Lore; m. Ernest Andrew Palladino, May 30, 1981. B.A. in Communications, Fordham U., 1977; M.A. in Journalism, NYU, 1980. Intern reporter Staten Island Advance (N.Y.), 1974-77, gen. assignment reporter, 1977-80, feature columnist, 1979—, edn. editor, 1980—; adj. prof. journalism L.I. U., Bklyn., 1980—. Co-editor poetry anthology New York Through Lyrics and Lens, 1977. Recipient scholarship Deadline Club N.Y., 1976, Scripps-Howard Found., 1978-80; Outstanding Grad. in Journalism award Soc. Profl. Journalists, 1977. Mem. N.Y. Press Club, Newswomen's Club N.Y., Deadline Club N.Y. (dir. 1979—), Soc. Profl. Journalists. Home: 273 Fingerboard Rd Staten Island NY 10305 Office: Staten Island Advance 950 Fingerboard Rd Staten Island NY 11103

LOREN, PAMELA JAN, telecommunications co. exec.; b. Paris, Jan. 11, 1944; d. Theodore and Mattie (Ephron) Loren; B.S., in Sociology, Columbia U., 1964; M.S. in Sociology, U. Madrid, 1968, M.S. in Langs., 1970; m. Morton P. Levy, June 2, 1963; children—Cristopher Aram, Stirling Brett, Cristina Sahula. Pres., Pamela Loren, Ltd., N.Y.C., 1964-74, Loren Communications Internat., Ltd., N.Y.C., 1972-74; chmn. bd. Loren Communications Internat., Ltd., Caracas, Venezuela, London, Milan, Italy and N.Y.C., 1974—; exec. v.p. Cinnamon World Trade Corp., 1974—; dir. Panda Internat. Export Corp., Durable Housing Internat., Crespi, Rosann & Ponti, Loren Group Constrn. and Mgmt., Danbury, Conn., 1981—; lectr. in field. Recipient Humanitarian award, Community Service Soc., 1972, Burden Center Aging, 1977, Soc. Order Helpers, 1978, 82. Mem. Am. Arbitration Assn., Am. Mgmt. Assn., Soc. Latin Am. Bus. Owners, N.Y. Assn. Women Bus. Owners, Women's Econ. Round Table. Club: Columbia. Author: The Generation In-Between Looking Ahead to Thirty-Five, 1978. Home: 1125 Park Ave New York NY 10028 Office: 235 E 57 St New York NY 10022

LORENO, ANNE ELIZABETH, business woman, skating instructor; b. Chgo., Sept. 24, 1946; d. Charles James and Mary Elaine (Keller) Bahr; m. Ronald Edward Loreno, May 18, 1968; 1 child, Amy Lynn. Grad. high sch., Chgo. Owner, operator R & R Roller Rink, Greenville, Pa., 1978—. Mem. Roller Skating Rink Operators Am., Soc. Roller Skating Tchrs. Am. Democrat. Avocations: photography; designing creative skating costumes. Office: R & R Roller Rink 28 Conneaut Lake Rd Greenville PA 16125

LORENZI, NANCY M., university official; d. Louis L. and Mary A. Lorenzi; A.B., Youngstown (Ohio) State U., 1966; M.S., Case Western Res. U., 1968; M.A., U. Louisville, 1975; Ph.D., U. Cin., 1980; m. Robert T. Riley. Dir. med. library Saint Elizabeth's Hosp., Youngstown, 1963-67; reference librarian, head info. services U. Louisville Med. Center, 1968-71; dir. med. center libraries U. Cin., 1972-84; assoc. sr. v.p. U. Cin. Med. Ctr., 1984—. Mem. Med. Library Assn. (pres. 1982-83), Am. Soc. Personnel Adminstrs., Cin. Personnel Assn., Ohio Acad. Scis. Contbr. articles to profl. jours. Office: U Cin 231 Bethesda Ave Cincinnati OH 45267

LORENZON, TERRI ANNE, lawyer; b. Rock Springs, Wyo., Nov. 26, 1950; d. Ray A. and Thelma (Oikari) L. B.A., U. Wyo., 1972, J.D., 1976. Bar: Wyo. 1976, U.S. Dist. Ct. Wyo. 1976. Staff atty. Wyo. Supreme Ct., Cheyenne, 1977-80; adminstrv. aide Environ. Quality Council, Cheyenne, Wyo., 1980—; faculty advisor Nat. Jud. Coll., Reno, 1983, 85. Mem. arts and sci. adv. council U. Wyo., 1980-81; bd. dirs. Cheyenne Planned Parenthood Assn., 1982—. Mem. ABA, Wyo. Bar Assn. Democrat. Roman Catholic. Office: Environmental Quality Council Emerson Bldg Room 304 2001 Capitol Ave Cheyenne WY 82002

LORING, PAULA LEVINE, information systems specialist; b. N.Y.C., June 18, 1947; d. Leon Lewis and Rose (Marcus) Levine; m. Denis Wallace Loring, Aug. 23, 1969. B.S.E.E., Rensselaer Poly. Inst., 1968; M.S.E.E., U. Ill.-Urbana, 1969; M.B.A., Boston U., 1977. Sr. engr. Honeywell, Billerica, Mass., 1969-74; mem. tech. staff The Mitre Corp., Bedford, Mass., 1974-79; sr. cons. Arthur D. Little & Co., Cambridge, Mass., 1979-83; dir. info. systems Cushman & Wakefield, N.Y.C., 1983—. Mem. IEEE (sect. vice-chmn. 1980-83), Am. Mgmt. Assn. (adv. com. 1985), Soc. Women Engrs. (sr.; pres. 1978-79; Disting. New Engr. 1979), Tau Beta Pi, Eta Kappa Nu, Beta Gamma Sigma. Democrat. Jewish. Home: 15 W 72d St 34F New York NY 10023 Office: Cushman & Wakefield 1180 Ave of Americas New York NY 10036

LORION, DIANE ALISON, computer company manager, editor, graphic artist; b. Fitchburg, Mass., July 1, 1955; d. Harold Arthur and Alice Mary (LeBlanc) Lacroix; m. Dennis Francis Lorion, Aug. 16, 1975; 1 child, Alison Judith. Student Lake Erie Coll., Painesville, Ohio, 1973-74, Fitchburg State Coll., 1974; A. in Bus. Adminstrn., Mount Wachusett Community Coll., Gardner, Mass., 1979; B.B.A., Fitchburg State Coll., 1980; M.B.A., Suffolk Coll., Boston, 1983. Cert. stage presence judge. Hostess, cashier, asst. buyer Old Mill Restaurant, Westminster, Mass., 1974-75; inventory control clk., stockroom attendant Digital Equipment Corp., Westminster, 1975-78, bill of material engr., Westminster and Marlboro, Mass., 1978-81, new products mfg. planner, 1981-82, sr. engring. tech. support adminstr., 1982, corp. newsletter editor, 1980-84, product mgr., 1982-86, sr. product mgr., 1986—. Editor, graphic artist: The Key-Note, 1984—, Harmony From Our Hearts, 1985. Chmn. troop com. Montachusett council Girl Scouts U.S.A., 1985—. Mem. Harmony, Inc., (chpt. pres. 1983-84, area parliamentarian 1984—, internat. bd. asst. 1984—), Fitchburg State Alumni Assn., Suffolk U. Alumni Assn. Democrat. Roman Catholic. Home: 143 S Ashburnham Rd Westminster MA 01473 Office: Product Mgmt/Mktg Digital Equipment Corp 200 Forest St MRO1-1/M23 Marlboro MA 01752

LORMAN, BARBARA K., state senator; b. Madison, Wis., July 31, 1932; 3 children. Student U. Wis., Whitewater and Madison. Pres. metal recycling firm. Mem. Wis. State Senate from 13th Dist., 1980—. Past pres. Ft. Atkinson Devel. Council, Wis. Republican. Office: Wis State Capitol Bldg Madison WI 53702

LORSCH, SUSAN ELAINE, banker; b. Chgo., Jan. 10, 1958; d. Bert and Hannah (Lazarus) L. B.S. magna cum laude in Fin., U. Ill., 1979; M.S. in Mgmt., Fin. Acctg. and Mktg., Northwestern U., 1985. Mgmt. assoc. LaSalle Nat. Bank, Chgo., 1979-80, portfolio asst., 1980-82, trust officer, 1982-84, asst. v.p., 1984—. Mem. Assn. Investment Mgmt. Sales Execs., Nat. Assn. Female Execs. Avocations: reading; jogging. Office: LaSalle Nat Bank 135 S LaSalle St Chicago IL 60690

LOSHIN, ANDREA LEE, lawyer; b. Cin., Oct. 23, 1955; d. Jerome and Betty (Moses) L.; m. Michael E. Colby, July 20, 1986. B.S. Environ. Engring., Rensselaer Poly. Inst., 1977; J.D., Albany Law Sch.-Union U., 1980. Bar: N.Y. 1981, U.S. Patent and Trademark Office, 1981, U.S. Dist. Ct. (so. and ea. dists.) N.Y. 1982. Legal intern N.Y. State Pub. Service Commn., Albany, 1979-80; patent atty. Union Carbide Corp., N.Y.C., 1980-82; assoc. Morgan & Finnegan, N.Y.C., 1982—. Editor: Albany Law Rev., 1979-80. Mem. ABA, N.Y. Patent, Trademark and Copyright Law Assn. Office: Morgan & Finnegen 345 Park Ave New York NY 10154

LOS MANSMANN, CAROL, federal court judge; b. 1942. B.A., J.D., Duquesne U. Bar: Pa. 1967. Former dist. judge Western Pa. Dist.; judge 3d Circuit Ct., U.S. Ct. Appeals, 1985—. Office: US Court of Appeals Federal Bldg Pittsburgh PA 15222*

LOTAS, JUDITH PATTON, advertising executive; b. Iowa City, Apr. 23, 1942; d. John Henry and Jane (Vandike) Patton; B.A., Fla. State U., 1964; children—Amanda Bell, Alexandra Vandike. Copywriter, Liller, Neal, Battle and Lindsey Advt., Atlanta, 1964-67; Grey Advt., N.Y.C., 1967-72; creative group head SSC&B Advt., N.Y.C., 1972-74, assoc. creative dir., 1974—, v.p., 1975-79, sr. v.p., creative exec., 1979-81; exec. v.p. creative, 1981-86; founder Lotas Minard Patton McIver, Inc., 1986—. Bd. dirs. Samuel Waxman Cancer Research Found. Recipient Clio Venic Film Festival, 1969, Graphics award Am. Inst. Graphic Arts, 1969, 70, Effie awards, 1985. Mem. Advt. Women N.Y., (1st v.p.). Democrat. Home: 45 E 89th St New York NY 10028 Office: The Chrysler Bldg 405 Lexington Ave New York NY 10174

LOTLIKAR, SAROJINI DATTARAM, university librarian; b. Bombay, Hindu, India, Apr. 26, 1930; came to U.S. 1969; d. Dattaram V. and Laxmibai D. Lotlikar. B.A. with honors, Bombay U., 1951; diploma in library sci. Bombay Library Assn., 1966; M.S.L.S., Villanova (Pa.) U., 1970; student Internat. Grad. Summer Sch., Aberystwyth, Wales, U.K., 1985. Asst. librarian Khalsa Coll., Bombay, 1966-69; catalog librarian Ganser Library, Millersville (Pa.) U., 1971—; cons. Balodyan, Sch. libraries, Bombay, 1966—. Compiler bibliography on India, 1983. Grantee Millersville U. Trust Fund, 1979. Mem. ALA, Assn. Coll. and Research Libraries, Smithsonian Assocs., AAUP. Office: Helen Ganser Library Millersville N George St PA 17551

LOTMAN, ARLINE JOLLES, lawyer, writer; b. Phila., Feb. 5, 1937; d. Samuel and Sarah (Schiffrin) Jolles; m. Maurice Lotman, Sept. 27, 1959 (dec.); 1 child, Maurice. B.A., Temple U., 1960, J.D. with honors, 1977, M.A. in Communications, 1984. Bar: Pa. 1977, D.C. 1980. Pres., Gen. Models, Bala Cynwyd, Pa., 1969-74; exec. dir. Pa. Gov.'s Commn. on Status of Women, Harrisburg, 1972-74; policy expert HEW, Washington, 1978; sole practice law, Phila., 1977—; lectr. in law Temple U., Phila., 1983, Villanova Law Sch., 1985. Author Jewish Nostalgia column Jewish Exponent, 1971-74; author articles in field. Bd. dirs. Americans for Democratic Action, 1977-80; exec. bd. Com. of 70, 1969—; mem. Am. Jewish Congress, 1980—; bd. dirs. Jewish Community Relations Council, 1979—, Nat. Inst. on the Holocaust, 1982—; mem. Com. to Elect Women Judges, 1983—; chmn. Montgomery County Democratic Com., 1977-78. Recipient Legion of Honor award Chapel of the Four Chaplains, 1980; Outstanding Service award N. Atlantic region Soroptimist Internat., 1975; Louise Waterman Wise award Am. Jewish Congress, Phila., 1974; co-recipient award Pa. LWV, 1973; named Outstanding Young Woman of Pa., 1972; 1st hon. mem. NOW, Phila.; editorial citations Phila. Inquirer, Main Line Times. Mem. ABA, Pa. Bar Assn., Phila. Bar Assn. (bd. govs. 1983-84, jud. selection and retention commn. 1983, chmn. pub. sch. edn. com. 1982, assoc. editor The Shingle 1978-79, chmn. com. jud. appointments 1979-81), Assn. Trial Lawyers Am., Assn. Bond Lawyers, Women in Communications, Temple U. Law Alumni Assn. (exec. com. 1979—), Gen. Alumni Assn. Temple U. (dir. 1983—). Office: 1608 Walnut St Philadelphia PA 19103

LOTMAN, SHELLY HOPE, exercise center executive, consultant; b. Phila., May 21, 1958; d. Herbert and Karen Andrea (Levin) L.; m. Scot Adam Fisher, Apr. 5, 1986. B.S., Syracuse U., 1980; M.E.D., U. N.C., 1982. Asst. dir. pub. relations and advt. Altomose Assocs., Valley Forge, Pa., 1982-83; owner, dir. Fitness Factory, Bryn Mawr, Pa., 1983—, also dir. corp. fitness, 1985—; cons., resource person Young Pres. Assn., Phila., 1984, London, 1985; instr. in exercise Bryn Mawr Coll., 1985—. Tchr. CPR, ARC, Bryn Mawr, 1979-82; foster parent Foster Parents Assn., 1980—; founder fundraising dance marathon Children's Hosp., Phila., 1985, 86. Mem. Am. Coll. Sports Medicine, Internat. dance Exercise Assn., Aerobics and Fitness Assn. Am., Assn. Fitness in Bus., Alpha Chi Omega (pres. 1979-80). Avocations: guitar; tennis; collecting miniatures, picture frames; singing. Office: Fitness Factory 931 Haverford Rd Bryn Mawr PA 19010

LOTRECK, SYLVIA MARGUERITE, lawyer; b. Boston, Oct. 17, 1955; d. Richard Leigh and Elsa Marguerite (Myers) Lotreck; m. Thomas Jasper Mahaffey, May 20, 1979. A.B summa cum laude, Bryn Mawr Coll., 1977; J.D. with honors, U. Tex.-Austin, 1980. Bar: Tex. 1980, D.C. 1984. Assoc. firm Akin, Gump, Strauss, Hauer & Feld, Dallas and Washington, 1980-84; assoc. firm Shaw, Pittman, Potts & Trowbridge, Washington, 1984—. Editor articles Am. Jour. Criminal Law, 1979-80. Mem. ABA, State Bar Tex., D.C. Bar.

Office: Shaw Pittman Potts & Trowbridge 1800 M St NW Washington DC 20036

LOTT, ANNIE, communication company executive, interpersonnal communications consultant; b. Newport, Ark., Aug. 3, 1942; d. Julia (Lott). B.A., Fairleigh Dickerson U., 1979. Supr. Ohio Bell, Cleve., 1970-72, asst. mgr., 1972-74, mgr., Solon, Ohio, 1974-76; staff specialist AT&T, Basking Ridge, N.J., 1976-79; dist. mgr. Ohio Bell, Solon, 1979—, coordinator minority and women's bus. enterprise, 1983—. Mem. Citizens League Greater Cleve., 1982—. Mem. Women Edn. Service Assn., Nat. Assn. Investment Clubs, Women's City Club Investment Group (treas. 1982-83, v.p. 1983-84). Democrat. Methodist. Club: Zonta Internat. (v.p. 1981-82), Women's Exec. Home: 13553 Cedar Rd University Heights OH 44118 Office: Ohio Bell Telephone Co 32200 Aurora Rd Solon OH 44139

LOTZE, BARBARA, physicist; b. Mezokovesd, Hungary, Jan. 4, 1924; d. Matyas and Borbala (Toth) Kalo; came to U.S., 1961, naturalized, 1967; Applied Mathematician Diploma with honors, Eotvos Lorand U. Scis., Budapest, Hungary, 1956; Ph.D., Innsbruck (Austria) U., 1961; m. Dieter P. Lotze, Oct. 6, 1958. Mathematician, Hungarian Central Statis. Bur., Budapest, 1955-56; tchr. math., Iselsberg, Austria, 1959-60; asst. prof. physics Allegheny Coll., 1963-69, assoc. prof., 1969-77, prof., 1977—, chmn. dept., 1981-84; lectr. in history of physics; speaker to civic groups. Mem. Am. Phys. Soc., Am. Assn. Physics Tchrs. (sect. rep. Western Pa., chmn. nat. com. on women in physics 1983-84, Disting. Service award 1986), AAUP, AAUW, Am. Hungarian Educators Assn. (pres. 1980-82), Wilhelm Busch Gesellschaft (Hanover, Germany). Editor: Making Contributions: An Historical Overview of Women's Role in Physics, 1984; co-editor The First War Between Socialist States: The Hungarian Revolution of 1956 and Its Impact, 1984; contbr. articles to profl. jours.; research in theoretical physics. Home: 462 Hartz Ave Meadville PA 16335 Office: Dept Physics Allegheny Coll Meadville PA 16335

LOUCKS, URSULA Z., venture capitalist; b. Springs, South Africa, Nov. 27, 1951; came to U.S., 1960, naturalized, 1976; d. Chester A. and Cecylia Zawistowski; m. Terry Lee Loucks, Apr. 16, 1977. B.A. in Biochemistry, U.Calif.-Berkeley, 1976; M.B.A., Wright State U., 1982; stepchildren—Todd L., Tadd L., Jon D. Mem. tech. staff Rockwell Internat., Thousand Oaks, Calif., 1974-77; pres. Priority Assocs., Red Bank, N.J., 1977—; sr. assoc. UNC Ventures, Inc., Boston, 1983—; v.p. UNC Realty, Inc., Boston, 1986—; dir. Azurdata, Inc., Redmond, Wash., Rana Systems, Inc., Chatsworth, Calif. Home: 15 Hopewell Farms Rd South Natick MA 01760

LOUDEN, FLORENCE MORLEY, research and development company executive; b. N.Y.C., May 21, 1925; d. George Bennett and Dora Huntington (Spencer) Morley, B.A., Smith Coll., 1946; m. William Gordon Louden, Apr. 10, 1948; children—Katherine, Stuart, David, Ann. Fgn. traffic dept. McCann Errickson, N.Y.C., 1946-47; production dept. N.W. Ayer, Phila., 1948-49; owner, treas. Tinicum Research Co., Frenchtown, N.J., 1968—. Bd. dirs. ARC, SE Pa. chpt., 1965-66; sch. dir Palisader Sch. Dist., Kintnersville, Pa., 1976-82, v.p., 1976-77; Democratic Committeewoman Tinicum Twp., 1981-84; mem. Tinicum Twp. Planning Commn., 1982—; Bucks County Council on Alcoholism, 1983—. Home: Roaring Rocks Erwinna PA 18920 Office: Box K Frenchtown NJ 08825

LOUGHNEY, JANET RITA, nurse, anesthetist; b. Pittston, Pa., Nov. 15, 1920; d. William Patrick and Genevieve C. (Reardon) L. R.N., Mercy Hosp., Wilkes-Barre, Pa., 1942; Anesthetist, St. Francis Hosp., U. Pitts., 1944. Anesthetist, Mercy Hosp., 1944-46, Gen. Hosp. Sch. Anesthesia, Wilkes-Barre, 1946-60; anesthetist VA Hosp., Wilkes-Barre, 1960-76, chief anesthetist, 1976-82, ret., 1982. Democrat. Roman Catholic.

LOUIE, MARCIA FUJIMOTO, tax lawyer; b. Papaaloa, Hawaii, July 10, 1951; d. Frank Shigeo and Shizue (Inomoto) Fujimoto; m. Martin Louie, June 2, 1978; 1 dau., Beth. B.B.A., U. Mich., 1973; J.D., 1978. Bar: Wash. 1978; C.P.A., Wash., Mich. Sr. auditor, Coopers & Lybrand, Detroit, 1973-78; EDP auditor State of Wash., Seattle, 1979-81; tax mgr. Deloitte Haskins & Sells, Seattle, 1981-84; pvt. practice, 1984—. Bd. dirs. Asian Mgmt. and Bus. Assn., Seattle, 1983-84, Asian Counselling and Referral Service, Seattle, 1984-86. Mem. ABA, Am. Inst. C.P.A.s, Wash. Soc. C.P.A.s, Wash. State Bar Assn., Wash. Women in Tax, Estate Planning Council, Seattle-King County Bar Assn. Office: Deloitte Haskins & Sells 999 3d Ave Suite 2525 Seattle WA 98104

LOUSBERG, SISTER MARY CLARICE, hospital executive; b. Fleming, Colo., Aug. 21, 1929; d. Edward P. and M. Irene (Berg) L. R.N., St. Joseph Hosp., Denver, 1952; B.S. in Nursing Edn., St. Mary Coll., Leavenworth, Kans., 1969; M.P.A. in Health Care Adminstrn., U. So. Calif., 1971. Mem. Sisters of Charity, Roman Cath. Ch. Nursing supr. St. John's Hosp., Helena, Mont., 1954-59, supr. obstetrics, Santa Monica, Calif., 1959-63; operating room supr. Providence Hosp., Kansas City, Kans., 1963-66; dir. nursing service DePaul Hosp., Cheyenne, Wyo., 1966-68, pres., 1979—; adminstr. St. James Community Hosp., Butte, Mont., 1972-79; dir. St. Joseph Hosp., Denver, 1980—, Laramie County Health Planning Com., Cheyenne, 1980-84. Mem. Wyo. State Cert. of Need Rev. Bd., Cheyenne, 1982-83, Cheyenne MX Impact Com., 1982—. Named Boss of Yr., Am. Bus. Women's Assn., Cheyenne, 1980. Fellow Am. Coll. Hosp. Adminstrs. (Regent Wyo. 1982—); mem. Wyo. Hosp. Assn. (chmn. bd. dirs.1985-86), Catholic Hosp. Assn., Mont. Hosp. Assn. (pres. 1976-77).

LOUTHIAN, SANDY LYNN, educator; b. Stockton, Calif., Dec. 11, 1946; d. Albert and M. Jayne (McCurry) Hauser; m. Russell Earl Louthian, July 31, 1971; 1 child, Jeremy Wyatt. B.A. in English, San Jose State U., 1968; postgrad., 1969. Tchr. Berry Sch., Los Gatos, Calif., 1969-79, tchr. elem. sch. Van Meter Sch., Los Gatos, 1979-85; remediation specialist Los Gatos Elem. Dist., 1985—; tour dir. Sta. KTEH TV San Jose, Calif., 1984-85; mem. dist. negotiations team Los Gatos Elem. Tchrs., 1981-85, chmn., 1983-85. Chmn. Los Gatos Cultural Resource Commn., 1977-81; sec. Los Gatos Mus., 1978-82; vice chmn. Forbes Mill Regional Mus., 1981-82; project coordinator Los Gatos Community Services for Youth Commn., 1983-84. Recipient Mayor's Commendation, Los Gatos, 1982; named Tchr. of Yr., Masonic Lodges, 1982, Tchr. of Yr. Los Gatos Elem. Tchrs. Assn., 1985. Mem. Jr. League of San Jose, Calif. Tchrs. Assn., Heritage Preservation Soc. (sec. 1978-80). Democrat. Avocations: gardening; reading. Home: 129 Loma Alta Ave Los Gatos CA 95030 Office: Blossom Hill Sch 16400 Blossom Hill Rd Los Gatos CA 95030

LOVAAS (BECK), CONSTANCE WINNIFRED, publishing company executive; b. Fort Dauphin, Madagascar, July 28, 1927; came to U.S., 1931; d. David and Emma (Hogie) Lovaas; m. Victor William Beck, Sept. 4, 1981. B.A., St. Olaf Coll., 1949. Parish worker St. Timothy Lutheran Ch., Chgo., 1949-51; parish missionary Am. Luth. Ch., Bekily, Madagascar, 1952-58; curriculum writer Malagasy Luth. Ch., Madagascar, 1959-67, 1974-75; audience relations mgr. Radio Voice of Gospel, Antsirabe, Madagascar, 1968-73; assoc. editor Augsburg Pub. House, Mpls., 1977-79, Am. Luth. Ch. Women SCOPE editor, 1979—. Author, editor 13 ednl. booklets in Malagasy lang., 1968-75. Contbr. articles to profl. jours. Ch. sch. workshop tchr. Malagasy Luth. Ch., 1961-75, nat. exec. sec., Sunday schs., 1961-64. Mem. Associated Ch. Press, Evang. Press Assn., LWV. Avocation: golf. Office: Augsburg Pub House 426 S 5th St Box 1209 Minneapolis MN 55440

LOVE, APRIL GAYE MCLEAN, librarian; b. San Jose, Calif., Apr. 28, 1947; d. Frederick F. and Geneva A. (Gmelin) McL.; m. Glen Bolinger, 1974 (div. 1984). B.A., U. Oreg., 1969, M.L.S., 1970, M.A. in Biology, 1976; postgrad. U. Calif.-Irvine, 1976-81. Research asst. Oreg. State U., Corvallis, 1972-74; sci. illustrator Smithsonian Inst., La Jolla, Calif., 1974; sci. bibliographer U. Calif.-Irvine, 1975—. Mem. ALA (conf. attendant, 1981), Calif. Acad. Research Librarians, Sci. and Engring. Acad. Librarians, Am. Soc. Limnology and Oceanography, Pacific Estuarine Research Soc., Med. Tech. Librarians Orange County. Choreographer: Everyone Gets the Blues, 1980; contbr. article to popular mag. Office: Acquisitions Library University of California PO Box 19557 Irvine CA 92713

LOVE, DOROTHY CATLETT, educator; b. Selmer, Tenn., Jan. 12, 1949; d. Oscar Woodrow and Elsie Mae (Boleyn) Catlett; B.S., Lamar U., 1972; M.Ed., North Tex. State U., 1976, Ph.D., 1984; m. Ronald Wayne Love, June 8, 1974. Tchr., Northside Ind. Sch. Dist., San Antonio, 1973-74; tchr. Richardson (Tex.) Ind. Sch. Dist., 1974-79, elem. tchr. cons., 1979—, sch. adminstr., 1981—. Asst. dir. Camp Whispering Pines, East Tex. council Girl Scouts U.S.A., 1971; vol. Project Head Start, Beaumont, Tex., 1970-72; mem. adv. bd. YWCA, 1979-80. Mem. Assn. for Supervision and Curriculum Devel., North Tex. Council Internat. Reading Assn., Tex. Elem. Prins. and Suprs. Assn., Phi Delta Kappa. Home: 2408 Decator St Plano TX 75075 Office: 400 S Greenville Richardson TX 77000

LOVE, DOROTHY MAE, minister, nurse; b. Worcester, Mass., May 22, 1922; d. Joseph Wilfred and Lillian Mary (Fagga) Fournier; m. Robert L. Love, Apr. 13, 1963 (div. Feb. 1983); children—Helen F. Hunter, Joseph Wayne Jodrey. Diploma in nursing, St. Mary's Hosp., 1963; ministerial diploma Religious Sci. Internat., 1973, D.Div., 1982. R.N., Ga.; ordained to ministry Ch. of Religious Sci., 1980. Dir., Southeast States region VIII, United Ch. of Religious Sci., Beverly Hills, Calif., 1980; staff minister World Ministry of Prayer, United Ch. of Religious Sci., Los Angeles, 1980-81, dir., v.p., Los Angeles, 1983—; minister, dir. Golden Circle Ch. of Religious Sci., Santa Ana, Calif., 1981-83; ministerial staff cons. alcohol recovery services Tustin Community Hosp. (Calif.), Villa Recovery Home for Women, Santa Ana. Author: A Time for Healing, 1975. Mem. Southeast Clergy of Religious Sci. (sec., v.p., pres. 1974-77). Republican. Club: Toastmaster (treas., sec., v.p., pres. 1971-72). Home: 249 S Lafayette Park Pl #305 Los Angeles CA 90057 Office: Founder's Church of Religious Science 3281 W 6th St Los Angeles CA 90075

LOVE, JANE HAZELTON, media specialist, educator; b. N.Y.C., Sept. 24, 1931; d. Paul Higham and Mildred Mignon (Fay) Hazelton; B.A., U. Md., 1971; M.Ed., W.Va. U., 1974, Ed.D., 1977; m. Thomas McAdoo Love, June 5, 1952 (dec.). Mem. staff Anne Arundel County (Md.) Public Schs., 1959—, media specialist, 1972-77, media generalist, 1977—; adj. prof. Western Md. Coll., Westminster, 1981—; chmn. legis. com. ALA-Am. Assn. Sch. Librarians, 1980-82. Mem. Assn. Ednl. Communications and Tech. (council 1979-84, sec. steering com., bd. dirs. 1982-85, publs. chmn. 1981-85), Md. Ednl. Media Orgn. (pres. 1979-80, conf. chmn. 1979, 80, 82, publs. chmn. 1981-83), Ednl. Media Assn. Anne Arundel County (pres. 1979-81), W.Va. U. Coll. Human Resources Alumni Assn. (pres. 1981-82). W.Va. U. Alumni Assn. (bd. dirs. 1979-84, bd. dirs. Balt. chpt. 1983-84, pres. 1985-86), Am. Assn. Sch. Adminstrs., Phi Delta Kappa (founds. chmn. U. Md. 1981-82). Home: 1736 Trent St Crofton Woods MD 21114 Office: 600 Old Mill Rd Millersvilles MD 21108

LOVE, LOIS, entertainment management company executive; b. New Haven; d. Kalil Bachara and Sara Louise (Magliola) Haddad; student Sacred Heart U., 1964-66, U. New Haven, 1966-67; m. Noel Love, Aug. 10, 1980; 1 dau., Krista Nicole. Traffic and public service dir. to asst. dir. music Sta. WNHC, New Haven, 1968-70; nat. sales service rep. Sta. WBZ-TV, Boston, 1970-71; local rep. Cin. region United Artist Records, 1973-74; regional dir. Chelsea Records, Detroit, Chgo., Cleve. and Cin., 1974-75; with Pvt. Stock Records, 20th Century Fox and Leber-Krebs Mgmt., Boston, 1975-78, N.E. regional mgr. Arista Records, Boston, 1978-83; pres. Love-Affair mgmt.-entertainment. pres. Alternative Programming, Inc., Love Affair Mgmt. Chmn. Loring Sch. Vol. Com., 1980-81; mem. Sudbury Valley Trustees, 1981-82. Named Promotion Person of Yr., Confidential Report, 1977, 78; recipient gold and platinum records Rec. Industry Assn. Am. Columnist Lovenotes in Cosmic Muffin Newsletter., 1980-83. Office: 6 W 57th St New York NY 10019

LOVE, MICHAEL, design company executive, facilities management consultant; b. Summit, N.J., May 21, 1925; d. Michael and Ethel (Sears) Sliver; m. Edwin P. Love (div.); children—Pamela, Michele. Student Traphagen Sch. Design, 1943-45, U. Miami (Fla.), 1946, Pratt Inst., 1949-50, Parsons Sch. Design, 1980-82. Pres. Quadric Inc., N.Y.C., 1970-78, 82—; v.p. design and constrn. Bankers Trust, N.Y.C., 1978-82; dir. Crestview of Am., Scotch Plains, N.J., 1980—. Lamp designer Am. Soc. Interior Designers; editor articles on interior design Home Mag. Mem. Chief Exec. Officers Club, Am. Soc. Interior Designers (dir.), Constrn. Specifications Inst., Assn. Real Estate Women, Internat. Facilities Mgmt. Assn., Art Deco Soc. N.Y. (pres. 1984—), Profl. Women in Constrn., Met. Mus. Art. Club: City (N.Y.C.). Home: 215 E 24th St New York NY 10010 Office: Quadric Inc 686 Lexington Ave New York NY 10022

LOVE, MILDRED LOIS (JAN), public relations executive; b. Iowa City, July 9, 1928; d. Joseph R. and Gladys M. (Parsons) Casey, B.S. in Bus. Adminstrn., U. Iowa, 1951; m. Gerald Dean Love, Apr. 4, 1952; children—Laura Anne Love Parris, Cynthia Love-Hazel, Gregory Alan, Linda Love Mesler, Geoffrey Dare. Vocal soloist Sta. KXEL, Waterloo, Iowa, 1944-46; sec. to lawyer, La Porte City, Iowa, 1944-46; administrv. aide Office of Supt., La Porte City High Sch., 1947-48; office mgr. Minn. Valley Canning Co., Iowa div. offices, LaPorte City, 1947-48; sec. dept. mktg. U. Iowa, 1948-51; asst. dept. public relations Chgo. Bd. Trade, 1949-51; exec. sec. patent dept. Collins Radio Co., Cedar Rapids, 1951-52; vol. VA Hosp., Albany, N.Y., 1965-73; adminstrv. dir. Tri-Village Nursery Sch., Delmar, N.Y., 1960-61; participant Internat. Lang. Teaching Exchange, Cambodia, 1961; vol. hosps. in Concord, N.H., 1963-64; vol. Chgo. Maternity Center, 1973-74; mgr. Wolf Trap Assos. Gift Shop, Vienna, Va., 1975-80; gen. mgr. Travelhost of Washington, 1980-81; cons. mgmt., 1980—; chair Nat. Cherry Blossom Festival, Washington. Participant community pageants on local and dist. levels, Iowa, 1950-51; Sunday sch. tchr. Meth. Ch., 1941-61; mem. Flossmoor (Ill.) Planning and Zoning Commn., 1973-74, McLean (Va.) Planning and Zoning Commn., 1975—; precinct worker in Iowa, 1946-52, N.Y., 1956-61, N.H., 1963-64, Va., 1979—; pres. I.O.W.A. Inc., Washington, 1980-81; active various community fund raising drives. Mem. AAUW, Am. Mkgt. Assn., Nat. Assn. Female Execs., Nat. Conf. State Socs. (pres. 1983); LWV, Delta Zeta. Republican. Clubs: Princeton (Washington); Normanside Country, Olympia Fields Winter. Home: 121 E Greentree Ln Lake Mary FL 32746

LOVE, PAULINE BODE, business management service owner; b. Salt Lake City, Oct. 24, 1923; d. Paul Andrew and Rosario (Muñoz) Bode; m. James Howard Love, Sept. 20, 1984; m. Claude E. Love, Apr. 12, 1947 (dec. Sept. 1982); children—Cheery Rae, Claudia Love Lee, Lisa Ann. Student U. Utah, 1940-43. Credit mgr. Deseret Book, Salt Lake City, 1944-47; v.p., gen. mgr. Doctors Bus. Mgmt. Service, Salt Lake City, 1951—. Mem. Nat. Assn. Female Execs., Radiology Bus. Mgrs. Assn. Republican. Mem. Ch. of Jesus Christ of Latter-day Saints. Clubs: Altrusa (Salt Lake City) (bd. dirs. 1970-71); Credit Women's Breakfast (treas. 1945-47). Avocations: scrapbooks; reading; needlework; organ lessons. Office: Doctors Bus Mgmt Service 508 E S Temple St Salt Lake City UT 84102

LOVE, SANDRA RAE, information specialist; b. San Francisco, Feb. 20, 1947; d. Benjamin Raymond and Charlotte C. Martin; B.A. in English, Calif. State U., Hayward, 1968; M.S. in L.S., U. So. Calif., 1969; m. Michael D. Love, Feb. 14, 1971. Tech. info. specialist Lawrence Livermore (Calif.) Nat. Lab., 1969—. Mem. Spl. Libraries Assn. (sec. nuclear sci. div. 1980-82, chmn. div. 1983-84), Beta Sigma Phi. Democrat. Episcopalian. Office: Lawrence Livermore Nat Lab PO Box 808 L-389 Livermore CA 94550

LOVEJOY, BEVERLY HARRIS, plumbing company and restaurant executive; b. Devils Lake, N.D., Oct. 8, 1935; d. Franklin E. and Frances Marion (Schneider) Harris; m. Floyd M. Lovejoy, June 8, 1952; children—Floyd M. II, Sonja, Marcia, Daniel, Herbert. Vice-pres., Yellowstone Plumbing Co., Inc., 1963—, JSA Corp., Billings, Mont., 1978—. Counselor youth groups Apostle Lutheran Ch., Billings, 1976-77, 79-82. Democrat. Lutheran. Avocations: writing novels; dress designing; skiing; camping. Home: 5040 Rimrock Rd Billing MT 59106

LOVELAND, HOLLY STANDISH, information systems manager; b. Slater, S.C., Aug. 28, 1947; d. Albert C. and Lucille E. (Standish) L.; A.A., Macomb Coll., 1974; B.B.A., Siena Heights Coll., 1985. Applications analyst Burroughs Corp., Detroit, 1977-79; programmer analyst Ford Hosp., Detroit, 1979-80, project leader applications support, 1980, project mgr. applications support, 1980-82, mgr. systems services, 1982-84; dept. exec. VI, info. services Wayne County, Detroit, 1984—; computer cons. Mem. Data Processing Mgmt. Assn. Home: 1068 Lakepointe Grosse Pointe Park MI 48230 Office: 900 W Lafayette Detroit MI 48226

LOVELAND, SUSAN CAROL, air force officer; b. Boston, Sept. 25, 1959; d. Richard William and Ruth Allene (Waite) Fletcher; m. Gary M. Barrette, June 7, 1980 (div. May 1984); m. A.D. Loveland, Sept. 22, 1984. A.S., Troy State U., 1981, B.S., 1983; A.Applied Sci., Community Coll. Air Force, Montgomery, Ala., 1982. Commd. 2d lt. U.S. Air Force, 1978, advanced through grades to 1st lt., 1985; adminstrv. specialist Air Force Data Systems Design Ctr., Gunter Air Force Sta., Ala., 1978-81, programming specialist, 1982; office automation specialist space div., Los Angeles, 1982-83, system mgr., 1983; chief computer assisted instrn. Sch. Health Care Scis., Sheppard AFB, Tex., 1984-85; chief med. systems U.S. Air Force Regional Hosp., Sheppard AFB, 1985—. Big sister Big Bros. and Sisters, Wichita Falls, Tex., 1985; arts and crafts dir. Elizabeth Gwynn Session Camp for Handicapped, Tupelo, Miss., 1985. Decorated Air Force Commendation medal. Mem. Nat. Assn. for Female Execs., Federally Employed Women, Am. Soc. Mil. Comptrollers, Company Grade Officers Council. Club: Gib Band Era Dance (Wichita Falls). Avocations: dancing; tennis; aerobics; hand and needle work. Office: US Air Force Regional hospital/SGC Sheppard AFB TX 76311

LOVELESS, JANE BRYAN, educator, communications consultant; b. Dallas, May 28, 1948; d. Lewis Calvin and Lucy Jane (Nunn) Bryan; B.A., So. Meth. U., 1970, M.L.A., 1974; m. Thomas Norman Loveless, May 17, 1980; 1 child, Lewis Bryan. Adminstrv. supr., legal librarian Jenkens, Spradley & Gilchrist, 1971-73; asst. to v.p., dir. mktg. Dallas Fed. Savs. & Loan, 1973-74; dir. communications, editor Alumni Mag., So. Meth. U. Alumni Assn., 1974-75; office mgr., recruitment coordinator Jenkens & Gilchrist, Dallas, 1975-77; salesperson Bonwit Teller, Boston, 1977; public info. supr. Dallas Fire Dept., 1977-79; salesperson Neiman Marcus, Dallas, 1979-80; press rep. Lone Star Gas, Dallas, 1979; mgr. product mktg. Tex. Fed. Savs. & Loan Assn., Dallas, 1979-82; advt. mgr. Mrs. Baird's Bakeries, Inc., 1982-85; tchr. English and journalism Hillcrest High Sch., Dallas, 1986—; cons. Support Systems Inc., Dallas, 1981. Bd. dirs., mem. exec. com., pub. relations rep. Nat. Arthritis Found., North Tex. chpt., 1981-84; pub. relations com. ARC, Dallas, 1983-84. Mem. Tex. Bakers Assn. (conv. publicity chmn. 1983-85), Women in Communications (Matrix award Dallas chpt. 1980), Dallas Advt. League (dir. 1984—), So. Meth. U. Alumni Assn., Jr. League of Dallas, Dallas Press Club, Pi Beta Phi. Methodist. Office: 9924 Hillcrest Rd Dallas TX 75230

LOVELL, EMILY KALLED, journalist, educator; b. Grand Rapids, Mich., Feb. 25, 1920; d. Abdo and Louise Marie (Claussen) Kalled; m. Robert Edmund Lovell, July 4, 1947. B.A., Mich. State U., 1944; M.A., U. Ariz., 1971. Asst. traffic mgr. Radio Sta. WOOD, Grand Rapids, Mich., 1944-46; traffic mgr. Radio Sta. KOPO, Tucson, 1946-47; reporter, city editor Alamogordo News (N.Mex.), 1948-51; journalist, editor local, regional and nat. papers, mags., wire service, Ariz., Colo., N.Mex., Tex., 1950-81; editor, pub., founder Otero County Star, Alamogordo, 1961-65; asst. dir. English Skills Program, Ariz. State U., Tempe, 1976; writer, editor, lectr. U. Pacific, Stockton, Calif., 1981—; nat. bd. dir. Hospitalized Vets. Writing Project, Mission, Kans., 1972—; interpreter cts., schs., state various cities Calif., 1982—. Author: Personalized History of Otero County, 1963; Weekend Away, 1964; Lebanese Cooking Streamlined, 1972; A Reference Handbook for Arabic Grammar, 1974, 77; contbg. author: The Muslim Community in N.Am., 1983; author booklet Elementary History of Otero County, New Mexico, 1959. Third v.p., publicity Community Concerts, Otero County, 1950-65; vice chmn. Nat. Found. for Infantile Paralysis, Otero County, 1958-61; mem. Am. Mothers, Inc., Ariz. Assn., 1969-81. Mem. Women in Communication (nat. v.p.), N.M. Press Women (sec.), Ariz. Press Women (state pres. 1969-70), Bus. and Profl. Women's Club (state pres. 1959-60). Clubs: Women's (dist. pub. relations chmn. 1957-60) (Alamogordo, N.M.); Pan American Round Table (Alamogordo). Home: PO Box 7152 Stockton CA 95207

LOVELL, RUTH MOSES, jewelry designer; b. Arab, Ala., Jan. 12, 1943; d. Clifton Morgan and June Evelyn (Oden) Moses; m. Donald G. Lovell, Nov. 23, 1969 (div. 1975). B.S., Auburn U., 1964; postgrad. Pa. State U., 1971. Systems analyst Dept. Army and Dept. Treasury, 1965-73; spl. agt. U.S. Treasury Dept., 1973-82; dir. SASC, Tampa, Fla., 1977-82; pres., chmn. bd. Houseware Rentals, Inc., Tampa, 1982—, RML Designs, Inc., Tampa, 1983—, Incahoots Designs, Tampa, 1983—. Recipient various awards for jewelry design. Mem. Gatlinburg Craftsmen Tenn., Art Assn. N.C., Eastern Shore Art Assn., Virginia Beach Art Assn., ALA. Office: PO Box 10098 Tampa FL 33679

LOVELY, HELEN TENNYSON, nursing care executive; b. Thomastown, Ireland, Apr. 16, 1939; came to U.S., 1963, naturalized 1963; d. James Gerald and Helena Sarah (Carr) Tennyson; m. Warren L. Lovely, July 13, 1963; children—James Warren, Helen Elizabeth, David Patrick. R.N., Bedford Gen. Hosp.-Eng., 1961; cert. midwife, Gables Maternity Hosp.-Eng., 1962; B.S. in Health Services Adminstrn. with honors, Fla. Internat. U., 1979, M.S. in Edn. with honors, 1981. Instr. Dade County Sch. System, Miami, Fla., 1981-82; dir. nursing services Nursefinders of Miami, 1982-84; cons. Miami Springs Sr. Ctr., 1983—; devel. coordinator preferred provider orgn. Gulf Life Ins., 1984-85, founder, chief exec. officer Nat. Council Licensure Examination Rev., 1983—; pres. Profl. Pvt. Nursing Care, Miami, 1983—, dir. nursing services, 1983—; cons. Mactown-Miami Facility for adult mentally retarded and Sunrise Sch. Retarded Children, 1975-84; cons. Miami Springs Sr. Ctr., 1983—; mem. profl. adv. bd. Advanced Human Studies Inst., Coral Gables. Vol., Am. Heart Assn., 1980—; mem. adv. bd. Advanced Human Studies Inst., Coral Gables, 1985-86; mem. Harvard Med. Survey Research Team, 1976—. Mem. Nat. Assn. Female Execs., Mental Health Assn. Greater Miami, Center Fine Arts Miami, Pi Lambda Pi, Kappa Delta Pi. Roman Catholic. Home: 18555 SW 94th Ave Miami FL 33157

LOVERRO, DOROTHY AGNES, fashion illustrator; b. Columbus, Ohio, Mar. 21, 1943; s. Angelo and Ruth (Dragunas) L.; cert. Parsons Sch. Design, N.Y.C., 1963. Staff fashion illustrator Women's Wear Daily, N.Y.C., 1963-77, Vogue mag., N.Y.C., 1975-77; adj. instr. Fashion Inst. Tech., N.Y.C., 1973—; pvt. tchr., freelance illustrator, 1963—. Robert Esehak Meml. scholar, summer 1962. Office: Fashion Inst Tech 227 W 27th St New York NY 10001

LOVETRI, JEANNETTE LOUISE, voice teacher; b. Southampton, N.Y., Apr. 2, 1949; d. James John and Aline Rita (Zimmer) Lovetri; student Manhattan Sch. Music, 1967-68, Juilliard Sch., 1971-72; pvt. dance, piano and vocal study. Singer opera, cabaret, summer stock, oratorios, jazz, 1966-80; owner voice studio, Greenwich, Conn., 1970-75, N.Y.C., 1975—; tchr. voice music dept. Upsala Coll., East Orange, N.J., 1976-81; founder, dir. The Voice Workshop, pub. speaking seminar, 1983—; guest lectr., workshop leader, U.S. and abroad; numerous appearances with Bklyn. Contemporary Chorus, Chapman Roberts Singers, Mid-Hudson Opera, others; chmn. Music Theatre Com. Ann. Symposium. Mem. N.Y. Singing Tchrs. Assn. (dir.), Nat. Assn. Tchrs. Singing, Women Bus. Owners N.Y. Home: 317 W 93d St New York NY 10025

LOVETT, CLARA M., university administrator, historian; b. Trieste, Italy, Aug. 4, 1939; came to U.S., 1962; m. Benjamin F. Brown. B.A. equivalent, U. Trieste, 1962; M.A., U. Tex.-Austin, 1967, Ph.D., 1970. Prof. history Baruch Coll., CUNY, N.Y.C., 1971-82, asst. provost, 1980-82; chief European div. Library of Congress, Washington, 1982-84; dean Columbian Coll., George Washington U., Washington, 1984—; vis. lectr. Fgn. Service Inst., Washington, 1979-85; bd. dirs. Inst. for Research in History, N.Y.C., 1981-82; exec. council Conf. Group on Italian Politics, 1980-83, others. Author: The Democratic Movement in Italy 1830-1876, 1982 (H.R. Marraro Prize, Soc. Italian Hist. Studies); Giuseppe Ferrari and the Italian Revolution, 1979 (Phi Alpha Theta book award); Carlo Cattaneo and the Politics of Risorgimento, 1972 (Soc. for Italian Hist. Studies Dissertation award); co-editor: Women, War, and Revolution, 1980; contbr. sects. to publs. U.S., Italy. Fellow, Guggenheim Found., 1978-79, Woodrow Wilson Internat. Ctr. for Scholars, 1979, Am. Council Learned Socs., 1976, Bunting Inst. of Radcliffe Coll., 1975-76, others. Mem. Am. Hist. Assn., Am. Assn. Higher Edn., Council for European Studies, Soc. for Italian Hist. Studies, Conf. Group on Italian Politics, others. Democrat. Episcopalian. Office: Office of Dean Columbian Coll George Washington U Washington DC 20052

LOVETT, JUANITA PELLETIER, clinical psychologist; b. Youngstown, Ohio, Mar. 9, 1937; d. Joseph Acadia and Alice Beatrice (Davis) Pelletier; m. James Emmett Lovett Jr., Aug. 9, 1958; children—Laura Ann, James Emmett. B.A. with honors in Psychology summa cum laude, Fairleigh Dickinson U., 1975; M.A., Tchrs. Coll. Columbia U., 1979; Ph.D., Columbia, 1980. Free lance fashion cons., 1958-70; psychology fellow Westchester Div. N.Y. Hosp. Cornell Med. Ctr., White Plains, 1977-80; program dir. inpatient service Fair Oaks Hosp., Summit, N.J., 1980; clin. psychologist, Summit, 1983—; adj. asst. prof. psychology and edn., dept. psychology Tchrs. Coll. Columbia U., N.Y.C., 1980—; field supr. grad. sch. applied profession psychology Rutgers U., 1981—; asst. dir. med. research Ciba Geigy Pharms., Summit, N.J., 1982-83; cons. AT&T Bell Labs., 1983—. Bd. dirs. Union County Mental Health, 1974-76; trustee N.J. Forensic Psychiatry Hosp., Trenton; coll. companion

Overbrook Hosp., Cedar Grove, N.J., 1972-75. Mennen scholar, 1975. Recipient Laurie Shavel award 1975. Mem. Am. Psychol. Assn., N.Y. State Psychol. Assn., Soc. Personality Assessment, N.J. Acad. Psychology, N.Y. Acad. Scis., N.J. Psychol. Assn., Sigma Xi, Phi Omega Epsilon. Home: 15 Norwood Ave 5B Summit NJ 07901 Office: 86 Summit Ave Summit NJ 07901

LOVIN, JOYCE FISHER, county official; b. Sylva, N.C., Oct. 24, 1931; d. Don and Dallie Edna (Gunter) Fisher; m. Thomas Lyndon Clayton, Dec. 29, 1946 (dec. Oct. 1978); 1 child, Thomas David; m. James Denman Lovin, May 4, 1980. Student Western Carolina U., 1955. Exec. sec. to mgr. The Mead Corp., Sylva, 1956-75; tax collector Jackson County, Sylva, 1975—. Mem. State Democratic Exec. Com., Raleigh, N.C., 1978-79; exec. bd. Jackson County Health Dept., Sylva, 1978—. Mem. N.C. Tax Assn., Western N.C. Tax Assn. (v.p. 1981-85). Baptist. Home: PO Box 177 Sylva NC 28779 Office: County of Jackson Courthouse Sylva NC 28779

LOVVORN, JOELLA, newspaper editor; b. Pep, Tex., Mar. 20, 1934; d. Alford Marion and Emma (Daniel) L. B.S., Wayland Bapt. Coll., 1969. Ch. news editor Plainview (Tex.) Daily Herald, 1957-60, typesetter, proofreader, 1965-67; offset printer, photographer Muleshoe (Tex.) Jours., 1960-64; asst. editor Ariz. Bapt. Beacon, Phoenix, 1964-65; society editor Lamb County Leader-News Littlefield, Tex., 1967-69, editor, 1969—. Bd. dirs. United Way Fund, 1979-85, Salvation Army, 1976—; dir. Lamb County Spelling Bee, Littlefield, 1980—; judge Regional Spelling Bee, Lubbock, 1980—; chmn. public info. Am. Cancer Soc., 1968—, Am. Heart Assn., 1976-79; chmn. publicity county chpt. ARC, 1976. Recipient appreciation cert. Am. Cancer Soc., 1974, 80, 83, Am. Heart Assn., 1974, appreciation plaque Distributive Edn. Classes Am., 1983. Mem. Soc. Profl. Journalists, Nat. Press Photographers Assn., Tex. Press Assn., West Tex. Press Assn. (contest chmn. 1970), West Tex. Competitive Shooters, Nat. Rifle Assn., Littlefield C. of C. (chmn. publicity). Democrat. Baptist. Lodge: Woodmen of World. Office: Lamb County Leader-News 313 W 4th St Littlefield TX 79339

LOW, LUCINDA ANN, lawyer; b. Denver, Nov. 30, 1951; d. John Wayland and Marian Elizabeth (Roth) Low; m. Daniel B. Magraw, Jr., Jan. 3, 1981; children—Kendra Elizabeth Low Magraw, Caitlin Barstow Low Magraw. B.A., Pomona Coll., 1973; J.D., UCLA, 1977. Bar: Calif. 1977, D.C. 1979, Colo. 1984. Assoc. Covington & Burling, Washington, 1977-83; legal cons., Boulder, Colo., 1983-84; ptnr. Sherman & Howard, Denver, 1984—; adj. prof. law Am. U. Sch. Law, 1983; lectr. Internat. Law Inst., 1982, U. Va. Law Sch., 1981, 82. Am. Field Service scholar, 1968-69. Editor in chief UCLA Law Rev., 1977; assoc. editor, 1976-77. Mem. ABA, Am. Soc. Internat. Law. Democrat. Congregationalist. Home: 728 10th St Boulder CO 80302 Office: 633 17th St Suite 2900 Denver CO 80202

LOW, MARY ELIZABETH, lawyer; b. Detroit, Dec. 25, 1946; d. William John and Alice (Koster) Low. B.A., U. Mich., 1968; J.D., Thomas Cooley Law Sch., 1978. Tchr., Royal Oak Sch. Dist. (Mich.), 1968-69; adminstrv. asst. Office of Gov., Detroit and Lansing, Mich., 1969-71; asst. to dir. Mich. Dept. of Labor, Lansing, 1971-72; exec. dir. Gov. Commn. on Employment of Handicapped, Lansing, 1973-74; exec. dir. Mich. Adv. Council on Spanish Speaking, Lansing, 1974-75; exec. dir. Mich. Commn. on Agrl. Labor, Lansing, 1975-77; chief Govs. Grant Program, Dept. of Labor, 1977-78; atty. Mich. Pub. Service Commn., Lansing, 1978—. Bd. dirs. Mich. Project on Equal Edn. Rights, Ann Arbor, 1979—, Mich. Ptnrs. of the Ams.; mem. Mich. Women's Commn., 1977-84, vice chmn., 1977, chmn., 1978; mem. Youth for Understanding Alumni Assn., Ann Arbor, 1964-84. Recipient History award DAR, Highland Park, Mich., 1960. Mem. ABA, Mich. Bar Assn., Cooley Law Sch. Alumni Bd. (bd. dirs. 1982-84), Alpha Chi Omega. Republican. Club: Zonta. Office: PO Box 833 East Lansing MI 48823

LOW, WILLA FRANCES, writer, editor; b. Boston, Nov. 4, 1912; d. Clifton Eliot and Hilia Signe (Paakonen) Belknap; B.S. in Edn., Framingham State Coll., 1952; m. George Malcolm Low, Sept. 10, 1932; 1 son, Malcolm Eliot. Tchr. Am. and ancient history Dana Hall Sch. for Girls, Wellesley, Mass., 1943-45, 1959-63; tchr. Vt. pub. schs., Barre, 1947-49, Wellesley pub. schs., 1951, 54-56; free lance writer, 1940—; author: Winthrop Sargent: Soldier and Statesman, 1976; editor Doric Column, 1971-77, women's aux. sect. Addison Gilbert Hosp. newsletter, 1974-76; editor: Tides of Essex (Edward T. Sanderson), 1977. Gen. chmn. Festival of the Arts, Wellesley Congregational Ch., 1965, Wellesley C. of C. Art Festival, 1968; participant Bicentennial Women's Capsule, Gloucester, Mass., 1976. Recipient Order of Paul Revere Patriots citation Gov. of Mass., 1974; Morgan Meml. Goodwill Industries vol. service citation, 1984. Mem. Nat. League Am. Pen Women (pres. North Shore br. 1976-78), Brit. Bronte Soc., World Affairs Council, Mass. State Fedn. Women's Clubs (12th dist. dir. 1966-68), AAUW (Named Gift award 1982-83), Doric Dames, Inc. Mem. Congregational Ch. Club: Wellesley Hills Woman's Club (pres. 1961-63, trustee 1975-76). Address: 16 Hillside Ct Gloucester MA 01930

LOWE, ADELE VIRGINIA (MRS. ALBERT ST. CLAIR LOWE), pharmacist; b. Indpls., June 27, 1919; d. Michael Angelo and Ivy Opal (Wilson) Lobraico; B.S. Indpls. Coll. Pharmacy, 1941; m. Albert St. Clair Lowe, Dec. 10, 1942; 1 dau., Judith A. (Mrs. Robert Frank Campbell). Chemist, E.I. duPont de Nemours & Co., Pryor, Okla., 1942-43; registered pharmacist Lobraico's Broad Ripple Pharmacy, Indpls., 1943—. Mem. Nat. Assn. Retail Druggists, Womens Orgn. Nat. Assn. Retail Druggists (pres. chpt. 20, 1977-79, chmn. legis. com.) Indpls. Assn. Pharmacists, Broad Ripple Bus. and Profl. Womens Club, Lambda Kappa Sigma (mem. grand council, supr. Midwest region 1948-50, 66-68, supr. So. region 1958-60, 4th v.p. 1950-54, grand v.p. 1968-70, grand pres. 1970-74, mem.-at-large 1974-78, chmn. ednl. trust com. 1975—, hon. adv. 1978-84, Disting. Service citation 1982). Clubs: Order Eastern Star, Daus. of Nile. Home: 12610 Brookshire Pkwy Carmel IN 46032 Office: 902 E Westfield Blvd Indianapolis IN 46220

LOWE, DOROTHY ANN, library technician; b. Gibson, N.C., Dec. 20, 1939; d. H. Bruce and Inez Campbell; B.S. in Media Tech., Fed. City Coll., 1975; M.S. in Media Sci., U. D.C., 1979; grad. Foster Inst. Real Estate, 1985; m. John Lowe, Jan. 18, 1958 (div. Dec. 1975); children—Donna, Steven, Inez. Personnel clk. FCC, 1972-76; microfilm photographer Library of Congress, Washington, 1976-77, personnel clk., 1977, library technician, 1977—. Pres., Pentecostal Ch. Missionaries, 1974—. Recipient letter of commendation FCC, 1976. Mem. D.C. Library Assn., U. D.C. Alumni Assn. Democrat. Office: Library of Congress 10 1st St SE Washington DC 20540

LOWE, ETHEL BLACK, artist; b. Kiowa County, Okla., Jan. 30, 1904; d. Benjamin Alonzo and Harriet Ann (Heaton) Black; B.A., Central State U., Okla., 1926; M.A., U. Tulsa, 1937; postgrad. U. Okla., U. Colo., Columbia, U. Hawaii; m. William Glenn Lowe, June 5, 1939 (dec. 1942). Tchr. pub. schs., Okla., 1922-39, N.Y., 1942-49, 50-68, ret.; teaching prin. Dragon Sch., Sasebo, Kyushu, Japan, 1949-50; works exhibited 1945—; exhbns. include Nat. Assn. Women Artists, 1953, 55, 71, 75, 77, Terry Nat. Art Exhibit, 1952, Provincetown Art Assn., 1952-53, Nassau Community Coll., 1971. Reproductions of works in newspapers, mags. Mem. N.Y. State Ret. Tchrs. Assn., Nat. Assn. Women Artists, Am. Watercolor Soc., Nat. Ret. Tchrs. Assn., Delta Kappa Gamma. Home: 48-50 44th St Woodside NY 11377

LOWE, FLORENCE SEGAL, government arts association executive; b. N.Y.C.; d. Samuel I. and Rose (Cantor) Segal; B.S. in Edn., U. Pa., 1930; postgrad. Sch. Social Service, 1935-36; m. Herman Albert Lowe, June 27, 1935; children—Lesley Ellen Lowe Israel, Roger Bernard. Guidance counsellor Phila. Public Schs., 1935-41; Washington corr. Variety and Daily Variety, Phila. Daily News, Manchester Union Leader, TV Guide, 1942-58; spl. public relations Radio Sta. WIP, Phila. and Metromedia, 1958-60; coordinator spl. projects Metromedia, 1960-70; dir. media relations, spl. projects Nat. Endowment for Arts, Washington, 1970—. Mem. public relations and advt. com. Nat. Symphony, 1952-56; mem. Sec. State's Commn. on Travel, 1970-71; mem. Coordinating Com. for Ellis Island, 1982—. Recipient All-Army Entertainment Contest award, 1958, spl. achievement award NEA, 1980, 83. Mem. Am. Women in Radio and Television (founder, pres. 1954-55), Govt. Communicators, Council Jewish Women, Women in Communications (citation for meritorious reporting 1962). Republican. Clubs: Washington Press (v.p. 1957-58, 63-64, bd. dirs. 1981-84), Am. News Women's (v.p. 1969-70), B'nai B'rith Women. Home: 2801 New Mexico Ave NW Washington DC 20007 Office: Nat Endowment for Arts Washington DC 20506

LOWE, KATHLENE WINN, lawyer; b. San Diego, Dec. 1, 1949; d. Ralph and Grace Lily (Rodes) Winn; m. Russell Howells Lowe, Oct. 3, 1977; 1 son, Taylor Rhodes. B.A. magna cum laude, U. Utah, 1971, M.A., 1973, J.D., 1976. Bar: Utah 1976. Assoc. firm Parsons, Behle & Latimer, Salt Lake City, 1976-79, mem., 1980-84; v.p. law Skaggs Alpha Beta, Inc., 1984—. Contbr. article to law rev., mem. Utah Law Rev., 1974-75, comment editor, 1975-76. Mem. ABA, Utah State Bar (chmn. legal econs. com. 1983-84), Salt Lake County Bar Assn., Phi Kappa Phi. Office: Skaggs Alpha Beta Inc PO Box 30658 Salt Lake City UT 84130

LOWE, LORETTA DAPHNE, art broker, oil and real estate investor; b. Lubbock, Tex., Sept. 12, 1948; d. Brady Mark and Pauline (Barrier) Lowe. B.Art, Tex. Tech U., 1970, postgrad. in art, 1972; postgrad. So. Meth. U., 1980. Tchr. art Dallas Pub. Schs., 1970-71; area dir. Campus Crusade for Christ, Boulder, Colo., 1972-80; cons. Lowe Land Co., Lubbock, Tex., 1970-84; owner, pres. Interior Investments Fine Art, Houston, 1980—. Mem. C. of C., Nat. Assn. Female Execs., Pi Beta Phi. Republican. Presbyterian. Home: PO Box 27303 Houston TX 77227 Office: Five Post Oak Park Suite 1825 Houston TX 77027

LOWE, MARY FRANCES, federal government official; b. Ft. Meade, Md., Apr. 15, 1951; d. Benno Powers and Peggy Catherine (Moore) L. B.A., Coll. William and Mary, 1972; M.A., Fletcher Sch. Law and Diplomacy, 1974, M.A. Law and Diplomacy in, 1975; diplome, Grad. Inst. Internat. Studies U. Geneva, Switzerland, 1975. External collaborator ILO, Geneva, 1974; legis. asst. to U.S. Senator Richard S. Schweiker, Washington, 1975-76; profl. staff mem. health and sci. research subcom. U.S. Senate Com. Labor and Human Resources, Washington, 1976-81; exec. sec. U.S. Dept. Health and Human Services, Washington, 1981-85; sr. asst. program policy U.S. FDA, 1985—; rep. U.S. delegations 34th and 35th World Health Assemblies, Geneva, 1981, 82; alt. trustee Woodrow Wilson Internat. Ctr. Scholars. Home: 7920 Spotswood Dr Alexandria VA 22308 Office: US FDA 5600 Fishers Ln Rockville MD 20857

LOWE, MARY JOHNSON, fed. judge; b. N.Y.C., June 10, 1924; B.A., Hunter Coll., 1952; J.D., Bklyn. Law Sch., 1954; LL.M., Columbia U., 1955; children by previous marriage—Edward H., Leslie H.; m. Ivan A. Michael, Nov. 4, 1961; 1 dau., Bess J. Michael. Admitted to N.Y. State bar, 1955; practiced law, N.Y.C., 1955-71; judge N.Y.C. Criminal Ct., 1972-73; acting justice N.Y. State Supreme Ct., 1973-77, justice, 1st Jud. Dist., 1978; judge U.S. Dist. Ct. for So. Dist. N.Y., 1978—. Recipient award for outstanding service to criminal justice system Bronx County Criminal Cts. Bar Assn., 1974, award for work on narcotics cases Asst. Dist. Attys., 1974. Mem. Women in Criminal Justice, Harlem Lawyers Assn., Bronx Criminal Lawyers Assn., N.Y. County Lawyers Assn., Bronx County Bar Assn., N.Y. State Bar Assn. (award for outstanding jud. contbn. to criminal justice Sect. Criminal Justice 1978), NAACP, Nat. Urban League, Nat. Council Negro Women, NOW. Office: US Dist Ct Foley Sq New York NY 10007*

LOWE, RUTH REEVE, librarian; b. Provo, Utah, June 27, 1929; d. Fenton West and Rhea Luthenia (Dixon) Reeve; m. Howard D. Lowe, Sept. 4, 1951; children—Kevin Howard, Linda Ann Lowe Weaver, David Jordan, Alan, Mark. B.S., Brigham Young U., 1951; M.L.S., U. Hawaii, 1969, M.Ed., 1970. Exec. sec. Geneva Steel Co., Orem, Utah, 1949, Bell Telephone Co., Provo, 1951, Gen. Foods Co., Chgo., 1951-52, Abadan Inst. (Iran), 1961-63; sch. librarian Univ. Lab., Honolulu, 1968-69, Blanche Pope Sch., Waimanalo, Hawaii, 1970—; participant Waimanalo Country TV Program, 1983; librarian Latter-Day Saints Ch., Kaneohe, Hawaii, 1970-74, Kailua, Hawaii, 1973-74. Author: A Penny Earned, 1964; artist oil paintings. Active PTA, Utah, Ariz., Hawaii, 1958—; coordinator Multiple Sclerosis, Waimanalo, 1978—; vol. Am. Cancer Soc., Kailua, 1976-78; leader Boy Scouts Am. Fed. Govt. grantee U. Hawaii, 1967-68. Mem. AAUW, ALA, Hawaii Sch. Library Assn. (chmn. 1974-75), Windward Library Assn. (chmn. 1976-78). Republican. Mormon. Clubs: Faculty, Tamaris (Provo). Home: 192 Alala Rd Kailua HI 96734 Office: Blanche Pope Elem Sch 41-133 Huli St Waimanalo HI 96795

LOWER, JAN ELLA, utility spokesperson, communications consultant; b. Milford, Del., Jan. 24, 1949; d. Paris Mills and Marie (Emory) Sharp; m. Brenton Ray Lower, Apr. 25, 1975. Student Del. State Coll., 1967-68; Shephard Coll., 1968-71. With tng. and devel. Lazarus Dept. Store, Columbus, Ohio, 1971-76; tng. video producer Gen. Telephone and Electronics, Ft. Wayne, Ind., 1976-79; media relations, Indpls Power & Light Co., 1979—; communications cons. non-profit orgns. including Salvation Army, United Way Greater Indpls., Urban League, Lakes At The Crossing Homeowner's Assn., Ind. Lung Assn. Fundraiser Indpls Opera Co., 1983-84, Humane Soc., 1984; publicity com. 500 Festival Assocs., 1983—; mem. Circle Theatre Media Adv. Com., 1983-84, Opening Night Planning Com., 1984; mem. Indpls. Sr. Citizen Bd., mem. hospitality com. City Assets Conf., 1985. Mem. LWV, Women in Communications (v.p. Indpls. profl. chpt.), Press Club of Indpls., Indpls. C. of C. Methodist. Club: Sycamore Golf. Office: Corp Communications Indpls Power & Light 25 Monument Circle Indianapolis IN 46204

LOWERY, NANCY ALBRIGHT, nursing educator; b. Monroe, La., Dec. 14, 1939; d. Ira Clay and Frances Adelia (Maxey) Albright; B.S., Northwestern State U., 1960; M.S., Emory U., 1964; m. Oliver Powell Lowery, Jr., July 9, 1966; children—Clay Patrick, Katherine Elise, John Oliver. Gen. staff nurse, La., N.J., 1961-63; faculty U. Tenn. Coll. Nursing, Memphis, 1964-66; faculty N.E. La. U. Sch. Nursing, Monroe, 1968—, mem. bd. nursing, 1976—, assoc. prof. nursing, pres. bd. nursing, 1982, 83; item writer Nat. State Bd. Test Pool Exam, 1976, 77; lectr. in field. Officer, Riverfield Acad. Parents Club, 1980-81; trustee, catechism instr. Sacred Heart Cath. Ch., 1978—. Named Outstanding Educator N.E. La. U., 1985-86. Mem. La. Nurses Assn., Am. Nurses Assn., Am. Assn. Critical Care Nurses, AAUW. Roman Catholic. Home: Route 5 Box 111 Rayville LA 71269 Office: NE La Univ Sch of Nursing Monroe LA 71201

LOWERY, SANDRA SCOGGINS, computer parts exchange company official; b. Oklahoma City, Jan. 15, 1949; d. William Albert and Lucile Dean (Perkins) S.; m. Leslie William Tompkins, Apr. 6, 1974 (div. 1983); m. Charles Leon Lowery, Apr. 7, 1984. B.S., Tex. Tech. U., 1971. Pre-hearing examiner Indsl. Accident Bd. State of Tex., various locations, 1971-82; regional sales mgr. CPX-Computer Parts Exchange, Houston, 1982—. Club: Briar. Home: 3509 Rice Blvd Houston TX 77005

LOWMAN, MARY BETHENA HEMPHILL (MRS. ZELVIN D. LOWMAN), civic worker, realtor, former educator; b. Lewis, Kans., Feb. 10, 1922; d. Frederick William and Gladys (Follin) Hemphill; A.B., Western State Coll., Colo., 1945; m. Zelvin D. Lowman, Oct. 24, 1943; children—Freda Ruth (Mrs. Neal Frink), James Fredrick, William Martin, Elizabeth June (Mrs. Joseph Herbst) (dec.). Tchr., Stout Creek Sch., Colo., 1942-43, San Diego City Sch. Dist., 1944-45, Los Angeles City Sch. Dist., 1948-50; pvt. sch. tchr. So. Inst. Music, 1956-57. Troop leader Frontier council Girl Scouts U.S.A., 1957-70, mem. exec. bd., 1961-73, 2d v.p., 1962-63, pres., 1968-71, recipient Thanks Badge, 1964, chmn. established camp com., 1963-67, dir. Camp Foxtail, 1965, 67, mem. Girl Scouts U.S.A. Region VI Com., 1973-75, chmn. Region VI Com., mem. nat. bd., mem. exec. com. and councils com., 1975-78; mem. Am. Field Service Exchange Student Bd. So. Nev., 1961. Parliamentarian, West Charleston PTA, 1957-59, Nev. Congress, 1960-61; chmn. Christian Edn. Commn., 1964-65; chmn. Commn. on Mission of Church, 1966; chmn. exec. com. Clark County Bicentennial Commn., 1974-76; chmn. bd. First Presbyterian Pre-Sch. Day Care Ctr., 1982-85. Family chosen as Nev. All-Am. Family, 1960. Mem. Gen. Fedn. Women's Clubs (dir. 1958-60, 62-64, 72-78, chmn. scholarships and student aid 1974-76, chmn. family living div., 1976-78; treas. Western States Conf. 1968-70, sec. 1970-72, pres. 1972-74), Nev. Fedn. Women's, Clubs, (past pres.), Md. fedn. women's Clubs (past jr. dir.), Clark County Pan-Hellenic Assn., So. Nev. Alumni Club (pres. 1961-62), Internat. Platform Assn. Presbyterian (elder). Clubs: Las Vegas Mesquite (past pres.); Jr. Women's (past pres.) (College Park, Md.); Newcomers (past pres.), Nat. Presbyterian Mariners; (past pres.), Nevada-Sierra District Mariners; Las Vegas Nautilus Mariners. Home: 1713 Rambla Ct Las Vegas NV 89102

LOWRANCE, MURIEL EDWARDS, program specialist; b. Ada, Okla., Dec. 28, 1922; d. Warren E. and Mayme E. (Barrick) Edwards; B.S. in Edn., East Central State U., Ada, 1954; 1 dau., Kathy Lynn Lowrance Gutierrez. Accountant, adminstrv. asst. to bus. mgr. East Central State U., 1950-68; grants and contracts specialist U. N.Mex. Sch. Medicine, Albuquerque, 1968-72, program specialist IV, dept. orthopaedics, 1975-86; asst. adminstrv. officer N.Mex. Regional Med. Program, 1972-75. Bd. dirs. Vocat. Rehab. Center, 1980-84. Cert. profl. contract mgr. Nat. Contract Assn. Mem. Am. Bus. Women's Assn. (past pres. El Segundo chpt., Woman of Yr. 1974), AAUW, Amigos de las Americas (dir.). Democrat. Methodist. Club: Pilot (pres. 1979-80, dir. 1983-84, dist. treas. 1984-86, gov.-elect S.W. dist. 1986-87) (Albuquerque). Home: 3028 Mackland Ave NE Albuquerque NM 87106

LOWREY, ELEANOR BLODWYN LANE, special education administrator; b. Mpls.; d. George Emerson and Eunice Blodwyn (Owen) Lane; student Macalester Coll., 1942-44, U. Minn., 1944-45; B.S., U. Denver, 1965, Ed.D., 1973; m. Jack B. Lowrey, Sept. 15, 1945; children—Susan, Gretchen, Georgia, John, David. Tchr., Fort Logan Mental Health Center, Denver, 1965-67; ednl. specialist Jefferson County Schs., Lakewood, Colo., 1968-71, coordinator spl. edn., learning disabilities, behavioral disorders, 1973-80, asst. dir. spl. edn., 1980—; facilitator and cons., group devel., organizational devel., 1982—; mem. bd. Gifted and Talented Colo., 1977-78. Bd. dirs. Indian Hills (Colo.) Water Dist., 1973—. Mem. Children with Learning Disabilities, Colo. Assn. Gifted and Talented, Soc. Learning Disabilities and Remedial Edn., Council Exceptional Children (dir.), Assn. Supervision and Curriculum Devel., Phi Delta Kappa, Kappa Delta Pi. Home: Box 977 Indian Hills CO 80454 Office: 3115 Kipling St Lakewood CO 80227

LOWREY, SARA NELLE, writer, film producer; b. Gatesville, Tex., Oct. 6, 1949; d. Oliver Wendell and Nelle (Goodall) Lowrey; B. Journalism, U. Tex., 1971; postgrad. So. Meth. U., 1972-73; m. Donald J. Mackie, Apr. 6, 1974; 1 child, Anna Kathleen. Gen. assignments reporter, anchorperson Sta. KDFW-TV, Dallas, 1972-74; gen. assignments reporter, 6 o'clock anchor person Sta. KPRC-TV, Houston, 1974-78, weekend anchorperson, 1979-80; prin. Lowrey Assos., Gatesville, 1978—, B-L-S Media Devel. Co., Houston, 1981—. Cons. Tex. press office George Bush for Pres. Campaign, 1979; bd. dirs. Coryell Meml. Hosp. Aux., 1980-82. Recipient Addy award-1st place for TV comml., 1980; 1st place award for documentary on childbirth Tex. Public Health Assn., 1977; Sch. Bell award, Tex. State Tchrs. Assn., 1973. Mem. Soc. Profl. Journalists, Women in Communication, Chi Omega. Presbyterian. Home: 806 Hilltop Circle Salado TX 76571 Office: 3328 Walnut Bend Ln Houston TX 77042

LOWRIE, PAMELA BURT, art educator, artist; b. Geneva, Ill., May 12, 1937; d. Morris Nathan and Helyn (Beetlestone) B.; m. Edmund G. Lowrie, June 25, 1960 (div. 1969); children—Edmund Gale, Matthew Burt; m. 2d, Michael Hammer, Aug. 14, 1982. B.A., U. Mich., 1959; M.S. in Edn., No. Ill. U., Dekalb, 1970; M.A., Claremont Grad. Sch. (Calif.), 1979. One women shows: Loyola U. Gallery, Chgo., U. Ill. Med. Ctr. Gallery, 1978, Elmhurst (Ill.) Coll. Gallery, 1980, Kankakee (Ill.) Coll. Gallery, 1981, The Edge Gallery, Villa Park, Ill., 1984; group shows include: Five Women Artists from Ill., Notre Dame U., 1979, Springfield (Ill.) Art Assn. Gallery, 1981, Am. Cultural Ctr., Taipei, Taiwan, 1982; represented in permanent collections: Coll. DuPage, Glen Ellyn, Ill.; art cons. Sch. Dist. 41, Glen Ellyn, Ill., 1970-72; instr. art Coll. DuPage, Glen Ellyn, 1972—; dir., staff Nat. Great Tchrs. Seminars, Williams Bay, Wis., 1976—; staff Calif. Great Tchrs. Seminar, Santa Barbara, 1979. Bd. dirs. Fine Arts Rev. Com., DuPage County, Ill., 1982. Home: 926 N Scott St Wheaton IL 60187 Office: Coll DuPage Lambert St and 22d St Glen Ellyn IL 60137

LOWRY, BARBARA JEAN, nursing educator; b. Rockford, Ill., Apr. 14, 1938; d. Albert Rudolph and Barbara Jean (Slater) Isoz; m. Clark Graydon Lowry, Dec. 16, 1961; 1 son, Andrew Karl. B.S., Rockford Coll., 1976, M.A. in Teaching with distinction, 1980. R.N., Ill. Staff nurse Rockford Meml. Hosp. (Ill.), 1960-61, nursing instr., 1964—, lectr., 1981—, curriculum chmn., 1983; staff nurse Copley Meml. Hosp., Aurora, Ill., 1961-62, asst. head nurse, 1962-64; lectr. Rockford Coll., 1983; moderator Alzheimer's Program. Student coordinator Am. Field Service, Rockford, 1983. Named Am. Field Service Mother, 1982, 84. Mem. Am. Nurses Assn., Nat. League Nursing (accreditation visitor 1986), Am. Assn. Critical Care Nursing, Alzheimers and Related Disease Assn., Ill. Nurses Assn. (pres.-elect 3d Dist. 1986), Rockford Meml. Nurses Alumni Assn. (meml. chmn. 1980—). Baptist. Club: Charter of Rockford Coll. Home: 2902 E State St Rockford IL 61108 Office: Rockford Meml Sch Nursing 2400 N Rockton Ave Rockford IL 61101

LOWRY, JOAN MARIE DONDREA, broadcaster; b. Weirton, W.Va., June 8, 1935; d. Rudolph and Mary (Telmanik) Dondrea; m. Robert William Lowry, June 15, 1957; 1 child, Christopher Scott. B.S. in Edn., Baldwin-Wallace Coll., 1956; student Ohio Sch. Broadcasting, 1977-79. Gen. mgr., news dir. Sta. WLRO, Lorain, Ohio, 1980-82; host 35 Live, Cinemavidio TV, Elyria, Ohio, 1980-83; TV show host Continental Cable, Cleve., 1983—; pub. relations dir. Sta. WZLE, Lorain, 1982-83; broadcaster, community relations dir. Sta. WRKG, Lorain, 1983—; performer commls.; speaker in field. Appeared in motion pictures: Those Lips Those Eyes, 1982, One Trick Pony, 1982. Mem. nat. steering com. Better Hearing and Speech, 1985-86; nat. philanthropy chair Delta Zeta Sorority and Found., 1980—, trustee, 1980—; mem. Lorain Litter Control Bd., 1981-83; bd. dirs. Lorain Conty Sr. Citizens Assn., 1982-85, Lorain Consumers Council, 1980—; v.p. Bay Village PTA Council, 1973-75; actige Multiple Sclerosis Soc., Am. Cancer Soc., Muscular Dystrophy Assn., others; grand marshal numerous parades. Named Woman of Achievement, Nat. YWCA and Lorain County Bus. and Industry Assn., 1983; U.S. Air Force award, 1982; U.S. Navy award, 1981; Media award Am. Cancer Soc., 1982; Communication award Easter Seals Soc., 1981; Community Service award Lorain County chpt. Am. Heart Assn., 1981; ofcl. hostess for U.S. Army in Lorain County, 1980-83; Mayor's Proclamation, 1982; hon. recruiter U.S. Army, 1981. Mem. Lorain County Arts Council, Baldwin-Wallace Alumni Assn. (nat. pres. 1979-81), LWV (chpt. pres. 1966-67), Cleve. Amateur Fencers (pres. 1965-67). Byzantine Catholic. Home: 578 Yarmouth Ln Bay Village OH 44140

LOWRY, NANCY JACKSON, industrial relations manager; b. Selma, Ala., Apr. 26, 1954; d. Ernest Frank and Doris (Bush) Jackson; m. Gregory L. Lowry, May 18, 1984. B.B.A., Augusta Coll., 1976. Personnel interviewer Sears, Roebuck & Co., Augusta, Ga., 1973-78; instr. Augusta Tech. Sch., 1979-81; faculty recruiter Med. Coll. Ga., Augusta, 1978-81; personnel rep. Pan Am. World Services, Ft. Gordon, Ga., 1981-84, mgr. indsl. relations, 1984—. cons. career devel., 1982—. Am. Business Women's Assn. scholar, 1972. Mem. Am. Soc. Personnel Adminstrn., Pan Am. Mgmt. Club (pres. 1982-84), C.S.R.A. Personnel Assn. (dir.), Phi Kappa Phi. Home: 2905 Arrowhead Dr E8 Augusta GA 30909 Office: Pan Am World Services PO Box 7506 Augusta GA 30909

LOWRY, PATRICIA KATHLEEN, educator; b. Chgo., Apr. 29, 1928; d. Robert Beardsley Fredrick and Kathleen Cleola (Heilman) Hardy; B.A., Ball State U., 1951, M.A., 1964, Ed.D., 1968; postgrad. Bowling Green State U., Sam Houston State U.; m. Douglas Lowry, Aug. 23, 1948; children—Fredrick Robert Hugh, Patricia Marjorie. Tchr. English and social studies various elem. and high schs., Ind., Ohio, and Tex.; now mem. faculty Coll. of Edn., Sam Houston State U., Huntsville, Tex.; poetry judge, ednl. cons., lectr. in field. Leader Girl Scouts U.S.A., 4-H, Campfire Girls; bd dirs. Deep E. Tex. Council Govts., Huntsville Leadership Inst.; mem. citizens rev. com. Huntsville Item; asst. chaplain Tex. Dept. Corrections. Recipient Outstanding Alumnus award Ball State U./Kappa Delta Pi, 1977. Mem. Internat. Reading Assn., Assn. Supervision and Curriculum Devel., Early Reading Research Council, Tex. Assn. Profs. of Reading, NEA, Internat. Congress on Arts and Communication, AAUW, AAUP, Tex. Assn. Tchr. Educators, Tex. Assn. for Improvement Reading, NOW, Tex. Women for ERA, Am. Quarterhorse Assn., Am. Poultrymen, Bulldog Club Am., Audubon Soc., Delta Sigma Theta. Christian Scientist. Clubs: Order Eastern Star, Bus. and Profl. Women. Author: Handbook for Parents of Kindergartners, 1964; Teacher Evaluation, 1968; contbr. articles to profl. jours.; author reports on literacy edn. in Indonesia. Office: Coll Edn Sam Houston State Univ Huntsville TX 77341

LOYD, DOLLY DIANE, marketing educator; b. Jackson, Miss., Sept. 13, 1943; d. Rufus E. and Lena Rai (Holloway) Purvis; m. Leonard Alan Loyd, June 15, 1967 (dec. Dec. 1968). B.S. in Bus. Adminstrn., U. So. Miss., 1965, M.B.A., 1979. Trainee McRaes Dept. Store, Jackson, 1965-66; buyer Gayfers Dept. Store, Pensacola, Fla., 1966-67, 69-76; procurement buyer Naval Air Sta., Honolulu, 1967-68; instr. mktg. U. So. Miss., Hattiesburg, 1979—. Vol. worker Spl. Olympics, Hattiesburg, 1982. Mem. Miss. Retail Mchts. (dir. 1982—, mem. legis. com. 1984—), Sales and Mktg. Execs., Am. Mktg. Assn. (advisor 1980—), Alpha Sigma Alpha (nat. alumnae province dir. 1982—), Phi Chi Theta (advisor 1980—), Beta Gamma Sigma. Democrat. Baptist. Clubs:

Women's (pres. 1976-77) (Pensacola); Alumnae Group (pres. 1980-84) (Hattiesburg). Home: 2300 Lincoln Rd Apt 140 Hattiesburg MS 39401 Office: Univ of So Miss Southern Station 8122 Hattiesburg MS 39406

LOZOWSKI, MARY, cytotechnologist; b. Bronx, N.Y., Oct. 9, 1953; d. William and Mary Charlotte (Kapustka) Lozowski; B.S., Fordham U., 1976; postgrad. Sch. Cytotechnology, Meml. Sloan-Kettering Cancer Center, 1974-75, Hofstra U., 1978, 83. Staff cytotechnologist, cons., lectr. J.F. K. Meml. Hosp. and Med. Center, Monrovia, Liberia, 1976-77; cytology supr. dept. pathology Nassau Hosp., Mineola, N.Y., 1978—; lectr. in field. Mem. Internat. Acad. Cytology, Am. Soc. Clin. Pathologists, Am. Soc. Cytology, Greater N.Y. Assn. Cytotechnologists, AAAS. Clubs: Kosciuszko Found., Polish Am. Mus. Found. Contbr. articles to profl. jours. Address: Pathology Dept Cytology Div Nassau Hosp 259 First St Mineola NY 11501

LUBEROFF, BONNIE LEE, personnel executive; b. Plainfield, N.J., Oct. 20, 1950; d. Michael John and Eleanore Joan (Hisko) Paccione; m. Paul Stephen Luberoff, Dec. 4, 1983; 1 child, Christopher Stephen. A.S., Brandywine Coll., 1970. Sales sec. Tenneco Chem. Inc., Piscataway, N.J., 1970-76; sr. sec. Warner Lambert Pharms., Morris Plains, N.J., 1976-81; exec. sec. to v.p. Airco Welding Products, Murray Hill, N.J., 1981-83; exec. sec. to pres. Multitone Electronics, Springfield, N.J., 1983-83, personnel mgr., 1983—. Mem. Nat. Assn. Female Execs., Am. Mgmt. Assn. Republican. Roman Catholic. Club: Sigma Iota Chi (social dir. 1969-70). Avocations: tennis; skiing; reading.

LUBETSKI, EDITH ESTHER, librarian; b. Bklyn., July 16, 1940; d. David and Leah (Aronson) Slomowitz; m. Meir Lubetski, Dec. 23, 1968; children—Shaul, Uriel, Leah. B.A., Blkyn. Coll., 1962; M.S. in L.S., Columbia U., 1965; M.A. in Jewish Studies, Yeshiva U., 1968. Judaica librarian Stern Coll., N.Y.C., 1965-66, acquisitions librarian, 1966-69, head librarian, 1969—; cons. Lawrence White Meml. Library, N.Y.C., 1970-72 Author: (with Meir Lubetski) Building a Judaica Library Collection, 1983. Mem. Assn. Jewish Libraries (corr. sec. 1980-84, pres. N.Y. chpt. 1984-86, nat. v.p. 1984-86, nat. pres. 1986-88), ALA, N.Y. Library Assn. Home: 1219 E 27th St Brooklyn NY 11210 Office: Stern Coll Hedi Steinberg Library 245 Lexington Ave New York NY 10016

LUBIC, BENITA JOAN ALK, travel executive; b. Green Bay, Wis., May 18, 1936; s. Isadore George and Marion (Segal) Alk; m. Robert Bennett Lubic, May 31, 1959; children—Wendy Alison, Bret David, Robin Kimberly. B.B.A., U. Wis. 1958. Cert. travel cons. Inst. Cert. Travel Agts. Pres., owner Transeair Travel, Inc., Washington, 1959—. Mem. adv. bd. Braniff Airlines, Republic Airlines, Sonesta Hotel Corp. Mem. Am. Soc. Travel Agts. (pres. Washington subchpt. 1985-87; bd. dirs. 1979), Prost Exec. Women in Travel (v.p. 1982-83, treas. 1984-85). Contbr. articles on incentive travel to mags. Democrat. Jewish. Avocations: golf; tennis; swimming; bicycling; travel. Home: 2813 McKinley Pl NW Washington DC 20015 Office: Transeair Travel Inc 4710 41st St NW Washington DC 20016

LUCAS, CAROL, gerontologist; b. Hewlett, L.I., N.Y., July 11, 1929; d. Irving William and Julia (Cutler) Lucas; B.S., Coll. William and Mary, 1949; M.A., Columbia U., 1951, Ed.D., 1953. Field dir. Greater N.Y. council Girl Scouts U.S.A., N.Y.C., 1949-51; recreation dir. Neponsit (N.Y.) Beach Hosp., 1951-53; cons. Nat. Council Jewish Women, N.Y.C., 1954-55; area coordinator Los Angeles County Heart Assn., Los Angeles, 1955-56; rehab. cons. City of Hope, Duarte, Calif., 1955-56, Los Angeles Tb and Health Assn., 1957-58; recreation cons. Fedn. Protestant Welfare Agys., N.Y.C., 1958-60; instr. Columbia, 1959—; dir. spl. pilot study in gerontology, N.Y.C., 1958-64; exec. dir. Five Towns Sr. Center; supr. adminstrn. on aging project Sr. Center of Nassau County, Uniondale, N.Y.; dir. Dept. Services for Aging, Town of Hempstead (N.Y.), 1968-78, commr., 1978—. Mem. Am. Recreation Soc., Nat. Assn. Social Workers, Nat. Recreation Assn., Acad. Cert. Social Workers, Royal Soc. Health (London), Kappa Delta Pi, Delta Psi Omega. Author: (with Josephine Rathbone) Recreation in Total Rehabilitation, 1958; Recreation Activity Development in Nursing Home, Homes for the Aging and Hospitals, 1962, rev. edit., 1982; Recreation in Gerontology, 1983. Contbr. articles to profl. jours. Home: 141 Wyckoff Pl Woodmere NY 11598

LUCAS, CAROL LEE, mathematician; b. Aberdeen, S.D., Feb. 13, 1940; d. Howard Cleveland and Sarah Ivy (Easterby) Nogle; B.A., Dakota Wesleyan U., 1961; M.S., U. Ariz., 1967; Ph.D., U. N.C., 1973; m. Richard Albert Lucas, Feb. 26, 1961; children—Wendy Lee, Sean Richard. Tchr. Spanish, Mitchell (S.D.) High Sch., 1960-61; tchr. math, English, sci. U.S. Army, Furth, Ger., 1961-62; systems analyst Cargill Inc., Mpls., 1962-65; research assoc. U. N.C., Chapel Hill, 1973-76, lectr., 1976-77, asst. prof. curriculum in biomed. engring. and math, 1977-84, assoc. prof., 1984—. NIH trainee, 1968-73. Mem. Am. Heart Assn., N.C. Heart Assn., Biomed. Engring. Soc. Democrat. Methodist. Contbr. articles to profl. jours. Home: 2421 Sedgefield Dr Chapel Hill NC 27514 Office: Burnett-Womack 229H Dept Surgery U NC Chapel Hill NC 27514

LUCAS, ELIZABETH HELENE, artist, calligrapher, educator; b. Pasadena, Calif., Aug. 21, 1936; d. Edward A. and Anona Marie (Snyder) Buse; m. Justice Campbell M. Lucas, Dec. 17, 1960; children—Scott, Stephen, Lisanne. A.A., Long Beach City Coll., 1956; B.A., Whittier Coll., 1958, M.A., 1984. Cert. gen. secondary tchr., Calif. Chmn. dept. sci. Bolsa Grande High Sch., Garden Grove, Calif., 1960-65; ind. tchr. calligraphy Long Beach, Calif., 1976—; instr. Sch. for Adults, Long Beach, 1978-80; asst. prof. calligraphy Calif. State U.-Long Beach, 1979—, coordinator cert. in calligraphy program, 1982—; instr. calligraphy and bookbinding U. Calif.-Riverside, 1982—; instr. calligraphy Whittier Coll., Calif., 1984-85; free-lance calligrapher and graphic designer, 1976—; designer, pub. line of calligraphy notecards, 1978—. Author: Calligraphy, The Art of Beautiful Writing, 1984; one-Woman calligraphy shows Long Beach Mus. Art Bookshop/Gallery, 1981, 84, Sr. Eye Gallery, Long Beach, 1982, 85, Gt. Western Savs. and Loan, Long Beach, 1983, David Scott Meier Gallery, Mendocino, Calif., 1983, Whittier Coll. Mendenhall Gallery, 1983; also group shows. Active, past mem. bd. dirs. Long Beach Law Aux., 1960—, Jr. League, Long Beach, 1968—; pres. Lowell Sch. PTA, Long Beach, 1972. Named Sci. Tchr. of Yr., So. Calif. Edison Co., 1963; recipient art awards, including First Place award Calif. State Lawyers' Wives, 1984. Mem. Soc. for Calligraphy (pres. 1982-83), Soc. Scribes and Illuminators, Friends of Calligraphy, Soc. Scribes, Profl. Writers League, Calif. State PTA (hon. life 1973—), Long Beach Mus. Art Found. (co-chairperson dir.'s circle 1985), Long Beach Art Assn., Pub. Corp. for Arts, Fine Art Affiliates of Calif. State U. at Long Beach. Republican. Lodge: Soroptimists (com. chairperson local club 1981—). Home: 518 Monrovia Ave Long Beach CA 90814 Office: PO Box 15276 Long Beach CA 90815

LUCAS, GEORGETTA MARIE SNELL, retired educator, artist; b. Harmony, Ind., July 25, 1920; d. Ernest Clermont and Sarah Ann (McIntyre) Snell; m. Joseph William Lucas, Jan. 29, 1943; children—Carleen Anita Lucas Underwood-Scrougham, Thomas Joseph, Joetta Jeanne Lucas Allgood. B.S., Ind. State U., 1942; M.S. in Edn., Butler U., 1964; postgrad. Herron Sch. of Art, Indpls., 1961-65, Ind. U., Indpls. and Bloomington, 1960, 61, 62, 65. Music, art tchr. Jasonville City Schs., Ind., 1942-43, Van Buren High Sch., Brazil, Ind., 1943-46, Plainfield City Schs., Ind., 1946-52, Met. Sch. Dist. Wayne Twp., Indpls., 1952-56, 1959-68; art tchr. Met. Sch. Dist. Perry Twp., Indpls., 1968-81. Illustrator: (book) Why So Sad, Little Rag Doll, 1963; artist (painting) Ethereal Season, 1966, (lithograph) Bird of Time, 1965-66: represented in permanent collections Ind. State U., Ind.-Purdue U.-Indlps.; lectr. Art Educators Assn. Ind., Ind. U.-Bloomington, 1976, Ind. Platform Assn., Washington, 1975, 77, 78, 82, 84 (Recipient Silver award 1978, appointed gov. 1983—). Named Best of Show, Nat. League Am. Pen Women State Show, 1983. Mem. Nat. Assn. Women Artist, Ind. Artist-Craftsmen, Inc. (pres. 1979-85), Ind. Fedn. Art Clubs (pres. 1986), Hoosier Salon, NEA, Art Edn. Assn. Ind., Nat. League Am. Pen Women (state art chmn. 1984—), Fine Art for State Ind. (Internat. Women's Yr. chmn. 1977), Internat. Platform Assn. (bd. dirs. 1983-85), Alpha Delta Kappa (Ind. state chmn. of art 1973-77, pres. 1972-74). Republican. Methodist. Clubs: Plainfield Art League, Marion County Art League. Lodge: Eastern Star. Avocations: genealogy; travel; numismatics. Home and Office: 9702 W Washington St Indianapolis IN 46231

LUCAS, IRENE CATALANO, sales executive; b. Boston, Feb. 23, 1954; d. Joseph Roy and Teresa Elizabeth (Lynch) Catalano; m. Raymond J. Lucas, Jr., Sept. 23, 1984. B.S., Boston U., 1976. Sales rep. Chilton Corp., Boston, 1976-78, EDP mgr., 1978-79, dir. tng., 1979-81; sales engr. ACDC Electronics Co., Sudbury, Mass., 1981-85, dist. sales mgr., 1985—. Mem. Nat. Assn. Female Execs., Internat. Fund Animal Welfare, World Wildlife Fund, Am. Protection Inst. Am. Roman Catholic. Avocations: fencing; running; art. Office: ACDC Electronics Co 39 Union Ave Sudbury MA 01776

LUCAS, JANE GARLAND, interior designer, educator; b. Poughkeepsie, N.Y., Aug. 24, 1951. B.A. in Studio Art, Sweet Briar Coll., 1973; M.S. in Interior Design, Drexel U., 1977. Designer, Anderson Notter Finegold Inc., Boston, 1977-81; designer/project mgr. Bennett Assocs., Boston, 1981-83; prin. JGL Interiors, Boston, 1983—; tchr. Boston Archl. Ctr., 1980—, Chamberlayne Jr. Coll., Boston, 1983—. Mem. Am. Soc. Interior Designers (bd. dirs.), Inst. Bus. Designers (bd. dirs.). Home: 63 Baldwin Charlestown MA 02129 Office: 10 Thacher St Suite 104 Boston MA 02113

LUCAS, LINDA DIANNE, skin care products manufacturing executive; b. Mpls., Nov. 1, 1942; d. Earl Winton and Shirley Grace (Holmgren) Skoog; B.S., Calif. Western U., 1981, M.B.A. candidate; m. Allen Joseph Lucas, Feb. 9, 1963; children—Teresa, Hollyanne, Scott (dec.), Jaime. Cons., Coppercraft Guild, Taunton, Mass., 1963-66; cons. Princess House, Inc., North Dighton, Mass., 1966-75, unit organizer, 1968-72, area dir., 1972-76; br. mgr. Leisure Home Parties, Inc., Racine, Wis., 1976-79, regional dir., 1976-79; dir. sales devel. Act II Jewelry, Inc., Bensenville, Ill., 1979-81; nat. mktg./sales mgr. Life Style Art, Inc., Kenyon, Minn., 1981-83; exec. v.p. Skin Care Internat., Peau Soin d'Amour, Sandy, Utah, 1983—; profl. instr. adult edn., St. Louis Park, Minn. Mem. Nat. Assn. Female Execs., Am. Soc. Profl. and Exec. Women. Lutheran. Author various co. publs. Home: 4730 Barbara Dr Minnetonka MN 55343 Office: 223 Cottage Ave Sandy UT 84070

LUCAS, SUZANNE, statistician; b. Baxter Springs, Kans., Jan. 16, 1939; d. Ralph Beaver and Marguerite (Sansocie) L.; B.A. in Math., Calif. State U., Fresno, 1967, M.A. in Ednl. Theory, 1969; M.S. in Stats., U. So. Calif., 1979; children—Patricia Sue Jennings, Neil Patric Jennings. Asst. to dir. NSF Inst., Calif. State U., Fresno, 1968; Tchr. secondary math. Fresno city schs., 1968-78; statistician corp. indsl. relations Hughes Aircraft Co., Los Angeles, 1979-80; personnel adminstr. Hughes Aircraft Co. Space and Communications Group, Los Angeles, 1981-82, mem. tech. staff in math., 1982-85, staff engr., 1985-86; lectr. in biostats. U. So. Calif., 1979. Kiwanis scholar, 1958. Mem. Soc. Women Engrs., Am. Statis. Assn., Am. Psychol. Assn., Internat. Assn. Parametric Analysts, Inst. Cost Analysis, U. So. Calif. Alumni Assn. (life), Kappa Mu Epsilon. Office: Hughes Aircraft Co PO Box 92919 Bldg C3 Mail Sta Z108 Los Angeles CA 90009

LUCCHETTI, LYNN, advertising manager, military officer, government executive; b. San Francisco, Calif., Aug. 21, 1939; d. Dante and Lillian (Bergeron) L. A.B., San Jose State U., 1961; M.S., San Francisco State U., 1967; grad. U.S. Army Basic Officer's Course, 1971, U.S. Army Advanced Officer Course, 1976, grad. U.S. Air Force Command and Staff Coll., 1982, U.S. Air Force War Coll., 1983, Sr. Pub. Affairs Officer Course, 1984. Media buyer Batten, Barton, Durstine & Osborn, Inc., San Francisco, 1961-67; producer-dir. Sta. KTVA-TV, Anchorage, 1967-68; media supr. Bennett, Luke and Teawell Advt., Phoenix, 1968-71; commd. 1st lt. U.S. Army, 1971; advanced through ranks to lt. col., 1985; officer U.S. Army, 1971-74, U.S. Nat. Guard, D.C., 1974-78, U.S. Air Force Res., 1978—, program advt. mgr. U.S. Navy Recruiting Command, 1974-76; exec. coordinator for the Joint Advt. Dirs. of Recruiting (JADOR), 1976-79; dir. U.S. Armed Forces Joint Recruiting Advt. Program (JRAP), Dept. Def., Washington, 1979—. Author: Broadcasting in Alaska, 1924-1966. Decorated U.S. Army Meritorious Service medal, Nat. Def. medal, U.S. Air Force Longevity Ribbon, U.S. Navy Meritorious Unit Commendation, Dept. Def. Joint Achievement medal, 1984. Sigma Delta Chi journalism scholar, 1960. Mem. Am. Women Composers, Women Officer's Profl. Assn., Dept. Def. Sr. Profl. Women's Group. Home: 5416 Barrister Pl Alexandria VA 22304 Office: Dir US Armed Forces Joint Recruiting Advt Program (JRAP) Dept of Defense 4015 Wilson Blvd (Code 020) Arlington VA 22203

LUCE, CLARE BOOTHE, playwright, former congresswoman, former ambassador; b. N.Y.C.; d. William F. and Ann (Snyder) Boothe; ed. St. Mary's, Garden City, N.Y., 1915-17, The Castle, Tarrytown, N.Y., 1917-19; Litt.D. (hon.), Colby Coll., Fordham U., Mundelein Coll.; LL.D. (hon.), Temple U., Creighton U., Georgetown U., Mt. Holyoke Coll., Seton Hall Coll., Boston U., Hamilton Coll., 1983, U.S.C. Med. Sch., 1984; A.F.D., St. John's U., Westminster Coll.; m. George Tuttle Brokaw, Aug. 10, 1923 (div. 1929); m. 2d, Henry R. Luce, Nov. 23, 1935 (dec.). Assoc. editor Vogue, 1930, Vanity Fair, 1931-32, mng. editor, 1933-34; newspaper columnist, 1934; playwright, 1935—; mem. 78th-79th congresses from 4th Conn. dist.; U.S. ambassador to Italy, 1953-57; mem. Pres.'s Fgn. Intelligence Adv. Bd., 1973-77, 82—; dir. Gray & Co.; cons. in Am. letters Library of Congress. Trustee Alfred E. Smith Meml. Fund, Honolulu Acad. Arts; bd. dirs. U.S. Strategic Inst., nat. adv. bd. U.S. Capitol Hist. Soc. Recipient Presdl. medal of Freedom, 1983, Dag Hammarskjold medal, Laeture medal, Am. Statesman medal, Fourth Estate award, Sylvanus Thayer award, Disting. Service to Congress award, Am. Eagle award, Woodruff award Assn. U.S. Army, Bob Hope 5-Star Civilian award, others. Mem. Acad. Polit. Sci., Nat. Fedn. Press Women, Internat. Platform Assn. Am. Inst. Fgn. Trade, Am. Security Council, Commn. on Present Danger, Ctr. for the Book, Internat. Rescue Commn., Nat. Intelligence Ctr., DAR, Hillsdale Assocs., others. Republican. Roman Catholic. Author: Stuffed Shirts, 1933; Europe in the Spring, 1940; (plays) Abide with Me; The Women, 1937; Kiss the Boys Goodbye, 1938; Margin for Error, 1939; Child of the Morning, 1951; Slam the Door Softly, 1970; (movie) Come to the Stable, 1947. Contbr. articles and fiction to mags. Collector, editor Saints for Now, 1952. •

LUCENTE, ROSEMARY DOLORES, educational administrator; b. Renton, Wash., Jan. 11, 1935; d. Joseph Anthony and Erminia Antoinette (Argano) Lucente; B.A., Mt. St. Mary's Coll., 1956, M.S., 1963. Tchr. pub. schs., Los Angeles, 1956-65, supr. tchr., 1958-65, asst. prin., 1965-69, prin. elem. sch., 1969-85, dir. instrn., 1985—; nat. cons., lectr. Dr. William Glasser's Educator Tng. Ctr., 1968—; nat. workshop leader Nat. Acad. for Sch. Execs.-Am. Assn. Sch. Adminstrs., 1980; Los Angeles Unified Sch. Dist. rep. for nat. pilot of Getty Inst. for Visual Arts, 1983-84, site coordinator, 1983-86. Recipient Golden Apple award Stanford Ave. Sch. PTA, Faculty and Community Adv. Council, 1976, resolution for outstanding service South Gate City Council, 1976. Mem. Nat. Assn. Elem. Sch. Prins., Los Angeles Elem. Prins. Orgn. (v.p. 1979-80), Assn. Calif. Sch. Adminstrs. (charter mem.), Assn. Elem. Sch. Adminstrs. (vice-chmn. chpt. 1972-75, city-wide exec. bd., steering com. 1972-75, 79-80), Asso. Adminstrs. Los Angeles (charter), Pi Theta Mu, Kappa Delta Pi (v.p. 1982-84), Delta Kappa Gamma. Democrat. Roman Catholic. Home: 6501 Lindenhurst Ave Los Angeles CA 90048 Office: Encino Elementary Sch 16941 Addison St Encino CA 91316

LUCERO, MARCELA, educator; b. Alamosa, Colo.; b. Agapito and Rose (Torres) Lucero; B.A. in English and Edn., Denver U., 1959; M.A. in Spanish and Linguistics, U. Kans., Lawrence, 1968; Ph.D. in Spanish and Linguistics, U. Minn., 1981; 1 dau., Patricia. Instr., Center for Students from Abroad, U. Denver, 1968-69, dir. Mexican Am. edn. program, 1969-72; teaching asst. U. Colo. and U. Kans., 1965-68; asst. dir. Pinto project, Denver, 1972-73; instr. U. Minn., Mpls., 1973-80; asst. prof. Mankato State U., 1980-81; asso. prof., dir Chicano studies Adams State Coll., Alamosa, Colo., 1981—; chmn. Hispanic adv. com. Mpls. pub. schs., 1976-78. Trustee, Mpls. YWCA; bd. dirs. United Way, 1980; mem. Gov.'s Appts. Commn., 1979. Named hon. citizen, Pueblo, Colo., 1976; Tchr. of Yr., U. Colo. Denver Center, 1971; named to Denver Post Gallery of Fame, 1971. Mem. Am. Assn. Tchrs. Spanish and Portuguese, MLA, Colo. Assn. Chicano Researchers (editorial bd.), Centro Cultural Chicano (dir.), Internat. Platform Assn., Kappa Delta Pi, Phi Sigma Iota. Author articles, poems. Office: Adams State College Alamosa CO 81102

LUCHT, SONDRA MOORE, state senator; b. Stumptown, W. Va., Dec. 12, 1942; d. Arthur Jackson and Lucille (Cain) Moore; m. William Lucht; 1 child, Carl Joseph. B.A., Glenville State Coll., M.A., Marshall U.; postgrad. James Madison U. Mem. W. Va. State Senate from Dist. 16, 1982—. Mem. W.Va. Orgn. Women (pres. 1977-82). Democrat. Address: 1013 Mill Race Dr Martinsburg WV 25401•

LUCIENE, SARA MCCLESKEY, banker; b. Atlanta, June 21, 1943; d. T. Waller and Doris (Reese) McCleskey; m. Robert Earl Luciene, Aug. 2, 1963; children—Sheri Lynn, John Stanley, Doris Elizabeth. Student Fla. Southern Coll., 1961-62, Fla. Sch. of Banking, Gainesville, 1983-86. Teller, Bank of Am., San Pedro, Calif., 1965-67; asst. cashier Exchange Bank, Tampa, Fla., 1968-80; asst. v.p., br. mgr. Barnett Bank of Tampa, 1980-86, v.p., br. mgr., 1986—. Mem., bd. dirs. YMCA Northwest, Tampa, 1983—; treas., bd. dirs. Womens Survival Ctr., Tampa, 1984—. Mem. Nat. Assn. Bank Women (Tampa chpt. pres. 1983-84, chair nominating com. 1984—), Am. Inst. Banking (Tampa chpt. dir. 1975). Democrat. Methodist. Avocations: bridge; reading; swimming. Home: 15611 Cashmere Ln Tampa FL 33624

LUCZ, CAROLYN ANN, communications company executive; b. Oskaloosa, Iowa, Apr. 12, 1936; d. Joseph A. and Marguerite M. (Votroubek) Abrahamson; m. Edward Francis Lucz, Nov. 25, 1955; children—Linda, Joanne Kay, Judy, Patricia, Diana. Student U. Ariz., 1965-82. Reporter, columnist Ariz. Cath. Diocesan Newspaper, Tucson, 1966-69; instr. Pima Community Coll., Tucson, 1980-81; v.p. Communications Skills, Inc., Washington, 1981—; dir. info. services Tucson Med. Ctr., 1969-75; exec. dir. Sunday Evening Forum, Tucson, 1976-83; coordinator career lifestyle dept. Levy's Dept. Store, Tucson, 1983-85; owner, pres. World Geog. Soc., Inc. Mem. Ariz. Adv. Council on Tourism, 1980—; active Ariz. Town Hall., Phoenix, 1981—, Tucson Com. Fgn. Relations, 1981-82, Tucson Tomorrow, Inc., 1981—; bd. dirs. Tucson Trade Bur., 1980-83, Tucson Assn. for Blind, 1978-83. Mem. Profl. Travel Film Lecture Assn. (v.p. 1979-81), Internat. Platform Assn., Ariz. Press Women, Exec. Women's Council So. Ariz. (founder 1979, pres. 1979-81), Nat. Alliance for Profl. and Exec. Women's Network (dir. 1981-83). Democrat. Roman Catholic. Office: Tucson AZ 85716

LUDERITZ, PAMELA ANN, educator; b. Burbank, Calif., Apr. 6, 1943; d. William Neil and Mary Alice (Dean) Salter; m. Kurt Paul Luderitz, Aug. 9, 1981. B.S., Boston U., 1964; M.Ed., U. San Francisco, 1981. Cert. tchr. secondary edn., adminstrn., Calif. Tchr. Fanning Trade Sch., Worcester, Mass., 1964-66, Watsonville High Sch., Calif., 1966—, mem. sch. improvement plan, 1980—, Dist. Curriculum Council, 1984—. Mem. Ben Lomond Fire Dept. Aux., Calif., Christmas Sharing Program. Mem. Internat. Motor Sports Assn. (Regional Exec. award 1984, scorer, timer), Sports Car Club of Am. (Regional Exec. award 1981, 82, Race Chmn. award 1981, Worker of Yr. 1981, scorer, timer 1968—), Calif. Assn. Health, Phys. Edn., Recreation & Dance (task force substance abuse 1985), AAHPER. Democrat. Club: Emblem (Santa Cruz, Calif.). Avocations: tennis; swimming; sports cars. Office: Watsonville High Sch 250 E Beach St Watsonville CA 95076

LUDVIGSON, GAIL ROSENBERG, investment company executive; b. Cambridge, Mass., Dec. 10, 1942; d. Joel and Ida Florence (Berenson) Rosenberg; m. Max Morris Ludvigson, Oct. 24, 1971; children—Laura, Deborah. B.A. in Econs. with honors, Conn. Coll., 1964; M.A. in Econs., Columbia U., 1965, Chartered fin. analyst. Arbitrageur, Smithers & Co., N.Y.C., 1971-72; sr. investment analyst Ticor, Los Angeles, 1972-79, sr. portfolio mgr., 1979-84; asst. v.p. Trust Services Am., Los Angeles, 1984—. Fellow Fin. Analysts Fedn., Los Angeles Soc. Fin. Analysts; mem. Women's Bus. and Profl. Group of South Bay (membership chmn. 1985—), Los Angeles Assn. Investment Women (pres. 1985—). Avocation: music.

LUDWICK, MARY KOPECKY, lawyer; b. Houston, Feb. 15, 1950; d. Roy Frank and Margaret Gillespie (Wilson) K.; m. David Chandler Ludwick, May 19, 1973 (div. July 1980). B.A., Rice U., 1971; J.D., So. Meth. U., 1974. Bar: Tex. 1974. Criminal prosecutor Dist. Attys. Office, Dallas, 1975-78, career criminal prosecutor, 1978-82, grand jury dir., 1982—. Phone bank dir. Dist. Attys. Campaign for Re-Election, Dallas, 1978, 82. Mem. ABA, Tex. Dist. and County Attys. Assn. Home: 12252 Montego Plaza Dallas TX 75230 Office: Dist Attys Office 600 Commerce St Dallas TX 75202

LUDWIG, KIMBERLY GAIL, marketing executive; b. Evanston, Ill., Mar. 20, 1951; d. Wesley Merrit and Hildegarde Christine (Rex) Keefer; m. Gary Raymond Crawford, Oct. 20, 1973 (div. May 1980); m. 2d, Marek William Ludwig, July 30 1983; 1 child, Andrew Rex. Student Jones Comml. Coll., Chgo., 1967-69, Oakton Coll., 1974-75. Market research sec. Kraft Foods Corp., Chgo., 1968-75; sales asst. Energy Absorption Systems, Inc., Chgo., 1975-78, sales adminstr., 1978-83, mktg. mgr., 1983—. Chmn. adv. Jones Bus. Coll., 1982-83. Mem. Am. Mgmt. Assn. (assoc.) ARTBA (assoc.), Inst. Transp. Engrs. (assoc.). Methodist. Office: Energy Absorption Systems Inc 1 E Wacker Dr Suite 3500 Chicago IL 60601

LUEKEN, PATTY WATSON, dietitian, business executive; b. Fayetteville, Ark., Oct. 20, 1953; d. Lavon Verdon and Evelyn Lucille (Bates) Watson; B.S., U. Ark., 1975, M.B.A., 1981; m. Thomas Whitten Lueken, Jan. 27, 1979. Adminstrv. dietitian VA Hosp., North Little Rock, 1976-77; dir. dietetics Central Bapt. Hosp., Little Rock, 1977-80; asst. dir. Nutritional Services, Ark. Children's Hosp., Little Rock, 1980—; asst. v.p. MultiMgmt. Services, Inc., 1984—; founder, prin. Lueken Consultants; adj. instr. Henderson State U., Arkadelphia, Ark. Mem. Am. Legion Aux., Am. Dietetic Assn., Ark. Interagy. on Nutrition, Am. Soc. Hosp. Food Service Adminstrs., Ark. Dietetic Assn. (Young Dietitian of Yr. 1982-83; treas. 1978-80, pres.-elect 1981-82, pres. 1982-83), Alpha Delta Pi. Baptist. Office: Suite 588 Medical Towers 9601 Interstate 630 Little Rock AR 72205

LUEPKE, GRETCHEN, geologist; b. Tucson, Nov. 10, 1943; d. Gordon Maas and Janice (Campbell) Luepke; B.S., U. Ariz., 1965, M.S., 1967; U. Colo., summer, 1962. With U.S. Geol. Survey, Menlo Park, Calif., 1967—, geologist, Pacific Br. of Marine Geology, 1976—. Registered geologist, Ore. Mem. Soc. Econ. Paleontologists and Mineralogists, Geol. Soc. Am., Ariz. Geol. Soc., Peninsula Geol. Soc., Bay Area Mineralogists (chmn. 1979-80), History of the Earth Scis. Soc., Internat. Assn. Sedimentologists, Sigma Xi. Editor: Stability of Heavy Minerals in Sediments; Econ. Analysis of Heavy Minerals in Sediments. Contbr. articles on heavy-mineral analysis to profl. jours. Office: 345 Middlefield Rd Menlo Park CA 94025

LUGINBUHL, ESTHER, recruiting and search company executive; b. Bklyn., Apr. 23, 1927; d. Ernst Gustav and Joyce (Van Buskirk) Heeren; m. Donald William Luginbuhl, June 5, 1948; children—Judith, Virginia, Joyce. Student Hofstra Coll., 1945-46. With depts. acctg. and data processing Benrus Corp., Ridgefield, Conn., 1967-72; mgr. Snelling & Snelling, Danbury, Conn., 1972-76; pres. Employment Opportunities Inc., Danbury, 1977—. Contbr. poetry to books. Mem. Conn. Assn. Personnel Cons. (sec. 1984-85, regional v.p. 1985—), Nat. Assn. Personnel Cons. Republican. Congregationalist. Avocations: clarinet playing; swimming; poetry. Home: 40 Marwick Manor New Milford CT 06776 Office: Employment Opportunities Inc 213 Main St Danbury CT 06810

LUHN, REBECCA ROSE, career educator, business consultant; b. Houston, Nov. 8, 1951; d. Reynold E. and Rose V. (DiDonna) L. Student U. Houston, 1971-74; B.B.A., Pacific Western U., 1981, D.B.A., 1983; postgrad. U. Houston, 1984. Real estate agt. P.L.S. Leasing Agy., Houston, 1971-73; law investigator S.J. Crumpton & Assocs., Houston, 1973-75; mgmt. devel. trainer Braniff Airlines Inc., Houston, 1975-77; communications analyst Continental Airlines Inc., Houston, Calif., 1977-82; instr. Houston Community Coll., 1982—; owner, pres. Innovative Tng. Acad., Houston, 1982—; pres., dir. Tng. and Devel., Houston, 1982—; owner, cons., ptnr. Innovative Tng., Houston, 1983-84; regional tng. coordinator Equitable Life Assurance Soc., Houston, 1984—; cons. Fairfield Corp., Houston, 1984—. Author: Building Business with Communication, 1983; Sales and Service Today, 1981; Careers in Travel, 1980; Management Motivation, 1981. Vol., Assistance League Houston, 1983, Arthritis Found., Houston, 1982-83, Tex. Assn. Pvt. Schs. Recipient Salesmanship award Delta Airlines, Houston, 1976, cert. of merit, 1982; Cert. of Approval, Tex. Edn. Agy., 1983; cert. of merit in mgmt. Rice U., 1983, cert. of merit in sales, mgmt. and tng. devel. Human Dimensions, Houston. Mem. Am. Soc. Tng. and Devel., Nat. Assn. Female Execs., Am. Assn. Women in Community and Jr. Colls., Women in Communication, Women in Edn., Tex. Assn. Pvt. Schs., Houston C. of C. Clubs: Elan, Pro Houston (Houston). Home: 14718A Perthshire St Houston TX 77079 Office: Innovative Tng Acad 14718A Perthshire St Houston TX 77079

LUIS, MARSHA J., banker; b. Somerville, Mass., Oct. 8, 1954; d. Joseph Paul and Carmela Jean (Correnti) Piraino; m. Duarte Arlindo Luis, Jan. 6, 1979. Student pub. schs. Boca Raton, Fla. Warranty clk. Ralph Buick, Delray Beach, Fla., 1972-73; sec., investigator Bay Bank Middlesex, Burlington, Mass., 1973-78, sr. investigator, 1978-80, asst. mgr., 1980-82, credit officer, mgr., 1982-85, asst. v.p., 1985—. Democrat. Roman Catholic. Avocations: drawing; bowling. Office: Bay Bank Middlesex 7 New England Exec Park Burlington MA 01803

LUITHLY, PHYLLIS CHRISTINE YANAGIHARA, property transfer specialist, business opportunities consultant; b. Kansas City, Mo., Sept. 23, 1950; d. Paul Leslie and Julie Anne (Lynn) Reed; m. Larry Kiyomi Yanagihara, Dec. 26, 1969 (div. Dec. 1970); 1 child, Robert Paul; m. James Henry Luithly, Apr. 1, 1984. Student Non-Commissioned Officers Acad., San Luis Obispo, Calif., 1976, Calif. Community Coll., 1981. Cert. escrow officer. Escrow officer, mgr. and sr. escrow officer with various title cos., bank, and ind. escrow cos., 1967-83; pres., owner Unicorn Escrow, Oxnard, Calif., 1983—; gen. ptnr. Exec. Unicorn, Oxnard, 1985—. Contbr. articles to newspapers and real estate periodicals. Active local Boy Scouts Am., 1979-80, United Way, Oxnard, 1984; coach Saticoy and Oceanview Little League, Ventura-Oxnard, 1980-81. Served with USAR, 1974-78. Recipient Commendation award City of San Bernardino, 1976. Mem. Ventura County Escrow Assn. (Spl. award 1980, charter pres. 1981, pres. 1982, dir. at large 1985), Calif. Escrow Assn. (state bd. dirs. 1981—, mktg. chmn. 1985), Am. Escrow Assn. (del. 1980—, hospitality chmn. 1982), Ventura County Profl. Women's Network (bd. dirs.), Women's Council Realtors (sec.), Channel Islands and Oxnard C. of C. Republican. Spiritualist. Club: Pacific Corinthian Yacht (Oxnard). Avocations: reading; power boating; parasailing; bowling. Home: 513 Ocean Dr Oxnard CA 93030 Office: Unicorn Escrow Inc 521 W Channel Islands Blvd Port Hueneme CA 93041

LUKAS, ELLEN, author, editor; b. Shenandoah, Pa.; d. Alexander J. and Margaret (McGuire) L.; A.B. in History, Coll. New Rochelle; student Pa. State U., Fordham U. UN corr. Newsweek mag., 1961-65; UN bur. chief Hearst Newspapers, 1965-67; with Harper's Mag., 1969; UNICEF press cons., 1971; press analyst to Sec. Gen. of UN, N.Y.C., 1977-81; editor, writer UN Dept. Info., 1982—. Mem. PEN, Authors Guild. Author: (with Mary Lukas) (biography) Teilhard de Chardin, 1977; contbr. Antiquity Mag., Cambridge U. Office: United Nations New York NY 10017

LUKE, BARBARA CAROL, lawyer; b. Hobbs, N.M., Apr. 24, 1939; d. Sam Price Jennings and Mary Hazel (Fannin) DeOcio; m. H. Douglas Luke, Apr. 27, 1963; children—Glee Carol, Heather Denise, Scott Douglas. B.S., Calif. State U.-Fullerton, 1972, teaching credential, 1973; J.D., Tex. Tech. Law Sch., 1980. Bar: Tex. 1981. Speech therapist Fullerton Elem. Sch. Dist. (Calif.), 1974-75; property mgr. Related Mgmt. Co., N.Y.C., 1975-77; assoc. law firm Allen Knuths & Cassell, Dallas, 1981-83; sole practice law, Dallas, 1983—; gen. counsel, dir. Transition Consultants, Inc., Dallas, 1981—. Vice-pres. Murfee Elem. Sch. PTA, Lubbock, Tex., 1978-79; newsletter editor LWV, Lubbock, 1978. Mem. ABA, Tex. Bar Assn., Dallas Bar Assn., Dallas Women Lawyers Assn. (pres. 1984, v.p. 1983, newsletter editor 1982), Phi Delta Phi. Republican. Club: Dallas Chamber Women's Network. Office: PO Box 38483 Dallas TX 75238

LUKE, DORETTE P. S., real estate development company executive; b. Honolulu, July 22, 1955; d. Theodore K.W. and Dorothy (J.) Luke. Student U. Hawaii, 1973-75; A.B. in Architecture, U. Calif.-Berkeley, 1977; M.B.A. in Fin., Columbia U., 1980. Fin. analyst Bellemead Devel., Roseland, N.J., 1980-81; sr. assoc. Security Pacific Realty Adv., N.Y.C., 1981-85; sr. v.p. Howco Investment Corp., Livingston, N.J., 1985—; ptnr., cons. Gaunt Ptnrs., N.Y.C., 1984—. Grantee Council on Grad. Minority Edn., 1979. Mem. Asian Mgmt. and Bus. Assn., Young Mortgage Bankers Assn., Real Estate Securities and Syndicators Inst., Nat. Assn. Corp. Real Estate Execs., Nat. Assn. Indsl. and Office Park Developers, Exec. Women of N.J. Democrat. Office: Howco Investment Corp 220 S Orange Ave Livingston NJ 07039

LUKER, KRISTIN, sociology educator; b. San Francisco, Aug. 5, 1946; d. James Wester and Bess (Littlefield) L. B.A., U. Calif.-Berkeley, 1968; Ph.D., Yale U., 1975. Postdoctoral fellow U. Calif.-Berkeley, 1974-75, asst. prof. sociology, San Diego, 1975-81, assoc. prof., 1981-85, prof., 1985—, dir. women's studies program, 1984—. Author: Taking Chances: Abortion and the Decision Not to Contracept, 1976 (hon. mention Jessie Bernard award); Abortion and the Politics of Motherhood, 1984 (Charles Horton Cooley award 1985). Bd. dirs. Ctr. for Women's Studies and Services, San Diego, Ctr. for Population Options, Washington. Recipient Outstanding Teaching award Warren Coll., U. Calif.-San Diego, 1985; Guggenheim Found. grantee, 1985. Mem. Am. Sociol. Assn., Sociologists for Women in Soc. Office: U Calif Dept Sociology San Diego CA 92093

LUKIN, JUDITH MICHELE, social service administrator, consultant; b. Bklyn., July 8, 1945; d. Max and Dinah (Goodman) L. B.A., Hunter Coll., 1967; M.S.W., Columbia U., 1970. Asst. program dir. Ednl. Alliance, N.Y.C., 1979-80; program dir. Mobilization for Youth, N.Y.C., 1980-81; freelance cons., N.Y.C., 1981-83; adj. faculty Mercy Coll., N.Y.C., 1982-83; assoc. dir. Andrew Glover Youth Program, N.Y.C., 1982-83; exec. dir. Caring Community, Inc., N.Y.C., 1983—; workshop speaker Networks Unltd., N.Y.C., 1982, Nat. League Nursing, N.Y.C., 1983; trainer Ctr. for Women in Govt., N.Y.C., 1982; cons. Little Sisters of the Assumption Family Health Services, N.Y.C., 1982. Bd. dirs. Northrop Meml. Nature Camp, N.Y.C., Andrew Glover Youth Program, 1979-82; com. mem. Am. Friends Service Com., N.Y.C.; mem. secretariat Lower East Side Neighborhood Coalition, N.Y.C., 1977-83. Mem. Nat. Assn. Social Workers, Women in Fin. Devel., Exec. Women in Human Services. Jewish. Office: Caring Community Inc 7 W 11th St New York NY 10011

LUMADUE, JOYCE ANN, hobby company executive; b. New London, Conn., Oct. 21, 1941; d. James E. and Camilla (Romeo) Hayes; student U. Conn.; m. Donald Dean Lumadue, June 28, 1958; children—Dawnia Jean, Donald Dean, Robert Ryan, Ronald Jeffrey. Partner, Joydon's Coin Shop, New London, 1958—, House of Leisure, New London, 1967—, Hobby Crafts, New London, 1969—; v.p. New Eng. Internat. Inc., New London, 1969-85, Lumadue Inc., New London, 1978—. Mem. Hobby Industry Assn. Am., Internat. Mgmt. Council, Nat. Assn. Female Execs., NOW. Methodist. Contbr. articles to profl. jours. Office: 78-88 Captains Walk New London CT 06320

LUMETTA, ROSEMARIE RENEÉ, management analyst; b. St. Louis, Feb. 25, 1948; d. Paul A. and Eleanor (Gallo) Lumetta; m. Randall Lynn Stuckey, Mar. 24, 1973 (div. 1984). A.A., Florissant Valley Community Coll., 1970; B.S., U. Mo.-St. Louis, 1971, M.B.A., 1976. Auditor, U.S. Army, St. Louis, 1971-72; agt. IRS, St. Louis, 1972-80; mktg. rep., St. Louis, 1980-81; systems acct., St. Louis, 1981-84; mgmt. analyst TROSCOM, Dept. Def., St. Louis, 1984—; tax cons., 1980—. Author: How Multi-level and Direct Salespeople Can Save Money on Their Income Taxes, 1970. Democrat. Roman Catholic. Home: 2034 Quiet Stream Maryland Heights MO 63043

LUMMEL, ONEVA MARIE, journalist; b. Nebr., May 18, 1937; d. Harry and Gertrude (Linnemann) Hoetfelker; m. Wendelin P. Lummel, May 4, 1955; children—Debra, Susan, Jim. Grad. high sch. Co-editor, owner Bridgeport News-Blade weekly newspaper (Nebr.), 1975—. Home: 501 5th St Bridgeport NE 69336 Office: News-Blade 801 Main St Bridgeport NE 69336

LUMMUS, CAROL TRAVERS, artist, printmaker; b. Hyannis, Mass., Nov. 2, 1937; d. Frank and Doris (Brown) Travers; student Walnut Hill Sch. Performing Arts, Natick, Mass., 1952-55; A.A., Colby-Sawyer Coll., New London, N.H., 1957; student U. Geneva (Switzerland), 1960-62; m. Bertrand W. Lummus, Jan. 27, 1962; children—Sarah Travers, Jonathan Ames. Artist and printmaker; one-woman shows include Hammerquist, N.Y.C., 1979, La Galeria, San Mateo, Calif., 1980, Alice Bingham, Memphis, 1980, P.S. Gallery, Ogunquit, Maine, 1980, 927 Gallery, New Orleans, Saint Gaudens Nat. Historic Site, Cornish, N.H.; group shows include All New Eng. show, 1975-76, Currier Mus., Manchester, N.H., 1976, 80, Fitchburg (Mass.) Mus., 1975-76, Instituto Brasil-Estadios Unidos, Brazil, 1978, Hobe Sound (Fla.) Gallery, 1976—, Payson-Waldron, Portland, Maine, 1982; mem. art adv. panel N.H. Commn. on Arts. Recipient Rosmond de Kalb award Currier Mus., 1975, 1st prize Fitchburg Mus. Art, 1973; N.H. Commn. on Arts grantee, 1980. Mem. Cape Cod Performing Arts Assn. (dir.), Artists Equity, Silvermine Guild Arts, Conn. League N.H. Craftsmen, Nat. Assn. Women Artists N.Y. Episcopalian. Club: Barnstable (Mass.) Yacht. Home: Lang Rd Cornish NH 03781 and Barnstable MA 02630

LUMPKIN, DIANE ARLINE, retail executive; b. Albany, Ga., Dec. 25; d. H. Hearn and Arline Lucile (Branch) Lumpkin; A.B. cum laude, Wesleyan Coll., 1963; postgrad. Emory U., 1963-64, Ga. State U., 1964-65. Tchr. public schs. Marietta, Ga., 1963-65, 66-68, Guantanamo Bay, Cuba, 1968-69, Atlanta, 1969-70; dept. mgr., asst. gen. mgr. ops. Saks Fifth Ave., Atlanta, 1970-74, asst. gen. mgr. merchandising, 1975-78, asst. gen. mgr. merchandising, Chgo., 1978-79, gen. mgr., Palm Beach, Fla., 1979-80. Springfield, N.J., 1980-81; store mgr. Macys's, Atlanta, 1981—. Dir., advisor Jr. Achievement, Atlanta; trustee Ga. chpt Leukemia Soc. Am. Mem. Atlanta Zool. Soc., Wesleyan U. Alumni Assn. Methodist. Office: Macy's Shannon Mall Union City GA

LUMPKIN, PENNY PALMER, wholesale periodicals company executive; b. Topeka, Aug. 20; d. William H. and Vivian J. Palmer; student U. Ariz., 1957-59, U. Kans., 1959-60; m. Joseph Henry Lumpkin, Nov. 26, 1960; children—William Henry, Kelley Kathleen. Buyer, merchandiser City News & Gift Shop, Topeka, 1954-57; mgr., buyer Vivian's Gift Shop, Topeka, 1961-76; book buyer Palmer News, Inc., Topeka, 1976-79, book buyer, personnel dir., 1979-80, dir. retail ops., treas., 1980-85, also dir.; co-owner Vivian's Gift Shop; dir. Ultra Fund-Security Benefit Life, Life Ins. Investors, The Palmer Cus. Bd. dirs. Mulvane Art Center, Topeka, 1968-80, Seven Step Found., Topeka, 1969-72; bd. dirs., charter mem. Mulvane Women, Topeka, 1969; div. chmn. United Way, Topeka, 1969; chmn. King of Hills Pro/Celebrity Tennis Benefit, 1977-79; spl. events chmn. Shawnee County unit Am. Cancer Soc., Topeka, 1976-78, v.p. bd. dirs., 1977, pres. bd. dirs., 1979; bd. dirs. Jayhawk Area council Boy Scouts Am., 1983-85, Topeka Civic Theatre, 1984—, Mt. Hope Cemetary; v.p. bd. dirs. Topeka Pub. Schs., bd. dirs. Stormont-Vail Hosp. Found.; co-chmn. Gala V Am. Cancer Soc. of Shawnee County. Named an Outstanding Woman Am., Jr. League of Topeka, 1975; recipient Outstanding Service award Am. Cancer Soc., 1976, Kans. div., 1978. Mem. Central States Periodicals Distbrs. Assn., Am. Booksellers Assn., Mid-Am. Periodicals Distbrs. Assn., Ind. Periodicals Distbrs. Assn., Topeka Friends of Zoo, Am. Heritage Assn., Kappa Kappa Gamma Alums. Republican. Episcopalian. Club: Jr. League (pres. Topeka 1971). Researcher, pub. fund-raising manual Assn. Jr. Leagues, 1974. Home: 3161 Shadow Ln Topeka KS 66604 Office: 1050 Republican Topeka KS 66604

LUMSDEN, LYNNE ANN, publishing comapny executive; b. Battlecreek, Mich., July 30, 1947; d. Arthur James and Ruth Julia (Pandy) L.; m. Jon B. Harden, May 3, 1986; B.A., Sarah Lawrence Coll., 1969; postgrad. U. Paris, 1967-69, NYU, 1970, CCNY, 1980-81. Cert. in mgmt. Am. Mgmt. Assn. Editorial asst. Harcourt Brace Jovanovich, N.Y.C., 1969-70, copy editor, 1970; acquisitions editor Appleton-Century Crofts, N.Y.C., 1971-73; editor coll. div. Prentice-Hall, Englewood Cliffs, N.J., 1973, Spectrum Books, Prentice-Hall, 1974-77, sr. editor, 1977-80, asst. v.p., editor-in-chief gen. pub. div. Prentice Hall, 1981, v.p., editorial dir., 1982-85; exec. v.p., pub. chief operating officer Dodd, Mead, 1985—; ptnr. Gamut Publ. Co.; lectr. Rutgers U. U.S., Europe, 1975—; pub. cons., 1979—. Mem. Am. Assn. Pubs. (co-chmn. stats. com.), Sarah Lawrence Alumnae Assn. (bd. dirs. 1980-82). Democrat. Episcopalian. Clubs: St. Barts Community, Sandbar, Jr. League. Home: 333 E 79th St New York NY 10021

LUNA, OLIVIA, educator, consultant; b. Los Angeles, May 21, 1932; d. Guadalupe Flores and Lorenza (Saenz) Velarde; m. Ralph Moreno Luna, June 24, 1951; children—Larry, Samuel, Leno. A.A., East Los Angeles Coll., 1960; B.A., Calif. State U.-Los Angeles, 1962; M.A., La Verne U., 1980, M.S., 1981. Tchr., counselor El Rancho Unified Sch. Dist., Pico Rivera, Calif., 1968—; bilingual specialist, 1972-81; owner, pres. Unlimited Potential Co., Whittier, Calif., 1980—; presenter workshops; ednl. cons., 1972-83. Author handbook. Co-founder Downey chpt. Failures Anonymous Internat., 1985. Recipient Fine Arts award Pico Rivera City Council, 1968. Mem. Calif. Council Adult Edn. (pres. 1980-82), Am. Fedn. Tchrs. (v.p. 1977-80), Calif. Assn. Bilingual Edn., ACLU (sec. Whittier chpt. 1981-83), Los Angeles Racewalkers, Whittier Democratic Club. Unitarian. Avocations: oil painting, writing, racewalking. Home: 1009 Guinea Dr Whittier CA 90601 Office: El Rancho Unified Sch Dist 9333 Loch Lomond Pico Rivera CA 90660

LUND, SISTER CANDIDA, college chancellor; b. Chgo.; d. Fred S. and Katharine (Murray) Lund Heck; B.A., Rosary Coll., River Forest, Ill., 1942; M.A., Cath. U. Am.; Ph.D., U. Chgo.; Litt.D., Lincoln (Ill.) Coll., 1968; LL.D. (hon.), John Marshall Law Sch., 1979; H.H.D. (hon.), Marymount Manhattan Coll., 1979. Pres., Rosary Coll., River Forest, Ill., 1964-81, chancellor, 1981—. Trustee Carnegie Found. for Advancement Teaching, 1970-78, Clarke Coll., Dubuque, Iowa, 1981—; council mem. Ill. Humanities Council, 1982—; mem. women's bd. U. Chgo.; bd. dirs. Chgo. Network, 1983—; bd. dirs. Am. Council on Edn., chmn. fin. com., 1977-81. Recipient Profl. Achievement award U. Chgo. Alumni Assn., 1974; U.S. Cath. award, 1984; Disting. Citizen award Protestant Found. Greater Chgo., 1980; Athena award for Disting. Bus. Woman of Yr., Oak Park-Lake Forest C. of C., 1980. Fellow Royal Soc. Arts (London); mem. Thomas More Assn. (dir. 1975—). Editor: Moments to Remember, 1980, The Days and the Nights, Prayers for Today's Woman; Nunsuch, 1982; Coming of Age, 1982; In Joy and in Sorrow, 1984; If I Were Pope, 1987. Address: Rosary Coll 7900 Division St River Forest IL 60305

LUND, DOLORES MARIE, psychologist; b. Mpls., Apr. 20, 1923; d. Albert Casmir and Leona Clara (Langlais) Kacher; m. Everett Ray Lund, Dec. 24, 1942 (div. 1968); children—Tracy, Mark, Laurie, Annette; m. Everett Ray Lund, Dec. 24, 1983. B.A., U. Minn., 1944; postgrad. U. Fla.-Orlando, 1973-74, Antioch Coll., Mpls., 1975; Addictions Specialist (hon.), St. Luke's Hosp., 1978. Mgr., All Service Placement, Mpls., 1969-71; job devel. specialist Opportunities Indsl. Ctr., Clearwater, Fla., 1972-73; coordinator Mental Health Assn., St. Petersburg, Fla., 1973; dir. Wilson House, Lakeland, Fla., 1974; with Wayside House, Mpls., 1975; dir. outpatients Abbott-Northwestern Hosp., Mpls., 1975-77; coordinator St. Luke Hosp. Chem. Abuse Ctr., Phoenix, 1977-78; psychologist Dolores Lund Inst., Phoenix, 1978—. Author primary outpatient programs, profl. confs., 1976, 77. Recipient Maharasahi award, Ariz. State U., 1981. Mem. Orgn. of Rehab. Ctrs. (sec. treas.), Bus. and Profl. Women (sec. treas.), Assn. Profl. Alcohol Specialists (treas.). Avocations: Tennis; swimming; horseback riding. Home: 3432 N 12th Pl 18 Phoenix AZ 85014

LUND, MARY WENDELL, lawyer; b. Washington, Sept. 3, 1944; d. Wendell Luther and Anne Catherine (Greve) L.; m. William James Lettice, III, Dec. 13, 1975. B.A. in Econs., Mary Baldwin Coll., 1966; postgrad. Calif. State U.-Northridge, 1970-71; M.A. in History of Art, U. Minn., 1974; J.D., George Washington U., 1981. Bar: D.C. 1981, D.C. Ct. Appeals 1981. Computer programmer/analyst Fed. Systems div. IBM 1966-70; grad. asst. Calif. State U.-Northridge, 1970-71; research asst. U. Minn., Mpls., 1972, teaching asst., 1973; asst. registrar Smithsonian Instn., Washington, 1975-82, program analyst, legal and mgmt. analyst, 1982-84; atty. advisor U.S. Dept. Justice, Washington, 1984—; bd. dirs. D.C. Computer Law Forum, 1984—, v.p. 1985. Mem. adv. bd. visitors Mary Baldwin Coll., 1983—; mem. Capitol Hill Women's Polit. Caucus. NEH fellow, 1972-73; Kress Found. grantee, 1972. Mem. ABA, Computer Law Assn., Assn. Fed. Info. Resources Mgmt., Am. Assn. Mus., Coll. Art Assn. Lutheran. Home: 323 N St Asaph St Alexandria VA 22314 Office: US Dept Justice Washington DC 20530

LUND, PATRICIA ADELE, food manufacturing company executive; b. Charleston, S.C., July 22, 1956; d. Benjamin Curtis and Clara Elizabeth (McCrory) Luna. B.S. in History, Auburn U., 1978, M.Ed. in History, 1980; M.A. in Adminstrn., U. Ala., 1981, Ed.S. in Adminstrn., 1984, Ph.D., A.B.D. in Adminstrn., 1986. Cert. tchr., Ga., Ala. History tchr. Harris County Middle Sch., Ga., 1978-79, head dept., 1979-81; residence hall dir. univ. housing U. Ala., 1981-83, asst. dir. residence life, 1983-85; intern Cornell U., Ithaca, N.Y., 1983; mktg. mgr. Golden Flake Snack Foods, Inc., Birmingham, Ala., 1985—; cons., lectr. in field. Author: Alcohol Awareness Programs, 1984; University Programming, 1984; Marketing Residential Life, 1985. Fundraiser, U. Ala. Alumni Scholarship Fund, Tuscaloosa, 1983, Am. Diabetes Assn., Tuscaloosa, 1984; fundraiser, com. chmn. Spl. Olympics, Tuscaloosa, 1985; bd. dirs. Cerebral Palsy Found., Tuscaloosa, 1985-86; com. chmn. Kairos Prison Ministry, Tutwiler State Prison, Ala., 1986; Recipient Dir. of Yr. award U. Ala., 1982, 83; Skeets Simonis award for Outstanding Contbns., U. Ala., 1984. Mem. Sales and Mktg. Execs. (chmn. com. 1985-86), Leadership Ala. (pres. 1982-83), Am. Mktg. Assn., Assn. Coll. and Univ. Housing Officers (com. chmn. 1983-85), Nat. Assn. Student Personnel Officers, Potato Chip and Snack Food Assn., Omega Rho Sigma (pres. 1983-84), Omicron Delta Kappa, Phi Delta Kappa, Phi Alpha Theta. Republican. Methodist. Clubs: Emmaus (chmn. com. 1985—) (Birmingham, Ala.); Sailing (Tuscaloosa). Avocations: skiing; racquetball; community work; public speaking. Home: 11 Vestavia Hills Northport AL 35476 Office: Golden Flake Snack Foods Inc 110 6th St S Birmingham AL 35201

LUND, SUSAN ELLEN, nurse consultant; b. Dayton, Ohio, Dec. 3, 1947; d. Joseph Edwin and Eva Lucille (Hollingsworth) Weiss. Diploma St. Patrick Sch. Nursing, Missoula, Mont., 1968; B.A. in Liberal Studies, Linfield Coll., 1976. R.N. Staff nurse St. Patrick Hosp., Missoula, Mont., 1965, Providence Hosp., Portland, Oreg., 1968-78, asst. head nurse, 1970-71, head nurse dialysis, 1971-75; nurse assoc. Dr. Fredrick Orether, Portland, 1971-75; pvt. practice nurse cons., Portland, 1978—; nurse cons. to ins. co. and lawyers, Portland; CPR instr. Am. Heart Assn., Portland, 1979—. Mem. City Council of Maywood Park, Oreg., pres., 1980-86. Democrat. Office: Sam Lund 1400 SW Montgomery Portland OR 97201

LUNDBERG, CONSTANCE K., law educator; b. Salt Lake City, July 1, 1947; d. Horace William and Nedra (Hurst) Lundberg; m. Boyd C. Erickson, Jan. 21, 1981. B.A. with distinction, Ariz. State U., 1968; J.D., U. Utah., 1972. Bar: Utah. Ptnr. Parson, Behle & Latimer, Salt Lake City, 1972-74, 77-82; counsel Council on Environ. Quality, Washington, 1975-76; assoc. prof. law Brigham Young U., Provo, Utah, 1982—; of counsel Parson, Behle & Latimer, 1982—. Co-author: Mineral Acquisition on the Public Domain, 1985; contbr. articles on mining and pub. lands to profl. jours. Vice chmn. Utah Bd. Oil, Gas and Mining, Salt Lake City, 1983—; mem. Utah Constnl. Revision Commn., Salt Lake City, 1978-79; trustee Rocky Mt. Mineral Law Found., Boulder, Colo., 1978—. Mem. Utah State Bar Assn. (chmn. natural resources sect. 1980-81), Salt Lake County Bar, Utah County Bar, ABA. Democrat. Mormon. Home: 749 W Sunny Ln Orem UT 84058 Office: J Reuben Clark Law Sch Brigham Young U 544 JRCB Provo UT 84602

LUNDBERG, ELLEN RAE WENDROW, med. technologist; b. N.Y.C., Aug. 11, 1942; d. Max and Martha (Miller) Wendrow; B.S., Fairleigh Dickinson U., 1964; children—Gregory, Andrew. Intern med. tech. Newark Presbyn. Hosp., 1963-64; med. technologist histology sect. Parke Davis & Co., Ann Arbor, Mich., 1964-65; supr. chemistry sect. pvt. lab., Ann Arbor, 1965-66; med. technologist pulmonary function and blood gas lab. VA Hosp., Ann Arbor, 1966-70; med. technologist pvt. labs., Durham, N.C., 1970-72; research technologist coagulation lab. Duke U. Med. Center, 1972-75, staff med. technologist blood bank, 1975-76, supr. nuclear medicine lab., 1976—, instr. Sch. Med. Tech., 1976—. Registered med. technologist. Asso. mem. Am. Soc. Clin. Pathologists; mem. Clin. Ligand Assay Soc. Home: 2813 McDowell St Durham NC 27705 Office: Duke U Med Center Box 3304 Durham NC 27710

LUNDBERG, SALLY, lawyer; b. Dallas, Aug. 17, 1949; d. Frederick Gordon and Corinne (Collins) Lundberg. B.A. in Biology, B.S. in Math., So. Meth. U., 1972; M.S. Environ. Biology, North Tex. State U., 1976; J.D., Baylor U., 1980. Bar: Tex. 1980. Acting asst. supr. Core Labs., Inc., Tyler, Tex., 1976; owner, dir. Math Skills SAT Prep Course, Dallas, 1975-80; chemistry/math. tchr., swim coach Dallas Ind. Sch. Dist., 1976-78; assoc. atty. Dalton, Moore, Forde, Dallas, 1980-82; atty. of counsel Baxter, Brown, Thomas, Dallas, 1982-83; pvt. practice law, Dallas, 1983—; dir. Loco Energy Corp., Lundberg Operating Co. Author: (with Elissa Sommerfield) Educational Skills PSAT-SAT Multi-Media Preparation Course, 1978. Co-chmn. Dallas Assn. Young Lawyers, 1982, dir. 1983, 84; sponsor 500, Inc., Dallas, 1977—. Mem. Dallas Assn. Young Lawyers (dir.), State Bar Tex., ABA, Kappa Mu Epsilon, Delta Theta Phi. Clubs: Dallas Jr. Garden, Slipper. Home: 6211 W Northwest Hwy 1500 Dallas TX 75225 Office: 7557 Rambler Rd Suite 1010 Dallas TX 75231

LUNDEN, JOAN, television host; b. Sacramento, Sept. 19, 1950; d. Erle Murray and Gladyce Lorraine (Somervill) Blunden; m. Michael Arthur Krauss, Sept. 10, 1978; children—Jamie, Lindsay. Student World Campus Afloat, Chapman Coll., 1967-68, U. of Americas, Mexico City, 1968-71; A.A., Am. River Coll., 1972; Calif. State U.-Sacramento, 1972-73. Weather reporter, consumer reporter, anchorwoman, writer, producer KCRA-TV, Sacramento, Calif., 1973-75; reporter, anchorwoman Sta. WABC-TV (Eyewitness News), N.Y.C., 1975-80; TV host ABC Good Morning Am., N.Y.C., 1980—, Mother's Day, Michael Krauss Prodns., Inc., White Plains, N.Y., 1983—, Mother's Minutes, 1984—; vis. instr. TV Montclair State Coll., N.J., 1977-78; nat. spokesperson Hasbro Toy Corp., Providence, R.I., Hasbro Children's Found., N.Y.C., 1985—. Host video cassette How to Use Your VCR, 1982; Newborn Baby: Everything You Need to Know, 1985. Chmn. smoking and pregnancy programs Am. Lung Assn., N.Y.C., 1983; spokesperson child car seat campaign Calif. Hwy. Patrol, Sacramento, 1983; hon. spokesperson Mothers Against Drunk Driving, Hearst, (Tex.); nat. spokesperson March of Dimes, N.Y.C., 1983. Recipient Today's Women award Council United Cerebral Palsy, 1981, Ace award nomination Nat. Cable TV Assn., 1984, 85; named Mother of Yr. Nat. Mothers Day Council, 1982. Mem. Am. Women in Radio and TV, Nat. Assn. TV Arts and Scis. Club: N.Y. Press. Office: ABC-TV Good Morning Am 1965 Broadway New York NY 10023

LUNDGREN, CLAUDINE WILMA, art director, button businenss owner; b. South Gate, Calif., Sept. 9, 1941; d. Melvin Martin Lundgren and Dora Wilma (Longuevan) Suttle. B.S., Linfield Coll., 1963. Cert. in teaching U. Oreg., 1967; Peace Corps. Cert., Mich. State U., 1964. Cert. secondary tchr. Spanish, physical edn., health. Artist, film stripper Your Town Press, Salem, Oreg., 1963-64, vol. U.S. Peace Corps., Chile, S.Am., 1964-66; Spanish tchr., coach Sch. Dist. 4J, Eugene, Oreg., 1968-75; co-owner, operator AtLund Press, Eugene, 1975-78; mgr., artist Oh Shirt!, Eugene, 1978-81, art dir., Springfield, Oreg., 1981—; Spanish cons. Lane County Sheriff Dept., Eugene, 1974-81, Eugene Police Dep., 1978-84; pres. Women's Network, Eugene, 1981-82; owner Lundgraph, Marcola, Oreg., 1980—. Co-author, illustrator: How to Create a Yearbook, 1964; illustrator: Selection of 33 Columbian Recipes, 1978; layout artist cassette cover: 7 Healing Stories, 1984; illustrator, co-author: Color Me Political, 1982. Vol. Bunker Hill Task Force, Marcola, 1985; hon. mem. Thespian Drama Soc., McMinnville, Oreg., 1963. Named Employee of Month, Springfield C. of C., 1984; grantee Sch. Dist. 4J, Eugene, 1973. Mem. Springfield Exec. Assn., Lambda Lambda Sigma (v.p. 1963). Avocations: photography, backpacking, bird watching, music, writing. Home: 94441 Marcola Rd Marcola OR 97454 Office: Oh Shirt! Inc 3320 Industrial St Springfield OR 97478

LUNDGREN, GAIL MARIE, lawyer; b. Tacoma, June 14, 1955; d. Arthur Dean and Vera Martha (Grimm) L. A.B. cum laude, Vassar Coll., 1977; J.D. cum laude, U. Puget Sound., 1980. Bar: Wash. 1981. Legal intern Reed, McClure, Moceri & Thonn, Seattle, 1979, Burgess & Kennedy, Tacoma, 1979-80; legal intern Lee, Smart, Cook, Martin & Patterson, P.S., Inc., Seattle, 1980-81, assoc., 1981—. Vestry com. Queen Anne Lutheran Ch., 1983—, mem. worship and music com., 1982-83, parish edn. com., 1983—. Recipient Am. Jurisprudence Book awards, 1980. Mem. ABA, Fed. Bar Assn., Wash. State Bar Assn., Seattle-King County Bar Assn., Wash. Assn. Def. Counsel, Order of Barristers. Democrat. Lutheran. Club: Wash. Vassar.

LUNDIE, LOUISE MARIE, customer service director; b. Meeme Twp., Wis., Mar. 2, 1940; d. Henry Joseph and Irene Theresa (Salm) Schwartz; A.A., Milw. Area Tech. Coll., 1978; B.S., Carroll Coll., 1982; m. Mel A. Lundie, Oct. 2, 1976; 1 dau. by previous marriage, Ann Louise Mathews. Sec. to gen. mgr. St. Regis Paper Co., Milw., 1961-65; asst. to pres. Wells Badger Corp., Milw., 1966-74; sec. to v.p. mktg. Everbrite Electric Signs, South Milwaukee, Wis., 1975, nat. sales adminstr., 1976-81, mgr. mktg. adminstrn., 1981, mgr. corp. planning, advt. and market research, 1981-84, dir. customer service, 1984—.

Pres., Adult AFS, Cudahy, Wis., 1982—. Mem. Nat. Secs. Assn. (pres. Milw. chpt. 1971-73), Adminstrv. Mgmt. Soc., Am. Assn. Individual Investors, Friends of Cudahy Library. Home: 5938 S Pennsylvania Ave Cudahy WI 53110 Office: Everbrite Electric Signs 315 Marion Ave South Milwaukee WI 53172

LUNDQUIST, LINDA ANN JOHNSON, engineering company representative; b. Iowa City, Iowa, Aug. 15, 1945; d. Elmer Clinton and Georgia Joan (Molloy) L.; m. Scott Arthur Johnson, Sept. 26, 1981. B.A., U. Iowa, 1968. Civil engring. drafter firm Shive-Hattery & Assocs., Iowa City, 1968-78; dir. drafting services firm Shoemaker & Haaland, Profl. Engrs., Coralville, Iowa, 1978-82; mktg. rep. firm Veenstra & Kimm, Inc., Engineers and Planners, Iowa City and West Des Moines, 1982—. Lic. foster parent, Iowa. Recipient Spl. Merit award Cedar Rapids Mus. Art, Iowa, 1979. Mem. Greater Iowa City Area C. of C. (chair environ. concerns com. 1984—), Greater Downtown Cedar Rapids Assn., Soc. Mktg. Profl. Services, Soc. Land Surveyors Iowa, Iowa Groundwater Assn., Nat. Assn. Women in Constrn., Cedar Rapids-Iowa City Architects Council, Am. Water Works Assn., Water Pollution Control Assn., Nat. Wildlife Fedn., Internat. Fund Animal Welfare, Alpha Gamma Delta. Avocations: figure drawing, plant studies, jazz dance, guitar. Office: Veenstra & Kimm Inc 1218 Highland Ct Suite 2 Iowa City IA 52240

LUNDQUIST, VIOLET ELVIRA, agency administrator; b. Bristol, Conn., Jan. 28, 1912; d. Otto Nimrod and Mabel Elvira (Lindeen) Ebb; diploma music Augustana Coll., Rock Island, Ill., 1932; postgrad. mgmt. systems U. Mo., 1969; m. Vernon Arthur Lundquist, May 14, 1935; children—Karen Ebb, Jane Christine. Tchr. music, public schs., Olds, Iowa, 1932-35; editor Warsaw (Mo.) Times, 1935-45, Anthon (Iowa) Herald, 1945-57; field dir. Iowa Heart Assn., Des Moines, 1957-66; exec. dir. S.E. Iowa Community Action Program, Burlington, 1966-74; adminstrn. dir. S.E. Ariz. Govts. Orgn. Community Services, Bisbee, Ariz., 1975-77; statewide advocate developmentally disabled adults, 1977—; adminstr. Arizona City Med. Center, part-time, 1979-80; adminstr. Dist. V Council on Developmental Disabilities, 1980—. Bd. dirs. Central Ariz. Health Systems Agy., 1979—; chmn. Arizona City Home and Property Owners Assn., 1979-82; bd. dirs. Ariz. State Health Planning Council, 1986—; mem. Ariz. Dist. V Human and Legal Rights Com. Recipient Carol Lane award Nat. Safety Council, 1956; USPHS scholar, Columbia U., summers 1963, 64; cert. vocat. rehab. adminstr. Mem. Nat. Soc. Community Action Program Dirs. (dir. 1966-75), Ariz. Fedn. Press Women. Lutheran. Clubs: Zonta (area dir. 1984-86), Women of Moose. Recipient 1st place awards Nat. Fedn. Press Women, 1952, 53, 55, 57. Home and Office: 609 W Cochise St Arizona City AZ 85223

LUNDY, JANET CECILE, histotechnologist; b. Laverty, Okla., May 20, 1942; d. Cecil LeRoy and Grace (Arnold) Parish; student pub. schs., Chickasha, Okla.; m. J.W. Lundy, Oct. 20, 1963. Histology technician Presbyterian Hosp., Oklahoma City, 1960-68; supr. histotech. Okla. Health Scis. Center, Oklahoma City, 1968-71; supr. histotech. Hillcrest Osteo. Hosp., Oklahoma City, 1972-75; supr., histotechnologist Bapt. Med. Center Okla., Oklahoma City, 1975-83; founder, operator Precision Histology Lab, 1983—; mem. adj. faculty Oscar Rose Jr. Coll., 1978-83. Mem. steering com. Linwood Pl. Neighborhood Assn., 1980-82. Mem. Okla. Soc. Histotechnologists, Nat. Soc. Histotech. Mem. Ch. Nazarene. Home: 3132 NW 22d St Oklahoma City OK 73107

LUNIA, RATNA, jewelry company executive; b. Gangashahr, India, Jan. 11, 1945; d. Than Mal and Jethi Devi (Sethia) Anchlia; m. P.C. Lunia, Mar. 9, 1970; 1 child, Anupama. Came to U.S., 1971. B.A., Maharni Coll., 1967; M.A. in Vocal Music, Sangeet Vharati, Ahmedabad, India, 1970. Exec. dir. Oriental Jewels Inc., N.Y.C., 1972—. Home: 301 E 47th St #14A New York NY 10017

LUNNY, ELLEN THERESE, data processing and personnel company executive; b. N.Y.C., Dec. 17, 1943; d. George Lawrence and Margaret Rita (Kennedy) Lunny; B.A. in Sociology, Coll. of New Rochelle, 1965; postgrad. N.Y.U., 1972. Personnel trainee United Med. Service, N.Y.C., 1966-67, asst. to dir. of personnel, 1967-69, mgr. benefits and services, 1969-72, automated records specialist ITT, N.Y.C., 1972-77, mgr. personnel adminstrn. center, 1977—; cons. to career edn. program Sacred Heart of Bayside. Mem. Tiana Shores Civic Assn., Hampton Bays, N.Y. Mem. Alumni Assn. of Coll. of New Rochelle, AMA, NAFE. Democrat. Roman Catholic. Contbr. to Diebold Automatic Data Processing Handbook for personnel mgmt. systems at ITT. Office: ITT 320 Park Ave New York NY 10022

LUNSFORD, MIDGE M., clinical social worker; b. Birmingham, Ala., May 25, 1943; d. Major and Effie (Oliver) Jones; m. Nathaniel Reeves Lunsford, Feb. 14, 1962 (div. 1975); children—Detra, Bruce. B.A., Bernard Baruch Coll., N.Y.C., 1976; M.S.W., Fordham U., 1982. Cert. social worker, N.Y. Coordinator minority recruitment Coll. Optometry, SUNY-N.Y.C., 1975-77; asst. to dean N.Y. Coll. Podiatric Med., N.Y.C., 1977-80; clin. social worker Central Bklyn. Med. Ctr., 1982-85; supr. counseling div. RCA Govt. Services, N.Y.C., 1985—; social work cons., Bronx, 1982—. Mem. Nat. Assn. Social Workers, Nat. Assn. Black Social Workers (mem. employment com. 1982—, recruiter voter registration drive 1984). Democrat. Avocations: theater, aerobics, tennis, jogging. Home: 3455 Corsa Ave Apt 2B Bronx NY 10469 Office: RCA Service Co 221 W 41st St New York NY 10036

LUNSFORD, WENDY JEANNE, lawyer; b. Sun Valley, Calif., July 31, 1950; d. David Whitfield and Marguerita D. (Pahl) Layer; m. Douglas L. Lunsford, Sept. 24, 1978. B.A., Occidental Coll., 1972; J.D., Duke U., 1975. Bar: Calif. 1975, N.Mex., 1979. Law clk. to judge U.S. Dist. Ct. (cen. dist.) Calif., Los Angeles, 1975-76; assoc. Romney, Schaap, Golant, Scillieri, Disner & Ashen, Beverly Hills, Calif., 1976-78; sole practice, Roswell, N.Mex., 1979-85; gen. counsel Midwest Royalties, Inc., Roswell, 1981-85. Pres. bd. dirs. Roswell Girls Club, 1982, bd. dirs., 1981-84, chmn. program devel. com., 1984; bd. dirs. United Way Chaves County, Roswell, 1983-85. Mem. ABA, N.Mex. Bar Assn., Chaves County Bar Assn., Professionally Oriented Women, Millionaires Anonymous Investment Club (treas. Roswell 1984-85), Phi Beta Kappa. Republican. Presbyterian. Home: PO Box 855 Roswell NM 88201 Office: PO Box 806 Roswell NM 88201

LUPICA, ANNE ELIZABETH HINKLEY, lawyer; b. Bainbridge, N.Y., Nov. 29, 1954; d. Charles Francis and Elizabeth Catherine (Church) Hinkley; m. Joseph Richard Lupica, June 2, 1979. B.A. cum laude, Vassar Coll., 1976; J.D. cum laude, Cornell U., 1979. Bar: Conn., Fla. Assoc. Alcorn, Bakewell & Smith, Hartford, Conn., 1979-83; ptnr. Pepe & Hazard, Hartford, 1983—. Mem. Charter Revision Commn., West Hartford, Conn., 1982-83; mem. West Hartford Fin. Adv. Bd., 1981-82. Republican. Roman Catholic. Office: Pepe & Hazard One Corporate Ctr Hartford CT 06103

LUPONE, PATTI, actress; b. Northport, L.I., N.Y., Apr. 21, 1949; d. Orlando Joseph and Angela Louise (Patti) DuP. B.F.A., The Juilliard Sch., 1972. Off-Broadway productions include The Woods, School for Scandal, The Lower Depths, Stage Directions; appeared in Broadway productions Next Time I'll Sing to You, The Time of Your Life, The Three Sisters, The Robber Bridegroom, The Water Engine, The Beggar's Opera, Oliver, 1984; star: Broadway play Evita, from 1979 (Tony award 1980); appeared in off-Broadway prodn. The Woods, 1982; other theatre appearances include: Company, Tyrone Guthrie Theater, Mpls., Edmond, Provincetown Playhouse, 1982, The Cradle Will Rock, The Acting Co., 1983, America Kicks Up its Heels, Playwrights Horizons, 1983. Office: care Internat Creative Mgmt 40 W 57th St New York NY 10019

LUPTON, MARY HOSMER, owner, operator rare book search service; b. Olympia, Wash., Jan. 2, 1914; d. Kenneth Winthrop and Mary Louise (Wheeler) Hosmer; student Gunston Hall Jr. Coll., 1932-33; B.S. in Edn., U. Va., 1940; m. Keith Brahe Wiley, Oct. 12, 1940 (dec. Apr. 1955); children—Sarah Hosmer Wiley Guise, Victoria Brahe Wiley; m. 2d, Thomas George Lupton, Nov. 27, 1965; 1 stepson, Andrew Henshaw. Ptnr., Wakefield Press, Earlysville, Va., 1940-55; owner, operator Wakefield Forest Bookshop, Earlysville, 1955-65, Forest Bookshop, Charlottesville, 1965-85, Wakefield Forest Tree Farm, 1955-85. Corr. sec. Charlottesville-Albemarle Civic League, 1963-64; sec. Instructive Vis. Nurses Assn., Charlottesville, 1961-62; chmn. pub. info. Charlottesville chpt. Va. Mus. Fine Arts, 1970-77; mem. writers' adv. panel Va. Center for Creative Arts, 1973-75, chmn. pub. info., 1976-77; mem. Albemarle County Forestry Com., 1961-62; bd. dirs. Charlottesville-Albemarle Mental Health Assn., 1980-82. Mem. AAUW, DAR (Am. Heritage com. chmn. 1983—), New Eng. Hist. Geneal. Soc., Conn. Soc. Genealogists, Va., Albemarle County hist. socs., Va. Soc. Mayflower Descs. (asst. state historian 1979-82), LWV, Soc. Mayflower Descs., Am. Soc. Psychical Research, Brit. Soc. Psychical Research, Nature Conservancy, Va. Forestry Assn., Chi Omega. Mem. Soc. of Friends. Address: La Casita Blanca PO Box 5206 Charlottesville VA 22905-0206

LURIA-COHEN, NANCY, lawyer; b. N.Y.C., Aug. 28, 1956; d. Leonard and Gloria (Biren) Luria; m. Dan Scott Cohen, Mar. 7, 1981. B.A. cum laude, Washington U., St. Louis, 1977; J.D., Boston Coll., 1981. Bar: Mass. 1981, Fla. 1982, Colo. 1983. Assoc. firm Volk & Clayman, Chelsea, Mass., 1981-82, O'Connor & Hannan, Denver, 1982-84, Cogswell & Wehrle, Denver, 1984—; assoc. investment banker Prudential-Bache Securities Inc., Los Angeles, 1984. Contbr. opinion to legal publ. Mem. ABA, Colo. Bar Assn., Denver Bar Assn., Fedn. Bus. and Profl. Women Assn. Office: Cogswell & Wehrle 1700 Lincoln St Denver CO 80203

LURIE, ALISON, author; b. Chgo., Sept. 3, 1926; children—John, Jeremy, Joshua. A.B. magna cum laude, Radcliffe Coll., 1947. Lectr. English Cornell U., 1969-73, adj. asso. prof., 1973-76, asso. prof., 1976-79, prof., 1979—. Author: V.R. Lang: a Memoir, 1959, Love and Friendship, 1962, The Nowhere City, 1965, Imaginary Friends, 1967, Real People, 1969, The War Between the Tates, 1974, Only Children, 1979, The Language of Clothes, 1981; Foreign Affairs, 1984. Recipient award in lit. Am. Acad. Arts and Letters, 1978; Yaddo Found. fellow, 1963, 64, 66; Guggenheim fellow, 1965; Rockefeller Found. fellow, 1967. Address: Dept English Cornell Univ Ithaca NY 14850

LURIE, DONNA ELLEN, lawyer; b. Fair Lawn, N.J., June 18, 1955; d. Stanley Jay and Shirley June (Levy) L.; m. Wesley Neal Sprague, Aug. 22, 1982. B.A. in Labor Studies summa cum laude, Pa. State U., 1977; J.D., U. Wis., 1980. Bar: Wis. 1980, U.S. Dist. Ct. (eastern and western dists.) Wis. 1980, Wash. 1983, U.S. Dist. Ct. (western dist.) Wash. 1983, U.S. Ct. Appeals (7th cir.) 1982. Law clk. Office of Atty. Gen., Madison, Wis., 1978; clk. firm Podell, Ugent & Cross, Milw., 1978-79; student intern Wis. Employment Relations Commn., Madison, 1979-80; project asst. U. Wis. Law Sch., Madison, 1980; atty. Shneidman Law Firm, Milw., 1980-82; assoc. exec. dir. Seattle Tchrs. Assn., 1982—; N.Y. dir. Frontlash, N.Y.C., 1977; labor edn. instr. Sch. for Workers, Milw., 1980-82. Author column: Grieve, Don't Gripe!, author research study: Facing Union Busters, 1982. Mem. Woodinville Design Rev. Com. Mem. ABA, Wash. Bar Assn., Seattle-King County Bar Assn., Wash. Women Lawyers, Nat. Audubon Soc., NOW. Phi Beta Kappa, Phi Kappa Phi. Democrat. Clubs: Downtown Athletic (racquetball awards 1980-82) (Milw.); Comparable Worth Project (Calif.). Office: Seattle Tchrs Assn 720 Nob Hill Ave N Seattle WA 98109

LURIE, KAREN ANN, electrical wholesale and distribution company executive; b. Jersey City, Oct. 24, 1957; d. Hilbert and Patricia Louise (McKnight) Lurie. B.S., U. So. Calif., 1980. Staff acct. Owens-Ill. Forest Products Div., Vernon, Calif., 1977-78; chief fin. officer Armstrong Pacific Corp., Santa Fe Springs, Calif., 1980—. Mem. Mensa, U. So. Calif. Orange County Young Alumni (pres. Newport Beach, Calif. 1984—), Pi Beta Phi. Republican. Presbyterian. Home: 14420 E Eastridge Dr Whittier CA 90602 Office: Armstrong Pacific Corp 11845 E Telegraph Rd Santa Fe Springs CA 90670

LURIE, MURIEL, psychiatric social worker; b. N.Y.C., June 16, 1915; d. Arthur and Celia (Nochimson) L.; B.A., SUNY, Albany, 1967, M.S.W., 1972; children—Daniel, Carolyn. Sec., fund raiser, fund-raising concerns, 1937-39; researcher/editor U.S. Senate Com. Investigating R.R.s, 1939-42; newswriter/editor OWI, London, 1942-45; mgr. advt. agy., N.Y.C., 1946-49; dir. social services depts. Childs Nursing Home and University Heights Health Center, Albany, 1972-79; legis./policy asso. N.Y. State chpt. Nat. Assn. Social Workers, 1979-83; dir. Cons. and Counseling Service to Older Adults and Their Families, 1983—; pvt. practice counseling and psychotherapy, Albany, 1978—; cons. area nursing homes, 1972—. Alt. del. White House Conf. on Aging, 1981; chmn. Long-Term Care Task Force, Health Systems Agy. N.E. N.Y., 1976—, chmn. Albany Sub-Area Council, 1985—. Mem. Nat. Assn. Social Workers, Long-Term Care Social Workers N.E. N.Y. (co-founder 1974), Acad. Cert. Social Workers, Urban League, LWV, Health Fdn. and Welfare Club Albany (dir. 1978—). Home: 21 Park Ln S Menands NY 12204 Office: Cons and Counseling Service to Older Adults and Their Families 919 Myrtle Ave Albany NY 12208

LURIE, NANCY OESTREICH, anthropologist; b. Milw., Jan. 29, 1924; d. Carl Ralph and Rayline (Danielson) Oestreich; B.A., U. Wis., 1945; M.A., U. Chgo., 1947; Ph.D., Northwestern U., 1952; LL.D., Northland Coll., 1976; m. Edward Lurie, 1951 (div. 1963). Instr. U. Wis.-Milw., 1947-49, 51-53, asst. prof., 1961-63, prof., 1963-72, chmn. dept. anthropology, 1967-70; curator anthropology Milw. Pub. Museum, 1972—; lectr. U. Mich., 1956-61, cons. expert witness for attys. representing tribal clients before U.S. Indian Claims Commn., 1957-64; Fulbright lectr. U. Aarhus, Denmark, 1965-66. Recipient (with co-editor) Anisfield-Wolf award for best scholarly book in intergroup relations, The American Indian Today, 1968; Gambrinus award Milwaukee County Hist. Soc., 1984. Fellow AAAS, Am. Anthrop. Assn. (exec. bd. 1977-80, pres. 1983-85); mem. Am. Ethnol. Soc., Soc. Applied Anthropology, Central States Anthrop. Soc. (pres. 1967), Sigma Xi. Editor, translator: Mountain Wolf Woman, The Autobiography of a Winnebago Woman, 1961; author: A Special Style: The Milwaukee Public Museum, 1882-1982, 1983. Home: 3342 N Gordon Pl Milwaukee WI 53212

LUROS, ELLYN CAROLE, nutritionist, computer software company executive; b. Bronx, N.Y., Jan. 15, 1947; d. Samuel Joseph and Ruth (Feld) Green; m. Richard Marc Luros, Nov. 28, 1968; children—Hilary, Jodi, Jason, Stephanie. B.S. in Food and Nutrition, U. Ala., 1968. Dietitian Holy Cross Hosp., Mission Hills, Calif., 1968-70, FSC Mgmt. Co., Chatsworth, Calif., 1970-80; pres., chief exec. officer Computrition, Inc., Chatsworth, 1980—. Author: How to Consult-A Guide to Success, 1979, Successfully Marketing and Selling to Nursing Homes, 1985; also articles. Bd. dirs. Heschel Day Sch., Northridge, Calif., 1984-85, chief fin. officer, 1985-87. Recipient Outstanding Alumni award U. Ala., 1985. Mem. Am. Dietetic Assn. (Outstanding Young Dietitian award 1976), Dietitians in Bus. and Industry, Roundtable for Women in Foodservice (Pacesetter award 1985), Home Econs. Soc., Cons. Dietitians in Health Care Facilities (chmn. 1976-82, bd. dirs., treas., nat. chmn. 1979-81). Jewish. Avocations: cooking; traveling. Office: Computrition Inc 21049 Devonshire St Chatsworth CA 91311

LUSCOMBE, WENDY, real estate consultant; b. Seend, Wilshire, Eng., Oct. 29, 1951; came to U.S., 1981; d. Norman Percival and Betty (Hall) Luscombe; diploma in estate mgmt., Oxford Sch. Architecture, 1972. Investment analyst Taylor Woodrow Property Co., World Trade Center, London, 1972; surveyor N. European Regional Group, Chase Manhattan N.A., London, 1973-77; head research div. Knight Frank & Rutley, intern. property cons., London, 1977-78; property mgr. Nat. Coal Bd. Pension Funds, also pres., dir. subs. Pan-Am. Properties, Inc., N.Y.C., 1978—; dir. Buckingham Holding Inc., Rampac, Insilco Corp.; arbitrator London Small Claims Ct., 1976-79. Chartered surveyor; chartered arbitrator. Mem. Royal Instn. Chartered Surveyors (former dep. chmn. eastern U.S. region), Chartered Inst. Arbitrators (U.K.). Contbr. articles in field to profl. jours. Office: 521 Fifth Ave Suite 1407 New York NY 10175

LUSK, GLENNA RAE KNIGHT (MRS. EDWIN BRUCE LUSK), librarian; b. Franklinton, La., Aug. 16, 1935; d. Otis Harvey and Lou Zelle (Bahm) Knight; B.S., La. State U., 1956, M.S., 1963; m. John Earle Uhler, Jr., May 26, 1956; children—Anne Knight, Camille Allana; m. 2d, Edwin Bruce Lusk, Nov. 28, 1970. Asst. librarian Iberville Parish Library, Plaquemine, La., 1956-57, 1962-68; tchr. Iberville Parish Pub. Schs., Plaquemine, 1957-59, Plaquemines Parish Pub. Schs., Buras, La., 1959-61; dir. Iberville Parish Library, Plaquemine, 1969—; chmn. La. State Bd. Library Examiners, 1979—. Mem. Iberville Parish Econ. Devel. Council, Plaquemine, 1970-71; sec. Iberville Parish Bicentennial Commn., 1973—; mem. La. Bicentennial Commn., 1974. Named Outstanding Young Woman Plaquemine, La. C. of C., 1970. Mem. La. (sect. chmn. 1967-68), Riverland (sec. 1973-74) libraries assns., Capital Area Libraries (chmn. com. 1972-74). Democrat. Episcopalian. Author: (with John E. Uhler, Jr.) Cajun Country Cookin' 1966; Rochester Clarke Bibliography of Louisiana Cookery, 1966; Royal Recipes from the Cajun Country, 1969; Iberville Parish, 1970. Home: 206 Pecan Tree Ln Plaquemine LA 70764 Office: 1501 J Gerald Berret Blvd Plaquemine LA 70764

LUSK, SYLVIA ANN, railroad car manufacturing executive; b. Lubbock, Tex., July 27, 1940; d. William Ray Headstream and Catherine Clay (Cox) Spencer; m. Murry Thomas Lusk, Aug. 11, 1956 (div. Jan. 1970); children—Thomas Lynn, Deborah Lusk Robertson. B.B.A. in Acctg., Tex. Tech. U., 1962. Jr. acct. Howard T. Cox & Co., Austin, Tex., 1961-63; sr. acct. Bus. Funds, Inc., Houston, 1964-68; asst. controller Marathon Mfg. Co., Houston, 1968-73; corp. sec., asst. treas. Richmond Tank Car Co., Houston, 1973—; officer, dir. Richmond-Lox Equipment Co., Livermore, Calif., 1983—, Richmond Stimwell, Houston, 1983—; officer Richmond Leasing Co., Houston, 1973—, D & R R.R. Co., Dardanelle, Ark., 1978—, Richmon Carbon Alloy Co., Houston, 1979—. Treas., St. Giles Presbyterian Ch., Houston, 1967-68; woman mgr. So. Meth. U., Houston, 1979; founding dir. Richmond Employees Credit Union, 1981-82. Mem. Nat. Assn. Accts. Republican. Home: 5959 Donwhite Ln Houston TX 77088 Office: Richmond Tank Car Co 1700 W Loop S Houston TX 77027

LUSKIN, DONNA, lawyer; b. Balt., Dec. 18, 1956; d. Joseph and Mildred S. L. B.A., U. Iowa, 1977; J.D., U. Balt., 1979. Bar: Fla. 1980, N.Y. 1981. Counsel, Columbia Pictures Industries, Inc., N.Y.C., 1981-83; sole practice, N.Y.C. and Hollywood, Fla., 1984—. Mem. ABA. Office: 4150 N 28th Terr Hollywood FL 33022

LUSKY, CHRISTINA MARIE, lawyer; b. Uniondale, N.Y., Nov. 8, 1948; d. Joseph Stanley Lusky and Margaret (Frombach) Lusky Hafers. B.A., Hunter Coll., 1970; J.D., N.Y. Law Sch., 1978. Cert. TESL, 1971. Bar: N.Y. 1979, U.S. Dist. Ct. (ea. dist.) N.Y. 1981, U.S. Dist. Ct. (so. dist.) N.Y. 1981. Law clk. Abeles, Clark & Osterberg, N.Y.C., 1975-76; paralegal McCaulay, Fields, Fisher, Goldstein, 1976; negligence atty. Peck & Peck, Bronx, 1978; legal proofreader Skadden, Arps, Slate, Meagher & Flom, N.Y.C., 1978; legal researcher, writer Gersten & Tisch, N.Y.C., 1978-79; paralegal Davis, Polk & Wardwell, N.Y.C., 1979; law clk., atty. H. Stuart Klopper, Forest Hills, N.Y., 1979-80; law asst. to judge Civil Ct., N.Y.C., 1980-81; atty. Human Resources Adminstrn., N.Y.C., 1981—. Mem. exec. com. Barbizon Tenants Assn., N.Y.C., 1980—; bd. govs. Republican Vols., 1980—; Mem. N.Y. Law Sch. Alumni Assn., N.Y. County Lawyers Assn., ABA. Episcopalian. Office: Human Resources Adminstrn 220 Church St 6th Fl New York NY 10021

LUSKY, LOIS FREESE, public relations executive; b. Wahpeton, N.D., Sept. 28, 1931; d. James and Edna Elizabeth (Eckes) Freese; student N.D. Sch. Sci., 1949-52, U. Denver, 1953-55; m. Sam Lusky, July 14, 1966; 1 stepson, Mark. Pub. relations asst. United Bank Denver, 1958-60, asst. pub. relations dir., 1960-63, dir. pub. relations, 1963-65; exec. v.p. Sam Lusky Assocs., Inc., Denver, 1965-79; sr. v.p. Hill and Knowlton Inc., 1979—. Mem. pub. relations com. United Fund Agy., 1960-65; pub. relations counsel Boys Clubs Denver, 1963-65; mem. Gov.'s Com. Status of Women, 1969-71; bd. dirs. Auraria Community Center, 1958-62, Denver Partnership; co-chmn. media div. Mile High United Way; publicity/promotion chmn. Gov.'s and Mayor's Colo. Pro Sports Com.; bd. advisers Salvation Army; bd. dirs., v.p., mem. exec. com. Jr. Achievement Met. Denver, 1977-84; bd. dirs. Colo. Celebration of Arts, 1978; mem. adv. bd., exec.-in-residence U. Denver Sch. Bus. Adminstrn. Mem. Pub. Relations Soc. Am. (state v.p. 1966), Colo. Indsl. Press Assn. (past dir.), Am. Assn. Advt. Agencies, 1st Advt. Agy. Network, Denver Advt. Fedn., Denver C. of C. (past dir., exec. com., vice chmn. membership and communications group). Home: 6340 E 6th Ave Denver CO 80220 Office: 1050 17th St Suite 2200 Denver CO 80265

LUST, VIRGINIA, art gallery dir.; b. Chgo., July 23, 1930; d. Nathaniel K. and Helen (Dillmann) Wertheimer; B.A., Mundelein Coll., Chgo., 1952; m. Herbert C. Lust, Aug. 17, 1963. Freelance publicist, 1952-68; dir. Gallery Bernard, Chgo., 1968-73; owner, dir. Virginia Lust Gallery, N.Y.C., also Graphics Club, Ltd., N.Y.C., 1973—; dir. Delvaux Retrospective of Prints and Drawings, 1969, Bellmer Retrospective, 1970. Home: 54 Porchuck Rd Greenwich CT 06830 Office: 1356 Madison Ave New York NY 10028

LUTFI AL-SAYYID MARSOT, AFAF, Middle East history educator, author; b. Cairo, Nov. 1, 1931; came to U.S., 1968; d. Said Lutfi and Atiya (Rashwan) al-Sayyid; m. Alain-Gerard Marsot, July 29, 1964; children—Vanina Mona, Vanessa Atiya. B.A. in Sociology, Am. U., Cairo, 1952; M.A. in Polit. Sci., Stanford U., 1956; D.Phil. in Oriental Studies, Oxford U., U.K., 1963. Research fellow St. Antony's Coll., Oxford, 1963-65; asst. prof. Am. U., Cairo, 1965-68; vis. asst. prof. UCLA, 1968-70, assoc. prof., 1970-75, prof. Middle East history, 1975—. Author: Egypt and Cromer, 1967, Egypt's Liberal Experiment, 1977, Egypt in the Reign of Muhammad Ali, 1983, A Short History of Egypt, 1985. Mem. Middle East Studies Assn. (pres. 1977), Am. Research Centre in Egypt (bd. mem. 1971—). Democrat. Muslim. Avocations: writing; travel. Office: Dept History UCLA Hilgard Ave Los Angeles CA 90024

LUTHER, FLORENCE JOAN (MRS. CHARLES W. LUTHER), lawyer; b. N.Y.C. June 28, 1928; d. John Phillip and Catherine Elizabeth (Duffy) Thomas ; J.D. magna cum laude, U. Pacific, 1963; m. William J. Regan (dec.); children—Kevin P., Brian T.; m. 2d, Charles W. Luther, June 11, 1961. Admitted to Calif. bar; mem. firm Luther, Luther, O'Connor & Johnson, Sacramento, 1964—. Mem. faculty McGeorge Sch. Law, U. Pacific, Sacramento, 1966—, prof., 1968—. Judge Bank Am. Achievement awards, 1969-71. Bd. dirs. Sacramento Suicide Prevention League, 1969-70. Mem. ABA, Calif., Sacramento County bar assns., AAUP, Womens Legal Groups, Am. Judicature Soc., Order of Coif, Iota Tau Tau. Mem. bd. advisors Community Property Jour., 1974—, state decision editor, 1974—. Home: 11101 Fair Oaks Blvd Fair Oaks CA 95628 Office: PO Box 1030 Fair Oaks CA 95628

LUTKENHOUSE, ANN, administrator; b. S.I., N.Y., Feb. 18, 1957. B.A. magna cum laude, Wagner Coll., 1979; cert. Goethe Inst., N.Y.C., 1981. Supr. Credit Suisse, N.Y.C., 1979-85; dist. office adminstr. N.Y. City Council, 1985-86; legal asst., 1986—; contbg. cons. Wagner Coll. Study Program, Bregenz, Austria, 1978—. Photographer, producer photography show, 1984. Swimming instr. ARC, S.I., 1977; campaign aide council member Fossella, N.Y. City Council, S.I., 1985; pres., bd. dirs. S.I. Chamber Music Players, 1984-86. Mem. Nat. Assn. Female Execs., Norwegian-Am. C. of C. Democrat. Roman Catholic. Avocations: needlecrafts; ballet; swimming; skiing; travel. Home: 399 Yetman Ave Staten Island NY 10307

LUTTBEG, LINDA EISENSTATT, wholesale company executive, civic worker; b. Omaha, Dec. 30, 1948; d. Leo and Aileen Phyliss (Feder) Eisenstatt; B.S. in Edn., U. Nebr., Omaha, 1970, M.S. in Social Scis., 1971; m. Steven M. Luttbeg, June 14, 1970; children—David, Lisa. Social studies tchr. Central High Sch., Omaha, 1970-75; exec. dir. Girls' Club Omaha, 1975-78, developer advocacy for girls campaign, San Diego, Calif., 1979-80; partner L&L Products, San Diego, 1981-82; pres. A Thing or Two, Inc., San Diego, 1984—. Mem. Mayor's Task Force on Police and Community Relations., 1973-74; active LWV, 1971-78, Clarkson Hosp. Service League, 1972-78, Mayor's Commn. Status of Women, 1976-77, CETA Planning Council, 1976-77, San Diego Juvenile Justice Commn., 1979-81; chairperson Girls Rehab. Facility inspection team, 1980; adv. bd. Girls' Club Pasadena, 1979-81; bd. dirs. Western region Girls' Clubs Am., 1980-82; bd. dirs. Jewish Community Center, chairperson presch. com., 1980-81; Named hon. citizen of Omaha, 1975, Women of Yr. in human services Nebr. Women's Polit. Caucus, 1977; recipient nat. award Girls' Clubs Am., 1978, Founder's Day award Girls' Club Omaha, 1979. Club: Jr. League (San Diego). Office: 438 Camino Del Rio S Suite B209 San Diego CA 92108

LUTZKER, EDYTHE, historian, writer, researcher; b. Berlin, Germany, June 25, 1904; d. Solomon and Sophia (Katz) Levine; B.A., City Coll. N.Y., 1954; M.A., Columbia U., 1959; m. Philip Lutzker, June 14, 1924; children—Michael Arnold, Arthur Samuel, Paul William. Bookkeeper, sec., exec. for bus. cos., N.Y.C., 1922-49; research asst. to Prof. Edward Rosen, City Coll. N.Y., 1951-54; author: Women Gain a Place in Medicine, 1969; Edith Pechey-Phipson M.D., Story of England's and India's Foremost Pioneering Woman Doctor, 1973. Pres. Child Care Center Parents Assn., 1943-51. Grantee Am. Philos. Soc., 1964, 65, Nat. Library of Medicine, 1966, 68-71, 72-74. Fellow Royal Soc. Medicine; mem. Am. Assn. History of Medicine, Am. Soc. for Microbiology, Soc. Internat. History Medicine, History of Sci. Soc., Am. Hist. Assn., Jewish Acad. Arts and Scis., Fawcett Soc. Democrat. Contbr. articles profl. publs., lectr. profl. orgns. Founder, v.p. Waldemar M. Haffkine Internat. Meml. Com. Home and Office: 201 W 89th St New York NY 10024

LUXTON, JANE C(HARLOTTE), lawyer; b. Phila., June 25, 1951; d. Elvin L. and Charlotte M. (Herring) Luxton; m. Charles Matz Horn, May 29, 1976; 1 son, Andrew Luxton Horn. A.B., Radcliffe Coll.-Harvard U., 1973; J.D., Cornell U., 1976. Bar D.C. 1976. Atty. advisor Commr. FTC, Washington, 1976-78; trial atty. Dept. Justice, Washington, 1978-81; assoc. Steptoe & Johnson, Washington, 1981—. Mem. ABA, D.C. Bar Assn., Women's Bar Assn. Democrat. Office: Steptoe & Johnson 1330 Connecticut Ave NW Washington DC 20036

LUZADDER, BEVERLY ANNE, management information systems executive; b. Phila., June 20, 1946; d. David Edward and Geraldine Edith (Williams) Waters; m. James William Luzadder, Dec. 28, 1968. B.S. in Indsl. Mgmt., Purdue U., 1968; M.B.A., Mich. State U., 1972. Account rep. Gen. Electric Co., Indpls., 1968-70; mgmt. systems analyst Burroughs Corp., Detroit, 1972-76, mgmt. systems mgr., Wayne, Mich., 1976-78, Plymouth, Mich., 1980-81; prodn. control mgr., Detroit, 1978-80, mgmt. systems dir., Detroit, 1981-85, sr. program mgr., 1985—. Treas. Highland Lakes Condominium Assn., Northville, Mich., 1982—. Mem. Am. Prodn. and Inventory Control Soc., Phi Mu (pres. 1967-68). Avocations: reading; gardening; camping. Office: Burroughs Corp Burroughs Pl Detroit MI 48232

LUZIETTI-MYERS, DEBRA LYNNE, lawyer, naval officer; b. Chgo., Oct. 9, 1953; d. Bruno and Beverly Brown (Barbour) Luzietti; m. David Hale Myers, Aug. 19, 1978. B.A., Bradley U., Peoria, Ill., 1975; J.D., Valparaiso U. (Ind.), 1978. Bar: Ill. 1978. Commd. lt. USN, 1981; asst. officer U.S. Navy charge Office of Legal Counsel, Annapolis, 1981-84; mil. justice atty. Office of JAG, Alexandria, 1984—; mem. Jr. Officers' Adv. Group, 1982-84 , chmn. projects com., 1983-84, sec. Women's Law Ctr. Anne Arundel County (Md.), 1984-86. Commd. lt. USN, 1981—. Mem. ABA, Ill. State Bar Assn., Women Officers Profl. Assn., Phi Alpha Delta, Pi Sigma Alpha (pres. 1974-75). Clubs: Women Law Students Assn. (Valparaiso) (pres. 1976-78) Home: 606 Forest Hills Dr Annapolis MD 21403 Office: Office of JAG 200 Stovall St Alexandria VA 22332-2400

LUZURIAGA, ADEL, Realtor, investment counselor, developer; b. Philippines, Oct. 31, 1949; came to U.S., 1970; d. Laurie Trinidad; student Maryknoll Coll., U. Madrid, Glendale Coll.; m. Apr. 1, 1970 (div.). With Kramer Wilson Co., 1971-74, Barnes Ins. Agy., 1974-75; salesperson PRO Realty, 1975-80; assoc. Famous Real Estate Co., 1980; pres. Realty Benefit Systems Inc., 1980—. Mem. Nat. Assn. Realtors, Calif. Assn. Realtors, Glendale Bd. Realtors (dir., Pres.'s award 1985), Women's Council of Realtors (pres. Glendale chpt. 1985), C. of C. Roman Catholic. Club: Zonta (bd. dirs.). Office: 413 E Glenoaks Blvd Glendale CA 91207

LYBARGER, ADRIENNE REYNOLDS (MRS. LEE FRANCIS LYBARGER, JR.), development and fund raising consultant; b. Boston, Mar. 8, 1926; d. Joseph Anthony and Albertine Mouton (Drevet) Reynolds; B.A., Mills Coll., 1947; certificate Katharine Gibbs Sch., 1948; m. Lee Francis Lybarger, Jr., Sept. 15, 1955 (dec.); children—Linda, Lauretta, James (dec.), Lisa, Leslie (dec.), Jeffrey (dec.), Lucia, Lana. Asst. to dir. Mid-Century convocation M.I.T., Cambridge, 1949, asst. to dir. West Coast regional office Mid-Century devel. program, 1949-50, asst. dir. So. regional office, 1950-51; asst. to dir. convocation program Ithaca (N.Y.) Coll., 1951; asst. to dir., devel. program U. Buffalo (N.Y.), 1951-52; asst. to dir. Diamond Jubilee program Case Inst. Tech., Cleve., 1952-54; asst. dir., expansion and improvement program John D. Archbold Hosp., Thomasville, Ga., 1954-55; partner Lybarger Prodns., comml. films, N.Y.C., 1955-61; asst. dir., then dir. regional campaigns, Ohio, Boston, Mass., N.Y.C., also supr. all other nat. regional campaigns Mt. Holyoke Coll. Fund for Future, South Hadley, Mass., 1961-63; fund-raising cons. to capital programs, Vocation Service Center and Bronx-Westchester YMCA, YMCA Greater N.Y., 1963-65; dir. devel. and pub. relations Bank Street Coll. Edn., N.Y.C., 1965-79; cons. South Bronx Overall Econ. Devel. Corp., 1978-79; cons. Manhattan Community Coll., 1979—; v.p. for devel., dir. Capital Campaign, Wells Coll., Aurora, N.Y., 1981-83; Realtor-assoc. Century 21 Realtors, Clinton, N.J., 1979-82. Mem. Council for Advancement and Support Edn., Deferred Giving Group of N.Y.; trustee, pres. Birch Island Corp., 1978-79. Author: (with L.F. Lybarger) Proven Guides to Effective Soliciting (slide film), 1950, rev., 1960, 81; exec. producer, script writer Now More Than Ever (film). Home: Kings Manor Pittstown NJ 08867 Office: Wells Coll Aurora NY 13026

LYLE, JEROLYN ROSS, economist; b. Meridian, Miss., Sept. 12, 1937; d. Fred A., Sr., and Everette B. Ross; B.A., So. Meth. U., 1958; M.A., U. Md., 1966, Ph.D., 1970; spl. studies in Spanish, Inst. Francisco Marroquin, Guatemala, 1975; m. Frank Allen Lyle, June 21, 1958; children—Kathryn E., James Jeffrey. Tchr., Dallas Public Schs., 1958-59, Arlington County County Schs., Arlington, Va., 1961-62, 63-64; tchr., curriculum specialist Houston Public Schs., 1959-61; office mgr. No. Va. Fair Housing Assn., 1965-67; economist, program specialist Office of Edn. and HEW, 1966-68; economist EEO Commn., 1968-71; mem. faculty econs. Am. U., 1971-75, Smith Coll., 1971; sr. economist Inter-Am. Devel. Bank, 1974-75; sr. economist Office Mgmt. and Budget, Exec. Office of the Pres., 1975-76; sr. economist Fed. Emergency Mgmt. Agy., Washington, 1976—; mem. faculty U. Pitts., 1983—, U. Md., part-time 1983—; vis. scholar Wolfson Coll., Cambridge U., 1984; cons. Urban Inst., 1971-72, Office Statis. Policy, Office Mgmt. and Budget, 1972, Office of Edn. and HEW, 1974; research asso. 1963. Prin. investigator corp. affirmative action programs EEO, 1971-73; guest lectr. U.S. Army War Coll., Carlisle, Pa.; travel grantee to India and Brazil, Internat. Communications Agy., 1978-79. Mem. Am. Econ. Assn., Am. Statis. Assn., Soc. Govt. Economists (dir. 1979-80), Indsl. Relations Research Assn., Allied Social Sci. Assns. Methodist. Author: Women in Industry, 1973; The Dynamics of Recent Inflation in Latin America, 1975; (with E. Zabrowski) A Proposed Method for Estimating the Critical Characteristics of Stockpile Materials, 1979; Estimating the Employment Impact of Trade Deficits for Input-Output Sectors of the U.S. Economy, 1980; the 21st Century in America: Statistical Support for Long-Range Planning; contbr. articles to profl. jours. Home: 5512 Center St Chevy Chase MD 20815 Office: Federal Emergency Management Agency Washington DC 20407

LYLE, MARY FRANCES, lawyer, lobbyist; b. Texarkana, Tex., Feb. 22, 1936; d. Robert Lewis and Frances Dillahunty (DePrato) Hodges; m. Michael Charles Lyle, July 12, 1954; children—Elizabeth Anne Lyle Miller, Stephen Michael, Mary Carol Lyle Hollis, David Robert. B.A., U. Louisville, 1966; J.D., Vanderbilt U., 1979. Bar: Tenn. 1979. Elem. tchr. Jefferson County Bd. Edn., Louisville, 1966-69, Warren County Bd. Edn., McMinnville, Tenn., 1969-76; assoc. firm Bruce, Weathers, Dughman & Lyle, Nashville, 1984—; lobbyist for women in state legislature Tenn. Women's Polit. Caucus, 1982—. Columnist; contbr. articles to legal publs. Bd. dirs. Planned Parenthood, Nashville, 1983—, pres., 1985—; mem. Met. Transit Authority Adv. Council, Nashville, 1983, Fed. Regulatory Flexibility Act Task Force, Washington, 1981. Mem. ABA, Tenn. Bar Assn., Nashville Bar Assn., Lawyers Assn. for Women, Tenn. Trial Lawyers Assn., C. of C. (small bus. com.), Women in Bus. Inc. (pres.). Democrat. Roman Catholic. Clubs: Altrusa, Cable (dir. Nashville 1982-83). Home: 6626 Holt Rd Nashville TN 37211 Office: Bruce Weathers Dughman & Lyle 1610 Parkway Towers Nashville TN 37219

LYMAN, ELISABETH REED, educator; b. Bklyn., Sept. 13, 1912; d. Carl Sweetland and Florence Irene (Bemis) Reed; B.A., Smith Coll., 1933; postgrad. U. Calif.-Berkeley, 1933-38; m. Ernest McIntosh Lyman, June 12, 1934; children—Nancy Lyman Repp, Elisabeth Lyman Rachal, Richard, Jerome, Carl. Instr., Smith Coll., 1941; research asst. Mass. Inst. Tech., 1941, staff mem. Radiation Lab., 1942-46; research asst. prof. Computer-based Edn. Research Lab., U. Ill., Urbana-Champaign, 1962-84, emerita, 1984—. Mem. Urbana Bd. Edn., 1950-65, pres., 1955-60; chmn. Dist.-Wide Sch. Com., Urbana, 1969-70; mem. Urbana Park Dist. Adv. Com., 1971-73, chmn., 1972-73; mem. Urbana Park Bd. Commrs., 1973-79; mem. Boneyard Creek Commn., 1976—, pres., 1978-81, treas. exec. bd. Univ. YWCA, 1964-71; bd. dirs. Champaign County United Way, 1974-78. Named Mother of Year, Champaign News Gazette, 1962. Mem. Am. Soc. for Engring. Edn., LWV, Soc. Women Engrs., Ill. Assn. Sch. Bds., U. Ill. Athletic Assn. (bd. dirs. 1976-79, sec. 1977-78, vice chmn. 1978-79), Assn. Devel. Computer-Based Instructional Systems, Assn. for Women in Sci., Phi Beta Kappa, Sigma Delta Epsilon, Alpha Lambda Delta. Republican. Congregationalist. Contbr. numerous articles to profl. jours. Home: 1009 S Orchard St Urbana IL 61801 Office: 252 Engring Research Lab U Ill Urbana IL 61801

LYMAN, MARY VANETTA, review and publications specialist; b. Columbus, Ohio, Oct. 26, 1953; d. Chester Tynes and Willa Mary (Gross) L. Student Otterbein Coll., 1971-73, Bowling Green State U., 1973-75; B.A., Ohio State U., 1979, postgrad., 1981-83. Cosmetician, cashier Super X Drug Stores, Columbus, 1975-77; tour guide Battelle Meml. Inst., Columbus, 1977-79, editor, 1979-83, review and publs. specialist, 1983—; fashion bd. rep. Sears, Columbus, 1970-71. Mem. women's student governing bd. Otterbein Coll., 1971-72. Mem. Women in Communications, Inc., Soc. Tech. Communications (sec. 1982-83), Sigma Gamma Rho. Democrat. Roman Catholic. Office: Battelle Meml Inst 505 King Ave Columbus OH 43201

LYNCH, BEVERLY PFEIFER, librarian; b. Moorhead, Minn., Dec. 27, 1935; d. Joseph B. and Nellie K. (Bailey) Pfeifer; m. John A. Lynch, Aug. 24, 1968. B.S., N.D. State U., 1957, L.H.D. (hon.); M.S., U. Ill., 1959; Ph.D., U. Wis., 1972. Librarian Marquette U., 1959-60, 62-63; exchange librarian Plymouth Pub. Library, Eng., 1960-61; asst. head serials div. Yale U. Library, 1963-65, head, 1965-68; vis. lectr. U. Wis.-Madison, 1970-71, U. Chgo., 1975; exec. sec. Assn. Coll. and Research Libraries, 1972-76; univ. librarian U. Ill.-Chgo., 1977—; vis. prof. U. Tex., Austin, 1978. Editor: Priorities for Academic Libraries, 1982; Management Strategies for Libraries, 1985. Contbr. articles to profl. jours. Named Acad. Librarian of Yr., 1981. Mem. Acad. Mgmt., ALA (pres. 1985-86), Am. Sociol. Assn., Bibliog. Soc. Am., Phi Kappa Phi. Clubs: Caxton, Grolier. Home: 1859 N 68th St Milwaukee WI 53213 Office: Box 8198 Chicago IL 60680

LYNCH, BRENDA CLARK, lawyer; b. Toledo, June 10, 1954; d. Robert Ellwood and Rosalyn Jean (Meyer) Clark; m. John Edward Lynch, Jr., Nov. 16, 1984; 1 child John Edward III. B.Ed. cum laude, U. Toledo, 1975, J.D. magna cum laude, 1978; grad. Nat. Inst. Trial Advocacy, 1983. Bar: Ohio 1978, U.S. Dist. Ct. (no. dist.) Ohio 1978, U.S. Ct. Appeals (6th cir.) 1982. Summer clk. Advs. for Basic Legal Equality, Toledo, 1976; summer assoc. Shumaker, Loop & Kendrick, Toledo, 1977; assoc. Squire, Sanders & Dempsey, Cleve., 1978-84; assoc. Porter, Wright, Morris & Arthur, Cleve., 1984—. Note and comment editor U. Toledo Law Rev., 1977-78. Mem. Ohio State Bar Assn., Cleve. Bar Assn. Democrat. Office: Porter Wright Morris & Arthur 1500 Huntington Bldg Cleveland OH 44115

LYNCH, CAROLINE HIRTH, physicians, consultant; b. Hartford, Conn., Feb. 15, 1935; d. Richard William and Emilie (Kaleta) Hirth; m. John Clement Lynch, June 1, 1957; children—Richard John, Allison Emilie. Student Hillyer Coll., 1953-54, 55-58, U. Conn., Storrs, 1954-55. Office mgr. various physicians' offices, Tex., Conn., Ill., 1960-77; cons. MAC Mgmt. and Consulting Services, Vernon, Conn., 1977-79; owner, pres. A Doctor's Service Ctr., Bountiful, Utah, 1979—. Author tng. manuals, guides, Instr. water safety ARC, Dallas, 1963-75, instr. disaster services, Salt Lake City, 1983—, vol. caseworker. Mem. Nat. Assn. Female Execs. Morman. Lodges: Order Eastern Star, Order Amaranth. Avocations: music, travel. Home: 644 N 400 E Kaysville UT 84037 Office: A Doctor's Service Ctr PO Box 758 Bountiful UT 84010

LYNCH, CATHERINE GORES, social work administrator; b. Waynesboro, Pa., Nov. 23, 1943; d. Landis and Pamela (Whitmarsh) Gores; B.A. magna cum laude and honors, Bryn Mawr Coll., 1965; Fulbright scholar, Universidad Central de Venezuela, Caracas, 1965-66; postgrad. (Lehman fellow), Cornell U., 1966-67; m. Joseph C. Keefe, Nov. 29, 1981; children—Shannon Maria, Lisa Alison, Gregory T. Keefe, Michael D. Keefe. Mayor's intern, Human Resources Adminstrn., N.Y.C., 1967; research asst. Orgn. for Social and Tech. Innovation, Cambridge, Mass., 1967-69; cons. Ford Found., Bogota, Colombia, 1970; staff Nat. Housing Census, Nat. Bur. Statistics, Bogotá, 1971; evaluator Foster Parent Plan, Bogotá, 1973; research staff FEDESARROLLO, Bogotá, 1973-74; dir. Dade County Advocates for Victims, Miami, Fla., 1974—; guest lectr. local univs. Participant, co-chmn. various task forces rape, child abuse, incest, family violence, elderly victims of crime, nat., state, local levels, 1974—; developer workshops in field; mem. gov.'s task force on victims and witnesses, gov.'s task force on sex offenders and their victims; cert. expert witness on battered women syndrome in civil and criminal cts. Recipient various public service awards including WINZ Citizen of Day, 1979; Outstanding Achievement award Fla. Network Victim Witness Services, 1982; cert. police instr. Mem. Nat. Orgn. of Victim Assistance Programs (bd. dirs. 1977-83; Outstanding Program award 1984). Fla. Network of Victim/Witness Programs (bd. dirs., treas., 1980-81), Nat. Assn. Social Workers, Am. Soc. Public Adminstrs., Dade County Fedn. Health and Welfare Workers, Fla. Assn. Health and Social Services (Dade County chpt., treas., 1979-80). Contbr. writings in field to publs. Office: 1515 NW 7th St Suite 213 Miami FL 33125

LYNCH, DAWN AMACKER, lawyer; b. Victoria, Tex., Nov. 17, 1957; d. Elbert Monroe and Alice Faye (Corkern) Amacker; B.A., Southeastern La. U., 1978; J.D., La. State U., 1982. Bar: La. 1982. Spl. prosecutor Dist. Atty.'s Office, 22d Jud. Dist., Covington, La., 1982; law clk. 1st Circuit Ct. of Appeal, Baton Rouge, 1982—. Mem. ABA, La. State Bar Assn., Phi Delta Phi. Methodist. Home: 4097 Burbank #6 Baton Rouge LA 70808 Office: 1st Circuit Court of Appeal PO Box 430 508 N Border Dr Bogalusa LA 70427

LYNCH, LEANDRA, physician; b. Chgo., Feb. 14, 1950; d. Hugh Francis and Muriel Gace (Atkin) L.; m. Steven L. Ein, Nov. 26, 1983. Student So. Ill. U., 1968-70; B.S., Purdue U., 1973, M.S., 1975; M.D., Ind. U., 1980. Intern, M.S. Hershey Med. Ctr., Hershey, Pa., 1980-81, resident in gen. surgery, 1981-82; physician specializing in emergency medicine, Los Angeles, 1982—; mem. staff Granada Hills Community Hosp. (Calif.), Valley Park Med. Ctr., Canoga Park, Calif., Daniel Freeman Meml. Hosp., Inglewood, Calif.; instr. basic life support, advanced cardiac life support Am. Heart Assn., Los Angeles, 1982—. Mem. AMA, Phi Kappa Phi. Democrat. Home: 23153 Oxnard St Woodland Hills CA 91367

LYNCH, LINDA ZANETTI, market research executive; b. N.Y.C., Mar. 21, 1933; d. Giacomo and Elise (Linfert) Zanetti; m. David D. Lynch, Oct. 8, 1955 (div. 1984); children—Catherine, Jeffrey, Jonathan, Jennifer, B.A., Brown U., 1954. Asst. editor Good Housekeeping Mag., N.Y.C., 1954-57; freelance editor, N.Y.C., 1965-75; asst. to dir. Ridgefield Library (Conn.), 1975-80; bus. researcher Mktg. Corp. Am., Westport, Conn., 1980-82, bus. research group mgr., 1982—, Mem. Am. Mgmt. Assn., Am. Mktg. Assn., Assn. Info. Mgrs. Club: Brown (N.Y.C.). Office: Mktg Corp 325 Riverside Ave Westport CT 06880

LYNCH, (MARY) ANN BALLMAN, rental executive; b. Cin., July 25, 1949; d. Robert John and Marjory Ann (Brennan) Ballman; m. Howard T. Lynch. B.A. in Art Edn., U. Cin., 1972; advanced profl. courses in mgmt. Part-owner Rottinghaus Gallery, Cin., 1972-74; with Whitehall Labs., div. Am. Home Products Co., 1974-79, div. mgr., Atlanta, 1977-79; with Bausch & Lomb Inc., 1979-82, dist. sales mgr., Atlanta, 1980-82; with Merrell Dow Pharms. div. Dow Chem., 1982-84; owner Lynch Rental Enterprises, 1984—. Mem. Purple Isle Art Guild, Marathon Art Guild (v.p.), Marathon Garden Club, Marathon Art Guild (program chmn. 1985-86, v.p. 1986-87). Roman Catholic. Club: Marathon Garden. Office: 2691 Sombrero Blvd Marathon FL 33050

LYNCH, SISTER MARY DENNIS, librarian; b. Phila., Apr. 23, 1920; d. J. Raymond and Ida A. (Teal) L.; A.B., Temple U., 1941; B.S. in L.S., Drexel U., 1942; M.S. in L.S., Catholic U., 1956; M.A., Villanova U., 1970, St. Charles Sem., 1980. Joined Soc. Holy Child Jesus, 1942; tchr., librarian Sch. Holy Child Jesus, Sharon Hill, Pa., 1942-45, 53-62, Summit, N.J., 1945-47; tchr. social studies West Phila. Cath. Girls High Sch., 1947-53; librarian Rosemont (Pa.) Coll., 1962—, lectr. methods of social studies, 1963-71, chmn. Am. studies com., 1970-73, lectr. polit. sci., 1973—; instr. library sci. dept. Villanova U., summers 1964-65; mem. ednl. adv. bd. St. Charles Borromeo Sem., 1968-76, 78—; bd. dirs. Tri-State Coll. Library Coop., 1967—, pres., 1980-81, exec. sec., 1967-70; trustee PALINET, 1983—, v.p., 1986; mem. Pa. State Library Bibliog. Access Study Adv. Com., 1977-78. Mem. Am., Cath. (nat. exec. council 1975—, pres. 1983-85), Pa. (chairperson coll. and research sect. 1975-76, parliamentarian 1977-83) library assns., OCLC Users Council (del. 1978-83, exec. com. 1982-83), Am. Acad. Polit. and Social Scis., Acad. Polit. Sci., Am. Studies Assn., Nat. Cath. Ednl. Assn., Nat. Council Social Studies, Beta Phi Mu. Address: Rosemont Coll Library Rosemont PA 19010

LYNCH, PATRICIA ANN, state government official; b. N.Y.C., Aug. 21, 1953; d. Thomas P. and Alice (Flanagan) L. B.S., SUNY-Albany, 1975; M.S. Russell Sage U., 1977. From mgmt. trainee to dir. internal audit N.Y. State Dept. Social Services, Albany, 1977—. Mem. Assn. Govtl. Accts., Inst. Internal Auditors, Assn. Pub. Welfare Adminstrs. Home: 48 Point of Woods Dr Albany NY 12203

LYNCH, SHERRY KAY, counselor intern; b. Topeka, Kans., Nov. 20, 1957; d. Robert Emmett and Norma Lea Lynch. B.A., Randolph-Macon Woman's Coll., 1979; M.S., Emporia State U., 1980; postgrad. Kans. State U., 1983—. Vocat. rehab. counselor Rehab. Services, Topeka, 1980-81, community program cons., 1981-86. Mem. exec. com. Sexual Assault Counseling Program, Topeka, 1983-86, recruitment coordinator, 1983-86, counselor, 1981-86; area admissions rep. Randolph-Macon Woman's Coll., Lynchburg, Va., 1981—. Recipient Kans. 4-H Key award Extension Service of Kans. State U., 1974; named Internat. 4-H Youth Exchange Ambassador to France, 1977. Mem. Nat. Rehab. Counseling Assn. (bd. dirs. 1982—, chairperson br. devel. subcouncil 1982—), Gt. Plains Rehab. Counseling Assn. (newsletter editor 1982-85, bd. dirs. 1983-87, pres. 1984-85, sec. 1986-87), Gt. Plains Rehab. Assn. (bd. dirs. 1983-85, awards chairperson 1984-85), Kans. Rehab. Counseling Assn. (bd. dirs. 1983-86, pres. 1984-85), Kans. Rehab. Assn. (bd. dirs. 1982-85, advt. chairperson 1983-85), Topeka Rehab. Assn. (bd. dirs. 1982-85, sec. 1982-83, pres. 1983-84), Am. Assn. Counseling and Devel., Kans. Assn. Counseling and Devel., Am. Coll. Personnel Assn., Kans. Coll. Personnel Assn., Am. Rehab. Counseling Assn. Republican. Methodist. Avocation: tennis. Home: 140 Breezeale Winthrop Coll Rock Hill SC 29733 Office: Counseling Ctr Winthrop Coll 203 Crawford Health Ctr Rock Hill SC 29733

LYND, NANCY HELLMAN, editor; b. Bklyn., Nov. 10, 1944; d. Al and Esther Deborah (Kleinspiec) Hellman; B.S., N.Y. U., 1965; M.A., Calif. State U., Northridge, 1973, postgrad., Fullerton, 1978-79, Dominguez Hills, 1977-78; m. William Lynd, July 3, 1973; children—Allyn David Lynd, Barry Howard Lynd. Secondary sch. tchr., N.Y., La., Calif., 1965-67; free lance writer, 1968-72; tchr. Calif. State U., Northridge, 1972-73; programmer/tech. writer Logicon/Intercomp, Inc., Torrance, Calif., 1974-76; pres. Lynd Assos., Santa Ana, Calif., 1976-80; pres. Tech. Text, Inc., 1980-83; mng. editor Liberty Street Chronicle, 1984-85, Burroughs Corp., 1985—; asst. sec. Mfrs. Resources and Planning, Inc., Santa Ana, 1977-78; cons. Bauer's Mus., 1979—. Active Women for Polit. Action, Orange County Music Center, Inc., South Coast Repetorary Theater. Mem. NOW, Am. Bus. Women's Assn., Nat. Women's Network. Jewish. Office: 1232A S Village Way Santa Ana CA 92705

LYNDS-CHERRY, PATRICIA GAIL, psychologist; b. Woodlake, Calif., Feb. 7, 1950; d. Edgar David and Frances Jean (Eberle) L.; B.A., Calif. State U., Fresno, 1972; M.A., U. Nebr., Lincoln, 1975, Ph.D., 1977; postgrad. U. Calif., Davis, 1978—; m. Albert L. Cherry, Nov. 13, 1982; 1 son, Steven Christopher Cherry. Project coordinator SOMPA II, U. Calif., Davis, 1979-80; psychologist Sacramento County Office of Edn., 1980-81, Kings County Supt. Schs., Hanford, Calif., 1981-83, Bakersfield City Sch. Dist. (Calif.), 1984—. Chairperson, Kings County Child Abuse Com. Maude Hammond Fling fellow, 1973-74. Mem. Am. Psychol. Assn., Assn. Women in Sci. Democrat. Contbr. articles to profl. jours. Home: 6909 Klamath St Apt A Bakersfield CA 93309 Office: Bakersfield City Sch Dist 1300 Baker St Bakersfield CA 93305

LYNN, EVADNA SAYWELL, investment analyst; b. Oakland, Calif., June 1935; d. Lawrence G. Saywell; m. Richard Keppie Lynn, Dec. 28, 1962; children—Douglas, Lisa. B.A., U. Calif.-Berkeley, M.A. in Econs. Chartered fin. analyst. Vice pres. Paine Webber, N.Y.C., 1974-77, Wainwright Securities, N.Y.C., 1977-78, Merrill Lynch Capital Markets, N.Y.C., 1978—. Mem. N.Y. Soc. Security Analysts, San Francisco Security Analysts (treas. 1973-74). Club: Fin. Women's of San Francisco (pres. 1967). Office: Merrill Lynch Capital Markets 165 Broadway St New York NY 10080

LYNN, GERI DUNLAP, educator; b. Odessa, Tex., Sept. 30, 1954; d. Jerry Cecil and Laquita Adelia (Whisenhunt) Dunlap; m. A. Dale Lynn, June 18, 1983. Student Odessa Coll., 1972-74; B.S.Ed., U. Tex., 1982. Lic. tchr., Tex. Child care worker emotionally disturbed adolescents Mary Lee Sch., Austin, Tex., 1979-81; homebound tchr. Balcones Coop., Austin, 1982; tchr. severe and profound unit Round Rock (Tex.) High Sch., 1982-84; tchr. trainable mentally retarded, 1984—; tchr. sign lang. Vol., Tex. Spl. Olympics, 1982—, coach, mem. planning com., 1983—, head coach bowling, basketball and gymnastics, 1983—, head coach soccer and track & field, 1984—; vol. deaf and blind children Tex. Lions, 1981—; Hattie Hewlitt Found. scholar, 1979-81. Mem. Tex. Soc. Autistic Citizens. Address: 18504 Lakeview Dr E Jonestown TX 78641

LYNN, LOIS ANN, lawyer; b. Butler, Mo., July 25, 1953; d. George William Lynn and Lois Isabel (Donalson) Davidson. B.A. in Polit. Sci., Wichita State U., 1979; J.D., Washburn Law Sch., 1981. Bar: Kans. 1983. Staff atty. child support enforcement div. State of Kans. Social Rehab. Services, Wichita, 1984—. Campaign organizer Jack Williams for Congress, Wichita, 1976. Mem. Wichita Bar Assn., Kans. Bar Assn., ABA, Assn. Trial Lawyers Am., Am. Judicature Soc., Young Democrats. Home: 7032 Farmview St Wichita KS 67207 Office: Dept Social Rehab Services State of Kansas PO Box 1620 Wichita KS 67201

LYNN, LORETTA WEBB, singer; b. Butcher Hollow, Ky., Apr. 14, 1935; d. Ted and Clara (Butcher) Webb; student pub. schs.; m. Oliver V. Lynn, Jr., Jan. 10, 1948; children—Betty Sue Lynn Markworth, Jack Benny, Clara Lynn Lyell, Ernest Ray, Peggy, Patsy. Country vocalist with MCA records, 1961—; numerous gold albums; sec.-treas. Loretta Lynn Enterprises; hon. chmn. bd. Loretta Lynn Western Stores. Hon. rep. United Giver's Fund, 1971. Named Country Music Assn. Female Vocalist of Year, 1967, 72, 73; Grammy award, 1971; Entertainer of the Year,, 1972; named Top Duet of 1972, 73, 74, 75; Am. Music award, 1978; named Entertainer of Decade, Acad. Country Music, 1980. Recorded 1st album to be certified gold by a country female vocalist. Author: Coal Miner's Daughter, 1976, released as motion picture, 1979. Office: care United Talent Inc PO Box 23470 Nashville TN 37202*

LYNN, PATRICIA PIFER, educator; b. Winchester, Va., Oct. 24, 1954; d. William Earl and Edythe (Renner) Pifer; B.S. in Spl. Edn., James Madison U., Harrisonburg, Va., 1977, M.Ed. in Learning Disabilities, 1984; m. Thomas G. Lynn, Oct. 27, 1979; children—Matthew Reese, Scott Edward. Tchr. public schs., Stephens City, Va., 1977-80; tchr. learning disabled Berryville (Va.) Primary Sch., 1981-85; ednl. diagnostician, coordinator Clarke County Pub. Schs., 1985-86. Democrat. Methodist. Office: Berryville Primary Sch Berryville VA 22611

LYNN, PAULINE JUDITH WARDLOW, lawyer; b. Columbus, Ohio, Nov. 14, 1920; d. Charles and Helen P. (Christman) Wardlow; student Wellesley Coll., 1938-40; B.A., Ohio State U., 1942, J.D., 1948; m. Arthur D. Lynn, Jr., Dec. 29, 1943; children—Pamela Wardlow, Constance Karen, Deborah Joanne, Patricia Diane. Admitted to Ohio bar, 1948; practiced in Columbus, 1948-49. Troop leader Girl Scouts U.S.A., 1969-71. Mem. ABA, Columbus Bar Assn., Phi Beta Kappa, Kappa Kappa Gamma (mem. research com. Heritage mus.), Pi Sigma Alpha. Republican. Episcopalian. Club: Columbus Met. Home: 2679 Wexford Rd Columbus OH 43221

LYON, BERENICE IOLA CLARK, civic worker; b. Westfield, Pa., June 4, 1920; d. Stephen Artemus and Ruth Gertrude (Tubbs) Clark; m. Robert Louis Lyon, May 28, 1944. Pres., Twin Tiers Geneal. Soc., N.Y. and Pa., 1976—, pub. jour. Gemini; Pa. state pres. Colonial Dames XVII Century, 1981-83, hon. state pres., 1983—, state parliamentarian 1983—; state chmn. heraldry, 1977-79, organizer-pres. Tyoga Gateway chpt., 1973-75, Treaty Elm chpt., 1975-77, state yearbook-directory compiler, 1979-80; N.Y. state chmn. DAR, 1968-71, pres. N.Y. council of regents, 1968-71, regent Corning (N.Y.) chpt. 1965-68, Wellsboro (Pa.) chpt., 1977-80, Pa. state vice chmn., 1980-83, dist. dir. 1983—; N.Y. state chmn. Daus. Am. Colonists, 1968-76, 85—, Atlantic Coast chmn., 1970-79, organizer-regent Forbidden Trail chpt., 1967-76; condr. geneal. seminars; speaker to convs., meetings, TV, radio. Recipient medal of appreciation SAR, 1966. Mem. Ams. of Royal Descent, Descs. Knights of Garter, Magna Carta Dames, Old Plymouth Colony Descs., Order of Crown, Order of Washington, Plantagenet Soc., Mansfield Friends of Library (pres. 1980-81). Clubs: Kiwanis Ladies, Clionian Circle (Corning); Mansfield (Pa.) Garden (pres. 1979-80), N.Y. Fedn. Garden Clubs (sect. chmn. 1969-73). Author series of articles on heraldry 17th Century Rev., 1978-79; subject of article DAR Mag. Home: Lowenhof 168A Bailey Creek Rd Millerton PA 16936

LYON, CATHRYN CROWELL CONOVER, technical information services consultant; Student Harpur Coll., 1949-51, Trenton Jr. Coll., 1954-58, Okla.

U., 1965-69; B.A., U. No. Colo.; M.P.A., U. N.C., 1976. Mgr. Tech. Info. Ctr., 1961-79; document retrieval Wainer-Eddison, Cambridge, Mass., 1981-82; mgr. tech. info. services Inst. for Def. Analysis, Alexandria, Va., 1982-85; tech. info. services cons., Cocoa, Fla., 1986—. Sec., Sr. Citizens Council, Warren, Mass., 1979-81, vice chmn., 1981-82; Warren mem. of Worcester Transp. Council, 1981-82; organizer, chmn. Users Council for Mil. Pub. Retrieval, 1982-85. Recipient brass plaque Va. Microfilm Assn., 1972-73; pewter plaque Fed. Librarians Assn., 1972; others. Mem. Assn. Info. Mgrs., World Future Soc., CLASS, AFFIRM, Nat. Assn. Female Execs. Avocation: history; organ.

LYON, PATRICIA LOUISE, computer manufacturing company executive; b. Clarksdale, Miss., Sept. 4, 1948; d. Richard Bailey and Mignonne Louise (Stanford) L.; A.B. with distinction, Mary Baldwin Coll., 1970; M.Computer Sci., U. Va., 1972. Instr., U. Va., Charlottesville, 1970-72; with Honeywell, 1972-82, regional mktg. mgr., Atlanta, 1979-80, nat. mktg. product mgr., computers, 1980-82; supr. mgmt. info services product evaluation and support Ga. Power Co., Atlanta, 1982-84; account mgr. La. br. Honeywell, Lafayette, 1984-85; sales rep. Digital Equipment Corp., Lafayette, 1985—; dir. Am. Realty Mktg. Corp.; cons. CII-Honeywell Bull, Honeywell French affiliate. Past pres. Wieuca's Way single's program Wieuca Rd. Baptist Ch., Atlanta, 1981-82. Mem. Assn. Computing Machinery, Nat. Assn. Female Execs., Aircraft Owners and Pilots Assn., Republican. Club: Beech Aero. Home: 143 L'Ambiance Circle Lafayette LA 70508 Office: 2020 Pinhook Rd Layfettte LA 70508

LYON-RODMAN, SYLVIA, TV company executive; b. Santiago, Chile, June 25, 1946; came to U.S., 1971, naturalized, 1983; d. Arturo A. and Julie (Valverde) Lyon; student UCLA, 1971-73; m. John S. Rodman, June 6, 1980; children—Lindsay Lyon, Bryan Lyon, Arielle Lyon. Copywriter Eastman Advt., Chile, 1968-70, J. Walter Thompson Advt., Brazil, 1970-71; receptionist KMEX-TV, 1974, public relations exec., 1974-75; dir. advt. and public relations Spanish Internat. Network, Inc., N.Y.C., 1977, asst. to pres., 1978, dir. programming Galavision, 1979—. Trustee Burden Center for the Aged, N.Y.C., 1981—; pres. Cygnus Internat., Inc. Mem. Women in Cable, Parents League of N.Y. (program dir.). Home: 19 E 72d St New York NY 10021 Office: 250 Park Ave New York NY 10177

LYONS, MARGARET LEWIS, nurse, counselor; b. Orlando, Fla., Oct. 4, 1926; d. Herbert R. and Lyla Buck Lewis; A.A.S., Coll. Lake County, 1971; B.A., Northeastern Ill. U., 1975, M.A., 1978; cert. reality therapy, 1985; m. David Lyons, Jan. 14, 1948 (dec.); children—Peggy Scholtes, Cathy Spear, Elizabeth, Dave, Jon Lyons. Nurses aide Highland Park (Ill.) Hosp., 1961-65, operating room technician, 1965-66, L.P.N., 1966-71, staff R.N., 1971-72, critical care, trauma nurse, 1972-74, night adminstr., 1975—, crisis counselor, 1975-80, coordinator chaplaincy, 1975-80, founder, dir. Hospice, 1979—; dir. counseling services, assoc. dean student devel. King's Coll., Briarcliff Manor, N.Y., 1980—. Active Civil Def. Am. Cancer Soc. R.N., Ill. Mem. Audubon Soc., Nat. Hospice Assn., Assn. Christian Colls., Am. Nurses Assn., Christian Assn. Psychol. Studies, Assn. Personnel and Guidance. Democrat. Lutheran Brethren. Home and Office: King's Coll Briarcliff Manor NY 10510

LYONS, REBECCA RUTH, educator counselor; b. Taylor, Tex., Dec. 13, 1933; d. William Thomas and Ruth Ethel (Speegle) Morgan; m. Billy Joe Lyons, Dec. 20, 1954; 1 son, Morgan Joe. B.S., Baylor U., 1955; M.A., East Tenn. State U., 1962; Ed.D., East Tex. State U., 1982. Tchr., Bay County, Panama City, Fla., 1955-57, Carter County, Elizabethton, Tenn., 1958-62; tchr., counselor Dallas Ind. Sch. Dist., 1962—. Tchr., dir. Class for Handicapped Adults, Pleasant Grove First Bapt. Ch., 1977—. NSF scholar U. Houston, 1966; Mem. NEA, Tex. State Tchrs. Assn., Classroom Tchrs. Dallas, Dallas Counselors Assn., Delta Kappa Gamma (scholar Greater Dallas chpt. 1980). Democrat. Baptist. Lodge: Order Eastern Star. Home: 8744 Barclay St Dallas TX 75227 Office: Skyline High Sch 7777 Forney Rd Dallas TX 75227

LYONS-LEPKE, ELAINE MIRIAM, market researcher, sociology and business educator; b. Washington, Apr. 13, 1937; d. Matthew and Sylvia (Aronson) Lyons; m. Keith B. Gould, Feb. 5, 1955 (div. 1970); children—Amy Gould Forton, Victoria, Patricia; m. 2d, John R. Lepke, Nov. 13, 1982. B.A. with high honors in Sociology, Douglass Coll., 1972; M.A., Rutgers U., 1975, Ph.D., 1986. Teaching asst. Rutgers U., New Brunswick, N.J., 1972-74; adj. prof. sociology Douglass Coll., New Brunswick, 1974-76; asst. prof. sociology Valparaiso U. (Ind.), 1977-79; project mgr. market research Gerber Products Co., Fremont, Mich., 1979-81; research dir. Response Analysis Corp., Princeton, N.J., 1981-83; sr. research analyst Miles Labs., Elkhart, Ind., 1984; program evaluator Gerontol. Masters Nursing Program, U. Fla. Coll. Nursing, Gainesville, 1984-85, vis. asst. prof. dept. mktg. Coll. Bus. Adminstrn., 1986—; project evaluator Tng. Inst. for Sex Desegregation, Sponsor HEW-Douglass Coll., New Brunswick, 1976-77; research cons. BASF Wyandotte Corp., Parsippany, N.J., 1976-77; participant Conf. of Grad. and Undergrad. Sociology Students, U. Notre Dame, South Bend, Ind., 1978. Contbr. papers at profl. confs. Sec., Wauhob Lake Park Assn., Valparaiso, 1984. Mem. Am. Sociol. Assn., Am. Mktg. Assn., Am. Assn. Pub. Opinion Researchers. Home: 1100 SW 25th Place Gainesville FL 32601 Office: U Fla Coll Bus Adminstrn Dept Mktg 205 Matherly Gainesville FL 32610

LYSOVA, MARA, ballet company artistic director; b. Berlin, Germany, June 1, 1924; came to U.S., 1938; d. Kurt Hans and Edith M. (Pechner) Leiser; m. Max Newman, 1942 (dec. 1975); children—Leslie Milton, Ronald Peter. Lifetime teaching credential in theatre arts. Dir. and artistic dir. Ballet Academie, Oxnard, Calif., 1956—, Ballet Mime, Oxnard, 1954-70; artistic dir. Cabrillo Music Theatre, Oxnard, 1965-77; tchr. theatre arts Oxnard Union High Sch., 1974-77; artistic dir. Academie Ballet Theatre, Ventura County, Calif., 1978—; producer ballet The Nutcracker, 6 yrs.; judge ballet competition Nat. Soc. Arts and Letters, Santa Barbara chpt., 1970's. Choreographer (ballet) Wuthering Heights, 1958; Moods, 1961; Feelings 1984; Les Companions Lament, 1984. Mem. steering com. Oxnard Auditorium, 1964; bd. dirs. Acad. Nat. Theatre Assn. Dance Festival, Pilgrimage Bowl, Hollywood (Calif.), 1962-63. Mem. Dancer's Soc., Dance Assn. Jewish. Avocation: writing. Office: 136 W 1st St Oxnard CA 93030

LYSTAD, MARY HANEMANN (MRS. ROBERT LYSTAD), sociologist, author; b. New Orleans, Apr. 11, 1928; d. James and Mary (Douglass) Hanemann; A.B. cum laude, Newcomb Coll., 1949; M.A., Columbia, 1951; Ph.D., Tulane U., 1955; m. Robert Lystad, June 20, 1953; children—Lisa Douglass, Anne Hanemann, Mary Lunde, Robert Douglass, James Hanemann. Postdoctoral fellow social psychology Southeast La. Hosp., Mandeville, 1955-57; field research social psychology, Ghana, 1957-58, South Africa and Swaziland, 1968; chief sociologist Collaborative Child Devel. Project, Charity Hosp. La., New Orleans, 1958-61; feature writer African div. Voice Am., Washington, 1964-73; program analyst NIMH, Washington, 1968-78, assoc. dir. for planning and coordination div. spl. mental health programs, 1978-80; chief Nat. Center for Prevention and Control of Rape, 1980-83; chief Ctr. Mental Health Studies of Emergencies, 1983—; cons. on youth Nat. Goals Research Staff, White House, Washington, 1969-70. Author: Millicent the Monster, 1968; Social Aspects of Alienation, 1969; Jennifer Takes Over P.S. 94, 1972; James the Jaguar, 1972; As They See It: Changing Values of College Youth, 1972; That New Boy, 1973; Halloween Parade, 1973; Violence at Home, 1974; A Child's World As Seen in His Stories and Drawings, 1974; From Dr. Mather to Dr. Seuss: 200 Years of American Books for Children, 1980; At Home in America, 1984; Innovations in Mental Health Services to Disaster Victims, 1985; Violence in the Home: Interdisciplinary Perspectives, 1986. Home: 4900 Scarsdale Rd Washington DC 20016 Office: 5600 Fishers Ln Rockville MD 20852

LYTLE, BETTY LOUISE, archivist; b. Roff, Okla., June 11, 1940; d. Lee Fitzhugh and Lucy Ruby (Dunn) Hargis; m. Jack Witt, Apr. 4, 1958 (div. 1976); children—Rhonda Kaye Luker, Michael Jack Witt, Jenifer Denise Witt; m. James Elbert Lytle, June 22, 1977 (div. 1986). B.A. in Acctg., Okla. State U., 1965. Accountant, T.G. & Y Inc., Oklahoma City, 1968-73, Internat. Environ. Corp., Oklahoma City, 1974-78; auditor K & B Inc., New Orleans, 1979-83; audit supr. Oshman's Inc., Houston, 1983-85; archivist Pentecostal Holiness Hdqrs., Oklahoma City, 1985—. Contbg. author: (manual) Fine Arts of Audit, 1985. Contbr. papers to profl. jours. Mem. Nat. Assn. Female Execs. (network dir. 1980-83, 83-85), Nat. Assn. Internal Auditors, Nat. Soc. Am. Archivists, Soc. Okla. Archivists, Soc. Southwest Archivists, Soc. Houston Execs., Okla. Spl. Collections and Archives Network (bd. dirs.), Okla. Conservation Congress, Soc. Pentecostal Studies, Beta Sigma Phi. Republican. Pentacostal. Avocations: poetry writing; cross-country skiing; tennis; swimming; horses. Home: 7204 NW 36th St #220 Bethany OK 73008 Office: Internat Hdqrs Pentacostal Holiness Ch 7300 NW 39th Express Bethany OK 73008

LYTTLE, PAULINE SWAINE, trainer, author, lecturer; b. Birmingham, Eng., July 11, 1945; came to U.S., 1968, naturalized, 1978; d. George H. and Joan (Lyons) Burgess; m. H.L. Lyttle, Apr. 26, 1973 (div.). B.A. in Edn., Birmingham U., 1966, M.S.W., 1968. Vice pres. corp. relations Lyco Land Devel., Seattle, 1968-72; asst. dir. Community Systems Inst., Grand Junction, Colo., 1974-79; owner, prin. Pauline Lyttle Cons., Grand Junction, 1979-83; pres. Operational Politics, Grand Junction, 1983—; chmn. Pvt. Industry Council, Denver, 1983-85. Author: Why Jenny Can't Lead: Understanding the Male Dominant System, 1985. Bd. dirs. Nat. Displaced Homemakers Council, Washington, 1979; past mem. bd. dirs. Colo. Humanities Council, Denver. Democrat. Clubs: Cosmopolitan (pres.), Women's (Grand Junction). Avocations: skiing; sailing. Office: Operational Politics Inc 715 Horizon Dr Suite 485 Grand Junction CO 81506

MA, SYLVIA SEE-WAI, marketing educator, management consultant; b. Hong Kong, Sept. 11, 1949; d. Ting-Lun and Mai-Ying (Lau) Ma; m. Edward Kiyoshi Nabeta, Sept. 10, 1977; children—Erik, Kyra, Ryan. B.A., U. Toronto, 1973, M.B.A., 1975, Ph.D., 1981. Lectr., Ryerson Poly. Inst., Toronto, 1978-80; asst. prof. Wilfrid Laurier U., Waterloo, Ont., Can., 1981-83; asst. prof. mktg. U. Toronto, 1983—; mktg. and mgmt. cons., Toronto, 1978—. Contbr. articles to profl. jours. Margaret Brown Byron scholar, 1975-77; U. Toronto scholar, 1977-80. Mem. Am. Mktg. Assn., Admintrv. Scis. Assn. Can., Assn. Consumer Research, Can. Assn. Univ. Tchrs., Ont. Confedn. Univ. Faculty Assn. Liberal. Baptist. Club: Univ. Women's. Office: Univ Toronto Erindale Campus Mississauga Rd Misissauga ON L5L 1C6 Canada

MAAG, RACHEL MCCORMICK, human resources professional; b. Hartford, Conn., June 5, 1939; d. Ernest Winfred and Esther Roslyn (Mallory) McCormick; m. Daniel Joseph Maag, (div. 1967); children—Elizabeth Ellen, William Barclay, Daniel John, Kathryn Elva. B.A., U. Conn.-Storrs, 1968; M.S., U. Hartford, 1976. Coordinator patient care U. Conn. Health Center, Farmington, 1968-70, dir. record services, 1970-80; dir. employee relations and communications Conn. Gen. Life, Hartford, 1980-82, Cigna Corp., Hartford, 1982—; cons. in med. records tech. Yale U. Sch. Nursing, 1975, U. Conn. Health Ctr., 1976. Rep., Health Systems Agy. of Conn., 1977; parent leader Avon Old Farms Sch., 1979, Watkinson Sch., 1983; mem. Kingswood-Oxford Alumni Bd., West Hartford, 1982-84. Mem. Capitol Area Consortium of Med. Record Adminstrs., Am. Mgmt. Assn., Am. Soc. Personnel Adminstrs., Phi Kappa Phi. Home: 9 Fernridge Rd West Hartford CT 06107 Office: Conn Gen Life Ins Hartford CT 06152

MAARBJERG, MARY PENZOLD, office equipment company executive; b. Norfolk, Va., Oct. 2, 1943; d. Edmund Theodore and Lucy Adelaide (Singleton) Penzold; m. John Peder Maarbjerg, Oct. 20, 1966; 1 son, Martin Peder. A.B., Hollins Coll., 1965; M.B.A., Wharton Sch., Pa., 1969. Cons. bus. and fin., Stamford, Conn., 1977-78; corp. staff analyst Pitney Bowes, Inc., Stamford, Conn., 1978-80, mgr. pension and benefit fin. 1980-81, dir. investor relations, 1981-85; v.p. planning and devel. Pitney Bowes Credit Corp., Norwalk, Conn., 1985-86; v.p. planning, treas. Pitney Bowes Credit Corp., 1986—. Mem. adv. com. City of Stamford Mcpl. Employees Retirement Fund, 1980—; mem. fin. adv. com. YWCA, Stamford, 1982—; bd. dirs. Stamford Symphony, 1985—, Vis. Nurses Assn., 1984-86. Fellow Royal Statis. Soc.; mem. Fin. Execs. Inst., Phi Beta Kappa. Congregationalist. Office: Pitney Bowes Credit Corp 201 Merritt Seven Norwalk CT 06851

MAASS, SOPHIA HANTZES, advertising agency executive; b. Washington, Apr. 12, 1952; d. Harry Nicholas and Mary (Protos) Hantzes; m. Jeffery Maass, June 21, 1975; 1 son, Alexander Reilly. A.B., Conn. Coll., 1974; M.A., Northwestern U., 1978. Research ABA, Washington, 1974-75, Northwestern U., Evanston, Ill., 1975-78; analyst Am. Hosp. Supply Corp., Evanston, 1978-80; market research analyst Am. Heyer-Schulte Corp., Santa Barbara, Calif., 1980-81; projects dir. edn. div. Sieber & McIntyre, Inc., Chgo., 1982-83, account supr., 1983—. Co-editor: Connecticut College Cookbook, 1981. Pres. Conn. Coll. Club Chgo., 1981-84; active Jr. League Chgo. Mem. Midwest Pharm. Advertisers Council, Women in Healthcare. Office: Sieber & McIntyre Inc 625 N Michigan Ave Chicago IL 60611

MAASS, VERA SONJA, psychologist; b. Berlin, July 6, 1931; came to U.S., 1958, naturalized, 1970; d. Willy Ernst and Walli Elisabeth (Reinke) Keck; B.A., Monmouth Coll., 1971; M.A., Lehigh U., 1974; Ph.D., U. Mo., 1978. Cert. sex counselor. Teaching asst. Lehigh U., 1971-72; tutor in adult basic edn. Teaching Assistance Orgn., Kansas City, Mo., 1973-74; grad. research asst. U. Mo., Kansas City, 1974-76; intern U. Ky. Med. Sch., Lexington, 1975-76; psychologist-therapist Dunn Mental Health Center, Richmond, Ind., 1976-80, psychologist, br. dir., Winchester, Ind., 1980-83; psychologist, outpatient clinic supr. Tri-County Mental Health Ctr., Indpls., 1983—; pres., clin. dir. Living Skills Inst., Inc.; v.p. Vitatronics, Inc., N.J., 1969—. Mem. adv. bd. Sta. WXTZ-FM. Mem. Am. Psychol. Assn., Am. Personnel and Guidance Assn., Am. Assn. Sex Educators, Counselors and Therapists, Internat. Assn. Applied Psychology, Nat. Council Family Relations, Internat. Platform Assn., Indpls. Mus. Art. Contbr. in field. Home: 6221 N Keystone Ave #6 Indianapolis IN 46220 Office: 2511 E 46th St Bldg I Indianapolis IN 46205

MABEE, GWYNNE, corporation executive; b. Little Rock, Apr. 19, 1924; d. John and Doris (Nichols) Rouse; children—Dorinda Cheryl Marlborough, Ronald C., Debra Lynn Witt. B.A., U. Houston, 1944. C.P.A., Tex. Sec.-treas. Igloo Corp., Houston, 1958-65; gen. mgr. Modern Dynamics, Houston, 1969-71; pres. Yschek, Inc., Houston, 1975-80; cons. dir. Jacqueline Stallone, Ltd., Las Vegas, Nev., 1983—; pres. Score Sales & Mfg., Inc., Salt Lake City, 1984—; dir. Jacqueline Stallone, Ltd., Score Sales & Mfg., Inc., Salt Lake City, Record Systems, Inc., Las Vegas. Named one of Top 50 Business Women, Harvard Bus. Rev., 1962. Mem. Am. Inst. C.P.A.s, Nat. Data Processing Mgrs. Assn., St. Rose de Lima Soc. Republican. Presbyterian. Avocations: painting; writing; reading; dancing. Office: Score Sales and Mfg Inc 8 E Broadway Suite 328 Salt Lake City UT 84111

MABIE, RUTH MARIE, realtor; b. Pueblo, Colo., Feb. 7; d. Newton Everett and Florence Ellen Allen; M.B.A., La Jolla U., 1980, Ph.D., 1981; m. Richard O. Mabie, Nov. 29, 1946; 1 son, Ward A. Mgr., LaMont Modeling Sch., San Diego, 1962; tchr. Am. Bus. Coll., San Diego, 1964-66; free-lance modeling, 1960-72; owner, broker Ruth Mabie Realty, San Diego, 1972—; asst. v.p. Skil-Bilt, Inc., 1976—; dir. Mabie & Mintz, Inc. Bd. dirs. Multiple Sclerosis Dr., 1971—. Mem. San Diego Bd. Realtors, Nat. Assn. Female Execs. Republican. Office: 4481 Palo Verde Terr San Diego CA 92115

MABRY, MURIEL KAYLIN, personnel executive, career counseling consultant; b. Los Angeles, Oct. 21, 1930; d. Sam and Florence Kaylin; m. Robert Mabry, Aug. 18, 1950 (div. Mar. 1977); children—Leigh Ann Mabry Laughner, John Michael. Ph.D., Sci. of Mind Coll., Long Beach, Calif., 1983, Awareness Psychologist, 1984. Mktg. dir. Corp. Dynamics, Santa Ana, Calif., 1970-76; dir. pub. relations Bernard Haldane Co., Los Angeles, 1975-76; chief exec. officer J. Frederic Marcy, Los Angeles, 1976; pres., owner Woman's World Internat., Santa Ana, Calif., 1976—; speaker in field. Author: Woman's Key to the Executive Washroom, 1976; Here's Genius, 1978; Man's Key to the Executive Washroom, 1979. Contbr. articles to profl. jours. Mem. Women in Mgmt., Profl. Bus. Women, Women's Referral Service. Avocations: writing; public speaking. Office: Woman's World Internat Inc 2020 E 1st St Suite 224 Santa Ana CA 92705

MACAFEE, LYNDA SUE, commercial real estate development company executive; b. Chelsea, Mass., Feb. 13, 1955; d. Kenneth Adams and Diane Elirae (Lockwood) MacA. B.A. in Psychology, B.A. in Sociology, U. Colo., 1976. Project sec. Centric Corp., Lakewood, Colo., 1978-80, estimating asst., 1980-81, adminstrv. safety and EEO officer, 1980-81; constrn. specialist John Madden Co., Englewood, Colo., 1981-83, v.p. contract adminstrn., 1983—. Mem. Nat. Assn. Women in Constrn. (bd. dirs. Met. Denver chpt. 1979-80, 81-82, 84-85, pres. chpt. 1983-84, chmn. nat. constrn. com. 1984-85), Nat. Assn. Female Execs. Republican. Presbyterian. Home: 1811 S Quebec Way # 161 Denver CO 80231 Office: John Madden Co 7800 E Orchard Rd Suite 300 Englewood CO 80111

MACALISTER, KIM PORTER, advertising agency executive; b. Providence, Oct. 25, 1954; d. Bruce Barnes and Jeanne Marie (Cahill) Macalister; m. Bruce Phillip Person, Dec. 29, 1979 (div. June 1984). B.S., Skidmore Coll., Saratoga Springs, N.Y., 1976. Media planner, account exec. J.H. Dietz Advt., Providence, 1976-79; media planner Della Femina, Travisano, Los Angeles, 1979-80; media planner J. Walter Thompson-Entertainment, Los Angeles, 1980-82, assoc. media dir., 1982-83, v.p., media dir., 1983-85; v.p., media dir. Thompson Recruitment Advt. subs. J. Walter Thompson, 1985—; mem. AAAA Inst. Advanced Advt. Studies. Mem. Los Angeles Media Dirs. Council. Republican. Office: Thompson Recruitment Advt 4201 Wilshire Blvd #600 Los Angeles CA 90010

MACAULAY, ALICE ITTNER, physician; b. Bklyn.; d. William and Anna (Holzman) Ittner; B.A. cum laude, Barnard Coll., postgrad., 1944-46; M.D., N.Y. Med. Coll., 1950; postgrad. N.Y. U., 1952-53; M.Sc., L.I. U. at Mercy Coll., 1982, cert. in gerontology, 1983; m. David Harvard Macaulay, July 10, 1936 (dec. 1971). Tchr. N.Y.C. high schs., until 1946; actress Columbia Lab. Players, 1928—, Summer Stock, Roxbury, Conn., 1932-34, Old Vic, London, 1934-35; intern and resident Grasslands Hosp., Valhalla, N.Y., 1950-56, hosp. practice internal medicine Grasslands Hosp., 1956-74, dir. outpatient services, 1956-74, asso. attending internal medicine, 1958-76, chmn. pharmacy and therapeutics com., 1967-74, mem. adminstrv. team, 1961-74; hon. attending in internal medicine Westchester County Med. Center, 1976-84, attending emeritus, 1984—; liaison hosp. officer for devel. of Neighborhood Health Centers; chmn. med. adv. bd. Westchester County Public Health Nursing; med. cons., dir. med. affairs Westchester Community Coll.; cons. Office of Vocat. Rehab. and State Med. Programs; cons. hypertension, 1956—; med. adv. bd. Westchester Heart Assn., chmn. com. on hypertension, 1973-75; prof. medicine Pace U. Grad. Sch. Nursing, 1974-77; vocat. rehab. specialist, 1975—; adv. bd. Columbia U. Ctr. for Geriatrics. Bd. dirs., med. cons. Donald Reed Speech Center, 1976—. Mem. Westchester Acad. Medicine, N.Y. State Med. Soc., Westchester, Am. heart assns., AAAS Cor et Manus, Contin, Am. Lung Assn., N.Y. Trudeau Soc., Alpha Epsilon Iota, Sigma Phi Omega (award 1984). Clubs: Soroptimists; Ardsley Country. Address: Hudson House Ardsley-on-Hudson NY 10503

MACBETH, HELEN LOUISE FELL, educator, librarian; b. Ft. Wayne, Ind., Sept. 1, 1906; d. Royal Virgil and May Belle (Goshorn) Fell; widowed; 1 child, Joanna (dec.). B.S., Ind. U., 1957, M.S., 1959. Cert. life tchr., cert. life prin., Ind., Tex. Elem. tchr. Austin Pub. Schs., Tex., 1962-73; tchr. Resurrection Episc. Sch., Austin, 1978-81, librarian, 1981-85. Mem. adv. bd. Capital Metro Transp., Austin, 1984-85; mem. com. Austin Tomorrow Ongoing Com., 1981-86; organizer Travis County Lit. Council, Austin, 1983-85. Mem. Tex. State Tchrs. Assn. (sch. rep. 1970-73), NEA, Tex. Real Estate Assn. (broker), Travis County Democratic Women, Ind. U. Alumni Assn., U. Tex. Alumni Assn. AAUW, LWV, Presbyterian. Avocation: reading. Home: 1717 Palma Plaza Austin TX 78703 Office: Saint Francis Sch 908 Old Koenig Ln Austin TX 78756

MACCABEE, PAULA GOODMAN, lawyer; b. Mpls., Feb. 10, 1957; d. Ernest and Malka (Lotterstein) Goodman; m. Paul Fishman Maccabee, June 22, 1980; children—Leora, Nadia. Student Macalester Coll., 1973-75; B.A. summa cum laude, Amherst Coll., 1977; J.D., Yale U., 1981. Bar: Minn., 1981, Fed. Dist. Ct., 1981. Congl. intern Senator Walter Mondale, Washington, 1976; fiscal policy aide Mayor of St. Paul, 1977; law clk., lobbyist Dayton, Herman et al., Mpls., 1979-80; atty. litigation Robins, Zelle et al, St. Paul, 1981-83; pvt. practice law, Maccabee Law Office, Mpls., 1983—; vol. atty. Chrysalis Women's Center, Mpls., 1983—; trademark cons. Greenpeace, San Francisco, 1979; legislative cons. Natural Resources Def. Council, Washington, 1978-79. Community organizer Clamshell Alliance, New Haven, 1978-79; writer, cons. DFL Feminist Caucus, St. Paul, 1981; treas., bd. dirs. Harriet Tubman Women's Shelter, Mpls., 1981-83; del. Democratic-Farmer-Labor Party, Mpls., 1982, 84. John Simpson fellow Amherst Coll., 1977. Mem. Minn. Women Lawyers, Minn. Trial Lawyers Assn., Am. Trial Lawyers Assn., ABA, Minn. Bar Assn., Phi Beta Kappa. Democrat. Jewish. Home: 2304 30th Ave South Minneapolis MN 55406 Office: 580 Lumber Exchange Bldg Minneapolis MN 55402

MACCARRONE, RENEE BENNETT, communications company executive; b. Alexandria, La., June 6, 1943; d. William James and Amy Armintha (Jackson) Bennett; B.S., La. Poly. Inst., 1964; postgrad. N.Y. U., 1966-76, Adelphi U., 1977-78; m. Anthony Maccarrone, Nov. 9, 1968; 1 son, Joseph Anthony. With Davis Publs., N.Y.C., 1964-68, with Scholastic Inc., N.Y.C., 1968-83, editorial and advt. adminstr. publ. div., 1980-83; pres. Bennett Communications, Inc., 1983—; cons. in field. Nat. dir. Turn OFF!, Teenagers United to Resist Narcotics in Ourselves, Families and Friends, 1984—. Recipient Crystal Prism award 2d dist. Am. Advt. Fedn., 1983, New Am. Woman award Esquire mag., 1984. Mem. Advt. Women N.Y., (bd. dirs.). Editor: Co-ed's Guide to Getting Married, 1982, 83. Office: 455 Park Ave S New York NY 10016

MACCINI, MARGARET AGATHA, county official; b. N.Y.C., Dec. 6, 1931; d. Camillo and Mary (Varca) Vergano; m. Arthur Maccini, Sept. 25, 1955; children—Mark Robert, Alan Arthur, Deirdre Rose. Student NYU, 1949-51, CCNY, 1952. Cert. mcpl. clk. Exec. sec. Universal Pictures Inc., N.Y.C., 1952-55, Chipman Chem. Co., Bound Brook, N.J., 1956-57, corp. treas. Pyramid Bindery Inc., N.Y.C., 1957-73, pres., 1979-82; adminstrv. asst. Somerset County Bd. Chosen Freeholders, Somerville, N.J., 1973-75, dep. clk. of bd., 1975-76, clk. of bd., 1976—; mem. edn. com. Rutgers U. Dept. of Govt. Services, New Brunswick, N.J., 1983—. Bd. dirs. Voluntary Action Ctr., Somerville, 1977-80, N.J. Ctr. for the Performing Arts, Somerville, 1980-83, Camp Okee Sunokee, Bridgewater, N.J., 1980—; dir. Adult Day Care Ctr., Finderne, N.J., sec., 1977-84, commr., sec., treas. Somerset County Cultural and Heritage Commn., Somerville, 1983—; del. N.J. Counties Cultural and Heritage Assn., 1981—; co-founder, chmn. Van Wickle Dames, Somerset, 1977—; trustee Meadows Found., Inc., Somerset, 1977—, fin. chmn., grantsman, 1982—, pres. 1983-84; dep. registration clk. Franklin Township Election Bd., Somerset, 1970-75; mem. Somerset County Office on Aging Adv. Council, Raritan, N.J., 1978-83, LWV, 1970-71, St. Matthias Rosary Altar Soc., Somerset, 1975-83, Franklin Township Republican Club, Somerset, 1970-84, Hillsborough Township Rep. Club., Somerville, 1985; campaign sec. N.J. Assembly Candidate B. Williams, 1973. Mem. N.J. Assn. Freeholder Bd. Clks. (sec. 1977-78, v.p. 1979-80, pres. 1981-82), Somerset County Mcpl. Clks. Assn. (treas. 1980-81, sec. 1982, v.p. 1983, pres. 1984), Mcpl. Clks. Assn. of N.J. (county rep., alternate 1984—, county membership chmn. 1985), Internat. Inst. Mcpl. Clks. (mem. records mgmt. com. 1984, vice chmn. records mgmt. com. 1985), N.J. Assn. Counties (legis., pub. works and environ. coms. 1982—). Roman Catholic. Club: Zonta Internat. (sec. 1977-78). Avocations: cooking, traveling, gardening, farming. Home: 38 Murrary Dr Neshanic NJ 08853 Office: Somerset County North Bridge and High Sts PO Box 3000 Somerville NJ 08876

MACDONALD, ANNA KAY, nurse; b. Grahn, Ky., Dec. 18, 1950; d. Eaph and Cleo (Nolen) Lowe; m. Ronald Jerry MacDonald, Sept. 3, 1977 (div. 1982). B.S. in Nursing and Behavioral Sci., Loretto Heights Coll., 1983. Staff nurse intensive care unit and cardiac care unit King's Daus. Hosp., Ashland, Ky., 1971-73; commd. officer U.S. Air Force, 1973, advanced through ranks to maj., 1984; med. surg. staff nurse Rickenbacker AFB Hosp., Ohio, 1973-74; charge nurse intensive care unit and cardiac care unit U.S. Air Force Hosp., Colo., 1974-78, U.S. Air Force Med. Ctr., Wright-Patterson AFB, Ohio, 1978-80, cardiac catheterization lab. and rehab. coordinator, 1980-82; chief nurse internal medicine br. U.S. Air Force Sch. Aerospace Medicine, Brooks AFB, Tex., 1983—; instr. Am. Heart Assn., San Antonio, 1983—. Vol. United Way, San Antonio, 1985. Mem. Am. Assn. Critical Care Nurses, Sigma Theta Tau. Democrat. Baptist. Club: Barry's San Antonio Very Strange Manifans (pres. 1985—). Avocations: piano; macrame. Home: 6403 Ridgebrook San Antonio TX 78250 Office: USAF Sch Aerospace Medicine/NGI Brooks AFB TX 78235

MACDONALD, ELIZABETH HELEN, bassoonist, educator; b. Lancaster, Pa., July 5, 1942; d. Joseph Harold and Verna Elizabeth (Schaeffer) Bishop; B.Mus. in Music Edn., Eastman Sch. Music, Rochester, N.Y., 1964, M.Mus. in Music Lit. and Performance, 1966; m. William Dallas MacDonald, Aug. 17, 1968. Bassoonist, Music in Maine Woodwind Quintet, Bangor, 1966-67; dir. jr. high sch. band and elem. instrumental music, Brewer, Maine, 1967-69; instr. music history, woodwind class and bassoon No. Conservatory Music, Bangor, 1967-69; tchr. jr. high sch. gen. and instrumental music, Orono, Maine, 1969-72; tutor bassoon and oboe Colby Coll., Waterville, Maine, 1972-75; instr.

bassoon, woodwind ensemble coach U. Maine, Orono, 1977—; prin. bassoonist Portland (Maine) Symphony Orch., 1967—; pvt. woodwind instr., 1972—; recitalist, soloist, music adjudicator, 1966—. Mem. Music Educators Nat. Conf., Internat. Double Reed Soc., Maine Music Educators Assn. Republican. Methodist. Home: 48 Dillingham St Bangor ME 04401 Office: Lord Hall U Maine Orono ME 04473

MAC DONALD, ELLEN KAYE, hospital corporation executive; b. Visalia, Calif., Oct. 9, 1950; d. Ian Dunbar and Claudine (Burch) Stubbs. M.P.H., UCLA, 1984. Dir. med. records AMI, Los Angeles, 1972-75, cons. AMI/Stat Records, 1975-78, v.p. Stat Records, 1978-82, pres., 1984—, corp. asst. v.p. AMI, 1982, v.p., 1983—. Author: (with others) Physician's Guide to DRGS, 1984, Hospital Coding Guidelines, 1984. Mem. So. Calif. Med. Records Assn. (pres. 1985-86), Calif. Med. Records Assn. (chmn. pub. relations 1984-85), Am. Med. Records Assn., Calif. Med. Records Assn., So. Calif. Soc. Hosp. Risk Mgrs., Nat. Assn. Med. Staff Coordinators. Avocations: tennis, aerobics, skiing, reading, needlework. Office: AMI/STAT Records Inc 9601 Wilshire Blvd Suite 744 Beverly Hills CA 90210

MACDONALD, FLORA ISABEL, Canadian government official; b. North Sydney, N.S., Can., June 3, 1926; d. George Frederick and Mary Isabel (Royle) MacD. Attended Empire Bus. Coll.; grad., Nat. Def. Coll., 1972, D.H.L. (hon.), Mt. St. Vincent U., 1979. Formerly in various secretarial positions; with Progressive Conservative Party Hdqrs., Ottawa, Ont., Can., 1956-65, exec. dir., 1960-65; adminstrv. officer, tutor dept. polit. studies Queen's U., 1966-72; also adv. Student Vo. Bur.; mem. Can. Parliament (for Kingston and the Islands), Ont., 1972—, Progressive Conservative spokesman, 1972, 1974; chmn. Progressive Conservative Caucus Com. on Fed.-Provincial Relations, 1976, sec. of state for external affairs, 1979-80, for external affairs and nat. def., 1980-84; minister employment and immigration, 1984—. Vice pres. Kingston and Islands Progressive Conservative Assn., 1962-72; nat. sec. Progressive Conservative Assn. of Can., 1966-69; exec. dir. Com. for Ind. Can., 1971; pres. Elizabeth Fry Soc. of Kingston, 1968-70. Mem. Can. Inst. Fgn. Affairs (dir. 1969-73), Can. Polit. Sci. Assn. (dir. 1972-75), Can. Inst. Internat. Affairs, Can. Civil Liberties Assn. Mem. United Ch. of Canada. Office: House of Commons Ottawa ON K1A 0A6 Canada

MACDONALD, IMELDA CHRISTINA, emergency room physician; b. Sydney, N.S., Can., July 28, 1954; came to U.S., 1981; d. Douglas Andria Casuol and Imelda Celestine (MacGillivary) MacD. B.S., Dalhousie U., 1974, M.D., 1979. Intern, Univ. Hosp., London, 1979-80; gen. practice medicine Queen Elizabeth Hosp., Charlottetown, P.E.I., 1980-81; emergency room physician Laughlin Meml. Hosp., Greenville, Tenn., 1981-83, Park Ridge Hosp., Rochester, N.Y., 1983-85, Wyoming County Community Hosp., Warsaw, N.Y., 1985—. Mem. Am. Coll. Emergency Physicians. Roman Catholic.

MACDONALD, JUDITH ANN, county official, specialty advertising company executive; b. Brookline, Mass., July 14, 1942; d. James Henry and Mary Anne (Teece) Lewis; m. John Francis Carey, Jan. 14, 1962 (div. 1971); children—William Joseph, Judith Elizabeth; m. John Lawrence MacDonald, Aug. 12, 1972; stepchildren—Eileen, John, Susanne, Paul, William. Student Rivier Coll.; cert. advt. specialist U. Wis., 1978. Teacher's aide Paul Smith Sch., Franklin, N.H., 1968-69; office mgr. Union Central Life Ins. Co., Manchester, N.H., 1971-72; pres., sales person MacDonald Assocs., Manchester, 1972—; registrar of deeds County of Hillsborough, Nashua, N.H., 1981—. Mem. exec. com. Republican City Com., Manchester, 1980—; mem. steering com. Latin Am. Ctr., Manchester, 1984—. Splty. Advt. Assn. scholar U. Wis., 1978; recipient appreciation award Am. Bus. Women's Assn., Manchester, 1982, Rep. City Com., Manchester, 1984. Mem. N.H. Register of Deeds Assn. (v.p. 1973—), N.H. Assn. of Counties (exec. com. 1985), N.H. Title Assn., Manchester C. of C., Women's Investment Group. Served with USN, 1960-62. Roman Catholic. Avocations: gardening; interior decorating; reading; travel; cooking. Home: 2971 Brown Ave Manchester NH 03103 Office: Registry of Deeds 19 Temple St Nashua NH 03061

MACDONALD, KATHLEEN VOUTÉ 0, college official; b. N.Y.C., Jan. 13, 1937; d. Arthur Jerome and Josephine (Rolleston) Vouté; cert. Japanese Lang. Sch., Kyoto, 1963; B.S., Columbia U., 1968, M.A., 1969; M.B.A., Golden Gate U., San Francisco, 1979; doctoral candidate Tchrs. Coll., Columbia U.; m. Daniel Stuart MacDonald, Jr., May 21, 1972; children—Daniel Stuart, Christine Rolleston. Maryknoll missionary sister, 1956-72; dir. Day Care Center, Marin, Calif., 1978-79; mem. adj. faculty Coll. of New Rochelle, 1980; dir. continuing edn. Coll. of Mt. St. Vincent, Riverdale, N.Y., 1981—. Mem. Columbia U. Alumni Assn., Westchester Assn. Continuing Edn. (dir., co-editor newsletter 1985-86), Am. Adult and Continuing Edn., Am. Assn. Higher Edn., Assn. Continuing Higher Edn., N.Y. Assn. Continuing/Community Edn., LWV, AAUW. Author, actress children's TV puppet show Let's Talk about God, NBC, 1959-61. Home: 316 Pondfield Rd Bronxville NY 10708 Office: College of Mount Saint Vincent Riverdale NY 10471

MACDONALD, LINDA STEFANIK, lawyer; b. Perth Amboy, N.J., Sept. 29, 1955; d. John and Anna (Janocko) Stefanik; m. John Arch MacDonald, Sept. 17, 1983 (dec. Feb. 1984). A.B., Rutgers U., 1977; J.D., Western New Eng. Law Sch., 1981. Assoc. Manning, West Santianiello and Pari, Providence, 1981-82; spl. asst. atty. gen. Atty. Gen.'s Office, Providence, 1982—; sr. trial atty., civil div. Motor Vehicles Dealers Licensing Commn., 1982-83; mem. Bd. Med. Examiners, Providence, 1982-83; chmn. Auto Body Repair Shop Com., 1982-83; legal counsel Auto Wrecking and Sales of Commn., 1982-83. Bd. dirs. YWCA, R.I., 1983, Leukemia Soc. R.I., 1983-85; mem. Cancer Support Group R.I., 1983-85. Named Outstanding Woman, YWCA, R.I., 1983; Outstanding Bd. Mem., Leukemia Soc. R.I., 1984. Mem. ABA, Am. Trial Lawyers Assn., R.I. Bar Assn., R.I. Women's Network, LWV. Greek Catholic. Home: 26 Corey Ave Warwick RI 02818 Office: Office Atty Gen 72 Pine St Providence RI 02903

MACDONALD, MARY THOMAS, interior designer; b. Jamestown, N.Y., Mar. 4, 1947; d. David MacDonald and Helen (Hancock) MacDonald Smith; 1 dau., Stephanie Pearl. A.S., SUNY-Jamestown, 1967; B.A., Fla. Internat. U., 1975, M.A., 1977. Founder, dir. A Children's Place, Jamestown, 1970-72; designer Hilton Internat. Hotels, Brussels, 1977; v.p. Creative Environs, Miami, Fla., 1978-84; pres. The MacDonald Design Group, Miami and Los Angeles, 1984—; lectr. hotel/restaurant design and mktg. N.Y. State Appalachia Program grantee, 1972; recipient awards for design, including: Restaurant Hospitality mag. Editor's Choice award for Sheraton Bal Harbour (Fla.), 1981; Restaurant Hospitality mag. 2d place award for hotel restaurant Cartouche, Chgo., 1981; Lodging Hospitality mag. Grand award for Lalique retaurant, Bal Harbour, 1982; Restaurant Hospitality mag. 1st place award for Boccaccio Club, Houston, 1983; Gold Key award for Caberat, Am. Hotel Assn., New Orleans, 1983; Restaurant Hospitality mag. 1st place for Top of Riverfront restaurant, St Louis Clarion Hotel, 1984. Mem. Inst. Bus. Designers, Am. Soc. Interior Designers, Miami Design Preservation League, Greater Miami C. of C. Home: 1925 Brickell Ave D-1213 Miami FL 33129 Office: 3250 Mary St Coconut Grove FL 33133

MACDONALD, VIRGINIA B., state senator; b. El Paso, Tex.; d. Wendell Holmes and Dorothy (White) Blue; student U. N.Mex.; m. Alan Hunter Macdonald, 1941; children—Susan Macdonald, Alan H. Mem. Ill. Ho. Reps., sec. Ho. Republican Caucus in Gen. Assembly, 1972; mem. Ill. Senate, 1980—. Del. 6th Ill. Constl. Conv., 1970; pres. Ill. Fedn. Republican Women; chairwoman Cook County Republican Com., 1964-68; committeewoman Wheeling Twp. Rep. Com.; chmn. Statewide Women's div. Everett McKinley Dirksen's Campaign, 1968; mem. adv. council Community Counciling Center, Suburban Br. Salvation Army; mem. citizens' adv. com. Northwest Suburban Mental Health Assn.; pres. Ill. Fedn. Republican Women, 1972-74. Mem. Northwestern U. Guild Club: Arlington Heights Women's. Office: 1100 W Northwest Hwy Mount Prospect IL 60056*

MAC DOUGALL, GENEVIEVE ROCKWOOD, journalist, educator; b. Springfield, Ill., Nov. 29, 1914; d. Grover Cleveland and Flora Maurine (Fowler) Rockwood; B.S., Northwestern U., 1936, M.A., 1956, postgrad., 1963—; m. Curtis D. MacDougall, June 20, 1942; children—Priscilla Ruth, Bonnie MacDougall Cottrell. Reporter, Evanston (Ill.) Daily News Index, 1936-37; asso. editor Nat. Almanac & Yearbook, Chgo., 1937-38, News Map of Week, Chgo., 1938-39; editor Springfield (Ill.) Citizens' Tribune, also area supr. Ill. Writers Project, 1940-41; reporter Chgo. City News Bur., 1942; tchr. English-social studies Skokie Jr. High Sch., Winnetka, Ill., 1956-68, coordinator TV, 1964-68; tchr. English Washburne Sch., Winnetka, 1968-81; editor Winnetka Public Schs. Staff Newsletter, 1981—; dir. Winnetka Jr. High Archeology Field Sch., 1971-83; cons., lectr. in field. Winnetka Tchrs. Centennial Fund scholar, 1964, 68. Named Tchr. of Year, Winnetka, 1976; Educator of Decade Northwestern U. and Found. Ill. Archeology, 1981. Mem. Winnetka Tchrs. Council (pres. 1971-72), NEA, Ill. Edn. Assn., Ill. Assn. Advancement Archeology, Women in Communications (pres. N. Shore alumni chpt. 1949-53), Pi Lambda Theta. Author: Grammar Book VII, 1963, 68; (with others) 7th Grade Language Usage, 1963, rev. 1968. Contbr. articles to profl. publs. Home: 537 Judson Ave Evanston IL 60202 Office: 515 Hibbard Rd Winnetka IL 60093

MACE, SHARON ELIZABETH, physician; b. Syracuse, N.Y., Oct. 30, 1949; d. James Henry and Leona Helen (Bednarski) M.; B.S., Syracuse U., 1971; M.D., SUNY, 1975. Intern and resident in pediatrics Case-Western Res. U. Hosps., Cleve., 1975-77, fellow in cardiology, 1977-79, instr. dept. emergency medicine, 1980—; research assoc. div. investigative medicine Mt. Sinai Med. Center, Cleve., 1979-80, staff physician depts. emergency medicine and investigative medicine, 1980-86, coordinator emergency medicine residency program; asst. dir. dept. emergency medicine Mt. Sinai Med. Ctr.; dir. emergency dept. Saratoga Hosp., Saratoga Sprongs, N.Y., 1986—; former instr. Case Western Res. U. Sch. Medicine; helicopter flight physician; lectr. Lakeland Community Coll.; instr. Advanced Cardiac Life Support. Mem. Am. Coll. Emergency Physicians (edn. com., dir. Ohio chpt., bd. dirs. N.Y. chpt.), Soc. Tchrs. Emergency Medicine, Univ. Assn. for Emergency Medicine. Congregationalist. Contbr. articles to med. jours. Home: 33 Collins Terr Saratoga Springs NY 12866 Office: Saratoga Hosp 211 Church St Saratoga Springs NY 12866

MACEBUH, SANDY, freelance business seminar and consulting firm executive, writer, poet. B.S. in Psychology, U. Minn., M.A. in Communications, Wayne State U., Ph.D. in Communications, NYU. Instr., community liaison Bowling Green State U., Ohio,Stautzenberger Coll., Toledo, analyst, communications coordinator Kemper Ins. Co., 1980-82; asst. dir. media relations, internat. hostess Los Angeles Olympic Com., 1984; mktg. asst./staff asst. Bus. Strategy Inst., Tustin, Calif., 1984—; free-lance writer, 1984—. Contbr. articles, poetry to various publs., including Potpourri Press, Sunset Publs., Poetry Press, Penna Press, Am. Poetry Anthology, others; TV, radio appearances. Recipient awards including Most Disting. Young Am. Contbr. to Community Am. Bus. Inst., 1981, Poet Laureate award U. Mont., 1978, Third Place award Edward A. Fallot Poetry, 1985. Office: 415 Kelly St Apt B Orange CA 92666

MACEDA, REMEDIOS PAAT, nurse; b. Santa Ilocos Sur, Philippines, Jan. 19, 1943; came to U.S., 1967; d. Melquiades Palasigui and Eufrosina (Belmonte) Paat; m. Jaime M. Maceda, Oct. 19, 1974; 1 child, Therese Marie Juliet. B.S. in Nursing, U. St. Tomas, Manila, Philippines, 1965; postgrad. U. Ill., Chgo., 1970-72. Head nurse, supr. U. St. Tomas Hosp., 1965-67; staff nurse Hahneman Hosp., Phila., 1967-68; staff nurse Michael Reese Hosp., Chgo., 1968-72, adminstrv. coordinator for continuing edn., 1973-80, adminstrv. coordinator for fgn. grads., 1980-85, adminstrv. coordinator for acad. affiliations, continuing edn., and fgn. grads, 1985—. Contbr. article to profl. jour. Mem. Am. Nurses Assn., Ill. Nurses Assn., Philippines Nurses Assn. Chgo. (editor gazette 1968-70). Roman Catholic. Avocations: home-making, gardening, singing, piano, writing. Office: Michael Reese Hosp and Med Ctr Lakeshore Dr at 31st St Chicago IL 60616

MACEY, MARSHA CENTER, lawyer; b. Bklyn., Feb. 19, 1940; d. Jacob George and Thelma (Hackman) Center; m. Douglas E. Macey, Jan. 18, 1960 (div. 1971); children—Melinda Jeanne, Garrett Neil. B.S., summa cum laude, U. N.H., 1960; J.D. cum laude, Harvard U., 1977. Bar: Mass. 1977, Calif. 1983. Exec. dir. N.H. Commn. on Human Rights, Concord, 1968-81; cons. U.S. Commn. on Civil Rights, N.Y.C., 1971-74; assoc. Csaplar & Bok, Boston, 1977-82, San Francisco, 1982—. Mem. ABA, Mass. Bar assn., Calif. Bar Assn., Boston Bar Assn., Nat. Alliance Profl. and Exec. Women's Networks (dir. 1981-82, 83—), Bay Area Exec. Women's Forum, Phi Beta Kappa, Alpha Epsilon Delta. Club: Boston Luncheon (pres. 1980-82). Home: 4606 19th St San Francisco CA 94114 Office: Csaplar & Bok 655 Montgomery St Suite 1000 San Francisco CA 94111

MAC GILLIVRAY, MARYANN LEVERONE, marketing consultant; b. Mpls., Oct. 18, 1947; d. Joseph Paul and Genevieve Gertrude (Ozark) Leverone; B.S., Coll. of St. Catherine, St. Paul, 1969; Med. Technologist, Hennepin County Gen. Hosp., 1970; M.B.A., Pepperdine U., 1976; m. Duncan MacGillivray, Apr. 28, 1973; children—Duncan Michael, Catherine Mary and Monica Mary (twins), Andrew John. Med. technologist Mercy Hosp., San Diego, 1970-72; with Diagnostics div. Abbott Labs., South Pasadena, Calif., 1972-79, tech. service rep., 1972-74, sr. tech. service rep., 1974-75, product coordinator, mktg., 1975-77, mktg. product mgr., 1977-79; clin. diagnostic mktg. cons., Sierra Madre, Calif., 1979—. Recipient Pres.'s award Abbott Diagnostics Div., 1975. Mem. Biomed. Mktg. Assn., Am. Assn. Clin. Chemistry, Am. Assn. Clin. Pathologists, Am. Soc. Med. Tech., Calif. Assn. Med. Lab. Technologists. Roman Catholic. Home: 608 Elm Ave Sierra Madre CA 91024

MACGOWAN, CAROL ANN, med. technologist; b. Gt. Falls, Mont., June 27, 1932; d. James A. and Lila J. (Davis) MacGowan; B.S. in Chemistry, Coll. of Gt. Falls, 1954; A.S.C.P.M.T., Columbus Sch. Med. Tech., 1955; children—Shannon, Timothy. Generalist/hematology Columbus Hosp. Lab., Gt. Falls, 1954-68, now sect. chief, mem. teaching staff; work dir. hematology Arabian Am. Oil Co., Dhahran, Saudi Arabia, 1960-62; adminstrv. technologist Seattle Gen. Hosp., 1962-64; sect. chief MacGregor Clinic Lab., Gt. Falls, 19 - , part-time staff Coll. of Gt. Falls. Mem. Am. Soc. Clin. Pathologists, Am. Soc. Med. Technologists. Address: 1509 3d Ave N Great Falls MT 59401

MACHADO, ANN PATRICIA, personnel executive; b. Toronto, Ont., Can., June 26, 1947; came to U.S., 1970; d. James Roger and Sylvia Joyce (Barnard) Kiteley; m. Joseph A. Machado, Jr., Dec. 6, 1970; children—Joseph Christian, Christine Ann. Elem. teaching cert. London Tchrs. Coll., 1967. Tchr., London (Ont.) Bd. Edn., 1967-69; asst. office mgr. Peat Marwick Mitchell, London, 1969-70; constrn. loan clk. Am. Title, Miami, 1971-72; mktg. mgr. Court Line, Miami, 1972-74; v.p. Am. Temporary, Miami, 1974-81; area v.p. Adia Personnel Services, Miami, 1981—. Bd. dirs. YWCA, Miami, 1975, Dade Employ the Handicapped Com., Miami, 1975-82, New Directions for Handicapped, Miami, 1981-84; charter mem. New Women's Network, Miami, 1980-84. Named Br. Mgr. of Yr., Am. Temporary, Miami, 1976, Employee of Yr., 1977, $1,000,000 Club, 1979; named Woman of Yr., Beta Sigma Phi, Lambda Mu, Miami, 1979. Mem. Personnel Assn. Greater Miami, Greater Miami C. of C. (Miami's for Me Com. 1983-84). Home: 12646 SW 95th Ct Miami FL 33176 Office: Adia Personnel Services 9150 SW 87th Ave Suite 106 Miami FL 33176

MACHAMER, LAURIE ELIZABETH, technicial executive recruiter; b. Hartford, Conn., Sept. 26, 1957; d. Dean Elliott and Diane Paula (Magee) Machamer. Student U. N.H., 1975-77, Central Conn. State U, 1979-81. Engring. computist Pratt & Whitney Aircraft, East Hartford, Conn., 1978-80; office mgr. G. Fox & Co., Hartford, 1980-82; direct import coordinator Hollywood Accessories, Carson, Calif., 1982-83; mgr. arch./engring. adminstrn. The Elliott Group, Los Alamitos, Calif., 1983-84; exec. recruiter E & M Search Services, Torrance, Calif., 1984—. Mem. Nat. Assn. Fin. Execs. Avocations: water skiing; tennis; voice. Home: 75 61st Pl #2 Long Beach CA 90803 Office: E & M Search Services Inc 21213 B Hawthorne Blvd Suite 5356 Torrance CA 90509

MACHISAK, MAUREEN DOROTHY, editor, writer; b. Passaic, N.J.; d. John Christian and Dorothy Catherine (Donahue) M. B.Polit. Sci., Chestnut Hill Coll.; M.P.A., Notre Dame U. Legal editor Office Adminstrv. Law, State of N.J., Newark, 1980-81; editor Prentice-Hall, Inc., Paramus, N.J., 1983-84; communication and edn. assoc. Employee Benefit Research Inst., Washington, 1984, program analyst GAO, Washington, 1984—; reporter Work in Am. Inst., White Plains, N.Y., 1984; free-lance cons., 1977—. Recipient merit scholarships Chestnut Hill Coll., Notre Dame U. Mem. N.J. Paralegal Assn., Notre Dame Alumnae Assn.

MACHTIGER, HARRIET GORDON, psychoanalyst; b. N.Y.C., July 27, 1927; d. Michael J. and Miriam D. (Rand) Gordon; B.A., Bklyn. Coll., 1947; dipl. with distinction, U. London, 1966, Ph.D., 1974; m. Sidney Machtiger, Feb. 7, 1948; children—Avram Coleman, Marcia Gordon, Bennett Rand. Tchr., Phila. Public Schs., 1962-64; ednl. therapist Child Guidance Tng. Center, London, 1966-68; ednl. therapist Sch. Psychol. Service, Inner London Edn. Authority, 1968-70; therapist Paddington Day Hosp., London, 1970-71, London Centre for Psychotherapy, 1971-74, Staunton Clinic, U. Pitts., 1974-78; pvt. practice psychoanalysis, Pitts., 1976—; pres. C.G. Jung Center, Pitts., 1976-81; cons. in field. Mem. SW Pitts. Community Mental Health, 1976-78. Recipient award for Disting. Contributions to Advancement in Edn., Pa. Dept. Edn., 1962; Social Sci. Research Council award, 1973; cert. psychologist, Pa. Fellow Am. Orthopsychiat. Assn.; mem. Inter-Regional Soc. Jungian Analysts. (dir. Pitts. program 1975—), Am. Acad. Psychotherapists, Am. Psychol. Assn., N.Y. Assn. Analytical Psychologists, Internat. Assn. Group Psychotherapists, Pa. Psychol. Assn., Brit. Psychol. Soc., Brit. Assn. Psychotherapists, Assn. Child Psychology and Child Psychiatry, Western Pa. Group Psychotherapy Assn., Nat. Assn. for Advancement Psychoanalysis, NOW. Home: 207 Tennyson Ave Pittsburgh PA 15213 Office: 110 The Fairfax 4614 Fifth Ave Pittsburgh PA 15213

MACIAS, AMELIA, leasing company executive; b. Las Cruces, N.Mex., June 10, 1950; d. Jesus Tostado and Maria Teresa (Huizar) M. A.B., U. San Francisco, 1980. Chief planner Calif. Office Small Bus., Sacramento, 1976-78; v.p. Tech. Leasing Corp., Oakland, Calif, 1979-82, sr. v.p., 1982-84, chief ops. officer, 1984—, also dir.; dir. Gaylor Constrn., Oakland. Served to staff sgt. USAF, 1975-79. Recipient Design award Community Design Assocs., 1984. Mem. Oakland C. of C., Mexican-Am. C. of C. (v.p. 1980) Western Assn. Equipment. Democrat. Mormon. Avocation: interior decorating. Office: Tech Leasing Corp 621 MacArthur Blvd Oakland CA 94610

MACIVER, PEGGE FARMER (MRS. DONALD GORDON MACIVER), monodramatist, educator; b. Colon, C.Z.; d. Alfred Gibson and Minnie (Cuckler) Farmer; B.A., Ohio U., 1935; B.L.L., Cin. Conservatory Music, 1938; M.A., George Washington U., 1964; m. Donald Gordon MacIver, June 7, 1957; 1 stepson, Neil. Monodramatist, lectr., writer touring U.S., Can. writing, performing own plays for one woman theatre presentations, 1938-67; speech therapist D.C. Public Schs., 1959-67, tchr. in-service tng. programs, program coordinator Ednl. Resources Center, 1967-70, asst. dir. dept. spl. edn., 1970-72, supervising dir. for staff devel. dept. spl. edn., 1972-78; ret., 1978; tchr. in-service tng. programs D.C. Tchrs. Coll. TV moderator, panelist Its Your World and World Headliner programs; mem. speakers burs. Dayton (Ohio) Council World Affairs, LWV, 1950-57. Mem. Nat. League Am. Pen Women, Am. Speech and Hearing Assn. (cert. of clin. competence in speech pathology), D.C. Speech and Hearing Assn., Internat. Platform Assn., Phi Beta Kappa, Pi Beta Phi, Alpha Delta Kappa, Delta Kappa Gamma. Contbr. articles to profl. publs. Home: 8500 New Hampshire Ave Silver Spring MD 20903

MACIVER, SANDRA PAGE STERN, winery executive; b. New Orleans, May 13, 1949; d. Edgar Bloom and Pauline Isabel (Stewart) Stern; m. David A. Steiner, Dec. 21, 1968 (div. 1979); children—Erica Maurine, Lauren Elizabeth; m. William Bolen MacIver, Apr. 19, 1980. Student Mills Coll., 1967-69. Co-owner, mgr. Steiner Vineyard, Santa Rosa, Calif., 1969-79, Matanzas Creek Vineyards, Santa Rosa, 1979—; pres. Matanzas Creek Winery, Inc., Santa Rosa, 1977—; chmn. Sonoma County Wine Showcase and Auction, Calif., 1985, 86. Grand juror Sonoma County Grand Jury, 1978; campaign chmn. McDermott for Sheriff, 1979; trustee Stern Fund, N.Y.C., 1968—; bd. dirs. Santa Rosa Symphony Assn., 1985—. Mem. Knights of Vine (Master Lady 1984—), Women on Wine (industry mem.), Wine Inst., Sonoma Valley Vintners Assn. (bd. dirs. 1978—, v.p. 1982-84), Hospitality Industry Council San Francisco (bd. dirs. 1986—), Sonoma County Wine Growers Assn. (bd. dirs. 1980—, v.p. 1984-85, pres. 1985—). Democrat. Avocations: calligraphy; knitting; sailing; dollhouses; gardening. Office: Matanzas Creek Winery 6097 Bennett Valley Rd Santa Rosa CA 95404

MACK, BRENDA LEE, sociologist, public relations consulting company executive; b. Peoria, Ill., Mar. 24; d. William James and Virginia Julia (Pickett) Palmer; A.A., Los Angeles City Coll.; B.A. in Sociology, Calif. State U., Los Angeles, 1980; m. Rozene Mack, Jan. 13 (div.); 1 child, Kevin Anthony. Ct. clk. City of Blythe, Calif.; partner Mack Trucking Co., Blythe; ombudsman, sec. bus facilities So. Calif. Rapid Transit Dist., Los Angeles, 1974-81; owner Brenda Mack Enterprises, Los Angeles, 1981—; lectr., writer, radio and TV personality; co-originator advt. concept Vee/Dee Project. Past bd. dirs. Narcotic Symposium, Los Angeles. Served with U.S. WAC, 1960-61. Mem. Women For, Calif. State U. Los Angeles Alumni. Home: 8749 Cattaraugus Ave Los Angeles CA 90034 Office: Brenda Mack Enterprises PO Box 5942 Los Angeles CA 90055

MACK, CRISTINA IANNONE, accountant; b. Olean, N.Y., Sept. 25, 1940; d. Angelo M. and Rose M. (Sirianni) Iannone; m. John O. Mack, Nov. 19, 1967; children—Elizabeth, Andrew. B.A. in Math., U. Calif.-Santa Barbara, 1962; postgrad. U. San Francisco, 1978—, Golden Gate U., 1983. Exec. dir. Bar Assn. San Francisco, 1966-68; owner, acct. CIM Assocs., San Francisco, 1978—. Treas. Mothers Milk Bank, 1977—; bd. dirs. Am. Paralysis Assn. Aux., 1984; precinct adminstr. Rep. County Central Com., 1964-66; Coro Found. fellow, 1963. Mem. Chi Omega Sorority (pres. 1962, treas. 1984—). Roman Catholic. Club: San Francisco Lawyers Wives (pres. 1974, auditor 1978—). Lodge: Little Sisters of Poor Aux. Avocations: hunting; tennis. Home: 2963 23d Ave San Francisco CA 94132 Office: CIM Assocs 22 Battery Suite 505 San Francisco CA 94111

MACK, EVELYN WALKER, insurance company executive; b. Westbrook, Maine, 1930. Student Colby Coll., 1952. Second v.p. computer systems devel. New Eng. Mut. Life Ins. Co., Boston. Address: New Eng Mut Life Ins Co 501 Boylston St Boston MA 02117*

MACK, JUDI ANN, college administrator; b. Chgo., Aug. 27, 1951; d. Leonard P. and Annabelle R. (Clemes) Stolarski; m. Charles R. Mack, Feb. 17, 1973; 1 child, Erin. B.A. summa cum laude, in Journalism, Duquesne U., 1972; M.A. in Pub. Service and Pub. Adminstrn., Gov's. State U., 1985. Editor Palos Regional Newspaper, Palos Heights, Ill., 1973-75; dir. pub. info. Community High Sch. Dist. 218, Worth, Ill., 1975-78; dir. pub. relations Thornton Community Coll., South Holland, Ill., 1978—. Contbr. articles to profl. jours. Active South Suburban Assn., Harvey, Ill., 1980—. Duquesne U. scholar, 1969-72. Mem. Ill. Coll. Relations Council, Nat. Council for Community Relations (dist. dir. 1980-82, sec. 1982-83, v.p. 1983-84, pres. 1984-85; Communicator of Yr. 1985). Office: Thornton Community Coll 15800 S State St South Holland IL 60473

MACK, JUDITH ANN, data processing executive; b. Chgo.; d. Samuel Perlow and Bertha Shapiro; m. John M. Mack, Aug. 28, 1960; children—Susan, Lawrence. B.S., Northwestern U., 1958, M.S., 1959. Systems engr. IBM, Chgo., 1959-63; cons., Chgo., 1963-76; nat. projects mgr. Itel Corp., Chgo., 1976-80; pres. Data Directions, Inc., Skokie, Ill., 1980-84; pres. Data Group Ltd., Lincolnwood, Ill., 1984—. Mem. Skokie Cable TV Found., 1985; mem. planning com. Legal Adv. Council, 1985. Mem. Nat. Assn. Women Bus. Owners (edn. com. 1984—), Chgo. Area Users Group, Law Office Mgmt. Users Group. Avocations: art; tennis. Office: Data Group Ltd 7250 N Cicero Ave Lincolnwood IL 60646

MACK, MONA CATHERINE, lawyer; b. Washington, Sept. 10, 1956; d. Peter Francis and Romona (North) Mack. B.A., U. Md., 1978; J.D., John Marshall Law Sch., Chgo., 1981. Bar: Ill. 1981, D.C. 1983. Legal intern U.S. Atty.'s Office, Chgo., 1981, Fed. Defender Program, Chgo., 1981; atty. State's Atty.'s Appellate Service Commn., Springfield, Ill., 1982; law clk. to Judge P.F. McArdle, D.C. Superior Ct., Washington, 1982-83, to Judge S.S. Harris, U.S. Dist. Ct. D.C., Washington, 1983-84; asst. U.S. atty., Washington, 1984—. Vol. Children's Hosp. Nat. Med. Ctr., 1984—. Mem. ABA, Ill. Bar Assn., D.C. Bar Assn., Phi Delta Phi (vice magister 1980-81). Democrat. Roman Catholic. Clubs: Jr. League, Congressional (Washington). Office: Chambers Hon Stanley S Harris US Dist Ct 3d and Constitution Aves NW Washington DC 20001

MACK, PHYLLIS FRIEDMAN (MRS. DAVID MACK), interior designer, civic worker; b. N.Y.C., Apr. 15, 1941; d. Maurice and Anne (Price) Friedman; student Vassar Coll., 1958-60, Sorbonne, Paris, 1960; B.S., Columbia U., 1963; grad. N.Y. Sch. Interior Design; m. David Mack, Oct. 8, 1961; children—Alexander H., Nicholas R. Interior designer domestic interiors, N.Y.C., 1963—. Bd. dirs. Stanley Isaacs Community Center, 1965-67; bd. dirs. Children's Blood Found., 1978—, benefit chmn., 1980; chmn. Friends of Children's Blood Found., 1979-80; dance chmn. George Jr. Republic, also mem. jr. bd., 1966-69; bd. dirs. Yorkville Youth Council, 1974-77; mem. public relations com. Asso. YM-YWHA, N.Y.C. Mem. Allied Bd. Trade, Brearley Alumnae Assn. (reunion chmn.). Club: Bailiwick Tennis. also 800 Park Ave New York NY 10021

MACK, WILHELMENA, hospital executive; b. Miami, Fla., Oct. 1, 1951; d. Eugene and Gladys (Terry) Brown; 1 dau., Shannon Lynnette. B.A., U. Miami, 1972, M.Ed., 1973; Ed.S., Fla. Atlantic U., 1983. Personnel officer Dade County Personnel, Miami, Fla., 1973-74; personnel officer Jackson Meml. Hosp., Miami, 1974-76, edn. coordinator, 1976-79; asst. dir. dept. edn. Meml. Hosp., Hollywood, Fla., 1979, dir. dept. edn., 1979—; dir. Traintex Mgmt. Services, Miami, 1978—; adj. faculty Broward Community Coll., Nova U.; founder Comprehensive Tng. Inst. Bd. dirs. Lincoln Meml. Nursing Home, Goulds, Fla., 1977, Ptnrs. in Excellence, Ft. Lauderdale, Fla., 1983, the Chord; dir.-at-large bd. dirs. Fla. chpt. Am. Lung Assn., trustee Broward-Glades-Hendry chpt. Mem. Fla. Adult Edn. Assn., Nat. Assn. Female Execs., Am. Soc. Tng. and Devel., (v.p. 1977), South Fla. Nurse Educators (pres. 1983). Democrat. Baptist. Office: Meml Hosp 3501 Johnson St Hollywood FL 33021

MACKAIG, JANET BROWNLEE, artist, printmaker, educator; b. Santa Monica, Calif., July 16, 1931; d. Roy Edward and Lorna (Feckler) Murphy; A.A., Pasadena City Coll., 1964; B.A., Calif. State U., Los Angeles, 1969, M.A., 1971, postgrad., 1975; postgrad. UCLA, 1975; m. Richard Allaire Mackaig, Dec. 13, 1950; children—Janet (Mrs. William Chadwick), Steven Richard. Tchr., Creative Arts Group, Sierra Madre, Calif., 1965-75, Duarte (Calif.) Unified Sch. Dist., 1973-76; tchr. Otis Art Inst., Los Angeles, 1975-76, Saddleback Coll., Mission Viejo, Calif., 1976-78, Laguna Beach Sch. Art, 1980—; one-man shows: Upstairs Gallery, Claremont, Calif., 1969, U. Oreg., 1976, Fine Arts Gallery, Laguna Beach, Calif., 1981, Minot (N.D.) State Coll., 1981; group shows include: Colorprint U.S.A., Tex. Tech. U., 1975, U. Ala., 1975, Pioneer Press Traveling Print Show, Africa, 1975-76, Art-A Multi-Cultural Show, Calif. Mus. Sci. and Industry, 1978, Contemporary Korean Printmakers Assn. Print Show, 1978, Coos Art Mus., Coos Bay, Oreg., 1979, La Grange (Ga.) Coll., 1980, Trenton (N.J.) State Coll., 1980, Internat. Print Biennial, Miami, Fla., 1982, Nat. Printmaking Invitational, San Bernardino, Calif., 1983, Angeles Gate Cultural Ctr., San Pedro, Calif.; represented in permanent collections. Bd. dirs. Womanspace, 1974—. Recipient Calif. Purchase awards Santa Monica Coll., 1973, Calif. State U., Los Angeles, 1976, Calif. Poly. U., Pomona, 1979. Mem. Laguna Beach Art Assn., Calif. Soc. Printmakers, Los Angeles Printmaking Soc. (pres. 1977-78), Los Angeles Inst. Contemporary Art, Print Club Phila., Pasadena Artists Concern. Club: Pioneer Press. Home: 23821 Salvador Bay Laguna Niguel CA 92677

MACKAY, PATRICIA MCINTOSH, counselor; b. San Francisco, Sept. 12, 1922; d. William Carroll and Louise Edgerton (Keen) McIntosh; A.B. in Psychology, U. Calif., Berkeley, 1944, elem. teaching credential, 1951; M.A. in Psychology, John F. Kennedy U., Orinda, Calif., 1979; Ph.D. in Nutrition, Donsbach U., Huntington Beach, Calif., 1981; m. Alden Thorndike Mackay, Dec. 15, 1945; children—Patricia Louise, James McIntosh, Donald Sage. Elem. tchr. Mt. Diablo Unified Sch. Dist., Concord, Calif., 1950-60; exec. supr. No. Calif. Welcome Wagon Internat., 1960-67; wedding cons. Mackay Creative Services, Walnut Creek, Calif., 1969-70; co-owner Courtesy Calls, Greeters and Concord Welcoming Services, Walnut Creek, 1971—; marriage, family and child counselor, nutrition cons., Walnut Creek, 1979—; coordinator Alameda and Contra Costa County chpts. Parents United, 1985—; bd. dirs. New Directions Counseling Center, Inc., 1975—, founder, pres. aux., 1977—. Bd. dirs. Ministry in the Marketplace, Inc.; founder, dir. Turning Point Counseling. Recipient Individual award New Directions Counseling Center, 1978, awards Neo-Life Co. Am. Prestige Club, yearly, 1977-86. Mem. Christian Assn. Psychol. Studies, Calif. Assn. Marriage and Family Therapists, C. of C., Prytanean Alumnae, Delta Gamma. Republican. Mem. Zion Fellowship. Club: Soroptomist (dir. 1976, 86) (Walnut Creek). Home: 1101 Scots Ln Walnut Creek CA 94596 Office: 1399 Ygnacio Valley Rd Suite 12 Walnut Creek CA 94598

MACKENZIE, AMANDA FISK, training and development official; b. Buffalo, Jan. 18, 1936; d. Bradley and Erma (Johnson) Fisk; B.A., Smith Coll., 1957; children—Bradley John, Alice Fisk, Douglas Bain. Editor, NEA, Washington, 1957-58; research asst., Africa, 1958, sec. to pres. Charles Scribner's Sons, N.Y.C., 1959; writer, producer Washington Ednl. TV, 1961-64; pub. affairs coordinator Can. Performing Arts Festival, 1975; editor, publ. coordinator The Pa. Co., Penn Central Corp., 1970-80. Vol. co-ordinator Adams-Morgan Community Council, Washington, 1966-68; public liaison ethics adv. bd. HEW, 1979-80; public affairs asst. to dir. Select Panel on Child Health, Dept. Health and Human Services, 1980; tng. program and devel. dir. Nat. Center Clin. Infant Programs, 1981—; mem. Mayor's Inter-Agy. Com. on Beautification. Bd. dirs. Jr. League, Washington, 1969-70, Hillcrest Children's Center, 1972-74, Eagles Mere Assn., 1972-75, Woodley House, 1973-76, Inter/Met, 1973-75; trustee Washington Theater Club, 1969-72, also chmn.; trustee Opera Soc. Washington, 1969-76, exec. v.p., 1973-75; trustee Soc. for More Beautiful Nat. Capital, 1971-76, v.p., 1972-76; trustee Selma M. Levine Sch. Music, Lester Hereward Cooke Found., Greg Reynolds Dance Quintet, Lincoln Theater Found. Democrat. Episcopalian. Clubs: Women's Nat. Democratic, Internat., Smith Coll. (pres. 1972-74) (Washington); Eagles Mere Yacht (sec.-treas. 1968-72). Home: 3025 Ordway St NW Washington DC 20008

MACKENZIE, ANN STANSBURY, retired retail merchant; b. Chattanooga, May 14, 1918; d. Samuel Riley and Katherine (Gillespie) Stansbury; m. George Nelson MacKenzie, July 3, 1937 (dec. Dec. 1983); children—Stephen Stansbury, George David, Robert Scott. Student sociology Agnes Scott Coll., 1937-41. Sec., Allen Organ Studies Atlanta, Inc., 1958-81, pres., 1981-83; mgr., buyer The Jo-Ann Inc., Rossville, Ga., 1963-83, v.p., 1963-79, pres., 1980-83. Republican. Baptist. Home: 5850 Riverwood Dr NW Atlanta GA 30328

MACKENZIE, JILL ANNE, public relations executive; b. New Brunswick, N.J., May 28, 1957; d. William H. and Helen R. (Rotkewicz) Mac K. B.A. in Communications, U. Del., 1979. Writer, Rollins Cablevision, Wilmington, Del., 1979-80; pub. relations asst. Del. Art Mus., Wilmington, 1980-81; pub. relations officer Shipley Advt., Wilmington, 1981-82, Hagley Mus. and Library, Wilmington, 1982—. Mem. Am. Acad. Mgmt. (pub. relations com., treas.), Discover Brandywine Pub. Relations Assn. (chmn. advt. 1982—), Internat. Assn. Bus. Communicators, Advt. Club Del., Del. Press Women. Roman Catholic. Office: Hagley Mus and Library PO Box 3630 Wilmington DE 19807

MACKENZIE, KAREN GEORGIA, advertising account executive; b. Ft. Wayne, Ind., Sept. 11, 1956; d. John and Collette Marie (Reynolds) MacKenzie. Student Katherine Gibbs Sch., 1979-80; B.A., Boston Coll., 1984. Editor, Sta. WBZ-TV, Westinghouse Broadcasting & Cable, Inc., 1980-84, author employee handbook, 1982; mktg. dir., contbr. The Illustrated mag., 1984—; writer MacKenzie & Co., Newton, Mass., 1982—; profl. mentor Boston, U., 1983. Contbr. articles to Quilt Mag. Asso. producer Children's Hosp. Benefit Telethon, Boston, 1983. Mem. Women in Communications (Nat. Clarion award 1982), New Eng. Broadcasters Assn., Mayflower Soc., DAR. Democrat. Roman Catholic. Home: 186 Auburn St Newton MA 02166 Office: One Boston Pl Boston MA 02108

MACKENZIE, LINDA ALICE, computer company executive, consultant telecommunications; b. Bronx, N.Y., June 24, 1949; d. Gino Joseph and Mary J. (Damon) Arale; m. John Michael Lassoureille, Aug. 7, 1968 (div. 1975); 1 child, Lisa Marie Lassoureille; m. Donald John Mackenzie, July 2, 1978 (div. 1982). Student Richmond Coll., 1967-68, West Los Angeles Community Coll., 1978-81. Spl. rep. N.Y. Telephone Co., White Plains, 1968-71; asst. mgr. Paul Holmes Real Estate Inc., Richmond, N.Y., 1974-77; telcom applications specialist engring. Continental Airlines, Los Angeles, 1977-83; data transmission specialist Western Airlines, Los Angeles, 1983—; owner Computers on Consignment, El Segundo, Calif., 1984—; cons. Farwest Brokers, Los Angeles, 1984-85, Caleb Feb. Credit Union, Las Vegas, Nev., 1985, Nat. Dissemenators, Las Vegas, 1985; mktg. cons. AT&T, Los Angeles, 1984-85. Author: The World Within, 1983. Active Calif. Lobbyists for Conservation, 1986. Recipient Alexander award Met. Mus. Art, N.Y., 1967. Mem. Nat. Assn. Female Execs., El Segundo C. of C.; assoc. mem. Mgmt. Assocs. Republican. Clubs: Marina City, Manhattan Beach Women's. Avocations: painting; creative writing; aerobic dance; skiing; travel. Office: Computers on Consignment 531 Main St Suite 426 El Segundo CA 90245

MACKENZIE, MARY HAWKINS, hospitality placement company executive; b. St. Louis, July 27, 1936; d. Henry Goodheart and Elizabeth Cummings (Collins) Hawkins; m. Robert S. McGregor, Sept. 3, 1956 (div. May 1973); children—Robert B., Mary Catherine McGregor Ryan, Susan Leigh; m. Kenneth W. MacKenzie, Jr., Apr. 24, 1976; 1 son, Kenneth W. III. B.A., So. Methodist U., 1957. Ctr. dir. YWCA, Dallas, 1966-67; profl. cons. in personnel M. David Lowe, Houston, 1973-75; employment mgr. St. Joseph Hosp., Houston, 1976-78; personnel dir. Greater Houston Hosp. Council, 1978; personnel dir. exec. com. Dunfey Hotel, Houston, 1978-81; pres. The Hotelier Inc., Houston, 1981—. Chmn. bd. dirs. Houston Jazz Ballet, 1979; mem. vestry Ch. of the Epiphany, Houston, 1979-82. Mem. Houston Hotel Motel Assn. (assoc.), Tex. Assn. Personnel Cons., Tex. Exec. Women (pres. 1984-85), Houston Women on the Move (chmn. 1985), Houston Hotel Personnel Dirs. (founder, exec. 1980-81), Houston Area Assn. Personnel Cons. (chmn. 1985—), Delta Gamma. Episcopalian. Avocation: Running. Office: Hotelier Inc 10101 Southwest Freeway Suite 103 Houston TX 77074

MAC KENZIE, MELISSA TAYLOR, musician, music tchr.; b. Brownsville, Tenn., Sept. 23, 1925; d. Lee Bond and Rose Eleanor (Harwood) Taylor; B.A., Peabody Coll., 1946, postgrad., 1946; postgrad. Memphis State U., summers 69-70; div.; 1 dau., Donna m. Pfohl. Soprano, Memphis Open Air Theatre, summer 1948; soprano Episcopal Actors' Guild of N.Y., 1949-51, Am. Theatre Wing, N.Y.C., 1949-51; concert singer, 1948—; pvt. tchr. piano, voice and organ, 1953—; tchr. music edn. Haywood County Bd. Edn., Brownsville, 1953—; soprano soloist, dir. music Temple Adas Israel, Brownsville, 1952-83; dir. music Gay Valley Camp, Brevard, N.C., summers 1959-62; mem. Grace Moore Opera Scholarship, 1966-72; mem. Tenn. Bicentennial Com., 1976. Mem. Nat. Fedn. Music Clubs, Tenn. Fedn. Music Clubs (parliamentarian, v.p.), Nat. Guild Piano Tchrs. (faculty, accredited music tchr.), Am. Coll. Musicians (Hall of Fame 1969), Tenn. Music Tchrs. Assn. (v.p., program chmn. West Tenn. div.), DAR (chmn. Am. music, regent David Craig chpt.), Wednesday Morning Musicale Brownsville (pres.), Rehearsal Club Alumnae Assn. N.Y., UDC, Haywood County Hist. Soc., Alpha Delta Kappa. Home: 647 W Main St Brownsville TN 38012

MACKENZIE, SARA ROGERS, lawyer; b. Britton, S.D., July 25, 1945; d. John Norton and Majorie Ann (Jahnig) Henderson; m. Allen Kyle Rogers, Sept. 1, 1961 (div. 1973); 1 son, Kyle Richard; m. 2d, Ralph Sidney MacKenzie, Nov. 12, 1976; 1 dau., Kristeen Renee. B.A., San Diego State U., 1977; J.D., U. San Diego, 1980. Bar: Fla. 1982. Assoc. Michael Sigman, Orlando, Fla., 1983-84; sole practice, Maitland, Fla., 1984—. Author: (with J. Beveridge) On Lawful Money and Legal Tender, 1983. Mem. Central Fla. Assn. Women Lawyers (chmn. com. 1984), ABA, Orange County Bar Assn., Fla. Bar Assn. Republican. Office: 940A N Maitland Ave Maitland FL 32751

MACKETY, CAROLYN JEAN, nurse, consultant; b. Chgo., Feb. 27, 1932; d. Gerald James and Minnette (Buis) Kruyf; m. Robert J. Martin, Oct. 3, 1952 (div. 1959); children—Daniel, David, Steven, Laura. Diploma, Hackley Hosp. Sch. Nursing, 1969; B.S., Coll. St. Francis, 1977; postgrad. Exec. M.B.A. Program, Canadian Sch. Mgmt., Northland U., Toronto. Nursing coordinator operating room Grant Hosp., Columbus, Ohio, 1981-84, dir. operating room services, 1981—; pres., owner Laser Cons., Inc.; laser nurse specialist. Mem. Polit. Action Group for Nurses, Assn. Operating Room Nurses, Am. Soc. Laser Medicine and Surgery (chmn.). Republican. Mem. editorial bd. Clin. Laser Mag. Author: Perioperative Laser Nursing.

MACKEY-HARGADINE, JUDY RAE, neurosurgeon; b. Omaha; d. Clyde C. and Mildred I. (Higgins) Hargadine; m. W. Robert Mackey, Jr., Feb. 20, 1983. B.S., St. Mary's Coll., 1960; M.S., U. Cin., 1962; M.D., U. Ky., 1977. Intern in surgery and resident in neurosurgery Los Angeles Med. Center-U. So. Calif. and Huntington Meml., Los Angeles, 1971-77; fellow in pediatric neurosurgery Children's Hosp. of Phila., 1978; postgrad. fellow in neurosurgery Nation Hosp. Queen Sq., London, 1979-80; asst. prof. neurosurgery U. Calif., San Francisco, 1980-83; asst. prof. neurosurgery U. Tex. Med. Ctr., Houston, 1983—; cons. in field of electrophysiology. Contbr. articles to med jours., chpts. to books. Mem. Am. Acad. Sci., Soc. Neurosurg. Anesthesia, and Neurol. Supportive Care.

MACKIN, ANNETTE LORETTA, health care executive; b. Herkimer, N.Y., July 31, 1946; d. Leo Bernard and Carolyn (Guido) M.; m. Frank A. Svet, June 18, 1966 (div. Feb. 1980); 1 dau., Marie Suzanne. B.S., SUNY-Brockport, 1973; M.B.A., Rochester Inst. Tech., 1977. Acctg. clk., sec. Lapp Insulator Div., LeRoy, N.Y., 1967-73; assoc. asst. Xerox Corp., Rochester, N.Y., 1973-74; adminstrv. analyst Monroe Community Hosp., Rochester, 1974-77; dir. fiscal affairs Clifton Springs (N.Y.) Hosp., 1977-80; v.p. fin. Vis. Nurse Service, Rochester, N.Y., 1980—. Office: Vis Nurse Service 1609 E Main St Rochester NY 14609

MAC KINNON, LEITA KECK, real estate broker; b. Ralls, Tex., May 4, 1939; d. Clarence D. and Vergie (Russell) Mc Candless; student Tex. Inst. Tech., 1961-62, U. Houston, 1970-74; m. Robert L. Mac Kinnon, Feb. 4, 1974; children—Rhonda Dixon, Brenda Nicholson. Salesperson, Century 21 N.W. Properties Co., Houston, 1970-76, Century 21 Regional Properties Co., Houston, 1976-79; owner, mgr. Century 21 Pin Oak Properties, Houston, 1979—; dir. bus. devel. Guardian Title Co. of Houston, 1983—; tchr. real estate. Cert. broker, Tex. Mem. Women's Council Houston Bd. Realtors Houston C. of C., Nat. Assn. Realtors. Democrat. Baptist. Home: 9166 Larston Houston TX 77055 Office: 4120 Southwest Freeway Suite 100 Houston TX 77027

MACLAINE, SHIRLEY, actress; b. Richmond, Va., Apr. 24, 1934; d. Ira O. and Kathlyn (MacLean) Beatty; ed. high sch.; m. Steve Parker, Sept. 17, 1954 (div. 1982); 1 dau., Stephanie Sachiko. Broadway plays include Me and Juliet, 1953, Pajama Game, 1954; Shirley MacLaine on Broadway, 1984; actress movies The Trouble With Harry, 1954, Artists and Models, 1954, Around the World in 80 Days, 1955-56, Hot Spell, 1957, The Matchmaker, 1957, The Sheepman, 1957, Some Came Running, 1958 (Fgn. Press award 1959), Ask Any Girl (Silver Bear award as best actress Internat. Berlin Film Festival), 1959, Career, 1959, Can-Can, 1959, The Apartment (Best Actress prize Venice Film Festival), 1959, Children's Hour, 1960, Two for the Seesaw, 1962, Irma La Douce, 1963, What A Way to Go and The Yellow Rolls Royce, 1964, John Goldfarb Please Come Home, 1965, Gambit and Woman Times Seven, 1967, The Bliss of Mrs. Blossom and Two Mules for Sister Sara, 1969, Desperate Characters, 1971, The Possession of Joel Delaney, 1972, The Turning Point, 1977, Being There, 1979, A Change of Seasons, 1980, Loving Couples, 1980, Terms of Endearment (Acad. award 1984), 1983, Cannonball II, 1984; TV shows include: Shirley's World, 1971-72, If They Could See Me Now, 1974, The Other Half of the Sky: A China Memoir, 1975, Gypsy in My Soul, 1976, Shirley MacLaine at the Lido, 1979, Shirley MacLaine...Every Little Movement, 1980. Author: Don't Fall Off the Mountain, 1970; The New Celebrity Cookbook, 1973; You Can Get There From Here, 1975; Out on a Limb, 1984; Dancing in the Light, 1985; editor: McGovern: The Man and His Beliefs, 1972. Office: care Internat Creative Mgmt 8899 Beverly Blvd Los Angeles CA 90048*

MACLEAN, BARBARA BARONDESS, interior designer; b. N.Y.C., July 4; d. Benjamin Gregor and Stella (Sirkis) Barondess; m. Douglas MacLean, June, 1936 (dec.); m. 2d, Leonard J. Knaster, Aug. 22, 1955 (div. Aug. 1974). Student NYU, 1925-26, UCLA, 1937-38, Los Angeles Art Ctr. Sch. Design, 1939-40, Art Sch., Paris 1952-53. Appeared in stage plays including: Crime, Riddle Me This, A Thousand Summers, Topaze, 1929-31; featured in motion pictures including: Rasputin, Hold Your Man, Merry Widow, Tale of Two Cities, Faithfully Yours, Pursuit of Happiness, Queen Christina; starred in TV film The Open Cage, 1982; columnist Morning Telegraph, 1928-31; interior and textile designer, Beverly Hills, Calif., 1938—; pres. Barbara Barondess MacLean Ltd., Inc., 1947—, N.Y.C., 1952—, Discovery Unltd., Palm Beach, Fla., 1973—; created column Little Bo-Beep on Broadway; wrote and appeared in film documentary One Life is not Enough, donated to Ellis Island Mus., 1986; paintings exhibited in galleries, Beverly Hills, N.Y.C., 1949—. Founder Barbara Barondess Theatre Lab Found., 1983—; tchr. 1st aid ARC, 1941-46. Mem. AFTRA, Actors Equity, Am. Inst. Design, Screen Actors Guild. Author: Cooking on the Run; 8 Times Larger than Life; contbr. articles to newspapers, mags. Address: 630 Park Ave New York NY 10021

MACLENNAN, BERYCE W., psychologist; b. Aberdeen, Scotland, Mar. 14, 1920; came to U.S., 1949, naturalized, 1965; d. William and Beatrice (MacRae) Mellis; B.Sc. with honors, London Sch. Econs., 1947; Ph.D., London U., 1960; m. John Duncan MacLennan, Nov. 29, 1944. Group psychotherapist, youth specialist cons. N.Y.C. and Washington, 1949-63; dir. Center for Prevention Juvenile Delinquency and New Careers, Washington, 1963-66; sect. chief Mental Health Study Center, NIMH, Adelphi, Md., 1967-70, chief, 1971-74; regional adminstr. Mass. Dept. Mental Health, Springfield, 1974-75; sr. mental health adv. GAO, Washington, 1976—; prof. George Washington U., 1970—. Fellow Am. Psychol. Assn., Am. Orthopsychiat. Assn., Am. Group Psychotherapy Assn. Democrat. Club: So. Md. Sailing. Home: 6307 Crathie Ln Bethesda MD 20816 Office: GAO NIH Bldg 31 2B-11 Bethesda MD 20892

MACLEOD, DEBBIE EDWARDS, real estate executive; b. Gainesville, Fla., Feb. 26, 1951; d. Hugh Coleman Edwards and Lillian (Harden) Zucha; m. Darrelle C. Stewart, Dec. 31, 1970 (div. 1973); 1 child, Sonia Jo Stewart; m. Peter J. MacLeod, Oct. 27, 1979. Grad. Bert Rodger's Sch. Real Estate, 1972. Real estate broker, Fla. Property mgr. Ray E. Haufler & Co., Gainesville, Fla., 1973-78; pres. Contemporary Mgmt. Concepts, Inc., Gainesville, 1978—, Contemporary Concepts & Investments, Inc., Gainesville, 1983—. Sponsor Ducks Unlimited, Gainesville, 1984. Mem. Gainesville Bd. Realtors (Million Dollar Club 1984), Gainesville Homebuilders, Gainesville C. of C. Republican. Baptist. Avocations: sailing, fishing, interior decorating. Office: 6910 W University Ave Suite 2 Gainesville FL 32607

MACLEOD GRIFFIN, BONNIE HELENA, lawyer; b. Cambridge, Mass., Feb. 14, 1948; d. John Howard and Constance Deena (Fillios) MacLeod; m. John Michael Griffin, June 10, 1973; 1 son, Andrew Ryan. B.A., Regis Coll., 1969; J.D., Suffolk U., 1972. Bar: Mass. 1972. Pvt. practice law, Boston, 1972-73; asst. dist. atty. Middlesex County, Cambridge, Mass., 1973-76; asst. bar counsel Bd. Bar Overseers, Boston, 1976-80, 1st asst. bar counsel, 1981—; adj. prof. law Northeastern Sch. Law, Boston, 1982—, New Eng. Sch. Law, Boston, 1977—. Bd. dirs. Project Bread, Boston, 1976—. Mem. Boston Bar Assn. (mem. council 1980-83), ABA, Nat. Orgn. Bar Counsel. Democrat. Roman. Catholic. Home: 56 Rockwell St Malden MA 02148 Office: Office of Bar Counsel 11 Beacon St Boston MA 02108

MACMANUS, SUSAN ANN, political science educator, researcher; b. Tampa, Fla., Aug. 22, 1947; d. Harold Cameron and Elizabeth (Riegler) MacManus. B.A. cum laude, Fla. State U., 1968, Ph.D., 1975; M.A., U. Mich., 1969. Instr. Valencia Community Coll., Orlando, Fla., 1969-73; research asst. Fla. State U., 1973-75; asst. prof. U. Houston, 1975-79, assoc. prof., 1979-85, dir. (M.P.A.) program, 1983-85, research assoc. Ctr Pub. Policy 1982-85; prof., dir. Ph.D. program Cleve. State U., 1985—; vis. prof. U. Okla., Norman, 1981—; field research assoc. Brookings Instn., Washington, 1977-82, Columbia U., summer 1979, Princeton U., 1979—, Nat. Acad. Pub. Adminstrn., Washington, summer 1980, Cleve. State U., 1982-83, Westat, Inc., Washington, 1983—; Author: Revenue Patterns in U.S. Cities and Suburbs: A Comparative Analysis, 1978; (with others) Governing A Changing America, 1984; contbr. articles to jours., chpts. to books; writer manuals in field; editorial bds. jours. Bd. dirs. Houston Area Women's Ctr., 1977, past pres., v.p. fin., treas.; mem. LWV, Harris County (Tex.) Women's Polit. Caucus, Houston. Recipient U. Houston Coll. Social Scis. Teaching Excellence award, 1977, Herbert J. Simon Award best article in vol. 3, Internat. Jour. Pub. Adminstrn., 1981; Ford Found. fellow, 1967-68; grantee Valencia Community Coll. Faculty, 1972, U. Houston, 1976, 77, 79, 83. Mem. Am. Polit. Sci. Assn. (program com. 1983-84, chairperson sect. intergovtl. relations), So. Polit. Sci. Assn. (V.O. key award com. 1983-84), Midwest Polit. Sci. Assn., Western Polit. Sci. Assn., Southwestern Polit. Sci. Assn. (local arrangements com. 1982-83, profession com. 1977-80), Am. Soc. Pub. Adminstrn. (nominating com. Houston chpt. 1983), Policy Studies Orgn. (mem. editorial bd. jours. 1981—, exec. council 1983-85), Women's Caucus Polit. Sci. (portfolio pre-decision rev. com. 1982-83, projects and programs com. 1981, fin.-budget com. 1980-81), Acad. Polit. Sci., Mcpl. Fin. Officers Assn., Phi Beta Kappa, Phi Kappa Phi, Pi Sigma Alpha. Republican. Methodist. Home: 1417 Winchester Lakewood OH 44107 Office: Cleveland State U Coll Urban Affairs Cleveland OH 44115

MACMILLAN, MARGARET LAURIE, aerospace company administrator; b. Los Angeles, Nov. 28, 1960; d. Donald Bather and Olaug Margrthe (Myhr) M. Student, U. Calif.-San Diego, 1978-80; B.B.A., Calif. State U.-Chico, 1982; M.B.A., U. So. Calif., Los Angeles, 1988. Project control adminstr. Hughes Aircraft Co., Torrance, Calif., 1983—; aerobics instr., 1984-85; cons. Macola Record Co., Hollywood, Calif., 1984, Baby'O Recorders, Hollywood, 1983—. Mem. Phi Chi Theta, Phi Kappa Phi, Beta Gamma Sigma, Sigma Iota Epsilon. Republican. Christian. Avocations: skiing; reading; sky diving; racquetball, jogging. Home: 162 Hermosa Ave Hermosa Beach CA 90254 Office: Hughes Aircraft Co 2000 W Lomita Blvd Torrance CA 90509

MAC MILLAN, VELMA JEANNE, educator; b. Chgo., 1926; d. Ernest Wilfred and Velma Jennie (Paramore) B.M., Coe Coll., 1948, 1949; M.S. in Music Edn., U. Ill., 1959; Ph.D. (NDEA Title IV fellow), U. Wis., 1969. Instr. vocal music Buffalo Center (Iowa) Consol. Schs., 1948-49; music supr. Manchester (Iowa) Pub. Sch., 1949-52; music instr. Kenosha (Wis.) Pub. Schs., 1952-67; critic tchr., 1963-66; prof. ednl. adminstrn. U. Wis.-Superior, 1969-86, coordinator ednl. adminstrn. programs, 1978-82, dir. profl. experiences, 1984-86. Mem. pres.'s adv. council Coe Coll., 1980-83; trustee Carthage Coll., 1985—; bd. dirs. Superior Meml. Hosp., 1984-86; sec., 1985-86. Named Outstanding Educator, 1975. Mem. Gov.'s Commn. on Edn. Seminar, 1966; chmn. Regional Pub. Hearing Kellett Commn. Gov.'s Commn. on Edn., 1970. Mem. Assn. for Supervision and Curriculum Devel., Nat. (dir. 1965-67), Wis. fedns. bus. and profl. women's clubs (pres. 1965-67), Assn. Wis. Sch. Adminstrs., Assn. U. Wis. Faculty, Mu Phi Epsilon, Pi Kappa Lambda, Pi Lambda Theta, Phi Delta Kappa. Lutheran. Home: 4117 80th St Kenosha WI 53142 Office: Div Edn U Wis Superior WI 54880

MACNISH, LINDA J., theatrical producer, writer; b. Chatham, N.Y., May 10; d. Preston and Florence (Dick) MacN. B.A., Drew U. Asst. to art dir. Good Housekeeping mag., N.Y.C., 1966-69; freelance writer, producer, theatrical personal mgr., N.Y.C., 1966-69; producing artistic dir. Mac-Haydn Theatre, Chatham, N.Y., 1969—; editor, writer Panorama Mag., Sarasota, Fla., 1975. Author, composer musical play Call it Love, 1971; author, lyricist off-off Broadway musical Broadway Calling, 1985. Contbr. articles to gen. interest mags. Mem. Preserve and Improve Chatham, 1983—. Mem. Chatham Bus. and Profl. Women, Columbia County C. of C. (dir. 1983—). Republican. Avocations: writing, vocal coaching, piano. Office: MacHaydn Theatre Inc PO Box 204 Chatham NY 12037

MACON, IRENE ELIZABETH, designer, consultant; b. East St. Louis, Ill., May 11, 1935; d. David and Thelma (Eastlen) Dunn; m. Robert Teco Macon, Feb. 12, 1954; children—Leland Sean, Walter Edwin, Gary Keith, Jill Renee Macon Martin, Robin Jeffrey, Lamont. Student Forest Park Coll., Washington U., St. Louis, 1970, Bailey Tech. Coll., 1975, Lindenwood Coll., 1981. Office mgr. Cardinal Glennon Hosp., St. Louis, 1965-72; interior designer J.C. Penney Co., Jennings, Mo., 1972-73; entrepreneur Irene Designs Unltd., St. Louis, 1974—; vol. liaison Pub. Sch. System, St. Louis, 1980-82; cons. in field. Inventor venetian blinds for autos, 1981. Committeewoman Republican party, St. Louis, 1984; vice chair 4th Senatorial Dist. of Mo., 1984, vol. St. Louis Assn. Community Orgns., 1983; instr. first aid Bi-State chpt. ARC, St. Louis, 1984; block capt. Operation Brightside, St. Louis, 1984. Named one of Top Ladies of Distinction, St. Louis, 1983. Mem. Am. Soc. Interior Designers (assoc.), NAACP, Nat. Mus. Women in the Arts (charter), Nat. Council Negro Women (1st v.p. 1984), Invention Assn. of St. Louis (subcom. head 1985), Coalition of 100 Black Women. Methodist. Club: Presidents, (Washington). Avocations: reading; designing personal wardrobe; modeling; horseback riding; boating. Home and Office: 5469 Maple St Saint Louis MO 63112

MACPHERSON, JANET TAYLOR WOLFENDEN, civic worker; b. Phila.; d. Edward Musker and Annette (Robertson) Wolfenden; B.S., M.A., U. Pa.; postgrad. Columbia U.; m. Herbert Grenfell MacPherson, June 5, 1937; children—Janet Lynne MacPherson O'Donel-Browne, Robert Duncan. Pres., Franklin Sch. PTA, Lakewood, Ohio, 1954-56; bd. dirs. Oak Ridge chpt. AAUW, 1957-59; pres. Oak Ridge LWV, 1961-63, LWV of Tenn., 1967-69, Friends of Oak Ridge Pub. Library, 1966-67; bd. dirs. Oak Ridge Civic Music Assn., 1963-66, pres. Women's guild, 1963-64; mem. Nat. Com. for Support Pub. Schs., 1967-70; mem. Com. of 100, Found. for Better Govt. for Tenn., 1967-70; mem. Tenn. com. 1970 White House Conf. on Children and Youth, 1969-70; mem. salary structure study com. Bd. Edn. Oak Ridge, 1969-71; chmn. Youth Com. Oak Ridge, 1969-70; mem. state planning com. Air Quality Project for Tenn., 1970-71; bd. dirs. Awareness House Oak Ridge, 1970-73; mem. Oak Ridge Charter Commn., 1972-74; bd. dirs. Anderson County (Tenn.) Health Council, 1974-84, CONTACT, telephone counseling service,

Oak Ridge, 1975-79, Mental Health Assn. Oak Ridge Region, 1977-84, Planned Parenthood East Tenn., 1978-81; mem. mental health statewide planning adv. com. Tenn. Dept. Mental Health and Mental Retardation, 1981-84. Editor: This Is Oak Ridge, Tennessee, 1961. Home: 102 Orchard Circle Oak Ridge TN 37830

MACROE-WIEGAND, VIOLA LUCILLE, psychiatrist, psychoanalyst; b. Indiana, Pa., May 17, 1920; d. Joseph Cyprian and Lucy E. (Colson) Macro; B.A., St. Joseph's Coll. for Women, 1941; M.A., Columbia U., 1942, Ph.D., 1958; M.D., U. Hamburg (Germany), 1962; m. Thomas F. Gordon, Nov. 23, 1977. Instr. and chief psychologist Manhattan Eye and Ear Hosp., N.Y.U. Med. Sch., N.Y.C., 1952-58; lectr. dept. psychiatry SUNY, Bklyn., 1962-63; psychiat. fellow Creedmore State Hosp., Queens, N.Y. 1962-63; intern U. Hamburg, 1962-63; resident St. Georg's Hosp., Hamburg, 1963-64; research fellow in neurology Mt. Sinai Hosp., 1963-64; resident in psychiatry P.R. Inst. of Psychiatry, 1976-79; practice internal medicine and psychiatry, San Juan, P.R., 1974—; psychologist geriatrics Little Sisters of Poor Hosp., Bklyn., 1965-67; mem. staff dept. neurology Kingsbrook Med. Center, Bklyn., 1967-68; asst. prof. psychology Kingsborough Community Coll., N.Y., 1966-67, CCNY, summer, 1968; mem. staff psychiatry Rio Piedras State Hosp., San Juan, 1974-82, P.R. Inst. of Psychiatry, San Juan, 1976-82: psychiatrist dept. mental health Knud Hansen Meml. Hosp., St. Thomas, V.I., 1978-82; fellow L.I. Inst. Psychoanalysis, Nassau County Med. Clinic, East Meadow, L.I., 1982—. Fellow Am. Assn. Mental Deficiency; mem. Am. Psychol. Assn., Eastern Psychol. Assn., N.Y. State Psychol. Assn., AMA, Am. Psychiat. Assn., P.R. Med. Assn., Asociación Hermandad en las Carreteras de P.R. (v.p. 1975—), Pi Lambda Theta, Kappa Delta Pi. Roman Catholic. Contbr. articles on physiol. psychology to profl. jours.; research in visual and auditory perception. Home: 185 Clinton Ave Brooklyn NY 11205 Office: 110-45 Queens Blvd Forest Hills NY 11375

MACRORIE, CAROL ANN, mfg. co. ofcl.; b. Little Falls, N.Y., Feb. 14, 1946; d. Harold D. and Lena Irene (Grassel) MacR.; student Northeastern U., 1973-76, Holyoke Community Coll., 1977—; 1 adopted son, Francis Gulla. Inventory control clk. Salada Foods, Inc., Woburn, Mass., 1964-69; distbn. supr. Addison Wesley Publ. Co., Reading, Mass., 1969-73; with Digital Equipment Corp., Maynard, Mass., 1973—, inventory and prodn. control supr., Westfield, Mass., 1979-80, distibn. mgr., 1980—. Mem. Am. Mgmt. Assn., Delta Nu Alpha. Office: Digital Equipment Corp 1111 Southampton Rd Westfield MA 01085

MACTAGGART, BETTE KAY, air force officer; b. Dothan, Ala., Apr. 11, 1952; D. Philip Richard and Bette Joan (Burt) MacT. B.S., U. Minn.-Duluth, 1975; postgrad. Okla. U., 1981—, Miss. State U., 1985—. Commd. 2d lt. U.S. Air Force, 1976, advanced through grades to capt., 1979, air traffic control officer, Wichita Falls, Tex., 1976-78, pub. affairs officer, Fort Walton Beach, Fla., 1978-79, dir. pub. affairs, Honolulu, 1979-81, dep. chief pub. affairs div., Frankfurt, W.Ger., 1981-84, chief pub. affairs div., 1984, chief Office of Pub. Affairs, Columbus AFB, Miss., 1984—; media community relations broadcaster, producer Rhein-Main Gateway Radio Program, Frankfurt, 1981-84, German-Am. tricentennial project officer, 1983; Pacific mil. project officer, rep. King Kamehameha Parade, Honolulu, 1981. Contbr. photo and news articles on mil. activities, personalities and programs to profl. jours. Mem. Honolulu Symphony Chorus, 1979-81, Frankfurt German Am. Choir, 1981-84 , Frankfurt Opera, 1983-84; bd. dirs., pub. chmn. Columbus Concert Assn. Decorated two Air Force Commendation medal, Abby award for Best Pub. Service Announcement, TV., numerous awards on photo and news articles. Mem. Women in Communications, Inc., Pub. Relations Assn. Miss. Episcopalian. Club: German Am. (Frankfurt). Home: 5016 Hankerson Ave Edina MN 55436 Office: Office Pub Affairs Columbus AFB MS

MAC VICAR, MARGARET LOVE AGNES, materials physicist, educator, university dean; b. Hamilton, Ont., Can., Nov. 20, 1943; d. George Francis and Elizabeth Margaret (Thompson) MacV.; came to U.S., 1946, naturalized, 1953. S.B. in Physics, MIT, 1964, Sc.D. in Metallurgy and Materials Sci., 1967; Sc.D. (hon.), Clarkson U., 1985. NATO and Marie Curie postdoctoral fellow Cavendish Lab., U. Cambridge, Eng., 1967-69; instr. physics MIT, Cambridge, 1969-70, asst. prof., 1970-74, asso. prof., 1974-79, Class of 1922 Career Devel. prof., 1973-75, asso. prof. phys. sci., 1979-83, prof., 1983—, Cecil and Ida Green prof. edn., 1980—, dean for undergrad. edn., 1985—; Chancellor's disting. prof. U. Calif., Berkeley, 1979; cons. to univs., industry, non-profit orgns.; dir. W.H. Brady Co., Exxon Corp., Research Corp.; v.p. Carnegie Instn. Washington; mem. adv. com. to dir. for sci. and engring. edn. NSF; mem. adv. council on edn., sci., tech., and economy Carnegie Corp.; mem. corp. Draper Lab., Cambridge. Past trustee Carnegie Found. for Advancement Teaching; trustee Boston Mus. Sci.; past mem. Carnegie Council on Policy Studies in Higher Edn. Recipient Most Significant Contribution to Edn. award MIT, 1977; Young Faculty Research award Gen. Electric Found. 1976-79; Danforth Found. asso., from 1972. Mem. Am. Assn. Higher Edn., AAAS (co-chmn. nat. council for sci. and tech. edn.), Am. Women in Sci., Am. Phys. Soc. Clubs: Boston Women's City; Georgetown Women's. Patentee in field. Office: Dean Undergrad Edn MIT Mass Inst Tech Cambridge MA 02139 also Carnegie Instn of Washington Washington DC 20005

MACY, JANET, educator; b. Omaha, Nov. 9, 1935; d. Val and Marie (Letovsky) Kuska; B.S., U. Nebr., 1957; M.S., Kans. State U., 1961; M.Ed., S.D. State U., 1970. With Fed. Extension Service, U.S. Dept. Agr., Washington, 1956, Kans. State U. Sta. KSAC, 1957-61, U. Nebr. Sta. KUON, 1961-62, Iowa State U. Sta. WOI-TV, 1962-67, S.D. State U. Sta. KESD-TV, 1967-71; mem. faculty U. Minn. Sta. KUOM, Mpls., 1971—, now assoc. prof. dept. family Soc. Sci.; with Meredith Pubs., Better Homes & Gardens, 1972-73; cons. U.S. Consumer Product Safety Commn., 1978-79. Recipient U. Nebr. Masters award, 1973; Minn. Edn. Assn. Sch. Bell award, 1980, 81, 82, merit award, 1983; Agrl. Communicators in Edn. Superior awards, 1966, 68, 79, 81; Am. Women in Radio and TV Communication Nutrition award, 1977. Mem. Agrl. Communicators in Edn., Am. Soc. Tng. and Devel., Minn. Intergovtl. Tng. Council, Minn. Edn. Assn., NEA, Epsilon Sigma Phi. Home: 8121 34th Ave S Minneapolis MN 55420 Office: 282 McNeal Hall Saint Paul MN 55108

MACY MARCY, SUZANNE KAY, behavioral ecologist, educator, consultant; b. Seattle, Oct. 24, 1951; d. Marshall Eugene Macy and Kathleen Mae (Lobb) Macy Siedelhuber; m. Scott Colson Marcy, May 2, 1981. A.A., Shoreline Community Coll., 1971; B.S., U. Wash., 1974, Ph.D., 1981; postgrad. Sangamon State U., 1984-85. Research asst. dept. psychology U. Wash., Seattle, 1974-75, teaching asst. dept. psychology, 1976-79, instr. psychology, 1979-81, also instructional cons. Ctr. for Instructional Devel. and Research, 1979-81; biol. technician Nat. Marine Fisheries Service, Seattle and Pribilof Islands, Alaska, 1975-77; dir. graphic arts Leisure Press, Highland Falls, N.Y., 1982; writer, editor West Point Mus., N.Y., 1983; mem. vis. faculty in biology Vassar Coll., Poughkeepsie, N.Y., 1984; sci. researcher, sci. office Ill. Legis. Research Unit, Springfield, 1984-85; mem. adj. faculty biology Northwestern State U. of La. Fort Polk Ctr., Leesville, 1986—; legis. sci. intern Sangamon State U., Springfield, 1984-85; mem. faculty, leader Sch. for Field Studies, affiliate Northeastern U., Cambridge, Mass., 1985—; cons. Videodiscovery, Seattle, 1986. First author booklet: Alzheimer's Disease: Activity of the 84th Illinois General Assembly and appendix, 1985. Rep., Nat. Mil. Family Assn., Washington, 1986. Nat. Marine Fisheries Service dissertation grantee, 1976, 77. Mem. AAAS, Am. Inst. Biol. Scis. (congl. liaison 1985-86), Animal Behavior Soc., N.Y. Acad. Scis., Phi Beta Kappa, Sigma Xi, Phi Theta Kappa. Clubs: PEO (chpt. corr. sec. and ednl. loan fund chairperson 1983-84) (New City, N.Y.). Avocations: reading; book collecting; painting; drawing; crafts. Home and Office: 521 Lakeshore Dr Leesville LA 71446

MACZULSKI, MARGARET LOUISE, association executive; b. Detroit, Apr. 1, 1949; d. Bohdan Alexander and Olga Louise (Martinuick) M. B.S., Mich. State U., 1972. Meetings mgr. Nat. Assn. Realtors, Mktg. Inst., Chgo., 1977-82; regional sales mgr. Fairmont Hotels, Chgo., 1982; mktg. mgr. Nat. Assn. Realtors, Mktg. Inst., 1982-83; dir., mgr. trade shows and confs. Am. Broadcasting Co./Pub. Div., Wheaton, Ill., 1983-85; mgr. meeting and conf. planning Am. Soc. Personnel Adminstrn., Alexandria, Va., 1985 . Mem. Meeting Planners Internat., Gt. Washington Soc. Assn., Execs. Republican. Roman Catholic. Avocations: piano; swimming. Home: 5340 Holmes Run Pkwy #219 Alexandria VA 22304 Office: Am Soc Personnel Adminstrn 606 N Washington Alexandria VA 22314

MADDEN, BETTY CAMPBELL, media company executive, lawyer; b. Clinton, Iowa, Oct. 15, 1942; d. Merrill J. and Clarice M. (Hanson) Campbell; m. Joseph R. Wolf, June 10, 1965 (div. 1972); 1 dau., Kari M.; m. Lauren R. Madden, Nov. 21, 1976. B.A., Cornell Coll., Mt. Vernon, Iowa, 1965; J.D., Ill. Inst. Tech., 1970; M.B.A., U. Iowa, 1982. Bar: Ill. 1970, Iowa 1974. Sole practice, Antioch, Ill., 1970-74; atty. Meredith Corp., Des Moines, 1974-79, asst. sec., 1979-80, corp. sec., 1980—; dir. Better Homes and Gardens Ins. Agy., Inc., Meredith Internat., Sail Devel. Corp., Sail Publs., Inc. Contbr. articles to profl. jours. Bd. dirs. Des Moines Pastoral Counseling Service, 1983—, Des Moines Symphony, Des Moines Ballet, Young Women's Resource Ctr. Mem. Iowa Bar Assn., Polk County Bar Assn., Polk County Women's Bar Assn., Des Moines C. of C. (2000 com.). Baha'i. Clubs: Des Moines, Wakonda Country (Des Moines). Office: Meredith Corp 1716 Locust St Des Moines IA 50336

MADDEN, MADELINE MARY, advertising agency executive; b. Yonkers, N.Y., Oct. 27, 1951; d. Joseph Patrick and Ruth Ann (Jones) M.; m. Paul Ryan Gnabasik, Aug. 30, 1980. B.A., Coll. Mt. St. Vincent, 1973. Placement dir., instr. Phillips Coll., Augusta, Ga., 1978-79; personnel asst. Young & Rubicam, Inc., N.Y.C., 1981-82, personnel rep., 1982—; adviser secretarial sci. dept. Kingsborough Community Coll., N.Y.C., 1982—. Contbr. articles to newspapers. Mem. Advt. Agy. Personnel Assn. (pres. 1982—), Personnel and Guidance Assn. Home: 183 Park Ave Mount Vernon NY 10552 Office: Young & Rubicam Inc 285 Madison Ave New York NY 10017

MADDOX, GRACE BERYL, economist, former govt. ofcl.; b. Hayward, Wis.; d. McPherson C. and Grace (Bailey) Maddox; student U. So. Calif., 1926-27, U. Calif. at Los Angeles, 1927-28; A.B., Am. U., 1954, M.A. in Econs., 1958. With various U.S. govt. agys., 1937-67; staff of U.S. mem. Internat. Mil. Tribunal, Nuremberg, Germany, 1945-46; Near East polit. analyst CIA, Washington, 1947-51, East European economist, Washington, 1952-56; economist FTC, Washington, 1956-67; researcher in field industry and finance. Recipient Superior Service award FTC, 1961, 67. Mem. Am. Econ. Assn., D.A.R., Phi Delta Gamma. Contbr. articles to govt. publs. Home: 5796 Encina Rd Apt 5 Goleta CA 93117

MADDOX, PATRICIA ANN WATSON, manufacturing company office administrator; b. Bklyn., Dec. 3, 1956; d. William Gerard and Josephine T. (Merulla) Watson; m. John Thomas Martin, Jr., Jan. 10, 1975 (div. 1982); children—John T. III, Misty Dawn; m. Stephen James Maddox, Mar. 22, 1986. Student Central Ariz. Coll., 1979-81, Western Internat. U., 1984-86, Rio Salado Community Coll., 1985. Adminstrv. asst. U.S. Air Force, McGuire Air Force Base, 1974-77; VA asst. Central Ariz. Coll., Coolidge, 1979-81; adminstrv. asst. Ariz. Army Nat. Guard, Phoenix, 1981-83; office mgr. sales Accuracy Systems, Inc., Phoenix, 1984—. Leader Girl Scouts U.S.A., 1978-79; active Phoenix PTA, 1985—; state sec. Am. Def. Preparedness Assn., 1983—. Served to 2d lt. U.S. Army, 1983-84, to 2d lt. Ariz. Army N.G., 1981—. Decorated Good Conduct medal, 1977, Airmen of Month medal, 1976. Mem. Nat. Assn. Female Execs., N.G. Assn. Democrat. Roman Catholic. Avocations: needlepoint; reading; camping. Home: 2853 E Siesta Ln Phoenix AZ 85024 Office: Accuracy Systems Inc 15203 N Cave Creek Rd Phoenix AZ 85032

MADDOX, PATRICIA JEAN, trucking company executive; b. Wichita, Kans., July 28, 1939; d. Paul Joseph Massey and Mabel Genevieve (Ford) Massey Malcom; m. Paul L. Hutchison, Jan. 14, 1956 (div. Apr. 1961); 1 child, William Hale; m. Dennis W. Maddox (div.); children—John Kevin, Crystal Rene'. Student pub. schs., Wichita. Billing clk. Associated Cartage, Wichita, 1959-63, Transcon Lines, Wichita, 1963-65, Royal Transp., Montebello, Calif., 1965-67; freight rate clk. ONC, Los Angeles, 1967; rate clk., supr. Russell Truck Co., Los Angeles, 1967-83; pres., mgr. RPM Trucking Co. Ltd., Santa Fe Springs, Calif., 1983—. Democrat. Avocation: needlework. Home: 17350 E Temple Sp 236 La Puente CA 91744 Office: RRM Trucking Co Ltd 11753 E Slauson Suite 9 Santa Fe Springs CA 90670

MADDOX, ROTHA M., broadcasting company executive; b. Waltham, Mass., Mar. 30, 1946; d. Curtis A. and Rotha Maddox; B.S., Barnard Coll., 1967. Med. research asst. USPHS study, Bellevue Hosp., N.Y.C., 1967-69; media planner Grey Advt., N.Y.C., 1969-71, Wells, Rich, Greene Advt., N.Y.C., 1971-73; sales mktg. dir. ABC-FM, 1973-74; account exec. Sta. WPLJ-FM, N.Y.C., 1974-75, Sta. WINS-AM, N.Y.C., 1975-77; account exec. nat. sales CBS-FM, N.Y.C., 1977-78; sales mgr., Detroit, 1978-79; nat. sales mgr. Sta. WCBS-FM, N.Y.C., 1979-82; local sales mgr. WCAU-FM Radio, Phila., 1982-83, nat. sales mgr., 1983—. Mem. Internat. Radio and TV Soc., N.Y. Market Radio Broadcasters, Adcraft Club Detroit, Nat. Assn. Female Execs. Democrat. Methodist. Office: WCAU-FM City Line and Monument Aves Philadelphia PA 19131

MADDOX, YVONNE TARLTON, medical communications company executive; b. Lubbock, Tex., July 19, 1936; m. George Allman, Nov. 2, 1974. B.A., Okla. State U. Pres., World Health Info. Services, Inc., N.Y.C., 1970-83; v.p. Health Edn. Technologies, Inc. div. Batton, Barton, Durstine & Osborn, Inc., N.Y.C., 1984-86; pres. Maddox & Assocs. Med. Communications, N.Y.C., 1986—. Mem. Pharm. Advt. Council, Am. Women in Radio and TV (past dir.). Home: 245 E 50th St New York NY 10022 Office: Maddox & Assocs 475 Fifth Ave New York NY 10022

MADEJ, JOSEPHINE STEPHANIE, international marketing executive; b. Lubeck, Fed. Republic Germany, Oct. 26, 1949; came to U.S., 1951; d. Zygmunt and Jozefa (Szymanski) M.; m. Thomas Dynevor Rees, Apr. 8, 1978; 1 child, Thomas Dynevor Rees. B.A., Bryn Mawr Coll., 1971; M.B.A., U. Pa., 1974. Account exec. Young & Rubicam, N.Y.C., 1975-78; account exec. Lewis & Gilman, Phila., 1979; internat. product dir. NcNeil Consumer Product Co., Fort Washington, Pa., 1979—. Bd. dirs. Bryn Mawr Coll. Alumnae Fund, 1981-83. Republican. Episcopalian. Avocations: travel; reading. Office: McNeil Consumer Products Co Camp Hill Rd Fort Washington PA 19034

MADISON-HIMES, DEBRENIA FAYE, lawyer, consultant; b. Tuskegee, Ala., Dec. 23, 1954; d. Dee Collins and Bessie (Fuller) Madison; m. Stanley Wayne Himes, May 31, 1980. B.A., UCLA, 1977; J.D., Georgetown U., 1980. Bar: Calif. 1983, D.C. 1985, U.S. Dist. Ct. (no. dist.) Calif. 1983, U.S. Ct. Internat. Trade 1985. Assoc. Hayes & White, Washington, 1980-81; cons. South of Market Cultural Ctr., San Francisco, 1982; arts adminstr., legal adviser San Francisco Arts Commn., 1983; assoc. Staiger Santana Yank Molinelli & Preston, San Francisco, 1984-85; atty. Madison Family, Concord, Calif., 1985-86; sole practice, Emeryville, Calif., 1986; atty. Berkley, Rhodes & Schwartz, Oakland, Calif., 1986—; trustee, adviser World Affairs Council No. Calif., San Francisco, 1985—. Author: (poetry) Emotions In Motion, 1979; (children's book) The Teddy Bear and The Red Balloon, 1983. Editorial staff mem. Internat. Law Jour., 1980. Bd. dirs. San Francisco Senators, 1983-84, Friends of South of Market Cultural Ctr., 1984. Named to Outstanding Young Women Am., U.S. Jaycees, 1983. Mem. Charles Houston Bar Assn., Black Women Lawyers, ABA, Nat. Bar Assn., San Francisco C. of C. Democrat. Roman Catholic. Avocations: swimming; skiing; horseback riding; writing. Home: 6 Admiral Dr #477 Emeryville CA 94608 Office: Berkley Rhodes & Schwartz Berkley Plaza Bldg 630 20th St Oakland CA 94612

MADORE, SISTER BERNADETTE, college president; b. Barnston, Que., Can., Jan. 24, 1918; came to U.S., 1920, naturalized; d. Joseph George and Mina Marie (Fontaine) M.; A.B., U. Montreal, 1942, B.Ed., 1943; M.S., Cath. U. Am., 1949, Ph.D., 1951. Instr. math. and English, Marie Anne Coll., Montreal, Que., 1943-44; prof. biology, dean of coll. Anna Maria Coll., Paxton, Mass., 1952-76, v.p., 1975-77, pres., 1977—; fund-raising cons.; corporator Consumer Savs. Bank. Bd. dirs. Central Mass. chpt. ARC; bd. dirs. Worcester Coll. Consortium; trustee Worcester Boys Club. Mem. AAAS, Am. Soc. Microbiology, Nat. Assn. Biology Tchrs., AAUW, Am. Assn. Higher Edn., Worcester C. of C. Roman Catholic. Club: Soroptimist. Home and office: Anna Maria College Sunset Ln Paxton MA 01612

MADORSKY, MARSHA GERRE, lawyer; b. Detroit, June 12, 1951; d. Max and Anne Ruth (Korash) Madorsky. B.A., U. Fla., 1972, J.D., 1975; LL.M., U. Miami, 1983. Bar Fla. 1975. Asst. atty. gen. State of Fla., West Palm Beach, 1975-77; assoc. atty. Sandstrom & Haddad, Ft. Lauderdale, Fla., 1977-80; med. fraud atty. Auditor Gen.'s Office, State of Fla., Miami, 1980-81; asst. state's atty., Miami, 1981; assoc. Bercuson Cahan Weksler & Lasky, Miami, 1983—. Consumer mem. State of Fla. Ombudsman and Long Term Care Com., 1981—. Mem. Fla. Assn. Women Lawyers (program chmn.), Democrat. Home: 1440 S Bayshore Dr Apt 904 Miami FL 33133 Office: Bercuson Cahan Lasky Tarr & Madorsky 9100 S Dadeland Blvd Suite 1410 Miami FL 33156

MADORY, MARTICIA MOORE, writer, editor, public relations specialist; b. Kansas City, Mo., Oct 21, 1941; d. Albert Wilson Luce and Faith Marie (Coffman) Moore; B.Journalism, U. Mo., 1963; m. Edward Madory, June 15, 1968; children—Paul Edward, Douglas Carl. Coordinator communications Marist Coll., Poughkeepsie, N.Y., 1976-77; public relations regional asst. Civil Service Employees Assn., Fishkill, N.Y., 1977-78; interim dir. public relations Culinary Inst. Am., Hyde Park, N.Y., 1981; co-founder, creator Mid-Hudson Communicators, Poughkeepsie, 1980—, pres., 1981—; founder, dir. Madory & Assocs., 1982—; founder Hudson Valley Wine and Food Festival, Regional Wine and Food Festival, Inc.; pub. Hudson Valley Weekender. Mem. Women in Communications, Inc., Pub. Relations Soc. Am., Am. Mktg. Assn., Am. Wine and Food Inst. (membership sec.), Women's Foodservice Roundtable. Unitarian. Home: 13 Greenbush Dr Poughkeepsie NY 12601

MADSEN, LUANN VOLLENWEIDER, lawyer; b. Salt Lake City, Dec. 28, 1955; d. Henry Louis and Ardis Arlene (Anderson) Vollenweider; m. G. Michael Madsen, Aug. 23, 1980. Student Iowa Wesleyan Coll., 1973-74; B.S. summa cum laude, Southeast Mo. State U., 1975; J.D., U. Mo., 1979. Bar: Mo. 1979, U.S. Dist. Ct. (we. dist.) Mo. 1979. Law clk. Cooper County Pros. Atty.'s Office, Boonville, Mo., 1978-79; law clk. Powell and Seitz, Attys., Columbia, Mo., 1978-79; asst. dir. services Mo. Bar, Jefferson City, 1979-83, dir. services, 1984-86; govtl. cons., 1986—. Mem. Order of Barristers, ABA, Bar Assn. Met. St. Louis, Mo. Bar, Mo. Soc. Assn. Execs. (bd. dirs., sec.-treas. 1984-85, pres.-elect 1985-86), Bus. and Profl. Women (v.p. 1984, career day chmn. 1984-85), Phi Delta Phi. Zeta Tau Alpha. Methodist. Editor Communis Scriptura, 1979-84, Courts and CLE Bull., 1984—, Legis. Digest, 1984-86. Office: 221A E Capitol Ave Jefferson City MO 65101

MADSEN, MARTHA, pathologist; b. May 29, 1908; m. L.J. Zinterhofen, July 25, 1938; 1 son. B.A., Rice U., 1928; M.D., U. Tex., 1932. Resident in pediatrics Children's Hosp., Detroit, 1933-34, resident in pathology, 1934-35, pathologist, lab. dir., 1937-40; asst. pathologist Wayne County Hosp., Eloise, Mich., 1940-42; pathologist, lab. dir. Deaconess Hosp., Detroit, 1944-59, St. Joseph's Hosp., Detroit, 1949-53; research assoc. Cancer Research Inst., Detroit, 1944-53; pathologist, lab. dir. Midland Meml. Hosp. (Tex.), 1953—, Parkview Gen. Hosp., Midland, 1964—; pathologist Med. Center Hosp., Odessa, Tex., 1953-57; cons. pathologist M.D. Anderson Hosp. & Tumor Inst., Houston, 1956—. Diplomate Am. Bd. Pathology. Fellow Am. Coll. Pathologists, Am. Coll. Clin. Pathologists; mem. AMA, Internat. Acad. Pathologists, Am. Soc. Clin. Pathologists, Am. Soc. Cytology, Tex. Soc. Pathologists, Am. Nuclear Soc., Am. Thermography Soc., AAUW, Midland C. of C. Home: 4605 Andrews Hwy Midland TX 79704 Office: West Tex Pathology Lab 2203 W Tennesse St Midland TX 79701

MADSEN, MILA CORDERO, business executive; b. Lucena, Quezon, Philippines, Feb. 28, 1930; came to U.S., 1952, naturalized, 1956; d. Pablo and Maria Epifania (Arrieta) Cordero; m. Erik Kjaer Madsen, Jan. 30, 1954; children—Kenneth, Kirk, Lizbeth, Jeannine. B.A., Far Eastern U., Philippines, 1951; Cert. Grad. Studies, Smith Coll., 1953, M.A., 1954. Pres., Mila Corp., Nassau, Bahamas, 1969-71, Manila, Philippines, 1971-75; mgr. Brooks Fashions, Merrillville, Ind., 1977-78; pres. Mila Internat. Travel, Merrillville, 1981—; pres. Mila Internat., Inc., Valparaiso, Ind., 1981—; gen. ptnr. Mila Internat. Pacific Resorts, Merrillville, 1984—; pres. Mila Internat. Resort Mgmt. Inc., Tahiti, French Polynesia, 1984—. Author: Technique and Style of James Boswell, 1954; contbr. articles to profl. jours. Founder., dir. Am. Theater Co., Brussels, Belgium, 1968-71; bd. dirs. Mich. Cancer Found., Detroit, 1975-76. Smith Coll. fellow, 1952-54; Far Eastern U. scholar, 1947-52. Fellow Epsilon Gamma Pi; mem. Philippines Profl. Assn., Lakeshore Bus. and Profl. Women's Club. Roman Catholic. Club: Am. Women (Brussels, dir. 1969-70). Home: 412 Scarborough Rd Valparaiso IN 46383 Office: Mila Internat Travel 8300 Mississippi Suite D Merrillville IN 46410

MADURA, JALAINE MARIE, economic development executive; b. Grants Pass, Oreg., Jan. 14, 1955; d. Philip Leonard and Janet Bernadette (Jeremicz) Madura. B.A., Willamette U., 1976. Asst. mgr. Oreg. Pub. Transit Div., Salem, 1976-79; program mgr. Oreg. Dept. Gen. Services, Salem, 1979-80; asst. dir. Oreg. Arts Commn., Salem, 1980-85; editor Oreg. Arts News, 1983-84. Mem. State Mgmt. Assn. Clubs: Aska, Shito-Ryu. Office: Econ Devel Dept 595 Cottage St NE Salem OR 97310

MAGAFAN, ETHEL, artist; b. Chgo., Oct. 10, 1916; d. Peter J. and Julie (Bronick) Magafan; student Colorado Springs Fine Arts Center; m. Bruce Currie, June 30, 1946; 1 dau., Jenne Magafan. John Stacey scholar, 1947; Tiffany fellow, 1949; Fulbright grant recipient, 1951; painter of 8 murals including HEW Bldg., Washington, Recorder of Deeds Bldg., Senate Chamber, South Denver Post Office, Fredericksburg (Va.) Nat. Mil. Park, 1978; paintings exhibited Acad. Arts and Letters, 1961, 64, 69, Carnegie Inst. Corcoran Gallery, Pa. Acad. Fine Arts, NAD, Met. Mus., Denver Art Mus., San Francisco Mus., N.Y. Exhbn., 1950-51, 53, 55, 56, 59, 61, 63, 66, 69, 70, 73, 79, 81, Art Gallery, SUNY, Albany, 1981, Midtown Galleries, N.Y.C., 1984; represented in permanent collections, including Springfield (Mo.) Art Mus., Provincetown Art Assn., Met. Mus. Art, Denver Art Mus., Del. Soc. Fine Arts, Des Moines Art Center, Norfolk Mus., Columbia Mus., Butler Inst. Art, others, also pvt. collections; guest artist in residence Syracuse U., 1976. Recipient Collectors Am. Art award, 1947, 48, Adele Hyde Morrison prize San Francisco Mus., 1950, hon. mention Am. Painting Today exhbn., Met Mus. Art, 1950, 1st Hallgarten prize NAD, 1951, Ida Wells Stroud award, Am. Watercolor Soc., 1955, purchase prize Nat. Exhbn. Contemporary Arts, 1956, Altman prize for landscape NAD, 1956, Hallmark Art award, 1952, Purchase award, Ball State Tchrs. Coll. Art Gallery, 1958, Columbia (S.C.) Mus., 1959, Portland (Maine) Mus., 1959, 1st award Albany Inst. Art, 1962, Benjamin Altman award NAD, 1964, 73, Andrew Carnegie prize, 1977, award Conn. Acad. Fine Arts, 1965, purchase award Watercolor U.S.A., Springfield Mus., 1966, Kirk Meml. award NAD, 1967, Berkshire Art Assn. award, 1966, 67, 68, 75, jurors prize Albany Inst. Art, 1969, Grumbacher award, 1970, 75, Hassam Fund purchase, 1970, Arches Paper award Am. Watercolor Soc., 1973, Zimmerman award Phila. Watercolor Soc., 1973; Pres.'s award Audubon Artists, 1974, Emily Lowe award, 1979, Stefan Hirsch Meml. award Audubon Artists Ann., 1976, award Rocky Mountain Nat. Watermedia Exhbn., 1976; Condec award Silvermine Guild Artists, 1978, award, 1979; Cooperstown Art Assn. award, 1978, 83; drawing award Ball State U., 1981; High Winds award Am. Watercolor Soc., 1983; Silver medal Audubon Artists, 1983; others. Mem. NAD (2d v.p. 1975, Benjamin Altman award 1980). Home: RD Box 284 Woodstock NY 12498 Office: Midtown Galleries 11 E 57th St New York NY 10022

MAGALLANES, DEBORAH JEAN, business consulting company executive; b. Gary, Ind., May 22, 1951; d. Ray Daniel and Courtney Ann (Manders) M. Student pub. schs., Crown Point, Ind. Adminstrv. asst. Fasfax Corp., Nashua, N.H., 1971-75; adminstrv. mgr. Advanced Tech. Labs., Bellevue, Wash., 1975, part-time, 1975-77; sales asst. VMC Corp., Woodinville, Wash., 1975-76; personnel cons. Bus. Men's Clearing House, Bellevue, 1976-79; salesperson, gen. mgr. Cypress Steel, Inc., Bellevue, 1979, part-time, 1979-80; pres. Magallanes, Inc., Bellevue, 1979—; cons. in field. Author: (with others) Easy Money-Easy Relationships, 1985. Bd. dirs. Friends of Youth, Renton, Wash., 1984—; vol. Save the Elephants Campaign, Seattle, 1984—; bd. dirs. Bellevue Leaders, pres., 1984-85; mem. Up With People, 1969—; mem. Seattle-King County Conv. and Visitors Bur. Mem. Women's Bus. Exchange (bd. dirs. 1981-85, Networker of Yr. 1983), MIT Alumni Assn. (hon. nat. officer 1984). Club: Briefcase Brigade (Bellevue). Lodge: Soroptimists. Avocations: investments; canoeing; fishing; drill team. Office: Magallanes Inc 10900 NE 8th St Suite 900 Bellevue WA 98004

MAGANZINI, TERESA AVERSA, lawyer; b. Phila., Dec. 8, 1951; d. Mario Salvatore and Teresa Elena (Sava) Aversa; m. Paul John Maganzini, May 22, 1976. B.A., U. Notre Dame, 1973; J.D., Villanova U., 1976. Bar: Ill. 1976. Asst. state's atty Cook County (Ill.), Chgo., 1977—. Mem. adv. com. Parental Stress Services, Chgo., 1984. Contbr. chpt. to book. Mem. ABA, Ill. Bar Assn., Chgo. Bar Assn. (com. chmn.), Nat. Dist. Attys. Assn. Roman Catholic. Home: 1146 N Kenilworth Oak Park IL 60302 Office: States Atty Cook County 1100 S Hamilton Chicago IL 60612

MAGARGAL, BONNIE MADELINE, day care school administrator, consultant; b. Sellersville, Pa., Nov. 23, 1950; d. Willard Miller and Anna Agnes (Dugard) Berthold; m. Donald Herbert Magargal, July 31, 1971. B.S. in Elem. Edn. cum laude, Kutztown State U., Pa., 1972; M.S. in Edn. with disting. recognition, Temple U., 1975; Prin.'s cert., U. Pa., 1978. Elem. sch. tchr.

Reading Sch. Dist., Pa., 1972-79, summer sch. instr., 1972-79, workshop presenter, 1972-79, curriculum developer, 1974-79, adminstv. inter, 1977-79; owner, adminstr. Wooly Bear Day Care Sch., Lansdale, Pa., 1979—; cons. in field. Contbr. articles to mags. Early childhood conf. coordinator Montgomery County Community Coll., Blue Bell, Pa., 1985. Recipient Outstanding Tchrs. Am. award Bd. of Advisors, 1975; named Tchr. of Yr. Reading/Berks County C. of C., 1976; George B. Hancher scholar Kutztown State U., 1971. Mem. Montgomery/Bucks Assn. for Edn. of Young Children (pres. 1982-84), Nat. Assn. for Edn. of Young Children, Pa. Assn. for Edn. of Young Children, Pa. Assn. Child Care Adminstrs. Republican. Lutheran. Club: Newcomers. Avocations: piano, water sports, reading, constructing and designing learning materials. Home: 106 Holly Dr Lansdale PA 19446 Office: Wooly Bear Day Care Sch 128 S Broad St Lansdale PA 19446

MAGE, BETTY JEAN, parliamentarian consultant; b. Jamestown, Kans., June 15, 1921; d. Walter A. and Clara (Moe) Carlile; m. Charles Mage, Dec. 15, 1941; children—Ronna Sue Loewen Leggitt, Gary C. Diploma Strickler Bus. Coll., 1940; A.A. Clark Community Coll., 1966; B.A., Portland State U., 1968. Clk. Kans. State Tax Dept., Topeka, 1940-41; office mgr. J.A. Powers Contractor, Los Angeles, 1941-42, Cascade Saw and Tool, Chelalis, Wash., 1957; underwriter N.Y. Life Ins., Tacoma, Wash., 1958-60; exec. dir. Health and Welfare Planning Council, Vancouver, Wash., 1968-76; human resources dir. Clark County Govt., Vancouver, 1976-78; profl. parliamentarian serving local, state and nat. orgns., 1961—; chmn. dir. Columbia Health Services Corp., Vancouver, 1979-85; chmn. state council for postsecondary edn., Olympia, 1982—, Vancouver Housing Authority, 1985—; mem. nat. adv. com. for adult edn., Washington, 1976-80. Trustee Clark Coll., Vancouver, 1967-78; bd. dirs. Showcraft Sheltered Workshop, Vancouver, 1979-80; parliamentarian Democratic Central Com., Vancouver, 1980, 84; mem. parish relations com. United Methodist Ch., 1981-84, mem. pastoral relations com., 1982—; active Camp Fire Girls, YWCA, Boy Scouts Am., PTA, Hospice Adv. Com., Elderly Task Force for Southwest Wash. Hosp. Recipient Woman of Achievement award Profl. Womens Club, 1964, Wakan award Camp Fire Girls, 1960. Mem. Nat. Assn. Parliamentarians, Am. Inst. Parliamentarians, PTA (nat. life mem., Golden Acorn, Outstanding Achievement awards). Avocations: swimming; bowling; golf; creative handwork. Home: 6901 Corregidor Rd Vancouver WA 98664

MAGEE, CATHERINE LOUISE, marketing executive; b. Richmond, Va., July 13, 1954; d. Stanley Earl and Louise (Allman) Magee. B.A. in History, Westhampton Coll., 1976. Govt. bond trader Wheat First Securities Inc., Richmond, Va., 1977-78; mcpl. bond retail trader Wheat First Securities, 1978-80; mcpl. bond retail sales Dean Witter Reynolds, Inc., N.Y.C., 1980-81; dir. retail mcpl. bond mktg. Moseley, Hallgarten, Estabrook & Weeden Inc., N.Y.C., 1981-82; account exec. Dean Witter Reynolds, Inc., Richmond, Va., 1984; mktg. rep. HCW, Inc., Boston, 1985; mktg. rep. Liberty Securities Corp., Boston, 1986—; key career cons. U. Richmond, Va., 1978-80. Recipient Key award, U. Richmond, 1980. Mem. Nat. Assn. Securities Dealers, Nat. Honor Soc., Phi Alpha Theta. Republican. Baptist. Clubs: Richmond Municipal Bond, Municipal Bond of N.Y. Avocations: photography; painting; jazz dance; racquetball; tennis. Home: 21 Beacon St Apt 8H Boston MA 02108 Office: Liberty Securities Corp 600 Atlantic Ave Boston MA 02110

MAGEE-MASSON, CONNIE DEEN, marketing support manager; b. Bogalusa, La., Nov. 3, 1953; d. Robert Stanley and Miriam Day (Sandifer) Magee; m. Robert Paul Masson, Mar. 17, 1984; 1 child Rebecca Lynn. B.Edn., Southeastern La. U., 1975, M.A., 1976; Ed.D., East Tex. State U., 1981, Vocat instr. Irving Sch. Dist. (Tex.), 1977-79; mktg. support rep. Royal Bus. Machines, Dallas, 1979-80; office automation specialist Prime Computer Inc., Dallas, 1980-81; office info. systems cons. Peat Marwick Co., Dallas, 1981-83, Sperry Corp., Dallas, 1983—; instr. Northlake Coll., Irving, Tex., 1977-78, El Centro Coll., Dallas, 1979-82; adj. prof. E. Tex. State U., Commerce, 1982. Chpt. sponsor Vocat. Office Career Clubs Tex., Irving, 1977-78, YWCA, Irving, 1977-78. Recipient Gold award Southwestern Co., Franklin, Tenn., 1975; Tough Minded Bus. award, Southwestern Co., 1975. Mem. Assn. Info. Systems Profls., Vocat.-Tech. Edn. Devel. Found. (charter), Office Systems Research Assn., Women in Computing, Phi Delta Kappa. Republican. Baptist. Home: 7303 Blythdale Dallas TX 75218 Office: Sperry Corp 7540 LBJ Freeway Suite 300 Dallas TX 75231

MAGEE-WILLARD, CINDY LEA, property management executive; b. Tulsa, Jan. 3, 1958; d. Owen Chandler and Jacqueline (Hurst) Magee. A.A., Claremore Coll., 1978; B.A., U. Tulsa, 1980. Cert. property mgr., apt. mgr. Gen. property mgr. Talley Investment Co., Dallas, 1980-83; properties supr. King Laughlin Co., Dallas, 1983—. Cons. procedure manual. Mem. Tarrant County Apt. Assn., Dallas Apt. Assn., Nat. Assn. Female Execs., Phi Theta Kappa (scholar 1977-78). Democrat. Office: King Laughlin Properties 3725 McKinney Ave Dallas TX 75204

MAGGARD, SARAH ELIZABETH, educator, lawyer; b. Whittier, Calif., Nov. 17, 1948; d. William Alexander and Laura (Redford) M. B.A., Whittier Coll., 1970, M.A. in Ed., 1971; J.D., Western State U., Fullerton, Calif., 1981. Bar: Calif. 1982. Tchr., Rowland Unified Sch. Dist., Rowland Heights, Calif., 1971—, also sole practice, Whittier, 1982—. Recipient Am. Jurisprudence awards Bancroft-Whitney Co., 1979, 80. Mem. State Bar Calif., ABA, Los Angeles County Bar Assn., Lawyers Club Los Angeles. Republican. Presbyterian. Assoc. editor Western State U. Law Rev., 1980. Home: 10319 Tigrina Ave Whittier CA 90603 Office: Rowland Unified Sch Dist 1830 S Nogales St Rowland Heights CA 91748

MAGGIO, MARY ELIZABETH, technical writer; b. Mt. Carmel, Ill., Aug. 11, 1954; d. Charles Richard and Jimzonia Ann (Rowand) Talley; m. Dominick F. Maggio, Aug. 17, 1974 (div.); children—Dominick Talley, Matthew Charles. B.A., U. South Fla., 1976. Tech. writer GTE Data Services, Tampa, Fla., 1976-79, sr. tech. writer, 1979, pub. affairs asst., 1979-80; software tech. writer Porta-Printer Systems, Largo, Fla., 1983; adminstrv. analyst Fotomat Corp., St. Petersburg, Fla., 1983—. Mem. Soc. Tech. Communication, Women in Communications, Inc. (treas. 1983-84, newsletter editor 1979-80). Office: Fotomat Corp 205 9th St N Saint Petersburg FL 33701

MAGGIO, THERESA ELIZABETH, medical librarian, consultant; b. Shreveport, La., May 27, 1952; d. James Henry and Annie Laurie (Rosenblath) Griffin; m. Edward James Maggio, July 2, 1977; 1 child, Kelli Suzanne. B.S. in Social Studies Edn., La. State U., 1975, M.L.S., 1980; postgrad. Fla. State U., 1985—. Librarian La. State Library, Baton Rouge, 1980-82; med. library cons. 7th Ward Hosp., Hammond, La., 1984—; med. librarian Lallie Kemp Hosp., Independence, La., 1982-85. Recipient Baker and Taylor Grassroots award, 1980; La. Library Assn. scholar, 1979. Mem. ALA, Med. Library Assn., La. Library Assn., Health Sci. Assn. La., Baton Rouge Library Club. Democrat. Roman Catholic. Avocation: horse racing. Home: 10878 Alco 4 Baton Rouge LA 70816 Office: Lallie Kemp Hosp Hwy 51 S Independence LA 70443

MAGINNESS, BARBARA HOLLOWAY, insurance company executive; b. Jacksonville, Fla., July 11, 1954; d. Barry Victor and Rudell Ramona (Bacon) Holloway; m. James Charles Maginness, Aug. 11, 1973. B.A. in Psychology, U. North Fla., 1980; M.A. in Mgmt., Central Mich. U., 1981. Mgmt. devel. specialist Blue Cross-Blue Shield Fla., Jacksonville, 1976-80; human resource devel. specialist Life of Ga. Co., Atlanta, 1981; asst. v.p. human resources Am. Security Ins. Group, Atlanta, 1981—; dir. employee benefits AMEV Holdings, Inc. Mem. mktg. and distributive edn. bus. adv. com. Ga. State U., Atlanta, 1983—. Mem. Am. Soc. for Tng. and Devel. (sec.-treas. N.E. Fla. chpt. 1976-78, pres. 1980, v.p. fin. and adminstrn. Atlanta chpt. 1984—). Democrat. Episcopalian. Home: 81 Montclair Ave Montclair NJ 07042 Office: 1 World Trade Ctr New York NY 10048

MAGLADRY, JEAN, lawyer; b. Balt., Sept. 15, 1957; d. Robert Eddy and Esther Janet (Struxness) Magladry; m. Cleveland David Jarvis III, Apr. 9, 1983. B.A. with honors, U. Md., 1979; J.D. cum laude, Gonzaga Law Sch., 1982. Bar: Wash. 1982. Law clk. City of Spokane (Wash.), 1980-82, city prosecutor, 1982-83; assoc. Burns & Ricketts, Seattle, 1983—. Mem. Wash. State Bar Assn., Spokane County Bar Assn., King County Bar Assn., Wash. Trial Attys. Assn., ABA (criminal justice com. 1983—). Republican. Lutheran. Office: Burns & Ricketts 500 Times Sq Bldg 414 Olive Way Seattle WA 98101

MAGLALANG, FLOR DALOCANOG, educational administrator; b. Cebu City, Philippines, Sept. 22, 1942; came to U.S., 1978, naturalized, 1984; d. Daniel Peras and Fructuosa (Jerusalem) Dalocanog; m. Demetrio Mendoza Maglalang, July 3, 1965; children—Herman, Alfred Kevin, Dmitiri, Maurice. B.S.B.A. summa cum laude, U. St. Charles, Cebu City; M.B.A., Ind. U., M.B.A., M.A. in Econs., Ind. U. Fin. analyst Presdl. Econ. Staff, Manila, 1965-68; chief economist Dept. Industry, Manila, 1968-72; gen. mgr. Afra Trade Export-Import, Manila, 1973-78; dir. fin. aid St. Meinrad Coll., Ind., 1979—; tchr. Vincennes U., Jasper, Ind., 1980—. Mem. fin. com., v.p. St. Nicholas Parish, Santa Claus, Ind., 1985-86. Recipient Good Citizen award DAR, 1985. Mem. Nat. Assn. Student Fin. Aid Adminstrs., Midwest Assn. Student Fin. Aid Adminstrs., Ind. Student Fin. Aid Assn., Ind. U. Alumni Assn. Republican. Roman Catholic. Clubs: Christmas Lake Village Golf and Tennis, CLV Assn. Avocations: reading; movies; dancing; real estate; counseling. Home: 131 Silver Bell Terr Christmas Lake Santa Claus IN 47579 Office: St Meinrad College College Ave Saint Meinrad IN 47577

MAGNER, RACHEL HARRIS, banker; b. Lamar, S.C., Aug. 5, 1951; d. Garner Greer and Catherine Alice (Cloaninger) Harris; B.S. in Fin., U. S.C., 1972; postgrad. UCLA, 1974, Calif. State U., 1975; m. Fredric Michael Magner, May 14, 1972. Mgmt. trainee Union Bank, Los Angeles, 1972-75, comml. loan officer, 1975-77; asst. v.p. comml. fin. Crocker Bank, Los Angeles, 1978, asst. v.p., factoring account exec. subs. Crocker United Factors, Inc., 1978-81; v.p. comml. services div. Crocker Bank, 1981-82, v.p., sr. account mgr. bus. banking div., 1982-83; v.p. corporate banking Office of Pres., Sumitomo Bank Calif., 1983—. Mem. Los Angeles Bank Creditmen's Assn., Wilshire Women's Bus. and Profl. Assn., Los Angeles Women's Profl. Bank Assn., Textile Profl. Assn. Home: 2200 Pine Ave Manhattan Beach CA 90266 Office: Sumitomo Bank of Calif 101 S San Pedro Suite 1005 Los Angeles CA 90012

MAGNETTI, SANDRA MARIE, health researcher, administrator; b. San Francisco, Apr. 30, 1948; d. Nicholas J. and Ruth C. (Randles) M.; m. Sergio Augusto Bentes de Melo e Silva, June 25, 1972 (div. 1977). B.A., U. Calif.-Davis, 1971; M.S., U. Calif.-Berkeley and Davis, 1972; Dr.P.H., U. Tex.-Houston, 1982. Health survey mgr. Golden Empire Health Planning Council, Sacramento, 1971-72; program developer Fazendas Aquiqui Agro-Industria, Ltd., Belem, Para, Brazil, 1972-74; health planner Para State Health Dept., 1975-76; coordinator, founder student internship info. ctr. Sch. Pub. Health, U. Tex.-Houston, 1978-79, sr. research assoc., 1979-81; research assoc. Tex. Research Inst., Houston, 1982-83 chairperson quality assurance, 1982-85; project dir. dept. behavioral medicine U. Pitts., 1985—; clinic dir./founder rural family planning clinic, Almeirim, Para, Brazil, 1975-76; research cons. Research Stats., Inc., Houston, 1979-81. Author monographs and articles. Founder, Indigenous Women's Self Devel. Orgns., Para, 1973-76; editor Houston Community Resource Directory, 1973—; vol. Crisis Intervention, Inc., Houston, 1973. USPHS trainee, 1977-80; Sociodade de Bem Estar Familiar scholar, 1974. Mem. Am. Pub. Health Assn., AAAS, Houston Community Involvement Com., Tex. Econ. and Demographic Assn., Soc. Behavioral Medicine, Assn. Behavioral Medicine Third Coast Computer Graphics Group. Home: 3727 Parkview Ave Pittsburgh PA 15213 Office: 3811 O'Hara St Pittsburgh PA 15213

MAGNEY, DESIREE HOLUBOWICZ, lawyer; b. Ephrata, Pa., Aug. 14, 1956; d. John Joseph and Georgette (Shaffer) Holubowicz; m. John Stevenson Magney, July 26, 1980. B.A., Cath. U. Am., 1978, J.D., 1981. Bar: D.C. 1982. Tax law specialist IRS, Washington, 1979-80, atty. Office of Chief Counsel, 1981—; law clk. Comptroller of Currency, Washington, 1981. Mem. Fed. Women's Program, Washington, 1981-82; coordinator Combined Fed. Campaign United Way, 1983, Savings Bond Campaign, 1982. Recipient letter of commendation IRS, 1980, Sustained Superior Performance award, 1983, Superior Performance in Partnership Class, 1983; Corpus Juris Secundum award, Cath. U. Am., 1981. Mem. D.C. Bar Assn., ABA, NOW, Planned Parenthood. Home: 2733 Unicorn Ln NW Washington DC 20015 Office: IRS 1111 Constitution Ave NW Washington DC 20224

MAGNI, DEBRA KAY, public relations executive; b. Sunbury, Pa., Nov. 5, 1954; d. Wallace Theodore and Florence Dolores (Hendricks) Townsend; m. Anthony Michael Magni, July 2, 1982; 1 dau., Kelly Ann. B.S., York Coll. Pa., 1978, A.S., 1977. Office mgr. York Coll. Pa., 1973-78; ter. mgr. bus. mgmt. systems Burroughs Corp., Hunt Valley, Md., 1978-80; dir. pub. relations York Coll. Pa., 1980—. Bd. dirs. Am. Cancer Soc., York, 1981—; mem. pub. relations com. S. Central Pa. chpt. Am. Heart Assn.; v.p. York Alcohol and Drug Services, 1982—, Rape Crisis Center York, 1982-84; mem. programming com. Strand Capitol Performing Arts Center, York, 1981-84; mem. York YWCA Mktg. Task Force, 1985, mem. Hanover YWCA mktg. com., 1985—. Council Advancement and Support Edn. scholar, 1981. Mem. Council Advancement and Support Edn., Coll. and Univ. Pub. Relations Assn. Pa., York Coll. Pa. Alumni Assn. Republican. Lutheran. Home: RD 2 Box 851 E Berlin Rd Thomasville PA 17364 Office: York Coll Pa Country Club Rd York PA 17403

MAGNUS, LAVELLE GRABER, retired school principal; b. Ottumwa, Iowa, Jan. 3, 1920; d. Harold Wordworth and Opal (Funk) Graber; B.Ed., Chgo., Tchrs. Coll., 1942; M.A., Long Beach State U., 1956; m. Gordon Eugene Magnus, June 4, 1960 (dec.); 1 son, Larry Coffman; stepchildren—Joyce McQuade, Jack Magnus, Clark Magnus. Tchr. public schs., Chgo., 1942-44, Little Lake Sch. Dist., Norwalk, Calif., 1944-45; tchr. Lynwood (Calif.) Sch. Dist., 1947-65, elem. sch. prin. 1965-76. Mem. NEA (life), Nat. Assn. Elem. Sch. Prins. Assn. Calif. Sch. Adminstrs., AAUW, DAR (past dist. dir., past state rec. sec., state chaplain), Republican Women. Methodist. Clubs: Universe, Order Eastern Star (Past Matrons club), Gethsemane White Shrine. Home: 1221 Oakmont Rd 178-B Seal Beach CA 90740

MAGNUS, MARGARET MANNION, nursing educator; b. Anthenry, Galway, Ireland; came to U.S., 1954; d. Michael and Mary (Lynskey) Mannion; m. Joseph Magnus, Aug. 7, 1970; 1 dau., Tayna Marie. B.S. in Nursing, Incarnate Word Coll., 1961; M.S. in Nursing, Cath. U., Washington, 1965, Ph.D., 1969. Unit supr. Santa Rosa Children's Hosp., San Antonio, 1961-63; asst. prof. Incarnate Word Coll., San Antonio, 1965-66; asst. prof. New Rochelle (N.Y.) Hosp. Sch. Nursing, 1969-70; mem. faculty Hunter-Bellevue Sch. Nursing, N.Y.C., 1970—, prof. nursing, 1979—, dir. grad. program, 1975-80, dir. undergrad. progrm, 1981-82, assoc. dean, 1983-84; vis. prof. Tchrs. Coll., Columbia U., summer 1986. Author: Fundamentals of Nursing, 1972. Editor: Blood Groups, 1970. Mem. exec. bd. Ctr. to Promote Health Care Studies N.Y., 1975. Mem. Nat. Assn. Female Execs., Am. Nurses Assn., Deans, Directors, Faculty N.Y. State Nurses Assn. (vice chmn. 1982—), Sigma Theta Tau, Phi Beta Kappa. Democrat. Roman Catholic. Office: Hunter-Bellevue Sch of Nursing 425 E 25th St New York NY 10010

MAGNUSON, CONSTANCE FOSTER, banker; b. Madison, Wis., Mar. 29, 1952; d. Howard Clinton and Mertice Ethel (Johnston) Foster; m. Michael Swan Magnuson, Oct. 22, 1977; 1 child, Karen Marie. B.A., Northwestern U., 1974, M.B.A., 1978. Trust officer No. Trust Co., Chgo., 1974-78, 2d v.p., 1980, v.p., 1983—; speaker nat. confs. Mem. Northwestern Profl. Womens Assn. (exec. v.p. 1980, sec. 1981), Kappa Kappa Gamma Alumni Assn. (sec. 1981). Office: Northern Trust Co 50 S LaSalle St Chicago IL 60675

MAGNUSON, NANCY LEE, university official; b. Lincoln, Nebr., Aug. 16, 1948; d. Clifford Frank and Bonnie Lee (Price) M.; B.A., U. N.Mex., 1970, M.A., 1980. Tchr., Los Lunas (N.Mex.) Consol. Schs., 1970-73; alumni field rep. U. N.Mex., Albuquerque, 1973-76, spl. asst. to pres. for sch. relations, 1976-77, dir. sch. relations and prospective student services, 1977-84, assoc. dir. devel. for ann. giving, 1984—, mem. pres.'s com. on excellence, adv. Mortar Bd., 1978-81, chmn. univ. combined fund dr., 1982-83; mem. AUTOCAP of N.Mex., 1983—. Mem. Council Advancement and Support of Edn. (bd. dirs. dist. IV 1985-86), Nat. Assn. Women Deans, Adminstrs. and Counselors, Nat. Assn. Coll. Admission Counselors, Greater Albuquerque C. of C. (edn. com. 1977-82), Jr. League Albuquerque, Pi Alpha Alpha, Pi Beta Phi. Home: 3109 La Mancha NW Albuquerque NM 87104 Office: Univ N Mex Albuquerque NM 87131

MAGUIRE, CHARLOTTE EDWARDS, physician; b. Richmond, Ind., Sept. 1, 1918; d. Joel Blaine and Lydia (Betscher) Edwards; student Stetson U., 1936-38, U. Wichita, 1938-39; B.S., Memphis Tchrs. Coll., 1940; M.D., U. Ark., 1944; m. Raymer Francis Maguire, Sept. 1, 1948 (dec.); children—Barbara, Thomas Clair II. Intern Orange Meml. Hosp., Orlando, Fla., 1944-46; resident Bellevue Hosp. and Med. Center, N.Y.U., N.Y.C., 1955; instr. nurses Orange Meml. Hosp., 1947-57, staff mem., 1946-48; staff mem. Fla. Sanatarium and Hosp., Orlando, 1946-56, Holiday House and Hosp., Orlando, 1950-62; mem. courtesy and cons. staff West Orange Meml. Hosp., Winter Garden, Fla., 1952-67; active staff, chief dept. pediatrics Mercy Hosp., Orlando, 1965-68; med. dir. med. services and basic care Fla. Dept. Health and Rehab. Services, 1975—; chief of staff of physicians and dentists Central Fla. div. Children's Home Soc. of Fla., 1947-56; dir. Orlando Child Health Clinic, 1949-58; engaged in pvt. practice, medicine, Orlando, 1946-68; asst. regional dir. HEW, 1970-72; pediatric cons. Fla. Crippled Children's Commn., 1952-70, dir., 1968-70; med. dir. Office Med. Services and Basic Care, Fla. Dept. Health and Rehab. Services; clin prof. dept. pediatrics U. Fla. Coll. Medicine, Gainesville, 1980—. Mem. profl. adv. com. Fla. Center for Clin. Services at U. Fla., 1952-60; del. to Mid-century White House Conf. on Children and Youth, 1950; U.S. del. from Nat. Soc. for Crippled Children to World Congress for Welfare of Cripples, Inc., London, Eng., 1957; pres. of corp. Eccleston-Callahan Hosp. for Colored Crippled Children, 1956-58; sec. Fla. chpt. Nat. Doctors' Com. for Improved Med. Services, 1951-52; med. adv. com. Gateway Sch. for Mentally Retarded, 1959-62; bd. dirs. Forest Park Sch. for Spl. Edn. Crippled Children, 1949-54, mem. med. adv. com., 1955-68, chmn. 1957—; mem. Fla. Adv. Council for Mentally Retarded, 1965-70; dir. central Fla. poison control Orange Meml. Hosp.; mem. orgn. com., chmn. com. for admission and selection policies Camp Challenge; participant 12th session Fed. Exec. Inst., 1971; del. White House Conf. on Aging, 1980. Mem. Nat. Rehab. Assn., Am. Congress Phys. Medicine and Rehab., Fla., Central Fla. (dir. 1949-58, pres. 1956-57) socs. crippled children and adults, Am. Assn. Cleft Palate, Fla. Soc. Crippled Children (trustee 1951-57, v.p. 1956-57, profl. adv. com. 1957-68), Mental Health Assn. Orange County (charter mem.; pres. 1949-50, dir. 1947-52, chmn. exec. com. 1950-52, dir. 1963-65), Fla. Orange County heart assns., AMA, Am. Med. Women's Assn., Am. Acad. Med. Dirs., So. Fla. (chmn. com. on mental retardation), Orange County med assns., Fla. Orlando pediatric socs., Fla. Cleft Palate Assn. (counselor-at-large, sec.). Office: Rm 204 Lafayette Bldg 2551 Executive Center-West Tallahassee FL 32301

MAGUIRE, PATRICIA RUTH, interior design company executive; b. Buenos Aires, Argentina, July 17, 1954; d. Juan Alexander Wassermann and Eva (Gyorgy) Eliel; m. Steven Joseph Maguire, Dec. 22, 1975. B.S., Skidmore Coll., 1975; postgrad. Fla. Atlantic U., 1984—. Adminstrv. asst. Am. Express Co., Caracas, Venezuela, 1978-79, mgr. corp. relations, 1979-80, dir. services, 1980-83; pres. Advena Interiors, Boca Raton, Fla., 1983—; bd. dirs. Amexclusivas, Caracas, Turisol, Caracas, Aspen Air Conditioning, Delray Beach, Fla. Artist, paintings exhibited in solo exhbn. Contini Art Gallery, Caracas, 1977, 78, paintings and enamels at Valencia Salon Artes del Fuego, Valencia, Venezuelo, 1976, 77. Mem. Nat. Assn. Female Execs., Interior Design Guild, Boca Raton C. of C. Avocations: languages; tennis; golf. Home: 767 Coventry St Boca Raton FL 33431 Office: Advena Interiors 217 E Palmetto Park Rd Boca Raton FL 33432

MAGUIRE-KRUPP, MARJORIE ANNE, financial institution manager; b. Stamford, Conn., Apr. 29, 1955; d. Walter Reeves and Jean Elisabeth (Cook) M.; m. Paul C. Croarkin, July 15, 1978 (div. Feb. 1981); m. Joseph Michael Krupp, Jr., Nov. 26, 1983; stepchildren Theresa Margaret, Donna Marie, Maura Elizabeth. B.A. cum laude, Franklin and Marshall Coll., 1976; M.B.A. with distinction, NYU, 1983, cert. in real estate, 1986; cert. French U. Strasbourg, France, 1971. C.P.A., Conn.; lic. real estate sales agt., N.J. Supervisory auditor Arthur Young & Co., Stamford, Conn., 1976-80; mgr. fin. planning Combustion Engring., Stamford, 1980-84; adminstrv. officer, fin cons. Kidder Peabody & Co., N.Y.C., 1984—; real estate developer, 1986—. Advisor, Jr. Achievement, Stamford, 1979-80; mem. Met. Opera Guild, N.Y.C., 1985-86, Met. Mus. Art, N.Y.C., 1983-86, Mus. Modern Art, N.Y.C., 1983-86; treas., dir. Cliffhouse Condo Assn., Cliffside Park, N.J., 1983-85. Mem. Am. Inst. C.P.A.s, N.Y. State Soc. C.P.A.s, Nat. Assn. Female Execs., Am. Women's Soc. C.P.A.s, Phi Beta Kappa, Beta Gamma Sigma. Club: Stamford Jaycee Women (pres. 1980-81, chmn. bd. 1981-82, Disting. Service award, Outstanding Young Woman of Yr. award, both 1980). Republican. Presbyterian. Avocations: travel; skiing; sailing; gourmet cooking; piano. Home: 300 Gorge Rd Cliffside Park NJ 07010 Office: Kidder Peabody & Co 2 Broadway 4th Floor New York NY 10004

MAGUIREN, MARGARET L., lawyer, government official; b. Bklyn., Oct. 31, 1944; d. William L. and Elizabeth L. (Steinbugler) Maguire; B.A., Marymount Coll., 1965; M.A., Colgate U., 1969; J.D., U. Louisville, 1977; 1 child, William. Teaching, translation and interpretation of Spanish and English various schs. in U.S. and Colombia, 1968-74; admitted Ky. bar, 1977; counsel First Ky. Nat. Corp., Louisville, 1977-79; atty. Fed. Res. Bd., Washington, 1979-80; asst. to dir. FDIC, 1980-81, dep. to chmn., 1981—. Served with Peace Corps, 1965-67. N.Y. State Regents scholar, 1961-65, Higher Edn. Act fellow, 1967-69. Mem. ABA. Office: Federal Deposit Insurance Corp 550 17th St NW Washington DC 20429

MAHAFFEY, JOAN, nurse; b. Richmond, Utah, Feb. 7, 1926; d. Joseph Perry and Annie Marie (Christofferson) Peart; R.N., Meth. Hosp., Los Angeles, 1950; B.S. in Health Sci., Calif. State U., Northridge, 1971, M.P.H., 1976; m. J.B. Mahaffey, June 5, 1949 (div. Jan. 1967). Hosp. and office nurse, Calif., 1951-72; mem. staff Calif. Nurses Assn., 1972—, dir. Nurses Profl. Registry, 1972—, regional dir. epicenter region 3, Van Nuys, 1981—; cons., speaker in field. Mem. Nat. League Nursing, Am. Nurses Assn., Calif. Nurses Assn. (pres. 1983-85, bd. dirs. 1985—), Valley Nursing Edn. Council. Democrat. Mormon. Clubs: Soroptimist, San Fernando Emblem. Home: 6620 Glade Ave Canoga Park CA 91303 Office: 7417 Van Nuys Blvd Suite O Van Nuys CA 91405

MAHAFFEY, MARTHA PLUMMER, government official; b. Bryn Mawr, Pa., June 1, 1946; d. John Lewis Plummer and Gloria Joan (Donatelli) Richards; m. Wilton Larron Mahaffey, Nov. 29, 1974; children—Melinda Kathleen, Matthew Timothy. A.B., cum laude, Bryn Mawr Coll., 1968, M.B.A., U. Va., 1970. Mgmt. cons. Booz, Allen & Hamilton, Washington, 1970-72; self-employed cons., Washington, 1972-73; mgmt. cons. Arthur Young & Co., Washington, 1973; program analyst. Exec. Office of President of U.S., Washington, 1973-74; exec. officer Health Care Financing Adminstrn., Dallas, 1974-83, dep. regional adminstr., Boston, 1983—. Bd. dirs. Montessori Sch. Park Cities, 1981-82; Christian edn. counselor, tchr. St. Michael and All Angels Ch., 1979-83. Recipient Administr.'s citation Health Care Financing Adminstrn., 1979-81; Sr. Exec. Service Candidate Selection award HHS, 1983. Mem. Lychnds Honor Soc. Republican. Episcopalian. Home: 10121 Daria Dr Dallas TX 75229 Office: JF Kennedy Fed Bldg Room 1309 Govt Ctr Boston MA 02205

MAHAIRAS, EVELYN PHILLIPINE, clinical social worker, psychotherapist, educator, researcher; b. N.Y.C., Sept. 25, 1933; d. Otto and Henrietta (Dolman) Poestges; B.A. in Clin. Psychiatry, Queens Coll., 1954; tchr. cert. Eastern Nazarene Coll., 1972; M.S.W., Ohio State U., 1976; postgrad. Bryn Mawr Coll., 1979—; m. C. Gus Mahairas, June 27, 1954; children—Pamela Linda, Janet Susan, Karen Lee, Evelyn Jean. Psychiat. social worker N.Y. State Dept. Mental Hygiene, 1954-56; bus. rep. N.Y. Telephone Co., Jackson Heights, N.Y., 1956-57; substitute tchr. public schs., Mass., Conn., 1970-74; dir. social services Wives Self Help/City Police and Fire Counselling Service, Phila., 1976-81; research specialist social work service Coatesville (Pa.) V.A. Med. Center, 1981—, adminstrv. asst. geriatric research, edn. com., 1984—; Sec., Social Action Com., 1968-70; coordinator Headstart, W. Springfield, Mass., 1968-70; mem. Lake Champlain Com., Vt., 1968—. Mem. Nat. Assn. Social Workers (dir. Pa. chpt., exec. com., fin. com., program chmn., v.p. 1979-81, exec. bd., pres. Brandywine div. 1978-79, co-chmn. continuing edn. 1978-80, mem. social action com., legis. com.), Acad. Cert. Social Workers, Nat. Register Clin. Social Workers, Mental Health Assn. of Southeastern Pa. Presbyterian (youth fellowship adv.). Co-editor: The Aging Veteran: Interorganizational Relations; contbr. articles to profl. jours. Home: 650 W Wind Dr Berwyn PA 19312 also Thompson's Point Charlotte VT 19312 Office: Coatesville VA Med Center Coatesville PA 19320

MAHAN, GENEVIEVE ELLIS, sociologist; b. Canton, Ohio, Aug. 1, 1909; d. William and Lillian (Ellis) Mahan. A.B., Case Western Res. U., 1931, A.M., 1941; postgrad. (Ford Found. fellow) Yale U., 1952, Akademie für Politische Bildung, Tutzing, Germany, 1963. Tchr. high schs., Canton, 1937-52; research asst. dept. sociology Yale U., New Haven, 1953-55; lectr. dept. sociology Walsh Coll., Canton, 1970. Del., Instns. Atlantic and European Cooperation, Coimbra, Portugal, 1970; participant 6th World Congress Sociology, Evian, France, 1966. Trustee, Stark County Psychiat. Found., 1961-68. Fellow Am. Sociol. Assn.; mem. Eastern Sociol. Soc., Am. Acad. Polit. and Social Sci., Nat., Ohio (exec. bd. 1962-69, pres. 1965-66) councils for social studies, Internat. Sociol. Assn., Ohio Acad. Sci., Ohio Soc. N.Y., AAUW, AAAS. Clubs: Canton

College; Canton Woman's; Massillon Woman's. Research in polit. caricature, 1955—. Address: 804 5th St NW Canton OH 44703

MAHAN, LORETTA BOSSO, chemical company marketing services coordinator, consultant; b. Phila., Aug. 15, 1948; d. Joseph Vincent and Antoinette Josephine (Teti) B.; children—Shawn Adam, Patrick Glenn. Pub. relations writer Spiro & Assocs., Phila., 1966-70; reading aide Octorara High Sch., Atglen, Pa., 1978-79; project coordinator, cons. E. I. DuPont & Co., Wilmington, Del., 1980—. Mem. recreation com. Borough Council, Parkesburg, Pa., 1979-81. Mem. Nat. Assn. Female Execs. Democrat. Roman Catholic. Avocations: music; guitar; racquetball; tennis; softball. Home: 530 W 2d Ave Parkesburg PA 19365 Office: E I DuPont de Nemours Co Inc Concord Plaza Wilmington DE 19898

MAHARAS, MARIAN E., health care marketing executive; b. Cleve., Aug. 22, 1949; d. Albert and Georgiana Marie (Perry) M. B.S. in Journalism, Okla. State U., 1972; M.A. in Journalism, U. Tex.-Austin, 1980. News reporter Okla. Eagle Newspaper, Tulsa, 1972-73; advertiser Aurora Sun Newspaper (Colo.), 1973-74; program assoc. Sta. KLRN-TV, Austin, Tex., 1977-78; health info. specialist City Health Dept., Austin, 1978-82; mktg. mgr. Healthcare Internat., Austin, 1982—. NIMH fellow, 1974. Mem. Women in Communications, Inc. (press. 1970-71, Outstanding Woman in Journalism 1971, scholarship 1970), Phi Kappa Phi, Kappa Tau Alpha. Roman Catholic. Home: 4209 Marathon Apt 203 Austin TX 78756 Office: Healthcare Internat PO Box 4008 Austin TX 78765

MAHER, FRAN, advertising agency executive; b. Chgo., June 22, 1938; d. Edward Stephan and Virginia Rose (Harrington) M.; student (Univ. scholar) U. Minn., 1956-57; student Spectrum Inst., 1968-71; B.A. summa cum laude, Kean Coll. N.J., 1979; m. Anthony Peter Petrella, Sept. 17, 1957; children—Roland, Louis, Marcus. Office mgr. Lead Supplies, Inc., Mpls., 1957-59; free-lance artist and writer, Warren, N.J., 1968-72; prin. Visuals, Warren, N.J., 1974-79; pres. Fran Maher, Inc., Stirling, N.J., 1980—; dir. Parent Edn. Advocacy Tng. Center, Alexandria, Va., 1979-85, Officer Friends of Weigand Farm, Milton, N.J., 1977-80, Somerset County unit Assn. for Retarded Citizens; founding mem. Flintlock Boys' Club. Recipient N.J. Art Dirs. Show award, 1978, 1st place award in graphics Watchung Art Center, 1980. Mem. Women Entrepreneurs N.J., Art Dirs. Club N.J., Printmaking Council N.J., Am. Women's Econ. Devel. Corp., Advt. Agy. Network Internat., Internat. Platform Assn. Office: 1390 Valley Rd Stirling NJ 07980

MAHER, JEANMARIE, law office administrator; b. Coeur d'Alene (Idaho); d. Richard Bonaventure and Celine Katherine (Chainey) Maher; B.A., U. Santa Clara, 1964. Spl. asst. The Asia Found., San Francisco, 1965-69; exec. asst. to chmn. Calif. Democratic Party, 1971-74; owner JMaher & Assocs., San Francisco, 1974-75; staff Brobeck, Phleger & Harrison, San Francisco and Los Angeles, 1975-79; adminstr. Lasky, Haas, Cohler & Munter, San Francisco, 1979—; editor Systems and Tech. Newsletter Assn. Legal Adminstrs., 1983-86, Golden Gate chpt. newsletter, San Francisco, 1982-83; occasional lectr., cons., 1983—. Bd. dirs. The Irish Forum, 1982—; mem. Women's Council, Democratic Nat. Com., Washington, 1983—. Mem. Assn. Legal Adminstrs. (bd. dirs., pres. 1985-86), Am. Mgmt. Assn., ABA, Calif. State Bar Assn. Democrat. Home: 570 Union St #206 San Francisco CA 94133 Office: Lasky Haas Cohler & Munter PC 505 Sansome St #1200 San Francisco CA 94111

MAHER, KIM LEVERTON, museum administrator; b. Washington, Feb. 25, 1946; d. Joseph Wilson and Helen Elizabeth (Bell) Leverton; m. William Fredrick Maher, June 12, 1965 (div. 1980); 1 child, Lauren Robinson. Student Duke U., 1963-65, George Washington U., 1966; B.A. in English, U. Fla., 1969. Social worker Fla. Health and Rehab. Service, Gainesville, 1969-71, Delray Beach, 1972-74, fraud unit supr., West Palm Beach, 1974-76, direct service supr., 1977-78; ctr. dir. Palm Beach County Employment and Tng. Adminstrn., West Palm Beach, 1979-81; exec. dir. Discovery Ctr., Inc., Ft. Lauderdale, Fla., 1981—. Bd. dirs. Singing Pines Mus., Boca Raton, Fla., 1984—, Broward Art Guild, Ft. Lauderdale, 1985—; mem. Leadership Broward II, Ft. Lauderdale, 1983-84. Recipient Cultural Arts award Broward Cultural Arts Found., 1985. Mem. Am. Assn. Museums, Assn. Sci. and Tech. Ctrs., Southeastern Museums Conf., Leadership Broward Alumnae (curriculum com. 1984—), Fort Lauderdale Downtown Council, Ft. Lauderdale C. of C. (cultural affairs task force 1983—), Women's Exec. Club, Phi Kappa Phi. Republican. Methodist. Avocations: scuba diving; piano; creative writing; collecting art and antiques; painting. Office: Discovery Ctr Mus 231 SW 2d Ave Fort Lauderdale FL 33301

MAHER, MARY Z., drama educator; b. Mason City, Iowa, June 17, 1941; s. Jack Patrick and Maxine Darryl (Mills) M. B.A., U. Iowa, 1963, M.A., 1970; Ph.D., U. Mich., 1973. Asst. prof. drama Hofstra U., 1973-75; assoc. prof. U. Ariz., Tucson, 1975—; cons. Ormonde Pub. Co., London, 1983—. Contbg. author: Theatres of Interpretation, 1976. Contbr. articles, revs. to profl. jours. Mem. Speech Communication Assn., Western Speech Communication Assn., Ariz. Communication and Theatre Assn. (editor jour. 1980-82), Soc. Tchrs. Speech and Drama, Internat. Shakespeare Assn., Shakespease Assn. Am., Ariz. Alliance for Arts Edn., Arts Edn. Collaborative, Internat. Shakespeare Assn. Office: Dept Drama U Ariz Tucson AZ 85721

MAHERAS, CLAUDIA RACHE, bank executive; b. Chgo., Mar. 14, 1946; d. William and Bernice (Gedraitis) Rache; m. Kostas Ilias Maheras, Feb. 20, 1966 (div.); children—Laura, Louis. B.A., U. Ill.-Chgo., 1969; degree of distinction, Inst. Fin. Edn., Chgo., 1983. Communications designer U. Ill., Chgo., 1969-71; ptnr. New Dimension Realtors, Chgo., 1971-75; ptnr. Merchant Restaurant Chgo., 1975-79; adminstrv. asst. Unity Savs. Assn., Norridge, Ill., 1979, mgmt. trainee, 1979-80, teller mgr., corp. officer, 1980-83; corp. officer/br. mgr. Talman-Home Fed. Savs. & Loan Assn. of Ill., Chgo., 1983-84; loan officer, corp. officer Talman Home Mortgage Corp., 1984—. Mem. Nat. Assn. Female Execs. (network dir. 1983—), Am. Mgmt. Assn., AAUW, Women in Mgmt. Home: 6729 W Senior Pl Harwood Heights IL 60634 Office: Talman-Home Mortgage Corp 4901 W Irving Park Chicago IL 60641

MAHLAND, JANET CAROL POLING, transportation company executive; b. N.Y.C., Jan. 15, 1936; d. Robert L. and Carol V. (Jacobsen) Poling; student Syracuse (N.Y.) U., 1954-55; diploma Katherine Gibbs Sch., N.Y.C., 1955; cert. World Trade Inst., 1979; m. Robert H. Mahland, Apr. 22, 1960; children—June Carol, Jeanne Caron. With Am. Oil Co., N.Y.C., 1955-56, Sinclair Refining Co., N.Y.C., 1956-57; with Poling Transp. Corp., N.Y.C., 1958—, v.p., 1976-79, pres., dir., 1979—; pres., dir. other corps. Bd. dirs., v.p. alumni bd. Packer Collegiate Inst., 1980; a founder Staten Island Childrens' Mus.; trustee Adelphi Acad.; bd. dirs. Eger Found., Meth. Hosp., Bklyn. Mem. Am. Petroleum Inst., Assn. Energy Profls., N.Y. Oil Trades Assn., Maritime Assn. Port N.Y., S.I. C. of C., N.Y. Towboat and Harbor Carriers Assn. (dir.), S.I. Hist. Soc. Lutheran. Clubs: Downtown Athletic (N.Y.C.); Richmond County Country, S.I. Garden. Office: 1 Edgewater Plaza Staten Island NY 10305

MAHLUM, RHONDA LYNN, accountant, realty sales person; b. Crookston, Minn., Apr. 25, 1959; d. Werner Conway and Darlene Harriet (Benson) M. B.S. in Acctg., Moorhead State U., 1981. C.P.A., N.D. Resident asst. Moorhead State U., 1979-81; cons. Small Bus. Inst., Moorhead, 1980-81; auditor Tax Dept. State of N.D., Bismarck, 1981-84; Realtor Bianco Realty, Bismarck, 1984—; acct. Puklich & Eckroth, P.C., Bismarck, 1985-86. Officer Heart Butte Water Ski Shows, Lake Tschide, 1982-84. Mem. N.D. Soc. C.P.A.s, Nat. Assn. Realtors, N.D. Assn. Realtors (chmn. edn. 1985-86), Bismarck-Mandan Bd. Realtors (chmn. edn. 1985-86). Club: Supreme Court Racquet & Fitness (Bismarck). Home: 718 1/2 N 23d St Bismarck ND 58501 Office: Puklich Eckroth 2021 E Main St Bismarck ND 58501

MAHMOUDI, HOMA, clinical psychologist; b. Tehran, Iran, Apr. 24, 1941; came to U.S., 1959, naturalized, 1977; d. Jalil and Badri M.; grad. certificate Middle Eastern studies, U. Utah, 1967; Ph.D. in Clin. Psychology, 1970; 1 child, Jason. Tng. officer Peace Corps, 1962-68; dir. police selection research project County of Los Angeles, 1970-73, chief psychologist Occupational Health Service, 1977-85; psychologist Cedar-Sinai Med. Ctr., 1986—; pvt. practice, Los Angeles; asst. clin. prof. med. psychology Sch. Medicine UCLA, 1973-77. Mem. Am. Psychol. Assn., Western Psychol. Assn., Soc. for Intercultural Edn. Tng. and Research, Am. Soc. Tng. and Devel. Baha'i. Author: The Urban Policeman in Transition: A Psychological and Sociological Review, 1973; co-author: Persian Phrasebook & Dictionary, 1977; contbr. articles in field to publs. Home: 909 Stonehill Ln Los Angeles CA 90049

MAHNKE, SUSAN MARGARET, editor; b. Sheboygan, Wis., Feb. 28, 1947; d. Edward Anton and Margaret Emma (DeBack) M.; m. Gordon Peery. 1 dau., Margaret Rose. B.A., U. Wis., 1970; postgrad. U. Mass., 1976-77; Asso. editor Wis. Trails mag., Madison, 1970-74; asst. editor The Stephen Greene Press, Brattleboro, Vt., 1974-76; freelance editor and writer, 1976-77; sr. editor Yankee mag., 1977—, The Old Farmer's Almanac, 1977—. Town clk. Town of Nelson, N.H., 1981—; trustee Olivia Rodham Library, Nelson, N.H., 1983—. Author: Portrait of the Past (2 vols.), 1972-73; Looking Back: Images of New England 1860-1930, 1982; The Wellesley Cookie Exchange Cookbook, 1986. Editor: Wisconsin, A State for All Seasons, 1972. Contbr. articles in field, including 70 interviews for Gt. New Eng. Cooks series Yankee mag., 1978-86. Home: Old Stoddard Rd Nelson NH 03457 Office: Dublin NH 03444

MAHNKEN, DIANA LYNN, nurse; b. Freeport, N.Y., Jan. 23, 1960. B.S. in Nursing, Wagner Coll., Staten Island, N.Y., 1981; M.Nursing, UCLA, 1985. Charge nurse Kessler B. Meml. Hosp., Hermmonton, N.J., 1982-83, Placentia-Linda Hosp., Calif., 1983; assoc. primary nurse Children's Hosp. Orange County, Calif., 1983-85; primary nurse cardiovascular/surg. ICU; Children's Hosp. of Boston, 1985—; clin. preceptor B.S. Nursing Programs, Orange County, 1984-85; clin. instr. Mass. Bay Community Coll. Tech. cons. Jour. of Pediatrics, 1985—. Editor: (teaching plan) Teaching Intermittent Self Catheterization, 1985. Mem. Am. Nurses Assn., Sigma Theta Tau. Home: 516 Pincus Ave Northfield NJ 08225

MAHOLMES, VALERIE, adult education counselor, consultant; b. Detroit, June 23, 1959; d. Spencer Lee and Mary Elizabeth (Lewis) M. B.A. in English, Montclair State Coll., 1980, M.A. in Counseling, Human Services and Guidance, 1984. Cert. tchr. secondary edn., cert. tchr. devel. edn., N.J. English tutor Passaic County Coll., Paterson, N.J., 1980; admissions counselor Caldwell Coll., N.J., 1980-81; acad. adviser, 1981-82, dir. admissions, 1982-83; counselor Montclair State Coll., Upper Montclair, N.J., 1983-84; intake counselor N.J. Dept. Edn., Newark, 1984—; tchr. Christian edn. Zion Holy Ch., Newark, 1976—; cons. writing and reading, workshop facilitator Ednl. Opportunity Fund, Montclair, N.J., 1986—. Editor, creator From the Pres.'s Desk nat. newsletter, 1986. Contbr. pub. info. articles to newspapers, 1985-86. Nat. children's music dir. Nat. Youth Conv., Phila., 1981—, corr. sec., 1983—. Black Alumni Assn. scholar Montclair State Coll., Upper Montclair, 1977. Mem. Nat. Assn. Female Execs., N.J. Assn. Black Educators (newsletter editor 1981-82), Assn. Black Women in Higher Edn. Democrat. Mem. Pentecostal Ch. Avocations: public speaking; music; reading; researching. Home: 27 Halsey Ave Rockaway NJ 07866

MAHON, MARGARET MARY, manufacturing company executive; b. Crossmolina, Ireland, Nov. 19, 1928; came to U.S., 1951, naturalized, 1970; d. Patrick John and Mary Christina (McNamara) M.; B.S., Fordham U., 1974, M.B.A., 1977. Sec., NCR Corp., N.Y.C., 1951-54, 63-74, adminstrv. specialist, 1974-77, dist. sect. mgr., 1977-78, N.Y. dist. adminstrv. mgr., 1978—; mgr. family bus., 1954-63. Mem. Assn. M.B.A. Execs., Grad. Bus. Alumni Assn. Fordham U., N.Y. C. of C. and Industry. Roman Catholic. Club: Lake Isle Country. Home: 12 Yonkers Ave Tuckahoe NY 10707 Office: 50 Rockefeller Plaza New York NY 10020

MAHONE, BARBARA JEAN, labor relations exec.; b. Tuskegee, Ala., Apr. 19, 1946; d. Fred D. and Sarah Lou (Simpson) Mahone; B.S., Ohio State U., 1968; M.B.A., U. Mich., 1972; postgrad. Harvard U., 1980. Systems analyst Gen. Motors Corp., Detroit, 1968-71; staff assignment/sr. staff asst., 1973-75, mgr. career planning, 1975-77, exec.-in-tng., 1978, dir. personnel adminstrn., Rochester (N.Y.) Product Div., 1979-82, mgr. indsl. relations Packard Electric div., Warren, Ohio, 1982-83; chmn. Fed. Labor Relations Authority, Washington, 1983-84; dir. human resources mgmt. Gen. Motors Corp., 1984—. Bd. dirs. ARC, Rochester, 1979—, Urban League of Rochester, 1979—, Rochester Area Multiple Sclerosis, 1980—; mem. YMCA human resources com., 1979-82; mem. United Way allocation com., 1981-82. Named one of 10 outstanding women in Mich., Redbook Mag., 1978. Mem. Nat. Black M.B.A. Assn. (bd. dirs. 1975—, Outstanding M.B.A. of Yr. award 1981), Nat. Council Negro Women (exec. com., Mary McLeod Bethune award 1977). Home: 265 Orange Lake Dr Bloomfield Hills MI 48013

MAHONEY, COLETTE, college president, biologist; b. Jamaica, N.Y., July 19, 1926; d. Timothy and Lillian (Boylan) M.; B.S., Marymount Coll., 1949, LL.D. (hon.), 1973; M.S., Fordham U., 1952, Ph.D., 1961; H.H.D. (hon.), St. Francis de Sales, 1974; LL.D. (hon.), Manhattan Coll., 1982. Joined Religious of Sacred Heart of Mary, 1945; tchr. biology Acad. Sacred Heart of Mary, N.Y.C., 1947-57, prin., 1965-67; instr. biology Marymount Coll., Arlington, Va., 1957-61, also chmn. sci. dept.; assoc. prof. biology Marymount Coll., Tarrytown, N.Y., 1961-65; pres., trustee Marymount Manhattan Coll., N.Y.C., 1967—; dir. Manhattan Life Ins. Co., Jack Lenor Larsen, Inc.; nominating com. Am. Stock Exchange, 1980-82. Mem. Pres.' Adv. Com. Econ. Role of Women, 1973-74; mem. Commn. Status of Women; commr. Middle States Assn., Women's Coll. Coalition; bd. advisors China Inst. Am., Inc., Burn Ctr. of N.Y. Hosp., Com. for Adult Learning at Coll. Bd., Pres.' Commn. on White House Fellowships, 1983-84, scholars program William T. Grant Found., 1981-84 bd. dirs. Inst. Mediation and Conflict Resolution, Fordham Prep. Sch., 1979-82, Yorkville Civic Council, Council Career Planning, Inc., Council Ind. Colls.; pres. Women's Forum, 1979; trustee Coll. Boca Raton, Marymount Coll., Tarrytown, N.Y., 1980-82, Mt. St. Mary's Coll., 1979-82; mem. David Rockefeller's N.Y.C. Partnership Task Force for Youth Employment, 1980-82. Recipient Extraordinary Woman of Achievement award NCCJ, 1978, Brotherhood award NAACP, 1980, Pres.' award Malcolm-King Harlem Coll. Extension, 1980, Pres.' medal Hunter Coll., 1983, Hoey award for interracial justice, 1983; decorated Cavaliere Order of Merit (Italy). Fellow AAUW; mem. Am. Assn. Higher Edn. (dir.), Am. Inst. Biol. Scis., N.Y. Acad. Scis., N.Y. Bus. and Profl. Women's Assn., N.Y. State Legis. Inst. Contbr. articles on biology to sci. publs. Office: Marymount Manhattan College New York NY 10021

MAHONEY, CORA ELIZABETH, county official; b. Gandy, Nebr., Mar. 15, 1925; d. Charles W. and Sylvia G. (Kelley) Druery; m. Harry G. Hoenig, Feb. 7, 1945 (div. 1958); children—Shirley M., Jeanne M.; m. Thomas W. Mahoney, Dec. 17, 1955; 1 child, Thomas J. Grad. high sch., Gandy, Nebr. Tchr. sch. dist. #29, Logan County, Nebr., 1941-42; clk.-typist U.S. Army, Fort Belvoir, Va., 1942-43, Fort Warren, Wyo., 1944-45; office mgr. U.S. Govt. Office Price Stabilization, Stapleton, Nebr., 1943-44; legal sec. H.E. Dress, Stapleton, Nebr., 1948-52; dep. county clk. Logan County, Nebr., 1952-75, county clk., 1975—; pvt. practice bonded abstracter, Logan County, 1952-80. Mem. Nebr. Assn. County Ofcls., Nebr. Tax Research Council. Avocations: travel; music; reading. Home: PO Box 87 Stapleton NE 69163 Office: PO Box 8 Stapleton NE 69163

MAHONEY, HEIDI LYON, State higher education administrator; b. Buffalo, N.Y., Nov. 14, 1930; d. James Henry and Mary Dorothy (Kaiser) Lyon; m. David John Mahoney, Feb. 19, 1955; children—David, Neal, John. B.S. in Edn., SUNY Coll. at Buffalo, 1952; M.L.S., SUNY-Geneseo, 1968; Ph.D., SUNY-Buffalo, 1978. Librarian, SUNY Coll. at Buffalo, 1970-74, adminstr., 1974-83; asst. commr. postsec. edn. policy analysis Dept. Edn. State N.Y., Albany, 1983—; N.Y. state coordinator Am. Council on Edn. Nat. Indentification Program for Women Adminstrs., Albany, 1981—; panelist, seminars and confs. Contbr. articles to profl. jours. Bd. dirs. Blind Assn., Western N.Y., 1982. Mem. Am. Assn. Higher Edn., Assn. Instl. Research, Assn. for Study of Higher Edn. Roman Catholic. Office: N Y State Edn Dept Room 5B44 CEC Albany NY 12234

MAHONEY, JANE LAURA, real estate company executive; b. Danville, Ill., May 21, 1942; d. Niels Christian and Jane Ellen (Mellick) Nielsen; m. Robert L. Mahoney, May 23, 1964 (div. June 1981); children—Tamara Jane, Michael Timothy. A.A., Monticello Coll., 1962; student U. Colo. Real Estate Inst., 1962-63, U. Real Estate Inst., Denver, 1973-82. Sales, fashion show coordinator Neusteters, Boulder, Colo., 1963-64; saleswoman, buyer Elli of Aspen, Colo., 1964-66; owner, broker, mgr. Mahoney & Co. Realtors, Denver, 1973-83; pres., broker, founder, mgr. Preferred Properties, Inc., Denver, 1983—. Active, East Washington Park Neighborhood Orgn., Denver, 1970-76; originator Washington Park Early Learning Ctr., 1972; fund raiser, co-chmn. city life com. Denver Pub. Schs., 1983—; fund raiser Denver Symphony Marathon, 1984. Mem. Denver Bd. Realtors (co-chmn. city life com. 1983, chmn. 1984, bd. dirs.1984—, Salesperson of Yr. 1985), Nat. Assn. Realtors, Colo. Assn. Realtors. Republican. Club: Soroptimist. Avocations: gardening; cooking; biking; dancing; sailing. Office: Preferred Properties Inc 1041 S Gaylord Denver CO 80209

MAHONEY, MARGARET ANN, judge; b. Alliance, Nebr., Apr. 22, 1949; d. John Charles and Grace Margaret (Hoban) M.; B.A. (Nat. Merit scholar), Coll. of St. Catherine, 1971; J.D. cum laude, U. Minn., 1974; m. Peter B. Ogren, June 28, 1980. Admitted to Minn. bar, 1974, Fla. bar, 1975; shareholder firm Stringer, Courtney & Rohleder, Ltd., St. Paul, 1974-84; U.S. bankruptcy judge Dist. Minn., Mpls., 1984—. Mem. Fed. Bar Assn., Minn. Bar Assn., Ramsey County Bar Assn., Minn. Women Lawyers, Fla. Bar Assn., Phi Beta Kappa, Sigma Delta Pi. Office: US Bankruptcy Ct 600 Galaxy Bldg Minneapolis MN 55401

MAHONEY, MARGARET ELLERBE, foundation executive; b. Nashville, Oct. 24, 1924; d. Charles Hallam and Leslie Nelson (Savage) M.; B.A. magna cum laude, Vanderbilt U., 1946; L.H.D. (hon.), Meharry Med. Coll., 1977, U. Fla., 1980, Med. Coll. Pa., 1982. Williams Coll., 1983, Smith Coll., 1985, Beaver Coll., 1985. Fgn. affairs officer State Dept., Washington, 1946-53; exec. assoc., assoc. sec. Carnegie Corp., N.Y.C., 1953-72; v.p. Robert Wood Johnson Found., Princeton, N.J., 1972-80; pres. Commonwealth Fund, N.Y.C., 1980—; trustee John D. and Catherine T. Mac Arthur Found., 1985—, Hosp. Research and Ednl. Trust, 1983—, Dole Found., 1984—; vis. fellow Sch. Architecture and Urban Planning, Princeton U., 1973-80. bd. dirs. Council on Found., 1982—; mem. N.Y.C. Commn. on the Yr. 2000, 1985—, MIT Corp., 1984—, Johns Hopkins Nat. Forum for Medicine; vestrywoman Parish of Trinity Ch., 1982—; mem. nat. adv. council Johns Hopkins U. Sch. Medicine, 1983—. Recipient Frank H. Lahey Meml. award, 1984, Alpha Omega Alpha award, 1985. Mem. AAAS, Inst. Medicine, Council Fgn. Relations. Contbr. articles to profl. publs. Office: Commonwealth Fund 1 E 75th St New York NY 10021

MAHONEY, RUBY GEORGINA, nurse; b. Newark, Jan. 4, 1928; d. Mervyn Victor Thomas and Josephine Marion (Jewell) Haines; m. Edward Paul Mahoney, Sept. 11, 1948; children—Carol, Connie, Cristie, Donald. R.N., Mountainside Hosp., Montclair, N.J., 1948. Head nurse pediatrics Middlesex Hosp., New Brunswick, N.J., 1948-49; staff nurse Rutgers U., 1949-51; office nurse, surg. asst. to doctor, New Brunswick, 1951-55; part-time charge nurse Merry Heart Nursing Home, Succasunna, N.J., 1974-77; home nursing instr. vol. ARC, West Chester, Pa., 1982—; Southeastern Pa. sub chmn. ARC Plann II Bloodmobile Nurses; camp nurse Donegal Presbyn., South York County, Pa., 1982-84; owner operator Sandwich Shop, Sydney (Australia), 1969. Deacon, Kennett Presbyn. Ch., 1984—. Mem. Assn. Disaster Nurses (chmn. Brandywine br. 1986—). Republican. Clubs: Roxbury-Mt. Olive Newcomers (charter pres. 1974-75); Kennett S. Area Newcomers (v.p. 1982-83), Homesteaders (v.p. 1984-85); Am. Women's of Taunus (tour chmn. 1978-80) (Frankfurt, Germany). Avocations: swimming; flower arranging; golfing; aerobics; choir. Home: 409 Taylor Ln KennettSquare PA 19348

MAHOOD, HELEN MAYNARD, advertising company executive; b. Summit, N.J., Nov. 16, 1953; d. Joseph and Mildred Evelyn (Thompson) M. B.A., Bates Coll., 1975; M.B.A., U. Conn., 1984. Staff mgr. advt. So. New Eng. Telephone Co., New Haven, 1979-83; acct. supr. Young & Rubicam, Los Angeles, 1983-84; dir. mktg. Geneva Corp., Costa Mesa, Calif., 1984-85; v.p. Tracy-Locke Direct, Dallas, 1985—. Founder, pres. S. central chpt. Alzheimers Disease and Related Disorders Assn., New Haven, 1983, mem., speaker, Dallas, 1985—. Mem. Dir. Mktg. Assn., Nat. Assn. Female Execs. Avocation: classical piano. Office: Tracy-Locke Dir 600 N Pearl St Dallas TX 75201

MAIDES, SHIRLEY ALLEN, psychologist; b. Roanoke Rapids, N.C., Sept. 16, 1951; d. John Thomas and Mary Shirley (Allen) Maides; B.A. with honors in Psychology, U. N.C., 1973; M.A., Vanderbilt U., 1975, Ph.D., 1978; m. John Thomas Keane, Nov. 8, 1980. Clin. psychology intern U. Calif. Med. Center, Davis, 1977-78; USPHS fellow U. Chgo. and Michael Reese Hosp., 1978-79; sr. supervising psychologist Incentives Inst., Des Plaines, Ill., 1980-81; pvt. practice psychology, Chgo., 1981—; account exec. N.P.D. Research, Rosemont, Ill., 1982—. USPHS clin. psychology fellow, 1974-77; USPHS Nat. Research Scientist, awardee, 1978-79. Mem. Am. Psychol. Assn., Am. Assn. Biofeedback Clinicians, Assn. Women in Psychology, Ill. Psychol. Assn. Democrat. Methodist. Contbr. articles to various publs. Office: Psychol Resources 20110 Governors Dr Suite 200 Olympia Fields IL 60461

MAIER, PAULINE, history educator; b. St. Paul, Apr. 27, 1938; d. Irvin Louis and Charlotte (Winterer) Rubbelke; A.B., Radcliffe Coll., 1960; postgrad. London Sch. Econs., 1960-61; Ph.D. in History, Harvard U., 1968; m. Charles Steven Maier, June 17, 1961; children—Andrea Nicole, Nicholas Winterer, Jessica Elizabeth Heine. Asst. prof., then assoc. prof. history U. Mass., Boston, 1968-77; Robinson-Edwards prof. history U. Wis., Madison, 1977-78; prof. history MIT, Cambridge, 1978—; mem. council Inst. Early Am. History, 1982-84. Recipient Douglass Adair award Claremont Grad. Sch.-Inst. Early Am. History, 1976, Kidger award New Eng. History Tchrs. Assn., 1981; fellow Nat. Endowment Humanities, 1974-75; Charles Warren fellow, 1974-75. Mem. Orgn. Am. Historians (exec. bd. 1978-82), Am. Hist. Assn. (nominations com. 1983-85, chmn. 1985), Soc. Am. Historians, Am. Antiquarian Soc. (exec. council 1984—), Colonial Soc. Mass., Mass. Hist. Soc. Author: From Resistance to Revolution: Colonial Radicals and the Development of American Opposition to Britain, 1765-1766, 1972; The Old Revolutionaries: Political Lives in the Age of Samuel Adams, 1980; The American People: A History, 1986. Home: 60 Larchwood Dr Cambridge MA 02138 Office: MIT E51-216 Cambridge MA 02139

MAIL, PATRICIA DAVISON, public health specialist; b. Kamloops, B.C., Can., Dec. 10, 1940; d. George Allen and Constance (Davison) M.; B.S., U. Ariz., 1963, M.A., 1970; M.S., Smith Coll., 1965; M.P.H., Yale U., 1967; postgrad. Seattle U., 1974. Commd. officer USPHS, 1970—, chief health edn. br. Portland Indian Health Service, 1979—; mem. faculty Seattle U., 1974-78. Recipient Early Career award Public Health Edn. sect. Am. Public Health Assn., 1979; USPHS Service Plaque, 1979, 86; USPHS Commendation medal, 1981, 86; USPHS trainee Yale U., 1965-67; NDEA grantee, 1968-70. Mem. Am. Public Health Assn., Soc. Public Health Edn., Med. Anthropology Soc., Soc. Applied Anthropology, Am. Sch. Health Assn., AAAS, AAHPER, Commd. Officers Assn. USPHS, Smith Coll. Alumnae Assn. Episcopalian. Club: Dorian Group. Author: (with D.R. McDonald) Tulapai to Tokay, 1980; editor SOPHE Sounds, 1976-86; contbr. articles to profl. jours. Home: 35214 28th Ave S Federal Way WA 98003 Office: Fed Center S 4735 E Marginal Way S Seattle WA 98134

MAILMAN, VIRGINIA SHEVLIN ADDISON (MRS. NORTON W. MAILMAN), public relations executive; b. Bronxville, N.Y., Apr. 27, 1929; d. Matthew Joseph and Virginia Boyd (McMillan) Shevlin; student U. Colo., 1947-49; B.A., Stanford, m. Norton W. Mailman, June 17, 1965; children—Bruce Addison, Matthew Addison, Christopher. Recruiter with industry A.R.C. Blood Program, Los Angeles, 1951-52; reporter Life mag., N.Y.C., 1952-61; asso. editor, asst. New York Bur. chief Show Bus. Illustrated, 1961-62; formed pub. relations firm Addison, Goldstein & Walsh, Inc., N.Y.C., 1962, v.p., 1962-76; formed Syndicated Airtime, producer 5 minute radio series, 1970; producer James Beard Cook-Along cassette series, 1973; patient relations rep. N. Shore Univ. Hosp., 1977—. Bd. dirs. N.Y. affiliate Nat. Council Alcoholism, 1978—. Club: Piping Rock (Locust Valley, N.Y.). Home: 109 E 69th St New York NY 10021

MAIO, SUSAN JANE, cosmetology school executive; b. Potsdam, N.Y., June 15, 1943; d. Earl Bernard and Ruth Hartford (Halliday) Sullivan; m. Dominick Patsy Maio, Aug. 18, 1963 (div. 1978); children—Joseph Donald, Regina Ruth Maio Frijo. Student, Univ. Coll., 1961-62, SUNY-Oswego, 1983. Hairstylist DeToto's Beauty Salon, Syracuse, N.Y., 1973-74; admissions adminstr., tchr. LePonto's Beauty Sch., Syracuse, 1974-78; salon mgr. Haircrafters, Syracuse, 1978-80; asst. dir. Phillips Inst., Syracuse, 1980-84; salon owner, mgr. Profl. Image, Syracuse, 1981-85; sch. owner, dir. LePonto's Hairstyling Sch., Watertown, N.Y., 1984—. Mem. N.Y. State Fin. Aid Adminstrs. Assn., Nat. Assn. Cosmetology Schs., Nat. Hairdressers Assn., N.Y. State Hairdressers Assn., N.Y. State Beauty Sch. Assn. Office: LePonto's Hairstyling Sch of Watertown Inc 75 Public Square Watertown NY 13601

MAIORISI, CATHERINE THERESA, data processing consulting company executive; b. Hackensack, N.J., Mar. 23, 1938; d. George and Helen (Spagnuolo) M.; B.A., Douglass Coll., 1960; M.A., Fairleigh Dickenson U., 1966. Statis. analyst A. C. Nielsen Co., N.Y.C., 1960-63; programmer Home Ins. Co., N.Y.C., 1963-64; systems rep. Honeywell, Inc., N.Y.C., 1964-66; systems analyst, project leader Colgate-Palmolive, N.Y.C., 1966-70; asst. v.p. systems and programming Group Health, Inc., N.Y.C., 1970-76; mng. cons Data Architects, Inc., Waltham, Mass., 1976-79; owner, pres. Computer

Concepts, Inc., N.Y.C., 1979—; dir. Pension Parameters, Inc. Co-chmn. bd. dirs. Fund for Human Dignity; mem. N.Y. State Adv. Council Minority and Women-Owned Bus. Enterprise; del., co-chair N.Y. State del. to White House Conf. Small Bus. Recipient Women in Bus. Advocate of Yr. award N.Y. Chamber Commerce and Industry. Mem. Nat. Assn. Women Bus. Owners (pres. N.Y.chpt., dir.), Assn. Systems Mgmt., Networks Unltd., Inc., Soc. Mgmt. Info. Systems, Women in Info. Processing, Inc., NOW. Office: 928 Broadway New York NY 10010

MAIRE, SUSAN STIEN, lawyer; b. Cambridge, Mass., July 6, 1933; d. Joseph William and Dorothy (Cassedy) Stien; m. Max S. Maire, June 7, 1950 (div. 1975); children—Stephen T., Katherine E., Jennifer C.; m. Wilbert B. Fisher, 1985. B.A., Harvard U., 1968; J.D., Northeastern U., 1972. Bar: Mass. 1973, N.H. 1985. Clk. ROIT Corp., Westwood, Mass., 1972-73; assoc. Howard & Clancy, Westwood, 1973-76; sole practice, Dedham, Mass., 1976-84; ptnr. Maire and Fisher, P.A., Kensington, N.H., 1984—; lectr. law Lincoln Coll., Northeastern U., Boston, 1984—. Author: How To Raise And Train An English Setter, 1963. Mem. N.H. Bar Assn., Mass. Bar Assn., Norfolk County Bar Assn., Essex County Bar Assn., Assn. Trial Lawyers Am. Republican. Roman Catholic. Club: English Setter Club of New Eng. Avocations: skiing; golf; shooting. Home: Route 107 South Rd Kensington NH 03827 Office: Maire and Fisher PA PO Box 425 Seabrook NH 03874

MAISONET, BRICEIDA, esthetician; b. Pomona, Calif., Oct. 16, 1950; d. Fernando H. and Ruth (Godoy) Lopez; m. Carlos Daniel Vega, Aug. 9, 1975 (div. 1980); children—Rachel Ennette, Jason Scott; m. 2d, Carlos Antonio Maisonet, May 22, 1982. Contract adminstrv. asst. Kaiser, Fontana, Calif., 1972-75; personnel dir., 1975-77; model Calif. Girls, Santa Monica, Calif., 1975-77; esthetician, owner About Face Skin Care Clinic, Brea, Calif., 1977—. Bd. dirs. Am. Inst. Esthetics, Huntington Beach, Calif., 1978-83, Dirs. award of achievement, 1979, 81, 82, 83, award of merit, 1980. Mem. Asthetics Internat. Assn. (pres. 1981-82), Centre Internat. Des Etudes Esthetique, Berea C. of C. Democrat. Office: About Face Skin Care Clinic 1027 E Imperial Hwy D3 Brea CA 92621

MAISSEL, RAINA EVE, lawyer; b. London, Apr. 12, 1931; came to U.S., 1956; d. Louis and Golde Pearl (Crowne) Corren; m. Leon Israel Maissel, Jan. 22, 1956; children—Simon Joseph, Gerda Sharon, Joseph Saul. LL.B., Univ. Coll. London, 1952. Barrister-at-law Eng. 1953; bar: N.Y. 1977, U.S. Dist. Ct. (so. dist.) N.Y. 1979, U.S. Dist. Ct. (ea. dist.) N.Y. 1979, U.S. Supreme Ct. 1982. Pupil to Hon. S.C. Silkin, London, 1953-54; sole practice, Bournemouth, Eng., 1954-56; research assoc. Ballard, Spahr et al, Phila., 1956-58; counsel Moran, Spiegel, et al, Poughkeepsie, N.Y., 1977-80; sole practice, Wappingers Falls, N.Y., 1980—. Vice pres. Dutchess County Players, Poughkeepsie, 1962-64; pres. Merrywood Civic Assn., 1972-74; mem. 1st ward com. Democratic party, Poughkeepsie, 1973-74; mem. Poughkeepsie Zoning Bd. Appeals, 1982-83. Mem. ABA, N.Y. State Bar Assn., N.Y. State Bar (com. on mental and phys. disabilities), Dutchess County Bar (exec. com. 1984—). Jewish. Home and office: 16 Smoke Rise Ln Wappingers Falls NY 12590

MAISTROVICH, JANET ANN, human resources executive; b. Davenport, Iowa, Dec. 16, 1950; d. William Charles and Ann Adele (Kill) Leaf; m. Mark Frederick Maistrovich, Aug. 30, 1980; 1 child, Jesse. B.A., U. Minn., 1973. Counselor, St. Jospehs's Home for Children, Mpls., 1973-74; program asst. Employer Edn. Service, U. Minn., Mpls., 1974-75; v.p. Employee Relations Cons. Inc., Mpls., 1975-80; mgr. Brown & Bigelow, St. Paul, 1980-84; dir. human resources Opus Corp., Mpls., 1984—; assoc. dir. Minn. State Adv. Council for Vocat. Edn., Mpls., 1975-79. U. Minn., Coll. St. Teresa scholar, 1969. Mem. Am. Soc. Personnel Adminstrn., Am. Compensation Assn., Adminstrv. Mgmt. Soc., Nat. Assn. Female Execs., Twin Cities Personnel Assn. Avocations: piano; painting; reading; dancing. Home: 533 Arthur St Edina MN 55343 Office: Opus Corp 9900 Bren Rd E Minnetonka MN 55343

MAIXNER, NANCY W(HEELWRIGHT), rehabilitation coordinator; b. Washington, July 4, 1952; d. David Page and Arabelle (Leonard) Wheelwright; m. Richard Charles Maixner, Jan. 7, 1976 (div. 1980); 1 dau., Sara Elizabeth. B.F.A. in Journalism, So. Meth. U., 1974. Tennis profl. Bent Tree Country Club, Dallas, 1974-77; dir. advt. Nardis of Dallas, 1977-80, account exec. DDO & H Advt., Dallas, 1980-82; asst. mktg. Network Security, Dallas, 1982; rehab. coordinator Richard S. Gold, Dallas; facilitator Dallas Head Injury Found. Bd. dirs., sec. Freedom Ride Found., Southlake, Tex. Mem. Internat. Assn. Logopedics and Phoniatrics. Republican. Presbyterian. Home: 6740 Town Bluff Dallas TX 75240

MAJOROS, MARY ELIZABETH, nurse, emergency medical technician; b. Trenton, N.J., Aug. 26, 1946; d. Thomas Bernard and Jean Marie (Williams) Driber; m. John William Majoros, Nov. 16, 1968; 1 dau., Susan Ellen. Lic. practical nurse Trenton Tech. Nursing Sch., 1965; emergency med. technician Trenton Sch. Emergency Med. Tech., 1965. Cert. emergency med. technician, CPR. Staff nurse St. Francis Med. Center, Trenton, 1965-71; medication and charge nurse Green Wood House, Trenton, 1971-74; staff nurse Hamilton Hosp., Trenton, 1974-77, 80—; nurse Martin's Ambulance, Trenton, 1977-80, Patient's Ambulance Service, 1983-84; nurse Florence Crittenton Home, Trenton, N.J., 1985-86; emergency med. technician, life mem. Liberty Rescue Squad, Trenton, 1964—, sgt.-at-arms, 1973—, sec. 1964-73; nurse Florence Crittenton Home, 1985—; reading tchr. Holy Cross Sch., Trenton, 1981-84. Recipient Disting. Leadership award for contbns. to nursing, 1985— Mem. Hamilton Twp. Crime Watch Unit, 1984—. Mem. Notre Dame High Sch. Alumni Assn. (class rep. Lawrenceville 1980). Democrat. Roman Catholic. Club: Goebel Collectors. Home: 839 Lalor St Trenton NJ 08610

MAJORS, JUDITH SOLEY, writer, health educator; b. Portland, Oreg., June 17, 1946; d. Alford H. and Leora L. (Carpenter) Soley; B.A., Marylhurst Coll., 1980; A.A., Mt. Hood Community Coll., 1970; m. Jack B. Majors, Mar. 18, 1967; 1 dau., Carrie. Sr. editor Apple Press, Milwaukie, Oreg., 1978—; local TV personality; author; works include: Sugar Free—That's Me, 1978; Sugar Free—Kid's Cookery, 1979; Sugar Free—Microwavery, 1980; Diet Out—Oregon, 1981; Meatless Wonder, 1982; Sugar Free ... Sweets and Treats, 1983. Bd. dirs. Oreg. Diabetes Assn.; adv. bd. North Clackamas Sch. Dist.; mem. Milwaukie Citizens Adv. Com.; bd. dirs. Milwaukie Festival Daze. Mem. Am. Assn. Diabetes Educators, Am. Diabetes Assn. (profl.), Nat. Fedn. Presswomen, Women in Communications, Willamette Writers, Oreg. Community Edn. Assn. Democrat. Home and Office: 5536 SE Harlow St Milwaukie OR 97222

MAKER, LYNNE DIANE, editor, writer; b. St. Paul, Mar. 30, 1960; d. Julius Warren and Jeannette June (Topel) M. B.A. summa cum laude, Coll. of St. Thomas, 1982. Nat. editor Deluxe Check Printers Inc., St. Paul, 1982—. Participant U.S. Figure Skating Assn. Meml. Fund Benefit Shows, Bloomington, Minn., 1976-77; mem. North Starlettes Precision Team, St. Paul, 1979; pub. relations intern St. Paul Council Camp Fire, 1982. Lutheran Brotherhood scholar, 1979-80; St. Thomas Disting. scholar, 1978-82. Mem. Internat. Assn. Bus. Communicators (North Star chpt.), The Loft: A Place for Writing and Lit., Sierra Club, Delta Epsilon Sigma. Mem. United Ch. of Christ. Club: Roseville Figure Skating.

MAKI, PATRICIA CAROLINE, financial executive; b. Berwyn, Ill., July 15, 1951; d. Edward Stanley and Caroline Lillian (Zalewski) M. B.S. in Accountancy cum laude, U. Ill., 1973. C.P.A., Ill. Audit sr. Price Waterhouse & Co., Chgo., 1973-76; regional controller McDonald's, Dallas, 1977-79; corp. acctg. mgr. Sangamo Weston, Atlanta, 1979-80; dir. ops. fin. analysis Cox Cable Communications, Atlanta, 1980—. Mem. Am. Inst. C.P.A.s, Ga. Soc. C.P.A.s, Am. Women's Soc. C.P.A.s, Nat. Assn. Female Execs. Roman Catholic. Home: 2297 Macby Ct NE Marietta GA 30066 Office: Cox Cable Communications 1400 Lake Hearn Dr Atlanta GA 30319

MAKINO, RENEE CHARLOTTE, marketing research executive; b. Rotterdam, Holland, Feb. 23, 1945; came to Can., 1952, naturalized, 1958; d. Bernard and Johanna J. (DeWit) Schriel; m. Kenji Makino, Sept. 21, 1967; children—Naomi Kay, Julia Yumi. B.A. with honors, York U., Toronto, Ont., Can., 1967. Research asst. McDonald Research Ltd., Donn Mills., Ont., Can., 1967, McCann-Erickson, Toronto, 1967-68, Simpsons-Sears, Ltd., Toronto, 1968-69; exec. asst. Continental Grain Co., Tokyo, 1970-71; mgr. catalogue circulation mktg. Simpson-Sears Ltd., Toronto, 1972-76; mgr. mktg. research Levi Strauss Can. Ltd., Don Mills, 1976-79, Harlequin Enterprises, Don Mills., 1980-83; dir. mktg. research Royal Trust Corp., Toronto, 1984—. Mem. Am. Mktg. Assn., Profl. Mktg. Research Soc. Office: Royal Trust Corp Toronto Dominion Tower 45th Floor PO Box 7500 Sta A Toronto ON M5W 1P9 Canada

MAKINS, DICY OLIVIA, technical writer; b. Kansas City, Kans., July 7, 1951; d. Clifford Lloyd and Edna Mae (Chisholm) M.; B.A. in Biology, Claremont Coll., 1973; postgrad. Drexel U., 1979. Fellow spl. cancer virus group U. So. Calif., Los Angeles, 1972; adv. enrichment program for high sch. minority students interested in health professions U. So. Calif. Sch. Medicine, Los Angeles, 1973; bus. assoc. R. C. Med. Carrier, Phila., 1981-83. Instr. elem. sch. children Presbyn. Ch., Pasadena. Meth. Found. grantee, 1971-81. Mem. Soc. Tech. Communications (bibliography com.). Methodist.

MAKUPSON, AMYRE PORTER, TV exec.; b. River Rouge, Mich., Sept. 30, 1947; d. Rudolph Hannibal and Amyre Ann (Porche) Porter; B.A., Fisk U., 1970; M.A., Am. U., Washington, 1972; m. Walter H. Makupson, Nov. 1, 1975; children: Rudolph Porter, Amyre Nisi. Asst. news dir. Sta. WGPR-TV, Detroit, 1975-76; public relations dir. Mich. Health Maintenance Orgn., Detroit, 1974-76, Kirwood Gen. Hosp., Detroit, 1976-77; news and pub. affairs mgr. Sta. WKBD-TV, Southfield, Mich., 1977—. Mem. adv. com. Mich. Arthritis Found.; pres. bd. dirs. Detroit Wheelchair Athletic Assn.; mem. adv. com. Cystic Fibrosis Soc.; bd. dirs. Barat House, Kids In Need of Direction; exec. com. March of Dimes. Recipient numerous service awards, including: Arthritis Found. Mich., Mich. Mchts. Assn., DAV, Jr. Achievement, City of Detroit, Salvation Army. Mem. Pub. Relations Soc. Am., Am. Women in Radio and TV (Outstanding Achievement award 1981), Women in Communications, Nat. Acad. TV Arts and Scis., Pub. Relations Soc. Am., Detroit Press Club, Ad-Craft. Roman Catholic. Office: 26955 W 11 Mile Rd Southfield MI 48034

MALANEY, MARILYN SUE, educator; b. Perryton, Tex., Oct. 15, 1944; d. Dempsey E. and Ruby Lee (Jackson) M. B.B.A., West Tex. State U., 1967; M.A., Prairie View A&M, 1985. Tchr. Cy-Fair Ind. Sch. Dist., Houston, 1976-85, Houston Ind. Sch. Dist., 1967-76. Bd. dirs. Beekman Place Community Improvement Assn., Houston, 1982-85. Mem. Bus. Edn. Assn., Tex. Profl. Edn. Assn. Republican. Baptist. Clubs: Space City Ski, Westside Tennis, Houston Tennis Umpires Assn., Houston Livestock Assn. Home: 10214 Beekman Place Dr Houston TX 77043

MALAS, CORNELIA, ret. bus. exec.; b. Cin.; d. John C. and Katherine (Farres) Malas; student U. Cin., 1940-42; bus. cert. Littleford Nelson Bus. Coll., 1943; student Schuster Martin Sch. Drama, 1943; cert. Patricia Stevens Modeling Sch., 1944; student Campbell Bus. Coll., 1956. Head central filing dept. Gruen Watch Co., Cin., 1945-50; expediter purchasing dept. MacGregor Sport Products, Cin., 1950-57; personnel adminstr. Eagle-Picher Industries, Inc., Cin., 1957-79, indsl. relations sec., 1979-82. Chmn., Rosie Reds Night at Crosley Field, Rooters Organized to Stimulate Interest and Enthusiasm in Cin. Reds Baseball Team, 1967, v.p., 1971, trustee, 1971-79, pres., 1975-76; mem. women's com. Nat. Gov.'s Conf., 1968; mem. ticket com. Cin. Symphony Orch., 1968; publicity chmn. May Festival, 1969, mem. women's com., 1971-73; mem. Women's com. United Fine Arts, 1973-75; mem. women's com. Cin. Art Mus., 1983—; judge Jr. Achievement, 1965, 67; bd. trustees. Opera Guild, 1980-84. Mem. Profl. Secs. Internat. (pres. Ohio div. 1969-70), Internat. Assn. for Personnel Women, Cin. Personnel Assn., Adminstrv. Mgmt. Soc., Alpha Delta Pi. Clubs: Hyde Park Golf and Country, Wyoming (Ohio) Women's, Cincinnati, Internat. Toastmistress, Williams (pres. 1966-67). Home: 9303 Constitution Dr Cincinnati OH 45215

MALBOUVIER, KATHRYN ANNE VERONICA, microwave electrical engineer; b. N.Y.C., Apr. 18, 1954; d. William Henry and Patricia Anne (Lynch) Irwin; m. Alain Daniel Malbouvier, July 8, 1976. B.S., U. Calif.-Davis, Engr. Avantek, Folsom, Calif., 1985—. Served to lt. USAF, 1974-80, Air NG, 1980—. U. Calif.-Davis Ann. Fund scholar, 1984; Nat. Guard Assn. Calif. scholar, 1983; Elliott Kisson Meml. scholar Am. River Coll., 1981; Tenco Tractor Engring. scholar, 1983; Women's Social and Cultural League scholar, 1982; Soroptimist scholar, 1981. Mem. IEEE, Soc. Women Engrs. Republican. Roman Catholic. Avocations: architectural design; art; aerobics; weight training. Office: Avantek 104 Woodmere Rd Folsom CA 95630

MALCHON, JEANNE K., state senator; b. Newark, June 17, 1923; d. Leslie Stafford and Edith Katherine (Marcelle) Keller; m. Richard Malchon, 1946; 1 child, Richard Jr. A.A., Va. Intermont Coll., 1943. Draftsman, Curtis-Wright Propeller div., Caldwell, N.J., 1943-44; civilian employee U.S. Army, Hickam Field, Hawaii, 1944-45; merchandising rep. L. Bamberger & Co., Newark, 1946-49; with Office of Tech. Assessment Task Force, 1971; mem. Gov.'s Commn. on Criminal Justice Standards and Goals, 1981-82, Fla. Jud. Council, 1972-82; commr. Pinellas County (Fla.), 1975-82; mem. Supreme Ct. Dispute Resolution Alternatives Com., Nat. Com. and Nat. Air Quality Commn., 1978-82; mem. Fla. State Senate from Dist. 18, 1982—, chmn. Senate Select Com. on Aging, vice chmn. Senate Health and Rehab. Services Com. Mem. exec. com. Am. Lung Assn., 1977—, nat. pres., 1982-84; chmn. Nat. Air Conservation Com. 1978—. Recipient women in govt. award Soroptimists, 1979, outstanding equal opportunity efforts award Pinellas County Urban League, 1980, most effective sen. for law enforcement Fla. Sheriff's Assn., 1983, environment award, Fla. Sierra Club, 1984, outstanding legislator of the yr. Fla. Nurses Assn., 1985, legislator of the yr. Fla. Psychol. Assn., 1985, disting. service award Pinellas County Assn. Respiratory Care Mgrs., 1985. Mem. State Assn. County Commrs. (dir. 1975—, chmn. urban affairs com. 1979—), Nat. Assn.-County (criminal justice steering com. 1975—, chmn. law enforcement subcom. 1979—). Democrat. Address: 2400 Pinellas Point Dr S St Petersburg FL 33712

MALDEN, JOAN WILLIAMS, physical therapist; b. Bayshore, N.Y., Apr. 14; d. Sidney S. and Myrtle L. (Williams) Siegel; B.S., N.Y. U., 1957; m. Alan A. Chasnov, Jan. 20, 1951; children—Marc, Robin, Debra and David (twins); m. 2d, Miroslav Mladenovic, Sept. 14, 1967; 1 dau., Kristine. Phys. therapist hosps. and orgns. in N.Y.C. area, 1956-57; phys. therapist Brunswick Hosp. Center, Amityville, N.Y., 1968-69; pvt. practice phys. therapy, Wantagh, N.Y., 1968—; licensure examiner, N.Y. State; cons., tchr. in field. Contbr. articles to profl. jours. Pres. internat. scholarships com. Massapequa chpt. Am. Field Service, 1962-64. Mem. Am. Acad. Cerebral Palsy, Am. Phys. Therapy Assn. (chmn. polit. action com. N.Y. chpt., chmn. L.I. dist.), AAUW (pres. Massapequa chpt. 1962-64), N.Y. State Soc. Continuing Edn. in Phys. Therapy, Airplane Owners and Pilots Assn., Ninety-Nines, Exptl. Aviation Assn., Farmingdale Flyers (officer). Democrat. Unitarian. Home: 35 S Bay Ave Massapequa NY 11758 Office: Wantagh Med Bldg 1228 Wantagh Ave Wantagh NY 11793 also 158 E Main St Huntington NY 11743

MALDONADO-BEAR, RITA MARINITA, economist, educator; b. Vega Alta, P.R., June 14, 1938; d. Victor and Marina (Davila) Maldonado; B.A., Auburn U., 1960; Ph.D., N.Y.U., 1969; m. Larry Alan Bear, Mar. 29, 1975. With Min. Wage Bd. & Econ. Devel. Adminstrn., Govt. of P.R., 1960-64; asso. prof. fin. U. P.R., 1969-70; asst. prof. econs. Manhattan Coll., 1970-72; assoc. prof. econs. Bklyn. Coll., 1972-75; vis. assoc. prof. fin. Stanford (Calif.) Grad. Bus. Sch., 1973-74; assoc. prof. fin. and econs. Grad. Sch. Bus. Adminstrn., N.Y.U., N.Y.C., 1975-81, prof., 1981—; cons. Morgan Guaranty Trust Co., N.Y.C., 1972-77, Bank of Am., N.Y.C., 1982-84, Res. City Bankers, N.Y.C., 1978—, Swedish Inst. Mgmt., Stockholm, 1982—; dir. Medallion Funding Corp., 1985—. P.R. Econ. Devel. Adminstrn. fellow, 1960-65; Marcus Nadler fellow, N.Y.U., 1966-67, Phillip Lods Dissertation fellow, 1967-68. Mem. Am. Econs. Assn., Am. Fin. Assn., Metro. Econ. Assn. N.Y., Assn. for Social Econs. Author: Role of the Financial Sector in the Economic Development of Puerto Rico, 1970; contbr. articles to profl. jours. Home: 95 Tam o'shanter Dr Mahwah NJ 07430 Office: 100 Trinity Pl New York NY 10006

MALECEK, RITA BERNADETTE, accountant; b. St. Louis, Feb. 22, 1928; d. George Francis and Antoinette (Gebken) Malecek. B.B.S., St. Louis U., 1975, M.B.A., 1977; M.S. in Accountancy, U. Houston, 1984. C.P.A., Mo., Tex. Jr. to sr. auditor various C.P.A. firms, St. Louis, 1962-73; internal auditor Nationwide Fin. Services, St. Louis, 1973-74; acctg./office mgr. Don Lipton Realty, St. Louis, 1975-76; tchr. acctg. St. Louis U., U. Mo., St. Louis, 1977-79; pvt. practice pub. acctg., St. Louis, 1977-79; tax mgr. C.P.A. Firms, Houston, 1979-82; controller Lewis tyra Interests, Houston, 1982-84; pvt. practice acctg., Houston, 1984—; fin. cons. Parkway Gardens Condos, Creve Coeur, Mo., 1978-79; pres. Tymis Inc., Houston, 1982; pres., dir. Colonial Realty & Investment Co., St. Louis, 1965—. Active campaigns Whitmire for Mayor, 1981-83, Art Sullivan for Alderman, St. Louis, 1957-67, Cervantes for Mayor, St. Louis, 1957-67. LeClerc Coll. scholar, 1945. Mem. Am. Inst. C.P.A.s, Mo. Soc. C.P.A.s, Am. Women's Soc. C.P.A.s, St. Louis U. M.B.A. Women (v.p. 1975-76), Phi Delta Zeta. Republican. Roman Catholic. Home: 7047 Bissonnet #18 Houston TX 77074

MALECKI, JANET M., bank executive, business systems consultant; b. Erie, Pa., Feb. 23, 1957; d. Raymond John, Sr., and Alice Roberta (Harabedian) M. Student Edinboro State Coll., 1975-77; B.S. in Bus. Adminstrn., Gannon U., 1980; M.B.A., Cleve. State U., 1985; postgrad. Cleve. Marshall Law Sch., 1986. Systems engr. Electronic Data System, Dallas, 1980-81; acct. systems Glidden Div. SCM Corp., Cleve., 1981-84, bus. systems analyst, 1984-85; sr. planning analyst AmeriTrust, N.A., Cleve., 1985—. Big Sister, Big Bros./Big Sisters, Buffalo, 1980; mem. Nat. Wildlife Fedn., NOW. Mem. Am. Inst. Banking, Nat. Assn. Female Execs., Cleve. State U. M.B.A. Alumni Soc., Gannon U. Alumni Soc., Alpha Xi Delta. Democrat. Avocations: Classical piano; sailing; running; body building. Home: 2198 Rexwood Rd Cleveland Heights OH 44118 Office: AmeriTrust NA 900 Euclid Ave S-2 Cleveland OH 44114

MALESKI, CYNTHIA MARIA, lawyer; b. Natrona Heights, Pa., July 4, 1951; d. Richard Anthony and Helen Elizabeth (Palovcak) M.; m. Andrzej Gabriel Groch, Aug. 7, 1982; 1 child, Elizabeth Maria. B.A. summa cum laude, U. Pitts., 1973; student U. Rouen (France), 1970; J.D., Duquesne U., 1976. Bar: Pa. 1976, U.S. dist. ct. (we. dist.) Pa. 1976, U.S. Supreme Ct. 1980, U.S. Ct. Appeals (3d cir.) 1984. Indsl. relations adminstr. Allegheny Ludlum Industries, Inc., Brackenridge, Pa., 1972-74; law clk. Conte, Courtney, Tarasi & Price, Pitts., 1974, Paul Hammer, Pitts., 1974-76; sole practice Natrona Heights, Pa., 1978—; gen. counsel Mercy Hosp., Pitts., 1976—; bd. dirs. legal adv. bd. Catholic Health Assn., 1980-82; gen. counsel, vice chmn. nat. assembly of reps. Nat. Confedn. Am. Ethnic Groups, 1980—; health law cons. and lectr.; task force on Pa. Med. Malpractice Reform, Hosp. Assn. Pa. Co-author: The Legal Dimensions of Nursing Practice (Nurses' Book of Month Club award 1982), 1982; contbr. articles to publs. Corp. sec., legal counsel Tamburitzan Nat. Folk Arts Ctr., Pitts., 1979—; mem. Council Self-Insured Hosps. of Pa.; vice chmn. Czechoslovak room com. Nationality Rooms Program, U. Pitts., 1983; mem. Allegheny County Dem. Com., 1986—; candidate for del. Democratic Nat. Conv. 20th Pa. Congl. Dist., 1984; chmn. Com. to Re-elect U.S. Congressman Doug Walgren, 1982; Ethnic Com. for Pa. Atty. Gen., 1980, Ethnic Com. for Judge Peter Paul Olszewski, 1983; U.S. del 4th Slovak World Congress, 1981; mem. adv. bd. Children's and Youth Services, Allegheny County; soloist, speaker various groups, Pitts. Slovakians. Scholar U. Rouen, 1970; Allegheny Ludlum Industries scholar, 1969-73; Andrew Mellon scholar, 1969; tuition scholar U. Pitts., 1969-73; tuition remission grantee Duquesne U., 1975, 76; recipient acad. excellence award Duquesne U., 1976; Mem. ABA (forum com. on health law, tort and ins. sect.), Am. Soc. Hosp. Attys., Nat. Health Lawyers Assn., Soc. Hosp. Attys. of Hosp. Assn. Pa. (v.p.), Soc. Hosp. Attys. Western Pa., Pa. Bar Assn. (med.-legal com., long range planning com.), Allegheny County Bar Assn. (chmn. med.-legal com., council civil litigation sect., chmn. interprofl. code com. Allegheny County Bar Assn.-Allegheny County Med. Soc.), Slavic Edn. Assn. (nat. treas. 1981—), St. Thomas More Soc. (bd. govs. 1980—), First Cath. Slovak Union, 1st Cath. Slovak Women's Assn., Civic Club Allegheny Valley, Bus. and Profl. Women Allegheny Valley, Phi Beta Kappa. Roman Catholic. Home: 2413 Freeport Rd Natrona Heights PA 15065 Office: Mercy Hosp of Pitts 1400 Locust St Pittsburgh PA 15219

MALEY, BECKY SCHAFER, writer; b. Ashland, Ohio, July 30, 1949; d. R. Lee and Mary (McAdoo) Schafer; m. Richard Maley, Sept. 16, 1972; children—Kathryn Rebecca, Victoria Elizabeth. B.S. in Journalism, Ohio U., 1971. Past reporter Ashland (Ohio) Times-Gazette; adminstrv. asst., employment mgr. Samaritan Hosp., Ashland; community relations adminstr. Southeast Ohio Emergency Med. Service, Gallipolis, 1972-74; supr. med. communications Univ. Health Scis.-Chgo. Med. Sch., 1974-78; sr. assoc. William M. Young & Assocs., Oak Park, Ill., 1978-80; freelance writer, 1982—; prin. Kator Corners, Oak Park, 1984—. Active Oak Park PTA. Mem. Sigma Delta Chi.

MALHOTRA, TRUDI ANNE, shopping center executive; b. Muskogee, Okla., Mar. 31, 1943; d. William Penn Garnett and Helen Delia (Singerhouse) Garnett Cunniff; m. Jagmohan Krisham Malhotra, May 25, 1973 (div. Mar. 1983); 1 dau., Paige Anne. Student U. Wis.-Stout, 1961-62, Eau Claire State U., 1962-64. Mdse. buyer Mildred's Bridal, Menomonie, Wis., 1965-69; store mgr., buyer Ray's Bridal, Detroit, 1969-73; mdse. mgr., store mgr. Alvin's, Inc., Detroit, 1973-78; dir. mktg., asst. center mgr. Center Cos., Cin., 1978—. Mem. task force Great Rivers council Girl Scouts U.S., 1983—; bd. dirs. Southwestern Ohio Lung Assn., Cin., 1982—. Mem. Cin. C. of C., Am. Mktg. Assn., Advt. Club Cin. (dir. 1983—), Zonta Internat., Tourist Council, Profl. Bus. Women's Club, Beta Sigma Phi. Home: 6908 Rt 48 Springboro OH 45066 Office: 11700 Princeton Cincinnati OH 45246

MALLARD-WARREN, GAIL MAUREEN, obstetrician-gynecologist; b. Oakland, Calif., July 14, 1953; d. Mack Maurice and Alice Carter (Vaughan) Mallard; m. Joseph Warren, Dec. 16, 1978; children—Janelle Chavonne, Jolana Rochelle, Jaryn Lanée. B.S., U. Calif.-Riverside, 1974; M.D., U. Calif.-Davis, 1979. Intern ob-gyn Valley Med. Ctr., Fresno, Calif., 1979-80, resident, 1980-83; practice medicine specializing in ob-gyn, Fresno, 1983—; med. dir. Planned Parenthood Central Calif., Fresno, 1983-84. Mem. Calif. Med. Assn., Alpha Kappa Alpha. Baptist. Office: Valley Professional Plaza 1300 N Fresno St Suite 200A Fresno CA 93703

MALLARY, GERTRUDE ROBINSON, civic worker; b. Springfield, Mass., Aug. 19, 1902; d. George Edward and Jennie (Slater) Robinson; student Bennett Coll., 1921-22, U. Conn., 1941-42; m. R. DeWitt Mallary, Sept. 15, 1923; children—R. DeWitt, Richard Walker. Co-owner, ptnr. Mallary Farm, Bradford, Vt., 1936—; mem. Vt. Ho. of Reps., 1953-56, sec. agr. com., 1953, mem. appropriations com., 1955; mem. Vt. Senate, 1957-58, mem. appropriations com., clk. pub. health com., vice chmn. edn. com., mem. interim legis. com. for study nursing, 1958-59. Pres., Jr. League, Springfield, 1931-33; chmn. Springfield Council Social Agys., 1938-40; mem. Mass. Commn. Pub. Safety, 1941-42; mem. Vt. Bd. Recreation, 1959-65; trustee Fairlee (Vt.) Public Library, 1953-84, Asa Bloomer Found., 1963-71, Orange County 4-H Found., 1969-71; trustee Justin Smith Morrill Found., 1964-71, pres., 1968-71; pres. Vt. Holstein Club, 1951-53; mem. Vt. Gov.'s Commn. for Library Services, 1966; regional v.p. Nat. Beef Council, 1960-64; Vt. chmn. Nat. Library Week, 1973; chmn. Fairlee Bicentennial Com., 1974-77; mem. Com. for New Eng. Bibliography, 1971-84, vice chmn. for Vt., 1977; trustee Wesson Meml. Hosp., Springfield, 1937-42, chmn. nursing services, 1939-42; mem. planning com. Gov.'s Conf. Future of Vt.'s Heritage, 1982; Orange County Chmn. Vt. Achievement Ctr., 1985—. Recipient Theresa R. Brungardt award, 1979. Mem. Vt. Library Trustees Assn. (pres. 1965-67), Vt. (trustee), Bradford (pres. 1965-69), Fairlee (program chmn. 1976-83) hist. socs., Am. Antiquarian Soc. Editor New Eng. Holstein Bull., 1947-50. Address: Mallary Farm Bradford VT 05033

MALLERY, AGNES EVELYN, therapeutic recreation executive; b. Mpls., Dec. 30, 1920; d. Albert Valentine and Rose Camilia (Quelland) Williams; m. William (Bill) Bean Mallery, Mar. 2, 1941; children—Rosora, Mary, William (Bill), Bonnie, Joseph. Farmer, Mallery Jerseys Inc., Shafer, Minn., 1942—; foster mother Wayward Teenagers, Sahfer, 1970-75; developer, co-owner Camilia Rose Convalescent Ctr., Coon Rapids, Minn., 1976—; founder, co-developer Grasslands Inc., non-profit apartment bldg. for physically handicapped people, Coon Rapids, 1980—. Leader 4-H Club, Rapid Rushers, Coon Rapids, 1952-60, Dalles, Taylors Falls, Minn., 1960-70; active Chisago County Health, Shafer, 1970-75; sec. Sr. Center Council, Coon Rapids. Republican. Lutheran. Clubs: Minn. Jersey Cattle, Super Srs. (Coon Rapids). Avocations: walking; stamp collecting; reading; travel. Home: 3144 Polk St NE Minneapolis MN 55418 Office: Camilia Rose Convalescent Ctr 11800 Zeon Blvd Coon Rapids MN 55433

MALLERY, GLORIA TYLER, travel agency executive; b. Wharton, Tex., Oct. 30, 1948; d. Johnny Elmo Tyler and Vera Berniece (Whitehead) Rucker; m. Francis Joseph Mallery, Sept. 14, 1968 (div. 1981); 1 child, Francis Joseph. Student, San Diego City Coll., 1966-68, U.S. Internat. U. Sch. Performing Arts, 1970, Tex. So. U., 1974-76. Exec. sales Continental Airlines, Houston, 1977-83; spl. sales agt. Eastern Airlines, Houston, 1984-85; dir. bus. devel. Dunn & Becker Travel Agy., Houston, 1985—; pres., GTM Enterprises; chief exec. officer Global Travel Mgmt., Inc.; cons. Action Interprises Devel., San Diego, 1982—. Co-chmn. Nat. Assault on Illiteracy, Houston, 1982; cons. Tex. Women for the Eighties, Houston, 1985. Recipient Spl. Recognition award Nat. Conf. Black Mayors, Ala., 1982, Action Interprises Devel., 1983, Assault on Illiteracy, 1985. Mem. Airline Employees Assn. (chmn. 1978), Assn. Black Airline Employees (founder). Democrat. Baptist. Home: PO Box 1601 Humble TX 77338 Office: 20007 Dawn Mist Dr Humble TX 77338

MALLET, LAURIE HELENE, apparel company executive; b. Tunisia, Apr. 13, 1948; d. Rene and Emmeline (Aidan) Belhassen; student Faculté de Sciences Economiques, Paris, 1968-72, Institut d'Etudes Politiques, Paris, 1968-71; divorced; children—Clemetine, Arthur. Asst. designer, 1972-74; asst. desinger Ellen Tracy, 1974-75; owner, operator Laurie Mallet Inc., 1975-76; owner, pres. Williwear, Ltd., N.Y.C., 1976—. Bd. dirs. Bklyn. Acad. Music. Mem. Fashion Group, Young Pres.' Orgn. Office: 209 W 39th St New York NY 10018

MALLETT, DANA D., librarian. B.A. in Art History, Smith Coll., 1957; M.A. in Library and Info. Sci., Denver U., 1968; postgrad. Def. Lang. Inst., 1961, Instituto Mexicano-Norteamericano de Relationes Culturales, 1962, John F. Kennedy Ctr. for Spl. Warfare, 1974, Nat. War Coll., 1976, No. Va. Bus. Sch., 1978, Cath. U. Am., 1981. Head librarian, administrn., Howard AFB Library, C.Z., 1969-70; asst. librarian Holmes Intermediate Sch., 1970-71; tchr. Spanish and substitute tchr. J.E.B. Stuart High Sch., 1972-77; sec. Office of exec. dir.-Africa The World Bank, 1978-79; personal sec. to rector Falls Ch. (Va.), 1979-81; mgr. Info. Services Ctr., BOM Internat., McLean, Va., 1981—. Mem. vestry Falls Ch. Episcopal Ch., 1982; del. Republican State Conv., 1981, 86; pres. Ravenwood Civic Assn., 1979-80, 80-81, 81-82; rep. Mason Dist., Fedn. Civic Assns.; mem. ann. plan rev. task force Mason Dist., 1981-82. Mem. AAUP, ALA, Am. Soc. for Info. Sci., Spl. Libraries Assn., Va. Library Assn., D.C. Library Assn., Women in Def., Jr. League Washington. Office: BDM Internat Inc 7915 Jones Branch Dr McLean VA 22102

MALLETTE, LILA MOHLER (SRI LILANANDA), writer, editor; b. Fort Lauderdale, Fla., June 7, 1931; d. Marvin Francis and Silvia Ione (Kenney) Mohler; student U. N.Mex., 1963-65; divorced; children—Michael F., Polly A. Mallette McPeak, Jefferson A. Founder, dir. Council for World Community, Washington, 1975-82; coordinator Arlington Visitor Ctr.; dir. Metamorphosis, 1982—. Fellow Menninger Found. Mem. NOW, World Future Soc., Assn. Humanistic Psychology, Planetary Citizens, Internat. Platform Assn., Mensa. Office: 2601 S Adams St Suite 4 Arlington VA 22206

MALLORY, JANICE DIANNE DAVIS, lawyer; b. Forsyth, Ga., June 9, 1957; d. Larry M. and Ann Elizabeth (Pierson) Davis; m. Paul S. Mallory; children—Pierson Davis, Paul Steven, Jr. B.A. magna cum laude, U. Ga., 1978, J.D., 1982. Bar: Ga. 1982. Law clk. Coweta Superior Ct. Circuit, LaGrange, Ga., 1983-84; assoc. Mattox and Baldwin, LaGrange, Ga., 1984-85. Bd. dirs. LaFayette Soc. for Performing Arts, LaGrange, 1983-84. Mem. ABA, State Bar Ga., Coweta Circuit Bar Assn., Troup County Bar Assn. (sec.-treas. 1984-85), Golden Key Honor Soc., Psi Chi, Alpha Omicron Pi. Republican. Baptist. Home: PO Box 1208 LaGrange GA 30241

MALLOY, CHERYL PATTON, trade association administrator, financial analyst; b. Greensboro, N.C., Sept. 13, 1950; d. Daniel Clark and Violet Dorothy (Andrews) P.; m. Joseph Edward Malloy, Oct, 1, 1983; 1 child, Daniel Patton. B.A. in Econs., U. N.C., 1972; M.Pub. Adminstrn., U. So. Calif., 1981. Multifamily housing rep. HUD, Richmond, Va., 1974-75; housing devel. mgr. New Haven Housing Authority, 1975-77; housing programs specialist HUD, Washington, 1978-79, br. chief, 1979-82; fin. analyst Govt. Nat. Mortgage Assn., Washington, 1982-84, dir. policy, 1984-85; dir. policy Mortgage Bankers Assn. Am., 1985—. Mem. Women in Housing and Fin. Democrat. Lutheran. Avocations: historic preservation; collecting antiques. Office: MBA 1125 15th St NW Washington DC 20005

MALLOY, KATHLEEN SHARON, lawyer; b. Evergreen Park, Ill., Apr. 7, 1948, d. Clarence Edmund and Ruth Elizabeth (Petrini) M.; m. Randall Kleinman, Aug. 5, 1978; children—Brighid Malloy, Ellena Malloy. B.A. in Psychology, St. Louis U., 1970; J.D., Loyola U., Chgo., 1976. Bar: Ill. 1976, Calif. 1977. Account exec. Complete Equity Mkts., Wheeling, Ill., 1970-76, corp. counsel, 1976-80, v.p., gen. counsel, 1980-83, exec. v.p., gen. counsel, 1983, chief operating officer, gen. counsel, 1984—; founding ptnr. firm Malloy & Kleinman, P.C., Des Plaines, Ill., 1985—. Vol. atty. legal aid orgns., Calif., 1976-79. Mem. ABA, Calif. State Bar Assn. Office: Malloy and Kleinman PC 640 Pearson St Suite 206 Des Plaines IL 60016

MALM, RITA, securities executive; b. May 8, 1932; d. George Peter and Helen Marie (Woodward) Pellegrini; student Packard Jr. Coll., 1950-52, N.Y. Inst. Fin., 1954, Wagner Coll., 1955; m. Robert J. Malm, Apr. 19, 1969. Sales asst. Dean Witter & Co., N.Y.C., 1959-63, asst. v.p., compliance dir., 1969-74; v.p., dir. Securities Ind. Assocs., N.Y.C., 1969-72; chief exec. officer Muriel Siebert & Co., Inc., N.Y.C., 1981-83; pres. Madison-Chapin Assocs., N.Y.C., 1984—; art mktg. cons. Mem. Women's Bond Club N.Y. (dir., v.p., program chmn., pres. 1980-82), Am. Cancer Soc., Sales Execs. Club, Zonta Internat. Office: 3 Hanover Sq New York NY 10004

MALONE, BRENDA RICHARDSON, lawyer; b. N.Y.C., Nov. 8, 1954; d. Ernest Alexander and Olive Geraldine (John) Richardson; m. Merrick Theodore Malone, Aug. 25, 1979; 1 dau., Piper Chanelle. B.A., Swarthmore Coll., 1976; J.D., Hofstra U., 1979. Bar: Mich. 1981; legal intern Office of Ct. Adminstrs., State of N.Y., N.Y.C., 1978; legal asst. Goldman & Hefferman, N.Y.C., 1978-79; legal intern Community Legal Assistance Corp., Hempstead, 1979; labor relations specialist Wayne State U., Detroit, 1979-83, contract adminstr., 1983—. Mem. ABA, Mich. Bar Assn., NAACP, Indsl. Relations Research Assn. Home: 15004 Warwick Detroit MI 48223 Office: Wayne State U 5980 Cass Ave Detroit MI 48202

MALONE, CAMILLE, mathematics educator; b. Tulsa, Feb. 22, 1947; d. Oscar Howard and Faydelle (Scott) Shields; m. Hal Dennis Wilkerson; 1 son, Jay David. B.A., North Tex. State U., 1969; M.A., U. Tex.-Dallas, Richardson, 1981. Tchr. math. Dallas Ind. Sch. Dist., 1968-71, 75-86, Skyline High Sch., 1984—; asst. credit mgr. Trinity Valley Foods Co., Inc., Dallas, 1973-75; instr. math. Eastfield Coll. Campus, Dallas County Community Coll. Dist., Dallas, 1982—; chmn. supt.'s oversight com. on incentive pay plan Dallas Ind. Sch. Dist., 1983—; forum panelist Exec. Devel. Seminar, U. Tex., 1984; presentation speaker at doctoral seminar East Tex. State U., 1984, at Nat. Conf. on Ednl. Excellence and Econ. Growth, 1984. Recipient Achievement in Teaching award South Oak Cliff High Sch., Dallas, 1982, 83. Mem. Nat. Council Tchrs. Math. (rep. 1968-69, state conv. 1970-71, presenter Southwestern Regional Conf. 1986, Jim Collins Outstanding Tchr. award 1986), Nat. Congress Parents and Tchrs., Greenpeace U.S.A., Environ. Task Force, Internat. Fund for Animal Welfare. Mem. Ch. of Christ. Home: 6123 Symphony Ln Dallas TX 75227 Office: Skyline High Sch 7777 Forney Rd Dallas TX 75227

MALONE, CLAUDINE BERKELEY, financial and management consultant; b. Louisville, May 9, 1936; d. Claude McDowell and Mary Katharine (Smith) M.; B.A., Wellesley Coll., 1963; M.B.A., Harvard U., 1972. Systems engr. IBM Corp., Washington, 1964; sr. systems analyst Crane Co., Chgo., 1966; controller, mgr. data processing Raleigh Stores, Washington, 1967-70; asst. prof. Harvard U., 1972-76, assoc. prof., 1977-81; fin. and mgmt. cons., Bethesda, Md., 1981—; dir. Scott Paper Co., Houghton Mifflin Co., Campbell Soup Co., Boston Co., Dart Grove Inc., Limited Stores, Supermarkets Gen. Corp.; trustee Penn Mut. Life Ins. Co. Chmn. Bus. for Reagan-Bush Com. Mass., 1980; trustee Wellesley Coll., 1982—. Recipient Candace award, 1982. C.P.A., Md. Mem. Assn. Women C.P.A.s, UN Assn., Wellesley Coll. Alumnae Assn. Episcopalian. Club: Washington Wellesley. Office: 7570 Potomac Fall Rd McLean VA 22102

MALONE, DOROTHY ANN, insurance agent, marketing executive, consultant, lecturer; b. Logansport, Ind., June 19, 1931; d. Harry and Lena Estella Malone. B.B.A., McKendree Coll., Radcliff, Ky., 1981; postgrad. in humanities Webster Coll., 1981-84; M.Pub. Service Adminstrn., Western Ky. U., 1984, M.Pub. Counseling, 1985. Lic. life and health agt. Joined U.S. Army, 1952, advanced through grades to master sgt., 1972, ret., 1975; ind. life underwriter, Elizabethtown, Ky., 1977—; dir. mktg. and sales Dixie Rabbit, Inc., Ekron, Ky., 1981—; cons., lectr. minority and women's subjects. First v.p. Hardin County (Ky.) chpt. NAACP., 1975; mem. Hardin County Human Relations Com., 1977-78; chairperson Hardin County Blue Ribbon Com., 1977; trustee Embry Chapel African-Meth. Episcopal Ch., Elizabethtown, 1983—; mem. Ky. Gov.'s Council on Volunteerism. Decorated Army Commendation medal with 5 oak leaf clusters; recipient numerous letters of commendation and appreciation and awards, including cert. of appreciation NAACP, 1976, others. Mem. Federally Employed Women (chairperson program Ft. Knox Area chpt. 1978-79, v.p. Ft. Knox Area chpt. 1978-79), Ky. Assn. Ret. Mil., Nat. Assn. Exec. Women, Ky. Central Assn. Life Underwriters, Life Investors' Pacer Club, Am. Defender Life Ins. Co., NAACP (life), Am. Soc. Profl. and Exec. Women.

MALONE, GEORGIA JOAN, lawyer; b. Bklyn., May 3, 1953; d. Joseph F. and Emma (Giustra) Abbate; m. Peter Dechar, Dec. 21, 1985. B.S. with honors, Boston U., 1975; J.D., New Eng. Sch. Law, 1978. Bar: N.Y. 1979. Counsel, Arlen Realty Devel. Corp., N.Y.C., 1979-80; assoc. Finkelstein, Borah, Schwartz, Altschuler and Goldstein, P.C., N.Y.C., 1980-83; counsel Rent Stabilization Assn. of N.Y.C., Inc., 1983-85; mem. firm Finkelstein, Borah, Schwartz, Altschuler & Goldstein, P.C., 1986—; adj. prof. NYU, 1984—; lectr. in field. Author: (with others) Rent Stabilization Association Digest: Court Decisions and CAB Opinions 1969-82, 1983; Rent Registration, Tenant Challenges: An Owner's Handbook, 1985; Personal Use Evictions and The Twenty-year Rule, 1986. Mem. ABA, Assn. Bar City N.Y., N.Y. State Bar Assn. (landlord and tenant com.). Office: Finkelstein Borah Schwartz Altschuler & Goldstein PC 377 Broadway New York NY 10013

MALONE, JEAN HAMBIDGE, educational administrator; b. South Bend, Ind., Nov. 23, 1954; d. Craig Ellis and Dorothy Jane (Piechorowski) Hambidge; B.S. in Edn., Butler U., 1976, M.S. in Edn., 1977; m. James Kevill Malone, July 8, 1978. Tchr., Indpls. Public Schs., 1977-78; dir. student center and activities Butler U., Indspl., 1978—; Eisenhower Meml. scholarship trustee, 1977-80. Bd. dirs. Campfire of Central Ind., 1980-84, 86—, Heritage Place of Indpls., 1983-84, Ind. Office Campus Ministries, Intercollegiate YMCA Indpls., 1985—. Recipient Outstanding Faculty award, Butler U., 1980. Mem. Ind. Assn. Women Deans, Adminstrs. and Counselors (bd. dirs. 1982-83), Ind. Assn. Coll. Personnel Adminstrs., Nat. Assn. Women Deans, Adminstrs. and Counselors, Kappa Delta Pi, Phi Kappa Phi, Alpha Lambda Delta (nat. liaison officer), Mortar Bd. (nat. liaison officer), Kappa Kappa Gamma (Mu house corp. bd. 1981-83). Roman Catholic. Office: 4600 Sunset Ave Indianapolis IN 46208

MALONE, JUNE PATE, personnel management specialist; b. Osceola, Ark., June 18, 1939; d. Wylie and Peola (Thompson) Dickerson; children—Cheri M. Perron, Karen I. Malone. Student Harris Tchrs. Coll., St. Louis, 1957, Park Coll., Parkville, Mo., 1973, So. Bapt. Coll., Walnut Ridge, Ark., 1978. Supply specialist U.S. Army, St. Louis, 1957-64; data transcriber Yale & Towne Corp., Phila., 1964-65; supply specialist U.S. Army, Phila., 1965-72; supply specialist U.S. Air Force, Blytheville, Ark., 1972-77, safety technician, 1977-79, personnel mgmt. specialist, 1979—, EEO counselor, 1977-79, spl. emphasis program mgr., 1979-83, handicapped employment mgr., 1983—, Hispanic employment mgr., 1983—, black employment mgr., 1983—. Counselor Suspected Child Abuse and Neglect, Osceola, 1978; bd. dirs. County United Way, Osceola, 1982, County Resource Housing Bd., 1985; councilman City Govt., Osceola, 1984. Recipient Letter of Commendation, USAF, Blytheville AFB, 1980, Sustained Superior Performance award USAF, Blytheville AFB, 1983, Outstanding Black Elected Ofcl. award City of Osceola, 1984. Mem. Bus. and Profl. Women (bd. dirs. 1981—), Federally Employed Women (membership chmn. 1981-85). Republican. Roman Catholic. Clubs: Osceola Roundtable (asst. sec. 1983—), Rosenwald Reunited (sec. 1981—) (Osceola). Home: 105 Shippen St Osceola AR 72370 Office: 97CSG/DPC Blytheville AFB AR 72317

MALONE, LINDA SUE, nurse; b. Shelby, N.C., Sept. 19, 1944; d. Garther Albert and Lucille (Smith) Whisnant; m. Gary P. Malone, Jan. 7, 1965; children—Mark Patrick, Gary Michael, Christopher Matthew. Diploma in nursing Charlotte Presbyn., N.C., 1965; student St. Joseph's Coll., 1985—. R.N., N.C., N.J., Hawaii. Nurse Heilbronn Elem. Sch., Germany, 1967-68; nurse pvt. duty Long Branch Nurses Registry, N.J., 1972-73; staff nurse Cape Fear Valley Med. Ctr., Fayetteville, N.C., 1975-78, coordinator quality assurance, 1978-85, dir. quality assurance, 1985—. Vol. nurse Westover Jr. High Sch., Fayetteville, 1979; pres. Paramed. Service, Fayetteville, 1982-85. Republican. Methodist. Avocations: crafts; gourmet cooking; water sports. Home: 426 Dunmore Rd Fayetteville NC 28303 Office: Cape Fear Valley Med Ctr Fayetteville NC 28302

MALONE, MARY JOANNE, radiographer, educational administrator, consultant; b. Nathalie, Va.; d. Harold Foster and Sirlena (Perkins) Traynham; m. James A. Malone, Dec. 12, 1970. Diploma W.J. Marquis Sch. Radiol. Tech., 1965; B.S. in Allied Health Edn., Montclair State Coll., 1979; M.A. in Urban Edn., Jersey City State Coll., 1983. Registered profl. radiographer Am. Registry Radiol Technologists, N.J. Staff radiographer, supr. Hosp. Ctr., Orange, N.J., 1966-74; instr. Passaic County Coll., Paterson, N.J., 1974-77; dir. edn., chmn. health care scis. dept. Sch. Health-Related Scis., U. Medicine and Dentistry of N.J., Newark, 1977—. Mem., scholarship com. Bethel Bapt. Ch., Orange, 1983-84, treas., 1984-85, v.p., 1985-86. Hunterdone Health Fund grantee, 1985-86. Mem. Am. Soc. Radiologic Technologists, N.J. Soc. Radiol. Technologist (pres. 1985—), Am. Soc. Radiol. Technologists (council radiol. tech. edn. of N.J.), Am. Registry Radiol. Technologists, Radiol. Technology Educators (pres. 1980-81). Office: U Medicine and Dentistry of NJ 100 Bergen St SHRP Room 322 Newark NJ 07103

MALONE, PERRILLAH (PAT) ATKINSON, state official; b. Montgomery, Ala., Mar. 17, 1922; d. Odolph Edgar and Myrtle (Fondren) Atkinson; B.S., Oglethorpe U., 1956; M.A.T., Emory U., 1962. Asst. editor-acting editor Emory U., 1958-64; asst. project officer Ga. Dept. Pub. Health, Atlanta, 1965-68; asst. project dir. Ga. Ednl. Improvement Council, 1968-69; assoc. dir. Ga. Edn. Improvement Council, 1970-71; dir. career services State Scholarship Commn., Atlanta, 1971-74; rev. coordinator Div. Phys. Health, Ga. Dept. Human Resources, Atlanta, 1974-79; project dir. So. Regional Edn. Bd., 1979-81; cons. Div. Family and Children Services, Atlanta, 1982—; mem. Gov.'s Commn. on Nursing Edn. and Nursing Practice, 1972-75; book reviewer Atlanta Jour.-Constn., 1962-79. Recipient Recognition award Ga. Nursing Assn., 1976, Korsell award 1974), Alumni Honor award Emory U., 1964. Mem. Am. Pub. Health Assn., Am. Pub. Welfare Assn. Methodist. Club: Atlanta Press. Home: 1146 Oxford Rd NE Atlanta GA 30306 Office: Suite 503 878 Peachtree St Atlanta GA 30309

MALONEY, CHRISTINE CAROLYNE, development company executive; b. Albany, Ga., Aug. 27, 1950; d. Wilfred James and Elsbeth M. (Hartmann) Poggi; 1 child, Kristin Lindsey Vance; m. Joseph J. Maloney, July 28, 1976 (div. 1982). B.S., Central Mo. State U., 1972; student Regional Police Acad., Kansas City, Mo., 1980. Parole officer Mo. State Parole, Kansas City, 1973-74; probation officer Jackson County Juvenile Ct., Kansas City, 1974-79; officer Kansas City Police Dept., 1979-82; pres. Poggi Devel. Co., Independence, Mo., 1982—; vol. tchr. Mo. State Parole, 1973; officer Res. Unit Kansas City Police Dept., 1979. Bd. dirs. Community Alcohol Program, Kansas City, 1979-80; mem. Interagy. Council Child Abuse, Kansas City, 1976-80. Recipient 2 Commendation Certs. Kansas City Police Dept., 1980, 81. Mem. Alpha Sigma Alpha. Lutheran. Office: Poggi Devel Co Inc 2905 Lees Summit Rd Independence MO 64055

MALONEY, KAREN MARIE, librarian; b. Tucson, Sept. 12, 1951; d. Joseph Leo Maloney and Marie Ellen (Billert) Maloney Bekoff; m. Dennis Vincent Saluti, May 26, 1979. B.A., U. Mass., 1976; M.Ed., Bridgewater State U., 1984; M.L.S., Simmons Coll., 1982. Cert. sch. librarian, media specialist, Mass. Reference asst. Lamont Library, Harvard U., Cambridge, Mass., 1978-82; librarian Brewster Elem. Sch. Mass., 1982-84; chmn. media ctr. Wellesley Middle Sch., Mass., 1984-85; media specialist William Mason Elem. Sch., N.J., 1985—; storyteller South Shore Storytellers, Braintree, Mass., 1982—. Contbr. book revs. to mags. for children. Mem. ALA, Mass. Library Assn. (continuing edn. award 1983), Am. Assn. Sch. Librarians, Mass. Assn. Ednl. Media, New Eng. Ednl. Media Assn., New Eng. Storytelling Center, Simmons Coll. Alumni Cape Cod. Home: 1160 Phinney's Ln Apt 4D Centerville MA 02632

MALONEY, LUCILLE TINKER, civic worker; b. Twin Falls, Idaho, Mar. 13, 1920; d. Edward Milo and Lillian (Schaefer) Tinker; tchr.'s cert. Idaho State U., 1940; student U. Wash., 1941; m. Frank E. Maloney, Feb. 20, 1943 (dec.); children—Frank E., JoAnn Maloney Smallwood, Elizabeth Maloney Hurst. Pres., U. Fla. Women's Club, 1960-61, Gainesville Women's Club, 1974-75, Friends of Five Sta. WUFT-TV, Public Broadcasting, 1976-77; chmn., organizer Gainesville Spring Pilgrimage, 1976; founder, pres. Thomas Center Assos., 1978-80; v.p. U. Fla. Art Gallery Guild, 1981, pres., 1982-84; mem. Fla. Gov.'s Challenge Program Com., 1981; trustee Fla. House, Washington; patron, organizer, trustee Hippodrome State Theatre; chmn. Santa Fe Regional Library Bd., 1980-81; pres. Gainesville Women's Forum, 1984-85; mem. Exec. Commn. Fla. for Statue of Liberty-Ellis Island Centennial; trustee Displaced Homemakers, Santa Fe Community Coll.; bd. dirs. Friends of Payne's Prairie, Inc. Recipient Fla. Leadership pin Gov. LeRoy Collins, 1961; Disting. Service award Women in Communication, Inc., 1975, Appreciation plaque Sta. WUFT-TV, 1977, Community Service award Gainesville Sun, 1979, Appreciation cert. Rotary Club Gainesville, 1980, Outstanding Service award Jr. League, 1980, Bicentennial plaque Alachua County Bicentennial Com., 1976. Mem. Friends of Library, Fla. Mus. Assocs. (pres. 1985—), Friends of Music, Hist. Gainesville, Inc., Found. for Promotion Music, Civic Chorus, Fla. Trust for Hist. Preservation, Fla. League Conservation Voters (bd. dirs. 1983—), Gainesville C. of C. (pub. affairs com. 1983-84), Altrusa Internat., Fla. Women's Network. Clubs: Gainesville Garden, Heritage (bd. govs.), Designer, Christmas Wreath So. Living mag., 1982. Home: 1823 N W 10th Ave Gainesville FL 32605

MALONEY, THERESE ADELE, insurance company executive; b. Quincy, Mass., Sept. 15, 1929; d. James Henry and F. Adele (Powers) M.; B.A. in Econs., Coll. St. Elizabeth, Convent Station, N.J., 1951; A.M.P., Harvard U. Bus. Sch., 1981. With Liberty Mut. Ins. Co., Boston, 1951—, asst. v.p., asst. mgr. nat. risks, 1974-77, v.p., asst. mgr. nat. risks, 1977-79, v.p., mgr. nat. risks, 1979—, also dir., pres. subs. Liberty Mut. (Bermuda) Ltd., 1981—; dir. Liberty Mut. Fire Ins. Co.; mem. faculty Inst. Inst., Northeastern U., Boston, 1969-74; mem. adv. bd., risk mgmt. studies Ins. Inst. Am., 1977-83; mem. adv. council Suffolk U. Sch. Mgmt., 1984—; mem. adv. council to program in internat. bus. relations Fletcher Sch. Law and Diplomacy, 1985—. C.P.C.U. Mem. Soc. C.P.C.U.s (past pres. Boston chpt.). Club: University (Boston). Office: Liberty Mutual Ins Co 175 Berkeley St Boston MA 02117

MALOOF, JANET LOUISE, lawyer; b. Springfield, Mass., July 16, 1952; d. Samuel R. and Salwa J. (Malouf) Maloof. B.A. magna cum laude, Tufts U., 1974; J.D., Suffolk Law Sch., 1979. Bar: Mass. Librarian, caseload mgmt. U.S. Attys. Office, Boston, 1976-83; mem. firm Williams & Jackson, Boston, 1983-85, Coulter, Daley & White, Boston, 1985—. Mem. licensing and zoning bd. Beacon Hill Civic Assn., 1977—. Mem. ABA, Mass. Bar Assn. (bd. dirs. young lawyers div., Suffolk del. 1984—), Boston Bar Assn., Acad. Trial Lawyers Am., Mass. Assn. Women Lawyers, Women's Bar Assn., Suffolk Law Sch. Alumni (bd. dirs. 1984—), ACLU. Office: Coulter Daley & White One Beacon St Boston MA 02108

MALOTT, ADELE RENEE, publishing company executive; b. St. Paul, July 19, 1935; d. Clarence R. and Julia Ann (Christensen) Lindgren; m. Gene E. Malott, Oct. 25, 1957. B.S., Northwestern U., 1957. Assoc. dir. pub. relations St. Paul C. of C., 1960-64; editor Daily Local News, West Chester, Pa., 1965-67; owner, editor Boutique Village Newspaper, Burlingame, Calif., 1967-76; sr. editor Webb Co., St. Paul, 1978-85; cons., editor GEM Pub. Group, Reno, Nev., 1985—. Recipient Gold medal Radio-TV Mirror, 1960, Radio Script 1st place award Calif. Press Women, 1960, Radio Script 1st place award Nat. Press Women, 1960, Community Service Series 3d place award Nat. Newspaper Assn., 1974, Editing award 3d place Nat. Fedn. Press Women, 1981, Disting. Editorial Excellence award Profl. Ins. Communicators Am., 1982, Spl. Issue 1st place award Nat. Fedn. Press Women, 1984. Mem. Press Women of Minn. (2d v.p. scholarship com. 1978-80, numerous writing and editing awards), Internat. Assn. Bus. Communicators (Merit award 1984). Republican. Office: GEM Pub Group 250 E Riverview Circle Reno NV 89509

MALSON, NANCY CARLEEN, educator; b. Jeffersonville, Ohio, Apr. 10, 1940; d. Carl Russell and Virginia Lois (Griffith) Allen; R.N., Riverside-White Cross Sch. Nursing, Columbus, Ohio, 1961; B.A. in Elem. Edn., Cedarville Coll., 1975; m. Donald W. Malson, Dec. 21, 1975; 1 child, Karla Elise Johnson. Clin. instr. psychiat. nursing Columbus (Ohio) State Hosp., 1962-67; staff/sch. nurse Fayette County Health Dept., Washington Court House, Ohio, 1967-70; Title I remedial reading tchr. Miami Trace Local Sch. Dist., Washington Court House, 1970-73, elem. tchr., 1973-75; coordinator, instr. orientation to health occupations Morris County Vocat.-Tech Sch., Denville, N.J., 1978-79, coordinator, instr. practical nursing program, 1979-81, mem. self-evaluation steering com. and conf. planning com.; tchr. 5th grade Mt. Olive Twp. Sch. System, N.J., 1982—; free lance writer including curriculum notebook for practical nursing, Morris County Vocat.-Tech. Sch., 1980; co-author articles on internat. muzzle loading competition and hunting; contbr. articles to publs., 1976—; active profl. nurses assn., Ohio, 1965-75. Mem. Nat. Muzzle Loading Rifle Assn. Am., Ohio Gun Collectors Assn., U.S. Internat. Muzzle Loading Team (silver medal for marksmanship, Madrid, 1978, fund raising chmn., gold medal, Bisley, Eng. 1977, silver and bronze medals, Bisley 1979, officer, 1979-82). Republican. Presbyterian. Club: North Morris County Women's.

MALSON, VERNA LEE, educator; b. Buffalo, Wyo., Mar. 29, 1937; d. Guy James and Vera Pearl (Curtis) Mayer; m. Jack Lee Malson, Apr. 20, 1955; children—Daniel Lee, Thomas James, Mark David, Scott Allen. B.A. in Elem. Edn. and Spl. Edn. magna cum laude, Met. State Coll., Denver, 1975; M.A. in Learning Disabilities, U. No. Colo., 1977. Cert. tchr., Colo. Tchr.-aide Wyo. State Tng. Sch., Lander, 1967-69; spl. edn. tchr. Bennett Sch. 29J, Colo., 1975-79, chmn. health, sci., social studies, 1977-79; spl. edn. tchr. Deer Trail Sch., Colo., 1979—, chmn. careers, gifted and talented, 1979-85; mem. spl. edn. parent adv. com. East Central Bd. Coop. Ednl. Services, Limon, Colo. Colo. scholar Met. State Coll., 1974; Colo. Dept. Edn. grantee, 1979, 81. Mem. Council Exceptional Children, Bennett Tchrs. Club (treas. 1977-79), Kappa Delta Pi. Republican. Presbyterian. Avocations: coin collecting; reading; sports. Home: PO Box 403 Deer Trail CO 80105 Office: Deer Trail Pub Schs 26J PO Box 129 Deer Trail CO 80105

MALTHOUSE, NANCY SIBBLES, computer systems engr.; b. Mobile, Ala., Nov. 16, 1943; d. Grant B. and Elma Sibbles; student Fla. State U., 1962-65, U. S.C., 1965-66, Clemson U., 1966-68; B.S., U. Tenn., 1969, M.S., 1975; m. June 26, 1965. Research and lab. technician ORTEC, Inc., Oak Ridge, 1969-72; programmer Oak Ridge Nat. Lab., 1972-75; programmer Boeing Computer Services, McLean, Va., 1975-78; systems engr. The MITRE Corp., McLean, 1978-85, LOGICON Inc., Washington, 1985—; pres. M-Squared Systems, Inc., Springfield, Va., 1982—; vice chmn. task force on edn. and tng. software profls. Commn. on Software Issues for 80's. Mem. Assn. Computing Machinery, IEEE, Women in Info. Processing, Nat. Council Career Women, Nat. Assn. Female Execs. Club: Toastmasters (past pres.). Home: 5918 Veranda Dr Springfield VA 22152 Office: 475 School St SW Washington DC 20024

MALUM, DONNA JEANNE, dietitian; b. Oklahoma City, May 27, 1947; d. Donald E. and Doris A. (Roushkolb) Malum; divorced; children—Michael David, Kristen Aimee. B.S., Stout State U., 1969; postgrad. St. Cloud State U., 1981—. Dietetic intern Milwaukee County Instns., 1969-70; sr. dietitian U. Minn. Hosp., Mpls., 1971-73; nursing home cons., central Minn., 1973-74; dietetic traineeship coordinator, clin. relief dietitian St. Cloud (Minn.) Hosp., 1974-80, adminstrv. dietitian, 1980—; asst. dir. Minn. dietetic internship consortium U. Minn., 1980-84; chief clin. dietetics VA Med. Ctr. St. Cloud, 1984—; instr. Coll. of St. Benedict's, St. Joseph, Minn., 1984—. Mem. Am. Dietetic Assn., Minn. Dietetic Assn., Central Minn. Dietetic Assn. (pres. dist. 83), AAUW. Home: 1546 12th Ave SE Saint Cloud MN 56301 Office: VA Med Ctr Saint Cloud MN 56301

MAMIN, ESTHA LEE GINSBERG (BEBE), real estate broker; b. Dallas; d. Jacob B. and Hinda (Bernstein) Ginsberg; B.A., U. Tex., 1945; student Lumbleau Sch. Real Estate, 1955-56; children—Cynthia Anne, Victoria Lynn, H. Jonathon, Marshall Timothy. Research asst. Cancer Lab., U. Tex. Med. Coll., Galveston; biochemist, pathology lab. James Walker Meml. Hosp., Wilmington, N.C., Tex. Children's Hosp., Dallas, 1946-47; research asst., pathology dept. Harvard Med. Coll., 1947-48; med. technologist, bus. mgr. doctor's office, Pasadena, Calif., 1948-56; real estate salesman H. H. Armistead Co., Pasadena, 1956-64, broker Mamin Co., Pasadena, 1964—. Mem. Women's Civic League. Mem. Pasadena Bd. Realtors (edn. com. 1966, mem. com. 1967, sec. womens council, 1967), Calif. Real Estate Assn., Nat. Assn. Real Estate Bds., World Affairs Council Los Angeles, Town Hall, LWV, AAUW. Clubs: Officers Wives, Curtain Raiser. Home and Office: 161 S Oak Knoll Ave Pasadena CA 91101

MAMLOK, URSULA, composer; b. Berlin, Germany, Feb. 1, 1928. Student, Mannes Coll.; M.M., Manhattan Sch. Music. Mem. faculty theory dept. City U., N.Y.U. Composition dept. Manhattan Sch. Music. Composer: Concerto for Oboe and Orchestra, 1976; Sextet, 1977; When Summer Sang, 1980; Panta Rhei, 1981, Concertino for Wind Quintet, 1984-85; From My Garden, 1983, others. CUNY Faculty Research grantee; NEA fellow; Nat. Fedn. Music Club awards; Internat. Soc. Composers Music award. Commissions; Parnassus, Jack Kreiselman, Jacob Glick, Da Capo Players, Group for Contemporary Musia. Am. Acad. and Inst. Arts and Letters grantee, 1981. Mem. Sigma Alpha Iota. Address: 315 E 86th St New York NY 10028

MAMON, DORIS ELAINE, laboratory administrator; b. Chgo., Jan. 31, 1943; d. Julius S. and Helen M. Bonk; B.S., Mundelein Coll., 1976; M.B.A., Marquette U., 1981; M.T., St. Mary of Nazareth Sch. Med. Tech., 1964; children—Deborah, Vincent. Sect. head immunohematology Alexian Bros. Med. Center, Elk Grove Village, Ill., 1969-78; supr. implementation Medistat, Milw., 1978-80; supr. product analyst Tymshare Med. Systems, Brookfield, Wis., 1980-81; sr. mgmt. cons. The Kennedy Group, Menlo Park, Calif., 1981-83; lab. mgr. Sherman Hosp., Elgin, Ill., 1984—. Mem. Am. Hosp. Assn., Am. Soc. Clin. Pathologists, Clin. Lab. Mgmt. Assn., Am. Assn. Blood Banks.

MANARY, ADRIA HILBURN, sports production company executive; b. Arlington, Va., Apr. 10, 1956; d. John Lawrence and Doris Mae (Christensen) Hilburn; m. Joel Maurice Manary, Mar. 22, 1986. B.A. in Communications, Va. Poly. Inst. and State U., 1978. Profl. singer and dancer, 1976-82; mktg. communications specialist Westinghouse Electric Corp., Pitts., 1978-81; dance instr. Arthur Murray, Alexandria, Va., 1982; account exec. Jack Morton Prodns., Washington, 1982; dir. devel. N.Y. Spl. Olympics, N.Y.C., 1983-86; co-founder, ptnr. Challenge-The Ultimate Corp. Games, Dallas. Mem. Advt. Women N.Y., N.Y.C. Lutheran. Avocations: tennis; dance. Home and Office: 604 A S 15th St Arlington VA 22202

MANATT, KATHLEEN GORDON, publishing company executive; b. Boone, Iowa, June 3, 1948; d. Richard Condon and Lewise Ryan (Gordon) M.; B.A., Coll. Wooster, 1970. Prodn. coordinator Scott, Foresman & Co., Glenview, Ill., 1970-73, editor, 1973-81, product mgr., 1981—. Mem. Nat. Council Social Studies, Ill. Council Social Studies, Nat. Assn. Bilingual Educators, Am. Council Tchrs. Fgn. Langs., Common Cause, So. Poverty Law Ctr., Amnesty Internat. Presbyterian. Home: 3270 N Lake Shore Dr Chicago IL 60657 Office: Scott Foresman & Co 1900 E Lake Ave Glenview IL 60025

MANCALL, JACQUELINE COOPER, library and information science educator; b. Phila., Mar. 31, 1932; d. Morris and Bertha Cooper; 1953; m. Elliott Lee Mancall, Dec. 27, 1953; children—Andrew Cooper, Peter Cooper. B.A., U. Pa., 1954; M.S., Drexel U. Sch. Library and Info. Sci., 1970, Ph.D., 1979. Adminstr., Miquon (Pa.) Sch., 1966-67, librarian, 1967-76; teaching asst. Drexel U., Phila., 1976-78, research assoc., 1979, asst. prof., 1979-85, assoc. prof., 1985—; chair Phila. Children's Reading Round Table, 1982-84, mem. steering com., 1984—mem. sch. library survey com. State Library Pa., 1983; cons. Author: (with M. Carl Drott) Measuring Student Information Use: A Guide for Sch. Library Media Specialists 1983; research editor Sch. Library Media quar., 1982—; editorial bd. Jour. Library and Info. Sci. Edn., 1981-86; contbg. editor Catholic Library World, 1981-85; contbr. chpts. to books, articles to profl. jours. Bd. dirs. Friends of William Jeannes Meml. Library, Plymouth Meeting, Pa., 1976-79; pres. bd. dirs. Miquon Sch., 1964-66. Mem. ALA (chair research com. 1983—), Pa. Sch. Librarians Assn. (bd. dirs. 1984—, chmn. tech. com. 1982—, chmn. profl. standard com. 1980-82), Assn. Am. Library Schs. Democrat. Jewish. Home: Harts Ln Miquon PA 19452 Office: Drexel U Coll Info Studies Philadelphia PA 19104

MANCHESTER, MELISSA TONI, singer, song writer; b. Bronx, N.Y., Feb. 15, 1951; d. David and Ruth M.; m. Kevin DeRemer, May 1, 1982. Grad., High Sch. Performing Arts, N.Y.C., 1969. Pres., owner Rumanian Pickleworks Music. Singer with, Bette Midler, 1971-72; recordings include: Bright Eyes (debut album), 1973, Melissa (Gold Album award), For the Working Girl, Mathematics, 1985; co-writer Midnite Blue, Come in from the Rain, Whenever I Call You Friend; co-writer, guest appearance TV series Fame. Recipient Best New Female Vocalist of Year award Cashbox mag., 1974; New Female Vocalist of Year award Billboard mag., 1975; Wright award for Midnight Blue, Broadcast Music Inc., 1975; Grammy award for best female vocal, 1982. Mem. Broadcast Music Inc., AFTRA, Screen Actors Guild, Am. Fedn. Musicians. Address: care Creative Artists Agy Inc 1888 Century Park E Los Angeles CA 90067

MANCHESTER, NORMA WINN, retired court reporter; b. Norfolk, Va., Aug. 9, 1923; d. Hunter Epps and Vercy (Grubbs) Winn; student William and Mary Coll., Williamsburg, Va., 1943-46, Durham Bus. Coll., 1960, Rice U., 1961-62, Robert Krippner Sch. for Reporting, 1963; divorced; children—Vickie L., Diane Virginia. Various secretarial positions, 1937-61; ct. reporter Allied Reporters, Houston, 1963-64; ofcl. ct. reporter U.S. cts., Houston, 1965-84. Pres. Manchester, Perry, Jamison, Maspero, Inc., 1975—; chmn. U.S. Fed. Ct. Reporter's Conv., 1974. Registered profl. ct. reporter. Mem. U.S., Greater Houston ct. reporters assns., Nat., Tex. shorthand reporters assns. Democrat. Baptist. Home: 505 Westcott St #208 Houston TX 77007 Office: 1400 Lubbock Room 224 Houston TX 77002

MANCHESTER, SUSAN JEAN, lawyer, artist; b. Oklahoma City, July 15, 1950; d. Frederick J. and Jean (Ball) Hoyt; m. Robert A. Manchester, III, Jan. 28, 1984. B.A. in Art Edn., Okla. State U., 1972; J.D., Okla. U., 1980. Bar: Okla. 1980, U.S. Dist. Ct. (we. dist.) Okla. 1981, U.S. Ct. Appeals (10th cir.) 1981. Profl. artist, Oklahoma City, 1973-80; atty./asst. atty. gen. Okla. Atty. Gen's. Office, Oklahoma City, 1980-81, dep. chief criminal div., 1981-82, chief criminal div., 1982-83; assoc. McClelland, Collins, Bailey, Bailey & Manchester, Oklahoma City, 1983—. Named to Outstanding Young Women of Am., 1983-84; invitational artist Okla. Bi-Centennial Showing, 1983. Mem. ABA, Oklahoma County Bar Assn., Okla. Bar Assn., Assn. Trial Lawyers Am., Phi Delta Phi. Democrat. Presbyterian. Office: McClelland Collins et al 11th Floor Colcord Bldg Oklahoma City OK 73102

MANCINA-BATINICH, MARY ELLEN, sch. adminstr.; b. Eveleth, Minn.; d. James V. and Mary (Noldin) Mancina; B.S. in Music Edn., Northwestern U., 1946, M.A., 1958, Ph.D., 1963; M.A., DePaul U., 1980; m. Alex Batinich. Tchr., Chgo. Public Schs., 1949-62, master tchr., 1962-65, adminstr., 1965-80; dir. Italians in Chicago Oral History Project, U. Ill., Chgo., 1979-82. Pres., founder Ill. State Reading Council, 1970-71. Mem. Joint Civic Com. Italian Americans (founder women's div. 1965, scholarship com. 1968), Am. Italian Hist. Assn. (founder, pres. Midwest chpt. 1974, editor newsletter 1977-82), Am. Italian War Veterans Aux. (founder, pres. Victor Arrigo Post 1974-78, scholarship com. 1972—, pres. Dept. Ill. 1978-79), Soc. History Edn., Internat. Reading Assn., Midwest Women's Center Ill. Agenda, Chgo. Hist. Soc., Range Hist. Soc., Inst. Plurality and Group Identity, Phi Delta Kappa. Author: Minnesota Souvenir Coloring Book for Children, 1965; Italian American Ethnic Studies Guide, 1972; Historic City: Settlement of Chicago, 1978; Invest in the Future: A College Education, 1974; The Italian Immigrant Women in North America, 1980. Office: 228 N La Salle St Chicago IL 60601

MANCOSKE, DEBRA ROSE, lawyer; b. Manitowoc, Wis., Sept. 24, 1958; d. Clifford Jacob and Marion Margaret (Rolland) M. A.A., U. Wis. Ctr., Manitowoc, 1978; B.S., U. Wis.-Oshkosh, 1980; J.D., St. Louis U., 1983. Bar: Mo. 1983, U.S. Dist. Ct. (so. dist.) Ill. 1983, Ill. 1984. Law clk. Chackes & Hoate, St. Louis, 1983; assoc. Ripplinger, Dixon & Hoffman, Belleville Ill., also St. Louis County, Mo., 1983-84; assoc. UAW Legal Services Plan, St. Louis, 1984—. Chairperson, Campaign Disability Rights Through Increased Voter Enrollment, St. Louis, 1984; mem. exec. com. Disabled Voters Council, St. Louis, 1983-84. AAUW scholar, 1978. Mem. ABA, Mo. Bar Assn., Bar Assn. Met. St. Louis, Women Lawyers Assn. St. Louis. Democrat. Roman Catholic.

MANCUSO, LYNN DENISE, radio station executive; b. Waynesburg, Pa., July 14, 1959; d. James Patrick and Helen Kay (Bystry) M. B.S., W.Va. U., 1981. Cashier Shop-N-Save, Waynesburg, 1974-77; receptionist Pierpont House, Morgantown, W.Va., 1979-81; news, program dir. Sta. WANB, Waynesburg, 1981—. organizer Cystic Fibrosis Walk-A-Thon, Waynesburg, 1984 (vol. award 1984); organizer, promoter Sta. KDKA Food Drive, Waynesburg, 1983. Democrat. Roman Catholic. Avocations: tennis; water sports; researching organized crime.

MANDEL, ELLEN DEBORAH, hospital administrator, nutritionist; b. Newark, Feb. 26, 1957; d. Morris and Ida (Schindel) M.; m. Mitchell Bruce Germansky, Mar. 22, 1979. B.S. in Foods and Nutrition, Montclair State U., 1979; M.P.A., Seton Hall U., 1985. Registered dietitian, N.J. Dietetic intern Univ. Medicine and Dentistry N.J., Newark, 1979-80, clin. instr., 1980-84, clin. dietitian Univ. Hosp., 1980-81; asst. dir. food services United Hosps., Newark, 1981-84; dir. food services Raritan Bay Med. Ctr., Perth Amboy, N.J., 1984-86; program coordinator diabetes treatment ctr. Newark Beth Israel Med. Ctr., 1986—. Bd. dirs. No. N.J. Community Relations Com., 1979-82. Mem. Am. Dietetic Assn., N.J. Dietetic Assn. (Young Dietitian of Yr. 1986-87, advt. chair 1986—), Am. Diabetes Assn., Am. Assn. Diabetes Educators, N.J. Met. Dist. Dietetic Assn. (chair legis. com. 1983-85, chair nominating com. 1985-86). Avocations: sports, needlework, gardening, gourmet cooking. Home: 131 River Bend Rd Berkeley Heights NJ 07922

MANDEL, KARYL LYNN, accountant; b. Chgo., Dec. 14, 1935; d. Isador J. and Eve (Gellar) Karzen; m. Fredric H. Mandel, Sept. 29, 1956; children—David Scott, Douglas Jay, Jennifer Ann. Student U. Mich., 1954-56, Roosevelt U., 1956-57; A.A. summa cum laude, Oakton Community Coll., 1979. Pres. Excel Transp. Service Co., Elk Grove, Ill., 1958-78; tax mgr. Chunowitz, Teitelbaum & Baerson, Northbrook, Ill., 1981-83, ptnr., 1984—; sec., treas. Lednam Inc., sec., treas. Trimark, Inc., Chgo. Recipient State Israel Solidarity award 1976, Mem. Am. Inst. C.P.A.s, Am. Soc. Women C.P.A.s, Women's Am. ORT (nat. bd. 1961-77, pres. Chgo. region 1972-74, nat. investment adv. bd. 1985—), Ill. C.P.A. Soc. (mem. estate and gift tax com., mem. legis. contact com. 1981-82, pres. North Shore chpt., award for excellence in acctg. edn., vice chmn. estate and gift tax com. 1985—), Chgo. Soc. Women C.P.A.s, Chgo. Estate Planning Council. Office: 401 Huehl Rd Northbrook IL 60062

MANDEL, MRS. LEON (CAROLA PANERAI MANDEL), foundation trustee; b. Havana, Cuba; d. Camilo and Elvira (Bertini) Panerai; ed. pvt. schs., Havana and Europe; m. Leon Mandel, Apr. 9, 1938. Mem. women's bd. Northwestern Meml. Hosp., Chgo. Trustee Carola and Leon Mandel Fund Loyola U., Chgo. Life mem. Chgo. Hist. Soc., Guild of Chgo. Hist. Soc., Smithsonian Assos., Nat. Skeet Shooting Assn. Frequently named among Ten Best Dressed Women in U.S.; chevalier Confrerie des Chevaliers du Tastevin. Capt. All-Am. Women's Skeet Team, 1952, 53, 54, 55, 56; only woman to win a men's nat. championship, 20 gauge, 1954, also high average in world over men, 1956, in 12 gauge with 99.4 per cent; European women's live bird shooting championship, Venice, Italy, 1957, Porto, Portugal, 1961; European woman's target championship, Torino, Italy, 1958; woman's world champion live-bird shooting, Sevilla, Spain, 1959. Named to Nat. Skeet Shooting Assn. Hall of Fame, 1970. Mem. Soc. Four Arts. Club: Everglades (Palm Beach, Fla.), The Beach. Home: 324 Barton Ave Palm Beach FL 33480

MANDELBAUM, DOROTHY ROSENTHAL, psychologist; b. N.Y.C., May 18, 1935; d. Benjamin Daniel and Rachael (Osofsky) Rosenthal; A.B. cum laude, Hunter Coll., 1956; Ph.D., Bryn Mawr Coll., 1975; m. Seymour Jacob Mandelbaum, Aug. 19, 1956; children—David Gideon, Judah Michael, Betsy Daniella. Tchr., Valley Road Sch., Princeton, N.J., 1956-59; instr. ednl. psychology dept. Temple U., Phila., summer 1970; asst. prof. dept. edn. Rutgers, The State U., Camden, N.J., 1974-80, asso. prof., 1980—, dir. women's studies, 1981-86, chair edn. dept., 1986—. AAUW predoctoral fellow, 1973-74. Mem. Am. Psychol. Assn., AAUP, Soc. Research in Child Devel. Contbr. articles on psychology of women and med. edn. to profl. publs. Author: Work, Marriage, and Motherhood: The Career Persistence of Female Physicians, 1981. Home: 2290 N 53d St Philadelphia PA 19131 Office: Rutgers U Camden NJ 08102

MANDELBAUM, JUDITH, business executive; b. Newark, May 2, 1940; d. Morris and Millicent (Piper) Solomon; m. Barry Richard Mandelbaum, June 13, 1960 (div. Jan. 1980); children—Kenneth, Lisa. B.A., Barnard Coll., 1961; M.A., NYU, 1973. Tchr. English, Chatham Jr. High Sch. (N.J.), 1961-62; adj. prof. English, Morris County Coll., Denville, N.J., 1979-80; asst. dir. Anti Defamation League, Livingston, N.J., 1980-84; dir. research and communications Louis Hoffman Assocs., Randolph, N.J. Author poem: Christmas Special (Acad. Am. Poets award 1976), 1974. Mem. MLA. Home: 24 Edgar Rd West Orange NJ 07052

MANDELL, ARLENE LINDA, public relations executive; b. Bklyn., Feb. 19, 1941; d. George and Esther Kostick; m. Lawrence W. Mandell, May 23, 1982; children by previous marriage—Bruce R. Rosenblum, Tracey B. Rosenblum. B.A. magna cum laude, William Paterson Coll., 1973. Newspaper reporter Suburban Trends, Riverdale, N.J., 1972-73; writer Good Housekeeping mag., N.Y.C., 1976-78; account exec. Carl Byoir & Assocs., N.Y.C., 1978—. Contbr. articles to profl. jours. and newspapers. Recipient 1st place women's interest writing N.J. Press Assn., 1973; named John W. Stahr Writer of Yr., Carl Byoir & Assocs., N.Y.C., 1981. Mem. Women in Communications. Club: Newswomen's. Office: Carl Byoir & Assocs 380 Madison Ave New York NY 10017

MANDELL, FRAN GARE, writer, publishing company executive; b. Jersey City, Dec. 5, 1939; d. David A. and Henrietta (Rich) Rhein; B.A., Fairleigh Dickinson U., 1963, M.A., 1965; cert. N.Y. Sch. Interior Design, 1966; M.S., U. Bridgeport, 1980, Naturopathic Dr., Braintridge Forest Sch., Eng., 1977; m. Marshall Mandell, Oct. 21, 1979; children by previous marriage—David Gare, Marc Gare. Owner, Wynken, Blynken & Nod, Englewood, N.J., 1967-70; pres. Nutri-Plan, Inc., N.Y.C., 1975—; pres. MarFran Publs., Inc. (name now Gare Inc.), Basket Magic, Norwalk, Conn., 1979—. Mem. Assn. Food Technologists, Am. Soc. Journalists and Authors, N.Y. Acad. Scis. Jewish. Club: Atrium. Author: (with Atkins and Monica) Dr. Atkins Diet Revolution, 1972; (with Monica) Dr. Atkin's Diet Cook Book, 1974; (with Monica) The Super Energy Diet Cook Book, 1978; (with Bomser) Dr. Mandell's Allergy Cookbook, 1980; (with Alan Pressman) A Complete Guide to Chiropractic, 1981; The Nutrition Cookbook, 1982; (with Marshall Mandell) It's Not Your Fault You're Fat; contbr. articles to profl. jours. Office: 3A Brush St Norwalk CT 06850

MANDELL, MADELINE ANN, child care agency executive; b. El Paso, Tex., Oct. 20, 1935; d. Humboldt C. and Mary E. (Smith) M. B.A., U. Tex., 1958; M.S.W., U. Denver, 1964. Cert. Social Worker, Tex. Dist. dir. Girl Scouts U.S.A., Mile Hi council, Denver, 1958-62; staff supr. San Francisco Bay Girl Scout Council, 1964-69; regional mgr. Day Care Ctrs. Am., Dallas, 1969-71; exec. dir. Child Care Dallas, 1971—. Past pres. Dallas Classic Guitar Soc.; pres. Women's Issues Network, Inc.; mem. Women's Council of Dallas County (Tex.), Inc.; mem. adv. bd. Women's Ctr. of Dallas, Inc.; founding mem. Women's Found. of Dallas, 1985. Recipient Women Helping Women award Women's Ctr. Dallas, 1982; Woman of Achievement award Working Women's Mag., 1983; Leadership Tex. award. Women's Found., Austin, 1984. Mem. Tex. Daycare Providers Assn. (past chmn.), Dallas Assn. Edn. Young Children (past sec.), Child Care '76 of Greater Dallas (past v.p.).

MANDIBERG, MYRTLE, psychologist; b. N.Y.C., July 1, 1918; d. Samuel and Sadie (Friedman) M.; B.A., Bklyn. Coll., 1938; M.A., U. Pa., 1940. Intern Wayne County Gen. Hosp., Eloise, Mich., 1940-41, staff psychologist, 1941-42; tchr. nursery sch. Detroit Bd. Edn., 1942-44; staff psychologist Detroit Recorders Ct. Psychopathic Clinic, 1944-49; psychotherapist Devereux Ranch Sch., Santa Barbara, Calif., 1949-51; supr. Reiss-Davis Child Guidance Clinic, Los Angeles, 1959-62; cons., coordinator profl. services Los Angeles Child Devel. Center, 1979-86, v.p., dir. clin. service, 1986—, also pvt. practice child psychology, 1951—; assoc. in psychology UCLA, 1978—. Mem. Am. Psychol. Assn., Calif. State Psychol. Assn., Los Angeles County Psychol. Assn., Assn. Child Psychoanalysis. Home and Office: 1470 Glendon Ave Los Angeles CA 90024

MANDRELL, BARBARA ANN, entertainer; b. Houston, Dec. 25, 1948; d. Irby Matthew and Mary Ellen (McGill) M.; grad. high sch.; m. Kenneth Lee Dudney, May 28, 1967; children—Kenneth Matthew, Jaime Nicole, Nathaniel. Country music singer and entertainer, 1959—; performed throughout U.S. and in various fgn. countries; mem. Grand Ole Opry, Nashville, 1972—; appeared in TV variety series The Barbara Mandrell Show, 1980-82, TV movie Burning Rage, various TV spl.; albums include Greatest Hits, Meant for Each Other, He Set My Life to Music (Grammy award for inspirational performance and rec.). Named Miss Oceanside (Calif.), 1965; Most Promising Female Singer, Acad. Country Music, 1971, Female Vocalist of Year, 1979; Female Vocalist of Year, Music City News Cover awards, 1979, Country Music Assn., 1979, 81; entertainer of the Year Country Music Assn., 1980, 81. Mem. Musicians Union, Screen Actors Guild, AFTRA, Country Music Assn. (dir.), Assn. Country Entertainers. Mem. Order Eastern Star. Office: care World Class Talent 1522 Demonbreux Nashville TN 37203*

MANDRELL, REGINA ANGELA MORENO, genealogist; b. Mobile, Ala., Mar. 10, 1906; d. Cameron Anderson and Seana Barkley (Crary) Moreno; A.B., Birmingham-So. Coll., 1926, postgrad., 1960; postgrad. U. Ky., 1964, Smith Coll., Northampton, Mass., 1965; m. George F. Kirchoff, Oct. 4, 1930 (dec.); children—George F., Margaret A. Kirchoff Pennington; m. 2d, William F. Mandrell, Oct. 20, 1971 (dec.). Tchr., attendance supr. Birmingham (Ala.) Public Schs., 1926-71; adminstrv. asst. Jefferson County Mental Health Assn., Birmingham, 1956-59; mem. Ala. Devel. Bd. for Health Survey, 1930; writing and geneal. research compiling family history, 1932—. Recipient George Washington medal Freedom Found., 1961. Mem. Ala. Hist. Soc., Baldwin County (Ala.) Hist. Soc. (officer), Writers Group, Baldwin County Writers Club, Pensacola (Fla.) Hist. Soc., DAR, Nat. Soc. Colonial Dames XVII Century, Alpha Chi Omega, Kappa Delta Epsilon, Pi Gamma Mu, Chi Delta Phi. Methodist. Author: Reminiscences of the Old South 1834-1866 (3 vols.), 1985. Contbr. articles to profl. jours., story to anthology Women of the South. Home: PO Drawer AM Fairhope AL 36532

MANES, BELLE, painter; b. N.Y.C., Mar. 22, 1930; d. Raphael and Hilda (Kurtz) Marder; m. Myron M. Manes, Sept. 10, 1949; children—Orianne Manes Davis, Alan Peter. B.F.A., Cooper Union, 1950. One woman shows include: Deal Gallery, Vassos Gallery, Greenwich Art Barn, Barrett Gallery, N.J., Branchville Soho Gallery; exhibited group shows: Rotunda Gallery, Naples Art Gallery, Fla., Bridge Gallery, Allbright Knox Mus., Laurel Gallery, N.Y., Argent Galley, N.Y., Feiner Gallery, N.Y., Book Gallery, Aldrich Mus. Contemporary Art, Bklyn. Mus.; represented in pub. and pvt. collections.

MANFORD, BARBARA ANN, contralto; b. St. Augustine, Fla., Nov. 13, 1929; d. William Floyd and Margaret (Kemper) Manford; Mus.B. in Voice, Fla. State U., 1951, Mus.M., 1970; studied with L. Palazzini, A. Strano, Japelli, E. Nikolaidi, E. Joseph. Appearances in Europe, performing major roles in 12 leading opera houses, 1951-68, with condrs. including Alfred Strano, Felice Cilario, Robert Shaw, Arnold Gamson, Guiseppe Patané, Ottavio Ziino, also numerous concerts and recitals in Paris and throughout Italy and Belgium; performed in world premiere Fugitives (C. Floyd), Fla. State U., Tallahassee, 1950; chosen by Gian Carlo Menotti for leading role in world premiere The Leper, Fla. State U., 1970; numerous radio, TV, and concert appearances, U.S., 1968—; artist-in-residence, asso. prof. voice Ball State U., Muncie, Ind., 1970—; numerous recs. Semi-finalist vocal contest, Parma, Italy, 1964; winner contest, Lonigo, Italy, 1965. Mem. Nat. Assn. Tchrs. Singing, Chgo. Artists Assn., Am. Tchrs. Nat. Assn., Sigma Alpha Iota, Pi Kappa Lambda. Christian Scientist. Home: 104 Colonial Crest Apts Muncie IN 47304 Office: Ball State Univ Muncie IN 47306

MANGAN, EDITH DUELL, nurse; b. Rutland, Vt., May 30, 1913; d. Francis Wheeler and Martha Marcelline (Bushey) Perry; m. Francis A. Mangan, Jan. 27, 1938 (dec. Jan. 1971); 1 child, Edmund. R.N., St. Francis Hosp., Jersey City, 1935; postgrad. Margaret Hague Maternity Hosp., Jersey City, 1935. Supr. obstetrics Columbus Hosp., N.Y.C., 1936-38, Polyclinic Hosp., N.Y.C., 1940-44; pvt. nurse film industry, Hollywood, Calif., 1938-40; staff and pvt. nurse Holy Name Hosp., Teaneck, N.J., 1944-71; dir. nursing St. Michael Villa, Englewood Cliffs, N.J., 1971-82, asst. dir. nursing, 1982—; del. Internat. Council Cath. Nurses to World Health Conf., Brussels, 1958. Recipient Cert. Recognition, Sisters of St. Joseph of Peace, 1982. Mem. Am. Nurses Assn., N.J. State Nurses Assn., Gerontol. Soc. Am., Rutland Hist. Soc. Republican. Roman Catholic. Club: Women of Moose (Rutland, Vt.). Office: St Michaels Villa Hudson Terr Englewood Cliffs NJ 07632

MANGAN, MAUREEN KENNEDY, survey research executive; b. Washington, Feb. 15, 1946; d. Daniel Bernard and Ann (Caldwell) Kennedy; m. James Harrison Mangan, Sept. 10, 1977. Student Coll. Steubenville, 1964-66; B.A., U. Md., 1970. Statis. asst. personnel Georgetown U., Washington, 1974-76; pres. Classic Photos Inc., Washington, 1976; research dir. for Daniel J. Edelman, 1976-79; instr. Va. Commonwealth U., Richmond, 1980-82; v.p., research dir. N.Am. Mktg., Richmond, 1980-83; pres. Mangan & Smith Research, Richmond, 1983—; lobbyist Va. Gen. Assembly, 1980-82. Vol. 222-Much Program for prevention drunken driving, Richmond, 1983-84; evaluator wider opportunities program Commonwealth council Girl Scouts U.S., 1983; bd. dirs. Richmond Theatre Co., 1984; bd. dirs. Va. affiliate Am. Heart Assn., 1982—, recipient Spl. Pub. Info. award, 1982, cert. Appreciation, 1983. Mem. Am. Mktg. Assn. (com. chmn. 1982—), Va. Press Assn. Club: Chestnut Oaks Recreation Assn. (Richmond). Home: 1921 Greenhurst Dr Richmond VA 23229 Office: Mangan & Smith Research Services 8100 Three Chopt Rd Suite 146 Richmond VA 23288

MANGE, JUDITH, physical therapist, hospice administrator; b. St. Louis, July 8, 1946; d. Willard Lesman and Bernice (Quicksilver) M.; student Ind. U., 1961-66; B.S., Washington U. Med. Sch., St. Louis, 1968; M.B.A. (grantee), U. Mo., St. Louis, 1980. Staff phys. therapist Jewish Hosp., St. Louis, 1968-71, supr. phys. therapy, 1971-78; housing coordinator Convenant House, St. Louis, 1980; dir. phys. therapy services Irene Walter Johnson Inst. Rehab., St. Louis, 1980-82; hospice cons., St. Louis, 1982—, pres., dir., adminstr. Community Hospice Care, Inc., St. Louis; mem. admissions com., phys. therapy program Washington U., 1979-82, lectr., 1979—. Bd. dirs. Am. Cancer Soc. Mem. Mo. Hospice Orgn. (pres., treas.), Nat. Hosp. Organ. (chmn. planning ann meeting), Am. Phys. Therapy Assn. (treas. Mo., chmn. St. Louis), Mo. Phys. Therapy Assn., Gerontological Soc., Jewish. Office: 2510 S Brentwood Suite 216 Saint Louis MO 63144

MANGOLD, LANA CAROLE, financial counselor, account executive, educator; b. San Antonio, July 30, 1943; d. Durtis E. and Bennie J. (Dockery) Paramore; m. William Johnson Mangold, July 17, 1965; m. 2d, James L. Clark, Nov. 17, 1978; 1 son, Justin Lowell. B.S., Tex. Woman's U., 1965; M.A., U. Tex.-Austin, 1972, Ph.D., 1974. Tchr., Dallas, 1965-66, Austin Ind. Sch. Dist., Tex., 1967-70; supr. Brazosport Ind. Sch. Dist., 1971; research assoc. U. Tex.-Austin, 1970-74; prof. North Tex. State U., Denton, 1974-82; account exec., fin. counselor H.C. Copeland & Assocs., Dallas, 1982—. Author/editor: Bulletin Board Ideas-Teaching Home Economics, 1980. Office: HC Copeland & Assocs Irving TX

MANGOLD, MARY LINDA, newspaper company official; b. Cin., June 18, 1956; d. Donald Roy and Thelma Lorrayne (Moore) M. B.S., Xavier U., 1978; cert. U. Vienna (Austria), 1977; Exec. sales mgr. Federated Dept. Stores, Cin., 1978; video cameraperson Scripps-Howard Broadcasting, Cin., 1978-79, asst. producer, 1979-80, pub. service dir., 1980-84; asst. dir. promotion Scripps-Howard Newspapers, Cin., 1984—. Bd. govs. Xavier U., Cin.; trustee Cin. br. Am. Lung Assn.; Mem. BRAVO! council Cin. Ballet Co.; Mem. Cin. Police Chief's Community Adv. Council. Recipient awards for pub. service announcements, 1981-83. Mem. Women in Communications (job exchange co-chair 1981—), Nat. Broadcast Assn. for Community Affairs, St. Ursula Acad. Alumnae (pres. 1981). Home: 8790 Foxboro Ct Cincinnati OH 45236 Office: Scripps-Howard Newspapers 1100 Central Trust Tower Cincinnati OH 45202

MANGUBAT, JUDITH RÉGNIER, customs inspector; b. Washington, Mar. 12, 1949; d. Cornelio and Ann Elizabeth (Price) M.; B.A., Mich. State U., 1971. Substitute tchr. Prince George's County Bd. Edn., Md., 1970-71; customs insp. trainee U.S. Customs Service, Phila., 1971-73, journeyman insp., 1973-77, sr. customs insp., 1977-80, supervisory customs insp., 1980-82, asst. chief insp., 1981, customs insp. (program officer), Washington, 1982—, instr. treasury enforcement communications system Phila. dist., inspection and control field rep. customs effectiveness measurement program, Hispanic employment coordinator Phila. dist., 1973-80. Bd. dirs. Pa. SER/JOBS for Progress Inc., 1974-82; devel. council Mich. State U., 1975-79; bd. advisors Acción Puertorriqueña (later Hispanic Orgn. for Profl. Devel.), 1975-82; task force on Hispanic concerns Fed. Regional Council; adv. bd. Nat. Ednl. Services Ctr., League of United Latin Am. Citizens, Phila., del. nat. conv., 1975-79; steering com. Society Hill Towers Condominium Buyers Assn.; life mem. Pearl S. Buck Found. Recipient Spl. Achievement award U.S. Dept. Treasury, 1976; named to Mich. State U. Kedzie Assocs., 1976, 77, 78. Mem. Nat. Assn. Female Execs., Am. Mgmt. Assn., Nat. Treasury Employees Union, ACLU (life), Mich. State U. Alumni Assn. (life), NOW, Phila. Zool. Soc. (life), Mensa, Assn. for Systems Mgmt., Internat. Platform Assn., Women's Transp. Seminars, Internat. Assn. Law Enforcement Intelligence Analysts, Phi Beta Kappa. Lutheran. Clubs: Mich. State U. President's, Fraternal Order Police. Home: 3514 55th Ave Hyattsville MD 20784 Office: US Customs Service Inspection and Control 1301 Constitution Ave NW Washington DC 20229

MANGUM, GINGER GAIL, insurance agent; b. Abilene, Tex., Aug. 5, 1947; d. Wilmer Wilford and Mildred Marie (Nelson) Allen; m. Robert Lee Mangun, Feb. 19, 1965 (div. Feb. 1979); 1 child, Sheri Lyn. Cert. oil and gas well drilling and exploration, Hardin-Simmons U., 1980. Ins. mgr. Freyschlag Ins., Eastland, Tex., 1967-75; co-owner Mangum Service Ctr., Eastland, 1968-79; prodn. supr. Western Co., Eastland, 1979-81; sta. mgr. Sta. KERC Radio, Eastland, 1981-83; ins. agt. Tex. Farm Bur., Eastland, 1983—. Campaign worker Republican Party, Eastland, 1984; county chmn. Tex. Sesquicentennial, Eastland, 1985-86. Named Girl of Yr., Beta Sigma Phi, 1973. Lutheran. Home:

PO Box 624 Eastland TX 76448 Office: Eastland County Farm Bur Hwy 80 East Eastland TX 76448

MANGUS, DEBBIE DEE, marketing executive; b. Fort Wayne, Ind., May 29, 1955; d. Kenneth R. and M. Irene Miller; m. Charles D. Lewis; children—David R., Carrie A.; m. John T. Mangus, Dec. 19, 1981; children—John T. III, April L., Brandon M., Ryan E. Nurse aide Parkview Meml. Hosp., Fort Wayne, Ind., 1973; waitress Newport Creamery, Groton, Conn., 1976—; store activities rep. McDonald's Systems, Newport News, Va., Fort Wayne, Ind., 1978, community relations rep. Fort Wayne, Columbus, Ohio, 1979-81; regional mktg. mgr. Arby's, Inc., Columbus, 1982-83; mktg. dir. McNeill Enterprises, Inc., Chillicothe, Ohio, 1984—; trainer regional mktg. mgrs. Arby's, Columbus, 1982-83; mktg. cons. MEI Franchisees, Inc. Franchisees, Ohio, Ill., Ky., 1984—. Fund raiser Ronald McDonald House, Columbus, Indpls., 1980-81; v.p. Parent Tchr. Orgn. Rose Ave. Sch., Washington Court House. Recipient Best Bets awards McDonald's-Indpls. region, 1980, 81. Mem. Nat. Assn. Female Execs. Methodist. Avocations: reading; softball; bicycling; crafts. Office: McNeill Enterprises 14 S Paint St 4th Floor Chillicothe OH 45601

MANIATIS, CHARLYNN CAROL, lawyer, physician, consultant; b. Bridgeport, Conn., Nov. 23, 1949; d. William Richard and Ada Mae (Wicks) M. B.A., Wellesley Coll., 1969; J.D., Harvard U., 1972, M.P.H., Johns Hopkins U., 1978, M.D., 1979. Bar: N.Y. 1973, Md. 1975, U.S. Ct. Mil. Appeals 1976, U.S. Supreme Ct. 1977, U.S. Dist. Ct. Md. 1978. Assoc. Dewey, Ballantine, Bushby, et al., N.Y.C., 1972-74, Semmes, Bowen & Semmes, Balt., 1975-80, Garbarini, Scher & DeCicco, P.C., N.Y.C., 1980-83, Morris J. Eisen, P.C., N.Y.C., 1983-84; cons. Med. Malpractice and Negligence, Cos Cob, Conn., 1984—; asst. prof. radiology Cornell U. Med. Coll., N.Y.C., 1983—; attending radiologist N.Y. Hosp., N.Y.C., 1983—, St. Vincents Med. Ctr., S.I., N.Y., 1984-85, Bayley-Seton Hosp., S.I., 1984-85, Our Lady of Mercy Med. Ctr., Bronx, N.Y., 1984—. Served with USNR, 1975—. Fellow Am. Coll. Legal Med.; mem. ABA. Republican. Episcopalian. Clubs: N.Y. Wellesley Coll. (bd. dirs. 1983—); Harvard (N.Y.C.); Army and Navy (Washington). Home: 11 River Rd Cos Cob CT 06807

MANKE, JUDITH (JUDI) MARION, insurance agent; b. Portland, Oreg., Mar. 9, 1938; d. Ross William and Erma (Asberry) Bruce; m. David L. Granteer, Dec. 6, 1956 (div. Apr. 1964); m. 2d, John Albert Manke, Apr. 14, 1967; adopted children—Susan Marie Manke Roberts, Donald Mark (dec.). Student Portland State Coll., 1962, Washington U., St. Louis, 1963-64. Lic. ins. agt. Owner, Portland Clinic, 1956-59, Medicare sec., 1964-73; appointment sec. Medford Radiol. Group (Oreg.), 1973-78; owner Manke Ins. Agy., Medford, 1978—; ptnr. Dove Ins. Agy., Medford, 1980—; propr. Judi's Typing Service, Medford, 1981—. Contbr. articles to religious publs. Mem. Ins. Women Medford. Republican. Nazarene (robarian 1980-82, mem. choir). Home: 2570 Rosewood Medford OR 97504 Office: Manke Ins Agy 1180 Crater Lake Medford OR 97504

MANKILLER, WILMA PEARL, principal chief Indian tribe; b. Stilwell, Okla., Nov. 18, 1945; d. Charley and Clara Irene (Sitton) M.; m. Hector N. Olaya, Nov. 13, 1953 (div. 1975); children—Felicia Marie Olaya, Gina Irene Olaya. Student Skyline Coll., San Bruno College, Calif., 1973, San Francisco State Coll., 1973-75; B.A. in Social Sci., Flaming Rainbow Coll., Okla., 1977; postgrad. U. Ark., 1979. Community devel. dir. Cherokee Nation, Tahlequah, Okla., 1977-83, dep. chief, 1983-85, prin. chief, 1985-87; pres. Inter-Tribal Council Okla.; mem. exec. bd. Council Energy Resource Tribes; bd. dirs. Okla. Indsl. Devel. Commn. Bd. dirs. Okla. Acad. for State Goals, 1985—. Recipient Donnanigh First Lady award Okla. Commn. for Status of Women, 1985. Mem. Cherokee County Democratic Women's Club, Nat. Tribal Chairmen's Assn., Nat. Congress Am. Indians. Avocations: reading; writing. Office: Cherokee Prin Chief PO Box 948 Tahlequah OK 74465

MANKIN, RUTH LARSON, association executive; b. Conrad, Mont., Nov. 14, 1932; d. Roy E. and Leila V. (McCartney) Larson; m. Hart Tiller Mankin, Aug. 14, 1954; children—Margaret, Theodore, Susan. B.S., Northwestern U.-Ill., 1954. Press sec. U.S. Rep. Tom Evans, Wilmington, Del., 1976-81; pub. affairs dir. U.S. Dept. HHS, Phila., 1981-83; v.p. Del. C. of C., Wilmington, 1983—. Cand. Republican Party of Del., 1978, dist. chmn., 1978-81; exec. com. March of Dimes, Wilmington, 1983—, Vice chmn. Del.; sec. Wilmington Waterways; bd. dirs. Wilmington Waterways, 1983—; co-chmn. Child Care Connection. Mem. Brandywine Valley Press Club, Pub. Relations Roundtable Del. (chmn.). Episcopalian. Club: Greenville Country. Home: 1101 Westover Rd Wilmington DE 19807 Office: Del State C of C 1 Commerce Ctr Wilmington DE 19801

MANLEY, BARBARA LEE DEAN, hospital administrator, consultant; b. Washington, Nov. 5, 1946; d. Robert L. Dean and Mary L. (Jenkins) Smallwood; m. Major Otis Manley, Nov. 16, 1969; 1 child, Laura Selena. B.S., St. Mary-of-the-Woods, Terre Haute, Ind., 1973; M.A., Central Mich. U., 1981. Indsl. nurse Ford Motor Co., Indpls., 1973-80; employee health nurse Starplex, Inc., Washington, 1981-84, Doctor's Hosp., Lanham, Md., 1984-85; regional occupational health nurse coordinator Naval Hosp., Long Beach, Calif., 1985—; project mgr. Health Care Network, Inc., Washington, 1980-84; cons. Health and Human Services, Washington, 1980-84; pvt. practice contract nurse specialist, Washington, 1980-84. Vol. ARC, Ft. Lewis, Wash., 1974-76, Ft. Harrison, Ind., 1978-80; counselor Crisis Hot-Line, Laurel, Md., 1981-83, Laurel Boy's and Girls Club, 1981-84. Fellow Acad. Ambulatory Nursing Adminstrs. (Honor plaque 1981); mem. Assn. Exec. Females, Am. Pub. Health Assn., Am. Nurses Assn., Am. Assn. Occupational Health Nurses, Central Mich. U. Alumni Assn. (sec. 1985—), Chi Eta Phi. Presbyterian. Avocations: reading; crocheting; traveling; roller skating. Office: Regional OHN Coordinator Branch Med Clinic Naval Sta Long Beach CA 90822

MANLEY, JOAN ADELE DANIELS, publisher; b. San Luis Obispo, Calif., Sept. 23, 1932; d. Carl and Della (Weinmann) Daniels; B.A., U. Calif., Berkeley, 1954; D.B.A. (hon.), U. New Haven, 1974; LL.D. (hon.), Babson Coll., 1978; m. Jeremy C. Lanning, Mar. 17, 1956 (div. Sept. 1963); m. Donald H. Manley, Sept. 12, 1964 (div. 1985). Sec., Doubleday & Co., Inc., N.Y.C., 1954-60; sales exec. Time Inc., 1960-66, v.p., 1971-75, group v.p., 1975-84, dir., 1978-84; circulation dir. Time-Life Books, 1966-68, dir. sales, then pub., 1968-76, chmn. bd., 1976-80, ret., 1984; dir. Sara Lee Corp., Borg Warner Co., Activision Inc., Lehigh Press. Mem. adv. council Stanford U. Bus. Sch., Berkeley Bus. Sch. Former trustee, Babson Coll., Bennington Coll; bd. dirs. Scholastic Inc., Combined Internat. Corp., Mayo Found., Keystone Ctr., Friends of Photography, Yosemite Nat. Inst. Clubs: Pubs. Lunch, Hemisphere. Home: Keystone CO Office: 888 8th Ave New York NY 10019

MANLY, CAROL ANN, speech-lang. pathologist; b. Canton, Ohio, Nov. 21, 1947; d. William George and Florence (Parrish) M.; B.S. in Edn. (PTA scholar, 1965, Penhellenic scholar, 1965), Kent State U., 1969; M.A. (VA fellow), U. Cin., 1970; postgrad. NYU. Instr., U. Cin. Med. Center, 1970-72; staff speech pathologist, NYU Med. Center, Goldwater Meml. Hosp., N.Y.C., 1972-75, sr. speech pathologist, 1975-78, supr., 1978-81, asst. dir., 1981-83; pvt. practice, 1983—; cons. speech pathologist Mary Manning Walsh Nursing Home, 1974-85, Drs. Hosp., 1983—; speaker profl. convs. Jr. asso. mem. Solomon R. Guggenheim Mus., 1976—. Contbr. articles to profl. jours. Mem. Am. Speech-Lang.-Hearing Assn., N.Y. State Speech-Lang.-Hearing Assn. (com. communication problems of aging), N.Y.C. Speech-Lang.-Hearing Assn.

MANN, ANGELA BIGGS, educational administrator; b. Atlanta, Apr. 4, 1951; d. Homer Daniel and Jewel (McCoy) Biggs; m. Justin S. Mann, Sept. 21, 1971; children—Justina, Alexis, Rahman. Degree in psychology and edn. Fisk U., 1968-72; postgrad. U. Minn., 1984—. Dir. edn. U. Islam, Nashville, 1973-75; math. instr. U.L. St. Acad., St. Paul, 1975; edn. coordinator Head Start, St. Paul, 1976; dir. child care Phyllis Wheatley Sch., Mpls., 1978-79; pub. relations mgr. Town Square, St. Paul, 1980-82; dir. Head Start, Ramsey Action Program, St. Paul, 1983—; resource access rep. Portage Project, Wis., 1984—. Bd. dirs. Minn. Assn. for Edn. Young Children, St. Paul, 1986; rules rev. mem. Dept. Human Services State Child Care Rules Rev., St. Paul, 1985—; chmn. arts enrichment St. Anthony Park Sch. Assn., St. Paul, 1984-85; active Loft Teen Ctr., St. Paul, 1985—. Recipient Outstanding Service award Child Care Council, 1977. Mem. Nat. Assn. Edn. Young Children, Resources for Child Caring (v.p. 1977), Nat. Head Start Assn., Minn. Head Start Dirs. Assn. (v.p. 1986—), Nat. Black Child Devel. Inst., Nat. Assn. Female Execs., Fisk U. Alumni Assn. (sec. 1981—). Democrat. Baptist. Home: 428 W Central Ave Saint Paul MN 55103 Office: Ramsey Action Program Head Start 586 Fuller Ave Saint Paul MN 55103

MANN, DOROTHY JOAN, accountant; b. Ventura, Calif., Sept. 25, 1941; d. Louis D. Chapel and Evelyn T. Mann Chapel; m. Wayne L. Boatman, Apr. 18, 1959 (div. 1971); children—Robert, Barry. A.A. Coastline Community Coll., 1982. Asst. controller Ferro Properties Co., Ventura, 1966-69; controller, Glover Properties Co., Ventura, 1970-75, John Taft Electric Co., 1975-78; staff accountant Dunlap & Litton Accountancy Corp, Ventura, 1979-80, Wierks and Munson C.P.A.s, Fullerton, Calif., 1980-81; fin. mgr. Electrend, Inc., Fullerton, 1981-85; chief fin. officer, shareholder Martin Electric Co., Inc., 1985—. Mem. Am. Assn. Women Accts., Nat. Assn. Female Execs., Am. Mensa Ltd., Beta Sigma Phi. Democrat. Home: 2445 El Rancho Vista Dr Fullerton CA 92633 Office: Martin Electric Co Inc 6351 Burnham Ave Buena Park CA 90621

MANN, ELVA JAMES, dietitian, educator; b. Truxno, La., June 20, 1904; d. Abner and Lavada (Tugwell) James; m. John F. Kahrs, Jan. 11, 1934 (dec. 1953); m. Gus G. Kindervater, Dec. 14, 1955 (dec. 1963); m. Curt F. Mann, Oct. 10, 1968 (dec. 1973); B.S., La. Poly. Inst., 1927. Dietetic intern Johns Hopkins Hosp., Balt., 1927-28; dietitian Girl Scout Camp, Annapolis, Md., 1928, 29, Johns Hopkins Hosp., 1928-29; staff dietitian Touro Infirmary, New Orleans, 1929-35, dir. dietary dept., 1935-40, 42-49, dir. dietetic intern program, 1945-49; dir. dietetics Dept. Instns. State La., Baton Rouge, 1940-42; dietitian Morrison Food Service, Baptist Hosp., Crippled Children's Hosp., 1954. Bd. dirs. Silver Cross Nursing Home, 1973-76, King's Daus. Hosp., 1977-80. Mem. Am. Dietetic Assn., Brookhaven C. of C., DAR, King's Daus. Aux. Republican. Presbyterian (elder 1977—). Clubs: Little Theater, Garden (pres. 1981-82). Avocations: gardening; theater; reading; gourmet cooking. Home: 631 S Church St Brookhaven MS 39601

MANN, FLORENCE MARGARET, librarian, educator; b. Balt., July 17, 1923; d. Carl Clarence and Amy Gertrude (Coulbourn) Drafts; m. Eugene Reinolt Mann, Sept. 4, 1949; children—Liza Gene M. A.B., Goucher Coll., 1946; M.L.S., Rutgers U., 1966; postgrad. Tex. Woman's U., 1979—. Program dir. YWCA, U.S. and Australia, 1946-52; pub. librarian, Brisbane, Australia, 1954-56; assoc. librarian Bloomfield Coll. (N.J.), 1957-66; librarian Dunellen High Sch., (N.J.), 1966-71, Moses Brown Sch., Providence, 1971-74; supr. sch. libraries North Kingstown, R.I., 1974-76; jr. high sch. media specialist Woonsocket Edn. Dept. (R.I.), 1980-82; tchr. English conversation Friends Sch., Tokyo, 1983-85; librarian Johnston (R.I.) Schs., 1985—; instr. Grad. Library Sch., U. R.I., Kingston, 1972-73; chmn. Nat. Library Week Com., Essex County, N.J., 1958-60; dir. reading Day Camp Program, Cranston, (R.I.) schs., summer 1972. Contbr. articles to profl. jours.; joint author: Rhode Island Quakers During the American Revolution, 1976. Chmn., Mayor's Com. for UN Day, Dunellen, 1970; mem. hospitality com. Tall Ships Bicentennial, Newport, R.I., 1976; chmn. Ch. Women United, World Community Day, Providence, 1977; bd. dirs. UNESCO, Tokyo, 1984—, Fellowship of Reconciliation. Peabody Conservatory of Music scholar, 1937-44. Mem. ALA, N.J. Library Assn., New Eng. Library Assn., Assn. Profl. Librarians of Tokyo, YWCA, Beta Phi Mu. Democrat. Quaker. Clubs: Goucher, R.I. Short Story. Home: 20 Colonial Rd Providence RI 02906 Office: Johnston Bd Edn Johnston RI

MANN, GRACE CARROL, ballerina, choreographer; b. Berkeley, Calif, Nov. 30; d. Robert H. and Nell Jeanette (Curry) M.; B.A., U. Calif., Berkeley, 1941; student Theodore Kosloff. Dancer, San Francisco Ballet and Opera, 1940, 41, Kosloff Ballet, Hollywood, Calif., 1942-46, film Spectre of the Rose for Ben Hecht, 1945; prin. dancer Original Ballet Russe of Col. de Basil including season Covent Garden, 1947-48; founder Studio of Dance Art, 1951; dir. Ballet Center, Oakland, Calif., 1971—; co-founder Ballet Valmann also choreography; instr. master classes; judge regional ballet auditions; choreography includes: Concerto in D (Poulenc), Concerto (Mendelssohn), Mikrocosmos (Bartok). Mem. Delta Epsilon. Home: 5960 Margarido Dr Oakland CA 94618 Office: 452 Santa Clara Ave Oakland CA 94610

MANN, HELENE DAVIS POWNER (MRS. CECIL W. MANN), psychologist; b. Greensburg, Ind., June 30, 1899; d. Charles Tracy and Olive (Davis) Powner; student U. Ariz., 1917-19; A.B., U. Calif., Berkeley, 1922; M.A., U. So. Calif., 1927; postgrad. U. So. Calif., Sorbonne, Paris, U. Madrid, 1927; pvt. study, France, U.S.A.; m. Cecil William Mann, Oct. 16, 1937; 1 dau., Jennifer O. Psychologist, tchr. gifted children Pasadena (Calif.) City Schs., 1926-29; chief psychol. examiner Los Angeles County Juvenile Hall Clinic, 1929-39; spl. lectr. U. Denver, 1939-41; psychologist Bur. Testing and Guidance, also Specialized Tng. and Reassignment Unit, U.S. Army, La. State U., 1943-45; dir. Tulane U. reading improvement program, 1953-57; editor Charles T. Powner Corp., Regan Pub. Co., Chgo., 1922-60; pvt. practice psychology, New Orleans, 1945-61; pvt. practice, research, Jackson County, N.C., 1961-74; psychol. cons. Western N.C. U. Mental Health Center, 1969-70, Dept. Interior Bur. Indian Affairs, Cherokee, N.C., 1962-70; pvt. practice psychology, Henderson County, 1974-79. Mem. AAUW, LWV, Am., Southeastern, N.C. psychol. assns., Pi Beta Phi. Club: Book. Contbr. articles to profl. jours.; also children's stories. Address: 11 Quail Trail Hendersonville NC 28739

MANN, HILDAGARDE EDYTHE, county commissioner of jurors; b. N.Y.C., Jan. 3, 1935; d. Albert C. Bunner and Hildegarde Caroline Perdoch; separated; children—Philip, Jr., Jeffrey, Caroline, Heidi. Sec. Am. Locomotive Co., Schenectady, N.Y., 1952-55; ski instr. West Mountain Ski Club, Gore Mountain Ski Club, Glens Falls, 1969-74; commr. jurors Warren County, State of N.Y., Lake George, 1979—. Mem. Warren County Republican Exec. Com., 1975—; mem. Queensbury Planning Bd., N.Y., 1975—; Lake Champlain-Lake George Regional Environ. Council, N.Y., 1975—. Bd. dirs. Warren County Coop. Extension; past pres. Warren County Children's Com. Mem. N.Y. State Assn. Jury Commrs. (v.p.), Adirondack Regional C. of C., Warren County Women's Rep. Club. Episcopalian. Clubs: Zonta, Glen Falls Country. Avocations: golf; skiing; politics; gardening. Home: 9-101 Regency Park Glens Falls NY 12801 Office: Lake George Municipal Ctr Lake George NY 12801

MANN, JOYCE PEARL, personal care facility administrator; b. Coopersburg, Pa., Apr. 22, 1928; d. Russell Isaac and Dorothy Helen (Baus) Mann. Cert. of Christian Edn., Pinebrook Jr. Coll., Coopersburg, Pa., 1956. Sec. to pres. Pinebrook Jr. Coll., 1955-70; asst. adminstr. Bible Fellowship Home for Aging, Nazareth, Pa., 1970-76; adminstr. Mannco Manor, Inc., Emmaus, Pa., 1976—; mem. Emmaus Ambulance Corp. Mem. Personal Care Providers Assn., Nat. Assn. Residential Care Facilities, Nat. Council on Aging, Nat. Woodcarvers Assn. Woodcarvers (Cin.), Nat. Carver's Mus. Avocations: woodcarving; sewing. Home: 659 Broad St Emmaus PA 18049 Office: Mannco Manor Inc 659 Broad St Emmaus PA 18049

MANN, KAREN, administrator, educator; b. Kansas City, Mo., Oct. 9, 1942; d. Charles and Letha (Anderson) M. B.A., U. Calif.-Santa Barbara, 1964; M.P.A., Golden Gate U., 1975, Ph.D. candidate, 1984—. Tchr. Sisters of Immaculate Heart, Los Angeles, 1964-68; group counselor San Francisco and Marin County Juvenile Halls, 1968-70; parole agt. Calif. Dept. Corrections, Sacramento and San Francisco, 1970—, unit supr., 1982—. Co-author: Prison Overcrowding, 1979; Community Corrections: A Plan for California, 1980. Active Buddhist Peace Fellowship, Berkeley, 1984—, Buddhists Concerned for Animals, San Francisco, 1983—, Fellowship of Reconciliation, N.Y., 1970—; co-founder, faculty Network Ctr. for Study of Ministry, San Francisco, 1982-84; pres. San Francisco Network Ministries, 1980-82. Mem. Am. Correctional Assn. Office: Calif Dept Corrections 759 S Van Ness Ave San Francisco CA 94110

MANN, KATY, city official; b. Seattle, Oct. 25, 1944; d. James Francis and Rosalyn Mae (Miller) Horan; m. Robert Bruce Mann, Dec. 10, 1965. Student U. Americas, 1965, U. Wash., 1964, U. Calif.-Santa Barbara, 1962-63; grad. Mpcl. Treas. Inst., Mich. State U., 1985. Cert. mcpl. treas. With loan dept. Park State Bank, Loves Park, Ill., 1966-73; controller Wabeek Country Club, Bloomfield Hills, Mich., 1974-79; staff acct. Spacht & Co., P.C., Troy, Mich., 1979-81; city clk., treas. City of Keego Harbor, Mich., 1981—, acting city mgr., 1985—. Mem. Sylvan-Otter Environ. Protection Group, Sylvan Lake, Mich., 1976—. Mem. Mcpl. Fin. Officers Assn., Oakland County Treas. Assn., Mich. Mcpl. Fin. Officers Assn., Internat. Assn. Mcpl. Clks., Oakland County Clks. Assn., Mich. Mcpl. Clks. Assn. Avocations: skiing; sailing; boating. Home: 2496 Garland Sylvan Lake MI 48053 Office: City of Keego Harbor 2025 Beechmont Keego Harbor MI 48033

MANN, LYNDA, management consultant; b. Maywood, Calif., July 13, 1947; d. Paul and Anne Hoover. B.S. in Edn., So. Ill. U., 1975; M.A. in Social Sci., Pacific Lutheran U., Tacoma, 1977; postgrad. U. Tex. Joined U.S. Army, 1971, advanced through grades to maj., 1985; exec. officer Madigan Army Med. Ctr., Tacoma, 1974-77; chairperson personnel activities 9th Inf. Div. Tacoma, 1978-79; chief orgn. effectiveness NATO-SHAPE, Casteau, Belgium, 1980, 21st Support Command, Kaiserslautern, W.Ger., 1981; resigned, 1981; pres. Mann & Assocs., Austin, Tex., 1982—. Bd. dirs. Austin Mil. Charity Ball, 1984, 85, 86. Served with Tex. N.G., 1982—. Decorated Meritorious Service medal; recipient MacArthur Found. Leadership Writing award, 1986. Mem. Am. Soc. Tng. and Devel. (chpt. v.p. programs 1985), Intergovtl. Tng. Council, Tex. N.G. Acad. Alumni Assn., N.G. Assn. Tex. (life), NOW, Phi Kappa Phi. Republican. Unitarian. Avocations: running; golf; writing; gourmet cooking. Home and Office: 7707 Islander Dr Austin TX 78749

MANN, MARY ANNEETA, author; b. Rockhampton, Queensland, Australia, Dec. 30, 1930; came to U.S., 1965; d. Willie Augustus and Dorothy Louisa M.; 1 child, Attica Andrew. B.A., Sydney U., Australia, 1964; M.A., U. Calif.-Berkeley, 1970; Ph.D., U. So. Calif., 1982. Author: Los Angeles Theatre Book, 1978, Los Angeles Theatre Book, 1984, The Construction of Tragedy, 1985; author plays: Tortoise Shell, Diana Devereaux, The Senator's Daughter, Maria and the Comet, 1983, Anzac I and II, 1984. Mem. Australian Soc. Accts.

MANN, PANSY HUDLER, school administrator; b. Beulaville, N.C., Feb. 27, 1944; d. Sammie Washington and Julia (Smith) Hudler; m. William Edgar Mann, Jr., Sept. 3, 1966; children—Susette Michele, Constance Lynn. B.A. in Sociology, Meredith Coll., Raleigh, N.C., 1974; M.A. in Ednl. Adminstrn., E. Carolina U., 1983. Tchr., Craven County Schs., N.C., 1966-67, Onslow County Schs., Jacksonville, N.C., 1967-78, asst. prin., tchr., 1978—; asst. prin. Morton Sch., Jacksonville; instr. in service workshops Onslow County Schs., Jacksonville, 1974-76. Pres., v.p., treas. Jacksonville Jaycettes, 1973-74. Named Onslow Tchr. of Yr., 1973. Mem. Assn. Supervision and Curriculum Devel., N.C. Prins., Onslow County Prins. Assn. Democrat. Baptist. Avocation: homemaking. Home: 1017 Beech Tree Rd Jacksonville NC 28540

MANN, SHARON ANN, food corporation executive; b. Detroit, Dec. 12, 1943; d. William Harold and Barbara Mary (Luckas) Gibson; m. R. Rodman Mann, Dec. 26, 1964; children—Christopher D'Arcy, Cynthia Ann. A.A. in Liberal Arts, Immaculata Coll., 1963; cert., McDonald's Hamburger U., Oak Brook, Ill., 1968. Acctg. clk. Nat. Assn. Home Builders, Washington, 1963-65; asst. to comptroller EAK Mgmt. Co., Bethesda, Md., 1965-68; sec., treas. G & M Food Corp., Arnold, Md., 1968—, Fox Chase, Inc., Arnold, 1981—; asst. treas. Chesapeake Acad., Arnold, Md., 1980—, mem. adv. bd., 1980—; pres. CRCS Corp., Arnold, 1981—. Creator, coordinator Chesapeake Assocs. Ltd. Partnership, 1981. Mem. Assn. Ind. Md. Schs., Immaculata Prep. Alumnae (treas. 1976-80). Home: 21 Pocono Dr Arnold MD 21012 Office: G & M Food Corp 21 Pocono Dr Arnold MD 21012

MANN, WENDY GAYLE, newscaster; b. Longview, Wash., June 13, 1956; d. Ernest Wayne and Donna Mae (Thompsen) Mann. B.A. in Communications, U. Wash., 1980. Reporter KNDU-TV (NBC), Kennewick, Wash., 1980-81, weather person, 1980-81; reporter, anchor KEPR-TV (CBS), Pasco, Wash., 1981-83; reporter, anchor KSTW-TV, Tacoma, 1983—. Hostess, Muscular Dystrophy Telethon, KNDU-TV, Kennewick, 1982; rep. U. Wash. Rose Bowl Parade Float, 1979. Mem. Women in Communications, Pi Beta Phi. Republican. Office: KSTW-TV Box 11411 2320 S 19th St Tacoma WA 98411

MANNELLY, KATHY OLSON, management consultant; b. Lawrence, Mich., Jan. 24, 1945; d. Willie Edward and Marjorie Ellen (Holton) Olson; A.B. in Behavioral Sci., Grand Rapids (Mich.) Jr. Coll., 1971; B.S. in Psychology, Grand Valley State Coll., Allendale, Mich., 1973; M.Pub. Adminstrn., Pacific Luth. U., 1985; m. Patrick K. Mannelly, Apr. 9, 1980; stepchildren—Brian, Michael. Coordinator edn., coordinator Sunrise Program, Grand Rapids, 1974-75; trainer Dymaxion Corp., 1974-78; supr. Employee Assistance Resource, Grand Rapids, 1975-77; personnel and mktg. mgr. Project REHAB, Grand Rapids, 1977-78; sr. citizen and substance abuse specialist Mich. Dept. Mgmt. and Budget, 1978-80; mem. faculty Profl. Update, 1980-82; dir. coop. edn. Pacific Luth. U., Tacoma, 1981-82, assoc. dean student life, 1983-86; faculty assoc., cons. in field. Mem. Active Tacoma Crisis Clinic, 1980-81; mem. program com. ARC, 1975-77; mem. placement, site and legis. coms. Coop. Edn. Assn., 1981-82; mem. exec. com. N.W. Coop. Edn. Assn., 1980-81; mem. adv. bd. N.W. Coop. Edn. Tng. Center, 1981-82; mem. work study adv. bd. Wash. State Council for Post Secondary Edn., 1981-82. Recipient various service awards; lic. social worker, Mich. Mem. Nat. Assn. Women Deans, Adminstrs. and Counselors, ASTD, Nat. Assn. Female Execs., South Sound Womens Network. Network, Internat. Platform Assn. Author articles, manuals in field.

MANNI, ELEANOR THERESA, social worker, counselor, consultant; b. San Antonio, Jan. 20, 1951; d. Anthony Joseph and Sofia Matilda (Elia) Piccolo; m. Kenneth Allen Manni, June 28, 1975; children—Nathan Matthew, Jessica Marie, David Michael. B.A., U. Conn., 1973. Cert. social worker, Idaho; cert. counselor, Wash. Coordinator, co-founder Road to Recovery, Inc., Dept. Health and Welfare, Blackfoot, Idaho, 1975; occupational program cons. Dept. Health and Welfare, Lewiston, Idaho, 1976-79; coordinator, counselor pregnancy program March of Dimes, Oak Harbor, Wash., 1983-84; instr., counselor Natural Family Planning, Couple-to-Couple League, Cin., 1979—. Bd. dirs. March Dimes, Oak Harbor, Wash., 1984—; v.p. North Whidbey Republican Women's Club, Oak Harbor, 1984-85, pres., 1986—; oblate Our Lady of Rock Monastery, Order of St. Benedict, Shaw Island, Wash., 1979. Mem. Am. Assn. Counseling and Devel., Couple-to-Couple League, Assn. Labor and Mgmt. Administrn. and Cons. on Alcoholism, Nat. Council on Alcoholism, Bus. and Profl. Women's Club. Roman Catholic. Avocations: interior design; horticulture wildlife photography; medieval history. Home and Office: 6767 675th Ave W Oak Harbor WA 98277

MANNILLO, PAULA ANNE, resort owner, business development specialist; b. Altus, Okla., Feb. 16, 1944; d. Joe Dial and Orlynn (Anciaux) McKibbin; m. Richard William Mannillo, July 1, 1966; children—Lynn Marie, Rya Clare, Richard Paul. B.A., Macalester Coll., 1966; M.A., U. Minn., 1975. Prin., Mannillo Co., St. Paul, 1973-74; owner Clothes Works, Inc., St. Paul, 1976-78; broker Gen. Brokerage, Inc., St. Paul, 1979-83; cons. Growth Ventures, Inc., St. Paul, 1981-84; resort owner Northland Lodge, Inc., Leech Lake, Minn., 1981—; fin. dir. Women's Econ. Devel. Corp., 1984—. Chair Small Bus. Adv. Council 916 Vo Tech, White Bear Lake, Minn., 1980-84; treas., Ramsey County Hist. Soc., St. Paul, 1979-82; co-chair Grand Old Days-Grand Ave. Bus. Assn., St. Paul, 1978; treas. Minn. Women's Trade Fair, 1984; bd. dirs. St. Paul Progress Housing Corp., 1985—. Mem. Nat. Assn. Women Bus. Owners (treas. 1980-82, nat. rep. 1980-84). Office: Women's Econ Devel Corp 1885 University Suite 395 Saint Paul MN 55104

MANNING, DIANE LOIS, winery executive; b. Bklyn., Dec. 21, 1940; d. William and Louise Margaret (Backer) Pfuhl; m. Thomas Frank Manning, Apr. 9, 1960; children—Craig, Scott, Dawn, Corey. Student Hofstra U. Assoc., Manning and Assocs., San Francisco, 1976-80; controller custom bottling Chateau Diana Cellars, Healdsburg, Calif., 1980-86, owner, controller, 1986—. Office: Chateau Diana 6195 Dry Creek Rd Healdsburg CA 95448

MANNING, DONNA DILLON, lawyer; b. Huntington, W.Va., July 7, 1941; d. Evan Frederick and Betha Irene (Brumfield) Dillon; m. Bayless Manning, Mar. 7, 1972. B.A., Westmount Coll., 1963; M.S., SUNY, 1971; J.D., Columbia U., 1977, M.B.A., 1978. Bar: N.Y. 1978. Tutor, Montreux, Switzerland, 1963-64; tchr. U.S. Air Force, Eng., 1964-65; tchr. Central Valley High Sch., N.Y., 1969-71; ednl. cons., tchr. Boise Sch. Dist. (Idaho), 1971-72; mem. firm Brown, Wood, Ivey, N.Y.C., 1978—; dir. Am. Ind. Reins. Co., Stamford, Conn. Bd. govs. Fgn. Policy Assn. OTR, N.Y.C., 1974—; chmn. spl. events com. Carnegie Hall, 1983—; mem. Central Park Conservancy, 1983—. Mem. ABA, Assn. Bar City N.Y. Democrat. Clubs: Cosmopolitan, Nat. Arts. Home: One Lexington Ave New York NY 10010 Office: Brown Wood Ivey Mitchell & Petty One World Trade Center New York NY 10048

MANNING, ELISSA LENORE, human resources manager; b. Seattle, July 5, 1954; d. Lorrin E. and Martha L. Lenore (Wells) Carl; m. Thomas Michael Manning, June 27, 1981. B.A., U. Wash., 1982. Tribunal adminstr. Am. Arbitration Assn., Seattle, 1975-78; personnel specialist Providence Med. Ctr., Seattle, 1978-79; asst. dir. personnel St. Cabrini Hosp., Seattle, 1980-81;

compensation analyst ISC Systems Corp., Spokane, Wash., 1981; human resources mgr. W. Coast Grocery Co., Spokane, 1982—. Chmn. adv. com. personnel YWCA, Spokane, 1982-84; bd. dirs. YWCA, 1983-86, v.p., 1986—. Mem. Am. Soc. Personnel Adminstrs., Pacific N.W. Personnel Assn. Office: West Coast Grocery Co T A Box 2808 Spokane WA 99220

MANNING, LORA JEANE, school board administrator; b. Bradenton, Fla., Apr. 11, 1946; d. Paul Joseph Manning and Leloa (Rhodes) Chestnut. B.S., Fla. A & M U., 1969; M.S., Nova U., 1977, Ednl. Specialist, 1979. Tchr., Dade County Sch. Bd., Miami, 1969-77, tchr. reading resources, 1974-77, tchr., 1977-79, ednl. specialist, 1979-81, community sch. adminstr., 1981-83, elem. sch. adminstr., 1983—. Mem. AAUW, The Exec. Female, Nat. Allegiance of Black Educators, Dade Dist. Citizens Adv. Com. Democrat. Baptist. Avocations: reading; traveling; crafts; music; cooking. Office: Treasure Island Elementary Sch 7540 E Treasure Dr Miami FL 33141

MANNING, MARGARET LOUISE, psychotherapist; b. Tucson, June 2, 1956; d. William Herman and Carole Eleanor (Musgrove) McBratney. B.A., U. Ariz., 1981; M.A., Calif. Grad. Inst., 1983. Lic. marriage, family and child counselor. Asst. to pres. Western Psychol. Services, Los Angeles, 1978-81; crisis counselor Cedars-Sinai Med. Ctr., Los Angeles, 1980-84; counselor South Bay Therapeutic Clinic, Hawthorne, Calif., 1982-84; psychotherapist PMC Treatment Systems, Los Angeles, 1984-85; psychotherapist Comprehensive Care Corp., Los Angeles, 1985—; counselor Brotman Med. Ctr., Los Angeles, 1982-83, Julia Ann Singer Ctr., Los Angeles, 1984. Mem. Women in Health, Bus. and Profl. Women, Am. Anorexia-Buimia Assn., Nat. Assn. Female Execs., Calif. State Psychol. Assn., Calif. Assn. Marriage and Family Therapists. Democrat. Office: 911 W Pico Blvd Suite 670 Los Angeles CA 90035

MANNING, MARGUERITE, univ. dean, clergywoman; b. Phoenix; d. Walter Jerald and Elizabeth (Smith) Manning; A.B., Scarritt Coll., 1942; M.A., Boston, 1943; M.Div., Union Theol. Sem., 1957; M.A., Columbia Tchrs. Coll., 1966, Ed.D., 1975. Ordained to ministry Congregationalist Ch.; dir. student activities U. Tenn., 1943-46; ednl. asst. Riverside Ch., N.Y.C., 1947-55; parish worker East Harlem Protestant Parish, 1955-57; minister East Congl. Ch. and Waits River Meth. Ch., Vt., 1958-61; tchr. English and phys. edn. Baghdad (Iraq) High Sch., 1961-62; adminstrv. asst. dept. guidance and student personnel adminstrn. Columbia Tchrs. Coll., 1962-66; research asso. Bank St. Coll. Edn., N.Y.C., 1966-68; with Bur. Research, N.Y.C. Bd. Edn., 1968-69; sec. personnel United Bd. Christian Higher Edn. in Asia, 1969-71; dean student affairs Rutgers U., Newark, 1971—. Active Red Feather drive; social worker ARC, Camp Shanks, N.Y., World War II; moderator Grafton-Orange Assn. Congl. Chs.; mem. minister's assn. Vt. Congl. Conf., 1958; pres. Women of Grace Ch., Newark; bd. dirs. YWCA. Mem. Nat. Assn. Women Deans and Counselors, Am. Assn. Ednl. Research, Am. Personnel and Guidance Assn., NEA, Am. Assn. Higher Edn., Am. Assn. U. Adminstrs., Bus. and Profl. Women's Club, Pi Lambda Theta (pres. Alpha Epsilon chpt. 1966-68, treas., 1969-72, chmn. nat. nominating com. 1966-67), Kappa Delta Pi, Phi Delta Kappa. Home: 351 Broad St Apt 1009 Newark NJ 07104

MANNING, SHERRY FISCHER, college president emerita, business executive; b. Washington, Apr. 28, 1943; d. Fred W. and Eleanor A. (Mertz) Fischer; B.A. cum laude, Western Md. Coll., 1965, L.H.D., 1980; M.A., William and Mary Coll., 1967; D.B.A., U. Colo. 1973; m. Charles W. Manning, Dec. 23, 1966; children—Shannon Marie, Charles Fischer, Kelly Eleanor. Mktg. rep., systems engr. IBM, 1967-71; staff assoc. Nat. Center for Higher Edn. Mgmt. Systems, 1971-72; exec. asst. to exec. dir. Nat. Commn. of the Financing of Postsecondary Edn., 1972-73; adj. prof. U. Colo., 1973-74; asst. prof. U. Kans., 1975-77; cons. to pres. for acad. planning Universidade Fed. de Ceara, 1976-77; exec. v.p. Colo. Women's Coll., 1977-78, pres., 1978-81, pres. emerita, 1981—; chief exec. officer John Madden Co., Englewood, Colo.; dir. United Bank Services Co., Imperial Am. Energy Inc. Trustee Adopt-A-School 1978-81, Denver Symphony 1978-81, Colo. Council on Econ. Edn., 1984—, Colo. Assn. Commerce and Industry Ednl. Found., 1984—Recipient DAR Outstanding Citizen award, 1961, Faculty Devel. award U. Kans., 1976, Soroptimists Women Helping Women award, 1980. Mem. Nat. Women's Coalition, Women's Forum, Zonta, Altrusa. Republican. Presbyterian. Club: Denver Met. Host: Community Affairs program Sta. KHOW 1979-80; contbr. articles in field. Office: John Madden Co 6312 S Fiddler's Green Circle Suite 150-E Englewood CO 80111

MANNING, SHIRLEY ANN, distribution executive; b. Utica, N.Y., Nov. 6, 1939; d. Arthur R. and Stella C. (Wiklac) Boxall; m. Michael C. Manning, Sr., Jan. 14, 1967 (div. Sept. 1978); children—Christi Lynn Manning DiStefano, Michael, Greg, Sean, Heather; m. Edward P. Thierbacker, Aug. 31, 1985. Student Albany Bus. Coll., 1963, Fulton Coll., 1972, Albany Jr. Coll. Lic. real estate broker; notary pub. Mgr., Manning Constrn. Co., Clifton Park, N.Y., 1968-76; mgr. Van Mar Realty, Saratoga, N.Y., 1976-77; adminstrv. asst., account exec. HMC Funding, Albany, N.Y., 1976-77; sales engr. Oxford Chems., Albany, 1977—; pres. SAM Distbrs., Schenectady, 1979—. Mem. social com. Country Knolls Civic Assn., Ballston Lake, N.Y., 1975. Recipient cert. of merit Police Benevolent Assn., Schenectady, 1986, others. Mem. Nat. Assn. Female Execs., Capital Region World Trade Council, Nat. Assn. Female Execs., Trade Assn. Albany Port. Democrat. Roman Catholic. Clubs: Wolfert's Roost (Albany); Hi Tech (Clifton Park). Avocations: tennis; skiing; reading; needlepoint; oil painting; decorating. Office: SAM Distbrs 2010 Maxon Rd Schenectady NY 12308

MANNING, SYLVIA, English studies educator; b. Montreal, Que., Can., Dec. 2, 1943; came to U.S., 1967; d. Bruno and Lea Bank; B.A., McGill U., 1963; M.A., Yale U., 1964, Ph.D. in English, 1967; m. Peter J. Manning, Aug. 20, 1967; children—Bruce David, Jason Maurice. Asst. prof. English Calif. State U., Hayward, 1967-71, assoc. prof., 1971-75, assoc. dean, 1972-75; assoc. prof. U. So. Calif., 1975—, asso. dir. Center for the Humanities, 1975-77, chmn. freshman writing, 1977-80, chmn. dept. English, 1980-83, vice provost, 1984—. Woodrow Wilson fellow, 1963-64, 66-67. Mem. MLA, Dickens Soc. Author: Dickens as Satirist, 1971; Hard Times, An Annotated Bibliography, 1984; contbr. essays to mags. Office: Department of English University of Southern California Los Angeles CA 90089

MANNIS, VALERIE SKLAR, lawyer; b. Green Bay, Wis., May 26, 1939; d. Phillip and Rose (Aaron) Sklar; m. Kent Simon Mannis, Dec. 28, 1958; children—Andrea, Marci. B.S., U. Wis., 1970; J.D., 1974. Bar: Wis. 1974. Staff atty. Legis. Council, Madison, Wis., 1974-75; sole practice, Madison, 1975-84; asst. to pres. Bank of Shorewood Hills (Wis.), 1984—; founding mem. Legal Assn. for Women, Madison, 1975—. Pres. Nat. Women's Polit. Caucus Dane County, Madison, 1984; bd. dirs. Madison Estate Planning Council, 1980-84, bd. dirs. Madison Jewish Community Council, 1975-79, 82-84. Mem. ABA, Dane County Bar Assn. (chmn. property com. 1978-84), State Bar. Wis. (gov. 1980-86), Nat. Assn. Banking Women. Democrat. Jewish. Club: Hadassah. Office: Asst to Pres Bank of Shorewood Hills Madison WI 53705

MANNS, SCOTTE HARRIS, newspaper executive; b. Phillippi, W.Va., Jan. 25, 1937; d. William Alvin and Gracelyn Anna (Reed) Harris; grad. Elizabeth (Pa.) High Sch., 1953; m. Don Franklin Manns, Sept. 23, 1961. Adminstr. classified advt. Des Moines Register & Tribune, 1962-63; adminstr. classified advt. Washington Post, 1963-65, supr., 1965-71, asst. mgr., 1971-73, mgr., 1973-76, asst. to v.p. sales, 1976—, advt. mgr., 1976—, dir. advt. sales, 1985—. Mem. Washington Bd. Trade, Advt. Club Washington. Home: 4203 38th Rd N Arlington VA 22207 Office: 1150 15th St NW Washington DC 20071

MANOCCHIO, AIMEE LOUISE, lawyer; b. Boonton, N.J., Sept. 22, 1957; d. Armando B. and Mary C. (Quackenbush) M. B.A. with high honors, Rutgers Coll., Rutgers U., 1979; J.D. cum laude, Seton Hall U., 1982. Bar: N.J. 1982. Law sec. Superior Ct. N.J. appellate div., 1982-83; assoc. Wilentz, Goldman & Spitzer, P.C., Woodbridge, N.J., 1983—. Notes and comments editor Seton Hall Law Rev., 1981-82; contbr. article to publ. Mem. ABA, N.J. Bar Assn., Middlesex County Bar Assn., Queen's Chorale Alumni Assn., Phi Beta Kappa, Omicron Delta Epsilon. Office: Wilentz Goldman & Spitzer 900 Route 9 Box 10 Woodbridge NJ 07095

MANOFF, DINAH BETH, actress; b. N.Y.C., Jan. 25; d. Arnold and Lyova (Rosenthal) M. Student public schs., N.Y. and Calif. Appeared in: TV series Soap, 1977-78; TV movies: For Ladies Only, 1981, Flight 90: Disaster on the Potomac, 1984; TV miniseries Celebrity, 1984; appeared on stage in I Ought To Be In Pictures (Tony award), 1980, Gifted Children, 1983, Leader of the Pack, 1985; motion pictures include: Grease, 1977, Ordinary People, 1979, I Ought To Be In Pictures, 1982. Mem. Screen Actors Guild, Actors Equity, AFTRA. Jewish. Home: New York NY Office: care The Gersh Agy Inc 222 N Cannon Dr Beverly Hills CA 90210

MANOLI, CHERYL ELLEN, mathematics educator; b. Framingham, Mass., Nov. 21, 1946; d. Anthony Gene and Mildred Sargent (Simmons) Manoli. B.S., Boston U., 1968, M.Ed., 1972; M.A., Boston Coll., 1976, postgrad. in ednl. research, measurement and evaluation, 1984. Cert. tchr., Mass. Tchr. math. North Quincy (Mass.) High Sch., 1968—. Boston U. trustee scholar, 1964-68; NSF math. grantee Boston Coll., 1972-76. Mem. Nat. Council Tchrs. Math., Quincy Edn. Assn., Mass. Tchrs. Assn., NEA, Pi Lambda Theta. Methodist. Home: 48 Bostonia Ave Brighton MA 02135 Office: North Quincy High Sch 316 Hancock St North Quincy MA 02171

MANOV, EILEEN MILLENA, engineering marketing specialist; b. Sofia, Bulgaria, Aug. 22, 1962; came to U.S., 1967; d. Vladimir and Elly (Nedeva) M. B.A., Cornell U., 1984. Bus. devel. coordinator VEP Assocs., Inc., West Caldwell, N.J., 1984—. Mem. Soc. Mktg. Profl. Services, Nat. Assn. Female Execs., LWV (dir. Livingston, N.J. chpt. 1985—), Smithsonian Inst., Cornell Club. Eastern Orthodox. Avocations: travel, tennis, skiing. Home: 16 Mount Vernon Ct Livingston NJ 07039 Office: VEP Assocs Inc 1140 Bloomfield Ave West Caldwell NJ 07006

MANSELL, KATHLEEN ANN, nursing administrator; b. Evergreen Park, Ill., Mar. 25, 1954; d. Partick Joseph and Jane Elizabeth (Dwyer) Gill; m. Edward Thomas Mansell, Jan. 17, 1981; 1 child, Jane Therese. B.S. in Nursing, St. Xavier Coll., Chgo., 1977; M.S. in Nursing, Loyola U., Chgo., 1979. Registered nurse, Ill. Staff nurse Mercy Hosp., Chgo., 1977-80; instr. St Xavier Coll., Chgo., 1980-81; dir. nursing Alma Med. Clinic, Maywood, Ill., 1981-82; dir. maternal child nursing Silver Cross Hosp., Joliet, Ill., 1982—; cons. Boring, Seattle, 1984—. Contbr. articles to profl. jours. Mercy Scholar Mercy Hosp., 1975; Nurse traineeship Loyola U., 1978. Mem. Met. Birth Environ. Network, Assn. Care of Children in Hosps., Nat. Assn. Ob-Gny Nurses, Sigma Theta Tau. Roman Catholic. Home: 1028 Forest Ln Lemont IL 60439

MANSFIELD, JOYCE COPELAND, mathematician, educator; b. Dallas, Apr. 23, 1926; d. James Robert and Hazel Marie Copeland; B.A., Baylor U., 1947, M.A. in Math., 1948; postgrad. U. Wash., 1952-53, 1978—; m. Barney Stiles Mansfield, June 28, 1953; children—Charles R., Steven B., John S. Instr. math., Baylor U., Waco, Tex., 1948-52, asst. dean women, 1951-52; dist. exec. Seattle-King County Girl Scouts, 1953-55; instr. math. San Antonio Coll., 1957-58, Everett (Wash.) Community Coll., 1962—. Membership chmn., newsletter editor Pilchuck Audubon Bd., 1977-80; membership chair Women's Polit. Caucus, Snohomish County. Mem. AAUP, Assn. Supervision and Curriculum Devel., Nat. Council Tchrs. Math., Assn. Women in Math., Research Council for Diagnostic and Prescriptive Math., AAUW (chmn. Ednl. Found. Edmonds br., individual projects grantee, 1980, pres. Edmonds br. 1983-85), Baylor U. Alumni Assn. (dir. 1979-81), Kappa Kappa Gamma. Democrat. Baptist. Office: Everett Community Coll Math Dept 801 Wetmore St Everett WA 98201

MANSFIELD, LOIS EDNA, mathematics educator, researcher; b. Portland, Maine, Jan. 2, 1941; d. R. Carleton and Mary (Bowdish) M. B.S., U. Mich., 1962; M.S., U. Utah, 1966, Ph.D., 1969. Vis. asst. prof. computer sci. Purdue U., 1969-70; asst. prof. computer Sci. U. Kans., Lawrence, 1970-74, assoc. prof., 1974-78; assoc. prof. math. N.C. State U., Raleigh, 1978-79; assoc. prof. applied math. U. Va., Charlottesville, 1979-83, prof., 1983—; mem. adv. panel computer sci. NSF, 1975-78; cons., vis. scientist Inst. Computer Applications in Sci. and Engring., Hampton, Va., 1976-78. Mem. editorial bd. Jour. Sci. Statis. Computing, 1979—; contbr. articles to profl. jours. Mem. Am. Math. Soc., Soc. Indsl. and Applied Math., Assn. Computing Machinery (dir. SIGNUM 1980-83). Office: Univ Va Dept Applied Math Thornton Hall Charlottesville VA 22901

MANSFIELD, NANCY, psychologist, business exec.; b. Milw.; d. John and Melanie Szeremeta; Ph.D., U. Chgo., 1971; children—Alison, John. Staff psychologist Vernon Psychol. Lab., Chgo., 1954-70; founder, prin. Hume Mansfield Silber, Chgo., 1970-77; founder, pres. Mansfield Human Resources, Chgo., 1977—; indsl./orgnl. cons.; cons. on test devel., assessment. Mem. Am. Psychol. Assn., Midwest Psychol. Assn., Ill. Psychol. Assn., Indsl. Orgn. Psychologists of Ill. (pres. 1976), Acad. Health Care Educators (adv. bd.), Nat. Orgn. Women Bus. Owners. Office: 950 Lee St Suite 203 Des Plaines IL 60016 also 811 E Wisconsin Ave Suite 231 Milwaukee WI 53202

MANSOUR, CAROLYN MARIE, marketing specialist, realtor; b. Greenville, Miss., Jan. 17, 1957; d. Abraham and Gloria Ann (Curry) Mansour. B.B.A. in Acctg.-Data Processing, U. S.Miss., 1979. Asst. mgr. data processing Coca-Cola Bottlers, Hattiesburg, Miss., 1978; systems analyst Texaco, Inc., Houston, 1979-82, software support analyst Oil & Gas Intelec, Inc., Houston, 1982; mktg. rep. Control Data Corp., Dallas, 1983-84; computer cons., sales Mansour Interests, 1984—; real estate agent/investor, fin. cons., Houston and Dallas. Republican. Roman Catholic. Home: 5981 Arapaho Rd #1405 Dallas TX 75248 Office: Mansour Interests 5290 Beltline Suite 152 Dallas TX 75240

MANTELL, SUZANNE RUTH, editor, writer; b. East Orange, N.J., Nov. 26, 1944; d. Milton A. and Florence B. (Braun) M.; married, 1985; 1 child, Erica. B.F.A., Pratt Inst., 1967. Prodn. editor Harper's Mag., N.Y.C., 1967-73, assoc. and exec. editor, 1977-80; editor in chief Harper's Bookletter, N.Y.C., 1973-77; freelance editor Calif. Living Mag., Phila. Mag., 1982-83; manuscript editor Family Learning Mag., Belmont, Calif., 1983-84; freelance writer, N.Y.C., 1984—; ediltor Travel Book Catalogue, Banana Republic, 1985—; guest lectr. U. Calif.-Santa Cruz, 1981, Stanford U., Palo Alto, Calif., 1980-81. Mem. P.E.N., Nat. Book Critics Circle. Home: 302 W 12th St Apt 4C New York NY 10014

MANTHEY, MERRILY RUTH, psychotherapist, educator, consultant; b. Seattle, Mar. 25, 1943; d. Russell S. and Ruth B. Kolemaine; B.A., Evergreen State Coll., 1976; postgrad. m. Arnold E. Manthey, Mar. 29, 1962 (dec.); 1 son, Scott. Research publs. supr. Stanford Research Inst., Huntsville, Ala., 1965-67; communications dir. Marine Constrn. & Design Co., Seattle, 1967-71; pvt. practice therapy, 1971—; instr., public affairs dir. Seattle Acad., 1971-72; owner, dir., tchr. Kent (Wash.) Montessori Sch., 1972-76; instr. Green River Coll., 1974—; dir., therapist Inst. Exec. Stress Mgmt., Kent, 1976—; cons. human relations; legis. aide to Wash. senator Kent Pullen, 1977-79, cons., 1977—. Ednl. div. chmn., communications dir. Wash. Taxpayers Assn., Citizens Taxpayers Assn.; supr. King Tut Exhbn., Seattle Art Museum, 1978; mem. Kent Arts Commn., 1985—; singer The Rainier Chorale. Recipient Torch award Nat. Honor Soc., 1961; cert. Internat. Found. Human Relations, Amsterdam, Holland, 1980. Mem. Am. Soc. Group Psychotherapy and Psychodrama, Internat. Stress and Tension Control Assn., Assn. Transpersonal Psychology, Internat. Assn. Progressive Montessorians (cert. 1971), Am. Personnel and Guidance Assn. Club: Psychodrama of Wash. Author: Editorial Standards Guide, 1965; How to Promote Your Cause, 1975; editor: The Sou'Wester, 1961; research on stress. Home: PO Box 5918 Kent WA 98064 Office: 1819 S Central Ave Suite 100 Kent WA 98032

MANTHORNE, JACKIE ANN, writer, adminstr.; b. Halifax, N.S., Can., Dec. 3, 1946; d. Ralph Eugene and Mildred Freda (Rhuland) M.; B.A., Dalhousie U., 1968, B.Ed., 1970. Teaching asst. Miriam Sch. for the Exceptional, Montreal, Que., Can., 1972-73; tchr. Peter Hall Sch. for the Exceptional, Montreal, 1973-75; info. officer Women's Info. and Referral Centre, Montreal, 1975-78, asst. dir., 1978—, adult edn. tchr. of women and fin. and women's discussion group, 1974—; editor-in-chief Les Editions Communiqu' Elles, 1981—. Mem. Feminist Party of Can., Internat. Women's Writing Guild, Women's Info. and Referral Centre, Federation des femmes du Quebec, Centre Investigative Journalism. Editor Communiqu' Elles. (French and English), 1975—, Montreal Women's Directory (French and English), 1977, 80, 82, Newcomer's Handbook (French, English, Greek, Portuguese, Hindi), 1979. Office: 3585 St-Urbain Montreal PQ H2X 2N6 Canada

MANTON, DEBORAH JEAN, chemist; b. Phila., Feb. 16, 1955; d. Russell Frederick and Lois Eileen (Lord) M.; B.A., Franklin and Marshall Coll., 1976; B.S. in Engring. Physics, Washington U. 1978; postgrad. Rochester Inst. Tech., 1981—. Devel. engr. Corning Glass Works, Erwin, N.Y., 1978-80; mfg. devel. engr. Xerox Corp., Webster, N.Y., 1980-82; project mgr. Schlegel Corp., Rochester, N.Y., 1982-83; chief chemist Delco Products div. Gen. Motors, 1983—. Chmn. Rochester area alumni admissions asst. program Franklin and Marshall Coll., 1981-82. NSF fellow, 1976. Mem. Soc. Women Engrs., Nat. Soc. Profl. Engrs., Am. Electroplating Soc. Democrat. Episcopalian. Home: 110 Southland Dr Rochester NY 14623 Office: 1555 Lyell Ave Rochester NY 14606

MANTOVANI, JUANITA MARIE, univ. dean, educator; b. Chgo., Sept. 18, 1943; d. Norman Bert and Marie Frances (Byczkowski) Watson; A.B. summa cum laude, Marymount Coll., 1965; A.M., UCLA, 1966; Ph.D. in English, U. So. Calif., 1974; m. Robert Albert Mantovani, June 6, 1970. Acting chmn. freshman English program U. So. Calif., 1972-73, asst. dean student affairs, 1973-75, asst. dean humanities, 1975-81, chmn. ethnic studies program, 1980-81, mem. English faculty, 1966-75, mem. adj. faculty, program for study women and men in society, 1975-81; dean undergrad. studies, asso. prof. English, Calif. State U., Los Angeles, 1981—; mem. English faculty Long Beach City Coll., 1974-77, Pepperdine U. Liberal Studies Program, 1975-77; lectr., condr. workshops on profl. devel. for women, career devel. and liberal arts edn., images of women and ethnic minorities in lit. and media; panelist Nat. Endowment for Humanities Research Seminar on Feminism, 1979. Office: ADM 707 Calif State U 5151 State University Dr Los Angeles CA 90032

MANTZURANIS, VIRGINIA LEE, fashion consultant; b. Jacksonville, Tex., Oct. 6, 1948; d. Cole and Rachel (Edwards) Butler; m. Christos Dimitri Mantzuranis, Dec. 6, 1981; children—Christina Alexandra, James Christos. A.A., Lon Morris Coll., 1969; B.F.A. in Theatre, So. Meth. U., 1973. Exec. dir. Jay Jacks Internat., Dallas, 1975-78; v.p. mktg. and sales Victor Costa Inc., Dallas, 1978-82, dir., 1981; fashion cons., Dallas, Mem. Daus. of Penelope of Holy Trinity Greek Orthodox Ch., Dallas, 1984, Philoptochos Soc., 1983-84. Mem. The Fashion Group, Delta Psi Omega. Republican.

MANUSZAK, CAROLYN, college president. Pres. Willa Julie Coll., Stevenson, Md. Office: Villa Julia Coll Green Spring Valley Rd Stevenson MD 21153*

MANUTI, ANNABELLE THERESA, advertising agency financial executive; b. Bklyn., Sept. 11, 1928; d. Decio Dan and Anna Michelle (Vanacore) Assorto; m. John Thomas Manuti, Dec. 31, 1958. B.S., Hunter Coll., 1950, postgrad. in real estate sch. Continuing Edn., 1980-82. Lic. real estate broker, N.Y. Statis. auditor Am. Fore Ins. Group, N.Y.C., 1950-55; bookkeeper Picard Advt., N.Y.C., 1955-60; supr. dept. acctg. Moquel Williams & Saylor Advt., N.Y.C., 1960-65; comptroller's asst. Frolich Advt., N.Y.C., 1965-70; supr. accounts payable Miller Advt., N.Y.C., 1970-80; v.p. fin. Jaffe Communications, N.Y.C., 1980—; real estate sales mgr. Gen. Devel. Corp., 1980-85. Roman Catholic. Office: Jaffe Communications 122 E 42d St New York NY 10168

MANZ, BETTY ANN, nurse administrator; b. Paterson, N.J., Nov. 30, 1935; d. James Albert and Elsie (Basse) Brown; diploma Newark Beth Israel Hosp. Sch. Nursing, 1955; B.S.N., Seton Hall U., 1964; children—Laura, Richard, Garry. Staff nurse operating room Newark Beth Israel Hosp., 1955-56, recovery room head nurse, 1956-57, operating room head nurse, 1957-58, supr. operating room, 1958-60; substitute tchr. pub. schs. Harding Twp., 1966-70; charge nurse St. Barnabas Med. Center, Livingston, N.J., 1965-70, head nurse emergency room, 1970-72; operating room supr. St. Clares Hosp., Denville, N.J., 1972-77; asst. dir. for operating rooms and post anesthesia rooms Newark Beth Israel Med. Center, 1977-82; asst. dir. nursing operating room care program Thomas Jefferson U. Hosp., Phila., 1982-84; asst. dir./assoc. nursing dir. operating room, anesthesia ICU, ambulatory surgery Univ. Hosp., SUNY-Stony Brook, 1984—; faculty mem. postgrad. course in microsurgy for Am. Coll. Obstetricians and Gynecologists, Newark, 1982; profl. cons. operating room products, also health cons. Henry E. Wessel Assos., Moraga, Calif.; profl. tech. cons., lectr. Surgicot, Inc., Smithtown, N.Y. Dep. dir. Harding Twp. CD, 1967-75. Recipient Service award Essex County Med. Soc., 1979. Mem. Am. Nurses Assn., N.Y. State Nurses Assn., Assn. Operating Room Nurses, Am. Soc. Post Anesthesia Nurses, Newark Beth Israel Hosp. Nursing Alumnae Assn., Seton Hall U. Alumnae Assn., Harding Twp. Civic Assn., Am. Field Service. Republican. Club: Mt. Kemble Lake Community. Editor operating room sect. SCORE mag. Home: 12 Hampton Ct Coram NY 11727 Office: SUNY Univ Hosp Stony Brook NY 11759

MANZANO, SONIA, actress, writer; b. N.Y.C.; d. Bonifacio and Isidra (Rivera) M. Ed., Carnegie Mellon U. Actress, play Godspell Lansbury Duncan Prodns., N.Y.C., 1972-73; actress-writer Children's TV Workshop, N.Y.C., 1972—. Recipient Cert. of Merit, Nat. Acad. TV Arts and Scis., 1976, Emmy award, 1983-84.

MANZARI, JOSEPHINE R., construction and land development company executive; b. Balt., June 23, 1941; d. Mary (Re) M.; children—George, Mary Jo. Student Essex Coll. Bookkeeper Mars Super Markets, Balt., 1958-70, Merry-Go-Round, Balt., 1970-75; bookkeeper, v.p. Gatlif Builders/Charles VanOver, Inc., Middletown, N.J., 1976—. Office: Charles VanOver Inc PO Box 4154 Middletown NJ 07748

MAPLE, MARILYN JEAN, coordinator educational media; b. Turtle Creek, Pa., Jan. 16, 1931; d. Harry Chester and Agnes (Dobbie) Kelley; B.A., U. Fla., 1972, M.A., 1975, Ph.D., 1985; 1 dau., Sandra Maple. Journalist various newspapers, including Mountain Eagle, Jasper, Ala., Boise (Idaho) Statesman, Daytona Beach (Fla.) Jour., Lorain (Ohio) Jour.; account exec. Frederides & Co., N.Y.C.; producer hist. films Fla. State Mus., Gainesville, 1967-69; writer, dir., producer med. and sci. films and TV prodns. for six medically related colls. U. Fla., Gainesville, 1969—; pres. Media Modes, Inc., Gainesville. Recipient Blakslee award, 1969, spl. award, 1979, Monsour Lectureship award, 1979. Mem. Health Edn. Media Assn. (dir., awards, 1977, 79), Phi Delta Kappa, Kappa Tau Alpha. Columnist: Health Care Edn. mag.; contbr. Fla. Hist. Quar. Home: 6722 SW 53d Ave Gainesville FL 32608 Office: University of Florida Box J-16 Gainesville FL 32610

MAPLES, GLORIA JEAN, artist; b. Memphis, May 18, 1949; d. Hassel Dixon and Ruby Gwendolyn (Garner) Rudd; m. Thomas Roy Maples, July 22, 1973. B.F.A., U. Houston, 1981. Respiratory therapist, various med. instns. and physicians, Dallas, 1970-74; dental asst., Houston, 1975-78; efficiency organizer Harper Oil Tool Co., Houston, 1978-80; artist in clay and fiber, 1978—; propr. G.J.R.M. Designs, Houston, 1983—. Exhibited one-woman retrospective of weavings Mancuso Houston Library, 1983; group shows including Sarah Campbell Gallery, Houston, 1980, 82, Glassell Sch. Art, 1982, Lawndale Art Annex Gallery, Houston, 1982. Mem. Ceramic Assn. (pres. Houston 1981-82, promoter, coordinator juried exhibit 1982), Am. Craft Council. Office: G J R M Designs 7507 Hereford St Houston TX 77087

MAPP, RAMONA HARTLEY, college official; b. Hartleys Corners, Ala., Jan. 18; d. Smith Culp and Annie Bess (Owens) Hartley; student Ind. U., 1956-57, City Lit. Inst., London, 1959-61, Huntingdon Coll., 1961-62; B.A., Old Dominion U., 1965, M.A., 1966; Ed.D., Va. Poly. Inst. and State U., 1980; m. Malcolm Conner Hamby, June 26, 1949 (dec. Jan. 1967); children—Gregory Stuart, Geoffrey Alan; m. 2d, Alf Johnson Mapp, Jr., Aug. 1, 1971. Instr. English, Old Dominion U., Norfolk, Va., 1966-69, 70-71; instr. English, Tidewater Community Coll., Portsmouth, Va., 1971-73, English coordinator, 1973-74, chmn. div. humanities and social scis., 1974—; judge internat. essay contest Nat. Assn. Tchrs. of English, 1974; profl. devel. coordinator Southeastern Conf. English in Two-Year Coll., 1981, state rep., 1977-82, asst. program chmn., 1983, program chmn., 1984. Mem. Portsmouth Public Library Bd., 1978-81, chmn., 1978-80; bd. dirs. Tidewater Child Care Assn., 1974-81, pres., 1975-77; v.p. Tidewater Literacy Council, 1971-72; corr. sec. Poetry Soc. Va., 1975-76; bd. dirs. Va. Opera Guild, 1980-86, Met. Arts Congress, 1980-82, Cultural Alliance Hampton Roads, 1984-86, Tidewater Assembly Family Life. Recipient Nat. Service award Family Found. Am., 1980; named Outstanding Profl. Woman of Hampton Roads, 1984. Mem. Nat. Council Tchrs. of English, South Atlantic MLA (sec. two-yr. coll. sect. 1982, program chmn. 1983, chmn. nominating com. 1986), Am. Assn. Colls. and Jr. Colls. (nat. com. internationalizing the curriculum 1976-80), South Atlantic Assn. Depts. English (adminstrv. com. 1983—, v.p. and pres.-elect 1986—), AAUW (v.p. Portsmouth chpt. 1983-85), Internat. Intercultural Consortium, Phi Kappa Phi, Phi Theta Kappa (hon.), Delta Kappa Gamma. Club: Internat. Assn. Torch Clubs. Home: Willow Oaks 2901 Tanbark Ln Portsmouth VA 23703 Office: Tidewater Community College Portsmouth VA 23703

MARANTZ, BABY RITA FILIPINAS B., fashion designer; b. Manila, May 17, 1942; came to U.S., 1969; d. Eustaquio and Rita (Berona) Bumanglag; m. Michael Moldero Marantz, July 25, 1965; 1 child, Gordon Michael. B.S. in Edn., U. of the East, 1964; B.S. in Fashion Design, Slims Design Sch., Philippines, 1985. Social worker Social Welfare Adminstrn., Manila., 1960-64; beauty cons. Shiseido Co. Ltd., Manila, 1965-69; adminstrv. asst. Organically Grown, Los Angeles, 1969-70; propr. Babco Sales, Los Angeles, 1970-75; importer, designer Calif. Babe, Los Angeles, 1976—; cons. in field. Mem. Nat. Assn. Female Execs. Democrat. Roman Catholic. Avocations: singing; piano. Office: Calif Babe Inc PO Box 15599 Los Angeles CA 90015

MARAVEGIAS, CAMILLE SCALERE, commercial artist; b. Bronx, N.Y., Oct. 24, 1948; d. Thomas M. and Phyllis (Pasquale) Scalere; m. George Maravegias, Nov. 17, 1973; 1 child, Jennifer. B.A., Hofstra U., 1979; M.S. candidate Pratt Inst., 1983—; cert. in packaging London U., 1985. Design cons., owner CGM Paste-UP & Design, Jamaica, N.Y., 1974—; lectr. museums. Pratt Inst. grantee, 1985-86. Mem. Nat. Assn. Female Execs., Alliance of Queens Artists (dir. 1983), Smithsonian Assocs., Mus. Modern Art. Avocations: painting; jogging; tennis.

MARAVICH, MARY LOUISE, realtor; b. Fort Knox, Ky., Jan. 4, 1951; d. John and Bonnie (Balandzic) M. A.A. in Office Adminstrn., U. Nev., Las Vegas, 1970; B.A. in Sociology and Psychology, U. So. Calif., 1972; grad. Realtors Inst. Cert. residential specialist. Adminstrv. asst. dept. history U. So. Calif., Los Angeles, 1972-73; asst. personnel supr. Corral Coin Co., Las Vegas, 1973-80; Realtor, Americana Group div. Better Homes and Gardens, Las Vegas, 1980-85, Jack Matthews and Co., 1985—. Mem. Nev. Assn. Realtors (cert. realtors inst.), Las Vegas Bd. Realtors, Nat. Assn. Realtors, Women's Council of Realtors, Am. Bus. Women's Assn., Nat. Assn. Female Execs. Club: Million Dollar. Office: 3100 S Valley View Blvd Las Vegas NV 89102

MARCALI, JEAN GREGORY, chemist; b. Jermyn, Pa., May 29, 1926; d. John Robert and Anna Marie Gregory; student U. Pa., 1948-52, U. Del., 1971-72; m. Kalman Marcali, Oct. 6, 1956; children—Coleman, Frederick. Microanalyst E. I. du Pont de Nemours & Co., Deepwater, N.J., 1943-60, tech. info. analyst, Jackson Lab., Deepwater, N.J. also Wilmington, Del., 1960-67, sr. adviser tech. info., Wilmington, 1967-70, supr. tech. info., 1970-82, 85—, supr. adminstrv. services, 1982-85. Sec., Alfred I. DuPont Elem. PTA, 1971, pres., 1972; pres. PTA of Brandywine Sch. Dist., 1973; mem. Wilmington Dist. Republican Com., 1976—. Mem. Am. Chem. Soc. (treas. div. chem. info. 1976-81, chmn.-elect 1981, chmn. 1982, div. councilor 1983—). Lutheran. Clubs: Order Eastern Star, Du Pont Country, United Health. Home: 312 Waycross Rd Wilmington DE 19803 Office: E I du Pont de Nemours & Co Central Research & Devel Dept Barley Mill Plaza P141212 Wilmington DE 19898

MARCANTEL, SILVA COOPER, educational administrator, counselor; b. Portola, Calif., July 16, 1940; d. Clarence Laborn Alton and Vivian (Ratcliff) Cooper; m. Wesley Marcantel, Oct. 19, 1961; children—Dawn, Laura. B.A., McNeese State U., Lake Charles, La., 1963, M.Ed., 1967, Ed.D., 1981. Cert. in elem. edn., secondary social studies, guidance, sch. psychology, child welfare and attendance, adminstrn. and supervision, La. Tchr. Calcasieu Parish Pub. Schs., Lake Charles, 1963-76; asst. dir. Health Counseling Service, Lake Charles, 1976; counselor Calcasieu Parish Pub. Schs., 1976-81, supr. child welfare and attendance, 1981—; vis. lectr. McNeese State U., 1982. Bd. dirs. La. Epilepsy Assn., 1980-83; mem. scholarship com. McNeese State U., 1975-76. Acad. scholar, 1958; T.H. Harris scholar, 1958; Phi Delta Kappa research grantee. Mem. NEA (nat. conv. del. 1980), Calcasieu Counselors Assn. (pres. 1978-79), La. Assn. Suprs. Child Welfare and Attendance, La. Assn. Sch. Execs., Phi Delta Kappa. Democrat. Baptist. Club: Lake Charles Quota.

MARCH, CHRISTINE ANN, lawyer; b. Chgo., Nov. 2, 1953; d. Thomas Donald and Mary (Trabka) March. B.S., So. Ill. U., 1975, M.S., 1976; J.D., La. State U., 1980. Bar: La. 1980, U.S. Dist. Ct. (we. dist.) La. 1980, U.S. Dist. Ct. (mid. dist.) La. 1984. Grad. asst. So. Ill. U., Carbondale, 1975-76; asst. prof. No. State U., Natchitoches, La., 1976-77; law clk. to presiding judge U.S. Bankruptcy Ct. (we. dist.) La., Opelousas, 1980-82, estate adminstr., 1982-83; assoc. Broadhurst, Brook, Mangham & Hardy, Lafayette, La., 1983-85, ptnr., 1986—; contbg. author La. Appellate Ct. Handbook, 1983-86, v.p., 1986. Bd. dirs. Hospice of Acadiana, Lafayette, 1983-84. Mem. ABA, La. State Bar Assn., La. Assn. Women Attys., Acadiana Assn. Women Attys., Phi Delta Phi. Republican. Roman Catholic.

MARCH, JACQUELINE FRONT, chemist; b. Wheeling, W.Va., July 10, 1914; d. Jacques Johann and Antoinette (Orenstein) Front; B.S., Case Western Res. U., 1937, M.A., 1939; Wyeth fellow med. research U. Chgo., 1940-42; postgrad. U. Pitts., 1945, Ohio State U., 1967, Wright State U., 1970-76; M.B.A., U. Dayton, 1979; m. Abraham W. Marcovich, Oct. 7, 1945 (dec. 1969); children—Wayne Front, Gail Ann March Cohen. Chemist, Mt. Sinai Hosp., Cleve., 1934-40; med. research chemist U. Chgo., 1940-42; research analyst Koppers Co., also info. scientist Union Carbide Corp., Mellon Inst., Pitts., 1942-45; propr. March. Med. Research Lab., etiology of diabetes, Dayton, Ohio, 1950-70; guest scientist Kettering Found., Yellow Springs, Ohio, 1953; Dayton Found. fellow Miami Valley Hosp. Research Inst., 1956. mem. chemistry faculty U. Dayton, 1959-69, info. scientist Research Inst., 1968-79; prin. investigator Air Force Wright Aero. Labs., Wright-Patterson AFB Tech. Info. Center, 1970-79; chem. info. specialist, div. tech. services Nat. Inst. Occupational Safety and Health, HHS, Cin., 1979—; propr. JFM Cons., 1980—; designer info. systems, speaker in field. Trustee Village Condominium Assn., treas., 1985—. Recipient Recognition cert. U. Dayton, 1980. Mem. Am. Soc. Info. Sci. (treas. South Ohio 1973-75), Am. Chem. Soc. (pres. Dayton 1977, Patterson-Crane award com.; nat. councilor 1982-85), Soc. Advancement Materials and Process Engrng. (pres. Midwest chpt. 1977-78), Affiliated Tech. Socs. (Outstanding Scientist and Engr. award 1978), Am. Congress Govtl. Indsl. Hygienists (rev. com. toxic chemicals 1983—), AAUP (exec. bd.), Sigma Xi (treas. Dayton 1976-79, Conrad P. Straub lectr. 1982, pres. Cin. Fed. chpt. 1986—). Contbr. articles to profl. publs. Home: 154 Stillmeadow Dr Cincinnati OH 45245 Office: 4676 Columbia Pkwy Cincinnati OH 45226

MARCH, POLLY LYNN, nurse, air force officer; b. Corpus Christi, Tex., May 14, 1955; d. Leonard Dale and Zola May (Thacker) March; m. Phillip Paul Tudich, Nov. 25, 1981. B.S. in Nursing, Tex. Woman's U., 1977; diploma Air U., 1981, Sch. Aerospace Medicine, 1983; diploma nursing service mgmt. U.S. Air Force Sch. Health Care Scis., 1985. R.N., Tex.; cert. operating room nurse. Staff nurse operating room Meth. Hosp., Houston, 1977-78; commd. 2d lt. USAF, 1978, advanced through grades to capt., 1981; staff nurse operating room Fairchild AFB, Wash., 1978-82; supr. operating room Beale AFB, Calif., 1982-84, infection control surveillance officer, 1979-82, 83-84, 84—, flight nurse 9th Aeromed. Evacuation Squadron, Clark Air Base, Philippines, 1984—. Sponsor, Christian Children's Fund, 1983—; vol. archery program Outdoor Recreation Ctr., Clark Air Base, 1985—. Decorated Humanitarian Service medal USAF; Air Force Commendation medal with oak leaf cluster. Mem. Air Force Assn., Assn. Operating Room Nurses. Home: PSC 5 Box 10623 APO San Francisco CA 96410 Office: 9th Aeromed Evacuation Squadron SGN Clark Air Base Philippines

MARCHAND, NANCY, actress; b. Buffalo, June 19, 1928; d. Raymond L. and Marjorie F. M.; m. Paul Sparer, July 7, 1951; children—David, Kathryn, Rachel. B.F.A., Carnegie Inst. Tech., 1949. Vol. actress, Am. Theater Wing, N.Y.C.; TV appearances include A Touch of the Poet; series regular on: Lou Grant, 1977-82; theater engagements at, Circle in the Sq., N.Y.C., Los Angeles Music Center, Lincoln Center, N.Y.C., Am. Shakespeare Festival, Goodman Theater, Chgo.; appeared on Broadway in: Mornings at Seven; in: Off Broadway play Children, Sister Mary Ignatius. Recipient Obie award, 1960, Emmy award, 1978, 80, 81, 82. Office: care William Morris 1350 Ave of the Americas New York NY

MARCHAND, ROBERTA ANGELA, company sales executive, consultant; b. Phila., July 4, 1942. B.A., Temple U., 1963; postgrad. IBM Education Ctr., Govt. Mgmt. System, Inst. of Energy Devel. Data processing specialist U.S. Govt., Phila., 1963-67, exec., Washington, 1967-73; cons. colorgraphics Ramtek Corp., Dallas, 1981-84; regional sales mgr. Uniras Inc., Dallas, 1984—; ptnr. Tamm Properties, Dallas, 1980—; co-owner Ensulcap Corp., Dallas, 1983—; cons. oil industry, state govt.; univ. instr. data processing, Washington, 1968-69. Coach, adv. Tex. Spl. Olympics, Dallas, 1982; active LWV, Dallas, 1982; sponsor, vol. Dallas Theater Ctr., 1982. Recipient Outstanding Achievement U.S. Govt., Washington, 1970. Mem. Nat. Assn. Computer Graphics, Desk and Derrick, Siggraph. Clubs: Christian Women's, Aerobics, Doberman Pinscher of Am.

MARCHANT, LINDA DARLENE, business owner; b. Vancouver, B.C., Can., arrived in U.S., June 1978; d. Clarence Leo and Margaret (Swailes) M.; m. George Darrell Wade, Feb. 5, 1968 (div. Jan. 1972); m. Roger Merrill Poor, Dec. 9, 1977. B.B.A. magna cum laude, Temple U., 1979; M.B.A. (scholar), NYU, 1981. Sales support coordinator Burroughs (NZ) Ltd., Auckland, N.Z., 1972-75; head office mgr. Printrite (HK) Ltd., Hong Kong, 1976-77; customer info system mgr. Saks Fifth Ave., N.Y.C., 1981-82; owner/pres. Words To Go, N.Y.C., 1982—; alumni contact for entrepreneurs NYU Alumni Assn., 1984—. Mem. Am. Mktg. Assn., Am. Women Entrepreneurs, Nat. Assn. Female Execs., Nat. Assn. Cottage Industries. Office: Words To Go 18 E 16th St #202 New York NY 10003

MARCHESANO, CAROLE VIRGINIA, advt. co. exec.; b. Des Moines, July 30, 1940; d. Samuel Thomas and Geneva Carol (Horner) Mazza; ed. Catholic U.; m. Martin R. Marchesano, Aug. 7, 1956 (div. July 1963); children—Michele, Richard. Office mgr. Kieffer Assos., Des Moines, 1963-65; comptroller W.A. Lemer Advt., Inc., Washington, 1966-69; owner Goldberg, Marchesano & Assos., Inc., Washington, 1970—, pres., 1978—; cons. advt. office systems. Media dir. Mayor Washington's campaign, 1974, also Congressman McClosky Presdl. Nomination Orgn. Mem. Met. Washington Bd. Trade, Advt. Club Met. Washington, League Advt. Agys., Nat. Acad. TV Arts and Scis. Home: 2139 N St NW Washington DC 20036 Office: 1910 Sunderland Pl Washington DC 20036

MARCIANO, K. L., tube and pipe manufacturing company executive; b. Charleston, W.Va., Aug. 12, 1955; d. William Calvin Haynes and Jerri Louise Haynes Wilson; 1 child, Christopher H. B.S. in Chem. Engrng., La. State U., 1978; student Calif. Bible Coll., Lake Elsinore, Calif., 1979-80. Owner, pres. Gulf States Tubular, Houston, 1982—. Author: With Love, Sara, 1986. Contbr. short stories and articles to local newspapers. Mem. Nat. Assn. Female Execs., Nat. Women's League of Bus. and Engrng. Republican. Home: 1303 Vassar St Houston TX 77098 Office: Gulf States Tubular PO Box 770876 Houston TX 77215

MARCIN, MARIETTA, writer, real estate consultant; b. Chgo., Aug. 4, 1932; d. William August and Marietta (Calderini) Marshall; m. Anthony A. Marcin, June 20, 1953 (separated 1979); 1 dau., Marietta. B.A., U. Wis., 1953. Editor, Cuneo Topics, Cuneo Press, Chgo., 1953-55, NARDA News, Nat. Appliance Assn., 1956-62, Internat. Design Conf. in Aspen (Colo.), 1963-67; writer Walker Report Rights in Conflict, 1968; cons. Nash Realty, Winnetka, Ill., 1969-85; Midwest editor Kasmar Publs., 1985—. Author: A Zoo in Her Bed, 1963; Profitable Rental Merchandising, 1982; Complete Book of Herbal Teas, 1983. Editor: Great American Short Stories: 1954; Stories of America's Past, 1955. Contbr. articles to profl. jours. and mags. Bd. dirs. Chamber Music Chgo., 1964—, v.p., 1981-83; bd. dirs. Contemporary Concerts Inc., 1976—, sec., 1978-82. Mem. Women in Communications, Midwest Writers Assn., Soc. Midland Authors (dir. 1982—), Chgo. Press Club. Home: 425 Sunset Rd Winnetka IL 60093

MARCINEK, JOYCE E., business executive; b. Nevada, Ohio, July 28, 1930; d. W. Frank and Bernice Marie McCallister; student Newark Coll. Engrng., 1952-53, Sinclair Community Coll., 1968-69. With sales, service, public relations depts. Standard Oil Co., Canton and Akron, Ohio, 1957-63; with TRW Supermet, Dayton, Ohio, 1966-70, sales engr., 1972-75; acct. Texaco Inc., Atlanta, 1970-72; asst. to pres. Hot Sam div. Internat. Host, Troy, Mich., 1975-76; accounts rep. Kelly Services, Lexington, Ky., 1976-77, br. mgr., 1977-80; v.p. Career Mgmt., Inc., Lexington, 1980-82; dir. personnel EBS Inc., subs. Traveler's Ins. Co., Lexington, 1982-83; pres. Kelleher Wholesale Div., and Joymar Corp., Orlando, Fla., 1984-86, gen. mgr. Joymar Corp. Temp. Resources, Inc., Southfield, Mich., 1986—. Active Urban League, Todd Trease Teddy Bear Fund; bd. dirs. Jr. Achievement, program chmn., 1981-82, also contest judge; sponsor, coordinator secretarial scis. Explorer troop Bluegrass council Boy Scouts Am.; team capt. United Way, 1978-81; mem. Better Bus. Bur. Recipient Distributive Edn. award Lexington Edn.-Work Council, 1978. Mem. Sales Mktg. Execs. (dir., coordinator seminar 1979), Adminstrv. Mgmt. Assn. (dir.), Lexington C. of C. (dir., mem. pres.'s council). Club: Zonta (regional dir. public relations). Home: 18309 W 13 Mile Rd Apt 21 Southfield MI 48075 Office: Joymar Corp Temp Resources Inc 19189 W 10 Mile Rd Southfield MI 48075

MARCINEK, MARGARET ANN, nursing educator; b. Uniontown, Pa., Sept. 29, 1948; d. Joseph Hugh and Evelyn (Bailey) Boyle; m. Bernard Francis Marcinek, Aug. 11, 1973; 1 dau., Cara Ann. R.N., Uniontown Hosp., 1969; B.S. in Nursing, Pa. State U., 1970; M.S., U. Md., 1973; Ed.D., W.Va. U., 1983. Staff nurse Presbyn. U., Pitts., 1970-71; instr. nursing W.Va. U., Morgantown, 1973-77, asst. prof., 1977-80, assoc. prof., 1980-83; assoc. prof. California U. of Pa., 1983—, dept. chmn., 1985—. Contbg. author: Critical Care Nursing. Contbr. articles to profl. jours. Mem. adv. council Mon Valley Cancer Soc., Pa., Valley Home Health, Inc. Mem. Am. Nurses Assn., Am. Assn. Critical Care Nurses, Sigma Theta Tau, Phi Kappa Phi. Office: California U of Pa Dept Nursing California PA 15419

MARCOTTE-MONTALBANO, TERRY ANN, finance company executive; b. New Orleans, Aug. 31, 1954; d. Maurice Harry and Doris May (Salzer) Marcotte; m. Nat. Montalbano, Jr., June 9, 1984. B. Music Edn., Southeastern La. U., 1976. Asst. mgr. McKenzie's Bakery, New Orleans, summers, 1972-75; cashier, asst. mgr. Avco Fin. Services, New Orleans, 1976-79; asst. mgr. Assocs. Fin. Service, New Orleans area, 1979-80, br. mgr., Chalmette, La., 1980, Kenner, La., 1980—, mgr. seminar attendant, 1980-83. Recipient Green S award Southeastern La. U., 1975. Mem. Am. Music Tchrs., Womens Internat. Bowling Congress, Delta Omicron for Women (pres. 1975-76), Phi Kappa Phi, Kappa Delta Pi. Democrat. Roman Catholic. Home: 229 Kilgore Pl Kenner LA 70065 Office: Assocs Financial Service 2560 Williams Blvd Kenner LA 70062

MARCUM, KIM MARIE, fashion editor; b. Rolla, Mo., Dec. 11, 1956; d. Larry Gene and Joan Dorothy (Schweizer) M. B.Journalism, Northwestern U., 1978. Asst. feature editor Kansas City Times (Mo.), 1978-79, feature editor, 1979-81; fashion editor Kansas City Star (Mo.), 1981, Dallas Times Herald, 1981—; cons. Poynter Inst., St. Petersburg, Fla., 1984. Recipient Lulu awards Men's Fashion Assn., 1983, 84, 85. Office: Dallas Times Herald 1101 Pacific Dallas TX 75202

MARCUS, LYNNE, accountant; b. Bklyn., June 13, 1945; d. Samuel and Estelle F. (Diamond) M.; B.A. in Acctg., Queens Coll., 1970; M.B.A., St. John's U. Acct., Price, Waterhouse & Co., C.P.A.s, 1970-71, Willkie, Farr & Gallagher, N.Y.C., 1971-74, Western Union Internat. Co., N.Y.C., 1975-77, N.Y.C. Bd. Edn., 1977-79, Citibank, N.Y.C., 1979-83; self-employed C.P.A., 1983—; adj. asst. prof. acctg. Adelphi U., 1984, Queensborough Community Coll., 1984—; adult edn. tchr., cons. in field. C.P.A., N.Y. Mem. Am. Inst. C.P.A.s, Am. Woman's Soc. C.P.A.s, N.Y. State Soc. C.P.A.s, Am. Mgmt. Assn., N.Y. State Soc. C.P.A.s, Omicron Delta Epsilon (life). Club: Hadassah. Home: 65-84 Booth St Rego Park NY 11374 Office: 65-77 Booth St Rego Park NY 11374

MARCUS, MELINDA, advertising consultant; b. New Orleans, Nov. 20, 1954; d. Irwin M. and Dorothy Francine (Mann) Marcus; m. Joseph Jacobson, June 9, 1979. B.A., Northwestern U., 1976; M.F.A., So. Meth. U., 1982. Copywriter, Tracy-Locke Advt., Dallas, 1977-79; sr. copywriter Kerss, Chapman, Bua & Norsworthy, Dallas, 1979-80; sr. copywriter The Richards Group Advt., Dallas, 1980-85, creative dir., 1983-85; pres. Marcus & Assocs., Inc., Dallas, 1985—; guest lectr. profl. confs.; copywriter TV commls.: Mercantile Bank Campaign (CLIO award), Haggar Slacks Campaign (U.S. TV Comml. Festival Gold award), 1979, MPACT Automatic Teller (CLIO award, Golden Radio award), 1984; print advt.: Richards Group Promotion (N.Y. Art Dirs. Gold award), 1983, MPACT Automatic Teller ads (Communication Arts award), 1982. Project mgr. and writer: Dallas Area Rapid Transit Bond Issues, 1983, Dallas Concert Hall Bond Issue, 1982, Jewish Fedn. Young Leadership, 1983-84, The 500 Inc., Dallas, 1983; chmn. lecture series Temple Emanu-El, Dallas, 1983-84. Vol. Action nominee Pres. U.S., 1982; recipient awards Outstanding Vol. Service, State of Tex., 1982, Vol. of Yr., Goodwill Industries, Dallas, 1980, Meals on Wheels/United Way, Dallas, 1979; recipient ADDY award Am. Advt. Fedn., 1979, 80, TELLY award, 1983, Tops awards Dallas Advt. League, 1980-85, awards Dallas Soc. Visual Communications, 1983-84. Mem. Women in Communications (Matrix awards 1980, 82-85), Northwestern Alumni Assn., So. Meth. Alumni Assn. Clubs: Aerobics Center (tennis champion 1980), Brookhaven (tennis champion 1978), USA Film Festival Hollywood 100, 1984. Office: Marcus & Assocs Inc 6022 Meadow Crest Dr Dallas TX 75230

MARCUS, RUTH BARCAN, philosopher; d. Samuel and Rose (Post) Barcan; B.A., N.Y. U., 1941; M.A., Yale U., 1942, Ph.D., 1946; children—James Spencer, Peter Webb, Katherine Hollister, Elizabeth Post. AAUW fellow, 1947-48; vis. prof. Northwestern U., 1950-57, Guggenheim fellow, 1953-54; asst. prof., asso. prof. Roosevelt U., Chgo., 1957-60; NSF fellow, 1963-64; prof. philosophy U. Ill., Chgo. Circle, 1964-70, head philosophy dept., 1964-68, Center for Advanced Study, 1968-69; prof. philosophy Northwestern U., 1970-73; Halleck prof. philosophy Yale, 1973—; fellow Center Advanced Study Behavioral Scis., 1979; vis. fellow Inst. Advanced Studies, U. Edinburgh, 1981; vis. fellow, Oxford U., 1985, 86. Fellow Am. Acad. Arts and Scis.; past mem. Council Philos. Studies, Assn. Symbolic Logic (past exec. council, exec. com. 1973, v.p. 1980, pres. 1983-86, council 1986—), Am. Philos. Assn. (past sec.-treas., nat. dir. 1967-83, pres. 1982, chmn. nat. bd. officers 1976-83), Internat. Union History and Philosophy of Sci. (past chmn. U.S. nat. com.), Institut International de Philosophie (v.p. 1985-88), Phi Beta Kappa. Editorial bd. The Monist, Jour. Philos. Logic, Philos. Studies, Jour. Symbolic Logic, others. Editor of, contbr. to to books and profl. jours. Office: Dept Philosophy Box 3650 Yale U New Haven CT 06520

MARCUS, SUZANNE GAIL, independent film producer; b. Jamaica, Queens, N.Y., Oct. 26, 1959; d. William B. Marcus and Beverly Sarah (Miller) M. B.F.A., NYU, 1981. Prodn. coordinator Hurrah Prodns., N.Y.C., 1981-82; post-prodn. adminstr. Devlin Video, N.Y.C., 1982-83; ops. and prodn. adminstr. Showtime Entertainment, N.Y.C., 1983-84; founder, chief exec. officer Electric Images Ltd., N.Y.C., 1984—; cons. and lectr. in field. Dir. theater prodn. Shade/Acad. of Desire, 1980. Grantee in field from numerous profl. orgns. Fellow Nat. Assn. Female Execs., Am. Film Inst., Assn. Ind. Video and Film Makers, NYU Tisch Sch. Arts Alumni Assn. Jewish. Avocations: Running; swimming; cooking; photography; writing poetry. Home: 33 Gold St Apt 712A New York NY 10038

MARDIAN, SUSAN CHRISTINE, journalist, artist; b. Phoenix, Aug. 10, 1947; d. Aram Stephen and Grace M.; student Ind. U., 1967-68, Stanford U., 1967, 68; B.A., Ariz. State U., 1970; postgrad. U. Calif., 1977-78. Stringer, NBC, ABC Radio News, AP Radio, NBC-TV News Program Service, 1973-75; reporter, city desk Phoenix Gazette, 1971-72; reporter, anchor, producer Sta. KTAR, KBBC and KTAR-TV (now Sta. KPNX-TV), Phoenix, 1973-75; asst. editor public info. office, Washington, 1972; researcher, writer: Call for Action, Sta. KGTV, San Diego, 1976-77; reader Ariz. Senate, 1973. Recipient 1st Pl. Media Excellence award San Diego County Med. Soc., 1982. Mem. Am. Women in Radio and TV, Nat. Fedn. Press Women (nat. award 1974), Ariz. Press Club (award 1973), Ariz. Press Women (2 awards 1974), Phoenix Press Club, Calif. Press Women (1st place state writing award 1982, leadership award 1983), Nat. Acad. TV Arts and Scis., Ind. U. Alumni Assn. (life), Ariz. State U. Alumni Assn., Soc. Profl. Journalists-Sigma Delta Chi. Mem. United Ch. of Christ. Radio documentaries: Alcohol Abuse (first pl. nat. competition 3M Corp.), 1974; Child Abuse (nat. award), 1974; contbr. articles to various publs. Address: 6622 N 40th St Phoenix AZ 85018

MARDIS, VERDENA ARLINE, educator, psychologist; b. Franklin, Ohio, Oct. 10, 1914; d. Frank M. and Grace Florence (Johnson) Fox; m. Jack Wadsworth Mardis, Aug. 26, 1946; raised nieces and nephew, Kathleen, Jerry, Rita Jean. B.S. in Elem. Edn., Wittenberg U., 1942; M.A. in Adminstrn. and Supervision, U. Dayton, 1949; M.S. in Sch. Psychology, Miami U., Oxford, Ohio, 1958. Cert. tchr., prin., sch. psychologist, Ohio. Tchr. Mad River Twp. Sch., Dayton, Ohio, 1934-38, prin., 1938-57; sch. psychologist Montgomery County Schs., Dayton, 1958-62, dir. pupil personnel, 1962-70; dir. psychology Children's Med. Ctr., Dayton, 1970-72; psychologist, intake coordinator Montgomery County Mental Retardation, Dayton, 1972-85; retired. Recipient Profl. of Yr. award Montgomery County Bd. Mental Retardation, 1980; Outstanding Service award Montgomery County Bd. Mental Retardation, 1984; Doers award Dayton Area Citizens Com. for Spl. Edn., 1984. Mem. Nat. Assn. Pupil Personnel Adminstrs. (hon. life), Ohio Assn. Pupil Personnel Adminstrs. (sec. 1966-68, hon. life), Montgomery County Ret. Tchrs. Assn. (v.p. 1985), Ohio Ret. Tchrs. Assn., Am. Assn. Ret. Tchrs., Alpha Delta Kappa. Democrat. Mem. Ch. of Christ. Home: 4209 White Oak Dr Dayton OH 45432

MAREK, ANN ARMSTRONG, marketing and public relations executive; b. N.Y.C., Feb. 20, 1935; d. Andrew F.H. Armstrong and Florence Elizabeth (White) Bowen; A.A.S., N.Mex. State U., 1956; B.A., U. Tex., Arlington, 1975; postgrad. U. Dallas, 1977; m. Gabriel Robert Marek, July 28, 1956; children—Andrew Vincent, Elizabeth Marek West, Melissa Marek Wheeler. Sales rep. Parker Bros., Ft. Worth, 1979, George Farha Toy Distbr. Co., Oklahoma City, 1980; area mgr. retail merchandising Mattel Sales Corp., Dallas, 1980-81; dir. community affairs Family Service Inc., Ft. Worth, 1981-84; dir. mktg./pub. relations Circle T, Girl Scouts U.S.A., Ft. Worth, 1984—; lectr. U. Tex., Arlington, 1973—. Chmn., Tarrant County Study Commn. on Children and Youth, 1973; vice chmn. Ft. Worth Utility Bd., 1976; mem. task panel on the family Pres.'s Commn. on Mental Health, 1977. Recipient Newsmaker of Yr. award Ft. Worth Press Club, 1973, Child Advocacy award Ft. Worth Mayor's Council on Youth Opportunity, Potter award for outstanding communication program, 1983. Mem. Network Exec. Women, Internat. Assn. Bus. Communicators, Forum Ft. Worth, Ad Club. Episcopalian. Author report: The Enhancement of Parenting Skills, 1977. Home: 2324 Edwin St Fort Worth TX 76110 Office: 4901 Briarhaven Fort Worth TX 76109

MARESCA, ROSALIA LORETTA, opera company director; b. N.Y.C., Aug. 16, 1923; d. Salvatore and Elizabeth M.; hon. grad. Cin. Conservatory of Music, 1958; studied voice with Carmen du Belier and Mario Laurenti; 1 dau., Rena Laurenti. Operatic debut as Adalgisa in Norma, Acad. Music, N.Y.C., 1944; performances with opera cos. throughout U.S. including those of Cin., Phila., Hartford, Chautauqua, New Orleans, Bklyn., Tampa, Rochester, Washington and Syracuse; appearances in theatres throughout U.S., Europe, Japan; prof. voice Manhattan Sch. Music, 1967-73; mgr., dir. San Carlo Opera, Fla. Lyric Opera, Matinee Opera Theatre, Clearwater, Fla., 1973—; voice tchr., head voice faculty Fla. Performing Arts Studio, St. Petersburg; organizer Fla. Artists Mgmt. Enterprise (FAME). Mem. Am. Guild Mus. Artists, Am. Guild Radio and TV Artists. Home: 1183D 85 Terrace N St Petersburg FL 33702 Office: Fla Performing Arts Studio 8th St and 4th Ave N St Petersburg FL

MARGOLIES, ALLISON, clinical psychologist; b. N.Y.C., Feb. 11, 1953; d. Sol and Bunny (Wertans) M.; M.A., Hofstra U., 1976, Ph.D., 1979. Psychologist, Bernard Fineson Developmental Ctr., Queens Village, N.Y., 1979-82; cons. psychologist Aurora Concept, Flushing, N.Y., 1981-84; assoc. psychologist Queens Children's Psychiat. Hosp., Bellerose, N.Y., 1982-85; assoc. psychologist Creedmoor Psychiat. Ctr., Queens Village, 1985—; pvt. practice clin. psychology, Lawrence, N.Y., 1982—. Lic. psychologist N.Y. State; cert. sch. psychologist N.Y. State. Mem. Am. Psychol. Assn., N.Y. State Psychol. Assn., Nassau County Psychol. Assn., Phi Beta Kappa. Qualified expert witness, N.Y. Supreme Ct. Home: 611 Arbucke Ave Woodmere NY 11598 Office: 360 Central Ave Lawrence NY 11559

MARGOLIN, ANN, real estate developer; b. Newark, Aug. 27, 1952; d. Morris and Edith (Zimring) Epstein; m. Fred Harold Margolin, Sept. 4, 1977. B.S. in Speech, Northwestern U., 1974, M.A. in Speech, 1974; M.B.A. in Fin., Columbia U., 1977. Trainee, Standard Oil of Ohio, Cleve., 1977-78; owner Intercon Gen. Agy., Dallas, 1978-82, Margolin Properties, Dallas, 1982—. Author newspaper column: How to Succeed, 1982. Bd. dirs. Anti-Defamation League, Dallas, 1983—, Women's Ctr. Dallas, 1980-82, Dallas Women's Found. Recipient Young Career Women award Dist. #15 Bus. and Profl. Women's Clubs, 1980. Mem. Exec. Women of Dallas, North Dallas C. of C. (govt. affairs chair 1985-86). Republican. Jewish. Club: Dist. #15 Bus. and Profl. Women's (legis. chmn.). Home: 10515 Lennox Ln Dallas TX 75229 Office: Margolin Properties 4100 Spring Valley Rd #400 Dallas TX 75234

MARGOLIS, ESTHER LUTERMAN, court management analyst; b. Pitts., Jan. 12, 1939; d. Nathan and Belle (Fogel) Luterman; B.S., Ariz. State U., 1976, M.S., 1978; m. Herbert Marvin Margolis, Apr. 15, 1962; children—Ruth Lys,

Judith Lyn. Statistician, court planners office Ariz. Supreme Ct., 1976-77; planner Ariz. Dept. Corrections, 1979; adminstrv. asst. planning and research bur. Phoenix Police Dept., 1979-82, police research analyst, 1982-83; ct. mgmt. analyst Calif. Jud. Council, Adminstrv. Office of Cts., San Francisco, 1983-84; asst. ct. adminstr., jury commr. Contra Costa County Superior Ct., 1984—; instr. Phoenix Community Coll., 1980-82; presenter paper ann. meeting Acad. Criminal Justice Scis., Phila., 1981. Mem. textbook selection com. Roosevelt Sch. Dist., Phoenix, 1975; chmn. bd. YMCA, South Mountain br., 1977-81; bd. mgrs. Phoenix and Valley of the Sun YMCA, 1978-81; pres. bd. dirs. Do it Now Found., 1978-80; bd. dirs. Boys' Clubs Phoenix, 1982—; fin. officer Pinole Ridge Homeowners Assn. Mem. Am. Soc. Public Adminstrn. (program com., panel coordinator regional conf. 1983; panel discussant ann. meeting N.Y.C. 1983), Am. Soc. Criminology, Nat. Council Crime and Delinquency, Nat. Assn. Women in Criminal Justice, Profl. Women for Kennedy. Editor ann. report Phoenix Police Dept., 1979-82. Home: 1417 Greenfield Circle Pinole CA 94564 Office: 725 Court St Room 124 Martinez CA 94553

MARGOLIS, GWEN LIEDMAN, state senator, developer; b. Phila., Oct. 4, 1934; d. Joseph and Rose Liedman; m. Allan Block Margolis, 1953; children—Edward, Ira, Karen, Robin. Student Temple U., 1951-54; A.A. (hon.), Miami Dade U., 1983. Owner, broker Gwen Margolis Real Estate, North Miami Beach, 1965—; mem. Fla. Ho. of Reps., Tallahassee, 1974-80; mem. Fla. Senate, 1980—; dir. Lincoln Savs. and Loan Assn. realtor, appraiser. Bd. dirs. Anti-Defamation League of B'nai Brith. Recipient Outstanding Woman in Politics award Bus. and Profl. Women's Assn.; Woman of Yr. award North Miami Beach C. of C.; awards Women in Communication, Fla. Women's Polit. Caucus, Profl. Firefighters of Fla.; Legis. Friend of Arts award Gov.'s Arts Com., 1982; Spirit of Life Humanitarian award City of Hope, 1974, 79, established Margolis Cancer Research fellowship. Mem. North Miami C. of C. (dir.). Home: 1891 NE 164th St North Miami Beach FL 31162 Office: Fla Senate State Capitol Tallahassee FL 32301*

MARGOLIS, NANCY KROLL, marketing and advertising executive; b. N.Y.C., Sept. 12, 1947; d. Herman and Florence (Yondorf) Kroll; m. Paul D. Margolis, Nov. 12, 1972; children—Kara, Seth. Student Parsons Sch. Design, 1964-65; B.A., Ohio State U., 1969. Traffic coordinator Wells, Rich, Greene, N.Y.C., 1970-72; asst. producer Nadler & Larimer, N.Y.C., 1972-73; pres. Nancy Britton Agy., Greenwich, Conn., 1973-75; v.p. Joseph Jacobs Orgn., N.Y.C., 1976-84; assoc. pub. advt. dir. Hadassah Mag., N.Y.C., 1984-86; prin. Margohs & Kroll Mktg. Mem. Advt. Women N.Y., Mag. Pubs. Assn. (speakers bur.). Democrat. Jewish. Lodge: Hadassah (life mem.).

MARGOSIAN, LUCILLE K. MANOUGIAN (MRS. ERVIN M. MARGOSIAN), artist, educator; b. Highland Park, Mich.; d. George Krikor and Vera Varsenig (Jernukian) Manougian; B.F.A., Wayne State U., 1957, M.A., 1958; postgrad. Calif. State U., Fresno, 1959-60, U. Calif. at Berkeley, 1960-61; m. Ervin M. Margosian, Oct. 28, 1960; children—Rebecca L., Rachel L. One-man show at Jackson's Gallery, Berkeley, Calif., 1961; exhibited in group shows at Detroit Art Inst., 1958, Oakland (Calif.) Art Museum, 1961, Wayne State U. Community Arts Center, Detroit, 1965, San Francisco Ann. Art Festivals, 1967, 68, 69, Jack London Square Arts Festival, Oakland, 1969, 70, Judah L. Magnes Meml. Mus., Berkeley, 1970, Kaiser Center Gallery, Oakland, 1970, Oakland Mus. Changing Gallery, 1969, Olive Hyde Art Center, Fremont, 1971, 73, Richmond (Calif.) Art Center, 1972, Villa Montalvo Galleries at Phelan Estate, Saratoga, Calif., 1976, others; faculty Peralta Community Colls., Laney campus, Oakland, 1967—, prof. art, 1970—, chmn. dept., 1982—. Charter mem. univ. art mus. council U. Calif. at Berkeley, 1965—. Recipient Certificate of Distinguished Achievement, Am. Legion, 1950; Best of Show 1st prize 5th Ann. Textile Exhbn., Fremont, Calif., 1973; Merit award City of Fremont, 1973, Zellerbach Bldg. Gallery, San Francisco, 1975. Mem. Calif. Art Edn. Assn., Oakland Museum Assn., Richmond Art Center, Women of Wayne, Wayne State U. Alumni Assn., East Bay Watercolor Soc., Internat. Platform Assn., Am. Fedn. Tchrs., Peralta Fedn. Tchrs. Office: Laney Coll Art Dept 900 Fallon St Oakland CA 94607

MARGULES, GABRIELE ELLA, publishing company executive; b. Tachov, Czechoslovakia, May 30, 1927; d. David Samuel and Rosa Zerlina (Leinwand) Margules; came to U.S., 1954. Student Cambridge Sch. Art (Eng.), 1944-47; diploma in fine art Royal Acad. Sch., London, 1950; postgrad. New Sch., N.Y.C., 1961-62. Direct mail asst. Harper's mag., 1959-67; direct mail mgr. Forbes mag., 1967-73; promotion mgr. Cath. Digest, 1973-79; circulation dir. Gernsback Publs., N.Y.C., 1979-81, Criminal Justice Publs., N.Y.C., 1981-82, Archaeology Mag., 1983—. Illustrator: Out of the Ark, 1968; Bird Song, 1970; also for Harper's mag. Painting exhibited, 1957-81. One man show (paintings and drawings): Garrison Art Ctr., N.Y., 1985. Recipient 1st prize life drawing Royal Acad., 1949; Meyers Art scholar, 1948, 61. Mem. Artists Equity, Women's Direct Response Group, Direct Mail Mktg. Assn., Mag. Pubs. Assn., Putnam Hist. Assn., Garrison Art Ctr., Barrett House. Democrat. Jewish. Home: 7 High St Cold Spring NY 10516 Office: 15 Park Row New York NY 10038

MARGULIS, LYNN ALEXANDER, biologist, educator; b. Chgo., Mar. 5, 1938; d. Morris and Leone (Wise) Alexander; A.B., U. Chgo., 1957; A.M., U. Wis., 1960; Ph.D., U. Calif., Berkeley, 1965; m. Carl Sagan, 1957; children—Dorion, Jeremy; m. Thomas N. Margulis, Jan. 18, 1967; children—Zachary, Jennifer. Mem. faculty Boston U., 1963—, asst. prof. biology, 1967-71, assoc. prof., 1971-77, prof., 1977—; coordinator biology Colombia program Peace Corps, summer 1965, 66; Sherman Fairchild Disting. scholar Calif. Inst. Tech., 1976-77; mem. adv. com. NASA. Guggenheim fellow, 1979. Fellow AAAS; mem. Nat. Acad. Sci. (chmn. com. planetary biology and chem. evolution 1977-81). Author: Origin of Eukaryotic Cells, 1970; Symbiosis in Cell Evolution, 1981; (with K.V. Schwartz) Five Kingdoms, 1982; (with D. Sagan) Origins of Sex, 1986; (with D. Sagan) Microcosmos, 1986; contbr. articles to profl. jours. Office: 2 Cummington St Boston MA 02215

MARIAKIS, JAN IRENE, ins., estate and fin. co. exec.; b. Portland, Oreg., May 28, 1951; d. Lyle Henry and Juanita Jean Vandercook; student Ga. So. Coll., 1971-72; B.S. in Adminstrn. of Justice/Sociology, Portland State U., 1975. C.L.U.; chartered fin. cons. M. J. Nick Mariakis, Oct. 5, 1985; children—Jennifer Spring, Katherine Nichole. Saleswoman, Lincoln Nat. Life Ins. Co., San Mateo, Calif., 1975-81; owner, mgr. Fiscal Design, San Mateo, 1981—; corp. treas. Material Handling Corp.; dir. Oreg. Handling Equipment Co., Inc., speaker in field. Charter mem. Friendly Acreas Neighborhood Bd.; local chairwoman Life Underwriters Polit. Action Com. C.L.U. Mem. Nat. Assn. Life Underwriters, Peninsula Assn. Life Underwriters (v.p.), Calif. Assn. Life Underwriters (mem. State Consumer Edn. Task Force), Internat. Assn. Fin. Planners. Christian Scientist. Club: Friends of Winemakers (Santa Clara). Office: Box 2399 Redwood City CA 94064

MARIE, GERALDINE, writer; b. Kew Gardens, N.Y., Sept. 9, 1949; d. Salvatore Astor and Louise Annette (Ingargiola) Lettieri; m. Alan Julian Marcus, 1984; children—Pamela Stacey, Elizabeth Kara. B.A., Queens Coll., 1971; M.S. in Edn., C.W. Post Coll., 1976. Cert. tchr., N.Y. Tchr. St. Patrick's Sch., Bay Shore, N.Y., 1971-81, Gt. Neck (N.Y.) Sch. Dist., 1981-83; author books including: The Magic Box (named Children's Choice for 1982), 1981; adaptation of The Hound of the Baskervilles (Arthur Conan Doyle), 1980; writer short stories; author cassettes: Children's Fairy Tales, 1979; author reading comprehension games. Mem. Soc. Children's Book Writers. Address: 873 Manor Ln Bay Shore NY 11706

MARIEL, photographer, former fabrication company executive; b. Pasadena, Calif., Aug. 5, 1938; d. Oscar Branche and Mary Lincoln (Hicks) Jackson; adopted dau. William Nathan Turner; m. Donald E. Coombes, June 13, 1957 (div. June 1972); children—William Cullen, Anna Maria, Joel Howard; 1 son by previous marriage, Scott Craig Goodwin. Co-incorporator, Mineral Harvesters Inc., Salem, Oreg., 1966-71, Ariz. Custom Mfg. Inc., Phoenix, 1971-81, bus. mgr., pres., 1972-81; pres. Ariz. Custom Steel, Phoenix, 1976-81, Eagle Erectors, Phoenix, 1979-81; now with Lazarus Enterprises; former co-owner WCS Constrn., Inc. Asst. dist. coordinator Oreg. Republican Party, 1964. Mem. Nat. Assn. Women Bus. Owners, Nat. Assn. Female Execs., Ariz. Network Profl. Women, Women Emerging, Internat. Platform Assn., Tolsum Farm Homeowners Assn., Ariz. Steel Fabricators Assn. (past pres.). Republican. Mem. Reorganized Ch. Jesus Christ of Latter-day Saints. Clubs: Intertel, Mensa. Home: PO Box 69325 Portland OR 97201

MARIEN, GAIL DOLORES, printing distributor sales executive; b. N.Y.C., July 29, 1942; d. Vito E. and Ann (Casdia) Ingoglia; m. Albert J. Marien, Jr., Jan. 15, 1966; children—Angela, Natalie. R.N., St. Vincent's Hosp., 1963; B.A. in Psychology summa cum laude, Marymount Coll., 1978; M.S.W., Adelphi U., 1980; cert. Creedmoor Family Therapy Inst., 1983. R.N., Fla., N.Y., N.J.; cert. social worker, N.Y. Indsl. nurse United Airlines, N.Y.C., 1966-71; salesperson Coredata Inc., N.Y.C., 1980-81; EAP dir. Creedmoor Hosp., N.Y.C., 1981-84; sales dir. Human Concepts, Union, N.J., 1984; v.p. sales Covedata, Inc., N.Y.C., 1984—; EAP cons., Franklin Lakes, N.J., 1983—. Adv. Parents for a Better Edn., Glen Cove, N.Y., 1976-78; mem. Parents Adv. Council for Spl. Children, Franklin Lakes, 1986. Mem. Acad. Cert. Social Workers, Assn. of Labor-Mgmt. Adminstrs. and Cons. on Alcoholism, Nat. Assn. Social Workers (cert.), Employee Assistance Soc. of N.Am., Alpha Chi. Avocations: dancing; singing. Home: 812 Linden Way Franklin Lakes NJ 07417 Office: Covedata Inc 230 W 41 St New York NY 10036

MARIGOLD, LYSBETH ALLYN, business executive; b. N.Y.C., Dec. 9, 1940; d. Allen Montague Marigold and Virginia (Davis) Emerson. B.A., Conn. Coll., New London, 1962. Jr. copywriter Glamour Mag., N.Y.C., 1962-65; food editor Ingenue Mag., N.Y.C., 1965-68; copy editor McCalls Mag., N.Y.C., 1968-73; account exec. Burson-Marsteller, N.Y.C., 1973-75; copy chief Ladies Home Jour., N.Y.C., 1975-82; pres. Wings Products Co. Inc., N.Y.C., 1982—; copy dir. BrainReserve, Inc., N.Y.C., 1982-84 , v.p., dir. creative services, 1984—. contbr. articles to mags. Publicity dir. Ladies Village Improvement Soc. of East Hampton (N.Y.), 1976-82, cookbook chmn., 1982-84. Clubs: Metropolitan (N.Y.C.); English Toy Spaniel (historian 1982); Rolls Royce Owners. Home: 410 E 57th St New York NY 10022 Office: Wings Products Co Inc PO Box 680 Georgica Assn East Hampton NY 11937

MARILAO, ROSELLA QUERUBIN, personnel director; b. Manila, Philippines, Mar. 10, 1939; came to U.S., 1969; d. Anastacio and Pelagia (EspirituSanto) Querabin; (div.); children—George, Willk, Frank, Mary Rose. A.B.A., St. Theresa's Coll., 1957; B.S.B.A., Calif. State U.-Hayward, 1976, M.P.A., 1979. Sales circulation mgr. Philippines Internat. Pub. Co., Manila, 1959-66; personnel analyst City of Oakland (Calif.), 1972-76; asst. to dean Chabot Coll., Hayward, 1976-79; personnel adminstr. Chaffey Coll., Alta Lana, Calif., 1979-82; dir. personnel Lakeland Community Coll., Mentor, Ohio, 1982—; cons. Peralta Community Coll. Dist., Oakland, 1976-79. Trustee, Lake County Mental Health Center, Mentor, 1982; bd. dirs. Family Tutorial Services, 1978; trustee, treas. Lake County Community Services Council, Mentor, 1983; vol. tutor Project LEARN. Mem. Am. Soc. Personnel Adminstrs., Internat. Personnel Mgmt. Assn., Am. Assn. U. Adminstrs., Internat. Assn. Quality Circles, Colls. Univ. Personnel Assn. Roman Catholic. Clubs: Altrusa of Lake (Mentor), Philippine Am. Soc. Ohio. Lodge: Legionarios del Trabajo in Am. Office: Lakeland Community Coll Mentor OH 44060

MARIN, ROSA CELESTE, research consultant, social work educator; b. Arecibo, P.R., June 1, 1912; d. Angel M. and Justa (Marin) Marin; B.S., U. P.R., 1933; M.S., U. Pitts., 1944, D.S.W., 1953. Social welfare officer, acting dist. dir., supr. Fed. Emergency Relief Adminstrn., 1933-36; social worker, gen. supr. in charge of research P.R. Reconstrn. Adminstrn., 1936-40; supr. spl. projects and head research sect. Div. of Pub. Welfare P.R., 1940-44; asst. prof. U. P.R. Sch. Social Work, 1944-59, assoc. prof., 1959-67, dir. Grad. Sch. Social Work, 1967-74, dir. research unit, 1955-74, prof., 1967-74, prof. emeritus, 1980—; cons. on research to supr. ednl. council cons. VA, Dept. Services Against Addiction, Coll. Pharmacy, Municipal Govt. San Juan; chmn. Welfare Devel. Corp.; mem. Council Human Resources. Mem. Assn. Tchrs. P.R., Nat. Assn. Social Workers, Nat. Conf. on Social Welfare, Coll. Social Workers, Soc. Newspaperwomen, Am. Acad. Polit. and Social Scis., Am. Assn. Statisticians, Assn. Research Centers Adminstrn. Editor: Revista Servicio Social, 1949-50, 52-65. Author: Compilation of Adminstrative Cases: Study of dependent Multiproblem Families in Puerto Rico, The Female Drug Addict in Puerto Rico, Fraudulent Medical Prescriptions of Controlled Substances in Puerto Rico; co-author: Manpower Resources and Projections; Effectiveness of the Rehabilitation of Drug Addicts in Puerto Rico. Editor Jour. Humanidad. Contbr. articles to profl. jours. Home: PO Box 6679 Santurce PR 00914 Office: 2153 Teniente Lavergne St Santurce PR 00913

MARINE, ANITA, retail menswear company executive; b. N.Y.C., May 11, 1921; d. Robert and Florence (Belkin) Smith; m. James A. Marine, Jan. 7, 1950; children—Carol A., Nancy J. B.S., N.Y. U., 1942. Advt. dept. G. Fox & Co., Hartford, Conn., 1942-43; treas. Quality Shop, Torrington, Conn., 1957—. Concert master Torrington Symphony, 1934-58; publicity Heart Assn., Torrington, 1955-56; Northwest Conn. council Girl Scouts; mem. Econ. Devel. com., Torrington, 1979. Mem. Mu Kappa Tau. Avocations: musical groups; symphony orchestra; quartets. Home: 122 Chestnut Hill Rd Torrington CT 06790 Office: Quality Shop 69 Main St Torrington CT 06790

MARING, MARY MUEHLEN, lawyer; b. Devils Lake, N.D., July 27, 1951; d. Joseph Edward and Charlotte Rose (Schorr) Muehlen; m. David Scott Maring, Aug. 30, 1975; 1 son, Christopher David. B.A. in Polit. Sci. summa cum laude, Moorhead State U., 1972; J.D., U. N.D., 1975. Bar: Minn., N.D. Law clk. Hon. Bruce Stone, Mpls., 1975-76; assoc. Stefanson, Landberg & Alm, Ltd., Moorhead, Minn., 1976-82, Ohnstad, Twichell, Breitling, Rosenvold, Wanner, Nelson, Neugebauer & Maring, P.C., West Fargo, N.D., 1982—; women's bd. mem. 1st Nat. Bank, Fargo, 1977-82; career day speaker Moorhead Rotarians, 1980-83. Contbr. note to legal rev.; note editor, N.D. Law Rev., 1975. Mem. ABA (del. ann. conv. young lawyers sect. 1981), Minn. State Bar Assn. (pres. young lawyers sect. 1981-82, bd. govs. 1982-83), Minn. Women Lawyers, N.D. State Bar Assn., Minn. Trial Lawyers, Clay County Bar Assn. (v.p. 1983-84). Roman Catholic. Clubs: Fargo Country, Southgate Racquetball. Office: Ohnstad Twichell Breitling Rosenvold Wanner Nelson Neugebauer & Maring PC 901 13th Ave E West Fargo ND 58078

MARINO, JOANNE MARIE, psychotherapist, consultant; b. Greenwich, Conn., Feb. 15, 1951; d. Frank Dominic and Matilda (Salvatore) M. B.A., U. Conn., 1973, M.A. in Ednl. Psychology/Rehab. Counseling, 1975. Counselor, program dir. Liberation Programs, Inc., Stamford, Conn., 1977-83; gen. practice psychotherapy, Cos Cob, Conn., 1983—; ptnr., cons. The Learning Exchange, Cos Cob, 1984—. Mem. Am. Assn. Counseling and Devel., Am. Mental Health Counselers Assn. Avocations: films; traveling; computers; reading.

MARION, WINIFRED ZENORINI, educator; b. Fairview, N.J., Oct. 12, 1929; d. Leopold and Anna (Saldarini) Zenorini; m. Louis William Marion, Nov. 29, 1952; children—William Harvey. B.A. with honors, Ladycliff Coll., N.Y., 1951; M.Ed. with honors, Paterson State Coll., 1968; M.Ed., Fairleigh Dickinson U., 1975-78; student Caldwell Coll., 1977, Monmouth Coll., 1980. Cert. tchr., N.J. Elem. sch. tchr., Tenafly, Ramsey and Franklin Lakes, N.J., 1951-54, 59-60, 61, 62—; piano tchr.; condr. ednl. and UNICEF workshops. Tchr., Confrat. of Christian Doctrine, Mt. Carmel Ch., Tenafly, 1962-72; active UN Assn., 1980—, chair edn. dept., 1985-86; mem. planning bd. Mt. Carmel Ch., Tenafly, 1975, parish lay minister, 1975-77; mem. parish renewal group St. Mary's Ch., Dumont, N.J., 1981—; active UNICEF card program League of Women/Jr. Women's Club, Tenafly, 1980—. Recipient award Northern Valley-Englewood/Tenafly chpt. UN Assn., 1980; Ladycliff Coll. scholar, 1950. Mem. Tenafly Edn. Assn. (negotiations rep. 1973-78), NEA, N.J. Edn. Assn., Bergen County Edn. Assn., AAUW, Smithsonian Inst., World Vision, Nat. Geographic Soc., Met. Opera Fund and Guild. Republican. Roman Catholic. Avocations: opera; ballet; travel; painting. Home: 9 Cambridge Rd Tenafly NJ 07670

MARK, ANN BELLA, computer services executive; b. Haifa, Israel, Mar. 8, 1949; came to U.S., 1962, naturalized, 1968; d. Paul and Dora (Tasma) Radzynski; m. Barry Mark, Aug. 23, 1969; children—Felicia, Eric, Jacqueline. B.A. in Econs., Bklyn. Coll., 1969; M.B.A., Pace U., 1972. Programmer, E.F. Hutton, N.Y.C., 1969-72, Home Ins., N.Y.C., 1972; cons. in field, N.Y., N.J., 1973-78; pres. Tekmark Computer Services, Inc., N.Y., N.J., 1979—. Mem. Nat. Assn. Women Bus. Owners. Republican. Jewish. Avocation: work on behalf of handicapped. Office: Tekhark Computer Services Inc 37 E 29th St New York NY 10016

MARK, LILLIAN GEE, school official; b. Berkeley, Calif., Mar. 18, 1932; d. Pon Gordon and Sun Kum (Wong) Gee; m. Richard Muin Mark, June 20, 1954; children—Dean, Kim, Faye, Glenn, Lynne. A.B. in Psychology, U. Calif.-Berkeley, 1954; postgrad. Pensacola Coll., 1985—. Sec., Western Life Ins. Co., San Francisco, 1944-54; child care tchr. San Diego Child Care Ctr., 1954-55; dir. pre-sch. ABC Nursery, San Mateo, Calif., 1969-76; founder, prin. Alpha Beacon Christian Sch., San Carlos, Calif., 1976—. Author: Handbook for Parents and Students, 1983. Mem. Assn. Christian Schs. Internat. Republican. Mem. Pentacostal Ch. Avocations: tennis; piano; Bible study. Home: 182 Exbourne Ave San Carlos CA 94070 Office: Alpha Beacon Christian Sch 750 Dartmouth Ave San Carlos CA 94070

MARK, MELISA GAYLE, office administrator; b. Ada, Okla., Aug. 8, 1962; d. Jim Daniel and Alice Larue (Henry) Kryza M. B.A. in History, George Mason U., 1984. Invoicing clk. Ebsco Subscription Services, Springfield, Va., 1979-81; clk. typist, sec. B & B Refrigeration Co., Inc., Fairfax, Va., 1981-84; field facilities supr. Epic Residential Network, Inc., Falls Church, Va., 1984-85; office adminstrn. coordinator CIT-Alcatel, Inc., Reston, Va., 1985—. Asst. editor Alca-Tells, 1985—. Mem. Nat. Assn. Female Execs., Nat. Historic Preservation Soc. Presbyterian. Avocations: travel; reading history; drawing.

MARKAS, PATRICIA ANNE, personnel executive; b. Shelby, N.C., May 11, 1931; d. John M. and Ruth Vere (Harmon) Markas. A.B., U. N.C.-Greensboro, 1953; M.S., U. N.C.-Chapel Hill, 1962. Psychologist, N.C. State Hosp., Butner, 1953-56; exec. dir. Rowan Cabarrus council Girl Scouts U.S., Kannapolis, N.C., 1956-58, Bright Leaf council, Durham, N.C., 1958-63, Pines of Carolina council, Raleigh, 1963-68; dir. personnel devel. N.C. Assn. Electric Coops., Inc., Raleigh, 1968—. Girl Scouts U.S.A. fellow, 1961. Mem. N.C. Adult Edn. Assn., Am. Soc. Personnel Adminstrn., Soc. Assn. Execs. Methodist. Home: 2909 Hope Valley Rd Durham NC 27707 Office: NC Assn Electric Cooperative PO Box 27306 Raleigh NC 27611

MARKEY, KATHLEEN, lawyer; b. Teaneck, N.J., Mar. 5, 1946; d. Thomas Francis and Catherine (Dillon) Markey; m. Kenneth Niejadlik, June 26, 1971; children—Kenneth Michael, Kara Michele. B.A. cum laude, Syracuse U., 1971; M.A., U. Miami, 1974, J.D. cum laude, 1978, LL.M., 1980. Bar: Fla. 1978, U.S. Tax Ct. 1980. Ptnr., Myers, Kenin, Levinson & Richards, Miami, 1980—. Mem. ABA, Fla. Bar. Episcopalian. Office: 1428 Brickell Ave Suite 700 Miami FL 33131

MARKHAM, EMILY DAY, home management consulting company executive; b. Dyer, Tenn., Mar. 1, 1943; d. Odis Fredrick and Vera Virginia (Powell) Day; m. Ronald Lee Markham II, Aug. 13, 1966; children—Kristin Day, Ronald Lee III. B.S. in Home Econs., U. Tenn., 1965. Chmn. home econs. dept. Englewood High Sch., Jacksonville, Fla., 1965-70; instr. DDD Appliances, Naples, Fla., 1980—; pres. Enthusiasm, Inc., Naples, 1982—; cons. sr. adults So. Bapt. Conv., Naples, 1986. Author: Microwave Simplicity, 1982. Sr. adult coordinator 1st Bapt. Ch., Naples, 1984—; adv. bd. Pine Ridge Middle Sch., 1985—. Mem. Am. Home Econs. Assn., Fla. Home Econs. Assn. (pres. dist. H 1986—, Outstanding Fla. Home Economist in Bus. 1984), Collier County Home Econs. Assn. (treas. 1983—). Republican. Avocation: playing piano. Home: 107 Westwood Dr Naples FL 33942 Office: Enthusiasm Inc PO Box 7142 Naples FL 33941

MARKHAM, JUDITH ELLENE, editor; b. Niagara Falls, N.Y., Sept. 21, 1941; d. Edward W. and Edith J. (Weimer) Errick; m. Robert L. Markham, Sept. 19, 1970. B.A., Houghton Coll., 1963. Curriculum editor Union Gospel Press, Cleve., 1963-65; asst. editor Child Evangelism Mag., Grand Rapids, Mich., 1965-68; asst. book editor Zondervan Pub. House, Grand Rapids, 1968-73, project editor, 1973-78, gen. editor trade books, 1978-80, editor-at-large, 1980-83, editor Zondervan Books, 1983—; editor Markham Books, 1982—; mem. faculty Sch. Christian Writing, Mpls., 1981, 82; vis. lectr. Houghton Coll., 1986. Author short stories. Named Houghton Coll. Alumna of Yr., 1985. Mem. Grand Rapids Symphonic Choir, 1968-78. Mem. Women's Nat. Book Assn. (chpt. dir. 1975-76), Profl. Women's Network. Presbyterian. Office: Zondervan Publishing House 1415 Lake Dr SE Grand Rapids MI 49506

MARKHAM, MARY ELIZABETH THORNTON (MRS. REGINALD A. MARKHAM), state ofcl.; b. Haverhill, Mass.; d. John W. and Mary E. (Murphy) Thornton; B.A., Regis Coll., 1937; M.Ed., Salem State Coll., 1968; m. Reginald A. Markham, Feb. 26, 1954 (dec. 1981). With Mass. Div. Employment Security, 1937-81, prin. counselor N.E. area Mass., Lawrence, 1965-70, mgr. concentrated employment program, Lowell, 1970-71, supervising mgr., 1971-73, supervisory mgr., Lowell, 1973-75, Haverhill Newburyport area, 1975-77, Lawrence, 1977-81. Bd. dirs. Merrimack River council Girl Scouts Am., 1965-73, chmn. personnel com., 1965-73, v.p., 1972-75; sec. Medford Ancillary Manpower Planning Bd., 1972-73; mem. steering com. project vol. power Malden Mayor's Com. for Employment of Handicapped, 1972-73; bd. dirs. No. Essex Regional Community Action Commn., Area Manpower Planning Bd.; mem. advisory bd. Whittier Regional Vocat. and Tech. Sch.; mem. Merrimack Valley Econ. and Devel. Com., Greater Lawrence, Haverhill coms. employment of handicapped, Greater Lawrence Community Service Assos., Haverhill Hist. Soc., Friends of Haverhill Pub. Library. Address: 180 Water St Apt 503 Haverhill MA 01830

MARKHAM, ROSEMARY, lawyer; b. Pitts., June 12, 1946; d. Chester James and Elizabeth Helen (Seger) Markham; m. Wayne Joseph Pfrimmer, Sept. 11, 1965 (div. 1975); 1 dau., Adriene. B.A., U. Pitts., 1968; J.D., Duquesne U., 1978. Bar: Pa. 1978; adminstrv. asst. West Pa. Conservancy, Pitts., 1969-70; law clk. Girman & DelSole, 1975-76, Watzman & DeAngelis, 1976-78; serious injury rep. Travelors Ins., 1978-79; assoc. Manifesto & Doherty, 1979-81; individual practice law, 1981—. Mem. ABA, Assn. Trial Lawyers Am., Pa. Bar Assn., Pa. Trial Lawyers Assn., Allegheny County Bar Assn. Democrat. Roman Catholic. Club: Rivers. Office: Rosemary Markham 320 Allegheny Bldg 429 Forbes Ave Pittsburgh PA 15219

MARKLEY, KAROL JEAN, mfr., designer riding apparel, exec. constrn. co.; b. Los Angeles, Mar. 26, 1939; d. Ashby V. Pearce and Jean (Xuma) Pearce Himes; B.A. cum laude, UCLA, 1968; M.A. in Psychology, U. Calif., Riverside, 1971; m. Francis Edward Markley, July 20, 1957; children—Teal Len, Tawne Anne. Research asst. to psychologist Arthur Janov, Los Angeles, 1967-70; dir., officer Francis E. Markley Corp., Francis E. Markley & Co., Inc., Palm Springs, Calif., 1971—, Milmark Painting, Inc., Milmark Corp., Talmarka Corp., Mark KD Inc., 1985—; exec. mgr. Markley Mgmt. Services, Palm Springs, 1971—; co-designer, builder Francis E. Markley Corp., constrn. co., Palm Springs, 1971—; designer, coordinator, mfr. riding apparel Karol Markley Enterprises, Palm Springs, 1975—; owner The Final Touch, Scottsdale, Ariz., 1975—; guest speaker horsemanship clinics. Mem. Am. Horse Shows Assn. (stock seat equitation com. 1977-85, vice chmn. 1982-84), Internat. Arabian Horse Assn. (equitation com. 1971—). Address: 2966 Via Vaquero Palm Springs CA 92262

MARKOVICH-TREECE, PATRICIA HELEN, economist; b. Oakland, Calif.; s. Patrick Joseph and Helen Emily (Prydz) Markovich; B.A. in Econs.; M.S. in Econs., U. Calif.-Berkeley, postgrad. (Lilly Found. grantee) Stanford U., (NSF grantee) Oreg. Grad. Research Center; children—Michael Sean, Bryan Jeffry, Tiffany Helene. With public relations dept. Pettler Advt., Inc.; pvt. practice polit. and econs. cons.; aide to majority whip Oreg. Ho. of Reps.; lectr., instr., various Calif. instns., Chemeketa (Oreg.) Coll., Portland (Oreg.) State U. Commr., City of Oakland (Calif.), 1970-74. Mem. Mensa.

MARKS, CAROL PAGE, nurse; b. Jackson, Miss., Dec. 13, 1961; d. Simon Seelig and Rose (Walley) M. B.S. in Nursing U. Miss., 1983. Lic. R.N., Miss. Staff nurse U. Miss. Med. Ctr., 1982-83; commd. staff nurse U.S. Navy, Groton, Conn., 1983—, ensign, 1982-85, lt. (j.g.), 1985—. Mem. Sigma Theta Tua. Republican. Roman Catholic. Club: Pi Beta Phi. Home: 150 Yantic St #204 Norwich CT 06360 Office: Naval Hosp Groton Box 600 P-Code 49 Groton CT 06349

MARKS, DEBORAH BRANDSTATTER, lawyer; b. Hollis, N.Y., Sept. 28, 1958; d. Edward and Evalyne (Manchik) Brandstatter; m. Evan Richard Marks, May 31, 1982. B.A. magna cum laude, Vanderbilt U., 1959; J.D. cum laude, U. Miami, 1982. Bar: Fla. 1982. Law clk. Young, Stern & Tannenbaum, P.A., North Miami Beach, Fla., 1981-82, assoc., 1982-83; assoc. Atkinson, Golden, Jenne, Diner & Stone, P.A., Hollywood, Fla., 1983—. Assoc. editor Lawyer of the Americas, 1980-82. Bd. dirs. Spencer Youth Ctr. Correctional Facility for Juveniles, Nashville, 1978-79. Presdl. scholar, 1975; Reid scholar, 1979-82. Mem. ABA, Assn. Trial Lawyers Am., Acad. Fla. Trial Lawyers, Fla. Bar, Am. Judicature Soc., Dade County Bar Assn., Fla. Assn. Women Lawyers, Bar and Gavel, Phi Alpha Delta (treas. 1980-81), Omicron Delta Epsilon. Clubs: Miami Vanderbilt (dir. 1983—); Turnberry Isle Yacht and Racquet (North Miami, Fla.). Home: 2020 S Hibiscus Dr North Miami FL 33181 Office: Atkinson Golden Jenne Diner & Stone PA 1946 Tyler St Hollywood FL 33022

MARKS, DOROTHY LIND, mathematics tutor; b. N.Y.C., Apr. 30, 1900; d. Alfred Daniel and Martha (Herzog) Lind; m. Norman Lincoln Marks, May 29, 1923 (dec. 1959); 1 son, Alfred Lind (dec. 1980). B.A., Barnard Coll., 1921. Substitute tchr. N.Y. high schs., 1921-28; math tutor The Brearley Sch., N.Y.C., 1953-62, The Marlborough Sch., Los Angeles, 1973—, pvt. and pub. secondary schs., Los Angeles, 1973—, NYU, 1965-72; chmn. math dept. The Lenox Sch., N.Y.C., 1960-70. Bd. dirs. women's orgn. Temple Rodeph Sholem, N.Y.C., 1925-50, fin. sec., 1925-47. Mem. Phi Beta Kappa (recipient Kohn Math. Prize 1921, sec.-treas. Barnard chpt. 1925-50, chartermem. alumnae in N.Y.). Republican. Jewish. Avocations: reading, music, theatre, concerts, ballet.

MARKS, ELAINE, foreign language educator; b. N.Y.C., Nov. 13, 1930; d. Harry and Ruth (Elin) M.; A.B. magna cum laude, Bryn Mawr Coll., 1952; M.A., U. Pa., 1953; Ph.D., NYU, 1958. Instr. French, NYU, 1957-60, asst. prof., 1960-62; assoc. prof. dept. French, U. Wis., Milw., 1963-65; prof. French, U. Mass., Amherst, 1965-66, 72-73, vis. prof., 1971; prof. dept. French and Italian, U. Wis., Madison, 1966-68, 80—, dir. Women's Studies Research Ctr., 1977-85, lectr., 1977; manuscript reader several book pubs., 1980-82; mem. grad. record exams. com. Examiners for Advances Test in French, 1978-82; mem. Council French Social and Cultural Affairs, NYU, 1981—. Panelist, Nat. Endowment for the Humanities, 1973-77. Mem. MLA (exec. com. div. women's studies in lang. 1977-82, exec. council 1984—), Midwest MLA (exec. com. 1978-81), Am. Assn. Tchrs. French, Nat. Women's Studies Assn. Author: Colette, 1960; Encounters with Death: An Essay on the Sensibility of Simone de Beauvoir, 1973; contbr. numerous articles and revs. on French lit. and women's studies to profl. publs.; editorial bd. Signs: Jour. of Women in Culture and Society, 1976—; co-editor Homosexualities and French Literature, 1979; New French Feminisms, 1980. Home: 2040 Field St Madison WI 53713 Office: 618 Van Hise Hall U Wis Madison WI 53706

MARKS, HELENA LIN, med. technologist; b. Peking, China, Oct. 6, 1935; came to U.S., 1955, naturalized, 1961; d. Kung and Shu-Fan (Lee) Lin; B.A. in Math. and Physics, Hunter Coll., N.Y.C., 1972; m. John S. Marks, Nov. 28, 1958 (dec. 1973); children—John Lin, Paul Lee; m. 2d J.B. Celleri 1977. Supr. chemistry lab. Tompkins County Hosp., Ithaca, N.Y., 1962-64; supr. labs. Calvary Hosp., Bronx, N.Y., 1964-67; med. technologist N. Central Hosp., Bronx, N.Y., 1977—; real estate saleswoman. Mem. Am. Soc. Clin. Pathologists, N.Y.C. Med. Lab. Suprs. Home: 4 Raleigh Dr New City NY 10956 Office: Blood Bank 3424 Kossuth Ave Bronx NY 10467

MARKS, JEANETTE, mktg. research agy. exec.; b. Bklyn., Nov. 4, 1929; d. Abraham and Sophie (Kessler) Fine; student Bklyn. Coll.; children—Rhonda, Craig, Alan. Nat. field dir. N.E. Field Facts, Natick, Mass., 1961-76; mktg. mgr. Market Research Agy., 1976—; mgr. Quick Test Opinion Center, Mesa, Ariz. Mem. Mktg. Research Assn. (pres. S.W. chpt. 1983-85), Am. Mktg. Assn. Jewish. Club: Jewish Bus. and Profl. Women. Home: 1216 E Vista Del Cerro Apt 2089 Tempe AZ 85281 Office: 1327 N Scottsdale Rd Scottsdale AZ 85257

MARKS, JILL STEINER, lawyer; b. Richmond, Va., Dec. 25, 1952; d. Leroy and Roberta Jean Thalia (Oresman) Steiner. B.S., N.C. State U., 1975; J.D., South Tex. Coll. Law, 1980. Bar: Va. 1980. Video Staff mem. South Tex. Coll. Law, Houston, 1978-79; legal asst. Lawsearch, Houston, 1979-80; assoc. firm Bowles & Bowles, Richmond, 1980-84, Steve Burcin, Richmond, 1984-85, Taylor, Hazen & Kauffman, Richmond, 1986—; dir. Richmond Theatre Co. Mem. ABA, Va. State Bar Assn., Va. Trial Lawyers Assn., Richmond Bar Assn., Richmond Jaycees. Delta Theta Phi. Office: Suite 1104 700 E Main St PO Box 1-P Richmond VA 23202

MARKS, JUDITH ANGELA, communication consultant; b. Milw., Aug. 11, 1949; d. Alois A. and Lucille M. Casper. B.S., U. Wis., Milw., 1972, M.A., 1976; m. James Arthur Marks, Aug. 18, 1972; 1 child Jonathan Casper. Teaching asst., then lectr. interpersonal communication U. Wis., Milw., 1974-78; guest lectr. Marquette U. Sch. Nursing Office Continuing Edn., spring 1981, Med. Coll. Wis., Wauwatosa, 1984; cons. High Ridge Health Care Ctr., Racine, Wis., Belleview Extended Care, Milw.; lectr. U. Wis., Whitewater, 1976-77, 78-83; workshop leader, judge, cons. in field. Scholar AAUW, 1974. Mem. Speech Communication Assn., Central States Speech Assn., Wis. Profl. Speakers Assn. Home: W247 S7465 Scotland Dr Waukesha WI 53186

MARKS, KAYE RYAN, information systems consultant; b. Norristown, Pa., Mar. 16, 1948; d. Francis Thomas and Rose Anne (Gnagy) Ryan; m. James Elliott Marks, June 20, 1981. Student Northeastern U., 1974-79. Cert. systems profl. Inst. Cert. Computer Profls. Programmer, analyst GTE Sylvania, Needham, Mass., 1974-79; cons., Acton, Mass., 1979-83; mgr. fin. systems Boston U., 1983-84; prin. programmer-analyst D E C, Marlboro, Mass., 1984-85; sr. systems analyst Tech. Mgmt. Corp., Norfolk, Va., 1985—. Mem. Data Processing Mgmt. Assn. (chpt. pres. 1982, 85), Am. Arbitration Assn., Am. Inst. Cert. Computer Profls., D.A.R. Republican. Roman Catholic. Lodge: Toastmistress. Avocations: building furniture; cooking; creative electronics. Home: 1124 Birdneck Lake Dr Virginia Beach VA 23457

MARKS, LILLIAN SHAPIRO, educator; b. Bklyn., Mar. 16, 1907; d. Hayman and Celia (Merowitz) Shapiro; B.S., N.Y. U., 1928; m. Joseph Marks, Feb. 21, 1932; children—Daniel, Sheila Blake, Jonathan. High sch. tchr., N.Y.C., 1929-30; tchr. Evalina de Rothschild Sch., Jerusalem, Palestine, 1930-31; social worker United Jewish Aid, Bklyn., 1931-32; tchr. Richmond Hill High Sch., 1932-40, Andrew Jackson High Sch., Cambria Heights, N.Y., 1940-71; mem. faculty New Sch. Social Research, N.Y.C., 1977—; staff Vassar Summer Inst., 1946. Mem. Am. Fedn. Tchrs., English-Speaking Union, Inst. Ret. Profls. Democrat. Jewish. Am. editor: Teeline, A System of Fast Writing, 1970; author: College Teeline, 1977; College Teeline Self-Taught, 1983; Touch Typing Made Simple, 1985. Home and Office: 117-16 Park Lane S Kew Gardens NY 11418

MARKS, MARGUERITE MCBURNEY, university administrator, educator; b. Binghamton, N.Y., Feb. 11, 1919; d. William Henry and Grace (Richardson) McBurney; B.S. in History, Portland State U., 1963, M.S.T. in History, 1965; Ph.D., U. Oreg., 1980; m. Kenneth Arthur Marks, Feb. 4, 1940; 1 dau., Diane M. Reader, dept. history Portland State U., 1962, grad. asst., 1963-65, dir. internat. student services, 1964-73, asst. prof. English as a Second Lang. Center, 1964—, mem. summer session faculty, 1967—, asst. prof. history, 1972-78, asst. prof. edn., 1977-83, prof. emerita, 1983—, admissions officer internat. students, 1973—, coordinator fgn. student alumni Portland State U., cons. in field; producer Foreign Student Friends, Local Public Radio, 1965-75, mem. adv. council for community listening, 1967—; mem. com. for UN, City of Portland; mem. Portland Pan-Am. Com., 1965-74; adv. internat. relations com. Portland Jr. C. of C., 1968-70; evaluator Nat. Liaison Com. Fgn. Students. Recipient Leader commendation Campfire Girls, 1959, Pres.'s award Portland Jr. C. of C., 1971, 72. Mem. Oreg. Congress Parents and Tchrs. (legis. dir. 1961-64; life), Nat. Assn. Fgn. Student Affairs, Am. Assn. Collegiate Registrars and Admission Officers, Pacific Coast Assn. Collegiate Registrars and Admissions Officers, Am.-Mideast Ednl. and Tng. Services. Author: Handbook on the Placement of Foreign Graduate Students, 1979; contbg. author: The Country Index, vol. 1, 1984; contbr. numerous poems to children's publs., 1959—. Home: 3033 NE Hancock Portland OR 97212 Office: Portland State U ESL Ctr PO Box 751 Portland OR 97207

MARKS, RENEE LEE, educator; b. Chgo., Nov. 20, 1936; d. Sol and Celia (Freund) Kaplan; B.S.J., Northwestern U., 1958, postgrad. (Chgo. Bd. Edn. scholar), summer 1978; B.J.S., Spertus Coll., 1972; M.A., Mundelein Coll., 1975; M.Ed. with distinction, De Paul U., 1981; postgrad. in ednl. adminstrn. Northeastern Ill. U., 1980-81; cert. in adminstrn. and supervision Nat. Coll. Edn., Evanston, Ill., 1982, postgrad., 1985—; postgrad. in computer sci. U. Ill.-Chgo., 1982-85; doctoral student in instrnl. leadership Nat. Coll. of Edn., 1984—; m. Donald Norman Marks, June 22, 1958; children—Robin Debra Marks Dombeck, Steven Michael, Jody Ilene. Tchr. Chgo. Bd. Edn., 1976—; lectr. on Holocaust. Mem. Nat. Council for Social Studies, Chgo. Council for Social Studies, Assn. for Supervision and Curriculum Devel., Am. Ednl. Research Assn., Nat. Soc. for Study of Edn., Phi Delta Kappa. Jewish. Author, Holocaust curriculum for Chgo. Bd. Edn., 1980. Home and Office: 9036 N Menard Morton Group IL 60053

MARKSON, HADASSAH BINDER, music administrator; b. N.Y.C., Aug. 9, 1927; d. Abraham W. and Anna (Freidman) Binder; B.A., Queens Coll., 1949; postgrad. Hunter Coll., 1976-80; m. Martin Markson, Feb. 6, 1949; children—Naomi Steinberger, Dina Markson. Dir., producer Lyrics and Lyricists series 92d St. Y Sch. Music, N.Y.C., 1969—; artistic dir., producer Jewish Opera at Y, N.Y.C., 1978—; producer Jazz in July. Sec., then v.p. Nat. Guild Community Schs. Arts; bus. mgr. Musica Judaica Jour., 1977—. Mem. Am. Soc. Jewish Music (sec.). Office: Sch Music 1395 Lexington Ave New York NY 10028

MARKUM, ARLENE, banker; b. N.Y.C., June 15, 1942; d. John Thomas and Mary Louise McAllister; student Pace U., 1975—; m. Onzelo Markum Jr., July 28, 1960; children—Onzelo III, Andrea Gail. Credit adminstrn. clk. Franklin Simon, N.Y.C., 1963; supr. Lord & Taylors, N.Y.C., 1963-68; with Citibank N.Y., N.Y.C., 1969—, asst. mgr., 1974-81, mgr., 1981-85, asst. v.p., 1986—. Mem. Nat. Assn. Female Execs. Republican. Home: 8400 Shore Front Pkwy Rockaway Beach NY 11693

MARKUM, GLORIA ANN, psychotherapist, consultant; b. Los Angeles, May 18, 1945; d. Isaac Robert and Lela Faye (Hamilton) M.; m. Allan Ray Huffaker, Feb. 1, 1964 (div. Dec. 1976); children—David Donley, Lindi Lauran, Jonathan Jared. B.S. magna cum laude, Hardin-Simmons U., 1966; M.Ed., E. Tex. State U., 1975. Speech and hearing therapist Dean Sch., Inc., Fort Worth, 1971-74; tchr. Child Study Ctr., Fort Worth, 1974-75; tchr. spl. edn. Plano Ind. Sch. Dist. (Tex.), 1975-77, ednl. diagnostician, 1977-79; psychotherapist, Dallas, 1979-80; cons. psychotherapy, Dallas, 1980—; trainer, pres. Options Unlimited, Inc. Author: poetry Soul's Landscaping, 1984. Participant, Concerned Americans, 1984. Mem. Nat. Speakers Assn., North Tex. Speakers Assn., Am. Assn. Profl. Hypnotherapists, Nat. Assn. Female Execs., Am. Assn. Marriage and Family Therapists, AAUW, Alpha Chi. Democrat. Mem. Unity Ch. Club: Women of Unity (pres. 1981-82, v.p. 1981—) (Dallas). Office: Options Unlimited Inc 5709 Forest Ln Dallas TX 75230

MARKUN, RACHEL, lawyer; b. Des Moines, Sept. 7, 1957; d. Ray O. and Marjorie (Campbell) Brandenburg; m. Paul Markun, Sept. 24, 1983; 1 child, Peter Ryan. B.A., U. Chgo., 1977; J.D., U. Calif.-San Francisco, 1981. Bar: Calif., 1981. Assoc. firm Morrison & Foerster, San Francisco, 1981—; adj. prof. taxation U. San Francisco, 1984—; lectr. taxation sect. Bar Assn. San Francisco, 1984; Calif. Continuing Edn. of Bar, 1984; tax cons. San Francisco Commn. on Status Women, San Francisco, 1984—. Editor-in-chief Hastings Law Jour., 1980-81. Mem. ABA, Calif. Bar Assn., Western Pension Conf., Bar Assn. San Francisco. Home: 613 Eucalyptus Way Mill Valley CA 94941 Office: Morrison & Foerster 345 California St San Francisco CA 94105

MARLBOROUGH, JANET LYNN, hospital administrator, consultant, author; b. Long Beach, Calif., Mar. 23, 1951; d. Malvin Joseph and Marion Josephine (Zolper) M. B.S. in Nursing, Calif. State U.-Los Angeles, 1973; postgrad. U. San Diego, 1981-82; M.B.A. in Mktg., U.S. Internat. U., San Diego, 1983. Registered nurse. Adminstrv. supr. Alvarado Hosp., San Diego, 1977-78; supr., dir. ambulatory care, asst. hosp. adminstr. Mercy Hosp. & Med. Ctr., San Diego, 1978—; prin. Marlborough & Assoc., San Diego, 1983—; dir. Specialty Home Health, San Diego. Author: Nursing Management: Patterns for Excellence, 1986; (with E. McLachlan and M. Silbur) Nursing Management. Contbr. article Contbr. article to RN mag. (Best Service Innovation award 1983). Mktg. com. San Diego Hospice, 1983. Served to lt. USN, 1971-76. Recipient Zanville Helping Hand award United Way, 1982; Pregnant Minor Program grantee Considine Found., 1983. Mem. Am. Mtkg. Assn. (v.p. 1984-85), Community Relations Mktg. Assn. (chair 1982-84, Nat. Highest hons. 1983, 84), Agy. Execs. Assn. (v.p. 1983-85, Zanville award 1982), Am. Hosp. Assn., Health Care Execs. Assn., U.S. Internat. U. Alumni. Democrat. Avocations: skiing; sailing. Office: Mercy Hosp & Med Ctr 4077 Fifth Ave San Diego CA 92103

MARLER, LINDA SUSAN, clinical microbiologist; b. Bloomington, Ind., May 28, 1951; d. Lynne Lionel and Lucille Elizabeth (Widman) Merritt; B.S. in Med. Tech., Ind. U., 1973, M.S. in Allied Health Edn., 1978; m. David William Marler, May 21, 1977 (div.); children—Brian David, Brittney Lynne. Med. technologist, then sr. med. technologist Ind. U. Med. Center, Indpls., 1973—, edn. coordinator dept. microbiology, 1974—, asst. prof. div. allied health Sch. Medicine, 1978-84, assoc. prof., 1984—; speaker in field. Mem. Am. Soc. Microbiology, Am. Soc. Med. Tech., South Central Assn. Clin. Microbiologists (area dir., assn. dir.). Methodist. Office: Fesler 416 1120 South Dr Indianapolis IN 46223

MARLEY, VICTORIA PILZ, banker; b. Flushing, N.Y., Oct. 26, 1954; d. Hanns Joachaim and Gertrude Margaret (Lindenberg) Pilz; m. Everett Barry Marley, July 22, 1977; Student pub. schs., Ft. Lauderdale, Fla. Exec. sec. Fingerhut Corp., Minnetonka, Minn., 1977-78; security mgr. First Bank Systems, Mpls., 1978-79; security/credit mgr. NorWest Banks, Mpls., 1979-82; v.p. bank ops. Home Fed. Bank, St. Petersburg, Fla., 1983—. Republican. Lutheran. Office: Home Federal Bank of Fla 1901 Central Ave Saint Petersburg FL 33713

MARLIN, ALICE TEPPER, research organization administrator; b. Long Branch, N.J., Aug. 10, 1944; d. Walter L. and Grace A. (Comins) Tepper; m. John Tepper Marlin, Sept. 25, 1971; children—John Joseph, Caroline. Ed. The Baldwin Sch., 1962; B.A., in Econs., Wellesley Coll., 1966; postgrad. in Bus. Adminstrn., N.Y.U. Securities analyst Drexel Burnham, N.Y.C., 1966-68; scheduler, advance planner McCarthy for Pres. Campaign, 1968; fin. analyst T. O'Connel Mgmt. and Research, N.Y.C., 1968-69; exec. dir. Council on Econ. Priorities, N.Y.C., 1969—; bd. dirs. Gathering Internat. Families Together, N.Y.C., 1982—; chmn. investment com. fund for Constl. Govt., Washington, 1983—; trustee Winston Found., N.Y.C., 1985—; v.p. Social Investment Forum. Author: Good Business: Shopping for a Better World, 1986. Editor: (monthly) Council Econ. Priorities Newsletter; editor more than 30 books. Contbr. articles to profl. jours. Mem., Com. for Nat. Security, Club of Rome, Women's Forum. Recipient Inventory of Hope award Saturday Review, disting. alumnae award The Baldwin Sch.; named woman of Yr., Mademoiselle mag.; Point fellow, 1972; Japan Soc. Leadership fellow, 1985-86. Democrat. Unitarian. Club: Harvard (N.Y.C.). Avocations: tennis; gardening. Address: Council on Econ Priorities 30 Irving Pl New York NY 10003

MARLOW, AUDREY SWANSON, artist, designer; b. N.Y.C., Mar. 3, 1929; d. Sven and Rita (Porter) Swanson; student (scholarships) Art Students League, 1950-55; spl. courses SUNY (Stony Brook), L'Alliance Française m. Roy Marlow, Nov. 30, 1968. With Cohn-Hall-Marx Textile Studio, 1961-65, R.S. Assos. Textile Studio, 1965-73; freelance designer, illustrator Prince Matchabelli, Lester Harrison Agy., J. Walter Thompson Agy., 1957-78; portrait and fine artist, Wading River, N.Y., 1973—; instr. Phoenix Sch. Design (N.Y.C.); exhibits include: Nat. Arts Club, NAD, Parish Art Mus., South Hampton, N.Y., Guild Hall, East Hampton, N.Y., Portraits Inc., Lincoln Ctr., Chung-Cheng Art Gallery, St. John's U., Mystic (Conn.) Art Assn., Harbour Gallery, St. Thomas, V.I. Trustee, Middle Island Public Library, 1972-76. Recipient John W. Alexander medal, 1976, award Council on Arts, 1978, award of excellence Cork Gallery, Lincoln Center, 1982; Grumbacher Bronze medal, 1983; Grumbacher Silver medal 1986; Best in Show award N.Y. Arts Council, 1986. Mem. Pastel Soc. Am. (award 1977, 80), Am. Artists Profl. League (2 1st prize awards), Hudson Valley Art Assn. (award), Knickerbocker Artists (2 awards), Catharine Lorillard Wolfe Art Club (award 1982), Salmagundi Club (5 awards), Nat. League Am. Pen Women (Gold award, Gold medal of Honor). Works represented at N.Y. U., pvt. collections; one-woman show Salmagundi Club, 1982. Home: 76 Northside Rd Wading River NY 11792

MARLOW, DOROTHY RUTH, nurse, educator; b. Phila.; d. William and Lillian (Shisler) M.; diploma Children's Hosp., Phila., 1942; B.S., U. Pa., 1948, M.S., 1956; Ed.D., Columbia U., 1958. Various nursing edn. and nursing service positions Children's Hosp., Phila., 1943-45; supr. pediatric dept., instr. pediatric nursing Hosp. U. Pa., 1945-53; instr. pediatric nursing Sch. Nursing, U. Pa., 1953-56, asst. prof., 1958-61, asso. prof., 1961-65, chmn. grad. program, 1962-64; prof. pediatric nursing, asst. dean. Coll. Nursing, Villanova (Pa.) U., 1965-68, dean Coll. Nursing, 1968-76; cons. curriculum in nursing to various schs. nursing. Mem. Nat. League Nursing, Am. Nurses Assn., Kappa Delta Pi, Sigma Theta Tau, Pi Lambda Theta. Author: Textbook of Pediatric Nursing (best book in coll. textbook group Phila. Book Show, 1962), 1961; Textbook of Pediatric Nursing, 2d edit., 1965 (certificate of award, coll. textbook group Phila. Book Show 1966), 3d edit., 1969, 4th edit., 1973, 5th edit., 1977. Home: 106 E Sylvan Ave Rutledge PA 19070

MARLOWE, HELEN LOUISE, customs service official; b. Newberry, Fla., July 11, 1938; d. Guilbert Daniel and Nellie Mae (McComb) M. A.A. with honors, Santa Fe Jr. Coll., 1968; B.S. in Bus. Adminstrn. with honors, U. Fla., 1970. Clk. Life Ins. Co. of Ga., Greenville, 1958-61; fiscal asst. U. Fla., Gainesville, 1961-68; acct. U.S. Customs Service, Houston, 1970-73, mgmt. analyst, Washington, 1973-79, program analyst, Miami, Fla., 1979-85, intelligence analyst, Tampa, Fla., 1985—; dir. Miami Fed. Credit Union, 1984—. Mem. Assn. Govt. Accts. (Miami chpt.; pres. 1983, bd. dirs. 1984), Fla. Genealogy Soc., Greater Miami Hist. Soc. Democrat. Baptist. Avocation: genealogical research. Home: 9728 NW PO Box 646 Tampa FL 33601-0646

MAROSCHER, BETTY JEAN, librarian; b. Ashland, Ky., Aug. 12, 1934; d. Raymond and Virginia Dell (Staten) Boggs; student Columbus Coll. (Ga.), 1963-64; B.S., Hardin-Simmons U., 1967; M.S. in L.S., Our Lady of Lake U., San Antonio, 1970; M.Ed., Trinity U., 1975; m. Albert G. Maroscher Mar. 21, 1955 (dec.). Tchr., McAllen (Tex.) Ind. Sch. Dist., 1967-68; tchr. Northside Ind. Sch. Dist., San Antonio, 1968-69, librarian, 1969-71; reference librarian ednl. media Trinity U., San Antonio, 1971-76; reference librarian St. Philip's Coll., San Antonio, 1976, audiovisual librarian, mgr. audiovisual dept., 1977—; lectr., cons. in field; chmn. subcom. programming and scheduling Univ. and Fine Arts Cable TV Com., 1980-81. Active ARC; sec., trustee Compañía de Arte Español, 1982-84. Recipient Minter/Medal Hardin-Simmons U., 1965, 66. Mem. Tex., S.W., Bexar County, Catholic library assns., Tex. Jr. Coll. Tchrs. Assn., Tex. Assn. Chicanos in Higher Edn. (sec. St. Philip's chpt. 1982-84), Audiovisual Instructional Media Services Group, Council Research and Acad. Libraries Coop. Circulation Group (sec.-treas. 1977-79), Pi Gamma Mu (sec. chpt. 1965-67), Alpha Chi (historian 1965-67), other orgns. Republican. Home: 5230 Galahad Dr San Antonio TX 78218 Office: 2111 Nevada St San Antonio TX 78203

MAROT, LOLA, printing administrator; b. Providence, Oct. 6; d. Frank and Iola (Lombardi) Ansuini; m. Joseph Marot (div. 1973); 1 child, David Joseph. B.A. with distinction, U. R.I., 1973; postgrad. Bryant Coll. Bookkeeper, Diamond Paper Box Co., Providence, 1958-69; export sales adminstr. Brite Industries, Providence, 1973-77; property services asst. Met. Property and Liability Ins. Co., Warwick, R.I., 1977-79, buyer, 1979-83, sr. buyer, 1983-86, supr. printing adminstrn., 1986—. Mem. Univ. Soc. Providence (pres. 1978). Office: 700 Quaker Ln Warwick RI 02886

MARQUARDT, CHRISTEL ELISABETH, lawyer; b. Chgo.; d. Herman A. and Christine M. (Geringer) Trolenberg; B.S., Mo. Western Coll., St. Joseph, 1970; J.D. with honors (Mabee scholar), Washburn U., 1974; children—Eric, Philip, Andrew, Joel. Bar: Kans. 1974, U.S. Supreme Ct. 1979, U.S. Ct. Appeals (10th cir.) 1980. Ptnr. firm Cosgrove, Webb & Oman, Topeka, 1970-86, Palmer, Marquardt & Snyder, 1986—; lectr. Kans. Bar Assn., Kans. Trial Lawyers, Menninger Found.; mem. Kans. Bd. Discipline for Attys., 1984—. Bd. dirs. YWCA; mem. Topeka Mayor's Commn. on Status of Women; bd. dirs. Sheltered Living for Retarded Citizens, Topeka Lutheran Sch.; 2d dist. sec. Kans. Republican Exec. Com., 1983—; asst. sec. Kans. Rep. Com., 1983—; bd. govs. Def. Research Inst., 1984—. Recipient disting. alumni award Mo. Western Coll., 1983; named Topeka Woman of Yr., 1982. Mem. Kans. Bar Assn. (chmn. sect. on corp., bus. and banking, chmn. legal services for elderly 1982-83, pres.-elect 1986—; pres.' outstanding service award 1980), Topeka Bar Assn. (chmn. public relations com., chmn. continuing legal edn.), Kans. Trial Lawyers Assn. (bd. govs. 1983-85), Am. Bar Assn., Am. Bus. Women's Assn. (edn. chmn. 1981-83, corr. sec. 1983-84), Greater Topeka C. of C. (bd. dirs. 1982—, v.p. govt. affairs 1983-84), Kans. Women's Polit. Caucus, Topeka Women's Polit. Caucus, Exec. Women's Forum, Phi Kappa Phi, Phi Alpha Delta. Lutheran. Mng. editor Washburn Law Jour., 1973-74; contbr. articles to legal jours. Home: 3121 Briarwood Circle Topeka KS 66611 Office: 112 SW 6th St Topeka KS 66603

MARQUARDT, KATHLEEN P., business executive; b. Kalispell, Mont., June 6, 1944; d. Dean King and Lorraine Camille (Buckmaster) Marquardt; children—Shane Elizabeth, Montana Quinn. Purser, Pan Am. World Airways, Washington, 1968-75; info. specialist Capital Systems Group, Kensington, Md., 1979-81; dir. pub. affairs Subscription TV Assn., Washington, 1981-83, exec. dir., 1983—; pres. Internat. Policy Studies Orgn., 1983—. Bd. dirs. Am. Tax Reduction Movement, 1983—; chmn. bd. Friends of Freedom, 1982—. Mem. Nat. Women's Polit. Caucus, NOW, Women in Communications, Nat. Assn. Women Bus. Owners. Home: 11 E Irving St Chevy Chase MD 20815 Office: 7201 Wisconsin Ave Suite 705 Bethesda MD 20814

MARQUIS, GERALDINE MAE HILDRETH (MRS. FORREST W. MARQUIS), educator; b. Ankeny, Iowa, Aug. 8; d. Vernon Otto and Alma Leona (Woods) Hildreth; student U. No. Iowa; M.A., Drake U., 1972; m. Forrest William Marquis; 1 son, Robert William. Elementary tchr., Ankeny and Ft. Dodge, Iowa, 1944-49, 56—; organizer Ft. Dodge Coop. Nursery Sch. Mem. NEA, Iowa Ft. Dodge edn. assns., Assn. Childhood Edn. Internat. (Iowa pres. 1974-77), Nat. Assn. Edn. Young Children, Civic Music Assn., TTT Nat. Soc. (pres. chpt.), Delta Kappa Gamma (pres. Kappa chpt. 1974-78), World Orgn. Early Childhood Edn., Phi Sigma Alpha. Republican. Methodist. Home: 2602 Williams Dr Fort Dodge IA 50501 Office: 615 N 16th St Fort Dodge IA 50501

MARQUIS, SARAH LYNNE, public relations firm executive, writer; b. Elgin, Ill., June 27, 1950; d. Paul Leslie and Mary Irene (Beck) Ecker. Student Elgin Community Coll., 1968-70; B.A. in Communications, Fla. State U., 1975. Broadcaster Sta.-WCTV, Tallahassee, 1973-74; legis. aide Fla. Ho. of Reps., West Palm Beach, 1975-76; broadcaster Sta.-WPOM, Palm Beach, Fla., 1976-77; account exec. Eason Dobbs Assocs., Fort Lauderdale, Fla., 1977-79; pres., owner Marquis Mktg. Inc., Fort Lauderdale, 1979—; cons. Fort Lauderdale Hist. Dist., 1977-78, South Fla. Symphony, Fort Lauderdale, 1985; dir. publicity Stranahan House Restoration, Fort Lauderdale, 1981. Contbr. articles to mags., 1980—. Mem. Fort Lauderdale Sign adv. Bd., 1978—. Mem. Prime Plus Real Estate Assn. (bd. govs. 1986). Office: Marquis Mktg Inc 2200 W Commercial Suite 305 Fort Lauderdale FL 33309

MARRERO, MYRIAM, real estate broker; b. Lares, P.R., July 25, 1930; d. Guillermo and Marina Marrero (Casanas) Villela; children—Marina Ziel Dias, Patricia Ziel Brenninkmeyer, Yvonne. A.A., Miami-Dade Community Coll., 1982; B.A.S., Fla. Internat. U., 1984. Mng. dir. Ziel Paint Store, Paramaribo Suriname, 1950-73; with Drimoziel Paint Factory, Paramaribo Suriname, 1965-73; mng. dir. S.L.O. Air-Cargo, Paramaribo Suriname, 1970-73, N.V. Guco, Paramaribo Suriname, 1973-78; pres. Carmaltha Realty, Inc., Miami Beach, Fla., 1980—; pub. relations officer Dynavest BHDN, Kuala Lumpur, Malaysia, Bangkok, Thailand, Singapore, and Hong Kong, 1980—. Bahai. Home: Albergastraat 48 Paramaribo Suriname Office: PO Box 807 Paramaribo Suriname

MARRIE-WORMAN, PAULA ANN, veterinarian; b. Youngstown, Ohio, Jan. 22, 1956; d. Patrick Joseph and Laura Jean (Lewis) Marrie; m. John Ludwig Worman, Sept. 26, 1981. D.V.M., Ohio State U., 1981. Veterinarian, Greenacres Animal Hosp., Canton, Ohio, 1981-82; owner, veterinarian Gahanna Animal Hosp. (Ohio), 1982—. Sec. Scholarship House Alumnae, Columbus, Ohio, 1984—. Mem. Am. Animal Hosp. Assn., AVMA, Ohio Vet. Med. Assn., Columbus Acad. Vet. Medicine (v.p. 1984-85), Ohio State U. Alumni Assn., Am. Fedn. Aviculture, Pilot Dogs Inc., Capital Area Humane Soc., Phi Kappa Phi. Democrat. Roman Catholic. Clubs: Columbus All Breed Tng., Canton All Breed Tng. Home: 4639 Shull Rd Gahanna OH 43230 Office: Gahanna Animal Hosp 144 Johnstown Rd Gahanna OH 43230

MARRIOTT, ALICE SHEETS, hotel corp. exec.; b. Salt Lake City, Oct. 19, 1907; d. Edwin Spencer and Alice (Taylor) Sheets; B.A., U. Utah, 1927, D.H.L., 1974; D.H.L., Mt. Vernon Coll., 1980; m. John Willard Marriott, June 9, 1927; children—John Willard, Richad Edwin. Co-founder Marriott Corp., Washington, 1927—, v.p., 1927—. Committeewoman D.C. Republican Nat. Com., 1959-76, vice chmn., 1965-76; chmn. Pres.'s Adv. Commn. on Arts for John F. Kennedy Center, 1970-76; trustee J. F. Kennedy Center, also mem. exec. com., 1971—. Mem. Arthritis and Rheumatism Assn. Washington, Am. Newspaper Women's Assn., Phi Kappa Phi, Chi Omega. Republican. Mormon. Clubs: Capitol Hill, Washington, Capitol Speakers, F Street. Home: 4500 Garfield St NW Washington DC 20007 Office: 1 Marriott Dr Washington DC 20058

MARRIOTT, GLADYS, state legislator; b. Spearman, Tex., Jan. 3, 1922; student pub. schs., Kansas City; m. Lloyd H. Marriott, Sept. 28, 1941; 2 daus. Mem. Mo. Ho. of Reps., 1967—, sec. Democratic Caucus, 77th Gen. Assembly, chmn. Dem. Caucus, 78th Gen. Assembly. Mem. U.S. Task Force on

Retirement and Pensions, 1965—; committeewoman 23d Ward, Kansas City; past vice chmn. Mo. 4th Congressional Dist.; past deaconess New Hope Ch.; past bd. dirs. Kansas City Council PTA. Mem. Nat. Order Women Legislators (past pres.), Chi Omega Alumnae, Am. Bus. Women's Assn. Club: Order of Eastern Star. Office: Mo State Ho of Reps Jefferson City MO 65101*

MARRON, DARLENE LORRAINE, real estate development executive, financial and marketing consultant; b. Auburn, N.Y., July 20, 1946; d. William Chester and Elizabeth Barbara (Gervaise) Kulakowski; m. Edward W. Marron, Jr., Apr. 28, 1973. B.S., Rider Coll., 1968; M.B.A., NYU, 1970. Lic. securities broker. Dir. mktg. Am. Airlines, N.Y.C., 1970-79; asst. v.p. Merrill Lynch, N.Y.C., 1979-83; v.p. Kidder, Peabody & Co., N.Y.C., 1983-86; prsn. Marron Cos., Upper Saddle River, N.J., 1986—; fin. and mktg. cons. to real estate devel. industry. Avocations: pianist; flutist; skiing; fly fishing. Home: 743 W Saddle River Rd Ho-Ho-Kus NJ 07423 Office: Marron Cos, 118 Hwy 17 Upper Saddle River NJ 07458

MARRON, KATHLEEN ANNE, lawyer; b. Mpls., Apr. 29, 1957; d. Richard Gregory and Carol Elaine (Aamoth) Marron. B.A. summa cum laude, U. Minn., 1979, J.D. cum laude, 1982. Bar: Minn. 1982, U.S. Ct. of Appeals (8th cir.) 1982. Tchr. sociology U. Minn., Mpls., 1979-80; research analyst Univ. Minn. and bur. of Crime Prevention, 1978-80; writing instr. U. Minn. Law Sch., Mpls., 1981-82; assoc. firm Robins, Zelle, Larson & Kaplan, Mpls., 1982—. Served with USAR, 1975-79. Mem. Internat. Law Soc. (co-chmn., dir. 1981-82), Internat. Law Moot Ct. (1st place Midwest region 1980-81), ABA, Minn. Trial Lawyers Assn., Am. Trial Lawyers Assn. Def. Research Inst., Phi Beta Kappa, Phi Kappa Phi. Club: Twin Cities Jazz Soc. (Mpls.). Office: Robins Zelle Larson & Kaplan 33 S 5th St Minneapolis MN 55402

MARRS, RITA BERNARDETTE, special education administrator; b. Vallejo, Calif., Feb. 22, 1925; d. Cecil Carl and Frances Bernardette (Campbell) Marrs; div.; children—Lisa Ann, Melanie Bernadette, Colleen Loretta. B.A., Calif. State U.-Long Beach, 1968; M.A., 1972, postgrad. 1973-78. Tchr. spl. edn. Westminster (Calif.) Sch. Dist., 1968-72, San Diego Unified Sch. Dist., 1972, Tustin (Calif.) Unified Sch. Dist., 1973-80, adminstr. spl. edn., 1980-84, adminstrv. program specialist spl. edn., 1980—. Mem. Council Exceptional Children (rec. sec. 1983-84), Women in Ednl. Leadership, So. Counties Women in Ednl. Mgmt., Pi Lambda Theta, Phi Delta Kappa (pres. Orange County chpt. 1982—), Delta Kappa Gamma. Republican. Roman Catholic. Home: 12691 Hazel Ave Garden Grove CA 92641 Office: Tustin Unified Sch Dist 300 S C St Tustin CA 92680

MARSCHALL, MARTHA REYNOLDS, antique shop executive; b. Oil City, Pa., Nov. 14, 1913; d. Frederick Benedict and Florence Ruth (Crahan) Reynolds; m. John Raymond Marschall, Jan. 23, 1931; children—Barbara Lynn, Martha Ray, John Raymond Jr. R.N., St. Mary's Hosp., Galveston, Tex., 1932; student Draughn's Bus. Sch., 1941-42. Nurse, Galveston, 1932-42; asst. mgr. Sherwin-Williams Co., Galveston, 1942-45; office, credit mgr. Climatic Engring., Galveston, 1949-52; head acctg. control unit fin. and acctg. br. U.S. Army C.E., Galveston, 1952-66; purchasing, supply rep. 2578th Air Base Group, Ellington AFB, Tex., 1966-72; owner antique shop, Galveston, 1980—. Recipient Turn Out Perfection award U.S. Air Force, Ellington AFB, 1967, Sustained Superior Performance award, 1969, Outstanding Performance award, 1970. Mem. Am. Bus. Women's Assn. (pres. 1955-56, membership chmn. 1955—, Woman of Yr. 1986-87), Galveston Archeology Soc., Pilot Internat. Democrat. Roman Catholic. Avocations: antique collecting, archeology. Home: 2201 31st St Galveston TX 77550

MARSDEN, ELIZABETH HARLOW, educator; b. Nashville, Mar. 17, 1923; d. Frank Ernest and Harriet Ellsworth (Rees) Harlow; Mus.B., U. Miami, 1944; M.A., Columbia U., 1945; m. Edward Derwood Marsden, Dec. 23, 1946 (div. Jan. 1971); children—Elizabeth Rhys Marsden Marmion, Margaret Lee Marsden Brown, Cathrine Harlow Marsden Mayhew, Harriet Ann Marsden Rice. Tchr., Southeastern La. Coll., 1945-47; asst. prof. music U. Miami, 1947-52; supr. music Penn Hills Sch., Pitts., 1954-59; tchr. piano, voice, Pitts., 1959-61; judge Music Educators Nat. Conf., Miami, 1953, Tampa, Fla., 1953; tchr. Dade County (Fla.) Schs., 1961, Brevard County (Fla.) Schs., 1966-72; minister of music Coral Way Presbyn. Ch., Miami, 1964-66, First Presbyn. Ch., Titusville, 1966-72; music coordinator Marietta (Ga.) City Schs., 1972—; lectr. U. South Fla., 1967-72, Rollins Coll., 1971, U. Ga., 1972—; condr. workshops, music programs for profl. assns., music tchrs., also coll. events; mem. Cobb County Symphony Guild; chmn. Cobb County Artist Series, founder Young Artist Series, both Cobb County Arts Council; chmn. Cobb County Jr. League, Cobb County Parks and Recreation Bd. Recipient Outstanding Contbn. to Arts award YWCA, 1981; Lillian Bennett Sullivan award Cobb County Arts Council, Marietta, 1982; Supt.'s award Marietta City Schs., 1985; Japan-China travel grantee Marietta Bd. Edn., 1986. Mem. AAUP, AAUW, Am. Guild Organists, Music Educators Nat. Conf., NEA, Classroom Tchrs. Assn., Fla. Elem. Tchrs. Assn., Brevard Edn. Assn., Ga. Music Educators Assn. (chmn. 12th dist., mem. study com.), Ga. Assn. Curriculum and Instrnl. Suprs., Ga. Music Edn. Adminstrs. Assn. (pres., steering com. 1977-78, v.p. 1978-79), Brevard Music Edn. Assn. (v.p.), DAR, Internat. Platform Assn., Delta Kappa Gamma, Chi Omega, Sigma Alpha Iota. Clubs: College, Tuesday Music, Mt. Lebanon Women's (Pitts.); Coral Gables Garden, Flamingo Dinner. Home: 335 Vineyard Dr Marietta GA 30064 Office: 145 St Box 1265 Marietta GA 30061

MARSDEN, MELISSA CARLSON, communication designer; b. Rockford, Ill., June 10, 1951; d. G. Albert and Bonnie Eileen Carlson; m. Bradd Weber Marsden, Apr. 29, 1979. B.A. in Edn. with honors, U. Ill., 1973. Tchr. Lutheran High Sch., Rockford, 1974-75; adminstr. repairwoman Sundstrand Corp., Rockford, 1976-78, adminstr. contracts, 1978-80, supr. contract group, 1980-83, communication designer, 1983, sr. communication designer, 1984—. Bd. dirs. YWCA, Rockford, 1977-79; co. campaign chmn. United Way Services, Rockford, 1982. Recipient Gold Plaque award United Way Services, 1982. Mem. Nat. Contract Mgmt. Assn. (1981-83). Internat. Assn. Bus. Communicators. Republican Lutheran. Club: Quota (dir. 1981-84). Home: 5836 Shelford Ln Rockford IL 61107 Office: Sundstrand Corp 4747 Harrison Ave Rockford IL 61101

MARSEN, LOUISE ATKINSON, librarian; b. Hibbing, Minn., Nov. 5, 1922; d. Marc Dumont and Roxaline (St. John) A.; m. Richard Allen Marsen, Feb. 21, 1948 (dec. Oct. 1974); children—James Richard, Betty Martha, Roxaline. A.A., Hibbing Jr. Coll., 1942; B.S., U. Minn., 1944; M.L.S., Rutgers State U., 1982. Asst. librarian U.S. Navy Civil Service, Oakland, Calif., 1943-44; librarian N.Y. Hosp., White Plains, N.Y., 1944-48; assoc. prof., media specialist Brookdale Community Coll., Lincroft, N.J., 1972—. Pres., Friends of Library Middletown, N.J., 1959-60; sec. Friends of Library of Monmouth County (N.J.), 1960-61; trustee Unitarian Ch., Middletown, N.J., 1975-76. Mem. ALA, Spl. Libraries Assn., Health Scis. Library Assn. N.J. Unitarian. Home: 10 Middlebrook Ct Red Bank NJ 07701 Office: Brookdale Community Coll Newman Springs Rd Lincroft NJ 07738

MARSH, CAROLE, author, photographer, publisher; b. Marietta, Ga., Dec. 22, 1946. Pres. Carole Marsh Books, Bath, N.C., 1979—. Author: (children's ednl. series) History Mystery Books, Lost Colony Collection; (single titles) The Teddy Bear's Annual Report, A Kid's Book of Smarts, Meet in the Middle, and others. Author various corp. annual reports and econs. communications. Named Communicator of Yr., Assn. Bus. Communicators; recipient Top Honors, Nat. C. of C. Office: Carole Marsh Books Gen Delivery Bath NC 27808

MARSH, CAROLYN O'NEAL, state administrator; b. Florence, S.C., Dec. 28, 1926; d. Charles O'Neal and Effie (Buzhardt) Marsh. B.A. in Psychology, U. Richmond, 1947, M.A. in Psychology, 1948. Lic. profl. counselor, Va. Grad. asst. U. Richmond (Va.), 1947-48, vocat. counselor, 1948-51; employment interviewer Miller & Rhoads, Richmond, 1951-53, personnel counselor, 1953-55, employment mgr., 1955-61, personnel mgr., 1961-71; pres. Carolyn Marsh Personnel Mgmt., Inc., Richmond, 1971-78; dir. State of Va. Employee Relations Counselors, Richmond, 1978—; mem. Va. Gov.'s Personnel Adv. Bd., Richmond, 1978—, vice chmn., 1978-79, chmn., 1980—, adv. bd. Bank of Richmond, 1974-80. Pres. bd. dirs. Goodwill Industries Richmond, 1971-77; trustee U. Richmond, 1972-76; v.p. Redeemer Lutheran Ch., Richmond, 1981-83. Recipient Disting. Westhampton Coll. Alumna award, 1975, Outstanding Woman in Va. award James Madison U. Faculty Women's Caucus, 1979. Mem. Am. Psychol. Assn., Am. Soc. Personnel Adminstrn., Westhampton Coll. Alumnae Assn. (nat. dir. 1969-79, 83-86), Omicron Delta Kappa. Club: Willow Oaks Country (charter mem.; dir. 1980-81). Office: Dept of Employee Relations Counselors 110 S 7th St Richmond VA 23219

MARSH, CHARLOTTE SKALSKI, advertising executive; b. Phila., July 6, 1950; d. Charles E. and Stephanie T. (Marek) Skalski; m. August John Marsh, Sept. 16, 1977. B.S., Phila. Coll. Art., 1972. Graphic designer Hay Assocs., Phila., 1972-77; creative dir. Photo Lith Inc., Stanton, Calif., 1977-78; owner Graphic Images, Santa Ana, Calif., 1979-81; pres., creative dir. Serling/Marsh, Irvine, Calif., 1981—; judge Maggie Awards, Los Angeles, 1983, 84. Recipient awards Orange County Advt. Fedn., 1983 (2), Western Art Dirs. Club, 1983 (2), Los Angeles Advt. Women, 1983, Advt. Club N.Y., 1984, CLIO, 1984, Advt. Club Los Angeles, 1985. Mem. Nat. Assn. Female Execs., Advt. Club Los Angeles, Am. Inst. Graphic Arts, Orange County Advt. Fedn., Art Dirs. Club Los Angeles. Office: 1124 Main St Suite C Irvine CA 92714

MARSH, DORIS ELAINE, dance educator; b. Saginaw, Mich., Sept. 14, 1931; d. William Henry and Elizabeth Ann (Bates) M.; B.A., U. Mich., 1953, M.A., 1956. Tchr., Saginaw Pub. Schs., 1957-70, Doris Marsh Sch. Ballet, Saginaw, 1956—; dir. Delta Coll. Summer Sch. Dance, 1964-84; dir. Saginaw Valley Dancers, 1975—. Choreographer: Nutcraker, 1979; Summer, 1982; Bluebird of Happiness, 1982; Five Lyric Pieces, 1983. Pres. Saginaw Valley Dance Council, 1972-74; bd. dirs. Saginaw Community Concert Assn., 1958-78; program com. mem. Temple Theatre Arts Assn., Saginaw, 1982—. Mem. Imperial Soc. Tchrs. of Dancing, Mich. Dance Assn., Temple Theatre Arts Assn. (program com. 1982—), Saginaw Valley Dance Council (pres., bd. dirs. 1972-74). Avocations: photography, sewing; hiking; canoeing. Office: Doris Marsh Sch Ballet 6410 Normandy St Saginaw MI 48602

MARSH, ELLA JEAN, pediatrician; b. Chgo., Dec. 16, 1941; d. Charles and Eleanor (Canfield) M.; B.A., St. Mary of Woods (Ind.) Coll., 1963; D.O., Chgo. Coll. Osteo. Medicine, 1971. Intern, Doctor's Hosp., Columbus, Ohio, 1971-72; resident in pediatrics, then asst. prof. Chgo. Coll. Osteo. Medicine, 1972-78, assoc. prof. pediatrics, 1978-82; assoc. prof. W.Va. Coll. Osteo. Medicine, 1975-77; now chmn. pediatric and newborn nursery, assoc. dir. med. edn. Orlando (Fla.) Gen. Hosp.; mem. staff Orlando Regional Hosp., Fla. Hosp.; pediatric cons. Nat. Bd. Osteo. Examiners; lectr., cons. in field. Donald Bucknar Moore scholar, 1963; diplomate Am. Coll. Osteo. Pediatricians (chmn. evaluating com. 1981-86), Nat. Osteo. Bds. Fellow Am. Coll. Osteo. Pediatrics (v.p. 1986); mem. Am. Osteo. Assn., Fla. Osteo. Assn., AMA, Women's Med. Assn., Chgo. Coll. Osteo. Medicine Alumni Assn., Orlando C. of C., Delta Omega. Roman Catholic. Home: 8210 Imber St Orlando FL 32825 Office: 7824 Lake Underhill Rd Orlando FL 32822

MARSH, JOAN KNIGHT, educational filmstrip and computer software company executive; b. Butler, Mo., Apr. 8, 1934; d. E. Lyle and Ruth (Hopkins) Knight; m. Alan Reid Marsh, Sept. 27, 1958; children—Alan Reid, Clayton Knight. B.A., Tex. Tech. U., 1956. Owner, mgr. Marshfilm, Kansas City, Mo., 1969—; dir. Mark Twain Plaza Bank, Kansas City. Bd. dirs., sec. Crittenton Ctr., Kansas City, 1983—; mem. council Family Study Ctr., U. Mo., Kansas City, 1983—, Children's Relief Assn. Mercy Hosp., Kansas City, 1984—. Mem. Gamma Phi Beta. Republican. Presbyterian. Club: Jr. League (sustaining chmn. 1982-84). Avocation: Egyptology.

MARSH, JULIE MAUREEN, lawyer; b. Muncie, Ind., Aug. 24, 1957; d. Roger Francis and Patricia May (Foster) Marsh; m. Jack Enterkine, Aug. 17, 1984. B.S. cum laude, Purdue U., 1979; J.D., George Washington U., 1982. Bar: D.C. 1982, Idaho 1983. Legal intern U.S. Dist. Ct. D.C., 1981; law clk. Washington Legal Found., 1982; summer assoc. Boise Cascade Corp., 1981, legal counsel, 1982—; adj. prof. Boise State U., 1985. Mem. exec. com. Nat. Fedn. Republican Women, Washington, 1977-82; intern Rep. Nat. Com., 1977; advisor Bus. Week, Idaho Assn. Commerce and Industry, Boise, 1983. Burmaster scholar Purdue U., 1975-79. Mem. ABA, Am. Corp. Counsel Assn. (young lawyers com. 1983—), Idaho Bar Assn., D.C. Bar Assn., Phi Beta Kappa, Phi Kappa Phi, Beta Gamma Sigma, Alpha Lambda Delta, Omicron Delta Kappa, Mortar Bd., Kappa Alpha Theta (exec. com. Boise alumni chpt.). Republican. Presbyterian. Club: Boise Jr. League. Office: Boise Cascade Corp One Jefferson Sq Boise ID 83728

MARSH, MARGARET, historian; b. Roanoke, Va., Nov. 30, 1945; d. Frank and Mildred (Hansborough) Sammartino; m. Robert H. Marsh, Mar. 21, 1970. B.A., Rutgers U., 1967, M.A., 1969, Ph.D., 1974; postgrad. U. Pa., 1967-68. Instr. history Richmond Coll., CUNY, 1973-74; asst. prof. Stockton State Coll., Pomona, N.J., 1975-79, assoc. prof., 1980—, chair div. arts and humanities, 1984—; vis. scholar Am. Civilization, U. Pa., Phila., 1983; mem. bd. State of N.J. Com. for Humanities, 1983—. Author: Anarchist Women, 1981; contbr. articles to profl. jours. Vice-pres., trustee Richard Stockton Found., Pomona, 1977-81. Samuel S. Fels scholar, U. Pa., 1967-68; research grantee Rutgers U., 1973-74, Stockton State Coll., 1978-81; NEH fellow, 1983. Mem. Penn Mid-Atlantic Seminar for Study of Woman and Soc. (program com. 1983-84), Women in Hist. Profession (coordinating com.), Am. Studies Assn., Orgn. Am. Historians, Am. Hist. Assn., Columbia U. City Seminar.

MARSH, RITA M., linguist, educator, researcher; b. Muncie, Ind., June 10, 1945; d. Edward M. and Edith M. (Swaim) Marsh; m. Wade G. Birch, Dec. 23, 1976; stepchildren—Dean W. Birch, Cynthia C. Birch. A.B., Ind. U., 1966; student Universidad Nacional Mayor de San Marcos, Lima, Peru, 1965; M.A., Ball State U., 1972; postgrad. U. Hawaii, 1967, NYU Ctr., Paris, summer 1980, Tex. A&M U., 1983; postgrad. Russian Lang. Workshop, Ind. U., summer 1984. Tchr. Spanish, French Crown Point, Ind., 1966-67, Honolulu Pub. Schs., 1968, Benton Central Schs. (Ind.), 1969-70, Leo High Sch. (Ind.), 1971-74; translator, interpreter, Hawaii, 1967-68, Dana World Trade, Ft. Wayne, Ind., 1970; supr. govt. export sales Stewart & Stevenson Services, Inc., Houston, 1974-77; adminstr., asst. treas. Tex. A&M Research Found., Coll. Station Tex., 1977-83; ptnr. B&M Cons., Bryan, Tex., 1981—; lectr. English Lang. Inst., Tex. A&M U., 1983—. Mem. Parks and Recreation Adv. Bd. City of Bryan, 1982—; v.p., 1983—; bd. dirs. LWV, Brazos County, Tex., 1981-83; mem. steering com. Award for Outstanding Woman of Brazos County, 1977—; mem. Brazos County Sequicentennial Com., 1983—. Mem. Nat. Council Univ. Research Adminstrs., Soc. Research Adminstrs., Nat. Assn. Women Deans, Adminstrs. and Counselors, Am. Assn. Tchrs. Spanish and Portuguese, Am. Bus. Women's Assn., Am. Council Tchrs. Fgn. Langs., Am. Assn. Tchrs. Slavic and Eastern European Langs., Tchrs. of English to Speakers of other Langs., AAUW (bd. dirs. chpt.), Phi Delta Gamma (Alpha Alpha chpt. pres. 1982-83), Kappa Alpha Theta (chpt. fin. advisor, mem. house corp. bd.). Home: 3109 Rolling Glen Bryan TX 77801 Office: Tex A&M Univ College Station TX 77843

MARSH, SHARON DEBORAH, medical management firm executive; b. Jacksonville, Fla., Feb. 20, 1951; d. Theodore Franklin and Blannie Evelyn (Barrow) Marsh. B.A. in Social Sci., U. West Fla., Pensacola, 1977. Patient accounts mgr. Med. Ctr. E.N.T., Houston, 1982-83; asst. bus. mgr. Diagnostic Ctr. Hosp., Houston, 1983-85; co-owner Med. Services Cons., Houston, 1983—. Bd. dirs. March of Dimes, Bay County, Fla., 1975-76. Served with U.S. Army, 1972-74. Mem. Nat. Assn. Female Execs., AAUW, Am. Soc. Notaries, Phi Kappa Phi.

MARSH, SHARON JANE, nurse; b. Portsmouth, Va., Nov. 26, 1948; d. Andrew Garfield and Jane Alvina (Fournier) M. B.S., No. Ill. U., 1970; M.S., St. Joseph's U., Phila., 1983. Commd. officer Nurse Corps, USN, advanced through grades to comdr., 1984; charge nurse U.S. Naval Hosp., Charleston, S.C., 1970-73, U.S. Naval Dispensary, Kenitra, Morocco, 1973-75, U.S. Naval Hosp., Quantico, Va., 1975-77, U.S. Naval Regional Med. Ctr., Portsmouth, Va., 1977-79; health care coordinator Naval Air Sta., Willow Grove, Pa., 1979-81; outpatient supr. Naval Regional Med. Ctr., Phila., 1981-83; charge nurse Naval Hosp., Bethesda, Md., 1983-84, patient care coordinator, 1984-85, dept. head hosp. corpsmen staffing, 1985—. Mem. Assn. Med. Surgeons U.S., Naval Inst. Roman Catholic.

MARSH, SHIRLEY M., state senator; b. Benton, Ill., June 22, 1925; d. Dwight Sidney and Margaret Reese (Hager) McVicker; m. Frank Marsh, Mar. 5, 1943; children—Sherry Anne Marsh Tupper, Stephan Alan, Dory Michael, Corwin Frank, Mitchell Edward, Melissa Lou. B.A., U. Nebr., 1972, M.B.A., 1978; hon. diploma Lincoln Sch. Commerce, 1975. Placement asst. U. Nebr., Lincoln, 1966-70; caseworker practicum Lancaster County Welfare Dept., Lincoln, 1971-72; vis. prof. Nebr. Wesleyan U., Lincoln, 1978, Doane Coll., Crete, Nebr., 1979; state senator Nebr. Legislature, Lincoln, 1972—, mem. appropriations com., 1972—, mem. Gov.'s Task Force on Child Abuse, 1984—; mem. adv. com. Am. Coll. Obstetricians and Gynecologists, Washington, 1980-86. Author: A Standard of Need for the State of Nebraska Relating to Aid to Dependent Children, 1978. Mem. exec. com. Nat. Republican Legislators Assn., 1982-86; mem. Nat. Fedn. Bus. and Profl. Women, 1972—. Recipient Centennial award for service to child health U. Nebr. Coll. Medicine, 1981; Cert. of Appreciation, Nebr. Women for Hwy. Safety, 1981; Safety award Nebr. Safety Council, 1984. Mem. Nat. Conf. State Legislatures (exec com. 1980-83), Nat. Order Women Legislators (pres. 1978), Nat. Conf. State Legislatures Women's Network. Republican. Methodist. Club: PEO (pres. 1972-73). Office: Nebr Legislature #29 Capitol Bldg Lincoln NE 68509

MARSHAL, NELLIE JEAN, financial executive; b. Pulaski, Tenn., Jan. 30, 1933; d. William Vernon and Elsie Beatrice (Glover) DeRamus; student Baxter Sem.; children—Jerami A., Roberta M. Goldstein. Owner, Trailestate Realty, Reno, 1957-60; v.p. Bank Mortgage Loan Co., Los Angeles, 1960-66; mgr. first trust deed dept. Union Home Loans, Los Angeles, 1966-69; owner Marshal Plan, Inc., Santa Monica, Calif., 1969—; chmn. bd. Golden State Holding Co., Inc., 1980—; speaker in field. Mem. Internat. Platform Assn., Santa Monica Bd. Realtors, Santa Monica C. of C. Democrat. Office: 3231 Ocean Park Blvd Suite 208 Santa Monica CA 90405

MARSHALL, ANN ENID, field analyst; b. Marshall, Tex., Nov. 14, 1959; d. Ray Reagan and Robbie Lee Marshall. B.B.A., U. Tex., 1981. Real estate agt. Commerce Austin Realty. Austin, Tex., 1981—; field analyst Gen. Electric Credit Corp., Dallas, 1983—. Recipient Lyndon B. Johnson Family Found. award, 1978; Tex. Achievement scholar, 1978-81. Mem. Real Estate Soc., Univ. Fin. Assn.

MARSHALL, ANNE BRADLEY, lawyer; b. Hartford, Conn., May 29, 1952; d. George A. and Anne Elizabeth (Bradley) M.; m. Bruce Rea Elworthy, Aug. 25, 1979. B.A., Wellesley Coll., 1974; J.D., Yale U., 1977. Bar: Calif., Tex. Assoc. firm Bracewell and Patterson, Houston, 1977-79. Pettit and Martin, San Francisco, 1981-82, Bronson, Bronson & McKinnon, San Francisco, 1982-83; ptnr. firm Elworthy and Marshall, Carmel, Calif., 1983—; lectr. World Trade Inst., N.Y.C., 1978-80, Am. Mgmt. Assn., 1979, Calif. Continuing Edn. of Bar, Berkeley, 1982. Durant scholar, Wellesley Coll., 1974; trustee scholar, 1974. Mem. ABA, Bar Assn. San Francisco, Monterey County Bar Assn., State Bar Calif. (estate planning sect., cert. tax specialist), Greater Carmel Valley C. of C. (bd. dirs.), Phi Beta Kappa. Clubs: Elizabethan (New Haven), Monterey Peninsula Country, Yale of Monterey, Monterey Bay Wellesley (bd. dirs.). Office: Elworthy and Marshall 24000 Robinson Canyon Rd Carmel CA 93923

MARSHALL, ANNE MARIE, association official, graphic artist; b. Detroit, Dec. 19, 1945; d. John Francis and Mildred Clara (Youngblood) Marshall. B.A. cum laude in Profl. Journalism, Calif. State U.-Long Beach, 1975; postgrad. UCLA, 1976-77, U. Santa Clara, 1980, San Jose State U., 1981. With pub. relations dept. Pacific Hosp., Long Beach, Calif., 1974-75; pub. relations coordinator Nat. Computer Conf., Anaheim, Calif., 1975; mem. editorial staff Bus. Life Newspaper, Gardena, Calif., 1975-76; advt. coordinator Person & Covey Pharm. Co. Inc., Glendale, Calif., 1975-79; asst. mgr. Greater Van Nuys Area C. of C. (Calif.), 1979—; freelance graphic artist for Newsletter pub. by Internat. Soc. Clin. Plastic Surgeons, 1976-85. Bd. dirs., rec. sec. Mid Valley Community Police Council, Van Nuys, 1980—; chmn. adv. com. Van Nuys Community Adult Sch. Mem. Nat. Am. Med. Writers Assn. (chpt. rep. 1975-79), Nat. Assn. Membership Dirs., Pub. Relations Roundtable of San Fernando Valley. Roman Catholic. Home: 465 Ivy St Apt 102 Glendale CA 91204 Office: Greater Van Nuys Area C of C 14545 Victory Blvd Van Nuys CA 91411

MARSHALL, CONSUELO BLAND, judge; b. Knoxville, Tenn., Sept. 28, 1936; d. Clyde Theodore and Annie (Brown) Arnold; m. George Edward Marshall, Aug. 30, 1959; children—Michael Edward, Laurie Ann. B.A., Howard U., 1958, LL.B., 1961. Bar: Calif. 1962. Atty., City of Los Angeles, 1962-67; assoc. mem. firm Cochran & Atkins, Los Angeles, 1968-70; commr. Los Angeles Superior Ct., 1971-76; judge Inglewood Mcpl. Ct., 1976-77, Los Angeles Superior Ct., 1977-80, U.S. Dist. Ct. Central Dist. Calif., Los Angeles, 1980—. Contbr. articles to profl. jours.; notes editor Law Jour. Howard U. Mem. adv. bd. Richstone Child Abuse Center. Research fellow Howard U. Law Sch., 1959-60. Mem. State Bar Calif., Calif. Women Lawyers Assn., Calif. Assn. Black Lawyers, Calif. Judges Assn., Black Women Lawyers Assn., Los Angeles County Bar Assn., NAACP, Urban League, Beta Phi Sigma, Alpha Phi Alpha. Mem. Ch. Religious Science. Office: US Courthouse 312 N Spring St Los Angeles CA 90012*

MARSHALL, DARLENE OLGA, retail executive; b. Park Rapids, Minn., Aug. 14, 1931; d. Robert Livingston and Olga Marie (Olson) Marshall; student St. Olaf U., 1949-50; m. K. N. Hanson, Nov. 23, 1950; children—Bruce K., Marshall Brad. Owner, operator 2 gift shops, Park Rapids and Nevis, Minn., 1955-58; saleswoman Holmes Realty Co., Fargo, N.D., 1959-61; owner, mgr. Perkins Pancake Houses Fla., St. Petersburg and Clearwater, 1961-66; investment advisor Fin. Programs Inc., St. Petersburg, 1966-67; personnel and purchasing mgr. Clairmont Personnel, Clairmont and La Jolla, Calif., 1967-68; office mgr. Eleo Med. Corp., Sorento Valley, Calif., 1968-69; owner, operator Candy Casa, San Diego, 1969-79, Candy Casa Too, St. Petersburg Beach and Madeira Beach, Fla., 1972-73, Vanilla Villa, 1981—; bldg. supr., leasing agt., mgr. Squibob Sq. Shopping Center, Old Town, San Diego, 1969-79; mem. planning com. Old Town, San Diego, 1973-78; dir. Perkins Pancake Houses Fla., 4 Seasons. Bd. dirs., v.p. C. of C. Pinellas County (Fla.), 1961-66. Recipient 7 service awards Kiwanis Club, St. Petersburg, 1961-66; named to Top 10 for real estate sales Fargo Bd. Realtors, 1961. Office: 3759 Avocado Blvd La Mesa CA 92041

MARSHALL, HOLLY R., data processing executive; b. Chgo., Sept. 28, 1945; d. Welton E. and Ferne Louise (Templeton) Richburg; student Macalester Coll., 1963-65. Various positions, data processing and sales Hartford, Conn. and Chgo., 1965-75; regional v.p. sales Advanced Systems Inc., Elk Grove, Ill., 1975-77, v.p. mktg., 1977-78; pres. Merit Assos., Schaumburg, Ill., 1978-81; chief exec. officer Universal Bus. Computing, Schaumburg, 1981—; dir. Ken Garen Inc., Skokie, Ill., Keys to the City, Los Angeles. Regular chorister Lyric Opera Chgo., 1967-69; founding mem. Chicagoans Choir, 1970. Office: PO Box 1519 Barrington IL 60011

MARSHALL, JEANIE, organization consultant; b. Cambridge, Mass., Jan. 21, 1944; d. Wilfred James and Mary (Cadwallader) Combellack; B.A. in Sociology, Boston U., 1966; M.S. in Human Resource Devel., am. U., 1982; m. Donald W. Marshall, Aug. 8, 1970. Owner, Marshall House, Inc., human resource devel. cons., Ballston Lake, N.Y., 1971-80, pres., 1971—; human relations trainer continuing edn. program Sch. Social Welfare, SUNY, Albany, 1979-81; tchr. parliamentary procedures Schenectady County Community Coll., 1980; tchr. career devel., presentation techniques Union Coll., Schenectady, 1980-82. Mem. AAUW (pres. Schenectady br. 1977-78, grantee Ednl. Found. 1978-79), Am. Soc. Tng. and Devel., Am. Inst. Parliamentarians, Assn. Creative Change, Assn. Psychol. Type, Nat. Assn. Female Execs., Hudson-Mohawk Soc. Tng. and Devel. Author articles, tng. manuals, modules, cassette/workbook Am. Mgmt. Assn. Home: 15 Ashley Dr Ballston Lake NY 12019 Office: Northway 10 Executive Park Ushers Rd Ballston Lake NY 12019

MARSHALL, KATHRYN SUE, lawyer; b. Decatur, Ill., Sept. 12, 1942; d. Edward Elda, Jr. and Frances Maxine (Minor) Lahniers; m. Robert Stephen Marshall, Sept. 5, 1964; children—Stephen Edward, Christine Elizabeth. B.A., Lake Forest Coll., 1964; J.D., John Marshall Law Sch., 1976. Bar: Ill. 1976, U.S. Dist. Ct. (no. dist.) Ill. 1976, U.S. Ct. Mil. Appeals 1977, U.S. Supreme Ct. 1979; lic. real estate agt., Ill. Intern Office of U.S. Atty. No. Dist. Chgo., Ill., 1974-76; mng. ptnr. Marshall and Marshall, Ltd., Waukegan, Ill., 1976-84; sole practice, Waukegan, 1984—; adj. tchr. John Marshall Law Sch., Chgo., 1980-81, Nat. Coll. Edn., Evanston, Ill., 1981—; legal adviser Nat. Coll. Paralegal Program, Evanston, Ill., 1981—; lectr. on various subjects internationally, 1978—. Contbg. author: New Tricks for Old Dogs: Managing A Family Law Practice; Flying Solo, 1984; also articles, manuals. Mem. alumni council John Marshall Law Sch., Chgo., 1977-81; mem. adv. com. on vets. for Senator Adeline J. Geo-Karis; intervenor Lawyer's Assistance Program, Inc. Fellow Ill. Bar Found.; mem. ABA (chm. various coms. sect of econs. of law practice 1976—, chmn. com. on econs. of practice 1981, mem. long planning com. 1982—, sect. family law), Ill. State Bar Assn. (com. on econs. of law practice 1981-82), Women's Bar Assn. Ill. (com. on family law 1980-82), Ill. Trial Lawyers Assn., Lake County Bar Assn (com on circuit clk.'s office 1976-77, com. on family law 1977—, chmn. com. on econs. of law practice

1979-80, chmn. com. on fee grievances 1979-80), Chgo. Bar Assn., Assn. Women Attys. of Lake County (com. on award of reasonable atty.'s fees 1982, bd. dirs. 1983—, chmn. com. on family law 1984—). Office: Law Offices of Kathryn S Marshall 224 Washington Waukegan IL 60085

MARSHALL, LINDA RAE, cosmetic company executive; b. Provo, Utah; Aug. 1, 1940; d. Arvid Otto and Tola V. (Broderick) Newman; divorced; children—James E., John N. Student, Brigham Young U., 1958-59, U. Utah, 1960-61. Buyer, Boston Store, Milw., 1961-62; sec. Milw. Gas & Light, 1962-64; mktg. rep. Elysee Sci. Cosmetics, Madison, Wis., 1971-75, pres., 1975—; mem. exec. com. Cosmetic, Toiletry and Fragrance Assn., Washington, 1979—, dir., 1977—, chmn. small cosmetics, 1978—; dir. Aesthetcians Internat. Fragrance Found.; cons. in field. Author: Discover The Other Woman In You, 1980; (with others) Cosmetic Industry Scientific and Regional Foundation, 1984. Contbr. articles to Beauty Fashion Mag. Pres., PTA, Madison, 1968-69. Club: Dental Wives. Avocations: piano, knitting, reading, skiing, dancing. Office: Elysee Sci Cosmetics 6804 Seybold Rd Madison WI 53719

MARSHALL, LOIS VANA, personnel placement executive; b. St. Paul, Aug. 9, 1947; d. William Herald and Sophie Francis (Antos) Vana; children—Justin, Joelle, Jordan. Supr. engring. dept. Pacific Telephone Co., San Diego, until 1968; co-founder Career Personnel, Can., 1968—, Career Personnel Internat., Carmel, Calif., 1979—; now with Marshall Group. Mem. Am. Mgmt. Assn., Nat. Assn. Personnel Cons., Am. Soc. Personnel Adminstrs. (dir., bd. dirs.), Am. Soc. Personnel Cons., Internat. Franchise Assn., Calif. Assn. Personnel Cons. Home: PO Box 1662 Carmel Valley CA 93924 Office: Marshall Group 2959 Monterey Salinas Hwy Monterey CA 93940

MARSHALL, MARILU (CLAUDETTE), corporate executive, lawyer; b. N.Y.C., Feb. 8, 1945; d. Albert and Louise C. Marshall. B.B.A. cum laude, U. Miami (Fla.), 1966, J.D. with honors, 1969. Bar: Fla. 1969, N.Y. 1982. Trial atty. Dept. Justice, Washington, 1970-74; dep. dir. Nat. Gambling Commn., Washington, 1974-76; v.p., spl. counsel Playboy Enterprises, Inc., N.Y.C., 1976-82, Playboy-Elsinore Assocs., Atlantic City, 1982-84; v.p. regulatory adminstrn. and gen. counsel Golden Nugget Hotel and Casino, Atlantic City, 1984—. Trustee NCCJ South Jersey, 1983—. Mem. ABA (council gaming law com. 1983—), Nat. Assn. Gaming Attys. (trustee 1983—). Republican. Roman Catholic. Office: Golden Nugget Hotel and Casino PO Box 1737 Atlantic City NJ

MARSHALL, MARTHA MAY, real estate broker, music publisher; b. Quincy, Mass., Aug. 3, 1939; d. Melvin Fayette and Ethel Mae (Randall) LeMay; m. Harold Xavier Marshall, Aug. 5, 1963 (div. 1965). Student schs. Quincy. Retail security officer Met. Secret Service, Boston, 1958-60, J.M. Fields, Boston, 1960-65; letter carrier U.S. Post Office, El Monte, Calif., 1966-73; real estate saleswoman Town & Country Properties, Los Angeles, 1973-81; real estate broker Marshall Realty, Los Angeles, 1981—. Bd. dirs. Van Ness Recovery House Inc., Los Angeles, 1982-83. Mem. Calif. Assn. Realtors (dir. 1975-78), Los Angeles Bd. Realtors (dir. 1975-78, Realtor Assoc. of Yr. 1975), Northeast Multiple Listing Service Los Angeles (dir. 1982, pres. bd. 1983—). Democrat. Office: Marshall Realty 5317 N Figueroa St Room 2 Los Angeles CA 90042

MARSHALL, MARY AYDELOTTE, state legislator; b. Cook County, Ill., June 14, 1921; d. John A. and Nell. A. Rice; B.A. with highest honors, Swarthmore Coll., 1942; m. Roger Duryea Marshall, Mar. 3, 1944; children—Nell Aydelotte, Jenny Winslow Marshall Davies, Alice Marie. Economist anti-trust div. Dept. Justice, Washington, 1942-46; mem. Va. Ho. of Dels., 1966-70, 72—, mem. privileges and elections com., rds. and internal nav. com., chmn. counties, cities and towns com., health, welfare and instns. com.; chmn. Legis. Study Commn. on Needs Elderly Virginians, 1973-78; chmn. Legis. Commn. Monitoring Long Term Care, 1983—; mem. No. Va. Transp. Commn., 1974-80; mem. exec. com. Nat. Conf. State Legislators, 1981—, also chmn. long term care task force; mem. Legis. (Bagley) Commn. on Mental Health and Mental Retardation, 1977-79; chmn. Task Force on Social Security for Women, Fed. Council on Aging, 1978-81; bd. dirs. Washington Met. Council Govts., 1978, 80. Pres., Va. Assn. Mental Health, 1970-73, Va. Fedn. Democratic Women's Clubs, 1971-72; bd. dirs. Nat. Assn. Mental Health, 1972-78; mem. Dem. Central Com. Va., 1976-78. Recipient Achievement award Va. Assn. Mental Health, No. Va. Assn. Mental Health, Va. Fedn. Bus. and Profl. Women's Clubs, Va. Assn. Ind. Retail Gasoline Dealers, No. Va. Altrusa, No. Va. Retarded Citizens Assn.; named WETA Disting. Woman. Mem. AAUW, LWV. Congregationalist. Clubs: Bus. and Profl. Women's, Home Demonstration, No. Va. Dem., Downtown.

MARSHALL, MERYL CORINBLIT, broadcasting executive, lawyer; b. Los Angeles, Oct. 16, 1949; d. Jack and Nita (Green) Corinblit; B.A., UCLA, 1971; J.D., Loyola Marymount U., Los Angeles, 1974. Bar: Calif. 1974. Dep. pub. defender County of Los Angeles, 1975-77; sole practice, Los Angeles, 1977-78; ptnr. Markman and Marshall, Los Angeles, 1978-79; sr. atty. NBC, Burbank, Calif., 1979-80, dir. programs, talent contracts bus. affairs, 1980, asst. gen. atty., N.Y.C., 1980-82, v.p., compliance and practicies, Burbank, 1982—. Chmn., Nat. Women's Polit. Caucus, Westside, Calif., 1978-80; mem. Calif. Democratic Central Com., 1978-79. Mem. Acad. TV Arts and Scis. (trustee 1985), Women in Film. Democrat. Jewish. Office: NBC 3000 W Alameda Ave Burbank CA 91523

MARSHALL, MIRA NAN, lawyer; b. Long Branch, N.J., Nov. 26, 1951; d. Donald Stanley and Shirley (Morrow) M. B.A. magna cum laude, U. Mass.-Amherst, 1975; J.D., Stanford U., 1982. Bar: D.C. 1982. Housing specialist Ednl. Fund LWV, Washington, 1976-77, project dir., 1978-79; assoc. dir. Equal Housing Opportunity, Met. Washington Planning and Housing Assocs., 1977-78; research asst. Stanford Law Sch. (Calif.), 1980-82; pvt. practice cons., Washington, 1982-83; assoc. firm Hewes, Morella, Gelband & Lamberton, P.C., Washington, 1984; counsel Nat. Com. against Discrimination in Housing, 1985; assoc. Fried, Frank, Harris, Shriver & Jacobson, Washington, 1986—; cons. Am. Friends Service Com. Community Relations Div., Phila., 1983. Assoc. editor Stanford Jour. Internat. Law, 1981-82; author pamphlet, 1977. Commonwealth scholar, U. Mass., 1971-75; summer intern Stanford Pub. Interest Law Found., 1980. Mem. ABA, Women's Bar Assn. D.C., Phi Kappa Phi. Office: Fried Frank et al 600 New Hampshire Ave NW Suite 1000 Washington DC 20037

MARSHALL, NANCY HAIG, library administrator; b. Stamford, Conn., Nov. 3, 1932; d. Harry Percival and Dorothy Charlotte (Price) Haig; m. William Hubert Marshall, Dec. 28, 1953; children—Bruce Davis, Gregg Price, Lisa Reynolds, Jeanine Haig. B.A., Ohio Wesleyan U., 1953; M.L.S., U. Wis.-Madison, 1972. Reference librarian U. Wis., Madison, 1972; dir. Wis. Inter Library Services, 1972-79; assoc. dir. U. Wis. Libraries, 1979—; mem. adv. com. Copyright Office, Washington, 1978-82; trustee Online Computer Library Service Ctr., Dublin, Ohio, 1982—; dir. USBE, Inc., Washington. Bd. editors Jour. Acad. Librarianship, 1981-85. Contbr. articles to profl. jours. Mem. ALA (council 1980-88), Wis. Library Assn. (Librarian of Yr. 1982), Am. Soc. Info. Sci., Beta Phi Mu. Office: U Wis Meml Library 728 State St Madison WI 53706

MARSHALL, NANCY LOU, lawyer; b. Biloxi, Miss., July 25, 1957; d. Joseph John and Ruth Elaine (Glidden) Marshall. A.A., St. Clair County Community Coll., 1977; B.A., U. Mich., 1979; J.D., Thomas M. Cooley Law Sch., 1982. Bar: Mich. Assoc. firm Dietrich & Cassavaugh, Port Huron, Mich., 1983—; atty., referee St. Clair County Probate Ct., Port Huron, 1984—. Deaconess 1st Congregational Ch., Port Huron, 1975-77; campaign worker William T. Fischer for County Commr., 1983. Mem. ABA, Mich. Bar Assn., St. Clair County Bar Assn., St. Clair County Council for Prevention of Child Abuse and Neglect, Women Lawyers Assn., Assn. Trial Lawyers Am., Phi Theta Kappa. Republican.

MARSHALL, NATALIE JUNEMANN, coll. ofcl.; b. Milw., June 13, 1929; d. Harold E. and Myrtle B. (Findlay) Junemann; A.B., Vassar Coll., 1951; M.A., Columbia U., 1952, Ph.D., 1963; widow; children—Frederick S., Alison B. Mem. faculty Vassar Coll., Poughkeepsie, N.Y., 1952-54, 58-60, prof. econs. 1973—, dean studies, 1973-75, v.p. student affairs, 1975-80, v.p. adminstrv. and student services, 1980—; mem. faculty Wesleyan U., Middletown, Conn., 1955-56, SUNY, New Paltz, 1964-73. Bd. mgrs. Children's Home, Poughkeepsie, N.Y., 1968-71; trustee St. Francis Hosp., Poughkeepsie, 1979—, Dutchess Area Fund, 1983—. Mem. AAUW (chpt. pres. 1961-63, v.p. N.Y. State 1964-66), Am. Econ. Assn. Am. Assn. Higher Edn. Author: The History of Economic Thought, 1968; Keynes Updated or Outdated, 1970; Collective Bargaining, 1971. Office: Box 3 Vassar Coll Poughkeepsie NY 12601

MARSHALL, SALLY JEAN, biomaterials scientist; b. Racine, Wis., Jan. 8, 1949; d. Charles and Adele Ruth Rimkus; B.S. with distinction in sci. engring., Northwestern U., 1970, Ph.D. in Materials Sci. and Engring., 1975; m. Grayson William Marshall, Jr., July 4, 1970; children—Grayson William III, Jonathan Charles. Instr. biol. materials Northwestern U., Chgo., 1974-75, asst. prof., 1975-80, assoc. prof., 1980-86, prof., 1986—; varsity swimming coach Northwestern U., Evanston, Ill., 1970-81; vis. fellow U. Melbourne (Australia), 1981. Recipient spl. dental research award Nat. Inst. Dental Research, 1977. Fellow Acad. Dental Materials (treas. 1983-85, v.p. 1985—, bd. dirs. 1983—); mem. Am. Soc. Metals, AIME, Soc. Women Engrs., Am. Swimming Coaches Assn., Ill. Swimming Assn. (Women's Collegiate Coach of Year 1978-79), Internat. Assn. Dental Research, Am. Assn. Dental Research (1st place research award Chgo. sect.), N.Y. Acad. Scis., Am. Coll. Sports Medicine, Soc. Biomaterials, AAHPER, Sigma Xi, Tau Beta Pi, Omicron Kappa Upsilon. Contbr. articles sci. jours. Home: 116 Maple Ave Wilmette IL 60091 Office: 311 E Chicago Ave Chicago IL 60611

MARSHALL, SIMONE SHERRY, auditor, accountant; b. St. Albans, N.Y., June 22, 1960; d. Calvin Lee and Shirley Ann M. B.B.A., Hofstra U., 1983. Internal auditor Chase Manhattan Bank, Lake Success, N.Y., 1984-85; auditor Office of Insp. Gen., Met. Transit Authority, N.Y.C., 1985—; dir. Fuschia Network Group, Queens, N.Y. Mem. Nat. Assn. Female Execs. Democrat. Lutheran. Avocations: photography, dance, horticulture, interior design. Home: 115-20 225th St Cambria Heights NY 11411

MARSHALL, STEPHANIE ANNE, superintendent schools; b. N.Y.C., July 19, 1945; s. Dominick Martin and Anne (Price) Pace; B.A., Queens Coll., 1967; M.A., U. Chgo., 1971; Ph.D., Loyola U., Chgo., 1983; m. Robert Marshall, Dec. 23, 1977. Tchr., Public Schs. Alsip (Ill.), 1967-74, gifted coordinator, 1971-74; nat. social studies cons., 1973-76; asst. curriculum dir. Public Schs. Naperville (Ill.), 1974-76; asst. supt. schs., then supt. Batavia (Ill.), 1976—; adj. prof. Nat. Coll. Edn.; assoc. prof. Loyola U., Chgo.; asst. dir. I/D/E/A; mem. Ill. Textbook Adv. Com., Ill. Adv. Com. Gifted Edn.; cons. Named One of Top 100 Sch. Execs. in N. Am., Exec. Editor Mag., Kone County (Ill.) Adminstr. of Yr. Mem. Assn. Supervision and Curriculum Devel., Am. Assn. Sch. Adminstrs., Ill. Assn. Supervision and Curriculum Devel. (pres.-elect), Nat. Assn. Gifted Children, Nat. Council Exceptional Children, Nat. Council Social Studies, AAUW, Phi Delta Kappa, Pi Lambda Theta. Home: 1145 Wheaton Oaks Dr Wheaton IL 60187 Office: 12 W Wilson St Batavia IL 60510

MARSHALL, SUSAN, lawyer; b. Ellsworth, Kans., July 8, 1950; d. Daniel Benjamin and Elizabeth Jean (Bailey) M. B.A., U. Kans., 1972; J.D. with honors, Washburn U., 1976. Bar: Kans. 1976. Summer legal intern, Campbell, Erickson, Cottingham, Morgan & Gibson, Kansas City, Mo., 1975; research asst., lobbyist Kans. County and Dist. Attys. Assn., Topeka, 1975-76; assoc. Metz & Metz, Lincoln, Kans., 1977-83; county atty. Lincoln County, Kans., Lincoln, 1980-85; sole practice law, Lincoln, 1983—; atty. position Kans. Commn. on Civil Rights, Topeka, 1978-86. Pres. Lincoln Carnegie Library, 1982—. Mem. ABA, Kans. Bar Assn., Kans. County and Dist. Attys. Assn., Nat. Dist. Attys. Assn., Nat. History Soc. Republican. Office: 113 S 4th St Lincoln KS 67455

MARSHALL, SUSAN LOCKWOOD, civic worker; b. Orange, N.J., Dec. 2, 1939; d. Richard Douglas and Helen Lockwood (Stratford) Nelson; B.E., Wheelock Coll., 1961; m. William Pendleton Marshall, Aug. 20, 1960; children—Jill, James. Vol., Newton-Wellesley (Mass.) Hosp., 1962-63, New Eyes for the Needy, Inc., 1963-64, amblyopia screening program, Short Hills, N.J., 1969-71; bd. dirs. Jr. League of Oranges and Short Hills, Inc., 1967-69, 70-72, corr. sec., 1970-72; fund raising vol. Children's Aid and Adoption Soc. N.J., 1969-73, dir., 1970-73, asst. sec., 1970-72, 1st v.p., 1972-73; bd. dirs. Jr. League Stamford-Norwalk (Conn.), 1974-78, asst. treas., 1976-77, treas., 1977-78; bd. dirs. Program One to One, Inc., 1975-76, also treas.; vol. Voluntary Action Center 1975-76; bd. dirs. Episcopal Churchwomen of St. Luke's Parish, 1974-75, 76-80, 2d v.p., 1976-77, asst. treas., 1977-78, treas., 1978-80, pres., 1980-81; bd. dirs. Lockwood Mathews Mansion Mus., 1979—, treas., 1979—, v.p., 1983—; mem. council Darien Sch. Parent Bd., 1978-83, 84-85, chmn., 1984-85; bd. dirs. Middlesex Jr. High Parents Assn., 1979-83, treas., 1982-83; mem. Darien High Sch. Parents Assn., 1982-85, chmn., 1984-85; bd. dirs. Darien United Way, 1984—; mem. vol. mgmt. assistance program adv. com. Darien chpt. Am. Field Service, 1984-86. Address: 358 Hollow Tree Ridge Rd Darien CT 06820

MARSHALL, VALERIE ANN, lawyer; b. Evansville, Ind., Aug. 26, 1954; d. Arthur Elliot and Jacqueline Jane (Maixner) Marshall. B.B.A., Stetson U., 1976; J.D., Stetson U., 1979. Bar: Fla. 1979. Assoc. law firm Clayton & Landis, Orlando, Fla., 1980-81; corp. counsel Walt Disney World Co., Lake Buena Vista, Fla., 1981-83; jr. ptnr. Haas, Boehm, Brown, Rigdon & Seacrest, Orlando, Fla., 1983—. Mem. ABA, Corp. Counsel Assn. (sec.-treas. 1982-83), Central Fla. Assn. Women Lawyers (sec. 1982-85), Fla. Bar (conv. com. of young lawyers sect. 1983, workers compensation rules com. 1985-86), Orange County Bar Assn. (vice chmn. workers' compensation com.), Stetson Lawyers Assn., NOW, Alpha Chi Omega. Republican. Methodist. Office: Haas Boehm Brown Rigdon & Seacrest 801 N Magnolia Orlando FL 32814

MARSHALL, WILMA, vocational counselor; b. Denmark, Tenn., Apr. 15, 1949; d. Tommy Lee Marshall and Margaret (Bond) Patrick. B.A., Lane Coll., Tenn., 1970; M.S., Pepperdine U., 1980. Social worker trainee Chs. United, Chgo., 1970-72; cons. Archdiocese Chgo., 1972-74; program coordinator Castle Drug Program, Los Angeles, 1974-77; vocat. counselor Rehab., Pasadena, 1977-80, A&M Counselors, Cons., Santa Monica, 1980-82, WLM & Assocs., Los Angeles, 1982—, San Gabriel Assn., Whittier, Calif., 1984—; cons. and lectr. in field. Chmn. Dance Gallery Guild, Los Angeles, 1985-86. Recipient Coll. Achievement award Lane Coll., 1970, Outstanding Leadership award, 1981. Mem. Worker's Compensation Claims Assn., Nat. Assn. Female Execs., Calif. Assn. Rehab. Profls., NAACP, Soroptimist, YMCA, Sigma Gamma Rho. Democrat. Baptist. Avocations: golf; collecting sculptures. Home: PO Box 6133 Beverly Hills CA 90212

MARSHALL-BAKER, DEBRALYN SANDRA, water resources engineer; b. Lebanon, N.H., July 6, 1956; d. Donald Stuart and Janet Margorie (Raymond) Marshall; m. Bernard Frederick Baker, Mar. 17, 1979. B.S.C.E., U. Vt., 1979; M.S. in Environ. Engring., U. Conn., 1982. Registered profl. engr., Conn. Engr. Electric Boat, Gen. Dynamics, Groton, Conn., 1979-80; asst. supt. water and sewer maintenance City of New London, Conn., 1980-82; supt. water and sewer maintenance, 1982—. Mem. Am. Water Works Assn. (Conn. sect. tech. com. chmn. 1982—, mem. edn. com. 1983—), Conn. Water Works Assn. (bd. dirs. 1985—), U.S. Power Squadron (pres. Alpha Mates, 1982—), Chi Epsilon. Universalist. Avocations: sailing; gardening. Home: 41 Woodlawn Rd New London CT 06320 Office: Water Div City of New London 111 Union St New London CT 06320

MARSHALL-NADEL, NATHALIE, humanities educator, artist; b. Pitts., Nov. 10, 1932; d. Clifford Benjamin and Clarice (Stille) Marshall; m. Robert Alfred Van Buren, May 1, 1952 (div. June 1965); children—Christine Van Buren Popovic, Clifford Marshall, Jennifer Van Buren Lake; m. David Arthur Nadel, Dec. 30, 1976. A.F.A., Silvermine Coll. Art, New Canaan, Conn., 1967; B.F.A., U. Miami, Coral Gables, 1977, M.A., 1982, Ph.D. in English and Fine Art, 1982. Instr. humanities Miami Ednl. Consortium, Miami Shores, Fla., 1977-79, Barry U., Miami Shores, 1979-81, U. Miami, Coral Gables, 1977-81; sr. lectr. Nova U., Ft. Lauderdale, Fla., 1981-84, assoc. prof. humanities, 1985—; chief artist Rockefeller U., N.Y.C., 1973-75; asst. registrar Lowe Art Mus., Coral Gables, 1976-78; co-founder, dir. The Bakehouse Art Complex, Miami, 1984—; mem. adv. bd. New World Sch. Arts, Miami, 1985—. One-woman shows: Silvermine Coll. Art, New Canaan, Conn., 1968, Ingber Gallery, Greenwich, 1969, Capricorn Gallery, N.Y.C., 1969, Pierson Coll. at Yale U., New Haven, 1970, The Art Barn, Greenwich, 1972, Art Unltd., N.Y.C., 1973, Benevy Gallery, N.Y.C., 1974, Richter Library, U. Miami, 1985, Nova U., Ft. Lauderdale, 1985, Ward Naarse Gallery, N.Y.C., 1985; group shows include: Capricorn Gallery, N.Y.C., 1968, Ingber Gallery, Greenwich, 1968, Compass Gallery, N.Y.C., 1970, Optimums Gallery, Westport, Conn., 1970, Finch Coll. Mus., N.Y.C., 1971, Town Hall Art Gallery, Stamford, Conn., 1973, 74, Jewish Community Ctr., Miami Beach, 1981, Continuum Gallery, Miami Beach, 1982, South Fla. Art Inst., Hollywood, Fla., 1984, Met. Mus., Coral Gables, Fla., 1985, Ward Nasse Gallery, N.Y.C., 1985, Brunner Mus., U. Iowa, Ames, 1986. Author, artist: Vibrations on Revelations, 1973, The Firebird, 1982, numerous artist books, 1968—. Author: Be Organized for College, 1980. Artist: (children's book) The Desert: What Lives There?, 1972. Editor, designer: Court Theaters of Europe, 1982. Contbr. poems to poetry mags., articles to profl. jours. Recipient Sponsor's award for Painting Greenwich Art Soc., 1967; Steven Buffton Meml. award Am. Bus. Women's Assn., 1980. Mem. Coll. Art Assn., MLA, Nat. Women's Studies Assn., Women's Caucus for Art (nat. adv. bd. 1983—, pres. Miami chpt. 1984-86, southeast regional v.p. 1986—). Home: 5708 SW 69th Ave Miami FL 33143 Office: Nova Univ 3301 College Ave Fort Lauderdale FL 33314

MARSHIK, JUDITH ANNE, market research consultant; b. Pierz, Minn., Apr. 13, 1941; d. Joseph Clarence and Julia Loretta (Kulla) Marshik Peters; m. Joseph Emil Bisso, June 30, 1966 (div. Oct. 1971); children—Joel, Jeffrey; m. Chester Gustafson, Jr. Dec. 26, 1973 (div. Apr. 1984); 1 child, Dawn. B.S. in Nursing, Coll. St. Catherine, 1962. Staff nurse St. Josephs Hosp., St. Paul, 1961-62, U. Minn., Mps., 1962-63; head nurse U. Minn., 1963-65; tchr. English, Shenker Inst., Rome, 1965-66; instr. nursing Naeve Hosp., Albert Lea, Minn., 1966-67; nurse clinician U. Minn., Mpls., 1967-68; nurse instr. St. Marys Jr. Coll., Mpls., 1968-70; instr. U. Minn., 1970-72, North Hennepin Community Coll., Mpls., 1972-73; dir. nursing program Normandale Community Coll., Bloomington, Minn., 1973-76; project dir. Found. for Health Care Evaluation, Mpls., 1976-79, dir., div. long term care evaluation, 1979-81; pres. Quality Decisions, Inc., Minnetonka, Minn., 1981—. Mem. evaluation task force United Fund, Mpls., 1985; mem. adv. bd. Chez Nous Home for Developmentally Disabled, 1981-85. Mem. Nat. Found. Women Bus. Owners (bd. dirs. 1984-85), Nat. Assn. Women Bus. Owners (bd. dirs., pres. Minn. 1984-85), Minn. Assn. Homes for the Aged, Minn. Assn. Health Care Facilities, NOW, ACLU, Minn. Council Strategic Health Planning, Pi Lambda Theta, Sigma Theta Tau. Avocations: philosophy; sailing; gardening; science fiction; drawing and painting. Office: 15612 Hwy 7 Suite 340 Minnetonka MN 55364

MARSLAND, AMY LOUISE, publishing company executive, writer; b. Saskatoon, Sask., Can., Mar. 23, 1924; came to U.S., 1945; d. Richard Albert and Alberta Georgina (Amy) Downey; m. William Marsland, Sept. 8, 1951; children—Alicia Marsland Geromel, Stephen, David, Adam. B.A., U. Sask., 1944; M.A., U. Mich., 1945, Ph.D. (Rackham fellow 1945-47), 1949. Instr., Carleton Coll., Northfield, Minn., 1949-50; sec. to Brit. Ambassador, Caracas, Venezuela, 1951; editor Chenango Am., Greene, N.Y., 1958-63; instr., asst. prof. SUNY-Binghamton, 1963-67; treas. Twin Valley Pubs., Greene, 1967—. Author: Venezuela Thru Its History, 1954; Cache Cache, 1981; Snow White, The Wolf and the Unicorn, 1982; A Classic Death, 1985; contbr. articles to profl. jours. Chmn. Doctor's Com., Greene, 1968, Bicentennial Celebration, Greene, 1976. Mem. Phi Beta Kappa, Phi Kappa Phi. Episcopalian. Home and Office: PO Box 366 Greene NY 13778

MARSTELLER, ANN YACKA, dietitian; b. Plainfield, N.J., June 21, 1950; d. Anthony P. and Ann L. (Monzione) Yacka; m. Franklin D. Marsteller, May 15, 1976 (div. Aug. 1982). B.S., Marywood Coll., Pa., 1972; M.S. in Nutrition, Hunter Coll., 1979; M.B.A. candidate Temple U., 1984—. Registered dietitian. Relief dietitian N.Y. Hosp., N.Y.C., 1973-75, research dietitian, 1975-77; coordinator nutrition Hosp. U. Pa., Phila., 1978-79, asst. dir. nutrition, 1979-81; regional dietitian Custom Mgmt. Corp., Kingston, Pa., 1981—, dist. mgr., 1983—; adj. prof. Drexel U., 1979-81. Editor: Manual of Nutritional Care, 1980. Marywood Coll. scholar, 1968-72. Mem. N.J. Dietetic Assn. (dist. licensure chair 1983-85), Am. Dietetic Assn., Phila. Dietetic Assn., Dietitians in Critical Care (publs. com. 1983-85), Nat. Assn. Female Execs., Pa. Acad. Fine Arts. Roman Catholic. Avocations: skiing; sailing; reading. Home: 111-6 Echelon Rd Voorhees NJ 08043 Office: Custom Mgmt Corp 844 Market St Kingston PA 18704

MARSTELLER, LINDA SUE, marketing executive; b. Cleve., June 19, 1956; d. James H. and Doris (Patterson) M. B.S. in Biol. Scis. with honors), Miami U., Oxford, Ohio, 1978. Cert. tchr., Ohio. Naturalist trainee Nat. Audubon Soc., Dayton, Ohio, 1977; researcher law dept. Goodyear Corp., Akron, Ohio, 1978, field sales rep. Indsl. rubber products div., Cleve., 1979-81, area sales mgr. Films div., Chgo., 1981-82; mktg. mgr. plastics div. Teepak Corp., Chgo., 1982-85; mgr. indsl. packaging Clearview Plastics div. Hanoschy Industries, 1985—. Women's Club scholar. Mem. Nat. Audubon Soc., Smithsonian Instn., Am. Meat Inst., Nat. Assn. Female Execs., Graphic Arts Tech. Found., Flexible Packaging Assn., Package Engring. Assn., Miami U. Alumni Assn., Phi Kappa Tau. Roman Catholic. Home: 1122 Schneiber St Oak Park IL 60302 Office: Clearview Plastics 120 25th Ave Bellwood IL 60104

MARSTERS, IRENE A., medical center executive; b. New Britain, Conn., Oct. 19, 1925; d. Eugene J. and Julia (Blogoslawski) Albro; m. Robert I. Lyman, Dec. 2, 1950 (div. Sept. 10, 1960); children—Sherry, Janet, Susan; m. 2d, Theodore N.V. Marsters (div.). B.S., Mary Washington Coll., U. Va., 1947. Dir. vol. services Conn. Mental Health, New Haven, 1966-69, Blue Hills Hosp., Hartford, Conn., 1969-71, Middlesex Hosp., Middletown, Conn., 1971-76; dir. vol. services St. Vincent's Med. Ctr., Bridgeport, Conn., 1976—. Inventor "1955. Mem. Republican State Central Com. Middlexex County, 1956-60. Mem. Bridgeport Assn. Vol. Adminstrs. (pres. 1983—), Am. Soc. Dir. Vol. Services, Nat. Ctr. Vol. Involvement. Republican. Roman Catholic. Home: 105 E Wharf Rd Madison CT 06443 Office: St Vincent's Med Ctr 2800 Main St Bridgeport CT 06606

MARSZALEK, GEORGIA, marketing executive; b. Buffalo, Nov. 14, 1946; d. Edward Stanley and Helen Ann (Rudick) Marszalek. B.A., SUNY-Buffalo, 1969; M.B.A., Pepperdine U., 1979. Mgr. mktg. communication Atari Inc. div. Warner Communications, Inc., Santa Clara, Calif., 1979-83, Convergent Techs., Santa Clara, 1983-84; dir. mktg. communications CAE Systems div. Tektronix, Sunnyvale, Calif., 1984-85, AIDA Corp., Santa Clara, 1985—. Home: 773 Widgeon St Foster City CA 94404 Office: AIDA Corp 3375 Scott Blvd Santa Clara CA 95054

MARTELL, RUTH, educational adminstrator; b. Cologne, Germany; came to U.S., 1939; d. Samuel and Elise (Silberberg) Rubinstein; m. Raymond Martell, June 24, 1953 (div. 1986); children—Erica Ellen, Madeline Ann. B.A. cum laude, Bklyn. Coll., 1951; M.S. in Edn., Queens Coll., 1967; M.S. in Adminstrn., Pace U., 1980. Co-chmn. Nat. Tay Sachs Fund Raising, 1963-67; kindergarten tchr. N.Y.C. Bd. Edn., 1970-78, head tchr. early childhood, 1978, test liaison, 1979—. Asst. to candidate Bess Myerson Senate Campaign, N.Y.C., 1980; vol. Guggenheim Mus., Nat. Tay-Sachs Assn., N.Y.C., English-in-Action, Doctors Hosp., N.Y.C. Mem. Nat. Council Adminstrv. Women in Edn., N.Y.C. Assn. Tchrs. English, Phi Beta Kappa. Jewish. Home: 505 E 14th St New York NY 10009 Office: Sch Dist 10 3961 Hillman Ave New York NY 10009

MARTENS, PATRICIA ANN, univ. adminstr.; b. Chadron, Nebr., July 18, 1952; d. Lloyd Ernest and Glendene (Wallingford) M.; B.S., Chadron State Coll., 1973, M.S., 1978. Phys. edn. tchr. Hot Springs (S.D.) High Sch., 1973-75, Sterling (Colo.) High Sch., 1975-76; state tng. mgr. Nebr. Head Start, Chadron, 1976-77; grad. asst. Chadron (Nebr.) State Coll., 1977-78; asso. dir. admissions Eastern N.Mex. U., Portales, 1978-79; admissions counselor N.Mex. State U., Las Cruces, 1979—, recruitment and publicity chmn., evening degree program com. chmn., 1980-82; sec. N.Mex. Coll. Day Com., 1979-81. Recipient Scholarships, Elks, 1970, Chadron State Coll., 1970, Chadron C. of C., 1970. Mem. Am. Assn. Collegiate Registrars and Admissions Ofcls., Rocky Mountain Assn. Counselors and Admissions Counselors, Rocky Mountain Assn. Collegiate Registrars and Admissions Ofcls., N.Mex. Assn. Collegiate Registrars and Admissions Ofcls. N.Mex. Sch. Counselors Assn. (secondary v.p. 1979-81), Am. Legion Aux., Am. Assn. Female Execs., Chadron State Coll. Alumni Assn., Phi Delta Kappa, Cardinal Key, Sigma Delta Nu, Kappa

Mu Epsilon. Republican. Baptist. Club: Pentax Owners. Office: Box 3A N Mex State U Las Cruces NM 88003

MARTENSON, RITA BRITT-MARIE, marketing educator, researcher; b. Hassleholm, Skane, Sweden, Dec. 8, 1950; came to U.S., 1985; d. Sven Gunnar and Elsa Margareta (Ogren) M. Grad. gymnasium, coll. Tech. Sch., Hassleholm, 1969; M.B.A. in Mktg. and Econs., U. Gothenburg, Sweden, 1976, D.Bus. Adminstrn., 1981. Ednl. asst. U. Gothenburg, 1976-77, assoc. prof., 1980-85, Calif. State U. Los Angeles, 1985—; supr. doctoral program U. Gothenburg, 1982—, dir. 14 univ. courses, 1980—, creator 3 new MBA courses, 1982-84; cons. mktg. Author: Market Communications/MC, 1984 (recipient Swedish Mktg. Exec. prize 1985); MC by fires in Sweden, 1985; Services Marketing, 1986; Contbr. numerous articles to profl. jours. Grantee in field. Mem. Swedish Mktg. Execs., Am. Mktg. Assn. Avocation: international contacts with people from different cultures. Home: Fassbergsgatan 16 Molndal Sweden S-43139

MARTHE, SISTER MARY, college president. Pres. Notre Dame Coll. of Ohio, Cleve. Office: Notre Dame Coll of Ohio 4545 College Rd Cleveland OH 44121*

MARTIKAINEN, A(UNE) HELEN, former health education specialist; b. Harrison, Maine, May 11, 1916; d. Sylvester and Emma (Heikkinen) M.; A.B., Bates Coll., 1939, D.Sc. (hon.), 1957; M.P.H., Yale, 1941; D.Sc., Harvard U., 1964, Smith Coll., 1969. Health edn. sec. Hartford Tb and Public Health Assn., 1941-42; cons. USPHS, 1942-49; chief health edn. WHO, Geneva, 1949-74, now mem. expert adv. panel. Trustee, Bridgton Acad., North Bridgton, Maine; mem program adv. bd., also membership com. U.S. Assn. Club of Rome; mem. N.C. Citizens Council Public Health; bd. dirs. Orange County Council Women, N.C. Center of Laws Affecting Women, Inc.; mem. adv. bd. Sch. Pub. Health, U. N.C., Chapel Hill; mem. Commn. on Women's Issues of Episcopal Diocese of N.C.; chmn., mem. com. N.C. Council Women's Orgns. Recipient Delta Omega award Yale; Nat. Adminstrv. award Am. Acad. Phys. Edn.; Bates Key award; Internat. Service award, France, 1953; Prentiss medal, 1956; spl. medal, certificate for internat. health edn. service Nat. Acad. Medicine for France, 1959; profl. award Soc. Public Health Educators, 1963. Fellow Am. Public Health Assn. (chmn. health edn. sect., Excellence award 1969); mem. AAUW (rep. to N.C. Council Social Legis.), U.S. Soc. Pub. Health Educators, Internat. Union Health Edn. (Parisot medal, tech. adviser), Acad. Phys. Edn. (asso.), Phi Beta Kappa. Episcopalian. Home: PO Box 3059 Chapel Hill NC 27514

MARTIN, ALICE LOUISE MCCLURE, manufacturing company official; b. Ottumwa, Iowa, Mar. 23, 1926; d. Floyd Edgar and Lena Olive (Shepherd) McClure; student Iowa State Coll., 1946-47; m. George Kenneth Martin, Oct. 19, 1947; 1 son, Douglas Bruce. Draftsman, engring. dept. Ottumwa Iron Works (Iowa), 1944-46; order receiver John Morrell & Co., Ottumwa, 1946-50; clk. production control Proto Tool div. Ingersoll-Rand Co., Portland, Oreg., 1970-72, steel inventory planner, 1972-77, steel buyer, 1978-83, steel and parts buyer, 1983—; buyer Stanley-Proto Indsl. Tools, Portland, 1984—. Mem. Clackamas County Election Bd., 1961-70; pres. women's assn. Oak Hills Presbyn. Ch., 1965-66. Mem. Nat. Assn. Female Execs., Inc., Sigma Kappa. Republican. Presbyterian. Home: 5332 SE El Centro Way Portland OR 97267 Office: 10330 SE 32d Ave Portland OR 97222

MARTIN, ANITA ELLEN, nurse; b. Chgo., Aug. 5, 1925; d. Cornelius James and Sophie Ann (Bruczyk) M.; diploma DePaul Hosp. Coll. Nursing, St. Louis, 1949; B.S.N., Mt. St. Mary's Coll., Los Angeles, 1955; postgrad. UCLA, 1955-56, Rutgers U., 1969. Supr. pediatrics St. Mary's Hosp., Evansville, Ind., 1950-52; supr. medicine St. Vincent's Hosp., Los Angeles, 1952-56; supr. pediatrics Hotel Dieu Hosp., El Paso, 1956-60; head nurse Hanson's Disease, USPHS Hosp., Carville, La., 1960-62; head nurse, night supr. gen. surgery Hines (VA) Hosp., 1962-65, head nurse oncolgy, 1965-68, head nurse Restoration Center, 1968-72, community health nurse hosp.-based home care, 1972-74, coordinator hosp.-based health care, 1974-85, counselor alcoholic treatment program Restoration Center, 1968-72, cons. palliative care com., 1979-85; Alzheimer's disease nurse Family Alliance Adult Day Care Ctr., Woodstock, Ill.; lectr. high schs., civic orgns. Mem. Am. Nurses Assn., Nat. Orgn. VA Nurses, Am. Assn. Rehab. Nurses, Ill. State Hospice Assn. (charter). Roman Catholic. Contbr. articles to profl. jours. Home: 3419 W John St McHenry IL 60050 Office: Family Alliance 248 N Throop St Woodstock IL 60098

MARTIN, CAROLANN FRANCES, educator, conductor, cellist; b. Woodward, Okla., Nov. 20, 1935; d. John C. Martin and Leah Mae (Heaston) Shilling; B.Mus.Edn., Oklahoma City U., 1957; M.A. (fellow), Ohio State U., 1964; D.M.A., U. Ariz., 1979. Tchr. music, pub. schs., Okla., 1957-58; asst. prof. Wilson br. Chgo. City Coll., 1964-67; assoc. prof. Morningside Coll., Sioux City, Iowa, 1969-76; dir. opera theater, cellist Oklahoma City Symphony, 1954-58, 67-69, Norfolk Symphony, 1958-59, Columbus (Ohio) Symphony, 1962-64; prin. cellist Chgo. Chamber Orch., 1965-67, Chgo. Civic Orch., 1966-67; prin. cellist Sioux City Symphony; condr. Siouxland Youth Symphony; asst. prin. cellist Tucson Symphony and Ariz. Opera Co., 1976-77; condr. S.E. Kans. Symphony and Pittsburg State U. Opera Theater, also Mid-Am. Youth Symphony, 1977—; mem. faculty Pittsburg State U., Kans., 1977—; asst. condr. Eastern Music Festival, 1983-84; guest condr. Bournemouth Sinfonietta, Eng., Victoria Symphony, Tex. Served to 1st lt. USMCR, 1958-61. Winner Nat. Conducting Competition, 1980. Mem. Am. String Tchrs. Assn., Music Educators Nat. Conf., Condrs. Guild, Kans. Music Tchrs. Assn. (exec. bd.), Am. Legion (post comdr.), Delta Zeta, Sigma Alpha Iota. Roman Catholic. Home: 107 E Carlton Pittsburg KS 66762 Office: Dept Music Pittsburg State U Pittsburg KS 66762

MARTIN, CECILIA ANN, educator; b. Broken Bow, Okla., Nov. 10, 1934; d. Cecil C. and Faye (Burks) Martin; B.S., Baylor U., 1955; M.Ed., North Tex. State U., 1962; Ed.D., U. No. Colo., 1975. Instr. phys. edn. Stripling Jr. High Sch., Ft. Worth, 1955-65; cons. in phys. edn. Ft. Worth Ind. Sch. Dist., 1965-74; dir. profl. preparation dept. phys. edn. Colo. State U., Fort Collins, 1974—, asst. dean Coll. Profl. Studies, 1979-80. Mem. Tex. Tchrs. Assn., Am., Tex. (asso. conv. mgr. 1970-71), Colo. (sec. elect) assns. health, phys. edn. and recreation, Nat., Central (membership chmn.) assns. phys. edn. in higher edn., Colo. Assn. Health, Phys. Edn., Recreation and Dance (sec., pres.), Phi Delta Kappa, Kappa Delta Pi, Delta Psi Kappa. Home: 1977 17th Ave Greeley CO 80631 Office: Moby Gymnasium Colo State Univ Fort Collins CO 80523

MARTIN, CHIPPA, counseling psychologist; b. Bronx, N.Y., Sept. 6, 1942; d. Murray and Rose (Kaplan) Riback; B.A., Queens Coll., 1964; M.A., Goddard Coll., 1978; children—Tara, Beth. Tchr., Manhasset (N.Y.) High Sch., 1964-65; tchr., humanities cons. Millbrook (N.Y.) High Sch., 1972-74; certifier Cambridge (Mass.) Govt. Housing, 1975-77; dir., counselor Aradia Counseling, Boston, 1978—. Vice-pres., League Preservation of Hudson Valley, 1972. Lic. social worker, Mass. Mem. Am. Personnel and Guidance Assn., Assn. Specialists in Group Work, Mass. Mental Health Counselors Assn., Am. Assn. Counseling and Devel., Assn. Women in Psychology. Home: 2150 Old Kings Hwy W Barnstable MA 02668 Office: 520 Commonwealth Ave Boston MA 02215

MARTIN, CLEO EILEEN, educator; b. Goldfield, Iowa, Aug. 5, 1925; d. Roy Bertram and Fannie Grace (Zinser) Martin; B.A., U. No. Iowa, 1946, M.A., 1954; postgrad. U. Iowa, 1961. Tchr. English, high schs., New Hampton and E. Waterloo, Iowa, 1946-53; teaching asst., instr., asst. prof., writing supr. freshman rhetoric program U. Iowa, Iowa City, 1954—, dir. summer writing workshops Iowa Writing Project, 1978—; cons. high sch. and coll. writing programs; dir. Writing Workshop Iowa Inst. on Writing, 1979, 80. Mem. Iowa Council of Tchrs. of English (Disting. Service award 1986), Nat. Council of Tchrs. of English, Coll. Conf. on Composition and Communication. Democrat. Home: 405 Crestview Ave Iowa City IA 52240 Office: 72 English-Philosophy Bldg Iowa City IA 52242

MARTIN, CONNIE RUTH, lawyer; b. Clovis, N.Mex., Sept. 9, 1955; d. Lynn Latimer and Marian Ruth (Pierce) M. B.U.S., Eastern N.Mex. U., 1976, M.Ed., 1977; J.D., U. Mo.-Kansas City, 1981. Bar: N.Mex. 1981, U.S. Dist. Ct. N.Mex. 1981. Substitute tchr. Clovis (N.Mex.) Mcpl. Schs., 1978; paralegal specialist IRS, Kansas City, Mo., summer 1980; dep. med. investigator Office Med. Investigator, Farmington, N.Mex., 1981-84; asst. dist. atty. Dist. Atty. Office, Farmington, 1981-84, head juvenile div., 1981-82, mem. criminal/felony prosecution div., 1982-84; assoc. firm Tansey, Rosebrough, Roberts & Gerding, P.C., 1984—. Bd. dirs., exec. com. San Juan County Econ. Opportunity Council, Farmington, 1982, 83; bd. dirs. Four Corners Substance Abuse Council, 1984-85; guest lectr. Farmington Police Dept., Aztec Police Dept., 1981-83; community lectr. sex crimes, drug abuse, child abuse, San Juan County. Recipient Am. Jurisprudence award Bancroft-Whitney Co., 1980; Moot Ct. Bd. award U. Mo., 1980-81; named Outstanding Young Woman, San Juan County Jaycees, 1984. Mem. ABA, Christian Legal Soc. (treas. law sch. chpt. 1979-80), State N.Mex. Bar Assn., San Juan County Bar Assn. (treas. 1985-86). Democrat. Baptist. Office: 621 W Arrington Farmington NM 87401

MARTIN, CORA ARLETA, retired equal opportunity specialist; b. Dean, Tenn., Sept. 30, 1923; d. Thomas Crawford and Florice (Gardner) Martin; cert. Bowling Green Bus. U., 1943. Clk.-typist War Dept., Tullahoma, Tenn., 1943-46; payroll clk. VA and U.S. Dept. Agr., Atlanta, 1946-51; personnel rep. U.S. Army Corps of Engrs., Tullahoma, 1951-60; placement and employee mgmt. relations specialist Army Rocket and Guided Missile Agy. and U.S. Army Missile Support Agy., 1960-69; personnel staffing specialist, equal opportunity specialist and fed. women's program mgr. U.S. Army Missile Command, 1969-85. Chmn., Bedford County Heart Unit, 1967-75, vice chmn., 1964-67. Mem. Internat. Personnel Mgmt. Adminstrn., Shelbyville Bus. and Profl. Women's Club, Tenn. Fedn. Bus. and Profl. Women's Clubs, Inc. (pres. 1963, parliamentarian 1965-66, 71-72), Bedford County African Violet Soc., Federally Employed Women (chpt. pres. 1971-72), Am. Bus. Women's Assn. Club: Altrusa Internat. (pres. 1983-85), Flat Creek Home Demonstration Club (sec. 1985—). Home: 502 Riverview Dr Shelbyville TN 37160

MARTIN, CYDNEY CAPELL, editor; b. Jacksonville, Fla., Dec. 20, 1956; d. Ernest Clary and Alice Rae (McGinnis) Capell; m. Garrick Philip Martin, July 16, 1983. B.A., Furman U., 1977. Mktg. rep. E.C. Capell & Assocs., Greenville, S.C., 1977-80; sales rep. Prentice-Hall Publs., Cin., 1980-81; sales, mktg. rep. Benjamin/Cummings, Houston, 1981-83; sales rep. McGraw-Hill Book Co., Houston, 1983-85, engring. editor, N.Y.C., 1985—; editor lit. mag. Talon, 1972; news editor Paladin newspaper, 1977. Named Rookie of Yr., McGraw-Hill Book Co., 1985. Mem. Women in Pub., Women in Communications, NOW, Nat. Assn. Female Execs., Mensa. Republican. Avocations: tennis, ballet.

MARTIN, DEBRA JO, marketing director, human resources consultant; b. Estherville, Iowa, June 21, 1948; d. Jerald Percy Godden and LaVonne Gertrude (Rosenstiel) Godden Martin; adopted dau., Claude Harold Martin. B.A., Calif.-Lutheran U., 1971; M.B.A., Dun & Bradstreet Fin. Analysis Tng. Program, Los Angeles, 1973. Cert. tchr., Calif. Bus. analyst Dun & Bradstreet, Inc., Los Angeles, 1972-74; tchr. gifted children Pilgrim Sch., Los Angeles, 1974-75; dir. county-wide program Moorpark Coll., Calif., 1975-78; tchr. Birmingham High Sch., Van Nuys, Calif., 1978-79; agy. dir. TransAm. Personnel Service, Canoga Park, Calif., 1979-83; dir. protocol adminstrn. Los Angeles Olympics Organizing Com., 1983-84; recruitment-tng. cons. CPI & Assocs., Canoga Park, 1983—; dir. mktg. and corp. devel. Los Angeles Bus. Labor Council, 1983—; employment and tng./mktg. cons. Los Angeles Community Coll. Dist., Los Angeles, 1984—. Recipient Achievement award Bank of Am., Oxnard, Calif., 1966; Brett Meml. award, Oxnard, 1966; Achievement award Calif. Luth. U. Honor Soc., 1971. Mem. Nat. Assn. Female Execs. Democrat. Baptist. Home: 7320 Darby Pl Reseda CA 91335 Office: Los Angeles Business and Labor Council Los Angeles CA 90084

MARTIN, DIANE TAYLOR, school administrator; b. Tucson, Feb. 2, 1954; d. L.C. Taylor and Edith Jackson; m. Edmund Donald Martin, Apr. 18, 1981. B.A. in History, Journalism, East Carolina U., 1976. Account exec., Surrey Broadcasting Inc., Tucson, 1976-79; gen. mgr. St. Thomas Investments Inc., Virgin Islands, 1979-81; prodns. asst. United Way of Am., Alexandria, Va., 1982, asst. to pres., 1983, asst. dir. Spl. U.S. Congl. Program, 1983-85; exec. dir. Tunon Internat. Hospitality Sch., Orlando, 1985—. Recipient Letter of Recognition, Fed. Emergency Food and Shelter Program Bd. Dirs., 1985. Mem. Central Fla. Hotel/Motel Assn., Greater Orlando C. of C., Orlando/Orange County Conv. and Visitors Bur., Indsl. Devel. Commn., Nat. Assn. Female Execs. Republican. Avocations: writing; scuba diving; skiing; sailing. Home: 4905 Hidden Springs Blvd Orlando FL 32819 Office: Tunon Internat Hospitality Sch 7061 Grand National Dr Orlando FL 32819

MARTIN, DOROTHY EVERETT, social work educator, consultant; b. Verona, N.J., Aug. 5, 1919; d. Frank Norton and Edith Sarah (Baker) Everett; m. Donald Darrow Matson, Sept. 11, 1943 (dec. May 1969); children—Martha, Donald E., James Edward, Barbara B.; m. Samuel Preston Martin, III, Sept. 5, 1970. B.S., St. Lawrence U., 1940; M.S.W., Case Western Res. U., Cleveland, 1946. Field dir. Planned Parenthood League Mass., 1966-70; dir. counseling Phila. Family Planning, 1971-72; supr. social work Daroff Hosp.-Albert Einstein Med. Ctr., Phila., 1973-76; supr. social work, sch. age parents program Phila. Sch. Dist., 1976-77; lectr. Sch. Social Work, U. Pa., Phila., 1977—; sex edn. cons., 1975—. Mem. Nat. Assn. Social Workers, Acad. Cert. Social Workers, Am. Assn. Sex Educators, Counselors and Therapists (cert.), Soc. Sci. Study of Sex, NOW, LWV. Democrat. Office: School Social Work Univ Pa 3701 Locust Walk Philadelphia PA 19143

MARTIN, DOROTHY MAE, retail drapery firm executive; b. Coatesville, Pa., May 3, 1951; d. Joseph and Martha (Smoker) Engel; m. Larry G. Martin, Apr. 18, 1970; children—Shawn E., Stacy R. Student pub. schs. Pres., Martin's Draperies & Interiors, Ltd., Intercourse, Pa., 1978—. Vol., Hospice, Lancaster, Pa., 1983; treas. Bus. and Profl. Women's Commn., Lancaster, 1986—. Avocations: sewing, crafts making, reading, biking. Home: 131 Fieldcrest Ln Gordonville PA 17529 Office: Martin's Draperies & Interiors Ltd 3611 Old Philadelphia Pike Intercourse PA 17534

MARTIN, EDITH KINGDON GOULD (MRS. GUY MARTIN), pianist, volunteer; b. N.Y.C., Aug. 20, 1920; d. Kingdon and Annunziata (Lucci) Gould; student Barnard Coll., N.Y.C., 1939-40; pvt. study piano; m. Guy Martin, Oct. 12, 1946; children—Isaiah Guyman III, Jason Gould, Christopher Kingdon, Edith Maria Theodosia Burr. Actress, Barter Theater, 1941, Summer Stock, Nyack, 1942, A Young American, 1946, Louis Brombfield's West of the Moon, 1946, Agatha Christie's Hidden Horizons, 1946; guest pianist Werner Lywen Quartet, 1965—. Bd. dirs. Paul VI Inst. for Arts, 1979—; trustee, past pres. Washington Opera. Served with USNR, 1942-46. Decorated Navy Expert Pistol medal. Clubs: City Tavern, Sulgrave (Washington). Author: Poems, 1934. Composer: Song Cycle on Poems of Lenau and Schiller, 1968. Home: 3300 O St NW Washington DC 20007

MARTIN, EDITH WAISBROT, electronics company executive; b. Chgo., June 25, 1945; d. Alexander Joseph and Helen Mae (Hance) Waisbrot; m. Charles Samuel Martin, Dec. 16, 1967 (div. Jan., 1982); children—William McNutt, Christine Katherine; m. Douglas Carter Montgomery, Sept. 2, 1982. B.A., Lake Forest Coll., 1967; postgrad., Universitat Karlsruhe, W. Ger., 1971-72; M.S. in Info. and Computer Sci., Ga. Inst. Tech., 1975-76, Ph.D., 1980. Dir. computer sci. tech. lab. Ga. Inst. Tech., Atlanta, 1976-80; corp. exec. dir. Control Data Corp., Atlanta, 1980-82; pres. EWM & Assocs., Inc., Atlanta, from 1982; dep. undersec. Dept. Def. for research and advanced tech., Washington, from 1982; U.S. prin. Non-Atomic Research and Devel. Com., from 1982, NATO Def. Research Group, Brussels, Belgium, from 1982; now v.p. technology assessment Boeing Electronics Co., Seattle. Contbr. articles to profl. jours.; editorial reviewer: Mil. Electronics Eountermeasures, 1976-80; mem. editorial bd.: IEEE Software, 1983—. Bd. dirs. Ga. Inst. Tech., Atlanta, 1983. Recipient numerous awards Dept. Def., 1982—; Appreciation award Pres. Ronald Reagan, 1983. Mem. IEEE (exec. bd. dirs. tech. com. on software Computer Soc. 1982—, award of appreciation-recognition 1983), Assn. Computing Machinery, Electronics Industries Assn. (subcom. chmn. 1981, recognition award 1976-82), Sigma Xi. Republican. Presbyterian. Office: Boeing Electronics PO Box 3707 MS 7J-20 Seattle WA 98124

MARTIN, EMILY FRANCES, accountant; b. Bklyn., Oct. 14, 1958; d. Henry F. and Emiko E. (Endo) Stanfield. A.A., St. Petersburg Jr. Coll., 1977; B.A. in Acctg., U. South Fla., 1982; M.Acctg., Nova U., 1985. File and systems clk. GTE Directories, St. Petersburg, Fla., 1975-81; bookkeeper Dara-Hennessy, St. Petersburg, 1981-83; staff acct. Spence Marston & Bunch, Clearwater, Fla., 1983; staff acct. Aero Systems, Miami, Fla., 1983-85, acctg. supr., 1985; chief acct., dep. dir. fin. Pan Am World Services, Medley, Fla., 1985—. Coordinator Neighborhood Crime Watch, St. Petersburg, 1982. Mem. Nat. Assn. Accts., Nat. Assn. Female Execs., Nat. Notary Assn. Avocations: reading; dancing; sewing. Home: PO Box 8125 Fort Lauderdale FL 33310 Office: Allmat Internat 9202 NW 101 St Medley FL 33178

MARTIN, GRACE BURKETT, psychologist; b. Sumter, S.C., Aug. 27, 1939; d. John Hazel and Grace Thomasine (Briggs) Burkett; B.A. magna cum laude, Armstrong State Coll., 1976; M.S., Fla. State U., 1979, Ph.D., 1980; m. H. Russell Martin, Jr., Oct. 9, 1957; children—H. Russell, Carolyne, Melinda. Hist. preservationist, 1962—; dir. Christian edn. St. Thomas Parish, Savannah, Ga., 1970-74; asst. prof. psychology Armstrong State Coll., Savannah, 1980—, dept. head; pres. Orgn. Cons.; lectr.; radio and TV appearances. Bd. dirs. Coastal Empire YMCA, 1972-75; mem. Savannah Symphony Soc.; mem. commn. on mission Episcopal Diocese of Ga., 1972-74, mem. liturg. commn., 1972-74, also lic. lay reader; pres. Operation Return, 1972-76. Named Mrs. Ga., 1962. Mem. Am. Psychol. Assn., Southeastern Psychol. Assn., Soc. Indsl. Organizational Psychology, Am. Mgmt. Assn., Commerce Club Savannah (charter), Ga. Ednl. Research Assn. Cons. editor Jour. Supplementary Abstract Service, 1980, 81. Home: 111 Herb River Dr Savannah GA 31406 Office: Armstrong State Coll Savannah GA 31406

MARTIN, HELEN ELIZABETH, educator; b. West Chester, Pa., Feb. 19, 1945; d. Thomas Edwin and Elizabeth Temple (Walker) M.; B.A., King's Coll., Briarcliff Manor, N.Y., 1967; M.Ed., West Chester U., 1970; postgrad. Goethe Inst., Freiberg, Fed. Republic Germany, 1979, Oxford U., 1979. Tchr. math. and sci. Unionville (Pa.) High Sch., 1967—. Mem. Pa. Republican State Com., Rep. Com. of Chester County. Fellow Am. Sci. Affiliation; mem. AAAS, Nat. Sci. Tchrs. Assn., Nat. Council Tchrs. Math., History Sci. Soc., So. Chester County Rep. Women's Council (pres.), Red Clay Valley Assn., Brandywine Valley Assn. Clubs: Delaware Camera, Women's Rep. of Chester County. Home: 329 Lambortown Rd West Grove PA 19390 Office: Unionville High Sch Unionville PA 19375

MARTIN, JANE ZIGLAR, marketing executive; b. Winston Salem, N.C., Sept. 7, 1949; d. Zeb Otis and Della Sue (Conrad) Z.; m. Ken L. Martin, Mar. 22, 1969 (div. Dec. 1983); 1 child, K. Taylor. M.B.A., Wake Forest U., 1982. Research asst. mktg. R.J. Reynolds Industries, Winston Salem, N.C., 1968-75; mktg. research analyst Hanes Corp., Winston Salem, 1975-77, asst. mgr. mktg. research, 1977-78; mgr. mktg. research dept. Kayser Roth Hosier Corp. No Nonsense Fashions div., Greensboro, N.C., 1978-82, asst. brand mgr., 1982-84, brand mgr., 1984-86, mgr. spl. Project on telemktg., 1986—. Mem. Am. Mktg. Assn. (chmn. student relations 1982-83, membership chmn., v.p. 1984). Republican. Home: 3535 New Delhi Dr Winston Salem NC 27101 Office: No Nonsense Fashions Inc PO Box 77057 Greensboro NC 27407

MARTIN, JOANNE, utility company executive; b. Akron, Ohio, Feb. 2, 1941; d. John and Ann M. (Capp) Martin; A.Secretarial Sci., U. Akron, 1968. Stenographer, Gen. Tire & Rubber Co., Akron, 1958-61; with Ohio Edison Co., Akron, 1961—, sec. to corp. sec., 1968-72, asst. corp. sec., 1972—. Cert. profl. sec., 1972. Mem. LWV of Akron, Women's Network Akron, U. Akron Alumni Assn., U. Akron John R. Buchtel Soc., Nat. Council Career Women, Nat. Assn. Female Execs., Bus. and Profl. Women's Club. Home: 520 Meredith Ln Apt 305 Cuyahoga Falls OH 44223 Office: 76 S Main St Akron OH 44308

MARTIN, JOSEPHINE WALKER, educator; b. Charleston, S.C., Jan. 15, 1927; d. George Archibald and Josephine Isabel (Walker) M.; A.B., U. S.C., 1946, M.Ed., 1950, Ph.D. (Stoddard fellow), Coll. Edn., 1971; M.A., Columbia U. Union Theol. Sem., 1952; postgrad. C.G. Jung Inst., Zurich, Switzerland, 1954-56. Nat. cert. counselor. Tchr., St. Andrew's Parish High Sch., Charleston, 1947-50; dir. Christian edn. Ch. of St. Edward the Martyr Episcopal, N.Y.C., 1952-54, 56-57; tchr., guidance counselor Crayton Jr. High Sch., Richland County (S.C.) Public Schs., 1957-67; instr. Coll. Edn., U. S.C., Columbia, 1968-71, asst. prof., 1971-77, asso. prof. ednl. founds., 1977-84, prof. emerita, 1984. Mem. vestry Trinity Episcopal Cathedral, Columbia, 1976-79. Mem. AAUP, AAUW, Am. Ednl. Studies Assn., S.C. Hist. Soc., South Caroliniana Soc., LWV, Common Cause, Phi Delta Kappa, Delta Kappa Gamma (pres. chpt. 1980-82). Club: Analytical Psychology of N.Y. Editor: Dear Sister Letters Written on Hilton Head Island 1867, 1977. Home: 1403 Haynsworth Rd Columbia SC 29205 Office: Coll Edn U SC Columbia SC 29208

MARTIN, JOYCE ADAMS, newspaper publisher; b. Moab, Utah, Nov. 13, 1929; d. Joseph William and Dora (Black) Adams; m. Gerald G. Martin, June 17, 1950 (div. Mar. 1967); children—Rae Jean Martin Melton, Steven K., Calvin Lawrence, Douglas L. B.A., U. Utah, 1951. Fashion model Wolf & Dessauer, Ft. Wayne, Ind., 1965-69; acct. Heritage House, Ft. Wayne, 1969-74; tchr. English Utah Pub. Schs., Monticello, 1974; substitute tchr. Indpls. Pub. Schs., 1975-80; co-pub. San Juan Record, Monticello, Utah, 1980—. Mem. adv. bd. Bur. Land Mgmt., 1984—. Recipient Best Editorial award Utah Press Assn., 1983. Mem. C. of C. (dir.), Apmin Fine Arts (hon.), Beta Delta Mu. Office: San Juan Record 937 E Hwy 666 Monticello UT

MARTIN, JUDITH M., lawyer; b. Ann Arbor, Mich., Feb. 10, 1943; d. D. Lawrence and Donna E. (Webb) Moran; m. E. Michael Martin, Sept. 28, 1963 (div.); children—Laura Claire, Paul Michael, Ann Lindsay; m. Daniel B. Ventres, Jr., Dec. 27, 1984. B.A., U. Mich., 1963; student Université de Jean Moulin, France, 1981; J.D., U. Minn., 1982; Ch.F.C., Am. Coll., Bryn Mawr, Pa., 1986. Bar: Minn. Assoc. CFTC Clayton Brokerage, Mpls., 1979-81; tax assoc. Coopers & Lybrand, Mpls., 1981-83, asst. to nat. dir. personal fin. planning 1982-84, mem. nat. steering com., 1982-84; instr. personal fin. planning tng. course, Minn. Soc. C.P.A.s 1983; dir. fin. planning services IDS/Am. Express, 1984-85, tax mgr., dir. fin. planning, 1985—. Mem. Mpls. Downtown Council, 1983-85, bd. dirs. Am. Field Service, Edina, Minn., 1983-84; dir. Hennepin County Gen. Hosp. Service League, 1969-72. Mem. ABA, Minn. Bar Assn. (estate planning council), Hennepin County Bar Assn., Minn. World Trade Assn., U. Minn. Law Sch. Ptnrs. in Excellence, Kappa Kappa Gamma. Presbyterian. Office: KMG Main Hurdman 1200 TCF Tower Minneapolis MN 55402

MARTIN, JUNE JOHNSON CALDWELL, journalist; b. Toledo, Oct. 6; d. John Franklin and Eunice Imogene (Fish) Johnson; A.A., Phoenix Jr. Coll., 1939-41; B.A., U. Ariz., 1941-43, 53-59; student Ariz. State U., 1939, 40; m. Erskine Caldwell, Dec. 21, 1942 (div. Dec. 1955); 1 son, Jay Erskine; m. 2d, Keith Martin, May 5, 1966. Free-lance writer, 1944—; columnist Ariz. Daily Star, 1956-59; editor Ariz. Alumnus mag., Tucson, 1959-70; fashion editor, book editor, gen. feature writer Ariz. Daily Star, Tucson, 1970—; panelist, co-producer TV news show Tucson Press Club, 1954-55, pres., 1958. Mem. Tucson CD Com., 1961; vol. campaigns of Samuel Goddard, U.S. Rep. Morris Udall, U.S. ambassador and Ariz. gov. Raul Castro. Recipient award Nat. Headliners Club, 1959, Ariz. Press Club award, 1957-59, Am. Alumni Council, 1966, 70. Mem. Jr. League of Tucson, Tucson Urban League, Pi Beta Phi (dir. Clarion, women's newspaper). Democrat. Methodist. Club: Tucson Press. Contbg. author: Rocky Mountain Cities, 1949; contbr. articles and stories to World Book Ency. and mags. Home: PO Box 2631 Tucson AZ 85702 Office: PO Box 26807 Tucson AZ 85726

MARTIN, KATHERINE A., county administrator; b. Jamaica, N.Y., June 9, 1947; d. James Thomas Martin and Kathleen (Howson) M.; B.A., SUNY, New Paltz, 1970; M.S., U. Utah, 1976; children—Dove Francoise Gordon, Sky Martin-Green. Organizer, Ulster County Community Action, Inc., Highland, N.Y., 1971-72; dir. Ulster County Friends of Farm Workers, Kerhonkson, N.Y., 1972-73; youth counselor, then program coordinator Dutchess County Neighborhood Youth Corps, Poughkeepsie, N.Y., 1973-74; manpower services specialist Rensselaer/Columbia Bd. Coop. Ednl. Services, Castleton, N.Y., 1974-75; project dir. Program Funding, Inc., Rochester, N.Y., 1975-77; grants adminstr. County of Ulster, Kingston, N.Y., 1978—, sr. mgmt. analyst, 1982—; cons. Chmn. bd. dir. Wawarsing Econ. Opportunity Center, 1971-75; mem. Gov.'s Adv. Council on Migrant Workers and Rural Poor, 1976-78; sec. bd. dirs. Ulster County Community Action Com., 1973-76; bd. dirs. Nat. Council Intergovtl. Coordinators, 1981—. Mem. Am. Mgmt. Assn., Am. Soc. Public Aminstrn., Nat. Assn. Counties, N.Y. State Assn. Counties, LWV, Assn. Native Americans. Home: 60 Old Ford Rd New Platz NY 12561 Office: County Adminstrs Office 244 Fair St Kingston NY 12401

MARTIN, KATHLEEN ANNE, librarian; b. Rochester, N.Y., Aug. 19, 1942; d. Edwin Wilkins and Hilda Ellen (Hartell) Martin; B.A., Marygrove Coll., Detroit, 1964; M.A. in L.S. (Josenhans scholar 1965), U. Mich., 1965; advanced online tng. cert. Nat. Library Medicine, 1979; m. Oliver Kalman Peterdy, Oct. 15, 1971 (div. 1981); children—Elizabeth, Matthew. Librarian, Detroit Public Library, 1964-66; bibliographer, then asst. tech. services librarian Edward G. Miner Med. Library, U. Rochester, 1969-72; librarian lab. indsl. medicine Eastman Kodak Co., Rochester, 1966-69, librarian health, safety and human factors lab., 1972-78, tech. info. analyst, 1978-84, health and environment lab., 1984—. Mem. AAUW (treas. Rochester br. 1979-80), Spl. Libraries Assn. Med. Library Assn. Home: 4 Belmont Rd Rochester NY 14612 Office: Eastman Kodak Co Kodak Park Div Bldg 320 Rochester NY 14650

MARTIN, KATHRAN JONANA, financial services executive; b. Pleasanton, Calif., Jan. 16, 1954; d. Gerald Lee and Detta Joan (Morris) Sutton; m. Jack L. Martin, Mar. 1, 1980. B.A., U. Calif.-Santa Barbara, 1975. Asst. buyer Silverwoods, Los Angeles, 1975-76; buyer Robinsons, Los Angeles, 1977; divisional mgr. Security 1st Group, Los Angeles, 1977-80; v.p. Am. Diamond, San Diego, Calif., 1980; pres. Designed Planning Cons., Dallas, 1980—. Author: Retirement Plans, 1978; (with others) Training Sales Personnel, 1982. Mem. Internat. Assn. Fin. Planners, Inst. Cert. Fin. Planners, Nat. Assn. Securities Dealers, Nat. Assn. Female Execs., Assn. Women Entrepreneurs. Democrat. Home: 10027 Silvertree St Dallas TX 75243 Office: Designed Planning Consultants 11910 Greenville Ave Suite 505 Dallas TX 75243

MARTIN, LAURA PAEZ REED, clinical psychologist; b. Los Angeles, May 18, 1935; d. Howard Richard and Laura (Paez) Reed; B.A., UCLA, 1958; M.A. (NIMH fellow), U. So. Calif., 1974, Ph.D., 1974; m. Warren Leicester Martin, Aug. 24, 1957; children—Laura, Susan, Warren. Instr. psychology Los Angeles Community Coll. Dist., 1975-77; pres. Laura Martin, Ph.D., Inc., 1977—; psychotherapist Psychiat. Assocs. Med. Group, Covina, Calif., 1976—; chief psychologist (adolescence) Sierra Royale Hosp., Azusa, Calif., 1976—; hosp. cons. nursing edn.; lectr. women's issues. Mem. Am. Psychol. Assn., Calif. Psychol. Assn., Assn. Mex.-Am. Psychologists, Assn. Women in Sci. Republican. Roman Catholic. Club: U. So. Calif. Golden Circle, Flintridge Riding. Home: 4172 Forest Hill Dr La Cañada CA 91011 Office: Psychiat Assos Med Group 750 Terrado Plaza Suite 245 Covina CA 91723

MARTIN, LESLIE ANN, oncologist, educator; b. N.Y.C., July 8, 1948; d. Edward Charles and Marjorie (Hyslop) Martin. B.A., Brown U., 1970; M.D., Tufts Med. Sch., 1975. Intern St. Elizabeth's Hosp., Brighton, Mass., 1975-76, resident in internal medicine, 1976-78, staff hematologist, oncologist, 1980—; asst. prof. medicine, Tufts U., Boston, 1981—; sr. investigator Eastern Co-op. Oncology Group, 1980—; med. dir. The Good Samaritan Hospice, Brighton, 1982—. Mem. ACP, Am. Cancer Soc. Office: St Elizabeths Hosp Brighton MA 02135

MARTIN, LILLIAN ANN, nurse, realtor; b. Purcell, Okla., Aug. 28, 1944; d. Joseph Cleo and Hassie Estelle (McClure) Marcotte; m. Robert Frederick Martin, Mar. 11, 1967. Diploma Mercy Hosp. Sch. of Nursing, 1962. R.N., Okla. Company nurse Hertz Corp., Oklahoma City, 1971-72; staff nurse critical care Mercy Health Ctr., Oklahoma City, 1970-74, charge nurse, critical care 1974-80, coordinator critical care edn., 1980-83, team leader monitoring services, 1983—, instr. cardiology rural hosps., 1979—. Mem. profl. adv. group AmCare, Oklahoma City Ambulance Trust, 1984—. Mem. Am. Heart Assn., Am. Assn. Critical Care Nurses (cert., program com. 1975-76, annual workshop com. Oklahoma City chpt. 1981—). Republican. Roman Catholic. Avocations: sewing; gardening. Office: Mercy Health Ctr 4300 W Memorial Rd Oklahoma City OK 73120

MARTIN, LISA DIANE, insurance agent; b. Victoria, Tex., July 26, 1957; d. Benjamin E. and Mary E. (Harp) Haning; m. John W. Martin, Jr., Feb. 23, 1978 (dec. 1980). B.S. in Mgmt., Oklahoma City U., 1987. Exec. sec. Fidelity Bank, Oklahoma City, 1978-83; profl. ins. agt. State Farm Ins. Co., Midwest City, Okla., 1983—. Mem. membership com. Oklahoma City YWCA, 1984-85; bd. dirs. Bapt. Med. Ctr. Assocs., Oklahoma City, 1985-86. Mem. Downtown Bus. and Profl. Women's Club (dir., recording sec. 1983, 1st v.p. 1984, pres. 1984-86; named Young Career Woman 1983), Nat. Assn. Life Underwriters, Civic Music Assn., Alpha Phi (Outstanding chpt. adv. 1982-84, Outstanding Alumnae Service award 1981, 82, 83, state day chmn. 1982, 85, dist. gov. 1986—). Democrat. Baptist. Avocations: music, reading, needlework, tennis. Office: State Farm Ins 1160 S Douglas Blvd Midwest City OK 73130

MARTIN, LYNN MORLEY, congresswoman; b. Chgo., Dec. 26, 1939; d. Lawrence William and Helen Catherine (Hall) Morley; B.A., U. Ill., 1960; children—Julia Catherine, Caroline. Former tchr., public schs.; mem. Ill. Ho. of Reps., 1977-79, Ill. Senate, 1979-81; mem. 97th-99th Congresses from 16th Ill. Dist. Mem. Winnebago County Bd., 1972-76. Named to Outstanding Young Women Am., U.S. Jaycees. Mem. AAUW, C. of C. of Rockford, Jr. League, Phi Betta Kappa. Republican. Office: 1208 Longworth Office Bldg Washington DC 20515

MARTIN, MARION ELIZABETH, consultant; b. N.Y.C., July 7, 1911; d. John Henry and Marion Elizabeth (Smith) M.; A.B., Coll. Mt. St. Vincent, 1931; A.M., Columbia U., 1937. Lab. technician, legis. rep. Assn. Lab. Technicians, N.Y.C., 1931-37; employment interviewer Div. Employment, N.Y. State Dept. Labor, 1937-44; counselor, supr., adminstr., asst. commr. vocat. rehab. Office Vocat. Rehab., N.Y. State Edn. Dept., Albany, 1944-77; rehab. cons. United Cerebral Palsy N.Y.C., 1977—; lectr. vocat. rehab. Syracuse U., 1950, N.Y.U., 1955-65; cons. Rehab. Service Adminstrn., U.S. Dept. Human Services, 1978—. Mem. Nat. Rehab. Assn. (com. chmn.), N.Am. Soc. Rehab. Engring., AAAS, Am. Personnel and Guidance Assn., Am. Assn. Mental Deficiency, Council Exceptional Children, AAUW, Bus. and Profl. Women's Club, N.Y. Acad. Sci. Roman Catholic. Home: 110 Fernbank Ave Delmar NY 12054

MARTIN, MARY JILL LOCKWOOD, accounting educator; b. Wichita, Kans., Jan. 10, 1948; d. Raymond Max and Yolanda (Gigliotti) Lockwood; m. Ronald Douglas Martin, June 29, 1969; 1 son, Jared Lockwood. B.A., U. Fla.-Gainesville, 1969; J.D., Emory U., Atlanta, 1974, LL.M. in Taxation, 1979. Bar: Ga. 1976. Sole practice, Atlanta, 1979-81; asst. prof. acctg. Ga. State U., Atlanta, 1981-84; assoc. prof., coordinator tax program Ga. So. Coll., Statesboro, 1984—; cons. Tax Research Inc., Atlanta, 1983—. Contbr. articles to profl. jours. Mem. ABA, Ga. Bar Assn. Democrat. Episcopalian. Home: 632 Washington Ave Savannah GA 31405

MARTIN, MAUREEN KATHERINE, health maintenance organization executive, nurse; b. Long Beach, Calif., Dec. 28, 1951; d. William Joseph and Elizabeth Josephine (Lins) M. B.A., Lone Mountain Coll., San Francisco, 1975; R.N., Evergreen Valley Coll., San Jose, Calif., 1980. R.N., Calif., Nev., Tex., Ga., Mass. Nurse St. Marys Hosp., Reno, Nev., 1980-82, Flying Nurses Inc., 1982-83; mgr. field supervision Health Examinetics, San Diego, 1984-85; mktg. rep. Gen. Med, San Diego, 1985—; owner, prin. Med Pro Network, San Diego, 1985—; founder Success Unltd., San Diego, 1986—. Inventor auto safety device. Mem. La Jolla Town Council, Calif., 1985—. Served with U.S. Army Res., 1976-78. Recipient Outstanding New Program award Kaiser Permanente Hosp., San Francisco, 1977; Outstanding Contbn. award Cambrian YWCA, Calif., 1979. Mem. Greater San Diego C. of C., La Jolla Mus. Contemporary Art. Avocations: skiing; writing; community activities for safety and social awareness. Home: 1110 Woodlake Dr Cardiff by the Sea CA 92007 Office: General Med 3333 Camino del Rio S Suite 420 San Diego CA 92108

MARTIN, MONA HELEN, university administrator; b. Corning, N.Y., June 24, 1951; d. Clayton Arlinton II and Ramona Louise (Herbert) Teator; student Alfred U., 1981—; m. Thomas J. Martin, Dec. 21, 1968; children—James H., Tina M. Univ. relations records clk. Alfred U., 1974-75, supr. records, 1975-76, records clk., 1976-78, assoc. for devel. research, 1978, supr. research and records, 1979-84, dir. devel. services, 1984—. Vol., CD Disaster Preparedness, Steuben County, United Way, Am. Heart Fund; instr. religious edn. program St. Ignatius Loyola Ch.; bd. dirs. Alfred/Allegany Ednl. Fed. Credit Union. Mem. Alpha Kappa Omicron. Republican. Roman Catholic. Home: 263 Grand St Hornell NY 14843 Office: PO Box 1165 Alfred NY 14802

MARTIN, NELDA MOORE, information systems specialist; b. Corsicana, Tex., Feb. 16, 1941; d. Teener Erskine and Mary Frances (Gay) Moore; m. Glenney Dial Martin, III, Dec. 15, 1961 (div. Apr. 1978); children—Glenney Dial, Bruce Patrick. B.S., Arlington State Coll. (Tex.), 1962. Tchr. algebra Mansfield High Sch. (Tex.), 1962; computer programmer Great Am. Res. Ins. Co., Dallas, 1963-69, systems cons., 1983-85, asst. v.p. systems analysis, 1985—; project leader J.C. Penney Life Ins., Dallas, 1974-82. Deaconess, 1st Christian Ch., Duncanville, Tex., 1982—. Fellow Life Mgmt. Inst. Office: Great Am Res Ins Co PO Box 388 2020 Live Oak St Dallas TX 75221

MARTIN, REBECCA JEAN, lawyer; b. Kansas City, Mo., Nov. 20, 1954; d. Glen Emerson and Alice Louise (Brown) M. B.A. in Classical Archaeology, Kans. U., Lawrence, 1977, B.A. in Geology, 1977; J.D., So. Meth. U., Dallas, 1980. Bar: Tex. Assoc. Locke, Purnell, Boren, Laney & Neely, Dallas, 1980—; adj. prof. So. Meth. U., 1981—. Vol., Dallas Zoo, 1981—, Office of Protocol, Dallas, 1983—. Mem. ABA, State Bar Tex., Mortar Bd., Phi Beta Kappa, Phi Kappa Phi. Republican. Presbyterian. Office: Locke Purnell Boren Laney & Neely 3600 Republic Bank Tower Dallas TX 75201

MARTIN, ROSALIE VINCENT, wholesale goods, apparel company executive; b. Chgo., July 25, 1941; d. Leo and Leslye (Vincent) Mc Henry; m. Robert Martin, Mar. 23, 1961; children—Steven, Carla Denise, Calvin Maurice. Student Art Inst. Chgo., 1960-62; A.A., San Diego City Coll., 1977. Recreational leader U.S. Navy, Memphis, 1967-70; spl. educator San Diego Unified Schs., 1972-79; tchr. Camolot Sch., Poway, Calif., 1979-80; sales rep. Shoffeitt Corp., Healdsburg, Calif., 1980-81; telemktg. sales rep. Cordura Publ., San Diego, 1981-84; co-owner, co-mgr. Sparkles of Calif., Escondido, 1984—. Editor: Tightwad Times, 1979. Chmn. dedication ceremony com. Hickman Elem. Sch., 1973; historian PTA, Hickman Elem. Sch., 1974, pres., 1975-77; mem. dist. adv. com. San Diego Unified Schs., 1974. Recipient Yes for Kids award San Diego Unified Schs., 1974; named to Calif. Hon. Soc., Hickman Elem. PTA, 1977. Mem. Nat. Assn. Female Execs. (Excellence award 1985). Home: 1160 S Hale Ave Escondido CA 92025 Office: Sparkles of Calif 200 W El Norte Pkwy Suite 201 Escondido CA 92026

MARTIN, ROSE, government law information specialist; b. Pozsony, Hungary, Aug. 25, 1928; came to U.S., 1949, naturalized, 1954; d. Ferenc and Zsuszanna (Nehai Szabo) Kocsis; m. Donald L. Martin, Aug. 23, 1961; 1 child, Virginia Kim. Student Seton Hall U., 1960-61; B.B.A., Kensington U., Glendale, Calif., 1968-69; cert. Cath. U. Am. 1981, George Washington U., 1982. Documents librarian Seton Hall U., South Orange, N.J., 1958-61; mem. office staff Dept. Def., Washington, 1962-63, Dept. Agr., Washington, 1963-67; info. specialist-law Office Adminstrv. Law Judges, Dept. Labor, Washington, 1976—. Active Republican Club, Great Falls, Va., 1986—. Recipient Meritorious award Dept. Agr., 1966, Outstanding award Dept. Labor, 1977. Mem. Am. Assn. Law Libraries, Gt. Falls Woman's Club. Roman Catholic. Club: River Bend Golf and Country (Great Falls). Avocations: travel; tennis; reading; swimming; cooking. Home: PO Box 405 Great Falls VA 22066

MARTIN, SALLY SYKES, technical writer, editor, audio-visual producer; b. St. Louis, Feb. 4, 1953; d. William Graham III and Winifred Estelle (Hamilton) M.; m. David Carlton Williams, May 15, 1977. B.A. in English Lit., Washington U., St. Louis, 1975; postgrad. U. Mo.-St. Louis, 1982-85. Data processing editor Emerson Electric Co., St. Louis, 1976-77; asst. editor Facts and Comparisons, St. Louis, 1977-78; procedurs writer/analyst McDonnell Douglas, St. Louis, 1978-82; tech. writer Ralston Purina, St. Louis, 1982-84; supr. communications-product assurance McDonnell Douglas Astronautics Co., St. Louis, 1984—; editor Catalyst newsletter Women in Bus., St. Louis, 1983. Mem. Lafayette Sq. Restoration Com., St. Louis, 1983—, editor Marquis newsletter, 1983-84; treas., mem. vestry, mem. worship com. St. Stephen's Episcopal Ch., St. Louis, 1984—. Recipient 2d Place award Assn. for Multi-Image Festival, 1983, Elizabeth Cook award Lafayette Sq. Restoration Com., 1984. Mem. IEEE (assoc.), Soc. Tech. Communications (Achievement award for brochure 1984), KETC, Zoo Friends. Avocation: piano (classical music). Home: 1526 Mississippi Saint Louis MO 63104 Office: McDonnell Douglas Astronautics Co PO Box 516 Saint Louis MO 63166

MARTIN, SHARON JAFFE, waterproofing company executive; b. Elyria, Ohio, June 20, 1944; d. Edward Gilbert and Sylvia Sophia (Werner) Jaffe; m. David Richard Martin, May 8, 1965; 1 child, Jeffrey Ross. Student Miami U., Oxford, Ohio, 1962-64, Lorain Community Coll., 1966, 73-74. Cashier Elyria Meml. Hosp., 1964-67; asst. tchr. Westshore Montessori Sch., North Ridgeville, Ohio, 1973-75, Montessori Cooperative of Vienna, Va., 1975-76; v.p., sec., treas. Reston Pressure Seal, Inc., Va., 1977—. Mem. Reston Community Players, Inc., treas., 1981-84. Nominated Reston Woman of Yr., 1983. Jewish. Avocations: dancing; acting. Home: 11281 Spyglass Cove Ln Reston VA 22091 Office: Reston Pressure Seal Inc PO Box 2292 Reston VA 22090

MARTIN, SUSAN KATHERINE, librarian; b. Cambridge, Eng., Nov. 14, 1942; came to U.S., 1950, naturalized, 1961; d. Egon and Jolan (Schonfeld) Orowan; m. David S. Martin, June 30, 1962. B.A. with honors, Tufts U., 1963; M.S., Simmons Coll., 1965; Ph.D., U. Calif.-Berkeley, 1983. Library intern Harvard U. Library, Cambridge, Mass., 1963-65, systems librarian, 1965-73; head library systems office Gen. Library, U. Calif., Berkeley, 1973-79; dir. Milton S. Eisenhower Library, Johns Hopkins U., Balt., 1979—; cons.; instr. U. Md., College Park, 1981. Author: Library Networks, 1986-87. Editor Jour. Library Automation, 1973-77. Contbr. articles to profl. jours. Trustee Phila. Area Library Network, 1980-81; bd. dirs. Universal Serials and Book Exchange, 1981-82, pres., 1984. Recipient Simmons Coll. Disting. Alumni award, 1977; Council on Library Resources fellow, 1973. Mem. ALA, Library and Info. Tech. Assn. (pres. 1978-79), Am. Soc. Info. Sci., Phi Beta Kappa. Home: 3518 Garrett Ct Ellicott City MD 21043 Office: Milton S Eisenhower Library Johns Hopkins Univ Baltimore MD 21218

MARTIN, THEODORA FURST, educator; b. White Plains, N.Y., Sept. 22, 1942; s. Robert George Laurence and Annette Alfreda (Morse) Furst; m. Jeffrey Max Martin, July 18, 1964; children—Andrew, Cynthia. B.S., Bucknell U., 1964; M.A., Rutgers U., 1971. Tchr., Cranford Schs., N.J., 1964-66; adj. prof. Bucks County Coll., Newtown, Pa., 1975-76; affirmative action coordinator N.J. Dept. Edn., Trenton, 1976-80, project supr., 1980—; v.p., founder N.J./Northeastern Coalition Ednl. Leaders, 1982-85. Mem. Clinton Twp. Sch. Bd., Annandale, N.J., 1972-77; mem. exec. com. Hunterdon County Sch. Bds. Assn., Flemington, N.J., 1976-77. Mem. Nat. Coalition for Sex Equity in Edn. (budget com. 1983-85), N.J. Assn. Supervision and Curriculum Devel., Phi Beta Kappa, NOW (leader task force 1972-74). Avocations: gourmet cooking; travel; reading; Nautilus. Home: 1 Spruce Rd Clinton NJ 08809

MARTIN, TONI LYNN, physician; b. Chgo., Nov. 22, 1951; d. Louis Emanuel and Gertrude (Scott) Martin; m. Earl Michael Darby, Mar. 30, 1974; 1 son, Andrew Darby. A.B., Radcliffe Coll., 1973; M.D., U. Calif.-San Francisco, 1977. Diplomate Am. Bd. Internal Medicine. Intern Moffitt Hosp., San Francisco, 1977-78; resident in internal medicine U. Calif.-San Francisco, 1978-80; practice medicine specializing in internal medicine, Oakland, Calif., 1980—; mem. staffs Providence Hosps., Merritt Hosp. Author: How to Survive Medical School, 1983. Mem. Alameda-Contra Costa Med. Assn. Episcopalian. Office: 3223 Telegraph St Oakland CA 94609

MARTIN, VIOLA VELMA, lawyer; b. Sweetwater, Tex., June 15, 1934; d. Ben Earl and Joe Helen (French) Wilson; m. G.W. Martin, Jan. 15, 1951 (div. Oct. 1980); children—Lester Earl, Valerie Sue, Gaylon Wade. A.S. with distinction, N.Mex. Jr. Coll., 1969; B.S. cum laude, Coll. Southwest, 1970; M.A., Eastern N.Mex. U., 1974; J.D., Baylor U., 1979. Bar: Tex., 1979, N.Mex., 1980. Case worker State N.Mex., Hobbs, 1970-74; atty. K.B. Wilson, P.A., Roswell, N.Mex., 1979-85; ptnr. Wilson and Martin, Roswell, 1985—; instr. Eastern N.Mex. U., Roswell, 1982. Mem. Zia council Girl Scouts Am., Lovington, N.Mex., 1963; city chmn. March of Dimes, Lovington, 1964; mem. steering com. Com. for Justice, Albuquerque, 1982. Mem. ABA, Am. Trial Lawyers Assn., N.Mex. Trial Lawyers Assn., Tex. State Bar, N.Mex. State Bar. Demomcrat. Office: Wilson and Martin 215 W 6th St PO Box 849 Roswell NM 88201

MARTINEZ, BETTY ELNORA, chem. co. exec.; b. Oklahoma City, Jan. 7, 1947; d. Jim and Jewell Frances Smith; B.S., Oklahoma City U., 1974, M.B.A., 1975; m. June 29, 1966 (div. July 1968). Pvt. booking agt. and bus. mgr., rock and roll bands, Okla., Colo., 1960-67; with Kerr McGee Corp., Oklahoma City, 1965-81, acct., 1974-76, solvent sales rep., from 1975, asso. sales rep. until 1981; petrochems. sales rep. No. Petrochem. Co., Ramsey, N.J., 1981—; sales rep. Allied/Signal Corp., Morristown, N.J., 1985—. Del. Okla. Democratic Conv., 1972. Mem. M.B.A. Club Oklahoma City U. (pres. 1975), ACLU. Home: 10 Sherwood Ln SE Marietta GA 30067 Office: PO Box 70426 Marietta GA 30007

MARTINEZ, ELENA RAQUEL, physician; b. Pinar del Rio, Cuba, Sept. 4, 1932; d. Maximo and Clara Maria (Aguiar) M.; B.S., U. Pinar del Rio, Cuba, 1950; M.D., U. Madrid (Spain), 1958, U. Havana, Cuba, 1959. Intern, Columbus Hosp., N.Y.C., 1965-66; resident in surgery St. Barnabas Med. Center, Livingston, N.J., 1966-67; resident in orthopaedic surgery USPHS Hosp., S.I., 1967-68, Met. Hosp., N.Y.C., 1969-70, Flower Hosp., N.Y.C., 1969-70, 5th Ave Hosp., N.Y.C., Hosp. Crippled Children, Newark, N.J., 1968-69; clin. instr. orthopedic surgery U. Miami; practice medicine specializing in orthopaedic surgery, Miami, Fla., 1970—. Diplomate Am. Bd. Orthopaedic Surgery. Fellow Am. Coll. Surgeons, Cuban Soc. Orthopaedic Surgery; mem. Am. Acad. Orthopaedic Surgery, Dade County Med. Assn., Fla. Med. Assn., AMA, Miami Orthopaedic Soc., Fla. Orthopaedic Soc., Am. Profl. Practice Assn. Home: 65 Shore Dr W Miami FL 33133 Office: Mercy Professional Bldg Suite 801 3661 S Miami Ave Miami FL 33133

MARTINEZ, ELIZABETH GERTRUDIS, sales, public relations and marketing executive, researcher; b. Bayamo, Oriente, Cuba, Nov. 17, 1951; came to U.S., 1967; d. Jose Ramon and Roselvi Kathy (Lau) M.; m. Jose Ramon Argiz, Aug. 9, 1952 (div.); m. Justo Ernesto Montero, Nov. 7, 1950. Student Miami Dade Jr. Coll., 1973-75, U. Miami, 1985—. Exec. sec. Union Fin., Miami, Fla., 1972-75; export sales mgr. Inter City Auto Stores, Miami, 1975-80; salesman A.G.E. Paper, Miami, 1982—. Mem. Nat. Assn. Female Execs., Pacific Inst. Alumni Assn. Republican. Roman Catholic.

MARTINEZ, EVA IRIS, controller; b. Ponce, P.R., Oct. 31, 1948; d. Julio and Rita Julia (Santiago) Martinez. B.B.A., Cath. U., Ponce, 1970; M.Acctg., Fla. State U., 1979. C.P.A., P.R. Auditor, Peat, Marwick, Mitchell, Ponce, P.R., 1971-77; instr./asst. dean U. P.R., Mayaguez, 1977-81; gen. acctg. mgr. Inspiron div. C.R. Bard, Cucamonga, Calif., 1981-83; asst. controller Inspiron Corp., Cucamonga, 1984—. Govt. P.R. and Cath. U. scholar, 1967-70. Mem. Am. Inst. C.P.A.s, Am. Acctg. Assn., Nat. Assn. Accts. (dir. profl. devel., sec. 1972-73), Colegio C.P.A.s de P.R. Roman Catholic. Home: 134 N Canyon Blvd Apt B Monrovia CA 91016 Office: Inspiron Corp 8600 Archibald Ave Rancho Cucamonga CA 91730

MARTINEZ, HERMINIA S., banker, economist; b. Havana, Cuba; came to U.S., 1961, naturalized, 1972; d. Carlos and Amelia (Santana) Martinez Sanchez; B.A. in Econs. cum laude, Am. U., 1965; M.S. in Fgn. Service (Univ. fellow), M.S. in Econs., Georgetown U., 1967; postgrad. Nat. U. Mex. Instr. econs. George Mason Coll., U. Va., Fairfax, 1967-68; researcher World Bank, 1967-69, indsl. economist, industrialization div., 1969-71, loan officer, Central Am., 1971-79, loan officer, economist, Mex., 1973-74, Venezuela and Ecuador, 1973-77, sr. loan officer in charge of Panama and Dominican Republic, Washington, 1977-81, sr. loan officer for Middle East and North Africa, 1981-84, sr. loan officer for Western Africa region, 1985—. Mem. Am. Econ. Assn., Soc. Internat. Devel., Brookings Inst. Latin Am. Study Group. Roman Catholic. Contbg. author: The Economic Growth of Colombia: Problems and Prospects, 1973. Home: 4734 Massachusetts Ave NW Washington DC 20016 Office: 1818 H St NW Washington DC 20037

MARTINEZ, LINDA VALENCIA, vocational education administrator; b. Farmington, N.Mex., Oct. 2, 1948; d. Peter Joseph and Fedelina (Trujillo) Valencia; m. Theodore Abuid Martinez, May 24, 1971; 1 child, Maria Teresa. B.A., N.Mex. Highlands U., 1971. Telephone operator, Santa Fe, 1968-69; pub. info. specialist N.Mex. Highlands U., Las Vegas, 1972-73; social worker N.Mex. Social Service Agy., Las Vegas, 1973-74; planner N.Mex. Adv. Council on Vocat. Edn., Albuquerque, 1974-83, exec. dir., 1983—; host Aspiracion program Sta. KGGM-TV, Albuquerque, 1979-81; workshop speaker, cons. to vocat. tchrs., women and minority orgns. throughout N.Mex., 1976—. Editor legis. and pub. relations guides. Chairperson vocat. adv. com. New Futures Sch., Albuquerque, 1984—; bd. regents N.Mex. Highlands U., 1983—; bd. dirs. Peanut Butter & Jelly Pre-Sch., Albuquerque, 1984—, New Futures Sch., Inc., 1985—. Recipient Communication Contest award N.Mex. Press Women, 1978; Women At Work award Council on Working Women, Denver, 1983. Mem. Women in Communications, Am. Vocat. Assn., Nat. Assn. Vocat. Edn. Communicators, N.Mex. Vocat. Assn. (Spl. Appreciation award 1983), Nat. Fedn. Press Women, Nat. IMAGE, Inc. (nat. sec. 1977-79, editor nat. newspaper 1977-79, Contbn. to Hispanics award 1979, pres. Albuquerque chpt. 1979-80), Mexican-Am. Women's Nat. Assn. Democrat. Roman Catholic. Home: 1509 Florida NE Albuquerque NM 87110 Office: New Mex Adv Council on Vocat Edn 600 2d St NW Suite 810 Albuquerque NM 87110

MARTINEZ, SUSANNE, lawyer; b. San Francisco, Mar. 3, 1945; d. Floyd W. and Mary Katherine (Grier) Sitton; B.A., U. Calif., Davis, 1967; J.D., U. Calif., San Francisco, 1970; 1 dau., Jennifer Sue. Admitted to Calif. bar, 1971, U.S. Supreme Ct. bar, 1976; legal asst. San Francisco Neighborhood Legal Assistance Found., 1968-70; staff atty. Youth Law Center, 1970-77; counsel Subcom. on Child and Human Devel., Com. Labor and Human Resources, U.S. Senate, Washington, 1977-80; legis. asst. Senator Alan Cranston, 1980—. Mem. ACLU, San Francisco Bar Assn., Order of the Coif. Democrat. Office: Senate Office Bldg 112 Hart Washington DC 20510

MARTINEZ, VILMA SOCORRO, lawyer; b. San Antonio, Oct. 17, 1943; d. Salvador and Marina (Pina) M.; m. Stuart R. Singer, Nov. 1968; children—Carlos, Ricardo. B.A., U. Tex., 1964; LL.B., Columbia U., 1967. Bar: N.Y. 1968, Calif. 1975. Staff atty. gen. civil rights litigation NAACP Legal Defense and Edn. Fund, 1967-70; EEO counsel N.Y. State Div. Human Rights, 1970-71; litigation assoc. Cahill, Gordon & Reindel, 1971-73; pres., gen. counsel Mexican-Am. Legal Defense and Ednl. Fund, Inc., 1973-82; ptnr. Munger, Tolles & Rickershauser, Los Angeles, 1982—; dir. Anheuser-Busch Cos., Inc.; cons. U.S. Commn. on Civil Rights, 1969-74, U.S. Census Bur., 1975-81, U.S. Treasury Dept., 1976, Calif. Fed. Jud. Selection Com., 1977-80, Presidential Adv. Bd. on Ambassadorial Appointments, 1977-81, U.S. Hispanic-Mexican Govt. Internat. Commn., 1980-82. Regent U. Calif., 1976—, chmn. 1984—; dir. Southwestern Voter Registration and Edn. Project; trustee Edward W. Hazen Found. Recipient Lex award Mexican-Am. Bar Assn., 1983, Jefferson award Am. Idst. Pub. Service, 1976, John D. Rockefeller III Youth award Rockefeller Found., 1977, univ. medal of excellence, Columbia U., 1978, Valerie Kantor award Mex. Am. Legal Defense Edn. Fund, Inc., 1982; John Hay Whitney fellow, 1964, Samuel Rubin fellow Columbia U. Sch. Law, 1983. Address: 612 S Flower St Los Angeles CA 90017

MARTÍNEZ, YOLANDA R., social services administrator; b. San Bernardino, Calif., Feb. 11, 1936; d. Eduardo R. and Consuelo (Rincon) M.; A.A., San Bernardino Valley Coll., 1959; B.A., U. Wash., 1974; m. William Edward Hawkins, Mar. 27, 1963 (div. Mar. 1983); children—Ricardo, Eduardo, William T. Tchr. public schs., Calif., 1958-59; parole adviser, project dir., counselor Active Mexicanos, Seattle, 1972-76; instr. Everett Community Coll., Everett, Wash., 1975-76; research, translator Wash. State Council Crime and Delinquency, Seattle, 1977; program asst., minority affairs Seattle Central Community Coll., cons. to community offenders programs 1977-81; sr. community service rep. Seattle Dept. Human Resources, 1981—; cons. Chicano mental health. Democratic precinct committeeman, 1968, 70; vol. worker various local and state polit. campaigns; translator Am. Red Cross Lang. Bank, 1975—; chmn. Region 10 Chicano Task Force on Drug Abuse, 1977-79; mem. Seattle Women's Commn., 1977-81; v.p. Concilio for Spanish Speaking; state dir., mem. nat. exec. bd. League United Latin Am. Citizens, 1980-82; chmn. Hispanic adv. bd. Seattle Community Coll. Dist. 6, 1981-83, chair Seattle/Mazatlan Sister City Assn., 1981-83; bd. dirs. United Way of King County; dist. adv. com. group health Northgate Clinic; del. White House Conf. on Families, Los Angeles, 1980. Recipient Gov.'s citation, 1974, award for committment to higher edn. Seattle Community Coll. Dist., 1983; award as One of 10 Unsung Heroes in Seattle, Radical Women, 1983; Community Service award Am. G.I. Forum, 1984; named assoc. mem. Eastern Washington U. Found., One of 100 Women Role Models for Pub. Schs., State Office Pub. Instrn. Mem. MUJER Hispanic Woman's Orgn. Author: Usted y La Ley, 1977. Home: 15532 11th St NE Seattle WA 98155 Office: Dept Human Resources City of Seattle 12707 30th St NE Seattle WA 98125

MARTING, LEEDA POLLOCK, management consultant; b. Birmingham, Ala., June 28, 1945; d. Lester Euler and Edytha (Chastain) Pollock; m. Rodger A. Marting, July 24, 1971 (div. Dec. 1976); 1 dau., Kristin Roselle. B.S., U. Ala.-Tuscaloosa, 1967, M.A., 1970; Ph.D., Ohio State U., Columbus, 1973; P.M.D., Harvard U., 1983. Asst. dir. Columbus Found., 1973-76; dir. Needmor Fund, Toledo, 1976-79; mgr. Levi Straus & Co., San Francisco, 1979-80; exec. dir. John Hay Whitney Found., N.Y.C., 1980-83; pvt. practice mgmt. cons., N.Y.C., 1983—. Mem. exec. com., bd. dirs. Pub. Broadcasting Service, Washington, 1979—; sec. Bank St. Coll., N.Y.C., 1979-83, chmn. bd. dirs., 1983—; trustee Enterprise Found., Columbia, Md., 1983—. Named Disting. Alumnus in Communications U. Ala., 1978. Democrat. Club: Harvard (N.Y.C.).

MARTIN NIEVES, KATHALEEN, bank administrator; b. Reno, Nev., Apr. 18, 1961; d. Tilden and DeVona Aileene (Burfield) Martin Scott; m. Kevin Nieves, Dec. 29, 1984. B.A., U. Nev., 1983; postgrad. U. Nev.-Reno. Customer service mgr. First Interstate Bank, Reno, 1984—. Vol. Temporary Assistance for Domestic Crisis, Las Vegas, 1981, 82, 83, Planned Parenthood, Reno, 1985. Mem. Nat. Assn. Bank Women, Am. Inst. Banking, Nat. Assn. Female Execs., NOW, U. Nev.-Las Vegas Alumni Assn., Phi Lambda Alpha (pres. 1981-82), Alpha Kappa Delta (award 1983), Phi Kappa Phi (award 1983). Democrat. Avocations: raquetball; bowling; aerobics; reading; writing. Home: 1877 El Rancho Apt 188 Sparks NV 89431 Office: First Interstate Bank 2405 Vassar Dept 139 Reno NV 89502

MARTINO, DIANNE MARIE, procurement administrator, jeweler; b. Norristown, Pa., July 21, 1954; d. James Martin and Nancy Jane (Heyser) M.; m. Lloyd Jerald Campbell, July 4, 1980 (div. June 1984), Richard Joseph Scafuto, July 21, 1984. B.S., Calif. State Poly. U., 1976; postgrad. Bus. Adminstrn., Pepperdine U., Malibu, Calif., 1983. Documentation coordinator Mitsubishi Internat., Los Angeles, 1976-78; material coordinator McDonnell Douglas Corp., Long Beach, Calif., 1978-81; system coordinator C.F. Braun, Alhambra, Calif., 1981-82; subcontract adminstr. Rockwell Internat., El Segundo, Calif., 1982-84; procurement adminstr. Northrop Corp., Pico Rivera, Calif., 1984—. Republican. Club: Mensa. Avocations: reading; horseback riding; skiing. Home: 11123 Arroyo Dr Whittier CA 90604 Office: Northrop Corp 8900 E Washington Blvd Rico Rivera CA 90660

MARTINY, ARDYTH LOUISE, air traffic controller, quality assurance executive; b. Aurora, Ill., July 11, 1956; d. Victor Albert and Marie (Martiny) Hamman. B.S., Purdue U., 1979. Cert. flight instr. Lineman/mechanic Reid Airways, Inc., Lafayette, Ind., 1977-80; co-pilot Ind. Airways, Inc., Lafayette, 1978-80; chief flight instr. Lafayette Aviation, Inc., 1980-84; chief pilot Plainfield Aviation, Inc., Plainfield, Ind., 1984—; air traffic controller FAA, Indpls., 1981—; quality assurance specialist FAA, Indpls., 1985—; mgr. Fed. Woman's Program, Indpls., 1985—. Author: Biennal Flight Review, 1981. Block capt. Neighborhood Crime Watch, Hadley Acres, 1986. Recipient Letter of Appreciation, FAA, 1984, 85. Mem. Aircraft Owners and Pilots Assn., The Exec. Female. Presbyterian. Clubs: Westwood Country, Friendswood Golf. Avocations: golf; racquetball; swimming; softball; waterskiing. Home: 1150 E Hadley Rd Plainfield IN 46168 Office: Indpls Air Route Traffic Control Center 2000 Bauman Dr Indianapolis IN 46241

MARTOCCIA, JOYCE SGRO, ednl. adminstr.; b. Cleve., Aug. 24, 1939; d. Santo M. and Johanna Mathilda (Lienerth) Sgro; B.A. in Bus. Edn., Baldwin-Wallace Coll., 1959; M.A. in Guidance and Counseling, Case Western Res. U., 1967; M.A., John Carroll U., 1974; m. William R. Martoccia, Mar. 28, 1968; 1 son, Marc William. Legal sec. Van Aken, Arnold, Bond and Withers, Cleve., 1959-62; bus. tchr. Cleve. Public Schs., 1963-66, guidance and placement counselor high schs., 1966-73; adminstr., asst. prin., unit prin. Audubon Jr. High Sch., Cleve., from 1973; now spl. projects counselor Damascus High Sch. and Sligo Intermediate Sch., Gaithersburg, Md.; mem. accrediting team N. Central Assn. High Schs. and Colls. Fine arts chmn. Cleve. Ballet, 1976—; co-chmn. vols. Shaker Lakes Regional Nature Center, 1975—; mem. Cleve. Opera Assn., Cleve. Mus. Art, Smithsonian Soc.; women's com. Cleve. Orch.; hon. v.p. Lincoln Jr. High Sch. PTA; adv. bd. John Carroll U.; vol. fundraising Am. Cancer Soc., Muscular Dystrophy Assn. Honored for best tutorial program in City of Cleve., 1975-78; honored as Outstanding Asst. Prin., 1978. Mem. Am., Ohio, NE Ohio (pres. 1976-77) personnel and guidance assns., Cleve. Council Adminstrs. and Suprs., Ohio, Nat. (commn. on profl. employment practices, co-author handbook 1977) assns. women deans, adminstrs. and counselors, Ohio Sch. Counselors Assn., Montgomery County Counselors Assn., Ohio Assn. Secondary Sch. Adminstrs., Indsl. Edn. Club of Cleve., Greater Cleve. Prins. Discussion Group (pres.), John Carroll U. Educators Alumni Assn. (pres., educators cons.), Delta Phi Alpha, Phi Delta Kappa, Alpha Delta Kappa. Republican. Roman Catholic. Home: 84 Pontiac Way Gaithersburg MD 20760 Office: 850 Hungerford Rd Gaithersburg MD 20760

MARTONE, JOANNE, accountant; b. Yonkers, N.Y., Mar. 3, 1951; d. August Jerome and Winnie (Rudolf) M.; B.A. in History, Centre Coll. Ky., 1973; postgrad. Ariz. State U., 1979-81. Tchr., basketball coach Junction City (Ky.) Elem. Sch., 1973-77; staff analyst Met. Life Ins. Co., 1975-77; tchr. Glendale Elem. Sch., 1977-78, Camelback Desert Sch., 1978-79; C.P.A., De Marcus & Assos. P.C., Phoenix, 1979-82; individual practice, 1982—; ptnr. Investment Co. Acres, 1978—, The Lucky Leopard, 1977—, dir. Adaman Mut. Water Co., 1981-82, sec.-treas., 1981-82. Bd. dirs. Impact... for Enterprising Women, 1983—, North Community Behavioral Health Center, Inc., 1984—, North Star, 1985—. Cert. tchr., Ky., Ariz.; C.P.A., Ariz. Mem. Am. Inst. C.P.A.s, Ariz. Soc. C.P.A.s, Am. Woman's Soc. C.P.A.s. Women C.P.A.s Phoenix. Club: Metro Bus. Network (treas.). Home: Route 1 Box 348 Litchfield Park AZ 85340 Office: 7112 N 55th Ave Suite B Glendale AZ 85301

MARTONE, PATRICIA ANN, lawyer; b. Bklyn., Apr. 28, 1947; d. David Andrew and Rita Mary (Dullmeyer) Martone. B.A. in Chemistry, NYU, 1968; M.A. in Phys. Chemistry, Johns Hopkins U., Balt., 1969; J.D. NYU, 1973. Bar: N.Y. 1974, U.S. Dist. Ct. (so. and ea. dists.) N.Y. 1975, U.S. Dist. Ct. (ea. dist.) Mich. 1985, U.S. Ct. Appeals (2d cir.) 1975, U.S. Ct. Appeals (1st cir.) 1981, U.S. Ct. Appeals (fed. cir.) 1984, U.S. Patent and Trademark Office 1983, U.S. Supreme Ct. 1984. Tech. rep. computer timesharing On-Line Systems Inc., N.Y.C., 1969-70; assoc. Kelley Drye & Warren, N.Y.C., 1973-77, Fish & Neave, N.Y.C., 1977-82; ptnr. Fish & Neave, N.Y.C., 1983—; lectr. (guest) litigation, patent law NYU Sch. Law, 1977, 81—; participating atty. Community Law Offices, N.Y.C., 1974-78; atty. Pro Bono Panel U.S. Dist. Ct. (so. dist.) N.Y., N.Y.C., 1982-84; lectr. Practising Law Inst., N.Y.C., 1984—. Mng. editor NYU Law Sch. Rev. Law, Social Change, 1972-73, contbr. articles to profl. jours. NYU scholar, 1964-68; NSF grad. trainee John Hopkins U., 1968-69; recipient Founder's Day award NYU Sch. Law, 1973; Environ. Law Note Prize, Assn. Trial Lawyers Am. Mem. Assn. Bar City N.Y. (environ. law com. 1978-83, trademarks, unfair competition com. 1983—), N.Y. Women's Bar Assn. (profl. ethics, discipline com. 1981-85), ABA, Am. Chem. Soc., N.Y. Patent, Trademark & Copyright Law Assn. Club: Club at Citicorp Ctr. (N.Y.C.) Office: Fish & Neave 875 3d Ave New York NY

MARTUCCI, CAROL THERESE, insurance agency executive; b. Mastic Beach, N.Y., Apr. 26, 1951; d. Vincent Peter and Carolyn Martha Ann (Garrett) Brunone; m. Richard Louis Martucci, June 7, 1970; children—Richard Louis, Vincent Anthony. Student SUNY-Stony Brook, 1968-70. Lic. property/casualty, life/health ins. agt., broker, Nev. Cosmetician, salesclk. Macy's, Lake Grove, N.Y., 1969-74; personal lines rater Hartford Ins., Reno, 1978-79; sec., agt. EA Stovall Ins., Reno, 1979-81; sec., agt. Valley Oaks Ins. Ctr. (named changed to Granite Hills Ins. Agy.), Reno, 1981-82, owner, pres., 1982—. 1st soprano Moriches Choral Soc., 1968-78; dir. bowling Spl. Olympics, Reno, 1978-82, state event, Las Vegas, 1982. Mem. Ins. Women Reno (v.p. 1980-81, pres. 1981-82), Ind. Ins. Agts. No. Nev., No. Nev. Assn. Life Underwriters. Clubs: Ad Libs Toastmasters (Reno). Home: 2990 Rustic Manor Circle Reno NV 89509 Office: PO Box 12730 1755 E Plumb Ln Suite 101 Reno NV 89510

MARTY, LORI SHELQUIST, medical practice group executive; b. Sioux Falls, S.D., Nov. 8, 1958; d. Virgil W. and Jacqueline D. (Hind) Shelquist; m. Dean A. Marty. B.A., Augustana Coll., 1981. Bus. mgr. Surg. Assocs., Ltd., Sioux Falls, 1981—. Membership vol. S.D. PAC/Am. PAC, Sioux Falls, 1984—; asst. leader Brownie troop Girl Scouts U.S., 1985—; youth leader Springdale Luth. Ch., 1985—; del. Lake Shetek Youth Camp, 1986. Mem. Med. Group Mgmt. Assn., S.D. Med. Group Mgmt. Assn. (sec.-treas. 1984), Sioux Falls Med. Practice Assn. (pres. 1983), Am. Coll. Med. Group Adminstrs. Democrat. Club: Sioux Falls Toastmasters. Avocations: travel, jogging. Office: Surg Assocs Ltd Suite 201 1201 S Euclid Sioux Falls SD 57105

MARTYN-NEMETH, PAMELA ANN, nurse; b. Chgo., Jan. 13, 1956; d. Leonard M. and Kyra V. (Hitz) Martyn; m. John P. Nemeth, Nov. 27, 1982; 1 child, A. Martyn. M.S., U. Mich., 1982. Registered nurse, Ill. Clin. specialist Northwestern Meml. Hosp., Chgo., 1982—; mem. Clin. faculty Northwestern U., Chgo., 1982—; cons. Mem. Am. Soc. Parenteral and Enteral Nutrition, Sigma Theta Tau (rec. sec. 1979-80, Nursing Excellence award 1985).

MARTZ, MIRIAM COBB, data processing executive; b. LaGrange, Ga., Dec. 5, 1938; d. Robert C. and Marie R. Cobb; diploma Marsh Bus. Coll., Atlanta, 1959; div.; 1 dau., Julie. Supr. computer ops. Equafax, Atlanta, 1959-70; mgr. data processing Crum & Forster Ins. Co., Atlanta, 1974-81; owner Accuracy Plus, word processing and data processing service and sch., Alpharetta, Ga., 1981-84; ptnr., ops. mgr. Laser Mail, Norcross, Ga., 1984—. Mem. Nat. Assn. Female Execs. Mem. Unity Truth Ch. Office: 21 N Main St Alpharetta GA 30201

MARUMOTO, BARBARA CHIZUKO, state legislator; b. San Francisco, July 21, 1939; d. Takeo and Kathleen (Tsuchiya) Okamoto; B.A., U. Hawaii, 1971; student U. Calif., 1957-60, UCLA, 1957; children—Marshall, Jay, Wendy, Megan. Legis. aide, researcher, Honolulu, 1972-78; mem. Hawaii Ho. of Reps., 1978—, minority floor leader, 1981; elected del. to Constl. Conv., 1978; real estate agt., 1979—. Mem. exec. bd. Hist. Hawaii Found.; bd. dirs. Pacific council Girl Scouts U.S.A.; active Rep. Party, Common Cause, LWV, PTA, Ripon Soc. Clubs: Honolulu, Jr. League Honolulu. Contbr. various news columns to publs. Office: Capitol Room 322 Honolulu HI 96813

MARVEL, FRANCES JEAN, librarian, travel consultant, real estate manager; b. Ferndale, Calif., July 12, 1933; d. Shirley Allison and Meriam Grace (Soule) Boyd; m. Lee Marvel, Aug. 30, 1953; children—Cheryl Kathleen, Donna Lee, John Emery. B.A. in Bus. Edn., Humboldt State U., 1967, M.A., 1976; postgrad. San Francisco State U., U. So. Oreg., Brigham Young U. Tchr. Arcata High Sch., Calif., 1968-83; librarian McKinleyville High Sch., Calif., 1983-84; pres. Marvel Mgmt. Co., Bayside, Calif., 1980—; travel cons. Sunsets Unltd., Arcata, Calif., 1982—; div. sec. Humboldt State U., 1958-64; sec. Presidio, San Francisco, State Bd. Equalization, Cal Trans div. hwys. Stephen Bufton Meml grantee, 1967. Mem. Arcata High Sch. Faculty Assn., Am. Bus. Women's Assn. (Woman of Yr. 1981), ALA, Nat. Bus. Edn. Assn., Humboldt Hist. Soc., Calif. Scholarship Fedn. (life), Calif. Bus. Educators Assn., Calif. Parent Tchrs. Assn., Humboldt State U. Alumni Assn., NEA, Calif. Media and Library Educators Assn. Democrat. Clubs: Exchangettes, Soroptimists. Home: 1380 Clipper Ln Bayside CA 95524 Office: Marvel Mgmt Co PO Box 112 Bayside CA 95524

MARVIN, HELEN RHYNE, state senator; b. Gastonia, N.C., Nov. 30, 1917; d. Dane S. and Tessie (Hastings) Rhyne; B.A. magna cum laude, Furman U., 1938; M.A., La. State U., 1938; postgrad. Winthrop Coll., U. N.C.-Chapel Hill, U. N.C.-Charlotte, U. Colo., U. Vt., U. Oslo; m. Ned Marvin, Nov. 21, 1941; children—Kathryn Nisbet, Richard Morris, David Rhyne. Part-time instr. polit. sci. Gaston Coll.; pres. Gaston County Democratic Women, 1973-75; mem. Gaston County Dem. Exec. Com., 1973-76; mem. N.C. State Dem. Exec. Com., 1973-76; del. Nat. Dem. Conv., 1972, 84; mem. N.C. Senate, 1977—, vice chairperson edn. com., 1979-82, vice-chairperson law enforcement and crime control com., 1981-82, appropriations com., 1981-82, chmn. congl. redistricting com., 1981-82, constl. amendment com., 1983-84, chmn. legis. study com. on social, econ. and legal needs of women, 1981—, chmn. pensions and retirement com., 1985—, vice chmn. children and youth com., 1985—. Bd. dirs. Gaston County United Way, Gaston County Mental Health Assn., Gaston County Family Planning Council, Gaston County Council for Children with Spl. Needs, Gaston County Cardiac Rehab. Council, Gaston County Children's Council; past mem., sec. So. Piedmont Health Services Agy.; past mem. N.C. State Health Coordinating Council, N.C. State Textbook Commn.; past chairperson N.C. Council on Status of Women, N.C. State Social Services Commn., N.C. Day Care Adv. Council; mem. N.C. Commn. on Yr. 2000; mem. Gov.'s Advocacy Council on Children and Youth; mem. N.C. Apprenticeship Council; trustee Vagabond Sch. Drama, Sacred Heart Coll., Flat Rock Playhouse; mem. bd. N.C. Child Advocacy Inst., N.C. Child Support Council; elder 1st Presbyterian Ch., 1983—. Mem. So. Polit. Sci. Assn., N.C. Polit. Sci. Assn., Delta Kappa Gamma. Club: Altrusa. Office: NC State Legislature Bldg Raleigh NC 27611

MARWELL, EMILY, lawyer; b. Mt. Kisco, N.Y., May 27, 1950; d. Edward Marvin and Grace (Glass) M. A.B. magna cum laude, Radcliffe Coll., 1972; J.D., Catholic U., 1976; cert. Harvard U., 1983. Bar: N.Y. 1977, D.C. 1979. Atty., U.S. Commn. on Civil Rights, Washington, 1977-79, U.S. Office Personnel Mgmt., Washington, 1979-81; spl. asst. to insp. gen. U.S. Treasury Dept., Washington, 1981-84, acting insp. gen., 1984, exec. asst. to gen. counsel, 1985; sr. atty. Office Comptroller of Currency, 1986—. Mem. D.C. Bar Assn.

MARX, GERTIE FLORENTINE, anesthesiologist; b. Frankfurt, Fed. Republic Germany, Feb. 13, 1912; came to U.S., 1937, naturalized, 1943; d. Josef and Elsa (Scheuer) M.; m. Eric P. Reiss, Sept. 26, 1940 (dec. Apr. 1968). Abitur, Gymnasium (Germany), 1931; M.D., U. Bern (Switzerland), 1937. Diplomate Am. Bd. Anesthesiology. Intern, resident Beth Israel Hosp., N.Y.C., 1939-42, attending anesthesiologist, 1942-55; asst., assoc. prof. Albert Einstein Coll. Medicine, Bronx, N.Y., 1955-70, prof. anesthesiology, 1970—; dir. obstetric anesthesia Hosps. affiliated with Albert Einstein Coll. Medicine, 1970—. Editor: Parturition and Perinatology, 1973; Clinical Management of Mother and Newborn, 1979; (with G.M. Bassell) Obstetric Analgesia and Anesthesia, 1980; author: (with L.R. Orkin) Physiology of Obstetric Anesthesia, 1969. Recipient Gold medal Obstetric Anaesthetists Assn. 1980. Fellow Am. Coll. Anesthesiology, Am. Coll. Obstetrics and Gynecology, N.Y. Acad. Medicine; mem. Soc. Obstetric Anesthesia and Perinatology; Am. Soc. Anesthesiology, AMA. Home: 642 A Heritage Village Southbury CT 06488 Office: Albert Einstein Coll Medicine Dept Anesthesiology 1300 Morris Park Ave J 1226 Bronx NY 10461

MARX, GILDA, exercise studio chain executive, clothing company executive, fashion designer; b. Pitts., Nov. 25, 1935; d. Herman and Ruth (Small) Wilstein; m. Leo N. Guzik, 1955 (div.); children—Laura Lynn, Mitchell Allan; m. 2d Robert Stuart Marx, June 30, 1973. Student Los Angeles City Coll., 1953-55. Founder, owner, operator Gilda's of Encino (name changed to Body Design By Gilda), Encino, Calif., 1960—, also Los Angeles, N.Y.C., Manhasset, N.Y., Stamford, Conn., Washington; founder, v.p., head designer Flexatard, Inc., Los Angeles, 1976—, Gild Marx Swimwear, 1984—, GMI Cycle-Wear, 1985—, Body, 1985—. Trustee, City of Hope, Scripps Clinic. Author: Body Design By Gilda Studios, Inc. Training Manual, 1979; Body by Gilda—Redesign Every Line, 1984; contbr. numerous articles to Harpers, Vogue, Glamour, Mademoiselle, McCalls, N.Y. Times, Cosmopolitan, others. Recipient award of Merit Bullocks Wilshire-Children's Home Soc., 1977; Fashion Design award Bullocks Wilshire, 1980; Woman of Yr. Spirit of Life award City of Hope, 1984; named Calif. Designer of Yr., Atlanta Apparel Mart, 1984; Legend of Aerobics award, 1985; 60 Distination award Woman Exec. and Entrepeneur, Savvy mag., 1984, 85. Mem. The Fashion Group, Blue Ribbon Soc. of Los Angeles Music Ctr. Democrat. Jewish. Clubs: The Women's Guild. Office: Flexatard Inc 11755 Exposition Blvd Los Angeles CA 90064

MARXER, DONNA, graphic design company executive; b. Miami, Fla., Apr. 15, 1934; d. Robert William and Kathryn Alice (Schmidt) M.; m. John David Rafferty, May 30, 1981; stepchildren—David, Colin, Brendan, Brian. B.Design, U. Fla., 1954; M.A., Tchrs. Coll., Columbia U., 1958; grad. Am. Women's Econ. Devel. Corp., 1983. Asst. art dir. Ruder & Finn Graphics, 1960-63; art dir. Zeneth Eidel Assocs., 1964-66; free-lance art dir., designer, N.Y.C., 1966-81; founder, pres. On Paper, N.Y.C., 1981—; lectr. on art, design to colls., univs., profl. orgns. Clients include Life, Money and People mags., N.Y. Times Book Rev., Internat. Paper Co., Renault Corp., Hill & Knowlton, Celanese, ABC, CBS; exhibited paintings in one-woman shows, including: York Gallery, N.Y.C., 1967, 20th Century Gallery, Williamsburg, Va., 1976, Marden Fine Arts, N.Y.C., 1979; group shows include: Bklyn. Mus., 1975, Summit Gallery, N.Y.C., 1977; represented in permanent collections. Author, illustrator: The Boatcook, 1983; contbr. to Arts, S.W. Art, Sail, Crusing World. Mem. Women in Design (pres. N.Y. chpt. 1982-83), Soc. Illustrators, Type Dirs. Club, Am. Inst. Graphic Artists. Office: On Paper 12 E 46th St New York NY 10017

MASARANI, MARCELIA CRUZ, gemologist; b. Baliwag, Bulacan, Philippines, Aug. 30, 1949; came to U.S., 1973, naturalized, 1982; d. Lazaro Alamazar Cruz and Petronila Labao Jimenez Cruz; B.S. in Bus. Adminstrn., St. Theresa's Coll., Quezon City, 1972; postgrad. child psychology, Columbia U., 1973; diploma in gemology Gemological Inst. Am., 1974; m. Fathi Masarani, Nov. 22, 1979. Jewelry appraiser P.J. Cruz Pawnshop, Manila, 1969-71; loan processor, bookkeeper First Nat. City Bank, Makati, 1972-73; gemologist, saleswoman Rupperthal-Am., Ltd., N.Y.C., 1974-75; head colored stone and gem identification dept., diamond grader, lectr. Gemological Inst. Am., 1975-78; gemologist, saleswoman, diamond grader, buying cons. Diaco Internat., N.Y.C., 1978—; instr., cons. in field. Mem. Am. Gem Soc., Nat. Assn. Female Execs., Coalition Asian-Am. Pacific Women. Club: N.Y. Health and Racquet. Office: 1185 Ave Americas New York NY 10036

MASENG, MARI, government official; b. Chgo., Mar. 15, 1954; d. Leif Eric and Betty (Hagen) M.; B.A. in Journalism, U. S.C., 1975. Reporter, Charleston (S.C.) Eve. Post, 1976-78; polit. aide various Republican senatorial and presdl. campaigns, 1978-80; presdl. speechwriter, 1981-83; asst. sec. pub. affairs U.S. Dept. Transp., 1983-85; v.p., dir. corp. relations Beatrice Co., Chgo., 1985-86; dir. pub. liaison communications dept. White House, Washington, 1986—. Mem. U. S.C. Alumni Assn., Women's Transp. Seminar, Sigma Delta Chi, Chi Omega. Presbyterian. Office: Communications Dept White House Office 1600 Pennsylvania Ave NW Washington DC 20500*

MASI, JANE VIRGINIA, marketing and sales consultant; b. N.Y.C., June 6, 1947; d. Vincent Joseph and Virginia Marie (Beddow) Masi; m. Charles Walter Friedman, Feb. 14, 1976. B.A. in Communications and Psychology, Mercy Coll., N.Y., 1969; M.A., New Sch. Social Research, 1979, now Ph.D. candidate. Asst. sales mgr. Chevron Chem., N.Y.C., 1969-71; writer, 1973-75; ptnr. Masi-D'Angelo Constrn. and Devel. Assocs., N.Y.C., 1979-83; pres., founder Beddow Mills Inc., N.Y.C., 1982-85, Beddow Mfg. Ind., 1983-85; co-pres. TRS Mktg. Inc., N.Y.C., 1985—; founder Energy Works, 1985. Author 38 novellas. N.Y. Regents scholar, 1965-69. Mem., Trans-Species Unltd., N.Y. Avicultural Soc. (co-founder), Soc. Ethical Treatment of Animals. Avocations: woodworking; carpentry; animal rights; design psychology. Office: TRS Mktg Inc 295 Fifth Ave New York NY 10016

MASIN, HELEN LOUISE, physical therapist; b. Berwyn, Ill., July 23, 1948; d. John Luton and Mary Louise (Fahy) M. B.S., NYU, 1970; M.M.Sc., Emory U., 1977. Pediatric phys. therapist Hope Ctr., Temple Hills, Md., 1979. Prince Georges County Pub. Schs., Forestville, Md., 1979-80; dir. phys. therapy Mailman Ctr. for Child Devel., U. Miami (Fla.), 1980-82, cons. phys. therapist, 1982-85, dir. phys. therapy, 1985—; dir. pediatric rehab. Ctr. for Phys. Rehab., Hollywood, Fla., 1982-85. Active Women's Profl. Network, Hollywood, 1982-83. Served with USPHS, summer 1969. Emory U. grad. sch. trainee, 1976-77; NYU univ. scholar, 1966-70. Mem. Am. Phys. Therapy Assn., World Confedn. Phys. Therapy, Perinatal Network. Democrat. Episcopalian. Club: Savant. Researcher in field. Office: Mailman Ctr for Child Devel PO Box 016820 Hollywood FL 33101

MASK, ROSE MARY, reading specialist; b. Newport News, Va., Nov. 1, 1955; d. Curtis Van and Mary Ella (Pearson) M. B.A., Utica Coll. of Syracuse U., 1976; M.S., Morgan State U., 1984. Cert. tchr., N.Y., Ohio, Md. Asst. Liberty Street Day Care, Newburgh, N.Y., 1969; jr. counselor Neighborhood Youth Corps, Newburgh, 1974; tutor, counselor Higher Edn. Opportunity Program, Utica, N.Y., 1976; tchr. English Balt. Pub. Schs., 1977-79; police agt. Balt. Police Dept., 1979—; reading clinician Towson State U., Balt., 1984; reading tutor Utica Free Acad., 1975. Counselor YWCA, Utica, 1974. Recipient award Merit Sonitrol Security Systems, 1983; Ottawa Found. grantee, 1973, Higher Edn. Opportunity Program, Utica Coll. grantee, 1973. Mem. Vanguard Justice Soc. (sec. 1980-82), Alpha Kappa Alpha, NAACP. Democrat. Baptist. Avocations: reading; sewing; singing; dancing; tennis.

MASKER, AUDREY HILDA, marketing research executive; b. St. Louis, July 19, 1933; d. Henry Ernst and Vera Lucille (Vennemann) Kuhlman; m. Donald Ray Masker, May 29, 1959 (div. June 1974); children—David Ray, Steven Grant. B.S. in Edn., Southeast Mo. State U., Cape Girardeau, 1959. Research asst. Doane Agrl. Services, St. Louis, 1974-77, project analyst, 1977-79, multiclient coordinator, 1979-80; prodn. mgr., project dir. Doane-Western Inc., St. Louis, 1980-82; research services mgr. Doane Mktg. Research Inc., St. Louis, 1982—. Mem. Nat. Assn. Female Execs. Lutheran. Club: Friendship Circles (treas. 1963-65) (St. Louis). Home: 11080 Golf Crest Dr Saint Louis MO 63126 Office: Doane Marketing Research Inc 12140 Woodcrest Executive Dr Saint Louis MO 63141

MASLONA, HALINA A., accounting executive; b. Sieradz, Poland, Apr. 26, 1957; came to U.S., 1966, naturalized, 1979; d. John and Anna (Banas) Krzyminski; m. George John Maslona, Apr. 28, 1979. B.S., U. Ill.-Chgo., 1979. C.P.A., Ill. Staff acct. Chgo. Coll. Osteo. Medicine, 1979-81, sr. acct., 1981-83, asst. mgr. of 3d party reimbursement, 1983-84; acctg. mgr. Southeastern Coll. Osteo. Medicine, North Miami Beach, Fla., 1984—. Mem. Am. Inst. C.P.A.s, Nat. Assn. Coll. and Univ. Bus. Officers, Nat. Assn. Female Execs. Democrat. Roman Catholic. Avocations: reading; needlepoint; aerobics. Home: 6600 Cypress Rd Apt 110 Plantation FL 33317 Office: Southeastern Coll. Osteo. Medicine 1750 NE 168th St North Miami Beach FL 33162

MASLOW, MELANIE JANE, physician; b. N.Y.C., Mar. 11, 1952; d. Morris and Rosalie (Kaufman) Schwartz; m. James Edward Maslow, June 17, 1973 (div. 1977); m. David Tice, Sept. 12, 1985. B.A., Barnard Coll., 1973; M.D., NYU, 1977. Diplomate Am. Bd. Internal Medicine. Intern NYU Med. Ctr.-Manhattan VA Hosp., N.Y.C., 1977-78, resident, chief resident, 1978-81, fellow, 1981-83; co-physician-in-charge infectious disease L.I. Coll. Hosp., Bklyn., 1983—; asst. prof. medicine SUNY-Downstate Med. Ctr. Mem. ACP, Am. Soc. for Microbiology, N.Y. Acad. Sci. Democrat. Jewish. Office: Long Island Coll Hosp 340 Henry St Brooklyn NY 11201

MASON, AIMEE HUNNICUTT ROMBERGER, retired educator; b. Atlanta, Nov. 3, 1918; d. Edwin William and Aimee Greenleaf (Hunnicutt) Romberger; B.A., Conn. Coll., 1940; postgrad. Emory U., 1946-48; M.A., U. Fla., 1979, Ph.D., 1980; M.A., Stetson U., 1968; m. Samuel Venable Mason, Aug. 16, 1941; children—Olivia Elizabeth (Mrs. James Butcher), Christopher Leeds. Jr. exec., merchandising G. Fox & Co., Hartford, Conn., 1940-41; air traffic controller CAA, Atlanta, 1942; partner Coronado Concrete Products, New Smyrna Beach, Fla., 1953-81; adj. faculty Valencia Jr. Coll., Orlando, Fla., 1969; instr. philosophy and humanities Seminole Community Coll., Sanford, from 1969, now ret. Area cons. ARC, 1947-50; del. Nat. Red Cross, Washington, 1949; founding mem. St. Joseph Hosp. Aux., Atlanta, 1950-53; v.p., treas. New Smyrna Beach PTA 1955-60. Bd. dirs. Atlanta Symphony Orch., Fla. Symphony Orch., 1954-59. Served to lt. USCGR, 1943-46. Recipient award in graphics Nat. Assn. Women Artists, 1939, 41, Golden Hatter award Stetson U., 1973, 74. Mem. Am. Philos. Assn., AAUP, AAUW (founding mem. New Smyrna Beach, exec. bd. 1984-85, chmn. scholarship com. 1984—), Fla. Philos. Assn. (exec. council 1978-79), Collegium Phenomenologicum, Soc. Existential and Phenomenological Philosophy, Soc. Phenomenology in Human Scis., Merleau-Ponty Circle, Fla. Assn. Community Colls. Home: 2103 Ocean Dr New Smyrna Beach FL 32069

MASON, BOBBIE ANN, novelist, educator; b. Mayfield, Ky., 1940; married. B.A., U. Ky.; M.A., SUNY-Binghamton; Ph.D., U. Conn. Asst. prof. English and journalism, Mansfield State Coll., Pa. Author: Nabokov's Garden, 1974; Shiloh and Other Stories, 1982 (Ernest Hemingway award, Nat. Book Critic's Circle award nominee, Am. Book award nominee, PEN Faulkner award nominee). Contbr. regularly: The New Yorker, 1980—. Contbr. articles to: The Atlantic, Redbook, Vanity Fair, N.Am. Rev., Va. Quar. Rev.,; contbr. works: Best American Short Stories, 1981; The Pushcart Prize: Best of the Small Presses, 1983; Best American Short Stories, 1983. Pa. Arts Council grantee, 1983; Guggenheim fellow, 1984; Am. Acad. and Inst. grantee in lit., 1984. Address: Box 340-C RD #1 Metztown PA 19539

MASON, CAROLYN, automobile club executive, psychotherapist, consultant; b. Buffalo, July 1, 1927; children—Gilbert D. Sylva, Nickolas A. Sylva, Christopher D. Mason. B.A., George Williams Coll., 1976, M.S.W., 1978; Ph.D., Southeastern U., 1980. Cert. clin. social worker. Pvt. practice psychotherapist, Oakbrook Terrace, Ill., 1973-79; v.p. human resources AAA/Chgo. Motor Club, Chgo., 1980—; cons. Chgo., Milw., 1975—. Author: Synthesis of Physiology and Psychology: Toward Wholism, 1978; artist retrospective aquatints (1st place Ill. Sesquicentennial, 1976). Co-founder All the Way House, Lombard, 1970. AAUW scholar, 1978, Hinsdale Bus. and Profl. Womens Assn. scholar, 1978; winner 1st place Oakbrook Artists Invitational, 1977. Mem. Am. Mgmt. Assn., Am. Assn. Tng. and Devel., AAUP. Democrat. Roman Catholic. Office: AAA Chicago Motor Club 66 E South Water St Chicago IL 60601

MASON, COLLEEN SUZANNE, medical technologist; b. San Diego, Mar. 8, 1952; d. Albert Michael and Pauline (Whitaker) Ross; student San Diego State U., 1970-72; B.S., Calif. Poly. Inst., 1975; M.S., U. Calif., Dominguez Hills, 1980; m. Alan James Mason, Apr. 8, 1972; children—Danielle Christine, Jennifer Suzanne. Med. technology trainee City of Hope Med. Center, Duarte, Calif., 1974-75; med. technologist U. Calif., Irvine, 1975-76, City of Hope Med. Center, Duarte, 1976-77; sr. med. technologist Victor Valley Hosp., Victorville, Calif., 1977-83; SBB intern San Bernardino Blood Bank (Calif.), 1984-85, PM supr., 1986—, dir. processing lab., 1986—; PM supr. San Bernardino Community Hosp., 1985-86. Recipient Outstanding Student award Calif. Poly. Inst., 1974. Mem. Am. Soc. Clin. Pathologists, Calif. Soc. Med. Technologists, Am. Soc. Med. Technologists, Beta Beta Beta, Phi Kappa Phi. Office: 399 Blood Bank Rd San Bernardino CA 92412

MASON, DEBBIE A., hospital marketing director, consultant; b. Perry, Fla., Nov. 24, 1959; d. Nathaniel Joseph and Verlyn (Tedder) M. B.S., U. Fla., 1981. Campus donor cons. Civitan Regional Blood Ctr., Gainesville, Fla., 1981-82; asst. promotion dir. Oaks Mall, Gainesville, 1982-83; dir. pub. relations Port St. Lucie Hosp., Fla., 1983-84, dir. mktg., 1984-85; dir. mktg. Martin Meml. Hosp., Stuart, Fla., 1985—; cons. Images Too, Port St. Lucie, 1984—. Author, producer direct mail piece: Emergency, 1985 (1st place award 1985), in-house publ.: Patient Information, 1984 (1st place award 1984). Dir. St. Lucie County United Way, 1984—, St. Lucie County Cancer Soc., 1985—. Leadership Fla. grad. Fla. C. of C., 1985. Mem. Pub. Relations Soc. Am. (task force 1985—), Am. Mktg. Assn., Fla. Hosp. Assn. (coms.), Nat. Assn. Female Execs., Am. Bus. Women Assn., Women in Communications, St. Lucie County C. of C. (dir. 1985—), Port St. Lucie C. of C. (dir. 1984—), U. Fla. Alumni Martin County (dir. 1985—). Republican. Methodist. Club: Gator Club of St. Lucie County. Avocations: Sailing; reading; skiing; swimming. Office: Martin Memorial Hospital PO Bin 2396 Stuart FL 33495

MASON, ELIZABETH JANE, educational administrator, consultant; b. Uniontown, Pa., Aug. 22, 1935; d. William Sherman and Margaret Catherine (Luman) M.; B.S. in Nursing, U. Pitts., 1959; M.S., Wayne State U., 1962; Ph.D. (USPHS predoctoral nurse fellow 1970-72), U. Wis., Madison, 1972; Instr. med.-surg. nursing U. Pitts., 1962-66; asst. prof. med.-surg. nursing U. Wis., Madison, 1966-70; assoc. prof. med.-surg. nursing and ednl. planning and devel. Va. Commonwealth U., Richmond, 1972-76; asst. dir. undergrad. edn. Ohio State U., Columbus, 1976-80; program dir. grad. program in nursing adminstrn. edn. U. Pitts., 1980-85; cons. nursing standards, quality assurance, pricing of nursing care. Mem. Am. Nurses Assn., Council Nurse Researchers, Am. Ednl. Researchers Assn., Pi Lambda Theta, Sigma Theta Tau. Author: How to Write Meaningful Nursing Standards, 1978, 2d edit., 1984.

MASON, GLADYS, accountant, cattlewoman; b. Camden, Ala., Aug. 11, 1951; d. William Jasper and Ida Cornelia (Bowman) M. B.S., Livingston U., 1973. Clk. Wilcox County Commn., Ala., 1973-75, chief clk., 1975-84; acct. James Bonner Real Estate, Camden, Ala., 1984—; co-ptnr. M-Z Red Angus Farm, Grampion Hills, Camden, 1983—; mem. exec. com. Ala. Assn. County Commns. Clks. and Adminstrs., 1983-84. County chmn. Jim Folsom U.S. Senate Campaign, Montgomery, Ala., 1980; pres. Baptist Young Women, Enon Bapt. Ch., Camden, 1985-86; clk. Pine Barren Bapt. Assn., Wilcox and Monroe counties, Ala., 1984-86. Named to Outstanding Young Women Am. 1983, 84. Mem. Camden Study Forum, Livingston U. Nat. Alumni Assn. (v.p. 1979-81, pres. 1981-83), Wilcox County Livingston U. Alumni Assn. (pres. 1976-83), Wilcox County Cattlemen's Assn., Ala. Cattlemen's Assn., Zeta Tau Alpha (chpt. sec. 1972). Democrat. Home: Route 2 Box 327 Camden AL 36726

MASON, JANE ELIZABETH, confectionery mfg. co. exec.; b. Chgo., Oct. 21, 1924; d. Albert Eugene and Mary Ellen (Egan) Paque; student Ohio State U., 1942-43, Triton Coll., 1954-55; student exec. course U. Chgo., 1953; m. James Thomas Mason, Sept. 8, 1945 (dec.); 1 dau., Dale Anne. Editor, Elmwood Park (Ill.) Herald, 1943-45; sec. Standard Wire Draw, Chgo., 1945-46; owner, operator secretarial and ghostwriting service, Chgo., 1946-49; sec. Leaf Confectionery, Inc., Chgo., 1949-54, asst. sales mgr., 1955-59, dir. sales, 1960—, gen. mgr. U.S. Chewing Gum Co. subs. Leaf Confectionery, Inc., Chgo., 1981—; mgr. nat. accounts Leaf Inc., 1986—; speaker to industry groups. Vol. for battered wives, 1970—, LaRibida Children's Hosp., Chgo., Spl. Olympics, Chgo.; election judge Democratic Party, Oak Park, Ill. Named Salesman of Yr., Hotel Corp. Am., 1963, Newsmaker of Yr., Billboard Pub. Co., 1959; recipient cert. Optimist Clubs, 1968. Mem. Nat. Bulk Vendors Assn. (Exec. Sec. award 1961, 64, 68, nat. pres. 1981—), Nat. Candy Wholesaler's Assn., Nat. Automatic Merchandising Assn. (asso.), Nat. Candy Brokers Assn. (asso.), Nat. Secs. Assn., Women's Share (Ill. Speakers Bur.). Roman Catholic. Club: Bus. and Profl. Women (Woman of Achievement award). Founder and dir. Tasters Club, children's consumer testing group Leaf Confectionery, Inc., 1980—. Office: 1155 N Cicero Ave Chicago IL 60651

MASON, JANE SOMMER, computer company executive; b. Chgo., Jan. 12, 1928; d. Armand and Leah (Bottigheimer) Sommer; m. Arthur K. Mason, July 5, 1953; children—Kent A., Thomas B., Peggy. A.M., U. Chgo., 1950; postgrad. George Washington U., 1980-82. Owner, dir. Cellar Art Scene, Bethesda, Md., 1965-82; dir. edn. ctr. Computer Workshop, Rockville, Md., 1982; owner, pres. Computer-Ease, Inc., Washington, 1983—; cons. in field of computers. Mem. Assn. for Women in Computing (publicity v.p. Nat. Capital chpt. 1983-84). Home: 1815 Kalorama Sq NW Washington DC 20008 Office: Computer-Ease Inc 5100 Wisconsin Ave NW Washington DC 20016

MASON, JOAN ELLEN, nurse; b. Reading, Pa., June 29, 1947; d. Richard Lenhart and Mary Jane (Miller) Fritz; m. W. Davis Mason, Feb. 12, 1977. R.N., Temple U. Hosp. Sch. Nursing, 1968; B.S. in Nursing Edn., Temple U., 1971, Ed.M. in Health Edn., 1981; postgrad. U. Pa. Staff nurse Temple U. Hosp., 1968-71; nursing instr. Phila. Gen. Hosp. Sch. Nursing, 1971-76; coordinator staff devel. Meml. Hosp., Roxborough, Phila., 1976-84; clin. editor Springhouse Corp., Pa., 1984—; instr. cardiopulmonary resuscitation Am. Heart Assn. Co-developer patient edn. workshop; developer self-learning packages for orientation, continuing edn. programs; author workbook: Assertiveness: Skills for Women on Becoming Assertive. Mem. Am. Nurses Assn., Pa. Nurses Assn. (mem. continuing edn. approval panel), Delaware Valley Inservice Assn. (mem. steering com.), Temple U. Nurses Alumni Assn., Am. Assn. Critical-Care Nurses (council continuing edn.), Phila. Hist. Soc. (dir., house tour com., v.p.), Franklin Inst., Phila. Mus. Art, U. City Arts League, Spruce Hill Community Assn. Republican. Home: 430 S 42d St Philadelphia PA 19104 Office: 1111 Bethlehem Pike Springhouse PA 19477

MASON, JOANNE ELISSA, coordinator corporate events, realtor, consultant; b. Troy, N.Y., May 10, 1952; d. William Charles and Veronica Laverna (Harris) Whitney; m. Thomas August Zink, July 17, 1970 (div. 1971); m. Robert L. Mason, May 4, 1974. Diploma, Albany Inst. Banking, 1977, Jim Russell Internat. Sch. Racing, Can., 1978. Accredited by Rensselaer County Bd. Realtors, N.Y. Operator, N.Y. Telephone, Albany, 1970-71; acting mgr. Bankers Trust Co., Albany, 1971-79; owner, mgr. Bob Mason Enterprises, East Greenbush, N.Y., 1973-85; salesperson Gillespie Real Estate, East Greenbush, 1978—; events coordinator Surplus Freight, Inc., Albany, 1985—; cons. Gasoline Retailers Assn., 1981-84. Contbr. articles to popular mags. Registrar Nassau Women's Rep. Club, 1968-69. Recipient Pyramid Club award Bankers Trust Co., 1971. Share the Spirit award Bankers Trust Co., 1976, numerous 1st pl. racing awards from racing orgns., 1973—. Mem. Nat. Council Corvette Clubs (regional competition dir. 1983—, founder, chmn. Interclub Assn. 1984—, hold nat. drag race records and regional competition awards), Tri-Vettes, Ltd. (social dir. 1976-80, gov. 1979—, editor Corvette Courier 1979—, author East Region Corvette Jubilee Program 1984-85, Corvette Jubilee award 1984). Methodist. Home: 3 Apricot Ct Clifton Park NY 12065

MASON, LUCILE GERTRUDE, fund raiser, consultant; b. Montclair, N.J., Aug. 1, 1925; d. Mayne Seguine and Rachel (Entorf) M. A.B., Smith Coll., 1947; M.A., NYU, 1968, 76. Editor, ABC, N.Y.C., 1947-51; asst. casting dir. Compton Advt., Inc., N.Y.C., 1951-55, casting dir. dept. head, 1955-65; conf. mgr. Camp Fire Girls, Inc., N.Y.C., 1965-66; exec. dir. Assn. of Jr. Leagues of Am. Inc., N.Y.C., 1966-68; dir. div. pub. affairs Girl Scouts of U.S.A., N.Y.C., 1969-71; dir. pub. relations YWCA of City of N.Y., 1971-73; dir. community relations and devel. Girl Scout Council of Greater N.Y., N.Y.C., 1973-76; dir. devel. Montclair Kimberley Acad., Montclair, N.J., 1976-78, Ethical Culture Schs., N.Y.C. and Riverdale, N.Y., 1978-80; pres. Lucile Mason & Assocs., Montclair, 1980-83; devel. officer founds. and corps. Fairleigh Dickinson U., Rutherford, N.J., 1983-85; dir. devel. Whole Theatre, Inc., Montclair, N.J., 1985-86. Bd. counselors Smith Coll., 1964-74, chmn. theatre com., 1969-74, exec. com. bd. counselors, 1969-74. Mem. Am. Women in Radio and TV (pres. N.Y.C. chpt. 1955-56), Community Agys. Pub. Relations Assn. (membership chmn. 1973-76), Nat. Soc. Fund Raising Execs. (dir. N.J. chpt. 1983—). Home: 142 N Mountain Ave Montclair NJ 07042

MASON, MARGARET PENDLETON PEARSON, lawyer; b. Radford, Va., Mar. 6, 1944; d. Charles Almond, Jr. and Margaret (Keller) Pearson; m. Charles Taft Mason, Jr., Sept. 7, 1963; children—Sarah St. Clair, Amy Grey. Student Randolph-Macon Woman's Coll., 1962-63; B.A., Goucher Coll., 1975; J.D., Yale U., 1978. Bar: Conn., 1978, U.S. Dist. Ct. Conn., 1978, U.S. Ct. Appeals (2d cir.) 1980, U.S. Supreme Ct., 1982. Mem. firm Tyler Cooper & Alcorn, New Haven, 1978—; sec. Weaver Bros., Inc., Washington, 1963-66; dir. Madison & Madison, Inc., Bethany, Conn., 1976—. Sec. Haddonfield (N.J.) Fortnightly, 1970-72; dir. Del. Valley Citizens Council Clean Air, Phila., 1970-72; mem. Democratic Town Com., 1980-82. Danforth Found. fellow, 1975; Eleanor Voss fellow Goucher Coll./Voss Trust, 1975; NSF grantee, 1973. Mem. ABA, Conn. Bar Assn., New Haven County Bar Assn. (dir. 1980—), Conn. Def. Lawyers Assn. (mem. com.). Democrat. Lutheran. Office: Tyler Cooper & Alcorn 205 Church St PO Box 1936 New Haven CT 06509

MASON, MARILYN GELL, library administrator, writer; b. Chickasha, Okla., Aug. 23, 1944; d. Emmett D. and Dorothy (O'Bar) Killebrew; m. Carl L. Gell, Dec. 29, 1965 (div. Oct. 1978); 1 son, Charles E.; m. Robert M. Mason, July 17, 1981. B.A., U. Dallas, 1966; M.L.S., North Tex. State U., Denton, 1968; M.P.A., Harvard U., 1978. Librarian, N.J. State Library, Trenton, 1968-69; dept. head Arlington County Pub. Library, Arlington, Va., 1969-73; chief library program Metro Washington Council of Govts., 1973-77; dir. White House Conf. on Library and Info. Service, Washington, 1979-80; v.p. Metrics Research Corp., Atlanta, 1981—; dir. Atlanta-Fulton Pub. Library, Atlanta, 1982—; Evalene Parsons Jackson lectr. Div. Librarianship, Emory U., Atlanta, 1981. Author: The Federal Role in Library and Information Services, 1983; editor: Survey of Libeary Automation in the Metro Washington Area, 1977. Bd. visitors Sch. Info. Studies, Syracuse U., 1981—, Sch. Library and Info. Sci., U. Tenn., Knoxville, 1983-85. Recipient Disting. Alumna award N. Tex. State U., 1979. Mem. ALA, Am. Assn. Info. Scis., Ga. Library Assn., D.C. Library Assn. (pres. 1976-77). Office: Atlanta Fulton Pub Library 1 Margaret Mitchell Square Atlanta GA 30303

MASON, MARSHA, actress; b. St. Louis, Apr. 3, 1942; d. James and Jacqueline M.; m. Gary Campbell, 1964 (div.); m. Neil Simon, Oct. 25, 1973 (div. 1983). Grad., Webster (Mo.) Coll. Mem.: cast Broadway and nat. tour Cactus Flower, 1968; other stage appearances include The Deer Park, 1967, The Indian Wants the Bronx, 1968, Happy Birthday, Wanda June, 1970, Private Lives, 1971, You Can't Take It With You, 1972, Cyrano de Bergerac, 1972, A Doll's House, 1972, The Crucible, 1972, The Good Doctor, 1973, King Richard III, 1974, Mary Stuart, Ahmanson Theatre, Los Angeles, 1980-81, Old Times, 1983-84, Twelfth Night, Old Globe Theatre, San Diego, 1983; film appearances include Blume in Love, 1973, Cinderella Liberty, 1973, Audrey Rose, 1977, The Goodbye Girl, 1977, Promises in the Dark, 1979, Chapter Two, 1979, Only When I Laugh, 1981, Max Dugan Returns, 1983. TV credits include; daytime series Cyrano de Bergerac, 1974, films The Good Doctor, 1978, The Cheap Detective, 1978, Lois Gibbs and the Love Canal, 1982, Surviving, 1985, Trapped in Silence, 1982. Recipient Golden Globe award for Cinderella Liberty, 1974, The Goodbye Girl 1978. Address: care Creative Artists Agy Inc Suite 1400 Los Angeles CA 90067

MASON, SANDRA ATKINSON, government contract negotiator; b. Newport News, Va., Oct. 18, 1951; d. George W. and Hula Grey (Bynum) Atkinson; B.A., Dillard U., New Orleans, 1973. Mgmt. auditor GAO, N.Y.C., 1973-75; auditor Dept. Energy, N.Y.C., Houston and Los Angeles, 1974-80; contract auditor Def. Contract Audit Agy., Los Angeles, 1980-82; contract price analyst Dept. Air Force, 1982-85, contract negotiator, 1985-86. Mem. Phi Gamma Nu, Delta Theta Phi.

MASON, TRUDY LEA, public transportation, government official; b. Bklyn., June 27, 1942; d. Sidney and Frances (Poel) M. B.A., cum laude, Wheaton Coll., Norton, Mass., 1963; postgrad. Columbia U., NYU. Asst. supr. N.Y. World's Fair Info. Ctr., 1963-64; asst. mgr. publicity and promotion Praeger Pubs., N.Y.C., 1964-65; asst. to pres. N.Y. City Council, 1966-70, community affairs cons., 1970-72; dep. asst. adminstr. N.Y.C. Econ. Devel. Adminstrn., 1972-76; dep. dir. N.Y.C. Mayor's Office of Service Coordination, 1976-78; dir. govt. affairs and community relations Met. Transp. Authority, N.Y.C., 1978—. Mem. N.Y.C. Commn. on Status of Women, 1982—; adv. bd. N.Y.C. Dept. Records and Info. Services, 1980—; mem. adv. bd. Marymount Manhattan Coll. Lifelong Learning Ctr., 1981—; New York County coordinator Carter/Mondale Campaign, 1980; N.Y. adv. com. Women's Campaign Fund, 1981—; mem. Met. council Am. Jewish Congress; mem. Nat. Women's Polit. Caucus. Mem. Am. Pub. Transit Assn. (vice chair women in transit com. 1984—), N.Y. Women's Transp. Seminar (exec. bd. 1982—), N.Y. Women in Communications, Am. Polit. Items Collectors (exec. bd. 1983—), 1979), Pub. Relations Officers Soc., Mcpl. Art Soc., N.Y. Press Club. Club: Bklyn. Jr. League. Home: 205 E 78th St New York NY 10021

MASON, VICTORIA ANNE, vocational and rehabilitation consultant; b. Seattle, Sept. 19, 1948; d. Gerald William and Barbara Lou (Stertz) Mason; m. Roy D. Larsen, Feb. 14, 1976; children—Matthew Evald, Katherine Janette. B.A., U. Tex., 1970; M.S., U. Wis.-Stout, 1974. Cert. rehab. counselor, vocat. evaluation specialist. Vocat. evaluator Dallas Rehab. Inst., 1974-75; chief vocat. evaluator North Tex. State U., Denton, 1975-77; pres. RSA, Inc., Dallas, 1978-81; cons. trainer McCarron-Dial Systems, Dallas, 1979—; asst. instr. U. Tex. Health Sci. Ctr., Dallas, 1981-83; pvt. practice vocat. and rehab. cons., Austin, Tex., 1977—; sec., dir. Commn. Cert. of Work Adjustment and Vocat. Evaluation Specialists, Chgo., 1981-83; vocat. cons. Office of Hearing and Appeals, SSA, Dallas, 1978—. Contbr. articles to profl. jours. Mem. Tex. Rehab. Assn. (sec. 1978-79, Presdl. Meritorious Service award 1978), Vocat. Evaluation and Work Adjustment Assn. (sec. 1976-77), Tex. Assn. Rehab. Profls. in Pvt. Sector (v.p. 1983-84, pres. 1984-85). Democrat. Episcopalian. Home and Office: 6804 Rearden Rd Austin TX 78745

MASQUELETTE, MELISSA FANCHER, self-employed; b. Canton, Miss., Sept. 29, 1955; d. Joseph Roderick, Jr., and Elsie (Robinson) Fancher; m. Philip Edward Masquelette, Nov. 25, 1978; child, Grace Fancher. B.B.A., U. Miss., 1977. C.P.A., Tex., Miss. Sr. auditor Arthur Andersen & Co., Houston, 1977-81; sect. supr. Superior Oil Co., Houston, 1981-85. Active Republican polit. campaigns. Mem. Tex. Soc. C.P.A.s, Miss. Soc. C.P.A.s, DAR, Beta Alpha Psi, Beta Gamma Sigma, Phi Kappa Phi, Alpha Lambda Delta, Chi Omega. Episcopalian. Home: 4027 Branard St Houston TX 77027

MASSENGILL, ELLEN WEBB, librarian; b. Littlefield, Tex., Mar. 6, 1932; d. Lester L. and Bessie (Webb) M.; B.S., Tex. Tech U., 1953, M.S., 1959; M.A., North Tex. State U., 1969. Homemaking tchr., Floyd, N.Mex., 1953-55, Crane, Tex., 1955-56, Seminole, Tex., 1956-68, Littlefield, Tex., 1971-73; librarian Odessa (Tex.) High Sch., 1969-71, Littlefield Jr. High Sch., 1973-82, Littlefield Ind. Sch. Dist., 1982-83, Littlefield High Sch. and Jr. High Sch., 1983-84, Littlefield High Sch., 1984—; dist., area, state adv. bd. mem. Future Homemakers Am., N.Mex., Tex., 1954-68, adv. mem. nat. exec. council, 1954-55; adv. Young Homemakers Tex., 1958-73; co-leader Girl Scouts U.S.A., 1948-49; del. Nat. Citizenship Council, 1954. Recipient Home Econs. Scholarship award Borden Co., 1953, Panhellenic award Lubbock (Tex.) Panhellenic Soc., 1953; Forum award Tex. Tech. U., 1953. Mem. AAUW (reporter, historian, sec., parliamentarian 1956-68), Sch. Library and Info. Sci. Assn., NEA, Am. Home Econs. Assn., Am. Vocat. Assn., PTA, Tex. State Tchrs. Assn. (life), ALA, Tex. Library Assn. (life; sec. dist. 9), Tex. Classroom Tchrs. Assn., Vocat. Homemaking Tchrs. Assn. Tex., Tex. Home Econs. Assn., Lamb County Tchrs. Assn. (treas.), Littlefield Classroom Tchrs. Assn. (treas.), Phi Kappa Phi, Phi Upsilon Omicron, Alpha Lambda Delta, Alpha Chi, Alpha Lambda Sigma, Beta Phi Mu, Delta Kappa Gamma (sec.). Democrat. Baptist. Home: 510 E 6th St Littlefield TX 79339 Office: 1100 W 10th St Littlefield TX 79339

MASSETTE, DOLORES CATANDO, advertising executive; b. Woodbury, N.J., July 4, 1934; d. Ralph A. and Anne Rita (Campellone) Catando; B.A., U. Pa., 1953; postgrad. Dickenson Coll., 1957-58; student Juilliard Sch. Music, 1946-54, Am. Acad. Fine Arts, 1949-52. Singer, Phila. Opera Co., 1946-54; appeared in Broadway theatrical prodns., 1952-56; with Eastern Airlines, 1960-65; with Parker Allen, Phila., 1965-70, Scanforms, Inc., 1970-76; mktg. cons. Advt. Specialization Inst., Trevose, Pa., 1976-78; v.p. direct response div. Smith-Langerman Agy., Phila., advt. dir. Nan Duskin Store, Phila., 1978-81; mktg. and sales promotion/advt. specialist RCA Service Co., Cherry Hill, N.J., 1981—; Pres. Our Lady of Lourdes Hosp. Aux., 1953-63. Recipient various awards for advt. campaigns. Mem. Direct Mail Mktg. Assn. (award), Nat. Assn. Female Execs., Phila. Direct Mail Club (award), Advt. Women, Nat. Retail Mchts. Assn., AAA Advt. Assn., Postal Forum, Lambda Sigma Chi. Republican. Roman Catholic. Clubs: Oaklands Trenton Country, Greate Bay Country. Home: 1215 Elm Ave West Collingswood NJ 08107 Office: RCA Service Co Route 38 Cherry Hill NJ 08358

MASSEY, DOROTHY BUTLER (MRS. GUY M. MASSEY), accountant; b. LaFayette, Ga.; d. R. Maihue and Cora (Sisemore) Butler; student U. Chattanooga, 1949; LL.B., Atlanta Law Sch., 1957, LL.M., 1958; B.B.A., Ga. State Coll., 1966; m. Guy M. Massey, Feb. 21, 1953. Accountant Gulf Oil Corp., Chattanooga, 1944-53, Crawford and Porter, Atlanta, 1953-54; accountant Baker Audio Assos., 1955-70, sec.-treas., 1955-70, also dir.; accountant Glenkaron Assos., Inc., 1955-68, sec.-treas., 1957-68; pres. Massey Co., 1971—, also dir.; pres. Profl. Credit Bur., Inc., 1977—; real estate agt. Shotz Assos. Mem. Am. Soc. Women Accountants (dir.), Ga. Soc. C.P.A.'s, Notaries Pub. Assn., Bus. and Profl. Women, Kappa Delta. Home: 1534 Peachtree Battle Ave NW Atlanta GA 30327

MASSEY, ELEANOR NELSON, school librarian, media specialist; b. Providence, Apr. 1, 1930; d. Walter K. and Jeanette (Perlman) Nelson; m. Marvin Donald Massey, June 29, 1952; children—Henry, David, Michael, Jonathan. B.A., Douglass Coll., New Brunswick, N.J., 1952; postgrad. Rutgers U. Cert. ednl. media specialist. Children's librarian Westfield (N.J.) Pub. Library, 1952-55; librarian Franklin Jr. High Sch., Metuchen, N.J., 1959-61; media specialist Campbell Sch., Metuchen, 1962—; coordinator libraries Metuchen Pub. Schs., 1982—; dir. Woodbridge-East Brunswick Area Coordination Council, 1982-85; mem. interim planning com. N.J. Library Network, 1984-85; cooperating tchr. Kean Coll. and Rutgers U., 1975—; speaker; bibliographer. Author. Vice pres. Sisterhood Neve Shalom, Metuchen, 1960; dir. Neve Shalom, 1959-60; bd. dirs. Union-Middlesex Regional Library Cooperative, Region IV, Inc., 1985—. Title II Demonstration Library grantee State of N.J., 1974-76. Mem. Ednl. Media Assn. N.J. (exec. bd. 1976-78), ALA, N.J., Library Assn., Ednl. Media Assn. Middlesex County (treas. 1982-83). Office: Campbell School Talmadge Ave Metuchen NJ 08840

MASSEY, LENICE LEETTA, state government administrator, building contractor; b. Kinsley, Kans., Apr. 8, 1919; d. Arthur Beryl and Mora E. (Lovette) Stevens; m. Ralph Milliard Massey, Jan. 30, 1939 (dec. Mar. 1945); children—Arthur, Donald. B.A. in Polit. Sci., Washburn U., Topeka, Kans., 1970; M.B.A., U. Kans.-Lawrence, 1979. Prin. acct. Dept. Health and Environ. State of Kans., Topeka, 1954-62, bus. mgr., chief of adminstrv. services, 1962-83, dir. personnel/employment services, 1983—, dir. personnel suggestion award com. div. personnel, 1979-82. Mem. com., acct. Topeka Day Care Assn., 1968-72. Mem. Am. Bus. Women. Republican. Episcopalian. Office: Kans Dept Health and Environment Forbes Field Bldg 740 Topeka KS 66620

MASSEY, PEGGY YVONNE, lawyer; b. Rock Hill, S.C., May 4, 1951; d. Nelson and Nannie (Lytle) Massey. B.S. in Polit. Sci. and English, Xavier U., 1973; J.D., Boston Coll., 1977. Bar: S.C., D.C. Instr. research and writing Council Legal Ednl. Opportunities Program, N.C. Central U. Sch. Law, Durham, summer 1977; instr. bus. dept. Central Piedmont Community Coll., Charlotte, N.C., spring 1977; atty. Palmetto Legal Services, Columbia, S.C., 1977-79; atty.-adviser U.S. Commn. Civil Rights, Washington, 1979—. Co-author reports on legal system in area of domestic violence. Reginald Heber Smith fellow, 1977. Mem. S.C. Bar Assn., Nat. Conf. Black Lawyers, ABA, Washington Bar Assn., Xavier U. Alumni Assn. Democrat. Roman Catholic. Office: US Commn Civil Rights 1121 Vermont Ave NW Washington DC 20425

MASSEY, W(ILMET) ANNETTE, nurse, former educator; b. Big Chimney, W.Va., June 30, 1920; d. Robert Lee and Twila Augusta (Pringle) M.; student Morris Harvey Coll., 1938-39; R.N., Phila. Gen. Hosp., 1943; B.S. in Edn., U. Pa., 1948; M.S. in Nursing, Yale U., 1959. Nurse cadet instr. U.S. Cadet Nurse Corps, Huntington (W.Va.) Meml. Hosp., 1943-45; nurse instr. St. Mary's Sch. Nursing, Huntington, 1948-51; WHO nurse cons. Govt. Ceylon, 1951-55; staff nurse instr. VA Hosp., Ft. Thomas, Ky., 1955-57; asst. prof. nursing Brigham Young U., Provo, Utah, 1959-61; assoc. prof. nursing W.Va. U., Morgantown, 1961-85, chmn. dept. psychiat. nursing, 1968-72; cons. Appalachian Regional Hosp., Beckley, W.Va., W.Va. Dept. Mental Health, Charleston, Valley Community Mental Health Center, Kingwood, W.Va.; group leader med.-nursing group to India, Expt. Internat. Living, Brattleboro, Vt., 1965. Mem. Appalachian Trail, Morgantown Hospice. NIMH grantee, 1964-75. Mem. Am. Nurses Assn., League Nursing, Am. Orthopsychiat. Assn., Internat. Transactional Analysis Assn., Am. Counseling Assn. (dir. 1981-82, v.p. 1982), Am. Soc. Profl. and Exec. Women, Tarrytown Group, Nat. Registry Psychiat. Nurse Specialists (edn. and resources com.), Internat. Acad. Cancer Counselors and Cons., Nat. Alliance Family Life, Inc. (founding), AAUP, Nat. Hist. Soc., Hastings Center, Nat. Wildlife Fedn., Smithsonian Assos., Phila. Gen. Hosp. Sch. Nursing Alumni, U. Pa., Yale U., W.Va. U. Sch. Nursing (hon.) alumni assns., Sierra Club, Appalachian Trail, Sigma Theta Tau. Republican. Methodist. Club: Alpine Lake Recreation Community (Terra Alta, W.Va.). Home: 432 Western Ave Morgantown WV 26505 Office: WVa U Sch Nursing Med Center Morgantown WV 26506

MASSON, ANNA MARGARET, court clerk; b. Rawlins, Wyo., Oct. 29, 1927; d. Carl Alfred and Charlotte Louise (Irving) Pearson; m. Robert Alden Masson, Sept. 1, 1947; children—Sandra Lee Masson Ferry, Cheryl Ann Masson Ingold, Gregory Robert, William John. Grad. high sch., Rawlins. County supt. of schs. deputy, 1945-47; sec. Sta. KRAL Radio, 1968-72; deputy clk. Dist. Ct., 1972-79; clk. Dist. Ct. Carbon County Seat, Rawlins, 1979—. Mem. Assn. Clks. Ct. of Wyo. (pres. 1984-85). Democrat. Presbyterian. Lodges: P.E.O. (pres. 1966-67, 75-76), Daughters of Nile Tamah Temple #73. Avocations: reading; travel camping. Home: 159 LaPaloma Dr Rawlins WY 82301 Office: Clk of Dist Ct PO Box 67 Rawlins WY 82301

MASSUCCO, DIANA LOU, educational media producer; b. Seattle, July 3, 1943; d. Louis and Bianca Amabile (Catuzo) M. B.A., U. Puget Sound, 1966, B.S., 1974; cert. respiratory therapy tech. Swedish Hosp., Seattle, 1972; student U. Wash., 1972-73, City U., Seattle, 1981—. Tchr. Federal Way Pub. schs. (Wash.), 1966-67; tchr. sci. St. Anthony Middle Sch., Renton, Wash., 1967-69; respiratory therapist, pulmonary function technologist Swedish Hosp., Seattle, 1970-72; research technologist U. Wash., Seattle, 1972-74; ednl. media producer Health Scis. Ctr. Ednl. Resources, Seattle, 1975—; ednl. cons. Puget Sound Blood Ctr., Seattle, 1980-82, Children's Orthopedic Hosp., 1984. Recipient honorable mention Nat. Ednl. Film Festival, 1984, Silver award Merit Internat. TV Assn., 1985. Ross Labs. grantee, 1982-83. Mem. Women in Communications, Health Scis. Communication Assn. (1st Place award for slide/audiotape 1982, 1st Place award for videotape 1983, award of Merit for slide/audiotape 1983), Am. Assn. Respiratory Therapy. Office: Health Scis Ctr Ednl Resources Health Scis Bldg T-252 SB-56 Seattle WA 98195

MASSY, PATRICIA GRAHAM BIBBS (MRS. RICHARD OUTRAM MASSY), social worker, author; b. Newbury, Eng., Mar. 21, 1918; came to U.S., 1963, naturalized, 1969; d. Oswald Graham and Dorothy (French) Bibbs; m. Richard Outram Massy, July 22, 1944; children—Patricia Lynn Massy Holmes, Julie Suzanne, Shaun Adele Massy Brink. B.A., U. B.C., 1941, M.S.W., 1962. With B.C. Welfare Field Service, Vancouver, Kamloops, Abbottsford, 1942-44; social worker Brandon Welfare Dept., Man., Can., 1945; with Children's Aid Soc., Vancouver, 1948-62; supr. Dept. Pub. Social Service, Los Angeles, 1963-70, staff devel. specialist-mgmt., 1970-77; lectr. colls. and bus. Author: A Study Guide for a Course in Miracles, 1984; One, 1985. Mem. AAUW (treas. 1970), Nat. Assn. Social Workers, Alpha Phi. Mem. Religious Sci. Ch. Home: 18936 Upper Cow Creed Rd Azalea OR 97410

MASTERS, BRENDA A., construction company executive; b. Mt. Clemens, Mich., July 28, 1951; d. Chester E. and Eleanor V. (Squire) Schmidt Masters; m. Peter V. Hoebee, Apr. 1980 (div. 1981); m. Kerry L. Wheeler, Feb. 21, 1986. B.A. in Social Work with high honors, Mich. State U., 1972; postgrad. Lansing Community Coll., Mich., 1976, IBM/Tandy Learning Ctr., Phoenix, 1983-84, Ariz. State U. Social worker Social Services, Battle Creek, Mich., 1972-76; bookkeeper Simplified Bookkeeping, East Lansing, Mich., 1977-78; asst. to controller Delta Electric & Air, Phoenix, 1978; client work-up Bolan Vassar & Barrows C.P.A., Phoenix, 1981-82; v.p. Elite Electric Inc., Phoenix, 1981-85; controller Fitch Corp., Mesa, Ariz., 1985—. Contbr. article to profl. jour. Vol. hiking dir., newsletter pub. Squaw Peak Hiking Club, Phoenix, 1984-85. Mem. Nat. Assn. Female Execs., Women Emerging, Nat. Assn. Women in Constrn., Ariz. Subcontractors Assn. (legis. com. 1986), Ariz. Networking Assn., Phi Alpha. Avocations: hiking; sailing; horses; computers. Home: 344 E Washington St Gilbert AZ 85234

MASTERS, JOAN, business and communications services company executive; b. DeKalb, Ill.; d. Charles Henry and Margaret Ann (McCabe) Corey; m. Charles H. Masters (div. Apr. 1972); children—Susan Jean, John Hal, Thomas Charles, William Lyle. Grad. high sch., DeKalb, Ill. Pres., owner Preferred Bus. Ctrs., Inc., Chgo., 1973—, Washington, 1981—; cons. women-owned businesses, 1977—. Mem. Experiment in Internat. Living, 1961-66, Am. Field Service, 1963-66; mem. steering com. for orgn. curriculum com. Kishwaukee Community Coll., DeKalb, Ill., 1964-66; mem. Council Fgn. Relations, Chgo., 1978. Mem. Nat. Press Club. Avocations: family; sports; reading. Home: 175 E Delaware Pl Chicago IL 60611 Office: Preferred Bus Ctrs Inc 875 N Michigan Ave Chicago IL 60611 also Nat Press Bldg 14th and F Sts NW Washington DC 20045

MASTERSON, PEGGY BELL, advertising executive; b. N.Y.C., Mar. 25, 1943; d. Richard Francis and Frances Dolores (Manning) Bell; grad. cum laude Dominican Coll. of Blauvelt, 1964; m. Patrick Masterson, May 20, 1972. Tchr. jr. high sch. history and art, 1965-69; copywriter Foote, Cone and Belding, 1969-74; with Ted Bates Advt., N.Y.C., 1974-75, creative supr., 1975-76, v.p., 1976-79, sr. v.p., creative dir., 1979-81; sr. v.p., creative dir. Benton & Bowles Advt., N.Y.C., 1981—; tchr. copywriting Tobe Coburn Sch., N.Y.C. Winner copywriting awards. Mem. Nat. Assn. Female Execs., Am. Soc. Profl. and Exec. Women. Office: Benton & Bowles Advertising 909 3d Ave New York NY 10022

MASTERTON, NANCY NYE, state legislator; b. Newton, Mass., Nov. 28, 1930; d. Harold Edward and Mabel Evelyn (Roberts) Nye; B.A. in English Lit. and Lang., Boston U., 1952; postgrad. U. Maine, 1964-65; m. Robert R. Masterton, Jr., May 23, 1953; children—Peter R., Laurie. Engaged in retail advt. bus., 1952-53, 55-56; mem. Maine Ho. of Reps., 1976-84, Maine Task Force on State Govt. Reorgn., 1967-69, Gov.'s Commn. on Senate Reapportionment, 1971; chmn. House Apportionment Commn., 1972. Bd. dirs. Portland (Maine) YWCA, 1963-71; pres. Portland area LWV, 1965-67, Maine LWV, 1971-73; mem. Cape Elizabeth (Maine) Planning Bd., 1973-76, Cape Elizabeth Town Council, 1984—; mem. Maine Bd. Environ. Protection, 1985—. Mem. LWV, Maine Audubon Soc., Natural Resources Council, Maine Hist. Soc. (trustee). Republican. Author: Maine: How We Govern; The Law and the Land. Home: 36 Delano Park Cape Elizabeth ME 04107

MATALAMAKI, MARGARET MARIE, educator, consultant; b. Hampton, Iowa, May 10, 1921; d. Byron Jacob and Vera Margaret (Wheaton) Myers; m. William Matalamaki, Sept. 11, 1942 (dec. 1978); children—Judith Marie Gerlinger, William Micheal. A.A., Itasca Community Coll., 1941; student U. Minn., 1941-42, 72. High sch. instr. Sch. Dist. 1, Bigfork, Minn., 1942-45, U. Minn. Sch. Agr., Grand Rapids, Minn., 1955-58; high sch. substitute Sch. Dist. 318, Grand Rapids, 1967-69; vocat. instr. Itasca Community Coll., Grand Rapids, 1970-78. bd. dirs. Blandin Found., Grand Rapids, trustee, 1981—, v.p., 1985, chmn. elect 1986; bd. dirs. Christus Home, Grand Rapids; cons. to Keewatin Community Devel. Corp., Grand Rapids, 1985; mem. consumer adv. bd. Land of Lakes Inc., St. Paul, 1984—; pres. Kooch-Itasca Action Council, Grand Rapids, 1981-84; adv. council mem. Women's Econ. Devel. Corp., Mpls., 1984—; bd. dirs. Itasca Meml. Hosp., 1975-85, Itasca County Nursing Home, 1975-85, No. Itasca Nursing Home, 1982-85, Itasca County Social Services, 1975-85; county commr. Itasca County, 1981-85; legis. coordinator Lutheran Ch. Am., 1983—, staff, advocacy coordinator Minn. Synod, 1983—; chmn. legis. com. Inst. Agr., Forestry and Home Econ. U. Minn., 1981—; 4-H club leader, Esko, Minn., 1945-49, Grand Rapids, Minn., 1949-63; home extension leader, Esko, 1945-49, Grand Rapids, 1949-63; county fair judge No. Minn., 1950-84; bd. dirs. United Way Grand Rapids, 1980-84; mem. Grand Rapids Citizen's League, 1980—, League Women Voters, 1977-84, Minn. Women for Agr., 1982—, Joint Religious Legis. Coalition, Mpls., 1977-78; mem. adv. bd. Luth. Social Services North Eastern Minn., 1986—; mem. Minn. Child Abuse Team, 1986—; pres. Luth. Ch. Women, 1959-62, Luth. Ch. Women Synodical Bd., 1972-76, dist. chmn., 1964-65; com. mem. Commn. for a New Lutheran Ch., 1985, chmn. transition team, 1986—, mem. exec. com. Synod Council, 1976-79; pres., sec. PEO Sisterhood, 1964—, Recipient Good Govt. award Grand Rapids Jr. C. of C., 1977, Good Neighbor award WCCO Radio, 1976. Avocations: cross country skiing, canoing, traveling. Home and Office: 3734 Sunny Beach Rd Grand Rapids MN 55744

MATAN, LILLIAN KATHLEEN ARCHAMBAULT, designer, educator; b. Boston, Aug. 18, 1937; d. George Frances and Lillian May (Herbert) Archambault; B.S., Seton Hill Coll., 1960; postgrad. U. Tex., 1972, Tex. A&I, 1971, Towson (Md.) State U., 1973, Rudolph Schaeffer Sch. Design, 1977-80; M.A. in Home Econs. Housing and Interior Design, San Francisco State U., 1985; m. Joseph Anthony Matan, Aug. 6, 1960; children—Maria, Meg, Tony, Lisabeth, Joan. Tchr. home econs., Surrattsville, Md., 1961-62; ednl. cons. Head Start, Frederick County, Md., 1971-72; head dept. home econs. Brunswick (Md.) High Sch., 1971-72, tchr. adult edn., 1972-73; designer Dudley Kelly & Assos., San Francisco, 1977-82, prin. Kay Matan Antiques and Interiors, Ross, Calif., 1982—. Chmn. Seconds to Go, resale shop Convent of Sacred Heart, San Francisco, 1975-76; bd. dirs. Cath. Social Services Marin County. Mem. Marin County LWV, Ecumenical Housing Assn., Women in Design, Am. Home Econs. Assn. Home Economists in Bus., Calif. Home Econs. Assn., Ross Valley Ecumenical Housing Assn. Democrat. Office: PO Box 1140 Ross CA 94957

MATCHETTE, PHYLLIS LEE, editor; b. Dodge City, Kans., Dec. 24, 1921; d. James Edward and Rose Mae (McMillan) Collier; A.B. in Journalism, U. Kans., 1943; m. Robert Clarke Matchette, Dec. 4, 1943; children—Marta Susan, James Michael. Reporter, Dodge City Daily Globe, 1944; tchr. English, Dodge City Jr. High Sch., 1944-45; asst. instr. Coll. Liberal Arts, U. Kans., Lawrence, 1945-47; dir. Christian edn. Southminster United Presbyn. Ch., Prairie Village, Kans., 1963-65; editor publs., dir. communications, supr. in-plant printing Village United Presbyn. Ch., Prairie Village, 1965—. Hon. mem. Commn. of Ecumenical Mission and Relations, United Presbyn. Ch., U.S.A.; ordained elder Village United Presbyn. Ch., 1964. Mem. Women in Communications, Kans. U. Dames (pres. 1946), Kansas City Young Matrons, Alpha Chi Omega (pres. edn. found. Phi chpt. 1951). Republican. Club: Order of Eastern Star. Home: 7405 El Monte Rd Prairie Village KS 66208 Office: 6641 Mission Rd Prairie Village KS 66208

MATECHAK-BLACK, TESSIE, nursing administrator, educator; b. Peckville, Pa., Mar. 19, 1926; d. Wasil and Anna (Horbal) Matechak; A.A. (scholarship), Keystone Jr. Coll., 1947; diploma nursing (scholarship) Sinai Hosp., Md., 1953; B.S. in Nursing, Johns Hopkins U., 1962; M.S. in Nursing, U. Md., 1970; m. James Franklin Black, Jan. 27, 1974. Staff nurse Sinai Hosp., Balt., 1953-54, instr. med.-surg. nursing, 1959-67, asst. dir. inservice edn., 1967-70; head nurse Johns Hopkins Hosp., Balt., 1954-59, asst. instr. emergency service, 1956-56; asso. dir. patient care services Balt. City Hosp., 1970-71; dir. nursing services Bon Secours Hosp., Balt., 1971-73; asso. prof. nursing U. Md., Balt., 1971-73; dir. nursing service Taylor Manor Hosp., Ellicott City, Md., 1974-75; asso. dir. nursing service King Faisal Specialist Hosp., Saudia Arabia, 1975, asst. adminstr. nursing, 1975-77; med. surg. clin. specialist Md. Gen. Hosp., Balt., 1977; asst. dir. nursing service Balt. City Hosps., 1978-79, dir. nursing services, 1981—; asst. prof. nursing Community Coll., Balt., 1981—, asst. chmn. nursing dept., 1985—. Sec., VFW Ladies Aux., 1947-48; fund raiser Jewish Charities, 1970-74. Recognition award King Faisal Hosp., 1977. Mem. Am. Nurses Assn., Md. Nurses Assn. (pres. dist. 2 1978-82), Cancer Soc. Md., Am. Bus. Women's Profl. Orgn., Johns Hopkins U. Alumni Assn., Sinai Nurses Alumni (pres. 1973-75), Keystone Jr. Coll. Alumni. Democrat. Greek Catholic. Home: 3619 Lochearn Dr Baltimore MD 21207 Office: Community College of Baltimore Baltimore MD 21215

MATEER, SHIRLEY ANN, public relations executive; b. Punxsutawney, Pa., June 14, 1937; d. Robert E. and Ruth (Haugh) M. A.B., Ohio U., 1957; M.A., Northwestern U., 1958. Market reseacher Procter & Gamble Co., 1958-60; asst. personnel dir. John Wanamaker, Phila., 1960-62; ednl. advisor Scott Paper Co., Phila., 1962-67; account supr. Bozell & Jacobs, Inc., N.Y.C., 1967-72; dir. publicity Nestle Co., White Plais, N.Y., 1972-78; pres. Mateer Mktg. Communication, Nyack, N.Y., 1978—. Recipient Graphic Arts award Printing Industries Am., 1978. Mem. Women Execs. Pub. Relations, Women in Radio and TV. Office: 48 Burd St Nyack NY 10960

MATERIA, KATHLEEN PATRICIA AYLING, nurse; b. Jersey City, Nov. 7, 1954; d. Donald Anthony and Muriel Cecilia (Joyce) Ayling; m. Francis Peter Materia, June 5, 1983. B.S. in Nursing, Fairleigh Dickinson U., 1976. R.N., N.J. Critical care nurse Palisades Gen. Hosp., North Bergen, N.J., 1976—, grad. nurse, 1976-77; nurse CCU, North Hudson Hosp., Weehawken, N.J., 1977-78. Mem. Alpha Sigma Tau. Democrat. Roman Catholic. Avocations: bowlings; dancing. Home: West New York NJ

MATES-BENTON, KATHIE ANN, nurse; b. Greensburg, Pa., July 27, 1952; d. John Andrew and Ruth Elizabeth (Shrader) Mates; B.S.N., U. Pitts., 1975; m. James G. Benton, Jr., Dec. 18, 1976; 1 son, Michael Thomas. Staff nurse Eye & Ear Hosp., Pitts., 1975-77; staff nurse Carson-Tahoe Hosp., Carson City, Nev., 1977, night supr., 1977-79, clin. coordinator surg. floor, 1979-80, charge nurse, 1980-84, operating room Surg. nurse, 1984—. Recipient Award of Clin. Excellence, Surg. Floor Staff, Carson-Tahoe Hosp., 1979—. Mem. Carson-Tahoe Employees' Assn. Methodist. Club: United Meth. Young Adults. Home: PO Box 394 Dayton NV 89403 Office: 1201 N Mountain St 2nd E Carson City NV 89701

MATESICH, SISTER MARY ANDREW, college president; b. Zanesville, Ohio, May 5, 1939. B.A., Ohio Dominican Coll., 1962; M.S., U. Calif.-Berkeley, 1963, Ph.D. in Chemistry, 1966. Asst. prof. chemistry Ohio Dominican Coll., Columbus, 1965-70, assoc. prof., from 1970, chmn. dept., 1965-73, acad. dean, 1973-78, pres. coll., 1978—. Petroleum Research Fund grantee Ohio Dominican Coll., 1965-68; NSF grantee Case Western Res. U. and Ohio Dominican Coll., 1969-72. Mem. Council Ind. Colls. (bd. dirs. 1985—), Nat. Assn. Ind. Colls. and Univs. (bd. dirs. 1986—), Assn. Ind. Colls. and Univs. Ohio (chmn. 1984-86). Office: Ohio Dominican Coll Office of Pres 1216 Sunbury Rd Columbus OH 43219

MATHER, SUSAN HOWARD, physician; b. Salisbury, Md., Feb. 6, 1940; d. Dalton Bailey and Jenny Louise (Whaley) Howard; B.S. with honors, U. Md., 1961, M.D., 1965; M.P.H., Johns Hopkins U., 1978; m. John H. Mather, June 17, 1967; children—Stephen, Alexandra. Instr. ambulatory medicine/student health physician U. Md., 1971-75; dir. adult health and epidemiology Prince George's County, Md., 1975-79; program chief pulmonary and infectious diseases VA, Washington, 1979—. Pres., Am. Lung Assn. Md., 1978-80, Am. Lung Assn. So. Md., 1980-82. Mem. Am. Pub. Health Assn., Am. Thoracic Soc. Presbyterian. Home: 12144 Long Ridge Ln Bowie MD 20715 Office: VACO 810 Vermont Ave Washington DC 20420

MATHERS, MARGARET, charitable agency administrator, consultant; b. Ada, Okla., Feb. 16, 1929; d. Robert Lee and Josiephine Margaret (Reed) Erwin; m. Coleman F. Moss, Sept. 1956 (div. 1966); children—Carol Lee Doria, Marilyn Frances; m. Boyd Leroy Mathers, Apr. 10, 1967. B.S. in Music, Tex. U., 1950. Service rep. Gen. Telephone Co., Santa Monica, Calif., 1955-58; tchr. pvt. sch., Santa Monica, 1958-60; computer program and data analyst System Devel. Corp., Santa Monica, 1961-66; computer programmer Inst. Def. Analyses, Arlington, Va., 1966-70; typist, transcriber, Edgewater, Md., 1971-80; dir. San Juan Catholic Charities, Farmington N.Mex., 1984—; asst. treas. San Juan Council Community Agys., 1985—; pres. Davidsonville-Mayo Health Assn., Edgewater, 1973-76, 77-80; cons. in field, 1983—. Chmn. county Libertarian Party of N.Mex., San Juan County, 1985; asst. sec. Our Lady of Perpetual Health, Parish Council, Edgewater, 1979-82; sec. River Club Community Assn., Edgewater, 1975-82. Roman Catholic. Avocations: nature study; birdwatching; reading; music. Office: San Juan Cath Charities 119 W Broadway Farmington NM 87401

MATHERSON, THALIA FAE, public school administrator; b. Dallas, Oct. 4, 1941; d. George Leonard and LaVurne (Cole) Brown; m. Arthur Matherson, Jr., Dec. 23, 1967; children—Aaron, Keith. B.A., Huston-Tillotson, 1963; M. Liberal Arts, Southern Meth., Dallas, 1972; D. Edn. Adminstrn., East Tex. State, 1982. Tchr. Dallas Ind. Schs., 1963-81, asst. prin., 1981-84, prin., 1984—; facilitator workshop Dallas Sch. Dist. Adminstrs., 1980—, presenter workshop, 1980—. Advanced Study grantee Dallas Ind. Sch. Dist., 1978-80. Named Woman of Year, Interdenominational Ministers Alliance, 1978. Mem. Tex. State Tchrs. Assn., Nat. Elementary Prins. Assn., Dallas Sch. Adminstrs. Assn., Phi Delta Kappa, Delta Sigma Theta. Democrat. Methodist. Advocation: reading. Home: 6416 Forest Knoll Trail Dallas TX 75232 Office: José A Navarro Community Learning Ctr 3530 Kingbridge St Dallas TX 75212

MATHESON, LINDA, social worker; b. Martna, Estonia, Dec. 29, 1918; came to U.S., 1962, naturalized, 1969; d. Endrek and Leena Endrekson; Diploma, Inst. for Social Scis., Tallinn, Estonia, 1944; M.S., Columbia U., 1966, D.S.W., 1974; m. Charles McLaren Matheson, Feb. 5, 1955. Social work officer UN Rehab. and Resettlement Assn., Germany, 1946-48; social worker Victorian Mental Hygiene, Australia, 1955-62; research assoc., social work project dir. Arthritis Midway Ho., N.Y.C., 1966-68; researcher Columbia Presbyn. Med. Center, N.Y.C., 1971-75, now social worker; field instr. Columbia U. Sch. Social Work, 1977-79. Family Found. fellow, 1966; NIMH grantee, 1969-72. Mem. Nat. Assn. Social Workers, Am. Security Council, Nat. Wildlife Fedn., Center for Study of Presidency, Smithsonian Assn., English Speaking Union, Alliance Francaise, Columbia U. Alumni Assn., Internat. Platform Assn., Nat. Trust Historic Preservation, Met. Mus. of N.Y. Lutheran. Home: 30-95 29th St Astoria NY 11102

MATHEWS, BARBARA EDITH, gynecologist; b. Santa Barbara, Calif., Oct. 5, 1946; d. Joseph Chesley and Pearl (Cieri) Mathews; A.B., U. Calif., 1969; M.D., Tufts U., 1972. Intern, Cottage Hosp., Santa Barbara, 1972-73, Santa Barbara Gen. Hosp., 1972-73; resident in ob-gyn Beth Israel Hosp., Boston, 1973-77; clin. fellow in ob-gyn Harvard U., 1973-76, instr., 1976-77; gynecologist Sansum Med. Clinic, Santa Barbara, 1977—. Bd. dirs. Meml. Rehab. Found., Santa Barbara, Channel City Women's Forum, Santa Barbara, Music Acad. of West, Santa Barbara; mem. citizen's continuing edn. adv. council Santa Barbara Community Coll. Diplomate Am. Bd. Ob-Gyn. Fellow ACS, Am. Coll. Obstetricians and Gynecologists; mem. AMA, Am. Soc. Colposcopy and Cervical Pathology (dir. 1982-84), Harvard U. Alumni Assn., Tri-counties Obstet. and Gynecol. Soc. (pres. 1981-82), Phi Beta Kappa. Clubs: Birnam Wood Golf (Santa Barbara). Author: (with L. Burke) Colposcopy in Clinical Practice, 1977; contbg. author Manual of Ambulatory Surgery, 1982. Home: 2105 Anacapa St Santa Barbara CA 93105 Office: 317 W Pueblo St Santa Barbara CA 93102

MATHEWS, JANE YOUNG CHREKJIAN, lawyer; b. Hackensack, N.J., May 12, 1953; d. George Peter and Ruth Helen (Young) Chrekjian; m. Paul Patrick Mathews, July 10, 1982. B.A., Sarah Lawrence Coll., 1975; J.D., Syracuse U., 1978; LL.M., NYU, 1979. Bar: N.Y. 1979, N.J. 1981. Law clk. U.S. Bankruptcy Ct., Bklyn., 1979-80; law clk. U.S. Ct. Appeals (2d cir.), N.Y.C., 1980-81; assoc. Haight, Gardner, Poor & Havens, N.Y.C., 1981-83, Hannoch, Weisman, Stern, Besser, Berkowitz & Kinney, P.A., Newark, 1983—; legal writing and research instr. Syracuse U. Sch. Law, 1977-78. Editor Syracuse Law Rev., 1977-78. Mem. ABA, Fed. Bar Council, N.Y. County Lawyers Assn. Home: 15 Skyview Rd Ringwood NJ 07456 Office: Hannoch Weisman Stern Besser Berkowitz & Kinney PA 744 Broad St Newark NJ 07102

MATHEWS, JEAN ANN H., state legislator; b. Ogden, Utah, Oct. 17, 1941; d. Walter H. and Connie Laverne (Jorgenson) Holbrook; m. John Phillip Mathews, Sept. 8, 1960; children—Michael, Mark, Nanette. Student, Weber Coll., Ogden, Utah, 1959-61; A.A., Florissant Community Coll., 1973; B.S. in Edn. magna cum laude, U. Mo.-St. Louis, 1980. Cert. tchr., Mo. Tchr., Mathews Vocal Studio, Florissant, 1964-80; profl. sales evaluator Edison Bros., Inc., St. Louis, 1971-73; mem. Mo. Ho. of Reps., 1981—. Author: Letting Go Is the Hardest, 1972; Repeat Drunken Driver Slips Through the System, 1982. Vice chmn. Florissant Bd. Appeals, 1976-80; committeewoman Florissant Twp., 1979—; sec. Mo. State Republican Party, Jefferson City, 1982—; mem. Gov.'s Commn. on Crime, 1984—. Recipient Golden Gleaner award Ch. Jesus Christ Latter-day Saints, 1969; Rookie Legislator of Yr. award Capitol City Press Corp., Jefferson City, 1981; Eagle award Eagle Forum, 1982; Americanism award VFW, 1983. Mem. Nat. Order Women Legislators, Am. Legis. Exchange Council (state chmn., Outstanding State Legislator 1984), Nat. Fedn. Republican Women, Kappa Delta Pi. Club: Rep. Women North St. Louis County (pres. 1978-82).

MATHEWS, JUDY CAROL, reporting service executive, consultant; b. Chgo., Sept. 29, 1957; d. Elliott A. and Jacqueline V. (Carter) M. B.A., Eastern Ill. U., 1978. Researcher James Lowry and Assocs., Chgo., 1977-78, cons., 1982—; intern U.S. C. of C., Washington, 1978; cons. Capitol Personnel, Washington, 1979-80; co-owner, prin. Carter Reporting Service, Chgo., 1980—; cons. James H. Lowry & Assocs., 1982—; profl. newsletter editor. Active, Chgo Urban League, NAACP, Young Dems., Citizens Choice, Washington. Mem. Nat. Assn. Female Execs. Roman Catholic. Office: Carter Reporting Service 179 W Washington St Chicago IL 60602

MATHEWS, MARGARET CARRYL, accountant; b. Albuquerque, Sept. 14, 1954; d. James Joseph and Catherine Jane (Vogel) Carryl; student Mercer U., 1972-73; A.A., Fla. State U., 1974, student, 1974-75; B.B.A., U. North Fla., 1976. Jr. acct. Alexander Grant & Co., C.P.A.s, Orlando, Fla. and Tallahassee, 1976-78; internal auditor Barnett Bank of Jacksonville (Fla.), 1978-79; sr. internal auditor Seaboard Coast Line Industries (now CSX Corp.), Jacksonville, 1979-80; sr. acct. Arthur Andersen & Co., C.P.A.s, Jacksonville and Bermuda, 1980—. Dansforth award for excellence, 1972; C.P.A., Fla.; cert. internal auditor. Mem. Inst. Internal Auditors (chpt. bd. dirs. 1979-81), Acctg. Alumni Assn. of U. N. Fla. (sec. 1981-82), Am. Inst. C.P.A.s, Fla. Inst. C.P.A.s, Am. Woman's Soc. C.P.A.s, Beta Alpha Psi. Home: Rosemont Ct #2 Rosemont Ave Pembroke Bermuda Office: PO 1553 129 Front St Hamilton 5 Bermuda

MATHEWS, PATRICIA ANN, food and beverage company executive; b. North Tonawanda, N.Y., Oct. 20, 1945; d. Daniel and Elizabeth Marian (Kassay) Por; m. Gregory Robert Mathews, Nov. 20, 1966; 1 child, Christopher Robert. B.A., SUNY-Fredonia, 1967; MBA, SUNY-Buffalo, 1982. Tchr., Wheelock Sch., Fredonia, 1967-68; library intern SUNY-Binghamton, 1968-73; office mgr. Bell and Howell, Buffalo, 1973-76; mgr. college relations Occidental Chem. Co., Niagara Falls, N.Y., 1977-82; mgr. recruitment and devel. Rochester Telephone Co., N.Y., 1982-83; sr. career devel. specialist Anheuser-Busch Co., 1983—. Cons. in human resources, St. Louis, 1983—. Chmn. spl. awards YWCA Leader Lunch, St. Louis, 1985-86. Mem. Personnel Assn. St. Louis (v.p. 1985-86). Internat. Assn. Personnel Women, Am. Soc. Personnel Adminstrs. Lutheran. Avocations: exercise; reading; women's issues. Home: 1013 Hollybend Dr Ballwin MO 63021 Office: Anheuser Busch Co Inc 1 Busch Pl St Louis MO 63118

MATHEWS, SHARON WALKER, ballet instructor, artistic director; b. Shreveport, La., Feb. 1, 1947; d. Arthur Delmar and Nona (Frye) Walker; m. John William (Bill) Mathews, Aug. 14, 1971; children—Rebecca, Elizabeth, Anna. B.S., La. State U., 1969, M.S., 1971. Dance grad. asst. La. State U., Baton Rouge, 1969-71; 6th grade tchr. East Baton Rouge Parish, 1971-72, health phys. edn. tchr., 1972-74; dance instr. Magnet High Sch., Baton Rouge, 1975—; artistic dir. Baton Rouge Ballet Theatre, 1975—; dance dir. Dancers' Workshop, Baton Rouge, 1971—. Mem. Southwestern Regional Ballet Assn. (bd. dirs. 1981—). Republican. Baptist.

MATHEWS, WILMA, public relations manager; b. Danville, Va., Dec. 23, 1945; d. Clarence Blanchard and Tina Collins (Powell) Kendrick; A.A., Stratford Coll., 1966, B.A., 1970; student East Carolina U., 1966-67, U. Md., European div., 1967-68, Guilford Coll., 1978-80. Asst. editor The Commonwealth Mag., Richmond, Va., 1970-72; news editor The Comml. Appeal, Danville, Va., 1972-73; pub. relations mgr. Danville C. of C., 1973-74; publs. officer Bowman Gray Bapt. Hosp. Med. Center, Winston-Salem, N.C., 1974-78; sr. pub. relations specialist Western Electric, 1978-82; mgr. pub. relations AT&T Internat., Basking Ridge, N.J., 1982-84; media relations mgr. AT&T Techs., N.Y.C., 1984-85; media relations mgr. AT&T Network Systems, 1985—; sr. pub. relations adv. N.C. Epilepsy Info. Service, 1979-80. Co-author: On Deadline: Managing Media Relations, 1985; Inside Organizational Communications, 2d edit. Mem. Danville Bicentennial Commn., 1972-74, bd. dirs. Nat. Tobacco-Textile Mus., 1973-74; mem. Danville City Beautiful Com., 1973-74, Maplewood Cultural Commn., 1986-87. Mem. Danville Hist. Soc. (dir. 1973-74), N.C. Zool. Soc., Smithsonian Instn., Internat. TV Assn. (sec. N.C. chpt. 1979-80), Internat. Assn. Bus. Communicators (dir. 1978-81, pres. N.C. chpt. 1977, 78, dir. Found. 1984—), Internat. Pub. Relations Assn., Council for Communications Mgrs., Internat. Platform Assn., Friends of Maplewood Library (pres. 1985-86), Stratford Coll. Alumni Assn. Republican. Baptist. Lodge: Internat. Order Job's Daus. Home: 65 Hudson Ave Maplewood NJ 07040 Office: 475 South St Morristown NJ 07960

MATHIAS, ALICE IRENE, health plan company executive; b. N.Y.C., Mar 2, 1949; d. Murray and Charlotte (Kottle) M. B.S. in Math., Western New Eng. Coll., 1972. Programmer, Carnation Co., Los Angeles, 1973-78; programmer/analyst Cedars Sinai Med. Ctr., Los Angeles, 1978-79, Union Bank, Los Angeles, 1979-81; group leader Kaiser Found. Health Plan, Pasadena, Calif., 1981—. Mem. Nat. Assn. Female Execs., Am. Mgmt. Assn., Kaiser Mgmt. Assn., Kaiser Women in Mgmt., Los Angeles County Mus. Art (patron), Los Angeles Philharm. Assn., Soc. Preservation Variety Arts. Home: 4210 Via Arbolada Unit 311 Los Angeles CA 90042 Office: Kaiser Found Health Plan Info Services Dept 393 E Walnut St Pasadena CA 91188

MATHIAS, BETTY JANE, communications and community affairs consultant, lecturer; b. East Ely, Nev., Oct. 22, 1923; d. Royal F. and Dollie B. (Bowman) M.; student Merritt Bus. Sch., 1941, 42, San Francisco State U., 1941-42; 1 dau., Dona Bett. Asst. publicity dir. Oakland (Calif.) Area War Chest and Community Chest, 1943-46; public relations Am. Legion, Oakland, 1946-47; asst. to public relations dir. Central Bank of Oakland, 1947-49; public relations dir. East Bay chpt. of Nat. Safety Council, 1949-51; propr., mgr. Mathias Public Relations Agy., Oakland, 1951-60; gen. assignment reporter and teen news editor Daily Rev., Hayward, Calif., 1960-62; free lance public relations and writing, Oakland, 1962-66, 67-69, dir. corp. communications Systech Fin. Corp., Walnut Creek, Calif., 1969-71; v.p. corp. communications Consol. Capital companies, Oakland, 1972-79, v.p. community affairs, Emeryville, Calif., 1981-84, v.p. spl. projects, 1984-85; v.p., dir. Consol. Capital Realty Services, Inc., Oakland, 1973-77; v.p., dir. Centennial Adv. Corp., Oakland, 1976-77; communications cons., 1979—; bd. dirs. Oakland YWCA, 1944-45, ARC, Oakland, So. Alameda County chpt., 1967-69, Family Center, Children's Hosp. Med. Center No. Calif., 1982-85, March of Dimes, 1983-85; adult and publs. adv. Internat. Order of the Rainbow for Girls, 1953-78; communications arts adv. com. Ohlone (Calif.) Coll., 1979-85, chmn., 1982-84; mem. adv. bd. dept. mass communications Calif. State U.-Hayward, 1985; pres. San Francisco Bay Area chpt. Nat. Reyes Syndrome Found., 1981-86. Recipient Grand Cross of Color award Internat. Order of Rainbow for Girls, 1955. Mem. East Bay Women's Press Club (pres. 1960-61, 83-85). Club: Order Eastern Star (publicity chmn. Calif. state 1955). Editor East Bay Mag., 1966-67, Concepts, 1979-83. Home: 20575 Gopher Dr Sonora CA 95370

MATHIAS, CORINNE FLORENCE, consultant company executive; b. Buffalo, June 10, 1926; d. Sidney and Florence (Vincent) O'Neill; m. Richard Charles Mathias, Sept. 6, 1947 (dec. Apr. 20, 1972); children—Richard Charles, Micheal William, Corinne Mary, Marc Francis. A.A., Citrus Coll., 1979. Dir. Universal Product Code and Direct Store Set-UP, Vons Grocery Co., El Monte, Calif., 1958-78; pres., owner Direct Delivery Data, Glendora, Calif., 1978—. Author receiving clerk's manual, 1966. Fellow mem. Los Angeles Art Mus., 1984—, Com. Against Govt. Waste, Washington, 1984—, Redlands Community Music Assn., Calif., 1984—. Women in Mgmt. scholar, 1979. Fellow So. Calif. Grocers Assn., Bus. and Profl. Women. Democrat. Roman Catholic. Avocations: bridge; golf; tennis; travel; photography.

MATHIESEN, ANNA PAULINE, social worker; b. Carroll, Iowa, Apr. 28, 1932; d. Matthew Raymond and Eileen Mercedia (Murphy) Murtogh; B.S., Creighton U., 1963; m. R.J. Mathiesen, Feb. 16, 1952; children—Roberta J. Mathiesen Behm, R.J., Raymond Joseph. Tchr., St. Peter's Sch., Omaha, 1964; with Douglas County Social Services, Omaha, 1966-83, social services supr., 1970-76; unit mgr. income maintenance, 1976-83; unit mgr. income maintenance Nebr. Dept. Social Services, 1983—. Mem. Nat. Assn. Social Workers, Nebr. Welfare Assn., Nat. Eligibility Workers Assn. Roman Catholic. Home: 3564 Poppleton Ave Omaha NE 68105 Office: 1909 Burt St Omaha NE 68102

MATHIEU, MAUREEN RITA, telephone company executive; b. N.Y.C., Oct. 24, 1951; d. Richard F. and Rita O. (O'Brien) Hofsaes; m. Alfred C. Mathieu, III, Oct. 23, 1976. B.S. in Edn., East Stroudsburg State Coll., 1973; M.A. in Math., Trenton State Coll., 1976. Tchr. Manville Bd. Edn., N.J., 1973-80; data base mgr. N.J. Bell Telephone Co., New Brunswick, 1980—. Pres. Bradford-Myrtle Block Assn., Plainfield, N.J., 1980-82; sec. Myrtle Block Assn., Plainfield, 1981. Republican. Club: Ski (N.J.). Avocations: skiing; sailing; reading; gardening.

MATHIEU, MICHELE SUZANNE, association executive; b. Chgo., Mar. 24, 1950; d. Joseph Edward Mathieu and Mary Ellen (Knapp) Fisher. Student DePaul U., 1971, 74-76; B.S. in Bus., Regents Coll., Albany, N.Y. 1987. Broadcast coordinator Grey-North Advt., Chgo., 1967-71; head drama dept.

Patricia Stevens Coll., Chgo., 1972; instr. beginning acting Ted Liss Sch. of Performing Arts, Chgo., 1973-75; project coordinator grants and contracts Am. Dietetic Assn., Chgo., 1974-81, adminstr. govt. affairs, 1981-86, mgr. licensure communications, 1986—; grant proposal cons. various performance arts, Chgo., 1978-81. Editor Legis. Newsletter, 1981-86; contbg. editor Nutrition Forum, 1986. Contbr. articles to profl. jours. Treas. Am. Dietetic Assn. polit. action com., Washington, 1981-86. Ill. Arts Council grantee, 1981. Mem. Nat. Assn. Female Execs. Roman Catholic. Avocations: reading; jazzercise. Office: Am Dietetic Assn 430 N Michigan Ave Chicago IL 60611

MATHIS, BETTY, public relations counsel; b. Atlanta, Oct. 5, 1918; d. Walter Rylander and Evelyn Battle (Epting) M.; student Agnes Scott Coll., 1934-36. Sports writer, columnist Atlanta Constitution, 1936-39; gen. news and feature writer, then editor spl. supplements, 1939-40; dir. public relations Atlanta Housing Authority, 1940; feature writer, asst. city editor, daily by-line columnist Atlanta Constitution, 1941-43; asst. regional info. exec. OPA, 1943-45; partner Mathis, Murphey & Bondurant public relations counsel, Atlanta, 1945-50; editor Sun Colony Mag., Fort Lauderdale, Fla., 1950-53; partner Mathis & Bondurant public relations, Ft. Lauderdale, 1953-82, owner, 1982—. Bd. dirs. ARC; mem. coms. United Way; sec. vestry All Saints Episcopal Ch., 1974-76, mem. vestry, 1978-80, 85—, treas., 1979, sr. warden, 1980, del. Diocesan Conv., 1975, 79, 80. Nominee, Pulitzer prize, 1937. Mem. Public Relations Soc. Am., Am. Soc. Hosp. Public Relations (profl. advancement com. 1980), Public Relations Council Fla. Hosp. Assn. (dir. 1977-79, pres. 1977-78), Women in Communications (pres. county 1968, 69, Atlantic Fla. chpt. 1979, named Woman of Yr. 1979), Gold Coast Hosp. Public Relations Council (founding, pres. 1981-82), Am. Hosp. Assn. Democrat. Club: Tower. Home and office: 1628 NE 15th Ave Fort Lauderdale FL 33305

MATHIS, LAURELLE SHEEDY, entrepreneur; b. Southampton, N.Y., Aug. 29, 1948; d. Edmund Sheedy and Tatiana (Widrin) Brooks; m. Robert Trimble Mathis, Oct. 20, 1979; children—Liliana Sheedy, Bronwyn Trimble. B.A., Stephens Coll., Columbia, Mo., 1970; M.B.A., Harvard U., 1977. Spl. asst. Congressman Ed Foreman, Washington, 1970; staff asst. Senator James L. Buckley, Washington, 1971-72; staff asst. to pres. U.S., Washington, 1973-75; v.p. Blyth Eastman Paine Webber, N.Y.C., 1977-81; v.p. Merrill Lynch Capital Markets, N.Y.C., 1981-84. Bd. curators Stephens Coll., 1981-83, Putnam Indian Field Sch., Greenwich, Conn., 1986—. Recipient Alumni Achievement award Stephens Coll., 1980. Republican. Episcopalian. Home: 22 Pecksland Rd Greenwhich CT 06831

MATHIS, SALLY LOUISE, utility company official; b. Baytown, Tex., July 9, 1957; d. James Warner and Wilma Lorene (Buchner) M. B.S. in Edn., La. State U., 1979. Cert. tchr., La., Tex. Receptionist, Chotin Transp. Co., New Orleans and Baton Rouge, 1976-78, ins. clk., Baton Rouge, 1978-79; tchr. Houston Ind. Sch. Dist., 1979-81; comml. rep. Houston Lighting & Power, Houston, 1981-82, conservation cons., 1982-83, supr., 1983—, instr., 1982—; cons., instr. Houston Community Coll., 1982; commentator Sta. KTSU, Houston, 1983-84. Editor: Angelette, 1978-79. Mem. Republican Women Houston, 1980—; vol. Greater Houston Alliance of Bus., 1982—; communications vol. Tex. Chamber Orch., 1983—; sponsor Fiestas Patrias, Houston, 1983—. Recipient Nat. Info. Officer award Nat. Angel Flight, 1978-79, Outstanding Sr. Mem. award, 1979; Outstanding Young Tchr. award Houston Ind. Sch. Dist., 1980. Mem. Women Profls. in Govt., Illuminating Engring. Soc., Soc. Consumer Affairs Profls., Women in Energy, Assn. Energy Engrs. (assoc.). Home: 2010 Winrock St Apt 653 Houston TX 77057 Office: Houston Lighting & Power Co PO Box 1700 Houston TX 77001

MATHIS, THELMA ATWOOD, artist; b. Creal Springs, Ill.; d. Hubert L. and Mima (Hutchison) Atwood; B.S., So. Ill. U., 1955, M.F.A., 1957; student Art Students League, 1957-59; m. John A. Mathis, Sept. 1, 1928 (div. 1950); children—John Atwood, Shirley (Mrs. Frank Woosley), James Stevens. One-man shows So. Ill. U., 1957, 59, Sparta (Ill.) Pub. Library, 1960, Art Mart, Inc., St. Louis, 1961, St. Louis Artists Guild, 1962, Midwestern Coll. (Iowa), 1967; two-man show Madison Galleries, N.Y.C., 1963; juried N.Y.C. Center, 1958, 59, Madison Sq. Garden, N.Y.C., 1958, Nat. Old Testament, St. Louis, 1961, 62, Mo. Art Show, St. Louis City Art Mus., 1954, 55, Nat. Arts & Crafts, Wichita, Kans., 1953, 55; instr., asst. prof. art dept. Midwestern Coll., Denison, Iowa, 1965-70. Recipient Grand prize oil and drawing DuQuoin State Fair, 1955, 56, 58, 59. Mem. St. Louis Artists Guild, AAUW, Pi Lambda Theta. Baptist. Home: Box 13 Pinckneyville IL 62274

MATHIS, VIOLETTE ELEANOR, sauna and hydrotherapy mfg. exec.; b. Kouts, Ind., Feb. 14, 1933; d. Benjamin John and Elnora (Egli) Kaufmann; student Kellberg Inst. Phys. Therapy, 1952-53, No. Bapt. Sem., 1954-55, U. Calif., 1955-57; m. Cleo Donald Mathis, Nov. 5, 1961. Youth dir. 1st Bapt. Ch., Garden Grove, Calif., 1955-57; pvt. practice phys. therapy, Long Beach Calif., 1957-59; owner Rita LeRoy franchise, Long Beach, 1959-60; partner Otto C. Klaye Real Estate Investments, Encino, Calif., 1960-61; co-founder, exec. v.p. Vico Products Mfg. Co. Inc., South El Monte, Calif., 1961—; cons. sauna and hydrotherapy to archtl. and mech. engring. firms. Mem. Bldg. Industry Assn. Republican. Composer designer tech. manuals in field. Home: 609 Howard St Montebello CA 90054 Office: 1808 Potrero St South Elmonte CA 91733

MATHISEN, RHODA SHARON, communications consultant; b. Portland, Oreg., June 25, 1942; d. Daniel and Mildred Elizabeth Annette (Peterson) Hager; m. James Albert Mathisen, July 17, 1964 (div. 1977). B.A. in Edn., Music, Bible Coll., Mich., 1964. Community Relations officer Gary-Wheaton Bank, Wheaton, Ill., 1971-75; br. mgr. Stivers Temporary Personnel, Chgo., 1975-79; v.p. sales Exec. Technique, Chgo., 1980-83; prin. Mathisen Assocs., Downers Grove, Ill., 1983—; presenter seminars; lectr. various profl. orgns.; cons. Haggai Inst., Atlanta; adv. mem. Nat. Bd. Success Group, 1986. Pres. chancel choir Christ Ch. of Oak Brook, 1985-87. Mem. Bus. and Profl. Women (charter mem. Woodfield chpt.), Execs. Club Oak Brook, Women in Communications, Nat. Assn. Female Execs., Single Profl. Soc., Chgo. Assn. Commerce and Industry (named Ambassador of Month N.W. suburban chpt. 1979), Art Inst. Chgo. Republican. Office: Mathisen Assocs Box 9208 Downers Grove IL 60515

MATHUS, NINA DAMEREL, marketing executive; b. N.Y.C., July 31, 1941; d. George Sarles and Nina (Tetamo) Damerel; m. John F. Mathus, Apr. 26, 1958; children—David Lackey, Diane Kristi. Student, Fairleigh Dickinson U., 1966-67, County Coll., Morris, 1968-70. Tchr. remedial math., substitute tchr., N.Y. and N.J., 1967-75; with Salisbury Research and Info. System (Conn.), 1975, mgr., 1976; project dir. Market Probe Internat., Inc., N.Y.C., 1977; mng. dir. Central Telephone Interviewing System, 1978, pres., 1978—; exec. v.p. CTIS, 1980—; v.p. Audits & Surveys, Inc., N.Y.C., 1980—. Bd. dirs. Sharon Creative Arts Found., 1976-77; active Boy Scouts Am., Girl Scouts U.S.A., 1965-72. Mem. Am. Mktg. Assn., Market Research Assn. Republican. Clubs: Bus. and Profl. Women's, Twin Lakes Beach, Snarks. Office: 1 Park Ave New York NY 10016

MATIS, NANCY JOY, speech pathologist; b. Chgo., Sept. 20, 1954; d. Jacob David and Rosalie Bette (Metzger) Matis; B.A., Columbia U., 1976; M.S., Tchrs. Coll., Columbia U., 1978. Staff speech pathologist diagnosis, program planning, treatment of multiply handicapped pre-sch.-age children St. Agnes Hosp., White Plains, N.Y., 1978-82; sr. speech pathologist infant/toddler devel. program North Shore Univ. Hosp., Westbury, N.Y., 1982—. Chmn. Young Adults Forum, Congregation Rodeph Sholom, 1983—. Mem. N.Y. Speech and Hearing Assn., Am. Speech and Hearing Assn. (cert. clin. competence), NE Communication Enhancement Group. Home: 25 Central Park W New York NY 10023 Office: North Shore Univ Hosp Dryden St Westbury NY

MATLACK, ARDENA LAVONNE, former state legislator; b. Carlton, Kans., Dec. 20, 1930; d. Walter D. and Bessie B. (Major) Williams; student Kans. Wesleyan U., 1940, Kans. State U., 1949-51, Washburn U., 1955; B.A. cum laude, Wichita State U., 1969; m. Don Matlack, June 10, 1951; children—Lucinda Dawn, Roxanne, Terry Clyde, Rex William, Timothy Alan. Tchr., Carlton Grade Sch., 1948-49; substitute tchr. Clearwater (Kans.) Schs., 1969-74; mem. Kans. Ho. of Reps., 1974-84. Democratic precinct committeewoman, 1966-68, 85—; mem. Dem. State Com., 1974-78; pres. Kans. State Dem. Club, 1978; chmn. Clearwater March of Dimes, 1980, Clearwater Area United Fund, 1980; project leader 4-H, 1962-71; mem. Adv. Council Kans. Arts Commn., 1985—. Recipient Gold Star Legis. award Assn. for legis. action by Rural Mayors, 1981. Mem. Clearwater United Methodist Women (hon. life; pres. 1972), Dist. United Meth. Women (hon. life, dist. coordinator social involvement 1975-76), Kans. Press Women, Gold Key, Mu Phi Epsilon, Alpha Xi Delta. Clubs: Clearwater Federated Women's Study (pres. 1966-67); Kans. Federated Women's Dem. (pres. 1985— Disting. Achievement award 1977), Clearwater Bus. and Profl. Women's (pres. 1985-86), West Side Dem. Home: 615 Elaine St Clearwater KS 67026 Office: State Capitol Bldg Topeka KS 66612

MATLOCK, EDITH, electronic test instruments company executive; b. N.Y.C., Aug. 5, 1947; d. Jack and Theresa (Michielli) Perna; m. Donald M. Matlock, Jr., June 28, 1969 (div. 1976); 1 son, Donald M. B.S., Rider Coll. Tchr., Newfield High Sch., Centereach, N.Y., 1970-73; dir. Jefferson Shores Sch., Port Jefferson, N.Y., 1973-77; adminstrv. asst. Bank Hapoalim, N.Y.C., 1977-81; asst. to pres. Leader Instruments Corp., Hauppauge, N.Y., 1981—. Mem. Task Force Gov. N.J., 1969; sec., Sachem Youth Soccer League, Lake Ronkonkoma, N.Y., 1980. Mem. Alumni Assn. Dowling Coll. Democrat. Roman Catholic. Office: Leader Instruments Corp 380 Oser Ave Hauppauge NY 11788

MATROSS, JEANNE KUKURA, lawyer; b. N.Y.C., Dec. 29, 1946; d. Emmett and Helen (Grekulinski) Kukura; m. Ronald Philip Matross, Aug. 14, 1971; children—Robin, Daniel. B.A., Barnard Coll., 1968; J.D., NYU, 1971. Bar: Minn. 1972, D.C. 1978. Atty. HUD, Mpls., 1972-86; atty. Met. Waste Control Commn., 1986—; instr. U. Minn., 1978—; mem. Mayor's Blue-Ribbon Personnel Issues Task Force, St. Paul, 1983—; mem. jud. liaison Minn. Women's Polit. Caucus, 1976-78. Freelance columnist on legal issues Minn. Women's Press, 1985—. Pres. St. Paul LWV, 1982-83, 2d v.p., 1982, chairperson action com., 1979-82; mem. com. to develop Minn. real estate licensure exam. Minn. Dept. Commerce, 1986; comml. arbitrator Am. Arbitration Assn., 1983—. N.Y. State Regents scholar, 1964-71. Mem. Minn. Bar Assn., Ramsey County Bar Assn., Minn. Women Lawyers, Nat. Assn. Women Lawyers, ABA, Phi Beta Kappa. Roman Catholic. Home: 486 Frontenac Pl Saint Paul MN 55104 Office: 350 Metro Sq Bldg St Paul MN 55101

MATSA, LOULA ZACHAROULA, social services adminstr.; b. Piraeus, Greece, Apr. 16, 1935; came to U.S., 1952, naturalized 1962; d. Eleftherios Georgiou and Ourania E. (Fraguiskopoulou) Papoulias; student Pierce Coll., Athens, Greece, 1948-52; B.A., Rockford Coll., 1953; M.A., U. Chgo., 1955; m. Ilco S. Matsa, Nov. 27, 1953; 1 son, Aristotle Ricky. Marital counselor Family Soc. Cambridge, Mass., 1955-56; chief unit II, social service Queen's (N.Y.) Children's Psychiat. Center, 1961-74; dir. social services, supr.-coordinator family care program Hudson River Psychiat. Center, Poughkeepsie, N.Y., 1974—; field instr. Adelphi, Albany and Fordham univs., 1969—. Fulbright Exchange student, 1952-53; Talcott scholar, 1953-55. Mem. Internat. Platform Assn., Internat. Council on Social Welfare, Nat. Assn. Social Workers, Assn. Cert. Social Workers, Civil Service Employees Assn., Pierce Coll. Alumni Assn. Democrat. Greek Orthodox. Contbr. articles to profl. jours.; instrumental in state policy changes in treatment and court representation of emtionally disturbed and mentally ill. Home: 81-11 45th Ave Elmhurst NY 11373 Office: Hudson River Psychiat Center Branch B Poughkeepsie NY 12601

MATSON, FRANCES SHOBER, social worker; b. Cin., Mar. 21, 1921; d. Frank Lyford and Florence Leone (Bridgeford) Shober; student U. Cin., 1939-41, B.A., 1951, postgrad., 1951-52; M.S.W., U. Calif., 1956; m. John Alan Matson, Dec. 2, 1942 (dec.). Councillor, County of San Mateo, 1956-57; therapist, supr. Center for Treatment and Edn. on Alcoholism, Oakland, Calif., 1957-63; pvt. practice social worker, Berkeley, Calif., 1960-64; supt. dept. social service County of Marin, Calif., 1966; psychotherapist Marin Inst., 1966-70, Oaknoll Naval Hosp., 1969; public health social worker Dept. Health County of Contra Costa (Calif.), 1972; psychotherapist Day Care Center for Schizophrenics, Contra Costa County Med. Services, 1972-74; dir. Martinez Mental Health Clinic, Contra Costa County Med. Services, 1974-81; coordinator adult outpatient services, edn., group therapy Contra Costa County Mental Health Center, 1981—. Lic. clin. social worker. Mem. Nat. Assn. Social Workers, Acad. Cert. Social Workers, Internat. Transactional Analysis Assn., Marin Assn. Mental Health, Contra Costa County Mental Health Assn., Soc. Clin. Social Work. Home: Box 2073 Martinez CA 94553 Office: 2025 Port Chicago Hwy Concord CA

MATSUKAGE, FAY MARIKO, lawyer; b. Honolulu, Sept. 1, 1955; d. Daniel Ryuzo and Nobuko M. B.A. summa cum laude, Colo. Coll., 1976; J.D., U. Denver, 1979. Bar: Colo. 1980. Assoc. firm McKie and Assocs., Denver, 1980-81, Olsen & Guardi, Denver, 1981-83; ptnr. Olsen & Matsukage, Denver, 1984-86; sole practice, Denver, 1986—. Mem. ABA, Denver Bar Assn., Colo. Bar Assn., Phi Beta Kappa. Office: 1433 17th St Suite 300 Denver CO 80202

MATSUMOTO, SHIGEMI, soprano, educator; b. Denver; d. Moriichi and Suki Matsumoto; B.A. in Mus. Performance, Calif. State U., Northridge; m. Martin J. Stark, Apr. 27, 1967. Performances with opera companies in Brussels, San Francisco, Phila., Portland, Oreg., Wolf Trap, Va., Kansas City, Mo., Tucson, San Antonio, Toledo/Dayton, Ohio, Augusta, Ga., Little Rock, Lake George, N.Y., also Spring Opera Theatre; with symphonies in Antwerp, Belgium, Lourdes, France, Mexico City, San Francisco, Mpls., Pitts., St. Louis, Houston, Denver, New Orleans, Memphis and Wichita, other cities; numerous internat. recitals including Tokyo, Washington, Chgo., Los Angeles, San Francisco, Houston, Vancouver, B.C., Kansas City, San Antonio, Milw.; lectr. demonstrations, master classes coll. campuses; guest artist, lectr. Can. Fedn. Music Tchrs.; guest soloist 25th Anniversary Celebration Founding UN, 1970. Recipient 1st prize Western Regional Met. Opera Auditions, 1967; grand winner San Francisco Nat. Opera Auditions, 1968; award winner Geneva Internat. Music Competitions, 1971; grantee Nat. Opera Inst., Internat. Inst. Edn., Los Angeles Bur. Music; named Japanese Woman of Year in So. Calif., Japanese-Am. Soc., 1969-70. Mem. Am. Guild Mus. Artists. Republican. Presbyterian. Home: 18342 Chatham Ln Northridge CA 91326 also 18142 Arminta St Reseda CA 91335

MATSUMURA, VERA YOSHI, pianist; b. Oakland, Calif.; d. Naojiro and Aguri Tanaka; B.A. in Piano Pedagogy, Coll. of Holy Names, Oakland, 1938; pvt. studies with F. Moss, M. Shapiro, L. Kreutzer, P. Jarrett; m. Jiro Matsumura, Aug. 8, 1942; 1 son, Kenneth N. Staff mem., pianist Radio Sta. KROW, Oakland, 1938-39; numerous concert performances in Far East (Japan, Thailand), 1940—; numerous teaching appointments, 1940—; dir. Internat. Music Council, Berkeley, Calif., 1969—. Named to Hall of Fame, Piano Guild, 1968. Mem. Music Tchrs. Nat. Assn., Music Tchrs. Assn. Calif., Internat. Platform Assn., Alpha Phi Mu. Methodist. Home: 2 Claremont Crescent Berkeley CA 94705

MATSUSHIMA, JANICE E., catering coordinator; b. Honolulu, Oct. 30, 1956; d. Ronald S. and Betty T. (Konishi) M. Student Kapiolani Community Coll., Honolulu, 1974-75. Lei greeter, tour guide Hawaiian Adventure Tours, Honolulu, 1975-76, tour coordinator, 1976-80; sales rep. Roberts Hawaii Tours, Honolulu, 1980-81; chief purser, paymaster Am. Hawaii Cruises, Honolulu, 1980-85; catering sales mgr. Westin Ilikai Hotel, Honolulu, 1985—. Mem. Am. Bus. Women Assn., Nat. Assn. Catering Execs., Hawaii Internat. Hospitality Ctr., Hotel Sales and Mktg. Assn., Network of Mktg. Women. Baptist. Avocations: handcrafts, cooking, sewing, sailing, swimming. Home: 3247 Catherine St Honolulu HI 96815 Office: Westin Ilikai Hotel 1777 Ala Moana Blvd Honolulu HI 96815

MATSUYAMA, MARILYN NIWAO, lawyer, accountant; b. Hilo, Hawaii, Sept. 24, 1951; d. Jitsuo and Masako (Kamitaki) Niwao; m. Leighton K. Matsuyama, Oct. 11, 1980. B.S., U. Wash., 1973, M.S. in Pub. Health Biostats., 1975; J.D., U. Mich., 1978. Bar: Hawaii; C.P.A., Hawaii. Sr. tax specialist Coopers & Lybrand, Honolulu, 1978-80; tax mgr. Deloitte Haskins & Sells, Wailuku, Hawaii, 1980-85; ptnr. Matsuyama, Niwao & Assocs., Wailuku, 1985—; corp. sec., dir. Maui Fin. Co., Wailuku, 1983-84. Mem. fin. com., treas. capital devel. campaign steering com. YMCA, Wailuku, 1985—; bd. dirs. Maui YMCA, 1986—. Mem. ABA (sect. on taxation), Hawaii Bar Assn., Maui Bar Assn., Am. Inst. C.P.A.s, Maui Estate Planning Council, Hawaii Assn. Public Accts. (pres. Maui chpt. 1986—). Office: Matsuyama Niwao & Assocs 2145 Wells St Suite 402 Wailuku HI 96793

MATTA, LORENE GENEVA, electronics firm executive; b. San Jose, Calif., Aug. 27, 1943; d. Willie Manuel and Lorene (Baxter) Dean; m. Dallas Joseph, May 18, 1959; children—Tina Lynn, Heidi Ann, Preston Joseph (dec.). Electronic assembler Sylvania, Santa Cruz, Calif., 1961-63; motel mgr., Santa Cruz, 1963-64; waitress Santa Cruz Holiday Inn, 1969-70; co-owner, operator Dallas Union 76 Service Sta., Bainbridge, Ga., 1973-74; electronic assembly contractor, Santa Cruz, 1975-81; pres., co-owner, Dallas Electronics, Santa Cruz, 1981—. Mem. Santa Cruz PTA, 1968-82, Bainbridge, 1973-74. Democrat. Avocations: writing; sewing; knitting; gardening. Home: 1351 High St Santa Cruz CA 95060 Office: Dallas Electronics 1201 Shaffer Rd Sect B Santa Cruz CA 95060

MATTE, JEANINE LOUISE, lawyer; b. Ridgewood, N.J., Apr. 18, 1949; d. Lucien J. and Anne T. M.; B.S., Va. Poly. Inst., 1971; J.D., U. N.C., 1974. Bar: N.C. 1974, D.C. 1978, U.S. Supreme Ct. 1978. Atty., U.S. Dept. Agr., Washington, 1975-80; sr. atty. U.S. Dept. Energy, Washington, 1980-82; asst. gen. counsel U.S. Synthetic Fuels Corp., Washington, 1982—. Recipient Exceptional Service award U.S. Dept. Energy, 1982; Outstanding Performance award Am. Lawyer mag., 1982; Superior Service award U.S. Synthetic Fuels Corp., 1983. Mem. ABA (synthetic fuels com., natural resources com., corp., banking and bus. law com.) Fed. Bar Assn., D.C. Bar Assn., N.C. Bar Assn., Mortar Bd. Home: 10221 Forest Lake Dr Great Falls VA 22066 Office: 2121 K St Washington DC 22206

MATTEUCIG, IOLE LOUISE, library consultant; b. San Francisco, Mar. 1, 1926; d. Anselmo and Rosminda (Stefanini) Cagnoni; m. Giacinto Matteucig, June 26, 1948; children—Catherine, Michael, Laurence. B.A., U. Calif.-Berkeley, 1947, B.L.S., 1948. Instr. library sci., U. San Francisco, 1968-69; instr., librarian City Coll. of San Francisco, 1968-72, dean Library Services, 1972-83, dean, emeritus, 1983—; ind. cons. library mgmt., San Francisco, 1983—; cons. San Francisco Community Coll. Dist., 1983—. HEW grantee, 1970. Mem. ALA (mem. legis. network Washington, 1980-83), Calif. Library Assn., Spl. Library Assn., Assn. Calif. Community Coll. Adminstrs. Home: 55 Aerial Way San Francisco CA 94116

MATTHES, BETSY DURKIN, lyricist, actress; b. Ft. Benning, Ga., Mar. 11, 1942; d. Edwin Joseph and Marjorie (Flynn) Ostberg; m. Gerald Stephen Rutter Matthes, Aug. 22, 1965 (div.); children—Peter, Charlton. Grad. Am. Theatre Wing, 1961. Appeared in various TV commls.; appeared in plays including: Cactus Flower (Broadway), Mary Mary (nat. co.); appeared in day-time series Dark Shadows, Hidden Faces; lyricist Love Express, Love is Holdin' On, Slip Into Somethin' Comfortable, Pleasure Man, Let's Get Down to Doin' It Tonight, Let's Go Another Dound, Chocolate Shake, Someone Just For Me, Veronica, I Was Made for You, Not In the Same Way, Do You Love Him, Looking Back, Crazy In Love, Right Before My Eyes, She's Gonna Love Ya to Death. Mem. Actors Equity Assn., Screen Actors Guild, AFTRA, ASCAP, NOW, Nat. Assn. Female Execs. Democrat. Home and office: 211 E 35th St New York NY 10016

MATTHEW, LYN, art marketing consultant and educator; b. Long Beach, Calif., Dec. 15, 1936; d. Harold G. and Beatrice (Hunt) M.; m. Wayne Thomas Castleberry, Aug. 12, 1961 (div. Jan. 1976); children—Melanie, Cheryl, Nicole, Matthew. B.S., U. Calif.-Davis, 1958; M.A., Ariz. State U., 1979. Pres., Davlyn Cons. Found., Scottsdale, Ariz., 1979-82; cons. The Art Business, Scottsdale, 1982—; vis. prof. Maricopa Community Coll., Phoenix, 1979—, Ariz. State U., Tempe, 1980-83; cons. Women's Caucus for Art, Phoenix, 1983—. Author: The Business Aspects of Art, Book I, 1979, Book II, 1979; Marketing Strategies for the Creative Artist, 1985. Mem. Women Image Now (Achievement and Contbn. in Visual Arts award 1983), Women in Higher Edn., Nat. Women's Caucus for Art (v.p. 1981-83), Ariz. Women's Caucus for Art (pres. 1980-82), Vocat. Edn. Assn. (sec. 1978-80).

MATTHEWS, AGNES CYNTHIA, state senator; b. Washington, Pa., Feb. 1, 1924; d. Spero and Harriet Kosmas; m. Phathon James Matthews, Dec. 5, 1946; children—Denise, Spero. B.S., Barnard Coll., 1946. Dep. mayor (1 term) Wethersfield, Conn., 1980—, mayor (2 terms), council woman, 1973-81; mem. Conn. Senate (representing 9th dist.), 1982-84; v.p., dir. Pie-O-Neer Corp., East Hardford, Conn., 1980—, Out O'Mystic Schooner Cruises, Mystic, Conn., 1967—, Sargent's Head Realty Corp., East Lyme, Conn., 1959—. Office: Out of Mystic Schooner Cruises 7 Holmes St Mystic CT 06109

MATTHEWS, ANNE LAMB, educational administrator, state official; b. Florence County, S.C., Nov. 3, 1942; d. Alex B. and Mettie (Nettles) L.; B.S. in Bus. Edn., Coker Coll., 1964; M.A. in Econs., Appalachian State U., 1968; Ed.D. in Ednl. Adminstrn., U. S.C., 1975; m. Glenny Jeff Matthews, Sept. 2, 1967. Tchr. bus. edn. dept. Hannah-Pamplico High Sch., Pamplico, S.C., 1964-67; instr. dept. bus. adminstrn. and secretarial sci. Florence-Darlington Tech. Edn. Coll., Florence, S.C., 1967-69; tchr.-counselor Youth Study Center, Greenville, S.C., 1970-71; dist. cons. Office Occupations Edn., Anderson (S.C.) Dist. Office, 1971-73; adj. prof. Coll. Bus. Adminstrn. U. S.C., Columbia, 1975-78; state supr. bus. and office edn. S.C. Dept. Edn., Columbia, 1973-80, chief supr. program planning and devel., 1980—, mem. various coms., 1975—; mem. Nat. Adv. Council for Career Edn., Nat. Commn. Employment Policy, Practitioners Task Force; nat. speaker over 300 confs. Vol. Vets Hosp., Columbia, 1978—; trustee Coker Coll., Hartsville, S.C.; bd. dirs. Richland County Am. Cancer Soc. Recipient Hulda Erath award, 1978, 79. Mem. Nat. Bus. Edn. Assn. (chmn. policies com. on bus. and econ. edn. 1979-80, pres. elect 1984, pres. 1985-86), So. Bus. Edn. Assn. (pres. 1984-85), Nat. Assn. State Suprs. of Bus. and Office Edn. (pres. 1977-79), S.C. Office Occupations Assn. (mem. exec. bd. 1973-76), Internat. Soc. for Bus. Edn., Am. Vocat. Assn. (mem. policy and planning com. 1977—), Adminstrv. Mgmt. Soc., S.C. Vocat. Dirs. Assn., S.C. Bus. Edn. Assn. (pres. 1969-70, mem. exec. bd. 1965-77), S.C. Vocat. Assn. (mem. program com. 1975-76), S.C. State Employees Assn., Internat. Word Processing Assn., S.C. Council for Adminstrv. Women in Edn., Nat. Speakers Assn., S.C. Hist. Soc., Friends of State Mus., Delta Kappa Gamma, Phi Delta Kappa. Baptist. Contbr. numerous articles to profl. jours.; author word processing materials; editor and reviewer various manuals and instructional guides on bus. and office occupations programs. Office: 904 Rutledge Bldg State Dept Education Columbia SC 29209

MATTHEWS, BURNITA SHELTON, judge; b. Burnell, Miss., Dec. 28, 1894; d. Burnell and Lora Drew (Barlow) Shelton; LL.B., George Washington U., (formerly Nat. U.), 1919, LL.M., 1920, LL.D. (hon.), 1950; LL.D. (hon.), Am. U., 1966; m. Percy Ashley Matthews, Apr. 28, 1917. Admitted to D.C., Miss., U.S. Supreme Ct. bars; practice in Washington, 1920; active in securing equal rights for women; formerly mem. faculty Washington Coll. Law; judge U.S. Dist. Ct. for D.C. (1st woman fed. dist. judge), 1949-68, sr. judge, 1968—. Past mem. Com. Experts Women's Work ILO; formerly mem. research com. Inter-Am. Commn. Women; former mem. Nat. Woman's Party. Mem., past 1st v.p. nat. bd. Med. Coll. Pa. (formerly Woman's Med. Coll. Pa.); nat. devel. com. Am. U. Recipient Alumni Achievement award George Washington U., 1968; Distinguished Service award Bar Assn. D.C., 1968. Mem. ABA, Nat. Assn. Women Lawyers (past pres.). Drafted many laws sponsored by Nat. Woman's Party. Home: 5420 Connecticut Ave NW Washington DC 20015 Office: US Courthouse 3d and Constitution Ave NW Washington DC 20001

MATTHEWS, CARYL EVE, radio station executive; b. Grand Rapids, Mich., Jan. 20, 1937; d. Walter Ray and Mary Elizabeth (Grant) Matthews. B.Music, Ind. U., 1958, M.Music, 1959. Vis. instr. Ark. State Coll., Conway, 1959-61; instr. Drury Coll., Springfield, Mo., 1961-65; program producer WBAA-Radio, West Lafayette, Ind., 1969-70, music supr., 1970-77, program dir., music supr., 1977—. Soloist, collaborative artist harpsichord and piano; producer, organizer 3 multiple piano festivals, Monster Concerts, Lafayette, 1979-82. Artistic cons. Bach Chorale Singers, 1982-85; bd. dirs. Tippecanoe Arts Fedn., Lafayette, 1982-86; mem. Worship and Music Commn., Episc. Diocese of Indpls., 1985—. Mem. Sigma Alpha Iota, Pi Kappa Lambda, Alpha Lambda Delta. Episcopalian. Office: WBAA Purdue U West Lafayette IN 47907

MATTHEWS, DORIS BOOZER, educator; b. Lexington, S.C., Aug. 18, 1932; d. Otto Raymond and Ruth (Sox) Boozer; B.S., Newberry Coll., 1952; M.Ed., U. S.C., 1955, advanced cert., 1971, Ph.D., 1972; m. Charles L. Matthews, Aug. 20, 1952; children—Shirley Ruth, Charles Ray, Sylvia Ann. Tchr., Brennen Sch., Columbia, S.C., 1952-64; supr. counseling S.C. State Employment Service, Columbia, 1964-66; counseling supr. and basic edn. specialist S.C. Com. for Tech. Edn., Columbia, 1966-68; instr. elem. edn. U. S.C., Columbia, 1968-72; asst. prof. Coll. of S.C. State Coll., Orangeburg, 1972-75, asso. prof., 1975-79, prof., 1979—; profl. lectr. Chmn., Columbians Youth Com., 1968-72, treas., 1966-72; chmn. Cayce Neighborhood Center, 1967-70. Mem. S.C. Edn. Assn., Assn. Supervision and Curriculum Devel., Employment Counselors Assn., Am., S.C. (pres. 1976-77) vocat. guidance assns., Am., S.C. personnel and guidance assns., Am. Communications and Tech. Assn., AAUP (pres. chpt. 1976-79, pres. S.C. conf. 1981-83), Assn. Tchr.

Educators, Assn. for Individually Guided Edn., Am. Vocat. Assn., Am. Humanistic Edn. and Devel., Internat. Stress and Tension Control Soc., Delta Kappa Gamma, Phi Delta Kappa (v.p. local chpt. 1978-79, pres. 1979-81). Lutheran (pres. ch. women 1971-74). Clubs: Cayce Womens (pres. 1965-67), Fashion Rose Garden (pres. 1962-64). Contbr. numerous articles to profl. jours. Home: 101 Deliesseline Rd Cayce SC 29033 Office: SC State Coll Orangeburg SC 29117

MATTHEWS, DOROTHEA ELIZABETH, lawyer; b. Englewood, N.J., June 12, 1947; d. John Clark and Dorothea (Kidd) Matthews; A.B., Smith Coll., 1969; J.D., Fordham U., 1974. Bar: N.Y. Assoc., Reid & Priest, N.Y.C., 1974-82, ptnr., 1983—. Mem. exec. com. Met. Republican Club; N.Y. County Rep. committeewoman. Mem. ABA. Presbyterian. Club: Smith Coll. Contbr. articles to profl. jours. Office: 40 W 57th St New York NY 10019

MATTHEWS, GAIL THUNBERG, marketing executive; b. Hartford, Conn., July 29, 1938; d. Harold Einar and Mildred (Wentland) Thunberg; student Boston U., 1958-59; m. Glenn Holbrook Matthews, Aug. 9, 1959; children—Scott Holbrook, Brett Holbrook. Hostess show, copywriter Sta. WJDA, Boston, 1956-58; fashion coordinator Jordan Marsh, Boston, 1958-59, Miller & Rhoades, Richmond, Va., 1959-60, Sage Allen, Hartford, 1960-61; columnist Boston Globe, 1962-63, Hartford Times, 1961-63; free-lance writer, contbr. articles to New Englander mag., Christian Sci. Monitor, Yankee, 1961-65; v.p., treas. Coll. Mktg. Group, Inc., Winchester, Mass., 1968—; corporator Reading Savs. Bank; mem. adv. council Baybank Middlesex. Choral dir. Barrows Sch., Reading; pres. local PTA; chmn. Heart Fund Reading; founder, chmn. Reading chpt. Am. Cancer Soc., named citizen of yr., 1983-84. Recipient Service to Youth award Reader's Digest, 1962; CAP award 1965; Spl. award Am. Cancer Soc., 1981, 82; Citizenship award Reading Tchrs. Assn., 1980. Mem. Antiquarian Soc. Club: Dartmouth Coll. Women's (bd. dirs.). Author: Hor'doeuvre Cooking, 1966; Gourmet Cooking, 1966; Birthday Fortune Book, 1967; (children's series) The Adventures of a Shih Tzu The Good Luck Puppy, 1980. Office: The Mill 1873 50 Cross St Winchester MA 01890

MATTHEWS, JEANNE PEARSON, logistic support analyst, company executive; b. Marietta, Ga., July 2, 1941; d. Silas Leon and Edith Mae (Rich) Pearson; m. William Dean Bottoms, Apr. 2, 1960 (div. 1973); 1 child, William Dave; m. William Glenn Matthews, Sept. 4, 1976. Typist, stenographer, sec. Lockheed-Ga. Co., Marietta, 1962-82, gen. acct., price estimator, 1982-84, logistic support analyst, 1984—; pres. J&B Office Service, Inc., Villa Rica, Ga., 1984—. Named Hon. Lt. Col. Aide-de-Camp Ala. State Militia, 1976; named Ms. Lockheed, Lockheed-Ga. Co., 1972, 74. Mem. Nat. Assn. Female Execs., Nat. Assn. Mature People, Paulding County C. of C. Democrat. Baptist. Clubs: Kennesaw Mountain Beagle (sec.-treas. Dallas, Ga. 1980—), Atlanta Braves Fan. Lodge: Order Eastern Star (rec. sec. Smyrna chpt. 387 1973-79). Avocations: Beagles; baseball; swimming. Home: Route 2 Box 519 Villa Rica GA 30180

MATTHEWS, JUDITH ELIZABETH, apparel industry executive; b. Pittsfield, Mass., June 9, 1948; d. Joseph Gordon and Florence Catherine (Sisson) Matthews; m. Griffith Ross McSwine, Aug. 8, 1970 (div. 1978). B.A., U. Fla., 1970. Counselor SP/Amcell, Jacksonville, Fla., 1972-73; researcher Freeman, Richardson, Watson, Jacksonville, 1973-74; sr. cons. Summerour & Assocs., Atlanta, 1974-84; assoc. Werner Mgmt., N.Y.C., 1984-85; mfg. mgr. Thomas Textile Co., Athens, Ga., 1985—. Contbr. articles to profl. jours. Fin. counselor Employee Assistance Program, Athens, 1986. Mem. Am. Apparel Mfrs. Assn., Indsl. Mgmt. Assn., Athens C. of C., Alpha Omicron Pi (pres. 1968-69). Democrat. Episcopalian. Avocations: racquetball; reading.

MATTHEWS, KAY CARROLL RAY, former educational services administrator; b. Meridian, Miss., Nov. 6, 1949; d. Charles E. and Barbara L. (Wilson) Ray. B.S., Bethune-Cookman Coll., Daytona Beach, Fla., 1971; M.A., Columbia U., 1984, M.Ed., 1984. Supr. tng. Opportunities Industrialization Ctr., Meridian, Miss., 1972-73, employment advisor, 1973-78, supr. student service, Bronx, N.Y., 1980-82; career advisor Youth Employment Tng. Program, Bronx, 1978-80; supr. counseling psychology dept. Tchrs. Coll. Columbis U., 1984-86, also teaching asst. Mem. Nat. Assn. Female Execs., Am. Psychol. Assn. Democrat. Baptist. Avocations: traveling; writing; bicycling; reading.

MATTHEWS, LINDA LLEWELLYN FINK, profl. assn. adminstr.; b. LaPort, Ind., Oct. 29, 1950; d. Omar Ray and Marianne Denham (Smith) Fink, Jr.; student U. N.C., Greensboro, 1968-70; B.A., George Washington U., 1973; m. Daniel G. Matthews, Oct. 25, 1975; children—Strelka Jamila, Francesca Alina. Admnstrv. asst. African Bibliog. Center, Washington, 1974-75, adminstrv. editor, 1975-79, adminstrv. dir., 1979—; adminstrv. dir. African Devel. Info. Assn. U.S.A., 1981—; treas., bd. dirs. African Communications Liaison Services, Washington, 1978—. Asso. mem. Women's Inst. for Freedom of Press, Washington, 1977—; coordinator communications liaison com. Washington Task Force on African Affairs, 1975-78; cons. article on Rhodesia, Nat. Geog. Mag., 1975. Mem. African-Am. Women's Assn. Editorial bd. and reviewer A Current Bibliography on African Affairs, 1974—; editor AMA: Women in African & American Worlds, An Outlook, 1975-80, HABARI Special Reports, 1978—; asso. producer Film Leopold Sedar Senghor, 1975; cons., writer Changing Africa, NBC/WRC-TV, 1976; asst. editor Am-South African Relations: Bibliographic Essays, 1975; compiler, co-author: Burundi: A Selected Bibliography & Resource Guide, 1975. Mem. Am. Mgmt. Assn., Internat. Platform Assn., African Studies Assn. Home: PO Box 13096 Washington DC 20009

MATTHEWS, MARY WEAKLEY, reading specialist, educator; b. St. Louis, Mar. 17, 1923; d. Jesse Anderson and Betelene (Joiner) Weakley; m. Arminous Rudolph Matthews, Sr., Jan. 3, 1943; children—Arminous Rudolph, Ronald J., Michael A., Carolyn E. B.A., Harris-Stowe Coll., St. Louis, 1959; M.Ed., St. Louis U., 1968. Cert. reading specialist, Mo. Elem. tchr. Madison Sch., St. Louis, 1959-65, Carroll St. Sch., 1965-67, Clinton Sch., 1967-73; remedial reading tchr. L'Ouverture Sch., St. Louis, 1973—; tchr. rep. sch. com. council St. Louis U., 1977-80; PTA tchr. rep., 1973—; del. tchr. corps St. Louis U. Conf., 1979. Mem. St. Peters African Methodist Episcopal Ch., St. Louis, sec. to steward bd., 1972—, dir. promotion missionary edn., local and conf. br. del. A.M.E. Ch. Bishops Council, Jamaica, 1978. Mem. NEA (team leader) 1965, Mo. State Tchrs. Assn., Nat. Council Tchrs. of English, Phi Delta Kappa, Iota Phi Lambda (Apple for Tchr. award 1983), Sigma Gamma Rho. Club: Fidelity (sec. 1983-84, treas. 1980-82). Home: 4646 Kossuth Ave Saint Louis MO 63115 Office: Toussaint L'Ouverture Middle Sch 3021 Hickory St Saint Louis MO 63104

MATTHEWS, NANCY LOU, librarian; b. Texarkana, Ark., July 8, 1931; d. Edgar and Wilhelmina (Mulhearn) Matthews. B.A., U. Ark.-Fayetteville, 1953; M.S., UCLA, 1984. Research assoc. Baylor U. Hosp., Dallas, 1953-55, Wadley Research Inst., Dallas, 1955-57, Rockefeller Inst., N.Y.C., 1957-60, UCLA Med. Sch., 1960-74; freelance writer, Los Angeles, 1974-82; info. specialist Arco Petroleum, Los Angeles, 1983-84; staff writer Los Angeles Community Coll. Dist., 1979-80, Research Assistance Inc., 1977-79; assoc. librarian Los Angeles Times, 1984—. Contbr. articles to profl. jours. Mem. NOW, ALA, Am. Soc. Info. Sci. Democrat. Ishtarian. Home: 17447 Tiara St Encino CA 91316

MATTHEWS, PATRICIA ANN, retail company executive; b. Victorville, Calif., Jan. 8, 1957; d. Samual Rosevelt Jones and Rose Marie (Hasty) Jones Williams; m. Richard Patrick Matthews, Nov. 24, 1978; children—Angela Lynne, Sonnie James, Richard Paul Samual. Student in psychology U. N.Mex., 1982-84. Personnel specialist Lovelace Med. Ctr., Albuquerque, 1977-79; personnel dir. Richardson Med. Ctr., Tex., 1979-80; asst. mgr. Lionel Playworld, San Antonio, 1980-81; zone mgr. Circle K Corp., Albuquerque, 1981-84, dist. mgr., Farmington, N.Mex., 1984—. Fundraising coordinator Muscular Dystrophy, Albuquerque, 1982-84, United Cerebral Palsy, Farmington, 1984—. Recipient awards Circle K Corp., 1983. Mem. Nat. Assn. Female Execs., Bloomfield C. of C., U.S. C. of C. Republican. Roman Catholic. Avocation: physical conditioning. Home: 4301 Windsor Dr Farmington NM 87401 Office: Circle K Corp 110 N 4th St Suite 2 Bloomfield NM 87413

MATTHEWS, PATRICIA CORNWELL, lawyer, labor relations specialist; b. Washington, Aug. 30, 1953; d. Edward Eugene and Shirley (Nims) Cornwell; 1 dau., Sheryl Yvette. B.A., Am. U., 1974; J.D., Georgetown U., 1977. Bar: D.C. 1977, U.S. Ct. Appeals (3d, 4th, 5th, 6th, 7th, 8th, 9th and 10th cirs.), U.S. Supreme Ct. 1982. Appellate atty. NLRB, Washington, 1977-79, trial atty., Atlanta, 1980-81; labor relations counsel McDonald's Corp., Chgo., 1981-84; labor relations officer Washington Met. Area Transit Authority, 1984—. Mem. ABA, Nat. Bar Assn. Office: METRO 600 5th St NW Washington DC 20001

MATTHEWS-FLOYD, MARY ETTA, vocational school administrator; b. Sparta, Tenn., Nov. 18, 1925; d. Ransom E. and Lily (Williams) Howard; m. Warren G. Matthews, Apr. 30, 1946 (dec. 1969); children—Fayetta Littrell, Jean Wellman. A.A., Truman Coll., 1965. Cert. dir. vocat. schs., Ill. Corr., Time-Life mag., Chgo., 1954-68; edn. dir. Cosmopolitan Style Team, Washington, 1971-75; adminstr. Onyx Vocat. Sch., Chgo., 1979—; exec. dir. Mathis/Matthews Prodns., Chgo., 1983—; lectr. in field. Author: (play) Jesus Called, Lazarus Come Forth, 1985. Producer, producer: (stage play) A Man Called Jesue, 1983-85. Moderator, producer: (radio serial) Gospel Theater, 1984. Recipient Cert. Drop Out Prevention Program, Ill., 1983. Mem. Am. Women Radio and TV, Allied Cos. Ill. Democrat. Baptist. Office: Onyx Vocat Sch 17 N State St #910 Chicago IL 60602

MATTHIES, MARY TILLMAN, lawyer; b. Baton Rouge, Mar. 22, 1948; d. Allen Douglas and Mazie (Poche) Tillman; 1 son, Alexander Douglas Martin. B.S. in Microbiology, Okla. State U., 1969; J.D., U. Tulsa, 1972. Bar: Okla. 1973, U.S. Supreme Ct. 1976. Assoc. and ptnr. firm Kothe, Nichols & Wolfe, Tulsa, 1972-78; sr. prin., pres. Matthies Law Firm, P.C., Tulsa, 1978—. Contbr. articles to profl. jours. Staff mem. Law Jour., U. Tulsa Coll. Law, 1971-72. Mem. ABA (co-chmn. subcoms. equal employment com.), Okla. Bar Assn. (chmn., sec., council mem. labor law sect.), Tulsa County Bar Assn., Tulsa Women Lawyers Assn. Presbyterian. Office: Matthies Law Firm PC Reunion Ctr Suite 300 Tulsa OK 74103

MATTHYS, ELIZABETH KLEIN, distributive edn. educator, coordinator; b. Stamford, Conn., Sept. 10, 1927; d. Henry and Emily Catherine (Weir) Klein; B.S., Simmons Coll., 1949; M.A., Framingham State Coll., 1978; m. Leon T. Matthys, Aug. 29, 1949; children—Lynne, Donna, Beth. Asst. buyer Jordan Marsh Co., Boston, 1949-51; asst. sales mgr. Curity Nursery Products, 1951-52; dir. comml. continuity Gen. Electric Co., Sta. WGY, Schenectady, 1952-53; retail mgmt. program coordinator Henry O. Peabody Sch., Norwood, Mass., 1970—; advisor Tri-County Regional Vocat. Tech. Sch., 1975—. Leader, Girl Scouts Am., Walpole, Mass., 1951-52, Acton, Mass., Norfolk, Mass., 1960-70; chmn. study group LWV, Acton, Mass., 1962-68. Mem. Fashion Group, NEA, Am. Vocat. Assn., Mass. Vocat. Assn., Norfolk County Tchrs. Assn., Nat. Assn. Distributive Edn. Tchrs., Distributive Edn. Clubs Am. Republican. Baptist. Home: 11 King Philip Trail Norfolk MA 02056 Office: HO Peabody Sch Peabody Rd Norwood MA 02062

MATTINGLY, SHEILA KAY STEWART, proprietor, marketing representative; b. Levelland, Tex., Apr. 18, 1953; d. Jack Merlin Stewart and Barbara June (Latch) Birchfield; m. William Allen Gresham, Apr. 23, 1976 (div. June 1978); m. Joseph Harold Mattingly, June 14, 1979; children—Wendy Gayle, Heidy Lane, Chase Stewart. Assoc., Tex. Tech U., 1973. Level I cert., American Inst. Banking. Mktg. sec. Houston Citizens Bank, 1973-76; adminstrv. asst. Capital Nat. Bank, Houston, 1976, Union Bank, Houston, 1976-78; mktg. dir. Excello Circuits, Inc., Houston, 1978-80; mktg. officer Commonwealth Bank, Houston, 1980-82; owner/propr. Unique Corner, Houston, 1982—; advisor cons. various retail orgns., Houston, 1982—. Active mem. Houston Heights Assn., Tex., 1981—; formation com. mem. Heights Mchts. Assn., Houston Heights, Tex., 1984—. Mem. Texas Bankers Assn., Nat. Assn. Banking Women. Republican. Bapt. Office: Unique Corner 355 W 19th St Houston TX 77008

MATTISON, JOAN TOMPKINS, educator, real estate executive; b. Mount Kisco, N.Y., Sept. 2, 1938; d. Henry William Tompkins and Margaret (Davies) Tompkins Wago; m. George Pratt Mattison, Mar. 28, 1959; children—Barbara Jean, Scott Joseph. B.S., Oswego State Coll., 1960; M.S., Potsdam State Coll., 1967. Cert. tchr. kindergarten-9th grade, N.Y. Elem. tchr. Ogdensburg Bd. Edn., N.Y., 1960—; landlord, broker The Cabinet Shop, Ogdensburg, 1974—. Test chmn. St. Lawrence Figure Skating Club, Canton, N.Y., 1974-81, pres., 1976-78, pres. North country council, 1981-83; pres., founder Ogdensburg Figure Skating Club, 1970-80. Mem. NEA, Ogdensburg Edn. Assn. (bldg. rep. 1960—). Republican. Episcopalian. Avocations: reading; bridge; sports. Home and Office: 627 Morris St Ogdensburg NY 13669

MATT MADDREY, ANN MARIE C., med. diagnostic company executive; b. Pittston, Pa., May 25, 1953; d. Andrew Joseph and Sophie Theresa (Loncala) M.; B.A. in Biology, Johns Hopkins U., 1975, M.S. in Communicative Disorders, 1976; m. Willis C. Maddrey, Apr. 18, 1981; 1 son, Thomas Blake. Mem. pharm. sales staff E.R. Squibb & Sons, Princeton, N.J., 1975-78; mktg. specialist Ortho Diagnostics, Raritan, N.J., 1978-80; clin. specialist Boehringer Mannheim Diagnostics, Houston, 1981-82; dir. biols. diagnostics and devices Pharmakinetic Labs. Inc., Balt., 1982-85; pres. Advanced Clin. Trials Systems, Inc., 1985—; tchr. ednl. seminars for hosps. Bd. dirs. Balt. Women's Health Coalition; mem. Balt. Assn. Retarded Citizens; mem. woman's bd. Thomas Jefferson U. Mem. Am. Assn. Clin. Chemistry, Nat. Assn. Female Execs., NOW, Assn. Profl. and Exec. Women, Am. Bus. Assn., Woman's Med. Study Research Group, AAUW. Roman Catholic. Office: 8355 Lorretto Ave Philadelphia PA 19152

MATTSON, CARMEN JOYCE, pharmacist, clinical pharmacist; b. Crosby, Minn., June 30, 1950; d. Julian Sanford and Alice Irene (Hippe) Morstad; m. Craig Niles Mattson, Oct. 12, 1974; 1 child, Erika Leigh. B.S. in Pharmacy, U. Minn., 1973. Staff pharmacist St. Mary Hosp., Rochester, Minn., 1973-74; Mercy Hosp., Iowa City, Iowa, 1974-76; clin. pharmacist, computer liaison Beth Israel Hosp., Boston, 1976-85, St. Mary's Hosp., Rochester, Minn., 1986—. Contbr. articles to profl. jours. Mem. League Women Voters, 1982-84; mem. elec. com. for town govt. candidate, Winchester, 1985. Named Pharmacist of Year, Mass. Soc. Hosp. Pharmacists, Boston, 1981. Mem. Mass. Soc. Hosp. Pharmacists (chmn. com. 1980-81), Am. Soc. Hosp. Pharmacists. Club: Minuteman Samoyed (Boston) (treas. 1978-81). Avocations: sewing; decorating. Home: 923 9th Ave SW Rochester MN 55902 Office: St Mary's Hosp 1216 2d St SW Rochester MN 55902

MATTSON, ESTHER JOAN, chemical company personnell executive; b. Worcester, Mass., Mar. 5, 1935; d. John Arthur and Mary Ann (Falcone) Santomenno; A.S., Becker Jr. Coll., Worcester, Mass., 1954; B.S., Pace U., 1977. Personnel programs adminstr. Crompton & Knowles, N.Y.C., 1969-70, mgr. employee benefits, 1970-73, mgr. benefits and compensation, 1973-78, dir. compensation, benefits and career planning, 1978-84, dir. human resources, 1984—. Mem. Am. Soc. Personnel Adminstrn., Am. Soc. Tng. and Devel., N.Y. Personnel Mgmt. Assn. (treas.), Am. Compensation Assn., Am. Arbitration Assn. Home: 301 E 63d St New York NY 10021 Office: 345 Park Ave New York NY 10154

MATUJA, MARY, city official; b. Habbura, Czechoslovakia, Jan. 4, 1939; came to U.S., 1949, naturalized, 1949; d. Julian and Anne (Shafron) Bobak; m. Robert D. Matuja, Sept. 17, 1960; children—Leslie, Jennifer, Nicole. Student Macomb County Community Coll., 1958-60, Oakland U., 1978. Councilwoman, City of Roseville (Mich.), 1975—, mayor pro tem, 1981, chmn. hobby shows, 1979-80; mem. Macomb County Planning Commn. Chmn., Patton Sch. PTA, Roseville, 1969-70; exec. v.p. Women for United Found., Detroit, 1969, dir., 1970-76; bd. dirs. Mich. Cancer Found. Mem. Detroit Inst. Arts. Democrat. Presbyterian. Clubs: Detroit Women's Symphony Assn., St. Joseph Aux., Mich. Dem. Home: 865 Lakeshore Dr Grosse Pointe MI 48236

MATULICH, MARILYN ALENE, educational administrator; b. Spokane, Wash., Dec. 14, 1931; d. Lyndell Lloyd and Florence Genevieve (Anderson) Shields; B.A. in Edn., Wash. State U., 1954; M.A., Whitworth Coll., 1973; m. Mark Anthony Matulich, May 15, 1954; children—Robert Allan, Paul Shields, James Christopher. Dir. Pre-Sch. of Port Townsend (Wash.), 1961-63; library media specialist Spokane Sch. Dist. 81, 1967-76, asst. instructional media coordinator, 1976-83, instructional media coordinator, 1983—. Chairperson, LWV, Spokane, 1964; drive chmn. Port Townsend Cancer Soc., 1962. Mem. AAUW, Assn. Supervision and Curriculum Devel., Wash. Library Media Assn., Assn. for Ednl. Communications and Tech., Northeast Wash. Assn. Sch. Adminstrs., Adminstrv. Women in Edn., Wash. Assn. Sch. Adminstrs., Delta Kappa Gamma, Phi Kappa Phi, Pi Lambda Thelta. Democrat. Home: N 7231 Fotheringham Spokane WA 99208 Office: E 4714 8th Ave Spokane WA 99212

MATURIN, THERESA POIRIER, nurse; b. St. Martinville, La., Apr. 21, 1932; d. Leopold and Emilie (Poche) Poirier; Cosmetician, Lafayette (La.) Beauty Sch., 1963; diploma Teche Area Nursing Sch., New Iberia, La., 1975; m. Joseph Newby Maturin, Aug. 23, 1953; 1 son, Roland Joseph. Staff nurse Lafayette Gen. Hosp., 1974, Oakwood Village Nursing Care Center, Lafayette, 1975-80; pvt. duty nurse, Lafayette, 1980—. Pres. La. chpt. Nat. Fedn. Democratic Women, 1979-83; mem. La. Dem. Fin. Council, 1982; pres. St. Mary's Guild, Lafayette. Mem. Lafayette Town House, Am. Bus. Women's Assn. (chmn. local membership 1964), La. Hist. Soc., Smithsonian Assos., Nat. Trust Hist. Preservation, Right to Life, Attakapas Hist. Assn., Am. Security Council, U.S. Capitol Hist. Soc., Nat. Hist. Soc., L'Heure de Musique, France Amerique de la Louisiane (v.p. 1982-83), DAR, Soc. Dames Ct. of Honor, Lafayette Ballet Assn., Soc. Confederacy, Beta Sigma Phi. Roman Catholic. Clubs: Catholic Daus. Ams. (ct. regent 1975-79), UDC (corr. sec. chpt. 1982-83). Home: 2710 Pinhook Rd Lafayette LA 70508

MATUSEWICZ, MICHELE, air traffic control project planner; b. N.Y.C., Apr. 4, 1961; d. Richard Robert and Olga (Oshva) M. B.A. in Internat. Relations and Econs., Am. U., Washington, 1983. Export lic. adminstr. IBM World Trade Corp., Washington, 1982-83; statistician's asst. U.S. Dept. Commerce, 1983-84; sta. clearance coordinator Mut. Broadcasting Network, Arlington, Va., 1984-85; jr. engr., project planner Engring. and Econs. Research, Inc. tech. div. Martin Marietta Corp., Washington, 1985—. Mem. Nat. Assn. Female Execs., Air Traffic Controller Assn. Republican. Russian Orthodox. Office: Martin Marietta Corp ATC Div 475 School St SW Washington DC 20024

MATUSON, LYNDA BRANDT, travel agency executive; b. N.Y.C., Nov. 30, 1940; d. Milton and Edythe (Goldstein) Brandt; m. Martin Jay Matuson, Nov. 19, 1960; children—Andrew Forrest, Marlyn Sue. B.A., William Paterson Coll., 1972. Tchr. Westwood Schs., N.J., 1972-74; librarian Paramus High Sch., N.J., 1974-76; pres. Adventours, Maywood, N.J., 1976—; adj. faculty Bergen Community Coll., Paramus, N.J., 1984—. Mem. Am. Soc. Travel Agts., Kappa Delta Pi. Jewish. Avocations: knitting; snorkeling; photography; collecting antique English automobiles. Office: Adventours 68A W Pleasant Ave Maywood NJ 07607

MATZ, KAY ELAINE, savings and loan executive; b. Warren, Ohio, Apr. 18, 1946; d. Nick M. and Julia H. (Petrulak) Kovic; m. Howard C. Matz, Jr., Oct. 11, 1969. Student in bus. mgmt. Hiram Coll., 1984—. Staff acct. R.M. Robbins & Assocs., Warren, 1964-73; with 1st Fed. Savs. & Loan Assn. Warren, 1973—, asst. treas., 1980-81, controller, 1982—; ann. fin. auditor Children's Rehab. Ctr., Warren, 1970-74. Mem. Am. Soc. Women Accts. (pres. Youngstown chpt. 1975-76), Fin. Mgrs. Soc. (pres. Pa.-Ohio chpt. 1983-84). Democrat. Clubs: Emblem, Warren Women's Networking. Avocation: travel. Home: 1406 Maplewood St NE Warren OH 44483 Office: 1st Fed Savs & Loan Assn Warren 185 E Market St PO Box 551 Warren OH 44481

MAUCERI, VALERIE FRANCES, lawyer; b. N.Y.C., Nov. 23, 1948; d. Arthur Angelo and Stephanie Frances (Guastella) M. A.B. magna cum laude, St. Peter's Coll., Jersey City, 1970; J.D. (scholar), Rutgers U.-Newark, 1974. Bar: N.J. 1975, N.Y. 1976, U.S. Dist. Ct. N.J. 1974, U.S. Dist. Ct. (ea. dist.) N.Y. 1976, U.S. Dist. Ct. (so. dist.) N.Y. 1976, U.S. Ct. Appeals (2d cir.) 1975, U.S. Ct. Appeals (3d cir.) 1978. Underwriter, Equitable Life Assurance Soc., N.Y.C., 1970-71, summer assoc. Kraft & Hughes, Newark, 1973; assoc. White & Case, N.Y.C., 1974-77, Bourne, Noll & Kenyon, Summit, N.J., 1977-78; asst. U.S. atty. Dept. Justice, Newark, 1978—. Mem. Salem Ridge Assn., 1977—. Mem. ABA. Office: Office of US Atty 970 Broad St Newark NJ 07102

MAUCK, DIANE JO, marketing and communication consulting company executive; b. San Diego, Dec. 4, 1943; d. Ralph Lewis and Mary Jane (French) Grossmiller; m. Gary Lee Mauck, Sept. 3, 1971. Student Tex. Women's U., 1961-62, Ariz. State U., 1963-67. Network editor, Phoenix Tee Vee Mag., 1967-68; dir. pub. relations Ariz. Lumber Assn., 1968-73; dir. Ariz. Banking Acad., Phoenix, 1973-78; v.p. Scottsdale Ednl. Ctr., Phoenix, 1978-85; v.p., owner Mauck & Assocs., Inc., Phoenix, 1985—. Mem. Nat. Assn. Female Execs., Am. Soc. Bus. & Profl. Women, Midtown Bus. & Profl. Women, Meeting Planners Internat., Nat. Assn. Women Bus. Owners (dir. 1985—), Ariz. Pvt. Sch. Assn. (bd. dirs. 1973-84). Republican. Methodist. Club: Consulting of Am. Avocations: skiing; animal welfare activities. Office: Mauck & Assocs Inc 5717 N 7th St Phoenix AZ 85021

MAUCK, JANET MARIE, newspaper editor and administrator, photographer; b. Rensselaer, Ind., Aug. 14, 1953; d. Ray Myron and Rita Pauline (Sullivan) M. B.A. in Elem. Edn., Anderson Coll. (Ind.), 1975. Reporter, Rensselaer Republican (Ind.), 1976-81; editor, mgr. Morocco Courier (Ind.), 1981—. Youth leader United Ch., Morocco, 1983—. Co-recipient Best News Story Under Deadline award Hoosier State Press Assn., 1977. Mem. Am. Bus. Women's Assn. (bull. chmn. 1985-86) (Rensselaer). Office: Morocco Courier 173 E State St Morocco IN 47963

MAUGER, PATRICIA ANN, TV producer; b. Allentown, Pa., Dec. 21, 1937; d. Von Edgar and Ruth (Kreitz) Mauger; ed. Berkeley Sch. With NBC, 1964—, now producer religion unit Network News. Recipient Silver Angel award for Christmas at Washington Cathedral, 1985; award excellence Media in Religion, 1985; Emmy nominee, 1986. Mem. Nat. Acad. TV Arts and Sci. Presbyterian. Office: NBC 30 Rockefeller Plaza New York NY 10020

MAUL, SUSAN KATHLEEN, nursing educator; b. Englewood, N.J., July 16, 1951; d. Ronald and Bernice (Moody) Sandbach; m. Robert J. Maul, June 30, 1973 (div. 1983); 1 dau., Kimberly Ann. B.S.N., Indiana U. Pa., 1973; M.S.N., U. Pa., 1978; postgrad. Tex. A&M U., 1982—. Lic. nurse, Tex., Pa. Asst. prof. U. Tex.-Houston, 1981—; staff nurse Toms River Community Meml. Hosp. (N.J.), 1976-77; pediatric clin. nurse specialist M.D. Anderson Hosp., Houston, 1978-81; condr. workshops. Author: Childhood Cancer: A Nursing Overview, 1984; contbr. articles to profl. jours. Girl Scout leader, Houston, 1983-85; vol. Spl. Olympics, Houston, 1983-84. Served to maj. U.S. Army, 1973—. HEW trainee, 1977-78. Mem. Sigma Theta Tau, Am. Nurses Assn., Assn. Care for Children's Health, Nat. Assn. Pediatric Nurse Assocs. and Practitioners, Assn. Pediatric Oncology Nurses (research com.). Republican. Home: 5523 Duxbury Houston TX 77035 Office: Univ Tex Sch Nursing 1100 Holcombe Blvd Houston TX 77030

MAULDIN, ANNA MARIE MARINO, design company executive, financial consultant; b. Dallas, Oct. 15, 1945; d. Samuel and Marie Rita (Petta) Marino; m. H.R. Mauldin, Dec. 18, 1964 (div. Apr. 1972). B.B.A., North Tex. State U., Denton, 1968. Treas., controller Web Thomas Aircraft, Dallas, 1971-75, Dahlgren Mfg. Co., Dallas, 1975-77, Jack Day Constrn. Co., Dallas, 1977-81; controller Southwestern Gage, Dallas, 1981-82; sec., controller Joyce K. Wynn, Inc., Dallas, 1982—; treas. Web Thomas Aircraft Sales, Dallas, 1975—; fin. cons. Dean Property, Dallas, 1981—, Shettle & Assocs.-Attys., Dallas, 1979—; comml. research and analysis fin. cons. Mem. Park Cities League. Republican. Roman Catholic. Home: 4133 Druid Ln Dallas TX 75205 Office: Joyce K Wynn Inc 2211 N Lamar St 200 Dallas TX 75202

MAULDIN, JEAN HUMPHRIES, aviation company executive; b. Gordonville, Tex., Aug. 16, 1923; d. James Wiley and Lena Leota (Noel-Carin) Humphries; B.S., Hardin Simmons U., 1943; M.S., U. So. Calif., 1961; postgrad. Westfield Coll., U. London, 1977-78, Warnborough Coll., Oxford, Eng., 1977-78; m. William Henry Mauldin, Feb. 28, 1942; children—Bruce Patrick, William Timothy III. Psychol. counselor social services 1st Baptist Ch., 1953-57; pres. Mauldin and Staff, public relations, Los Angeles, 1957-78; pres. Stardust Aviation, Inc., Santa Ana, Calif., 1962—. mem. Calif. Democratic Council, 1953-70; mem. exec. bd. Calif. Dem. Central com. exec. bd., 1957—, Orange County Dem. Central Com. exec. bd., 1960—; del. Dem. Nat. Conv., 1974, 78; Calif. State adv. U.S. Congressional Adv. Bd., 1982—; mem. U.S. Congressional Adv. Bd.; rep. 37th Senate Caucus; pres. Santa Ana Friends of Public Library, 1973-76, McFadden Friends of Library, Santa Ana, 1976-80; chmn. cancer crusade Am. Cancer Soc., Orange County, 1974; mem. exec. bd. Lisa Hist. Preservation Soc., 1970—; lay leader Protestant Episcopal Ch. Am., Trinity Ch., Tustin, Calif.; founder Pacific Opera, Orange County Performing Arts Ctr. Named Woman of Yr., Key Woman in Politics, Calif. Dem. Party, 1960-80. Am. Mgmt. Assn. (pres.'s club), Bus. and Profl. Women Am., Exptl. Aircraft and Pilots Assn., Nat. Women's Polit. Caucus, Dem. Coalition Central Coms., Calif. Friends of Library (life), Women's Missionary Soc. (chmn.), World Affairs Council, LWV, Nat. Fedn. Dem. Women, Dem. Assocs. (exec. bd.), Calif. Fedn. County Central Com. Mems., Internat. Platform Assn., Nat.

Women's Pilot. Caucus Club: U. So. Calif. Ski. Author: Cliff Winters, The Pilot, The Man, 1961; The consummate Barnstormer, 1962; The Daredevil Clown, 1965. Home: 1013 W Elliott Pl Santa Ana CA 92704 also 102 E 45th St Savannah GA 31405 Also 112 8th St Seal Beach Ca 90740

MAUPIN, CAROL GRINSTEAD, food consultant; b. Pawhuska, Okla., Jan. 31, 1936; d. Randolph Henry and Mildred Asilee (Pfaff) Grinstead; B.A., U. Okla., 1958. Asst. to food dir. Neiman Marcus, Dallas, 1958-62; asst. to food dir. So. Meth. U., Dallas, 1963-64; asso. dir. food ops. Mut. of Omaha, 1964-69; dir. tearoom, parties and spl. events Denver Dry Goods, 1970-74; dir. food and party services Jr. League of Houston, 1974-81; partner Jackson and Co., catering service, 1981-83; head food research and devel. Neiman Marcus, Dallas, 1983—; Entertaining columnist Dallas Morning News; food cons. Mus. Food Arts; cooking instr. Batterie de Cuisine Cooking Sch., Foleys, Gourmet Kitchens; food lectr.; food and party cons. protocol office City of Houston; food service cons., bd. dirs. Alley Theatre of Houston. Mem. Am. Home Econs. Assn., Nat. Assn. Cooking Schs., Internat. Food and Wine Soc., Houston Culinary Guild. Republican. Episcopalian. Home: 4423 Westway Ave Dallas TX 75205 Office: Neiman Marcus Dallas TX 75201

MAURA, DAISY B., educator; b. Beaumont, Tex., Nov. 10, 1937; d. Clarence and Eddie Mae (Murphy) Graham; m. Freddie Maura III, Mar. 22, 1959; children—Robert James, Craig Anthony, Kimberly Yvette. B.S., Tex. So. U., 1959, M.S. in Edn., 1968; postgrad. U. Calif-Berkeley, 1966. Cert. tchr., Tex. With Houston Ind. Sch. Dist., 1961—, asst. prin., 1973-81, prin. Dowling Middle Sch., 1981—. Pres. Madison PTA, Houston, 1975; mem. Hiram Clarke Civic Club, 1970—; bd. dirs. St. Benedict Cath. Council, 1982—. Named Outstanding Prin., Houston Ind. Sch. Dist., 1982-83, Outstanding Educator Houston Bus. and Profl. Women, 1983; named to Prin.'s Inst., Harvard Grad. Sch. Edn., 1985. Mem. Houston Profl. Assn., Tex. Edn. Assn. Tex. PTA (life), NEA, Tex. Assn. Secondary Sch. Prins., Nat. Assn. Secondary Sch. Prins., Top Ladies of Distinction, Alpha Kappa Alpha, Iota Phi Lambda. Democrat. Avocations: cooking; jogging; gardening. Home: 3827 Cheryl Lynne St Houston TX 77045 Office: Dowling Middle Sch 14000 Stancliff St Houston TX 77045

MAURER, JANET RAE, physician; b. Great Falls, Mont., Nov. 26, 1947; d. Cedric Albert and Elfriede Emilie (Riebhoff) Maurer; m. David Ives Kent, Sept. 27, 1980; children—Rachel, Jeremy. B.A., U. Mont., Missoula, 1968; M.A., U. Oreg., Eugene, 1969; M.D., U. Minn., 1976. Diplomate Am. Bd. Internal Medicine. Resident in medicine Emory U., Atlanta, 1976-79; fellow in pulmonary medicine U. Calif.-San Diego, 1979-81; staff physician Bronx (N.Y.) VA Hosp., Mt. Sinai Med. Ctr., CUNY, 1981-84, Toronto Gen. Hosp. (Ont., Can.), 1984—; instr. Mt. Sinai Med. Ctr., 1981-84; asst. prof. U. Toronto, 1984—. Author: How To Talk to Your Doctor, 1986. Contbr. articles on pulmonary medicine to med. jours. Fellow Royal Coll. Physicians and Surgeons Can.; mem. ACP, Am. Thoracic Soc., Am. Coll. Chest Physicians, Alpha Omega Alpha. Home: 56 Foursome Crescent Willowdale ON M2P 1W4 Canada Office: Toronto Gen Hosp Toronto ON M5G 2C4 Canada

MAURER, LUCILLE DARVIN, state legislator; b. N.Y.C., Nov. 21, 1922; d. Joseph Jay and Evelyn (Levine) Darvin; student U. N.C.-Greensboro 1938-40; B.A., U. N.C.-Chapel Hill, 1942; M.A., Yale U., 1945; H.L.D. (hon.), Hood Coll., 1984; m. Ely Maurer, Apr. 29, 1945; children—Stephen Bennett, Russell Alexander, Edward Nestor. Economist, U.S. Tariff Commn., 1942-43; econ. and market research for pvt. firms, 1957-60; cons. Nat. Center for Ednl. Stats., 1969-70; mem. Md. House of Dels., 1969—, mem. ways and means com., 1971—, chmn. joint com. on fed. relations, 1983—; mem. intergovtl. adv. council U.S. Dept. Edn., 1980-82. Del., Md. Constl. Conv., 1967-68; mem. Montgomery County Bd. Edn., 1960-68; trustee Montgomery Community Coll., 1960-68; vice chmn. nat. planning com., advanced leadership program of seminars on edn. and ednl. policy for state legislators Edn. Commn. of States, 1979-81; mem. exec. com. of edn. com. Nat. Conf. of State Legislatures, 1975-84, chmn., 1978-79, chmn. com. on taxes, trade and econ. devel., 1985-86; mem. adv. com. Servicemems. Opportunity Colls., 1978-82; mem. nat. adv. bd. Inst. for Ednl. Leadership, 1979-81; co-chmn. Md. Commn. on Intergovernmental Cooperation, 1976-82; mem. Nat. Com. on Postsecondary Accreditation, 1974-1979; bd. dirs. Montgomery United Way, 1971-76, 84—; mem. Commn. Higher Edn. of Middle States Assn., 1982-85; mem. Gov.'s Employment and Tng. Council, 1983—. Recipient Legislator of Yr. award Md. Assn. for Retarded Children, 1972; John Dewey award Montgomery County Fedn. Tchrs., 1972; Hornbook award Montgomery County Edn. Assn., 1972; Legislator of Yr. award Md. Assn. Counties, 1984; Willis award for outstanding service Md. Assn. Bds. Edn., 1984. Mem. LWV (past dir. Montgomery County, past dir. Md.), AAUW (Internat. Women's Yr. award Silver Spring 1975), Bus. and Profl. Women's Club (Woman of Yr. 1984), NOW (Legis. Excellence award 1981), Women's Equity Action League, Women's Polit. Caucus, Montgomery County Hist. Soc., Order Women Legislators, Delta Kappa Gamma. Jewish. Office: 223C Lowe Ho of Dels Bldg Annapolis MD 21401

MAURER, VIRGINIA GALLAHER, legal educator; b. Shawnee, Okla., Nov. 7, 1946; d. Paul Clark Gallaher and Virginia Ruth (Watson) Abernathy; m. Ralph Gerald Maurer, July 31, 1971; children—Ralph Emmett, William Edward. B.A., Northwestern U., 1968; M.A., Stanford U., 1969, J.D., 1975. Bar: Iowa 1976. Tchr. social studies San Mateo (Calif.) High Sch. Dist., 1969-71; spl. asst. to pres. U. Iowa, Iowa City, 1976-80, adj. asst. prof. law, 1979-80; affiliate asst. prof. law U. Fla., Gainesville, 1981, asst. prof. bus. law, 1980-85, assoc. prof., 1985—; cons. Gov.'s Com. on Iowa 2000, Iowa City, 1976-77, Fla. Banker's Assn., Gainesville, 1982. Contbr. articles to profl. jours. Mem. fundraising com. Pro Arte Musica, Gainesville, 1980-84. Mem. ABA, Am. Bus. Law Assn., Southeastern Bus. Law Assn. (sec.-treas. 1985-86), Iowa State Bar Assn., LWV, Kappa Alpha Theta, Delta Sigma Pi. Club: Univ. Women's (Gainesville, Fla.). Home: 2210 NW 6th Pl Gainesville FL 32603 Office: Coll Bus Adminstrn U Fla Gainesville FL 32611

MAUS, BETTY JEAN, hosp. adminstr.; b. Balt., July 13, 1929; d. Howard Arrington and Edna May (Brown) Smith, Jr.; student Strayer's Bus. Coll., 1946-47; m. Bernard Harvey Maus, Sept. 24, 1950. Asst. cashier Sykesville State Bank, 1950-53; head teller Randallstown (Md.) State Bank, 1953-55; med. records staff Springfield Hosp. Center, Sykesville, 1955, prin clk. purchasing office, 1960-67, coordinator vol. services, 1967—. Bd. dirs. Vol. Action Carroll County, 1975-80, Vol. Action Central Md., 1977-79, v.p., 1980; mem. Ad Hoc. Com. for Health Systems Central Md.; sec. Westminster Recreational Council; leader 4-H; instl. rep. Boy Scouts; den mother Cub Scouts, treas. St. Paul's United Methodist Ch., also Sunday sch. tchr., counselor Meth. Youth Fellowship, chmn. council of ministries. Named Outstanding Woman of Carroll County, 1976; recipitn Rotary Internat. award, 1971; South Carroll Community award, 1980; numerous others. Mem. Am. Soc. Dirs. Vol. Services, Md. Council Dirs. Vol. Services, Assn. Vol. Action Scholars, Assn. Vol. Adminstrn., Carroll County Assn. Retarded Citizens, Washington County Mental Health Assn. Democrat. Clubs: Bonnette (Sykesville); Order Eastern Star; Soroptimist (pres. Westminster 1973-75, treas. 1975-77, v.p. 1977-78, pres. 1978-80). Home: 7344 Springfield Ave Sykesville MD 21784 Office: Springfield Hosp Center Sykesville MD 21784

MAU-SHIMIZU, PATRICIA ANN, lawyer; b. Honolulu, Jan. 17, 1953; d. Herbert G.K. ad Leilani (Yuen) Mau; m. John B. Shimizu, Aug. 15, 1981; 1 child, Melissa Rose. B.S., U. San Francisco, 1975; J.D., Golden Gate U., 1979. Bar: Hawaii 1979. Law clk. State Supreme Ct., Honolulu, 1979-80; atty. Bendet, Fidell & Sakai, Honolulu, 1980-81; legis. atty. Honolulu City Council, 1981-83; legis. atty. House Majority Research Office, Honolulu, 1983—. Mem. Hawaii State Bar Assn., Hawaii Young Lawyers, Hawaii Women Lawyers. Democrat. Roman Catholic. Home: 7187 Hawaii Kai Dr Honolulu HI 96825 Office: State House of Representatives House Majority Research Office State Capitol Room 308A Honolulu HI 96813

MAVILLE, PAULINE BRIGGS, industrial engineer; b. Lebanon, N.H., Jan. 29, 1924; d. Clifton Charles and Grace Francis (Lovering) Briggs; student U.S. Naval Aviation Tech. Tng. Sch., 1944; grad. Plus Sch. Bus., 1968; student Stonehill Coll., 1975-76, Massassoit Community Coll., 1978-79; m. Feb. 24, 1945 (div.); 1 son, Thomas Briggs. Machinist, various cos., Lebanon, N.H. and Waltham, Mass., 1946-68; jr. indsl. engr. Compo Industries, Inc., Waltham, 1968-70; scheduling coordinator Heath Cons., Inc., Stoughton, Mass., 1971-72; cost estimator Metal Bellows Co., Sharon, Mass., 1972-75; sr. cost estimator Bird-Johnson Co., Walpole, Mass., 1975-79; sr. cost estimator MAPO div. Disney Prodns., Glendale, Calif., 1980-81, indsl. engr. WED div., Glendale, 1981-84; sr. indsl. engr. Allied Bendix Aerospace, North Hollywood, Calif., 1984—. Served with USN, 1944-45, Mem. Am. Inst. Indsl. Engrs., Am. Legion. Democrat. Club: Bus. and Profl. Women's. Home: 1231 N Verdugo Rd Glendale CA 91206 Office: Bendix Electrodynamics Div Allied Aerospace 11600 Sherman Way North Hollywood CA 91605

MAVRONIKOLAS, RUTH THORP HARVEY, educator, real estate company official; b. Phila., July 3, 1931; d. Cyril Hingston and Ruth Sharpless (Thorp) Harvey; B.F.A. in Art Edn., Phila. Coll. Art, 1956; M.S. in Edn., U. Pa., 1964; m. Christopher George Mavronikolas, Nov. 27, 1958; children—Elia Ruth, George Christopher. Tchr., Baldwin Sch., Bryn Mawr, Pa., 1957-66, chmn. art dept., 1960-66; assoc. prof. art edn. Phila. Coll. Art, 1966-74, registrar, 1956-57; tchr. Moorestown (N.J.) Friends Sch., 1974-76, chmn. art dept., 1974-76; tchr. Franklin Learning Center, Phila., 1976-82; salesperson Colonial Realty Co., Westmont, N.J., 1982—. T. Wistar Brown Fund Endl. grantee, 1952-64; Mary Jeannes Fund Ednl. grantee, 1952-53; Anne Townsend Fund grantee, 1952-53. Mem. Nat. Trust for History Preservation. Republican. Home: 208 West End Ave Haddonfield NJ 08033 Office: 142 Haddon Ave Westmont NJ 08108

MAWYER, MARGARET JOHNSON, consumer finance company executive, consultant; b. Nottoway County, Va., July 7, 1930; d. Clifton Corbett and Nannie (Dalton) Johnson; m. Jesse Osten Mawyer, July 30, 1948; children—Diane Mawyer Terrell, Thomas Michael, Brenda Mawyer Cramer. Student Washington Bible Sch. Extension, 1947-48, 78-80, Lynchburg Bible Coll. Extension, 1975-77. In sales and credit Western Auto Supply, Richmond, Va., 1944-47, Miller & Rhoads, Richmond, 1947-48; with statis. dept. Thalhimers, Richmond, 1948-49; mgr. Security Pacific Fin. Corp., Richmond, 1951—, also notary pub., 1955—; credit cons. Credit Women Internat., Richmond, 1978—; 1st v.p. pub. relations Assn. Retarded Children, Richmond, 1979—; pub. relations exec. Mortgage Bankers Assn., Richmond, 1982—. Contbr. articles to Managing Arts, 1980—. Presenter Assn. Retarded Children, 1980—, Richmond Pub. Schs., 1984-85; active Women's Missionary Soc., Richmond. Recipient Outstanding Achievement award Security Pacific Fin. Corp., 1979-85, Gabriel award Am. Fin. Services Assn., 1985, Round Table award Internat. Consumer Credit Assn., 1985. Mem. Nat. Assn. Female Execs., Credit Women Internat. (1st v.p. chpt. 1978-86, 5R Club 1984, Boss of Yr. 1984), Cert. Consumer Credit Execs. (cert. consumer credit exec., Network 1982-86), Women's Resource Ctr. of U. Richmond (Network 1983-86), Women Council Realtors (Outstanding Accomplishment award 1985), Career Club. Republican. Mem. Ch. of the Nazarene. Avocations: horseback riding; bowling; camping. Home: 816 Circlewood Dr Richmond VA 23224 Office: Security Pacific Fin Corp PO Box 24294 Richmond VA 23224

MAXEY, CATHERINE ANNETTE, human resource executive, consultant, trainer; b. Carbondale, Ill., Dec. 12, 1938; d. J. Ellsworth and Catherine (Crossno) Tucker; m. James H. Maxey, Aug. 20, 1961; 1 son, Gregory Scott. B.A., Ill. Wesleyan U., Bloomington, 1960; M.A., U. Chgo., 1962. Dir. Gwinnett-Rockdale Mental Health Mental Retardation Services, Lawrenceville, Ga., 1973-76; supt. Ga. Regional Hosp., Decatur, 1977-82; exec. dir. Nat. Assn. Social Workers, Silver Springs, Md., 1982-83; instr. U. Ga., Athens from 1984; mem. exec. bd. Health Systems Agy., Atlanta, 1980-82; dir. Health Planning Agy., State of Ga., 1984—; mem. task panel Pres. Commn. on Mental Health, Washington, 1978; del. Internat. Fedn. Social Workers, 1982. Recipient Disting. Alumnus award Ill. Wesleyan U., 1978. Mem. Nat. Assn. Social Workers, Mental Health Assn., Assn. for Retarded Citizens, NOW, Acad. Cert. Social Workers. Democrat. Club: Ansly Golf (Atlanta). Office: Health Planning Agy 4 Executive Park Dr NE Suite 2100 Atlanta GA 30329

MAXEY, JUANITA NELMS, motion picture theater owner; b. Isola, Miss., Oct. 12, 1925; d. Elmer and Ida (Byrd) Nelms; m. Paul Maxey, Nov. 21, 1943; children—Paula Maxey Bostic, Kathy Maxey Schexnayder. Student N.W. Jr. Coll., Senatobia, Miss., 1978. Owner, mgr. Tobie Twin Cinema, Senatobia, 1970—. Author: (poetry) White Sycamore, 1980 (Library Week award 1984). Mem. adv. bd. City Schs. of Senatobia, DeSoto Schs., Miss.; mem. aux. Baddour Meml. Ctr., Senatobia, Tate County Arts Council, Senatobia; col., dir. and ednl. dir. Miss. Gov.'s Staff, 1976-80; mem. com. Miss. State Extension Adv. Council Launch Miss., 1986. Mem. Tri-State Theatre Owners Miss.-Tenn.-Ark. (pres. 1979-81, bd. dirs. 1985); Showman of Yr. award 1978), Nat. Assn. Theatre Owners (pres. Miss. chpt. 1981-83, sec.-treas. Miss. chpt. 1985, mem. adv. bd.), Senatobia C. of C. (pres. 1984-85), Variety Club Internat. Republican. Baptist. Avocation: ceramics. Office: Tobie Twin Cinema 226 Main St Senatobia MS 38668

MAXEY, LOIS BRUNSON, clinical social worker; b. DeKalb County, Ind., Jan. 6, 1929; d. Tom Bennett and Clara Lodell (Bash) Brunson; student Cin. Bible Sem., 1946-49; A.B., SW Christian Sem., Phoenix, 1951; postgrad. Phoenix Coll., 1953-54, Catherine Spalding Coll., Louisville, 1963-64; M.S.S.W., U. Louisville, 1966; m. Victor L. Maxey, Sept. 14, 1949; children—Thomas, Victor L., David. Oral proof reader Am. Printing House for the Blind, Louisville, 1959-63; group worker Neighborhood House, Louisville, 1963-64; social service dir. Headstart, 4 schs., Louisville, 1966; caseworker Family and Children's Agy., Louisville, 1966-68; clin. social worker Comprehensive Care Center No. Ky., Newport, 1968-72, 75-80, team leader 5 offices, 1972-75, coordinator children's services Catchment B, 1980-83, clin. social worker, 1983—. Active No. Ky. Chpt. Mental Health Assn. Named Social Worker of Yr., No. Ky., 1978; lic. clin. social worker, adminstrn. and mgmt., Ky. Mem. Nat. Assn. Social Workers, Acad. Cert. Social Workers. Mem. Ch. of Christ. Home: 5119 Grossepointe Ln Cincinnati OH 45238 Office: 18 N Fort Thomas Ave Fort Thomas KY 41075

MAXFIELD, ELIZABETH FONDA, lawyer; b. Dallas, Aug. 7, 1954; d. Jack George and Louise (Gribble) M. B.F.A. magna cum laude, So. Meth. U., 1976; J.D., U. Tex., 1979. Bar: Tex. 1979. Atty., FCC, Washington, 1979-80, dep. dir., 1980-81; adj. prof. telecommunications law Antioch Ctr. Legal Studies, Washington, 1983; atty. Becker, Gurman & Raiser, P.C., Washington, 1981—. Editor: Broadcasting and Government, 1981; adminstrv. editor Tex. Internat. Law Jour., 1978-79. Mem. spl. events com. Arthritis Found., Washington, 1982. Mem. ABA, State Bar Tex., Fed. Communications Bar Assn., Women in Communications, Inc. Democrat. Presbyterian. Office: Becker Gurman & Raiser PC One Thomas Circle Washington DC 20005

MAXSON, NANCY O'NEAL, veterinarian; b. Bklyn., Dec. 15, 1954; d. George W. and Jean (Jourdan) O'Neal; 1 dau., Marian A. B.S., La. State U.-Baton Rouge, 1975, D.V.M., 1980. Veterinarian, Veterans Veterinary Hosp., Metairie, La., 1980-83, Broadmoor Animal Hosp., New Orleans, 1983-84, Dale Mabry Animal Hosp., Tampa, Fla., 1984—. Recipient Outstanding Sr. award Phi Kappa Phi, 1980. Mem. AVMA.

MAXWELL, CATHY LYNN, trucking company executive; b. Kansas City, Mo., Nov. 26, 1953; d. John Charles and A.F. Sue (Forbes) Picardy; m. Korb Winter Maxwell, May 23, 1975; 1 child, Korb Winter II. B.S., Kans. State U., 1975, M.S., 1976. Salesman All States div. PIE, Walnut Creek, Colo., 1978-80, Kansas City, Kans., 1980; pres. C. Maxwell Trucking, Overland Park, Kans., 1980—. Mem. WTX, Kans. Motor Carriers Assn., Beta Sigma Phi (treas. 1985). Avocations: running; swimming; scuba. Office: C Maxwell Trucking Co Inc 10551 Barkley St Suite 100 Overland Park KS 66212

MAXWELL, FLORENCE HINSHAW (MRS. JOHN WILLIAMSON MAXWELL), civic worker; b. Nora, Ind., July 14, 1914; d. Asa Benton and Gertrude (Randall) Hinshaw; B.A. cum laude, Butler U., 1935; m. John Williamson Maxwell, June 5, 1936; children—Marilyn, William Douglas. Coordinator, Sight Conservation and Aid to Blind, 1962-73, nat. chmn., 1969-73, active various fund drives; chmn. jamboree, hostess coms. North Central High Sch., 1959, 64, Girl Scouts U.S.A., 1937-38, 54-56; mus. chmn. Sr. Girl Scout Regional Council, 1956-57; scorekeeper Little League, 1955-57; bd. dirs. Nora Sch. Parents' Club, 1958-59, Eastwood Jr. High Sch. Triangle Club, 1959-62; bd. dirs. women's com. Ind. State Symphony Soc., 1965-67, 76-79; vision screening Indpls. innercity public sch. kindergartens, pre-schs., 1962-69; chmn. vision screening Head Start, 1967—, health adv. com., 1976—, sec., 1980—; assessment team of compliance steering 1978-79, 84; asst. glaucoma screening clinics Gen. Hosp., Glendale Shopping Center, City County Bldg., Am. Legion Nat. Hdqrs., Ind. Health Assn. Conf., 1962-73; chmn. sight conservation and aid to blind Nat. Delta Gamma Found., Indpls., Columbus, Ohio, 1969-73; mem. telethon team Butler Univ. Fund, 1964; Symphoguide hostess Internat. Conf. on Cities, 1971, Nat. League of Cities, 1972; Symphoguide chmn. Gray Line Symphony City Tours, 1976-79; bd. dirs. Ind. Soc. to Prevent Blindness, 1962—, exec. com., sec., 1971-83, v.p., hon. life v.p., 1983-86; mem. women's com. Ind. State Symphony Soc. Recipient Key to City of Indpls., 1972; Those Spl. People award Women in Communications, 1980; Head Start Appreciation award, 1983. Mem. Ind., Nat. (Sight-Saving award 1974) socs. to prevent blindness, People of Vision Aux. (founder 1981), Delta Gamma (Cable award 1969, Outstanding Alumna award 1973, chmn. communication and decades com. 50th anniv. celebration Alpha Tau chpt. 1975, treas. Alpha Tau House Corp., 1975-78, nat. chmn. survey and coordination parents clubs 1976-77; Service Recognition award 1977, Shield award 1981, scholarship named in her honor 1981). Republican. Address: 1502 E 80th St Indianapolis IN 46240

MAXWELL, GAIL, nurse educator; b. Muskogge, Okla., May 10, 1951; d. Eulis and Margaret (Weir) LaFave; m. Larry Allen Maxwell, Oct. 13, 1969 (div. Oct. 1977); 1 son, Barry Wayne; m. 2d, Frank Charles Simpson, Feb. 4, 1984. B.S. in Nursing (pres.' honor roll), Central State U., Edmond, Okla., 1975; M.S. in Nursing, U. Okla., 1980. Dir. nursing Haskell County Hosp., Stigler, Okla., 1976-77; instr. nursing Westark Jr. Coll., Ft. Smith, Ark., 1977-78, Central State U., Oklahoma City, Okla., 1978-80; instr. nursing U. Okla., Oklahoma City, 1980-82; asst. prof., 1983—; coordinator health occupations Francis Tuttle Vocat. Tech., Oklahoma City, 1982-83; staff nurse Bapt. Med. Ctr.; cons. Indian Health Service, Pawnee, Okla., 1983; lectr. in field. CPR instr. Am. Heart Assn., Oklahoma City, 1977-83. Named Nurse of Day, Oklahoma City, 1983. Mem. Okla. Nursing Assn. (del. 1982, by-laws com. 1983), Am. Nursing Assn., U. Okla. Alumni Assn. (exec. council 1982-83), Okla. League Nursing, Sigma Theta Tau. Democrat. Baptist. Reviewer John Wiley & Sons Pub. Co., 1982; contbr. articles to profl. jours. Home: 2913 Fairfield Dr Edmond OK 73034 Office: U Okla Box 26901 Oklahoma City OK 73190

MAXWELL, KATHERINE GANT, school psychologist, educational consultant; b. El Paso, Tex., Nov. 27, 1931; d. Leslie and Lillian (Beard) Gant; B.S., Abilene Christian U., 1955; M.S., Miss. State U., 1967, Ph.D., 1974; m. Fowden Gene Maxwell, July 14, 1955; children—Steve, Becky Harvey, Randy. Teaching asst. Miss. State U., Starkville, 1969-72, practicum in sch. psychology, 1973-74; adminstr. psychol. tests Starkville Pub. Schs., 1974-75; sch. psychologist Dixie & Gilchrist (Fla.) County Schs., 1977-79; instr. continuing edn. dept. U. LaVerne (Calif.), 1979-80; sch. psychologist Bryan (Tex.) Ind. Sch. Dist., 1979-80; owner, dir. Reading Improvement Center, College Station, Tex., 1979-80, Assn. Interpersonal Devel., Inc., 1982—; sch. psychologist, ednl. diagnostician Temple (Tex.) Ind. Sch. Dist., 1980-81; sch. psychologist Franklin (Tex.) Ind. Sch. Dist., 1981-82; ednl. cons., College Station, Tex., 1982—. Cub Scout leader Boy Scouts Am., Starkville, 1960; Brownie leader Girl Scouts U.S.A., Starkville, 1961-64; pres. Starkville Overstreet PTA, 1962; sec. Starkville Civic League, 1962-65; active Mental Health Assn. Alachua County (Fla.), 1976-77; treas. Citizens Com. for Mental Health in Bryan, 1979-80. Mem. Nat. Assn. Female Execs., Mid-South Ednl. Research Assn., Miss. Psychol. Assn., AAAS, Am. Psychol. Assn., Tex. Psychol. Assn., Brazos Valley Psychol. Assn., Council for Exceptional Children, AAUW (women's com. 1984—), Bryan-College Station C. of C., Opera and Performing Arts Soc., Arts Council Brazos Valley, Nat. Edn. Honor Soc., LWV, Phi Delta Kappa. Clubs: Sorosis (sec. 1962-65), Tex. A&M Faculty Wives, Tex. A&M Newcomers, Altrusa, Extension Service (1st v.p. 1984), Exec. Wives, Campus Study, Book Rev., Brazos Beautiful. Address: Redmond Terr Sta PO Box CJ College Station TX 77841

MAXWELL, KATHERINE LUMPKIN, financial planner; b. N.Y.C., Oct. 13, 1943; d. John H. and Margaret (Harper) Lumpkin; (div.); 1 dau., Jennifer Lee. B.A., Kans. U.-Lawrence, 1965, B.S., 1967; M.A., Tex. A&I U.-Kingsville, 1971. Cert. fin. planner; lic. stockbroker and prin. Asst. dept. mgr. Vandervoorts, St. Louis, 1965-66; tchr. Topeka, Kans. also Corpus Christi, 1967-69, 70-71; spl. edn. tchr. Dallas Ind. Sch. Dist., 1972-78, sch. counselor, 1978-81; self-employed ins. sales and fin. planner, Dallas, 1981—; fin. planner Asset Mgmt., Dallas, 1983-84; adj. faculty Coll. Fin. Planning, Denver, 1983—; instr. Dallas Community Colls., 1980—; bus. systems cons. Mem. adv. bd. Multiple Careers Magnet Ctr., Dallas Ind. Sch. Dist., 1981—. Mem. Internat. Assn. Fin. Planners (dir. 1983-84), Am. Bus. Womens Assn., Inst. Cert. Fin. Planners, Nat. Assn. Female Execs. Home: 10536 Countess Dr Dallas TX 75229 Office: 14940 Venture Dr Dallas TX 75234

MAXWELL, KATHRYN, financial consultant; b. South St. Paul, Minn., Dec. 10, 1952; d. Alfred R. and Doris A. (Meaden) McCormick; m. Charles H. Maxwell, Oct. 26, 1980. Student, Canada Coll., Redwood City, Calif., 1972-74. Mgr. payroll and benefit acctg. dept. Pacific Telephone Co., San Francisco, 1970-79; nat. sales trainer Neo-Life Co., San Francisco, 1979-81; owner, mgr. Creative Flow Mgmt. Co., Marin County, Calif., 1981-82; ptnr. Ross Fin. Group, Marin County, 1981-82; ptnr., fin. cons. Maxwell-Chesus Personal Fin. Systems, Marin County, 1982—; instr. Coll. of Marin, Kentfield, Calif., 1981-84, Ctr. of Excellence, San Francisco, 1986—. Vol., Werner Erhard & Assocs., San Francisco, 1979-83; bd. advisers Wingham Ministries, Mill Valley, 1982—. Recipient GoldKey award Neo-Life Co., 1981-83. Mem. Internat. Assn. Fin. Planners, Nat. Assn. Female Execs., Nat. Assn. Profl. Saleswomen, San Rafael C. of C. Club: Lew Epstein Women's (San Francisco). Avocations: cycling; hiking; spiritual studies; southwest U.S.A. studies. Office: Maxwell-Chesus Personal Fin Systems 60 E Sir Francis Drake Blvd Larkspur CA 94941

MAXWELL, LINDA RYAN, hair salon executive; b. New Britain, Conn., Aug. 28, 1951; d. James Alexander and Patricia Ann (Noel) Ryan; m. Dennis Gray Maxwell, Jr., Apr. 25, 1973 (div. Oct. 1984); 1 child, David Ryan. B.A. in Edn., Boston Coll., 1973. Asst. mgr. Food Service Assocs., Weston, Mass., 1973-79; salon coordinator Great Beginning, Weston, 1980-83, bus. mgr., 1984; dir. edn. Food Service Assocs., Weston, 1985—; dir. mgmt., corp. officer C.J. Maxwell & Co., Newtonville, Mass., 1985—. Mem. Nat. Assn. Female Execs., Avocations: photography; writing. Home: 16 Clifton Rd Wellesley MA 02181 Office: C J Maxwell & Co 39 Austin St Newtonville MA 02160

MAXWELL, MADALYN, lawyer; b. Nashville, Ill., Jan. 9, 1926; d. Ralph Lester and Beulah Madalyne (House) M.; m. Thomas H. McGary, July 4, 1968. A.A., Whitworth Coll., Brookhaven, Miss., 1945; B.S. in Law, U. Ill.-Urbana, 1948, M.A. in History, 1949. Law clk., Ill. Supreme Ct., Nashville, 1951-53; asst. atty. gen. State Ill., Springfield, 1953-55, 56—; asst. to treas. Sangamo Electric Co., Springfield, 1955-56. Bd. dirs. Sojourn Women's Ctr., Springfield, 1980—, chmn., 1982-83; bd. dirs. Springfield Symphony Orch., 1979—. Mem. ABA, Ill. State Bar Assn., Central Ill. Women's Bar Assn. (pres. 1986—). Episcopalian. Office: Ill Atty Gen 500 S 2d St Springfield IL 62704

MAXWELL, MARCIA GAIL, insurance company executive; b. Polk County, Ga., Aug. 15, 1948; d. Morris Lee and Mildred Ruth (Head) Martin, Sr.; m. Larry O. Maxwell, July 31, 1970; 1 child, Mischelle D. Sec., Ga. Income Tax Unit, Atlanta, 1969-72; sr. sales rep. Fed. Nat. Mortgage Assn., Atlanta, 1972-83; secondary mktg. acct. exec. Gen. Electric Mortgage Ins. Co., Atlanta, 1983—; rep. GECC Capital Markets Group, Atlanta, 1985—. Recipient #2 Secondary Trader award Gen. Electric Credit Corp., 1984, Winner's Circle award Gen. Electric Credit Corp., 1985, Outstanding Achievement award Gen. Electric Mortgage Ins. Co., 1985. Mem. Nat. Assn. Female Execs., Am. Mgmt. Assn., Nat. Assn. Profl. Mortgage Women (mem. publicity com. 1985—). Democrat. Baptist. Clubs: Toastmasters Internat. (pres. 1976-77), Fed. Nat. Mortgage Assn. Recreation (pres. 1980-81). Avocations: camping; boating; flower arranging. Home: 652 Stillwaters Dr Marietta GA 30064 Office: Gen Electric Mortgage Ins Co 400 Perimeter Ctr Terr Atlanta GA 30346

MAXWELL, NANCY PHILLIPS, lawyer; b. Manchester, Conn., Oct. 11, 1951; d. Paul Francis and W. Norene (Spurlin) P. B.A., So. Conn. State Coll., 1973; J.D., Stetson U., 1979. Bar: Conn. 1980, Fla. 1980. Computer programmer Hartford Ins. Group (Conn.), 1974-77, Conn. Bank & Trust, Hartford, 1976-77; law clk. U.S. Ct. Appeals for 2d circuit, N.Y.C., 1979-80; assoc. firm Walton, Lantaff, et al, West Palm Beach, Fla., 1980-83, Horty Springer & Metzger, West Palm Beach, 1983-84, Metzger & Sonneborn, West Palm Beach, 1984—. Chmn., Commn. on Status of Women, West Palm Beach, 1983-84. Mem. ABA, Conn. Bar Assn., Fla. Bar Assn., Palm Beach County Bar Assn., Guild Catholic Lawyers (v.p.). Democrat. Roman Catholic. Office: Metzger & Sonneborn 1615 Forum Pl West Palm Beach FL 33401

MAXWELL, PATRICIA JOY, association executive; b. Belle Plaine, Iowa, Feb. 7, 1937; d. Verne Edwin and Julia Inez (Beem) M.; student Pepperdine Coll., 1954-55; B.S., Iowa State Tchrs. Coll., 1958; M.P.A., Roosevelt U., 1982; m. Martin E. Sodetz, Jan. 21, 1984. Dir. resource devel. Boys Clubs Am., Chgo., 1978-81; exec. dir. Westlake Health Services Found., 1981-84; dir. devel.

and alumni affairs U. Ill. Coll. Medicine, 1984—; dir. profl. services Ency. Britannica Ednl. Corp.; cons. Prentice Hall Inc., U.S. State Dept. Mem. Am. Mktg. Assn., Chgo. Area Pub. Affairs Group, City Club of Chgo., Women Health Execs. Methodist. Clubs: Eastern Star, Rebekah, Order White Shrine. Office: 1130 S Michigan Ave Chicago IL 60605

MAXWELL, RUBY HOOTS, county official; b. Hendersonville, N.C., July 4, 1924; d. James Few and Nora Adlaide (Capps) Hoots; m. Foy Judson Maxwell, Apr. 24, 1944; 1 child, Terry Chandler. Supr. Spinning Wheel Rugs, Hendersonville, 1943-48; nurse aid ARC, Hendersonville, 1954-55; asst. Optician, Hendersonville, 1963-64; dep. register of deeds Henderson County, N.C., 1964-78, registrar, 1978—; instr. notary pub. edn. Blue Ridge Tech. Coll., Flat Rock, N.C., 1978—. Active Women's Democratic Club, Hendersonville, 1978—; asst. treas. Faith Bible Ch., Hendersonville, 1974—, sec. missionary com., 1980—. Mem. N.C. Register of Deeds Assn., Am. Soc. Notaries. Avocations: art; music. Office: Register of Deeds Courthouse Hendersonville NC 28739

MAXWELL, SHARON LEE REYNOLDS, government official, consultant; b. Taft, Calif., Mar. 2, 1939; d. Theodore Roosevelt Reynolds and Adelaide Velma (Johnson) Reynolds Sikola; B.A., U. Ariz., 1966, M.A., 1969; divorced; children—Maurynne Ruth, Edward Stuart. Asst. cataloger Tucson Public Schs., 1966-68, tchr., librarian, 1968-72; teaching asst. U. Ariz., 1971-72; with City of Tucson, 1972—, citizen participation adminstr., 1978—. Mem. Pima area adv. group Health Systems Agy. So. Ariz., 1978-80. Mem. Internat. Reading Assn., NEA, AAUW, Tucson Community Food Bank, Ariz. Edn. Assn., Am. Soc. Public Adminstrn., Am. Soc. Tng. and Devel., Nat. Assn. Female Execs., Exec. Women's Council of So. Ariz., Altrusa Internat., Pi Lambda Theta. Avocations: music; reading; counseling. Home: PO Box 13388 Tucson AZ 85732 Office: City of Tucson PO Box 27210 Tucson AZ 85726-7210

MAXWELL-BRODGON, FLORENCE, school administrator; b. Spring Park, Minn., Nov. 11, 1929; d. William Frederick and Florence Ruth (LaBrie) Maxwell; m. John Carl Brogdon, Mar. 13, 1957; children—Carole Alexandra, Cecily Ann, Daphne Diana. B.A., Calif. State U.-Los Angeles, 1955; M.S., U. So. Calif., 1957; postgrad. Columbia Pacific U., San Rafael, Calif., 1982-86. Cert. tchr., Calif. Dir. Rodeo Sch., Los Angeles, 1961-64; lectr. Media Features, Culver City, Calif., 1964—; dir. La Playa Sch., Culver City, 1968-75; founding dir. Venture Sch., Culver City, 1974—, also chmn. bd.; bd. dirs., v.p. Parent Coop. Preschools, Baie d'Urfe Quebec, Calif., 1964—. Author: Let Me Tell You, 1973; Wet 'n Squishy; 1973; Balancing Act, 1977; (column) What Parents Want to Know, 1961—. Editor: Calif. Preschooler, 1961-74. Contbr. articles to profl. jours. Treas. Democrat Congl. Primary, Culver City, 1972. Mem. Calif. Council Parent Schs. (bd. dirs. 1961-74), Parent Coop. Preschools Internat. (advisor 1975—). Libertarian. Home: 10814 Molony Rd Culver City CA 90230 Office: Venture Sch 5333 S Sepulveda Blvd Culver City CA 90230

MAXWELL-WILLIAMS, GWEN, nurse; b. Starkville, Miss., July 4, 1947; d. Charlie Will and Annie Bell (Cannon) Maxwell; m. C.E. Williams, Mar. 19, 1976 (dec. Mar. 25, 1985); 1 child, David Keith. A.A. in Nursing, Union U.-Jackson, Tenn., 1971; B.S.N., Seattle Pacific U., 1976; M.Nursing Adminstrn., U. Wash., 1977; Cert. Interior Design, Am. Acad. Interior Design, 1984. Cert. operating rm. nurse, cert. nursing adminstr. Operating rm. nurse Pub. Health Hosp., Seattle, 1973-76; operating rm. supr. U. Wash. Hosp., Seattle, 1977-79; operating rm. dir. Stanford U. Med. Ctr., Palo Alto, Calif., 1979-82; div. dir. nursing Good Samaritan Hosp., Puyallup, Wash., 1982-84; nursing adminstrn. supr. Harborview Med. Ctr., Seattle, 1985—; pres., owner Distinctive Images Boutique, Inc., Redmond, Wash., 1982—; cons. Kimberly Clark Corp., Atlanta, 1980-82. Contbg. editor: Medical Surgical Nursing, A Psychophysiological Approach, 1980; contbr. articles to profl. jours. Bd. dirs. 101 Black Women, Seattle, 1986—, Central Area Mental Health Ctr., 1983-85. Mem. Nat. Assn. Female Execs., Women's Bus. Exchange, Delta Sigma Theta. Clubs: Soroptomist (sec., bd. dirs.), Mary Mahoney Registered Nurses. Democrat. Baptist. Avocations: reading; gourmet cooking; travel. Home: 14134 110th NE Kirkland WA 98034 Office: Distinctive Images Inc 16150 NE 85th St Redmond WA 98052

MAY, AVIVA, educator; b. Tel-Aviv; naturalized Am. citizen, 1958; d. Samuel and Paula (Gordon) Rabinowitz; B.A., in Piano Pedgogy, Northeastern Ill. U., 1979; married; children—Rochelle, Alan, Risa, Ellanna. Tchr., pianist, 1948—; tchr. adult B'nai Mitzva, 1973; tchr. music, dir. McCormick Health Centers, Chgo., 1978-79, Cove Sch. Perceptually Handicapped Children, Chgo., 1978-79; prof. Hebrew and Yiddish, Spertus Coll. Judaica, Chgo., 1980—; tchr. continuing edn. Northeastern Ill. U., 1978-80, also Jewish Community Centers. folksinger, guitarist, 1962—; composer classical music for piano, choral work, folk songs. Recipient Magen David Adom Public Service award, 1973; Ill. State grantee, 1975-79; Ill. State Congressman Woody Bowman grantee, 1978-79. Mem. Music Tchrs. Nat. Assn., North Shore Music Tchrs. Assn. (a founder, charter mem., sec.), Ill. Music Tchrs. Assn., Organ and Piano Tchrs. Assn., Am. Coll. Musicians, Ill. Assn. Learning Disabilities, Sherwood Sch. Music, Yivo Inst. Yiddish. Democrat. Contbr. articles to profl. jours. Home: 3600 North Lake Shore Dr Chicago IL 60613 Studio: Fine Arts Bldg 410 S Michigan Ave Chicago IL

MAY, BARBARA CATHERINE, nurse; b. N.Y.C., July 20, 1937; d. Nathan and Thelma Ella Lucille (Kirkwood) Jones; R.N., Manhattan State Hosp. Sch. Nursing, 1957; B.S.N., N.Y. U., 1972; M.P.S., C.W. Post Coll., 1975; postgrad. Columbia Pacific U., 1982—; m. William Canty, Jr., Dec. 12, 1982; 1 dau. by previous marriage, Cynthia Joelle Webster. Mem. staff, Bronx Mcpl. Hosp. Center, 1961—, nursing clinician psychiatry, 1961—; cons. in field; commr. deeds, N.Y.C., 1980—. Bd. visitors Bronx Children's Psychiat. Center, 1981—; co-leader Girl Scouts. Am., 1981-83; mem. Nat. Bd. Funeral Dirs., 1983. Recipient Psychiat. Nurse award, Manhattan State Hosp. Sch. Nursing, 1957; NIMH grantee, 1971, others. Mem. C.W. Post Alumni Assn., Am. Nurses Assn. (cert. nursing adminstr.), N.Y. State Nurses Assn., Caribbean Nurses Assn., N.Y. Zool. Soc., Sigma Theta Tau. Democrat. Episcopalian. Co-author manuals in field; contbr. articles to profl. jours. Home: 100 10 Coop City Blvd Bronx NY 10475 Office: Pelham Pkwy S and Eastchester Rd Bronx NY 10461

MAY, BARBARA JEAN, public relations administrator, journalist; b. Cuyahoga Falls, Ohio, Feb. 2, 1948; d. James Lennon and Edna Grace (Lamb) Misock; m. Thomas O. May, June 22, 1968; children—Thomas Leon, Steven James. Student, Villa Maria (Pa.) Convent, 1962-68; student in English and speech Kent State U., 1968-71; A.A. in Media Technology, Ferris State U., 1974. Tchr., St. Joseph's Sch., Suffield, Ohio, 1968-70, Southeast High Sch., Edinburg, Ohio, 1970-71; freelance journalist, Big Rapids, Mich., 1971-74; news broadcaster Sta. WLBC, Muncie, Ind., 1974-76, Stas. WMDH and WHLN, New Castle and Anderson, Ind., 1976-79; community relations dir. Comprehensive Mental Health Services, Muncie, 1979—; spl. corr. Muncie Star newspaper, 1977—; freelance journalist T.J. Lennon/Assocs., Muncie, 1980—; mem. pub. relations com. Council of Community Mental Health Ctr., Indpls., 1980—; mem. media relations com. Community Concerns Council, Muncie, 1981—. Author: (video-tape) Muncie, A Great Place to Live, 1980; contbr. articles to profl. jours., newspapers, trade publs. Mem. disaster action team ARC, Muncie, 1980—; leader Legis. Awareness Seminar, Indpls., 1984. Recipient Accurate Reporting award Ind. State Tchrs. Assn., 1977-78. Mem. Women in Communications (pres. 1983-85), Internat. Assn. Bus. Communicators, Muncie C. of C. (community leader 1979-80). Clubs: Muncie Tennis; Skiers Assn., Racquetball, Freelancers (Denver). Home: Route 12 446 Parkwood Muncie IN 47302 Office: Comprehensive Mental Health Services 309 N High St Muncie IN 47305

MAY, DAPHINE G., business machines company executive; b. Hazlehurst, Miss., Jan. 31, 1952; d. Josie Mae (Gordon) Coley; m. Reginald Forsythe May, Sept. 8, 1974; children—Khalilah, Sonceira. B.A. in Acctg., Millsaps Coll., 1974. Accounts payable specialist IBM, Jackson, Miss., 1974-77, account adminstr., Atlanta, 1977-81, adminstrv. ops. mgr., Houston, 1981-83, divisional automatic document generation coordinator, Atlanta, 1983, adminstrv. instr., Atlanta, 1984—. Active PTA, Atlanta. Baptist. Home: 140 Roswell Farms Ct Atlanta GA 30075 Office: IBM 6151 Powers Ferry Rd Atlanta GA 30055

MAY, JANICE EVELYN CHRISTENSEN, political science educator; b. Mpls., May 29, 1923; d. Arnold Michael and Bernice Evelyn (Schauer) Christensen; B.A. summa cum laude, U. Minn., Mpls., 1944, M.A., 1946, Ph.D., 1952; m. Francis Barns May, June 9, 1956. Asst. instr. U. Minn., 1947-48; instr. U. Tex., 1948-53; instr., asst. prof. U. Okla., 1953-56; lectr. U. Tex., Austin, 1959, 64-65, instr., 1965-72, asst. prof., 1972-74, assoc. prof. govt., 1974—; lectr. U. Minn., Mpls., 1960; researcher Office Gov., State Tex., 1966, Inst. Public Affairs, U. Tex., 1969, 71, Tex. Adv. Commn. Intergovtl. Relations, 1972, Inst. Urban Studies, U. Houston, 1974. Pub. mem. bd. dirs. State Bar Tex., 1979-82; mem. Austin Commn. Status of Women, 1975-80, vice-chmn., 1978-79; mem. Tex. Constl. Revision Commn., 1973-74, 67-68; mem. S.W. Regional Panel, Pres. Commn. White House Fellows, 1970. Recipient Teaching Excellence award U. Tex., Austin, 1983. Mem. LWV (mem. state bd. 1964-70, nat. com. rep. govt. 1974-75), AAUW (award 1980, nat. legis. com. 1967-73), Am. Polit. Sci. Assn., Am. Acad. Polit. and Social Sci., Am. Judicature Soc., Nat. Mcpl. League, So. Polit. Sci. Assn., Southwestern Polit. Sci. Assn. (sec.-treas. 1980—), Southwestern Social Sci. Assn., Women's Polit. Caucus, Austin World Affairs Council. Author: Amending the Texas Constitution, 1951-72, 1973; The Texas Constitutional Revision Experience in the 70's, 1975; (with Stuart A. MacCorkle and Dick Smith) Texas Government, 7th edit., 1974, 8th edit., 1980; also articles in profl. publs. Office: Dept Govt U Tex Austin TX 78712

MAY, JOSEPHINE, banker; b. Cologne, Germany, Mar. 21, 1922; came to U.S., 1926, naturalized, 1939; d. Curt and Eva M. (Bungartz) Hartog; m. Herman E. May, Nov. 8, 1942; children—Linda J., James E. B.A., George Williams Coll., 1982; postgrad., 1982—. Asst. v.p. Bank of Yorktown, A Cole-Taylor Bank, Lombard, Ill., 1954-56, v.p., cashier, 1957-83, sr. v.p., 1983; pres., 1984—, also dir. Mem. fin. com. Good Samaritan Hosp., Downers Grove, Ill., 1984-85; mem. task force DuPage Pvt. Indsl. Council, 1985; charter mem. West Suburban Council, Downers Grove, 1984-85. Mem. Oak Brook C. of C., Lombard C. of C., Women in Mgmt. (treas. Oak Brook chpt. 1980), DuPage Bank Adminstrn. Inst. (bd. dirs. 1981), Yorktown Mchts. Assn. (bd. dirs. 1983—). Clubs: Oak Brook Breakfast; DuPage (bd. govs. 1985). Avocations: gardening; reading. Office: Bank of Yorktown 1 Yorktown Ctr Lombard IL 60148

MAY, LOIS MARIE, lawyer; b. Rockville Center, N.Y., July 24, 1951; d. Bernard Francis and Dorothy Marie (Schmitt) M.; m. George Raymond Dieter, June 15, 1980; 1 child, Christine Elizabeth. B.A., Coll. New Rochelle, 1973; Ph.D., St. John's U. Sch. Law, 1981. Bar: N.Y. 1982. Social security adv. claims engr., Huntington, N.Y., 1973-79; student legal asst. Western Electric, N.Y.C., 1979-80, U.S. Atty.'s Office, N.Y.C., 1980-81; asst. corp. counsel N.Y.C. Law Dept., 1981—. Mem. N.Y. Bar Assn. Roman Catholic. Home: 35-39 161 St Flushing NY 11358 Office: NYC Law Dept 100 Church St New York NY 10007

MAY, MELANIE GIVEN, lawyer; b. Lake Worth, Fla., Jan. 13, 1952; d. William Samuel and Martha (Rhoades) May; m. Gregory William Kehoe, May 7, 1983. B.S., Fla. Atlantic U., 1973; J.D., Nova U., 1981. Bar: Fla. 1981; U.S. Dist. Ct. (so. dist.) Fla. 1981, (mid. dist.) Fla. 1982; U.S. Ct. Appeals (5th and 11th cirs.) 1981. Tchr., St. Thomas Aquinas High Sch., Ft. Lauderdale, Fla., 1973-77; law clk. U.S. Ct. Appeals (11th cir.), Atlanta, 1981-82; assoc. Bunnell, Denman & Woulfe, P.A., Ft. Lauderdale, 1982—, adj. prof. law Nova Law Ctr., Ft. Lauderdale, 1982—. Mem. Fla. Bar Assn. (admiralty law com. 1983—, unauthorized practice law com. 1983—), Broward County Bar Assn., ABA. Republican. Episcopalian. Office: Bunnell Denman & Woulfe PA 1080 SE 3d Ave Fort Lauderdale FL 33316

MAY, PHYLLIS JEAN, adult foster care corporation executive; b. Flint, Mich., May 31, 1932; d. Bert A. and Alice C. (Rushton) Irvine; grad. Dorsey Sch. Bus., 1957; cert. Internat. Corr. Schs., 1959, Nat. Tax Inst., 1978; M.B.A., Mich. U., 1970; m. John May, Apr. 24, 1971; children—Phillip, Perry, Paul. Office mgr. Comml. Constrn. Co., Flint, 1962-68; bus. mgr. new and used car dealership, Flint, 1968-70; controller 6 corps., Flint, 1970-75; fiscal dir. Rubicon Odyssey Inc., Detroit, 1976—; acad. cons. acctg. Detroit Inst. Commerce, 1980-81; pres. small bus. specializing in adminstrv. cons. and acctg., 1982—; owner Pieces and Things, catalog sales, 1983—; notary public, 1968—. Pres. PTA Westwood Heights Schs., 1972; vol. Fedn. of Blind, 1974-76, Probate Ct., 1974-76. Recipient Meritorious Service award Genesee County for Youth, 1976, Excellent Performance and High Achievement award Odyssey Inc., 1981; lic. real estate broker. Mem. Am. Bus. Women's Assn. (treas. 1981, rec. sec. 1982, v.p. 1982-84, Woman of Yr. 1982), Nat. Assn. Profl. Female Execs. (network dir.), Internat. Platform Assn., Tau Alpha Gamma. Baptist. Home: 12050 Barlow St Detroit MI 48205 Office: Rubicon Odyssey Inc 7441 Brush St Detroit MI 48202

MAY, YVONNE, lawyer; b. N.Y.C., Aug. 4, 1946; d. Santiago S. and Margarita Blanca (de la Torres) Sanchez; m. Farnsworth R. May, Dec. 21, 1981; 1 dau., Andrea Lee. B.A., Marymount Manhattan Coll., N.Y.C., 1974; R.N., Mt. Sinai Sch. Nursing, N.Y.C., 1968; J.D., NYU, 1977. Bar: N.Y. 1978, Fla. 1981. Assoc., Gair, Gair & Conason, N.Y.C., 1977-79; staff nurse Morton Plant Hosp., Clearwater, Fla., 1980-81; assoc. James Helinger, P.A., Clearwater, 1981-82; ptnr. Carrion & May, P.A., Clearwater, 1982-83; sole practice, Clearwater, 1983—; health cons. Head Start curriculum dept. HEW, Washington, 1971; guest lectr. on operating room trends, Clearwater, 1983. Author: Medical Malpractice, 1978. Mem. ABA, Fla. Bar, N.Y. Bar, Acad. Fla. Trial Lawyers, Clearwater Bar Assn., Pinellas County Bar Assn. Democrat.

MAYANS, DORIS KAISER, ednl. adminstr.; b. St. Clair County, Ill., Jan. 14, 1931; d. Leonard Andrew and Luella Lillian K.; m. Frank Mayans; 6 stepchildren. B.S. Ed., Miami U., Oxford, Ohio, 1953, M.Ed., 1960. Tchr., Public Schs. Aurora (Colo.), 1953-54; tchr. Oak Hills Local Sch. Dist., Hamilton County, Ohio, 1954-63, intermediate supr., 1963-68, T.E.S.T. Project curriculum specialist, 1968-70, tchr. S.W. Local Sch. Dist., 1970-72; curriculum coordinator Sycamore Community Schs., Cin., 1972—; mem. tchr. edn. redesign com. Miami U., Oxford, 1979-81; mem. adv. com. Grad. Sch. Adminstrn., Xavier U., Cin., 1977-81. Mem. Assn. Supervision and Curriculum Devel., Cin. Council Social Studies (pres. 1978), Kappa Alpha Theta Methodist. Home: 6795 Marblehead Dr Cincinnati OH 45243 Office: Sycamore Community Schs 4881 Cooper Rd Cincinnati OH 45242

MAYBERRY, PATRICIA MARIE, lawyer; b. St. Louis, Aug. 25, 1951; d. Samuel G. Mayberry and Shirley (Mayberry) Hawkins. B.A., U. Mo., 1973; M.S.W., U. Houston, 1976; J.D., Thurgood Marshall Law Sch., 1979. Bar: Tex. 1979. Outreach counselor Juvenile Justice, Houston, 1978-79; sr. law intern Community Legal Services, Houston, 1978-80; law clk. Shell Oil, Houston, 1979-80; commd. capt. U.S. Air Force, 1980; asst. staff judge adv., Denver, 1980-84, resigned, 1984; assoc. Alvin Dillings, P.C., Denver, 1984—. Friend, Denver Girls, Inc., 1981—; usher Chapel One Lowry AFB, Denver, Shorter AME Ch.; mem. Protestant Chapel Council, Denver. Decorated commendation medal with cluster USAF. Mem. ABA, State Bar Tex., State Bar Colo., Assn. Trial Lawyers Am., Air Force Assn., Phi Alpha Delta, Delta Sigma Theta. Democrat. Methodist. Home: 3412 S Eagle Apt 102 Aurora CO 80014 Office: 1120 Lincoln St Suite 809 Denver CO 80203

MAYBURY, MARY-ELLEN LIVERMORE, state senator; b. Portland, Maine, Nov. 28, 1943; d. Hervey Claflyn and Barbara (Tuttle) Livermore; m. Michael William Maybury, 1965; children—Mark, Penny. Student Gorham State Tchrs. Coll., 1962-64, U. Maine, 1972, 84, 85. Mem. Brewer Bd. Appeals, Maine, 1977-79, Maine Ho. of Reps. from Dist. 74, 1982-84, Maine Senate from Dist. 11, 1984—. Pres., Bangor-Brewer LWV, 1975-77, Maine LWV, 1978-79; chmn. Brewer Community Action Group Against Drug and Alcohol Abuse, 1982-83. Mem. Bangor Bus. and Profl. Women (1st v.p. 1984-86). Congregationalist. Club: Brewer City (bd. dirs.). Republican. Office: Maine State Capitol Bldg Augusta ME 04333

MAYCOCK, RONNIE LEE, computer software company executive; b. Seoul, South Korea, Mar. 25, 1953; came to U.S., 1973, naturalized, 1979; d. Sang-Hoon and Keum-Nock (Hong) Lee; m. Roger Maxwell Maycock, July 1, 1984. Student Sogang U., Seoul, 1973; B.A., UCLA, 1976. Instr. Northrop U., Inglewood, Calif., 1977-78; tech. staff adviser Summation, Los Angeles, 1978-80, dir. tech. services, 1980-83, project mgr., 1983-84, mgr. spl. projects, 1984—, also dir. Developer various software packages. Mem. Nat. Assn. Female Execs. Avocations: classical guitar; piano; music transcription; drawing. Office: Summation 5801 E Slauson Ave Suite 220 Los Angeles CA 90040

MAYER, BEATRICE CUMMINGS, civic worker; b. Montreal, Que., Can., Aug. 15, 1921; came to U.S., 1939, naturalized, 1944; d. Nathan and Ruth (Kellert) Cummings; B.A. in Chemistry, U. N.C., 1943; postgrad. U. Chgo. Sch. Social Service Adminstrn., 1946-47; D.H.L. (hon.), Spertus Coll. Judaica, 1983; m. Robert Bloom Mayer, Dec. 11, 1947 (dec.); children—Robert N., Mrs. Stephen P. Durchslag. Mem. vis. com. Sch. Social Service Admnstrn. U. Chgo., 1964—, dept. art, 1972; dir. women's bd., 1973—; governing life mem. Art Inst. Chgo., life trustee, 1985—, also mem. women's bd.; trustee Michael Reese Hosp. and Med. Center, Chgo., 1974-85; bd. dirs. Michael Reese Found., 1983—; Trustee Kenyon Coll., Gambier, Ohio, 1976—; bd. fellows Brandeis U., Waltham, Mass., 1977—; mem. womens bd. Northwestern U., 1978—; trustee Anshe Emet Synagogue, Chgo., 1974-86, v.p., 1978-86; trustee Mus. Contemporary Art, Chgo., 1974—, v.p., 1978—; bd. dirs. Spoleto Festival U.S.A., 1981—; dir. Consol. Foods Corp., former chmn. public responsibility com. Recipient Brandeis U. Disting. Community Service award, 1972; Am. Jewish Com. Human Rights medallion, 1976; YMCA Leadership award, 1979; Woman of Year in Arts, YWCA Met. Chgo., 1979; Alumni Laureate award Loyola Coll. Balt., 1984; Centennial Gold medal for disting. community service Jewish Theol. Sem., 1986. Clubs: Tavern, Standard (Chgo.); Lake Shore Country (Glencoe, Ill.). Home: Chicago IL 60611

MAYER, CATHERINE ANNE, psychiatrist; b. Evanston, Ill., Oct. 10, 1945; d. George Andrew and Lorna (Lindsay) M.; B.A. cum laude, Stanford U., 1967; M.D., U. Wis., 1978. Diplomate Am. Bd. Psychiatry and Neurology. Intern, C. F. Menninger Meml. Hosp., Topeka, 1978-79, resident in psychiatry, 1979-82, staff psychiatrist, 1982—. Mem. AAAS, Am. Psychiat. Assn., Alpha Omega Alpha. Office: Box 829 Topeka KS 66601

MAYER, DIANA LYNNE KIARSIS, investment banker; b. Hanover, N.H., Oct. 17, 1946; d. Victor and Barbara Evelyn (McFee) Kiarsis; m. George Lindsay Mayer, Aug. 28, 1971 (div. Dec. 1983). B.A., Wellesley Coll., 1968; M.B.A., Harvard U., 1971. Portfolio mgr. Merrill Lynch, Pierce, Fenner & Smith, Inc., N.Y.C., 1968-69; cons. McKinsey & Co., N.Y.C., 1970; asst. v.p. Citicorp, N.Y.C., 1971-74, v.p., 1974-81; sr. v.p. Marine Midland Bank, N.Y.C., 1981—. Alt. del. Republican Nat. Conv., Detroit, 1980. Mem. Fin. Women's Assn. Clubs: Downtown Athletic (N.Y.C.). Home: 211 Central Park W Apt 10K New York NY 10024 Office: Marine Midland Bank 140 Broadway New York NY 10015

MAYER, EDITH PEACOCK, county official; b. Cin., July 24, 1929; d. Howard William and Serene (Allan) Peacock; student Ind. U.; m. Charles D. Mayer, Apr. 24, 1959; children—Sandra, Charles D. Tchr. math. and English, Madison County, Ala., 1951-53; staff asst. toilet goods product research Procter & Gamble, Cin., 1956-59; mem. Ohio Ho. of Reps., 1977-82; rural zoning commr., Hamilton County, Ohio, 1982—; dir. Enterprise Fed. Savs. & Loan, Cin. Mem. Greenhills-Forest Park Bd. Edn., 1968-77, pres., 1969, 71, 73; parliamentarian Great Oaks JVS Bd. Edn., 1972-77; mem. Ohio PTA Bd. Mgrs., 1972-77; mem. Ohio Adv. Council for Vocat. Edn. Recipient Outstanding Leadership awards Ohio Sch. Bds. Assn., 1976, Ohio Elem. Adminstrs., 1980, Ohio Twp. Trustees Assn., 1980, Humane Soc. U.S., 1981, Ohio Assn. Gifted and Talented, 1981. Republican. Episcopalian. Club: Cin. Woman's. Home: 10120 Winstead Ln Cincinnati OH 45231

MAYER, ELIZABETH BILLMIRE, educational administrator; B.Ed., Nat. Coll. Edn., Evanston, Ill., 1953; M.A. in Liberal Studies, Wesleyan U., 1979. Teaching asst. Hull House, Chgo., 1950-51; teaching scholar Nat. Coll. Edn. Demonstration Sch., 1952-53; pre-sch. tchr. St. Matthew's Sch., Pacific Palisades, Calif., 1959-63, tchr. 2d grade, 1963-67; librarian Chandler Sch., Pasadena, Calif., 1971-72, tchr. 4th grade, 1972-80, curriculum coordinator 1st-8th grades, 1979-80; tchr. 4th-6th grades Inst. for Experimentation in Tchr. Edn., SUNY-Cortland, 1980; asst. prof. edn. SUNY-Cortland, 1980-82; founder, headmistress The Mayer Sch., Ithaca, N.Y., 1982—. Mem. Nat. Council Tchrs. Math., Nat. Council Tchrs. English, Nat. Sci. Tchrs. Assn., Calif. Assn. Ind. Schs., N.Y. State Assn. Ind. Schs., Phi Delta Kappa (officer 1980-81). Office: The Mayer Sch 416 Cayuga Heights Rd Ithaca NY 14850

MAYER, KAY, writer; b. Chgo.; d. Frank J. and Harriet (Schnell) Magnor; m. Kenneth W. Mayer, May 2, 1943; children—Michael J., Patricia A., Mark T. Student Northwestern U., 1938-43. News reporter Tampa Times, 1943; advt. copywriter Marshall Field & Co., Chgo., Earle Ludgin & Co., Chgo., Henri, Hurst & McDonald, Chgo., 1944-58; spl. editor, writer Scott, Foresman & Co., Glenview, Ill., 1966-71; freelance writer Art West, Ariz. Hwys., Southwest Art, Am. Artist, Am. Way, 1971—. Recipient Nat. and State Press Women's 1st place awards, 1983, 84, 85. Mem. Nat. Fedn. Press Women, Ariz. Press Women, Nat. Council Social Studies, Western History Assn., Soc. Southwestern Authors (dir. 1981-83). Home: 3525 N Millard Dr Tucson AZ 85715

MAYER, MARILYN GOODER, steel company executive; b. Chgo.; d. Seth MacDonald and Jean (McMullen) Gooder; m. William Anthony Mayer, Nov. 14, 1959; children—William Anthony Jr., Robert MacDonald. grad. Career Inst. Chgo., 1941; student Lake Forest Coll., Ill., 1942. Adminstrv. asst. Needham, Louis & Brorby, Chgo., 1949-53; v.p. RMB Corp., Chgo., 1963-71, Mayer Motors, Ft. Lauderdale, Fla., 1965-74, Gooder-Henrichsen, Chicago Heights, Ill., 1975—; dir. Barnett Bank, West Palm Beach, Fla. Trustee Gulf Stream (Fla.) Sch., St. Andrew's Sch., Boca Raton, Fla.; bd. dirs. Bethesda Hosp. Assn., Boynton Beach, Fla., pres. 1981-82; bd. dirs. Gulf Stream Civic Assn. Mem. Soc. Four Arts. Republican. Episcopalian. Avocation: travel. Home: 2925 Polo Dr Gulf Stream FL 33444

MAYER, MARY JANE AMANDA, nursing company executive, nurse; b. Milw., June 13, 1934; d. Carl Bernard and Delores M. (Rauk) M. B.S.N., Marquette U., 1961, M.N., 1965. Instr. nursing of children Milw. Children's Hosp., 1961-63; instr. med.-surg. nursing Milw. Tech. Coll., 1963-67; instr. pub. health Alverno, Milw., 1967-68; asst. prof. pub. health nursing U. Wis.-Oshkosh, 1968-69; dir. edn. Vis. Nurse Assocs., Milw., 1969-72, exec. dir., 1972—. Recipient Vocat. Recognition award Milw. Rotary Club, 1984. Mem. Med. Soc. Milw. County, Am. Pub. Health Assn., Wis. Homecare Assn. (pres. 1979-81), Wis. Employee Benefits Assn. (bd. dirs. 1979—, sec. 1981-82, v.p. 1983—), Nat. Assn. Home Care (bd. dirs. 1982-84), Vis. Nurse Assns. (dir. Am. affiliation 1983). Office: Visiting Nurse Assocs 1540 N Jefferson Milwaukee WI 53202

MAYER, PATRICIA HATFIELD, secretary to governor; b. Schenectady, Feb. 23, 1933; d. G. Elliott and Lucille Roipequet (Goedde) Hatfield; m. Donald Franklin Mayer, Feb. 26, 1955; children—Kathleen Patricia, Leslie Susan, Elliott Hatfield. B.S. in Chemistry, Mary Washington Coll., U. Va.-Fredericksburg, 1954. Dept. mgr., asst. buyer Woodward & Lothrop, Washington, 1968-77; confidential sec. Gov. Va. Charles S. Robb, Richmond, 1977—. Mem. Mary Washington Coll. Alumni Assn. (2d v.p. 1981-83), Achievement Rewards for Coll. Scientists Inc. Presbyterian. Clubs: Jr. Women's of Fairfax County (Fairfax, Va.); DAR (state chmn. 1983—). Office: Office of Governor The State Capitol Richmond VA 23219

MAYER, RITA MCDERMOTT, writer, writers consortium executive; b. Beaumont, Tex., July 25, 1942; d. William Herd and Pina Mae (Brown) McDermott; m. Terry Lee Mayer, Dec. 26, 1971 (dec. mar. 1978). B.J., U. Tex., 1964; postgrad. East Tex. State U., 1971. Reporter, editor, columnist Beaumont Jour., 1964-70; tchr. English, Highlands High Sch., San Antonio, 1970-71; feature writer East Tex. State U., 1971; editorial cons. Bd. World Missions Presbyterian Ch. U.S., Nashville, 1972-73; creative dir. Lee Harrison Agy., Nashville, 1973-75; co-owner Total Graphics Corp., Nashville, 1975; creative dir. Peppy Martin & Assocs., Louisville, 1976-77, Jack Guthrie & Assocs., Louisville, 1977-78, Christiansen & Assocs., Nashville, 1978; founder, pres. Cumberland Group, Nashville, 1978—; cons. Hosp. Corp. Am., Nashville, Fin. Instns. Services, Inc., Nashville, others. Author and editor corporate publications. Contbr. articles to profl. jours. Vice pres. Operation Get Well, Beaumont, Tex., 1967-70; dir. pub. relations Piney Woods TB Assn., Beaumont, 1968; vol. United Services Orgn., San Antonio, 1970-71, Norton's Childrens Hosp., Louisville, 1977, United Way Nashville, 1973, 81, Oasis House, Nashville, 1983—; big buddy Buddies of Nashville, 1982-84; bd. dirs. Nashville Child Ctr., Inc., 1986—. Mem. Nashville Advt. Fedn. (Diamond award 1973, 83, 84, 85), Nat. Acad. TV Arts and Scis., Tenn. Literary Assn., Internat. Assn. Bus. Communicators (Gold Quill award of Merit 1981). Methodist. Avocations: reading; cooking; entertaining; music. Office: Cumberland Group 1161 Murfreesboro Rd Nashville TN 37203

MAYER, SUSAN LEE, nurse; b. N.Y.C., Feb. 10, 1946; d. Hans and Frieda (Schein) Abramson; B.S.N., Hunter Coll., 1968; M.A., N.Y.U., 1974, postgrad., 1974; cert. in gerontology Yeshiva U.; m. Steven Mayer, June 24, 1973; children—Jason, Stuart, Richard, Deborah. Staff nurse ICU-CCU, Montefiore Hosp., Bronx, N.Y., 1968; organizer CCU, Jewish Meml. Hosp., N.Y.C., 1968; supr., adminstr. Morrisania City Hosp., N.Y.C., 1969-76; instr. Adelphi Univ.,

Garden City, N.Y., 1977-78; substitute nurse Great Neck (N.Y.) Public Schs., 1980—; tchr. CPR, 1972-80, 85—; lectr. PTA groups, 1981-82. Bd. dirs. Great Neck Synagogue, 1981—, v.p. Sisterhood, 1978-79, pres., 1979-81; former bd. dirs. Russell Gardens Assn.; founder Work for Share, Zedek Hosp., 1977—. N.Y. State Regents scholar, 1963. Mem. Am. Nurses Assn., Assn. Orthodox Jewish Scientists, Nat. League Nursing, N.Y. Counties Registered Nurses Assn., N.Y. Heart Assn., Sigma Theta Tau. Democrat. Club: New York University. Home: 28 Laurel Dr Great Neck NY 11021

MAYER, VELIA ANN, lawyer; b. nr. Mt. Pleasant, Tex., Feb. 13, 1943; d. Velia John and Opal (Dale) Mayer; B.A. cum laude, U. Miss., 1965, J.D., 1968. Admitted to Miss. bar, 1968; practiced in Jackson, 1971—; law clk. for judge of Miss. Supreme Ct., Jackson, 1968-69; spl. asst. atty. gen. State of Miss., Jackson, 1969-71; assoc. firm Watkins and Eager, attys. at law, Jackson, 1971-75, partner, 1975-82. Mem. Am., Miss., Hinds County bar assns., Am. Judicature Soc. Home: 787 Arlington St Jackson MS 39202 Office: Box 650 Jackson MS 39205

MAYERSON, HOLLIS LYNNE, psychiatrist; b. N.Y.C., Feb. 25, 1948; d. Saul J. and Dorothy (Davis) Mayerson. A.B. cum laude, Vassar Coll., 1968; M.D., Hahnemann Med. Coll., 1972. Diplomate Nat. Bd. Med. Examiners. Med. intern, Albert Einstein Med. Ctr., Phila., 1972-73, resident in radiology, 1973-74; family practice and diagnostic work, N.Y.C., 1974-79; with Med-Dental Resource Bank, 1979-80; resident in psychiatry Upstate Med. Center, Syracuse, N.Y., 1980-82; staff psychiatrist Hutchings Psychiat. Ctr., Syracuse, 1982—; asst. clin. prof. psychiatry SUNY-Syracuse, 1982—. Vol. The Caring Coalition, Syracuse, 1983—. Mem. Am. Psychiat. Assn. Club: Vassar. Office: Hutchings Psychiatric Center Unit TU4 618 Madison St Syracuse NY 13210

MAYERSON, SANDRA ELAINE, lawyer; b. Dayton, Ohio, Feb. 8, 1952; d. Manuel David and Florence Louise (Tepper) Mayerson; m. Scott Burns, May 29, 1977 (div. 1978). B.A. cum laude, Yale U., 1973; J.D., Northwestern U., 1976. Bar: Ill. 1976, U.S. Dist. Ct. (no. dist.) Ill. 1976, U.S. Ct. Appeals (7th cir.) 1977. Counsel, Washington Nat. Corp., Evanston, Ill., 1974-79; assoc. gen. counsel JMB Realty Corp., Chgo., 1979-80; assoc. law firm Chatz, Sugarman, Abramsetal, Chgo., 1980-81; mem. firm Gottlieb & Schwartz and predecessor firm, Chgo., 1981-83; dep. gen. counsel, asst. sec. AM Internat. Inc., Chgo., 1983-85; ptnr. Kirkland & Ellis, Chgo., 1985—; dir. Mordine & Co., Chgo. Bd. dirs. Jr. Med. Research Inst. Council, Dysfunctioning Child Ctr. Michael Reese Hosp. Mem. Ill. State Bar Assn. (mem. governing council corp. securities sect.), Chgo. Bar Assn. (mem. com. to revise Ill. uniform ltd. partnership act), ABA. Democrat. Jewish. Clubs: Yale of New York, Met. (Chgo.). Home: 1550 N Lake Shore Dr Apt 9B Chicago IL 60610 Office: Kirland & Ellis 200 E Randolph Dr 59th Floor Chicago IL 60601

MAYES, BERNICE ELIZABETH, dietitian; b. Oxford, N.C., Feb. 5, 1937; d. Garland Sherwood and Maggie (Richards) Mayes. Student Va. State Coll., 1954-58; B.S., Fairleigh Dickinson U., 1982. Staff dietitian Clara Maass Hosp., Belleville, N.J., 1960-62, therapeutic dietitian, 1962-68, tng. dietitian, 1965-66; cafeteria mgr. Newark Bd. Edn., 1968-72, asst. dir., 1972-76, dir., 1976—; weekend dietitian St. Barnabas Hosp., Livingston, N.J., 1970-72, project supr., summer 1971; commr. East Orange Bd. Health. Author handbook for employees and food-service tng. manual. Past pres. Essex County (N.J.) Adv. Bd. on Status of Women, 1983; mem. concerned set TLC Day Care Ctr., East Orange, N.J. 1983; mem. Women in Support Essex County Coll. Adv. Bd., Newark, 1983; bd. dirs. Carver Youth and Family Ctr., Trenton, 1983. Mem. U.S. Dept. Agr. Commodity Adv. Bd. (chmn. major cities sect.), Assn. Sch. Bus. Ofcls., Adminstrv. Employees Assn., Nat. Assn. Colored Women's Clubs (life mem., chmn.), Essex County Nutrition Council, AAUW, Va. State Alumni Assn., Fairleigh Dickinson Alumni Assn., Roundtable for Women in Foodservice, N.J. Sch. Food Service Assn. (legis. chmn., pres.), Nat. Assn. Female Execs. Democrat. Episcopalian. Clubs: Garnetts (Plainfield, N.J.); St. Ann's Guild (Newark). Office: Newark Bd Edn 2 Cedar St Newark NJ 07102

MAYESKI, FRAN ELIZABETH, educational consultant; b. Rolla, Mo., Nov. 6, 1941; d. Charles Emil and Katherine Dorothy (Parker) Gelven; B.S. in English, St. Louis U., 1964; postgrad. U. Wash., Seattle, 1974; M.B.A., City Coll., Seattle, 1980; m. John Kent Mayeski, May 21, 1966; 1 son, Mark Edward. Publs. asst. St. Louis U., 1965-66; tchr. St. Charles Schs., Spokane, Wash., 1967-68, Holmes Jr. High Sch., Colorado Springs, 1969, Sacred Heart Sch., Bellevue Wash., 1971-74, Interlake High Sch., Bellevue, 1974-76, area chairperson social studies, 1976-77; tchr., project leader Bellevue Public Schs., 1979-80; dir. staff devel. and spl. projects Ednl. Service Unit 10, Kearney, Nebr., 1980-83; dir. curriculum and instrn. Holdredge City Schs. (Nebr.), 1983-85; ednl. cons.; pres. Promoting Effective Growth, Inc., 1985—; instr. Seattle Pacific U., Kearney State Coll. Mem. Assn. Supervision and Curriculum Devel., Nebr. Assn. Supervision and Curriculum Devel., Women in Mgmt. Assn., Am. Ednl. Research Assn., Am. Soc. Tng. and Devel., Nat. Speakers Assn., Phi Delta Kappa. Club: Kearney State Coll. Faculty Wives.

MAYFIELD, LORI JAYNE, automobile club administrator; b. Newport Beach, Calif., Sept. 11, 1955; d. John Vincent and Marilyn Jane (Huish) M. Student Linn-Benton Community Coll., 1973-75, N.W. Coll., 1975-76. Gen. ins. cert. Ins. Inst. Am. Cashier Auto Club So. Calif., Anaheim, 1977-80, ins. clk., sec., Fullerton, 1980-81, ins. rep., 1981, field coordinator, Costa Mesa, Calif., 1981—. Recipient Outstanding Citizenship award YMCA, Santa Ana, Calif., 1984. Mem. Nat. Assn. Female Execs. Democrat. Office: Auto Club So Calif 3333 S Fairview St Costa Mesa CA 92626

MAYFIELD, MARY KATHRYN, commercial real estate firm executive; b. Waco, Tex., Aug. 25, 1948; d. Ray V. and Nita (Robbins) M. Student Shakespeare Inst., Statford-Upon-Avon, Eng., 1970; B.A. in English and History, Houston Bapt. U., 1970; M.Ed. in Adminstrn. and Supervision, U. Houston, 1973, postgrad. in edn., 1974. Secondary tchr. English, Aldine Ind. Sch. Dist., Houston, 1970-74; dir. leasing Shindler/Cummins, Inc., Houston, 1974-81; owner, pres. Mayfield Interests, Inc., Houston, 1981—. Pres., Pres.'s Advisers of Houston Bapt. U., 1981-82; bd. dirs. Salvation Army, Houston, 1983-84, Theatre Under the Stars, Houston, 1981-82. Recipient awards including Assoc. of Yr., Comml. Div. Shindler/Cummins, Inc., 1978; Outstanding Alumnus award Houston Bapt. U., 1980. Mem. Houston Bapt. U. Alumni Assn. (pres. 1980-81), Houston C. of C. (edn. com. 1974-81), Houston Bd. Realtors, Houston Office Leasing Brokers Assn., Am. Bus. Women's Assn., Profl. Women Execs., Nat. Assn. Women in Comml. Real Estate (a founder; v.p. 1980-81, mem. adv. bd. 1981-82), Ballet Guild, Cultural Arts Council, Encorps, Heritage Soc., Mus. Fine Arts, Opera Guild. Clubs: Afton Oaks Civic University (sec. Women's Assn.), Ladies Reading, LTG (dir. 1982-83, pres. 1984—). Office: 10333 Harwin Suite 201 Houston TX 77036

MAYHEW, KATHLEEN ANN, nonprofit organization executive; b. Corpus Christi, Nov. 12, 1948; d. James T. and Shirley (Strangward) Maher; m. Lewis Baltzell Mayhew, Jr., July 15, 1972. B.A. in Psychology, Santa Clara U., 1970; M.A., San Jose State U., 1973. Cert. counselor community coll., Calif. Instr., Modesto Jr. Coll., 1975-80; social worker asst. Omnicare, Modesto, 1978; social service worker Drs. Med. Ctr., Modesto, 1979; exec. dir. Via, supporting those living with death and life-threatening illness, Modesto, 1980—; counselor Family Service Agy., Modesto, 1974-75; mem. steering com., trainer, bd. dirs. Community Hospice, Modesto, 1979-81; mem. Dirs. of Vols. in Agys., 1981-83; cons., lectr. Bd. dirs. Stanislaus County chpt. Am. Cancer Soc., 1978-83; trustee Stanislaus Meml. Soc., 1979-83, pres., 1983; mem. Title IX Leadership Com., 1976; v.p., rec. sec. Stanislaus County Commn. for Women, 1982-84. Bd. dirs., mem. editorial bd., contbr. Woman's Compendium, 1985. Rotary Club scholar, 1966. Mem. Women's Network, Modesto C. of C. (Leadership Modesto). Democrat. Avocations: photography; cross-country skiing; weaving; mountain climbing. Office: Via 1700 McHenry Village Way Suite 4 Modesto CA 95350

MAYNARD, VIRGINIA MADDEN, association executive; b. New London, Conn., Jan. 29, 1924; d. Raymond and Edna Sarah (Madden) Maynard; B.S., U. Conn., 1945; postgrad. Am. Inst. Banking, 1964-66, Cornell U., 1975. With Nat. City Bank (now Citibank), N.Y.C., 1954-79, asst. cashier, 1965-69, asst. v.p., 1969-74, v.p. internat. banking group, 1974-76, comptroller's div., 1976-79; v.p. First Women's Bank, N.Y.C., 1979-80; Internat. Fedn. Univ. Women rep. UN, 1982—; cons. in field. Trustee fellowships endowment fund AAUW Ednl. Found., Washington, 1977-80, Va. Gildersleeve Internat. Fund Univ. Women, Inc. Mem. AAUW (fin. chmn. N.Y.C. br. 1976-79, bylaws chmn. 1979-83, adminstr. Meml. Fund 1983—, Woman of Achievement 1976). Republican. Congregationalist. Home: 601 E 20th St New York NY 10010

MAYNE, LUCILLE STRINGER, finance educator; b. Washington, June 6, 1924; d. Henry Edmond and Hattie Benham (Benson) Stringer; B.S., U. MD., 1946; M.B.A. (grad. scholar), Ohio State U., 1949; Ph.D. (fellow), Northwestern U., 1966; children—Patricia Anne, Christine Gail, Barbara Marie. Asst. to promotion mgr. NBC, Washington, 1946-48; instr. fin. Utica (N.Y.) Coll., 1949-50; analytical statistician Air Materiel Command, Dayton, Ohio, 1950-52; lectr. fin. Roosevelt U., Chgo., 1961-64; lectr. Pa. State U., State College, 1965-66, asst. prof., 1966-69, assoc. prof., 1969-70; assoc. prof. banking and fin. Case Western Res. U., Cleve., 1971-76, prof., 1976—, dean Sch. Grad. Studies, 1980-84; dir. Horizon Savs., Cleve.; staff economist Pres.'s Commn. Fin. Structure and Regulation, 1970-71; economist FDIC, 1977-78. Bd. dirs. Cleve. Citywide Devel. Corp., 1981—. Mem. Am. Fin. Assn., Midwest Fin. Assn., Fin. Mgmt. Assn. (dir. 1982-83), Phi Kappa Phi, Beta Gamma Sigma. Episcopalian. Assoc. editor Jour. Money, Credit and Banking, 1980-83, Bus. Econs., 1980-85; contbr. articles to profl. jours. Office: Case Western Reserve U Weatherhead Sch Mgmt University Circle Cleveland OH 44106

MAYO, CORA LOUISE, educator; b. Chgo., Oct. 31, 1925; d. Charles Amos and Mary (Elder) Scott; m. Marion Wesley Mayo, July 21, 1948; children—Lynne, Janice, Jo Ann, Thomas. B.S., U. Ill.-Urbana, 1949, advanced degree in adminstrn. and supervision, 1973; M.A., U. Chgo., 1961; Ph.D., Heed U., Fla., 1981. Program facilitator Chgo. Bd. Edn., 1955—; owner/pres. From the Black Experience, Inc., Chgo., 1979—; dir. pub. relations Afro-Am. Pub. Co., Chgo., 1972-73; ednl. cons. Ednl. Leadership Inst., Chgo., 1976-78; community prof. Govs. State U., Park Forest, Ill., 1975—. Author: Developmental Skills Activities Guide, 1982; columnist Teaching Black Positively; editor Human Relations Digest; author/pub.: (early childhood learning kit) Mwenzi Companeros, 1982. Bd. dirs. Woodson Delany Ednl. Fund, Chgo., 1975—, House of the Black Madonna, Chgo., 1978—; cons. Head Start, St. Stephen's Ch., Chgo., 1982-83; organizer Women for Washington, 1982-83, Women for Jackson, 1984; vol. instr. parenting House of the Black Madonna; proposals cons. Du Sable Mus. Afro-Am. History, Chgo. Recipient Leadership award Boy Scouts Am., 1971; named Outstanding Educator of Yr., Woodson-Delany Ednl. Fund, 1976; others. Mem. Nat. Assn. Media Women (fin. sec. 1983—, sec. chpt. 1982—, v.p. 1973), Women in Communications, Phi Delta Kappa. Democrat. Congregationalist. Club: Debonnettes (pres. 1984) (Chgo.). Home: 1618 E 85th Pl Chicago IL 60617

MAYO, FLORENCE BAKER, newspaper publisher; b. Denver, Sept. 5, 1904; d. Andrew Martinius and Inga Marie Baker; m. Richard Wheeler Mayo, Sept. 12, 1927 (dec. Jan. 1975); children—Richard Wheeler, James Watie, Andrea. B.A. cum laude, U. Colo., 1926. Tchr. math. Delta High Sch., (Colo.), 1926-27; tchr. math Sallisaw High Sch. (Okla.), 1928-29; founding publisher Sequoyah County Times, Sallisaw, 1932—; pres. Cookson Hills Publishers Inc., Sallisaw, 1978—. Fellow Internat. Soc. Weekly Newspaper Editors; mem. Okla. Press Assn. (50 yr. award 1982), U. Okla. Found., U. Colo. Alumni Assn., Colo. Head Injury Found. Clubs: Friday Forum (past pres.), Garden. Office: Sequoyah County Times 111 N Oak St PO Box 370 Sallisaw OK 74955

MAYO, REATA FRANCES, nurse; b. Marquette, Mich., Aug. 18, 1959; d. William Joseph and Doloris Joan (Froberg) Mayo. A.A.S. with honors, Mich. Technol. U., 1979; B.S.N. magna cum laude, No. Mich. U., 1981. Charge nurse, supr. Norlite Ctr., Marquette, 1979-80; staff nurse Marquette Gen. Hosp., 1980-81, asst. head nurse orthopedics dept., 1981—. Mem. Nat. Assn. Orthopedic Nurses. Democrat. Roman Catholic. Home: Rural Route 1 PO Box 203 Republic MI 49879 Office: Marquette Gen Hosp 420 W Magnetic St Marquette MI 49855

MAYR, KAY FAYSTINE, radio station executive; b. Lansdale, Pa., June 17, 1939; d. Russell Myers and Frances M. (Stauffer) Swartley, m. Ronald Batson, 1961 (div. 1963); 1 child, John Tracy; m. William Fred Mayr, July 28, 1965; children—Tiffany Lynn, Christina Noelle. B.A. magna cum laude, Western Conn. State U., 1976. Reservation ticket agent Trans World Airlines, Phila., 1960-65; head tchr. Hamilton Nursery Sch., Conn., 1970-73; with Sta. WLAD/WDAQ, 1977—; asst. sales mgr. Berkshire Broadcasting, Danbury, Conn., 1979-81, sales mgr., 1981-83, gen. sales mgr., 1983—. Pres. Vol. Bur. Greater Danbury, 1983—, Ridgefield Civic Ballet Bd., 1984—; v.p. Ridgefield Workshop, 1984—; trustee United Way of No. Fairfield County, 1983—. Recipient Sales Breakthrough award Radio Advt. Bur., 1979. Mem. AAUW, Am. Women in Radio and TV (pres. New Eng. chpt. 1983-84, found. chmn. 1984-85, state broadcasting chmn. 1985—), Danbury C. of C. (task force on women on the move 1982—). Republican. Avocations: singing; acting; writing; travel. Office: WLAD/WDAQ 198 Main St Danbury CT 06810

MAYS, GENEVA, government administrator; b. N.Y.C., Mar. 17; d. John and Clara (Lancaster) Wise; B.A., Bernard Baruch Sch. Bus. Adminstrn., N.Y.C., 1959; m. Paul Mays, Aug. 29, 1959; children—Paul Eric, Jon William. Various secretarial and adminstrv. asst. positions, 1957-71; EEO specialist, mgr. fed. women's program Dept. Transp., Washington, from 1971—, now EEO mgr. Recipient Meritorious Achievement Honor award Dept. Labor, 1966, Outstanding Performance award, 1983. Mem. Nat. Assn. Minority Polit. Women (founder, pres.), Am. Soc. Public Adminstrn., Federally Employed Women, Urban League, Blacks in Govt., Black Women's Agenda, Suitland Civic Assn., Links, Jack and Jill Am. (founder, 1st pres. Prince George's County chpt. 1974). Home: 5010 Luci Ln Suitland MD 20746 Office: 2100 2d St SW Washington DC 20593

MAYS, PATRICIA ELAINE, educator; b. Dallas, June 24, 1944; d. Wilfred S. Means and Ruby (Carter) Means-Barton; m. Isaiah White, Feb. 20, 1966 (div. 1976); children—Brian, Kimberly; m. Stanley R. Mays, Dec. 6, 1978. Mus.B., No. Tex. State U., Denton, 1963; M.S., East Tex. State U., Commerce, 1976. Tchr. Garland (Tex.) Ind. Sch. Dist., 1972-78; asst. prin. Q. Mills Sch., Dallas, 1978-82, William Limpscomb Sch., Dallas, 1982-83, David G. Burnet Sch., Dallas, 1983—, demonstration tchr. dist., 1978-79. Vice-pres. LWV, Garland, 1972; bd. dirs. City of Garland Library, 1976, YMCA, YWCA. Recipient award for teaching excellence Dallas schs., 1979. Mem. Delta Sigma Theta. Democrat. Methodist. Home: 4928 G Burnet Sch 3200 Kinkaid Dallas TX 75227 Office: David G Burnet Sch 3200 Kinkaid Dallas TX 75227

MAYSON, BETTY ANNE PEEPLES, medical consultant; b. Aiken, S.C., Dec. 23, 1943; d. Junius Black Peeples and Edna Earle (Sandifer) Peoples McKnight; m. Richard Grey Mayson, Sept. 23, 1959 (div. Sept. 1968); children—Richard Grey, Elizabeth Boatwright. Cert. operating room technician Adjust Edn., Augusta, Ga., 1973; A.S. in Nursing with high honors, U. S.C., 1975, B.S. in Nursing cum laude, 1978. R.N., Ga., S.C. Mgr. car rental co., Augusta, Ga., 1966-70; ward clk. Plantation Gen. Hosp., Fla., 1970-72; staff nurse St. Joseph Hosp., Augusta, Ga., 1975-76; teaching assoc. U. S.C., Columbia, 1978; cons. O.F. Furr, Esquire, Columbia, 1977-82; med. cons. Solomon, Kahn, Smith & Baumil, attys., Charleston, S.C., 1982—. Vol. Med. U. S.C., Charleston, 1985, Hospice, Charleston, 1986. Panhellenic scholar, 1975; Bus. and Profl. Women's Found. Lady Clairol scholar, 1976-78; Lettie Mae Whitehead Meml. scholar U. S.C., 1976-78. Mem. Sigma Theta Tau. Methodist. Home: 27 Lamboll St Charleston SC 29401 Office: Solomon Kahn Smith & Baumil 39 Broad St Charleston SC 29402

MAYSTEAD, SUZANNE RAE, optometrist; b. Hillsdale, Mich., Sept. 30, 1955; d. Marvin Charles and Helen Alberta (Glendenning) Patrick; m. Ivan Karl Maystead, III, June 4, 1977. O.D., Ferris State Coll. Optometry, 1979. Research asst. to optometrist, Big Rapids, Mich., 1979-80; clin. assoc. Ferris State Coll. Optometry, Big Rapids, 1979-84; pvt. practice optometry, Portland, Mich., 1980—. Recipient Contact Lens Achievement award Bauch & Lomb, 1979. Mem. Mich. Optometric Assn., Portland C. of C. Avocations: indoor gardening, interior decorating. Club: Am. Chesapeake. Home: 7667 Peckins Rd Lyons MI 48851 Office: 1311 E Bridge St Portland MI 48875

MAY-WHALEY, JAYRE DIANNE, advertising agency executive, accessory designer and executive; b. San Berito, Tex., Jan. 3, 1953; d. William Edward and Ella Katheryn (Sparks) May; m. David Landus Whaley, Aug. 29, 1984. Student San Miguel de Allende Inst., Mex., 1970-71, Sam Houston State U., 1971-73. Real estate agt. David Gayne & Assoc., Houston, 1973-74; salesperson East Asiatic Corp., Houston, 1974-80, Lone Star Wholesale Co., Houston, 1980-81; pres. Henson-May & Assocs., Houston, 1981—, Jayre/Tex., Inc., 1985—; mem. indsl. bd. Allied Fairbanks Bank, Houston. Mem. Splty. Advt. Assn., Advt. Splty. Inst., Houston C. of C., Better Bus. Bur. Republican. Avocations: hunting; fishing; horses; skiing. Home: 701 Bering Dr #1705 Houston TX 77057

MAZER, GWEN VERNEA, image consultant; b. N.Y.C., May 23, 1937; d. Theodore Roosevelt and Edythe Belle (Winfrey) Goodman; student Hunter Coll., 1952-54, N.Y. U., 1954-57. Fashion dir. Advt. Images, N.Y.C., 1961-68; fashion editor Harper's Bazaar, N.Y.C., 1968-73; founder Narcissa, boutique, N.Y.C., 1970-75; mktg. dir. Nazareno Gabrielli, fashion co., N.Y.C., 1976-78; creative dir. Espirt de Corp, San Francisco, 1978-80; prin. Gwen Mazer and Assocs., San Francisco, 1980—; lectr. U. Calif., Berkeley, 1980-81; instr. Skyline Coll., 1981-82. Trustee Magic Theatre, Ft. Mason, San Francisco. Recipient Excellence award Communication Arts mag., 1979, Excellence cert. Am. Inst. Graphic Arts, 1979. Mem. Women's Roundtable-San Francisco, Profl. Women's Network, WAIF, The Fashion Group, Assn. Image Cons. Address: 2210 Jones St San Francisco CA 94133

MAZER, NORMA FOX, writer; b. N.Y.C., May 15, 1931; d. Michael and Jean (Garlen) F.; m. Harry Mazer, Feb. 12, 1950; children—Anne E., Joseph D., Susan R., Gina B. Author: I, Trissy, 1971, A Figure of Speech, 1973 (Nat. Book award nominee 1974); Saturday, the Twelfth of October, 1975 (Lewis Carroll Shelf award 1976); Dear Bill, Remember Me? and Other Stories, 1976 (N.Y. Times Notable Book 1976, Am. Library Assn. Notable Book 1976, Sch. Library Jour. Best Books of Yr. 1976, Christopher award 1976, Lewis Carroll Shelf award 1977); (with Harry Mazer) The Solid Gold Kid, 1978 (Am. Library Assn. Best Books for Young Adults 1978); Up in Seth's Room, 1979 (Am. Library Assn. Best Books for Young Adults 1979); Mrs. Fish, Ape and Me, The Dump Queen, 1980 (German Children's Literature prize 1982); Taking Terri Mueller, 1981 (Edgar award 1982, Calif. Young Readers' award 1985), Summer Girls, Love Boys and Other Short Stories, 1982, When We First Met, 1982; Someone to Love, 1983 (Am. Library Assn. Best Books for Young Adults 1983), Downtown, 1984 (Am. Library Assn. Best Books for Young Adults 1984, N.Y. Times Notable Book 1984), Supergirl, 1984, Three Sisters, 1986, A, My Name Is Ami, 1986. Home: Brown Gulf Rd Jamesville NY 13078

MAZERO, JOYCE GREENBURG, lawyer; b. Tulsa, Sept. 28, 1955; d. Sidney Thomas and Susan Marie (Bernstein) Greenburg; m. John R. Mazero, Jr., July 20, 1980. B.A., S.W. Tex. State U., 1976; J.D., St. Mary's U., 1979. Bar: Pa. 1979, U.S. Dist. Ct. (we. dist.) Pa. 1979, Tex. 1983. Assoc. Swensen & Perer, Pitts., 1979-83; counsel Pitts. Hearing Speech and Deaf Services, Inc., Westmoreland County Deaf Services, Beaver County Deaf Services, Pitts., 1981-83; gen. counsel, corp. sec. Curtis Mathes Corp., Dallas, 1983—; dir. Curtis Mathes Found., Dallas, 1983—; cons., Dallas, 1983—. Mem. ABA (antitrust, litigation, forum on franchising sect. 1982—), Internat. Franchise Assn. (co. rep.), Tex. Bar Assn. (Young Lawyers Assn. antitrust, litigation, corp. banking and bus. sect. 1983—), Dallas Bar Assn. (antitrust sect. 1983—), Pa. Bar Assn., Am. Corp. Counsel Assn., Am. Trial Lawyers Assn. Republican. Roman Catholic.

MAZUR, GAIL BECKWITH, poet, educator, journalist; b. Cambridge, Mass., Nov. 11, 1937; d. Manuel and Sylvia Mildred (Rosenberg) Beckwith; m. Michael Burton Mazur, Dec. 28, 1958; children—Daniel Isaac, Kathe Elizabeth. B.A., Smith Coll., 1959; M.A., Lesley Coll., 1983. Poet-in-residence Emerson Coll., Boston, 1979-80; mentor Lesley Coll., Cambridge, Mass., 1983-84; mem. faculty U. Mass., Boston, 1985; dir. Blacksmith Poetry Program, Cambridge, 1973—. Author: Nightfire, 1978, The Pose of Happiness, 1986. Contbr. articles to profl. jours. Editor Ploughshares, 1980, 83. Recipient award Nat. Endowment for Arts, 1978. Mem. Poetry Soc. Am. (Celia Wagner prize 1981), PEN New Eng. (mem. steering com. 1983—), New Eng. Writers (mem. steering com.); New Eng. Writers for Survival. Home: 5 Walnut Ave Cambridge MA 02140

MAZUR, MEREDITH (MARGIE ELLA) HANDLEY, reading educator; b. Tulsa, Mar. 27, 1941; d. Joyce Samuel and MaryPaul (Ellsworth) Handley; m. Don Leroy Mazur, Aug. 31, 1962 (div. Nov. 1974); children—Susan Diane, Michael. B.A. in Art, U. Tulsa, 1962, M.Teaching Arts in Spl. Edn., 1967; postgrad. Calif. State U.-Los Angeles, UCLA, Purdue U.-Calumet, Ind., San Jose State U. Accredited tchr., reading specialist, adminstr., Calif. Classroom tchr. Tulsa Pub. Schs., 1963-65; fellow, clinician, diagnostician, instr. Mabee Reading Clinic, U. Tulsa, 1965-67; instr. So. Meth. U. Reading Clinic, Dallas, fall 1969; classroom tchr. Los Angeles Unified Sch. Dist., 1975-76; reading specialist Sierramont Middle Sch., Berryessa Union Sch. Dist., San Jose, Calif., 1976—; pvt. tutor, San Jose, 1976—; owner, operator Eastside Learning Ctr. and Reading Clinic, San Jose, 1978-82. Cons., activist in women's and children's rights in child-support enforcement; chmn. child-support enforcement task force San Jose-South Bay chpt. NOW, 1984-85. Entrance Exam. scholar U. Tulsa, 1959, John Mabee grad. fellow, 1966. Mem. Santa Clara County Reading Council, Calif. Reading Assn., Internat. Reading Assn., Women Leaders in Edn., Lantern Hon. Soc., Scroll Hon. Soc., Mortar Bd., Alpha Delta Kappa, Kappa Alpha Theta (chpt. pres. 1961-62). Mem. Bahái Faith, San Jose Community. Avocations: ballroom dancing; skiing; sailing; reading; sewing. Home: PO Box 32744 San Jose CA 95152 Office: Sierramont Middle Sch 3155 Kimlee Dr San Jose CA 95132

MAZUR, STELLA MARY, former organization administrator; b. Lowell, Mass.; d. Stanley and Katherine (Cichowicz) M.; B.S. in Edn., U. Lowell; student ARC Mgmt. Tng. Sch., 1962, Nat. Tng. Lab. for Applied Behavioral Sci., 1963. USO club dir., Windsor Locks, Conn., 1942; gen. field rep. ARC, 1944, exec. dir., Waltham, Mass., 1944-79. Spl. assignment State Dept. USIA Graphic Arts Cultural Exchange Program, Eastern Europe, Poland, 1965. Mem. Pres.' Circle, Lowell U. Recipient Waltham Rotary Club spl. citation, 1952; Waltham Community 25 Year Service award, 1969; Recognition award Waltham chpt. ARC, 1971; Outstanding Woman, Waltham News Tribune, 1974; Woman of Today, Waltham Bus. and Profl. Women's Club, 1976; Outstanding Service award ARC New Eng., 1979; Disting. Alumni award U. Lowell, 1979. Mem. Internat. Platform Assn., ARC Retiree Assn., Am. Assn. Ret. Persons, Smithsonian Assos., Lowell U. Alumni Assn. (hon. life). Seton Guild Lowell, Lowell Hist. Soc., Lowell Mus. Corp. Clubs: Vesper Country (Tyngsboro, Mass.); Longmeadow Golf, Country, Lowell U. Pres.' Univ. Circle (Lowell). Author, pub.: Roots and Heritage of Polish People in Lowell, 1976. Home: 170 Andover St Lowell MA 01852

MAZUY, CAROL A., software company executive; b. Boston, Aug. 19, 1942; d. William Joseph and Beatrice L. (Rodde) Cox; B.S., Boston Coll., 1964; M.Ed., Fitchburg State Coll., 1972; Ed.D., Nova U., 1980; m. Jon Claude Mazuy, May 14, 1979; children—Kelly Marie Dolan, Sean William B. Dolan Tchr., Littleton (Mass.) public schs., 1964-73; dir., grad. advisor Elem. Master Program, Fitchburg State Coll., 1977-80, adj. faculty, 1975—; dir. Title III Tchr. Tng. and dir. Mentorship Gifted Title IVC Program, Lexington, Mass., 1979-80; dir. staff devel. Merrimack (Mass.) Edn. Center, 1977-80; cons., mgr. Honeywell Info. Systems, Waltham, Mass., 1980-83; dir. corporate communications and mktg. services Software Research Corp., Natick, Mass., 1983—. adj. faculty mem. U. Laverne (Calif.), 1976—. Bd. dirs. Walker Sch. Named Woman Achiever in Bus. and Industry, 1982. Mem. NEA, Am. Mgmt. Assn., Nat. Assn. Female Execs. Contbr. articles to profl. jours. Home: 77 Strawberry Hill Rd Acton MA 01720 Office: One Natick Exec Park Natick MA 01760

MAZZAFERRO, JOAN, telephone company executive; b. Greenport, N.Y., Jan. 1, 1956; d. Joseph Anthony and Sophia (Kroleski) M. B.S., SUNY-Brockport, 1978; M.S., Purdue U., 1980. Sr. tech. assoc. Bell. Tel. Labs., Whippany, N.J., 1978-79, mem. tech. staff, 1979-83; staff analyst Pacific Bell Co., San Francisco, 1983-84, staff mgr., 1984-85, dist. staff mgr., San Ramon, Calif., 1985—. Kodak scholar, 1978. Mem. Nat. Assn. Female Execs., Summit Orgn. Roman Catholic. Club: Young Adults (San Ramon). Avocations: Skiing; sailing; aerobics; theatre; dance. Office: Pacific Bell 2600 Camino Ramon 4E503 San Ramon CA 94583

MAZZANTI, MAXINE ELLEN, educator; b. Bklyn., May 14, 1947; d. Louis Hendelman and Lillian (Kaplan) Hendelman Sherry; m. Albert Dino Mazzanti, Aug. 11, 1973 (div. Feb. 1982); 1 child, Jamie Benjamin; m. John George Homentosky, Sept. 10, 1983. B.A., Queens Coll., 1971; M.S. in Edn., Hofstra U., 1974; learning disabilities tchr. cons. cert. Montclair State Coll., 1986. Various ednl. certs., N.Y., N.J. Driver Main Cab Co., L.I. City, N.Y., 1968-72; spl. edn. tchr. Pub. Sch. 206, N.Y.C., 1978-81, Lincoln Sch., Lake Hiawatha, N.J., 1981-83, Jr. High Sch. 45, N.Y.C., 1983—; actress regional theater, 1978-85; appearances include World According to Garp, 1980, Falling in Love, 1984, Guiding Light, 1984. Coordinator Taxi Drivers for McGovern/Shriver, N.Y., 1972. Mem. United Fedn. Tchrs., AFTRA. Democrat. Jewish. Avocations: whitewater rafting; camping. Home: 80 Wall St Rockaway NJ 07866 Office: Jr High Sch 45 2351 First Ave New York NY 10035

MCADAM MCPHERSON, LORETTA MORRIS, business systems specialist, business educator; b. Roanoke, Va., Dec. 14, 1941; d. James Thurman and Ruby (Anderson) Morris; m. Lawrence A. McAdam, Dec. 15, 1984; Bernard A., david. Jr. B.A. cum laude, U. Central Fla., 1971, M.Ed. cum laude, 1976. Chmn. bus. div. Lake Sumter C. of C., Leesburg, Fla., 1971-76; office mgr. May Zima & Co. C.P.A.s, Daytona Beach, Fla., 1977-78; bus. instr. Seminole/Valencia Colls. 1978-82; adminstr. C.H. Hamilton & Co. C.P.A.s, Houston, 1982-84; adminstr. Ballas, Bersch & Co., P.A., C.P.A.s, Orlando, Fla., 1984—; bus. instr. Nat. Edn. Ctr., Houston, 1983-84, Valencia Community Coll., 1979-84, Seminole Community Coll., Daytona Beach Community Coll.; pvt. practice cons. in office orgn., personnel, 1971-83; presenter workshops; mem. Fla. Edn. Com., 1971-82. Mem. Fla. Inst. C.P.A.s, Fla. Vocat. Assn., Fla. Assn. Community Colls., Legal Adminstrs., Nat. Assn. Female Execs., Jayceettes. Democrat. Methodist. Club: Woman's (Fla.). Home: 104 Winding Ridge Dr Sanford FL 32771

MCADAMS, SHEILAH HELEN, lawyer; b. Lima, Ohio, Aug. 27, 1951; d. Richard Albert and Mary Patricia (Burke) McAdams; m. Michael W. Pettit, Sept. 24, 1976 (div. 1981). Student Ohio Wesleyan U., 1969-70; B.A., Ohio U., 1973; postgrad. Emory U., 1973; J.D., U. Toledo, 1978. Bar: Ohio 1978. Assoc. Ritter, Boesel, Robinson & Marsh, Toledo, Ohio, 1979—; pros. atty. City of Maumee (Ohio), 1979—, Village of Whitehouse (Ohio), 1981—; lectr. in law U. Toledo, 1985—. Mem. Lucas County Dem. Party, Toledo. Emory U. fellow, 1973; U. Toledo acad. scholar, 1976-77. Mem. ABA, Ohio State Bar Assn., Toledo Bar Assn. (jr. bar exec. com. 1983—), Toledo Women's Bar Assn. (co-chmn. publs. com. 1985—), Ohio Mcpl. Attys. Assn., Northwest Ohio Suburban Mcpl. Prosecutors Assn. (pres. 1981—). Democrat. Editorial bd. U. Toledo Law Rev., 1977-78. Office: Ritter Boesel Robinson & Marsh 610 United Savs Bldg Toledo OH 43604

MCADEN, MARY CATHERINE OVERFELT, educator; b. Franklin County, Va., Oct. 22, 1931; d. Walter Madison and Lizzie Oberson (Angel) Overfelt; A.A., Ferrum Coll., 1951; B.A., High Point Coll., 1953; postgrad. Scarritt Coll., 1956; M.A. (Phi Epsilon Omega grantee), U. Va., 1977; m. Robinson H. McAden, Aug. 21, 1954; children—Marcella, James, Ellen, John, Robert. Dir. Christian edn. Mt. Vernon Meth. Ch., Danville, Va., 1953-54, First Meth. Ch., Gainsville, Ga., 1955-56; ednl. missionary Meth. Ch., Bolivia, 1957-67; reading tchr. Callaway (Va.) Elem. Sch., 1974-76, Sandhills Youth Center, McCain, N.C., 1976-79; resource tchr. Samarkand Manor, Eagle Springs, N.C., 1979-81; learning disabilities resource tchr. Western Albemarle High Sch., Crozet, Va., 1981-86; resource tchr. Candor Elem. Sch., N.C., 1986—. Trustee, Ferrum Coll., 1974-75. Named Outstanding Leader in Elem.-Secondary Edn., Callaway Elem. Sch., 1976. Mem. NEA, Va. Edn. Assn. Methodist. Contbr. religious writings to mags., youth publs. Home: 140 Williams Rd Southern Pines NC 28387 Office: Candor Elem Sch Candor NC 27229

MCAFEE, FLORA ELAINE, educational administrator; b. Danville, Va., Aug. 30, 1939; d. David Lee and Lillie Mae (Coates) Cantrell; m. A. C. McAfee, Dec. 25, 1959; children—Ashley Craig, Katherine, Christie, Kimberly. Student Eastfield Jr. Coll., Mesquite, Tex., 1985—. Tchr. A-1 Towneast Daycare, Mesquite, 1969-75; owner, dir. Northwest Day Care, Dallas, 1975—. Bd. dirs. Child Care Protective Action Dallas, 1983—; chairperson adv. com. Mesquite Ind. Sch. Dist., 1985-86. Mem. Tex. Lic. Child Care Assn. (rec.-sec. 1978-79), Dallas Assn. Edn. Young Children, Dallas C. of C., Better Bus. Bur. Clubs: Women's Missionary Aux. (pres. 1973-75), Order Eastern Star. Democrat. Baptist. Avocations: volleyball, horseback riding, bicycling. Home: 2902 Potomac Mesquite TX 75149 Office: Northwest Day Care 8620 McKavett Dallas TX 75238

MCALEER, MARY JEAN, cardiac transplant coordinator, nurse; b. Bangor, Maine, Nov. 29, 1955; d. Curtis and Mary Rita (Smith) Tackett; m. Owen Kevin McAleer, June 18, 1977 (div. Aug. 1983); children—Michael Kevin, Leah Marie. B.S.N., U. Ariz., 1977. Asst. head nurse U. Med. Ctr., Tucson, 1977-79, ICU nurse, 1980-82, cardiac transplant coordinator, 1982—. Mem. planning com., nurses symposium Internat. Soc. Heart Transplantation, Cambridge, Eng., 1984—; lectr. U. Med. Ctr., Stockholm and Göteborg, Sweden, 1984. Mem. editorial bd. Am Jour. Cardiovascular Nursing. Contbr. articles to profl. jours. Mem. Internat. Soc. Heart Transplantation, N. Am. Transplant Coordinators Orgn., European Transplant Coordinators Orgn., So. Calif. Transplant Soc. Democrat. Roman Catholic. Home: 4273 N River Grove #233 Tucson AZ 85719 Office: Dept Surgery 1501 N Campbell Ave Tucson AZ 85724

MCALESTER, VIRGINIA SAVAGE, historic preservationist; b. Dallas, May 13, 1943; d. Wallace Hamilton and Dorothy (Harris) Savage; m. Clement McCarty Talkington, Nov. 25, 1965 (div. 1976); children—Clement McCarty, Jr., Amy Virginia; m. 2d, Arcie Lee McAlester, July 11, 1977. B.A., Harvard U., 1965. First v.p. Historic Preservation League, Inc., Dallas, 1972-75, pres., 1975-76, bd. dirs., 1978—; chmn. Historic Dallas Fund, 1976-80; ptnr. McAlester and Assocs., Dallas, 1981—; bd. advisors Nat. Trust for Historic Preservation, Washington, 1973-82; bd. dirs. Central Bus. Dist. Assn., Dallas, 1976-79; mem. Dallas Historic Landmark Preservation Com., 1973-76, Tex. Nat. Register Bd. Rev., Austin, 1979-82. Author: The Making of an Historic District: Swiss Avenue, 1975; A Field Guide to American Houses, 1984. Phys. devel. chmn. East Dallas Design Com., 1972-77. Recipient Honor citation AIA, Dallas, 1977; Community Service award Lakewood Bank & Trust Co., Dallas, 1977. Mem. Dallas County Heritage Soc., Soc. Archtl. Historians, Dallas Hist. Soc., Tex. Historic Found. Episcopalian. Clubs: Jr. League, Harvard (Dallas). Office: McAlester and Assocs 12700 Hillcrest Rd Suite 201 Dallas TX 75230

MC ALISTER, LINDA LOPEZ, university administrator, philosopher; b. Long Beach, Calif., Oct. 10, 1939; d. Manuel Lee and Elena Maria (Sherwood) McAlister; A.B., Barnard Coll., 1962; postgrad. Coll. City N.Y., 1963-64; Ph.D., Cornell U., 1969. Mem. faculty, adminstr. Bklyn. Coll., 1968-77, CUNY. Grad. Center, 1970-77; prof. humanities, dean campus Imperial Valley campus San Diego State U., 1977-82; prof. philosophy, campus dean U. South Fla., Ft. Myers, 1982-85; spl. asst. to vice chancellor for acad. programs State Univ. System Fla., 1985—; Fla. state coordinator Am. Council Edn. Nat. Identification Project, 1983—. Franz Brentano Found. grantee, 1968-72; Fulbright-Hays research grantee, 1973-74. Mem. Am. Philos. Assn., Soc. Women in Philosophy, Assn. von Philosophinen in Deutschland (founding) Author: The Development of Franz Brentano's Ethics, 1982. Contbr. articles to profl. jours. Editor and translator: Psychology From an Empirical Standpoint (Franz Brentano), 1973; Sensory and Noetic Consciousness (Franz Brentano), 1980; editor: The Philosophy of Brentano, 1976; translator: On Colour (Ludwig Wittgenstein), 1977. Office: 107 W Gaines St Tallahassee FL 32301

MCALLISTER, JILL, real estate broker; b. Allentown, Pa., Sept. 2, 1938; d. John Raymond and Helen (Hartzell) Fuehrer; m. Willis Eugene McAllister, July 4, 1959; children—John Willis, David Ray, Stephen Charles. Student Cedar Crest Coll., 1956-58, Mt. San Antonio Coll., 1969-71; grad. Realtors Inst., 1973. Sec., Ivar Lovret, Pomona, Calif., 1962-64; salesperson LaVerne Realty (Calif.), 1965-69, Wheeler/Steffen Real Estate Claremont, Calif., 1969-72; pres. Jill McAllister, Realtor, Inc., Claremont, Calif., 1972—. Bd. dirs. Boy Scouts Am., 1978—, Foothill Philharmonic, 1977—, Pilgrim Place, 1979—, Curtain Raisers, 1975—, Scripps Fine Arts, 1980—. Mem. Pomona Valley Bd. Realtors (dir. 1981—, pres. 1986), Calif. Assn. Realtors (state dir. 1982—), Nat. Assn. Realtors (nat. dir. 1985—, edn. com.). Republican. Presbyterian. Home: 508 W 11th St Claremont CA 91711 Office: Jill McAllister Inc Realtor 508 W 11th St Claremont CA 91711

MCALLISTER, LINDA MCCALLA, dietitian; b. Kansas City, Mo., Mar. 18, 1944; d. Howard Lewis and Faye Louise (Teas) McCalla; divorced; 1 child, James Douglas. B.A., San Diego State U., 1967, M.S., 1976. Registered dietitian. Clin. dietitian VA Med. Ctr., La Jolla, Calif., 1972-73, chief nutritional dietetics, 1973-77; chief adminstrv. dietetics VA Med. Ctr., Loma Linda, Calif., 1977-79; chief dietetic service VA Med. Ctr., Phoenix, 1979-81, VA Med. Ctr., Albany, N.Y., 1981-84, VA Med. Ctr., Palo Alto, Calif., 1984—. Author: (with others) Patient Care Audit: A Quality Assurance Procedure Manual for Dietitians, 1979. Loaned exec. United Fund, Phoenix, 1980. Served to capt. Med. Specialists Corps, U.S. Army, 1967-69. Recipient Dir.'s commendation VA Med. Ctr., Phoenix, 1981; Dir.'s commendation VA Med. Ctr., Albany, 1984, Achievement award, 1982. Mem. Am. Dietetic Assn., Calif. Dietetic Assn., Dietitians With Mgmt. Responsibilities, Dietitians in Bus. and Industry, Internat. Assn. of Quality Circles (chpt. organizer and treas. North Eastern chpt. Albany 1983-84), Nat. Assn. Miniature Enthusiasts, Women's Army Overseas Service League, Am. Legion. Lodge: Zonta. Avocations: miniatures; piano; gardening; arts; crafts. Home: 921 Willow Rd Menlo Park CA 94025 Office: VA Medical Center 3801 Miranda Ave Palo Alto CA 94304

MCALLISTER, MARY JEAN LEONE, lawyer; b. N.Y.C., Sept. 21, 1942; d. Joseph J. and Helen (Midolla) Leone; m. Edward John McAllister, July 7, 1962 (div. 1980); children—Janine Patrice, Celeste Helene. B.S. summa cum laude in Health Edn., SUNY-Stony Brook, 1974, M.A. in Sociology, 1975; J.D. (Moot Ct.; honor roll), Stetson U., 1981. Bar: Fla. 1982. Devel. officer Am. Cancer Soc., Melville, N.Y., 1974-76; adj. prof. sociology Suffolk Community Coll., Selden, N.Y., 1975; dir. community devel. S. Central Fla. Health Systems Agy., Sarasota, 1976-77; asst. state project dir. Fla. Mental Health Systems Tng. Program, St. Petersburg, Fla., 1977; sole practice, St. Petersburg, 1982—; adj. prof. bus. adminstrn. Tampa Coll., Clearwater, Fla.; mem. bd. arbitrators Nat. Assn. Securities Dealers, Inc., 1986—. Mem. Carriage House Players Community Theatre Assn., Stony Brook, 1972-75; bd. dirs. Pinellas County unit Am. Cancer Soc., 1984-85. Mem. Fla. Bar Assn., ABA, St. Petersburg Bar Assn., Stony Brook Alumni Assn., Phi Delta Phi.

MCALPINE, LINDA ANN, nurse; b. Buffalo, Feb. 22, 1958; d. Ralph and Margaretta (Matecko) McA. B.S. in Nursing summa cum laude, SUNY-Buffalo, 1980. Registered nurse, N.Y.; cert. basic cardiac life support and advanced cardiac life support Am. Heart Assn. Nurses aide Manor Oak Skilled Nursing Facility, Cheektowaga, N.Y., 1979; staff nurse med-surg. unit specializing in renal transplants, Buffalo Gen. Hosp., 1980-84, staff nurse med.-surg. ICU, 1984—; chief steward Nurses United-Communication Workers Am. Local 1168, Buffalo, 1983—. Mem. Am. Assn. Critical-Care Nurses. Democrat. Roman Catholic. Avocations: dancing; racquet sports.

MCANALLY, MARY ELLEN, poet; b. Vandalia, Ill., Jan. 21, 1939; d. Virgil Pafford McAnally and Mary Frances (Handy) Ruble; m. Etheridge Knight, June 11, 1973; children—Mary Tandiwe, Etheridge Bambata. B.A., U. Tulsa, 1962; B.D., Princeton Theol. Sem., 1965; M.A., Columbia U., 1968, postgrad., 1965-68; postgrad. in journalism and creative writing New Sch. for Social Research, 1969-70. Asst. to chaplain Rutgers U., New Brunswick, N.J., 1963; dir. Christian edn. 1st Presbyn. Ch., Bartlesville, Okla., summer 1963; adminstrv. asst. Office Student World Relations, United Presbyn. Ch. in U.S.A., N.Y.C., 1965-69; instr. African religions Spelman Coll., Atlanta, summer 1967; counselor for Vietnam vets. S.I. Community Coll., 1969-70; assoc. editor Am. Report, N.Y.C., 1970-72, instr. black studies Upward Bound Program, Lincoln U., Jefferson City, Mo., summer 1972; VISTA supr. Legal Services Orgn., Indpls., 1972-73; sr. citizens supr. Indpls. Settlements, Inc., 1973-74; state edn. supr. Assoc. Migrant Opportunity Services, Inc., Indpls., 1974-75; dir. Suburban South YWCA, Bloomington, Minn., 1975-77; dir. Women's Ctr., Tulsa Met. Ministry, 1977-78; poet-in-prisons for Okla. Arts and Humanities Council and instn. programs, 1978-84; research assoc. asst. dir. Nat. Indian Child Abuse and Neglect Research/Resource Ctr., Tulsa, 1979-80; state coordinator Head Start, Claremore, Okla., instr. prisons, 1980-81; state coordinator Okla. Religious Coalition for Abortion Rights, 1982—; dean of students Okla. Jr. Coll., 1986—. Author books of poetry including: We Will Make a River, 1979; Poems From the Animal Heart, 1981; The Absence of the Father and the Dance of the Zygotes, 1982; editor anthologies: New Black Writing, 1978; Warning: Hitchhikers May Be Escaping Convicts, 1980; Family Violence: Poems on the Pathology, 1982; We Sing Our Struggle, 1982; assoc. editor Am. Report; poetry editor: Sister Advocate and Nimrod; contbg. editor: Sez, South & West, Okla. Free Press, others; contbr. essays, articles, revs., research to publs. including Jour. Internat. Studies, Africa Today, Am. Report, Christian Sci. Monitor, Internat. Library Jour., over 50 lit. jours. Vol. counselor, organizer, tchr. orgns. N.Y.C., Indpls., Mpls., Tulsa including: counselor, bd. mem. Harriet Tubman Shelter, Mpls., Domestic Violence Intervention Services, Tulsa; organizer, bd. mem. Open Door Arts Coop., Tulsa; bd. mem. Individual Artists Okla., Oklahoma City, 1982-84, Women's Ctr., Tulsa, 1983-84; mem. Poets for Peace, Artists Call, Tulsa Poetry Alliance. Recipient Beuadoin prize for Poetry, 1978, Carl Sandburg poetry prize, 1979, Nat. Endowment for Arts creative writing fellow, 1981-82. Mem. Nat. Writers Union (nat. exec. bd. 1983-85, state organizer Okla. 1982-84). Democrat. Presbyterian. Home: 76 N Yorktown Tulsa OK 74110

MC ANULTY, MARY CATHERINE CRAMER (MRS. CHARLES GILBERT MCANULTY), retired educator; b. Braddock, Pa., June 26, 1909; d. Albert R. and Sara (Kelly) Cramer; A.B., Fla. So. Coll., 1929; M.A., Tchrs. Coll. Columbia, 1937; postgrad. Fla. State U., 1946-50; m. Charles Gilbert McAnulty, Dec. 25, 1937. Elem. tchr. Lake Ann Sch., Lake Garfield, Fla., 1930-31, elem. prin., 1932-34; prin. South Winter Haven Elem. Sch., Winter Haven, Fla., 1935-55; adminstrv. asst. to supervising prin. Winter Haven Area Schs., 1956-60; prin. Fred Garner Elem. Sch., Winter Haven, 1961-68, Lake Alfred Elem. Sch., 1969-70. Asst. chmn. vols., asst. tng. chmn., local chpt. ARC, 1967-68, 2d v.p., also chmn. vols., 1969-70, bd. mem., chmn. service to mil. families, 1970-71, chmn. coll. youth, 1971-72; treas. Imperial Harbours Condominium, 1980-82, pres., 1984; v.p. Beymer United Methodist Women, 1973, 74, 75, pres., 1976, 77; lay del. ann. conf. Meth. Ch., 1978, 79; pres. Lake Region Extension Homemaker's Club, 1974, 75; trustee Winter Haven Hosp. Aux., rec. sec., 1985-86, corr. sec., 1986-87. Mem. Am. Assn. Supervision and Curriculum Devel., Internat. Reading Assn. (Polk County chmn.), NEA, Fla. Edn. Assn. (dir. dept. elem. sch. prins. 1965-67), Polk County Elem. Prins. Assn. (sec.), LWV (local dir. 1962), AAUW (local br. chmn. status women com. 1963), DAR (chpt. treas. 1967-68, historian 1969-70, regent 1970-72, state chmn. jr. Am. citizens 1972—, dir. dist. VI 1973-74), Fla. So. Coll. Alumni Assn. (sec.), Internat. Platform Assn., P.E.O. (chpt. treas. 1970-74, 80—, chaplain 1976, 77, chpt. pres. 1978-79), Ch. Women United (v.p. 1977—, chmn. adv. bd. 1980-81), Pi Gamma Mu, Delta Kappa Gamma (State Achievement award 1964, Fla. pres. 1962-63, chpt. parliamentarian 1968-73, pres., v.p., treas.). Methodist (choir mem., chmn. commn. edn. 1959-60, supt. study program 1969-70, organist 1970-77, pres. Wesley fellowship class 1972-73, chmn. adminstrv. bd. 1980, 81, 83-85 trustee 1983-88), lay leader 1985, 86, fin. com., workshop com. Clubs: Pilot (charter, pres. 1954-55, 61-62), Poinsettia Garden (pres. 1984-85). Lodge: Order Eastern Star. Winter Haven Woman's (edn. chmn. 1967-68, v.p. 1983-84, pres. 1984-85). Home: 333 W Lake Howard Dr Apt 104D Winter Haven FL 33880

MCARTHUR, VICKI HOLLOWAY, music educator, school administrator; b. Richmond, Calif., Jan. 20, 1949; d. Winford Byron and Helen Irene (Smith) Holloway; m. Charles Clayton McArthur, III, Mar. 1, 1969. B.A., Fla. State U., 1971, M.Ed., 1972, Ph.D. candidate. Cert. in piano and theory. Class piano instr. Fla. State U., Tallahassee, 1971-72; pvt. piano instr., Tallahassee, 1970—; dir. owner McArthur and Musical Assocs., Tallahassee, 1980—; dir. Urban Waste, Inc., Birmingham, Ala. Top 10 Finalist Miss Ala. Pagent, 1969; fellow Fla. State U., 1971. Mem. Fla. State Music Tchrs. Assn., Music Tchrs. Nat. Assn., Tallahassee Music Tchrs. Assn. (v.p. 1971-73, 83-85), Phi Kappa Lambda, Phi Kappa Phi. Republican. Club: Capital City Music. Avocations: foreign travel, gourmet food. Home: 1104 Terrace St Tallahassee FL 32303

MCATEE, MARY LEE, utility company executive; b. Detroit, Nov. 22, 1930; d. Homer Leroy and Lenore (Denson) Fowler; m. Jack Damon Prutsman, June 19, 1951 (div. Sept. 1969); children—Jeffrey D., John D.; m. Charles Oliver McAtee, Dec. 26, 1969. B.S., Barry U., 1985. Dir., Acad. Las Delicias, Maracay, Venezuela, 1962-65; asst. to pres. GAC Utilities, Inc., Miami, 1969-74; pres. Fla. Water & Utilities, Miami, 1975-77; grants coordinator Miami Dade Water & Sewer Authority, Miami, 1977—. Grey lady ARC, Homested, Fla., 1959. Republican. Methodist. Office: Miami Dade Water & Sewer 3575 S LeJeune Rd Miami FL 33133

MC ATHIE, MARYLOU, nursing consultant, educator; b. Huron, S.D., July 9, 1927; d. John and Agnes Virginia (Mangan) McA.; diploma Oak Park Hosp. unit Loyola U., Chgo., 1948; B.S. in Nursing, DePaul U., 1954, M.S. in Nursing, 1956; Ed.D., U. San Francisco, 1980. Cons. Calif. State Dept. Health, 1961-68; dir. nursing San Joaquin Gen. Hosp., Stockton, Calif., 1960-68; regional nursing cons., spl. asst. Pacific Basin affairs USPHS, HEW, San Francisco, 1968—; prof. Sonoma State U.; ex officio mem. exec. com. Western Council on Higher Edn. for Nursing. Mem. scholarship com. San Joaquin March of Dimes, 1964-68. Recipient award HEW Region IX, 1974, commendation March of Dimes, 1968, citizen's commendation San Joaquin County, 1967, cert. of merit UCLA, 1972, cert. in leadership tng. Western Council on Higher Edn. in Nursing, U. Calif., San Francisco, 1962, cert. in pub. health nursing Calif. Dept. Pub. Health, U. San Francisco, 1964, spl. recognition award USPHS, 1984. Mem. Am., Calif. (conv. del. 1972, 85) nurses assns., Nat., Western (chmn. com. nursing service adminstrs.) leagues for nursing, AAUW, Am. Pub. Health Assn., Western Soc. Research in Nursing, Sigma Thetas Tau. Speaker, convs., confs.; contbr. to audio and TV tapes, articles to profl. publs. Home: 8109 Arroyo Way Stockton CA 95209 Office: Sonoma State U Rohnert Park CA 94928

MCBATH, AUDREY MARTINA, civil engineer; b. Cleve., Aug. 4, 1954; d. Harry Martin and Lelia (Smith) McB.; B.S. in Engring. (Nat. Achievement scholar 1972), Duke U., 1976. Engrs. aid Woodruff, Inc., Beachwood, Ohio, 1975; cost engr. Arthur G. McKee & Co., Cleve., 1976; constrn. project engr. Gt. Lakes Constrn. Co., Cleve., 1976-77; environ. engr. EPA, Durham, N.C., 1977-79, Cin., 1979-83, program mgr. fed. women's program, Cin., 1981-83; cost engr. U.S. Army C.E., Los Angeles, 1983-85; Consortium for Grad. Study in Mgmt. fellow U. So. Calif., 1985—. Mem. Nat. Tech. Assn. (v.p. Cleve. chpt. 1977, Cin. chpt. 1981), Blacks in Govt. (del. 1982), Federally Employed Women, Soc. Women Engrs., Nat. Black M.B.A. Assn., Los Angeles Council Black Profl. Engrs. ASCE, MENSA. Mem. United Ch. Christ. Home: 3613 Kalsman Dr #4 Los Angeles CA 90016

MCBEE, SUSANNA BARNES, journalist; b. Santa Fe, Mar. 28, 1935; d. Jess Stephen and Sybil Elizabeth (Barnes) McBee; A.B., U. So. Calif., 1956; M.A., U. Chgo., 1962. Staff writer Washington Post, 1957-65, 73-74, 77-79, asst. nat. editor, 1974-77; asst. sec. for public affairs HEW, 1979; articles editor Washingtonian mag., 1980-81; assoc. editor U.S. News & World Report, 1981—; Washington corr. Life mag., 1965-69; Washington editor McCall's mag., 1970-72. Recipient Penney-Missouri mag. award, 1969; Sigma Delta Chi Public Service award, 1969. Club: Nat. Press. Home: 3834 T St NW Washington DC 20007 Office: 2400 N St NW Washington DC 20037

MCBIRNEY, JAMELYN BLAIR, retail executive; b. Lubbock, Tex., Aug. 11, 1957; d. James Early and Laura Jean (Fry) Blair; m. Edwin T. McBirney, Jan. 23, 1982. B.S., So. Meth. U., 1979. Sales clk. Down the Street, Victoria, Tex., 1974-76, buyer, 1976-79, pres., 1982—, cons., 1979—; sales rep. Twins Swimwear, Dallas, 1979-80; office mgr. Amstar Fin., Dallas, 1980-82; ptnr., dir. Heather Morgan Inc., Dallas, 1983—; v.p. Lease Plan, Dallas, 1980-84. Patron Jr. League, Victoria, 1982-84; patron St. Labre Indian Sch., Montana, 1983, 84. Mem. Tri-Delta.

MCBRIDE, BETTY JEAN, county government official; b. Pittsburg, Kans., Sept. 21, 1936; d. Santo and Filomena (Torchia) Sandella; m. Ray Earnest McBride, Apr. 24, 1954; children—Ruth Ann McBride Hall, Wesley Ray. Student pub. schs. Sec., Barker Ins. Co., Columbus, Kans., 1965-66; receptionist, bookkeeper to physician, Columbus, 1966-68; treas. Cherokee County, Columbus, 1968—. Precinct committeewoman Cherokee County Democratic party, 1966-71, 83—, sec. Cherokee County Dem. Central Com., 1968—. Mem. Kans. County Treas. Assn. (pres. 1984-85), S.E. Kans. County Ofcls. Assn. (pres. 1979, 83), S.E. Kans. County Treas. Assn. (pres. 1972, 76, 82), Am. Legion Aux. Roman Catholic. Home: 429 S Delaware Columbus KS 66725

MCBRIDE, DONNA JANNEAN, publisher; b. Kansas City, Kans., July 3, 1940; d. Donald Merle and Hazel Frances (Williams) McBride. A.B., Central Coll., 1962; M.L.S., U. Mo.-Columbia, 1969. Tchr., Pilot Grove High Sch. (Mo.), 1961-62; corr. Bus. Men's Assurance Co., Kansas City, Mo., 1962-66; acctg. clk. Prudential of Eng., Sydney, Australia, 1966-67; head tech. processes Kansas City Pub. Library (Mo.), 1967-77; customer rep. C.L. Systems, Inc., Newtonville, Mass., 1977-80; dir. support services Leon County Pub. Library, Tallahassee, 1980-82; dir. ops. The Naiad Press, Inc., Tallahassee, 1982—; dir. The Naiad Press, 1976—, Sappho's Library, 1983—. Mem. ALA, Nat. Gay Task Force, Am. Booksellers Assn., Nat. Women's Studies Assn. Home: Rt 1 PO Box 3319 Havana FL 32333 Office: The Naiad Press Inc PO Box 10543 Tallahassee FL 32302

MCBRIDE, EMMA PEARL, civic worker, educator; b. Abbyville, Kans., Feb. 23, 1927; d. Perry Claude and Eva Pearl (Benson) Bachus; m. Frank J. McBride, June 4, 1950; children—Steven F., Susan D., Scott M., Mark D. B.S., Kans. U., 1948, postgrad., 1949. Cert. tchr. Instr. Adela Hale Bus. Coll., Hutchinson, Kans., summers 1947-48, Clay Ctr. High Sch., Kans., 1948-50, Brown-Mackie Bus. Coll., Salina, Kans., 1950-52. Tchr., 1st Methodist Ch., Salina, 1955-70; bd. dirs. YWCA, Salina, 1973-79, fin. chmn., 1976; treas. Jr. High PTA, Salina, 1976; registrar United Methodist Women Kans. W. Conf. Sch. Missions, Salina, 1981; vol. Asbury Hosp., Salina, 1985—; docent Salina Art Gallery, 1985—. Mem. AAUW (corr. sec. 1971-72, exec. bd. 1983-84; named Outstanding Br. Mem. 1985). Republican. Club: Helianthus (pres. 1972-73). Avocations: foreign and domestic travel, arts, crafts, quilting, sewing.

MCBRIDE, JOYCE BROWNING, accountant; b. Ga., May 28, 1927; d. Eph and Zula (Harden) Browning; grad. So. Bus. U., 1947; children—Jan Burge, Gary McBride, Kandie Lysse. Asst. controller Hampton Court Knits, Los Angeles, 1967-78; owner, mgr. McBride & Assocs. Bookkeeping Service, 1978—. Address: 1766 Sinaloa Rd #180 Simi Valley CA 93065

MCBRIDE, VIRGINIA BASILEA, accountant; b. Staten Island, N.Y., Oct. 11, 1941; d. Mario and Elizabeth Stevenson (Reid) Basilea; m. Robert William McBride, June 9, 1962; children—Kathleen, Amy. A.A. in Med. Sci., Potomac State Coll., 1961; B.S. in Bus. Adminstrn., Roger Williams Coll., 1982. Med. sec. Continental Ins. Co., Newark, 1961-62; sec. to prin. Harwich Pub. Schs., Mass., 1973-84; tax preparer McBrides Acctg. Service, Balt., 1972-73, acct., Harwich, Mass., 1973—. Speaker Nat. Assn. Future Women, Hyannis, Mass., 1984-85, Shaklee, Hyannis, 1985; cons. James Trainor & Assocs., Orlean, Mass., 1984-85. Author: Accounts Payable 2000 System, 1983; How to Save Money on Your Taxes - Legally, 1985. Treas. Sandy Shore Assn., Harwich, 1983-85; teller Town of Harwich, 1980-85; mem. Town Computer Study Com., Harwich, 1984-85. Mem. Nat. Assn. Future Women. Democrat. Methodist. Clubs: Harwich Junior Women (chmn. fgn. affairs 1976-77); Harwich Fire Aux. (treas. 1975-80). Avocations: reading; gardening; biking; canoeing. Home: 325 Oak St PO Box 986 Harwich MA 02645 Office: McBrides Accounting Service 325 Oak St Box 986 Harwich MA 02645

MCCABE, ANITA KYRIAKOS, health services executive; b. Clarksville, Tenn., Jan. 12, 1953; d. Peter Leon and Juanita (Dunn) Kyriakos; student Austin Peay State U., 1971-74; B.S. Bus. Adminstrn., U. Tenn., Knoxville, 1976; m. Thomas J. McCabe, Dec. 29, 1979. Sales staff IBM, Knoxville, 1976-78, Stimtech div. Johnson & Johnson Co., Houston, 1978-79; ter. mgr. Electro-Biology, Inc., Dallas, 1980-83, nat. sales trainer, 1981-83; pres. HiTech Med., Inc., Dallas, 1983—. Mem. Dallas Symphony Orch. League, Chi Omega. Republican. Baptist.

MCCABE, ANN ELIZABETH, psychologist, educator; b. Green Bay, Wis., Feb. 13, 1942; d. Paul Edward and Elizabeth Jane (Jacobs) Miskella; B.S., St. Norbert Coll., 1964; M.S., Iowa State U., 1966; Ph.D., U. Wis., Madison, 1973; m. Bernard Oliver McCabe, Nov. 26, 1966 (dec.); 1 son, Brian. Asst. prof. Trinity Coll., Dublin U., 1967-69; asst. prof. U. Windsor (Ont., Can.), 1973-77, assoc. prof. devel. psychology, 1977—; vis. asso. prof. U. Toronto, 1979-81. Bd. dirs. Childrens Achievement Centre, 1978-80. Recipient grant Royal Commn. Study Violence in Communications Industry, 1976, Gerontology Research Council of Ont., 1983. Mem. Am. Psychol. Assn., Soc. Research in Child Devel., Can. Psychol. Assn. Clubs: U. Windsor Faculty, U. Windsor Faculty Women's. Asso. editor Can. Jour. Early Childhood Edn., 1980-86; contbr. articles to profl. jours. Home: 7 Elderfield Crescent Etobicoke ON M9C 3K6 Canada Office: Dept Psychology Univ Windsor Windsor ON N9B 3P4 Canada

MC CABE, ELIZABETH GAILEY, bank ofcl.; b. Troy, N.Y., Nov. 5, 1928; d. William and Jean (McKay) Gailey; grad. Rochester (N.Y.) Inst. Tech., 1949; m. Raymond J. McCabe, Sept. 30, 1960. Club teller Troy Savs. Bank, 1951-53, paying and receiving teller, 1953-58, gen. ledger bookkeeper, 1958-62, acct., 1962-66, asst. auditor, 1966-67, auditor, 1967—, v.p., 1982—. Cert. internal auditor Inst. Internal Auditors. Mem. Savs. Bank Auditors and Controllers of N.Y. State, Eastern N.Y. chpt. Bank Adminstrs. Inst., Nat. Assn. Bank Women, Am. Inst. Banking (life), Nat. Assn. Mut. Savs. Banks. Office: 2d and State Sts Troy NY 12180

MCCABE, GAY LOYCE EVANS, securities company executive; b. Tuscaloosa, Ala., Feb. 27, 1943; d. Walter H. and Loyce Roena (Park) Evans; m. James W. McCabe, Jr., July 7, 1977. B.A., David Lipscomb Coll., 1965; postgrad. George Peabody Coll., Vanderbilt U., 1968. Tchr., Houston Ind. Sch.

Dist., 1970-71, Bolles Sch., Jacksonville, Fla., 1971-75; advt. account exec. William H. Coleman, Inc., Jacksonville, 1975-76, Bozell, Jacobs, Atlanta, 1976-77; test specialist Telemedia, Inc., Isfahan, Iran, 1977-79; with McCabe Petroleum Corp., San Antonio, 1979-81; advt. dir. San Anco Energy Corp., San Antonio, 1981-83; pres. McCabe Communications, San Antonio, 1981-83; pres. San Anco Securities Co., San Antonio, 1983—. Mem. Nashville Symphony Chorus, 1968, Jacksonville Symphony Chorus, 1972; vol. Texans War on Drugs, 1982-83; bd. dirs. Trinity U. Tennis Found., 1981-83. Mem. Am. Mktg. Assn., Am. Mgmt. Assn., S.W. Research Found. Forum, San Antonio C. of C. Republican. Mem. Ch. of Christ. Clubs: Retama Polo Ctr.; (San Antonio); Dominion Country; Sawgrass (Ponte Vedra, Fla.). Office: San Anco Securities Co 100 Sandau Ste 201 San Antonio TX 78216

MCCABE, LINDA I., insurance consultant; b. Phila., June 8, 1949; d. Leoanrd Edgar and Grace Alma (Strang) McDermott; m. Dennis James McCabe, Dec. 12, 1977 (div. July 1984); 1 child, Melissa; m. Gerald P. McMenamin, Apr. 18, 1970 (div.); 1 child, Patrick. Grad. Life Underwriters Tng. Council, Pa. Asst. mgr. Caplans Inc., Phila., 1977-78; mgr., instr. World Odyssey Co., Phila., 1978-81; sales rep. Met. life and Affiliated Companies, 1982—; gen. agt. Keystone Profl. Planning Co., Phila., 1985—. Mem. Nat. Assn. Underwriters Phila., Nat. Assn. Female Execs., Faternal Order Police Phila. (assoc.) Republican. Avocations: scene painting; violin and piano; writing; beach. Office: McCabe Ins Cons 6502 Rising Sun Ave and 12446 Wyndom Rd Philadelphia PA 19154

MCCABE-SCHMIDT, CARROLL LOUISE, lawyer; b. Washington, Oct. 27, 1953; d. Eugene Anthony and Louisa Carroll (Wright) McCabe; m. Bruce Edward Schmidt, Jan. 21, 1983; 1 son, Kyle Edward Schmidt. B.A. in Social Scis. and Edn., U. No. Colo., 1976; J.D., U. Balt., 1982. Bar: Md. Tchr. Lareine High Sch., Suitland, Md., 1977-78, St. Peter's Sch., Waldorf, Md., 1978-79; law clk. Robert Ades & Assocs., P.C., Landover, Md., 1980-82, assoc., 1982-85; sole practice, 1985—; guest lectr. U. Md., College Park, 1983—. Contbr. articles to newspapers. Mem. ABA, Md. Bar Assn., Prince George's County Bar Assn. Democrat. Roman Catholic. Office: PO Box 492 Seabrook MD 20706

MCCAFFERTY, BELINDA SUE, accountant; b. Columbia, S.C., Dec. 24, 1951; d. Edward Earle and Dorothy (Devaney) McCafferty. B.B.A., Delta State U., 1973. Auditor IRS, Jackson, Miss., 1973-77. 78-79, revenue agt., Clarksdale, Miss., 1977, tax auditor, group mgr., Lafayette, La., 1979-80, regional analyst, Dallas, 1980-83, revenue agt., Dallas, 1983-85, revenue agt. group mgr., 1985—, mem. EEO com., Dallas, 1981-82. Mem. Assn. Govt. Accts. (pres. 1975). Baptist. Home: 5930 Arapaho Dallas TX 75248

MCCAHAN, JOAN HELEN, business executive; b. Balt., June 12, 1951; d. Anthony Joseph and Frances Helen (Waclawski) Bartynski; A.A. in Mental Health Human Services, Anne Arundel Community Coll., 1973; B.A. in Edn., Music, Fine Arts, U. Md., 1977; postgrad. in bus. U. Balt., 1980-84; conservatory diploma Peabody Inst. of Peabody Conservatory, 1969; 1 dau., Valerie Kay. Instr. music Stringer Music Center, Balt., 1969-73; musician, pianist, organist, Balt., 1975-77; instr. music Acad. Music, Glen Burnie, Md., 1973-77; acctg. clk. Johns Hopkins Hosp., Balt., 1979-80, cash mgr., 1980-83; cash mgr. Md. Casualty Co., Balt., 1983—. Mem. Am. Risk and Ins. Assn., Nat. Assn. Accts., Inst. Mgmt. Acctg., Mid-Atlantic Cash Mgmt. Assn. Office: 3910 Keswick Rd Baltimore MD 21211

MCCAIN, BETTY LANDON RAY (MRS. JOHN LEWIS MCCAIN), political party official; b. Faison, N.C., Feb. 23, 1931; d. Horace Truman and Mary Howell (Perrett) Ray; student St. Marys Jr. Coll., 1948-50; A.B. in Music, U. N.C., Chapel Hill, 1952; M.A., Columbia U., 1953; m. John Lewis McCain, Nov. 19, 1955; children—Paul Pressly, III, Mary Eloise. Courier, European tour guide Ednl. Travel Assocs., Plainfield, N.J., 1952-54; asst. dir. YWCA, U. N.C., Chapel Hill, 1953-55; chmn. N.C. Democratic Exec. Com., 1976-79; mem. Dem. Nat. Com., 1976-79, 80-85, mem. com. on Presdl. nominations, 1981-82; mem. Winograd Commn., 1977-78; pres. Dem. Women of N.C., 1971-72, dist. dir., 1969-72; pres. Wilson County Dem. Women, 1966-67; precinct chmn., 1972-76; del. Dem. Nat. Conv., 1972; dir. Carolina Tel. & Tel. Co. Sunday sch. tchr. First Presbyn. Ch., Wilson, 1970-71, mem. chancel choir, 1985—; mem. Council on State Goals and Policy, 1970-72, Gov.'s Task Force on Child Advocacy, 1969-71, Wilson Human Relations Commn., 1975-78; charter mem. Wilson Edn. Devel. Council; active Arts Council of Wilson, Inc., N.C. Art Soc., N.C. Lit. and Hist. Assn.; regional v.p., bd. dirs. N.C. Mental Health Assn.; pres., bd. dirs., legis. chmn. Wilson County Mental Health Assn.; bd. dirs. Friends of U. N.C.-TV, Country Doctor Mus., Wilson United Fund; bd. govs., sec. personnel and tenure com. U. N.C.; bd. regents Barium Springs Home for Children; bd. dirs., pres. N.C. Mus. History Assocs., 1982-83; co-chmn. Com. to Elect Jim Hunt Gov., 1976, 80, co-chmn. senatorial campaign, 1984; mem. N.C. Adv. Budget Com., 1981-85; bd. visitors Peace Coll., Wake Forest U. Sch. Law, U. N.C., Chapel Hill; co-chmn. fund drive Wilson Community Theatre; state bd. dirs. N.C., Am. Lung Assn., 1985—. Recipient state awards N.C. Heart Assn., 1967, Easter Seal Soc., 1967, Community Service award Downtown Bus. Assocs., 1977, award N.C. Jaycettes, 1979, 85; Order of Old Well and Valkyries, U. N.C., 1952; named Dem. Woman of Yr., N.C., 1976. Mem. U. N.C. Chapel Hill Alumni Assn. (dir.), St. Marys Alumni Assn. (regional v.p.), AMA Aux. (dir., nat. vol. health services chmn., aux. liaison rep. Council on Mental Health, aux. rep. Council on Vol. Health Orgns.), N.C. (pres., dir., parliamentarian) med. auxs., UDC (historian John W. Dunham chpt.), DAR, N.C. Soc. Internal Medicine Aux. (pres.), Pi Beta Phi. Contbg. editor History of N.C. Med. Soc. Clubs: Book (pres.); Little Book; Wilson Country. Home: 1134 Woodland Dr Wilson NC 27893

MCCAIN, LENDA HAYNES, librarian; b. Roanoke, Ala., Oct. 19, 1929; d. Crawford Clift and Gulema (Harrod) Haynes; m. Marvin Enloe McCain, May 19, 1949; children—Eleanor, Allen Haynes. B.A., Peabody Coll., 1949, M.A., 1951; Ed.S., Fla. State U., 1975. Librarian Cheatham County Schs., Ashland City, Tenn., 1949-53; librarian Bay County Schs., Panama City, Fla., 1953-69, county media specialist, 1969—. Mem. DAR, Phi Delta Kappa, Delta Kappa Gamma. Democrat. Presbyterian. Avocation: genealogy. Home: 2206 Country Club Harbour Lynn Haven FL 32444 Office: Bay County Ednl Media Ctr 1310 E 11th St Panama City FL 32401

MCCAIN, SARAH SULLIVAN, banker; b. Reading, Pa., July 1, 1938; d. Robert J. and Caroline H. (Horst) S.; B.A., Vassar Coll., 1960; children—Anna Tobin, Robert Sullivan. Programmer/analyst Bankers Trust Co., N.Y.C., 1960-65; v.p. Morgan Guaranty Trust Co. N.Y., N.Y.C., 1974—; ptnr. Sheerlund Properties, Reading, Pa. Home: 40 E 10th St New York NY 10003 Office: 23 Wall St New York NY 10015

MCCALL, CANDACE SMITH, medical supply company executive; b. Grand Rapids, Mich., Sept. 3, 1947; d. Gerald Robert Smith and Helen (Swanson) Saylor; m. Herbert A. M. McCall, June 25, 1967; 1 child, Brian Eric. B.A., Mary Washington Coll. U. Va., 19; M.S. in Adminstrn., George Washington U., 1981. Exec. Garfinckel, Brooks Bros. Miller & Rhoads, 1975-78; exec. May Dept. Stores, Washington, 1978-81; owner Potomac Profl. Pharmacy Inc., Woodbridge, Va., 1981-86, Fairfax Profl. Pharmacy Inc., Annandale, Va., 1981-86, Potomac Med. Supply, Inc., Vienna, Va., 1984—. Medi-Spec, Inc., Vienna, 1984-86. Bd. dirs. Hunter Mill Country Day Sch., 1983-86. Mem. Societe Cybernetique. Republican. Presbyterian.

MCCALL, CAROLYN MARIE, technical representative; b. Houston, Oct. 14, 1951; d. Joseph Pleasant and Annie Mae (Allen) Cochran; m. Arthur Lee McCall, Jr., Feb. 4, 1949. A.A.S., Arapahoe Jr. Coll., 1970; B. Bus. Tech., U. Houston, 1980. Supr. 3-11 Sam Houston (Tex.) Meml. Hosp., 1978-80, lab. dir., 1980-83, asst. lab. dir., 1983; fin. broker EIBA Internat., Houston, 1983, credit service mgr., 1983-84; tech. rep. Datalab Lab. Computer Info. System, 1984—; tchr. Sam Houston Meml. Hosp., 1979-83. Med. scholar Western Med. Br., Houston, 1978-79. Mem. Am. Soc. Clin. Pathology, Clin. Lab. Mgmt. Assn., Tex. Soc. Med. Tech., Nat. Certification Agy. for Med. Lab. Personnel. Democrat. Methodist. Home: 1903 Aldsworth Houston TX 77088

MCCALL, LINDA DEANNE, flexible packaging company official; b. Hickory, N.C., Apr. 6, 1947; d. James Horace and Lucille Marie (Daniels) McC.; m. Jerome Perry Abernethy, Jr., Mar. 15, 1968 (div. 1971). Student Am. Mgmt. Assn., 1982. Nat. accounts mgr. Plastic Packaging, Inc., Hickory, N.C., 1966—. Mem. Packaging Inst. U.S.A. (mem. exec. com. Va./Caroline chpt. 1982-83, regional coordinator so. region 1983-84, chpt. of yr. 1983), Nat. Assn. Female Execs., Hampton Heights Ladies' Golf Assn. (pres. 1982). Republican. Methodist. Office: Plastic Packaging Inc 1246 Main Ave SE Hickory NC 28601

MCCALL, PATSYE, association executive; b. Bainbridge, Ga., June 1, 1939; d. Wilma Carlton and Nelle (Raker) McC.; children—Daniel Patrick Owens, Maury Luff Owens. B.S., Fla. State U., 1969, M.S., 1970. Exec. dir. Fla. Epilepsy Found., Tallahassee, 1972-76; dep. exec. dir. U.S. Commn. on Epilepsy, Washington, 1976-78; pub. health adviser NINCDS/NIH/HEW, Bethesda, Md., 1978-79; exec. dir. Epilepsy Internat., Milan, Italy, 1980-85; exec. dir. Internat. Bur. for Epilepsy, Heemstede, Holland, 1985—. Editor: Florida 5-Year Plan for Epilepsy, 1972; (with R.L. Masland) U.S. Report for Control of Epilepsy and Its Consequences, 1977. Assoc. chmn. Gov.'s Task Force Health, Tallahassee, 1970; sec. bd. dirs. Fla. Vol. Health Assn., 1974; council mem. Gov.'s DDPA Council, Tallahassee, 1973-76; dir. Epilepsy Internat., Geneva, Switzerland, 1977-80; v.p. Internat. Bur. Epilepsy, Geneva, 1977-80. Recipient 1st place spl. award, Epilepsy Found. Am., 1974; Ambassador for Epilepsy, Epilepsy Internat., 1978. Avocations: languages, creative writing. Address: Route 1 Box 18-A Sopchoppy FL 32358

MCCALLA, SANDRA ANN, high sch. principal; b. Shreveport, La., Nov. 6, 1939; d. Earl Gray and Dorothy Edna (Adams) McC.; B.S., Northwestern La. State U., 1960; M.S., U. No. Colo., 1968. With Caddo Parish Sch. Bd., Shreveport, 1960—, asst. prin. Capt. Shreve High Sch., 1977-79, prin., 1979—; instr. math La. State U., evenings 1979-81. Danforth fellow, 1982; named Educator of Yr., Shreveport Times-Caddo Tchrs. Assn., 1966, Times-Caddo Educators Assn., 1984; Capt. Shreve High Sch. recipient Excellence in Edn. award, 1982-83. Mem. Nat. Assn. Secondary Sch. Prins., La. Assn. Prins., La. Assn. Sch. Execs., NEA, La. Assn. Educators, Caddo Assn. Educators, Phi Delta Kappa. Democrat. Club: Altrusa.

MCCALLION, HAZEL, mayor; b. Port Daniel, Que., Can.; m. Samuel McCallion; children—Peter, Linda, Paul. Grad. secretarial program. With Canadian Kellogg, asst. to gen. mgr., after 1942, then officer mgr., Toronto; with printing bus.; reeve, reeve, editor Streetsvile Booster (Ont., Can.). Former dep. mayor, Streetsville, pres. Anglican Young People's Assn. Can.; mem. Mississauga and Peel Relgional Councils, 1974, ward councillor, mayor City of Mississauga, 1978—; chmn. Mississauga Taxicab Authority, Mississauga Planning Com., Site Com.; vice chmn. adv. com. on local govt. mgmt.; mem. Mcpl. Liaison Com; 1st v.p. and past pres. Assn. Municipalities of Ont.; chmn. Provincial Mcpl. Subcom. on Transp. of Dangerous Goods; mem. Credit Valley Hosp. Bd.; Govt. No. 51 of Can. Jaycees; hon. mem. Mississauga Kinsmen. Paul Harris fellow, Mem. Can. Fedn. Municipalities (dir.), Polish Alliance of Can., Mississauga Real Estate Bd., Mississauga Kinsmen. Address: Office of Mayor 1 City Centre Dr Mississauga ON L5B 1M2 Canada

MCCALLUM, PATRICIA ANN, public relations specialist, consultant; b. Cleve., Apr. 25, 1944; d. Jacob and Ruth (Eckert) Palomaki; B.S.J., Northwestern U., 1966, postgrad., 1966; m. James S. McCallum, July 2, 1966; children—Julie Lynn, David James. Reporter, New Brunswick (N.J.) Daily Home News, 1966-68; mng. editor Central Post, Kendall Park, N.J., 1969-70; govt. reporter Stewart Citizen, Walden, N.Y., 1972-75; editor Army Community Services Bull., Schweinfurt, Ger., 1976; pub. info. officer No. Va. Community Coll., Woodbridge campus, 1978-81; pub. affairs specialist, vol. cons. Directorate of Personnel and Community Activities, Ft. Sill, Okla., 1981—. Bd. dirs. Greentree Village Homeowners Assn., 1981. Recipient 1st place award govt. news feature N.J. Press Assn., 1970; Community Achievement award Schweinfurt Mil. Community, 1976, 77, hon. mention Nat. Sch. Pub. Relations Assn., 1980, cert. of achievement Dept. of Army, 1983, 86, awards for publs. Improvements Sec. Army, 1985, others. Mem. Women in Communications, Internat. Assn. Bus. Communicators, European Council Parents and Tchrs. (life mem.). Home: 521 Lauman Ave Fort Sill OK 73503

MC CANDLESS, ANNA LOOMIS, club woman; b. Aspinwall, Pa., July 21, 1897; d. George Wilberforce and Estella (Loomis) McC.; B.S., Carnegie-Mellon U., 1919. Pres., Vis. Nurses Assn. of Allegheny County, 1955-57; mem. vis. com. Margaret Morrison Carnegie Coll., 1962-66; v.p. Alumni Fedn. Carnegie Inst. Tech., 1963-66. Trustee Carnegie-Mellon U., 1966—. Mem. AAUW. Clubs: Coll., Univ., Twentieth Century (pres. 1956-58) (Pitts.); Appalachian Mountain. Home: Park Plaza Apts Craig St Pittsburgh PA 15213

MCCANDLESS, BARBARA J., tax and home economics consultant; b. Cottonwood Falls, Kans., Oct. 25, 1931; d. Arch G. and Grace (Kittle) McCandless; B.S., Kans. State U., 1953; M.S., Cornell U., 1959; postgrad. U. Minn., 1962-66, U. Calif., Berkeley, 1971-72; m. Allyn O. Lockner, 1969. Enrolled agt. IRS. Home demonstration agt. Kans. State U., 1953-57; teaching asst. Cornell U., 1957-58, asst. extension home economist in marketing, 1958-59; consumer mktg. specialist, asst. prof. Oreg. State U., 1959-62; instr. home econs. U. Minn., 1962-63, research asst. agrl. econs., 1963-66; asst. prof. U. R.I., 1966-67; asso. prof. family econs., mgmt., housing, equipment dept. head S.D. State U., 1967-73; asst. to sec. Dept. Commerce and Consumer Affairs, S.D., 1973-79; now cons. Mem. Nat. Council Occupational Licensing, dir., 1973-75, v.p., 1975-79. Mem. Am. Mktg. Assn., Am. Agrl. Econs. Assn., Am. Home Econs. Assn., Nat. Council on Family Relations, Am. Council Consumer Interests, LWV, Kans. State U. Alumni Assn., Pi Gamma Mu. Club: Brookings (S.D.) Country. Research on profl. and occupational licensing bds. Address: 2114 Potomac Dr Topeka KS 66611

MC CANN, JOAN CELIA, school administrator; b. Malden, Mass., Jan. 23, 1936; d. Vincent Jacob and Helen Lorraine (Pontone) Celia; A.B. cum laude, Tufts U., 1957; M.A., U. Mich., 1968; Ed.D., Fordham U. 1986; m. William J. McCann, Aug. 23, 1958; children—Susan, Peter. Tchr. 1st grade Gleason Sch., Medford, Mass., 1957-58, Hutchinson Sch., Pelham, N.Y., 1958-61; tchr. 1st grade Siwanoy Sch., Pelham, 1968-69, reading cons., 1969-71, prin., 1971-75; prin. Fox Meadow Sch., Scarsdale, N.Y., 1975—; mem. adminstrv. adv. com. internship St. John's U., 1973—. Mem. Pelham Bicentennial Com., 1974—, sch. cons. Between the Lines publ., 1975; mem. adv. bd. Scarsdale Hist. Soc., 1975—; chmn. Pelham Bicentennial Ball, 1976; adv. com. Westchester County Office of Aging; adv. bd. Prins. Forum at Fordham U. Recipient award in appreciation for cooperation Pelham Manor Fire Dept., 1974; IDEA fellow Charles Kettering Found., 1976, 77. Mem. Internat. Reading Assn., N.Y. State Adminstrs. Assn., Nat. Assn. Elementary Sch. Prins., Nat. Congress Parents and Tchrs. (life), Am. Assn. sch. Adminstrs., Beatrix Potter Soc., Jean Piaget Soc., Jackson Coll. Alumnae Assn., U. Mich. Alumni Assn., Phi Delta Kappa, Chi Omega. Club: Internat. Garden. Home: 242 Eastland Ave Pelham NY 10803 Office: Fox Meadow Sch Brewster Rd Scarsdale NY 10583

MCCANN, MARIE ANDREW, aquarist; b. Jonesboro, Ark., Mar. 10, 1914; d. Francis Marion and Grace (Clark) Andrew; m. Hughes Sanford McCann, Aug. 28, 1932 (div. 1960); children—Andrew Hughes, Patricia Grace. Hort. designer, builder Cotton Carnival, Memphis, 1931-32; vocalist Breakfast Club, WREC, Memphis, 1928-32; owner McCann's, Dallas, 1945-56; owner, mgr. McCann's Tropical Fish Shop, Dallas, 1950-63, McCann's Aquarium Service, Dallas, 1951—; owner, designer Decorative Accents, Dallas, 1978—; cons. Dallas Pub. Aquarium, 1948-70. Contbr. articles to Hobby Publs., 1950-65. Mem. Dallas Aquarium Soc. (editor mag. 1945-70), Fedn. Tex. Aquarium Soc., Internat. Fedn. Aquarium Socs. (editor publ. 1959-63). Democrat. Methodist. Address: 3012 McFarlin Blvd Dallas TX 75205

MCCANN, MARY CHERI, medical technologist, horse breeder and trainer; b. Pensacola, Fla., July 29, 1956; d. Joseph Maxwell and Cora Marie (Underwood) McC.; m. Robert Lee Spencer, July 20, 1977 (div. Nov. 1983). A.A., Pensacola Jr. Coll., 1975; student U. Md., 1977-78; B.S. in Biology, Troy State U., 1979; postgrad. U. Fla., 1979. Med. technologist Cape Fear Valley Med. Ctr., Fayetteville, N.C., 1981-85, Doctors Diagnostic Centre, Fayetteville, 1985-86; sales rep. Waddell & Reed, Fayetteville, 1985-86; med. technologist Roche Biomed. Lab., Burlington, N.C., 1986—. Served with U.S. Army, 1976-77. Mem. Am.Soc. Clin. Pathologists (registrant), Nat. Assn. Female Execs., Am. Quarter Horse Assn., Appaloosa Horse Club, Pinto Horse Assn. Am. Republican. Avocations: horses; karate; guns; oil painting. Home: Route 2 Box 571 Hope Mills NC 28348 Office: Roche Biomed Lab Burlington NC 27215

MCCARLEY, MARGARET ONEIDA MAY, business executive; b. Dallas, May 31, 1947; d. Fred and Mary Lou (McGowan) May; 1 son, James Daniel. Sec., office mgr. Security Realty, Irving, Tex., 1965-68; bldg. mgr. Carpenter Freeway Med. Center, Irving, 1968-69; office mgr. Runaway Bay, Bridgeport, Tex., 1970-71; v.p., corp. sec. Metro Warehouse, Carrollton, Tex., 1971-81; mng. dir., v.p. dir. fin. +nternat. Airline Passengers Assn., Irving, Tex., 1981-84; v.p. ops. B-Komp, Inc., Dallas, 1984—. Mem. Am. Warehousemen's Assn., Nat. Assn. Female Execs., Nat. Assn. Exec. Secs., Notable Women of TX. Mem. Ch. of Christ. Home: 3302 Pritchett Irving TX 75061 Office: 800 W Airport Freeway Irving TX 75062

MCCARTER, KATHERINE SAUTER, association executive; b. Nyack, N.Y., Nov. 12, 1942; d. William Charles and Josephine Rosina (Schoenle) Sauter; B.A. in Biology, Cedar Crest Coll., Allentown, Pa., 1964; M.H.S. (EPA trainee), Johns Hopkins U., 1973; m. Robert James McCarter, Dec. 6, 1969; 1 dau., Emily Katherine. Chmn. sci. dept. Arundel (Md.) Jr. High Sch., 1964-68; program asso. career devel. program Am. Lung Assn., N.Y.C., 1968; air conservation cons. Mass. Lung Assn., 1968-69; exec. dir. Met. Boston Citizen's Coalition Clean Air, 1968-69; community health educator Environ. Health Adminstrn., Md. Dept. Health, 1971-76; dir. govt. relations Am. Public Health Assn., Washington, 1976-80, asst. exec. dir., 1980-83, assoc. exec. dir., 1984—; bd. dirs. Nat. Coalition Health and Environ., 1980-82; bd. dirs. Coalition for Health Funding, 1983—, treas., 1983—; mem. nat. air pollution manpower devel. adv. com. EPA, 1973-76. Mem. Nat. Environ. Health Assn., Am. Public Health Assn., Health on Wednesday. Home: 9027 Billow Row Columbia MD 21045 Office: 1015 15th St NW Washington DC 20005

MCCARTER, MARGIE JOHNSON, investments and travel consultant; b. Bosqueville, Tex., Nov. 7, 1929; d. Joseph Bernard and Bettie Ruth (McNamara) Johnson; m. Jack McCarter, Dec. 13, 1952 (div. 1975); children—Jack III, Bettie M. Boyd, Parnell; m. William Richard Thompson, Sept. 1, 1982. Student Mary Baldwin Coll., 1947-48, U. Tex., 1948-51; B.A., Baylor U., 1951; postgrad. So. Meth. U., 1952. Saleswoman Viking Travel Agy., 1975, Unimark Travel, Dallas, 1976; ind. agt. T.H.E. Travel Agy., Dallas, 1977—. Mem. Highland Park PTA Sch. Bd.; active Crystal Charity, Dallas Summer Musicals, Symphony League, Les Femmes du Monde, Maureen Connally Brinker Found., Dallas Theater Center, Baptist. Clubs: Headliner's, T-BAR-M Racquet. Home: 3631 Asbury St Dallas TX 75205 Office: 11353 Emerald St Dallas TX 75229

MCCARTER, RENATE BOHNE, publisher; b. Berlin, Feb. 9, 1939; came to U.S., 1957, naturalized, 1963; d. Wilhelm and Regina (von Boyens) Bohne; B.A., in Philosophy, U. Americas, Mexico City, 1963; m. Thomas N. McCarter III, June 22, 1976. Lit. agt., N.Y.C., 1976—; pub. UN Plaza mag., N.Y.C., 1979-82, UN Weekly Report, 1982—; rep. state of Morelos, Mex., 1986—. Mem. Nat. Council Women, World Affairs Council (bd. dirs. 1986). Clubs: Mid-Atlantic; River (N.Y.C.); Meadow, (South Hampton, N.Y.). Address: 823 Park Ave New York NY 10021

MCCARTHY, CATHERINE FRANCES, lawyer; b. N.Y.C., Feb. 13, 1921; d. Joseph J. and Eva E. (Berger) McC.; m. Peter Donald Andreoli, Aug. 25, 1945; children—Peter, Brian, Catherine, Christine, Francine. B.S., St. John's U., 1941, LL.B., 1943. Bar: N.Y. 1943, U.S. Supreme Ct. 1966. Assoc. Spencer, Ordway and Wierum, 1942-50; sole practice, N.Y.C., Pelham, N.Y., 1950-67; real estate atty. Gen. Foods Corp., White Plains, N.Y., 1967-68, trademark atty., 1968-73, chief trademark counsel, 1973-81, dir. legal services-trademarks, 1981—. Mem. ABA, Assn. Bar City N.Y., N.Y. State Bar Assn., Westchester County Bar Assn., Westchester-Fairfield Corp. Counsel Assn., U.S. Trademark Assn. (dir. 1976-80). Office: 250 North St White Plains NY 10625

MCCARTHY, DONNA LEE, electronics company official; b. Woburn, Mass., Jan. 14, 1951; d. William Joseph and Lorraine (Collins) McC.; m. Henry Thaddeus Wrobel, Feb. 29, 1976. Student Inst. European Studies, Paris, 1971-72; B.A. with honors, Brandeis U., 1973; M.B.A. with honors, Northeastern U., 1982. Cert. tchr., Mass.; cert. Pratique de Langue Française, U. Paris, 1971. Secondary tchr. Woburn Pub. Schs. (Mass.), 1973-79; distbn. analyst Digital Equipment Corp., Northboro, Mass., 1980-82, distbn. mgr., Hudson, Mass., 1982-84, customs planner, Acton, Mass., 1984—. Observer LWV, Acton, 1982—. Fulbright grantee, Ger., summer 1975. Mem. Woburn Tchrs. Assn. (v.p. 1977-78, newsletter editor 1977-79), Beta Gamma Sigma. Baptist. Office: Digital Equipment Corp Nagog Park Acton MA 01720

MCCARTHY, GAIL ELIZABETH, consulting mechanical engineer, b. San Francisco, Sept. 27, 1952; d. Lloyd Wilson and Vanda (Sargentini) Kendall; m. Roger Lee McCarthy, Jan. 6, 1979. B.S., U. Calif.-Berkeley, 1973, M.S., 1974; Ph.D., MIT, 1978. Registered profl. engr., Calif. Asst. prof. U. Calif.-Berkeley, 1978-81; pres. Gail E. McCarthy, Inc., Belmont, Calif., 1982—. Contbr. articles to profl. jours. Mem. Nat. Safety Council, ASME, Nat. Soc. Profl. Engrs. Office: Gail E McCarthy Inc 1007 Misty Ln Belmont CA 94002

MCCARTHY, HANNAH M., college president. Pres. Daniel Webster Coll., Nashua, N.H. Office: Daniel Webster Coll University Dr Nashua NH 03063*

MCCARTHY, JACKQUELYN SUE ELLIS, construction company executive, consultant; b. Beech Grove, Ind., May 21, 1947; d. George Edward and Mary Frances (Clevenger) Ellis; m. Thomas Patric McCarthy (div. 1973). Student Purdue U., 1965-66, Ind. U., 1968, Ind. Central U., 1982-83, Butler U., 1971. Sales staff L.S. Ayres, Indpls., 1968-69; rental agt. Turtle Creek Mana, Indpls., 1966; sec., treas. George Ellis Excavating Engr., Inc., Indpls., 1963—; also dir.; sec., treas. DWC Corp., Indpls., 1976-83, Multi-Phase Corp., Indpls., 1977-80. Mem. Southside bd. dirs. Indpls. Symphony Com., 1974-84, Christian Women's Club, Indpls., 1966-73; bd. dirs. Southport High Sch. Alumni, Indpls., 1980-85; docent Indpls. Children's Mus., 1985. Mem. Nat. Assn. Women in Constrn. (com. mem.), Assn. Builders and Contractors. Republican. Avocations: reading, skiing, racquetball, tennis. Home: 7600 E 126th St Noblesville IN 46060 Office: George Ellis Excavating Engr 2222 Bluff Rd Indianapolis IN 46225

MCCARTHY, JEAN CATHERINE, city parks, playgrounds and forestry official; b. Fitchburg, Mass., Jan. 3, 1925; d. Charles H. and Catherine I. (Beer) McC.; grad. mgmt. course U. Mass. Inst. Govtl. Services, 1980. Clk.-typist Fitchburg Park-Recreation-Forestry Dept., 1948-53, prin. clk., 1953-70, adminstrv. asst., 1970-76, supt. parks and playgrounds, city forester, 1976-82, adminstrv. asst. and city forester, 1982—. Founder, 1st pres. Montachusett unit Am. Cancer Soc., 1970—, chmn. public info., 1976-77, mem. cancer crusade com., 1981—, bd. dirs., 1970-84, chmn. Montachusett Unit Cancer Prevention Study II, 1982—; bd. dirs. Micah Housing Rehab. Program, 1974-76; mem. adv. com. for adult and occupational edn. Fitchburg Public Sch. System, 1979-82; U.S. Nat. Council Catholic Laity rep. World-Wide Consultation of Cath. Laity, Rome, 1975; bd. dirs. founding assembly Nat. Council Cath. Laity, 1971-82, sec. exec. bd., 1974-78; bd. dirs. U.S. Cath. Mission Council, 1980-82; mem. Worcester Diocesan Council, Worcester, Mass., 1966-76, pres., 1968-74; mem. Worcester Diocesan Pastoral Council, 1972-74; internat. conv. clk. Daus. of Isabella, 1970, 74, sec. Mass. Circle, 1961-62, regent Jeanne d'Arc Circle, 1959-60, trustee Jeanne d'Arc Circle, 1979-82, chmn. liturgy Jeanne d'Arc Circle, 1979-84; lay dir. Worcester Diocesan Cursillo Secretariat and Leaders' Sch., 1983—, mem. Team for Women's Weekends; mem. adv. bd. Gov.'s Commn. on Women's Issues, 1984—. Recipient State award Am. Cancer Soc., 1972, 77, state cert. appreciation, 1976, award for 25 yrs. of service, 1985; cert. for advancement public service in Commonwealth Mass., U. Mass. Inst. Govtl. Services, 1980; cert. appreciation United Neighbors of Cleghorn Inc., 1980, Brain Injured Children Softball Marathon Com., 1980. Home: 294 Madison St Fitchburg MA 01420 Office: Park and Recreation-Forestry Dept City Hall 718 Main St Fitchburg MA 01420

MCCARTHY, JOANNE ELIZABETH, educator, consultant; b. Allentown, Pa., May 6, 1943; d. Robert Franklin and Sarah Elizabeth (Knauss) Schall; m. William James McCarthy, June 21, 1969. B.A., UCLA, 1966; M.Ed., U. Rochester, 1974; M.S., U. LaVerne, 1981; M.A., Mills Coll., 1983. Elem. tchr. Centralia Sch. Dist., Buena Park, Calif., 1968-70; reading specialist elem. sch. Spencerport (N.Y.) Sch. Dist., 1973-74, Wayne Central Sch. Dist., Ontario, N.Y., 1974-75; tchr. State Demonstration Project, Pittsburg (Calif.) Unified Sch. Dist., 1977-78; English and reading tchr. Vallejo (Calif.) City Unified Sch. Dist., 1978—; staff devel. cons. Profl. Devel. Ctr. Mem. NEA, Assn. Supervision and Curriculum Devel., Calif. Assn. Tchrs. English, Nat. Council Tchrs. English, Phi Delta Kappa, Pi Lambda Theta; Nat. Audubon Soc. Author publ. in field. Home: 105 Poshard St Pleasant Hill CA 94523 Office: Vallejo City Unified School District 840 Nebraska St Vallejo CA 94591

MCCARTHY, KAREN, state legislator; b. Haverhill, Mass., Mar. 18, 1947; d. Lawrence A. and Barbara V. McCarthy; B.S., U. Kans., 1969, M.B.A., 1984;

M.A., U. Mo.-Kansas City, 1975; Tchr. English, Shawnee Mission South High Sch., Overland Park, Kans., 1969-75; tchr. upper sch. humanities Sunset Hill Sch. for Girls, Kansas City, Mo., 1975-76; mem. Mo. Ho. of Reps., 1976—, chmn. ways and means com., vice chmn. energy com.; mem. platform drafting subcom. Dem. Nat. Com., 1984, mem. Dem. Policy Com., 1985-86. English Speaking Union grantee, Stratford-upon-Avon, Eng., 1974. Mem., del. Am. Council Young Polit. Leaders to Yugoslavia, 1978, to People's Republic of China, 1979; bd. dirs. Com. for County Progress, Jackson County, Mo., Citizens Assn., Kansas City, Mo. Named an Outstanding Young Woman Am., U.S. Jaycees, 1979; recipient Mo. award Phi Chi Theta, 1979; European Community Visitors grantee alternative energy research, 1982; Harvard U. Inst. Politics fellow, 1982. Mem. Nat. Conf. State Legislatures, Phi Delta Kappa. Office: House PO Jefferson City MO 65101

MC CARTHY, MARY, author; b. Seattle, June 21, 1912; d. Roy Winfield and Therese (Preston) McC.; A.B., Vassar Coll., 1933; hon. degrees Syracuse U., 1973, U. Hull (Eng.), 1974, Bard Coll., 1976, U. Aberdeen (Scotland), 1979; Bowdoin Coll., 1981, U. Maine-Orono, 1982; 1 child, Reuel K. Wilson; m. James Raymond West, Apr. 15, 1961. Editor Covici Friede, 1936-37; editor Partisan Rev., 1937-38, drama critic, 1937-48; instr. lit. Bard Coll., 1945-46; instr. English, Sarah Lawrence Coll., 1948; Northcliffe lectr. Univ. Coll., London, 1980; holder Stevenson chair of lit. Bard Coll., 1986—. Guggenheim fellow, 1949-50; recipient Horizon prize, 1949, Nat. Medal for Lit., 1984, MacDowell medal, 1984, Lit. award Friends of Rochester Pub. Library, 1985; Nat. Inst. grantee, 1957; Guggenheim fellow, 1959-60. Mem. Nat. Inst. Arts and Letters, Phi Beta Kappa. Author: The Company She Keeps, 1942; The Oasis, 1949; Cast a Cold Eye, 1950; The Groves of Academe, 1952; A Charmed Life, 1955; Sights and Spectacles, 1956; Venice Observed, 1956; Memories of a Catholic Girlhood, 1957; The Stones of Florence, 1959; On the Contrary, 1961; The Group, 1963; Mary McCarthy's Theatre Chronicles, 1963; Vietnam, 1967; Hanoi, 1968; The Writing on the Wall, 1970; Birds of America, 1971; Medina, 1972; The Seventeenth Degree, 1974; The Mask of State, 1974; Cannibals and Missionaries, 1979; Ideas and the Novel, 1980; (adaptation) La Traviata, 1983; Occasional Prose, 1985. Contbr. articles to nat. mags. Address: Main Street Castine ME 04421

MCCARTHY, MARY PHYLLIS MASCITTI, family center director; b. Leominster, Mass., Oct. 12, 1928; d. Pelino and Anna Pelina (DiNino) Mascitti; m. Walter Joseph McCarthy, May 21, 1955 (dec.). B.S., UCLA, 1954; M.S.W., Catholic U. Am., 1963; Ph.D., Bryn Mawr Coll., 1976. Lic. clin. social worker, Calif. Psychometrist, Student Counselint Center, UCLA, 1953-55; caseworker Catholic Social Service, Vallejo, Calif., 1959-61; med. social worker Georgetown U. Hosp., Washington, 1962-63; psychiat. social worker Cath. U. Child Guidance Clinic, Washington, 1961-62; pvt. practice clin. social worker, 1965—; instr. courses Immaculate Heart Coll., Hollywood, Calif., and Mt. St. Mary's Coll., Los Angeles, 1963-68; dir. profo. services Holy Family Adoption Service, Los Angeles, 1963-70; liaison for Los Angeles Archdiocese Dept. Health and Hosps. and Natural Family Planning Research Project, 1976-80; co-prin. investigator Natural Family Planning Research Study, Nat. Inst. Child Health and Human Devel., NIH, Cedars-Sinai Med. Center and 6 other Los Angeles hosps., 1976-80; social systems analyst Local and Internat. Systems, Los Angeles, 1976—; dir. Quo Vadis Family Center, Torrance, Calif., 1980—; condr. workshops, lectr. in field, 1965—; cons. Regis House Settlement House Program, 1974-76; cons. WHO, 1977; apptd. Calif. Social Welfare Task Force for Study of Services to Unmarried Parents, 1968-69; mem. Com. on Community Devel. of Services in Child Welfare, Los Angeles Welfare Planning Council, 1966-71. NIMH grantee, 1962, 71. Mem. Nat. Assn. Social Workers (nat. publs. com. 1978-80, local bd. dirs. 1966-71, nat. del. to nat. assemblies 1967, 69), Acad. Cert. Social Workers (nat. cert. bd. 1970-74), Nat. Conf. Social Welfare, Internat. Conf. Social Work, Am. Assn. Social Welfare History, Nat. Conf. Cath. Charities Los Angeles, Sisters of Social Service (local dir. 1968-71, del. to gen. chpts. 1968, 74, gen. councilor, treas. 1974-76), Sigma Kappa. Author: Home Visitors: A Dynamic of Christian Witness, 1971; Drastic Social Change of a Closed Community, 1977; contbr. articles to profl. jours., papers to confs. in field; condr. workshops U.S., Colombia. Home: 1120 Westchester Pl Los Angeles CA 90019 Office: 3715 W Lomita Blvd Suite 129 Torrance CA 90505

MCCARTHY, REGGIE LUCILLE, business educator; b. Petoskey, Mich., Mar. 21, 1947; d. Frank James and Inez (Diquigiovanni) Gregory; m. Gary Robert Neal, July 1, 1966 (div. May 1972); children—Keri Lynn, Kevin Robert, Michael Ernest; m. Keith Richard McCarthy, Aug. 7, 1982. Student Winona State U., 1964-66; B.S., Mankato State U., 1975; M.S., Bemidji State U., 1984. Sec., purchasing agt. Continental Nonferrous Foundry, Albert Lea, Minn., 1970-71; sec., receptionist Kevco of Minn., Albert Lea, 1972-73; instr. bus. edn. Albert Lea AVTI, 1973-75; exec. sales sec. Holes-Webway Co., St. Cloud, Minn., 1982-83; instr. bus. edn. Brainerd AVTI, Minn., 1975—, yearbook advisor, 1974-75; advisor Future Sec. Assn., 1984—. Supt. Sunday sch. First United Ch., Brainerd, 1978-80, tchr., 1975-78. Mem. Minn. Bus. Educators (treas. 1985—, bd. dirs.), Brainerd Edn. Assn. (pres. 1979-80), Minn. Edn. Assn., NEA, Pi Omega Pi. Methodist. Clubs: Lioness (Little Falls, Minn.); Profl. Secs. (advisor) (Brainerd). Avocations: sewing; aerobics; reading. Office: Brainerd Vocat Sch 300 Quince St Brainerd MN 56401

MCCARTHY, SANDRA GIFFORD, stockbroker; b. Decatur, Ala., July 16, 1946; d. William and Elizabeth (Cox) Long; student Lurleen B. Wallace Jr. Coll., 1964-66, Tallahassee Jr. Coll., 1968-69, Personnel Sch., Am. Banking Inst., 1973, Merrill Lynch Extended Study, 1980; m. James M. McCarthy, Aug. 15, 1980; 1 dau., Lori Lynn. Asst. v.p., asst. personnel dir. First Nat. Bank Mobile (Ala.), 1973-75; property mgr. Bryson Realty, Tallahassee, 1975-76; sales mgr. NASCO, Inc., Springfield, Tenn., 1976-79, personnel recruiter cons., 1980—; stockbroker Merrill Lynch, Nashville, 1980—. Fund raising chmn. Robertson County (Tenn.) Republican Party, 1981. Named Top Salesman NASCO, Inc., 1977, Top Rookie in Sales, 1977; recipient Exceeding Sales Quota award 1978. Mem. SEC Brokers. Baptist. Club: Key to City (chmn. arts fund raising 1981, 1st v.p. 1982, pres. 1983, adviser 1984—) (Hendersonville, Tenn.) Rock Castle Ball (chmn. 1984). Home: 106 Surrey Hill Point Hendersonville TN 37075

MCCARTHY, SHARON MURPHY, purchasing agent; b. Syracuse, N.Y., Oct. 6, 1956; d. John Daniel and Colleen (Stapleton) Murphy; m. Robert Raynolds McCarthy, June 19, 1982. B.S., LeMoyne Coll., Syracuse, 1978; M.B.A., Rochester Inst. Tech., N.Y., 1982. Prodn. scheduler Carrier Fin. Corp., Syracuse, 1978, buyer, 1978-79; buyer Mobil Chem. Co., Macedon, N.Y., 1979-81; buyer Gen. Electric Co., Syracuse, 1981-83, purchasing agt., 1983—. Mem. Nat. Assn. Female Execs. Home: 104 Old Lyme Rd Syracuse NY 13224 Office: Gen Electric Co Count St Plant Bldg 2 Room 16 Syracuse NY 13221

MCCARTNEY, SHIRLEY LEONE, telecommunications company official; b. Salt Lake City, Nov. 12, 1945; d. Clarence Eldon and Thora Leone (Johnson) Williams Campbell; m. Marvin Dwayne McCartney, Apr. 24, 1971 (div. Apr. 1980); children—Ty, Shannon, Lauren. A.S., Brigham Young U., 1967; B.S., U. Utah, 1970. Exec. sec. Company Enterprises, Salt Lake City, 1968-70; dept. mgr. Robinson's Newport Beach, Calif., 1970-71; exec. sec. Segerstrom & Sons, Costa Mesa, Calif., 1971-72, Bonneville Internat. Corp., Salt Lake City, 1979-83, Bonneville Telecommunications, Salt Lake City, 1983—. Mem. Exec. Women Internat. (sec. 1983-84). Mem. Ch. of Jesus Christ of Latter-day Saints. Office: Bonneville Telecommunications Co 19 W S Temple Salt Lake City UT 84101

MCCARTY, BARBARA SMITH, county official; b. Andalusia, Ala., Sept. 7, 1940; d. Egbert L. and Gladys (Hartin) S.; m. Lucius Edard McCarty, Apr. 21, 1961; children—Debra McCarty Slaughter, Lucius Edward, Donna McCarty Swilley. Student South Ga. Tech. Coll., 1958-60, U. Ga.-Athens, 1964—. Office mgr. to county tax commr., Americus, Ga., 1966-76; clk.-treas. Sumter County Bd. Commrs., Americus, 1976-85, chief adminstrv. officer, treas., 1985—; v.p. Assoc. Industries of Americus. Mem. County Adminstrs. Assn. Ga., Ga. County Clks. Assn., Inst. Mcpl. Clks. Ga. Democrat. Baptist. Lodge: Order Eastern Star (worthy matron 1979-80). Avocations: reading; walking; music. Home: PO Box 1664 Americus GA 31709 Office: County Courthouse Americus GA 31709

MCCARTY, EMILY HOLCHIN, librarian; b. Cleve., Mar. 30, 1949; d. Frank John and Emilie (Benko) Holchin; m. Patrick Shane McCarty, Oct. 7, 1973 (div. 1984). B.S., Baldwin-Wallace U., 1971; M.S. in L.S., Case Western Res. U., 1973; grad. in learning disabilities/behavorial disorders Notre Dame U., 1977; cert. in sign lang. Fairmount Theatre for Deaf, 1980. Tchr. Cleve. Pub. Schs., 1971-72; head librarian Griswold Inst., Cleve., 1972-73; head childrens room Lakewood (Ohio) Pub. Library, 1973-76, Cuyahoga County Pub. Library, Cleve., 1976-81; librarian for physically impaired Queens Borough Pub. Library, Jamaica, N.Y., 1982—; book reviewer Children's Book Rev. Service, 1972—. Asst. editor periodical Library High Tech., 1983—. Mem. ALA, N.Y. Library Assn. Lutheran. Home: 84-20 Austin St Apt 2L Kew Gardens NY 11415 Office: Queens Borough Pub Library 89-11 Merrick Blvd Jamaica NY 11432

MCCARVER, BETTY LOUISE, nurse, educator; b. Hurley, N.Mex., Oct. 12, 1932; d. Carl Thomas and Stella Alberta (Kreamer) McLendon; m. Robert Roy McCarver Jr., Sept. 3, 1954 (div. Jan. 1975); children—Robert Roy III, Deborah Lynn McCarver Stenberg. Diploma in nursing U. Okla., 1954; B.S., Ariz. State U., 1972, postgrad., 1974-76; postgrad. No. Ariz. U., 1983—. R.N. Supr. U. Okla. Childrens Hosp., Oklahoma City, 1954; instr. Research Hosp., Kansas City, Mo., 1954-55; charge nurse U.S. Army Dispensaries, Sendai, Japan, 1956-57; owner, mgr. Hallmac Foods and Camping Supplies, Scottsdale, Ariz., 1965-68; asst. exec. dir. Ariz. Nurses Assn., Phoenix, 1976-82; tng. dir. Ariz. Family Planning Council, Phoenix, 1983—. Author: Once Upon A Time: A Complete Guide to Baby Sitting, 1965; Dear Gussie: The 1-2-3 of G.E.M.S., 1968. Editor Caduceus Crier, 1972-73. Chmn. various coms. Maricopa County Med. Aux., 1963-73, Ariz. Med. Aux., 1970-73; wilderness survival counselor Theodore Roosevelt council Boy Scouts Am., Scottsdale, 1971. Recipient award of honor Nat. Safety Council, 1965, 66. Mem. Maricopa County Med. Aux. (hon. life), Council Continuing Edn., Am. Nurses Assn. (dist. 18 nominating com. 1983), Ariz. Nurses Assn., Ariz. Vocat. Edn. Assn. Republican. Mem. Ch. of Jesus Christ of Latter-day Saints. Avocations: hiking; backpacking; painting; sewing; travel. Home: 7124 N Via De Amigos Scottsdale AZ 85258 Office: Ariz Family Planning Council 316 W McDowell Phoenix AZ 85258

MCCAUGHRIN, WENDY BORDOFF, educator; b. Windsor, Ont., Can., Nov. 24, 1944; d. Jack and Tillie (Starker) Bordoff; B.A., Wayne State U., 1967; B.A. with honors, U. Windsor, 1974; M.A., Merrill Palmer Inst., 1977; M.S., U. Ill., 1981, now postgrad; m. Scott Jame McCaughrin, July 1, 1972. Guidance counselor, instr. high sch., Chatham, Ont., 1967-70; reading therapist, instr., Windsor, Ont., 1971-77; reading and lang. therapist The Reading Group Program, Urbana, Ill., 1980-81; now ednl. cons. learning abilities program Mercy Hosp., Urbana. Mem. Cousteau Soc., Am. Speech-Lang.-Hearing Assn., Orton Soc., Internat. Reading Assn., Kappa Delta Pi. Jewish. Author reading and writing tests. Office: Mercy Hosp 1400 W Park Ave Urbana IL 61801

MCCAULEY, ELFRIEDA BABNEY, media educator; b. Milw., Aug. 11, 1915; d. Rudolph Babney and Louise (Hetzel) Babney; m. Leon McCauley, June 10, 1938; children—Brian, Christopher, Kevin, Matthew. B.S.Ed., U. Wis.-Milw., 1948; M.S., Columbia U., 1965, D. Library Sci., 1971. Librarian Milw. Pub. Library, 1935-40; reporter Religious News Service, N.Y.C., 1941-43; freelance pub. relations, N.Y.C., 1943-46; sec.-treas. McCauley Enterprises, Greenwich, 1961-65; librarian Greenwich Pub. Schs., 1965-69, coordinator media services, 1969—. vis. lectr. Columbia U., N.Y.C., 1972-73; assoc. prof. Pratt Inst., Bklyn., 1975-76, Fairfield U. (Conn.), 1977-78; del. White House Commn. on Libraries and Info. Services, 1979-80; cons. Ednl. Mission to Teheran, 1975; mem. doctoral com. Columbia U. Sch. Library Sci., 1972-74; mem. library/media suprs. group State Dept. Edn., 1981—, mem. adv. council on computers in edn., 1982—. Author: Book of Prayers, 1955; Treasury of Faith, 1957; Mill Girl Libraries of New England, 1971; Reading for Young People: New England, 1985. Recipient Sch. Library Program of Yr. award Am. Assn. Sch. Librarians/Britannica, Inc., 1979, Rheta Clark award Conn. Ednl. Media Assn., 1982. Mem. Ednl. Film Library Assn. (bd. dirs. 1981-83), ALA (John Cotton Dana award 1970, 75), Assn. Ednl. Data Systems, Am. Assn. Sch. Librarians (chmn. suprs. sect. 1982), Phi Delta Kappa, Beta Phi Mu Contbr. articles to profl. jours. Home: 32 Longmeadow Rd Riverside CT 06878 Office: Greenwich Public Schs 290 Greenwich Ave Greenwich CT

MCCAULEY, MARGARET MEIER, retail malls leasing representative; b. Takoma Park, Md., July 25, 1943; d. Robert Henry and Elizabeth Dewees (Shanaman) Meier, Jr.; m. James Edward McCauley, Jr., Sept. 12, 1964 (div. Dec. 1972); 1 child, Christopher Dewees. B.A., Pa. State U., 1965; M.Ed., Temple U., 1975. Cert. tchr., Pa., Tex. Tchr. English, Hampton City Schs. (Va.), 1966-67; tchr. 4th grade Phoenixville Sch. Dist. (Pa.), 1967-68, Springfield Sch. Dist. (Pa.), 1973-74; tchr. 5th grade Phila. Bd. Edn., 1974-80, tchr. lang. arts Alief Sch. Dist., Houston, 1980-81; leasing rep. in Tex. for Rouse Co., Columbia, Md., 1981—. Republican election judge, Phila., 1973-74; vol. Tex. Inst. Research and Rehab., Houston, 1980-81; bd. dirs. Kerry Glen III Condominiums, Houston, 1983—. Pa. Senatorial scholar Pa. State U., 1961-65. Mem. Internat. Council Shopping Centers (affiliate). Republican. Episcopalian. Home: 6495 Bayou Glen Houston TX 77057 Office: Rouse Co 10001 Westheimer St Suite 1310 Houston TX 77042

MCCAULEY, MARY ANN JACKSON, communications co. exec.; b. Moline, Ill., Feb. 20, 1947; d. Alvin Southern and Helen Ruth (Reamy) Jackson; B.J., U. Mo., 1969; m. Gary W. McCauley, Nov. 2, 1973. Reporter, editor Mason City (Iowa) Globe Gazette, 1969-71; editor Hallmark, Cards, Inc., Kansas City, Mo., 1971-72; asso. editor Am. Nurses Assn., Kansas City, Mo., 1972-76; pres., editor Galena Sentinel-Times, Kans., 1976-78; cons. Bi-State Region ARC BloodCenter, 1978; mgr. public relations First Union Bancorp./First Nat. Bank in St. Louis, 1978-81, Gen. Dynamics Communications Co., St. Louis, 1981—. Mem. grant proposal com. Galena Congregate Meals Program/Meals-on-Wheels. Mem. Public Relations Soc. Am., Internat. Assn. Bus. Communications (dir.), Women in Communications, Galena Merchants Assn. Office: Gen Dynamics Communications Co 12101 Woodcrest Exec Dr St Louis MO 63141

MCCAULEY, PATRICIA ANN, health care administrator; b. Harrisonburg, Va., June 30, 1946; d. Auston Garfield and Rose Ann (Wood) McC.; R.N., Roosevelt Hosp. Sch. Nursing, 1967; student (Alumni scholar) Columbia U., 1968-71; B.A., U. So. Calif., 1972; M.B.A., Pepperdine U., 1980. Staff nurse Columbia-Presbyn. Med. Center, 1967-71; nurse with adolescents UCLA, 1971-72, supr. Neuropsychiat. Inst., 1972-73; nursing adminstr. Central City Community Mental Health Center, Los Angeles, 1973-75; staff nurse in neurology Los Angeles County Med. Center, 1976; staff nurse, nursing coordinator Cedars-Sinai Med. Center, Los Angeles, 1976-80, clin. dir. nursing, 1980—; cons. practical aspects, Los Angeles, 1974—.

MCCLAIN, ELSIE TALLEY, diversified co. exec.; b. Bascom, Fla., Oct. 6, 1927; d. William Russell and Hattie Mae (Benton) Talley; student Jacksonville U., Harvard Bus. Coll., 1975-76, U. N. Fla., 1978-79; children—Elizabeth McClain Jenkins, Leslie Wayne. Sec., USDA, 1945-47; sec., bookkeeper Duval County Sch. Bd., 1959-60; with Patterson Enterprises, Jacksonville, Fla., 1960—, exec. sec., adminstrv. asst., 1971-73, controller, 1973—. Mem. Jacksonville Equal Opportunity Council; bd. dirs. USO Internat.; auctioneer Public TV, 1973-79; tchr. Sunday sch. Presbyterian Ch., ruling elder, 1980-83. Mem. Exec. Women Internat., Women in Constrn., NCR Computer Users Group, Nat. Users Constrn. Group, Adminstrv. Mgmt. Soc., Am. Soc. Personnel Adminstrn. Winner 1st place cooking contest Jacksonville Jour., 1979, 80, 81. Office: Patterson Enterprises PO Drawer 2699 Jacksonville FL 32203

MCCLAIN, JUDITH KATHERINE, marketing executive; b. Fort Smith, Ark., Sept. 30, 1943; d. Harry L. and Katherine (Ritchie) Adams; m. Jerry C. McClain, Mar. 8, 1965 (div. Feb. 1976); children—John Adams, Scott Clowers. B.S. Ed., U. Ark., 1966. Fin. pub. relations Allied Bancshares, Houston, 1975-77; dir. advt. Mecca Devel., Houston, 1977-78; dir. devel. Am. Productivity Ctr., Houston, 1978-79; self-employed mktg. cons., Houston, 1979-81; dir. bus. planning ISD Inc., Houston, 1981-85; mktg. cons. Central Houston, Inc., 1985—. Mem. Buffalo Bayou Sesquicentennial Park Com. Mem. Internat. Facility Mgmt. Assn., Soc. Mktg. Profl. Services, Downtown Houston Assn. Houston C. of C. (mem. downtown com. 1982-84, chairperson subcom.). Episcopalian. Clubs: River Oaks (sec. 1981), Bus. Women's Exchange (sec. 1981) (Houston).

MCCLAIN, LENA IRENE, educator; b. Brenham, Tex., Nov. 3, 1941; d. Earnest and Bertha (Clemons) Jones; m. Will Judge McClain, Nov. 2, 1963; children—Willene Renee, Christopher Bernard. B.S., Tex. So. U., 1971, M.Ed., 1973. Tchr., Burbank Elem. Sch., Houston, 1971-72, tchr. Houston Gardens Elem. Sch., 1972— math. coordinator, 1976—, grade chairperson, 1979—; supervising tchr. Houston Ind. Sch. Dist., 1976-81, demonstration tchr., number sense sponsor, 1977-83; mem. Task Force for Ednl. Excellence, Houston, 1982-83. Author: Hands on Mathematics, 1982. Leader, Camp Fire Girls, Houston, 1979. Recipient Acad. Excellence award Tex. So. U., Houston, 1969; NSF award U. Houston, 1978, Tchr. of Yr. award Houston Ind. Sch. Dist., 1982; named Outstanding Young Educator, Houston Jr. C. of C., 1974. Mem. NEA, Ednl. Leadership Inst., Houston Tchrs. Assn., Bus. and Profl. Women (v.p. 1983), Tex. State Tchrs., Houston Council Edn. Democrat. Pentecost. Clubs: Women's Christian Econ. (pres. 1971-83); Century; Shepherd Park Plaza Civic (Houston). Home: 1033 Richelieu Houston TX 77018 Office: Houston Gardens Elem Sch 6820 Homestead Rd Houston TX 77028

MCCLAIN, SHIRLA ROBINSON, teacher educator; b. Akron, Ohio, Feb. 4, 1935; d. Dumas Defoe and Marcella Carolyn (Macbeth) Robinson; B.S. in Edn. with distinction, U. Akron, 1956, M.S. in Edn., 1970, Ph.D. in Edn., 1975; m. Henry Lee McClain, Apr. 6, 1957; children—Kelli Jesselyn, Scott Jay. Tchr. Akron Pub. Schs., 1956-65, remedial tchr., 1966-71, ednl. specialist, 1971-76; asst. prof. edn. Kent (Ohio) State Univ., 1976-81, asso. prof. edn., 1981—; multicultural edn. cons. Gt. Rivers council Girl Scout U.S.A., 1981-82; mem. State of Ohio Library Bd., 1979-84; bd. dirs. Summit County Hist. Soc., 1981-84, 2d v.p., 1982-84; mem. City of Akron Human Relation Commn., 1982-83; trustee Akron Urban League, 1980-83; mem. WAKR Community Relations Bd., 1976-81. Recipient Black Applause award for outstanding achievement in edn., Phi Beta Sigma, 1980; Achievement award Akron Urban League, 1975. Mem. Nat. Council Social Studies, Assn. for Tchr. Edn., Am. Assn. for Colls. of Tchr. Educators, Multicultural Edn. Spl. Interest Group, Phi Delta Kappa. Episcopalian. Home: 865 Packard Dr Akron OH 44320 Office: 404 White Hall College of Edn Kent State Univ Kent OH 44242

MCCLAY, MERI JANE, med. technologist; b. Colorado Springs, Colo., May 9, 1944; d. Charles David and Alice (Livengood) McC.; B.A., U. Oreg., 1966. Med. technologist Sacred Heart Hosp., Eugene, Oreg., 1966-67, Highland Alameda County Hosp., Oakland, Calif., 1967-68; chief technologist Arlington (Tex.) Community Hosp., 1968-72, chief technologist Fannin County Hosp., Bonham, Tex., 1972—. Mem. Am. Soc. Clin. Pathologists (registered, affiliate). Presbyterian. Home: PO Box 273 Bonham TX 75418 Office: 504 Lipscomb St Bonham TX 75418

MCCLEAN, LENORA JAMES, dean, nursing educator; b. Jesup, Ga., Apr. 22, 1937; d. Ealey and Mary (Howard) Hayes; diploma St. Vincent's Hosp. Sch. Nursing, Jacksonville, Fla., 1958; B.S., Fla. State U., 1961; M.A., Tchrs. Coll., Columbia U., 1963, Ed.D., 1972; m. Robert William McClean, July 13, 1963; children—Anne-Marie St. John, Sharman Danielle, Tara Lauren, Marshall Hayes. Asst. prof. nursing Fla. State U., Tallahassee, 1963, Tchrs. Coll., Columbia U., N.Y.C., 1964-73; clinician Bronx Psychiat. Center, 1966-73; prof. SUNY, Stony Brook, 1973-81, dean Sch. Nursing, 1981—; cons. intervention in self-destructive behavior. Vis. fellow Sturt Coll. Advanced Edn., Bedford Park, South Australia, 1981-82; grantee. Mem. N.Y. State Nurses Assn. (v.p. 1980-82), Am. Nurses Assn. Democrat. Episcopalian. Author: (with Dorothy Anderson) Indentifying Suicide Potential, 1976; contbg. author: Comprehensive Psychiatric Nursing, 1979, 2d edit., 1982; also articles. Office: SUNY Stony Brook NY 11794

MCCLELLAN, JOAN LURELLE, marketing executive; b. Santa Monica, Calif., Aug. 13, 1946; d. Clarence S. and Virginia L. (Woodruff) McC.; m. Kurt Parnell Kupper, June 18, 1966 (div. 1974); children—Kristopher Parnell, Damon Stuart; m. Benedictus Hubertus H. Bolsman, Feb. 6, 1983. B.S. with honors, Calif. Poly. State U., 1973. Dir. ops. McClellan Corp. Internat., Woodland Hills, Calif., 1974-78, v.p., 1978-81, pres., chief exec. officer, 1981—. Editor/pub. newsletters and research surveys. Mem. exec. com. Calif. Gov.'s Conf. on Tourism. Mem. Hotel Sales and Mktg. Mgmt. Assn. (dir. 1981-83; Outstanding Mem. of Yr. 1981), Travel and Tourism Research Assn. (chair 1986, dir. 1983-84), Calif. Travel Industry Assn. (treas. 1986, dir. 1984), Postal Customer Council (sec. 1980-84), Pacific Area Travel Assn., Am. Soc. Travel Agts., Assn. Travel Mktg. Execs., Caribbean Tourism Assn. Democrat. Presbyterian. Avocations: sports; dance; antique clock collecting; Japanese print collecting; languages. Home: 4935 Serrania Ave Woodland Hills CA 91364 Office: 21318 Dumetz Rd Woodland Hills CA 91364

MCCLELLAND, SHARON ELIZABETH, nurse; b. Milw., May 2, 1945; d. Henry William and Caroline Elizabeth (Kuehn) Luedtke; m. Donald Arthur McClelland, Oct. 14, 1967; children—Kristina, Matthew, Mark, Kimberly, Kari Lynn. B.S., U. Wis., 1967; M.S. in Nursing, U. Calif.-San Francisco, 1970. R.N. Nursing instr. Mt. Sinai Hosp. Sch. Nursing, Chgo., 1967-68; staff nurse Mills Meml. Hosp., San Mateo, Calif., 1969-70; instr. clin. nursing DeAnza Coll., Cupertino, Calif., 1972-73, coordinator, nursing asst. program, 1973-77. Author: Manual for Implementing a Nursing Assistant Program, 1975; Basic Patient Care, 1977, 3rd edit., 1984. Leader Santa Clara County council Girl Scouts U.S.A., Los Gatos, Calif., 1977, 79. Mem. Health Services Edn. Council (dir. 1977-78), Mortar Bd., Sigma Theta Tau. Republican. Mormon.

MCCLENDON, BETTY JEAN, physical education resource educator; b. Closplint, Ky., Feb. 24, 1933; d. Bennie and Ophelia (Copeland) McC. B.S., Tuskegee Inst., 1955; M.S., Mich. State U., 1964; cert. in instructional supervision, Ga. State U., 1974. Cert. phys. edn. supr., Ga. Tchr. phys. edn. Coweta County, Newnan, Ga., 1955-63, Atlanta Pub. Schs., 1963-64, 66-68, 68-74, Area I Office, Atlanta, 1974—; basketball ofcl. nat. and state tournaments. Inducted into Tuskegee Inst. Athletic Hall of Fame, 1983; named Coach of Yr. Atlanta Pub. Schs., 1963-64, First and only State Girls' Track Starter, 1967-84; recipient Outstanding Track and Field Service plaques, 1981-82; 1st female to officiate men's NCAA basketball. Mem. Nat. Assn. Sport Ofcls., Amateur Basketball Assn. of U.S. A. Ofcls. Assn., Ga. Assn. Inter-collegiate Athletics for Women Ofcls., Ga. Assn. for Health, Phys. Edn., Recreation and Dance, Women's Am. Basketball Assn., Atlanta Assn. of Educators, AAHPER, So. Coaches and Ofcls. Assn., Atlanta Quarterback Club, Ga. Women Basketball Assn., Amateur Softball Assn., Athletic Congress, Phi Delta Kappa. Mem. African Methodist Episcopalian. Ch. Avocation: fishing. Home: 3560 Hogan Rd SW Atlanta GA 30331 Office: Atlanta Pub Schs Area I Office 711 Catherine St SW Atlanta GA 30310

MC CLENDON, MAXINE, artist; b. Leesville, La., Oct. 21, 1931; d. Alfred Harry and Clara (Jackson) McMillan; student Tex. U., 1948-50, Tex. Woman's U., 1950-51, Pan Am. U., 1963-64; m. Edward Edson Nichols, Mar. 28, 1967; children—Patricia Ann, Joan Terri, Christopher, Jennifer. One-man shows include: Art Mus. S. Tex., Corpus Christi, 1971, McAllen (Tex.) Internat. Mus., 1976, Amarillo (Tex.) Art Center, 1982 group shows in Wichita, Kans., 1972, Marietta, Ohio, 1975, Dallas, 1977; represented in permanent collections: Mus. Internat. Folk Art, Santa Fe, Ark. Mus. Fine Art, Little Rock, McAllen Internat. Mus., Lauren Rogers Mus., Laurel, Miss.; commns. include: Caterpillar Corp., Peoria, Ill., Union Bank Switzerland, N.Y.C., Crocker Bank, Los Angeles, Tarleton U., Tex., Hyatt Regency, Ft. Worth Forbes Inc., San Francisco, First Savs. & Loan, Shreveport, La., Continental Plaza, Ft. Worth. curator Mexican folk art McAllen Internat. s., 1974-80. Recipient judges award 4th Nat. Marietta, 1975, numerous others. Mem. World Crafts Council, Am. Crafts Council (Tex. rep. 1976-80), Tex. Designer/Craftsmen (pres. 1973-74). Christian Scientist. Home and Studio: 2018 Sharyland St Mission TX 78572

MCCLENDON, RUTH ANN, psychotherapist, consultant; b. Cleve., Mar. 22, 1943; d. James Edward and Jeanne Ruth (Moore) Surrell; m. Leslie B. Kadis, Dec. 29, 1978. B.A., U. Mich., 1965, M.S.W., 1967. Lic. social worker, marriage, family, and child counselor, Calif. Asst. clin. prof. Langely Porter Neuropsychiat. Inst., U. Calif.-San Francisco, 1976—; clin. faculty The Fielding Inst., Santa Barbara, Calif., 1974—; dir. Family Devel. Ctr., Aptos, Calif., 1980—. Contbr. articles to profl. jours. Mem. Internat. Transactional Analysis Assn. (past pres.), Am. Group Psychotherapy Assn. (past dir.), Am. Acad. Psychotherapists, Nat. Assn. Social Workers, Am. Family Therapy Assn., Am. Marriage and Family Therapy Assn. Author: Chocolate Pudding and other Approaches to Intensive Multiple Family Therapy, 1983. Address: PO Box 190 Aptos CA 95003

MCCLESKEY, MELISSA DANNELLY, public relations executive; b. Dallas, Apr. 16, 1959; d. Charles Rosser and Wanda Lane (Jones) Dannelly; m. Dennis Wayne McCleskey, Sept. 18, 1982. B.J., U. Tex.-Austin, 1979; postgrad. U. Dallas, 1980-81. Asst. dir. communications North Tex. Commn., Dallas/Ft. Worth, 1980; account supr. Pharr Cox Communications, Dallas, 1980—. Vol., Tri-Delta Alum Group/Tri-Delta Charity Antique Show, Dallas, 1981—; mem. com. Big D Beat Charity Ball-Heart Assn., Dallas, 1983—; vol.

Backstagers, Dallas, 1983—. Recipient Matrix award for internal corp. communications/print, 1984. Mem. Women in Communications (chmn. scholarship 1984, chmn. fundraising 1985, treas. 1985-87). Republican. Roman Catholic. Home: 4206 Valley Ridge Rd Dallas TX 75220 Office: Pharr Cox Communications 7067 Twin Hills Suite 400 Dallas TX 75231

MC CLINTOCK, BARBARA, scientist; b. Hartford, Conn., June 16, 1902; B.S., Cornell U., 1923, M.A., 1925, Ph.D. in Botany, 1927; Sc.D. (hon.), U. Rochester, 1947, Western Coll., 1949, Smith Coll., 1958, U. Mo., 1968, Williams Coll., 1972. Asst. in botany Cornell U., Ithaca, N.Y., 1924-27, instr., 1927-31; asst. in plant breeding, 1934-36, Andrew D. White prof.-at-large, 1965; NRC fellow Calif. Inst. Tech., 1931-33; Guggenheim fellow Bot. Inst. U. Freiburg, 1933-34; asst. prof. botany U. Mo., 1936-41; staff mem. Carnegie Inst., Washington, 1941-67, Disting. Service mem., from 1967; researcher Cold Spring Harbor (N.Y.) Lab. Recipient Kimber Genetics award, 1967; Nat. Medal Sci., 1970; Rosenstiel award, 1978; Lasker Prize for basic med. research, 1978; Nobel Prize in physiology or medicine, 1983. Mem. Nat. Acad. Sci., Am. Soc. Naturalists, Am. Philos. Soc., Bot. Soc. Am., Genetics Soc. Am. (v.p. 1939, pres. 1945). Research in cytogenetics of maize. Office: Cold Spring Harbor Lab Cold Spring Harbor NY 11724*

MCCLINTOCK, SHIRLEY SPRAGUE, govt. ofcl.; b. Flushing, N.Y., Jan. 3, 1928; d. George Wilkie and Mary Dorothea (O'Rourke) Sprague; student Cornell U., 1949-51; m. John William McClintock, Sept. 22, 1951; children—Barton, Charles, Scott. Personnel adminstr. Gen. Motors Co., 1952-54, analyst, overseas ops., N.Y.C., 1965-68; mem. U.S. Govt. Transition Com., 1968-69; housing adminstr. HUD, N.Y.C., 1969-79, 82—, Buffalo, 1979-82. . Bd. dirs. Soc. Prevention Cruelty to Children Mass., 1962-64; sec. LWV, N.Y.C., 1960-62. Recipient Cert. Superior Service, HUD, 1975. Mem. Cornell Club Greater Buffalo (pres. 1981—), Cornell U. Alumni Assn. Club: Cornell (N.Y.C.). Home: 541 E 20th St New York NY 10010 Office: 26 Federal Plaza New York NY 10278

MCCLINTON, EDNA GRACE, real estate broker; b. Windom, Kans., Jan. 2, 1925; d. Ira Francis and Ella Nancy (Joslin) Hites; m. Arthur LeRoy Copeland, Feb. 20, 1943 (div. 1948); children—Clair Arthur, Richard Wade; m. Raymond Arthur McClinton, May 26, 1952 (div.); children—Roxane Dora, Renee Ella, Tamara Yvonne, James Ray, Phillip Lee. Grad. high sch., Albion, Pa. Owner, broker McClinton Real Estate, Meadville, Pa., 1967-70; owner McClinton Co., Meadville, 1968—; beauty tchr. Wel Mar, Meadville, 1983—; owner rooming house, Meadville, 1975—. Mem. Bus. and Profl. Women, Grange. Methodist. Avocations: rebuilding older homes; fishing; travel. Home: 827 Water St Meadville PA 16335 Office: Meadville-McClinton Real Estate and Notary Service 827 Water St Meadville PA 16335

MCCLINTON, SUZANNE YVETTE, financial service firm executive, consultant; b. Chgo., Sept. 8, 1955; d. Willie B. and Essie (Pugh) McDonald; m. Marlon McClinton, Sept. 3, 1977; 1 child, Jamila Makini. B.A., U. Ill.-Chgo., 1976; M.B.A., U. Chgo., 1978. Security analyst, portfolio mgr. First Nat. Bank Chgo., 1977-79; co-mgr. CEDCO Capital Corp., Chgo., 1979-81; mgr. CEDCO Comml. Credit, Chgo., 1981-82; pres., owner McClinton Mgmt. Services, Chgo., 1981—; prof. Chgo. State U., 1983-85; dir. Fin. Ind. Inst., Chgo., Kelly Chem. Co., Chgo., Internat. Women's Econ. Devel. Corp., Chgo., Kelly Chem. Co., Chgo. Contbr. articles to profl. publs. Mem. steering com. South Shore Community Credit Union, Chgo., 1980-82; mem. Chgo. Regional Purchasing Council, 1984—, Probe, Inc., Chgo., 1982. Recipient Leadership award Images, 1984, Kizzy award Black Women's Hall of Fame, 1985. Mem. Nat. Black M.B.A. Assn., Black Alumni Assn., Soc. Fin. Analysts, Cosmopolitan C. of C. Avocations: reading; travel. Home: 7217 S Crandon Ave Chicago IL 60649 Office: McClinton Mgmt Services 407 S Dearborn Suite 1150 Chicago IL 60605

MCCLISH, C. POLLY, finance executive; b. Lubbock, Tex., May 30, 1933; d. Hershell Lee and Carrie Maude (Johnson) Ward; four children by previous marriage. A.A. in Bus. Psychology, Amarillo Jr. Coll., Tex., 1966; B.Acctg., West Tex. State U., 1968, B.B.A., 1970. Asst. credit mgr., collection mgr. Woolco Inc., Amarillo, Tex., 1968-74; credit mgr. Sakowitz Inc., Amarillo, 1974-79; sales mgr. Med. and Profl. Mgmt. Service, Galveston, Tex., 1979-82, v.p., gen. mgr., 1982-83; pres., bd. dirs. Colelli & Assocs., Galveston, 1983—; cons. and lectr. in field. Mem. adv. bd. Tex. Edn. Commn.; mem. aux. U. Tex. Med. Br.; mem., div. chmn. United Fund. Named Outstanding Credit Exec. of Yr., Tex., 1976. Mem. Internat. Consumer Credit Assn. (legis. adv. council), Am. Collectors Assn. (legis. adv. com., condr. numerous seminars), Asso. Credit Bur., Retail Mchts. Assn. Tex. (pres.), Nat. Assn. Female Execs., Soc. Cert. Consumer Credit Execs., Exec. Career Women, Bus. and Profl. Women (past pres.), C. of C. (pres.'s club, honor guard, Galveston chpt.), Credit Mgmt. Assn. Tex. (past pres.), Credit Women Internat. (past pres. Lone Star council), Am. Collectors Assn. Tex. (pres.), Forgery Investigation Assn. Tex. Club: Propeller (Galveston). Address: 3220 69th St F-2 Galveston TX 77551

MCCLOSKEY, SARAH HELEN, psychiatric nurse specialist; b. Bellwood, Pa., Aug. 6, 1943; d. Charles William and Bertha A. (Bell) McCloskey; m. Richard J. Webb, Dec. 22, 1967 (div. 1975). Grad. Polyclinic Hosp. Sch. Nursing, 1964; B.S. in Nursing, Pa. State U., 1973. R.N., Pa. Emergency room nurse Polyclinic Hosp., Harrisburg, Pa., 1964-69; sch. nurse Bellwood Sch. Dist. (Pa.), 1969-72; psychiat. nurse supr. Altoona Ctr. Mental Health (Pa.), 1976—; cons. Altoona Area Sch. Dist., 1983. Instr. CPR and first aid ARC, Altoona, 1982-84. Mem. Am. Nurses Found. Century Club, NOW, Sigma Theta Tau, Republican. Presbyterian. Lodge: Order of Eastern Star. Home: 525 7th St Bellwood PA 16617 Office: Altoona Ctr 1515 4th St Altoona PA 16602

MCCLOUD, SARAH LEE, nurse; b. Blanche, N.C., Mar. 11, 1936; d. James Lindsay and Rosa Estelle (Mecks) Saunders; m. Jack Raeford McCloud, Jan. 2, 1957; children—Sheryl Jean, Jacqueline Merle, Jack. Diploma in nursing, Lincoln Hosp. Sch. Nursing, 1956. Staff nurse Duke U. Med. Center (N.C.), 1956-61, Washington Hosp. Center, 1962-70, Capitol Hill Hosp., Washington, 1978—. Democrat.

MCCLUNG, CHRISTINA JUNE, training company executive; b. Newark, N.J., Jan. 19, 1948; d. Frederick and Maria (Dallinger) Palensar; m. Kenneth Austin McClung, Mar. 21, 1975. B.A., Kean Coll., 1970; M.A. in Edn., Seton Hall U., 1973; Ed.D. in Instructional Tech., U. So. Calif., 1976. Tchr. Chatham Twp. (N.J.) pub. schs., 1970-74; instructional designer Tratec Co., Los Angeles, 1976-79; asst. prof. Lehman Coll., Bronx, N.Y., 1977-79; ind. cons., 1978-80; v.p., bd. dirs. Instructional Design Group, Morristown N.J., 1980—. Mem. Nat. Soc. Performance Instrn. (program chmn. N.J. chpt.), Phi Delta Kappa. Author 5 book series Computers for Professionals, 1983. Office: Instructional Design Group 20 Community Pl Morristown NJ 07930

MCCLUNG, SISTER ROSE ANNELLE, univ. dean; b. Oklahoma City, Dec. 16, 1925; d. Guy Lamont and Gladys T. (Noret) McClung; B.S. in Bus. Adminstrn., Our Lady of Lake Coll., 1946; M.A. in Econs., Cath. U. Am., 1965. Tchr. bus. St. Francis Xavier High Sch., Alexandria, La., 1948-49, Providence Central High Sch., Alexandria, 1949-56, Providence High Sch., San Antonio, 1956-62; chmn. dept. bus. adminstrn., Our Lady of Lake U., San Antonio, 1962-74, dir. div. bus. studies, 1974-80, dean Sch. Bus. and Public Adminstrn., 1980—. Recipient Outstanding Alumna in Profession award, Our Lady of Lake U., 1979; named Coll. Bus. Tchr. of Yr. Tex. Bus. Edn. Assn., 1979. Mem. AAUP, Am. Acctg. Assn., Am. Econ. Assn., Nat. Assn. Female Execs., Data Processing Mgmt. Assn., Freedom Found., Univ. Aviation Assn., Soc. Logistics Engrs., World Future Soc., Nat. Bus. Edn. Assn., Nat. Assn. Bus. Tchr. Edn. Am. Soc. Tng. and Devel. Roman Catholic. Home and Office: 411 SW 24th St San Antonio TX 78285

MCCLURE, ANGELINE KITCHENS, human resource management executive, consultant; b. Macon, Ga., Dec. 26, 1945; d. Benjamin Grady and Reba (Atkins) Kitchens; m. Donald Wayne McClure, Nov. 2, 1974; children by a previous marriage—Leanna Kay Oliver Linnekohl, Gregory Alan Oliver. B.A. in Social Sci., Hollins Coll. (Va.), 1971; postgrad. U. Va., 1972, Commonwealth U. of Va., 1972. Tchr., Roanoke City Pub. Schs. (Va.), 1971-73, Twiggs County Pub. Schs., Jeffersonville, Ga., 1973-75; human resource specialist Charter Med. Corp., Macon, 1975-79; personnel cons. Mut. Personnel Service, Macon, 1980-81; human resource mgr. So. Trust Ins. Co., Macon, 1981-84; mgmt. cons., owner Motivational Mgmt. Resources, Macon, 1984—; mem. employer's relation com. Ga. Dept. Labor, 1983. Mem. Gov.'s Leadership Forum for Post-Secondary Edn., State of Ga., 1983; co-chmn. employers' relations com. Am. Cancer Soc., Macon, 1984, 85; Mem. Middle Ga. Personnel Assn. (pub. relations dir. 1982, v.p. 1983, pres. 1984, bd. dirs. 1985), Am. Soc. Personnel Adminstrs., Nat. Assn. Female Execs., Career Women's Network, Middle Ga. Employers Assn., Bus. and Industry Relations Com., Macon C. of C. Baptist. Home: 3076 Tiffin Circle Macon GA 31204 Office: Motivational Mgmt Resources PO Box 6735 Macon GA 31208

MCCLURE, ANN ELKINTON, trade association executive; b. Ames, Iowa, June 21, 1936; d. Charles Moore and Cecelia (Daniels) Elkinton; m. Stanley G. McClure, June 9, 1957; children—Kevin George, Michael Bruce. B.A. with honors in Journalism, Wash. State U., 1958. News editor Pullman Herald (Wash.), 1958; copywriter Sta. KSSS, Colorado Springs, 1969-70; pub. relations/tournaments dir. Broadmoor Hotel and Golf Club, Colorado Springs, 1970-71; program dir. YMCA, Bowie, Md., 1971-73; tennis teaching pro Annapolis Racquet Club/Arlington Tennis Club, 1971-80; club gen. mgr. Ct. Control, Inc., Arlington, Va., 1980-84; dir. meetings and membership Assoc. Landscape Contractors Am., 1985—; dir. Prince George's County Jr. Tennis League, Bowie, 1971-73; sec. Bowie Recreation Council, 1975-77. Author: Prince George's County, 1973. Mem. Women in Communications, Inc. (pres. 1970-71), U.S. Profl. Tennis Assn. (local rep. 1980-82, D.C. pro of yr. 1981), Phi Beta Kappa, Phi Kappa Phi. Club: Bowie Women's Tennis (pres. 1975-76). Home: 200 N Maple Ave #617 Falls Church VA 22046 Office: Assoc Landscape Contractors Am 405 N Washington St Falls Church VA 22046

MCCLURE, ANN L., lawyer; b. Mt. Vernon, Ohio, Dec. 26, 1946; d. W. Roger and Marian E. (McBurney) Levering; m. J. Kenneth McClure, Apr. 6, 1981; children—Andrew Daniel, James Stephen, Mark Ian. B.A., Hanover Coll., 1968; M.L.S., Ind. U., 1970, M.B.A., 1973; J.D., South Tex. Coll. Law, 1976. Bar: Tex. 1976; librarian Southwestern Consol. Sch. Dist. Ind., Hanover, 1968-69; reference librarian Ind. State Library, Indpls., 1970-71; individual practice of law, Wichita Falls, Tex., 1976—; instr. Midwestern State U., 1982—; city atty., Holliday, Tex., 1984-86. Bd. dirs. Northside Girls Club, 1983-86, KIDZ-Channel 13, 1983—, Library Bd., Wichita Falls, 1986—. Mem. ABA, Tex. Bar Assn., Wichita Falls Bars Assn., AAUW (pres. 1981-83), Bus. and Profl. Womens Club, LWV. Democrat. Presbyterian. Office: Ann L McClure 1907 Kemp St Wichita Falls TX 76309

MCCLURE, BROOKE RICE, marketing research consultant; b. Biloxi, Miss., May 25, 1954; d. Brooks Terry and Marilyn (May) Rice; m. Thomas James McClure; children—Conner Hale, Scott Thomas. B.A. in Psychology, U. Ark., 1975; M.A. in Clin. Psychology, U. Mo., 1977. Account exec. New Product Insights, Kansas City, Mo., 1977-79; pres. BRM Research, Inc., Conway, Ark., 1979—. Active United Way, Conway, 1985; Mem. Qualitative Research Cons. Assn., Conway C. of C., Phi Beta Kappa. Clubs: Altrusa (Conway). Jr. Aux. Home: 836 Donaghey Conway AR 72032 Office: BRM Research Inc 915 Oak St Conway AR 72032

MCCLURE, DOROTHY MAE, truck paint and body shop executive; b. Corsicanna, Tex., June 24, 1924; d. Jess Austin and Fannie Mae (Robinson) Clift; m. Rhumelous Leroy McClure, Dec. 17, 1941; children—Lee Roy, Karen Darlene, Debbie Laura, Jess Austin. Student pub. schs., Shamrock and Shallowater, Tex. Self-employed interior painter and designer, Whittier, Calif., 1945-51; co-owner/operator truck paint and design co., 1951-55; owner, operator Roy & Dot's Truck Specialties, Montebello, Calif., 1955—. Recipient award of appreciation Crippled Children's Soc., Pomona, Calif., 1982, 1st Place award for truck design Orange County Raceway, 1982, 1st Place award for truck paint and design Sierra Sids, 1983, award of elegance for truck paint and design R.C. Canning, 1985. Mem. Montebello C. of C. Avocations: taking jet powered truck to shows; baseball. Office: Roy & Dot's Truck Specialties 825 S Maple Ave Montebello CA 90640

MCCLURE, FLORENCE HELEN, savings and loan executive, human resource consultant; b. Chgo., July 21, 1930; d. George and Minnie (LaBarbara) Torre; m. Richard D. McClure, Feb. 16, 1952; children—Kimbert, Brian, Douglas, Ronald. Student Ind. U., 1948-50, Kent State U., 1967-68, Lake Erie Coll., Ohio, 1969-70. Elem. sch. tchr., Geneva, Ohio, 1966-71; coordinator traffic dept. True Temper Corp., Saybrook, Ohio, 1971-72; mktg. dir. Peoples Savs. & Loan, Ashtabula, Ohio, 1973-82; pres. Chem. Seal, Inc., Grand Junction, Colo., 1982-85; mktg./personnel dir. Valley Fed. Savs. & Loan, Grand Junction, 1982—; human resource cons., 1985—. Commr., Colo. Housing Authority, Grand Junction, 1985-86; bd. dirs. Alternative Housing Assocs., Grand Junction, 1982—. Mem. Am. Soc. Personnel Adminstrn., Western Slope Personnel Assocs., Grand Junction C. of C. (pub. relations com. 1985—, coll. edn. com. 1983-85). Republican. Roman Catholic. Avocations: walking; reading; travel. Home: 374 1/2 Ridge View Dr #1 Grand Junction CO 81503 Office: Valley Fed Savs & Loan PO Box 400 Grand Junction CO 81502

MC CLURE, MARY ANNE, state senator; b. Milbank, S.D., Apr. 21, 1939; d. Charles Cornelius and Mary Lucille (Whittom) Burges; B.A. magna cum laude, U. S.D., 1961; postgrad. U. Manchester (Eng.), 1961-62; M.P.A., Syracuse U., 1981; m. D.J. McClure, Nov. 17, 1963; 1 dau., Kelly Joanne. Mem. staff U.S. Senator Francis Case, 1959-61; sec. to Lt. Gov. Nils Boe, 1963; exec. sec. to Lewis Dymond, pres. Frontier Airlines, 1963-64; tchr. public schs., Pierre, S.D., 1965-66, Redfield, S.D., 1968-70; mem. S.D. Senate, 1975—, pres. pro tem, 1979-86. Mem. sch. bd. Redfield Ind. Dist., 1970-75. Fulbright scholar; Bush Leadership scholar. Mem. Phi Beta Kappa. Republican. Congregationalist.

MCCLURE, MARY ELLEN, general contractor, restaurant and bar owner; b. Havana, Ark., Apr. 4, 1942; d. Luther Edward and Wilda (Harger) Vaughn; m. Clinton Eugene McClure, Oct. 5, 1960; children—Victoria Lynn, Tonya Renee, Charles Eugene. Cosmetologist, Arroyo Grande, Calif., 1960-64; caterer, Porterville, Calif., 1968-78; real estate broker, Porterville, 1968—; gen. contractor, Porterville, 1969—; owner restaurant and bar, Porterville, 1985—. Republican. Avocations: talking with people; boating. Home: 22665 Ave 178M Porterville CA 93257 Office: Charlie's 1531 N Main St Porterville CA 93257

MCCOLLOM, LESLIE LOUISE, lawyer; b. Oklahoma City, July 5, 1949; d. Raymond Dayton and Christine Ovlla (McCullough) McCollom; m. William Fred Hughes, Jan. 7, 1978 (div. 1982). B.A., Rice U., 1972, M.A., 1975; A.B.D., Rice U., 1975; J.D. with honors, U. Tex.-Austin, 1980. Bar: Tex. 1980. Law clk. Feeney, O'Hanlon & Moore, Austin, Tex., 1980; shareholder atty. 1300 Guadalupe, Austin, 1980-81; pvt. practice law, San Antonio, 1982-83; ptnr. Wood & McCollom, San Antonio, 1984—; asst. coordinator, mem. steering com. 10th Nat. Conf. on Women and the Law, U. Tex. Law Sch., Austin, 1978-79. Mem. Women's Law Ctr., San Antonio, 1982—; vol. Lloyd Doggett for Senate campaign, 1983-84. Rice U. grantee, 1974-75; Rice U. Women's Club scholar, 1972-73. Mem. State Bar Tex., ABA, Bexar County Women's Bar Assn. (chmn. com. on women's law ctr.), San Antonio Bar Assn., Travis County Women Attys. Assn. Democrat. Office: Wood and McCollom Interfirst Financial Ctr NW Suite 575 6243 1-H 10 West San Antonio TX 78201

MCCOLLUM, ADRIENNE MARIE, consulting company executive; b. Los Angeles, Sept. 14, 1937; d. Luther Slayton and Joe Ann Marie (Goodson) Slayton Hale; m. Rubin Dale McCollum, June 14, 1959; children—Cheryl Kimberly, Kristin Elise, Kacie Charmion. A.A., Los Angeles City Coll., 1957; B.S., Calif. State U., 1972; Ed.D., U. Mass., 1975. Grad. asst. U. Mass., Amherst, 1972, assoc. to dir. urban edn., 1972-74; exec. dir. Springfield Day Nursery (Mass.), 1974-75; sr. assoc. Roy Littlejohn and Assocs., Washington, 1975-77; v.p. Thomas Buffington & Assocs., Washington, 1977-79; pres. Research Assessment Mgmt., Inc., cons., Silver Spring, Md., 1980—; cons. Dept. Edn., Washington, 1978-82, Child Devel. Assn., Washington, 1973-74, D.C. Sch. System, 1980. Contbr. articles to profl. jours. Active Tots 'n Teens, Howard County, Md., 1981—. Mem. exec. bd. trustees Benedict Coll. Recipient Appreciation award Bur. Edn. Handicapped, Washington, 1978. Mem. Am. Assn. Black Women Entrepreneurs, Nat. Council Negro Women (service award 1981), Zeta Phi Beta (meritorious award 1981, 85). Presbyterian. Office: Research Assessment Mgmt Inc 1320 Fenwick Ln Silver Spring MD 20910

MCCOLLUM, SHIRLEY WISURI, executive suite company executive; b. Iron River, Mich., Dec. 1, 1932; d. William Leonard and Anna Lydia (Makela) Wisuri; m. Samuel Clayton McCollum, Nov. 10, 1951; children—Sandra Lee, Deed Annette McCollum Broholm. M.A., Sangamon State U., 1975. Coordinator, Big Brother/Sister Orgn., Springfield, Ill., 1975-76; adminstr. Sangamon-Cass CETA, Springfield, 1976-78; pres. Bus. World, Atlanta, 1979—, Bus. World Office Network, Atlanta, 1985—. Pres. LWV, Springfield, 1967-69; mem. Ill. adv. com. U.S. Commn. Civil Rights, Chgo., 1974-78; chmn. 4 County Mental Health Survey, Springfield, 1974-75; mem. North Fulton Mental Health Adv. Com., Atlanta, 1980-82. Mem. Women Bus. Owners (sec. 1985—), Ga. Secretarial Services Assn., Jr. League (pres. Springfield chpt. 1970-71), Assn. Jr. Leagues (N.Y. area dir. 1970-73). Republican. Presbyterian. Avocations: golf; bridge; gardening. Office: Bus World 5901-B Peachtree Dunwoody Suite 500 Atlanta GA 30328

MCCONNELL, LORNA ANN, insurance agent; b. Weehawken, N.J., Oct. 15, 1948; d. Joseph Washington and Florence Mary (Sunkel) McC. B.S., Trenton State Coll., 1971. Tchr., North Plainfield High Sch., N.J., 1972-73; personnel dir. Canrad-Hanovia Inc., Newark, 1973-76; ins. agt. Schlitt Ins. Services, Inc., Vero Beach, Fla., 1976—. Drive chmn., bd. dirs. United Way, Vero Beach, 1977-83; pres. River Trees Property Owners Assn., Roseland, Fla., 1985. Mem. Indian River Assn. Ins. Agts. (pres. 1985—). Democrat. Roman Catholic. Avocations: tennis; bicycling; boating. Office: Schlitt Ins Services Inc 321 21st St Vero Beach FL 32960

MCCONNELL, MARGARET LEE, management consulting company executive; b. Hazard, Ky., Mar. 31, 1937; d. Wallace Mason and Levisa Mae (Goff) Combs; m. John Joel Watson, Oct. 5, 1968 (div. 1970); children—Kevin, Alissa, Michelle, Patrick; m. Kent Rawls McConnell, Apr. 23, 1970 (div. 1977); 1 child, Fiona Siobhan. B.A., summa cum laude, U. Ky., 1961; postgrad. U. Mass., 1967-68, U. Oxford (Eng.), 1968. Sci. editor, researcher Vanderbilt Med. Ctr., Nashville, 1976-85; spl. rep. George S. May Internat. Co., Park Ridge, Ill., 1986—. Author research papers. Sec. Charity League of Ashland, 1967; exec. sec. Nashville Arts and Edn. 1971; active Nashville Symphony Guild, 1972; vol. counselor Ednl. Found. Fgn. Study, 1986. NDEA fellow, 1967. Mem. Nat. Assn. Exec. Females, AAUW, Phi Beta Kappa. Democrat. Presbyterian. Avocations: travel; needlework; writing; reading; skin-diving. Home: 10 Shady Ln Covington LA 70433 Office: George S May Internat Co 111 S Washington St Park Ridge IL 60068

MC CONNELL, MARGARET MAHLER (MRS. J.H. TYLER MCCONNELL), civic worker; b. Wilmington, Del., July 3, 1944; d. John Anthony and Maggie Naomi (Davis) Mahler; A.A., Marjorie Webster Coll., 1964; m. James Hoge Tyler McConnell, Apr. 25, 1973. Sec., CIA, Washington, 1964-65, Hercules, Inc., Wilmington, 1965-66; with Delaware Trust Co., Wilmington, 1966-73, asst. corp. sec., 1969-72, asst. v.p., 1972-73. Bd. dirs., corp. sec. Del. Mus. Natural History, Wilmington, 1969-79; asst. sec., treas. Cecil County (Md.) Breeders' Fair, 1969-75; sec., mem. exec. com. Fair Hill (Md.) Races, 1969-75; bd. dirs. Wilmington Vis. Nurse Assn., 1974—, sec., 1982-85; bd. dirs. Brandywine YMCA, Wilmington, 1977-82, Del. Art Mus., 1983—, Soc. Four Seasons. Mem. Nat., Del. assns. bank women, Nat. Steeplechase & Hunt Assn., Del. Soc. Fine Arts. Democrat. Episcopalian. Clubs: Farmington Country, (Va.), River, Bath and Tennis; Everglades (Palm Beach, Fla.). Home: 805 Snuff Mill Rd Wilmington DE 19807 also 400 S Ocean Blvd Palm Beach FL 33480

MCCONNELL, MARILYN LEIGH, lawyer; b. Cheltenham, Pa. Jan. 16, 1957; d. William John and Joan Marilyn (Floyd) McC. B.A., Miami U., Oxford, Ohio, 1978; J.D., Ohio State U., 1981. Bar: Ohio 1982. Staff asst. Honorable Charles A. Vanik, Washington, 1979; sole practice, Columbus, Ohio, 1982—. Mem. ABA, Ohio Bar Assn., Columbus Bar Assn., Creditors' Rights Com. Republican. Mem. Grace Brethren Ch. Home: 78 W California St Columbus OH 43202 Office: 999 S High St Columbus OH 43206

MCCONNELL, SHARON DIANE, construction company executive, consultant; b. Providence, Oct. 13, 1945; d. David Harold and Florence Sarah (Stabenow) Cashman; m. William Andrew McConnell, Sept. 19, 1964; 1 child, David Andrew. Student R.I. Sch. Nursing, 1963-64, Newburgh City Coll., 1964-65, R.I. Jr. Coll., 1965, Mohegan Coll., 1980. Med. sec., nursing asst. Kent County Hosp., Warwick, R.I., 1968-71; owner Craft Cottage, Warwick, 1971-74; community service dir. ARC, Providence, 1974-76, cons., Hartford, Conn., 1977-79, exec. dir., New London, Conn., 1979-81, cons., Palm Beach, Fla., 1982—; pres. Tri-M-Services, Inc., West Palm Beach, Fla., 1982—; activities dir. Casa Del Monte, West Palm Beach, 1981-84. Author weekly column on crafts Warwick Beacon. Organizer Program TAP-Telephone Assurance Program R.I., 1975, Volunteer Program, Warwick, Family Ct. Program, Providence; founder Troop LymeCt; youth chmn. ARC, Warwick, 1972, bd. dirs., 1968—; steering com. Rape Crisis Ctr., Providence, 1972; den leader, coach Narragansett Council Boy Scouts Am., 1970—; bd. dirs. Camp Fire R.I., Conn., Fla., J.F.K. Hosp. Aux., 1968—; disaster asst. ARC. Recipient Hidden Heroine award Girl Scouts U.S.A.; Dist. Award of Merit Boy Scouts Am.; Commendation, Gov. Noel Saint of R.I.; various commendations ARC. Mem. Palms W. C. of C. Republican. Presbyterian. Avocations: ceramics; crewel; swimming; reading. Home: 290 Akron Rd Lake Worth FL 33467 Office: Tri-M-Services Inc 7641 Hooper Rd West Palm Beach FL 33467

MCCORD, CAROL MCCRACKEN, personnel executive; b. Pitts., June 26, 1949; d. Ellis Ray and Ruth (Thomas) McCracken; A.A., So. Sem., 1969; postgrad. Elon & Albright Coll.; m. Thomas McCord, Sept. 4, 1970; 1 son, Jeffrey. Loan asst. Franklin State Bank, Princeton, N.J., 1974-76; cons. Associated Personnel, Humble, Tex., 1978-80; owner Kingwood (Tex.) Personnel, 1980—. Active, Kingwood Community Theater. Mem. Women in Action (dir.), Houston Area Assn. Personnel Cons., Better Bus. Bur., Humble C. of C. Republican. Presbyterian. Office: Kingwood (Tex) Personnel 4802 Shore Hills Kingwood TX 77345

MCCORD, JULIA ANN, internal auditor; b. Waurika, Okla., May 22, 1924; d. William Solon and Eurah Pearl (Watson) Osteen; B.S., Okla. Coll. Liberal Arts, 1968; M.B.A., U. Tampa, 1980; cert. internal auditor; m. Elmer C. McCord, Jr., June 10, 1943 (div. 1974); children—Perry Houston, Linda Ann. Bookkeeper, Dyer & Watkins Ins. Agy., Durant, Okla., 1947-50, Thornton Ins. Agy., Oklahoma City, 1950-51, Gene Strauss Ins. Agy., Kansas City, Mo., 1951-52; controller Fla. Div., Am. Cancer Soc., Tampa, 1968-71; supr. auditing Sch. Bd. Hillsborough County, Tampa, 1973—; tchr. acctg., adult edn. Recipient Disting. Mem. of Yr. award Pres. Round Table of Orgns. of Greater Tampa, 1985. Mem. Inst. Internal Auditors (chpt. bd. govs. 1978-86), Nat. Assn. Accts. (chpt. sec. 1977), Fla. Assn. Sch. Bus. Adminstrs. (pres. 1984-85), LWV, AAUW (ednl. founds. chmn. 1981-82, corr. sec. 1983-86, pres. Tampa br. 1986-88), Limetree Beach Resort Homeowners Assn. (treas., bd. dirs. 1984-86). Methodist. Home: 4209 W Sevilla St Tampa FL 33629 Office: 901 E Kennedy St Tampa FL 33601

MCCORD, LINDA DEYTON, veterinarian, educator; b. Knoxville, Tenn., May 19, 1952; d. James Wendell and Clara Gayle (Doggett) Deyton; m. Patrick Blake McCord, June 17, 1978. B.A. in Biology, West Ga. Coll., Carrollton, 1974; D.V.M., U. Ga.-Athens, 1978. Veterinarian, Glenwood Small Animal Clinic, Decatur, Ga., 1978-79; veterinarian Briarcliff Animal Clinic, Atlanta, 1979-80; asst. prof. animal sci. Ft. Valley State Coll. (Ga.), 1980—. Recipient Gordon Watson award West Ga. Coll., 1970; Tchr. of Yr. award Agri-Demic Forum Ft. Valley State Coll., 1982. Mem. Am. Vet. Med. Assn., Am. Assn. Feline Practitioners, Am. Assn. Sheep and Goat Practitioners, Ga. Vet. Med. Assn., Middle Ga. Vet. Med. Assn. Methodist. Home: Route 4 Box 494 Salem VA 24153 Office: Technology Program PO Box 4370 Fort Valley State Coll Fort Valley GA 31030

MCCORD, MARILYN, marketing executive; b. Dallas; d. A. Ray and Sybil Gloria (Ramey) McCord. B.S., Tex. Tech U., 1974; M.B.A., So. Meth. U., 19. Sales and mktg. engr. Texas Instruments, Austin, 1976-82; sales support specialist Info. Gen., Dallas, 1982; mgr. office automated products InteCom, Plano, Tex., 1983; mgr. bus. planning Mitel, Boca Raton, Fla., 1984-85; dept. mgr. planning Microtel, Boca Raton, 1985—. Methodist. Avocations: numerology; stained glass; walking; reading.

MCCORMACK, GRACE LYNETTE, engineering technician; b. Dallas, Nov. 2; d. Audley and Janice Meredith (Metcalf) McC. Tech. degree, Durham's Coll., 1958; grad. in civil engring., El Centro Coll., 1972; grad. in advanced surveying, Eastfield, 1975. Cert. sr. engr. technician. Contract design technician various engring firms, Dallas, 1958-70; sr. design engr. technician City of Dallas Survey Div., 1970-80, street light div., 1980—. Mem. Nat. Assn. Female Execs., Women's Forum of Am. Mem. Unity Ch. Avocations: numerology, astrology, aerobics, boating, metaphysics. Home: 1428 Meadowbrook Ln Irving TX 75061 Office: 320 W Jefferson St Dallas TX 75203

MCCORMACK, JUDITH GAIL, medical technologist; b. Chgo., Oct. 4, 1939; d. Milton and Marie Hedwig (Schroeder) Srail; B.S., Roosevelt U., Chgo., 1960; Med. technologist Mt. Sinai Hosp., Chgo., 1960; m. Robert George McCormack, Sept. 17, 1960. Med. technologist Mt. Sinai Hosp., 1962-65; serology supr. Meml. Hosp. DuPage County, Elmhurst, Ill., 1965-69; immunovirology supr. Lutheran Gen. Hosp., Park Ridge, Ill., 1969-82, immunology supr. Elmhurst Meml. Hosp., 1982-84; lab. info. systems mgr. Health Techs., Inc., 1984-85; exec. v.p. mktg. and edn. Bion Enterprises, Ltd., 1985—. Mem. Am. Soc. Clin. Pathologists, Am. Soc. Microbiology, South Central Assn. Clin. Microbiology, Ill. Soc. Microbiology. Mem. Ind. Fundamental Chs. Am. Home: 5 Oak Brook Club Dr Oak Brook IL 60521 Office: 656 Busse Hwy Park Ridge IL 60068

MCCORMACK, LOWELL RAY, accountant, document examiner, graphoanalyst, oil producer; b. Ladonia, Tex., Oct. 2, 1925; d. Lowell and Orianna (McDonnold) Coney; m. Paul H. McCormack, June 4, 1948; children—Sharron Ann, Lowell Henry. Student, Rutherford Met. Coll., 1962, U. Tex.-Arlington. Bookkeeper, Jot-Em Down Gin Corp., Pecan Gap, Tex., 1947, Shedd Bartush Foods, Dallas, 1948-52; acct., credit mgr. J.P. Ashcraft Co. Inc., Dallas, 1956-65; sec., treas. Safari Oil Corp., Dallas, 1954—; owner crude oil properties; chief fin. officer, v.p., sec., treas. Dallas Title Co., 1965-83; instr. graphoanalysis Brookhaven Coll., 1980; acctg. cons. to atty.; lectr. Mem. Internat. Platform Assn., Positive Thinkers Club, North Tex. Oil and Gas Assn., Internat. Graphoanalysis Soc. (life; pres. Tex. chpt. 1979), World Assn. Document Examiners, Ind. Assn. Questioned Document Examiners (assoc.), Baptist. Clubs: Zonta (co-chmn. fin. com. 1982, dir., v.p. 1983-84), Soroptimist, Toastmistress (pres. 1981). Home: 2712 Blanton St Dallas TX 75227

MCCORMACK, MARJORIE GUTH, communications educator, public relations consultant; b. Jersey City, Dec. 27, 1934; d. Joseph Leo and Vera Marie (Clossey) Guth; m. Kevin T. McCormack, Nov. 11, 1961. B.A., St. Peter's Coll., 1974; postgrad. Jersey City State Coll., 1983—. Editor, AT&T, N.Y.C., 1952-60, librarian, 1960-67; librarian St. Peter's Coll., Jersey City, 1967-71; pub. relations mgr. Blue Cross of N.J., Newark, 1971-81; instr. history, econs. St. Aloysius High Sch., Jersey City, 1981-82; pub. relations cons. Creative Pub. Relations Assocs., Jersey City, 1981—; adj. instr. communications St. Peter's Coll., 1982—. Bd. mgrs. Am. Cancer Soc., Jersey City, 1978-79; mem., sec. parish council St. Aloysius Ch., 1981-85; mem. Jersey City Tenants Orgn., 1981—, Rent Leveling Bd. Jersey City, 1983—. Mem. AAUP, Nat. Assn. Female Execs. (pub. relations chmn. 1980-82), Jersey City Bus. and Profl. Women's Assn. (legis. chmn. 1975-77, Nat. Program award 1976, State Press award 1982). Hudson County Women's Network. Avocations: music, theater, gourmet cooking. Office: St Peter's Coll 2641 Kennedy Blvd Jersey City NJ 07306

MCCORMACK, MARYANNE TERESA, hair salons executive; b. N.Y.C., Oct. 13, 1946; d. William and Annabelle (Conroy) Warren; m. John M. McCormack, Mar. 8, 1976. Student Queens Beauty Inst., 1964-65, Advanced Precision Cutting Sch., Paul Mitchell, N.Y.C., 1973-75, Advanced Cutting Sch., Vidal Sassoon, N.Y.C., 1975, 76. Mgr., hairstylist Beauty Spot, Valley Stream, N.Y., 1965-72; owner Hair We Are, Franklin Square, N.Y., 1972-77; v.p., ednl. dir. Visible Changes/Fascination, Houston, 1977—; U.S. rep. World Congress Intercoiffure Mondial, Rio de Janeiro, Brazil, 1983. Mem. Intercoiffure Am. and Can., Congress of Colorists, Orgn. Creative Colorists. Democrat. Roman Catholic. Office: Visible Changes/Fascination 1303 Campbell St Houston TX 77055

MCCORMICK, ADOREEN, government official; b. Helena, Mont., Aug. 20, 1936; d. Walter Nelson and Cecilia (Burke) McC. B.A., Seattle U., 1958; M.A., Georgetown U., 1962. Info. and editorial asst. Library of Congress, Washington, 1958-59, info. and editorial specialist, 1960-61, adminstrv. asst., 1961-66, legis. liaison officer, 1966—. Contbr. articles to profl. jours. Bd. dirs. Deborah's Place, Washington, 1981-85; mem. Archdiocesan Pastoral Council, Washington, 1982-85; mem. council, v.p. Holy Trinity Ch., Washington, 1983—. Recipient Superior Service award Library of Congress, 1985. Mem. Kappa Gamma Pi. Home: 4799 Crescent St Bethesda MD 20816 Office: Library of Congress 101 Independence Ave SE Washington DC 20540

MCCORMICK, ALMA HEFLIN, writer, retired educator, psychologist; b. Winona, Mo., Sept. 2, 1910; d. Irvin Elgin and Nora Edith (Kelley) Heflin; B.A., E. Wash. Coll., 1936, Ed.M., 1949; Ph.D., Clayton U., 1977; m. Archie Thomas Edward McCormick, July 14, 1942; children—Thomas James, Kelly Jean. Press relations Eastern Wash. Coll., Cheney, 1948-49; instr. Wash. State U., Pullman, 1952-53; instr. East Los Angeles Coll., Monterey Park, Calif., 1972-73; originator dept. severely mentally retarded Tri-City Public Schs., Richland, Wash., 1953, Parkland, Wash., 1955; co-founder, dir. Adastra Sch. for Gifted Children, Seattle, 1957-64; writings include: Adventure Was The Compass, 1942, Merry Makes a Choice, 1950; contbr. articles to various publs., 1937—. Mem. Am. Psychol. Assn., Kappa Delta Pi. Republican. Episcopalian. Clubs: Women's Internat. Bowling Congress, Citrus Belt Women Bowlers, OX 5 Aviation Pioneers. Editor: Cub Flyer. First Am. woman test pilot, 1942. Home and Office: Apple Valley CA 92308

MCCORMICK, LINDA KAY, realty broker, owner; b. Garden City, Kans. Sept. 6, 1947; d. Kenneth Dean and Clora Anita (Norris) Ray; m. Larry Patrick McCormick, May 2, 1970; children—Shawn Patrick, Kelli Rae. A.A. in Psychology, Dodge City Community Coll., 1967; B.S. in Elem. Edn., Ft. Hays Kans. State U., 1970. Grad. Realtors Inst. Realtor assoc. Brady Stevens Co., Joplin, Mo., 1978-80; broker, owner PRO 100, Inc., Realtors, Joplin, 1980—. Mem. adv. com. Franklin Tech. Sch. Vocat. Edn., Joplin, Mo., 1981-83; mem. adv. bd. Oakhill Hosp. Home Health Agy, 1984. Named Realtor of Yr., Joplin Bd. Realtors, 1983. Mem. Mo. Assn. Realtors (bd. dirs. 1982—; mem. com. 1982-84; mem. edn. council 1984), Joplin Bd. Realtors (edn. chmn. 1982-84), Joplin C. of C. (bd. dirs. 1982-84; mem. exec. com. 1983-84; div. chmn. 1983-84). Republican. Presbyterian. Office: PRO 100 Inc Realtors 1329 E 32nd St Joplin MO 64801

MCCORMICK, LOUISE L., insurance company executive; b. Miami, Fla., 1942. Student U. Fla., 1964, in law, U. Conn., 1975. Sec., counsel Aetna Life and Casualty Co., Hartford, Conn. Mem. ABA, Am. Soc. Corporate Secs. Address: Aetna Life and Casualty Co 151 Farmington Ave Hartford CT 06156*

MCCORMICK, MARIANN HONOR, advertising executive; b. Phila., Mar. 21, 1942; d. John A. and Honor (Cullen) McCormick; adopted dau. of Nancy Cullen Olmer. Ed. St. Joseph's U., 1963-67. Asst. promotion dir. Sta. WFIL-TV-FM, Phila., 1967-69; promotion dir. Rumrill-Hoyt, Phila., 1970-71, media dir., 1971-72; dir. advt. Cottman Systems, Phila., 1972-76; planning dir. Nat. Media Group, Phila., 1976-77; media/mktg. cons. Kalish & Rice, Inc., Phila., 1977-79, Mel Richman, Inc., Phila., 1979-80; v.p. media and research Blair/BBDO, Rochester, N.Y., 1980—. Adult leader Girl Scouts Am., Phila., 1966-69; vol. advt. coordinator Effective Parent Info. for Children. Mem. Am. Women in Radio/TV (pres. Rochester chpt.), Rochester Advt. Council, Mktg. Com. Rochester, Mensa. Democrat. Roman Catholic. Club: Poor Richard (1st v.p. 1978-79) (Phila.). Home: 533-7 Stowell Dr Rochester NY 14616 Office: Blair/BBDO Inc 96 College Ave Rochester NY 14607

MCCORMICK, MARJORIE, horticulture co. exec.; b. Baker, Oreg., Nov. 10, 1928; d. William Everett and Hulda Alice (Scantlin) Price; student Met. Bus. Coll., Seattle, 1952, Yakima Bus. Coll., 1955; m. Charles W. McCormick, Nov. 6, 1958; children—Stephen, Victoria, Cheryl. owner, v.p., sec., Sec., mgr., partner Antles & Price, Yakima, Washington, 1954-58; Callahan Nursery, Inc., Yakima, Wash., 1976—; owner, mgr. McCormick Fruit Tree Co., Inc., Yakima, Wash., 1958—, pres., sec. 1982—; owner, broker McCormick Realty, Yakima, 1961—; cons. in field. Sec.-treas. Naches Pass Tunnel Hwy. Assn., Miracle Mile Assn.; dir., founder Spring Acres Group Home for Retarded, 1969-76; v.p. Young Republican Club, 1957. Recipient Top Nat. Salesman award Stark Bros. Nurseries, 1962, 64, award Zonta Women's Club, 1959. Mem. Nat. Peach Council, Wash. State Hort. Assn. (life), Yakima Bd. Realtors, Yakima C. of C. (chmn. agr. com.). Republican. Presbyterian. Club: Altrusa Internat. (recording sec. 1963-65). Author: The Golden Pollen, 1960, 73, 84; patentee on Silverspur red delicious, 1977, Firmgold delicious apple, 1977, Rose Red delicious apple, 1972, Superclone apple, 1982, Flamespur Rome apple, 1983, Deli-Jon apple, 1983. Office: 6111-A Englewood Blvd Yakima WA 98908

MCCORMICK, SHARON ANASTASIA, radio station executive; b. Detroit, June 8, 1935; d. Charles Callahan and Loretta Marie (Elsliger) Isbill; m. Robert Charles McCormick, Nov. 15, 1958; children—Suzanne A., Marjorie Melissa. Student Wayne State U., 1954-57. Editor, TV Guide Mag., Detroit, 1956-59; asst. to pres. for pub. affairs Saginaw Valley Coll., Mich., 1963-67; ctrs. dir. Macomb County OEO, Mt. Clemens, Mich., 1972-73; traffic mgr. Sta. KVOA-TV, Tucson, 1973-76; spl. asst. Project 1st Chance U. Ariz., Tucson, 1976-78; promotion dir. Sta. KUAT AM/FM U. Ariz., Tucson, 1978—. Bd. dirs., pres. Planned Parenthood of Saginaw, Mich., 1964-66; bd. dirs. Concerned Citizens for Action, Utica, Mich., 1968-72. Recipient Pub. Awareness award Corp. Pub. Broadcasting, 1982. Mem. Ariz. Press Women (sec. 1984-85, bd. dirs. 1985—, 1st place award Pub. Relations 1984), Nat. Fedn. Press Women, Tucson Jazz Soc. (bd. dirs. 1985—). Democrat. Episcopalian. Club: Tucson Balloon. Avocations: hot-air ballooning; hiking. Home: 9701 E Sunburst Dr Tucson AZ 85748 Office: KUAT Univ Ariz Modern Langs Bldg Room 222 Tucson AZ 85721

MC CORMICK, WILLIE MAE WARD (MRS. WALTER WITTEN MCCORMICK), city ofcl., ret. tech. specialist; b. Centerville, Tex. Oct. 17, 1908; d. William Sylvester and Lucy (Marshall) Ward; B.A., Mary Hardin Baylor Coll., 1929; M.A., Hardin Simmons U., 1931; postgrad. So. Methodist U., Tex. Woman's U.; m. Walter Witten McCormick, May 29, 1929; 1 dau., Elizabeth Ward McCormick Wilcox. Tchr. chemistry and algebra Big Spring (Tex.) High Sch., 1941-44, 45-48; weather observer for Dept. Commerce, Big Spring, 1943-44; analytical chemist Dow Chem. Co., Freeport, 1944-45; calculator Chance Vought (now Ling-Temco-Vought), Dallas, 1951-55, structural engr., 1955-63, sci. programmer, 1963-67, tech. specialist, 1967-69; sr. program analyst Univ. Computing Co., Arlington, Tex., 1970-73; adv. council 1st City Savs. of Euless (Tex.); dir. Mbank of Euless, 1985—. Mem. Euless City Council, 1973-85, mayor pro tem, 1975-85; chmn. Trinity River Authority Central Wastewater System; mem. Water Resources Council N. Central Tex.; bd. dirs. Euless Pub. Library. Mem. AAAS, Am. Chem. Soc., Math. Assn. Am., Fedn. Am. Scientists, AAUW, Trainmen's Aux. (pres. 1940-41), Internat. Platform Assn., LWV (publicity chmn.), Metro Bus. Profl. Womens Club, Acad. Scis., Inst. Am. Chemists, Soroptimist (hon.). C. of C. (dir.). Democrat. Baptist (tchr. adult dept. Sunday sch.). Clubs: Order Eastern Star (past worthy matron), Oakcrest Woman's, Altrusa. Home: 2300 N Main Euless TX 76039

MCCORMICK BUSSE, MARY FONETTA, broadcasting executive; b. Butte, Mont., Sept. 16, 1952; d. Manly Kirkwood and Margaret Idale (Harris) McCormick; m. David Robert Busse, Dec. 31, 1983. B.A. in Radio-TV Mgmt., Eastern Wash. State Coll., 1974. Comml. ops. mgr. Sta. KING-TV, Seattle, 1974-75, broadcast standards and ops. dir., chief news film and tape editor, 1975-76, cameraperson, 1976-80; mini-cam engr. Sta. KABC-TV, Los Angeles, 1980-83; network news producer NBC, Burbank, Calif., 1983; dir. spl. projects Merrimack Prodns., Los Angeles, 1984—. Bd. dirs., founder Drug Info. and Mobile Crisis Orgn., Cheney, Wash., 1973. Recipient 2 Emmy awards Nat. Acad. TV Arts and Scis., Seattle, 1979-80. Mem. Nat. Press Photographers Assn. (awards 1978, 80), Women in Film, Women in Cable, Am. Film Inst., Internat. Documentary Assn., Sierra Club. Home: 21368 Broken Arrow Dr Diamond Bar CA 91765

MCCOY, BARBARA S., database marketing specialist, consultant; b. Paterson, N.J., Sept. 28, 1950; d. Richard and Mary Ann (Rizzello) Studer. B.A., William Paterson Coll., 1972; M.L.S., Rutgers U., 1979. Tchr. Randolph Twp. Bd. Edn., N.J., 1972-75; asst. librarian Pandullo Quirk Assoc., Wayne, N.J., 1976-78; v.p. adminstrn. Bramble Assoc., Flanders, N.J., 1977-79; info. service adminstr. RCA Corp., Somerville, N.J., 1979-81; communication service mgr. Engring. Info., N.Y.C., 1981-85; cons., owner Barbara S. McCoy, Morganville, N.J., 1985—; cons. Marquis Who's Who, Chgo., 1983-84. Editor: Compende Search Manual, 1981, 83; Prosthetics, Orthotics and Bionics, 1985 (Award of Excellence 1985); Compendex Search Manual, 1981, 83; Tech. Bull.; (newsletter) Notes and Comments, 1981-85. Mem. Spl. Libraries Assn., Am. Soc. Info. Sci., Am. Soc. Engring. Edn. Avocations: sailing; reading. Home: 219 Applegate Ln East Brunswick NJ 08816 Office: 481 Hwy 79 Morganville NJ 07751

MCCOY, DEBRA POPINEAU, lawyer; b. Victorville, Calif., June 23, 1953; d. Frank Dennis and Mattie Sue (Blackard) Popineau; m. Michael F. McCoy, May 5, 1979. B.A. in History and Polit. Sci., So. Calif. Coll., 1975; J.D., Yale U., 1978. Bar: Calif. 1978, U.S. Dist. Ct. (cen. dist.) Calif. 1978. Assoc. atty. Parker Milliken Clark & O'Hara, Los Angeles, 1978-80; individual practice law, 1980-83; assoc. Tuohey & Prasse, P.C., Santa Ana, Calif., 1983—. Mem. ABA, Calif. Bar Assn. Republican. Home: 2277 Pacific Ave B103 Costa Mesa CA 92627 Office: Tuohey & Prasse 1200 N Main St Suite 800 Santa Ana CA 92701

MCCOY, ELEANOR LOUISE RICE, communications executive, b. Wichita, Kans., May 29, 1928; d. Claude R. and Gwen Laura (Palmer) Rice; student Wichita State U., 1946-48, 60, Kans. U., 1978, 80—; m. Dale Wesley McCoy, Aug. 10, 1948; children—Cathi Lynn McCoy Robillard, Michael Wesley, Marc Alan, Timothy John, Dale Wesley III. Women's dir. Sta. KKOY-KQSM Radio Chanute, 1970-85, news dir., 1985—. Docent, Wichita Art Mus., 1964-68, bd. dirs. 1967-68, chmn. art auction, 1966; cofounder Chanute Art Gallery, 1973, chmn., 1973—; docent Wichita Hist. Mus., 1967-68; chmn. Cancer Crusade, Neosho County, Kans., 1969-75; pres. Martin Johnson Safari Mus., Chanute, 1976; mem. vestry Grace Episcopal Ch., Chanute, 1976-79; mem. Supreme Ct. nominating commn. State of Kans., 1975-81; bd. dirs. Kans. Childrens Service League; pres. Four County bd. Tri-Valley Devel. Center, 1979-84; pres. Neosho County Republican Com., 1983—. Republican. Clubs: Art and Lit. (pres. 1976), St. Cecelia Music. Author: Ellys Cookbook, 1977. Home: 1009 Windsor Rd Chanute KS 66720 Office: PO Box 788 Chanute KS 66720

MCCOY, FRIEDA ANN, mgmt. cons.; b. Casper, Wyo., July 15, 1945; d. William B. and Helen C. (Brattis) Noell; A.A., Casper Coll., 1965; B.S., U. Wyo., 1967; M.L.S., U. Denver, 1968; M.B.A., U. Utah, 1975; m. Gerald E. McCoy, Oct. 12, 1968. Social sci. librarian U. Utah Marriott Library, Salt Lake City, 1968-71, govt. documents dept. head, 1971-75; document control supr. Alyeska Pipeline Co., Fairbanks, 1975-77; document control supr. N.W. Alaskan Pipeline Co., Salt Lake City, 1977-78, records and data mgmt. mgr., 1978-80, records and methods dir., 1980-82; owner, pres. CRM, cons., Salt Lake City, 1982—; instr. mgmt. U. Utah Coll. Bus., 1973-75; mgmt. cons., 1972-75. Mem. Am. Mgmt. Assn., Alaska Pipeline Builders Assn. (v.p. 1982—), Assn. M.B.A. Execs., Assn. Records Mgrs. and Adminstrs., Nat. Micrographics Assn., Project Mgmt. Inst. Contbr. articles to profl. jours. Home: 1192 S 9th St E Salt Lake City UT 84105 Office: 1192 S 9th E Salt Lake City UT 84105

MCCOY, HELEN LEE, warehouse corporation executive; b. Dallas, July 8, 1939; d. Bird Pierce and Eletha Thelma (Guynes) Thomas; m. James Kent McCoy, Dec. 11, 1979; children by previous marriage—Gregory Scott Odell, Mark Aaron Odell. Student schs. Redondo Beach, Calif. Sales mgr. Stretch & Sew Fabrics, Santa Rosa, Calif., 1972-73; teller Bank of Am., Napa, Calif., 1984; bd. dirs. Stor-it Mini Warehouse, Napa, 1981—, sec., treas. Stor-it Mini Warehouse Corp., Napa, 1981—, supr., 1981—. Active Home Owners Assn., Napa. Mem. Self Service Storage Assn., Nat. Assn. Female Execs., Napa C. of C. Republican. Avocations: Reading; bicycling; crocheting. Office: Stor-in Mini Warehouse Corp 1775 Industrial Way Napa CA 94558

MCCOY, JOENNE R., psychiatric clinic adminstrator; b. Detroit, Jan. 26, 1941; d. Harlan and Dorothy (Simpson) Heinmiller; children—Harlan Craig, Cathi-Jo. B.A., Mich. State U., 1966; M.S.W., U. Mich., 1983. Cert. social worker. Tchr. Owosso and Garden City pub. schs., Mich., 1962-73; psychotherapist, group leader Wayne County Hosp., Mich., 1981-82; psychotherapist East Point, Westland, Mich., 1982-83, Midwest, Dearborn, Mich., 1982-83; owner, dir. Personal Devel. Ctrs., Inc., Plymouth, Mich., 1981—; bd. dirs. Hospice Suport Services, Inc., Livonia, Mich., 1981—; cons. Westland Convalescent Ctr., Mich., 1983—; cons., facilitator Women-the Emerging Entrepreneurs, Wayne State U. and Small Bus. Assn., 1985—; chmn. Substance Abuse Com., Plymouth Schs., 1982; cons. Salvation Army, Plymouth. Mem. steering com. for neighborhood programs YWCA. Soroptimist scholar, 1982. Mem. Internat. Assn. Pediatric Social Workers, Mich. Assn. Bereavement Counselors, Families in Crisis: Domestic Violence Inc., Nat. Assn. Social Workers, Nat. Assn. Female Execs., Am. Entrepreneurs Assn., Women's Network (pres.). Club: Agora. Avocation: flying. Home: 41607 Bedford Dr Canton MI 48187 Office: Personal Devel Ctrs Inc 40400 Ann Arbor Rd Plymouth MI 48170

MCCOY, KATHLEEN LYNNE, writer; b. Dayton, Ohio, Apr. 25, 1945; d. James Lyons and Ethel Elizabeth (Curtis) McC.; B.S. in Journalism, Northwestern U., 1967, M.S. in Mag. Journalism, 1968; m. Robert Miles Stover, May 28, 1977. Free lance writer, 1965—; contbr. to Glamour, Mademoiselle, Woman's Day, Redbook, Family Circle, Cosmopolitan, TV Guide, Readers Digest, Families, Bride's, Seventeen; feature editor 'TEEN Mag., Los Angeles, 1968-77; columnist Sex and Your Body, Seventeen mag., 1983—; frequent guest various TV, radio talk shows. Mem. Screen Actors Guild, AGVA, AFTRA, NOW, Women in Communications, Soc. Profl. Journalists. Author: Discover Yourself, 1976; Discover Yourself II, 1978; The Teenage Body Book, 1979; Your Guide to Planning Your Future, 1979; The Teenage Survival Guide, 1982, Coping with Teenage Depression: A Parents Guide, 1982; The Teenage Body Book Guide to Sexuality, 1983; The Teenage Body Book Guide to Dating, 1983; The New Teenage Body Book, 1984; Growing and Changing: A Handbook for Pre-Teens, 1986. Home: 25665 Rancho Adobe Rd Valencia CA 91355

MC COY, LEE BERARD, paint company executive; b. Ipswich, Mass., July 27, 1925; d. Damase Joseph and Robena Myrtle (Bruce) B.; student U. Ala., Mobile, 1958-60; m. Walter Vincent de Paul McCoy, Sept. 27, 1943; children—Bernadette, Raymond, Joan, Richard. Owner, Lee's Letter Shop, Hicksville, L.I., N.Y., 1950-56; mgr. sales adminstrn. Basila Mfg. Co., Mobile, Ala., 1957-61; promotion mgr., buyer Mobile Paint Co., Inc., Theodore, Ala., 1961—. Bd. dirs. Friends of Mus., 1978-81, Monterey Tour House, Mobile, 1972-78, Miss Wheelchair Ala., 1980—; mem. gov.'s com. Pres.'s Com. Employment of Handicapped, 1981—; del. Civic Roundtable, 1978-80, v.p., 1980-81, pres., 1981-82. Mem. Spectromatic Assos., Color Mktg. Group, Nat. Paint Distbrs. Republican. Methodist. Clubs: Bienville, Quota (pres. Mobile chpt. 1978-80). Home: 1553 Monterey Pl Mobile AL 36604 Office: 4775 Hamilton Blvd Theodore AL 36582

MCCOY, LOIS CLARK, county ofcl.; b. New Haven, Oct. 1, 1920; d. William Patrick and Lois (Dailey) Clark; B.S., Skidmore Coll., 1942; student Nat. Search and Rescue Sch., 1974; m. Herbert I. McCoy, Oct. 17, 1943; children—Whitney, Kevin, Marianne, Tori, Debra Jill, Sally Gay., Daniel. Asst. buyer R.H. Macy & Co., N.Y.C., 1942-44, assoc. buyer, 1944-48; instr. mountain medicine and survival U. Calif., San Diego., 1973-74; cons. editor Search and Rescue mag., 1975; coordinator San Diego Mountain Rescue Team, LaJolla, 1975-80; disaster officer, San Diego County, 1980—; editor-in-chief Response mag., 1981-86. Chmn. search and rescue com. Calif. Seismic Safety Commn., 1982-84; pres. San Diego com. Los Angeles Philarm. Orch., 1978-79; chmn. search and resuce com. Gov.'s Task Force on Earthquakes, 1981-82. Recipient Hal Foss award, 1982. Mem. Nat. Assn. Search and Resucue (dir. 1980—, pres. 1985—), Am. Astron. Soc., AIAA, Council Survival Edn., Mountain Rescue Assn., Nat. Jeep Search and Rescue Assn., IEEE, Am. Soc. Indsl. Security. Episcopalian. Author handbooks in field. Office: 5201-Q Ruffin Rd San Diego CA 92123

MCCOY, MARY ANN, state ofcl.; b. Duluth, Minn., Oct. 13, 1924; d. Homer Burke and Avis (Woodworth) Hursh; B.A., Grinnell Coll., 1946; postgrad. Laval U., 1946, Mankato State U., 1964-65, U. Minn., 1970-73; m. Charles Ramon McCoy, June 11, 1949; children—Jeffrey, Mary, Jeremy. Exec. trainee Younkers, Inc., Des Moines, 1946; advt. copywriter Des Moines Register & Tribune, 1947; field dir. Duluth (Minn.) Girl Scout Council, 1947-49; with merchandising dept. Dayton's, Inc., Mpls., 1966-75; dir. election and legis. manual div. Office of Sec. of State of Minn., St. Paul, 1975-81; exec. dir. Minn. State Ethical Practices Bd., St. Paul, 1981—. Mem. exec. council Minn. Hist. Soc., 1972-81, 82—; mem. Minn. Supreme Ct. Bd. for Continuing Legal Edn., 1981—; sec. State Rev. Bd. for Nominations to Nat. Register, 1976—. Mem. Am. Judicature Soc., Women Historians of Midwest, Am. Assn. State and Local History. Editor, Minn. Legis. Manual, 1975-81. Office: Ethical Practices Bd 41 State Office Bldg St Paul MN 55155

MCCOY, MARY JO, management analyst; b. Boise, Idaho, July 6, 1938; d. Charles Herbert and Evelyn (Horgan) Buckel; student U. Oreg., 1957, Alaska Meth. U., 1967, Cochise Coll., 1973-75; M.A., U. No. Colo., 1978; m. Joseph G. McCoy, June 13, 1979; children—David, Susan, Joseph. With U.S. Army, Fort Huachuca, Ariz., 1972—, program analyst, communication command, 1979-83, fed. women's program mgr., 1983—; family counselor Cath. Social Services, Sierra Vista, Ariz., 1978-81; counselor Cochise County Conciliation Ct., 1980-81; cons. Success Strategies; instr. Cochise Coll., part time, 1981—. Mem. Oblate Order St. Benedict, 1971—; founder Community of the Holy Trinity, 1964; mem. Anchorage Council Chs., 1966-70; bd. dirs. Cath. Charities Anchorage, 1966-70. Mem. Am. Soc. Mil. Comptrollers. Republican. Club: Jobs Daus. Home: 2116 Elmwood Ln Sierra Vista AZ 85635 Office: Comdr US Army Info Systems Command A0 PER IIA Fort Huachuca AZ 85613

MCCOY, MARY LOU, manufacturing company executive; b. Ridgeway, Mo., Oct. 19, 1934; d. Earl Richard and Rowena (McCollum) McC. Student, Detroit Bus. Inst., 1952, Wayne State U., 1967, 79, 80, Oakland U., Rochester, Mich., 1968. Mgr. materials Cox Instrument, Lynch Corp., Detroit, 1970-76, dir. personnel and materials, 1976-81, dir. ops., 1981-82; mgr. materials Ametek, Schutte & Koerting, Cornwells Heights, Pa., 1982-83, product coordinator, 1983—. Recipient Appreciation plaque Am. Prodn. and Inventory Control Soc. Democrat. Office: Ametek Schutte & Koerting Div 2233 State Rd Cornwells Heights PA 19020

MCCOY, MEREDITH, lawyer; b. Little Rock, Jan. 21, 1949; d. Travis Walton and Evelyn Lois (Greene) McC.; m. Scott Enos Slaughter, Sept. 9, 1972; children—Garrett Crawford, Evelyn McMath. B.A., U. Ark., 1971; B.S., Simmons Sch. Library Sci., Boston, 1972; J.D., George Washington U., 1976. Bar: Va. 1977, D.C. 1978. Counsel, Mergers and Acquisitions, Inc., McClean, Va., 1977; atty. Congl. Research Service, Washington, 1977-86; mng. atty. Washington office Arnold Grobmyer & Haley, Little Rock, 1985—; cons. ABA Project on Attys.' Fees, 1978-79. Editor: Clayton Act and Mergers (ABA), 1976, Mergers and Acquisitions Jour., 1977, Fed. Bar News & Jour., 1980—. Sec., Capitol Hill Women's Polit. Caucus, Washington, 1981. Mem. Fed. Bar Assn. (sec. Younger Lawyers div. 1980, Dist. Service award 1982), Women's Bar Assn., Bar Assn. D.C., Va. Bar Assn., Women's Legal Def. Fund. Democrat. Methodist. Home: 3916 Aspen St Chevy Chase MD 20815 Office: Arnold Grobnyer & Haley 1101 Connecticut Ave Washington DC 20036

MC COY, PATRICIA ALICE, deaf interpreter; b. Cheverly, Md., Feb. 18, 1952; d. George Dudley and Louise Adeline (Waterholter) McC. Student Gallaudet Coll., 1973, 86—; A.A. in Arts and Scis., Prince George's Community Coll., 1983; student U. Md., 1984-86. Cashier, G. C. Murphy Co., Hyattsville, Md., 1969-73; sec., George's Radio and TV, Washington, 1973-77; sec., interpreter Gallaudet Coll., Washington, 1978—; chmn. consultancy com. Deaf Media Council, 1974-77. Recipient cert. of appreciation Nat. ARC, 1976. Mem. Registry Interpreters for Deaf (Potomac bd. mem.), Nat. Assn. Deaf, Md. Assn. Deaf, Washington Met. Deaf Alliance (v.p.), Met. Washington Assn. for Deaf, Internat. Platform Assn., World Poetry Soc., Telecommunicators for Deaf, Inc., Nat. Geog. Soc., Am. Biog. Research Assn., Deaf Awareness. Home: care I Hear Your Hand PO Box 26 6025 Springhill Dr Greenbelt MD 20770 Office: Gallaudet Coll Office of Admissions 800 Florida Ave NE Washington DC 20002

MCCOY, ROXANNE ELISE, electronic executive; b. Tigua, Tex., Apr. 20, 1952; d. Herbert Kenneth and Dorothy Lou (Cowan) McCoy; m. William Faulkner Doherty, Mar. 11, 1978; children—Debra, Mike, Donna, Doug. Student, Foothill Coll., 1970-72. Supr., Intech, San Jose, Calif., 1970-71; electronics exec. Sierra Systems, Sunnyvale, Calif., 1971-75; v.p. Emco High Voltage Co., Sunnyvale, 1975—. Mem. Am. Assn. Breeders of Peruvian Horses, Am. Horse Council, Aircraft Owners and Pilots Assn. Club: South Bay Yacht (v.p. 1980, treas. 1979, sec. 1978). Address: Emco High Voltage Co 556 Weddell Dr Suite 4 Sunnyvale CA 94086

MCCOY, VIRGINIA LEE, practical nurse, civic worker; b. Washington, Ill., Mar. 8, 1944; d. Emory Leon and Nell Creole (Watkins) O'D.; m. Dale Clifton McCoy, May 27, 1967; 1 child, Daryl Craig. Grad. Peoria Sch. Practical Nursing, 1964. Nurse, Proctor Community Hosp., Peoria, 1964-65; charge nurse Washington Nursing Ctr., Ill., 1965-67; office nurse G.F. Mori, M.D., Washington, 1967-76, G.W. Giebelhausen M.D., Peoria, 1977—. Alderman, City Council Washington, 1985—. Mem. Am. Med. Assistance Assn. Republican. Home: 106 S Lawndale St Washington IL 61571

MCCOY-GAINES, ADRIANE THERESA, broadcasting executive; b. Mt. Vernon, N.Y., Aug. 27, 1947; d. James and Dorothy (Williams) McCoy; m. Thomas E. Gaines, Oct. 16, 1965 (div. 1973). B.A. cum laude, Fordham U., 1978. Securities and safekeeping dep. Marine Midland Bank, Poughkeepsie,

N.Y., 1965-68; investment and securities dep. State Nat. Bank El Paso, 1968-71; asst. info. specialist Rochester Inst. Tech., 1971-72; asst. librarian Culinary Inst. Am., Hyde Park, N.Y., 1972-73; dir. corp. adminstrn. Unity Broadcasting Network, N.Y.C., 1973-82, v.p., 1982—; interim gen. mgr. KATZ-AM/WZEN-FM Radio, St. Louis, 1982. Co-founder, bd. dirs. World Inst. Black Communications/CEBA Awards, N.Y.C., 1978-84. Mem. Women in Cable, Advt. Women Radio and TV, Coalition of 100 Black Women (bd. dirs.), Nat. Acad. TV Arts and Scis. Home: 218 W 138th St New York NY 10030 Office: Unity Broadcasting Network Inc 10 Columbus Circle New York NY 10019

MC CRACKEN, ALICE IRENE, psychotherapist; b. Indpls., May 4, 1942; d. Neal and Falma Dorothy (Rice) McC.; B.A. with honors, Mills Coll., 1963; M.A., U. Calif.-Davis, 1965; Ph.D., Tulane U., 1968; M.Counseling, Ariz. State U., 1975; 1 child, Tammy Maru. Library asst., head current periodicals service Ariz. State U. Library, 1968-70; community program specialist City of Scottsdale, Ariz., 1971-72; women's editor Scottsdale Daily Progress, 1972-74; activities therapist Camelback Hosp., Phoenix, 1972-74, dir. public relations, psychotherapist, 1975-78; psychotherapist Family Service Agy., Tempe, Ariz., 1978-81; pvt. practice psychotherapy, Scottsdale, Ariz., 1981—; owner Dynamic Video, Scottsdale. Served with USAR, 1976-78. Recipient Ariz. Press Women editing and writing awards, 1972-75; Ariz. Bus. Communicators editing award, 1975. Mem. Am. Group Psychotherapy Assn., Phoenix Psychoanalytic Study Group, Ariz. Group Psychotherapy Soc., Am. Assn. for Counseling and Devel., Am. Mental Health Counselors Assn. Office: Dynamic Counseling Assocs 6741 E McDowell Rd Scottsdale AZ 85257

MCCRACKEN, LINDA, librarian, commercial artist; b. Rochester, N.Y., Apr. 13, 1948; d. Frederick Hugh Craig and Shirley Betty (Shacter) Bickford; m. Alan Cheah, June 13, 1972 (div. 1978); m. Bruce E. McCracken, Sept. 23, 1978 (div. 1985); 1 child, Karen Elizabeth. B.A. in History, SUNY-Geneseo, 1970, M.L.S., 1970. Reference librarian Northeastern U., Boston, 1971-72; asst. librarian Burlington Pub. Library, Mass., 1972-74; research asst. Data Resources, Inc., Lexington, Mass., 1974-76; comml. artist McCracken's, Wolfeboro, N.H., 1973—; asst. librarian N.H. Vocat.-Tech. Coll., Manchester, 1985—. Participant paintings Horseheads Mall Art Show (3rd place award 1968); graphic artist Rare Coin Rev. mag., 1983; layout artist quar. book: Market Media Guide, 1979; author Burlington Times-Union, 1973. Treas. Village Players, Wolfeboro, 1982-83; pub. relations com. Gov.'s Arts Council, Wolfeboro, 1982; mem. Clearlakes Chorale, Jefferson Chorus, Wolfeboro Chorus. Mem. Health Scis. Librarians, Nat. Assn. Female Execs., State Employees Assn. N.H. Unitarian. Avocations: Skiing; gardening; singing; acting; hiking; reading; computers. Home: Box 1906 Pine Hill Rd Wolfeboro NH 03894 Office: NH Voc-Tech College 1066 Front St Manchester NH 03102

MCCRARY, EUGENIA LESTER (EUGENIA CAMPBELL LESTER), civic worker, writer; b. Annapolis, Md., Mar. 23, 1929; d. John Campbell and Eugenia (Potts) Lester; A.B. cum laude, Radcliffe Coll., 1950; M.A., Johns Hopkins U., 1952; postgrad. Harvard U., spring 1953, Pa. State U., 1953-54, Drew U., 1957-58, Inst. Study of USSR, Munich, W.Ger., 1964; m. John Campbell Howard, July 15, 1955 (dec. Sept. 1965); m. 2d, Dennis Daughtry McCrary, June 28, 1969; 1 son, Dennis Campbell. Grad. asst. dept. Romance langs. Pa. State U., 1953-54; tchr. dept. math. The Brearley Sch., N.Y.C., 1954-57; dir. Sch. Langs., Inc., Summit, N.J., 1958-69, trustee, 1960-69. Dist. dir. Eastern Pa. and N.J. auditions Met. Opera Nat. Council, N.Y.C., 1960-66, dist. dir. publicity, 1966-67, nat. vice chmn. publicity, 1967-71, nat. chmn. public relations, 1972-75, hon. nat. chmn. public relations, 1976—; chmn. Van Cortland Mansion Mus., 1985—. Mem. Nat. Soc. Colonial Dames Am. (bd. mgrs. N.Y.), Playhouse Assn. Summit, Met. Opera Nat. Council, Soc. Mayflower Desc. (bd. dirs. N.Y. soc., chmn. house com.), Soc. Daus. of Holland Dames (bd. dirs., 3d directress gen.), Huguenot Soc. Am. (governing council). Republican. Episcopalian. Club: Colony. Home: 24 Central Park S New York NY 10019

MCCRAVEN, EVA STEWART MAPES, health service administrator; b. Los Angeles, Sept. 26, 1936; d. Paul Melvin and Wilma Zech (Ziegler) Stewart; B.S. magna cum laude, Calif. State U., Northridge, 1974, M.S., 1976; m. Carl Clarke McCraven, Mar. 18, 1978; children—David Anthony, Lawrence James, Maria Lynn Mapes. Dir. spl. projects Pacoima Meml. Hosp., 1969-71, dir. health edn., 1971-74; asst. exec. dir. Hillview Community Mental Health Center, Lakeview Terrace, Calif., 1974—, dir. Hillview Center dept. Consultation and Edn., dir. long-term resdl. program, 1986—. Pres., San Fernando Valley Coordinating Council Area Assn.; mem., past pres. Sunland-Tujunga Coordinating Council; bd. dirs. Northeast Valley Health Corp., 1970-73, Golden State Community Mental Health Center, 1970-73. Recipient Cert. tribute community service city of Los Angeles, 1982, 83; Commendation Los Angeles Bd. Suprs., 1981. Fellow Assn. Mental Health Administrs.; mem. Am. Pub. Health Assn., Health Services Adminstrn. Alumni Assn., Bus. and Profl. Women, LWV. Office: 11600 Eldridge Ave Lake View Terrace CA 91342

MCCRAY, DOLORES ROSELYN, banker; b. Youngstown, Ohio, Jan. 14, 1940; d. Cleo W. and Ada (Polnett) LaCalleaux; m. Charles Earle McCray, Jan. 18, 1957 (div.); children—Charles Earle Jr., Dolores Roselyn. A.A., B.B.A., Pace U. From teller to ops. officer Chem. Bank, N.Y.C., 1967-78; acct. Combustion Equipment Inc., N.Y.C., 1979-80; asst. treas., br. mgr. Anchor Savs. Bank, N.Y.C., 1980—. Mem. East Midtown C. of C. (bd. dirs.), Urban Bankers Coalition (bd. dirs.), Coalition of 100 Black Women (bd. dirs.), Soc. Profl. and Exec. Women, Nat. Assn. Female Execs. Democrat. Lutheran. Home: 345 E 93d St New York NY 10128 Office: Anchor Savs Bank 404 5th Ave New York NY 10018

MC CRAY, EVELINA WILLIAMS, librarian, researcher; b. Plaquemine, La., Sept. 1, 1932; d. Turner and Beatrice (Gordon) Williams II; m. John Samuel McCray, Apr. 7, 1955; 1 dau., Johnetta McCray Russ. B.A., So. U., Baton Rouge, 1954; M.S.L.S., La. State U., 1962. Librarian, Iberville High Sch., Plaquemine, 1954-70, Plaquemine Jr. High, 1970-75; proofreader short stories, poems Associated Writers Guild, Atlanta, 1982-86; library cons. Evaluation Capitol High Sch., 1964, Iberville Parish Educators Workshop, 1980, Tchrs. Core/Iberville Parish, 1980-81. Vol. service Allen J. Nadler Library, Plaquemine, 1980-82; librarian Local Day Care Ctr., Plaquemine, 1978-79. Mem. ALA, La. Library Assn., Nat. Ret. Tchrs. Assn., La Ret. Tchrs. Assn., Iberville Ret. Tchrs. Assn. (info. and protective services dir. 1981—). Democrat. Baptist. Home: PO Box Q Plaquemine LA 70765

MCCREA, PATRICIA ANNE, noncommissioned army officer; b. Riverside, Calif., Oct. 7, 1945; d. Clarence Edwin and Mathilda Anne (Pfarr) McC.; m. William Louis Pagels, Oct. 7, 1963 (div. June 1982); children—Susan, Theresa, Kathryn, William Patrick. Student U. Md., Evreux, France, 1962-63; B.S., SUNY-Buffalo, 1983; postgrad. Genesee Community Coll., 1982-83. Served as enlisted person U.S. Army, USAR, 1974—, personnel mgmt. supr. for ops. and tng. 390th Personnel and Adminstrn. Bn., Richmond, Va., 1985—; program asst. Coop. Extension, Batavia, N.Y., 1980-82; unit adminstr. U.S. Army Res., Richmond, Va., 1984-85; substitute tchr. Alexander Central Sch., N.Y., 1982-84; adj. faculty Genesee Community Coll., Batavia, 1982-84. Tutor, officer Literacy Vols. of Am., Batavia, 1982-84. Decorated Army Commendation medal, others. Mem. Assn. U.S. Army, Nat. Assn. Female Execs., DAV (life), Mensa. Republican. Roman Catholic. Avocations: needlework; fencing; reading; quilting. Home: 1910 Repp St Highland Springs VA 23075 also 11269 E Bennett Rd Grass Valley CA 95945 Office: 390th Personnel and Adminstrn Bn 1305 Sherwood Ave Richmond VA 23220

MCCREADIE, MARIAN CHRISTINE, software engineer; b. Midland, Mich., Oct. 24, 1951; d. Gordon and Sarah Lee (Rainey) MacBeth; m. Robert Manning McCreadie, July 8, 1972; children—Elizabeth, Lydia. B.A. in Computer Sci., U. Calif.-Santa Cruz, 1983. Ops. officer Bank Am., San Bruno, Calif., 1972-76; proprietor Prestige Plants, Aptos, Calif., 1979-81; software engr. Litton Mellonics, Sunnyvale, Calif., 1983—. Troop leader Girl Scouts Am., Aptos, 1982—. Club: Welcome Wagon (Aptos) (v.p. 1978-79). Home: 463 Los Altos Dr Aptos CA 95003 Office: Litton Mellonics Systems Devel 1001 W Maude Ave Sunnyvale CA 94088-340/

MCCREADY, FLORINE A., employment administrator; b. Balt., Apr. 29, 1945; d. Pinkney W. and Nazerine (Spicer) McC. B.S. in Bus. Adminstrn., Morgan State U., M.B.A. in Mgmt. and Mktg. Social worker Dept. Social Services, Balt., 1968-75; recruitment and employment advisor Mobil Oil Corp., Valley Forge, Pa., 1975-80; mgr. employment Washington Gas Light, 1980—; task force mem. Nat. Alliance Bus., Youth Motivation, Washington, 1982—. Recipient cert. employee relations law Inst. Applied Mgmt. and Law, 1982; practitioners cert. law relations PTI Mgmt. Ctr., Inc., 1983. Mem. Am. Soc. Personnel Adminstrn. (D.C. legis. rep. 1983), Washington Personnel Assn., Assn. M.B.A. Execs., Mid-Atlantic Placement Council, Coll. Placement Council, Nat. Assn. Blacks in Energy, Delta Sigma Theta. Office: Washington Gas Light Co 1100 H St Washington DC 20080

MCCREIGHT, LILLIAN MOOD, state commissioner; b. Columbia, S.C., Aug. 12, 1940; d. Francis Palmer and Lula Sue (Rigby) Mood; children—Lillian Wynn, Susan Maria, Elizabeth Mood. B.S. in Nursing, U. S.C.-Columbia, 1962, M.P.H., 1976. Staff nurse Georgetown Hosp. (S.C.), 1969-70; program supr, evaluator Home Health Services Dept. Health and Environ. Control, State of S.C., Columbia, 1970-78, project dir. community long-term care, 1979, dir. pub. health nursing, 1979—, asst. commr., 1980—; adj. prof. Sch. Pub. Health U. S.C., Columbia, 1976—. Mem. editorial rev. bd. Nursing & Health Care, 1983—. Mem. chancel choir Shandon United Methodist Ch., Columbia, chmn. worship commn., 1984. Mem. Assn. State & Territorial Dirs. Nursing (sec., treas. 1982-83, pres.-elect 1983-84), S.C. Pub. Health Assn. (pres. 1978-79), Nat. League for Nursing (dir. 1982-83), Am. Pub. health Assn., Sigma Theta Tau, Delta Omega. Office: SC Dept Health and Environ Control 2600 Bull St Columbia SC 29201

MCCRICKARD, RUBY ASHWELL, hospital administrator; b. Huddleston, Va., Apr. 19, 1931; d. Harry Odell and Nellie (Cundiff) Ashwell; diploma Riverside Hosp. Sch. Nursing, 1953; cert. health care adminstrn. U. So. Calif., 1976; B.A., Goddard Coll., 1975; M.S., Med. Coll. Ga., 1977; Ph.D., Walden U., 1985; m. George T. McCrickard, Aug. 9, 1952; 1 son, George T. Operating room staff nurse, head nurse med. unit Riverside Hosp., Newport News, Va., 1953-55; asst. operating room supr., operating room staff nurse, acting operating room supr., Kecoughtan Vets. Hosp., Hampton, Va., 1955-60; intensive care and central supply supr. Lynchburg (Va.) Gen.-Marshall Lodge Hosps., 1962-66, asst. dir. nursing services, 1966-69, dir. nursing services, 1969-78, dir. nursing service, asst. adminstr., 1978-84, v.p. hosp. adminstrn., 1984-85, sr. v.p. hosp. adminstrn., 1985—; mem. Va. Bd. Health, 1981-85, chmn., 1984-85; mem. Lynchburg Coll. Nursing Edn. Adv. Council, 1979-80; mem. adv. com. respiratory therapy Central Va. Community Coll., 1978—; mem. Central Va. Health Planning Emergency Med. Adv. Council, 1975-77; mem. primary care com. S.W. Va. Health Systems Agy., Inc.; hosp. coordinator United Way, 1983. Recipient Ella T. Whitten award Registered Nurses Associated Alumnae Assn. Lynchburg, Va., 1966; Phoebe Kandel Rohrer Founders award Med. Coll. Ga., 1986. Mem. Am. Nurses Assn. (past mem. membership and by-laws coms.), Nat. League Nursing, Nat. Forum Adminstrn. Nursing Services, Am. Soc. Hosp. Nursing Service Adminstrn. (pres. Va. chpt. 1981, dir. Va. chpt. 1982, candidate, program for excellence in nursing adminstrn. 1980), Nat. Soc. Lit. and Arts, AAUW, Va. Nurses Assn. (chmn. profl. nursing practice com.), Va. League Nursing com., pres.-elect 1986—, chmn. membership com. 1984-85), Va. Hosp. Assn. (com. on nursing, com. emergency med. services), Piedmont Heart Assn. (past dir., chmn. nursing com.), Riverside Hosp. Sch. Nursing Alumnae (pres. 1959-60), Sigma Theta Tau. Baptist. Clubs: Order Eastern Star, Scottish Rite Women's Nobletts. Home: Route 1 Box 483 Rustburg VA 24588 Office: Tate Springs Rd Lynchburg VA 24506

MCCRIMMON, BARBARA SMITH, writer, librarian; b. Anoka, Minn., May 3, 1918; d. Webster Roy and Jessie (Sargeant) Smith; m. James McNab McCrimmon, June 10, 1939; children—Kevin Mor, John Marshall. B.A., U. Minn., 1939; M.S.L.S., U. Ill., 1961; Ph.D., Fla. State U., 1973. Asst. librarian Ill. State Nat. Hist. Survey, Champaign, Ill., 1961-62; research assoc. Bur. Community Planning, U. Ill., Champaign, 1962-63; librarian Ill. Water Survey, Champaign, 1964-65; librarian Am. Meteorol. Soc., Boston, 1965-67; editorial asst. Jour. Library History, Tallahassee, 1967-69, 73-74; adj. assoc. prof. Sch. Library Sci., Fla. State U., Tallahassee, 1976-77. Author: Power, Politics and Print, 1981; editor: American Library Philosophy, 1975; contbr. articles to profl. jours. Mem. ALA, Bibliog. Soc. Am., Pvt. Libraries Assn., Beta Phi Mu, Manuscript Soc. Democrat.

MC CRORY, ELLANN, radiologist; b. Butler Springs, Ala., Mar. 22, 1936; d. William Bryant and Eva Estelle (Stabler) McCrory; B.S., U. Ala., 1956; M.D., Med. Coll. Ala., 1960. Rotating intern Univ. Hosp., Birmingham, Ala., 1960-61; resident Bapt. Meml. Hosp., Memphis, 1961-64; instr. radiology U. Fla., 1964-65; pvt. practice radiology, Fort Payne, Ala.; speaker; chief of med. staff DeKalb County Hosp., 1977. Trustee, Landmarks Inc., pres., 1978-79. Recipient Bausch and Lomb sci. award, 1953. Mem. Am. Coll. Radiology, Radiol. Soc. N.A., AMA, Am. Med. Women's Assn., So. Radiol. Assn., Am. Roentgen Ray Soc., Am. Assn. Women Radiologists, Mid-South Med. Assn., Med. Assn. Ala. (v.p. 1986-87), DeKalb County Med. Soc. (pres. 1977), So. Med. Assn., Ala. Radiol. Soc., Fort Payne C. of C. (dir., pres. 1979-80) Ala. Hist. Soc., U. Ala. Alumni Assn. (pres. elect DeKalb County chpt. 1977, nat. dist. v.p.), Phi Beta Kappa, Alpha Lambda Delta. Methodist. Home: 1408 Alabama Ave SW Fort Payne AL 35967 Office: 1215 Alabama Ave N Fort Payne AL 35967

MCCROSKEY, ELIZABETH WEAR, lawyer; b. Dallas, Oct. 19, 1937; d. J. B. and Helen Elizabeth (Ginn) Wear; m. William James McCroskey, Jan. 31, 1960; children—Nancy Elizabeth, Susan Carol. B.A., U. Tex.-Austin, 1959; M.A., Rutgers U., 1965; J.D., U. Santa Clara, 1981. Bar: Calif. 1981. Coordinator low-moderate income housing Mid-Peninsula Citizens for Fair Housing, Palo Alto, Calif., 1972; assoc. Fuller, Glickman, Mousalam & Barton, Palo Alto, 1981-82; ptnr. Gullixson, Hollman & McCroskey, Palo Alto, 1983—. Incorporator, bd. dirs. Mid-Peninsula Access Corp., Santa Clara County, Calif.; co-chmn. City Cupertino (Calif.) Goals Com. Housing Task Force, 1970-71. Mem. ABA, Calif. State Bar Assn., Santa Clara County Bar Assn., AAUW (dir. 1983-84). Democrat. Presbyterian. Office: Gullixson Hollman & McCroskey 720 University Ave PO Box 1041 Palo Alto CA 94302

MCCUBBIN, KATHRYN O'BRIEN, computer science educator; b. Chgo., Feb. 26, 1936; d. Gaetano T. and Mary (Perzia) Buttice; B.S., Marquette U., 1958, M.S., 1960; postgrad. Ill. Inst. Tech., 1959-66; m. T. Roderick McCubbin, Feb. 22, 1980; 1 dau., Mary Catherine O'Brien. With Ill. Inst. Tech. Research Inst., 1959-66, asst. mathematician, 1959-62, research mathematician, 1962-66; cons. mathematician Gen. Electric Missile and Space Div., 1966-68; dir. faculty Computer Programming Inst. of Delaware-Chgo., Inc.; pres. DIDO, Inc., Joliet, Ill., 1968-75; div. mgr. Merck Co., Rahway, N.J., 1975-79; dir. mgmt. info. services Washington Met. Area Transit Authority, 1979-83; asst. prof. Christopher Newport Coll., Newport News, Va., 1983—. Contbr. articles to sci. jours. Home: 15 Autumn E Williamsburg VA 23185 Office: 15 Shoe Ln Newport News VA 23606

MCCUE, DONNA CAPRARI, advertising and public relations executive; b. Scranton, Pa.; d. Samuel R. and Teresa M. Caprari; B.A., Rosemont Coll., 1974; m. Timothy P. McCue. Program dir. hypertension screening Am. Heart Assn., Binghamton, N.Y., 1974-75; owner, pres. McCue Advt. & Pub. Relations, Inc., Binghamton, 1975—; lectr. Broome Community Coll., SUNY-Binghamton. Bd. dirs., officer Am. Heart Assn., Binghamton, 1982-86; bd. dirs. Broome County Child Devel. Council, 1986; mem. pub. relations com. Broome/Tioga Pvt. Industry Council. Mem. Pub. Relations Soc. Am., Broome County C. of C. Office: 407 Press Bldg 19 Chenango St Binghamton NY 13901

MCCULLAR, AUDREY TISDALE, retail/rental store executive; b. Bklyn., Oct. 30, 1948; d. Burie Edward and Marie (Plaia) Tisdale; m. Newton DeCial McCullar, Dec. 23, 1981 and Mar. 6, 1982. Student in bus. Grace Downs Inst., N.Y.C., 1965-66, Hunter Coll., 1970-71. In adminstrv. positions Finley Kumble Wagner, N.Y.C., 1976-81; sec.-treas. Vandervoort Thoroughbreds, Atlanta, 1981-83, cons., 1983; pres., owner ATM Enterprises, Inc., Lithonia, Ga., 1983—; sec./treas. TRIB Group, Ltd., Atlanta, 1983—. Mem. dinner com. Nat. Asthma Found., Colo., 1981—; supporting patron High Mus. Art, Atlanta, 1985-86; mem. Positive Action Lithonia, 1983-86, Atlanta Ballet, 1984-86. Mem. DeKalb C. of C. (edn. council 1984-86). Home: 3371 Waterford Lithonia GA 30058 Office: ATM Enterprises 6958 Main St Lithonia GA 30058

MCCULLOUGH, PHYLLIS (HOGOBOOM), marketing executive; b. St. Louis, Aug. 6, 1936; d. Lester Robert and Gladys Helen (Sollar) Hogoboom; grad. Hickey's Bus. Sch., St. Louis, 1955; children—Maureen, Megan, Sean. Exec. sec., adminstrv. asst. Gardner Advt., St. Louis, 1955-60, adminstrv. asst. internat. div., art buyer, prodn. mgr., acct. exec., 1964-78; corp. advt. mgr. Huffy Corp., Dayton, Ohio, 1978-83; mktg. mgr. Raleigh Cycle Co., Seattle, 1983—. Mem. Am. Mgmt. Assn., Nat. Assn. Exec. Womens, Am. Soc. Profl. and Exec. Women, Internat. Assn. Bus. Communicators, Oreg. Hist. Soc., Dayton Advt. Club (dir.), Bicycle Fedn., Ohio Bicycle Fedn., League Am. Wheelmen, Bike Centennial. Republican. Club: Dayton Cycling. Home: 14006 13th Ave SW Seattle WA 98166 Office: 22701 72d Ave S Kent WA 98032

MCCULLOUGH-WIGGINS, LYDIA STATORIA, pharmacist, consultant; b. Chgo., May 14, 1948; d. George Robert and Isabell (King) Boulware; m. Robert Dale McCullough, Aug. 1, 1970 (div. Oct. 1977); m. 2d, James Calvin Wiggins, Nov. 3, 1979. Student Wis. State U.-Whitewater, 1966-69; B.S. in Pharmacy, U. Ill.-Chgo., 1972; cert. UCLA, 1976-78. Registered pharmacist, Ill. Registered pharmacy apprentice Lefel Drugs, Chgo., 1971-72; pharmacy mgr. Fernwood Pharmacy, Chgo., 1972-73, Sapstein Bros. Pharmacy, Chgo., 1973-74; dir. pharmacy Martin Luther King Neighborhood Health Ctr., Chgo., 1974-80; pharmacist-in-charge Walgreens, Chgo., 1980—. Author: M.L.K. Drug Formulary, 1978. Bd. dirs. NIA Comprehensive Ctr. Recipient Cert. of Leadership, YMCA Met. Chgo., 1979; Kizzy award 1980 Black Women Hall of Fame Found., Chgo., 1981; Ann. Med. Achievement award Greater Chgo. Met. Community, 1981. Mem. Nat. Pharmacists Assn. (bd. dirs.), Chgo. Pharmacists Assn., Am. Pharm. Assn., Ill. Pharm. Assn., Nat. Assn. Female Execs., U. Ill. Alumni Assn. Democrat. Baptist. Club: Christian Novice (pres. 1977-78) (Chgo.). Office: Walgreens 1650 W Chicago St Chicago IL 60622

MCCULLY, RUTH ALIDA, educator; b. Port Huron, Mich., Feb. 13, 1933; d. Leon Eugene Lounsberry and Rachel Elizabeth (DeSerano) Lounsberry-Maser; m. Donald Cecil McCully, Feb. 8, 1952; children—Stephen Donald, Robert Leon, Julie Ann. B.S., Eastern Mich. U., 1976, M.A., 1980. Asst. children's librarian Monroe County Library, Mich., 1962-64; dir. Weekday Nursery Sch., Youngstown, Ohio, 1964-71; dir. children's programs Lake-in-the-Woods, Ypsilanti, Mich., 1974-76; tchr. 1st grade Dundee Community Schs., Mich., 1976—. Lay speaker Ann Arbor Dist., United Meth. Ch., 1979—; chmn. Dundee Community Caring and Sharing, 1982—; active Monroe County Food Bank, 1983—, Dundee Interfaith Council, 1984—, Dundee Area Against Substance Abuse, 1984—. Named Woman of Yr., United Meth. Women, Dundee United Meth. Ch., 1983. Mem. NEA, Mich. Edn. Assn., Monroe County Edn. Assn., Mich. Reading Assn. Club: Dundee School Employees (sec. 1985-86). Avocations: playing piano/guitar; needlework; sketching/painting; gardening; reading. Home: 510 E Monroe St Dundee MI 48131

MCCUNE, MARY LOU, psychiatric nurse; b. Greensburg, Pa., Oct. 7 1937; d. John Joseph and Margaret Katherine (Finfrock) Carr; m. William Carl McCune, Dec. 24, 1952; children—Deborah Lynne, William Carl, Jr., Marshal Kay. Diploma nursing, U. S.C., 1981. Staff nurse adolescent unit S.C. Dept. Mental Health, Columbia, 1981, nurse clinician, 1982; head nurse forensic unit S.C. State Hosp., Columbia, 1983, dir. nursing I, 1984—. Mem. Murrayview Homeowners Assn., Columbia, 1983—. Mem. S.C. State Nurses Assn. Democrat. Roman Catholic. Club: Garden (pres.). Avocations: bridge; painting; swimming. Home: 1424 Murrayview Dr Columbia SC 29210 Office: SC State Hosp PO Box 119 Columbia SC 29202

MCCURLEY, LEANNE, insurance agent; b. Oakland, Calif., May 8, 1948; d. A. Leo and Martha Dittman Bridges; m. Robert L. McCurley, Jan. 28, 1984; children—Holly L., Robert; m. Daniel L. Santos, June 29, 1969 (div. 1984). Student LaSalle U., 1981. Cert. ins. counselor. Loan officer 1st Inter Bank, Lake Tahoe, Calif., 1972-75; mgr. Evergreen Fed. Savs. & Loan, Brookings, Oreg., 1975-78; ins. agt., owner, pres. Brookings Harbor Ins. Agy., Harbor, Oreg., 1978-83; agt., mgr. Abel & Swank Ins. Co., Harbor, 1983; agt., mgr. Allstate Ins. Co., Harbor, 1985—. Mem. Soc. Cert. Ins. Counselors, Brookings Harbor C. of C. (pres. 1982-84). Republican. Lodge: Order Eastern Star (matron 1981-82), Jobs Daughters grand rep; guardian. Avocations: singing; bowling; reading. Home: 15525 Winriver Rd Harbor OR 97415 Office: PO Box 2927 Harbor OR 97415

MCCURRY, VIRGINIA MARIE, funeral home executive; b. Brunswick, Mo., Aug. 13, 1928; d. Otto John and Bertha S. (Reigelsberger) Reichert; m. Laurance Elmo McCurry, Jan. 10, 1949; (dec. Dec. 1971); children—Gregory, Kenneth, Carolyn, Debra, Laurance, Richard, Kelly, Mark. Student pub. schs., Brunswick. Funeral dir. McCurry-Berry Funeral Home, Brunswick, 1965—. Active St. Mary's Alter Soc., Brunswick. Mem. Mo. Funeral Dirs. Assn., Nat. Funeral Dirs. Assn., TTT Soc. Democrat. Roman Catholic. Home: 309 Vine Brunswick MO 65236 Office: McCurry-Berry Funeral Home 511 W Broadway Brunswick MO 65236

MCCUTCHAN, JEAN ANNALEE, family counselor; b. Cleve., Aug. 20, 1952; d. H. Robert and Myrna Jean (Flory) Gemmer; B.A., Manchester Coll., North Manchester, Ind., 1974; M.A., Ball State U., Muncie, Ind., 1975; postgrad. Ind. U., South Bend, Andrews U., Berrien Springs, Mich.; cert. Human Devel. Tng. Inst., 1979, Effectiveness Tng. Inst., 1979; m. Larry J. McCutchan, Dec. 24, 1973; 1 son, Eric Daniel. Sch. psychologist Baugo-Concord-Wa-Nee Spl. Edn. Coop., Wakarusa, Ind., 1975-80, dir. spl. edn., 1980-85; family counselor Family Learning Ctr., Elkhart, Ind., 1985—; lectr. Andrews U., Berrien Springs, Mich., 1977, 80; vis. instr. Ind. U., South Bend, 1979; coordinator Elkhart (Ind.) County Pediatric/Ednl. Survey, 1978-79; coordinator Elkhart County Presch. Screening Com., 1982-85; mem. Elkhart County Schs. Comprehensive System of Personnel Devel., 1980-85, chair., 1982-85. Bd. dirs. H.C. Gemmer Family Christian Found., 1977—, Family Counseling Service, Elkhart County, 1980-85; mem. Elkhart County Adv. Council Children and Youth, 1979—. United Christian Missionary Soc. scholar 1970; Gt. Books scholar, 1965. Mem. Am. Assn. Counseling and Devel., Nat. Assn. Sch. Psychologists, Council Exceptional Children, Ind. Council Administrs. Spl. Edn., Am. Orthopsychiat. Assn. Home: 22660 Remington Ct Elkhart IN 46514 Office: 301 W Franklin Elkhart IN 46516

MCCUTCHEN, CHARLOTTE BARNWELL, neurologist, neurosciences educator; b. Camp Lejeune, N.C., Oct. 31, 1944; d. James Malcolm and Emily Strother (Dunovant) McC. B.S., U. S.C.-Columbia, 1966; M.D., Med. Coll. Va.-Richmond, 1970. Intern, Med. U. S.C., Charleston, 1970-71, asst. resident in neurology, 1971-72; asst. resident in neurology Vanderbilt U. Hosp., Nashville, 1972-73, resident, 1973-74; staff neurologist Electroencephalographer and neurologist in charge Seizure Clinic, Seattle VA Hosp. Epilepsy Ctr., 1974-76; acting instr., cons. U. Wash. Hosp., 1976-77; asst. clin. prof. neurosci. U. Calif.-San Diego, 1977-84, cons. in neurology Internal Medicine Group, 1980-84; staff neurologist VA Med. Ctr., San Diego, 1977-84; dir. epilepsy program San Diego VA Med. Ctr., 1977-84, dir. EEG Lab., 1977-84; assoc. prof. neurology Georgetown U. Sch. Med., 1984—; staff neurologist VA Med. Ctr., Washington, 1984—, dir. epilepsy program, 1984—, chief neurophysiology lab., 1984—. Bd. dirs. Epilepsy Found. for Nat. Capital Area, 1985-88. Contbr. articles to profl. jours. Mem. San Diego County Epilepsy Soc. (mem. profl. adv. bd. 1978, bd. dirs. 1978), Western EEG Soc. (bd. dirs. 1982—), Am. Epilepsy Soc. (sec. 1982—). Episcopalian.

MCDANIEL, AUDREY MAY, author, radio personality, non-profit foundation executive; b. Washington, Feb. 24, 1908; d. Dwight David and Jenette Marie (Nolan) Stansell; m. Valrie Shields McDaniel, 1941; 1 child, Val. Pres. Audrey McDaniel Faith and Hope Found., Arlington, Va., 1974—; featured personality Sta.-WFAX, Falls Church, Va., and other stas., 1963—, Abiding Love, 1974—. Featured in series Faith and Life, Sta.-WRC-TV, NBC, Washington, 1973, A Christmas Rose spl., Sta.-WTKK-TV, Manassas, Va., 1982, in series Capital Life, Sta.-WTKK-TV, 1973. Author books, including: (inspirational) The Greatest of These is Love, 1962, Forget-Me-Nots of Love, 1964, Garden of Hope, 1966, God is There, 1969, A Christmas Rose, 1971, Abiding Love, 1973, Only Believe in Him, 1977, Love's Promise, 1980, Hope for Every Heart, 1986; (autobiography) Touched by the Master, 1975; author words: Hymn Gems From Sacred Memory Time, 1967. Author, narrator audiocassette: Faith, Hope and Love, 1986. Mem. Nat. League Am. Pen Women (D.C. br.) (past nat. chaplain, Disting. Pen Woman award 1979), ASCAP. Methodist. Home and Office: 5800 N 11th St Arlington VA 22205

MCDANIEL, DEBRA LYNN, personnel representative; b. Racine, Wis., Oct. 28, 1954; d. Kenneth Arthur and Dorothy Jane (Kuhlman) Stofen; m. Jesse Lynn McDaniel, Dec. 17, 1983. B.A. in Psychology, Carthage Coll., 1976; M.S. in Indsl. Relations, U. Wis., 1978. Personnel adviser Consumers Power Co., Jackson, Mich., 1978-79, personnel asst., Pontiac, Mich., 1979-80; employee relations analyst Exxon Chem. Co., Baytown, Tex., 1980-83; personnel assoc. Eli Lilly & Co., Indpls., 1983, personnel rep., 1983—; cons. Blue Cross/Blue Shield, Chgo., 1978. Recipient acad. scholarships, 1972-76. Mem. Indsl. Relations Assn., Acad. Mgmt., Psi Chi. Mem. Lutheran Ch. Am. Office: Eli Lilly & Co 1200 Kentucky 328/1 Indianapolis IN 46285

MC DANIEL, JEANNE ADELE, school administrator; b. Battle Creek, Mich., Aug. 26, 1914; d. Arnold Herman and Viola May (Rice) Kambly; R.N., Michael Reese Hosp. Sch. Nursing, Chgo., 1935; m. Lloyd G. McDaniel, Feb. 6, 1937 (dec. 1980); children—Lloyd Kambly, Stephanie McDaniel Wirt, Patricia McDaniel Paddock. Asst. to dir. Lanham Fund Day Care Centers, Battle Creek Pub. Schs., 1945-46; dir., pres. bd. dirs. Kambly Sch. Retarded Children, Battle Creek, 1959—. Bd. dirs. Woodlawn Nursery; sponsor troop Boy Scouts Am. Mem. Michael Reese Nurses Alumnae Assn., D.A.R., Council Exceptional Children, Calhoun County Assn. Retarded Children, Beta Sigma Phi. Republican. Presbyn. Home: 115 Irving Park Dr Battle Creek MI 49017 Office: 1003 North Ave Battle Creek MI 49017

MCDANIEL, JUANITA SUE, utility company executive; b. Caney, Kans., Aug. 20, 1946; d. Wiley A. and Juanita Frances (Dawson) Wilson; m. Charles R. Palmer, Jan. 10, 1967 (div.); 1 child, Wendy Ranae McDaniel; m. Clifford McDaniel, Apr. 14, 1972 (separated). Student Northwestern U., Talequah, Okla., 1964-65, La. State U., 1970-72. With South Central Bell Telephone Co., 1967-83, test desk foreman, Covinton, La., 1976-77, bus. office mgr., Hammond, La., 1977-83; mgr. phone ctr. store AT&T Telephone, Covington, 1983—, New Orleans, 1984—. Adviser Jr. Achievement, Hammond, 1978-79; charter mem. Hammond Mayor's Commn. on Needs of Women, 1981-82. Named to Outstanding Young Women Am., U.S. Jaycees, 1980. Mem. Bus. and Profl. Women's Club (state treas. 1985-86), Nat. Assn. Female Execs., New Orleans C. of C. Republican. Baptist. Office: AT&T Telephone 7052 Read Rd New Orleans LA 70127

MCDANIEL, LORETTA MARIE, ednl. adminstr.; b. LaGrande, Oreg., Dec. 21, 1938; d. Wilfred J. and Margaret F. (Briggs) Lyon; B.S., Eastern Oreg. State Coll., 1978; m. Gale E. McDaniel, July 28, 1956; children—Larry B., Peggy S., Kevin K. Dep. county clk. Union County, LaGrande, 1964-77; juvenile ct. counselor Union County, 1977-79; dir. student services Modern Bus. Coll., Kennewick, Wash., 1980, dir., 1980—. Mem. Sch. Bd., Cove Sch. Dist., 1974-76; mem. Union County Republican Central com., 1974. Mem. Union County Legal Secs. Assn. (v.p. 1968), Nat. Assn. Female Execs., Pacific N.W. Personnel Mgrs. Assn., Am. Soc. Personnel Adminstrn., Am. Soc. Tng. and Devel. (exec. bd. Columbia Basin chpt.). Republican. Club: Zonta. Home: 1601 S Nelson St Kennewick WA 99336 Office: 3311 W Clearwater Suite 1201 Kennewick WA 99336

MCDANIEL, MYRA ATWELL, lawyer, state official; b. Phila., Dec. 13, 1932; d. Toronto Canada and Eva Lucinda (Yores) Atwell; m. Reuben Roosevelt McDaniel, Jr., Feb. 20, 1955; children—Diane Lorraine, Reuben. B.A., U. Pa., 1954; J.D., U. Tex.-Austin, 1975. Bar: Tex., U.S. Dist. Ct. (ea. dist.) Tex. 1979, U.S. Dist. Ct. (we. dist.) Tex. 1977, U.S. Dist. Ct. (no. dist.) Tex. 1978, U.S. Dist. Ct. (so. dist.) Tex. 1978, U.S. Ct. Appeals (5th cir.) 1978, U.S. Supreme Ct. 1978. Asst. atty. gen. State of Tex., Austin, 1975-79, chief taxation div., 1979-81, gen. counsel to gov., 1983-84; asst. gen. counsel Tex. R.R. Commn., Austin, 1981-82; gen. counsel The Wilson Cos., San Antonio and Midland, Tex., 1982; assoc. Bickerstaff, Heath & Smiley, Austin, 1984; sec. of State of Tex., Austin, 1984—; bd. dirs. Nat. Leadership Conf. for Exec. Women in State Govt., Washington, 1983-84, Episcopal Found. Tex., 1986—; dir. Austin Cons. Group, Inc., 1983-86; lectr. Bd. visitors U. Tex. Law Sch., 1983—, vice-chmn., 1983-84; bd. dirs. Friends of Ronald McDonald House Central Tex., 1983-86, chmn. house ops. com., 1983-84; trustee Tex. Bar Found., 19896-89; clk., vestry bd. St. James Episcopal Ch., 1976-79, 81-83. Recipient medal West Phila. Citizens League, 1950; honoree Serwa Yetu chpt. Mt. Olive Grand chpt. Tex. Order Eastern Star, 1979. Fellow Tex. Bar Found., Am. Bar Found.; mem. State Bar Tex. (chmn. subcom. profl. efficiency and econ. research 1978-84), Tex. Bar Assn., ABA, Travis County Bar Assn., Austin Black Lawyers Assn., Travis County Women Lawyers Assn. Democrat. Clubs: Soroptimists, Women in Mgmt. (Austin). Office: State Capitol Bldg PO Box 12697 Austin TX 78711

MCDANIEL, WANDA J., educational administrator; b. Las Cruces, N.Mex., Aug. 10, 1931; d. William Howell and Lena Josephine (Fowler) Hand; m. Carl M. McDaniel; children—Timothy, Robert McDaniel. B.S., Anderson Coll., Ind., 1954; M.Ed., Fla. Atlantic U., 1968; Ph.D., Syracuse U., 1976. Cert. ednl. adminstr. Ohio. Tchr. pub. schs., Mich., Ind., Fla., N.Y., 1954-68; asst. prin. Clay County Pub. Schs., Green Cove Springs, Fla., 1968-70; tchr. spl. assignments Dade County Pub. Schs., Miami, Fla., 1970-72; prin. Allentown Pub. Schs., Pa., 1976-82; dir. Intermediate Unit, Schnecksville, Pa., 1982-85; asst. supt. Dayton Pub. Schs., 1985—; staff assoc. Syracuse U., 1974-76; adj. assoc. prof. Lehigh U., 1978-83. Author. (manual) Perceptual Motor Training, 1976. Contbr. articles to profl. jours. Mem. Nat. Conf. U. Pa. (presenter 1984), Nat. Assn. Elem. Sch. Prins. (presenter 1980), S.E. Regional Reading Conf. (presenter 1980), Pa. Women's Caucus (exec. com. 1984-86), Pa. Elem. Sch. Prins. (exec. bd. 1982-84). Republican. Club: Prin. Assoc. (Allentown, pres. 1980-82). Avocations: golf; music. Home: 2133 University Pl Dayton OH 45406 Office: Dayton Pub Schs 4280 Western Ave Dayton OH 45427

MCDANIELS, DELORES PAULINE, community services adminstrator; b. Bakersfield, Calif., Jan. 29, 1941; d. A. Paul and Florentina Minnie (Tisch) Schwartz; m. Clifford Frank Anderson, Dec. 13, 1958 (div.); children—Martin Lee Anderson, Cindy Lou Evans. Cert. in Psychology and Edn., U. Calif.-Riverside, 1967; Cert. in Bldg. and Safety, Calif. Poly. Inst., 1979. Enforcement officer, dir. vehicle abatement and weed abatement, acting fire marshall, 1979-81; disaster preparedness co-ordinator City of Lake Elsinore, Calif., 1980, dir. community services, 1978—, grants mgr., 1986—; human resource specialist Inland Service Ctr., Riverside, Calif., 1986—. Recipient Cert. of Honor, City Council, 1980; commendations Fed. Govt. Ordinance Officer, Dept. Air Force, Gov.'s Office, Calif. Conservation Corp. Mem. So. Calif. Assn. Govts. (Riverside-San Bernardino County com. for transp. 1985—), Nat. Assn. Female Execs., Bus. and Profl. Women (corr. sec. 1985-86, pres. 1986-87), Rescue Squad Four (sec. 1965), C. of C. (bd. govs. 1980—). Avocations: oil painting, swimming, horseback riding. Home: 19810 Gustin Rd Perris CA 92370 Office: City of Lake Elsinore/Transit System 130 S Main St Lake Elsinore CA 92330

MCDANIELS, LINDA CAROL, contract analyst; b. Horry, S.C., Oct. 24, 1955; d. Thomas Hughy and Letha (Smith) McD. B.A., N.C. State U., 1978. Research asst. N.C. Energy Inst., Research Triangle Park, 1978-81; contracts adminstr. N.C. Alternative Energy Corp., Research Triangle Park, 1981-84; contract analyst Blue Cross Blue Shield, Durham, N.C., 1984—. Tchr., Intense Bible Study, Raleigh, N.C., 1983-84. Democrat. Methodist. Home: 606F Chateau Apt 606 Powell Dr Raleigh NC 27606

MCDARGH-ELVINS, EILEEN, communications consultant; b. Denver, Sept. 5, 1948; d. H. J. and Mary S. (Reineberg) McDargh III; B.A. in Speech Communications, U. Fla., 1969; postgrad. U. Calif., Irvine, 1978—; m. W. T. Elvins, May 18, 1980; children by previous marriage—Todd, Holly, Heather. Public relations, mktg. dir. Amelia Island Plantation, Amelia Island, Fla., 1973-78; corp. communications exec. Comprehensive Care Corp., Newport Beach, Calif., 1978-79; sr. account exec. Gloria Zigner & Assos., Newport Beach, 1979-80; pres. McDargh Communications, Laguna Niguel, Calif., 1980—; lectr. U. Calif., Irvine, 1980—, Orange Coast Community Coll., Costa Mesa, Calif., 1980—. Author: How To Work for a Living & Still Be Free To Live. Reading tutor South Coast Literacy Council, Laguna Niguel, Calif., 1981—. Recipient Outstanding Tchr. award Nassau County, 1972. Mem. Women in Communications (dir. Orange County chpt. 1979), Assn. Profl. Cons. (founding mem. 1980, dir. 1980-82), Calif. Press Women, Public Relations Soc. Am., Internat. Assn. Bus. Communicators. Contbr. articles in field to profl. publs. Home and Office: 23731 Montego Bay Laguna Niguel CA 92677

MCDAVID, JANET LOUISE, lawyer; b. Mpls., Jan. 24, 1950; d. Robert Matthew and Lois May (Bratt) Kurzeka; m. John Gary McDavid, June 9, 1973; 1 child, Matthew Collins McDavid. B.A., Northwestern U., 1971; J.D., Georgetown U., 1974. Bar: D.C. 1975, U.S. Supreme Ct., 1980, U.S. Ct. Appeals D.C. 1976, U.S. Ct. Appeals (5th cir.) 1983. Assoc. Hogan & Hartson, Washington, 1974-83, ptnr., 1984—; gen. counsel ERAmerica, 1977-83. Contbr. articles to profl. jours. Mem. ABA (vice chmn. civil practice com. antitrust sect.), Washington Council Lawyers, D.C. Bar Assn., Fed. Bar Assn., Womens Legal Def. Fund, ACLU. Democrat. Office: Hogan & Hartson 815 Connecticut Ave Washington DC 20006

MC DERMID, ALICE MARGUERITE CONNELL (MRS. RALPH MANEWAL MCDERMID), civic and political worker, lectr.; b. Sterling, Ill., May 25, 1910; d. William Hayes and Margaret (Durr) Connell; A.B., U. Ill., 1931; m. Ralph Manewal McDermid, Nov. 28, 1931; children—Ralph Manewal, Jane Dillon (Mrs. Anders Wiberg), Michael Metcalf, John Fairbanks. Bd. dirs. Scarsdale (N.Y.) Woman's Exchange, 1953-60; mem. social service bd. N.Y. Infirmary, 1960-76, vice chmn., 1964-76; trustees team United Hosp. Fund, 1965-75; case policy bd. Spence-Chapin Adoption Service, 1960—; fund raising Greer Sch., 1958-73, Vis. Nurse Assn., 1960-64; co-chmn. UN Program, Westchester County; founder Jane Todd Meml. Scholarship, 1966; mem. adv. council Morse Gallery of Art, Winter Park, Fla., 1974—; sec. exec. com. Morse Gallery Art Assocs., 1977-78, v.p., 1978-80, pres., 1980-82; bd. dirs. Council Arts and Scis. Central Fla., 1975—, v.p., 1976-78; bd. dirs. Charles Hosmer Morse Found., 1980-82. Sec., Young Republicans Ill., 1930-31; bd. dirs. Scarsdale (N.Y.) Women's Rep. Club, 1961-67, pres., 1965-67, legis. chmn., 1981—; del. Washington Conf. Nat. Fed. Rep. Women, 1965-72; mem. council Fedn. Women's Rep. Clubs N.Y. State, 1967-76; Rep. dist. leader, 1967-75; del. Rep. Jud. Conv., 1969-71; vice chmn. Rep. Town Com., 1969-75, mem. Rep. Presidents Club, Scarsdale; mem. N.Y. State Rep. Com., 1970-72; N.Y. Rep. committee woman 90th Assembly Dist., 1970-72. Recipient Rep. Woman of Yr. award, Scarsdale, 1974, other awards. Mem. Women's Rep. Federated Club of Winter Park (pres. 1978-80), Lock Haven Art Center, Friends of Winter Park Library, Orlando Opera Guild, Winter Park Hist. Soc., English Speaking Union U.S., Friends of Cornell Fine Arts, Loch Haven Arts Soc., Alpha Xi Delta. Episcopalian. Clubs: Scarsdale Women's, Ladies Harvard, Women's Nat. Rep. (N.Y.C.); Women's of Winter Park (dir. 1977-79), Racquet (Winter Park). Home: 1445 Granville Dr Winter Park FL 32789

MCDERMOTT, LYNDA CARYL, human resources consultant; b. Columbus, Ohio, Sept. 23, 1950; d. Ned Roland and Marian Carlotta (Johnson) Green; m. William W. Waite, May 30, 1975. B.A. in Psychology, Miami U., Oxford, Ohio, 1972; M. Orgn. Devel., Bowling Green State U., 1983. Mgr. data processing Ohio Bell Telephone, Columbus and Cleve., 1972-78; cons. AT&T, Denver and N.Y.C., 1976; mgmt. cons. Ernst & Whinney, Cleve. and N.Y.C., 1978-82; dir. human resources cons. KMG Main Hurdman, N.Y.C., 1982-86; exec. v.p., prin. Corp. Resources, Inc., N.Y.C., 1986—; chmn. Equipro Devel., Inc., 1985—. Contbr. articles to profl. jours. Program com. Women Bus. Owners of N.Y., N.Y.C., 1983; mem. resource com. Girls Clubs Am.; bd. dirs. Friends of the Joffrey Ballet. Mem. Am. Soc. Personnel Adminstrs., Am. Compensation Assn. (bd. dirs.), N.Y. Human Resources Planners, Am. Soc. Tng. and Devel. (dir. orgn. devel. and bd. dirs. 1977-86), Orgn. Devel. Network. Republican. Clubs: Atrium, Saugatuck Yacht. Office: Corp Resources 18 E 48th St New York NY 10017

MCDERMOTT, PAMELA GILLMAN, public relations and marketing company executive; b. Buffalo, Mar. 12, 1951; d. Harry Abram and Phyllis Joy (Pettys) Gillman; m. Terence Patrick McDermott, May 12, 1984. Student Inst. European Studies, Vienna, Austria, 1971-72; B.E., U. Vt., 1973; postgrad. Suffolk U., 1976-78. Lic. real estate broker, Mass. Spl. asst. to fed. co-chmn. New Eng. Regional Commn., Boston, 1974-77; cons. U. Mass., Amherst, 1977; spl. asst. to Lt. Gov. Commonwealth of Mass., Boston, 1977-79, coordinator Coalition of Northeastern Govs., 1977-78, Gov's. rep. to New Eng. Regional Commn., 1978-79; assoc. producer D.H. Sawyer & Assocs., N.Y.C., 1979, dir. Boston office, 1979-80; project dir. Office of Mktg. and Devel., City of Boston, 1980-81; pres. Northeast Mgmt. & Mktg. Co., Boston, 1981—. Columnist, Boston Herald, 1980-82. Mem. Mass. Women's Bus. Devel. Council, 1983—; candidate for Boston City Council, 1981; bd. dirs. Big Sister Assn. of Greater Boston, 1984—; mem. Dems. for Ward 5 Com., 1981-82; mem. fin. com. Kennedy for Pres., 1980; patron The Laboure Ctr., 1984-86, Pope John XXIII Nat. Seminary, 1984-85; active numerous polit. campaigns at local and state levels. Mem. Greater Boston C. of C. (Execs. Club 1982—). Avocations: golf; skiing; swimming; reading. Home: 201 Milton St Dorchester MA 02124 Office: Northeast Mgmt and Mktg Co One Boston Pl Suite 3400 Boston MA 02108

MCDERMOTT, PATRICIA ANN, nurse; b. Bklyn., July 10, 1943; d. John J. and Lillian E. (Sweeney) Skelly; m. Joseph Kevin McDermott, Oct. 5, 1963; children—Colleen Mary, John Joseph. Diploma, Kings County Hosp. Ctr. Sch. Nursing, Bklyn., 1963; B.S. in Health Care Adminstrn., St. Francis Coll., Bklyn., 1979. Staff nurse Kings County Hosp., Bklyn., 1963-66, head nurse outpatient dept., 1966-74; evening supr. Park Nursing Home, Rockaway Park, N.Y., 1974-83; day supr. Hyde Park Nursing Home, Staatsburg, N.Y., 1984-85, dir. nursing, 1985—; propr. retail liquor bus. Active local Girl Scouts U.S.A., 1971-78, Boy Scouts Am., 1978-82, Stella Maris Parents Club, 1978-82, St. Francis de Sales Altar and Rosary Soc., 1970-83, St. Francis de Sales Little League, 1978-80, also softball coach, 1974-77. Republican. Roman Catholic. Avocations: knitting; crocheting; roller skating; bowling; oil painting. Home: 286A Shadblow Ln Clinton Corners NY 12514 Office: Hyde Park Nursing Home Route 9 Staatsburg NY 12580

MCDERMOTT, STEPHANIE ANASTASIA, real estate investment consultant; b. Balt., July 9, 1953; d. Francis James and Angelina Anastasia (Burnett) Geppi; m. Peter Samuel McDermott, Jan. 27, 1978 (div. 1983); 1 child, Jeffrey Scott. B.A., UCLA, 1974, Calif. Arts Sch., 1976. Broker, Coldwell Banker, Los Angeles, 1974-78; adminstrv. v.p. Ashwill-Burke, Los Angeles, 1978-83; developer, Los Angeles, 1983-84; real estate investment specialist, dir. Morton Capital Co., Los Angeles, 1984—; cons. Trust Deed Investment Services, Los Angeles, 1980—. Chmn., ARC, Los Angeles, 1978; docent Calif. Inst. Arts, Valencia, 1980; participant U.S. Olympic Com., Ventura, Calif., 1984. Mem. Mortgage Brokers Inst. Republican. Roman Catholic. Avocations: Tennis; water sports; art; art history; music.

MC DEVITT, ELLEN, physician; b. Shubuta, Miss., Sept. 3, 1907; d. James Andrew and Alma (McManus) McDevitt; A.B., Miss. State Coll. for Women, 1930; M.D., U. Utah, 1949. Chief technician vascular clinic N.Y. Post Grad. Hosp., 1934-46; intern Meadowbrook Hosp., Hempstead, N.Y., 1949-50; asst. resident Hackensack (N.J.) Hosp., 1950-51, Bellevue Hosp., N.Y.C., 1953-54; research asso. medicine N.Y. Hosp.-Cornell U. Med. Coll., 1951-52; provisional asst. physician out patient dept. N.Y. Hosp., 1951-52; mem. staff, chief 2d med. div. vascular clinic Bellevue Hosp.; instr. medicine Cornell U., 1954-56, asst. prof., 1957-63, asso. prof., 1963-72; former asso. attending N.Y. Hosp., dir. vascular sect., 1968-72, now hon. mem. med. staff. Recipient award for excellence Miss. U. for Women, 1984. Fellow Am. Soc. Geriatics; mem. AMA, Miss., East Miss. med. socs., Am. (fellow council on circulation, fellow council on stroke), N.Y., Miss. heart assns., Sigma Xi. Contbr. articles to profl. jours. Home: 1520 Olive St Gulfport MS 39501

MCDONALD, ALICE COIG, state education department adminstrator; b. Chalmette, La., Sept. 26, 1940; d. Olas Casimere and Genevieve Louise (Heck) Coig; m. Glenn McDonald, July 16, 1967; 1 child, Michel. B.S., Loyola U., New Orleans, 1962, Ed.M., 1966; postgrad., Spalding Coll., 1975. Tchr. St. Bernard Pub. Sch., Chalmette, 1962-67; counselor, instrn. coordinator Jefferson County Schs., Louisville, 1967-77; ednl. advisor Jefferson County Govt., Louisville, 1977-78; chief exec. asst. Office of Mayor, Louisville, 1978-80; dep. supt. pub. instruction Ky. Dept. Edn., Frankford, 1980-83, supt. pub. instruction, 1984—; bd. dirs., com. mem. Ky. Council Higher Edn., 1984—, Ky. Juvenile Justice Com., 1984—, Ky. Ednl. TV Authority, 1984—; So. Regional Council Ednl. Improvement, 1984—. Contbr. articles to profl. jours. Democratic nat. committeewoman, Ky., 1976-79; mem. Pres. Adv. Com. on Women, 1978-80; mem. exec. com. Dem. Nat. Com., 1977—; del., alternate platform com. Dem. Nat. Conv., 1972, 76, 80, 84. Mem. Council Chief State Sch. Officers, Edn. Commn. of States, Women in Sch. Adminstrn., NEA, Ky. Edn. Assn., Dem. Women's Club of Ky. (pres. 1974-76). Office: Ky Dept Edn 1st floor Capital Plaza Tower Frankfort KY 40601

MC DONALD, BARBARA ANN, psychotherapist; b. Mpls., July 15, 1932; d. John and Georgia Elizabeth (Baker) Rubenzer; B.A., U. Minn., 1954; M.S.W., U. Denver, 1977; m. Lawrence R. McDonald, July 27, 1957; adopted children—John, Mary Elizabeth. Day care cons. Minn. Dept. Public Welfare, St. Paul, 1954-59; social worker Community Info. Center, Mpls., 1959-60; exec. dir. Social Synergistics Co., Littleton, Colo., 1970—; cons. to community orgns., Indian tribes. Family therapist Am. Inst. Public Service, Washington, 1979—. Named 1 of 8 Women of Yr. and featured on TV spl. Ladies Home Jour., 1974; Clairol scholar, 1974; Am. Bus. Women's Assn. scholar, 1974; Alpha Gamma Delta scholar, 1974; lic. psychotherapist, Colo. Mem. Minn. Pre-Sch. Edn. Assn. (hon. life), Nat. Assn. Social Workers, Am. Bus. Women's Assn., Alpha Gamma Delta (Disting. Citizen award 1975). Club: Altrusa (hon.). Author: Selected References on the Group Day Care of Pre-School Children, 1956; Helping Families Grow: Specialized Psychotherapy with Hearing Impaired Children and Their Families, 1984. Office: 13720 Franciscan Dr Sun City West AZ 85375

MCDONALD, BARBARA BLACK ROBERTSON, packaging and product design consultant; b. N.Y.C., Mar. 7, 1951; d. Donald Black Robertson and Elizabeth Morton (Stout) McD. Student Western New Eng. Coll., 1969-70, Fashion Inst. Tech., N.Y.C., 1970-71, Sch. Visual Arts, N.Y.C., 1971-72. Designer, Unique Studios, N.Y.C., 1972-74; assoc. art dir. CBS, N.Y.C., 1974-77; creative dir. Remco Toys, N.Y.C., 1977-80; sr. design mgr. Lever Bros., N.Y.C., 1980-81; pres., owner B. McDonald, N.Y.C., 1981—. Canvaser, recruiter Re-Election for Ed Koch, N.Y.C., 1985. Mem. Graphic Artists Guild, Package Designers Council, Nat. Assn. Female Execs. Democrat. Avocations: wind surfing; racquetball; canoeing; writing; reading. Office: 1123 Broadway Suite 817 New York NY 10010

MCDONALD, CAROL ANN, dentist; b. Schenectady, Feb. 6, 1957; d. Arthur Earl McDonald and Lucy Marie (Wiggins) McDonald Boyles; m. James Paul Rappenecker, Apr. 9, 1983. D.D.S., U. Tex., Houston, 1981. Staff dentist Carl C. Boyles, D.D.S., Houston, 1981-83; pvt. practice dentistry, Houston, 1983—. Home: 2610 Montrose St Apt 4 Houston TX 77006 Office: 6410 Fannin St Suite 706 Houston TX 77030

MC DONALD, COLLEEN, social work administrator; b. Duluth, Minn., Mar. 17, 1950; d. Thomas Joseph and Lillian Clara (Hedlund) Mc Donald. B.F.A., U. Wis., 1973. Adminstrv. asst. British Steel Corp., London, 1973-75, CBS News, N.Y.C., 1976-77; coordinator CBS, Inc. Sch. of Mgmt., N.Y.C., 1977-81; social worker, supr. Westside Cluster, N.Y.C., 1981-83, project dir. Ctr. for Homeless Women, 1983—; mem. Coalition for Homeless, N.Y.C., 1981—, speaker, 1984—. Founding mem. Com. for Women in Crisis, N.Y.C., 1986; mem. Ansonia Dems., N.Y.C., 1985, West 71st St. Assn., N.Y.C., 1986. Democrat. Office: Westside Cluster 257 W 30th St New York NY 10001

MCDONALD, FLORENCE SANCHEZ, facility manager; b. Houston, Oct. 27, 1950; d. Joe R. and Rachel (Lopez) S. B.S., U. Colo., 1979. Plant reports clk. Mountain Bell, Boulder, Colo., 1972-75; student staff supr. U. Colo., Boulder, 1976-79; teaching asst. Boulder Valley Schs., 1977-79; tchr. Denver Pub. Schs., 1979-80; mgr. Am. TV & Communications Corp., Englewood, Colo., 1980—. Mem. Women in Cable, Women in Communications, Colo. Telecommunications Assn. Roman Catholic.

MC DONALD, GAIL FABER, musician, educator; b. Jersey City, Oct. 24, 1917; d. Samuel and Jennie (Weiss) Faber; diploma Mannes Music Sch., N.Y.C., 1938; B.A., U. Md., 1962; Mus.M., Cath. U., 1968; D.Mus. Arts, U. Md., 1977; m. Angus McDonald, Nov. 10, 1946; children—Lora McDonald Ferguson, Charles, Henry. Legis. asst. Capitol Hill, 1943-46; pvt. tchr. piano and music theory, Washington and Md., 1950—; piano soloist Nat. Gallery Art, 1977; rec. artist Educo Records; lectr., performer Bach Sinfonias and Mendelssohn's Complete Songs Without Words; recorder complete solo piano works of Daniel Gregory Mason. Mem. D.C., Md. (pres. 1977—) music tchrs. assns., D.C. Fedn. Music Clubs, Nat. Guild Piano Tchrs. (performing mem., adjudicator 1972—), Friday Morning Music Club. Author: Muzio Clementi and the Gradus Ad Parnassum, 1968. Address: 6807 Farmer Dr Fort Washington MD 20744

MCDONALD, GLORIA DRAKE, town councilwoman; b. Buffalo, Dec. 7, 1928; d. Harold and Vera Katherine (Seitz) Drake; B.S. in Commerce, D'Youville Coll., Buffalo, 1949; m. Thomas C. McDonald, Oct. 1, 1951 (dec. 1979); children—Paul H., Mary Kay. Various secretarial positions, 1949-55; dist. congressional asst., 1965-74; legal asst. to husband, 1956-79; councilwoman Town of Tonawanda (N.Y.), 1976—, chmn. bldg. dept., mem. taxes, assessments, energy conservation, econ. devel., bldg. dept., planning, parks and recreation, sr. citizens and boat harbor coms., also youth bd.; bd. dirs. Tonawanda Devel. Corp., Tonawanda Housing Authority. Past pres. Green Acres Republican Women's Club; mem. women's aux. Salvation Army. Named Woman of Yr. Green Acres Rep. Women's Club, 1977. Mem. Western N.Y. Paralegal Assn. (asso.), N.Y. State Fedn. Women's Clubs (dist. dir., treas. elect 1982-84), Buffalo Fedn. Women's Clubs (dir.), Honorarians (2d v.p. 1982-84, past treas.). Roman Catholic. Club: Kenmore Zonta (chmn. status women com. 1980-82). Home: 350 Grayton Rd Tonawanda NY 14150 Office: 2919 Delaware Ave Kenmore NY 14217

MCDONALD, JANE F., insurance company executive; b. Winthrop, Mass., Dec. 19, 1940; d. William Francis and Isabelle Frances (Mythen) Moran; m. James Joseph McDonald, Aug. 21, 1965 (div. 1976); children—Maureen Lynn, Susan Jill, Kevin James. B.S. in Edn., Salem State Coll., Mass., 1962; Assoc. in Underwriting, Ins. Inst., Malvern, Pa., 1983. Tchr., East Hartford Sch. System, Conn., 1962-66; acct. Watkin Bros. Piano & Organ, Hartford, 1975-76; policy analyst Hartford Steam Boiler Insp. & Ins., 1976-80; supervising underwriter Am. Nuclear Insurers, Farmington, 1981—. Mem. Nat. Assn. Ins. Women, Am. Nuclear Soc., Nat. Assn. Female Execs., N.Y. Acad. Scis., Hartford Assn. Ins. Women (by-laws chmn. 1984-85). Democrat. Roman Catholic. Avocations: reading; handwriting analysis; travel. Home: 675 Graham Rd South Windsor CT 06074 Office: Am Nuclear Insurers 270 Farmington Ave Farmington CT 06074

MCDONALD, JOANNE, high technology company executive; b. San Diego, June 10, 1947; d. Paul and Dolores (Paganucci) McD. B.A., U. Md., 1970. High tech. exec. ENSCO Inc., Springfield, Va., 1981—. Bd. dirs. Yorktowne Sq., Falls Church, Va., 1981. Mem. Am. Soc. Tng. and Devel., Internat. Assn. Personnel Women, Am. Soc. Personnel Adminstrs., Internat. Assn. Bus. Communicators. Office: ENSCO Inc 5400 Port Royal Rd Springfield VA 22151

MCDONALD, JUDY A., television advertising and promotion manager; b. Louisville, Jan. 13, 1955; d. George T. and Helen R. (Effinger) McD. Student Jefferson Community Coll., 1972-73, U. Louisville, 1974-75; B.A. in Radio and TV, Ind. U., 1977. News asst. Sta. WLKY-TV, Louisville, 1977-78, promotion asst., producer, 1978-80; promotion producer Sta. WKRC-TV, Cin., 1980-81; creative series dir. Sta. WAVY-TV, Norfolk, VA., 1982-83; advt., promotion mgr. Sta. WOTV, Grand Rapids, Mich., 1983—; com. mem. NBC Affiliate Promotion Com., 1985—. Writer, exec. producer WOTV 35th Anniversary, 1984 (BPME Gold award 1985); writer, exec. producer WOTV News Performance, 1983 (ADDY award 1984); contbr. writer, producer WAVY-TV Daily News Spooky, 1983 (BPME Gold award 1984). Event coordinator Va. Prevention Child Abuse, Norfolk, 1983. Recipient Ad Club Cert. Merit Ad Club, 1983, 1984. Mem. Broadcast Promotion and Mtg. Execs., Press Club Grand Rapids. Democrat. Roman Catholic. Avocations: bicycling; tennis; volleyball; reading. Office: WOTV 120 College SE PO Box B Grand Rapids MI 49501

MCDONALD, JULIE JENSEN, writer, journalism educator; b. Iowa, June 22, 1929; d. Alfred Julius Jensen and Myrtle Petra (Faurschou) Jensen Petersen; m. Elliott Raymond McDonald, Jr., May 6, 1952; children—Beth McDonald Pearson, Elliott R. III. B.A., U. Iowa, 1951; Litt.D. (hon.), St. Ambrose Coll., 1972. Womans' editor Rockford Newspapers, Ill., 1951-52; arts reviewer, features Quad-City Times, Davenport, Iowa, 1962-83; lectr. in journalism St. Ambrose Coll., Davenport, 1974—; art and dance critic Rock Island Argus,

Ill., 1983—; artist-in-the-schs. Iowa Arts Council, 1974—. Author: Amalie's Story, 1970; Petra, 1978 (Friends of Am. Writers award 1979); The Sailing Out, 1982 (Johnson Brigham award 1983). Bd. dirs. Davenport Hospice, 1984; pres. Friends of Davenport Pub. Library, 1983-85; trustee Davenport Art Gallery, 1985—. Mem. Am. Authors Guild, Iowa Press Women (nat. 1st prize for novel 1983), PEO, Danish Sisterhood of Am. Republican. Presbyterian. Avocations: clarinetist (Bettendorf Park Band); Scottish Deerhound fancier. Home: 2802 E Locust St Davenport IA 52803

MCDONALD, KATHRYN JACKSON, public speaker; b. Glendale, Calif., Mar. 21, 1949; d. James Lawrence and Marjorie (Hoofnagle) Jackson; m. Lawrence Patton McDonald, June 19, 1976 (dec. Sept. 1983); children—Lawrence Patton, Lauren Aileen. Student Glendale Coll. Lectr. on KAL 007, nat. defense, central am. women's econs., aid and trade with communist countries, Marietta, Ga., 1983—; ptnr. Southeastern Services, Rome, Ga., 1984—. Pres., Larry McDonald Meml. Found., Inc., Marietta, Ga., 1984—; hon. nat. chmn. Larry McDonald Crusade to Stop Financing Communism, San Marino, Calif., 1983—. Named to 10 Most Admired Women in Am., Readers Conservative Digest, 1984. Mem. Am. Civil Def. Assn. Republican. Methodist. Office: Larry McDonald Meml Found Inc PO Box 745 Marietta GA 30061

MCDONALD, MARIANNE, classicist; b. Chgo., Jan. 2, 1937; d. Eugene Francis and Inez (Riddle) McD.; B.A. magna cum laude, Bryn Mawr Coll., 1958; M.A., U. Chgo., 1960; Ph.D., U. Calif., Irvine, 1975; m. Torajiro Mori, Aug. 12, 1978; children—Eugene, Conrad, Bryan, Bridget, Kirstie, Hiroshi. Teaching asst. classics U. Calif., Irvine, 1972-74, instr. Greek, Latin and English, mythology, modern cinema, 1975-79, researcher Thesaurus Linguae Graecae Project, 1979—; dir. Centrum. Bd. dirs. Am. Coll. of Greece, 1981—, Scripps Hosp., 1981—, LaJolla Country Day Sch., 1971-73; nat. bd. advisors Am. Biog. Inst., 1982—. Mem. Am. Philol. Assn., Am. Classical League, Philol. Assn. Pacific Coast, MLA, Am. Comparative Lit. Assn., Modern and Classical Lang. Assn. So. Calif., AAUP, Hellenic Soc., Calif. Fgn. Lang. Tchrs. Assn., Internat. Platform Assn. Republican. Buddhist; Greek Orthodox. Clubs: KPBS Producers, Hellenic Univ. (dir.). Author: Terms for Happiness in Euripides, 1978; Semilemmatized Concordances to Euripides' Alcestis, 1977; Cyclops, Andromache, Medea, 1978; Heraclidae, Hippolytus, 1979; Hecuba, 1982; Euripides in Cinema: The Heart Made Visible, 1983; Hercules Furens, 1984; translator Hoshi Shinichi: The Cost of Kindness and Other Fabulous Tales, 1985; Video Tape: Business Negotiations with the Japanese: A Practical Guide, 1985; contbr. numerous articles to profl. jours. Home: Box 929 Rancho Santa Fe CA 92067 Office: Thesaurus Linguae Gracae Project U Calif Irvine CA 92717

MCDONALD, PATRICIA ANNE, lawyer; b. Kansas City, Mo., Apr. 24, 1943; d. Robert Ralph and Lucille Frances (Bannon) McDonald. B.A., St. Mary Coll., Leavenworth, Kans., 1972; J.D., U. Kans., 1982. Bar: Kans. 1982. Payroll clk. Southwestern Bell Co., Kansas City, Mo., 1969-71; payroll clk. H.D. Lee Co., Lenexa, Kans., 1971-72; payroll supr. TeleCommunications, Inc., Denver, 1973-74; exec. sec. to Mayor of Kansas City (Kans.), 1975-79; sole practice, Kansas City, Kans., 1983; ct. trustee Wyandotte County Dist. Ct., Kansas City, 1983—. Bd. dirs. Parents' Time Out, Kansas City, 1983—. Mem. ABA, Wyandotte County Bar Assn., Kans. Bar Assn., Phi Delta Phi, Kansas City Area C. of C. (bd. dirs. 1983-84), Kansas City Women's C. of C. (pres. 1983—). Democrat. Roman Catholic. Club: Pilot Internat. (Kans. City, Kans.). Office: CT Trustee 710 N 7th St Kansas City KS 66101

MCDONALD, PEGGY ANN STIMMEL, automobile company official; b. Darbyville, Ohio, Aug. 25, 1931; d. Wilbur Smith and Bernice Edna (Hott) Stimmel; missionary diploma with honor Moody Bible Inst., 1952; B.A. cum laude in Econs. (scholar), Ohio Wesleyan U., 1965; M.B.A. with distinction, Xavier U., 1977; m. George R. Stich, Mar. 7, 1953 (dec.); 1 son, Mark Stephen (dec.); m. Joseph F. McDonald, Jr., Feb. 1, 1986. . Missionary in S. Am., Evang. Alliance Mission, 1956-61; cost acct. Western Electric Co., 1965-66; acctg. mgr. Ohio Wesleyan U., 1966-73; fin. specialist NCR Corp., 1973-74, systems analyst, 1974-75, supr. inventory planning, 1975, mgr. material planning and purchasing control, 1976-78; materials mgr. U.S. Elec. Motors Co., 1978; with Gen. Motors Corp., 1978—, shift supt. materials, Lakewood, Ga., 1979-80, gen. ops. supr. material data base mgmt. Central Office, Warren, Mich., 1980, dir. material mgmt. Gen. Motors Truck and Bus. div., Balt., 1980-86; vis. lectr. Inst. Internat. Trade, Jiao Tung U., Shanghai, China, 1985. Mem. Am. Prodn. and Inventory Control Soc., Am. Soc. Women Accts., AAUW, Balt. Exec. Women's Network, Balt. Council on Fgn. Relations, Baptist. Home: 125 Arbutus Ave Baltimore MD 21228 Office: Gen Motors Truck and Bus 2122 Broening Hwy PO Box 148 Baltimore MD 21203

MCDONALD, PENNY S(UE), educational administrator; b. Portland, Oreg., May 1, 1946; d. Norman James and Edna (Kaufmann) McD. B.A., Oreg. State U., 1968, M.Ed., 1974; Ed.D., Portland State U./U. Oreg., 1981. Tchr. English, Fleming Jr. High Sch., Los Angeles, 1968-69; tchr. lang. arts and social studies Highland View Jr. High Sch., Corvalis, Oreg., 1970-72; tchr. English, dir. student activities Crescent Valley High Sch., Corvallis, 1973-78; grad. asst. Portland State U., Oreg., 1978-80; evaluation intern N.W. Regional Edn. Lab., Portland, 1980; Nat. Inst. Edn. assoc., edn. policy fellow Nat. Commn. on Excellence in Edn., Washington, 1981-83; prin. Inza R. Wood Middle Sch., West Linn Sch. Dist., Wilsonville, Oreg., 1983—; cons. Oreg. Dept. Edn., 1980-81; sr. counselor Oreg. Assn. Student Councils Camps, 1976-78, 80. Named to Outstanding Young Woman Am., U.S. Jaycees; AFL-CIO scholar Oreg. State U., Corvallis, 1964; Univ. scholar Oreg. State U., 1965-68; nat. Alpha Delta Pi scholar Oreg. State U., 1967-68. Mem. Nat. Assn. Student Councils, Oreg. Assn. Activities Advisors (chmn. 1976-77, bd. dirs. 1977-78), Oreg. Assn. Student Councils, Confedn. Oreg. Sch. Adminstrs., Nat. Assn. Secondary Sch. Prins., N.W. Women in Ednl. Adminstrn., Am. Ednl. Research Assn., Nat. Sch. Pub. Relations Assn., Assn. Supervision and Curriculum Devel., Edn. Policy Fellowship Alumnae, Delta Kappa Gamma (chpt. rec. sec.), Phi Delta Kappa. Democrat. Office: Inza R Wood Middle Sch 11055 SW Wilsonville Rd Wilsonville OR 97070

MCDONALD, PRISCILLA ANN, nurse, educator; b. New Brunswick, N.J., Sept. 15, 1953; d. John Sherlock and Louise Bertha (Marcks) Hilman; m. Francis Leo McDonald, June 24, 1978; children—Elizabeth Louise, Colleen Ann. B.S., Salve Regina Coll., 1975; M.A., Central Mich. U., 1980; postgrad. in gerontology U. Mass.-Amherst, 1984—. Staff nurse Med. Coll. Va., Richmond, 1975-76; staff nurse Queens Med. Ctr., Honolulu, 1978; pub. health nurse Upjohn Home Health Agy., Honolulu, 1979-80; staff nurse Hardin Meml. Hosp., Kenton, Ohio, 1981; charge nurse Hardin County Home, Kenton, 1982, Poet Seat Nursing Home, Greenfield, Mass., 1983; instr. clin. nursing Greenfield Community Coll., 1983—. Vol. sch. nurse Holy Trinity Nursery Sch., Greenfield, 1983-84; vol. nurse YMCA Health Clinic, Greenfield, 1983; sec.-treas. New Eng. Fedn. Coll. Republicans, Boston, 1973-75; sec. Ohio No. U. Law Wives and Assocs., Ada, 1982-83; vol. mgr. Girl Scouts U.S.A., Hardin County, Ada, 1981-82; bd. dirs. Franklin County Home Care Corp., 1984—. Served to lt. (j.g.) USN, 1976-78. Mem. Am. Nurses Assn. (mem. com. on gerontol. nursing 1986), Mass. Nurses Assn. Res. Officers Assn. Democrat. Roman Catholic. Home: PO Box 295 62 Peabody Ln Greenfield MA 01302 Office: Dept Nursing Greenfield Community Coll College Dr Greenfield MA 01302

MCDONALD, RITA THERESE, clinical psychologist, educator; b. Milw., Sept. 3, 1929; d. Peter Matthew and Elizabeth Lucille (Gonia) Kluczny; B.A. magna cum laude, Alverno Coll., 1962; M.S., Marquette U., 1969; Ph.D. Loyola U., Chgo., 1971; m. James Charles McDonald, Jan. 18, 1970. Tchr. pvt. schs., Milw. and Green Bay, Wis., 1950-65; chief psychologist Curative Rehab. Center, Milw., 1970-72; dir. Marquette U. Honors Program, Milw., 1975-78, asst. prof., 1972-75, 78-80, assoc. prof., 1981—; pres. R.T. McDonald & Assocs. Inc., 1984—; cons. Milw. Public Schs.; mem. adv. bd. St. Camillus Health Center, Milw.; chmn. subcom. on health needs United Way of Greater Milw., 1980-81, subcom. on allocations, 1981-82. Mem. Goals for Milw. 2000, 1981-82; bd. dirs. Cardinal Stritch Coll., YWCA of Greater Milw., 1983-84. Recipient Teaching Excellence award Marquette U., 1980. Mem. Am. Psychol. Assn., Wis. Psychol. Assn., Milw. Area Psychol. Assn., Forum for Death Edn. and Counseling, Nat. Forum for Women (bd. dirs. 1984—). Contbr. articles to profl. jours. Home: 1229 N Jackson St Milwaukee WI 53202 Office: Psychology Dept Marquette U Milwaukee WI 53233

MCDONALD, ROSA NELL, research and development budget administrator; b. Boley, Okla., Feb. 12, 1953; d. James and Beatrice Irene (Hayes) McD. B.S., Calif. State U.-Long Beach, 1975; M.B.A., Calif. State U.-Dominquez Hills, 1980, also postgrad. Acct., The Aerospace Corp., El Segundo, Calif., 1976-77; analytical accountant, 1977-79, budget analyst, 1979-81, sr. budget analyst, 1981-84, budget adminstr., 1984—. Vol., Youth Motivation Task Force, El Segundo, 1980—, Holiday Project, El Segundo, 1984, 85. Recipient Adminstrn. Group Achievement award The Aerospace Corp., 1985. Mem. Am. Bus. Woman's Assn., Nat. Assn. Female Execs., Beta Gamma Sigma. Democrat. Avocations: dancing; aerobics; reading; contests. Office: 2350 E El Segundo Blvd El Segundo CA 90245

MC DONALD, RUTH DUNCAN, pianist, educator; b. St. Joseph, Mo., May 26, 1921; d. Harry E. and Muriel G. (Hockett) Duncan; B.Mus., Kansas City (Mo.) Conservatory Music, 1942; grad. diploma Juilliard Sch. Music, 1946; m. Patrick Sandys, Aug. 11, 1948; children—Patricia, Karen, Michael; m. 2d, Charles McDonald, Feb. 19, 1966. Concert tours, 1950-55; jazz pianist, Montgomery, Ala., 1956-57, Roosevelt Hotel, Jacksonville, Fla., 1957-60, DeSoto Hotel, Savannah, Ga., 1960-64, Dinkler Hotel, Atlanta, 1964, Hilton Inn, Atlanta, 1965; mem. faculty Ga. State U., Atlanta, 1966—, asst. prof. piano, 1971-77, assoc. prof. piano, 1977-86, prof., 1986—, coordinator Internat. Congress on Women in Music, 1986; performed at Keele U., U. Sussex (Eng.), 1978, Internat. Piano Workshop, Honolulu, 1981, Innsbruck, Austria, 1982. Mem. Nat. Fedn. Music Clubs (state student adviser, audition chmn.), AAUP (Internat. Women's Year award in performing arts 1975), Music Educators Nat. Conf., Mu Phi Epsilon. Author articles; pianist tapes for blind students; performed N.Y. premier of Meyer Kupferman Sonata, 1976, Am. Women Composers in Mexico City, 1984; also rec. performed Am. music Wigmore Hall, London, 1977. Home: 751 Briar Park Ct Atlanta GA 30306 Office: Ga State Univ Univ Plaza Atlanta GA 30302

MCDONALD,, SAMMANTHA LYNNE MARIE HAYWARD, customer service official; b. Pasadena, Calif., Nov. 18, 1949; d. Louis George and Ethelyn Georgia (Hale) Nichols; A.S., San Diego Mesa Coll., 1976; B.B.A., Nat. U., 1980, M.B.A., 1983; m. Jerry Boone McDonald, July 31, 1983; 1 dau., Nicole Charise. Customer info. rep. San Diego Gas and Electric, 1970-72, 1974-80, customer info. analyst, 1980-81, customer service supr. Beach Cities Dist. Office, 1981-85, regional customer tng. supr. No. Region, 1985—. Seminar leader, trainer Energy Speakers Corps, 1980—. Mem. citizens adv. com. Sandburg Elem. Sch., San Diego, 1974-75, v.p., 1974, pres., 1975; area coordinator San Diego Sch. Bond Election, 1974. Recipient Sch. Citizens Adv. Com. Service award San Diego City Schs., 1975. Mem. Mira Mesa Scripps Ranch C. of C. (bd. dirs., membership chmn., pres. 1985), Am. Mgmt. Assn. Democrat. Mem. editorial bd. Women's Basic Tng. Manual, 1981-82. Home: 13530 Longfellow Ln San Diego CA 92129 Office: PO Box 1831 San Diego CA 92112

MCDONALD, SUSAN ELIZABETH, editor, educator; b. Detroit, Aug. 19, 1952; d. Robert William and Patricia Ann (Titus) Blohm; m. Patrick McDonald, June 22, 1973 (div. Feb. 1981). B.S., Wayne State U., 1976. Reporter, Grosse Pointe News, Grosse Pointe Farms, Mich., 1976-81, editor, 1981—; instr. Wayne State U., 1983—. Recipient Sch. Bell award, 1977. Mem. Indian Village Assn., Detroit, 1977—. Mem. Soc. Profl. Journalists. Office: Grosse Pointe News 99 Kercheval Ave Grosse Pointe Farms MI 48236

MCDONALD-FUNK, IDA LEWIS, travel agency executive; b. Four Oaks, N.C., Aug. 10, 1931; d. William Carl and Adna Leigh (Bailey) Lewis; m. Richard Lee McDonald, Jr., Sept. 30, 1951 (div. 1963); children—Richard Lee III, Martha Carle; m. Larry Theodore Funk, Mar. 31, 1979. Student Greensboro Coll., 1949-50; A.B., U. N.C., 1952. Br. mgr. AAA Carolina Motor Club, Durham, N.C., 1954-79; pres. McDonald Travel, Inc., Durham, 1980—; sec. Vanguard Cellular Systems, Inc. Mem. Durham C. of C., Sales and Mktg. Execs., Am. Soc. Travel Agts., Travel Agts. of Carolinas (bd. dirs. 1984—), Delta Delta Delta. Democrat. Baptist. Avocations: bridge; music. Home: 4231-E American Dr Durham NC 27705 Office: McDonald Travel 1904 Front St Suite 610 Durham NC 27705

MC DONNELL, HELEN MARGARET, educator; b. Bogata, N.J., July 31, 1923; d. Maurice Martin and Helen (Vollmer) McD.; B.A., Monmouth Coll., 1958; M.A., Seton Hall U., 1959; postgrad. Oxford (Eng.) U., summer 1964; Ph.D., (Woodrow Wilson fellow) Rutgers U., 1970. Civil service employee, Ft. Monmouth, N.J., 1942-58; tchr. English, Asbury Park (N.J.) High Sch., 1958-59; chmn. English dept., tchr. English, Wall High Sch., Wall Twp., N.J., 1959-64; chmn. English dept., tchr. English Ocean Twp. High Sch., Oakhurst, N.J., 1965—; lectr. English, Monmouth Coll., part-time, 1960-62. Recipient Ford Found. grant summer study, 1959. Mem. N.J., Monmouth County edn. assns., N.J. Secondary Sch. Tchrs. Assn., Assn. Secondary Sch. Dept. Heads N.J., N.J. Assn. Tchrs. English, Nat. Council Tchrs. English (mem. com. on comparative and world lit. 1966—, assoc. chmn. 1970-74, chmn. 1975-77, mem. commn. on lit. 1979-82). Author: Nobel Parade, 1975. Co-author: (anthology series) Man in Literature, 1970; England in Literature, 1972, rev. edit., 1979, 84; Literature and Life, 1979; Travels, 1983; Traditions in Literature, 1984. Address: 2927 Bangs Ave Neptune NJ 07753

MC DONNELL, KATHLEEN MARIE, manufacturing company executive; b. London, Eng., May 16, 1947; d. John Joseph and Mary Bridget (Lunney) McDonnell; A.S. in mktg., Westchester Community Coll., 1967. With W.T. Grant Co., various locations, 1963-70, asst. buyer N.Y. Office, 1970-71, buyer, 1971-76; v.p. Mothercare Stores Inc., 1976-81; dir. Merchandising Borg Textile, 1981-82; v.p. sales and mktg. First Phillips Mfg. Co., Sunbury, Pa., 1983—. Office: First Phillips Mfg Co Sunbury PA 17801

MC DONNELL, LORETTA WADE, educator; b. San Francisco, May 31, 1940; d. John H. and Helen M. (Tinney) Wade; B.A., San Francisco Coll. for Women, 1962; M.A., Stanford U., 1963; grad. Coro Pub. Affairs Tng. Program for Women, 1976; m. John L. McDonnell, Jr., Apr. 27, 1963 (div.); children—Elizabeth, John L. III, Thomas. High sch. tchr. East Side Union High Sch. Dist., San Jose, Calif., 1962-63; project coordinator Inter Agency Collaboration Effort, Oakland, Calif., 1977—; legal asst. Pacific Gas and Electric Co., 1980—. Bd. dirs. Carden Redwood Sch., 1975-77, St. Paul's Sch., 1974-75; budget panelist United Way of Bay Area, 1975-77; community v.p. Jr. League, 1976-77, nat. conv. del., 1976; bd. dirs. Alameda County Vol. Bur., 1973-74; chmn. speakers panel Focus on Am. Women, 1973-74. Mem. Jr. League of Oakland-East Bay, Inc., Stanford Alumni. Democrat. Roman Catholic. Club: Stanford San Francisco Luncheon. Assoc. editor The Antiphon, 1971-74.

MCDONNELL, MARIA SUZANNE, real estate agent; b. Munich, Fed. Republic Germany, Aug. 27, 1951; came to U.S., 1951, naturalized, 1978; s. Stephen Pekary and Maria (Cseh) Pekary Csemez; divorced; children—Tomas, Eva. A.A.S., SUNY-Morrisville, 1971; B.S., Cornell U., 1974; tchr.'s cert. Colgate U., 1975. Vice pres., comptroller Tri-County Implement Co., Earlville, N.Y., 1975-81; pub. McDonnell Pub. Inc., Fredericksburg, Va., 1981-85; real estate agt. William A. Middleton Realtors, Fredericksburg, 1985—. Founder, photographer, feature writer Farm & Country, 1981-85. Recipient award Va. Horse Council, 1982-86. Mem. Va. Arabian Horse Assn., Internat. Arabian Horse Assn. (region 15 v.p., del. and directory chmn. 1983-85). Roman Catholic. Home: 700 Harrison Rd Fredericksburg VA 22401 Office: William A Middleton Realtors 5604 Courthouse Rd Spotsylvania VA 22553

MCDONOUGH, SANDRA MARTIN, lawyer, administrator; b. Albany, N.Y., Feb. 5, 1939; d. Stevens John and Louise Jane (Minshall) Martin; 1 child, Lora Elizabeth Couture. B.A., SUNY-Regents Coll., Albany, 1979; J.D., U. Bridgeport, 1982. Bar: Conn. 1982, U.S. Dist. Ct. 1983; lic. comml. pilot, flight inst. Research assoc. Yale U., New Haven, 1958-61; service rep. Conn. Blue Cross, New Haven, 1962-67; project dir. Bridgeport Hosp. (Conn.), 1967-68; dir. patient accounts Park City Hosp., Bridgeport, 1968-74; adminstr., pres. Med. Personnel Pool, Fairfield, Conn., 1975—; sole practice, Fairfield, 1982—. Adult advisor Safe Rides of Fairfield, 1984; active legis. affairs Conn. Community Care, Bristol, Conn., 1982—. Mem. Fairfield Bar Assn. (treas. 1983—), Assn. Trial Lawyers Am., Lawyer-Pilots Bar Assn., Conn. Trial Lawyers Assn., Conn. Home Health Services Assn. (sec., gen. counsel 1982—), SUNY Alumni Assn. (trustee Regents Coll. 1983—), Ninety-Nines (chmn.-elect 1983), Mensa. Republican. Episcopalian. Home: 427 Morehouse Hwy Fairfield CT 06430 Office: 1210 Post Rd Fairfield CT 06430

MCDOUGALL, BARBARA JEAN, Canadian government financial official; b. Toronto, Ont., Can., Nov. 12, 1937; d. Robert James and Margaret Jean (Dryden) Leamen; m. Peter McDougall, Sept. 5, 1963 (dec.). Student U. Toronto. Former exec. dir. Can. Council Fin Analysts; v.p. Dominion Securities Ames Ltd., A.E. Ames & Co. Ltd.; former mgr. Portfolio Investments, Northwest Trust Co.; former investment analyst Odlum Brown Ltd.; market research analyst Toronto Star Ltd.; econ. analyst Can. Imperial Bank Commerce; fin. columnist Chatelaine mag.; fin. commentator CBS program Take Thirty; bus. columnist City Woman mag.; bus. journalist CITV Edmonton, Vancouver Sun; past pres. Rosedale P. Cons. Assn.; elected to House of Commons, 1984; now minister of state for fin., 1984—. Chmn., City of Toronto Salvation Army Red Shield Appeal, 1984; bd. dirs. Community Occupational Therapy Assoc., chmn., 1982-84; bd. dirs. Second Mile Club, United Way, Enoch Turner Schoolhouse; vice chmn. Elizabeth Fry Soc.; counsellor Oakhalla Province Prison for Women. Progressive Conservative. Club: Albany. Office: Ministry of State for Finance Pl Bell Canada 169 Elgin St Ottawa ON K1A 0G5 Canada*

MCDOW, HOLLY ANNE, field engineer; b. Portsmouth, Va., Oct. 28, 1953; d. Louis Anthony and Joanne Marie (Fox) Socorso; A.A., Seminole Jr. Coll., 1973; student Fla. Tech. U., 1974, Hinds Jr. Coll., 1976; B.S., Middle Tenn. State U., 1979; m. B. David McDow, Dec. 28, 1977. Chief chemist Tenn. Oil & Refining, Portland, 1979-80; tech. rep. Recra Environ. & Health Scis., Nashville, 1980-81; ind. cons. oil re-refining, Nashville, 1981; mgr. mktg. Gulf Coast ops., Canonie Environ. Services, Houston, 1981-82; prin., oil recycling cons. H.A. Assocs., Houston, 1982-84; field engr. Hewlett Packard, Dallas, 1984—. Mem. Houston C. of C., ASTM (vice chmn. P-VI and P III of subcom. P 1979-84, sec. subcom. P 1983-84), Am. Petroleum Inst., Sales and Mktg. Execs. Houston, Nat. Assn. Female Execs., Beta Beta Beta. Republican. Contbr. articles to profl. jours. Office: 930 Campbell Rd Richardson TX 75081

MCDOWELL, DONNA SCHULTZ, lawyer; b. Cin., Apr. 23, 1946; d. Robert Joseph and Harriet (Parronchi) Schultz; m. Dennis Lon McDowell, June 20, 1970; children—Dawn Megan, Donnelly Lon. B.A. with honors in English, Brandeis U., 1968; M.Ed., Am. U., 1972; C.A.S.E. with honors, Johns Hopkins U., 1979; J.D. with honors, U. Md., 1982. Bar: Md. 1982. Instr., Anne Arundel & Prince George's Community Coll., Severna Park and Largo, Md., 1977-78; coll. adminstr. Bowie State Coll. (Md.), 1978-79; assoc. Miller & Bortner, Lanham, Md., 1982-83; sole practice, Lanham, 1983—; ednl. cons. Chmn. Housing Hearing Com., Bowie, 1981-83; trustee Unitarian-Universalitst Ch., Silver Spring, Md., 1979-83; bd. dirs. New Ventures, Bowie, 1983, Second Mile (Runaway House), Hyattsville, Md., 1983. Recipient Am. Jurisprudence award U. Md., 1981. Mem. ABA, Assn. Trial Lawyers Am., Md. Trial Lawyers Assn., Prince George's Bar Assn. Democrat. Club: Soroptimist. Home: 24308 Hipsley Mill Rd Gaithersburg MD 20879 Office: Donna McDowell 9332 Annapolis Rd Lanham MD 20706

MC DOWELL, JENNIFER (MRS. MILTON LOVENTHAL), editor, sociologist, composer; b. Albuquerque, May 19, 1936; d. Willard A. and Margaret Frances (Garrison) McDowell; B.A., U. Calif., 1957; M.A. in English, San Diego State U., 1958; M.L.S., U. Calif., Berkeley, 1963; Ph.D. (fellow) in Sociology, U. Oreg., 1973; m. Milton Loventhal, July 2, 1973. Tchr. English, Abraham Lincoln High Sch., San Jose, Calif., 1960-61; free lance editor in Soviet field, 1961-63; research asst. dept. sociology U. Oreg., Eugene, 1964-66; reader for the Jour. for Sci. Study of Religion, 1974-75, 79—; co-producer radio shows for Sta. KALX, 1971-72; tchr. numerous workshops in writing, 1969-73; research cons., 1973—; editor and publisher Merlin Press, San Jose, 1973—; music pub. Lipstick & Toy Balloons Pub. Co., 1978—; composer for Paramount Pictures, 1982—. Calif. Arts Council grantee, 1976-77. Mem. Am. Sociol. Assn., Soc. for Sci. Study of Religion, Soc. for Study of Religion and Communism, Phi Beta Kappa, Sigma Alpha Iota, Beta Phi Mu, Kappa Kappa Gamma. Democrat. Author: Black Politics, 1971; Contemporary Women Poets, an Anthology, 1977; contbr. poems, essays and short stories to lit. mags., articles to profl. jours.; composer songs Money Makes a Woman Free, 1976, My Love Is Stronger than Life Itself, 1979; composer music for play Simple Gifts, 1980; co-creator mus. comedy Russia's Secret Plot to take Back Alaska, 1983; co-creator (play) The Estrogen Party to End War, 1986. Office: PO Box 5602 San Jose CA 95150

MCDOWELL, PAT LEWIS, entrepreneur; b. Bronaugh, Mo., July 7, 1933; d. Clarence L. and Mary Bell (Pitts) Lewis; student public schs., Shreveport; La.; m. E. A. McDowell, June 4, 1954; children—David Albert. Adminstrv. asst. Cities Service Oil Co., Shreveport, 1950-54; with Riley-Beaird, Inc., Shreveport, 1956-58, Pitney & Bowes, Inc., Shreveport, 1958-70; pres. Pat McDowell & Assos., Inc., Shreveport, 1970—; partner Stoner Co., Shreveport, 1975-80; The Gordian Knot, Shreveport, 1979—; pres. Tapes 'n Thoughts, Inc., Shreveport, 1982—; v.p. public relations Accu-Med Corp., Shreveport, 1982—; pres., chmn. bd., chief exec. officer Self-Devel. Inst. Inc., Shreveport, 1983—; lectr. in field. Pres. bd. dirs. La. Assn. for Blind, Shreveport, 1978-80, 79-80, chmn. bd., 1980-81; adv. bd. Nat. Industries for the Blind, Bloomfield, N.J., 1977-82, bd. dirs. Community Action for Corrections in La., 1975, Youth Advocates, Inc., 1976. Recipient J. Cheshire Peyton award; numerous awards Success Motivation Inst. Mem. Sales and Mktg. Execs., Am. Soc. for Training & Devel. Episcopalian. Clubs: Positive Mental Attitude Breakfast (bd. dirs., founding mem.), Toastmasters Hi-Noon. Home: 427 Pennsylvania St Shreveport LA 71105 Office: 3722 Youree Dr Shreveport LA 71105

MC DUFFIE, DEBORAH JEANNE, composer; b. N.Y.C., Aug. 8, 1950; d. Thomas Elliott and Nan Ruth (Woods) McD.; B.A., Western Coll. Women; children—Kijana Babatu, Kemal. Music producer, composer McCann-Erickson Advt., Inc., N.Y.C., 1971-81; music dir. Mingo-Jones Advt., 1981—; pres. Jana Prodns, Inc., Janée Music Co., Great Music Mgmt. Co., N.Y.C., 1977—; profl. singer, composer, arranger, producer. Recipient numerous advt. awards. Mem. ASCAP, Screen Actors Guild, AFTRA, Am. Fedn. Musicians, Nat. Acad. Rec. Arts and Scis., Nat. Assn. Female Execs. Vocal arranger: I'd Like to Teach the World to Sing, 1972; composer producer Miller High Life campaigns, 1980-83; album: I Am an Illusion, 1981, Damaris, 1984; composer Hooray for Love. Office: 485 Lexington Ave 26th Floor New York NY 10017

MCDUNN, KATHLEEN EVELYN, nurse, nursing educator; b. Chgo., Apr. 29, 1954; d. William Dorcey and Evelyn Sylvia (Drabik) McDunn. B.S., DePaul U., 1976; M.S., No. Ill. U., 1985. Staff nurse U. Ill. Hosp., Chgo., 1976-78, asst. head nurse, 1978-80, acting head nurse, 1980; instr. nursing Little Co. of Mary Hosp. Sch. Nursing, Evergreen Park, Ill., 1980-84, acad. advisor, 1980-84; hosp.-home care coordinator Health Care at Home, Hinsdale, Ill., 1985-86; nurse cons. Infant Mortality Reduction Inst., Cook County Dept. Pub. Health, 1986—; instr. cardiopulmonary resuscitation Chgo. Heart Assn., 1982—. Mem. Am. Nurses' Assn., Assn. for Care of Children's Health, Ill. Nurses Assn., DePaul U. Dept. Nursing Alumni Assn. Roman Catholic. Home: 5362 S Maplewood Ave Chicago IL 60632 Office: Cook County Dept Pub Health 16501 S Kedzie Pkwy Markham IL 60426

MCELROY, CHARLOTTE, electrical contracting company executive, consultant; b. Doss, La., Sept. 6, 1923; d. John Elijah and Ida Belle (Welch) Caldwell; m. C.G. McElroy, Apr. 30 1962; children—Pamela Denise McElroy McCunn, Rebecca Layne McElroy Redmond; 1 stepchild, Bob G. McElroy. Grad. high sch., Chatham, La., 1941. Pres., McElroy Elec. Supply Co., West Monroe, La., 1957—; owner Mrs. Mac's Books, West Monroe, 1972—; ptnr. McElroy & Elias, West Monroe, 1980—. Mem. Delta Rho Delta. Democrat. Mem. Assembly of God Ch. Office: McElroy Elec Supply Co PO Box 657 West Monroe LA 71291

MCELROY, COLLEEN JOHNSON, English educator, poet; b. St. Louis, Oct. 30, 1935; d. Jesse Dalton and Ruth Celeste (Long) Johnson; m. David Fairfield McElroy, Nov. 29, 1968 (div. 1978); children—Kevin Duane, Vanessa Colleen. A.A., Harris-Stowe Tchrs. Coll., 1956; B.S., Kans. State U., 1958, M.S., 1963; Ph.D., U. Wash., 1973. Cert. speech clinician Chief speech clinician Rehab. Inst., Kansas City, Mo., 1963-66, dir. speech, hearing clinic, 1963-66; talkshow moderator KVOS-TV, Bellingham, Wash., 1967-70; instr. Projects Upward Bound, Bellingham, 1968, 70; asst. prof. speech Western Wash. U., Bellingham, 1966-71, dir. speech clinic, 1966-71; assoc. prof. English, U. Wash., Seattle, 1973-79, prof. English, 1983—, dir. freshman composition, 1973-81, dir. creative writing, 1984—. Author: (textbook) Speech and Language Development of the Pre-School Child, 1972; (poems) Music From Home: Selected Poems, 1976; Winters Without Snow, 1979; Lie and Say You Love Me, 1980; Queen of the Ebony Isles (Am. book award 1985), 1984. Recipient Women of Achievement award Theta Sigma Phi-Matrix Table, 1985; NEA fellow, 1978. Mem. Writers Guild Am., United Black Artist Guild (lit. editor). Avocation: visual arts. Home: 2616 4th North 406 Seattle WA 98109 Office: English Dept GN-30 Creative Writing Program U Wash Seattle WA 98196

MCELROY, JUNE PATRICIA, sales consultant; b. Atlantic City, Sept. 26, 1929; d. Edmund N. and Dorothy R. (McDowell) Ricchezza; m. David Waycott Carson, Apr. 8, 1947 (div. 1954); m. 2d, Ottavio Gelmi, Dec. 16, 1954 (div. 1964); 1 dau., Alessandra; m. 3d, Robert Joseph McElroy, Oct. 16, 1970 (dec. May 1974). Student Temple U., 1947-48, Inst. Linguistics, Georgetown U., 1951-53. Mem. staff Am. consulate gen., Milan, Italy, 1954; legis. asst. U.S. Senate, Washington, 1956; social sec. to ambassador of Finland, Washington, 1958; legis. asst. to congressman, Washington, 1960-65; sr. assoc. Gillmore M. Perry Co., Washington, 1965-76; sales exec./cons. furniture industry, Hilton Head, S.C., 1981—; govt. sales rep. in Washington A. Brandt Co., Inc., Ft. Worth, 1985—. Mem. Georgetown U. Alumni Assn. Republican. Roman Catholic. Club: Army Navy (Washington). Home: 65 Wood Duck Rd Hilton Head SC 29928

MCELROY, PATRICIA LEE, trucking company executive; b. Tarentum, Pa., Sept. 13, 1955; d. Calvin Wilson and Clara Valjean (Powell) McE.; m. Anthony G. Butch, Feb. 14, 1976 (div. Sept. 1982). Grad. high sch., Vandergrift, Pa. Sr. sec. U. Pitts., 1974-76; office mgr. Perrysville Coal Co., Apollo, Pa., 1976-81, pres., 1981—; ptnr. North Washington office Rossi & Co., Apollo, 1984—; assoc. agt. Nationwide Ins. Co., Avonmore, Pa., 1985—. Democrat. Methodist. Avocations: golf; camping; sewing. Home: 644 Grange Dr Apollo PA 15613 Office: Perrysville Coal Co 751 Route 66 Apollo PA 15613

MCELROY, SUZANNE ELAINE, nurse, educator; b. Windber, Pa., Dec. 17, 1943; d. Donald Frank and Edna Alice (McDowell) Shaffer; m. Daniel Joseph McElroy, Dec. 22, 1973; 1 child, Erin Kathleen. B.S. in Nursing, Ohio State U., 1965, M.S. in Nursing, 1972; A.A.S. in Early Childhood Devel., Northland Pioneer Coll., 1984. Psychiat. head nurse 98th KO Med. Detachment, Nha Trang, Vietnam, 1969-70; asst. chief nursing service for evenings and nights Madigan Army Med Ctr., Tacoma, 1970-71; dir. psychiat. nurse clinician course Walter Reed Army Med. Ctr., Washington, 1972-75; clin. nurse expert NIH Clin Ctr., Bethesda, Md., 1977-80; mental health counselor Community Counseling Ctr., Showlow, Ariz., 1984-85; nurse educator in psychiatry Presbyn. Hosp., Dallas, 1985—; vol. nurse Navy Psychiat. Ops. Mission, Nha Trang, 1969-70; CPR instr. U.S. Army Res. Hosp., Rockville, Md., 1979-80; pre sch. tchr. Pinetop Presch., Ariz., 1982-84. Asst. leader Girl Sout U.S.A., 1966; counselor Suicide Prevention Line, Columbus, 1971; Sunday sch. tchr. Good Shepherd Episcopal Ch., Burke, Va., 1976-79, Community Presbyn. Ch., Pinetop, 1983-85. Served to capt. Nurse Corps, U.S. Army, 1964-75. Decorated Bronze Star. Mem. Am. Nurses Assn., Ohio State U. Alumni Assn., Humane Soc. of White Mountains, Phi Theta Kappa, Sigma Theta Tau. Club: Ariz. White Mountain Kennel (Lakeside). Avocations: aerobics; Am. and English history; child development education; church choir; oil painting. Home: 921 Thistle Ridge Ln Arlington TX 76017 Office: Presbyn Hosp of Dallas 8200 Walnut Hill Ln Dallas TX 75231

MCELWAIN, JUANITA MURIEL, music therapy educator; b. Geneva, Ohio, Jan. 17, 1928; d. George Myron and Muriel Maude (Randolph) Stilwell; B.M.E., Fla. State U., 1958, M.M.E., 1959, M.Mus., 1974, Ph.D., 1978; m. O.D. McElwain, Aug. 21, 1948; 1 son, Thomas George. Tchr., Jennings (Fla.) Public Sch., 1961-62; tchr. piano, organ Monterey Bay Acad., Watsonville, Calif., 1962-67; tchr. organ, piano Antillian Union Coll., Mayàguez, P.R., 1967-69; music therapist Sunland Tng. Center, Marianna, Fla., 1978-80; asst. prof., dir. music therapy Sch. Music, Eastern N.Mex. U., Portales, 1980-85; assoc. prof., dir. music therapy Phillips U., Enid, Okla., 1985—; condr. workshops on music in spl. edn. Mem. profl. adv. com. Community Services Portales, 1981-85; bd. dirs. Campfire Girls, Portales, 1982-85. Mem. Nat. Assn. Music Therapy, Pi Kappa Lambda. Adventist. Home: Route 4 Box 127R Enid OK 73701 Office: Phillips U Enid OK 73702

MC ENROE, PATRICIA SOLON, assn. exec.; b. Algona, Iowa, Nov. 19, 1922; d. John Edward and Kathryn Leone (Solon) McE.; student (scholar) Briar Cliff Coll., Sioux City, Iowa, 1942-44; B.Mus.Edn., Northwestern U., 1946, Mus.M., 1948; postgrad. Am. Conservatory of Music, Chgo. With Iowa Sch. for Braille and Sight Saving, Vinton, 1948-51; various positions Chgo. Bd. Edn., 1952-54, 56-57, 65-70; tchr. jr. high sch., Dover, Minn., 1954-55; music tchr. Ft. Carson, Fountain, Colo., 1955-56; v.p., program chmn. AAUW, Algona, 1976—. Founder, Kossuth County Democratic Women's Club, Algona, 1958; recreation leader ARC, Evanston, Ill., 1951; rep. Archdiocese Chgo. in pub. schs., Chgo., 1965-70. Mem. NOW, LWV, Iowa Women's Polit. Caucus, Internat. Platform Assn., Delphion Soc., Nat. Historic Preservation. Home and Office: 400 N Thorington Algona IA 50511

MCENTEE, JOAN MARIE, lawyer; b. N.Y.C., June 3, 1948; d. C. and Virginia (Nolan) McEntee; m. Thomas A. Brooks, June 6, 1981; 1 son, Daniel Nolan. B.A. cum laude, Marymount Coll., 1969; M.A., Am. U., 1972, J.D., 1982. Bar D.C. 1984. Asst. for legis. affairs HUD, 1971-73, spl. asst. to undersec., 1974-75; spl. asst. to assoc. dir. Office Mgmt. and Budget, Washington, 1975-77; cons. Consumer Product Safety Commn., Washington, 1977-78; minority staff dir. Subcom. on Intergovtl. Relations, U.S. Senate, Washington, 1978-80, staff dir., chief counsel Govt. Affairs Com., 1980—. Mem. James S. Brady Presdl. Found., 1982, Georgetown Civic Assn., Washington, 1981; friend Washington Project for Arts, 1981. Am. U. disting. and hon. fellow, 1981. Mem. D.C. Bar, Marymount Coll. Alumnae Assn. Republican. Roman Catholic. Home: 2820 N St NW Washington DC 20007

MCENTEGART, EILEEN FRANCES, oil company executive; b. N.Y.C., July 1, 1929; d. Thomas Emmet and Mary Amelia (Dewhurst) McE.; B.A. in Math., Coll. New Rochelle, 1951; M.B.A. in Fin., N.Y.U., 1980. Jr. engr., math. asst., programmer M.W. Kellogg Co., N.Y.C., 1951-62; programmer, analyst, supr. sci. applications Mobil Corp., N.Y.C., 1962-69, mgr. systems support, mgr. computer services dept., 1969-75, sr. industry analyst, supr. planning assos. corp. planning, 1975-81, controller payroll, benefits and personnel systems, Dallas, 1981-86, mgr. planning and adminstrn. corporate employee relations, 1986—. Trustee Manhattan Coll., N.Y., 1980—; mem. Pres.' adv. bd. Coll. New Rochelle, 1975-79. Mem. Mobil Polit. Action Com. (vice chairperson 1978—). Roman Catholic. Home: 45 W 60th St Apt 34D New York NY 10023 Office: 150 E 42d St New York NY 10017

MCEVOY, PAMELA THOMPSON, psychotherapist; b. Forest Hills, N.Y., Mar. 8, 1937; d. Reynolds Thomas and Pamela Shipley (Sweeny) McE.; B.A., U. La Verne, 1978, M.S., 1980; Ph.D., U.S. Internat. U., 1982; children—Michael B. Anderson, Jeffery A. Thomas, Candy L. Anderson Nott, Kenneth L. Anderson. Data processing coordinator Ernest Righetti High Sch., Santa Maria, Calif., 1974-78; instr. psychology-sociology Allan Hancock Coll., Santa Maria, 1977-78; mental health asst. Santa Barbara City Alcoholism Dept., 1977-78; gen. mgr. Profl. Suites, San Diego, 1978-81; therapist Chula Vista Community Counseling Center, San Diego, 1978—; assoc. dir. Acad. Assoc. Psychotherapists, 1982—; research asst. U.S. Internat. U., 1979-82. Bd. dirs. San Diego County Mental Health Assn., 1978-80; pres. Chula Vista (Calif.) Counseling Center, 1978; mem. Delinquency Prevention Commn., 1978. State fellow, 1979, 80, 81, 82, Calif. State scholar, 1976-77. Mem. Am. Psychol. Assn., Am. Assn. Marriage and Family Therapists, Christian Assn. Psychol. Counselors, Calif. Assn. Marriage and Family Therapists. Republican. Roman Catholic. Home: 17452 Ashburton Rd San Diego CA 92128 Office: 16776 Bernardo Center Dr Suite 204 San Diego CA 92128

MCFADDEN, MARY, lawyer; b. Bethlehem, Pa., Nov. 7, 1950; d. Joseph B. and Catherine M. McFadden; B.A. magna cum laude, Boston U., 1972; J.D. cum laude, Suffolk U., 1978; m. Lawrence T.P. Stifler, Nov. 25, 1977. Research asso. Med. Found., Inc., Boston, 1973-78; admitted to Mass. bar, 1978; trial atty. for Child Welfare Unit, Mass. Dept. Public Welfare, Boston, 1978-80, Mass. Dept. Social Services, 1980-82; exec. sec. Mass. Commn. on Jud. Conduct, Boston, 1982—. Mem. Am. Bar Assn., Mass. Bar, Mass. Bar Assn., Boston Bar Assn., Women's Bar Assn., Phi Beta Kappa, Psi Chi, Phi Delta Phi. Co-author articles on alcohol use; editorial referee Jour. Studies on Alcohol. Home: 150 Mountfort St Brookline MA 02146 Office: 14 Beacon St Suite 102 Boston MA 02108

MC FADDEN, MARY JOSEPHINE, fashion designer; b. N.Y.C., Oct. 1, 1938; d. Alexander Bloomfield and Mary Josephine (Cutting) McFadden; student Columbia U., New Sch. Social Research, Traphagen Sch. Design; D.F.A. (hon.), Internat. Fine Arts Coll., Miami, Fla.; 1 dau., Justine Emma Harari. Pub. relations dir. Christian Dior, N.Y.C., 1962-64; merchandising editor Vogue mag. in S. Africa, 1964; polit. and travel columnist Rand (S. Africa) Daily Mail, 1965-68; founder, dir. Vukutu, sculptural workshop for African artists, Inyanga Province, Rhodesia, 1968-70; spl. project editor Vogue mag., N.Y.C., 1970-73; designer of dresses, jewelry, fabric, accessories, stationary and home furnishings, 1973—; pres., owner Mary McFadden, Inc., N.Y.C., 1976—; pres. Mary McFadden Jewels, 1978—; curator Lannan Mus., Palm Beach, Fla., 1970-83, now curator emerita. Mem. Lannan Found.; trustee New Mus., N.Y.C.; founding dir., trustee Sundance Inst., Utah; trustee Eugene O'Neill Meml. Theatre Ctr., Waterford, Conn., Pub. Sch. No. 1, N.Y.C.; mem. policy panel arts design program Nat. Endowment for Arts, mem. Com. for Nat. Arts Week, 1986; mem. profl. com. Cooper-Hewitt Mus., N.Y.C. Recipient Fashion Hall of Fame award, 1977; Coty award, 1976, 78, 79; President's award R.I. Sch. Design, 1979; Albert Einstein award of achievement; Tommy award for fabric design; Rex award; Gold Coast award; named to Coty Hall of Fame, 1979. Mem. Council Fashion Designers Am. (v.p., bd. dirs.). Office: 264 W 35th St New York NY 10001

MCFADDEN, MATTIE FLORENCE, author, materials and standards engineer; b. West Windsor, Vt., Mar. 22, 1918; d. Berton Jerry and Julia Ann (Snide) McFadden. Grad. Vought Aero. Engring., NYU, 1943; student metall. engring. New Haven Coll., 1951-53. Registered profl. engr., Mass. Asst. engr. Vought Aircraft, Stratford, Conn., 1943-49; with Hubbard, Lawless, New Haven, 1950-51; mgr. materials engring. Norden Co., Norwalk, Conn., 1951-54; mgr. materials and standards engring. Raytheon Co., Bedford, Mass., 1954-74, staff to mgr., 1974-81, dir. corp. standards, 1974-81; cons. engr., author, South Dennis, Mass., 1981—. Author: Women in Engineering, 1986. Contbr. articles to profl. jours. Treas., Dennis Com., South Dennis, 1984—; sec. South Dennis Village Assn., 1984—; grants com. Charles A. Lindbergh Fund, Inc., Mpls., 1984—. Recipient Author's awards, Raytheon Co., 1965-80; Glen L. Martin Gold Wings, Women's Flyers of Am., 1951. Mem. Am. Soc. Metals, AIAA, Soc. Women Engrs. (pres. Boston chpt. 1972), Standards Engrs. Soc. (dir. pub. relations 1983-84), Cape Cod Writers Conf. (bd. dirs. 1985—, com. 1985—). Club: Pilot Internat., Women Flyers of Am. Avocations: travel; rock-hound; watercolor painting; reading. Address: 23 Holly St PO Box 257 South Dennis MA 02660

MCFADDEN, ROSEMARY THERESA, mercantile exchange executive; b. Scotland, Oct. 1, 1948; came to U.S. 1951, naturalized 1967; s. John and Winifred (Quinn) McFadden.; m. Brian Doherty, May 26, 1973. B.A., Rutgers U., 1970, M.B.A., 1974; J.D., Seton Hall U., 1978; hon. doctorate St. Elizabeth's Coll.-Convent Station, N.J., 1985. Spl. Asst. office of the Mayor, Jersey City, 1973-76; exec. dir. Hudson Health System, Jersey City, 1976-81; assoc. legal counsel N.Y. Merc. Exchange, N.Y.C., 1981-82, exec. v.p., 1982-84, pres., 1984—; mem. deans adv. council Rutgers U. Grad. Sch. Mgmt., Newark, 1985. Bd. dirs. Jersey City Med. Ctr., 1985—. Named Alumna of Yr., Rutgers U., 1985. Mem. N.J. Bar Assn., ABA, Am. Petroleum Inst., Soc. Ind. Gas Mktg., Rutgers U. Alumni Assn. Roman Catholic. Avocations: travel; antique collecting. Office: New York Mercantile Exchange 4 World Trade Center New York NY 10048

MC FADDEN, SYBILL MARTIN, museum curator; b. Pitts., Mar. 22, 1918; d. Alfred Nicholas and Rachel (Church) Martin; B.A. in Journalism, Pa. State U., 1941; m. William Patrick McFadden, Aug. 19, 1942; children—Suzanne Sybill, William Patrick, Gary J. Public relations dir. advt. ARC, Eastern Area Hdqrs., Alexandria, Va., 1941-46; owner, curator Mus. Antique Dolls and Toys, Lakewood, N.Y., 1960—; artist, one-woman shows, N.Y. and Fla.; writer, photographer nat. doll and toy mags., antiques mag.; writer, columnist Hobbies Mag. Mem. United Fedn. Doll Clubs, Inc., Western N.Y. Doll Club, Fla. West Coast Doll Collectors, Doll Study Club Jamestown (founder), Doll Collectors Am. Author: Portraits in Porcelain. Home and Office: 96 W Summit Ave Lakewood NY 14750

MC FADDEN, WILMOT CURNOW HAMM, chief librarian; b. Lead, S.D., Oct. 3, 1919; d. William and Ingeborg (Christianson) Curnow; student S.D. State Coll., 1938-41; m. Kenneth G. Hamm, Jan. 8, 1944 (div. 1963); 1 dau., Wilmot Christine; m. 2d, John Stinson McFadden, Mar. 1965. Asst. librarian Rock Springs (Wyo.) Pub. Library, 1947-48, head librarian, 1953—; exec. dir. Wyo., Nat. Library Week, 1969; mem. Wyo. Adv. Council for Libraries, 1977. State committeewoman Democratic Party, 1952—, also state vice chmn. Mem. adv. bd. Fed. Commn. Civil Rights, 1963—; treas. Dist. 4 Sch. Bd., 1966-78, clk. dist. 1, 1969—; adv. bd. Western Wyo. Community Coll. Bd. dirs. State Library Archives and Hist. Bd., 1959-64, 66-71, 77—, mem., 1967—; mem. Wyo. Community Coll. Commn., 1983—, honored as co-founder coll. Recipient Grolier Nat. Library Week award 1969, award for outstanding service to Sweetwater County, 1975. Mem. Federated Woman's Club, Am. Legion Aux., Mountain Plains (Wyo. rep. 1967-68, v.p. 1972, pres. 1972-73), Am., Wyo. (chmn. conf. 1966, v.p. 1972, pres. 1972-73, Librarian of Yr. award 1977, Georgia Shovlain spl. projects award 1980, Outstanding Librarian award 1985) library assns., Am. Library Trustees Assn., Wyo. Sch. Bds. Assn. (hon., commendation 1979), Alpha Delta Kappa. Author: Handbook Wyoming Library Trustees. Home: 28 Cedar St Rock Springs WY 82901 Office: 400 C St Rock Springs WY 82901

MC FALL, GENE PAULIN (MRS. JAMES C. MC FALL), social worker; b. Dallas, Nov. 19, 1907, d. Vasco Ferdinand and Elizabeth (Britain) Hallum; A.B., San Diego State Coll., 1931; M.S.W., U. So. Calif., 1948; m. James C. McFall, Feb. 14, 1928. Psychiat. social worker, div. chief Dept. Pub. Welfare, San Diego, 1936-44; home service field rep., psychiat. social worker western region A.R.C., San Francisco, 1944-46; exec. dir. San Diego County council Girl Scouts U.S.A., 1947-63; chief psychiat. social worker Douglas Young Clinic, San Diego, 1964-67; clin. social worker State of Calif., 1967-72; pvt. practice as social worker, 1972—; case work cons. First Presbyn. Ch., San Diego; guest lectr. social work San Diego State Coll. Organizer Camp Safari, 1960, adminstr., 1960-63. Chmn. San Diego City Social Work Commn., 1953-58; U.S. rep. Nobel prize presentation, Stockholm, 1962; docent Fine Arts Gallery San Diego; bd. dirs. San Diego Community Welfare Council, Assistance League San Diego, Calif. Assn. Health and Welfare, Mental Health Assn. San Diego, Am. Field Service, San Diego-Yokohama Sister City Program, San Diego Hist Soc.; bd. govs. United Fund San Diego; mem. San Diego Com. of 100. Recipient certificate of commendation as med. field agt. S.S.S., U.S. Pres., 1945; named San Diego Woman of Year, 1956, Citizen of Week, 1963; licensed clin. social worker, Calif. Mem. Nat. Assn. Social Workers, (past chmn. San Diego chpt.), Acad. Cert. Social Workers, Mus. of Photography, Friends of San Diego Pub. Library, Smithsonian Instn., Chi Omega. Clubs: Wednesday, Altrusa (past pres. San Diego). Home: 666 Upas St San Diego CA 92103

MCFARLAND, CAROLINE HARVEY, data processing manager; b. Reserve, N.Mex., Sept. 5, 1948; d. Earl Simpson and Lois M. (McCarty) Harvey; m. Robert G. Krause, May 7, 1979 (dec. 1984). B.S., N.Mex. State U., 1970; postgrad., McGill U., 1968, U. N.Mex., 1976-77. Systems, sales rep. IBM Corp., Albuquerque, 1973-77; systems analyst State of N.Mex., Santa Fe, 1977-81; project mgr. Mgmt. Resources, Inc., Santa Fe, 1981-84; project leader Gas Co. N.Mex., Albuquerque, 1984-85, mgr. engring. distrbn. support, 1985-86. Cons. United Way, Albuquerque, 1986—. Mem. Data Processing Mgmt. Assn., Audubon Soc. Republican. Presbyterian. Office: Gas Co NMex 2444 Louisiana NE Albuquerque NM 87110

MCFARLAND, DONNA REYNE, illustrator, educator, consultant; b. Charleston, W.Va., Oct. 24, 1948; d. Clyde Freeman and Ruby June (Summerfield) Armstrong; m. Elmer Reace McFarland, Oct. 28, 1966; children—Kelli Reyne, Jay Reace, B.A. in Art cum laude, W.Va. State Coll., 1985. Art dir. Calvary Bapt. acad., Hurricane, W.Va., 1980-84; art judge State Accelerated Christian Edn. High Sch. Competition, Jacksons Mill, W.Va., 1981—; owner, tchr. art Donna McFarland Studio, Scott Depot, W.Va., 1983—; art cons. Brandywine, Hurricane, W.Va., 1985—. Illustrator Wonderful W.Va. Mag., 1983. Pres. Teays Village Homeowners Assn., Scott Depot, 1986. Fellow Allied Artists W.Va.; mem. W.Va. Artists and Craftsmen's Guild. Republican. Baptist. Avocations: reading; classical music; walking; cooking. Home and Studio: 23 Barbara Circle Scott Depot WV 25560

MCFARLAND, J. RUTH, state senator, biologist; b. Zita, Okla., June 10, 1925; d. Albert and Dorotha Anne (Patterson) McF.; B.S., U. Okla., 1954; B.A., Central Wash. State U., 1960; M.S., U. Oreg., 1966, Ph.D., 1970; children—Linda J. Blanchard, Nancy R. Logan, Janice L. McFarland. Tchr., Wash. and Oreg. public schs., 1961-67; instr. biol. scis. Mt. Hood Community Coll., Salem, Oreg., 1970—; mem. Oreg. Senate from 12th Dist., 1981—. Mem. Multonamah County Econ. Devel. Commn., 1976—; pres. E. Multnomah County chpt. LWV, 1975. Mem. AAUW, Bus. and Profl. Women, Oreg. Women's Polit. Caucus (Mary Rieke award 1978). Democrat. Club: Order Eastern Star. Office: Box 68 Salem OR 97308

MCFARLAND, JACLANEL MOORE, lawyer; b. Dawson, Tex., June 6, 1952; d. Jack Leon and Frances Junell (Linch) Moore; m. Allen Keith McFarland, Aug. 14, 1976; children—Allen Keith, Jr., Linch Moore. B.A., Baylor U., 1974, J.D., 1977; postgrad., Oxford U., 1974. Bar: Tex. 1977, U.S. Dist. Ct. (so. dist) Tex. 1979. Atty. Tarrant Title Co., Ft. Worth, 1977-78; assoc. Gerald L. King and Assocs., Inc., Spring, Tex., 1978-79; sole practice, Houston, 1979—; prof. govt. bus. law North Harris County Coll., 1979-80. Mem. legal com. South Main Bapt. Ch., 1979-83. Mem. ABA, Tex. Bar Assn., Houston Bar Assn. (family law sect.), Baylor U. Alumni Assn. (life), Harvey M. Richey Moot Ct. Soc., Assn. Women Attys., Phi Alpha Delta, Pi Sigma Alpha. Home: 542 Pine Walk Trail Spring TX 77373 Office: 400 FM 1960 W Suite 111 Houston TX 77090

MCFARLAND, KAY ELEANOR, state justice; b. Coffeyville, Kans., July 20, 1935; d. Kenneth W. and Margaret E. (Thrall) McF.; B.A. magna cum laude, Washburn U., Topeka, 1957, J.D., 1964. Admitted to Kans. bar, 1964; pvt. practice, Topeka, 1964-71; probate and juvenile judge Shawnee County, Topeka, 1971-73; dist. judge, Topeka, 1973-77; justice Kans. Supreme Ct., 1977—; owner, operator Quilts by Kay McFarland, Topeka, 1961-64. Mem. Am., Kans., Topeka bar assns., Dist. Judges Assn., Nat. Assn. Juvenile Judges, Nat. Assn. Probate Judges. Office: Supreme Ct Kansas State House Topeka KS 66612

MC FARLAND, MARTHA ANN, educator; b. Natchitoches, La., Aug. 6, 1940; d. Charles I. and Virginia (Watson) McF.; B.A., Northwestern State U., 1967; M.Ed., U. Miss., 1971; postgrad. W.Va. U., 1972-73; Ph.D., Fla. State U., 1979. With Caddo Parish Sch. Bd., Shreveport, La., 1967-70; tchr. W. Shreveport Acad., 1970, Natchitoches (La.) Acad., 1971; regional dir. early childhood Region VI, Ednl. Service, Wheeling, W.Va., 1971-73; instr. edn., dir. kindergarten Berry Coll., Mt. Berry, Ga., 1973-78; prof. edn. Liberty U., Lynchburg, Va., 1979—; condr. numerous workshops, W.Va., Ga., La. Mem. Assn. Childhood Edn. Internat., Fla. Assn. Childhood Edn., Leon County Assn. Childhood Edn., Nat. Assn. Edn. Young Children, Va. Assn. Young Children, Ga. Assn. Young Children, So. Assn. Children Under Six, Piedmont Area Assn. Young Children (pres. 1986-88), Assn. Christian Educators of Tchrs., W.Va. Assn. Childhood Edn. (v.p. infants 1972-73), Phi Delta Kappa. Contbr. articles to profl. jours. Office: Div Edn Liberty U PO Box 1401 Lynchburg VA 24506

MCFARLAND, VIOLET VIVIAN, author; b. Seattle, Feb. 26, 1908; d. Judson Loring and Annie (Conners) Sweet; M. J. Lamar Butler, 1944 (div. 1953); m. Glen W. McFarland, 1958 (div. 1965). B.A., Wash. State U., 1928; M.A., Columbia U., 1933. Tchr., Konawaena High Sch., Kealakekua, Hawaii, 1928-30, Am. Sch. in Japan, Tokyo, 1930-31; soc. editor Japan Times, Tokyo, 1930-31, Hong Kong Telegraph, 1940; real estate assoc. Long Beach Bd., Calif., 1961—. Author (as Violet Sweet Haven): Hong Kong for Weekend, 1939; Many Ports of Call, 1940; Gentlemen of Japan, 1944. Contbr. articles to profl. jours. Mem. Nat. Press Club, Calif. Bd. Realtors, Delta Zeta. Avocations: travel; curator Oriental art and lit. Address: PO Box 872 Lake Elsinore CA 92330

MCFARLANE, BETH LUCETTA TROESTER, mayor; b. Osterdock, Iowa, Mar. 9, 1918; d. Francis Charles and Ella Carrie (Moser) Troester; M. George Evert McFarlane, June 20, 1943 (dec. May 1972); children—Douglas, Steven (dec.), Susan, George. B.A. in Edn., U. No. Iowa, 1962, M.A. in Edn., 1971. Cert. tchr. Tchr. rural and elem. schs., Iowa, 1936-50, 55-56; elem. tchr. Oelwein Community Schs., Iowa, 1956-64, jr. high reading tchr., 1964-71, reading specialist, 1971-83; mayor of Oelwein, 1982—; evaluator North Central Accreditation Assn. for Ednl. Programs. Mem. Planning Team for Confs. for Iowa Cities, N.E. Iowa, 1985; mem. Area Econ. Devel. Com. N.E. Iowa, 1985. Named Iowa Reading Tchr. of Yr., Internat. Reading Assn. Iowa, 1978; recipient Outstanding Contbrn. to Reading Council Activities award Internat. Reading Assn. N.E. Iowa, 1978. Mem. N.E. Iowa Reading Council (pres. 1975-77), MacDowell Music and Arts Orgn. (pres. 1978-80). Oelwein Bus. and Profl. Women (Woman of Yr. 1983), Delta Kappa Gamma (pres. 1980-82). Republican. Mem. Reorganized Ch. of Jesus Christ of Latter Day Saints. Avocations: bicycling, refinishing antiques, gardening. Home: 512 7th Ave NE Oelwein IA 50662 Office: City of Oelwein 20 2d Ave SW Oelwein IA 50662

MCFARLANE, KAREN WEISKOPF, lawyer; b. N.Y.C., Dec. 22, 1946; d. Moe and Pauline (Landesberg) Weiskopf; m. Alex McFarlane, July 6, 1973 (div. 1984). B.A., U. Wis., 1967; M.A., Columbia U., 1974; J.D., Bklyn. Law Sch., 1981. Bar: N.Y. 1982, Fla. 1983, U.S. Dist. Ct. (so. and ea. dists.) N.Y. 1982. Tchr., edn. specialist N.Y.C. Bd. Edn., 1970-77; clin. assoc. Dist. Atty. N.Y. County, N.Y.C., 1979-80; summer assoc. Newman & Adler, N.Y.C., 1980; mem. firm Greenhill, Speyer & Thurm, N.Y.C., 1981-84, Hendler & Murray, P.C., N.Y.C., 1984—. Chpt. chmn. United Fedn. Tchrs., 1974-77. Recipient Am. Jurisprudence award, 1979, 80; Ely Trachtenberg award United Fedn. Tchrs., 1977. Mem. Moot Ct. Honor Soc., N.Y. County Lawyers Assn., ABA. Home: 20 Garden Pl Brooklyn NY 11201

MC FATE, PATRICIA ANN, foundation administrator, educator; b. Detroit, Mar. 19, 1936; d. John Earle and Mary Louise (Bliss) McF.; B.A. (Alumni Scholar), Mich. State U., 1954; M.A., Northwestern U., 1956, Ph.D., 1965; M.A. (hon.), U. Pa., 1977. Asso. prof. English, asst. dean liberal arts and scis. U. Ill., Chgo., 1967-74, asso. prof. English, asso. vice chancellor for acad. affairs, 1974-75; asso. prof. folklore Faculty of Arts and Scis., U. Pa., Phila., 1975-81, prof. tech. and soc. Coll. Engring. and Applied Sci., 1975-81, vice provost, 1975-78; dep. chmn. Nat. Endowment for Humanities, Washington, 1978-81; exec. v.p. Am. Scandinavian Found., N.Y.C., 1981-82, pres., editor, pub. Scandinavian Rev., 1982—; vis. asso. prof. dept. medicine Rush U., Chgo., 1970—; dir. Associated Dry Goods Corp., CoreStates Fin. Corp., Phila. Nat. Bank. Bd. dirs. Inst. for Cancer Research. Decorated officier Ordre de Leopold II, comdr.'s cross Icelandic Order of Falcon, comdr. Royal Order Polar Star (Sweden), comdr. Order of Lion (Finland); comdr. Royal Order of Merit (Norway); knight 1st class Royal Order of Dannebrog (Denmark); Bishop Anderson House Found. U. Ill. Grad. Coll. faculty fellow, 1968. Fellow N.Y. Acad. Scis.; mem. Acad. Scis. Phila. (founding mem., corr. sec. 1977-79), AAAS, Am. Com. on Irish Studies, Can. Assn. for Irish Studies, Internat. Assn. for Anglo-Irish Studies, MLA, Theta Alpha Phi, Omega Beta Pi. Club: Cosmopolitan (Phila.). Author: The Writings of James Stephens, 1979; editor: Uncollected Prose of James Stephens, 1983; contbr. articles to various jours.

MCFAUL, PATRICIA LOUISE, editor; b. Jersey City, June 28, 1947; d. James Leo and Ethel Louise (Shea) McF.; 1 child, Jennifer Jeanne. Student Nassau Community Coll., 1969-70. Pub. info. officer L.I. Cath. Newspaper, Hempstead, N.Y., 1967-68, researcher, 1968-70, staff writer, 1970-73, copy editor, 1973-78, layout and copy editor, 1978—, readership surveyor, Rockville Centre, N.Y., 1971, 75; mem., com. chmn. Diocesan Family Life Bd., Rockville Centre, 1978-82. Researcher: Mission to Latin America, 1976. Pres. Florence A. Smith Sch. P.T.A., Oceanside, N.Y., 1982-84; chmn. talented and gifted com. Oceanside Council P.T.A.s, 1984-85; mem., sec.-treas. L.I. Interfaith Council, Rockville Centre, 1977-80. Recipient Citation, Diocese of Rockville Centre, 1984. Mem. Cath. Press Assn. U.S. and Can. (mem. research com. 1975-80, mem., chmn. credentials and inspectors of elections com. 1976—, 1st place award design 1978, citations 1980, 81, 82, 83, 84). Democrat. Roman Catholic. Avocations: flying; classical music. Office: The LI Catholic 115 Greenwich St Hempstead NY 11550

MCGAFFEY, EDNA MILDRED, journalist; b. Riverton, Utah, Apr. 15, 1920; d. Wilford Thomas and Florence Clements (Bills) Silcock; m. Harold Lavon Monteer, 1939 (div.); 1 son, David Harold; m. 2d, Claude Weldon McGaffey, Jr., Aug. 21, 1948. B.A., St. Mary's U., 1955; postgrad. in journalism, photography, radio-TV, San Antonio Coll., 1976-79. From writer to office chief Hist. Office, San Antonio Air Material Area, Kelly AFB, Tex., 1947-73; spl. writer San Antonio Express-News, 1973—. Recipient Outstanding Clubwomen San Antonio award Express-News, 1971. Mem. Tex. Press Women (state pres. 1979-81, Woman of Achievement award 1973), Women in Communications (headliner award 1969, chpt. pres. 1966-68), Nat. Fedn. Press Women (region 6 dir. 1982-84, edn. fund bd. 1984—), AAUW (pres. San

Antonio br. 1978-80). Clubs: Zonta (pres. 1984-86), Women's (San Antonio). Home: 6701 Blanco Apt 1114 San Antonio TX 78216

MCGAFFIGAN, PEGGY WEEKS, former legislative assistant; b. Houlton, Maine, June 27, 1952; d. Francis P. and Ruth Conrad (Steeves) Weeks; B.A., U. Maine, Orono, 1974; M.A., Tufts U., 1975; m. Edward McGaffigan, Jr., July 3, 1982; 1 son, Edward Francis. Analyst div. nat. security and internat. affairs Congl. Budget Office, Washington, 1975-79; legis. asst. to Senator William S. Cohen, Washington, 1979-84. Mem. Phi Beta Kappa. Home: 4818 N 37th St Arlington VA 22207

MC GANN, GERALDINE, government official; b. Bklyn., Dec. 21, 1937; d. Daniel and Geraldine (LeGrande) Essex; B.A. with honors, Hofstra U., 1974; M.Profl. Studies in Health Care Adminstrn. with honors, C.W. Post Coll., L.I. U., 1978; m. Edward J. McGann, Apr. 7, 1956; children—Daniel, Kevin, Kerrie, Jacqueline. Tchr., Hempstead and East Rockaway Schs.; coordinator sr. citizen services Town of Hempstead, N.Y., 1974-78, dep. commr. dept. services for aging, 1978-81; spl. asst. to regional adminstr. HUD, N.Y.C., 1981-83, exec. asst. to regional adminstr., 1983—. Chairperson Island Park (N.Y.) Housing Authority, 1975-81; village trustee, Island Park, N.Y., 1982—; mem. Republican Nat. Com. Mem. Am. Soc. Public Adminstrn., Assn. Pub. Adminstrn. and Health Care Profls., Women in Housing and Fin., Pi Alpha Alpha. Republican. Home: 42 Roosevelt Pl Island Park NY 11558 Office: 26 Federal Plaza New York NY 10278

MCGARRAH, KAREN, medical facility administrator; b. Columbus, Ga., Apr. 24, 1947; d. William Marion and Margaret (Evans) McG. B.S., Ala. Coll., 1969; M.Ed., U. Montevallo, 1974; grad. in hosp. service adminstrn. devel. U. Ala.-Birmingham, 1983; M.B.A., Samford U., 1984. Cert. hosp. adminstr. Tchr., Jefferson County, Birmingham, Ala., 1969-74; dir. Camp Fire West, Camp Fire, Inc., Birmingham, 1974-75; dir. donor resources ARC, Birmingham, 1975-78; dir. materials East End Hosp., Birmingham, 1978-81; materials mgr. Bapt. Med. Ctrs., Birmingham, 1981—. Mem. exec. com. YWCA, Birmingham, 1981-83, also treas. Mem. Young Men's Bus. Club. Democrat. Baptist. Home: 836 August Dr Birmingham AL 35215 Office: Baptist Med Ctrs 800 Montclair Rd Birmingham AL 35213

MCGARRY, MARCIA LANGSTON, probation and parole officer; b. Washington, Dec. 9, 1941; d. Emil Sylvester and Bernice B. (Bland) Busey. B.S., Morgan State U., 1964. Cert. tchr., law enforecment officer, Fla. Payroll clk., jr. acct. U.S. Dept. Labor, Washington, 1964-65; English tchr., Taiwan, 1968-70; tchr. Monroe County Sch. Bd., Key West, Fla., 1971-81; exec. dir. Monroe Assn. Retarded Citizens, Key West, 1977-79; dep. sheriff Monroe County Sheriff's Dept., Key West, 1979-83; probation/parole officer Fla. State Dept. Corrections, Key West, 1983—; instr. Fla. Keys Community Coll., 1983—. Active local polit. campaigns; co-founder day schs. for underprivileged children. Recipient cert. of appreciation Lions Club, 1978, 79; Career Week award Harris Elem. Sch., 1981. Mem. Nat. Assn. Female Execs., Fla. Police Benevolent Assn., Big Bros./Big Sisters Am. (membership com. 1985—), Spouse Abuse, Key West Profls., Lutheran Ch. Women. Home: 3220 Pearl Ave PO Box 2648 Key West FL 33040 Office: 424 Fleming St Key West FL 33040

MC GAURAN, MADELEINE R., social worker; b. Providence; d. Michael J. and Mary (Flanagan) McGauran; B.S., U. R.I., 1938; postgrad. Boston Coll., 1943-46; M.S., Boston U., 1949. Social worker Providence Dept. Public Welfare, 1939-41, asst. dist. supr., 1941-42, dist. supr., 1942-43; casework supr. R.I. Div. Public Assistance, Providence, 1943-48; field supr. sch. social work Boston Coll., 1946-48, Boston U., 1947-48; area supr. div. public assistance R.I. Dept. Social Welfare Div., 1949-64, chief med. assistance for aging, 1964-68, chief of field ops., 1968-71; chief casework supr., chief field ops., div. mgmt. services and assistance payments R.I. Dept. Social and Rehab. Services, Granston, 1971-76, asst. adminstr., 1976-78. Mem. Newport Council Social Agys., 1950-58, Warwick Council Community Services, 1958-60, R.I. Council Community Services, 1962-64. Mem. Nat. Assn. Social Workers, Acad. Cert. Social Workers, Pinewoods Inst., Am. Pub. Welfare Assn., Nat. Conf. Social Work. Home: 73 Mount View Dr Cranston RI 02920 Office: 600 New London Ave Cranston RI 02920

MC GAW, JESSIE BREWER, author, educator; b. Clarksville, Tenn., Oct. 17, 1913; d. Lewis Vernon and Birdie (Basford) Brewer; A.B., Duke U., 1935; M.A., Peabody Coll., 1940; postgrad. Columbia U., 1948-50, (Fulbright scholar) Am. Acad. Rome, 1959; m. Howard Franklin McGaw, Dec. 28, 1939 (div. 1958); children—Miriam Katherine, Vernon Howard; m. 2d, Harold L. Geis, Aug. 1964 (div. 1972); m. George P. Bickford, May 24, 1986. Tchr. Latin, Ward Belmont Sch., Nashville, 1938-40; tchr. Lausanne Sch., Memphis, 1940-42; asso. prof. English and Latin, U. Houston, 1952—. Bd. dirs. YWCA, 1957-59, Day Care Assn., 1956-61, Houston Civic Music Assn., 1958-60, Houston Council Human Relations. Recipient Cokesburg Juvenile award; Theta Sigma Phi lit. award. Fulbright grantee Am. Acad. in Rome, 1959; research grantee, 1964, 72; Delta Kappa Gamma ednl. grantee, China, 1981. Mem. Tex. Folklore Soc., South Central Modern Lang. Assn., Houston Council, Tchrs. Fgn. Lang. (treas.), League Women Voters, AAUW, Tex. Inst. Letters, U. Houston Women's Assn. (pres. 1967-68), Mus. Fine Arts (asso.), Delta Kappa Gamma, Kappa Kappa Gamma. Democrat. Methodist. Club: University Houston Woman's (pres. 1954-55, 67-68). Author: How Medicine Man Cured Paleface Women, 1956; History of Houston YWCA, 1957; Painted Pony Runs Away, 1958; Little Elk Hunts Buffalo, 1961; Chief Red Horse Tells About Custer, 1981. Translator: Heptaphus (Pico delia Mirandola), 1977. Home: 2405 Dickey Pl Houston TX 77019

MCGEE, BETTY JEANNE, editor; b. Lubbock, Tex., Dec. 15, 1929; d. Thomas Anderson and Hester Vianna (Parrack) Baber; m. J.C. McGee, Oct. 25, 1946 (div. May 1983); children—Jerry D., Barbara R., Delores Dianne. Student Cisco Jr. Coll., 1983. Proofreader, Lubbock Avalanche Jour. (Tex.), 1966-67; bookkeeper, sec. Harper Printing Co., Garland, Tex., 1967-72; advt. mgr. Montgomery Ward Co., Lubbock, 1972-73; editor, mgr. Ranger Times (Tex.), 1976-84; editor Everman Times (Tex.), 1984—. Mem. Soc. Profl. Journalists. Democrat. Methodist. Home: 300 Georgetown Dr Everman TX 76140

MCGEE, CAROLYN MARIE, computer services co. exec.; b. Pottstown, Pa., Jan. 8, 1947; d. John Joseph and Beverley Valeria McGee; B.S., Carnegie Mellon U., 1968, M.S., 1970; Ph.D., U. Ala., 1971; m. Denis J. Bogan, June 7, 1969; children—Kathleen Bogan, John Bogan. Mem. faculty Kans. State U., Manhattan, 1972-74; v.p. Am. Mgmt. Systems, Arlington, Va., 1974—. Recipient Cert. of Merit, GAO, 1979. AAUW fellow, 1970. Mem. AAUW. Contbr. articles to profl. jours. Home: 5110 Althea Dr Annandale VA 22003 Office: 1777 N Kent St Arlington VA 22209

MCGEE, DEBRA DIANE, interior designer, consultant; b. Johnson City, Tenn., Dec. 30, 1959; d. Robert Guy and Lula Janette (Rose) McG. B.S., U. N.C.-Greensboro, 1981. Inerior designer Carolina Office Equipment, Hickory, N.C., 1981; salesperson, interior designer Miller Services, Charlotte, 1981—; project designer Joseph t. Ryerson & Son, Charlotte, 1983-84; space planner Internat Paper Co., Charlotte, 1984-85. Mem. Inst. Bus. Designers, Am. Soc. Interior Designers, Nat. Assn. Female Execs. Republican. Baptist. Club: Charlotte Contact Exchange (v.p. 1983). Avocations: golf; tennis; water skiing. Home: 7324-8 Lakefront Dr Charlotte NC 28210 Office: 100 E Park Ave Charlotte NC 28203

MCGEE, DOROTHY HORTON, author, historian; b. West Point, N.Y., Nov. 30, 1913; d. Hugh Henry and Dorothy (Brown) McG.; ed. Sch. of St. Mary, 1920-21, Green Vale Sch., 1921-28, Brearley Sch., 1928-29, Fermata Sch., 1929-31. Asst. historian Inc. Village of Roslyn (N.Y.), 1950-58; historian Inc. Village of Matinecock, 1966—. Author: Skipper Sandra, 1950; Sally Townsend, Patriot, 1952; The Boarding School Mystery, 1953; Famous Signers of the Declaration, 1955; Alexander Hamilton—New Yorker, 1957; Herbert Hoover: Engineer, Humanitarian, Statesman, 1959, rev. edit., 1965; The Pearl Pendant Mystery, 1960; Framers of the Constitution, 1968; author booklets, articles hist. and sailing subjects. Chmn., Oyster Bay Am. Bicentennial Revolution Comm., 1971—; historian Town of Oyster Bay, 1982—; mem. Nassau County Am. Revolution Bicentennial Commn. Dir., The Friends of Raynham Hall, Inc.; treas. Family Welfare Assn. Nassau County, Inc., 1956-58; dir. Family Service Assn. Nassau County, 1958-69. Recipient Cert. of award for outstanding contbn. children's lit. N.Y. State Assn. Elem. Sch. Prins., 1959; award Nat. Soc. Children of Am. Revolution, 1960; award N.Y. Assn. Supervision and Curriculum Devel., 1961; hist. award Town of Oyster Bay, 1963; Cert. Theodore Roosevelt Assn., 1976. Fellow Soc. Am. Historians; mem. Soc. Preservation L.I. Antiquities (hon. dir.), Nat. Trust Hist. Preservation, N.Y. Geneal. and Biol. Soc. (trustee), Oyster Bay Hist. Soc. (pres. 1971-75, chmn. 1975-79, trustee), Theodore Roosevelt Assn. (trustee), Townsend Soc. Am. (trustee), others. Republican. Address: Box 142 Locust Valley NY 11560

MCGEE, LINDA MACE, lawyer; b. Marion, N.C., Sept. 20, 1949; d. Cecil Adam and Norma Jean (Hogan) Mace; m. B. Gary McGee, Dec. 19, 1970; 1 son, Scott Adam. B.A., U. N.C.-Chapel Hill, 1971, J.D., 1973. Bar: N.C. 1973. Exec. dir. N.C. Acad. Trial Lawyers, Raleigh, 1973-78; assoc. Finger, Watson & di Santi, Boone, N.C., 1978-80; ptnr. Finger, Watson, di Santi & McGee, Boone, 1980—; mem. trustee's panel U.S. Bankruptcy Ct., Greensboro, N.C., 1980—; dir. Northwest Savs. and Loan, Boone, 1982-83; bd. dirs. Legal Services of N.C., Raleigh, 1982—. Trustee Caldwell Community Coll. and Tech. Inst., Hudson, N.C., 1982—; exec. bd. N.C. Assn. Community Coll. Trustees, 1983—; vice chmn. Watauga County Council on Status of Women, 1979-82; chmn. polit. action study com. N.C. Bus. and Profl. Women's Clubs, 1982-83; mem. Watauga County Ext. Adv. Bd., 1981—; state parliamentarian LWV, 1980, bd. dirs., Boone, 1981-82. Named Young Career Woman, N.C. Fedn. Bus. and Profl. Women's Clubs, 1980, Woman of Yr., Boone Bus. and Profl. Women's Club, 1980; mem. N.C. Women's Forum, Chapel Hill, 1981. Mem. ABA (com.), N.C. Bar Assn. (bd. govs. 1983—), N.C. Assn. Women Attys. (charter treas. 1980—), N.C. Acad. Trial Lawyers (editor mag. 1973-78), Watauga County Bar Assn. (sec.-treas. 1984), Assn. Trial Lawyers Am., N.C. State Assn. Trial Lawyers, C. of C. (bd. dirs.), AAUW (pres. Boone 1980-82). Democrat. Presbyterian. Home: PO Box 1423 Boone NC 28607 Office: PO Box 193 102 E King St Boone NC 28607

MCGEE, PATRICIA ANN, computer management consultant; b. N.Y.C., July 22, 1939; d. Patrick James and Bridget Mary (O'Leary) Brennan; B.A., CCNY, 1961; 1 dau., Ayn Maureen. Sr. cons., analyst Western Ops., Inc., San Francisco, 1968-71; data processing mgr. R. H. Lapin & Co., San Francisco, 1971-73; project leader, systems analyst Transmaerica Corp., San Francisco, 1973-74; systems analyst United Vintners, Inc., San Francisco, 1974-75; systems planner Fiberboard Corp., 1975-76; customer rep. Computer Scis. Corp., 1976-78; project mgr. Crocker Nat. Bank, 1978-80; cons. Bechtel Co., 1980, Mason-McDuffie & Co., 1980, Pacific Telephone Co., 1980-81; partner The Profls., San Francisco, 1981-83; computer cons. Risk Mgmt. Applications, San Francisco, 1983-84; cons. Bank of Am., Wells Fargo Realty Fin., 1985. Mem. Am. Mgmt. Assn., Republican Women San Francisco, Women Entrepreneurs, World Affairs Trade Council, Profl. Women's Network, Assn. System Mgrs. Republican. Roman Catholic. Clubs: Commonwealth of California; San Francisco Bay. Home: 430-10th Ave San Francisco CA 94118 Office: 430-10th Ave San Francisco CA 94118

MC GEORGE, CONSTANCE JEANNE, personnel executive; b. Pitts., Aug. 23, 1946; d. Paul Eugene and Margaret Agnes (McLaughlin) McG.; B.A. in English, Carnegie-Mellon U., 1968; postgrad. U. Pitts., 1969, U. Minn., 1976-79, 83—; m. Neil Wallace, June 14, 1978. Asst. wage and salary adminstr. Levinson Steel Co., Hays div., Pitts., 1968-69; personnel asst. Clifton div. Litton Industries, Clifton Heights, Pa., 1970-72; adminstr. prof. staff personnel policies Bank St. Coll. Edn., N.Y.C., 1973-74; spl. projects coordinator personnel Fed. Reserve Bank, Mpls., 1974-77, mgr. compensation and personnel adminstrn., 1977-79, mgr. human resource utilization, 1979-83, mgr. planning, 1983—. Mem. Falcon Heights Human Rights Commn., 1980—, Project with Industry Adv. Com. Multi Resource Centers, Mpls., 1977-79; mem. Mayor's Adv. Com. on Handicapped, Mpls., 1977; mem. Mpls. Area Council Employment Handicapped, 1974-76, chmn., 1976; chmn. Falcon Heights Human Rights Commn., 1984—. Mem. Am. Soc. Personnel Adminstrs., Human Resource Planning Soc., Minn. Women's Network, AAUW, Amnesty Internat., Phi Kappa Phi. Home: 2099 W Hoyt Ave St Paul MN 55108 Office: 250 Marquette Ave Minneapolis MN 55460

MCGERITY, MARGARET ANN, lawyer; b. Boston, Aug. 23, 1949; d. Francis Charles and Margaret Mary (Ford) McG.; m. Max Folkenflik, Apr. 3, 1971; 1 son, Alexander. B.A., Columbia U., 1978; J.D., Benjamin N. Cardozo Sch. Law, 1981. Artist, 1970-75; law clk. Seward & Kissel, N.Y.C., summer, 1979; asst. U.S. atty. U.S. Atty.'s Office for So. Dist. N.Y., N.Y.C., summer 1980; asst. dist. atty. Bronx Dist. Atty.'s Office, 1981-84; assoc. Wistendahl & Folkenlfik, N.Y.C., 1984—. Mem. ABA, N.Y. County Bar Assn., N.Y. Woman's Bar Assn., Assn. Bar City of N.Y. Democrat. Roman Catholic. Home: 320 Riverside Dr New York NY 10025 Office: 777 3d Ave New York NY 10017

MCGHEE, CONNIE BENTLEY, lawyer, association executive; b. Indpls., Dec. 27, 1947; d. Charles Edward and Myrtle Jean (Thompson) Bentley; m. Samuel Timothy McGhee, Jr.; children—Samuel Timothy III, Jeffrey Charles. B.S. in Edn., Ball State U., 1969; postgrad. in student personnel, Columbia U., 1973; J.D., Seton Hall U., 1977. Bar: N.J. 1982. Tchr. social studies Mineola High Sch., Garden City, N.Y., 1969-72, N.Y. Bd. Edn., Bklyn., 1972-77; sr. labor relations specialist Newark Bd. Edn. (N.J.), 1977-79; dir. employee relations Jersey City State Coll., 1979-84; asst. corp. counsel City of Newark, 1985—; v.p. pub. colls., sec. N.J. Assn. Affirmative Action Higher Edn., 1979—; legis. com. Affirmative Action Council, State of N.J., 1983-84. Mem. Coalition for a United Hillside (N.J.), 1983—; trustee Nat. Urban League Hudson County, Jersey City, 1983-86, Action Sickle Cell, Jersey City, 1981—. Mem. ABA, Nat. Assn. Women Lawyers, N.J. Assn. Black Women Lawyers, Alpha Kappa Alpha. Home: 1548 Maple Ave Hillside NJ 07205

MC GHEE, PATRICIA LOUISE OHLSEN, educator; b. Monticello, Wis., Sept. 14, 1934; d. Michael Peter and Alicia Alma (Ellefson) Ohlsen; B.A., U. Ariz., 1956; M.A., Marquette U., 1958; postgrad. U. Wis-Madison, 1972-74; m. John Ferdinan; 2 children. Tchr. social studies pub. schs., Milw., 1960-62, Fox Point-Bayside (Wis.), 1963-67, Shorewood, Wis., 1971-72, Waukesha, Wis., 1974—; tchr. social studies Milw. Area Tech. Coll., 1968-74; participant NEH-Carnegie-Mellon project on social history, summer 1981. Sec. Ozaukee County Democratic party, 1973; participant Wis. Conf. on Arms Control, Wingspread, 1978; mem. adv. com. Wis. Pub. TV Network, 1985-86. Taft fellow, 1975; Newspaper in Edn. scholar, 1980. Mem. Historians Film Com., Internat. Assn. for Audio-Visual Media in Hist. Research and Edn., Am. Ednl. Research Assn., Assn. for Ednl. Communications and Tech., Smithsonian Assocs., Ednl. Film Library Assn., Gamma Phi Beta, Pi Gamma Mu. Home: 31258 W Century Dr Mukwonago WI 53149 Office: 401 E Roberta Ave Waukesha WI 53186

MCGILL, LILLIE C., educator; b. Kingstree, S.C., Dec 26, 1943; d. James and Lucile (Strong) Cunningham; m. Norman McGill, Apr. 29, 1967; children—Norman Carlton, Lynn Vanessa. B.S., Tuskegee Inst., 1964; M.Ed., S.C. State Coll., 1972. Tchr., Williamsburg County Schs., Kingstree, S.C., 1964-83, curriculum coordinator, 1983—. Sec., Green Acre-Woodland Acres Community Action, Kingstree, 1980-86; mem. vis. com. So. Assn. Colls. and Schs. Mem. Williamsburg Edn. Assn., Assn. for Supervision and Curriculum Devel., Nat. Am. Female Execs., NEA, NAACP, Alpha Kappa Alpha. Methodist. Lodge: Order Eastern Star (assoc. matron). Home: 901 Eastland Ave Kingstree SC 29556 Office: Kingstree Elementary Sch 500 Academy St Kingstree SC 29556

MCGILLEY, SISTER MARY JANET, college president; b. Kansas City, Mo., Dec. 4, 1924; d. James P. and Peg (Ryan) McG.; B.A., St. Mary Coll., 1945; M.A., Boston Coll., 1951; Ph.D., Fordham U., 1956; postgrad. U. Notre Dame, 1960, Columbia U., 1964. Social worker, Kansas City, 1945-46; joined Sisters of Charity of Leavenworth, Roman Catholic Ch., 1946; tchr. English, Hayden High Sch., Topeka, 1948-50, Billings (Mont.) Central High Sch., 1951-53; faculty dept. English, St. Mary Coll., Leavenworth, Kans., 1956-64, pres. coll., 1964—; mem. bd. North Central Assn. Colls. and Schs., 1985—, exec. bd., 1983—, v.p., 1985-87; Roman Cath. rep. Nat. Congress on Ch.-Related Colls. and Univs., 1979. Bd. dirs. Kans. Ind. Colls. Assn., pres., 1985-86; bd. dirs. Kansas City Regional Council for Higher Edn., United Leavenworth Way, 1965-85, edn. v.p., 1986-87; trustee at large Ind. Coll. Funds Am., 1975-76, exec. com., 1974-77; bd. dirs. Kans. Ind. Coll. Fund, pres., 1964—, chmn. bd., 1977, 78; mem. Leavenworth Planning Commn., 1977-78; mem. Commn. on Women in Higher Edn., Am. Council on Edn., 1980—; trustee-at-large Nat. Assn. Ind. Colls. and Univs., 1982-85, fin. chmn., 1985. Recipient Alumnae award St. Mary Coll., 1969; Disting. Service award Baker U., 1981. Mem. Nat. Assn. Ind. Colls. and Univs. (dir. 1982-83), Nat. Council Tchrs. English, Am. Assn. Higher Edn., Leavenworth C. of C. (bd. dirs.), Assn. Am. Colls. (commn. liberal learning 1970-73, com. curriculum and faculty devel. 1979—), St. Mary Alumnae Assn. (hon. pres.), Delta Epsilon Sigma. Democrat. Contbr. articles, fiction, poetry to various jours. Address: St Mary Coll 4100 S 4th Street Leavenworth KS 66048

MCGILVRAY, JOAN BAILEY, stockbroker; b. Monrovia, Calif., Nov. 4, 1926; d. William James and Helen Jane (Davis) Bailey; student Stanford U., 1944-47; divorced; children—Alexander Crane, Jr., Mark Rankin, Lynn. Asso. v.p. Dean Witter & Co., Pasadena, Calif., 1966-76; 1st v.p. Bateman Eichler Hill Richards, Los Angeles, 1976-84; v.p. investments Dean Witter Reynolds Inc., Carlsbad, Calif., 1984—. Mem. Nat. Options Soc. (founding dir.), So. Calif. Options Soc. (pres. 1978). Republican. Club: Live Oak Tennis. Home: 76 St Malo Beach Oceanside CA 92054 Office: 3150 El Camino Real Suite 102 Carlsbad CA 92008

MCGINLEY, NANCY ELIZABETH, lawyer; b. Columbia, Mo., Feb. 29, 1952; d. Robert Joseph and Ruth Evangeline (Garnett) McG. B.A. with high honors, U. Tex., 1974, J.D., 1977. Bar: Tex. 1977, U.S. Dist. Ct. (no. dist.) Tex. 1979. Law clk. U.S. Dist. Ct. (no. dist.) Tex., Fort Worth, 1977-79; assoc. Crumley, Murphy and Shrull, Fort Worth, 1979-81; staff atty. SEC, Fort Worth, 1981—. Mem. editorial staff Urban Law Rev. Mem. Tarrant County Young Lawyer's Assn., Women Lawyers of Tarrant County, Fort Worth Bus. and Profl. Women's Assn., Mortar Bd., Phi Beta Kappa, Phi Kappa Phi, Alpha Lambda Delta. Home: 2222 Irwin Ave Fort Worth TX 76110 Office: SEC 411 W 7th St 8th Floor Fort Worth TX 76102

MCGINNIS, CYNTHIA WOLF, microbiologist; b. Lancaster, Pa., Jan. 17, 1949; d. H. LeMar and Rosemary A. (Snyder) Wolf; student Millersville Coll., 1979—. Staff technician St. Joseph Hosp., Lancaster, 1966-67; staff technician Lancaster Osteo. Hosp., 1968-72, microbiology supr., 1972—, mem. infection control com., 1973—; mem. adv. panel Med. Lab. Observer, 1979-81, 85—. Mem. Am. Med. Technologists, Am. Soc. Microbiology, Central Pa. Microbiology Assn., Pa. Soc. Med. Technologists, N.Y. Acad. Scis., Nat. Cert. Agy. Med. Lab. Personnel. Roman Catholic. Office: 1175 Clark St Lancaster PA 17604

MCGINNIS, LYNNE G(REIFINGER), lawyer; b. Los Angeles, Feb. 18, 1956; d. Carl and Phyllis Harriet (Stoliar) Greifinger; m. Wayne C. McGinnis, July 25, 1978. B.A. in Polit. Sci., UCLA, 1978; J.D., Loyola U.-Los Angeles, 1981. Bar: Calif. 1981. Summer law clk. firm Stutman, Treister & Glatt, Los Angeles, 1980; assoc. firm Ball, Hunt, Hart, Brown & Baerwitz, Los Angeles, 1981-82; vol. atty. Westside Legal Services, Los Angeles, 1982-83; assoc. Law Office of Byron Pesin, Los Angeles, 1983, firm Pain, Pippin, Cluff & Olson, San Diego, 1983, Law Offices of Deane B. Houston, San Diego, 1984; now sole practice. Note and comment editor, contbr. articles Loyola Law Rev., 1979-81. Vol. Carter campaign, Los Angeles, 1976; publicity chmn. Democratic Club, Pacific Palisades, 1972. Thomas V. Girardi scholar, 1979, 80; recipient Bur. Nat. Affairs Law Week award, 1981, award Am. Jurisprudence Constl. Law and Corps., West's Pub. Co., 1980. Mem. ABA, Calif. State Bar Assn., San Diego Trial Lawyers Assn., Assn. Trial Lawyers Am., Calif. Trial Lawyers Assn., San Diego County Bar Assn. Club: San Diego Swim Masters. Home: 2625 Tonto Way San Diego CA 92117 Office: 701 B St Suite 800 San Diego CA 92101

MCGINTY, BARBARA BURCH, cabinet manufacturer; b. Savannah, Ga., Mar. 18, 1928; d. Charles Breckenridge and Dorothea (Brodman) Burch; m. John Kennedy McGinty, Apr. 14, 1949; children—Lynda, Geoffrey. A. Bus., Armstrong Jr. Coll., Savannah, 1948. Mortgage loan officer Harry D. Gurley Co., Savannah, 1948-50, First Fed. Savs. & Loan Assn., Savannah, 1950-55; v.p., co-owner Wilmington Cabinet Co., Savannah, 1955—. Vice chmn. Chatham County (Ga.) Hosp. Authority, 1980—; pres. Fedn. Democratic Women, Chatham County, 1978—; del. Nat. Conv. Dem. Party, 1980. Mem. Ga. Hosp. Assn., LWV, Home Builders Assn. (service award 1976), Bldgs. Material Mchts. Assn., Bus. and Profl. Women's Club, Savannah C. of C. (dir. 1981-84). Home: 2024 Walthour Rd Savannah GA 31410 Office: Wilmington Cabinet Co Inc 211 Johnny Mercer Dr Wilmington Island Savannah GA 31410

MCGINTY, MARGARET ANNE, nursing educator; b. Balt., Apr. 6, 1940; d. Jack Buckley and Anne Elizabeth (Matthai) Maguire; m. James Joseph McGinty, May 10, 1969. Diploma, Mercy Hosp. Sch. Nursing, Balt., 1961; B.S. in Nursing, U. Md., 1961, M.S., 1976. Staff nurse Mercy Hosp., Balt., 1961-66, mem. faculty Sch. Nursing, 1966-75; instr. U. Md. Mercy Ctr., Balt., 1976-77, asst. prof. nursing, 1977-80; asst. prof. U. Md. Sch. Nursing, Balt., 1980—. Mem. Women's Commn. Balt. County, 1982-83; bd. dirs. Dundalk Heritage Assn., 1983. Named Faculty Mem. of Yr., U. Md. Class of 1983. Mem. Sigma Theta Tau, Phi Kappa Phi. Democrat. Roman Catholic. Home: 1911 Sunberry Rd Baltimore MD 21222 Office: U Md Sch Nursing 655 W Lombard St Baltimore MD 21201

MCGINTY, MARILYN RICHARDS, mental health center administrator; b. Carbondale, Pa., June 6, 1936; d. Edward Laverne Richards and Florence Cora (Mackle) Richards Rogers; m. John Joseph McGinty, Sept. 1, 1956 (div. 1984); children—Maureen, Patricia, Michael, Margaret, Jack. B.A., Antioch U., 1984. Credit investigator Phila. State Hosp., 1971-73; revenue officer Woodhaven Ctr., Phila., 1973-84, dir. reimbursement, 1984-85, asst. fin. dir., 1985—; pres., dir. Benjamin Rush Mental Health/Mental retardation Ctr., Phila., 1980—; sec., dir. The Northwestern Corp., Erdenheim, Pa., 1984—; vice chmn. Phila. Mental Health/Mental Retardation Bd., 1981—. Author: (mag.) The Rush Hour, 1980-82. Coordinator Bill Green for U.S. Senate campaign, Phila. 1976, Lewis for Senate compaign, Phila., 1978, Bill Green for Mayor, Phila., 1979. Recipient Citation City of Phila., 1980. Mem. Am. Assn. for Mental Deficiency. Democrat. Roman Catholic. Avocations: music; creative writing. Home: 3140 B Grant Ave Wimbledon Ct Philadelphia PA 19114 Office: Woodhaven Ctr 2900 Southampton Rd Philadelphia PA 19154

MCGIRR, SARAH ELIZABETH, advertising executive, real estate development consultant; b. Pocatello, Idaho, Jan. 19, 1938; d. Clark Lowell Edwards and Sarah Elizabeth Pederson; m. Richard G. McGirr, Jr., Mar. 23, 1958; children—Richard G. III, Michael. Student U. Pacific, 1956-58. Clin. grants coordinator Pfizer, Inc., Groton, Conn., 1964-79; owner, operator The Quellen Group, Groton, 1980—; chmn. Women's Bus. Ownership Conf., Hartford, Conn., 1984. Mem. rep. town meeting Town of Groton, 1977-79, town councilor, 1975-77; chmn. Rep. City Com., 1984-85; mem. Rep. Town Com., 1977-85; treas. Thames East LWV, 1977-85; moderator 1st Congl. Ch. Christ, 1983-85; pres. bd. dirs. YWCA of Southeastern Conn., 1981-84; mem. Conn. Conf. on Sm. Bus., 1985; alt. U.S. Senate Com. on Sm. Bus. Adv. Council; co-chair 4th Ann. Women's Congress, 1985. Mem. Mistick River Bus. & Profl. Women (Woman of Yr. 1977, charter pres.), Conn. Fedn. Bus. Profl. Women (pres. 1983-84), Nat. Fedn. Bus. Profl. Women (leadership trainer 1984). Home: 25 Circle Ave Groton Ct 06340 Office: The Quellen Group 349-B Mitchell St Groton CT 06340

MCGIRT, SHERRI LYNN, lawyer; b. Charlotte, N.C., May 3, 1949; d. Joseph Ward and S. Pearl (Gasaway) McG.; m. Lawrence D. Farber, 1984. B.A., U. N.C., 1971, J.D., 1974. Bar: N.C.; C.P.A., N.C. Estate and gift tax atty. IRS, Greensboro, N.C., 1974-79; tax supr. Touche, Ross & Co., Charlotte, 1979-81; assoc. firm Weinstein & Sturges, P.A., Charlotte, 1981-83, mem., 1983—; mem. planning com. U. N.C. Annual Tax Inst., 1980—; lectr. probate and fiduciary seminar N.C. Bar Assn., Charlotte Estate Planning Council, Charlotte Pension Forum. Bd. dirs. Latta Place, Inc., Charlotte, 1982-84. Contbr. articles to legal publs. Mem. ABA, N.C. Bar Assn., Mecklenburg County Bar Assn. (chmn. legal services for elderly 1983-85, nominating com. 1984-85), Am. Inst. C.P.A.s, N.C. Assn. C.P.A.s. Presbyterian. Office: Weinstein & Sturges PA 810 Baxter St Charlotte NC 28202

MCGIVERN, MARY ELIZABETH, chemical engineer; b. Parkersburg, W.Va., Jan. 28, 1954; d. William Edward and Glenda Louise (Bowers) McGivern; B.Chem.Engrng., W. Va. U., 1975; M.B.A., U. Houston, 1982; m. James R. McKinley, Feb. 29, 1980. Process engr. Gulf Oil Chem. Co., Baytown, Tex., 1975-76, ops. specialist, 1976-79, zone supr., 1979-80, bus. analyst, Houston, 1980-85, asst. product mgr., 1985—. Vol. advisor Jr. Achievement, 1975-78. Recipient Woman of the Yr. award, YWCA, Houston, 1980. Mem. Houston Bus. Forum, Am. Inst. Chem. Engrs. Republican. Roman Catholic. Address: 5611 Arenas Timbers Humble TX 77346

MCGLAMERY, BARBARA COGGINS, homebuilder; b. Atlanta, Aug. 19, 1939; d. Robert Allen and Minnie (Reed) Coggins; m. Gerald G. McGlamery, Nov. 26, 1960; children—Gerald G. Jr., George L. B.A., Auburn U., 1961.

Sales assoc. Ronald Warren Real Estate, Florence, Ala., 1978-83, property mgr., 1984-86; v.p. So. Heritage Homes, Florence, 1985—. Mem. adv. bd. Kennedy-Douglass Ctr. for Arts, Florence, 1976-83; bd. dirs. Kennedy-Douglass Vols., 1976-83; mem. Salvation Army Aux. Mem. Nat. Assn. Homebuilders, Nat. Assn. Realtors, Ala. Assn. Realtors, Alpha Omicron Pi (adv. bd. Alpha Kappa chpt. 1970-82). Presbyterian. Home: 214 Robin Hood Dr Florence AL 35630 Office: So Heritage Homes PO Box 674 Florence AL 35630

MC GLASSON, CHRISTINE LOUISE, advertising director, consultant; b. Glendale, Calif., Nov. 13, 1944; d. Howard Allen and Christine (Fee) McGlasson; B.A. in Radio and TV, Fla. State U., 1966; M.A. in Communications, Calif. State U., 1980; student Am. Acad. of Dramatic Arts, 1964. Asst. dir. of news program Sta. WFSU-TV, Fla. State U., Tallahassee, 1965-66, radio announcer Sta. WFSU-FM, 1964-66; copywriter and programming asst. Sta. WSB-AM-FM, Atlanta, Ga., 1966; continuity dir., announcer and promotion dir. Sta. KCTC, Sacramento, Calif., 1968-72; copy supr. and account exec. Brown, Clark & Elkus Co., Sacramento, 1972-73; writer and comml. producer for Sta. KCRA-TV, Sacramento, 1974-75; propr., creative dir. Chris McGlasson & Assos., Communications Cons., Sacramento, 1976—; mktg. dir. Rancho Murieta Properties, Inc., near Sacramento, 1976-80, also gen. mgr. Rancho Murieta Country Club, 1977-78; Western region media mgr. Seven-Up U.S.A., 1982-85; dir. advt. and sales promotion Blue Diamond Almonds, Sacramento, 1985—; guest lectr. on communications and broadcasting to local secondary schs. and jr. colls., 1972—; dir. Sacramento Better Bus. Bur., 1975-76. Broadcast chmn. Sacramento Red Cross, 1970-73; publicity chmn. Soc. for the Prevention of Cruelty to Animals, 1976-77; music festival chmn. Sacramento Symphony Assn., 1977-80, bd. dirs., 1979-82; mem. publicity com. Sacramento Opera Guild, 1977-79. Served to capt. USAF, 1966-70; lt. col. with Calif. State Info. Office Air NG, 1972—. Recipient Sacramento C. of C. award, 1970, Nat. Retail Advt. award, 1972, Am. Radio/TV Commls. awards (Clios), 1972-73, Am. Advt. Fedn. award, 1973, Calif. Assn. Realtors award (3), 1978, Superior Calif. Builders Assn. awards (4), 1978, 79; Cable Car awards San Francisco Ad Club, 1979; mktg. Dir. of Yr. award Superior Calif. Bldg. Industries, 1979; Appreciation awards for public service by various community and civic orgns., 1973-77; named Sacramento Advt. Person of Yr., 1974; High Achievement Award Seven-Up, 1985. Mem. Am. Acad. of Advt., Sacramento Advt. Club (past pres.; 80 awards for creativity 1971-82), Sacramento Women in Media, Sacramento Women in Advt., Women in Communications, Internat. Communications Assn., Sacramento Press Club, Nat. Guard Assn. Episcopalian. Contbr. feature articles to local publs. Home: 2805 Adirondack Way Sacramento CA 95827

MCGLONE, MARY ELLEN, columnist, fashion editor; b. Cin., Jan. 2, 1943; d. Morris S. and Rose Caroline (Fremmel) Hermann; m. Samuel D. McGlone, Nov. 4, 1967; children—Michael, Molly, Michelle. B.A., Barat Coll., 1964; postgrad. U. Minn., Mankato State U., Troy State U., Northeastern Ill. State U. Freelance fashion coordinator, cons., model, 1967—; asst. dir. fashion merchandising and self-improvement Lowthian Coll. (formerly Patricia Stevens Sch.), Mpls., 1968-70; mgr. Patricia Stevens Modeling Agy., Mpls., 1970; instr., dir. fashion merchandising ITT-Minn. Sch. Bus., Mpls., 1971-81, asst. dir. placement, 1981-82, student services coordinator, 1982-86; columnist Skyway News, Mpls., 1978—, fashion editor, 1986—; editor Fashion Quarterly, 1986—; fashion writer and coordinator Where mag., 1986—; fashion editor Active Seniors, 1986—; originator Reach Out & Touch Me, ann. fashion for blind and handicapped. Bd. dirs. Minn. Heart Assn., 1970-71; publicity chmn. cookie drive Girl Scouts U.S.A., 1983. Barat scholar, 1960-64; Ill. State scholar, 1960-64; NDEA fellow, 1965. Mem. Minn. Press Club, Fashion Group (dir., program chmn. 1982-83, past treas.), Sales and Mktg. Execs. Club: N.W. Pilots Wives (past pres.). Author: (with others) The Person You Are, 1978, 2d edit., 1985; (with Mayer) Kids' Chic, 1984; columnist Entourage, Rapport; guest editor MSB News, Minn. Fashion Group News, Placement World; contbr. articles to Woman's World, Creative Service, WITT's. Home: 4457 Gaywood Dr Minnetonka MN 55343 Office: Skyway News 2104 Park Ave S Minneapolis MN 55414

MCGONIGAL, PEARL, Canadian province official; b. Melville, Sask., Can., June 10, 1929; d. Fred and Kathryne Kuhlman; ed. in Melville, Sask. LL.D., U. Man.; m. Marvin A. McGonigal, Nov. 3, 1948; 1 dau., Kimberly Jane. Formerly engaged in banking; then mdse. rep.; mem. St. James-Assiniboia (Man.) City Council, 1969-71; mem. Greater Winnipeg (Man.) City Council, 1971-81, chmn. com. on recreation and social services, 1977-79, dep. mayor and chmn. exec. policy com., 1979-81; lt. gov. Man., 1981—. Bd. dirs. Winnipeg Conv. Centre, 1975-77, Red River Exhbn., 1975-81, Rainbow Stage, 1976-81; ex-officio mem. Man. Theatre Centre, 1977-81; mem. Winnipeg Conv. and Visitors Bur., 1973-75, Man. Environ. Council, 1974-76, Man. Aviation Council, 1974-77; mem. selection com. Faculty Dental Hygiene, U. Man., 1970-80, bd. mgmt. Winnipeg Home Improvement Program, 1979-81; chmn. adv. com. Sch. Nursing, Grace Gen. Hosp., 1972—; past chmn. St. James-Assiniboia Inter-faith Immigration Council; former mem. vestry St. Andrew's Anglican Ch.; former vol. Lions Manor, Sherbrook Day Centre. Decorated dame of grace Order of St. John; recipient award Dist. 64 Toastmasters, 1974, Winnipeg lodge Elks, 1975; Humanitarian award B'nai B'rith, 1984; named hon. col. 735 Communications Regt. Liberal. Club: Winnipeg Winter. Author: Frankly Feminine Cookbook, 1975; weekly columnist Reliance Press Ltd. Newspapers, 1970-81. Home: 10 Kennedy St Winnipeg MB R3C 1S4 Canada Office: Room 235 Legislative Bldg Winnipeg MB R3C 0V9 Canada

MCGOUGAN, CAROLYN SPRUILL, corrections adminstrator; b. St. Joseph, La., Nov. 20, 1937; d. Harvey Lee and Maedy (Cowan) Spruill; m. John Marshall McCougan, Aug. 9, 1968; 1 son, Scott. B.S., Northwestern U., 1960; C.S.W., La. State U., 1966, M.S.W., 1973. Welfare visitor, welfare caseworker, welfare dir., caseworker for blind children Dept. Health and Human Resources, Baton Rouge, La., 1973-76; chief social services, supt., asst. sec., corrections program adminstr., dir. div. instns. Dept. Corrections, Baton Rouge, 1976—. Recipient Cert. of award Dept. Corrections, 1978, 83; Maharish award Transcendental Meditation Orgn., Baton Rouge, 1982. Mem. Nat. Assn. Juvenile Corrections Agys. (bd. dirs. 1982—), Am. Correctional Assn., Nat. Assn. Social Workers, La. Juvenile Probation and Parole Officers Assn. (mem. exec. bd. 1983—), La. Assn. Minority Criminal Justice Workers, LWV Democrat. Baptist. Office: Dept Corrections Box 44304 Capitol Sta Baton Rouge LA 70804

MCGOUGH, ALICE MARIE, chem. co. purchasing agt.; b. Tarentum, Pa., June 25, 1937; d. Edward Albert and Frances Amelia (Gross) Gase; B.A. magna cum laude, Carlow Coll., Pitts., 1957; postgrad. U. Pitts., 1958-59; children—Mary Gase, Paul Aidan, Daniel John. Research asst. in biophysics U. Pitts., 1957-59; lab. technician GAF Corp., Wayne, N.J., 1973, chems. buyer, 1973-76; buyer organic chems. div. Am. Cyanamid Co., Bound Brook, N.J., 1976-78, purchasing agt. materials planning and procurement div., 1978-81, purchasing agt. chems. group, 1981—. mem. exec. bd. LWV of Wayne Twp., N.J., 1969-72; vol. Paterson (N.J.) Task Force, Day Care Center, 1972. Mem. Smithsonian Assos. Democrat. Roman Catholic. Club: Sierra. Office: One Cyanamid Plaza Wayne NJ 07470

MCGOUGH, SHEILA, lawyer, editor; b. Pulaski, Va., Apr. 20, 1944; d. Thomas Francis and Irene Elizabeth (Kennedy) McGough. B.S., Georgetown U., 1964; J.D., George Mason U., 1982. Bar: Va., 1982, D.C., 1982. Editor Carnegie Instn., Washington, 1968-72, publs. officer, 1972-79; sole practice law, Alexandria, Va., 1982—; bd. dirs. Council Biology Editors, 1969-70. Contbr. articles to various publs; editor sci. reports Carnegie Inst. Year Book, 1968-78. Mem. exec. com. Alexandria Republican City Com., 1976-79, Alexandria Fedn. Civic Assns., Alexandria, 1976-80; City Alexandria rep. Met. Washington Council Govts. Citizens Adv. Com. Transp., 1977-79. Recipient Am. Jurisprudence award, Lawyers Coop. Pub. Co., 1982. Mem. Alexandria Bar Assn., D.C. Bar Assn., Assn. Trial Lawyers Am., Women's Bar Assn. D.C., Va. Women Attys. Assn. Club: Nat. Press (Washington). Office: 218 N Lee St Alexandria VA 22314

MCGOVERN, MAUREEN THERESE, singer, actress; b. Youngstown, Ohio, July 27, 1949; d. James T. and Mary Rita (Welsh) McG.; diploma Boardman (Ohio) High Sch., 1967. Recorded The Morning After, 1973, We May Never Love Like This Again, 1974, Can You Read My Mind, 1979, Different Worlds, 1979; cameo appearance in movie The Towering Inferno; appeared as singing nun in movie Airplane, 1979, as Mabel in stage play The Pirates of Penzance, N.Y.C., 1981, as Lusia Contini in Nine, 1982-83, as Mary in Brownstone, 1984. Mem. Com. of Performing Artists for Nuclear Disarmament, Celebrity Com. of UNICEF; bd. dirs. Osmond Found. for presentation of Children's Hosps. Miracle Network Telethon. Recipient Grand prize Tokyo Music Festival, 1975. Mem. Actors Equity Assn., Screen Actors Guild, Am. Fedn. Musicians, AFTRA, Am. Soc. Composers and Performers. Composer (with lyricist Judy Barron) You Love Me Too Late, 1978, Thief In the Night, 1978, Don't Stop Now, 1979, (children's album) I Want to Learn to Fly, 1981. Office: care Internat Creative Mgmt 40 W 57th St New York NY 10019

MCGOVERN, PATRICIA, state senator. Mem. Mass. State Senate from Dist. 2. Mem. Mass. State Democratic Com. Office: Mass Senate State Capitol Boston MA 02123*

MCGOVERN-HEHMAN, PATRICIA ELLEN, securities analyst; b. N.Y.C., May 2, 1947; d. Albert Michael and Mary Francis (Broderick) McGovern; B.S., U. Dayton, 1970, M.A., 1973; m. Thomas W. Hehman, May 17, 1980; children—Marisa McGovern, Broderick John. Teaching asst. U. Dayton; instr. English schs. V.I., Jamaica, 1970-75; adminstrv. asst. Standard Security Life Ins. Co., 1976-77; research asst., fin. editor E.F. Hutton & Co., Inc., 1977-80; sr. fin. writer, editor Smith Barney, Harris Upham & Co., N.Y.C., 1980-84, telecommunications industry securities analyst, 1984—; cons. E.F. Hutton & Co. Mem. AAUP, Nat. Assn. Female Execs. Republican. Roman Catholic. Contbr. articles to profl. jours. Home: 301 E 78th St New York NY 10021 Office: 1345 Ave of Americas 47th Floor New York NY 10105

MCGOWAN, JAN CAROL, nurse; b. Evansville, Ind., Oct. 20, 1953; d. Robert Eugene and Mary Edith (Nicholson) McG.; B.S. in Nursing, U. Evansville, 1975, M.S., 1978. With St. Mary's Hosp., Rochester, Minn., 1975-76; with CCU, Welborn Hosp., Evansville, Ind., 1976-78; instr. emergency room, emergency med. technician Deaconess Hosp. Sch. Nursing, Evansville, Ind., 1978-86; nurse surg. ICU, Vanderbilt U. Med. Ctr., Nashville, 1986—; instr. CPR. Cert. advanced cardiac life support. Mem. Emergency Dept. Nurses Assn., Tri-State Emergency Med. Technician Assn., Phi Mu, Alpha Tau Delta. Club: Single Civitans. Home: 2601 Hillsboro Rd Apt F-4 Nashville TN 37212 Office: Vanderbilt U Med Ctr Nashville TN 37212

MCGOWAN, KATHLEEN KEER, artist; b. Newark, Mar. 8, 1918; d. Theodore F. and Florence (MacRae) Keer; B.A., Smith Coll., 1940; postgrad. Columbia U., 1943, N.J. Tchrs. Coll., 1946-49; m. B.C. Breeden, June 29, 1940 (div. 1943); 1 dau., Kathy; m. Harold F. Allenby, July 28, 1949 (div. 1977); m. John Francis McGowan, Apr. 24, 1981. (dec. Apr. 28, 1986). Kindergarten tchr. Kimberly Sch., Montclair, N.J., 1946-49; tchr. art to handicapped Kessler Inst. Rehab., West Orange, N.J., 1961-77. Exhibited one-man shows Woman's Club Montclair, 1st Savs. & Loan Bank, Cedar Grove, N.J., Music Sch., Cedar Grove, Piggins Art Gallery, Montclair, N.J., all 1972; 2-man show 1st Nat. Bank of Palm Beach, 1978; exhibited in group shows N.J. State Fedn. Women's Clubs, Art Center of Oranges. Leader, Girl Scouts U.S.A., Little Falls, N.J., 1955-56; social dir. PTA, Great Notch, N.J., 1955-56. Recipient art awards Upper Montclair Women's Club; cert. of merit in art N.J. Fedn. Women's Clubs, 1st place essay award, 1973; 2 awards for oil paintings Lighthouse Art Gallery, Tequesta, Fla. Mem. Art Center Oranges, West Essex Art Assn., N.J. State Fedn. Women's Clubs (7th dist. art chmn. 1973-74), West Palm Beach Coin Club (sec. 1978-81). Clubs: Glen Ridge Country (N.J., handicap chmn. 1970, past publicity chmn. women's golf group); Upper Montclair Women's (dir. art dept. 1971-72, garden chmn. 1976-77); Little Falls Women's (treas. 1959-61); Quill (sec. 1985—), Beach (Palm Beach); Smith of the Palm Beaches (treas. 1976-77); Palm Beach Yacht, Jonathan's Landing Golf. Home: Apt G 331 The Waterford 603 South US Hwy 1 Juno Beach FL 33408

MCGOWAN, PHYLLIS GRACE, computer specialist; b. Saco, Maine, Mar. 21, 1933; d. Walter Clarence and Sophie Marie (Fritzberger) Grace; m. Eric David McGowan, Apr. 30, 1953; 1 child, Adele Marie McGowan Healy New (dec.). Student U. Md. Computer specialist Johnson, Mirmiran & Thompson, Silver Spring, Md., 1983—, Dept. of Justice, Washington, 1975-83. Treas. Love People, Inc., Silver Spring, 1982—. Served with USAF, 1951-53. Democrat. Roman Catholic. Avocations: sports; crocheting; sewing; bingo; travel. Home: 9810 Braddock Rd Silver Spring MD 20903 Office: Johnson Mirmiran & Thompson 1751 Elton Rd Silver Spring MD 20903

MCGOWEN, MARCIA ANN, insurance company executive; b. Prairie Grove, Ark., Feb. 1, 1941; d. Arthur Doyal and Dorotha Loucille (Brown) Mullins; B.Music Edn., Mo. So. State Coll., 1969; M.Music Edn., N.E. La. U., 1972; postgrad. U. So. Miss.; m. Jerry J. McGowen; children—Michael A. Taylor, Alicia A. Bohn, Tonya L. Howell, Scott S., Randall L., Robert T. Music dir. choral and band Rogers (Ark.) public schs., 1961-63; dir. chorus and orch. Joplin (Mo.) public schs., 1969-71; instr. music edn. and piano N.E. La. U., 1971-72, music instr., instr. dance drill team Vernon Parish (La.) public schs., 1973-76; curriculum coordinator William Carey Coll., Hattiesburg, Miss., 1976-77; sales rep., then dist. mgr. Profl. Mktg. Am., 1977-78, regional mgr., 1978-79, area v.p., Hattiesburg, 1979-81, v.p. recruiting, Ruston, La., 1979-81, dir., 1980-81; owner, pres. Reagan Ins. Agy., 1981-83; gen. agt. for south Miss., Transam. Occidental, 1983—. Music scholar U. Ark., 1958, U. So. Miss., 1976; recipient numerous service and sales awards. Home: Route 7 Box 987 Hattiesburg MS 39401 Office: 206 W Front St PO Box 1653 Hattiesburg MS 39401

MCGRADY, CORINNE YOUNG, design company executive; b. N.Y.C., May 6, 1938; d. Albert I. and Reda (Bromberg) Young; m. Michael Robinson McGrady; children—Sean, Siobhan, Liam. Student, Bard Coll., Annandale-on-Hudson, N.Y., 1960, Harvard U., 1968-69. Founder, pres. McGrady Corp., East Northport, N.Y., 1970—. Acrylic works exhibited in group shows at Mus. Contemporary Crafts, N.Y.C., 1969-70, Smithsonian Instn., 1970-71, Pompidou Ctr., Paris, 1971, Mus. Sci. and Industry, 1970; sculpture exhibited at Guild Hall Show, Southampton, N.Y., 1968, Hecksher Mus., 1968. Vice pres. Woman's Internat. League for Peace and Freedom, Huntington, N.Y., 1971. Recipient Design Rev. award Indsl. Design, 1969, 70; Instant Supergraphic Indsl. Design Rev. award, 1971. Patentee cookbook stand. Home: 95 Eatons Neck Rd Northport NY 11768 Office: Corinne McGrady Designs The McGrady Corp 29 Brightside East Northport NY 11731

MCGRAIL, JEAN KATHRYN, artist, educator; b. Mpls., May 1, 1947; d. Robert Vern and Mary Virginia (Kees) McGrail; m. Theodore Esser III, Sept. 28, 1985. B.S., U. Wis.-River Falls, 1970; M.F.A., Cranbrook Acad. Art, 1972; postgrad. Sch. of Art Inst. of Chgo., 1985. One woman shows include Gallery at the Commons, Chgo., 1982; group exhbns. include Saginaw Art Mus., Mich., 1972, Met. Mus. Art, Miami, Fla., 1974, Lowe Mus. Art, Coral Gables, Fla., 1974, 76, Miller Galleries, Coconut Grove, Fla., 1978, 80, Cicchinelli Gallery, N.Y.C., 1980-82, Harper Coll., 1984; represented in permanent collections at Miami-Dade Pub. Library, U. Wis.-River Falls, MacGregor Found., others. Cranbrook Acad. Art scholar, 1971; recipient Poster Competition award Vizcaya Mus., 1974; Print award Auction WPBT, 1979. Mem. Coll. Art Assn., Chgo. Artists Coalition. Democrat. Home: 607 Columbia Ave Elgin IL 60120 Office: PO Box 1425 Elgin IL 60121

MCGRAIL, SUSAN KING, travel agency executive, accountant; b. Richmond, Va., Mar. 7, 1952; d. William Jr. and Anne Winn (Gibson) King; m. John Patrick McGrail, Jr., June 2, 1979; 1 child, Katharine Anne. B.B.A., Coll. William and Mary, 1974. C.P.A., Va. Employment counselor Avante Gard of Richmond, Inc., 1970-73; staff acct. Touche Ross & Co., Washington, 1974-75, Richmond, 1975-78; controller Continental Cablevision, Richmond, 1978-81; v.p. fin. Warner Amex Cable Communications, Cin., 1981-85; prin. Travel Agts. Internat., Cin., 1985—; sec., treas. Warner Amex Minority Loan Fund, Cin., 1981-85; dir. Warner Amex Cable Communications of Cin. Inc., 1981—. Alumni career adviser Coll. William and Mary, Williamsburg, Va., 1982—, fund raiser ann. fund, 1984—. Fellow Am. Inst. C.P.A.s, Va. Soc. C.P.A.s; mem. Women in Cable, Nat. Assn. Female Execs., Am. Soc. Travel Agts., Pi Beta Phi. Republican. Episcopalian. Avocations: scuba diving; snorkeling; reading. Home: 2207 Spinningwheel Ln Cincinnati OH 45244 Office: Travel Agts Internat Montgomery 10778 Montgomery Rd Cincinnati OH 45242

MCGRATH, CORA ELISIA, educator; b. Mora, N.Mex., Apr. 29, 1922; d. Tom and Guadalupe McG.; student Hunter Coll., summer 1943, Okla. A&M U., 1943, N.Mex. Highlands U., 1940-43, 62-80, B.A., 1964, M.A., 1967; postgrad. U. N.Mex., 1969-70; m. George O. Maloof, Dec. 23, 1943; children—Wardie J. Hennessy, George O., Zian H. Swanson. Tchr., Guadalupe County, N.Mex., 1942-43; tchr. West Las Vegas Schs., 1964-69, 70-79, 80-82, dir. spl. edn., 1979-80; tchr. Albuquerque City Schs., 1969-70; ret., 1982. Democratic precinct chairwoman; presiding election judge; mem. San Miguel County Central Com.; commd. dep. sheriff; mem. E. Romero Hose and Fire Dept. Aux.; leader 4-H, Girl Scouts; den mother Boy Scouts Am.; dist. rep. PTA. Roman Catholic. Club: Order of Does. Composer songs. Served with USNR, World War II. Mem. Council for Exceptional Children, Retarded Children Assn., Internat. Reading Assn., NEA, Am. Legion, Nat. League Am. Pen Women, DAV.

MCGRATH, ELEANOR BURNS, magazine editor, journalist; b. Gloucester, Mass., July 28, 1952; d. Edward James and Julie Ann (Holloran) McGrath, m. Paul A. Witteman, May 5, 1984. A.B. magna cum laude, Mt. Holyoke Coll., 1974. Researcher Time-Life Books, N.Y.C., 1974-76; reporter-researcher Time Mag., N.Y.C., 1976-78, staff writer, 1978-81, edn. writer-editor, 1981-86; sr. editor Women's Sports & Fitness mag., Palo Alto, CAlif., 1986—. Trustee, Mt. Holyoke Coll., 1976-79; pres. Greater N.Y. Athletic Assn., N.Y.C., 1980-83. Time fellow Duke U., 1981; recipient Journalist-in-Residence award Nat. Endowment Humanities, U. Mich., 1984-85. Home: 199 Caselli Ave San Francisco CA 94114 Office: 310 Town and Country Village Palo Alto sco CA 94301

MCGRATH, SANDY ANN, nurse; b. Plattsburgh, N.Y., Sept. 29, 1946; d. Ralph Griffin and Rose Marie (Pauone) Sindo; m. James William McGrath, Oct. 13, 1973. Student Champlain Valley Sch. Nursing, 1966; A in Nursing, Pima Community Coll., 1980; Student Northwestern State U., 1984-85. Lic. practical nurse, N.Y., Ariz. Lic. practical nurse Plattsburgh AFB Hosp., 1967-76, Davis Monthan AFB Hosp., Tucson, 1976-80; R.N. Davis Monthan AFB Hosp., Tucson, 1980-83; R.N., staff nurse VA Med. Ctr., VA Adminstrn., Alexandria, La., 1983—; vol. worker Ronald McDonald House, Tucson, 1980-82. Mem. Arthritis Found. Republican. Roman Catholic. Home: 4228 Blalock Rd Pineville LA 71360

MCGRATH, SAREPTA ROYAN, medical supplies company executive; b. Oklahoma City, May 28, 1957; d. William R. and Royetta R. McG.; student Tex. Tech U., 1981. Adminstrv. sec. U. Tex. Health Sci. Center, Dallas, 1977-79; tech. sales rep. Cardiovascular Systems Inc., San Antonio, 1979-81; owner, operator Cardiovascular Spltys., Inc., Lubbock, Tex., 1981—. Mem. Am. Bus. Women's Assn., Nat. Assn. Female Execs., Nat. Audubon Soc., Nat. Geog. Soc., Am. Inst. Cancer Research, Nat. Humane Socs. Republican. Episcopalian. Office: PO Box 64906 Lubbock TX 79464

MCGRATH, VALENE KAREN, vocational training center director; b. Salt Lake City, Aug. 23, 1942; d. Albert Clark and Violet (Robinson) Robison; m. Mikel Eugene McGrath, Dec. 1, 1957; children—Cynthia McGrath Buchanan, Karen McGrath Hill, Kimberlie, Mikelene McGrath Driver, JoDell, Mathew. Student U. Idaho, 1959-60, Samaritan Sch. Nursing, Nampa, Idaho, 1961-62; L.P.N. U. Oreg., 1967-69; student U. Utah, 1978-79. Lic. practical nurse, Idaho. In various nursing positions, 1962-66; surg. floor supr., med. nurse U. Oreg. Tongue Point Job Corps, Astoria, 1966-69, residential supr., 1974-75; motel operator, Long Beach, Wash., 1972-73; coordinator student govt. and religious coordinator Thiokol Corp. Clearfield Job Corps (Utah), 1975-79, mgr. health services, 1979-80; residential dir. tng. and mgmt. resources Denison Job Corps. (Iowa), 1980; center dir. Tng. and Mgmt. Resources Inc., 1980-83, with corporate office tng. and mgmt. resources, Atlanta, 1983—. Capt., CAP, 1965—, mem. Rocky Mountain Staff, Ogden, Utah, 1976-80, mem. staff Regional Staff Coll., Portland, Oreg., 1979; franchise cons. Sav-A-Buc Internat., Jacksonville, Fla., 1984-85; dir. programs Brunswick Job Corps., 1983-84; co-owner, v.p. Diamond M Enterprises, mktg. and indsl. tng., 1984—; sales rep. Brunswick br. Fla. region Jim Walter Homes, 1985—. Mem. Assn. Supervision and Curriculum Devel., Nat. Assn. Vietnamese Am. Edn. Home and Office: 21 Windsor Circle Brunswick GA 31520

MCGRAVEY, CAROL HAJJAR, lawyer; b. Methuen, Mass., Dec. 31, 1954; d. James G. and Evelyn (Haddad) Hajjar; m. James A. McGravey, Nov. 24, 1979. B.A., Merrimack Coll., 1976; student St. John's U. Law Sch., 1976-77; J.D., Boston U., 1979. Bar: Mass. 1979, U.S. Dist. Ct. Mass. 1980. Sole practice, Methuen, Mass., 1979-81; spl. counsel City of Lawrence, Mass., 1979—, Lawrence Econ. Devel. and Indsl. Corp., 1980—; spl. asst. dist. atty. Essex County Dist. Atty.'s Office, Lawrence, Mass., 1983—; spl. counsel City of Somerville, Mass., 1984—; practice affiliated with Hyatt & Hyatt Law Offices, Lawrence, Mass., 1981—; bd. dirs. Merrimack Valley Legal Services, Lowell, Mass. Del. Mass. State Dem. Conv., 1983. Recipient Merrimack Coll. Trustees' Scholarship, 1972-76, St. Thomas More Scholarship, 1976-77. Mem. ABA, Mass. Bar Assn., Lawrence Bar Assn., Women's Bar Assn. Mass., Mass. Assn. Women Lawyers. Democrat. Roman Catholic. (religious edn. coordinator 1980—, mem. parish council, 1980—). Club: Methuen Women's Civic. Office: Hyatt & Hyatt Law Offices 8 Jackson Ct Lawrence MA 01840

MCGRAW, ANN LAVITCHKA, nursing home administrator, nurse; b. Lansing, Ohio, Dec. 26, 1916; d. Joseph and Freda Lavitchka; m. Robert N. McGraw; 1 son, Donald J. Diploma Grant Hosp. Sch. Nursing, Columbus, Ohio, 1939; student Coll. of Steubenville (Ohio), 1947, Case Western Res. U. Sch. Pub. Health, Cleve., 1948, West Liberty State Coll., Wheeling W.Va., 1948-49. Nursing supr. Martins Ferry Hosp. (Ohio), 1944-45; R.N., ARC and Met. Life Ins. Co., 1945; pub. health nurse Belmont County, Ohio, 1945-57; owner, operator McGraw Nursing Home, Adena, Ohio, 1957—, also sec.-treas., 1957—; instr. health care Belmont County Schs., 1945-57, geriatric rehab. nurse Ohio State U., Columbus. Trustee, Bellaire Med. Clinic (Ohio), 1964—; developer programs for teaching in pub. schs. and in nursing home industry. Served to 2d lt. U.S. Army Nurse Corps, 1942-43; ETO. Recipient pub. service awards Belmont County. Fellow Am. Coll. Nursing Home Adminstrs.; mem. Nursing Home Adminstrs., Ohio Health Care Assn. (sec. dist. #10 1979-83), Nat. Health Care Assn., Crippled Children's Assn., Am. Legion (adj. sec.-gen. St. Clairsville, Ohio). Home: PO Box 178 Bannock OH 43972 Office: RD 2 Adena OH 43901

MCGRAW, RACHAEL ANNE, communications specialist, consultant; b. Abington, Pa., July 25, 1957; d. Robert Jackson and Helen Sarah (Walter) McGraw. B.S., Lock Haven U., 1979; M.S., Syracuse U., 1981; postgrad. Shippensburg U., 1984. Tchr. English, Holicong Jr. High Sch., Buckingham, Pa., 1981-82; communication specialist Adams Electric Co-Op, Gettysburg, Pa., 1982—; Recipient A.D. Stainbrook award, 1983. Mem. Women in Communications. Roman Catholic. Office: Adams Electric Coop Inc 153 N Stratton St Gettysburg PA 17325

MCGREEVY, (LYNDA) DIANNE, personnel agency owner; b. Buffalo, Oct. 9, 1946; d. Paul Joseph and Hazel Annette (Gould) McG.; m. Gerald Jerome Wozniak, Oct. 7, 1969 (div. Aug. 1974). B.A., SUNY-Fredonia, 1968; M.A., SUNY-Buffalo, 1974. Tchr. Spanish, Tonawanda (N.Y.) High Sch., 1970-78; spl. agt. trainee FBI, Washington, 1978; personnel cons. M. David Lowe, Houston, 1978-81; personnel cons. Joseph Chris Personnel, Houston, 1981-83; owner Lyndian, Inc., Houston, 1983—; sch. rep. curriculum planning, Tonawanda, N.Y., 1974-76. Co-author: Programmed Learning for Secondary Foreign Language Instruction, 1973. Fund raiser Channel 17 Ednl. TV, Buffalo, 1975-77. Mem. Tex. Personnel Assn. Mem. Unity Ch. Home: 9090 S Braeswood St Apt 45 Houston TX 77074 Office: 5373 W Alabama #500 Houston TX 77056

MCGREW, RUTH LOUREA, personnel relations representative; b. McKeesport, Pa., Aug. 29, 1936; d. John Clair and Grace Elizabeth (Whitfield) McG. Clk. typist Westinghouse Credit Corp., Pitts., 1954-55, posting machine operator, 1955-56, gen. duty clk., 1956-57, sec. to controller, 1957-71, employee relations adminstr., 1971-73, personnel relations rep., 1973—. Republican. Presbyterian. Home: 2249G Ridge Rd McKeesport PA 15135 Office: Westinghouse Credit Corp One Oxford Centre Pittsburgh PA 15219

MCGROARY, MARY ELLEN, management executive; b. Far Rockaway, N.Y., Nov. 8, 1941; d. John and Ann (Waters) McG. Grad. Kaupert Secretarial Inst., Jamaica, N.Y., 1960. Vice pres. confs. and spl. services Nat. Retail Mchts. Assn., N.Y.C., 1984—. Mem. Gibson Civic Assn., Valley Stream, N.Y., 1970—. Mem. Meeting Planners Internat. (chpt. membership com. 1984—). Club: Sun and Surf Beach (Atlantic Beach, N.Y.). Avocations: reading; French; travel. Office: Nat Retail Mchts Assn 100 W 31st St New York NY 10001

MCGRORY, SUSAN ALICE, social service administrator; b. Trenton, N.J., July 22, 1947; d. Arthur Anthony and Marian Isabelle (Young) Salvatore; m. Robert Kevin McGrory, Aug. 16, 1969 (div. Mar. 1984); children—Regan Young, Erin Elizabeth. B.A., Georgian Court Coll., 1969; M.A. summa cum laude, Rider Coll., 1985. Social worker Div. of Youth and Family Services, Trenton, 1969-73, asst. social work supr., 1973-74, regional supr., 1974-77, coordinator, instl. abuse, 1980-83, statewide supr. instl. abuse, 1983—. Author, (with others) Institutional Abuse "1978-80", manual, 1982. Active, Glen Afton Civic Assn., Trenton, 1980-82; mem. planning com. Human Services, Mercer County, Trenton, 1978-79; mem. adv. bd. Greater Trenton Community Mental Health Ctr., 1979-80, Cath. Welfare Bur., Trenton, 1983—. Democrat. Club: Ravine. Avocations: piano; reading mystery novels. Home: 102 School Ln Trenton NJ 08618 Office: State of New Jersey Div of Youth and Family Services 1 S Montgomery St Trenton NJ 08625

MCGUCKIN, D. PATRICIA, drug researcher, nurse; b. Somers Point, N.J., Mar. 9, 1948; d. Rowland Fellman Jr. and Nina Ann (Aucott) Snyder; m. Hugh Patrick McGuckin, Sept. 20, 1969; children—Susan L., Betsy J., Robert H. Student Pa. State U., 1965-66; R.N., Abington Meml. Hosp., Pa., 1968; B.B.A. with honors, Montgomery County Community Coll., Blue Bell, Pa., 1986; postgrad. Phila. Coll. Textile and Sci., 1986—. R.N., Pa. Staff nurse Abington Hosp., Pa., 1968-77, North Pa. Hosp., Lansdale, 1978-82; clin. research assoc. Rorer Pharm. Co., Ft. Washington, Pa., 1982—; tng. cons. Rorer Group, Inc. Ft. Washington, 1986. Author, editor tng. manuals. Tchrs. aid Perkiomen Valley Sch. Dist., Skippack, Pa., 1978-82; mem. Perkiomen Home and Sch. Assn., Neighborhood Civic Assn.; active Girl Scouts U.S., Skippack, 1982—. Mem. Assocs. Clin. Pharmacology, Am. Heart Assn., Abington Nurses Alumnae Assn. Democrat. Episcopalian. Avocations: decorating, writing. Home: PO Box 427 Skippack PA 19474 Office: Rorer Group Inc 500 Virginia Dr Fort Washington PA 19034

MCGUFFEE, CORA JEAN, medical legal consultant; b. Beaumont, Tex., Aug. 24, 1943; d. James DeeWitte and MayBelle Agnes (Stafford) McGuffee; m. Richard Leonard Rodriguez, Apr. 10, 1965; children—James, Karen. B.S., La. State U., 1965; M.S., Cath. U. of Am., 1979. R.N., Va., D.C. Head nurse pediatric unit Shawnee Mission Hosp. (Kans.), 1966-67; obstet. nurse Weibaden (W.Ger.) Hosp., U.S. Air Force 1973-74; pub. health nurse Fairfax County Health Dept., Fairfax, Va., 1975-77; head nurse labor and delivery Washington Hosp. Ctr., 1979-80; nurse cons. Med.-Legal Cons. Service, Chevy Chase, Md., 1980-86; nurse cons. Blue Cross/Blue Shield Group Hospitalization Inc., Washington, 1983—; lectr. med.-legal issues in nursing, 1980-83. Author chpt. in book. Canvaser, Am. Heart Assn., Reston, Va., 1980, Nat. Children's Hosp., Washington, 1981; tchr. Youth Group, United Christian Parish, Reston, 1981. Mem. Am. Nurses Assn., Va. Nurses Assn., Va. Nurses Coalition for Action in Politics (treas. 1978-80), Nurses Assn. Am. Coll. Obstetrics and Gynecology. Democrat. Presbyterian. Home: 6306 Friendship Ct Bethesda MD 20817

MCGUINNESS-MUKERJEE, JEANNE HELENE, nurse, administrator, consultant; b. Providence, Aug. 22, 1942; d. John William and Helen Louise (McCormack) McGuinness; m. Dilip K. Mukerjee, Feb. 6, 1975 (div. 1979). B.S.N., Simmons Coll., 1979; M.Ed., Cambridge Coll., 1982. Clin. specialist Lawrence Gen. Hosp., Mass., 1980-81; asst. dir. nursing Essex Hall, Beverly, Mass., 1981-82, Greenery Rehab. Ctr., Brighton, Mass., 1982-83; dir. nursing Elder Care Services, Tewksbury, Mass., 1983-84; asst. adminstr. Webster Manor, Mass., 1984-85, adminstr., 1985—; lectr. in field. Author: An Understanding of Policy Analysis, 1982. Mem. Am. Coll. Health Care Adminstrs., Mass. Nurses Assn., Mass. Fedn. Nursing Homes (program chair 1984-85), Am. Nurses Found., Am. Nurses Assn. Roman Catholic. Avocations: private pilot rating; golf; collecting French antiques. Home: 97 Larch Row Wenham MA 01984 Office: Webster Manor 745 School St Webster MA 01570

MCGUIRE, KATHLEEN IRENE, lawyer; b. Emmetsburg, Iowa, Aug. 19, 1944; d. James Neilon and A. Irene (Molloy) McGuire. B.F.A., Drake U., 1966; M.A., Tex. Tech. U., 1973; J.D., Calif. Western Sch. Law, 1979. Bar: Alaska 1981. Tchr., Judson Sch. Dist., Converse, Tex., 1969-70, Edgewood Sch. Dist., San Antonio, 1970-76; teaching asst. Calif. Western Sch. Law, San Diego, 1977-79; law clk. Alaska Ct. System, Anchorage, 1979-81; asst. atty. gen. State of Alaska for Natural Resources, Anchorage, 1981—. Del., State Democratic Conv., Fairbanks, 1980. Recipient Dean's award, Calif. Western Sch. Law, 1979; others. Mem. ABA, Alaska Bar Assn., Nat. Assn. Women Lawyers, Anchorage Assn. Women Lawyers, Zeta Phi Eta, Theta Alpha Phi. Democrat. Home: 1241 I St Anchorage AK 99501 Office: 1031 W 4th Ave Suite 200 Anchorage AK 99501

MCGUIRE, KAY C(LABOUGH), therapist, human service center administrator; b. Champaign, Ill., Feb. 9, 1941; d. Charles Wesley and Eleanor (Noll) Clabaugh; m. Richard Lee McGuire, June 23, 1962; 1 child, Donna Kay. B.A. in Sociology, Sangamon State U., 1974, M.A. in Human Devel. Counseling, 1976; M.S.W., U. Ill., 1982. Cert. social worker, Ill. Mental health counselor Community Mental Health, Paxton, Ill., 1976-82; dir., owner Ctr. for Creative Communication, Urbana, Ill., 1982—; instr. Women Helping Women, Menominee, Wis., 1979—; cons. Performax Internat., Mpls., 1984—, Personal Performance Cons., St. Louis, 1984—. Mem. Nat. Assn. Social Workers, Nat. Speakers Assn., Nat. Assn. Female Execs., Beta Sigma Phi (sec.). Methodist. Avocations: reading; spectator sports; travel. Home: 206 E Holmes Urbana IL 61801 Office: Ctr for Creative Communication Lincoln Sq Suite 6 Urbana IL 61801

MCGUIRE, MAUREEN A., designer of architectural stained glass; b. Flushing, N.Y., July 13, 1941; d. Leo Thomas and Cecilia A. (Danz) McG. B.F.A., N.Y. State Coll. of Ceramics at Alfred U., 1963; M.A., Pope Pius XII Inst., Florence, Italy, 1964. Apprentice designer Crafts, Glassart Studio, Scottsdale, Ariz., 1964-68; ind. designer, Phoenix, 1968—. Mem. Inter-faith Forum on Religious Art and Architecture, Stained Glass Assn. Am. Republican. Roman Catholic. Avocation: bike touring. Home and Office: 924 E Bethany Home Rd Phoenix AR 85014

MCGUIRE, MAUREEN MONICA, arts administrator, writer; b. Newark, Nov. 4, 1955; d. John Henry and Janet Anne (Verze) McG.; m. Keith Robert Jones, Sept. 29, 1984. B.A. in Polit. Sci., Rutgers Coll., 1977, cert. Women's Studies Program, 1977. Project dir. Hosp. Audiences of N.J., Inc., Trenton, 1978; adminstrv. asst. Bruns, Nordeman, Rea & Co., N.Y.C., 1980; artist rep., New Brunswick, N.J., 1980-82; project dir. Middlesex County Neighborhood Arts consortium, North Brunswick, 1982—; cons., 1985—. Founding mem. Women's Crisis Ctr., New Brunswick, 1974-77; ERA outreach coordinator Women's Studies program Rutgers Coll., New Brunswick, 1976; legis. lobbyist Pub. Interest Research Group, Trenton, 1975. Mem. Women's Network of N.J. Avocations: mountain climbing and hiking; reading; piano. Home: 52 Wertsville Rd Neshanic Station NJ 08853

MCGUIRE, SANDRA LYNN, nursing educator; b. Flint, Mich., Jan. 28, 1947; d. Donald Armstrong and Mary Lue (Harvey) Johnson; B.S.N., U. Mich., 1969, M.P.H., 1973; m. Joseph L. McGuire, Mar. 6, 1976; children—Matthew, Kelly, Kerry. Staff nurse Univ. Hosp., Ann Arbor, Mich., 1969; public health nurse Wayne County Health Dept., Eloise, Mich., 1969-72; instr. Madonna Coll., Livonia, Mich., 1973; public health coordinator Plymouth Center for Human Devel., Northville, Mich., 1974-75; asst. prof. community health nursing Sch. Nursing, U. Mich., Ann Arbor, 1975-83; asst. prof. Coll. Nursing, U. Tenn., Knoxville, 1983—; resource person Gov.'s Com. Unification of Mental Health Services in Mich.; speaker profl. assns. and workshops. Bd. dirs. Mich. chpt. ARC, 1980-83, Knoxville chpt., 1984—. USPHS fellow, 1972-73. Mem. Nat., Mich. leagues nursing, Am., Mich. (chmn. mental health sect. 1976) public health assns., Nat., Mich. (dir., co-chmn. residential services com. 1976-79, chmn. health services 1979-82), Plymouth (chmn. residential services com. 1975-77) assns. retarded citizens, Sigma Theta Tau, Phi Lambda Theta, Phi Kappa Phi. Author: (with S. Clemen. and D. Eigsti) Comprehensive Family and Community Health Nursing, 1981, 2d edit., 1986. Home: 11008 Crosswind Dr Concord TN 37922 Office: 1200 Volunteer Blvd Knoxville TN

MCGUIRL, MARLENE DANA, lawyer, educator, librarian; b. Hammond, Ind., Mar. 22, 1938; d. Daniel David and Helen Elizabeth (Baludis) Callis; A.B., Ind. U., 1956; J.D., DePaul U., 1963; M.A. in L.S., Rosary Coll., 1965; LL.M., George Washington U., 1978; postgrad. Harvard U., 1985; m. James Franklin McGuirl, Apr. 24, 1965. Law library asst. DePaul Coll. Law Library, 1961-62, asst. law librarian, 1962-65; admitted to Ill. bar, 1963, Ind. bar, 1964, D.C. bar, 1972; reference law librarian Boston Coll. Sch. Law Library, 1965-66; law librarian D.C. Bar Library, 1966-70; library cons. Nat. Clearinghouse on Poverty Law, OEO, 1967-69, Northwestern U. Nat. Inst. for Edn. in Law and Poverty, 1969, D.C. Office Corp. Counsel, 1969-70; instr. legal librarianship Grad. Sch., Dept. Agr., 1968; lectr. legal lit., law for librarians, advanced legal lit. grad. dept. library sci., Cath. U., 1972-73, adj. asst. prof., 1973—; asst. chief Am.-Brit. law div. Library Congress Law Library, Washington, 1970, div. chief, 1970—; instr. Ph.D. program in Am. civilization George Washington U., 1976, 79, lectr. environ. law, 1979—; pres. Hamburger Heaven, Inc., Palm Beach, Fla., 1981—. Mem. Georgetown Citizens Assn.; del. Ind. Democratic Conv., 1964; trustee D.C. Law Students in Ct. Recipient Meritorious Service cash award Library Congress, 1974. Mem. Am. (facilities of Law Library of Congress com. 1976-85), Fed. (mem. council Capitol Hill chpt. 1972-76), Ill., D.C. (inter-Am. bar relations com. 1968-70, memls. com. 1969-70), Women's (treas. 1970-72, pres. 1972-73, exec. bd. 73-77, parliamentarian 1975, chmn. constn. and by-laws com. 1975-76) bar assns., D.C. Bar (election bd. 1973-75, specialization com. 1975-76), Am. Bar Found. (library service com. 1969-72), Nat. Assn. Women Lawyers (co-chmn. legis. com. 1976-77), Internat. (program chmn. 1974), Am. (co-chmn. stats. com. 1970-72, chmn. legis. and legal devels. 1972-73, exec. bd. 1973-77, chmn. indexing periodical lit. com. 1979-82) assns. law libraries, Law Librarians Soc. Washington (pres. 1971-73), Brit. and Irish Assn. Law Librarians, Assn. Am. Library Schs. (prison libraries com. 1975-76), Exec. Women in Govt. Clubs: Nat. Lawyers, Zonta. Contbr. articles to profl. jours. Home: 3416 P St NW Washington DC 20007 Office: Law Library Am-Brit Law Div Library Congress Washington DC 20540

MCGUIRL, SUSAN ELIZABETH, lawyer; b. Providence, Sept. 10, 1952; d. John Raymond and Rita Mary (Ryan) McGuirl. B.A., R.I. Coll., 1974; J.D., Suffolk U. Law Sch., 1977. Bar: R.I. 1977. Prosecutor R.I. Dept. Atty. Gen., Providence, 1977-79, chief county offices, Warwick, 1979-80, Providence, 1980—. Mem. R.I. Women's Polit. Caucus, 1974-82; pres. R.I. Young Democrats, Providence, 1974-76; mem. Gov.'s Adv. Com. Aging, Providence, 1978-80; mem. Gov.'s Election Reform Com., Providence, 1977; bd. dirs. The Women's Ctr., Providence, 1981—. Recipient Woman's Achievement award Gov.'s Adv. Com. Women, 1980; named Woman of Yr., YWCA, 1980-83; Woman of Yr., R.I. Jaycees, 1984. Mem. R.I. Bar Assn., Fed. Bar Assn., Am. Jud. Assn., Women Lawyer's Assn., Am. Trial Assn. Democrat. Roman Catholic. Office: Dept of Atty Gen 72 Pine St Providence RI 02903

MCGUNIGLE, DOROTHY GREENE, interior designer, artist; b. Providence, Jan. 24, 1914; d. Dutee Thomas and Carrie May (Stewart) Greene; m. Douglas Campbell McGunigle, June 14, 1941 (dec. 1958); children—Jane Douglas (dec.), Bruce Campbell. Grad. R.I. Sch. Design, 1935. Interior designer Healy & Helgeson, Providence, 1935-36, Merriam Co., Providence, 1936-43; mgr. interior decorating dept. Shepard Co., Providence, 1960-69; owner Dorothy McGunigle Interiors, East Greenwich, R.I., 1970—; tchr. adult edn. Providence YMCA, 1958-59, Cranston High Sch., 1962, Warwick High Sch., 1964, East Greenwich High Sch., 1970-71; art shows include: Providence Art Club, 1972, 74, 76, 78, 80, 82; Indsl. Nat. Bank, Providence, 1974, 76; Warwick Pub. Library, 1980; cons. hist. restoration Varnum House Mus., 1963—. Bd. dirs. East Greenwich Preservation Soc., 1972-77, chmn. consultation com. hist. restoration; active East Greenwich Civic Club. Recipient Hon. Mem. award Continental Ladies, Varnum House Mus., 1970. Mem. AID, ASID, R.I. Hist. Soc. Clubs: Providence Art (picture custodian 1976—, chmn. ladies bd. 1978-79), Providence Pottery and Porcelain (pres. 1981-83), Colonial Dames, Mayflower Descendants, DAR.

MCHALE, MAGDA CORDELL, educator, trend analyst; b. June 24, 1921; widow. Sr. research assoc. Ctr. for Integrative Studies, SUNY-Binghamton, 1968-76; sr. research assoc. Ctr. for Integrative Studies, U. Houston, 1977-79; dir. Ctr. for Integrative Studies, SUNY-Buffalo, 1980—. Contbr. articles, papers, reports in field; mem. editorial bd. profl. publications. Grantee UN Environ. Programme, Ctr. for Econ. and Social Studies of Third World, Intergovernmental Bur. for Informatics, Hubert H. Humphrey Inst. Pub. Affairs, Aspen Inst., Population Reference Bur. Fellow World Acad. of Art and Sci., Royal Soc. Arts; mem. N.Y. Acad. Scis., U.S. Assn. for Club of Rome, World Future Soc., Assn. Internationale Futuribles (hon.), World Futures Studies Fedn. (v.p.). Office: Ctr for Integrative Studies 108 Hayes Hall SUNY Buffalo NY 14214

MCHALE, MARY MARGARET, columnist, librarian; b. Detroit, Mar. 12, 1929; d. Richard D. and Rose M. (Krummack) Mudd; m. John Edward McHale, Jr., Jan. 3, 1951; children—Kathleen McHale Shearer, Michael Joseph, Therese McHale Gallegos, John Edward, Brian Kennedy, Mary Elaine, Mary Sheila. B.A. in Spanish, Saint Mary's Coll., (Ind.), 1950; M.L.S., Cath. U. Am., 1982. Columnist, Mill Valley (Calif.) Review, 1953-58, Enquirer-Gazette, Upper Marlboro, Md., 1976—, So. Prince George's Ind., Clinton, Md., 1978-85, Clinton Times, 1985-86, South County Times, Clinton, 1986—, Post-Sentinel, Hyattsville, Md., 1985—; librarian Saint Philip's Sch., Camp Springs, Md., 1970—; library cons., 1982—. Active Skyline Citizens Assn., Suitland, Md., Charles County (Md.) Heritage Commn., Dr. Samuel A. Mudd. Soc., La Plata, Md.; Morningside-Skyline Park and Recreation Council (Dedicated Service award, 1982). Recipient Disting. Service award, Fraternal Order Police Ladies Aux., 1983; Laddie Beardmore award Morningside (Md.) Sportsmens Club, 1980. Mem. ALA, D.C. Library Assn. Republican. Roman Catholic. Club: Andrew's A.F.B. Officers. Author: History of Saint Philip the Apostle Church, 1982. Home and Office: 4304 Skyline Dr Suitland MD 20746

MC HUGH, MARGARET ANN GLOE, psychologist; b. Salt Lake City, Nov. 8, 1920; d. Harold Henry and Olive (Warenski) Gloe; B.A., U. Utah, 1942; M.A. in Counseling and Guidance, Idaho State U., 1964; Ph.D. in Counseling Psychology, U. Oreg., 1970; lic. psychologist; nat. cert. counselor; m. William T. McHugh, Oct. 1, 1943; children—Mary Margaret McHugh-Shuford, William Michael, Michelle. Tchr. kindergarten, Idaho Falls, Idaho, 1951-62, tchr. high sch. English, 1962-63; counselor Counseling Center, Idaho State U., Pocatello, 1964-67; instr. U. Oreg., Eugene, 1967-70; asst. prof. U. Victoria (B.C., Can.), 1970-76; therapist Peninsula Counseling Center, Port Angeles and Sequim, Wash., 1976-81, McHugh & Assocs. Counseling Center, 1981—. Served with WAVES, 1943-44. Mem. Am. Psychol. Assn., Am. Assn. for Counseling and Devel., Am. Assn. Marriage and Family Therapy, Western Psychol. Assn., Wash. Psychol. Assn. Research on women in relationships, also depression and women, sexual abuse. Home: 249 F Cameron Rd Sequim WA 98382

MCHUGH, TONI WALTER, civic worker; b. Milw., Nov. 25, 1946; d. Harland Anton Walter and Elizabeth (Abel) Walter Adamson; m. Harry Miller McHugh, Aug. 31, 1968; children—Meagan Elizabeth, Hilary Barbree. B.B.A., U. Wis., 1968; M.B.A., Fairleigh Dickinson U., 1985. Exec. trainee, asst. buyer B. Altman & Co., N.Y.C., 1968-69; spot TV buyer J. Walter Thompson, N.Y.C., 1969-72; founder, mgr., owner The Cheese Shop, Ridgefield, Conn., 1972-75; chairperson membership LWV, Chester, N.J., 1976; chairperson March of Dimes Mothers March, Vernon, N.J., 1978; pres. Edna Gladney N.Y. Area Aux., N.Y.C., 1980; founder, chairperson N.J. Com. for Adoption, 1980-83; bd. dirs. Nat. Com. for Adoption, Washington, 1980-86, chairperson, 1983-85; fundraiser New Vernon Vol. Fire Dept., N.J., 1982; chairperson Adoption Fair, N.J., 1982, 83; fundraiser Peck Sch., Morristown, N.J., 1982-85; chairperson Family Services Ball, Morristown, N.J., 1985. Named Friend of Adoption, Nat. Com. for Adoption, 1985. Mem. Jr. League of Columbus (Ohio). Republican. Avocations: tennis; golf; reading; cooking. Home: 1261 Clubview Blvd N Worthington OH 43085

MCINERNEY, JANET MARIE, financial editor; b. Boston, Jan. 22, 1944; d. Timothy Joseph and Marguerite Patricia (Kirby) McI. B.A., Newton Coll. Sacred Heart, 1965; M.B.A., Fordham U., 1981. Social worker N.Y. Foundling Hosp., N.Y.C., 1965-68; research asst. A. G. Becker, N.Y.C., 1968-69; researcher Boyden Assocs., N.Y.C., 1969-71; research asst. Middendorf Colgate, N.Y.C., 1971-72, Estabrook, N.Y.C., 1972-73; mng. editor, v.p. Morgan Stanley, N.Y.C., 1973—. Mem. Money Marketeers. Republican. Roman Catholic. Home: 424 E 52d St New York NY 10022 Office: Morgan Stanley 1251 Ave of Americas New York NY 10020

MCINNIS, CAROLYN CRAWFORD, real estate broker; b. Fayetteville, Tenn., Oct. 30, 1937; d. Sidney Johnson and Winnie Grace (Jean) Crawford; m. Bobby Jack Graben, June 30, 1960 (div. Aug. 75); children—Niles Crawford, Nancy Carol, Norman Curtis. B.S., No. Ala. U., 1960; M.A. in Edn., Tenn. State U., 1972. Real estate agt. McKinney Realty World, Dallas, 1979-80; tchr. Comstock Middle Sch., Dallas, 1976-82; real estate broker Carolyn McInnis, Inc., Realtors, Dallas, 1982—. Membership chmn. Buckner Terr. Homeowners Assn., Dallas, 1983—, publicity chmn., 1980-81. Mem. Greater Dallas Bd. Realtors, Kappa Omicron Phi. Republican. Baptist. Home: 4847 Ashbrook Rd Dallas TX 75227 Office: Carolyn McInnis Realtors 8238 ERL Thornton St Suite 200B Dallas TX 75228

MCINTEE-LARENAS, TERRI LEE, compensation specialist; b. Cleve., Nov. 9, 1955; d. Edward Franklin and Janet Rae (Porter) McIntee; m. Romulo David Larenas, Jan. 3, 1980. B.A., Ohio State U., 1978; postgrad. Hunter Coll., 1983, Baruch Coll., 1985—, NYU, 1985—. Benefit approver Equitable Life Ins. Co., Cleve., 1978-79, mem. flying squad, N.Y.C., 1979-80, coverage coordinator, system specialist, 1970-82; clin. adminstr. Lenox Hill Hosp., N.Y.C., 1982-84; compensation specialist Securities Industry Automation Corp., N.Y.C., 1984—. Mem. AAUW, Internat. Assn. Personnel Women, Am. Compensation Assn., Wall St. Compensation Assn., Ecuadorean Am. Assn., Nat. Assn. Female Execs. Jehovah's Witness. Avocations: swimming, horseback riding, reading. Home: 6908 3d Ave Brooklyn NY 11209 Office: Securities Industry Automation Corp 55 Water St New York NY 10041

MCINTIRE, THERESA JEAN, traffic engineer; b. Gustine, Calif., Dec. 14, 1952; d. Tony Joseph Medeiros and Marie Joan (Braza) Dixon; m. Robert Keith McIntire, Mar. 30, 1973; children—Tessa Marie, Aaron Keith. A.A., Merced Jr. Coll., 1973; postgrad. in trans. engring. U. Calif.-Berkeley, 1980-85, U. Calif.-Irvine, 1982. Draftsman, City of Merced, Calif., 1973-74, engring. aide, 1974-75, engring. technician I, 1975-76, engring. technician II, 1976-79, engring. technician III, 1979-84, engring. asst., 1984—. Dance coach Merced Coll. Cheerleaders, 1979-81. Recipient Appreciation cert. Summer Youth Employment Program, 1984. Mem. Inst. Transp. Engrs. (assoc.), Bus. Profl. Women (young careerist chmn.), Internat. Right of Way Assn., Urban Traffic Engrs. Council, Merced City Employees Assn., Merced Coll. Basketball Boosters (chmn. luncheon 1982-83), AAUW. Democrat. Roman Catholic. Office: City Merced Dept Engring 561 W 18th St PO Box 2068 Merced CA 95344

MCINTOSH, LOUISA AICHEL, interior design firm, art gallery executive; b. Atlanta, June 1, 1925; d. Siegfried Louis and Margaret Katura (Rosser) Aichel; m. Alexander Preston McIntosh, Sept. 2, 1947 (dec. Jan. 1966); children—Alexa Louis McIntosh Selph, Preston Stuckey, Peter Aichel, Patricia Amelia. B.A., Agnes Scott Coll. Owner, Louisa McIntosh Interiors, Atlanta, 1967—; owner, dir. McIntosh Gallery, Atlanta, 1982—; design cons. Fed. Res. Bank, Atlanta, 1975-78, Sci. Atlanta, 1976-80, English Lang. Sch., Atlanta, 1980-82, Nat. Bank of Ga., 1984-85, Lantel Co., 1985. Treas., Midtown Bus. Assn., Atlanta, 1978, pres., 1979; trustee Atlanta Pub. Library, vice chmn. bd., 1981-82; trustee Atlanta Fulton Pub. Library, chmn. bd., 1983-85. Mem. Inst. Bus. Design. Episcopalian. Home: 75 Inman Circle NE Atlanta GA 30309 Office: Louisa McIntosh Interiors 1421 Peachtree St NE Atlanta GA 30309

MCINTOSH, MICHAELE D., group controller; b. Warsaw, Ind., Mar. 12, 1946; d. Paul E. and Dorothy E. (Seiffert) Hodges; B.B.A., U. Miami (Fla.), 1968; cert. in acctg. UCLA, 1976; m. J.W. McIntosh, Apr. 8, 1972; 1 son, James Kyle. Asst. dist. credit mgr. W.T. Grant Co., Los Angeles, 1969-70; v.p., treas. R & B Enterprises, Los Angeles, 1970-80; pres., exec. dir. L.I.F.E. Inc., Warsaw, Ind., 1981; recreational vehicles group controller Coachmen Industries, Middlebury, Ind., 1981—; mgmt. cons. City of Warsaw; real estate broker, Ind. Trustee, Kosciusko Leadership Acad.; mem. Madison Sch. Parent-Tchr. Orgn. Mem. Nat. Bd. Realtors, Ind. Bd. Realtors, Kosciusko County Bd. Realtors, Chi Omega. Club: Women of Moose. Home: 718 Front St Syracuse IN 46567

MCINTOSH, RHODINA COVINGTON, lawyer, international development analyst; b. Chicago Heghts, Ill., May 26, 1947; d. William George and Cora Jean (Cain) Covington; m. Gerald Alfred McIntosh, Dec. 14, 1970; children—Gary Allen, Garvey Anthony, Ayana Kai. B.A., Mich. State U., 1969; J.D., U. Detroit, 1978. Asst. to dir. Office Equal Opportunity Program, Mich. State U., East Lansing, 1969-70; law clk. Bell & Hudson, P.C., Detroit, 1977-79; lectr. U. Swaziland and Botswana, Kwaluseni, 1981-83; chief info. and tech. assistance Office Pvt. and Vol. Cooperation, U.S. AID, Washington, 1983—; founding bd. mem. Women's Justice Ctr., Detroit, 1975-77; coordinator women's leadership conf. Wayne State U., Detroit, 1979; main rapporteur 1st All-Africa Law Conf., U. Swaziland and Botswana, Kwaluseni, Swaziland, 1981. Urban program coordinator Mich. Republican party, Lansing, 1979-81; bd. mem. Mayor's Com. to Keep Detroit Beautiful, 1980, Detroit Urban League, 1981; chairperson fgn. relations subcom. Nat. Black Women's Polit. Caucus, Washington, 1984; bd. mem. Am. Opportunity Found., Washington, 1984—. Nat. achievement scholar Ednl. Testing Service, Princeton, N.J., 1965; scholar Martin Luther King, Jr. Ctr. for Social Change, Atlanta, 1976; recipient award Detroit Edison, 1980, New Republicans, Mich., 1981. Mem. Delta Sigma Theta. Republican. Roman Catholic. Office: US AID Room 333 SA-B 320 21st St NW Washington DC 20533

MCINTYRE, CHARSHEE CHARLOTTE LAWRENCE, historian, educator, consultant; b. Andover, Mass., May 14, 1932; d. Harold Shipman Lawrence and Anne (Sutton) Oliver; m. Ken Arthur McIntyre, Sept. 8, 1958; children—Kaijee, Kheil. B.A. in History, Wesleyan U., Middletown, Conn., 1971; M.A. in Philosophy, SUNY, 1975, M.A. in History, 1978, Ph.D. in History, 1984. Asst. Newport Jazz Festival, N.Y.C., 1958-67; assoc. prof. humanities SUNY, Old Westbury, 1971—; dir. FIPSE-Grant, Washington, 19; cons. Black History Mus., Hempstead, N.Y., 1980—, L.I. Hist. Soc., Bklyn., 1985. Author: African-American Music The Creative Process, 1978. Nat. conf. chmn. African Heritage Studies Assn. N.Y., 1978—; mem. N.Y. Network for Progress, N.Y., 1983-85; mem. polit. action com. Coalition of 100 Black Women, N.Y.C., 1984-85. Served with USAF, 1953-56. Danforth fellow, 1978. Fellow Soc. Values Higher Edn., African Am. Heritage Assn. L.I. (mem. bd.). Roman Catholic. Avocations: painting; bowling; poetry. Home: 159-34 Riverside Dr West #1E New York NY 10032 Office: State Univ NY at Old Westbury Box 210 Storehill Rd Old Westbury NY 11568

MCINTYRE, JOAN CAROL, computer software company executive, author; b. Portchester, N.Y., Mar. 1, 1939; d. John Henry and Molly Elizabeth (Gates) Daugherty; m. Stanley Donald McIntyre, Aug. 24, 1957 (div. Jan. 1986); children—Michael Stanley, David John, Sharon Lynne. Student Northwestern U., 1956-57, U. Ill., 1957-58. Assoc. editor Writer's Digest, Cin., 1966-68; instr. creative writing U. Ala.-Huntsville, 1975; editor Strode Pubs., Huntsville, 1974-75; paralegal Smith, Huckaby & Graves (now Bradley, Arant, Rose & White), Huntsville, 1976-82; exec. v.p. Micro Craft, Inc., Huntsville, 1982-85, pres., 1985—; also dir. and co-owner. Author 8 computer-operating mans. for law office software, 1978-85; co-author: Alabama and Federal Complaint Forms, 1979; Alabama and Federal Motion and Order Forms, 1980; also numerous articles, short stories, poems, 1955-84. Editor: Alabama Law for the Layman, 1975. Bd. dirs. Huntsville Lit. Soc., 1976-77. Hon. scholar Medill Sch. Journalism, Northwestern U., 1956. Republican. Methodist. Office: Micro Craft Inc 688 Discovery Dr Huntsville AL 35806

MCINTYRE, JOY ADELE, public relations executive, journalist; b. Mt. Holly, N.J., Aug. 4, 1952; d. Arthur Francis and Mary Adele (Zuczek) McI.; m. William Harris Tobolsky, Oct. 14, 1978. A.B. in English, Princeton U., 1974; student Mansfield Coll., Oxford, Eng., summer 1972; postgrad. Seton Hall Law Sch., 1977-78. Reporter, intern Home News, New Brunswick, N.J., summer 1973; reporter Bergen Record, Hackensack, N.J., 1974-76, N.Y. Daily News, West Orange, N.J. and N.Y.C., 1976-79, Phila. Bull., 1979; reporter Phila. Daily News, 1979-82; dir. info. services div. Ednl. Testing Service, Princeton, N.J., 1982—. Mem. Women in Communications, Sigma Delta Chi (1st prize award 1973). Office: Ednl Testing Service Rosedale Rd Princeton NJ 08541

MCINTYRE, KAYE, nonprofit organization executive; consultant; b. Hartford, Conn., Oct. 13, 1950; d. Richard Arthur and Helen Marie (von Richter) Tillotson; m. Daniel Brian McIntyre, Feb. 21, 1969; (div. Dec. 1979). A.S. in Human Services, Northwest Conn. Community Coll., Winsted, 1983; B.S. in Bus. Adminstrn., Charter Oak Coll., Hartford, 1985. Counselor, McCall House, Torrington, Conn., 1979-80; freelance photographer, Torrington,

1980—; exec. dir. Warner Theatre, Torrington, 1982-84; exec. dir. Elderly Health Screening Service, Inc., Waterbury, Conn., 1982—; cons. in field. Asst. coordinator Conn. Earth Action Group, Litchfield, 1971; regional coordinator Conn. Citizens Action Group, Litchfield County, Conn., 1971-72; pres. Northwest Conn. Assn. for the Arts, Inc., Torrington, 1981-84; bd. dirs. Torrington Trust for Historic Preservation, Inc., 1981—; 6th dist. coordinator Office of Protection and Advocacy for the Handicapped and Developmentally Disabled, Litchfield County, 1982; chairperson adult programming com. YWCA of Waterbury, 1985—; v.p. Thomaston Opera House Found., 1985—. Recipient citation Conn. Soc. Prevention of Blindness, 1984; citation Conn. Gen. Assembly, 1984. Mem. Nat. Assn. Female Execs., Am. League Historic Theatres, Conn. Assn. Historic Theatres (pres. 1984—). Republican. Taoist. Club: Mensa (Litchfield County coordinator). Avocations: photography; writing; hiking. Office: Elderly Health Screening Service Inc 24 Central Ave Waterbury CT 06702

MC INTYRE, MARY ARNETTA, computer systems analyst; b. Canon City, Colo., May 16, 1938; d. David Taggart and Mary Arnetta (Forney) McIntyre; A.S., Chemeketa Community Coll., Salem, Oreg., 1971, A.A., 1974; postgrad. Oreg. State U., 1974-77. Prototype assembly technician Nortronics Co., Hawthorne, Calif., 1961-63; elec., electronic and mech. assembly technician C.T. Engring. Corp., Lawndale, Calif., 1963-64, engring. technician, 1964-67, quality control technician, 1963-67; bookkeeper, accountant, tax preparer Valley Bookkeeping Service, Dallas, Oreg., 1971-75; scale house operator Stayton Canning Co., Dayton, Oreg., 1968-79; computer systems analyst Oreg. Dept. Employment, Salem, 1979—; dir. Inform-Facts, Amity, Oreg., 1975—; acctg. clk., computer operator City of McMinnville, Oreg., 1978. Served with USMC, 1956-60. Democrat. Mem. Assembly of God Ch. Author: Mailorder Handbook, 1978. Home: 14850 SE 1st St McMinnville OR 97128 Office: PO Box 285 Amity OR 97101

MC INTYRE, RAE MORSE, real estate services exec., fin. planner; b. Lowell, Mass., May 26, 1945; d. Walter Silas and Regina Marie (Trudel) Morse; student Coll. Fin. Planning, 1980—; children—Eugene, Regina. Sales asso. Paul Revere Cos., Miami, Fla., 1978—; owner, pres. R/R Discovery, Inc., Miami, 1979—; resident mgr. Palm Lakes, Ltd., 1983—; participant seminars on fin. mgmt. Recipient various ins. sales awards, 1979; certified Fin. Planners Inst. Mem. Nat. Assn. Female Execs., Nat. Assn. Security Dealers, Mensa. Pub. Newsletter for Profl. Women - State of Fla. Home: 1200 102d Ave N Saint Petersburg FL 33702

MCIVER, KATHY ANN, accountant; b. Las Vegas, July 12, 1957; d. Paul Holloway and Martha Ann (Brandon) McI. B.S. in Bus. Adminstrn., U. Nev.-Las Vegas, 1979. C.P.A., Nev. Tax auditor IRS, Las Vegas, 1977-79; staff acct. Fox & Co. C.P.A.s, 1979-80; auditor State of Nev. Gaming Control Bd., Las Vegas, 1980-84; sr. auditor, acct. Kaiser Aluminum & Chem. Corp., Oakland, Calif., 1984—. Active Girl Scouts U.S.A., Las Vegas, 1981-84. Mem. Am. Inst. C.P.A.s, Nev. Soc. C.P.A.s, Nat. Assn. Female Execs. Democrat. Pentecostal. Home: 499 Estudillo St Apt 307 San Leandro CA 94577 Office: Kaiser Aluminum and Chem Corp 300 Lakeside Dr Oakland CA 94643

MCIVER, SUSAN BERTHA, zoology educator; b. Hutchinson, Kans., Nov. 6, 1940; d. Ernest Dale and Thelma Faye (McCrory) McIver; B.A., U. Calif., Riverside, 1962; M.S., Wash. State U., 1964, Ph.D., 1967. Asst. prof. dept. parasitology U. Toronto (Ont.), 1967-72, assoc. prof., 1972-81, prof. dept. zoology, 1981-84; prof., chmn. dept. environ. biology U. Guelph (Ont., Can.), 1984—; cons., surgeon gen., U.S. Army, 1977-82; cons. tropical med. parasitology NIH; mem. exec. Biol. Council Can. Recipient C. Gordon Hewitt award Entomol. Soc. Can., 1978; Vis. Scientist award Med. Research Council Can., 1978; InterAm. Fellow in tropical medicine NIH, 1973. Mem. Entomol. Soc. Ont. (pres. 1981), Entomol. Soc. Can. (dir. 1975-78, pres. 1984), Entomol. Soc. Am. (chmn. sect. 1982), Canadian Soc. Zoologists, Am. Soc. Parasitologists, Micros. Soc. Can. Contbr. articles to various publs. Office: Dept Environ Biology Univ Guelph Guelph ON N1G 2W1 Canada

MC KAIG, DIANNE L., lawyer, former soft drink company executive; b. Massillon, Ohio, Nov. 17, 1930; d. Sherman J. and Kathryn (Blaidough) McKaig; B.A., U. Ky., 1952, J.D., 1954; LL.M., Harvard U., 1955. Admitted to Ky. bar, 1954, Mass. bar, 1976, D.C. bar, 1984; law clk. Ky. Ct. Appeals, Frankfort, 1954; atty. firm Palmer, Dodge, Gardner & Bradford, Boston, 1955-56; practice law, Boston, 1956-58; atty.-adviser Office of Solicitor, U.S. Dept. Labor, Washington, 1958-62; regional dir. Women's Bur., Atlanta, 1963-66, chief div. legislation and standards, Women's Bur., Washington, 1966-68; spl. asst. to sec. (consumer interests) HEW, Washington, 1968, dir. Office Consumer Services, 1968-69; exec. dir. Mich. Consumers Council, 1969-72; asst. v.p. consumer affairs Coca-Cola Co., Atlanta, 1972-74, v.p., 1976-83; v.p. Coca-Cola U.S.A., 1974-76; mem. firm Jones and McKaig, Washington, 1983—; mem. Major Appliance Consumer Action Panel, 1970-72; dir. Fleet Fin. Group Inc.; spl. lectr. Coll. Indsl. Mgmt., Ga. Inst. Tech., 1975. Bd. dirs. Nat. Council for Family Fin. Edn., 1970-72, Nat. Council Better Bus. Burs., 1971-72, Girl Scouts U.S.; bd. govs. chpt. ARC, 1980-83; chmn. pub. affairs com. Food Safety Council, 1977-79; trustee Pace Acad., Atlanta, 1979-83; mem. vis. com. U. Ky. Law Sch., 1978-83. Mem. Ky., Fed., Mass., D.C. bar assns., Soc. Consumer Affairs Profls. (dir. 1973-77), Bus. Profs. Assn. (chmn. found. 1984-85), Grocery Mfrs. Am. (consumer rep. task force 1978-80), U.S. C. of C. (consumer affairs com. 1978-80), U. Ky. Alumni Assn. (pres. Washington 1962), Bus. and Profl. Women's Clubs, Order of Coif, Mortar Bd., Alpha Delta Pi (chpt. outstanding alumna 1965), Eta Sigma Phi, Phi Beta. Asso. editor Ky. Law Jour., 1953. Home: 3256 Jones Ct Georgetown Washington DC 20007 Office: Jones and McKaig 1819 H St NW Suite 800 Washington DC 20006

MCKAY, CONSTANCE GADOW, hotel executive; b. Aurora, Ill., Mar. 7, 1928; d. William H. and Esther E. (Olson) Gadow; student U. Ill., U. Wis.-Madison, U. Wis.-Milw.; widow; children—Richard A., Scott A., Mark G. Dir. catering Arlington Park (Ill.) Race Track, 1966-68, Arlington Park Hilton Hotel, Arlington Heights, Ill., 1969-85, O'Hare Kennedy Holiday Inn, 1985—. Commr., Arlington Heights Bd. Local Improvements, 1979—; Arlington Heights Relocation of Post Office Comm., 1958-59, Arlington Heights Zoning Bd., 1959-60; commr. Youth Commn., 1981—. Named Outstanding Bus. Woman, Paddock Publs., Arlington Heights, 1977. Mem. Catering Execs. Club Am. Republican. Home: 604 S Waterman Ave Arlington Heights IL 60004 Office: O'Hare Kennedy Holiday Inn Hotel 5440 N River Rd Rosemont IL 60018

MCKAY, JOY H., real estate executive; b. Warrenville, N.J., June 14, 1914; d. Arthur and Helen (Milius) Hofheimer; grad. Sarah Lawrence Coll., 1934; m. Joseph J. Siccardi, Sept. 5, 1934 (div. 1978); children—Helen Gay, Arthur J. Siccardi, Carol Ann Roberts, Marilyn Jill Iuliucci; m. Raymond Roth, Aug. 25, 1955 (dec.); m. Samuel J. McKay, Dec. 1970. Mem. Bd. Edn. Warren Twp., N.J., 1940-47, pres., 1947; chmn. Warren Twp. ARC, v.p. Mental Hygiene Soc. Union County, N.J., 1946-49, pres., 1949-51; bd. mgrs. N.J. Neuropsychiat. Inst., Princeton, N.J., 1951-55, v.p., 1953-54; pres. N.J. Assn. for Mental Health, 1951-56, mem. bd., 1951-64, exec. com. 1951-63, chmn. planning com. 1958-62; chmn. com. orgn. Nat. Assn. Mental Health, 1953-57, dir., 1951-62, mem. exec. com., 1953-62, chmn. planning com. 1959-61, mem. program com., 1961-63, chmn. direct services com., 1961-63; exec. dir. Somerset County Assn. for Mental Health, 1965-67; dir. div. services N.J. Heart Assn., 1967-70; supvr. Heart Sunday Broward County (Fla.) Heart Assn., 1970-71, dir. fund raising, 1971-72; assoc. J.G. Realty, Deerfield, Fla., 1972-73; assoc. Gold Palm Realty, Boca Raton, Fla., 1973—, v.p., 1976—; broker, dir. Homes Internat. Realty, Inc., 1980—; v.p. Robert Kerber Realty Inc., 1976-77; sec. Ratner Assocs., Inc., 1977-78, Boca Real Estators Inc., 1978-81; pres. Ocean Plaza Realty Inc., 1981-82; Forsini Realty Corp., 1985—, Coldwell Banker Real Estate, 1985—. Trustee Nathan Hofheimer Found., 1945-70. Mem. Fla. Assn. Realtors (dir. 1981-84, profl. standards com. 1981-82, membership com. 1982-83), Boca Raton Bd. Realtors (membership com. 1976, chmn. 1979, mem. grievance com. 1977-79, treas. 1980-81, chmn. budget and fin. com. 1980-81, Realtor of Yr. award 1981, pres. 1983, chmn. long range planning com. 1984, dir. 1980-85), Women's Council Realtors (sec. Boca Raton chpt. 1975—, v.p. 1976-77). Home: 750 NE Spanish River Blvd Boca Raton FL 33431

MCKAY, LOLA MERLE, marketing executive, consultant; b. Jacksonville, Tex., Jan. 6, 1930; d. Clarence Malcom and Joe Dee (Rountree) Reagan; m. Lawrence Brian McKay, Mar. 10, 1950 (dec. Oct. 1982). A.A., Jacksonville Jr. Coll., 1948; B.A., So. Meth. U., 1950. Pub. relations asst. to pres. city council and acting mayor, N.Y.C., 1950-54; corp. sec., dir. Exec. Search and Tech.

Recruiting Co., N.Y.C., 1954-59; adminstrv. asst. internat. relations Nat. Acad. Sci.-NRC, Washington, 1959-62; ptnr., mgmt. cons. Mktg. Innovations Co., Washington and Arlington, Va., 1962-70, Houston, 1977-83, owner, mgmt. cons., Alexandria, Va., 1983—; gen. services adminstr. Ferris & Co., Inc., Washington, 1970-77. Sustaining mem. Republican Nat. Com., 1976—; mem. Rep. Senatorial Com., 1980—; mem. Commonwealth Rep. Women's Club, Alexandria, Va., 1984—. Mem. Am. Mktg. Assn., Alexandria C. of C. Methodist. Home and Office: 375 S Reynolds Apt 502 Alexandria VA 22304

MCKAY, NAN A., management consultant, training company executive; b. Peoria, Ill., Aug. 14, 1942; d. John S. Norton and Mary Ann (Brewer) Norton Jameson; m. Patrick McKee, May 10, 1963 (div.); m. James David McKay, June 15, 1968; children—Molly, John. A.A., Bradley U., 1962; B.A., Met. State U., Minn., 1976; postgrad. Mankato State U., 1976-78, Fed. Exec. Inst., 1978. Cert. housing mgr. Flight attendant Am. Airlines, Chgo.-63; sec., adminstrv. asst. Mpls. Housing Authority, Mpls., 1963-67; adminstrv. asst., mgr., asst. exec. dir. South St. Paul Housing Authority, Minn., 1967-72; exec. dir. Dakota County Housing Authority, Hastings, Minn., 1971-80; pres. Nan McKay and Assocs., Inc., St. Paul, 1980-85; pres. Nan McKay and Assocs., Inc., San Diego, 1985—, McKay Computer Services, Inc., San Diego, 1985—; cons. Rauenhorst Corp., Mpls., 1971-73; cons., tchr. Nat. Leased Housing Assn., Washington, 1982—; instr. U. Minn.-St. Paul, 1978-80, Nat. Ctr. for Housing Mgmt., Washington, 1980-82; cons. instr. HUD, Washington, San Francisco, 1983; mem. Senator Durenberger's Task Force on Housing, 1980-81; vice chmn. Met. Council Housing Adv. Bd., 1977-79. Author: Creative Supervisor; Creating Positive Performance; A Guide to Assisted Housing Management, How To Do It Guide, Multifamily Housing Management, Executive Director Handbook; 5 coursebooks. Contbr. articles to profl. jours. Mem. adv. bd. Inver Grove Heights Jr. Coll., 1978-80, Profl. Ethics Com. for Attys., Dakota County, 1978-80; pres. adv. bd., founder Dakota Area Referral and Transp. for Srs., 1973-75; chmn. adv. bd. Pub. Service Bd. for Vocat. Tech. Sch., Coop. Community Manpower Planning Commn., Twin Cities Camps, 1968-69. Recipient Cert. of Appreciation Met. Council, 1979; named Hon. Citizen West St. Paul City Council, 1980. Mem. Nat. Assn. Housing and Redevel. Ofcls. (Minn. pres. 1981-83, v.p. region 1982, chmn. nat. com. sect. 1978-81, Nan McKay Bldg. 1970, Nan McKay Manor 1980, Allan Anderson award 1981), Nat. Leased Housing Assn. (bd. dirs. 1978—), Women In Housing (founder 1978), Am. Soc. for Tng. and Devel., Nat. Assn. Female Execs., Nat. Assn. Women Bus. Owners, Kiwi Club (v.p., treas. 1964-66), Mrs. Jaycees (bd. dirs. 1964-66), LWV. Avocation: bridge. Home and Office: Nan McKay and Assocs Inc 1544 Shadow Knolls Dr San Diego CA 92020 also McKay Computer Services Inc 3855 Avocado St Suite 110 La Mesa CA 92041

MCKAY, NANCY JANE FOLAND, county commissioners clerk; b. Wilmington, Ohio, June 2, 1955; d. Dan Boyland and Marjorie M. (Haidet) Foland; m. Roderick Stephen McKay, July 30, 1983. Student Ohio U., 1973-75. Deputy clk. Clinton County Commrs., Wilmington, 1977-80, clerk, 1980—. Active Wilmington area Jaycettes, 1982-83, Clinton County Hist. Soc. (nominating com. 1983). Clubs: DAR (chpt. chmn. jr. membership 1979-85), Snow Hill Country (New Vienna). Republican. Baptist. Home: 371 E Vine St Wilmington OH 45177 Office: Clerk to Govn Bd Clinton County Seat County Courthouse Wilmington OH 45177

MC KAY, RENEE, artist; b. Montreal, Que., Can., came to U.S., 1946, naturalized, 1954; d. Frederick Garvin and Mildred Gladys (Higgins) Smith; B.A., McGill U., 1941; m. Kenneth Gardiner McKay, July 25, 1941; children—Margaret Craig, Kenneth Gardiner. Tchr. art Peck Sch., Morristown, N.J., 1955-56; one woman shows: Pen and Brush Club, N.Y.C., 1957, Cosmopolitan Club, N.Y.C., 1958; group shows include: Weyhe Gallery, N.Y.C., 1978, Newark Mus., 1955, 59, Montclair (N.J.) Mus., 1955-58, Nat. Assn. Women Artists, Nat. Acad. Galleries, 1978. N.Y. World's Fair, 1964-65, Audubon Artists, N.Y.C., 1955-62, 74-79, N.Y. Soc. Women Artists, 1979-80, Provincetown (Mass.) Art Assn. and Mus., 1975-79; traveling shows in France, Belgium, Italy, Scotland, Can., Japan; represented in permanent collections: Slater Meml. Mus., Norwich, Conn., Norfolk (Va.) Mus., Butler Inst. Am. Art, Youngstown, Ohio, Lydia Drake Library, Pembroke, Mass., many pvt. collections. Recipient Jane Peterson prize in oils Nat. Assn. Women Artists, 1954, Famous Artists Sch. prize in watercolor, 1959, Grumbacher Artists Watercolor award, 1970; Solo award Pen and Brush, 1957; Saalie-Max Tesser award in watercolor Audubon Artists, 1975, Peterson prize in oils, 1980; Michael Engel prize Nat. Soc. Painters in Casein and Acrylic, 1983. Mem. Nat. Assn. Women Artists (2d v.p. 1969-70, adv. bd. 1974-76), Audubon Artists (pres. 1979), Artist Equity (dir. 1977-79, v.p. 1979-81), N.Y. Soc. Women Artists, Pen and Brush, Nat. Soc. Painters in Casein and Acrylic M.J. Kaplan prize 1984, Nat. Arts Club, Provincetown Art Assn. and Mus. Club: Cosmopolitan. Address: 200 E 66 St New York NY 10021

MCKAY, TERRI ANNE, radio station executive; b. Pitts., Oct. 2, 1954; d. James William and Helen Anne (Jordan) McK. B.A., Allegheny Coll., 1976; M.A., Edinboro State Coll., 1978. Instr. English Brandon Hall Sch., Dunwoody, Ga., 1977-79; travel counselor Am. Express Co., Atlanta, 1979-80; instr. freshman composition Community Coll. of Allegheny County, Pa., 1982—; promotion dir. Sta. WEEP/WDSY, Pitts., 1981—. Editor co. newsletter Entercom Intercom, 1982—. Mem. NOW, Pitts. Radio and TV Club, Alpha Chi Omega. Democrat. Presbyterian. Avocations: camping; reading; oil painting. Home: 604 Forest Ave Pittsburgh PA 15202 Office: Sta WEEP/WDSY Radio 107 6th St Pittsburgh PA 15222

MCKEE, DYANA CARLYNE, home health company executive, consultant, lecturer, educator; b. Springfield, Ohio, June 26, 1941; d. Carl Golden and Betty Mae (Kunkle) McK.; m. James C. Shepherd, Nov. 17, 1958 (div. Mar. 1980); children—Carlton Shepherd, James Shepherd, Roy-J. Shepherd. Adminstrv. asst. cert. MATA, Dayton, Ohio, 19—; secretarial cert. Inst. Tech., Dayton, 1963; cert. in acctg. Met. Coll., Knoxville, Tenn., 1965; student Jefferson State Jr. Coll., Center Point, Ala., 1981-83. Co-owner, co-operator Rex-James Assocs., Trussville, Ala., 1962-71; owner, operator Dreamway Inc., Trussville, 1973-80; control coordinator St. Vincent Hosp., Birmingham, Ala., 1980-81; v.p. Medicare Convalescent Aids, Birmingham, 1981—; cons. in field. Author: I Was Abused, 1979. Vol. cons. Cerebral Palsy, Birmingham, 1969-78, St. Jude Children's Research, Memphis, 1970-80; mem. Toys for Tots, 1970-78; instr. Am. Cancer Soc. of Ala., 1971-76; lectr. Medaids, Birmingham, 1984—. Named to Outstanding Young Women Am., 1977; recipient Birmingham Woman of Yr. award Profl. Women, 1978; Fund Raiser of Yr. award St. Jude Children's Research, 1978. Mem. Med. Social Services Orgn. (charter mem., audio visual chairperson 1986—), Epsilon Sigma Alpha (chpt. pres. 1978-79, state Girl of Yr. award 1976). Republican. Lutheran. Home: 29 M Pinewood Dr Trussville AL 35173 Office: Medicare Convalescent Aids 237 Oxmoore Circle Birmingham AL 35209

MCKEE, EDITH MERRITT, geologist; b. Oak Park, Ill., Oct. 9, 1918; d. Eustis Ewart and Edith (Frame) McK.; B.S., Northwestern U., 1946. Geologist, U.S. Geol. Survey, 1943-45, Shell Oil Co., 1947-49, Arabian Am. Oil Co., 1949-54, Underground Gas Storage Co. Ill., 1956-58; ind. cons. geologist, Winnetka, Ill., 1958—; mem. environ. adv. com. Fed. Energy Adminstrn., 1974; mem. Nat. Adv. Com. Oceans and Atmosphere, 1975; speaker, cons. in field. Commr., Winnetka Park Bd., 1976-79. Fellow Marine Tech. Soc., Geol. Soc. Am.; mem. Am. Geol. Inst., Am. Inst. Profl. Geologists (cert., charter), Assn. Engring. Geologists, Ill. Geol. Soc., Am. Oceanic Orgn. Research on shore erosion, mapping of Gt. Lakes basins and deep ocean basins, global econ. devel. programs and mineral exploration. Address: 4225 Pine Hill Dr Harbor Springs MI 49740

MCKEE, ELIZABETH BROOKS THAYER, civic leader; b. Bklyn.; d. John Van Buren and Elizabeth B. (Chatfield) Thayer; grad. Bklyn. Heights Sem., 1914; m. Waldo McCutcheon McKee, Oct. 3, 1925; children—Elizabeth Brooks, M. Jean. Hon. dir. Orphan Asylum, Bklyn.; past chmn. social service com. Cumberland Hosp., Bklyn.; past treas. Bklyn. Community Met. Opera; past mem. com. N.Y. Philharmonic Soc.; mem. Cheshire Com. Am. Revolution Bicentennial Adminstrn., 1976, Cheshire Bicentennial Com., 1980. Bd. dirs. Womens Republican Club, Cheshire. Mem. Bklyn. Jr. League (past pres.), Nat. Soc. Colonial Dames (past v.p. N.Y.), L.I. Cheshire (dir.), New Haven Colony Hist. Socs., Conn. Antiquarian and Landmarks Soc. Clubs: Civitas (past v.p.), Mrs. Fields Literary (past v.p.). Home: 532 S Brooks Vale Rd Cheshire CT 06410

MCKEE, KATHRYN DIAN, banker; b. Los Angeles, Sept. 12, 1937; d. Clifford William and Amelia Rosalia (Shacher) Grant; m. Paul Eugene McKee,

June 17, 1961; children—Scott Alexander, Grant Christopher. B.A., U. Calif.-Santa Barbara, 1959; grad. Exec. Program, UCLA, 1979. Mgr., Mattel, Inc., Hawthorne, Calif., 1963-74; dir. 20th Century Fox Film Corp., Los Angeles, 1975-80; sr. v.p. First Interstate Bancorp, Los Angeles, 1980—; pres. Personnel Accreditation Inst., Washington, 1986—. Contbr. articles to profl. jours. Bd. dirs. Garden Grove Assn. for the Arts, 1985—, Vis. Nurses' Assn., Los Angeles, 1984—. Named Outstanding Sr. Woman, U. Calif.-Santa Barbara, 1959. Mem. Internat. Assn. Personnel Women (past pres., Mem. of Yr. 1986), Orgn. Women Execs., Women in Bus., Am. Compensation Assn., Am. Soc. Personnel Adminstrs. (bd. dirs. 1986—). Club: Los Angeles Athletic. Office: First Interstate Bancorp 707 Wilshire Los Angeles CA 90017

MC KEE, MARGARET JEAN, federal agency executive; b. New Haven, June 20, 1929; d. Waldo McCutcheon and Elizabeth (Thayer) McKee; A.B., Vassar Coll., 1951. Staff asst. United Republican Fin. Com., N.Y.C., 1952; staff asst. N.Y. Rep. State Com., N.Y.C., 1953-55; staff asst. Crusade for Freedom (name later changed to Radio Free Europe Fund), N.Y.C., 1955-57; researcher Stricker & Henning Research Assocs., Inc., N.Y.C., 1957-59; exec. sec. New Yorkers for Nixon (name later changed to N.Y. State Ind. Citizens for Nixon Lodge), N.Y.C., 1959-60; asst. to Raymond Moley, polit. columnist, N.Y.C., 1961; asst. campaign com. Louis J. Lefkowitz for Mayor, N.Y.C., 1961; research programmer, treas. Consensus, Inc., N.Y.C., 1962-67; spl. asst. to U.S. Senator Jacob K. Javits, N.Y., 1967-73, adminstrv. asst., 1973-75; dep. adminstr. Am. Revolution Bicentennial Adminstrn., 1976, acting adminstr., 1976-77; chief of staff Perry B. Duryea (minority leader) N.Y. State Assembly, 1978; public affairs cons., 1979-80; dir. govt. relations Gen. Mills Restaurant Group, Inc., 1980-83; exec. dir. Fed. Mediation and Conciliation Service, 1983—; dir. Interam. Life Ins. Co. Mem. N.Y. State Bingo Control Commn., 1965-72, U.S. Adv. Commn. on Public Diplomacy, 1979-82; pres. Bklyn. Heights Slope Young Republican Club, 1955-56; co-chmn. Bklyn. Citizens for Eisenhower-Nixon, 1956; chmn. 2d Jud. Dist. Mem. N.Y. State Young Rep. Clubs, Inc., 1957-58, vice-chmn., mem. bd. govs., 1958-60, v.p. 1960-62; pres., 1962-64; mem. exec. com. Fedn. Women's Rep. Clubs N.Y. State, Inc., 1960-64, mem. council, 1964-70; mem. exec. com. N.Y. Rep. State Com. 1962-64; co-chmn. spl. assts. Rockefeller for Pres. Nat. Campaign com., N.Y.C., 1964; co-dir. N.Y. Rep. State Campaign Com., 1964; asst. campaign mgr. Kenneth B. Keating for Judge Ct. Appeals, N.Y., 1965; dir. scheduling Gov. Rockefeller campaign, 1966, Sen. Charles E. Goodell campaign, 1970; dir. scheduling and speakers' bur. N.Y. Com. to Re-elect the Pres., 1972; dir. planning, strategy and women's programs Reagan-Bush campaign. Mem. bd. govs. Women's Nat. Rep. Club, N.Y.C., 1963-66. Mem. Jr. League of Bklyn. (past dir.), Exec. Women in Govt., Nat. Women's Edn. Fund (mem. bd.), Am. Newspaper Women's Club, Nat. Soc. Colonial Dames Am. Episcopalian. Club: Vassar (past dir.) (Bklyn.). Home: 3001 Veazey Terr NW Washington DC 20008

MCKEE, MARLENE SUE, educational administrator, consultant; b. Houston, May 31, 1936; d. Ed Tyndale and Daisy Mae (Bishop) McKee. B.A., Tenn. Temple U., Chattanooga, 1958; M.Ed., U. Houston, 1970. Tchr. Blvd. Christian Sch., Pensacola, Fla., 1958-61; coordinator Tenn. Temple U., 1961-63; tchr. Fairyland Elem. Sch., Lookout Mountain, Ga., 1963-64, Keswick Christian Sch., St. Petersburg, Fla., 1964-68; sec. Harris County Dept. Edn., Houston, 1968-69, disseminator, 1969-70, psychol. assoc., 1970-72, coordinator, 1972-73, dir., 1973-81, exec. dir., 1981—; psycho-edn. cons. Summer Inst. Linguistics, Huntington Beach, Calif., 1971—; cons. workshops for profl. orgns., Tex., 1970—. Sunday sch. tchr. Bethel Ind. Presbyn. Ch., Houston, 1968—, singer, 1970—. Mem. Tex. Psychol. Assn. (outstanding assoc. award 1983, treas., 1978, assoc. dir. exec. com. 1981), Council Exceptional Children (chpt. pres. 1978-79, pres.'s award 1982). Republican. Presbyterian. Office: Harris County Dept Edn 6515 Irvington Houston TX 77022

MCKEE, NANCY ANN, fgn. service officer; b. Tulsa, Mar. 12, 1933; d. Charles and Estelle Marie (Larrieu) McK.; student U. Tulsa, 1950-52. Sec., Jones & Laughlin Supply Div., Tulsa, 1952-63; sec. Am. Embassy, Bonn, W.Ger., 1963-66, Lagos, Nigeria, 1963-68, Dept. State, Washington, 1968-70, 71-72, Am. Embassy, Nicosia, Cyprus, 1970-71; commd. fgn. service officer Dept. State, 1972, consular officer Am. Embassy, Manila, 1972-74, Mexico City, 1975-79, Nairobi, Kenya, 1979-82; supr. visa sect., dept. prin. officer Am. Consulate Gen., Juarez, Mex., 1982—. Republican. Roman Catholic.

MCKEEMAN, CHRISTINE ELAINE, lawyer; b. Austin, Tex., Apr. 23, 1953; d. Bruce Bingham and Wanda Lee (Dunlap) Batchelor; m. Leland Paul McKeeman, May 25, 1985; children—John Edward Potter, Ryan Keith McKeeman. B.A. with highest honors, U. Tex., 1975; J.D., 1982. Bar: Tex. 1982. Planner, City of Austin (Tex.), 1977-79; briefing atty. Tex. Supreme Ct., Austin, 1982-83; assoc. Rinehart & Nugent, Austin, 1983-85; with McKeeman, Tuttle & Hein, Austin, 1985—. Mem. ABA, State Bar Tex., Travis County Bar Assn., Austin Young Lawyers Assn., Phi Beta Kappa, Phi Kappa Phi. Office: McKeeman Tuttle & Hein 5407 N Interregional Hwy Suite 300 Austin TX 78723

MCKEEN, LYNN MARIE, insurance company executive; b. Mars Hill, Maine, June 26, 1951; d. Theodore Frank and Lois Marie (Hubbard) Durost; m. James Elwood McKeen, Apr. 18, 1970 (div. Aug. 1980). Cert. profl. ins. woman. Legal sec. Stewart, Griffiths & Quigley, Presque Isle, Maine, 1969-71; sec., file clk. Maine Mut. Group, Presque Isle, 1971-75, policy typist, 1975-76, rating clk., 1976-77, asst. underwriter, 1977-82, staff underwriter, 1982-83, underwriting supr., 1983-85, underwriting mgr., 1986—; officer Maine Mut. Fire Ins. Co. Mem. Nat. Assn. Ins. Women. (pres. Aroostook 1981-82, state dir. 1983-85, Ins. Woman of Yr. 1982, state Speak-off winner 1983). Home: 68 Barton St Presque Isle ME 04769 Office: Maine Mutual Group Ins Cos 551 Main St Presque Isle ME 04769

MCKELVEY, JEANNE WOLFORD, lawyer, oil company executive; b. Johnstown, Pa., Feb. 10, 1947; d. Donald Ralph and Wilma Miller Wolford; B.S. in Med. Tech., U. Pitts., 1967; M.S. in Biochemistry, Indiana U. of Pa., 1976; J.D., Dickinson Sch. Law, 1983; m. William Graham McKelvey, Sept. 29, 1979. Bar: Pa. 1984. Chief technologist Conemaugh Valley Meml. Hosp., 1967-72, Johnstown Regional Blood Center, 1972-73; instr. med. tech. Johnstown Vocat.-Tech. Sch., 1973-76; asst. dir. pub. affairs U. Pitts. at Johnstown, 1976-78; v.p. McKelvey Oil Co., Inc., Harrisonville, Pa., 1978—, McKelvey Petroleum, Inc., Somerset, Pa., 1978—; sole practice, 1983—; dir. Summit Bank; mem. Pa. State Bd. Med. Edn. and Licensure. Bd. dirs. Windber (Pa.) Hosp., Cumberland Valley Humane Soc. Mem. ABA, Pa. Bar Assn., Fulton County Bar Assn., Cambria County Bar Assn., Allegheny County Bar Assn., Am. Soc. Clin. Pathologists, Lawyer-Pilot's Bar Assn., Pa. Student Bar Assn., Mensa. Presbyterian. Club: Sunnehanna Country, Indian Lake Golf, Great Cove Golf. Home: Tall Timbers Farm McConnellsburg PA 17233 Office: Box 105 SR 3 Harrisonville PA 17228

MCKELVEY, JUDITH GRANT, lawyer, educator; b. Milw., July 19, 1935; d. Lionel Alexander and Bernadine R. (Verdun) Grant; B.S. in Philosophy, U. Wis., 1957, J.D., 1959. Bar: Wis. 1959, Calif. 1968. Atty./adviser FCC, Washington, 1959-62; adj. prof. U. Md. (Europe), 1965; prof. law Golden Gate U. Sch. Law, San Francisco, 1968-74, 81—, dean Sch. Law, 1974-81. Bd. dirs. San Francisco Neighborhood Legal Assistance Found. Fellow Am. Bar Found.; mem. ABA, Wis., Calif., San Francisco (dir. 1975-77, chmn. legis. com. 1977, pres.-elect 1983, pres. 1984) bar assns., Calif. Women Lawyers (1st pres.), Law in a Free Soc. (cons.), Continuing Edn. of Bar (chmn. real estate subcom., mem. joint adv. com.). Democrat. Contbr. to Damages Book, 1975, 77. Office: Golden Gate U Sch Law 536 Mission St San Francisco CA 94105

MCKENDALL, RHONDA NABONNE, journalist; b. New Orleans, Ag. 23, 1951; d. Warren Joseph and Margaret Masaline (Danna) Nabonne; m. Larry Joseph McKendall, July 6, 1974. B.A., Loyola U., New Orleans, 1973. Staff writer Times Picayune, New Orleans, 1973—, now edn. writer. Recipient Outstanding News Coverage award La. Assn. Educators, 1982; Sch. Bell award La. Fedn. Tchrs., 1981, Outstanding News Coverage award Greater Slidell C. of C., 1981; Community Service to Edn. award Phi Delta Kappa, 1984. Mem. Press Club New Orleans (1st place investigative reporting 1977). Democrat. Roman Catholic. Home: 7820 Trapier Ave New Orleans LA 70127 Office: Times Picayune 3800 Howard Ave New Orleans LA 70140

MCKENNA, BARBARA ST. CLAIR, food columnist; b. Latrobe, Pa., June 21, 1922; d. Thomas and Emma Maria (Herrmann) St. Clair; m. Frank Shirley

McKenna, June 19, 1943 (dec.); children—Pamela McKenna Smith, Jenifer, Thomas, Megan. Student Barnard Coll., Columbia U.; B.A., DePauw U., 1964. Food columnist Sunday Courier & Press, Evansville, Ind., 1982—. Bd. dirs. Ind. Council for Humanities, Ind. Family Halth Council, Indpls., Evansville Philharmon. Orch., Planned Parenthood, Channel 9, Youth Service Bur., Leadership Evansville, U. Evansville Press, U. Evansville Samuel Johnson Soc. Named Woman of Yr. YWCA, 1975. Mem. LWV (bd. dirs.). Democrat. Methodist. Clubs: Evansville Country, Evansville Kennel, Social Lit. Lodge: PEO (officer 1968-80). Home: 726 S Willow Rd Evansville IN 47714

MCKENNA, FAY ANN, electrical manufacturing company executive; b. Bennington, Vt., Jan. 7, 1944; d. George Francis and Barbara Mae (Youngangel) Hoag; m. James Dennis McKenna, Sept. 3, 1963 (div. 1983); children—Russell (dec.), Laura, James, Sean, Michael. Student, Mercy Coll. Key punch operator N.Y. State Taxation and Fin. Dept., Albany, 1960-61; receptionist Trine Mfg./Square D Co., Bronx, 1972-76; clk. Square D Co., Bronx, 1976-78, exec. sec., 1978-79, personnel mgr., 1979—. Fund raiser YMCA, Bronx, 1979—; mem. Community Bd. #9, Bronx, 1984—; Recipient Service to Youth award YMCA, 1985. Mem. Adminstrv. Mgmt. Soc. Republican. Roman Catholic. Avocations: physical fitness; reading; interior decorating. Home: 4100-20 Hutchinson River Pkwy E Bronx NY 10475 Office: Square D Co 1430 Ferris Pl Bronx NY 10461

MCKENNA, MARY CATHERINE, nutritional biochemist, educator; b. Bethesda, Md., Dec. 17, 1945; d. John Reilly and Mary Cusack (McManus) McK.; B.A., U. Md., 1968, Ph.D., 1979; m. Alan Mink, Dec. 18, 1974. Stewardess, Overseas Nat. Airways, N.Y.C., 1969-72; grad. teaching and research asst., dept. chemistry U. Md., College Park, 1973-78, affiliate asst. prof. dept. food, nutrition and inst. adminstrn., U. Md., College Park, 1983—; research asst. prof. dept. pediatrics U. Md. Sch. Medicine, Balt., 1982—; staff fellow, nutritional biochemistry sect. Lab. of Nutrition and Endocrinology, Nat. Inst. Arthritis, Diabetes, Digestive and Kidney Disease, NIH, Bethesda, Md., 1979-82. Sigma Xi research excellence awardee and research grantee, 1977. Mem. Am. Inst. Nutrition, Am. Chem. Soc., Am. Oil Chemists Soc., N.Y. Acad. Scis., AAAS, Am. Forestry Assn., Sigma Xi. Home: 13088 Williamfield Dr Ellicott City MD 21043 Office: Div Pediatric Research Dept Pediatrics U Md Sch Medicine Baltimore MD 21201

MCKENZIE, FLORETTA DUKES, supt. schs.; b. Lakeland, Fla.; d. Martin and Ruth Jeter Dukes; B.S. in History, D.C. Tchrs. Coll., 1956, postgrad., 1967-69; M.A. (grad. sch. fellow 1957), Howard U., 1957; Ed.D., George Washington U., Am. U. 1985; postgrad. Catholic U. Am., Union Grad. Sch., Balt.; children—Kevin Donald, Dona Ruth. Tchr., Balt. and Washington Schs., 1957-67; from asst. supt. charge secondary schs. to dep. supt. ednl. programs and services D.C. public schs., 1969-74; area asst. supt. Montgomery County (Md.) public schs., 1974-77, dep. supt. schs., 1978-79; asst. dep. supt. schs. State of Md., 1977-78; with U.S. Dept. Edn., 1979-81, dep. asst. sec. Office Sch. Improvement, 1980-81; edn. cons. Ford Found., 1981; supt. D.C. public schs., 1981—; adv. com. Washington office Coll. Entrance Exam. Bd., 1970—; trustee Ednl. Products Info. Exchange, 1970; cons., speaker in field. Recipient various service awards; hon. life mem. Md. PTA. Mem. Am. Assn. Sch. Adminstrs., Urban League, Gamma Theta Upsilon, Phi Alpha Theta, Phi Delta Kappa. Baptist. Address: Presdl Bldg 415 12th St NW Washington DC 20004

MCKENZIE-WHARTON, LOU BERTHA VIOLA, educational administrator; b. Chgo., Aug. 15, 1939; d. Joseph Leonidas and Myrtle Arlene (Ellison) McKenzie; student Howard U., 1956-58; B.A., Roosevelt U., 1961; M.A., 1969, M.A., 1970; M.Ed., Columbia U., 1971, Ed.D., 1973; m. Richard G. Wharton, July 15, 1972; children—Jonathan, Joseph. Tchr., Chgo. Sch. Dist., 1961-73; ednl. cons. Wharton & McKenzie-Wharton, N.Y.C., 1973-74; dir. title VI and VII govtl. programs West Hartford (Conn.) Public Schs., 1974-81, dir. title VI govtl. program, 1981-82, dir. compensatory edn. programs, 1982—; vis. scholar Tchrs. Coll., Columbia U., 1986-87. Bd. dirs. YWCA, 1979-81, treas., 1980-81. Mem. Am. Assn. Sch. Adminstrs., Hartford Womens Network, League Voters, Tchrs. Coll.-Columbia U. Alumni Council, Sperling Soc., Chgo. No. Dist. Assn. Club Women, Hartford Symphony Aux., Phi Alpha Theta, Alpha Kappa Alpha. Home: 292 Steele Rd West Hartford CT 06117 Office: West Hartford Public Schs 211 Steele Rd West Hartford CT 06117

MCKEON, DONNA FORILL, journalist; b. Cleve., Dec. 18, 1927; d. Paul John and Helen Ann (Winkel) Forill; m. John Vincent McKeon, Nov. 3, 1951; children—Mary Christine, Paul, Patrick. B.A., St. Mary-of-the-Woods Coll., 1949; M.A., Marquette U., 1951. Pub. relations chmn. Easter Seal Soc., Madison, Wis., 1952-56, Christmas Seal Soc., Madison, 1952-56; editor Smilin'Thru, Madison, 1952-56; society asst. Madison Capital Times, Wis. State Jour., Madison, 1953-56; advt. clk. Western Auto Supply, Cleve., 1951; gen. assignment reporter West Life, Cleve., 1967-69; asst. society editor Cleve. Press, 1969-71; freelance writer Richmond (Va.) LifeStyle, 1979-82; contbg. editor Met. Woman, Richmond, 1982—. Author: This Is Sister, 1968; contbr. articles to profl. jours. Trustee St. Mary-of-the-Woods Coll., 1971-73, mem. nat. alumnae bd., 1964-68. Recipient editing and writing award Am. Newspaper Guild, 1948; service award Wis. Easter Seal Soc., 1955. Mem. Nat. League Am. Pen Women (pres. 1982-84), Women in Communications (pres. 1953-55), Va. Press Women. Roman Catholic. Home: 4122 Old Gun Rd E Midlothian VA 23113

MCKEON, JANE F., nurse, health management consultant; b. Cleve., Sept. 11, 1941; d. John Thomas and Mary Jane (Werwage) McK.; R.N., Good Samaritan Hosp. Sch. Nursing, Dayton, Ohio, 1969; B.S., Mt. St. Joseph Coll., 1971; M.Ed., Loyola U., Chgo., 1975; Instr., Wesley/Passavant Sch. Nursing, Chgo., 1971-75; asst. dir. nursing Franklin Blvd. Hosp., Chgo., 1975-76; dir. nursing, staff devel. and quality assurance Children's Meml. Hosp., Chgo., 1976-77; mgr. A. T. Kearney Inc., Health Services Cons., Chgo., 1977-83, Coopers and Lybrand Health Services Cons., 1983-84; dir. nursing Edgewater Hosp., Chgo., 1984—; Seminar leader. Mem. Chgo. Heart Assn., 1978—; patron Lyric Opera of Chgo., 1981-82; vol. Horizon Hospice, Chgo., 1984—. Mem. Women in Mgmt. Inc. (chmn. program com. 1982-83), Women Health Execs. Network. Home: 777 N Michigan Ave Chicago IL 60611 Office: 5700 N Ashland Ave Chicago IL 60660

MCKEOWN, HELEN GAIL, laboratory administrator; b. Hartford, Ky., June 11, 1947; d. Ivan Dennie and Ovelia (Pillow) Allen; B.S., Western Ky. U., 1973; m. Earl Glenn McKeown, June 25, 1966; children—Cary Reid, Adam Kyle. Med. technologist Sacred Heart Hosp., Idaho Falls, Idaho, 1968, Cytomed. Lab., Norwich, Conn., 1969-71, Med. Lab., Bowling Green, Ky., 1971-72, Western Ky. U., Bowling Green, 1972-74, Newell & Assos., Chattanooga, 1976-80; lab. supr. Red Bank (Tenn.) Community Hosp., 1980-83, North Park Hosp., Hixson, Tenn., 1983—; instr. microbiology rev. Chattanooga State Community Coll. Pres. Chattanooga PTA Council, 1979-81; historian Hixson Elem. Sch. PTA, 1977-79. Recipient cert. of appreciation City of Idaho Falls, 1968. Mem. Am. Soc. Clin. Pathologists, Tenn. Soc. Med. Tech. (sec. 1985-86), Chattanooga Soc. for Med. Tech. (pres. 1984-85), Chattanooga Edn. in Music Arts Assn., Inc., Children's Internat. Summer Village, Sister City Assn. of Chattanooga, Inc., Hixson C. of C. (chmn. 1983). Democrat. Methodist. Home: 6515 Grubb Rd Hixson TN 37343 Office: 2051 Hamill Rd Hixson TN 37343

MCKEOWN, KATHLEEN MARY, business consultant; b. New Haven, Dec. 11, 1941; d. Edward J. and Elizabeth Grace (Sullivan) McK. B.A., Notre Dame of Md., 1963; postgrad. San Francisco Art Inst., 1967, Acad. Art, 1968. Art supr. pub. schs., Wolcott, Conn., 1963-66; interior decorator, San Francisco, 1966-69; office mgr. Multiple Line Engring. Service, San Francisco, 1970-73; bus. mgr. Uniplan Corp., San Francisco, 1973-74, dir. prodn. control, 1974-75, dir. client services, 1976-77, v.p., 1977-78; dir. franchise resales Swensens, Inc., San Francisco, 1979; mgmt. cons. China Books & Periodicals, San Francisco, 1980—, also dir.; cons. Chinese papercuts exhibit Berkshire Mus. Art, Lenox, Mass., 1982—; graphics cons. Fgn. Lang. Press, Beijing, 1983—, New World Press, Beijing, 1983—; photographer Terwiliger Found., Tiburon, Calif., 1981—. Bus. affiliate Citizens Adv. Com. to San Francisco Police Dept., 1976-77. Mem. Embarcadero Ctr. Forum (pres. 1978), Book Publicists No. Calif., Grey Panthers. Democrat. Roman Catholic. Home: 35 Iris Ave San Francisco CA 94108

MC KEOWN, MARY ELIZABETH, educator; d. Raymond Edmund and Alice (Fitzgerald) McNamara; B.S., U. Chgo., 1946; M.S., DePaul U., 1953; m. James Edward McKeown, Aug. 6, 1955. Supr. high sch. dept. Am. Sch., 1948-68, prin., 1968—, trustee, 1975—, v.p., 1979—. Mem. Nat. Assn. Secondary Sch. Prins., Central States Assn. Sci. and Math Tchrs. Nat. Council Tchrs. Math., Assn. for Supervision and Curriculum Devel., LWV, Adult Edn. Assn. Home: 1469 N Sheridan Rd Kenosha WI 53140

MCKEOWN, PATRICIA LUCAS, radio news director, columnist; b. N.Y.C., Jan. 8, 1939; d. Gordon Maskell and Ruth (Lounsbery) Lucas; B.A., Moravian Coll., 1963; postgrad. Lehigh U., 1964; children—Matthew, Adam, Joshua. Library asst. Moravian Coll., 1961-63; acct. Durkee Foods div. Glidden Co., 1958-61; tchr. Bethlehem (Pa.) Schs., 1963-67; news corr. Bethlehem Globe-Times, 1973-74; reporter Park Newspapers, St. Lawrence, N.Y., 1975-77; editor Massena (N.Y.) Observer, 1977-82; news and public affairs dir. North Country Public Radio, Canton, N.Y., 1982—; columnist Syracuse Post-Standard & Herald Am.; lectr. sch. dists. Liaison Tchrs. Union, 1966-67; treas., fin. chmn. LWV, 1969-72; bd. dirs. Moravian Coll. Alumni, 1968, Renewal House; chmn. Mayor's Task Force on Drug Abuse, 1979-80; bd. dirs. North Country Women's Shelter, Inc., 1977-79; bd. dirs. Massena Salvation Army, 1982; mem. program on gifted children N.Y. Bd. Coop. Edn. Services, 1981. Mem. Massena C. of C. (dir. 1982), Nat. Women's Polit. Caucus, St. Laurence Press Assn. (treas. 1983—), Massena Bus. and Profl. Women, Moravian Coll. Alumni Assn. (pres. 1966-67). Home: RD 3 339 Massena NY 13662 Office: Payson Hall Saint Lawrence U Canton NY 13617

MC KERNAN-MARKOFF, JANIS LEIGH, nurse, former union official; b. New London, Conn., June 17, 1949; d. Joseph Bernard and Shirley Mae (Kenyon) McKernan; m. Henry Markoff. R.N., Hartford (Conn.) Hosp., 1972; student R.I. Coll., 1978 B.S. in Mgmt., Salva Regina Coll., 1984. Nurse hosps. in R.I., 1972—; charge nurse, supr. registered nurses Inst. Mental Health, Cranston, 1974-77, supr. registered nurse rehab. unit, 1977-80; nat. v.p. Nat. Assn. Nurses, Nat. Health Care Union, 1980-82; staff nurse coronary intensive care, care unit Our Lady of Fatima, unit St. Joseph's Hosp., 1982—; dir. inservice Cedar Crest Nursing Ctr., Cranston, R.I., 1984-85; investigator Medicaid Fraud Control Unit, R.I. Dept. Atty. Gen., 1982—. Served with Nurse Corps, U.S. Army, 1975; capt. Res. Mem. Am. Nurses Assn., R.I. State Nurses Assn., Am. Soc. Law and Medicine Res. Officers Assn., Assn. U.S. Army, Nat. Assn. Govt. Employees (pres. unit collective bargaining 1976-81), Nat. Fedn. Republican Women. Home: 28 Mozart St Cranston RI 02920

MCKILLIP, MARY ELIZABETH, publishing company executive; b. Gary, Ind., July 3, 1950; d. Milton G. and Mary Louise (McEnery) Thomas; B.A., Coll. St. Teresa, Winona, Minn., 1971; m. Michael R. McKillip, Aug. 15, 1970. Adminstrv. coordinator U. Chgo. Med. Center, 1971-80; mgr. adminstrv. services Am. Hosp. Pub., Inc., Chgo., 1980-83, circulation dir., 1983—. Campaign dir. Crusade of Mercy, Chgo., 1979-83. Mem. Nat. Assn. Female Execs., Direct Mktg. Assn., Chgo. Circulation Round Table, Women in Mgmt. Office: 211 E Chicago Ave Suite 700 Chicago IL 60611

MCKILLOP, LUCILLE, college president; b. Chgo., Sept. 28, 1924; d. Daniel and Catherine (Hamill) McK. B.A., St. Xavier Coll., 1951; M.S., U. Notre Dame, 1959; Ph.D., U. Wis., 1965. Vis. prof. Ill. Inst. Tech., Chgo., 1969; faculty St. Xavier Coll., Chgo., 1958-59, 63-73; pres. Salve Regina Coll., Newport, R.I., 1973—; dir. Old Colony Coop. Bank, Providence, 1976-81; mem. Gov's Adv. Commn. Ednl. TV, 1977-82, R.I. Postsecondary Edn. Commn., 1979—, Gov's Commn. on Taxation, 1981—, Gov.'s Commn. on R.I. Legis. Compensation, 1980—. Trustee Newport Hosp., 1976-80; mem. corp. R.I. Blue Cross/Blue Shield, 1980—; bd. dirs. Council for Advancement Small Colls., 1978-82, Newport Music Festival, 1978—. Mem. Nat. Assn. Ind. Colls. and Univs. (dir. 1977-82), R.I. Ind. Higher Edn. Assn. (exec. com.), Associated Cath. Colls. and Univs. (exec. com. coll. and univ. dept. 1977-80). Address: Salve Regina Coll Office of Pres Ochre Point Ave Newport RI 02840

MCKILLOP, MARIE ALICE, hair salon owner; b. Glasgow, Scotland, May 19, 1938; came to U.S., 1963, naturalized, 1986; d. Joseph M. and Mary Jospehine (Hamilton) Imlah; m. Daniel Macauley McKillop, Dec. 26, 1966; 1 child, Janine Lara. Student, U. Md., 1974-75; A.A., Montgomery Coll., 1978. Hair stylist Vincent & Vincent, Takoma Park, Md., 1963-66; hair stylist, owner Marcel of Bethesda, Chevy Chase, Md., 1966-74, Touch of Class, Olney, Md., 1974—. Mem. adv. bd. Guide Youth Ctr., Olney, 1984-85; mem. parent council Sandy Spring Friends Sch., Md., 1983-85; chmn. Olney Parade, 1984, 85, 86. Mem. Olney C. of C. (1st v.p. 1984-86, pres.-elect 1986, Bus. Person of Yr. 1984), Greater Olney Civic Assn. (Bus. Person of Yr. 1984). Avocations: travel; theatre; reading; classes of all kinds. Office: Touch of Class Hairstylist Inc 3308 Route 108 Olney MD 20832

MCKINLEY, ELLEN BACON, priest; b. Milw., June 9, 1929; d. Edward Alsted and Lorraine Goodrich (Graham) Bacon; m. Richard Smallbrook McKinley, III, June 16, 1951 (div. Oct. 1977); children—Richard IV, Ellen Graham, David Todd, Edward Bacon. B.A. cum laude, Bryn Mawr Coll., 1951; M.Div. Yale U., 1976; S.T.M., Gen. Theol. Sem., N.Y.C., 1979; postgrad. Union Theol. Sem., N.Y.C., 1981—. Ordained deacon Episcopal Ch. 1980, priest, 1981. Intern St. Francis Ch., Stamford, Conn., 1976-77; pastoral asst. St. Paul's Ch., Riverside, Conn., 1979-80, curate, 1980-81; priest assoc. St. Saviour's Ch., Old Greenwich, Conn., 1982—. Sec., Greewich Com. on Drugs, 1970-71; bd. dirs. Greenwich YWCA, 1971-72. Mem. Conn. Clergy Assn. (Episcopal), Episcopal Women's Caucus, New Eng. Women Ministers Assn., Greenwich Fellowship of Clergy, Colonial Dames Am., Jr. League. Clubs: Sulgrave, Rocky Point. Avocations: theatre, concerts, swimming, sailing, reading, architecture--building and remodeling houses. Office: St Saviour's Ch 350 Sound Beach Ave Old Greenwich CT 06870

MCKINLEY, LOIS ANN, nursing educator; b. Pitts., Nov. 6, 1943; d. Charles Andrew and Irene Ann (Kirk) McK. B.S. in Nursing with distinction, Pa. State U., 1981. Nurse, St. Francis Hosp., Pitts., 1964-67, nursing supr., 1977-80; mem. faculty Sch. Respiratory Therapy, 1976-80, mem. faculty Alvernia Sch. Practical Nursing, 1967—, asst. dir., 1978-83, audio-visual coordinator, 1976-83, level I coordinator, 1979-83, coordinator gerontology, 1979-83, coordinator pediatrics, 1967-83, faculty sec.-treas., 1980-83. Author, editor film: Care of the Patient with a Fractured Femur, 1977. Mem. adminstrv. bd. Emory United Meth. Ch., Pitts., 1983-86. Recipient Leadership cert. St. Francis Hosp., 1966. Mem. Pa. State U. Alumni Assn., St. Francis Hosp. Sch. Nursing Alumni, Sigma Theta Tau. Democrat. Methodist. Home: 826 Farragut St Pittsburgh PA 15206 Office: Alvernia Sch Practical Nursing 4400 Penn Ave Pittsburgh PA 15201

MCKINLEY, RUTH JOANN, hospice administrator, psychotherapist; b. Los Angeles, Sept. 24, 1933; d. Ward Ivan and Lilah May (Conger) Hallin; B.A., Calif. State U.-Northridge, 1966; M.S.W., U. So. Calif., 1972; Ph.D. cum laude, Am. Western U., 1981; m. John Clyde McKinley, Nov. 19, 1954 (dec. 1972); children—Terance Phillip Green, Mark Stuart. Adminstr., Pacoima (Calif.) br. San Fernando Valley Child Guidance Clinic, 1965-68; dependency supr. placement services Los Angeles County Juvenile Ct., Van Nuys, Calif., 1968-72; psychotherapist Simi Valley and Conejo Mental Health, Ventura County Mental Health Services, Thousand Oaks, Calif., 1972—; exec. dir. Hospice of the Conejo, 1984—, pvt. practice psychotherapy Capper Psychiat. Med. Group, Camarillo, Calif., after 1979; exec. dir. Hospice of Conejo, 1984—; pvt. practice Mc Kinley Assocs., 1983—; cons., tng. cons. Conejo Community Hotline. Dir., Lifeline, Westlake Village, Calif., 1972-75; mem. White Ho. Conf. on Children and Youth, 1970; mem. Ventura County Coalition Against Household Violence, 1980. Children's Bur. Fed. grantee, 1970-72. Mem. Acad. Cert. Social Workers, Soc. Clin. Social Work. Office: 199 E Thousand Oaks Blvd Thousand Oaks CA 91361

MCKINNEY, BARBARA ANN, lawyer, business executive; b. Wyandotte, Mich., May 27, 1950; d. Robert and Roselyn Marie (Weers) Budjac; m. William Smith McKinney, Sept. 24, 1977 (div. Nov. 1982). B.S.C. in Acctg., U. Louisville, 1972; J.D., George Washington U., 1979, M.B.A., 1981. Bar: Va. 1979; C.P.A., Mich., Va., D.C. Jr. acct., teller Firestone Employee Fed. Credit Union, Wyandotte, Mich., 1968-71; tax asst. Touche Ross & Co., Louisville, Ky., 1971-72; sr. auditor Arthur Andersen & Co., Detroit, 1972-74, sr. systems analyst, Washington, D.C., 1974-75; controller NEA, Washington, D.C., 1975-77; div. mgr. Forbes & Assoc., Inc., Springfield, Va., 1978-79; East Coast regional counsel Centex Homes, Inc., Manassas, Va., 1979-80; v.p. fin., gen. counsel EPIC Holdings, Ltd., Falls Church, Va., 1980—, also dir.; asst. prof. Grad. Sch. Bus. George Washington U., Washington, D.C. 1981—; dir. Prune Leasing, Ltd., Fairlane Corp., Encore Corp., Bonneville Corp., EPIC Fin. Services, Inc., all Falls Church, Va., Dist. Realty Title Ins. Co., Washington; cons. repurchase program Phi Sigma Epsilon Nat., Richmond, Va., 1984—. Author: (instrn. and ops. manual) Executing the Section 1031 Tax Free Exchange, 1980; (course instrn. manual) New Venture Initiation, 1982; (programs) Expandable Partnerships, 1982; EPIREM, 1982. Mem. ABA, Va. Bar Assn., Fairfax Bar Assn. Am. Inst. C.P.A.s, Va. Inst. C.P.A.s, Aircraft Owners and Pilots Assn., Am. Woman's Soc. C.P.A.s, Am. Mgmt. Assn., George Washington U. Alumni Assn., Phi Kappa Phi, Pi Omega Pi, Alpha Xi Delta, Phi Alpha Delta. Repubican. Lutheran. Office: EPIC Holdings Ltd 5113 Leesburg Pike Suite 901 Falls Church VA 22041

MCKINNEY, BETTY JO, publisher; b. Maryville, Mo., July 16; d. Joseph Glenn and Virginia Joy (Schubert) Thomas; student N.W. Mo. State U., 1959, Tarkio (Mo.) Coll., 1960-62, Colo. State U., 1967-69; m. George Wendell McKinney, Jan. 29, 1966. Asst. dir. office public relations, Tarkio Coll., 1963-65; publ. specialist office univ. communications, Colo. State U., Ft. Collins, 1966-81; founder, pres., partner Alpine Publs., Loveland, Colo., 1975-80, pub., 1980—. Mem. Dog Writers Assn. Am., Am. Kennel Club. Am. Shetland Sheepdog Club, Com. Small Mag. Editors and Pubs., Rocky Mountain Pubs. Assn. Author: Sheltie Talk, 1976, rev., 1985; Beardie Basics, 1978. Address: 1901 S Garfield St Loveland CO 80537

MCKINNEY, BEVERLY SUE, banker; b. Charleston, W.Va., May 7, 1946; d. John A. and Norma Sue (Brewer) Castle, Jr.; m. Robert Lee McKinney, Feb. 8, 1969; children—Robert L. II, Heather Sue. Student Morris Harvey Coll., 1964-66. With Bank of St. Albans (N.Y.), 1965-69, Chem. Bank & Trust Co., South Charleston, W.Va., 1969-70; customer service rep. C & S Nat. Bank, Atlanta, 1971-75; consumer affairs dir., mortgage loan officer First Bank Ceredo (W. Va.), 1976-80; v.p. First Huntington Nat. Bank (W.Va.), 1980—; instr. Marshall U., Huntington, parttime, 1981, 83; pres., dir. Appalachian Craftsmen, Inc., Huntington. Bd. dirs., sec. Cabell County Tailgate Farmers Market, Huntington, 1981—. Mem. Huntington Bus. Assn. (com. mem. 1983), Promote Huntington Downtown Assn., Advt. Club Huntington (dir.), Internat. Assn. Bus. Communicators (chpt. sec. 1981-82), W.Va. Bankers Assn. (automation com. 1983—), Am. Mgmt. Assn., Nat. Assn. Bank Women. Republican. Episcopalian. Club: Quota (Huntington). Lodge: Order Eastern Star. Home: 6101 Clark Dr Huntington WV 25705 Office: 1st Huntington Nat Bank 1000 5th Ave Huntington WV 25701

MCKINNEY, DEBRA HILL, educator, adminstrator, musician; b. Kansas City, Kans., July 11, 1950; d. Benton Fisher and Midge Varnese (Pearce) Hill; m. William Ray Townsend, III, July 17, 1971 (div. June 1979); 1 dau., Laurie Michelle; m. 2d, Richard George McKinney, June 19, 1982. B.Mus., Converse Coll., Spartanburg, S.C., 1972. Cert. tchr., Tex. Tchr. music Houston Ind. Sch. Dist., 1972-78; dir. childrens choir First Presbyn. Ch., Houston, 1973—, child care coordinator, dir. children's ministries, 1983—, dir. Mother's Day Out program, 1980—. Mem. Choristers Guild. Republican. Club: Tuesday Mus. Home: 301 Piney Point Houston TX 77024 Office: First Presbyterian Ch 5300 S Main St Houston TX 77004

MCKINNEY, JEAN CARLEEN, educational administrator; b. Paducah, Ky., Apr. 7, 1935; d. Eugene and Lillian M. (Ballard) Brown; m. George D. McKinney, June 15, 1957; children—George A., Grant A., Gregory A., Gordon A., Glenn A. B.A., San Diego State U., 1973; M.S. in Counseling, 1977. Cert. tchr., Calif.; lic. missionary Ch. of God in Christ, 1982. Founder/dir. St. Stephen's Nursery Sch., San Diego, 1963-73; tchr. San Diego City Schs., 1973-78; founder/dir. St. Stephen's Christian Sch., San Diego, 1978—. Author: The Advantages of Nursery Education, 1979. Recipient spl. commendation City Council San Diego, 1983; proclamation San Diego County Bd. Suprs., 1983. Democrat. Avocations: travel; reading; arts and crafts. Home: 5848 Arboles St San Diego CA 92120

MCKINNEY, PHYLLIS LOUISE KELLOGY HENRY, school administrator, bank director, education and management consultant; b. Mason City, Iowa, May 3, 1932; d. Wilbur Rhode and Dorothy Margaret (Bauer) K.; children—Curtis Dean, Catherine Rose Henry Jones, David Russell. A.A. in Elem. Teaching, U. No. Iowa, 1953; B.A. Calif. State U.-Los Angeles, 1963, M.A., 1968. Cert. elem. tchr., cert. reading specialist, sch. adminstrn. credential. Tchr., Arlington pub. schs., Iowa, 1951-52, St. Louis Park pub. schs., Minn., 1953-55; tchr., supr. ABC Sch. Dist., Cerritos, Calif., 1963-69; cons. in reading State Dept. of Calif., Sacramento, 1969-70; cons. in edn. Orange County Dept. Edn., Santa Ana, Calif., 1970-75; sch. adminstr. McKinney Sch., Long Beach, Calif., 1975—; dir. New City Bank, Orange, Calif.; cons. in field. Author: Song of Sounds, 1969; (with others) Beginnings for Christian Schools, 1976. Conf. coordinator State Dept. Edn., Calif., Sacramento, Santa Barbara, 1970 (Outstanding Leadership award 1974-75). Mem. Nat. Ind. Pvt. Sch. (v.p. 1982-83, dir. seminars 1983), Pre-Sch. Assn. Calif. (legis. chair 1978-84), Reading Specialists Calif. (pres. 1970-73). Republican. Baptist. Avocations: sking; scuba diving; painting; photography; travel. Home: 4438 Heather Rd Long Beach CA 90808 Office: McKinney Sch 2951 Long Beach Blvd Long Beach CA 90806

MCKINNEY, RITA ESTELLE, needlework designer, instructor; b. Los Angeles, Oct. 25, 1946; d. Virgil William and Herticina (Russell) McCue; m. Edward Derrell McKinney, Mar. 20, 1969; 1 child, Jason Bowden. Student Cerritos Coll., Calif., 1970-71, El Camino Coll., Torrance, Calif., 1966-68; cert. of completion Acad. of Arts, San Francisco, 1965. Asst. art dir. Kierulff Electronics, Los Angeles, 1970-76; prodn. mgr. EPI Advt., Los Angeles, 1972-76; artist, designer The Garden, Downey, Calif., 1976-79; owner, artist, designer Etcetera Designs, Los Angeles, Hanford, Visalia, Calif., 1979-82, Rita Designs, Tulare, Calif., 1982—; pub. relations dir. SDA Orgn., Kings County, Calif., 1980-83. Contbr. articles to Sun Newspapers. Mem. Embroiderers Guild Am., Am. Needlepoint Guild. Home and office: Rita Designs 448 W Allstar Ave Tulare CA 93274

MCKINNEY, RUBY BURT, radio station copywriter; b. Monticello, Ark., Nov. 1, 1958; d. Fred Charles Burt and Maybelle Jenette (Elliott) Burt Brayden; m. Bryce Baker McKinney; 1 child, Bryce Baker Jr. Student Ark. State U., 1977. Lic. radio operator. News reporter Sta. KTAL-TV, Shreveport, La., 1979, pub. service dir., 1979-81; copywriter Sta. KWRF, Warren, Ark., 1983—. Avocations: oil painting; needlepoint; plate collecting. Home: PO Box 971 Warren AR 71671 Office: Sta KWRF PO Box 480 Warren AR 71671

MCKINNIS, DORIS CHRISTINE, lawyer; b. Marshall, Minn., July 10, 1951; d. James Christian and Joan Christine (Sand) Otto; m. Randall Kent McKinnis, July 17, 1970. B.A. magna cum laude, U. Minn., 1975; J.D., William Mitchell Coll. Law, 1982. Bar: Minn. 1982, U.S. Dist. Ct. Minn. 1982, U.S. Ct. Appeals (8th cir.) 1982. Sec. women's programs Coll. Continuing Edn., Drake U., Des Moines, 1974-76; med. sec. Univ. Hosps., U. Minn., Mpls., 1977-78; research asst. William Mitchell Coll. Law, St. Paul, 1980-82, teaching asst., 1981; assoc. Kurzman, Manahan & Partridge Law Offices, Mpls., also Mankato, Minn., 1982—. Mem. Minn. Trial Lawyers Assn., Assn. Trial Lawyers Am., ABA, Minn. Bar Assn., Hennepin County Bar Assn. Home: 11160 Anderson Lakes Pkwy Unit 316 Eden Prairie MN 55344 Office: 600 1st Ave N Suite 260 Minneapolis MN 55403

MCKINNISS, PATRICIA PERKINS, bank executive; b. Glendale, Calif., Jan. 15, 1955; d. Edwin Ray and Dolores (Vogelsang) Perkins; m. Steven Wayne Mount, July 26, 1975 (div. July 1977); m. Michael Jones McKinniss, Nov. 30, 1979; 1 child, Caroline Greenleaf. Student Mt. San Antonio Coll., 1973-78, Calif. State U.-Los Angeles, 1978-80. Part-time salesperson Sears Roebuck, Covina, Calif., 1973-75; personnel interviewer United Calif. Bank, Los Angeles, 1975-79; recruiter, personnel officer Coast Fed. Savs. & Loan Assn., Los Angeles, 1979-80; personnel officer Crocker Nat. Bank, Los Angeles, 1980-82; asst. v.p., personnel officer Security Pacific Bank, Glendale, Calif., 1983, v.p., employment mgr., 1983-85; human resources mgr. Security Pacific Brokers, Inc., 1985—. Vol., SecuriTeam, Glendale, 1984. Mem. Assn. Personnel Adminstrn., Human Resource Planning Soc. Republican. Congregationalist. Office: Security Pacific Brokers Inc 155 N Lake Ave Suite 260 Pasadena CA 91101

MCKINNON, DOROTHY ELAINE, automobile association executive; b. Oakland, Nebr., Sept. 20, 1946; d. Charles Clarke and Dorothy Margaret (Corbin) Jewell; student Prince George Community Coll., 1964-65, U. Md., 1971-72, N. Va. Community Coll., 1975-76, Rochester Inst. Tech., 1984—; 1 child, Rebecca Long. Prodn. analyst Am. Automobile Assn., Falls Church, Va., 1966-71, club cons., 1971-74, mgmt. analyst, 1974-78, mgr. spl. projects, 1978-79, mgr. credit card ops., 1979-81, mng. dir. adminstrv. services, Madison, Wis., 1981-82; v.p., asst. gen. mgr. Auto Club, Rochester, N.Y., 1983—; bd. dirs. N.Y. State Automobile Assn., 1983—; treas. bd. dirs.

Wisconsin Safety Patrols, 1981-83. 4-H instr., 1977; v.p. bd. dirs. Loudoun County (Va.) Citizens Assn., 1975-79; mem. Va. Taxpayers Assn., 1977-79; chmn. bd. dirs. Loudoun County Taxpayers Assn., 1978-79; adv. budget com. Loudoun County Bd. Suprs., 1979. Mem. Data Processing Mgmt. Assn., Women in Communications (bd. dirs.), Women's Coalition for Downtown Rochester, Genesee/Finger Lakes Hwy. Users Council, Rochester Conv. and Visitors Bur. Home: 60 Cathaway Park Rochester NY 14610 Office: 777 Clinton Ave S Rochester NY 14620

MCKINNON, MARY THOMASON, lawyer; b. El Dorado, Ark., July 20, 1953; d. Virgil Lemuel and Emma Jean (Ritchie) Thomason; m. Walter Corbin McKinnon, Jr., May 1, 1982. B.A., U. Ark.-Monticello, 1975; J.D., U. Ark.-Fayetteville, 1980. Bar: Ark. 1980. Tchr., El Dorado Pub. Sch., 1975-77; mem. Law Office of Worth Camp, El Dorado, 1980—; atty. Union County Child Support Enforcement, El Dorado, 1980-83. Pub. relations chmn. Union County Young Democrats, 1982; bd. dirs. YWCA, El Dorado, 1983—, Pilot Club of El Dorado, 1982—; sponsor El Dorado Anchor Club, 1981—; chmn. South Ark. Jr. Miss Program, 1981-83. Recipient Jack Yates Meml. scholar U. Ark., 1978. Mem. Ark. Bar Assn., ABA, Am. Trial Lawyers Assn., Union County Bar Assn., Alpha Chi, Delta Theta Phi. Methodist. Home: 1403 Briarwood St El Dorado AR 71730 Office: Law Office of Worth Camp 304 E Peach St El Dorado AR 71730

MCKINSTRY, BONNIE MARIE, banker; b. Kenmore, N.Y., Mar. 30, 1956; d. Robert James and Joanne Mary (Harrington) McK. Student U. Houston. Asst. loan adminstr. Wells Fargo Realty Advisors, Inc., Houston, 1981-85; asst. v.p. First City Nat. Bank of Austin, Tex., 1985—; assoc. Renaissance Bus. Assocs., Loveland, Colo., 1985—; founder, co-owner Quality Assessments, Austin, 1986—. Office: First City Nat Bank 9th and Congress Austin TX 78767

MCKNIGHT, BARBARA ANN FERRELL, land development company executive; b. Austin, Tex., June 28, 1938; d. Floyd E. Ferrell and Virginia Louise (Casparis) Ferrell Edwards; divorced; children—William Keith, Wendy Kay, Wesleye Karen. Student Baylor U., 1956-57, Durham Bus. Coll., 1967, Houston Community Coll., 1979-80. Lic. real estate assoc., Tex. Adminstrv. asst. Ryland Group, Houston, 1973-80; project mgr. Gibraltar Savs. Assn. of Tex., Houston, 1980-84; v.p. Rheinhold Corp., Houston, 1984-85, Texindevco, Inc., Houston, 1985—; owner, mgr. Barbara McKnight Cons., Houston, 1985—. Alternate, Tex. Republican Conv., Houston, 1976, del., Austin, 1980. Mem. Nat. Assn. Female Execs. Baptist. Office: Texindevco Inc 5555 Fellowship Ln Spring TX 77379

MCKNIGHT, JO-ANNE MARY, communication association executive; b. Washington, Jan. 26, 1948; d. Herbert Vincent and Alma Maye (Mitchell) McK. B.F.A, Howard U., 1970. Dir. cdnl. unit, co-ordinator Human Kindness Day, Compared to What, Washington, 1973-74; drama tchr. Durham Council for the Arts, Durham, N.C., 1977-78; guest lectr. N.C. Central U., Durham, 1978-79; writer Assn. for Study Afro-Am. Life and History, Washington, 1979-80; pres. Omni Communications Arts, Washington, 1981—; playwright New Theatre Sch. Washington, 1976-80; dir. Young Peoples Theater, Durham, 1977-79; tech. writer John F. Kennedy Ctr., Washington, 1979-80. Author record album: (with others) Feelings of Love not Yet Expressed, 1975, (book) The Inverted Crow, 1984; writer various dramas. Chmn. ch. com. Durham chpt. N.C. Black Polit. Women's Caucus, 1978; chmn. program com. Washington chpt. Nat. Black Ind. Polit. party, 1981-82. Democrat. Baptist. Office: Omni Communication Arts PO Box 1328 Washington DC 20013

MCKNIGHT, JOYCE SHELDON, college official, counselor; b. Meadville, Pa., Oct. 12, 1949; d. Seth Carlyle and Juanita Bessie (Sheets) Sheldon; B.A. in Psychology and Sociology, Allegheny Coll., 1971; M.Ed. in Counseling, Gannon Coll., 1977; m. Hugh Frank McKnight, Aug. 22, 1970; children—Frank Nathan, Joanna Michelle. Asst. met. dir. Ecumenical Inst., Chgo. and Tulsa, 1970-73; health planner East Okla. Devel. Dist., Muskogee, 1973; juvenile counselor Tulsa County Aftercare Program, 1973; program specialist psycho-social rehab. Counseling Services Center, Corry, Pa., 1975-77; counselor for Adult Diploma Program, Corry, 1974-79; dir. Anchor House Agy., Corry, 1977-78; community programs dir. Warren-Forest Counties Econ. Opportunity Council, Warren, Pa., 1979-80; dir. Corry Enrichment Center, Mercyhurst Coll., 1981—, adj. faculty, 1981—; adj. faculty Allegheny Coll., 1984. Pres., Corry Concerned for Youth, Inc., 1975-77; pres. Community Care Council of Agys., Corry, 1976-79, sec., 1975; mem. steering com. Vol. Action Center, Corry, 1977; bd. dirs. Erie County Citizens Coalition for Human Services, Erie, 1979-80. Horizon House for Women, 1981—; mem. coordinating bd. Corry Reindustrialization Council, 1983—. Mem. Pa. Assn. Public Continuing Adult Edn. (dir. 1977-78), Nat. Assn. Public Continuing and Adult Edn., Pa. Assn. for Adult Continuing Edn. (bd. dirs. 1985—), Pa. Community Edn. Assn., Nat. Community Edn. Assn., Rural Mental Health Assn., Am. Assn. for Counseling and Devel., Corry C. of C., Corry Bus. and Profl. Women, Zonta. Methodist. Contbr. research. papers in field. Home: 217 Fairview St Corry PA 16407 Office: 16 E Park Pl Corry PA 16407

MCKNIGHT, SONJA DISMUKES, judges confidential assistant; b. Dothan, Ala., Mar. 4, 1946; d. Davis Lee and Mary Selma (Speigner) Dismukes; m. William Gaines McKnight, Sept. 6, 1969; children—Miriam Leigh, William Gaines, Jr. Legal sec. Ala. Farm Bur., Montgomery, 1976-77; confidential asst. to presiding Judge William M. Bowen, Jr., Ala. Ct. of Criminal Appeals, Montgomery, 1977—. Leader Southeast Ala. council Girl Scouts U.S., 1981-82; tchr. Whitfield Meth. Ch., Montgomery, 1983-85, mem. kindergarten com., 1981—; pres. Peter Crump Elem. PTA, Montgomery, 1983-85, leg. rep., 1983-85; pres. Cloverdale Jr. High PTA, Montgomery, 1985—; mem. Cloverdale Community Ctr. Council, Montgomery, 1983—. Recipient Disting. Service award Montgomery County Edn. Assn., 1983; named Hon. Mem. Lt. Govs. Staff State of Ala., 1983. Mem. Spring Valley Garden Club (pres. 1981-82), Wallace' 82 Govs. Club. Democrat. Avocations: tennis; piano. Home: 3704 Hunting Creek Rd Montgomery AL 36116 Office: Ala Ct Criminal Appeals 455 Dexter Ave Montgomery AL 36104

MCKNIGHT, SUSAN KAREN, market researcher, manufacturers' distributor, entrepreneur; b. Detroit, Aug. 30, 1954; d. William Ross and Jean Marie Lydia (Thompson) McKnight. B.A. cum laude, Eastern Mich. U., Ypsilanti, 1975, postgrad., 1975-77. Grad. asst. Eastern Mich. U., 1975-77, instr., 1976-77; instr. Henry Ford Community Coll., Dearborn, Mich., 1976-78; adminstrv. asst. coordinator County of Lake, Waukegan, Ill., 1978-81; research assoc., project mgr. No. Ill. U., DeKalb, Ill, 1981-83; ptnr. Quality Flow Co., Waukegan, 1983—; v.p., owner On Tap Premium Quality Waters Inc., 1985—; author slide presentation water quality. Bd. dirs. Crime Stoppers, Waukegan, 1981-82; precinct committeewoman Democratic Party, 1986—. Eastern Mich. U. teaching fellow, 1976-77. Mem. Nat. Assn. Counties (award 1979, 81), Lake County Tng. Assn. (v.p. 1981-85), Water Quality Assn., Lake County Barter Exchange, Chgo. Assn. Commerce and Industry. Lutheran. Home: 1500 Westmoreland Waukegan IL 60085

MCKOWEN, DOROTHY KEETON, librarian; b. Bonne Terre, Mo., Oct. 5, 1948; d. John Richard and Dorothy (Spoonhour) Keeton; m. Paul Edwin McKowen, Dec. 19, 1970; children—Richard James, Mark David. B.S., Pacific Christian Coll., 1970; M.S. in Library Sci., U. So. Calif., 1973; M.A. in English, Purdue U., 1985. Librarian-specialist Doheny Library, U. So. Calif., 1973-74; asst. librarian Pacific Christian Coll., 1974-78; serials cataloger Purdue Univ. Libraries, 1978—. Bd. dirs. Purdue Christian Campus House, 1985—; vice chmn. Christian edn. com. Brady Lane Ch. of Christ, Lafayette, Ind., 1986—, pianist, 1978—. Mem. ALA (resources and tech. services div. council of regional groups 1983—, resources sect. micropublishing com. 1986—), Ind. Library Assn. (vice chmn. tech. services div. 1983-84, chmn. 1984-85), Ohio Valley Group Tech. Services Librarians (vice chmn. 1984-85, chmn. 1985-86). Republican. Home: 7625 Summit Ln Lafayette IN 47905 Office: Purdue Univ Libraries West Lafayette IN 47907

MCKUSICK, ANN STARK, nonprofit association executive; b. Coral Gables, Fla., Sept. 27, 1950; d. Marwood Wellington and Nora (Levin) Stark; m. Richard Alan McKusick, Dec. 10, 1983. B.A. in English magna cum laude, Spring Hill Coll., 1972; M.A. in Human Devel., Pacific Oaks Coll., 1977; student in theology Fuller Theol. Sem., 1980-81. Resident dir. Regency Park Retirement Home, Pasadena, Calif., 1978-80; dir. festival devel. Pasadena Arts Council, 1980-81; dir. donor communication World Vision, Pasadena, 1981-84, dir. pub. relations, 1984-85, dir. resource devel., 1985—; advisor Diakonos, Pasadena, 1985—; mem. adv. bd. for devel. edn. Overseas Devel. Council/Interaction, Washington, 1985—; co-chmn., founder Africa Crisis Employee Response, Monrovia, Calif., 1984-85. Recipient Best Media Materials award Pub. Relations Soc. Los Angeles, 1985. Mem. Nat. Assn. Exec. Females, Publicity Club. Republican. Mem. Swedish Evangelical Covenant Ch. Office: World Vision 919 W Huntington Dr Monrovia CA 91016

MCLAIN, EMMA LILIA MENDIOLA, social service agency administrator; b. San Juan, Tex., Sept. 10, 1956; d. Maximo and Maria Guadalupe (Tijerina) Mendiola; m. J. Scott McLain, Mar. 11, 1977. B. Social Work, U. Tex., 1980. Cert. social worker, Tex. Counselor Planned Parenthood of Austin, Tex., 1980; edn. dir. Planned Parenthood of Hidalgo County, McAllen, Tex., 1980-84, asst. exec. dir., 1985—, mem. bd. dirs., 1984-85; rape crisis program coordinator Women Together Inc., McAllen, 1984-85; exec. dir. Xochil Art Inst., Mission, Tex., 1985. Chmn. Hidalgo County 4-H and Youth Com., Edinburg, Tex., 1981-83; bd. dirs. Casa Mirasol Home for Troubled Youth, McAllen, 1982, Rio Grande Valley Cancer Awareness League, McAllen, 1986—. Mem. Nat. Assn. Female Execs., Tex. Family Planning Assn. Democrat. Roman Catholic. Avocations: gardening; reading; sewing; singing; art films. Office: Planned Parenthood of Hidalgo County 1017 Pecan St McAllen TX 78501

MCLAIN, SUSAN LYNN, law educator; b. Chestertown, Md., May 6, 1949; d. Joseph Howard and Margaret Ann (Hollingsworth) McLain; m. Bryson Leitch Cook, May 21, 1977. B.A., U. Pa., 1971; J.D., Duke U., 1974, postgrad., 1976-77. Bar: Md. 1974. Assoc. firm Piper & Marbury, Balt., 1974-76; John S. Bradway Grad. fellow in clin. edn. Duke U. Sch. Law, Durham, N.C., 1976-77; asst. prof. law U. Balt., 1977-80, assoc. prof., 1980-83, prof., 1983—; hearing officer Md. Atty. Gen.'s Office, Consumer Protection Div., Balt., 1982-84; reporter on evidence Md. Trial Judges' Bench Book, 1981—; bd. dirs. Balt. City Bar Found., Inc., 1984—. Recipient U. Balt. Best Full-Time Faculty Mem. award, 1984. Co-editor supplement to book: Discovery Opinions, 1983; contbr. articles to profl. jours. Mem. ABA (chmn. sect. patent, trademark and copyright law, com. 307, subcom. on copyright and non-copyright protection for authors 1983-84, asst. to reporter sect. litigation trial evidence com. study on fed. rules of evidence 1982-83), Md. Bar Assn. (chmn. fed. cts. com. sect. litigation 1983-84). Republican. Episcopalian. Home: 5704 Stony Run Dr Baltimore MD 21210 Office: Univ Balt Sch Law 1420 N Charles St Baltimore MD 21201

MCLAINE, ALICE JEANETTE, athletic trainer, educator; b. Caribou, Maine, July 17, 1958; d. Robert Eugene and Melba Fern (Davis) McN.; m. Lawrence West McLaine, Nov. 24, 1985. B.Edn., Ohio U., 1980; M.S., W.Va. U., 1981. Grad. asst. athletic trainer W.Va. U., 1980-81; head women's athletic trainer Iowa State U., Ames, 1981—. Recipient Al Hart Scholarship award, 1979-80. Mem. Nat. Athletic Trainers Assn., Iowa Athletic Trainers Assn. Methodist. Home: 505 25th St Ames IA 50010 Office: 111 Phys Edn Bldg Iowa State U Ames IA 50011

MCLANE, NANCY BAXTER, medical writer; b. Grand Rapids, Mich., Oct. 3, 1950; d. Robert Emerson and Mary (Knoblauch) Baxter; m. Edward Timothy McLane, May 23, 1982. B.A. in Journalism, Am. U., 1972. Asst. dir. publs. Am. Speech, Lang. and Hearing Assn., Washington, D.C., 1973-77; mng. editor Biomedia, Inc., Princeton, N.J., 1977-79; editor A.M. Best Co., Oldwick, N.J., 1979-81; mng. editor Continuing Profl. Edn. Ctr., Inc., Princeton, N.J., 1981-82; med. writer/editor Biomed. Info. Corp., N.Y.C., 1982-83; pres. McLane Media, Inc., Greenwich, N.J., 1983—. Mem. Am. Med. Writers Assn., Women in Communications. Home: PO Box 380 Ye Greate St Greenwich NJ 08323 Office: McLane Media Inc PO Box 380 Ye Greate St Greenwich NJ 08323

MCLANE, SUSAN, state legislator. Mem. N.H. Ho. of Reps., 1983-84; now mem. N.H. Senate. Republican. Office: NH Senate State Capitol Concord NH 03301*

MCLANE, WILHELMINA, pianist, educator; b. Franklin, Ohio, Sept. 30, 1910; d. George and Margaret (Brannon) McLane; B.M., Coll. Conservatory of Music Cin., 1932, M.M., 1934; student of Nadia Boulanger in France, 1963; student Am. Conservatory of Music, Chgo.; m. Edwin Sidney Vinnell, Jan. 22, 1957. Tchr. piano, Middletown, Ohio, 1950—; organist United Meth. Ch., Franklin, 1968—; asso. tchr., adjudicator Am. Scholarship Assn.; adjudicator Nat. Guild Piano Tchrs. Recipient Springer Gold Merit award, George Ward Nichols award. Mem. Am. Guild Piano Tchrs., Nat. Music Tchrs. Assn., Dayton Music, Am. Matthey Assn. (workshop mem.), Club. Home and studio: 1618 Gage Dr Middletown OH 45042

MCLANEY, PATRICIA HART, state official; b. New Haven, Apr. 23, 1945; d. Lloyd Garrison and Leone (Mathews) Hart; m. C. Knox McLaney III, Aug. 12, 1967; children—Laura Hayden, Tryon Mathews. B.S., U. Ala.-Tuscaloosa, 1967, M.A., 1969, postgrad., 1970. Tchr. pub. schs., Tuscaloosa and Montgomery, Ala., 1968-72; cons. Ala. Commn. on Higher Edn., Montgomery, 1972; asst. to dir. postsecondary services Ala. Dept. Edn., Montgomery, 1975-79, coordinator program for exceptional children, 1979-84, coordinator profl. devel. services, 1984—; cons. in field; adv. mem. Ala.'s Plan for Excellence in Edn., 1984-85. Bd. dirs. Jr. Coll. Prison Program, Alexandria City, Ala., 1977-80, Ala. Child Welfare Com., 1983-84. Delta Delta Delta scholar, 1978; recipient Outstanding Service award Ala. Assn. Jr. and Community Coll., 1980. Mem. Ala. Council Exceptional Children, Ala. Jr. Coll. Assn., Nat. Assn. State Dirs. Spl. Edn., Kappa Delta Epsilon. Democrat. Methodist. Avocations: travel; antique collecting. Home: Route 1 Box 448 Hope Hull AL 36043 Office: Ala Dept Edn Div Profl Services State Office Bldg Room 520 Montgomery AL 36106

MCLAREN, KETHA, library administrator. Head tech. services div. Hamilton Pub. Library, Ont., Can. Office: Hamilton Pub Library Tech Services Div 55 York Blvd Hamilton ON L8R 3K1 Canada

MCLAREN, MARILYN PATRICIA, packaging company administration and human resources manager, aviatrix, b. Jamaica, N.Y., July 5, 1942; d. Raymond Lionel and Katherine Marie (Doepp) Cowan; student public schs., also various aviation schs.; m. Richard Edward McLaren, July 17, 1976; 1 son, Paul William Hibner. Exec. sec. to chief design Wiedersum Assos., architects and engrs., Valley Stream, N.Y., 1960-61; officer mgr., interior designer Keith I. Hibner, architect, Hicksville and Garden City, N.Y., 1961-73; owner, pres. Hibner Atelier, Ltd., interior design and gen. constrn., Garden City, 1968-75; office mgr. Ward Assos./Planning Assos., architects and engrs., Bohemia, N.Y., 1975-76; flight/ground aviation instr. Islip Aviation, Ltd. (N.Y.), 1974-77; asst. to pres. Arkay Packaging Corp., Hauppauge, N.Y., 1977-86, in-house constrn. mgr., 1980-82, adminstrn. and human resources mgr., 1986—; ind. aviation flight/ground instr. airplane and instrument, 1977—; safety counselor FAA, 1974—, Eastern Region Counselor Coordinator, 1985-86; past bd. dirs., officer Aviation Council L.I.; founder Seminar on Air Travel for Everyone (S.A.F.E.), 1975, Fly-C-Cure/We Air Condition People, 1979. Mem. nat. panel Consumer arbitrators Nat. Consumer Arbitration Program, Better Bus. Bur. Lic. comml. pilot, flight and ground instr. Mem. Ninety-Nines (past chmn. L.I. chpt., founding internat. chmn. safety edn., Amelia Earhart Bronze medal 1975), Aircraft Owners and Pilots Assn., Nat. Assn. Flight Instrs., Am. Soc. Personnel Adminstrn. Specialist on fear of flying; author articles, seminar syllabus. Home: 3 Park St Lake Grove NY 11755 Office: 22 Arkay Dr Hauppauge NY 11787

MCLAUGHLIN, ANN DORE, govt. ofcl.; b. Newark, Nov. 16, 1941; d. Edward Joseph and Marie (Koellhoffer) Lauenstein; B.A., Marymount Coll., Tarrytown, N.Y., 1963; m. John Joseph McLaughlin, Aug. 23, 1975. Supr. network comml. schedule ABC, N.Y.C., 1963-66; dir. alumnae relations Marymount Coll., 1966-69; account exec. Meyers-Infoplan Internat., Inc., N.Y.C., 1969-71; dir. communications Presdl. Election Com., 1971-72; asst. to chmn., press sec. Presdl. Inaugural Com., 1972-73; dir. Office Pub. Affairs, EPA, 1973-74; with govt. relations dept., asst. dir. communications dept. Union Carbide Corp., Washington, N.Y.C., 1974-77; propr. McLaughlin & Co., pub. affairs, 1977-81; asst. sec. pub. affairs Treasury Dept., 1981-84; under sec. Dept. Interior, 1984—; dir. Nat. Savs. & Trust Co., Washington, 1977-78. Mem. Nat. Fedn. Republican Women (adv. com.). Clubs: Nat. Press, Fed. City (Washington). Office: Dept Interior 18th and C Sts NW Washington DC 20240

MCLAUGHLIN, CLARA JACKSON, television station executive; b. Brunswick, Ga., Oct. 22, 1946; d. Dave and Arnetta (Lundy) Jackson; m. Richard A. McLaughlin, Oct. 1968; children—Rinetta A., Ricky A. B.A., Howard U., 1972. Founder, chmn., chief exec. officer Sta. KLMG-TV, Longview, Tex., 1980—. Author: Black Parents' Handbook—A Guide to Healthy Pregnancy, Birth and Child Care, 1976. Bd. dirs. United Cerebral Palsy, Houston, 1976-80, chmn. bd., 1978-80; trustee Tex. So. U., Houston, 1978—; mem. Aux. to AMA, 1974—. Mem. Leadership Tex. Home: PO Box 91094 77291 Office: KLMG-TV East Texas Television Network Suite 430 10303 Northwest Freeway Houston TX 77092

MC LAUGHLIN, EMILY LYNN, cosmetic company executive; b. Fairmont, W.Va., Feb. 17, 1939; d. Albert Lynn and Martha Edith (Jenkins) Springston; B.A. in Elem. Edn., Fairmont State Coll., 1961; m. John Richard McLaughlin, June 17, 1961; children—Randy, Timothy, Steven. Elem. and nursery sch. tchr., 1961-63, 67-68; with Mary Kay Cosmetics Inc., 1971—, unit sales dir., Somerville, N.J., 1972-78, nat. sales dir., 1979—. Recipient numerous sales awards; mem. Mary Kay's Millionaire Club. Republican. Methodist. Address: 111 Flanders Dr Somerville NJ 08876

MCLAUGHLIN, KATHLEEN, educator; b. Paterson, N.J., Mar. 17, 1946; d. John George and Madeline Elizabeth (Morbell) McL. B.A. in Anthropology and Sociology, Bloomfield Coll., 1968; M.A.T. in Edn., Wm. Paterson Coll., 1972; 6th Yr. Degree in Edn., Fairfield U., 1984. Tchr. Paterson Bd. Edn., 1968-74, Wilton Bd. Edn., Conn., 1974—. Foster home for Danbury Animal Welfare Soc., Conn., 1978—. Mem. NEA, Wilton Edn. Assn. (bldg. rep. 1984—). Avocations: reading, sewing, needlework, gardening. Home: 138 Redding Rd Georgetown CT 06829 Office: Driscoll Sch 336 Belden Hill Wilton CT 06897

MCLAUGHLIN, KATHLEEN LOUISE, air force officer, logistician; b. Portchester, N.Y., June 18, 1954; d. Edward John and Carmel Dian (Carretta) McL.; m. Robert Bruce Monzie, Aug. 12, 1980. B.S. in Biology, N.Mex. State U., 1976; M.S. in Logistics, Air Force Inst. Tech., 1985; also various mil. courses. Commd. 2d lt. U.S. Air Force, 1978, advanced through grades to capt., 1985; squadron aircraft maintenance officer 438 Mil. Airlift Wing, McGuire AFB, N.J., 1978-79, C-141B Beddown Project officer, 1979-80, avionics flight control systems/instruments br. officer in charge, 1980-81, wing maintenance control duty officer, 1981, wing maintenance job control officer, 1981-82; comdr. Air Tng. Command Field Tng. Detachment 211, Griffiss AFB, N.Y., 1982-84; logistics plans and programs officer San Antonio Air Logistics Ctr., 1985—, also social activities coordinator, 1985—; sponsor Saudi Arabian officer aircraft maintenance officers course, Chanute AFB, Ill., 1978; crime prevention officer Griffiss AFB, 1983; mem., report consolidator Worldwide Comdrs. Conf., Sheppard AFB, Tex., 1983. Carpenter's asst. Champaign County His. Mus., Champaign, Ill., 1978; hugger N.J. Spl. Olympics, Wrightstown, 1979, 80; ofcl. base tour guide Jr. Air Force ROTC Cadets, McGuire AFB, 1980; base housing block capt. Wright-Patterson AFB, 1985. Named to Outstanding Young Woman Am., U.S. Jaycees, 1983; N.Mex. Rotary Club scholar N.Mex. State U., Las Cruces, 1972-73. Mem. Soc. Logistics Engrs., Nat. Assn. Female Execs., Air Force Inst. Tech. Assn. of Grads., Mil. Order of World Wars, Air Force Assn., Central Assn. of Miraculous Medal, Assn. Old Crows of Electronic Def. Assn., Strategic Air Command 200 Mile Club, Jr. Council World Affairs (Outstanding Mem. award 1971). Democrat. Roman Catholic. Club: Internat. Fitness Ctr. Avocations: running; weight training; reading; stamp collecting; writing. Home: 9935 Birch Field San Antonio TX 78245 Office: San Antonio Air Logistics Ctr MMTMC Bldg 171 San Antonio TX 78241

MCLAUGHLIN, THERESA DORSEY, lawyer; b. Biloxi, Miss., Apr. 30, 1944; d. Robert Dorsey and Helen Theresa (Maher) McLaughlin; m. Asim Hashim Al-Azzawi, Sept. 3, 1965 (div. 1979); children—Sarah A., Karim A.; m. 2d, Philip Walker Shaw, Jr., Nov. 19, 1983. B.A., Mich. State U., 1966, M.A., 1969; Ph.D., Mich. State U., 1973; J.D., Thomas M. Cooley Law Sch., 1982. Bar: Mich., Miss. Computer programmer Auto Owners Ins. Co., Lansing, Mich., 1966-68; instr. Lansing Community Coll., 1968-69; instr. Mich. State U., 1969-72, research assoc., 1972-74; analyst State of Mich., Lansing, 1974-82; atty. Levi & Denham, Ltd., Ocean Springs, Miss., 1983—. Mem. ABA, Mich. Bar Assn., Miss. Bar Assn., Miss. Trial Lawyers Assn., Gulf Coast Women Lawyers Assn. (treas.). Democrat. Unitarian Universalist. Office: Levi and Denham Ltd 424 Washington Ave Ocean Springs MS 39564

MCLAURIN, BARBARA PERRY, home economist, and nutrition specialist; b. Phila., Jan. 8, 1950; d. Allen Glenn and Doris Mae (Beery) Perry; m. Prentiss Cortez McLaurin, Jr., Aug. 23, 1970; 1 son, Prentiss III. B.S., Miss. State U., 1971, M.S., 1974. Registered dietitian Am. Dietetic Assn. Dietary supr. Felix Long Meml. Hosp., Starkville, Miss., 1971-72; research asst. Miss. State U., 1972-73, temporary instr., 1974, food and nutrition specialist Coop. Extension Service, 1976-84, staff coordinator and extension food and nutrition specialist, 1984—; instr. nutrition Miss. U. for Women, Columbus, 1974-76. Mem. exec. bd. Am. Diabetes Assn., Jackson, Miss., 1979-80. Mem. N.E. Miss. Dietetic Assn. (pres. 1977-78, named Outstanding Young Dietitian 1978), N.E. Miss. Home Econs. Assn. (pres. 1981-82), Gamma Sigma Delta (sec. 1982-83), Epsilon Sigma Phi (state rep. 1982). Baptist. Office: PO Box 5446 Mississippi State MS 39762

MCLAY, MARTHA, educational administrator; b. Portland, Maine, Sept. 18, 1939; d. Doric Preston and Annabelle Violet (Clark) C.; m. Daniel Allan McLay, Oct. 16, 1965; 1 child, Jason Allan. Student Bouve-Boston Coll., 1962; B.S. in Edn., Tufts U., 1962; M.S. in Edn., Nova U., 1982. Cert. tchr., adminstr. Instr. Harpur Coll., N.Y. State U., Binghamton, 1962-65; tchr. Burlington High Sch., Vt., 1965-66, Ganesha High Sch., Pomona, Calif., 1966-67, Enterprise High Sch., Redding, Calif., 1968-76, chmn. implementation of Title IX, 1973; tchr. Adirondack-Southern Sch., St. Petersburg, Fla., 1977-84, dean (headmistress), 1980-85; dir. academics Cedu Sch., Running Springs, Calif., 1985—; lectr. in field. Contbr. articles to profl. jours., poetry to mags. Debator LWV, Redding, 1968; active PTA, various locations. Recipient Service award Mid-Day Bus. and Profl. Women, St. Petersburg, 1984, Dedication awards Adirondack-Southern Sch. Yearbook, 1978, 85. Mem. AAHPER Fla. Council Ind. Schs., Bus. and Profl. Women (1st v.p. 1982-83, 84-85, pres. 1983-84). Republican. Club: WISP (Women Investors of St. Petersburg) (sec. 1982-83). Avocations: tennis; snow skiing; archery; fly-fishing; hiking. Office: Dir Academics Cedu Sch PO Box 1176 Running Springs CA 92382

MCLEAN, B(ONNIE) HEATHER, manufacturing company executive, photographer, ski instructor; b. Nyack, N.Y., Mar. 28, 1958; d. C. Clifford and Carol (Hunsicker) McL. A.A.S., Rochester Inst. Tech., 1978, B.F.A., 1980. Photog. sales person Blumenthals, Olean, N.Y., 1976-78; night mgr. clothing sales The Silo, Mt. Kisco, N.Y., part-time 1980-83; tech. sales rep. Majestech, Somers, N.Y., 1981-84; ski instr. Catamount, Hillsdale, N.Y., part-time 1981-84; regional mgr. Autotype USA, Elk Grove, Ill., 1984—; condr. screenmaking seminar Rochester Inst. Tech., 1986. Recipient Internat. Sales award Stretch Devices, Phila., 1983. Mem. Screen Printing Assn. Internat., Conn. Screen Printers Assn. (chpt. bd. dirs. 1982-83, sec. 1983-84), Profl. Ski Instrs. Am., Exec. Female. Episcopalian. Avocations: skiing, golf, music, aerobics, racquetball, sewing, photography. Office: 1525 Greenleaf Ave Elk Grove IL 60007

MCLEAN, RHONDA JOY, lawyer; b. Chgo., Aug. 15, 1952; d. John Wesley and Georgianna Virginia (Coles) McL. B.S., Aurora Coll., 1972; M.S., N.C. A&T State U., 1980; J.D., Yale U., 1983. Bar: Mich. Tng. coordinator Learning Inst. N.C., Greensboro, 1973-79; assoc. dir. State Tng. Officer for Head Start, Greensboro, 1979-80; law clk. to U.S. Dist. Judge, Detroit, 1983—; tutor Wayne State Law Sch., Detroit, 1984-85. Mem. N.C. Legal Services Bd., Raleigh, 1976-77; sec.-treas. Greensboro Legal Aid Bd., 1976-79; sec. NAACP Voter Edn. Project, Greensboro, 1977; mem. Trinity Ch. Soup Kitchen Staff, Detroit, 1984-85. Named Woman of Yr., Greensboro NAACP, 1978. Democrat. Presbyterian. Avocations: music; reading. Office: US Dist Ct 231 W Lafayette Blvd Suite 257 Detroit MI 48207

MCLEE, ANNA J., teacher; b. Chatman, Ala., Apr. 2, 1949; d. John Theodore Price and Clara Louise (Smith) Price Yarborough; m. Charles Dale McLee, Aug. 20, 1974. B.S. in Edn., Calif. State U., 1970; M.Ed., U. Pitts., 1983, postgrad., 1983—. Speech and hearing clinician Western State Sch. and Hosp., Cannosburg, Pa., 1970-71; tchr. Uniontown Sch. Dist., Pa., 1970-74, Penn Hills Sch. Dist., Pa., 1974-78; curriculum specialist Allegheny Intermediate Unit, Pitts., 1980-81; reading specialist Penn Hills Sch. Dist., Pa., 1979—; cons. Bidwell Trng. Ctr. Inc., Pitts., 1985—. Sunday sch. tchr. 6th Mt. Zion Baptist Ch., Pitts., 1980—. Mem. Am. Assn. Curriculum Devel., NEA, Pa. State Edn. Assn., Delta. Democrat. Club: College (Uniontown). Avocations: Reading;

working out at spa; travel. Home: 36 Nancy Dr Pittsburgh PA 15235 Office: Penn Hills High Sch 12200 Garland Dr Pittsburgh PA 15235

MCLELLAN, MARY THERESA, assistant state librarian, legislative researcher; b. Quincy, Mass., Feb. 25, 1927; d. John Patrick and Theresa Mary (O'Reilly) Johnson; m. George Bernard Savage, Nov. 2, 1947 (div. 1969); 1 dau., Kathleen Mary; m. 2d, Vincent Bernard McLellan, May 13, 1971; children—Vincent, Elaine, Mary Joy, Mark, Anne, Christopher. Student U. Mass. Extension, Boston, 1944-46, 63-65, Boston U., 1946-47, Inst. Govtl. Services, Boston, 1983-84, Suffolk U., Boston, 1976-78. Cert. librarian, Mass.; lic. real estate broker, Mass. Jr. asst. Thomas Crane Pub. Library, Quincy, 1944-46, sr. asst., 1947, 1962-69; asst. librarian Bethlehem Steel Co., Quincy, 1946; pvt. practice as real estate broker, 1953-62; reference librarian Mass. State Library, Boston, 1969-73, legis. reference librarian, 1973-82, asst. state librarian, 1982—. Author: Interns Guide to Legislative Research, 1973; Guide to Massachusetts Legislative and Government Research, 1981. Contbr. chpt. to Handbook of Legal Research in Massachusetts. Mem. Assn. Boston Law Libraries. Democrat. Roman Catholic. Office: Mass State Library 341 State House Boston MA 02133

MCLELLAN, SHIRLEY ANN, clinical nurse specialist; b. Franklin, N.C., July 2, 1935; d. Clifford B. and Callie L. (Stewart) Lawrence; m. Hebert C. White, June 10, 1957 (div. June 1976); children—Herbert, Linda D., Tina M.; m. 2d, Lee McLellan, Sept. 1, 1979. B.S., SUNY-Plattsburg, 1957, M.S. in Edn., 1966; M.S.N., Russell Sage Coll., 1975; M.S. in Ednl. Adminstrn., SUNY-Albany, 1976. R.N.; cert. specialist. Head nurse Physicians Hosp., Plattsburgh, 1959; tchr. New Lebanon Central Sch. (N.Y.), 1963-70; ESEA Title I dir. Pittsfield Pub. Schs. (Mass.), 1970-72; staff nurse Berkshire Med. Ctr., Pittsfield, 1966-73; clin. nurse specialist VA Med. Ctr., Albany, 1974—; mem. adj. faculty Russell Sage Coll., Troy, N.Y., 1983—. Mem. Assn. for Health Services Research, Am. Nurses Assn. Clin. specialist, nurse researcher, Am. Nurses Found., Assn. Internat. Urol. Sci. Inc., Am. Soc. for Parenteral and Enteral Nutrition. Club: Kripalu Yoga (Albany). Home: 249 Birdsall E Ave Battle Creek MI 49017

MCLENDON-MCCULLOUGH, BEVERLY J., city official; b. Daytona Beach, Fla., July 28, 1949; d. George McLendon Jr. and Bernice Lillian (Wiley-McLendon) Thompson; m. Tyrone L. McCullough, June 28, 1980; 1 dau., Kendle Joi. B.Sc., Ky. State U., 1971; M.Sc., Howard U., 1973. Adult edn. tchr. Washington Sch. Dist., 1972-73; curriculum specialist Howard U., Washington, 1971-73; price stabilization analyst Cost of Living Council, Washington, 1973-75; housing mgr. Community Devel. Div., City of Houston, 1975-79, housing adminstr., 1979-82; community liaison aide Police Dept., Houston, 1982—; cons. Social Systems Intervention, Washington, 1972-74. Co-author: (tng. manual), Training of Community Personnel in Health Maintenance Organizations, 1972. Mem. Am. Assn. Pub. Adminstrs., Omicron Nu. Democrat. Office: Office of Police Chief 61 Riesner Houston TX 77002

MCLEOD, BARBARA ANN, television producer; b. Chgo., Apr. 19, 1945; d. John Francis and Mignonne Elinor (Huffman) Burke; m. E. Bruce McLeod, Feb. 5, 1982. Student U. Chgo., summers 1964, 65; B.A. (univ. scholar), Purdue U., 1967; M.A. in Journalism, U. Ga., 1980. Programmer, data processing Time, Inc., Chgo., 1967, interviewer personnel dept., 1967-69, asst. employment mgr., 1969-70, dept. head mag. subscriber relations, 1970-72, mem. adminstrv. staff, 1972-76; promotion exec. Paul Harris Stores, Inc., Indpls., 1976-77; TV news producer Sta. WSB-TV, Atlanta, 1979-82; TV news producer Sta. WTSP-TV, St. Petersburg, Fla., 1982—; mng. dir. Ron Nielsen Photography, Nielsen Communications Team, Four Quarters, Chgo., 1973-76. Vol. Children's Meml. Hosp., 1969-72, Rehab. Inst. Chgo., 1973-76. Mem. Women in Communications, Inc. (2d v.p. membership 1974-75, chmn. hospitality com. 1973-74), U. Ga. Alumni Assn., Purdue Alumni Assn., Mortar Bd., Sigma Delta Chi, Zeta Tau Alpha. Presbyterian. Club: Tampa Bay Bulldog. Address: 5505 Seminary Rd 1603-N Falls Church VA 22041

MCLEOD, DEBORAH JACKSON, museum official; b. Little Compton, R.I., Aug. 20, 1915; d. Eugene Bailey and Caroline Wilbour (Patten) Jackson; grad. pvt. schs.; m. Harry McIntosh McLeod, June 19, 1934 (dec.); 1 dau., Penelope McLeod Beekman; m. 2d, Wilfred A. Dunderdale, May 19, 1980. With dept. reprodns. Met. Mus., N.Y.C., 1962-63; adminstrv. asst. U.S. Com. for UNICEF, 1955-59; mem. exec. com. Bklyn. Mus., 1974-77, gov., 1975-77; mem. exec. com. council of friends Inst. Fine Arts, N.Y. U. Pierpont Morgan Library fellow, 1975. Mem. Am. Assn. Museums (asso.), Internat. Council Museums, Friends of Asia Soc., Albert Gallatin Assos. Presbyterian. Club: Colony (N.Y.C.).

MCLEOD, MARILYNN HAYES, educational administrator, farmer; b. Lake View, S.C., Jan. 2, 1924; d. Cary Victor and Benna (Price) Hayes; B.A., Furman U.; M.Ed., U. S.C., 1952, postgrad., 1975; m. Charles Edward McLeod, Aug. 24, 1947; children—Cary Franklin, Mary Marilynn. Tchr., Hamer-Kentyre Sch., Hamer, S.C., 1944-45, Bennettsville (S.C.) City Schs., 1946-59, Clio (S.C.) Elem. Sch., 1960-63; asst. prof. elem. edn. St. Andrews Presbyn. Coll., Laurinburg, N.C., 1964-67; instr. U. S.C., Florence, 1971; reading supr. Marlboro County Sch. Dist., Bennettsville, S.C. 1967—; farmer, 1960—. Chmn. adminstrv. bd. Trinity United Meth. Ch., 1982—, chmn. pastor-parish relations com., 1979—. Mem. NEA, Internat. Reading Assn., S.C. Edn. Assn., S.C. Internat. Reading Assn., Marlboro County Edn. Assn., Pee Dee Internat. Reading Assn., Delta Kappa Gamma. Democrat. Methodist. Home: PO Box 38 S Main St Clio SC 29525 Office: 122 Broad St Bennettsville SC 29512

MCLEOD, NANCY JANE, city official; b. St. Louis, June 19, 1946; d. Kenneth Leroy and Velma Jane (Muchmore) McL.; B.A., U. Ariz., 1967, M.B.A., 1970; postgrad. Ariz. State U., 1981—. Adminstrv. aide LEAP dept. City of Phoenix, 1972-73, planning asst., 1973-74, chief program planner, 1974-75, planning coordinator dept. human resources, 1975-83, asst. dir. dept., 1983—. Mem. Bus. and Profl. Women's Club of Phoenix (1st v.p. 1978-80, pres. 1980-82), Soc. Advancement of Mgmt. (dir. 1977-81), Am. Mgmt. Assn., Am. Soc. Pub. Adminstrn., Am. Planning Assn., Acad. Polit. Sci., Internat. City Mgmt. Assn. Club: Toastmasters. Home: 3753 E Bloomfield Rd Phoenix AZ 85032 Office: 302 W Washington St Phoenix AZ 85003

MCLEOD, RENEE PARNELL, health association executive, nurse, educator, consultant; b. Winston-Salem, N.C., Nov. 13, 1953; d. Charles Edward and Edith Erline (Preston) Parnell; m. Eric Scott McLeod, June 14, 1975; children—Erin Erline, Logan Scott. B.S. in Nursing, U. Tenn.-Memphis, 1976, Pediactric Nurse Practitioner, 1976; M.S. in Nursing, U. Calif.-San Francisco, 1978. R.N.; cert. pediatric nurse practitioner. Faculty, U. LaVerne, San Francisco, 1978-81; propr. Kitsap Family Services, Poulsbo, Wash., 1982-83; dir. St. Joseph Hosp. Pediatric Diagnostic Ctr., Memphis, 1983-85, adminstrv. dir. St. Joseph Family Health Ctr., 1984-85; pres. Associated Health Mgmt., Germantown, Tenn., 1985—; LaLeche leader, LaLeche League, Philippines, Wash., San Francisco, 1978-81; instr. Preparation for Childbirth, Am. Acad. Husband Coached Childbirth, Seattle, 1978-82; counselor Child Abuse T.A.L.K. Line, San Francisco, 1976-78. Chmn.-elect Mid-South chpt. Nat. Multiple Sclerosis Soc., Temphis, 1986; co-chmn. legis. com. Memphis/Shelby County Children and Youth Council, chmn. early childhood care com., 1985; bd. dirs. Mayor's Com. for Handicapped, Memphis, 1985-86. Mem. Am. Nurses Assn., Tenn. Nurses Assn., Council Primary Care Nurse Practitioners, Am. Acad. Husband Coached Childbirth, Nat. Assn. Nurse Assocs. and Practitioners, Sigma Theta Tau. Democrat. Methodist. Avocations: Reading; swimming; scuba diving; bicycling. Home: 153 Country Pl Cordove TN 38018 Office: Associated Health Management Inc 1924 Exeter Suite 4 Germantown TN 38138

MCLIN, RHINE LANA, funeral director, educator; b. Dayton, Ohio, Oct. 3, 1948; d. C. Josef, Jr., and Bernice (Cottman) McL. B.A. in Sociology, Parsons Coll., 1969; M.Ed., Xavier U., Cin., 1972; postgrad. in law U. Dayton, 1974-76. Lic. funeral dir. and notary pub.; cert. tchr., Ohio. Tchr. Dayton Bd. Edn., 1970-72; divorce counselor Domestic Relations Ct., Dayton, 1972-73; law clk. Montgomery Common Pleas Ct., Dayton, 1973-74; v.p., mgr. McLin Funeral Homes, Dayton, 1972—; instr. Central State U., Wilberforce, Ohio, 1982—; speaker Dayton Pub. Schs., 1980—. Author 6-series article: Death and Dying, 1980. Adv. bd. Dayton Contemporary Dance Co., 1977, Montgomery County Welfare and Social Services, Dayton, 1983, Nat. Council on Women's Edn. Programs, 1980; mem. Democratic Voters League, Dayton, 1969; mem. Ohio Lottery Commn., 1983—. Recipient Friendship award St. Mark's Masonic Lodge 165, 1980, Brotherhood award Upshaw African Meth. Episcopal Ch., 1983, Recognition award Fed. Women's Program, Dayton, 1981; One in a Million award Columbus 10-City Rally of Nat. Council Negro Women, 1984. Mem. Nat. Funeral Dirs. Assn., Ohio Funeral Dirs. Assn., Montgomery County Funeral Dirs. Assn., Women Bus. Owners Assn., Delta Sigma Theta (recognition award 1981). Home: 1130 Germantown St Dayton OH 45408 Office: McLin Funeral Home Inc 1130 Germantown St Dayton OH 45408

MCLOON, MARILYN FOGG, real estate broker, executive; b. Norwood, Mass., Nov. 8, 1931; d. Lester Burton and Gertrude Emelia (Thompson) Fogg; m. Richard Fisher McLoon, May 23, 1953; children—Lauren, David, Amy Beth, Christopher, Wendy. Student Boston U., 1949-52. Tchr. br. Northeast Cons., Hamilton, Mass., 1968-76; sales assoc. Baribeau Agy., Wiscasset, Maine, 1980-81, Peter Coe Realty, Damariscotta, Maine, 1981-83; broker, owner Marilyn McLoon Real Estate, Damariscotta, 1984—; real estate broker Community-Home Improvement Project, Damariscotta, 1985-86. Mem. Lincoln County Realtors (pres. 1986—), Maine Assn. Realtors (2 coms.), Nat. Assn. Realtors, Realtor Nat. Mktg. Inst. (CRB candidate), Lincoln County Bd. (Realtor of Yr. 1985). Democrat. Episcopalian. Club, Hospital League (Damariscotta). Avocations: chamber music; needlework; raising labrador retrievers. Home: Shore Rd HC60 PO Box 119 Bremen ME 04551 Office: Marilyn McLoon Real Estate Bus Route 1 Water St Damariscotta/Wiscasset ME 04543

MCLOONE, JEANNE HOWE, interior designer, salesperson; b. Newark, Aug. 18, 1950; d. William Benjamin and Gloria Mae (Vela) Howe; m. Mark Edward McLoone, July 8, 1975 (div. July 1982); 1 child, Angus Howe. B.A., Mary Baldwin Coll., Staunton, Va., 1972. Asst. office mgr. Baker & Botts, Washington, 1973-74; asst. interior designer Jane Zivney Interiors, Phoenix, 1975-78; pres. Jeanne McLoone Designs, Inc., 1979—; interior design, sales Barrow's Furniture, Phoenix, 1983—; interior design Rosson House. Mem. Phoenix Art Mus., 1978—, league bd., 1982, co-chmn. Festival of Trees, 1982. Recipient cert. Assuidité Institut de Touraine, Tours, France, 1967. Mem. Inst. Bus. Designers. Republican. Episcopalian. Avocations: tennis; skiing; backpacking; gourmet cooking. Office: Barrow's Exec Furniture 2301 E Camelback Phoenix AZ 85016

MCLOUD, PATRICIA ANN, district court clerk; b. Ft. Dodge, Iowa, Jan. 10, 1938; d. Clifford Merle and Kathryn Elizabeth (Welch) Naser; m. Dennis James McLoud, Aug. 6, 1957; children—Steven James, Michael Dennis. Student pub. schs., Ft. Dodge. Asst. to county clk. Webster County Clerk's Office, Ft. Dodge, 1956-58; sec., bookkeeper Lazy Ike Corp., Ft. Dodge, 1959-60; legal sec. Hamilton & Schill, Ft. Dodge, 1960-61, Albert Habhab, Ft. Dodge, 1962-70; asst. to city clk. City Clerk's Office, Ft. Dodge, 1972-77; dist. ct. clk. Webster County, Ft. Dodge, 1977—. Mem. Webster County Democratic Central Com., Ft. Dodge, 1976—, Webster County Dem. Women's Com., 1976—; precinct chairperson Dem. party, Ft. Dodge, 1980-84; mem. Trinity Regional Hosp. Aux., Ft. Dodge, 1977—, Corpus Christi Ladies Aux., Ft. Dodge, 1948—. Mem. Iowa Clerk's of Dist. Ct. Assn. (dist. 1 pres. 1978-81, state pres. 1984—; Appreciation awards), Cath. Daus. of Am. Avocations: knitting; crocheting; fishing; antiquing. Home: 2715 N 13th Pl Fort Dodge IA 50501 Office: Clerk of Ct Webster County Courthouse Fort Dodge IA 50501

MC LOUGHLIN, ELLEN V(ERONICA), ret. editor; b. Utica, N.Y.; d. James Henry and Mary Frances (Riley) McLoughlin; student Utica Free Acad.; A.B., Smith Coll., 1915; postgrad. Radcliffe Coll., 1921-22; L.H.D., Lincoln Coll., 1949. Asst. editor woman's page Country Gentleman, 1915-17; circulation promoter Crowell Pub. Co., 1922-24; asst. advt. mgr. Grolier Soc., 1924-34, advt. mgr., 1934-41, editorial dir., 1947-59, v.p., 1956-64; mng. editor Book of Knowledge, Children's Ency., 1936-42, editor Book of Knowledge Annuals, 1940-53, Book of Knowledge, 1942-60, Story of Our Time, 1947-53, L'Encyclopedie de la Jeunesse, 1948-60, Le Livre de l'Annee, 1950-60, La Science Pour Tous, 1960-64. Pres. bd. trustees Cragsmoor (N.Y.) Library, 1967-70. Roman Catholic. Author: The Murder of Doctor Casenova (with Lucile Rathbun, Anetia McLoughlin), 1934. Contbr. verse to mags., articles to encys. Home: 500 Osceola Ave Apt 202 Winter Park FL 32789

MCMAHAN, ANNA PRINCE, songwriter, music publisher, construction company executive; b. Isabella, Tenn., May 28, 1935; d. Ulysses Gordon and Della Carrie (Hawkins) Prince; m. Robert L. McMahan, Apr. 6, 1972; children—Sandra, Teresa, Vandi. Student Carolina Sch. Broadcasting, 1963-66; Zion Diploma, Israel Bible Sch., Jerusalem, 1970; student United Christian Assn., 1976; Diploma Southwestern Tech. Coll., 1970. Songwriter Hank Locklin Music Co., Nashville, 1963-70; entertainer 1982 World's Fair, Knoxville, Tenn., 1982; ptnr., owner Prince Wholesale Bait Co., Canton, N.C., 1976-82, Grad Builders, Canton, 1982—; music publisher Broadcast Music, Inc., Nashville, 1982—. Songs recorded on RCA: I Feel a Cry Coming On, 1965 (#1 in Eng.), Best Part of Loving You, (#1 in Eng.), Anna, 1969 (Billboard 1970, recorded in Ireland 1974, hit in Europe); over 20 songs recorded to date. Cand. for county commnr. Democratic party Macon County, N.C., 1984; bd. dirs. Macon County Taxpayers Assn., Inc., 1984-84, vice pres. 1984—, bd. dirs. Head Start, Topton, N.C., 1969-73. Nominated Disting. Women N.C., N.C. Council on Status of Women, 1984, Jefferson award WYFF TV and Am. Inst. for Pub. Service, Outstanding Bus. Woman Small Bus. Adminstrn., 1984. Mem. Nashville Songwriters Assn. Internat. (moderator, tchr. 1984—), Fraternal Order Police. Democrat. Avocations: public speaking, fishing, bear hunting, walking, writing poetry. Home: 2131 Elm Hill Pike Apt F 134 Nashville TN 37210 Office: Grad Builders 9 Mingus Hill Rd Canton NC 28716

MCMAHAN, CELESTE TINA, architect, construction executive; b. Denver, Jan. 1, 1948; d. Frank McMahan and Jean Dolores (Graves) Kauno; m. George Cardinal Richards, Dec. 2, 1977. B. Urban Studies, U. Colo., 1976, M. Urban and Regional Planning, 1977, postgrad. in architecture, 1977. Cert. lymphologist; lic. real estate sales person. Housing sales coordinator Gt. Western United, Colorado City, 1970-74; dir. parks and recreation City Edgewater (Colo.), 1975-76; planner City Aurora (Colo.), 1976-77; project mgr., architect Stanford (Calif.) U., 1977-79; designer, facilities planners Sacramento Savs. & Loan, 1979-80; project mgr. Crocker Bank, San Francisco, 1980-81; team mgr. corp. real estate Bank of Am., San Francisco, 1981—; owner, mgr. McMahan Cons., Vallejo, Calif., 1979—. Author: A Market Analysis of Downtown Aurora, 1976; Housing Market and Population Projections, 1976; photographer: Tales from the Old Country, 1984. Mem. commn. Archtl. Rev. Bd., Environ. Beautification Commn., Menlo Park, Calif., 1978; mem. com. Gov.'s Housing Policy Com., Denver, 1976; archtl. com. San Francisco Traditional Jazz Found., 1984; bd. dirs. San Francisco Friends of Art Commn., 1984-86. Recipient Exceptional Performance award Bank Am., 1984, 86. U. Colo. grantee, 1974-77; WICHE intern, 1976. Mem. Nat. Assn. Female Execs., Orgn. Women Architects, AIA (assoc.), Nat. Assn., Corp. Real Estate Execs., Stanford U. Alumni Assn. Episcopalian. Club: Commonwealth. Home: 550 Battery 406 San Francisco CA 94111 Office: Bank America Corp Real Estate 560 Davis St San Francisco CA 94111

MCMAHON, CANDACE ANNE, bank security manager, educator; b. Chgo., Oct. 24, 1948; d. Frances Anthony and Alice Mary (Wilson) Zawaski; m. John Richard McMahon, Jan. 23, 1971, 1 dau., Galen Kathleen. B.S.E., No. Ill. U., 1971, M.S.E., 1981. Cert. tchr. Office mgr. car salesperson The Pit Stop, DeKalb, Ill., 1971-73; jr. and sr. high sch. tchr. Elgin Sch. Dist. (Ill.), 1973-81; agt FBI, 1981-82; asst. dir. security Sears Bank & Trust Co., Chgo., 1982-84; dir. security, asst. v.p. Exchange Nat. Bank, Chgo., 1984—; cons. Constl. Rights Found., Chgo., 1976-78. Co-founder criminal justice program Elgin Sch. Dist. Mem. Assn. Fin. Crime Investigators (research com.), Ex-FBI Agts. Assn., Spl. Agts. Assn., NEA. Democrat. Roman Catholic. Office: Exchange Nat Bank Security Div 120 S LaSalle St Chicago IL

MCMAHON, CATHERINE DRISCOLL, lawyer; b. Mineola, N.Y., Apr. 28, 1950; d. Matthew Joseph and Elizabeth (Driscoll) McM.; m. Gregory Arthur McGrath, Sept. 10, 1977; children—Elizabeth Driscoll, Kerry Margaret. B.A., Simmons Coll., 1972; J.D., Boston Coll., 1975; postgrad. Suffolk U., 1972-73; LL.M., NYU, 1980. Bar: N.Y. 1976, D.C. 1979, U.S. Supreme Ct. 1980. Tax atty. asst. Exxon Corp., N.Y.C., 1975-76, asst. tax atty., 1976-77, sr. tax atty., 1979-81; tax atty. Exxon Internat. Co., N.Y.C., 1977-79; tax mgr. Exxon Research & Enging. Co., Florham Park, N.J., 1981—. Bd. dirs. Southeast Morris chpt. ARC, Madison, N.J., 1983. Recipient TWIN award YMCA, Plainfield/Westfield, N.J., 1983. Mem. ABA, N.Y. State Bar Assn., D.C. Bar Assn. Roman Catholic. Office: Exxon Research & Engring Co PO Box 251 Florham Park NJ 07932

MCMAHON, LINDA SORRELL, state official; b. Raleigh, N.C., Sept. 8, 1946; d. Russell and Valeria (Garlington) Sorrell. B.A., Coll. William and Mary, 1968. Sec., NEH, Washington, 1968-69; legal sec. Williams, Eklund & Brown, Washington, 1969-70; legis. asst. U.S. Congressman William L. Dickinson, Washington, 1970-78; assoc. dir. U.S. C. of C., Washington, 1978-79; profl. staff mem. U.S. Senate Com. on Fin., Washington, 1979-81; assoc. commr. for family assistance Social Security Adminstrn., U.S. Dept. Health and Human Services, Washington, 1981-83; dir. Calif. Dept. Social Services, Sacramento, 1983—; subcom. chmn. Commn. on Child Support Devel. and Enforcement, Sacramento, 1983-84; mem. Life Care Contracts Adv. Bd., Sacramento, 1983-84; Calif. mem. Gov.'s Task Force on Child Abuse Prevention, 1984—, Gov.'s Com. for Employment of Handicapped, 1983—; mem. Gov.'s Task Force on Child Care, 1984-85; mem. Rep. Women's Forum, Washington, 1982-83. Recipient Commr.'s citation for creative mgmt. Social Security Adminstrn., 1982; Spl. Act or Service award for Outstanding Performance, U.S. Dept. Health and Human Services, 1983, Medallion award, 1983. Mem. Am. Pub. Welfare Assn., Am. Soc. Profl. and Exec. Women, Sacramento Urban League, Capitol Network. Office: Calif Dept Social Services 744 P St Sacramento CA 95814

MCMAHON, MARY FRANCES, state legislator, lawyer; b. Providence, Apr. 2, 1955; d. Paul Bernard and Mary Patrice (Schuette) McM.; B.A., St. Mary's Coll., 1977; J.D., Suffolk U., Boston, 1980. Bar: R.I., Mass. 1980. Assoc., McMahon, Hendel & Mc Mahon, Pawtucket, R.I., 1980—; mem. R.I. Ho. of Reps., 1981—. Chmn., Adv. Bd. Library Commrs., 1981—; mem. energy com. Nat. Conf. State Legislatures, 1981—. Mem. rules com. Democratic Nat. Com., 1984—. Mem. R.I. Bar Assn., Mass. Bar Assn. Roman Catholic. Office: 200 Main St Pawtucket RI 02860

MCMAHON, MARY JANE, rancher; b. Sonora, Calif., June 4, 1938; d. Wilbur Morgan and Mary Jane (Nicholson) McMahon. B.A., San Francisco State U., 1960; postgrad. San Jose State U., 1961-65. Tchr., Mountain View Unified Sch. Dist., Calif., 1960-69; owner, ptnr. Clothing Store, Ft. Bragg, Calif., 1969-84, J-J Ranch, Potter Valley, Calif., 1984—. Chmn. Am. Cancer Soc., Ft. Bragg, 1975; advisor Downtown Redevel. Agy., Ft. Bragg, 1978-80. Mem. Men's Wear Retail Assn., Am. Quarter Horse Assn., Pacific Coast Quarter Horse Assn., C. of C. Execs., Calif. Tchrs. Adv. Com., Mendocino County C. of C. (pres. 1984-85), Ft. Bragg-Mendocino Coast C. of C. (dir.). Democrat. Roman Catholic.

MCMAHON, YVONNE WADDELL, educational consultant; b. East Bernard, Tex., Nov. 23, 1940; d. William Robert and Ruth (Bernard) Waddell; m. Thomas Carter McMahon, Jan. 17, 1970 (div. Oct. 1978); children—Simone, Nicole. B.S., Lamar U., 1963; postgrad. St. Thomas U., 1968-69; M.Ednl. Psychology, U. Houston, 1972. Tchr., Houston Ind. Sch. Dist., 1963-70; ednl. diagnostician, 1972—; cons. spl. edn. and ednl. diagnostics, Houston, 1977—; cons. Harris County Dept. Edn., Houston, 1977. Teller, Nat. Women's Conf., Houston, 1977. Mem. Tex. Assn. Ednl. Diagnosticians (pres. 1978-79), Houston Met. Assn. Ednl. Diagnosticians (pres. 1976-77), Council Exceptional Children. Republican. Episcopalian. Clubs: Space City Ski, Sierra, Houston Ski, Single Profl. Men and Women (Houston). Home: 5123 Forest Haven Houston TX 77066

MCMANAMA, TRUDY E., psychologist; b. Pitts., Mar. 30, 1945; d. Francis J. and Mary Margaret (McDonough) Figura; m. Patick J. McManama, Nov. 25, 1967 (div. 1977); 1 child, Steven Patrick. B.S., Mansfield U., 1967; M.S., So. Conn. U., 1973, 6th yr. degree, 1974. Tchr. New Milford Schs., Conn., 1967-69; tchr. Shepaug Valley High Sch., Washington Depot, Conn., 1969-72; tng. cons. Danbury Area Unified Social Services, Conn., 1971-72; psychologist Bd. Coop. Services, Poughkeepsie, N.Y., 1974-75; psychologist Berrien County Ind. Sch. Dist., Berrien Springs, Mich., 1975—; cons. Stanley Clark Sch., South Bend, Ind., 1981—; adj. prof. Ind. U., South Bend, 1979—; instr. St. Joseph Hosp., South Bend, 1985—. Pres., Neighborhood Watch Program, South Bend, 1982-83; hospice vol., South Bend; bd. dirs. Child Abuse and Neglect Coordination Orgn., South Bend, 1986—; mem. Handicapped Camping Bd., 1986—; mem. Democratic Precinct Com., South Bend, 1980-82; del. Ind. Dem. State Conv., 1984. Berrien County Task Force grantee, 1979. Mem. Assn. Supervision and Curriculum Devel., Nat. Assn. Female Execs., Nat. Assn. Sch. Psychologists. Democrat. Roman Catholic. Avocations: Jogging; reading; cross country skiing. Home: 2725 Erskine Blvd South Bend IN 46614 Office: Berrien County Intermediate Sch Dist 711 St Joseph Ave Berrien Springs MI 49103

MCMANN, MARY ELIZABETH, counseling educator, consultant; b. Potsdam, N.Y., Aug. 24, 1954; d. John George and Catherine Burr (Tobin) McM. B.A., St. Lawrence U., 1976; M.A.T., Colgate U., 1977; M.S., Ed.S., SUNY-Albany, 1981. Continuing edn. media coordinator State U. Coll., Potsdam, 1977-78; caseworker Madison County Social Services, Wampsville, N.Y., 1978-79; coordinator undergrad. vols. SUNY, Albany, 1979-81; counselor SUNY Coll. Tech., Utica, 1981-82; asst. dir. career ctr. Hamilton Coll., Clinton, N.Y., 1982; devel. services coordinator, asst. prof. Onondaga Community Coll., Syracuse, N.Y., 1982—; career planning cons. to various community orgns., Syracuse, 1981—; assertiveness trainer YWCA, Utica, 1981-82; cons., trainer Anorexia-Bulimia Support Inc., Syracuse, 1983—, bd. dirs., 1984—. Mem. N.Y. State Assn. Two Yr. Colls., N.Y. State Personnel and Guidance Assn., Nat. Assn. Female Execs., Community Coll. Gen. Edn. Assn. Home: Westbrook Hills Syracuse NY 13215 Office: Dept Counseling Onondaga Coll Syracuse NY 13215

MCMANNIS, CYNTHIA ANN, dietitian; b. Canton, Ohio, Mar. 3, 1942; d. Georgia Alberta McM.; B.S. in Home Econs., Ohio U., 1964, M.B.A., 1984; dietitian cert. Drexel U., 1965. Therapeutic dietitian Lankenau Hosp., Phila., 1965-68; chief therapeutic dietitian Whelan Food Service at St. Mary Hosp., Phila., 1969-72; patient service dietitian Inst. Pa., Phila., 1972-75; patient service dietitian St. Vincent Hosp. and Med. Center, Toledo, 1975—; adv. Northwest Ohio Hosp., Institutional, Ednl. Food Service Soc. Committee woman Republican Party, Phila., 1972-74. Cert. food service mgr., vocat. tchr., Ohio. Mem. Am. Dietetic Assn. (registered dietitian), Ohio Dietetic Assn., Am. Mgmt. Assn. Republican. Methodist. Club: Pilot. Home: 1805 Brownstone Toledo OH 43614 Office: 2213 Cherry St Toledo OH 43608

MCMASTER, GLORIA MAE BUGNI, mezzo-soprano, educator; b. Montreal, Wis., Oct. 22, 1926; d. Anton George and Rose (Gatto) Bugni; m. Chester L. McMaster (dec. 1972); children—Chester Anthony, Raymond Dale, Brian Monroe, Maureen Anne, Heather Lynn; m. 2d, Martin Juhn, July 30, 1977. Student U. Minn.; B.S., Juilliard Sch. Music, N.Y.C.; postgrad. Columbia U., U. Detroit, SUNY-Brockport; Mus.M., Eastman Sch. Music, U. Rochester. Lic. real estate broker, Fla. Performed in concert, oratorio, opera throughout U.S., including solo appearances with Juilliard Opera Theater, Chautauqua Opera Assn., Rochester Opera Theater; appeared as soloist with Mpls. Symphony, Rochester (N.Y.) Philharm. Buffalo Philharm. Music Theater of Rochester, Eastman Rochester Symphony, Rochester, Hornell (N.Y.) Symphony; recitals at Youngstown, Ohio, Ironwood, Mich., Hornell, Alfred and Rochester, N.Y.; concerts Nazareth Art Ctr., Nat. Opera Assn., New Orleans; dir. Dansville (N.Y.) Music Theater; asst. prof. Youngstown State U., State U. Coll., Geneseo, N.Y.; assoc. prof. Houghton (N.Y.) Coll.; prof. music Alfred

(N.Y.) U.; co-owner, broker, salesperson Sarasun Properties, Sarasota, Fla. Appeared in title role Nat. Edn. Television prodn. The Medium. Mem. exec. com. Livingston County Young Republicans; mem. pres.'s leadership council U. Rochester. Mem. AAUW (pres. Dansville area br.), AAUP (chpt. exec. bd.), Nat. Opera Assn., Nat. Assn. Tchrs. Singing, Juilliard Alumni Assn., Eastman Alumni Assn., N.Y. Music Tchrs. Assn. Home: 8470 Mt Morris Rd Dansville NY 14437 also 2732 Proctor Rd Sarasota FL 33581

MCMATH, DORIS JEANNETTE BACCUS, instructional resource educator, consultant; b. Dallas, Aug. 12, 1927; d. Jasper and Edna (Nixon) Baccus; m. LeRoy McMath, Dec. 18, 1954; 1 dau., Linda. B.S., Tuskegee Inst., 1948; M.A., So. Meth. U., 1971; Dr. Metaphysics (hon.), Am. Bible Inst., 1981. Tchr. 3d grade Dallas Ind. Schs., 1948-51; instr. sci. Southwestern Christian Coll., Terrell, Tex., 1952-54; tchr. 5th grade Waco (Tex.) Pub. Schs., 1954-56; dir. early childhood Am. Sch., Phalsbourg, France, 1957-60; tchr. 2d grade Dallas Sch. Dist., 1965-71, instructional resource tchr., 1972—; curriculum writer Dallas Ind. Schs., 1975-76. Vol. dep. registrar Dallas County Tax Office, Dallas, 1979-81; membership chmn. YWCA, United Way, Dallas, 1983. Recipient Meritorious award Dallas Ind. Sch. Dist., 1977; Merit award Southwestern Christain Coll., 1978; Dedicated Service award Tex. State Tchrs. Assn., 1982; Goodwill People Travel Program award People to People Internat., 1983. Mem. NEA (del. conv. 1978-79), Internat. Reading Assn. (sec. 1978-79, mem. com. Tex. council 1984), Tex. Assn. Childhood Edn. (v.p. 1983-84), Dallas Assn. Childhood Edn. (pres. 1981-82), Classroom Tchrs. Dallas (faculty rep. 1979-82, service award 1979), Dallas Hist. Soc., Dallas Mus. Art, Internat. Platform Assn., Epsilon Delta Chi. Republican. Mem. Ch. of Christ. Club: Tuskegee (v.p. 1980-81) (Dallas). Home: 1817 Goldwood Dr Dallas TX 75232

MCMENAMIN, JOAN STITT, headmistress; b. N.Y.C., May 7, 1925; d. William Britton and Josephene Lloyd (White) Stitt; m. Edward B. McMenamin, Jan. 24, 1953. A.A. in Econs., Smith Coll., 1946. With Econ. Cooperation Adminstrn., Paris, 1949-50; office mgr. Ford Found., N.Y.C., 1951-52; history tchr. Nightingale-Bamford Sch., N.Y.C., 1962-63, asst. to headmistress, 1963-65, asst. headmistress, 1965-71, headmistress, 1971—; mem. adv. council for nonpub. schs. N.Y. State Commr. of Edn., 1985—; pres. Guild Ind. Schs. N.Y., 1983-85; mem. admissions com. Nat. Assn. Ind. Schs., 1977-79. Former vice chmn. English-Speaking Union Exchange Scholarship Program; former spl. advisor Parents League N.Y.; bd. dirs. Council for Religion in Ind. Schs., 1976-79, Ind. Sch. Orchs., Inc., 1980-84; trustee A Better Chance, Inc., 1977-83, The Town Sch., 1975-77, Buckley Sch., 1977—, Council for Basic Edn., Washington, 1978—, N.Y. State Assn. Ind. Schs., 1978—, Clark Found., 1979—, Robert Coll. of Istanbul, Turkey, 1979—, Ind. Ednl. Services, 1985—, WICAT Founds., 1976—. Mem. Nat. Assn. Prins. of Girls' Schs. (pres. 1983-85), Headmasters Assn., Country Day Sch. Headmasters Assn., Headmistresses Assn. of East. Democrat. Presbyterian. Club: Cosmopolitan (N.Y.-C.). Avocation: reading. Home: 14 E 90th St New York NY 10128 Office: Nightingale-Bamford Sch 20 E 92d St New York NY 10128

MCMICHAEL, BRENDA, financial executive; b. Raleigh, N.C., Aug. 7, 1953; d. Otis and Pearlena Mae (Dunn) McM. B.S.C., N.C. Central U., 1975; M.B.A., Atlanta U., 1978; grad. Sherrill's U. Cosmetology, Raleigh, N.C., 1985. Asst. sr. auditor Deloitte Haskins & Sells, Chattanooga, 1978-81; sr. fin. auditor Bullock's, Los Angeles, 1981-82; state auditor I Office of Auditor, Raleigh, N.C., 1983; acct. I, Div. of Health, Raleigh, 1984; owner Nails by Brenda, Raleigh, 1985—, M&L Acctg. and Fin., Raleigh, 1982—. Arbitrator Better Bus. Bur., Raleigh, 1985. Mem. Nail Aesthetician and Nail Artist Assn., Nat. Assn. Black Accts., Nat. Assn. Accts., N.C. Central Alumni Assn. (chmn. networking com. 1983—), Alpha Kappa Alpha. Democrat. Baptist. Clubs: Fletcher Grove Homemakers (pres.), Wake County Geneal. Soc. (Raleigh). Avocations: playing piano; tole painting; ceramics. Home: 5328 Montclair Dr Raleigh NC 27609 Office: PO Box 18743 Raleigh NC 27619

MCMILLAN, CAROLYN C(ECELIA), state official; b. Mobile, Ala., Aug. 16, 1946; d. Aaron and Rosina (Kinney) McM.; children—Brian, Caryn. Vet. rep. disabled vets. outreach program State of Calif., Los Angeles, 1977-78, local vets. employment rep., 1978-80; asst. state dir. vets. employment Dept. Labor, San Bernadino/Riverside County, Calif., 1980—; cons. in field. Bd. dirs. Calif. Vets. Affairs, Sacramento, 1982-83. Named to Outstanding Young Women Am., U.S. Jaycees, 1981; recipient Outstanding Community Achievement award Pres. Jimmy Carter, 1979, Fed. Exec. Bd., Los Angeles, 1982. Democrat. Office: Dept Labor 2160 Orange St Riverside CA 92501

MCMILLAN, LOIS EARGLE, lawyer, administrator; b. Columbia, S.C., Jan. 1, 1948; d. Claude Von and Miriam Lois (Campbell) Eargle; m. Thomas Sanders McMillan, III, Jan. 28, 1970; 1 son, Thomas Sanders IV. B.S., U. S.C., 1976, J.D., 1979. Bar: S.C. 1979. Acct., U. S.C., Columbia, 1968-72; ptnr. Shine, Graab & McMillan, Columbia, 1979-80; sole practice, Lexington, S.C., 1980-81; adminstrv. atty. Richbourg's Sales & Rentals, Columbia, 1981-83; loan adminstrn. officer State of S.C., Columbia, 1983—. Newsletter chmn. Lexington Republican Women's Club, 1983; den mother St. Stephen's Lutheran Ch., 1982-83. Mem. ABA, S.C. Bar Assn., Hist. Columbia Found., Riverbanks Zool. Soc. U. S.C. Alumni Assn. 1976—. Phi Beta Phi. Presbyterian. Office: South Carolina Jobs Economic Development Authority 1 Main Bldg 1203 Gervais St Columbia SC 29201

MC MILLAN, MARIE ELIZABETH (MRS. JAMES BATES MCMILLAN), casino executive, aviation director; b. Exeter, Calif., Aug. 1, 1926; d. James Martin and Eva Marie (Cash) Stever; student Calif. Sch. Fine Arts, 1943, U. Calif., 1944-45, San Jose State U., 1956; U. Nev., 1966, 75-76; m. James Bates McMillan, June 20, 1964; children—Michelle (dec.), John, Jeffrey. Sec., U. Calif. Radiation Lab., 1956-60; adminstrv. sec. AEC, Las Vegas, Nev., 1960-65; employment interviewer State of Nev. Employment Security, Las Vegas, 1965-67; mgr. McMillan Ranches, Reedley, Calif., also aviation lectr. and ferry pilot, 1974-80; v.p., aviation dir. Presdl. Casino, Port Harcourt, Nigeria, 1980—. Recipient Amelia Earhart medals, 1974, 76; named Woman Pilot of Yr., 1976-77, S.W. sect. 99's, Las Vegas chpt., 1973-76. Mem. The Ninety-Nines, Nat. Aero. Assn., All Woman Transcontinental Air Race Assn., Soaring Soc. Am., Aircraft Owners and Pilots Assn., CAP, Nev. Safety Council (aviation com.). Democrat. Holder world and U.S. nat. records for speed over recognized course between Fresno and Las Vegas, 1978, for time to climb 3,000 meters, 1979, holder 656 world and U.S. nat. aviation speed records from Las Vegas to Hermosillo, Mazatlán, Puerto Vallarta, Guadalajara, Mexico City, Acapulco (all Mexico) and return to Las Vegas, 1981, others. Home: 705 Twin Lakes Dr Las Vegas NV 89107 Office: Presidential Casino PMB 5141 Port Harcourt Nigeria

MCMILLAN, MARIE HUDSON, nursing home administrator, beautician; b. Lucedale, Miss., Aug. 30, 1931; d. Jessie Dewitt and Mollie Lonize (Mitchell) Dickson; m. Lynn Junior Brown, Aug. 9, 1947 (div. 1961); children—Jessie Dale, Lynda Gale, Jackie Jean, Lynn Junior, James Doug; m. Walter Wilson Hudson, Sept. 9, 1963 (div.); m. Mitchell Elwood McMillan, Aug. 27, 1982. Diploma Ala. Beauty Coll., 1956. Owner, operator Marie's Beauty Shop, Lucedale, 1957-63; bar tacker Lucedale Garment Co., 1961-63; owner, mgr., stylist Step-N-Style, Ocean Springs, Miss., 1963—; owner, stylist Ave. of Style, Ocean Springs, 1975-82; owner, mgr. T.L.C. Nursing Home, Ocean Springs, 1979—, Ocean Springs Manor, 1981—. T.L.C. nursing home featured on Sta. WLOX-TV, 1979; named Outstanding Citizen, Miss. Press, 1980. Democrat. Methodist. Avocation: fishing. Home: 9002 Travis Ave Ocean Springs MS 39564 Office: Ocean Springs Manor 614 Washington Ave Ocean Springs MS 39564

MCMILLEN, LINDA LOUISE, lawyer; b. Ft. Worth, Dec. 20, 1947; d. James M. and Helen Dorrace (Taylor) McM.; m. Burke William Biow, Dec. 30, 1968 (div. 1973); 1 child, Heather Lyn McMillen. B.S. with high honors, Tex. Wesleyan Coll., 1977; J.D., Baylor U., 1980. Bar: Tex. 1980. Collections sec. Ryan Mortgage Co., Arlington, Tex., 1973-75; law clk. Wash, Hodges & Segrest, Waco, Tex., 1978-79; atty. Kinkead Law Offices, Amarillo, 1980; lectr. bus. law, U. Tex.-Arlington, 1984-86; sole practice, Arlington, 1981—. Sec. bd. dirs. Am. Thai Found. for Edn., Arlington, 1983—, Am.-Thai Christian Found., Arlington, 1983—. Author: The Shadow of Man, 1983; Eiphaun, 1986. Mem. State Bar Tex., ABA, Tarrant County Family Bar Assn., Tarrant County Women Lawyers, Tarrant County Bar Assn., Arlington Bar Assn., others. Mem. Christian Ch. Address: 3605-A W Pioneer Pkwy Arlington TX 76013

MCMILLIN-WOOD, JEANIE BYRD, educator, scientist; b. Spartanburg, S.C., Sept. 26, 1939; d. Walter Louis and Frances Elizabeth (Austell) McMillin; B.A., Converse Coll., 1961; Ph.D. in Biochemistry, U. N.C., 1967; children—Elizabeth, David Emerson. Research assoc., instr. U. N.C., Chapel Hill, N.C., 1967-68; research assoc. Cornell Med. Coll., N.Y.C., 1968-69; instr. Baylor Coll. Medicine, Houston, 1969-72, asst. prof., 1972-80, assoc. prof. medicine, biochemistry and pediatrics, 1980-85, prof., 1985-86; prof. medicine and cell biology, dir. cardiac biochemistry U. Ala.-Birmingham, 1986—; cons. NIH, 1979—, mem. cardiovascular pulmonary study sect., 1982-86; mem. central research rev. com. Am. Heart Assn., 1981—, mem. exec. bd. Basic Sci. Council. Fulbright fellow in chemistry, 1961-62; NASA fellow, 1962-66; USPHS fellow, 1966-67; grantee Am. Heart Assn., 1978-81, Muscular Dystrophy Assn., 1980—, NIH, 1977—. Mem. Internat. Study Group for Research in Cardiac Metabolism, Biophys. Soc., Cardiac Muscle Soc., Am. Soc. Biol. Chemists, Am. Physiol. Soc., N.Y. Acad. Scis., Bioenergetics Club. Democrat. Editorial bd. Am. Jour. Physiology, 1980—, Circulation contbr. articles to various publs. Office: Dept Medicine Div Cardiovascular Disease U Ala Univ Station Birmingham AL 35294

MCMINN, TAMZIN MACDONALD, lawyer; b. N.Y.C., July 22, 1936; d. James R. and Jean (Scull) MacDonald; m. Robert William McMinn, July 2, 1958; children—Virginia, Donald R. B.A., Swarthmore Coll., 1958; M.A., Drew U., 1978; J.D., Rutgers U., 1981. Bar: N.J. 1981, U.S. Dist. Ct. N.J. 1981, U.S. Ct. Appeals (3d cir.) 1982. Fellow Drew U., Madison, N.J., 1980-82; assoc. Pitney, Hardin, Kipp & Szuch, Newark, also Morristown, N.J., 1981-84. Chmn. 25th Reunion fund drive Swarthmore Coll (Pa.), 1983; v.p. Chatham Twp. Bd. Edn. (N.J.), 1972-75; mem. Chatham Twp. Bd. Adjustment, 1975-77; bd. dirs. SE Morris unit ARC, Madison, 1984—. Named Vol. of Yr., Jr. League Morristown, 1976. Mem. ABA, N.J. Bar Assn. mem. spl. com. on plain lang. constracts 1981—), Morris County Bar Assn. Republican. Episcopalian. Clubs: Morris County Golf (Morristown); Chatham Colony (N.J.). Office: 375 Wychwood Rd Westfield Morristown NJ 07090

MC MONIGLE, PATRICE ANN, psychologist; b. Pitts., Sept. 27, 1949; d. Bernard and Anita (Bromberg) McM.; B.A. in Psychology, Radford Coll., 1971, M.A., 1972; Ph.D. in Indsl.-Organizational Psychology (fellow), Rice U., 1975; m. John Vaillant Gaudreau, May 19, 1973. Cons. psychologist Lifson, Wilson, Ferguson & Winick, Houston, 1975-78, Reid, Merrill, Brunson & Assocs., Denver, 1979-80; corp. psychologist Rohrer, Hibler and Replogle, Inc., Denver, 1980-84; cons. psychologist McMonigle Cons., 1984—; tchr. Denver U., Colo. Women's Coll., Loretto Heights Coll.; dir. Bayard Industries. Mem. nominating com. for bd. dirs. Mile High council Girl Scouts U.S. Mem. Am. Psychol. Assn., Colo. Indsl.-Organizational Psychol. Assn., Phi Kappa Phi, Denver C. of C., Leadership Denver. Contbr. articles to profl. jours. Home: 6551 Elaine Rd Evergreen CO 80439 Office: 1726 Cole Blvd Suite 325 Golden CO 80401

MCMORRIS, GRACE ELIZABETH, bank exec.; b. Malden, Mass., Feb. 6, 1922; d. John Edward and Selma Florence (Swanson) O'Brien; B.A., Boston U., 1944; postgrad. Ariz. State U., 1962; m. William Michael McMorris, May 14, 1944 (dec.); children—Sheila Elizabeth McMorris Christenson, Michael, James, John. Clk., Parlin Meml. Library, Everett, Mass., part-time, 1938-40; clk. student post office Boston U., 1941-42; supr. classified advt. desk The Boston Post, 1942-44; substitute tchr. public schs., Randolph, Mass., 1956-57; with Valley Nat. Bank Ariz., Phoenix, 1960—, trust adminstr., 1969-73; trust officer, 1973-75, asst. v.p., 1975-78, v.p., 1978—, corp. trust mgr., 1977—. Active PTA, Little League. Mem. Nat. Assn. Bank Women (sec. 1974-75, dir. 1973-75), North Central Ariz. Group, Western Stock Transfer Assn. (chair Rocky Mountain Sunbelt group 1983-84), Stock Transfer Assn. N.Y., Am. Soc. Corp. Secs., Valbanqueras, Pi Lambda Sigma. Roman Catholic. Home: 1936 N Illinois St Chandler AZ 85224 Office: 241 N Central Ave Phoenix AZ 85004

MCMULLEN, BARBARA ELIZABETH, data processing company executive, writer; b. Phila., Aug. 2, 1942; d. Walter Woodrow and Nellie Elizabeth (Rojewski) Ludman; m. John F. McMullen, May 12, 1978; stepchildren—Claire Ann, Luke John. B.S. in Math., Pa. State U., 1963; postgrad. Pratt Inst., 1971, N.Y. Sch. Interior Design, 1973; M.P.A. in Pub. Fin., NYU, 1976. Supr. AT&T, Mt. Kisco, N.Y., 1963-65; sr. programmer Pan Am. World Airways, N.Y.C., 1965-67; analyst N.Y. Stock Exchange, N.Y.C., 1967-69; project leader Bache Halsey Stuart, N.Y.C., 1974-76; mgr. Morgan Stanley & Co., N.Y.C., 1976-78; pres. McMullen & McMullen, Inc., Jefferson Valley, N.Y., 1978—; mem. faculty NYU, 1980-82, New Sch. for Social Research, N.Y.C., 1981—. Author: (with John F. McMullen) Microcomputer Communications, 1982. Contbg. editor Computers & Electronics, 1981-85, Computer Living, 1985—, Computer Shopper, 1985—. Contbr. chpt. to book, articles to profl. jours. Recipient Lepesqueur award N.Y.U., 1976. Bd. dirs. Osceola Heights Assn., Jefferson Valley, 1984. Mem. Big Apple Users Group (sec. and bd. dirs. 1981-84), Boston Computer Soc., Assn. for Computing Machinery, N.Y. Personal Computer Club (sec., bd. dirs. 1982—), N.Y. Amateur Computer Club, Westchester IBM Users Group. Roman Catholic. Clubs: Downtown Athletic (N.Y.C.); Jefferson Valley Racquet (N.Y.). Avocations: private pilot; painting; needlework; tropical fish breeding; amateur radio. Home: Perry St Jefferson Valley NY 10535 Office: McMullen & McMullen Inc McM Plaza Jefferson Valley NY 10535

MCMULLEN, CAROL BUECHNER, manufacturing company human resource executive; b. Jersey City, Sept. 3, 1929; d. Clarence A. and Elsie (Erdman) Buechner; m. Randolph B. McMullen, June 16, 1951; children—Gail, Carolyn, Randolph. B.A., Moravian Coll., 1951. System service supr. Info. Sci., Montvale, N.J., 1970-76, systems analyst, 1976-79; human resource systems supr. Grand Met. U.S.A., Montvale, 1979-84; personnel systems mgr. Lehn & Fink Products Group, Sterling Drug Inc., Montvale, 1984—. Mem. Assn. for Women in Computing (v.p. program 1983-84), Human Resource Systems Profession, NOW, AAUW, LWV. Republican. Home: 55 Montebello Rd Suffern NY 10201 Office: Lehn & Fink Products 225 Summit Ave Montvale NJ 07645

MCMULLEN, CAROLINE LOVELL, foundation executive; b. St. Petersburg, Fla., June 25, 1954; d. Richard Park McMullen and Caroline Lovell (Johnson) McMullen Pyott. A.B., Smith Coll., 1976. Program officer John M. Olin Found., N.Y.C., 1979-82, spl. asst. to dir., 1983—; spl. asst. to chmn. Nat. Endowment for Arts, Washington, 1982-83. Vice pres. N.Y. Jr. League, N.Y.C., 1985; bd. dirs. Halt-Ams. for Legal Reform., 1986—. Republican. Episcopalian. Club: Cosmopolitan (N.Y.C.). Home: 301 E 87th St New York NY 10128 Office: John M Olin Foundation 100 Park Ave Room 2701 New York NY 10017

MCMULLEN, SUSAN MARIE, business services company executive; b. Hartford, Conn., Nov. 11, 1951; d. Walter Joseph and Helen Frances (Hay) McM.; m. Thaddeus Carlo Pencikowski, May 10, 1974; children—Zachariah, Christopher. Student Albertus Magnus Coll., 1970-71; B.A., Trinity Coll., Hartford, Conn., 1974; student Ecole des Sciences Politiques, Paris, 1972-73; postgrad. Sch. Law, U. Conn., 1974-76. Owner, operator Simsbury Telephone Answering Service, Conn., 1976-82; pres. Advance Communications, Inc., Farmington, Conn., 1982—. Mem. Simsbury Democratic Town Com., 1982-83. Mem. Conn. Assn. Telephone Answering Services (pres. 1985-86, bd. dirs. 1983-85), Nat. Assn. Secretarial Services, Nat. Assn. Female Execs., Farmington C. of C., Simsbury C. of C. Roman Catholic. Home: 19 Riverside Rd Simsbury CT 06070 Office: Advance Communications Inc 790 Farmington Ave Farmington CT 06032

MCMULLIN, MARY JO, nurse; b. Sedalia, Mo., July 8, 1933; d. Robert Henry and Rose Mary (Alt) Welliver; R.N., St. Mary's Hosp., Kansas City, Mo., 1954; m. Jesse Francis McMullin, Nov. 26, 1955; children—James, Tom, Rose, Jane. Staff nurse St. Mary's Hosp., 1954-55; night nursing staff Bothwell Hosp., Sedalia, Mo., 1955-58, head nurse, 1958-70, asst. dir. nursing, 1970-83, dir. patient care services, 1983-85, dir. nursing, 1985—, tchr. stoma care, 1976—. 4-H Club leader, 1975—; pres. Pettis County Extension Council, 1983-84. Mem. Am. Nursing Assn., Mo. Nursing Assn., 10th Dist. Nursing Assn. (v.p. 1982), Profl. Nurses Assn. Bothwell Hosp. Roman Catholic. Home: Route 2 La Monte MO 65337 Office: PO Box 1706 Sedalia MO 65301

MCMURDO, MARY-JANE, state legislator. State denator democrat, Hawaii dist. 15, 1985—. Office: Hawaii State Senate State Capitol Honolulu HI 96813*

MCMURRAY, DEBORAH HANSON, financial public relations and marketing consultant; b. Willmar, Minn., Sept. 24, 1953; d. Willard Julian and Muriel Joy (Jones) Hanson; m. Allan Ray McMurray, July 9, 1977 (div. Nov. 1980); m. Boyd J. Tomasetti, May 4, 1984. B.A., Gustavus Adolphus Coll., 1975; M.Mus., U. Mich., 1977. Registered rep., Nat. Assn. Security Dealers. Instr. Interlochen Arts Acad., Mich., 1977-78; dir. spl. events March of Dimes, Denver, 1978-81; dir. mitg. Granite Corp., Denver, 1981-82; cons. fin. pub. relations and mktg., Denver, 1982—; fin. pub. relations specialist EMCOR Petroleum, Denver, 1984; cons. Arthur Andersen & Co., Denver, 1985—. Vol., adv. mem. March of Dimes, Denver, 1981—; mem. Denver Ctr. Players. Mem. Nat. Investor Relations Inst. Republican. Methodist. Club: PEO (pres. 1984-85). Avocations: aerobic exercise, reading, cooking, outdoor activities. Office: 1600 Stout St Suite 1100 Denver CO 80202

MCMURRIN, TRUDY ANN, university press director; b. Los Angeles, May 28, 1944; d. Sterling Moss and Natalie (Cotterel) McMurrin; B.A. in History and Philosophy, U. Utah, 1981; m. William M. Howard, Mar. 9, 1963 (div. 1967); m. 2d. Robert Bruce Evans, Sept. 24, 1969 (div. 1971); m. 3d, Mick McAllister, June 16, 1982; 1 dau., Natalie Roberta Howard. Editor U. Utah Press, Salt Lake City, 1967-74, asst. dir., 1974-80, editor-in-chief, 1980-83; dir. So. Meth. U. Press, 1983—; cons., lectr. for groups and agys., 1967—; art dir., co-designer award winning books, 1972—. Mem. Coalition to Save Our Sch. Libraries, 1981—; mem. adv. bd. Children's Mus. Utah, 1979-81; mem. Com. for Rowland Hall-St. Mark's Sch. Centennial Symposium Quality in Pre-Coll. Edn., 1980-81. Nat. Endowment Humanities fellow, Am. Assn. State and Local History 1977; Inst. Am. West fellow, 1981, 82. Mem. Assn. Utah Pubs. (pres. 1978-83), Assn. Am. Univ. Presses, Western Univ. Presses, Western Lit. Assn., Western Writers Am., Medieval Acad. Am., Dallas Opera Guild, Dallas Symphony Orch. League, Colophon, Friends Dallas Pub. Library, Tex. Hist. Assn., Tex. Folklore Soc., Southwestern Booksellers' Assn., Tex. Pub. Assn., Friends Archives. Office: So Meth U Press Box 415 Dallas TX 75275

MCMURRY, CHERYL SUZANNE, health care planner, lawyer; b. Selma, Ala., June 24, 1950; d. James Clive and Martha Sue (Walton) McM. B.S., Auburn U., 1972; M.A.T., Winthrop Coll., 1974; M.P.A., U. S.C., 1977, J.D., 1977. Bar: S.C. 1977. Ptnr., Kohn, McMurry & Wengrow, Columbia, S.C., 1978-80; dir. pub. affairs FHWA, U.S. Dept. Transp., Washington, 1980, chief counsel, 1980-81; dir. client service MetPath, Inc., Teterboro, N.J., 1981-82, spl. counsel to chmn., 1982-83, planning dir., 1983—; cons. Airport Enterprises, Inc., Chgo., 1983—. Contbg. author: Yearbook of Law and Edn., 1976, 77; Jour. Law and Edn., 1980. Mem. ABA, S.C. Bar Assn., Phi Kappa Phi, Kappa Kappa Gamma. Democrat. Presbyterian. Home: 770 Anderson Ave Apt 9P Cliffside Park NJ 07010 Office: MetPath Inc 1 Malcolm St Hackensack NJ 07608

MCMURTRY, CLARA LOUISE, educator; b. Clarence, Iowa, Jan. 17, 1916; d. William Frederick and Bertha Caroline (Lightjohann) Keller; m. Glen Eldon McMurtry, Nov. 25, 1938; children—Ronald, Larry, Anita. B.S., Mankato State U., 1967; Diploma, Mankato State Tchrs. Coll., 1936. Elem. tchr. Rural Sch., Triumph, Minn., 1936-37, Welcome, Minn., 1937-40, Dunnell, Minn., 1940-42; tchr. grade 5, Ceylon Pub. Sch., Minn., 1954-74, grades 5-6, 1974-83. Mem. Minn. Edn. Assn., Ceylon Edn. Assn. (pres. 1970-71). Methodist. Address: Welcome MN 56181

MCNAB, SUSAN ELIZABETH, human resources executive; b. Chgo., Nov. 4, 1949; d. James Orville and Betty Edith (Westlake) McN. B.A., Purdue U., 1971; M.A, U. Md., 1977; M.B.A., U. Puget Sound, 1984. Assoc. buyer Procter & Gamble, Cin., 1971-72; counselor U. Md.-College Park, 1972-73; personnel cons. Girl Scouts U.S.A., Burlingame, Calif., 1973-76; personnel and safety supt. Monsanto Corp., Seattle, 1976-80, mgr. personnel, St. Louis, 1980-82; dir. personnel Lanoga Corp., Seattle, 1982-85, v.p., 1986—; cons. Performex Corp., 1983—, Pacific N.W. Personnel Assn., 1983; lectr. Contbg. author: Strike Preparation Manual, 1982; contbr. articles to profl. jours. Pres. Totem council Girl Scouts U.S.A., Seattle, 1983; bd. dirs. Seattle Seafair Orgn., 1980, Gov.'s Com. for Handicapped, St. Louis, 1980-82. Named Time Mag. Newsmaker of Tomorrow, 1978; Community Action award, Girl Scouts U.S.A., 1980; Outstanding Sr. Woman, Purdue U., 1971. Mem. Am. Soc. Personnel Adminstrn. (nat. com. employee and labor relations), Pacific N.W. Personnel Mgmt. Assn., Pacific N.W. Personnel Assn. (dir. 1979-80). Roman Catholic. Club: Wash. Athletic. Home: 2515 20th Ave E Seattle WA 98112 Office: Lanoga Corp 1400 Norton Bldg Seattle WA 98104

MCNAIR, LOIS I. D., speech therapist; b. New Brunswick, Can.; d. George W. and Mary (McColl) McN.; B.Sc., Emerson Coll., 1967; M.Ed., Boston State Coll., 1969, postgrad., 1969-70; postgrad. Boston U., 1975-76; Ph.D., Heed U., Fla., 1982. Radiologic technician Can. Dept. Vets. Affairs, 1947-62, 67-68; tchr. speech and hearing Boston Sch. System, 1969; radiographer Radiologic Group Greater Boston, 1970-71; counselor, tchr. speech and hearing Manchester (N.H.) Sch. System, 1970-71; tchr. speech therapy Houlton (Maine) Sch. System, 1972—; mem. Nat. Stuttering Project. Cert. tchr., Maine, Mass., N.H. Mem. Can. Med. Radiation Technologists, Royal Soc. Health, Nat. Council Family Relations, NEA, Am. Personnel and Guidance Assn., Maine Personnel and Guidance Assn., Maine Speech and Hearing Assn., Am. Public Health Assn., AAAS, Speech Communication Assn. Home: PO Box 393 Houlton ME 04730

MCNAIR, ODESSA HARDISON, educator; b. Ft. Valley, Ga., Jan. 14, 1931; d. John and Fannie Mae (Hamilton) Hardison; m. Raymond McNair, Jan. 20, 1960. B.S., Ft. Valley State Coll., 1954; M.S., Ph.D., Internat. Coll., Los Angeles, 1981. Instr., Harris County Bd. Edn. (Ga.), 1954-56; sec. Ft. Valley State Coll., 1956-60; instr. Los Angeles Unified Sch. Dist., 1962—. Mem. adv. council Washington Adult Sch.; bd. dirs. Fremont Adult Sch., acad. chairperson, gen. chairperson accreditation com.; sec. bd. stewards St. James A.M.E. Ch., Los Angeles, 1st v.p., local lay orgn., mem. sr. choir, sec. quar. conf., Central Los Angeles-San Bernardino Dist.; asst. to pres. 5th Dist. Lay Orgn., chairperson edn. dept.; sec. So. Calif. Conf. Econ. Devel. Fund; pub. relations dir. So. Calif. Conf. Lay Orgn. Recipient certs. Recognition, City of Los Angeles, 1977, 79, State of Calif., 1980; cert. of merit County of Los Angeles, 1979; Outstanding Tchr.'s award, 1981; Outstanding Service award St. James A.M.E. Ch., 1977-81; Community Service award Watts Health Found., 1983; cert. spl. recognition Congress of U.S. Mem. Classroom Tchrs., Adult Edn. Assn. Democrat. Club: Community Improvement. Home: 636 W 80th St Los Angeles CA 90044

MCNAIR, RITA HADLEY, education educator, consulant; b. Mobile, Ala., Aug. 8, 1939; d. William Moore and Wilma (Funchess) Hadley; m. Donald Wesley McNair, Dec. 1968; children—Gary, Amy, Scott. B.E., Nat. Coll. Edn., Chgo., 1968; M.Ed., U. South Ala., 1982; Ed.D., Auburn U., 1985. Owner, McNair Antiques, Glen Ellyn, Ill., 1970-78; sales assoc. 1st United Realtors, Glen Ellyn, 1972-73; tchr. pub. schs., Glen Ellyn, 1973-77; teaching fellow early childhood and elem. edn. U. South Ala., Mobile, 1982-84, adj. prof. early childhood and elem. edn., 1985—, instr. continuing edn., 1984—; cons. Mobile Consortium, 1984-85; curriculum specialist South Ala. Inst., Mobile, 1984—. Contbr. articles to profl. pubs. Dir. South Baldwin Chamber Theater, Gulf Shores, Ala., 1982—; mem. altar guild St. Paul's Episcopal Chapel, Magnolia Springs, Ala., 1982—; sec. Magnolia Springs Community Assn., 1982—. Recipient Outstanding Achievement award Glen Ellyn Jr. Women's Club, 1972. Named Outstanding Cast Mem., South Baldwin Theater, Gulf Shores, 1983. Mem. Ala. Council Computers in Edn., Assn. Supervision and Curriculum Devel., Internat. Reading Assn., Ala. Reading Assn., Met. Mobile Reading Assn., Foley Performing Arts Assn., Kappa Delta. Democrat. Home: Box 173 Magnolia Springs AL 36555 Office: South Ala Inst 254 Old Bay Front Dr Mobile AL 36615

MCNAIR-DOCKE, JULIA LYNN, editor, writer; b. Meridian, Miss., June 6, 1946; d. Robert Edward and Pauline Jean (Hicks) Brewer; m. Henry L. McNair III, Jan. 18, 1967 (dec. July 1972); 1 dau., Sonya Lynn; m. 2d, John Docke Jr., June 5, 1982. B.A. in English, Miss. State U., 1966; M.A. in Journalism, U. Miss., 1979. Spl. investigator Juvenile Ct. Travis County, Austin, Tex., 1966-67; yearbook adviser U. Tex., Austin, 1969-72; freelance copywriter, Dallas, 1973-79; communications dir. Southwest Homefurnishings Assn., Dallas, 1980-82; mng. editor Profl. Furniture Mcht., Coral Springs, Fla., 1982-83, editor, 1983—. Mem. Women in Communications, Nat. Home Fashions League, Sigma Delta Chi. Episcopalian. Club: Toastmasters (Fla.).

MCNALLY-CURTIS, PATRICIA ANN, travel company executive; b. Worcester, Mass., Oct. 16, 1945; d. James Irving and Loretta Alice (Girard) McNally; m. Geoffrey John Padfield Curtis, May 25, 1980. B.S., Clark U., 1970; M.Ed., U. Mass., 1975, Ed.D., 1980. Pres., treas. Travel Concepts, Inc., Boston, 1982—. Author: From Decadence to Paradox, 1981. Democrat. Avocations: writing; skiing.

MCNAMARA, ANN DOWD, medical technologist; b. Detroit, Oct. 17, 1924; d. Frank Raymond and Frances Mae (Ayling) Sullivan; B.S., Wayne State U., 1947; m. Thomas Stephen Dowd, Apr. 23, 1949 (dec. 1980); children—Cynthia Dowd Restuccia, Kevin Thomas Dowd; m. Robert Abbott McNamara, June 15, 1985. Med. technologist Woman's Hosp. (now Hutzel Hosp.), Detroit, 1946-52, St. James Clin. Lab., Detroit, 1960-62; supr. histo-pathology lab. Hutzel Hosp., Detroit, 1962-72, Mt. Carmel Mercy Hosp., 1972—. Mem. Am. Soc. Clin. Pathologists, Am. Soc. Med. Technology, Mich. Soc. Med. Technology, Nat. Soc. Histotechnology, Mich. Soc. Histotechnologists, Wayne State U. Alumni Assn., Smithsonian Assos., Detroit Inst. Arts Founders Soc. Home: 29231 Oak Point Dr Farmington Hills MI 48018 Office: 6071 W Outer Dr Detroit MI 48235

MCNAMARA, JANET L., real estate broker; b. Rossville, Pa., d. Willard Lucian and Alice (Bream) McMurtrie. Student York Coll., 1963-66. Grad. Realtors Inst. Instr., Concord, N.H., 1980-84; owner, mgr. Hampton Marine, East Hampton, N.Y., 1969-70; mgr. Vt. Equities, Ltd., 1970-79; owner, mgr. McNamara Real Estate, Wilmington, Vt., 1979—. Co-chmn. Windham County Republican Com. for Gov. and State Rep., 1984, also Town of Wilmington Com. Mem. Phi Theta Kappa, Sigma Tau Sigma. Lutheran. Avocations: skiing; sailing; hiking; cycling; golf. Home: Box 231 Wilmington VT 05363 Office: McNamara Real Estate Route 100 Box 575 Wilmington VT 05363

MC NAMARA, MARY ELLEN, marketing executive; b. Long Branch, N.J., May 26, 1942; d. Edward Ward and Alice Marie (Reynolds) McN.; B.A., Glassboro State U., 1965; M.B.A., N.Y.U., 1975, Advanced Profl. Cert., 1980. Tech. asst. Bell Labs., Holmdel, N.J., 1965-66, sr. tech. asst., 1966-68; programming writer, analyst IBM, N.Y.C., 1968-71, systems programmer, 1971-72, bus. planner, 1972-74, industry planning adminstrn., Princeton, N.J., 1974-77, industry mktg. adminstr., 1977-81, product mktg. adminstr., White Plains, N.Y., 1981-83, mgr. engrng. sci. programming, Boca Raton, Fla., 1983-84, mem. market research staff, White Plains, N.Y., 1984-85, mgr. market devel., Valhalla, N.Y., 1986—. Mem. IEEE (sr. mem., vice chmn. Palm Beach sect. 1984), AAAS, Assn. Computing Machinery, AAUW, Assn. Women in Computing, Nat. Council Women U.S.A., Women's Econ. Roundtable, Exec. Women of Palm Beaches, N.Y. Acad. Sci., N.Y. U. Alumni Assn., Glassboro State U. Alumni Assn., Beta Gamma Sigma. Republican. Roman Catholic. Home: PO Box 21 Allenhurst NJ 07711 Office: 400 Columbus Ave Valhalla NY 10595

MCNAMEE, SISTER CATHERINE T., nun, educational association administrator; b. Troy, N.Y., Nov. 13, 1931; d. Thomas Ignatius and Kathryn Elizabeth (Quinn) McN.; B.A., Coll. of St. Rose, 1953, D.H.L., 1975; M.Ed., Boston Coll., 1955, M.A., 1958; Ph.D., U. Madrid, 1967. Joined Sisters of St. Joseph of Carondelet, Roman Catholic Ch., 1957; tchr. Spanish and Latin, Gilbertsville (N.Y.) Central Sch., 1953-54; asst. registrar Boston Coll. Grad. Sch., Chestnut Hill, Mass., 1955-57; tchr. Spanish and history McCloskey Meml. High Sch., Albany, N.Y., 1960-61; assoc. prof. Spanish, Coll. of St. Rose, Albany, 1961-75, v.p. acad. affairs, 1968-75; dir. liberal arts Thomas Edison State Coll., Trenton, N.J., 1975-76; pres. Trinity Coll., Burlington, Vt., 1976-79, Coll. St. Catherine, St. Paul, 1979-84; dean Dexter Hanley Coll., U. Scranton, 1984-86; pres. Nat. Cath. Ednl. Assn., Washington, 1986—. Bd. dirs. Kotz Grad. Sch. Mgmt., 1984—, United Chs. N.E. Pa., 1985-86, UN Assn. Greater Scranton, 1985—. Mem. Am. Assn. Higher Edn., Assn. Cath. Colls. and Univs. (chmn. 1982-84), Internat. Fedn. Cath. Univs. (v.p. 1980—), AAUW, Delta Epsilon Sigma. Club: Zonta. Office: Nat Cath Ednl Assn 1077 30th St NW Suite 100 Washington DC 20007

MCNAUGHT, JUDITH, author; b. San Luis Obispo, Calif., May 10, 1944; d. Clifford Harris and Rosetta (Prince) Spath; m. J. Michael McNaught, June 1, 1974 (dec. 1983); children—Whitney, Clayton. B.S., Northwestern U., 1966. Pres. Pro-Temps, Inc., St. Louis, 1983-84. Author Tender Triumph, 1983 (Critics Choice award 1983); Double Standards, 1984; Whitney, My Love (Best Hist. Novelist 1985). Mem. Romance Writers Assn. Roman Catholic. Club: Gleneagles Country (Plano, Tex.). Avocations: racquetball, skiing.

MCNAUGHTON-JONES, LINDA B., talent and model agency executive, consultant; b. Atlanta, Jan. 5, 1948; d. B.H. and Elwanda (Sims) Bagley; m. W.S. Jones, Sept. 1979 (div. Sept. 1983) children—April Felice, William Bradford Samuel. B.A., Emory U.; Ph.D., Fla. State U. Pub. relations Hyatt Hotel Corp., Los Angeles, 1967-71; adminstrv. asst. Wells, Rich, Greene Advt., N.Y.C., 1971-77; pres. The Talent Shop, Inc., Atlanta, 1978—; cons. in field; dir. Atlanta Skylarks. Contbr. articles to profl. publs. Judge, Am. Pagentry, Columbia, S.C., 1980, Tampa, Fla., 1982, N.Am. Youth Festival, Louisville, 1984, Miss S.C. Teen, 1985, Miss S.C., 1986. Mem. Screen Actors Guild (agt. 1978—), AFTRA (agt. 1978—), S.E. Assn. Talent Judges (judge 1980—), Bus. and Profl. Women, Women in Film (v.p.), Nat. Acad. TV Arts and Scis., Women Bus. Owners, Ansley Park Homeowners Assn. Avocations: tennis; reading; playwrite. Episcopalian. Home: 130 Montgomery Ferry Dr NE Atlanta GA 30309

MCNEAL, MARY ANN, fine art consultant; b. Miami, Fla., Oct. 8, 1942; d. Sidney Earl and Mary Marcella (Feldkamp) McNeal. Student U. Cin., 1960-64, Cin. Art Acad., 1985-86. Art dir. Ralph Jones Advt., Cin., 1964-66, Integon Corp., Winston-Salem, N.C., 1966-68, Coalition Advt., Fayetteville, N.C., 1970-72; realtor Plessinger & Co., Denver, 1973-74, Mary Rae & Assocs., Denver, 1974-76; pres., realtor Vintage Properties Ltd., Denver, 1976-84; fine art cons. William Havu Fine Art, 1984-85, Laura Pollak Galleries, 1986:13 . Contbr. articles to profl. publs. Mem. bd. dirs. Civic Centre E., Denver, 1980—, N. Capitol Hill Devel. Corp., Denver, 1981—; mem. bd. realtors City Govt. Com., Denver, 1980—. Mem. Denver Bd. Realtors (1st pl. Denver Inner Elegance award 1980), Hist. Denver, Denver C. of C. Office: 855 W Narbor Dr San Diego CA

MCNEALY, BETHENE ELAINE, training executive, research and development engineer; b. Sacramento, Calif., July 28, 1953; d. Delbert Dean and Marjorie Ester (Shorten) McN. B.S., Tex. Woman's U., 1975, M.S., 1981 now postgrad. Grad. tchr., researcher Tex. Woman's U., Denton, 1975-81; tng. rep. Ford Aerospace and Communications Corp., Houston., 1981-83, research and devel. engr., 1983-84; tng. mgr., sr. research and devel. engr., 1984—; NASA astronaut candidate, 1984, 85. Mem. AAAS, AIAA, NAFE, Univ. Women's Assn., Houston Scout Soc., Tex. Woman's U. Alumnae, Audubon Soc., Iota Sigma Pi (chpt. v.p., sec., treas.), Phi Delta Gamma. Roman Catholic. Office: Rockwell Shuttle Ops Co RS19-4 600 Gemini Ave Houston TX 77058

MC NEESE, BETTY ALLISON, school administrator; b. Shreveport, La., Jan. 26, 1927; d. John Richard Preston and Leora (Byram) Allison; B.A., Northwestern State U., 1947; M.Ed., U. Miss., 1965, Ed.D. (teaching fellow), 1968; m. Robert L. McNeese, June 10, 1951 (div.); children—Sara Allison, Robert Hilliard. Tchr. English, Rodessa High Sch., 1947-50, Ida High Sch., 1950-51, Fair Park High Sch., Shreveport, 1957-66; guidance counselor Oak Terr. Jr. High Sch., Shreveport, 1967-68; parish supr. English and social studies Central Staff, Caddo Parish Sch. System, Shreveport, 1968-71, dir. secondary edn., 1971-79, asst. supt. curriculum and instrn., 1979-84; prin. Trinity Heights Christian Acad., 1985—; adj. prof. La. State U., Shreveport. Trustee, exec. com. La. Council Econ. Edn.; trustee CUP adv. bd. La. Tech. U.; edn. com. La. Div. Arts; minuteman youth task force Bicentennial Com., 1976. Recipient award Phi Alpha Theta, 1944. Mem. La. Council for Social Studies (exec. bd., pres.), La. Council Econ. Edn. (exec. com., bd. trustees), Caddo Adminstrs. Club, La. Assn. Educators, Nat. Assn. Educators, La. Assn. Sch. Suprs., PTA. Democrat. Baptist. Author: Factors Influencing College Choice of University of Mississippi Freshmen, 1968; The Story of American History, 1969; History of the Fifty States, 1970; Elementary Story Starters, 1971; Advanced Story Starters, 1971. Home: 233 Pierremont Rd Shreveport LA 71105

MCNEIL, BARBARA JOYCE, radiologist, educator; b. Cambridge, Mass., Feb. 11, 1941. A.B., Emmanuel Coll., 1962; M.D., Harvard Med. Sch., 1966; Ph.D., Harvard U., 1972. Diplomate Am. Bd. Nuclear Medicine, Nat. Bd. of Med. Examiners. Intern pediatrics Mass. Gen. Hosp., Boston, 1966-67; resident radiology Peter Bent Brigham Hosp., Children's Hosp. Med. Ctr., Boston; instr. radiology Harvard Med. Sch., Cambridge, 1974-75, asst. prof., 1975-78, staff radiologist nuclear medicine joint program nuclear medicine, 1974—, assoc. prof. radiology, 1978-83, prof. radiology and clin. epidemiology, 1983—; dep. dir. for residency training joint program in nuclear med., Harvard Affiliated Hosps.; dir., Ctr. for Cost-Effective Care, Brigham, Women's Hosps., 1980—; mem. radiopharm. adv. com. FDA, HEW, 1976-80; Kieckhefer lectr. Harvard-MIT div. health sci. and tech., 1978-79. Mem. editorial bds. Harvard Med. Sch. Health Letter, Jour. of Health Care Tech.; assoc. ed Radiology. Recipient Research Career Devel. award NIH, 1976-81; NIH fellow, 1967-70, special fellow 1970-71. Mem. Assn. Univ. Radiologists, AAAS, Am. Coll. Radiology, Mass. Radiology Soc., Soc. for Med. Decision Making, Am. Coll. Nuclear Physicians, Fleischner Soc., Nat. Council on Radiation, Inst. Medicine. Address: 538 Lewis Wharf Boston MA 02110

MCNEIL, JEAN ANNE, lawyer; b. Boone, Iowa, June 23, 1954; d. Ronald Dean and Marjorie Ruth (Minson) McNeil; m. David W. Dunn. B.S. in Microbiology, U. Iowa, 1976; J.D., U. Ill., 1981. Bar: Iowa 1981. Ptnr., Davis, Hockenberg, Wine, Brown & Koehn, Des Moines, 1981—; part-time instr. Des Moines Area Community Coll., Ankeny campus, 1983. Mem. instructional rev. com. Mercy Hosp. Med. Ctr., Des Moines, 1983—; active YMCA. Recipient Freshman Chemistry award Des Moines Area Community Coll., 1973. Mem. ABA, Iowa State Bar Assn., Polk County Bar Assn., Polk County Women's Bar Assn., Phi Delta Phi. Democrat. Baptist. Office: Davis Hockenberg Wine Brown & Koehn 2300 Financial Ctr Des Moines IA 50309

MC NEILL, CARMEN MARY, business broker; b. Charles City, Iowa, July 16; d. Benjamin T. and Mary (Orvis) McN.; M.B.A., U. Chgo., 1957. Sec.-treas., Old Rep. Life Ins. Co., 1943-62; cons., officer life cos., 1962-70; broker-finder, owner Am. Cons.'s, Chgo., 1970—. Methodist. Home: 918 Argyle Ave Flossmoor IL 60422 Office: Suite 1314 30 N Michigan Ave Chicago IL 60602

MCNEILL, M(ARY) JANET, university administrator; b. Austin, Tex., Nov. 9, 1945; d. Robert B. and Jeanne Lancaster McN.; B.A., Oberlin Coll., 1967; postgrad. Columbia U., 1968. Asst. to artist mgr. Baldwin Piano & Organ Co., N.Y.C., 1970-71; performer Minn. Opera Co., 1973-75; dir. pub. relations St. Paul Chamber Orch., 1973-76, Eastman Sch. Music, Rochester, N.Y., 1978-79; dir. pub. info. and publs. U. Redlands (Calif.), 1980-82; dir. publs. Stanford U., 1983—; cons., editor, writer, designer various promotional materials for colls. and univs. Nat. Merit Corp. scholar, 1963-67; Am. Field Service scholar, 1962; NSF scholar, 1961. Mem. Council for Advancement and Support of Edn. (2 Grand and Gold awards for publ. excellence), Coll. and Univ. Designers Assn., Am. Symphony Orch. League. Office: Publs Stanford U Press Courtyard Santa Teresa St Stanford CA 94305

MCNEILL, VICKI, city official. Mayor, Spokane, Wash., 1986—. Address: Office of the Mayor W 808 Spokane Falls Blvd Spokane WA 99201*

MCNELLY, DIANE LYNN, educator; b. East Chicago, Ind., Dec. 27, 1954; d. George Winfield and Beverly Louise (McMains) McN. B.S., Ball State U., 1978. Cert. in elem. edn., early childhood edn., Tex. Tchr. Cumberland Elem. Sch., West Lafayette, Ind., 1978-79, Mayflower Mill Elem. Sch., Lafayette, Ind., 1979-80; Chpt. 1 resource tchr. Lorenzo de Zavala Sch., Dallas, 1980-83; Chpt. 1 resource tchr., ESL specialist O.M. Roberts Sch., Dallas, 1983—. Theatre and dramatics instr. Gt. Pretenders, Inc., Carrollton, Tex., 1983—, Childrens Arts and Ideas Found., Dallas, 1980-83; mem. Greater Lafayette Civic Theatre; mem. STAGE. Recipient sch. award Dallas Ind. Sch. Dist., 1981; cert. of appreciation Cinco de Mayo Program, 1982-83. Mem. Bus. and Profl. Women, NEA, Assn. for Childhood Edn., P.E.O. Republican. Presbyterian. Home: 5919 Velasco Ave Dallas TX 75206

MC NITT, MIRIAM ELIZABETH, craft artist; b. Syracuse, Kans., Feb. 13, 1916; d. Frank Dunham and Nina (Kirkpatrick) Davis; student Coll. of Sequoias, 1952—; m. William O'Neal McNitt, June 30, 1934; children—Nela (Mrs. David J. Dunaway), Nancy (Mrs. Bernard K. Knoll). Accountant, office mgr. Delta Mosquito Abatement Dist., Visalia, Calif., 1951-56; office mgr. Hathaway Nursery, Visalia, 1956-58; office mgr. Anchor of Calif., Fresno, 1958-62; personal studio craft artist, Fresno, 1962-68, 75—; adminstrv. asst. Yosemite Nat. Park, Calif., 1968-72, Merced Coll., 1972-75. One-man show McHenry Mus., Modesto, Calif., 1985, Carnegie Ctr. for Arts, Turlock, Calif., 1986, U. Pacific, 1984; exhibited Elders Gallery, Fresno, 1980, Ansel Adams Studio, Yosemite Nat. Park, 1976, 81, Le Entrepreneur Gallery, Fresno, Bank of Calif., Modesto, 1982, Farmers & Mchts Bank, Modesto, 1982; exhibited juried shows ACC S.W. Crafts Fair, San Francisco, Presdl. Mus., Odessa, Tex., The Art Place, Pen Women's Art Show, Modesto, Gallo Winery, Modesto, Yosemite Nat. Park, Fresno Arts Center, McHenry Mus., Modesto, Calif., Profl. Artists Show, Fresno, Needlework Show, Woodlawn Plantation, Mt. Vernon, Va., No. Calif. Artists Show, Crocker Mus., Sacramento; exhibitor Manteca Quilt Show (Calif.); exhibitor, acquisition chmn. Luncheon and Quilt Show, McHenry Found.; commd. work Yosemite Nat. Park, McHenry Mus., Modesto, Calif. Vol. mem. Area 4 Neighborhood Council, Fresno, 1979—; Christmas Seal sale chmn. Tulare Kings Counties Tb Assn., 1956-57, sec.-treas., 1954-58; v.p. Fresno County Epilepsy Soc., 1965-68; mem. docent council McHenry Mansion Found., 1983-86; active Camp Fire Girls, Reseda, Calif., Van Nuys and North Hollywood (Calif.) Girl Scouts, Visalia and El Portal (Calif.) 4-H Clubs. Mem. Calif. Congress Parents and Tchrs. (life), Visalia Bus. and Profl. Women (radio TV chmn. 1956-58), Am. Craftsmans Council N.Y., Central Calif. Art League, Modesto Symphony Assn., Turlock (Calif.) Regional Arts Council, Benicia (Calif.) Community Arts. San Joaquin Valley Town Hall, Yosemite Natural History Assn. Republican. Club: Calif. Fedn. Women's Clubs (art chmn. 1965-67). Address: 1141 Cambridge Ct Modesto CA 95350

MCNULTY, DOROTHY GUINN, home health agency executive; b. Tuscaloosa, Ala., May 14, 1930; d. Lewis Luther and Dorothy Louise (Norton) Guinn; m. Harvey McNulty, Oct. 15, 1955; children—Robert Lewis, Colleen McNulty See. R.N., Erlanger Sch. Nursing, Chattanooga, 1951. Nurse-anesthetist Anesthesiologists Assn., Chattanooga, 1952-53; nursing supr. Mt. Edgecumbe (Alaska) Hosp., 1953-56, Alaska Pioneer Home, Sitka, 1963-68; dir. nursing Sitka Community Hosp., 1956-63, 68-78, Profl. Home Health, Chattanooga, 1979-81; exec. dir. nursing Superior Home Health Care, Chattanooga, 1981—; instr. Sitka Community Coll., 1974-76. Contbr. articles to profl. jours. Sec., chmn. In-Home Services Council Greater Chattanooga. Mem. Am. Nurses Assn. (cert. nursing adminstr.), Nat. Assn. Home Caring. Democrat. Methodist. Home: 628 Mohawk St Rossville GA 30741 Office: Superior Home Health Care Inc 6227 Lee Hwy Chattanooga TN 37421

MCNULTY, NANCY GILLESPIE, business writer, consultant; b. Greenville, Pa., May 1, 1919; d. Stanley A. and Bess (Anthony) Gillespie; m. Arthur P. McNulty, July 16, 1942 (dec. 1961); 1 son, Terence. B.A., Thiel Coll., 1940; M.A., NYU, 1948. Industry analyst Equity Corp., 1940-42; writer spl. devel. project Time Inc., N.Y.C., 1942-45; freelance bus. writer/researcher, 1957-67; ind. bus. cons., N.Y.C., 1967—; founder, dir. Internat. Survey of Mgmt. Edn., N.Y.C., 1968—. Author: Management Education to Meet the Challenge of Tomorrow, 1968; Training Managers: The International Guide, 1969; Markets of the Seventies, 1970; Newspaper Publishing, 1972; Kamaz, the Billion Dollar Beginning, 1974; European Management Education Comes of Age, 1975; Business Education and Training of Americans for Business Relations with Japan, 1977; Management Development by Action Learning, 1979; Management Development Programs: The World's Best, 1980; Action Learning's International Adaptation, 1983; The International Directory of Executive Education, 1985. Ford Found. scholar, 1968, 78. Mem. Acad. Mgmt., N.Am. Mgmt. Council (bd. dirs.), Internat. Cons. Found., European Found. Mgmt. Devel., Internat. Found. Action Learning. Episcopalian. Club: Yale of N.Y.C. Home and Office: 55 W 89th St New York NY 10024

MCNULTY, PATRICIA LOGAN, hospital official; b. Huntington, W.Va., Apr. 21, 1937; d. Patrick Henry and Ethel (Rowland) Vincent; m. John Michael McNulty, Aug. 10, 1963; children—John Patrick, Bernard, Andrew Logan. B.A. cum laude, Centre Coll., 1958; M.A., U. Va., 1960. Chmn. English dept. Sullins Coll., Bristol, Va., 1960-63; instr. English, U. Cin., 1968-71, Sinclair Coll., Dayton, Ohio, 1979-80; assoc. editor Nursing Life Mag., Dayton, 1980-82; sr. editor Miami Valley Hosp., Dayton, 1982-83, publs. mgr., 1983-86; account mgr. Ireland Cancer Ctr., Univ. Hosps. of Cleve., 1986—. Bd. dirs. Friends of Dayton Ballet, 1982—, parish liaison St. George's Episcopal Ch., 1982—. Recipient over 15 awards for excellence in pub. relations and advt. Mem. Internat. Assn. Bus. Communicators, Am. Soc. Hosp. Pub. Relations, Women in Communication, Ohio Hosp. Assn., Ohio Soc. Hosp. Pub. Relations, LWV, AAUW. Home: 31008 Clarewood Bay Village OH 44140 Office: Pub Relations Univ Hosps 2074 Abington Rd Cleveland OH 44106

MCNUTT, ALICE HITE, state legislator; b. Henderson, Ky., June 22, 1917; d. Leslie Peyton and Mary Gladys (Flaherty) Hite; student Paducah Community Coll., 1934-36, Am. Acad. Dramatic Art, 1936-37; m. S. H. McNutt, Feb. 25, 1941. Pres., Royal Crown-Nehi Bottling Co., 1942-73; city commr., Paducah, Ky., 1968-70; mayor, City of Paducah, 1973-76; mem. Ky. Ho. of Reps., 1976—; exec. dir. Paducah Tourist Commn., 1980—; dir Paducah Bank & Trust Co. Chmn., McCracken County Red Cross; mem. Civic Beautification Bd.; active McCracken County Tb Assn., McCracken County Mental Health Assn. Recipient Mrs. Lyndon B. Johnson Community Service award Keep Am. Beautiful, 1980, Clyde W. Ware Leadership award Hands Found., 1981; named Paul Harris fellow Rotary Internat., 1986, Outstanding Kentuckian, 1986. Democrat. Roman Catholic. Office: 417 Washington St Paducah KY 42001

MCPEAK, BRENDA MAE, food company executive; b. Raysal, W.Va., Mar. 10, 1939; d. Luther Muncy and Rhoda Opal (Burks) Muncy Koger; m. Gerald Melvin McPeak, Feb. 28, 1956; children—Rickie Allen, Mark David, Robert Scott, Jeri Ann. Grad. high sch., Welch, W.Va., 1957. Operator asst. Bell Telephone Co., Welch, 1957-61; sec. AAA Corp., Richmond, Va., 1965-68, Manpower Corp., Richmond, 1970-77; with Pocahontas Foods, USA, Richmond, 1977—, mgr. meetings, exhibits and travel, 1981—. Named Sweetheart of Yr., First Freewill Baptist Ch., Richmond, 1963. Mem. Meeting Planners Internat., Am. Soc. Assn. Execs., Nat. Assn. Female Execs., Richmond Profl. Women in Travel, Va. Soc. Assn. Execs., Beta Sigma Phi. Baptist. Lodge: Order of Easter Star. Avocations: singing; exercising; traveling. Home: 3101 Trail Dr Richmond VA 23228 Office: PO Box 9729 7420 Ranco Rd Richmond VA 23228

MCPEEK, MARY LIMING, lacemaker, educator, lecturer, author, consultant; b. Bethel Ohio, Dec. 4, 1909; d. Ora Lee and Elizabeth Pearl (Earhart) Liming; m. Gwynn Spencer McPeek, Sept. 11, 1937; children—John Spencer, Mary Ann. B.S. in Edn., Ohio State U., 1930, M.A., 1935. Exhibitor, Bowling Green State U., Ohio, 1964, Pub. Library, Detroit, 1976; lectr. Hist. Mus., Ypsilanti, Mich., 1972; demonstrator Medieval Fair, U. Mich., Ann Arbor, 1975-84; lectr., workshop Embroidery Guild, Dallas, 1975, Lace Group, Pitts., 1982; bobbin lace tchr. Abbey of Regina Laudis, Bethlehem, Conn., 1980; workshops Internat. Old Lacers, P.R., 1985. Author: A Bobbin Lace Sampler, 1977, Studies in Cantu' Bobbin Lace, 1985. Translator: Les Dentelles aux Fuseaux, 1974, Encyclopedia of Needlework, 1976. Contbr. articles to Spinning Wheel mag., 1978. Lectr. Art Mus., Moose Jaw, Sask., Can., 1969; exhibitor lace Pub. Library, New Orleans, 1957, miniature bobbin lace, Hist. Mus., Plymouth, Mich., 1982; demonstrator bobbin lacemaking Mediterranean Festival, Madison, Wis., 1965, Am. Acad. Rome, 1978. Recipient Bobbin Lace First prize Mich. State Fair, 1975-84, Bobbin Lace Best of Show, 1983-84; Essay Competition First place Internat. Old Lacers, 1984. Conbr. to Lace by Virginia Churchill Bath and Bobbin Lacemaking by Doris Southard, Promoter of Lace Postage Stamps for 1986. Mem. Great Lakes Lace Group (founder 1976), Internat. Old Lacers (sec. 1970-72), AAUW (dir. 1943-45). Club: Faculty Wives. (chmn. 1950-59). Avocation: music. Home and Office: 1257 Island Dr Apt 201 Ann Arbor MI 48105

MCPHAIL, ELIZABETH CLAY, stockbroker; b. Dayton, Ky., Feb. 6, 1948; d. Glenn Washington and Margaret Elizabeth (Randle) Clay; B.S., U. Ky., 1970; M.S., Kans. State U., 1977; m. James Dupont McPhail, Aug. 16, 1970. Home econs. tchr., Bourbon County Jr. High Sch., Paris, Ky., 1970-71, Manhattan (Kans.) Jr. High Sch., 1975-76; home econs. tchr. Manhattan High Sch., 1976-77, occupational home econs. tchr., coordinator, 1978-84; stockbroker Edward D. Jones & Co., Cary, N.C., 1984—. Charter ambassador Cary C. of C., 1985—, mem. State of Kans. Adv. Council for Vocat. Edn., 1981-84. Author: Motivation Plus, 1983. Named Outstanding Young Woman, Manhattan Jaycee Women, 1983. Mem. Kans Assn. Vocat. Home Econs. Tchrs. (Educator of Yr. 1984), Kans. Vocat. Assn. (Outstanding Vocat. Educator 1984), Phi Upsilon Omicron, Omicron Nu, Alpha Xi Delta. Presbyterian. Home: 119 W Park St Cary NC 27511

MCPHEE, PENELOPE L. ORTNER, television producer, writer; b. Louisville, Nov. 24, 1947; d. Alvin B. and Loyce (Levenson) Ortner; m. Raymond Hunter McPhee, Aug. 25, 1973; 1 child, Cameron Brook. B.A. with honors, Wellesley Coll., 1969; M.S. in Journalism, Columbia U., 1970. Pub. relations dir. Am. Sch. in Switzerland, Lugano, 1970-71; writer, researcher Sta. WTVJ-TV, Miami, Fla., 1972-73; prof. journalism and film Fleming Coll., Florence, Italy, 1972-73; freelance writer, producer, Miami, 1973-80; writer, cons. Burger King Corp., Miami, 1979; exec. producer for cultural programming Sta. WPBT-TV, Miami, 1980—, Author: Martin Luther King, Jr.: A Documentary, Montgomery to Memphis (Best of Best Books award ALA 1983), 1976; Beauty Ency., 1978; King Remembered, 1986; contbg. author: Underwater Photography for Everyone, 1978. Recipient Iris award Nat. Assn. TV Program Execs., 1983, Children's Programming award Corp. for Pub. Broadcasting, 1982 local program award Corp. Pub. Broadcasting, 1984, Emmy award, 1984, N.Y. State Martin Luther King, Jr. medal of freedom, 1986. Sackett scholar Columbia U., 1970. Mem. Women in Communications. Club: Miami Wellesley (v.p. 1976-80, admissions rep. 1980—). Office: Sta WPBT-TV PO Box 2 Miami FL 33261

MCPHERSON, MARY PATTERSON, college president; b. Abington, Pa., May 14, 1935; d. John B. and Marjorie Hoffman (Higgins) McP.; A.B., Smith Coll., 1957, LL.D. (hon.), 1981; M.A., U. Del., 1960; Ph.D., Bryn Mawr Coll., 1969; LL.D. (hon.), Juniata Coll., 1975; Litt.D. (hon.), Haverford Coll., 1981; L.H.D., Lafayette Coll., 1982. Instr. philosophy U. Del., 1959-61; asst., fellow and lectr. dept. philosophy Bryn Mawr Coll., 1961-63, asst. dean, 1964-69, asso. dean, 1969-70, dean Undergrad. Coll., 1970-78, assoc. prof., from 1970, acting pres., 1976-77, pres., 1978—; bd. dirs. Agnes Irwin Sch., from 1971, Shipley Sch., from 1972, Phillips Exeter Acad., 1973-76, Wilson Coll., 1976-79, Greater Phila. Movement, 1973-77, Internat. House of Phila., 1974-76, Josiah Macy, Jr. Found., from 1977, Carnegie Found. for Advancement Teaching, from 1978, Univ. Museum, Phila., 1977-79, Univ. City Sci. Center, Phila., from 1979, Am. Council on Edn., from 1979; dir. Provident Nat. Bank of Phila., Provident Nat. Corp., Bell Telephone Co. Pa. Mem. Soc. for Ancient Greek Philosophy. Clubs: Fullerton, Cosmopolitan. Address: Taylor Hall Bryn Mawr College Merion Ave Bryn Mawr PA 19010*

MCPHERSON, REBEKAH JO, mental health executive; b. West Frankfort, Ill., Sept. 3, 1947; d. Joseph and Gladys Leona (Davis) McP. m. Walter Thomas Ogle, June 1968 (div. 1971). B.S., Case Western Res. U., 1976; M.S., U. Ill., 1978. Textbook editor C.V. Mosby Co., St. Louis, 1966-71; pub. relations dir. Presidential Mgmt. Corp., St. Louis, 1971-72; cons. Psychol. Research Services, Cleve., 1972-76; clin. social worker St. Elizabeth Hosp., Washington, 1978-80; dir. consultation/edn. Maryview Hosp., Portsmouth, Va., 1980-83; exec. dir. Alcoholic Rehab., Inc., Arlington, 1983—. Mem. Nat. Assn. Social Workers, Am. Mktg. Assn., Democrat. Home: 228 N Thomas St #4 Arlington VA 22203 Office: Alcoholic Rehab Inc 506 N Pollard St Arlington VA 22203

MCPHETRIDGE, EMMIE RICHESON, insurance company representative; b. Kobe, Japan, Nov. 5, 1951; came to U.S., 1953; d. James Edward Lloyd and Kazue (Tanaka) Fuller; m. Ronald Wayne McPhetridge, Apr. 27, 1985; 1 child, David Keith. Student Middle Tenn. State U., 1967-71, U. South Fla., 1972, U. Tenn., Chattanooga, 1982. Adminstrv. asst. ARC, Tampa, Fla., 1972-75; office services rep. Manpower Inc., Chattanooga, 1975-81; supr. records and retention Blue Cross Blue Shield, Chattanooga, 1981-84, supr. claims control, 1984-86; provider service rep. Blue Cross Care Choice, Knoxville, 1986—. Vol. tchr. Chattanooga Area Literacy Movement, 1981-85, Outstanding Contbn. award, 1983. Mem. Nat. Assn. Female Execs., Am. Records Mgrs. Assn., Chattanooga C. of C. (vice chmn. diplomat corps, program chmn.), Adminstrv. Mgmt. Soc. (past pres., chmn. bd.), Acad. Cert. Adminstrv. Mgrs. Republican. Baptist. Avocations: writing; dancing; reading. Home: 6822 Cochise Dr Knoxville TN 37918 Office: Blue Cross Blue Shield CareChoise 1611 Magnolia Ave NE Knoxville TN 37917

MCQUADE, KAREN MARIE, plant biologist; b. Cleve., Sept. 10, 1952; d. Lawrence Edward and Colette Marie (Lynch) McQ.; B.S., U. Dayton (Ohio), 1974; M.S., Northwestern U., 1975. Research asst. Northwestern U., 1974-75; tech. rep. Meistergram, Inc., Cleve., 1975-76; tchr. sci. Magnificat High Sch., Rocky River, Ohio, 1976-77; dir. quality control Bonne Bell Co., Lakewood, Ohio, 1977-79; project asso. plant biochemistry/genetic engring. research and devel. Standard Oil of Ohio, Cleve., 1979—; judge high sch. sci. fairs, 1981—. Asst. Nat. Spl. Olympics Danceathon, 1981; fitness cons., aerobic dance instr. Grantee Huntington Fund, 1970-72. Mem. AAAS, Plant Molecular Biology Assn., Tissue Culture Assn., Nat. Assn. Female Execs. Democrat. Roman Catholic. Clubs: Ski West Ski (activities chmn. 1976-77), Fagowees Internat.

Ski, North Coast Volleyball Assn. (sec.), U.S. Volleyball Assn. Office: 4440 Warrensville Center Rd Cleveland OH

MCQUADE, PATRICIA ANN, nursing educator, interpreter; b. Terre Haute, Ind., Aug. 20, 1945; d. Joseph R. and Florence L. (Stoike) M. B.A., Ind. U., Bloomington, 1968; student U. San Marcos, Lima, 1967; postgrad., Mich. State U., 1982—. Lic. nurse, Ind., Mich. Ward sec. Meml. Hosp., South Bend, Ind., 1963-68, charge nurse, geriatric unit, 1979-80, critical care float nurse, 1980-81, nursing educator, 1981—, co-founder nursing image com., 1984-86; tchr. Spanish, Latin Am. history Bloomington pub. schs., 1969-73; office mgr. J.A. McQuade, M.D., Inc., South Bend, 1979-80. Co-author brochure. Active Hilltop Luth. Ch. South Bend, 1980—. Sigma Theta Tau scholar, 1985-86. Mem. No. Ind. Research Consortium, Nat. League Nursing, Assn. Critical Care Nurses, Ind. Council Hosp. Schs. Nursing (sec., treas. 1982-83). Home: 2345 Arrowhead Circle Apt 27 South Bend IN 46628

MCQUEARY, CHERYL LEE BATH, technical company executive; b. Long Beach, Calif., July 31, 1944; d. Philip Raymond and Rosa Lee (Barnett) Bath; B.A., Drew U., 1978; M.P.A., Fairleigh Dickinson U., 1980; m. Charles Everette McQueary, July 8, 1972. Pricing analyst McDonnell Douglas Astronautics Corp., Santa Monica, Calif., 1966-70; teaching asst. Drew U., Madison, N.J., 1977-78; staff mgr. AT&T, Basking Ridge, N.J., 1980-84; tech. supr. Bell Labs., Holmdel, N.J., 1984—. Mem. exec. com., v.p., bd. dirs. Regional Health Planning Council; mem. exec. com. N.J. Statewide Health Coordinating Council; mem. corp. Morristown Meml. Hosp., Mem. Am. Health Planning Assn. (dir., exec. com.), Am. Pub. Health Assn., Am. Soc. Pub. Adminstrs., Am. Hosp. Assn., N.J. Hosp. Assn., Beta Beta Beta. Republican. Presbyterian. Office: Crawfords Corner Rd Holmdel NJ 07733

MCQUEEN, BEATRICE DORATHEA, slip ring assemblies manufacturing company executive; b. Houston, Jan. 17, 1917; d. John and Teresa M. (Gross) da Silva (Silvey); m. Joe B. McQueen, Jan. 19, 1935; children—Cynthia McQueen Barrow, Diana McQueen Hudson. Student pub. schs., Houston. Corp. sec. IEC Corp., Austin, Tex., 1968-78, pres., 1978—; Murray Grey cattle rancher, Austin, 1975—. Mem. Travis County Grand Jury Assn., Austin, 1958—, Catholic Daus. Chromocik Ct., Fayetteville, Tex., 1950—. Mem. Am. Murray Grey Assn., Am. Murray Grey Aux. (pres. 1977-79). Republican. Avocation: travel. Home: Lake Austin 5213 Tortuga Trail Austin TX 78731 Office: IEC Corp 3100 Longhorn Blvd Austin TX 78759

MCQUEEN, SANDRA MARILYN, educator; b. Greenville, S.C., Nov. 30, 1948; d. Clement Edgar and Sara Elizabeth (Gentry) McQ.; B.A., Presbyn. Coll., Clinton, S.C., 1970; M.A., Presbyn. Sch. Christian Edn., Richmond, Va., 1972; postgrad. Ga. State U., 1986—. Dir. Christian edn. Rock Spring Presbyn. Ch., Atlanta, 1972-74; tchr. Thomasville Heights Elem. Sch., Atlanta, 1974-80; tchr. gifted students Sutton Middle Sch., Atlanta, 1980—, chmn. dept. spl. edn., 1982—; cons. in field. Mem. chancel choir Rock Spring Presbyn. Ch.; mem. camps and confs. Presbyn. Synod S.E.; mem. Women's Advocacy Task Force, Atlanta Presbytery, 1980—, co-pres., 1985-86; elder Rock Spring Presbyn. Ch., 1986-88; sec. Calvin Task Force, 1974-79. Named Sutton Tchr. of Yr., 1985. Mem. Assn. Supervision and Curriculum Devel., NEA, Ga. Edn. Assn., Atlanta Assn. Educators, Ch. Sch. Tchrs., Presbyn. Coll. Alumni Assn. (pres. Atlanta club 1982-83), Ga. State U. Doctoral Fellows, Sigma Kappa, Kappa Delta Pi. Office: 4360 Powers Ferry Rd NW Atlanta GA 30327

MCQUILLA, KATHLEEN ROSE, law enforcement official; b. Jersey City, July 4, 1957; d. Richard and Mary (Glover) McQ. B.A., St. Peter's Coll., Jersey City, 1979; M.A., Seton Hall U., 1983. Asst. sociol. researcher St. Peter's Coll., Jersey City, 1978-79; youth counselor Hudson County C.E.T.A., Bayonne, N.J., 1978-82; tchr. Bayonne Bd. Edn., 1979-80; mgr. Smitty's Auto Repair, Bayonne, 1979—; alcohol counselor Womanpower Projects, Newark, 1982; probation/hearing officer Hudson County Probation Dept., Jersey City, 1983—. Co-coordinator NAACP Youth Group, Bayonne, 1980—; big sister Hudson County Big Bros./Sisters, Jersey City, 1978-80. Mem. Hudson County Reading Council, Nat. Black Alcohol Council, Nat. Soc. Notaries. Baptist. Office: Hudson County Probation Dept 595 Newark Ave Jersey City NJ 07306

MCQUILLAN, FRANCES CARROLL, artist; b. Chgo.; d. Thomas William and Jane Ellen (Connors) Carroll; B.A., Caldwell Coll., 1975; postgrad. Parsons Sch. Design, 1932; m. Edward J. McQuillan, Apr. 23, 1941; children—Thomas, Kathleen. Fashion artist, N.Y. and Chgo. papers, 1932-35; freelance window display, N.Y. and N.J., 1936-38; instr. art Yard Art Sch., 1967-69, 83-84, Montclair Art Mus. Sch. Art (N.J.), 1950—; one person shows Argent Galleries, N.Y.C., Seton Hall U., Newark; exhibited in group shows Nat. Arts Club, N.Y.C., Dayton Art Inst., Conn. Acad. Fine Arts, Seton Hall U., Paris, Exposition Continental, Monaco and Dieppe, France, Mus. Fine Arts, Springfield, Mass. Mem. Am. Artists Profl. League, N.J. Watercolor Soc., Montclair Art Mus., Art Centre N.J. Home: 3 Godfrey Rd Upper Montclair NJ 07043 Office: South Mountain Ave Montclair Mus Montclair NJ 07042

MC QUILLAN, MARGARET MARY, publishing company executive; b. N.Y.C.; d. John A. and Margaret (Higgins) McQ., A.B., Coll. New Rochelle, 1945; M.A. Columbia U., 1948. With Harcourt Brace Jovanovich, Inc. (formerly Harcourt, Brace & World), N.Y.C., 1949—, asst. sec., 1960-70, sec., 1971—, v.p. 1975-78, adminstrv. v.p., 1978-80, sr. v.p., 1980—. Home: 125 Crestwood Ave Tuckahoe NY 10707 Office: Orlando FL 32887

MCRAE, DEE (DOROTHY SUE), writer, editor; b. Huntsville, Ala., May 29, 1939; d. Alan and Dorothy Adel (Heffernan) McR., Jr.; student Florence (Ala.) State Coll., 1957-59; B.J., U. Mo., Columbia, 1961; m. Paul W. Chesser, May 29, 1973; 1 son, Timothy Paul. With Florence Herald, 1962-63; newsroom writer-editor USIA, Washington, 1963-64, editor, writer Am. Illustrated mag., 1964-67, picture editor Topic mag., 1967-69, mem. pamphlets staff, editor, writer, 1969-72; freelance writer, editor, picture editor, 1972-74; asst. editor Smithsonian Mag., Washington, 1974-77, asso. editor, 1977-81; freelance writer/editor, 1981—; assoc. for revs. Smithsonian mag. Mem. NOW. Home: Dragonlair Saint George Island MD 20674

MCRAE, NORA FRANCES STONE, lawyer; b. Columbus, Miss., Nov. 2, 1955; d. Douglas Clyde and Betty Ruth (Boyls) Stone; m. Vaughan Watkins McRae, Apr. 17, 1982. B.A., U. of South, 1977; J.D., U. Miss., 1980. Bar: Miss. 1980. Law clk. Miss. Supreme Ct., Jackson, 1980-81; assoc. firm Barnett, Alagia & Pyle, Jackson, 1981-82; in house counsel Miss. Power & Light Co., Jackson, 1983—. Mem. Galloway Players; v.p. Miss. Opera Guild, 1984; bd. dirs. Young Jacksonians for Symphony, Jackson, 1984; provisional mem. Jr. League Jackson, 1984-85; mem. Jackson Symphony League, 1983-84, Jackson Ballet Guild, 1983-84. Mem. ABA, Miss. Bar Assn., Miss. Women Laywers Assn., Hinds County Bar Assn., Miss. Mus. Art Aux., Jackson Young Lawyers Assn. Methodist. Home: 4054 Eastwood Dr Jackson MS 39211 Office: Miss Power & Light Co PO Box 1640 Jackson MS 39205

MCREYNOLDS, MARY ARMILDA, lawyer; b. Carthage, Mo., Sept. 2, 1946; d. Allen and Virginia Madeliene (Hensley) McR.; m. John DeQuedville Briggs, III, Jan. 1, 1972. B.A., Mt. Holyoke Coll., 1968; J.D., Georgetown U., 1971; LL.M., Harvard U., 1973. Bar: D.C. 1971, U.S. Ct. Appeals (D.C. cir.) 1971, U.S. Ct. Appeals (2d cir.) 1975, U.S. Ct. Appeals (4th Cir.) 1979, U.S. Ct. Appeals (1st, 5th, 6th, 9th, 10th cirs.) 1980, U.S. Supreme Ct. 1980, U.S. Ct. Appeals (11th cir.) 1981, U.S. Ct. Appeals (3d, 7th, 8th cirs.) 1983. Law clk. U.S. Ct. Appeals for D.C. cir., 1971-72; assoc. Wilmer, Cutler & Pickering, Washington, 1973-77; sr. trial atty. civil div. fed. program br. U.S. Dept. Justice, 1977-79, mem. appellate staff, 1979-81; ptnr. McReynolds & Mutterperl, Washington, 1981-83, Wilner & Scheiner, Washington, 1983—. Contbr. articles to profl. jours. Chmn. bd. dirs. Washington Bach Consort, 1981-83. Mem. ABA, Bar Assn. D.C., Fed. Bar Assn., Am. Soc. Legal History. Episcopalian. Clubs: Racquet (Washington); Kenwood (Bethesda, Md.). Home: 2101 Connecticut Ave Apt 26 Washington DC 20008

MCREYNOLDS, MARY MAUREEN, municipal environmental administrator, consultant; b. Tacoma, July 15, 1940; d. Andrew Harley and Mary Leone (McGuire) Sims; m. Gerald Aaron McReynolds, Dec. 10, 1964; Student Coll. Puget Sound, 1957-59; B.A., U. Oreg., 1961; Ph.D., U. Chgo., 1966; postgrad. San Diego State U., 1973-75. NIH postdoctoral fellow U. Tex., Austin, 1966-68, mem. adj. faculty, 1980-82, mem. biohazards com., 1981—; research assoc. Stanford U., Calif., 1968-71; chemist assoc. Syva Co., Palo Alto, Calif., 1972; environ. specialist County of San Diego, Calif., 1973-75; dept. head City of Austin, 1976-84, chief environ. officer, 1984-85, environ. mgr., 1985—; cons. enologist Mirassou Vineyards, San Jose, Calif., 1969-72; lectr. Wright Inst., Berkeley, Calif., 1971-72; instr. San Diego State U., 1974-75. Contbr. articles to profl. pubs. USPHS tng. grantee U. Chgo., 1961-64; univ. fellow U. Chgo., 1961-66. Mem. Water Pollution Control Fedn., Am. Planning Assn., Am. Inst. Cert. Planners (cert.), Assn. Environ. Profls., AAAS, Am. Water Resources Assn., Austin Soc. Pub. Adminstrn., Nat. Assn. Female Execs., Zeta Tau Alpha. Lodges: Soroptimists (dir. Soroptimist Manor 1978-80, 83-85, v.p. chpt. 1983-85, pres. chpt. 1985-86), Toastmasters (club pres. 1981, area gov. 1981-82, div. lt. gov. 1983-84, Able Toastmaster award 1984). Avocations: gourmet food and wine. Office: City of Austin PO Box 1088 Austin TX 78704

MCROY, RUTH GAIL, social worker, educator; b. Vicksburg, Miss., Oct. 6, 1947; d. Horace David and Lucille A. (McKinney) Murdock; B.A. in Sociology and Psychology, U. Kans., 1968; M.S.W., 1970; Ph.D. in Social Work (Danforth Found. fellow 1980-81, Black Analysis, Inc. fellow 1980-81), U. Tex.- Austin, 1981; m. June 5, 1968 (div.); children—Myra Louise, Melissa Lynn. Marriage counselor Family Consultation Service, Wichita, Kans., 1970-71; adoption specialist Kans. Children's Service League, Wichita, 1971-73; asst. prof. social work U. Kans., Lawrence, 1973-77; asst. prof. sociology and social work Prairie View A&M U., 1977-78; tech. asst. specialist Region VI Adoption Resource Center, Austin, 1979-81; assoc. prof. social work U. Tex., Austin, 1981—; guest speaker in field; cons. adoptions; instr. in continuing edn.; pres. bd. dirs. Black Adoption Program and Services, Kansas City, Kans., 1976-77; pres. bd. dirs. George Washington Carver History Mus., 1983—. Mem. Nat. Assn. Social Workers, Council Social Work Edn., Phi Delta Kappa, Phi Kappa Phi. Episcopalian. Author: Black Homes for Black Children, 1974; Instructor's Guide to Accompany Human Responses to Social Problems, 1981; Transracial and Inracial Adoptees: The Adolescent Years, 1983. Contbr. articles to profl. jours. Office: 2609 University Ave Austin TX 78712

MCSHAN, LOIS HILDRETH, savings and loan executive; b. Magnolia, Ark., Nov. 14, 1951; d. Eddie Lee and Garnies Lee (Stevenson) Parsha Hildreth; m. Gary Anthony McShan, Nov. 14, 1971; 1 dau., Kimberly Dawn. A.A., Mountain View Jr. Coll., 1976; B.A., Dallas Bapt. Coll., 1977. Central supply technician Dal-Tec/Vets. Hosp., Dallas, 1968; insp. Tex. Instruments, Inc., Richardson, Tex., 1969-70; computer operator, librarian Southwestern Bell Telephone Co., Dallas, 1970-79; coordinator/student tchr. United Way/Dallas Ind. Sch. Dist., Mountain View Coll., Dallas, 1978-79; supr. info. systems Gibraltar Fed. Savs. & Loan, Beverly Hills, Calif., 1979—; advisor Aubudon Jr. High Computer Ctr., Los Angeles, 1982-83. Solicitor, Voter Registration, Dallas, Los Angeles, 1975—; coordinator/solicitor United Way Fund/Red Cross Blood Dr., Dallas, Los Angeles, 1970—; pres. Audubon Jr. High Sch. PTA, Los Angeles, 1981-83; mem. exec. bd. Project Citizen, Los Angeles, 1981-83. Crown Zellerbach Found. scholar, 1975, Dallas Personnel Assn. scholar, 1976. Fellow Zeta Phi Beta (life, outstanding young woman of yr. 1967-69), Phi Theta Kappa (life); mem. Nat. Assn. Female Execs., Nat. Assn. Univ. Women. Democrat. Baptist. Clubs: Women in Mgmt. (sec. 1979-80), Women in Data Processing. Home: 4710 Coliseum St Apt 38 Los Angeles CA 90016 Office: Gibraltar Fed Savs & Loan Assn 9111 Wilshire Blvd Beverly Hills CA 90213

MCSHERRY, JOYCE ANN, broadcasting executive, radio program host; b. York, Pa., June 25, 1946; d. Vernon Eugene and Edna Ellen (Noel) McMaster; m. Gordon Phillip Moul, Apr. 17, 1965; 1 child, Gordon Phillip. Student pub. schs., York. Announcer Sta.-WRHY, Starview, Pa., 1971-76, Sta.-WSBA, York, 1976; ops. mgr., talk show host Sta.-WNOW, York, 1978—. Republican. Lutheran. Club: Quota. Avocations: gourmet cooking. Office: Sta-WOBG PO Box 2506 York PA 17405

MCSHIRLEY, SUSAN RUTH, gift industry company executive, consultant; b. Glendale, Calif., July 31, 1945; d. Robert Claude and Lillian Dora (Mable) McS. B.S., U. Calif.-Berkeley, 1967. Nat. sales dir. McShirley Products, Glendale, Calif., 1967-71, Viade Products, Camarillo, Calif., 1972-80; pres. SRM Press, Inc., Los Angeles, 1980—; nat. sales cons. Warner Bros. Records, Burbank, Calif., 1985. Author: Racquetball: Where to Play, USA, 1978. Patentee picture pen. Creator novelty trademarks including Collectable Critters, Preppy Pen, Dependable Heart. Mem. Calif. Alumni Assn., Alpha Omicron Pi. Avocations: travel; photography; tennis; foreign languages. Home: 15947 Temecula St Pacific Palisades CA 90272 Office: SRM Press Inc 4216 1/2 Glencoe Ave Marina del Rey CA 90292

MCSWEEN-BROOKS, CAROL ANGELA, personal computer specialist, educator, consultant, writer; b. Washington, Mar. 2, 1950; d. Clarence and Dorothy (Erskine) Yancey McSween; m. Charles Edward Brooks, Jan. 1, 1972; children—Brandy Heather McSween Brooks, Rebecca Elizabeth McSween Brooks and Michelle Celeste McSween Brooks (twins). Student in biochemistry Brown U., 1968-72; student in bus. adminstrn. Clark U., 1981-82; student in design and graphics Sch. Worcester Art Mus., 1982-84. Computer operator, jr. programmer Mass. Eye and Ear Infirmary, Cambridge, 1973-75; office staff Nortech, Clinton, Mass., 1980-82; owner, advt. coordinator Communications, Worcester, Mass., 1982-84; office mgr. Horizon Systems Corp., Reston, Va., 1984-85; owner, instr., cons., writer Writing By Design, Reston, 1985—. Editor Parents' Turn newsletter Minorities Achieve Excellence, Forest Edge Elem. Sch., Reston, 1984-85, 85-86; co-chmn. Forest Edge Elem. Sch. Minorities Achieve Excellence Com., 1984-85; lectr., participant Forest Edge Elem. Sch. Young Authors' Conf., 1985, Forest Edge Career/Role Model Series, 1986; chaplain chorus choir John Wesley African Meth.-Episc. Zion Ch., Washington, 1985-86, also active March Club; mem. Fairfax County Pub. Schs. Area III Community Parent Adv. Com., Va., 1985-86. Univ. scholar Brown U., Providence, 1968; U.S. Dept. Commerce jr. fellow, 1968-72. Mem. Nat. Assn. Female Execs. Avocations: writing poetry and short stories; creative sewing; graphic design; photography. Office: Writing By Design PO Box 3151 Reston VA 22090

MCSWEENEY, JUNE ELIZABETH, printing company executive; b. Boston, June 18, 1932; d. William Earnest and Mabel Evelyn (Ricker) Mortimer; m. Charles Edward McSweeney, June 21, 1952; children—David Charles, Donna Marie, Diane June. Student Boston U., 1948-52; A.S., Northeastern U., 1970, B.S., 1974. Policywriter, T.C. Curran Ins., Hyde Park, Mass., 1948-56; office mgr. Slattery Ins., Abington, Mass., 1954-70; v.p., treas. Fairmount Press, Inc., Rockland, Mass., 1967—. Chmn. edn./bus. community Alliance Rockland pub. schs., 1982—; bd. dirs. White Island Pond Conservation Alliance, East Wareham, Mass., 1986—. Mem. Printing Industries Am., Sigma Epsilon Rho. Club: Mass. State Fedn. Women's Clubs (trustee endowment fund 1982-84, dir. evening membership 1986—) (Quincy). Home: 250 Barker Rd East Wareham MA 02538 Office: Fairmount Press Inc 496 Union St Rockland MA 02370

MCTEER, MAUREEN ANNE, lawyer; b. Cumberland, Ont., Can., Feb. 27, 1952; d. John J. and Beatrice E. (Griffith) McT.; B.A., U. Ottawa (Ont.), 1973, LL.B., 1977; m. Charles Joseph Clark, June 30, 1973; 1 dau., Catherine Jane. Called to Ont. bar, 1980. Bd. govs. U. Ottawa, 1980—. Named Woman of Future, Ladies Home Jour., 1979, Chatelaine Woman of yr., 1984. Mem. Nat. Council Women of Can. (hon. pres.), Nat. Assn. Women and Law, Nat. Action Com. on Status of Women. Progressive Conservative. Roman Catholic.

MCTIERNAN, MIRIAM, government executive; b. Limerick, Ireland, May 2, 1952; came to Can., 1973; d. Michael and Marjorie (Woulfe) Lynch; m. Timothy Patrick McTiernan, Oct. 31, 1972; 1 child, Leah Rhiannon. B.A. with honors, Nat. U. Ireland, U. Coll. Dublin, 1972, diploma in archival studies, 1973; diploma in pub. sector mgmt. U. Victoria, 1985. Coll. archivist Douglas Coll., New Westminster, B.C., 1973-76; univ. archivist U. B.C., Vancouver, 1975; credit union archivist B.C. Central Credit Union, Vancouver, 1976-79; govt. records archivist Govt. of Yukon, Whitehorse, Yukon Ter., 1979-80, territorial archivist, 1980-84, dir. libraries and archives, 1984—. Contbr. articles to profl. jours. Mem. Assn. Can. Archivists (bus. archives com. 1976-79, treas. 1981-83, v.p. 1983-84, pres. 1984-85), Bur. Can. Archivists, Assn. B.C. Archivists (sec.-treas. 1976-78, pres. 1978-80), Yukon Hist. and Mus. Assn. (treas. 1981), Soc. Am. Archivists, Assn. Records Mgr. and Adminstrs., Inst. Pub. Adminstrn. Can.

MCVAY, PATTI, travel agency executive. B.A., Aqinas Coll., 1968. Formerly real estate salesperson, acctg. tchr. Ind. Coll. Bus. Tech.; salesperson Fifth Season Travel, Indpls., 1977-79, pres., 1979—. Address: Fifth Season Travel 4930 N Pennsylvania Indianapolis IN 46205

MCVEY, MARCIA ALICE, educational administrator; b. San Jose, Calif., Aug. 31, 1934; d. Charles Thurston and Thelma (Hackett) McV.; B.A., Pomona Coll., 1955; M.A., Claremont Grad. Sch., 1959; Ed.D. (Delta Kappa Gamma Scholar), U. So. Calif., 1978. Tchr., Glendora Sch. Dist., 1955-59; tchr. Covina Valley Unified Sch. Dist., 1959-65, counselor, jr. high sch., 1965-67, asst. prin. jr. high, 1967-68, prin., 1968-72, 73-79; dir. curriculum and instruction Norwalk (Calif.) LaMirada Unified Sch. Dist., 1979-83; asst. supt. Centralia Sch. Dist., Buena Park (Calif.), 1983-86, Duarte Unified Sch. Dist., Calif., 1986—; ednl. cons.; mem. Calif. Dept. Edn. task force on conflict resolution in secondary schs., 1972-73. Bd. dirs. HEAR Center, Pasadena, 1976—; community vol. Pomona Coll. Assocs.; mem. Calif. Curriculum Devel. and Supplemental Materials Commn., 1984—. Kettering IDEA fellow, 1981. Mem. Assn. Calif. Sch. Adminstrs., Calif. Assn. Gifted, Profl. Advocates for Gifted Edn., Assn. Supervision and Curriculum Devel., AAUW, Phi Delta Kappa, Delta Kappa Gamma. Contbr. articles to profl. jours. Office: 1427 Buena Vista Ave Duarte CA 91010

MCVICAR, ANN LAMONT, librarian; b. Seattle, Sept. 1, 1935; d. Ralph Howell and Vivian Hazel (Effinger) Lamont; m. Forrest B. McVicar, Mar. 21, 1959; children—Mary, Helen, Bruce Lamont. B.A. in Am. Lit., U. Wash., 1957, M.L.S., 1960; postgrad. N. Tex. State U. Profl. Librarian's cert., N.J.; State Bd. Cert. for Librarian, Wash. Br. librarian and reference librarian Library Assn. Portland, 1971-74; head reference dept. Old Bridge Pub. Library, N.J., 1975-79; dir. library Nat. Office Boy Scouts Am., Irving, Tex., 1979—; adminstrv. asst. to pres. Tex. Library Assn., Dallas, 1984—. Precinct committeeperson Republican Party, Portland, 1972; pres. P-TSA George Smith Elem. Sch., Portland, 1972-73. Mem. Am. Library Assn., Tex. Library Assn., Special Libraries Assn. Club: Church Women United (vice pres. 1975-76). Office: Boy Scouts Am 1325 Walnut Hill Ln Irving TX 75038-3096

MCVICKER, MARY ELLEN HARSHBARGER, business executive, art history educator; b. Mexico, Mo., May 5, 1951; d. Don Milton and Harriet Pauline (Mossholder) Harshbarger; m. Wiley Ray McVicker, June 2, 1973; children—Laura Elizabeth, Todd Michael. B.A. with honors, U. Mo., 1973, M.A., 1975, postgrad. Adminstrv. sec. Engring. Surveys, Columbia, Mo., 1976-77; instr. Columbia U., Mo., 1977-78, Central Methodist Coll., Fayette, Mo., 1978-85; mus. dir. Central Methodist Coll., Fayette, 1980-85; project dir. Mo. Com. for Humanities, Fayette, 1981-85, Mo. Dept. Natural Resources Office Hist. Preservation, 1978-79; co-owner Memories of Mo. Inc., 1986—. Author: History Book, 1984. Vice pres. Friends Hist. Boonville, Mo., 1982—; bd. dirs. Mus. Assocs. Mo. U., Columbia, 1981-83, Mo. Meth. Hist. Soc., Fayette, 1981-84; chmn. Bicentennial Celebration Methodism, Boonville, Mo., 1984. Mem. Mo. Heritage Trust (charter mem.), AAUW (treas. 1977-79), Am. Assn. Museums, Centralia Hist. Soc. (project dir. 1978), Mus. Assocs. United Methodist Ch. (charter mem., bd. dir. 1981-83), Phi Beta Kappa, Mortar Bd. Democrat. Clubs: Women's (treas. 1977-79), United Methodist Women's Group (charter mem.). Avocations: collecting antiques; gardening; family farming; singing; travelling. Home: 813 Christus Dr Boonville MO 65233 Office: PO Box 228 Boonville MO 65233

MCWHERTER, DORIS NEWTON, brokerage firm executive, financial consultant; b. Newcastle, Tex., Dec. 30, 1936; d. Marion Orville and Dannie (Burns) Newton; m. Tom A. McWherter, Jr., Mar. 23, 1965 (div. 1977); children—David, Ronald, Julia Diane; m. 2d, Robert Bernet Williams, Sept. 20, 1978. Student N.Y. Inst. Fin., 1961-63. Ops. mgr. Eddleman, Pollock & Fosdick, Houston, 1956-60; br. mgr. E. F. Hutton & Co., Houston, 1960-79; account exec. Merrill Lynch, Houston, 1979-81; v.p. Dean Witter Reynolds, Houston, 1981—; writer rules com. N.Y. Stock Exchange, N.Y.C., 1977-80. Precinct sec. Republican party, Houston, 1975-76. Mem. Nat. Assn. Security Dealers, N.Y. Stock Exchange (assoc.), Chgo. Bd. Trade (assoc.), Chgo. Mercantile Exchange (assoc.). Republican. Episcopalian. Home: 7114 Redding Rd Houston TX 77036 Office: Dean Witter Reynolds 1616 S Voss St Suite 620 Houston TX 77057

MCWHINNEY, MADELINE H. (MRS. JOHN DENNY DALE), economist; b. Denver, Mar. 11, 1922; d. Leroy and Alice (Houston) McW.; B.A., Smith Coll., 1943; M.B.A., N.Y.U., 1947; m. John D. Dale, June 23, 1961; 1 child, Thomas Denny. Economist, Fed. Res. Bank N.Y., 1943-73, chief fin. and trade statis. div., 1955-59, mgr. market stats. dept., 1960-65, asst. v.p., 1965-73; pres. First Women's Bank, N.Y.C., 1974-76; trustee Retirement System Fed. Res. Bank, 1955-58; vis. lectr. N.Y.U. Grad. Sch. Bus., 1976-77; pres. Dale, Elliott & Co., Inc., N.Y.C., 1977—, mem. N.J. Casino Control Commn., 1980-82; bd. govs. Am. Stock Exchange, 1977-81. Trustee, Carnegie Corp. N.Y., 1974-82, Central Savs. Bank of N.Y., 1980-82, Charles F. Kettering Found., 1975—, Inst. Internat. Edn., 1975—, Investor Responsibility Research Center, Inc., 1974-81; asst. dir. Whitney Mus. Am. Art, 1983—; dir. Atlantic City Electric Co., 1983—; trustee Mgr. of Mgr. Funds, 1983—; adv. bd. Grad. Sch. Bus., Denver U.; mem. adv. com. prof. ethics N.J. Supreme Ct., 1983—. Recipient Smith Coll. medal, 1971, Alumni Achievement award N.Y.U. Grad. Sch. Bus. Adminstrn. Alumni Assn., 1971; N.Y.U. Crystal award, 1982. Mem. Am. Fin. Assn. (past dir.), Money Marketeers (v.p. 1960, pres. 1961-62), Nat. Assn. Bank Women, Alumni Assn. Grad. Sch. Bus. Admin. N.Y.U. (dir. 1951-63, pres. 1957-59), Am. Econ. Assn., Soc. Meml. Center, Phi Beta Kappa Assos. (v.p. 1979—). Home: 24 Blossom Cove Rd Red Bank NJ 07701 Office: PO Box 458 Red Bank NJ 07701

MCWHIRTER, DIANE BALTZELLE, lawyer; b. Miami Beach, Fla., Sept. 12, 1958; d. Conner and Mary Athria (Marney) Baltzelle; m. John McWhirter. B.A. in Philosophy, Duke U., 1979; J.D., U. Fla., 1982; postgrad. in comparative law Magdalen Coll., Oxford, Eng., summer 1980. Bar: Fla. 1983, U.S. Dist. Ct. (mid. dist.) Fla. 1983, U.S. Ct. Appeals (11th cir.) 1984. Asst. pub. defender, Pub. Defender's Office, Lake City, Fla., 1983-84, Orlando, Fla., 1984—; teaching fellow Holland Law Ctr., Gainesville, Fla., 1982; lectr. Pub. Defender Spring Conf., 1985. Editor family law, Legal Aid Handbook, 1981-82. Mem. Fla. Symphony League, Orlando, 1983-84, Columbia Assn. for Retarded Children, Lake City, 1984; mem. choir 1st United Presbyn. Ch., Lake City, 1984; Sunday sch. tchr. 1st United Methodist Ch., Orlando, 1983, 85; trustee Fla. United Meth. Children's Home, Enterprise, 1985—. Mem. Bus. and Profl. Women's Club Lake City, ABA, Fla. Bar Assn. (evidence com. 1985-86), Orange County Bar Assn. (vice chmn. law and edn. com. 1986—), Central Fla. Women Lawyers Assn., Phi Delta Phi (clk. 1981-82, historian 1982, cert. of merit 1981, 82). Democrat. Home: 2517 Oak Park Way Orlando FL 32822 Office: Public Defender's Office 1 N Orange Ave Suite 500 Orlando FL 32801

MCWHORTER, SHARON LOUISE, business executive, inventor, consultant; b. Detroit, Feb. 22, 1951; d. Leroy Byron Harris Jr. and Josiebell (Richards) Harris Aaron; m. Abner McWhorter II, Mar. 15, 1969 (div. Aug. 1974); 1 child, Abner III. Student Wayne State U., 1975-79; cert., SBA, Detroit, 1978; cert. in sound engring. Detroit Rec. Inst., Warren, Mich., 1982. Directory asst. Mich. Bell Telephone Co., Detroit, 1969; quality control clk. Chevrolet Gear & Axle, Detroit, 1971-74; circulation clk. Wayne County Community Coll., Detroit, 1977-85, mem. library standing com. and open house com., 1983-84; pres. Galactic Concepts & Designs, Detroit, 1977—, cons., 1983—; gen. ptnr., mgr. S.M.J. Corridor Devel., Detroit, 1982—, hist. researcher, 1982; del. Small Bus. Conf., 1981; ad-hoc mem. Minority Tech. Council, 1981-82; elected alt. Mich. del. White House Conf. on Small Bus., Washington, 1985-86. Author, editor Creative Dilemma newsletter, 1985—. Co-patentee cup holding apparatus. Vol. counselor Barat House/March of Dimes, Detroit, 1977; active Concerned Citizens Cass Corridor, Detroit, 1982, Cass Corridor Citizen's Patrol, Detroit, 1983-84; v.p. Wayne County chpt. Mothers Against Drunk Driving, Mich., 1984—. Recipient Hist. Landmark award Dept. Interior, 1983, cert. appreciation Tri-County Substance Abuse Awareness Com., 1984. Mem. Inventors Council Mich. (bd. dirs. 1985—), Black Women in Bus. (sec. 1984-85), Greater Detroit C. of C., Detroit Econ. Club. Democrat. Methodist. Avocations: inventing; writing; re-adaptive furniture design; photography; video production. Office: Galactic Concepts & Designs 453 Myrtle Suite 102 Detroit MI 48201

MCWILLIAMS, BETTY CARROL, state official; b. Princeton, Ind., July 11, 1934; d. Herbert C. and Helen Elizabeth (Short) Miller; m. Charles Edward McWilliams, Feb. 18, 1956; children—David Kevin, Theresa Lynn, Michael Edward. Grad. high sch., Spurgeon, Ind. Installment loan clk. Old Nat. Bank, Evansville, Ind., 1953-56; installment loan teller Mercantile Bank, Hammond, Ind., 1956-61; data processor Calumet Nat. Bank, Hammond, 1969-70, Kuhn, Olson & West, Munster, Ind., 1970-76; pvt. practice acctg., 1976-83; procurement outreach specialist Pvt. Industry Council, Hammond, 1983-84; pres. Ptnrs. in Contracting, Hammond, 1984-85; asst. dir. fed. mktg. devel. div. Ind.

Dept. Commerce, 1985—. Editor Robur Editor news booklet, 1979, 80. Mem. Nat. Contract Mgmt. Assn., VANI (bd. dirs.), The Inventor and Entrepreneurs Soc. Ind., Inc., Sigma Alpha (nat. pres. 1982-83). Home: 7858 Hunters Path Indianapolis IN 46224 Office: Ind Dept Commerce One N Capitol Suite 700 Indianapolis IN 46204

MCWILLIAMS, CANDYCE LYNN, account representative; b. Johnstown, Pa., June 24, 1950; d. Howard Clifton and Phyllis Irene (Keener) McW.; m. Blair Sidney Allen, July 2, 1971 (div. Feb. 1978); 1 son, Thageron Linere Allen. B.A., Pa. State U., 1971; postgrad. in internat. bus. adminstrn. Golden Gate U., 1980—; student in computer programming Computer Learning Ctr., San Francisco, 1982. Animal researcher Pa. State U., University Park, 1973-74; sr. sec. Levi Strauss Internat., San Francisco, 1980; sr. sec. Matson Nav. Co., San Francisco, 1980-81, tng. coordinator, 1981-82; adminstrv. asst. in fin. DHL Corp., San Bruno, Calif., 1982-83; office systems analyst Indsl. Indemnity, San Francisco, 1983-84; account rep. Southwestern Bell Publs., 1985—; mem. teen. adv. bd. Penn Traffic Co., Johnstown, Pa., 1967-68. Contbr. articles to profl. publs. Vice pres. bd. dirs. Paul Scardina Dance Co., San Francisco, 1981-82; v.p. bd. dirs. Advs. for Women, San Francisco, 1983-84; entertainment chmn. Russian Hill Neighbors. Fellow Office Automation Research Forum (pres. 1981-82, award 1983); mem. Profl. Assn. Diving Instrs. (basic diver scuba cert.), Jr. League San Francisco. Republican. Home: 1550 Bay St Apt 303 San Francisco CA 94123 Office: Southwestern Bell Publs 1900 Powell Suite 255 Emeryville CA 94608

MCWILLIAMS, CONNIE OPAL, insurance company executive; b. Magnolia, Iowa, June 28, 1947; d. Thomas E. and Ila M. (Vore) Chatburn; m. Dale Roy McWilliams, Sept. 29, 1973. Sec. Kovar Agy., Inc., Missouri Valley, Iowa, 1965-76; owner McWilliams Enterprises, Missouri Valley, 1976—. Chairperson, Harrison County (Iowa) March of Dimes, 1970-73; commr. Iowa Jud. Qualifications Commn., 1981—. Mem. Assn. Life Underwriters, (past pres. chpt.), Christian Legal Soc., Toppers Club of Farmers Ins. Group, Lifemasters Club, Comml. Masters Club. Democrat. Mem. Reorganized Ch. of Jesus Christ of Latter-day Saints. Club: Community Band and Chorus (dir. 1981). Home: Rural Route 2 Box 172 Logan IA 51546 Office: 301 E Erie St Missouri Valley IA 51555

MEAD, CATHERINE SMITH, librarian; b. Sharon Springs, N.Y., July 11, 1924; d. Elmer Charles and Marguerite (Brady) Smith; B.A. in English, N.Y. State Coll. Tchrs., Albany, 1944, B.S. in L.S., 1947; m. John Mead, Feb. 6, 1947; 1 son, Gregory. Post librarian Camp Drake, Japan, 1953-55; cataloger post library Fort Hood, Tex., 1955-63, Pa. State Library, Harrisburg, 1964-65; asst. state librarian info. resources State Library Ohio, Columbus, 1971-83, head reference and info services. Mem. ALA, Ohio Library Assn., Ohio Assn. Archivists. Office: 65 S Front St Columbus OH 43215

MEAD, GRETCHEN MARIE, business executive; b. Westhampton Beach, N.Y., June 29, 1943; d. Karl Hans and Wanda Elisabeth Guttmann; married. Student Baylor U., 1961; B.A., U. Tex., Austin, 1963, M.S. in Mktg., 1964, in Comparative Lit., 1965, M.B.A., 1967. Account exec. HG&A Assos., Austin, Tex., 1965-68, J.J. Henry & Assos., Alexandria, Va., 1968-71; dir. mktg. Emersons Ltd., Rockville, Md., 1971-73; account supr. Ketchum, MacLeod & Grove, Inc., Pittsburgh, 1973-76; mgmt. supr. W.B. Doner & Co., Balt., 1976-79; sr. mgmt. cons. Resource, Balt., 1979-80; v.p. communications Tab Books, Inc., 1980-82; mng. ptnr. Resource Unltd., San Antonio, 182—; horse trainer and shower; breeder Rotweiler dogs. Vol., United Way, Cystic Fibrosis Assn. Recipient Clio award, 1974, Addy award, 1975. Mem. Am. Mktg. Assn., MENSA, Advt. Club Met. Washington, Md. Mus. Ceramic Arts (founding Sponor), Somali Cat Club Am., Internat. Somali Cat Club. Jewish. Author: the W.B. Doner Leave-Behind Folder, 1978. Home: 227 Lively Dr San Antonio TX 78213

MEAD, HARRIET COUNCIL, librarian, author; b. Franklin, Va., Jan. 11; d. Hutson and Ollie (Whitley) Council; m. Berne Matthews Mead, Jr., Dec. 2, 1940; children—William Whitley, Charles Council. B.A., Coll. William and Mary, 1935; postgrad. Rollins Coll., 1966, 70, 84; student Fla. State U., 1958-62. County librarian Carroll County, Hillsville, Va., 1935-36; city librarian Suffolk City Schs., Va., 1936-41; librarian, media specialist Orange County Schs., Orlando, Fla., 1961-80. Author: The Irrepressible Saint, 1983. Contbr. article to mag., 1983. Sustaining mem. Jr. League Orlando, Winter Park, 1985, Soc. Colonial Dames in State of Fla., Orlando, 1985, Orange County Hist. Soc., 1985, LWV, Orlando, 1985. Mem. Friends of Library, Fla. Council Libraries, Orange County Media Specialists (pres. 1968-69), Nat. Soc. Colonial Dames, DAR, Orange County Ret. Educators. Democrat. Episcopalian. Avocation: watercolor painting. Home: 500 E Marks St Orlando FL 32803

MEAD, SUSAN PHELPS, leasing manager; b. Berkeley, Calif., Nov. 9, 1947; d. John Heaton and Betty Bernadine (Bakke) Phelps; m. Harold Eugene Rhineberger, Sept. 27, 1975 (div. 1982). A.A., Diablo Valley Coll., 1967; B.S. in Sociology, Calif. State U.-Hayward, 1970, B.S. in Recreation, 1971; postgrad. Calif. State U.-San Jose. Registered recreation therapist, Calif., U.S. Ward clk., nurses aide Herrick Meml. Hosp., Berkeley, Calif., 1969-72; dir. adjunctive therapy, coordinator continuing med. edn., cons. Walnut Creek Hosp., Calif., 1972-81; leasing mgr., dir. pub. relations Trans-West Capital, Lafayette, Calif., 1981-83; personnel officer Calif. First Bank, 1984—. Author: Mental Health Concepts Applied to Nursing, 1978. Mem. Jr. League of East Bay, AAUW, Nat. Assn. Female Execs., Lafayette C. of C. Club: Soroptimists.

MEADE, SISTER ELLEN PATRICIA, hospital consultant; b. N.Y.C.; d. Patrick and Ellen (Sullivan) Meade; B.S. in Adminstrn., Coll. St. Elizabeth Convent, 1953; M.S., St. Louis U., 1958. With HOLC, 1937-46; adminstrv. asst., office mother gen. Sisters of Charity of St. Elizabeth, 1946-54; asst. adminstr. St. Elizabeth Hosp., Elizabeth, N.J., 1954-57, adminstr., 1957-77; hosp. cons., 1977—. Trustee, v.p. Union County Mental Health; trustee Hosp. and Health Council Region 3. Fellow Am. Coll. Hosp. Adminstrs.; mem. Am. Hosp. Assn., N.J. Hosp. Assn., N.J. Cath. Hosp. Conf., St. Louis U. Hosp. Adminstrn. Alumni Assn. (exec. council, pres.), Mental Health Assn. Union County, Union County Social Planning Council, Am. Assn. Maternal and Child Health, Hosp. Personnel Mgmt. Assn., Nat. Conf. Cath. Charities, Am. Assn. Hosp. Accts. Address: 6 Oak Ridge Ave Summit NJ 07901

MEADE, VIOLET ARLENE, nurse; b. Pikeville, Ky., Feb. 19, 1948; d. Fred and Evelyn (Harrison) Damron; m. Joseph G. Raucci, Feb. 24, 1968 (div. 1976); 1 son, James; m. 2d. Roger Lowell Meade, Dec. 17, 1976. Grad. Mayo Vocat. Sch., 1976. Carhop Parkmoor Restaurant, Fairborn, Ohio, 1966; waitress Frisch's Restaurant, Fairborn, 1966-67; clk. Johnson's Cleaners, Colonial Heights, Va., 1972; cashier Wards Bakery, Colonial Heights, Va., 1972-73; dispatcher Pike County Detective Bur., Pikeville, Ky., 1974-75; nurse Meth. Hosp., Pikeville, 1976—; dir. dist. 9 unit 3 Ky. State Assn. Licenced Practical Nurses, 1985—. Sec. Parent Tchrs. Orgn., Robinson Creek, Ky., 1980-83. Democrat. Home: Route 4 Box 747 Pikeville KY 41501

MEADORS, GAYLE M(ARLEEN), lawyer; b. Chgo., Sept. 13, 1946; d. Howard C. and Eileen M. (Baker) M.; m. William F. Fortuna, II, June 11, 1983. A.B. in English, U. Ill., 1969; M.A. in Library Sci., U. Chgo., 1973; J.D. magna cum laude, DePaul U., 1977. Bar: Ill. 1977. Cons. Hewitt Assocs., Lincolnshire, Ill., 1976-83; sr. counsel Am. Hosp. Supply Corp., Evanston, Ill., 1983—. Mem. ABA, Ill. Bar Assn., Chgo. Bar Assn., Phi Beta Kappa. Home: 530 E Prospect Ave Lake Bluff IL 60044 Office: Am Hosp Supply Corp One American Plaza Evanston IL 60201

MEADOW, SUSAN ELLEN, magazine editor and publisher; b. N.Y.C., Dec. 17, 1936; d. Sol and Betty (Greene) Raunheim; m. Alvin Harvey Meadow, Aug. 17, 1958; children—Eric, Douglas, Peter. B.A. in English, U. Mich., 1958; M.S. in Edn., Iona Coll., 1967. Asst. editor N.Y. State Pharmacist, N.Y.C., 1958-60; mng. editor Westchester mag., White Plains, N.Y., 1969-70; editor, pub. Westchester Spotlight, Rye, N.Y., 1977—. Bd. dirs. ARC, Rye, 1981—; Westchester-Putnam div. Diabetes Assn. Am.; mem. adv. council Westchester Community Coll. Found., 1984-85. Recipient plaque Leukemia Soc., 1983, Am. Cancer Soc., 1984. Mem. Westchester Women in Communications (excellence in periodicals award 1982), Advt. Club Westchester. Democrat. Jewish. Office: 18-20 Purdy Ave Rye NY 10580

MEADOWS, SANDRA KAY, lawyer, air force officer; b. Mobile, Ala., Nov. 19, 1956; d. James Jack and Alice Louise (Manry) M. B.A., U. Ala., 1979, J.D., 1982. Bar: Ala. 1982, U.S. Ct. Mil. Appeals 1983. Research asst. U. Ala., University, 1979-81, grad. asst., 1981-82; commd. 2d lt., U.S. Air Force, 1982, advanced through grades to capt. 1982, chief civil law JAGC, Blytheville, AFB, Ark., 1982-84; area def. counsel Plattsburgh AFB, N.Y., 1984—; working group chmn. Drug and Alcohol Abuse Control Com., 1983-84; mem. Jr. Officers Council, 1982—, v.p., 1984—. Mem. ABA, Ala. Bar Assn., Nat. Assn. Female Execs., Assn. for Women and the Law (pres. University 1981-82), Federally Employed Women. Democrat. Roman Catholic. Home: 9A Sandra Ave Plattsburgh NY 12901 Office: HQ USAF Area Def Counsel Plattsburgh AFB NY 12901

MEADS, PATRICIA JANE, chemical company executive; b. Midland, Mich., Oct. 17, 1946; d. Bryce James and Ada Jean (Boggs) Parkinson; m. Thomas Floyd Meads, July 27, 1968; 1 child, Jeffrey Thomas. B.A., Mich. State U., 1968. Mktg. acct. Dow Corning, Midland, 1975-76, plant acct., 1977, mgr. office and tech. personnel, 1981-82, personnel devel. mgr., 1983-85, mgr. compensation, 1985—; controller Hemlock Semiconductor Corp. subs., Hemlock, Mich., 1978-81. Mem. Am. Compensation Assn., Nat. Assn. Female Execs. Home: 1002 West Park St Midland MI 48640 Office: Dow Corning Box 994 Midland MI 48640-0994

MEADS, PATRICIA JEAN, marketing specialist; b. Fargo, N.D., Apr. 10, 1950; d. Raymond Byron and Isabel Edith (Barrett) Whiting; student So. Meth. U., 1968-69; B.A., U. Minn., 1971. Advt. coordinator Sun Newspapers, also mng. editor Zenith Express, 1973-74; dir. consumer communications A.S. Industries, Mpls., 1974-76; sales promotion coordinator Carlson Mktg. Group div. Carlson Cos., Mpls., 1976-79, dir. mktg. services, 1979—. Mem. Women in Communications (pres. Twin Cities chpt.), Internat. Tng. in Communications, Minnetonka Chorale. Contbr. to Pro-Con Mag. Home: 18900 Shady Ln S Minnetonka MN 55345 Office: 12755 Hwy 55 Minneapolis MN 55441

MEAGHER, CYNTHIA NASH, journalist; b. Detroit, Dec. 24, 1947; d. Frederick Copp and Carolyn (Coffin) Nash; 1 dau., Lydia Anne. B.A., U. Mich., 1969. Reporter, Detroit News, 1970-75, sports columnist, 1975-77, Life Style columnist, 1977-79, Life Style editor, 1979-82; news features editor Seattle Times, 1983, asst. mng. editor Sunday Seattle Times, 1983-86, assoc. mng. editor, 1986—. Mem. Women in Communications. Office: Seattle Times PO Box 70 Seattle WA 98111

MEALING, ISABEL THORPE, retired social worker; b. Townsend, Ga., Oct. 4, 1907; d. Elisha McDonald and Maude (Davis) Thorpe; student Ga. State Tchrs. Coll., 1924-26; A.B., Randolph-Macon Woman's Coll., 1928; M.S.W., Tulane U., 1943; postgrad. U. Va., 1929; m. John Pace Mealing, Jr., Aug. 15, 1929 (div. Dec. 1939); children—Elisha Thorpe, Margaret Mae (Mrs. Wayne Frederick Orlowski). Visitor, Fulton County Dept. Pub. Welfare, Atlanta, 1937-38; dir. McIntosh County Dept. Pub. Welfare, Darien, Ga., 1938-40; child welfare cons. State of Ga., Atlanta, 1941-44; social worker ARC, Lawson Gen. Hosp., Atlanta, 1944-45; asst. field dir. Lawson Gen. Hosp., and Sta. Hosp., Ft. Benning, Ga., 1945-46; chief social work service VA Regional Office, Ft. Jackson, S.C., 1947-48; pub. welfare officer Dept. Army, Japan, 1949-51; sr. social worker Valley Forge Army Hosp., 1951; chief social work service VA Hosp., Richmond, Va., 1951-52, VA Center, Wadsworth, Kans., 1952-68, Dublin, Ga., 1968-77; ret., 1977; Peace Corps vol., Morocco, 1978-80. Mem. Social Planning Council, Leavenworth, Kans., 1952-68, v.p., 1955-56, 67-68, pres., 1956-57; bd. dirs. ARC, Leavenworth, 1960-68; bd. govs. United Fund, Leavenworth, 1967-68; bd. dirs. YWCA, Leavenworth, 1962-68, pres., 1964-65; chmn. welfare com. Mayor's Adv. Com., Leavenworth, 1968; mem. organizational bd. Leavenworth Community Action Program, 1966; adviser Explorer Scouts Am., 1972; bd. dirs. Dublin Mental Health Assn., v.p., 1971-72, pres., 1972-74. Mem. Nat. Assn. Social Workers (exec. bd. Mo.-Kans. chpt. 1954-56, pres. central Ga. chpt. 1970-71, del. to assembly 1971), Am. Assn. Med. Social Workers (pres. Mo.-Kans. chpt. 1954-55), Nat., Internat., Ga. (nominating com. 1945) confs. on social welfare, Hist. Soc. McIntosh County (v.p. 1982-84), Daus. Am. Colonists (regent), Colonial Dames 17th Century (treas. Golden Isles chpt. 1982-84), Magna Charta Dames, DAR (regent St. John's Parish 1982-84, state com. on accreditation 1984—, vice regent St. Andrews 1982-84, registrar 1984—), Community Resource Forum (pres. 1971-73). Club: Dublin Pilot (charter). Address: PO Box 1118 Darien GA 31305

MEANS, MARIANNE, columnist; b. Sioux City, Iowa, June 13, 1934; d. Ernest M. and Else Marie (Andersen) Hansen; m. Warren Weaver, Jr., Feb. 10, 1977. B.A., U. Nebr., 1956; J.D., George Washington U., 1977. Copy editor Lincoln Jour., Nebr., 1955-57; sect. editor No. Va. Sun, Arlington, 1957-59; congl. corr. The Hearst Newspapers, Washington, 1959-61, White House corr., 1961-66, syndicated nat. affairs columnist, 1966—; commentator various TV and radio programs, 1977—. Author: The Woman in the White House, 1963. Recipient Front Page award N.Y. Newspaper Womens Club; Headliners Club award. Mem. White House Corrs. Assn. Clubs: Gridiron; Nat. Press. Office: The Hearst Newspapers Suite 420 1701 Pennsylvania Ave NW Washington DC 20006

MEARA, ANNE, actress; b. Bklyn.; d. Edward Joseph and Mary (Dempsey) Meara; student Herbert Berghoff Studio, 1953-54; m. Gerald Stiller, Sept. 14, 1954; children—Amy, Benjamin. Apprentice in summer stock, Southold, L.I. and Woodstock, N.Y., 1950-53; off-Broadway appearances include Ulysses in Nighttown, 1958, Maedchen in Uniform (Show Bus. Off-Broadway award), 1955, A Month in the Country, 1954, The House of Blue Leaves, 1970; mem. Shakespeare Co., Central Park, N.Y.C., 1957; film appearances include The Out-of-Towners, 1968, Lovers and Other Strangers, 1969, Nasty Habits, 1976, The Boys From Brazil, 1978, Fame, 1979; comedy act (with husband Jerry Stiller), 1963—, syndicated TV series Take Five With Stiller and Meara, 1977-78; appearances include Happy Medium and Medium Rare, Chgo., 1960-61, Village Gate, Phase Two and Blue Angel, N.Y.C., 1963, The Establishment, London, 1963; numerous appearances on TV game and talk shows, also spls. and variety shows; rec. numerous commls. for TV and radio; star TV series Kate McShane, 1975, Archie Bunker's Place, 1979. Co-recipient Voice of Imagery award Radio Advt. Bur., 1975. Address: care William Morris Agy 151 El Camino Beverly Hills CA 90212*

MEBANE, BARBARA MARGOT, service company executive; b. Sylacauga, Ala., July 21, 1947; d. Audrey Dixon and Mary Ellen (Yaikow) Baxley; m. James Lewis Mebane, Dec. 31, 1971; 1 child, Cieson Brooke. Grad. high sch., Albany, Ga. Line performer J. Taylor Dance Co., Miami, Fla., 1964-65; sales mgr. Dixie Readers Service, Jackson, Miss., 1965-67; regional sales mgr. Robertson Products Co., Texarkana, Tex., 1967-75; owner, pres. Telco Sales, Service and Supply, Dallas, 1976—; mem. Dance Masters, Miami, 1975—; cons. Lewisville Ballet, Gallerie Dance Ensemble, 1982; choreographer music videos for pay/cable TV, 1985. Author: Paper on Positive Thinking, 1983. Sponsor, St. Jude's Research Hosp., Memphis, Cancer Research Ctr., Dallas. Mem. Nat. Fedn. Ind. Businesses, Female and Minority Owned Bus. League, Assoc. Gen. Contractors (assoc.), Female Exec. Club N.Y.C. Avocations: working with children; teaching dance; writing. Home: 3701 Twin Oak Ct Flower Mound TX 75028 Office: Telco Sales Service and Supply 11163 Shady Trail Suite 102 Box 29763 Dallas TX 75229

MECHANIC, JANET LOVE (MRS. MELVIN OLIVER ARONSON), optometrist; b. Cambridge, Mass., June 30, 1921; d. Leon and Clarice Olga (Hameson) Mechanic; Dr. Optometry, New Eng. Coll. Optometry, 1942; postgrad., U. Maine, 1942-43, Frankfort Arsenal, 1943-44; m. Melvin Oliver Aronson, Oct. 25, 1953; children—Leanne Ruth, Joyce Merle. Chief optical insp. Boston Ordnance Dept., 1942-45; editor sci. optical material M.I.T., Cambridge, 1945-46; pvt. practice optometry, Brookline, Mass., 1947—; head optometrist New Eng. Hosp., 1949-70; cons. indsl. optometrics, 1949-70; optometrist for various rehab. instns. Cert. in gen. and ocular pharmacology, Mass. Trustee, Inst., 1980—. Mem. Mass. (contact lens com.), Boston socs. optometrists, Am. Optometric Assn., New Eng. Coll. Optometry Alumni Assn. (class agt. 1967-69), Epsilon Omicron Sigma. Contbr. articles to profl. jours. Home: 105 Gardner Rd Brookline MA 02146 Office: 1146 Beacon St Brookline MA 02146

MECHANIK, REBECCA FERN, electronics company executive; b. Plainfield, N.J., June 22, 1961; d. Harvey Kenneth and Harriet Isabel (Harrison) M. B.A. summa cum laude, Tufts U., 1983; M.Mgmt., Northwestern U., 1985. Fin. analyst Zenith Electronics Corp., Glenview, Ill., 1985—. F.C. Austin scholar, 1983. Mem. Nat. Assn. Female Execs., Assn. M.B.A. Execs., Northwestern Mgmt. Club of Chgo. Home: 5431 N East River Rd #707 Chicago IL 60656

MECKLER, MARLYS E., speech pathologist; b. Chgo., Mar. 11, 1939; d. Isadore D. and Betty (Shaine) Alpert; m. Milton Meckler, Aug. 15, 1959; children—Ilyce, Renee. B.A., U. Mich., 1960; M.A., Calif. State U.-Northridge, 1970. Cert. in gerontology UCLA, 1982; lic. speech pathologist. Pres., dir. Tarzana Speech and Lang. Ctr., Encino, Calif., 1975—. Mem. Am. Speech, Lang. and Hearing Assn., Calif. Speech and Lang. Assn., Calif. Assn. Speech Pathologists in Pvt. Practice. Club: Am. Field Service (Sepulveda, Calif.) (past pres.). Office: Tarzana Speech and Lang Ctr 17525 Ventura Blvd Suite 307 Encino CA 91316

MEDARIS, FLORENCE ISABEL, osteopathic physician and surgeon; b. Kirksville, Mo.; d. Charles Edward and Nellie (Finley) Medaris; B.A., Coll. Wooster, 1932; D.O., Kirksville Coll. Osteopathy and Surgery, 1939; postgrad. U. Wis., Marquette U. Pvt. practice osteo. medicine and surgery, Milw., 1940—. Active Milwaukee County Mental Assn., Milw. Art Center, Friends of Art; mem. med. bd. dirs. Milw. Soc. Multiple Sclerosis Soc., 1973—; mem. Mayor's Beautification Com., 1968—. Dir. Zonta Manor, 1957-67, Brace Fund Bd. of Advt. Women of Milw., 1958-64, pres. bd., 1962-63, 77—; bd. mem. Bookfellows Milw.; finance com. Coll. Womens Club Found., 1971-78. Mem. Am. Osteo. Assn. (com. mental health 1964), Wis. Assn. Osteo. Physicians and Surgeons, Milw. Dist. Soc., Osteo. Physicians and Surgeons, Am. Coll. Gen. Practitioners, Applied Acad. Osteopathy, Am. Assn. U. Women, Inter-Group Council Women (pres. 1947-49, dir.), Wis. Pub. Health Assn., Council for Wis. Writers, Photog. Soc. Am., Wis. Acad. Scis., Arts and Letters, Delta Omega (nat. pres. 1952-53). Presbyn. Club: Zonta (bd. mem. Milw. 1968-69). Home: 1121 N Waverly Pl Milwaukee WI 53202 Office: 161 W Wisconsin Ave Milwaukee WI 53203

MEDEARIS, ELIZABETH ANNE, educator; b. Jackson, Tenn., Nov. 17, 1948; d. Leroy A. and Evelyn Angeline (Threadgill) Holmes; m. Walter Medearis, Sept. 8, 1968; children—Brent Hartwell, Matthew Holmes. B.S. in Edn., U. Tenn., 1970, M.S. in Edn., 1974, postgrad., 1974-82. Cert. elem. spl. edn. and mental retardation tchr., Tenn. Tchr. remedial reading Beaver Sch., Lexington, Tenn., 1971-73; spl edn. tchr. Paul G. Caywood Sch., Lexington, 1974—. Devotional leader Lexington Civic League, 1984-85. Mem. Council for Exceptional Children, Tenn. Edn. Assn., Lexington Edn. Assn., Henderson City U. Tenn. Alumni Assn. (sec. 1983-84, v.p. 1984-85, pres. 1985-86), Delta Kappa Gamma (com. profl. affairs 1984-85). Methodist. Avocations: family; church activities; education; canoeing. Home: Route 2 Box 72-C Lexington TN 38351 Office: Paul G Cavwood Sch 162 Monroe Lexington TN 38351

MEDEROS, CAROLINA LUISA, government official; b. Rochester, Minn., July 1, 1947; d. Luis O and Carolina (delValle) M. B.A., Vanderbilt U., 1969; M.A., U. Chgo., 1971. Adminstrv. asst. to lt. gov. State of Ill., Chgo., 1972; sr. research assoc. U. Chgo., 1972; project mgr./cons. Urban Dynamics/Inner City Fund and Community Programs Inc., Chgo., 1972-73; legis. asst. to pres. Ill. Senate, Chgo./Springfield, 1973-76; program analyst U.S. Dept. Transp., Washington, 1976-79, chief transp. assistance programs div., 1979-81, dir. programs and evaluation, 1981—. Recipient Sec.'s Meritorious Achievement award Dept. Transp., 1980, Superior Achievement award, 1981. Mem. Am. Assn. Budget and Program Analysis, Sr. Execs. Assn., Exec. Women in Govt., Womens Transp. Seminar. Office: Dept Transp 400 7th St SW Washington DC 20590

MEDICE, ROSE ANN, nurse; b. Greenville, Pa., May 13, 1956; d. Francis Stephen and Marjorie Joan (Malson) McElhinny; m. Arthur Lynn Medice, June 21, 1980. Diploma, Jameson Meml. Sch. Nursing, New Castle Pa., 1977. Staff nurse Greenville Hosp., Pa., 1977—. Democrat. Methodist. Avocations: Aerobics; biking; gardening; camping; latchhook. Home: 41 Glenn Ave Greenville PA 16125

MEDLEY, SHERRILYN, auditor; b. Oneida, Ky., Sept. 7, 1946; d. Ora E. and Rheba (Allen) Rice; m. James F. Laughlin, Sept. 20, 1966 (div. Apr. 1969); m. James Silas Medley, Jan. 25, 1980. B.S. in Acctg., U. Ky., 1975; M.B.A., Xavier U., 1986. Cert. internal auditor. Tchr., Ky. Bus. Coll., Lexington, 1976-78; claims approver Met. Life Ins. Co., Lexington, 1967-73; staff acct. Jerrico, Inc., Lexington, 1976-77, acctg. supr., 1977-80, sr. auditor, 1980-82, internal audit supr., 1982—. Vol., Central Baptist Aux., Lexington, 1984. Mem. Inst. Internal Auditors (chpt. pres. 1985-86), Nat. Assn. Accts., Beta Alpha Psi. Republican. Home: 118 Dundee Dr Lexington KY 40503

MEDLEY-MOORE, BETTE JEANNE, marketing executive; b. Tulsa, Mar. 20, 1950; d. William Charles and Betty (Howell) Moore; grad. with distinction Inst. Fin. Edn., 1978; 1 child, Tanya Ann. Teller, Hawaii Thrift & Loan, Honolulu, 1970-71; savs. supr. Am. Savs., Tucson, 1972-73; asst. br. mgr. Albuquerque Fed. Savs., 1973-78, asst. sec.; asst. v.p. Am. Savs., Albuquerque, 1978; solicitor, underwriter Van Schaack Mortgage, Albuquerque, 1978-79; real estate and fin. mgr. Nu-West, Inc., Phoenix, 1979-82; mktg. dir. Fausett Mgmt. Co., Little Rock, 1982-84; pres. Vesta Mktg. Group, Inc., Little Rock, 1984—; lectr. in field. Mem. Am. Bus. Women's Assn., Inst. Fin. Edn. (dir. 1973-78). Republican. Episcopalian. Club: Civitan (Duke City 1977, 78). Home: 112 Midland Little Rock AR 72205

MEECH, SONJA ROSEMARY, interior design studio owner; b. Mpls., Jan. 16, 1950; d. Frank Mike and Elvira Gertrude (Stolzman) Schumm; m. Frank Otis, Feb. 17, 1968 (div. 1975); 1 child, Christopher. Student schs. Robbinsdale, Minn. Non-foods mgr. Red Owl, Mpls., 1968-71; real estate agt. Centruy 21, Mpls., 1976-79; teller Valley Nat. Bank, Tucson, 1981-85; owner Sonja's, Tucson, 1981—. Telephone solicitor Republican Party, Tucson, 1982. Mem. Assn. Gen. Contractors (spl. events Tucson 1985-86). Home: 4826 N Los Altos Pl Tucson AZ 85704 Office: Sonjas 2730 E Grant Rd Tucson AZ 85716

MEEDER, JEANNE ELIZABETH, food technologist; b. Erie, Pa., Mar. 5, 1950; d. Theodore Roosevelt and Linnie Loretta (Drury) M. B.A., Houghton Coll., 1972; postgrad. Kent State U., 1978-81. Product devel. technician Welch Foods Inc., Westfield, N.Y., 1972-73, tech. asst., 1973, assoc. tech. asst., 1973-76, sr. tech. asst., 1976; research and devel. technologist Stouffer Foods Corp., Solon, Ohio, 1976-77, entree team leader, 1977-82; sr. food technologist Del Monte Corp., Walnut Creek, Calif., 1982-84, prin. food technologist, 1984-85, mgr. product devel., 1985-86, mgr. exploratory devel., 1986—. Mem. Home Economists in Business (treas. San Francisco sect. 1986—), Am. Home Econs. Assn., Inst. Food Technologists, Nat. Assn. Female Execs., Women's Network of Contra Costa County, D.A.R., West County Hist. Soc. Republican. Presbyterian. Lodge: Order of Eastern Star. Avocations: antiques; refinishing furniture; gardening; literature; travel. Office: Del Monte Corp 205 N Wiget Ln Walnut Creek CA 94598

MEEHAN, EILEEN MARY, association executive; b. Hartford, Conn., May 19, 1951; d. John Joseph and Eileen (Tromley) M. B.A. cum laude, Albertus Magnus Coll., New Haven, 1973; M.P.A., Roosevelt U., Chgo., 1981. Membership rep. Ill. State Med. Soc., Chgo., 1976-77; survey analyst Joint Commn. Accreditation of Hosps., Chgo., 1977-79; asst. dir. Accreditation Assn. Ambulatory Health Care, Skokie, Ill., 1979—. VISTA vol. Pembroke Exceptional Children's Ctr., Hopkins Park, Ill., 1973-74; vol. fire fighter Pembroke Fire Dept., Hopkins Park, 1973-74. Hartford Bus. and Profl. Woman's Club scholar, 1969; Conn. Scholarship Commn. scholar, 1969-73; Nat. Merit scholar, 1969. Mem. Chgo. Bus. and Profl. Women's Club, Chgo. Soc. Assn. Execs., Chgo. Assn. Med. Soc. Execs., Nat. Assn. Female Execs.,

Assn. Adminstrs. Ambulatory Health Services. Office: Accreditation Assn for Ambulatory Health Care Westmoreland Bldg Skokie IL 60077

MEEK, CARRIE P., state legislator. Formerly mem. Fla. Ho. of Reps.; now mem. Fla. Senate. Democrat. Office: Fla Senate State Capitol Tallahassee FL 32301*

MEEKS, BILLIE ALLEN, college dean; b. Winston-Salem, N.C., Feb. 25, 1948; d. William Myers and Angeline (Wagoner) Allen; m. Kerdis Edgar Meeks, Jan. 26, 1974; 1 child, Mark Allen. B.A., Appalachian State U., 1969; M.Ed., U. N.C.-Greensboro, 1971, Ed.S., 1977. Vocat. rehab. counselor Vocat. Rehab., Greensboro, 1971-74; guidance counselor Guilford County Schs., N.C., 1974-78; counselor Western Piedmont Community Coll., Morganton, N.C., 1978-82, dean of student services, 1982—. Mem. Burke Arts Council, Morganton, 1983—; active Community Concert Assn., Morganton, 1983—. Mem. N.C. Assn. Developmental Studies (pres. 1983-84), Student Services Personnel Assn. (sec. dean's div. 1982-83, exec. bd. dean's div.), AAUW. Democrat. Presbyterian. Home: 410 Bost Rd Morganton NC 28655 Office: Western Piedmont Community Coll 1001 Burkemont Ave Morganton NC 28655

MEEKS, CONSTANCE MARIE, banker; b. Ft. Wayne, Ind., May 10, 1929; d. Harold Ray and Viola Margaret (Mason) Wells; student Internat. Bus. Coll., 1947-49, Grad. Sch. Banking U. Wis., 1976-78; m. Ronald Lawrence Meeks, Aug. 28, 1948; children—Cynthia Kay Meeks Murphy, Rhonda Sue Meeks Gulley, Brian Keith, Kevin Scott. Sec., Radio Equipment Co., Ft. Wayne, 1948-51; exec. sec. Anthony Wayne Bank, Ft. Wayne, 1965-72, adminstrv. asst., 1972-74, asst. cashier, 1974, asst. v.p., 1974-78, v.p. adminstrn. and ops., 1978-79, v.p. ops., personnel dir., 1979-84, corp. bus. devel. and sr. personnel adminstr., 1984—. Active Big Bros./Big Sisters, Ft. Wayne, Small Bus. Council; treas., bd. dirs. YWCA of Ft. Wayne; bd. dirs. Park Ctr., ArkLink. Mem. Ft. Wayne C. of C., Ft. Wayne Women's Bur., Ind. Bankers Assn., Nat. Assn. Bank Women, Am. Inst. Banking, Am. Bus. Women's Assn., Nat. Assn. Female Execs., Am. Soc. Personnel Adminstrn., Toastmasters. Republican. Methodist. Clubs: Pine Valley Country, Scottish Rite Ladies, Mizpah Shrine Ladies. Home: 6824 Kanata Ct Fort Wayne IN 46815 Office: 203 E Berry St Fort Wayne IN 46802

MEEKS, JOANNE, accountant; b. Plainfield, N.J., Jan. 29, 1956; d. Richard Smith and Janet (Martin) Meeks. B.S., Kean Coll., 1982, B.A., 1982. Asst. supr. Schering-Plough, Kenilworth, N.J., 1983-84, supr., 1984—. Pres. Ladies Aux. Exempt Fire Dept., Watchung, N.J., 1986-87; pres. Union County chpt. Nat. Multiple Sclerosis Soc., 1985—. Mem. Nat. Assn. Credit and Fin. Execs. (chmn. Accounts Payable Interchange div.), Nat. Assn. Female Execs., Sierra Club, Phi Kappa Phi. Office: Schering-Plough 2000 Galloping Hill Rd Kenilworth NJ 07033

MEELHEIM, HELEN DIANE, nurse, nursing administrator; b. Charleston, W.Va., Mar. 25, 1952; d. Richard Young and Dolores (Frick) M. B.S.N., U. N.C., 1974; M.S.N., E. Carolina U., 1982. Charge nurse Pitt County Health Dept., Greenville, N.C., 1974-77; nursing adminstr. E. Carolina U. Sch. of Med., Greenville, N.C., 1978—; cons. Eastern Area Health Edn. Ctr., Greenville. Served to 1st lt. Army Nurse Corps, U.S. Army Res. Mem. Oncology Nurses Soc., Am. Nurses Assn., N.C. State Nurses Assn., Hospice of E. Carolina. Republican. Episcopalian. Avocation: painting. Home: 107 Speight Dr Greenville NC 27834 Office: East Carolina U Sch Medicine Dept Surgery Greenville NC 27834

MEESE, CELIA EDWARDS, pharmaceutical and nutritional supplement company executive; b. San Diego, May 10, 1938; d. Roy Clifford Edwards and Bessie Lucille (Lang) Hill; m. Jed D. Meese, July 6, 1963; 1 son, Scott Edwards. Student U. Calif.-Sacramento, 1958-60; B.A., U. Wis., 1964; B.A. (hon.), U. Taiwan, 1965. Office mgr. Pacific Telephone, San Jose, Calif., 1965-72; pres. Vitaline Corp., Incline Village, Nev., 1972—; v.p. RenalChem, Inc., San Jose, Calif., 1982—, Formulations Tech., Inc., Oakdale, Calif., 1982—; dir. Spectra Diagnostics, San Jose. Bd. dirs. Sierra Council on Alcoholism, Kings Beach, Calif., 1980—. English-Chinese Exchange Council, Taipei, 1964-65, vol. Brandon House, San Jose, 1965—, Children's Home Soc., San Jose, 1965—; mem. steering com. U.S. Rep. Mineta, Calif., 1974. Mem. Pharm. Mfrs. Assn., Am. Soc. Bariatric Physicians, Mensa (proctor 1985). Avocations: drug rehabilitation counselor; travel; the study of languages. Home: PO Box 4772 Incline Village NV 89450 Office: Vitaline Corp PO Box 6757 Incline Village NV 89450

MEESE, JUDITH ANNE, design company executive; b. Lewistown, Pa., Feb. 6, 1942; d. William Musser and Verla Mary (Wilson) Heintzelman; m. Charles Richard Meese, Dec. 22, 1962; children—Susan Patricia, Sally Anne. Owner, instr. Creative Mouse House, Wilmington, Del., 1977-80; interior decorator Habersham Plantation Corp., Augusta, Ga., 1981-83; prin. officer Dept. of Interiors, Augusta, 1983—. Fellow Augusta C. of C.; mem. Nat. Soc. of Tole and Decorative Painters (v.p. 1977-78). Club: Landsdowne Garden (pres. 1973-75) (Wilmington). Avocations: piano; organ; decorative painting; flower arranging; decorative arts. Home: 3505 Lost Tree Ct West Lake Augusta GA 30907 Office: Dept of Interiors Inc 3540 Wrightsboro Rd Augusta GA 30909

MEGDAL, SHARON BERNSTEIN, state commissioner, economics educator; b. Newark, Apr. 4, 1952; d. William B. and Ann (Kopatonsky) Bernstein; m. Ronald G. Megdal, Aug. 18, 1974. A.B. in Econs., Rutgers U., 1974; M.A. in Econs., Princeton U., 1977, Ph.D. in Econs., 1981. Asst. prof. econs. U. Ariz., Tucson, 1979—; commr. Ariz. Corp. Commn. Contbr. articles on econs. to profl. jours. Vol., United Way of Greater Tucson, 1982-85. Richard D. Irwin fellow, 1977-78; fellow Princeton U., 1974-78. Mem. Am. Econs. Assn. (com. on status of women 1983—), Western Econ. Assn., Women Execs. in State Govt., Nat. Assn. Regulatory Utility Commrs. (com. on electricity), Phi Beta Kappa, Beta Gamma Sigma. Office: Ariz Corp Commn 1200 W Washington Phoenix AZ 85007

MEGLINO, JOSEPHINE, home improvement products company executive; b. Bklyn., Dec. 28, 1928; d. Donato and Olimpia Buglione; m. Nicholas Meglino, May 13, 1951; children—Patricia, James, Don. B.A., Hunter Coll., 1949, M.A., 1951. Cert. tchr., N.Y. Engring. aide Bell Labs., N.Y.C., 1951-52, tchr. N.Y.C. Pub. Schs., 1950-53; v.p. Jodee Plastics, Inc., Westbury, N.Y., 1953—; pres. Patrician Products, Inc., Westbury, 1965—. Mem. AAUW (bd. dirs. local chpt.). Roman Catholic. Avocation: duplicate bridge. Home: 91 Lipton Ave Williston Park NY 11596 Office: Patrician Products Inc 468 Union Ave Westbury NY 11590

MEGOFNA, C(HRISTINE) GAIL, medical corporation manager, nurse; b. New Britain, Conn., Aug. 12, 1949; d. Edward Lucian and Mary Dorothy (Cappello) Jacynowicz; m. William John Megofna, Mar. 23, 1974; 1 child, William John, Jr. A.Bus. Adminstrn./Med. Scis., Briarwood Coll., Southington, Conn., 1969; R.N., Tunxis Sch. Nursing, Farmington, 1981; postgrad., 1981-86. Cert. in counseling and human services. Kinetic therapist Kinetic Concepts, San Antonio, Tex., 1981-83; mktg. cons. JM Mktg., Rocky Hill, Conn., 1983—; area mgr. PCS div. EMPI, Fridley, Minn., 1984-85; asst. mktg. mgr. H.L. Moore Med. Corp., New Britain, 1985—. Pres., Briarwood Coll., Southington, 1967-69. Mem. Nat. Assn. Female Execs., Sales and Mktg. Execs., Conn. Bus. and Industry Assn. Democrat. Roman Catholic. Club: New Britain Jr. Woman Club (health chmn. 1977, treas. 1977, sec. 1978). Avocations: golf; reading music; coaching little league. Home: 422 Clinton St New Britain CT 06053 Office: H L Moore Med Corp 370 John Downey Dr New Britain CT 06050

MEGRATH, ROSANNE, company sales executive; b. Mt. Vernon, N.Y., Oct. 7, 1947; d. Vincent James and Antonina (LaRocca) Costantino; 1 dau., Catherine Anne. B.A., U. Bridgeport, 1969. Sec. John Carey, Architect, Pleasantville, N.Y. 1973-75; instr. Manatee Jr. Coll., Bradenton, Fla., 1978-80; sec. Tropicana Products, Bradenton, 1975-79; adminstrv. asst. to v.p., sales and mktg. Tropicana Products Sales, Inc., Bradenton, 1979-83, mgr. mil. sales, 1983—. Mem. PTA, Bradenton, 1977-84. Mem. Am. Logistics Assn. Am. Mgmt. Assn. Republican. Roman Catholic. Home: 3212 21st Ave Drive West Bradenton FL 33505 Office: Tropicana Products Sales Inc PO Box 338 Bradenton FL 33506

MEHERIN, MARGARET WILSON, acct.; b. Mobile, Ala., Jan. 5, 1955; d. Joseph Henry and Rose Patricia (McNamara) Wilson; B.S.C., Spring Hill Coll., 1975; m. Dennis Peter Meherin, May 31, 1975; 1 dau., Bridget Claire. Staff acct. L.E. Nicholas & Co., Mobile, 1975, Morrison & Smith, C.P.A., Mobile, 1975-77; pvt. practice public acctg., Mobile, 1977-80; pvt. practice C.P.A., Mobile, 1980—; sec.-treas. Wilson Electric Co., Inc., Mobile, 1980—, Gulf Coast Electronics, Inc., Mobile, 1980-81. Sec.-treas., Med. Clinic Bd. Second City of Mobile, 1980-82. C.P.A., Ala. Mem. Am. Inst. C.P.A.s, Am. Soc. Women Accts., Am. Women's Soc. C.P.A.s, Ala. Soc. C.P.A.s. Roman Catholic. Home: 1283 Skywood Dr Mobile AL 36609 Office: 32 Tacon St Mobile AL 36607

MEHRMANN, CRAIGANN, nurse; b. Hershey, Pa., Jan. 6, 1953; d. Charles Craig and Martha Arlene (Shepler) M.; B.S., Bloomsburg State Coll., 1974; A.A. in Nursing, Harrisburg Area Community Coll., 1979; B.S. in Nursing, Pa. State U., 1985, postgrad., 1985—. R.N., Pa. Substitute tchr., Derry Twp., Central Dauphin, and Middletown Area sch. dists., 1974-77; nursing asst. Milton Hershey Med. Center, 1978; staff nurse Holy Spirit Hosp., Camp Hill, Pa., 1979, Milton Hershey Med. Center, Hershey, Pa., 1979-80; clin. coordinator Hillcrest Women's Med. Ctr., Harrisburg, Pa., 1980-85. Vol., Am. Cancer Soc., ARC. Mem. Am. Bus. Women's Assn., Am. Nurses Assn., Am. Coll. Obstetricians and Gynecologists (Nurses Assn.), Pa. Nurses Assn. (past dist. treas. and pres.), Harrisburg Area Community Coll. Alumni Assn., Bloomsburg State Coll. Alumni Assn., Sigma Theta Tau. Methodist. Home: 426 W Granada Ave Hershey PA 17033

MEHTA, EILEEN ROSE, lawyer, landscape contracting executive; b. Colver, Pa., Apr. 1, 1953; d. Richard Glenn and Helen (Wahna) Ball; m. Abdul Rashid Mehta, Aug. 31, 1973. Student Miami U., Oxford, Ohio, 1971-73; B.A. with high distinction, Fla. Internat. U., 1974; J.D. cum laude U. Miami (Fla.), 1977. Bar: Fla. 1977. Law clk. U.S. Dist. Ct. (so. dist.) Fla., Miami, 1977-79; asst. county atty. Dade County Atty.'s Office, Miami, 1979—; v.p., dir. Shalimar Trucking, Inc., 1984—, Coral Reef Cruises, Inc., 1984—, Mehtatron Enterprises, Inc., 1985—; guest lectr. U. Miami Law Sch., Coral Gables, Fla., 1982, 83. Alumni scholar Miami U., Oxford, 1971-73. Mem. ABA, Fla. Bar Assn. Office: Dade County Atty's Office Met-Dade Ctr Suite 2810 111 NW 1st St Miami FL 33128

MEIER, KAREN LORENE, educator; b. Davenport, Iowa, Aug. 17, 1942; d. Charles Frank and Minnie Louise (Arp) Meier; B.A., U. Iowa, 1963, M.A., 1974. Tchr., librarian Plano (Ill.) High Sch., 1963-67; tchr. social studies Moline (Ill.) High Sch., 1967—; coordinator Moline Secondary Social Studies, 1978—. Bd. dirs. Quad-City World Affairs Council; active LWV. Mem. Nat., Iowa, Ill. (sec. 1973-74, v.p. 1974-75, dir. 1982-84) councils social studies, NEA, Ill. (sec.-treas. regional council 1975-79, legis. chmn. 1980-81, treas. 1984-86), Moline (pres. 1977-78) edn. assns., Social Studies Suprs. Assn., Assn. for Supervision and Curriculum Devel., Women in Ednl. Adminstrn. (dir. 1983-84, pres. 1985-86), Iowa Women in Ednl. Leadership, Am. Soc. Profl. and Exec. Women, AAUW, Alpha Delta Kappa. Office: Moline High Sch 3600 23d Ave Moline IL 61265

MEIERHENRY, JUDITH KNITTEL, state official, lawyer; b. Burke, S.D., Jan. 20, 1944; d. Adolph John and Anna Elizabeth (Voos) Knittel; m. Mark Vernon Meierhenry, May 14, 1961; children—Todd, Mary. B.A. in English, U. S.D., 1966, M.A., 1968, J.D., 1977. Bar: S.D. 1977. Tchr. English, Plattsmouth pub. schs. (Nebr.), 1966-67; instr. U. S.D., 1968-70, Hiram Scott Coll., Scottbluff, Nebr., 1970; tchr. Todd County Pub. Schs., Mission, S.D., 1971-74; ptnr. Meierhenry, DeVaney, Krueger & Meierhenry, Vermillion, S.D., 1977-79; dir. S.D. Econ. Opportunity Office, Pierre, 1979-80; cabinet sec. S.D. Dept. Labor, Pierre, 1980-83, Dept. Edn. and Labor, 1983—. Author: The Comic Hero in the Modern American Novel, 1968; mem. bd. law rev. editors S.D. Law Rev., 1977. Bd. dirs. S.D. Ednl. TV, 1983—. Mem. ABA, S.D. Bar Assn., S.D. Trial Lawyers Assn., Interstate Conf. of Employment Security Agys, Exec. Women in State Govt. (dir. 1983—). Office: SD Dept Labor and Edn 700 Illinois N Pierre SD 57501

MEIERS, RUTH LENORE, state official; b. Parshall, N.D., Nov. 6, 1925; d. Axel and Grace Mary (Williams) Olson; B.S., U. N.D., 1946; m. Glenn E. Meiers, June 28, 1950; children—David, Michael, Monte, Scott. Mem. Mountrail County Welfare Bd., 1947-71; mem. N.D. Ho. of Reps., 1975-84; lt. gov. State of N.D., 1985—; mem. Disciplinary Bd., N.D. Supreme Ct., 1978-85. Bd. dirs. Upper Mo. Dist. Health Unit, 1958-84. Mem. Women Execs. in State Govt., Nat. Assn. Lt. Govs., Order Women Legislators, N.D. Public Health Assn. Democrat. Lutheran. Club: Sew and So Homemakers.

MEIFU, VALERIE SUZANNE, personnel representative; b. Los Angeles, Oct. 22, 1959; d. Hiroshi and Jane Tokiko (Maruno) M. B.S. in Bus. Adminstrn., Mktg., Calif. State U.-Northridge, 1982. Clk. typist Golden State Service, Van Nuys, Calif., 1977-80; nat. promotional dir. Columbia Sch. of Broadcasting, Hollywood, Calif., 1981-83; pub. relations, advt. adminstr. MicroComputer Accessories, Culver City, Calif., 1983-84; client service rep. Thompson Advt., Los Angeles, 1984-85; personnel rep. FutureNet Corp., Chatsworth, Calif., 1985—. Recipient Scholarship award Alpha Gamma Sigma Bus., 1979. Mem. Am. Mktg. Assn., Nat. Assn. Female Execs., Delta Sigma Pi, Alpha Mu Alpha, Beta Gamma Sigma. Avocations: music; reading; travel.

MEIJER-HIRSCHLAND, JOAN ELLEN, writer, lecturer; b. N.Y.C., May 19, 1939; d. Richard Simon and Bonnie (Prudden) Hirschland; B.A. in History, U. Vt., 1961; student Stella Adler Theatre Studio, 1963, Emergency Care Inst., Beekman Downtown Hosp., 1978; m. Hans Meijer, Apr. 6, 1964; children—Peter Jan, Richard Simon, Jacqueline Cristina. Emergency med. technician, paramedic, N.Y., 1975-82; instr. ARC, Woodstock, Vt., 1976—, Vt. affiliate Am. Heart Assn., 1976—; founder, pres. Nat. Emergency Care Adv. Council, Barnard, Vt., 1977—; cons. emergency care nat. TV, 1977—; also actress, opera singer. Mem. Vt. Democratic State Com., 1972-74. Mem. Nat. Assn. Female Execs., N.Y.C. Assn. Paramedics, League Vt. Writers, Nat. Registry Emergency Med. Technicians. Author: Student Workbook of Cardiopulmonary Resuscitation, 1983; Disaster Jones Children's Stories, 1982; EMS Coloring Book for State of Connecticut, 1983; also articles. Home and Office: 880 Lexington Ave New York NY 10021

MEIKLEJOHN, (LORRAINE) MINDY JUNE, political organizer; b. Staunton, Colo., June 9, 1929; d. Edward H. and Erna E. (Schwabe) Mindrup; student Ill. Bus. Coll., 1948, Red Rocks Community Coll., 1980-81; m. Alvin J. Meiklejohn, Apr. 25, 1953; children—Pamela, Shelley, Bruce, Scott. Pvt. sec. Ill. Liquor Commn., 1948-51, David M. Wilson, Ill. Sec. of State's Office, 1951-52; flight attendant Continental Airlines, 1952-53, pvt. sec. to mgr. flight services office, 1953-54; organizational dir. Colo. Republican Party, Denver, 1981-85; campaign coordinator Hank Brown's Exploratory Campaign for Gov., 1985; mgr. Hank Brown for Congress, 1985-86; dep. campaign dir. Steve Schuck for Gov., 1985-86; active campaigns; del., alt. to various, county, state, dist. and nat. assemblies and convs. Mem. Jefferson County Hist. Commn., Colo., 1974-82, pres., 1979; vol. Jefferson County Legal Aid Soc., 1970-74; vice chmn. Jefferson County Rep. Party, 1977-81; vice chmn. Colo. State Rep. Party, 1981-85; chmn. Rep. Nat. Pilot Project on Volunteerism, 1981; mem. adv. council U.S. Peace Corps, 1982-84; sect. chmn. Jefferson County United Way Fund Dr.; mem. exec. bd. Colo. Fedn. Rep. Women; pres. Operation Shelter, Inc., 1983—. Lutheran. Club: Jefferson County Women's Rep. Home: 7540 Kline Dr Arvada CO 80005

MEIL, KATE, accountant; b. N.Y.C., June 15, 1925; d. Jacob and Becky (Lichtman) Meil; 1 child, Maria Rebecca Black. B.B.A. in Acctg., CCNY, 1949. Acct. chem., printing, garment, machine and tool, film industries, 1943-73; office mgr., acct. Barrie Imports, Inc., Upper Saddle River, N.J., 1973—. Sculptor: Mein Kind, 1976, Determined to Be, 1977, Inner Mirror, 1979, Zeyda, 1980, Meydele, 1985. Leader Hudson Ave Area Residents Assn., Edgewater, 1973. Mem. Salute to Women in Arts, Whittle Ones, Ethical Culture Soc. Clubs: Dumont Chessmates (N.J.); Palisades Nature Assn. (Alpine, N.J.). Avocations: chess; theater; folk dancing. Office: Barrie Imports Inc 145 Route 17 Upper Saddle River NJ 07458

MEILAHN, ELAINE NATHALIA, epidemiologist, horse farm owner; b. Northfield, Minn., Sept. 22, 1947; d. Melford Henry Docken and Mabel Anne (Falkenberg) Adams; M. Michael Meilahn, June 10, 1970 (div. 1975). B.S., U. Wis., 1969; M.P.H., U. Pitts., 1975, also postgrad. Peace Corps vol., Bolivia, Ecuador, 1970-72; intervention dir. for nat. heart study Pitts. Ctr., U. Pitts., 1975-82, project dir., study of epidemiology of cardiovascular disease in women, 1983—; mem. adv. bd. Mon Valley Health Ctr., Monessen, Pa., 1979-82; cons. to Nat. Pulmonary Function Study, Pitts., 1985. Contbr. chpts. to books. Vol. paramedic Tri-Community Ambulance Service, Monongahela, Pa., 1981-83; dir. community-based risk reduction program, Pitts., 1981-82; speaker for Health Edn. Ctr., Pitts., 1980-82. Noyes Found. grantee U. Pitts., 1974-75; USPHS grantee, 1973-74, 82-83. Mem. Soc. for Epidemiologic Research, Combined Tng. Assn. Western Pa. Avocation: training and competing combined training horses. Office: Dept Epidemiology Grad Sch Pub Health U Pittsburgh 5th Ave Pittsburgh PA 15261

MEILINGER, DOMENICA MARIE (DOLLY), nurse; b. Bklyn., Oct. 18, 1937; d. Louis Andrew and Cosmas Jeanette (Cavallaro) S.; m. Arthur Thomas Meilinger, Apr. 8, 1961; children—Thomas, William, Louis, Michael. Diploma, Bellevue Sch. Nursing, N.Y.C., 1959; student Greenville Tech., S.C., 1980-81; B.S. in Nursing, U. S.C., 1983; postgrad. Clemson U., 1983—. R.N., S.C. Staff nurse Huntington Hosp., N.Y., 1959-63, Greenville Meml. Hosp., S.C., 1978—; pvt. duty nurse Upjohns Agy., Hicksville, N.Y., 1970-73; clin. instr. Greenville Inst. Tech., 1983; instr; grad. asst. Clemson U., S.C., 1984, clin. instr., 1985—. Contbr. articles to newspaper. Vol. health worker Mauldin Elem. Sch., S.C., 1973-76; vol. library asst. Mauldin Library, 1980—; vol. cons. USC-S Health Fair Screening, Spartanburg, S.C., 1983; screening cons. Sterling Day Care Ctr., Greenville, 1984. Mem. Am. Nurses Assn., Gerontol. Soc. Am., Bellevue Alumnae Assn., U. S.C. Alumni Assn., Sigma Theta Tau. Republican. Avocations: stamp collecting; gardening; reading; painting; arts and crafts. Home: 102 Royal Oak Rd Route 10 Greenville SC 29607 Office: Clemson U Room 432 Clemson SC

MEIN, ELAINE LOGAN, interior designer; b. Carlisle, Pa., Nov. 9, 1934; d. Arthur Gerald and Helen (Hall) Logan Jacob; m. Gardner Williams Mein, Oct. 26, 1963; children—Gardner Logan, Gardner Williams. Student So. Sem., Buena Vista, Va., 1954, Columbia U., 1955-56, Traphagen Sch., 1959. Designer, Yale R. Borge, N.y.C., 1959-60, Val Arnold, San Francisco, 1960-61, 62-64, Don McApee, Washington, 1961-62; owner, designer Mein Prodns., San Francisco, 1964-82; designer, ptnr. A.D.D., San Francisco, 1982—. Cover editor Nob Hill Gazette, 1975—. Mem. Am. Soc. Interior Design (assoc.), San Francisco Art Inst. (council 1972—), San Francisco Mus. Modern Art (council 1974—).

MEINE, EVELYN DE VIVO, orchestra executive; b. New Castle, Pa., Apr. 27, 1926; d. Joseph and Helen (DeMasi) DeVivo; m. Kenneth Meine, July 15, 1950; (div. May 1973); children—Kenneth, Glenn, Lee, Curt. A.A., Oakton Community Coll., 1973, B.A., DePaul U., 1975. Pvt. sec. med. office New Castle, Pa., 1944-63; part time sec., Balt., Detroit, Chgo., 1963-73; arts adminstr. Nederlander Assn., Balt., 1966-67; mgr. spl. services Chgo. Symphony, 1973—. Mem. adv. bd. Chgo. Artists Coalition, 1982—, Sheffield Winds, 1981—; bd. dirs. Old Town Sch. Folk Music, 1982—, Ill. Arts Alliance, Chgo. Coalition Arts in Edn., Chgo. Music Alliance, 1985. Presdl. scholar Oakton Community Coll., 1973. Recipient Gov.'s award for arts Ill. Arts Council, 1984; spl. service award Chgo. Council Exceptional Children, 1984; disting. alumni award Oakton Community Coll., 1984, DePaul U., 1984. Mem. Am. Symphony Orch. League, Music Educators Nat. Conf., Ill. Council Orchs. (2d v.p.), Delta Gamma. Roman Catholic. Office: Chicago Symphony Orch 220 S Michigan Ave Chicago IL 60614

MEINHARDT, LAURA LEE, publisher, publicist; b. San Pedro, Calif., July 27, 1954; d. Ben William and Myrna Loris (Piepkorn) M. B.S., U. Minn., 1978. Mem. advt. sales staff Dollars & Sense, St. Paul, 1981-82; owner, writer, pub. Schpitfeir Pub., Seattle, 1980—; owner, publicist Inner Circle Promotions, Seattle, 1986—. Author: Olga's Frumpy Folds,, 1980. Mem. Ind. Pubs. Assn. (charter), Book Publicist N.W. (charter), Enological Soc., N.W. Culinary Alliance, Pacific N.W. Book Pubs. Assn., Women's Nat. Book Assn. (charter), PCjr. Users Group Seattle (pres.). Avocations: outdoor walks; racquetball; wine tastings-studying. Office: Schpitfeir Pub PO Box 4253 Seattle WA 98104

MEINTZER, C. ELLA, new toy planner; b. Bklyn., Apr. 3, 1955; d. John Willis Parris and Anna Gladys (Gilreath) Maner; m. Gerard C. Martyn, Jr., June 23, 1973 (div. Jan. 1978); 1 child, Gerard Calvin Martyn, III; m. John Raymond Irwin, Dec. 3, 1981 (div. 1985); m. James Peter Meintzer, Jan. 25, 1986. Ged. Edn. Diploma, State of Va., 1979. Cert. basic project mgr. Documentation clk. C.C.S. Hatfield Wire & Cable, Cranford, N.J., 1979-80; reporting typist Twincoast Newspaper, Terminal Island, Calif., 1980; internat. schedule coordinator Tomy Corp., Carson, Calif., 1980-81, internat. data processing coordinator, 1982-83, new toy planner, 1983—, dept. word processor, 1981-83. Mem. Nat. Assn. Female Execs. Avocations: Computer programming; reading; writing poetry; dancing. Office: Tomy Corp 901 E 233d St Carson CA 90745

MEISEL, BARBARA, leasing company official; b. N.Y.C., Apr. 16, 1955; d. Samuel J. and Renee V. (Goldman) M. B.A. with honors, U. Pa., 1977; M.B.A., NYU, 1980. C.P.A., N.Y. With Coopers & Lybrand, N.Y.C., 1980-82; asst. treas. Chase Manhattan Bank, N.Y.C., 1982-83; mgr. asset acquisition lequity sales Allied Corp./Equilease, N.Y.C., 1983—. Mem. Am. Inst. C.P.A.s, N.Y. State Soc. C.P.A.s. Office: Equilease Corp 750 3d Ave New York NY 10018

MEISINGER, SUSAN, federal government administrator. Dep. under sec. employment standards Dept. of Labor, Washington. Office: Dept of Labor Employment Standards 200 Constitution Ave NW Washington DC 20210*

MEISLER, BARBARA ALTMAN, speech pathologist; b. Wilkes-Barre, Pa., Oct. 5, 1943; d. Julius and Ann (Garber) Altman; B.A. in Speech Correction, George Washington U., 1965, M.A., 1967; m. Jules Murray Meisler, July 4, 1965; children—Marc Alan, Jan David. Speech clinician and lectr. George Washington U., Washington, 1967-68; tchr. Silver Spring (Md.) Nursery Learning Center, 1973-75, speech-lang. pathologist, 1972-79; speech pathologist Silver Spring Speech and Lang. Center, 1974-77; pvt. practice speech pathology, 1977—; cons. Learning Diagnostics, Inc., Silver Spring, 1976-79; guest lectr. Montgomery County public schs., 1979; v.p. Speech and Hearing Discussion Group, 1971-73. Liaison to bd. dirs. Silver Spring Jewish Center, 1975-79, sisterhood pres. 1975-79; bd. dirs., v.p. Hebrew Day Inst., Rockville, Md., 1979-82, pres., 1982-84, exec. dir., 1985—, pres. day sch., 1982—; bd. dirs. Sisterhood Young Israel Shamrei Emunah, Silver Spring, United Jewish Appeal Fedn., 1982—; mem. women's div. United Jewish Appeal Fedn., recipient award of merit, 1980, 81; co-chmn. Marge Freedman Mus. Endowment Talented Children, 1984—. Recipient Service award Silver Spring Jewish Center, 1978; award Hebrew Day Inst., 1984; award of merit Hebrew Day Inst., 1985. Mem. Am. Speech and Hearing Assn., Md. Speech and Hearing Assn., D.C. Speech and Hearing Assn., Sigma Alpha Eta (pres. 1964-65, hon. mem. award 1965), Am. Mizrachi Women. Democrat. Jewish. Home: 11411 Monticello Ave Silver Spring MD 20902 Office: care Hebrew Day Inst 11710 Hunters Ln Rockville MD 20852

MEIXNER, BECKI, cosmetic company executive, make-up artist; b. Cookville, Tenn., May 15, 1956; d. Epi Stephan and Reba (Denny) Bilak; m. Timothy Mark Meixner, July 10, 1976; children—Jeffrey Paul, Nicole Marie. Student Abilene Christian U., 1973-76. Field exec. Aloetta Cosmetics, Niagra Falls, Ont., Can., 1981-85; pres. Aloette Cosmetics So. Mich., Dearborn, 1985—. Mem. Nat. Assn. Female Execs. (network dir. 1985-86), Women's Assn. Vital Ednl. Services, Ladies Assocs. Mich. Christian Coll., Greater Detroit C. of C. Office: Aloette Cosmetics 24103 Dartmouth St Dearborn Heights MI 48125

MEKULA, JANICE ALEXIS, educator, poet; b. Detroit, June 27, 1952; d. Alexander Carl and Jane Kathleen (Plisak) M. B.A., U. Mich., 1974; M.A., Wayne State U., 1978. Cert. tchr., Mich. Spanish tchr. Livonia Pub. Schs., Mich., 1974; English tchr. West Bloomfield Pub. Schs., Mich., 1974—, chmn. dept. English, 1981-84; seminar leader U. Mich.-Dearborn, 1977—; judge writing awards Detroit News and Detroit Free Press, 1978-85; grader SAT exams Ednl. Testing Service, Princeton, N.J., 1981-83. Author: Frozen Sunshine, 1980; contbr. poetry to various jours., anthologies. Recipient Whitney award U. Mich., 1974; named tchr. of yr. West Bloomfield Pub. Schs., 1985. Mem. Nat. Mensa Soc., Nat. Council Tchrs. English, Mich. Edn. Assn. (crisis chairperson 1982), Phi Beta Kappa. Democrat. Jewish. Avocations: reading; piano; guitar; songwriting; photography.

MELAMED, CAROL DRESCHER, lawyer; b. N.Y.C., July 12, 1946; d. Raymond A. and Ruth W. Drescher; A.B. magna cum laude with high honors in English Lit., Brown U., 1967; M.A.T., Harvard U., 1969; J.D., Cath. U. Am., 1974; m. A. Douglas Melamed; children—Stephanie Weisman, Deborah Weisman, Kathryn Melamed. Admitted to Md. bar, 1974, D.C. bar, 1975; law clk. U.S. Ct. of Appeals, D.C. Circuit, Washington, 1974-75; assoc. firm Wilmer, Cutler & Pickering, Washington, 1975-79; assoc. counsel Washington Post, 1979—. Mem. D.C. Bar, Md. Bar, Phi Beta Kappa. Office: 1150 15th St NW Washington DC 20071

MELCHIONNE, LAURA ANNE, graphics engineer, illustrator; b. Belleville, N.J., Aug. 19, 1958; d. Anthony Joseph and Yvette Marie (Santos) M. B.F.A., Rochester Inst. Tech., 1980, M.S., 1986. Supr. art dept. Rochester Inst. Tech. Print Shop, N.Y., 1978-81; graphics engr. Xerox Corp., Fremont, Calif., 1981—; free-lance illustrator, San Francisco. Mem. Nat. Assn. Female Execs., Graphics Arts Guild, U.S. Ski Assn. Club: Far West Masters (Incline Village, Nev.). Avocations: running; skiing. Office: Xerox Corp/Electronic Typewriter Printer Div 901 Page Ave Fremont CA 94537

MELCONIAN, LINDA JEAN, state senator, lawyer; b. Springfield, Mass.; d. George and Virginia Elaine (Noble) Melconian. B.A., Mt. Holyoke Coll., 1970; M.A., George Washington U., 1976, J.D., 1978. Bar: Mass. Chief legis. asst. to Ho. of Reps. Speaker Thomas P. O'Neill, Jr., U.S. Congress, Washington, 1971-80; pros. atty. Hampden County Dist. Atty., Springfield, Mass., 1981-82; state senator Mass. Gen. Ct., Boston, 1983—; instr. Western New Eng. Coll., Springfield, 1978-82; Our Lady of the Elms Coll., Springfield, 1982-83. Chmn., Heart Fund Ball, Western Mass., 1983; incorporator Springfield Coll., 1982—; ex officio trustee Ella T. Grasso Found., Conn., 1982—; active Democratic State Com., Mass., 1983, Hampden County Dems. Recipient Appreciation award Vietnam Vets. of Greater Springfield, 1983; Equal Edn. for All Children award Bilingual Parents of Springfield, 1983; Appreciation award Vets.-Hampden County Council, 1984. Mem. Hampden County Bar Assn., Zonta. Club: Mt. Holyoke. Office: State House Room 504 Boston MA 02133

MELDON, GERI MICHELLE, jewelry designer; b. Cleve., Feb. 4, 1944; d. Paul E. and Rhoda (Goldberg) M.; student Stephens Coll., 1962-63, Parsons Sch. Design, 1963-64; 4 yr. diploma in silversmithing Cleve. Inst. Art, 1968; Grad. Gemologist-in-residence diploma Gemological Inst. Am., Santa Monica, Calif., 1969; Calif. lifetime teaching credentials in adult edn. UCLA, 1972; B.A., Calif. State U., 1974. Tchr. jewelry and design Los Angeles Dept. Recreation and Parks, 1970-76; retail sales May Co. Fine Jewelry, Los Angeles, 1974-75, Tiffany and Co., Beverly Hills, Calif., 1975-77, Slavicks Jewelers, Los Angeles, 1977; instr. jewelry retailing and Am. Gem. Soc. selling and merchandising program Gemological Inst. Am., 1977-78; free-lance jewelry designer, 1970—. Sec. ch. guild, art editor newsletter Ventura County Ch. of Religious Science, Ventura, Calif., 1980-81. Recipient 2d Pl. award Oxnard (Calif.) Cake Decoration Competition, 1980, 1st pl. and 2d pl. for most original, 1981, 1st pl. and Best in Show, 1982. Mem. Nat. Assn. Jewelry Appraisers, Calif. Jewelers Assn., Nat. Assn. Female Execs. Office: 1187 Coast Village Rd 1 Suite 316 Montecito CA 93108

MELE, JOANNE THERESA, dentist; b. Chgo., Dec. 5, 1943; d. Andrew and Josephine Jeanette (Calabrese) M. Diploma, St. Elizabeth's Sch. Nursing, Chgo., 1964; diploma in Dental Hygiene, Northwestern U., 1977; A.S., Triton Coll., 1979; D.D.S., Loyola U., 1983. Registered nurse, dental hygienist. Staff nurse in medicine/surgery St. Elizabeth's Hosp., Chgo., 1964-66, operating room nurse, 1966-67; head nurse operating room Cook County Hosp., Chgo., 1967-76, head nurse ICU, 1976-77; dental hygienist Mele Dental Assocs., Ltd., Oakbrook, Ill., 1977-79, practice dentistry, 1983—. Recipient Northwestern U. Dental Hygiene Clinic award, 1977; Dr. Duxler Humanitarian award scholar Loyola U., 1982. Mem. Chgo. Dental Soc., Ill. State Dental Soc., Acad. Gen. Dentistry, Am. Assn. Women Dentists, Psi Omega (Kappa chpt.). Roman Catholic. Avocations: reading; music; golfing; jogging; skiing.. Office: Mele Dental Assocs Ltd 120 Ctr Mall Suite 610 Oakbrook IL 60521

MELICK, KATHERINE, publishing company official; b. Carteret, N.J., Feb. 4, 1924; d. Stephen and Mary (Ginda) M.; m. Stanley R. Niemiec, Apr. 24, 1948 (dec. 1973). B.L., Rutgers U., 1944. Manual writer G.M. Corp., Linden, N.J., 1944-46; news asst., sec. Wall Street Jour., N.Y.C., 1946-55; exec. sec. Dow Jones & Co., Inc., N.Y.C., 1955-72, asst. to promotion mgr., 1972-74, adminstrv. mgr. mktg. services, 1975—. pres., N.J. Fedn. Women's Clubs, Carteret, 1953-55. Mem. Advt. Women N.Y., Japan Soc., AAUW, Am. Mgmt. Assn. Clubs: Rutgers (N.Y.C.), Douglass Coll. Alumnae Assn. (New Brunswick, N.J.). Office: Dow Jones & Co Inc 420 Lexington Ave New York NY 10170

MELIN, NANCY JEAN, editor, consultant; b. Cleve., Feb. 15, 1941; d. Myron Alexander and Irma (Sell) M.; m. 2d, Milo Gabriel Nelson, Feb. 15, 1980. B.A., Mt. Union Coll., Alliance, Ohio, 1962; M.A., Wayne State U., 1972; M.L.S., Simmons Coll., 1972. Serials librarian U. Vt., Burlington, 1972-75, Central Mich. U., Mt. Pleasant, 1975-78; library systems analyst Research Library Group, Stanford, Calif., 1979, Online Computer Library Ctr., Columbus, Ohio, 1980; serials librarian CUNY Grad. Ctr., N.Y.C., 1981-82; editor-in-chief Library Hi Tech, 1982-83, Library Hi Tech News and Library Software Rev., 1982—, Serials Rev., 1978-83, Ref. Services Rev., 1980-83, Small Computers in Libraries, 1984—, Optical Info. Systems Update, 1986—. Editor: Serials Collection, 1982; Serials Management in an Automated Age, 1982; International Subscription Agents, 1978; Serials and Microforms, 1983; Library Standards 1984; author: Essential Guide to the Library IBM PC, 1985; contbr. articles profl. jours. Mem. ALA. Democrat. Office: 42 Grandview Dr Mount Kisco NY 10549

MELLO, SHEILA MARLENE, software company executive; b. Boston, Mar. 6, 1943; d. Solomon Barnett and Roslyn (Schenker) Jacobson; m. Leonard Mello, May 7, 1966 (div. 1976); children—Michelle Renee, Matthew Jay; m. Lawrence Paul Smetana, Sept. 9, 1984. B.S. in Math. magna cum laude, Tufts U., 1965. Data processing mgr. GCA Corp., Bedford, Mass., 1964-67; mgr. comml. systems PHI Corp. subs. Wang Labs., Arlington, Mass., 1967-72; mgr. small bus. systems Arthur D. Little Systems, Burlington, Mass., 1972-78; v.p. ops. Distbn. Mgmt. Systems, Lexington, Mass., 1978-83; dir. software distbn. Wang Labs., Lowell, Mass., 1983-84, dir. software cons., 1984-85; dir. customer support Palladian Software Inc., Cambridge, Mass., 1985—. Recipient Pres.' award Arthur D. Little, 1977. Mem. Nat. Council Phys. Distbn. Jewish. Club: Sun Valley Swim and Tennis (Lexington) (pres. 1975-76). Office: Palladian Software Inc 4 Cambridge Ctr Cambridge WA 02142

MELLO, SUSAN H., lawyer; b. South Bend, Ind., May 3, 1955. Student Beloit Coll. Wis., 1972-74; A.B., Washington U., St. Louis, 1976; J.D. magna cum laude, Ind. U., 1979. Bar: Ariz. 1981, Mo. 1981, Mass. 1979, U.S. Dist. Ct., U.S. Ct. Appeals (8th cir.). Congl. asst. to John Brademas, Washington, 1973; research assoc. Rand Corp., 1974; research assoc. Trans Century Corp., Washington, 1975; legal analyst U.S. Dept. of Labor OSHA, Washington, 1976; law clerk to town solicitor, Lincoln, R.I.; assoc. Nutter, McClennen & Fish, Boston, 1979-80; Lewis & Roca, Phoenix, 1981-82; Law Offices Louis Gilden, St. Louis, 1983-84; Green, Kehr, Kanefield & Hoffman, St. Louis, 1984; sole practice, 1984—. Mem. ABA (contbr. Real Property Probate & Trust Jour. 1981), Mo. Bar Assn., Women Lawyers Assn. St. Louis, Met. Bar Assn. St. Louis (Young Lawyer award of merit 1986, treas. young lawyers sect. 1986—), Assn. Am. Trial Lawyers, Plaintiff Employment Lawyers Assn., Mortar Bd., Order Coif, Pi Sigma Alpha. Office: 111 S Bemiston Saint Louis Clayton MO 63105

MELLON, JOAN ANN, educator; b. Massena, N.Y., Nov. 29, 1932; d. Leo Herbert and Irene (Tyo) French; m. Donald Emmett Mellon, Aug. 24, 1963. B.A., Coll. St. Rose, 1954; M.Ed., St. Lawrence U., 1956; M.Ed., Tchrs. Coll. Columbia U. 1972, Ed.D., 1985. Tchr. math. Copenhagen Sch. Dist., N.Y., 1954-57, Massena Sch. Dist., N.Y., 1957-62; supr. student tchrs. SUNY-Albany, 1962-63; asst. prof. math SUNY-Potsdam, 1963-67; tchr. math. Long Beach Sch. Dist. (N.Y.), 1967-70; chmn. math. dept. Edgemont Sch. Dist., Scarsdale, N.Y., 1971—; instr. inservice course for elem. tchrs. SUNY-Potsdam, 1965; instr. Inst. for Jr. High Sch. Tchrs., 1966; vis. com. Middle States Assn., 1973, 76, 79. Vice grand regent Cath. Daus. Am., Norwood, N.Y., 1959, grand regent, 1960; treas. St. Lawrence Deanery of Council Cath. Women, Ogdensburg, N.Y., 1958; chmn. Jr. Cath. Daus., Norwood, 1964. Mem. Assn. Math. Tchrs. N.Y. State (exec. council 1977-78), N.Y. Assn. Math. suprs. (v.p. 1978-79), Nat. Council Tchrs. Math., Math. Assn. Am., Edgemont Tchrs. Assn. (pres.), Delta Kappa Gamma. Republican. Roman Catholic. Home: 8 Woodhaven Dr New City NY 10956 Office: Edgemont High Sch White Oak Ln Scarsdale NY 10583

MELNIKOFF, SARAH ANN, gem importer, jewelry designer; b. Chgo., Feb. 12, 1936; d. Harry E. and Marie Louise (Straub) Caylor; m. Casimir Adam Jestadt, Feb. 27, 1959 (div. Sept. 1972); 1 child, Christina Marie Jestadt-Russo; m. Sol Melnikoff, July 31, 1981. Student Gemol. Inst. Am., 1968-69, Am. Acad. Art, Chgo., 1952-56, Art Inst. Chgo., 1953, Mundelein Coll., Chgo., 1953-54. Pres., Casmira Gem, Inc., Chgo., 1963—; comml. artist, Chgo., 1957-78; U.S. del. Internat. Colored Gemstone Dealers Assn., W.Ger., 1985; lectr., cons. in field. Mem. Chgo. Salesman's Alliance, MINK Inc., Am. Gem Trade Assn. (nat. sec. 1982-86), Am. Horse Show Assn., Am. Saddlebred Horse Show Assn., Mid-Am. Horse Show Assn. (dir. 1980-83). Republican. Roman Catholic. Avocation: horses. Office: Casmira Gems 5 N Wabash Ave Suite 1100 Chicago IL 60602

MELON, PATTY ANN, tractor company treasurer; b. Thermopolis, Wyo., Apr. 25, 1951; d. Amon William and Mary Nancy (Stull) Davis; m. Bennie Lee McDonald, Apr. 10, 1970 (div. 1983); 1 child, Lee McDonald; m. Gaston Desiree Melon, Nov. 1, 1983. Exec. Sec. Diploma, Draughons Bus. Sch., Oklahoma City, 1970; postgrad. U. Okla. Ass. ops. mgr. C.I.T. Corp., Oklahoma City, 1970-83; loan officer First Nat. Bank, Oklahoma City, 1983-84; treas. Gaston Melon Ford, Purcell, Okla., 1984—. Republican. Mem. Ch. of Christ. Avocations: writing fiction; short stories. Home: Route 3 Box 158 A Lexington OK 73080 Office: Gaston Melon Ford Tractor Inc 1700 N Green Ave Purcell OK 73080

MELOY, SYBIL PISKUR, lawyer; b. Chgo., Dec. 1, 1939; d. Michael M. and Laura (Stevenson) P.; B.S., U. Ill., 1961; J.D., Chgo.-Kent Coll. Law, 1965; m. Paul W. Meloy, June 29, 1963 (div. 1979), children—William, Bradley. Bar: Ill. 1965, U.S. Supreme Ct. 1972, Fla. 1985. patent chemist G.D. Searle & Co., Skokie, Ill., 1961-65, patent atty., 1965-69, sr. patent atty., 1969-71, dir. internat. legal affairs, 1971-72; regional counsel Pacific and Far East, Abbott Labs., North Chicago, Ill., 1972-78; pvt. practice, Arlington Heights, Ill., 1978-79; asst. gen. counsel Alberto-Culver Co., Melrose Park, Ill., 1979-83; of counsel Palmer, Blackman, Mancini & Riebandt, Park Ridge, Ill., 1980-83; corp. counsel Key Pharms., Inc., Miami, Fla., 1983—; adj. prof. U. Miami Sch. Law, 1986—. Mem. Am. Chem. Soc., Am., Chgo. bar assns., Am. Patent Law Assn., Licensing Execs. Soc., Phi Beta Kappa, Phi Kappa Phi, Iota Sigma Pi, Kappa Beta Pi, Sigma Kappa. Home: 1915 Brickell Ave Apt C-1108 Miami FL 33129 Office: 4400 Biscayne Blvd Miami FL 33137

MELROY, LUELLA ELIZABETH, ins. agy. exec.; b. Churchs Ferry, N.D., May 22, 1920; d. Roy Arthur and Grace Alma (Dingman) Noltimier; student Dakota Bus. Coll., 1938-39; m. Richard Melroy, May 25, 1957. With various ins. offices, Fargo, N.D., 1939-51, Mpls. and St. Paul, 1951-53, Toledo, 1953-61; with Manhattan Ins. Service, Inc., Toledo, 1961—, pres., owner, 1971—. Bd. dirs. Toledo YWCA, 1963-76, pres., 1973-75; bd. dirs., treas. Girls Club of Toledo, 1981-82; chmn. Community Planning Council Com. on Battered Women; bd. dirs., treas. Rescue-Crisis Bd., 1979-81. Named Woman of Yr., Toledo chpt. Nat. Mgmt. Assn., 1975; Bus. Woman of Yr., Dist. 2 Bus. and Profl. Women, 1978; Ins. Woman of Yr., Toledo Assn. Ind. Ins. Agts., 1967. Mem. Ohio Assn. Profl. Ins. Agts. (dir. 1980-83, membership chmn. 1981-83), Toledo Assn. Ind. Ins. Agts. (pres. 1980-81, dir. 1973-82), Nat. Assn. Ins. Women (v.p. 1978-79, regional dir. 1976-77), Inst. Cert. Profl., Mgrs. (cert. profl. mgr.), Women Bus. Owners, Nat. Mgmt. Assn. (nat. dir. 1982—, vice chmn. midwest area 1984, 85, nat. sec.-treas. 1986), Women Involved in Toledo. Republican. Office: 709 Madison Ave Toledo OH 43624

MELTON-SCOTT, MARY MEULI, hospital administrator, consultant; b. Dec. 4, 1943; d. August Martin and Vada Irene (Matthews) Meuli; m. James Lynn Bell, May 23, 1961 (div. 1964); 1 child, James Lynn; m. Charles David Scott, Jr., Sept. 18, 1964 (div. 1969); 1 child, Charles David III; m. Charles Tabb, Jr., June 23, 1970 (div. 1973); 1 child, Erika Elizabeth; m. Johnny Wayne Scott, 1983. B.A., McMurry Coll., 1971; M.S., Wright State U., 1978; Ph.D., Columbia Pacific U., 1983; M.B.A., Xavier U., Cin., 1986. Cert. alcoholism counselor, 23 states, including Ohio. High sch. tchr. Dayton pub. schs., Ohio, 1972-74; therapist Greene Hall, Greene Meml. Hosp., Xenia, Ohio, 1975-77; clin. dir. Bus. Alcoholism Services, Dayton, 1978-83; v.p. Dettmer Hosp./Upper Valley Med. Ctr., Troy, Ohio, 1983—; owner, pres. Melton-Scott Enterprises, Tipp City, Ohio, 1983—; cons. WORAC, Dayton, 1978-83; exec. dir. Miami County Mental Health, Ohio, 1984—. Mem. Nat. Assn. Female Execs., Assn. Mental Health Adminstrs., Nat. Assn. Alcoholism Counselors, Nat. Council on Alcoholism (Ohio chpt.), Am. Coll. Health Care Adminstrs., Sigma Delta Tau. Avocations: writing; gardening; needlework; sports. Home: 227 N Hyatt St Tipp City OH 45371 Office: Dettmer Hosp Inc 3130 N Dixie Hwy Troy OH 45373

MELTZER, MIRIAM SCHLESINGER, social worker, administrator; b. Pitts., Oct. 3, 1938; d. Hymen and Ida Rose (Mirowitz) Schlesinger; m. Donald Meltzer, Apr. 15, 1961; children—Deborah, Alan. B.A., U. Mich., 1960; M.S.W., U. Md., 1966. Counselor, Counseling and Testing, So. Ill. U., Carbondale, 1966-67, dir. social service Meml. Hosp., 1973-75; social worker Sch. Dist. No. 95, Carbondale, 1975-76; field ops. asst. U.S. Census Bur., Belleville, Ill., 1980; dir. truancy alternate program Regional Supt. Schs., Murphysboro, Ill., 1983—; mem. panel specialists Ill. Dept. Rehab., 1985—. Advisor Welfare Rights Orgn., Carbondale, 1973; pres. Beth Jacob Sisterhood, Carbondale, 1979, 80, 81, Lincoln Jr. High Sch. PTA, Carbondale, 1981-82; bd. dirs. Temple Beth Jacob, 1979-80-81. Home: 3007 W Kent Dr Carbondale IL 62901 Office: Regional Supt Schs Courthouse Murphysboro IL 62966

MELVILLE, JANE ELLEN, engineer; b. St. Louis, Sept. 19, 1957; d. Edwin George and Mary Belle (McClure) Mathae; m. Frank Allen Melville, Jr., Oct. 29, 1983. B.S. in Indsl. Engring., U. Mo., 1979. Planning engr. Western Electric Co. Repair Planning and Devel., St. Louis, 1979—, chmn. Tech. Excellence Recognition Award Com. Western Electric Co. Southwestern Region, St. Louis, 1983-84. Chmn. bd. youth Epiphany Lutheran Ch. Council, St. Louis, 1982-83. Recipient Engring. Cost Reduction Achievement award Western Electric Co. Engring., Southwestern Region, St. Louis, 1983. Mem. St. Louis Women's Commerce Assn., Nat. Assn. Female Execs. Republican. Lutheran. Compiler, catalog of current repair planning projects—Repair Plan Book—Business/Residence Products, 1983. Office: Western Electric Co Dept 421420 1111 Woods Mill Rd Saint Louis MO 63011

MELVIN, JOYCE ANN, lawyer; b. Newport News, Va., July 23, 1951; d. George Jackson and Virginia Lee (Washington) M.; m. Carter Kevin Jones, Nov. 6, 1982. B.S. with honors Hampton Inst., 1973; J.D., Coll. William and Mary, 1979. Bar: Va. 1980. Revenue officer IRS, Newport News, Va., 1973-77; mem. firm Scott, Coles, Brown & Melvin, Newport News, 1980—; instr. bus. law Hampton Inst. (Va.), 1980-81; bd. dirs. young lawyers conf. Va. State Bar, Richmond, 1983—. Bd. dirs. Youth Services Commn., Newport News; v.p. NAACP, Newport News, 1976; campaign coordinator Robert C. Scott, Va. Ho. of Dels., 1977; del. Democratic State Conv. U.S. Senate, Williamsburg, Va., 1978. Honoree in field of law Madam Daniels' Sch., Newport News, 1984. Mem. ABA, Va. Women Attys., Newport News Bar Assn. (bd. 1982—), Nat. Assn. Black Women Attys., Delta Sigma Theta (parliamentarian 1982-83). Home: 734 Longleaf Ln Newport News VA 23602 Office: Scott Coles Brown & Melvin 247 28th St Newport News VA 23607

MEMMER, MARY MARGARET, nursing educator; b. St. Paul, Apr. 23, 1936; d. Philip Loren and Georgia Mildred (Rose) Kelly; m. David Jay Memmer, June 24, 1972. B.S. in Nursing, U. Nebr., 1958; M. in Nursing Edn., U. Minn., 1960; postgrad. U. Wash., 1966-67. R.N., Calif., Nebr.; cert. pub. health nurse, Calif. Staff nurse U. Nebr. Hosp., Omaha, 1958-59, U. Minn. Hosp., Mpls., 1959; instr. U. Nebr., Omaha, 1961-62; instr., then asst. prof. U. Mich., Ann Arbor, 1962-66; instr. U. Wash., Seattle, 1967-68; from asst. prof. to prof. nursing Calif. State U.-Chico, 1968—. Author of learning modules (5) Intercampus Nursing Project. Contbr. articles to profl. jours. Mem. Chico Symphony Orch., 1975—. Grantee U. Mich., 1965, Calif. U. and Coll. System, 1974-75, 73-74, Calif. State U.-Chico, 1977-78, 81. Mem. Nat. League Nursing, Calif. State Employees Assn. (chpt. treas. 1972-73, nominating com. 1977-78), U. Nebr. Sch. Nursing Alumnae Assn., Sigma Theta Tau. Democrat. Methodist. Club: Sierra. Office: Calif State U Chico CA 95926

MEMMING-FRIEDENSON, INGRID, business information analyst; b. Jan. 26, 1945; d. Gerrit H.R. Memming and A. Katherine (Blikslager) Memming-Fischer; m. Jay P. Friedenson. B.S., Rutgers U., 1976, M.L.S., 1980. Tech. info. specialist Engelhard Corp., Menlo Park, N.J., 1967-77; med. info. researcher, supr., internat. div. Merck & Co., Rahway, N.J., 1977-79; bus. info. analyst BASF Wyandotte Corp., Parsippany, N.J., 1980—. Contbr. articles to profl. jours. Mem. Spl. Libraries Assn. (edn. chmn. N.J. chpt. 1981-83, program chmn. 1982-83, 1st v.p. 1983-84, pres. 1984-85), Am. Mktg. Assn., Am. Mgmt. Assn., Assoc. Info. Mgrs. Office: BASF Wyandotte Corp 100 Cherry Hill Rd Parsippany NY 07054

MEMORY, CATHERINE ANN, psychologist; b. Boston, Sept. 8, 1939; d. Roger and Mary (Loftus) Keane; A.B. magna cum laude, Regis Coll., 1960; Ed.M., Harvard U., 1961; postgrad. Boston U., 1964-69; m. Robert Edward Memory, Oct. 12, 1969; 1 son, Robert James. Tchr. public schs., Stoneham, Mass., 1961-63, sch. counselor, 1963-68; sch. counselor, Brookline, Mass., 1968-70; psychologist, public schs., Attleboro, Mass., 1970—; cons. Bridgewater State Coll. spl. edn. workshop, 1974; instr. Bristol Community Coll., Fall River, Mass., 1972-73; guest panelist Boston Catholic Family Life program, 1970—; lectr. Project Interserv Tchr. and Parent Tng. Program, 1975—; presenter Project IMPACT Parent Edn. Program, 1978-79. Mem. City of Attleboro Social Services Com., 1970-74; South Attleboro residential chmn. Attleboro United Fund, 1973; com. pack mem. Cub Scouts Am., 1981—. NDEA grantee, San Diego State Coll., 1965; recipient Stoneham Jaycees Outstanding Young Educator award, 1967. Mem. Am. Psychol. Assn., Mass. Psychol. Assn., Mass. Sch. Psychologists Assn., Delta Epsilon Sigma. Club: Regis Coll. Alumnae Assn. Researcher with hyperkinetic children; contbr. paper on subject to profl. confs. Home: 145 Park Circle South Attleboro MA 02703

MENAKER, SHIRLEY ANN LASCH, psychology educator; b. Jersey City, July 22, 1935; d. Frederick Carl and Mary Elizabeth (Thrall) Lasch; m. Michael Menaker, June 4, 1955; children—Ellen Margaret, Nicholas. B.A., Swarthmore Coll., 1956; M.A., Boston U., 1961, Ph.D., 1965. Adminstrv. asst. N.J. State Fedn. Dist. Bds. Edn., Trenton, 1956-59; trainee clin. psychology Mass. Mental Health Ctr., Boston, 1960-61; intern clin. psychology Thom Guidance Clinic for Children, Boston, 1961-62; research assoc. ednl. psychology U. Tex.-Austin, 1964-67, asst. prof. edn. psychology, 1967-70. assoc. prof. ednl. psychology, 1970-79, assoc. dean grad. sch., 1975-77, psychology cons. Research and Devel. Ctr. for Tchr. Edn., 1965-67, faculty investigator, 1967-74; assoc. prof. counseling psychology U. Oreg., Eugene, 1979-85, prof., 1985—, assoc. dean grad. sch., 1979-84, acting dean grad. sch., 1980-81, 82-83, dean grad sch., 1984—. Bd. dirs. Nat. Grad. Record Exam. Bd. and Policy Council-Test of English as Fgn. Lang., Ednl. Testing Services, 1984-87. Contbr. articles to profl. jours. NIMH fellow, 1963-64. Mem. Am. Psychol. Assn. Home: 2955 McKendrick St Eugene OR 97405 Office: Grad Sch U Oreg Eugene OR 97403

MENALDI-SCANLAN, NANCY LEE, librarian, puppeteer, educator; b. Youngstown, Ohio, Mar. 20, 1950; d. Arthur Felix and Evelyn Florence (Chiody) Menaldi; m. Michael Joseph Scanlan, Aug. 21, 1976. B.F.A. summa cum laude, Kent State U., 1972; M.A., Northwestern U., 1973; M.S., Simmons Coll., 1979; postgrad. NYU, London, 1982. Cert. tchr. elem., speech, sch. librarian. Child drama tchr. Ark. Arts Ctr., Little Rock, 1973-74; fine arts tchr. St. James Sch., Arlington, Mass., 1976-78; children's librarian Lexington Pub. Library (Ky.), 1979-80; dir. pub. arts programs, U. Ky., Lexington, 1980-81; librarian/tchr. St. Andrew's-Sewanee Sch., St. Andrews, Tenn., 1981-83; children's librarian Providence Pub. Library, 1983—, juvenile, young adult reviewer, 1983—; library asst. Melrose Pub. Library (Mass.), 1978-79; dir. Puppet Playhouse, Youngstown, Ohio, 1968-72, Lexington, 1979-81, Providence, 1983—. Contbr. book revs. to various profl. jours. Bd. dirs. Thurmond Library, Sewanee, Tenn., 1982-83. Recipient Town Hall Players award, Kent State U., 1972. Mem. ALA, Am. Theatre Assn., Southeastern Theatre Assn., R.I. Library Assn. Roman Catholic. Home: 55 Parkside Dr Cranston RI 02910 Office: Providence Pub Library 708 Hope St Providence RI 02906

MENDEL, LOUISE A., interior design co. exec.; b. New Orleans, Nov. 3, 1896; d. Jacob and Stella (Bloom) Abraham; m. Walter Scott Mendel, Aug. 2, 1916; children—Louise Stella, Charles. With The Strassel Co., Louisville, 1929—, pres., 1946-79, chmn. bd. dirs., 1979—. Mem. Am. Soc. Interior Decorators Nat. Antique and Art Dealers Assn.of AM., Inc. Republican. Home: 6114 Longview Ln Louisville KY 40222

MENDEL, MARSHA DELONG, insurance company executive; b. Reading, Pa., Aug. 23, 1952; d. William Marsh and Jane Eaches DeLong; m. Michael Thomas Mendel, Sept. 5, 1982. B.A., Duke U., 1974; C.P.C.U., Ins. Inst. Am., 1980. Coach swimming and diving Kutztown (Pa.) Swim Assn., summers 1968, 69; mem. pub. relations staff Kutztown Folk Festival, summers, 1970-74; mktg. rep. Aetna Life & Casualty, Reading, 1974-77, personal lines account exec., 1977-83; personal lines underwriting mgmt. CNA Ins., Reading, Pa., 1983—; nat. exam. grader Ins. Inst. Am., 1981—. Vol. Easter Seal Soc., Reading, 1976-81, coordinator pledge ctr., 1979; co. chmn. United Way of Berks County, 1981-82; bd. dirs. Flint Hill Water Co., Bowers, Pa., 1974—; vol. speaker Center City Devel. Corp., Reading, 1980—. Named Ins. Woman of Yr., 1980, Brace for an Ace award Easter Seal, 1978. Mem. Ins. Women of Reading (past pres.), Nat. Assn. Ins. Women (regional legis. chmn. 1981), Soc. C.P.C.U.s (chpt. pres. 1984-85), Nat. C.P.C.U. Soc. (bd. dirs. 1986—), Junior League of Reading. Republican. Mem. United Ch. of Christ. Office: CNA Ins 401 Penn St Reading PA 19601

MENDEZ, CAROLYN COX, insurance broker; b. Denver, June 22, 1952; d. William Miller Cox and Anne (Todaro) Cox Lowrey; m. Angelo Carlos Mendez, Mar. 27, 1982. Assoc. Nursing, U. Tex., 1973; property and casualty ins. license Pohs Inst., White Plains, N.Y., 1976. Property and casualty underwriter Meadowyork Agy., Elmsford, N.Y., 1975-76; property underwriter L. Newman Agy., White Plains, 1977-78; account rep. Marsh & McLennan, Inc., N.Y.C., 1979-81; account exec. Franey & Parr, Dallas, 1981-83, K. Murchison & Co., Dallas, 1983—. Mem. Tex. Cable Assn., Nat Cable TV Assn., Women in Cable. Republican. Roman Catholic. Club: Baylor Wives (Dallas).

MENDEZ, JANA LYNN, state senator; b. Moscow, Idaho, Jan. 18, 1944; d. Earl Dean and Alverta (Dalberg) Hall; m. Richard Albert Mendez, Sept. 16, 1965; children—Amy, Jennifer, Christopher. B.S. in Journalism, U. Colo., 1981. Community and issue activist Boulder County Housing Authority and Citizens for the Right To Vote, Longmont, Colo., 1975-83; legis. asst. Senate Minority Leader, Denver, 1982-84; mem. Colo. Senate, Denver, 1985—. Author: (with others) Chile From The Ground Up, 1982. Democratic precinct leader, area coordinator, senate dist. chmn. Boulder County, Colo., 1975-84; chmn., commr. Boulder County Housing Authority, 1974-83. Regents scholar, 1963, Cervi scholar, 1980; U. Colo. Women's Ctr. grantee, 1980; named Outstanding Freshman Senator Colo. Social Legis. Com., 1985. Mem. Kappa Tau Alpha. Avocations: gardening; reading; photography; cooking. Office: State Capitol Room 274 Denver CO 80203

MENDOZA, CRISTINA LAGUERUELA, lawyer; b. Havana, Cuba, July 27, 1946 came to U.S., 1960; d. Benito Javier and MaryAnn (Pollis) Lagueruela; m. Victor G. Mendoza, Jr., Dec. 28, 1967; children—Cristi, Victor, Nicole, Andres. B.A., Chatham Coll., 1966; M.A., U. Miami, 1967, J.D., 1982. Bar: Fla. 1982. Instr., Law Sch. U. Miami (Fla.), 1981-84; law clk. U.S. Dist. Co. (so. dist.) Fla., Miami, 1982-83, U.S. Ct. Appeals (11th cir.), Miami, 1983—. State crime task force chmn. Jr. Leagues of Fla., 1983-85; sec. Coral Gables Khoury League, Miami, 1982-84; mem. Ransom Everglades Mothers Bd., Miami, 1983-84. Mem. ABA, Cuban-Am. Bar Assn., Fla. Bar Assn., Fed. Bar Assn., Order of Barrister, Wig and Robe, Bar and Gavel, Phi Kappa Phi. Democrat. Roman Catholic. Home: 1528 Robbia Ave Coral Gables FL 33146 Office: US Court of Appeals 300 NE 1st St Miami FL 33131

MENDOZA, JEANNE MATHIAS, educational administrator; b. Mpls., July 6, 1932; d. Paul F. and Irene J. (Kunitz) Bartholoma; m. Russell Mathias, Oct. 29, 1955 (dec.); children—Mark, Jeff; m. Clifford Mendoza, June 28, 1974; children—Robyn, David. B.S., U. Minn., 1954; M.S. in Counseling, St. Cloud State U., 1971; Ph.D. in Psychology, Internat. Coll., Los Angeles, 1984. Tchr., Mpls., 1968-74; counselor San Diego City Schs., 1974-77, adminstr., 1977—; project coordinator San Diego State U., 1984—; adj. prof. San Diego State U., 1983—; lectr. Fin. Focus, San Diego, 1975-83; cons. Author: Connections Developmental Skills for Families, 1981; Search: Exploring the Systems of Survival, 1985; Learning Styles, 1981. Group trainer LaJolla Presbyn. Ch., 1979-83; bd. dirs. Ednl. Talent Search, San Diego, 1984-85; mem. nat. adv. bd. Fed. Project: TAPP, Boston, 1984—, Multi-Cultural Trainer of Trainers, Los Angeles, 1982—. March of Dimes grantee, 1984, 85; recipient profl. awards. Fellow San Diego Assn. Women in Adminstrn., Parent/Community Bd.; mem. Commn. Coop. Interagy. Agreements (funding chair). Republican. Club: LaJolla Tennis. Avocations: skiing; biking; tennis. Home: 5552 Via Callada LaJolla CA 92037

MENG, DOROTHY SMITH, nurse, administrator; b. Oak Creek, Colo., Jan. 10, 1927; d. William M. and Nellie (Berere) Smith; m. Ernest Meng, 1946; children—Terese, Adrienne, Marilyn, Carter, Kevin, Brian, Eric. A.A. with honors, Daley Coll., 1976; B.A. with honors, Roosevelt U. Staff nurse Michael Reese Hosp., Chgo., 1977; Rush-Presbyn. St. Luke's Hosp., Chgo., 1979—; registry nurse Staff Builders, Inc., 1977-80. Active Christian Family Movement. Mem. Internat. Flying Nurses Assn., Daley Coll. Nursing Alumni (editor 1980-84). Home: 6039 S Mobile Ave Chicago IL 60638

MENGE, DANNETTE MARIE, petroleum engineer; b. New Orleans, Feb. 26, 1958; d. Laurence Hewitt and Gloria (LouViere) Menge; m. Melvin August Mueller, Sept. 4, 1982. B.S. in Mech. Engring., U. New Orleans, 1981; M.S. in Petroleum Engring., Tulane U., 1986. Petroleum engr. Chevron USA, Inc., New Orleans, 1981—. Mem. ASME (treas. 1980-81), La. Engring. Soc. (assoc.), Soc. Petroleum Engrs., Am. Welding Soc. (charter mem.). Democrat. Roman Catholic. Avocations: scuba diving, swimming, camping, fishing, sewing. Home: 801 Sena Dr Metairie LA 70005 Office: Chevron USA Inc 935 Gravier St New Orleans LA 70112

MENK, PAULINE AYERS, account executive; b. Jefferson Twp., Mo., Dec. 18, 1941; d. Walter McKinley and Margaret (Wescoat) Ayers; m. Merlin H. Menk, Feb. 1, 1979. B.A. in Liberal Arts, U. Colo., 1977; postgrad. Stetson U., 1981. Asst. supr. Sinclair Refining, Kansas City, Mo., 1960-66; exec. sec. Inexco Oil Co., Denver, 1968-71; with B.C. Christopher & Co., 1972-74; asst. exec. v.p., Nat. Health Labs. Denver, 1973-77; cons., Denver, 1977-78; account exec. Blinder, Robinson, Denver, 1982—; pres. Ascend Investments, Denver, 1980-82. Clubs: U. of Colo. Dirs., Flatirons (Boulder), Elks. Republican. Office: Blinder Robinson 700 Broadway Suite 961 Denver CO 80203

MENNELL, CONSTANCE JACKSON, advertising and marketing executive; b. Boston, July 26, 1940; d. Frederick M. and Josephine P. Jackson; B.A. in Psychology, Skidmore Coll., 1962; m. Michael A. Mennell, Oct. 26, 1968 (div.). Advt. mgr. Lake Tahoe Assos., San Francisco, 1967-68; account exec. in land devel. Don Frank & Assos., Los Angeles, 1968-69; media dir., account exec. Wilton, Coombs and Colnett, Inc., Los Angeles, 1969-71; media dir., account service exec. Meyers & Muldoon Advt., San Francisco, 1972-74; free-lance account exec., San Francisco, 1975-76; advt./mktg. mgr. Geyser Peak Winery subs. Joseph Schlitz, San Rafael, Calif., 1976-80; advt./mktg. dir. Buck Stove West, Inc., Benicia, Calif., 1980-82; account exec. Jamison & Assocs., San Francisco, 1983—. Home: 72 Corte Real Greenbrae CA 94904

MENNEN, DOROTHY RUNK (MRS. HAROLD E. MENNEN), retired performing arts educator; b. Marshfield, Wis., July 17, 1915; d. Jon Cleveland and Minnie Pearle (Walker) Runk; B.S. in Edn., Kent State U., 1938; M.A., Purdue U., 1964; m. Harold E. Mennen, Jan. 5, 1943; children—Ferol, Laurel (Mrs. Bruce Miller Robb). Tchr., choral dir. Twinsburg (Ohio) pub. sch., 1938-41; tchr. speech, English Aurora (Ohio) High Sch., 1941-42; tchr. Cuyahoga Falls (Ohio) High Sch., 1941-42; tchr. English, Wea High Sch., Tippecanoe County, Ind., 1951-53; tchr. vocal music West Lafayette (Ind.) pub. schs., 1957-60; assoc. prof. theatre Purdue U., West Lafayette, Ind., also vocal coach, from 1964, chmn. senate, 1979-80. Now prof. emeritus; contralto soloist, 1946—. Editor: Directory of Voice and Speech Specialists in Actor Training Programs in U.S. and Canada, 1981. Bd. dirs. Lafayette Symphony, 1958-60, Civic Theatre, Lafayette, 1972-73. Mem. Am. Theatre Assn. (nat. chairperson theatre, speech and voice 1968-71, 73-75, Outstanding Leadership and Performance award Univ.-Coll. Theatre div. 1985), Nat. Assn. Tchrs. of Singing (treas. Ind. chpt.), Speech Communication Assn., AAUP (chairperson com. W on Status of Women 1972-74, pres. chpt. 1974-75, 75-77), LWV. Democrat. Methodist. Home: 1804 Ravinia Rd West Lafayette IN 47906 Office: Theater Dept Creative Arts Stewart Center Purdue U West Lafayette IN 47907

MENNOR, BETTINA ANN, nurse; b. Lancaster, Pa., Sept. 13, 1947; d. Marvin Elliot and Doreen (Derr) Hamblin; m. Fernando Antonio Nazario, Nov. 6, 1965 (dec. 1970); children—Fernando Antonio, Rebecca Elaine; m. Charles Douglas Mennor, June 11, 1970; children—Douglas Paul, Steven Michael. Assoc. Edn., Central Tex. Coll., A.Nursing, 1970. R.N., Tex. Staff nurse Scott & White, Temple, Tex., 1970-71, staff nurse, 1971-74, therapist, 1974-77, infection control clinician, 1977-79, staff nurse orthopedics, 1979-82; staff nurse E.R. Metroples Hosp., Killeen, Tex., 1978-82; field supr. A. Jackson Health Care Systems, Temple, Tex., 1983—. Health chmn. PTA, Harker Heights, 1980-81. Mem. Nat. Assn. IV Therapists, Tex. Assn. IV Therapists, Assn. Practitioners in Infection Control, Central Tex. Infection Control Assn., others. Republican. Mem. Ch. of Jesus Christ of Latter Day Saints. Club: Harker Heights Police Ladies Aux. (past treas., sec.). Home: 202 E Cherokee St Harker Heights TX 76543 Office: A Jackson Health Care Systems PO Box 4005 Temple TX 76501

MENSCH, LINDA SUSAN, lawyer, educator; b. N.Y.C., Mar. 12, 1951; d. Max Robert and Judith (Keller) M.; m. Michael Gerald Heyman, Aug. 28, 1977. Student, U. Salzburg, Austria, 1971-72, Collegium Palatinum, Heidelberg, Ger., 1972, Caius and Gonville Colls., Cambridge U. (Eng.), 1972; B.A., Hamilton Coll., 1973; J.D., NYU, 1976. Bar: N.Y. 1977, Ill. 1977. Law clk. Snadowsky & Fox, N.Y.C., 1974-76, Women's Rights Project, ACLU, N.Y.C., 1975; adj. prof. Columbia Coll., Chgo., 1978—; assoc. law firm Shelton, Kalcheim & Cotnoir, Chgo., 1977-82, Katten, Muchin, Zavis, Pearl & Galler, Chgo., 1982-84, Linda S. Mensch, P.C., 1985—; v.p., gov., gen. counsel Nat. Acad. Rec. Arts and Scis., Chgo., 1979—, nat. trustee, 1985—; bd. dirs. Lawyers for Creative Arts, Chgo., 1982—; entertainment mgmt. cons. Chgo. Entertainment Network, 1983—. Exec. producer record album Back to Chicago Duke Tumatoe, 1983, Heavy Manners, 1983. Vice-pres., bd. dirs. Midwest Rec. Arts Found., Chgo., 1983—. N.Y. State Regents scholar, 1969-73. Mem. Chgo. Bar Assn. (creative arts com., patent, trademark and copyright com. 1983—), Nat. Assn. Women Bus. Owners, ABA, Ill. State Bar Assn., Nat. Acad. Rec. Arts and Scis., Women in Film (founding mem. sec. 1984). Home: 1158 S Plymouth Ct Chicago IL 60605 Office: 33 N Dearborn Suite 506 Chicago IL 60602

MENTZ, BARBARA ANTONELLO, lawyer; b. Kans. City, Mo., July 4, 1944; d. John Francis and Eleanor Barbara (Vagnino) Antonello; m. Lawrence Mentz, Nov. 10, 1973; children—Kathleen Elizabeth, Lawrence Goodwin. B.A. in Econs., U. Kans., 1965; J.D. magna cum laude, U. Notre Dame, 1973. Bar: N.Y. 1974. Assoc. Sullivan & Cromwell, N.Y.C., 1973-77; assoc. Forsyth Decker Murray & Hubbard, N.Y.C., 1977-79; ptnr. Hall, McNicol, Hamilton & Clark, N.Y.C., 1979-86; atty. CBS Inc., N.Y.C., 1986—; mem. panel arbitrators N.Y. Stock Exchange. Contbr. articles to profl. jours. Mem. ABA (mem. Sect. 7), Bar Assn. City of N.Y. (mem. com. on profl. discipline), Securities Industries Assn. (mem. legal and compliance div.). Office: Hall McNicol Hamilton & Clark 220 E 42nd St New York NY 10017

MENTZER, MERLEEN MAE, adult education educator; b. Kingsley, Iowa, July 25, 1920; d. John David and Maggie Marie (Simonsen) Moritz; m. Lee Arnold Mentzer, June 1, 1944. Student Westmar Coll., 1939, Wayne State U., Nebr., 1942, Bemidji State U., 1950, Mankato Coll., 1978, U. Minn.-St. Paul, 1979. Tchr., Kingsley, Iowa, 1938-41; owner, mgr. Mentzer's Sundries, Hackensack, Minn., 1946-76, House of Mentzers, Pine River, Minn., 1974-77; instr. Hennepin Tech., Eden Prairie, Minn., 1978—. Mem. Mpls. C. of C., Hackensack C. of C., (v.p. 1970-76), Northern Lights Federated Woman's Club (pres. 1958-59). Republican. Lutheran. Avocations: dancing; bowling; reading; theatre; seminars. Home: 6781 Tartan Curve Eden Prairie MN 55344

MENYUK, PAULA, educator; b. N.Y.C., Oct. 2, 1929; d. Louis and Helen (Weissman) Nichols; B.S., N.Y.U., 1951; M.Ed., Boston U., 1954; D.Ed., 1961; m. Norman Menyuk, Mar. 5, 1950; children—Curtis R., Diane E., Eric D. Chief lang. clinic Mass. Gen. Hosp., Boston, 1952-54; lectr., teaching fellow Boston U., 1955-58, predoctoral fellow, 1958-61; postgrad. fellow M.I.T., 1961-64, mem. research staff, 1964-72; mem. faculty Boston U., 1972—, prof. psycholinguistics, 1973—, dir. reading and lang. devel. div., 1982—; cons. in field. Fulbright fellow, 1971; NIMH fellow, 1958-64. Fellow Am. Speech, Lang. and Hearing Assn.; mem. Soc. Research Child Devel., Linguistic Soc. Am., Internat. Soc. Study Behavioral Devel., Internat. Soc. Phonetic Scis., Internat. Child Lang. Assn., AAAS. Author: Sentences Children Use, 1969; Acquisition and Development of Language, 1971; Language and Maturation, 1977; also monographs. Office: 605 Commonwealth Ave Boston MA 02215

MENZIES, JEAN STORKE (MRS. ERNEST F. MENZIES), retired newspaperwoman; b. Santa Barbara, Calif., Dec. 30, 1904; d. Thomas More and Elsie (Smith) Storke; B.A., Vassar Coll., 1927; M.A. in Physics, Stanford, 1931; m. Ernest F. Menzies, Oct. 20, 1937; children—Jean Storke (Mrs. Dennis Wayne Vaughan), Thomas More. Teaching asst. dept. physics Stanford, 1927-29; instr. of physics Vassar Coll., 1929-30; tchr. math., chemistry, gen. sci. Sarah Dix Hamlin Sch., San Francisco, 1931-34; sec. to Dr. and Mrs. Samuel T. Orton, N.Y.C., 1935-36; press reporter, spl. writer Santa Barbara News-Press, 1954-63. Rec. sec. nat. YWCA, India, Burma and Ceylon, 1941-42; rec. sec., Calcutta YWCA, 1942-47, v.p., 1949-51; sec. Tri-County adv. council Children's Home Soc., Santa Barbara, 1952-54; founding dir., sec. corp. Santa Barbara Film Soc., Inc., 1960-66. Bd. dirs. Santa Barbara County chpt. Am. Assn. UN, 1954-59, Friends U. Calif. at Santa Barbara Library, 1970-74, Small Wilderness Area Preservation, 1971-79; sec. bd. trustees Crane Country Day Sch., 1955-57; trustee Mental Hygiene Clinic of Santa Barbara, 1956-60, U. Calif. Santa Barbara Found., 1974-80, Santa Barbara Mus. Natural History, 1977-81; adv. council Santa Barbara Citizens Adult Edn., 1958-62, v.p., 1960-62; bd. dirs. Internat. Social Sci. Inst., sec., 1963-68, mem. adv. bd., 1969; bd. dirs. Planned Parenthood Santa Barbara County, Inc., 1964-65, adv. council, 1966-67; trustee Santa Barbara Botanic Garden, 1967-81, hon. trustee, 1981—; trustee. Santa Barbara Trust for Historic Preservation, 1967-68, 72-77; mem. affiliates bd. dirs. U. Calif. at Santa Barbara, 1960-61, 67-70, 72-77; sec. Santa Barbara Mission Archive-Library, 1967—; mem. Santa Barbara Found., 1977-81. Mem. Santa Barbara Hist. Soc. (dir. 1957-62, founding mem. women's projects com. 1959-63, sec. 1961-62), Channel City Women's Forum (v.p. 1969-73, bd. dirs. 1973—), Phi Beta Kappa, Sigma Xi. Club: Vassar of Santa Barbara and the Tri-Counties (1st v.p., founding com. 1956-57, 2d v.p. 1959-61, chmn. publicity com. 1961-73). Home: 2298 Featherhill Rd Santa Barbara CA 93108

MÉRAS, PHYLLIS LESLIE, journalist; b. Bklyn., May 10, 1931; d. Edmond Albert and Leslie Trousdale (Ross) M.; B.A., Wellesley Coll., 1955; M.S. in Journalism, Columbia U., 1954; Swiss Govt. Exchange fellow, Inst. Higher Internat. Studies, Geneva, 1957; m. Thomas H. Cocroft, Nov. 3, 1968. Reporter, copy editor Providence Jour., 1954-57, 59-61; feature writer Ladies Home Jour. mag., 1957-58; editor Weekly Tribune, Geneva (Switzerland), 1961-62; copyeditor, travel sect. N.Y. Times, 1962-68; mng. editor Vineyard Gazette, Edgartown, Mass., 1970-74, contbg. editor, 1974—; asso. editor Rhode Islander, Providence, 1970-76; travel editor Providence Jour., 1976—; editor Wellesley Alumnae mag., 1979—; assoc. in journalism U. R.I., 1974-75; adj. instr. Columbia U. Sch. Journalism, 1975-76; author: First Spring: A Martha's Vineyard Journal, 1972; A Yankee Way With Wood, 1975; Miniatures: How to Make Them, Use Them, Sell Them, 1976; Vacation Crafts, 1978; The Mermaids of Chenonceaux and 828 Other Tales: An Anecdotal Guide to Europe, 1982; co-author: Christmas Angels, 1979; Carry-out Cuisine, 1982; Exploring Rhode Island, 1984. Pulitzer fellow in critical writing, 1967. Mem. Soc. Am. Travel Writers. Home: Sunnyside Ave Vineyard Haven MA 02568 Office: Providence Jour Providence RI 02902

MERCADO, JESSICA THERESA, marketing representative; b. Fontana, Calif., Oct. 29, 1954; d. Raul Joseph and Rose (Caballero) M. A.A. in Fashion Merchandising, Brooks Coll., Long Beach, Calif., 1974; B.A., Calif. State U., Fullerton, 1980. Mktg.-sales support staff Pacific Bell, Los Angeles, 1982—. Mem. Nat. Assn. Female Execs., Statue of Liberty Found., Beta Sigma Phi (mem. exec. bd., v.p., treas.). Avocations: cooking; aerobics; nutritional awareness. Office: Pacific Bell 1010 Wilshire Blvd Los Angeles CA 90017

MERCE, ANNE MARIE, insurance underwriter; b. Denison, Ohio, Nov. 5, 1947; d. Russel and Leona (Berry) M.; student Alderson Broaddus Coll., 1967-68; B.Mus. Edn., Westminster Choir Coll., 1972. Cons., tchr. Nat. Keyboard Arts Assocs., Princeton, N.J., 1972-73; homeowners underwriting clk. Walter B. Howe, Inc., Ins., Princeton, 1973; adminstrv. asst. E.D. Sayer, Inc., Princeton, 1974-79, asst. v.p., underwriter, 1979-84; treaty under-writer GRE-Re of Am. Corp., Princeton, 1984-85; account rep. GRE/Albany-Atlas Ins. Group, Princeton, 1985—. Mem. Nat. Assn. Female Execs., Soc. Profl. and Exec. Women, Assn. Profl. Ins. Women. Republican. Baptist. Home: 189 Princeton Arms N Cranbury NJ 08512 Office: 1020 US Route 1 Princeton NJ 08540

MERCER, JUNE GREER, retail company executive, consultant, b. Homerville, Ga., Sept. 27, 1953; d. Mack Varnedoe and Betty (English) Greer; m. Jerry L. Mercer, Dec. 11, 1981; 1 child, Thomas Greer. B.S. in Journalism and Home Econs., U. Ga., 1975, M.S., 1976. Account exec. So. Bell, Griffin, Ga., 1976-78; office mgr. Jerry Mercer, Valdosta, Ga., 1981—; image cons. Beauty for All Seasons, Valdosta, 1982—; owner, buyer Big and Tall Man's Store (Unique Image, Inc.), Valdosta, 1985—, pres. Unique Image, Inc.; sec., treas. South Ga. Emergency Physicans, Inc. Recipient Outstanding Sales Achievement award So. Bell, 1977; named one of 10 Top Cons. in Southeast, 1984. Mem. Am. Council Consumer Issues, Am. Home Econs. Assn., Ga. Home Econs. Assn., DAR, Phi Kappa Phi, Phi Upsilon Omicron, Gamma Sigma Delta, Pi Kappa Alpha, Kappa Delta. Presbyterian. Clubs: Valdosta Jr. Women's (pres.); Wymodausis Woman's (3d v.p.) (Valdosta). Avocations: sports; sewing; meeting people. Home: 809 Millpond Rd Valdosta GA 31602

MERCHANT, MARILYN WALSH, entrepreneur, manufacturing company executive; b. Bklyn., June 13, 1948; d. James Joseph and Wanda Josephine (Zelenski) Walsh; student U. Ottawa, 1977-79, N.Y.U., 1967-68; m. Brian Taylor Merchant, June 11, 1986; children—Thérèse-Marie, Elizabeth-Marie. Mem. staff purchasing dept. Simmonds Precision Co., N.Y.C., 1967-68; exec. sec. Bronson Imports, N.Y.C., 1968-75; photo-reporter Ottawa Jour. and Emporium Echo, 1975-77; chief acct. Arcila and Assos., N.Y.C., 1973-75; pres., gen. mgr. Mich. Etching Inc., Grand Rapids 1979-85; chmn. bd. Electroluminescent Displays Tech. Inc., 1982-85; gen. mgr. Orr Industries, 1985—. Dir. Confraternity of Christian Doctrine, Okla. and Pa. Roman Catholic Ch.; mayor, Borough of Driftwood, Cameron County, Pa., 1976; adviser N.Y. State Assembly, 1974. Mem. Nat. Assn. Female Execs., Nat. Fedn. Ind. Bus., Soc. Automotive Engs. (subcom. 1979—), Soc. Mfg. Engrs., Am. Soc. Women Accts. Republican. Office: PO Box 261 Ada MI 49301

MERCOUN, DAWN DENISE, human resources executive; b. June 1, 1950; d. William S. and Irene (Micci) M. B.S., Fairleigh Dickinson U., 1978. Personnel payroll coordinator Bentex Mills Inc., East Rutherford, N.J., 1969-72; employment mgr. Inwood Knitting Mills, Clifton, N.J., 1972-75; gen. mgr. Consol. Advance, Inc., Passaic, N.J., 1975-76; dir. human resources Wesray Electronics, Inc., Clifton, N.J., 1976—. Mem. Am. Soc. Personnel Adminstrn., Am. Compensation Assn., Internat. Found. Employee Benefits. Republican. Episcopalian. Office: Wesray Electronics Inc 215 Entin Rd Clifton NJ 07014

MERDINGER, SUSAN, communications executive; b. Boston, Oct. 5, 1943; d. J. George and Bertha (Lotten) Greenfield; m. Edward Franklin Merdinger, Dec. 21, 1963; children—Mindy Beth, Matthew Joseph. A.A., Green Mountain Coll., 1963. Asst. dir. pub. relations Filene's, Boston, 1963; real estate sales, Marlboro, N.J., 1970-78; nat. dir. edn. Network of Homes, Babylon, N.Y., 1978-79; v.p. homefinding Employee Transfer Co., Chgo., 1979-81; dir. mktg. Merrill Lynch Realty, Stamford, Conn., 1981-83, asst. v.p. communications and promotional services, 1983-84, dir. mktg. communication, 1984—; founder, pub. mgr. Fine Homes, 1982—; lectr. in field. Pres., founder Hadassah, Marlboro, N.J., 1972-75, mem. nat. membership com., 1972-75. Mem. N.J. Realtors Assn., Nat. Speakers Assn., Mag. Pubs. Assn., Am. Mgmt. Assn. Jewish. Office: Merrill Lynch Realty Assocs 10 Stamford Forum Stamford CT 06901

MEREDITH, BARBARA BELLE, nursing home administrator; b. Sinks Grove, W.Va., May 16, 1941; d. William Brown and Hazel B. (McPeak) Skelton; m. Ward Stockton Meredith, Mar. 19, 1970; children—William, Melody, James, Jason, Lisa. Lic. nurse Camden Vo-Tech., 1958; cert. Montclair Coll., 1983. Nurse Rancocos Valley Hosp., Willingboro, N.J., 1961-65, Mt. Holly Hosp., N.J., 1965-71; bookkeeper Gulf Gate Water, Sarasota, Fla., 1971-75; adminstr. Garden State Nursing Home, Burlington, N.J., 1975—; cons. Burlington County Welfare Bd., Mt. Holly, 1980—, Homeless Bd./Burlington County, Mt. Holly, 1985—; mem. Gov.'s Adv. Bd., Trenton, N.J., 1984—; mem. Burlington County Mental Health Bd., 1986. Mem. Am. Health Care Assn. (exec. bd. dirs., chairwoman). Avocations: walking bowling. Home: 1141 Railroad Ave Edgewater Park NJ 08010

MEREY, DAISY, physician; b. Tangiers, Morocco, Feb. 1, 1949, came to U.S., 1961; d. Theodore and Lilly (Roth) Breuer; m. John Howard Merey, Dec. 26, 1967; children—DeAnne, Andrew. B.A., Barnard Coll., 1964; Ph.D., NYU, 1971; M.D., St. George's U., 1979. Resident Broward Gen. Med. Ctr., Ft. Lauderdale, Fla., 1979-80; practice medicine, West Palm Beach, Fla., 1981—; med. cons. Vis. Nurse Assn., 1981-83. Recipient Founder's Day award NYU, 1970. Fellow Am. Soc. Bariatric Physicians, Interam. Physicians Assn.; mem. AMA (Physicians Recognition award 1982, 86), Am. Bariatric Assn., Internat. Bariatric Assn., Internat. Acad. Bariatric Physicians (internat. pres.), Am. Soc. Clin. Nutrition, Am. Soc. Contemporary Medicine and Surgery, Exec. Women Palm Beaches. Office: 900 N Olive Ave West Palm Beach FL 33401

MERIDITH, DENISE PATRICIA, government official; b. N.Y.C., Apr. 14, 1952; d. Glenarva C. and Dorothy (Sawyer) M. B.S., Cornell U., 1973. Cert. wildlife biologist. With Bur. Land Mgmt., various locations, 1973—, chief div. resources, Alexandria, Va., 1980-83, dep. state dir., 1983—. Vol., Insect Zoo, Smithsonian, Washington, 1980-82. Recipient Ray Gildea Conservation award Soil Conservation Service, 1972; Spl. Achievement award, Bur. land Mgmt., 1980. Mem. Wildlife Soc., Soc. Am. Foresters, Audubon Soc., Wilderness Soc., Nat. Wildlife Fedn., Friends of Nat. Zoo, Natural History Soc., Federally Employed Women, Nat. Assn. Female Execs., Smithsonian Residents Assn., Washington Performing Arts Soc. Club: Latent Image Photography. Avocations: photography; writing; movies; art; public speaking. Home: 8711 Leonard Dr Silver Spring MD 20910 Office: Bur Land Management 350 S Pickett St Alexandria VA 22304

MERJOS, ANNA, financial analyst, securities researcher; b. N.Y.C., Apr. 1, 1923; d. Stavros and Helen (Papavasiliou) M. B.A., Hunter Coll., N.Y.C., 1944. Vice pres. Merrill Lynch, Pierce, Fenner & Smith Inc., N.Y.C., 1951—. Contbr. articles to profl. jours. Mem. Pi Mu Epsilon, Phi Beta Kappa. Greek Orthodox. Office: Merrill Lynch Pierce Fenner & Smith Inc 165 Broadway St New York NY 10080

MERKEL, JOANN KAYE, personnel services executive; b. Bottineau, N.D., Jan. 18, 1949; d. Kenneth Harlan and Joyce Suzanne (Larson) Kornkven; m. Donevan A. Mortenson, May 28, 1971 (div. Mar. 1978); children—Alexia, Ryan; m. 2d, Arnold Elroy Merkel, May 29, 1980; children—Brian, Brad, Barry. Student U. N.D., 1967-68, N.D. State U., 1968-69, N.D. State U., 1970, Minot State Coll., 1970-71, Moorhead State U., 1981—. Adminstrv. asst. Involved, Inc., Minot, N.D., 1973-75; coll. placement specialist Job Service N.D., Minot, 1975-81; owner, mgr. Personnel Service Systems, Minot, 1982—. Bd. dirs. Minot Winterfest Assn., 1983—, Minot Art Gallery, 1984—, Friends of Minot Art Gallery, 1983—, Souris Valley United Way, 1985—, Women's Symphony League, 1985—; publicity chmn. Artfest, 1984—; sec. North Hill Sch. PTA, 1984-86; media chmn. Summer Youth Employment Campaign, 1984—; v.p. Easter Seal Campaign, 1984—, chmn., 1986. Mem. Am. Soc. Personnel Adminstrs., Minot Area Personnel Assn. (pres.), Minot C. of C. (chmn. com. 1985-86), Am. Bus. Women's Assn. Republican. Lutheran. Club: Quota (v.p. 1986) (Minot). Home: 1812 Highland Dr Minot ND 58701 Office: Personnel Service Systems Inc 1542 S Broadway Minot ND 58701

MERKER, DAWN GAY, nurse; b. Phillipsburg, Kans., July 8, 1940; d. Merle E. and Marjorie Gwendolyn (Logan) Brush; m. Jerry Wheeler Merker, Sept. 3, 1961; children—Scott, Melissa. B.S., Kans. State Coll., 1961; B.S. in Nursing, U. Tex., 1981, M.S. in Nursing, 1984. Surgery staff nurse Meml. Hosp., Manhattan, Kans., 1961-64; office nurse Dr. George Bascom, Manhattan, 1964-68; surgery staff nurse St. Mary Hosp., Manhattan, 1968-70; staff nurse Lake Shore Gen. Hosp., Pointe Claire, Quebec, Can., 1973-75; asst. dir. nursing services St. Joseph Hosp., Bryan, Tex., 1976-83, dir. operating room, 1983—. Mem. Assn. Operating Room Nurses, Tex. Nurses' Assn. (sec.-treas. 1983—). Home: 1401 Village St College Station TX 77840 Office: St Joseph Hosp 2801 Franciscan Bryan TX 77801

MERKER, MATHILDA SUE, nursing educator, nursing consultant; b. Richmond, Va., Oct. 23, 1942; d. Frank F. and Edith Marjorie (Greer) Merker; m. Robert C. Acuff, Feb. 7, 1970 (div. Oct. 1982). B.S. in Nursing, Med. Coll. Va., 1965; M.S., Va. Commonwealth U., 1975. Asst. dir. nursing Mid-Mo. Mental Health Ctr., Columbia, 1980-81; staff devel. instr. Sheppard and Pratt Hosp., Balt., 1981-82, cons., 1981—; instr. psychiat. nursing Sch. Nursing, U. Md., Balt., 1982—; cons. Resource Applications, Balt., 1982—, A Safe Place, 1983—. Served to lt. U.S. Navy, 1967-70. Mem. Am. Nurses Assn., Md. Nurses Assn., Sigma Theta Tau Psi. Democrat. Methodist. Office: U Md Sch of Nursing 655 W Lombard Baltimore MD 21201

MERKLE, HELEN LOUISE, hotel executive; b. Carrington, N.D., May 23, 1950; d. Orville F. and Lillian M. (Argue) Merkle; B.S., N.D. State U., 1972. Asst. dir. food mgmt. Stouffer's Atlanta Inn, Atlanta, 1972-74; dir. food mgmt. Stouffer's Indpls. Inn, 1974-78; adminstrv. dir. food mgmt. Stouffer's Riverfront Towers, St. Louis, 1978-80; food mgmt. cons. Fraser Mgmt., Westlake, Ohio, 1980-83; exec. chef Marriott Hotel, Cleve., 1983—. Recipient First Place award for soups Taste of Indpls., 1976. Mem. Am. Culinary Fedn., Cleve. Culinary Assn., Food Service Execs. Assn., Nat. Assn. Female Execs. Democrat. Lutheran. Home: 27618 B Caroline Circle Westlake OH 44145 Office: Marriott Hotel 4277 150th St Cleveland OH 44135

MERKLE, JUDITH ASTRAIA, political science educator, writer; b. Brunswick, Maine, Jan. 14, 1942; d. Theodore Charles and Helene Rafaela Antonia (Suarez) M.; m. W. Parkes Riley, II, June 19, 1971; children—Elizabeth Antonia, Marlow Francis Parkes. B.A., U. Calif.-Berkeley, 1962, Ph.D., 1974; A.M., Harvard U., 1964. Mgmt. intern Dept. Def., Washington, 1964-65, research mgr., 1965-66; research and teaching asst. U. Calif., Berkeley, 1967-69, acting instr., 1969-70, lectr. pub. adminstrn., 1970-71; asst. prof., dir. Russian and East European Studies Ctr., U. Oreg., Eugene, 1971-82; assoc. prof. polit. sci. Claremont McKenna Coll., Calif., 1982—; mem. faculty Claremont Grad. Sch.; cons., guest lectr., book reviewer; books include: Management and Ideology: The Legacy of the International Scientific Management Movement, 1980; contbr. articles to profl. jours. Vice pres. Lane County Diabetes Assn., 1981; pres. Oreg. State Employees Assn., 1981. NSF grantee; 1969; Deutscher Akademischer Austauschdienst, Council European Studies, 1975. Mem. Acad. Mgmt., Am. Polit. Sci. Assn., Am. Soc. Pub. Adminstrn., Am. Assn. Advancement Slavic Studies, Phi Beta Kappa, Alpha Mu Gamma, Pi Sigma Alpha. Democrat. Episcopalian. Home: 1776 Essex Ave Laverne CA 91750 Office: Dept Political Science Claremont McKenna College Claremont CA 91711

MERKLE, LINDA L., legal administrator; b. Washington, Apr. 6, 1947; d. Robert Clifton, Shreeves II and Esther A. (Harrison) Cumming; lic. real estate, Prince Georges Community Coll., Largo, Md., 1972; children—Christina L., Regina L. Various secretarial positions, 1964-65, 67-72; real estate saleswoman, 1973-74; div. sec. Prince Georges Community Coll., 1974-75; real estate saleswoman Harvest Realty Inc., Clinton, Md., 1974-75; legal adminstr., property mgr., investment mgr. firm Tucker, Flyer, Sanger, Reider & Lewis P.C., Washington, 1975-84; legal adminstr. Anderson, Heibey, Nauheim & Blair, Washington, 1984-85; chief adminstrv. officer Barnes, Morris & Pardoe, Inc., Washington, 1985—; dir. Md. Corp.; pres. Lawtabs Inc. Del. Corp.; cons., speaker Mem. Assn. Legal Adminstrs. (chmn. new adminstrs. and gen. adminstrn. sect. 1984-85), ABA (asso.). Home: 8715 Baskerville Pl Upper Marlboro MD 20772 Office: 919 18th St NW Washington DC 20006

MERLIN, BEVERLY ROBERTS, distributing company executive; b. Atlanta, June 2, 1941; d. William R. and Martha (Carreker) Roberts; m. Michael Pattillo, June 19, 1965 (div.); m. 2d Arthur Merlin, Mar. 24; 1 dau., Dara Rachel. Mus. B., Shorter Coll., 1963; postgrad. Ga. State U., 1965. Asst. buyer Rich's, Inc., Atlanta, 1963-67; buyer Saks Fifth Ave., Atlanta, 1967-73; pres., chmn. bd. Sweeper Supply Co., Inc., Atlanta, 1973—. Pres. B'nai Brith Women, 1976; chmn. Women's Plea for Soviet Jews, 1977. Recipient Superior Achievement award Am. Lincoln, Bowling Green, Ohio, 1979, 80, 81; superior achievement award Star Industries, Inc., Chgo., 1983. Jewish. Office: Sweeper Supply Co Inc 3565 McCall Pl Atlanta GA 30340

MERMELSTEIN, ISABEL MAE ROSENBERG, adminstrative financial planner; b. Houston, Aug. 20, 1934; d. Joe Hyman and Sylvia (Lincove) Rosenberg; m. Robert Jay Mermelstein, Sept. 6, 1953 (div. July 1975); children—William, Linda, Jody. Student U. Ariz., 1952, Mich. State U., 1974, Lansing (Mich.) Community Coll., 1975. Exec. dir. Shiawassee County YWCA, Owosso, Mich., 1975-78; real estate developer F & S Devel. Corp., Lansing, Mich., 1978-79, Corum Devel. Corp., Houston, 1979-81; adminstrv. fin. planner Investec Asset Mgmt. Group, Inc., Houston, 1981-85. Author: For You! I Killed the Chicken, 1972. Recipient State of Mich. Flag, 1972, Key to City, City of Lansing, 1972-73. Republican. Jewish. Lodges: Zonta, Licoma,

B'nai B'rith, Hadassah, Nat. Fedn. Temple Sisterhoods. Avocations: flying; gourmet cooking; needlepoint; knitting; snow skiing. Home: 4030 Newshire Houston TX 77025

MERMELSTEIN, PAULA, TV executive; b. N.Y.C., Nov. 8, 1947; d. Robert and Dorothy (Asch) Mermelstein; B.A. in Speech and Theater cum laude, Bklyn. Coll., 1968; m. Francis W. James, Jr., Nov. 23, 1975; 1 son, Robert Austin James. Editorial staff various game shows including Joe Garagiola's Memory Game, 1969; writer/producer On-Air promotion NBC, N.Y.C., 1970-78, supervising writer/producer, 1978-79, dir., 1979, v.p., 1979-82, creative dir. East coast, 1982-85, exec. dir. copy, 1985—. Recipient First Place News award U.S. TV Commls. Festival for NBC Profile, David Brinkley, 1977. Mem. Writers Guild Am. Author protest column, Glamour Mag., 1970. Office: NBC 30 Rockefeller Plaza New York NY 10020

MEROLA, MARY LOUISE FRANCES, physician; b. N.Y.C., Oct. 9, 1950; d. John A. and Mary T. (Guidera) Merola. B.S. in Biology, St. John's U., Jamaica, N.Y., 1972; M.D., U. Bologna (Italy), 1979. Resident in family practice Community Hosp., Glen Cove, N.Y., 1979-82, asst. dir. family practice residency program, 1982—. Mem. Am. Assn. Family Practitioners, AMA, Am. Med. Women's Assn., N.Y. Acad. Scis., Nassau Acad. Medicine.

MERRELL, DOLORES ALEXANDER, business executive; b. Norristown, Pa., Feb. 25, 1949; d. Raymond Stanley and Stephanie (Kozikowski) Alexander; m. Norman E. Merrell, Jr., Mar. 26, 1976. B.A., Temple U., 1971; M.A., Villanova U., 1975, M.B.A., 1985. Benefits coordinator Zapata Haynie, Houston, 1978-79; real estate agt. Paul Hemby & Co., Houston, 1979-80; sales rep. Newport Realty, Crosby, Tex., 1980-81; personnel cons. M. David Lane, Houston, 1981-82; v.p. NEMCO, Inc., Royersford, Pa., 1982—, also dir. Mem. Nat. Assn. Female Execs., Am. Mgmt. Assn., Assn. of MBA Execs. Avocations: stained glass; volleyball.

MERRIAM, MARY-LINDA SORBER, college president; b. Jeannette, Pa., May 31, 1943; d. Everett S.C. and Madeleine (Case) Sorber; B.A., Pa. State U., 1965, M.A., 1967, Ph.D., 1970. Spl. asst. to pres. Emerson Coll., Boston, 1977-78, asst. prof. speech and communication, 1972-79, v.p. adminstrn., 1978-79; asst. to pres. Boston U., 1979-81; pres. Wilson Coll., Chambersburg, Pa., 1981—; cons. in field. Bd. dirs. Boston/New England Nat. Acad. TV Arts and Scis., 1980-81, Sta. WITF, Inc., South Central Pa. Fgn. Study Group, 1982—, Chambersburg Hosp., 1984—; trustee Scotland Sch. for Vet. Children. Named Disting. Alumna, Pa. State U., 1984. Am. Council Edn. fellow, 1977-78. Mem. AAUW, Speech Communication Assn., Am. Assn. Higher Edn., Phi Kappa Phi, Rho Tau Sigma, Phi Delta Kappa, Pi Kappa Delta. Presbyterian. Office: Wilson College Chambersburg PA 17201

MERRICK, MELISSA TOOPS, nurse; b. Munich, Germany, Oct. 10, 1958; came to U.S. 1959; d. Alan Toops and Salee (Fain) Horwedel. Diploma in Nursing, Burge Sch. Nursing, 1980; B.S.N., So. Mo. State U., 1985. Staff nurse Cox Med. Ctr., Springfield, Mo., 1980-81, asst. head nurse, 1981-82; charge nurse Springfield Community Hosp., Mo., 1982-85, part-time shift supr., 1984-85; coordinator ICU, Park Central Hosp., Springfield, 1985—. Lester E. Cox Meml. scholar, 1977; Roy T. Wilcox Meml. scholar, 1982. Mem. S.W. Mo. State U. Nursing Alumni Assn. (dir.), Phi Kappa Phi, Sigma Theta Tau. Republican. Lodge: Order Eastern Star. Avocations: bridge; reading; bowling; softball. Office: Park Central Hosp 440 S Market St Springfield MO 65806

MERRILL, DALE MARIE, computer company executive; b. Melrose, Mass., Feb. 21, 1954; d. Richard Paul and Rosemarie Reine (Porelle) M. B.A. in English, U. Iowell, 1976; M.A. in Am. Studies, Boston Coll., 1982. Sales rep. A-Copy Inc., Natick, Mass., 1976-77; sales mgr. Jan Optical Co., Waltham, Mass., 1977-78; researcher Decision Research Co., Lexington, Mass., 1979-81; sales rep. Henco Software Co., Waltham, 1981-82; account mgr. Univ. Computing Co., Chgo., 1982-83; regional sales mgr. Software House, Cambridge, Mass., 1983—; dir. M.T. Corp., Woburn, Mass. Contbr. poetry Seeds mag., 1971-72, co-editor, 1972, Poetry award, 1972; contbr. poetry to mags. Recipient Top Sales awards A-Copy Inc., 1976, 77, Software House, 1985, 86, Interviewer award Decision Research Corp., 1981. Mem. Nat. Assn. Profl. Women, NOW, Digital Equipment Corp. User Soc. Democrat. Avocations: skiing, photography, painting, sculpturing, karate. Home: PO Box 2586 Woburn MA 01888 Office: Software House 1105 Massachusetts Ave Cambridge MA 02138

MERRILL, LYNNE BARTLETT, public relations and advertising executive; b. Southampton, N.Y., Mar. 17, 1953; d. William Stuart and Marilyn (Bake) Bartlett; m. John Albee, June 1, 1974. B.S., Boston U., 1975. Intern. U.S. Congress 1974; account exec. Creative Promotions Co., Dover, N.H., 1974-75; pres., owner Merrill Assocs., Inc., Kingston, N.H., 1975—; salesperson Kingston Real Estate, N.H., 1974—. Chmn., Kingston Recreation Commn., 1975-77; program chmn. Kingston Bus and Profl. Women's Club, 1978-80, chmn. young career women, 1979—, recipient young career woman award, 1979, Graniteer awards, 1982, 84. Mem. Pub. Relations Soc. Am. (by-law chmn. Yankee chpt. 1985), Seacoast Communications Network (charter), Portsmouth C. of C., Greater Haverhill C. of C., Ad Club N.H. (exec. bd. 1982-83, pres. 1984-85). Republican. Congregationalist. Avocations: Boating; swimming; sewing; reading; traveling. Home: 89 Ball Rd Kingston NH 03848 Office: Merrill Assocs Inc 153 Main St Kingston NH 03483

MERRIMAN, AMY IRENE, steel company executive; b. Rochester, N.Y., Dec. 14, 1951; d. William Thomas and Irene (Peschan) Hochreiter; m. Martin Aloi Merriman, July 8, 1977 (separated Dec. 1983). Supr. prodn. control Columbia Mills, Minetto, N.Y., 1973-77; systems analyst Lipe Rollway, Syracuse, N.Y., 1978; mgr. systems and adminstrn., instr. statis. process control Crucible Inc. div. Colt Industries, Syracuse, 1978—. Performer Clay Towne Players, Syracuse, 1983-85; vol. reader WCNY Readout for the Blind, Syracuse, 1984-85. Mem. Am. Prodn. and Inventory Control Soc. (dir. publicity 1984-85). Republican. Roman Catholic. Avocations: dancing; skiing; real estate; golf; filmmaking.

MERRIMAN, BETTY LOU, city official; b. LaGrange, Ind., Mar. 25, 1953; d. Moyne Whitcomb and Hyacinth Lillian (Strayer) Fuller; m. Glenn Calvin Merriman, Nov. 3, 1973 (div. 1985); children—Joel, Gavin. Student Ball State U., 1971-72, Ind. U., 1976-84. Outreach worker City Bloomington, 1973-74, relocation specialist, 1974-76, fiscal analyst, 1976-78, asst. dir., 1978-82, dep. controller, 1982, controller, 1982—. Treas. McCloskey for U.S. Congress Com., Bloomington, Ind., 1984-86. Mem. Ind. Controller's Assn. (pres. 1984), Ind. Assn. Cities and Towns Legislative Com., Ind. Govt. Fin. Officers Assn. (bd. dirs. 1986—), Nat. Assn. Accts. Democrat. Methodist. Club: Democrat Women's (Bloomington, Ind.). Avocations: reading; tennis; softball. Office: City of Bloomington 220 E 3d St Bloomington IN 47401

MERRITT, DORIS HONIG, pediatrician, former university dean; b. N.Y.C., July 16, 1923; d. Aaron and Lillian (Kunstlich) Honig; B.A., City U. N.Y., 1944; M.D., George Washington U., 1952; children—Kenneth Arthur, Christopher Ralph. Pediatric intern Duke Hosp., 1952-53; teaching and research fellow pediatrics George Washington U., 1953-54; pediatric asst. resident Duke U. Hosp., 1954-55, cardiovascular fellow pediatrics, 1955-56, instr. pediatrics, dir. pediatric cardiorenal clinic, 1956-57; exec. sec. cardiovascular study sect., gen. medicine study sect. div. research grants NIH, 1957-60; dir. med. research grants and contracts Ind. U. Sch. Medicine, 1961-62, asst. prof. pediatrics, 1961-68, asst. dean med. research, 1962-65, asst. dir. med. research, aerospace research application center, 1963-65, asso. dir. med. research, 1965-68, asst. dean for research, office v.p. research and dean advanced studies, 1965-67, dir. sponsored programs, asst. to provost, 1965-68, asso. dean for research and advanced studies, office v.p. and dean for research and advanced studies, 1967-71, asso. prof. pediatrics, 1968-73, prof., 1973-80; spl. asst. to dir. NIH, 1978—, research tng. and research resource officer, 1980—, acting dir. Nat. Ctr. for Nursing Research, 1986—; cons. USPHS, NIH div. research grants, Div. Health Research Facilities and Resources, Nat. Heart Inst., 1963-78, Am. Heart Assn., 1963-67, Ind. Med. Assn. Commn. Vol. Health Orgns., 1964-67, Bur. Health Manpower, Health Profession's Constrn. Program, 1965-71, Nat. Library Medicine, Health Center Library Constrn. Program, 1966-72; dir. office sponsored programs Ind. U.-Purdue U. Indpls. Office Chancellor, 1968-71, dean research and sponsored programs, 1971-79; mem. Nat. Library Medicine biomed. communications rev. com., 1970-74. Chmn. Indpls. Consortium for Urban Edn., 1971-75; v.p. Greater Indpls. Progress Com., 1974-79; mem. Community Service Council, 1969-75; bd. dirs. Bd. for Fundamental Edn., 1973-77, Ind. Sci. Edn. Found., 1977-78, Community Addiction Services Agy., Inc., 1972-74; trustee Marian Coll., 1977-78; exec. com. Nat. Council U. Research Adminstrs., 1977-78; bd. regents Nat. Library Medicine, 1976-80; chmn. adv. screening com. for life scis. Council Internat. Exchange of Scholars, 1978-81. Served to lt. (j.g.), USNR. Diplomate Nat. Bd. Med. Examiners, Am. Bd. Pediatrics. Fellow Am. Acad. Pediatrics; mem. AAAS, George Washington U., Duke U. med. alumni assns., Phi Beta Kappa, Alpha Omega Alpha. Contbr. articles to profl. jours. Office: Bldg 1 Room 209 NIH Bethesda MD 20014

MERRITT, JUDITH ANN, educator; b. Pitts., Feb. 6, 1937; d. Albert Alphonse and Margaret Louise (Reiland) Pschirer; m. Richard Frederick Boland, Feb. 9, 1957 (div. 1971); children—Richard Frederick, Jr., David Todd; m. Lloyd Wesley Merritt, Feb. 18, 1984; stepchildren—Lori Merritt, Lisa Merritt. B.S., Indiana U. of Pa., 1963; M.S., Pa. State U., 1976. Tchr. Millvale Sch. Dist., Pitts., 1963-68, Shaler Area Sch. Dist., Glenshaw, Pa., 1968—. Mem. Carnegie Inst. Soc., Pitts., 1982-84, Pitts. History Landmarks Soc., 1985—. Carlow Coll. grantee, 1985. Mem. NEA, Pa. State Edn. Assn., Shaler Area Edn. Assn. (bldg. rep. 1984—, mem.-at-large 1985—). Democrat. Roman Catholic. Clubs: North Hills Jr. Woman's (Glenshaw, Pa.); Oakmont Yacht. Avocations: golf; swimming; aerobics. Home: 206 Mary Ave Pittsburgh PA 15209 Office: Shaler Area Sch Dist 1800 Mount Royal Blvd Glenshaw PA 15116

MERRITT, PATRICIA ANNE, data processing exec.; b. Rochester, N.Y., Jan. 12, 1945; d. Richard Henry and Florence Elizabeth (Adams) M.; student Long Beach (Calif.) City Coll., 1972-74, Foothill Jr. Coll., 1974-77; grad. Bryman Paramed. Sch., San Jose, Calif., 1977; m. Steve Verderber. Data processing clk. Lincoln Rochester Trust Co., Rochester, N.Y., 1965-67; keypunch operator Eastman Kodak, Rochester, 1967-70; keypunch and verify operator Reliance Steel Co., Los Angeles, 1971; keypunch operator Automatic Data Processing, Long Beach, 1971, Fed. Civil Service, Los Alamitos, Calif., 1971-73, Varian Assos., Palo Alto, Calif., 1973-78; tech. typist, word processor lead-operator Watkins Johnson, Palo Alto, 1978-79, 79-81; supr. office systems Smith Kline Instruments, Sunnyvale, Calif., 1981-82; owner I.P.S. Info. Processing Systems, 1982—; word processor sr. operator Palo Alto Unified Sch. Dist., 1979. Leader, Monroe County council Girl Scouts U.S.A., Rochester, 1969-70, Santa Clara County council, Mountain View, Calif., 1978-83; commr. City of Santa Clara Hist. Commn., 1983—. Mem. Beta Sigma Phi. Office: 3579 Mauricia Santa Clara CA 95051

MERROW, TONI SUE, secretary; b. Springfield, Mo., Mar. 24, 1940; d. Haldene Kemp and Ruth Darlene (Jordan) Holt; m. Maesil LeGrand Merrow, May 13, 1961; children—Dene O., Scott J., Regina L. Student pub. schs., Denver. Exec. sec. Colo. Brick Co., Denver, 1959-60; sec. Stanley Aviation, Denver, 1960-61; sec. to service specialist Ford Motor, Tractor div., Denver, 1961-77; sec. to v.p. advt. communications KWAL Paints, Inc., Denver, 1979-84; sec., asst. to v.p. Intermountain Network, Denver, 1985—; pub. relations cons. The Osburn Band, Denver, 1977—. Vice pres. Hallet Sch. PTA, Denver, 1971-73; active various charitable orgns.; mem., pub. relations cons. Blue Knights Drum and Bugle Corps Parents Orgn., Littleton, 1983-84; historian, pub. relations cons. Highland High Sch. Booster Assn., Thornton, 1983-84. Cert. of Commendation, City of Thornton, 1975. Mem. Nat. Assn. Female Execs., Scholastic Gold Key. Avocations: antiques; geneology; reading; camping. Home: 2502 E 90th Pl Thornton CO 80229

MERSEL, MARJORIE KATHRYN PEDERSEN (MRS. JULES MERSEL), lawyer; b. Manila, Utah, June 17, 1923; d. Leo Henry and Kathryn Anna (Reed) Pedersen; A.B., U. Cal., 1948; LL.B., U. San Francisco, 1948; m. Jules Mersel, Apr. 12, 1950; 1 son, Jonathan. Admitted to D.C. bar, 1952, Calif. bar, 1955; Marjorie Kathryn Pedersen Mersel, atty., Beverly Hills, Calif., 1961-71; staff counsel Dept. Real Estate State of Calif., Los Angeles, 1971—. Mem. Beverly Hills Bar Assn., Los Angeles County Bar Assn., Trial Lawyers Assn., So. Calif. Women Lawyers Assn. (treas. 1962-63), Beverly Hills C. of C., World Affairs Council. Club: Los Angeles Athletic. Home: 13007 Hartsook St Sherman Oaks CA 91403 Office: Dept Real Estate 107 S Broadway Los Angeles CA

MERSEREAU, BOBBI, claims manager, administrator; b. Boston, Dec. 30, 1945; d. George William and Nellie (David) M. Cert., Vesper George Sch. Art, Boston, 1972-73; Cert. Legal Prins., Am. Ednl. Inst., Basking Ridge (N.J), 1983. With Fireman's Fund Ins. Co., Boston, 1963—, claims rep., 1972-76, claims supr., 1976-78, sr. claims supr., 1978-82, line sr. Fidelity & Surety, 1982-84; asst. claims mgr. administration, 1984—; arbitrator Ins. Arbitration Forums, Woburn, Mass., 1982—. Account exec. United Way Mass. Bay, Boston, 1982, 83, sect. chmn., 1984; mem. com. Boston Paralympic Com., 1983; vol. Spl. Olympics, Boston, 1983; vol. Nikee Pikee Roadrace for Spl. Olympics, 1982, 83. Republican. Home: 108 Myrtle St Apt 12A Boston MA 02114

MERSKEY-ZEGER, MARIE GERTRUDE FINE, retired librarian; b. Kimberley, South Africa, Oct. 10, 1914; came to U.S., 1960, naturalized, 1965; d. Herman and Annie Myra (Wigoder) Fine; m. Clarence Merskey, Oct. 8, 1939 (dec. 1982); children—Hilary Pamela Merskey Nathe, Susan Heather Merskey Sinistore, Joan Margaret Merskey Schneiderman; m. Jack I. Zeger, July 15, 1984. Grad. Underwood Bus. Sch., Cape Town, South Africa, 1934; B.A., U. Cape Town, 1958, diploma librarianship, 1960. Sec. to Chief Rabbi Israel Abrahams, South Africa, 1945-49, Jewish Sheltered Employment Council, 1954-56; reference librarian New Rochelle Pub. Library, 1960-63; research librarian Consumers Union, Mt. Vernon, 1963-66; asst. readers services, head union catalog Westchester Library System, 1966-69, mem. adult services com., 1973-74; dir. Harrison Pub. Library and West Harrison Br., 1969-84. Pub. edn. officer USCG Aux. Flotilla 63. Author: History of the Harrison Libraries, 1980. Trustee Mamaroneck Free Library; bd. dirs. Shore Acres Point Corp., Mamaroneck. Recipient Brotherhood award B'nai B'rith, 1974; named Woman of Yr., Harrison, 1984. Mem. ALA, Westchester Library Assn., N.Y. Library Assn. (adult edn. com. for continuing edn. 1971-75, adult services com. 1973-75, vice chmn., 1975, exec. bd. 1981-82), Pub. Library Dirs. Assn. (tech. services com. chmn. Westchester County 1971, exec. bd. 1974-75, vice chmn. 1975), Clubs: Harrison Women's, YMCA, Harrison Hist. Soc. (bd. dirs. Charles Dawson History Ctr. (founder), Hadassah, (Cape Town), USCG Aux. Contbr. articles to local newspapers. Home: 316 S Barry Ave Mamaroneck NY 10543

MERWIN, JANE HURLEY, printing, mailing and data processing company executive; b. Clinton County, Ohio, Sept. 4, 1934; d. Alton Brock and Ethel Marie (Davis) Hurley; m. Roy Layton Merwin, July 24, 1954; children—Minda Jane, Maureen Jo, Brock Layton. B.A. in History, Stetson U., 1966. Sec. Brown-Brockmeyer Co., Dayton, Ohio, 1951-53, Gen. Electric Co., Dayton, Ohio, 1953-54, First Bapt. Ch., Sarasota, Fla., 1962; sales rep. Capitol Homes, Schenectady, N.Y., 1957-58; owner The Spinning Wheel, Indialantic, Fla., 1960-61; tchr. Daytona Beach (Fla.) Jr. High Sch., 1966-67, Athens (Ala.) High Sch., 1967; newscaster Sta. KTMF, New Prague, Minn., 1970-72; sales rep. Sta. KYMN, Northfield, Minn., 1972-74; profl. bldg. mgr. Apple Valley Exec. Offices, Apple Valley, Minn., 1974-75; service rep. Nat. Bus. Lists, Apple Valley, 1975-77; v.p. adminstrn. EU Services, Rockville, Md., 1977—; sec., treas. Hurley Industries, Inc., Rockville, Md., 1965—; co-owner Clockwork Computers, Rockville. Mem. Mid-Montgomery Bus. and Profl. Women, Am. Soc. Personnel Adminstrn., Am. Soc. Profl. and Exec. Women. Presbyterian. Office: EU Services 649 N Horners Ln Rockville MD 20850

MESEK, JEANIE MAY, therapist; b. Omaha, May 18, 1926; d. Archie Mason and Lela May (Lanning) Schreiber; B.S., George Williams Coll., 1976; postgrad. No. Bapt. Theol. Sem., 1976; M.S. in Social Work, U. Louisville, 1978; m. Fred Mesek, Nov. 18, 1944; children—Fred, Randelyn, Gary. Advocate, Ill. Status Offenders Services, DuPage County, 1975-77; social worker Riveredge Hosp., Forest Park, Ill., 1978; child care worker Fox Hill Home for Girls, Batavia, Ill., 1979; clin. therapist Guardian Angel Home, Joliet, Ill., 1979—; dir. social service Westmont (Ill.) Health Centre, 1978-81; prin. May Cons. Service, Downers Grove, Ill., 1978-80. Vol. Hinsdale Hosp., 1965-72; v.p. Clyde Estates Property Owners, 1967. Cert. tchr., Ill.; cert. social worker, Ill. Mem. Nat. Assn. Social Workers, Acad. Cert. Social Workers.

MESHEL, PAMELA ELIZABETH, human resources executive, consultant; b. Oakland, Calif., Sept. 15, 1952; d. Donald Edward Loy and Joyce Ellen (Thomas) Loy Rose; m. Robert Stephen Moore, Sept. 22, 1973 (div.); children—Robert Aaron, Stephen Randall; m. 2d, Barry Meshel, Jan. 8, 1983. Student U. Calif.-Fullerton, 1972-74. Premium audit clk. Hartford Ins. Co., Santa Ana, Calif., 1971-72; office mgr. H. Cliff Ivester, Fullerton, Calif., 1972-76; personnel dir. Naugles, Inc., Fullerton, 1980—; counselor networking groups, Orange County, Calif., 1981. Resume counselor U. Calif.-Irvine, Women's Opportunity Ctr., 1981-84. Mem. Personnel and Indsl. Relations Assn., Am. Mgmt. Assn., Orange County Women in Bus. (chairperson outreach), Am. Soc. Personnel Adminstrs. Democrat. Office: Naugles Inc 2932 E Nutwood Ave Fullerton CA 92634

MESHUN, JANICE SOPHIA, marketing association executive; b. Chgo., Jan. 20, 1962; d. Richard Arthur and Mary Georgia (Harris) M. Student No. Ill. U., 1980-81, Harper Coll., 1981-83. Sec. Nat. Assn. Realtors, Chgo., 1983; designation coordinator Realtors Nat. Mktg. Inst., Chgo., 1983-84, edn. coordinator, 1984-85, mem. services mgr., 1985—. Editor: Education Resource Manual, 1984. Mem. Am. Soc. Assn. Execs., Nat. Assn. Female Execs. Democrat. Greek Orthodox. Avocations: skiing; camping; rafting; sailing. Home: 519 S Falmouth Ln Schaumburg IL 60193 Office: Realtors Nat Mktg Inst 430 N Michigan Ave Chicago IL 60611

MESICK, JUDITH ESTHER, fund raising corp. ofcl.; b. Paw Paw, Mich., June 12, 1948; d. Morris James and Jean Evelyn (Holm) M.; student Mich. State U., 1966-68; B.S. in Elem. Edn., U. Tex., El Paso, 1972, M.Ed., 1976. Tchr., Ysleta Ind. Sch. Dist., El Paso, 1973-78; Tex. dist. mgr., outside sales rep. Nationwide Fund Raisers, Inc., of Tucker, Ga., 1978—, recruiter, mgr. confs., cons. Mary Kay Cosmetics, 1982—. Active Robert Kennedy campaign, 1967. Served with U.S. Army, 1968-70. Mem. Nat. Assn. Female Execs. Republican. Baptist. Office: Nationwide Fund Raisers Inc 2649 Mountain Ind Blvd Tucker GA 30084

MESKE, EUNICE BOARDMAN, educator; b. Cordova, Ill., Jan. 27, 1926; B.M., Cornell Coll., Mt. Vernon, Iowa, 1947; M.M.E., Tchrs. Coll. Columbia U., 1951; Ed.D., U. Ill., 1963; m. Delmar Meske. Elem. music specialist, high sch. choral dir. Iowa Public Schs., 1947-56; instr. music edn. No. Ill. U., 1956-57; prof. music edn. Wichita State U., 1957-72; vis. prof. Ill. State U., Normal, 1972-74, Chgo. Mus. Coll. Roosevelt U., 1974-75; prof. music edn. U. Wis., Madison, 1975-80, dir. Sch. Music. Grantee in field. Mem. Music Educators Nat. Conf., Wis. Music Educators, AAUP, NEA, Assn. Suprs. Student Tchrs., Coll. Music Soc., Mu Phi Epsilon, Pi Kappa Lambda. Home: 314 Lake Shore Dr Lake Mills WI 53551 Office: 455 N Park St Madison WI 53706

MESNEY, DOROTHY TAYLOR, mezzo-soprano, pianist, composer, educator; b. Bklyn., Sept. 15, 1916; d. Franklin and Kathryn Munro Taylor; diploma Berkeley Inst., 1934; B.A., Sarah Lawrence Coll., 1938; postgrad. Columbia U., 1938-41, Juilliard Sch. of Music, 1963-71, Manhattan Sch. Music, 1971-73; m. Peter Michael Mesney, Oct. 15, 1942; children—Douglas, Kathryn, Barbara. Mezzo-soprano, operetta, mus. comedy, concert and oratorio; ch. soloist, N.Y.C., 1956—; debuts include: N.Y. Cultural Center, 1971, Carnegie Recital Hall, 1974; leading roles with local opera and Gilbert and Sullivan groups; dir. a-capella vocal quintet The Notebles; rec. artist Folkways Records, Musicanza Records; dir. American Experience ensemble, also An Elizabethan Encounter; tchr. piano and singing, Douglaston, N.Y., 1958—, also tchr. introduction music classes; founder, dir. children's series Concerts for Children; founder Introduction to Music for Preschoolers; performer early Am. music for mus., hist. socs., schs., colls.; performer Renaissance music N.Y. State Renaissance Festival, 9 yrs.; 2c authority on Am. and Renaissance music. Com. chmn. PTA, Douglaston, 1952-55; den mother Greater N.Y. council Cub Scouts Am., 1953-56; Brownie leader Greater N.Y. council Girl Scouts U.S.A.; bd. dirs. Community Concerts Assn. of Great Neck, N.Y. Mem. Nat. Piano Tchrs. Guild, Nat. Fedn. Music Clubs (N.Y. chpt.), Met. Opera Guild, Tuesday Morning Music Club (pres. 1979-81). Democrat. Congregationalist. Composer hymns, songs, instrumental quartets and trios, ballades also songs for children.

MESSALL, SANDRA KAY, marine corps officer; b. St. Louis, July 2, 1943; d. Richard Dudley and Onieda Barbara (Haberberger) Messall; student various mil. schs. Revenue coordinator Am. Airlines Co., N.Y.C., 1962-65; enlisted USMC, 1966, commd. warrant officer, 1975, chief warrant officer, 1977, advanced through grades to capt., 1983, air traffic controller, supr. instr. Marine Corps Air Sta., Kaneohe, Hawaii, 1969-72, air traffic controller, facility operator, instr., Cherry Point, N.C., 1972-75, asst. fiscal officer Marine Corps Base, Camp Lejeune, N.C., 1975-77, asst. budget officer, 1977, fiscal acctg. officer 4th Marine Aircraft Wing, New Orleans, 1977-78, fiscal officer Consol. Acctg. Office, 1978-80; acctg. officer Camp H.M. Smith, Hawaii, 1980-82; acctg. officer Marine Corps Air Sta., Kaneohe Bay, Hawaii, 1982-83; fin. mgr. SABRS Devel. Team, Washington, 1983—. Mem. Soc. Mil. Controllers (chpt. sec. 1976-77, 78-79, reporter, staff asst. New Orleans chpt. newsletter), Women's Mil. Assn. Roman Catholic. Office: Code FDA-57 Washington DC 20380

MESSER, SONIA, collector toys designer, manufacturer and importer wholesale toys; b. Los Angeles, Nov. 23, 1932; d. George Messer and Milena Messer-Brozovich; m. Anthony Randazzo, June 21, 1970; one child, Monica Milena. Student pub. schs., Alhambra. Head bookkeeper Seaboard Fin. Co., Los Angeles, 1950-59; owner, operator Stuyvesant Travel, N.Y.C., 1959-65; owner, operator, designer Sonia Messer Imports, Los Angeles, 1965—. Designer numerous pieces of collector dollhouse furniture, 1969—, ltd. edit. collector dolls, 1982-85. Active Nat. Charity League, Los Angeles, 1983—, Jr. Tennis League, Los Angeles, 1984—. Mem. Western States Toy Assn., Los Angeles Gift Assn., Hobby Assn. Am. Republican. Episcopalian. Avocations: miniature collector; tennis; skiing; classical music. Home: 4811 Glencairn Rd Los Angeles CA 90027 Office: Sonia Messer Imports 4115 San Fernando Rd Glendale CA 91204

MESSERLE, JUDITH ROSE, hospital official librarian; b. Litchfield, Ill., Jan. 16, 1943; d. Richard Douglas and Nelrose (Davis) Wilcox; m. Darrell Wayne Messerle, Apr. 26, 1968; children—Kurt Norman, Katherine Lynn. B.S. in Zoology, So. Ill. U., 1966; M.L.S., U. Ill., 1967. Cert. med. librarian Grade I. Librarian, St. Joseph's Sch. Nursing, Alton, Ill., 1967-73; med. librarian St. Joseph's Hosp., Alton, 1973-77, dir. info. services, 1977-79, dir. ednl. resources and community relations, 1979-84, dir. adminstrv. services, 1984-85; dir. med. ctr. library St. Louis U., 1985—; cons. Alton Mental Health Ctr., 1972-81, Idaho State Library, Boise, 1978; coordinator Areawide Hosp. Library Consortium of Southwestern Ill., Alton, 1974-78; cons. Nat. Library of Medicine Planning Panel, 1985-86; instr. Lewis and Clark Community Coll., Godfrey, Ill., 1975-76; chmn. Lewis and Clark Regional White House Conf. on Libraries, 1979; mem. Ill. State Library Adv. Com., 1979-81. Co-editor: Hospital Library Management, 1984; contbr. articles to med. jours. Bd. dirs. Family Service Vis. Nurse Assn., Alton, 1976-79, Alton chpt. Am. Cancer Soc., 1983-85. Mem. Med. Library Assn. (dir. 1981-84, pres. 1986-87), St. Louis Med. Librarians (pres. 1975, 76), Beta Phi Mu. Home: 5100 Candy Ln Alton IL 62002 Office: St Louis U Med Ctr Library 1402 S Grand Saint Louis MO 63104

MESSERSCHMITT, NORMA FLORINE, nurse; b. Long Beach, Calif., Jan. 3, 1928; d. John Homer and Bernice Mildred (Miller) Mauk; m. John Arthur Messerschmitt, Nov. 8, 1947; children—John, James, Jarrett. R.N., Long Beach City Coll., 1972. Nurse, Pioneer Hosp., Artesia, Calif., 1972-73; lab. nurse supr. Clin. Lab. St. Mary's Hosp., Long Beach, 1973—, instr. health technologies Long Beach City Coll., 1976—. Mem. Nat. Phlebotomy Assn., Internat. Platform Assn. Republican. Home: 8001 Ring St Long Beach CA 90808 Office: 1050 Linden Ave Long Beach CA 90813

MESSIER, KATHLEEN MARIE, academic counselor; b. Nashua N.H., June 19, 1953; d. Paul and Theresa M. (Dube) M. B.A., U. Tex., 1978, M. Ed., U. Houston, 1983. Adminstrv. asst. U. Houston, 1979-80, coordinator clinic adminstrn., 1980-81, coordinator academic advising, 1981-83, academic counselor, 1983—. Served with U.S. Army, 1975-77. Mem. Am. Assn. Counseling and Devel., Am. Psychol. Assn., Am. Coll. Personnel Assn., Nat. Vocat. Guidance Assn. Republican. Home: 7500 Pinemont Dr Apt 1604 Houston TX 77040 Office: University of Houston 4800 Calhoun Houston TX 77004

MESSIN, MARLENE ANN, fine gifts store executive; b. St. Paul, Oct. 6, 1935; d. Edgar Leander and Luella Johanna (Rahn) Johnson; m. Frank Messin; children—Rick, Debora, Ronald, Lori, Carlson; 5 stepchildren. Bookkeeper Jeans Implement Co., Forest Lake, Minn., 1952-53, part-time bookkeeper, 1953-57; bookkeeper Great Plains Supply, St. Paul, 1960-62; bookkeeper Plastic Products Co., Inc., Lindstrom, Minn., 1962-75, pres., major owner,

1975-81; co-owner Gustaf's Fine Gifts, Lindstrom, Minn., 1985—. Bookkeeper, Trinity Lutheran Ch., Lindstrom, 1976-81. Mem. Nat. Assn. Women Bus. Owners, Soc. Plastic Engrs. (chmn. membership com.), Swedish Inst. Home: 28940 Olinda Trail Lindstrom MN 55045 Office: 30355 Akerson St Lindstrom MN 55045

MESSNER, ALETHA JOANNE BRAGG, nursery school educator, author, poet; b. Buffalo, Mar. 19, 1939; d. Lester William and Helen Aleetah (Rich) Bragg; m. Howard Myron Messner, Aug. 21, 1959 (div. 1982); children—Jennifer, Linda, David. Student Antioch Coll., 1957-60; B.A., U. Md., 1978; postgrad. Johns Hopkins U. Asst. tchr., dir. afternoon daycare Kindercare/Columbia Montessori; sec., tchr. United Martial Arts Sch., Columbia, Md., 1984-85; substitute tchr. Baltimore County, Carroll County, Howard County. Religious edn. coordinator, cons. Howard County Unitarian Soc.; vol. Howard County Gen. Hosp. Recipient Martial Arts award, 1984. Mem. Nat. Wildlife Assn. Home: 5689C Harpers Farm Rd Columbia MD 21044 Office: Kindercare/Columbia Montessori Marble Faun Lane Columbia MD 21044

MESSNER, KATHRYN HERTZOG, civic worker; b. Glendale, Calif., May 27, 1915; d. Walter Sylvester and Sadie (Dinger) Hertzog; B.A., UCLA, 1936, M.A., 1951; m. Ernest Lincoln, Jan. 1, 1942; children—Ernest Lincoln, Martha Allison. Tchr. social studies Los Angeles schs., 1937-46, 58-73; mem. Los Angeles County Grand Jury, 1961. Mem. alumni council UCLA, 1942-46; mem. exec. bd. Los Angeles Family Service, 1959-62; mem. Dist. Atty.'s Adv. Com., 1965-82, chmn. San Marino chpt. Am. Cancer Soc.; bd. dirs. Pasadena Rep. Women's Club, 1960-62, San Marino dist. council Girl Scouts U.S.A., 1959-68; pres. San Marino High Sch. PTA, 1964-65; bd. dirs. Pasadena Vol. Placement Bur., 1962-68, Los Angeles Women's Philharmonic Com., 1972-84, 86—; mem. adv. bd. Univ. YWCA, 1956—, bd. dirs., 1960—; co-chmn. Dist. Atty's. adv. bd. Young Citizens Council, 1968-81; mem. San Marino Red Cross Council, 1966—, chmn., 1969-71, vice chmn., 1972-73; mem. San Marino bd. Am. Field Service, 1971—; bd. dirs. Reachout com. Los Angeles Music Center, 1975—; trustee Pacificulture Art Mus., 1973-79; mem. Atty. Gen.'s Vol. Adv. Council, 1972-78; mem. adv. bd. Beverly Hills-West Los Angeles YWCA, 1973-84, Los Angeles Met. YWCA, 1975-84; mem. San Marino Community Council, 1964-73; hon. bd. Pasadena chpt. ARC, 1978-82, vice chmn., 1980-83; bd. dirs. Vol. Action Center, West Los Angeles, 1980-84, Pasadena Philharm. Com., 1980—, Stevens House, 1980—, San Marino Hist. Soc., 1977-83; bd. dirs. Friends Outside, 1982—, sec., 1984. Recipient spl. commendation Am. Cancer Soc., 1961, 73; Community Service award UCLA, 1981; Community Service award West Los Angeles Coordinating Council, 1985. Mem. DAR, Pasadena Philharmonic, Los Angeles Lawyers' Wives (dir. 1973—), Las Floristas, Huntington Meml. Clinic Aux., Nat. Charity League, Law Wives of Los Angeles (mem. bd. 1976—), Pasadena Dispensary Aux., Gold Shield (co-founder), Mortar Bd., Prytanean Soc., Pi Lambda Theta, Pi Gamma Mu. Home: 1786 Kelton Ave Los Angeles CA 91108

MESTAS ALVAREZ, CHRISTINE ESTELLE, lawyer; b. LaJunta, Colo., July 10, 1951; d. Tony and Josephine (Peña) Mestas; m. Raul Alvarez, June 30, 1973; children—Raquel, Adan. B.A. in Polit. Sci., Stanford U., 1973, J.D., 1976. Bar: Calif. 1976, D.C. 1978, Colo. 1981. Staff atty. Nat. Ctr. Youth Law, San Francisco, 1976-78; legis. counsel to U.S. Sen. Gary Hart, Washington, 1978-79; dep. counsel U.S. Senate Subcom., Washington, 1979-81; cons., lobbyist Nat. Child Labor Com., N.Y.C., 1981; ptnr. firm Baron, Faulkner & Alvarez, Denver, 1981—;adj. prof. law U. Colo., Boulder, 1983-84; lectr. George Washington U., 1979-81; counsel Am. Friends Service Com., San Francisco, 1976-78; lectr. Kwame Forum, Palo Alto, Calif., 1978. Colo. del. Democratic Mid-Term Conv., Phila., 1982; chmn. Cranston for Pres. Com., Colo., 1983-84; bd. dirs. U. Houston Inst. Law and Govt., Houston, 1982—; co-founder Nat. Migrant Edn. Coalition, San Francisco, N.Y.C., Washington, 1977-78; mem. com. to investigate discrimination against imigrant children Office Civil Rights. Mem. ABA, Colo. Bar Assn., D.C. Bar Assn., Calif. Bar Assn., Hispanic Bar Assn., Stanford U. Alumni Assn., Hispanic C. of C., Denver C. of C. (steering com.), Latin Am. C. of C. (dir. 1984—). Democrat. Roman Catholic. Office: Baron Faulkner and Alvarez 550 Writer Sq 1512 Larimer St Denver CO 80202

METCALF, JO ANN HOFFMANN, municipal official; b. Longview, Tex., May 22, 1931; d. John Richard and Eila Mae (Wilson) Hoffmann; m. Jesse Virgil Metcalf, Mar. 21, 1954; 1 child, Eric Shawn. Student pub. schs., Longview. Clk.-typist City of Longview, 1947-64, asst. city sec., 1964-77, city sec., dir. mcpl. services, 1977—; treas., bd. dirs. Firemen's Relief and Retirement system, Longview, 1977—; sec., bd. dirs. Gee-Tex Fed. Credit Union, Longview, 1984-87. Recipient cert. merit City of Longview, 1977. Mem. Internat. Inst. Mcpl. Clks., Mcpl. Treas. Assn. U.S. and Can., Assn. City Clks. and Secs. Tex. Christian Scientist. Lodge: Order Eas Star (past local sec.). Home: 1215 Columbia Dr Longview TX 75601 Office: City of Longview 300 W Cotton St Longview TX 75601

METCALF, LYNNETTE CAROL, naval officer, journalist; b. Van Nuys, Calif., June 22, 1955; d. William Edward and Carol Annette (Keith) M. B.A. in Communications and Media, Our Lady of Lake, 1978; M.A. in Human Relations, U. Okla., 1980; M.A. in Mktg. Webster U., 1986. Enlisted U.S. Air Force, 1973, advanced through grades to sgt., 1975; intelligence analyst, Taiwan, Italy and Tex., 1973-76; historian, journalist, San Antonio, 1976-78; commd. officer U.S. Navy, 1978, advanced through ranks to lt., 1982; pub. relations officer, Rep. of Panama, 1979-81; personnel adminstr., London, 1981-82; ops. plans/tng., McMurdo Sta., Antarctica, 1982-84; exec. officer transient personnel unit Naval Tng. Ctr., Great Lakes, Ill., 1984-86, comdg. officer transient personnel unit, 1986—; anchorwoman USN-TV CONTACT, 1986—. Contbr. articles to profl. jours.; editor Naval Station Anchorline, 1979-81, WOPN Caryatides, 1985—; author: Winter's Summer, 1983. Sec. San Vito Dei Normanni theatre group, Italy, 1975-76; coordinator Magic Box Theater, Zion, Ill., 1984—. Decorated Antarctic Service medal, 1983, Sec. Navy Letter of Commendation, 1984, Expert Marksman medal, 1985. Mem. Nat. Assn. Female Execs., Women Officers' Prof. Network. Clubs: McMurdo; Soc. of South Pole. Avocations: scuba diving; travel; reading; writing; performing.

METRAILER, ANN MARIE, lawyer; b. Little Rock, June 15, 1950; d. William Joseph and Anna Jane (Fulmer) M.; m. Bernard Joseph Sharkey, Jr., June 11, 1983. B.F.A., Newcomb Coll., Tulane U., 1972; M.P.A., La. State U., 1981, J.D., 1981. Bar: La. 1981. Claims examiner State of La., Baton Rouge, 1974-76, research statistician, 1976-77; atty. U.C.C.S., Inc., Baton Rouge, 1981-84; in-house counsel Sentry Ins. Co., Baton Rouge, 1984—. U.S. Dept. Edn. fellow, 1977-78. Mem. Baton Rouge Assn. Women Attys. (treas. 1984, pres. 1985), Baton Rouge Bar Assn., La. State Bar Assn., ABA, La. Trial Lawyers Assn., Phi Alpha Delta. Democrat. Office: PO Box 80013 2237 S Acadian St Baton Rouge LA 70898

METROS, MARY TERESA, librarian; b. Denver, Nov. 10, 1951; d. James and Wilma Frances (Hanson) Metros. B.A. in English, Colo. Women's Coll., 1973; M.A. in Librarianship, U. Denver, 1974. Adult services librarian Englewood Pub. Library (Colo.), 1975-81, adult services mgr., 1983-84; library systems cons. Dataphase Systems, Kans. City, Mo., 1981-82; circulation librarian Westminster Pub. Library (Colo.), 1983; profl. services supr. Tempe Pub. Library, 1984—. Mem. ALA, Pub. Library Assn., Ariz. Library Assn., Nat. Mgmt. Assn. Democrat. Home: 1001 N Pasadena 28 Mesa AZ 85201 Office: Tempe Pub Library 3500 S Rural Rd Tempe AZ 85202

METROSE, CYNTHIA JANE, surgical sales executive; b. Pitts., July 10, 1959; d. Stacey Theodore and Anastasia (Manolas) M. Student U. Salamanca, Spain, 1980; B.A. in Psychology with honors, Pa. State U., 1981. Dir. bus. ops. Process Skills, Inc., University Park, Pa., 1980-81; intern Ryan Homes, Pitts., 1981; hosp. rep. E.R. Squibb and Sons, Pitts., 1982-84; surg. sales rep. Precision-Cosmet Co., Pitts., 1984—. Author: (with others) Test Taker's Survival Guide, 1981. Vol., Salvation Army, Pitts., 1982—. Mem. Nat. Assn. Female Execs., Pa. State Alumni Assn., Phi Beta Kappa. Republican. Greek Orthodox. Avocations: racquetball; water sports; flea marketing; theater; music. Home: 803 St James Pittsburgh PA 15232

METTEE-MCCUTCHON, ILA, army officer; b. Mobile, May 1, 1945; d. John Martin and Anna Ruth (Cleveland) Mettee; B.S., Auburn (Ala.) U., 1967, M.S., 1969; grad. various army schs.; m. John Robert McCutchon, Oct. 13, 1974; 1 dau., Erin Tempest. Research psychologist VA Hosp., Tuskegee, Ala., 1967-69; clin. psychologist U. Ala. Med. Center, Birmingham, 1969-71; commd. 1st lt. U.S. Army, 1971, advanced through grades to maj., 1981; OIC, Alcohol and Drug Abuse Rehab. Center, Presidio, San Francisco, 1971-73; strategic intelligence officer 8th Psychol. Bn., 1973-75; tactical intelligence officer, ops. officer, co. comdr. 525th MI Group CEWI (Airborne), Ft. Bragg, N.C., 1976-79; project officer Command, Control, Communications and Intelligence Directorate, Combined Arms Combat Devel. Activity, Ft. Leavenworth, Kans., 1979-82; instr. U.S. Mil. Acad., 1975; student Command and Gen. Staff Coll., 1982-83; ops. officer Army Spl. Security Group, Washington, 1983—. Decorated Army Commendation medal, Meritorious Service medal (2), Army Achievement award. Mem. Assn. U.S. Army. Home: 6732 Anders Terr Springfield VA 22150 Office: Hdqrs US Army Spl Security Group Pentagon Washington DC 20310

METTLER, MARILYNN VIRGINIA, nurse educator; b. Topeka, Kans., Feb. 23, 1926; d. Isaac Webb and Dickey Jewell (Fish) Vernon; m. Marvin Dean Mettler, Apr. 6, 1947 (div. 1969); 1 son, Max Vernon. Diploma Hutchinson Jr. Coll., 1946, William Newton Sch. Nursing, 1959; B.S. in Nursing, U. Mo., 1962; M.S., U. Colo., 1965; postgrad. in computer sci. U. So. Colo., 1982-84. Cashier, acct. Barton Salt Co., Hutchinson, Kans., 1948-56; staff nurse, supr. William Newton Meml. Hosp., Winfield, Kans., 1959-60, instr. nursing, 1960-61; staff nurse U. Mo. Med. Ctr., Columbia, 1961-62; dir. nursing edn. Butler County Community Coll., El Dorado, Kans., 1965-74, St. Johns Coll., Winfield, Kans., 1974-80; mem. faculty U. So. Colo., Pueblo, 1980—, assoc. prof., interim asst. dean, 1980-81, assoc. degree nursing coordinator, 1981—. Mem. Am. Nurses Assn., Nat. League for Nursing (assoc. degree nursing accreditation visitor 1983—, bd. rev. 1984—), NEA, Sigma Theta Tau. Democrat. Methodist. Club: Soroptimist (Winfield, Kans.). Home: 1243 Ln 28 Pueblo CO 81006 Office: Univ of So Colo 2200 Bonforte Blvd Pueblo CO 81006

METTLER, MARY A., business executive; b. Akron, Ohio, Oct. 9, 1937; d. William M. and Margaret E. (Young) M.; B.A. with distinction in Econs., Stanford U., 1959; postgrad. program in bus. adminstrn. Harvard U.-Radcliffe Coll., 1960; M.B.A., Am. U., 1962. Dir. research Ferris & Co., Washington, 1960-63; systems engr. IBM, San Francisco, 1964-68; pres. Western Ops., Inc., San Francisco, 1968-74; dir. fin. United Vintners, San Francisco, 1975-79; sr. v.p., chief fin. officer Lawrence Systems Inc., San Francisco, 1979-84; v.p. fin. San Francisco Newspaper Agy., 1984—. Recipient Elijah Watt Sells award, 1974. Club: Commonwealth of Calif. Home: 4462 24th St San Francisco CA 94114 Office: 925 Mission St San Francisco CA 94103

ME TWYMAN, MICHELE ELIZABETH, budget analyst; b. Hampton, Va., Mar. 26, 1950; d. Bennie and Celestine E. (Ward) Baker; m. David Robert Twyman, June 27, 1970; children—Sherele Evangeline, David DuVal. Student Va. Union U., 1967-69, No. Va. Community Coll., 1985, Nat. Coll. Edn., 1986—. Buyer's asst. House & Hermann, Washington, 1972-73; service rep. Am. Security Bank, Washington, 1973-75; collection officer Pentagon Fed. Credit Union, Arlington, Va., 1978-80, Nat. Credit Union Adminstrn., Washington, 1980-81; dep. comptroller Dept. Army, Alexandria, Va., 1981-85, budget analyst, 1985—. Recipient profl. awards. Mem. Am. Assn. Budget and Program Analysts (cert. 1985), Am. Soc. Mil. Comptrollers (cert. 1985), Nat. Assn. Female Execs. (cert. 1984), Democrat. Baptist. Avocation: reading. Home: 2344 Old Trail Dr Reston VA 22091 Office: Dept Army Bldg 15 Cameron Sta Alexandria VA 22304

METZ, MARY SEAWELL, college president, educator; b. Rockhill, S.C., May 7, 1937; d. Columbus Jackson and Mary (Dunlap) Seawell; B.A. summa cum laude in French and English, Furman U., 1958, H.H.D., 1984; postgrad. Institut Phonetique, Paris, 1962-63, Sorbonne, Paris, 1962-63; Ph.D. magna cum laude in French, La. State U., 1966; LL.D. (hon.), Chapman Coll., 1985; m. F. Eugene Metz, Dec. 21, 1957; 1 dau., Mary Eugena. Instr. French, La. State U., 1965-66, asst. prof., 1966-67, 68-72, assoc. prof., 1972-76, dir. elem. and intermediate French programs, 1966-74, spl. asst. to chancellor, 1974-75, asst. to chancellor, 1975-76; prof. French, Hood Coll., 1976-81, provost, dean acad. affairs, 1976-81; pres. Mills Coll., Oakland, Calif., 1981—; vis. asst. prof. U. Calif., Berkeley, 1967-68; dir. Lucky Stores, Pacific Gas & Electric; dir. Rosenberg Found., 1985-87; assoc. Gannett Ctr. Media Studies, 1985—. NDEA fellow, 1960-62, 63-64; adv. council Stanford Research Inst. Internat., 1985—, Fulbright fellow, 1962-63; Am. Council Edn. fellow, 1974-75. Mem. Western Coll. Assn. (v.p. 1982-84, pres. 1984-86), Assn. Ind. Calif. Colls. and Univs. (exec. com. 1982—), So. Conf. Lang. Teaching (dir. 1975-78, vice chmn. 1975-76, chmn. 1976-77), Bus.-Higher End. Forum, Women's Forum West, World Affairs Council No. Calif. (dir. 1984—), Women's Coll. Coalition (exec. com. 1984—), Nat. Assn. Ind. Colls. and Univs. (govt. relations adv. council 1982-85). Phi Kappa Phi, Phi Beta Kappa. Author: Reflets du monde français, 1971, 78, Cahier d'exercices: Reflets du monde français, 1972, 78; (with Helstrom) Le Français à découvrir, 1972, 78; Cahier d'exercices: Le Français à découvrir, 1972, 78; Le Français à vivre, 1972, 78; Cahier d'exercices: Le Français à vivre, 1972, 78; editorial bd. Liberal Edn., 1982—; author standardized tests. Office: Mills College Oakland CA 94613

METZ, NANCY HERRON, med. technologist; b. Guthrie County, Iowa, Nov. 8, 1940; d. Raymond E. and Lillian M. Herron; B.S., Wheaton Coll., 1962; cert. in med. tech. U. Kans., 1964; m. William Mason Metz, Aug. 14, 1966; children—Steven James, Gail Leanne, Marcia Jane. Staff technologist Blood Bank Lab., U. Kans. Med. Center, Kansas City, 1964-70; staff technologist lab. and x-ray Lookout Meml. Hosp., Spearfish, S.D., 1971—. Mem. Am. Soc. Clin. Pathologists. Home: 821 10th St Spearfish SD 57783

METZ, ROXIE ANNE, art educator; b. New Rochelle, N.Y., July 2, 1955; d. Calvin Leon and Dorothy May (Belton) Metz. B.F.A., Coll. New Rochelle, 1978, M.A. in Art/Psychology, 1984. Asst. residence supr. Westchester Assn. for Retarded Citizens, White Plains, N.Y., 1978-79; art tchr. New Rochelle City Sch. Dist., 1979—. Vol. New Rochelle Hosp. Med. Ctr., 1977—; active New Rochelle Community Action Agy., 1973-74. Mem. Nat. Assn. Female Execs., Smithsonian Instn., N.Y. State United Tchrs., Am. Fedn. Tchrs. Democrat. Christian. Address: 80 Guion Pl Apt 8T New Rochelle NY 10801

METZEL, REBECCA ANN, city executive; b. Cardington, Ohio, Feb. 21, 1936; d. William Harrison and Violet (Glass) Casto; m. Edward Carl Metzel, June 29, 1957; children—Anne E. Metzel Linc, Linda S. Metzel Alderfer, Edward C., III. Student Malone Coll., 1954-56. Mem. secretarial pool Hydraulic Mfg. Co., Mt. Gilead, Ohio, 1956-57; sec. credit dept. Johns-Manville, Cleve., 1957-58; sec. Cleve. Heights, Ohio, 1978; asst. commr. central services, City of Cleveland Heights, 1978-80, supr. central services, 1980—. Mem. Task Force for Devel. of Minority Bus. Enterprise Plan. Mem. Nat. Assn. Govt. Purchasing. Methodist. Avocations: gardening; sewing; antique collecting; cut glass; traveling. Office: Supr of Central Services 40 Severance Circle Cleveland Heights OH 44118

METZGER, EVELYN PETERSEN, publisher, editor; b. Sandstone, Minn., Apr. 27, 1921; d. Hjalmar and Rigmor (Wosgaard) Petersen; m. Evron Maurice Kirkpatrick, 1950 (div. 1953); 1 child, Anna Marie; m. Arthur Zelig Metzger, Feb. 18, 1955; children—Lise Kai, Jon Frederick. B.A. cum laude, U. Minn., 1942. Staff writer/editor Nat. Geog. Mag., Washington, 1952-57; Washington editor Doubleday & Co., Inc., N.Y.C., 1957-73; founder, pres., pub., editor EPM Publs., Inc., McLean, Va., 1973—; dir. McLean Savs. & Loan Assn. Mem. Nat. Press Club, Phi Beta Kappa, Theta Sigma Phi. Office: EPM Publs 1003 Turkey Run Rd McLean VA 22101

METZGER, LAURA HELEN, advertising agency executive; b. N.Y.C., June 20, 1950; d. Robert Louis and Ann (Rittenberg) M. B.A., U. Pa., 1971. Research analyst Bank of Am., San Francisco, 1971-73, systems liaison officer, 1974; mktg. research Crown Zellerbach Corp., San Francisco, 1975-76; project dir. Grey Advt., Los Angeles, 1976-78, sr. project dir., 1978-81, v.p., dir. research services, 1981-82; v.p. so. ops., research dir. Ogilvy & Mather, Houston, 1982-85, v.p., dir. strategy devel., 1985—; guest lectr. local univs., 1981—. Recipient EFFIE award for advt. effectiveness, 1983, 85. Mem. Am. Mktg. Assn., Research Round Table. Office: Ogilvy & Mather 1415 Louisiana Houston TX 77002

METZGER-CAMPBELL, LINDA ARLENE, educator; b. Orange, Calif., Nov. 15, 1957; d. Vernon Arthur and Beth Arlene (Wilson) Metzger; m. James Lee Campbell, Nov. 26, 1983. A.A., Orange Coast Community Coll., 1976; B.A., Long Beach State U., 1978; M.A., Azusa Pacific U., 1985. Trainer, Santa Ana Unified Schs. (Calif.), 1979—; tchr. 1st grade health curriculum, 1983, trainer gifted and talented individuals, 1985-86. Mem. Kappa Delta Pi (social v.p. 1979).

METZLER, YVONNE LEETE, travel agent; b. Bishop, Calif., Jan. 25, 1930; d. Ben Ford and Gladys Edna (Johnson) Leete; student U. Calif., Berkeley, 1949; m. Richard Harvey Metzler, June 2, 1950; children—David Grant, Regan M., Erin E. Vocat. instr. Ukiah (Calif.) Jr. Acad., 1962-63; bookkeeper Sid Beamer Volkswagen, Ukiah, 1963-64; acct. Ukiah Convalescent Hosp., 1964, Walter Woodard P.A., Ukiah, 1964-66; assoc. dir. Fashion Two Twenty, Ukiah, 1966-67, dir., Santa Rosa, Calif., 1967-71; acct. P.K. Marsh, M.D., Ukiah, 1971-72, Walter Woodard P.A. and Clarence White C.P.A., Ukiah, 1972-74; ptnr., travel agt. Redwood Travel Agy., Ukiah, 1973-76; owner, mgr. A-1 Travel Planners, Ukiah, 1976—; owner A-1 Travel Planners of Willits (Calif.), 1979—. Commr., Ukiah City Planning Commn., 1979-84, vice chmn., 1981, chmn., 1981-83; mem. Republican County Central Com., 1978-80. Mem. Ukiah C. of C. (1st v.p. 1980, pres. 1981-83), Mendocino County C. of C. (dir. 1981), Mendocino County Vintners Assn. (assoc.). Internat. Platform Assn. Clubs: Soroptimist (pres. 1977-78), Bus. and Profl. Women (treas. 1977-78). Office: 505 E Perkins St Ukiah CA 95482

MEUSE, ANN TERRELL, insurance company executive; b. Massillon, Ohio, Jan. 16, 1943; d. Douglass Fuqua and Jane (Chidester) Terrell; B.A. magna cum laude, Coll. White Plains (N.Y.), 1974; diploma paralegal edn. N.Y. U., 1975; m. Lewis Andrew Meuse, Apr. 16, 1960; children—Ann W., Laura A. Corp. sec., compliance dir. Gerber Life Ins. Co., White Plains, 1974-78; dir. legis. and policy research services Colonial Penn Group, Inc., Phila., 1978-82; asst. v.p. bus. devel. Montgomery Ward Life Ins. Co., Chgo., 1982—. Mem. Chgo. Headline Club, Chgo. Women's Direct Response Group, Soc. Ins. Research, Sigma Delta Chi. Club: Toastmasters. Office: 200 N Martingale Rd Schaumburg IL 60194

MEYER, ALICE SHERMAN, fashion marketing director writer; b. N.Y.C., Mar. 22, 1936; d. Sidney and Rose (Cheiten) Sherman; m. Norman Meyer, Dec. 20, 1953 (dec. 1978). B.A., NYU, 1956; grad. Profl. Program in Bus. and Mktg., NYU, 1978. Fashion researcher Lord & Taylor, N.Y.C., 1956-66; fashion coordinator Bloomingdales store, N.Y.C., 1966-76; fashion dir. R.H. Stearns, Boston, 1976-78; v.p. Abbracci, Ltd., U.S. and Italy, 1978-80; pres. Fashion Dirs., N.Y.C., 1980—; cons. to Italian and Israeli fashion industries, 1980-86; U.S. fashion mktg. dir. Govt. of Israel, 1986—. Author: Clotheswise, 1982; Stop the Clock Dressing, 1987. Contbr. articles in field to publs. Mem. Fashion Group, Fashion's Inner Circle. Democrat. Mem. Religious Sci. Ch.

MEYER, ANNE STRINGER, association executive; b. Decatur, Ala., Nov. 20, 1930; d. William Lowe Stringer and Corinne Annabelle (Stritzinger) Stringer Stanton; m. William Andrew Meyer, Sept. 9, 1949 (div. Jan. 1977); children—William Andrew, Jr., Robert Moore, Anne Elizabeth. B.A., Tulane U., 1976. Real estate agt. Stan Weber & Assocs., Metairie, La., 1971-76; owner Chateau Florist, Kenner, La., 1978-82; pub. relations dir. Goodwill Industries, New Orleans, 1982-84; community relations coordinator East Jefferson Gen. Hosp., 1984-86; prin. Anne Meyer and Assoc., Pub. Relations Cons., 1986—; free-lance artist, writer. Chmn. bus. and profl. group Goodwill Industries Vol. Services, 1984-85; chmn. thank you com. United way, 1985; mem. mayor's adv. com. City of Kenner. Recipient awards for drawings, 1971-72. Mem. Women in Communications (local v.p. 1983—), Pub. Relations Soc. Am., Kenner Bus. Assn. (co-founder, 1st v.p. 1979), Internat. Assn. Bus. Communicators (v.p. programs 1985), Kenner Women's Profl. Assn., Friends of Zoo, McGehee Sch. Alumnae Assn. (sch. class rep. 1950—), Newcomb Alumnae Assn., Republican. Roman Catholic. Club: Press (New Orleans). Home: 3408 Connecticut Ave Kenner LA 70065 Office: Anne Meyer and Assocs 3408 Conn Ave Kenner LA 70065

MEYER, BETTE EUNICE, historian, museologist, preservationist; b. Chgo., Apr. 18, 1930; d. Henry Hahneman and Pearl Eunice (Kane) Wagner; m. Robert Edward Meyer, Feb. 3, 1951; children—Robert Daniel, Kathleen Lynn, Susan Joan. B.A., De Paul U., Chgo., 1956; M.Ed., Eastern Wash. U., Cheney, 1967, B.A. magna cum laude, 1971; postgrad. Wash. State U., 1981—. Curator history and edn. Eastern Wash. State Hist. Soc., Spokane, 1967-71; chief Office of Archeology and Historic Preservation, Wash. State Parks, Olympia, 1971-73; exec. dir. Congress of Valley Agys., Livermore, Calif., 1975-77; historic preservation planner Benton Franklin Govtl. Conf., Richland, Wash., 1978-79; researcher Wash. State U. Found., Pullman, 1981-84, also past mem. mus. adv. com.; devel. and mktg. coordinator Holy Names Ctr. at Ft. George Wright Historic Dist., Spokane, 1984—; exec. com. Wash. State Geog. Names Bd., Olympia, 1971-73. Author: Ainsworth, A Railroad Town, 1983, also articles. Chmn. Pullman Civic Arts Commn., 1981-82; mem. Wash. Land Use Plan Commn., Olympia, 1971-72. NEH fellow. Mem. Am. Assn. Mus., Am. Assn. State, Local History (grantee), Can. Mus. Assn., Nat. Trust Historic Preservation, Whitman County Hist. Soc. (bd. dirs. 1981-83). Mont. Hist. Soc., Inland N.W. Tourism Coalition, AAUW (pub. info. chmn. Wash. div. 1972), Washington Trust for Historic Preservation, Council Am.'s Mil. Past, Victorian Soc. Am. Home: W 903 Westover Rd Spokane WA 99218 Office: Holy Names Ctr Fort George Wright W 4000 Randolph Rd Spokane WA 99204

MEYER, BETTY ANNE (MRS. JOHN R. BASKIN), lawyer; b. Cleve.; d. William Henry and Monica (McSherry) Meyer; student Denison U., 1941-43; A.B., Flora Stone Mather Coll., Western Res. U., 1946, LL.B., 1947; m. John R. Baskin, 1967. Admitted to Ohio bar, 1947; asst. to dean Adelbert Coll., Western Res. U., 1948-49; assoc. Kiefer, Hunter, Knecht & Williams, Cleve., from 1965; now mem. firm Knecht, Rees, Meyer, Mekedis & Shumaker. Mem. Alpha Phi. Home: 2679 Ashley Rd Shaker Heights OH 44122 also East Chop Martha's Vineyard MA 02557 also Key Largo FL 33037 Office: Terminal Tower Cleveland OH 44113

MEYER, BETTY JANE, librarian; b. Indpls., July 20, 1918; d. Herbert and Gertrude (Sanders) M.; B.A., Ball State Tchrs. Coll., 1940; B.S. in L.S., Western Res. U., 1945. Student asst. Muncie Public Library (Ind.), 1936-40; library asst. Ohio State U. Library, Columbus, 1940-42, cataloger, 1945-46, asst. circulation librarian, 1946-51, acting circulation librarian, 1951-52, adminstrv. asst. to dir. libraries, 1952-57, acting asso. reference librarian, 1957-58, cataloger in charge serials, 1958-65, head serial div. catalog dept., 1965-68, head acquisition dept., 1968-71, asst. dir. libraries, tech. services, 1971-76, acting dir. libraries, 1976-77, asst. dir. libraries, tech. services, 1977-83, instr. library adminstrn., 1958-63, asst. prof., 1963-67, asso. prof., 1967-75, prof., 1975-83, prof. emeritus, 1983—; library asst. Grandview Heights Public Library, Columbus, 1942-44; student asst. Case Inst. Tech., Cleve., 1944-45; mem. Ohio Coll. Library Center Adv. Com. on Cataloging, 1971-76, mem. adv. com. on serials, 1971-76, mem. adv. com. on tech. processes, 1971-76; mem. Inter-Univ. Library Council, Tech. Services Group, 1971-83; trustee Columbus Area Library and Info. Council Ohio, 1980-83. Ohio State U. grantee, 1975-76. Mem. ALA, Assn. Coll. and Research Libraries, AAUP, Ohio Library Assn. (nominating com. 1978-81), Ohioana Library Assn., Ohio Valley Group Tech. Services Librarians, No. Ohio Tech. Services Librarians, Franklin County Library Assn., Acad. Library Assn. Ohio, PEO, Beta Phi Mu, Delta Kappa Gamma. Club: Ohio State U. Faculty Women's. Home: 970 High St Unit H2 Worthington OH 43085

MEYER, BEVERLY BARRY, sightseeing excursion company executive; b. N.Y.C., Oct. 18, 1938; d. Francis Joseph and Ellen (Slevin) Barry; children—Catherine Seaton, John Barry, Dana DeBard. Student Dunbarton Coll., 1957-58. Vice-pres. Circle Line Sightseeing Yachts, Inc., N.Y.C., 1982—, also dir.; v.p. Hudson River Day Line, Inc., N.Y.C., 1982—, also dir; corp. sec. Circle Line Statue of Liberty Ferry, Inc., N.Y.C., 1974—, also dir. Bd. dirs. Harbor Festival Found.; mem. adv. com. travel and tourism adminstrn program New Sch. for Social Research, N.Y.C. Mem. West Side Assn. Commerce (bd. dirs.), Hotel Assn. N.Y., Am. Soc. Travel Agts., Nat. Tour Brokers Assn., Hotel Sales Assn. N.Y., N.Am. Travel Assn., Am. Bus Assn., Travel Industry Assn. Am., N.Y. Conv. and Visitors Bur. Clubs: Westhampton Country (admissions com.) (Long Island); Whitehall, Le Club (N.Y.C.). Office: Circle Line Plaza W End of 42d St New York NY 10036

MEYER, CATHY LYNN, lawyer; b. Springfield, Ill., Oct. 29, 1957; d. William Harold and Sandra Joan (Unsell) Meyer. B.A., Sangamon State U., 1979; J.D., St. Louis U., 1982. Bar: Tex. 1982. Assoc. firm George Chandler & Assoc., Baytown, Tex., 1982; asst. city atty. City of Abilene, Tex., 1983-86, City of Irving, Tex., 1984—. Mem. ABA, Tex. Bar Assn., Dallas Bar Assn., Tex. Young Lawyers Assn., Abilene Writers Guild. Office: City of Irving 825 W Irving Blvd Irving TX 75060

MEYER, CYNTHIA LOU, interior designer, oriental rug expert, investment art dealer; b. Kansas City, Mo., May 31, 1944; d. Edwin and Hazel Kathleen (George) M.; student Kansas City Art Inst. and Sch. Design, 1962-64, N.Y. Sch. Interior Design, 1973; 1 dau., Kimberly Ann Nowak. With Baumritter Corp.-Ethan Allen, 1973-74, Design Forum Assos., Wilbraham, Mass., 1973-76, Hayden-Wayside Furniture, Inc., Enfield, Conn., 1974-76, 78-81, Cynthia Meyer, Bowler, Jones & Page, Keene, N.H., 1976-78; owner, operator Creative Design, Inc., East Longmeadow, Mass., also partner Park Trading, Ltd., 1980—; tchr., lectr. career days for young people, interior design seminars, design, rug and art investment. Mem. Am. Soc. Interior Designers (asso.), Springfield Art Mus. (patron). Office: 38 Center Sq East Longmeadow MA 01028

MEYER, IVAH GENE, social worker; b. Decatur, Ill., Nov. 18, 1935; d. Anthony and Nona Alice (Gamble) Viccone; A.A. with distinction, Phoenix Coll., 1964; B.S. with distinction, Ariz. State U., 1966, M.S.W., 1969; postgrad. U.S. Internat. U.; m. Richard Anthony Meyer, Feb. 7, 1954; children—Steven Anthony, Stuart Allen, Scott Arthur. Social worker Florence Crittendon Home, Phoenix, 1969-70; social worker Family Service of Phoenix, 1970-73; faculty asso. Ariz. State U., 1973; field supr. Pitzer Coll., Claremont, Calif., 1977—; social worker Family Service of Pomona Valley, Pomona, Calif., 1975—; field supr. Grad. Sch. Social Services, U. So. Calif., 1978—; pvt. practice Chino (Calif.) Counseling Center. Lic. clin. social worker, Calif. Mem. Nat. Assn. Social Workers, Acad. Cert. Social Workers. Republican. Roman Catholic. Home: 778 Via Montevideo Claremont CA 91711 Office: 12632 Central Ave Chino CA 91710

MEYER, JANE, personnel executive; b. Boston, Mar. 2, 1949; d. Eric Lothar and Thelma (Ralston) Meyer; m. Robert C. Braiotta, Nov. 15, 1969 (div. 1975). B.S. magna cum laude in Mgmt., Mercy Coll. 1982. Personnel asst. Clairol Inc., Stamford, Conn., 1974-76; asst. personnel mgr. Louis Dreyfus Corp., Stamford, 1977-80, personnel mgr., 1980-84; affirmative action mgr. Frank B. Hall Inc., Briarcliff Manor, N.Y., 1984—. Mem. Internat. Assn. Personnel Women (v.p. profl. devel.), Am. Soc. Personnel Adminstrn., Delta Mu Delta. Democrat. Mem. Christian Ch. Office: Frank B Hall Inc 549 Pleasantville Rd Briarcliff Manor NY

MEYER, JUDITH TURNER, marketing firm executive; b. Washington, Aug. 12, 1945; d. Melvin Harvey and Wilsie (Riggin) Turner; m. Lawrence Howard Meyer, May 29, 1968 (div. Apr. 1974). B.A., U. Md., 1968. Mem. pub. relations staff USAF, various locations, Tex., Va. and Ohio, 1968-73; co-founder, sr. v.p. McFaddin Kendrick/McFaddin Ventures, Houston, 1973-83; owner Meyer Mktg. Concepts, Houston, 1984—. Staff supr. Conf. for Econ. Progress, Washington, 1967-68; regional chmn. Families of POW/MIA, Alexandria, La., also Columbus, Ohio, 1969-71; mem. vol. staff Sand Dollar Home, Houston, 1983—, Democratic Nat. Com., Washington, 1964-68; bd. dirs. Delia Stewart Sch. Dance, Houston, 1982—. Mem. Houston Advt. Fedn., Sales and Mktg. Execs., Nat. Assn. Pub. Relations. Roman Catholic. Club: LTG (dir. 1982-83) (Houston). Office: Meyer Marketing Concepts 605 Colquitt St Houston TX 77006

MEYER, KAREN ANN GRITZAN, speech/language pathologist; b. Bronx, Nov. 7, 1947; d. Stephan and Pauline Theresa (Linkiewicz) Gritzan; B.A., Herbert H. Lehman Coll., 1969; M.A. (fellow), Northwestern U., 1971; m. Charles J. Meyer, Oct. 17, 1970; children—Matthew, Thomas. Speech and lang. pathologist Mt. St. Ursula Speech Center, Bronx, 1971; speech and lang. pathologist Westchester Assn. Retarded Children (N.Y.), 1971-72; clin. communicologist, instr. rehab. medicine Mental Retardation Inst., N.Y. Med. Coll. and Flower Fifth Ave. Hosp., N.Y.C., 1972-75; pvt. practice speech and lang. pathology for children, Brewster, N.Y., 1980—; adj. lectr., clin. supr. Hunter Coll. Center for Communication Disorders, 1980—, asst. to coordinator Inst. Lang. and Learning Disabilities, 1981. Mem. Am. Speech Lang. and Hearing Assn. (moderator 2 sessions 1981 conf.), N.Y. State Speech Lang. and Hearing Assn. (chmn. com. career devel/student concerns and continuing edn. conv. 1984), Westchester Speech Lang. and Hearing Assn., Phi Beta Kappa. Roman Catholic. Home: 506 Village Dr Brewster NY 10509

MEYER, LYNN NIX, lawyer; b. Vinita, Okla., Aug. 10, 1948; d. William Armour and Joan Manners (Ross) Nix; m. Lee Gordon Meyer, Mar. 14, 1980; children—Veronica Lynn, Victoria Lee, David Gordon. Student U. Tex., 1966-68, 76-77; B.A., Baldwin Wallace Coll., 1978; J.D., Case Western Res. U., 1981. Bar: Ky. 1982, Colo. 1984. Asst. dept. mgr. U. Tex. Bookstore, Austin, 1967-74; co-owner Tex. Voting Systems, Austin, 1974-76; paralegal Texaco Devel. Co., Austin, 1976-77; legal asst. Alcan Aluminum Co., Cleve., 1977-79; assoc. Wyatt, Tarrant & Combs, Lexington, Ky., 1982-83; Founding ptnr. Meyer Legal Advisors, Englewood, Colo., 1984—. Mem. ABA. Republican. Home: 10487 E Ida Ave Englewood CO 80111 Office: DTC Pkwy Suite 317 Englewood CO 80111

MEYER, M. KATHERINE, sociologist, educator; b. Balt., Apr. 4, 1943; d. Walter Francis and Winifred Marie (Kenney) M.; A.B., Trinity Coll., Washington, 1964; M.A., U. N.C., Chapel Hill, 1971, Ph.D., 1974; m. John Seidler, June 25, 1978; children—Anne Meyer Seidler, Elizabeth Meyer Seidler. Tchr. jr. high sch., Balt., 1964-67, Hyattsville, Md., 1967-68; assoc. prof. sociology Ohio State U., 1974—. NIMH trainee, 1969-73, fellow, 1979; Johns Hopkins Deans fellow, 1979; NSF grantee, 1970-74; Ohio State U. grantee, 1977. Mem. Am. Sociol. Assn., N. Central Sociol. Assn., So. Sociol. Assn. Democrat. Roman Catholic. Contbr. articles to profl. jours. Home: 1179 Middleport Dr Columbus OH 43220 Office: Dept Sociology Ohio State U Columbus OH 43210

MEYER, MARION M., editor; b. Sheboygan, Wis., July 14, 1923; d. Herman O. and Viola A. (Hoch) M.; B.A., Lakeland Coll., 1950; M.A., N.Y.U., 1957. Payroll clk. Am. Chair Co., Sheboygan, 1941-46; tchr. English and religion, dir. athletics Am. Sch. for Girls, Baghdad, Iraq, 1950-56; mem. edn./publ. staff United Ch. Bd. for Homeland Ministries, United Ch. Press/Pilgrim Press, 1958-64, sr. editor, 1965—; cons. to religious orgns. on editorial matters, copyrights, hymnals. Incorporating mem. Contact Phila., Inc., 1972, bd. dirs., 1972-75, v.p., chmn. com. to organize community adv. bd., chmn. auditing com., editor newsletter, 1972-74, pres., 1974-75, assoc. mem., 1977—. Mem. ofcl. bd. Old First Reformed Ch., Phila., 1984—. Honored as role model United Ch. of Christ, 1982, 85. Mem. AAUW. Mem. United Ch. of Christ (deacon 1984—). Contbr. articles to various publs. Home: 1900 JF Kennedy Blvd Philadelphia PA 19103 Office: 132 W 31st St New York NY 10001

MEYER, MARY-LOUISE, art gallery owner; b. Boston, Feb. 21, 1922; d. Alonzo Jay and Louise (Whitledge) Shadman; m. Norman Meyer, Aug. 9, 1941; children—Wendy C., Bruce R., Harold Alton, Marilee, Laurel. B.A., Wellesley Coll., 1943; M.S., Wheelock Coll., 1965. Head tchr. Page Sch., Wellesley Coll., Mass., 1955-60; instr. early childhood edn. Pine Manor Coll., Brookline, Mass., 1960-65; chaplain/counselor Charles St. Jail, Boston, 1974-79; Christian Sci. practitioner, Wellesley, Mass., 1974—; owner Alpha Gallery, Boston, 1972—; cons. Living & Learning Centers, Boston, 1966-69; 2d reader Christian Sci. Ch., 1979-82. Contbr. articles to profl. jours. Trustee Sturbridge Village, 1981—, trustee, 1986—; visitor Am. Decorative Arts dept. Mus. Fine Arts, Boston, 1973—; chmn. Wellesley Voters Rights Com., 1983-84; state organizer Edml. Channel 2 Group, Boston, 1960; co-founder Boston Assn. for Childbirth Edn., 1950. Mem. Farnsworth Mus., Waldoboro Hist. Soc., Soc. for Pres. New Eng. Antiquities. Club: Wellesley Coll.

MEYER, NANCY J., financial executive; b. Iowa; d. Frank Jacob and Marjorie Estelle (Duhme) M.; B.A., Barnard Coll., 1969; Dipl. Supérieur, Alliance Francaise, Paris, 1980; m. Charles Linzner, Nov. 14, 1970. With Krambo Corp., N.Y.C., 1969-76, San Francisco, 1976-77, v.p. and treas., 1973-77, also dir.; 2d v.p., sr. budget officer Chase Manhattan Corp., N.Y.C., 1977, 2d v.p., project mgr. system support, 1980-81, div. exec./ops. fin. planning, 1981-83, v.p., 1982-83; sr. fin. officer Rainier Nat. Bank, Seattle, 1983-85, v.p., 1985; asst. v.p. strategic planning, mergers and acquisitions CIGNA Corp., Phila., 1985—; asst. v.p. strategic planning/mergers and acquisitions CIGNA Corp., Phila., 1985—. Chartered fin. analyst, 1976; Nat. Merit scholar, 1965-69. Fellow Fin. Analysts Fedn.; mem. Inst. Chartered Fin. Analysts, N.Y. Soc. Security Analysts, mem. Barnard Coll. Alumnae Assn. Home: PO Box 6539 Lawrenceville NJ 08648 Office: One Logan Sq 29th Floor Philadelphia PA 19103

MEYER, NATALIE, state official; b. Henderson, N.C., May 20, 1930; d. Ranie and Mary Osborne (Johnson) Clayton; m. Harold Meyer, June 17, 1951; children—Mary, Becky, Amy. B.A., U. No. Iowa, 1951. Tchr., Jefferson City Schs.; tchr., prin. Ascension Lutheran Ch., Littleton, Colo., 1965-78; exec. dir. Ronald Reagan Presdl. Campaign, Colo., 1976; mgr. Phil Winn for Republican State Chmn., Colo., 1978; dir. Rep. State Legis. Races, Colo., 1980; polit. dir. 1980 Colo. Reps., 1980; sec. state State of Colo., Denver, 1983—. Rep. precinct committeeman, Littleton, 1960-82; vice chmn. Arapahoe County Reps., Littleton, 1967-74. Mem. Nat. Assn. Secs. of State, AAUW. Lutheran. Office: Office Sec of State 1560 Broadway Suite 200 Denver CO 80202

MEYER, PATRICIA HANES, psychiatric social worker; b. Champaign, Ill., Feb. 10, 1947; d. Walter Ernest and Mary Kathryn (Kemp) Hanes; B.A., Carroll Coll., Waukesha, Wis., 1969; M.S.W., Cath. U. Am., 1976; m. Scott Kimbrough Meyer, June 15, 1969; children—Jennifer Suzanne, Claire Catherine, John Andrew. Dir. family therapy program Fairfax County Juvenile Ct., Fairfax, Va., 1970-77; clin. instr. Georgetown U. Med. Sch., Washington, 1976-84; pvt. practice family psychiatry, 1976—. Mem. Am. Orthopsychiat. Assn., Am. Family Therapy Assn., Nat. Assn. Social Workers. Adv. editor The Family, 1977-84. Home: 3419 Tilton Valley Dr Fairfax VA 22033 Office: 2233 Wisconsin Ave Suite 214 Washington DC 20007

MEYER, PRISCILLA ANN, Russian language and literature educator, writer, translator; b. N.Y.C., Aug. 26, 1942; d. Herbert Edward and Marjorie Rose (Wolff) M.; m. William L. Trousdale, Sept. 15, 1974; 1 dau., Rachel V. B.A., U. Calif.-Berkeley, 1964; M.A., Princeton U., 1966, Ph.D., 1971. Lectr. in Russian lang. and lit. Wesleyan U., Middletown, Conn., 1968-71, asst. prof., 1971-75, assoc. prof., 1975—; vis. asst. prof. Yale U., 1973; tchr. John Lyman Elem. Sch., Middlefield, 1982-83. Editor: Dostoevsky and Gogol, 1979; Life in Windy Weather (by Andrei Bitov), 1986; translator stories; contbr. articles to profl. jours. Sr. scholar exchange Internat. Research and Exchange Bd., 1973; Ford Found. grantee, 1964-68, 70. Mem. Am. Council Tchrs. Russian (dir. 1983—), Am. Assn. Tchrs. Slavic and East European Langs., Am. Assn. for Advancement of Slavic Studies, Conn. Acad. Arts and Scis. Office: Russian Dept Wesleyan Univ Middletown CT 06457

MEYER, RUTH KRUEGER, museum administrator, art historian, critic; b. Chicago Heights, Ill., Aug. 20, 1940; d. Harold Rohe and Ruth Halbert (Bateman) Krueger; m. Kenneth R. Meyer, June 15, 1963 (div. 1978); 1 child, Karl Augustus. B.F.A., U. Cin., 1963; M.A., Brown U., 1968; Ph.D., U. Minn., 1980. Lectr., Walker Art Ctr., Mpls., 1970-72; instr. U. Cin., 1973-75; curator Contemporary Arts Ctr., Cin., 1976-80; dir. Ohio Found. on the Arts, Columbus, Ohio, 1980-83, Taft Mus., Cin., 1983—. Author (exhibition catalogues) Brad Davis: The Pines, 1984, The Am. Weigh, 1983, New Epiphanies, 1982; David Black: An American Sculptor, 1985; Sandy Rosen: Vestal Vases, 1986, Rick Paul, 1986. Pub. Dialogue Mag., 1980-83. Trustee Cin. Sculpture Council, 1984; mem. adv. Coll. Design, Architecture, Art and Planning, U. Cin., 1983—; adv. com. Friends of William Howard Taft Birthplace. Recipient Kress Found. Research award Brown U., 1967, Kress Found. Research award U. Minn., 1976. Mem. Assn. Art Mus. Dirs., Internat. Assn. Art Critics, Coll. Art Assn., Am. Assn. Mus. Democrat. Office: Taft Museum 316 Pike St Cincinnati OH 45202

MEYER, SHEREL LYNNE, business executive; b. Covington, Ky., Sept. 24, 1945; d. William P. and Viola Meyer; A.S., U. Cin., 1965. With Xerox Corp., 1966-85, br. mktg. support mgr., 1976-85 sales mgr., 1976-78, Cin. region supply products mktg. mgr., 1978-79, regional low vol. sales ops. mgr., Washington, 1980, mktg. program mgr. office products div., Dallas, 1980-82, mgr. advanced products/mktg. support, office products div., 1982-83, mktg. support mgr. info. products div., 1983-85; owner, pres. L'Executive, Dallas, 1985—. mem. adv. bd. Brookhaven Coll. Named Citizen of Day, Sta. WLW, 1969. Mem. Nat. Assn. Women Bus. Owners, NOW, Nat. Assn. Female Execs. Home: 1105 Whispering Oaks Ln Richardson TX 75081 Office: Village on the Pkwy 5100 Beltline Rd Suite 704 Dallas TX 75240

MEYER, URSULA, librarian; b. Free City of Danzig, Nov. 6, 1927; came to U.S., 1941, naturalized, 1949; d. Herman S. and Gertrude (Rosenfeld) M.; B.A., UCLA, 1949; M.L.S., U. So. Calif., 1953; postgrad. U. Wis.-Madison. County librarian Butte County (Calif.) Library, 1961-68; asst. div. library devel. N.Y. State Library, Albany, 1969-72; coordinator Mountain Valley Coop. System, Sacramento, 1972-73; dir. library services Stockton (Calif.)-San Joaquin County Public Library, 1974—; chair 49-99 Coop. Library System, 1974-84. Higher Edn. Title II fellow, 1968-69. Mem. ALA (council 1979-83, chmn. nominating com. 1982-83, mem. COL 1985-87), Am. Assn. Public Adminstrs., Freedom to Read Found., Calif. Library Assn. (pres. 1978, council 1974-79), AAUW, LWV, Common Cause, NOW. Club: Soroptimist. Home: 6423 Monitor Pl Stockton CA 95209 Office: 605 N El Dorado St Stockton CA 95202

MEYERS, CHRISTINE LAINE, publishing executive, consultant; b. Detroit, Mar. 7, 1946; d. Ernest Robert and Eva Elizabeth (Laine) M.; m. Kenneth Adamski, Feb. 12, 1972; 1 child, Kathryn Laine. B.A., U. Mich., 1968. Editor, indsl. relations Diesel div. Gen. Motors Corp., Detroit, 1968; nat. advt. mgr. J.L. Hudson Co., Detroit, 1969-76, mgr. internal sales promotion, 1972-73, dir. pub., 1973-76; nat. advt. mgr. Pontiac Motor div., Mich., 1976-78; pres., owner Laine Meyers Assocs., Troy, Mich., 1978—; dir. Internat. Inst. Met. Detroit, Inc. Contbr. articles to profl. pubs. Mem. bus. adv. council Central Mich. U., 1977—. Named Mich. Ad Woman of Yr., 1976, One of Top 10 Working Women, Glamour Mag., 1978. Mem. Women in Communications (Vanguard award 1986), Internat. Assn. Bus. Communicators, Adcraft Club, Women's Advt. Club (1st v.p. 1975), Women's Econ. Club (pres. 1976-77), Women's Forum Mich. Detroit C. of C., Mortar Board, Quill and Scroll, Pub. Relations Com. Women for United Found., Founders Soc. Detroit Inst. Arts, Fashion Group, Pub. Relations Soc. Am., First Soc. Detroit (exec. com. 1970-71), Kappa Tau Alpha. Home: 1780 Kensington Bloomfield Hills MI 48013 Office: Laine Meyers Assocs Inc 3645 Crooks Rd Troy MI 48084

MEYERS, DIANE MARIE, diabetes association executive; b. Detroit, Aug. 6, 1943; d. Raymond Paul and Charlotte (Masserant) Aumann; m. Gary Lee Meyers, Mar. 14, 1964; 1 child, Brian Lee. Student Sherwood Coll., 1962-64, Macomb Coll., 1973-75. Lic. cosmetologist, Fla., Mich. Coordinator spl. projects, Mich. Cancer Found., Detroit, 1978-83; exec. dir. Am. Cancer Soc., Wayne County, Mich., 1983-85; dir. income devel. Am. Diabetes Assn., Mich., 1985—. Owner, mgr. Linda's Beauty Salon, St. Clair Shores, 1964—. Author: Volunteerism, 1979. Mem. Nat. Female Execs. Assn., Econs. Club Detroit. Republican. Roman Catholic. Club: Zonta. Home: 25819 Jefferson Saint Clair Shores MI 48081 Office: Am Diabetes Assn 23100 Providence Dr Southfield MI 48075

MEYERS, DOROTHY, gerontologist, writer; b. Chgo., Jan. 9, 1927; d. Gilbert and Harriet (Levitt) King; B.A., U. Chgo., 1945, M.A., 1961, also postgrad.; postgrad. Columbia U., New Sch. Social Research, Northwestern U.; m. William J. Meyers, Oct. 9, 1947; children—Lynn, Jeanne. Instr. sr. adults, Chgo. Bd. and/City Colls. Chgo., 1961-78; coordinator pub. affairs forum and health maintenance program City Colls. Chgo.-Jewish Community Centers, Chgo., 1975-78; lectr. adult program City Colls. Chgo., 1984; tchr. Dade County Adult Edn. Program, Miami, Fla., 1983-85; discussion leader Brandeis U. Adult Edn., 1985-86; cons., lectr. in field. Chmn. legislation PTA; chmn. civic assembly Citizens Sch. Com.; v.p. community relations Womens Fedn. and Jewish United Fund; discussion leader LWV, Gt. Decisions, Fgn. Policy Assn.; program chmn. Jewish Community Centers, 1966-67, also mem. sr. adult com.; bd. dirs. council Jewish Elderly, Open U.; mem. art and edn. com. Chgo. Mayor's Com. for Sr. Citizens and Handicapped; mem. com. on media Met. Council on Aging. Mem. Am. Sociol. Assn., Gerontol. Assn., Nat. Council Aging, Chgo. Met. Sr. Forum (media com.), Council Women Chgo. Real Estate Bd., Women in Communications, Chgo. Real Estate Bd., Nat. Assn. Real Estate Bds., Art Inst. Chgo., Mus. Contemporary Art, Soc. Contemporary Art. Contbr. articles to profl. jours. Office: 77 Washington St W Chicago IL 60602

MEYERS, JAN, Congresswoman; b. Superior, Nebr.; m. Louis Meyers; children—Valerie, Philip. A.A. in Fine Arts, William Woods Coll., 1948; B.A. in Communications, U. Nebr.-Lincoln, 1951. Mem. Overland Park City Council, 1967-72, pres. City Council; mem. Kans. Senate, 1972-84, chmn. pub. health and welfare com. and local govt. com., vice chmn. transp. and utilities com., reapportionment com., 1972-84; mem. 99th Congress from 3d Kans. Dist.; mem. sci. and tech. com., small bus. com., select com. on aging, congl. caucus and task force memberships, house Republican policy com., house Rep. research com., v.p. 1984 Rep. freshmen class. Active Larry Winn for Congress com., Overland Park City Chmn., 1966; 3rd dist. co-chmn. Bob Dole for U.S. Senate, 1968; chmn. Johnson County Bob Bennett for Gov., 1974. Recipient Outstanding Elected Ofcl. of Yr. award Assn. Community Mental Health Ctr. Kans.; Woman of Achievement Matrix award Women in Communications, Inc.; Disting. Service award Bus. and Profl. Women Kansas City; Community Service award Jr. League Kansas City; 1st Disting. Legislator award Kans. Assn. Community Colls.; Outstanding Service award Kans. Library Assn.; Disting. Service award United Community Services; Legis. award Assn. Retarded Citizens Johnson County; 1st Legis. award Gov.'s Conf. Child Abuse and Neglect; Outstanding Legis. award Kans. Action for Children; Outstanding Mem. award League Women Voters; Friend of Edn. award Shawnee Mission, cert. of appreciation; Friend of Edn. award Phi Delta Kappa; Vis. Prof. award Baker U.; Outstanding Service award Kans. Pub. Health Assn., Outstanding Vol. award Mental Health Assn.; Most Outstanding Women in Johnson County award. Mem. Johnson County Community Coll. Found., Johnson County Mental Health Assn. (bd. dirs.), Shawnee Mission LWV (past pres.). Methodist. Offices: 204 Federal Bldg Kansas City KS 66101 and 1407 Longworth House Office Bldg Washington DC 20515

MEYERS, KAREN LORAYNE DONNELL, work therapist; b. Augusta, Ga., Aug. 11, 1952; d. James Moncie and Ruby Lorayne (Bartlett) Donnell; m. Joseph Arthur Meyers, July 2, 1982. B.A. in Psychology, Augusta Coll., 1974. Instr. YWCA, Augusta, 1971, asst. dir. summer camp, 1971; recreation leader II, Gracewood State Sch. and Hosp., Ga., 1972-74, work therapist, 1974-84, med. librarian, 1984, work therapist, 1984—, investigator EEO devel. team, 1979-84; mem. women's guild Doctors Hosp., Augusta, 1982. Jr. bd. dirs. USO, Augusta, 1971; bd. dirs. Augusta Tng. Shop for Handicapped, 1979-80. Mem. Zeta Tau Alpha (Eta Mu chpt.). Republican. Episcopalian. Avocations: reading; sewing; gardening. Home: 2827 Fairmount St Augusta GA 30906 Office: Gracewood State Sch Hosp Resident Work Tng Program Gracewood GA 30812

MEYERS, MARIAN CATHERINE, college administrator; b. Lackawanna, N.Y., Nov. 25, 1934; d. Walter Rojek and Bernice (Kocan) Palka; m. Donald George Meyers, Sept. 22, 1956; children—Donald, Mary, Margaret, John. Diploma in nursing, Mercy Hosp. Sch. Nursing, 1955; B.S. in Nursing, SUNY-Buffalo, 1967, M.S. in Nursing, 1970, also postgrad. Gen. duty nurse, head nurse, supr. Mercy Hosp., Buffalo, 1957-64; instr. Erie County Bd. Coop. Services, Buffalo, 1965-66, Deaconess Hosp. Sch. Nursing, Buffalo, 1967-70; chmn. nursing program Trocaire Coll., Buffalo, 1970-73, acting chmn. radiologic tech. programs, 1973-79, dean div. health sci., 1973-79, acting chmn. div. natural sci. and math., 1976-79; dir. devel. and pub. relations, 1979-81, dir. devel., 1981-85; v.p. for devel., 1985—, numerous coms. and other activities; clin. assoc. faculty SUNY-Buffalo Sch. Nursing, 1971-79; cons. in field. Planning coordinator Western N.Y. for Am. Council on Edn. nat. identification program for Advancement Women Higher Edn. Mem. Am. Assn. Community Jr. Colls., Am. Assn. for Higher Edn., Am. Council Edn. Nat. Identification Program, Buffalo C. of C., Council for Advancement Support Edn., N.Y. State Assn. Two Yr. Colls. (commn. adminstrn.), Nat. Council for Resource Devel. Home: 70 Therin Hamburg NY 14075 Office: Trocaire Coll 110 Red Jacket Pkwy Buffalo NY 14220

MEYERS, PATRICIA ANN, newspaper mgr.; b. Forreston, Ill., Nov. 20, 1932; d. Elmer Wilbur and Marie Leona (Abels) Brockmeier; student No. Ill. U., 1950-51; m. Richard Meyers, Mar. 17, 1956; children—Joey, Stuart, William, Robert. Acct., Micro Switch, Freeport, Ill., 1951-57; office asst. Forreston Jour., 1974-80, mgr., news dir., 1980—. Methodist. Home: 9744 Townline Rd Forreston IL 61030 Office: Box 237 Forreston IL 61030

MEYLOR, COLLEEN BETH, foundry product development specialist, educator; b. Milw., Nov. 29, 1957; d. Michael Bernard and Karole Joan (Kabbeck) M. B.S. in Chem. Engring., U. Wis.-Madison, 1979. Registered profl. engr. Devel. engr. Foseco, Inc., Cleve., 1980-82, product specialist, 1982-85, sr. product devel. specialist, 1985—; instr. Cast Metals Inst., Am. Foundry Soc., Chgo., 1984—. Soc. Mem. Am. Foundrymen's Soc., Am. Women in Metal Industries, Nat. Assn. Female Execs., U. Wis. Alumni Assn. Avocations: piano; sports. Home: 32747 Willowbrook Ln North Ridgeville OH 44039 Office: Foseco Inc 20200 Sheldon Rd Cleveland OH 44142

MEYNER, HELEN STEVENSON, former congresswoman, co. dir.; b. N.Y.C., Mar. 5, 1929; d. William Edward and Eleanor (Bumstead) Stevenson; B.A. in History, Colo. Coll., 1950, LL.D. (hon.), 1973; m. Robert B. Meyner, Jan. 19, 1957. With ARC, Korea, 1950's; later with UN, N.Y.C. then consumer adv. TWA; staff Adlai E. Stevenson; columnist Newark Star Ledger, 1962-69; hostess TV interview program, 1965-68; mem. 94th and 95th Congresses from 13th N.J. Dist.; dir. Prudential Ins. Co., 1979—, Allied Co., 1979. Opened N.J. gov.'s mansion Morven to public; mem. N.J. Rehab. Commn., 1961-75. Bd. dirs. Newark Mus. Mem. N.J. Democratic Policy Council; congressional candidate from 13th N.J. Dist., 1972. Home: 16 Olden Ln Princeton NJ 08540

MEYNINGER, RITA, civil engineer; b. Newark; B.S. in Civil Engring., Newark Coll. Engring., 1958; M.S. in Civil Engring., NYU, 1973; candidate D.Eng., N.J. Inst. Tech. With Clinton Bogert Assocs., Ft. Lee, N.J., 1970-74; v.p., gen. mgr. Resource Planning div. Hydrosci., Inc., Emerson, N.J., 1974-78; regional dir., region II, Fed. Emergency Mgmt. Agy., N.Y.C., 1979-81; now sr. v.p. Enviresponse, Inc., Foster Wheeler Corp., Livingston, N.J.; fed. coordinating officer in emergency declaration at Love Canal, N.Y. State, 1980; fed. coordinating officer in drought emergency declaration in N.J., 1980. Recipient Alumni Honor Roll award N.J. Inst. Tech., 1980; Tau Beta Pi Eminent Engr. award, 1986. Mem. ASCE, Am. Water Works Assn., Water Pollution Control Fedn. Home: 300 Winston Dr Cliffside Park NJ 07010

MEZEY, LUCINDA SANDFORD, banker; b. Plainfield, N.J., June 24, 1947; d. Joseph Webster and Barbara (Tracy) Sandford; m. William Lewis Mezey, Nov. 29, 1969. B.A., Wilson Coll., 1969. Chartered fin. analyst. Vice-pres., investment analyst Provident Nat. Bank, Phila., 1970-84, dir. equity research, 1984—. Pres. Jr. League Phila., 1984-85, exec. com., 1979-85; bd. dirs. Maternal and Family Activities, Phila., 1985—, Greater Phila. Cultural Alliance, 1985—. Mem. Fedn. Fin. Analysts, Fin. Analysts Phila. Club: Cosmopolitan (Phila). Avocations: classical music; opera; needlepoint; sports. Office: Provident Nat Bank PO Box 7648 Philadelphia PA 19101

MEZZULLO, KAREN ANN, grant coordinator; b. Mt. Vernon, N.Y., July 28, 1955; d. John N. and Terry (Agostino) M. B.A., Trinity Coll., Vt., 1977; M.A., U. Md., 1983. Cert. spl. edn. tchr. Spl. edn. tchr. Continuing Edn., Rocky Mount, Va., 1977-80, Wassaic Devel. Ctr., N.Y., 1980-81; research asst. U. Md., College Park, 1981-83, vocat. coordinator, 1983-84; grant coordinator Nassau County Bd. Coop. Ednl. Services, Westbury, N.Y., 1985—; curriculum cons. Mem. Assn. Severely Handicapped, Nat. Assn. Female Execs. Avocations: theater; music; reading; hiking. Home: 43 S Baldwin Pl Massapequa NY 11758 Office: 2850 N Jerusalem Ave Wantagh NY 11793

MICCHELLI, MARYANNE PATRICIA, radio station executive; b. Newark, June 15, 1959; d. Mario R. and Lucy C. (Attunasio) Micchelli. B.A., Rutgers

U., 1981. Sales asst. Sta.-WNBC, N.Y.C., 1981-84, account exec., 1985—; account exec. Sta.-WHN, N.Y.C., 1984-85; speaker Fairleigh Dickenson U., Teaneck, N.Y., 1985-86, career seminars YWCA, N.Y.C., 1985-86. Mem. Advt. Club North Jersey, Nat. Assn. Female Execs., Internat. Radio and TV Soc., N.Y. Market Radio Broadcasters Assn., Rutgers Alumnae Assn. Roman Catholic. Club: Rutgers of N.Y. (N.Y.C.). Avocations: photography; tennis; travel; music. Home: 199 Westminster Pl Lodi NJ 07644 Office: NBC 30 Rockefeller Plaza Room 293 New York NY 10020

MICELI, DOROTHY, publishing company executive, editorial associate, business administrator; b. Bklyn., Dec. 20, 1939; d. Howard Clifford and Helen Clare (Mangold) Werber; m. Frank Joseph Miceli, Sept. 24, 1960; children—Frank Albert, Carolyn Louise, Stephen Joseph, Andrew James. Student Los Angeles City Coll., 1958-59. Typist, Savoy Real Estate, South Ozone Park, N.Y., 1956-57; stenographer/typist Western Electric, N.Y.C., 1957, sec., 1958; sec. Coldwell Banker & Co., Los Angeles, 1958-61; biller, typist Microfilm Pub. Inc., New Rochelle, N.Y., 1976, circulation mgr., 1976—; editorial assoc. Badler Group, New Rochelle, 1976—; bus. mgr. Internat. Micrographics Source Book, New Rochelle, 1976—; asst. pub.-editor Micrographics Newsletter, New Rochelle, 1985—. Typist New Rochelle Little League, 1980-82; eucharistic minister Ch. of Holy Family, New Rochelle, 1984—. Democrat. Roman Catholic. Clubs: Salesian High Sch. Parents Guild (v.p. 1986—), Salesian Cooperators (v.p. 1982—) (New Rochelle). Home: 333 Mayflower Ave New Rochelle NY 10801 Office: Microfilm Publishing Inc PO Box 950 Larchmont NY 10538

MICHAEL, COLETTE VERGER, educator; b. Marseille, France, May 3, 1937; d. Raymond Marc and Fanny (Kindler) Verger; B.Phil., U. Wash., 1969, M.A. in Roman Langs., 1970; M.S. in History of Sci., U. Wis., 1975, Ph.D. in French, 1973; children—Barbara, Peggy, Monique, Alan, David, Gerard. Tchr. French, U. Wis., 1973-75, Shimer Coll., Mt. Carroll, Ill., 1976; prof. French, No. Ill. U., DeKalb, 1977. Fellow Ford Found., 1970-73, NEH, summer 1977. Mem. Am. Assn. Tchrs. French, Fedn. Internat. Professeurs Francais, Am. Philos. Assn., 18th Century Studies Assn., Aircraft Owners and Pilot Assn. Author: Choderlos de Laclos: The Man, His Work and His Critics, 1982; (poetry) Intemperies, 1982, Sens Dessus Dessous, 1984; Choderlos de Laclos, Les Milieux Philosophiques et le Mal, 1984; The Marquis de Sade: The Man, His Works, and His Critics, 1986. Home: 5 Moraine Terr DeKalb IL 60115 Office: 315 Weston Hall No Ill U DeKalb IL 60115

MICHAEL, DOROTHY ANN, nurse, naval officer; b. Lancaster, Pa., Sept. 20, 1950; d. Richard Linus and Mary Ruth (Hahn) Michael. Diploma, R.N., Montgomery Hosp. Sch. Nursing, Norristown, Pa., 1971; B.S. Nursing, George Mason U., 1980; postgrad. U. Tex. Health Sci. Ctr., 1984—. Joined U.S. Navy, 1970, advanced through grades to lt. comdr. Nurse Corps, 1980; staff nurse Nat. Naval Med. Ctr., Bethesda, Md., 1971-73; charge nurse Naval Hosp., Guantanamo Bay, Cuba, 1973-74, Naval Regional Med. Ctr., Phila., 1974-76, Naval Hosp., Keflavik, Iceland, 1977, Naval Hosp., Bethesda, 1980-84; splty. advisor to dir. Navy Nurse Corp., Navy Med. Command, Washington, 1983—. Vice pres. Deepwood Homeowners Assn., Reston, Va., 1978-82; advisor, com. mem. Reston Found., 1979. Mem. Am. Nurses Assn. Roman Catholic.

MICHAEL, PHYLLIS CALLENDER, hymnwriter; b. nr. Berwick, Pa., Dec. 24, 1908; d. Bruce Miles and Emma (Harvey) Callender; grad. Bloomsburg Coll., 1928; B. Mus., U. Extension Conservatory, Chgo., 1953; m. Arthur L. Michael, Aug. 21, 1933; children—Robert Bruce, Keith Winton. Elem. tchr. Berwick Schs., 1928-33; substitute tchr. Shickshinny and Northwest Area, Pa., 1954-66; tchr. Northwest Area High Sch., 1966-71; gen. tchr. piano, organ, theory and voice, 1943—; hymnwriter, poet, author, composer, 1943—. Recipient first place in Nat. Favorite Hymns contest for Take Thou My Hand, 1953, Cert. of Merit for disting. service to composition outstanding hymns, 1967, and others. Adv. mem. MBLS. Mem. Nat. Ret. Tchrs. Assn., Internat. Platform Assn., Nat. Soc. Lit. and the Arts, Hymn Soc. Am. Author: Poems for Mothers, 1963; Poems From My Heart, 1964; Beside Still Waters, 1970; Fun to Do Showers, 1971; Bridal Shower Ideas, 1972; Is my Head on Straight, 1976; contbr. songs, articles, poems to books, hymn-books, booklets, mags. Address: Oak Haven RFD 3 Shickshinny PA 18655

MICHAELS, CATHERINE MARIE, museum dir., artist; b. Newport Beach, Calif., Mar. 13, 1953; d. Donn Owen and Marian Marie (Melandri) M.; B.F.A., U. Calif., Irvine, 1975. With retail sales and display dept. J. C. Penney Co., Newport Beach, 1972-77; retail display asst. mgr. Neiman-Marcus, Newport Beach, 1978-79; graphics cons. Mus. N. Orange County, Fullerton, Calif., 1977-79; dir. La Habra (Calif.) Children's Mus., 1979—. Mem. Mus. Educators So. Calif., Orange County Arts Alliance, Calif. Confedn. of Arts, La Habra Cultural Arts Council, Am. Assn. Mus. Office: La Habra Mus 301 S Euclid La Habra CA 90631

MICHAELS, DONNA L., imported bed linens company executive; b. Providence, Aug. 28, 1952; d. Lloyd Frederick and Pearl Ellen (Sibya) Sprague; m. John Thomas Michaels, Sept. 16, 1978; children—Devon Leigh, Kelsey Lynn, Kyle Patrick. A.B., Boston Coll., 1974; M.Ed., Rhode Island Coll., 1976. Tchr. Walpole Schs., Mass., 1974-78; sales rep., dist. field rep. Procter & Gamble, North Quincy, Mass., 1978-81; pres., owner The Comforter Connection, Inc., Westwood, Mass., 1981—; cons. various cos., 1982—; speaker devel. mail order bus. Am. Marketing Assn., 1985. Mem. New Eng. Direct Mktg. Assn., New Eng. Mail Order Assn., Direct Mktg. Assn., New Eng. Women Bus. Owners, Catalog Council Direct Mktg. Assn. Roman Catholic. Advocations: swimming; tennis; reading; crafts; jogging. Office: 555 High St Westwood MA 02090

MICHAELS, JOANNE, editor; b. N.Y.C., Dec. 30, 1950; d. Lawrence William and Renee M.; B.A., U. Conn., Storrs, 1972; m. Stuart A. Ober, Sept. 20, 1981; 1 child, Erik Michaels-Ober. Asst. editor Viking Press, N.Y.C., 1972-74; editor David McKay Co., N.Y.C., 1974-76, St. Martin's Press, N.Y.C., 1977-78; v.p. mktg. and dir. Beekman Pub., Woodstock, N.Y., 1978-82; editor-in-chief Hudson Valley mag., Woodstock, 1982—; instr. Marist Coll., Poughkeepsie, N.Y., 1985. hostess Speak Out Show, Sta. HV-TV, Port Ewen, N.Y., 1982-83. Mem. Women in Communications, Authors Guild, Internat. Women Writers Guild, Woodstock C. of C., Ulster County C. of C., Ulster County Coalition for Free Choice, Catskill Alliance for Peace. Author: Living Contradictions: The Women of the Baby Boom Come of Age, 1982. Home: PO Box 888 Woodstock NY 12498 Office: PO Box 425 Woodstock NY 12498

MICHAELS, KAYE R., advertising executive; b. Evansville, Ind., June 6, 1949; d. Guy and Nancy Alice (Jackson) Johnston; m. Stuart Tyler Smith, Jan. 24, 1973; 1 son, Michael Tyler. Student U. Evansville, 1968, Ind. State U., 1969-72. Prodn. Coordinator Keller Crescent Co., Evansville, 1969-78; advt. mgr. H&R Devel. Co., 1978-81; owner, pres. Kaye Michaels, Inc., Casselberry, Fla., 1981—; cons. in field. Recipient Outstanding Mktg. awards Bank Systems and Equipment Assn., 1982; award Am. Banking Assn., 1982. Mem. Orlando Advt. Fedn., Orlando Tourist and Trade Assn., Fla. C. of C. Republican. Home: 516 Birdsong Ct Longwood FL 32779 Office: 316 Live Oaks Blvd Casselberry FL 32707

MICHAELS, SHARON LEE, lawyer; b. Chgo.; d. Robert Anthony and Marjorie (Richardson) M. B.S. in Journalism, Northwestern U., 1975; M. Pub. Adminstrn., Govs. State U., Park Forest South, Ill., 1980; J.D. magna cum laude, U. Houston, 1983. Bar: Tex. 1983. Caseworker Ill. Dept. Pub. Aid, Harvey, Ill., 1975-80; briefing atty. Tex. 1st Ct. Appeals, Houston, 1983-84. Recipient Am. Jurisprudence award, 1983. Mem. Houston Trial Lawyers Assn., Houston Bar Assn., Tex. Young Lawyers Assn., Kappa Tau Alpha. Democrat. Roman Catholic. Club: University (Houston). Office: 3810 Westheimer Suite 2030 Houston TX 77027

MICHAK, HELEN BARBARA, educator, nurse; b. Cleve., July 31; d. Andrew and Mary (Patrick) Michak; Diploma Cleve. City Hosp. Sch. Nursing, 1947; B.A., Miami U., Oxford, Ohio, 1951; M.A., Case Western Res. U., 1960. Staff nurse Cleve. City Hosp., 1947-48; pub. health nurse Cleve. Div. Health, 1951-52; instr. Cleve. City Hosp. Sch. Nursing, 1952-56; supr. nursing Cuyahoga County Hosp., Cleve., 1956-58; pub. info. dir. N.E. Ohio Am. Heart Assn., Cleve., 1960-64; dir. spl. events Higbee Co., Cleve., 1964-66; exec. dir. Cleve. Area League for Nursing, 1966-72; dir. continuing edn. nurses, adj. assoc. prof. Cleve. State U., 1972—. Trustee, Northeast Ohio Regional Med. Program, 1970-73; mem. adv. com. Dept. Nursing Cuyahoga Community Coll., 1967—; mem. long term care com. Met. Health Planning Corp., 1974-76, plan devel. com. 1977—; mem. policy bd. Center Health Data N.E. Ohio, 1972-73; mem. Rep. Assembly and Health Planning and Devel. Commn., Welfare Fedn. Cleve., 1967-72; mem. Cleve. Community Health Network, 1972-73; mem. United Appeal Films and Speakers Bur., 1967-73; mem. adv. com. Ohio Fedn. Licensed Practical Nurses, 1970-73; mem. tech. adv. com. TB and Respiratory Disease Assn. Cuyahoga County, 1967-74; mem. Ohio Commn. on Nursing, 1971-74; mem. Citizens com. nursing homes Fedn. Community Planning, 1973-77; mem. com. on home health services Met. Health Planning Corp., 1973-75. Mem. Nat. League Nursing (mem. com. 1970-72), Am. Nurses Assn. (accreditation visitor 1977-81, 83-84), Ohio Nurses Assn. (com. continuing edn. 1974-86, chmn. com. 1984-86), Greater Cleve. Nurses Assn. (joint practice com. 1973-74, trustee 1975-76), Cleve. Area Citizens League for Nursing (trustee 1976-79, nominating com. 1982-85), Am. Soc. Tng. and Devel., AAUP, Zeta Tau Alpha. Home: 4686 Oakridge Dr North Royalton OH 44133 Office: Cleve State U 2344 Euclid Av Cleveland OH 44115

MICHALS, LEE MARIE, travel agency executive; b. Chgo., June 6, 1939; d. Harry Joseph and Anna Marie (Monaco) Perzan; B.A., Wright Coll., 1959; children—Debora Ann, Dana Lee, Jami. Internat. travel sec. E.F. MacDonald Travel, Palo Alto, Calif., 1963-69; pres. Travel Experience, Santa Clara, Calif., 1973—; ptnr. Cruise Connection, Mountain Valley, Calif., 1983—. Mem. Am. Soc. Travel Agts., Inst. Cert. Travel Agts., Bay Area Travel Assn., Pacific Area Travel Agts. Office: Travel Experience 3255 7F Scott Blvd Santa Clara CA 95051 also 1622 El Camino Real Mountain View CA 94040

MICHALSKI, DOLORES PATRICIA, tool and machine manufacturing company executive; b. Detroit, Jan. 10, 1932; d. Joseph and Mary Anne (Cryulewska) Obezil; m. Thomas Gerald Michalski, Oct. 10, 1953; children—James, David, Mary, Thomas. B.S. in Elem. Edn. cum laude Oakland U., 1975, M.A. in Teaching, 1976. Cert. elem. tchr., Mich. Corp. sec. Applies Industries, Warren, Mich., 1965-75, 78-80, also dir.; supr. student teaching Oakland U., Rochester, Mich., 1976-78; pres., chief operating officer Major Mfg., Inc., Pompano Beach, Fla., 1981—, also dir.; corp. sec. C.I.D., Inc., Inglis, Fla., 1980-81. Mem. Nat. Tool and Machining Assn. (chpt. chmn. 1984). Republican. Roman Catholic. Avocations: computer science; literature. Home: Apt 6D 250 S Ocean Blvd Boca Raton FL 33432 Office: Major Mfg Inc 4100 N Powerline Rd E3 Pompano Beach FL 33067

MICHAM, NANCY SUE, systems consultant; b. Toledo, May 15, 1956; d. Charles Edward and Dorothy Ruth (Bittner) Linker; m. Donald Thomas Kerner, June 20, 1975 (div. June 1980); m. Ray David Micham, III, May 19, 1984. A.S. with high honors, U. Toledo, 1980; B.S.M. cum laude, Pepperdine U., 1983. Cert. systems profl. Programmer, Owens-Ill., Toledo, 1973-80; programmer analyst Smith Tool Co., Irvine, Calif., 1980-82; systems analyst Denny's, Inc., La Mirada, Calif., 1982-83; mgr. corp. systems group Libbey-Owens-Ford Co., Toledo, 1983-86; Mem. Nat. Mgmt. Assn., Assn. Systems Mgmt., Nat. Assn. Female Execs., Assn. for Cert. Computer Profls. Republican. Roman Catholic. Avocations: running, travel, backpacking, bicycling, racquetball.

MICHEL, KAREN RAE, employment services company executive; b. Macomb, Ill., Dec. 30, 1946; d. Harry Dale and Jeanette Elvina (Stoke) Shannon; m. Thomas Edward Michel, Apr. 15, 1967 (div. Mar. 1977). Student Paricia Stevens Sch., Milw., 1965-66. Freelance model, Milw., 1967-71; sales promotion mgr. Charles Levy Co., 1972-75; photographer Karen's Kamera, Jefferson, Iowa, 1975-77; co-owner Mgmt. Recruiters, Janesville, Wis., 1977-78; ops. mgr. Mgmt. Recruiters Internat., Cleve., 1978-83, nat. sales trainer, 1978-83, corp. office mgr., San Francisco, 1983—; photography judge State of Iowa, 1976-77; cons. in field. Tchr., cons. Jr. Womens Club Retarded Child Program, Milw., 1969; mem., worker Young Republican Womens Group, Charleston, Ill., 1971; leader, tchr. Christian Youth Fellowship, Jefferson, Iowa, 1976; leader Master Mariner council Girls Scouts U.S.A., Milw., 1967-71. Named Hon. Citizen Gov. State Tex., 1979. Mem. Am. Mgmt. Soc., Sales and Mktg. Execs. Assn., Calif. Assn. Personnel Cons. (dir. 1980-81, program dir. 1981). Club: Shorewood Jr. Womens (program chmn. 1968-70) (Milw.). Lodge: Toastmasters Internat. (sec. 1976-77). Home: 105 3d St #1 Sausalito CA 94965 Office: Mgmt Recruiters/Internat Office Mates 5 of San Francisco Div 44 Montgomery St Suite 1350 San Francisco CA 95104

MICHELSON, BETTY MURDEN, lawyer; b. Norfolk, Va., May 24, 1935; d. Joseph David and Louise (Darden) Murden; m. Ronald Keith Michelson, Apr. 25, 1959 (div. 1972); 1 son, David Keith. A.B., Sweet Briar Coll., 1957; pvt. study Rhodes and Watson, Virginia Beach, Va., 1975-78. Bar: Va. 1978. Assoc. law firm Rhodes and Watson, Virginia Beach, 1978-86, Pickett, Lyle, Drescher, Segal, and Crowshaw, P.C., 1986—; mem. adv. bd. Bank of the Commonwealth, Virginia Beach, 1983—. Mem. ABA, Va. State Bar, Virginia Beach Bar Assn., Assn. Trial Lawyers Am., Democrat. Episcopal. Clubs: Princess Anne Garden, Colonial Circle of Kings Daus., Princess Anne Country, Princess Anne Hunt. Home: 110 45th St Virginia Beach VA 23451 Office: Pickett Lyle Drescher Segal and Crowshaw PC One Columbus Ctr Virginia Beach VA 23462

MICKA, SALOMEA SOPHIE (SALLY), information systems executive; b. Milford, Conn., May 9, 1940; d. Stanley John and Sophie Frances (Ignatowski) Kamykowski; m. Edward John Micka, June 16, 1962; children—Edward John, Sally. B.A. in Physics, Cath. U. Am., 1962. Data base cons., various orgns., 1968-76; br. chief Energy Research and Devel. Agy., Germantown, Md., 1976-77; mgr. Internat. Atomic Energy Agy., UN, Vienna, 1977-81; asst. to dir. Dept. Energy, Germantown, 1981-83; office dir. Technassociates, Inc., Rockville, Md., 1983—; pres. SEMCOM Assocs., Inc., Gaithersburg, Md., 1984—. Mem. AIMS-2K Data Base Mgmt. Users Group (pres. 1976-77), Nat. Assn. Women Bus. Owners, Montgomery County C. of C. Democrat. Roman Catholic. Club: Women's Golf Montgomery County. Avocations: golf; reading; hiking. Home: 8307 Warfield Rd Gaithersburg MD 20879

MICKINS, ANDEL WATKINS, retired educational administrator; b. Central, S.C., Oct. 28, 1924; d. Ernest Samuel and Estelle Charlotte (Jamison) Watkins; B.S., Tuskegee Inst., 1946; M.A., Columbia, 1962; postgrad. Iowa State Coll., 1948, U. Miami, m. Isaac C. Mickins, July 11, 1952; 1 son, Isaac Clarence, II. Head home econs. dept. Anderson County Tng. Sr. High Sch., Pendleton, S.C., 1946-52; classroom tchr. Holmes Elem. Sch., Miami, Fla., 1952-62; asst. prin. for curriculum Liberty City Elem. Sch., Miami, 1962-67; prin. R.R. Moton Elem. Sch., Miami, 1967-71, Rainbow Park Elem. Sch., Miami, 1971-81; supervising tchr. U. Miami, summer 1965. Pres., Friendship Garden and Civic Club, 1969-75; 1st v.p. Bapt. Women's Council, 1966—; pres. Ministers Wives and Ministers Widors Council Greater Miami; chmn. exec. bd. Fla. Gen. Bapt. State Conv.; bd. dirs. Black Archives History and Research Found. South Fla. Recipient Sarah Blocker award Fla. Meml. Coll., 1966; plaques Liberty City Elem. Sch., 1967, Rainbow Park Elem. Sch., 1974, Friendship Garden and Civic Club, 1969, Meml. Temple Bapt. Ch., 1965; citation Fla. Gov. Mem. NEA (life), Dade County Admintrs. Assn., Nat. Assn. Elem. Sch. Prins., Alpha Kappa Alpha, Phi Delta Kappa, Kappa Delta Pi, Pi Delta Kappa. Democrat. Clubs: Jack and Jill of Am., Order of Eastern Star. Home: 16300 NW 44th Ct Miami FL 33054

MICKLE, KATHRYN ALMA, security company executive; b. Pittsfield, Mass., May 17, 1946; d. Frederick Louis and Bertha Laura (Webster) Wick; m. William Joseph Mickle III, May 11, 1968; children—William J. IV, Deborah Sharon. R.N., Cooley Dickinson Hosp., Northampton, Mass., 1967. Charge nurse Berkshire Med. Ctr., Pittsfield, 1967-75; intensive and coronary care nurse, 1975-81; nursing cons. Springside Nursing Home, Pittsfield, 1974-76; owner New Eng. Security, Pittsfield, 1978—. Active Western Mass. council Girl Scouts U.S., 1975—; dir., tchr. Dalton Bible Sch., Mass., 1979-83; vice chmn. bd. Berkshire County Christian Sch., 1984-86, sec. bd. dirs., 1982-84; chmn. pub. relations exec. com. Billy Graham Crusade, Pittsfield area, 1982; Dalton coordinator Silvio O. Conte Re-election Campaign, 1984. Recipient numerous sales awards Dynamark Inc., 1980—; Appreciation award Dalton Vacation Bible Sch., 1983. Fellow Central Berkshire C. of C., No. Berkshire C. of C., Cooley Dickinson Alumni Assn. Congregationalist. Avocations: arts and crafts, swimming, reading, gardening, camping. Home: 72 Braeburn Rd Dalton MA 01226 Office: New England Security 14 Dalton Ave Pittsfield MA 01201

MIDDAUGH, KAREN LEE LAWRENCE, greeting card company executive; b. Joplin, Mo., Oct. 1, 1942; d. William Clifford and Lucille Josephine (Sigler) Lawrence; B.A., Tchrs. Coll. Emporia (Kans.), 1964; M.A., U. Kans., 1969; m. Richard Lowe Middaugh, Sept. 2, 1967; 1 dau., Marian Elizabeth. Vol. Peace Corps, Loja, Ecuador, 1964-66; editor Hallmark Cards, Kansas City, Mo., 1969-72, sr. editor, 1972-75; editorial dir. Rust Craft Greeting Cards, Dedham, Mass., 1975-77; mng. editor Am. Greetings Corp., Cleve., 1977-81, editorial dir., 1982-85, exec. dir. editorial, 1985—. Asst. instr. English, U. Kans., 1966-69. Bd. dirs. Norfolk Bristol Home Health Services, Walpole, Mass., 1976-78. U. Kans. honors fellow, 1966-69. Democrat. Editor: The Art of Happiness: Selected Writings of Andre Maurois, 1971; Pathways to Happiness: Inspiration from the World's Great Religions, 1972; Faith for Our Times: Contemporary Prayers, Poetry and Prose, 1973. Office: 10500 American Rd Cleveland OH 44144

MIDDLEBROOK, GRACE IRENE, nurse/educator; b. Los Angeles, Mar. 5, 1927; d. Joel P. and Betty (Larson) Soderberg; dip. West Suburban Hosp., 1950; B.S. in Nursing, Wheaton Coll., 1951; M.A. in Edn., Ariz. State U., 1965, Ed.D., 1970; m. Albert William Middlebrook, July 7, 1950; children—Alberta Elizabeth, Jo Anne. Office nurse, Dr. G.A. Hemwall, Chgo., 1950-51; supr. Bates Meml. Hosp., Bentonville, Ark., 1955-58; instr. Sparks Meml. Hosp. Sch. Nursing, Ft. Smith, Ark., 1959-61; instr., coordinator med.-surg. nursing Sch. of Nursing, Good Samaritan Hosp., Phoenix, 1961-64, asst. dir. Sch. Nursing, 1964-73, dir. edn. and tng., 1968-80; corp. dir. edn. Samaritan Health Service, Phoenix, 1969—; adj. prof. Samaritan Coll. Nursing, Grand Canyon Coll. Bd. dirs. Ariz. Bus. Edn. Adv. Council Mem. speakers bur. Sch. Career Days, 1970—. Recipient award for leadership co-op programs Phoenix Union High Sch., 1980, Sammy award Samaritan Health Service and Samaritan Med. Found., 1981. Mem. Ariz. Nurses in Mgmt. (bd. dirs. 1983-85), Am. Hosp. Assn., Nat. League Nursing, Ariz. League for Nursing, Adult Edn. Assn., Pi Lambda Theta, Kappa Delta Pi, Sigma Theta Tau. Home: 4242 N 15th Dr Phoenix AZ 85015 Office: Samaritan Health Service Edn Center 1500 E Thomas Rd Phoenix AZ 85014

MIDDLETON, CAROLE FOSTER, insurance broker, consultant; b. Weymouth, Mass., Dec. 24, 1946; d. David Warren and Hazel Margaret (McRae) Foster; m. Finley Norman Middleton II, Mar. 23, 1974. B.A. in Speech and Drama, Coll. St. Catherine, St. Paul, 1968; B.S. in Bus. Mgmt., Rutgers U., 1974; postgrad. Coll. Ins., N.Y.C., 1977-79. Claims supr. Allstate Ins., Minn. and N.Y., 1969-74; asst. account exec. Johnson & Higgins, Rio de Janeiro, Brazil, 1974-76, asst. v.p., N.Y.C., 1977-81; mgr. new bus. prodn. Edward Lumley & Sons, Johannesburg, South Africa, 1976-77; asst. v.p. Alexander & Alexander, N.Y.C., 1981-83; pres. Lynmar Internat., N.Y.C., 1983—; pres. Foxberry Press, Gourmet Internat. and Expat!; speaker in field to various ins., internat., women's groups. Columnist Wall Street Woman, Wall Street Bus. and Profl. Women mag., 1979-80; contbr. articles to profl. jours. Vol. Young Republicans, Ariz., Minn., 1961-68; active various coms., fundraiser Retarded Infants Service, N.Y.C., 1977-83; bd. dirs. YWCA, Bklyn., 1980-83, treas., 1982-83. Mem. Assn. Profl. Ins. Women N.Y.C. (adviser 1982-83), Women's Econ. Round Table, Am. Mgmt. Assn., Nat. Fedn. Bus. and Profl. Women. Clubs: Wall Street Bus. and Profl. Women's (1st v.p. 1978-80, pres. 1980-81, 19 Membership awards 1978-81), Am. Women's of Denmark (pres. 1986-87, editor Chronicle mag. 1985-86). Presbyterian. Office: Lynmar Internat 45 Ridge St Yonkers NY 10707

MIDDLETON, CATHERINE ELISA, insurance broker; b. N.Y.C., Aug. 15, 1949; d. John Warren and Clarita Elisa (Birch) M. Student Stetson U., 1966-68; B.A., La. State U., 1971; postgrad. Golden Gate U., 1976-81. Tchr., Andrew Jackson High Sch., Chalmette, La., 1971-73; office mgr. Star Nat., Miami, 1973-74; asst. mgr. Am. Savs. Bldg., San Francisco, 1974-75; comml. acctg. rep. Aetna Casualty, San Francisco, 1975-78; comml. acctg. mgr. Earl Goldman Ins., Concord, Calif., 1978-83; comml. lines mgr. Joseph Bobba Co., Inc., Dublin, Calif., 1983—. Mem. C.P.C.U.S. (treas. 1981-83), Cert. Profl. Ins. Women, Ins. Women's Assn. Contra Costa County (v.p. 1982-83, pres. 1984-85), Ind. Ins. Agts. Contra Costa Councy (dir. 1980-82). Republican. Episcopalian. Office: Joseph Bobba Co Inc 7950 Dublin Blvd Dublin CA 94568

MIDDLETON, PAULETTE BAUER, atmospheric chemist; b. Beeville, Tex., Dec. 8, 1946; d. Paul Wylie and Lillian Grace (Schoppe) Bauer; B.A., U. Tex., Austin, 1968, M.A., 1971, Ph.D., 1973; m. John William Middleton, July 12, 1970; children—Mären Katherine, Erin Ann. Research asst., then instr. chemistry U. Tex., 1968-73, research asso. chem. engring., 1973-75; postdoctoral fellow Nat. Center Atmospheric Research, Boulder, Colo., 1975-76, sci. visitor, 1977-79, spl. project scientist, 1979, staff scientist, 1979—; research assoc. Atmospheric Scis. Research Center, SUNY, Albany, 1976-77; lectr., seminar leader in field. Grantee EPA, 1982. Mem. Air Pollution Control Assn., AAAS. Author papers. Home: 2385 Panorama Ave Boulder CO 80302 Office: Box 3000 Boulder CO 80307

MIDGETT, LYNDA FAYSSOUX, county official; b. Greensboro, N.C., Dec. 6, 1943; d. Robert Gardner and Viola (Kendrick) Fayssoux; m. Arvin Alexander Midgett, May 1, 1964; 1 child, Allison Arlene. Grad. high sch., Danville, Va. Driver for blind, caseworker Social Services, Manteo, N.C., 1961-63; sec. Manteo Bd. Edn., 1963-68; dep. tax collector Dare County, N.C., 1970-79, tax collector, 1979-82; supr. Bd. Elections, Dare County, 1983—. Pres. Sea N Sounds Arts Council, Manteo, 1982-83, 84—; com. mem. Dare Day, 1977—; adv. council Bus. Edn. Dept. Manteo High Sch., 1983—; chmn. Dare County Christmas Parade, 1970-82. Mem. N.C. Assn. Legal Secs. (state chmn. scholarship com. 1982-84), Dare County Legal Secs. (Legal Sec. of Yr. 1977, 79), Manteo Woman's Club (Clubwoman of Yr. 1979-80), N.C. Suprs. Assn. (scholarship com. 1985—). Democrat. Methodist. Avocations: travel; cooking; attending plays, concerts. Home: PO Box 723 Manteo NC 27954 Office: Supr Bd Elections Dare County Administration Bldg Manteo NC 27954

MIDKIFF, MARTHA L., psychotherapist; b. Indpls., May 21, 1939; d. Louis A. and Clara A. (Miller) Lukenbill; m. L. Michael Midkiff, July 9, 1960; children—Gregory A., Andrew M. B.A. in Sociology, Ind. U., 1971, M.S.W., 1973. Sch. social worker Indpls. pub. schs., 1973-79; med. social worker Riley Hosp., Indpls., 1979-80; pres./founder Supportive Systems, Inc., Indpls., 1980—; cons. University Heights Hosp., Indpls., 1973-75; field instr. Grad. Sch. Social Work, Ind. U.-Indpls., 1979-80. Mem. exec. com., women's com., membership devel. Indpls. Symphony, 1977—. Fellow Nat. Assn. Social Workers; mem. Acad. Cert. Social Workers, Nat. Register Clin. Social Workers. Avocations. hiking; camping; travel; gourmet cooking. Home: 634 Grand Mesa Ct Indianapolis IN 46217 Office: Supportive Systems 539 Turtle Creek S Dr Indianapolis IN 46227

MIDLER, BETTE, singer, actress, entertainer; b. Honolulu, 1945; m. Martin von Haselberg. student U. Hawaii, 1 year. Debut as actress film Hawaii, 1965; mem. cast Fiddler on the Roof, N.Y.C., 1966-69, Salvation, N.Y.C., 1970, Tommy, Seattle Opera Co., 1971; nightclub concert performer on tour U.S., 1972-73; appearance Palace Theatre, N.Y.C., 1973; TV appearances include David Frost Show, Tonight Show; appeared revue Clams on The Half-Shell Revue, N.Y.C., 1975; rec. The Divine Miss M, 1972; Bette Midler, 1973; Broken Blossom, 1977, Live at Last, 1979, New Thighs and Whispers, 1979, New Depression, 1979, Divine Madness, 1980, No Frills, 1984, Mud Will Be Flung Tonight, 1985; star motion picture The Rose, 1979, Jinxed, 1982, Down and Out in Beverly Hills, 1986. Recipient After Dark Ruby award, 1973, Grammy award, 1973, spl. Tony award, 1973, Tony award for One Woman Show on Broadway, 1974, Emmy award, 1978, Grammy award, 1981, Golden Globe awards (2), 1980, Walk of Fame Star on Hollywood Blvd. Author: A View from Abroad, 1979; The Saga of Baby Divine, 1983. Address: care Atlantic Records 75 Rockefeller Plaza New York NY 10019*

MIEGEL, JANET PIERCE, marketing executive; b. Little Rock, Ark., Jan. 4, 1951; d. Richard Reid and Betty Jean (Simpson) Pierce. B.A., U. Tex. Programmer, Chilton Corp., Dallas, 1973-76; system rep. Pansophic System, Dallas, 1976-78, mktg. services coordinator, 1978-79, nat. mgr. mktg. services, 1980-81, mgr. spl. projects, 1981-82, tng. mgr., Oak Brook, Ill., 1982-84; sales rep., dir. mktg. services Henco Software, Inc., Waltham, Mass., 1984—. Mem. Alpha Pi. Methodist. Office: Henco Software Inc 100 5th Ave Waltham MA 02154

MIESSE, MARGARET ELIZABETH, marketing professional; b. Chgo., Nov. 17, 1957; d. Winston Charles and Mary Aurelia (Luckhardt) M. B.S. in Bus. Adminstrn./Mktg., U. Ill., 1979; student Drake U. 1982-83. Mktg. analyst Maytag Co, Newton, Iowa, 1979-83, asst. to mgr. sales promotion, 1982-83, sr. sales stats. analyst, 1983-84; div. ops. staff mgr. L.M. Berry & Co., New Orleans, 1984-85, premise sales rep., 1985—; dir. Grand Res. Ltd., Bridgeview, Ill.; seminar leader. Troop leader Moingona council Girl Scouts U.S.A., Newton, Iowa, 1979-81; v.p. Jaycee-Ettes, Newton, 1980-81; mktg. advisor Jr. Achievement, Newton, 1981; publicity chmn. City Anti-Drug Abuse Campaign

Telethon, Newton, 1983. Mem. Am. Mktg. Assn. (chpt. treas. pro tem 1980-81, sec./treas. 1981—), Sales and Mktg. Execs., Maytag Mgmt. Club/Nat. Mgmt. Assn., Am. Bus. Women's Assn. Club: Newton Country. Office: PO Box 8466 Metairie LA 70011

MIESSE, MARY ELIZABETH (BETH), educator; b. Amarillo, Tex.; M.Ed. in Guidance and Counseling, M.A., W. Tex. State U., Canyon, 1952, M.B.A., 1960; M.Personnel Service, U. Colo., Boulder, 1954. With various bus. firms and radio stas., 1940-47; prof. Amarillo (Tex.) Coll., 1947-63; tchr. pvt. and pub. schs., also TV work, 1963-78; spl. edn. cons., writer, 1978—. Mem. NEA, Tex. State Tchrs. Assn., Am. Psychol. Assn., North Plains Assn. for Children with Learning Disabilities, AAUP Pioneered in ednl. TV in West Tex.; recipient awards in typewriting and ednl. TV; elected to Top Ten Women of Yr., Am. Bus. Women's Assn., 1962. Certified in spl. edn. supr., spl. edn. counselor, ednl. diagnostician, spl. edn. (lang. and/or learning disabled, mentally retarded) tchr., profl. counselor, profl. tchr., supt., prin., Tex. Editor, Tex. Jr. Coll. Tchrs. Assn. publ., 7 yrs. Home and Office: PO Box 3133 Valle de Oro Boys Ranch TX 79010

MIESZALA, PATRICIA T., nurse, consultant; b. Chgo., Sept. 27, 1946; d. Joseph Walter and Eugenia Rose (Mocarski) M. R.N., St. Mary of Nazareth Health and Hosp. Ctr., Chgo., 1968; postgrad. in psychology and psychiatry, Northeastern Ill. U., 1974-78. Lic. nurse, Ill. Psychiat. staff nurse Ill. State Psychol. Inst., Chgo., 1968-69; psychiat. staff nurse St. Joseph's Hosp., Chgo., 1969-70; pediatric office nurse Suburban Pediatrics Ltd., Des Plaines, Ill., 1970-71; research nurse Cook County Hosp. Burn Ctr., Chgo., 1971; psychol. burn nurse clinician Cook County Hosp. Burn Ctr., 1972-81; pres., founder Burn Concerns Inc., Chgo., 1981—; cons. and lectr. in field. Contbr. articles to profl. jours.; editor Jour. Burn Care and Rehab., 1981—; tech. cons. Film Communicators, 1976—. Nat. Juvenile Firesetter Project Mgr., FEMA, 1981-86. Recipient Outstanding Fire/Burn Prevention Educator of Yr. award U.S. Fire Adminstrn., 1979; Dr. Curtis P. Artz Disting. Service award Am. Burn Assn., 1983; Dir.'s award FEMA, 1984. Mem. Internat. Soc. Burn Injuries, Am. Burn Assn., Am. Nurses Assn., Phoenix Soc. Recovered Burn Victims (adv. bd.), Nat. Assn. Female Execs., Ind. Order Foresters, Ill. Nurses Assn., Ill. Fire Chiefs and Insps. Assn. Avocations: music box collecting; golf. Home and Office: 4218 N Pulaski Rd Chicago IL 60641

MIGALA, LUCYNA, radio station executive; b. Krakow, Poland, May 22, 1944; d. Joseph and Estelle (Suwala) M.; came to U.S., 1947, naturalized, 1955; student Loyola U., Chgo., 1962-63, Chgo. Conservatory of Music, 1963-70; B.S. in Journalism, Northwestern U., 1966; m. Kazimierz Wieclaw, Nov. 27, 1971 (div. Jan. 1978). Radio announcer, producer sta. WOPA, Oak Park, Ill., 1963-66; writer, reporter, producer NBC news, Chgo., 1966-69, 1969-71, producer NBC local news, Washington, 1969; producer, coordinator NBC network news, Cleve., 1971-78, field producer, Chgo., 1978-79; v.p. Migala Communications Corp., 1979—; program dir., on-air personality Sta. WCEV, Cicero, Ill., 1979—; lectr. Chgo. City Colls., 1981; soloist, mgr., 1965—; artistic dir., gen. mgr. Lira Singers, Chgo., 1986—. Mem., chmn. various cultural coms. Polish Am. Congress, 1970—; bd. dirs. Nationalities Services Center, Cleve., 1973-78, Ill. Humanities Council, 1983—. Washington Journalism Center fellow, spring 1969; v.p., bd. dirs. Cicero-Berwyn Fine Arts Council, 1980—; pub. mem. Ill. Humanities Council, 1983—; bd. dirs. Polish Women's Alliance Am., 1983—; v.p. Kosciuszko Found., Chgo., 1983-84; gen. chmn. Midwest Chopin Piano Competition, Kosciusko Found., 1984. Office: Sta WCEV 5356 W Belmont Ave Chicago IL 60641

MIGDAIL, RHONDA GLORIA, lawyer; b. N.Y.C., Feb. 14, 1955; d. Leonard and Herta (Ismann) Laskow; m. Evan Michael Migdail, June 2, 1979. B.S. in Econs., Wharton Sch. U. Pa., Phila., 1977, B.A., 1977, J.D., 1980. Bar: D.C. 1981. Intern, U.S. Congressman Coughlin, Washington, summer 1976; summer clk. U.S. Dept. Justice, Washington, summer 1978; law clk. Pope, Ballard & Loos, Washington, summer 1979; teaching asst. acctg. Wharton Sch., U. Pa., 1978-80; assoc. law firm Galland, Kharasch, Calkins & Morse, P.C., Washington, 1980-83; assoc. law firm Golden, Freda & Schraub, P.C., Washington, 1983—. Campaign worker Congressman Lawrence Coughlin, Pa., 1976, 78. Mem. Women's Transp. Seminar, ABA, Phi Beta Kappa, Beta Alpha Psi. Democrat. Office: Golden Freda & Schraub PC 1625 Massachusetts Ave NW Washington DC 20036

MIHAJLOVIC, MARY JANE, nurse; b. Sheboygan, Wis., May 18, 1954; d. Matthew Joseph and Irene Ann (Zywicki) Rehberger; m. Dusan Milan Mihajlovic, May 4, 1974; children—Daniel, Michael. Assoc. degree in Nursing, Milw. Area. Tech. Coll., 1976. Registered nurse, Wis. Staff nurse I, St. Luke's Hosp., Milw., 1976-77, staff nurse III, 1982-84; staff nurse St. Francis Hosp., Milw., 1984—; camp nurse Gracanica Monastery Summer Camp, Graylake, Ill., 1984. Room mother Glenwood Sch., Greenfield, Wis., 1984-85. Mem. Assn. Operating Room Nurses. Serbian Orthodox. Avocations: karate; biking; calligraphy. Home: 3929 S 41st St Greenfield WI 53221

MIHALY, JANET LOUISE, entrepreneur; b. Camp Blanding, Fla., July 13, 1945; d. Harry Raymond and Mary Elizabeth (Rawdon) Harris Doyle; m. Robert Andrew Mihaly, Mar. 6, 1965 (div. July 1974); children—Elizabeth, Robert, September, Tara. B.A., Capital U., 1981. Owner Pandora Restaurant, Akron, Ohio, 1969-72; co-owner Mihaly Hauling Service, Akron, 1965-74, A.J. Rubbish Service, Akron, 1975-77; co-owner Green Mansions Statuary, Akron, 1975-81; sr. sales service coordinator for Cavalier, B.F. Goodrich, Akron, 1977—, co-instr. B.F. Goodrich Learning Ctr., Akron, 1980—; resume writer, career counselor, Akron, 1980—. Mem. Am. Mktg. Assn. (newsletter editor 1982-83). Home: 2116 Lee Dr Akron OH 44306 Office: BF Goodrich Bldg 25C Dept 0611 500 S Main St Akron OH 44306

MIHRAM, DANIELLE, curator, bibliographer, educator; b. Alexandria, Egypt, July 23, 1942; came to U.S., 1965; d. Albert and Aimee (Seidman) Redibaum; m. George Arthur Mihram, Dec. 22, 1965. B.A. with honors, U. Sydney (Australia), 1964; diplôme d'études supérieures, Ecole des Hautes Etudes, Paris, 1965; Ph.D., U. Pa., 1970; M.L.S., Rutgers U., 1982. Vis. lectr. Swarthmore (PA.) Coll., 1971; asst. prof. Haverford (Pa.) Coll., 1971; vis. lectr. U. Pa., 1974; bus./research assoc. G. A. Mihram, Cons., Haverford, Pa., 1974-79; library staff Princeton U., 1980-82; reference librarian NYU, N.Y.C., 1982—; adj. asst. prof. NYU, 1985—. Contbr. articles to profl. jours. British Commonwealth scholar Australian Govt., U. Sydney, 1959-65; NATO travel grantee, 1977. Mem. ALA, Assn. Internat. de Cybernétique, (Titre Scientifique), Assn. Coll. and Research Libraries, Modern Lang. Assn. Home: PO Box 1188 Princeton NJ 08542 Office: EH Bobst Library NYU 70 Washington Square S New York NY 10012

MIKA, MARY JANE, physician; b. Chgo., Mar. 8; d. John and Mary (Milas) M.; student U. Ill., 1960-62; B.S. (scholar), Roosevelt U., 1965, M.S. 1970; Ph.D., U. Ill. Med. Center, Chgo., 1973; M.D., Universidad Autonoma de Ciudad Juarez (Mexico) Escuela de Medicina, 1978. Reviewer current gas chromatography lit. Preston Tech. Abstracts Co., Evanston, Ill., 1968-73; contbg. editor Internat. Jour. Pharm. Abstracts, Am. Soc. Hosp. Pharmacists, Washington, 1972-73; asst. in chemistry U. Ill. Coll. Pharmacy, Chgo., 1970-73; biochem. researcher VA Hosp., North Chicago, Ill., 1975-76; intern in internal medicine Cook County Hosp., Chgo., 1978-79, fellow in gastroenterology, 1981-83; resident in internal medicine St. Francis Hosp., Evanston, 1979-81. Mem. ACP. Research in gaso-chromatography in flavor volatiles, mass spectrometric analysis of aromatic amines.

MIKEL, CHARLENE ANN, social worker, consultant, lecturer, editor; b. Oswego, Kans., Sept. 30, 1938; d. Warren Fowler and Gladys Maude (Hoke) Hardwick; m. Robert Andrew Mikel, Oct. 22, 1960 (div. July 1979); children—Cassandra, Mark. B.S. in Edn., Kans. State Coll., 1960; M.S.S.W., U. Mo., 1968. Social worker State of Kans., Topeka, 1964-66, 67-69, med. social worker 1976-82; social worker S.E. Kans. Mental Health, Humboldt, 1970-74; cons. Charlene Mikel Cons., Oswego, 1982—, editor, 1984—; lectr. Labette Community Coll., Parsons, Kans., 1983—, Barton County Community Coll., Great Bend, Kans., 1982—. Active 4-H. Mem. Nat. Assn. Social Workers, Kans. Soc. Clin. Social Workers (membership com. 1985—), Am. Legion Aux. (past pres. local chpt.). Republican. Methodist. Avocations: sewing; reading; travel. Home and Office: PO Box 204 Oswego KS 67356

MIKEL, SARAH ANN, librarian; b. Bklyn., Aug. 29, 1947; d. Robert H. M. and Sarah A. (Saver) Whalen; m. John R. Mikel, Oct. 21, 1977; 1 dau., Katherine Ann. B.A., U. Miami, 1969; M.A., U. Fla., 1971; M.A.L.S., Rosary Coll., River Forest, Ill., 1973. Editorial researcher Field Ednl. Enterprises, Chgo., 1971-72; librarian Purdue U., West Lafayette, Ind., 1973-75, U.S. Army Corps of Engrs., Rock Island, Ill., 1975-76, chief librarian, Washington, 1976—; chmn. FEDLINK Users Group, 1980—; program chmn. Fed. Interagy. Field Librarians Workshop, 1983-84. Mem. Spl. Library Assn. (chmn. mil. librarians 1978-79). Home: 10516 Gainsborough Rd Potomac MD 20854 Office: US Army Chief of Engineers Library 20 Massachusetts Ave NW Washington DC 20314

MIKELSONS, NANCY BERKS, school administrator; b. N.Y.C., Dec. 6, 1939; d. William Morris and Rose Natalie (Cohen) Rubin; 1 child, Adam Chaney. B.A., Boston U., 1963. Dir. social services Maryhaven Nursing Home, Glenview, Ill., 1976-78; investigator Legal Assiatance Found., Chgo., 1979-82; dir. DuPage Community Sch., Downers Grove, Ill., 1982—; vice chmn. DuPage County Child Welfare Consortium, Downers Grove, 1982—. Bd. dirs. John Howard Assn., Chgo. (co-editor training namual 1983, 85), 1978—, Chgo. Law Enforcement Study Group, 1983—, Chgo. Com. to Defend the Bill of Rights, 1983—; consumer rep. West Suburban Health Systems Agy., Oak Park, Ill., 1981-83. Mem. Am. Correctional Assn., Ill. Correctional Assn. Avocation: research in mythology of all nations.

MIKESELL, MARY (JANE), communication and human systems specialist; b. Rockledge, Fla., Oct. 29, 1943; d. John and Mary C. (Leighty) Wagner. B.A., Calif. State U.-Northridge, 1967; M.A., Pacific Oaks Coll., 1980; postgrad. Calif. Grad. Inst. Psychology, 1984—. Tchr., Los Angeles pub. schs., 1966-69; photog. lab. dir. Oceanograficos de Honduras, Roatan, 1969-70; supr. Los Angeles Life Ins. Co., 1970-72; customer service rep. Beverly Hills Fed. Savs. & Loans, Calif., 1972-73; mem. staff counseling ctr. Calif. State U.-Northridge, 1974-78; head office services Pacific Oaks Coll., Pasadena, Calif., 1978-79; prodn. supr. Frito-Lay, Inc., Los Angeles, 1979-81; circulation supr. Daily News, Van Nuys, Calif., 1981-82; ednl. therapist/intern Barr Counseling Ctr. and Victory-Tampa Psychol. Ctr. (now Reseda Psychol. Ctr.), San Fernando Valley, Calif., 1982—; project coordinator Carlson Rockey & Assocs., Brentwood, Calif., 1983-84; project coordinator/communications and systems specialist Student Ins. div. William F. Hooper, Inc., Brentwood, 1985—; cons. Designer Collection by Pingy, 1985, others. Photographer. Vol., San Fernando Valley Democratic Com. Mem. Nat. Assn. Female Execs., Planetary Soc., Calif. Scholarship Fedn., Calif. Inst. Psychology Grad. Student Assn. (v.p. 1985-86). Democrat. Judeo-Christian. Club: CSUN Anthropology. Avocations: photography; writing; laser research; astronomy; sports. Office: 11661 San Vicente Blvd Brentwood CA 90049

MIKIEWICZ, ANNA DANIELLE, marketing representative; b. Chgo., Dec. 22, 1960; d. Zdislaw and Lucy (Magnusewska) K. B.S. in Mktg., Elmhurst Coll., 1982; postgrad. Triton Coll. Asst. to Midwestern regional mgr. Meister Pub. Co., Chgo., 1983; sales rep. First Impression, Elk Grove, Ill., 1984; mktg. and customer services rep. Airco Ind. Gases, Broadview and Carol Stream, Ill., 1985, Yamazen USA, Inc., Schaumburg, Ill., 1985—. Named Chgo. Polish Queen, Polish Am. Culture Club, 1983-84. Mem. Nat. Assn. Female Execs. Republican. Roman Catholic.

MIKKO, DAGMAR CHRISTINE, lawyer; b. Detroit, Apr. 24, 1952; d. Karl Emil Mikko and Marcella (Lewandowski) Vance; m. Samuel John Fortier, Sept. 15, 1983; 1 dau., Nova Marie. B.A., Mich. State U., 1974; postgrad. land survey tech. U. Alaska, 1979; J.D., Northwestern Sch. Law, Portland, Oreg., 1982. Bar: Alaska 1982. Land surveyor Bur. Land Mgmt., Anchorage, 1977, Bell and Assocs., Anchorage, 1978; law librarian Northwestern Sch. Law, 1980-82; legal intern Northwestern Legal Clinic, 1981-82; law clk. Lynch, Farney & Crosby, Anchorage, 1980, 81; assoc. Cummings & Routh, Anchorage, 1982-84; asst. municipal atty. Municipality of Anchorage, 1984; ptnr. Fortier & Mikko, 1985—. Named Survey Student of the Yr., Am. Congress of Surveying and Mapping, 1978. Mem. ABA, Alaska Bar Assn., Anchorage Assn. Women Lawyers. Democrat. Home: 8650 Pioneer Dr Anchorage AK 99504 Office: Suite 101 600 W Internat Airport Rd Anchorage AK 99502

MIKOLAITIS, SANDRA MUCOWSKI, lawyer; b. May 2, 1952; d. Stanley C. and Jeannette (Aleszczyk) Mucowski; d. Joseph F. Mikolaitis, Dec. 30, 1972; children—Justine Ann, Kristin Marie. B.A. in Econs., Holy Family Coll., Phila., 1974; J.D., U. Balt., 1977. Bar: Pa. 1978. Analyst Health Care Financing Adminstrn., Balt., 1974-78; legal counsel Inter-County Hospitalization Plan, Inc., Jenkintown, Pa., 1979-81; assoc. counsel Blue Cross Greater Phila., 1982—. Mem. Phila. Bar Assn., Pa. Bar Assn. ABA (sect. torts, ins. practice), Nat. Health Lawyers Assn. Am. Corp. Counsel Assn., Jagiellonian Soc. Republican. Roman Catholic. Office: Blue Cross Greater Philadelphia 1333 Chestnut St Philadelphia PA 19107

MIKULSKI, BARBARA ANN, congresswoman; b. Balt., July 20, 1936; d. William and Christina Eleanor (Kutz) Mikulski; B.A., Mt. St. Agnes Coll., 1958; M.S.W., U. Md., 1965; LL.D., Goucher Coll., 1973, Hood Coll., 1978. Tchr., Mt. Saint Agnes Coll., 1969, Community Coll. Balt., 1970-71, VISTA Tng. Center, 1965-70; with Balt. Dept. Social Services, 1961-63, 66-70, York Family Agy., 1964, Asso. Cath. Charities, 1958-61; city councilwoman 1st dist. Balt., 1971-76; mem. 96-99th Congresses from 3d Md. Dist.; mem. interstate and fgn. commerce com., energy and commerce com., mcht. marine and fisheries com.; mem. Congressional Steel Caucus, Congresswomen's Caucus, Democratic Study Group, Environ. Study Conf., Mems. Congress for Peace Through Law; cons. orgns. including Nat. Center Urban Ethnic Affairs. Mem. Polish Women's Alliance, Polish Am. Congress, Citizen Planning and Housing Assn., S.E. Community Orgn.; chmn. commn. community devel. Archiocesan Urban Commn. Mem. Nat. Women's Polit. Caucus; mem. nat. com. Muskie for Pres., 1971-72; chairperson 1973 commn. del. selection and party structure Dem. Nat. Com.; Dem. nominee U.S. Senate, 1974, Ho. of Reps., 1976; mem. Dem. Nat. Strategy Council; nat. bd. dirs. Urban Coalition; bd. dirs. Valley House. Named One of Outstanding Young Women in Am.; Md. Outstanding Young Women of Year, 1968; recipient hon. degrees Hood Coll., Goucher Coll., Pratt Inst. Mem. Am. Fedn. Tchrs., Nat. Assn. Social Workers, LWV. Contbr. articles to N.Y. Times, U.S. Steelworker Jour., Red Book and others. Home: Fell's Point Baltimore MD 21231 Office: 1414 Federal Bldg Baltimore MD 21201 also 2404 Rayburn House Office Bldg Washington DC 20515

MILAM, MARY JUSTINA GRATTAN, sociologist, writer; b. Kansas City, Kans., May 10, 1930; d. Francis Patrick and Cathrein Catherine Mary Lyonsgrattan (Byrnes) G.; Grattan; student U. Mo., Kansas City, 1947-49; B.A. with honors, N. Tex. State U., 1969, M.A., (fellow), 1971; Ph.D. in Sociology and Liguistics (fellow), Tex. Woman's U., 1977; m. David Leake Milam, Sr., Nov. 23, 1950 (div. 1979); children—Melinda Sue, David Leake, Barnaby Walker (Twins). Freelance writer and stringer Kansas City Star, Kansas City Kansan, Prom mag.; radio continuity Sta. KCMO; author short stories, articles and interviews for various mags. and jours.; instr. sociology N. Tex. State U. and Laredo State U.; research scholar London Sch. Econs., 1983-85; sociolinguistic research cons. Active Girl Scouts Am., Cub Scouts. Mem. Internat. Sociol. Assn., Am. Sociol. Assn., S.W. Sociol. Assn., Mid-South Sociol. Assn., Soc. Study of Social Problems, Internat. Sociolinguistics Research Com., Alpha Kappa Delta. Roman Catholic. Author: An Axiomatic Theory of Adolescence. Papers collected at Kinsey Inst., Ind. and Lockwood Meml. Library, Buffalo. Address: 6222 Malcolm Dr Dallas TX 75214

MILANO, HEATHER CASEY, educator; b. St. John, N.B., Can., Mar. 2, 1934; B.A. in L.S., St. Francis Xavier U., Antigonish, N.S., Can., 1956; M.Sc. in Audiovisual Edn., Western Conn. State Coll., Danbury, 1976; married, 2 children. Librarian various schs., 1957-59; library media specialist Putnam Valley (N.Y.) Central Sch. Dist. 2, 1972—. Mem. cultural com. Putnam Valley Pub. Library, 1972-74; media council rep. to Bd. Coop. Ednl. Services, Yorktown Heights, N.Y., 1973—. Mem. N.Y. State United Tchrs., Sch. Librarians of Southeastern N.Y. Pi Lambda Theta. Certified library media specialist, N.Y. State. Home: 2730 Quaker Church Rd Yorktown Heights NY 10598 Office: Putnam Valley Jr High Sch Peekskill Hollow Rd Putnam Valley NY 10579

MILANO, PAMELA CREESE, systems and software company executive, b. Ensenada, P.R., Sept. 28, 1947; d. Philip Guy and Jean Craig (Cooper) Creese; grad. Bixby Bus. Coll., 1965; student St. Petersburg Jr. Coll., 1965-72, Tampa Coll., 1976-78; student Thomas A. Edison State Coll., 1986—; spl. courses; m. Richard Nicholas Milano, May 26, 1973; children—Saria Pattan, Richard Creese. Platform sec. Barnett Bank, St. Petersburg, Fla., 1967-73; asst. cashier Ellis N.E. Nat. Bank, St. Petersburg, 1967-73; corp. officer Cheezem Devel. Corp., St. Petersburg, 1973-74; legal sec. Marlow, Shofi, Ortmayer, Smith & Spangler, Tampa, Fla., 1974-76; office mgr./acct. SHS Assocs., Inc., St. Petersburg, 1977-81; group v.p. loans and v.p., dir. mortgage loans Fla. Software Services, Inc., Orlando, 1979-82; v.p., tech. dir. Digital Systems, Inc., Pensacola, Fla., 1982-85; v.p. electronic mortgage systems Citicorp Person-to-Person, Inc., St. Louis, 1985—; condr. banking seminars for students; cons. seminars on lending instruments. Formerly active League to Aid Retarded Children, Young Republicans. Lic. real estate asso., Fla.; cert. profl. sec. Mem. Am. Inst. Banking, Am. Bus. Women's Assn., Nat. Assn. Female Execs., Fla. Soc. Cert. Profl. Secs., Data Processing Mgmt. Assn., Pensacola Arts Council, North Hills Preservation Dist. (bd. dirs.). Episcopalian. Home: 1 Claiborne Pl Webster Groves MO 63119 Office: 670 Mason Ridge Center Dr Saint Louis MO 63119

MILBOURNE, PAULA DENISE, commercial auditor; b. Phila., Jan. 10, 1956; d. Norman J. and Doris Eleanor (Albritton) M. B.S. in Internat. Studies, Am. U., 1978; M.B.A. in Fin., LaSalle U., 1983. Payroll supr. Quality Caulking Co. Inc., Southampton, Pa., 1978-80; advanced underwriter Liberty Mut. Ins. Co., Bala-Cynwyd, Pa., 1980-84; auditor asset based group BancAmerican Comml. Corp., Allentown, Pa., 1984—; cons. Seal Tite Co., Glenside, Pa., 1984—. Mem. publicity com. 100 Coalition of Black Women, Phila., 1985—. Mem. Black M.B.A. Assn., Alpha Kappa Alpha (black history com., calendar girl, fin. and budget treas. 1977, media liaison for undergrads local chpt. 1986). Democrat. Episcopalian. Clubs: Between Friends of Phila. (chmn. entertainment com., co-chmn. civic com.), Blazers Ski (Phila.). Avocations: skiing, dancing; reading; fashion; horticulture. Office: BancAmerican Comml Corp 1621 Cedar Crest Blvd Suite 101 Allentown PA 18104

MILBY, SHEILA GALE, marketing-communications firm executive, consultant; b. Liberty, Ky., May 24, 1953; d. Leslie Kenneth and Juanita Faye (McFarland) Porter; m. Gary D. Milby, May 10, 1974. A.A., U. Louisville, 1979, B.S., 1982; M.A., Webster U., 1984. Mktg. dir. Ky. Telco Fed. Credit Union, Louisville, 1982-83; pres. SGM Mktg.-Communications, Inc., Louisville, 1983—. Mem. Am. Mktg. Assn., Sales and Mktg. Execs. of Louisville, Nat. Assn. Female Execs. Democrat. Methodist. Avocations: tennis; biking; walking; aerobics; needlepoint. Office: SGM Mktg-Communications Inc 1313 Lyndon Ln Suite 215 Louisville KY 40222

MILDON, MARIE ROBERTA, association executive; b. Pittsburg, Calif., Apr. 18, 1935; d. Samuel Ward and Roberta Alice (Trumpower) Wilson; m. James Lee Mildon, Sept. 17, 1958; 1 dau., Laura Marie. B.S., U. Nev.-Reno, 1983. News editor Seaside News Sentinel (Calif.), 1956-58; adminstrv. asst. for corp. devel. Crown Zellerbach, San Francisco, 1959-64; assoc. dir. Nat. Council Juvenile and Family Ct. Judges, Reno, Nev., 1969—; tng. dir. Nat. Coll. Juvenile Justice, Reno, 1971-72; apptd. cons. to task force on abused and neglected children Mo. Supreme Ct. Alt. trustee John Shaw Field Found., Reno, 1979-85. Co-author: Model Statute for Termination of Parental Rights, 1976; Model Statute on Juvenile and Family Court Records, 1981; My World To Share, 1982. Editor: Judicial. Concern for Children in Trouble, 1974; Juvenile and Family Ct. Jour., 1986—; prodn. editor Juvenile and Family Law Digest, 1986—. Office: Jud Coll Bldg U Nev Campus Reno NV 89557

MILENKI, JANET CHESTELYNN, financial broker; b. Albany, Ky., Nov. 24, 1953; d. Kathleen (Stearns) Conner. Student, Purdue U. Vice pres. mktg. Brandon Polo Club, Fla., 1981-82; asst. Puller Mortgage, Indpls., 1982-83; pres., owner Excalibur Fin., New Castle, Ind., 1983—. Appointed mem. Ind. Venture Capital Conf., Indpls., 1983. Named Hon. Lt. Gov., Lt. Gov. Mutz of Ind., 1983. Mem. Nat. Assn. Women Bus. Owners, Network Women in Bus., Nat. Assn. Sec. Services, Internat. Entrepreneurs Assn., Delta Sigma Pi. Republican. Methodist. Clubs: Brandon Polo (Fla.); Ind. Sanyo Users (Chmn.) (Indpls.). Avocations: polo, business, fox-hunting, computers, airplanes. Home: PO Box 48 New Castle IN 47362

MILES, BARBARA ANN, health care facility administrator, nurse; b. Huron, S.D., July 4, 1940; d. Marvin Christian and Lucy Johanna (DeYoung) Roesch; m. Frederick Dean Miles Jr., May 6, 1967; 1 child, Frederick Dean III. R.N., Presbyn.-St. Luke's Hosp. Sch. of Nursing, Chgo., 1961; student U. Ill.-Chgo., 1965, Case Western Res. U., 1963-65. R.N., Ill., Ohio, Ariz. Asst. head nurse Tucson Med. Ctr., 1971-72; supr. Desert Samaritan Hosp., Mesa, Ariz., 1972-74; nurse mgr. McDowell facility Cigna Health Plan of Ariz., Phoenix, 1974-83, assoc. adminstr., 1983-85, adminstr., 1985—; state chairperson nursing contest Vocat. Indsl. Clubs of Am., Phoenix, 1984—, nat. chairperson nursing contest, 1985—. Mem. Am. Acad. Ambulatory Nursing Adminstrs., Chandler C. of C. Methodist. Avocations: playing piano; reading; crafts. Home: 1019 E Vinedo Ln Tempe AZ 85284 Office: Cigna Health Plan of Ariz 1349 W Chandler Blvd Chandler AZ 85224

MILES, BARBARA LOUISE, economist; b. Gustine, Calif., July 5, 1944; d. William Pitt and Mabel Elizabeth (Harrison) M. B.A., Occidental Coll., 1966; M.A., U. Wash., 1968. Instr. econs. St. Martin's Coll., Olympia, Wash., 1969; economist Wash. State Planning Agy., Olympia, 1969, Bur. Econ. Analysis, Washington, 1969-75, Congl. Research Service, Library of Congress, Washington, 1975—. Contbr. articles to profl. jours. Mem. fin. com. Episcopal Diocese of Washington, 1983—; warden Ascension Parish, Gaithersburg, Md., 1985—; asst. dir. Browningsville Band, Md., 1980—. Mem. Am. Real Estate and Urban Econs. Assn., Congl. Research Employees Assn. (pres. 1984—), Sigma Alpha Iota (life), Omicron Delta Epsilon. Episcopalian. Avocations: bicycling; music. Home: 19831 Wheelwright Dr Gaithersburg MD 20879 Office: Congl Research Service Library of Congress Washington DC 20540

MILES, BETTY LOU LABUFF, oil company executive; b. Dayton, Tex., June 4, 1936; d. James Jefferson and Barbara Loucille (White) LaBuff; m. Roger Williams Simmons, Aug. 1956 (div. 1961); 1 child, Kirby Madden Simmons; m. 2d Ellison Miles, Aug. 15, 1964; children—Merry Meagan Miles, Bradford Tyson Miles, Mark Joseph Miles. Student U. Alaska, 1954-55; B.B.A., U. Tex., 1958. Sec. to col. U.S. Corps Engrs., Anchorage, 1954-55; sec. to oil operator, Houston, 1957-58; sec. to pres. Permian Oil Co., Houston, 1959-61; actress Hawaii-5-0, Honolulu, 1968-70; sr. oil and gas lease rental analyst, head rentals sect. Monsanto Oil Co., Houston, 1982—; assoc. travel editor, spl. events editor Travelog Mag., Vol., Tex. Children's Hosp., Houston, 1957-64, St. Luke's Hosp., Houston, 1957-64, Clin. Pathology Clinic, Houston, 1962-64; mem. ofcl. staff J.F. Kennedy campaign for Pres. U.S., 1961. Mem. Houston Livestock Show and Rodeo (life mem., mem. internat. com.), Cattlemen's Internat. Assn.-Greater Am., Desk and Derrick Club. Democrat. Roman Catholic.

MILES, CANDICE ST. JACQUES, writer, editor; b. Chgo., Sept. 4, 1951; d. Omer Alcide and Marilyn Elizabeth (Scholl) St. Jacques; m. Bruce Fraley Miles, Apr. 1, 1972. B.A., Ariz. State U., Tempe, 1972. Freelance writer, San Diego, 1972-76; assoc. editor MESA (Ariz.) Mag., 1976-77; creative coordinator State Fair Ariz., Phoenix, 1977-78; mng. editor Ariz. Living Mag., Phoenix, 1978-82; Freelance writer, Phoenix, 1982—. Ghost writer: (by Howard Adams) Quad, 1984; contbr. numerous articles to publs. Pub. relations person Central Ariz. chpt. ARC, Phoenix, 1982-84, Planned Parenthood, 1982-84. Recipient Appreciation award Ariz. State U., 1972. Mem. Women in Communications (pres. Phoenix Chpt. 1984-85, nat. chmn. publs. rev. com.), Ariz. Authors Assn., Southwest Writers Conf., Ariz. Press Women, AAUW. Home: 6329 N 13th St Phoenix AZ 85014

MILES, DORI ELIZABETH, lawyer; b. Bklyn., Jan. 3, 1953; d. Sidney and Beatrice (Lehman) Miles. B.A., NYU, 1974; J.D., Southwestern U., Los Angeles, 1982. Bar: Calif. 1982, U.S. Ct. Appeals (9th cir.) 1982, U.S. Dist. Ct. (cen. dist.) Calif. 1982. Student extern U.S. Dist. Ct. (cen. dist.) Calif., Los Angeles, summer 1981, U.S. Ct. Appeals (9th cir.), Los Angeles, 1982; assoc. Fonda & Garrard, Los Angeles, 1982—. Mem. ABA, Calif. Bar Assn., Los Angeles Bar Assn., Southwestern U. Sch. Law Dean's Circle (founding). Home: 1048 14th St Apt 202 Santa Monica CA 90403 Office: Fonda & Garrard 12301 Wilshire Blvd Los Angeles CA 90025

MILES, DOROTHY MARIE, air force officer; b. Gary, Ind., May 10, 1950; d. Isaac and Lattie (Durden) M. B.S., Oakland City Coll., Ind., 1973; M.A., Central Mich. U., 1981. Commd. 2d H. U.S. Air Force, 1979, advanced through grades to capt., 1983; div. chief equal opportunity Mil. Personnel Ctr., Randolph, Tex., 1983-85, liaison officer, Joint Def. Dept., Patrick AFB, Fla., 1985—. Mem. Tuskegee Airmen, Nat. Assn. Female Execs. Democrat. Baptist. Home: 258 Versailles Dr Melbourne Beach FL 32951

MILES, ELIZABETH NESTOR, speech and language pathologist; b. Medford, Mass., Nov. 10, 1923; d. James Francis and Agnes Agatha Nestor; B.S., Salem State Coll.; M.Ed., Boston U., 1951, CAGS in Speech Pathology, 1960; m. E. Robert Miles, May 29, 1955; 1 dau., Lisa Marie. Speech and hearing cons. West Hartford (Conn.) schs., 1952-55; speech pathologist Lexington (Mass.) Sch. Dept., 1966-67; speech and hearing specialist Medford Sch. Dept., 1967-73, supr. instrn. and related services, 1973-76, dir. Chpt. I, ESEA, 1976—; lectr. speech pathology Boston U., 1962-63, supr. clin. practicum, 1962-67. Recipient award Tri-City Council for Children, 1976. Mem. Am. Speech and Hearing Assn. (cert. clin. competence, mem. legis. council 1974-76), Am. Assn. Clin. Counselors, Mass. Speech and Hearing Assn. (sec. 1970-74, exec. bd. 1970-76, pres. elect 1984-85, pres. 1985-86, award 1975), Council Adminstrs. of Compensatory Edn., Boston U. Osgood Hill Alumni (exec. bd.). Pi Lambda Theta. Roman Catholic. Home: 32 Catherine Rd Reading MA 01867 Office: 215 Harvard St Medford MA 02155

MILES, SUE KELTY, childhood development educator, guidance consultant, public speaker; b. Henderson, Tex., Oct. 5, 1940; d. Charles W. and Clara W. Kelty; m. George D. Miles, Aug. 26, 1961 (div. July 1973); 1 son, Joel Scott; m. Roger Kern, Jan. 1985. B.S. in Edn., Sam Houston U., 1961; M.Ed., U. Houston, 1964; postgrad. Tex. A&M U., 1967, No. Ill. U., 1976—, Northwestern U., 1975, Harvard U., 1977, Nova U., 1986. Cert. tchr., Tex., Ill. Elem. tchr. Deepwater Sch., Deer Park Sch. Dist., Pasadena, Tex., 1961-63, 68-73, substitute tchr., 1963, 64; part-time instr. Lamar U., Beaumont, Tex., 1972-73; tchr. 1st and 2d grades Hinsdale (Ill.) Sch. Dist. 181, 1973-75; coordinator, instr. early childhood devel. program Waubonsee Community Coll., Sugar Grove, Ill., 1975—, coll. mgr. Waubonsee Coll. Child Devel. Ctr., sponsor student service club, also coordinator Extension Ctr. Child Care; mem. Mid-Valley Vocat. Adv. Com.; mem. adv. com. Waubonsee Child Devel. Ctr.; cons. in field. Mem. adv. com. Family Focus, Indian Valley Vocat. Ctr., Aurora Home Econs. Adv. Bd.; mem. child care com. United Way. Recipient Outstanding Service awards Waubonsee Community Coll. Child Devel. Club, 1975-79. Mem. Nat. Assn. for Edn. of Young Children, Chgo. Assn. for Edn. of Young Children, Am. Fedn. Tchrs., Tex. Tchrs. Assn., Ill. Soc. Early Childhood Profls., Fox Valley Child Care Com., Nat. Orgn. Future Women, Downers Grove (Ill.) Jaycee-ettes, Zeta Tau Alpha. Episcopalian. Author several booklets in field. Home: 959 Meadowlawn St Downers Grove IL 60516 Office: Waubonsee Community Coll Route 47 at Harter Rd Sugar Grove IL 60554

MILFORD, PATRICIA POLINO, drapery company executive, interior designer; b. Detroit, June 2, 1940; d. John and Madeline Rose (Graham) Polino; m. Laurence Milford, Apr. 18, 1959 (div. Nov. 1983); children—Laurence, Sherri Lynne, Jeffrey Shane. With James Renfrew & Snook & Assocs., Royal Oak, Mich., 1956-58; legal sec. Renfrew & Assocs., Royal Oak, 1958-60; v.p. Spring Crest Draperies, Naples, Fla., 1975-83, pres., 1983—. Inventor solarium shade. Mem. Am. Bus. Womens Assn., C. of C., Nat. Fed. Ind. Bus., Collier County Builders and Contractors Assn. Avocations: tennis; aerobics; reading. Office: Spring Crest Draperies 7600 Trail Blvd N Naples FL 33963

MILGRAM, GRACE, housing economist; b. Phila., Mar. 13, 1915; d. William Morris and Anna (Steinberg) Smelo; m. Morris Milgram, June 26, 1937 (div. Mar. 1969); children—Gene, Elizabeth Milgram April. B.A. with honors, Antioch Coll., Yellow Springs, Ohio, 1937; M. City Planning, U. Pa., 1960, Ph.D. in City Planning, 1967. Research asst. prof. Inst. for Environ. Studies, U. Pa., Phila., 1960-67; asst. dir. for research Inst. of Urban Envirornment, Columbia U., N.Y.C., 1967-71; project dir. N.Y. State Urban Devel. Corp., N.Y.C., 1971-75; specialist in housing Library of Congress Congl. Research Service, Washington, 1975—; staff mem. housing econs. Presdl. Task Force on Urban Problems, Washington, 1965-66; mem. HUD Task Force on Housing Costs, Washington, 1977-78; cons. in field. Author (with others) Institutional Investors and Corporate Stock, 1973. Editor (with others) Urban Housing, 1966. Contbr. articles to profl. publs. Mem. Am. Real Estate and Urban Econs. Assn., Am. Inst. Cert. Planners, Nat. Assn. Housing and Redevel. Ofcls., Lambda Alpha. Club: National Economists. Avocations: enameling on copper or steel; reading. Home: 201 Eye St SW Washington DC 20024 Office: Library of Congress Congl Research Service-Economics Washington DC 20340

MILKS, SALLY ANN, food service district manager, dietitian; b. Bradford, Pa., Nov. 29, 1949; d. John David and Pearl Marie (Meier) Morrison; m. Frank Elmer Milks, Aug. 18, 1973 (div. 1978); 1 child, Jason Michael. B.S. in Edn., Mansfield State Coll., 1971; student Indiana U. of Pa., 1969-71. Registered dietitian. Clin. dietitian St. Vincent Med. Ctr., Erie, Pa., 1971-72, 73-74; dietetic intern Shadyside Hosp., Pitts., 1972-73; cons. dietitian Sheridan Manor Nursing Home, Buffalo, 1975-77; nutrition instr. E.J. Meyer Sch. Nursing, Buffalo, 1975-77, chief clin. dietitian, 1977-78; asst. dir. food services ARA Services, Erie County Med. Ctr., 1978-79, dir. food services, 1979-82, dist. mgr., Phila., 1982—; mem. adv. council Buffalo State U., 1985—; guest lectr. food and nutrition dept., 1980—. Ho. of dels. United Way of Buffalo and Erie County, 1983—. Mem. Am. Dietetic Assn., Erie County Assn. for Retarded Children (2d v.p. 1983-85, chmn. residential services com. 1981—). Home: 17 Apollo Dr Amherst NY 14120 Office: ARA Services 11103 Pepper Rd Hunt Valley MD 21031

MILLANE, LYNN, town official; b. Buffalo, N.Y. 10/14/28; d. Robert P. Schermerhorn and Justine A. (Ross) m. J. Vaughan Millane, Jr.; Aug. 16, 1952 children—Maureen, Michele, John, Mark, Kathleen Ed.B. Grad., U. Buffalo, 1949, Ed.M., in Health Education 1951. Mem. Amherst Town Bd., 1982—. Pres., E. J. Meyer Hosp. Jr. Bd., 1962-64; pres. Aux. to Erie County Bar Assn., 1966-68; pres. Women's Com. of Buffalo Philharm. Orch., 1976-78, v.p. adminstrn., 1975-76, v.p. pub. affairs, 1974-75, chmn. adv. bd., 1979-82; v.p. Buffalo Philharm. Orch. Soc., Inc., 1976-78, mem. council trustee, 1974— 1st v.p. Fans for 17, 1980-82; 1st. v.p. Friends of Baird Hall, SUNY-Buffalo, 1980-82; exec. bd. mem. Longview Protestant Home for Children, 1979-85, 2d v.p., 1982-85; bd. dirs. ARC, Town of Amherst br., 1982-87, by-laws com., 1981, 84, chmn. sr. concerns com., 1982-87; bd. dirs. Amherst Symphony Orch. Assn., 1981-86, roster chmn., 1982-84, nominating chmn., 1985-86; nat. music com. Women's Assn. for Symphony Orchs. in Am. and Can., 1977-79; council mem. Am. Symphony Orch. League; sec. Amherst Sr. Citizen's Adv. Bd., 1980-81, liaison from Amherst Town Bd., 1982—; dir.-at-large community adv. council SUNY-Buffalo, 1981—; co-assoc. chmn. maj. gift div. capital campaign Daemen Coll., 1983-84; co-chmn. Women United Against Drugs Campaign, 1970-72; founding mem. Lunch and Issues, Amherst, 1981—; mem. edn. com. Network in Aging of Western N.Y., Inc., 1982-86, bd. dirs., 1985-86; bd. dirs. Amherst Elderly Transp. Corp.; committeeman dist. Town of Amherst Republican Com.; treas. Town and Country Rep. Club, 1980-81; mem. nominating com. Fedn. Rep. Women's Clubs Erie County, 1980; exec. bd. mem. Women's Exec. Council of Erie County Rep. Com., 1969-71; dir. Amherst Rep. Women's Club, 1963-65. Pi Lambda Theta National Honorary-1950. Named Homemaker of Yr., Family Circle Mag., 1969; Woman of Substance, 20th Century Rep. Women, 1983; Woman of Yr., Buffalo Philharm. Orch. Soc., Inc., 1982; Outstanding Woman in Community Service, SUNY-Buffalo, 1985; recipient Good Neighbor award Courier Express, 1978; Merit award Buffalo Philharm. Orch., 1978; award Fedn. Rep. Women's Clubs Erie County, 1982; Disting. Service award Town of Amherst Sr. Ctr., 1985. Mem. Amherst C. of C. (VIP dinner com. 1984), LWV, SUNY-Buffalo Alumni Assn. (life, presdl. advisor 1977-79). Club: Zonta (Amherst) (dir. 1984-86, 1st v.p. 1985-86, pres. 1986-87). Office: 5583 Main St Williamsville NY 14221

MILLAR, SALLY GRAY, nurse; b. Madison, Wis., Dec. 8, 1946; d. W. Llewellyn and Janet Josephine (Dean) M. R.N., St. Joseph Hosp. Sch. Nursing, Joliet, Ill., 1968; M.B.A., Simmons Coll., Boston, 1985. Staff nurse Bryn Mawr Hosp., Pa., 1968-69; surg. ICU, Mass. Gen. Hosp., Boston, 1969-78, head nurse, respiratory, surg. ICU, 1978-81, supr. intensive care nursing service, 1981-85; project dir., 1985—. Editor: Methods in Critical Care, 1980, AACN Procedure Manual for Critical Care, 1985. Contbr. chpts. to books, articles to profl. jours. Mem. Am. Assn. Critical-Care Nurses (dir. 1976-82, pres. 1980-81). Republican. Roman Catholic. Office: Mass Gen Hosp 32 Fruit St Boston MA 02114

MILLARD, LAVERGNE HARRIET, free-lance artist; b. Chgo., July 8, 1925; d. Lewis and Julia (Smolk) Bassmire; student Chgo. Art Inst., 1937-39; m. Samuel Costales, Jan. 31, 1943 (div. 1957); m. 2d, Bailey Millard, Mar. 9, 1958 (div.); children—Bryan Lewis Costales, Julie Crump, Candace Lynn Millard. Cocktail waitress Verdis, Grant Street, Concord, Calif., 1955-61; mgr. used book shop Joyce Book Shop, Concord, 1964-79; free-lance artist, 1979—. Recipient ribbons local fairs, art shows. Republican. Copyright holder for pastel art work. Home and Office: 1890 Farm Bureau Rd #11 Concord CA 94519

MILLBERRY, KIMBERLEE WHITNEY, geological scientist, educator; b. N. Adams, Mass., Apr. 3, 1959; d. Donald Robert and Joan (Whitney) Millberry; B.A. in Geology with highest honors; Williams Coll., 1981; M.A. in Geology U. Tex., Austin, 1984; postgrad. Ohio State U., 1984—. Summer research asst. to govtl. sponsored study of the coastal erosion of Saco Bay, Maine, 1979; tutor, teaching asst. geology Williams Coll., 1977-81; assoc. instr. Ind. U., Bloomington, 1981; teaching asst. U. Tex., Austin, 1981-83, tutor for geology/petroleum engring. students; sr. hydrogeologist New Eng. Pollution Control Co. Inc., Norwalk, Conn., 1986—. Active Big Bros. and Big Sisters, 1978-81. Williams Coll. grantee, 1977-81; Nat. Assn. Geology Tchrs. and Amax Corp. scholar, 1980; Bronfman Sci. research grantee, 1980-81. Mem. Nat. Assn. Women in Sci. Found., Internat. Assn. Sedimentologists, Soc. Econ. Paleontologists and Mineralogists, Am. Assn. Petroleum Geologists, Assn. Women Geoscientists, Nat. Water Well Assn., Geol. Soc. Am., Phi Beta Kappa. Episcopalian. Contbr. articles to profl. jours. Home: 84 Maple Ave S Westport CT 06880 Office: NEPCCO 81 Seaview Ave Norwalk CT 06855

MILLER, ADELE ENGELBRECHT, educator; b. Jersey City, July 31, 1946; d. John Fred and Dorathea Kathryn (Kamm) Engelbrecht; B.S. in Bus. Edn., Fairleigh Dickinson U., 1968, M.B.A. magna cum laude, 1974; cert. in public sch. adminstrn. and supervision Jersey City State Coll., 1976; m. John M. Mamone, Apr. 3, 1971; m. William A. Miller, Jr., Dec. 21, 1981. Bus. tchr. Jersey City Bd. Edn., 1967—, coordinator coop. office edn. programs, 1973—, acting v.p., 1985—, prin. of summer sch., 1985; adj. instr. St. Peter's Coll., 1974-75; curriculum cons. Cittone Bus. Sch., 1981-82; mem. adv. council Dickinson High Sch., 1973—, chmn., 1978-80; organizer, bd. dirs. Frances Nadel and Cooke-Connolly-Coffey-Witt Faculty Meml. Scholarships, 1978—; trustee Dickinson High Sch. Parents Council, 1985—. Mem. Citizens Adv. Council to Mayor of Jersey City, 1968-71; organizer, dir. Jersey City Youth Week, 1970-72; mem. juvenile conf. com. Hudson County Juvenile Ct., 1978—; active annual telethon Stevens Inst. Tech., 1978-80; trustee Jersey City Coll.-Community Orch., 1979—; adv. bd. Hudson-Hamilton council Boy Scouts Am., 1985—. Recipient Dickinson High Sch. Key Club Tchr. of Yr. award, 1971. Mem. NEA, N.J. Edn. Assn., Jersey City Edn. Assn., N.J. Coop. Office Edn. Coordinators Assn. (dir., treas., v.p.), N.J. Fedn. Women's Clubs, Jersey City Women's Club (scholarship chmn., adviser Jr. Woman's Club), AAUW (edn. chmn. N.J. div., sec., del. to White House briefing on edn., women's issues, arms control); AAUW-Coll. Club of N.J. (pres., v.p., sec., treas.). Clubs: Jersey City (pres.), N.J. Fedn. Women's (jr. membership dept.), Jersey City Jr. Woman's (v.p., sec., treas.). Co-author: New Jersey Cooperative Office Education Coordinators Resource Manual, 1984; author coop. office edn. study course Jersey City Public Schs., 1980, 84. Home: 91 Sherman Pl Jersey City NJ 07307 Office: Dickinson High School 2 Palisade Ave Jersey City NJ 07306

MILLER, ADELIA DUHON, nurse, educator; b. Conroe, Tex., Jan. 20, 1936; d. Lawrence Bradford and Angel Emilanne (Gigout) Duhon; R.N., Lamar U., 1956; B.S.N., U. Tex., Tyler, 1978, M.S., 1982; m. Robert Lloyd Miller, Aug. 19, 1956; children—Kurt Bradford, Eve Marie, Karl William. Staff nurse Mother Frances Hosp., Tyler, Tex., 1966-70, dir. nursing service, 1970-75; office nurse, Shreveport, La., 1957-59; instr. nursing Tyler Jr. Coll., 1978-79, chmn. dept. vocat. nursing, 1979—; gov.'s appointee State Bd. Vocat. Nurse Examiners, 1984-89. Mem. Am. Nurses Assn., Tex. Nurses Assn., Tex. Jr. Coll. Tchrs. Assn., Tex. Assn. Vocat. Nurse Educators. Methodist.

MILLER, ANGELA PEDRAZINE, hospice, home health care coordinator; b. San Antonio, Jan. 21, 1933; d. Roman and Godelva (Salinas) Pedrazine; m. Robert E. Miller, June 17, 1955; children—Kenneth W., Kara M. Kissick, Kevin B., Kristen G. R.N., Parkland Hosp., Dallas, 1955. Inservice educator St. Catherine Hosp., Garden City, Kans., 1976-79; instr. geriatrics Garden City Community Coll., 1979-83; staff nurse Trinity Assn., Garden City, 1981-83; hospice home health care coordinator Mobile Agy. Southwest Health, Garden City, 1983—; founder Jeanne B. Corley Hospice, Garden City, 1981, coordinator, 1981-83. Bd. dirs., sec. Finney County Com. on Aging, Garden City, 1983-86. chmn. Am. Lung Assn., Garden City, 1977-79; mem. Belles of St. Catherine Hosp., 1976-86; pres. PTA, Aurora, Colo., 1969-70. Named Mil. Wife of Yr., Fitzsimmons Officers Wives, Denver, 1977. Mem. Kans. State Nurses Assn. (bd. dirs., Kans. Nurse of Month, 1982), Mobile Agy. for Southwest Health (bd. dirs.), Southwest Kans. Med. Soc. Aux. (bd. dirs., pres. 1979). Democrat. Episcopalian. Club: Ret. Officers Wives (Denver). Home: 1703 Crestway Dr Garden City KS 67846 Office: Mobile Agy for Southwest Health 608 N 6th St Garden City KS 67846

MILLER, BARBARA, phys. therapist; b. Lakewood, N.J., Dec. 31, 1954; d. Robert and Carolyn (Seiden) M.; m. Joel Behar, Dec. 22, 1986. B.S.P.T., Washington U., 1977. Staff therapist, then sr. therapist Nassau Hosp., Mineola, N.Y., 1977-82; sr. phys. therapist Jewish Inst. Geriatric Care-Geriatric Community Health Center, New Hyde Park, N.Y., 1982—; pvt. practice, Mineola, 1977—; guest lectr.; cons. Coma Recovery Assn., Internat. Coma Recovery Inst. Current researcher in efficacy of helium neon laser stimulation on wound healing. Mem. Am. Phys. Therapy Assn. Home: 11 Clement St Glen Cove NY 11542

MILLER, BARBARA ANN, computer consulting firm executive; b. N.Y.C., July 5, 1952; d. Charles John and Catherine (Ponkrashoff) M. B.A., U. Vt., 1974. Systems analyst Honeywell Info. Systems, Billerica, Mass., 1978-80, sr. systems rep., Houston, 1980-82, Tandem Computers, Houston, 1983-84; tech. support rep. Allied Data Research, Houston, 1982-83; sr. v.p. Neu-Sound of Houston, 1984—; cons. Honeywell Info. Systems, Tallahassee, Fla., 1985—; dir. Neu-Sound of Houston. Recipient Pacemaker award Honeywell Info. Systems, 1981, 82. Roman Catholic. Avocations: sailing; skiing; tennis; raquetball; photography. Home: 3700 Watonga Blvd #406 Houston TX 77092 Office: Neu-Sound of Houston PO Box 271569 Houston TX 77277

MILLER, BARBARA ANN, freelance writer/editor; b. Ft. Bragg, N.C., Feb. 3, 1955; d. James Housten and Ada (Neil) Rutan; div. 1978; children—Naomi, Rebecca; m. 2d, Timothy P. Miller, May 28, 1983. A.A., Pikes Peak Community Coll., 1979; B.A. in Communications, U. Colo., 1983; cert. LaSalle Ext. U., 1975, Writer's Digest Sch., 1983. Photog. lab. asst. Pikes Peak Community Coll., Colorado Springs, Colo., 1980-81; editorial work U. Colo., Colorado Springs, 1981-83; graphic artist Counseling Ctr., Colorado Springs, 1982; assoc. editor Colo. Springer mag., 1983; graphic designer Media Ctr., Colorado Springs, 1983; freelance journalist, photographer, Colorado Springs, 1984—; photographer Penrose Pub. Library, Colorado Springs, 1980; editor newsletter Colorado Springs Police Dept., 1980-81. Mem. Nat. Writers Club, Women in Communications. Home: 1514 N El Paso Colorado Springs CO 80907

MILLER, BARBARA ANNE, social work therapist; b. N.Y.C., May 1, 1930; d. Herbert and Rena Hortense (Heyman) Strauss; m. Arthur Zinkin Jr., Mar. 21, 1960 (div. 1974); 1 dau., Anne Frances; m. 2d, Roger Rowles Miller, Dec. 31, 1977. A.B., Barnard Coll., Columbia U., 1952, M.S.W., 1956; Ed.D., U. Mass., 1984. Tchr. Oceanside Pub. Schs. (N.Y.), 1952-54; clin. social worker Community Service Soc., N.Y.C., 1956-61; clin. social work supr. Jewish Family Service, Paterson, N.J., 1964-66, 68-71; social worker Campus Sch., Paterson State Coll. (N.J.), 1966-68; clin. social work supr. Northampton State Hosp. (Mass.), 1971-74, unit dir., 1976-78; assoc. area dir. Commonwealth of Mass. Dept. Mental Health, Northampton, 1974-76; clin. social work supr. Children's Aid and Family Service, Northampton, 1978-81; dir. mental health services Westfield area Dept. Mental Health, 1981-82; clin. social worker U. Mass. Med. Sch., Northampton, 1980-82; clin. social work supr. McLean Hosp., program at Northampton State Hosp., 1982—; clin. asst. prof. Smith Coll. Sch. Social Work. Lic. ind. clin. social worker, Mass. Mem. Nat. Assn. Social Workers, Am. Group Psychotherapy Assn., Orthopsychiatry Assn., Acad. Cert. Social Workers. Democrat. Unitarian. Office: McLean Northampton State Hosp PO Box 389 Northampton MA 01060

MILLER, BARBARA JANE, lawyer; b. Milw., June 12, 1951; d. Lawrence Martin and Mary Magdalene (McGinley) Miller. B.A. in Communications, U. Ky., 1973; J.D., U. San Francisco, 1978. Bar: Calif. 1978. Paralegal Ga. Indigents Legal Services, Inc., Atlanta, 1973-74; juvenile counselor City and County of San Francisco, 1974-75; legal asst., clk. firm Hall, Henry, Oliver & McReavy, San Francisco, 1975-77; law clk. firm Walker, Schroeder, Davis & Brehmer, Monterey, Calif., 1977-78; assoc. firm Thelen, Marrin, Johnson & Bridges, San Francisco, 1978-84; assoc. firm Knox, Ricksen, Snook, Anthony & Robbins, Oakland, Calif. and San Francisco, 1984—, lectr., panelist on estate planning. Recipient commendation State Bar Calif., 1983. Mem. San Francisco Bar Assn. (vice chmn. estate planning com. 1979-80, chmn. 1980-82), Barristers (dir. 1982-83). Democrat. Home: 1374 El Centro Ave Oakland CA 94602 Office: Knox Ricksen Snook Anthony & Robbins 1 Kaiser Plaza Suite 850 Oakland CA 94612

MILLER, BARBARA JEAN, savings and loan executive, banker; b. Honolulu, May 16, 1943; d. Genaro D. Alipio and Hilda E. (Espiritu) Alipio Uu; div.; children—Gina, Byard. Student, Am. Banking Inst., San Diego, 1973-1979, Am. Bankers Assn., Northwestern U., 1980. Ops. adminstr. San Diego Trust & Savs. Bank, 1969-81; acctg. supr. Bank of the West, San Jose, Calif., 1981-82; asst. v.p. San Diego Trust & Savs. Bank, 1982-83; v.p. Founders Savs. & Loan, Los Angeles, 1983-84; adminstrv. asst. First Interstate Bank of Hawaii, Honolulu, 1984—; conversion coordinator San Diego Trust & Savs. Bank, 1974-83; cons. Founders Savs. & Loan, Los Angeles. Leader, sec. Blue Birds, Cub Scouts Boy Scouts Am., 1972-74; coordinator, family ministries United Methodist Ch., San Diego and Honolulu, 1981-82; vol. Spl. Olympics, San Diego, 1982-84; master tabulator Muscular Dystrophy, San Diego, 1982-84, fin. chmn., 1985. Republican. Lodge: Soroptimist Internat. of Am. (v.p. 1981-82). Avocations: crafts, doll making, sewing. Home: 2014-H Fern St Honolulu HI 96826 Office: First Interstate Bank of Hawaii 2 N King St Honolulu HI 96817

MILLER, BARBARA STALLCUP, foundation executive; b. Mayten, Calif., Sept. 4, 1919; d. Joseph Nathaniel and Maybelle (Needham) Stallcup; B.A., U. Oreg., 1942; m. Leland Frank Miller, May 16, 1946; children—Paula, Susan, Daniel, Alison. Women's editor Eugene (Oreg.) Daily News, 1941-43; law clk. J. Everett Barr, atty., Yreka, Calif., 1943-45; mgr. Yreka C. of C., 1945-46; dir. public relations Columbia River Girl council Scouts U.S.A., Portland, Oreg., 1962-67; dir. pub. relations and info. U. Portland, 1967-78; dir. devel. U. Portland, 1978-79, exec. dir. devel., 1979-83; assoc. dir. St. Vincent Med. Found.; 1983—. Pub. relations cons. Portland Jr. Civic Theatre, 1964-71, Women for Agr., 1970-71. Bd. dirs., mem. edn. com. Portland Civic Theatre, 1964-71; bd. dirs., public relations chmn. Portland Columbia River council Girl Scouts U.S.A., 1960-62, leader, 1954-72; public relations cons. Vols. Am. of Oreg., 1968-71, pres. bd. dirs., 1980-83, nat. bd. dirs., 1984—; bd. dirs. Oreg. Black History Project, Providence Child Care Center, 1980-82, Southeast Mental Health Network. Recipient Rose award Alpha Xi Delta, Presdl. Citation, Oreg. Editors and Communicators, Miltner award U. Portland, 1977; named Woman of Dedication, Portland Fedn. Women's Clubs, 1978. Mem. Women in Communications Inc. (N.W. regional v.p. 1973-75, Matrix award 1976, 80), Public Relations Soc. Am. (accredited, accreditation chmn. Columbia River chpt. 1981—), Oreg. Assn. Editors and Communicators (dir. 1975-76), Oreg. Press Women (dist. v.p. 1977-79), Oreg. Fedn. Women's Clubs (public relations chmn. 1978-80), Alpha Xi Delta. Clubs: Portland Zenith (pres. 1975-76, 81-82), City Club of Portland. Home: 5930 SW Meadows Rd Lake Oswego OR 97034 Office: 9205 SW Barnes Rd Portland OR 97225

MILLER, BERNADETTE JANE, businesswoman, financial consultant; b. Dayton, Ohio, Nov. 30, 1947; d. Carl Burdette and Betty Jane Miller; student Wright State U., Dayton, 1966. With Am. Bankers Life Ins. Co., 1976-81, regional career cons., 1980-81; dir. women's mktg. Universal Guaranty Life Ins. Co., Columbus, Ohio, 1981-82; pres. Money Concepts Internat. of Miami Valley, Dayton, Ohio, 1982—; mem. Industry Task Force Women and Minorities in Ins., 1981—; seminar instr. in field. Recipient various sales awards; mem. Millionaires Club, 1976-80; named Internat. Woman of Yr., Am. Bankers Life, 1977, 79. Mem. Am. Bus. Women's Assn. (chpt. pres. 1979, 81, nat. del. 1978, chmn. area council 1983), Nat. Assn. Life Underwriters, Women in Ins., Ohio Assn. Life Underwriters, Dayton Assn. Life Underwriters (chmn. 1981), Columbus Assn. Life Underwriters, Ohio Forestry Assn. Republican. Lutheran. Clubs: Zonta, Order Eastern Star. Office: 7940 N Main St Dayton OH 45415

MILLER, BERNADETTE MARIE, banker; b. Phila., Apr. 13, 1958; d. John William and Genevieve Theresa (Carpitella) M. B.A., Chestnut Hill Coll., 1980; student Fairleigh Dickinson U., 1980-81, M.A. in Ednl. Psychology Temple U., 1986. Bank teller, new accounts rep. Phila. Saving Fund Soc., 1979-80, with Howard Savs. Bank, Short Hills, N.J., 1980-81; br. loan ops. specialist Industrial Valley Bank, Jenkintown, Pa., 1981—. Mem. Am. Psychol. Assn., Pa. Psychol. Assn., Psi Chi. Republican. Roman Catholic. Club: Psychology Interest Group (pres. 1979-80). Avocations: reading; jogging; swimming; wood working. Home: 408 Waring Rd Elkins Park PA 19117 Office: Industrial Valley Bank & Trust Co Old York Rd and West Ave Jenkintown PA 19046

MILLER, BETH FORESMAN, security investments firm operations manager, model, horsetrainer; b. Newark, Feb. 8, 1954; d. George A. and Helen H. (Harter) Forsman; m. E. Randall Miller, Mar. 10, 1973 (div. 1977); 1 child, Dawn Kimberly. Student Delaware Valley Coll., 1972. Modeling instr., make-up artist, horse trainer-instr., 1970-85; service rep. Summit Trust, N.J., 1984-85; ops. mgr. E.A. Moos, N.Y.C., 1985—. Mem. Profl. Horseman Assn. Avocations: Horses; sailing; travel. Home: 71 West End Ave Summit NJ 07901 Office: EA Moos 350 Springfield Ave Summit NJ 07901

MILLER, BETTY BROWN, writer; b. Altus, Ark., Dec. 21, 1926; d. Carlos William and Arlie Gertrude (Sublett) Brown; B.S., Okla. State U., 1949; M.S., U. Tulsa, 1953; student Am. U., 1966-68; m. Robert Wiley Miller, Nov. 15, 1953; children—Janet Ruth, Stephen Wiley. Tchr., LeFlore (Okla.) High Sch., 1947-48, Osage Indian Reservation High Sch., Hominy, Okla., 1948-50, Jenks (Okla.) High Sch., 1950-51; instr. Sch. Bus., U. Tulsa, 1950-51; tchr. Tulsa public schs., 1951-54; instr. Burdette Coll., Boston, 1954-55; reporter Bethesda-Chevy Chase Tribune, Montgomery County, Md., 1970-73; freelance writer, contbr. newspapers and mags., 1973—. Vice-pres. Kenwood Park (Md.) Citizens Assn., 1960; mem. Ft. Sumner Citizens Assn., editor newsletter, 1969; mem. Md. State PTA, editorial coordinator leadership conf., 1973-74; chmn. Montgomery County Forum for Edn., 1970—; trustee Friends of Valley Forge Nat. Hist. Park. Mem. Nat. Soc. Arts and Letters (past editor mag., dir. public relations, past nat. corr. sec.), Nat. League Am. Pen Women (former budget chmn., former nat. treas.), PEO, Pilot Inst. Montgomery County Press Assn., Internat. Platform Assn., Capital Speakers Club of Washington (past pres.), Adventures Unltd., U.D.C., Soc. Descs. of Washington's Army at Valley Forge (past nat. sec.), past nat. dir., historian gen., now inspector gen.), DAR, Huguenot League (Pa. state dir.). Republican. Clubs: Washington; Sedgeley (pres.) (Phila.). Address: PO Box 573 Valley Forge PA 19481

MILLER, BETTY JO, machine manufacturing company executive; b. Pitts., July 27, 1924; d. Paul Haines and Ella Irene (Berkey) Young; m. Clifford Miller, Feb. 16, 1946; 1 child, Paul David. B.S. in Bus., Burdett Coll., 1950; postgrad. MIT, 1960. With engring. dept. Armstrong Cork, Braintree, Mass., 1942-44; pvt. sec. F.S. Webster Co., Boston, 1944-46; acct., treas. Braintree Tool Co., Inc., 1952-75, pres., 1975—; acct. Blackburn Sheetmetal, Braintree, 1954-78, Micro Hydraulic Valves, Braintree, 1955-80, Mandel E. Cohen, M.D., Boston, 1964—, Howie and Cramond, Inc., Quincy, Mass., 1974—, Smith Harrison Co., Inc., 1969—; notary pub. Mass., 1970—; IRS rep. Holtsville, N.Y., 1984. Patentee electric undercutter and armature turning tools. Clk. of the polls, Braintree, 1964—; sec. Hampshire Shores Assn., 1967—; acct., tax specialist Braintree gardeners guild, 1983—. Mem. Braintree Bd. Trade, Nat. Fedn. Ind. Bus., South Shore C. of C., U.S. SBA, Nat. Bus. Assn., Braintree Women's Club (pres. 1982-83) treas., auditor 1968—), Gen. Fedn. Women's Clubs, State Fedn. Womens Clubs. Republican. Avocations: golf; bowling; bridge. Office: Braintree Tool Co Inc 121 Hancock St PO Box 253 Braintree MA 02184

MILLER, BLANCHE ESTHER, cytologist; b. Georgetown, N.Y., July 28, 1915; adopted d. Ralph Raymond and Mary Margaret (Hetrick) M.; A.B., Fairleigh Dickinson U., 1976. Cytotechnologist, Roosevelt Hosp., N.Y.C., 1953-55, screener cytotechnologist, 1955-56; with R.I. Hosp., Providence, 1956; mem. staff Newark City Hosp., 1957-68, chief cytology lab., 1960-66, co-dir. cancer detection center, 1966-68; sect. head cytology lab. N.J. Coll. Medicine and Dentistry, 1968-75; supr. continuing edn. in cytology Gyn Cytology and Pathology Assos., Leonia, N.J., 1975-78; teaching supr. cytology dept. Metpath, Teterboro, N.J., 1979-83; with Bus. Sci. Internat., 1984—. Mem. Am. Soc. Cytology, Am. Soc. Clin. Pathologists (cert. technologist, med. technologist), Pan Am. Cancer Cytology Soc., N.J. Assn. Cytology (founder mem., sec.-treas., mem. exec. bd., service award). Methodist. Home: 369 Tenafly Rd Apt 369E Tenafly NJ 07670 Office: Research Assoc Inc and Concept Testing Bus Sci Internat 270 Sylvan Ave Englewood Cliffs NJ 07632

MILLER, BLANCHE RUTH, insurance agency executive; b. Perth Amboy, N.J., Mar. 18, 1920; d. Arthur and Regina (Klein) Berkowitz; m. Leonard D. Miller, May 13, 1952; children—Henry, Cary S., Eric R., Ilene C. A.B., N.J. Coll. Women, 1940. Fin. analyst Lefkowits-Elias Corp., New Brunswick, N.J., 1940-41, U.S. Govt. War Dept., Washington, 1941-42; office mgr. Otten, Liskey & Rhodes, Washington, 1942-44; advt. mgr. Nat. Indsl. Stores Assocs., Washington, 1944-46; office mgr. Tobacco Jobber Publs., N.Y.C., 1946-52; ins. mgr., agt. Miller Ins. Agy., Highland Park, N.J., 1952—. Mem. Middlesex County Ins. Women (treas. 1979-80). Democrat. Jewish. Home: 154 N 10th Ave Highland Park NJ 08904 Office: Miller Agy 431 Paritan Ave Highland Park NJ 08904

MILLER, BONNIE GRACE JENKS, library media specialist; b. Miami, Fla., July 26, 1949; d. Philip and Arlean Pearl (Kagel) Jenks; m. Warren Hal Maltzman (div.); m. Stephen E. Miller, Dec. 17, 1977; 1 son, David Michael. B.A. in English, U. Calif.-Santa Barbara, 1971; M.L.S., U. Calif.-Berkeley, 1973, cert. in library adminstrn., 1975. Cert. elem. and secondary tchr., Calif. Librarian, U. Calif.-Berkeley, 1973-75; sch. library media specialist, computer curriculum coordinator Mt. Diablo Unified Sch. Dist., Concord, Calif., 1975—; dir. Diablo Valley Montessori Sch., Lafayette, Calif., 1983—; cons. computer edn., 1983—; instr. Chapman Coll., 1985-86. Author: Coastal Zone Bibliography, 1974; contbg. author: Visions and Prophecies for New Age, 1981. Mem. Nat. Women's Polit. Caucus, Berkeley, 1974-76; conf. coordinator Assn. for Research and Enlightenment, Virginia Beach, Va., 1976-82; mem. team cursillos in Christianity, Oakland Diocese, Calif., 1982—. Mem. ALA, Computer-Using Educators, Calif. Media and Library Educators Assn., Diablo Valley Fedn. Tchrs. (elem. v.p. 1980-82), AAUW, Alumni Assn. U. Calif.-Berkeley Sch. Library and Info. Sci., Beta Phi Mu, Phi Sigma Sigma (treas. 1968-69). Democrat. Roman Catholic. Pine Hollow Intermediate Sch 5522 Pine Hollow Rd Concord CA 94521

MILLER, BONNIE JEAN, lawyer, journalist; b. Lansing, Mich., July 29, 1946; d. John Francis and Irene (Valerina) M. B.A. in Journalism, Mich. State U., 1969; J.D., Cooley Law Sch., 1978. Bar: Mich. 1979. Research/info. asst. Mich. League Human Service, Lansing, 1971-72; info. specialist Mich. Consumer Commn., Lansing, 1973-76; asst. editor Mich. State U. Alumni Mag., East Lansing, 1975-76; project dir. Pros. Attys. Assn. Mich., Lansing, 1978-80; assoc. firm Kizer, Reader, Howell, Mich., 1980-82; sole practice law, Howell, 1982—. State trustee Child/Family Services Mich., 1983—, bd. dirs. Spouse Abuse Council Livingston County, Mich., 1982—; pres. Housing Assistance Found., Lansing, 1979. Named Disting. Alumna, Cooley Law Sch., 1983. Mem. ABA (family law sect.), Mich. Bar Assn. (family law sect.), Livingston County Bar Assn. (sec. 1981-82), Women Lawyers Mich. (region pres. 1982-84), Assn. Trial Lawyers Am., NOW. Home: 120 S Maple Box 324 Fowlerville MI 48836 Office: Parker & Miller 611 E Grand River #202 Howell MI 48843

MILLER, BONNIE KAY, banker; b. Lake Odessa, Mich., Dec. 15, 1938; d. Arthur H. and LaVerne A. (Fogleson) Johnson; m. Arthur W. Miller, Dec. 12, 1964 (div. Sept. 1978). Student Grand Rapids (Mich.) Jr. Coll., 1957; B.B.A., U. Mich., 1961; grad. U. Mich. Sch. Bank Mgmt., 1981, ABA Sch. Bank Investment, Norman, Okla., 1983. Mgmt. trainee First Nat. Bank, Kalamazoo, 1961-64; sec., receptionist Lawton (Okla.) C. of C., 1965-66; bookkeeper Wayland (Mich.) State Bank, 1966-70, adminstrv. asst. to pres., 1971-75, adminstrv. v.p., 1976-82; v.p. funds mgmt. United Community Bank, Wayland, 1983—; instr. Davenport Coll., Grand Rapids, Mich., 1978-80. Writer local news column Fedn. Focus, 1982-83. Trustee Heinika Pub. Library, Wayland, 1977-83; bd. dirs. Mich. State Fedn. Women's Clubs, Lansing, 1976-83, Girlstown Found., Belleville, Mich., 1980-83; bd. dirs., treas. Fontana Chamber Music Ensemble, Shelbyville, Mich., 1982-83. Mem. Am. Inst. Banking, West Mich. Women Execs., Mich. State Fedn. Women's Clubs (1st v.p. 1984—). Club: Wayland Ladies Library (pres. 1982-83). Office: United Bank 6140 28th St SE Suite 220 Grand Rapids MI 49506

MILLER, BONNIE LEE, engineering technician; b. Whidbey Island, Feb. 26, 1958; d. Donald Arthur and Diana Joanne (Spence) M. B.S. in Indsl. Tech., Calif. Poly. State U., 1980. Mfg. devel. engr. Convair div. Gen. Dynamics Corp., San Diego, summer 1978; prodn. supr. Clorox Co., Los Angeles, summer 1979; prodn. team mgr. Procter and Gamble Co., Modesto, Calif., 1980-83; bottling and warehouse mgr. Robert Mondavi Winery, Woodbridge, Calif., 1983-84; engring. technician Calaveras County Dept. Pub. Works, San Andreas, Calif., 1985—. Coach, Modesto Youth Soccer Assn., 1980, 82; mem. Nat. Found. for Ileitis and Colitis, San Francisco, 1983—, Met. Players Theatre Group Calaveras County, 1985—. Named Outstanding Graduating Sr., Calif. Poly. Sch. Engring., 1980; recipient Platinum Key award for cost savs. Procter & Gamble Co., 1981. Mem. Nat. Assn. for Female Execs., Stanislaus County Young Profls., Modesto Adult Soccer Club. Democrat. Avocations: skiing, soccer, reading, sewing, photography.

MILLER, CATHY LYNN, insurance company executive; b. Spokane, Wash., Apr. 27, 1948; d. Robert E. Barton and Betty Lou (McClung) Barton Paxton; m. William B. Miller, Oct. 23, 1971. Student U. Idaho, 1966-67. Claims clk. Unigard Ins. Co., Portland, Oreg., 1967-69; personal ins. asst. Ralph W. Fullerton Ins. Co., Portland, 1969-71; office mgr. Ward Cook Ins. Co., Portland, 1971-79; ins. agt. Gacek Ins. Co., Portland, 1979-81; co-owner, ptnr., Wilson-James Ins. Co., Tualatin, Oreg., 1981—. Vice chmn. United Cerebral Palsy, Portland, 1979; bd. dirs. YWCA, Portland, 1981, Cystic Fibrosis Found., Portland, 1976-83; mem. adv. bd. West Hotel Woman's Shelter, Portland, 1983; active Portland Art Assn., 1979; regional safety chmn. Women Hwy. Safety Leaders, Portland, 1972-73. Mem. Ins. Women Portland (sec. 1972-73, pres. 1976-77; Ins. Woman of Yr. award 1974), Washington County Ind. Agts., Oreg. Assn. Ind. Ins. Agts. (honorarium 1975), Nat. Assn. Ins. Women (cert. profl.; regional pub. relations chmn. 1975-76), Western Ins. Info. Service (Century award 1980). Democrat. Christian Scientist. Club: 50-50. Lodges: Eagles Aux., Elks. Home: 18010 S Anderson Rd Oregon City OR 97045 Office: Wilson-James Ins Co 8101 SW Nyberg Rd Tualatin OR 97062

MILLER, CONSTANCE LYNN, brokerage executive; b. Auburn, Ind., Jan. 11, 1956; d. Frederick Bernard and Frances Celena (Hoff) M. Student Ind. U., 1974-76; B.A. in Bus. Adminstrn., Nat. U., Sacramento, 1985. Registered rep. N.A.S.D., 1983, Life and Disability and Variable Annuities Licenses, 1984. Mktg. asst. Sacramento Bus. Mgmt., 1978-79; media buyer/mktg. asst. Valleycore Co., Sacramento, 1979-80; sales asst. Merrill Lynch, Pierce, Fenner and Smith, Sacramento, 1980-83, account exec., 1983-85; brokerage exec. The Garrick Fin. Group, 1985—. Recipient San Francisco Regional Emmy award Nat. Acad. TV Scis., No. Calif. area, 1979. Mem. Nat. Assn. Profl. Saleswomen, Sacramento Comstock Club, Sacramento Women's Network, Nat. Speakers Assn. Roman Catholic. Office: The Garrick Fin Group 1495 River Park Dr Suite 200 Sacramento CA 95815

MILLER, CYNTHIA ANN, mathematics educator; b. Thomasville, Ga., Oct. 17, 1951; d. James Peyton and Mildred Virginia (Simpson) M.; m. Michael Leroy Duggar, Dec. 30, 1978 (div. 1986). B.S., U. Tenn.-Chattanooga, 1972; M.Ed. cum laude, West Ga. Coll., 1978; Ed.S., Ga. State U., 1980, Ph.D., 1983; postgrad. Ga. Inst. Tech., 1980-81. Math. tchr. Cobb City Bd. Edn., Marietta, Ga., 1978-80; prof. math. edn. Ga. State U., Atlanta, 1981-82, prof. math., 1982-83; prof. math. and computer sci., DeKalb Coll., Atlanta, 1980-84; prof. math. Spelman Coll., Atlanta, 1984—, Mercer Coll., Atlanta, 1985—; researcher NASA Jet Propulsion Lab., Pasadena, Calif., 1985, 86, cons., 1985—. Nat. Merit scholar, 1969. Mem. Nat. Council Tchrs. Math., Math. Assn. Am., Ga. Council Tchrs. Math., Assn. for Women in Math., Internat. Orgn. Women in Math., Mensa, Pi Mu Epsilon, Kappa Delta Pi. Club: Met. Atlanta Math. Avocations: water skiing; hiking; reading; travel; photography. Office: Spelman Coll Box 4 Atlanta GA 30314

MILLER, DARLENE, microbiologist; b. Boston, Aug. 28, 1951; d. Fred Lee and Carrie Lee (Jones) M.; 1 child, Crispin Stanley. B.S. in Med. Tech., U. Miami, 1978; M.A. in Microbiology, U. Miami, 1984. Med. technologist clin. microbiology South Miami Hosp., Fla., 1977-80, Mercy Hosp., Miami, 1981-83; supr. microbiology Bascom Palmer Eye Inst., Anne Bates Leach Eye Hosp., U. Miami, 1983—, cons., 1983—. Contbr. articles to profl. jours. Mem. Am. Soc. Microbiology, Am. Soc. Clin. Pathologists, Fla. Soc. Med. Technologists, Woodson Williams Marshall Assn., Nat. Council Negro Women, Nat. Assn. Female Execs. Avocations: cycling; bowling; chess; reading; music. Home: 14780 Monroe St Miami FL 33176 Office: AR Abrams Ophthalmic Microbiology Lab Bascom Palmer Eye Inst Anne Bates Leach Eye Hosp U Miami Dept Ophthalmology 900 NW 17th St Miami FL 33176

MILLER, DEANE GUYNES, beauty, cosmetic company executive; b. El Paso, Tex., Jan. 12, 1927; d. James Tillman and Margaret Anne (Brady) G.; B.B.A., U. Tex.-El Paso, 1963; m. Richard G. Miller, Apr. 12, 1947; children—Jay Michael, Marcia Deane. Pres., owner The Velvet Door, Inc., El Paso, 1967—; pres., owner Merle Norman Cosmetic Studios, El Paso, 1975—; dir., Mountain Bell Tel. Co. Bd. dirs., treas. El Paso Mus. Art; chmn. bd. dirs. El Paso Internat. Airport; bd. dirs. Fgn. Trade Zone; pres. Pan Am. Roundtable; bd. dirs. Armed Services YMCA; v.p. Sun Carnival Assn., 1965-66. Republican. Episcopalian. Club: Junior League of El Paso. Address: 1 Silent Crest El Paso TX 79902

MILLER, DEBORAH LEE, laboratory manager; b. Teaneck, N.J., Sept. 1, 1953; d. Henry Thomas and Dorothy Grace (Davison) Miller. B.S. in Med. Tech., Caldwell Coll., 1975; diploma in Med. Tech. Mountainside Hosp., Montclair, N.J., 1975; M.S. in Med. Tech. and Lab. Adminstrn., St. John's U., Jamaica, N.Y., 1984. Med. technologist Bergen Pines County Hosp., Paramus, N.J., 1975; med. technologist Holy Name Hosp., Teaneck, N.J., 1975-82, mgr. out-patient lab. services, 1982-83, supr. immunochemistry, 1983; dir. mktg. Clin Path Inc., Hackensack, N.J., 1983-85; lab. mgr. St. Francis Hosp., Jersey City, 1985—. Mem. Am. Soc. Clin. Pathologists, Am. Soc. Med. Tech., N.J. Soc. Med. Tech., Md. Geneal. Soc., Md. Hist. Soc. Roman Catholic. Home: 52 Phelps Ave Bergenfield NJ 07621 Office: 25 McWilliams Pl Jersey City NJ 07302

MILLER, DEBRA LEE, insurance agency executive; b. Tulsa, Nov. 4, 1955; d. Raymond L. and Vivian Lee Moreland; m. Greg Miller, June 5, 1982 (div. Apr. 1985); 1 child, Tishey Lee. B.S., Okla. State U., 1977. Adminstrv. asst. United Gen. Agy., Inc., Tulsa, 1977-79, exec. v.p., 1979-84, pres., 1984—; mem. ins. task force Nat. Grocers Assn., Washington, 1985. Cert. ins. counselor Soc. Cert. Ins. Counselors. Mem. Profl. Ins. Agts. of Okla., Ins. Women of Tulsa, Ind. Ins. Agts. of Tulsa, Tulsa C. of C., Okla. Retail Grocers Assn. Republican. Club: Tulsa Panhellenic Soc. Home: 1506 E 68th Pl Tulsa OK 74136 Office: United Gen Agy Inc 1212 E 58th St Tulsa OK 74105

MILLER, DIANE DORIS, real estate executive, consultant; b. Sacramento, Calif., Jan. 18, 1954; d. George Campbell and Doris Lucille (Benninger) M. B.A., U. Pacific, 1976; B.A., Golden Gate U., 1985, M.B.A., 1986. Mgr., A.G. Spanos, Sacramento, 1977-81, Lee Sammis, Sacramento, 1981-83; vice pres. Consolidated Capital, San Francisco, 1983-85; pres. D. Miller & Co., Sacramento, 1986—. Bd. dirs. Sacramento Symphony, 1982-84, Sacramento Ballet, 1983-84, Oakland Ballet, Calif., 1984-85. Named Vol. of Yr. Junior League, 1983. Mem. U. Pacific Alumni Assn. (bd. dirs. 1978-85). Republican. Avocations: ballet; water sports.

MILLER, DIANE DROPSEY, hospital administrator; b. Gary, Ind., Apr. 29, 1929; d. Lawrence Alton and Tirzah Catherine (Butler) Dorsey Dropsey; children—Michael, Phillip, William, David. R.N., Gary Meth. Hosp. Sch. Nursing, 1952. Staff nurse Gary Meth. Hosp., Ind., 1952-53, asst. head nurse, 1960, night supr., 1961-62; office nurse Dr. H.M. English, Gary, 1953-54; pvt. duty nursing, Gary, 1954-60; nursing services adminstr. Harrison County Hosp., Corydon, Ind., 1962-70, assoc. exec. dir., 1970—; cons. Accreditation Standards for Hosps., Ind. and Ky., 1978-85. Mem. adv. com. Ind. U. Sch. Nursing, 1981-83; mem. Fed. Relations Com., Ind., 1984; bd. dirs. Harrison County Hosp. Found., 1985—. Mem. Am. Soc. Nursing Service Adminstrs. (membership com. 1981-82), Am. Nurses Assn., Bus. and Profl. Women's Assn. (v.p. 1976; Outstanding Woman of Yr. 1985), Nursing Adminstrn. Council, Meth. Hosp. Sch. Nursing Alumni (past pres.), Ind. Soc. Nursing Service Adminstrs. (past pres., bd. dirs. 1976-77, 79, 80, 81, 83), Ind. State Bd. Nursing (registration and edn. com.), Ind. State Nurses Assn. (commn. on practice 1983), Ind. Hosp. Assn., Southeastern Ind. Soc. Hosp. Nursing Service Adminstrs. (past pres.). Democrat. Methodist. Home: 425 Williar Ave Corydon IN 47112 Office: Harrison County Hosp 245 Atwood St Corydon IN 47112

MILLER, DIANE MARIE, financial planning company executive; b. Burbank, Calif., July 18, 1945; d. Garnett Addison and May (Hope-Doeg) Smith; m. Floyd George Miller, Sept. 10, 1965 (div. 1979); children—Jeanne Nicole, Anthony Michael. B.A. in History, U. Calif.-San Diego, 1972, postgrad., 1974. Cert. financial planner. Probation officer, family counselor San Diego County, 1974-78; fin. planner Conn. Gen., San Diego, 1978-80, Capital Growth Planning, El Cajon, Calif., 1980-81; pres. Exec. fin. planning, San Diego, 1981—; cons. Home Fed. Savings and Loan Trust Dept., San Diego, 1982-84. Editor and contbr. to newsletter Investor Outlook. Mem. Internat. Assn. for Fin. Planners (pub. relations com. 1982-83), Inst. for Cert. Fin. Planners, Women Bus. Owners Assn. (pres. 1983-84), Nat. Assn. Women Bus. Owners (nat. membership chmn. 1984-85), San Diego C. of C. (nominated outstanding bus. owner of yr. 1983). Club: Atlas (San Diego). Avocations: tennis, aerobics, weight lifting, skiing. Office: Exec Fin Planning 2650 Camino del Rio N #302 San Diego CA 92108

MILLER, DORIS DERFLINGER, county official; b. Front Royal, Va., Jan. 28, 1944; d. Irvin R. and Otis (Sealock) Derflinger; m. Larry Ralph Miller, June 12, 1965; 1 child, Cindy Jo. A.S. in Bus. and Acctg., Roller Bus. Coll., Front Royal, 1964. Sec. Office Commonwealth Atty., Front Royal, 1964-66; dep. treas. County of Warren, Va., 1966-76, treas., 1976—; mem. Warren County Fin. Com., 1976—. Mem., poll worker Warren County Democratic Com., 1976—; treas. Bennett's Chapel Methodist Ch., Warren County, 1978—. Recipient cert. appreciation Am. Heart Assn., 1980, cert. appreciation Robb for Gov. Campaign, 1982. Mem. Treas.'s Assn. Va., Local Govt. Ofcls. Conf., Front Royal/Warren County C. of C., Jefferson Club Va. Avocations: gardening; cooking; pottery. Home: Route 4 Box 415 Front Royal VA 22630 Office: Warren County Treas's Office Warren County Courthouse Front Royal VA 22630

MILLER, DORIS MARIE, veterinary pathologist; b. Sylvester, Ga., Apr. 5, 1951; d. Otis Zack and Rita Mary (Andrew) Miller, Sr. D.V.M., U. Ga., 1976, M.S. in Vet. Pathology, 1979, Ph.D., 1981. Diplomate Am. Coll. Vet. Pathologists. Vet. practitioner Blanding Blvd. Animal Clinic, Jacksonville, Fla., 1976-77; instr. Tifton Diagnostic Lab. (Ga.), 1977-78; asst. prof. Coll. Vet. Medicine, U. Ga., Athens, 1981—, organizer, dir. pet visitation-pet therapy program, 1984—. Contbr. articles, revs. and tutorial programs to profl. lit. Advisor Explorer post Athens council Boy Scouts Am., 1983—. Faculty Improvement grantee U. Ga., 1983; reproductive pathology in swine grantee Vet. Med. Expt. Sta., Athens, 1978, 82, 83. Mem. Am. Coll. Vet. Pathologists, Ga. Vet. Med. Assn., Fla. Vet. Med. Assn., AVMA, Athens Kennel Club, Am. Legion Aux., AAUW, Omega Tau Sigma (alumni treas. 1981—, council sec. 1981—), Phi Zeta. Office: Athens Diagnostic Lab Coll of Veterinary Medicine U of Ga Athens GA 30602

MILLER, DORIS PARSONS, artist; b. Bangor, Pa., Aug. 6, 1927; d. Alfred H. and Evelyn May P.; student Baum Sch. Art, Allentown, Pa., 1955-58; pvt. studies in art; m. Lewis E. Miller, June 10, 1946; 1 son, Alex Lewis. Portrait artist, 1955-63; pvt. studio artist, Wyomissing, Pa., 1977—; works represented in pvt. and permanent collections in U.S.; one-woman shows include: Nat. Bank of Boyertown, Jacksonwald, Reading, Pa., 1981; group shows: Berks Art Alliance, 1978-80, Nat. Portrait Seminar, N.Y.C., 1979, Catherine Lorillard Wolfe Art Club, N.Y.C., 1980. Sec. women's com. Reading Symphony Orch., 1972-77. Mem. Berks Art Alliance, Berks Art Council (1st prize 1980), Portrait Club Am., Catherine Lorillard Wolfe Art Club (asso.), DAR (Nat. award of excellence 1982), Daus. Am. Colonists (chpt. librarian 1982—). Episcopalian. Home: 19 Birchwood Rd Wyomissing PA 19610

MILLER, ELEANOR CARROLL, broadcasting company executive; b. Asheboro, N.C., June 7, 1949; d. Garnet Edward and Willie Berte (Upchurch) M.; B.A. magna cum laude, Duke U., 1971; postgrad. Université de Bordeaux, 1972-73. Translator, Algerian Embassy, Washington, 1973-74; public affairs projects coordinator Corp. for Public Broadcasting, 1974-76, asst. to publs. mgr., 1976-78, publs. mgr., 1981-83, acting dir. corporate communications, 1984—; editor Public Telecommunications Letter, Nat. Assn. Ednl. Broadcasters, 1978-79, Public Telecommunications Review, 1980-81. Mem. Am. Women in Radio and TV, Women in Communications, Broadcast Promotion Mkgt. Execs., Phi Beta Kappa. Club: Nat. Press. Office: Corp for Public Broadcasting 1111 16th St NW Washington DC 20036

MILLER, ELIZABETH CAVERT, oncologist, educator; b. Mpls., May 2, 1920; B.S., U. Minn., 1941; M.S., U. Wis., 1943, Ph.D. in Biochemistry, 1945; D.Sc. (hon.) Med. Coll. Wis., 1982. Finney-Howell Found. med. research fellow in oncology Med. Center, U. Wis., Madison, 1945-47, instr. to asso. prof., 1947-69, prof. oncology, 1969-80, Van Rensselaer Potter prof., 1980—, WARF sr. disting. research prof., 1984—. Co-recipient Teplitz-Langer award Ann Langer Cancer Research Found., 1963, Lucy Wortham James award James Ewing Soc., 1965, Papanicolaou Research award Papanicolaou Cancer Research Inst., 1975, Lewis S. Rosenstiel award Brandeis U., 1976, nat. award basic sci. Am. Cancer Soc., 1977; Bertner award in cancer research M.D. Anderson Hosp. and Tumor Inst., 1971, Wis. Nat. Div. award Am. Cancer Soc., 1973, Founders award Chem. Industry Inst. Toxicology, 1978, Bristol-Myers award Cancer Research, 1978, internat. ann. award Gairdner Found., 1978, Griffuel prize, 1978, Lewis and Bert Freedman award in biochemistry N.Y. Acad. Sci., 1979, Mott award Gen. Motors Found., 1980. Fellow Wis. Acad. Scis.; mem. Nat. Acad. Sci., Am. Soc. Biol. Chemists, Am. Assn. Cancer Research. Researcher exptl. chem. carcinogenesis. Office: McArdle Lab University of Wisconsin 450 N Randall Ave Madison WI 53706

MILLER, ELIZABETH G., realty executive; b. Columbus, Ind., Mar. 2, 1948; d. J. Irwin and Xenia S. (Simons) M.; B.A., Goucher Coll., 1970; M.A., Courtauld Inst. Art, U. London, 1972; M.B.A., Columbia U., 1976; m. R. Alan Melting May 3, 1980; children—Benjamin Simons Melting, Andrew Wellons Melting, AnnaCatherine Solberg Miller. Chester Dale fellow Met. Mus. Art, N.Y.C., 1972-73; program dir. Archtl. League N.Y., N.Y.C., 1973-74; bus. mgr. Fawcett Books Group, CBS Publs., Inc., N.Y.C., 1976-78; bus. mgr. Mus. Contemporary Art, Chgo., 1978-80; project mgr. Tishman Realty & Constrn. Co., Inc., N.Y.C., 1980-82; v.p. constrn. Battery Park City Authority, N.Y.C., 1982-84; v.p. constrn. The Georgetown Group, 1984-86; ptnr. ER Assocs., 1986—. Bd. dirs. Irwin-Sweeney-Miller Found. (Ind.), 1976—, Archtl. History Found., N.Y.C., 1978—, Goucher Coll., Md., 1981—. Mem. Mcpl. Art Soc. N.Y., 1981—. Address: 610 West End Ave Apt 5B New York NY 10024

MILLER, ELIZABETH LOUISE, hypnotist, business consultant; b. Chattanooga, May 12, 1930; d. Cecil C. and Carolyn Windom (Mayton) Noecker; student Mich. State U., 1948; grad. Williams Inst. Hypnological Sci. and Research, 1969; m. Robert Andrew Miller, July 1949 (dec.); 1 dau., Pamela Kay Miller Painschab. Owner, operator Mondovi Theatre (Wis.), 1949-69; woman's editor Eau Claire (Wis.) Leader, 1965-66, La Crosse (Wis.) Tribune, 1966-69; exec. editor Skyway News, Mpls., 1970-71; promotional mgr. Barberio Corp., Mpls., 1972-73; assoc. Culler & Assos., Mpls., 1975—; pres. Hypnotism Inst. Inc., La Crosse, 1974—, Mpls., 1978—; tchr., lectr., cons. in field. Active Republican Party. Recipient Showmanship citation Allied Theatre Owners, 1964, citation Biafran Govt., 1967, award USAF, 1967. Mem. Assn. Advancement Ethical Hypnosis, Bus. and Profl. Women, Wis. Regional Writers Assn. Methodist. Author: Just People of the Friendly Valley, 1965; I Am the Mississippi, 1975. Home: 4516 58th Ave N #120 Minneapolis MN 55429

MILLER, ELMA FRANCES, nurse; b. Connersville, Ind., Apr. 2, 1926; d. Charles Elmer and Bessie Belle (Haley) Winkle; m. Lawarence A. Miller, Jr., Feb. 10, 1951; (div. May 1966); children—Vicki Ann, Deborah S., Edward E. Grad., Reid Meml. Hosp. Sch. of Nursing, Richmond, Ind., 1949; qualified mental retardation profl. Wright State U., 1985-86. R.N., Ind., Ohio. Surg. nurse Reid Meml. Hosp., 1950-51; office nurse, Richmond, 1951-74; charge nurse Friends Fellowship, also Heritage House Nursing Home, Richmond, 1974-81, Heartland Cedar Springs, New Paris, Ohio, 1981—. Republican. Lutheran. Lodges: Order of Eastern Star (past matron, past grand page Ind. Grand chpt.), White Shrine of Jerusalem (past worthy high priestess Manetho Shrine 15, supreme instr. Manetho Shrine 15, 1985—). Avocations: knitting, crocheting. Home: 224 SW 19th St Richmond IN 47374

MILLER, ELOUISE DARLENE, educator; b. Alton, Kans., Nov. 24, 1930; d. Clarence Sylvester and Laura Areta (Sparks) M. B.S., Ft. Hays State U., 1956, M.S., 1961, Ed.S., 1970; postgrad. Temple U., 1966. Tchrs. cert., Kans. Tchr. Liberty Sch., Alton, Kans., 1948-49, Mt. Hope Sch., Osborne, Kans., 1949-50, Woodston Grade Sch., Kans., 1950-55; 1st grade tchr. United Sch. Dist. 489, Hays, Kans., 1956-65, tchr. kindergarten, 1965—, kindergarten chmn., 1983—; tchr. remedial reading, fed. program, Hays, summers, 1970—. Primary supt. Meth. Sunday Sch., Hays, 1976—. Mem. Internat. Reading Assn. (charter pres. 1965-67, NEA (pres. Hays 1962-63, del. Kans. 1980—), AAUW, Meth. Ch. Women, Kans. Hist. Soc., Hays Arts Council, Delta Tau (pres. Hays 1959-61), Delta Kappa Gamma, Phi Delta Kappa, Phi Kappa Phi. Avocations: traveling; reading; jogging; bicycling. Home: 2729 Hickory St Hays KS 67601 Office: Lincoln Sch 1906 Ash St Hays KS 67601

MILLER, ELVA RUBY CONNES (MRS. JOHN R. MILLER), civic worker; b. Joplin, Mo.; d. Edward and Ada (Martin) Connes; student Pomona Coll., part-time, 1936-56; m. John R. Miller, Jan. 17, 1934 (dec. Nov. 1968). Entertainer various night clubs, supper clubs, also Hollywood Bowl, 1967; tv appearances; rec. artist Capitol Records, from 1966, Amaret Records, from 1969; appeared in motion pictures. Active Girl Scouts U.S.A., 1933-58; hon. mem. Mayor's Com. for Sr. Citizens, Los Angeles, 1966active Los Angeles Mus. of Art, Music Ctr. of Los Angeles County. Recipient awards including Thanks badge Girl Scouts U.S.A., 1956, Key to City, Mayor San Diego, 1967, plaque Dept. of Def. for trip to Viet Nam, 1967. Mem. Gen. Alumni Assn. U. So. Calif. (life), DAV Comdrs. Club. Republican. Clubs: Northridge Rep. Women, Calif. Rep. Home: 9585 Reseda Blvd Northridge CA 91324

MILLER, ERICA T(ILLINGHAST), aesthetician, skincare and cosmetics company executive, writer; b. Laramie, Wyo., Oct. 17, 1950; d. Walter McNab and Martha (Brown) M. Student Sophia U., Tokyo, 1969-72, U. Md., Tokyo, 1969-72, Simultaneous Interpreting Acad. Tokyo, 1974; cert. Christian Shaw Sch. Beauty, London, 1973, Kanebo Total Beauty Acad., 1974; internat. diploma CIDESCO, 1977. Instr., Nakano Am. English Ctr., Tokyo, 1969-72; instr., researcher Kanebo Cosmetics Inc., Tokyo, 1973-76, internat. cons., 1976—; dir. edn. Aestheticians Internat., Dallas, 1976-79; pres. Correlations Inc., Dallas, 1979—; cons. Nieman Marcus Greenhouse, Arlington, Tex., 1981—. Assoc. pub., editor Aesthetics World Mag., 1980-85. Contbr. articles to various publs.; translator tech. film. Mem. Aestheticians Internat. (dir. edn. 1976-79), Am. Inst. Esthetics (lectr.), Nat. Hairdressers and Cosmetology Assn. (co-dir. skin care sect. aesthetics com.), Dallas C. of C., North Dallas C. of C. Republican. Episcopalian. Avocations: tennis; English riding; swimming; care and training of animals. Office: Correlations Inc 4803 W Lovers Ln Dallas TX 75209

MILLER, EUGENIA PORRETTA, educational and training specialist, researcher; b. Silver Creek, Pa., July 12, 1928; d. Vincent James and Pietrina (Calabrese) Porretta; m. George David Miller, Oct. 15, 1966 (dec. July 1980). B.S., Mansfield U., 1950; M.S., SUNY-Albany, 1956; profl. diploma Columbia U., 1965; Ph.D., U. N.Mex., 1979. Cert. sch. dist. adminstr., tchr. English, French, Spanish, English supr., N.Y. Tchr. Stratford Sch. Dist., N.Y., 1950-55, Johnstown High Sch., N.Y., 1955-56; tchr. Clarkstown Sch. Dist., New City, N.Y., 1956-60, chmn. English dept., 1960-68, sch. adminstr., 1968-78; tng. specialist BDM Corp., Albuquerque, 1980—; cons. in field, 1960-75; researcher S.W. Research, Albuquerque, 1976-77. Author: (children's book) Pedro and Tony, 1950. Author, dir. films: Detour, 1963, The Junk Yard, 1964, Fiesta and Siesta, 1972. Active United Way, Albuquerque, 1982. Edn. Profl. Devel. Act grantee U. Iowa, Iowa City, 1969; N.Y. State grantee Columbia U., 1963. Mem. Am. Soc. Tng. and Devel., Met. Opera Guild, Nat. Soc. for Performance Inst., Querque Crows, Alpha Psi Omega, Kappa Delta Pi, Phi Delta Kappa. Republican. Roman Catholic. Home: 1801 Sunset Rd Rio Rancho NM 87124 Office: BDM Corp 1801 Randolph Rd Albuquerque NM 87106

MILLER, FRANCES HALL, lawyer, educator; b. Boston, Dec. 25, 1938; d. Addison Smith and Frances Winston (Ivey) Hall; m. Hugh Miller, June 3, 1961; children—Hugh III, Christopher Graham. A.B., Mt. Holyoke Coll., 1960; J.D. cum laude, Boston U., 1965; postgrad. London Sch. Econs. (Eng.), 1965-66. Bar: Mass. Prof. law Boston U., 1968—, prof. Med. Sch. 1983—; assoc. Powers & Hall, Boston, 1973-76; of counsel Bowker, Elmes, Perkins, Mecsas & Gerrard, Boston, 1976—; commr. Mass. Rate Setting Commn., 1974; mem. ethical-legal bd. Urban Med. Group, Inc., Boston, 1983-85; mem. adv. bd. Adolescent Consultation Service, Inc., Cambridge, 1980—; chmn. Mass. Health Facilities Appeals Bd., 1986—. Contbr. articles to profl. jours. Trustee Mt. Holyoke Coll., South Hadley, Mass., 1976-81; mem. human rights rev. com. Judge Baker Clinic of Children's Hosp., Boston, 1976—; bd. dirs. New Eng. Legal Found., Boston, 1982—. W.K. Kellogg Found. fellow, Battle Creek, Mich., 1983-86. Mem. ABA (spl. com. on profl. med. liability reform). Club: Longwood Cricket (sec. 1981, gov. 1980-83). Office: Boston U Sch of Law 765 Commonwealth Ave Boston MA 02215

MILLER, GENEVIEVE, medical historian; b. Butler, Pa., Oct. 15, 1914; d. Charles Russell and Genevieve (Wolford) M. A.B., Goucher Coll., 1935; M.A., Johns Hopkins U., 1939; Ph.D., Cornell U., 1955. Asst. in history of medicine Johns Hopkins Inst. of History of Medicine, Balt., 1943-44, instr., 1945-48, research assoc., 1979—; asst. prof. history of medicine Sch. Medicine, Case Western Res. U., Cleve., 1953-67, assoc. prof., 1967-79, assoc. prof. emeritus, 1979—; research assoc. in med. history Cleve. Med. Library Assn., 1953-62, curator Howard Dittrick Mus. of Hist. Medicine, 1962-67, dir. Howard Dittrick Mus. Hist. Medicine, 1967-79. Author: William Beaumont's Formative Years: Two Early Notebooks 1811-1821, 1946; The Adoption of Inoculation for Smallpox in England and France (William H. Welch medal Am. Assn. for History of Medicine 1962), 1957; Bibliography of the History of Medicine of the U.S. and Canada, 1939-1960, 1964; Bibliography of the Writings of Henry E. Sigerist, 1966; Letters of Edward Jenner and Other Documents Concerning the Early History of Vaccination, 1983; assoc. editor Bull. of History of Medicine, 1944-48, acting editor, 1948, mem. adv. editorial bd. 1960—; mem. bd. editors Jour. of History of Medicine and Allied Scis., 1948-65; editor Bull. of Cleve. Med. Library, 1954-72; contbr. articles in field to profl. jours. Am. Council Learned Socs. fellow, 1948-50; Dean Van Meter fellow, 1953-54. Alumna trustee Goucher Coll., Balt., 1966-69. Hon. fellow Cleve. Med. Library Assn.; mem. Am. Assn. for History of Medicine (pres. 1978-80, mem. council 1960-63), Am. Hist. Assn., Internat. Soc. for History of Medicine, Soc. Archtl. Historians, Phi Beta Kappa; corr. mem. fgn. socs. for history of medicine. Democrat. Club: Johns Hopkins (Balt). Home: 914 Dulaney Valley Ct Apt 4 Towson MD 21204 Office: Johns Hopkins Institute of the History of Medicine 1900 E Monument St Baltimore MD 21205

MILLER, GERALDINE, clinical psychologist; b. Jersey City, Nov. 30, 1946; d. Gerard and Nora M.; m. Walter Greenberg. B.A., magna cum laude, CCNY, 1971; M.Ph., CUNY, 1979, Ph.D., 1980. Clin. intern Columbia Presbyn. Med. Center, N.Y. State Psychiat. Inst., N.Y.C., 1974-75; staff psychologist Albert Einstein Med. Coll. Substance Abuse Service, Bronx, 1978-79; assoc. psychologist Pilgrim Psychiat. Center, West Brentwood, L.I., 1980—, treatment team leader, 1985—. Sec., patient relations com. Presbyn. Hosp. Community Health Council, 1979-82. Recipient numerous awards CCNY, Employee Recognition award Pilgrim Psychiat. Center, 1981, 84. Lic. psychologist, N.Y. Mem. Am. Psychol. Assn. (div. membership chmn. clin. psychology sect. 1982—), Eastern Psychol. Assn., N.Y. State Psychol. Assn. (Ph.D. dissertation award 1982), N.Y. Soc. Clin. Psychologists, Suffolk County Psychol. Assn., Phi Beta Kappa.

MILLER, GLORIA M., county govt. ofcl.; b. Mercer County, Pa., Oct. 24, 1940; d. Cecil F. and Edith H. (Bittler) Gill; B.S. in Bus. Adminstrn., Youngstown (Ohio) State U., 1966; divorced; 1 son, Mark William. Sr. acct. Mort-Bohn Assos., C.P.A.s, Sharon, Pa., 1963-67; asst. controller Hynes Steel Products Co., Youngstown, 1967-70; exec. dir. Crawford County Community Action Agy., Meadville, Pa., 1970-73; planning and devel. dir. Multi-County Human Resources Corp., Meadville, 1973-76; adminstr., chief exec. officer Mercer County Consortium Services, Inc., Clark, Pa., 1976—; bd. dirs., regional rep. Nat. Assn. County Employment and Tng. Adminstrn., 1978-81; bd. dirs., sec. Mercer County Area Agy. Aging, 1976-82; v.p. Mid-Atlantic Manpower Profl. Assn., 1979-80; gen. adv. com. Mercer County Area Vocat. Tech. Sch., Mercer, 1979-82, Venango County Area Vocat. Tech. Sch., Oil City, Pa., 1981-82. Recipient various certs. appreciation. Mem. Am. Mgmt. Assn., Am. Soc. Tng. and Devel. Democrat. Presbyterian. Home: PO Box 171 12 N Main St Greenville PA 16125 Office: PO Box 462 3665 Valley View Rd Clark PA 16113

MILLER, HARRIET SANDERS, art center executive; b. N.Y.C., Apr. 18, 1926; d. Herman and Dorothy (Silbert) Sanders; m. Milton H. Miller, June 27, 1948; children—Bruce, Jeffrey, Marcie Miller Homer. A.B., Ind. U., 1947; M.A., Columbia U. Tchrs. Coll., 1948; M.S. in Painting, U. Wis., 1962, M.F.A. in Sculpture, 1967; grad. mus. mgmt. seminar U. Calif.-Berkeley, 1981. Founder, dir. Madison Art Ctr. Sch., Wis., 1963-72; instr. painting, sculpture Douglas Coll., Vancouver, B.C., Can., 1972-78; acting dir. continuing edn. humanities U.B.C., Vancouver, 1976-77; exec. dir. Palos Verdes Art Ctr., Calif., 1978-84; dir. City Los Angeles Jr. Art Ctr., 1984—; exec. council Los Angeles Cultural Affairs Dept., 1984—; adv. bd. Children's Mus., Los Angeles, 1984—, Performing Tree, Los Angeles, 1984—. Exhibiting artist painting Gallery Allen, Vancouver, 1974, exhibiting artist sculpture Gallery One, Toronto, Can., 1977, Linda Farris Gallery, Seattle, 1978, Gallery One, Los Angeles, 1979. Recipient Events award Internat. Congress World Fed. Mental Health, Vancouver, 1977, Playboard Cover Yo-Yo-Ma, Vancouver, 1974. Mem. Am. Assn. Mus., We. Assn. Mus. Office: City of Los Angeles Jr Arts Ctr 4814 Hollywood Blvd Los Angeles CA 90027

MILLER, HEATHER ROSS, author, educator; b. Albemarle, N.C., Sept. 15, 1939; d. Fred E. and Geneva (Smith) Ross; m. Clyde H. Miller, Feb. 14, 1960; children—Melissa, Kirk. B.A., U. N.C.-Greensboro, 1961, M.F.A., 1969; Litt.D. (hon.), Meth. Coll., Fayetteville, N.C., 1985. Instr. English, Southeastern Community Coll., Whiteville, N.C., 1969-71, Stanly Tech. Coll., Albemarle, N.C., 1973-76; assoc. prof. Pfeiffer Coll., Misenheimer, N.C., 1976-83; assoc. prof. dept. English, U. Ark., Fayetteville, 1983—. Author: (novels) The Edge of the Woods, 1964, Tenants of the House, 1966, Gone A Hundred Miles, 1968, A Spiritual Divorce, 1975, Love Offering, 1985; (poetry) The Wind Southerly, 1967, Horse, Horse, Tyger, Tyger, 1974, Adam's First Wife, 1983. Nat. Endowment for Arts fellow, 1968, 73, 79; recipient N.C. medal for lit. State of N.C., 1983. Office: U Ark Dept English Fayetteville AR 72701

MILLER, HEINRICH BONNIE, state senator; b. Dec. 6, 1938. B.S., Valley City State Coll., 1959. Mem. N.D. Senate. Del. Democratic Nat. Conv., 1976. Office: ND Senate State Capitol Bismarck ND 58505*

MILLER, HELEN MARIE DILLEN (MRS. J. CARTER MILLER), bus. exec.; b. Sedalia, Mo.; d. John Barney and Lulu (Blume) Dillen; student Central Coll., 1936-37; m. J. Carter Miller, Dec. 3, 1941; 1 son, J. Carter. Sec.-treas. Midwest Supply Co., Lansing, Ill., 1946—, Midwest Supply Co. of Can., 1946—; sec.-treas. Carter Controls, Inc., Lansing, also Livonia, Mich., 1952—, v.p., 1956—; v.p. Carter Controls Internat., Windsor, Can., Antwerp, Belgium, 1960—; sec.-treas. Carter Controls U.K. Ltd., Sheffield, Eng., Carter Controls, GmbH, Busingen, Germany, Carter Controls, A.G., Schaffhausen, Switzerland. Social worker ARC, Hammond, Ind., 1942-44. Mem. Principia Patrons No. Ind. (pres. 1963-65), Chgo. Symphony, Sarah Siddons Soc., Chgo. Art Inst. Christian Scientist. Clubs: Principia Mothers (dir. Chgo. 1962-64); Fortnightly, Woman's Athletic (Chgo.); Woodmar Country (Hammond); Everglades (Palm Beach, Fla.). Home: 1731 Wilson Ave Munster IN 46321 also Ibis Isle Rd Palm Beach FL Office: 2800 Bernice Rd Lansing IL 60438

MILLER, JACQUELINE K. THOMSON, education/development consultant; b. Flora, Inc., March 5, 1940; d. Jack O. and Betty L. (Tolen) T.; children—Elizabeth Ann Miller-Frederick, Victoria Lynne Miller. Assoc. Sci., Mankato State U., 1978; B.A., Metro State U., St. Paul, 1980; M.A., St. Mary's Coll., 1982. Instr. adult edn. Iowa Community Colls. and YMCA, 1970-75; dir. aquatics Faribault Family YMCA and Faribault Community Services, Minn., 1975-78; tech. sales/tng. rep. Ames div. Miles Labs., Mpls., 1978-80; med. lab. instr. Normandale Community Coll., Boomington, Minn., 1978-80; staff edn. coordinator St. Joseph's Hosp., Marshfield, Wis., 1981-84; dir. edn. services Fairview Ridges Hosp., Burnsville, Minn., 1984-85; owner, prin. J. Miller Assocs., Burnsville, 1979—. Developer wellness program Life Styling, 1979, mobile fitness test ctr. Health on Wheels, 1982; author-dir. video programs Body Mechanics, 1982. Chmn. Girl Scouts, Kokomo, Ind., 1964-69; vol. swim instr. ARC, Corning, Iowa, 1970-75, Faribault, Minn., 1975-78. Recipient Traveling Art awards Ia. State Lending Library, Des Moines, Iowa, 1973-74; artist in residence Corning Community Schs., Iowa, 1972. Mem. Am. Soc. Tng. and Devel. (bd. dirs. Central Wis. 1982-83, mem. career devel. task force So. Minn. 1986, mem. program com. 1985-86), Nat. Wellness Assn. (nat. membership chmn. 1983-85), Am. Soc. Health Edn. and Tng., Am. Soc. Med. Technologists, Am. Soc. Clin. Pathologists, Nat. Assn. Female Execs., Delta Kappa Gamma. Episcopalian. Avocations: art; swimming; gardening; sailing. Home: 12139 Oak Leaf Ct Burnsville MN 55337 Office: J Miller Assocs Box 1377 Burnsville MN 55337

MILLER, JACQUELINE WINSLOW, library administrator; b. N.Y.C., Apr. 15, 1935; d. Lynward Roosevelt and Sarah Ellen (Grevious) Winslow; B.A. in English, Morgan State Coll., 1957; M.L.S., Pratt Inst., N.Y.C., 1960; m. Percy St. Clair Miller, June 29, 1968; 1 son, Percy Scott. Young teen librarian trainee Bklyn. Pub. Library, 1957-59, reading improvement instr., 1959-60, young teen specialist, 1960-63, br. librarian, 1963-64; dir. young teen services, 1964-68; head extension services New Rochelle Public Library (N.Y.). 1969-70; br. adminstr. Yonkers Pub. Library (N.Y.) 1970-75, dir. library, 1975—; mem. Commr.'s Com. on State-Wide Library Devel., 1980; resource person N.Y. State task force on fed. depository library service, 1982. Mem. Colonial Heights Assn. Taxpayers, Yonkers Employment Service for Srs., Inc.; mem. adv. com. Work Opportunity Referrals for Kids; mem. Westchester adv. council Pratt Inst., 1978-84, pres., 1978; mem. budget crisis subcom. METRO, 1976; mem. adv. bd. Sta. WEBS, 1980—; mem. Westchester Ednl. Brokering Service, Citizens Library Council N.Y. State; bd. dirs. Class of '88 Community Planning Council of Yonkers. Honored Citizen of Yonkers, Ch. of Our Saviour, 1980; recipient Ann. award Westchester County club Nat. Assn. Negro Bus. and Profl. Women's Clubs, 1981; Community Service award Women's Civic Club of Nepperhan, 1982. Mem. ALA (chpt. pubs. relations com. 1969-70; dir. pub. library assn. div. 1976-80, div. nominating com. 1980-81, div. planning com. 1980-82), Pub. Libraries Assn. N.Y., N.Y. Library Assn. (2d v.p. 1980-81, dir. 1967-68, scholarship and grants com. 1982-84, legis. com. 1978, membership com. 1984, chmn. 1985, 86), Pub. Library Dirs. Assn. (N.Y. State exec. bd. 1976-84), Coalition for Pub. Library Legislation, Westchester Library Assn. (v.p. 1978, pres. 1979), N.Y. Library Club (council 1969-70, 79-82, chmn. publicity com. 1977-78), Nat. Citizens for Pub. Libraries. Home: 219 Grandview Blvd Yonkers NY 10710 Office: 7 Main St Yonkers NY 10701

MILLER, JANE RUTH, poet, creative writing educator; b. N.Y.C., Apr. 27, 1949; d. H. Walter and Florence (Freed) m. B.A., Pa. State U., 1970; M.A., Calif. State U.-Humboldt, 1975; M.F.A., U. Iowa, 1977. Asst. prof Goddard Coll., Plainfield, Vt., 1977-81; writer in residence Writers Community, N.Y.C., 1983-84; assoc. prof. U. Iowa, Iowa City, 1984—. Author: Many Junipers, Heartbeats, 1980; The Greater Leisures, 1983; Black Holes, Black Stockings, 1985. Avocation: piano.

MILLER, JANEL HOWELL, psychologist; b. Boone, N.C., May 18, 1947; d. John Estle and Grace Louise (Hemberger) Howell; B.A., DePauw U., 1969; postgrad. Rice U., 1969; M.A., U. Houston, 1972; Ph.D., Tex. A&M U., 1979; m. C. Rick Miller, Nov. 24, 1968; children—Kimberly, Brian, Audrey, Rachel. Asso. sch. psychologist Houston Ind. Sch. Dist., 1971-74; research psychologist VA Hosp., Houston, 1972; assoc. sch. psychologist Clear Creek Ind. Sch. Dist., Tex., 1974-76; instr. psychology, counseling psychology intern Tex. A. and M. U., 1976-77; clin. psychology intern VA Hosp., Houston, 1977-78; coordinator psychol. services Clear Creek Ind. Sch. Dist., 1978-81, assoc. dir. psychol. services, 1981-82; pvt. practice, Houston, 1982—; faculty U. Houston-Clear Lake, 1984—; adolescent suicide cons., 1984—. DePauw U. Alumni scholar, 1965-69; NIMH fellow U. Houston, 1970-71; lic. clin. psychologist, sch. psychologist; lic. profl. counselor, Tex. Mem. Am. Psychol. Assn., Tex. Psychol. Assn., Houston Psychol. Assn. (media rep. 1984-85), Am. Assn. Marriage and Family Therapists, Tex. Assn. Marriage and Family Therapists, Houston Assn. Marriage and Family Therapists, Tex. Psychotherapy Assn., Tex. Sch. Psychol. Affiliates, Houston Behavior Therapy Assn. Home: 806 Walbrook Dr Houston TX 77062 Office: Southpoint Psychol Services 11550 Fugua St Suite 450 Houston TX 77034

MILLER, JEAN DIENER, training coordinator; b. Chgo., Feb. 20, 1926; d. Eugene Irl and Marian Roberts (Wentworth) Diener; m. Richard Paul Miller, June 21, 1947; children—Timothy E., Patrick R., Thomas E., Peter D., Leslie Anne. B.S., Northwestern U., 1947; M.A. in Teaching, U. Notre Dame, 1967. Cert. secondary tchr., Ind., systems profl. Quality analyst asst. Miles Labs., Inc., Elkhart, Inds., 1943-47, sec. to chief chemist, 1947-48, tech. writer, 1979-80, tng. coordinator, 1980—; sci. tchr. Elkhart Community Schs., 1966-79. Bd. dirs. Elkhart YMCA, 1955-60, Elkhart Family Counseling, 1962-66, Elkhart Mental Health Assn., 1960-62; sec., treas. Trucker's Helper, Inc., 1979—. Nolan scholar, 1946-47. Mem. Assn. Systems Mgmt.; Kappa Kappa Kappa, Delta Zeta (sec. 1946-47). Republican. Methodist. Avocations: backpacking, music, gardening. Home: 51585 Winding Waters Ln Elkhart IN 46514 Office: Miles Labs Inc 1127 Myrtle St Elkhart IN 46515

MILLER, JEANIE, account executive, real estate broker; b. Clovis, Calif., June 26, 1946; d. Kenneth Lynn and Vida Bessie (Wilkinson) Harris; m. Drake Boyce Edward, Sept. 4, 1963 (div. Apr. 1978); children—Steve, Cyndy; m. John Allen Miller, July 16, 1983. Student Fresno City Coll., 1964-66, U. So. Calif., 1980-81, MIT, 1984-85. Real estate broker, Calif. Service rep. Pacific Telephone, Fresno, 1965-75; owner Calif. Design Assoc., Fresno, 1976-77; realtor assoc. Rana Mead Real Estate, Fresno, 1977-81; real estate broker Central Real Estate, Fresno, 1981-82; account exec. ATT, Fresno, 1982-86; loan officer First Interstate Mortgage, 1986—; owner Miller Real Estate, Clovis, 1982—. Mem. Nat. Assn. Female Execs., Fresno C. of C., Western States Corvette Council (bd. dirs. 1982-84), Fresno Bd. Realtors. Democrat. Clubs: Corvettes of Fresno, Women in Bus. Lodge: Jobs Daus. Avocations: car shows; charity events; racquetball; aerobics. Home: 1476 W Locust St Fresno CA 93711

MILLER, JEANNE-MARIE ANDERSON (MRS. NATHAN JOHN MILLER), English educator; b. Washington, Feb. 18, 1937; d. William and Agnes Catherine (Johns) Anderson; B.A., Howard U., 1959, M.A., 1963, Ph.D., 1976; m. Nathan John Miller, Oct. 2, 1960. Instr. dept. English, Howard U., Washington, 1963-76, also asst. dir. Inst. for Arts and Humanities, 1973-75, asst. prof. English, 1976-79, asso. prof., 1979—, asst. to v.p. acad. affairs, 1976—, grad. asst. prof., 1977-79, grad. assoc. prof., 1979—; cons. Am. Studies Assn., 1972-75; cons. several ednl. book pub. cos. Mem. Washington Performing Arts Soc., 1971—, Friends of WETA-TV, 1971—, Mus. African Art, 1971—, Arena Stage Assos., 1972—; chmn. theatre and poetry com. D.C. Public Library for Arts, 1976-79. Ford Found. fellow, 1970-72, So. Fellowships Fund fellow, 1972-74; Am. Council Learned Socs. grantee, 1978-79; NEH grantee, 1981-84. Mem. Nat. Council Tchrs. of English, Coll. English Assn., Am. Studies Assn., Am. Theatre Assn. (editor Black Theatre Bull. 1977—), AAUP, AAUW, LWV, ACLU, Am. Acad. Polit. and Social Sci., Nat. Assn. Women Deans, Adminstrs. and Counselors, Coll. Lang. Assn., MLA, Nat. Assn. Advancement Humanities, Am. Assn. Higher Edn., Assoc. Writers Guild Am., Friends Kennedy Center for Performing Arts. Democrat. Episcopalian. Editor: Realism to Ritual: Form and Style in Black Theatre, 1983. Contbr. articles to profl. jours. Home: 1100 6th St SW Washington DC 20024

MILLER, JILL A., software executive; b. Hanover, N.H., May 8, 1943; d. Ralph K. and Vivian M. (Witt) Andrist; m. A. Richard Miller, Sept. 12, 1965. B.A. in Botany, Conn. Coll., 1965. Programmer, Liberty Mut. Ins. Co., Boston, 1966-67, systems analyst, 1968-69; systems programmer Zayre Corp., Framingham, Mass., 1969-75; ind. cons., Natick, Mass., 1975-78; owner, ptnr. Miller Microcomputer Services, Natick, 1978—. Avocations: quilting; sailing; whales. Home: 61 Lake Shore Rd Natick MA 01760

MILLER, JO CAROLYN, family and marriage counselor, educator; b. Gorman, Tex., Sept. 16, 1942; d. Leonard Lee and Vera Vertie (Robison) Dendy; m. Douglas Terry Barnes, June 1, 1963 (div. June 1975); children—Douglas Alan, Bradley Jason; m. Walton Sansom Miller, Sept. 19, 1982. B.A., Tarleton State U., 1964; M.Ed., N. Tex. State U., 1977. Tchr., Mineral Wells (Tex.) High Sch., 1964-65, Weatherford (Tex.) Middle Sch., 1969-74; counselor, instr. psychology Tarrant County Jr. Coll., Hurst, Tex., 1977-82; pvt. practice family and marriage counseling, Dallas, 1982—. Author: (with Velma Walker, Jeannene Ward) Becoming: A Human Relations Workbook, 1981. Vol. Am. Heart Assn. in Tex., Dallas chpt., 1983-84. Mem. Tex. State Bd. Examiners Profl. Counselors, Tex. Assn. Counseling and Devel., Am. Assn. Counseling and Devel., Am. Mental Health Counselors Assn., North Central Tex. Assn. for Counseling and Devel. Methodist. Clubs: Highland Park Sports, So. Meth. U. Mothers (Dallas). Home: 3556 Binkley Ave Dallas TX 75205

MILLER, JOYCE MCDANIEL, urban planner; b. Jamaica, W.I., June 17, 1930; d. Arthur McDaniel and Laura (Williamson) Hunter; m. Roy P. Miller, Apr. 23, 1949; children—Darryl P., Sharon M. Student Hunter Coll., 1948-50, 71; B.A., Fordham U., 1975; M. Urban Planning, NYU, 1979. Asst. to exec. dir. The Roosevelt Hosp., N.Y.C., 1968-75; asst. dir. Adelphia Hosp., Bklyn., 1976-78; boro coordinator Community Service Soc., N.Y.C., 1979-82; dir. govt. affairs and grants coordinator Harlem div. Urban Devel. Corp., N.Y.C., 1982—; cons. in field. Pres. Convent Neighborhood Assn., Manhattan, N.Y., 1975-80; mem. Community Bd. 9, Manhattan, 1980—; active Democratic Party, Manhattan. Mem. Am. Planning Assn. Clubs: Am. Tennis Assn.; N.Y. Tennis Assn. Inc. (exec. sec. 1979—). Home: 310 Convent Ave Apt 4D New York NY 10031

MILLER, JUDITH ANN, computers in medicine company executive, educator; b. Abilene, Tex., June 14, 1944; d. Frederick William and Mary Jo (Carter) Smith; m. Howard Stanley Miller, Nov. 9, 1963 (div. 1972); children—Phillip, Darrell. A.S., YMCA Community Coll., 1972; B.S., Northeastern Ill. U., 1982; postgrad. Central Mich. U., 1977—. Med. asst. Baylor Med. Ctr., Houston, 1963-65; Rush-Presbyn.-St. Luke's Med. Ctr., Chgo., 1969-74; dir., prof., med. asst. programmer Triton Coll., River Grove, Ill., 1974-79; product specialist Am. Optical Co., Buffalo, 1979-82; dir. customer service, dealer support Bio-logic Systems Corp., Northbrook, Ill., 1982—. Author: Medico-legal Handbook for the Medical Office; contbr. articles to profl. jours. Founder med. asst. curriculum Triton Coll., 1972-78; active NOW, Chgo.; leader Boy Scouts Am., River Forest, Ill., 1972-75. Mem. Am. Assn. Med. Assts. (sec. Chgo. chpt. 1973-74, founder, pres. Triton chpt. 1975), Nat. Network of Women Sales, IBM User's Group, Chgo. Computer Soc., Delta Gamma. Office: Bio-logic Systems Corp 425 Huehl Rd Northbrook IL 60062

MILLER, JUDITH ROBINSON, accountant; b. Danville, Ill., Aug. 25, 1944; d. Walter Kenneth and Ellsbeth (Cepl) Robinson; m. Frederick Thomas Miller, June 21, 1969; children—Scott Michael, Justine Elizabeth. B.S. in Acctg. and Bus. Edn., Ind. U., 1966; M.B.A. in Acctg., Northwestern U., 1969. C.P.A., N.Y. Mem. audit staff Arthur Andersen & Co., Chgo., 1967-68; acct., treas. Bd. Coop. Edn. Services, Port Chester, N.Y., 1972-74, adult edn. instr., 1974-77; fin. analyst Exxon Internat., N.Y.C., 1974-76; mgr. fin. analysis PepsiCo, Inc., Purchase, N.Y., 1976-79, mgr. credit union, 1979-81, mgr. corp. payroll, 1981-85; comptroller Dowling & O'Neil Ins. Agy., 1985—. Bd. dirs. Valhalla Methodist Nursery Sch., N.Y., 1973-75; treas. Valhalla United Meth. Ch., 1974-77, mem. fin. com., 1983-85. Named Credit Union Mgr. of Yr., Nat. Assn. Fed. Credit Unions, Washington, 1980. Mem. Assn. Payroll Mgmt. (pres. bd. dirs. 1982-83), Am. Payroll Assn., Am. Inst. C.P.A.s, N.Y. State Soc. C.P.A.s, Am. Women's Soc. C.P.A.s. Republican. Home: 285 Main St Chatham MA 02633 Office: Dowling & O'Neil Ins Agy Inc 222 W Main St Hyannis MA 02601

MILLER, JUDY ANN FRANCES, county ofcl.; b. Cleve., Sept. 16, 1940; d. Frank Albert Jagoda and Antoinette (Serba) Parise; B.S. in Public Adminstrn., U. Ariz., 1963. Supr. social services dept. Contra Costa County, Calif., 1969-72, dir. allied services/projects adminstrn., 1972-76, dir. community services adminstrn., 1976-77, dir. dept. manpower programs, 1977—. Mem. exec. com. Combined Assn. Prime Sponsor Adminstrs. Recipient for services integration Nat. Assn. Counties, 1974; award for job placements Dept. Labor, 1978. Mem. Am. Mgmt. Assn., Am. Soc. Public Adminstrs., Nat. Assn. Employment and Tng. Adminstrs. (v.p. 1980-81), Phi Chi Theta. Roman Catholic. Office: 2425 Bisso Ln Suite 100 Concord CA 94520

MILLER, JUNE FASESKY, retail department store public relations executive; b. Bethlehem, Pa., June 27, 1955; d. Walter Franklin and Frances Helene (Broczkowski) Fasesky; m. Michael David Miller, Jan. 1, 1977. B.A. in Journalism, Lehigh U., 1977. Exec. trainee Bamberger's, Newark, 1977, employee communications asst. mgr., 1977-78; mdse. tng. coordinator Chas. A. Stevens, Chgo., 1978-80, fashion events coordinator, 1980, media/mktg. coordinator, 1980-81; employment communications supr. J. W. Robinson's, Los Angeles, 1981, mdse. promotions mgr., 1981-82, spl. programs mgr., 1982-84; sr. mgr. spl. events The Broadway, Los Angeles, 1984-86; div. v.p. pub. relations and spl. events Los Angeles div. The Broadway, 1986—. Home: 1014 Arroyo Dr #1 South Pasadena CA 91030 Office: The Broadway 3880 N Mission Rd Los Angeles CA 90031

MILLER, KAREN BAREDZIAK, chem. co. exec.; b. Chgo., Feb. 12, 1951; d. Joseph Henry and Alice Ann (Tatosian) Baredziak; B.A., Ill. State U., 1973; m. Craig Stephen Miller, Nov. 24, 1973. With Velsicol Chem. Corp., Chgo., 1973—, internat. acctg. clk., 1973-76, asst. credit mgr., 1976-78, corp. credit mgr., 1978—, vice-chmn. Agri Export Credit Group, 1981—. Mem. VFW Aux. (treas.), Nat. Assn. Credit Mgrs., Nat. Chem. Credit Assn. (div. sec.-treas. 1982-83), Internat. Credit Execs., Fgn. Credit Interchange Bur., Agri Export Credit Group. Office: 341 E Ohio St Chicago IL 60611

MILLER, KAREN FARISH, clergywoman; b. Fredericksburg, Va., Oct. 3, 1955; d. Joseph Key and Ruby Jess (Galloway) Farish; m. Perry Stanton Miller, May 3, 1980. B.S., So. Methodist U., 1977; M.Div., Duke U., 1981. Minister of edn. Highland United Meth. Ch., Raleigh, N.C., 1979-81; assoc. minister Lambuth Meml. United Meth., Jackson, Tenn., 1981-83; minister Maple Spring United Meth. Ch., Benton, Ky., 1983—; trustee Lakeshore United Meth. Assembly, Camden, Tenn., 1982—; supervising pastor for candidates to United Meth. Ministry, 1984—. Bd. dirs. Purchase Area Spouse Abuse Ctr., Ky., 1985—; sponsor Parents Anonymous of Marshall County, Ky., 1985. Named Young Career Woman 1984, Ky., Fedn. Bus. and Profl. Women; Woman of Achievement, Marshall County Bus. and Profl. Women, 1985. Mem. Aurora Area Ministerial Alliance, Bus. and Profl. Women (mem. state legis. com. 1985—). Democrat. Avocations: writing; liturgical and modern dance; camping; tennis; travel; drama; gardening; fishing.

MILLER, KAREN-ANN, naval officer; b. Washington, Aug. 31, 1949; d. Clair Leon and Dorothy Genevieve (Fink) M.; m. David Manuel Gonzalez, Apr. 11, 1970 (div. June 1979); 1 child, Kevin Manuel. A.A., St. Petersburg Jr. Coll., 1969; B.A., Northeastern Ill. U., 1977. Long distance operator Gen. Telephone Co., Clearwater, Fla., 1969-70; enlisted woman U.S. Navy, 1972-77, commd. ensign 1977; sporting goods mgr. Navy Exchange, San Diego, 1971-73; electronics technician Naval Air Sta., Glenview, Ill., 1974-77, ground tng. officer, 1978-79; maintenance/material control officer HT 8, Milton, Fla., 1980-82; asst. maintenance officer Patrol Squadron 44, Brunswick, Maine, 1982-85; avionics div. officer AIMD Rota, Spain, 1985; prodn. control officer, 1986—. Mem. Soc. Logistics Engrs., U.S. Naval Inst., AAUW, Dunedin Hist. Soc. (life). Republican. Episcopalian. Office: Box 15 AIMD USNS FPO New York NY 09540

MILLER, LADONNA JEAN, design engineer, computer software writer; b. Nazareth, Tex., Mar. 7, 1960; d. Ernest Godfrey and Florine Marie (Wilhelm) Brockman; m. William Gregory Miller, Nov. 26, 1983. B.S., Tex. A&M U., 1982. Design engr. Narco Bio-Systems, Houston, 1978—. Roman Catholic. Home: 8329 A Constellation Houston TX 77075 Office: Narco Bio Systems 7651 Airport Blvd Houston TX 77061

MILLER, LANORA ETOILE (TILLIP), real estate broker; b. Lubbock, Tex., Aug. 7, 1929; d. Robbie Roy and Wanda Lavelle (Smith) Graham; m. Harry Eugene Miller, Aug. 12, 1951; children—Robert Eugene, Thomas Allen, Gary Edward. B.A., Eastern N.Mex. U., 1950. Tchr. Coronado Elem. Sch., Hobbs, N.Mex., 1951-52, elem. sch., House, N.Mex., 1952-53; substitute tchr. Inst. Logopedics and Stanley Elem. Sch., Wichita, Kans., 1976-77; real estate agt. Carl Chuzy Co., Wichita, 1977-78; ptnr. Holleman, Price & Miller Realty, Nacogdoches, Tex., 1978—. Mem. Nacogdoches County Bd. Realtors (pres. 1984, bd. dirs. 1985—), Nat. Assn. Realtors, Tex. Assn. Realtors, Nacogdoches County C. of C. (Ambassadors Club). Republican. Mem. Ch. of Christ. Club: Stephen F. Austin Univ. Women's. Home: 1604 Victoria St Nacogdoches TX 75961 Office: Holleman Price & Miller Realty 920 University Dr Nacogdoches TX 75961

MILLER, LILLIAN RUTH, offshore oil and gas technologist, tech. writer; b. Des Moines, Dec. 5, 1948; d. Charles N. and Marjorie R. (Hammons) Miller; A.A. in Petroleum Tech., Nichols State U., Thibodaux, La., 1977. Galley hand Offshore Foods & Services Co., Houma, La., 1973-74; with Ocean Drilling & Exploration Co., New Orleans, 1974—, jr. gauger, 1975-77, gauger, 1977-79, lead gauger, 1979-82, project coordinator offshore field tng. com., 1979-82; pres. SPEC Internat., Inc., 1982—. Publicity chmn. 1st Bapt. Ch.; capt. Daniel

Little, Inc.; publicity dir. Friends of Library, Thibodeux, La.; publicity coordinator Martha Sowell Utley Meml. Library and Cultural Center. Mem. Nichols State U. Alumni Assn., DAR (chmn. conservation com.), Soc. Mayflower Descs., Friends of Library, Terrebonne Writers Guild. Republican. Research on oil field history and offshore devel. Home: 1414 W Main St Houma LA 70360 Office: PO Box 956 Gray LA 70359

MILLER, LINDA LOUISE, sales training executive; b. Bay City, Mich., Aug. 14, 1945; d. Victor Hugo and Dolores Juanita (Martin) Floyt; B.A. in Communication Arts, Mich. State U., 1967. Speech tchr. Southfield (Mich.) Bd. Edn., 1967-68; sales rep. Revlon, Inc., N.Y.C., 1971-76; sales rep. Security First Group, Inc., Los Angeles, 1976-77, regional sales dir., 1977-84; founder, dir. Sales Tng. Inst., Encino, Calif., 1984—. Recipient Glen A. Holden Mgr. of Yr. award Security First Group, 1980. Mem. Internat. Platform Assn., Nat. Assn. Female Execs., Am. Soc. for Tng. and Devel. Lutheran. Home: 16727 Bosque Dr Encino CA 91436

MILLER, LISA ANN, healthcare agency executive; b. Englewood, N.J., Mar. 23, 1959; d. Alfred and Janet (Pelton) M. B.A. in English, Douglass Coll., Rutgers U., 1981. Adminstrv. asst. Klemtner Advt. Inc., N.Y.C., 1982, asst. account exec., 1983, account exec., 1983-84; account exec. Botto, Roessner, Horne & Messinger Inc., N.Y.C., 1984-85; account mgr. Baxter, Gurian & Mazzei Inc., Mountain View, Calif., 1985—. Mem. Med. Mktg. Assn., Nat. Assn. Female Execs., The Mus. Soc. Avocations: tennis; crafts; cultural and historical site explorations; creative writing. Office: Baxter Gurian and Mazzei Inc 1580 W El Camino Real Suite 14 Mountain View CA 94040

MILLER, LOIS LEA, artist; b. Texarkana, Tex., Sept. 16, 1929; d. George Newton and Daisy Rena (Alford) Gage; m. Jack Curtis Miller, Sept. 1, 1950 (div. 1963); 1 child, Jackie Lee. B.F.A., U. Houston, 1977, M.A., 1983. Artist, NASA, Johnson Space Ctr., Houston, 1960—; judge art scholarship com. Houston Rodeo and Stock Show, 1983—. Chmn. bd. dirs. Krishen Found. for Arts and Scis., 1981—. Mem. Am. Fedn. Govt. Employees (1st v.p. legis. coordinator, 1980—), Soc. for Tech. Communications, Am. Bus. Women's Assn., AAUW, U. Houston Alumni Assn. Democrat. Roman Catholic. Clubs: Toastmasters, Mensa. Home: 9702 Palmfield St Houston TX 77034 Office: NASA Johnson Space Ctr Mail Code JM2 Houston TX 77058

MILLER, LYNN MARIE, secretarial and word processing service executive; b. Cleve., June 25, 1958; d. Richard Robert and Frances Marie (Hoskin) M.; m. Michael Gerald Berendsen, Nov. 1977 (div. May 1979); 1 child, Marie Diane Miller. Student pub. schs., Cleve. Asst. sec. to pres. R.O. Hull Co., Cleve., 1976; customer service coordinator Lott & Geckler, Cleve., 1978-81; sec., customer service coordinator Brown Derby, Inc., Walton Hills, Ohio, 1981-83, Midwestern Land Devel. Corp., Cleve., 1983-85; sec. Johnston, Leach, McDonough & Eddy, A.C., Parkersburg, W.Va., 1985—; ptnr., v.p. F & L Enterprises, Caldwell, Ohio, 1985—. Co-producer Noble County Performing Arts, 1986. Publicity chmn. Community Christmas, Noble County Jr. Women's League, Caldwell, 1985, sec., 1986; treas.-elect Lit. Club, Caldwell; youth leader Meth. Youth Fellowship. Mem. Noble County Bus. and Profl. Women (Young Careerist chmn. 1986, Young Careerist award 1985, 86), Nat. Assn. Female Execs., Farmingdale C. of C., Caldwell Mchts. Assn., Ohio Office Edn. Assn. (historian and voting del. 1974-75), Ohio Geneal. Soc. (v.p. Noble County chpt. 1986). Lodge: Order Eastern Star (assoc. conductress 1986). Avocations: amateur and semi-professional theatre; cross stitching. Home: RD 4 Caldwell OH 43724 Office: Johnston Leach McDonough & Eddy AC PO Box 184 Parkersburg WV 26102

MILLER, LYNNE CATHY, parasitologist; b. Washington, Dec. 25, 1951; d. Albert and Lorraine Shirley (Sweet) M.; m. Gary Franklin Clark, July 25, 1982; 1 child, Nicole Beth. B.S. in Pharmacy, U. R.I., 1974; M.S. in Biol. Scis., U. Tex., El Paso, 1977; Ph.D. in Biology, N.Mex. State U., 1980. Registered pharmacist Meml. Gen. Hosp., Las Cruces, N.Mex., 1979; postdoctoral research asso. dept. entomology and plant pathology N.Mex. State U., Las Cruces, 1980-81; assoc. prof. biology and allied health Bloomsburg U. (Pa.), 1981—; Giardiasis cons., 1983—; parasitology and pub. health field worker, Mexico, El Paso, Tex. Sponsor, Creature-Feature program, 1981—. Recipient Disting. Faculty Teaching award Bloomsburg U., 1985; Bloomsburg U. faculty research grantee, 1981—; Commonwealth of Pa. grantee, 1981—. Mem. AAAS, Rocky Mountain Conf. Parasitologists, Entomol. Soc. Am., Helminthological Soc. Washington, Sigma Xi, Beta Beta Beta, Phi Kappa Phi. Contbr. sci. articles to profl. jours. Office: Biology and Allied Health Bloomsburg U Bloomsburg PA 17815

MILLER, MADELYN SUE, advertising executive; b. Chgo., Mar. 4, 1947; d. Seymour and Estelle (Klotwogg) Jensky; student NYU, 1966-67; B.A. in Journalism, U. Mich., 1968; m. Howard Brian Miller, May 26, 1968; children—Mallorie Ann, Gregory Scott. Copywriter, Young & Rubicam, Detroit, 1968-69, Yaffe Stone August, Huntington Woods, Mich., 1969-70, Dancer Fitzgerald Sample, N.Y.C., 1970-71, Neiman-Marcus, Dallas, 1975-76; sr. copywriter Tracy, Dallas, 1976-81; pres. Madelyn Miller, Inc., Dallas, 1982—. Adv. bd. Dallas Art Inst. Recipient Clio award, 1981; Matrix award Outstanding Dallas Woman in Advt., 1981; Effie award, 1980; Addy award (2), 1980; cert. of merit Dallas Soc. Visual Communications, 1979, Dallas Ad League, 1979; Bronze medal Dallas Soc. Visual Communications, also Bronze award, 1979; Bravo award (4) Detroit Art Dirs. Club, 1981; numerous others. Mem. Dallas Soc. Visual Communications, Women in Communications (student pres. 1968), Dallas Advt. League, Women in Communications, Internat. Assn. Bus. Communicators, Bus. and Profl. Advt. Assn., Am. Inst. Graphic Artists, Northwood Inst. Am. Women in Radio and TV. Jewish. Club: Hadassah Nat. Fedn. Jewish Women. Home: 9619 Rocky Branch Dallas TX 75243 Office: 10100 N Central Expressway Suite 430 Dallas TX 75231

MILLER, MARGARET ANN, real estate executive, handwriting analyst; b. Custer, Okla., June 26, 1937; d. Eddie Arthur and Pansy Opal (Harrall) Friesen; m. Marvin James Miller, May 20, 1955 (div.); children—Wayne Douglas, James Russell, Richard Don. Student in social work, U. Okla., 1972-74. Legal asst. U. Okla., Norman, 1972-74; contract adminstr. Pizza Inn, Inc., Dallas, 1974-77; real estate saleswoman Joe Chitwood Real Estate, Arlington, Tex., 1977-80, Hamilton Owen Real Estate, Dallas, 1980-83; office mgr., legal asst. Brown & Shapiro, Dallas, 1983-84; dir. real estate Lone Star Lubrications, Dallas, 1985—. Asst. chmn. Neighborhood Crime Watch, Dallas, 1983; chmn. Gov.'s com. Employment Handicapped Archtl. Barriers, 1980-82; mem. Dallas Mayor's Com. Employing Handicapped; chmn. AID/Handicapped Housing Com., 1979-82; mem. City Dallas 1981 Internat. Yr. Disabled Persons Access Com.; mem. credit rev. com. Women's S.W. Fed. Credit Union. Recipient Lois Hair Bernays award Dallas Bd. Realtors, 1980. Mem. Tex. Assn. Realtors, Dallas Assn. Realtors, Greater Dallas Bd. Realtors, Nat. Assn. Realtors, Comml. Real Estate Women Dallas and Tarrant County. Democrat. Home: 425 E Harwood Apt 1110 Euless TX 76039

MILLER, MARGARET HAIGH, librarian; b. Ashton-under-Lyne, Lancashire, Eng., Feb. 26, 1915; came to U.S., 1915, naturalized, 1919; d. Errwood Augustus and Florence (Stockdale) Savage; m. Mervin Homer Miller, June 30, 1940; children—Nancy Elaine Reich, Edward Stockdale, Jame Elizabeth Miller-Dean. B.S. in Edn., Millersville U. (Pa.), 1937; M.S. in L.S., U. So. Calif., 1952; postgrad. in supervision Calif. State U.-Northridge, 1957-59. High sch. librarian Phoenixville Sch. Dist. (Pa.), 1937-40; jr. high sch. librarian Los Angeles Unified Sch. Dist., 1952-55, coordinating librarian, 1955-62, coll. head librarian, 1959-62, supr. library services, 1962-83; lectr. children's lit. U. So. Calif., Los Angeles, 1959-76, advisor Sch. Library and Info. Sci., 1980-83; resource person Nat. Council for Accreditation Tchr. Edn., Washington, 1976—; cons. Pied Piper Prodns., Glendale, Calif., 1978—, David Sonnenshein Assocs., Los Angeles, 1983—, Baker & Taylor Co., Inc., N.Y.C., 1979-83, H.W. Wilson Co., N.Y.C., 1975—, Mook & Blanchard, La Puente, Calif., 1985—. Editor: Book List for Elementary School Libraries, 1966; Books for Elementary School Libraries, 1969; Children's Catalog, 13th edit., 1976; Multicultural Experiences in Children's Literature, Grades K-6, 1978; Periodicals for School Libraries, Grades K-12, 1977; Multicultural Experiences in Literature for Young People, Grades 7-12, 1979; School Selection Guide, K-12, 1980, 81, 82, 83; Supplement to Multicultural Experiences in Children's Literature, 1982; Special Books for Special People: A Bibliography about the Handicapped, 1982. Bibliographer: Concepts in Science, Levels 1 through 6 students' edits. (P. Brandwein et al), 1972; Concepts in Science, 1972. Columnist, book reviewer Los Angeles Times, various jours. Mem. Los Angeles Sch. Library Assn. (cons. 1952-83), Calif. Assn. Sch. Librarians (pres. So. sect. 1971-72, state pres. 1975-76, many coms. 1952-77), Calif. Media and Library Educators Assn. (various coms. 1977—), ALA (many coms. young adult services div.), Am. Assn. Sch. Librarians, Assn. Library Service to Children, Friends Children and Lit. (dir. 1979—, pres. 1986), So. Calif. Council on Lit. for Children and Young People (dir. 1961—, pres. 1973-74, 1st v.p. 1986), Calif. Library Assn., Young Adult Reviewers Booklist Com., Assn. Adminstrs. Los Angeles Unified Sch. Dist., Beta Phi Mu (dir. 1977-79, 84—, pres. 1979-80), Pi Lambda Theta (chpt. pres. 1964-66), Delta Kappa Gamma (chpt. sec. 1962-64). Republican. Home: 4321 Matilija Ave Sherman Oaks CA 91423

MILLER, MARGERY SILBERMAN, speech and language pathologist; b. Roslyn, N.Y., May 7, 1951; d. Bernard and Charlotte (Schatzberg) Silberman; m. Mark Howard Miller, Sept. 5, 1971; children—Kip Lee, Tige Justice. Lic. speech pathologist, N.Y., Md.; cert. tchr. nursery-6th grades, spl. edn., N.Y., advanced profl. tchr. speech and hearing, Md. B.A., Elmira Coll., 1971; M.A., NYU, 1972; Ed.S., M.S., SUNY-Albany, 1975; postgrad. in psychology Georgetown U., 1984—. Speech and lang. pathologist Mental Retardation Inst., Flower and Fifth Ave. Hosp., N.Y.C., 1971-72; community speech/lang. pathologist N.Y. State Dept. Mental Hygiene, Troy, dir. speech and hearing services, 1972-74; instr. communication disorders dept. Coll. of St. Rose, Albany, N.Y., 1975-77; clin. supr. U. Md., College Park, 1978; speech/lang. pathologist Md. Sch. for Deaf, Frederick, 1978-84; auditory devel. specialist Montgomery County Pub. Schs., Rockville, Md., 1984—; instr. sign lang. program Frederick Community Coll.; dance instr. for deaf adolescents; diagnostic cons. on speech pathology; mem. editorial rev. com. Gov.'s Devel. Disabilities Council of Md., 1984; presenter at confs. Author: It's O.K. To Be Angry, 1976; contbr. chpt. to Cognition, Education, and Deafness: Directions for Research and Instruction, 1985. Former vol. Am. Cancer Assn., Heart Assn., Muscular Dystrophy Assn.; vol. Emergency Interpreting for Deaf; choreographer Miss Deaf Am. Pageant, 1984. Office of Edn. Children's Bur. fellow, 1971. Mem. Am. Speech, Lang. and Hearing Assn. (cert. clin. competence in speech/lang. pathology), Md. Speech, Lang. and Hearing Assn., D.C. Speech, Lang. and Hearing Assn., Assn. for Retarded Citizens, Nat. Assn. of Deaf. Jewish. Home: 12316 Triple Crown Rd Gaithersburg MD 20878 Office: 14615 Bauer Dr Rockville MD 20853

MILLER, MARIAN HOGAN, accountant; b. Lake Charles, La., Jan. 13, 1941; d. Mike L. and Minnie Mae Hogan; 1 child, Carla. B.B.A., Tex. A&M U., 1978. Acct., Lanier, Locke & Ritter, Austin, Tex., 1978-80; chief fin. officer Gillingwater Interests, Inc., Austin, 1980-85; chief exec. officer Ultra Systems Design Inc., Austin, Tex., 1985—. Mem. Am. Inst. C.P.A.s, Tex. Soc. C.P.A.s, Nat. Assn. Female Execs., Austin Bus. Womens League (founder). Democrat. Home: 4908 Bob Cat Run Austin TX 78731 Office: Ultra Systems Design Inc 1204 S Congress St Austin TX 78704

MILLER, MARION HELEN, consultant; b. Chgo., Aug. 8, 1940; d. Chester Albert and Dorothy Marcella (Chaneske) M.; student DePaul U., Chgo., also various ins. courses. With Amalgamated Ins. Agy. Services, Inc., Chgo., 1960-83, claims mgr. dental/vision depts., 1968-73, claims dir. accident, health, dental, vision and prescription claims, 1973-83; spl. cons. subsidiary Meridian Agy., Fed. Computer Systems Inc., 1984-85; cons., project coordinator Group Adminstrs., Schaumburg, Ill., 1985—. Sec., bd. dirs. Lakeside Condominium D Assn., 1978-79, 81-82, v.p., 1982-83, author newsletter, 1979-83. Ill. State scholar, 1958; Mayor Daley Youth Found. grantee, 1958. Mem. Nat. Assn. Female Execs.

MILLER, MARJORIE CAVINS LEEPER (MIDGE), educator, state legislator; b. Morgantown, W.Va., June 8, 1922; d. Lorimer V. and Neva (Adams) Cavins; student Spokane Jr. Coll., 1939-40, Morris Harvey Coll., 1940-41; B.A., U. Mich., 1944; M.S., U. Wis., 1962; m. Harry Dean Leeper, Nov. 5, 1944 (dec. 1954); children—Steven Lloyd, David Dean, Linda Jean, Kenneth Chandran; m. Edward Ernst Miller, May 12, 1963; stepchildren—Mark, Sterling, Jeffrey, Nancy, Randy. Teen-age program dir. Ann Arbor YWCA, 1944-45; married women's program dir. New Haven YWCA, 1945-46; teaching asst. U. Wis., Madison, 1957-60, asst. dean letters and sci., 1960-66, coordinator univ. religious activities, 1966-68; mem. Wis. Assembly, 1970-84, chmn. commerce and consumer affairs, 1977-82, state affairs com., 1975-76, higher and vocat. edn., family and econ. assistance, 1983-84; co-chmn. law revision com., 1979-84; vice chmn. Dane County Democratic Com., 1967-68; mem. Dem. Nat. Com., 1975-84; mem. nat. adv. bd. Interchange Resource Center; founder Nat. Council Alternative Work Patterns; founder, chmn. The Madison Inst. Mem. Nat. Orgn. Women Legislators (nat. adv. com.), Nat. Women's Polit. Caucus. Methodist.

MILLER, MARJORIE LOIS, business executive; b. Mineola, N.Y., Aug. 14, 1937; d. J. Kenneth and Margaret (Campbell) M.; B.A. magna cum laude, Muskingum Coll., New Concord, Ohio, 1959; M.Litt., U. Pitts., 1960; M.A., Princeton Theol. Sem., 1965. Tchr., Jericho (N.Y.) High Sch., 1960-63; area rep. United Presbyn. Ch., Kansas City, Mo., 1965-68; exec. Am. Bible Soc., 1968-72; fellowship program dir. United Bd. Christian Higher Edn. in Asia, 1973-76; evening sch. dir. Katharine Gibbs Sch., N.Y.C., 1977-80; bus. adminstr. Miller Bus. Services, 1980—. Mem. Fifth Ave. Presbyterian Ch., N.Y.C. Republican. Home: 170 West End Ave New York NY 10023

MILLER, MARLA JO, lawyer; b. Chgo., Dec. 5, 1954; d. Arnold and Beverly (Shayne) Miller; m. David Harrison Kremer, Dec. 6, 1981. A.B. cum laude, Harvard U., 1976, J.D. cum laude, 1980; postgrad. London Sch. Econs., 1976-77. Bar: Calif. 1981. Law clk. to judge U.S. Ct. Appeals 9th Cir., San Francisco, 1980-81; atty. Howard Rice Nemerovski Canady Robertson & Falk, San Francisco, 1981—; teaching fellow Harvard U., 1979-80. Contbr. articles to profl. jours. Bd. dirs. Chamber Symphony of San Francisco, 1985—. Rotary Found. fellow, 1976-77. Mem. ABA, San Francisco Bar Assn., San Francisco Women Lawyers' Alliance (treas., bd. dirs. 1985—), Calif. Women Lawyers Assn., Phi Beta Kappa. Democrat. Office: Howard Rice Nemerovski Canady Robertson & Falk 3 Embarcadero Ctr San Francisco CA 94111

MILLER, MARTHA BROWN, courier service company executive; b. Mobile, Ala., Oct. 18, 1946; d. Cecil Hamilton and Bessie Lois (Clark) B.; m. Leonard Eugene Miller, May 3, 1973 (div. Feb. 1977). M.S., Auburn U., 1969. Billing clk. Internat. Paper Co., Mobile, 1967, 68 summers, Gulf States Paper Co., Tuscaloosa, 1969-70; math. technician So. Research Co., Birmingham, Ala., 1971-73; sr. evaluator U. S. Ala., Mobile, 1973-74; office mgr. Sharpe's Icemaker Dist., Mobile, 1974-81 owner, pres. Specialty Couriers, Inc., Mobile, 1981—. Home: 7100 Ivywood Dr Mobile AL 36619 Office: Specialty Couriers Inc 7100 Ivywood Dr Mobile AL 36619

MILLER, MARY JEANNETTE, records management consultant; b. Washington, Sept. 24, 1912; d. John William and David Evangeline (Hill) Sims; student Howard U., 1929-30, U. Ill., 1940-42; real estate cert. LaSalle U., 1969; student U. Md., 1975, 77, Dept. Agr. Grad. Sch., 1958-59; m. Cecil Miller, June 17, 1934; children—Sylvenia Delores, Ferdi Agusto, Cecil. Chief mail clk., records supr. AID, records mgmt. cons., mail clk. Dept. Interior, 1943-57; records supr. AID, Washington, 1957-71, records mgmt. cons., 1971—; real estate sales assoc. Hugh T. Peck Co., Wheaton, Md., 1976-78; office mgr. Bechtel Assocs., Washington, 1976-78; tchr. ESL, Ministry Edn., Seoul, Korea, 1959-60; cons. AID, Liberia, 1980-81, Yemen, Sudan, and Somalia, 1982, Sri Lanka, 1985-86. Bd. dirs. U.S. Embassy Seoul, Korea, 1959-60; appointee Mayor's Internat. Adv. Council, 2-yr. term. Mem. Soc. Am. Archivists, Records Mgmt. Assn., Am. Mgmt. Assn., Am. Fgn. Service Assn., Montgomery Bd. Realtors, Zeta Phi Beta. Roman Catholic. Author: Secretaries Handbook, 1972; Records Management Handbook, 1974; Principles and Practices of Records Management and Paperwork Control, 1974; Index for Alpha-Numeric Filing System and Records Disposal Manual, 1974; Manual of Instructions for Official Bio-data Card, 1973; Secretarial Handbook USAID/Liberia, 1981; editor-in-chief Club 8953 Employee's Newsletter, 1977-78. Home: 1008 Avery Pl Largo MD 20772

MILLER, MELISSA GAIL UNDERWOOD, print journalist; b. Kingsport, Tenn., Mar. 4, 1955; d. Julian Clifford and Clara Mae (Lamie) Underwood; m. Lawrence Russell Miller, May 28, 1983. B.S. in Communications, U. Tenn., 1977, postgrad., 1978-81. Publs. editor Kingsport Press Inc., Tenn., intermittently, 1973-76; job devel.-pub. relations dir. Assn. for Retarded Citizens, Knoxville and Nashville, 1977-79; editor Knoxville Lifestyle mag., 1979-80; mktg. and publs. cons., 1981-83; news-feature writer Johnson City Press, Tenn., 1983-84; tourism com. dir. Columbus Conv. and Visitors Bur., Ga., 1984—; pub., editor So. Open Inc., Columbus, 1984—; bd. dirs. W. Central Ga. Tourism Assn., 1984—. Contbr. articles to numerous newspapers and mags. Trainer, fund-raising and pub. relations cons. Girls Scouts Am.; communications dir. various polit. campaigns. Recipient awards in field. Mem. Pub. Relations Soc. Am. (Ga. chpt.), Ga. Hospitality and Travel Assn., Travel Industry Assn. Am., Historic Columbus Found., Nat. Tour Assn., Columbus C. of C., S.E. Tourism Soc., Sigma Delta Chi. Methodist. Avocations: hiking; backpacking; reading; entertaining; regional history. Office: Columbus Conv and Visitors Bur 801 Front Ave Box 2768 Columbus GA 31902

MILLER, MERSHON BROWNLEE, packaging engr.; b. Fortress Monroe, Va., June 13, 1940; d. Laurance Hilliard and Mary Mershon (Kessler) Brownlee; student U. Ariz., 1957-59, Coll. of San Mateo, 1961-67, Coll. Notre Dame, 1967-69; m. Patrick Bernard Miller, Mar. 18, 1967. Prodn. artist Fortune House Pub., San Francisco, 1959; theatre costume design instr. Nat. Music Camp, Interlochen, Mich., 1959; display artist Halle Bros., Cleve., 1959-60; asst. buyer Sterling Lindner Davis, Cleve., 1960-61; with Maurice Roberts Jewelry, Cleve., 1961, Joseph Magnin, San Francisco, 1961-63; with Carlisle Litho div. Litton Industries, San Francisco, 1963-66, Western Family Foods, Inc., San Francisco, 1966-69; prodn. mgr. Albert Frank Guenther Law Advt., San Francisco, 1969-73; with Fortune House Pub., San Francisco, 1973; prodn. mgr. David W. Evans Advt., San Francisco, 1974-76; purchasing agt. Raychem Corp., Menlo Park, Calif., 1976-79, packaging engr., purchasing agt., 1979-82, packaging engr., purchasing sect. mgr. graphics/packaging, 1982—; lectr. in field. Performing mem. Claypipers Melodrama Theatre, Drytown, Calif., 1968—, asst. play dir., 1979; mem. adv. bd. Food Adv. Service/Gallery Faire, Brisbane, Calif., 1978—. Mem. Soc. Litho and Printing House Craftsmen, In-Plant Printing Mgmt. Assn., Peninsula Women in Advt., Soc. Packaging and Handling Engrs., Prodn. Women's Club (past pres.). Author: Fast But Fancy Secrets to Gourmet Entertaining, 1976. Office: 300 Constitution Dr Menlo Park CA 94025

MILLER, MURIEL AGNES, professional parliamentarian, educator, consultant, professional presider; b. St. Paul, Minn.; d. Edward William and Mayme Blanche (Vandelac) Oestreich; m. Carl Stinson Miller, Aug. 19, 1944; children—Suzanne Marie Rechtzigel, Dennis William. B.S., St. Catherine's Coll., 1937; postgrad. U. Minn., 1939-60. Cert. registered parliamentarian. High sch. tchr. Minn. Edn. Assn. high schs. Murray, Monroe, St. Paul, 1937-47; profl. vol. AAUW, Bus. and Profl. Women, Interclub Council, Minn. Federalists, Minn. U., Library St. Paul, numerous others; parliamentarian, pres. St. Paul Branch AAUW, St. Paul Bus. and Profl. Women, Friends of Pub. Library, St. Paul, St. Paul City Club, St. Paul's Womans Club; dir. St. Paul YWCA, Twin Cities Opera Guild, Minn. Opera; served as nat. parliamentarian White House Conf. on Families, Minn., Am. Assn. Hosp. Adminstrs., Am. Assn. Social Workers, Nat. Bus. and Profl. Women, numerous nat. coms.; state parliamentarian Minn. LPNs, Minn. Dental Assts. Assn., Minn. LWV, AAUW, Minn. Nurses Assn., Minn. Soil and Water Conservation Dists.; pres. Minn. State Assn. Parliamentarian, 1973-75, 77-79, v.p., chmn. coms., in charge of two state seminars and two convs.; charter pres. St. Paul Unit Parliamentarians, chmn. numerous coms.; instr. parliamentary procedure St. Thomas Coll., St. Catherine's Coll., St. Paul Sch. System Adult Edn.; served as parliamentary procedure judge Office Edn. Assn. (Bus. and Service award 1979); tchr. high sch. Author parliamentary tests on nat. level. Author several papers on parliamentary procedure, AAUW fellow. Mem. Nat. Assn. Parliamentarians (dist. V bd. dirs.), Assn. of Parliamentarians (pres. St. Paul unit), Minn. Assn. Parliamentarians (pres. 1960). Republican. Unity Unitarian. Avocations: travel, drama, theatre. Home and Office: 44 Miller Crest Ln St Paul MN 55106

MILLER, NAN LOUISE, real estate development executive; b. Atlanta, Aug. 6, 1948; d. William Mitchell and Harriet Irene (Wilkie) Schotanus; B.S., Kans. State U., 1970; postgrad. UCLA, 1979-80, Media Communications, 1981, West Barron Sch. TV, 1982, East Tenn. State U., 1982-83; m. Robert W. Miller Jr., Oct. 31, 1981. Buyer, Jones Store Co., Kansas City, Mo., 1971-75, Harzfeld's, Kansas City, 1975-76; exec. sales rep. Monet, Los Angeles, 1976-80; mgr. corp. buying offices Trifari, N.Y.C., 1980-82, field mktg. coordinator and media pub. relations rep., 1981-82; co-owner, v.p. mktg./sales Devel. Resources Corp., Kingsport, Tenn., 1982—; interior designer Willowbrook Devel. Corp., 1981—. Kingsport Grocery Co. Restaurant, 1985; TV comml. actress; media/pub. relations cons. Willowbrook Devel. Corp. Publicity chmn. Kingsport Fun Fest Festival. Mem. Nat. Assn. Female Execs., Fashion Group of N.Y., Am. Mgmt. Assn., Kingsport Home Builders Assn., Kingsport C. of C. (v.p.), Jr. League of Kingsport, Chi Omega. Presbyterian. Club: Altrusa of Met. Kingsport (publicity chmn.). Home: 108 Willowbrook Dr Kingsport TN 37660 Office: Devel Resources Corp 453 E Main St Suite 301 Kingsport TN 37660

MILLER, NANCY, art educator; b. Tulsa, Sept. 16, 1942; d. Chester Elbert and Margie Wasalee (Delozier) Miller. B.S. in Art Edn., Tex. Woman's U., Denton, 1964, M.S., 1970, postgrad., 1976; postgrad. Sam Houston State U., Huntsville, Tex., summer 1974. Art tchr., chairperson creative art dept. Bryan Adams High Sch., Dallas Ind. Sch. Dist., 1968—; secondary art curriculum writer Tex. Edn. Agy., Austin, summer 1978. Group shows include: Richardson Civic Art Soc. (Tex.), 1974, 76; Dallas Art Edn. Assn., 1974, 75 (Best of Show award), 77, 78, 82 (Merit award), U. Tex., Arlington, 1976, Tex. Fine Arts Assn. 1976, 81 (tour); Northlake Coll., Irving, Tex., 1981. Recipient Recognition award Dallas Ind. Sch. Dist., 1979. Mem. Tex. Art Edn. Assn., Inc. (pres. 1982-83, outstanding contbn. to art edn. in Tex. award 1980). Home: 723 Dumont St Dallas TX 75214 Office: Bryan Adams High Sch 2101 Millmar St Dallas TX 75214

MILLER, NANCY ELIZABETH, librarian; b. Campbellsville, Ky., Sept. 17, 1916; d. Isaiah K. and Mallie (Davis Graham) M.; student S.D. State Coll., 1934-36; A.B., U. Ky., 1938; B.S. in Library Sci., U. Ill., 1942, M.S., 1947; M.A., Western Res. U., 1960. Librarian, Campbellsville (Ky.) High Sch., 1938-40; librarian, sect. reviser dept. library sci. U. Ky., 1940-43; head reference dept. Canton (Ohio) Public Library, 1943-49; asso. prof. library sci. Kent State U. (Ohio), 1949-55; head Chamberlain br. Akron Public Library, 1955-56, head extension dept., 1956-59; asst. dir. Law Library Ohio State U., Columbus, 1959-86, instr. cataloging, 1955-74. Mem. Ohio Regional Assn. Law Librarians (pres. 1964-65), Am. Assn. Law Librarians (chmn. cataloging and classification com. 1962-64, 67-68, 71-72), Beta Phi Mu. Democrat. Methodist. Club: Pilot (pres. 1971-72). Home: 1995 Tewksbury Rd Columbus OH 43221 Office: 1659 N High St Columbus OH 43210

MILLER, NANCY ELLEN, health care administrator; b. Long Beach, N.Y., Aug. 20, 1947; d. Jerome H. and Kathy P. M.; m. Walter A. Romanek, Aug. 25, 1983. B.A., N.Y.U., 1969; M.A., Harvard U., 1970; Ph.D., U. Chgo., 1978; cert. Washington Sch. Psychiatry, 1981; postgrad. Washington Psychoanalytic Inst., 1981—. Clin psychologist City of Chgo. Dept. Mental Health, 1971-77; research asst. U. Chgo., 1972-75, research assoc., 1975-77; exec. sec. Sci. Rev. Group NIMH, 1977-79, chief clin. research program Center for Studies of Mental Health Aging, 1977—; dir. NIMH clin. research ctrs. program on psychopathology of elderly, 1984; instr. clin. geriatric psychiatry Georgetown U. Sch. Medicine; del. White House Conf. on Aging, 1981. USPHS fellow, 1972-76; HEW fellow, 1975-77. Mem. AAAS, Am. Orthopsychiat. Assn., Am. Psychol. Assn., Alzheimer's Disease and Related Disorders Assn., Am. Psychoanalytic Assn., Boston Soc. Gerontologic Psychiatry, D.C. Psychol. Assn., Gerontol. Soc. Am., Internat. Assn. Gerontology, Internat. Neuropsychol. Soc., Soc. Neurosci. Soc. Psychotherapy Research, Phi Delta Kappa, Pi Lambda Theta. Author: Clinical Aspects of Alzheimer's Disease & Senile Dementia, 1981; Life Span Research on the Prediction of Psychopathology, 1985; mem. editorial bd. Jour. Ednl. Gerontology, 1976-80, Neurobiology of Aging, 1980—, Profl. Psychology, 1980—, Psychoanalytical Psychology, 1984—; contbr. numerous articles to profl. jours. Home: 9 Logan Circle NW Washington DC 20005 Office: NIMH Aging Research Br 5600 Fishers Ln Rockville MD 20857

MILLER, NELDA WEST, mail order executive; b. Wilkesboro, N.C., July 19, 1947; d. Arlie Wilson and Irene B. (Nichols) West; m. Jerome D. Miller, Apr. 20, 1974. B.S., Appalachian State U., 1967; M.B.A., Temple U., 1977. With Corning Glass Works, N.Y., 1977-81, mgr. systems devel., Medfield, Mass., 1981 84; data processing mgr. The Stitchery, Wellesley, Mass., 1984-85, v.p. ops. and MIS, 1985—. Mem. Nat. Assn. Female Execs., Data Processing Mgmt. Assn. Avocations: golf; needlecrafts; ceramics; reading. Home: 4 Timberline Dr Norfolk MA 02056 Office: The Stitchery 204 Worcester St Wellesley MA 02181

MILLER, NICKOLA ELLEN, communications company executive, medical advertising writer; b. Massillon, Ohio, June 16, 1942; d. Douglas Babcock Miller and Nancy Jane (Miller) Goorey. Cert. dental hygiene Ohio State U.,

1963. Registered dental hygienist, Ohio, N.Y. Pvt. practice dental hygienist, Ohio, 1963-69, N.Y.C., 1969-71; copywriter John Wiley & Sons, N.Y.C., 1971-76; sr. copywriter William Douglas McAdams, N.Y.C., 1977-78; v.p., copy supr. Rolf, Werner, Rosenthal, N.Y.C., 1979-81, Botto, Roessner, Horne & Messinger, Inc., N.Y.C., 1981-83; pres. Nickola Miller Communications, N.Y.C., 1983—; creative cons. Rolf Werner Rosenthal Advt., Burson-Marstellar, Sudler & Hennessey, Squibb-Connaught Labs., all. N.Y.C., 1983—. Photographer: numerous ednl. texts, 1975-84, Internat. Festival Women Artists exhibit, 1980, Women Photograph Men, 1977. Mem. Am. Med. Writers Assn., Women in Communications, Am. Women Entrepreneurs, Profl. Women Photographers (bd. dirs.), Pharm. Advt. Council. Address: 320 W 83d St New York NY 10024

MILLER, NORMA JEAN, banker; b. Cashton, Wis., July 8, 1936; d. Bernard J. and Nora C. (Schmitz) Brueggen; grad. Grad. Sch. Banking, U. Wis., 1978; m. Levi Miller, Sept. 7, 1959; 1 foster child, Iris McAloney. With Bank of Cashton, 1955—, cashier, dir., 1976—. Chmn., treas. Cashton Centennial; treas. Monroe County Bicentennial, PCCW, Roman Cath. orgn.; sec.-treas. Cashton Scholarship Fund, 1986-88. Mem. Nat. Assn. Bank Women (chmn. Mississippi Valley group 1983-85, state pub. affairs chmn.), Monroe County Hist. Soc., Bank Administrn. Inst., Bankers Installment Loan Assn. Office: PO Box 70 Cashton WI 54619

MILLER, PAMELA GARDINER, lawyer; b. Newark, May 29, 1948; d. Herbert and Adele (Hoffman) Gardiner; m. David Edward Miller, Dec. 28, 1974. B.A., U. Wis., 1971; M.A., Columbia U., 1972; J.D., Case Western Res. U., 1975. Bar: Ohio 1975, Wis. 1982. Legal intern Pub. Defender Office, Cleve. 1973-75; asst. trust officer Cleve. Trust Co., 1975-78; asst. dean student acad. affairs Coll. of Letters and Sci., U. Wis., Madison, 1978-84; exec. dir. Madison Festival of the Lakes, Inc., Madison, 1984—. Mem. Wis. Bar Assn., ABA.

MILLER, PAMELA GUNDERSEN, city official; b. Cambridge, Mass., Sept. 7, 1938; d. Sven M. and Harriet Adams Gundersen; A.B. magna cum laude, Smith Coll., 1960; m. Ralph E. Miller, July 7, 1962; children—Alexander, Erik, Karen. Feature writer Congressional Quar., Washington, 1962-65; dir. cable TV franchizing Storer Broadcasting Co., Louisville, Bowling Green, Lexington, and Covington, Ky., 1978-80, 81-82; mem. 4th Dist. Lexington, Fayette County Urban Council, 1973-77, councilwoman-at-large, 1982—, vice-mayor, 1984—; dep. commr. Ky. Dept. Local Govt., Frankfort, 1980-81; pres. Pam Miller, Inc., 1984—, Community Ventures Corp., 1985—. Mem. Fayette County Bd. Health, 1975-77, Downtown Devel. Commn., 1975-77; alt. del. Dem. Nat. Conv., 1976; bd. dirs. YMCA, Lexington, 1975-77, 85—, Fund for the Arts, 1984—, Council of Arts, 1978-80, Sister Cities, 1978-80; treas. Prichard Com. for Acad. Excellence, 1983—. Named Woman of Achievement YWCA, 1984, Outstanding Woman of Blue Grass, AAUW, 1984. Mem. LWV (dir. 1970-73), Profl. Women's Forum, NOW, ACLU, Land and Nature Trust of the Bluegrass. Home: 140 Cherokee Park Lexington KY 40503 Office: 200 E Main St Lexington KY 40507

MILLER, PATRICIA CROUGH, physician; b. Cleve., Feb. 8, 1925; d. Thomas Anthony and Hilda May (Sampier) Crough; student Syracuse U., 1952-53, B.A. cum laude, 1961; student U. Wis., Madison, 1955-56; M.D., SUNY Upstate Med. Center, Syracuse, N.Y., 1964; m. George H. Miller, 1947 (div. 1962); children—Bruce Douglas (dec.), Brian Scott, Jeffrey Burke; m. 2d, Paul F. Swarthout, Jr., Feb. 9, 1967. Med. sec. to Arthur D. Ecker, M.D., Syracuse, N.Y., 1946-50; intern SUNY, Upstate Med. Center, Syracuse, N.Y., 1964-65; house physician Community Gen. Hosp., Syracuse, N.Y., 1965-67; pvt. practice medicine specializing in family practice, Manlius, N.Y., 1967—; mem. staff Community Gen. Hosp., Crouse Irving Meml. Hosp. Mem. med. adv. bd. Planned Parenthood, Syracuse, 1977—; bd. dirs. Rape Crisis Center, 1982—. Diplomate Am. Bd. Family Practice. Mem. Onondaga County Med. Soc., AMA (Physician's Recognition award 1979-82, 82-85), Am. Med. Women's Assn., N.Y. Acad. Scis., NOW, SUNY Alumni Assn. (dir. 1973-80, sec. bd. 1974-76). Office: Fairgrounds Dr Manlius NY 13104

MILLER, PATRICIA ELIZABETH, construction company executive; b. Bremerton, Wash., Sept. 20, 1945; d. Raymond Franklin and Amelia Celia (Warnock) Stevens; m. Richard L. Miller, Nov. 27, 1971; children—Pamela Jean, Richard G., Christopher R. Student Olympic Coll., 1963-65, U. Wash., 1968-70. Computer specialist Blue Cross, Inc., Seattle, 1966-71; exec. sec., contract specialist Foutch Miller Corp., Bremerton, 1979-81; owner, gen. mgr Miller Sheetmetal, Inc., Bremerton, 1981—. Mem. Sheet Metal and Air Conditioning Contractors Nat. Assn. Republican. Roman Catholic. Office: Miller Sheetmetal Inc PO Box 123 Manette Station Bremerton WA 98310

MILLER, PATRICIA LOUISE, state senator, nurse; b. Bellefontaine, Ohio, July 4, 1936; d. Richard William and Rachel Orpha (Williams) Miller; m. Kenneth Orlan Miller, July 3, 1960; children—Tamara Sue, Matthew Ivan. R.N., Meth. Hosp. Sch. Nursing-Indpls., 1957; B.S., Ind. U., 1960. Office nurse A.D. Dennison, M.D., 1960-61; staff nurse Meth. Hosp., Indpls., 1959, Community Hosp., Indpls., 1958. Representative, State of Ind., Dist. 50, Indpls., 1982-83, senator, State of Ind., Dist. 32, Indpls., 1983—, mem. edn., health welfare and aging, labor and pension, legis. apportionment and elections coms. Mem. Bd. Edn., Met. Sch. Dist. Warren Twp., 1974 82, pres., 1979-80, 80-81; mem. Warren Twp. Citizens Screening Com. for Sch. Bd. Candidates, 1972-74, 84, Met. Zoning Bd. Appeals, Div. I, City-County Council, 1972-76; bd. dirs. Central Ind. Council on Aging, Indpls., 1977-80; mem. State Bd. of Voc. and Tech. Edn., 1978-82, sec., 1980-82; mem. Gov.'s Select Adv. Commn. for Primary and Secondary Edn., 1983; precinct committeeman Republican Party, 1968-74, ward vice chmn., 1975-78, ward chmn., 1978-85, twp. chmn., 1985—; del. Rep. State Conv., 1968, 74, 76, 1980, sgt. at arms, 1982, mem. platform com., 1984; del. Rep. Nat. Conv., 1984; active various polit. campaigns; bd. dirs. PTA, 1967-81; pres. Grassy Creek PTA, 1971-72; state del. Ind. PTA, 1978; mem. child care adv. com. Walker Career Center, 1976-80, others; bd. dirs. Ch. Fedn. Greater Indpls., 1979-82, Christian Justice Center, Inc., 1983-85, Gideon Internat. Aux., 1977—; mem. United Meth. Bd. Missions Aux. of Indpls., 1974-80, v.p., 1974-76; bd. dirs. Lucille Raines Residence, Inc., 1977-80; exec. com. S. Ind. Conf. United Meth. Women, 1977-80, lay del. S. Ind. Conf. United Meth. Ch., 1977—, fin. and adminstrn. com., 1979—, planning and research com., 1980—; sec. 'Indpls. S.E. Dist. Council on Ministries, 1977-78, pres., 1982; chmn. council on ministries Cumberland United Meth. Ch., 1969-76; chmn. stewardship com. Old Bethel United Meth. Ch., 1982-85, fin. com., 1982-85, adminstrv. bd., mem. council on ministries, 1981-85. Recipient Phi Lambda Theta Honor for outstanding contbr. in field of edn., 1976; Woman of the Year, Cumberland Bus. and Profl. Women, 1979; Ind. Voc. Assn. citation award, 1984, others. Mem. Indpls. Dist. Dental Soc. Women's Aux., Ind. Dental Assn. Women's Aux., Am. Dental Assn. Women's Aux., others. Clubs: Warren Twp. Rep. Franklin Rep., Lawrence Rep., Center Twp. Rep., Fall Creek Valley Rep., Marion County Council Rep. Women, Ind. Women's Rep., Indpls. Women's Rep., Ind. Fedn. Rep. Women, Nat. Fedn. Rep. Women, Beech Grove Rep., Perry Twp. Rep. Address: 1041 S Muesing Rd Indianapolis IN 46239

MILLER, PATRICIA LYNN, clinical psychologist; b. Chgo., Jan. 27, 1938; d. Joseph L. and Gertrude R. Lynn; student Carleton Coll., 1955-56; A.B., U. Chgo., 1958; M.S., Ill. Inst. Tech., 1971, Ph.D. in Psychology, 1979; m. Eric E. Miller, Feb. 27, 1960; children—Kurt, Nathan, Peter. Pub. relations dir., field dist. dir. Chgo. Area council Camp Fire Girls, 1958-68, asst. exec. dir., 1966-68; task force tchr., mem. assessment team for 45-15 yr. 'round sch. plan Valley View Sch. Dist., Romeoville, Ill., 1968-70; sch. psychologist Lockport (Ill.) Area Spl. Edn. Coop., 1971-80; pvt. practice psychology, Joliet, Ill., part-time 1977-80; pvt. practice psychology, diagnostics and treatment of children and women, Joliet, 1980—; cons. sch. psychology program Ill. Inst. Tech., Chgo., 1975-77, instr. dept. psychology, 1975; condr. tng. seminars crisis line vols. and agy. staffs; field supr. Chgo. Sch. Profl. Psychology, 1981-82. Mem. Tribune Charities Youth Com., Chgo., 1958-60; former mem. Com. To Repeal Ill. Personal Property Tax, Citizen's Com. for Wider Use of Schs., Mayor Daley's Youth Commn.; former mem. Women's Network for ERA. State of Ill. grad. fellow. Mem. Am. Psychol. Assn., Ill. Psychol. Assn., Internat. Neuropsychol. Soc., Nat. Sch. Psychologists Assn., Ill. Sch. Psychologists Assn., Sigma Xi. Club: Zonta (charter) (Joliet). Co-developer Psy-Dx, electronic Halstead neuropsychol. test battery. Home: 3510 Bankview Ln Joliet IL 60435 Office: 310 N Hammes Ave Joliet IL 60435

MILLER, PAULINE KAMEN, educational administrator, counselor; b. N.Y.C., Dec. 8, 1952; d. Edward Robert and Evelyn (McMullen) Kamen; m. Frederick A. Miller, June 19, 1982. B.S. in Biology, Coll. William and Mary, 1974; M.S., Ed.S., SUNY-Albany, 1977. Cert. guidance counselor. Counselor, dept. human resources, City of Albany (N.Y.), 1977-78, dir. tng. and ednl. advisement, 1978-79; asst. dir. career devel. Russell Sage Coll., Troy, N.Y., 1979-83, dir. career devel., 1983-85; dir. career devel. Albany Law Sch., 1985—; cons. Schenectady Pub. Library (N.Y.), 1981. Vol. career counselor YWCA, Albany, 1981-82, v.p., 1981-83, pres., 1983-85; mem. steering com. Albany Women's Forum, 1980-81. Mem. Albany Bus. and Profl. Women's Club, Capital Dist. Personnel and Guidance Assn., Eastern Coll. Personnel Officers, Nat. Assn. Law Placement. Office: Career Devel Albany Law Sch Albany NY 12203

MILLER, PHYLLIS FOREMAN, nurse; b. Pitts., Aug. 1, 1929; d. William Arthur and Ruthadel (Rollier) Foreman; diploma Hosp. of U. Pa., 1950; B.S., Millersville U., 1963, M.Ed., 1968; m. Edwin Garvin Miller, Aug. 26, 1950; children—Edwin Randall, Geoffrey Blair. Staff nurse St. Joseph Hosp., Lancaster, Pa., 1950; office nurse, Lancaster, 1950; indsl. nurse RCA, Lancaster, 1955-56; pediatric staff nurse Lancaster Gen. Hosp., 1960, pediatric head nurse, 1960-61, supr., 1961-62; sch. nurse Manheim Twp. Sch. Dist., 1962-73; asst. dir. nursing, staffing and staff devel. Ephrata (Pa.) Community Hosp., 1974-76; asst. dir. nursing, staff devel. Hershey Med. Center, 1976-79, asso. hosp. dir., dir. nursing Milton S. Hershey Med. Center, Hershey, Pa., 1979-86; cons. Nurse Exec. Services. Mem. Pa. Nurses Assn., Am. Nurses Assn. (cert. nursing adminstr. advanced), Nat. League Nursing, Pa. League Nursing, Am. Nurses Found., Pa. Orgn. Nurse Execs., Am. Orgn. Nurse Execs. Hosp. Assn. Pa., Am. Heart Assn. Republican. Methodist.

MILLER, RHOETA BETH, nurse; b. Plainfield, N.J., Aug. 14, 1927; d. Reginald Bazil and Ruth Naugle; B.R.E., Arlington Bapt. Coll., 1971; A.D. in Nursing, El Centro Coll., 1974; postgrad. Northwestern State U., 1981, La. Inst. Tech.; B.A. in Counseling and Psychology, La. Tech. U., 1986; m. Harold Stanley Miller, Oct. 31, 1980; children—Dawn H. Butler, W. David Butler, Paul D. Butler, Clay D. Butler, Dwight A. Broach, Gregg M. Miller. Staff nurse Brookhaven Hosp., Dallas, 1974-75; charge nurse Bossier Med. Center, Bossier City, La., 1975-77; public health nurse Shreveport, La., 1977-79; dir. nursing Midway Manor Nursing Home, Shreveport, 1979-80; sch. nurse Caddo Parish Sch. Bd., Shreveport, 1980—. Vol., ARC, 1974—; mem. Substance Abuse Team for Prevention by Edn., 1981-82; active PTA, 1953-82. Sue Armstrong Nursing scholar, 1972, 73, 74; recipient Service award, B.T. Washington High Sch., Shreveport, 1981. Mem. Am. Nurses Assn., La. Sch. Nurses Assn. (exec. bd. 1983—, sec. 1983-84, editor-in-chief publ. 1984—), Nat. Sch. Nurses Assn. Democrat. Baptist. Contbr. articles to profl. jours. Home: 1810 Pollyanna St Bossier City LA 71112 Office: 7600 Cornelius Ln Shreveport LA 71109

MILLER, ROSE MARIE, nursing educator; b. Leonardtown, Md., Mar. 31, 1955; s. Robert Bernard and Helen Gertrude (Clark) Norris; m. Bobby Glenn Miller, Mar. 31, 1975. A.S., Wallace Community Coll., 1979; B.S.N., Troy State U., 1981; M.S.N., U. Ala., 1983. Relief charge nurse Flowers Hosp., Dothan, Ala., 1980-81, head nurse surg. intensive care unit, 1981-83; nursing instr. Wallace Coll., Dothan, 1983—. Mem. nursing scholarship com. Troy State U., Ala., 1983. Served with USAF, 1974-78. Mem. U. Ala. Birmingham Alumni Soc., Wiregrass Critical Care Assn. (v.p. 1981-82), Republican. Roman Catholic. Avocations: motorcycle riding; reading; raising doberman pinschers. Home: Route 2 49 Wynnwood Acres Midland City AL 36350 Office: Nursing Dept Wallace Coll Napier Field Dothan AL 36303

MILLER, ROSEMARY MARGARET, accountant; b. Jersey City, Jan. 3, 1935; d. Joseph John and Marguerite (Delatush) Corbin; student Barnard Coll., 1953-54, Rutgers U., Newark, 1954-56, Howard U., 1962-63, No. Va. Community Coll., 1976-83, U. Md., 1984—; A.A., Thomas A. Edison State Coll., 1981; cert. H & R Block, 1981; m. James Noyes Orton, 1956 (div. 1977); children—Alexandria Lynn Orton Pollard, Jennifer Ann Orton; m. Julian Allen Miller, Oct. 14, 1978. Cost acct. Radiation Systems, Inc., Sterling, Va., 1973-80; acct. Bilsom Internat., Inc., Reston, Va., 1980-83; sales mgr. Bay Country Homes, Inc., Fruitland, Md., 1984; sr. staff acct. Snow & Powell Accts., Salisbury, Md., 1985—; owner, prin. RCOM Cons., acctg., bookeeping, taxes, Princess Anne, Md. Mem. Accreditation Council for Accountancy (accredited 1981), Nat. Soc. Public Accts., Nat. Acctg. Assn., Nat. Student Bus. League, Alpha Kappa Mu. Democrat. Lutheran. Home: Route 2 Box 255 B 27 Princess Anne MD 21853 Office: 111 Baptist St Suite 100 Salisbury MD 21801

MILLER, ROXANNE HARDWICK, manufacturers representative; b. Meridian, Tex., Sept. 13, 1939; d. Milton Riddle and Helen Drusilla (Warren) Hardwick; m. Jack Donald Elder, Jr., July 14, 1958; children—Kellie Anne, Ginger Leigh; m. Roger Eugene Miller, Nov. 13, 1979. B.A., Baylor U., 1961. Cert. secondary edn. tchr. Tchr., Levi Fry Jr. High Sch., Texas City, Tex., 1964-66; tchr., therapist div. child psychology John Sealy Hosp., Galveston, Tex., 1966-70; regional mgr. Attitude Control Inst., Houston, 1970-82; owner, pres. Double R Enterprises, Houston, 1980—; tchr. ALIEF Individualized Study Ctr., 1984. Contbr. articles to profl. jours. Pres. bd. dirs. Beaumont Ballet (Tex.), 1973; treas. Beaumont Symphony, 1973; v.p. Beautify Tex. Council, Austin, 1977. Named First Lady of Kilgore, Beta Sigma Phi, 1977. Mem. DAR. Republican. Mem. Unity Ch. Lodges: New Atlantis, Rosicrucians. (Houston).

MILLER, RUTH LOYD, lawyer, author; b. Ida, La., May 29, 1922; d. Cecil A. and Gladys (Means) Loyd; m. Minos D. Miller, Jr., Dec. 22, 1942; children—Bonner M. Hunter, Minos D., James Valcour. B.A. in Speech, La. State U., 1942. Bar: La., 1957. Sole practice, Jennings, La., 1957—; sec. Jennings Gas Co., 1959—. Author, editor Shakespeare Indentified, 3rd edit., 1975; Hidden Allusions in Shakespeare's Plays, 34d edit., 1975: A Hundreth Sundrie Flowers, 2d edit., 1975. First v.p. La. Constl. Conv., 1973; mem. La. Mineral Bd., 1972-73; mem. bd. suprs. La. State Univ. System, 1974—, chmn., 1983-84; active polit. campaigns, La. Named Nat. Woman of Yr., Delta Zeta, 1983. Mem. ABA, La. State Bar Assn. Republican. Methodist. Home: PO Box 1309 Jennings LA 70546

MILLER, SALLY ANN, plant pathologist; b. Canton, Ohio, Apr. 11, 1954; d. Stanley A. and Eileen T. (Larke) M.; m. Donald James Styer, II, June 26, 1976; children—Allison Miller Styer, Carolyn Miller Styer. B.S., Ohio State U., 1976; M.S., U. Wis.-Madison, 1979, Ph.D., 1982. Research scientist I, DNA Plant Technology Corp., Cinnaminson, N.J., 1982-84, research scientist II, 1984-85; unit head Agri-Diagnostics Assocs., Cinnaminson, 1985—. Contbr. articles to profl. jours., chpts. to books. Ohio State U. grantee, 1976. Mem. Am. Phytopath. Soc. (chair com. women in plant pathology 1985-86), AAAS, Sigma Xi, Gamma Sigma Delta, Phi Kappa Phi. Roman Catholic. Avocations: cross-country skiing; birdwatching; wildflower photography; gardening. Home: 6313 Wyndam Rd Pennsauken NJ 08109 Office: 2611 Branch Pike Cinnaminson NJ 08077

MILLER, SELAINA AUNOA LEVI, employment and training executive; b. Apia, Western Samoa, May 5, 1946; came to U.S., 1962, naturalized, 1969; d. Arius and Avasa (Niu) Levi; m. Charles M. Miller, Dec. 14, 1974; 1 child, Jamila Atamai. A.A., Chabot Coll., 1969; B.A., Calif. State U.-Hayward, 1971. Cert. tchr., Calif. Program developer/coordinator Alameda County Assn. Mentally Retarded, Oakland, Calif., 1969-71; program dir., tchr. Contra Costa Assn. Retarded/Richmond Calif. Sch. Dist., Walnut Creek, Calif., 1971-74; mgr. regional services MidWillamette Jobs Council, Pvt. Industry Council, Salem, Oreg., 1975—; mem. adv. bd. study on unemployment problems of Samoans, N.W. Regional edn. Lab., Portland, Oreg., 1982-83; participant vocation extern program for tchrs. and trainers Oreg. State U. and Oreg. Alliance for Program Improvement, Corvallis, 1985-86. Participant region 9-Oreg. Joint Action for Community Service, 1982-85; bd. dirs. Green Bhumb Agy. for Older Workers, Oreg.-Wash., 1985-86, Community Action Orgn. Info. and Referral, Stayton, 1985-86. Mem. Oreg. Employment and Tng. Assn. Avocations: sewing; gardening; swimming. Home: 18874 Old Mehama Rd SE Stayton OR 97383 Office: Mid Willamette Jobs Council 1495 Edgewater NW Suite 225 Salem OR 97304

MILLER, SHARON KAY, university official, public relations specialist; b. Tyler, Minn., Mar. 14, 1947; d. Dandrew C. and Elna H. (Kittelson) Lickness; m. Grant Larry Miller, Oct. 11, 1969 (div. Apr. 1976); 1 child, Jeffrey Grant. B.S. in Bus., Mankato State U., 1980; A.A., Worthington Community Coll., Minn., 1967. Exec. sec. State Univ. System, St. Paul, 1967-76, exec. asst. to chancellor, 1976-83, dir. pub. info., 1983—; mem. State Govt. Info. Council, 1985, 86. Mem. Minn. Women's Network, 1976—. Named Outstanding State Employee, Gov. Minn., 1981. Mem. Minn. Assn. Govt. Communicators (dir. 1985-86). Democrat. Avocations: reading; gardening; sewing; biking. Office: State Univ System 555 Park St Suite 230 Saint Paul MN 55103

MILLER, SHARON MONAHAN, medical technologist, educator; b. Oak Park, Ill., Jan. 1, 1942; d. Douglas and Elaine Iva (Markuson) Monahan; B.A., Northwestern U., 1963, M.S., 1965; Ph.D., U. Calif., Santa Cruz, 1972; postgrad. Stanford U., 1968; diploma Sch. Med. Tech., Silver Cross Hosp., Joliet, Ill., 1975; m. Thomas Raymond Miller, May 29, 1965. Asst. prof. med. tech., dir. allied health programs Coll. St. Francis, Joliet, 1969-75; edn. coordinator med. tech. program Northwestern U. Med. Center, 1975; asso. prof., coordinator med. tech. program Sch. Allied Health Professions, No. Ill. U., DeKalb, 1975—, acting assoc. dean Coll. Profl. Studies, 1983-84; mem. bd. Comprehensive Health Planning N.W. Ill., 1980—; CPR instr. ARC, 1980-84; bd. dirs. Adv. Bd. Vocat. and Career Edn., Regional Office Edn., Boone-Winnebago Counties, 1978—. Comdr. USNR. NSF fellow, 1965-66, 68-69; Arctic Inst. N. Am. grantee, 1971-73; Peace Corps tng. grantee, 1982. Mem. Am. Soc. Med. Tech. (trustee edn. and research fund 1980-83, chmn. scholarship com. 1981-82, regional chmn. biochemistry sci. assembly 1981-86), AAAS, Am. Assn. Clin. Chemists, Am. Soc. Clin. Pathologists (affiliate), Am. Soc. Allied Health Professions, Ill. Med. Tech. Assn. (chmn. coms. 1979-84, pres. Rockford br. 1981-82), Ill. Acad. Sci., Naval Res. Assn., Forest City Dog Tng. Club, Pine Tree Pistol Club, Phi Beta Kappa, Omicron Sigma, Beta Beta Beta., Phi Kappa Phi, Alpha Eta. Republican. Episcopalian. Club: Order Eastern Star. Author, editor in field. Home: 1604 Homewood Dr Rockford IL 61108 Office: Williston Hall Room 217 No Ill U DeKalb IL 60115

MILLER, SHIRLEY JEAN, automotive products company sales manager; b. Bennington, Okla., Nov. 19, 1936; d. Claude James and Mildred (Beames) Cleveland; m. Robert Clark Miller (div.); children—Lyndy Miller Riley, Micah Dawn. Sales rep. Curtis Industries, Eastlake, Ohio, 1977, cert. trainer, 1977-78, area mgr., 1978-83, dist. sales mgr., 1983—. Republican. Methodist. Home: 1130 Havner St Houston TX 77037

MILLER, SUSAN MCCALLUM, city official, accountant; b. Cheboygan, Mich., Oct. 13, 1945; d. Donald Hugh and Dorothy Jean (Becks) McCallum; m. Larry Alan Miller; children—David Albert, Heide Nicole. B.S. in Acctg., N.Y. Inst. Tech., 1977. C.P.A., Fla. Pvt. practice acctg., 1964-76; acct. IV, Bd. of County Commrs., Broward County, Fla., 1976-81; fin. dir. City of Boca Raton, Fla., 1981—, mem. pension bd. trustees, 1981—, chmn. indsl. revenue bond screening com., 1983—. Mem. Beautification Blue Ribbon Com., Boca Raton, 1983, 84. Mem. Gov. Fin. Officers Assn. (fin. reporting achievement award 1981, 82, 83, 84, profl. achievement recognition award 1982, 83, 84), Am. Inst. C.P.A.s (state and local govt. acctg. com.), Govt. Accts. Assn., Fla. Govt. Fin. Officers Assn. (chmn. tech. resources com. 1985-86), Fla. Inst. C.P.A.s (chmn. state and local govt. acctg. conf., mem. state and local govt. com.), Boca Raton C. of C. (mem. acctg./fin. and econ. devel. coms. 1983-85). Club: Woman's Forum (Boca Raton). Avocations: autocrossing Corvettes; cats; orchids; Grand Prix races. Office: City of Boca Raton 201 W Palmetto Park Rd Boca Raton FL 33432

MILLER, SUZANNE MELANIE, psychologist, educator; b. Montreal, Que., Can., May 28, 1951; came to U.S., 1977; d. Gerald and Joanne Miller; B.S. (Univ. scholar), McGill U., Can., 1972; Contbr. Inst. Psychiatry, U. London, 1976. Asst. prof. dept. psychology U. Western Ont. (Can.), 1976-77; research fellow div. family studies dept. psychiatry U. Pa., Phila., 1977-79; vis. scholar dept. psychology Stanford (Calif.) U., 1978-79; asst. prof. dept. psychology Temple U., 1979-83, assoc. prof., 1983—, adj. prof. dept. medicine, 1985—. Recipient Young Scientist award Brit. Psychophysiol. Soc., 1975; Nat. Research Council of Can. grantee, 1976; Temple U. research grantee, 1979-85; Robert Wood Johnson Found. scholar, 1983-86. Mem. Am. Psychol. Assn., Assn. of Behavior Therapists, Assn. for the Advancement of Behavior Therapy, Soc. of Psychophysiol. Research, AAAS, Soc. Behavioral Medicine. Mem. editorial bd. Cognitive Research and Therapy, Health Psychology. Contbr. numerous articles on behavior therapy, stress and depression to profl. jours. Home: 120 Broadmead St Princeton NJ 08540 Office: Dept Psychology Temple Weiss Hall Philadelphia PA 19122

MILLER, VIRGINIA IRENE, fine art galleries executive; b. Tampa, Fla., May 29, 1943; d. Chester Howard and Marie M.; A.A., Miami-Dade Community Coll., 1969; B.A. in Psychology, U. Miami, 1973; m. William Robert DuPriest, June 16, 1974. Art cons., organizer, dir. numerous art exhbns. for leading charities, fin. instns., Dade County, Fla., 1969-73; owner, dir. Virginia Miller Galleries, Inc., Coconut Grove, Fla., 1974-84; owner, dir. ArtSpace/Virginia Miller Galleries, Coral Gables, Fla., 1981—; guest lectr. Miami-Dade Community Coll. Ctr. Continuing Edn. of Women, 1984, U. Miami, 1985, Fla. Internat. U., 1985; pres. MACH I, Met. Mus. and Art Ctrs., Coral Gables, 1979-80, also mem. community relations com.; panelist, New Sch., N.Y.C., 1978; juror Artist's Day Competition, Coconut Grove 110th Birthday Celebration, 1984, Mus. of Sci. Left Bank Art; curator Miami ARTSfest, 1985; guest panelist Spl. Assignment: The Outlook for the Arts, WLRN-TV, 1985, art writer Women's Almanac newspaper, 1978-79; del. Gov.'s Conf. on Small Bus., 1983; community relations com., dir. Met. Mus. and Art Centers, 1979-80, mem. loan com. Fla. Feminist Credit Union, Miami, 1978-79; mem. adv. bd. The Coral Gables City Beautiful mag., 1983-85; bd. dirs. Miami Forum, 1984—; mem. exec. com. South Fla. Wilderness Camp, 1983, Jack and Ruth Eckerd Found.; press delegate White House Conf. on small bus., Washington. Mem. Coral Gables C. of C. (mem. beautification com., 1977, chmn. cultural affairs com. 1979-81), Coconut Grove C. of C. (dir., chmn. cultural affairs com. 1978-79, chmn. tourism com. 1979-80), Greater Miami C. of C. (mem. econ. devel. com., 1985-86), Nat. Found. for the Advancement of the Arts (mem. Com. of 1000, panelist Fla. Cultural Conf., 1984), Art Dealers Assn. South Fla. (treas. 1978-79), Phi Kappa Phi, Psi Chi. Address: ArtSpace 169 Madeira Ave Coral Gables FL 33134

MILLER, ZOYA DICKINS (MRS. HILLIARD EVE MILLER, JR.), civic worker; b. Washington, July 15, 1923; d. Randolph and Zoya Pavlovna (Klementinovska) Dickins; grad. Stuart Sch. Costume Design, Washington, 1942; student Sophie Newcomb Coll., 1944, New Eng. Conservatory Music, 1946; grad. Internat. Sch. Reading, 1969; m. Hilliard Eve Miller, Jr., Dec. 6, 1943; children—Jeffrey Arnot, Hilliard Eve III. Fashion coordinator, cons. Mademoiselle mag., 1942-44; instr. Stuart Summer Sch. Costume Design, Washington, 1942; fashion coordinator Julius Garfinckel, Washington, 1942-43; star TV show Cowbelle Kitchen, 1957-58, Flair for Living, 1958-59; model mags. and comml. films, also nat. comml. recs., 1956—; dir. program devel. Webb-Waring Lung Inst., Denver, 1973—. Mem. exec. com., bd. dirs. El Paso County chpt. Am. Lung Assn., 1954-63; bd. dirs., mem. exec. com. Colo. chpt., 1965—, chmn. radio and TV council, 1963-68, mem. med. affairs com., 1965-70, pres., 1961-68, procurer found. funds, 1965-72; developer nat. radio ednl. prodns. for internat. use Nat. Tb and Respiratory Disease Assn., Am. Lung Assn., 1963-68, coordinator statewide screening programs Colo., other states, 1965-72; chmn. benefit fund raising El Paso County Cancer Soc., 1963; founder, coordinator Colorado Springs Debutante Ball, 1967—; coordinator Nat. Gov.'s Conf. Ball, 1969; mem. exec. com. Colo. Gov.'s Comprehensive Health Planning Council, 1967-76, chmn., 1973-75; chmn. Colo. Chronic Care Com., 1969-73, chmn. fund raising, 1970-72, chmn. spl. com. congressional studies on nat. health bills, 1971-72; mem. Colo.-Wyo. Regional Med. Program Adv. Council, 1969-73; mem. Colo. Med. Found. Consumers Adv. Council, 1972-78; mem. decorative arts com. Colorado Springs Fine Arts Center, 1972-75; nat. founder, coordinator benefit fund raising Noel, 1973—. Recipient James J. Waring award Colo. Conf. on Respiratory Disease Workers, 1963; Zoya Dickins Miller Vol. of Yr. award established Am. Lung Assn. of Colo., 1978; Nat. Public Relations award Am. Lung Assn., 1979, Gold Double Bar Cross award, 1980, 83. Lic. pvt. pilot. Mem. Nat. (chmn. nat. father of year contest 1956-57), Colo., El Paso County (pres. 1954, TV chmn. 1954-59) cowbelle assns. Club: Broadmoor Garden (ways and means chmn. 1967-69, civic chmn. 1970-71, publicity chmn. 1972)(Colorado Springs, Colo.). Contbr. articles, lectures on health care systems. Home: 74 W Cheyenne Mountain Blvd Colorado Springs CO 80906

MILLER-BREIDENBACH, LYNNE ALCOTT, broadcasting executive, lobbyist; b. New Haven, Jan. 6, 1957; d. Bradford Alcott and Georgianna Lilia (Wicks) Miller; m. William Holmes Breidenbach, Aug. 12, 1978; children—Jonathan Alcott, Michael David. Student U. Central Fla. Producer talk show WKIS-Radio, Orlando, Fla., 1977-78; news dir. WWKE/WMFQ, Ocala, Fla., 1978; news reporter WRMF Radio, Melbourne, Fla., 1978-79; program dir. WAJL Radio, Orlando, 1979-80; news dir. WCIE Radio, Lakeland, Fla., 1981-86; coordinator Central Fla. Freedom Council, 1986—, Editor Focus,

1980. Lobbyist Concerned Women of Am., Washington and Lakeland, 1984—. Mem. Sigma Delta Chi. Republican. Episcopalian. Avocations: world vision international sponsor, prison ministry. Office: 2224 Magnolia Ave Lakeland FL 33803

MILLER-MCMILLEN, KAREN JO, personnel executive; b. Allentown, Pa., June 10, 1956; d. Paul Henry and Ruth Ann (Bartholomew) Miller; m. Robert Glenn McMillen, Oct. 14, 1978. B.S., Pa. State U., 1978; M.A., Ind. U. Pa., 1982. Caseworker, Indiana County Children and Youth, Pa., 1978-83, supr., 1983-84; human services coordinator Indiana County Planning Commn., Pa., 1984; testing and assessment specialist Susquehanna Employment & Tng. Corp., Lebanon, Pa., 1984-85; personnel dir. Cedar Haven, Lebanon, 1985—; personnel cons., Indiana, Pa., 1979-84. Reviewer book reviews Jour. Home Econs., 1981-83. Pub. relations chmn. Bus. and Profl. Women's Club, Lebanon, 1985-86; bd. dirs. Indiana County Head Start, 1979-83. Mem. Am. Soc. Personnel Administrn., Am. Soc. Tng. and Devel., Nat. Assn. Female Execs., Lebanon Area Personnel Assn., Pa. State U. Alumni Assn., Am. Bus. Women's Assn. Democrat. Presbyterian. Clubs: Zonta, Pa. State. Avocations: Jafra skin care cons.; aerobics; antique doll collecting. Home: 1425 E Walnut St Annville PA 17003 Office: Cedar Haven 590 S 5th Ave Lebanon PA 17003

MILLET, NAOMI CASSELL, mathematician; b. Washington, Nov. 15, 1923; d. Smith Maxwell and Eva (Hill) Cassell; B.S., Howard U., 1945; m. James Joseph Millet, Apr. 5, 1948; children—James Joseph, Andre Anthony, Michael Gregory, John Adler, Philip Avery. Mathematician, Dept. Def., 1951-63, mathematician/systems analyst, 1963-73; mathematician, analyst Dept. Agr., Kansas City, Mo., 1973-85; tech. mgr. SIMCAS, 1985—. Home: 3227 Vista St NE Washington DC 20018 Office: 1008 Avery Pl Largo MD 20772

MILLETT, KATHERINE MURRAY (KATE), feminist leader, author; b. St. Paul, Sept. 14, 1934; B.A. magna cum laude, U. Minn., 1956; postgrad. St. Hilda's Coll. Oxford (Eng.), 1956-58; Ph.D., Columbia, 1970; m. Fumio Yoshimura, 1965. Instr. English, U. N.C. at Chapel Hill, 1958; sculptor, Tokyo, 1961-63; file clk., N.Y.C., then kindergarten tchr. N.Y.C.; tchr. Barnard Coll., 1964-68; formerly tchr. English Bryn Mawr (Pa.) Coll.; distinguished vis. prof. Sacramento (Cal.) State Coll., from 1973; co-producer, co-dir. film Their Lives, 1970; one-woman shows of sculpture: Minami Gallery, Tokyo, Judson Gallery, Greenwich Village, 1967, Noho Gallery, N.Y.C., 1976, 78, 80, Levitan Gallery Soho, N.Y.C., 1978. Mem. Congress Racial Equality, from 1965; chmn. edn. com. N.O.W., 1966; active supporter women's liberation groups. Mem. Phi Beta Kappa. Author: Sexual Politics, 1970; The Prostitution Papers, 1973; Flying, 1974; Sita, 1977; The Basement, 1979; Going to Iran, 1981. Address: care Putnam Pub Group 200 Madison Ave New York NY 10016*

MILLHOUSE, NANCY CATHERINE, sales executive; b. Cleve., Sept. 21, 1954; d. Edward Leopold and Rose Marie (Cepek) Lah; m. Scott Alden Millhouse, Oct. 30, 1982; 1 child, John Creighton. B.A. in Chemistry, St. Louis U., 1977. Market mgr. Calgon Corp., subs. Merck & Co., Inc., Pitts., 1980-85; sr. tech. sales rep. Mobay Corp., Pitts., 1985—. Research fellow Monsanto Chem. Co., St. Louis, 1976. Mem. Nat. Assn. Female Execs., Alpha Sigma Nu. Democrat. Roman Catholic. Club: Mt. Lebanon Jr. Women's (pres. 1986-87). Home: 175 Markham Dr Pittsburgh PA 15228 Office: Mobay Corp Mobay Rd Pittsburgh PA 15205-9741

MILLIKEN, SUSAN JOHNSTONE, mathematician, educator, govt. ofcl.; b. Woodstock, Conn.; d. Francis U. and Violet Floyd (Ward) Johnstone; A.B., Vassar Coll.; M.A., Columbia U.; m. Peter H. Milliken, Dec. 15, 1950; children—Peter H. III, Frances U. Johnstone Balsam. Chief statistician, research analyst E. W. Axe & Co., investment counsel, N.Y.C., 1940-42, 48-52; economist War Prodn. Bd., Washington, 1943-44; chief economist for sugar and allied products OPA, 1945-46; head sugar price control in U.S. and its possessions U.S. Dept. Agr., 1947; profl. genealogist, 1953—; tutor in stats., math., French, econs. Columbia U., 1962—; instr. math. N.Y. Bd. Edn., 1966-83. Life mem. Gov. William Bradford Compact, editor bull., 1963-69. Mem. Colonial Dames Am. (docent, co-chmn., house com. mus., hospitality com.), Soc. Daus. Holland Dames, N.Y. Geneal. and Biog. Soc. Episcopalian. Club: Barnard. Author articles in field. Home: 423 W 120th St New York NY 10027

MILLIKIN, PATRICIA ANN M., real estate broker, developer; b. Milw., Nov. 3, 1958; d. Arthur D. Millikin and Hazel Maxine (Rogers) Millikin McEven. Student U. Fla., 1976-80, Buster's Sch. Constrn., Gainesville, Fla., 1983. Salesman, Benton and Brewer Realty, Gainesville, 1977-79, Wallace Cain Realty, Alachua, Fla., 1979-80; owner, broker Henry Matthews and Co., Alachua, 1980—; dir. D'Angelo Constrn., Inc., Alachua; pres. Real of Alachua, Inc., 1983—. Mem. Alachua C. of C., High Springs C. of C., Gainesville Bd. Realtors (bd. dirs. 1984), Farm and Land Inst., Multiple Listing Service (exec. com. 1982, 84). Republican. Methodist. Avocations: horses; snowskiing; sport fishing. Home: Route 2 Box 450 Alachua FL 32615 Office: Henry Matthews and Co 4020 N Hwy 441 PO Box 520 Alachua FL 32615

MILLMAN, MADELINE KERMAN, insurance company executive, educator; b. N.Y.C., Jan. 15, 1942; d. Samuel and Sylvia (Bass) Teich; m. Kenneth L. Kerman, Sept. 2, 1962 (div.); children—Marc Ira, Melissa Beth; m. 2d, Arthur J. Millman, Mar. 27, 1983. Student Syracuse U., 1959-61; B.S., NYU, 1963; M.Ed., Rutgers U., 1973, postgrad. 1973-74. Cert. tchr. N.J. Tchr. Manalpan-Englishtown (N.J.) Schs., 1971-72; grad. asst. N.J. Dept. Edn., Trenton, 1973-74; forums coordinator Nat. Health Council, N.Y.C., 1974-77; coordinator provider relations Bradford Adminstrv. Services, N.Y.C., 1977-78; adminstr. product devel. Blue Cross/Blue Shield, N.Y.C., 1978-79, adminstr. govt. relations, 1979—; chmn. Health Occupations Edn. Task Force, N.Y. State Dept. Edn., 1981-83; preceptor, selection day judge Coro Found., N.Y.C., 1981. Mem. Bus. Adv. Council, Black and Puerto Rican Caucus, N.Y. State Legislature, 1983-84. Mem. Consumer Assembly (dir. 1982—), Govt. Affairs Profls. (pres. 1983-85), N.Y. Area Pub. Affairs Profls., Am. Pub. Health Assn., Fin. Women's Assn., Creative Alternatives (dir. 1984—), Phi Delta Kappa, Kappa Delta Pi. Office: Blue Cross Blue Shield of Greater New York 3 Park Ave New York NY 10016

MILLNER, DIANNE MAXINE, lawyer; b. Columbus, Ohio, Mar. 21, 1949; d. Charles Nelson and Barbara Rose (Johnson) M. A.A., Pasadena City Coll., 1970; A.B., U. Calif.-Berkeley, 1972; J.D., Stanford U., 1975. Assoc. Pillsbury, Madison & Sutro, San Francisco, 1975-80; ptnr. Alexander, Millner & McGee, San Francisco, 1980—; dir. Star Seven Broadcasting, San Francisco, Black TV Workshop, Santa Rosa, Calif. Recipient Pres.'s award Nat. Bar Assn. Women, 1980. Mem. Calif. State Bar Assn., Charles Houston Bar Assn., Black Women Lawyers Assn., Bar Assn. San Francisco, Phi Beta Kappa. Office: Alexander Millner & McGee 353 Sacramento St San Francisco CA 94111

MILLS, ANNE, residence executive, therapist, administrator; b. Trieste, Italy, Nov. 24, 1923; came to U.S., 1930; d. Joseph and Clementine (DiMaquois) Stegos; m. Joseph Devlin (div. 1974); children—Joseph, Tom, Mark, Adam. B.A., Hunter Coll., 1946; M.S.W., U. Pa., 1981. Cert. social worker. Free lance writer, N.Y.C. and Montreal, 1947-61; instr. Immaculate Coll., Malvern, Pa., 1961-64; pub. Millshire Bus. Directory, Spring City, Pa., 1964-72; social worker Life Centers, Phila., 1972-74; pres., adminstr. Tri County Respites, Inc., Warwick and Southampton, Pa., 1974—; cons. to nursing homes, lawyers, individuals. Contbr. articles to publs. Mem. Nat. Assn. Social Workers. Unitarian-Quaker. Avocations: aging; mental health mental retardation; travel; real estate devel. Home: 171 N Broad St Doylestown PA 18901 Office: Tri County Respites Inc 1460 Meetinghouse Rd Warwick PA 18974

MILLS, ANNETTE CAROL, transportation engineer; b. Evanston, Ill., Nov. 17, 1939; d. Charles Elmer and Helen Bertha (Moen) Palmgren; m. Lawrence William Savre, Dec. 28, 1958 (div. Dec. 1966); children—Kimberly Ann Savre Harris, Scott Lawrence; m. William Teel Mills, Apr. 24, 1972. B.S.C.E., Bradley U., 1962; M.Engring. Adminstrn., 1975. Registered profl. engr., Ill. Engr., Ill. Dept. Transp. (formerly Dept. Pub. Works), Peoria, 1964—. Mem. Peoria Traffic Commn., 1973—. Mem. Ill. Assn. Hwy. Engrs. (Engr. of Yr. 1973), Ill. Soc. Profl. Engrs., ASCE. Avocations: golf, fishing, general outdoor activities. Office: Ill Dept Transp 6035 N Knoxville Peoria IL 61614

MILLS, CAROL MARGARET, trucking company executive; b. Salt Lake City, Aug. 31, 1943; d. Samuel Lawrence and Beth (Neilson) M.; B.S. magna cum laude, U. Utah, 1965. With W.S. Hatch Co., Woods Cross, Utah, 1965—, corp. sec., 1970—, traffic mgr., 1969—, dir. publicity, 1974—; dir. Hatch Service Corp., Nat. Tank Truck Carriers, Inc., Washington; chmn. bd. dirs. Intermountain Tariff Bur. Inc. Fund raiser March of Dimes, Am. Cancer Soc., Am. Heart Assn.; active senatorial campaign, 1976. Mem. Nat. Tank Truck Carriers, Utah Motor Transport Assn. (dir. 1982—), Transp. Club Salt Lake City, Am. Trucking Assn. (pub. relations council), Internat. Platform Assn., Beta Gamma Sigma, Phi Kappa Phi, Phi Chi Theta. Home: 77 Edgecombe Dr Salt Lake City UT 84103 Office: 643 S 800 W Woods Cross UT 84087

MILLS, DENISE YVONNE, librarian; b. Compton, Calif., July 19, 1946; d. Clifford Clinton and Lois Catherine (Eaton) Mills; children—Randall, Marisa, Nicholas. B.A. in Sociology, Calif. State U.-Long Beach, 1968; profl. diploma in elem. edn. U. Hawaii, 1976, M.L.S., 1980. Sch. librarian Stevenson Intermediate Sch., Honolulu, 1981-82, Bloomington (Calif.) High Sch., 1983—; librarian San Bernardino County Library, Fontana br., 1985—; research sec. Johns Hopkins U., Balt., UCLA, U. Calif.-Irvine, 1972-74. Mem. steering com. ednl. media task force San Bernardino County Supt. Schs., Calif., 1983-84. Mem. ALA, Calif. Media Library Educators Assn., Am. Assn. Sch. Librarians. Republican. Presbyterian. Home: 6615 Churchill St San Bernardino CA 92407 Office: Bloomington High Sch 10750 Laurel St Bloomington CA 92316

MILLS, ELIZABETH ANN, librarian; b. Cambridge, Mass., Apr. 1, 1934; d. Ralph Edwin and Sylvia Elizabeth (Meehan) McCurdy; m. Albert Ernest Mills, July 6, 1957; 1 dau., Karen Elizabeth. B.A., Duke U., 1956; M.S., Simmons Coll., 1973; postgrad. Boston Coll., Framingham State U., Bridgewater State U. Sec. Lowell House, Harvard U., Cambridge, 1956-57; substitute librarian, tchr. Wellesley High Sch. (Mass.), 1972-73, Needham High Sch. (Mass.), 1972-73; librarian Tucker Sch. Media Ctr., Milton Pub. Schs. (Mass.), 1973—, chmn. computer com., bldg. coordinator gifted program, 1981—. Contbr. articles to profl. jours. Active Girl Scouts U.S.A., U.S. Power Squadron, Gt. Blue Hill, Mass., 1974—. Mem. ALA, Am. Assn. Sch. Librarians, Assn. Library Service Children, Mass. Assn. Ednl. Media, Beta Phi Mu, Kappa Delta. Republican. Episcopalian. Home: 177 Jarvis Circle Needham MA 02192 Office: Tucker Sch 187 Blue Hills Pkwy Milton MA 02187

MILLS, EVELYN HURST, educator; b. Macon, Ga., Oct. 22, 1923; d. Wyatt Clark and Alma Evelyn (Andrishok) Hurst; m. James Arthur Mills (div.); 1 child, Barbara Alma. B.S., Memphis State U., 1945. Cert. tchr., Tenn. Tchr. Haywood County Schs., Brownsville, Tenn., 1945-47, Mississippi County Schs., Osceola, Ark., 1947-48; Memphis City Schs., 1959—; mem. state com. to write curriculum guides, 1985; mem. com. to write curriculum guides Memphis City Schs., 1985. Active Girl Scouts U.S., ARC. Fulbright Found. grantee, 1982. Recipient Award for Tchr. Excellence, Memphis Rotary, 1982. Mem. Am. Classical League, Classical Assn. Middle West and South, Tenn. Classical League (v.p. 1982-83), Vergilian Soc., Alpha Delta Kappa (pres. 1970-72). Republican. Episcopalian. Avocations: travel, reading. Office: White Sta High Sch 514 S Perkins St Memphis TN 38117

MILLS, FRANCES JONES, state official; b. Gray, Ky.; d. William Harrison and Bertie (Steely) Jones; student Union Coll., Barbourville, Ky., Eastern Ky. U., Richmond; grad. Cumberland Coll., Williamsburg, Ky.; m. Gene Mills, 1949. Mem. Ky. Ho. of Reps., 1961-62, asst. to speaker, 1963-65; dir. women's activities Ky. CD, 1965-72; clk. Ky. Ct. of Appeals, 1972-76; treas. Commonwealth of Ky., Frankfort, 1976-79, sec. state, 1979-83; treas. Commonwealth of Ky., 1984—; mem. Personal Service Contract Rev. Commn., 1976-80, Ky. Tchrs. Retirement Bd., 1976-80; del. Democratic Nat. Convs., 1964, 68, 76, 80, alt. del., 1972. Named Woman of Achievement, Bus. and Profl. Women's Club, 1976; Outstanding Alumna, Cumberland Coll., 1978; Outstanding Woman of Yr. in Ky., 1973; recipient Pub. Service award Ky. Fedn. Bus. and Profl. Women, 198; named one of eight Disting. Women of Knox County. Mem. Nat. Assn. State Treas. (v.p., So. region chairperson 1976-78), Nat. Conf. Appellate Ct. Clks. (pres. 1975-76), Nat. Assn. State Auditors, Comptrollers and Treasurers, AMA Aux., Whitley County Med. Aux. Baptist. Clubs: Williamsburg Order Eastern Star (Williamsburg); Bus. and Profl. Womens. Author CD booklet, What Would You Do?. Office: Dept Treasury Capitol Annex Frankfort KY 40601

MILLS, HELEN SLABY, English language educator, writing consultant; b. Cleve., Apr. 8, 1923; d. Ollie F. and Nettie J. (Hejl) Slaby; B.A. magna cum laude, Western Res. U., 1944; M.A., Calif. State U., Sacramento, 1965; m. LeRoy Kenneth Mills, June 12, 1948 (dec. Aug. 1983); children—Marilyn Antoinette, David Ellsworth. Women's editor Cleve. Citizen, 1945-48; tchr. (part-time) Western Res. U., Cleve., 1945-48; sec. to dir. Cleve. Inst. Art, 1948-50; x-ray technician and mgr. pvt. med. office, Sacramento, 1957-65; prof. English, Am. River Coll., Sacramento, 1965-84, part-time instr., 1984—; instr. U. Calif. Extension, Davis, 1972; instr. various workshops for tchrs., 1972—; writing cons. for bus. and govt., 1984—; book reviewer Harper & Row Publishers, 1972, Scott Foresman & Co., 1974—, Holt, Rinehart and Winston Co., 1975; free-lance writer, 1984—. Mem. Calif. State U. Alumni Assn., Kappa Delta Pi. Author: Commanding Communication, 1972; Commanding Sentences, 1974, 3d edit., 1983; Commanding Paragraphs, 1977, 2d edit., 1981; Commanding Essays, 1978, 2d edit., 1982; Commanding Composition, 1980; Connecting and Combining in Sentence and Paragraph Writing, 1982; contbr. articles on learning to profl. jours.; editorial bd. Jour. Personalized Instruction, 1974-81. Home: 3157 Oak Cliff Circle Carmichael CA 95608

MILLS, JOSEPHINE JAYNES, librarian; b. Greeneville, Tenn., Oct. 8, 1914; d. James Shipley and Azubah Earnest (Lyon) Jaynes; m. Kyle E. Mills, July 19, 1942; 1 child, Rebecca Josephine. B.S., East Tenn. State U., 1941, M.S., 1954. Cert. tchr., Tenn. Tchr., Greene County Schs., Greeneville, 1936-42, Greeneville City, 1944-51; librarian, 1951-75, ret., 1975; vol. librarian Nolachuckey Sch., Greene County, 1982—; lectr. in field. Sec., Andrew Johnson Meml. Assn., Greeneville, 1983—. Recipient Tchr. of Yr. award Greeneville C. of C., 1964; Appreciation plaque PTA, 1982, Greene County Bd. Edn., 1984. Mem. Nat. Ret. Tchrs. Assn., Local Ret. Tchrs. Assn., Tenn. Edn. Assn., Delta Kappa Gamma (pres. 1974-76, membership chmn. 1984—), DAR (regent 1980-82, chaplain 1982—). Democrat. Methodist. Club: Andrew Johnson Christian Women's. Avocations: doll collecting; swimming; sewing. Home: Route 4 Golf Course Circle Greeneville TN 37743

MILLS, MARCIA JOAN, lawyer; b. Evanston, Ill., Dec. 14, 1948; d. Fred Edward and Faye Henrietta (Kohn) Ryherd; m. Gerald Edward Mills, Mar. 5, 1977; children—Michael E., Amanda S. B.A., U. Ill., 1970; J.D. with honors, Fla. State U., 1975. Bar: Fla. 1975, Wis. 1977. Research asst. Fla. Ct. of Appeals (1st dist.), Tallahassee, 1975-76; ptnr. Glinski, Haferman, Ilten, Mills & Dreier, S.C., Stevens Point, Wis., 1976—. Bd. dirs. Community Alcohol Drug Abuse Ctr., Inc., Stevens Point, 1979—, Women's Resource Ctr., Stevens Point, 1980—; rep. Pvt. Industry Council Cen. Wis., Wisconsin Rapids, 1983—; adv. Community Alcohol Drug Abuse Council, Stevens Point, 1979—. Mem. ABA, Fla. Bar Assn., Wis. State Bar Assn., Portage County Bar Assn. (sec.-treas. 1984-85), Stevens Point Womens Forum. Roman Catholic. Club: Zonta.

MILLS, MARGARET MARY HOWARD, association executive; b. Levenshulme, Eng., Dec. 16, 1921; came to U.S., 1953, naturalized, 1973; d. Leonard and Katharine (Howard) M.; student U. London, 1939-42, Colegio Superior de Vicosa, Minas Gerais, Brazil, 1943-45. Translator, writer O Observador Economico, Rio de Janeiro, 1945-47; researcher Brazilian embassy, London, 1948-53; asst. dir. purchasing commn. Brazilian Treasury del., N.Y.C., 1954-64; asst. Cheryl Crawford Prodns., 1965-67; asst. to dir. Am. Acad. Arts and Letters, N.Y.C., 1968-73, exec. dir., 1973—; adv. com. Am. Art Directory, 1978. Bd. advisers Community Environments, N.Y.C., 1978. Recipient various certs. merit. Democrat. Office: American Academy of Arts and Letters 633 W 155th St New York NY 10032

MILLS, MARSHA SUE, auto manufacturing company executive; b. Hillsboro, Ohio, Oct. 23, 1949; d. Clarence V. and Edna (Toler) M. B.S., Ohio State U., 1972; M.A., Mich. State U., 1975. Personnel rep. Mich. State U., Lansing, 1977, compensation analyst, 1977-78; with Volkswagen of Am. Corp., various locations, 1978—, personnel adminstrv. mgr., Englewood Cliffs, N.J., 1982-83, corp. employee relations mgr., Troy, Mich., 1983—. Mem. adj. faculty Macomb Community Coll., Warren, Mich., 1985—; personnel cons. L.W. Norman & Assocs., Oak Park, 1979—. Vol. Big Brothers Big Sisters, Lansing, 1977-78. pres. Leadership scholar Ohio State U., 1972. Mem. Womens Econ. Club Detroit, Nat. Black MBA Assn., NAACP, (life), Phi Delta Kappa. Democrat. African Methodist Episcopal. Avocations: tennis; racquetball; antique collecting; travel. Home: 15700 Providence Dr Apt 911 Southfield MI 48075 Office: Volkswagen Am Inc PO Box 3951 Troy MI 48007

MILLS, MITZI TADE, textile company executive, designer; b. Highland, Ill., Jan. 9, 1949; d. George Thomas and Wilma Jean (Daily) Tade; m. Donald Bjorn Mills, July 24, 1970; children—George Robert, Jessica McCandlish. B.F.A., Tex. Christian U., 1971. Dir. mktg. A. Brandt Co., Inc., Fort Worth, 1974-82, Gilbert Internat., Fort Worth, 1982-83; pres. Stratford Hall, Inc., Fort Worth, 1983—; freelance artist for advt. industry, Fort Worth; 1970-74. Mem. Women of the West, 1978-80, Fort Worth Historic Preservation Council, 1984—, The Arts Orgn., 1984—; sect. pres. Fort Worth Jr. Womans Club, 1979—. Recipient Bevey award Jr. Womans Club Sect., 1982, 83. Mem. Inst. Bus. Designers (silver award for Conquistador textile design 1985), Am. Soc. Interior Designers (industry found.), Color Mktg. Group, Chi Omega Alumnae (officer 1979-81, Best Alumnae award 1982). Avocation: art. Home: 4104 Harlanwood Dr Fort Worth TX 76109 Office: Stratford Hall Inc 2946 Stuart Dr Fort Worth TX 76104

MILLS, NANCY LOUISE, accountant; b. Coral Gables, Fla., Sept. 29, 1960; d. Alfred Preston and Josephine Elizabeth (Sullivan) M. B.S. in Acctg., U. Fla., 1983; M.Profl. Acctg., U. Miami, Fla., 1984. C.P.A., Fla. Intern, Occidental Chem. Co., White Springs, Fla., 1982; staff auditor Touche, Ross & Co., C.P.A.s, Miami, 1985—. Mem. Am. Inst. C.P.A.s, Fla. Inst. C.P.A.s, Nat. Assn. Female Execs., Am. Women's Soc. C.P.A.s, U.S. Tennis. Assn., Beta Gamma Sigma. Clubs: Royal Palm Tennis, Tropical Rose Soc. (Miami). Avocations: tennis; water sports; camping; roses; cactus. Home: 7540 SW 28 St Miami FL 33155 Office: Touche Ross & Co CPAs 100 Chopin Plaza Miami FL 33131

MILLS, PATRICIA WILLIAMS, lawyer; b. Johnstown, N.Y., Sept. 18, 1940; d. Virginia Mills Howard; m. Samuel Williams (div.); children—Vincent Michael, Valerie Michelle. A.B. in Math., Carthage Coll., 1970; M.Math., U. So. Calif., 1974; J.D., U. Calif., 1978. Bar: Calif. 1979, U.S. Dist. Ct. (no. dist.) Calif. 1979, U.S. Dist. Ct. (ea. dist.) Calif. 1983. With Pacific Bell Telephone Co., 1963-70, Ill. Bell Telephone Co.; tchr. math. Los Angeles Unified Sch. Dist., 1970-75; assoc. Long & Levit, San Francisco, Breon, Galgani, Godino & O'Donnel, San Francisco, 1980-84; sole practice, San Francisco, 1984—. NSF grantee, 1974-75. Mem. Calif. Assn. Black Lawyers (historian 1982, treas. 1983), Calif. Bar Assn., No. Dist. Calif. Black Women Lawyers (treas. 1981, v.p. 1982). Democrat. Roman Catholic. Home: 3301 Morcom Ave Oakland CA 94619 Office: 703 Market St Suite 306 San Francisco CA 94103*

MILLS, REBECCA ANN, advertising executive; b. Storm Lake, Iowa, May 11, 1950; d. Omer H. and Awanda Lucille (Mathison) Roth; B.A. with honors in Journalism, Drake U., 1972; m. Timothy Lemar Mills, Dec. 22, 1973; 2 daus., Sarah Rebecca, Abby Elizabeth. Editor, The Spirit, Des Moines Register & Tribune, 1972-73; coordinator Iowa Credit Union League Mktg. Services, 1973-74; account exec. The Prescott Co., 1974-75; pres. The Mills Agy., Storm Lake, 1975—; guest lectr. Buena Vista Coll.; conf. speaker. Bd. dirs. Faith, Hope and Charity, 1982-85; mem. Lake Creek Ladies Bd., 1983-86, pres., 1985. Mem. Women in Communications, Am. Soc. Exec. and Profl. Women, Internat. Platform Assn., Am. Fedn. Ind. Bus., Ad Club Sioux Cities, Internat. Soc. Bus. Communicators, Iowa Soc. Bus. Communicators, Storm Lake C. of C. (dir. 1980-82, pres. 1983), AAUW (mem.-at-large), DAR (regent 1981-82). Republican. Presbyterian. Clubs: Keystone (pres. 1983), Eastern Star (past officer), Taekwondo (4th deg. decided blue belt). Home: 131 N Emerald Dr Storm Lake IA 50588 Office: PO Box 28 Storm Lake IA 50588

MILLS, ROBIN KATE, law librarian; b. Chgo., Jan. 10, 1947; d. Dumont Cromwell and Virginia Anne (Nordeng) M.; A.B., Ind. U., 1969, M.L.S., 1970; J.D., U. S.C., 1976. Circulation/reference librarian Ind. U. Sch. Law, Bloomington, 1970-73; asst. law librarian U. S.C. Sch. Law, Columbia, 1973-76, asst. prof. law and law librarian, 1976-81, asso. prof. law and law librarian, 1981-84; asso. prof. law and law librarian Emory U. Sch. Law, Atlanta, 1984—. Mem. Am. Assn. Law Libraries (chpt. pres. 1980-82), Am. Bar Assn., S.C. Bar Assn., S.C. Library Assn. Author: South Carolina Legal Research Handbook, 1976. Office: Emory U Law Library Gambrell Hall Atlanta GA 30322

MILLS, STEPHANIE, singer, actress; b. N.Y.C., 1959. Studied at Juilliard Sch. of Music. Rec. artist; Broadway debut in The Wiz, 1975, revival, 1984. Recipient Grammy award for best rhythm and blues recording for female vocalist for Never Knew Love Like This Before, 1980. Address: care Casablanca Records Polygram Classics Inc 810 7th Ave New York NY 10019*

MILLS, SUSAN KATHLEEN AHEARN, medical technologist; b. St. Cloud, Minn., Sept. 11, 1951; d. Clarence and Kathleen (Siverling) Ahearn; m. Richard Cameron Mills, May 19, 1977. B.S., Concordia Coll., Moorhead, Minn., 1973. Lic. clin. lab. technologist Fla.; registered med. technologist Am. Soc. Clin. Pathologists. Med. technologist Bapt. Hosp., Pensacola, Fla., 1973-75, Hyland Plasmapheresis, Pensacola, 1975-76, No. Central Labs., St. Cloud, Minn., 1976-79; tech. specialist Technicon Instruments, Chgo., 1979-81; tech. dir. Instrumentation Lab., Elk Grove, Ill., 1981—; guest lectr. U. Ill. Med. Sch., S.D. Med. Tech. Soc., Wis. Med. Technologists, Minn. Soc. Med. Tech. Home: 445 Oxford Pl Roselle IL 60172 Office: 2901 Higgins Rd Elk Grove Village IL 60007

MILNE, ROBIN JAYN LAUTENBACH, sales executive; b. El Paso, Tex., Nov. 2, 1955; d. William Earl and Jacqueline Renee (Whitt) Lautenbach; m. Richard William Milne, Jr., Apr. 20, 1985. B.A. in Bus. Adminstrn., Ariz. State U., 1978. Sales rep., interior designer TOTAL/Interiors, Scottsdale, Ariz., 1975-79; sales rep. Am. Hosp. Supply, San Francisco, 1979-81, sales mgr., 1981-82, sales mgr., Sacramento, 1982-83; region mgr. H.B.O. & Co., San Francisco, 1983-85, sales dir., Scottsdale, 1985—. Mem. Nat. Assn. Profl. Saleswomen (founding pres. San Francisco 1981-82, nat. pres. 1983-85, Cross Pen Outstanding Sales Woman award 1982, rep. Am. Bus. Women's Day White Ho. Luncheon 1983), Bus. and Profl. Women's Assn. (Young Careerist award 1985, Young Career Woman award 1986), Am. Acad. Med. Adminstrs. Republican. Club: Soroptomists. Avocations: racquetball, public speaking. Home: 4551 N 65th St Scottsdale AZ 85251 Office: HBO & Co 901 Mariner's Island Blvd #700 San Mateo CA 94404

MILNER, BRENDA ATKINSON LANGFORD, psychologist; b. Manchester, Eng., July 15, 1918; emigrated to Can., 1944; d. Samuel and Leslie (Doig) Langford. B.A., Cambridge (Eng.) U., 1939, M.A., 1949, Sc.D., 1972; Ph.D., McGill U., 1952; LL.D. (hon.), Queen's U. Exptl. officer U.K. Ministry of Supply, 1941-44; prof. agrégé Institut de Psychologie, Université de Montréal, 1944-52; research asso. psychology dept. McGill U., Montreal, 1952-53, lectr. dept. neurology and neurosurgery, 1953-60, asst. prof., 1960-64, asso. prof., 1964-70, prof. psychology, 1970—; head neuropsychology research unit Montreal Neurol. Inst., 1953—; Clothworkers fellow Girton Coll., Cambridge, 1972-73. Mem. editorial bd.; Neuropsychologia, 1973—, Behavioral Brain Research, 1980. Assoc. Med. Research Council Can., 1964—; recipient Disting. Sci. Contbn. award Am. Psychol. Assn., 1973; Karl Spencer Lashley award Am. Philos. Soc., 1979; Izaak Walton Killam Meml. prize Can. Council, 1983. Fellow Royal Soc. London, Royal Soc. Can., Am. Psychol. Assn., AAAS, Can. Psychol. Assn.; mem. Am. Epilepsy Soc., Am. Neurol. Assn., Association de Psychologie Scientifique de Langue Française, Brit. Soc. Exptl. Psychology, Psychonomic Soc., Eastern Psychol. Assn., Internat. Neuropsychology Symposium, Soc. Neurosci., Nat. Acad. Scis. (fgn. asso.), Am. Acad. Neurology (asso.), Assn. Research in Nervous and Mental Diseases (asso.), Royal Soc. Medicine (affiliate), Sigma Xi. Office: Montreal Neurol Inst 3801 University St Montreal PQ H3A 2B4 Canada

MILNER, ZELDA WINOGRAD, government executive; b. Cleve., Dec. 17, 1919; d. Maurice Aaron and Rae (Garber) Winograd; m. Irvin Myron Milner, Aug. 15, 1943. A.B magna cum laude, Case Western Res. U., 1941. Tchr., Cleve. Pub. Schs., 1941-42; economist War Labor Bd., Cleve., 1943-46; asst. editor ency. World Pub. Co., Cleve., 1946; economist Wage Stabilization Bd., Cleve., 1946-47; with U.S. Dept. Commerce, 1947—, dep. dir., Cleve., 1970-80, dir., 1980—, mem. field ops. mgmt. council, 1980-81, regional mgr., 1980-81; dep. dir. U.S. Aircraft Trade Mission, Sudan, Kenya, Nigeria, 1978; writer, voice radio scripts Sta. WGAR, 1961-77. Editor: Bull. of Commerce, 1947-64, Bus. America-Ohio, 1965—. Mem. adv. com. Cleve. State U., 1985—, Cuyahoga Community Coll., Cleve., 1965—; mem., exec. sec. Minority Bus. Opportunity Com., Cleve., 1970-80; exec. sec. No. Ohio Dist. Export Council, Cleve., 1980—; exec. sec. Nat. Def. Exec. Res., Cleve., 1980—; mem. vis. com. Western Res. Coll., 1979—; bd. overseers Case Western Res. U., 1982—. Recipient Silver medal Sec. of Commerce, 1957, Creative Communication award, 1965; Fed. Career Service award Greater Cleve. Growth Assn., 1968;

Spl. Achievement award Bur. of Census, 1971; Outstanding Achievement award Fed. Exec. Bd., 1976-83; Case Centennial scholar Case Inst. Tech., Case Western Res. U., 1980. Mem. Cleve. Bus. Economists Club, Phi Beta Kappa (pres. Cleve. chpt. 1968-69). Club: Women's City Cleve. (bd. dirs. 1978-83, bd. dirs. found. 1984—). Office: US Dept Commerce 666 Euclid Ave Cleveland OH 44114

MILOWE, LAYNE KIMBERLY, caterer; b. Cin., Aug. 31, 1958; d. Irvin Donald and Milowe and Roberta Sue Greene. B.S., Salem Coll., W.Va., 1980. Dir. Reston Riding Ctr., Va., 1980; supr. Telecheck, Inc., Bethesda, Md., 1980-81; mgr. Le Souperb, Washington, 1981-82; asst. mgr. Zim's Restaurants, San Francisco, 1982-83; owner, pres. Swan Caterers Inc., Washington, 1983—; riding instr., Md. and Va., 1980-82; instr. Open U., Washington, 1986—. Mem. Inst. Off-Premise Catering, Nat. Assn. Female Execs., Nat. Restaurant Assn. Democrat. Jewish. Avocations: skiing, hiking, camping, photography, singing. Home: 1622 Florida Ave NW Washington DC 20009 Office: Swan Caterers Inc 1532 U St NW Washington DC 20009

MILSK, BARBARA SILVERMAN, personnel executive; b. Chgo., June 5, 1947; d. Lewis and Rose (Brown) Levin; m. Stephen G. Silverman, Aug. 8, 1971 (dec. Aug. 1974); m. David S. Milsk, Dec. 2, 1984; children—Laura, Susan. B.A., Am. U., 1969; M.A., NYU, 1971; postgrad. Leningrad U. (USSR), 1967. Research assoc. Russell Reynolds Assocs., N.Y.C., 1972-74; dir. research Booz-Allen & Hamilton, Chgo., 1975-78; asst. dir. personnel Needham Harper & Steers, Chgo., 1978-83; dir. profl. personnel Sonnenschein Carlin Nath & Rosenthal, Chgo., 1983-84; v.p. human resources Bozell, Jacobs, Kenyon & Eckhardt, Chgo., 1985—. Mem. Chgo. Symphony Soc., Am. Jewish Congress & Com., Chgo., N.Y.C. Mem. Am. Soc. Personnel Adminstrs., Nat. Assn. Law Placement. Clubs: Chgo. Advt., Women's Advt. Office: 625 N Michigan Ave Chicago IL 60611

MILTON, PATRICIA ANN, journalist; b. Rockville Centre, N.Y., Mar. 14, 1948; d. Arthur G. and Marie F. (Landis) Milton; B.A. in History/Polit. Sci., C.W. Post Coll., 1970; M.Pub.Adminstrn., L.I. U., 1973; postgrad. St. John's U., 1971; m. Charles Roy Steinfort, June 28, 1980. Reporter gen. news The AP, N.Y.C., 1971-76, corres., L.I. Bur. chief, 1976—. Democratic leader Village of Westbury, L.I., 1971-73. Recipient writing award Am. Acad. Physicians. James Gordon Bennett scholar, 1967-70. Mem. Women in Communications, Sigma Delta Chi. Roman Catholic. Clubs: Deadline, Overseas Press. Author: For Mercy Sake (booklet), 1966; contbr. articles to profl. jours. Home: 1333 Carper's Farmway Vienna VA 221802 Office: AP State Supreme Ct Mineola NY 11501

MILTON, PATRICIA ANNE, educator, consultant; b. Frederick, Md., May 26, 1939; d. Raymond Guynne Brown and D. Edith (Baker); m. James Douglas Milton (dec.); children—Vicki Denise, Hollie Vanessa, Jami Elizabeth. A.A., Brevard Community Coll., 1974; B.A. in English and Phys. Edn. with honors, Rollins Coll., 1976; M. in Phys. Edn. with honors, U. Central Fla., 1978; M.Ed. with honors, Nova U., 1978. Instr. athletic injuries Brevard Community Coll., Cocoa, Fla., 1979—; cons. diet and nutrition, Satellite Beach, Fla., 1981—, Cheerleaders Assn., Brevard County, Fla., 1975—; cons., pres. Project READS, Southeastern States, 1984—; tchr. Melbourne High Sch., Fla.; instr. aerobics, Fla., 1974—; clinician Women's Volleyball, Brevard County, 1974—. Writer, cons. adult edn. module program, 1985—. Coordinator Spl. Olympics, Merritt Island, Fla., 1980-84. Recipient Hon. aware Brevard Community Coll., 1982. Mem. AAUW, Fla. Adult Edn. Assn., Am. Inst. Athletics For Women, Am. Writers Guild, Phi Delta Kappa. Club: Merritt Island Women's (chmn. program 1973-75). Home: 3040 Clearlake Ct Weston Park Melbourne FL 32940 Office: Melbourne High Sch 74 Bulldog Blvd Melbourne FL 32901

MIMS, DONNA THERESA, educator; b. Washington, July 17, 1953; d. Oscar Lugrie and Barbara (Crockett) M. B.A., U. Md., 1975; M.A., Trinity Coll., 1977; postgrad. U. Houston, 1983—. Tchr. French and Spanish, Prince George's County Sch. Dist. (Md.), 1975-81; internat. student advisor Tex. So. U., Houston, 1981, internat. admissions officer, 1981-82; instr. English, San Jacinto Coll., Pasadena, Tex., 1982-83; tchr. English, Houston Ind. Sch. Dist., 1983—, English as a Second Lang. tchr. Ithaca City Sch. Dist., N.Y., 1984—. Mem. NEA, Nat. Assn. Fgn. Student Affairs, U. Md. Alumni Assn.

MIMS, JOYCE ELAINE, lawyer; b. Chgo., Mar. 6, 1942; d. Thomas Samuel Mims and Hortense Bernice (Wade) Miller. B.A., U. Wis., 1964; M.A., Northwestern U., 1965; J.D., NYU, 1975. Bar: Ill. 1976. Tchr. lang. Lane Tech. High Sch., Chgo. Bd. Edn., 1965-67; edn. specialist IBM World Trade Corp., N.Y.C., 1968-69; adminstr. lectr. CUNY-Brooklyn, 1969-75; assoc. firm Bell, Boyd & Lloyd, Chgo., 1975-78; atty. Am. Hosp. Supply Corp., Evanston, Ill., 1978-82, div. counsel, 1982-83, asst. gen. counsel, 1983—. Mem. Evanston Zoning Bd. Appeals, 1977-82; bd. dirs. Evanston Community Devel. Corp., Evanston Hosp. Corp.; Anderson del. Rep. Nat. Conv., 1980. NAACP Scholar, 1960; Chessmen Men's Club scholar, 1960. Mem. ABA, Chgo. Bar Assn., Nat. Slavic Honor Soc. Office: Am Hospital Supply Corp One American Plaza Evanston IL

MIMS, SUZANNE LOWERY, advertising executive; b. Akron, Ohio, July 17, 1954; d. Martin K. and Anne (Legan) Lowery; m. Gary Brooks Mims, Apr. 26, 1980; B.S. magna cum laude, Kent State U., 1976. Reporter, anchor Sta.-WKSU-FM, Kent, Ohio, 1973-76; asst. press sec. Riegle for Senator campaign, Detroit, 1976, press sec. Senator D. W. Riegle, Washington, 1976-79; pub. info. officer U.S. Metric Bd., Washington, 1979; account exec. H.J. Kaufman & Assocs., Washington, 1980-81, v.p., 1981-83, sr. v.p., 1983—. Active Nat. Women's Dem. Club, Washington. Recipient Marjorie M. Block award Women in Communications, Inc., 1976. Mem. Pub. Relations Soc. Am., Women in Advtg. and Mktg., Sigma Delta Chi. Roman Catholic. Office: Henry J Kaufman & Assocs 2233 Wisconsin Ave NW Washington DC 20007

MINARIK, ELSE HOLMELUND (BIGART), author; b. Aarhus, Denmark, Sept. 13, 1920; d. Kaj Marius and Helga Holmelund; B.A., Queens Coll., 1940; m. Walter Minarik, July 14, 1940 (dec.); 1 dau., Brooke Ellen; m. 2d Homer Bigart, Oct. 3, 1970. Tchr. 1st grade, art, pub. schs., Commack, N.Y., 1950-54; author children's books: Little Bear, 1957; Father Bear Comes Home, 1959; Little Bear's Friend, 1960; Little Bear's Visit, 1961; No Fighting, No Biting, 1958; Cat and Dog, 1960; The Winds That Come From Far Away, 1960; The Little Giant Girl and the Elf Boy, 1963; A Kiss for Little Bear, 1968. Mem. PEN Club. Home: Rural Delivery Barrington NH 03825 Office: care Harper & Row Inc 10 E 53d St New York NY 10022

MINCEY, BONNIE DIANE, telecommunications company official; b. Metter, Ga., Feb. 8, 1947; d. Ralph and Rose Lee (Daniel) M.; m. Clifton R. Groves, July 18, 1970 (div. 1979); 1 son, Rajah. B.B.A., Bernard Baruch Coll., 1979. Proof clk. Textile Banking Co., N.Y.C., 1965-68; long distance operator N.Y. Tel. Co., N.Y.C., 1968-69; asst. treas. Savings Banks Trust Co., N.Y.C., 1969-84; sales/mktg. staff Coradian Telecommunications Systems, 1984—. Mem. Savs. Banks Women, Exec. Female Assn., 100 Black Women. Democrat. Baptist. Home: 210 W 251st St Riverdale NY 10471

MINCHK, ELLEN KAY, community action agency executive; b. Danville, Ill., June 14, 1950; d. John Wiley and Helen Therese (McAndrews) Garrett; m. William Kerry Minchk, Aug. 16, 1980; m. Harry E. Egli, Aug. 21, 1971 (div. Nov. 1977). B.A., U. Dubuque, 1973. Mgr., Mr. Steak Restaurant, Dubuque, 1970-77; substitute tchr. Galena Middle Sch., Ill., 1973-74; employment coordinator Operation: New View, Peosta, Iowa, 1978-79, employment program mgr., 1979-82, dep. dir., fiscal officer, 1982-83, exec. dir. 1983—. Bd. dirs. Dubuque Girls Club, 1984. Mem. Iowa Community Action Assn. (bd. dirs. 1983—, chmn. tng. com. 1983—), Iowa Assn. Community Action Dirs., Regional and Nat. Assn. Community Action Dirs., Women in Mgmt., Dubuque Area C. of C., Iowa Youth Employment Assn. (sec. 1979-82). Democrat. Roman Catholic. Office: Operation New View PO Box 152 Peosta IA 52068

MINCIS, PHYLLIS GRECKEN, psychiatric social worker; b. Bklyn., Apr. 16, 1926; d. Jacob and Mamie (Liebman) Grecken; m. Albert Stephen Mincis, May 24, 1953; children—Mira Joan, Jonathan Jay. B.A., Bklyn. Coll., 1948; M.S.W., U. Minn., 1949; postgrad. Yeshiva U., 1982-85, D.S.W. (hon.), 1985. Cert. alcoholism counselor, N.J. Caseworker, Jewish Family Service, Phila., 1949-51, Bklyn. Bur. Social Service and Children's Aid, 1951-53; psychiat. social worker San Diego Dept. Pub. Health, 1957-59; family and marriage counselor Bergen County Jewish Family Service, Hackensack, N.J., 1965-68; sr. psychiat. social worker, alcohol counselor Bergen Pines County Hosp., Paramus, N.J., 1973-85. Recipient Eugene H. Adelman Social Worker of Yr. award Bergen Pines County Hosp., 1985. Mem. Nat. Assn. Social Workers (com. on alcoholism), Acad. Social Work, Clin. Social Work Directory, Internat. Transactional Assn., N.J. Assn. Alcoholism Counselors, Women's Task Force on Alcoholism. Jewish. Home: 54 Smithfield Rd Waldwick NJ 07463 Died Nov. 19, 1985.

MINDEL, ADRIENNE RAUCHWERGER, historian, educator; b. Bayonne, N.J.; d. Joseph and Blanche (Vitriol) Rauchwerger; m. Robert G. Spivack, 1940 (dec. 1970); children—Lorna Ellen Spivack, Miranda Sheila Spivack; m. 2d, Joseph Mindel, 1975. B.A., NYU, 1941; M.A., Am. U., 1966, Ph.D., 1976. Editorial assoc. Roscoe Drummond, newspaper columnist, Washington, 1960-63; teaching asst. Am. U., Washington, 1966-68, Massey fellow, 1968-69, univ. fellow, 1969-70; asst. prof. history Hood Coll., Frederick, Md., 1970-76, assoc. prof., 1976-84, prof., 1984—; commentator Duquesne U. History Forum, 1985; mem. Wye faculty seminar Aspen Inst., 1983; cons. town planning Town of Reston (Va.), 1963-64; humanities scholar and panelist Md. Com. for Humanities, 1977, 78, com. mem., 1979—. Assoc. editor Contemporary Affairs, 1963-64; contbg. editor: China and U.S. Far East Policy, 1967; contbr. articles to profl. jours. Mem. Va. Gildersleeve Internat. Fund for Univ. Women, 1981—; mem. Md. br. Nat. Coordinating Com. for Promotion of History, 1982—, AAUW Coll. Faculty Program scholar, 1964. Mem. Am. Hist. Assn., French Hist. Studies Assn., AAUP, AAUW, So. Assn. Women Historians, Phi Alpha Theta. Office: Dept History Hood Coll Frederick MD 27101

MINEMIER, BETTY M(ITCHELL), educational media specialist, computer consultant; b. Dansville, N.Y., July 13, 1928; d. Marshall Bradley and Joyce (Kenney) Mitchell; m. Robert Stansbury Minemier; children—Diana, Robert Stansbury, Ronald, Leah, Martin. B.S. in Edn. summa cum laude, SUNY-Geneseo, 1961, M.L.S., 1965, M.S. in English, 1971. Cert. library media specialist, N.Y. Library media specialist Central Sch., Arkport, N.Y., 1961-64; library media specialist Central Sch., Dansville, 1964—, dist. coordinator, 1981—; presenter computer workshops, 1979—; mem. Rochester Area Resource Exchange (N.Y.), 1979—; cons. microcomputers, 1979—. Reviewer for reference books Instr., 1964-80; mem. adv. council Scholastic, Inc., 1980-83. Clk. of session Presbyterian Ch., Dansville, 1979—; jour. clk. Genesee Valley Presbytery; mem. coll. council SUNY Coll.-Alfred, 1981—; mem. alumni council SUNY-Geneseo, 1983—. Mem. ALA, N.Y. Library Assn., Greater Rochester Area Sch. Media Sect. (mem. RESOURCES), N.Y. State Tchrs. Assn., Genesee Valley Tchrs. Assn., Am. Assn. Sch. Librarians, Dansville Tchrs. Assn., Assn. Council Mems. and Coll. Trustees of SUNY, Delta Kappa Gamma (parliamentarian), Kappa Delta Pi. Home: 20 Chestnut Ave Dansville NY 14437

MINER, CAROL SPALDING, educator; b. Louisville, Jan. 6, 1950; d. Wallace H. and Martha Lee (Ratterree) S.; B. in Internat. Studies, U. Louisville, 1972; M.A. in Human Resource Mgmt., Pepperdine U., 1976; m. John Boyd Miner, Oct. 2, 1971. Instr., Fla. Jr. Coll. at Jacksonville, 1972—, coordinator/counselor offender assistance program, 1975-77; assoc. dir. Jacksonville Community Council, 1977-81; dir. continuing edn. Fla. Jr. Colls., 1981-85, dean Open Campus, 1985—. Mem. United Way rev. com., 1977-78; pres. Spring Homeowners Assn., 1980-83; chmn. state public affairs com. Jr. League; host Politics is Your Business, LWV; bd. dirs. Leadership Jacksonville; v.p. Goodwill Industries; bd. dirs. Tree Hill, pres., 1985. Mem. Am. Soc. Public Adminstrn. (dir.), Am. Planning Assn., Jacksonville Women's Network (v.p.). Home: 1968 Largo Pl Jacksonville FL 32207 Office: Florida Junior College 101 W State St Jacksonville FL 32202

MINER, JACQUELINE, political consultant; b. Mt. Vernon, N.Y., Dec. 10, 1936; d. Ralph E. and Agnes (McGee) Mariani; B.A., Coll. St. Rose, 1971, M.A., 1974; m. Roger J. Miner, Aug. 11, 1975; children—Laurence, Ronald Carmichael, Ralph Carmichael, Mark. Ind. polit. cons., Hudson, N.Y.; instr. history and polit. sci. SUNY, Hudson, 1974-79. Republican county committeewoman, 1958-76; vice chmn. N.Y. State Ronald Reagan campaign, 1980; candidate for Rep. nomination for U.S. Senate, 1982; chmn. Coll. Consortium for Internat. Studies; mem. White House Outreach Working Group on Central Am.; co chmn. N.Y. State Reagan Roundup Campaign, 1984—; mem. nat. steering com. Fund for Am.'s Future. Mem. U.S. Supreme Ct. Hist. Soc., P.E.O. Address: Route 2 Hudson NY 12534

MINERVINI, MARIE ELEANOR, physical education teacher; b. Yonkers, N.Y., May 5, 1927; d. Charles Michael and Josephine Eleanor (Daniele) Parrotta; m. George August Minervini, Jan. 21, 1953; 1 dau., Lucia Maria. B.S., James Madison Coll., 1949; M.A., Columbia Tchrs. Coll., 1950. Tchr. phys. edn. Lexington Sch. Deaf, N.Y.C., 1949-50, Memphis Sch. Dist., 1952, Norfolk County Sch. (Va.), 1953, Mt. Vernon Sch. (Va.), 1951-53, 54, Yonkers Pub. Schs. (N.Y.), 1957—. Trustee Yonkers Pub. Library, 1978—, pres., 1980-82; pres. aux. Yonkers Gen. Hosp., 1980-82; trustee Women's Inst., Yonkers, 1980—; chairperson devel. speakers bur. Hudson River Mus., 1983-84. Recipient Humanitarian award Ch. of Our Savior, Yonkers, 1975. Mem. Sigma Sigma Sigma, Alpha Delta Kappa. Republican. Roman Catholic.

MINGA, BERNICE EQUILLA, chemist; b. Spring Hope, N.C., Nov. 11, 1952; d. John Eugene and Bernice Benford (Terrell) M.; m. Walter Perry Smith, Jr., Dec. 30, 1984. B.S., Meredith Coll., 1974. Sr. specialist chemistry Carolina Power & Light Co., Raleigh, N.C., 1974-84; sr. engr. Impell Corp., Norcross, Ga., 1985—. Mem. Am. Nuclear Soc., Am. Chem. Soc. Avocations: tennis; swimming; cooking; reading. Home: 100 Perch Point Peachtree City GA 30269 Office: Impell Corp 333 Research Ct Technology Park Atlanta Norcross GA 30092

MINGIN, MARGARETMARY ANDREA, educational media specialist; b. Perth Amboy, N.J., Oct. 23, 1942; d. Joseph John and Cecilia (Stolarik) Bakaisa; m. Gerald C. Mingin, Aug. 22, 1964; 1 son, Gerald C. A.B., Douglass Coll., 1964; M.L.S., Rutgers U., 1980. Cert. med. librarian, elem. tchr., ednl. media specialist. Med. librarian Muhlenberg Hosp., Plainfield, N.J., 1978-79; info. specialist N.J. Occupational Resource Ctr./Ednl. Resources Info. Clearinghouse, Edison, N.J., 1979-80; library media specialist East Brunswick (N.J.) High Sch., 1980-84; head librarian Columbia (N.J.) High Sch., 1984—. Trustee South Plainfield Free Pub. Library, 1973-83, pres., 1981-83. Mem. ALA, N.J. Ednl. Assn., N.J. Library Assn., N.J. Library Trustee Assn., Internat. Assn. Sch. Librarians, Beta Phi Mu. Home: 87 Laurel Hollow Ct Edison NJ 08820 Office: Columbia High Sch 17 Parker Ave Maplewood NJ 07040

MINICK, PHYLLIS BRIDGE, editor; b. Los Angeles, Jan. 15, 1929; d. Louis A. and Gertrude E. Bridge; m. Stanley R. Minick, Jan. 25, 1951; children—Lloyd Scott, Ricky Patrice. B.A., UCLA, 1952. Freelance editor, writer, 1967—; contbr. articles to Dive Mag., Skin Diver, Genie, San Diego Mag, Aquarius, Atlante; oceanographic statis. researcher, scuba diver Fathoms Plus, Inc., 1967-70; sci. writer Health Communications, Inc., 1973-74; sr. house editor Scripps Clinic and Research Found., La Jolla, Calif., 1974—; instr. extension div. U. Calif., San Diego; lectr. tech. English. Mem. Soc. Tech. Communications (past chmn. San Diego chpt.), Am. Med. Writers Assn. (nat. bd. dirs.), Council Biology Editors. Home: 5860 Cactus Way La Jolla CA 92037 Office: 10666 N Torrey Pines Rd La Jolla CA 92037

MINK, MARJORIE LEE, interior designer; b. Los Angeles, Apr. 20, 1944; d. DeWitt and Marjorie Vernon (West) McIver; student Willamette U., Salem, Oreg., 1964, Calif. State U., San Jose, 1966; m. Douglas Hamilton Barr, Oct. 24, 1981; children by previous marriage—Jason C., Marne Anne. Textile cons. J.H. Thorpe Co., Los Angeles, 1967-68; designer Sally Sirkin Interior Design, Beverly Hills, Calif., 1968-71; pres. Lee Mink & Assocs., interior design and planning, Beverly Hills, 1971—; propr. Lee Mink Sch. Interior Design, Laguna Hills, Calif.; designer children's clothes under name Bunwarmers, 1985—; author weekly newspaper column Ask Lee; prin. works include corp. hdqrs. Occidental Petroleum Co., UNOCAL N.Y. Hdqrs. Active local Young Life, Cystic Fibrosis drives. Recipient Community Service award LaSertoma Club Internat., 1962; named Cook of Year, 17 mag., 1958. Mem. Alpha Chi Omega. Democrat. Presbyterian. Home: 66 Balsam Ave Toronto ON M43B7 Canada Office: 3722 Green Gables Dr Tarzana CA 91356

MINK, MAXINE MOCK, public relations executive; b. Lakeland, Fla., Jan. 17, 1938; d. Idus Frank and Elizabeth (Warren) Mock; student Fla. So. Coll.; children—Lance Granger, Justin Chandler. With Union Fin. Co., Lakeland, Fla., 1956-62; partner/owner S & S Ent. & Arrow Lake Mobile Home Pk., Lakeland, Fla., 1957-66; head bookkeeper Seaboard Fin., Lakeland, 1964-68; partner Custom Chem., Inc., Lakeland, 1968-75; partner Don Emilio Perfumers, Newport Beach, Calif., 1978-79; owner Maxine Mink Public Relations, Newport Beach, 1978-84; fine homes and relocation specialist Merrill Lynch Realty, Newport Beach, 1985—. Bd. dirs. Guild of Lakeland Symphony Orch., 1972-75; mem. Lakeland Gen. Hosp. Aux., 1974-76. Mem. Newport Beach C. of C., Hoag Hosp. Aux., NOW, Nat. Assn. Female Execs., Orange County Music Center Guild. Republican. Clubs: Lido Isle Woman's, Balboa Bay, Lido Isle Yacht. Home: 115 Via Undine Newport Beach CA 92663 Office: PO Box 1262 Newport Beach CA 92663

MINKLEY, SUZANNE SAWYER, educator; b. Middletown, Ohio, May 15, 1915; d. Clifford Louis and Harriett May (Logan) Sawyer; A.B., John B. Stetson U., 1937, M.A., 1942; B.L.S., George Peabody Coll. of Vanderbilt U., 1940; postgrad. Manatee Jr. Coll., 1960, Fla. So. Coll., 1966, U. South Fla., 1966-67; m. Carl Henry Minkley, Apr. 3, 1943; children—Elizabeth Suzanne Jarrard, Philip Carl. Tchr., librarian Mt. Dora High Sch., 1937-41, Leesburg High Sch., 1941-43, Delray Beach High Sch., 1943-45, Samsula Elem. Sch., 1955-56, Sarasota High Sch., 1956-57; reading specialist Bayshore Jr. High Sch., 1963-74, chmn. lang. arts dept. Bayshore Middle Sch., 1967-74; tchr. social studies Bradenton Middle Sch., 1974-84; cons. tchr. tng. program Edn. Professions Devel. Act of U.S. Dept. Edn., 1970-71; parliamentarian Manatee County Edn. Assn., 1968-72; mem. Volusia County Continuing Council on Edn., 1954-56; parliamentarian Bradenton Middle Sch. PTA, 1976-78. Chmn. bd. Deland (Fla.) Children's Mus., 1954-56; state bd. dirs. Am. Cancer Soc., 1954-61. Recipient citation Am. Cancer Soc., 1952-55; cert. of profl. acceptance NEA, 1966-67. Mem. Volusia County Fedn. Women's Clubs (legis. chmn. 1952-54), Fla. Fedn. Women's Clubs (chmn. radio and TV 1962-66), DAR, NEA, Fla. Edn. Assn., AAUW (chmn. edn. com. Deland br. 1943-45, Sarasota br. 1960-62), Am. Inst. Parliamentarians (cert. mem. Gulfcoast chpt., pres. 1984-85), Nat. Assn. Parliamentarians (pres. Sarasota unit 1973-77, 79-82, membership chmn. Sarasota unit 1982-84, parliamentarian Bradenton unit 1982-84, edn. chmn. Bradenton unit 1980-82), Fla. Assn. Parliamentarians, Gen. Fedn. Women's Clubs, Leonardy Gaveliers (pres. 1972-73), Mu Omega Xi, Sigma Kappa. Democrat. So. Baptist. Clubs: Primrose Garden (pres., founder 1953-55), Orange Blossom Garden (pres. 1962-63), DeLand Women's (pres. 1951-53), Woman's of Sarasota (pres. 1960-61), Fla. Fedn. Women's Clubs (dist. dir. 1960-63, parliamentarian dist. 1963-65). Coordinator Have Gavel, Will Travel panels for civic and social orgns., 1959-65. Home: 2540 Hibiscus St Sarasota FL 33579

MINNELLI, LIZA, singer, actress; b. Los Angeles, Mar. 12, 1946; d. Vincente and Judy (Garland) M.; m. Peter Allen, 1967 (div. 1972); m. 2d, Jack Haley, Sept. 15, 1974 (div.); m. 3d, Mark Gero, Dec. 4, 1979. Appeared in Off Broadway revival of Best Foot Forward, 1963; recorded You Are for Loving, 1963; appeared with mother at London Palladium, 1964; appeared in Flora, The Red Menace, 1965 (Tony award), The Act, 1977 (Tony award), The Rink, 1984; nightclub debut at Shoreham Hotel, Washington, 1965; appeared in numerous films including Charlie Bubbles, 1967, The Sterile Cuckoo, 1969, Tell Me That You Love Me, Junie Moon, 1970, Cabaret, 1972 (Oscar award), Lucky Lady, 1975, A Matter of Time, 1976, New York, New York, 1977, Arthur, 1981; appeared on TV in own spl. Liza With a Z, 1972, The Princess and the Pea, Showtime, 1983. Address: care Creative Mgmt Assos 40 W 57th St New York NY 10022*

MINNER, RUTH ANN, state senator; b. Milford, Del., Jan. 17, 1935; m. Roger Minner. Student Del. Tech. and Community Coll. Former mem. Del. Ho. of Reps.; now mem. Del. Senate. Democrat. Office: Del State Capitol Bldg Dover DE 19901*

MINNICH, NANCY LOUISE PHARR, librarian; b. Norristown, Pa., Feb. 5, 1927; d. John D. and Marjorie E. (Ries) Pharr; m. C. Stewart Minnich, May 29, 1948; children—Keith R., Ronald G. David L. B.A., Ursinus Coll., 1949; M.S.L.S., Drexel U., 1965; M.S. in Edn. Media, Temple U., 1971. Tchr. Primos Sch., Upper Darby, Pa., 1952-56; elem. sch. librarian, Haverford (Pa.) Sch., 1965-68; library dir. Tower Hills Sch., Wilmington Del., 1968—; del. Del. Gov.'s Conf. on Libraries, 1978; library cons., 1983—; cons. Ptnrship. Library Project. Contbr. articles to profl. jours. Pres. Friends of Wilmington Library, 1980-81. Del. Humanities Forum grantee, 1979; Del. Div. Libraries grantee, 1982. Mem. Del. Sch. Library Media Assn. (past pres.), Ind. Sch. Tchrs. Assn. (past pres.), Nat. Assn. Ind. Schs. (com. chmn.), Libraries in New Castle County (governing bd. rep., 1981-83), ALA, Am. Assn. Sch. Libraries (past com. chmn., chmn. non-pub. schs. sect. 1986-87), AAUW, LWV. Home: 2613 Deepwood Dr Wilmington DE 19810 Office: Tower Hill School Library 2813 W 17th St Wilmington DE 19806

MINNIER, TAMRA ELIZABETH, nursing administrator; b. Salamanca N.Y., Dec. 9, 1961; d. Glenn Ellwood and Marilyn Joan (Morrison) M.; A.S., U. Pitts., 1981, B.S., 1984, M.S. in Nursing, 1985. Staff and charge nurse Bradford Hosp., Pa., 1981-85, nursing supr., 1985—; teaching asst. U. Pitts., 1984-85. Mem. Am. Nurses Assn., Pa. Nurses Assn., Bradford Profl. Nurses Orgn., Grad. Student Nurses Orgn. (pres. 1984—), Sigma Theta Tau. Democrat. Episcopalian. Avocations: skiing; golf; reading; boating. Home: 78 Fiske Ave Bradford PA 16701 Office: Bradford Hosp 116-156 Interstate Pkwy Bradford PA 16701

MINTER, JIMMIE RUTH, medical corporation administrator; b. Greenville, S.C., Sept. 28, 1941; d. James C. and Lois (Williams) Jannino; B.S. Acctg., U. S.C., 1962; m. Charles H. Minter, Nov. 3, 1972; 1 dau., Regina M. Asst. controller Package Supply & Equipment Co., Greenville, 1964-70, Olympia Knitting Mills, Spartanburg, S.C., 1970-72; controller Diacou Knitting Mills, Spartanburg, 1972-74; adminstr. Atlanta Med. Specialists, P.C., Riverdale, Ga., 1974-79; adminstr., corp. sec. David L. Cooper, M.D. P.C., Riverdale, 1979—. Program chmn. 4th of July Celebration and Beauty Pageant, City of Riverdale; active local and state election campaign fund raising. Mem. Am. Bus. Women's Assn. (chpt. Bus. Woman of Yr. 1969), Nat. Assn. Female Execs. Home: 1244 Branchfield Ct Riverdale GA 30296 Office: 150 Med Way Suite C-2 Riverdale GA 30274

MINTZ, GILDA YOLLES, public relations company executive; b. N.Y.C.; d. Naftali and Sarah Pearl (Langner) Yolles; B.A., Hunter Coll., 1956; children—Louis Neil, Stephen Matthew. With Ruder Finn & Rotman Inc., N.Y.C., 1960-85, account supr., 1970-85, sr. v.p., 1978-85; pres. Gilda Yolles Mintz & Assocs., Inc., pub. relations and mktg., 1986—. Chmn. pub. relations adv. bd. Twp. of Teaneck (N.J.). Mem. Pub. Relations Soc. Am. (Silver Anvil 1978), Nat. Home Fashions League (v.p., past dir.), Am. Soc. Interior Designers. Office: 240 Madison Ave New York NY 10016

MINTZER, DORIAN, psychotherapist; b. Pitts., Feb. 19, 1946; d. Oscar A. and Minna (Giffen) M.; B.A. in Social Scis., U. Calif., Berkeley, 1968; M.S.W. with honors, U. Pitts., 1970; Ph.D., Smith Coll., 1979. Group worker Assn. Retarded Citizens Allegheny County, Pitts., 1970-72; chief social worker devel. clinic Children's Hosp., Pitts., 1972-75; research asso. child devel. unit Children's Hosp. Med. Center, Boston, 1977-78; clin. cons. Learning Therapies, Inc., Newtonville, Mass., 1977-81; research asso. social work and child psychiatry Beth Israel Hosp., Boston, 1980-82, also pvt. practice psychotherapy, Boston and Newton Centre, Mass., 1977—; lectr. Allegheny Community Coll., 1971-75; instr. U. Pitts., 1970-75; lectr. in psychiatry Cambridge Hosp., Harvard Med. Sch., 1983—. Cert. Nat. Registry Health Care Providers in Clin. Social Work; lic. clin. social worker, lic. clin. psychologist, Mass. Mem. Boston Ctr. for Study of Groups and Social Systems (program chair), Nat. Assn. Social Workers, Am. Assn. Mental Deficiency, Am. Orthopsychiat. Assn., Soc. Research in Child Devel., Am. Psychol. Assn. (assoc.), A.K. Rice Inst. Author: The Psychoanalytic Study of the Child, vol. 39. Home: 43 W Boulevard Rd Newton Centre MA 02159 Office: 82 Marlborough St Boston MA 02116

MINUZZO, ANTOINETTE, educator; b. Lake Forest, Ill., Nov. 20, 1938; d. Frank and Maria Minuzzo; B.A., Lake Forest Coll., 1960; M.A., Northwestern U., 1967. Tchr., Oak Terrace Sch., Highwood, Ill., 1960—; cons. Xerox Ednl. Publs., My Weekly Reader. Local and state edn. lobbyist; chmn. Ill. Polit. Action Com. for Edn., 1974-80. Bd. dirs. Literacy Vols. of Lake County, 1983-86. Recipient Those Who Excel award, 1974. Mem. NEA, Ill. Edn. Assn. (dir. 1972-80), Highwood-Highland Park Edn. Assn., Nat. Assn. Female Execs., AAUW, Phi Delta Kappa, Delta Kappa Gamma (pres. chpt. 1982-84, state legis. chmn. 1981-85, state rec. sec. 1985—). Home: 813 Jenkisson Rd Lake Bluff IL 60044

MIRANDA, JACQUELINE FRY, former management consulting company executive; b. St. Anthony, Idaho, Nov. 3, 1953; d. Jack P. and Noreen (Daugherty) Fry; A.A., Cottey Coll., 1974; A.B., U. Calif., Berkeley, 1975; postgrad. Chgo.-Kent Coll. Law, 1983—; m. Daniel F. Miranda, Dec. 28, 1975; children—David F., Kate. Research assoc. Paul R. Ray & Co., N.Y.C., 1975-79; cons. Bartholdi & Co., Chgo., 1979-80; v.p. Houze, Shourds & Montgomery, Chgo., 1980-82.

MIRCI, SELMA ERK, clinical psychologist; b. Turkey; came to U.S., 1969; d. Kamil and Faika Erk; B.S., Middle East Tech. U., 1965; M.A., Hacettepe U., Turkey, 1968; Ph.D., U.S. Internat. U., 1976. Instr. psychology Hacettepe U., 1966-69; psychol. intern Orange County Mental Health, 1974-75; pvt. practice clin. psychology, Irvine, Calif., 1975—; cons. to women's groups. Mem. Am. Psychol. Assn., Calif. Psychol. Assn., Internat. Soc. Polit. Psychology, Orange County Art Alliance, Laguna Beach Chamber Music Soc., NOW. Office: 2070 Business Center Dr Irvine CA 92715

MIRELL, SANDEE LYNN, counselor, educator; b. New Haven, May 31, 1943; d. J. R. and Ruth B. White; A.B., Chapman Coll., 1964; postgrad. Calif. State U., Fullerton, 1965; m. Michael A. Mirell, Apr. 7, 1973; 1 dau., Hope. Tchr. English, Villa Park High Sch., Orange, Calif., 1965-67; adminstrv. asst. World Campus Afloat, Orange, 1968; law librarian City Atty. Law Library, Los Angeles, 1971-82; sch. counselor, tchr. Vivian Webb Schs., Claremont, Calif., 1982—. Mem. Assn. Ind. Sch. Counselors, ALA. Democrat. Mem. Christian Ch. (Disciples of Christ). Office: Webb Schs 1175 W Baseline Rd Claremont CA 91711

MIRKIN, MARSHA PRAVDER, psychologist; b. N.Y.C., Apr. 14, 1953; d. Sidney and Ann Toby (Goldman) P.; m. Mitchell I. Mirkin, Oct. 2, 1983; 1 child, Allison Sarah. B.A. (Regents scholar 1969-73, Sullivan award 1973), SUNY, Stony Brook, 1973; Ph.D., SUNY, Albany, 1979. Tchr. high sch. English, 1973-74; unit psychologist O.D. Heck Devel. Center, Schenectady, 1976-77; group home supr. Bosco House of St. Catherine's Center Children, Albany, 1977-78; intern Children's Psychiat. Center, Red Bank, N.J., 1978-79; adolescent clin. cons. Charles River Counseling Center, Newton, Mass., 1979-81; coordinator adolescent psychotherapy Charles River Hosp., Wellesley, Mass., 1981, dir. adolescent psychotherapy, 1981-84, dir. adolescent internship tng., 1984-85, dir. psychology tng., 1985; pvt. practice psychotherapy, consultation and tng., Newton; clin. instr. psychiatry Boston U. Med. Sch., 1981-84, asst. clin. prof., 1984—; guest lectr., cons., workshop leader in field. Mem. Am. Psychol. Assn., Am. Orthopsychiat. Assn., Soc. Family Therapy and Research, Women's Action for Nuclear Disarmament. Jewish. Co-editor: Handbook of Adolescents and Family Therapy. Author papers in field. Office: 53 Langley Rd Suite 300 Newton Center MA 02159

MIRLOCCA, NAOMI CECILE, computer software company official; b. Elizabeth, N.J., Feb. 17, 1937; d. Benedetto and Dorothy Ann (Mandelbaum) Mazza; m. Matthew Joseph Mirlocca, Dec. 28, 1957; children—Joseph Matthew, Scott David. A.A., Union County Coll., Cranford, N.J., 1957; B.S., Rutgers U., 1975; M.B.A., Fairleigh Dickinson U., 1977. Programmer, analyst Union Carbide Corp., N.Y.C., 1959-69; project mgr. Schering-Plough, Kenilworth, N.J., 1970-76; sr. systems analyst Am. Cyanamid, Wayne, N.J., 1976-77; mgr. profl. tech. tng. Mobil Corp., N.Y.C., 1977-84; mgr. tech. edn. ADR Ameritech, Princeton, N.J., 1984—; pres., New Computer Methodologies, Union, N.J., 1983—. Pres., Democratic Club, Union, 1981; 2d v.p. Union Twp. Dem. Com., 1981-82; leader Union County Dem. Dist., 1979—; bd. dirs. Union Twp. Bd. Edn., 1976—; bd. govs. Union County Coll., 1981—, trustee, 1981-82; founder, pres. Union chpt. Juvenile Diabetes Found., 1978; commr. Spl. Services Commn. Union County, 1982—; co founder Joseph Mirlocca Meml. Found., 1979—; past pres. mother's aux. Cub Scouts, 1977. Harrison A. Williams Congl. scholar, 1955; Humanitarian of Yr. award UNICO, 1983. Mem. Tri State Info. Mgmt. Educators, Regis 4 Computer Based Tng. User's Group, Fairleigh Dickinson U. Alumni Assn., Rutgers U. Alumni Assn., N.J. Sch. Bds. Assn. (governance com. 1981-82, del. 1977—), Alpha Sigma Lambda, Phi Chi. Roman Catholic. Club: Toastmasters (chmn. 1976-77). Home: 1866 Quaker Way Union NJ 07083

MIRON, RHODA PASCO, club woman; b. Cornwall, Eng., Feb. 16, 1902; brought to U.S., 1904, naturalized, 1940; d. William and Jane (Dymond) Pasco; student pub. schs., Hancock, Mich.; m. William E. Miron, June 19, 1926 (Dec. Jan. 1962); children—William E., John, Mary Miron Cota. Dep. sheriff, Escanaba, Mich., 1933-57; pres. House and Senate Club, Lansing, Mich., 1961-62; historian, chaplain Am. Legion Aux., Escanaba, Mich.; guide Daus. of Isabella, Escanaba; mem. Mich. Democratic Central Com.; mem. St. Francis Hosp. Aux. Club: Women's (Escanaba, Mich.). Home: 518 8th St Escanaba MI 49829

MIRSKY, SONYA WOHL, librarian, curator; b. N.Y.C., Nov. 12, 1925; d. Louis and Anna (Steiger) Wohl; m. Alfred Ezra Mirsky, Aug. 24, 1967 (dec. June 1974). B.S. in Edn., CCNY, 1948; M.S.L.S., Columbia U., 1950. Asst. librarian Rockefeller U., N.Y.C., 1949-60, assoc. librarian, 1960-77, univ. librarian, 1977—, curator spl. collections, 1979—; v.p., trustee Med. Library Ctrs. N.Y., 1980—; cons. library mgmt. Mem. Bibliog. Soc. Am., Bibliog. Soc. Can., Bibliog. Soc. Gt. Britain, Soc. Bibliography of Natural History. Home: 500 E 63d St Apt 15C New York NY 10021 Office: Rockefeller U Library 1230 York Ave New York NY 10021 6399

MIRZA, LEONA LOUSIN, educator; b. Chgo., July 1, 1944; d. Max B. and Opal Lousin; B.A. in Math., North Park Coll., Chgo., 1965; M.A. in Edn., Western Mich. U., Kalamazoo, 1967, Ed.D. in Edn., 1972; m. David B. Mirza; children—Sara Anush, Elizabeth Ann. Tchr. Kalamazoo Pub. Schs., 1965-69; asso. prof. edn. North Park Coll., 1969—. Chmn. adv. com. on edn. in Ill., 1975-77. Mem. Nat., Ill. assns. supervision and curriculum devel., Ill. Assn. Colls. of Tchr. Edn., Ill. Assn. Tchrs. Edn. in Pvt. Colls. (officer 1974-86). Contbr. articles to profl. jours. Specialist in elem. curriculum and adminstrn. Home: 795 Lincoln Ave Winnetka IL 60093 Office: 5125 N Spaulding Ave Chicago IL 60625

MISCHELL, PATRICIA LUCILLE, author, minister; b. Hurricane, W.Va., July 5, 1936; d. William and Gladys Lou (Tabor) Chapman; children—Rene Victoria, Cynthia Ann, Steven Joseph Zang. Student pub. schs., Blue Ash, Ohio. Founder, Hope Ministries and Positive Living Ctr.; pres. World of ESP; cons. Sci. Bur. of Investigation in N.Y.; affiliated with Tour Crafters of Cin.; lectr. in field; parapsychologist. Author: Beyond Positive Thinking, 1985. Mem. PSI Center, Positive Living Found., Assn. for Spiritual Devel. and Research, Spiritual Frontiers Fellowship, The Rosicrucian Order, Assn. for Research and Enlightenment, Internat. Entrepreneurs Assn., Nat. Fedn. Ind. Bus., Noohra Found. Office: Positive Living Center-Hope Ministry 8425 Vine St Cincinnati OH 45216

MISCHIARA, PAMELA LEE, business educator; b. Passaic, N.J., Apr. 23, 1945; d. Ernest Robert and Jeanne de la Montaigne Betz; master cosmetologist Jos. Paterno Coll. Beauty, 1973; postgrad. Pasco-Hernando Community Coll., 1979-82, Nova U., 1982-84; m. Richard Mischiara, May 19, 1965; 1 son, Timothy. Pvt. practice cosmetology, Andover, N.J., 1973, Holiday, Fla., 1974-79; office mgr. Forguson Real Estate, New Port Richey, Fla., 1979-81, Ednl. Service Bur., New Port Richey, 1979-81; exec. dir. Nat. Assn. Ednl. Negotiators, Brooksville, Fla., 1980-85; bus. instr. Pasco-Hernando Community Coll., 1985—. Sec., Shady Hills Little League Assn., Brooksville, 1979, v.p., 1980-82. Mem. Nat. Assn. Female Execs., Fla. Soc. Assn. Execs., Fla. Ednl. Negotiators, Pasco-Hernando Community Coll. Alumni Assn. (v.p.), West Pasco Bus. and Profl. Women's Assn., Suncoast Vets. Council (del.), NOW, LWV, Phi Theta Kappa (charter sec. 1979-80). Home: 225 Shirla Rae Dr Spring Hill FL 33526 Office: Pasco-Hernando Community Coll 7025 Moon Lake Rd New Port Richey FL 33553

MISCHKE, NYLA JEANNE, graphic arts company executive; b. Junction City, Kans., Mar. 18, 1956; d. James Nels and Lorraine Adell (Gleason) Aspelin; B.S. in Journalism and Mass Communications, Kans. State U., 1977; postgrad. U. Mo., 1978; m. Karl Reynolds Mischke, Nov. 24, 1978. Chief copywriter Burstein-Applebee Co., Kansas City, Mo., 1978-80; advt. coordinator Clinic Masters, Inc., Independence, Mo., 1980-81; mgr. advt. Am. White Goods Co., Kansas City, 1981-85; account exec. L&J Graphic Arts Corp., Kasas City, 1985—. Mem. Direct Marketing Club Kansas City, Advt. Club Kansas City, Print Prodn. Club. Club: German Shepherd Dog, Greater Kansas City Dog Tng. (Kansas City); White German Shepherd. Editor: The Schaferhunde News, 1982. Home: 5438 NE Carmel Rd Kansas City MO 64119

MISHKIN, HERMINE PENNY, occupational therapist; b. N.Y.C., Nov. 4, 1949; d. Sidney and Jeanne (Silverstein) Mishkin. B.A., NYU, 1971; M.S., Columbia U., 1978. Registered occupational therapist. Publicity asst. Grosset & Dunlap, N.Y.C., 1972-73; editorial asst. Random House, N.Y.C., 1973-75; supr. occupational therapy Blueberry Sch., Bklyn., 1979-81; sr. occupational therapist St. Vincent's Hosp., N.Y.C., 1981—, Mt. Sinai Hosp., 1985—. Mem. Am. Occupational Therapy Assn., Met. N.Y. Dist. Occupational Therapy Assn., N.Y. State Occupational Therapy Assn., Ctr. for Study of Sensory Integration Dysfunction. Clubs: Atrium, East River Tennis.

MISKEL, ANNAMAE DICKIE, former medical research technologist; b. St. Louis, Dec. 20, 1918; d. Roy Alexander and Marie Elizabeth (Schlamp) Dickie; m. John Albert Miskel, June 29, 1949; 1 son, Roy Elliot. Student Washington U., St. Louis, 1936-37, U. Mo., 1937-38, also credits at Washington U. Med. Sch., NYU, San Francisco State Coll., Med. Sch., U. Calif.-San Francisco, Chabot Coll., U. Calif-Hayward, intermittently, 1956-68. Med. technologist Los Alamos Nat. Lab., 1943-46, Washington U. Med. Sch., St. Louis, 1939-43, 46-49, Central Suffolk Hosp., Riverhead, N.Y., 1950-53, Lawrence Livermore Nat. Lab., Calif., 1956-59, 77-83, Sandia Lab., Livermore, 1967-68, Murietta Allergy Lab., Livermore, 1969-70; tchr. elem. and jr. high grades Alameda County Sch. Dist., Calif., 1959-70. Discoverer and honored in naming of Dickie Bodies, particles in lymphocytes that correlate with exposure to radiation, 1943-49. Home: 23 Castledown Rd Pleasanton CA 94566

MISSEL, ESTHER BARBARA, artist; b. Hartford, Conn., Apr. 4, 1926; d. Gasper and Lucy (Melandrillo) Lissandrello; A.A., Bay Path Coll., 1949; student in gen. studies Columbia U., 1949-52; m. Frederick F. Missel, July 16, 1949; children—Deborah, Gillian, Frederick Allen. Exhibited paintings in one-woman shows: Framer's Gallery, Moorestown, N.J., 1973, Perkins Center for Arts, 1979, Newman Galleries, Phila., Kalyn's Fine Arts, Princeton, N.J., Cannon House Office Bldg., Washington, 1985, also numerous pub. bldgs.; group shows include: Burlington County (N.J.) Art Guild, 1974, South Jersey All-Profl. Art Show, Cape May, 1973, Rider Coll., 1973, Nat. League Am. Pen Women Club House, Washington, 1977, N.J. Center for Performing Arts, 1974, Haddon Fortnightly, Haddonfield, N.J., 1970, Am. Artists Profl. League, Princeton, N.J., 1981, Perkins Center for Arts, Moorestown, N.J., 1982; represented in public collections: 1st. Presbyn. Ch., Moorestown, Squibb Co., Princeton, Farmers & Mechanics Bank, Moorestown, N.J., also pvt. collections, U.S., abroad. Recipient awards, including 1st Pl. in oils Burlington County Art Guild, 1970, 2d Pl., 1972, 1st in oils Haddonfield Fortnightly, 1973, Popular Vote award Cape May Art League Nat. Summer Art Show, 1969. Mem. Nat. League Am. Pen Women, Inc. (Women in the Arts), Am. Soc. Marine Artists, Am. Artists Profl. League, Inc. Presbyterian. Home and Office: 264 E Main St Moorestown NJ 08057

MITCHAM, KAREN JO, skin care, cosmetics direct selling executive; b. Erie, Pa., Nov. 12, 1946; d. Chrstian Niels and Marguerite Lucille (Shaffer) Blumensaadt; B.F.A., Mercyhurst Coll., 1969; m. John B. Stoeckley, Nov. 14, 1981; 1 son, Clark Shaffer; children by previous marriage, Aaron Urie, M. Denton; 1 stepson, Reed B. Owner, The Crow's Nest, retail store, Oil City, Pa., 1973-77; pres. Karen Mitcham Assos., mfrs. rep., Monroeville, Pa., 1974-78; mktg. dir., culinary cons. Cousances div. Schiller & Asmus, Inc., Chgo., 1978-80; exec. adminstr. Ingrid At Home, direct selling, North Chicago, Ill., 1980-83; v.p. mktg. and sales Wicker World Enterprises Inc., Bensenville, Ill., 1984-85; exec. dir. Skin Care Internat. (doing bus. as Peau Soin Internat.), direct selling, Sandy, Utah, 1985—; freelance pub. speaker. Vice pres. Assn. Promotion Oil City, 1976; bd. dirs. Greater Pitts. Mdse. Mart, 1977; vestrywoman Calvary Episcopal Ch., Louisiana, 1986—. Mem. Democrat. Home: Route 1 Box 193A Louisiana MO 63353

MITCHAM, PATRICIA HAMILTON, educator; b. El Paso, Tex., Sept. 8, 1942; d. Leverett Chandler and Annabelle (Cunningham) Hamilton; B.A., Tex. Western Coll., 1964; m. Eugene L. Mitcham III, Apr. 19, 1968; children—Shirley Dianne, Steven Craig. Teaching asst. U. Tex., El Paso, 1965-67; instr. English, Hardin Simmons U., Abilene, Tex., 1967-68; tchr. El Paso (Tex.) public schs., 1968-70, 75-79; vol. supr. Army Community Service, Fort Bliss, Tex., 1971-74; tchr. Bret Harte Sch., Los Angeles, 1979-81, Washington High Sch., Los Angeles, 1981-85, Gardena High Sch., 1985—. Mem. DAR, Am. Bus. Women's Assn., Assn. for Supervision and Curriculum Devel., Internat. Platform Assn., Assn. Calif. Sch. Adminstrs. Episcopalian. Home: 6082 Hardwick Circle Huntington Beach CA 92647 Office: 1302 W 182d St Gardena CA 90248-3398

MITCHELL, ALICE SCHAFFER, oil company executive; b. Mobile, Ala., Jan. 23, 1950; d. William James and Alice Martii (Ford) Schaffer; m. Timothy Allen Mitchell, Mar. 6, 1976; 1 dau., Meghan Ann. B.S., U. Ala.-Tuscaloosa, 1971, J.D., 1974. Bar: Okla. 1976. Contractman, Texaco, Inc., Tulsa, 1974-77; landman, atty. Sabine Corp., Oklahoma City, 1977-79; trial examiner Corp. Commn., Oklahoma City, 1979, conservation atty., 1980-82; atty. Linn & Helms, Oklahoma City, 1979-80; div. atty. Inexco Oil Co., Oklahoma City, 1982—; lectr. Okla. U., Norman, 1982. Mem. Okla. Bar Assn. Internatate Oil Compact Commn., Oklahoma City Mineral Lawyers, Oklahoma City Title Attys., DAR. Democrat. Roman Catholic. Club: Zonta. Home: 1101 Woodford Ct Edmond OK 73034 Office: Inexco Oil Co 3030 Northwest Expressway Oklahoma City OK 73112

MITCHELL, ANDREA LOUISE, journalist; b. N.Y.C., Oct. 30, 1946; d. Sydney and Cecile Mitchell; B.A., U. Pa., 1967. Polit. reporter KYW Newsradio, Phila., 1967-76; polit. corr. Sta. KYW-TV, Phila., 1972-76; corr. Sta. WTOP-TV, Washington, 1977-78; gen. assignment and energy corr. NBC News, Washington, 1978-81, White House corr., 1981—; co-anchor Summer Sunday U.S.A., NBC News; instr. Gt. Lakes Colls. Assn., 1974-76. Recipient award for public affairs reporting Am. Polit. Sci. Assn., 1969; Public Affairs Reporting award AP, 1976, Chesapeake award, 1977; Communicator of Yr. award Phila. chpt. Women in Communications, 1976; award for broadcast reporting Phila. chpt. Sigma Delta Chi, 1975. Club: Washington Press. Office: 4001 Nebraska Ave NW Washington DC 20016

MITCHELL, ARELYA JANET, broadcasting executive; b. Columbus, Miss., May 19; d. W.B. and Martha (Rice) M. B.A., Miss. U. for Women, 1971; M.Polit. Sci., Memphis State U., 1982. Pub. relations writer Stax Records, Inc., Memphis, 1971-75; continuity dir. Sta. WMC, Memphis, 1975-76; asst. community relations dir. Sta. WKNO-TV-FM, Memphis, 1976-78; pub. info. dir. Sta. WKNO-TV-FM, Memphis, 1978—; cons. Memphis Visitors and Conv. Ctr., 1982. Mem. com. Am. Soc. Am., Memphis, 1980, Memphis Jobs Corps, 1981. Recipient nat. promotion award Pub. Broadcasting Service, Washington, 1983. Mem. Women in Communications (program co-chmn. 1983—), Pub. Relations Soc. Am. (accredited pub. relations specialist), Broadcasters Promotions Assn., So. Ednl. Communications Assn. (council 1978-80, 83—, awards 1978, 80). Methodist. Home: 347 S Pauline St Apt 6 Memphis TN 38104 Office: WKNO-TV and FM Box 80000 Memphis TN 38152

MITCHELL, BARBARA JEAN ELLIS DONEGAN, elementary school principal; b. Chgo., Mar. 22, 1933; d. C.B. and Hilda (Davis) Ellis; B.E., Chgo. Tchrs. Coll., 1952; M.A., Roosevelt U., 1955; postgrad. U. Chgo., 1955, Chgo. State U., 1959, 68-69; m. Leon A. Donegan, Nov. 25, 1960 (div. 1963); 1 son, Leon Ellis; m. 2d, Ivory D. Mitchell, Apr. 16, 1966 (div. 1969); 1 son, Brian DeWitt. Tchr., Betsy Ross Sch., Chgo., 1952-57, Andrew Carnegie Sch., Chgo., 1957-62; tchr. 61st and University Sch., Chgo., 1962-63, asst. prin., 1963-68; asst. prin. Robert A. Black Mini-Magnet Sch., Chgo., 1968-71; prin. Charles S. Brownell Sch., Chgo., 1971-77; prin. Henry Clay Sch., Chgo., 1977-80, Edward Dunne Sch., Chgo., 1980—; adult edn. tchr., 1964-66; adjustment counselor, 1964-68; sch. librarian, 1964-68; curriculum coordinator, 1970. Recipient merit certificate Carnegie Sch. PTA, 1959, Distinguished Service recognition Ill. Congress Parents and Tchrs., 1961, recognition award for outstanding community service, Park Manor Neighbors Community Council, 1975. Mem. Chgo. Prins. Assn., Nat. Council Adminstrv. Women, Phi Delta Kappa. Episcopalian. Author: A Comparative Study of Faculty Meeting Procedures, 1955. Home: 18844 S May Ave Homewood IL 60430 Office: 10845 S Union Ave Chicago IL 60628

MITCHELL, BETTY JO, writer, publisher; b. Coin, Iowa, May 2, 1931; d. Edith Darrah McWilliams; B.A., S.W. Mo. State U., Springfield; M.S.L.S., U. So. Calif. Asst. acquisitions librarian Calif. State U., Northridge, 1967-69, librarian for personnel and fin., 1969-71, acting asso. library dir., 1971-72, asso. dir. univ. libraries, 1972-81; owner Viewpoint Press, Tehachapi, Calif.; cons. Western Interstate Commn. for Higher Edn. USOE Inst. for Tng. in Staff Devel. Problem Solving; participant workshops in field. Bd. dirs. San Fernando Valley council Girl Scouts U.S.A., 1974-77, employed personnel com., 1979—; bd. dirs. Bear Valley Springs Condominium Owners Assn., 1978, Empyrean Found., 1978—. Mem. ALA (mem., chmn. various coms.), Nat. Library Assn., Calif. Library Assn., Assn. Calif. State U. Profs. (sec., exec. com., 1971-72), AAUP, Pi Beta Chi, Alpha Mu Gamma. Co-author: Cost Analysis of Library Functions: A Total System Approach, 1978; author: ALMS: A Budget Based Library Management System, 1982; co-author: How to See the U.S. on $12 a Day; speaker profl. confs.; contbr. writings to profl. publs.; editor Staff Development column in Special Libraries, 1975-76. Home: Star Route 3 Box 4600-7 Tehachapi CA 93561 Office: PO Box P Tehachapi CA 93561

MITCHELL, BETTY NELL, government agency executive; b. Marshall, Tex., Feb. 3, 1947; d. Johnnie Dean Mitchell and Elvia Lean Mitchell-Nickerson; adopted daughter Janella Conley Mitchell. Student, Bishop Coll., Dallas, 1965-68, U.S. Dept. Agr., 1970-71, U. D.C., 1972-78. Personnel asst. Dept. State, Washington, 1968-73, personnel mgmt. specialist, 1973-76, chief personnel br., 1976-79; chief personnel and adminstrv. service br. HUD, Milw., 1979-83, personnel officer, 1983—; external adviser Alverno Coll., Milw., 1984—. Mem. parent adv. bd. St. Rose Sch., Milw., 1984, YMCA, Milw., 1985; typist reading dept. Elm Creative Arts Sch., Milw., 1985—. Served as sgt. USAR, 1974-78. Recipient Sustained Superior Performance award HUD, 1983, 85, Cert. for Spl. Achievement, HUD, 1983, Highly Successful Performance award 1984. Mem. Fed. Ofcls. Assn., Ptnrs. in Investment (asst. treas. 1985—), Nat. Assn. Female Execs. Baptist. Avocations: working with youth; reading; movies. Office: HUD 310 W Wisconsin Ave Milwaukee WI 53203

MITCHELL, CAROL BRYANT, county tax commissioner; b. Covington, Ga., Jan. 27, 1943; d. Thomas Cook and Mary Inez (Holifield) Bryant; m. Robert Scales Mitchell, July 21, 1962; children—Robin Spivey, Kerri Anne, Julie Carol. Sec. Oxford Industries, Atlanta, 1961-62, Western Elec. Co., Conyers, Ga., 1962-66; dep. tax commr. Newton County, Covington, 1967-80, tax commr., 1980—. Treas. Covington-Newton County United Fund, Ga., 1980—; mem. Covington-Newton County Clean Community Commn., 1983—; chairperson Ga. Easter Seal Soc., del. Dem. Nat. Conv., 1984. Mem. County Officers Assn., Ga. Assn. Tax Ofcls., Newton County C. of C. Methodist. Avocations: water skiing; fishing; football. Home: 4171 Rebecca St Covington GA 30209 Office: Newton County Tax Commr 1105 Usher St Covington GA 30209

MITCHELL, CONSTANCE AYER, design analyst; b. Painesville, Ohio, Oct. 9, 1952; d. Russell Ayer and Jean Ann (Hanna) Poxon; m. Leslie Olan Mitchell, Feb. 15, 1972; children—Bryan, Brandon. A.A., Lakeland Coll., Ohio, 1973. Programmer, analyst Curtis Industries Inc. div. Congoleum, Eastlake, Ohio, 1973-79; asst. to sr. v.p. Lake Nat. Bank, Painesville, 1979-81; sr. programmer analyst Picker Internat., Highland Heights, Ohio, 1981-83; sr. analyst George Worthington Co., Mentor, Ohio, 1983—; cons. and lectr. in field. Co-author: data processing systems. Mem. Nat. Assn. Female Execs. Episcopalian. Avocations: reading; photography. Home: 91 Chatfield Dr Painesville OH 44077 Office: George Worthington Co 8100 Tyler Blvd Mentor OH 44060

MITCHELL, EDNA STEINER, educator; b. Sacramento, June 29, 1931; d. Howard F. and Thelma (Johnson) Steiner; B.A., William Jewell Coll., Liberty, Mo., 1952; M.A., Kansas City U., 1956; Ph.D., U. Mo., Kansas City, 1971; children—Debra, Tom, Kris. Tchr. elem. schs., Independence, Mo., 1953-55; from instr. to prof. dept. edn. William Jewell Coll., 1955-71; asst. prof. Smith Coll., Northampton, Mass., 1969-73; prof., head dept. edn. Mills Coll., Oakland, Calif., 1973—; research asso. MidContinent Regional Ednl. Lab., Kansas City, Mo., 1967; spl. asst. to Congressman Tom Lantos, 1981-82. Congressional Sci. fellow, 1980-81; NSF grantee, 1978-80, Spencer Found. grantee, 1981, AEI grantee, 1982. Mem. Soc. Research in Child Devel., Assn. Supervision and Curriculum Devel., Calif. Council Edn. Tchrs., Am. Edn. Research Assn., Phi Delta Kappa. Democrat. Contbr. articles in field. Office: Mills College Oakland CA 94613

MITCHELL, ELIZABETH FERGUSON, nurse; b. Bklyn., Feb. 1; d. Wilbur Paul and Alice (Wilson) Ferguson; R.N., Methodist Hosp., Bklyn., 1948; student NYU; cert. occupational health nurse; m. Donald P. Mitchell, Oct. 3, 1953; children—Brett, Todd. Staff nurse, supr. hosps. in N.Y., Oreg. and N.J., 1948-53; occupational health nurse Freightliner Corp., 1974-80; coordinator occupational health program St. Vincent Hosp., Portland, Oreg., 1980-82; hosp. loss prevention rep. St. Paul Fire & Marine Ins. Co., Portland, 1982—. Pres., Maplewood (N.J.) Sch. PTA, 1966; v.p. Women's Soc., United Methodist Ch., Maplewood, 1967. Mem. Columbia River Assn. Occupational Health Nurses (pres. 1982-84), Am. Soc. Health Care Risk Mgrs. Republican. Presbyterian. Home: 9460 SW Martha St Tigard OR 97224 Office: 825 NE Multnomah Portland OR 97232

MITCHELL, GAIL ELLEN, utility company executive; b. N.Y.C., Sept. 23, 1951; d. Howard Bernard and Veronica Thelva (LeDoux) M.; B.A., Boston U., 1973; M.U.P., N.Y. U., 1975. Transp. planner Office Upper Manhattan Planning and Devel., 1974-75; sr. planner N.J. Dept. Community Affairs, 1975-78; sales rep. Xerox Corp., N.Y.C., 1978; market adminstr. N.Y. Tel., N.Y.C., 1978-83, sales commn. control specialist Info. Systems, 1983-84, adminstrv. supr., 1984—. Recipient various awards N.Y. Tel.; grantee Boston U., N.Y. U. Mem. Nat. Council Negro Women, NAACP, Nat. Urban League, Delta Sigma Theta. Office: 1 Penn Plaza Floor 2 New York NY 10119

MITCHELL, GENEVA BROOKE, hypnotherapist; b. Ringgold, Tex., Feb. 15, 1929; d. Roy Banks and Willie Jewel (Lemons) Shaw; m. Roy David Mitchell, Nov. 30, 1947; children—Ronald, Donald, Joel, Pamela, Annette. Cert. master hypnotist Hypnosis Tng. Inst., Los Angeles, 1980, cert. hypnotherapist, 1983; cert. in advanced investigative and forensic hypnosis Tex. A&M U., 1982. Chiropractic asst. Alamogordo, N.Mex., 1962-79; hypnotherapist Alamogordo Hypnosis and Counseling Ctr., 1980—; pres. Reco Corp., Albuquerque, 1980—, M&M Horses Corp., Tularosa, N.Mex., 1985—; pres. N.Mex. Chiropractic Aux., 1984-85; mem. Am. Council Hypnotist Examiners, 1980-85; hypnotist for tape series. Charter pres. La Sertoma, Alamogordo, 1957; pres. Oregon sch. PTA, Alamogordo, 1958, La Luz Sch. Parents Club, N.Mex., 1962; sec. N.Mex. Jr. Rodeo Assn., 1964; co-founder Pre-Sch. La Luz, 1969; mem. N.Mex. Gov.'s Council on Youth, 1969; bd. dirs. Otero County Jr. Rodeo Assn., N.Mex., 1968. Recipient Speakers award Life Found., 1984. Mem. Am Assn. Profl. Hypnotherapists, Ladies for Life (appreciation award 1984), N.Mex. Ladies Life Fellowship (pres. 1983, bd. dirs. 1985). Avocations: golf; painting; swimming; martial arts. Office: Alamogordo Hypnosis and Counseling Ctr 9th and Porto Rico Alamogordo NM 88310

MITCHELL, GLADYS MARIE, real estate broker; b. Chilton, Tex., Sept. 26, 1931; d. Fred and Thelma Mae (Spivey) Kilgore; m. William Henry Mitchell, Dec. 21, 1951; 1 dau., Lisa Ann. Sec. to Dist. Atty., Marlin, Tex., 1948-49; sec., office mgr. Tex. Dept. Pub. Welfare, Marlin, 1949-51; real estate saleswoman Ranchers Realty, 1974-75, Price Real Estate, 1975-76; ptnr., broker Mitchell & Walker Realtors, Inc., 1976—. County dir. Tex. High Sch. Rodeo Assn., 1983—; mem. St. John's Marlin Sch. Bd., 1974-76, pres., 1976-78. Mem. Nat. Assn. Realtors, Tex. Assn. Realtors, Tex. Fedn. Profl. and Bus. Women. Democrat. Baptist. Home: Rural Route 1 Box 63 Marlin TX 76661 Office: Mitchell & Walker Realtors Inc 119 Live Oak Marlin TX 76661

MITCHELL, GWENDOLYN VAN DERBUR, lawyer; b. Denver, Aug. 29, 1931; d. Francis Stacy and Gwendolyn (Olinger) Van D.; m. Robert L. Falkenberg, Jr., Feb. 6, 1954 (div. Aug. 1971); children—Robert L. III, Nancy Elaine; m. Ernest Albert Mitchell, May 14, 1972. B.A., U. Colo.-Boulder, 1953; J.D., U. Mo.-Kansas City, 1957. Bar: Kans. 1957, Calif. 1974, U.S. Dist. Ct. (no. dist.) Calif. 1978; cert. family law specialist. Assoc., Henry Shankel Gilman, Falkenberg & Rainey, Overland Park, Kans., 1957-72; asst. to exec. dir. San Francisco Neighborhood Legal Assistant Found., 1973-75; assoc. Lawrence Stotter Law Offices, San Francisco, 1975-82; assoc. Carr, McClellan, Ingersoll, Thompson & Horn, Burlingame, Calif., 1982-85, v.p., sec., corp. counsel European Asiatic Mktg., San Mateo, Calif., 1986—. Pres. Family Service Agy. of San Mateo County, Burlingame, 1986. Mem. ABA, Calif. State Bar Assn., Bar Assn. San Francisco, San Mateo County Bar Assn. Republican. Methodist. Club: Francisca (San Francisco). Office: European Asiatic Mktg 2000 Alameda de las Pulgas Suite 160 San Mateo CA 94403

MITCHELL, HESTER LOUISE, retired librarian; b. Plainfield, N.J., Dec. 8, 1915; d. Henry Sayen and Maude Frances (Raymond) Mitchell; spl. courses U.

Va., 1937, London Regent Inst., 1939, U. N.H., 1939, 40, 48, 51, Harvard U., 1941, 42, Boston U., 1941, 46, 47, 50, 52, 53, University Okla., 1961-62 and 64. Asst. high sch. library, Beverly, Mass., 1934, children's asst. pub. library, 1935-40, adult asst., 1940-48; literary staff Springfield (Mass.) Rep. Newspaper, 1941-45; head children's dept. pub. library, Everett, Mass., 1948-51; head librarian pub. library, Ipswich, Mass., 1951-67; librarian Addison-Wesley Pub. Co., Inc., Reading, Mass., 1967-80. Pres. Cable Meml. Hosp. Auxiliary, 1958. Mem. ALA, N.E., Mass. (exec. bd. 1952, 53, 56, com. mem. (1963-64), Merrimac Valley (past pres.) library assns., Mass. State Aid to Libraries (sec. to adv. bd. N. Met. region 1963-64), Spl. Libraries Assn., Ipswich Hist. Soc., Women's Nat. Book Assn., Am. Security Council, Internat. Platform Assn., D.A.R., Marquis Biog. Soc. (adv. mem.), Linus Pauling Inst. Sci. and Medicine, Nat. Wildlife Fedn. (assoc.), Nat. Audubon Soc., Swampscott Hist. Soc., Mass. Chiefs of Police Assn. (assoc.). Mem. Order Eastern Star. Clubs: Woman's (Ipswich, Mass.); Book Review (treas. 1957) (Boston). Author articles in mags. and newspapers. Book reviewer ALA Reference Quar., 1969-80. Home: 88 Stetson Ave Swampscott MA 01907 also 7503 NW 70th Terr Ft Lauderdale FL 33319

MITCHELL, JANET ALDRICH, fund raising executive, reference materials publisher; b. Providence, Jan. 12, 1928; d. Norman Ackley and Janet (Gordon) Aldrich; m. Raymond Warren Mitchell, Jan. 9, 1954 (div. 1967); children—Lydia Aldrich, Polly Burbank. A.B., Smith Coll., 1949; M.Ed., Rutgers U., 1975. Engaged in devel. various non-profit orgns., 1954-72; dir. devel. Wilson Fellowship Found., Princeton, N.J., 1972-74; dir. spl. projects N.J. Dept. Higher Edn., Trenton, 1974-76; pub., editor-in-chief Mitchell Guide, Princeton, 1976—; cons. to numerous non-profit orgns., 1976—; lectr. Adult Sch., Princeton, 1983-84. Editor: Directory of Woodrow Wilson Fellows, 1968; Guide to Federal Aid to Higher Education, 1975; Higher Education Exchange, 1978; A Community of Scholars, 1980. Exec. officer Princeton Community Democratic Orgn., 1984—; candidate Princeton Twp. Com., 1984; mem. NAACP Legal Def. Fund, 1980—; trustee N.J. Hist. Soc., 1984—. Episcopalian. Clubs: Smith Coll. (pres. 1968-70), Princeton Dog (bd. dirs. 1962-68). Avocation: breeding and showing standard poodles. Home: 418 Franklin Ave Princeton NJ 08540 Office: Mitchell Guide PO Box 413 Princeton NJ 08542

MITCHELL, JANET PATRICIA, technical writer, consultant; b. Union Level, Va., Nov. 29, 1954; d. Lewis Elmer and Iris Lee (Phillips) Mitchell. Student U. Md., 1974-79. Sec. I, U. Md., College Park, 1974-79; adminstrv. asst. Am. Econ. Devel. Corp., Washington, 1979; word processing operator, ops. center sec. Syscon, Inc. (formerly Systems Cons.), Washington, 1979-80; sr. word processing specialist Automated Bus. Systems, Hyattsville, Md., 1980; mgmt. analyst IMR Systems Corp., Arlington, Va., 1981—, cons., adminstrv. asst., Washington, 1979-81; cons., proposal writer CEE Systems Engring., Landover, Md., 1982-83, C & M Systems Corp., Landover, 1983; cons. word processing specialist Systems Group Assocs., Washington, 1978-80. Co-author manual: A Quick and Easy Guide to Keypunching, 1976. Vol. art therapy St. Elizabeth's Hosp., Washington, 1975. Recipient Appreciation award Systems Group Assocs. Mem Internat. Word Processing Assn., Nat. Assn. Female Execs., Inc., Entrepreneurship Inst. Alumni. Baptist.

MITCHELL, JAYNE FRANCIS, lawyer; b. Great Falls, Mont., Feb. 8, 1951; d. William Howard and Dorothy Elizabeth (Lane) Mitchell; m. Clair Russell Tempero, June 23, 1973 (div. 1978); m. Doug Randell James, June 26, 1981 (div. 1983). B.S., Mont. State U., 1973; J.D., U. Mont., 1981. Bar: Mont. 1981. Tchr. Edgar (Mont.) Pub. Sch., 1973-78; legal intern Office Pub. Instrn., Helena, Mont., 1980; research asst. Mont. Criminal Law Research Info. Ctr., Missoula, 1979-81; assoc. Robinson & Doyle, Hamilton, Mont., 1981; chief counsel Mont. Ins. Dept., Helana, 1981-83; asst. Mont. Dept. Adminstrn., Helena, 1983—. Mem. ABA, Mont. Bar Assn. Club: Toastmistress. Office: Dept Adminstrn Mitchell Bldg Helena MT 59601

MITCHELL, JEANNE OLSON, mining and minerals company executive; b. Orlando, Fla., Oct. 10, 1959; d. Carl Howard and Mary Jane (Jattuso) Olson; m. Douglas Keith Mitchell, Feb. 16, 1985. A.A., Lake-Sumter Community Coll., Leesburg, Fla., 1978; B.S., U. Fla., 1980, M.S., 1981. Grad. asst., U. Fla., Gainesville, 1981, interium dir. instr. materials, 1982; info./press relations staff mem. Future Farmers Am., Alexandria, Va., 1982-83; dir. pub. relations Fla. Sugar Cane League, Clewiston, Fla., 1983-86; pub. relations advisor Mobil Mining & Minerals Co., Nichols, Fla., 1986—. Author and editor curriculum guides. Sec., treas. Hendry County City-Farm Tour Council, Labelle, Fla., 1983-86, Everglades Fair Com., South Bay, Fla., 1983-86. Mem. U. Fla. Alumni Assn., Nat. Assn. Female Execs., Pub. Relations Soc. Am., Fla. Pub. Relations Assn. (bd. dirs. 1986, chmn. publicity Palm Beach chpt. 1983-84, Golden Image award 1983, 84, 85). Baptist Club: Women Involved in Farm Econs. (BelleGlade, Fla.). Office: Mobil Mining & Minerals Co PO Box 311 Nichols FL 33863

MITCHELL, JO BENNETT, educator, civic worker; b. Laredo, Tex., Jan. 14, 1928; d. Hilary Joseph and Inez Bell (Drake) Bennett; B.A., N.Mex. State U., 1949; postgrad. Hartford Sem. Found., 1951-52, U. Wash., 1973; M.A., Pacific Oaks Coll., 1981; m. Robert Curtis Mitchell, Aug. 30, 1949; children—Drake Curtis, John Douglas, Mary Cecilia. Day care tchr. Seattle Day Nursery, 1949-50, University Heights Sch., 1950-51; nursery sch. and kindergarten tchr. Campus Sch., N.Mex. State U., 1961-65; child care cons. HELP, Albuquerque, 1965; teaching assoc. Central Wash. U., Ellensburg, 1970-82; dir. Alaska/N.W. Extension Center, San Francisco Theol. Sem., Seattle, 1982—. Mem. policy bd. Kittitas County Head Start, 1967-70; trustee Westminster Found. United Presbyterian Ch. Synod Alaska N.W., 1979-82; bd. dirs. United Ministries in Higher Edn., Central Wash. U., 1975-82; bd. dirs. Christian Century Lectureship Northwest, 1984—, United Ministries in Higher Edn. Pacific Northwest, 1985—; mem. Family Life Task Force of Ch. Council Greater Seattle. Mem. AAUW, NOW, LWV, Coalition on Women and Religion, Fellowship of Reconciliation, AAUP, Nat. Assn. Edn. of Young Children, Soc. for Advancement Continuing Edn. for Ministry, Phi Delta Kappa. Office: Alaska Northwest Extension Center San Francisco Theological Seminary 720 Seneca St Seattle WA 98101

MITCHELL, JOAN, artist; b. Chgo., 1926; d. James Herbert and Marion (Strobel) M.; student Smith Coll., 1942-44; M.F.A., Art Inst. Chgo., 1950; hon. degrees Western Coll. Ohio, 1972, Miami U., Oxford, Ohio, 1971. One-person shows: Galerie Fournier, Paris, 1967-86, Everson Museum, Syracuse, N.Y., 1972, Whitney Mus. Am. Art, N.Y.C., 1974, Arts Club, Chgo., 1974, Carnegie Mus., Pitts., 1974, Gloria Luria Gallery, Bay Harbor Fla., 1981, Janie Lee Gallery, Houston, 1981, Musee d.'Art Moderne de la Ville de Paris, 1982, Xavier Fourcade Inc., N.Y.C., 1976-86; group shows include: M.I.T., 1962, Pa. Acad. Fine Arts, 1966, Mus. Modern Art, N.Y.C., Japan, India and Australia, 1967, U. Ill., 1967, Mus. Modern Art, N.Y.C., 1971, Corcoran Gallery Art, Washington, 1975, N.Y. State Mus., Albany, 1977, Albright-Knox Art Gallery, Buffalo, 1978, Hirshhorn Mus. and Sculpture Garden, Washington, 1980; represented in permanent collections: Basel (Switzerland) Mus., Albright-Knox Art Gallery, Art Inst. Chgo., Mus. Modern Art, Phillips Collection, Washington, Corcoran Gallery Art. Recipient Premio Lissone, Milan, Italy, 1961, Brandeis award, 1974; Art Inst. Chgo. travel fellow, 1947. Office: care Xavier Fourcade Inc 36 E 75th St New York NY 10021

MITCHELL, JONI, singer, songwriter; b. Ft. MacCleod, Alta., Can., Nov. 7, 1943; d. William A. and Myrtle M. (McKee) Anderson; student Alta. Coll. Art. m. Chuck Mitchell, 1965 (div.); m. 2d, Larry Klein, Nov. 21, 1982. Albums include Clouds; For the Roses; Blue; Miles of Aisles; Court & Spark; Joni Mitchell; Hissing of Summer Lawns; Hejira; Ladies of the Canyon; Don Juan's Reckless Daughter; Mingus (Jazz Album of the Year and Rock-Blues Album of the Year, Downbeat Mag., 1979); Shadows and Light; compositions include Both Sides Now, Michael from Mountains, Urge for Going, Circle Game. Recipient Grammy award for best folk artist, 1971, 75; Playboy award for best female artist, 1974; 1st Ann. Rocky award for best female vocalist, 1975. Address: care Warner Communications Inc 75 Rockefeller Plaza New York NY 10019*

MITCHELL, JOSEPHINE GRAY, musician; b. Bonham, Tex.; d. Moses Vashti and Bertie (Hoy) Gray; B.S., Tex. Woman's U., 1926, M.A., 1971; m. T.A. Mitchell, Mar. 21, 1929; children—Richard Gray, Thomas Albert. Pianist in profl. concerts in Tex., Okla., and Colo., 1927—; tchr. music Port Arthur (Tex.) High Sch., 1928-29; lectr. on Tex. music and composers; established Southwestern Folk Music Archive in Ft. Worth Library; chmn. in establishment of Tex. Composers Manuscript Archives in Dallas Pub. Library; mem. bd. Tex. Girls' Choir Youth Orch. Greater Ft. Worth; chmn., adv. Tex. Composers Commn. Fund, 1978—, founder, chmn., 1980-82; mem. contest Van Cliburn Piano Quadrennial Contest, 1976-82; bd. dirs. Fine Arts Soc. Tex., 1980—, S.W. Ballet Assn.; presented hist. ballet with commd. composers and choreographers Tex. Women's U., 1980; established Modern Dance-Ballet Archive, Lyndon Baines Johnson Library, Austin, Tex., 1980; bd. dirs. S.W. Ballet Ctr.; chmn. Tex. Composers Commn. Fund, 1984—. Recipient various citations; named 1st Lady of Music in Ft. Worth, 1967. Mem. Am. Coll. Musicians, Ft. Worth League Composers (founder 1958, pres. 1958-76), Fine Arts Guild, Nat. Fedn. Music Clubs (folk music archivist 1963-65, research chmn. 1956-68), Tex. Fedn. Music Clubs (dist. pres. 1964-65), Tex. Composers Guild (pres. 1952-76, adv. 1978-82), Tex. Woman's U. Alumnae Assn. (past pres.), Ft. Worth Ballet Assn. (charter), Symphony League (charter), Ft. Worth Opera Guild (charter), Fine Arts Soc. Tex. (charter dir.), Tex. Hist. Assn., Tarrant County Hist. Soc., Nat. Guild Piano Tchrs. (nat. adjudicator), Sigma Alpha Iota (pres. 1961-62). Episcopalian. Clubs: Ft. Worth Piano Forum, Ft. Worth Women's, Euterpean Music (pres. 1952-54), E. Clyde Whitlock Music (charter, past pres.). Editor: Texas Composers Handbooks, 2d edit., 1974; author: Creative Music of Texas, 1836-1986. Column editor Tex. Composers News, 1978—.

MITCHELL, JUDITH MARIE, psychology researcher; b. Los Angeles, Oct. 1, 1950; d. Glen H. and Carla J. (Bilderback) Taylor; m. Paul F. Mitchell, Dec. 29, 1969 (div. Apr. 1971); 1 child, Jennifer Ann. B.A. summa cum laude, Calif. State U.-Northridge, 1976, M.A. in Clin. Psychology, 1980; postgrad. UCLA, 1980—. Rehab. counselor Valley Assn. for Retarded, Los Angeles, 1979-80; adminstrv. asst. Assn. Child Passenger Safety, Los Angeles, 1980-81; vocat. counselor VA Hosp., Sepulveda, Calif., 1981-82; researcher Neuropsychiat. Inst., Los Angeles, 1982-85, Grad. Sch. Edn., UCLA, 1985—; intern Airport-Marina Counseling Ctr., Los Angeles, 1983-84. Author article in field. Mabel Wilson Richards scholar, 1974-77; Univ. Women's Club fellow, 1977-78; UCLA Grad. Sch. Edn. fellow, 1981-85. Mem. Am. Psychol. Assn., Am. Assn. Counseling and Devel., UCLA Ctr. for Study of Women. Home: PO Box 5064 Mission Hills CA 91345 Office: Grad Sch Edn UCLA Moore Hall Room 132 Los Angeles CA 90024

MITCHELL, LAURA ANN, lawyer; b. Miles City, Mont., Oct. 21, 1952; d. Wilmer Ashford and Avis Jean (Baldwin) M.; m. John Walker Ross, Nov. 21, 1981. B.A., U. Mont., 1975; J.D. with honors, George Washington U., 1978. Bar: Mont. 1978. Law clk. U.S. Dist. Ct., Billings, Mont., 1978-79; assoc. Crowley Law Firm, Billings, 1979-83, ptnr., 1984—. Mem. adv. panel/spl. projects Mont. Arts Council, Billings, 1980-82. Mem. Am. Judicature Soc., ABA, Mont. Bar Assn., Yellowstone County Bar Assn. Presbyterian. Home: 2104 Elm St Billings MT 59101 Office: Crowley Haughey et al 490 N 31st St Billings MT 59101

MITCHELL, MARGARET ANN, banker; b. Newton, Mass., Dec. 22, 1953; d. John Oscar and Anna Sophia (Honekamp) Mitchell. B.A., Catholic U. Am., 1976; M.B.A., Iran Ctr. Mgmt. Studies, Tehran, 1978. Fin. analyst Polaroid Corp., Cambridge, Mass., 1978-79; mgmt. cons. Peat, Marwick, Mitchell Co., Washington, 1979-82; 2d v.p. Chase Manhattan Bank, N.Y.C., 1982—. Treas., v.p. 440 E. 79th St. Owners Corp., N.Y.C., 1983-84. Iran Ctr. Mgmt. Studies scholar 1977; Catholic U. Am. scholar, 1970-75. Democrat. Roman Catholic. Club: Vertical (N.Y.C.). Home: 440 E 79th St Apt 17 I New York NY 10021 Office: 1 Chase Manhattan Plaza New York NY 10081

MITCHELL, MARY, retail store advt. exec.; b. Cheery Ridge, La., July 25, 1934; d. W. C. and Ora Mae (Henderson) Webb; student St. Louis Bus. Coll., 1961; m. Bill H. Mitchell, May 15, 1966. Womens' dir., noontime hostess KTHV-TV, Little Rock, 1964-73; v.p. Holland & Assocs., Little Rock, 1973-76; nat. merchandise mgr. Jimmy Dean Foods, 1973-76; mdse. mgr. Ole South Foods, Little Rock, 1974-76; corp. broadcast advt. dir. Dillard Dept. Stores, Inc., Little Rock, 1976—. Active Christmas program Salvation Army, United Fund, ARC and Am. Cancer Soc. local units. Mem. Ark. Advt. Fedn., S.W. Regional Advt. Sales and Mktg. Execs. Assn., Internat. Platform Assn. Office: 900 W Capitol St Little Rock AR 72203

MITCHELL, MIANNE SUE, radio station executive, broadcasting company executive; b. Des Moines, Feb. 9, 1958; d. Forrest James and Joan Diane (Dianis) M.; m. James Ronald Bultendorp, May 7, 1983 (div. Aug. 1984). B.Gen. Studies, U. Iowa, 1980. Journalism instr. United Sch. Dist. 428, Great Bend, Kans., 1980-82; radio sta. mgr. WMCW Radio, Mitchell Broadcasting Co., Harvard, Ill., 1982—; v.p. Mitchell Broadcasting Co., Grinnell, Iowa, 1984—. Pub. relations dir. steering com. edn., Harvard, Ill., 1984-85. Mem. Nat. Assn. Broadcasters, Ill. Assn. Broadcasters. Republican. Lutheran. Clubs: Jaycees (Woodstock, Ill.); P.E.O. (Grinnell). Avocations: work; golf; travel. Home: 603 C Abbey Springs Fontana WI 53125 Office: WMCW Radio 67 N Ayer St Harvard IL 60033

MITCHELL, NANCY BROWN, psychologist; b. Chgo., Mar. 7, 1931; d. Edward Berrien and Jeannette (Landes) B.; B.A., Montevallo U., 1967; M.S., U. Ga., 1974, Ph.D., 1976; m. James Evans Mitchell, Jr., July 29, 1951 (dec.); children—James Evans, Thomas Edward, Janet Lucille. Tchr., Coosa County Bd. Edn., Goodwater, Ala., 1967-71; research asst., grant coordinator U. Ga., 1971-75; asst. to head spl. projects So. Regional Edn. Bd., Atlanta, 1977; psychologist Ala. Dept. Youth Services, Birmingham, 1977; mem. tech. adv. team U.S. Army Inf. Sch., Ft. Benning, Ga., 1977-80; psychologist Army Research Inst. Advanced Simulation Tech., Alexandria, Va., 1980-84; human factors specialist Lockheed Missiles and Space, Sunnyvale, Calif., 1984-85; sr. tech. analyst for human factors Decisions & Designs, Inc., McLean, Va., 1985—. Mem. Am. Psychol. Assn., Women in Sci. and Engring., Human Factors Soc., Sigma Xi, Psi Chi, Kappa Delta Pi. Office: Decisions & Designs Inc McLean VA 22101

MITCHELL, NANCY DENICE, nurse anesthetist; b. Houston, Sept. 27, 1956; d. Carl Dewie and Marlene (Eakin) Mitchell. A.S. in Nursing, San Jacinto Coll., Pasadena, Tex., 1976; dipl. Harris County Sch. Nurse Anesthesia, Houston, 1981. R.N., cert. registered nurse anesthetist. From staff nurse to head nurse surg. intensive care, Ben Taub Hosp., Houston, 1976-79; nurse anesthetist, cardiovascular operating room Fondren-Brown Meth. Hosp. Houston, 1981—; clin. inst. Baylor Coll., 1981—. Mem. Gulf Coast Assn. Nurse Anesthetists, Am. Assn. Nurse Anesthetists, Tex. Assn. Nurse Anesthetists. Home: 8327 Sandy Glen Ln Houston TX 77071 Office: Baylor Coll Med 1200 Moursund Houston TX 77030

MITCHELL, PAULA RAE, nursing educator; b. Independence, Mo., Jan. 10, 1951; d. Millard Henry and E. Lorene (Denton) Gates; m. Ralph William Mitchell, May 24, 1975. B.S. in Nursing, Graceland Coll., 1973; M.S. in Nursing, U. Tex., 1976. R.N., Tex., Mo.; cert. childbirth educator. Commd. capt. U.S. Army, 1972; ob-gyn nurse practitioner U.S. Army, Seoul, Korea, 1977-78; resigned, 1978; instr. nursing El Paso Community Coll. (Tex.), 1979-85, dir. nursing, 1985—, acting div. chmn. health occupations, 1985—; ob-gyn nurse practitioner Planned Parenthood, El Paso, 1981—. Founder, bd. dirs. Health-C.R.E.S.T., El Paso, 1980—; mem. pub. edn. com. Am. Cancer Soc., El Paso, 1983-84. Decorated Army Commendation medal, Meritorious Service medal. Mem. Nat. League for Nursing, Am. Soc. for Psychoprophylaxis in Obstetrics, Nurses Assn. of Am. Coll. Obstetricians and Gynecologists (cert. in ambulatory women's health care; chpt. coordinator 1979-83, nat. program rev. com. 1984-86), Am. Nurses Assn., Advanced Nurse Practitioner Group El Paso (coordinator 1980-83 legislative committee 1984), Orgn. for Advancement of Assoc. Degree in Nursing (membership chmn. 1985-86), Am. Vocat. Assn., Am. Assn. Women in Community and Jr. Colls., Sigma Theta Tau. Mem. Christian Ch. (Disciples of Christ). Home: 4616 Cupid Dr El Paso TX 79924 Office: El Paso Community College PO Box 20500 El Paso TX 79998

MITCHELL, RIE ROGERS, psychologist, counselor educator; b. Tucson, Feb. 1, 1940; d. Martin Smith and Lavaun (Peterson) Rogers; student Mills Coll., 1958-59; B.S., U. Utah, 1962, M.S., 1963; postgrad. San Diego State U., 1965-66; M.A., UCLA, 1969, Ph.D., 1969; m. Rex C. Mitchell, Mar. 16, 1961; 1 child, Scott Rogers. Tchr., Coronado (Calif.) Unified Sch. Dist., 1964-65; sch. psychologist Glendale (Calif.) Unified Sch. Dist., 1968-70; psychologist Glendale Guidance Clinic, 1970-77; asst. prof. ednl. psychology Calif. State U., Northridge, 1970-74, assoc. prof., 1974-78, prof., 1978—, chmn. dept. ednl. psychology, 1976-80, acting exec. asst. to pres., 1981-82; acting exec. asst. to pres. Calif. State U., Dominguez Hills, 1978-79; cons. to various Calif. sch. dists.; pvt. practice psychology, Calabasas, Calif. Recipient Outstanding Educator award Maharishi Soc., 1978, ACFS Presdl. award, 1986; Woman of Yr. award U. Utah, 1962. Mem. Calif. Assn. Counselor Edn., Supervision and Adminstrn. (dir. 1976-77), Western Assn. Counselor Edn. and Supervision (officer 1978-82, pres. 1980-81), Assn. Counselor Edn. and Supervision (dir. 1980-81, program chmn. 1981-82, treas. 1983-86), UCLA Doctoral Alumni Assn. (pres. 1974-76), Am. Psychol. Assn., Am. Ednl. Research Assn., Calif. Women in Higher Edn. (pres. chpt. 1977-78), Calif. Concerns (treas. 1984-86), Pi Lambda Theta (pres. chpt. 1970-71, chairwoman nat. resolutions 1971-73). Contbr. numerous articles on group process, juvenile delinquency, adminstrn., counselor edn. to profl. jours. Home: 22945 Paul Revere Dr Calabasas CA 91302 Office: Calif State U Northridge CA 91330

MITCHELL, ROSE MARIE, educational administrator; behavior consultant; b. Columbia, Mo., Feb. 12, 1939; d. James Arthur and Aldonia (Jones) (Lee) M.; m. Robert L. Washington, Aug. 17, 1956 (div. Mar. 1976). Student, S.W. Coll., 1974-75, Calif. Sch. Psychology, 1977; M.A. in Human Devel., Pacific Oaks Coll., 1980. Librarian, Ft. McArthur, San Pedro, Calif., 1975; behavior cons. Kedren Mental Health, Los Angeles, 1975-77; dir. Brotherhood Assn., Santa Ana, Calif., 1976-77; program dir. Neighborhood Youth, Venice, Calif., 1977-79; children's service worker Dept. Social Services, Los Angeles, 1979-80; dir., prin. Exceptional Children's Opportunity Sch., Los Angeles, 1980—; cons. Los Angeles Unified Sch. Dist., 1977-84. Mem. adv. bd. Regional Ctr., Los Angeles, 1982—. Recipient Merit award Calif. Sch. Profl. Psychology, 1978. Mem. Nat. Assn. Social Workers, Nat. Assn. Female Execs., Neighborhood Justice Ctr., Los Angeles Bar Assn., Am. Mgmt. Assn., Nat. Assn. Psychologists. Democrat. Methodist. Office: Exceptional Children's Opportunity Sch 12204 S San Pedro St Los Angeles CA 90061

MITCHELL, RUTH ELLEN (BUNNY), advertising executive; b. Mpls., Jan 2, 1940; d. Burt and Helen (Bolnick) Horwitz; children—Cathy Ann, Thomas Charles, Andrew Robert. Student UCLA, 1957, U. Minn., 1960. Substitute tchr. Holy Innocents' Sch., Atlanta, 1972-76; mem. staff Issues Dept., Carter-Mondale, Atlanta, 1976; office mgr. Atlanta Area Psychiatry Clinic, 1976-79; account exec. Am. Advt. Distributors, Atlanta, 1979-81, Brown's Guide Ltd., Atlanta, 1981-82; account mgr. Billian Pub., Atlanta, 1983-85; regional sales dir. Am. Hosp. Pub., Inc., Chgo., 1985—; cons. G.C.C., Inc., Atlanta, 1982-83. Bd. dirs. Nat. Council Jewish Women, Mpls., 1963-70, Temple Israel Sch., Mpls., 1964-68, Minn. Symphony Assn., Mpls., 1963-71; The Temple Sisterhood, Atlanta, 1972-77, Holy Innocents' Sch., Atlanta, 1973-77; vol. fundraiser KTCA-TV Pub. Broadcasting Service, Mpls., 1968-71, WETV-TV, Atlanta, 1976-80; vol. Northside Hosp., Atlanta, 1971-77, Arts Festival of Atlanta, 1971-80, Holy Innocents' ch. summer program, 1974-76, Buckhead Mental Health Clinic, Atlanta, 1975-77. Mem. Nat. Assn. Profl. Saleswomen, Atlanta Advt. Club, Mag. Advt. Reps. of the South (sec. 1982-83, v.p. 1983-84), High Mus. Art., Atlanta Symphony Orch. Assn., Atlanta Ballet. Home: 255 Blackwater Cove NW Atlanta GA 30328 Office: 1117 Perimeter Ctr W 5th Floor-E Atlanta GA 30338

MITCHELL, SOPHY MAE, JR., food service official; b. Sebring, Fla., Oct. 10, 1931; d. Thomas McKinnon and Sophy Mae (Smith) M. B.S. in Agr., U. Fla., 1953; M.S. in Bus. and Hotel and Restaurant Adminstrn., Fla. State U., 1959. Unit mgr. Morrison's Food Service, New Orleans, 1960-62; dist. mgr. Interstate United, Houston, then food service specialist, St. Louis, 1962-71, food service specialist, sch. adminstr., 1981, food service dir. Interstate United, SUNY Maritime Coll., Bronx, N.Y., 1981—; asst. prof. bus. Fla. State U., Tallahassee, 1971-75; guest lectr. U. New Haven Hospitality Dept.; adv. council Bur. Home Econs., N.Y.C. Pub. Schs., 1983; treas., past dir. Research & Devel. Assocs. for Mil. Food and Packaging. Mem. Nat. Restaurant Assn., N.Y. State Restaurant Assn. (dir.), N.Y.C. Restaurant Assn. (v.p.), Internat. Food Service Execs. Assn. (v.p. N.Y. br., cert.), Inst. Food Technologists, Am. Bus. Women's Assn., Beta Sigma Phi, Tau Beta Sigma. Republican. Presbyterian. Contbr. articles trade jours. Office: 1633 Broadway Suite 1603 New York NY 10019

MITCHELL, SUE YVONNE, preschool and kindergarten owner; b. New Lexington, Ohio, July 26, 1934; d. Robert Benson and Mae Elizabeth (Rowe) Hall; m. David Robert Mitchell, June 28, 1952; children—Steven Allen (dec.), Susan Debra, Shauna Lyn, Scott Evan. B.A., Kean Coll., Union, N.J., 1971. Cert. elem. tchr., N.J., cert. tchr. handicapped; cert. nursery sch. tchr. Elem. tchr. Parsippany Schs., N.J., 1965-77, owner, dir. Kiddie Korner, Parsippany, 1977—. Author children's stories, numerous poems. Supt., Presbyterian Ch. Sch., Morris Plains, N.J.; elder Presbyn. Ch., Morris Plains; commr. Newton Presbytery, N.J. Republican committeeman, Parsippany. Ednl. grantee State of N.J. 1974. Mem. N.J. Ednl. Assn. (bldg. rep. 1972-77), N.J. Assn. Edn. Young Children (v.p. local chpt. 1979-81, pres. 1981-83, v.p. state 1983-85). Clubs: Square Dance, Couple's, Parsippany Rep. Avocations: reading, knitting, crocheting, photography, aerobics, swimming. Home: 29 Dodie Dr Parsippany NJ 07054 Office: Kiddie Korner 29 Dodie Dr Parsippany NJ 07054

MITCHELL, SUSAN MILLER, insurance executive; b. Appleton, Wis., Apr. 13, 1945; d. James Frederick and Bernice Eileen (Bleick) Miller; B.A. magna cum laude, Lawrence U., Appleton, 1967; M.A. in Journalism, U. Wis., 1970; m. George Allen Mitchell, Oct. 28, 1973; children—Margaret Kim, Mary Eleanor. Tchr., Wakefield (Mass.) Elem. Schs., 1967-68; reporter Wall St. Jour., Chgo., 1970-72, San Francisco Examiner, 1972-73, Riverside (Calif.) Press Enterprise, 1973; exec. asst. Wis. Dept. Regulation and Licensing, 1975-78, sec., 1978-79; commr. ins. State of Wis., 1979-82; exec. v.p. adminstrn. Milw. Ins., 1983-86, sr. v.p. ops. gen. life, 1986—. Mem. Milw. Council on Alcoholism, Wis. Hosp. Rate Rev. Com. Recipient award Center Public Representation, Madison, 1981. Home: 4516 N Ardmore Ave Shorewood WI 53211 Office: 803 W Michigan St Milwaukee WI 53202

MITCHELL, SUSAN WEAMAH EMMA, psychologist, unite executive; b. Stamford, Conn., Sept. 27, 1953; d. John Payne and Esther Arvilla (Harrison) M.; B.A., Fisk U., 1982. Workshop supr. South Middlesex Assn. for Retarded Citizens, Framingham, Mass., 1976-77; mental retardation specialist Wrentham (Mass.) State Sch., 1977-83, asst. staff psychologist, 1983-86, asst. unit dir., 1986—. Mem. Nat. Assn. Female Execs., Alpha Kappa Alpha. Home: 65 E Washington St Apt 2203 North Attleboro MA 02760 Office: Wrentham State Sch Box 144 Wrentham MA 02093

MITCHELL, VELDA JEAN, filter manufacturing company personnel executive; b. Alton, Ill., July 27, 1937; d. Glenn Kessinger and Eunice Ruth (Jarvis) Saxton; m. Spencer L. Middlecoff, Oct. 20, 1957 (div. 1980); children—Laura A. Middlecoff Decker, Mark S. m. Robert E. Mitchell, May 31, 1986. Student in bus. mgmt. Sinclair Coll., Dayton, Ohio, 1986—. Exec. sec. Sinclair Refining, Hartford, Ill., 1955-58, Laclede Steel Co., Alton, Ill., 1958-71; personnel specialist Fram Corp., Greenville, Ohio, 1974-80, personnel adminstr., 1980-83, supr. human resources, 1983-84; supr. employee relations Fram Corp. div. Allied Aftermarket, Greenville, 1984—; mem. adv. bd. Blue Cross/Blue Shield, 1978—. Mem. adv. bd. Ansonia Schs. Bus. Edn., 1980—, Greenville Schs. Bus. Edn., 1982—. Mem. Personnel Assn. SW Ohio. Office: Fram Allied Aftermarket Martz & Jackson St Greenville OH 45331

MITCHELL, VERNICE VIRGINIA, nurse, poet, author; b. Scott, Miss., Mar. 11, 1921; d. Isaiah and Martha Magdalene (Edwards) Smith; m. Willis Mitchell, Aug. 17, 1940; children—Elaine, Kenneth, Liethia, John, Ransom, Paul. Diploma Princeton Continuation Coll., 1955. Lic. practical nurse. L.P.N. Cook County Sch. Nursing, Chgo., 1951-59, U. Ill. Hosp., Chgo., 1959-67, Grant Hosp., Chgo., 1967-78, Northwestern Meml. Hosp., Chgo., 1979-84, Aetna Nurse's Registry, Chgo., 1984—. Author poetry and musical lyrics. Recipient merit cert. Am. Poetry Assn., 1982, World of Poetry, 1983, 85; Golden Poet award World of Poetry, 1985. Club: 6700 Emerald Ave. Block (pres. 1971—). Avocations: reading; writing; cooking; traveling; sewing; crocheting.

MITCHELL-CHINN, GLADYS COMMORA, government administrator; b. Washington, Jan. 29, 1942; d. Wallace and Gladys (Aylor) Mitchell; m. Thomas Malachi, June 26, 1959 (div.); children—Karen, Kevin; m. Harold B. Chinn, Jr., Feb. 1, 1973 (div.). B.S. in Early Childhood Edn., D.C. Tchrs. Coll., 1978; M.P.A., Am. U., 1985. Asst. pre-sch. dir. D.C. Therapeutic Ctr., Washington, 1977-78; budget and account analyst D.C. Recreation Dept., 1976-79; chief adminstrn. support D.C. Office Fin. Mgmt., 1979-81; exec. mgmt. asst. D.C. Dept. Human Services, 1981-83, payments and collections officer, 1983—. Recipient Cert. of Excellent D.C. Govt., 1979-84; named Employer of Yr., Nat. Rehab. Assn., 1984. Mem. Nat. Rehab. Assn., Nat. Women's Polit. Caucus, Theta Sigma. Democrat. Baptist. Avocations: profl. swimmer; diver; tennis. Home: 2806 13th St NE Washington DC 20017 Office:

DC Dept Human Services Payments & Collections Div 1170 12th St NW Washington DC 20005

MITELMAN, BONNIE COSSMAN, writer, lecturer; b. Flint, Mich., Feb. 15, 1941; d. Maurice B. and Frieda H. (Ragir) Cossman; student U. Mich., 1958-61; B.A., Northwestern U., 1969; M.A., Manhattanville Coll., 1977; m. Stanley D. Lelewer, Mar. 12, 1961 (div. 1969); children—Joanne, Stephen; m. 2d, Alan N. Mitelman, July 23, 1972; 1 son, Geoffrey. Copywriter trainee Dancer-Fitzgerald-Sample, Inc., Chgo., 1956-60; advt. copywriter Spiegel, Inc., Chgo., 1961-63; freelance advt. and public relations writer, Chgo., N.Y., 1963—; co-founder Mitelman & Assocs., Briarcliff Manor, N.Y., 1972—; adj. lectr. dept. history Mercy Coll., Dobbs Ferry, N.Y., 1979—; contbr. articles to N.Y. Times, Reform Judaism, 1977—. Mem. Am. Hist. Assn., Women in Communications, Authors Guild. Author: Mothers Who Work: Strategies for Coping; mem. editorial bd. Reform Judaism, 1977—. Home: 639 Pleasantville Rd Briarcliff Manor NY 10510

MITRE, BLIMA KIRMAYER, pathologist; b. Romania, Aug. 15, 1942; came to U.S., 1968, naturalized, 1978; d. Moses and Regina Kirmayer; m. Ricardo J. Mitre, Oct. 7, 1967; children—Edward, Sandra, Marcie, Richard James. Grad. Universidad Mayor de San Simon, 1967. Intern Viedma Hosp., Cochabamba, Bolivia, 1967-68; resident in pathology Bapt. Meml. Hosp., Jacksonville, Fla., 1968-70; with Presbyn. Hosp., Pitts., 1970-72, Children's Hosp., Pitts., 1972-73; assoc. pathologist St. Margaret Meml. Hosp., Pitts., 1974-83, Suburban Hosp., 1983—; clin. instr. pathology U. Pitts. Med. Sch., 1970—. Mem. Internat. Acad. Pathology, Am. Soc. Clin. Pathologists, Coll. Am. Pathologists, Pa. Assn. Clin. Pathologists. Office: Suburban Gen Hosp S Jackson St Pittsburgh PA 15202

MITTELSTAEDT, JOAN NAOMI, educator, consultant; b. Fond du Lac, Wis., Feb. 9, 1950; d. H. Arthur and Naomi Genevieve (Maltby) Steiner; B.S. in Edn., U. Wis., Stevens Point, 1972, M.S. in Edn., 1978; 1 son, Robert John. Tchr., Menasha (Wis.) High Sch., 1972—, also owner Fox Valley Bus. Cons., Neenah, Wis., 1978—; tchr. English, facilitator Wis. Dept. Edn.; tchr. positive mental attitude classes for bus. people; leader sales tng. seminars; curriculum and sales tng. system developer; public speaker on free enterprise, entrepreneurship and assertiveness, 1978—. Cert. tchr. English and speech, Wis.; cert. Amway Gold Direct Distbr. Mem. Republican Presdl. Task Force, 1982. Mem. Nat. Council Tchrs. of English, Wis. Council Tchrs. of English, Assn. Supervision and Curriculum Devel., Wis. Regional Writers, Worldwide Diamond Assn., Nat. Assn. Female Execs. (network dir.), Am. Mgmt. Assn., Citizens Choice, Am. Fedn. Tchrs. (local sec. 1974-76), Assn. Supervision and Curriculum Devel., Delta Zeta, Delta Kappa Gamma. Episcopalian. Research on imagists influence on contemporary poets. Home: 304 Quarry Ln Neenah WI 54956

MITTLER, DIANA, music educator and administrator, pianist; b. N.Y.C., Oct. 19, 1941; d. Franz and Regina (Schilling) Mittler; m. Victor Battipaglia, Sept. 5, 1965 (div. 1982). B.S., Juilliard Sch., 1962, M.S., 1963; D.M.A., Eastman Sch. Music, 1974. Choral dir. William Cowper Jr. High Sch. and Springfield Gardens Jr. High Sch., Queens, N.Y., 1963-68, coordinator of music Flushing High Sch., Queens, 1968-79; asst. prin. music Bayside High Sch., Queens, 1979—; assoc. condr. Queens Borough-Wide Chorus, 1964-70; pianist, founder Con Brio Chamber Ensemble, 1978; faculty So. Vt. Music Festival, 1979-83; soloist with N.Y. Philharmonic, 1956; solo and chamber music appearances; examiner N.Y.C. Bd. Edn. Bd. Exams., 1985—. Author: 57 Lessons for the High School Music Class, 1983. Choral dir. and accompanist various charitable, religious, mil., civic holiday functions. N.Y. State Regents scholar, 1958-62; scholarships, Juilliard Sch. and Eastman Sch. Music. Contbr. articles to music publs. Mem. Music Edn. Nat. Conf., Delta Kappa Gamma. Democrat. Home: 108-57 66th Ave Forest Hills NY 11375 Office: Bayside High Sch 208th St and 32d Ave Bayside NY 11361

MIX, ESTHER, U.S. magistrate; b. Warner, Okla., Dec. 21, 1920; d. Burk and Bertie (Hawkins) Markham; student U. Okla., 1937-39, McGeorge Coll. Law, 1948; children—Sarah Jane, Richard, Jr. Pvt. practice law, 1951-71; U.S. magistrate, Sacramento, 1971—. Mem. ABA, Nat. Council Fed. Magistrates, Calif. Bar Assn., Women Lawyers Sacramento. Office: US Courthouse Rm 1034 650 Capitol Mall Sacramento CA 95814

MIXON, ROSALIE WARD, social work consultant; b. Maysville, Mo., Feb. 17, 1908; d. Luther Thomas and Mary (Bray) Ward; A.B., Park Coll., 1929; postgrad. (Univ. scholar 1929-30, 32-35), U. Chgo., 1929-34; M.S.W., U. So. Calif., 1944; postgrad. UCLA, 1965, Riverside, 1970, San Diego, 1975-76; m. John Lewis Mixon, Dec. 20, 1929; children—Rosemary Mixon Snow, John Lindley, David Lewis, Robert Nelson. Dir. med. social service Children's Meml. Hosp., Chgo., 1951-52; researcher in religious demography, 1952-58; instr. social work La Verne Coll. (Calif.), 1958-59; with Calif. Dept. Mental Hygiene, San Bernardino and Pomona, 1959-66, 69-74; Fulbright lectr., cons. psychiat. and med. social work Med. Sch., Pahlavi U., Shiraz, Iran, 1966-67; lectr. Sch. Social Work, Teheran, Iran, 1966-67; social researcher Meth. Bd. World Missions, Lima, Peru, 1968-69; pvt. practice psychiat. social work cons., Redlands, Calif., 1974—; vis. prof. Alaska Pacific U., Anchorage, 1978-79. Active Chgo. Community Fund Adv. Com., 1951, Claremont Community Services Com., 1960-75, Redlands A.B.L.E. Com., 1975—. Lic. clin. social worker, Calif. Mem. Nat. Assn. Social Workers, Nat. Acad. Cert. Social Workers, Register Clin. Social Workers, Soc. Internat. Devel. Club: Browser's Book. Author: The Methodist Churches of Arizona, 1966; The Barriadas of Lima, Peru, 1969; contbr. chpt. to Choice and Change, 1966. Address: 716 Plymouth Rd Claremont CA 91711

MIXON, VERONICA, editor; b. Phila., July 11, 1948; d. Mathew and Bertha Lee (Goodwine) Mixon. Student L.I. U., 1970-74. With Food Fair, 1966-68, Social Security Adminstrn., 1968-70; editor Starlight Romances, Doubleday & Co. Inc., N.Y.C., 1970—; reviewer VM Media Service. Democrat. Baptist. Co-editor: Freshtones: Women's Anthology, 1979; The World of Octavia Butler, Essence mag., 1979. Home: PO Box 694 Grand Central Sta New York NY 10163 Office: Doubleday & Co Inc 245 Park Ave New York NY 10167

MIYASAKI, ELLEN KAZUKO, telecommunications cons.; b. Kalopa, Hawaii, June 10, 1930; d. Uichi and Tsuyako (Yamada) M.; student U. Hawaii, 1948-49; cert. Sawyer Sch. Bus., Los Angeles, 1950. Med. sec. U.S. Dept. Army, Dept. Air Force, Japan, Okinawa, Germany, Morocco, 1951-57; med. sec. dept. psychiatry Jackson Meml. Hosp., Miami, 1958-62; med. asst. Jim S. Jewett, Internist, 1963-66; med. research asst. Dome Labs., N.Y.C., 1966-67; field office asst. ARC, Japan, Korea, Okinawa, 1967-69; adminstr. MCA Engring. Corp., Rockville, Md., 1969-73; with The Mktg. Programs and Services Group, Inc., Gaithersburg, Md., 1973—, corp. sec., 1975, corp. v.p., 1976—, also dir. Notary public, Md. Mem. Nat. Fedn. Bus. and Profl. Women's Club, Nat. Assn. Female Execs., Nat. Registry Med. Secs. Home: 9145 Centerway Rd Gaithersburg MD 20879 Office: 1350 Piccard Dr Suite 300 Rockville MD 20850

MIZE, MARY MAHON, child care centers chain executive, consultant; b. Eustis, Fla., Sept. 29, 1945; d. David Parker and Vesta Virginia (Bragg) Mahon; m. H. Raymond Self, June 25, 1965 (div 1971); 1 child, Tara; m. C. Vernon Mize, Feb. 24, 1973; children—Debra, Sandra. A.A., Troy State U., 1965; B.A. in History and Edn., Columbus Coll., Ga., 1970; M.S. in Child Care Adminstrn., Nova U., 1983; M.A. in Am. Studies, Stetson U., 1985. Tchr., Muscogee Sch. Bd., Columbus, 1969-71, Seminole Sch. Bd., Sanford, Fla., 1971-73; pres., owner Sanford Child Care, 1973—; validator Nat. Assn. Edn. Young Children, Fla., 1985. Vice pres. Seminole County Youth Services, Sanford, 1982-83; mem. Fla. Gov.'s Conf. on Youth and Aged, Tallahassee, 1984; mem. Fla. Gov.'s Constituency for Children, Tallahassee, 1985; bd. dirs. Seminole County United Fund, 1984-85; mem. adv. bd. Seminole Community Coll. Child Devel., 1985—. Mem. Nat. Assn. Children Under Six, Community Coordinated Child Care (bd. dirs. 1984-85, spl. dir. 1984—, 6 Gold Seal of Excellence awards 1983, 84), Fla. Assn. Children Under Six, Nat. Assn. Child Care Mgrs., Fla. Assn. child Care Mgrs., World Orgn. Children Under Eight, Seminole County Assn. Children Under Six, Sanford C. of C. (chairwoman membership drive 1978-85). Democrat. Presbyterian. Avocations: reading; tennis; sewing; writing. Office: Sanford Child Care Inc PO Box 1814 Sanford FL 32771

MIZELL, CAROL LYNN, life insurance agent; b. San Diego, Oct. 27, 1945; d. Marvin Carroll and Ethelyn Clark McGowan; m. Robert Griffin Mizell, Aug. 9, 1969; children—Michelle, Jennifer. B.Mus. with honors, North Tex. State U., 1868, M.Music Edn., 1970, postgrad. 1970-73; student Abilene Christian U., 1965, U. Colo., Boulder, 1966. Pub. sch. music tchr. Arapaho Elem. Sch., Richardson, Ind. Sch. Dist. (Tex.), 1968-69; grad. fellow Sch. Music, North Tex. State U., Denton, 1969-73; instr., dir. instrumental activities Tex. Woman's U., Denton, 1975-76, 76-78; agt. Fidelity Union Ins. Co., Denton, 1978, Northwestern Nat. Life Ins. Co., Denton, 1979—, Metroplex Fin. Services, Inc., Denton, 1983—. Conductor, Denton Community Band, 1978—; bd. dirs. Greater Denton Arts Council, The Arts Guild; rec. sec. Denton Benefit League, 1975-76; cultural arts chmn. Woodrow Wilson PTA, 1982-84; festival coordinator Denton Festival of Carols, 1981, 82. Mem. Nat. Assn. Life Underwriters, Tex. Assn. Life Underwriters, Denton Assn. Life Underwriters, Denton Alumnae (pres. 1974-76), Mortar Bd., Phi Kappa Lambda. Sigma Alpha Iota, Kappa "B" Province (v.p. 1978-81), Kappa Delta. Methodist. Composer: The Prince of Peace. Home: 2722 Crestwood Pl Denton TX 76201 Office: 109 E Oak St Denton TX 76201

MIZER, KAREN MARY, rehabilitation specialist, business executive; b. Bklyn., Sept. 13, 1954; d. Joseph Peter and Lois (Swenson) McCafferty; m. Jay McGowan, Dec. 19, 1976 (div. 1978); m. Orville Charles Mizer, Jan. 20, 1979; children—Thomas Aquinas, Catherine Ann Marie, Elizabeth Ann. B.B.A. summa cum laude, U. Md.-Okinawa, 1982. Cert. ins. rehab. specialist Mgr. Em-R's Jewelers, Rockaway Beach, N.Y., 1974-76; adminstrv. officer U.S. Marine Corps, Okinawa, Japan, 1979-82; mgr., counselor AAA Employment, Gainesville, Fla., 1982-84; rehab. specialist, owner TMS Assocs., Gainesville, 1984—; rehab. specialist Orlando Cons., Gainesville, 1983-84. Author, photographer mag. articles. Vol. United Way, Gainesville, 1985. Served with USN, 1976-79. Mem. Fla. Assn. Rehab. Providers, Nat. Assn. Female Execs., Gainesville C. of C. (ambassador 1985—), Phi Kappa Phi. Republican. Roman Catholic. Club: Navy Wives (pres., pub. relations officer Okinawa 1979-82, Navy Wife of Yr. 1981). Avocations: Reading; swimming; boating. Home: 8304 SW Williston Rd Gainesville FL 32608 Office: TMS Associates Rehabilitation Management 8308 SW Williston Rd Gainesville FL 32608

MIZWA, MARY JANE HOUSE, publishing executive, antique dealer; b. Nacogdoches, Tex., Oct. 16, 1936; d. Garnet Reed and Johnnie Rhae (Simons) House; m. Tad S. Mizwa, Mar. 12, 1965; children—John, Michael, Michelle, Stephen; m. Barnett J. Jones, Sept. 1, 1957 (div. May 1964). A.A., Lon Morris Coll., 1955; B.Ed., U. Tex., 1958. Advt. and editorial asst. Horseman Mag., Houston, 1967-70; advt. salesman, 1970-73; assoc. editor Western Outfitter, Houston, 1973-75, editor, 1975-80; ops. mgr. Cordovan Corp., Houston, 1980-82, mgr. circulation adminstrn., 1982-85; circulation dir. Southwest Art, 1985—; owner Past Tense Antiques, Houston, 1983-85; v.p. Antique Panache Inc., 1984—. Republican. Presbyterian. Home: 1205 Krist Dr Houston TX 77055 Office: Southwest Art Nine Greenway Plaza Suite 2010 Houston TX 77046

MLAY, MARIAN, government official; b. Pitts., Sept. 11, 1935; d. John and Sonia M.; A.B., U. Pitts., 1957; postgrad. (Univ. fellow) Princeton U., 1969-70; J.D., Am. U., 1977. Mgmt. positions HEW, Washington, 1961-70, dep. dir. Chgo. region, 1971-72, dir. div. consol. funding, 1972-73, dep. dir. office policy devel. and planning USPHS, Washington, 1973-77; dir. program evaluation EPA, Washington, 1978-79, dep. dir. Office of Drinking Water, 1979-84, dir. Office of Ground Water Protection, 1984—. Bd. dirs. D.C. United Fund, 1979-80. Recipient Career Edn. award Nat. Inst. Public Affairs, 1969. Mem. ABA, D.C. Bar (steering com. energy, environment and natural resources div.), Exec. Women in Govt., D.C. Women's Bar, Nat. Cathedral Choral Soc. Eastern Orthodox. Author articles in field. Home: 3747 1/2 Kanawha St NW Washington DC 20015 Office: 401 M St SW Washington DC 20460

MMAHAT, ARLENE CECILE, steel company executive, civic activist; b. New Orleans, Oct. 5, 1943; d. John Alden and Margaret Therese (Nuccio) Montgomery; m. John Anthony Mmahat, Aug. 12, 1967; children—Arlene, Amy, John Anthony, Jr. B.A., La. State U., 1965. Clk., Shell Oil Co., New Orleans, 1965; claims rep. Social Security, New Orleans, 1966-67; chmn. bd. New Era Tubulars, New Orleans, 1979-84; chief exec. officer Olympia Tubular Corp., New Orleans, 1984—. Bd. dirs. New Orleans Symphony, 1983—, chmn. musicians adv. com., 1984, 85, membership chmn., 1985, oil and gas chmn. devel. com., 1983, devel. chmn. pub. sector, 1984; mem. Houston Bus. Council, 1980—, Ind. Women's Orgn., 1968—; mem. adv. bd. Kennedy Ctr. for Performing Arts, 1980, Loyola U. Sch. Music, 1982—; fin. advisor New Orleans Symphony Soc. Jr. Com., 1977-79, fin. chmn., 1976; bd. dirs. Young Audiences, Inc., 1985—; mem. nat. adv. bd. on tech. and the disabled U.S. Dept. HHS; bd. dirs. Leukemia Soc. Am., Inc., 1978, corp. del., 1979; founder Ladies Leukemia League; Odyssey Weekend chmn. New Orleans Mus. Art, 1985, fellows, 1983; mem. adv. com. St. Michael's Sch. for Spl. Students, 1978—, fin. chmn., 1977, mem. fin. com., 1973-76; fin. chmn. La. Landmarks Soc., 1973-75; bd. dirs. Preservation Resource Ctr., 1980, ways and means com., 1979, Christmas Benefit advisor, 1975, 76. Named One of 10 Outstanding Persons, New Orleans Inst. Human Understanding, 1977; One of 83 People to Watch in 1983, New Orleans Mag.; recipient Vol. Activist award Germain Monteil and D.H. Holmes Co., Ltd., 1977. Democrat. Roman Catholic. Home: 1239 1st St New Orleans LA 70130 Office: Olympia Tubular Corp 348 Baronne St Suite 602 New Orleans LA 70112

MOATTS, FRANCES SUSAN, nurse; b. Clanton, Ala., Aug. 31, 1937; d. Ray and Marjorie Lee (Price) Mizell; R.N., Sylacauga Sch. Nursing, 1959; postgrad. U. Ala., 1979; m. Thomas Raymond Moatts, July 9, 1965; 1 son, Michael Thomas. Staff nurse Chilton County Hosp. (now Central Ala. Community Hosp.), Clanton, Ala., 1959-65, 65—, asst. dir. nursing, 1978-81; staff nurse Jackson Hosp., Montgomery, Ala., 1965. Vol. ARC Blood Program, 1959—. Recipient Good Citizenship award, 1953; Kiwanis scholar, 1956. Republican. Baptist. Club: Progressive Woman's Orgn. Home: Route 5 PO Box 157 Clanton AL 35045 Office: Laydam Rd Clanton AL 35045

MOBLEY, MONA LEJEUNE, writer, lecturer, Bible educator; b. Lucedale, Miss., Aug. 29, 1933; d. Cecil and Birdie Lee (Adams) McLeod; m. Harold Dean Mobley, Dec. 19, 1952; children—Stephen, Tamara, Twayne, Timothy. Student Freed-Hardeman Coll., 1952; French lang. cert. Grenoble Inst., Florence, Italy, 1970. Legal sec. for various attys., Wichita Falls, Tex., 1975-79; missionary Ch. of Christ, Florence, Italy, 1961-71, Montreal, Can., 1961-75; lectr., writer, 1961—; tchr. Ch. of Christ, Channelview, Tex., 1979—, counselor, Tex., Italy, Can., 1961—; lectr. various religious functions, Europe and U.S., 1961—. Author: Joyful Hospitality, 1983; Because I'm a Woman ... Please Understand, 1983; From Mom With Love, 1985, also articles. Sec. Forest River Estates Civic Club, Channelview, 1980. Democrat. Avocations: painting; various crafts; homemaking; volunteer work.

MOCK, KATHERINE GWENDOLYN, county court official; b. Meadowview, Va., June 19, 1925; d. Matthew Floyd and Mary Edith (Neff) M. Student Mary Dalton Frye Pvt. Secretarial Sch., Abingdon, Va., 1955. Sec. hosp., Abingdon, 1956-57; dep. clk. Washington County Circuit Ct., Abingdon, 1957-80, clk., 1980—. Mem. Bus. and Profl. Women's Club. Republican. Baptist. Avocations: Music; cooking; flower arranging; gardening; reading. Office: Circuit Ct Washington County Court St Abingdon VA 24361

MOCK, LEILANI ANN, adult education administrator, consultant; b. Boston, July 18, 1944; d. Raymond Clayton and Audrey Mary (MacDonald) Lunde; children—Dean, Cheryl, Vicki, Jennifer. Dir. religious edn. St. Jerome Cath. Ch., Houston, 1974-78, Christ the Good Shepherd, Spring, Tex., 1978-84, St. Pius Cath. Ch., Pasadena, Tex., 1984—; ptnr. South West Ctr. for Ministry, Houston, 1985—. Contbr. articles to profl. jours. Mem. edn. com. Conf. of Catholic Women, Houston, 1984—; vice chmn., organizer Girl Scouts U.S.A., Houston, 1974-78. Mem. Am. Soc. Tng. and Devel., Nat. Assn. Lay Ministry, Religious Edn. Assn., Nat. Assn. Dir. Religious Edn. (rep. 1981—, pres. 1982-86), Diocesan Assn. of Dir. Religious Edn. (pres. Houston 1979-82). Roman Catholic. Avocations: travel; reading; art; music. Home: 601 Cypress Station Dr #1302 Houston TX 77090 Office: St Pius Cath Ch 824 S Main Pasadena TX 77506

MOCK, MELINDA SMITH, medical costs consultant, nurse; b. Austell, Ga., Nov. 15, 1947; d. Robert Jehu and Emily Dorris (Smith) Smith; m. David Thomas Mock, Oct. 20, 1969. A.S. in Nursing, DeKalb Coll., 1972. R.N., Ga.; cert. orthopedic nurse specialist. Nursing technician Ga. Baptist Hosp., Atlanta, 1967, staff nurse, 1979; asst. corr. Harcourt, Brace & World Pub. Co., Atlanta, 1968-69; receptionist-sec. Goodbody & Co., Atlanta, 1969-70; nursing asst. DeKalb Gen. Hosp., Decatur, Ga., 1970-71; staff nurse Doctor's Meml. Hosp., Atlanta, 1972-73; staff nurse Shallowford Community Hosp., Atlanta, 1973, relief charge nurse, 1973, charge nurse, 1973-76, head nurse, 1976-79, orthopedic specialist emergency room, 1979; rehab. specialist Internat. Rehab. Assocs., Inc., Norcross, Ga., 1981, sr. rehab. specialist, 1981, rehab. supr., 1981-82; cons., founder, propr. Healthcare Cost Cons., Alpharetta, Ga., 1982-83; cons., founder, pres. Healthcare Cost Cons., Inc., Alpharetta, 1983—; mem. legis. com. of adv. council Ga. Bd. Nursing, Atlanta, 1984-85. Dep. voter registrar Fulton County Voter Registration Dept., Atlanta, 1983—. Mem. Nat. Assn. Orthopedic Nurses (nat. policies com. 1981-82), Orthopedic Nurses Assn. (nat. bd. dirs. 1977-79, nat. treas. 1979-81), Council Splty. Nursing Orgns. Ga. (nominating com. 1976-77), Assn. Rehab. Nurses (bd. dirs. Ga. chpt. 1980-81, del. people-to-people program to People's Republic China 1981), Nat. Assn. Female Execs., Ga. Jaycees (dist. 4C rep. Ga. Jaycee Legis. 1984, 85, adminstrv. asst. 1985), North Fulton C. of C. (vice chmn. health service effectiveness alliance 1984-85, chmn. 1985—, co-chmn./editor periodical 1985), Alpharetta Jaycees (adminstrv. v.p. 1984-85), internal v.p. 1985-86), Alpharetta Jaycee Women (bd. dirs. 1983—). Democrat. Baptist. Avocations: reading; boating; community service activities. Home: 424 Michael Dr Alpharetta GA 30201 Office: Health Cost Cons Inc 26 Milton Ave Suite W-4 Alpharetta GA 30201

MOCK, PATRICIA ELIOT, advertising executive; b. Charlston, W.Va., Oct. 22, 1940; d. Philip Samuel and Erma Lousie (Patterson) Skaff; m. Richard Basil Mock, Oct. 24, 1982; m. David Anthony McQueen, Apr. 1, 1962 (div. 1969); children—Ron Alexander, Juliet Maude May. B.F.A., U. Tex., 1969. Designer, Steck Vaughn Publs., Austin, Tex., 1967-68; owner, 1st Family Gallery, Houston, 1968-70; art dir. Pacifica Radio, Houston, 1970-71; designer Gulf State Advt., Houston, 1972-74; registrar Menil Found., Houston, 1977-81; art dir. Rod Serling's Twilight Zone Mag., N.Y.C., 1982-84; owner, mgr. Creative Zone, Inc., N.Y.C., 1984—; cons. Am. Assn. Museums, 1966-81, Hadassah, N.Y.C., 1985. Office: Creative Zone Inc 149 W 27th St New York NY 10001

MOE, BARBARA ANN, counselor, educator; b. Grand Forks, N.D., June 24, 1955; d. Robert Alan and Ruth Ann (Wang) M.; m. William Martin Fishback, June 1986. B.S. in Psychology, U. N.D., 1977, M.A. in Counseling and Guidance, 1979, B.S. in Elem. Edn., 1984. Cert. elem. tchr. and counselor, S.D., N.D. Sales clk. Vold Drug Store, Grand Forks, 1972-79; tchr. United Day Nursery, Grand Forks, 1977-78; social worker Cavalier County Social Services, Langdon, N.D., 1979-83; skin care cons. Jafra Cosmetics, Westlake Village, Calif., 1983—; elem. sch. counselor Douglas Sch. System, Ellsworth Air Force Base, S.D., 1984—. Vol. Big Sister Program, Grand Forks, 1978-84; leader Pine to Prairie Girl Scout Council, Langdon, N.D., 1980-82; tchrs. asst. Head Start Program, Grand Forks, 1979. Mem. Am. Assn. Counseling and Devel., NEA, AAUW (local branch newsletter editor 1980-81, branch sec. 1981-83), S.D. Edn. Assn., Am. Sch. Counselor Assn., S.D. Assn. Counseling and Devel., S.D. Sch. Counselor Assn., West River Personnel and Guidance Assn., Kappa Alpha Theta (newsletter, magazine article editor 1976-77). Club: Jaycettes (Landgon) (dir. 1982-83). Avocations: cooking; camping; curling; ceramics; creative writing. Home: 4633 Capital St Rapid City SD 57701 Office: Francis Case School Ellsworth Air Force Base SD 57706

MOE, VIDA DELORES, civic worker; b. Ryder, N.D., Feb. 29, 1928; d. John Nelson and Inga Marie (Lewis) Ahlgran; m. Placido Ferdinand, July 28, 1950 (div.); children—Terrence Paul, Star Marie; m. Edgar Louis Moe, May 24, 1970 (dec. 1983). Student Minot State Coll., 1964-66; diploma interior decorating LaSalle Extension U., 1976. Clk.-stenographer various divs. Minot AFB, N.D., 1960-70, 73-76, housing assignment clk., 1974-75, sec., various divs., 1975—; historian Minot Republican Women, 1984-86; chmn. decorations com. 40/50 Rep. Women, Minot, 1983, v.p., 1982; bd. dirs. Patrons of the Library, Minot, 1978-88, sec., 1979-80, v.p., 1981, pres., 1982-83; chmn. Carnegie Restoration and Art Ctr. Project City Art League, 1980-88, pres., 1977-79. Recipient Superior Performance award 5th Bomb Wing, Minot AFB, 1968; Devotion to Vol. Duty award USAF Regional Hosp., Minot, 1983, 86. Mem. Minot Bus. and Profl. Women's Club (pres. 1981-82), N.D. Bus. and Profl. Women's Club (rec. sec. 1978-79, 81-82), Am. Legion Aux. (pres. 1982-84, judge jr. art posters 1980-82), Minot Shrine Hosp. Aux. (pres. 1986), Beta Sigma Phi (pres. Laureate chpt. 1983-85, Valentine Girl 1985, Girl of Yr. 1984). Lutheran. Club: MidState Porcelain Artists Guild (pres. 1984). Lodge: Order Eastern Star (Grand Martha 1984-85, Grand Electa 1985-86, Worthy Matron chpt. 14, 1976). Avocations: china painting, oil painting, sewing, tennis, embroidery. Home: 705 25th St NW Minot ND 58701

MOEDER, CLAUDIA NELL, career college executive; b. Athens, Tex., Jan. 25, 1941; d. Herschel A. and Eunice I. (Mayfield) Munday; m. Virgil Joseph Moeder, Oct. 24, 1964; 1 child, Ty Jeffrey. Owner/tchr. Claudia Mundy's Sch. of Dance, Wichita, Kans., 1956-60; instr., salesperson Patricia Stevens Sch., Wichita, 1961-71, owner, dir., 1975—; sec. Moeder Constrn. Co., Wichita, 1971-75; chair adv. commn. Kans. State Bd. Edn. Proprietary Schs., 1982—. Mem. Kans. Assn. Pvt. Career Schs. (sec. 1984—), Nat. Assn. Women Bus. Owners (treas. 1984—), Modeling Assn. Am., Internat. Model and Talent Competition. Roman Catholic. Avocations: yard work; boating. Office: Patricia Stevens School 2823 E Douglas St Wichita KS 67211

MOELLER, BEVERLEY BOWEN, agribusiness executive; b. Long Beach, Calif., Oct. 12, 1925; d. George Walter and Agnes Ruth (Coffey) Bowen; B.A., Whittier Coll., 1956; M.A., UCLA, 1965, Ph.D., 1968; m. Roger David Moeller, Dec. 11, 1955; children—Roger Bowen Shelton, Wendell Shelton, Claire Agnes, Barbara Bowen, Thomas David. Writer, Valley News and Green Sheet, Van Nuys, Calif., 1961-64; scholar-tchr. Valley Coll., Los Angeles, 1968-69, UCLA, 1970; instr. Petróleos Brasileiros, Salvador, Bahia, Brazil, 1972-73; pres. Nova Pioneira Agroindustrial Ltda., Belém Pará, Brazil, 1982—; dir. Associacão Cultural Brasil-Estados Unidos, 1972-73. Mem. Calif. Regional Water Quality Control Commn., 1970-71. Mem. IEEE (history com., chmn. region 2 com. on profl. opportunities for women), Soc. History of Tech., Internat. Soc. Tropical Foresters, Forest History Soc. Republican. Author: Phil Swing and Boulder Dam, 1971. Home: 7802 Glenn Eagle Dallas TX 75248

MOELY, BARBARA E., psychology researcher, educator; b. Prairie du Sac, Wis., July 17, 1940; d. John Arthur and Loretta Ruth (Giese) M.; m. Gerald Wiener, May 21, 1974; children—John Jacob, David Andrew. Student Carroll Coll., 1958-60; B.A., U. Wis., 1962, M.A., 1964; Ph.D., U. Minn., 1968. Asst. prof. U. Hawaii, Honolulu, 1967-71; research psychologist UCLA, 1971-72; asst. prof. Tulane U., New Orleans, 1972-75, assoc. prof. psychology, 1975-85, prof., 1985—; cons. New Orleans Pub. Schs., 1973-75. Contbr. articles to profl. jours. Grantee La. Commn. Extension and Continuing Edn., 1973-74, U.S. Office Edn., Handicapped Personnel Preparation, 1977-80, Tulane U., 1973, 75, 77, 78, 83-84, Inst. for Mental Hygiene, City of New Orleans, 1983-84, Nat. Inst. Edn., 1983-84. Mem. Soc. Research in Child Devel., Am. Psychol. Assn., Am. Ednl. Research Assn., Southwestern Soc. for Research in Human Devel. (pres.-elect 1984—), Phi Beta Kappa (pres. Alpha chapter La. 1981-82). Office: Dept Psychology Tulane Univ New Orleans LA 70118

MOENCH, ELIZABETH ANN, pharmaceuticals company executive; b. Bristol, Eng., May 5, 1958; arrived U.S., 1975; d. Edward Charles and Phyllis Winnifred (Johnson) Cross; m. Frederick Emil Moench, Dec.30, 1978. Student, Lamar U., 1976-77. Owner, pres. Moench Advt., Tampa, Fla., 1978-80; product mgr. Boots Pharms., Shreveport, La., 1981-82, dir. communications, 1982—; speaker profl. assns., Food and Drug Law Inst., 1983, Pharm. Advt. Council, 1983. Bd. dirs. Arthritis Found., Barnwell Arts Centre. Mem. Pharm. Mfrs. Assn., Internat. Assn. Bus. Communicators, Shreveport C. of C. (mem. leadership council 1982—). Anglican. Home: 6131 N. Weatherby St Shreveport LA 71129 Office: Boots Pharmaceuticals Inc 6540 Line Ave Shreveport LA 71106

MOERSCH, DEWEENTA CONRAD (MRS. HERMAN J. MOERSCH), former banker, club woman; b. Omaha; d. James Harvey and Lila (Weeks) Conrad; student pvt. schs., Wellesley, Mass.; m. Howard Kramer Gray, Sept. 2, 1925 (dec. 1955); children—Howard Kramer, DeWeenta Russell (Mrs. Walter Bones, Jr.); m. 2d, Herman J. Moersch, Jan. 3, 1973 (dec. 1981). Women's rep. first Nat. Bank, Rochester, Minn., 1956-64. Vice pres. YWCA, Rochester, 1933-36, bd. dirs., 1930-36; pres. U.S.O., Rochester, 1942-45; bd. dirs. Art Center, Rochester, 1956-64, v.p., 1959-61; sec., bd. dirs. YMCA, Rochester, 1957-60; mem. women's exec. com. Minn. Statehood Centennial, 1958; mem. Minn. hospitality com. WHO Internat. Meeting, Mpls. Bd. dirs. Rochester Community Chest, 1962-64, Christmas Anonymous, Rochester, 1956-64, Ability Bdlg. Center, Rochester, 1957-64. Trustee St. Mary's Hosp., Rochester, 1968-76, Tyrone Guthrie Theatre Found., Mpls., 1962-68. Recipient Service to Mankind award Sertoma Internat., 1965. Mem. Nat. Assn. Bank

Women (chmn. regional meeting Rochester 1961), UN Assn., U.S.A. (Minn. bd. dirs. 1958-62, Rochester chpt. bd. dirs. 1959-62, pres. 1960-62), League Women Voters (dir., pres. Rochester 1948-49), Minn. Hist. Soc. (women's bd. dirs. 1952-55, chmn. 1954-55, exec. council 1955-57), Bus. and Profl. Women's Club (Bus. Woman of Yr. Rochester 1961), Rochester C. of C. (priorities com. 1966). Methodist. Clubs: Woman's (Mpls.); Country; Rochester Golf and Country. Home: 2221 Hillside Ln SW Rochester MN 55902

MOFFAT, MARYBETH, automotive company executive; b. Pitts., July 25, 1951; d. Herbert Franklin and Florrence Grafe (Knerem) M.; m. Brian Francis Soulier, Nov. 30, 1974 (div.). B.A., Carroll Coll., 1973. Indsl. engring. technician Wis. Centrifugal Co., Waukesha, Wis., 1976-77; indsl. engr. Utility Products, Inc., Milw., 1977-79; indsl. engring. mgr. Bear Automotive, Bangor, Pa., 1980—. Group home house parent Headwaters Regional Achievement Ctr., Lake Tomahawk, Wis., 1974. Mem. Am. Inst. Indsl. Engrs., MTM Assn. for Standards Research, Indsl. Mgmt. Soc., Alpha Gamma Delta (standards chmn. 1971-72). Republican. Methodist. Avocations: skiing; horseback riding; swimming; reading. Home: Spring Ridge Apts #P-23 Whitehall PA 18052 Office: Bear Automotive Service Equipment Co South Main and Werner Sts Bangor PA 18013

MOFFETT, HOPE MERLETTI, trade publication executive; b. North Tonawanda, N.Y., June 25, 1938; d. Charles and Jennie (Weber) Guzzetta; grad. high sch.; children—Katherine, Mark, Robert Merletti; stepchildren—Andra, Timothy, Allison Moffett. Co-organizer, coordinator largest wine tasting in East, 1977—; v.p., partner Vineyard & Winery Mgmt., Watkins, N.Y., 1978—; coordinator Wineries Unltd., 1976—. Pres. Schuyler County LWV, 1985-86; chmn. ambulatory care subcom. Health Services Agy., 1975—. Mem. Soc. Wine Educators, Am. Wine Soc., N.Y. State Hort. Assn., Am. Soc. Enologists, Pa. Hort. Assn. Home and office: Box 329 Watkins Glen NY 14891

MOFFORD, ROSE, state official; b. Globe, Ariz., June 10, 1922; attended public schs. Sec. to Joe Hunt, Ariz. State Treas., 1941-43, Ariz. State Tax Commr., 1943-54, to Wesley Bolin, Ariz., Sec. of State, 1954-55; asst. sec. of state State of Ariz., Phoenix, 1955-79, sec. of state, 1979—. Democrat. Office: Office of Sec of State West Wing State Capitol Phoenix AZ 85007*

MOGFORD, SHARON MARIE, state official; b. Kerrville, Tex., Mar. 4, 1959; d. Harold Lamar, Sr., and Mary Elizabeth (Phipps) M. B.B.A., S.W. Tex. State U., 1981. Cert. scuba diver. With State Auditor's Office, Austin, Tex., 1981—, asst. state auditor, 1981-83, in-charge asst. state auditor, 1983-85, supervising asst. state auditor, 1985—. Republican. Baptist. Avocations: scuba diving; softball; snow skiing. Home: 2207 Hollybush 103 Dallas TX 75228

MOHLER, MARY, magazine editor. Mng. editor Ladies Home Jour., N.Y.C. Office: Ladies Home Jour Family Media Inc 3 Park Ave New York NY 10016*

MOHR, DIANE LOUISE, librarian; b. Fairbanks, Alaska, Nov. 24, 1951; d. Dean Burgette and Mary Louise (Leonard) M. Deuxieme degree, Alliance Francais, Brussels, 1971; B.A. in Black Studies Calif. State U.-Long Beach, 1977; M.S. in L.S., U. So. Calif. 1978. Indexer/reviewer Litigation Support Services, Getty Oil Co., Los Angeles, 1978-79; librarian in charge Woodcrest br., Los Angeles County Pub. Library, 1979-82, View Park br., 1982-83, Los Angeles County Pub. Library, 1982-83; sr. librarian-in-charge Compton br. Los Angeles County Pub. Library, 1983—; Mem. ALA, Calif. Black Librarians Caucus, NOW, U. So. Calif. Alumni, Links Inc., Alpha Kappa Alpha, Phi Kappa Phi. Democrat. Episcopalian. Club: Links. Home: 2354 N Indian Hill Blvd Claremont CA 91711 Office: Compton Pub Library 240 W Compton Blvd Compton CA 90220

MOHR, HARRIET, writer, author, researcher; b. N.Y.C., Oct. 27, 1939; d. Solomon and Jeanette (Shein) Baris; m. William L. Mohr, Oct. 26, 1962; 1 child, Tara Sophia. B.A. with honors in Psychology of Women, Lone Mountain Coll., 1977. Free-lance writer, researcher, Menlo Park, Calif. Author: (with husband) Quality Circles: Changing Images of People At Work, 1983, 84; contbr. articles to various publs.; Interviewer, film maker (documentary) Quality Circles in the United Kingdom. Mem. Am. Soc. Tng. and Devel. Internat. Assn. Quality Circles, Jewish Profl. Women's Orgn., Analytical Psychology Club, Orgn. Devel. Inst.

MOHR, JEAN HOLLY, newspaper account executive; b. New Rochelle, N.Y., Jan. 27, 1955; d. John Henry and Ethel Jane (Zimmerman) M. B.A. in Advt. and Pub. Relations, Tex. Tech. U., 1977; postgrad. U. Houston. Scheduling coordinator nat. advt. Houston Chronicle, 1977-78, account rep. retail advt., 1978-83, account coordinator advt. spl. event retail, 1983-85, retail advt. mktg. specialist southwest, 1985—; promotional asst. Houston Livestock Show and Rodeo, 1983; judge Mktg. Distbr. Edn. Competitions, Houston, 1978-79, 86. Vol. Ronald McDonald House, Houston, 1983. Named Salesperson of Month, 100 Club mem. Houston Chronicle, 1985. Mem. Nat. Assn. Female Execs., Tex. Tech. Ex-Students Assn., Delta Delta Delta (pres. Houston 1985—). Methodist. Avocations: jazzercise; tennis. Home: 8151 Misty Ridge Ln Houston TX 77071 Office: Houston Chronicle 10325 Landsbury Dr Suite 414A Houston TX 77099

MOHR, PATRICIA PRUDEN, educational administrator; b. Johannesburg, South Africa; naturalized U.S. citizen. R.N., Sacramento Jr. Coll. Sch. Nursing; student Claremont Grad. Sch., U. Calif., San Diego; M.A., Pacific Oaks Coll. Tchr. pre-sch., elem. sch., parent edn., community coll.; teaching fellow Pacific Oaks Coll.; assoc. prof., dir. student health and child devel. programs Chaffey Community Coll.; adminstr. child devel. programs Hacienda-LaPuente Unified Sch. Dist., Calif., 1982—; cons. in field. Bd. dirs. Channel of Love, Los Angeles, 1966-70; bd. dirs., pres. Claremont Civic Assn., 1972-73; mem. Community Coll. Chancellor's Task Force on Early Childhood, 1976-78; grants writer San Bernardino County Schs.; San Bernardino Title XX grantee, 1980-81. Mem. Assn. Community Coll. Adminstrs., Calif. Child Devel. Adminstrs. Assn. (bd. dirs., pres.), Nat. Assn. Edn. Young Children, So. Calif. Assn. for Edn. Young Children. Mem. Am. Friends Soc. Editor: Broadcasting for Children, 1979-81. Office: Hillgrove Ctr for Children and Parents Hacienda La Puente Sch Dist 1234 Valencia Hacienda Heights CA 91745

MOIR, BETTY SCOTT, heavy equipment, leasing and construction company executive; b. Columbus, Kans., July 14, 1934; d. William Howard and Esther Laura (Mitchell) Scott; R.N., St. Luke's Hosp., 1955; m. James Sterling Moir, Aug. 31, 1957; children—James Sterling, John Thomas, Heather Logan. Partner, B & T Equipment Co., Honolulu, 1958-61; partner Moir Ranch & Constrn. Co., Eugene, Oreg., 1971-80; sole proprietor Brown Bear Constrn. Co., Eugene, 1980—. Vol. docent U. Oreg. Art Mus., 1974-81. Republican. Lutheran. Clubs: Eugene Country, Town and Country Garden. Address: 86510 Pine Grove Rd Eugene OR 97402 also 10 Scenic Way 215 San Mateo CA 94403

MOLBERG, ANDREA, psychologist, educator; b. Mpls., Jan. 3, 1951; d. Allen Luther and Phillis Ann M.; B.A. summa cum laude, Ariz. State U., 1971; Ph.D. in Indsl. Orgn. and Counseling Psychology, U. Minn., 1976; m. Jeffrey Rogers Basford, Feb. 27, 1982. Teaching asst., teaching asso., instr. Gen. Coll., U. Minn., 1972-75, instr. dept. psychology, 1974, asst. prof. extended programs, 1976-77; instr. dept. psychology Coll. St. Thomas, St. Paul, 1974-77, asst. prof. counseling psychology, 1977-81, adj. prof., 1981—; pvt. practice cons. psychology, St. Paul, 1976—. Mem. Am. Psychol. Assn., Am. Assn. Counseling and Devel. Contbr. in field. Home: Route 2 Box 143 Kasson MN 55944 Office: PO Box 5901 Rochester MN 55903

MOLDEN, PATRICIA, college official; b. Council Bluffs, Iowa, May 6, 1936; d. Frank Glenwood and Marguerite (Hadell) Coover; m. John R. Molden, Oct. 15, 1959; children—Susan E. Rose, Michael J., Kathleen M. B.A., U. Nebr., 1958; postgrad. Universidad de los Andes, Bogota, Colombia, 1959. Reporter, editor Lincoln Jour., Nebr., 1954-59; writer Northwestern Bell Telephone Co., Omaha, 1961-64; communications mgr. Ortho Pharm., Raritan, N.J., 1973-79; freelance writer, 1980-81; dir. pub. info. and publs. Kean Coll., Union, N.J., 1982—. Chmn. Joint Civic Com., Westfield, N.J., 1972; active Parent-Tchr. Council, Westfield, 1965-73. InterAm. Press Assn. scholar, 1959. Mem. Pub. Relations Soc. Am., Council for Advancement and Support Edn. Democrat. Episcopalian. Avocations: tennis, swimming, gardening. Home: 701 E Brookside Ln Somerville NJ 08876 Office: Kean Coll of NJ Morris Ave Union NJ 07083

MOLDENHAUER, HELGA GISELA, travel agency executive; b. Frankfurt/Main, West Germany, Jan. 6, 1938, came to U.S., 1953; d. Max Albert and Maria Sophia (Herbold) M. B.A., U. Calif.-Berkeley, 1962, M.A., 1965. Ops. agent Scandinavian Airlines, Frankfurt, 1955-56; instr. U. Calif., Berkeley, 1962-65; mgr. See and Sea Travel, San Francisco, 1967-70; pres. Crossroads Travel, Inc., San Francisco, 1972—, All West Travel and Tours, San Francisco, 1980—. Mem. Assn. Retail Travel Agts., San Francisco Visitor and Conv. Bur., San Francisco C. of C., Nat. Honor Soc. Club: Metropolitan (San Francisco) Avocations: writing; painting. Office: Crossroads Travel Inc 235 Montgomery St #1111 San Francisco CA 94104

MOLER, ELIZABETH ANNE, lawyer; b. Salt Lake City, Jan. 24, 1949; d. Murray McClure and Eleanor Lorraine (Barry) M.; B.A., Am. U., 1971; postgrad. Johns Hopkins U., 1971, 72; J.D., George Washington U., 1977; m. Thomas Blake Williams, Oct. 19, 1979; 1 child, Blake Martin Williams. Admitted to D.C. bar, 1978; staff asst. Hon. Laurence J. Burton, 1967-69, Senator Mike Gravel, 1971-72; chief legislative asst. Senator Floyd K. Haskell, 1973-75; law clk. Sharon, Pierson, Semmes, Crolius & Finley, Washington, 1975-76; profl. staff mem. Com. Energy and Natural Resources, U.S. Senate, Washington, 1976-77, counsel, 1977—. Mem. Am. Bar Assn., D.C. Bar Assn. Democrat. Author: (with James T. Bruce) Mexico: The Promise and Problems of Petroleum, 1979. Office: Com Energy and Natural Resources US Senate Washington DC 20510

MOLITOR, SISTER MARGARET ANNE, college president; b. Milford, Ohio, Sept. 19, 1920; d. George Jacob and Mary Amelia (Lockwood) Molitor; B.A., Our Lady of Cin. Coll., 1942; M.Ed., Xavier U., 1950, LL.D. (hon.), 1981; M.A., Cath. U. Am., 1963, Ph.D., 1967. Joined Sisters of Mercy, 1943; tchr. elem. schs., Cin., 1946-50, secondary schs., Cin. and Piqua, Ohio, 1951-60; faculty Edgecliff Coll., Cin., 1962-73, pres., 1973-80; Research cons. various religious communities. Bd. dirs. Citizens Com. on Youth; trustee Chatfield Coll.; mem. Area Council Planning Task Force; mem. Cin. Commmunity Devel. Adv. Council. Recipient Woman of Yr. award Cin. Enquirer, 1977. Mem. Greater Cin. Consortium Colls. and Univs. (pres. 1980). Address: 2335 Grandview Ave Cincinnati OH 45206

MOLLISON, CHAR, women's rights activist; b. Michigan City, Ind., Mar. 31, 1945; d. Isaac and Mildred Ruth (Brooklyn) Jolles; m. Andrew Ramsay Mollison, Jr., Dec. 27, 1967. B.A, Mich. State U., 1972; M.A. in Comparative Lit., CUNY, 1985. Teaching fellow dept. English, Queens Coll., N.Y.C., 1977; with Women's Equity Action League, Washington, 1977—, exec. dir., 1980—. Bd. dirs. House of Ruth, Washington, 1983—, Planned Parenthood of Met. Washington, 1986—; speaker women's rights, nonprofit mgmt. and fundraising. Author articles. Sarah Lawrence Coll. and Smithsonian Instn. scholar Inst. Women's History, 1979. Office: WEAL 1250 I St NW Suite 305 Washington DC 20005

MOLLOY, ANGELA MARGARET, advertising, marketing, and public relations executive; b. Pitts., July 16, 1948; d. John Robert and Angela Margaret (Culotta) Fanto; m. William Francis Molloy, June 24, 1970 (div. Oct. 1978); 1 dau., Angela Margaret. B.A., Duquesne U., 1970. Editorial asst. Nat. Council Internat. Visitors, Washington, 1970-73; dir. devel. DeMatha High Sch., Hyattsville, Md., 1973-75; mktg. officer Washington Fed. Savs. & Loan, Washington, 1978-80; asst. v.p., dir. mktg. Md. Fed. Savs. & Loan, Hyattsville, 1980-83; asst. v.p., dir. mktg. and advt. B.F. Saul Co., Chevy Chase, Md., 1983-86; sr. v.p. Power House Communications affiliate Gray & Co., pub. relations, 1986—. Bd. dirs. So. Hills Child Guidance Ctr., Pitts., 1977-78, Hyattsville Local Devel. Assn., 1981-82. Mem. Soc. Profl. Journalists, Women in Advt. and Mktg., Advt. Club Met. Washington (bd. dirs. 1984—). Democrat. Roman Catholic. Club: Desiree (Washington). Office: Power House Communications 1000 Potomac St NW Washington DC 20007

MOLNAR-BONCELA, CATHERINE LEE, lawyer; b. Gary, Ind., Feb. 2, 1957; d. Robert Lee and Betty Lou (Murray) Molnar; m. Edward Carl Boncela, Sept. 24, 1982. B.A. magna cum laude in Communications, Valparaiso U., J.D., 1981; LL.M., DePaul U., 1983; postgrad. Ind. U.-Gary, 1983—. Bar: Ind. 1981. Research asst. Valparaiso (Ind.) U., 1980-81; law clk. Bankruptcy Ct., Gary, 1981-84; assoc. firm Goldsmith, Goodman, Ball & Van Bokkelen, Highland, Ind., 1984—, asst. Highland Forensics, Ind., 1980—; dir. ETX Systems, Inc., Griffith, Ind. Vol. ARC, 1976-81, various polit. campaigns, Lake County, Ind., 1984. Mem. Ind. State Bar Assn., ABA, Women Lawyers Assn., Moot Ct. Soc. Lutheran. Home: 1737 Solo Dr Schererville IN 46375 Office: Goldsmith Goodman Ball & Van Bokkelen 3737 45th St Highland IN 46332

MOLTENI, BETTY PHILLIPS, painter; b. Norfolk, Va., Dec. 15, 1913; d. William Henry and Margaret (Brownley) Phillips; A.B., Coll. William and Mary, 1938; student art U. Nev., Reno, 1966-71; m. Peter G. Molteni, Jr., July 22, 1939; children—Peter G. III, Margaret Elizabeth, Christopher Phillips, Marianne Stephanie. Founder, chmn. Armed Forces Art Show Hawaii, 1962; one-woman shows Artist Coop., Reno, 1978, 81, Mother Lode Nat. Art Exhbn., Sonora, Calif., 1977, 79, Delta Art Assn. Show, Antioch, Calif., 1978, Lodi (Calif.) Ann. Art Exhbn., Acampo, Calif., 1979, 84, Nev. Ann., 1977-86, Nev. Woman Art Show, 1979; two-person shows Artist Coop., Reno, 1966-79, 82, Las Vegas Mus., 1985; exhibited group shows Nev. Women Art Show Las Vegas, 1976, Nat. League Am. Pen Women, Salt Lake City, 1973, Sacramento, 1978, Washington, 1984, Nev. State Exhibit (Best of Show award), 1971, Lake Tahoe Ehrman Art Festival, 1980, 81, Sierra Nev. Mus., Reno, 1983; feature artist Brewery Art Ctr., Carson City; represented in permanent collection Sierra Nev. Mus. Art. Bd. dirs. Nev. Art Gallery, 1975-78; del. Sierra Arts Assembly, 1977-82. Mem. Nat. League Am. Pen Women (v.p. 1973, pres. Reno chpt. 1980-82, pres. Nev. 1982-84), Soc. Western Artists, Latimer Art Club (pres. 1974, art scholarship chmn. 1978, treas. 1978), Carson City Alliance (charter mem.), Nev. Artists Assn., Nev. Art Gallery, Nev. Watercolor Soc. (ann. 1984), Sierra Nev. Mus. Art Aux., Sierra Arts Assembly, Artist Co-op. (charter). Republican. Roman Catholic. Home: 1130 Alpine Circle Reno NV 89509

MOLTZAN, JANET ROZDIL, library administrator; b. Bridgeport, Conn., Jan. 6, 1945; d. Andrew Peter and Helen (Botsko) Rozdil; m. Herbert John Moltzan, July 30, 1976. B.S. in L.S., Tex. Woman's U., Denton, 1963-67, M.L.S., 1973. Spl. counselor Tex. Woman's U., 1967-68; children's librarian Dallas Pub. Library, 1968-74, asst. library mgr., 1974-76, mgr., 1976-85, asst. dir. pub. services, 1985—; cons. Lamplighter Sch., Dallas, 1971; mem. field staff Caldecott Award Jury, 1982-84; cons. on book Reminiscences: A Glimpse of Old East Dallas, 1983; ex-officio mem. Lakewood Library Friends Bd., Dallas, 1982-85; participant NDEA Inst. Pub. and Sch. Library Work with Gifted Children, Denton, 1970. Contbr. articles to profl. jours. Friends of Dallas Pub. Library scholar, 1973. Mem. ALA (col. chmn. 1978-79), Tex. Library Assn. (legis. coordinator 1976-78), (children's roundtable v.p. 1975-76, pres. 1976-77, recognition award 1980) Pub. Library Assn. (chmn. services to children com. 1976-77), Assn. Library Services to Children (nominating com. 1980, publs. com. 1984—), Lakewood-Skillman Bus. and Profl. Assn. (dir. 1980-82), Zonta Internat. Mem. Eastern Orthodox Ch. Office: Dallas Pub Library 1515 Young St Dallas TX 75201

MONACO-HALPERN, JEANNETTE, marketing executive, financial business analyst; b. N.Y.C., May 20, 1955; d. Rudolph Andrew and Louise Marie (Tabacco) Monaco; m. Stephen Laurence Halpern, Sept. 1, 1979. B.A. magna cum laude in Internat. Affairs, Lafayette Coll., 1977; M.S. in Acctg., NYU, 1978, M.B.A. in Fin., 1983. Staff acct. Peat Marwick Mitchell, N.Y.C., 1977-79; fin. analyst Avon Products, N.Y.C., 1979-81; sales promotion mgr. Bergdorf Goodman, N.Y.C., 1981-83; mktg. mgr. James River Traders, N.Y.C., 1984—; fin. cons. Monaco-Halpern Ltd., N.Y.C., 1983—. Author: The New Wave in Electronic Banking, 1984. Mem. Direct Mktg. Assn., Phi Alpha Theta, Beta Gamma Sigma. Roman Catholic. Office: James River Traders 9 W 57th St 14th Floor New York NY 10019

MONAGHAN, NANCY C., journalist; b. Olean, N.Y., May 13, 1945; d. Stephen Francis Cipot and June (Butler) Cipot Duffey; m. G. Patrick Monaghan Jr., June 24, 1967 (div. 1973). Student U. Rochester, 1974-75. Mng. editor City Newspapers, Rochester, N.Y., 1973-75; pres. Mill Sq. Communications, Rochester, 1975-77; reporter, day metro editor Democrat and Chronicle, Rochester, 1977-82, metro editor, 1982; nat. editor, day nat. editor USA Today, Washington, 1982-84, mng. editor, news, 1984—. Vice chmn. Nat. Communications Council, Va. Tech., Blacksburg, 1983—. Recipient Matrix award Women in Communications, 1982, Spot News Reporting award N.Y. State AP, 1979, 82, Legal Reporting award N.Y. State Bar Assn., 1981, Govt. Reporting, award N.Y. State Pubs. Assn., 1973, 74, Polit. Reporting award N.Y. State Pubs. Assn., 1975. Mem. AP Mng. Editors (gen. news com.), Nat. Soc. Profl. Journalists (nat. membership chmn. 1984-85), Rochester Soc. Profl. Journalists (pres. 1980-81). Office: USA Today PO Box 500 Washington DC 20044

MONAHAN, JEANETTE, hospital administrator, organizational development consultant; b. Dallas, May 9, 1949; d. John I. and Julia M. (Galloway) Welsh; B.A. in English, U. Tex., Austin, 1971; M.P.A., U. Colo., 1975; diploma Internat. Inst. Study of Systems Renewal, Seattle, 1981; m. Terence F. Meany, Mar. 17, 1977; 1 dau., Theresa K. Monahan. Intern, City of Boulder (Colo.), summer 1975, Colo. Dept. Regulatory Agys., Denver, summer 1976; tng. specialist Municipality of Met. Seattle, 1977-78; mgr. employee tng. and devel. U. Wash. Hosps., Seattle, 1978-82; dir. mgmt. devel. Virginia Mason Med. Center, Seattle, 1982—. Recipient Suggestion award Municipality of Met. Seattle, 1978. Mem. Am. Soc. Tng. and Devel. (Outstanding Contbr. award 1977, 78; region VIII conf. planning com. 1983), Am. Soc. Healthcare Edn. and Tng. (nat. program planning com. 1982, 83), World Futures Soc. Democrat. Roman Catholic. Club: Toastmasters (Seattle). Contbr. articles on organizational devel. to profl. jours. Office: PO Box 1930 Seattle WA 98111

MONAHAN, VIRGINIA, public relations counsel; b. N.Y.C., Apr. 13, 1928; d. Thomas Louis and Mary Margaret (Glynn) Smith; children—Maureen, Cathleen, Sharon, Elizabeth. Dist. rep. Congressman Richard Ottinger of N.Y., 1964-70; exec. asst. Builders Inst. of Westchester/Putnam Counties, 1971-73; dir. Westchester Found., White Plains, 1973-81; adminstr. Constrn. Industry Employee Assistance Program, White Plains, 1977-83; dir. communications Westchester County Bd. Realtors, Inc.; exec. dir. Bldg. Owners and Mgrs. Assn., 1985—. Editor: Impact, 1979-83, Builders Inst. ann. yearbook, 1978-83, Westchester Realtor, ann. yearbook, 1983.

MONAT, HELENE SPUNGIN, marketing executive; b. North Bergen, N.J., Feb. 25, 1947; d. Melvin and Dorothy (Smoller) Spungin; m. Ronald Monat, Mar. 24, 1974; 1 child Jeffrey, B.S., Rutgers U., 1968; M.S., Colo. State U., 1970. Research analyst ARC, Washington, D.C., 1970-72; mktg. research asst. Gen. Mills Corp., Mpls., 1972-74, mktg. research mgr., 1974-76; account research supr. Campbell Mithun, Mpls., 1976-78; client service supr. cons. Trim, Inc., Westport, Conn., 1978-80, regional sales/client service mgr., River Edge, N.J., 1980-83, chief operating officer, Los Angeles, 1983—, pres., 1984—; self-employed market research cons., Randolph, N.J., 1978-80. Mem. Am. Mktg. Assn., Phi Beta Kappa. Home: 231 S Barrington St Apt 4 Brentwood CA 90049 Office: Trim Inc 5455 Wilshire Blvd Los Angeles CA 90036

MONCRIEF, CAROL YVONNE, systems engineer; b. Coulee Dam, Wash., Apr. 19, 1950; d. Lawrence Edward and Mary Elizabeth (Haile) M.; B.S. in Systems Engring., Boston U., 1972; postgrad. Marist Coll. 1973; postgrad. in bus. adminstrn. George Mason U., 1976-80. Jr. programmer IBM, Poughkeepsie, N.Y., 1972-74; assoc. systems engr., Manassas, Va., 1974-78; systems engr. MITRE Corp., McLean, Va., 1978-80; staff systems test engr. Satellite Bus. Systems, McLean, 1980-84; systems engr. Tech. Applications Inc., Falls Church, Va., Chmn. sect. membership Nat. Council Negro Women, Washington, 1978-80, bd. dirs., 1982, treas., 1982-84; bd. dirs. Tanner's Cluster, Reston, Va. Recipient Community Action Program Inst. for Urban Affairs and Research award Howard U., 1979. Mem. Soc. Women Engrs. (treas. 1982-84), 1984—. Black Ski, Alpha Kappa Alpha (treas. chpt. 1976-78, parliamentarian chpt. 1982-83). Democrat. Baptist. Office: 5201 Leesburg Pike 3 Skyline Pl Falls Church VA 22041

MONCRIEF, SUSAN GLOGER, investments and real estate company executive; b. Houston, Mar. 17, 1944; d. Leroy Joseph and Reba Kay (Creppon) Gloger; m. John Arthur Moncrief, June 6, 1970; children—J. Arthur, Jr., Thomas S., Timothy S. B.A., Stephen F. Austin U., 1962. Vice pres. Sta. KIKK-AM-FM, Houston, 1963-73, Sta. KGKL, San Angelo, Tex., 1971-83, Sta. K-DOG-TV, Houston, 1976-78; owner, mgr. Gloger Properties, Houston, 1979—. Fund raiser Houston Livestock Show and Rodeo, Houston, 1968—. Republican. Roman Catholic. Home: 10003 Briar Forest St Houston TX 77042 Office: Gloger Properties PO Box 25214 Houston TX 77005

MONDAY, DONNA ARNOLD, newspaper editor; b. Greenfield, Ind., Dec. 8, 1942; d. Ephraim Ashton and Blanche Elizabeth (Monday) Arnold; m. James Stephen Edwards, Aug. 9, 1964 (div.); children—Charles Paul, April Suzanne; m. 2d, Max Ray Boles, July 24, 1982. B.A., Hanover Coll., 1964, postgrad. Butler U., 1976-77. Tchr. elem. schs. Indpls., 1964-66, Ft. Lewis, Wash., 1966-67; freelance writer, 1975-78; writer, photographer Sentinel Dispatch, Zionsville, Ind., 1978—, editor, 1979—; rep. journalism profession Hanover Connection, Ind., 1982-83. Author (poetry) Monsters and Moonbeams; composer, lyricist The Zionsville Street Song (cert. of appreciation 1983). Pres. Zionsville Boys Club, 1984; mem. steering com. Boone County IVY Tech., Lebanon, Ind. Recipient Community Service award Hoosier State Press Assn., Indpls., 1981; scholarship Greenfield Tri Kappa, 1960, Hanover Alumni, 1963. Mem. Zionsville C. of C. (dir. 1980-84, promotional com. 1982-84), Psi Iota Xi (chmn. Dollars for Scholars 1984), Alpha Omicron Pi (chaplain 1963-64), Gamma Sigma Pi. Methodist. Office: Sentinel Dispatch Box 291 Zionsville IN 46077

MONDAY, JANET TALLEY, medical technologist; b. Hopewell, Va., Jan. 31, 1953; d. John Harrison and Marie (LaForce) Talley; student Petersburg Gen. Hosp. Cert. Lab. Asst. Sch., 1972-73; m. William Gregory Monday, Aug. 17, 1974. Gen. bench technician John Randolph Hosp. Lab., Hopewell, Va., 1973-74; gen. lab. technician Lee Med. Lab., Inc., Richmond, Va., 1974-77; med. lab. technician Temporary Lab. Services, Richmond, 1981—; 3-11 lab. shift supr. John Randolph Hosp. Lab., Hopewell, Va., 1978-83, 85—; ind. mfrs. sales rep. Med. Arts Assocs., Tobyhanna, Pa., 1984—. Active Hopewell-Prince George chpt. ARC. Mem. Am. Assn. Med. Technologists (publicity chair Va. chpt. 1986, fin. team com. Virginian Technoscope, 1985-86, Area 10 membership rep. 1985-86, Va. state co-chair Nat. Lab. Week 1986, ways and means com. 1986, del. nat. meeting 1986, Gold Key award Va. State 1986, 3d place Add-A-Mem. contest 1985-86), Am. Soc. Clin. Pathologists, Internat. Soc. Clin. Lab. Tech., Clin. Lab. Mgmt. Assn. Methodist. Home: 3611 Settlers Ln Hopewell VA 23860 Office: 700 N 4th Ave Hopewell VA 23860

MONDRAGON-TIU, FE A., obstetrician, gynecologist, ultrasonologist; b. Ormoc City, Philippines, Jan. 4, 1946; d. Lapulapu and Ligaya (Areola) Mondragon; m. Amando S. Tiu, Apr. 17, 1971; children—Ronan Antonio, Bernadette, Christopher. B.S. magna cum laude, U. San Carlos, 1964; M.D., U. Santo Tomas, 1969. Resident Albany Med. Ctr. (N.Y.), 1976-79; supr. ob-gyn, ultrasound Albany Med. Coll., (N.Y.), 1981—; pvt. practice ob-gyn, Clifton Park, N.Y., 1981—. Mem. Med. Soc. N.Y., Am. Coll. Obstetricians and Gynecologists. Home: 61 Fairlawn Dr Selkirk New York 12158

MONDY, NELL IRENE, educator; b. Pocahontas, Ark., Oct. 27, 1921; d. D. Daley and F. Ethel (Carroll) M.; B.A. in Chemistry summa cum laude, Ouachita U., 1943, B.S. in Chemistry summa cum laude, 1943; M.A. in Biochemistry, U. Tex., 1945; Ph.D. in Biochemistry (Sigma Xi fellow), Cornell U., 1953. Asst. prof. chemistry Ouachita U., 1943-44; research asst. biochem. inst. U. Tex., 1944-45; research asst. in biochemistry and nutrition Cornell U., Ithaca, N.Y., 1945-46, instr. food and nutrition, 1948-51, asst. prof., assoc. prof., prof. food and nutrition and nutritional scis., 1953—; instr. chemistry Assoc. Colls. of Upper N.Y., 1946-47, asst. prof. chemistry, 1947-48; supervisory food specialist human nutrition research div. Food Quality Lab., U.S. Dept. Agr., Beltsville, Md., 1960-61; food cons. R.T. French, 1966-67; prof. food and nutrition Fla. State U., 1969-70; food cons. Holmen Brenderi - Gjovik, Norway, 1972-73; cons. S & B Shokuhim Co., Ltd., Tokyo, 1978-79, Nihon Kaken Co., Ltd., Tokyo, 1978-79, EPA, Washington, 1979-80; Birkett-Williams lectr., Ouachita, 1980—; vis. scientist Internat. Inst. Tropical Agr., Ibadan, Nigeria, 1983-84; participant confs., seminar, congresses in field, France, Poland, Switzerland, Scotland, Eng.; mem. N.Y. State Potato Adv. Council. Fund raiser United Way; active Cornell Centennial Campaign, Cornell Tower Club; vice chmn. Ouachita Baptist U. Campaign, Historic Ithaca. Recipient Danforth award, 1954, 58. Fellow AAAS, Am. Inst. of Chemists; mem. AAUP (exec. com. 1980—), Am. Chem. Soc., Inst. Food Technologists, N.Y. Acad. Scis., Am. Home Econs. Assn., European Assn. for Potato Research, Potato Assn. Am. (charter mem., hon. life, physiology com. 1974—, chmn. site selection com. N.Am. and S.Am. 1973—), Soc. for Cryobiology, Am. Dietetics Assn., N.Y. State Hort. Soc., Empire State Potato Assn., Am. Soc. Plant Physiologists, Internat. Platform Assn., Washington Women's Network, Grad. Women in Sci. (pres. nat. orgn. 1983-84; nat. historian 1978—, gen. coordinator nat. awards 1974-75), Sigma Xi, Iota Sigma Pi, Sigma Delta

Epsilon, Phi Kappa Phi, Omicron Nu, Pi Lambda Theta, Phi Tau Sigma. Democrat. Baptist. Clubs: Cornell Campus, Cayuga Trails (exec. bd.). Author: Experimental Food Chemistry, 1980; contbr. papers to profl. confs. in field in U.S., France, Japan, Korea, India, Poland; contbr. writings to publs. U.S., France, Ireland, Japan. Office: Div Nutritional Scis Cornell U N231 MVR Ithaca NY 14853

MONGAN, AGNES, administrator, art historian; b. Somerville, Mass. A.B., Bryn Mawr Coll., A.M., Smith Coll., L.H.D. (hon.), 1941; Litt.D. (hon.), Wheaton Coll., 1954; D.F.A. (hon.), U. Mass., 1970, LaSalle Coll., 1973, Colby Coll., 1973, U. Notre Dame, 1980. Research asst. Fogg Art Mus., Harvard U., Cambridge, 1928-37, curator drawings, 1937-75, assoc. dir., 1964-69, dir., 1969-71; vis. dir. Timken Art Gallery, San Diego, 1971-72; mem. adv. com. I Tatti; mem. Council of Fellows of Pierpont Morgan Library; vis. dir. Met. Mus. and Art Ctr., Coral Gables, Fla., 1979-80; lectr. fine arts Harvard U.; vis. prof. U. Tex.-Austin, 1981; vis. lectr. fine arts Mt. Holyoke Coll., 1966-67, Oberlin Coll., 1967—; vis. prof. Northwestern U., spring 1976, U. Louisville, fall 1976, U. Tex.-Austin, spring 1977, U. Calif.-Santa Barbara, 1979; Kress prof. in residence Nat. Gallery Art, Washington, 1977-78. Recipient Palms d'Acad. award French Govt., 1947; Cavaliere, Order of Merit award Republic of Italy, 1971; hon. fellow Morgan Library Assn.; Benjamin Franklin fellow Royal Soc. Arts. Mem. Coll. Art Assn. Am., Brit. Inst. U.S. (bd. dirs. 1982—), Assn. Art Mus. Dirs. Address: Fogg Art Mus Harvard U Cambridge MA 02138*

MONGAN, JANET, librarian; b. N.Y.C., July 14, 1931; d. Stephen Leo and Florence (Geary) M.; m. Frank Friedlander, Oct. 16, 1954 (div. 1977); children—Todd, Clare, Paul. B.A., Cornell U., 1963; M.L.S., U. Tex., 1957; Ph.D., Case Western Reserve U., 1970. Asst. dir. coll. devel. Cleve. State U. Library, 1977-84, asst. dir. info. service, 1985—; head reference librarian Case Western Res. U., Cleve., 1971-72. Office: Cleve State U Library 1860 E 22d St Cleveland OH 44115

MONGOLD, SANDRA K., corporate executive; b. Springfield, Ohio, Aug. 14, 1947; d. Robert Harold and Norma Jean (Fennessy) Rine; m. Alan Darrell Mabry, Aug. 18, 1968 (div. 1977); m. Danny Willard Mongold, Nov. 16, 1979; children—Brian Alan Mabry, Krista Marie Mabry. Student, Wright State U., Urbana Coll., So. State Coll., Ohio. Acctg. clk. Irwin Co., Wilmington, Ohio, 1968-80, asst. treas., 1980-85, treas., 1985—, new product com., 1985—. Mem. Nat. Assn. Accts., Nat. Assn. Female Execs., Am. Mgmt. Assn. Republican. Presbyterian. Avocations: golf; bowling. Home: 330 Washington Ave Wilmington OH 45177 Office: Irwin Co 92 Grant Wilmington OH 45177

MONICAL, MARY CHRISTINE, medical diagnostics sales executive; b. Cin., Apr. 6, 1950; d. Robert Duane and Carol Arnetha (Dean) M. B.S., U. Miami, 1972, postgrad., 1973; postgrad. Butler U., 1980. Tech. specialist Am. Dade div. Am. Hosp. Supply Corp., Miami, Fla., 1976-79; sales rep. Gen. Diagnostics Co., Morris Plains, N.J., 1980-81, microbiology specialist, 1981-83; sales rep. Coulter Immunology, Hialeah, Fla., 1983-85, regional sales mgr., 1985—. Recipient best sales tng. performance award Gen. Diagnostics, 1980; named to Pres.'s Club, Outstanding Sales Rep., Coulter Electronics, 1984-85, 85-86. Home: 1754 Laurance Ct Crofton MD 21114

MONIGAN, DAISY MAXINE, educator, poet; b. Flatwood, Ala., Mar. 18, 1949; d. Mildred L. Monigan. B.S., Ala. A&M U., 1971; M.S., U. Hartford (Conn.), 1975; also pvt. student voice; divorced; children—Maia N., Floyd V. Tutor music Ala. A&M U., 1969; with Conn. Dept. Community Affairs, 1971; tchr. English and music Weaver High Sch., Hartford, Conn., 1971—. Contbr. poetry to various anthologies. Vol. counselor Women in Crisis, 1978—. Mem. Conn. Edn. Assn. Am. Fedn. Tchrs. (mem. Black Caucus), Hartford Fedn. Tchrs., NAACP, Zeta Phi Beta. Democrat. Baptist. Address: 23 Hill Farm Rd Bloomfield CT 06002

MONK, JANICE WALLS, special education coordinator; b. Detroit, Oct. 29, 1954; d. George Oscar and June Pauline (Strohm) Walls; m. Charles Stanton Monk, Aug. 28, 1981. B.S. in Edn., U. Ga., 1974, M.Ed., 1975. Speech pathologist DeKalb County Schs., Decatur, Ga., 1975-77, 80, Health Authority, Gateshead, Eng., 1977-79, Cobb County Schs., Marietta, Ga., 1980-82; research asst. Ga. State U., Atlanta, 1982-83; coordinator spl. edn. Atlanta pub. schs., 1983—; adv. Ga. State U. Speech Pathology Program, Atlanta, 1984—; guest lectr., 1982—. Mem. Young Republicans, Ga., 1976, 80-81. Fellow Ga. State U., 1982-83, U. Ga., 1975. Mem. Am. Speech and Hearing Assn., Council for Exceptional Children, Ga. Council for Exceptional Children, (membership chmn. div. on career devel. 1983—), Phi Kappa Phi, Phi Delta Kappa. Presbyterian. Avocations: Duplicate bridge; gourmet cooking; wine tasting. Home: 1708 Hickory Grove Trail Acworth GA 30101 Office: Atlanta Pub Schs 2930 Forrest Hill Dr SW Atlanta GA 30315

MONKS, KAREN ELIZABETH, nursing educator; b. Grand Rapids, Mich., Nov. 3, 1936; d. Louis Francis and Evelyn Anne (Hammerschmidt) McGough; m. Patrick Joseph Monks, Nov. 26, 1966; children—Laura Anne, Joseph Patrick. Diploma in nursing Mercy Central Sch. Nursing, Grand Rapids, 1956; B.S. in Nursing, Marquette U., 1965; M.S. in Nursing, U. Tex. Med. Br., Galveston, 1984. R.N., Mich., Wis., Ariz. Staff nurse St. Mary's Hosp., Grand Rapids, 1957-58; staff nurse, then head nurse Kent County Hosp., Grand Rapids, 1958-62; staff nurse part-time St. Joseph's Hosp., Milw., 1962-65, head nurse, 1965-66; staff nurse, then house supr. Yuma Regional Med. Ctr. (Ariz.), 1966-72; nursing instr. Ariz. Western Coll., Yuma, 1972—, div. chmn. human services, 1984—; bd. dirs. Yuma Regional Med. Ctr., 1980—, chmn. personnel/nominations, 1981-84; chmn. Ariz. Council Assoc. Drgree Nursing Programs, 1985-86; co-chmn. Ariz. Council on Nursing Edn., 1985-86. Mem. Nat. League Nursing (legis. network). Democrat. Roman Catholic. Home: 1946 London Dr Yuma AZ 85364 Office: Ariz Western Coll Box 929 Yuma AZ 85364

MONO, MADELEINE, cosmetics company executive; b. London, Aug. 7, 1935; d. Arthur and Elizabeth Lillian (Emanuel) M.; m. Joseph Berry (div.); children—Gail Lynne, Louise Ann, Craig Justin, Grant Lloyd; m. 2d, Arthur Levene, Nov. 25, 1972. Stage actress, London, 1947; antique dealer, London, 1968-72; founder, pres., creative dir. Madeleine Mono Cosmetics Ltd., Great Neck, N.Y., 1972—; cons. on make-up to mags. Author: Make eyes With Madeleine Mono, 1980. Bd. dirs. Nassau Reperatory Theatre, L.I. Mem. Fragrance Found., Cosmetic/Toiletry Fragrance Assn., Am. Women's Devel. Corp., Foragers. Lodge: Daus Brit. Empire. Office: Madeleine Mono Cosmetics Ltd 1800 New Hwy Farmingdale NY 11735

MONROE, MARIAN LOUISE, educator; b. Wichita, Kans., Dec. 2, 1934; d. Everett C. and Opal Lois (Stover) Badgley; B.S. in Home Econs., U. Ark., 1955; M.S. in Child Devel., U. Ala., 1957; Ph.D. in Curriculum and Instrn., U. Tex., 1983; m. Gregory T. Monroe, Oct. 11, 1959; children—Stacey Terence, Tracey Lawrence, Patricia Lynn. Home economist agrl. extension service U. Ark., 1955-56; grad. asst. U. Ala., 1956-57; home economist agrl. extension service U. Ariz., 1957-59, Tex. A. and M. U., 1960-63; nursery sch. tchr. U. Houston, 1965-66; home mgmt. supr. Family and Children's Service, Houston, 1966-67, Harris County Community Action Assn., Houston, 1967-68; edn. dir. Head Start, Houston, 1968-70; contract mgr./program specialist Tex. Dept. Human Resources, Austin, 1970-80, child devel. dir., 1980—; mem. Austin Mayor's Commn. on Child Care. Mem. Nat. Assn. Edn. Young Children, So. Assn. Children Under Six, Assn. Childhood Edn. Internat., Tex. Public Employees Assn., Tex. Assn. Edn. of Young Children, Nat. Assn. State Dirs. Child Devel., Phi Upsilon Omicron, Kappa Delta Pi, Phi Kappa Phi. Methodist. Author articles in field. Mng. editor Tex. Child Care Quar., 1981—. Home: 6708 Notre Dame Dr Austin TX 78723 Office: 523-A TDHR PO Box 2960 Austin TX 78769

MONROE, NANCY, bank auditor; b. Wyoming, Pa., Mar. 24, 1936; d. Arthur Mitchell and Anna Elizabeth (Jones) Fritz; m. Edward Allan Hearn Sr., Nov. 22, 1956 (div. Oct. 1971); children—Diane Lynn Hearn Thurmond, Edward Allan Jr.; m. Robert Hamilton Monroe, Feb. 23, 1980. Student, Am. Inst. Banking, Las Vegas, 1969-71. From teller to utility clk. First Nat. Bank, Las Vegas, 1963-72; from utility clk. to ops. officer Pioneer Citizens Bank of Nev., Las Vegas, 1972-74, ops. officer, Reno, 1978—; from loan sec. to loan mgr. First Valley Bank, Kingston, Pa., 1974-78; asst. to the auditor Nev. Bankers Assn., Reno, 1983. Mem. Am. Inst. Banking. Republican. Baptist. Avocations: bowling; crocheting; bicycling. Office: Pioneer Citizens Bank of Nev 10 State St Reno NV 89505

MONSALVE, DAISY, systems specialist; b. Havana, Cuba, July 4, 1943; d. Vicente and Elvira De La Merced (Rodriguez) Bosquet; m. Erwin Monsalve, Dec. 12, 1971; 1 dau., Merced Therese. Student Havana U., 1958-61; A.S., Northeastern U., 1980; B.S., 1973; postgrad. bus. Lesley Coll. Exec. sec. Procter & Gamble Co., Havana, 1961-68; estimator Cambion Co., Boston, 1970-72; legal sec. Lazar Lowinger, Boston, 1972-73; data processor adminstr. Stone Webster Engring. Corp., Boston, 1973-76, budget specialist, 1977-80, data tech. coordinator, 1980—; cons., co-owner LeCardeau, West Somerville, Mass., 1983-84. Mem. Exec. Female, AAUW. Roman Catholic. Club: Toastmasters (adminstrv. v.p. 1983-84). Home: 77 Liberty Ave Apt 1 West Somerville MA 02144 Office: Stone & Webster Engring Corp 245 Summer St Boston MA 02144

MONSON, CAROL LYNN, osteopathic physician, psychotherapist; b. Blue Island, Ill., Nov. 3, 1946; d. Marcus Edward and Margaret Bertha (Andres) M.; m. Frank E. Warden, Feb. 28, 1981. B.S., No. Ill. U., 1968, M.S., 1969; D.O., Mich State Coll. Osteo. Medicine, 1979. Lic. physician, Mich. Expeditor-psychotherapist H. Douglas Singer Zone Ctr., Rockford, Ill., 1969-71; psychotherapist Tri-County Mental Health, St. Johns, Mich., 1971-76; pvt. practice psychotherapy, East Lansing, Mich., 1976-80; intern Lansing Gen. Hosp., Mich., 1979-80; pvt. practice osteo. medicine, Lansing, 1980—; mem. staff Ingham Med. Hosp., Lansing Gen. Hosp.; field instr. Sch. Social Work, U. Mich., 1973-76; clin. instr. Central Mich. Dept. Psychology, 1974-75; clin. prof. Mich. State U., 1980—; mem. adv. bd. Substance Abuse Clearinghouse, Lansing, 1983—, Kelly Health Care, Lansing, 1983-85, Americor Health Services, Lansing, 1984—. Bd. dirs. Am. Adoption Congress, 1984—. Mem. Am. Osteo Assn., Internat. Transactional Analysis Assn., Mich. Assn. Physicians and Surgeons, Ingham County Osteo. Assn., Nat. Assn. Career Women (conv. com. 1984—), Lansing Assn. Career Women. Lodge: Zonta (chmn. service com. Mid Mich. Capital Area chpt.). Avocations: gardening; orchid growing; antique collecting. Office: 3320 W Saginaw St Lansing MI 48917

MONTALBANO, ANGELA BROGNA, advertising executive; b. Bklyn., Nov. 4, 1942; d. Salvatore and Ann (Taibi) Brogna. Student New Sch. Social Research, 1970-71, Warren Robertson Sch. Drama, N.Y.C., 1968-70. Casting dir. Norman Craig & Kummel Advt. Co., N.Y.C., 1968-73, v.p., talent rep. Lester Lewis, N.Y.C., 1973-78, Bob Waters Agy., N.Y.C., 1978-80; ptnr., v.p., casting dir. City Limits Casting, N.Y.C., 1980-81; talent mgr. Curtis Brown Mgmt., N.Y.C., 1981-82; v.p., dir. casting, celebrating negotiator William Esty Co., N.Y.C., 1982—; new bus. cons. Show People, Inc., N.Y.C., 1982, Westside Arts, N.Y.C., 1984; comml. acting instr. seminars, schs. Mem. Nat. Assn. Talent Reps., Nat. Acad. TV Arts and Scis.

MONTANARI, MARION GOODRUM, treatment center adminstr.; b. McKeesport, Pa., Apr. 20, 1935; d. John Thomas and Edith (Lutz) Goodrum; B.A. in Psychology, Carlow Coll., Pitts., 1962; M.Ed. in Counseling, Duquesne U., Pitts., 1969; m. Adelio J. Montanari, Dec. 20, 1971; stepchildren—Gary, Adele. Tchr., then prin. pvt. elem. and jr. high sch., Pitts.; child care counselor, Pitts.; asso. dir. Montanari Residential Treatment Center, Hialeah, Fla., 1970—, also inservice staff tng. dir.; co-owner Marion Hills Thoroughbred Farm, Ocala, Fla.; cons. Troubled Children's Found., 1971—. Trustee Greater Miami Opera Assn. Mem. Am. Personnel and Guidance Assn., Fla. Group Child Care Assn., Am. Orthopsychiatric Assn., Inc., Dade County Mental Health Assn. Roman Catholic. Office: 291 E 2d St Hialeah FL 33010

MONTANT, JANE, editor. With Gourmet Mag., N.Y.C., 1958—, formerly editorial asst., travel editor, sr. editor, exec. editor, now editor-in-chief. Office: Gourmet Mag Conde Nast Publs Inc 560 Lexington Ave New York NY 10022*

MONTEAGUDO, MARITZA EMMA, export company executive; b. Havana, Cuba, Jan. 2, 1955; came to U.S., 1961; d. Felix M. and Merita L. (Valdes) Gonzalez; m. Pablo T. Monteagudo, Sept. 2, 1979; children—Marissa Christina, Diana Lynn. B.A. in Bus. Mgmt., Marymount Manhattan Coll., 1977. Sales adminstr. Bankers Trust Co., N.Y.C., 1977-78; internat. sales rep. Burlington Industries, N.Y.C., 1978-80; account exec. D'Arcy MacManus & Masius Advt. Agy., N.Y.C., 1980-81; N.E. sales rep. 3M Co., N.Y.C., 1981-83; pres. Mediquip Internat., Union City, N.J., 1984—. Mellon Found. women in mgmt. grantee, 1974-77. Republican. Roman Catholic. Home: 713 16th St Union City NJ 07087 Office: PO Box 1095 Union City NJ 07087

MONTEE-CHAREST, KAREN ANNE, lawyer, educator; b. Montclair, N.J., May 15, 1957; d. Bobby Dean and Barbara Joyce (Thatcher) Montee; m. Stephen Glenn Charest, Aug. 14, 1982. B.A. with distinction, U. Nebr., 1979, J.D. with distinction, 1982. Bar: Nebr. 1982, Ariz. 1984. Intern law dept. Union Pacific R.R., Omaha, 1981; exec. editor Nebr. Law Rev., Lincoln, 1981-82; research asst. U. Ariz. Coll. Law, Tucson, 1982; instr., program coordinator Chapman Coll., Tucson, 1983-84; ptnr. Elsken & Montee-Charest, Attys.-at-Law, Lincoln, 1985—; adj. prof. law Park Coll., Tucson, 1983-84; assoc. justice U. Nebr. Student Ct., Lincoln, 1981-82, Nebr. Model UN, Lincoln, 1981; 1st v.p., 1982; legal researcher, research asst. U. Nebr. Coll. Law, 1980. Editor student law rev., 1981-82. Contbr. article to law rev. Mildred F. Thompson fellow U. Nebr., 1985-86. Mem. ABA, Nebr. Bar Assn., Am. Judicature Soc., Phi Beta Kappa, Phi Alpha Theta, Alpha Lambda Delta, Phi Eta Sigma. Democrat. Roman Catholic. Club: SCA (chatelaine 1982—). Office: 304 S 13th St Suite One Lincoln NE 68508

MONTEMAYOR, GRACIELA DURAN-TROISE, biomedical consultant, cancer research scientist; b. Buenos Aires, Argentina, Sept. 14, 1943; d. Eduardo and Melida Ethel (Troise) Duran; M.S., U. Buenos Aires, 1969, Ph.D., 1973; m. Ernest A. Montemayor, May 24, 1974; 1 son, Diego. Fellow U. Buenos Aires, Argentina, 1969-70, Argentinian League for Fight Against Cancer, Buenos Aires, 1970-71; WHO fellow Curie Found. and Gustave Roussy Inst., Paris, France, 1971-73; postdoctoral fellow Nat. Cancer Inst., NIH, Bethesda, Md., 1973-76, vis. asso., 1976-78; sr. research scientist Meloy Labs., Rockville, Md., 1979-80; dir. DTM Cons., Bethesda, Md., 1981—. Bd. dirs. Hispanic Orgn. Profls. and Execs., 1981—; mem. Argentine Woman's Commn. Charity, 1978—. Mem. Am. Soc. Microbiology, AAUW, Tissue Culture Assn., AAAS, Assn. Women in Sci., Argentine Genetic Soc., Am. Translators Assn., N.Y. Acad. Scis., San Martin Soc. Washington. Contbr. numerous articles to various publs. Home: 3353 East-West Hwy Chevy Chase MD 20815

MONTES, MARIA ISABEL, lawyer; b. San Juan, P.R., Nov. 5, 1951; d. Ruben Edmundo and Maria B. (Montes) M.; m. David Neal Plotkin, June 20, 1976. Student U. P.R., 1969-70; B.A., U. Calif.-Santa Cruz, 1973; J.D., U. Calif. Hastings Coll. Law, 1977. Bar: Calif. 1980, U.S. Dist. Bar (no. dist.) Calif. Legal intern U.S. Immigration and Naturalization Service, San Francisco, 1976-77, SEC, San Francisco, 1977-78; law clk. to Alameda County/Counsel, Oakland, Calif., 1978-79, Farella, Braun & Martel, San Francisco, 1979-80; sole practice law, San Francisco, 1980-83; gen. counsel Office Adminstrv. Law Judges, U.S. Dept. Labor, San Francisco, 1983-84; legal writer editorial staff Matthew Bender & Co., Inc., Oakland, 1984—; pro bono immigration atty. vol., San Francisco, 1982-83. David E. Snodgrass meml. scholar, 1977, Hoberg scholar, 1977; Ft. Ord Thrift Shop scholar, 1969. Mem. ABA, State Bar Calif., San Francisco Bar Assn. Democrat. Roman Catholic. Club: San Francisco Barristers. Home: 488 Walnut Ave Walnut Creek CA 94598 Office: Matthew Bender & Co Inc 2101 Webster St Oakland CA 94604

MONTES, MARTA, laboratory executive, city official, nurse; b. Esperanza, Cuba, Feb. 23, 1948; came to U.S., 1955, naturalized, 1969; d. Carlos Aguila and Maria Martinez Leon de Aguila; children—Jose Antonio, Carlos Adrino. R.N., Columbia U., 1970. Registered nurse, N.Y. Account exec. MetPath Lab., Ft. Lauderdale, Fla., 1978—; nurse Latin Am. Med. Ctr., Miami, Fla., 1980—. Mem. City Council, City of Hialeah Gardens, Fla., 1983—, vice chmn., 1983; pres. Hialeah Gardens Civic Assn. Mem. Women in Govt. Service, Pan Am. C. of C. (v.p.). Roman Catholic. Avocation: working with children. Home: 10000 NW 80th Ct Apt 2409 Hialeah Gardens FL 33016 Office: MetPath Lab 4090 NE 6th Ave Fort Lauderdale FL 33334

MONTES, PEGGY ANN, counselor; b. Chgo., Oct. 17, 1938; d. Thomas and Myrtle (Thomas) Booker; student Howard U., 1956-58; B.Ed., Chgo. State U., 1960; postgrad. Gov.'s State U., Chgo., 1973-74; m. Paul Joseph Montes, Dec. 17, 1960; children—Paul, Pia. Elementary tchr. Chgo. Bd. Edn., 1960-71, adjustment tchr.-counselor, 1971-74, coordinator counseling services dept. Percy Julian High Sch., 1975—; cons. in field. Pres., Profl. Aux. Provident Hosp., 1973—; bd. dirs. Harriet Harris YWCA, 1972—, Chgo. Area Planned Parenthood Assn., 1974-76, Provident Med. Ctr., DuSable Mus. African Am. History; commr. Women's Affairs Commn. Named Woman of Year, Civic Aux. Planned Parenthood Assn., 1975. Mem. Am. Personnel and Guidance Assn., Council for Exceptional Children, Am. Assn. Supervision and Curriculum, League Black Women, Nat. Council Negro Women, Phi Delta Kappa, Phi Delta Kappa. Address: 9240 S Wabash Chicago IL 60619

MONTGOMERY, ADELE, lawyer; b. Detroit, Feb. 2, 1936; d. Adelbert Kirsten and Ruth May (Eldert) Toepfer; m. Richard Lee Montgomery, Aug. 6, 1980; children—Michelle Anne, Eric Gawaine, Alicia Renee. Student Scripps Coll., 1954-56; B.S., U. Mich., 1958, M.P.H., 1963; J.D., Rutgers U.-Newark, 1978. Bar: N.J. 1978. Pub. health educator Washtenaw County Health Dept., Ann Arbor, Mich., 1963-66; tng. dir. OEO Health Ctr., Baldwin, Mich., 1967-69; instr. Dental Sch., U. Mich., Ann Arbor, 1971-72; cons. Coll. Medicine, Newark, 1974-75; clk. firm Lanigan, O'Connell and Hirsh, P.A., Basking Ridge, N.J., 1977-78; sole practice law, Mendham, N.J., 1978—. Author articles. Chmn. Democratic Com. Mendham Twp., 1981-84; v.p. Bd. of Health, Mendham Twp., 1981-83; counsel Safe Rides, Mendham, 1982-84, Morris County Dem. com., 1984—; mem. LWV, Mendham, Chester; liaison rep. Morris County Office of Community Devel., 1979—; mem. policy adv. com. N.E. Water Quality Plan, 1976-80; active Morris County Office Consumer Protection, 1979—. Mem. Moot Ct. Bd., Rutgers Law Sch., 1977. Mem. ABA, N.J. State Bar Assn., Morris County Bar Assn., Assn. Trial Lawyers Am., Assn. Trial Lawyers N.J., Lawyers Encouraging Govt. and Law, AAUW (legis. chmn. Somerset Hills Br., Basking Ridge 1975-80), Sigma Phi Alpha. Club: Zonta. Home: 154 Route 24 Mendham NJ 07945 Office: 8 E Main PO Box 459 Mendham NJ 07945

MONTGOMERY, BARBARA ANNBURKE, business consultant; b. Greenville, S.C., May 7, 1940; d. Rufus and Lydia Mae (Brockmond) Burke; m. Marvin Leroy Cullens (div. 1967); children—Charlene Cullens, Darryl Keith Cullens. A.S. in Bus., Wayne County Community Coll., A.S. in Psychology. Exec. sec. in bank, Detroit, 1967; sec., dictaphone operator Dept. Social Services, Detroit, 1967-70; supr. sec. of State's Office, Detroit, 1970-72; social worker Wayne County Dept. Social Services, Detroit, 1972-80; bus. cons., Oak Park, Mich., 1980—. Author, editor poetry books: A Growing Woman, 1984; Religious Poems, 1985. Community activist, Detroit, 1975-77; mem. Com. for Barbara Rose Collins, Detroit, 1981-83; pres. Mix & Match, Oak Park, Mich., 1983—; community liaison March of Dimes, 1986. Recipient cert. Mich. Metaphys. Soc., 1978. Mem. NAACP, Black Women's Entrepreneurs, Nat. Assn. Female Execs. Democrat. Methodist. Avocations: reading; writing; travel; sports. Home and Office: 24281 Morton Oak Park MI 48237

MONTGOMERY, DENISE KAREN, nurse, N.Y.C., Dec. 23, 1951; d. Thomas Cornell and Dorothy Marie (Castine) Simons; m. Timothy Bruce Montgomery, July 19, 1974 (div. Feb. 1981); m. Joseph Samuel Montgomery, Aug. 20, 1983. A.D.N., San Jacinto Coll., 1971. R.N., Tex. Charge nurse Aaron's Women's Clinic, Houston, 1977; research asst. dept. ob-gyn Baylor Coll. Medicine, Houston, 1977-81, nursing supr., 1979-81, program coordinator population control program, 1979-81; nurse Dr. Eric J. Haufrect, Houston, 1982-83, Dr. Samuel Law, Houston, part-time, 1983-84. Contbr. articles to med. jours. Recipient Disting. Pub. Service award Am. Heart Assn., 1976; grantee in field. Mem. Nat. Assn. Coll. Ob-Gyn. Democrat. Roman Catholic. Home: 8014 Argentina Houston TX 77040

MONTGOMERY, ELIZABETH FLANAGAN (MRS. STEWART MAGRUDER MONTGOMERY), ch. and civic worker; b. Cary, Miss., July 25, 1898; d. Robert Edward Lee and Annie May (Purdy) Flanagan; grad. Northwestern Sch. Speech, 1918; A.B., Miss. State Coll. for Women, 1924; summer study Peabody Coll., U. Cal., Columbia; m. Stewart Magruder Montgomery, Jan. 5, 1935. Instr. elementary grades, high sch. English and dramatics, Cary, Miss., 1924-51. Mem. King's Daus. and Sons, state pres. 1949-51, 55-56, dir. Indian work, speaker internat. conv.; state pres. Miss. Women's Cabinet, 1954-55; mem. adv. council Miss. Children's Code Commn.; edn. com. Miss. Assn. Mental Health, 1958—, dir., exec. com., nominating com., 1963-66, dir., 1966—, sec., 1973—; chmn. Miss. Mental Health Conv., 1964; county commr. Fifth Region Mental Health Center, 1967—; del. Nat. Mental Health Conv., 1963, meeting, N.Y.C.; dir. State Mental Health Bd.; sec. Miss. Mental Health Assn., 1971-73; county campaign chmn. A.R.C., 1962. Mem. pub. relations com. Miss. Women's Cabinet, 1961—, now also recreation chmn.; mem. Gov.'s Ladies Staff, Miss., 1960-64; sec. Miss. Mental Health, 1969—; mem. Sharkey County Mental Health Commn., 1967—. Trustee King's Daus. Home, Natchez, Miss., 1948-52, pres. gov.'s bd., 1956—, gov.'s bd. trustees, 1965—. Recipient Woman of Achievement award Rolling Fork Bus. and Profl. Women, 1965; named Outstanding Civic leader Am., 1967; Community Leader award Hist. Preservation Am., 1979-80. Mem. Miss. King's Daus. and Sons (historian 1969—, parliamentarian), Internat. Platform Assn., Daus. Am. Colonists, Order of Washington, Daus. of 1812, Colonial Dames of XVII Century (chpt. pres. 1971-73, state 1st v.p. 1971-73, state pres. 1973—), Dames of Court Honor, Daus. Confederacy, Soc. Magna Charta Dames, Ams. Royal Descent, Zeta Phi Eta. Episcopalian (state pres., women's orgn., 1952-55; pres. IV province Episcopal Ch. 1957-60). Clubs: Highland (pres. aux. 1963-64), Delta Debutante (patron 1961—).

MONTGOMERY, EVANGELINE JULIET, exhibits and museum specialist, artist; b. N.Y.C., May 2, 1933; d. Oliver Paul and Carmelite Thompson. Student Calif. State U-Los Angeles, 1958-62, U-Calif., Berkeley, 1969-70; A.A., Los Angeles City Coll., 1958; B.F.A., Calif. Coll. Arts and Crafts, 1969. Ethnic art cons. Oakland (Calif.) Mus., 1968-74; freelance art and hist. exhibits and mus. specialist, Calif. and Washington, 1968—; exhibits and workshops coordinator Am. Assn. for State and Local History, Nashville, 1979; dir. community affairs WHMM-TV, Washington, 1980; v.p. bd. dirs. Ark Urban Systems Inc., 1973-77. Exhibited in one man shows including: Bowie State Coll., 1973, Hampton Inst. Mus., 1974, Taylor Gallery, 1974, De Paul U. Gallery, 1974, Seattle World Expo Black Pavilion, 1974; group shows include: travelling exhibit Mills Coll. Art Gallery, 1971-73; Oakland (Calif.) Mus., 1974; Berkeley Arts Center, 1975; Brook Meml. Gallery, Memphis, 1979; represented in permanent collections including: Los Angeles Bd. Edn., Oakland Mus., So. Ill. U., Normal, Mus. Afro-Am. Artists, Roxbury, Mass.; mem. San Francisco Art Commn., 1976-79, chmn. visual arts com., 1976-79. Smithsonian fellow, 1973; Nat. Endowment for Arts grantee, 1973; Third World Fund grantee, 1974. Mem. Am. Assn. Mus., Nat. Conf. Artists (nat. coordinator regions 1973-79), Am. Assn. for State and Local History, Am. Craftsmen Council, Nat. Assn. for Negro Bus. and Profl. Women (nat. fine arts dir. 1976-79), Metal Arts Guild Calif. (pres. 1972-74). Baptist. Home: 1237 S Masselin Ave Los Angeles CA 90019

MONTGOMERY, JEAN OLIVE, antique dealer; b. Springerville, Ariz., June 1, 1919; d. Henry T. and Cordelia Carol (Shideler) Miller; B.A. with honors, U. Pacific, Stockton, Calif., 1939; M.S. with honors, Simmons Coll., Boston, 1940; m. George W. Montgomery, Jr., Feb. 21, 1942. Owner, mgr. Montgomery Antiques, Los Gatos, Calif., 1948—; treas. Los Gatos Heritage Preservation Soc. Mem. Calif. Republican Central Com., 1962-64; officer, mem. bd. Los Gatos-Saratoga Rep. Assembly, 1950-68; founding mem. bd. Calif. Rep. League, 1960-73; bd. dirs. Bellringer Preservation Project. Mem. Antique Dealers Assn. Calif., Antique Dealers Orgn. No. Calif., U. Pacific Alumni Assn., Pi Kappa Delta, Pi Gamma Mu. Club: Wiscasset Yacht. Home: 262 E Main St Los Gatos CA 95030 also Middle St Wiscasset ME 04578 Office: 262 E Main St Los Gatos CA 95030

MONTGOMERY, JUDY G(LASS), child care executive; b. Jacksonville, Fla., July 19, 1945; d. Paul H. and Pearle V. (Greene) Glass; m. Jack T. Montgomery, Jan. 4, 1970; 1 child, Sean Christopher. B.S. in Math., La. State U., 1967. Group chief operator South Central Bell Telephone Co., Baton Rouge, 1967-69; systems analyst Sperry Univac, Baton Rouge, 1969-70; pres. M & M Playland Inc., Baton Rouge, 1973—, L'Ecole, Inc., Baton Rouge, 1976—, Child Care Info., Baton Rouge, 1984—; cons. in field. Author: Door To Learning, 1983; contbg. author and mem. adv. bd. for tng. manuals Day Care Directions, 1984. Chairperson La. Women's Conf. on Day Care, Baton Rouge, 1977; day care rep. Senator Thomas Hudson, Baton Rouge, 1977; mem. Gov.'s Council on Children, La., 1980; lobbyist children's services Baton Rouge, 1976—; bd. dirs. Baton Rouge Vocat. Tech. Sch., 1980—. Mem. Nat. Alliance Child Devel. Assns., La. Fedn. Child Devel. Ctrs. (lobbyist 1976-81, pres. 1978-81), Baton Rouge C. of C. (edn. com. 1980). Avocations: reading; sewing. Office: L'Ecole/M & M Playland PO Box 45212 Dept 223 Baton Rouge LA 70895

MONTGOMERY, OLIVE, writer, actress, musician, advt. exec.; b. West Hartford, Conn., Oct. 29, 1909; d. M. Goode and Katharine (Slayback) Wolfe; student piano Aurelio Giorni, Rome and N.Y.C., Bruce Simonds, New Haven; student (scholar) Smith Coll., 1932; m. Carl John Schmauss, May 14, 1960 (dec.); children—Joan Elise, Mary Ann, Daniel, John. Actress in summer stock, radio and films; last appeared in Man on the Swing, 1973; concert pianist, 1927-42; writer radio drama, serials, drama and commls.; founder Montgomery Agency, N.Y.C., 1942, now pres.; founder, dir., tchr. drama and music Silvermine Music and Drama Center, 1960—; a founder Am. Shakespeare Theatre (Stratford, Conn.), Lincoln Center for Performing Arts, N.Y.C., Norwalk (Conn.) Symphony Orch.; bd. dirs. New Haven Symphony Orch., 1932-42. Mem. Nat. League Am. Pen Women (pres. Greenwich br. 1972-77, treas. br. 1978-82, treas. Conn. 1982—), English Speaking Union, Jr. League Stamford-Norwalk, Inc., DAR, Wilton, Norwalk, Westport hist. socs. Republican. Presbyterian. Club: Silver Spring Country (Ridgefield, Conn.). Home: 1114 2d Ave S Tierra Verde FL 33715

MONTGOMERY, VELMANETTE, state senator; b. Tex. M.Ed., NYU; student U. Ghana. Mem. N.Y.C. Dist. 13 Sch. Bd., 1977-80, pres., from 1977; former co-dir. advocacy group Child Care Inc.; mem. N.Y. Senate, 1984—, mem. child care, consumer protection, health, social services, commerce and mental hygiene coms. Fellow Inst. Ednl. Leadership, 1981, Revson Found., 1984. Democrat. Office: NY State Capitol Blvd Albany NY 12224*

MONTGOMERY, VIRGIE CARRELL, realtor; b. Oakman, Ala., Nov. 4, 1928; d. Ernest Gordon and Essie Lois (Swindle) Carrell; m. James Newton Beck, Apr. 11, 1946 (dec. 1981); children—James, Joan, Charles, Ronald, Michael, Douglas; m. 2d, Howard Montgomery, Oct. 15, 1983. Student Walker Coll., 1977; grad. Realtor Inst. Sales mgr. Realty World-Simmons Realty Inc., Jasper, Ala., 1978-81; sales rep. Byars Realty, Jasper, Ala., 1981-82; sales assoc. Wilson, Yeager & Masterson, Inc., Fairhope, Ala., 1982-84, Island Realty, Gulf Shores, Ala., 1984—; pres. Jasper Area Multiple Listing Service, 1980-82. Pres. Redmill Sch. PTA, Jasper, 1955; v.p. Oakman Sch. PTA, 1975. Named Listing Leader of Month, Realty World Edn. and Awards Com., 1979, Top Sales Agt., 1980, Top Listing Agt., 1980. Mem. Walker Bd. Realtors (program chmn. 1979-80, Make Am. Better chmn. 1980-81), Baldwin County bd. Realtors, Women's Council Baldwin Bd. Realtors. Democrat. Baptist. Club: Dramatic (Oakman). Home: Route 2 Box 2644 Orange Beach AL 36561 Office: Island Realty 1415 Gulf Shores Office Park Gulf Shores AL 36542

MONTOYA, FRIEDA M., government official; b. Albuquerque, Oct. 14, 1923; d. Max Emiliano and Emilia (Gurule) Montoya; m. Frank Wolfel Montoya, June 20, 1945; children—Maxine Berea, Frank Wolfel. Student La. Junta Jr. Coll. (Colo.), 1943-45. Clk., interviewer U.S. Army and Air Force Recruiting Sta., Albuquerque, 1949-53; sales unit mgr. Stanley Home Products, Albuquerque, 1953-56; sec. ACF Industries, Inc., Albuquerque, 1956-57; sec. U.S. Dept. Energy, Albuquerque, 1967-80, mgr. fed. women's program, 1980; sec. to dir. VA Med. Ctr., Albuquerque, 1980-82; exec. dir. Fed. Exec. Bd., Albuquerque, 1982-84; with command sect. field command Def. Nuclear Agy., Kirtland AFB, N.Mex., 1984—; chmn. Fed. Women's Program, Albuquerque, 1974-75. Author: Upward Mobility for Women, 1974. Coordinator, U.S. Savs. Bonds, Albuquerque, 1983-84, Combined Fed. Campaign, Albuquerque, 1983-84, United Blood Service, Albuquerque, 1983-84, ARC, Albuquerque, 1983-84, commentator, lector, eucharistic minister St. Charle's Ch., Albuquerque. Mem. Am. Soc. Pub. Adminstrn. Roman Catholic. Club: Toastmistress Am. (sec./treas. 1960, v.p. 1961, pres. 1962, mem. council 1963, pres.). Office: IRS 517 Gold Ave SW Albuquerque NM 87106

MONTY, GLORIA, television executive; b. Union Hill, N.J., Aug. 12, 1927; d. Joseph and Concetta (Mango) Montemuro; m. Robert O'Byrne, Jan. 8, 1949; Student, U. Iowa, 1938-40; B.A., NYU, 1947; M.A., Columbia U., 1944. Instr., head speech dept. Dramatic Workshop, New Sch. Social Research, 1944-46; dir. Abbey Theater Workshop, N.Y.C., 1946-51, Columbia Broadcasting Co., 1952-60, numerous plays including: Deirde of the Sorrows, 1949, Shadow of a Gunman, 1950, Don't Go Away Mad, 1951, Rose in the Wilderness, 1952; dir. Secret Storm, CBS-TV, 1958-69, Bright Promise, NBC-TV, 1970, TV series This Child of Mine, 1969; producer TV series Gen. Hosp., 1978—; lectr. to actors Am. Theatre Wing. Recipient Emmy award for daytime drama series. Mem. Dirs. Guild Am. Office: care ABC/Gen Hosp 1451 N Gower Blvd Los Angeles CA 90028

MOODY, BARBARA GAREY, nursing administrator; b. Medford, Mass., June 23, 1931; d. DeMelle and Mildred (Holman) Garey; B.A., William Jewell Coll., Liberty, Mo., 1953; M.Ed., Northeastern U., Boston, 1964; M.B.M., Leslie Coll., Boston, 1983; m. Richard H. Moody, May 15, 1954; children—Meredith, Heather, Richard B., Janice. Dir. personnel P.W. Moody Co., Andover, Mass., 1954-70; guidance counselor Lawrence (Mass.) Gen. Hosp. Sch. Nursing, 1971-77, asst. dir. nursing, 1980-81; adminstrv. asst. in nursing New Eng. Deaconess Hosp., Boston, 1977-80, adminstrv. asst., 1981—; asso. dir. Lawrence Coop. Bank, 1976—. Dir., sec. Gale Systems, 1972-74; dir. Coulter Fibers, Inc., 1968-77. Pres. Andover Vis. Nurse Assn., 1964-74. Mem. Andover Sch. Com., 1963-66. Bd. dirs. Andover council Girl Scouts, 1956-60, Andover YMCA, 1968-73, bd. dirs. Greater Lawrence Family Service, 1972-77, v.p., 1971-78. Mem. Nat. Assn. Women Deans, Adminstrs. and Counselors, LWV, Mass. Assn. Hosp. Fin. Mgrs., Nat. League Nursing, Am. Personnel and Guidance Assn., Pi Kappa Delta. Mem. United Ch. Christ (clk., past mem. bd. Christian edn.). Club: Andover Tennis. Home: 95 Sunset Rock Andover MA 01810 Office: New Eng Deaconess Hosp Boston MA 02215

MOODY, DOLORES IRENE, nurse; b. Hazelhurst, Miss., Aug. 14, 1930; d. Med Roy and Lois Louise (Middleton) Ashley; m. Wallace Ross Williams, July 2, 1954 (div. 1963); children—Anthony Ross, Timothy Owen; m. 2d. Jack Wright Moody, May 17, 1974; 1 dau., Nancy E. R.N., Miss. Bapt. Hosp. Sch. Nursing, 1952. Cert. occupational health nurse. Mem. staff surgery Miss. Bapt. Hosp., Jackson, 1952-53; staff nurse Sch. Nursing, Houston, 1953-61; supr. nursing Meml. Hosp., Houston, 1961-64; surg. nurse G.S. Dowdy, M.D., Houston, 1964-69; occupational health nurse Bank of the Southwest, Houston, 1969-75; head nurse Pennzoil Co., Houston, 1975—. Mem. employee edn. com. Am. Cancer Soc., Houston, 1980—; instr. C.P.R. and first aid ARC, Houston, 1980—. Academic scholar Miss. Bapt. Hosp., Jackson, 1949; named Outstanding Employee Meml. Hosp., Houston, 1963; Outstanding Profl. Woman, Houston Assn. Occupational Health Nurses, Houston, 1983. Mem. Houston Assn. Occupational Health Nurses (program co-chmn. 1972-73), Tex. Assn. Occupational Health Nurses (continuing edn. chmn. 1983—), Am. Assn. Occupational Health Nurses. Democrat. Baptist. Office: Pennzoil Co 700 Milam St Houston TX 77001

MOODY, EVELYN WILIE, consulting geologist; b. Waco, Tex.; d. William Braden and Enid Eva (Holt) Wilie; student Baylor U., 1934-35; B.A. with honors in geology and edn. U. Tex., 1938, M.A. with honors in geology, 1940; children—John D., Melissa L., Jennifer A. Geologist, Ark. Fuel Oil Co., Shreveport, La., New Orleans and Houston, 1942-45; teaching asst. Colo. Sch. Mines, Golden, 1946-47; exploration cons. geologist Gen. Crude Oil Co., Houston, 1975-77; ind. cons. geologist, Houston, 1977—; exploration cons. geologist Shell Oil Co., Houston, 1979-81; faculty dept. continuing edn. Rice U., Houston, 1978. Cert. profl. geologist. Pres., Sipes Found., 1985, editor bull., 1985. Mem. Am. Assn. Petroleum Geologists, Soc. Ind. Profl. Earth Scientists (sec. 1978-79, vice chmn. 1979-80, chpt. chmn. 1980-81, nat. dir. 1982-85), Geol. Soc. Am., Watercolor Soc. Houston, Manhasset (N.Y.C.) Art Assn., Am. Inst. Profl. Geologists, Houston Geol. Soc., Pi Beta Phi (nat. officer 1958-60, 66-68). Republican. Presbyterian. Contbr. articles to profl. jours.; editor: The Manual for Independence, 1983. author: How (To Try) To Find An Oil Field, 1981. Office: 956 The Main Bldg 1212 Main St Houston TX 77002

MOODY, VIRGINIA LAREECE (GOODIN), commercial realtor; b. Oakland, Calif., Dec. 22, 1942; d. True Pete and Essie Mae (Lemons) Goodin; m. Robert Dean Walker, Sept. 15, 1962 (div. Sept. 1970); children—Kimberly, Kelly; m. William Francis Moody, Aug. 23, 1980; stepchildren—Eric, Brandon. Student Orange County Jr. Coll., 1963-65, Midwestern U., 1961-62, Tarrant County Jr. Coll., 1975-83. Clk., agt., dispatcher Chgo. Rock Island R.R., Fort Worth, 1967-80; v.p., mgr. farms ops. Moody Farms, Inc., North Richland Hills, Tex., 1980—; comml. realtor Roseberry Comml. Real Estate Co., North Richland Hills, 1985—. Mem. council City of North Richland Hills, 1984—; mem. Women in Govt., Nat. League of Cities, 1984; bd. dirs. Indsl. Devel. Council, NE Tarrant County, 1984—, North East Fin Arts League, 1986—. Mem. Nat. Assn. Female Execs., Fort Worth Bd. Realtors, Comml. Real Estate Women, Haltom-Richland C. of C. Democrat. Episcopalian. Avocations: historical areas; fine arts; video games. Home: 7720 Cedar Park Ave North Richland Hills TX 76180 Office: Roseberry Comml Real Estate Co 5013 Davis Blvd North Richland Hills TX 76118

MOOK, BARBARA HEER HELD, civic worker; b. Akron, June 9, 1919; d. Harold Edward and Helen Wilhelm (Heer) Held; student Coll. Wooster, 1937-39; diploma Actual Business Coll., 1941; m. Conrad Payne Mook, Sept. 6, 1941; children—Patricia Ann Mook Harris, Mary Ann Mook Barnum. Tchr., lectr. DAR Museum, Washington, 1973-79; sr. nat. asst. organizing sec. Children of the Am. Revolution, Washington, 1974-76, hon. sr. nat. v.p., 1977-83. Troop leader Girl Scouts U.S.A., Arlington, Va., 1951-53, neighborhood chmn., 1953-55, mem. program com. Arlington County council, 1955-56; rec. sec. Thomas Nelson chpt. DAR, Arlington, 1963-65, 73-75, librarian, 1967-69, regent, 1965-67. Recipient medal of appreciation SAR, 1981, Martha Washington medal, 1984. Mem. Va. Hist. Soc., Ohio Geneal. Soc., First Families Ohio, Soc. Descs. of Washington's Army at Valley Forge (charter v.p. 1976-78), Daus. of Union Vets. of Civil War 1861-65 (sr. v.p. 1978-80, pres. 1981-82), Children of Am. Revolution (sr. nat. officers club), Potomac Regents Club DAR (treas. 1974-75, librarian historian 1983-84), Aux. Sons Union Vets. of Civil War (patriotic instr. 1981-84, pres. 1984-85). Home: 5222 26th Rd N Arlington VA 22207

MOOK, SARAH, chemist; b. Bklyn., Oct. 29, 1929; d. Wong and Lie Won (Woo) M.; B.A., Hunter Coll., 1952; postgrad. Columbia U., 1954-57, 62-65, U. Hartford, 1958-59. Cartographic aide U.S. Geol. Survey, Dept. of Interior, Washington, 1952-54; research asst. Mineral Beneficiation Lab., Columbia U., N.Y.C., 1954-57; analytical chemist nuclear div. Combustion Engring., Inc., Windsor, Conn., 1957-59; research scientist Radiation Applications Inc., Long Island City, N.Y., 1959-62; chemist Marks Polarized Corp., Whitestone, N.Y., 1962-64; sr. chemist NRA Ins. subs. Nuclear Research Assos., Inc., New Hyde Park, N.Y., 1964-75; clin. chemist Coney Island Hosp., Bklyn., 1974-84, mem. community bd., 1978-84; chemist Bellevue Hosp. Ctr., N.Y.C., 1984—; mem. adv. com. to state assemblyman, State of N.Y., 1970-72. Trustee Park Avenue Christian Ch., 1973—, sec., 1973-80, vice chmn., 1980-81, chmn. bd. trustees, 1981-82, mem. ofcl. bd., 1962—, vice chmn., 1974-76, pres. Christian Women's Fellowship, 1962-65. Mem. Am. Chem. Soc., Am. Acad. Polit. and Social Sci., AAAS. Republican. Contbr. articles on inorganic chemistry to profl. publs. Home: 2042 E 14th St Brooklyn NY 11229 Office: 462 1st Ave New York NY 10016

MOON, GLORIA JEAN, sales executive; b. Springfield, Mo., Feb. 10, 1947; d. George Howard and Patsy Ruth (Simmons) Gray; m. Ronald Ellis Bunch, Feb. 9, 1967 (div. 1975); 1 son, Anthony Edward; m. Richard Leroy Moon, Oct. 25, 1975; children—Ricky, Connie O'Hara, Rob, Rolland. B.S., SW Mo. State U., 1967. With Southwestern Bell Telephone Co., Springfield, Mo., 1966-77; sec., v.p. mktg. Harter Corp., Sturgis, Mich., 1977-78, sales cons. Custom Communications, Kalamazoo, 1978-81, sales mgr., 1981—; presenter sales seminars. Mem. Kalamazoo Profl. and Exec. Assn., Kalamazoo-Grand Rapids C. of C., Kalamazoo Mgmt. Assn. (pres. 1986-87), Kalamazoo Network, Kalamazoo Bus. and Profl. Women's Club. Avocations: reading; piano; fishing; swimming; cooking. Office: Custom Communications 341 W Lovell St Kalamazoo MI 49007

MOON, KAY KAREN, nurse; b. Grove City, Pa., July 1, 1945; d. Kenneth Harvey and Marian Elizabeth (Burns) M. Diploma in Nursing, Trumbull Meml. Hosp. Sch. Nursing, 1967. Staff nurse Trumbull Meml. Hosp., Warren, Ohio, 1967-68, Bashline Hosp., Grove City, Pa., 1968-69, Warren Gen. Hosp., Warren, Ohio, 1969-70, Packard Electric div. Gen. Motors, Warren, 1970—. Republican. Home: 15 Arms Blvd Apt 5 Niles OH 44446 Office: Packard Electric Box 431 Warren OH 44486

MOON, LINDA ELLEN, medical center researcher; b. Corpus Christi, June 10, 1946; d. Troy William and Beatrice Claire (Cryer) Moon; m. Jerry Preston Reid, Oct. 29, 1965 (div. 1971); 1 son, James Troy; m. Jack James Flagg, Feb. 6, 1986. B.A., U. Tex., 1969. Research asst. Tex. A&M U. Research and Extension, Overton, 1969; lab. technician East Tex. Chest Hosp., Tyler, 1970-73; med. tech. James M. Gray & Assocs., Houston, 1974, Motley Clin. Labs., Inc., Houston, 1974-75, med. technician III, U. Tex. Cancer Ctr., M.D. Anderson Hosp., Houston, 1976-84; sr. research asst. dept. surgery/organ transplant U. Tex. Health Sci. Ctr., 1984—. Republican. Methodist. Home: 3215 Elmridge Houston TX 77025 Office: U Tex Health Sci Ctr 6431 Fannin HMSMB Room 6237 Houston TX 77025

MOON, LYNNE HARA, personnel and training executive; b. Honolulu, Dec. 3, 1950; d. James and Gladys (Nakama) Hara. B.A. magna cum laude in Communications and Sociology, U. Wash., 1972; M.A., U. Hawaii, 1979. Research assoc. Hawaii Employers Council, Honolulu, 1976-77; employee relations/tng. coordinator, 1978-79; personnel/tng. mgr. Liberty House, Honolulu, 1979-80, employee relations mgr., 1980-81; employee relations and mgmt. devel. mgr. Duty Free Shoppers, Honolulu, 1981-82, corp. dir. tng. and devel., 1982—. Bd. dirs. Jr. Achievement, Honolulu, 1982-84, advisor, 1976; coach J. Roger Basketball League, Honolulu, 1973. Wash. Advt. Scholar, 1972; East-West Ctr. degree scholar, 1972-74. Mem. Women in Communications, Am. Soc. Personnel Adminstrs., Am. Soc. Tng. and Devel., Internat. Platform Assn., Phi Beta Kappa, Alpha Kappa Delta, Alpha Lambda Delta. Address: 5340 Liwai St Honolulu HI 96821 Office: Duty Free Shoppers PO Box 29500 Honolulu HI 96820 also Duty Free Shoppers 655 Montgomery St 18th Floor San Francisco CA 94111

MOON, MARJORIE RUTH, state treasurer Idaho; b. Pocatello, Idaho, June 16, 1926; d. Clark Blakeley and Ruth Eleanor (Gerhart) M.; student Pacific U., Forest Grove, Oreg., 1944-46; A.B. cum laude in Journalism, U. Wash., Seattle, 1948. Reporter, Pocatello (Idaho) Tribune, 1944, Caldwell (Idaho) News-Tribune, 1948-50; bur. chief Boise, Deseret News, Salt Lake City, 1950-52; owner Idaho Pioneer Statewide weekly newspaper, Boise, 1952-55; founder, pub. Garden City (Idaho) Gazette, 1954-68; partner Sawtooth Lodge, Grandjean, Idaho, 1958-60; partner Modern Press, Boise, Idaho, 1958-61; treas. State of Idaho, Boise, 1963—. Del. nat. nominating com. Idaho Democratic Com., 1972, 76, 80, 84; chmn. Idaho Commn. on Women's Programs, 1971-74. Mem. Nat. Assn. State Treasurers (sec.-treas. 1976-78, regional v.p. 1978-79, 84-85). Nat. Fedn. Press Women, Idaho Press Women (past pres.). Congregationalist. Clubs: Soroptimist (past pres. Boise Club), Women's Ltd. (dir. 1983, pres. 1984) (Boise). Office: 102 Statehouse Boise ID 83720

MOONEY, DIANE THOMPSON, real estate broker, consultant; b. San Francisco, Nov. 15, 1941; d. Lowell Eldon and Esther Frances (Cano) Thompson; m. Thomas Patrick Mooney, Jr., July 30, 1966; children—Noelle, Tracy. B.S., San Jose State U., 1963, postgrad., 1964-66. Real estate salesperson Roger Maason Co., Sunnyvale, Calif., 1963, Lowell Thompson Co., Sunnyvale, 1963-64; real estate broker Diane Noel Thompson, Sunnyvale, 1964-76, R.V. Jones Co., Los Altos, Calif., 1976-77, Whitecliff Realty, Los Altos, 1977-78, Diane Thompson Mooney, Los Altos, 1978—. Bd dirs. Lakeview Pines Condo, South Lake Tahoe, Calif., 1982-84. Recipient Art awards Santa Clara County Fair, 1964. Mem. Los Altos Bd. Realtors (local govt. relations chmn. 1982, 84, legis. chmn. 1984), Calif. Assn. Realtors, Nat. Assn. Realtors, LWV (treas. Mt. View-Los Altos chpt. 1985-86). Roman Catholic. Office: Diane Thompson Mooney Realty PO Box 122 Los Altos CA 94022

MOONEY, JANICE MARIE, actuarial company executive; b. New Orleans, Oct. 17, 1958; d. Francis James and Flaudry Louis (Guidry) Mooney. B.S. in Bus. Adminstrn. and Fin., La. State U., 1981. Mktg. rep. Profl. Devel. Service, Inc., Baton Rouge, 1982—, Richard F. Camus & Assocs., New Orleans, 1982—. Author, editor: Actuarially Speaking (newsletter). Democrat. Roman Catholic. Home: 220 Oklahoma St Apt 209 Baton Rouge LA 70802 Office: Profl Devel Service Inc 2626 Myrtle Ave Baton Rouge LA 70806

MOONEY, LORI, county official; b. Atlantic City, Aug. 22, 1929; d. Joseph Aloysius and Alice Marie Inemer; m. Charles H. Calvi (div.); children—Joseph P., Stephen C., Christina L.; m. Thomas Christopher Mooney; children—Thomas C., Timothy C. Service rep. Bell Telephone Co., Atlantic City, 1950-58; sr. evaluator U.S. Census Bur., N.J., 1960-63; coordinator Nat. Small Bus. Com. for Johnson and Humphrey, Washington, 1964; owner, mgr. Lori Mooney & Co., Realtors, Atlantic County, N.J., 1965-77; commr. Atlantic County Bd. Elections, from 1970, also chmn. 5 yrs.; county clk. County of Atlantic, Mays Landing, 1978—; mem. Active Corps Execs., Nat. SBA; chmn. county clk. liaison com. N.J. Supreme Ct., 1984-86. Del. Democratic Nat. Conv., 1972, 76, 84; mem. study team N.J. Div. Youth and Family Services, 1982; mem. U.S. Senator Bill Bradley's Citizen Adv. Com. Recipient Woman of Achievement award N.J. Fedn. Bus. and Profl. Women, 1985. Mem. Internat. Assn. Clks., Recorders, Election Ofcls. and Treas., Atlantic County Realtors Assn., Bus. and Profl. Women Atlantic County (scholarship chmn. 1982-85), County Officers Assn. N.J. (bd. dirs. 1978—), N.J. Assn. County Clks. (chmn. 1984-86), N.J. Assn. Realtors, Nat. Assn. Realtors, N.J. League Municipalities, Assn. Records Mgrs. and Administrs., Atlantic City Women's C. of C., Nat. Assn. Female Execs. Home: 62 E Wright St Pleasantville NJ 08232 Office: Atlantic County Clerks Office Main St Mays Landing NJ 08330

MOONIE, LIANA MARIA, artist; b. Trieste, Italy, Mar. 22, 1922; came to U.S., 1947, naturalized, 1950; d. Angelo and Maria (Canciani) Gabrielli. B.A., U. Trieste, 1940; student Robert Brachman, Art Students League, Edgar Whitney. One-woman shows and numerous juried and invitationals in galleries and mus. throughout U.S. and Europe; works exhibited in pvt. and corp. collections; contbg. editor Beaux Arts mag., 1974-77; lectr. and juror in field. Chmn. Beaux Arts Project, Westchester, N.Y. Recipient numerous art awards. Mem. Am. Soc. Contemporary Artists (N.Y.C. watercolor award 1983, dir.), Nat. Assn. Women Artists (N.Y.C. oil award 1984, watercolor award 1983, 85, dir.), Allied Artists Am. (oil award 1985), Scarsdale Art Assn. N.Y., Silvermine Artists Guild, Hudson River Contemporary Artists (past pres.), Mamaroneck Artists Guild (past pres.). Club: Salmagundi (N.Y.C.). Address: 40 Taunton Rd Scarsdale NY 10583

MOOR, DINA MAVIS, advertising agency executive; b. Phoenix, Aug. 23, 1943; d. Isaac Lowery and Anna Mavis (Stinson) M.; student State U. Iowa, 1961-62; B.A., So. Meth. U., 1967; M.B.A., U. Dallas, 1976; 1 child, Aaron Michael. Freelance model, 1965-71; sec. to academic dean U. Dallas, 1971-72, asst. to dean, 1972-74, dir. affiliated programs, 1974-76; dir. Mgmt. Labs. Am., Exec. Edn. Inst., Center for Publishing, 1974-76; owner Moor and Assos., Inc., Dallas, 1976—; owner Standby Club, Highlands Trading Co.; dir. Lynn Weiss & Assos.; bd. dirs. Screen Actors Guild and AFTRA, 1967-70. Recipient Wall St. Jour. award, 1976. Mem. Savs. Instns. Mktg. Soc. Am., Sales and Mktg. Execs. Dallas, Women in Communications, Inc., North Dallas C. of C., Grad. Sch. Mgmt. Alumni Assn. (past pres.), Sigma Iota Epsilon. Episcopalian. Clubs: Slipper, 500 Inc. (past dir.). Office: 3721 27th Place W Seattle WA 98199

MOORE, ALDERINE BERNICE JENNINGS (MRS. JAMES F. MOORE), club woman; b. Sacramento, Apr. 17, 1915; d. James Joseph and Elise (Thomas) Jennings; A.B., U. Wash., 1941; m. James Francis Moore, Aug. 14, 1945. Sec. to div. Plant supr. Pacific Tel. & Tel. Co., Sacramento, 1937-39; exec. sec. Sacramento Community Chest Fund Raising Dr., 1941; sec. USAAF, Mather Field, Sacramento, 1942; statistician Calif. Western States Life Ins. Co., 1943; treas. Women's Aux. Stranger's Hosp., Rio de Janeiro, Brazil, 1964-65. Vice pres. Douglaston (N.Y.) Women's Club, 1955; mem. Douglaston Garden Club, 1951-55; pres. Nina Opland chpt. Women's Cancer Assn. U. Miami, 1960-61; corr. sec. Coral Gables (Fla.) Garden Club, 1960-62; pres. Miami Alumnae Club of Pi Beta Phi, 1961-62; mem. Putnam Hill chpt. D.A.R., Greenwich Conn., 1967-75, Palm Beach chpt., 1978—; mem. Woman's Club, Greenwich, Conn., 1967-75; mem. Women's Panhellenic Assn., Miami, 1961-62; internat. treas. Ikebana Internat., Tokyo, Japan, 1966-67, parliamentarian Tokyo chpt., 1966-67, N.Y. chpt., 1968-69; mem. Coll. Women Assn. Japan, 1965-66, mem. Tchrs. Assn. Sogetsu Sch. Japanese Flower Arranging, 1966—. Served to lt. USNR, 1943-45. Mem. Internat. Platform Assn., AAUW, Pi Beta Phi (local v.p. alumnae club 1969-71). Baptist. Club: Steamboat Investment (pres. 1972-73). Home: 316 Fairway Ct Atlantis FL 33462

MOORE, ALMA JEAN BROWN, cosmetologist; b. Knoxville, Jan. 15, 1933; d. Eugene Solomon Brown and Ruth Annabella (Bragg) Minor; m. Thomas Louise Coley Moore, July 6, 1951; children—Thomas, Yvonne, Dionee, Michael. Owner, Beautyrama Salon and Wig Boutique, Knoxville, 1960-82, Ru-Mal's Boutique, Knoxville, 1969-83, Diana Moore Beauty Salon, Knoxville, 1972—. Mem. Tenn. Beauticians Assn. (treas. 1968-72, state organizer 1972-78, pres. 1982—), Tenn. Top Ten Hairdressers (pres. 1974-82). Mem. African Methodist Episcopal Ch. Clubs: Top Ladies Distinction (Knoxville) (pres. 1982—), Links (Knoxville) (treas. 1970-74), Les Modernettes (pres. 1983—). Home: 4703 Westover Terr Knoxville TN 37914 Office: Diana Moore Inc 2309 Magnolia Ave Knoxville TN 37917

MOORE, BETTIE JO, designer, artist, consultant; b. Shawnee, Okla., July 4, 1928; d. Cedric and Verna H. (Avery) M. Student Ringling Art Sch., Sarasota, Fla., 1945; B.F.A., U. Colo., 1969; M. Vocat. Edn., Colo. State U., 1973. Cert. vocat. edn., Colo. Dir./designer Moore Display & Design Studio, Aurora, Colo., 1955—; sch. dir. Visual Merchandising Inst., Aurora, 1979-81; cons. sales dir. Goodwill Industries Denver, 1981-83; exhibited in one-woman shows: Okla. Bapt. U., Shawnee, 1945; group shows include: U. Colo., 1969, Salito (Mex.) Gallery, 1972; represented in permanent collections: Okla. Bapt. U., Ringling Mus., Sarasota, Fla.; cons. visual merchandising; lectr., seminar instr. Denver Merchandising Mart, 1980-83; instr. visual merchandising Colo. State U., Ft. Collins, 1973. Author: Basic Display And Advertising, 1970. Nat. rep. to Goodwill Conf. for Goodwill Aux. Denver, 1983. Recipient First place award for store design Visual Merchandising and Store Design Internat. Competition, 1951, 75, also 3 hon. mention awards, 1960-82; recipient numerous first, second and third place awards from various art shows, 1969-80. Mem. Bus. Women's Club Am. (chairperson speakers 1979), Aurora Art Guild, Rocky Mountain Graphologists, Kappa Pi. Office: Goodwill Industries 6850 N Federal Blvd Denver CO 80205

MOORE, BOBBIE JEANNE HENDERSON, mathematics educator; b. Newnan, Ga., Mar. 29, 1936; d. Joe Pete and Jennie Mae (Brown) Henderson; m. Roy William Moore, June 5, 1960 (div. 1972); 1 dau., Stacey Lynne. B.A., Clark Coll., 1957; M.S. in Edn., U. So. Calif., 1962; Ed.D. U. San Francisco, 1982. Tchr. math. Los Angeles City Schs., 1969—, math. coordinator, 1982—; tchr. Newnan (Ga.) Pub. Schs., 1957-58, Atlanta Pub. Schs., 1964; tchr., cons. Berkeley (Calif.) Unified Schs., 1964-69, Los Angeles City Schs., 1969-82; gifted coordinator Los Angeles Unified Schs., 1983—; coll. coordinator Clark Coll. Alumni, Los Angeles, 1978-80. Recipient Community Service award Clark Coll. Alumni, 1978; Community award United Negro Coll. Fund, 1974; named Tchr. of Yr., Berkeley ARC, 1967. Mem. Nat. Assn. Univ. Women, Clark Coll. Alumni (pres. 1972-78), NEA, Nat. Assn. Female Execs., Internat. Platform Assn., Nat. Council Tchrs. Math., Alpha Kappa Alpha (sec. 1983—), U. So. Calif. Alumni Assn. Democrat. Methodist. Home: 1933 Virginia Rd Los Angeles CA 90016 Office: Los Angeles Unified Schs 450 N Grand Ave Los Angeles CA 90012

MOORE, BRENDA BARFIELD, university official; b. Cabool, Mo., Aug. 11, 1956; d. Arnold Barto and Ruby Rose (Britzman) Barfield; m. L. Missildine, July 13, 1976 (div. Apr. 1979); 1 child, Hunter; m. Herff L. Moore, Jr., July 1, 1983; children—Terri, Christopher, Kimberley. B.B.A., East Tex. State U., 1983; postgrad. St. John Fisher Coll., 1984. Office mgr. Barfield Distbrs., New Boston, Tex., 1975-83; br. mgr. Manpower Temp. Services, Rochester, N.Y., 1984-85; acct. Div. Continuing Edn., U. Central Ark., Conway, 1985—, Indsl. Developers Ark., 1985—; dir. Barfield Distbg. Co. Editor in chief profl. newsletter: Continuing Edn. Horizons, 1986. Mem. U. Central Ark. Staff Assn., Bus. and Profl. Women. Avocations: reading, cross-stitching, ceramics. Home: 15 Smoking Oak Rd Conway AR 72032 Office: Div Continuing Edn U Central Ark Conway AR 72032

MOORE, CAROL J(EAN), software engineering firm executive; b. Ventura, Calif., July 15, 1940; d. John Munro and Maria (Hamburg) Bowie; m. Bruce W. Moore, Oct. 3, 1970 (div. 1980); 1 child, Ian David. B.S. in Math., Stanford U., 1962; postgrad. U. Colo., 1967-68, Calif. State U.-Fresno, 1974-77. Programmer Kaman Nuclear Corp., Colorado Springs, Colo., 1962-65, Wolf Research & Devel. Corp., Colorado Springs, 1965; systems analyst System Devel. Corp., Colorado Springs, 1965-69; asst. dir. computer ctr. Calif. State U. Fresno, 1969-77; project leader BDM Corp., Monterey, Calif., 1977-80; dir. projects Sterling Software, Palo Alto, Calif., 1980—. Co-author: Catalog of Instructional Programs, 1976; also co-author numerous proposals and feasibility studies. Vice chmn. Neighborhood Assn., Menlo Park, Calif., 1986—. Canfield Found. scholar and Calif. State Scholarship Fedn. scholar Stanford U., 1958-62. Mem. IEEE Computer Soc., Planetary Soc., Am. Mgmt. Assn. Democrat. Lutheran. Avocations: hiking; needlework; reading; tennis. Home: 254 Santa Margarita Menlo Park CA 94025 Office: Sterling Software 1121 San Antonio Rd Palo Alto CA 94303

MOORE, FAY LINDA, computer programmer; b. Houston, Apr. 7, 1942; d. Charlie Louis and Esther Mable (Banks) Moore; m. Noel Patrick Walker, Jan. 5, 1963 (div. 1967); 1 dau., Trina Nicole Moore. Student Prairie View A&M Coll., 1960-61, Tex. So. U., 1962. Instr., Internat. Bus. Coll., Houston, 1965; keypunch operator IBM Corp., Houston, 1965-67, sr. keypunch operator, 1967-70, programmer technician, 1970-72, asst. programmer, 1972-73, assoc. programmer, 1973—. Mem. Data Processing Mgmt. Assn., Nat. Assn. Female Execs. Inc. Democrat. Roman Catholic. Club: Clear Lake Osborne Group. Office: IBM Corp 1322 Space Park Dr Houston TX 77058

MOORE, HARRIET ANN, hospital assistant administrator; b. Keyser, W.Va., Sept. 22, 1946; d. Arnold G. and Hilda (Murphy) Clark; m. Carl E. Moore, June 13, 1975; children—Ron, Nancy, Angela, Derek, Jennifer, Kerry, Heidi. R.N., Meml. Hosp., Cumberland, Md., 1967; student Potomac State Coll., 1984; student in mgmt. St. Joseph Coll., North Windham, Maine, 1985—. Cert. nursing adminstrn. Am. Nurses Assn. Staff nurse Potomac Valley Hosp., Keyser, W.Va., 1968-73, ICU, CCU nurse, 1973-74, surg. nurse, 1974-79, infection control, discharge coordinator, 1979-84, asst. dir. nursing, 1982-85, asst. adminstr., 1985—. Chmn. adv. com. health careers Mineral County Vo Tech. Sch., Keyser, W.Va., 1983—. Vol., ARC, 1972-75. Methodist. Home: 91 Poplar St Westernport MD 21562 Office: Potomac Valley Hosp S Mineral St Keyser WV 26726

MOORE, JACQUELYN CHESTELL, association director; b. Kansas City, Mo., Oct. 8, 1944; d. Chester Randall and Jonnie Thelma (Nix) McAfee; m. Charles A. Moore, III, Aug. 27, 1966; 1 child, Charles A. Moore IV. B.A. in Sociology, Howard U., 1966; M.S. in Human Resources Mgmt., U. Utah, 1972. Counselor, Div. Employment Security, Kansas City, Mo., 1966-68; supportive service coordinator Concentrated Employment Program, Kansas City, 1968-71; dir. human resources Mid-Am. Regional Council, Kansas City, 1971-84, dir. aging, 1984—; planning chmn. Mo. Affirmative Action Assn., 1979-83, Mo. Adv. Council on Alcohol and Drug Abuse, 1977-83; sec. Mo. Alliance of Area Agys. on Aging Adminstrs., 1984—. Bd. dirs. Catholic Charities, Kansas City Diocese, 1979—, Kansas City Consensus, 1984—; govt. relations com. Heart of Am. United Way, Kansas City, 1981—; chmn. Career Fair, Urban League Greater Kansas City, 1978-83. Fellow Kansas City Tomorrow; mem. Nat. Caucus on Black Aged, Nat. Assn. Regional Councils (aging task force), Nat. Assn. Area Agys. on Aging, Mo. Mcpl. League (human resource policy com. 1979—). Office: Mid-America Regional Council 20 W 9th St Kansas City MO 64105

MOORE, JACQUELYN CORNELIA, labor union ofcl., editor; b. Balt., Dec. 25, 1929; d. James C. and Harriette I. (Conaway) Thomas; m. Clarence Carbin Moore, Jan. 19, 1947 (dec. Feb. 1970); children—Clarence Joseph, Janet Elizabeth Moore Oliver. Mail clk. U.S. P.O., Phila., 1966—; editor Local 509 Newsletter, Nat. Alliance of Postal and Fed. Employees, Washington, 1969-74, editorial newsletter chmn., 1969-74, sec. Dist. 5, 1972-74, nat. editor Nat. Alliance, 1974—, mem. exec. bd., 1974—, union photographer, 1974—, dir. 202 Housing for Elderly Corp. bds., Chattanooga, New Orleans, 1981—, sec. supervisory com. Nat. Fed. Credit Union, 1977-82. Vol. D.C. Voting Rights Corp., Washington, 1979—; sustaining mem. Democratic Nat. Com., 1977—. Mem. Coalition of Labor Union Women. Democrat. Roman Catholic. Clubs: Capitol Press, Nat. Bus. and Profl. Women's, Nat. Press. Home: 4040 B 8th St NW Washington DC 20011 Office: 1628 11th St NW Washington DC 20001

MOORE, JANE ROSS, librarian; b. Phila., Apr. 24, 1929; d. John William and Mary (McClure) Ross; m. Cyril Howard Moore, Jr., June 1, 1956 (div. Mar. 1967). A.B., Smith Coll., 1951; M.S. in L.S., Drexel U., 1952; postgrad., Columbia U.; M.B.A. with distinction, NYU, 1965; Ph.D., Case Western Res. U., 1974. Cataloguer, Yale U. Library, 1952-54; chief tech. processes librarian Lederle Labs., Am. Cyanamid Co., Pearl River, N.Y., 1954-58; chief serials catalog librarian Bklyn. Coll. Library, 1958-65, asst. prof., chief catalog div., 1965-70, asso. prof., chief catalog div., 1971-73, asso. prof. asso. librarian adminstrv. services, 1973-76; prof., chief librarian Grad. Sch. and Univ. Center, CUNY, 1976—; lectr. Syracuse U. Grad. Sch. Library Sci., summer 1967, 69, Queens Coll. Grad. Sch. Library and Info. Studies, 1967-69, adj. asso. prof., 1974-76, adj. prof., 1977—; HEW Title IIB fellow Case Western Res. U. Sch. Library Sci., 1970-72; trustee N.Y. Met. Reference and Research Library Agy., 1984—. Bd. dirs. Vis. Nurse Assn. of Bklyn., 1984—. Mem. N.Y. Library Assn. (pres. 1979-80, pres. resources and tech. services sect. 1966-67, councilor 1966-67, 75-76, 78-81, sec.-treas. acad. and spl. libraries sect. 1973-75), ALA (membership com. 1967-71, chmn. council regional groups, resources and tech. services div. 1968-69, dir. div. 1968-70, 75-76, chmn. div. cataloging and classification sect. 1975-76), N.Y. Tech. Services Librarians (pres. 1963-64, award 1976), Assn. Coll. and Research Libraries (chmn. univ. libraries sect. 1983-84), N.Y. Library Club (sec. 1964-66, pres. 1980-81, council 1966-70, 73-77, 79-82), OCLC Users Council (SUNY del. 1981-85), AAUP, AAUW, Am. Soc. Info. Sci., Archons of Colophon, Spl. Libraries Assn., NYU Grad. Sch. Bus. Adminstrn. Alumni Assn. (rec. sec. 1967-69, dir. 1969-70, 75-79), Phi Kappa Phi. Presbyterian (elder). Clubs: Smith Coll. (Bklyn.) (pres. 1966-67, 67-68, class treas. 1976-81); Civitas (Bklyn.)). Home: 35 Schermerhorn St Brooklyn NY 11201 Office: Mina Rees Library Grad Sch and Univ Center City U NY 33 W 42d St New York NY 10036

MOORE, JANET LYNN, fashion school administrator; b. Buffalo, Apr. 11, 1952; d. Donald Charles and Norma Ruth (Davis) Bradley; m. Edgar William Moore, Oct. 28, 1972; 1 child, Jaret William. B.A. in Econs., Old Dominion U., 1974; postgrad. Law Sch. SUNY-Buffalo, 1978. Paralegal, Williams, Worrel et al, Norfolk, Va., 1974-75; mgr. Stretch & Sew Fabrics, Buffalo, 1975-81; exec. dir. Barbizon Schs., Virginia Beach, Va., 1979-81; pres. Fashion Schs. Inc., Tysons Corner, Va., 1981—; sec. treas. Nordon Fabrics Amherst Inc., Buffalo, 1975—; dir. John Robert Powers Sch., Vienna, Va., 1981—; cons. About Faces Cosmetics, Towson, Md., Color Concepts, Amherst, N.Y. Author fashion column Washington Post, 1981. Editor: Fashion Schools Inc Student Manual, 1985. Field supr. Howard U. Fashion Interns, Washington, 1982-84; vol. dir. Cherry Blossom Princess Com., Washington, 1984-85. A.D. Morgan scholarship Old Dominion U., 1974. Mem. Modeling Assn. Am. Internat. (bd. dirs. 1981-85). Republican. Club: Profl. Bus. Women's Assn. Avocations: piano; swimming; lecturing. Home: 4508 Little River Run Dr Annandale VA 22003 Office: Fashion Schs Inc Suite 120 8027 Leesburg Pike Vienna VA 22180

MOORE, JANET MARIE, state official; b. Butler, Pa., Mar. 13, 1947; d. Jesse Robert and Katherine Mae (Pisor) Moore; Asso. in Specialized Bus., New Castle Bus. Coll., 1972. Cost accountant Package Products Inc., Pitts., 1967-68; audit clk. Liberty Mut. Ins. Co., New Castle, Pa., 1968-71; acct. S.R. Snodgrass & Co., C.P.A.s, New Castle, 1971-74; clerical supr. Pa. vital statistics Pa. Dept. Health, New Castle, 1974—; pvt. practice acctg., Volant, Pa., 1974—. Mem. Owner Handler Assn., Nat. Rifle Assn. (life). Democrat. Presbyterian. Club: New Castle Kennel (sec. 1978, dir. 1977-81, v.p. 1979-81). Home: RD 3 Box 101 Volant PA 16156 Office: PO Box 1528 New Castle PA 16103

MOORE, JEAN BANTE, lawyer; b. St. Louis, Oct. 26, 1955; d. John Delbert and Mary Garvin (Quinn) Bante; m. Stephen James Moore, Aug. 4, 1979; children—Michelle Marie, Colleen Garvin. B.S. in Bus. Adminstrn., Rockhurst Coll., 1977; J.D., St. Louis U., 1980. Bar: Mo. 1980, U.S. Dist. Ct. (we. dist.) Mo. 1980, U.S. Ct. Appeals (D.C. cir.). Atty., Union Electric Co., St. Louis, 1980—. Adminstrv. editor St. Louis U. Law Jour., 1979-80. Mem. ABA, Mo. Bar, Bar Assn. St. Louis. Republican. Roman Catholic. Office: PO Box 149 Code 1310 1901 Gratiot Saint Louis MO 63123

MOORE, JEANETTE EVELYN, cosmetics company executive; b. Terre Haute, Ind., Apr. 19, 1946; d. Earl Brown and Nola Helen (Griffen) McCarty; m. Frederick Steven Moore, Dec. 27, 1971; children—Carter Alan, Todd Jason. Student Brigham Young U., 1964-65; grad. Roper Sch. Real Estate, 1970, Dublin Beauty Coll., 1982. Coordinator, Charted Services Calif., Hayward, 1974-76; v.p. Ins. Rev. Agy., Hayward, 1975-76; loan officer Sierra Home Loans, Grass Valley, Calif., 1978-82; ins. broker Moore Ins. Agy., San Ramon, Calif., 1976-82; pres. Boughatti Internat., Pleasanton, Calif., 1983—, mktg. dir., 1983-85. Author: Boughatti Sales/Training Manual, 1983; 10 Steps of Basic Nail Care, 1983; My Nails-Sculptured Nail Manual, 1983. Den mother Boy Scouts Am., San Ramon, Calif., 1978. Mem. Nat. Assn. Female Execs., Nat. Write Your Congressman Orgn., Nat. Assn. Nail Artists. Republican. Avocations: waterskiing; snow skiing; dancing; bowling. Home: 9425 Alcosta Blvd San Ramon CA 94583

MOORE, JOANNE, quality control specialist; b. Newport News, Va., Nov. 1, 1943; d. Joseph and Mable (Williams) Jackson; m. Calvin Louis Moore, June 28, 1969; children—Nikisha Terri, Calvin Louis. B.A., U. Md.-Balt., 1982. Mgr., U.S. Postal Service, Balt., 1978-84, quality control specialist, 1984—. Active local Apostolic ch.; pres. youth dept. United House of Prayer, Balt., 1971-81; bd. dirs. McCollough Day Care Ctr., 1983-86; finalist Mrs. America Pageant, Balt., 1983. Mem. Nat. Assn. Female Execs., Am. Bus. Women's Assn., Nat. Assn. Postal Suprs. (newsletter editor 1983-84, area v.p. 1985-86), U. Md. Alumni Assn. Democrat. Avocations: writing; bowling; singing; fishing. Home: 7100 Hull Ct Baltimore MD 21207 Office: US Postal Service 900 E Fayette St Baltimore MD 21233

MOORE, JOYCE PAULLIN, advertising executive; b. Mattoon, Ill., Aug. 19, 1937; d. William J. and Jewell L. (Sowers) Paullin; m. David A. Moore, May 19, 1967 (div. 1983). Student Eastern Ill. U., 1955-56, Northwestern U., DePaul U., Chgo. Personnel adminstrv. asst. Booz-Allen & Hamilton, Chgo., 1967-72, corp. personnel adminstr., 1972-74, office and personnel mgr., 1974-79, v.p., dir. adminstrv. services Needham, Harper Worldwide, Chgo., 1979—, also chmn. adminstrv. task force, mem. bd. mgmt. Mem. Am. Mgmt. Assn., Chgo. Ad Club. Office: Needham Harper Worldwide 303 E Wacker Dr Chicago IL 60601

MOORE, JUDITH ANN, finance company executive; b. Boise, Idaho, Mar. 2, 1942; d. Lawrence deMeza and Ida Mae (Emerson) Jessen; m. Douglas Clayton Moore, Dec. 28, 1964 (div. May 1974); children—Jennifer Ann, Jeffrey Lawrence. B.A., Willamette U., 1964; postgrad. Portland State U., 1976-77. Mgr. accounts receivable Multnomah Athletic Club, Portland, Oreg., 1974-75; asst. to pub. info. officer Oreg. Dept. Environ. Quality, Portland, 1975-76; lang. arts educator Beaverton Sch. Dist., (Oreg.), 1976-77, Yamhill Sch. Dist. (Oreg.), 1977-79; sr. sec. Mercedes-Benz Credit Corp. (formerly Freightliner Credit Corp.), Portland, Oreg., 1979-82, exec. sec., 1982, corporate services supr., Norwalk, Conn., 1982—. Author, editor Line of Credit, 1980—. Mem. Mortar Board, Chi Omega. Office: Mercedes-Benz Credit Corp 201 Merritt 7 Suite 700 Norwalk CT 06851

MOORE, JUDITH MARIE, nurse; b. Evanston, Ill., June 2, 1947; d. Herbert Potter and Irene Ellen (Wagner) M.; B.S., Loma Linda (Calif.) U., 1970. Mem. staff White Meml. Med. Center, Los Angeles, 1970-80, coordinator edn. tng. MacPherson Applied Physiology Lab., 1979-80; critical care nurse Critical Care Services, Inc., Los Angeles 1980; dir. health edn. and rehab. tng. program St. Helena Hosp. and Health Center, Deer Park, Calif., 1981—; bd. dirs. Napa County chpt. Am. Heart Assn., 1980—; speaker in field. Mem. Am. Assn. Critical Care Nurses, Nat. Critical Care Inst., Am. Heart Assn., Calif. Soc. Cardiac Rehab., Am. Assn. Cardiovascular and Pulmonary Rehab. Seventh-day Adventist. Home: PO Box 154 Deer Park CA 94576 Office: HEART Program St Helena Hosp and Health Center Deer Park CA 94576

MOORE, JULIA MARTIN, restaurateur; b. Dec. 27, 1955; d. Carol Walton and Ruth (Hines) Martin; m. Gregory Allen Moore, Nov. 10, 1979; children—Junius Gregory, Margaret Burlie. Student St. Mary's Coll., Raleigh, N.C., 1974-76; B.A., U. N.C., 1978. Social worker John Umstead Hosp., Butner, N.C., 1978-79; customer service employee C & S Bank, Charleston, S.C., 1979-81; corp. sec. SCNB, Inc., Jacksonville, N.C., 1981—; owner, developer Smithfield's Chicken-n-Bar BQ, N.C., 1981—; co-officer Smithfield Devel. Co., 1985—. Mem. N.C. Restaurant Assn., Carteret County Restaurant Assn. (sec. 1985), N.C. C. of C. Republican. Episcopalian. Home: 2226 Warrenton Way Jacksonville NC 28540 Office: SCNB Inc Smithfield Devel PO Box 1634 Jacksonville NC 28541

MOORE, KARLEE PHIPPEN, nurse, researcher; b. Grace, Idaho, Apr. 15, 1936; d. Lloyd Williams and Edith (Smith) Phippen; m. James Bud Wardle, Nov. 11, 1953 (div. 1973); children—Danlet Wardle Kambich, Cora Lyn Wardle Meyer, Heidi Renee Wardle Rowland; m. Richard Francis Moore, Aug. 5, 1973. A.S. with high honors, Santa Rosa Jr. Coll., 1983; postgrad. Sonoma U., 1986—. Owner, operator Karlee's Beauty Salon, Randle, Wash., 1964-73; charge nurse Healdsburg Hosp., Calif., 1983—; intern tchr. Santa Rosa Jr. Coll., Calif., 1984—. Republican. Avocations: creative needle work design; reading; helping drug and alcohol abusers. Home: 404 Stameroff Cloverdale CA 95425

MOORE, LINDA GRACE, orch. mgr.; b. Monroe, Mich., May 18, 1948; d. Emmett R. and Mary E. (Scott) M.; B.Mus., Western Mich. U., 1971; M.Mus., Ball State U., 1973, D.A., 1976. Teaching fellow Ball State U., 1972-75; asst. prin. cellist Fort Wayne Philharmonic, 1975-79, adminstrv. asst., 1977-79; gen. mgr. Lexington (Ky.) Philharmonic Soc., 1979—; mem. performing arts review panel Ky. Arts Council, 1982; chmn. mem. com. Lexington Council Arts, 1979—. Recipient Future Scientist Am. award Ford Found., 1965; Carnegie Found. fellow Ball State U., 1975. Mem. Am. Symphony Orch. League, Met. Orch. Mgrs. Assn., AAUP, Music Educators Nat. Conf., S.E. Regional and Met. Orch. Mgrs. Office: 412 Rose St Lexington KY 40508

MOORE, LINDA PERIGO, writer; b. Evansville, Ind., Nov. 25, 1946; d. John Myrl and Loraine Jeannette (Hudson) Perigo; m. Stephen Howard Moore, Aug. 12, 1967; 1 child, Jackson Staurt Moore. B.S., Miami U., Oxford, Ohio, 1968; M.S., M.Ed., U. Louisville, 1973. Instr., St. Joseph Infirmary, Louisville, 1969-71; tng. dir. Park-DuValle Neighborhood Health Ctr., Louisville, 1971-74; counselor Charlestown High Sch. (Ind.), 1974-75; tng. dir. Midtown Mental Health Ctr., Indpls., 1977-79; freelance writer, 1980—; cons. Kelly & Assocs., Indpls., 1977-81; instr. Ind. U., Indpls., 1979-81. Bd. dirs. Jr. League Evansville, 1982-84, Mothers Assn. Evansville Day Sch., 1985-87. Author: Does This Mean My Kid's a Genius?, 1981; You're Smarter Than You Think, 1985; (with Bart Conner) Winning the Gold, 1985; (with Richard Simmons) Reach for Fitness, 1986; also articles in mags. and trade jours. Bd. dirs. Planned Parenthood Southwestern Ind., Evansville, 1983, Evansville Mus. Arts and Scis. Guild, 1983-86. Office: PO Box 489 Boonville IN 47601

MOORE, LISA ANN, lawyer; b. Dallas, May 4, 1954; d. Douglas Eugene and Jeannie Marie (D'Amato) M.; m. Mark S. Carnes, Aug. 23, 1980 (div. 1984). B.A. in Polit. Sci., U. Tex.-Austin, 1976; J.D., St. Mary's Sch. Law, San Antonio, 1980. Bar: Tex. 1981. Assoc. Sullivan, King & Sabom, Houston, 1982—; dir. Toyota Town, Inc., Dallas, 1979—. Fin. com. mem. Houston mayoral campaign, 1983; mem. steering and fin. coms. Bob Kruegar polit. campaign, Houston, 1984. Mem. ABA, State Bar Tex., Houston Bar Assn., Houston Young Lawyers Assn. Democrat. Roman Catholic. Home: 5110 San Felipe 71-W Houston TX 77056

MOORE, LOLA PEARL RAMSEY, realtor; b. Omaha, Ill., Oct. 14, 1910; d. Floyd and Fannie Ann (Dillard) Ramsey; certificate in real estate U. Calif. at Berkeley, 1967; student Long Beach Secretarial Coll., 1942, Diablo Valley Coll., 1961-63. Accountant various firms, 1940-61; with various real estate firms, 1961-64; owner Moore Realty, Concord, Calif., 1964-65; pres., gen. mgr. Moore Realty Inc., Concord, 1965-72; owner Loma Realty, Camarillo, Calif., 1972—. Recipient awards Contra Costa Bd. Realtors, 1965, 66. Mem. Contra Costa Bd. Realtors (chmn. library com. 1965-66), Calif. Real Estate Assn., Nat. Assn. Realtors (mem. woman's council 1964—; pres. Contbr. chpt. 1965), Nat. Inst. Real Estate Brokers, Camarillo Bd. Realtors (sec. 1973-75, treas. 1976), Concord C. of C. (dir. 1970-72, mem. com. Concord coordinated services project 1967-68), League Women Voters, DAR. Methodist. Clubs: Order Eastern Star, Soroptimists (pres. 1970-71) (Concord); Soroptimists (Camarillo). Author: Ramsey Families History, 1984. Home: PO Box 337 Camarillo CA 93010 Office: 1820 Ventura Blvd Camarillo CA 93010

MOORE, LYNNE ELISE, lawyer; b. Sterling, Colo., Sept. 28, 1957; d. James Hamilton and Mabel Louise (White) Moore. B.A. in Liberal Arts, Colo. Coll., 1979; J.D., U. Denver, 1983. Bar: Colo. 1983. Law clk. Dailey, Goodwin et al, Aurora, Colo., 1980-81; asst. to prof. U. Denver, 1981; law clk. Gorsuch, Kirgis et al, Denver, 1982; summer assoc. Kirkland & Ellis, Denver, 1982; intern to presiding justice Denver Dist. Ct., 1983; assoc. Montgomery, Little, Young, Campbell & McGrew, Denver, 1983—. Bd. dirs. Colo. Women's Employment and End., Inc. Contbr. articles to profl. jours, chpts. to book. Denver Panhellenic scholar, 1977. Mem. ABA, Denver Bar Assn., Colo. Bar Assn., Kappa Alpha Theta (Founders' Meml. scholar). Home: 2255 Leydon St Denver CO 80207 Office: Montgomery Little Young Cambell & McGrew 1120 Lenden St 1500 Denver CO 80203

MOORE, LYNNE SCHMITZ, moving and storage company executive; b. Little Falls, Minn., May 1, 1944; s. Everett Joseph and Margaret Maude (Proff) Schmitz; m. Laurie Walker Moore, Jr., Oct. 9, 1970; children—Phillip Schmitz, Zane Everett. B.S., U. Minn., 1966; M.S., UCLA, 1969. R.N., Va. Sch. nurse Oxnard Elem. Sch. System, Calif., 1966-68; adminstrv. asst. St. Mary's Hosp., Richmond, Va., 1970-72, asst. adminstr., 1972-74; dir. nursing service Hampton Gen. Hosp., Va., 1974-76, asst. adminstr., 1976-79; chmn. bd. Moore Moving & Storage Co., Newport News, Va., 1979—; chmn. Lynne N. Am., Newport News, 1984—. Recipient Sales Achievement award Burnham Van Services, Columbus, Ga., 1982; 1st place agy. award Interstate Van Lines, Springfield, Va., 1983; Domestic Mil. Sales award Suddath Van Lines, Jacksonville, Fla., 1984. Mem. Am. Movers Conf., Nat. Movers and Warehouseman's Assn., Va. Movers and Warehouseman's Assn., Peninsula Movers and Warehouseman's Assn. (v.p. 1981-83, pres. 1983-85). Republican. Methodist. Avocations: water sports; roses. Home: 4204 Chesapeake Ave Hampton VA 23669 Office: Lynne North American and Moore Moving & Storage Inc 4808 Commerce Dr Newport News VA 23607

MOORE, MARGARET ANN, rehabilitation services executive; b. Bayonne, N.J., Sept. 6, 1942; d. Andrew F.X. and Virginia Milton; A.A., Fullerton Coll., 1962; B.A., Calif. State U., Fullerton, 1965; 1 son, Brian Andrew. Claims adjustor State Compensation Ins. Fund, Santa Ana, Calif., 1965-73; sr. claims rep. Firemans Fund, Santa Ana, 1975-77; rehab. supr. Comprehensive Rehab. Services, Arcadia, Calif., 1977, dist. mgr., Brea, Calif., Phila., Southfield, Mich. and No. Oreg., 1977-85, tech. adminstrv. asst., spl. projects mgr., 1985—; instr. Mt. Hood Community Coll. Mem. Nat. Rehab. Assn., Nat. Rehab. Counselors Assn., Nat. Assn. Rehab. Profls. in Pvt. Sector, Pa. Assn. Pvt. Rehab. Profls. (dir. 1980, sec. 1981, 82, standards and ethics com. 1981, 82), Nat. Rehab. Adminstrs. Assn., Oreg. Rehab. Counselors Assn., Oreg. Rehab. Assn., Mich. Rehab. Assn., Mich. Rehab. Counselors Assn. Republican. Roman Catholic. Home: 9668 SW Siuslaw St Tualatin OR 97062

MOORE, (MARGARET) ELEANOR MARCHMAN, ret. librarian; b. Pinckard, Ala., Nov. 6, 1913; d. Robert Lee and Eleanor Rowena (Paris) Marchman; A.B., Fla. State Coll. for Women, 1936; B.S. in L.S., George Peabody Coll. for Tchrs., 1947, M.A. in Library Sci., 1962; m. James William Moore, Feb. 22, 1934 (div. 1940); 1 son, John Robert. Tchr. Alva (Fla.) High Sch., 1938-40, Wacissa (Fla.) Jr. High Sch., 1940-43; librarian Bartow (Fla.) Sr. High Sch., 1943-45, 48-67, Bartow Pub. Library, 1945-48; cataloger Roux Library, Fla. So. Coll., Lakeland, 1967-70, reference librarian, 1970-75; co-sponsor Polk County Student Library Assn., 1957-59; intern tchr. Fla. State U.; former mem. evaluating team So. Assn. Secondary Schs. and Colls. Recipient Polk County Career Increment award, 1961. Mem. NEA, Beta Phi Mu, Delta Kappa Gamma. Democrat. Baptist. Address: 251 Marilyn Dr Lafayette LA 70503

MOORE, MARJORIE SILCOX, dietitian; b. Mpls., Aug. 27, 1935; d. Walter Bruce and Ruth May (Davis) Silcox; m. Howard Warner Moore, June 29, 1957; children—Michael Howard, Meri Beth. B.S., Iowa State U., 1957. Therapeutic dietitian Luth. Hosp., Balt., 1957-61; pvt. practice as cons. dietitian, Nashville, 1972-75; clin. dietitian Bapt. Hosp., Nashville, 1975-83, chief clin. dietitian, 1983—; mem. adv. bd. Health Promotions and Fitness Ctr., Nashville, 1984—. Advisor, Care Line Social Action Group on Aging, Nashville, 1982—; bd. dirs., pres. Head's Up Child Devel. Ctr., Nashville, 1984—. Mem. Tenn. Dietetic Assn. (Vol. bus. mgr.), Nashville Dist. Dietetic Assn. (chmn. profl. materials). Democrat. Methodist. Avocations: needlework; knitting; music; reading; jogging; weight lifting. Home: 836 Clematis Dr Nashville TN 37205 Office: Baptist Hosp 2000 Church St Nashville TN 38236

MOORE, MARTHA BECK, financial consultant; b. Jackson, Miss.; d. Earl Crafton and Lorraine (Harrington) Beck; B.A., Duke U.; cert. bus. adminstrn., Harvard U.-Radcliffe Coll. Grad. Bus. Sch.; cert. N.Y. Sch. Interior Design; m. Edward S. Moore, III (dec.); children—Diana, John Donelson. Investment research analyst Tri-Continental Corp., also Union Service Funds, N.Y.C.; fin. asso. corp. fin. Smith, Barney & Co., Inc., investment bankers; interior designer Village Residential Design, Lost Tree Village, Fla.; designer, prin. Martha Smith, Inc., Palm Beach, Fla.; now with Citicorp Trust, Palm Beach; vol. restoration worker. Mem. Am. Soc. Interior Designers (asso.), Phi Beta Kappa. Republican. Episcopalian. Office: Royal Palm Way Palm Beach FL 33480

MOORE, MARY CHARLOTTE, banker; b. Washington, Iowa, Nov. 22, 1945; d. F. Burdette and Martha E. (Caldwell) M.; B.B.A. in Acctg., U. Iowa, 1968. From mem. audit staff to audit mgr. Arthur Andersen & Co., C.P.A.s, Chgo. and Milw., 1968-80; dir. acctg. Blue Cross/Blue Shield, Chgo., 1980-81, v.p. fin. ops., 1981-84; v.p., controller Am. Nat. Bank and Trust Co. Chgo., 1984—. C.P.A., Ill., Wis. Mem. Am. Inst. C.P.A.s, Am. Soc. Women C.P.A.s (nat. bd. dirs.), Ill. Soc. C.P.A.s, Chgo. Soc. Women C.P.A.s (dir.), Chgo. Fin. Exchange, Women's Forum. Presbyterian.

MOORE, MARY MELISSA, society administrator; b. Flint, Mich., Feb. 6, 1957; d. Maurice Malcolm and Marian Adelaide (Zierold) M. B.A. in Govt., Wells Coll., 1979; student Georgetown U., 1977-78. Legis. corr. Sen. Hayakawa, Calif., 1979-80, legis. aide, 1980-82; asst. dir. fed. govt. relations ASME, Washington, 1982—, dir. pub. affairs devel., 1984—; cons. in field. Mem. Women in Energy and Environ., Jr. League Washington. Republican. Episcopalian. Avocations: Horseback riding; sailing; snow & water skiing; swimming. Home: 5812 Merton Ct #183 Alexandria VA 22311 Office: Am Soc Mech Engrs Suite 216 1825 K St NW Washington DC 20006

MOORE, MARY TYLER, actress; b. Bklyn., Dec. 29, 1937; d. George and Marjorie Moore; m. Richard Meeker; 1 child, Richard (dec.); m. Grant Tinker, 1963 (div. 1981); m. Robert Levine, 1983. Appeared TV series Richard Diamond, Private Eye, 1957-59, Dick Van Dyke Show, 1961-66, Mary Tyler Moore Show, 1970-77, Mary, 1978, Mary Tyler Moore Hour, 1979, Mary, 1985—; TV movies Love Am. Style, 1969, Run a Crooked Mile, 1970, First You Cry, 1978; numerous other TV appearances; motion pictures include: X-15, 1961, Thoroughly Modern Millie, 1967, Don't Just Stand There, 1968, What's So Bad About Feeling Good?, 1968, Change of Habit, 1969, Ordinary People (Acad. Award nominee for best actress 1981), 1980, Six Weeks, 1982, Just Between Friends, 1986; TV spl. How to Survive the Seventies, 1978; TV films: Heartsounds, 1984, Finnegan Begin Again, 1984; chmn. bd. MTM Enterprises, Inc., Studio City, Calif. Recipient Emmy award Nat. Acad. TV Arts and Scis., 1964, 65, 73, 74, 76; Golden Globe award, 1965, 81; elected to TV Hall of Fame, 1985. Address: care MTM Enterprises 4024 Radford Ave Studio City CA 91604

MOORE, MELISSA LAIRD, public relations executive; b. Watertown, N.Y., Aug. 3, 1939; d. Alton Wilson and Marie Alice (Beardsley) Laird; B.A., Vassar Coll., 1961; m. Theodore Wayne Moore, Oct. 16, 1971. Asst. photo researcher Western Printing Co., N.Y.C., 1961-63; asst. to photo lab. mgr. Saturday Evening Post, N.Y.C., 1963-65; freelance photojournalist, N.Y.C., 1965-68; owner, mgr. Melissa Laird Public Relations, Phoenix, 1970-71; v.p., account supr. Joanne Ralston & Assos., Inc., Phoenix, 1971-81; pres. Moore Public Relations, Inc., Phoenix, 1981—. Lic. real estate agt. Mem. Nat. Assn. Realtors, Central Ariz. Bd. Realtors. Republican. Office: 2024 N 7th St Suite 200 Phoenix AZ 85006

MOORE, MUFFY (MARY FRENCH), potter, county official; b. N.Y.C., Feb. 25, 1938; d. John French and Rhoda Walker Teagle; B.A. cum laude, Colo. U., 1964; m. Alan Baird Minier, Oct. 9, 1982; children—Jonathan Corbet, Jennifer Corbet, Michael Corbet. Potter, Wilson, Wyo., 1969-82, Cheyenne, Wyo., 1982—; commr. County of Teton (Wyo.), 1976-83, chmn., 1981, 83, mem. dept. pub. assistance and social service, 1976-82, mem. recreation bd., 1978-80, water quality adv. bd., 1976—; mem. land quality adv. bd. Dept. Environ. Quality, 1983—. Bd. dirs. Teton Sci. Sch., 1968-82, vice chmn., 1979-81, chmn., 1982; bd. dirs. Jackson Hole Art Assn., vice chmn., 1981, chmn., 1982; bd. dirs. Teton Energy Council, 1978-80; mem. water quality adv. bd. Wyo. Dept. Environ. Quality, 1979-83; Democratic precinct committeewoman, 1978-81, mem. Wyo. Dem. Central Com., 1981-83, platform chmn. state conv., 1982, vice chmn. exec. com. Wyo. Dem. Com., 1985—; vice chmn. Laramie County Dem. Central Com., 1983; mem. Dem. Nat. Com., 1984—, mem. fairness commn., 1985; del. Dem. Nat. Conv., 1984, mem. Gov.'s Steering Com. on Troubled Youth, 1982; legis. aide to gov. Wyo., 1985, 86; project coordinator Gov.'s Com. on Children's Services, 1985. Mem. Nat. Assn. County Ofcls., Jackson Hole Bus. and Profl. Women (Woman of Yr. award 1981), Pi Sigma Alpha. Home and Office: 8907 Cowpoke Rd Cheyenne WY 82009

MOORE, PATRICIA ANN, hospital administrator; b. Moberly, Mo.; d. Jack Harold and Mary Ann (Lynch) M. B.A. in Polit. Sci., U. Mo.-Columbia, 1970;

M.P.A. in Health Services Adminstrn., U. Mo.-Kansas City, 1976. Sec. to Boone County Pros. Atty., Columbia, 1971-73; exec. sec. Citizens Conf. on State Legislatures, Kansas City, Mo., 1973-75; pub. relations counselor Blue Cross & Blue Shield, Kansas City, Mo., 1975, supr., 1977-78; adminstrv. intern Menorah Med. Center and Truman Med. Ctr., Kansas City, Mo., 1976; project analyst Mid-Am. Health Systems Agy., Kansas City, Mo., 1979-80; cons. Southeast Mo. Hosp., Cape Girardeau, 1981-82, adminstrv. asst. for planning and mktg., 1982—. Co-editor: Insights: Trends and Developments in Health Care Delivery, 1975-76. Vol. Am. Cancer Soc., United Way, John Wornall House; precinct worker Republican party, 1978-80; bd. dirs. ARC, Cape Girardeau, 1983-84. Univ. scholar U. Mo.-Columbia, 1966-67; Grad. fellow U. Mo.-Area Health Edn. Center, Kansas City, 1975-76. Mem. Am. Soc. Hosp. Planning, Am. Health Planning Assn., Am. Mktg. Assn., Zonta Internat., Sigma Rho Sigma, Pi Sigma Alpha, Kappa Alpha Theta (pres. alumni assn. 1970-71, mem. chpt. adv. bd. 1970-72). Roman Catholic. Home: 710 E Rodney St Cape Girardeau MO 63701 Office: Southeast Mo Hosp 1701 Lacey St Cape Girardeau MO 63701

MOORE, PATRICIA KAY, market research administrator; b. Peoria, Ill., Jan. 20, 1947; d. David Harold and Mary Jane (Gregoryk) Jenkins; m. James Christopher Moore, Jan. 11, 1980. B.S. in Bus. Adminstrn., U. Mo., 1978, M.B.A., 1981. Planning analyst Emerson Electric Corp., St. Louis, 1972-79; mgr. mktg. adminstrn. Emerson Electric WED, Houston, 1979; dir. mktg. adminstrn. HBE Corp., St. Louis, 1979-82; mgr. market research Emerson Electric ESD, St. Louis, 1982—; instr. U. Mo.; cons. project bus. Recipient Woman Leader award YWCA. Mem. Am. Mktg. Assn., U. Mo. Alumni Assn., Beta Gamma Sigma. Roman Catholic. Home: 3446 Bluff View Dr Saint Charles MO 63303 Office: Emerson Electric ESD 8100 W Florissant St MS 3216 Saint Louis MO 63136

MOORE, PATRICIA SUSAN, hairdresser, make-up artist; b. Toledo, Ohio, June 14, 1957; d. Wilford Henderson and Beatrice Ann (Otting) M. Lic. cosmetologist. Hairdesigner Country Charm Beauty Salon, Swanton, Ohio, 1975; mgr. Tory's Services, Inc., Swanton, 1975-80; owner Patty and Co. Hairdesigners, Swanton, 1980—; owner Jhirmack Lyceum, Redding, Calif., 1979; advisor Penta County Cosmetology Dept. Adv. Com., Penta County Vocat. High Sch., 1979—. Mem. Nat. Hairdresser and Cosmetology Assn. Democrat. Roman Catholic. Office: Patty and Co 137 Airport Hwy Swanton OH 43558

MOORE, PEARL B., nurse; b. Pitts., Aug. 25, 1936; d. Hyman and Ethel (Antis) Friedman; diploma Liliane S. Kaufmann Sch. Nursing, 1956; B.S. in Nursing, U. Pitts., 1968, M. Nursing, 1974; 1 dau., Cheryl. Staff nurse Allegheny Gen. Hosp., Pitts., 1957-60; instr. Liliane S. Kaufman Sch. Nursing, Pitts., 1960-70, asst. dir., 1970, dir., 1970-72; cancer nurse specialist Montefiore Hosp., Pitts., 1974-75; coordinator Brain Tumor Study Group, Pitts., 1975-83; exec. dir. Oncology Nursing Soc., 1983—; adj. asst. prof. U. Pitts., 1983—. Mem. Am. Nurses Assn., Oncology Nurses Soc., Am. Soc. Clin. Onoclogy, Am. Soc. Assn. Execs., Nurses Alumnae U. Pitts., Sigma Theta Tau. Contbr. articles in field to profl. publs. Home: 4221 Winterburn Ave Pittsburgh PA 15207 Office: 3111 Banksville Rd Pittsburgh PA 15216

MOORE, SANDRA, architect, environmental designer, educator, consultant; b. Charleston, S.C., June 30, 1945. B.A. in Architecture, Tuskegee Inst., 1967, M.Environ. Design, Yale U., 1973; Ed.D., Harvard U., 1982. Architect Clauss and Nolan, Architects, Planners, Trenton, N.J., 1968-72; founder, exec. dir. Trenton Design Ctr., 1970-73; asst. prof. Schs. Architecture and Edn., U. Wis.-Milw., 1973-75; dir. ctrs. for environ. edn. Edn. Devel. Ctr., Cambridge, Mass., 1975-76; asst. prof. environ. design Mass. Coll. Art, Boston, 1975-76; assoc. Alexander Cooper & Assocs., N.Y.C., 1976; adminstr. Dept. Housing Preservation and Devel., N.Y.C., 1978-79; asst. prof., asst. dean Fla. A&M U., Tallahassee, 1979-82; assoc. prof., assoc. dean Sch. Architecture, N.J. Inst. Tech., Newark, 1982-83, assoc. prof., 1983—; mem. policy panel Nat. Endowment Arts, Nat. League Cities. Author: Survey on Black Women in Architecture. Recipient citation N.J. Soc. Architects; Nat. Endowment Arts fellow, 1984, 85

MOORE, SHIRLEY THROCKMORTON (MRS. ELMER LEE MOORE), accountant; b. Des Moines, July 3, 1918; d. John Carder and Jessie (Wright) Throckmorton; student Iowa State Tchrs. Coll., summers 1937-38, Madison Coll., 1939-41, M.C.S., Benjamin Franklin U., 1944; m. Elmer Lee Moore, Dec. 19, 1946; children—Fay Moore-Sines, Lynn Dallas Moore Sherman. Asst. bookkeeper Sibley Hosp., Washington, 1941-42, Alvord & Alvord, 1942-46, bookkeeper, 1946-49, chief acct., 1950-64, fin. adv. to sr. partner, 1957-64; dir. Allen Oil Co., 1958-74; pvt. practice acctg., 1964—. Mem. sch. bd. Takoma Acad., Takoma Park, Md., 1970—; bd. dirs. Washington Adventist Hosp., 1971—; mem. Spl. Commn. to Pres., 7th Day Adventists, 1982—. Recipient Disting. Grad. award Benjamin Franklin U., 1961. C.P.A., Md. Mem. Am., D.C. insts. C.P.A.s, Am. Women's Soc. C.P.A.s, Bus. and Profl. Women's Club, Benjamin Franklin U. Alumni Assn. (Disting. Alumni award 1964), DAR, Md. Assn. C.P.A.'s (charter mem. Montgomery Prince George County), Assn. Seventh Day Adventist Women, Assn. Self-supporting Christian Workers. Mem. Seventh Day Adventist Ch. Contbr. articles to profl. jours. Home and Office: 1007 Elm Ave Takoma Park MD 20912

MOORE, SUE, clergywoman; b. Dodge City, Kans., July 14, 1941; d. James William and Mary Louise (Pollock) Pickle; m. Frederick Lewis Moore, May 1, 1966 (div. 1979); children—Polly Marie, Frederick William. B.S., Millikin U., 1978; postgrad. U. Ill., 1978-79; M.Div., Luth. Theol. Sem., 1984. Ordained to ministry Lutheran Ch., 1983. Pastor, St. Mark's Luth. Ch. of Snydersburg, Hampstead, Md., 1982—; resident rural ministry Town and Country Ch. Inst., Gettysburg, Pa., 1983-84; chairperson World Hunger Task Force, Md. Synod, Luth. Ch. Am.; organizer chem. abuse programs Snydersburg area; organizer, chief adminstr. Snydersburg Area Youth Program; organizer dir. Joyful Noise Handbell Chori; organizer, dir., adminstr. Local Mission Food, Clothing and Emergency Assistance Bank of Snydersburg; supr. community service Snydersburg area Carroll County ct. system; Recipient Millikin Dames award, Milliken U., 1978; Simon P. Eckard fellow, Gettysburg Sem. Home: 2812 Snydersburg Rd Hampstead MD 21074 Office: St Mark's Luth Ch of Snydersburg 1616 Capehorn Rd N Hampstead MD 21074

MOORE, SUSAN EVELYN, chemist, biologist; b. Mobile, Ala., July 20, 1954; d. Thurston Theodore and Evelyn (Patty) M. B.S. magna cum laude, Mobile Coll., 1976; postgrad. U. South Ala. Tech. dir. Ala. Lions Eye Bank, Birmingham, 1979-81; chem. cons. Merck & Co., Inc., Birmingham, 1981-84; indsl. chem. specialist Ashland Co., Huntsville, Ala., 1984-85; chemist/electron microscopist U. Ala., Birmingham, 1986—. Mem. choir Shades Mountain Baptist Ch., 1980—. U. South Ala. research grantee, 1977-79. Mem. Nat. Assn. Sports Ofcls. (charter), Nat. Fedn. Interscholastic Ofcls. Assn. (charter), Ala. High Sch. Athletic Assn. (basketball and football cert.), Amateur Softball Assn. (umpire), Nat. Assn. Female Execs. (charter). Republican. Baptist. Avocations: tennis; antique refinishing; softball; basketball. Home: 1219-I Beacon Pkwy E Birmingham AL 35209 Office: Dept Cell Biology U Ala Univ Sta Birmingham AL 35294

MOORE, SUSAN LYNN, county criminal investigation official; b. Freeport, N.Y., Mar. 21, 1949; d. Robert Emmett Moore and Margaret Ann (Moline) Reich; m. Frank Badalucco (div. Dec. 1974); 1 child, Lisa. m. Gary Wayne Sitton, May 22, 1981. A. in Gen. Studies, Pima Community Coll.; postgrad. U. Ariz. Lic. real estate salesperson, Ariz.; commd. peace officer, Ariz. Pvt. investigator, L.I., N.Y., 1969-73; investigator Office of Spl. Investigations, N.Y. Dept. Social Services, Bayshore, 1973-74; sgt. USAF, Davis Monthan AFB, Tucson, Ariz., 1974-77; sr. investigator criminal div., Pima County Atty.'s Office, Tucson, 1977-80, 88-crime program dir. (CrimeStoppers), 1980—; founding mem., dir. CrimeStoppers USA, 1980-82; hon. dir. La Hacienda Foster Care Resource Ctr., Tucson, 1985—. Mem. Republican Women's Club, Tucson, 1984—, U.S. Congressman Kolbe's Women's Issues Com., Tucson, 1985—, Gov. Bruce Babbitt's Crime Commn., Phoenix, 1984; dir. Tucson Community Found., 1985—; founder, chmn. Missing Children's Task Force, Tucson, 1985—. Named to Teaching Individuals Positive Solutions/Protective Strategies Adv. Council Ariz. Supreme Ct., 1985—. Mem. Am. Soc. Indsl. Security (Tucson chpt.), Tucson Met. C. of C. (Outstanding Community Service award 1984, prevention com. 1983—). Club: Soroptimist Internat. of Desert (Tucson). Lodge: Fraternal Order of Police. Avocations: aerobics; free weights; running. Home: 1871 S Skyview Pl Tucson AZ 85748 Office: Pima County Attys Office 110 W Congress Tucson AZ 85701

MOORE, VIRGINIA BRADLEY, librarian, educator; b. Laurens, S.C., May 13, 1932; d. Robert Otis Brown and Queen Esther (Smith) Bradley; m. David Lee Moore, Dec. 27, 1957 (div. 1973). B.S., Winston-Salem State U., 1954; M.L.S., U. Md., 1970. Cert. in library sci. edn. Tchr., John R. Hawkins High Sch., Warrenton, N.C., 1954-55, Happy Plains High Sch., Taylorsville, N.C., 1955-58, Young and Carver elem. schs., Washington, 1958-65; librarian Davis and Minor elem. schs., Washington, 1965-72, Ballou Sr. High Sch., Kramer Jr. High Sch., Washington, 1972-75, 78-80, Anacostia Sr. High Sch., Washington, 1975-77, 80—, class, club sponsor, 1975—; chmn. competency-based curriculum D.C. Pub. Schs., 1978—; speaker, presenter Ch. and Synagogue Library Assn., 1975, 80, 83; dir. ch. library workshops Asbury United Methodist Ch., Washington, 1972-74, 76. Author: (bibliography) The Negro in American History, 1619-1968, 1968; TV script for vacation reading program, 1971, sound/slide presentation D.C. Church Libraries' Bicentennial Celebration, 1976, A School Librarian Visits China, 1985; video script and tchr.'s guide for Nat. Library Week Balloon Launch Day, 1983; also articles, book revs. Rec. sec. Washington Pan-Hellenic Council, 1975; librarian Mt. Carmel Baptist Ch., Washington, 1984; del. People to People Citizen Ambassador Program, Peoples Republic China, 1985. Recipient certs. of award D.C. Pub. Library, 1980, for vol. service in support of pub. edn., 1983; NDEA scholar Central State Coll., Edmond, Okla., 1969, U. Ky., 1969; scholar Ball State U., 1969; grad. fellow U. Md., 1969. Mem. NEA (life), Am. Assn. Sch. Librarians (coms. 1973-85), D.C. Assn. Sch. Librarians (pres. 1971-73, citation 1973, newsletter editor 1971-75, 83, Freedom to Read Found., ALA (councilor-at-large 1983—), Internat. Assn. Sch. Librarians, Internat. Biographical Assn., D.C. Library Assn., Md. Ednl. Media Orgn., Internat. Platform Assn., People to People Internat., LWV, Zeta Phi Beta (v.p. chpt. 1972-74). Democrat. Club: S.E. Neighbors. Home: 2100 Brooks Dr Apt 721 Forestville MD 20747 Office: Anacostia Sr High Sch 16th and R Sts SE Washington DC 20020

MOORE, WANDA KATHERYNE, service assn. personnel exec.; b. Chgo., May 7, 1926; d. William Howard and Mary (Matthew) Williams; cert. in personnel N.Y. U., 19 ; m. Frank Moore, June 6, 1948; children—Ronald, Donald, Jill. Teletype operator N.Y. Telephone Co., N.Y.C., 1947-48; parent educator Moblzn. For Youth, N.Y.C., 1963-64; dir. personnel Planned Parenthood, N.Y.C., 1974—. Bd. dirs. N.E. Comprehensive Health Center, N.Y.C., 1968—, chmn. bd., 1972-79. Recipient Public Service award Nema Health Council, 1978. Mem. Am. Mgmt. Assn., Personnel Mgmt. Office: 380 2d Ave New York NY 10010

MOORE-COLLOM, PATRICIA ANNE, hospital administrator; b. N.Y.C., June 27, 1947; d. Edward J. and Elizabeth M. (Farrell) Kiernan; m. John A. Collom, Mar. 22, 1986. Student Fordham U., NYU, 1984—. Departmental mgr. NYU Med. Ctr., N.Y.C., 1972-76, adminstr., 1984—; spl. asst. to v.p. N.Y.C. Health and Hosp. Corp., 1976-78; asst. to dep. dir. Bellevue Hosp., N.Y.C., 1978-80; asst. to pres. S. Masuda, Inc., N.Y.C., 1980-82; departmental mgr. Beekman Downtown Hosp., N.Y.C., 1982-84. Mem. Nat. Assn. Female Execs., Am. Mgmt. Assn. Democrat. Roman Catholic. Avocations: painting; reading. Office: NYU Med Ctr Affiliation Office 550 1st Ave New York NY 10016

MOORHEAD, ROLANDE ANNETTE REVERDY, artist, educator; b. Périgueux, France, Sept. 24, 1937; d. RémyJean and Andrée Marcelle (Lavollée) Reverdy; liberal arts degree Coll. Technique, Nice, France, 1954; m. Elliott Swift Moorhead, III, Sept. 30, 1960; children—Edward Marc, Roland Elliott, Rémy Bruce. Bi-lingual sec., France, 1957-58, French Embassy, 1959-60, 1968-70; chmn. exhibit com. Lauderdale-By-The-Sea Art Guild, Ft. Lauderdale, Fla., 1972-75, v.p., 1972-74; charter mem. Gold Coast Water Color Soc., Ft. Lauderdale, 1976; mem. exhibit com. Broward Art Guild, Ft. Lauderdale, 1976; treas., dir. Alliance Française, Miami, Fla., 1973-75; one-man shows include: numerous banks Ft. Lauderdale area, 1971—, Ocean Club Art Gallery, Ft. Lauderdale, 1971-74, Pier 66 Gallery, Ft. Lauderdale, 1973, 75, 76, Ft. Lauderdale City Hall, 1974, 77, 78, 81, 82, 83, 84, 85, St. Basil Orthodox Ch., North Miami Beach, 1977, Galerie Vallombreuse, Biarritz, France, 1977, Galerie du Palais des Fêtes, Périgueux, 1978, Le Club Internationale, Ft. Lauderdale, 1979; exhibited in group shows: Broward Art Guild, Ft. Lauderdale, 1971, 73, 74, Point of Am. Gallery, Ft. Lauderdale, 1971, 73, Internat. Festival, Miami, 1976, Internat. Salon, Biarritz, 1977, Internat. Summer Salon, Paris, 1977, Fine Art Gallery Show and Competition, Long Galleries, Ft. Lauderdale, 1979, Pembroke Pines (Fla.) City Hall, 1982, Hollywood (Fla.) City Library, 1982, also area banks, chs. and libraries, numerous local art festivals; represented in permanent collections: Ft. Lauderdale City Hall, DAV Hdqrs., Washington, Associated Aircraft Co., March of Dimes Bldg. (both Ft. Lauderdale), U.S. Air Force Mus., Ohio, Main Line Fleets, Inc., Palm Beach, Fla., Creditre form, Dusseldorf, W.Ger., St. Front Cathedral, Périgueux, St. Sacerdoce Cathedral, Sarlat, France, also numerous pvt. collections, U.S. and Europe. Recipient Best in Show award Internat. Salon, Biarritz, 1977. Mem. Fla. Watercolor Soc., Am. Watercolor Soc., Palm Beach Watercolor Soc., Wo/Man's Showcase (dir. visual arts div. 1982—, chmn. edn. com. 1983), Am. Bus. Women's Assn., Nat. League Am. Penwomen, Lauderdale-By-The Sea Art Guild, Broward Art Guild, Boca Raton Center for Arts, Gold Coast Water Color Soc. (pres. 1984-86), Del Ray Beach Art Guild, Fla. League of Arts, Artists Equity, Everglades Artists, Çercle Français of Ft. Lauderdale, Alliance Française of Dade County, Internat. Platform Assn., Union des Français de l'Etranger. Office: PO Box 8692 Fort Lauderdale FL 33310

MOORHOUSE, LINDA VIRGINIA, symphony orchestra administrator; b. Lancaster, Pa., June 26, 1945; d. William James and Mary Viginia (Wild) Moorhouse. B.A., Pa. State U., 1967. Sec., San Antonio Symphony, Tex., 1970-71, adminstrv. asst., 1971-75, asst. mgr., 1975-76; gen. mgr. Canton Symphony, Ohio, 1977—. Mem. Ohio Arts Council Music Panel, 1980-82. Mem. Met. Orch. Mgrs. Assn. (pres. 1983-85), Orgn. Ohio Orchestras (pres. 1985—), Am. Symphony Orch. League (bd. dirs. 1983-85). Office: Canton Symphony Orch 1001 Market Ave North Canton OH 44720

MOOSBRUGGER, MARY COULTRIP, marketing research consultant; b. Urbana, Ill., Sept. 1, 1947; d. Donald Lyle and Charlotte Carol (Barber) Coultrip; m. John R. Moosbrugger, Apr. 24, 1971; children—Peter John, Kathryn Rose. B.A., U. Ill., 1969; M.B.A., U. Chgo., 1982. Research analyst Leo Burnett Co., Chgo., 1969-71; study dir. Booz Allen & Hamilton, Chgo., 1972-73; research supr. Quaker Oats Co., Chgo., 1974-75; mgr. mktg. research Kitchens of Sara Lee, Deerfield, Ill., 1975-77; pres., owner Moosbrugger Mktg. Research, LaGrange, Ill., 1977—; speaker profl. assn. confs. Mem. Am. Mktg. Assn. Roman Catholic. Home: 934 N Brainard Ave LaGrange Park IL 60525 Office: Moosbrugger Mktg Research 901 W Hillgrove LaGrange IL 60525

MOOSE, SANDRA OHRN, management consultant; b. Boston, Feb. 17, 1942; d. Fritz Andrew and Esther Helen (Bastey) Ohrn; m. Alan James Zakon, Nov. 26, 1972. Student U. Vienna, Austria, 1962; B.A. summa cum laude, Wheaton Coll., 1963; M.A., Harvard U., 1965, Ph.D., 1968. Tutor, Harvard U., Cambridge, Mass., 1964-65; cons. FDIC, Washington, 1966-68; pres. Sandra O. Moose, Inc., Chestnut Hill, Mass., 1981—; v.p., dir. The Boston Cons. Group, Boston, 1968-81, 84—; dir. GTE Corp., Rohm & Haas, New Eng. Life Mut. Funds. Contbr. articles to profl. jours. Trustee, Wheaton Coll., Norton, Mass., 1981—; bd. dirs., treas. Arts Boston, 1976—; corporator Northeast Deaconess Hosp., Boston, 1981— trustee Hampshire Coll., 1976-83. Woodrow Wilson fellow, 1963-64; recipient 100th Anniversary award, Wheaton Coll. Alumnae Assn., 1970. Mem. Am. Econs. Assn., Com. of 200. Club: Union. Home: 53 Beverly Rd Chestnut Hill MA 02167 Office: The Boston Cons Group Exchange Pl Boston MA 02109

MOOSNICK, MARILYN KILGUS, television performer; b. Jeffersonville, Ind., June 3, 1930; d. George Matthew and Golda (Lantz) Kilgus; m. Franklin Bernard Moosnick, Nov. 24, 1957; children—Jeffrey L., Gregory M., Madeline G., Ross A. A.B., U. Ky., 1952. Reporter, Lexington Leader (Ky.), 1952-58, edn. editor, 1955-58; women's program dir., hostess Blue Grass Personalities talk show Sta. WLEX-TV, Lexington, 1965—; pub. relations cons. Lexington Pub. Sch. System, 1958. Pres. Lexington Council Arts, 1976-77, Living Arts and Scis. Ctr., 1977-83; panel mem. Nat. Endowment for Arts, Washington, 1973-75; v.p. Central Ky. Jewish Assn., 1983—; mem. nat. bd. Hadassah, N.Y.C., 1969—, nat. v.p., 1982-83; bd. dirs. Ky. Arts Council, Frankfort, 1975—, Housing for Handicapped, Lexington, 1976—. Recipient City of Peace award Bonds for Israel, 1971; Service award Urban-County Parks and Recreation Div., Lexington, 1977; arts award Lexington Council Arts, 1978; Brotherhood award NCCJ, Lexington, 1980. Mem. Women in Communications, Nat. Soc. Arts and Letters (fund-raising chmn. 1979-81), Alpha Gamma Delta, Chi Delta Phi, Beta Sigma Phi (Outstanding Woman of Yr. 1968). Democrat. Jewish. Home: 755 Brook Hill Dr Lexington KY 40502 Office: WLEX-TV Russell Cave Pike Lexington KY 40505

MORA, JUDITH STEVENS, fin. instns. cons.; b. Oakland, Calif., Dec. 5, 1946; d. Russell Norman and Lorraine C. Stevens; B.A., U. Hawaii, 1969; M.A. in Mgmt., U. Redlands, 1980; m. Gilbert Mora, Feb. 26, 1977. Acting editor ofcl. publ. Navy Civil Engr. Corps. and Seabees, Pearl Harbor, Hawaii, 1967-70; mgr. public relations and advt. Bishop Trust Co. Ltd., Honolulu, 1970-73; mgr. mktg. and promotions Ala Moana Center (Dillingham Corp.), Honolulu, 1973-75; museum cons., Hilo, Hawaii, 1975-76; cons. Edward Carpenter & Assos., Los Angeles, 1976-79; pres. J. Mora & Assocs., Inc., cons. to fin. industry, Garden Grove, Calif., 1979—. Mem. spl. gifts and public relations coms. Am. Cancer Soc., 1973-76. Mem. Women in Communications (past chpt. pres.), Bank Adminstrn. Inst. (assoc.), Am. Heart Assn. Contbr. to Hawaii Ency., 1977. Office: 12459 Lewis St Suite 202 Garden Grove CA 92640

MORADIANS-GOSS, TANYA JOY, clinical social worker; b. Chgo.; B.A., U. Calif., Berkeley, 1958; M.S.W., U. So. Calif., 1971; Ph.D., Inst. Clin. Social Work, 1981. Clin. social worker Olive View Children's Psychiat. Service, Sylmar, Calif., 1974-77, Olive View Psychiat. Emergency Service, 1970-75, Olive View Adult Psychiat. Outpatient Clinic, 1970-81; pvt. practice psychotherapy, Sherman Oaks, Calif., 1971—; asst. clin. prof. Neuropsychiat. Inst., UCLA. Cert. group psychotherapist. Mem. Social Work Treatment Service (dir.; outstanding service award), Acad. Cert. Social Workers, Soc. Clin. Social Work (dir.), Los Angeles Group Psychotherapy Soc. (dir.), Nat. Assn. Social Workers, Am. Group Psychotherapy Assn. Office: 15422 Ventura Blvd Suite 204 Sherman Oaks CA 91403

MORAIN, MARY STONE DEWING, association executive; b. Boston, Mar. 18, 1911; d. Arthur S. and Frances (Hall Rousmaniere) Dewing; student Radcliffe Coll., 1930-33; B.S., Simmons Sch. Social Work, 1934; M.A., U. Chgo., 1937; cert. social work U. So. Calif., 1941; m. Lloyd L. Morain, July 6, 1946. Social worker, Calif., N.Y.C., 1941-45; tchr. social scis. Keuka Coll., N.Y., 1945-46; v.p. LWV, Boston, 1946-53; bd. dirs., v.p. Planned Parenthood League Mass., 1948-52; bd. dirs., pres. Planned Parenthood Assn. San Francisco, 1953-60; bd. dirs. Internat. Humanist and Ethical Union, 1953-65; bd. dirs., v.p. Assn. Vol. Sterilization, 1963-77, 79—, UNESCO Assn. U.S.A., 1977—, Monterey YWCA, 1975-80, UN Assn. San Francisco, 1961-69; pres. Internat. Soc. Gen. Semantics, 1976-86, v.p., 1986—. Fellow World Acad. Art and Sci.; mem. Am. Assn. Social Workers. Club: Altrusa. Author: (with Lloyd Morain) Humanism as the Next Step, 1954; contbr. articles to profl. jours. Editor: Teaching General Semantics, 1969; Classroom Exercises in General Semantics, 1980; Bridging Worlds Through General Semantics—selections from 40 years of Et cetera, 1984, Enriching Professional Skills Through General Semantics, 1986. Home: PO Box 7190 Carmel CA 93921 Office: PO Box 2469 San Francisco CA 94126

MORALES, CATHERINE RYAN, retail company official; b. Bklyn., July 31, 1934; d. Charles Augustus, Sr., and Catherine (Shaughnessy) Ryan; m. Henry Philip Morales, Mar. 21, 1953 (div. Apr. 1968); 1 son, Michael Patrick. Ed. CCNY, 1956, NYU, 1960, Manhattan Community Coll., 1970-71, Pace U., 1984. Notary pub., N.Y. With Citibank and Chem. Corn Exchange, N.Y.C., 1952-55; with personnel dept. J.C. Penney Co., N.Y.C., 1957-64, with adminstrv. services dept., 1964—, office support services mgr., 1982—. Second vice chmn. Community Planning Bd. 3, S.I., N.Y.; dist. leader 54 AD Democratic County Com., S.I., 1983-86; area rep. to staff N.Y. State Assemblywoman Connelly, S.I., 1982-86; chmn. constn. com. South Shore Dem. Club, S.I., 1983, 2d v.p., acting pres., 1986—; treas. Sea View Hosp. and Home Aux., 1986—; mem. Richmond County Econ. Devel. Council; mem. adv. bd. Richmond Meml. Hosp.; legal chmn. Groups, Inc. Mem. Bus. and Profl. Women's Orgn. Richmond County. Roman Catholic. Clubs: Lioness, Democratic Banner. Office: JC Penney Co 1301 Ave of Americas New York NY 10019

MORALES, DIANE KAY, marketing executive; b. Houston, July 11, 1946; d. Arthur Clement and Helen Mary (Araiza) M. B.A., U. Tex.-Austin, 1968. Advt./pub. relations account exec. Goodwin, Donnenbaum, Littman & Wingfield, Houston, 1968-71; mgr. Neiman-Marcus, Dallas, 1971-80; sr. assoc., mgr. mktg. 3D Internat., Houston, 1980-81; commr. Native Hawaiian Study Commn., Washington, 1981-83; dep. asst. sec. for policy, spl. asst. to sec. Dept. Interior, Washington, 1981-83; bd. mem. CAB, Washington, 1983-85; cons. Office of Mgmt. and Budget, Washington, 1985; cons. Consumer Product Safety Commn., Washington, 1985—. Bd. dirs. Dallas Council Republican Women's Clubs, 1980, Dallas County Men's Republican Club, 1980, Houston Inter-Am. C. of C., 1981; pres. Downtown Dallas Women's Republican Club, 1979, 80; mem. fiscal mgmt. task force, govt. relations com. Houston C. of C., 1981. Mem. Republican Women's Fed. Forum, Nat. Fedn. Republican Women, Exec. Women in Govt., Republican Nat. Hispanic Assembly. Presbyterian. Club: Internat. Aviation. Office: Consumer Product Safety Commn 5401 Westbard Ave Bethesda MD 20816

MORALES-GUDMUNDSSON, LOURDES ELENA, Spanish language educator; b. Los Angeles, Apr. 18, 1944; d. Rafael Casimiro and Carmen (Lopez) Morales; m. Reynir Gudmundsson, May 16, 1971; 1 child, Carmen Elena. B.A., Loma Linda U., 1966, M.A., U. de Valencia, 1968; Ph.D., Brown U., 1981. Chmn. modern lang. dept. Atlantic Union Coll., South Lancaster, Mass., 1968-79, dir. English Lang. Inst., 1975-79; chmn. Spanish dept. Antillian Coll., Mayaguez, P.R., 1979-84; asst. prof. Spanish lang. and lit. U. Conn., Stamford, 1984—; pres. El Taller, Inc., Harford, Conn., 1984—. Editor, dir.: El Taller Literario jour., 1986. Herbert A. Kenyon fellow, 1977-78. Mem. Assn. Internat. de Hispanistas, MLA, Alpha Mu Gamma (sponsor 1974-76). Democrat. Seventh-day Adventist. Club: Zonta Internat. (advisor 1983-84). Avocations: piano, guitar, voice, translating, yoga. Home: 3270 Old Town Rd Bridgeport CT 06606 Office: Dept Langs U Conn-Stamford Scofieldtown Rd Stamford CT 06903

MORAN, ANNE MARIE, accountant; b. Vancouver, B.C., Can., June 14, 1958; came to U.S., 1972; d. Michael Joseph and Elizabeth Mary (Roche) Moran. B.S., U. Conn., 1980. C.P.A., Tex. Staff auditor Laventhol & Horwath, Dallas, 1980-82, sr. auditor, 1982-83; ops. acct. Cadillac Fairview Urban Devel. Co., Dallas, 1983—. Mem. Am. Inst. C.P.A.s, Tex. Soc. C.P.A.s (young C.P.A. involvement com. Dallas chpt. 1983—), Delta Sigma Pi. Roman Catholic. Club: Greater Dallas Bicyclists. Home: 6060 Village Bend No 2508 Dallas TX 75206 Office: Cadillac Fairview Urban Devel Co 1910 Pacific Ave Suite 400 Dallas TX 75201

MORAN, DEBORAH LOUISE, manufacturing company executive; b. Chgo., Dec. 29, 1950; d. Theodore Emile and Irma Hattie (Rhyne) M. B.A., Western Coll., Oxford, Ohio, 1972; M.B.A., Washington U., St. Louis, 1974. With IBM, various locations, 1974—, sr. product planner, White Plains, N.Y., 1982-85, mgr. fin. and bus. planning, Bethesda, Md., 1985—. Instr. fin. U. Mo., St. Louis, 1975-76. Consortium for Grad. Study in Mgmt. scholar, 1972. Mem. Exec. MBA Assn., Black MBA Assn., Nat. Assn. Female Execs. Western Coll. Alumni Assn. (trustee 1984—). Methodist. Avocations: travel; tennis. Home: 33 Valerian Ct Rockville MD 20852 Office: IBM Corp 10401 Fernwood Rd Bethesda MD 20817

MORAN, JUDITH LYNN, insurance company executive; b. Orange, N.J., Aug. 31, 1951; d. Daniel P. and Grace E. (Dick) M. B.S. in Edn., Trenton State Coll., 1973; postgrad. Rutgers U., 1981. Cert. tchr., N.J., 1973. Tchr. Hazlet Twp. Pub. Schs. (N.J.), 1973-81; sales rep. Greenville Abstract Inc., West N.Y., N.J., 1981-82; pres., sales rep. Nuco Title Ins. Agy., Kearny, N.J., 1981-83; v.p. sales, Home Title Inc., Bloomfield, N.J., 1983—. Active YMCA (camp com. mem. 1977-81), Red Bank, N.J. Mem. Nat. Assn. Female Execs., Kappa Chi Omega. Democrat. Roman Catholic. Home: 203 Davis Ave Kearny NJ 07032 Office: Home Title Agy Inc 256 Broad St Bloomfield NJ 07003

MORAN, JULIETTE M., chemist, consultant; b. N.Y.C., June 12, 1917; d. James Joseph and Louise Moran; B.S., Columbia U., 1939; M.S., N.Y.U., 1948. Research asst., Columbia, 1941; jr. engr. Signal Corps. Lab. AUS, 1942-43; with GAF Corp. (formerly Gen. Aniline & Film Corp.), N.Y.C., 1943-82, successively jr. chemist process devel. dept., tech. asst. to N.Y. process devel. dept., tech. asst. to dir. Central Research Lab., tech. asst. to dir. comml. devel. 1953-55, supr. tech. service, comml. devel. dept., 1955-59, sr. devel. specialist, 1959-60, mgr. planning, 1961, asst. to pres., 1962-67, v.p., 1967-71, sr. v.p., 1971-74, exec. v.p., 1974-78, vice chmn., 1980-82, cons., 1974-83, also dir.; dir.

GAF Corp. and various subs., 1974-83; dir. Am. Savs. Bank; cons., 1982—. Bd. dirs. N.Y. State Sci. and Tech. Found. Fellow AAAS, Am. Inst. Chemists; mem. Am. Chem. Soc., Comml. Devel. Assn. Home: 10 W 66th St New York NY 10023

MORAN, KATHLEEN ROSE, advertising executive; b. Rochester, N.Y., May 4, 1957; d. Harry Joseph and Mildred Rose (Eberhard) M. B.A., St. Bonaventure U., 1979. Staff reporter Brador Publs. Inc., Rochester, 1975-79; advt. and pub. relations mgr. Honeoye Industries, Inc., Honeoye Falls, N.Y., 1979-80; advt./merchandising mgr. NAP Philips Consumer Electronics Corp., Knoxville, Tenn., 1980-85; advt. mgr. Eastman Kodak Co., Rochester, N.Y., 1985—. Recipient Addy award Knoxville region Am. Advt. Fedn., 1982, award Knoxville Ad Council, 1983, Mktg. Motivation award Nat. Sales Premium Execs., 1983. Mem. Am. Mktg. Assn., Creative Alliance of Communicators, Knoxville Ad Club (award 1983), Sigma Delta Chi. Democrat. Roman Catholic. Home: 1294 Emerson St Rochester NY 14606 Office: Eastman Kodak Co Rochester NY 14650

MORAN, LORI ELLEN, oil company manager; b. Albion, N.Y., Oct. 20, 1955; d. Ralph Joseph Babcock and Barbara Ellen (Lancto) Reynolds; m. John Gordon Moran, Apr. 30, 1983; 1 child, Jonathan MacKenzie. Student Plattsburgh State Coll., N.Y., 1973-74. Cert. applicator Structural Pest Control Bd. Tex. Office mgr. ABC Truck Rental and Leasing, Houston, 1979-80; with dept. accounts payable Forney Oil Co., Houston, 1980-81, accounts payable supr. with dept. accounts receivable, 1981-82, mgr. acctg. dept., 1982—. Mem. Nat. Assn. Female Execs. Democrat. Roman Catholic. Avocations: bicycling; gardening; reading; boating. Home: 11214 Crayford Ct Houston TX 77065 Office: Forney Oil Corp 5599 San Felipe St Suite 1200 Houston TX 77056

MORAN, PATRICIA KIELTY, government official; b. Wilkes-Barre, Pa., Dec. 11, 1927; d. Patrick Francis and Mary Flanagan Kielty; children—Patrick, Francis, Edward, Mary. B.A., Marymount Coll., Tarrytown, N.Y., 1949; M.A., Catholic U. Am., Washington, 1953. Reporter, Broadcasting mag., Washington, 1952-54, feature editor, N.Y.C., 1954-55; spl. projects editor Nat. Assn. Broadcasters, Washington, 1955-57; dir. info. Nat. Assn. Ednl. Broadcasters, Washington, 1966-71; dir. info. and editorial services Council of Better Bus. Burs., Inc., Washington, 1971-73; dir. corp. communications DATRAN, Washington, 1973-76; communications cons., Washington, 1976-80; dir. Office of Pub. Info., GAO, Washington, 1980—. Mem. Nat. Press Club, Nat. Assn. Govt. Communicators, Washington Women's Network, Woman's Nat. Democratic Club. Roman Catholic. Office: US Gen Acctg Office 441 G St NW Washington DC 20548

MORAN, THERESA ANN KUCKUCK, health care executive; b. Phila., June 13, 1945; d. Alan McCollough and Theresa Ann (Healy) Kuckuck; A.S., Gwynedd-Mercy Coll., Gwynedd Valley, Pa., 1965; student Va. Commonwealth U., 1970, Sangamon State U., Springfield, Ill., 1976-78; m. Timothy F. Moran, Jr., June 18, 1966; children—Kerry, Tracey (dec.), Jennifer, Stephanie, Monica, Kristen, Lindsay, Timothy F. III, Patrick. Med. sec., 1965-66; bus. mgr. Moran Eye Center, Springfield, 1972—. Pres. bd. dirs. Care Center, Springfield, 1979-80, outreach dir., 1982-86, mem. fin. com., 1982-86, chmn., 1983, benefit com., 1984-86, chmn., 1984, treas., 1984; regional legis. chmn. Ill. Caucus on Teen-Age Pregnancy, 1984; pres. Springfield Right-to-Life Com., 1976-79, legis. chmn., 1979-81; sec. Springfield Roman Catholic Diocesan Pastoral Council, 1977-78. Mem. Sangamon County Med. Wives Aux. (chmn. mental health com. 1976), Jr. League Springfield (co-chmn. impact com. 1977), Springfield Art Assn. Contbr. articles to profl. jours. Office: 1124 S 6th St Springfield IL 62703

MORANDO, JEANNE BUTLER, savings and loan association executive; b. Crystal River, Fla., Feb. 17, 1928; d. James Taylor and Lucile (Sparkman) Butler; m. Herbert O. Hope, June 12, 1951 (dec. 1958); m. Sil S. Morando, Jan. 13, 1961; children—Marta Lucile Hope Morando, James William Hope Morando. Student St. Helen's Hall Jr. Coll., 1945, U. Oreg. Extension Ctr.-Portland, 1949-50, San Joaquin Delta Coll., 1963-65. Lic. real estate broker, Calif. Asst. buyer Olds & Kings Western Dept. Stores, Inc., Portland, 1948-51; gen. mgr. Hadley's Inc., Stockton, Calif., 1958-61; with World Savs. and Loan Assn., 1972-77, regional mgr., Oakland and Stockton, Calif., 1974-76, mktg. coordinator, Oakland, 1977; v.p., savs. adminstr., mktg. dir. Stockton Savs. & Loan Assn., 1977—. Mem. exec. com., bd. dirs. Jr. Achievement San Joaquin County, 1984—; bd. govs. Stockton Civic Theatre, 1967-69, chmn. pub. relations and publicity, mem. steering com., 1967-69, 71-62, fin. v.p., trustee, 1982—; bd. dirs. San Joaquin County United Way, Calif., 1979—, pres., 1986—; mem. San Joaquin County Crime Awareness and Prevention Com., 1980; trustee Friends of Chamber Music, 1983—. Mem. Savs. Instn. Mktg. Soc. Am. (basic mktg. sch. cert.), San Joaquin County Zool. Soc. (life). Republican. Lutheran. Club: Exec. Women (Stockton). Home: 1202 McClellan Way Stockton CA 95207 Office: 212 N San Joaquin St Stockton CA 95201

MORAN-NELSEN, MARY ELIZABETH, banker; b. Bridgeport, Conn., Oct. 5, 1951; m. Keith Douglas Nelsen, July 31, 1982; 1 dau., Kelly Burr. Student U. New Haven, 1969-72, U. Bridgeport, 1975-79. With Peoples Bank, Bridgeport, Conn., 1970—, asst. treas., 1981-82, asst. v.p., 1982—; ptnr. Sporran Prodns., Shelton, Conn., 1982—; adv. council Fin. Instns. Services Inc. Bd. dirs. YMCA, Bridgeport, 1981-82. Mem. Nat. Assn. Bank Women, Am. Soc. Tng. and Devel., Bank Women, Am. Inst. Banking (dir. pub. relations 1973-77). Democrat. Episcopalian. Home: 184 Isinglass Rd Huntington CT 06484 Office: Peoples Bank 211 State St Bridgeport CT 06602

MORASKY, MARY ANN, mathematics educator; b. Scranton, Pa., May 23, 1950; d. Andrew Paul and Bernetta Gertrude (Bonavoglia) M. B.S. in Astronomy, Villanova U., 1972; M.S. in Math. Edn., Marywood Coll., 1979. Lab. asst. Villanova U. (Pa.), summer 1972; tchr. math. and sci. St. Anthony's Sch., Dunmore, Pa., 1973-76; asst. prof. math. Keystone Jr. Coll., La Plume, Pa., 1979—. Recipient Judges award Pa. Jr. Acad. Sci., Pa. State U., 1982. Mem. Am. Math. Soc., Math. Assn. Am., Nat. Council Tchrs. Math., Planetary Soc. Democrat. Roman Catholic. Office: Keystone Jr Coll College Ave La Plume PA 18440

MORATH, INGE, photographer; b. Graz, Austria, May 27, 1923; d. Edgar Eugen and Mathilde (Wiesler) M.; B.A., U. Berlin; D.F.A. (h.c.), U. Hartford, 1984; m. Arthur Miller, Feb. 1962; 1 dau., Rebecca Augusta. Formerly translator and editor ISB Feature Sect., Salzburg and Vienna, Austria, later editor lit. monthly Der Optmist, Vienna and Austrian editor Heute Mag.; former freelance writer for mags. and Red White Red Radio Network; with Magnum Photos, Paris and N.Y.C., 1952—, mem., 1953—; exhibited photographs one-woman shows: Wuehrle Gallery, Vienna, 1956, Leitz Gallery, N.Y.C., 1958, N.Y. Overseas Press Club, 1959, Chgo. Art Inst., 1964, Oliver Woolcott Meml. Library, Litchfield, Conn., 1969, Art Mus., Andover, Mass., 1971, U. Miami, 1972, U. Mich., 1973, Carlton Gallery, N.Y.C., 1976, Neikrug Galleries, N.Y.C., 1976, 79, Grand Rapids (Mich.) Art Mus., 1979, Mus. Modern Art, Vienna, 1980, Kunsthaus, Zurich, Switzerland, 1980; numerous group shows include: Photokina, Cologne, Ger. and World's Fair, Montreal, Que., Can.; represented in permanent collections: Met. Mus. Art, Boston Mus. Art, Art Inst. Chgo., Bibliothèque Nationale, Paris, Kunsthaus, Zurich, Prague (Czechoslovakia) Art Mus.; photographer for books: Guerre à la Tristesse (Dominique Aubier), 1956, Venice Observed (Mary McCarthy), 1956, (with Yul Brynner) Bring Forth the Children (Yul Brynner), 1960, From Persia to Iran (Edouard Sablier), 1961, Tunisia (Claude Roy, Paul Sebag), 1961, Le Masque (drawings by Saul Steinberg), 1967, In Russia (Arthur Miller), 1969, East West Exercises (Ruth Bluestone Simon), 1973, Boris Pasternak: My Sister Life (O. Carlisle, editor), 1976, In The Country (Arthur Miller), 1977, Chinese Encounters (Arthur Miller), 1979, Images of Vienna (Barbara Frischmuth, Pavel Kohout, Andre Heller, Arthur Miller), 1981, Salesman in Beijing (Arthur Miller), 1984; editor, co-photographer Paris/Magnum, Aperture Inc.; biography: Grosse Photographen unserer Zeit, 1975; contbr. numerous photographs to European, U.S., S. Am., Japanese mags., and to numerous anthologies including Life series on photography and photographic yearbooks; tchr. photography course Cooper Union, 2 years; lectr. at various univs. including U. Miami, U. Mich.; lectr. Smithsonian, 1985. Recipient various citations for shows. Mem. Am. Soc. Mag. Photographers. Home: Tophet Rd Roxbury CT 06783 Office: Magnum Photos 251 Park Ave S New York NY 10010

MOREHEAD, JEANNE BELLEW, advertising and public relations agency owner; b. Des Moines, Mar. 8, 1928; d. Chellis E. and Ethel C. (Cook) Bellew; m. Harry Turner Morehead, Feb. 2, 1952; children—Harry Turner, Julie J. B. Journalism, U. Mo., 1948. Writer, announcer Y&R KSD Radio, St. Louis, 1951-52; on-air talent WTAR, Norfolk, Va., 1952-54; writer promotion dept. ABC TV, Chgo., 1954-56, writer press dept., N.Y.C., 1956-58; writer, talent, promotion WRAL-TV, Raleigh, N.C., 1958-63; owner J. Morehead Advt. and Pub. Relations, Tampa, Fla., 1967—. Named Mem. of the Yr., Am. Women in Radio and TV, 1966-67; Advt. Profl. of Yr., Tampa Advt. Fedn., 1978. Mem. Am. Women in Radio and TV (pres. 1967-68), Tampa Advt. Fedn. (pres. 1975-76), U. Fla. Adv. Council, Fla. Pub. Relations Assn. Republican. Episcopalian. Office: Jeanne Morehead Advt Pub Relations 208 N Armenia Ave Tampa FL 33609

MOREHEAD, LOIS KATHRYN, educator; b. Columbus, Ohio, Jan. 4, 1944; d. Elwood and Kathryn ed. Chico State U.; m. Jon Franklin Morehead, June 28, 1963; chidren—Michael, Michele, Mindy, Matt. Sec., Track & Field News, Los Altos, Calif., 1959-60; sec. Sch. Planning Lab., Stanford U., 1961-62; tchr., Rosedale Elem. Sch., 1965-66, Chico Unified Sch. Dist., 1966-67; tchr. Citrus Sch., Chico, 1967—; Amway Corp. voting mem. Recipient awards for civic activities. Mem. NEA, Chico Unified Tchrs. Assn., Omega Nu. Clubs: Chico Racquet, Sports Medicine. Home: Route 2 Box 141 2200 Oak Park Ave Chico CA 95926 Office: Citrus Sch 1350 Citrus Chico CA 95926

MOREHEAD, PATRICIA STALDER, state legislator; b. Falls City, Nebr., July 21, 1936; d. Leo L. and Luella (Dowell) Stalder; m. Kenneth Edwin Morehead, 1967. Student, MacMurray Coll., Jacksonville, Ill., 1954-55; B.S., U. Nebr., 1958. Mem. Nebr. State Legislature from 30th Dist., 1983—. Mem. arts, tourism and culture resources com. Nat. Conf. State Legislatures; trustee Nebr. Council on Econ. Edn.; mem. statewide adv. council Nebr. Art Assn.; active Gage County Democratic Women. Mem. PEO, Blue Valley Home Economists, Am. Trap Shooting Assn., AAUW, Am. Legion Aux., Daus. of Nile, Eastern Star, Nat. Order Women Legislators, Beatrice Federated Women's Club, Phi Upsilon Omicron, Chi Omega. Office: Nebr State Capitol Bldg Lincoln NE 68509

MORELAND, OLGA BUDOR, public relations and public affairs cons.; b. Hamtramck, Mich., Mar. 19, 1939; d. William Anthony and Maria (Grabowska) B.; B.A. (Ford scholar), U. Mich., 1960, M.A., 1962; postgrad. Rutgers U. Sch. Law; m. Thomas Hawley Moreland, May 1, 1976; 1 son, William Lloyd. With pub. relations dept. Edison Electric Inst., 1962-66, NYU, 1966-68; public relations positions N.Y.C., 1968-78; dir. Citizen Advs. for Justice, Inc., N.Y.C., 1981-85. Adv. com. N.Y.C. Comm. Status of Women; mem. Women in Housing and Fin.; former mem. county exec. com. Democratic Party. Mem. Pi Alpha Kappa. Greek Catholic. Club: Women's City. Author book revs., grants proposals, tng. manuals. Home: 167 E 82d St New York NY 10028

MORELLI, THERESA ROSEMARIE, bibliographical retrieval services company executive; b. Albany, N.Y., Feb. 22, 1944; d. Anthony and Marie (Almendo) M.; ed. Fredonia State Coll., 1962-64, Russell Sage Coll., 1965-66; EDP cert. Cybernetics, 1965. Keypunch operator Research Found., Albany, 1968, programmer trainee, 1968; programmer, 1968, sr. programmer, 1969, asst. dir. data processing, 1970-77; dir. computer services Bibliographic Retrieval Services, Latham, N.Y., 1977-82, contract mgr., 1982-83, mgr. tech. support, 1983-84, software product mgr., 1985—. cons. Active Performing Arts Ctr., Saratoga, N.Y., 1972-82; speaker in field. Mem. Data Processing Mgmt. Assn. (dir., chmn. membership, sec. regional confs.). Roman Catholic. Office: 1200 Route 7 Latham NY 12110

MORENO, SUSAN KAY, financial services manager; b. Fargo, N.D., Aug. 22, 1946; d. Glenn William and Phyllis Elaine (Ellingson) Heaton; m. Carl A. Moreno, May 28, 1976 (div. 1980). Student, N.D. State U., 1964-68. Acct. asst. Bank of Am., San Francisco, 1969-75; credit analyst Central Bank of Colo., Colorado Springs, 1975-77; ops. mgr. Borg-Warner Acceptance, Palatine, Ill., 1978—. Republican. Home: 328 Woodbury Ct Schaumburg IL 60193

MORESKY, LANA, organization executive; b. Youngstown, Ohio, Feb. 23, 1946; d. Edward S. and Rose (Gelfand) Zatell; B.S., Pa. State U., 1967; m. Marc Moresky, July 30, 1967; children—Rachel, Joanna. Mem. NOW, 1970—, pres. Ohio chpt., 1974-75, mem. nat. bd. dirs., 1976-77, pres. Cleve. East chpt., 1980-81, cons., 1981—; mem. Ohio Atty. Gen. ERA Implementation Task Force Sexism in Edn., 1975, Ohio Internat. Women's Year Coordinating Com., 1977; mem. Cuyahoga County steering com. White House Conf. Families, 1979. Mem. platform com., del. Democratic Nat. Conv., 1980; mem. Cuyahoga County Dem. Exec. Com., 1978; chmn. 22d Congl. Dist. Caucus, 1980; bd. dirs. Cleve. chpt. Ams. for Democratic Action, 1982, pres., 1985, nat. bd. dirs., 1984—. Recipient Susan B. Anthony award NOW, 1975; Ohio and local women in bus. advocate award, 1984; named Woman of Yr., Coalition Labor Union Women, 1980; honored by Ohio Women's Hall of Fame, 1983. Jewish. Address: 3918 Washington Blvd Cleveland OH 44118

MORETTI, ARDEN WELLS, freelance writer; b. Orillia, Ont., Can., Jan. 18, 1932, came to U.S., 1973; d. Kenneth McNeill and Audrie (Sinkins) Wells; m. Frank Joseph Moretti, Sept. 10, 1955; children—John, Lauren, Lisa. B.A., U. Western Ont., 1955; postgrad. U. Houston, 1978-82. Freelance writer, Houston, 1978-84: contbr. articles to Ultra Mag., Houston City Mag., Houston Home and Garden mag.; editor, writer Houston Working Woman's Jour., 1980-81; contbr. Houston Downtown, 1978-82; columnist, feature writer Southwestern Argus, 1978-79; editor, writer, layout and photography Univ. Village Assn. News, 1979-83; reviewer Tex. Episc. Churchman, 1984-86; research asst. Mus. Fine Arts, Houston, 1986. Mem. Women in Communications (Matrix award 1982), Golden Key Honor Soc. Home: 2125 Goldsmith St Houston TX 77030

MORETTO, JANE ANN, nurse; b. Belgium, Ill., Apr. 9, 1934; d. Bernard James and Mildred Bertha (Sutton) Moretto; R.N., Mercy Hosp. Sch. Nursing, Urbana, Ill., 1955; B.S. in Nursing, St. Joseph Coll., Emmitsburg, Md., 1969. Relief head nurse, staff nurse Mercy Hosp., Urbana, Ill., 1955-57; staff nurse in psychiatry VA Hosp., Danville, Ill., 1957-59; staff nurse pulmonary disease VA Hosp., Long Beach, Calif., 1959-60, staff nurse surg. unit, Los Angeles, 1960-61, staff nurse operating room, 1961-64; staff nurse USPHS Hosp., Galveston, Tex., 1964-66, staff nurse tumor ICU, Balt., 1967, asst. operating room supr., New Orleans, 1969-71, operating room supr., Brighton, Mass., 1971-78, dep. dir. nursing, dir. inservice edn. Carville, La., 1978-80, dir. nurses Nat. Hansen's Disease Center, 1980—; cons. in field; lectr. in field. Commd. lt. comdr., USPHS, 1969, advanced through grades to capt., 1975—. Recipient Superior Performance award, USPHS Hosp., Galveston, 1966, Outstanding Service medal for exemplary performance of duty Dept. Health Human Services-Pub. Health Service, 1986. Mem. Am. Nurses Assn., La. Nurses Assn., La. Hosp. Assn., La. Soc. Nursing Service Adminstrs., Nat. Assn. for Uniformed Services, Assn. Mil. Surgeons of U.S., Assn. Operating Room Nurses, Alumnae Assn. of Schlarman High Sch., Alumnae Assn. of St. Joseph Coll., Commd. Officers Assn. USPHS. Roman Catholic. Home: 303 Bridgett St Westville IL 61883 Office: Nat Hansen's Disease Center Carville LA 70721

MORGAN, BARBARA JOAN, real estate broker, real estate company owner; b. Mattoon, Ill., July 5, 1940; d. Wendel Lewis and Helen Irene (Adkins) Huddlestun; m. David A. Morgan, Aug. 22, 1958; children—Wendy A., Eric W., D. Gregory. B.S. in Edn., Ea. Ill. U., 1962. Tchr. Lincoln Sch., Mattoon, Ill., 1962-66; real estate broker, Paris, Ill. 1974—; real estate broker, owner Paris Realty, 1978—; real estate tchr. Lakeland Jr. Coll., Mattoon, 1980—. Pres. Paris Newcomers club, 1974-75. Named Paris Woman of Yr., 1985-86. Mem. Ill. Assn. Realtors (inst. grad. 1977, cert. residential specialist 1979), East Central Ill. Bd. Realtors (pres. 1978-79), Bus. and Profl. Women Paris (pres. 1983-84), Paris C. of C. (v.p. 1984-86). Republican. Club: Prairies Edge Toastmaster's (charter mem.). Lodge: Order Eastern Star. Office: Paris Realty 207 N Central St Paris IL 61944

MORGAN, CHARLIE JO, nursing educator; b. Nashville, Ark., May 5, 1938; d. Edmond B. Green and Ernestine (Stuart) Green Williams; m. Willie Charles Morgan, Nov. 14, 1964 (div. June 1976); children—Vanessa Deanne, Shelton Charles. Nursing diploma Glendale Adventist Hosp., 1959; B.S., Andrews U., 1976; M.S., Loma Linda U., 1978; postgrad. Claremont Grad. Sch., 1981—. Staff nurse Meml. Hosp., Phoenix, 1960, Broadway Hosp., Los Angeles, 1960-62; asst. head nurse Los Angeles County Hosp., 1962-65, head nurse, 1965-71; nursing instr. Lake Michigan Coll., Benton Harbor, Mich., 1973-74; asst. prof. nursing Point Loma Coll., San Diego, 1979-81; instr. nursing Loma Linda (Calif.) U., 1977-79, asst. prof., 1981-84; chmn. dept. nursing Oakwood Coll., Huntsville, Ala., 1984—. Mem. sch. bd. Loma Linda Acad., 1982—. Mem. Nat. League Nursing, Assn. 7th Day Adventist Nurses, Sigma Theta Tau. Home: 184 Oldwood Rd Huntsville AL 35811 Office: Oakwood College Huntsville AL 35896

MORGAN, DEBRA (DELLE), newspaper editor; b. Houston, Aug. 5, 1950; d. Arthur Albert and Juanita Amelia (Couvillion) Rosenfelder; m. Cleveland McAlister Morgan, June 16, 1968; children—Kristina, Clayton, Joshua. Student Colo. State U., 1968-70, Aims Coll., 1970-71. Owner, mgr. bookstore, Hot Springs, Ark., 1976-79; mng. editor Ark. Real Estate Exchange, Hot Springs, 1976-79; editor The Grapevine, Waller, Tex., 1980-81; editor Attaway Newspaper Group publs., Waller County News-Citizen, Hempstead, Tex., 1981-82, Spring Times, Conroe, Tex., 1982-83, Daily Courier, Conroe, 1983—, supervising editor Pizzazz mag., Conroe, 1983—, cons. editor Spring Times, 1983—; lectr. in field. Leader Girl Scouts U.S.A., Hempstead, 1981-82; vol. Imperial Miss Beauty and Talent Show, Hempstead, 1981-82; vol. campaign Waller County Republican Women, Hempstead, 1981; mem. community adv. bd. Doctors Hosp., Conroe, 1984—. Recipient newspaper and design awards. Mem. Am. Bus. Women's Assn., Bus. and Profl. Women Assn., Conroe Art League. Methodist. Home: 6103 Crystal Forest Conroe TX 77302 Office: Daily Courier PO Box 609 Conroe TX 77305

MORGAN, DERNA VETRANO, publisher, printer; b. New Britain, Conn.; d. Carmine D. and Marie C. (Giardino) Vetrano; m. Robert S. Morgan, Apr. 15, 1965; children by previous marriage—Dennis M. Shaughnessy, Sheila Shaughnessy Karim, R. Brian Jaymes. Student graphics pub. NYU, 1954-56. With Printing Corp. Am., Bristol, Conn., 1950-54; dir. prodn., assoc. editor Advt. Agy. Mag., mng. editor Am. Printer Lithographer, Moore Pub. Co., N.Y.C., 1954-58; asst. to pres., mgr. directory dept., mng. editor Who's Who in Advt., Haire Pub. Co., N.Y.C., 1960-69, pub. Who's Who in Advt., Rye, N.Y., 1969-79; pres. Redfield Pub. Co., Rye, 1969-79, pres., owner Redfield Realty Assocs., Inc., 1969-79; chairperson, treas. Vt. Printing Co., Brattleboro, Vt. 1970-82; v.p. Marine Trading & Promotion Corp.; cons. graphic arts and pub., 1984—. Bd. dirs. Chester Hill Apt. Corp. Home: 395 Westchester Ave Port Chester NY 10573

MORGAN, EVELYN BUCK, nursing educator; b. Phila., Nov. 3, 1931; d. Kenneth Edward and Evelyn Louise (Rhineberg) Buck; m. John Allen McGeary, Aug. 15, 1958 (div. 1964); children—John Andrew, Jacquelyn Ann McGeary Keplinger; m. Kenneth Dean Morgan, June 26, 1965 (dec. 1975). R.N., Muhlenberg Hosp. Sch. Nursing, 1955; B.S. in Nursing summa cum laude, Ohio State U., 1972, M.S., 1973; Ed.D., Nova. U., 1978. R.N., N.J., Ohio, Fla., Calif.; cert. specialist Am. Nurses Assn. Psychiat.-Mental Health Clin. Specialists; advanced R.N. practitioner Fla. Bd. Nursing. Staff nurse Muhlenburg Hosp., Plainfield, N.J., 1955-57; indsl. nurse Western Electric Co., Columbus, Ohio, 1957-59; supr. Mt. Carmel Hosp., Columbus, 1960-65; instr. Grant Hosp. Sch. Nursing, 1965-72; cons. Ohio Dept. Health, 1972-74; prof. nursing Miami (Fla.)-Dade Community Coll., 1974—; family therapist Hollywood Pavilion Hosp., 1977-82; pvt. practice family therapy, Ft. Lauderdale, Fla., 1982—. Sustaining mem. Democratic Nat. Com., 1975—. Mem. Am. Nurses Assn., Fla. Council Psychiat.-Mental Health Clin. Specialists, Am. Nurses Found., Am. Holistic Nurses Assn., Sigma Theta Tau. Democrat. Roman Catholic.

MORGAN, FLORETTE FORD, talent agency executive; b. Detroit, Apr. 5, 1948; d. Jessie Monk and Leona Maria (Pelichet) Ford; m. Stanley Wilson Morgan, June 1, 1967; children—Stan'Lee Angela, Dion Paulette. Fashion trainee Saks Fifth Ave., San Francisco, 1966-67; hostess, co-producer disco Express TV show, Las Vegas, Nev., 1976-77; hostess, producer Florette With Friends, Honolulu, 1977-78; founder, dir. Ebony Wahine Models, Honolulu, 1978—; hostess Joffrey Ballet, Sta.-KHET pub. TV, Hawaii, 1978; pres., founder Morgan Talent Enterprise, Honolulu, 1979—, also tchr. drama, 1983; casting dir. Murder She Wrote, Universal Pictures, Honolulu, 1985; speaker, lectr. in field; tchr. Charisma Concept, Honolulu, 1981—. Author: How to Break In Modeling, Motion Pictures, and Television, 1985. Active Judy Baley Cancer Aux. Soc., Las Vegas, Nev., 1974—; chairperson NAACP, Honolulu, 1980. Recipient Minority Achiever award Black Bus. and Profl. Women, Honolulu, 1980, Women in Leadership award YWCA, Honolulu, 1981. Mem. Better Bus. Bur. Honolulu, Nat. Assn. Female Execs. Republican. Methodist. Avocations: photography; cooking; collecting handpainted plates and spoons. Home: 250 Kawaihae St Apt 10B Honolulu HI 96825 Office: Morgan Talent Enterprise 1750 Kalakaua Ave 706 Honolulu HI 96826

MORGAN, INGA BORGSTROM, educator, pianist; b. Amarillo, Tex.; d. August and Charlotte (Jonsson) Borgstrom; grad. Amarillo Jr. Coll., 1938; Mus.B., Eastman Sch. Music, 1940, Mus.M., 1944, performer cert., 1942; postgrad. Sommer Akademie, Mozarteum, Salzburg, Austria, 1969, 71; student Friederich Wuhrer, Max Landow, Lilly Larsen, Esther Jonsson, Radie Britain; m. Edwin Phillip Morgan, Aug. 23, 1942; 1 child, Kent August. Mem. faculty, dept. music Coll. Fine Arts, U. Tex., Austin, 1942-43, N. Tex. State U., Denton, 1944-45; prof. music and piano Sch. Music, U. N.C., Greensboro, 1946—; cons.; concert pianist, harpsichordist, lecture-recitalist, accompanist. Mem. Am. Liszt Soc., Coll. Music Soc., Music Tchrs. Nat. Assn., N.C. Music Tchrs. Assn., Greensboro Music Tchrs. Assn., Am.-Scandanavian Found., Vasa Order (officer), Pi Kappa Lambda, (past officer), Mu Phi Epsilon. Presbyterian. Club: Euterpe Music. Home: 1005 Guilford Ave Greensboro NC 27401 Office: 209 Music Bldg U NC Greensboro NC 27412

MORGAN, JANE HALE, library administrator; b. Dines, Wyo., May 11, 1926; d. Arthur Hale and Billie (Wood) Hale; B.A., Howard U., 1947; M.A., U. Denver, 1954; m. Joseph Charles Morgan, Aug. 12, 1955; children—Joseph Hale, Jane Frances, Ann Michele. Mem. staff Detroit Pub. Library, 1954—, exec. asst. dir., 1973-75, dep. dir., 1975-78, dir., 1978—; dir. Met. Affairs Corp.; mem. Mich. Library Consortium Bd., exec. bd. Southeastern Mich. Regional Film Library; mem. Mich. State Library Advisory Council; chmn. adv. council library sci. U. Mich., Wayne State U. Trustee New Detroit, Inc.; v.p. United Found.; pres. Univ.-Cultural Center Assn.; bd. dirs. Rehab. Inst., YWCA, United Community Services Met. Detroit. Recipient Anthony Wayne award Wayne State U., 1981; Detroit Howardite of Yr. award, 1983. Mem. ALA, Mich. Library Assn., Women's Nat. Book Assn., Assn. Municipal Profl. Women, NAACP, LWV, Alpha Kappa Alpha. Democrat. Episcopalian. Club: Women's Econ. Office: Detroit Public Library 5201 Woodward Ave Detroit MI 48202

MORGAN, KAREN ANN (FALCONER), state official; b. Rockford, Ill., Sept. 24, 1948; d. Duane Fay and Vivian Marie (Milani) Falconer. B.S. in Edn., Ill. State U., 1971. Cert. Ill. assessing ofcl. Spl. edn. tchr. Winnebago Co-op, Rockton, Ill., 1971-76; assessor Winnebago Twp., Ill., 1977-85; program coordinator Ill. Growth Enterprises, Rockford, Ill., 1977—. Pub. ofcl. Assessor-Winebago Twp., 1977-85. Mem. Twp. Assessor's Assn. (treas. 1985), Ill. Assessor Assn., Twp. Ofcls. Assn., North Central Assessor Assn., Nat. Assn. Female Execs. Roman Catholic. Club: Forest City Square Dancers. Avocations: square dancing; photography; bird watching; gardening; traveling; bicycling; ceramics; cross country skiing.

MORGAN, KATHY G., sales executive; b. Cin., Nov. 2, 1957; d. Jack Robert and Mae S. (Sams) Morgenroth. B.S. in Econs., No. Ky. U., 1983. Sales rep. Dodge, Datsun, and Chevrolet dealers, Cin., 1979-84; mfg. sales rep. State Chem., Cin., 1984-86; dist. sales mgr. Chevrolet Zone, Cin., 1986—. Advisor Jr. Achievement, 1984-85. Recipient 1st Timers award Ohio Jaycees, 1985. Republican. Methodist. Clubs: Cin. Ski, Hyde Park Methodist (Cin.). Avocations: water skiing; snow skiing; volleyball; softball. Home: 2902 Chalet Dr Apt 703 Cincinnati OH 45217 Office: Chevrolet Zone Office 155 Tri County Pkwy Cincinnati OH 45246

MORGAN, LILA KRESS, public relations executive; b. Chgo., Sept. 6, 1942; d. Ralph and Frances Lucille (Baker) Kress; m. Joseph Morgan, Feb. 16, 1959 (div. 1984); children—Lisa, Michele. Ed., Willis Bus. Coll., UCLA, Royal Acad. Dramatic Arts. Ind. contractor ops. mgmt. various firms in Southwest, 1966-71; legal sec. to numerous attys., Los Angeles, 1971-72; charter tour dir. C & L Services, Culver City, Calif., 1972-84; property traffic mgr., controller, exec. asst., corp. sec. bd. mem. various accounts, 1972-79; ops, and property mgr. various corp. offices and shopping ctrs., 1979-80; co-owner C & L Office Efficiency Services, Burbank, Calif., 1980-83; ops. mgr., mktg. dir. DNB Mfg. Inc., Riffler Services Inc., Jewelart Inc., Corner Arcades Inc., CMS-Robinson Ins. Brokers Inc., 1980-82; mgmt. cons. exec. search Corp. Mgmt. Services Inc., Los Angeles, 1982-84; exec. dir., mgr. Reseda C. of C., Calif., 1983-84; pub. relations cons. Kress-Morgan & Assocs., Culver City, Calif., 1978—; exec. dir. Greater Rancho Par C. of C., 1985—; newspaper columnist Rancho-Cheviot

Hills News; mag. writer Golden Chef. Author: The Disfranchised Students of California, 1971. Editor: The Reseda Business Review, 1983-84; The Reseda Round-Up, 1984—. Contbr. articles on dance to profl. publs. Mem. Culver City Guidance Clinic, 1973—, Culver City Friends of the Library, 1980—, Culver City Sister City Com., 1982—, Culver City Foster Children's Assn., 1982—, Culver City Hist. Soc., 1982—, Los Angeles County Commn. for Women, 1983—, Reseda Community Adult Sch. Adv. Com., 1983—; mem. 12th dist. council Calif. Citizen's Adv. Com., Los Angeles, 1983—; mem. adv. bd. Reseda Sr. Citizens Multi-Purpose Ctr., 1983—; mem. Culver City Landlord/Tenant Mediation Bd., 1981; mem. adv. com. West Valley Council Sr. Concerns, Reseda, 1984—; mem. Mayor Bradley's Edn. Adv. Com., Los Angeles, 1984—; mem. exec. bd. Calif. Rep. Party, 1978-82; pres. North San Fernando Valley unit Calif. Rep. Assembly; orgn. chmn. Rep. Party Los Angeles County, 1981-82; Mem. Nat Assn. Women Bus. Owners, Women in Mgmt., Nat. Fedn. Bus. and Profl. Women (1st v.p., legis. chmn. 1983—, pub. relations chmn. Los Angeles Sunset dist.), Am. Arbitration Assn., Nat. Notary Assn., Calif. Women's Savs. and Loan Assn., Calif. Women's Bus. Owners Assn., Calif. Assn. C. of C. Execs., Los Angeles World Affairs Council. Republican. Presbyterian. Clubs: Manuscripters' (speakers chmn. 1971-73), Venice Boys and Girls, Marina Republican, Sunset Republican, Fox Hills Rep. Federated Women's (precinct chmn. 1980-84). Address: 6210 Reseda Blvd Apt 206 Reseda CA 91335

MORGAN, LUCY WARE, newspaper reporter; b. Memphis, Oct. 11, 1940; d. Thomas Allin and Lucile (Sanders) Keen; m. Alton F. Ware, June 26, 1958 (div. 1967); children—Mary Kathleen, Andrew Allin; m. Richard Alan Morgan, Aug. 9, 1968; children—Lynn Elwell, Kent Morgan. A.A., Pasco Hernando Community Coll., 1975; student U. South Fla., 1975-80. Reporter, Ocala Star Banner, Fla., 1965-68, St. Petersburg Times, Fla., 1967—. Recipient Paul Hansel award Fla. Soc. Newspaper Editors, 1981, Pub. Service award Fla. Press Club, 1982, Pub. Service award Fla. Soc. Newspaper Editors, 1982, Pulitzer prize Columbia U., 1985, runner-up Pulitzer prize Columbia U., 1982. Republican. Presbyterian. Office: Saint Petersburg Times 490 First Ave S Saint Petersburg FL 33732

MORGAN, LYNN KASNER, library administrator, medical educator; b. N.Y.C., Oct. 13, 1950; s. Edward Paul and Michaela (Lipton) Kasner; m. Nicky N. Morgan, June 25, 1978. B.A., SUNY-Binghamton, 1972; M.L.S., SUNY-Albany, 1972. Coordinator N.Y. and N.J. Regional Med. Library, N.Y.C., 1976-78, dir., 1978-80; assoc. librarian N.Y. Acad. Medicine, N.Y.C., 1981-83; adj. lectr. Queens coll., N.Y.C., 1984—; Columbia U., Sch. Library Service, N.Y.C., 1985 ; dir. Levy Library Mt. Sinai Sch. Medicine, N.Y.C., 1983—, instr. med. edn., 1983—; trustee Med. Library Ctr. of N.Y., N.Y.C., 1985—, N.Y. Met. Reference and Research Library Agy., N.Y.C., 1985—; cons. N.Y. State Nurses Assn., Albany, 1978-79, SUNY-Albany, Sch. Library and Info. Service, 1975, Mt. Sinai Sch. Continuing Edn. in Nursing, N.Y.C., 1976-77. Editor: N.Y. and N.J. Regional Med. Library News, 1976-80; asst. editor Jour. N.Y. State Nurses Assn., 1975-76. Contbr. articles to profl. jours. Nat. Library of Medicine grantee, 1980. Mem. AAAS, ALA, Med. Library Assn. (cert.), Biomed. Communications Network (bd. dirs. 1983—), Assn. Coll. and Research Libraries, Beta Phi Mu. Home: 20 Marquette Rd Upper Montclair NJ 07043 Office: Levy Library Mount Sinai Med Ctr 1 Gustave L Levy Pl New York NY 10029

MORGAN, M. JANE, computer software consultant; b. Washington, July 21, 1945; d. Edmond John and Roberta (Livingstone) Dolphin; student U. Md., 1963-66, Montgomery Coll., 1966-70, SUNY, 1978-81; 1 dau., Sheena Anne. With HUD, Washington, 1965-84, computer specialist, 1978-84; pres., chief exec. officer Systems and Mgmt. Assocs., 1983—; dir. systems engring. Advanced Technology Systems, Inc., Vienna, Va., 1984—. Mem. Fed. Automatic Data Processing Users Group, Am. Mgmt. Assns. Episcopalian. Club: Order Eastern Star. Office: care Advanced Tech Systems Inc 8027 Leesburg Pike Vienna VA 22180

MORGAN, MARITZA LESKOVAR, painter; b. Zagreb, Yugoslavia, Nov. 20, 1920; came to U.S., 1929, naturalized, 1930; d. Josef and Paula Mihailovic (Yunkovic) Leskovar; M.A., Cornell U., 1944; m. Norman Charles Morgan, May 10, 1941, children—Vincent, Penelope, Jonathan, Christopher, Catherine. Music editor Chautauguan Dailey, Chautaugua, N.Y., 1969—; one woman shows: Central Cathedral, N.Y.C., 1982, Downtown Cathedral, Rochester, N.Y., 1982, Bryn Mawr (Pa.) Presbyn. Ch., 1982, 86, Univ. Christian Ch., Austin, Tex., 1986; represented in permanent collections Hurlbut Ch., Chautaugua, All Souls Unitarian Ch., Tulsa, Downtown Presbyn. Ch., Rochester, Presbyn. Ch., Warren, Pa., St. Joseph Ch., Erie, Pa.; executed mural Mellon Cathedral, Pitts. Transl.: The Cunning Little Vixen (Rudolf Tesnohildek), 1984. Home: 10 Forest Ave Chautaugua NY 14722

MORGAN, MARY ELISE, nurse; b. Middletown, N.Y., Oct. 1, 1935; d. Edward B. and Mary Elizabeth M.; diploma in nursing, White Plains (N.Y.) Hosp., 1956; A.A., Peralta Jr. Coll., Oakland, Calif., 1968; B.S. in Nursing, U. Calif., San Francisco, 1975, M.S. in Nursing, 1978. Staff nurse hosps. in Calif., 1959-69; evening supr., relief nurse San Leandro (Calif.) Hosp., 1969; evening charge nurse Herrick Hosp., Berkeley, Calif., 1969-75; in-service educator Brookside Hosp., San Pablo, Calif., 1975-77; dir. in-service edn. Oakland (Calif.) Hosp., 1977-79; dir. operating rm. services Presbyn. Hosp., Albuquerque, 1979-82; v.p. nursing service Meth. Hosp., Sacramento, 1982-85, USAF, 1985-86. Mem. Assn. Operating Rm. Nurses (nat. sec. 1966-69), Nat. League Nursing, Am. Nurses Assn., Am. Mgmt. Assn., Nat. Soc. Nursing Service Adminstrs., Calif. Soc. Nursing Service Adminstrs., Calif. Nurses Assn. (sec. nursing council 1973-75), N.Mex. Nurses Assn., Sigma Theta Tau. Roman Catholic. Contbr. articles to profl. jours. Address: 9809 Alta Mesa Rd Wilton CA 95693

MORGAN, MELIANE WELLS, mathematics educator; b. Madisonville, Tex., Aug. 21, 1956; d. Harold Gene and Patricia Sue (Wren) Wells. B.S., Tex. A&M U., 1978; M.Ed., U. Houston, 1984. Math. tchr. Madisonville Ind. Sch. Dist. (Tex.), 1978-79; math. tchr. Spring Branch Ind. Sch. Dist., Houston, 1979-86, chmn. dept., 1981-86; ednl. specialist Tex. Edn. Agy., Austin, 1986—; tchr., coordinator Computer Galleries, 1983; tchr. U. Houston-Park 10, 1984-85. Author curriculum materials. Chmn. Madisonville chpt. Am. Heart Assn., 1978; sponsor Pioneer Girls, Spring Branch Community Ch., 1980-81. PTA scholar U. Houston, 1982, 83; NSF grantee, 1980; named Tchr. of Yr., Landrum Jr. High Faculty, 1984, Spring Branch Tchr. of Year, 1984, Tex. Tchr. of Yr., 1985; a finalist for Nat. Tchr. of Yr., 1985. Mem. Tex. Computer Edn. Assn., NEA, Tex. State Tchrs. Assn., Spring Branch Edn. Assn., Nat. Council Tchrs. Math., Tex. Council Tchrs. Math., Spring Branch Council Tchrs. Math. (past sec., v.p., pres., Pres.'s award 1983), Delta Kappa Gamma, Beta Sigma Phi (past sec., v.p.). Democrat. Baptist. Home: 804A Rutherford Pl Austin TX 78704 Office: Tex Edn Agy 1701 N Congress Ave Austin TX 78701

MORGAN, NANCY, communications company executive; b. Covington, Ky., Sept. 7, 1952; d. John Henry and Maria Therese (Grimm) Van Wickler; m. Donal William Morgan, Feb. 14, 1980. Central office technician Contel of Ill., DeKalb, 1978-79; service ctr. dispatcher Contel of Calif., Victorville, 1979-81, service ctr. supr., 1981-83, quality circle facilitator, 1983—, computer ctr. specialist, 1983-85, service ctr. supr., trainer 911 sch. program presentations, distributive computerized records info. systems trouble coordinator, 1985—. Solicitor, Contel Polit. Action Com., Victorville and Barstow, 1981-83; blood donor solicitor San Bernardino County Blood Bank, 1984-85. Mem. Nat. Assn. for Female Execs. Office: Contel of Calif 15168 La Paz Dr Victorville CA 92392

MORGAN, REBECCA, state legislator. Mem. Calif. Senate dist. 11, 1985—. Republican. Office: Calif State Senate State Capitol Sacramento CA 95814*

MORGAN, RUTH ANN, publishing computers company executive; b. Chgo., June 4, 1958; d. Jimmy Louis and Esther Nancy (Sorensen) Sorensen; m. Bradford Rex Morgan, Aug. 11, 1979. Student Dana Coll., 1976-77, U. No. Iowa, 1977-79. With Deer Valley Dude Ranch, Nathrop, Colo., 1978, Am. Entertainment Prodns., Columbus, Ohio, 1979; typesetter, designer K&J Typographers, Streamwood, Ill., 1980-81; applications engr. Atex, Chgo., 1982-84; cons. Morgan & Assocs., Roselle, Ill. and King of Prussia, Pa., 1984—. Vol., Spl. Olympics, Phila., 1986. Nebr. Bd. Regents scholar, 1976. Mem. Nat. Assn. Female Execs., Multiple Computer Bull. Bds. Republican. Club: Medinah Country (Ill.). Avocation: jazz dance. Office: Suite A-803 Morgan & Assocs 251 DeKalb Pike King of Prussia PA 19406

MORGAN, RUTH MILDRED, medical technologist; b. Indpls., Mar. 8, 1917; d. James Franklin and Lula Floy (Heiny) M.; B.S. in Allied Health Edn., Ind. U.-Purdue U., Indpls., 1976; student Ind. U., 1954-57, 76-77, Butler U., 1958. Dental asst., med. asst. and med. technologist, Indpls., 1953—; tchr. hematology Med. Lab., 1970-79, supr. hematology, 1960-79, gen. supr., 1980—. Fin. chmn. 8th precinct 20th Ward of Indpls., 1977-79. Recipient citation Mayor Richard Lugar, 1976; registered med. technologist, lic. health facility adminstr. Mem. Am. Soc. Clin. Pathologists (affiliate), Am. Soc. Profl. and Exec. Women, Marion County Council Republican Women, Nat. Fedn. Republican Women, Am. Coll. Health Care Adminstrs. (assoc. Ind. chpt.), Brown County Art Gallery Assn., Ind. Soc. Med. Technologists. Club: Eastern Star (matron 1950). Inventor, patentee cabinets for indsl. use. Home: 3965 N Meridian Suite 6-D Indianapolis IN 46208 Office: 8801 N Meridian St Indianapolis IN 46250

MORGAN, SARA POSEY, business educator; b. Andrews, N.C., May 11, 1915; d. Garland Temple and Willabelle (Sandlin) Posey; m. Frank McConaughy Morgan (dec. Jan. 1981); 1 son, George William. B.S., Asheville Coll. (N.C.), 1942; M.S., U. Tenn., 1944; postgrad. U. N.C., 1945; J.D., Cumberland Sch. Law, 1969. Bar: Ala. 1969. Asst. cashier Citizens Bank & Trust Co., Murphy, N.C., 1935-41; tchr. Chapel Hill High Sch. (N.C.), 1942-43; teaching fellow U. Tenn., Knoxville, 1943-44; coordinator distbg. edn. Asheville Schs., 1945-46; prof. bus. U. Montevallo (Ala.), 1943-44, 48-80, asst. to pres., 1977-80, prof. emeritus, 1980—; dir. corp. bd. John C. Campbell Folk Sch., Brasstown, N.C., 1983. Case Inst. Tech. grantee, 1956; Fulbright scholar, 1974. Mem. Ala. State Bar Assn., ABA, AAUW (pres. Andrews chpt. 1982-84), Archibald D. Murphy DAR (treas. Cherokee County 1982-84), Delta Kappa Gamma, Phi Chi Theta, Omicron Delta Kappa, Democrat. Methodist. Home: PO Box 102 Corner 3d and Oak Sts Andrews NC 28901

MORGAN, SHERLI JO, religious educator; b. Guymon, Okla., Mar. 13, 1953; d. James Leslie and Zola Loyce (Fike) M.; student Panhandle State U., 1971, Amarillo Coll., 1972; B.S., Southwestern Assemblies of God Coll., 1977; M.B.A., Belmont Coll., 1979. Dir. computer data J.C. Penney Co., Dallas, 1975-77; dir. pub. relations Your Place Inc., Nashville, 1978-79; asst. dir. artists relations and sales IBC Records Inc., Nashville, 1979-80; dir. music and Christian edn. First Assembly of God Ch., Lakewood, Calif., 1980—; pvt. instr. voice and piano. Pres., Young Republicans, 1972, 73; vol., Rep. campaigns, 1980. Mem. Country Music Assn., Gospel Music Assn., Female Execs. Club, Ch. Music Dirs. Assn., Women So. Calif. Coll. Mem. Assembly of God. Club: Hope of our Heritage. Office: First Assembly of God Ch 6022 E Candlewood St Lakewood CA 90713

MORGAN, SUSAN MELINDA, computer programmer, retail salesperson; b. Parisburg, Va., May 11, 1957; d. Fred Allen and Druscilla (Roseman) M. Student U. N.C.; A.S. in Acctg., Cleveland Tech. Coll., Shelby, N.C., 1978, A.S. in Bus. Adminstrn., 1978; B.S. in Bus. Adminstrn., Gardner Webb Coll., Boiling Springs, N.C., 1980. Computer-aided engring. programmer Lockwood Greene, Spartanburg, S.C., 1980 ; sales clk. Waccamaw Pottery, Spartanburg, 1984—. Mem. Nat. Assn. Female Execs. Republican. Lutheran. Home: 801 N Vernon St Spartanburg SC 29303 Office: Lockwood Greene Engrs 700 I-26 Spartanburg SC 29304

MORGAN, THERESA BEASLEY, nurse; b. Pontotoc, Miss., Sept. 17, 1925; d. William C. and Mary V. (Lyon) Beasley; children—Mary Wise, Marguerite Chapman, John D. Morgan, Sherrie Farley, Barbara Halberg. B.S., Calif. Bapt. Coll., 1972; student Miss. State Coll. for Women, 1943-44, George Peabody Coll., 1948; R.N., Bapt. Meml. Hosp. Sch. Nursing, Memphis, 1947. Cert. nurse practitioner. Staff nurse Riverside Community Hosp., Calif., 1955-57; head nurse Riverside Gen. Hosp., 1957-59; dir. student health service Calif. Bapt. Coll., 1961-76; dir. nurses Beverly Enterprises, Riverside, 1976-79; adult nurse practitioner Parkview Indsl. Sports Clinic, Riverside, 1979-84; R.N. charge nurse Warner Brown Hosp., El Dorado, Ark., 1984—. Charter mem. Presdl. Task Force, 1984; sustaining mem. Republican Nat. Com., 1984-86; tchr. Bible study East Main Bapt. Ch., El Dorado, 1985—, dir. women's missionary union, 1985—. Recipient awards Easter Seal Soc., Am. Heart Assn., Am. Lung Assn. Mem. Ark. Nurses Assn., Diploma Nurses Ark., Nat. Assn. Female Execs. Club: Altrusa. Avocations: reading; golf; civic work. Home: 921 N Madison St El Dorado AR 71730

MORGAN, VALDA JUNE, educator; b. Houston, Apr. 17, 1931; d. Clarence Henry and Ola Dell (Smith) Sowells; m. Jack C. Morgan, Nov. 27, 1954; 1 child, Jack Clarence. B.A. in Music, Prairie View U., 1954, M.Ed., Tex. So. U., 1964. Tchr., Atlanta Ind. Sch. Dist., Tex., 1954-55, Bay City Ind. Sch. Dist., Tex., 1958-59; band tchr. Hearne Ind. Sch. Dist., Tex., 1960-61; tchr. Houston Ind. Sch. Dist., 1961 ; supr. student tchrs. U. Houston, 1972-76; coordinator Fail-Safe, Houston Ind. Sch. Dist., 1981-85; coordinator chpt. I, 8th Ave. Elem. Sch., Houston, 1980. Sec., West MacGregory Protective Assn., Houston, 1983-84, Wesley Chapel A.M.E. Ch. Choir, 1982-84. Recipient Service award Houston Ind. Sch. Dist., 1981; Tchr. of the Year, Holden Elem. Sch., 1985. Mem. NEA, Tex. Tchrs. Assn., Houston Area Tchrs. Assn., Assn. for Bilingual Edn. Democrat. Methodist. Avocation: bowling. Address: 3902 Charleston St Houston TX 77021

MORGAN, VIKKI D., clothing manufacturer, retailer; b. Ft. Thomas, Ky., Jan. 30, 1957; d. Harvey Williams and Janetta May (Bay) M.; m. David Allan Eagle, Oct. 10, 1980 (div. 1983). B.S. in Animal Sci., U. Mo., Columbia, 1979. Retail sales staff Cari's, Columbia, 1978-79; retail mgr. Action Fashions, Columbia, 1979-80; owner, designer You Gotta Be Kidding!, Columbia, 1980—; comedy writer Group W Cable, Columbia, 1983-85; lectr. schs. and churches, Columbia, 1982—; cons., writer. Writer TV situation comedy Shafted, 1983; writer, performer, Quarry, 1983-85. Mem. Central Columbia Assn., Columbia C. of C., North Village Assn. Baptist. Club: Columbia Athletic. Avocations: reading; sports; sculpture; travel; cooking. Home: 309 N William St Columbia MO 65201 Office: You Gotta Be Kidding! 1025 E Walnut St Columbia MO 65201

MORGAN (FERRY), CHRISTINE ADELE, pharmaceutical company researcher; b. Los Angeles, Dec. 8, 1952; d. Thomas Henry and Evelyn (Schmidt) M.; B.A., La Verne Coll., 1974, M.A. in Edn., 1976; m. Michael Corbett Ferry, June 28, 1981; children—James, Sara (twins). Tchr., Corona-Norco Sch. Dist., Corona, Calif., 1974-76; mktg. rep. Dun. & Bradstreet, Santa Ana, Calif., 1976-77; pharm. rep. Sandoz Pharms., East Hanover, N.J., 1977-78; hosp. research assoc. Miles Pharms., La Verne, Calif., 1978—, sales trainer, 1981—. Zonta Club scholar, 1970-71; La Verne Coll. scholar, 1970-71. Mem. Ins. Women of Inland Empire, Los Angeles County Pharm. Reps. Assn. Democrat.

MORGAN-ALSTON, VALERIE ETHEL, lawyer; b. San Francisco, June 4, 1951; d. Harvey Franklin and Dorothy Marie (Baynard) Morgan; m. Clifton Joseph Alston, July 28, 1984. B.A. in Biology and Psychology, Wellesley Coll., 1973; M.S. in Nursing, Pace U./N.Y. Med. Coll., 1976; M.S. in Parent-Child Nursing, U. Colo.-Denver, 1978; J.D., Georgetown U., 1983. Bar: Colo. 1983; lic. nurse, Colo., D.C. Staff nurse Denver Children's Hosp., 1976-77, Med. Personnel Pool, Denver, 1977-78; head nurse NICU, Rose Med. Ctr., Denver, 1978-79, asst. dir. nursing, 1979-80; staff nurse NICU, Kimberly Nurses, Washington and Colo., 1980-83; dep. dist. atty. Denver Dist. Attys. Office, 1983—; perinatal health care cons. Colo. Dept. Health, 1979-80; guest lectr. March of Dimes, U. Colo. Sch. Nursing, Am. Lung Assn. Recipient DAR Citizenship award, 1969. Mem. Colo. Nurses Assn., Nat. Dist. Attys. Assn., Colo. Perinatal Care Council (rep. 1979-80), Black Law Student Assn., Equal Justice Found., ABA, Sigma Theta Tau. Democrat. Episcopalian. Office: Denver Dist Atty 924 W Colfax Ave Denver CO 80204

MORGAN-PARSONS, JULIE ANN, investment management company executive; b. Inglewood, Calif., Feb. 22, 1960; d. Lester Morgan and Audrey Mae (Slusher) Morgan; m. Bob Parsons Jr., May 19, 1979; 1 child, Ashley Rae. Cert. in cosmetology Lompoc Beauty Acad., 1978 Haircutter, mgr. Supercuts, Walnut Creek, Calif., 1978-79, gen. mgr., dist. mgr., San Rafael, Calif., 1979-83; gen. ptnr. A Cup Sur, Salem, Oreg., 1981—; gen. ptnr. Progressive Investments, Dublin, Calif. and Chgo., 1983—; pres. Morgan-Parsons, Inc., Lafayette, Calif., 1984—; gen. ptnr. Abaws Investors, Fort Lauderdale, Fla., 1985—. Democrat. Baptist. Avocations: water skiing; horseback riding; traveling. Home: 855 N Oaks Tulare CA 93274

MORGANTHALER, MARY ELIZABETH, foundation executive; b. Ravenna, Mich., Dec. 3, 1906; d. Ferdinand Ambrose and Bessie Lynn (Hudson) Portzline; m. Otis Philip Morganthaler, Jan. 28, 1948 (dec. Dec. 1975); 1 child, Philip David. R.N., Presbyterian Hosp. Sch. Nursing, Chgo., 1930; B.S., U. Chgo., 1932; M.A., Columbia U., 1933; postgrad. U. Mich., 1939. Supt. nurses Methodist Hosp., Indpls., 1934-36; spl. nurse Dr. Henshaw, dean of dental sch., Indpls., 1936-38; pub. health nurse State Bd. Health, Carroll, Iowa, 1939-41; pres. O. P. Morganthaler Found., Inc., 1964—; dir. Open Door Sch. for Retarded and Handicapped, New Port Richey, Fla., 1977—. Avocations: bridge; bowling; reading. Home: 611 River Dr New Port Richey FL 33552 Office: Open Door Sch 330 E Vermont St New Port Richey FL 33552

MORGENTHAU, JOAN ELIZABETH, physician; b. N.Y.C., Oct. 9, 1923; d. Henry and Elinor M.; A.B., Vassar Coll., 1945; M.D., Columbia U., 1949; m. Fred Hirschhorn, Jr., Oct. 6, 1957; children—Elizabeth, Joan, Elinor. Intern, Maimonides Hosp., Bklyn., 1949-50; resident N.Y. Hosp., 1950-54; instr., then asst. prof. pediatrics Cornell U. Med. Sch., 1954-67; dir. adolescent health center Mt. Sinai Hosp., N.Y.C., 1968-81, prof. clin. pediatrics, 1975-81; assoc. dean Mt. Sinai Sch. Medicine, 1976-81; professional lectr. pediatrics and community medicine, 1982—; dir. health service Smith Coll., Northampton, Mass., 1981—, adj. prof. psychology, 1981—. Trustee, Henry J. Kaiser Family Found., Vassar Coll. Mem. Am. Acad. Pediatrics, Am. Public Health Assn., Soc. Adolescent Medicine, Ambulatory Pediatrics Assn. Club: Cosmopolitan (N.Y.C.). Contbr. articles to profl. jours. Home: 55 Binney Ln Old Greenwich CT 06870 Office: 69 Paradise Rd Northampton MA 01060

MORIARTY, JUDITH KAY SPRY, county official; b. Fairfield, Mo., Feb. 2, 1942; d. Earl Price and Blanche May (McDavitt) Spry; m. David Charles Moriarty, Oct. 21, 1961; children—Derek David, Michael Price, Timothy John. Student Central Mo. State U., 1959-61, State Fair Community Coll.; tng. cert. Elections and County Clks. Assn., Mo., 1985. Motor Vehicle agt. Sedalia Motor Vehicle Registration, Mo., 1977-81; county clk. Pettis County, Sedalia, 1982—. Vice regent Daus. Isabella, Sedalia, 1985-86; del. Mo. Democratic Conv., 1980, 84; active Women's Dem. Club Pettis County, Sacred Heart Catholic Ch.; bd. dirs. Salvation Army, Sedalia, 1978—, Am. Cancer Soc., Sedalia, 1982—, Sedalia Area Council for Arts, 1980-84. Named Outstanding Young Woman Sedalia, Sedalia Jaycees, 1959. Mem. LWV, Bus. and Profl. Women (legis. chmn. 1984-86), Sedalia Area C. of C. (v.p., bd. dirs. 1982-85), Women's Aglow. Avocations: reading; physical fitness; walking; pen and ink sketching; baking. Home: 3015 S Ohio Sedalia MO 65301 Office: Office Pettis County Clk 415 S Ohio Sedalia MO 65301

MORING, BARBARA JANE, business educator; b. San Gabriel, Calif., Feb. 17, 1952; d. Jack Leroy Moring and Vivian Olivia (Gardner) Pennington. B.A., Whittier Coll., 1974; M.B.A., U. LaVerne, 1983. Cert. secondary tchr., Calif. Tchr. bus. Baldwin Park Unified Sch. Dist., Calif., 1976—, curriculum writer, 1976, 80, 82. Mem. Calif. Bus. Edn. Assn., Nat. Assn. Female Execs. Republican. Avocations: antique collecting; cats. Home: 1645 Aspen Village Way West Covina CA 91791 Office: Baldwin Park Unified Sch Dist 3699 N Holly Baldwin Park CA 91706

MORIOKA, MIA SUSAN, sales representative, electrical engineering consultant; b. Orange, Calif., Apr. 1, 1962; d. F.K. and M. Morioka. B.S.E.E., U. Calif.-Irvine, 1984. Tech. sales rep. Control Data Corp., Irvine, 1984—; elec. engring. cons., 1985—. Recipient Critic's Circle award Nat. Piano Guild, 1976. Mem. IEEE, Nat. Assn. Female Execs., U. Calif.-Irvine Alumni Assn., Delta Delta Delta. Avocations: piano, skiing, tennis.

MORISSEAU, DOLORES SCHANNÉ, psychologist, govt. agy. ofcl.; b. N.Y.C., Dec. 1, 1936; d. Lawrence Charles and Anne Lucy (Jelincic) Schanné; B.A. summa cum laude, George Mason U., 1978, M.A. in Psychology, 1980; M. Kenneth Clay Morisseau, May 3, 1958; children—Anne Lavita, Kenneth Clay. Stewardship editor Luth. Woman's Quarterly, St. Louis, 1969-75; mng. editor patient newsletter Georgetown U. Center for Continuing Health Edn., Washington, 1975, faculty moderator, 1974-75; instr. activated patient skills Nat. Public Broadcasting, 1975; fed. intern, personnel psychologist, U.S. Office Personnel Mgmt., Washington, 1979; lectr. psychology No. Va. Community Coll,. Loudoun, 1981—; tng. and assessment specialist U.S. Nuclear Regulatory Commn., Washington, 1981—. Mem. Fairfax (Va.) Hosp., Aux., 1969-78, coordinator library service for patients, publicity dir., 1974-76. Mem. Am. Psychol. Assn., Human Factors Soc., AAUW, Alpha Chi, Psi Chi. Contbr. articles in field to profl. jours. Home: 11800 Breton Ct 32B Reston VA 22091

MORK, LAURA LUNDE, utility engineer; b. Seattle, Dec. 5, 1956; d. Marvin Conrad and Mary Anna (Dowman) Lunde; m. Loren Leslie Mork, Dec. 23, 1980. B.S. in Chem. Engring., U. Wash., 1980. Engring. intern EPA, Seattle, 1977-78; fuel engr. Bethlehem Steel Corp., Seattle, 1980-85; control engr. Seattle Steel Corp., Seattle, 1985, utility engr. Lederle Labs., Pearl River, N.Y., 1985—. Precinct committeeman. Republican Party, Seattle, 1980, mem. com. Assn. of Wash. Bus., Olympia, 1983-85. Mem. Assn. Iron and Steel Engrs., Am. Inst. Chem. Engrs., Soc. Women Engrs., Instrument Soc. Am., Nat. Assn. Female Execs.

MORLEY, RUTH, costume designer. Designer costumes for films including: The Miracle Worker (Oscar nomination), Annie Hall, Kramer vs. Kramer, Superman, One from the Heart, I Ought to Be in Pictures, Hammett, The Chosen, Tootsie; designer costumes for Broadway prodns.: Deathtrap, It's So Nice to be Civilized, A Thousand Clowns, Inherit the Wind, Moon for the Misbegotten, Twice Around the Park and others; designed prodns. for TV including: The Gardner's Son (Emmy nomination), Playing for Time. Address: 17 W 71st St New York NY 10023*

MORNINGSTAR, CARY PRICKETT, human resources manager; b. Greenville, S.C., July 26, 1943; d. Joseph and Lucille (McAdams) Prickett; m. Gary A. Morningstar, Nov. 15, 1985. A.A., North Greenville Jr. Coll., 1963; B.A. in Sociology, Carson-Newman Coll., 1965; M. Ed., Clemson U., 1972; post grad. Furman U., 1965-69. Tchr. Greenville County Pub. Schs., 1965-70; health careers cons. Appalachian Health Council, Greenville, 1970-72, child devel. coordinator, 1971-74; employer-supported child-care specialist, Appalachian Regional Commn., Washington, 1974—; mem. Fed. Interagy. Subcom. Early Childhood Edn. Mem. Nat. Assn. Female Execs. Address: 1002 Wilkins Ct Martinsburg WV 25401

MORO-BISHOP, DIANA LYNN, editor; b. Passaic, N.J., July 2, 1961; d. Remo J. and Aurelia (Macherone) Moro; m. Ronald C. Bishop III, Aug. 2, 1986. B.S. in Pub. Communications, Syracuse U., 1982. Mng. editor Del. County Times, Delhi, N.Y., 1982-83; arts and entertainment editor Paterson News, N.J., 1983-84; sr. desk editor Lebhar-Friedman, N.Y.C., 1984-85; mng. editor Ridgewood News, N.J., 1985—. Trustee Syracuse U. Met. N.Y. Alumni Club, 1985—. Recipient Lifesavers award Several Sources Found., 1986. Mem. ABA, Nat. Assn. Female Execs. Democrat. Episcopalian.

MOROZE, LINDA GALVANI, insurance company executive; b. Stockton, Calif., Sept. 24, 1955; d. Benjamin Robert and Isabel Constance (Lopez) Galvani; m. Chester Moroze, Feb. 2, 1985. B.A. cum laude, U. Pacific, 1977; postgrad. Columbia U. Law Sch., 1986—. Broker's asst. Stockton Ins. Exchange, 1978-80; program coordinator I, West Ins. Mgrs., Stockton, 1980-81; corp. ins./employee benefits mgr. Am. Savs., Stockton, 1981-84; asst. risk mgr. Fin. Corp. Am., Los Angeles, 1984; asst. to risk mgr. N.Y. Times, 1984-85. Contbr. articles to profl. jours. Mem. Risk and Ins. Mgmt. Soc., Ins. Women of San Joaquin County (rec. sec. 1978, bull. chmn. 1980). Democrat. Buddhist.

MORPHEW, DOROTHY RICHARDS-BASSETT, artist; b. Cambridge, Mass., Aug. 4, 1918; d. George and Evangeline Booth (Richards) Richards; grad. Boston Art Inst., 1949; children—Jon Eric, Marc Alan, Dana Kimball. Draftsman, United Shoe Machinery Co., 1937-42; blueprinter, advt. artist A.C. Lawrence Leather Co., Peabody, Mass., 1949-51; propr. Studio Shop and Studio Potters, Beverly, Mass., 1951-53; tchr. ceramics and art, Kingston, N.H., 1953—; two-man exhbn. Topsfield (Mass.) Library, 1960; owner, operator Ceramic Shop, West Stewartstown, N.H. Served with USNR, 1942-44. Recipient Profl. award New Eng. Ceramic Show, 1975; also numerous certificates in ceramics. Home: 608 Harbor Dr Venice FL 33595 Studio: Intervale Rd York Cliffs ME 03910

MORPHOS, DIANE BELOGIANIS (MRS. PANOS PAUL MORPHOS), civic worker; b. Chgo.; d. Demetrios and Alice (Rousseas) Belogianis; B.S., U. Chgo., 1937, M.A., 1938; m. Panos Paul Morphos, Dec. 11, 1948; children—Evangeline, Paul. Mem. faculty U. Chgo. Orthogenic Sch., 1938-45, U. Chgo.

Remedial Reading Clinics, 1945-48; vis. lectr. Tulane U., 1947. Bd. dirs. S.E. La. council Girl Scouts U.S.A., New Orleans, 1959-65, v.p., 1965-68, pres., 1968—; bd. dirs. AAUW, New Orleans, 1969, v.p., 1970-75, pres., 1975-80; Republican candidate for La. 2d Congl. Dist., 1974. Mem. Athenee Louisianais, France-Amerique. Mem. Greek Orthodox Ch. Home: 1404 Audubon St New Orleans LA 70118

MORRAN, MICHELLE, linguist; b. Paris, Dec. 30, 1933; d. Raymond and Yvette Perrotte; B.E.P.C., Baccalaureat, Staatliche Hochschule fur Musik, Munich, 1956; M.A., Stanford U., 1971; children—Stevan, Ivan-Pierre. Tchr. French, Coe Coll., Iowa, 1962, Monterey Inst. Fgn. Studies, Calif., 1963; sr. lectr. French, Stanford U., Calif., 1969—, coordinator French lang. program, 1983-84. Organist, dir. choir Our Lady of Mt. Carmel Ch., Redwood City, Calif., 1979—. Mem. Am. Guild Organists, Am. Assn. Tchrs. French, AAUP, Pi Delta Phi. Roman Catholic. Club: Stanford Faculty. Composer Motets, Missa Brevis, 1976, musical setting for mass; co-author APPEL. 1983. Home: 55 Belden Dr Los Altos CA 94022 Office: Dept French 287B Stanford U Stanford CA 94305

MORRILL, JOYCE MARIE, social worker, consultant; b. Rockland, Maine, Dec. 27, 1939; d. Henry Higgins and Julia Ellen (Philbrook) Thompson; B.A., U. Hartford, 1964; M.S.W., Hunter Coll., 1972; m. Edward Morrill, Sept. 7, 1972; 1 son, Gregory Hodgman. Co-host Today in Conn. Program, Sta. WHNB-TV, Hartford, 1964-65; clin. social worker, field instr. Rehab. Inst., N.Y., 1972-78; dir., founder Wellness Services, Jamaica Estates, N.Y., 1979—. Mem. Nat. Assn. Social Workers, Am. Women's Econ. Devel. Corp., N.Y. Bus. Group on Health. Home and Office: 181-38 Midland Pkwy Jamaica Estates NY 11432

MORRIN, VIRGINIA WHITE, retired educator; b. Escondido, Calif., May 16, 1913; d. Harry Parmalee and Ethel Norine (Nutting) Rising; B.S., Oreg. State Coll., 1952; M.Ed., Oreg. State U., 1957; m. Raymond Bennett White, 1933 (dec. 1953); children—Katherine Ann, Marjorie Virginia, William Raymond; m. Laurence Morrin, 1959 (dec. 1972). Social caseworker Los Angeles County, Los Angeles, 1934-40, 61-64; acctg. clk. War Dept., Ft. MacArthur, Calif., 1940-42; prin. clk. USAAF, Las Vegas, Nev., 1942-44; high sch. tchr., North Bend-Coos Bay, Oreg., 1952-56, Mojave, Calif., 1957-60; instr. Antelope Valley Coll., Lancaster, Calif., 1961-73; ret., 1974. Treas., Humane Soc. Antelope Valley, Inc., 1968—. Mem. Nat. Aero. Assn., Oreg. State U. Alumni Assn. (life). Office: PO Box 570 Lancaster CA 93539

MORRIS, BETTY JEAN, product designer, manufacturing company executive; b. Denver, Sept. 15, 1940; d. Ernest and Rose Elma (Prentice) Nassimbene; m. Charles Wilbert Morris, Aug. 24, 1962; children—Gregory Todd, Kendal Sue, Brenda Kay. Secretarial Degree, Colo. State U., 1960. Profl. ventriloquist, Denver, 1959-70; exec. sec. Stanley Aviation, Denver, 1960-62; owner pres. Playwise, Inc., Hartland, Wis., 1983—, K & B Innovations, Inc., Brookfield, Wis., 1971—. Author: Voodle Vision, 1984. Co-originator Shrinky Dinks, mfr., designer Belt Organizer, Beltzee, 1985. Vol., Young Life, Hartland, 1982—. Republican. Methodist. Clubs: North Lake Yacht (commodore 1984-85), Jr. Sailing (coordinator 1983-85). Home: W325 N7240 Clearwater Ct Hartland WI 53029 Office: K & B Innovations Inc 17258 W North Ave PO Box 66 Brookfield WI 53005

MORRIS, CARMEN ANN-MORINE, communications specialist; b. Kingston, Jamaica, Nov. 4, 1958; came to U.S., 1969; d. Victor Morris and Gloria Hamilton. A.A., Miami Dade Community Coll., 1977; B.A., Howard U., 1980; M.B.A., Barry U., 1981. News prodn. asst. Sta. WDVM-TV, Washington, 1978-80; mgr. trainee Storer Communication, Miami, Fla., 1980-81, community service dir., 1982-83; spl. project coordinator Southwestern Cable TV, San Diego, 1983-84; exec. dir. South Fla. Black Media Coalition, 1984—; pres. MEI Communications, Inc., 1984—; adj. lectr. Yates Sr. High Sch., Houston, 1982-83. Creator: (video prodn. series) Elem. Sch. Program, 1982-83, (documentary) George I. Sanchez Sch. Writer, producer, dir.: (video prodn.) Legacy, 1983. Founding mem., officer A.M.E. Prison Ministry Polit. Prisoners, Howard U., Washington, 1979; researcher Nat. Black Media Coalition, Washington, 1979; pub. relations chmn. Dawkins campaign, Miami, 1981; bd. dirs. Dade County Com. Status of Women, Miami, 1980-81, media relations Gulf Coast United Way, Houston, 1982; mem. Southwestern Bowling Team, San Diego, 1984. Recipient Cert. Appreciation Dade County Police Benevolent Assn., Miami, 1981, Outstanding Service award Houston Ind. Sch. Dist., 1983. Women in Communications scholar, 1978-79. Mem. Gulf Coast Assn. Minorities in Communication (founder, pres. 1982-83), Women in Communications, Nat. Assn. Black Journalists, Nat. Assn. TV, Houston Arts & Scis., Am. Women Radio & TV, Women in Cable (founder, pres. 1982-84, Outstanding Service award 1983), Houston C. of C. (dir. 1982-83), Howard U. Alumni Assn. (founder Miami chpt., pres. 1980-81). Office: MEI Communications Inc 3220 NW 169 Terr Carol City FL 33059

MORRIS, CAROLINE JANE MCMASTERS STEWART (MRS. FRANCIS J. MORRIS), librarian; b. Ridley Park, Pa., Sept. 14, 1923; d. James Sterrett and Mildred M. (McCloskey) Stewart; B.S. in Commerce, Drexel U., 1950, M.S. in L.S., 1964; m. Francis Joseph Morris, Feb. 3, 1951; 1 son, Edward James Stewart. Adminstrv. trainee John Wanamaker, Phila., 1946-50; serials librarian Penn Morton Colls., Chester, Pa., 1964-65; dir. libraries and archives Pa. Hosp., Phila., 1965—; cons., 1970—; instr., leader several library workshops Am. Hosp. Assn., Cath. Hosp. Assn., Med. Library Assn. Mem. Emergency Aid Pa., 1960—. Served with WAVES, 1943-45. Mem. Nat. Med. Library Assn. (sect. chmn. 1970 pres. local chpt. 1978—), ALA, Spl. Libraries Assn., Med. (local chpt. pres. 1969-70), Prospect Park library assns., AAUP, D. of R. (pres. Pa. 1947—), Victorian Soc. Am., Soc. Am. Archivists, Manuscript Soc., Delaware County Hist. Soc., Historic Delaware County, AAUW, Soc. Preservation Landmarks, Hist. Soc. Pa., Oral Hist. Soc., Geneol. Soc. Pa., Hort. Soc. Pa., Dames Loyal Legion (state pres. 1966-68), Phila. Mus. Art, Am. Assn. Records Mgrs., Am. Soc. Profl. and Exec. Women, Drexel U. Alumni Assn. (pres. 1969-71). Club: Art Alliance (Phila). Home: 555 13th Ave Prospect Park PA 19076 Office: 8th and Spruce Sts Philadelphia PA 19107

MORRIS, CAROLYN WILLIS, clergywoman; b. Atlanta, Feb. 23, 1931; d. Lewis Warner and Georgette (Covington) Willis; m. William E. Morris, Apr. 16, 1949; children—Beverly Morris Jones, Jeffrey, Clay. B.A. summa cum laude, Mercer U., 1976; M.Div., Candler Sch. Theology, Emory U., 1979. Ordained to ministry Methodist Ch., as deacon, 1974, as elder, 1980. Minister, Ebenezer United Meth. Ch., Alpharetta, Ga., 1973-77, Hinton Meml. United Meth. Ch., Dacula, Ga., 1977-80, Oconee St. United Meth. Ch., Athens, Ga., 1980-82, Trinity United Meth. Ch., Atlanta, 1982—. Bd. dirs. Wesley Found, U. Ga., Ga. State U.; Mem. status and role of women com. Meth. Ch., 1976-80, superintendency com., 1976-80, Episcopacy com., 1980-84, global ministries, 1980-85, dist. coordinator missions, 1982-84, Bd. Ordained Ministry, 1980—, dist. chairperson Council on Ministries, 1984—, dist. com. ministry, 1980—, alternate del. Gen. Conf., 1984, del. S.E. Jurisdictional Conf., 1984; dean Sch. of Christian Mission, 1983-85; chairperson People of Faith for ERA, Athens, Ga., 1981-82; bd. dir. Atlanta Recovery Ctr., 1982—, YWCO, Athens, 1980-82, Capitol Area Ministries, 1982—, Atlanta Urban Ministries, 1982—; mem. Atlanta Civilian Police Rev. Bd., 1984—; mem. adv. bd. Athens Gen. Hosp., 1980-82. Recipient John Owen Smith Preaching award 1979; named Woman of Yr., Pilot Club, 1981; named Outstanding Student in Religion, Mercer U., 1974. Avocations: gourmet cooking, reading, gardening, travel. Home: 3401 Casa Woods Ln Clarkston GA 30021 Office: Trinty United Methodist Ch 265 Washington St Atlanta GA 30303

MORRIS, DARLENE DOROTHY, kennel owner, dog breeder; b. Portland, Oreg., May 7, 1943; d. Raymond Jacob and Dorothy Elizabeth (Zollner) Decker; m. James Patrick Morris, Feb. 12, 1966. B.A. in Elem. Edn., Mt. Angel Coll., 1966; M.S. in Polit. Sci., Portland State U., 1970; postgrad., 1970-74. Cert. tchr., Oreg. Tchr. Redland Sch. Dist., Oregon City, Oreg., 1966-73; owner, restaurant mgr. Wicker Basket, Portland, 1974-75; sales rep. Brodie-Dohrman Hotel Supply, Portland, 1975-84; owner, German Shepherd breeder Archer's Kennels, Sherwood, Oreg., 1984—. Mem. German Shepherd Dog Club Am., Am. Boarding Kennel Assn., United Schutzhund Club Am., Columbia Working Dogs Assn., Nat. Fed. Ind. Bus. People, Oreg. Dressage Soc. (treas. 1972-78), U.S. Dressage Fedn.

MORRIS, DEBRA LYNN, city official; b. East Chicago, Ind., Aug. 6, 1961; d. Edward Lewis and Thelma (Comer) M. B.S., Ind. U., 1983, postgrad., Ind. U.-Gary, 1985—. Audio visual coordinator Public Sch. System East Chicago, Ind., 1978-79, tchr., 1979-83, substitute tchr., 1980-84; downtown mgr. Mcpl. Govt. East Chicago, 1984—. Editor, author: The East Chicago Mcht., 1986—, Ind. Harbor Newsletter, 1984—. Bd. dirs. Robertson Child Devel. Ctrs., East Chicago, 1985, ALSE Clemente Ctr., East Chicago, 1985. Hoosier scholar, 1979. Mem. Am. Soc. Public Adminstrs., Downtown Improvement Corp. (bd. dirs. 1986), Retail Adv. Bd. (bd. dirs. 1984—), Indiana Harbor Mchts. (bd. dirs. 1984—), Nat. Assn. Female Execs., East Chicago Mchts. (bd. dirs. 1984—), Alpha Kappa Alpha. Democrat. Baptist. Avocations: writing; fashion designing. Home: 645 Taft Pl Gary IN 46404 Office: City of East Chicago Bus Devel Dept 4525 Indianapolis Blvd East Chicago IN 46312

MORRIS, EDNA BROKAW, civic worker; b. N.Y.C., Nov. 13, 1908; d. Howard Crosby and Edna (Loew) Brokaw; m. John A. Morris, May 27, 1942; children—John A., Alfred H. Vice pres. Girl Scout Council Greater N.Y., 1970—, chmn. Gold Book com. and mem. exec. com., pres. Council Mus. of City of N.Y. Mem. Huguenot Soc., Colonial Dames Am. Republican. Episcopalian. Club: Colony. Home: 4 E 72d St New York NY 10021

MORRIS, ELIZABETH TREAT, physical therapist; b. Hartford, Conn., Feb. 20, 1936; d. Charles Wells and Marion Louise (Case) Treat; B.S. in Phys. Therapy, U. Conn., 1960; m. David Breck Morris, July 10, 1961 (div.); children—Russell Charles, Jeffrey David. Phys. therapist Crippled Children's Clinic No. Va., Arlington, 1960-62, Shriners Hosp. Crippled Children, Salt Lake City, 1967-69, Holy Cross Hosp., Salt Lake City, 1970-74; pvt. practice phys. therapy, Salt Lake City, 1975—. Mem. Am. Phys. Therapy Assn., Friendship Force Utah, Salt Lake Area C. of C., AAUW, U.S. Figure Skating Assn. Home: 4177 Mathews Way Salt Lake City UT 84124 Office: 2178 South 900 East Suite 3 Salt Lake City UT 84106

MORRIS, EMMA WARD, marketing director; b. Lafayette, Ind., Sept. 6, 1952; d. Curtis Howard and Charlotte Berkley (Reed) Ward; m. John Harry Morris, Jr., Sept. 12, 1975. Student Sorbonne, Paris, 1972-73; B.A. cum laude, Emory U., 1974; M.B.A., U. S.C., 1976. Tchr. math. and French, Ashley Hall Sch., Charleston, S.C., 1975-76; systems engr. IBM Corp. Columbia, S.C., 1976-79, mktg. rep., Charleston, 1979-81; v.p. mktg. Cambar Bus. Systems, Charleston, S.C., 1981-83; mgmt. cons. Ernst & Whinney, Atlanta, 1983-85; dir. industry mktg. Mgmt. Sci. Am., Inc., Atlanta, 1985—; co-owner, pres. Computer Catch Up, Charleston, 1982-83. Mem. adv. bd. Charleston County Vocat. Edn., 1981-83; mem. adv. bd. MIS, U. Ga., 1983—. Named Young Career Woman of Yr., Bus. and Profl. Women Charleston, 1981. Mem. Assn. Systems Mgrs., Assn. Small Computer Users (com. chmn.), Bus. and Profl. Women (pres. 1982-83), Atlanta C. of C., Nat. Assn. Elec. Distbrs. (chmn. nat. EDP fair com. 1982-83). Republican. Baptist. Home: 3791 Ridge Rd Smyrna GA 30080 Office: 3445 Peachtree Rd NE Atlanta GA 30326

MORRIS, GLORY HUCKINS, artist; b. Texarkana, Ark., Aug. 15; d. Joseph and Olive (Mills) Huckins; div. Student Smith Coll. Grad. Sch. Architecture, 1936-39, also Ecole des Beaux Arts, Fontainebleau, France, Art Students League, N.Y.C., Mus. Fine Arts Sch., Houston. One woman shows English Speaking Union, Houston, 1967, fine arts dept. Houston Pub. Library, 1970, Gallery Am. Art, Shreveport, 1971, River Oaks Garden Forum, Houston, 1976, Fidelity Bank, Oklahoma City, 1979, Town House, Houston, 1984, Palmer Fine Arts, Houston 1985; exhibited in group shows museums fine arts Dallas and Houston, Okla. Art Ctr., Okla. Mus. Art, Jr. League Gallery, Oklahoma City, McNey Mus., San Antonio; represented in permanent collections Okla. Art Ctr., Smith Coll. Recipient Ellen Goins Art award Children's Lit. Assn., Houston, 1982. Mem. Am. Watercolor Soc. (assoc.), Watercolor Art Soc., Tex. Watercolor Soc. Republican. Episcopalian. Home: 2241 Welch Ave Houston TX 77019

MORRIS, HELEN KNOX, oil company executive; b. Healdton, Okla., Apr. 2, 1918; d. Dewey Merle and Alta Belle (Barnett) Knox; m. Albert Earl Morris, Jr., July 2, 1939 (dec. July 1968). Student So. Methodist U., 1935-38. Draftsman Rollins & Forrest, Dallas, 1942, Core Labs., Dallas, 1943; geologist's asst. W. F. Krause, Graham, Tex., 1948-49; ptnr. Doc y Cia SRL, Asuncion, Paraguay, 1949-55, A. E. Morris Oil, Graham, Tex., 1960-74, 75; ptnr., operator D. M. Knox Oil Co., Weatherford, Tex., 1978—. Precinct sec., del. county conv. Republican party, Fort Worth, 1980, 84. Mem. Ind. Petroleum Assn. Am. Presbyterian. Clubs: Pan Am. Round Table I of Ft. Worth (custodian 1979-80, corr. sec. 1980-82, dir. 1981-83); Ninety-Nines, Inc. (sec. 1963-65, treas. 1965-67, v.p. 1967-68). Avocations: translating Spanish histories to English; needlework; painting. Home: 8504 Choctaw Trail Fort Worth TX 76116 Office: D M Knox Oil Co PO Box 625 Weatherford TX 76086

MORRIS, JANE EMELIA, research consultant; b. Texarkana, Tex., Oct. 5, 1950; d. S. J. and Mabel (Martin) Morris. B.F.A., U. Tex., 1973; M.S., E. Tex. State U., 1974; Ph.D., So. Meth. U., 1982. Curriculum, career dir. Cameron U., Lawton, Okla., 1975-76; asst. city adminstr. and grant coordinator, City of New Boston (Tex.), 1976-77; exec. dir. Northeast La. E.M.S. Found., Monroe, 1978-80; dir. Dallas Research Assocs., 1980—; cons. N. Tex. Commn., Dallas, 1983—. Author: Foundations, Funds and Trusts in Dallas, 1983; Major Women in Christian History, 1981; Employment Outlook for Careers Requiring a College Degree, 1976; author lecture series: Ten Weeks to a More Successful You, 1982. Exec. sec. Corinthian House, Dallas, 1982, 83; bd. dirs. Kids Club of Dallas, 1982, 83. Women's Studies Council So. Meth. U. grantee, 1981; Hillcrest Found. grantee, 1982; Robert W. Johnson Found. grantee, 1983. Mem. Gov.'s Commn. on Status of Women Com., State Regents Com. on Women and Higher Edn. Mem. Dallas Area Women's Polit. Caucus. Republican. Methodist. Club: Magna Charta (E. Tex. colony). Office: Dallas Research Assocs Suite 124 8950 N Central Expressway Dallas TX 75235

MORRIS, JANICE MARIE, nurse; b. Rocky Mount, Va., July 21, 1956; d. Brady Lee and Lena Love (Maxie) Morris. A.A.S., Va. Western Community Coll., 1976, postgrad., 1981. Staff nurse ICU, Community Hosp. of Roanoke Valley, Va., 1976-77; asst. head nurse ICU, 1977-78, head nurse pulmonary unit, 1979—, primary nursing cons., 1981—, nurse chairperson joint practice com., 1982—, instr. respiratory rehab. program, 1982—. Co-author booklet: Breathing Easier, 1980; editor info. cards: Respiratory Medications, 1982. Bd. dirs. Roanoke region of Va. Lung Assn., 1983—, vol., 1982—, chairperson nursing edn. com., 1983—. Baptist. Home: 4132 Avenham Ave Roanoke VA 24014 Office: Community Hosp of Roanoke Valley 101 Elm Ave Roanoke VA 24018

MORRIS, KAY WETZEL, psychotherapist, social worker; b. Salt Lake City, July 9, 1939; d. Nevin Frank Wetzel and Jane Rawlins Deakin; student U. Utah, 1957-59; B.A. with highest honors, U. Calif., San Jose, 1961; M.S.W. summa cum laude, Ohio State U., 1963; m. Richard L. Morris, July 9, 1966 (div.); 1 son, Michael David. Psychiat. social worker children's service Napa (Calif.) State Hosp., 1963-66; pupil personnel dir. Trinity County Supt. of Schs. Office, 1967-70; founder, social worker Trinity County Mental Health Services, 1970-76; pvt. practice psychotherapy and consultation, Redding, Calif., 1967—, Aptos, Calif., 1982-83; dir. Victor Residential Center, Inc. (Stepping Stones), 1976-80, now cons. to bd. dirs.; rural services com., cons. children's service com. Calif. Conf. Local Mental Health Dirs., 1972-77; mental health cons. plan devel. com. No. Calif. Health Systems Agy., 1976-81; cons. Task Force for Handicapped Children, Shasta County Supt. of Schs., 1971-74; cons. to Redding Med. Ctr., 1980—; Seattle Children's Home, 1982-83; lectr. Women's Career Network, Seattle, 1981, Learn to Live, Redding, Calif., 1986; developer Trinity County Mental Health Service, 1970; mem. com. on integration and coordination services to children and families Calif. Dept. Mental Health. Trustee, Redding Elem. Sch. Dist., 1977-82; vol. KIXE Public Broadcasting System; Trinity County chmn. McGovern for Pres., 1972; v.p. Redding Elem. Sch. Bd., 1979-81; bd. mem. Group Home Assn. Calif. NIMH fellow, 1961-62. Mem. Nat. Assn. Social Workers, AAUW, Psi Chi. Office: 2301 Park Marina Dr Suite 21 Redding CA 96001

MORRIS, LOIS LAWSON, educator; b. Antoine, Ark., Nov. 27, 1914; d. Oscar Moran and Dona Alice (Ward) Lawson; m. William D. Morris, July 2, 1932 (dec.); 1 child, Lavonne Morris Howell. B.A., Henderson U., 1948; M.S., U. Ark., 1951, M.A., 1966; postgrad. U. Colo., 1954, Am. U., 1958, U. N.C., 1968. History tchr. Delight High Sch., Ark., 1942-47; counselor Huntsville Vocat. Sch., 1947-48; guidance dir. Russellville Pub. Sch. System, Ark., 1948-55; asst. prof. edn. U. Ark., Fayetteville, 1955-82, prof. emeritus, 1982—; ednl. cons. Ark. Pub. Schs., 1965-78. Mem. Commn. on Needs for Women, 1976-78; pres. Washington County Hist. Soc., 1983-84. Named Ark. Coll. Tchr. of Year, 1972; recipient Plaque for outstanding services to Washington County Hist. Soc., 1984. Mem. Ark. Council Social Studies (sec.-treas.), Washington County Hist. Soc. (exec. bd. 1977-80), NEA, Nat. Council Social Studies, Ark. Edn. Assn., Ark. Hist. Assn., AAUW, U. Ark. Alumni Assn., Phi Delta Kappa, Kappa Delta Pi, Phi Alpha Theta. Democrat. Episcopalian. Address: 1601 W 3d Ct Russellville AR 72801

MORRIS, LUMMIE DENE, business manager; b. Elbert, Tex., Sept. 4, 1931; d. Conley Clarence and Lora Alma (Fulton) Smith; student St. Marys U., 1968-70; m. Edwin J. Morris, Sept. 15, 1955 (dec.); children—Robin Dee, Atiyeh, Tracy Lee Morris Hair. Instr. interior design St. Marys U., San Antonio, evenings, 1970-71; asst. dir. Faye Neri Modeling Studio, San Antonio, 1970-72; interior designer, San Antonio, 1972-77; v.p. Communications Services, Inc., San Antonio, 1977-79, pres., 1984—; gen. mgr. Nat. Electric Corp., San Antonio, 1979—; mgr. trucking div. Agribusiness Services, Inc., San Antonio, 1981—; v.p. Morton & Assocs., Inc., 1984—; lectr. San Antonio high schs. Coordinator family services program USAF, Zweibruecken, W. Ger., 1968. Mem. Internat. Guild Accredited Interior Designers, Beta Sigma Phi. Republican. Mem. Ch. of Christ. Home: 223 W Silversands #5 San Antonio TX 78216 Office: 4850 Whirlwind San Antonio TX 78217

MORRIS, LYNNE LOUISE, psychotherapist; b. Youngstown, Ohio, Nov. 5, 1946; d. Richard Davies and Elsie Margaret Raymond) M. B.A., Westminster Coll., Pa., 1969; postgrad. NYU, 1971. Social worker Community Service Soc., N.Y.C., 1971-74, Altro Health and Rehab. Services, Inc., N.Y.C., 1974-79; field instr. Hunter Coll. Sch. Social Work, NYU Grad Sch. Social Work, 1974-79; clin. coordinator Montefiore Hosp. and Med. Center, Bronx, N.Y., 1979-81; asst. dir. II, social service dept. Montefiore Hosp., Bronx, 1981-83; pvt. practice psychotherapy, N.Y.C., 1976—; sr. staff therapist Counseling and Human Devel. Center, N.Y.C., 1979—. Contbr. articles of profl. jours. including Jour. Geriatric Psychiatry, 1975; abstractor Abstracts for Social Workers, 1975. Fellow N.Y. State Soc. Clin. Social Work Psychotherapists; mem. Nat. Assn. Social Workers, Acad. Cert. Social Workers, Am. Assn. Pastoral Counselors (profl. affiliate). Mem. profl. adv. com. Cary Addis Meml. Found. Home and office: 161 W 75th St 2C New York NY 10023

MORRIS, MARILOU PLUMMER, real estate company executive; b. Wichita, Kans., Apr. 16, 1939; d. Hugh and Grace (Parker) Plummer. Student, Kilgore Coll., Tex., 1955-57; B.S., LA, State U., 1959; M.A. in Counseling. U. Denver, 1973, Ph.D. in Sch. Adminstrn., 1979. Lic. real estate broker, Colo. Owner, mgr. real estate co., Denver, 1977-80; co-owner Colo. Coll. Tech., Colorado Springs, 1980-81; asst. dir. Union Pvt. Sch., Port-au-Prince, Haiti, 1981-82; comml. real estate salesperson URBB, Denver, 1982-84; real estate broker, salesperson Jonathan's Landing Realty, Jupiter, Fla., 1984—. Bd. dirs. Gallery of Arts, Vernal, Utah, 1962-64, Little Theater Group, Vernal, 1963, Children's Show, Denver, 1982-83, Bow Mar Blakcouts Annual Prodn., Denver, 1966-68. Named English Tchr. of Yr., 1963; Peabody Vanderbilt fellow, 1969. Mem. South Suburban Bd. Realtors (chmn. 1974-75, treas. 1975, bd. dirs. 1976-79), Christian Women's Fellowshp Orgn. (pres. 1967-68), Jupiter Tequerton Bd. Realtors, Phi Delta Kappa.

MORRIS, MARJORIE HALE, truck driver, retail executive, appraiser; b. Chattanooga, Aug. 4, 1940; d. Laurie Everett and Marjorie (Hunt) Hale; 3 children. Student El Camino Jr. Coll., 1958-60. Stewardess, Am. Airlines, 1960-62, mem. staff nat. advt. and publicity, 1961-62; mgr. Viking Ski Shop, Pacific Palisades, Calif., 1963-64; Pepsi Cola Corp. rep. to Republican Nat. Conv., 1964; co-owner, mgr. Ready Room Restaurant, Los Angeles, 1967; architects adv., restaurant devel. and design, Honolulu, Dallas, Atlanta, Los Angeles, 1967-73; mgr., buyer Great Things, Honolulu, 1972-74; mgr. Braille Inst. Thrift Shop, Los Angeles, 1975-78, dir., 1978—, devel. officer, 1980—; account exec. Alexanders Moving & Storage, Atlas Van Lines, 1981-86, truckdriver, class 1, 1986—; U.S. promotional cons. Kids Only Market, Granville Island, Vancouver, B.C., Can., 1985; buyer Granville Island Toy Co., 1985; owner Marjorie Morris Arts, 1985—; partner Arrasmith & Morris, appraisers; freelance writer and photographer, 1974—; designer floats Pacific Palisades Parade, 1965, TransPac Race Com., Honolulu, 1972. Team mother Pacific Palisades Little League, 1974-76. Mem. Beverly Hills C. of C. (Outstanding Service to Community awards 1976, 77). Originator, dir. Christmas Tree Project, Beverly Hills; cover editor Calif. Yacht Club Mag., 1976; founder, editor Waterlines, newsletter of Flotilla 12-7, USCG Aux., 1979—. Mem. Am. Soc. Appraisers (panel speaker nat. conv. 1983), Brentwood C. of C., Western Mus. Registrars Com. (assoc.). Home: PO Box 71 Pacific Palisades CA 90272 Office: 125 N Western Ave Los Angeles CA 90004

MORRIS, MARY A., real estate executive; b. Wooster, Ark., Sept. 17, 1932; d. Doyle and Cordelia (Matchett) Holloway; m. Charles D. Powers (div. 1973); children—Carla, Steven, Daniel. Student, Ayers Sch. Bus., Shreveport, La., 1970, Tyler Jr. Coll., Tex., 1977. Legal sec. Atty. C.A. Marvin, Minden, La., 1970-73; sec. Webster Parish Sch., Minden, 1973-75, Howard Lumber, Minden, 1975-77; real estate sales ERA Homes, Longview, Tex., 1977-80, broker-owner-pres. ERA-AAA Real Estate Inc., Longview, 1980—. Mem., YMCA, Longview, 1980—. Recipient numerous awards for excellence in real estate. Mem. Nat. Assn. Female Execs., Nat. Assn. Realtors, Electronic Realty Assocs., C. of C. (pub. relations com. 1977—), Found. for Women (assoc.), Tex. Assn. Realtors, Longview Bd. Realtors (bd. dirs. 1983—, pres.-elect 1985-86). Episcopalian. Club: Toastmasters (Longview). Avocations: fishing; boating.

MORRIS, MARY ANN, real estate broker; b. Newton, Kans., Feb. 19, 1945; d. Jack Edmund and Lois (Richert) Morris; m. Robert C. Hamer, June 21, 1969 (div. 1972). m. Claude Edward Hooten, Oct. 1, 1981. B.A., U. Houston, 1969. Sales mgr. Sta. WKJQ, Houston, 1978-81; franchise dir. Charlie's Hamburgers, Houston, 1981-82; assoc. realtor Coldwell Banker Real Estate Services, Houston, 1982-83; prin., broker Conquistador Realty, Houston, El Paso, Tex., 1983—; cons. mktg. Keyboard Express, Houston, 1981—; ptnr. DJ Creative Services, El Paso, 1980—. Songwriter (as Mary Hamer) A Western Christmas, 1973; designer —Flowers— Jewelry, 1978. Mem. El Paso Bd. Realtors, Tex. Assn. Realtors, Nat. Assn. Realtors. Office: Conquistador Realty 22 Goodwin El Paso TX 79912

MORRIS, MARY LOUISE, university administrator; b. Birmingham, Ala., Oct. 14, 1947; d. Martin Azelle and Mary Elizabeth (Doolittle) M.; B.S., U. Montevallo, 1969, M.Ed., 1972; student U. Ida., 1979-82. Tchr., Birmingham (Ala.) High Sch. System, 1969-71; program dir. Birmingham Girls Club, 1971-72; dispatcher, officer in tng., patrol officer Boise (Idaho) Police Dept., 1973-77; prodn. line worker Skyline Corp., Boise, 1978; dir. spl. services U. Idaho, 1980—. Mem. N.W. Women's Studies Assn., N.W. Assn. Spl. Programs (parliamentarian, treas., v.p., pres.), Nat. Women's Polit. Caucus, Nat. Women's History Project, Assn. Children and Adults with Learning Disabilities, Nat. Council Ednl. Opportunity Assns. (bd. dirs., fin. com., nat. fund raising coordinator), Nat. Assn. Acad. Affairs Adminstrs. Home: RFD 01 Box 21 Desmet ID 83824 Office: U Idaho Phinney Hall 302 Moscow ID 83843

MORRIS, MICHELLE LOUISE, author; b. Los Angeles, July 21, 1941; d. Charles Burr and Norma Angeline (Nielson) Morris; m. Edward Lawrence Kerin III, June 14, 1974; 1 son, David Michael. A.A. in Journalism, Santa Ana Coll., 1962; B.A. in English, Calif. State U.-Fullerton, 1974; B.A. in Psychology, Calif. State U.-Los Angeles, 1965. Social caseworker Los Angeles County Dept. Pub. Social Services, 1965-66, Los Angeles County Dept. Adoptions, 1966-68; exec. dir. Orange County Community Referral and Info. Service, Santa Ana, Calif., 1970-72; asst. dir. Environ. Analysis Found., Newport Beach, Calif., 1972-74; child advocate, participating in seminars and lectr. on prevention and treatment of sexual abuse of children throughout U.S. Author: (novel) If I Should Die before I Wake, 1982 (transl. into French, Swedish 1983, Norwegian, Japanese and Dutch 1984); (stageplay) Carla's Song, 1983; (film script) Breaking Silence: Sexual Abuse of Children, 1984; co-author: Will the Circle Be Unbroken: Women Healing from Family Abuse, 1986. Mem. Authors Guild, NOW (chpt. pres. 1978-79), Internat. PEN. Democrat. Office: PO Box 1498 Costa Mesa CA 92628

MORRIS, MYRNA RHONDA, educator; b. Dallas, July 29, 1941; d. Travis Eugene and Ann Ellen (Williams) M. B.S.E., Abilene Christian Coll., 1963. Tchr., Christian Schs., Inc., Dallas, 1963-64, Wilmer-Hutchins Ind. Sch. Dist., Wilmer, Tex., 1964-67, Dallas Ind. Sch. Dist., 1967—. Mem. Old Oak Cliff Conservation League, Dallas, 1980—; trustee Maffett Fellowship Fund, Ft. Worth, 1982—. Recipient Perot Found. award Perot Found./Dallas Ind. Sch. Dist., 1971; Golden Apple award as Tchr. of Yr., 1985-86. Mem. Nat. Fedn. Bus. and Profl. Women, Inc. (program chmn. 1982-83), Tex. Fedn. Bus. and Profl. Women, Inc. (pres. 1980-81, outstanding dist. dir. 1975), Oak Cliff Fedn. Bus. and Profl. Women, Inc. (pres. 1971-72, woman of yr. 1974). Mem. Ch. of

Christ. Clubs: Cliff Toppers Toastmistress (pres. 1980-81; Council 2, Red River Region pres. 1983-84) (Dallas); Oak Cliff Parliamentary Law Unit (pres. 1970-71) (Dallas). Home: 723 Haines St Dallas TX 75208 Office: Edna Rowe Elementary Sch 4918 Hovenkamp St Dallas TX 75227

MORRIS, RAYLENE, fabric and fiber company personnel executive; b. McRae, Ga., July 13, 1956; d. Raymond Eugene and Martha Lenna (Watson) M. B.A. in Journalism, U. Ga., 1978; textile supr. cert. Ga. Inst. Tech., 1983. Prodn. trainee Amoco Fabrics & Fibers Co., Hazlehurst, Ga., 1978-80, employment supr., 1980-83, tng. mgr., 1983-84, employee relations mgr., Andalusia, Ala., 1984-86, employee relations mgr., Nashville, Ga., 1986—, also seminar instr., Hazlehurst, 1980-86; mem. adv. council Covington County Bank, Andalusia, 1985-86. Leader Altamaha Area council Girl Scouts U.S., 1979-84; pres. Jeff Davis Med. Services Ctr., Hazlehurst, 1982-85; chmn. Jury Commn., Hazlehurst, 1983-84; active Pilot Club, Andalusia, 1984-86; bd. dirs. United Fund, Andalusia, 1984-86. Named to Outstanding Young Women Am., U.S. Jaycees, 1981. Mem. Am. Soc. Personnel Adminstrs., Ala. Coll. Placement Assn., So. Coll. Placement Assn., Nat. Assn. Female Execs., Bus. Council Ala., Ala. Textile Mfrs. Assn., Ga. Textile Mfrs. Assn. Methodist. Home: PO Box 1053 Nashville GA 31639 Office: Amoco Fabrics & Fibers Co PO Box 477 Nashville GA 31639

MORRIS, RUTH FALLS (MRS. VESTAL L. MORRIS), educator; b. Gastonia, N.C., Jan. 23, 1913; d. Charles Newton and Bryte (Stroupe) Falls; B.S., East Carolina Coll., 1951; M.A., Tchrs. Coll. Columbia U., 1958; M.S., LaVerne Coll., 1975; m. Vestal L. Morris, Oct. 22, 1943. Tchr. Lucia Sch., Mt. Holly, N.C., 1935-40; typist U.S. Army Engr. Corps., Am. Consulate, Colon, Panama, 1943-45; tchr. Gatun Sch., Gatun, C.Z., 1946-54; tchr. primary, intermediate educable mentally handicapped children Margarita Sch., Margarita, C.Z., 1958-66; staff mem. Ft. Gulick Elem. Sch., 1967-70, tchr. acad. enhancement, 1970-72; ednl. prescriptionist, vis. tchr. spl. classes Atlantic and Pacific dists. Panama Canal Schs. Div., 1973-75; owner-dir. Morris Tutoring Service, 1975—. Patron Tallahassee Symphony Orch., Tallahassee Little Theatre. Named Outstanding Tchr. Panama Canal Zone Schs. Div., 1967, 73, 75; recipient Outstanding Service cert. Spl. Edn. Assn. C.Z., 1975. Mem. AAUW, Atlantic Tchrs. Guild (v.p. 1952, treas. 1953), Am. Assn. Mental Deficiency, Caribbean Assn. Edn. Young Children, C.Z. Med. Wives Soc., Council Exceptional Children, Internat. Platform Assn., Assn. Exceptional Children, Internat. Reading Assn. (v.p. 1975-76, pres. 1976-77), Nat. League Am. Pen Women (Caribbean br. at Panama Canal), Isthmian Anthropology Soc., Sierra Club, Common Cause, NOW, Federally Employed Women (Atlantic area coordinator), Friends of Library, Lemoyne Art Found., Tallahassee Jr. Mus., Beta Sigma Phi (life mem., v.p. 1956), Phi Delta Kappa (Isthmus of Panama chpt.). Presbyterian. Clubs: Cristobal Woman's (life), Caribbean Coll. (life mem., charter pres. 1952), Soroptimist (pres. 1960, vice gov. Costa Rica and Panama 1965-69) (Colon, Panama); Inter-Am. Women's (life mem., charter, Colon unit); Republican Women's of Leon County. Contbr. articles to profl. jours. Home: 2419 Castletowers Ln Tallahassee FL 32301

MORRIS, SUSAN ELIZABETH, computer company executive; b. Louisville, Jan. 10, 1952; d. Adam and Agnes Bertha (Huber) M.; B.S. in Commerce, U. Louisville, 1978. Paralegal law firm Wyatt, Grafton & Sloss, Louisville, 1973-79; systems installer HBO & Co., Inc., San Mateo, Calif., 1979-81; systems specialist Whittaker Medicus, Evanston, Ill., 1981-83; product installation mgr. Computer Synergy, Inc., Oakland, Calif., 1983; adv. analyst, mgr. Shared Med. Systems, Oakland, 1983—. Active Third Century, Louisville, 1978-79. Mem. Bus. and Profl. Women's Assn., NOW, Ky. Hist. Soc., U. Louisville Alumni Assn., U.S. Capital Hist. Soc., Greenpeace, Internat. Platform Assn., Calif. Hist. Soc., Sierra Club; Louisville Preservation Alliance. Democrat. Roman Catholic. Club: Filson. Home: 325 Kitty Hawk Rd #201 Alameda CA 94501 Office: 2201 Broadway Oakland CA 94612

MORRIS, SUSAN MARIE, government official; b. Newark, Sept. 3, 1944; d. Michael and Helen Krawchuk; A.A., Middlesex County Coll., 1972; B.A., Rutgers Coll., 1974; postgrad. New Sch. for Social Research, N.Y.C., 1977—. Adminstr. mgmt. devel. CETA, New Brunswick, N.J., 1974-77; pres. Pvt. Employment Agy., Metuchen, N.J., 1977-78; asst. to pres. Franco Mfg. Co., N.Y.C., 1978-79; pres. Susan Products, New Brunswick, N.J., 1979—; dep. regional dir. U.S. Dept. Interior World Trade Center, N.Y.C., 1979-83; fed. women's program mgr. Dept. Def., Ft. Monmouth, N.J., 1983-85, EEO officer, 1986—. pub., editor Women Sense mag., Metuchen, N.J. Mem. Nat. Assn. Female Execs., Central N.J. Profl. Women's Network, NOW. Club: World Trade Center. Office: DRSEL-EO Fort Monmouth NJ 07703

MORRIS, SUSAN MCDONALD, financial institution executive; b. Orange, Calif., Mar. 1, 1946; d. Coalson Clyde and Jesse Jean (Crawford) Morris; B.A., U. So. Calif., 1968. Press sec. Orozco for Congress, 1968; coordinator field services U. So. Calif., Los Angeles, 1969; dir. donor relations U. So. Calif., 1971, dir. event planning from 1976; pres., owner McDonald Morris & Assocs., Inc., Los Angeles, 1981-85; v.p. Perry Morris Corp., Newport Beach, Calif., 1985—. Mem. Los Angeles World Affairs Council, Town Hall Calif. Republican. Presbyterian. Club: Los Angeles Athletic. Office: PO Box 54123 Los Angeles CA 90054 also 567 San Nicolas 3d Floor Newport Beach CA 92660

MORRIS, UNA LORRAINE, physician; b. Kingston, Jamaica, W.I., Jan. 17, 1949; came to U.S., 1965; d. Arthur Samuel and Lydia (Reid) Morris; m. Charles Cecil Chong, Mar. 27, 1981; children—Keone Tremaine, Cheynne Jehon, Wei-Lin Lorraine Chong. M.D., U. Calif.-San Francisco, 1974. Diplomate Am. Bd. Radiology. Intern, Kaiser Permanente Hosp., Oakland, Calif., 1974; resident in radiology Martin Luther King Jr. Gen. Hosp, Los Angeles, 1975-79; fellow U. Calif.-Irvine; practice medicine specializing in radiology, Los Angeles, 1980—; asst. prof. radiology U. So. Calif., Los Angeles, 1984—; program coordinator San Gabriel Women Physicians Assn., 1982—; organizer, liaison Jamaican Med. Airlift, Los Angeles, 1982—. Contbr. articles to profl. jours. Named Sportswoman of Yr. for Jamaica, Jamaica Amateur Athletic Assn., 1964, 65, 66; mem. Olympic team 1964, 68, 72. Mem. Radiol. Soc. N.Am. Baptist. Address: 1617 Homewood Dr Altadena CA 91001

MORRIS, YOLANDA LILLIAN, state official; b. Louisville, June 7, 1956; d. Raymond and Lonnie Mae (Ellis) M.; A.A.S., U. Louisville, 1985; postgrad. Ky. State U., 1985—. Planner planning div. Ky. Transp. Cabinet, Louisville, 1979-81, sr. planner traffic div., 1981-84, program planner mass transp., Frankfort, 1984-85, sect. mgr. pub. transp., 1985-86, sec. planning div., Louisville, 1975-79; exec. dir. Office of Minority Affairs, Frankfort, 1986—. Recipient numerous awards and commendations for profl. and civic excellence; U.S. Dept. Transp. scholar, 1979-80. Mem. Nat. Assn. Female Execs. Democrat. Roman Catholic. Office: Ky Transp Cabinet State Office Bldg Frankfort KY 40601

MORRIS DAWKINS, MARGOT, advertising specialities executive; b. Atlanta, July 31, 1954; d. Marcus Mancel and Betty Jo (Curry) Morris; m. Marvin Henry Dawkins, Jr., Apr. 25, 1981; 1 child, Matthew David Dawkins. B.S. in Econs., Ga. So. Coll., 1976; cert. advt. specialist U. Wis., 1978. Vice pres. sales Atlanta Advt. Novelty Co., 1976—, dir., 1980—; sec. Cert. Advt. Specialists, 1979-82, Young Execs. in Splty. Advt., 1979—. Bd. dirs. March of Dimes of Metro Atlanta, 1983—; outreach leader Rainbow Park Baptist Ch., Decatur, Ga., 1983. Named Busy Beaver, Sta. WSB, 1982; named Silver Patron, Ga. So. Coll., 1981-83. Mem. Ga. Soc. Assn. Execs., Atlanta Women's C. of C. (chmn. 1984-85), Phi Delta Theta. Home: 2957 Blue Grass Ln Decatur GA 30034 Office: Atlanta Advertising Novelty Co 161 Spring St NW Suite 226 Atlanta GA 30303

MORRISON, AGNES KIRKLAND, corporate executive; b. Graceville, Fla., Aug. 3, 1911; d. Jeremiah Monroe and Alyce Laura (Casey) Kirkland; student Columbus U., 1935-37; m. Ralph L. Morrison, July 18, 1950; stepchildren—Betty Jane Church, Ralph L. Sec. to v.p. Charles H. Tompkins Co., Washington, 1955, sec. to sr. partner, 1956-68; v.p., asst. sec. Johnston, Lemon & Co., Inc., Washington, 1978-82, trustee profit sharing plan and stock option plan, 1977-82; adminstr. James M. Johnston Charitable and Ednl. Trust, 1982—. Service with WASP, 1943-44. Mem. Women's Syndicate Assn., 1968-82. Presbyterian. Clubs: Bus. and Profl. Women's, Coral Beach and Tennis, Order Eastern Star (trustee, 1978-81). Home: 3133 Connecticut Ave NW Washington DC 20008 Office: 1101 Vermont Ave NW Washington DC 20005

MORRISON, ALBA MARIE, social service agency executive; b. Aug. 25, 1926. B.S. with honors, U. Ark., 1953; M.S.W., Tulane U., 1958. Cert. social worker, N.Y.; lic. social worker, Okla. Tchr. high sch. English, Bradford Sch. Bd., Ark., 1953-54; caseworker La. Dept. Pub. Welfare Bur. for Blind and Sight Conservation, Baton Rouge, 1955-57, 58-61; dir. social services Blind Assn. Central Ohio, Inc., Columbus, 1961-66, acting dir., 1966; regional cons. Am. found. for Blind, Inc., N.Y.C., 1966-73; pvt. practice cons. and family counseling, Tulsa, 1975—; organizer, exec. dir. New View, Inc., Tulsa, 1980—; bd. dirs. League for Blind, Oklahoma City, 1974-80; bd. dirs., v.p., treas. Okla. Council of Blind; past del. White House Confs. on Handicapped; past mem. Okla. Coalition Citizens with Disabilities, Am. Coalition Citizens with Disabilities; past mem. adv. bd. Nat. Pub. Radio, Print Handicapped Services; past pres. consumer adv. bd. Dept. Human Services; past mem. Health Systems Agy. Bd.; past del. Affiliated Leadership League Agys. Serving Blind and Orgns. of Blind. Mem. Acad. Cert. Social Workers, Nat. Assn. Social Workers, Nat. Assn. Workers for Blind, U. Ark. Alumni Assn., Tulane U. Alumni Assn. Office: New View Inc 6734 E 51st Pl Tulsa OK 74145

MORRISON, ALEXIA, lawyer; b. Los Angeles, Apr. 9, 1948; d. Alexander and Edith (Blayney) M.; B.A., Rutgers U., 1969; J.D., George Washington U., 1972; m. Robert A. Shuker, Feb. 11, 1978; 1 dau., Amanda Meighan. Legal asst. Office Drug Abuse Law Enforcement, U.S. Dept. Justice, 1972-73; admitted to D.C. bar, 1973, D.C. Circuit bar, 1975, Supreme Ct., 1981; asst. U.S. atty., Washington, 1973-81, chief grand jury sect. Superior Ct., 1977-78, chief felony trial div., 1979-81; chief litigation counsel Div. Enforcement, SEC, Washington, 1981-85; ptnr. Swidler & Berlin, Chartered, Washington, 1985—; mem. faculty Nat. Inst. Trial Advocacy, 1976-81; mem. BNA Rico Adv. Bd. Recipient Dirs. award U.S. Dept. Justice, 1980; Presdl. rank award of Disting. Exec., 1985. Mem. D.C. Bar (chmn. steering com. litigation div., vice chmn. long-range planning com.). Republican. Office: 1000 Thomas Jefferson St NW Suite 500 Washington DC 20007

MORRISON, GRACE BLANCH SIMPSON, accountant, government official; b. Waterloo, Iowa, Dec. 18, 1933; d. Lyle Meredith and Grace Luella Blanch Simpson; B.S., So. Meth. U., 1956; M.Ed., U. Houston, 1973; C.P.A., Tex.; m. Glenn Harry Murphree, July 2, 1955 (dec.); children—Gregory Alan, Gina Grace; m. 2d, Henry Joseph Morrison, Jr., July 23, 1974. Tchr. math., Mesquite (Tex.) Ind. Sch. Dist., 1957-58, Clear Creek Ind. Sch. Dist., Seabrook, Tex., 1967-73, Richardson (Tex.) Ind. Sch. Dist., 1973-74; equal opportunity asst. Office for Civil Rights, HEW, Dallas, 1974-75; govt. relations specialist, consumer affairs officer Region VI, Dept. Energy, Dallas, 1975-81; audit acctg. aide IRS, Dallas, 1981-82, revenue agt., 1982-85. Mem. Mensa, Am. Amateur Press Assn., Commerce Bus. and Profl. Women's Club, Nat. Assn. Parliamentarians, Federally Employed Women, Tex. Assn. Parliamentarians, North Tex. Registered Parliamentarians. Unitarian. Home: 4865 Mistletoe Way Mesquite TX 75150 Office: DCAA 1100 Commerce St 3B17 Dallas TX 75242

MORRISON, HELEN LOUISE, forensic, general and child psychiatrist; b. Greensburg, Pa., July 9, 1942, student Franklin Sch. Sci. and Arts, Phila., 1960-61, Community Coll. Phila., 1967-68, Temple U., 1968-69; M.D., Med. Coll. Pa., 1972; postgrad. Chgo. Inst. Psychoanalysis, 1975-84; diplomate Am. Bd. Forensic Psychiatry, Am. Bd. Psychiatry and Neurology-Gen. Psychiatry, Am. Bd. Psychiatry and Neurology Child and Adolescent Psychiatry; m. George J. Dohrmann, III, Dec. 22, 1979. Research technician Johnson & Johnson Research Found., 1962-65; lab. personnel dir. AME Assos., Princeton, N.J., 1965-67; assoc. dir. Biosearch, Inc., 1967-70; intern U. Wis. Hosp., 1972-73, resident in psychiatry, 1972-75, fellow child psychiatry, 1975-76; research assoc. Wis. Psychiat. Research Inst., 1976-77; dir. child psychiatry Stritch Sch. Medicine, Loyola U., Chgo., 1978-80; mem. exec. bd. U. Wis. Hosps. Madison Center Health Scis., also pres. house staff assn., 1975-76. Mem. women's bd. Chgo. Heart Assn. Mem. Am., Ill. psychiat. assns., AMA, State Med. Soc. Ill., Am. Acad. Child Psychiatry, Am. Acad. Psychiatry and Law (program chmn., pres. chpt.), AAAS, Am. Acad. Forensic Scis. Clubs: Women's Athletic, Saddle and Cycle. Co-author: Contemporary Issues in the Treatment of Psychotic and Neurologically Impaired Children: A Systems Approach; editor: Children of Depressed Parents: A Comprehensive Study in Research and Treatment; contbr. articles to profl. jours. Office: 919N Michigan Ave Chicago IL 60611

MORRISON, JUDITH ANN, manufacturing company executive; b. Jersey City, Apr. 18, 1953; d. Herman William and Margaret Mary (Kiernan) M.; m. Duane Henry Boehler, Aug. 25, 1972 (div. Nov. 1982); 1 son, Matthew Duane. Student Fla. Jr. Coll., Jacksonville, 1972, Mpls. Community Coll., 1979. Sec., Fla. Div. Health, Jacksonville, 1972-73; sec. Honeywell, Inc., Mpls., 1973-79, work dir., 1979-80, supr. adminstrv. services, 1980-84, human resource info. systems specialist, 1984—. Mem. Assn. Info. Systems Profls., Honeywell Womens Council. Democrat. Roman Catholic. Clubs: Boxcar Investors (Mpls.); Toastmasters (new mem. coach, 1981, v.p. edn. 1982, speech winner 1981). Home: 7511 Logan Ave South 1A Richfield MN 55423 Office: Honeywell Inc MN 12-3166 Honeywell Plaza Minneapolis MN 55408

MORRISON, K. JAYDENE, education counseling firm executive; b. Cherokee, Okla., Aug. 22, 1933; d. Jay Frank and Kathryn D. (Johnson) Walker; m. Michael H. Morrison, Aug. 11, 1955; children—Jay, Mac. B.S., Okla. State U., 1955, M.S., 1957; postgrad. U. Colo., 1965, Central State U., Okla., 1968-70, 84, U. Denver, 1981-82. Tchr., Cushing Pub. Schs., Okla., 1955-57, Indpls. Pub. Schs., 1958-59; counselor, tchr. spl. edn. Helena-Goltry Pub. Schs., Okla., 1965-73; psychometrist Okla. State Title III Program, Alva, 1974-75; sch. psychologist Okla. State Dept. Edn., Enid, 1977-85; pres., dir. Ventures in Learning, Inc., Helena, 1984—, career counselor, Oklahoma City, 1985—. Chmn., Alfalfa County Excise and Equalization Bd., Cherokee, 1979-83; asst. state coordinator Okla. Am. Agr. Movement, Oklahoma City, 1982-83; co-chmn. Alfalfa County Democratic party, Cherokee, 1976-83, sec.-treas. 6th Dist. Dem. party, 1983—. Recipient Tchr. of Yr. award Helena Masonic Lodge, 1967, Spl. award Okla. Women for Agr., 1979. Mem. Biofeedback Soc. Am., Okla. Soc. for Advancement Biofeedback, Nat. Assn. Sch. Psychologists, Okla. Sch. Psychologists Assn., Garfield County Interagy. Task Force, Okla. Assn. Learning Disabilities, Delta Kappa Gamma, Chi Omega Alumni. Mem. Christian Ch. Office: Ventures in Learning Inc Box 585 Helena OK 73741 also 11212 N May St Suite 301A Oklahoma City OK 73120

MORRISON, LINDA, music educator; b. Fort Deposit, Ala., June 19, 1939; d. Clarence Alexander and Buena Ethyl (Murray) Morrison; Mus.B., Samford U., 1961; Mus.M., So. Bapt. Theol. Sem., 1965; D.M.A., North Tex. State U., 1984; children—Eric, Allen. Pvt. piano and organ tchr., 1963—; minister of music Crescent Hill Baptist Ch., Louisville, 1973-76; faculty La. Coll., Pineville, 1976-83, asst. prof. music, 1979-83; choral dir. Louisville Collegiate Sch, 1983-85; faculty Jefferson Community Coll. Mem. Am. Guild Organists. Baptist. Home: 401 Godfrey Ave Louisville KY 40206

MORRISON, LUCILE PHILLIPS, psychologist, author; b. Los Angeles, Sept. 8, 1896; d. Lee A. and Catherine (Coffin) Phillips; A.B., Vassar Coll., 1918; M.A. in Psychology, George Pepperdine Coll., 1958; Litt.D. (hon.), Calif. Sch. Profl. Psychology, 1978; m. Wayland Augustus Morrison, Dec. 27, 1917; children—Wayland Lee, Richard Holt, Lee Allen, Keith Norman; 1 adopted dau., Patricia Lee. Dir., Lee A. Phillips, Inc., 1930-49, v.p., 1938-42, pres., 1942-49; intern Am. Inst. Family Relations, Los Angeles, 1952-53, asso. counselor 1954-55, counselor, 1955-64, also v.p. bd. dirs., until 1964. Pres., founder mem. Duarte (Calif.) Community Service Council, 1946-48, editor newsletter, 1946-48, v.p., 1948-50, health chmn., 1951-54; bd. trustees Westminster Gardens Presbyn. Ch. U.S.A., Duarte, Calif., 1953-66, hon. life trustee, 1966; dir., mem. Duarte Community Center Bd., 1949-57; dir. Children's Hosp., Los Angeles, 1921-44; trustee, mem. coms. Scripps Coll., 1930—, trustee emeritus, 1972—, chmn. ednl. policy com., 1965-70, Ellen Browning Scripps Assos. award, 1976; constituent mem. bd. fellows Claremont (Calif.) U. Center, 1967-70, mem. grad. sch. com., 1968-70, mem. adv. bd. Inst. Antiquity and Christianity, Claremont Grad. Sch., 1968—, mem. bldg. and grounds com.; v.p., dir., mem. staff Psychol. Guidance Center, Anaheim, Calif., 1960-63; trustee Calif. Sch. Profl. Psychology, 1972-78, hon. life trustee, 1978—, exec. council, 1973-74, mem. acad. commr., 1974-78; dir. Psychol. Publs., Inc., Los Angeles, 1966—. Active mus., hist., archeol. socs., So. Calif. Symphony Assn., Founders, Music Center For Performing Arts, Calif. Hist. Soc., Hist. Soc. So. Calif. Named Woman of Yr., Marlborough Sch. Class of 1914, 1979; lic. psychologist, lic. marriage, family and child counselor, cert. psychologist, State of Calif. Mem. N.Y. Acad. Scis., Child Study Assn. Am., AAUW, Am. (asso.), Calif., Western psychol. assns., DAR, Am., Calif., So. Calif. assns. marriage and family therapists, Calif. State Marriage Counseling Assn., Am. Assn. Humanistic Psychology, Inst. Achievement Human Potential, Phi Beta Kappa, Delta Kappa Gamma, Psi Chi. Club: Women's University (Los Angeles). Author: Mystery Gate, 1928; The Attic Child, 1929; Blue Bandits, 1930; The Lost Queen of Egypt (Nat. Pen Women's award for fiction), 1938; (with Robert M. Taylor) Taylor-Johnson Temperament Analysis; Research and Development of Test and Manual, 1963-67; also articles. Editor: Doll Dreams (4 vols.), 1927-32; The World of Books (for Scripps Coll.), 1934. Home: 1134 Rancho Rd Arcadia CA 91006

MORRISON, SYLVIA HERMAN, publishing company executive; b. N.Y.C., Feb. 10, 1953; d. Edwin W. and Bess (Miller) Herman; m. Paul Stanley Morrison, Mar. 27, 1976; children—Dale Michele, Alan Ross. B.A., Ohio State U., 1974. Entertainment listings editor Cleve. Mag., 1974-76; asst. to pub. Cleve. Mag., 1976-85; editor Entertainment Guide, dir. circulation, 1986—; career cons. Pro Cleve., 1982—; with direct mktg. dept. Cleve. Advt. Club, 1980. Columnist Circulation Mgmt. mag., 1985, 86. Active United Way, Am. Cancer Soc. Mem. Alpha Lambda Delta. Democrat. Jewish. Address: 2126 Campus Rd Beachwood OH 44122

MORRISON, WINIFRED ELAINE HAAS, social services administrator, educator; b. Buffalo, Aug. 31; d. Edward Albert and Elaine Magdalene (McNamara) Haas; B.S. in Edn., SUNY, Buffalo, M.S. in Edn. magna cum laude, 1964; M.L.S., SUNY, Geneseo, 1969; Ph.D., SUNY-Buffalo, 1984; postgrad. SUNY Coll. at Buffalo, Harvard U., UCLA; m. Robert Charles Morrison; children—Robert Edward, James Richard. Instr., Genesee Community Coll., 1972-78, 80, also asst. prof. State U. Coll., Buffalo, 1973-77; corr. course instr. Empire State Coll., Saratoga Springs, N.Y., 1975-78; dir. early edn. div. Park Sch., Buffalo, 1960-74, dir. lower sch., 1974-78; mem. faculty ednl. studies, lectr. Coll. H, SUNY, Buffalo, also coordinator child care adv. service Early Childhood Research Center, Amherst campus, 1978-80; dir. children's services Erie County Assn. for Retarded Children, 1980—, now exec. dir.; chmn. early childhood com. Nat. Office Gifted and Talented, HEW, 1976; panelist symposium Chautauqua Inst., 1974. Pres. bd. dirs. Day Care Council Western N.Y., 1971-72; adv. com. parenthood edn. project Buffalo and Erie County council Girl Scouts U.S.A., 1972-76; child adv. com. child/adult edn. project Western N.Y. div. Salvation Army, 1977-82; TV and reading com. WNED-TV Public Broadcasting, 1977-79; chmn. community com. Erie Community Coll., 1971-72; hon. chmn. Week of the Young Child; pres. Erie County Adv. Council on Disabled, 1986. Recipient Outstanding Service award Villa Maria Coll. Child Devel. Adv. Council, 1979, 84; outstanding achievement award YWCA of Buffalo and Erie County, 1985. Mem. AAUW, Nat. Assn. Edn. of Young Children, Council Exceptional Children, World Orgn. Presch. Edn., Assn. Childhood Edn. Internat., Center Women in Mgmt. (bd. dirs. 1983—), ALA, Nat. Assn. Supervision and Curriculum Devel., N.Y. State Council for Children, Pi Lambda Theta (pres. Alpha Nu 1985—), Phi Delta Kappa Club: Zonta. Author: This Book Is About Your School, Early Education Unit, 1976, Primary Unit, 1977; You Are Your Child's First Teacher, 1974; (with Carol Woodard) You Can Help Your Baby Learn, 1979; (with Betty Jenkins) Kiddy Kards (screening materials), 1982. Home: 13 Karen Dr Tonawanda NY 14150 Office: 101 Oak St Buffalo NY 14203

MORRISSEY, JOANNE, insurance analyst; b. New Kensington, Pa., Nov. 5, 1947; d. Clair William and Elizabeth (Ewing) Stone; 1 son, Nathanial Joseph Cake; m. 2d, Michael Joseph Morrissey, June 5, 1982; 1 stepson, Scott Christopher. B.A., Westminster Coll., 1969; M.A., Case Western Res. U., 1974. Ins. claims Hartford Ins. Group, Parsippany, N.J., 1975-77, Crum & Forster, Morristown, N.J., various mgmt. positions, 1977-84; v.p., sr. investment analyst Firemark Cons., Inc., Morristown, N.J., 1984-85, pres., 1985—. Republican. Presbyterian. Office: Firemark Cons Inc PO Box 400 Morristown NJ 07960

MORRISSEY/HAVLIN, PAT ROSE, journalist; b. Flint, Mich., Aug. 3, 1946; d. William Henry and Sigrid Mabel (Zachariasen) Morrissey; m. Earl Richard Havlin, Oct. 31, 1981. A.A., A.S., Flint Community Coll., 1966; B.S., U. Miami (Fla.), 1968. Prodn. asst. Sta. WPBT-TV, Miami, Fla., 1970; account exec. Charles Cinnamon Assocs., Miami, 1970-74; pub. relations dir. Mus. Sci., Miami, 1973-75, Bascomb Meml. Broadcasting Found., Miami, 1974-78; editor Internat. Pub. Co. Am., Miami Springs, Fla., 1979-81; publs. mgr. Jackson Meml. Med. Center, U. Miami, 1982—. Author: A Career Guide to the Foodservice Industry, 1981; editor: Miami's Neighborhoods, 1982. Mem. Women in Communications (chpt. pres. 1984-85, chpt. Headliner award 1981, Nat. Publicity award 1973), S. Fla. Astrological Assn. (dir. 1978—, pres. 1980-82). Democrat. Home: 7260 SW 76th St Miami FL 33143 Office: U of Miami Jackson Meml Med Center 1611 NW 12th Ave The Alamo Miami FL 33136

MORROW, CHERYLLE ANN, accountant; b. Sydney, Australia, July 3, 1950; came to U.S., 1973; d. Norman H. and Esther A. E. (Jarrett) Wilson; m. Christopher Alan Oswald, Dec. 27, 1984. Student U. Hawaii, 1975; diploma Granville Tech. Coll., Sydney, 1967. Acct., asst. treas. Bus. Investment, Ltd., Honolulu, 1975-77; owner Lanikai Musical Instruments, Honolulu, 1980—, Cherylle A. Morrow Profl. Services, Honolulu, 1981—; fin. managerial cons. E.A. Buck Co., Inc., Honolulu, 1981-84; controller, asst. trustee THC Fin. Corp., Honolulu, 1977-84, bankruptcy trustee, 1984—. Mem. Small Bus. Hawaii PAC, Lanikai Community Assn., Arts Council Hawaii. Mem. Australian-Am. C. of C. (dir. 1985—), The Forum, Nat. Assn. Female Execs. Avocations: reading; music; dancing; sailing; gardening; computers. Office: 1001 Bishop St Pacific Tower Suite 772 Honolulu HI 96812

MORROW, MARY RUTH, bus. rep.; b. Eutaw, Ala., Dec. 17, 1941; d. Pearlie and Maggie Lee (Lavender) M.; student Los Angeles Met. Coll., 1961, Bryant & Stratton Bus. Inst., 1963; B.A., SUNY, 1980, cert. in materials mgmt., 1980, postgrad. in communications, 1980; With Buffalo Bisons Baseball Promotional, 1963-64, Hengerers' Dept. Store, Buffalo, 1964-65; clk.-typist Buffalo Distbg. Co., 1963-64; telephone operator N.Y. Telephone, Buffalo, 1964-65, jr. service asst., 1965-67, service asst., 1967-72, instr. tng. long distance operators, acting asst. mgr. operator services, customer service bur., 1972-73, rep. bus. service and sales, 1979—; chmn. Western Area Telephone Comml. Union, 1981; chmn. local 213, Telephone Comml. Union, also mem. raiding and edn. coms.; personnel interviewer S.M. Flickinger Co., 1974. Loan officer credit union St. John Baptist Ch., 1974-75, mem. youth adv. bd., 1970-75; tchr. Sunday sch., 1966-73; vol. Children's Hosp. Variety Club Telethon, 1981. Recipient Buffalo Bd. of Dirs. PUSH award, 1978; Black Achievers' award, 1979. Mem. Am. Bus. Women's Assn. (mem. hospitality com. and edn. com. 1974), Nat. Assn. Female Execs., Women in Communication, Buffalo Urban League (sec. guild 1976, co-chmn. golf com., entertainment chmn. 1981), NAACP (hon. chmn. 1978-80, dir.), PUSH Excel (dir.), PUSH (dir.), Delta Sigma Gamma, Alpha Kappa Alpha. Democrat. Baptist. Clubs: SUNY Buffalo Alumni, Golden Tee Golf (v.p. 1981-82), United Voices of St. John Booster. Office: NY Telephone 5th Floor Erie County Savings Bank Bldg Buffalo NY 14202

MORROW, SHARON M., university official; b. Pierce County, Wash., Aug. 26, 1953; d. Kenneth L. and Patsy R. (Cepicky) M. B.S., Ball State U., 1975, postgrad., 1975-77; postgrad. Miami U., 1977-79. Teaching grad. asst. English Ball State U., Muncie, Ind., 1975-76, publs. grad. asst., 1976-77; editorial asst. Old N.W. Miami U., Oxford, Ohio, 1977-79; admissions counselor Kans. Wesleyan U., Salina, 1979-80; publs. editor Western Mich. U., Kalamazoo, 1980-83; dir. publs. Bradley U., Peoria, Ill., 1983-86, mem. publs. council, 1983-86; publs. dir/editor Kans. State U., Manhattan, 1986—. Active Lakeview Mus. Arts and Scis., Peoria, 1983—; treas. Commn. Status of Women, Western Mich. U., 1981-82; conf. com. mem. Council Advancement and Support Edn., Dist. 5, 1984. Recipient Adams award Peoria Advt. and Selling Club, 1985. Mem. Women in Communications, (sec. 1981-83, chmn. 1986-87), Women in Mgmt. (v.p. pub. relations 1984-85), Internat. Assn. Bus. Communicators, Nat. Assn. Female Execs. Democrat. Office: Univ Relations Office Kans State U 8 Anderson Hall Manhattan KS 66506

MORROW, SUSAN DAGMAR, psychic, educator, writer, consultant; b. Harrisburg, Pa., July 10, 1932; d. William Lime and Margaret Louise (Deckard) Brubaker; m. Henry Taylor Morrow, June 9, 1952 (div. Mar. 1984); children—Quenby Anne Morrow Smith, Christopher Brian. Student Carnegie Inst. Tech., 1950-52, U. Ariz., 1952-54, U. Calif.-Berkeley Ext., 1960-72, Foothill Coll., 1980-81. Self-employed psychic, psychic tchr., Palo Alto, Calif., 1976-80, Mountain View, Calif., 1980—; psychic, tchr. Seekers Quest Profl. Ctr., San Jose, Calif., 1983—; tchr. San Andreas Health Council, Palo Alto, 1981-83; lectr. U. Calif.-Berkeley, 1979, Foothill Coll., Los Altos, Calif., 1980; lectr. in field; cons. in cases of mental disorientation to psychologists, Palo Alto and Mountain View, 1978-84. Contbr. articles on psychic awareness to various publs. Mem. Assn. Psychic Practitioners (co-founder, v.p. 1982-83, editor and writer newsletter 1982-83), Assn. Research and Enlightenment, Friends of the Animals. Democrat. Methodist. Avocations: mediumship; painting; swimming; sailing; skiing.

MORROW, SUSAN HOLLY, interior designer; b. N.Y.C., Aug. 27, 1943; d. Murray and Roslyn Jeanette Benjamin (Polsky) Chalkin; B.A. in Fine Arts, Syracuse U., 1964; M.A., N.Y.U., 1965; cert. in appraisal, Post Coll., 1981; divorced; 1 son by previous marriage—Christopher A. Morrow. Tchr., N.Y.C. Pub. Schs., 1965-69; interior designer Bagatelle Assos., Roslyn, N.Y., 1971-74, The Wallpaper Place, Unltd., 1974-75; pres. Apricot Designs, Ltd., Roslyn, 1974-79, Trio Design I and Trio Designs II, Inc., Huntington, N.Y., 1975-80, SHS Design Assocs., Ctd., Great Neck, N.Y., after 1980; ptnr. Designs for ..., 1980—; pres. Deja Va Designs, 1984—, Wallpapers And ..., 1985—; participant 1984 Designers Showcase; lectr. interior design adult evening programs. Vice pres. Roslyn LWV, Civic Assn., Norgate; co-chmn. budget adv. com. Roslyn Pub. Schs.; v.p. The Village Sch. Mem. Am. Soc. Interior Designers, 110 Bus. and Profl. Women's Assn. (designer Showcase 1985), Allied Bd. Trade, Internat. Soc. Interior Designers, Assn. Environ. Designers, Internat. Platform Assn., Mensa. Club: Roslyn Hadassah (v.p., Woman of Yr.). Editor in chief Hadassah Jour., 1981-82. Office: Designs For ... 1345 Old Northern Blvd Roslyn NY 11576 also Wallpapers And ... 1025 Oyster Bay Rd East Norwich NY 11732

MORSE, ALICE ANDREA, lawyer; b. New Orleans, Dec. 30, 1957; d. Arthur Snowman and Hilda (Mercado) Morse. B.S., Tex. A&M U., 1978; J.D., South Tex. Coll. Law, 1981. Bar: Tex. 1981. Assoc. Tex. Legal Assocs., Spring, 1982, Garza & Van Deilen, Houston, 1982; sole practice, Houston, 1983-84; mng. atty. Hyatt Legal Services, Memorial City-Houston, 1984—. Mem. ABA, Am. Trial Lawyers Assn., Order Barristers, Houston Bar Assn., Houston Trial Lawyers Assn., Houston Young Lawyers Assn., South Tex. Coll. Law Alumni Assn., Houston A&M Club, Inns of Ct., Delta Theta Phi. Home: 27 Litchfield Ln Houston TX 77024 Office: Hyatt Legal Services 9725 Katy Freeway Houston TX 77024

MORSE, ELEANOR MEREDITH, art dealer; b. Bklyn., June 2, 1926; d. Daniel and Salley Beatrice Hershey; B.B.A., CCNY, 1947; m. Mitchell Ian Morse, Dec. 24, 1947; children—Jeffrey Aslan, Andrea Urdang. Vice pres. Art Gallery on Wheels, Floral Park, N.Y., 1953-54; product designer, v.p. Wall Decorating, Inc., Cedarhurst, and Lawrence, N.Y., 1954-70; free-lance window designer, 1955-61; interior designer, 1961-68; sec./treas. Mann-Morse Graphics, N.Y.C., 1968-69, Morse-Sun Art Assocs., Inc., N.Y.C., 1972-75; v.p., Mitch Morse Gallery, Inc., N.Y.C., 1966-85, pres., 1985—; v.p. Art Spectrum, 1979—, Yogre Bldg. Assocs., Lawrence, 1964—; sec. China Spectrum, Inc., N.Y.C., 1981—; watercolorist; one-person show jewelry design, Annapolis, Md., 1983. Office: 334 E 59th St New York NY 10022

MORSE, EUGENIA MAUDE, architect, educator; b. Houston, Feb. 23, 1920; d. Robert Emmett and Eugenia Elizabeth (Maddox) Morse Fry; B.A. in Architecture, Rice U., 1941, B.S. in Architecture, 1942. Practicing architect, 1949—; asso. prof. U. S.W. La., 1954-59; prof. architecture Tex. Tech. U., Lubbock, 1959—. Pres. bd. dirs. Storm Def. Club, 1970-73. Mem. West Tex. Watercolor Assn. (treas., dir. 1971-72), Nat. Geog. Soc., Museum Natural History, Am. Forestry Assn., Smithsonian Instn. Prin. works include Seitter Photography Bldg., Corpus Christi, Tex., Miles Ramagosa Clinic, Lafayette, La., also residences. Home: 2621 33d St Lubbock TX 79410

MORSE, LOIS, advertising executive, lawyer; b. Boston, May 15, 1935; d. David and Rebecca (Wall) Weinstein; m. Norman Morse, Nov. 23, 1955; children—Peter L., Julie G. Student, Oberlin Coll., 1951-53; B.S. in Bus., Boston U., 1955; J.D., Suffolk U., 1972. Bar: Mass., 1973, U.S. Dist. Ct. for Mass., U.S. Ct. Appreals, U.S. Supreme Ct. Asst. pub. relations div. Filene's Store, Boston, 1957-61; founder, pres. The Morse Agy, Inc., Newton MA 1968—; corp. counsel, dir. Guardian Corp., Boston, 1973-83; sec., chmn., Automotive Advertisers Council, Chgo., 1983—. Mem. ABA, Women's Bar Assn., Nat. Assn., Nat. Assn. Women Lawyers, Automotive Pub. Relations Council, Mass. Assn. Women Lawyers (officer, 1973—). Jewish (treas. Temple Shalom Nursery Sch., Newton). Contbr. article to profl. jour. Home: 118 Kirkstall Rd Newtonville MA 02160 Office: Guardian Corp 145 N Beacon St Brighton MA 02135

MORSE, TAMARA ELEANOR, financial services consultant; b. Portland, Oreg., Feb. 4, 1945; d. Frederick Baker and Eleanor (Arkell) M. B.A. with highest distinction Purdue U., 1965, M.S. with distinction, 1968, M.B.A., 1978. Cert. tchr. Calif.; registered rep. Nat. Assn. Securities Dealers. Instr. Moraga Sch. Dist., Calif., 1968-75, Fluor Internat., Ahwaz, Iran, 1976-77; sales tng. program Chevron, U.S.A., Anchorage, Seattle, and Portland, 1978-79, orgn. cons., San Francisco, 1979-80, staff supr., Seattle, 1980-81, div. analyst, 1981-86; pres. Morse Mgmt. Services, Bellevue, Wash., 1983—; assoc. Fin. Resources Group, Bellevue, 1986—. Contbr. articles to profl. jours. Account exec. United Way of King County, Seattle, 1981. Mem. Am. Mktg. Assn., Am. Mgmt. Assn., ASTD, Internat. Assn. Fin. Planners, Delta Gamma, Delta Rho Kappa. Office: Financial Resources Group 10800 NE 8th St Suite 512 Bellevue WA 98004

MORT, VIRGINIA ANN, aerospace co. exec.; b. Steubenville, Ohio, Oct. 25, 1938; d. Frank L. and Mary C. (Lucas) Petrola; B.S. in English, Calif. State U., Long Beach, 1970; M.S. in Mgmt. and Adminstrn., Pepperdine U., Los Angeles, 1975; divorced; children—Robert M., Susan A. Tchr., then counselor Anaheim (Calif.) Union High Sch. Dist., 1970-79; human resources adminstr. Northrop Corp., Anaheim, 1980, mgr. tng. and communications, 1981—; lectr., cons. in field. Mem. AAUW (chpt. v.p. 1975-77), Northrop Mgmt. Club (v.p. 1981), Am. Soc. Tng. and Devel., Orgn. Devel. Network, Nat. Assn. Female Execs., Calif. State U. Long Beach Alumni Assn., Phi Beta Kappa, Phi Kappa Phi, Alpha Mu Gamma. Office: Northrop Corp 500 E Orangethorpe St Anaheim CA 92801

MORTHLAND, CONSTANCE AMELIA GRANT (MRS. ANDREW MORTHLAND), civic worker; b. Eng., Mar. 31, 1915 (came to U.S. 1919, naturalized 1940); d. Douglas Gordon and Maud (Smith) Grant; ; A.B. summa cum laude, Stanford, 1936; m. Andrew Morthland, Aug. 8, 1937; children—Joan (Mrs. Warren C. Hutchins), Patricia (Mrs. James F. Draper). Research asst. RKO Studios, 1936-39; story dept. analyst Paramount Studios, 1941-46; free lance writer, 1955-60; cons. overseas program Stanford U. Pres. Friends of Claremont Colls., 1976-78; mem. Friends of Radcliffe Coll., 1962-70; chmn. fin. com. Episcopal Ch. Women, 1959-60; mem. exec. bd. Assistance League, 1968-69; staff mem. Laguna-Moulton Community Playhouse, 1961-69, editor Callboard, 1955—; community adviser Jr. League, 1973-75. Trustee Pitzer Coll., Claremont, Calif.; bd. overseers Claremont Coll., 1965-73; bd. dirs. Lyric Opera Assn. Orange County, 1973-84, Continuing Edn. at Claremont Coll., 1973-77; trustee South Coast Med. Center, 1978-84; exec. bd. Assocs. of House Ear Inst., 1982-84; bd. dirs. Research Assocs. U. Calif.-Irvine Coll. Medicine, 1983—. Recipient Journalism award Sigma Delta Chi, 1936, Calif. Internat. Woman award 1971. Mem. Soc. Preservation Rural Eng. (hon.), Daus. Brit. Empire (regent 1972-73, 80—), Aircraft Owners and Pilots Assn., Ninety-Nines. Clubs: Stanford (Orange County sec.); Stanford Profl. Women's; Women's University (London); Newport Harbor Yacht; El Miguel Country; N.Y. Yacht. Home: 165 Moss Point Laguna Beach CA 92651

MORTIER, MARY PRESSLY LITZELMAN, clothing manufacturing company executive; b. Long Branch, N.J., Feb. 10, 1947; d. Karl Burns and Marjorie Watt (Pressly) Litzelman; B.A., Pratt Inst., 1970; m. Alain Daniel Mortier, Dec. 23, 1972. Knitwear stylist, coordinator Damon Creations, N.Y.C., 1970-78; mdse. mgr. knitwear H.I.S. Sportswear, N.Y.C., 1978-80; mdse. mgr. menswear Am. Argo Corp., N.Y.C., 1980-81, gen. mdse. mgr., 1981-82, v.p. merchandising, 1982—. Home: 236 Washington Ave Brooklyn NY 11205 Office: Am Argo Corp 350 5th Ave Suite 1400 New York NY 10118

MORTIMER, DELORES MINERVA, government official; b. N.Y.C., July 23, 1949; d. Nathaniel Granville and Lenora (McKinney) M.; student Macalester Coll., 1969-70; B.A. (grantee), Howard U., 1971; M. Profl. Studies (fellow 1971-72), Cornell U., 1973; 1 dau., Dominique Filostrat. Freelance publs. cons., 1967—; research coordinator/project supr. African Bibliog. Center, Washington, 1972-75; adminstr. Phelps Stokes Fund, Washington, 1974-75; broadcaster/tech. resource person HABARI Info. Service, Washington, 1973-84; social sci. analyst Smithsonian Instn., Washington, 1975-79; social sci. analyst U.S. Commn. on Civil Rights, Washington, 1979-81; sr. acad. exchange specialist USIA, Washington, 1981—. Mem. women's council Smithsonian Instn., 1976-79. Sponsors for Ednl. Opportunity grantee, 1970. Mem. Nat. Assn. Female Execs., African Studies Assn., Latin Am. Studies Assn. Co founder, editor AMA Women in African and Am. Worlds jours., 1976; contbr. articles to profl. jours. Office: USIA 301 4th St SW Washington DC 20547

MORTKOWITZ, MARSHA ILENE, lawyer; b. Newark, Aug. 12, 1957; d. Al and Ida (Fishkin) M. B.A., Cornell U., 1979; J.D., Seton Hall U., 1982. Bar: N.J. 1982. Polit. intern Union County Democratic Com., Rahway, N.J., 1974-75; piano and organ tchr. Linden Music Ctr. (N.J.), 1972-75; team leader CETA, Elizabeth Union County, N.J., 1976; adminstrv. aide Fed. Energy Regulatory Commn., Washington, 1978; with accounts payable Am. Cyanamid Co., Linden, 1980-82; atty. workers' compensation, family law Margolis & Gordon, Union, N.J., 1982—; commr. N.J. State Motor Vehicle Study Commn., Trenton, 1974-75; founding mem., bus. mgr. Nothing But Treble, Ithaca, N.Y., 1976-79. Mem. Child Placement Rev. Bd., Elizabeth, N.J., 1982—; advisor, interviewer No. N.J. chpt. Cornell Secondary Schs. Adv. Com., 1981—; condr., mem. Suburban Jewish Ctr. Choir, Linden, 1970—. Mem. NOW, Union County Bar Assn. (scholar 1979), Women Lawyers Union County. Democrat. Clubs: Collegiate Chorale (librarian N.Y.C. 1980-81), Cornell Chorus (v.p. 1978-79), Choral Art Soc. N.J. Contbg. author: N.J. State Motor Vehicle Commission Report, 1975; contbr. articles to profl. jours. Office: Lawrence Henry Bank 10 McKinley St Closter NJ 07624

MORTON, ANN MAYO TILDEN, civic worker, genealogist; b. Concord, N.H., Dec. 3, 1931; d. Sidney Edward and Wanda Louise (Tapp) Tilden; m. Robert Basil Brazil, Jan. 29, 1953 (div. 1956); m. 2d Donald John Morton, Aug. 16, 1958; children—Saundra Kay Morton Hannaford, Donald John, Mary Ann Morton Kasperson. B.S. in Biology, N.Mex. State U., 1953. Cert. Am. Lineage Research Specialist. Organizing chpt. regent Capt. Samuel Wood chpt. Nat. Soc. DAR, Northborough, Mass., 1972, state recording sec., Mass., 1974-77, state vice regent, 1977-80, state regent, 1980-83, v.p. gen. Nat. Soc. DAR, 1983-86; registrar gen. Soc. Descs. Colonial Clergy, 1986—; Nat. Soc. Old Plymouth Colony Descs., 1984—; state recording sec. Daus. of Colonial Wars in Commonwealth of Mass., Ind., 1980-83, state registrar, 1983—; state pres. Mass. Soc., Nat. Soc. Colonial Dames XVII Century, 1985—. Mem. Nat. Soc. of Dames of Ct. of Honor, Hereditary Order of Descendants of Colonial Govs., Nat. Soc. Daus. of Founders and Patriots of Am., Gen. Soc. Mayflower Descendants, Nat. Soc. New Eng. Women, Piscataqua Pioneers (asst. registrar 1985—), Nat. Geneal. Soc., Mass. Soc. Genealogists (state corr. sec. 1985—), Conn. Soc. Genealogists, New Eng. Hist. Geneal. Soc., Essex Soc. Genealogists, Knox County (Ill.) Geneal. Soc., Maine Old Cemetery Assn., Geneal. Soc. Vt. Episcopalian. Home: 12 Westchester Dr Auburn MA 01501

MORTON, BERNICE FINLEY, nurse; b. Detroit, Aug. 29, 1923; d. Virgil and Minnie Alice (Batchelor) Finley; B.S.N., Wayne State U., 1954, M.S.N., 1961; Ph.D., U. Mich., 1980; m. Donald Allen Morton, Oct. 1, 1949; children—Donna Jean, Mildred Ellen. Staff nurse Grace Hosp., Detroit, 1948; public health nurse Detroit Dept. Health, 1948-58; instr. Deaconess Sch. Nurses, Detroit, 1960-62; instr. med. terminology Highland Park (Mich.) Community Coll., 1962; asst. dir. Met. Hosp., Detroit, 1962-63; mem. faculty Wayne State U., 1963—, assoc. prof. nursing, chmn. community health nursing, 1973—, minority affairs officer, 1977—, also mem. speakers' bur. vis. prof. Howard U., 1983-84; dir. nursing service Model Neighborhood Comprehensive Health Care Center, 1969-72; mem. Mayor Detroit Adv. Com. Health, 1970-72; cons., reviewer in field. Horace Rachkam fellow, 1975; grantee USPHS, 1959. Mem. AAUP, Am. Nurses Assn., Nat. League Nursing, Am. Pub. Health Assn., Detroit Dist. Nurses Assn., Am. Assn. for History of Nursing, Mus. African-Am. History, Wayne State U. Wayne State U. Alumni Assn., Smithsonian Assocs., Sigma Theta Tau, Delta Sigma Theta, Chi Eta Phi. Author papers in field. Address: 3790 Sturtevant Ave Detroit MI 48206

MORTON, CAROLINE JULIA, devel. co. exec.; b. N.Y.C.; B.S. in Edn., U. Pa.; M.B.A., N.Y. U.; grad. cert. in profl. writing and effective communication, CCNY. Vice pres. mktg. mgmt. V-TEC Corp., Hopewell, Va.; pres. CMR Co., Hopewell; past cons. Advt. Women of N.Y. Mem. Am. Mktg. Assn. (past dir.), Advt. Women of N.Y., Fedn. Profl. Bus. Women, Am. Mgmt. Assn., AAUW. Contbr. articles to profl. jours. Address: PO Box 841 Hopewell VA 23860

MORTON, DONNA HARTWICH, public relations executive; b. Aransas Pass, Tex., Mar. 11, 1933; d. Harold Charles and Lavernia Arlene (Snow) Hartwich; m. Ralph Edward Morton, Jr., Aug. 18, 1956 (div.); 1 dau., Tracey Windsor. Sec. Aerojet-Gen., Washington, 1959-63; security adminstr. Teledyne Ryan Aero., Washington, 1964-74; adminstrv. exec. Doremus & Co., Washington, 1974—. Mem. Park Ctr. Tenant Assn., Alexandria, Va., 1982—. Mem. Mensa. Office: Doremus & Co 1090 Vermont Ave NW Washington DC 20005

MORTON, JOANNE MCKEAN, computer applications educator, consultant; b. New London, Conn., Dec. 3, 1953; d. Newton Hubbard and Lucille (Raganetti) McK.; m. Michael McNally Morton, Sept. 16, 1978. B.A., Conn. Coll., 1976; M.B.A., Rensselaer Poly. Inst., 1985. Dept. mgr. Great Atlantic & Pacific Tea Co., Inc., Springfield, Conn., 1976-84; research asst. Hartford Grad. Ctr., Conn., 1985, adj. lectr. Sch. Mgmt., 1986—; ind. small bus. computer cons. and trainer, 1986—. Republican. Avocations: personal investing; basketry; collecting watercolors. Office: The Hartford Grad Ctr 275 Windsor St Hartford CT 06220

MORTON, JUDITH BOOZE, consultant; b. Los Angeles, Apr. 29, 1945; d. Charles Phillips Booze and Eleanor (Warren) Miller; m. C. David Morton, June 12, 1975 (div. 1978); 1 child, Shannon Leigh. B.A., Fla. State U., 1967; M.A., Fairfax Inst. Behavioral Sci., 1982. Legis. aide Fla. Senate, 1965-68; research analyst Nat. Security Agy., 1967-68; state schedule dir. Fla. Gubernatorial campaign, 1969-70; press liaison U.S. Senate campaign, St. Petersburg, Fla., 1970, co-chmn., 1979-80; office mgr. law firm, Miami, Fla., 1971-73; office adminstr. ins. co., archtl. firm, Miami, 1973-78; dir. adminstrn. Internat. Automotive Design, Miami, 1978-79; dir. adminstrn. Century 21 Real Estate of So. Fla., Miami, 1980-81; legis. liaison, pub. affairs officer U.S. Govt. Printing Office, Washington, 1981-84; dir. environ. policy analysis council on Environ. Quality, Exec. Office of Pres., 1984-85: pub. affairs cons., Washington, Fla., 1978—. Contbr. articles to profl. publs. Staff, Republican Nat. Conv., Miami, 1968, 72; instr. United Way, Miami, 1971; bd. dirs. Met. Mus. Art, Miami, 1975-78; regional chmn. Easter Seals Telethon, Miami, 1981. Recipient Service award of appreciation, Combined Fed. Campaign, 1984. Mem. Am. soc. Profl. and Exec. Women, Exec. Women in Govt., Republican Women's Fed. Forum, Vizcayans (v.p. 1971-80). Presbyterian. Clubs: Coconut Grove Republican Women's (Miami) (pres. 1975-77), Beaux Arts (Miami). Home: 307 Yoakum Pkwy Alexandria VA 22304

MORTON, SALLIE MILLER, jeweler; b. Reno, Nov. 8, 1925; d. Meredith Raines and Sarah Ellen (Phillips) Miller; m. MacDonald Grant Morton, Sept. 24, 1949; 1 son, Philip Raines. B.S.B.A., U. Oreg., 1947; student U. Calif.-Berkeley, 1944-45. Jr. acct. Skinner & Hammond, C.P.A., San Francisco, 1947; bookkeeper Sherman & Clay, San Francisco, 1947-48; pub. acct. Gordon Penny, Reno, 1948; bookkeeper, Y-Teen dir. YMCA, Reno, Nev., 1948-49; pub. acct., San Jose, 1949-53; with Morton Jewlers, San Jose, Calif., 1953—, pres., 1970—. Mem. Am. Gem Soc. (pres. 1977-79, jeweler's vigilance com., treas. 1986 Hall of Fame award), Jewelers of Am., Calif. Jewelers Assn., San Jose C. of C. Republican. Club: San Jose Toastmasters. Home: 1333 Phelps Ave San Jose CA 95117 Office: 625 Town and Country Village San Jose CA 95128

MORVAK, DANA MARILYN, construction company executive; b. New Haven, Feb. 3, 1950; d. Claire (Fish) Rocco; m. Joseph John Morvak, Oct. 5, 1975; children—Teri Lynn, Shawn Michael. B. in Child Devel., U. Conn., 1972, M. in Spl. Edn., Ariz. State U., 1976. Sec. Walsh Bros., Phoenix, 1973-74; tchr. Upward Found., Phoenix, 1974-77; corp. officer JMC Homes, Inc., Apache Junction, Ariz., 1978—. Advisor Jr. Achievement, Phoenix, 1973-76. Mem. Home Builders Assn. Home: 5090 E Roosevelt Apache Junction AZ 85219 Office: JMC Homes Inc 5090 E Roosevelt Apache Junction AZ 85219

MORVAY, RUTH GANEK, advertising agency executive; b. Newark, Aug. 10, 1922; d. Benjamin and Sarah (Wexelman) Ganek; m. Leonard Samuel Morvay, Dec. 17, 1944; d. Roslyn Barbara, Judith Morvay Bridges, Steven Elliott. B.A., N.J. State Tchrs. Coll., 1943; M.A., Kean Coll., 1962, Ph.D., 1974. Tchr., Irvington Bd. Edn. (N.J.), 1946-47, Orange Bd. Edn. (N.J.), 1947-50; master tchr. So. Mountain Sch., Millburn, N.J., 1958-81, pres. Morvay Advt. Agy. Inc., South Orange, N.J., 1982—; therapist learning disability children, 1984—. Mem. Essex County Republican Com., 1982—; bd. dirs. Family Counseling, Child Guidance, 1983—. Mem. Alpha Delta Kappa (past pres.). Republican. Jewish (sec. sisterhood 1970). Home: 31 S Mountain Rd Millburn NJ 07041 Office: Morvay Advt Agy Inc 177 Valley St South Orange NJ 07079

MOSBACH, MARIE THERESA, educator, consultant; b. Bridgeport, Conn., July 27, 1928; d. William and Loretta (Lawrence) Schaefer; B.A., Albertus Magnus Coll., 1950; M.A., U. Conn., 1968, Ph.D., 1978; m. Thomas W. Mahan, 1952 (div.); m. 2d, Michael F. Mosbach, July 27, 1974; children—Maureen T. Mahan-Copolof, Brendan Mahan. Tchr. elem. and secondary schs., Fairfield, Conn., 1950-54; tchr. secondary schs., Griswold, Conn., 1962-64; tchr. Windsor (Conn.) Pub. Schs., 1966-86, supr. English dept., 1969-74; instr. U. Conn., 1970-73; cons. Intensive Jour. Dialogue House, N.Y.C., 1981-86, ednl. researcher on use of Intensive Jour. method of psychologist Ira Progoff; condr. mental health workshops. Named Windsor Tchr. of Yr., 1983-84. Mem. Windsor Edn. Assn., Conn. Edn. Assn. (Mahatma Gandhi peace award 1984), NEA, Assn. Supervision and Curriculum Devel., Nat. Council Tchrs. of English, World Future Soc., Inst. Noetic Scis. Home: 422 Salmon Brook St Granby CT 06035

MOSBACK, NANCY CLAIRE, media buyer, planner; b. Balt., Jan. 2, 1958; d. Thaddeus Joseph and Ida Marie (Harrison) Beck. A.A., Villa Julie Coll., Greenspring (Md.), 1979. Asst. prodn. mgr. Eisner & Assocs., Balt., 1979-81; media buyer, planner Smith Burk & Azzam, Balt., 1981-84; media buyer, planner Needham, Harper Worldwide, Washington, 1984-86; media buyer, media account exec. McCann-Erickson, N.Y.C., 1986—. Mem. Advt. Club Balt. Home: 130 Water St 11A New York NY 10003

MOSBY, CAROLYN BROWN, state legislator; b. Nashville, May 10, 1932; d. Alvin Thomas and Mary Elizabeth (Snelling) Brown; m. William Edward Jordan, Jr., 1950; 1 son, William Edward; m. 2d, John Oliver Mosby, Feb. 5, 1966; 1 dau., Carolyn Elizabeth. Adminstrv. asst. dept. econs. U. Chgo., 1961-80; mem. Ind. Ho. of Reps., 1979-82, Ind. Senate, 1982—; pres. Carolyn Mosby Enterprises, Inc., Gary, 1980—. Mem. com. on platform accountability Democratic Nat. Com. Recipient Women's Agenda for Action award, 1981; Omega Psi Phi Outstanding Citizen award, 1981; INFO Newspaper awards as Outstanding Citizen in Politics, 1983, in Govt., 1983; Outstanding Citizen award City of Gary, 1983. Mem. Gary C. of C. (dir. 1981-83), Nat. Assn. Minority Women in Bus. Baptist. Clubs: Toastmistress, Jack and Jill Am. Mem. editorial bd. AIM mag., 1980-82. Office: 465 Broadway Gary IN 46402

MOSCOVICH, ELIZABETH ANN, graphics company executive; b. Pleasant Hill, Mo., Feb. 18, 1950; d. Dennis Vernon and Mary Esther (Edmondson) Reeves; m. Edgard J. Moscovich, Nov. 21, 1976; 1 dau., Dawn Marie. Student pub. schs., Lee's Summit, Mo. Lic. real estate broker, Fla. Sec., Fordick Corp., Kansas City, Mo., 1970-72; office mgr. Dackus Tile & Marble Co., Fort Lauderdale, Fla., 1972-75; exec. v.p. Am. Graphics Corp., Fort Lauderdale, 1975—, prodn. dir. reference book, 1980. Hon. mem. Friends of Ft. Lauderdale Library, 1981—, U. Miami Sch. Medicine Friends for Life, 1984—. Mem. Ft. Lauderdale Area Bd. Realtors, Phi Theta Kappa.

MOSELEY, CATHERINE MYRTA, internal auditor, accountant; b. Painesville, Ohio, Apr. 8, 1955; d. Howard Andrew and Audrey May (Jerome) M. Assoc. degree in Acctg., Ohio Inst. Bus., 1974; B.B.A. cum laude, Ohio U., 1981. C.P.A.; charter bank auditor. Acctg. clk. R.W. Sidley, Inc., Painesville, Ohio, 1975-79; auditor Banc One Corp., Columbus, Ohio, 1981—; part time instr. acctg. Lakeland Community Coll., Mentor, Ohio, 1984-85, Columbus Community Coll., 1985—. Mem. Inst. Internal Auditors, Bank Adminstrn. Inst., Ohio Soc. C.P.A.s, Beta Alpha Psi. Republican. Methodist. Avocation: creative stitchery. Office: Bank One Corp 841 Greencrest Columbus OH 43081-0386

MOSELEY, DIANE MARIE CLEAR, telecommunications executive; b. Odessa, Tex., Mar. 13, 1956; d. E.E. and Mary Frances Clear; m. William R. Moseley, Sept. 25, 1983. B.S., Okla. State U.-Stillwater, 1978. Customer support rep. Fisk Telephone Systems, Tulsa, 1979, office mgr., 1979-80, recruiting/tng. coordinator, Houston, 1981; mgr. human resource devel. Central Bus. Systems, Houston, 1981—. Mem. Am. Soc. for Tng. and Devel. Office: Centel Bus Systems 2100 Travis St Suite 900 Houston TX 77002

MOSELEY, LAURICE CULP, music mcht.; b. Chilton County, Ala., Feb. 15, 1927; d. John Curtis and Alma Roma (Hand) Foshee; student Air U. Extension Course Inst., 1951-57; m. Charles W. Culp, Oct. 23, 1946; children—Randall D., Robert C.; m. 2d Ernest B. Moseley, Jr. May 21, 1966. Auditor, personnel clk. fed. govt., 1949-55; founder, chmn. bd. Culp Piano & Organ Co. Co. (doing bus. as Fairview Piano Co., Inc., Electronics Organ Service Co., Moseley Piano Co., Crown Gems Internat., Culp Internat. Inc.), Montgomery, Ala., 1955—, also dir.; dir. Dimensions Inc., Montgomery. Mem. Nat. Assn. Music Mchts., Am. Music Conf. Republican. Club: Soroptimist. Author: (with A.T. Thomas) 6 Lessons Toward Keyboard Mastery, 1978. Home: 2543 Wildwood Dr Montgomery AL 36111 Office: 634 E Patton Ave Montgomery AL 36111

MOSELEY-NERO, ROBERTA, lawyer; b. Hudson, N.Y., Dec. 7, 1957; d. Robert Joseph and Patricia (Montague) M. B.A. in Econs., Russell Sage Coll., 1978; J.D., Syracuse U., 1979. Bar: N.Y. 1980, U.S. Supreme Ct. 1984. Legal asst. to county atty. Columbia County, Hudson, N.Y., 1980-82; asst. dep. counsel N.Y. State Dept. Taxation and Fin., Albany, 1982—. Com. mem. Columbia County Democratic Com., Hudson, 1981—. Recipient Evans award Russell Sage Coll., 1976. Mem. ABA, N.Y. State Bar Assn., Columbia County Bar Assn., State Women's Bar Assn. (bd. dirs. Capital Dist. chpt., sec.), Zonta (charter mem., 1st pres. Columbia-Greene area), Omicron Delta Epsilon. Roman Catholic. Home: 736 Union St Hudson NY 12534 Office: NY State Dept Taxation and Fin State Campus Office Bldg Law Bur Albany NY 12227

MOSER, ROSEMARIE SCOLARO, psychologist; b. Hackensack, N.J., June 16, 1954; d. Giovanni Natale and Mary (Bellaera) Scolaro; B.A. magna cum laude in Psychology, U. Pa., 1976, M.S. in Psychol. Services, 1977, Ph.D. in Counseling Psychology, 1981; m. Robert Lawrence Moser, June 4, 1978; 1 dau., Rachel Ann. Psychol. counselor Phila. Interdisciplinary Health and Edn. Program, 1976-77; counselor intern Intercommunity Action Mental Health/Mental Retardation Center, Phila., 1977; psychologist, cons. intern Cath. Home for Girls, Phila., 1977-78; sch. psychologist intern New Castle County, Newark, Del., 1978-79; intern Towson (Md.) State U. Counseling Center, 1979-80; counselor Sch. Nursing U. Md., Balt., 1980—; cons. Towson State U. Day Care Center, 1979-80; coordinator Jr. year minority student retention project Sch. Nursing, U. Md., 1980—; vol. Children's Hosp. of Phila., 1974, Hahnemann Hosp., Phila., 1975. Cert. sch. psychologist, Md. Mem. AAAS, Am. Psychol. Assn., Am. Personnel and Guidance Assn., Eastern Psychol. Assn., Phi Delta Kappa, Pi Lambda Theta. Office: U Md Sch Nursing 655 W Lombard St Baltimore MD 21201

MOSES, BETTE J., artist; b. Blackwell, Okla.; d. Walter W. and Mary Jane (Kirkpatrick) Swingle; B.A., Northwestern State U., Alva, Okla., 1946; m. Edward R. Moses, June 9, 1966; children—Kirk Rodgers, Joell Ireland. Tchr. English and speech pub. high sch., Washington, Okla., 1947-48; kindergarten tchr., Oklahoma City, 1948-60, Oklahoma City and Gt. Bend, Kans., 1960-66; owner Bette Moses Art Gallery, Gt. Bend; one woman shows: Gt. Bend Pub. Library, 1976, 85, Hutchinson (Kans.) Pub. Library, 1976, Ft. Hays State U., Hays, Kans., 1977, Wichita (Kans.) Pub. Library, 1978, 1st Nat. Bank, Hutchinson, 1978; group shows include: Barton County Community Coll., Gt. Bend, 1970—, Kans. State U., Manhattan, 1970, Ft. Hays State U., 1976, Hays Pub. Library, 1979, Wichita Art Mus., 1979, Kans. Watercolor Soc., 1980-84; represented in permanent collections: Nelson Sales Gallery, Kansas City, Mo., Wichita (Kans.) Art Mus., numerous others. Founder, Art, Inc., Barton County Community Coll., 1970, mem. bd. advisers, 1972—. Mem. Kans. Watercolor Soc. (Hollidays Artist award 1984), Kans. Profl. Painters Assn. Republican. Mem. Christian Ch. Home: 3901 19th St Great Bend KS 67530

MOSES, BONNIE CLARK, travel agency executive; b. Phila., June 2, 1944; d. Ronald James and Anna (Alexander) Clark; m. Edward M. Moses, Oct. 23, 1977 (separated). Student Pierce Bus. Coll., Phila., 1967-69. Cert. travel counselor Inst. Cert Travel Agts. Travel cons. United Presbyn. Bd. Christian Edn., Phila., 1967-68, Admiral Travel Service, Phila., 1968-73; Midwest regional sales mgr. Fun-Tyme Tours, Cleve., 1973-75; account exec. Travelmart, Cleve., 1975-76; publs. mgr. Travel Agy. Adminstrn. Dept., Air Traffic Conf. Am., 1976-78; Middle Atlantic regional sales mgr. Gen. Tours, 1978-79; gen. mgr. Old Town Travel Agy., Alexandria, Va., 1979-85; pres., gen. mgr. Old Town Travel Agy., Travel Pointe Agy., Travel Pointe Meetings, Alexandria, 1982—. Bd. dirs. Old Town Bus. Assn., Alexandria, 1983-85. Recipient Outstanding Achievement award D.C. Fedn. Women's Clubs, 1981, Spl. Recognition award Air Traffic Conf. Am., 1980. Mem. Meeting Planners Internat., Profl. Women in Travel (dir. 1982), Am. Soc. Travel Agts., Nat. Assn. Female Execs., Nat. Assn. Women Bus. Owners, Alexandria C. of C. (new mem. com. 1985). Clubs: Zonta Internat. (Alexandria) (ways and means com. 1985); Potomac River Jazz (Arlington, Va.). Avocations: theater; reading; dancing; writing; community activities. Office: Profl Corporate Services Inc Travel Pointe/US Jet Exec Services 1800 Diagonal Rd Suite 170 Alexandria VA 22314

MOSES, ILENE RUTH, apparel manufacturing company executive; b. Highland Park, Mich., Aug. 24, 1936; d. Arthur H. and Helen Mary (Simon) Yalenezian; m. Anthony J. Moses, Sept. 1, 1956; 1 child, Michelle Moses Berlin. Student U. Detroit, 1954-57. Legal sec. Robbins & Christe, Detroit, 1954-56; exec. sec. Trans Continental Industries, Detroit, 1956-58; owner, operator Anthony's Supermarket, Detroit, 1960-66, Michelle's Boutique, Grosse Pointe, Mich., 1966-76; pres. SMS, Inc., Detroit, 1976—; owner Cranship, Ltd., London, Jolland Co., Ltd., Hong Kong, 1982—; pres. IRM, Inc., Detroit, 1982—. Named Michiganian of Yr., Detroit News, 1985. Mem. N.Y. Fashion Guild, Detroit Club. Democrat. Roman Catholic. Avocations: reading, music, theatre, art, history. Home: 180 Lewiston Rd Grosse Pointe Park MI 48236 Office: SMS Inc 16135 Harper Ave Detroit MI 48224

MOSES, MARY HELEN, law educator, lawyer; b. Atlanta, Aug. 18, 1953; d. Jack and Jean Elizabeth (Tollison) Moses. B.A., Furman U., 1975; J.D., U. Ga., 1978; LL.M., Georgetown U., 1981. Bar: Ga. 1978, D.C. 1980. Asst. prof. law N.C. Central U., Durham, 1978-79; counsel to John A. Penello, NLRB, Washington, 1979-81; asst. prof. law Albany (N.Y.) Law Sch., 1981-83, assoc. prof. law, 1984—; mem. com. on research involving human subjects Albany Med. Coll., 1981—. Author: (with Patricia J. Youngblood) A Guide to Research in the Common Law, 1982; contbr. articles to legal jours. Mem. ABA, State Bar Ga., D.C. Bar, Indsl. Relations Research Assn. Home: 337 Presidential Way Guilderland NY 12084 Office: Albany Law Sch of Union Univ 80 New Scotland Ave Albany NY 12208

MOSES, PAMELA ANN, lawyer, singer; b. DeRidder, La., Feb. 18, 1956; d. Elmer Wallace Moses and Betty Louise (Lanier) Mansell. B.A., U. S.W. La., 1978; J.D., La. State U., 1981. Bar: La. 1982. Mem. firm Blanche & Moses, Baton Rouge, 1982-84; sole practice, 1984—; researcher presentation for S.W. Polit. Sci. Assn., 1983. Mem. ABA, La. State Bar Assn., Greater Baton Rouge Assn. Women Attys. (pres. 1983). Democrat. Baptist. Home: 4904 Alvin Dark Dr Baton Rouge LA 70820 Office: Pamela A Moses 201 Napoleon St Baton Rouge LA 70802

MOSHER, SALLY EKENBERG, lawyer; b. N.Y.C., July 26, 1934; d. Leslie Joseph and Frances Josephine (McArdle) Ekenberg; m. James Kimberly Mosher, Aug. 13, 1960 (dec. Aug. 1982). B.Mus., Manhattanville Coll., 1956; postgrad. Hofstra U., 1958-60, U. So. Calif., 1971-73; J.D., U. So. Calif., 1981. Bar: Calif., 1982. Musician, pianist, tchr. N.Y., Los Angeles, 1957-74; music critic Pasadena Star-News, 1967-72; mgr. Contrasts Concerts, Pasadena Art Mus., 1971-72; rep. Occidental Life Ins. Co., Pasadena, 1975-78; v.p. James K. Mosher Co., Pasadena, 1961-82; pres., 1982—; pres. Oakhill Enterprises, Pasadena, 1984—; assoc. White-Howell, Inc., Pasadena, 1984—. Contbr. articles to various publs. Bd. dirs. Pasadena Arts Council, 1966-68, Jr. League Pasadena, 1966-67, Encounters Concerts, Pasadena, 1966-72, U. So. Calif. Friends of Music, Los Angeles, 1973-76, Pasadena Chamber Orch., 1986—. Manhattanville Coll. hon. scholar, 1952-56. Mem. ABA, Calif. Bar Assn., Los Angeles Bar Assn., Pasadena Bar Assn., Am. Assn. Realtors, Calif. Assn. Realtors, Pasadena Bd. Realtors, Assocs. of Calif. Inst. Tech., Kappa Gamma Pi, Mu Phi Epsilon, Phi Alpha Delta. Republican. Clubs: Pasadena Athletic; Athenaeum, Jr. League. Home: 1260 Rancheros Rd Pasadena CA 91103

MOSIER, JACQUELINE M. VENNELL, business entrepreneur; b. Chgo., Mar. 25, 1931; d. John Marshall and Edna M. (Alred) Vennell; m. William E. Mosier, Apr. 9, 1955; children—Jane, William, Elizabeth, Thomas. B.S., No. Ill. U., 1951. Stewardess United Airlines, 1952-55; mgr. Pubs. Resources, New Canaan, Conn., 1974-77; owner, mgr. New Canaan Graphic Arts, 1977—. Mem. Advt. Club Fairfield County, Advt. Club Greater Hartford, Women in Communications, New Canaan C. of C. Republican. Congregationalist. Clubs: New Canaan Lake, Hills of Lakeway, Airline Stewardess Alumnae Fairfield County. Home: 12 Drummond Ln New Canaan CT 06840 Office: New Canaan Graphic Arts 111 Cherry St New Canaan CT 06840

MOSIER, SUSAN (KAY), systems consultant, art broker; b. Manhattan, Kans., July 10, 1959; d. Jacob Eugene and Betty Jean (Willey) M. B.A., Kans. State U., 1980; M.B.A., U. Tex., Austin, 1983. Staff systems cons. Arthur Andersen & Co., Dallas, 1983-85, sr. systems cons., 1985—; broker watercolor originals and prints. Fundraiser pub. TV, Dallas, 1985. J. Andersen Fitzgerald scholar U. Tex., 1982. Mem. Nat. Assn. Female Execs., Grad. Bus. Women's Network (treas. 1982-83), PEO, Phi Beta Kappa, Phi Kappa Phi. Republican. Methodist. Research on workaholics. Avocations: handball; tennis; squash; jewelry-making. Home: 3502 Asbury Dallas TX 75205 Office: Arthur Andersen & Co 5600 Interfirst Plaza Dallas TX 75202

MOSK, SANDRA LEE, therapy educator; b. Worcester, Mass., Mar. 24, 1941; d. Edward and Rebecca (Gass) Budnitz; m. Richard Mitchell Mosk, Mar. 21, 1964; children—Julie Katharine, Matthew Alan. B.A. magna cum laude, Brown U., 1962; M.Ed., Harvard U., 1963. Cert. lifetime tchr., Calif. Tchr. Newton Sch. Dist., Mass., 1963-64, Jefferson Sch. Dist., Daly City, Calif., 1964-65, Beverly Hills Sch. Dist., Calif., 1965-66, home tchr., 1969-81, tutor, 1966-81; ednl. therapist Ednl. Resource and Services Ctr., Beverly Hills, 1984—; vol. tchr. Edison Sch., Santa Monica, Calif., 1973-74, Venice Day Care Ctr., Los Angeles, 1971-73, South Central Community Child Care Ctr., Los Angeles, 1974-81; asst. cross country coach Am. Sch. Hague, Netherlands, 1982-83. Commr., chmn. Calif. Equal Ednl. Opportunities Commn., Sacramento, 1978-82; active in Calif. State Dept. Edn., Sacramento, 1981-82; commr. Los Angeles Bd. Edn. Commn. Sex Equity, 1984—; exec. bd. Neighbors Watts, Los Angeles, 1975-82; bd. dirs., officer U. Elem. Sch., Los Angeles, 1969-82. Mem. League Women Voters (bd. dirs. 1966—), Phi Beta Kappa, Pi Lambda Theta. Avocations: long distance running; music; tennis; dance. Home: 1531 San Ysidro Dr Beverly Hills CA 90210

MOSKOWITZ, RANDI ZUCKER, nurse; b. N.Y.C., Oct. 19, 1948; d. Seymour and Gertrude (Levy) Zucker; R.N., Jewish Hosp. & Med. Center Sch. Nursing, 1969; B.A., Marymount Manhattan Coll., 1975; M.S., Hunter Coll., 1979; postgrad. in bus. Baruch Coll.; m. Marc N. Moskowitz, July 11, 1976. Gen. staff nurse neurosurgery unit, N.Y. Hosp., N.Y.C., 1969-71, sr. staff nurse Recovery Room, 1971-76, nurse coordinator utilization rev., 1976-79; health educator Office of Cancer Communications, Meml. Sloan-Kettering Cancer Center, 1979-81; adminstrv. nurse oncologist Bklyn. Community Hosp. Oncology Program, Meth. Hosp., 1981-83, grants coordinator radiotherapy dept., 1983-86; adminstr. Ambulatory Oncology Ctr., Columbia-Presbyn. Med. Ctr., N.Y.C., 1986—. instr. Div. Gen. Studies, Community Health and Health Adminstrn., St. Joseph's Coll., 1979—. Mem. Am. Public Health Assn., Oncology Nursing Soc. (sec. N.Y.C. chpt. 1983—), Soc. for Pub. Health Edn. (sec. tri-state chpt. 1982-84, membership chmn. 1984—), Nat. Hospice Orgn., City-Wide Adv. Council on Sch. Health (sec. 1983—), Patient Edn. Consortium, Am. Cancer Soc. Contbr. articles to profl. jours. Home: 222 E 80th St New York NY 10021 Office: 506 6th St Brooklyn NY 11215

MOSKOWITZ, RITA JOYCE, Realtor; b. Little Rock, Aug. 31, 1928; d. Sam and Celia (Granoff) Schlesinger; X-ray technologist, radiation therapist, U. Ark., 1947; m. Frank David Moskowitz, Oct. 28, 1951; children—Marcy Ann, Mitchell Ben, Shelley Rae. X-ray technologist, radiation therapist Mo. Pacific Hosp., St. Louis, 1947-48; radiation therapist Jewish Hosp., St. Louis, 1948-49; X-ray technologist for pvt. physician, Kansas City, Mo., 1949-50, Mt. Sinai Hosp., Miami Beach, Fla., 1950-51; sec.-treas. Moskowitz Realty Co., Tulsa, 1963—; free-lance writer, researcher, cons. Chairperson Okla. Real Estate Commn. 1973-76; mem. Okla. State Personnel Bd.; bd. dirs. Fenster Gallery Jewish Art; trustee Temple Israel, Tulsa. Mem. NCCJ, Am. Jewish Com. (nat. exec. council, pres. Tulsa chpt.), Nat. Council Jewish Women (life), Met. Tulsa Bd. Realtors, Nat. Assn. Realtors (nat. dir.), Okla. Assn. Realtors (dir.), Real Estate Securities and Syndication Inst. (past pres. Okla. chpt.), Internat. Real Estate Fedn., NOW, Okla. Writers Fedn. Jewish. Office: 3227 E 31st St Suite 100 PO Box 2875 Tulsa OK 74101

MOSLEY, MARIAN JUNE, lawyer, educator; b. Great Falls, Mont., Aug. 5, 1929; d. Theodore and Edith Aileen (Bowman) Kummerfeld; m. Edward Reynold Mosley, Dec. 26, 1965; children—Cary Jerome Hanson, Laura Dawn Hanson, Kia Marie, Edward Reynold, Christopher Reynold, Caroline Aileen. B.A., Calif. State U.-Fresno, 1960; postgrad. U. Costa Rica, San Jose, 1964; J.D., Humphreys Coll. Law, Fresno, 1980. Bar: Calif. 1980. Office mgmt. Air Am. Airlines, Los Angeles, 1948-50; area mgr. Tupperware Inc., Los Angeles, 1950-55; tchr. Fresno City Unified Dist., 1955-74; legal asst. Culy, Millett & Sanner, Fresno, 1977-80; sole practice, Fresno, 1980—; master tchr. Calif. State U., Fresno, 1963-73; mem. jud. evaluation commn. State Bar Calif., 1986; mem. com. Calif. Tchr. Preparation and Licensing, Sacramento, 1969-72. 1st v.p. Calif. Young Republicans, Sacramento, 1964-66; founder, 1st pres. La Paloma Guild, Fresno, 1974-76; bd. dirs. Fresno County Hist. Soc., 1974-76; v.p. White Ash Broadcasting, Inc., 1976, bd. dirs., 1983—; mem. Med. Polit. Action com. Fresno County Med. Soc., 1979—; NDEA scholar, 1963; Fulbright scholar, 1964. Mem. ABA, Calif. Bar Assn., Calif. Trial Lawyers Assn., Fresno County Bar Assn., Fresno County Women Lawyers (pres. 1984). Republican. Home: 3075 W Kearney Blvd Fresno CA 93706 Office: 808 M St Fresno CA 93721

MOSLEY, MARY FRANCIS, children's librarian; b. Bessemer, Ala., Sept. 11, 1951; d. King and Clara Virginia (Smoot) Mosley. B.A., Miles Coll., 1973; M.S., Atlanta U., 1974. Asst. reference librarian Ala. A. and M. U., Normal, 1975; serials, tech. services librarian Miles Coll., Birmingham, Ala., 1975-79; radio operator USAF Res., Maxwell AFB, Ala., 1976-82; circulation librarian Ala. A. and M. U., Normal, 1979-82; air cargo specialist USAF Res., Andrews AFB, Washington, 1982—; children's librarian D.C. Pub. Library, Washington, 1982—. Asst. leader Girl Scouts U.S.A., 1982—; asst. sec. Hosp. and Prison Ministry of Maple Springs Bapt. Ch., Capitol Heights, Md., 1982—. Recipient award for promoting Christianity, Help One Another Club, 1981, 83. Mem. ALA, Ala. Library Assn., D.C. Library Assn., Met. Washington Caucus Black Librarians, Delta Sigma Theta. Club: Scrabble Game Players (Holbrook, N.Y.). Home: 2107 Suitland Terrace SE Apt 301 Washington DC 20020 Office: Fort Davis Regional Br Library 3660 Alabama Ave SE Washington DC 20020

MOSLEY, MILDRED CATHERINE YONGUE, educator; b. Charlotte, N.C., Nov. 11, 1933; d. William Henry and Mildred Lenora (Grigg) Yongue; A.B., Johnson C. Smith U., 1954; M.S., N.C. Agrl. and Tech. U., 1966; postgrad. Fla. State U., 1974-75, Specialist Edn. (grad. fellow 1976-77), 1977, Ph.D., 1978; cert. in supervision and adminstrn. U. N.C.-Charlotte, 1981; m. Wade Hampton Mosley, Jr., Jan. 16, 1962; 1 son, Wade Yongue. Elem. tchr. Marie Davis Elem. Sch., Charlotte, N.C., 1954-75; Emergency Sch. Aid Act diagnostician Williams Jr. High Sch., Charlotte, 1975-76; grad. clin. asst. Fla. State U., Tallahassee, 1976-77; elem. resource tchr. Cornelius and Davidson Elem. Schs., Charlotte, 1977-78; Derita Elem. Sch., Charlotte, 1978-79; elem. tchr. Lincoln Heights Sch., Charlotte, 1979—; mem. tchr. adv. council Charlotte-Mecklenburg County Schs., 1980-81; instr. reading Johnson C. Smith U. Bd. dirs. Our Lady of Consolation Ch. and Sch., 1980-83; sec., bd. dirs. Second Ward High Sch. Nat. Alumni Found., 1980—. Robert Taft Inst. fellow, 1981. Mem. Assn. Supervision and Curriculum Devel., Internat. Reading Assn., Fla. State Alumni Assn., Johnson C. Smith U. Alumni Assn., Delta Sigma Theta. Home: 4348 Hyde Park Dr Charlotte NC 28216

MOSS, ANNA MARIE, textile co. exec.; b. Vienna, Austria, Apr. 20, 1904; came to U.S., 1922, naturalized, 1928; d. Wentzel and Maria (Rossler) Prevost; grad. Cleve. Sch. Art, 1930; student Max Reinhardt Sch. Acting, Austria, 1931; m. Theron Victor Moss, July 3, 1939; children—Theron Charles, Judith Ann. Artist-designer Lighting-Railley Corp., Cleve., 1933-39; plant. supr. South Eastern Cordage Co., Cleve., 1959-72, Cleveland, Tenn., 1972-80; exec. textile supr., SECO Industries, Inc., Cleveland, 1980—. Republican. Mem. Ch. of God. Club: Cleveland Country. Home: Holiday Inn Hilltop Interstate Cleveland TN 37311 Office: PO Box 234 Old Michigan Ave Rd Cleveland TN 37311

MOSS, CHARLOTTE ANN, interior design and decorative accessories executive; b. Jan. 24, 1951; d. Edward Joseph and Martha Clare (Skinner) M.; m. James Brian Hotze, Dec. 29, 1973 (div. May 1979); m. Barry Sewell Friedberg, Oct. 10, 1985; stepchildren—Benjamin, James. B.A., Va. Commonwealth U., 1973. Asst. dir. admissions Va. Commonwealth U., Richmond, 1973; ins. underwriter Frank B. Hall Co., Atlanta, 1975-77; freelance writer, 1978; v.p. mktg. Becker Paribas, N.Y.C., 1979-84, Merrill Lynch, N.Y.C., 1984-85; pres. Charlotte Moss & Co., Ltd., N.Y.C., since 1985—. Bd. dirs. Stepfamily Assn. Am., Balt., 1985, fundraising chairperson N.Y. chpt., 1983—; patron Met. Mus. Art, N.Y.C., 1986—. Mem. N.Y. Hort. Soc., Nat. Council Women, Victorian Soc. Am., Brit. Am. C. of C. (corp. mem.), Royal Oak Found. (corp. mem.). Home: 48 W 10th St New York NY 10011 Office: Charlotte Moss & Co Ltd 48 W 10th St Ground Floor New York NY 10011

MOSS, EVELYN MEDORA, accounting executive; b. Panama, July 17, 1939; came to U.S., 1962, naturalized, 1969; d. George Leopole and Eliza (Imogene) Lynch; m. Lonnie Frank Moss, May 15, 1965; 1 child, Marc Anthony. A.A. in Home Econs., Panama U., 1959; B.A. in Econs., Bklyn. Coll., 1977, B.S. in Acctg., 1978. Home econs. tchr. Christ Episcopal Sch., Colon, Republic Panama, 1959-60; asst. buyer La Inovacion, Panama City, 1961-62; asst. bookkeeper White Mark Stores, N.Y.C., 1962-68; acct. Ebasco Services, Inc., N.Y.C., 1968-80, acctg. supr., 1982—; real estate sales Gen. Devel. Corp., Bronx, N.Y., 1980-82; cons. advisor Save and Improve East Flatbush Assn., Bklyn., 1980-84. Editor: (Spanish cookbook) La Cocina al Dia, 1961. Sec., Ensearch Corp. Polit. Assn., N.Y.C., 1984—; mem. Harry S Truman New Way Democratic Club, Bklyn., 1982—, Nat. Polit. Congress Black Women, 1985—. Mem. Bklyn. Coll. Alumni Assn., Nat. Assn. Black Accts., Nat. Assn. Female Execs., Episcopal Ch. Women (sec.-treas. 1983-86), AAUW (chpt. fin. officer 1984-86, 2d v.p. 1985-86). Club: Toastmasters. Avocations: reading, golfing, cooking, decorating. Office: Ebasco Services Inc Two World Trade Ctr New York NY 10048

MOSS, KATHLEEN SUSAN, geneticist, patent lawyer; b. Washington, Dec. 21, 1950; d. Janet Daines McCowin; m. Dale Thomas Moss, Jan. 1, 1981; 1 child, Jan Alexis. B.A. in Genetics, U. Calif.-Berkeley, 1971; M.S. in Human Genetics, George Washington U., 1978; postgrad. Law Program, U. Va., Exeter, Eng., 1978, Am. U., Warsaw, Poland, 1979; J.D., George Mason U., 1980. Bar: D.C. 1980, U.S. Patent Bar 1980. Research fellow, asst. Med. Sch. George Washington U., Washington, 1971-75; law clk. Bd. Contract Appeals, NASA, Washington, 1976; law clk., atty. advisor FDA, Rockville, Md., 1976-79; assoc. Cotten, Day and Doyle, Washington, 1979-80, Bernard and Brown, Washington, 1980-81; patent examiner U.S. Patent Office, Crystle City, Va., 1981-85, Wegner & Bretschneider, Washington, 1985—; guest lectr. Med. Sch. George Washington U., 1974-75. Author draft decision, 1976-79; co-author jour. article. Pres. Marcheta Tenants Assn., Washington, 1981-83. Research fellow dept. urology Med. Sch. George Washington U., 1971-72; recipient letter of commendation chief adminstrv. law judge FDA, 1976. Mem. ABA, D.C. Bar Assn., Am. Patent Law Assn. Patent Office Profl. Assn., Woman's Patent Profl. Assn. Home: One Scott Circle NW Washington DC 20036 Office: 1233 20th St NW 3d Floor Washington DC 20036

MOSS, PATRICIA ARLENE, union official; b. Cleve., May 6, 1947; d. Shirley Leon and Pauline (Frelich) Moss. B.A., Ohio U., 1969; J.D., Cleve. Marshall Coll. Law, 1981. Bar: Ohio 1981. Adminstrv. specialist Cuyahoga County Welfare Dept., Cleve., 1969-72; gen. rep. Ohio Council 8, Am. Fedn. State, County and Mcpl. Employees, AFL-CIO, Cleve., 1972—, trustee Ohio Council 8 Health and Welfare Fund, Cleve., 1983—. Mem. Columbus (Ohio) Democratic Exec. Com., 1983—; trustee, sec. bd. Council for Econ. Opportunities Greater Cleve., 1980—. Mem. ABA, Ohio Bar Assn., Audubon Soc., Smithsonian Assoc., Cousteau Soc. Roman Catholic. Home: 1289 W 103d St Cleveland OH 44102 Office: Ohio Council 8 AFSCME AFL-CIO 2975 Superior Ave Cleveland OH 44114

MOSS, SANDRA HUGHES, law office administrator; b. Atlanta, Dec. 24, 1945; d. Harold Melvin and Velma Aileen (Norton) H.; m. Marshall L. Moss, May 1, 1965; children—Tara Celise, Justin Hughes. Student W. Ga. Coll., 1964-65. Legal sec. Smith, Cohen, Ringel, Kohler & Martin, Atlanta, 1965-78; real estate salesman Century 21-Phoenix, College Park, Ga., 1978-80; office mgr./personnel dir. Smith, Cohen, Ringel, Kohler & Martin, Atlanta, 1980-85; dir. adminstrn. Smith, Gambrell & Russell, Atlanta, 1985—. Bd. dirs., sec. North Clayton Athletic Assn., Riverdale, Ga., 1981-83; sec. E.W. Oliver PTA, Riverdale, 1981; exec. com. E.W. Oliver and N. Clayton Jr. PTA, Riverdale, 1980, 81, 82; den leader Cub Scouts, Pack 959, Riverdale, 1984. Mem. Am. Soc. Personnel Adminstrs, Assn. Legal Adminstrs. Home: 1627 Lauranceal Way Riverdale GA 30296 Office: Smith Gambrell & Russell 2400 First Atlanta Tower 2 Peachtree St Atlanta GA 30383

MOSSER, MARLA BIANCO, management consulting company executive; b. Easton, Pa., July 20, 1953; d. Thomas S. and Alvera (Tomaino) Bianco; m. Bart H. Mosser, Feb. 23, 1979. B.S. in Edn. cum laude, West Chester U., 1975, M.A. in Psychology, 1977; M.Mgmt., Northwestern U., 1986. Teaching asst. psychology dept. West Chester (Pa.) U., 1975-76, psychology intern Counseling Ctr., 1976-77; counselor-therapist Devereux Found., Exton, Pa., 1976-77, psychotherapist, 1977-78; cons. Crawford Rehab. Services, Phila., 1978-79, Boston, 1979-80; v.p. J.M. Boros and Assoc., Ltd., Chgo., 1980—; lectr. in field. Mem. Women in Mgmt. (career devel. com. Chgo. chpt. 1983-84), Assn. M.B.A. Execs., Am. Soc. Personnel Adminstrs., Northwestern U. Profl. Women's Assn., Kappa Delta Pi, Psi Chi. Home: 1 E Schiller St Chicago IL 60610 Office: JM Boros and Assocs Ltd 208 S LaSalle St Suite 1760 Chicago IL 60604

MOSSO, SANDRA MARIA, training specialist; b. Phila., Sept. 10, 1956; d. Alicia (Laguna) Spinks. B.S. in Bus. Adminstrn., Trenton State Coll. Mgmt. trainee McGraw-Hill, Inc., Hightstown, N.J., 1978-79, placement supr., 1979-81; employee relations rep. RCA Corp., Cherry Hill, N.J., 1981-83, sr. employee relations rep., 1983-84, tng. specialist, 1984—. Recipient Cherry Hill Employee Excellence Recognition award RCA Corp., 1983. Mem. Nat. Assn. Female Execs., Delta Sigma Theta. Democrat. Roman Catholic. Avocations: reading, travel, horseback riding, self-enrichemtn. Home: 2114 Ryan's Run E Maple Shade NJ 08052 Office: RCA Corp Route 38 Cherry Hill NJ 08358

MOST, KATHLEEN MARGARET, computer manufacturing administrator; b. Trenton, N.J., Dec. 2, 1948; d. John Joseph and Evelyn Marie (Criss) O'Hare; m. Eugene George Most, Nov. 22, 1969 (div. Nov. 1978); 1 child, Michele. Grad., Taylor Bus. Inst., Plainfield, N.J., 1967. Sec., IBM Corp., Princeton, N.J., 1967-73, staff asst., 1973-78, adminstrn. mgr., Indpls., 1978-81, adminstrn. ops. mgr., Southfield, Mich., 1981—. Mem. Nat. Assn. Female Execs. Republican. Roman Catholic. Avocations: writing poetry; reading; swimming; traveling. Home: 1815 Brentwood St Troy MI 48098 Office: IBM Corp 2800 Northwestern Hwy Southfield MI 48086

MOSTELLER, JEAN SNOW, librarian; b. South Gate, Calif., July 23, 1928; d. Bernhard B. Snow and Doris Snow Jorgensen; m. Roy Allen Mosteller, June 4, 1955; children—Richard Allen, Jan Alison Duke. B.S., San Diego State U., 1950; M.S., U. Wash., 1952. Librarian, Hawaii State Library, 1964-65; library cons. Hawaiian Electric Co., 1965-70; prof. East-West Ctr. Inst. Tech. Interchange, U. Hawaii, Honolulu, 1966-67; library cons. Woodward Clyde Engrng. Cons., San Diego, 1978-80; librarian San Diego Pub. Library, 1979—; library cons. San Diego Bd. Realtors, San Diego, 1978-79. Mem. ALA, Calif. Library Assn. (editor Briefings 1982), San Diego Pub. Library Staff Assn. (pres. 1957-58), San Diego Friends of Library for Children's Services (pres. 1982-86), San Diego Natural History Mus., San Diego Mus. Art, U. Wash. Alumni Assn., Alpha Sigma Chi, Delta Zeta. Home: 1141 Albion St San Diego CA 92106 Office: San Diego Public Library 820 E St San Diego CA 92101

MOTEN, SARAH ELIZABETH, Peace Corps administrator, educator; b. Norfolk, Va., Dec. 9, 1941; d. Woodrow Wilson and Mary Elizabeth (Peelich) Price; 1 child, Michele Denise Motem. B.S., Hampton U., 1964; M.A., George Washington U., 1970; Ed.D., Atlanta U., 1979. Tchr. D.C. Pub. Schs., Washington, 1964-67, tchr. reading, 1967-70, counselor, 1970-74, asst. prin., 1974-80; adminstr. research Howard U., Washington, 1980-82; country dir. U.S. Peace Corps, Swaziland, 1982—; lectr. Spelman Coll., Atlanta, 1977-78; asst. to pres. Morehouse Coll., Atlanta, 1978-79; chairperson Nat. Council for Accreditation Tchr. Edn., Washington, 1970-82. Speaker Nat. Black Republicans, San Francisco, 1980; mem. Coalition for Social and Econ. Change, San Francisco, 1980; mem. U.S. del. UN Conf. for Women, Nairobi, Kenya, 1985. Rockefeller Found. fellow, 1977. Episcopalian. Avocations: reading; bowling; playing cards. Office: US Peace Corps PO Box 362 Mbabane Swaziland

MOTHERSHEAD, ALICE BONZI (MRS. MORRIS WARNER MOTHERSHEAD), former college program administrator, civic worker; b. Milan, Italy, Dec. 25, 1914; came to U.S. 1920, naturalized 1925; d. Ercole and Alice (Spalding) Bonzi; pvt. pupil music and art; student Pasadena City Coll., 1958-60; m. Morris Warner Mothershead, Sept. 15, 1935; children—Warner Bonzi, Maria (Mrs. Andrei Rogers). Partner Floal Toy Co., Pasadena, Calif., 1942-44; community adv. Fgn. Student Program, Pasadena City Coll., from 1952, past dir. Community Liaison Center. Chmn., Am. Field Service Internat. Scholarships, Pasadena, 1953-55; mem. West Coast adv. com. Inst. Internat. Edn., San Francisco, 1957-70. Vice pres. San Rafael Sch. PTA, Pasadena, 1945-46; active Community Chest, ARC, Pasadena; chmn. Greater Los Angeles Com. Internat. Student and Visitor Services, 1962; mem. Woman's Civic League Pasadena, chmn. city affairs com., 1985, pres., 1986-87; bd. dirs. Fine Arts Club of Pasadena, 1983-85, Friends of Caltech Y, 1984—, Pasadena City Coll. Found., 1983-85. Decorated knight Govt. of Italy, 1975. Mem. Nat. Assn. Fgn. Student Affairs (chmn. community sect. and v.p. 1964-65, chmn. U.S. study abroad com. 1969-70), Am. Assn. UN (chpt. 2d v.p. 1964), Soc. Women Geographers, Am. Friends Middle East, Omicron Mu Delta. Club: International (Pasadena). Author: Social Customs and Manners in the United States, 1957; Dining Customs Around the World, 1982; co-author: 15 Years of the Foreign Student Program at Pasadena City College, 1965. Editor: Students to People to Future, 1971. Home: 675 Burleigh Dr Pasadena CA 91105 Office: Pasadena City Coll 1570 E Colorado Blvd Pasadena CA 91106

MOTLEY-LONG, JANABETH, public relations company executive, consultant; b. Littlefield, Tex., Mar. 13, 1952; d. Bill and Christene (Griffin) Smith; m. G.B. Long, Dec. 11, 1982; 1 child, Brandon Neeley. B.A. in Speech, Harding U., 1974; postgrad. So. Meth. U., 1975-76, Tex. Christian U., 1978-80, U. Dallas, 1980-82. Mem. sales staff Southwestern Pub. Co., Nashville, 1971-76; adminstrv. asst. to exec. v.p. PVI Industries, Inc., Ft. Worth, 1978-80; adminstrv. asst. to pres. Mid-Tex Mfg. Co., Inc., Ft. Worth, 1980; fin. v.p., dir. AFTECH Leasing, Inc., Dallas, 1980-81; v.p. ATS Investments, Inc., Ft. Worth, 1981-83, also dir.; v.p., dir. Maxum Stores, Inc., Ft. Worth, 1983-84; v.p., Long & Hulme, Inc., Ft. Worth, 1984—; dir. McKamy Enterprises, Inc., Ft. Worth, 1981—; corp. sec., cons. Hulme and Brooks, Inc., Ft. Worth, The Performance Devel. Group, Inc., Ft. Worth. Recipient Century Club Sales award Southwestern Pub. Co., 73, 74-75, Top 40 Sales award, 1973. Mem. Pi Kappa Delta, Alpha Phi Gamma. Republican. Presbyterian. Avocations: dog breeding and training, ranching, needlework and design, photography. Home: Route 1 Box 615 Springtown TX 76082 Office: Long & Hulme Inc 620 Water Gardens Pl 100 E 15th St Fort Worth TX 76102

MOTT, BETTY LOU, auto repair and painting company executive; b. Reynoldsville, Pa., Feb. 3, 1935; d. Earl H. and Emma (Guthrie) Johnston Swan; m. Ralph P. Mott, Feb. 16, 1951; children—Deborah L., Ralph P. Jr., Randy E., Ricky J. Student Jamestown Community Coll., intermittently. Owner, mgr. Ralph's Collision Service, Inc., Olean, N.Y., 1959—; samples assembler Am. Olean Tile Co., 1985—; real estate broker World Inc., Olean, 1980-82, Century 21, Olean, 1982-83, Turek Agy., Olean, 1983—. Guardian, Nat. Fedn. Small Bus., 1979—. Mem. U.S. C. of C., Greater Credit Bur. Olean. Mem. fin. bd. First Free Methodist Ch., Allegany, N.Y., 1985—. Avocations: Camping; snowmobiling; boating. Home: PO Box 204 Westone Mills NY 14788

MOTT, JOSEPHINE ELIZABETH, lawyer; b. Balt., Mar. 21, 1952; d. Albert W. and C. Lorraine (Alsop) Bialozynski; m. Robert Allan Bonaccorsi, June 6, 1973 (div. Feb. 1974); m. 2d, Marshall J. Mott, May 2, 1981; 1 child, Benjamin Abraham; stepchildren—Geoffrey Philip, Laura Nicole, Sharon Lee. A.A., Hartford Coll. for Women, 1972; B.A., Smith Coll., 1977; J.D., U. Conn., 1980. Bar: Conn. 1983, U.S. Dist. Ct. Conn. 1983. Legal asst., office adminstr. Law Offices of Marshall J. Mott, East Hartford, Conn., 1980-83; ptnr. firm Mott & Mott, East Hartford, 1983-84; staff legal atty. Legal Aid Soc. Hartford County, Inc., 1984-85; mng. ptnr. Mott & Mott, Hartford, Conn., 1985—. Mem. Democratic Town Com., Columbia, Conn., 1982-83, Columbia Safety Commn., 1982-83, Columbia Bd. Edn., 1982-83. Mem. ABA, Conn. Bar Assn., Hartford County Bar Assn. Jewish. Home: 75 Brainard Rd West Hartford CT 06117 Office: Mott & Mott 117 Oak St Hartford CT 06106

MOTT, JUNE MARJORIE, educator; b. Faribault, Minn., Mar. 8, 1920; d. David C. and Tillie W. (Nelson) Shifflett; B.S., U. Minn., 1943, M.A., 1948; m. Elwood Knight Mott, Oct. 18, 1958. Tchr. high schs. in Minn., 1943-46, 48-53, 54-57; script writer, Hollywood, Calif., 1953-54; tchr. English, creative writing and journalism Mt. Miguel High Sch., Spring Valley, Calif., 1957—, chmn. English dept. council, 1967-68; mem. Press Bur., Grossmont (Calif.) High Sch. Dist., 1958—; scriptwriter TV prodn. Lamp Unto My Feet, Jam Dandy Corp.; free-lance writer, Cons. travel writer, photographer. Vice chmn. polit. action San Diego County Regional Resource Center, 1980-81. Writing project fellow U. Calif., San Diego, 1978; named Outstanding Journalism Tchr., State of Calif., Outstanding Humanities Tchr., San Diego County, Tchr. of Yr. for San Diego County, 1978. Mem. Nat. Council Tchrs. English, Nat. Journalism Assn., NEA, AAUW, Assn. Supervision and Curriculum Devel., Calif. Assn. Tchrs. English, Calif. Tchrs. Assn., So. Calif. Journalism Assn., Grossmont Edn. Assn. (pres. 1978-80), Greater San Diego Council Tchrs. English, Nat. Writers Club, Am. Guild Theatre Organists, Sigma Delta Chi. Democrat. Lutheran. Club: Order Eastern Star. Author, editor in field. Home: 2885 New Jersey Ave Lemon Grove CA 92045 Office: Mt Miguel High Sch 1800 Sweetwater Spring Valley CA 92077

MOTT, MARY ELIZABETH, educator; b. West Hartford, Conn., July 10, 1931; d. Marshall Amos and Mary Salome (Herman) M. B.A., Conn. Coll. Women, 1953; M.A., Western Res. U., 1963. Cert. tchr., Ohio. Mgr. sales promotion Cleve. Electric Illuminating Co., 1953-60; tchr. Newbury Bd. Edn., Ohio, 1960-67, West Geauga Bd. Edn., Chesterland, Ohio, 1967—; chmn. state certification com. in computers ECCO, Mayfield, Ohio, 1983—, exec. bd., 1980—. Asst. dir. West Geauga Day Camp, Chesterland, 1968. Mem. Ednl. Computer Consortium Ohio, Delta Kappa Gamma. Republican. Clubs: MAC Users Group, NEO Apple Corps, Nat. Assn. Playing Card Collectors. Avocations: golf, travel, reading, gardening, computers. Office: Westwood Sch 13738 Caves Rd Chesterland OH 44026

MOTT, MELANIE MADGE, manufacturing industry consultant; b. Houston, Oct. 12, 1951; d. Manning Marshall and Leonia Dolores (Grant) M.; B.A., Smith Coll., 1973. Production control analyst Gen. Electric Co., 1973-75, supr. prodn. planning and inventory control, 1975-76, subcontract adminstr., 1976-77; intern cons. I, Rath & Strong, Inc., 1977; sales rep. Gen. Electric Info. Services Co., 1977-78, account rep., 1978-79; intern cons. II Rath & Strong, Inc., Lexington, Mass., 1979, assoc. cons. 1980-82, cons., 1982-84, sr. cons., 1985—. Mem. Inst. Mgmt. Cons., Am. Prodn. and Inventory Control Soc., NOW. Home: 132 Williams St Boston MA 02130 Office: 21 Worthen Rd Lexington MA 02173

MOTTER, ROBERTA LEE, marketing consulting firm executive; b. Honolulu, Mar. 8, 1936; d. Donald D. and Florence B. (Downie) Reed; student Cornell U., summer 1956, various other courses; children—Eddie, Lori, Lisa. Dir. personnel Hawaiian Village Hotel, Honolulu, 1956-59; office mgr. Fisher Constrn. Co., Honolulu, 1960-61; paymaster, computer specialist Gate City Steel, Omaha, 1961-64; payroll supr., accounts receivable supr. Mayflower Hotel, Washington, 1966-67; computer specialist, dir. personnel Alan M. Voorhees & Assos., McLean, Va., 1968-71, adminstrv. mgr. PRC Computer Center subs., 1972-73; conversion specialist accounts payable system Medenco, Inc., Houston, 1973-74; personnel dir., office mgr. Summit Ins. Co. of N.Y., Houston, 1974-75; dir. adminstrv. services N.Y. State Ins. Dept. Liquidation Bur., N.Y.C., 1975-80; program analyst Office of Customer and Industry Relations, GSA, Washington, 1980-81, supervisory procurement analyst Office Procurement Ops., Arlington, Va., 1981-84; owner Contacts Unltd., 1978—, pres., 1985—. Mem. Am. Soc. Personnel Mgrs., N.Y. Purchasing Mgmt. Assn., Adminstrv. Mgmt. Soc. (dir.), N.Y. Internat. Personnel Mgmt. Assn., Internat. Platform Assn., Community Entrepreneurs Orgn., Nat. Assn. Profl. Saleswomen, Sales and Mktg. Execs., Les Amis du Vin, Beta Sigma Phi. Republican. Home: 1168 Ravine View Dr Roseville CA 95678

MOTZ, ESTHER PAULINE, city official; b. Elkton, Mich., Sept. 21, 1918; d. Freeman Josiah and Bertha Pauline (Sparschu) M. Grad. high sch., Elkton, 1935. Sec. to supt. Elkton High Sch., 1935-36; Elkton news corr. Times Herald, Port Huron, Mich., 1933-36; bookkeeper Thumb Bottling Co., Bad Axe, Mich., 1936-57, asst. sec.-treas., 1952-57; office mgr. Fairmont Foods Co., Bad Axe, 1957-72; legal sec. Thomas R. McAllister, Bad Axe, 1972-76; personal sec. Ruth M. McAllister, Bad Axe, 1976-78; treas. City of Bad Axe, 1978—. Mem. Bad Axe Bus. and Profl. Women (pres. 1981-84, editor 1980-83), Hist. Soc. Huron County, Bad Axe Council of Arts, Nat. Travel Club, Nat. Arbor Day Found., Am. Assn. Ret. Persons, Nat. Geographic Soc. Republican. Avocations: Bible study; scrabble; reading; walking; travel. Office: City of Bad Axe 110 S Hanselman St Bad Axe MI 48413

MOTZKIN, EVELYN HERSZKORN, psychiatrist; b. Warsaw, Poland, Jan. 12, 1933; d. Joseph and Eda (Itzkowitz) Herszkorn; m. Donald Motzkin, 1955; children—Patricia, Linda, Neil, Nancy, Richard, Lisa. M.D., SUNY, 1958; Ph.D. in Psychoanalysis, So. Calif. Inst. Psychoanalysis, 1978. Intern, Vassar Bros. Hosp., 1958-59; fellow in endocrinology Baylor U., Houston, 1960-62, resident in psychiatry, 1962-64; resident in psychiatry VA Hosp., Sepulveda, Calif., 1965-67; practice psychiatry and psychoanalysis, Encino, Calif., 1967—; cons. Sepulveda VA Hosp., 1967-68, Jewish Home for Aged, 1968-71; clin. instr. UCLA Neuropsychiat. Inst., 1969-71; instr. So. Calif. Psychoanalytic Inst., 1980—; coordinator U. Judaism Extension Div. and So. Calif. Psychoanalytic Inst., 1983; mem. staff Woodview Calabasas Hosp., Med. Ctr. Tarzana, Calif., Encino Hosp., Calif., Rancho Encino Hosp. Initiator, chmn. psychiat. div. San Fernando Valley United Jewish Welfare Fund, 1977, 77; major gifts co-chmn. United Jewish Appeal, San Fernando, 1979; mem. community relations council United Jewish Fedn., 1982-86; bd. dirs. Assn. Mental Health Affiliation with Israel. Recipient Ben Gurion award San Fernando Valley State of Israel Bonds Med. Div., 1977. Mem. So. Calif. Psychoanalytic Soc. (exec. com. 1980-81, sec. treas. 1981-83, chmn. membership com. 1983), Am. Psychiat. Assn., So. Calif. Psychiat. Assn., Internat. Psychoanalytic Assn., Am. Psychoanalytic Assn., Israeli Med. Assn., Physicians for Israel. Home: Woodland Hills CA Office: Motzkin Med Corp 5353 Balboa Blvd Encino CA 91316

MOUCHKA, SUSAN ANNE (FOSSUM), govt. health planning ofcl.; b. Peoria, Ill., Nov. 18, 1941; d. Joseph L. and Bernadette Marie (O'Hearn) Hecht; B.S., Ind. U., 1964; M.S. in Clin. Psychology, San Francisco State U., 1974; postgrad. Fielding Inst., Santa Barbara, 1981—; m. G. Mouchka (div.); children—Catherine, Margaret; m. 2d Jim Fossum, May 18, 1980. Cons. on psychology of developmental disabilities, Sacramento, 1970—; clin. dir., Calif. Dept. Developmental Services, Sonoma State Hosp., 1977-78, cons. in program evaluation, 1979-80; coordinator Calif. Public Forums on Long Term Care and Aging, Calif. Health and Welfare Agy., Sacramento, 1981-82; project dir. NIMH grant Calif. Dept. Mental Health, Sacramento, 1982-84; chief spl. studies Calif. Dept. Devel. Services, 1984-85; pvt. practice individual and family counseling and organizational devel., 1985—. Lic. nursing home adminstr., lic. marriage, family, child counselor. Mem. Am. Psychol. Assn., Am. Acad. Family Mediators, Am. Assn. Marriage and Family Therapists. Contbr. papers and report to publs. in field. Home: 3400 Northrop Ave Sacramento CA 95864 Office: 1329 H St Sacramento CA 95814

MOULDING, MARY BAKER, civic worker; b. Peoria, Ill., Aug. 15, 1907; d. Murray Morrison and Mary (Lyman) Baker; m. Arthur Tilt Moulding, Apr. 9, 1932 (dec. 1977); children—Patricia Moulding Hibben, Murray. Student Marot Jr. Coll., Thompson, Conn., 1925-26, Bradley U., 1928. Mem. founders' council Field Mus. Natural History, Chgo.; mem. women's bd. Field Mus.; mem. Winnetka aux. Rush-Presbyn. St. Luke's Hosp., Chgo.; mem. orch. assn. Chgo. Symphony Orch. Antiquarian Soc., Art Inst., Chgo.; mem. governing bd. Art Inst., Chgo. Hort. Soc.; mem. Chgo. Hist. Soc., Ill. State Hist. Soc., Audubon Soc., Hawaiian Mission Children's Soc., Jr. League of Evanston, Bahamas Nat. Trust, Nature Conservancy, Nat. Soc. Colonial Dames of Am. in Ill., Lyman Mission House and Mus. Assn., vestry Ch. of St. Christopher, Lyford Cay, Nassau, Bahamas; Bishop's Assocs., Diocese of Chgo. Author: (with Arthur T. Moulding) Shells at Our Feet, 1967. Dedications: Two species of shells Field Mus. Natural History, Chgo., 1985. Republican. Episcopalian. Clubs: Chgo. Shell, Woman's Athletic, Fortnightly (Chgo.); Winnetka Garden; Nassau Garden (Bahamas); Lyford Cay; Indian Hill. Avocations: conchology; horticulture; conservation; music.

MOULTON, BARBARA MOORE, nurse; b. Brockton, Mass., Oct. 8, 1926; d. Lawrence Harold and Avis Evelyn (Moore) M. B.S.N.Ed., Fla. State U., 1963; M.S.N.Ed., U. Pitts., 1967. Staff nurse obstetrics St. Luke's Hosp., Jacksonville, Fla., 1947-50, asst. dir. nursing service, 1950-51, staff nurse clin. instr. obstetrics, 1951-53, instr. obstetrics nursing, 1956-57; office nurse Dr. C. J. Masters, Jacksonville, 1953-55; adminstrv. supr. obstetrics Bapt. Meml. Hosp., Jacksonville, 1955-61; instr. maternal-child St. Vincent's Hosp. Sch. Nursing, Jacksonville, 1964; health educator/cons. Maternal-Child Health Bur., Fla. State Bd. Health, Jacksonville, 1964-66; asst. prof. obstetric nursing U. Pitts. Sch. Nursing, 1968-69; dir. nursing Magee-Women's Hosp., Pitts., 1969-76; clin. assoc. prof., chmn. U. Pitts. Sch. Nursing, 1969-76; asst. prof. adj. faculty U. Minn. Sch. Nursing, Mpls., 1980—; asst. dir. nursing Rochester Meth. Hosp. (Minn.), 1976—; cons. Akron (Ohio) Gen. Hosp., Olmsted Community Hosp., Rochester, Minn., hosps. in southwestern Pa. and Fla. mem. profl. adv. bd. Childbirth Edn. Assn. Mem. nominating com., area del. Rivertrails council Girl Scouts Am., Rochester, Minn., 1985-86. Mem. Nurses Assn. Am. Coll. Ob-Gyn, Internat. Childbirth Edn. Assn., Assn. Care of Children's Health, Cybele Soc., Great Plains Orgn. Perinatal Health Care, Minn. Perinatal Orgn. (dir. 1982), Sigma Theta Tau. Democrat. Methodist. Home: 2301 Elton Hills Dr NW Rochester MN 55901 Office: Rochester Meth Hosp 201 W Center St Rochester MN 55902

MOULTRIE, RUBY LEE, music educator; b. Plainview, Tex., Feb. 11, 1955; d. Massie Lee Williams and Artie Mae (Green) Williams Moultrie. B.Music Edn., W. Tex. State U., 1977; M.Sacred Music, So. Meth. U., 1981, M.Music in Performance, 1981. Music tchr. Richardson Elem. Sch., Dimmitt, Tex., 1977-79; voice tchr. Sunset High Sch., Dallas, 1979-80, Music Masters, Plano, Tex., 1982—; adminstrv. asst. Gt. Am. Res. Ins. Co., Dallas, 1982—. Choir dir. 1st United Meth. Ch., Dimmitt, Tex., 1977-79, Brandon Ave United Meth. Ch., Dallas, 1980-82; vol. Phylis Wheatly Elem. Sch., Dallas, 1983-84. Bus. and Profl. Women's scholar W. Tex. State U., 1973; vocal scholar W. Tex. State U., 1973-77, acad. scholar, 1974-76. Mem. Mu Phi Epsilon. Democrat. Methodist. Office: Great Am Res Ins Co 2020 Live Oak St Dallas TX 75201

MOULTRIE, THELMA LARNETTA, office machines company sales executive; b. Plainview, Tex., Nov. 6, 1953; d. Albert and Artie Mae (Green) M. B.S. in Psychology, West Tex. State U., 1975. Sales rep. IBM, Big Spring, Tex., 1976-80, account rep., Dallas, 1978-80; cons. makeup, Dallas, 1981-83; dist. sales mgr. Xerox Corp., Southfield, Mich., 1983—. Winner Wilhelmenia Modeling Wilhelmina Run-Way Competition, Houston, 1977; recipient Misa Black Am. of Tex. award and Top Ten Miss Black Am. award Miss Black Am., Inc., 1978; Rotary Club and Kiwanis Club scholar West Tex. State U., Canyon, 1972. Mem. Delta Sigma Theta. Democrat. Methodist. Avocations: singing; tennis; writing music. Home: 29260 Pointe O'Woods Pl Apt 106 Southfield MI 48034 Office: Xerox Corp 26555 Evergreen Rd Southfield MI 48076

MOUNDS, LEONA MAE REED, educator; b. Crosby, Tex., Sept. 9, 1945; d. Elton Phillip and Ora Lee (Jones) Reed; m. Aaron B. Mounds Jr., Aug. 21, 1965; 1 dau., Lisa Nichelle. B.S. in Elem. Edn., Bridgewater State Coll., 1973; M.A. in Mental Retardation, U. Alaska, 1980. Cert. tchr. Alaska, Colo., Tex., Mass. Tchr., Sch. Dist. 11, Colorado Springs, Colo., 1973-75; tchr. Anchorage Sch. Dist., 1976-78, 80—, mem. math. curriculum com., reading contact tchr., mem. talent bank. Tchr. Del Valle (Tex.) Sch. Dist., 1979-80. Bd. dirs. Urban League, 1974; 1st v.p. PTA, Crosby, Tex.; del. Tex. Democratic Conv., 1980; tchr. religious edn., lay Eucharist minister St. Martin De Pores Roman Cath. Ch., St. Patricks Cath. Ch. Served with USAF, 1964-66. Alaska State Tchr. Incentive grantee, 1981; Ivy Lutz scholar, 1972. Mem. NEA (coordinator human relations Alaska chpt.), Anchorage Edn. Assn. (minority chmn. 1982—, mem. Black Caucus polit. action com.), Black Educators of Pikes Peak Region (pres. 1974), Anchorage Edn. Assn. (women's caucus, v.p. programs, bd. dirs.), Assn. Supervision and Curriculum Devel., Alaska Women in Adminstrn., Council for Exception Children, NAACP.

MOUNT, WARD (PAULINE WARD), painter, sculptor; b. Batavia, N.Y.; d. Fred Kendall and Nellie L. (Dowsey) Ward; grad. Flushing High Sch.; student N.Y.U., Art Students League; pvt. study with Gertrude Gardner, Kenneth Hayes Miller, Albert P. Lucas, Joseph P. Pollia; m. Elmer M. Mount; 1 son, Marshall Ward. Former head of dept. oil painting and sculpture N.J. State Tchrs. Coll.; founder, former dir. art classes Jersey City Med. Center, 1948-49; dir., instr. Ward Mount Art Classes. Represented by paintings and sculptures, Columbia U. Library, Irvington Pub. Library, Delgado Mus., New Orleans, Hudson River Mus., Montclair Art Mus., Provincetown Art Gallery, Trenton State Mus., Jersey City Mus., N.A.D., Marquis Biog. Library, Library of Congress, Nat. Sculpture Soc., Archtl. League (N.Y.), Verona Pub. Library, N.Y. Pub. Library, Municipal Art Galleries, Allied Artists Am., Allied Arts Mus. (N.Y.), Riverside Mus., Nat. Arts Club (N.Y.C.), Grand Central Palace, Acad. Allied Arts (N.Y.C.), Am. British Art Center, N.Y. Hist. Mus., Kearney Mus., N.J. Gallery, Macy Galleries, Fine Arts Bldg. (N.Y.C.), Essex, Sussex and Warren, Monmouth hotels (Spring Lake, N.J.), Berkley Carteret (Asbury Park, N.J.), Palm Beach (Fla.) hotel, Alford Hotel (East Orange, N.J.), Brentanos, Audubon Artists, Pa. Acad., Smithsonian Instn., Carlebach Galleries (N.Y.C.), Terry Art Inst. (Fla.), Worlds Fair, N.Y., 1965, Madison Sq. Garden, F. D. Roosevelt Mus., Archives Am. Art (Eng.), Westchester Art Galleries, Lever House, N.Y.C., Mus. Modern Art, also fgn. countries. Designed bronze Medal of Honor for Painters and Sculptors Soc. N.J.; designed and executed The Bell of Am., Bell Assn. Represented in many collections including Pres. Franklin D. Roosevelt, Hon. Charles B. Howard of Canada, Georgia Timken Fry, Bernard U. Gimbel. Recipient 1st prize for watercolor, Jersey City Art Exhbn.; 1st prize for oil painting, Jersey City Mus.; 1st prize for sculpture, Painters and Sculptors Soc.; Clayton E. Freeman 1st prize sculpture, ann. state exhbn., Montclair Air Mus.; 1st prize sculpture, N.J. Artists (Union, N.J.); 1st prize sculpture Asbury Park Soc. Fine Arts; first sculpture prize Kearney (N.J.) Mus; 1st prize bronze sculpture Art Fair, N.Y.C.,; Jersey Jour. Woman Achievement Gold medal, 1971; named Artist of Yr., Hudson Artists, 1985; decorated Knight Mark Twain. Past mem. faculty Acad. Allied Arts (N.Y.). Fellow Internat. Inst. Arts and Letters (life), Royal Soc. of Arts (Eng.); mem. N.Y. Soc. Painters, Artists Equity (founding mem.), N.Y., Painters and Sculptors Soc. N.J. (founder, hon. pres.), D.A.R., Acad. of Italy. Designed and executed Christmas card for Am. Heart Assn., 1971; one of 100 honorees from Hudson County for Miss Liberty celebration. Home and studio: 74 Sherman Pl Jersey City NJ 07307

MOUSER, MARCELLA, educator; b. Frontenac, Kans., Jan. 16, 1926; d. Frank and Lillie (Arkle) M.; B.S. in Edn., Pittsburg State U., 1947, M.S. in Edn., 1952; Ed.D. in Secondary Edn., U. Nebr., Lincoln, 1969. Tchr. bus. Louisburg (Kans.) High Sch., 1947-49, Yates Center (Kans.) High Sch., 1951-59; asst. prof. bus. and bus. edn. Emporia State U., 1959-69, asso. prof., 1969-73, prof., 1973—; bd. dirs. nat. Future Bus. Leaders Am./Phi Beta Lambda, Inc.; asst. chairperson Kans. Future Bus. Leaders Am. Capt., United Way, Sch. Applied Arts and Scis., Emporia State U., 1982. Emporia State U. Faculty Research and Creativity grantee, 1976, 82. Mem. NEA, Kans. Edn. Assn., Kans. Bus. Edn. Assn. (exec. bd.), Nat. Bus. Edn. Assn. (exec. bd.), AAUP, AAUW, Mountain-Plains Bus. Edn. Assn. (exec. bd.), Am. Bus. Women's Assn., Pi Omega Pi, Delta Pi Epsilon, Kappa Kappa Iota. Roman Catholic. Club: Am. Legion Aux. Advt. mgr. Kans. Bus. Tchr., 1976-82. Home: 1219 Merchant Emporia KS 66801 Office: 1200 Commercial Emporia KS 66801

MOUSSATOS, MARTHA ANN TYREE, librarian; b. Parris Island, S.C., Sept. 18, 1936; d. Frank La Prade and Vireen Florrie (Varn) Tyree; m. Apostolos Harilaos Moussatos, June 27, 1959; children—Vasiliana Vireen, Harilaos Apostolos. B.A., Columbia Coll., 1958; M.L.S., U. Ariz., 1974. Asst. reference librarian U. S.C., Columbia, 1958-59; librarian Fulton High Sch., Atlanta, 1962; substitute tchr. pub. schs., Sierra Vista, Ariz., 1967-68; librarian Naco Elem. Sch. (Ariz.), 1968-70, Benson High Sch. (Ariz.), 1970-75; head librarian Depot Library, Parris Island, S.C., 1975—. Author: Hagar (play), 1980; Young Eliza (play), 1958; Marshgrass and Muscadines (poetry), 1980; Scuppernong Wine at Room Temperature (poetry), 1984; contbr. articles to profl. jours. and popular mags. Mem. Historic Port Royal Found. (S.C.), 1976—, bd. dirs., 1981—. Recipient award as head of outstanding single parent family Beaufort County Homebuilders Assn. (S.C.), 1980. Mem. ALA, Library Assn. Beaufort County, S.C. Library Assn. (editorial com. 1979—), Poetry Soc. S.C. (bd. dirs. 1980-83). Methodist. Home: 3011 Hickory St Burton SC 29902 Office: Depot Library PO Drawer 5-055 Parris Island SC 29905

MOWERY, JOAN HARDY, oil company executive; b. Tulsa, Aug. 6, 1949; d. Homer Dwight, Jr. and Phyllis Joan (Love) Hardy; m. Jerry L.R. Mowery, July 11, 1980; 1 child, Scott Weston. B.B.A., Okla. U., 1971; M.B.A., So. Meth. U., Dallas, 1979. Acct. exec. Dean Witter Reynolds, St. Louis, 1976-78; internal auditor The Williams Cos., Tulsa, 1979-80; fin. analyst Peabody Coal Co., St. Louis, 1980-81; assoc. auditor Chevron Oil Co., San Francisco, 1981-82, telecommunications analyst, 1982-84, controls analyst, Tulsa, 1985—; v.p., dir. World Art services, Tulsa, 1978—. Vol. Domestic Violence Intervention Services, Tulsa, 1984—; adviser Jr. Achievement, Tulsa, 1985. Republican. Episcopalian. Mem. Jr. League of Tulsa, Kappa Alpha Theta. Avocations: needlepoint; snow skiing; jogging; swing dancing. Office: Chevron Oil Co 1350 S Boulder Tulsa OK 74102

MOXLEY, LINDA EDELMAN, orchestra administrator; b. Freeport, N.Y., Jan. 30, 1956; d. Herbert John and Lony Maria (Erler) Edelman; m. Harry Ethelberg Moxley, Oct. 19, 1985. Mus.B., Fredonia Coll., 1978; M. in Arts Mgmt., Cin. U., 1980. Dir. pub. relations and mktg. Va. Philharm., Norfolk, 1980-81; asst. dir. pub. relations San Francisco Symphony, 1981-83, asst. dir. mktg., 1983—, summer pops coordinator, 1983-84. Asst. producer documentary film Oberlin Dance Company: The Contemporary Move, 1984 (Cine Golden Eagle award 1984). Mem. Am. Symphony Orch. League, Nat. Acad. Rec. Arts and Scis., Nat. Assn. Female Execs. Avocations: classical pianist; dance; racquetball; photography. Office: San Francisco Symphony Davies Symphony Hall San Francisco CA 94102

MOXNESS, MARGARET ANN, psychiatrist; b. Lorain, Ohio, Oct. 31, 1953; d. John Brand and Irene (Stachowski) M.; Student Oberlin Coll., 1971-73; B.S. in Psychology, U. Cin., 1975, M.D., 1979; m. Robert J. Ward, May 19, 1984. Intern, St. Vincent's Hosp., N.Y.C., 1979-80, resident in psychiatry, 1980-83, fellow child and adolescent psychiatry, 1983-85; dir. consultation psychiatry Schneider's Children's Hosp., L.I. Jewish/Hillside Med. Ctr., New Hyde, N.Y., 1985-86; asst. to exec. med. dir. Pride of Judea Mental Health Ctr., Douglaston, N.Y., 1986—. Mem. Am. Psychiat. Assn. (mem. editorial bd. N.Y. and Area II Council 1983, chmn. com. on residents 1981-83), Am. Acad. Child Psychiatry, N.Y. Council on Child Psychiatry, N.Y. Acad. Medicine (chmn. seminar 1983), Phi Beta Kappa. Home: 123 Warwick Ave Douglaston NY 11363 Office: Pride of Judea Mental Health Ctr Douglaston NY 11363

MOY, AUDREY, retail buyer; b. Bronx, N.Y., May 6, 1942; d. Ferdinand Walter Melkert and Stella (Factorow) Schroff; m. Edward Moy, Aug. 16, 1974. B.A. in Biology, Hunter Coll., 1964, M.A. in Biology, 1966. Asst. buyer Bonwit Teller, N.Y.C., 1961-68; dept. mgr. Franklin Simon, N.Y.C., 1968; asst. buyer Saks Fifth Ave., N.Y.C., 1968-73; buyer Martins, Bklyn., 1973, Belk Store Services, N.Y.C., 1974—. Mem. Nat. Assn. Female Execs. Democrat. Avocations: cooking; bird watching; fishing.

MOY, JANE, leasing company executive, real estate agent, mortgage broker, consultant; b. Grovetown, Ga., May 2, 1956; d. William and Peggy (Eng) Moy; m. Raymond Shih Ying Yang, Aug., 1, 1976; one son, Simon. B.B.A., U. Miami, 1976. Exec. Federated Stores, Miami, 1976-81; pres., owner Pvt. Safe Deposit Box Co., Inc., Hollywood, Fla., 1981—; v.p. Appliance Leasing Systems, Inc., Ft. Lauderdale, Fla., 1985—. Mem. Hollywood Bd. Realtors, C. of C., Phi Kappa Phi. Baptist. Office: Appliance Leasing Systems Inc PO Box 2453 Hollywood FL 33022

MOYE, SANDRA ZIEGLER, food company official, businesswoman; b. Miami, Fla., Oct. 19, 1941; d. Louis Henry Torruella and Victoria Elizabeth (Posgay) Torel; m. Donald Atkins Moye, Dec. 24, 1966 (div. 1976); children—S. Allison, Shawn T. M.B.A., Columbia Pacific U., 1985. Adminstrv. mgr. Edgar H. Mueller Constrn., Buena Park, Calif., 1962-67; office mgr. Foundry div. Teledyne, Norwalk, Calif., 1967-70; adminstrv. asst. personnel and purchasing Best Foods unit CPC Internat., Inc., Santa Fe Springs, Calif., 1973-74, purchasing agt., 1974-78, purchasing mgr., 1978—; owner, pres. Petland, Big Bear Lake, Calif., 1981-83; cons. self-help guidance for teenagers and sr. citizens, Whittier, Calif., 1978—. Com. chmn. Republican Women's Orgn., Los Angeles, 1972; chmn. Residents Opposing Modification Zoning Ordinance, Whittier, 1982-83. Mem. Purchasing Mgmt. Assn. Orange County, Nat. Assn. Purchasing Mgrs. Presbyterian. Home: 13311 Danbrook Dr Whittier CA 90602 Office: Best Foods Unit of CPC International Inc 15700 Shoemaker Ave Santa Fe Springs CA 90670

MOYER, LAURENE FRANCES, professional recruiting executive; b. Balt., Sept. 6, 1940; d. Joshua E. Arrington and Dorothy M. (Rohleder) Arnold; m. Samuel Lee Moyer, Apr. 9, 1969; children—Kurt, Sheryll, Jodi, Paul, Tish, Christopher. Student Monterey Peninsula Jr. Coll., 1968-69, Chaminade U., 1976-77. Salesperson, Honolulu, 1971-77; br. mgr. Career Cons., Bailey's Crossroads, Va., 1977-80; pres. ExecuSearch, Inc., LaGrange, Ga., 1980-84, OmniSearch, Inc., Tampa, Fla., 1982—; owner References on Request, Tampa, 1986—. Mem. Nat. Assn. Female Execs. (network dir. Tampa 1984—), Fla. Assn. Personnel Cons. Avocations: golf; reading; board games; gourmet cooking. Office: OmniSearch 5444 Bay Center Dr Suite 110 Tampa FL 33609

MOZDIN, SHARON RAILING, computer systems analyst, lighting designer, photographer; b. Wilmington, Del., Sept. 13, 1951; d. Wilford Edward and Shirley Hogg (Sackett) Railing; m. David James Mozdin, Nov. 5, 1983. B.A. in Theatre, Lycoming Coll., 1973. Computer operator U. Del., Newark, 1973-74, coordinator user edn., 1974-80; jr. systems analyst Delmarva Power and Light, Newark, 1980-82, systems analyst, 1982—; instr. lighting Wilmington Drama League, Del., 1986. Photographer: Corporate Systems, 1977, The Animals of Africa, 1982. Lighting advisor Wilmington Drama League, lighting designer, 1980—; lighting designer Brandywiners, Ltd., 1986, Ardensingers, 1976—, Opera Del., 1984; lighting cons. Arden Hwy. Ensemble, 1984—; pres. Del. Assn. Theater, 1981-83. Recipient Hon. Mention award Delmarva Photo Club, 1982. Mem. Nat. Assn. Profl. Women. Republican. Episcopalian. Club: Delmarva Photo (pres. 1981-83). Avocations: travel; amateur theatre. Home: 505 Clearview Ave Woodside Hills Wilmington DE 19809 Office: Delmarva Power and Light Route 273 & I-95 Newark DE 19714

MOZER, DORIS ANN, writer; b. July 10, 1929; d. Charles Ross and Mary Margaret (Redmiles) Werner; B.A., N.Mex. State U., 1963, M.A. in English, 1970; postgrad. in English, U. Md., 1982; div.; children—Stephen, Judith, Mary Catherine, Laura, John. Grad. asst. N.Mex. State U., 1963-65, instr., 1969-75; free-lance editor, 1969—; editor Sibyl-Child, women's arts and cultural jour., 1976—; grad. asst. U. Md., College Park, 1976-78, dir. Writing Center, 1978-80, acad. adviser, internship coordinator, 1980-82; tech. writer Environ. Satellite Data, Inc., Suitland, Md., 1982-84, RCA, Morrestown, N.J., 1984—. Vice pres., publicity chmn. Las Cruces (N.Mex.) Children's Theatre, 1968; pres., publicity chmn. Las Cruces Theater Guild, 1969. Folger Shakespearean Inst. fellow, 1979. Mem. Phi Kappa Phi. Democrat. Unitarian. Author: (poetry) The Quickest Promise Home. Home: 48 Covered Bridge Rd Cherry Hill NJ 08034 Office: RCA Advanced Tech Labs Morrestown NJ

MRDEZA, JANET E DRAKE, sales executive; b. Chatham, Ont., Can., Nov. 5, 1948; came to U.S., 1968, naturalized, 1982; d. Cyril Edgar and Esther (Harlick) Srigley; m. George E. Mrdeza, Mar. 18, 1984. A.Arts and Sci. with honors, No. Collegiate Coll., 1967; A.B., Chamberlain Sch. Retailing, 1968; m. Millard Llewellyn Drake, July 27, 1968. Area rep. Internat. Playtex, Stamford, Conn., 1971-74; nat. field sales coordinator Burlington Hosiery, N.Y.C., 1974-77; dir. sales devel. Natural Wonder Div., Revlon, N.Y.C., 1977-80; dir. sales devel. Lord Jeff div. Gen. Mills, N.Y.C., 1980-81; mgr. sales tng. and merchandising Danskin div., Internat. Playtex, Stamford, 1981-83, regional sales mgr., 1983, nat. accounts mgr. Playtex, 1984—. Mem. Am. Mgmt. Assn., Fashion Group of N.Y. Clubs: Metropolitan, N.Y. Athletic (N.Y.C.); Canadian. Home: 41 Flying Cloud Rd Stamford CT 06902 Office: 700 Fairfield Ave Stamford CT 06904

MRKONICH, DOROTHY EVANSON, nursing educator; b. Echo, Minn., July 10, 1938; d. August Alfred and Tilda (Sollom) Evanson; B.S.N., St. Olaf Coll., 1960; M.Ed., U. Minn., 1961, Ph.D., 1982; m. Thomas Mrkonich, Aug. 15, 1959; children—Jana Kaye, Kirsten DeAnn, Jon Thomas. Mem. faculty dept. nursing Coll. of St. Catherine, St. Paul, 1961-62; mem. faculty dept. nursing St. Olaf Coll., Northfield, Minn., 1970—, assoc. prof., 1980—, chmn. dept. nursing, 1979-86; mem. Minn. Bd. Nursing, 1981—, pres., 1984; dir. Minn. Intercollegiate Nursing Consortium. Mem. Am. Nurses Assn., Minn. Nurses Assn., Sigma Theta Tau, Pi Lambda Theta. Office: St Olaf Coll Northfield MN 55057

MRUK, JILL ADAMS, radio station executive; b. Pitts., Oct. 14, 1957; d. William David Crawford and Rosemary Adele (Zimmerman) Crawford Schafer; m. Ronald Stephen Mruk, Apr. 14, 1982; 1 child, Ronald Stephen. B.A. in Speech Communications, Pa. State U., 1979. Announcer, Sta.-WGMR,

State College, Pa., 1978-79, Sta.-WXLR, State College, 1978-79, Stas.-WJPA/WYTK, Washington, Pa., 1980-82; program dir. Stas.-WNAT/WQNZ, Natchez, Miss., 1982—. Mem. Nat. Assn. Broadcasters, Miss. Broadcasters Assn. Republican. Lutheran. Office: Stas-WNAT/WQNZ 2 O'Ferral St Natchez MS 39120

MUCCIANO, STEPHANIE LYONS, travel and tourism executive; b. Pitts., Jan. 8, 1944; d. Ross Cooper and Catherine Dorothy (Perrone) Lyons; m. Richard Francis Mucciano, Apr. 17, 1963 (dec. 1972); 1 child, Stephanie Lynn. Student St. Petersburg Jr. Coll., 1963-64, Alamogorda Bus. Coll., 1970-71. Sales mgr. Bahama Cruise Line, Tampa, Fla., 1978-82; dir. mktg./sales AAA Holidays/St. Petersburg Motor Club, Fla., 1982-84; pres., dir. mktg./sales Travel and Tourism Resources, Inc., St. Petersburg, and Island Harbor Resort, Cape Haze, Fla., 1984—; mktg. cons., dir. Royal Fiesta Cruises, Tampa; seminar leader, internat. industry speaker. Mem. Fla. Gulf Coast Symphony Guild, St. Petersburg, 1975—, All Childrens Hosp. Guild, 1975—, Infinity League to Aid Abused Children, 1981—, Pinellas Assn. for Retarded Adults, 1975—. Recipient Cert. of Recognition, George Greer County Commr., Pinellas, 1986. Mem. Pacific Area Travel Assn. (dir.), Sun Coast Travel Industry Assn., Sales & Mktg. Execs. Internat., Travel & Tourism Research Assn., C. of C., Women Execs. in Travel, Nat. Assn. Female Execs., Fla. Women's Network, Am. Soc. Travel Agts., Am. Mktg. Assn. Republican. Clubs: Italian-Am., St. Petersburg Internat. Folk Fair Soc. Avocations: reading; volunteer work. Office: Island Harbor Resort 1124 S Myrtle Ave Clearwater FL 33516

MUCCIOLI, ANNA MARIA, artist; b. Detroit, Apr. 23, 1922; d. Anthony and Josephine (Coccardi) De Pascale; student Coll. Art and Design, 1970-75; student of Sarkis Sarkision, Detroit, 1962-66, Charles Culver, Detroit, 1963-67; m. Joseph E. Muccioli, Dec. 26, 1942; children—Ronald, Nathan, Edward, James. One-woman shows of sculpture and/or paintings include: Verve Gallery, 1965, Left Bank Gallery, Flint, Mich., 1969; group shows include: Ford Motor Co. Art Exhbn. (17 awards), 1961-65, 68, 69, 74, 76, 77, 78, 79, Birmingham (Mich.) Art Festival, 1966, Oakland Community Coll., 1967, Mich. Watercolor Soc. (honorable mention), 1968-71, Mich. State Fair, 1968, 69, 71, 73, 76, 78, Am. Watercolor Soc., N.Y.C., 1971, Nat. Art Club, N.Y.C., 1971, Ala. Water Color Soc., 1972, Detroit Inst. Arts Rental Gallery. Recipient numerous art awards, including Water Color award Oakland Community Coll. Mem. Founders Soc. Detroit Inst. Arts, Friends of Modern Art, Women's Caucus of Art, Mich. Watercolor Soc., Soc. Arts and Crafts. Home: 16194 Sprenger East Detroit MI 48021 Studio: 511 Beaubien Detroit MI 48226

MUCH, KATHLEEN, editor; b. Houston, Apr. 30, 1942; d. C. Frederick and Ortrud V. (Lefevre) M.; m. W. Robert Murfin, Aug. 17, 1963 (div. 1981); children—Brian C., Glen M. B.A., Rice U., 1963, M.A., 1971, postgrad., 1978. Clk., Tex. State Library, Austin, 1963-64; tchr. Kinkaid High Sch., Houston, 1964-66; editorial asst. Rice U., 1969-71, assoc. editor, 1972-81; freelance writer Houston, 1971—; dir. info. Meth. Hosp., Houston, 1981-84; sr. editor Addison-Wesley Pub. Co., Menlo Park, Calif., 1984-86; editor Ctr. for Advanced Study in Behavioral Scis., Stanford, Caalif., 1986—. dir. Tex. Wordworks, Inc. Active Houston Ballet Guild, Rice U. Fund Council, Friends of Stanford String Quartet, Bus. Vols. for Arts, Houston Grand Opera, Tex. Chamber Orchestra. Internat. Assn. Bus. Communicators, Pub. Relations Soc. Am., Soc. Tech. Communication, Phi Beta Kappa. Editor, contbr. profl. jours. Home: 2080 Marich Way #14 Mountain View CA 94040

MUCHMORE, PATSY WILLINE, author, photographer; b. Holdenville, Okla., June 28, 1937; d. Mennis Miller and Olive Faye (Ballard) Noblett; student Okla. State U., 1968, 74; m. Gareth Bruce Muchmore, Oct. 16, 1977 (dec. Sept. 22, 1983); children by previous marriage—Kerry James Redmond, Kathyrn Joy Pruitt, Darla Sue Duncan. Soc. editor Holdenville Daily News, 1960-62; news editor Wewoka (Okla.) Daily Times, 1962-63; reporter Kingfisher (Okla.) Free Press, 1964; aux. staffer Enid (Okla.) Morning News, 1965; news wire editor Ponca City (Okla.) Daily News, 1965-74, freelance writer Africa and Central Am., 1974-75; asst. and assoc. editor Dental Econs., Tulsa, 1975-77, editor, 1977-82, contbg. editor, 1983—; cons. dental firms, newspapers; speaker. Chmn. tourism Ponca City C. of C., 1974 bd. dirs. Ponca City Art Assn. Recipient hon. mention Golden Pen award, 1977, hon. mention Golden Pencil award, 1980; 1st runner-up AP Creative Writing award, 1969. Mem. Author's Guild, Am. League Authors, Okla. Writers Fedn., Sigma Delta Chi. Republican. Presbyterian. Author: Guide to Collections, 1979; (with others) As Your Practice Grows, 1977, How to Hire an Associate, 1982; contbr. numerous articles to newspapers, periodicals and jours. Office: 4405 S Columbia Ave Tulsa OK 74105

MUCHNICK, JEANNE RUTH, magazine executive; b. Balt., Aug. 8, 1961; d. Beryl Harry and Adele (Goldstein) M. B.A., Syracuse U., 1983. Editorial asst. Food Word, Columbia, Md., 1981-82; writer Balt. Jewish Tiimes, 1982; reporter Towson Times, Balt., 1981-82; writer Syracuse Mag., N.Y., 1980-82; editorial asst. Seventeen Mag., N.Y.C., 1983-84; asst. editor Good Housekeeping Mag., N.Y.C., 1984-85; bus. travel assoc. editor Travel Agt. Mag., N.Y.C., 1985—. Mem. Women in Communications, Soc. Profl. Journalists. Home: 462 W 58th St Apt 1C New York NY 10019 Office: The Travel Agt Mag 2 W 46th St New York NY 10036

MUCHOW, CHARLOTTE IRENE, engineer; b. Sioux Falls, S.D., Nov. 14, 1943; d. George W.F. and Irene Anna (Matthies) M.; B.S. in Engring. Physics, S.D. State U., 1965; postgrad. U. Ariz., 1970; M.S. in Geography, U. Calif., Riverside, 1980. Asso. engr. Westinghouse Research Labs., Pitts., 1965-67; engring. programmer Bell Telephone Labs., Whippany, N.J., 1967-69; sci. programmer Lockheed Aircraft Service, Ontario, Calif., 1971; physicist-mathematician for Bionetics at Jet Propulsion Lab., Pasadena, 1972-73; data analyst for Technicolor Graphics at EROS Data Center, Sioux Falls, 1974-76; tech. staff specialist Aerojet Electro-Systems, Azusa, Calif., 1980-81; systems engr. Measuronics, Gt. Falls, Mont., 1981-83; cons., 1983-85; prin. Muchow & Assocs., Gt. Falls, Mont., 1985—. Vol., Big Sisters, Gt. Falls. Mem. Soc. Women Engrs., IEEE, Am. Soc. Photogrammetry, Bus. and Profl. Women, AAUW. Lutheran. Home and office: PO Box 1375 Great Falls MT 59403

MUCKLER, JULIE ROBINSON, employee communications and development executive; b. Mpls., Jan. 4, 1951; d. William Joseph and Martha (Snider) Robinson; B.S., Iowa State U., 1973, M.S., 1978; m. Richard D. Muckler, June 1, 1974. Personnel rep. John Deere, Des Moines, 1975-77; dir. recruitment and selection Social Services, Des Moines, 1978-79, asst. dir. field ops., 1979-80; co-owner, prin. Applied Mgmt. Assocs., 1980—; compensation and devel. mgr. Pioneer Hi-Bred, Internat., Inc., Des Moines. Mem. Am. Soc. Tng. and Devel., Am. Soc. Personnel Adminstrn., Midwest Coll. Placement Assn. Republican. Methodist. Office: 6700 NW 62d Ave Johnston IA 50131

MUDD JOHNSON, JOANN LARAINE, nurse; b. Louisville, July 2, 1942; d. Richard Lawrence and Corrine (Ewing) Mudd; m. Bertram Gerard Johnson, Dec. 2, 1960; children—Gairon Gerard, Gayla Michelle. B.Health Sci. Calif. State Dominguez U., Carson, Calif., 1981; postgrad. Calif. State Coll.-Los Angeles. R.N. Asst. head nurse Los Angeles County-U. So. Calif. Med. Ctr., Los Angeles, 1970-73, nursing research asst., 1981-84; pub. health clinic nurse Los Angeles Dept. Community Health Services, 1973-78; nurse examiner Drew Postgrad. Med. Sch., Los Angeles, 1979-81; sch. nurse Los Angeles Unified Sch. Dist., 1984—. Mem. Council of Sch. Nurses, Beta Pi Sigma. Democrat. Mem. Religious Sci. Ch. Avocations: taking classes, traveling, aerobics, antiques, home decorating. Home: 3205 Griffith Ave Los Angeles CA 90011 Office: Foshay Jr High Sch 3751 S Harvard Blvd Los Angeles CA 90018

MUDGE, JEAN MCCLURE, writer, filmmaker; b. Fort Benning, Ga., Dec. 4, 1933; d. Robert Battey and Eva Eugenia (Colby) McClure; m. Lewis Seymour Mudge, June 15, 1957; children—Robert Seymour, William McClure, Anne Evelyn. B.A., Stanford U., 1955; M.A., U. Del., 1957; Ph.D., Yale U., 1973. Reader, Smith Coll., Northampton, Mass., 1963-65, lectr., 1972-73; curator Amherst (Mass.) Coll., 1965-76; filmmaker, Amherst, 1971—; vis. scholar China Trade Mus., Milton, Mass., 1977—; cons. Peabody Mus., Salem, Mass., 1980—, Essex Inst., Salem, 1980—; lectr. Field Mus., Chgo., 1982—. Author: Chinese Export Porcelain for the American Trade, 1785-1835, 1962, rev. edit., 1981; Emily Dickinson and the Image of Home, 1975; Chinese Export Porcelain in North America, 1986; author films: Emily Dickinson, 1978; Herman Melville, 1982; Sanctuary in Chicago, 1985. Winterthur fellow H. F. duPont Mus., Wilmington, Del., 1955-57; Danforth Found. fellow, 1969-71; recipient Red Ribbon, N.Y. Film Festival, 1978, finalist, 1982; Chris Plaque, Columbus Film Festival, 1978, 82. Mem. NOW, MLA, Oriental Ceramic Soc., Winterthur Grads. Assn. Democrat. Home: 1218 E Madison Park Chicago IL 60615

MUDGE, JOY JEAN NORTH (MRS. GLEN R. MUDGE), librarian; b. Cleve., Mar. 14, 1929; d. John Edward and Doris Eileen (McKinnon) North; A.B., Beaver Coll., 1951; postgrad. Kent State U., 1955; M.S., Wayne State U., 1962; m. Glen R. Mudge, Dec. 27, 1955 (dec. Aug. 1977). Tchr., Glenmoor Sch., East Liverpool, Ohio, 1951-55; librarian Wayne State U., Detroit, 1955-58; librarian Oak Park, Clinton Jr. high schs., Oak Park, Mich., 1958-68; dir. sch. librarian Charlevoix (Mich.) Schs., 1968—. Named Girl Scout Career Woman of the Year, East Liverpool, 1963. Mem. ALA, Mich. Sch. Librarians Assn., Alpha Delta Kappa, Pi Lambda Theta. Home: Box 96A Ellsworth MI 49729 Office: Charlevoix Pub Schs Garfield St Charlevoix MI 49720

MUDRON, MAUREEN DOLORES, lawyer; b. Joliet, Ill., June 7, 1948; d. Francis Raymond and Veronica Marie (McGuire) M. B.A., U. Ill.-Urbana, 1970; J.D., John Marshall Law Sch., Chgo., 1974. Bar: Ill. 1974. Staff atty. Ill. Dept. Mental Health and Devel. Disabilities, Chgo., 1974-78, asst. to chief counsel, 1978-80, chief legal counsel, 1980—; speaker in field. Mem. Nat. Abortion Rights Action League. Mem. ABA, Ill. Bar Assn., Chgo. Council Lawyers, NOW, NAT. Assn. State Mental Health Attys. (sec. 1981-82, v.p. 1982—). Roman Catholic. Office: Ill Dept Mental Health and Devel Disabilities 160 N LaSalle St Chicago IL 60601

MUEHLENTHAL, CLARICE KELMAN, travel consultant; b. Cleve., Nov. 16, 1924; d. William and Ann (Teitel) Kelman; m. Arnold G. Muehlenthal, Dec. 17, 1950 (dec. Sept. 1980); children—Shelley Muehlenthal Mitchell, David M. Cert., Draughons Bus. Coll., 1945; cert. travel counselor, Inst. Cert. Travel Agts., 1980. Owner, Cee-Jay Bus. Service, Riverhead, N.Y., 1952-55; travel cons. Journey House Travel, Dallas, 1967-73; ptnr. Alpha Travel, Dallas, 1973-76; owner World Wide Travel Service, Dallas, 1976—. Round Table chmn. Dallas North dist. Boy Scouts Am., 1971-73; charter mem. Tex. Cultural Alliance, 1975—; courier Hands Around the World, Tex., 1975—. Recipient Dist. Award of Merit, Boy Scouts Am., Circle Ten, Dallas, 1973; Internat. Fellowship, Tex. Cultural Alliance, Dallas, 1982; named Ambassador of Goodwill, State Tex., 1975. Mem. Am. Soc. Travel Agts., The 3020 Soc. (sec.-treas. 1982—), Inst. Cert. Travel Agts. (sec.-treas. 1982—, study group leader 1983, life 1982), Assn. Retail Travel Agts., Travel Agy. Council N. Tex. (sec. 1981-83), Phi Sigma Alpha. Home: 3030 Leahy PO Box 59327 Dallas TX 75229 Office: World Wide Travel Service 2860 Walnut Hill Ln Suite 106 PO Box 52327 Dallas TX 75229

MUEHLNER, SUANNE WILSON, library director; b. Rochester, Minn., June 29, 1943; d. George T. and Rhoda (Westin) Wilson. Student Smith Coll., 1961-63; A.B., U. Calif.-Berkeley, 1965; M.L.S., Simmons Coll., 1968; M.B.A., Northeastern U., Boston, 1979. Librarian, Technische Univ. Berlin, Germany, 1970-71; earth and planetary scis. librarian MIT Libraries, Cambridge, 1968-70, 1971-73; personnel librarian, 1973-74, asst. dir. personnel services, 1974-76, asst. dir. pub. services, 1976-81; dir. libraries Colby Coll., Waterville, Maine, 1981—. Mem. New Eng. Assn. Coll. and Research Librarians (v.p., pres. elect 1985—, sec.-treas. 1983-85), Maine Library Assn. (chmn. intellectual freedom com. 1984—), Nelinet (bd. dirs. 1985—), ALA. Office: Miller Library Colby Coll Waterville ME 04901

MUELLER, ALISON LEE, nurse, naval officer; b. Summit, N.J., Oct. 8, 1949; d. Charles Stanley, Jr. and Elizabeth Bleaker (Henry) Williams; student Cazinonia Coll., 1967-68, U. Calif. Sch. Medicine, San Diego; R.N., Mercy Hosp., Denver, 1971; B.B.A., Nat. U., Calif., 1983; children—Tiffany Leigh, Grant Williams. Commd. lt. comdr., Nurse Corps, U.S. Navy, 1970—; stationed at Naval Regional Med. Center, Oakland, Calif., 1971-74; surg. intensive care staff, charge nurse recovery room Naval Regional Med. Center, San Diego, 1974-77; charge nurse emergency room Patuxent River Naval Hosp., Md., 1977-80, family nurse practitioner Family Practice Clinic, Naval Regional Med. Center, Camp Pendleton, Calif., 1981, dir. EMT program; now dir. combat med. tng. unit 3d Med. Bn. 3d FSSG, Okinawa, Japan; tchr. nursing classes to LPN students; faculty Central Tex. Coll.; co-dir. Emergency Med. Tech. Sch., 1980—. Decorated Nat. Def. medal, Vietnamese Humanitarian medal; cert. family nurse practitioner, in advanced cardiac life support. Mem. Emergency Dept. Nurses Assn., Am. Nurses Assn., Uniform Nurse Practitioners Assn. Home: 3d Med Bn 3d FSSG FPO San Francisco CA 96604-8861

MUELLER, AUDREY EDNA, public relations specialist, psychic counselor; b. Nazeing, Essex, Eng., Oct. 2, 1932; came to U.S., 1954; d. William and Lilian Gertrude (Schirn) Hale; m. Robert Estes Hegwood, Sept. 22, 1952 (div. Jan. 1967); children—Robert, Beverly, Irene, Virginia, David; m. Larry Emerson Mueller, May 3, 1969 (div. July 1985). Ed. English schs. Copywriter, advt. sales rep. Springfield (Ohio) Advertiser, 1966-1967; copywriter, mng. editor New Carlisle (Ohio) Sun, 1967-79; advt. specialist Dayton Tire & Rubber Co. (Ohio), 1979-80; pub. relations and fund devel. dir. Am. Lung Assn., Dayton, 1980—; speaker; dir., coordinator Miami Valley Coalition Smoking Or Health, 1982—; pub. relations cons. Am. Lung Assn.; coordinator, promoter Stop Smoking Clinics, Dayton, 1983—; tchr. psychic devel. groups Greater Dayton area. Recipient Optimists Creed award New Carlisle Rotary Club, 1973; Voice of Democracy award VFW, Medway, Ohio, 1978; Recognition award Tire Rev. Mag., 1980, Nat. VFW, 1979. Mem. Pub. Relations for Health (pres. 1984), Ohio Congress Lung Assn. Staff (sec.-treas. 1982-84), Assn. Research and Enlightenment, Internat. Assn. Bus. Communicators (sec. 1984), Women in Communications, Inc. Democrat. Unitarian. Clubs: English Accents of New Carlisle (sec., founder, past pres.), Rotary (hon.) (New Carlisle). Home: 433 E Carpenter Dr New Carlisle OH 45344 Office: American Lung Assn Miami Valley 226 Belmonte Park E Dayton OH 45405

MUELLER, BETTY JEANNE, social work educator; b. Wichita, Kans., July 7, 1925; d. Bert C. and Clara A. (Pelton) Judkins; M.S.S.W., U. Wis., Madison, 1964, Ph.D. (E.B. Fred fellow, Nat. Inst. Child Health and Human Devel. fellow), 1969; children—Michael J., Madelynn J. Asst. prof. U. Wis., Madison, 1969-71; vis. assoc. prof. Bryn Mawr (Pa.) Coll., 1971-72; assoc. prof., dir. social work Cornell U., Ithaca, N.Y., 1972-78, prof. human services studies, 1978—; nat. cons. Head Start, Follow Through, Appalachian Regional Commn., N.Y. State Office Planning Services, N.Y. State Dept. Social Services, N.Y. State Div. Mental Hygiene, Council Internat. Exchange of Scholars, Nat. Congress PTA; adv. com. Nat. Social Work Research Inst. HEW grantee, 1974-76, 79-80; N.Y. State grantee, 1975-85. Mem. Am. Sociol. Assn., Nat. Conf. Social Welfare, Nat. Assn. Social Workers, Council Social Work Edn., Internat. Conf. Soc. Welfare, Chi Omega. Democrat. Unitarian. Author: (with H. Morgan) Social Services in Early Education, 1974; contbr. articles to profl. jours. Home: 11 Forest Ln Ithaca NY 14850 Office: Human Services Studies N135 MVR Hall Cornell U Ithaca NY 14853

MUELLER, JUDITH ANN, biologist; b. Tyler, Tex., Dec. 31, 1955; d. Charles Clarence and Lois Marie (Conlon) M. A.A., Tyler Jr. Coll., 1976; B.S., U. Houston, 1981. Sports dir. Pal Meadows Resort Ranch, Warda, Tex., 1977; lab. technician S.W. Research Instn., Houston, 1977-79; aquatic biology taxonomist Dames & Moore Consultants, Houston, 1979-81; research asst. U. Houston, 1980-81; biol. research asst. Houston Zool. Gardens, 1981-82; biologist, dir. edn. Bio Quantum Technologies, Houston, 1982—. Contbr. articles to profl. jours. Mem. AAAS, Oceanic Soc., Internat. Soc. Lasers in Neurosurgery, Soc. Microsurg. Specialists, Internat. Oceanographic Found., Cath. Newman Assn., Phi Theta Kappa. Roman Catholic.

MUELLER, LOIS M., psychologist; b. Milw., Nov. 30, 1943; d. Herman Gregor and Ora Emma (Dettmann) M.; B.S., U. Wis.-Milw., 1965; M.A., U. Tex., 1966, Ph.D., 1969. Postdoctoral intern VA Hosp., Wood, Wis., 1969-71; counselor, asst. prof. So. Ill. U. Counseling Center and dept. psychology, Carbondale, 1971-72, coordinator personal counseling, asst. prof., 1972-74, counselor, asst. prof., 1974-76; individual practice clin. psychology, Carbondale, 1972-76, Clearwater, Fla., 1977—; owner, dir. Adult and Child Psychology Clinic, Clearwater, 1978—; staff mem. Med. Center Hosp., Largo, Fla., 1979; mem. profl. adv. com. Mental Health Assn. Pinellas County, 1978, Alt. Human Services, 1979-80; cons. Face Learning Center, Hotline Crisis Phone Service, 1977—; advice columnist Clearwater Sun newspaper, 1983—; public speaker local TV and radio stas., 1978, 79; talk show host WPLP Radio Sta., Clearwater, 1980-83. Campaign worker for Sen. George McGovern presdl. race, 1972. Lic. psychologist, Ill., Fla. Mem. Am., Fla., Ill., Pinellas (founder, pres. 1978) psychol. assns., Assn. Advancement Psychology, Am. Soc. Clin. Hypnosis, Fla. Soc. Clin. Hypnosis, Acad. Family Psychology, Bus. and Profl. Women of Clearwater, Assn. Women in Psychology. Contbr. articles to profl. jours. Office: 2901 US 19 N Suite 202 Clearwater FL 33575-1806

MUELLER, MARGARET REID, social worker; b. Cleve., Aug. 20, 1929; d. James Sims and Felice (Crowl) Reid; B.A., Smith Coll., 1951; M.A., Case Western Res. U., 1969, M.S.W., 1973; m. Werner D. Mueller, Sept. 6, 1952; children—Fred, John, Lydia, Felice, Omar. Social worker Cleve. Soc. for the Blind, 1969-71; social worker Childrens Services, Cleve., 1973-75; social worker Cuyahoga County Juvenile Ct., Cleve., 1975—, supr. probation dept., 1975—. Candidate for U.S. Ho. of Reps. Mem. Acad. Certified Social Workers, Nat. Assn. Social Workers. Republican. Presbyterian. Clubs: Kirtland Country, Womenspace, Jr. League. Home: 8848 Music St Novelty OH 44072

MUELLER, MARY ELSIE, medical technologist; b. Buffalo, Nov. 10, 1939; d. Thomas Michael and Elsie Mary (Kienke) Rusch; B.A., diploma med. tech., U. Buffalo and Buffalo Gen. Hosp. Sch. Med. Tech., 1961; m. Peter M. Mueller, Mar. 21, 1964; 1 son, Thomas P. Microbiology technologist, then microbiology supr. Buffalo Gen. Hosp., 1961-71, microbiology teaching supr., 1971—; temporary supr. lab, West Seneca, 1983; computer writer Spirit Graphics, 1985—; clin. instr. area colls. and univs. Sunday Sch. supt. Resurrection Luth. Ch., Buffalo, 1983—. Mem. Am. Soc. Clin. Pathologists, Nat. Cert. Agy. Med. Lab. Personnel. Lutheran. Home: 75 Chesterfield Dr Buffalo NY 14215 Office: 100 High St Buffalo NY 14215

MUELLER, NANCY, speech and language pathologist; b. Cleve., May 26, 1952; d. Zolton Stephen and Eleanor (Tachar) Bitto; m. David Frederick Mueller, June 6, 1981; 1 dau., Sarah Anne. B.A. in Speech Pathology and Audiology, Cleve. State U., 1975, M.A. in Speech Pathology, 1977. Lic. speech pathologist, Ohio. Speech and lang. pathologist Deaconess Hosp., Cleve., 1977-80; dir. speech pathology Parma (Ohio) Community Gen. Hosp., 1980—. Mem. Ohio Council Speech and Hearing Execs., Am. Speech-Hearing-Lang. Assn. (cert. clin. competency), Ohio Speech and Hearing Assn. Home: 8210 Lanyard St Parma OH 44129 Office: Parma Community Gen Hosp 7007 Powers Blvd Parma OH 44129

MUELLER, PATTY, oil and gas engineering company executive; b. Laredo, Tex., Dec. 10, 1931; d. Valentine Lawrence and Sara Louise (Payne) Puig; m. Joseph Paul Mueller, Sept. 4, 1954; children—Michelle, Martha L., Mary Pat, J. Paul, Julianna. B.S., U. Tex., 1954. Tchr., Corpus Christi Ind. Sch. Dist., Tex., 1954-56; bookkeeper J.P. Mueller, Cons., Corpus Christi, 1957-70, acct., 1970-76; controller Mueller Engring. Corp., 1976-84, v.p. fin., controller, 1984—; v.p., treas. Mueller Exploration Inc., Corpus Christi, 1977—. Bd. dirs. Corpus Christi Pub. Library, 1975—, treas., 1975-77, chmn. bd., 1978-82; vice chmn. adv. council South Tex. Library Systems, 1980-81; rep. Gov.'s Conf. on Libraries, 1974; past pres., sec., children's services chmn. Friends of Corpus Christi Pub. Libraries, 1964—; leader Girl Scouts U.S.A.; bd. dirs. Am. Cancer Soc.; mem. prins. adv. com., various schs. Corpus Christi; trustee The Hearth, 1973-79; pres., fin. chmn., Amigos de las Americas, 1984-85; treas. Pan Am. Round Tables Tex., 1983-85. Republican. Roman Catholic. Clubs: Cotillion III (pres. 1982-83), Corpus Christi Town. Office: Mueller Engring Corp 1010 First City Tower II Corpus Christi TX 78478

MUENSTER, KAREN, state senator; m. Ted Muenster; children—Ted, Mary, Thomas. Mem. S.D. Senate 1985—. Democrat. Office: SD State Capitol Bldg Pierre SD 57501*

MUFF, JANET, nurse; b. Bombay, India, May 26, 1947 (parents Am. citizens); d. James Bertram and Fette K. (Britt) M.; R.N., St. Vincent's Coll. Nursing, Los Angeles, 1968; B.S. in Nursing, Columbia, 1976, M.S., 1977; m. James D. Boyce, July 26, 1975. Clin., teaching and adminstrv. positions, Los Angeles and N.Y.C., 1968-79; nurse psychotherapist, cons., South Pasadena, Calif., 1979—. Bd. dirs. Women's Bldg., Los Angeles. Recipient Sigma Theta Tau award, 1976. Mem. Am. Nurses Assn., Calif. Nurses Assn., Sigma Theta Tau. Author/editor: Socialization, Sexism and Stereotyping: Women's Issues in Nursing (Am. Jour. Nursing Book of Yr. award), 1982. Address: 202 Oaklawn Ave South Pasadena CA 91030

MUGGLI, CLARA DARDARA, civic worker; b. Hebron, N.D., Nov. 10, 1927; d. Matt and Mary (Schneider) Maershbecker; student Dickinson State Coll.; m. Ewald Muggli, Sept. 27, 1948; children—Allen, Linda, Joyce, Carol, Gary, Holly. Tchr. rural schs., 1945-48; county chmn. establishment Bookmobile, 1960, bd. dirs., 1960—, bd. dirs., librarian Glen Ullin (N.D.) Public Library, 1956—; social services home health aide, 1972-76; co-owner, mgr. Rock Mus., Glen Ullin, 1970—, also instr. rocks and minerals, 1970—; sec. Glen Ullin Hist. Soc., 1978—; tchr. Sacred Heart Ch., 1969—, dir. religious edn., 1982—, dir. family life, 1984—; weekly columnist Glen Ullin Times, 1977-84. Recipient State Homemakers award for Cultural Arts, 1975; KC Religious Edn. award, 1979; Best of Show award Dakota Gem and Mineral Show, 1979, 84. Mem. Morton County Hist. Soc., Glen Ullin Hist. Soc., Central Dakota Gem and Mineral Assn., Badlands and Knife River Rock Clubs, Art Assn., Am. Legion Aux. Club: Homemakers. Home: 701 Oak Ave Glen Ullin ND 58631

MUHAWI, EDWINA, food company executive; b. N.Y.C., Nov. 27, 1943; d. Edward Francis and Anne Helene (Breglia) Aquino; m. Elias Mahfuz Muhawi, Dec. 13, 1972; children—Halima, Michael, Sascha. Student, Raymond Coll., 1962-64; B.A., U. Calif.-Davis, 1965, M.A., 1971. Social worker County of Stockton, Calif., 1965-67; teaching asst. U. Calif.-Davis, 1968-71; instr. English U. Minn., Morris, 1971-74; pres. SinBad Sweets Inc., Clovis, Calif., 1981—. Democrat. Office: SinBad Sweets Inc 324 N Minnewawa St Clovis CA 93612

MUHLANGER, GILDA OLIVER, lawyer; b. Cienfuegos, Las Villas, Cuba, Sept. 26, 1951; came to U.S., 1969; d. Orlando Jaime and Gilda Violeta (Aloma) Oliver; m. Erich Muhlanger, July 13, 1973; 1 son, Erich. A.A., Hartford Coll. for Women, 1972; B.A., Wesleyan U., 1974; J.D., U. Conn.-W. Hartford, 1980. Bar: Conn. 1981. Tchr. Mercy High Sch., Middleton, Conn., 1974-79; lawyer Williams & Brooke, Hartford, Conn., 1981-82; atty. The Travelers Ins. Cos., Hartford, 1982—. Recipient Scott prize for modern lang. Wesleyan U., 1974. Mem. ABA, Conn. Bar Assn., Hartford County Bar Assn., Hartford Assn. Women Attys. Republican. Roman Catholic. Home: 13 Clemens Ct Rocky Hill CT 06067 Office: The Travelers Ins Cos 1 Tower Sq Hartford CT

MUHLEMAN, JANET CHRISTIE, design, marketing and advertising firm executive, designer; b. Dayton, Ohio, July 23, 1951; d. John Louis and Mary Griffith (Hallenbeck) M.; 1 son. B.S. in Indsl. Design, Ohio State U., 1973, M.A. in Design Planning, 1975. Grad. teaching assoc. Ohio State U., Columbus, 1973-75; exec. v.p. Group 243 Design, Columbus, 1974-75, Ann Arbor, Mich., 1975-81, pres., 1981—; pres., dir. Image Masters, Ann Arbor and Gulfport, Miss., 1981—, Portfolio Contract Furniture, Ann Arbor, 1983—; chmn. Denison Group, Atlanta, 1984—, Ashlar Devel., Ann Arbor, 1985—. Mem. art enrichment com. Catherine McAuley Health Ctr., Ann Arbor, 1984—; chmn. adv. bd. Washtenaw Community Coll., Ann Arbor, 1984—. Recipient various awards for creative work. Mem. Soc. Typographic Arts, Am. Inst. Graphic Arts, Am. Assn. Advt. Agys., Am. Mgmt. Assn., Advt. Research Found., Greater Detroit C. of C., Ann Arbor C. of C. (bd. dirs. 1985—). Republican. Clubs: Adcrafters, Economic (Detroit); The List (Ann Arbor). Office: Group 243 Design 4251 Plymouth Rd Bldg 1 Ann Arbor MI 48105

MUHLERT, JAN KEENE, director; b. Oak Park, Ill., Oct. 4, 1942. B.A., Albion Coll., 1964; M.A., Oberlin Coll., 1967; student Neuchatel U., Inst. European Studies, Paris, Sorbonne, Institut de Phonetique, Academie Grande Chaumière. Set designer Huntington and Manikiki Playhouses, Cleve., summer 1964; grad. asst. dept. art Oberlin Coll. (Ohio), 1964-65; curatorial asst. Allen Meml. Art Mus., Oberlin, Ohio, 1965-66, asst. curator, 1967-68; asst. curator 20th century painting and sculpture and White House rotating exhbn., program advisor Nat. Collection Fine Arts, Smithsonian Instn., Washington, 1968-73, assoc. curator, 1974-75; dir. U. Iowa Mus. Art, 1975-79, Amon Carter Mus. Western Art, Ft. Worth, 1980—; lectr. in field. Contbr., author various exhbn. catalogs. Assn. of Art Mus. Dirs./Nat. Endowment for Arts and Donner Found. grantee, 1979. Mem. Assn. Art Mus. Dirs. (trustee 1981-82, 84-86), Upper Midwest Regional Conservation Ctr. (trustee 1976-79), Nat. Endowment for Arts, Iowa Arts Council, Western Assn. Art Museums (regional rep. 1978-79), Am. Arts Alliance (bd. dirs. 1980-86). Address: The Amon Carter Museum PO Box 2365 Fort Worth TX 76113

MUHLNICKEL, ISABELLE, mental health counselor; b. Strong, Colo., May 11, 1931; d. Albert and Frances (Martinez) Quintana; m. Ludwig Albert Muhlnickel, Jan. 13, 1952; children—Ludwig Albert, Elizabeth, Mary Karolyn. B.A. in Sociology, Met. State Coll.-Denver, 1980. Lic. psychiat. technician, Colo. Ednl. loan officer Lowry Fed. Credit Union, Denver, 1972-76; mgr., dir. Teamsters Credit Union, Denver, 1980-81; psychiat. technician State of Colo., Wheatridge, 1981—; founder, exec. dir. Fathers Crisis Center, Denver, 1984—. Met. State Coll. Colo. Scholars award, 1977, 78, 79. Fellow Nat. Assn. Female Execs. Democrat. Roman Catholic. Avocations: travel; photography; skiing; hiking; painting.

MUHN, JUDY ANN, public relations director; b. Detroit, Dec. 29, 1952; d. Wilbur William and Dolores Eleanor (Sutinen) Nimer; B.S., Mich. State U., 1975; m. Dennis James Muhn, June 6, 1975. Research asst. Mich. State U., 1972-76; microbiologist Sacramento Med. Preventics Clinic, 1976-77; advt. mgr. J.C. Penney, Plattsburgh, N.Y., 1977-80; promoter Pepsi-Cola Bottling Co., Keeseville, N.Y., 1980; legal sec., 1980-81; legis. aide to Calif. state senator, 1982-84; dir. pub. relations Tierra del Oro Girl Scout Council, Rancho Cordova, Calif., 1984—. Bd. dirs., chmn. pub. affairs com. Planned Parenthood Clinton County (N.Y.), 1980-81; bd. dirs. Family Planning Advocates, Albany, N.Y., 1981; pres. bd. dirs. Planned Parenthood of Sacramento Valley, 1982—; mem. Sacramento Pro-choice Coalition, 1982—; adv. com. Lake Champlain (N.Y.) Com., 1981; founder Women's Roundtable, Plattsburgh, 1981. Mem. Downtown Capitol Bus. and Profl. Women's Club (pres., legis. chmn. 1982—, pub. relations vice chmn. 1982—), NOW, Sierra Club, Nat. Wildlife Fedn., Nat. Abortion Rights Action League, Common Cause. Home: 222 Branch Dr Mather AFB CA 95655 Office: Tierra del Oro Girl Scout Council 3005 Gold Canal Dr Rancho Cordova CA 95670

MUIR, HELEN, journalist, author; b. Yonkers, N.Y., Feb. 9, 1911; d. Emmet A. and Helen T. (Flaherty) Lennehan; student public schs.; m. William Whalley Muir, Jan. 23, 1936; children—Mary Muir Burrell, William Torbert. With Yonkers Herald Statesman, 1929-30, 31-33, N.Y. Evening Post, 1930-31, N.Y. Evening Jour., 1933-34, Carl Byoir & Assos., N.Y.C., and Miami, Fla., 1934-35; syndicated columnist Universal Service, Miami, 1935-38; columnist Miami Herald, 1941-42; children's book editor, 1949-56; woman's editor Miami Daily News, 1943-44; freelance mag. writer, numerous nat. mags., 1944—; drama critic Miami News, 1960-65. Trustee, Coconut Grove Library Assn., Friends U. Miami Library, Friends Miami-Dade Public Library; vis. com. U. Miami Libraries; bd. dirs. Miami-Dade County Public Library System; mem. State Library Council, 1979—, past chmn. Recipient award Delta Kappa Gamma, 1960; Fla. Library Assn. Trustees and Friends award, 1973; trustee citation ALA, 1984; named to Fla. Women's Hall of Fame, 1984. Mem. Women in Communications (Community Headliner award 1973), Soc. Women Geographers. Clubs: Florida Women's Press (award 1963); Cosmopolitan (N.Y.C.). Author: Miami, U.S.A., 1953. Home: 3855 Stewart Ave Miami FL 33133

MUJICA, BARBARA LOUISE, educator, author; b. Altoona, Pa., Dec. 25, 1943; d. Louis and Carol Freida (Kline) Kaminar; A.B., UCLA, 1964; M.A., Middlebury Coll., 1965; Ph.D., N.Y. U., 1974; m. Mauro E. Mujica, Dec. 26, 1966; children—Lillian Louise, Mariana Ximena, Mauro Eduardo Ignacio. Tchr. French, UCLA, 1963-64; asso. editor modern langs. Harcourt Brace Jovanovich, N.Y.C., 1966-73; instr., asst. prof. Romance langs. CUNY, 1973-74; assoc. prof. Spanish, Georgetown U., Washington, 1974—. Dir. El Retablo Spanish Lang. Theater Group, 1986—. Penfield fellow, 1971; NEH summer Inst. faculty, 1980. Mem. Writers Center, Brazilian Am. Cultural Inst., Am. Assn. Tchrs. Spanish and Portuguese, MLA, Women's Caucas MLA, S. Atlantic MLA, N.E. MLA, AAUP. Author: Readings in Spanish Literature, 1975; Calderon's Characters: An Existential Point of View, 1980; Pasaporte, 1980, 84; Aqui y ahora, 1979; Entrevista, 1982; Iberian Pastoral Characters, 1986; sr. editor Washington Rev.; editor, pub. Verbena: Bilingual Rev. of the Arts, 1979—. Home: 7811 Lonesome Pine Ln Bethesda MD 20817 Office: Dept Spanish Georgetown Univ Washington DC 20057

MUKA, BETTY LORAINE OAKES, lawyer; b. McAlester, Okla., Jan. 30, 1929; d. Herbert La Fern and Loraine Lillian (Coppedge) Oakes; m. Arthur Allen Muka, Sept. 6, 1952; children—Diane Loraine, Stephen Arthur, Christopher Herbert, Martha Ann, Deborah Susan. B.S., U. Okla., 1950; M.S., Cornell U., 1953; M.B.A., 1970; J.D., Syracuse U., 1980. Bar: R.I. 1983, U.S. Dist. Ct. 1984. Jr. acct. Maxfield, Randolph & Carpenter C.P.A.s, Ithaca, N.Y., 1970-71; income tax cons. H & R Block, Ithaca, 1971-73; salesman Investors Diversified Services, Ithaca, 1972-73; sole practice, Providence, R.I., 1983—. Co-editor mag. The Executive, 1970. Leader, Camp Fire Girls, Cub Scouts and 4-H, Ithaca, 1961-71; founding mem. Com. to Make N.Y. #1 Again, N.Y.C., 1983. Mem. ABA, New York State Bar Assn., R.I. Bar Assn., R.I. Trial Lawyer's Assn., Oikonomia (pres. 1948-49), Omicron Nu (pres. 1949-50), Mortar Bd., Sigma Delta Epsilon, Phi Delta Phi (J. Mark McCarthy award 1980), Delta Delta Delta (pres. alumnae chpt. Ithaca 1964-65). Home: 113 Kay St Ithaca NY 14850 Home and Office: 23 Carol Ct Providence RI 02909

MUKERJI, BETTY-LOU, mental health association executive, educator, vineyard executive; b. Buffalo, Feb. 14, 1930; d. Leroy Manley and Ethel Mae (Walker) Brumaghim; m. Sasanka Mukerji, June 28, 1948; children—Elizabeth Louise, Victoria Maya. B.A., Sonoma State Coll., 1972. Cert. tchr. anthropology, fine applied arts and pub. affairs and services, Calif. Rancher, v.p. Toribeth Vineyards, Inc., Napa, Calif., 1959—; tchr. Napa Valley Unified Adult Sch., Napa, 1980-83, coordinator/tchr. 1983—; exec. dir. Mental Health Assn. Napa County, Napa, 1985—; cons., tchr./trainer in field, Calif. Active Non-Profit Coalition, Napa County, 1985-86, Carneros Quality Alliance, 1985-86; bd. dirs. Ali Akbar Coll. Music Marin, Calif., 1986. Levi Strauss grantee, 1984, 85. Mem. Calif. Council Adult Edn., Correctional Educators Assn. (bd. dirs. 1985-86), Napa Valley Arts Council (bd. dirs. 1985-86), Am. Correctional Assn., Am. Soc. Aging. Democrat. Methodist. Club: World Trade (San Francisco). Home: 1 Mukerji Ave Napa CA 94559

MUKOYAMA, HELEN KIYOKO, social worker; b. Paia, Maui, Hawaii, Nov. 13, 1914; d. Ginichi and Shio (Takahashi) Takehara; B.A., Simpson Coll., 1937; postgrad. U. Denver, 1936; M.A., U. Chgo., 1943; m. Teruo Mukoyama, June 11, 1936 (div. 1956); children—Marshall H., Howard T., Wesley K. Caseworker, Chgo. Welfare Adminstrn., 1938-41, Cook County Dept. Welfare, Chgo., 1945-46; cons. to Japanese Ams. relocating to Chgo., Ill. Public Aid Commn., 1945-46, welfare adminstrv. aide supr., 1949-69; caseworker Travelers Aid Soc.-Immigrants Service, Chgo., 1951-65; intake worker Homemaker Service, Salvation Army Family Service, Chgo., 1957-65; social work supr. intake Ill. Dept. Children and Family Services, 1965-67; caseworker III, Salvation Army Family Service, Chgo., 1967-72; casework supr. Jewish Family and Community Services, Chgo., 1972-73; supr. intake Council for Jewish Elderly, Chgo., 1973-77, supr. community aides and welfare adminstrv. coordinator, 1977-79; coordinator elderly housing Japanese Am. Service Com and mgr. Heiwa Ter. Japanese Am. Elderly Housing, Chgo, 1980—; mem. Japanese Am. Housing Bd. Mem. Council of Ministries, Welfare Div. United Meth. Ch., 1963-69. Recipient award Japanese Am. Service com., 1963, others. Mem. Acad. Cert. Social Workers, Nat. Assn. Social Workers, Ill. Cert. Social Workers, Chgo. Human Relations Commn., Japanese-Am. Citizens League, Japanese-Am. Soc., Art Inst. Chgo., Epsilon Sigma, Pi Gamma Mu. Methodist. Contbr. articles to profl. jours. Home: 912 S Mason Ave Chicago IL 60644 Office: 920 W Lawrence St Chicago IL 60640

MULCAHY, ELLEN MARIE, nursing administrator; b. Rockville Centre, N.Y., Feb. 9, 1956; d. Daniel J. and Julia T (McKeown) Mulcahy. Diploma, Pilgrim Psychiat. Ctr., 1977; B.S., Long Island U., Greenvale N.Y., 1980. R.N., N.Y. Home health aide Upjohn Health Care Service, Hicksville, N.Y., 1976-77, nurse, 1977; nurse supr. Comprehensive Geriatric Service, Smithtown, N.Y., 1977-81; dir. nursing Bestcare Co., Garden City, N.Y., 1981—. Mem. Am. Nurses Assn., Am. Assn. Continuity Care, N.Y. State Hospice Assn., Long Island Profl, Bus. Womens Assn. Republican. Roman Catholic. Office: Bestcare Co 370 Old Country Rd Garden City NY 11530

MULDAUR, DIANA CHARLTON, actress, guild president; b. N.Y.C., Aug. 19, 1938; d. Charles Edward Arrowsmith and Alice (Jones) Muldaur; m. James Mitchell Vickery, June 26, 1969 (dec. 1979); m. Robert James Dozier, Oct. 11, 1981. B.A., Sweet Briar Coll., Va., 1960. Actress appearing in: Off-Broadway theatrical prodns., summer stock, Broadway plays including A Very Rich Woman, 1963-68; guest appearances on TV in maj. dramatic shows; appeared on: TV series Survivors, 1970-71; McCloud, 1971-73; Tony Randall Show, 1976; Black Beauty, 1978; star: Born Free, 1974; Hizzoner, 1979; Fitz & Bones, 1980; motion picture credits include: McQ. Gov., Acad. TV Arts and Scis., 1978-80, 2d v.p., 1978-80, 1st v.p., 1980-83, pres., 1983—; bd. advisers Nat. Ctr. for Film and Video Preservation, John F. Kennedy Ctr. Performing Arts, 1985—. Mem. Acad. Motion Picture Arts and Scis., Screen Actors Guild (bd. dirs. 1978), Conservation Soc. Martha's Vineyard Island.

MULDROW, TRESSIE WRIGHT, psychologist; b. Marietta, Ga., Feb. 1, 1941; d. Festus Blanton and Louise Williams Wright Summers; B.A., Bennett Coll., 1962; M.S., Howard U., 1965, Ph.D., 1976; 1 dau., DeJuan Denise. Research asst. W.C. Allen Corp., Washington, 1966-68; personnel research psychologist Dept. Navy, Washington, 1968-73, Office Personnel Mgmt., CSC, 1973-79; chief, adv. council on alternative selection procedures Office Personnel Mgmt., Washington, 1979—; lectr. Howard U., 1979. Mem. Washington Inter-Alumni council United Negro Coll. Fund, 1970—; trustee Bennett Coll., vice chmn., 1985—; v.p. Family Life Ctr. Br., Boys and Girls Clubs of Washington, 1984—. Named Alumnae of Yr., United Negro Coll. Fund, 1971, recipient Individual Achievement award, 1985; Outstanding Alumnae Morehouse Coll., 1978. Mem. Bennett Coll. Alumnae Assn. (nat. pres. 1978-85), Am. Psychol. Assn., Nat. Assn. Black Psychologists, D.C. Assn. Black Psychologists, Delta Sigma Theta. Presbyterian. Contbr. articles to profl. publs. Office: 1900 E St NW Washington DC 20415

MULHAUSER, KAREN, organization executive; b. Burlington, Vt., Nov. 5, 1942; d. Harold H. and Leta H. Webber; B.A. in Biology, Antioch Coll., 1965; m., Aug. 18, 1968; 1 child, Christopher. Research asso. Albert Einstein Coll. of Medicine, Bronx, N.Y., 1965-67; sci. tchr. Cambridge Sch., Weston, Mass., 1967-70; family planning trainer/educator HEW Region X, Seattle, 1970-73; lobbyist Nat. Abortion Rights Action League, Washington, 1973-75, exec. dir., 1975-81; polit. cons., 1981-82; exec. dir. Citizens Against Nuclear War, Washington, 1982—; adv. bd. Peace Media Project; dir. Ind. Action; v.p. Antioch U. Alumni Bd.; mem. exec. com. Nuclear Weapons Freeze Campaign. Mem. Planned Parenthood Met. Washington (past pres., dir.), Center for Population Options (dir.), Voters for Choice (sec., exec. com.), Friends of Family Planning (exec. com.). Democrat. Office: 1201 16th St NW Washington DC 20036

MULHERN, EILEEN M., Mfg. co. ofcl.; b. Queens, N.Y., Oct. 15, 1953; d. Patrick Joseph and Joan Francis (Cassidy) M.; B.A., Coll. New Rochelle (N.Y.), 1975; M.B.A., U. Notre Dame, 1977. Asst. met. banking div. Chem. Bank, N.Y.C., 1977-79; asst. to pres. First Nat. Bank, Houma, La., 1979, First Nat. Bank Colorado Springs (Colo.), 1980-81; sr. fin. supr. Colo. Telecommunications div. Hewlett-Packard, Colorado Springs, 1981—. Mem. Am. Soc. Profl. and Exec. Women, Nat. Assn. Female Execs., Kappa Gamma Pi. Office: Colo Telecommunications div Hewlett-Packard PO Box 7050 Colorado Springs CO 80933

MULL, PATRICIA BAYLEY, accountant; b. Bridgetown, Barbados, W.I., Aug. 12, 1940; came to U.S., 1960, naturalized, 1966; d. Harold Haynes Bayley and Iris (Bradshaw) Bannochie; m. Robert M. Mull, Sept. 18, 1972 (dec.); 1 child, Robert. B.S. in Bus. Adminstrn. with honors, Fla. Atlantic U., 1972. C.P.A., Fla. Auditor, Price Waterhouse & Co., Miami, Fla., 1972-73; pvt. practice acctg., Miami, 1974—. Mem. Am. Inst. C.P.A.s, Fla. Inst. C.P.A.s. Republican. Club: Palm Bay (Miami). Avocations: flying; sailing; fishing. Home and Office: 1122 NE 98th St Miami Shores FL 33138

MULLEEDY, JOYCE ELAINE, nursing service administrator, educator; b. Paterson, N.J., Aug. 30, 1948; d. Edward and Jane (Van De Weert) Schuurman; m. Philip Anthony Mulleedy, May 14, 1982. B.S., Paterson State Coll., 1970. R.N., cert. emergency nurse, emergency med. technician, paramedic. Pub. health nurse Vis. Nurse Assn. of No. Bergen County, Ramsey, N.J., 1970-72; health dir. Camp Fowler Assn., Speculator, N.Y., 1973-76; exec. dir. Am. Cancer Soc., Speculator, 1976-77; pub. health nurse Hamilton County Nursing Service, Lake Pleasant, N.Y., 1977-80, supervising pub. health nurse, 1980-82, dir. patient services, 1982—; cons. dir. Home Health Care of Hamilton County, Inc., Indian Lake, N.Y., 1979—. Author instructional booklet: Assessing Your Patients, 1983, (pamphlet) A Note to Parents, 1985. Bd. dirs. Am. Cancer Soc.-Hamilton County Unit, Speculator, 1972-76, Speculator Vol. Ambulance Corps, Inc., 1974-81, ARC-Hamilton County chpt., Lake Pleasant, N.Y., 1981—; mem. adminstrv. bd. dirs. Grace United Methodist Ch., Speculator, 1982—. Martha Hazen Scholar Am. Legion, 1966; recipient Service award Am. Legion, 1977. Mem. N.Y. State Assn. County Health Ofcls., Adirondack-Appalachian Regional Emergency Med. Services Council (chmn. 1982—), Emergency Nurses Assn., Hamilton County Emergency Med. Services Council (sec.-treas. 1974—, instr. 1974—), Dirs. of Northeastern N.Y. Home Health Agys. Republican. Home: PO Box 203 Elm Lake Rd Speculator NY 12164 Office: Hamilton County Pub Health Nursing Service Home Health Agy Route 8 County Office Bldg Lake Pleasant NY 12108

MULLEN, FRANCES ANDREWS, consulting psychologist, author, lecturer; b. Chgo., Nov. 27, 1902; d. Edmund Lathrop and Ethel (Baker) Andrews; Ph.B. in Math., U. Chgo., 1923, M.A. in Edn., 1929, Ph.D. in Ednl. Psychology, 1939; m. Urban Joseph Mullen, Oct. 12, 1929, (div. 1945); children—Urban Edmund, Mary Ann, William, Ethel Alice. Tchr. high sch. Chgo. Pub. Sch. System. 1925-39, sch., psychologist, 1939-47, prin. elem. sch., 1947-49, dir. Bur. Mentally Handicapped Children, 1949-53, asst. supt. schs. for spl. edn., 1953-66; pvt. practice psychol. cons., Chgo. and Los Angeles, 1966-75; pres. Internat. Council Psychologists, Inc., 1977, sec.-gen., 1977-79, emeritus, 1979—; cons. edn. and psychology of exceptional children, Sherman Oaks, Calif., 1975—; chmn. SHARE, program of hospitality for psychologists traveling internationally, 1973—; instr. Calif. State U., Northridge, 1978-80, bd. dirs. Inst. for Juvenile Research, Chgo.; mem. psychology adv. panel Office of Vocat. Rehab., HEW, 1961-63. Bd. dirs. Ill. Soc. for Crippled Children and Adults, United Cerebral Palsy of Chgo., Retarded Children's Aid, Girl Scouts U.S.A. of Chgo. Diplomate Am. Bd. Examiners in Profl. Psychology. Fellow Am. Psychol. Assn. (pres. div. sch. psychologists 1951-53); mem. Am. Orthpsychiat. Assn., Am. Assn. on Mental Deficiency, Council for Exceptional Children (life mem.), Internat. Council of Psychologists, Inc. Democrat. Presbyterian. Clubs: Am. Alpine, Can. Alpine, Sierra. Editor Internat. Psychologist, 1966-72; contbr. numerous articles to profl. jours. Home and Office: 4014 Cody Rd Sherman Oaks CA 91403

MULLENIX, LINDA SUSAN, lawyer, educator; b. N.Y.C., Oct. 16, 1950; d. Andrew Michael and Roslyn (Rosenthal) Marasco; m. James William Mullenix, Sept. 26, 1981; children—Robert Bartholomew, John Theodore, William Joseph. B.A., CCNY, 1971; M. Philosophy, Columbia U., 1974, Ph.D. (Pres.'s fellow), 1977; J.D., Georgetown U., 1980. Bar: D.C. 1981, U.S. Dist Ct. D.C. 1981, U.S. Supreme Ct. 1986. U.S. Ct. Appeals (D.C. cir.) 1981. Assoc. prof., lectr. George Washington U., Washington, 1977-80; asst. prof. Am. U., Washington, 1979; clin. prof. Loyola U. Law Sch., Los Angeles, 1981-82, vis. asst. prof., 1982-83; vis. asst. prof. Catholic U. Law Sch., Washington, 1983-84, asst. prof., 1984-86, assoc. prof., 1986—; assoc. Pierson, Ball & Dowd, Washington, 1980-81; adj. instr. Fordham U., N.Y.C., 1975-76, adj. asst. prof. 1977; adj. asst. prof. CCNY, 1977; adj. instr., adj. asst. prof. Cooper Union Advancement Sci., Art, N.Y.C., 1977; instr. N.Y. Inst. Tech., N.Y.C., 1976, U. Md. European div., Ramstein, Germany, 1974. Editor bibliographies Political Theory, A Jour. Polit. Philosophy, 1972-74; The Tax Lawyer Jour., 1978-80; contbr. articles to profl. publs. Alt. del. Va. Democratic State Conv., 1980. Fellow NDEA, 1971-74, Georgetown U. Law Sch., 1978; N.Y. State Regents scholar, 1967-71. Mem. D.C. Bar Assn., Women's Bar Assn. D.C., ABA, Phi Beta Kappa, Phi Alpha Delta. Home: 6221 Redwing Rd Bethesda MD 20817 Office: Catholic U Washington DC 20064

MULLER, ADELYN CAMERON, retired educator; b. Greenville, Tex., Mar. 5, 1913; d. Frank Clifton and Hortense (White) Cameron; B.A., B.A. in English and Math., E. Tex. State U., Commerce, 1934; M.A. in Math. Edn., U. Mo., Kansas City, 1968; Ph.D. in Math. Edn., Kans. State U., Manhattan, 1975; m. John G. Muller; children—Ken Cameron, Jon Tackaberry. Tchr., Greenville (Tex.) Pub. Schs., 1936-40; aero. liasion engr. Ft. Worth Consol.-Vultee, 1943-46; coordinator math. Valley View Sch. Dist., Overland Park, Kans., 1960-69, Shawnee Mission (Kans.) Pub. Schs., 1969-70; adj. prof. Kans. State U., U. Mo., Kansas City. Mem. AAUW, Shawnee Mission Pub. Sch. Adminstrs. Assn., Nat. Council Tchrs. Math., Phi Delta Kappa, Delta Kappa Gamma. Recipient Nat. Edn. Assn. Pacemaker award, 1969. Participant in HEW 3-month tour of India; Nat. Sch. Assn. people-to-people tour Russia, Switzerland, France, Eng. Contbr. articles in field to profl. jours. Home: 370 Terrace Trail W Lake Quivira KS 66106

MULLER, CHARLOTTE FELDMAN, economist; b. N.Y.C., Feb. 19, 1921; d. Louis and Lillian (Drogin) Feldman; A.B., Vassar Coll., 1941; A.M., Columbia U., 1942, Ph.D. in Econs., 1946; m. Jonas N. Muller, 1942 (dec.); children—Jeremy Lewis, Sara Linda; m. 2d, Carl Schoenberg. Instr. econs. Bklyn. Coll., 1943; lectr. Barnard Coll., 1943-46; asst. prof. Occidental Coll., 1947; asst. study dir. Survey Research Center, U. Mich., 1948; research asso. U. Calif., Berkeley, 1948-50; lectr. Yale U. Sch. Public Health, 1952-53; asst. prof. Columbia U. Sch. Public Health, 1957-67; assoc. dir. Center for Social Research, CUNY, 1967—, prof. econs., 1978—, prof. urban studies, 1967-78, prof. sociology, 1982—; prof. dept. community medicine Mt. Sinai Sch. Medicine, 1986—; v.p. CUNY Acad. Humanities and Scis., 1985—; bd. dirs. CUNY Research Found., 1985—; disting. alumna speaker Vassar Centennial, 1971; mem. N.Y.C. Mayor's Com. on Prescription Drug Abuse, 1970-73; bd. dirs. Alan Guttmacher Inst., 1972-82; v.p. Med. and Health Research Assn. N.Y.C.; mem. health care tech. study sect. Nat. Center Health Services Research, 1976-79; mem. commn. on nat. policy Am. Jewish Congress. Ford/Rockefeller Founds. grantee, 1972-73, 75-76; Russell Sage Found. grantee, 1985—. Mem. Am. Econ. Assn., Am. Public Health Assn., NOW. Jewish. Editorial bd. Am. Jour. Public Health, Inquiry, Research on Aging, Women, and Health; contbr. numerous articles on health econs. to profl. publs. Office: CUNY 33 W 42d St Room 625 New York NY 10036

MULLER, CLAUDYA BARBARA, librarian; b. Furth, Bavaria, Ger., Sept. 14, 1946; came to U.S., 1952; d. Ralph Leon and Elfriede Katerina (Hilpert) Burkett; m. William A. Muller, III, Dec. 12, 1965 (div. 1986); 1 dau., Martha Genevieve. B.A., Ga. So. Coll., 1967; M.L.S., Emory U., Atlanta, 1968. Dir., Jackson County Library, Ripley, W.Va., 1976-78; adminstr. Worcester County Library, Snow Hill, Md., 1978-83; state librarian State of Iowa, Des Moines, 1983-86; dir. Suffolk Coop. Library System, Bellport, N.Y., 1986—. Tommie Dora Barker fellow, 1967. Mem. ALA, Pub. Library Assn., Library Adminstrn. and Mgmt. Assn., Am. Soc. Pub. Adminstrn. Roman Catholic. Office: Suffolk Coop Library System 627 N Sunrise Service Rd Bellport NY 11713

MULLER, ELSIE FERRAR, psychotherapist, psychiatric social worker; b. Worcester, Mass., Apr. 7, 1913; d. Frederic and Anne (Binns) Bonnet; B.S., Alfred U., 1934; M.S.W., U. Mo., Columbia, 1969; postgrad. U. Mo., Kansas City, 1962-63; m. Frederick Wentworth Muller, Oct. 10, 1936 (div. 1961); 1 dau., Jean Ferrar Muller Mackimmie. Lic. clin. social worker. Art. instr. Alfred U., 1935-36; art therapist Gillis Home, Kansas City, Mo., 1958-70; psychotherapist Ozanam Home, Kansas City, Mo., 1970—; art therapy cons. Jackson County, Kansas City, Mo., 1975-78, Wyandotte County Sch. Social Workers, Kansas City, Kans., 1978—. Mem. Nat. Assn. Social Workers, Acad. Social Workers, Am. Art Therapy Assn. (hon. life), Am. Soc. Psychopath. Expression (editorial adv.), Nat. Register Clin. Social Workers. Episcopalian. Home: 9801 Lee Blvd Leawood KS 66206 Office: 421 E 137th St Kansas City MO 64145

MULLER, GEORGENE KAY, computer company public relations specialist, writer; b. Jamaica, N.Y., May 27, 1950; d. Robert Henry and Lois Alene (Kase) M.; m. Raymond Eric Classen, Dec. 19, 1969 (div. 1975); children—Rachel Marie, Amanda Lee. B.A., Western Conn. State U., 1979. Freelance writer, reporter, editor, Conn., N.Y., 1978-81; sr. writer Branson Sonic Power Co., Danbury, Conn., 1981-83; pub. relations asst. Data Switch Corp., Norwalk, Conn., 1983—; instr. writing Western Conn. State U., Danbury, 1982, Branson Sonic Power, 1982-83; editorial cons. Comics Collector, Iola, Wis., 1983; editorial coordinator Comics Spotlight, Bethel, Conn., 1983-84. Contbr. articles to hobby and comic publs., 1980-84. Mem. Internat. Assn. Bus. Communicators (sec. 1983, editor newsletter 1984), Women In Communications, Soc. Profl. Journalists, Danbury Area Women's Network, Women's Ctr. Greater Danbury Newtown Assn. for Gifted and Talented (newsletter editor). Home: 47 Walnut Tree Hill Rd Sandy Hook CT 06482 Office: Data Switch Corp 444 Westport Ave Norwalk CT 06851

MULLER, KATHLEEN HOFLAND, nursery school/day care centers executive, print shop executive; b. New Brunswick, N.J., Nov. 18, 1940; d. Robert and Winifred (Wood) Hofland; m. S. Albert Muller, June 9, 1962; children—Jeanne Elizabeth, Kenneth Whitney. B.A., Douglass Coll., 1964; postgrad. Rutgers U., 1969. Owner, exec. dir., Creative Nursery Sch., Highland Park, N.J., 1967—, North Brunswick, N.J., 1968—; owner, exec. dir. Creative Child Care Ctr., Highland Park, 1977—, North Brunswick, 1982—; co-owner Good & Quick Print Shop, North Brunswick, 1984—; lectr. in field. Author: Formulas for Fun & Learning, 1975. Pres. United Methodist Women, Highland Park, 1981-83. Mem. N.J. Assn. for Edn. of Young Children (pres. Kenyon chpt. 1975-78, mem. exec. bd. 1978-80). Avocations: tennis; art; literature. Home: 123 Happer St Highland Park NJ 08904 Office: Creative Nursery Schs Inc 123 Harper St Highland Park NJ 08904

MULLET, DARLENE MARILYN, rehabilitation educator; b. Butte, Mont., Oct. 16, 1935; d. Ernest John Onnela and Iva Eleanor Onnela Sullivan; B.S., Western Mich. U., 1960; m. Stanley Mullet, Feb. 24, 1961 (dec. 1973); 1 son, Kevin. Rehab. tchr. Ohio Commn. for Blind, Columbus, 1960-61, 62-63; occupational therapist Goodwill Industries, Denver, 1966-70; rehab. tchr. for adults Tex. Commn. for Blind, Galveston, 1973—. Recipient service pin and cert. Tex. Commn. for Blind, 1978, 84. Mem. Am. Assn. Workers for Blind, Assn. Edn. Visually Handicapped Alliance, Tex. Assn. Workers for Blind. Devised, conducted functional testing program for disability determination for social security, 1966-70.

MULLETTE, JULIENNE PATRICIA, research astrologer, author, lecturer, television personality and producer, editor, holistic health center administrator; b. Sydney, Australia, Nov. 19, 1940; came to U.S., 1953, naturalized, 1962; d. Ronald Stanley Lewis and Sheila Rosalind Blunden (Phillips) M.; m. Fred Gillette Sturm, Nov. 24, 1964 (div. Dec. 1969); m. Kenneth Walter Gillman, Dec. 27, 1971 (div. Dec. 1978); children—Noah Khristoff Mullette-Gillman, O'Dhaniel Alexander Mullette-Gillman. B.A., Western Coll. for Women, Oxford, Ohio, 1961; postgrad. Harvard U., 1964, U. Sao Paulo, Brazil, 1965, Instituto do Filosofia, Sao Paulo, 1965, Miami U., Oxford, 1967-69. Tchr. English, High Mowing Sch., Wilton, N.H., 1962-64, Stoneleigh-Prospect Hill Sch., Greenfield, Mass., 1964; seminar dir. Western Coll., Oxford, Ohio, 1967-69; pres. Family Tree, The Home Univ., Montclair, N.J., 1978-80; dir. Pleroma Holistic Health Ctr., Montclair, 1980—; dir. Astrological Research Ctr., Sydney, 1983; hostess You and the Cosmos talk show Sta.-WFMU-FM, East Orange, N.J., 1985, The Julienne Mullette Show, Connections TV, Newark, 1985—; pvt. astrology counselor, 1962—; lectr., speaker worldwide, 1968—; guest on radio and TV shows, U.S. and Can., 1962—. Author: The Moon—Understanding the Subconscious, 1973; also articles, 1968—. Founding editor KOSMOS mag., 1968-78, The Jour. of Astrological Studies, 1970, The Signs of the Times, 1986—. Founder local chpt. La Leche League, Montclair, 1972. Mem. Internat. Soc. Astrological Research (founding pres. 1968-78), Am. Fedn. Astrologers (cert.), Societe Belge d'Astrologie, Am. Assn. Humanistic Psychology, AAUW, Nat. Assn. Female Execs., Avocations: competitive tennis; local theatre; singing. Home: 70 Melrose Pl Montclair NJ 07042

MULLIGAN, CAROLYN LITTLEJOHN, social worker; b. Spartanburg, S.C., Dec. 12, 1927; d. Thomas Willard and Hazel (Traxler) Littlejohn; m. Charles Ray Mulligan, June 29, 1949 (div. June 1971); children—Debra Carol, Charles Ray, Jr.; m. Nicholas Stephen Parthemos, June 7, 1973 (div. June 1976). B.A., Limestone Coll., 1949; postgrad. U. Ga., 1966, Southeastern Conf. on Alcoholism, 1963, U. N.C., 1956. Caseworker, supr. Dept. Pub. Welfare, Spartanburg, S.C., 1949-59, 62-66; sch. home visitor Sch. Dist. 6, Spartanburg, 1966—. Mem. S.C. Assn. Social Workers. Baptist. Avocations: reading; gardening; listening music. Home: 221 Connecticut Ave Spartanburg SC 29302 Office: Sch Dist 6 1493 WO Ezell Blvd Spartanburg SC 29301

MULLINS, ELIZABETH IONE, sociology educator; b. Colemaine, Minn., Sept. 6, 1928; d. Edgar R. and Bess (Redhed) M. B.A., Miami U., Oxford, Ohio, 1950; M.A., U. Ill., 1954; Ph.D., Ind. U., 1975. Tchr., Blue Ash High Sch., Ohio, 1950-53; student personnel rep. Ind. U., Bloomington, 1954-57; coordinator activities devel. ctr. So. Ill. U., Carbondale, 1957-65; vis. lectr. Ind. U., 1972-73; asst. prof. sociology Kent State U., Ohio, 1973—. Co-editor Sociol. Focus, 1980—. Mem. ACLU, Common Cause, North Central Sociol. Assn. (exec. council 1980—), Am. Sociol. Assn. (com. 1972-75), NOW, Women Studies Assn., AAUP, Alpha Kappa Delta (v.p. 1974-78). Office: Kent State U Lowery Hall Kent OH 44242

MULLINS, OBERA, microbiologist; b. Egypt, Miss., Feb. 15, 1927; d. Willie Ree and Maggie Sue (Orr) Gunn; B.S., Chgo. State U., 1974; M.S. in Health

Sci. Edn., Governors State U., 1981; m. Charles Leroy Mullins, Nov. 2, 1952; children—Mary Artavia, Arthur Curtis, Charles Leroy, Charlester Teresa, William Hellman. Med. technician, microbiologist Chgo. Health Dept., Chgo., 1976—. Mem. AAUW, Am. Soc. Clin. Pathologists (cert. med. lab. technician). Roman Catholic. Home: 9325 S Marquette St Chicago IL 60617 Office: 3026 S California Ave Chicago IL 60623

MULLINS, RUTH GLADYS, pediatric nurse; b. Can., Aug. 25, 1943; naturalized 1954; d. William G. and Gladys (Page) Henderson; B.S., Calif. State U., Long Beach, 1966; M.Nursing, UCLA, 1973; m. Leonard E. Mullins, Jr., Aug. 27, 1963; children—Deborah, Catherine, Leonard E. III. Nurse, Los Angeles County Health Dept., 1967-68, Meml. Hosp. Med. Center, Long Beach, 1968-73; mem. faculty Calif. State U.,-Los Angeles, 1973; mem. faculty Calif. State U.-Long Beach, 1973—, asst. prof., 1974-80, assoc. prof., 1980—, program dir. pediatric nurse practitioner program, 1975—, chmn. grad. div. level, 1978-81, coordinator health services credential, 1979—; mem. Calif. Maternal, Child, Adolescent Health Bd., 1977—; vice chmn. Long Beach/Orange County Health Consortium. Fellow Nat. Assn. Pediatric Nurse Practitioners/Assocs. (exec. bd.); mem. Am. Pub. Health Assn., Ambulatory Pediatrics Assn., Nat. Assn. Faculties of Pediatric Nurse Practitioner Programs (sec.), AAUP. Democrat. Methodist. Author: (with Bobbie Nelms) Growth and Development: A Primary Health Care Approach, 1982; reviewer AAAS; contbr. articles to profl. jours., chpts. to textbooks. Home: 6382 Heil Ave Huntington Beach CA 92647 Office: 1250 Bellflower Blvd Dept Nursing Long Beach CA 90840

MULQUEEN, ELLEN, career consultant; b. Bklyn., Jan. 11, 1941; d. James C. and Jane E. (Jaenike) M.; A.B. in English, Pace U., 1962; M.A. in English, N.Y. U., 1967. Personnel clk. Book-of-the-Month Club, N.Y.C., 1962; activities sec. Pace U., N.Y.C., 1963; adminstrv. asst. Loeb Student Center, N.Y. U., N.Y.C., 1963-65; asst. dean students State U. N.Y., Geneseo, 1965-67; asst. dean students R.I. Coll., Providence, 1967-70; asst. dir. campus center Trinity Coll., Hartford, Conn., 1970-71, asst. dean student services, 1971-72, assoc. dean for student services, 1972-74, dean student services, 1974-76; dean student affairs Post Coll., Waterbury, Conn., 1976-80, also adj. instr. English; assoc. dean students Rider Coll., Lawrenceville, N.J., 1980-82; pvt. practice career cons., 1982—; asst. dir. career services Sch. Law, Western New Eng. Coll., Springfield, Mass., 1984—; mem. accrediting team New Eng. Assn. Colls. and Schs. Bd. dirs. Planned Parenthood Assn. Mercer Area, 1981-84, sec. bd. edn., 1983-84; bd. dirs. Planned Parenthood of Greater Waterbury, 1978-80, sec. bd., 1980; bd. dirs. LWV of Ewing Twp., 1981-84, 1st v.p., 1981-83, legis. chmn., 1985—. Recipient Trustees' award Pace U., 1962. Contbr. papers to publs., also nat., regional confs. profl. orgns. in field. Home: 112 Hermitage Dr Springfield MA 01129 Office: Sch Law Western New Eng Coll Springfield MA 01119

MULRONEY, MILA PIVNICKI, wife of Canadian prime minister; b. Sarajevo, Yugoslavia, 1953; d. Dmitrije and Bogdanka Pivnicki; m. (Martin) Brian Mulroney, May 6, 1973; children—Caroline Anne, Benedict Martin, Robert Mark, Daniel Nicolas Dimitri. Student Sir George Williams U. (now Concordia U.), Montreal, Que., Can. Office: care Office of Prime Minister Langevin Block Parliament Bldgs Ottawa ON K1A 0A2 Canada

MULVANEY, MARY JEAN, educator; b. Omaha, Jan. 6, 1927; d. Marion Fowler and Blanche (McKee) M.; B.S., U. Nebr., 1948; M.S., Wellesley Coll., 1951. Instr. phys. edn. Kans. State U., 1948-50; instr., then asst. prof. U. Nebr., 1951-62; asst. prof. U. Kans., 1962-66; mem. faculty U. Chgo., 1966—, prof. phys. edn. and athletics, 1976—, chmn. dept., 1976—; mem. council and long range planning com. Nat. Collegiate Athletic Assn. Mem. Internat. Assn. Phys. Edn. and Sport for Girls and Women, AAHPERD, Nat. Assn. Collegiate Dirs. Athletics, Nat. Assn. Phys. Edn. in Higher Edn., AAUP, Mortar Bd., Pi Lambda Theta, Alpha Chi Omega. Home: 5825 S Dorchester Ave Chicago IL 60637 Office: 5640 S University Ave Chicago IL 60637

MULVANEY, MAUREEN GAIL, speaker, counselor, educator; b. Norfolk, Va., Oct. 2, 1950; d. Paul Leo and Mary Patricia (Landry) M.; m. James Matthew Keith, July 10, 1976 (div. Nov. 1985). B.A., Troy State U., 1972; Ed.M., Boston U., 1980. Social services asst. U.S. Govt., Augsburg, W.Ger., 1980, clin. psychologist William Beaumont Army Med. Ctr., El Paso, Tex., 1984; counselor Adlerian Family Counseling Ctr., Litchfield Park, Ariz., 1984—; instr. Grand Canyon Coll., Phoenix, 1984—; profl. speaker, Phoenix, 1985—; cons. stress mgmt. corp. orgns., Phoenix, 1985-86; cons. Carl Hayden High Sch., Phoenix, 1986, Maryvale High Sch., Phoenix, 1986. Author: The Stress Strategists, 1986. Active Mothers Against Drunk Drivers, El Paso, 1985. Recipient Certs. of Achievement, Dept. of Army, 1981. Mem. Am. Personnel and Guidance Assn., Nat. Speakers Assn., Am. Assn. Female Execs., NOW, Phoenix C. of C. Democrat. Roman Catholic. Avocation: cons. to women's athletic teams. Home: 8118 N 38th Ave Phoenix AZ 85051

MULVEY, HELEN FRANCES, emeritus history educator; b. Providence, Feb. 22, 1913; d. William James and Anna (Nelson) M. A.B., Pembroke Coll., 1933; A.M., Columbia U., 1934; A.M., Radcliffe Coll., 1942; Ph.D., Harvard U., 1949. Instr. history Russell Sage Coll., Troy, N.Y., 1944-46; asst. prof. to prof. history, Conn. Coll., New London, 1946-83, prof. emeritus, 1983—, Brigida Pacchiana Ardenghi chair, 1975-78; vis. prof. Brit. history, U. Wis., Madison, 1971-72; vis. lectr. Yale U., 1974-83; lectr. Irish history, Pfizer Adult Edn., Groton, Conn., 1983-84; vis. scholar Phi Beta Kappa, Washington, 1982-83. Author articles, essays Irish and Brit. history; co-editor bibliog. vol. in A New History of Ireland, 9 vols. Anne Crosby Emery fellow, Brown U., 1933. Mem. Am. Hist. Assn., Am. Com. for Irish Studies, Conf. on Brit. Studies, AAUP (chpt. pres. 1962-64), Phi Beta Kappa. Club: Providence Art. Office: Conn Coll Box 1508 Mohegan Ave New London CT 06320

MULVIHILL, LINDA JOYCE, real estate executive; b. Houston, June 9, 1951; d. John William and Joyce Laverne (Bryant) M. Student Gulf Coast Sch. Real Estate, Houston, 1978. Lic. real estate salesman, Tex. Exec. sec. Musemeche/Assocs., Architect, Houston, 1969-70; personnel sec. A.B. Chance Co., Houston, 1970-72; property mgmt. sec. Gerald D. Hines Interests, Houston, 1972-76; property mgr. Kilburn G. Moore Co., Houston, 1976-78; project mgr. Mel Powers Investment, Houston, 1978-83; comml. leasing agt. Horne Co., Houston, 1983—. Mem. Young People in Real Estate, Houston Bd. Realtors. Republican. Roman Catholic. Office: The Horne Co Realtors 1801 Main St Suite 600 Houston TX 77002

MULZET, LYNDA ROSE, health care management consultant, nurse; b. Grand Rapids, Mich., July 2, 1946; d. Philip Paul and Dorothy Maxine (VanDragt) Bronkema; m. Mark Joseph Mulzet, Apr. 13, 1974 (div. Nov. 1981); 1 child, Matthew Joseph. B.S.N., U. Mich., 1967. Head nurse Good Samaritan Hosp., Phoenix, 1970-76; dir. nurses Mission Convalescent Hosp., Riverside, Calif., 1978-80; clin. dir. Scottsdale Meml. Hosp., Ariz., 1980-83; dir. patient care services Scottsdale Meml. Hosp.-North, 1983-84; dir. nurses Beverly Enterprises, Scottsdale, 1984-85; v.p. Patient Acctg. Mgmt. Services, Phoenix, 1985—; asst. coordinator LEADS, Phoenix, 1986. Democrat. Avocations: reading; skiing; writing poetry; scuba diving; movies; sewing. Home: 4704 E Paradise Village Pkwy N-121 Phoenix AZ 85032 Office: Patient Acctg Mgmt Services 5201 N 19th Ave Suite 118 Phoenix AZ 85032

MUMFORD, EMILY HAMILTON, medical sociologist; b. Cape Girardeau, Mo., Dec. 19, 1922; d. Barney A. and Dola (Stolzer) Hamilton; A.B., U. Tulsa, 1941; M.A., Columbia U., 1958, Ph.D., 1963. Research asst. Bur. Applied Social Research, Columbia U., N.Y.C., 1958-59; instr., maj. adv. Hunter Coll., N.Y.C., 1960-64; vis. prof. behavioral and social scis. New Coll., Sarasota, Fla., 1965-66; asst. prof. sociology in psychiatry Mt. Sinai Sch. Medicine, N.Y.C., 1966-68, assoc. prof., 1968-73, cons. dept. psychiatry, 1969-71; assoc. prof. sociology Grad. Center, City U. N.Y., N.Y.C., 1968-73, prof. sociology grad. program in med. sociology Lehman Coll., 1973-74; prof. psychiatry Downstate Med. Center, SUNY, Bklyn., 1974-77, spl. asst. to dean, 1976-77, cons. nat. survey renal patients, 1972, cons. med. edn., 1977, cons. edn. in ethics, 1978; prof. psychiatry and preventive medicine U. Colo. Health Scis. Center, Denver, 1977-84, mem. admissions com., 1978-84; prof. clin. sociomed. sci., psychiatry and pub. health Columbia Presbyn. Coll. Physicians and Surgeons, 1984—; chief div. health services and policy research N.Y. State Psychiat. Inst., 1984—; assoc. cons. in sociology to sci. adv. staff St. Luke's Hosp., N.Y.C., 1961; task force on studies devel. United Hosp. Fund N.Y., 1969-71; cons. Inst. for Study of Health and Soc., Georgetown, Md., 1972; co-chmn. panel, conf. on cancer rehab. Nat. Cancer Inst., Washington, 1972; mem. colloquium Am. Assn. Med. Colls., Washington, 1974; cons. on evaluation, dept. medicine Montefiore Hosp., N.Y.C., 1977; cons. Random House, 1978; cons., site visitor psychiat. edn. br. NIMH, 1978, mem. adv. council, 1979-82; mem. behavior sci. test com. Nat. Bd. Med. Examiners, 1983-86; charter mem. Alcohol, Drug Abuse and Mental Health Agy., Dept. HHS, 1985—; chmn. search com. for dir. Davis Inst. for Care and Study of Aging; mem. regent's monitoring bd. U. Riyadh, U. Colo. Travel grantee Milbank Meml. Fund, 1969; grantee Commonwealth Fund, 1968-70, NIMH, 1975-76, 77, project dir. HEW, 1978. Fellow Am. Public Health Assn., Am. Sociol. Assn. (med. sociology sect.), Am. Psychiat. Assn. (hon.); mem. Sigma Xi. Author: Interns: From Students to Physicians, 1970; (with J. Skipper, Jr.) Sociology in Hospital Care, 1967; editor Academic Guide, 1976-77; assoc. editor Jour. Health and Social Behavior, 1976—; mem. editorial bd. Jour. Med. Edn. cons. TV health series, 1976; contbr. invited book reviews to profl. pubs.; reviewer manuscripts for pubs.; contbr. articles to profl. publs. Home: 45 E 85th St New York NY 10028 Office: NY State Psychiat Inst 722 W 168th St New York NY 10032

MUNCASTER, BARBARA JEAN, educator; b. San Francisco, Dec. 22, 1943; d. Floyd Christopher and Era Mae (Peterson) Felkins; B.S. in Bus. Edn., Okla. State U., 1967, M.S., 1973; m. John Randolph Muncaster, III, Mar. 25, 1967; 1 son, Scott Christopher. Physician's sec., 1960-67; pianist First Baptist Ch., Stillwater, Okla., 1963-67; accounts payable clk. Borg-Warner Corp., Memphis, summer 1968; tchr. bus. edn. dept. chmn. high schs. in Tenn. and Okla., 1968-78; instr. bus. edn. Oscar Rose Jr. Coll., Midwest City, Okla., 1975-77, 78—. Adv. bd. Trinity Episcopal Sch., Oklahoma City, 1977-80; chmn. bd. dirs. Okla. Alliance Children, 1980-81. Consumer econs. scholar, 1971. Mem. Nat. Bus. Edn. Assn., Internat. Word Processing Assn., The Forum, Delta Pi Epsilon. Episcopalian. Author: Learning Basic and Business Math Using the Electronic Calculator, 1984. Home: 1707 Windsor Pl Oklahoma City OK 73116 Office: 6420 SE 15th St Midwest City OK 73110

MUNDEN, JULIA ANN, manufacturing company manager; b. Victoria, Va., Apr. 24, 1943; d. Richard and Julia (Robertson) Vreeland; m. James Munden, Feb. 24, 1962; children—Amelia, Brittany. B.A., U. So. Miss., 1966; postgrad. Syracuse U., 1969. Sales rep. Olovitti, Ruston, La., 1969-75; supr./mng. resource Dupont, Richmond, Va., 1975—. Contbr. poems to Christian mags. Mem. Nat. Assn. Female Execs. Republican. Methodist. Avocation: tennis. Office: Dupont Jefferson Davis PO Box 20071 Richmond VA 23234

MUNDHENKE, STEPHANIE ANN, lawyer, banker; b. Mpls., Oct. 8, 1951; d. Alden Runge and Nina Lavina (Hanson) Chester; m. Gary Wayne Mundhenke, Sept. 12, 1981. B.A. magna cum laude, Augustana Coll., 1973; J.D., U. S.D., 1977; postgrad. C.F.S.C., ABA Nat. Grad. Trust Sch., Evanston, Ill., 1984. Bar: S.D. 1977, Minn. 1979. Asst. counselor Minnehaha County Juvenile Ct. Ctr., Sioux Falls, S.D., 1972-73; child care worker Project Threshold, Sioux Falls, 1973-74; legal intern Davenport, Evans, Hurwitz & Smith, Sioux Falls, 1976; law clk. S.D. Supreme Ct., Pierre, 1977-78; originations dept. buyer Dain Bosworth, Inc., Mpls., 1978-79; v.p., trust officer 1st Bank of S.D., N.A., Sioux Falls, 1979-86; v.p. 1st Trust Co., Inc., St. Paul, 1986—; bd. dirs., pres.-elect mem. program com. Sioux Falls Estate Planning Council, 1983-85; Projects and research editor S.D. Law Rev., 1977; author law rev. comment. Mem. fund raising coms. S.D. Symphony, Sioux Falls Community Playhouse, Augustana Coll., 1982-83; mem. S.D. div. Nat. Women's Polit. Caucus; mem. events com. Augustana Coll. Fellows, Sioux Falls, 1984; bd. dirs. YWCA, Sioux Falls, 1984; mem. Sioux Falls Jr. Service League, 1984. Augustana Coll. scholar, 1969-73; Augustana Coll. Bd. Regents scholar, 1973. Mem. S.D. Bar Assn., Minn. Bar Assn., ABA, 2d S.D. Jud. Circuit Bar Assn., Nat. Assn. Bank Women (state conv. com. 1983-85), Phi Delta Phi, Chi Epsilon. Republican. Lutheran. Clubs: Network, Portia (Sioux Falls). Office: 1st Trust Co Inc 180 E 5th St Saint Paul MN 55102

MUNDTH, ANNE MICHELLE, journalist; b. Phoenix, Feb. 23, 1957; d. Lyman Kenneth and Hilda Marie (Phillips) M. B.A. in Journalism, San Diego State U., 1978. Midwest overnight editor UPI, Chgo., 1980-81; editor nat. desk Atlanta Constitution, 1981-82; editor gen. desk UPI, Atlanta, 1982-83, overnight editor, nat. desk, Washington, 1984—; Midwest alternate nat. com. Wire Service Guild, 1980, unit chmn., Atlanta, 1983, UPI drug and alcohol rehab. com., 1983—. Recipient Medallion of Merit award Ariz. State U., 1974; Copley Newspaper award, 1977; Eugene C. Pulliam fellow Indpls. Newspapers Inc., 1978. Mem. Women in Communications, Sigma Delta Chi (scholarship 1977), Kappa Tau Alpha, Phi Kappa Phi. Methodist. Home: 2225 40th Pl NW #3 Washington DC 20007 Office: United Press Internat 1400 I St NW Washington DC 20005

MUNHALL, RUTH BEATRICE, business and financial consultant; b. Mendon, Mass., Feb. 8, 1929; d. Lawrence B. and Elsie B. (Gaskill) M.; grad. Salvation Army Officers Coll., Bronx, N.Y., 1951; M.B.A., Calif. Western U., 1980, Ph.D., D.B.A., 1981. Civilian supr. U.S. Army and VA Hosp., Framingham, Mass., 1946-50; ordained clergywoman; officer Salvation Army centers in Mass., N.Y. and N.J., 1951-64; owner, operator acctg. and real estate firm, N.Y.C., 1964-68; supr. fiduciary and individual taxation Bank of N.Y., N.Y.C., 1968-79; cons. non profit orgns. founder R.M. Scholarship Info. Services, Ark., N.Y., Mass. and Israel, 1981—; pres., chief exec. officer Munhall, Monahan, Chapman Fiduciary Animal Charities, Inc., 1984—; pres. Munhall Research Sci. Corp., 1985—; cons. in field. Recipient 5 Yr. Civil Def. award Gov. N.Y. State. Mem. Am. Mgmt. Assn., DAR, Alumni Assn. Calif. Western U. Republican.

MUNRO, JUNE EDITH, librarian; b. Echo Bay, Ont., Can., June 20, 1921; d. Neil and Agnes (MacLeod) M.; B.J., Carleton U., 1961; B.L.S., U. Toronto 1962, M.L.S., 1972. Head children's library services Sault Ste. Marie (Ont., Can.) Public Library, 1941-51; children's librarian London (Ont.) Public Library, 1951-53; head children's library services Leaside Public Library, 1953-56; asst. to exec. dir., publs. prodn. editor Canadian Library Assn., 1956-61; supr. extension service, editor Ont. Library Rev., Ont. Provincial Library Service, 1961-70; book acquisition adv. Coll. Bibliocentre, Toronto, Ont., 1970-72; chief public relations div. Nat. Library Can., Ottawa, Ont., 1972-73; dir. library services St. Catharines (Ont., Can.) Public Library, 1973-82; sessional lectr. Sch. Librarianship, U. B.C., 1983. Past chmn. bd. dirs. Carousel Players, St. Catharines, Ont.; bd. dirs. YWCA, St. Catharines. Recipient Librarian of Year award Ont. Library Trustees Assn., 1971. Mem. ALA, Can. Library Assn., Ont. Library Assn. Clubs: Golf and Country, Univ. Women's (St. Catharines). Editor Ont. Library Rev., 1961-70.

MUNROE, PATRICIA HALSEY, lawyer, consultant, marine corps officer; b. Los Angeles, May 11, 1948; d. Charles Jesse and Nellie Jewel (Carter) Frederick; m. William Carley Halsey, Jan. 20, 1972 (div. 1980); m. 2d Leslie Joseph Munroe, July 30, 1983; children—Michelle, Lionel. A.A., Cerritos Coll., 1968; B.A., UCLA, 1970; J.D., Calif. Western Sch. Law, 1975. Bar: Calif. 1975; U.S. Ct. Mil. Appeals 1976, U.S. Supreme Ct. 1980. cert. Judge Adv. 1976. Legal intern, City Atty.'s Office, San Diego, 1974-75; commd. lt. U.S. Marine Corps, 1974, advanced through grades to maj., 1981, served U.S., Japan, judge adv., Washington, 1973-83; sole practice law, Berlin, W.Ger., 1983—; cons. HHS, Washington, 1978-80, ABA, Chgo., 1982-83. Editor: Domestic Violence in the Military, 1980; author pamphlets, articles. Witness on Domestic Violence Legis., U.S. Congl. Com., 1980; speaker Calif. State Atty. Gen. Conf. on Domestic Violence, 1979-80; bd. dirs. Women's Resource Ctr., Oceanside, Calif., 1979-81. Named Woman Marine of Yr., 1st Marine Div., 1976; life mem. student body Cerritos Coll. Mem. ABA (cons. 1975—), San Diego Lawyers Club, Mortar Board. Club: Internat. Women's (Berlin, dir. 1984-85). Home: 3026 Azahar Ct Carlsbad CA 92082 Office: Am Embassy US Ber Box E APO New York NY 09742

MUNROE, SHIRLEY ANN, hospital association executive; b. Mpls., Mar. 31, 1924; d. Laurence John and Esther (Tuttle) M.; pre-nursing cert. La Sierra Coll., Arlington, Calif., 1943; R.N., Glendale Sanitarium and Hosp. Sch. Nursing, 1946; postgrad. UCLA Extension, 1953-55, Los Angeles City Coll., 1948-51; cert. U. Calif. at Santa Cruz extension, 1971; m. Stanley G. Fjelstrom, Dec. 26, 1954 (div. June 1957). Chief nurse, office mgr. for pvt. practice physicians, Los Angeles, 1946-51; bus. mgr. Bolander Clinic and Emergency Hosp., Van Nuys, Calif., 1951-56, Mendocino Med. Ctr., Ukiah, Calif., 1956; adminstr. Hillside Community Hosp., Ukiah, 1956-78, sec., 1956-78; dir. Ctr. for Small or Rural Hosps., Am. Hosp. Assn., Chgo., 1978-79, dir. constituency programs, 1979-83, exec. dir. constituency sects., 1984-85, v.p., 1985—; mem. adv. and eval. com. Ukiah Dist. Sch. Vocat. Nursing, 1965-78; faculty U. Calif. extension at Berkeley, Basic Adminstrn. Hosp. Adminstrs. Program, 1966-70; dir., sec. Obs. Investment Co., Ukiah, 1957-67. Asst. dir. pub. relations alumni postgrad. assembly Loma Linda U., Los Angeles, 1949-55; dir. pub. relations world meeting Aerospace Med. Assn., Los Angeles, 1953; chmn. re-edn. nursing com. Calif. Dept. Employment, 1962; cons. lectr. nurse aide edn., adult edn. Willits, Ukiah high schs., 1962; chmn. Career Project for Sr. High Sch. Girls, 1962-64; mem. Mendocino-Lake adv. com. Regional Med. Program, 1969-73; mem. vocat. edn. adv. com. Ukiah Unified Sch. Dist., 1970-73. Soloist, Presbyn. Ch., Ukiah, 1956-69, Ukiah Oratorio Soc., 1958-65; supt. children's edn. Seventh-day Adventist Ch., 1961-64, dir. pub. relations, 1967-78, chmn. fin. com., 1967-78, mem. ch. bd., 1967-78, mem. exec. com. Ill. conf., 1983—, soloist, 1958-78; mem. ch. bd. Seventh-day Adventist Ch., Elmhurst, 1979—; co-chmn. edn. com. Mendocino County br. Am. Cancer Soc., 1961-62, bd. dirs., 1961-76, pres., 1963-65; mem. steering com. Am. Heart Assn., Mendocino County br. Calif. Heart Assn.; chmn. trustees Tri-County Pre-Payment Medi-Cal Pilot Project, State of Calif., 1969-71; trustee Nor Coa Health, 1967-76, 1st v.p. 1969-71, pres., 1971-72, chmn. South Planning council, 1972-74; mem. Mendocino-Lake counties council, 1966-76; bd. dirs. Mendocino County chpt. ARC, 1968-70; bd. dirs. Blue Cross No. Calif., 1971-78, exec. bd., 1973-78, hosp. provider rep., 1970-78; leader del. People to People Internat. U.S. Citizen Ambassador Program, 1981; mem. bd. Adventist Health System/North, 1981—, chmn. strategic planning com., 1983—; mem. bd. Hinsdale Hosp., 1979—, mem. joint conf. com., 1980—, chmn. strategic planning com., 1983—; bd. dirs. Broadview Acad., Lafox, Ill., 1983—. Recipient Civic Participation award, Outstanding Women in Professions award Calif. Fedn. Bus. and Profl. Women's Clubs, 1965; Outstanding Service award Mendocino-Lake br. Am. Cancer Soc., 1963, 64, 65, Notable Service award, 1968; Walker fellow, 1973. Mem. Am. Hosp. Assn. (ho. of dels. 1974-78, regional adv. bd. 1974-78, rural resource com. 1976-78, v.p.), Calif. Hosp. Assn. (membership com. 1960-61; legis. liaison 1960, panel hosp. peer rev. adminstrs. 1968-78; mem. ins. com. 1971-78), Redwood Empire Hosp. Conf. (ins. com. 1957-59, exec. com. 1968-71, 1st v.p. 1968, pres. 1969), Hosp. Council No. Calif. (bd. dirs. 1968-77, pres. 1975-76, chmn. com. on program and edn. 1968-70), Assn. Western Hosps. (edn. research found. council 1963-65), Glendale Sanitarium and Hosp. Sch. Nursing Alumni Assn. (pres. Glendale 1947-48), Bus. and Profl. Women's Club (exec. bd. 1957-61, pres. 1959-60, 3d v.p. 1960-61, career advancement com. 1961-62, chmn. personal devel. com. 1962-64, mem. bd. 1962-65, music chmn. Redwood Empire dist. 1960-61), Republican. Club: Soroptimist (pres. Ukiah 1971-72, music chmn. 1962-63, service com. 1961-78, editor bull. 1965-66, Woman of Achievement award 1965, dir. 1970-73). Home: 233 N Garfield St Hinsdale IL 60521 Office: 840 N Lake Shore Dr Chicago IL 60611

MUNSELL, ELSIE LOUISE, lawyer; b. N.Y.C., Feb. 15, 1939; d. Elmer Stanley and Eleanor Harriet (Dickinson) M.; A.B., Marietta Coll., 1960; J.D., Coll. William and Mary, 1972; m. George P. Williams, July 14, 1979. Admitted to Va. bar, 1972, U.S. Supreme Ct., 1980; asst. atty. Commonwealth of Va., Alexandria, 1927-74, asst. U.S. atty. Eastern Dist. Va., 1974-79, U.S. magistrate, 1979-81, U.S. atty., 1981-86; sr. trial atty. Office of Gen. Cousel, Dept. Navy, 1986—. Bd. visitors Coll. William and Mary, 1972-76. Mem. Am. Bar Assn., Alexandria Bar Assn., Va. Women's Attys. Assn., Va. Bar Assn., Fed. Bar Assn. Republican. Episcopalian. Office: Dept Navy Office Gen Counsel Washington DC 20360

MUNSEY, SANDRA GOSS, government official; b. Portsmouth, N.H., July 8, 1937; d. Robert Bennett and Frances Lawrence (Drake) Goss; B.A. in Govt., U. N.H., 1959; M.P.A., Northeastern U., 1976; m. Donald Tucker Munsey, Jr., Sept. 12, 1959; children—Suzanne Gail, Carol Elizabeth. Intern, N.H. State Planning Office, 1959; adminstrv. asst. Town of Rye, N.H., 1957-59; social studies tchr. Md. and Mass., 1966-69; revenue officer IRS, 1969-71; budget examiner Mass. Budget Bur., 1971; personnel mgmt. specialist, grant adminstrn. New Eng. region U.S. CSC, Boston, 1972-77, U.S. Dept. Army, 1983-85, U.S. Dept. Navy, 1985—; project mgr. Mass. Exec. Office for Adminstrn. and Fin., 1977-82; lectr. Suffolk U., mem. public mgmt. adv. council, 1980-84. Selectman, mem. charter commn., planning bd., zoning bd. appeals, growth policy com. Town of Medfield, 1969—; mem. Norfolk County Adv. Bd., 1977-80; treas. Norfolk County 4-H Leaders' Assn., 1975—. Recipient Norfolk County 4-H Alumni award, 1971; U.S. Army Performance award, 1984. Mem. Norfolk County Selectman's Assn., Internat. Personnel Mgmt. Assn., Am. Soc. Public Adminstrn. (Mass. chpt. pres., sect. on intergovtl. adminstrn. and mgmt., exec. council sect. on profl. devel., nat. council, membership chmn. 1981-83), Sigma Pi Epsilon. Clubs: Medfield Music Boosters, Narragansett Bay Quilter's Assn., New Eng. Quilters Assn. Lodge: Order Eastern Star. Contbr. articles to publs.; first woman as elected mem. Medfield chief exec. bd. Home and Office: 8 Clark Rd Medfield MA 02052

MUNSINGER, CELESTE, realtor; b. Oxford, Nebr., Aug. 21, 1939; d. Elvis Harry and Lucile Maxine (Hinze) Kinney; m. Larry Gene Munsinger, Dec. 28, 1958; children—Renee Celeste, Todd David. B.A., Ft. Hays State U., 1962; grad. Realtors Inst. Salesperson, Bob Finch & Assocs., Hays, Kans., 1974-81; broker Horizon Homes, Realtors, Hays, 1981—; sec.-treas. Hays Multi-List, Inc., 1978, 79. Leader Girl Scouts U.S.A., 1968-71; den mother Cub Scouts Am., Hays, 1973-75, den leader, coach, 1975-76. Mem. Nat. Assn. Realtors, Kans. Assn. Realtors, Hays Bd. Realtors (sec.-treas. 1981, pres.-elect 1982, pres. 1983 Realtor of Yr. award 1984), Women's Council Realtors (sec.-treas. Kans. chpt. 1980-81, pres. 1984), Realtors Nat. Mktg. Inst. Republican. Methodist. Home: 107 W 34th St Hays KS 67601

MUNSON, CATHERINE HAM, real estate development company executive; b. Omaha, Jan. 21, 1928; d. Aubrey Lawson and Hermine Anne (Thuman) Ham; m. William W. Munson, June 13, 1948 (dec. 1967); children—Lisa Allison, Shelley Anne, Adrienne Leigh; m. Eugene F. Sthymmel, Oct. 15, 1975. B.A. with distinction, U. Nebr., 1948, M.A. with distinction, 1950. Dir. microbiology research group Armour and Co., Chgo., 1950-53; research assoc. U. Calif. Med. Ctr., San Francisco, 1953-54; subdiv. mgr. Eichler Homes, Inc., Palo Alto, Calif., 1958-66; pres. Lucas Valley Properties, Inc., San Rafael, Calif., 1966—; real estate developer, syndicator; tchr. real estate investment analysis Coll. of Marin, Kentfield, Calif., 1972—. Project dir. Pixie Parents, Ross, Calif., 1956-58; fund raiser Sunny Hills, San Anselmo, Calif., 1960-72; bd. dirs. Boyd Mus. Natural History, San Rafael, 1960-63, Marin Symphony Assn., San Rafael, 1978-84, San Rafael Pub. Edn. Found., 1983—. Mem. Real Estate Div. of Nat. Mktg. Assn. (cert. comml. investment mgr.), Marin County Bd. Realtors (chmn. comml. investment com. 1985). Democrat. Avocations: travel; hiking; gardening; photography; music. Office: Lucas Valley Properties Inc 14 Commercial Blvd Suite 121 Novato CA 94947

MUNSON, CHERYL DENISE, advertising copywriter; b. Milw., Aug. 3, 1954; d. John James and Mattie Juanita (Waldon) M. B.A., U. Wis., 1975. Writer/producer Kloppenburg, Switzer & Teich Advt., Inc., Milw., 1977-80; copywriter Foote, Cone & Belding Advt., Inc., San Francisco, 1980—; pres., owner Love, Auntie Cheryl Greetings; free lance writer, San Francisco, 1980—. Communications cons. 3rd Bapt. Ch., San Francisco, 1980—. Recipient Fred Miller Meml. scholarship Milw. Braves, 1971-75; Pub. Service Advt. award San Francisco Advt. Club, 1981. Mem. Nat. Assn. Black Women Entrepreneurs, Nat. Assn. Female Execs. Democrat. Baptist. Office: Foote Cone & Belding 1255 Battery St San Francisco CA 94133

MUNSON, LUCILLE MARGUERITE (MRS. ARTHUR E. MUNSON), real estate broker; b. Norwood, Ohio, Mar. 26, 1914; d. Frank and Fairy (Wicks) Wirick; R.N., Lafayette (Ind.) Home Hosp., 1937; A.B., San Diego State U., 1963; student Purdue U., Kans. Wesleyan U.; m. Arthur E. Munson, Dec. 24, 1937; children—Barbara (Mrs. Charles Papke), Judith (Mrs. Judith Andrews), Edmund Arthur. Staff and pvt. nurse Lafayette Home Hosp., 1937-41; indsl. nurse Lakey Foundry & Machine Co., Muskegon, Mich., 1950-51, Continental Motors Corp., Muskegon, 1951-52; nurse Girl Scout Camp, Grand Haven, Mich., 1948-49; owner Munson Realty, San Diego, 1964—. Mem. San Diego County Grand Jury, 1975-76, 80-81. Mem. San Diego Bd. Realtors. Methodist. Home: 5765 Friars Rd #200 San Diego CA 92108 Office: 2999 Mission Blvd #102 San Diego CA 92109

MUNSON, NANCY KAY, lawyer; b. Huntington, N.Y., June 22, 1936; d. Howard H. and Edna M. (Keenan) Munson. Student Hofstra U., 1959-62; J.D., Bklyn. Law Sch., 1965. Bar: N.Y. 1966, U.S. Supreme Ct. 1970, U.S. Ct. Appeals (2d cir.) 1971, U.S. Dist. Ct. (ea. and so. dists.) N.Y. 1968. Law clk. to E. Merritt Weidner, Huntington, 1959-66; sole practice law, Huntington, 1966—; mem. legal adv. bd. Chgo. Title Ins. Co., Riverhead, N.Y., 1981—. Mem. ABA, Suffolk County Bar Assn., Bklyn. Bar Assn., N.Y. State Bar Assn., Nat. Rifle Assn. Republican. Christian Scientist. Club: Soroptimist (past pres.). Office: 197 New York Ave Huntington NY 11743

MUNSON, NORMA FRANCES, biologist, educator; b. Stockport, Iowa, Sept. 22, 1923; d. Glenn Edwards and Frances Emma (Wilson) M.; B.A., Concordia Coll., 1946; M.A., U. Mo., 1955; Ph.D. (NSF fellow 1957-58, Chgo. Heart Assn. fellow 1959), Pa. State U., 1962; postgrad. Ind. U., 1957, Western Mich. U., 1967, Lake Forest Coll., 1971, 72, 78; student various fgn. univs., 1964-71. Tchr., Aitkin (Minn.) High Sch., 1946-48, Detroit Lakes (Minn.) High Sch., 1948-54, Libertyville (Ill.) High Sch., 1955-79; researcher on nutrition, Libertyville, 1950—. Ruling elder First Presbyn. Ch., Libertyville, 1971-77; pres. Lake County Audubon Soc., 1971-86; Libertyville Edn. Assn., 1964-67; active Rep. Party of Ill., Citizens to Save Butler Lake, Citizens Choice, The Defenders. Recipient Hilda Mahling award, 1967, C. of C. award, 1971, Biology Tchr. of Yr. award, 1971 Ill. Best Teacher's award, 1974; Nat. Sci. fellow, 1957, 58, 60, 61, 62; Chgo. Heart Assn. fellow, 1959; NSF fellow, 1960-71. Mem. Nat. Biology Tchrs. Assn. (award 1971), AAAS, Am. Inst. Biol. Sci., Ill. Environ. Council, Nat. Audubon Soc., N.Y. Acad. Scis., Ill. Audubon Council, Nat. Health Fedn., Nat. Wildlife Fedn., Heritage Found., Parks and Conservation Assn., N.Y. Acad. Sci., Internat. Platform Assn., Holy Land Christian Mission Internat. Dirs. Club, Delta Kappa Gamma. Contbr. research articles to publs. Home and Office: 206 W Maple Ave Libertyville IL 60048

MUNSON, PATRICIA BASS, public relations specialist; b. Peoria, Ill., Jan. 16, 1944; d. Maxwell Burton and Dorothy Helen (Risen) B.; m. Elvin LeRoy Gentry, Aug. 14, 1965 (div. Feb. 1976); children—Alan Burton, William Seth; m. 2d Wayne Milo Munson, June 17, 1978 (div. Jan. 1986). B.F.A., Ill. Wesleyan U., 1966; M.A., U. No. Colo., 1982. Account exec. E.F. Hutton & Co., Colorado Springs, Colo., 1976-77, Bosworth Sullivan, Colorado Springs, 1976; communications supr. Colorado Springs Med. Ctr., 1977; trust officer First Nat Bank, Colorado Springs, 1977-81; dir. community involvement McDonald's of Colorado Springs, 1983—. Mem. Colorado Springs Jr. League, 1973-79; mem. Acacia Sr. Citizen Nutrition Task Force, 1984; pres. bd. trustees Pikes Peak Library Dist., Colorado Springs, 1982-83; mem. vestry St. Michael's Episcopal Ch., Colorado Springs, 1982-85; program coordinator Sch. Dist. 20 Sounding Bd., Colorado Springs, 1982-83; bd. dirs. Pikes Peak Hospice Inc.; bd. mgrs. Pikes Peak YMCA Camping Services; mem. Citizens Goals Leadership Com.; mem. Pub. Edn. Coalition of Pikes Peak Region. Mem. Internat. Assn. Bus. Communicators, Colorado Springs Execs. Assn., Pikes Peak Advt. Fedn., Kappa Kappa Gamma Alumni Assn. (pres. 1974-76). Office: McDonald's of Colorado Springs 210 N Corona Colorado Springs CO 80903

MUNTS, MARY LOU, public service administrator; b. Chgo., Aug. 21, 1924; d. T. Hunton and Elizabeth (Vinsonhaler) Rogers; student Swarthmore Coll.; M.A., U. Chgo., 1947; J.D., U. Wis., 1976; m. Raymond Munts, July 19, 1947; children—Lisa Munts Redburn, Polly, Andy. Research asst. U.S. Dept. Treasury, 1947-48; instr. Sch. Bus. Wilkes Coll., Wilkes Barre, Pa., 1949-50; asst. to congressman, Washington, 1960; econ. research assoc. Robert R. Nathan Assocs., Washington, 1964-66; admissions sec. Center for Devel., U. Wis., Madison, 1967-72; mem. conservation com. Nat. Assn. Regulatory Commrs.; mem. Wis. Assembly, 1972-84, chair environ. resources com., 1975-82, co-chair joint com. fin., 1983-84, mem. joint com. employment relations, 1983, mem. legis. council, 1983, chair legis. council spl. com. groundwater, 1982-83; now mem. Wis. Pub. Service Commn.; chair nat. resources and environ. com. of Nat. Conf. of State Legislatures, 1980-81; mem. Nat. Sea Grant Rev. Panel, 1978-81, Dept. Energy Environ. Adv. Com., 1980-81. Bd. dirs. Portal Foster Center, Madison; sec. Dane County (Wis.) Democratic Party. Recipient Dane County Assn. Retarded Children ann. recognition award, 1973, 74, 81; Wis. Assn. Mental Health Citizen of Yr. award, 1975; Public Service award Center for Public Representation, 1976; Disting. Service award Dane County Alliance for Mentally Ill, 1979; Legislator of Yr. award Wis. Wildlife Fedn., 1981; Wis. Assn. Marriage and Family Therapy ann. award, 1982; Woman of Yr., Wis. chpt. NOW, 1982; Environ. Leadership award Wis. Environ. Decade, 1976, 78, 80, 82; award Wis. Assn. Family and Children's Agys. and Wis. Council on Human Concerns, 1985. Office: 4802 Sheboygan Ave PO Box 7854 Madison WI 53707

MURALI, LAKSHMI, physician; b. Madras, India, Aug. 4, 1943; d. Rangaswami and Jeya Krisna Swami; m. Raj Murali, Apr. 7, 1972; children—Sujatha, Ram. M.B.B.S., U. Madras, 1967. Diploma child health Royal Coll. Physicians and Surgeons, Glasgow, 1974; diplomate Am. Bd. Phys. Medicine and Rehab. Intern, Govt. Gen. Hosp., Madras, 1967-68; sr. house officer internal medicine Bensham Gen. Hosp., Gateshead, Eng., 1968-69, 70-72; sr. house officer pediatrics Queen Elizabeth Hosp., Gateshead, 1971-72; sr. house officer, registrar phys. medicine and rehab. Astley Ainslie Hosp., Edinburgh, Scotland, 1972-75; resident in phys. medicine and rehab. Inst. Rehab. Medicine, NYU Med. Ctr., N.Y.C., 1975-77; clin. instr. rehab. medicine NYU Med. Ctr., 1977-82; assoc. attending rehab. medicine Bellevue Hosp Med. Ctr., N.Y.C., 1977—; cons. rehab. medicine Astoria Gen. Hosp. (N.Y.), 1982—; attending physician St. Vincent's Hosp. and Med. Ctr., N.Y.C., 1982—, dir. Amputee and Prosthetic Clinic, 1983—; asst. prof. rehab. medicine N.Y. Med. Coll., Valhalla. Mem. Am. Spinal Injury Assn., Gen. Med. Council Gt. Britain, Am. Acad. Phys. Medicine, Internat. Soc. Prosthetics and Orthotics, Am. Congress Phys. Medicine and Rehab., Internat. Rehab. Medicine Assn., Am. Spinal Injury Assn., N.Y. Acad. Medicine, N.Y. Soc. Phys. Medicine. Hindu. Office: 130 W 12th St Suite 2G New York NY 10011

MURAWSKI, ROBERTA LEE, lawyer, writer, editor; b. Staunton, Va., June 6, 1958; d. Norbert Thomas and Germaine Felicia (Lipinski) M.; B.A. magna cum laude SUNY-Buffalo, 1979; J.D., George Washington U., 1982. Bar: D.C. 1982, Md. 1984, Va. 1986. Legal researcher, editor, writer Samuel Green and John V. Long, Washington, 1981-83, Judge Joyce Hens Green and John V. Long, Washington, 1984-86; assoc. Herbert Rubenstein and Assocs., Washington, 1986—; clk. Samuel Green, Washington, 1981. Editor, researcher: Marriage and Family Law Agreements, Vol. 1, 1984, co-author Vol. 2, Divorce, Custody and Division of Property, 1986. Mem. ABA, D.C. Bar Assn., Md. Bar Assn., Va. Bar Assn., D.C. Women's Bar Assn., Phi Beta Kappa. Democrat. Roman Catholic.

MURCHISON, RUTH M. (PEGGI), publisher; b. Plattsburg, N.Y., Aug. 17, 1942; d. Donald Edward and Ruth Edna (Rivers) Marshall) m. John Robert Murchison, June 18, 1960; children—Robert William II, Lori Ann Nohea Murchison. Student U. Hawaii, 1983. Asst. mgr. printing dept. Pacific Telephone Co., Sacramento, 1961-65; med. asst. Mililani Med. Clinic, Hawaii, 1970-72; editor Mililani Town Assn., 1972-75; bookkeeper Gray, Rhee Assocs., Honolulu, 1975-78; pres., treas. PMP Co. Ltd., Wahiawa, Hawaii, 1978—. Editor Parade of Homes Guide, 1980—; Hawaii Architect, 1985—; Ka Nupepa O Mililani, newspaper, 1971-75, 81—. Mem. Wahiawa Bus. Assn., 1985—. Mem. Bldg. Industry Assn. (Assoc. Mem. of Yr. 1983, Life Spike 1983). Democrat. Club: Honolulu Press. Avocations: baseball fan; collecting glasses and dolls. Office: PMP Co Ltd 319B N Cane St Wahiawa HI 96786

MURDOCH-KITT, NORMA HOOD, clinical psychologist; b. Clinton, S.C., May 16, 1947; d. Bernard Constantine and Martha Grace (Hood) Murdoch; B.A. (Most Outstanding Student award 1968-69), Wake Forest U., 1969; M.S., U. Pitts., 1971, Ph.D. (USPHS fellow 1969-72), 1975; m. Jonathan Michael Murdoch-Kitt, Mar. 23, 1974; children—Kelly Michelle, Mark Jason, Sabrina Brittany, Laura Kristina. Psychology intern Eastern Pa. Psychiat. Inst., 1972-73; asst. prof., therapist campus counseling center Coll. William and Mary, Williamsburg, Va., 1973-74; staff psychologist child psychiatry dept. Med. Coll. Va., 1974-75; pvt. practice individual psychotherapy and family and marital therapy, Richmond, Va., 1975—. Mem. Richmond Democratic Com., 1976-79, 82—; pres. Richmond Dem. Women's Club, 1979-81; chmn. govtl. relations com. Ginter Park Civic Assn., 1977-82; mem. Richmond Human Relations Adv. Commn., 1976-80, Richmond Citizens Crime Commn., 1985-86; founder, 1st state chmn. polit. action com. ERA, 1977-78. Mem. Am. Psychol. Assn., Va. Psychol. Assn. (state legis. lobbyist 1978-79 (chmn. legis. com. 1981-83), bd. profl. affairs 1981-85, pres. 1986), Va. Acad. Clin. Psychologists (chmn. profl. affairs com. 1982-84), Richmond Area Psychol. Assn., LWV, ACLU, NOW. Presbyterian. Club: Richmond First (chmn. edn. com. 1979-80, dir. 1980-81). Home: 3408 Moss Side Ave Richmond VA 23222 Office: Murdoch-Kitt Profl Bldg 3217 Chamberlayne Ave Richmond VA 23227

MURDOCK, FRANCES LYNCH, county official; b. Gaston County, N.C., Mar. 25, 1923; d. Walter Robertus and Eva (Kiser) Lynch; m. John Carl Murdock, Jr., May 17, 1942 (dec. July 1966); children—John Carl, Nancy Anne; m. Gilmer Lethco Murdock, Dec. 26, 1981. A.B., Lenoir-Rhyne Coll., 1972. Tchr., Wayside Sch., Iredell County, Statesville, N.C., 1966-71, Celeste Henkel Sch., 1972-84; faculty rep. N.C. Assn. Tchrs., Statesville, 1966-84; Iredell County Democratic party precinct ofcl., 1959-76, party state officer, 1971-76, Iredell County commr., 1978—. Mem. NEA, N.C. Assn. Edn., Iredell County Edn. Assn., Classroom Tchrs. Assn. (pres. 1977-78), Nat. Assn. Counties (chmn. edn. sub.-com. 1983-84), Am. Bus. Women's Assn., Am. Univ. Women's Assn., Statesville Bus. and Profl. Women, Am. Legion Aux. Lutheran. Avocations: cross-stitching; needlepoint; crocheting; walking; golf. Home: Route 1 Box 604 Troutman NC 28166 Office: Office County Commr Statesville NC 28677

MURDOCK, JOAN H., state government official; b. Ross, Calif., Oct. 30, 1936; d. William John and Helen Sophie (Woldemar) Murdock; m. Elvin Dalla Stewart, Oct. 23, 1959 (div. 1967); children—John Dale, James Robert; m. 2d, Carlos Joaquin Canizares, Mar. 24, 1972 (div. 1976); m. 3d, James Roland Miller, July 15, 1977 (div. 1979). A.A., Shasta Coll., 1966; B.A., Calif. State U., Chico, 1974; pub. sector labor relations cert. U. Calif., Davis, 1980; postgrad. U. LaVerne, 1984—. Engring. aide Yolo County, Woodland, Calif., 1965-66; draftsman Caltrans-Dist. 2, Redding, Calif., 1966-67, engring. technician, 1967-70, adminstrv. officer, 1970-77, personnel/labor relations officer, 1977-81; dep. dist. dir. adminstrn. Caltrans-Dist. 9, Bishop, Calif., 1981-84; labor relations cons. City of Bishop, Calif., 1981-82; operator Hi Desert Photo, Bishop; counselor alcohol abuse, Bishop, Calif., 1981-83. Planning commr. Shasta County Planning Commn., Redding, Calif., 1974-78; trustee Buckeye Elem. Sch. Bd., Redding, 1978-81; treas. Shascade Assn. for Retarded Citizens, Redding, 1979-81; bd. dirs. Inyo-Mono Assn. for Handicapped, Bishop, Calif., 1981-82. Mem. Am. Mgmt. Assn., Sierra Desert Art Assn., San Francisco Mus. Modern Art. Democrat. Lutheran. Clubs: Death Valley 49ers, U.S. Citizens Band Radio Association. Lodge: Women of Moose. Office: Caltrans-Dist 9 500 S Main St Bishop CA 93514

MURDOCK, PAMELA ERVILLA, wholesale travel company executive, retail travel company executive; b. Los Angeles, Dec. 3, 1940; d. John James and Chloe Conger (Keefe) M.; children—Cheryl, Kim. B.A., U. Colo., 1962. Pres., Dolphin Travel, Denver, 1972—, Mile Hi Tours, Denver, 1974—. Named Wholesaler of Yr., Las Vegas Conv. and Visitors Authority, 1984. Mem. Am. Soc. Travel Agts. Republican. Office: Mile Hi Tours Inc 2120 S Birch Denver CO 80222

MURGA, ANNE, diabetes nurse therapist; b. Jersey City, Sept. 21, 1954; d. Anthony Steve and Mary Carol (Miksza) Genova; m. James Stuart Buckman, Apr. 7, 1979 (div. 1983); m. Witold Murga, May 20, 1984; stepchildren—Melissa, Michelle; 1 child, Jonathan Edward. B.S. in Nursing, St. Peter's Coll., N.J., 1983. Mgr. wallpaper dept. Siperstein Paint, Jersey City, 1969-78; staff nurse Christ Hosp., Jersey City, 1978-80, diabetes nurse therapist Christ Hosp., Jersey City, 1980—; cons. in field. Author: (book) In Control, 1982; (newsletter) Control It. Mem. Am. Assn. Diabetes Educators, Am. Diabetes Assn. (clin. soc.), Nat. Assn. Female Execs. Roman Catholic. Avocations: women's rights; books; self-help; subliminal learning; exercise. Home: 183 W 51st St Bayonne NJ 07002

MURNIN, BETTE F., retired government executive; b. Omaha, Mar. 10, 1918; m. Joseph Albert Murnin, Mar. 9, 1971; children—Robert Manning, Christopher Hill Maxwell. B.S., Baker U. 1940; M.S. in Edn., Ind. U.-Bloomington, 1960; postgrad. various schs. 1961-85. Field supr. Ind. Dept. Pub. Instruction; dir. guidance Merrillville, Ind.; tchr. Jr. high sch., Elkhart, Ind.; program officer Office Edn. Dept. HEW, 1968-84; pres. U.S. Dept. Edn. Region VIII Am. Fed. Govt. Employees Local Union #3898, 1977-82; nat. exec. bd. Am. Fed. Govt. Employees Nat. Council #252 U.S. Dept. Edn., 1982-84. Bd. dirs. Gary Players, 1961-64, Lake County chpt. Am. Cancer Soc., 1960-72, sec. 1962, 64, state bd. dirs. 1965, 72; pres. PTA, Merrillville, 1965; program chmn. 1964; nat. committeewoman Colo. Young Democrats, 1950; capt. Jefferson County Democrats, 1949-52; program chmn. Jefferson County Jane Jeffersons; bd. dirs. Jefferson County Community Chest 1949-55; chmn. Roosevelt Jr. High Sch. faculty. Baker U. scholar; U.S. Govt. grantee. Mem. Ind. Personnel and Guidance Assn. (founder), Alpha Chi Omega. Office: Fed Bldg 1961 Stout St Denver CO 80291

MUROVIC, JUDITH ANN, neurosurgeon; b. Chgo., Mar. 23, 1949; d. Henry Francis and Mary Ellen (Milosevich) Hmurovic. B.A., Northwestern U., 1971, M.D., 1975. Diplomate Nat. Bd. Med. Examiners. Intern in gen. surgery Northwestern U., 1976-77, resident in neurosurgery, 1978-79; resident in neurosurgery U. Miami, 1979-83; Fellow in neuro-oncology U. Calif.-San Francisco, 1983-86. Recipient Anne Addington research award Northwestern U., 1979. Mem. Alpha Chi Omega. Roman Catholic. Home: 601 Van Ness Ave Apt 123 San Francisco CA 94102 Office: U Calif HSW 783 501 Parnassus San Francisco CA 94143

MURPHREE, GWENDOLYN CRIBBS, retired business executive; b. Houston, May 13, 1921; d. Walter Lee and Lady Lois (Weller) Cribbs; B.A., Rice U., 1942; postgrad. U. Tex., 1941, U. Houston, 1952-53; m. Harold Edwin Murphree, Jr., Feb. 5, 1942; children—Sandra, Patricia (Mrs. Philip W. Smith), Harold Walter, Pres. League Women Voters, Dickinson, Tex., 1956-58, mem. Tex. State Bd., 1958-64, Ind. State Bd., 1965-68, mem. nat. bd., 1968-74, nat. v.p., 1970-72, nat. orgn. chmn., 1970-74, nat. chmn. energy task force, 1974-76; prin. partner cons. firm; v.p., founder Legislex Assos., Columbus, Ind., 1976-82; pub. affairs cons., 1982—; mem. Tex. Gov.'s Com. for Mental Health, 1963-64. Bd. dirs. Galveston County (Tex.) ARC, Human Relations Council, 1961-64; chmn. nat. devel. and fund raising Overseas Edn. Fund, LWV, 1976-77. Home: 1922 College Green Dr Houston TX 77058

MURPHY, BERNADETTE BARTELS, stock market analyst; b. N.Y.C., Apr. 9, 1934; d. Joseph Francis and Julia (Flynn) Bartels; m. Eugene F. Murphy, May 20, 1982. B.A., Our Lady of Good Counsel, White Plains, N.Y., 1955. Vice pres. Shaw & Co., N.Y.C., 1965-86; exec. dir. strategies and selections div. M. Kimelman & Co., N.Y.C., 1986—; panelist TV program Wall St. Week, Md. Ctr. for Pub. Broadcasting, 1979—; Lubin lectr. Pace U., 1981. Contbr. articles to profl. jours. Trustee Pace U., 1978-82. Mem. N.Y. Soc. Security Analysts (pres. 1984-85, dir. 1974—), Fin. Analysts Fedn. (bd. dirs. 1982—, sec.-treas. 1986—, vice chmn. investment analysis standards bd. 1985—, exec. com. 1985—, mem. admissions com.), Market Technicians Assn. (pres. 1977-78), Internat. Soc. Fin. Analysts (bd. dirs., chair membership com.), Fin. Womens Assn. (pres. 1973-74, dir. 1972-78). Home: Bronxville NY Office: M Kimelman & Co 100 Park Ave New York NY 10017

MURPHY, BLANCHE MAXINE, speech pathologist; b. Shandon, Ohio, Oct. 22, 1916; d. Elmer P. and Margaret (Hayes) Heitfield; A.A. (Rotary scholar 1954), Ventura Coll., 1954; B.A. in Speech Therapy, Los Angeles State U., 1956; M.A. in Edn., U. Santo Tomas (Philippines), 1970; M.A. in Counseling Psychology, Ball State U., 1975; m. Harry Blaisdell Murphy, Aug. 24, 1952. Tchr., Santa Paula (Calif.) Sch. Dist., 1954-55, speech therapist, 1956-57; speech therapist Oxnard (Calif.) Sch. Dist., 1957-58, Ventura County (Calif.) Schs., 1958-61, Dept. Def. Dependent Schs., Clark Air Base, Republic of Philippines, 1961-70; speech pathologist Dept. Def. Dependent Schs., European Area, Sembach, Germany, 1970-77, Dept. Def. Dependent Schs., Okinawa, Japan, 1977—; speaker edn. seminars, in-service tng. Pacific Area Command Air Force, 1963-70; condr. workshops for Am. tchrs. Am. Sch., Saigon, Viet Nam, 1963. Recipient Ofcl. commendation for outstanding performance Dept. Army, 1976, Outstanding Service and Conduct award Dept. Def. Dependent Schs., Sembach, 1976; Outstanding Contbn. award as sec. of conf. European Council Parents and Students, 1977; lic. speech pathologist State of Calif. Mem. NEA, Am. Speech and Hearing Assn. (cert. clin. competence in speech pathology 1969), Calif. Speech and Hearing Assn., Am. Personnel and Guidance Assn., Overseas Edn. Assn., Phi Delta Kappa, Pi Lambda Theta. Episcopalian. Author: Speech Improvement for First Grade Children, 1970; Speech Improvement of the Primary School Child Through Ear Training Techniques, 1975. Home: PO Box 833 FPO Seattle WA 98773 also 1804 Parkside Terr Okinawa Japan

MURPHY, BRENDA FETTIG, market research company executive; b. N.Y.C., Aug. 12, 1942; d. Ludwig and Anna (Jusits) Fettig; m. T. Jefferson Murphy, Feb. 17, 1968; 1 son, Christopher Harrington. B.A., Trinity Coll., 1963; M.A., Columbia U., 1969. Cert. tchr., N.Y. Tchr. math. Gt. Neck (N.Y.) Pub. Schs. 1965-73; instr. math. Western Mich. U., Kalamazoo, 1977-79; pres. Harrington Market Research Co., Kalamazoo, 1980—; speaker mktg. seminar Stryker Ctr., Kalamazoo Coll., 1982-83, Mktg./Advt. Round Table, Kalamazoo, 1983, South Central Mich. Planning Council, 1983. Contbr. articles on market research to profl. jours. Bd. dirs. Kalamazoo Inst. Art, 1984, Kalamazoo Symphony Soc., 1985, Jr. Achievement, 1985. Chmn. Legal Aid Soc.-Jr. Com., N.Y.C., 1971-73; bd. dirs. Kalamazoo Figure Skating Club, 1974-76. NSF grantee, 1966, 67-68. Mem. Am. Mktg. Assn., Mktg. Research Assn., Jr. League N.Y., Jr. League Kalamazoo. Office: Harrington Market Research 429 S Burdick Kalamazoo MI 49007

MURPHY, CAROLE DIANE, software mktg. co. exec.; b. Sacramento, Jan. 21, 1942; d. Carl G. and Mary T. (Domich) M.; student U. Calif., Berkeley, 1960, Am. Mgmt. Assn. Seminars, 1963, 69; m. Harris A. Herman, Oct. 5, 1973; children—Terri, Jami, Andria, Nick. Exec. sec. Mut. of New York, Sacramento, 1959-62, R. F. Brown & Assos., Sacramento, 1963-68; adminstrv. office mgr. Informatics Inc., Sacramento, 1968-72; v.p. Software Module Mktg. Co., Sacramento, 1974—, also dir. Mem. Software Industry Assn., Nat. Assn. Ins. Women, Am. Soc. Profl. and Exec. Women, Nat. Small Bus. Assn., Am. Mgmt. Assn. Democrat. Roman Catholic. Office: Software Module Mktg Co 1007 7th St Penthouse Sacramento CA 95814

MURPHY, CAROLE JOYCE, insurance sales executive, consultant; b. Chgo., Nov. 26, 1942; d. Adolph Orger and Frances Rose (Villa) Amundsen; m. Michael Brendan Murphy, Sept. 10, 1969; children—Angela Catherine, Martin Ignatius. Lic. life, accident, health, property and casualty ins. agt.; registered investment rep. Exec. sec. New Am. Library, N.Y.C., 1964-66; registrar M.B.A. Program, Northwestern U., Chgo., 1966-68; exec. sec. Mktg. Inst., Dublin, Ireland, 1968-70; analyst, supr. Motorola, Schaumburg, Ill., 1978-80; sales rep. Met. Ins. Co., Elgin, Ill., 1980-81; agt. Prudential Ins. Co., Niles, Ill., 1981-86; sales rep. Met. Ins., Schaumburg, 1986—. Council mem. St. Margaret Mary Roman Catholic Ch., Algonquin, Ill., 1980-83, religious edn. tchr., 1982-83; mem. adv. com. Medic Alert Found. Internat., 1983—. Mem. Nat. Assn. Life Underwriters, Ill. Life Underwriters Assn., Chgo. Area Life Underwriters, Women Life Underwriters Council, Nat. Assn. Female Execs., Ill. C. of C. (exec. mem. small bus. council), Crystal Lake C. of C. (editor Legis. Briefing 1983—). Republican. Home: 310 Crestwood Ct Algonquin IL 60102 Office: Met Life Schaumburg Corp Ctr 1501 Woodfield Rd Suite 114E Schaumburg IL 60195

MURPHY, CAROLYN LOUISE, insurance company executive; b. Chgo., Dec. 12, 1944; d. Frank Joseph and Louise Mary Tomecek; student U. Chgo., 1965-67; B.S. in Math., Coll. of St. Francis, Joliet, Ill., 1965. Mktg. mgr. IBM, Chgo., 1976-77; exec. asst. to chief exec. officer CNA Ins., Chgo., 1977-78, v.p. personnel, 1978-80, v.p. adminstrn., 1980-83, v.p. field ops., 1984—. Office: CNA Ins CNA Plaza Chicago IL 60685

MURPHY, COLLEEN MARIE, physical therapist; b. Yonkers, N.Y., July 10, 1959; d. Roger James and Jean Marie (Holzheimer) Murphy. B.S. with cert. Phys. Therapy, Simmons Coll., 1981. Lic. phys. therapist, Calif., Tex., Fla. Mem. staff Lifemark Phys. Therapy, Houston, 1982, dir.-in-tng., 1982-83, dir., 1983, ops. coordinator, 1983-84; Calif. sales rep. Phys. Tech., Inc., Calif., 1984; adminstr. Associated Health focus, Irvine, Calif., 1984—. Recipient Barbara J. Rosen award Simmons Coll., Boston, 1981, mem. Acad., 1979-81. Mem. Am. Phys. Therapy Assn., Am. Mgmt. Assn. Office: Associated Healthfocus 14795 Jeffrey Rd #100 Irvine CA 92714

MURPHY, DEBORAH JUNE, legal advisor; b. Clinton, Tenn., Dec. 19, 1955; d. Robert Carlton and Mary Ruth (Melton) M. B.S., U. Tenn., 1977; postgrad. Vanderbilt U., 1983; J.D., Nashville YMCA Law Sch., 1987. Bank officer C&C Bank, Oak Ridge, 1975-76; tax auditor State of Tenn., Knoxville, 1977-82, Nashville, 1983-85, legal advisor, 1985—; instr. Draughons Coll., Knoxville, 1978-81. Mem. Tenn. Homecoming 1986 Com. Mem. Internat. Assn. Auto Theft Investigators, Sigma Delta Kappa. Democrat. Methodist. Avocation: travel. Home: 712 Capitol Towers Nashville TN 37219 Office: Tenn Dept Safety CID 602 Andrew Jackson Bldg Nashville TN 37219

MURPHY, DIANA E., federal judge; b. Faribault, Minn., Jan. 4, 1934; d. Albert W. and Adleyne (Heiker) Kuske; B.A. magna cum laude, U. Minn., 1954, J.D. magna cum laude, 1974, postgrad., 1955-58; postgrad. Gutenberg U., Mainz, Germany, 1954-55; m. Joseph E. Murphy, July 24, 1958; children—Michael, John. Admitted to Minn. bar, 1974; asso. firm Lindquist and Vennum, Mpls., 1974-76; mcpl. judge Hennepin County (Minn.), 1976-78; dist. judge Minn., 1978-80; judge U.S. Dist. Ct. Minn., 1980—; instr. U.S. Dept. Justice Advocacy Inst., U. Minn. Law Sch., 1977—. Bd. regents St. John's U., 1978—; chmn. Mpls. Charter Commn., 1974-76; mem., chmn. bill of rights com. Minn. Constl. Study Commn., 1971-73; bd. dirs. Hennepin County Bar Found., 1981—, pres., 1983-84; bd. dirs. Bush Found., Spring Hill Conf. Center. Recipient Outstanding Achievement award U. Minn. Fulbright scholar, 1954-55. Fellow Am. Bar Found.; mem. Fed. Judges Assn. (dir. 1982—, v.p. 1984—), Am. Law Inst., ABA (ethics and responsibility judges adv. com. 1981—), Minn. Bar Assn. (bd. govs. 1976-81), U. Minn. Alumni Assn. (pres. 1981-82, dir. 1977-83), Am. Judicature Soc. (dir. 1982—), 8th Circuit Dist. Judges Assn., Nat. Assn. Women Judges, Minn. State Bar Assn., Hennepin County Bar Assn., Minn. Women Lawyers, Order of Coif, Phi Beta Kappa. Editor Minn. Law Rev., 1954-55. Office: 670 US Courthouse 110 S 4th St Minneapolis MN 55401

MURPHY, DONNA JEANNE, educator; b. Columbus, Ind., Nov. 27, 1954; d. George Calvin and Jacqueline (Drake) Murphy; B. Music Edn., Ind. Univ. Sch. Music, 1980. Asst. recreation supr. Res-Care, Inc.-Atterbury Job Corps, Edinburgh, Ind., 1979-80; mgr. Nkenge's Nightclub, Houston, 1980-81; tchr. band Houston Ind. Sch., 1980—; pvt. tchr. music, 1970—; rep. Avon Corp. Active Neighborhood Civic Club; mem. Houston Symphony Chorale, 1984—. Recipient Sword of Honor, Sigma Alpha Iota, 1978. Mem. Houston Tchrs. Assn., Tex. State Tchrs. Assn., NEA, Tex. Music Educators Assn., Music Educators Nat. Conf., Nat. Assn. Female Execs. Methodist. Home: 7125 Gammage Houston TX 77087 Office: 7111 Westover St Houston TX 77087

MURPHY, E. ANNE, business services and consulting company executive; b. Charleston, S.C., Feb. 26, 1936; d. Barnwell H. and Miriam Elizabeth (Hilton) Limehouse. Pres., Finders Internat. Ltd. Inc., 1968; v.p., dir. Comprehensive Acctg. Corp., Aurora, Ill., 1979-84; pres., chief operating officer Pop-In, Inc., Columbiana, Ohio, 1984-85; pres., chief exec. officer, chmn. bd. PMA Ent., Inc., Aurora, Ill., 1984—, PMA, Inc., Aurora, 1984—; pres., chief exec. officer Gen. Mgmt. Services, Elmhurst, Ill., 1986—. Contbr. articles to profl. jours. Author: Recruiting, Hiring and Training, 1983, Prairie State 2000 Authority, 1986. Served with USN, 1955-59. Mem. Women in Mgmt., Nat. Alliance of Female Execs., Womens Ednl. Services Assn. (Ill. Businesswoman of Yr. 1984). Mem. Pentecostal Assemblies of God. Avocations: music; theater. Home: 1110 N Farnsworth #213 Aurora IL 60505 Office: Gen Mgmt Services Inc 102 Haven Rd Elmhurst IL 60126

MURPHY, EDRIE LEE, hospital laboratory administrator; b. Redwood Falls, Minn., Dec. 4, 1953; d. Melvin Arthur and Betty Lou (Wenholz) Timm; m. David Joseph Murphy, July 28, 1984. B.S. in Med. Tech. summa cum laude, Mankato State U., 1976; M.B.A., Coll. of St. Thomas, 1984. Registered med. technologist. Med. technologist Children's Hosp., St. Paul, 1976-81, chemistry supr., 1981-85, lab. mgr., 1985—. Charles H. Cooper scholar, 1976. Mem. Am. Soc. Med. Tech., Minn. Soc. Med. Tech., Am. Assn. Clin. Chemists, Clin. Lab. Mgmt. Assn., Phi Kappa Phi. Club: Elan Vital Ski (v.p. membership 1981-82) (Mpls.). Avocations: photography; sailing; skiing; tennis; travel. Office: Children's Hosp 345 N Smith Saint Paul MN 55102

MURPHY, FELICIA STALLWORTH, nursing administrator; b. Sparta, Wis., Apr. 4, 1954; d. William David and Betty Lou (Woods) Stallworth; m. Stephen Jerome Murphy, Oct. 10, 1975 (div. Aug. 1983). B.S. in Nursing, U. Minn., 1977; M.S. in Nursing Adminstrn., DePaul U., 1982. Nurse, Michael Reese Hosp. and Med. Ctr., Chgo., 1977-79; supr. operating room, dir. nursing Louise Burg Hosp., Chgo., 1978-79; nursing supr. Franklin Blvd. Hosp., Chgo., 1979-80; infection control nurse, nursing supr. Chgo. Lakeshore Hosp., 1980-82; adminstr. Cons. for Home Health Care, Inc., Chgo., 1982-85; asst. dir. nursing South Shore Community Hosp., Chgo., 1985—; instr. nursing Chgo. Loop City-Wide Coll., 1981-82, Triton Coll., River Grove, Ill., 1981-82. Mem. State Nurses Active in Politics in Ill., Advocates of Child Psychiat. Nursing, Assn. Practitioners in Infection Control, Chgo. Nurses Assn., Am. Nurses Assn., Ill. Nurses Assn., Am. Holistic Nursing Assn. Democrat. Roman Catholic. Avocations: horseback riding; golf. Home: 821 E Anderson St Savannah GA 30907

MURPHY, GRACE ELIZABETH, clinical administrator hospital chemical dependency unit, therapist, nurse; b. Jersey City, July 8, 1942; d. Edward Leo and Gertrude Edith (Martell) Gallagher; children—Timothy Alan, Jeffrey Michael, Christopher David, Megan Grace. B.S. in Nursing, Seton Hall U., 1964; M.A., Azusa Pacific U., 1981. Lic. nurse, Calif.; cert. marriage, family, child counselor, Calif. Staff nurse emergency unit Jersey City Med. Ctr., 1964-65; co-chmn. maternal-child health dept. Holy Name Hosp., Teaneck, N.J., 1965-66; office mgr. Ob-Gyn, Jersey City, 1966-68; treatment team coordinator St. Mary Med. Ctr., Long Beach, Calif., 1981-83; developer family program Meml. Med. Ctr., Long Beach, 1983-84, supr., 1984-85, clin. program dir. chem. dependency unit, 1986—; pvt. practice marriage, family, child therapy; condr. community workshops, Los Angeles County, 1980-85. Recipient Margaret C. Haley award, Seton Hall U., 1965, awards Calif. State U., 1981, St. Mary Med. Ctr., 1982. Mem. Am. Assn. Marriage, Family Therapists (clin.), Calif. Assn. Marriage, Family Therapists, Am. Assn. Family Counselors and Mediators (cert. mediator), Am. Heart Assn. (basic life support instr.), Nat. Nurses Soc. on Addictions, Nat. Assn. Alcoholism and Drug Abuse Counselors, Calif. Assn. Alcoholism and Drug Abuse Counselors, Assn. Labor-Mgmt. Adminstrs. and Cons. on Alcoholism, Nat. Counsel on Family Relations, Assn. Family Conciliation Cts., Sigma Theta Tau. Roman Catholic. Home: 3641 Navajo Pl Palos Verdes Estates CA 90274 Office: Meml Med Ctr 455 Columbia St Long Beach CA 90801-1428

MURPHY, IRENE LYONS, policy analyst; b. N.Y.C., Oct. 23, 1920; d. George Vincent and Marie Agnes (Mackey) Lyons; m. Francis P. Murphy, Nov. 14, 1947 (div.); children—Diane Murphy Ramo, Bennett Justin. B.A., Barnard Coll., 1941; M.A., Columbia U., 1946, Ph.D., 1970. Editorial asst. Newsweek mag., N.Y.C., 1941-42, 46-47; asst. to dir. Horowitz Found., N.Y.C., 1947-49; postmaster Hicksville Post Office (N.Y.), 1961-66; adj. prof. George Wash. U., Washington, 1974-78; exec. dir. Fedn. of Orgns. for Profl. Women, Washington, 1974-76; policy analyst U.S. Dept. Interior, Washington, 1977—. Author: Public Policy on the Status of Women, 1973; co-author: Working Women, 1976; contbr. articles to profl. jours. Served with USNR, 1942-46. Eagleton Inst. of Politics fellow, 1972-73; recipient Superior Service award U.S. Interior Dept., Washington, 1980. Mem. Internat. Polit. Sci. Assn. (co-chmn. panel 1982—), Am. Soc. Pub. Adminstrn. (panelist 1978—).

MURPHY, JANET GORMAN, college president; b. Holyoke, Mass., Jan. 10, 1937; d. Edwin Daniel and Cahterine Gertrude (Hennessey) Gorman. B.A., U. Mass., 1958, postgrad. 1960-61, Ed.D., 1974; M.Ed., Boston U., 1961. Tchr. English and history John J. Lynch Jr. High Sch., Holyoke, 1958-60; tchr. English, Chestnut Jr. High Sch., Springfield, Mass., 1961-63; instr. English and journalism Our Lady of Elms Coll., Chicopee, 1963-64; mem. staff Mass. State Coll., Lyndonville, Vt., 1977-83, Mo. Western State Coll., St. Joseph, 1983—. Mem. campaign staff Robert F Kennedy Presdl. Campaign, 1967. Recipient John Gunther Tchr. award NEA, 1961, award Women's Opportunity Com., Boston Fed. Exec. Bd., 1963; named one of 10 Outstanding Young Leaders of Greater Boston Area, Boston Jr. C. of C., 1973. Address: Mo Western State Coll Office of President 4525 Downs Dr Saint Joseph MO 64507*

MURPHY, JO ANNE, lawyer; b. Binghamton, N.Y., Oct. 23, 1957; d. William T. and Shirley Anne (Merriam) Murphy. B.A., SUNY-Albany, 1978; J.D., Cornell U., 1981. Bar: N.Y. 1982, U.S. Dist. Ct. (so. dist.) N.Y. 1982. Asso. firm Cleary, Gottlieb, Steen, & Hamilton, N.Y.C., 1981—. Mem. ABA, N.Y. Bar Assn., Assn. Bar City N.Y., Order of Coif. Democrat. Office: Cleary Gottlieb Steen & Hamilton 1 State St Plaza New York NY 10004

MURPHY, JOANNE MARIE, health care equipment company sales executive; b. Chgo., Jan. 17, 1938; d. Charles John and Catherine Elizabeth (Nallon) M. Student, Clarke Coll., 1955-57, St. Francis Hosp. Sch. Med. Tech., Evanston, Ill., 1957-58. Registered med. technologist. Med. technologist J.B. Hartney, M.D., Oak Park, Ill., 1959-61; chem. lab. supr. St. Anne's Hosp., Chgo., 1961-67; tech. sales rep. Hycel, Inc., Chgo., 1967-72; adminstr. Gen. Med. Lab., Chgo., 1972-76; sales rep. Instrumentation Lab., Chgo., 1976-79, S.W. area sales mgr., Houston, 1979-84; central regional sales mgr. Radiometer Am., Inc., Dallas, 1985—. Bd. dirs. Bayou Woods Condo Assn., 1982-84. Recipient Pres.'s Club awards Instrumentation Lab., Lexington, Mass., 1978, 79. Mem. Am. Soc. for Med. Tech., Am. Assn. for Clin. Chemistry, Clin. Lab. Mgmt. Assn., Nat. Assn. Female Execs. Roman Catholic. Office: 2730 Northaven #305 Dallas TX 75229

MURPHY, JOANNE MILLER, marketing executive; b. Holyoke, Mass., Dec. 31, 1957; d. LeRoy Paul and Rose Marie (Danehey) Miller; m. Dennis Francis Murphy III, June 2, 1979; 1 child, Dennis Francis IV. A.S. in Bus. Studies, Holyoke Community Coll., 1979; B.A. in Mktg., U. Mass., 1980. Account rep. Xerox Corp., Hartford, Conn., 1980-82; sales rep. Lanier Bus. Products, East Hartford, Conn., 1982-83; sr. account exec. Exxon Office Systems, Stamford, Conn., 1983-85; area sales cons. ShareTech, Hartford, 1985-86; sr. mktg. rep. Honeywell Info. Systems, Glastonbury, Conn., 1986—. Editor shared tenant newsletter, 1985. Mem. Data Processing Mgmt. Assn., Orgn. for Profls. in Telecommunication. Republican. Roman Catholic. Avocations: tennis; jogging; reading; computer activities. Home: 20 Hilltop Dr West Hartford CT 06107 Office: Honeywell Info Systems 300 Winding Brook Dr Glastonbury CT 06033

MURPHY, KATHLEEN JOAN, macroproject development company owner; b. N.Y.C., Mar. 24, 1947; d. John Joseph and Frances Lepley (Spates) M.; m. Konstantine W. Tsombikos; 1 child, William Konstantine. B.A., Marymount Manhattan Coll., 1968; M.A., NYU, 1971. Cons. McKinsey & Co., Amsterdam, Netherlands, 1971-75, Mexico City, 1975-76, N.Y.C., 1976-82; owner Global Bus. Strategy & Mgmt., N.Y.C., 1982—; adj. prof. Marymount Manhattan Coll., 1984—. Author: Macroproject Development in the Third World, 1983; contbr. articles to profl. jours. Mem. Women Bus. Owners of N.Y., Am. Women's Econ. Devel. Corp. Avocations: swimming; running.

MURPHY, KATHRYN COCHRANE, lawyer; b. Chatham, Ont., Can., Apr. 17, 1949; came to U.S. 1949; d. John Romaine and Mary Emma (Suchta) Cochrane; m. Glenn E. Murphy, Jr., Aug. 19, 1972; 1 child, Glenn E. III. Student Mt. Holyoke Coll., 1967-69; A.B. in Urban Studies cum laude, Yale Coll., 1971; postgrad. Georgetown U., 1971-72; J.D. magna cum laude, Boston Coll., 1975. Bar: Mass. 1975. Assoc. Csaplar & Bok, Boston, 1975-83, ptnr., 1983—. Incorporator Children's Mus., 1983—; former trustee Boston YWCA, Soc. Preservation New Eng. Antiquities. Mem. ABA, Mass. Bar Assn., Boston Bar Assn., Mass. Conveyancers Assn., New Eng. Women in Real Estate (steering com.), Urban Land Inst., Order of Coif. Clubs: Yale of Boston (dir. 1983—, asst. treas. 1984-85, treas. 1985—), Boston Luncheon (dir., officer 1977-80). Office: Csaplar & Bok One Winthrop Sq Boston MA 02110

MURPHY, KATHRYN MARGUERITE, archivist; b. Brockton, Mass.; d. Thomas Francis and Helena (Fortier) M.; A.B. in History, George Washington U., 1935, M.A., 1939; M.L.S., Cath. U., 1950; postgrad. Am. U., 1961. With Nat. Archives and Records Service, Washington, 1940—, supervisory archivist Central Research br., 1958-62, archivist, 1962—, mem. fed. women's com. Nat. Archives, 1974, rep. to fed. women's com. GSA, 1975; lectr. colls., socs. in U.S., 1950—; lectr. Am. ethnic history, 1978-79. Founder, pres. Nat. Archives lodge Am. Fedn. Govt. Employees, 1965—, del. conv., 1976, 78, 80, recipient award for outstanding achievement in archives, 1980. Recipient commendation Okla. Civil War Centennial Commn., 1965; named hon. citizen Oklahoma City, Mayor, 1963. Mem. ALA, Soc. Am. Archivists (joint com. hosp. libraries 1965-70), Nat. League Am. Pen Women (corr. sec. Washington 1975-78, pres. chpt. 1978-80), Phi Alpha Theta (hon.). Contbr. articles on Am. ethnic history to profl. publs. Home: 1500 Massachusetts Ave NW Washington DC 20005 Office: Nat Archives and Records Service 7th and Pennsylvania Aves NW Washington DC 20408

MURPHY, LINDA SUE, city official; b. Lynchburg, Va., June 6, 1948; d. Carter P. and Dorothy L. (Clark) Tucker; m. Daniel K. Murphy, Mar. 25, 1972; 1 child, Krystal Grace. Student, Longwood Coll., 1966-68. Exec. sec. First Nat. Bank of Anchorage, Seward, Alaska, 1976-80; clk. of ct., asst. magistrate Alaska Ct. System, Seward, 1980-81; city clk., personnel officer City of Seward, 1981—. Sec., Seward Concert Assn., 1982; chmn. Seward Sch. Adv. Bd., 1983; v.p. bd. dirs. Seward Life Action Council, 1983-84, pres. bd. dirs., 1984—; chmn. Seward-Obihiro Sister City Com., 1984. Mem. Internat. Inst. Mcpl. Clks., Internat. Personnel Mgrs. Assn., Alaska Assn. Mcpl. Clks. (sec. 1984-85, v.p., pres. elect 1985-86, pres. 1986-87). Democrat. Home: NHN Salmon Creek Rd Seward AK 99664 Office: Seward City Hall PO Box 167 Seward AK 99664

MURPHY, MARCIA GAUGHAN, lawyer, educator; b. Cleve., Nov. 23, 1949; d. John James and Alma Marie (Friedman) Gaughan; m. James Paul Murphy, Sept. 5, 1975. A.B. with honors in English, Smith Coll., Northampton, Mass., 1972; J.D. summa cum laude, U. Notre Dame, 1975. Bar: Ohio 1975. Assoc., Jones, Day, Reavis & Pogue, Cleve., 1975-77; asst. prof. law Case Western Res. U., 1977-81, assoc. prof., 1981-83, prof., 1983; vis. prof. law Am. U., Washington Coll. Law, 1983, prof., 1984—, acting dep. dean, 1984—; referee Ct. Common Pleas, Cleve., 1980; participant Law & Econs. Conf. for Lawyers, Hanover, N.H., 1983. Assoc. editor: Couse's Ohio Form Book, 1985; contbr. articles to law jours. Div. chmn. Campaign for Notre Dame U., 1979; mem. Women's Com. Nat. Symphony Orch., Washington. Mem. ABA, Women's Bar Assn. D.C. Roman Catholic. Office: American U Washington Coll Law 4400 Massachusetts Ave NW Washington DC 20016

MURPHY, MARGARET ANN HENRY, English educator; b. Guntersville, Ala., Dec. 27, 1938; d. Marshall Cochran and Ruth Judson (Parnell) Henry; student Judson Coll., 1956-57; B.S. with honors, Auburn U., 1960; M.Ed., Livingston U., 1968; Ed.D., U. So. Miss., 1980; m. Cecil L. Murphy, Aug. 22, 1957 (div. Feb. 1983); children—Lee Ann Murphy Wasden, Sherry Lynn Murphy Gregson, Tammy Cecile, Cecil L., Margaret Ann. Instr. English, Livingston U., 1968-70, William Carey Coll., 1970-71; chmn. lang. and fine arts div. So. Union State Jr. Coll., 1972-74; chmn. lang. and fine arts div., instr. English, Patrick Henry State Jr. Coll., Monroeville, Ala., 1974—; instr. English, Troy State U., part-time, 1975-81. Mem. steering com., mem. exec. com. Com. of 100; chmn. Sumter County Cancer Crusade, 1970. Mem. Nat. Council Tchrs. English (life), Southeastern Conf. English in the Two-Yr. Colls., NEA, Patrick Henry Tchrs. Assn. (pres. 1983-84), Ala. Edn. Assn., Ala. Assn. Jr. and Community Coll. Chairpersons, Ala. Coll. English Tchrs. Assn., Phi Kappa Phi, Lambda Iota Tau. Democrat. Baptist. Home: PO Box 386 Monroeville AL 36461 Office: PO Box 2000 Monroeville AL 36461

MURPHY, MARGARETTE CELESTINE EVANS, educator, writer; b. Chgo., June 25, 1926; d. Crawford and Ethel Hazel (Cartman) Evans; Ph.B., U. Chgo., 1945, M.A., 1949, postgrad., 1950-79, Ph.D., Colo. Christian Coll., 1972; m. Robert H. Murphy, Sept. 25, 1949; children—Linda, Michelle. Tchr., English, Spanish and French, Willard Elem. Sch., 1950-52, McKinley High Sch., 1952-60, chmn. fgn. langs. dept. Crane High Sch., 1960-64, Harlan High Sch., Chgo., 1967—; tchr. TESL, Chgo. City Jr. Colls., 1976—. Mem. Women's Share in Pub. Service, Brazilian Soc. Chgo., Am. Security Council (nat. adv. bd.), U. Chgo. Alumni Assn., AAUW, Alpha Kappa Alpha. Republican. Roman Catholic. Club: 1200 of Chgo. Author: Note on Martinez Zuviria, Argentinian Novelist, 1949. Home: 8214 S Evans Ave Chicago IL 60619 Office: care Mrs Eva C Martin and Linda M Murphy 907 Polk Ave Memphis TN 38104

MURPHY, MARY C., state legislator. B.A., Coll. St. Scholastica; postgrad. U. Minn., Macalester Coll., U. Wis.-Superior, Am. U. High sch. tchr.; mem. Minn. Ho. of Reps., 1976—, vice-chmn. govtl. ops., health/welfare corrections, mem. commerce and econ. devel. com., labor-mgmt. relations com., chmn. negotiations and gen. labor legislation subcom. Trustee St. Mary's Hosp., Duluth, Minn.; bd. dirs. Minn. Alliance for Sci. and Tech.; mem. adv. com. Home Econs. Vocat. program Hermantown Community Schs.; active del. Duluth Central Labor Body AFL-CIO; mem., lector St. Raphael's Parish; dir. State Democratic Farmer-Labor Party, 1972-74, chmn. 8th Dist. credentials com., 1974—, chmn. St. Louis County Legis. Delegation, 1985-86. Mem. Duluth Fedn. Tchrs. (1st v.p. 1976-77, various coms.), Minn. Fedn. Tchrs. (legis. com. 1972-75), Am. Fedn. Tchrs. (del. nat. convs.), Coalition Labor Union Women, Minn. Hist. Soc., Alpha Delta Kappa. Office: State Office Bldg Saint Paul MN 55155

MURPHY, MARY ELIZABETH, business executive; b. Newton, Kans., Apr. 11, 1941; d. Paul Herbert and Ruby Mae (Thomas) Rutschman; m. Arthur Bradfield Campbell, Aug. 1962 (div. 1967); m. John Francis Murphy, Mar. 17, 1970. Student, Ft. Hays State U., 1959-60, U. Wichita (Kans.), 1959-60, 65-66, Emporia State U. (Kans.), 1960-61; cert. bank mktg. Temple U., 1981, tng. Inst. Legis. Assts., Washington, 1978, Coll. Fin. Planning, Denver, 1979. Lic. real estate agt., D.C., Va. Editing asst. Tech. Services Inc., exec. sec. United Van Lines Co., Denver, 1960-62; sec., office mgr. Nat. Distbg. Co., Denver, 1963; exec. sec. network election service-Kans., ABC-TV, Wichita, 1964; employees div. sec. United Fund, Council Sedgwick County, Wichita, 1965; exec. sec., news, asst. corp. security officer Sta. KOOL-AM, TV, Inc., Phoenix, 1966-70; sec. Vietnam Regional Exchange, Saigon, Vietnam, 1970; exec. sec. USO Pacific Command, Saigon, 1971, receptionist Sen. Barry Goldwater, Washington, 1973, staff asst. John J. Rhodes, U.S. Ho. of Reps., Washington, 1974-81; dir. mktg. and devel. Women's Nat. Bank, Washington, 1981-82; pres. The Murphy Registry, Washington, 1982-84. Mem. Planners, Women's Fed. Forum, Washington, 1972—; treas. League Rep. Women D.C. 1983; mem. Rep. Women Capitol Hill, 1973—, bd. dirs., editor newsletter, 1975; fin. com. Cathedral Park Council Co-Owner, Washington, 1982; editor, founder Cactus Chatter Newsletter Ariz. Soc., Washington, 1972, mem. 1972—; organist St. Christopher's Ch., Saigon, 1970-71. Mem. Women in Communications, Inc., D.C. Met. Chpt. Internat. Assn. Fin. Planers, (v.p. pub. affairs 1983). Episcopalian. Clubs: Capitol Hill, Exec. Link, Capitol Hill Toastmaster (all Washington). Lodge: Order Eastern Star. Home and Office: 4637 Fourth Rd N Arlington VA 22203

MURPHY, MARY KATHLEEN CONNORS (MRS. MICHAEL C. MURPHY), fund raiser, educational administrator, writer; b. Pueblo, Colo.; d. Joseph Charles and Eileen E. (McDermott) Connors; m. Michael C. Murphy, June 6, 1959; children—Holly Ann, Emily Louise, Patricia Marie. A.B., Loretto Heights Coll., 1960; M.Ed., Emory U., 1968; Ph.D., Ga. State U., 1980. Tchr. English pub. schs., Moultrie, Ga., 1959, Sacramento, 1960, Marietta, Ga., 1960-65, DeKalb County, Ga., 1966; tech. writer Ga. Dept. Edn., 1966-69; editorial asst. So. Regional Edn. Bd., Atlanta, 1969-71; dir. alumni affairs The Lovett Sch., Atlanta, 1972-75, dir. publs. and info. services, 1975-77; coordinator summer series in aging Ga. State U., 1979; dir. found. relations Ga. Inst. Tech., 1980—; state coordinator for Ga., Am. Council on Edn. nat. identification program for women in higher edn. administrn., 1983-85; presenter profl. confs.; freelance edn. writer, 1968—; contbr. and contbg. editor numerous articles on teaching, secondary edn., higher edn., and fund raising to profl. publs.; columnist Daily Jour., Marietta, 1963-67, The Atlanta Constn., 1963-68. Bd. advisors Bridge Family Counseling Center, 1981-86, Northside Sch. Arts, 1981-83; bd. dirs. Atlanta Women's Network, 1982-84, v.p., 1983-84; bd. dirs. Sch. Religion, Cathedral of Christ the King, 1979-84; publicity chmn. Phoenix Soc. Atlanta, 1981—; mem. allocations com., exec. com. United Way Met. Atlanta, 1983; bd. counseling Fulton Service Ctr., Met. Atlanta chpt. ARC, 1982-83; mem. Leadership Atlanta, class of 1983-84; group facilitator, 1984-85, co-chmn. edn. program, 1987. NDEA fellow, 1965-66; Adminstrn. of Aging fellow, 1977-79; recipient Image Maker award Atlanta Profl. Women's Directory, Inc. 1984. Mem. Council for Advancement and Support of Edn. (publs. com., dist. III bd. 1981-87, chmn. corp. and found. support conf. 1985, maj. donor research conf. Washington 1985, dist. III conf. chmn. 1986) Nat. Assn. Ind. Schs. (publs. com.), Edn. Writers Assn., Am. Vocat. Assn., Nat. Soc. Fund Raising Execs. (v.p. chpt. 1985, pres. 1986, mem.-at-large nat. bd. 1985—, chmn. pub. relations com. 1985—), Phi Delta Kappa, Kappa Delta Pi (pres. 1980-81). Co-author: Fitting in as a New Service Wife, 1966. Home: 2903 Rivermeade Dr NW Atlanta GA 30327

MURPHY, MARY KATHRYN, industrial hygienist; b. Kansas City, Mo., Apr. 16, 1941; d. Arthur Charles and Mary Agnes (Fitzgerald) Wahlstedt; B.A., Avila Coll., Kansas City, 1962; M.S., Central Mo. State U., 1975; m. Thomas E. Murphy, Jr., Aug. 26, 1963; children—Thomas E., III, David W. Indsl. hygienist Kansas City area office Occupational Safety and Health Adminstrn., 1975-78, regional indsl. hygienist, 1979—; asst. dir. safety office U. Kans. Med. Center, 1978-79. Summer talent fellow Kaw Valley Heart Assn., 1961; cert. in comprehensive practice indsl. hygiene. Mem. AAAS, N.Y. Acad. Scis., Am. Indsl. Hygiene Assn. (sec.-treas. Mid-Am. sect. 1978-79), Am. Chem. Soc., Am. Conf. Govt. Indsl. Hygienists (threshold limit value com. chem. agts.), Am. Coll. Toxicology (asso.), Internat. Soc. Environ. Toxicology, Am. Acad. Indsl. Hygiene, Am. Coll. Chem. Labeling. Home: 10616 W 123rd Street Overland Park KS 66213 Office: 911 Walnut St Suite 406 Kansas City MO 64106

MURPHY, PATRICIA, speech-language pathologist, learning specialist; d. Michael and Nora (Dennehy) M. B.A. in Speech Pathology and Audiology, Hunter Coll., 1968, M.A. in Communication Scis., 1970; M.A. in Learning Disabilities and Reading, NYU, 1977; postgrad. in Ednl. Psychology, Columbia U. Speech-lang. pathologist Goldwater Meml. Hosp. NYU Med. Ctr., 1970-78; lang. learning specialist in child and adolescent psychiatry N.Y. Med. Coll.; instr. psychiatry Met. Hosp., N.Y.C., 1980-85; learning disabilities-lang. specialist Pediatric Learning Ctr., Manhattan Eye, Ear and Throat Hosp., 1985—; cons. speech-lang. pathologist Mary Manning Walsh Nursing Home, N.Y.C., 1974—. Mem. Am. Speech Lang. and Hearing Assn., Orton-Dyslexia Soc., Internat. Reading Assn., NYU Alumni Assn., Hunter Coll. Alumni Assn. Club: Appalachian Mountain.

MURPHY, SARAJANE LEONARD, printing and mailing co. exec.; b. St. Petersburg, Fla., Sept. 19, 1924; d. John Lawson and Mabel Lillian (Houser) Leonard; student Jones Coll., 1941-42; m. Stanley W. Murphy, Sept. 26, 1946; children—Cynthia Louise, Amy Elizabeth, Peggy Leonard, Stanley W., William Stone, Patrick Francis. Copy writer Convention Press, 1960-65, Inland Waterway Guide, 1964-65; v.p. Stan Murphy Co., Jacksonville, Fla., 1955—. Past pres., v.p., dir. local and dist. bd. United Methodist Ch.; sec. local unit Am. Cancer Soc.; dir., mem. exec. com. State Cancer Sos.; dir., bd. mem. Theatre Jacksonville. Clubs: Belle Meade Hunt (Ga.); Garden of Jacksonville. Office: 705 American Heritage Life Bldg Jacksonville FL 32202

MURPHY, SHEILA ANNE, state official; b. Buffalo, May 18, 1945; d. Glenn Edward and Julia Mary (Byrne) M. B.A. in Speech Communications, SUNY-Buffalo, 1973. Radio news reporter Sta. WYSL, Buffalo, 1971-73; news reporter, asst. news dir. Sta. WGR, Taft Broadcasting, Buffalo, 1973-75; anchor, reporter Sta. WGR-TV Taft Broadcasting, Buffalo, 1975-81; common councilman City of Buffalo, 1982-83; asst. sec. of state N.Y. State, Buffalo, 1983—. Recipient 1st Place award N.Y. State Associated Press Broadcasters Assn., 1978. Democrat. Roman Catholic. Home: 226 Summit Ave Buffalo NY 14214 Office: NY Dept of State 65 Court St Buffalo NY 14202

MURPHY, SOLBRITT ELISABET, state health adminstr., pediatrician; b. Sweden, June 20, 1933; came to U.S., naturalized, 1966; d. Bo and Dagny Sundren; student U. Wash., 1953-54, M.D., 1960; candidate medicine Karolinska Inst. Medicine and Surgery, Stockholm, 1955-57; M.P.H., U. Calif., Berkeley, 1972; children—Kari, Stephen, Britt. Intern in pediatrics Children's Orthopedic Hosp., Seattle, 1960-61; resident in pediatrics, then resident in psychiatry U. Wash., 1961-63, resident in pediatrics, 1964-65, clin. instr. in pediatrics, 1965-67, 67-70, clin. asst. prof., 1970-71, pediatrician Child Devel. and Mental Retardation Center, 1967-71, asst. prof. pediatrics, 1965—; sch. physician sch. dists., Renton, Issaquah and Mercer Island, Wash., 1963-64, 65-67; dir. Children and Youth Project, Seattle, 1972-74; dir. Maternal and Infant, Children and Youth Project, Tri-County Dist. Health Dept., 1974-76, assoc. dir. Tri-County Dist. Health Dept., 1977-81; dir. Bur. Maternal and Child Health, N.Y. State Dept. Health, Albany, 1981—; asst. prof. U. Colo. Med. Center, co-dir. community pediatric fellowship; mem. N.Y. Gov.'s Citizen's Task Force on Child Abuse and Neglect, 1982; cons. in field. Diplomate Am. Bd. Pediatrics. Fellow Am. Acad. Pediatrics; mem. Am. Pub. Health Assn. Office: Bur Maternal and Child Health Tower Bldg Empire State Plaza Albany NY 12237

MURPHY, STEPHANIE GREEN, lawyer; b. Coral Gables, Fla., Oct. 6, 1950; d. Thomas Robert and Nilda (Lopez) Green; m. Gerald McBride, Dec. 2, 1978 (div. 1980); m. Terence Murphy, Feb. 8, 1986. B.A., U. Fla., 1973; J.D., U. Miami, 1978. Bar: Fla. 1980. Atty. firm Paige & Catlin, Miami, Fla., 1978-80; adminstrv. mgr. internat. div. Aeromexico, Miami, 1980-82, legal counsel internat. div., 1982—; dir. Corp. Counsel Assn. South Fla., 1980—. Active Am. Cancer Soc., 1983. Mem. ABA, Fla. Bar Assn., Dade County Bar Assn. Republican. Roman Catholic. Clubs: Surf, Aviation Exec. (dir.). Home: 600 Biltmore Way Apt 713 Coral Gables FL 33134 Office: Aeromexico 8390 NW 53 St Miami FL 33166

MURPHY, THERESA ROSE, compensation analyst; b. Oklahoma City, Jan. 30, 1958; d. Edward James and Margaret Mabel (Chase) Murphy. B.B.A., North Tex. State U., 1980, M.B.A., 1983. Compensation analyst Meth. Hosps. Dallas, 1980-83; corp. compensation analyst Tex. Instruments, Inc., Dallas, 1983—. Mem. Am. Compensation Assn., Dallas Mus. Art. Roman Catholic. Office: Tex Instruments Inc 13500 N Central Expressway Dallas TX 75234

MURPHY, VIVYAN PATRICIA, engineer; b. Birmingham, Ala., Oct. 25, 1948; d. William W. and Ellamai V. (Grizzard) M.; m. Ollie D. Kennedy, June 26, 1965 (div. Mar. 1976). B.S. in Engring., Auburn U., 1965, M.B.A., 1968. Environ. engr. J.B. Converse, Mobile, Ala., 1970-73; dist. rep. Nalco Chem., Mobile, 1973-77; foreman-in-tng. pulp and paper mill Container Corp. Am., Fernandina Beach, Fla., 1977-79, foreman pulp mill, 1979-82, asst. supt. power dept., 1982-84, group leader utilities Internat. Paper Co., Mansfield, La., 1984—. Editor: Auburn Engr., 1964-65. Drug abuse vol. United Way, 1966-82; leader candystripers Hosp. Aux., Opelika, Ala., and Fernandina Beach, 1978-81; membership chair Young Democrats, Fernandina Beach, 1980-82. Mem. Am. Inst. Aerospace and Aero. Engrs. (pres. 1963-64; Outstanding Engr. 1965), Nat. Assn. Female Execs., NOW, Soc. Am. Mgrs., Am. Bus. Women's Assn. (v.p. 1981-82; award 1981), AAUW, Pi Beta Phi, Tau Beta Phi. Democrat. Baptist. Avocations: painting; aerobics; tennis. Home: 1509 Lafitte Cove Shreveport LA 71105 Office: PO Box 999 Mansfield LA 71052

MURPHY-SUPPLE, LINDA ANN, personnel administrator; b. Bronx, N.Y., Sept. 3, 1955; d. James Leo and Katherine Susan (Conger) Murphy; 1 son, Devin Leo. B.A. in Sociology, Hunter Coll., 1977. Page N.Y. Pub. Library, N.Y.C., 1970-73, clk., library asst., 1973-76; office mgr. London Futures Ltd., N.Y.C., 1976-78; personnel adminstr. Diamond Internat., N.Y.C., 1978-82; sr. project specialist Burson-Marsteller, N.Y.C., 1982-83; personnel mgr. Tensolite Co div. Carlisle Corp., Buchanan, N.Y., 1983—; tutor Bd. Edn., N.Y.C., 1970-73. Mem. Am. Soc. Personnel Adminstrn. (chairperson 1982-83, dir. 1983—). Democrat. Office: Tensolite Co div Carlisle Corp Old Post Rd Route 9A Buchanan NY 10511

MURR, DEIRDRE ANN, data processing documentation consultant; b. Tulsa, Feb. 4, 1948; d. Hugh Orville and Pamela Hilda (Comley) Steavenson. B.A. in History, U. S.C., 1971. Data control mgr. Sterling Computers Co., Houston, 1977-78; ops. supr. Weingartens Co., Houston, 1978-80; cons. in data processing The Leslie Corp., Houston, 1981; documentarian, trainer, Barbour Computer Service, Houston, 1981-83; prin., owner Docutext Co., Houston, 1983—. Soc. Tech. Communication, Tex Hist. Soc., Women in Data Processing, Houston Assembly Delphian Chpts. Episcopalian. Club: Quitters Guild Houston. Office: Docutext PO Box 29089 Houston TX 77227

MURRAY, ANGIE ANNA ALICE, government official; b. Thibodaux, La., July 6, 1949; d. Edward Justin Paul and Anna Angelina (Himmler) Hebert; m. Walter Thomas Murray, Mar. 21, 1970; 1 child, Thomas Joseph. Speedwriting Cert., Sawyer Secretarial Sch., 1974. Mem. customer service staff European Exchange System, Ramstein, Ger., 1967-68; buyer, expeditor Thurow Electronics, Tampa, Fla., 1968-70; quotation clk. Thomas & Betts Co., Elizabeth, N.J., 1970-75; cost acct., girl Friday, Fulton Shirt Co., Elizabeth, 1975-76; office sec. Rapides Parish Police Jury, Alexandria, La., 1977-81, parish sec., 1981—; sec. Rapides Parish Stormwater Mgmt. and Drainage Dist., 1983—. Recipient Journalism award Noncommd. Officers Wives Club, 1967. Mem. Am. Soc. Notaries, Sec.-Treas. Orgn. of La. (region 8 exec. bd.), VFW Aux. Democrat. Roman Catholic. Avocations: reading; handicrafts. Home: PO Box 187 Elmer LA 71424 Office: Rapides Parish Police Jury PO Box 1150 Alexandria LA 71309

MURRAY, ANNE, singer; b. Springhill, Nova Scotia, Can., June 20, 1945; d. Carson and Marion (Burke) M.; B.Phys. Edn., U. N.B. (Can.), 1966; m. William Langstroth, June 20, 1975; children—William Stewart, Dawn Joanne. Country and pop singer, 1970—; appearances on stage and TV; appeared in 4 CBS-TV spls., 1981-85; rec. artist; songs rec. include Love Song (Grammy award for best country vocalist 1974), You Needed Me (Grammy award for best pop vocalist 1979), Could I Have This Dance (Grammy award for best country vocalist 1980), A Little Good News (Grammy award for best country vocalist 1983). Decorated companion Order of Can.; recipient numerous Juno awards Can. Acad. Rec. Arts and Scis., 1970-80; Country Music Assn. awards; Am. Music awards; named to Nashville Country Music Hall of Fame, 1974; star in Hollywood Walkway of Stars, 1980. Office: care Balmur Ltd 4881 Yonge St Suite 412 Toronto ON M2N 5X3 Canada

MURRAY, ARNETTE MARIE, ednl. cons.; b. Chgo., Dec. 17, 1934; d. Arnett Bedford Francis and Hazel Marie (Lumpkins) Murray; B.S., U. Ill.,

1957; M.S., Coll. Racine, 1974; Ph.D., So. Ill. U., 1981; div.; children—Victor, Vincent, Victoria. Tchr., Holy Child High Sch., Waukegan, Ill., 1957-60; tchr. Zion (Ill.) Elem. Dist. No. 6, 1969-70, Title I dir., 1970-76; ednl. cons. reading, tchrs. centers gifted edn. Ill. State Bd. Edn., Springfield, Ill., 1976—; cons. U.S. Dept. Edn., NEA; mem. dist. study com. on gifted and computer edn. Vol. workshop leader Springfield Housing Authority, 1980; Right-to-Read dir. Zion-Benton Twp., 1974-76; mem. Zion Environ. Commn., 1974; mem. civilian rev. bd. U.S. Selective Service. Mem. Am. Assn. Sch. Adminstrs., Assn. Tchr. Educators, Ill. Assn. Supervision and Curriculum Devel., Am. Assn. Supervision and Curriculum Devel., Ill. Writers Inc., Phoenician Artist Assn. Home: 2908 Woodward Ave Springfield IL 62703 Office: 100 N 1st St Springfield IL 62777

MURRAY, CHARMAINE EVADNEY, computer programmer; b. Kingston, Jamaica, Feb. 18, 1962; came to U.S., 1978; d. Clarence Enderby and Ivy Elfreda (Johnson) M. B.S., CCNY, 1984. Programmer, IBM Corp., N.Y.C., 1983-84, edn. specialist, White Plains, N.Y., 1984-85, assoc. programmer, 1985—, edn. cons., 1984—. Postgrad. U. Conn., 1985—. Author: (poetry) Something For Everyone, 1981; also songs. Democrat. Baptist. Avocations: tennis; swimming; reading; real estate; poetry. Home: 55 Newfield Ave #93 Waterbury CT 06708 Office: IBM PO Box 3332 Danbury CT 06813

MURRAY, CHERRY ROBERTS, artist, fine arts educator; b. Colfax, La., Jan. 3, 1921; d. John Bunyon and Mary (Procter) Roberts; student U. N.Mex., 1940-41; B.F.A., U. Tex., 1942; student Nagayama Studio, Tokyo, 1955; studied under numerous profl. artists, including Ward Lockwood, Best-Mougourd, Maynard Dixon, Millard Sheets, Peter Hurd, Georgia O'Keefe, Vincent Farrell; m. John Lewis Murray, May 2, 1942; children—John Roberts, James Procter (dec.), Cherry Ann, Nancy Lee. Tchr. painting, U.S., 1939-54, 70—, Japan, 1954-56, 60-64, Pakistan, 1957-60, Korea, 1965-68, Indonesia, 1968-70; instr. fine arts Pima Coll. East, Tucson, 1979—; exhbns. include: Baluche Regiment, Cherat, West Pakistan, 1965-68, Am. Embassy Residence, Seoul, Korea, 1965-68, Djarkarta, Indonesia, 1968-70, Abba Gallery, 1978-80, Kay Bonfoey Gallery, 1980, Rentschler Gallery, 1980, Casa Grande Art Gallery, Tucson, 1980; represented in permanent and pvt. collections: U. Tex., U. N.Mex., Nagayama Studio, Tokyo, Ayub Kahn, Baluche Regiment, West Pakistan, Mitha Collection, Lahore, Pakistan, Sir Ian McKensie, Brit. Isles, H. Allen Loomes, Australia, Ambassador Yehuda Horam, Israel, Chote-Kholgvista, Thailand, Kopper, Indonesia, Galbraith, Washington, USIS, Indonesia, Am. Embassy, Djarkarta, Am. Embassy, Seoul, Lathrum, Hicks, Woods, Elliott collections (all Washington), Valley Nat. Bank, City of Douglas, Old Adobe Patio Gallery, others. Recipient 56 awards, 1975-86, including: Creative Artist of Yr. award, 1976; 1st pl. award So. Ariz. Watercolor Guild, 1978; Merit award Watercolor Southwest III, Houston, 1978; Best of Show award Nat. League Am. Pen Women, 1978; Tchr. of Yr. award Pima Coll. East, 1983. Mem. U. Tex. Art Assn. (1st pres.), So. Ariz. Watercolor Guild, Tubac Center of the Arts, Santa Cruz Valley Art Assn., Sierra Vista Art Assn., Ariz. Watercolor Soc., Archeol. and Hist. Soc., Nat. Soc. Arts and Letters, Southwestern League Fine Arts, Gem and Mineral Soc., Nat. League Am. Pen Women, AAUW, Pilot Internat. Democrat. Presbyterian. Home: Route 8 Box 78 Tucson AZ 85748 Office: Pima Community College 8202 E Poinciana Dr Tucson AZ Office: Pima Coll E Tucson AZ 85710

MURRAY, CHERYL, fashion coordinator, hair designer, photo stylist; b. Chgo., Jan. 26, 1931; d. Henry and Emma (Severin) Petry; m. John Francis Murray, Nov. 10, 1971 (dec. 1973). Student Chgo. Acad. Fine Arts, 1945, U. Chgo., 1949-53, N.Y. Sch. Interior Design, 1970-72, Marinello, N.Y.C., 1972-74, Sassoon's, London, 1975. Photog. stylist Kravalle Studio, N.Y.C., 1955-61; photog. stylist, fashion coordinator Ogilvy & Mather, N.Y.C., 1961-63; interior designer, stylist Eastman Chem., N.Y.C., 1963-64; photo stylist, interiors and fashions, Pagano Studio, N.Y.C., 1964-67; head of styling Nugent-Christensen, N.Y.C., 1967-73; head children's dept. Pagano Studio, 1973-75; hair designer Cheryl of N.Y., Los Angeles, 1978-83; sr. fashion coordinator Allied Graphic Arts, N.Y.C., 1985—. Democrat. Avocations: painting; cooking; camping; walking; museums and old homes. Home: 33 Gold St Townhouse 1 New York NY 10038 Office: Allied Graphic Arts 1515 Broadway New York NY 10036

MURRAY, CHERYL LORAINE, real estate development company executive; b. Medford, Mass., Apr. 23, 1959; d. Paul Loraine and Anne Regina (Conlin) Bauguss; m. Richard Christopher Murray, July 8, 1978; children—Loraine Anne, Heather Marie. Student U. So. Maine, Northeastern U., U. Lowell. Office mgr. Great Bay Co., Portland, Maine, 1983, controller, 1983-84; project mgr., mktg. dir. Portland House, Inc., 1984-85; real estate devel. cons. A. David Rapaport, Bangor, Maine, 1985; fin. coordinator Donald R. Peters, South Portland, 1985; project mgr. Donalco, Inc., South Portland, 1986—; cons. Rapaport Fin., Bangor, 1985—, Realty Assocs., Old Orchard, Maine, 1985—, Portland House, Inc., 1985—. Leader Brownie scout troop Girl Scouts U.S.A., Cumberland, Maine, 1985—; exec. sec. Children's Coop. Nursery Sch., Portland, 1984-85. Recipient Excalibur award Maine Savs. Bank, 1986. Democrat. Roman Catholic. Club: Cumberland County Riding (treas. 1985—). Avocations: horses; painting; outdoor activities; music; literature. Home: 89 Depot Rd Gray ME 04039 Office: New Linwood Realty Trust Inc 33 E Grand Ave Old Orchard Beach ME 04064

MURRAY, CLAIRE ANNE, training and education consultant; b. Quincy, Mass., July 8, 1952; d. William Francis and Claire Mildred (Cunningham) M.; B.A. with honors, Northeastern U., 1976; M.Ed., Northeastern U., 1978. Staff specialist Northeastern U., Boston, 1972-78; cons. Newton, Mass., 1979-81; staff specialist, trainer Stone & Webster Engring., Boston, 1981-83; pres. C.A. Murray Assoc., 1983—. Regular contbr. The Tng. Scene, 1981—, guest editor June issue, 1986. Instr., ARC, Boston, 1977—, Easter Seal Soc., 1983. Mem. Am. Soc. Training and Devel. (bd. dirs. Mass. chpt. 1982—, regional liason, conf. dir.), New Eng. Assn. for Coop. Edn. and Field Experience, Am. Inst. Cancer Research. Democrat. Roman Catholic. Office: 3 Silverhill #2 Natick MA 01760

MURRAY, FLORENCE KERINS (MRS. PAUL F. MURRAY), justice Supreme Ct. R.I.; b. Newport, R.I., Oct. 21, 1916; d. John X. and Florence (MacDonald) Kerins; A.B., Syracuse U., 1938; LL.B., Boston U., 1942; student R.I. Coll., Edn., 1942, Ed.D. (hon.), 1956; LL.D., Bryant Coll., 1956, U. R.I., 1963, Mt. St. Joseph Coll., 1972, Providence Coll., 1974, Johnson-Wales Coll., 1977, Salve Regina Coll., 1977, Suffolk U.; m. Paul F. Murray, Oct. 21, 1943; 1 son, Paul F. Admitted to Mass., R.I. bars, U.S. Supreme Ct. bar; pvt. law practice with husband, under name Murray & Murray, Newport, R.I., 1952-56; mem. R.I. Senate, 1948-56; asso. justice R.I. Superior Ct., 1956-78, presiding justice, 1978-79; justice R.I. Supreme Ct., 1979—; first woman judge State of R.I.; staff, faculty adviser Nat. Coll. State Judiciary, 1971-72. Mem. Gov.'s Jud. Council, R.I. Alcohol Adv. Council Com., Adv. Council on Mental Health, Nat. Adv. Com. on Women in Service; mem. civil and polit. rights com. Pres.'s Commn. Status of Women, 1960-63; chmn. Newport Sch. Com., 1951-57; bd. dirs., mem., sec. R.I. Physicians Service; sec. R.I. Commn. on Jud. Discipline and Tenure; dir., sec. R.I. Blue Shield; chmn. R.I. Nat. Endowment Humanities com., 1972; bd. dirs. YMCA, Newport, Nat. Coll. Judiciary, Reno, 1975—, Inst. Ct. Mgmt., Denver, 1977; trustee Syracuse U., 1974—, Bryant Coll.; bd. visitors Boston U. Law Sch. Served as lt. col., WAC, World War II, now hon. Res. Recipient Legion of Merit, Army Commendation Ribbon, Arents Alumni award Syracuse U., 1956, Carroll award R.I. Inst. Instrn., 1956; Regina medal Salve Regina Coll., 1962; Alumni award Boston U., 1965; named to R.I. Heritage Hall of Fame, 1980. Fellow Inst. Jud. Adminstrn.; mem. Am. Bar Assn. (jud. adminstrn. div. council), Am. Judicature Soc. (dir. 1976-80), Am. Legion (judge adv. post 7, mem. nat. exec. com.), AAUW (chmn. state edn. com., 1954-56), Bus. and Profl. Woman's Club (past state v.p., past pres. Newport, past pres. nat. legis. com.), Alpha Chi Omega, Kappa Beta Pi. Club: Quota (past gov. internat., past pres. Newport). Office: 250 Benefit St Providence RI 02903

MURRAY, JANE ELLEN, advertising executive; b. Chgo., Aug. 21, 1927; d. Thomas F. and Mildred (Spacek) M.; m. Edwin R. Wentz, June 10, 1983. B.A., Vassar Coll., 1948. Sec., J. Walter Thompson, Chgo., 1948-58, group head, 1958-68, assoc. creative dir., 1968-70, v.p., 1970-75, creative dir., 1975—. Author musical: Fear of Filing, 1982; contbr. articles to profl. jours. Recipient award Chgo. Daily News Writing Contest; Spl. Citation, Vogue Prix de Paris Contest; Blue Ribbon award Chgo. Copywriter's Club, 1958; award Am. TV Commercial Festival, 1964; citation Bur. Advt. ANPA, 1968; named The Top 100, Heads-Up Headlines; Hermes award, 1969; cert. appreciation Sch. Journalism, No. Ill. U., 1975; Leadership award YWCA, 1977. Mem. Am. Advt. Fedn. (Advt. Woman of Yr., Ad Person of Yr. 5th dist. 1978, Chgo. Addy award and 6th dist. Addy 1980, chmn. 6th dist. Addy awards 1982), Women's Advt. Club Chgo. (pres. 1979-80, 80-81, bd. dirs. 1978-79), Jr. Women's Advt. Club (pres.). Republican. Roman Catholic. Club: Vassar (dir. 1978).

MURRAY, JILL CHARMIAN, information and publishing company executive; b. London, July 18, 1936; d. Frederick William and Phyllis Dorothy (Miller) Gordon-Hall; children—Sophie Claire Chapuisat, Tanya Louise Chapuisat; m. 2d, James Murray, May 8, 1982. Student Riante Rive, Lausanne, Switzerland, 1952-54. Asst. TV producer J. Walter Thompson London, 1956-58; pub. relations account exec. Link Info. Services (Unilever), London, 1958-60; asst. publicity dir. Conde Nast Glamour Mag., N.Y.C., 1960-61; internat. publicity dir. Jacques Heim Couturier, Paris, France, 1961-64; soft news editor Daily Jour., Caracas, Venezuela, 1970-73, U. Geneva, 1975-76; research mgr. Bus. Internat., Geneva and London, 1977-81, research dir., N.Y.C., 1982-85; sr. v.p. research Morag Hann & Co. tchr., Lima, Peru, 1965-70. Home: 220 Columbia Heights Brooklyn NY 11201

MURRAY, JULIA KAORU (MRS. JOSEPH EDWARD MURRAY), occupational therapist; b. Wahiawa, Oahu, Hawaii, 1934; d. Gijun and Edna Tsuruko (Taba) Funakoshi; B.A., U. Hawaii, 1956; cert. occupational therapy U. Puget Sound, 1958; m. Joseph Edward Murray, 1961; children—Michael, Susan, Leslie. Therapist, Inst. Logopedics, Wichita, Kans., 1958; sr. therapist Hawaii State Hosp., Kaneohe, 1959; part-time therapist Centre County Center for Crippled Children and Adults, State College, Pa., 1963; vice chmn. adv. bd. Hosp. Improvement Program, East Oreg. State Hosp., Pendleton, 1974; v.p. Independent Living, Inc., 1976-79; also job search instr.; mem. adv. com. Oreg. Ednl. Coordinating Commn., 1979-82; mem. Oreg. Bd. Engring. Examiners, 1979—; now occupational therapist Fairview Tng. Ctr., Salem, Oreg. Rep. from Umatilla County Commrs. to Blue Mountain Econ. Devel. Council, 1976-78; bd. dirs. Ashland LWV, 1967-71, v.p., 1970; mem. Ashland Park and Recreation Bd., 1972-73; vice chmn. adv. bd. LINC, 1978; mem. exec. bd. Liberty-Boone Neighborhood Assn., 1979-83. Mem. Am., Oreg., Hawaii (sec. 1960) occupational therapy assns., LWV (dir. Pendleton 1974, 77-78, pres. 1975-77; dir. Oreg. 1979-81). Address: 760 Ironwood Dr SE Salem OR 97306 Office: Fairview Tng Ctr 2250 Strong Rd SE Salem OR 97310

MURRAY, KATHLEEN ELLEN, editor; b. Chgo., Feb. 23, 1946; d. John Joseph and Marie (Stoltzman) M.; A.A. in Bus., Am. River Coll., 1968; B.A. in Journalism, Calif. State U., 1973. File clk. Allstate Ins. Co., Sacramento, 1964-66; clk. typist Calif. Hwy. Patrol, Sacramento, 1968-69; copy editor Sacramento Bee, 1971—; tchr. Calif. State U., 1975-76; tutor Calif. Youth Authority Camp. Mem. Sacramento Press Club. Democrat. Home: PO Box 606 Nevada City CA 95959 Office: PO Box 15779 Sacramento CA 95813

MURRAY, KATHLEEN VIRGINIA, editor; b. Charleroi, Pa., Nov. 7, 1939; d. William Albert Carney and Virginia (Behanna Carney) Clark; B.A. cum laude in Communications, Mundelein Coll., 1980; m. David Lee Murray, Dec. 29, 1961; children—Clark David, Timothy Lee. Div. sales mgr. Port-A-Bookstore, Palatine, Ill., 1973-74; editor Murray Communications, Evanston, Ill., 1975-81; assoc. editor The Guarantor, Chgo. Title & Trust Co., 1981-83, editor, 1983, editor, communications officer, 1984-85; tng. and communications cons. Career Exchange Network, Carlsbad, Calif., 1985—. Mem. Internat. Assn. Bus. Communicators, Women in Communications, North Shore Choral Soc. (dir.), Kappa Gamma Pi. Editor: You, Your Children and Divorce, New Decision, 1981; mng. editor PACE, 1980. Home: 4175 Bachman Pl 66 San Diego CA 92103 Office: 2111 Palomar Airport Rd Suite 350 Graham Internat Plaza Carlsbad CA 92008

MURRAY, LINDA IRENE, postmaster; b. Seattle, Oct. 23, 1947; d. Billie Burton and Irene (Abraham) M.; m. Alex Curt Alvarez, Mar. 10, 1967 (div. 1977); children—Alex Carlos, Candy Lynn, Billie Lee. Student U. Oreg., Eugene, 1965-66, Lane Community Coll., 1978-82, Southwestern Oreg. Community Coll., 1983. Clk., U.S. Postal Service, Eugene, 1969-83, postmaster, Gardiner, Oreg., 1983—; mem. women's adv. bd. U.S. Postal Service Mail Sectional Ctr., Eugene, 1985—. Bd. dirs. Latch Key, Eugene, 1980; soccer coach Southwestern Oreg. Youth Assn., Reedsport, 1984, 85. Mem. Nat. Assn. Postmasters of U.S., Southwest Coast Postmasters, Coast Women's Adv. Group, Bus. and Profl. Women. Club: Coast Cruisers (Reedsport). Lodge: Eagles. Avocations: reading; sewing; camping; fishing; rafting. Home: PO Box 12 Gardiner OR 97441 Office: US Postal Service 637 West St Gardiner OR 97441

MURRAY, LOIS A. HEIL, lawyer; b. Marshfield, Wis., June 3, 1953; d. Frank N. and Bertha J. (Hafenbreadl) Heil; B.A., B.S. in Acctg., U. Wis., River Falls, 1974; J.D. cum laude, U. Minn., 1978; m. Alan E. Murray, Aug. 18, 1973. Tax examiner Minn. Dept. Revenue, 1974-75; admitted to Wis. bar, 1978, Minn. bar, 1978, U.S. Dist. Ct. bar, 1978; law clk. firm Ralph Senn, River Falls, 1976; research asst. to prof. law and asso. dean Sch. Law, U. Minn., Mpls., 1976-78; law clk. Honeywell, Inc., Mpls., 1977; assoc. firm Heywood, Cari & Murray and predecessor, Hudson, Wis., 1978-80, partner, 1980—; mem. faculty Wis. Indianhead Tech. Inst., Hudson Community Edn. Bd. dirs. West Central Wis. Action Agy., 1984-85. Mem. State Bar Assn. Wis., State Bar Assn. Minn., Am. Bar Assn., St. Croix Valley Bar Assn., AAUW, LWV, Hudson Area C. of C. Roman Catholic. Home: 600 7th St Hudson WI 54016 Office: Micklesen Bldg 204 Locust St Hudson WI 54016

MURRAY, LYNN, lawyer; b. Paterson, N.J., Mar. 2, 1956; d. James Lindsay and Joan (Van Winkle) M. B.A., Purdue U., 1978; J.D., Rutgers U., 1981. Bar: Ind. 1981. Assoc. firm Sandy, Deets & Kennedy, Lafayette, Ind., 1981-82; staff atty. UAW legal services plan Gen. Motors Corp., Kokomo, Ind., 1983-86, supervising atty., 1986—. Contbr. articles to legal publs. Active Democtats of Howard County, Ind. Hist. Soc. Mem. ABA, Ind. Bar Assn., Howard County Bar Assn., Purdue U. Alumni Assn., Phi Alpha Delta, Pi Sigma Delta, Phi Alpha Theta. Methodist. Home: 323 N Berkley St Kokomo IN 46901 Office: UAW Legal Services Plan 1213 E Hoffer St Kokomo IN 46902

MURRAY, MARGOT SCOTT, nursing educator; b. Montreal, Que., Can., Sept. 13, 1940; came to U.S., 1968, naturalized, 1979; d. Russell Edward Bradley and Margaret Pearson Scott; m. Richard Ian Murray, Oct. 20, 1979; children—Deborah, Susan, Graham. A.S., U. Hawaii, 1974, B.S., 1977, M.S., 1981. Staff nurse intensive care unit St. Francis Hosp., Honolulu, 1974-78; staff nurse-psychiatry Queen's Med. Center, Honolulu, 1978-79, Castle Hosp., Kailua, Hawaii, 1980-81; instr. nursing Kapiolani Community Coll., Honolulu, 1981-82, Arapahoe Community Coll., Littleton, Colo., 1982—; faculty Ednl. Resources, Inc., 1986—; pvt. practice psychotherapy; now clin. specialist in adult psychiat. and mental health nursing. Mem. Hawaii Nurses Assn., Nat. League Nursing, Am. Nurses Assn., Colo. Soc. Clin. Specialists in Psychiat. Nursing, Colo. Nurses Assn., Sigma Theta Tau. Home: 6905 S Garfield Way Littleton CO 80122 Office: Arapahoe Community Coll 5900 Santa Fe Dr Littleton CO 80120

MURRAY, META RUTH, lawyer; b. Glens Falls, N.Y., Apr. 12, 1951; d. Russell Bernard and Marguerite Ruth (Merkel) M.; m. George B. Pfeiffer, Oct. 12, 1980; 1 dau., Meghan Ruth. B.A., St. Lawrence U., 1973; J.D., Albany Law Sch., 1977. Bar: N.Y., U.S. Dist. Ct. (no. dist.) N.Y. Adminstrv. asst. Ways and Means Com. N.Y. State Senate Assembly, Albany, 1973-75; legal intern N.Y. State Senate, Albany, 1976, N.Y. State Office of Ct. Adminstrn., Albany, 1977; sr. atty. N.Y. State Dept. Law, Albany, 1977-85, N.Y. State Dept. Environ. Conservation, Albany, 1986—. Mem. ABA, N.Y. State Bar Assn., Phi Alpha Theta. Republican. Jewish. Home: 25 Owen Ave Glens Falls NY 12801 Office: Environ Conservation 50 Wolf Rd Albany NY 12233-0001

MURRAY, NANCY SIEGEL, marketing executive; b. Chelsea, Mass., Nov. 20, 1947; d. Edward Isaac and Bertha (Greenberg) Siegel; m. Ronald Francis Murray, Aug. 8, 1976. B.A., Vassar Coll., 1970; M.Ed., Columbia U., 1975; M.B.A., So. Meth. U., 1980; cert. in Cobol programming, Columbia U., 1983. Cert. rehab. counselor, N.Y. Counseling intern Neurol. Inst., N.Y.C., 1974; supr. counseling Hosp. for Joint Diseases, N.Y.C., 1975-78; market research analyst Acclivus Corp., Dallas, 1980; market research analyst Suburban Assocs., Ridgewood, N.J., 1981; sr. market research analyst/internat. mktg. Mfrs. Hanover Trust Co., N.Y.C., 1982-84; mktg. officer Marine Midland Bank, N.Y.C., 1984—. Mem. Am. Mktg. Assn., Bank Mktg. Assn., Am. Soc. Tng. and Devel., Nat. Rehab. Assn. Democrat. Club: Vassar. Home: 289 Midvale St Ridgewood NJ 07450

MURRAY, PAULETTE JEAN, mortgage company underwriter; b. Chgo., Mar. 10, 1944; d. Paul John and Bonniejean (Foster) Schmiedl; m. Stanley R. Klepac, May 27, 1965 (div. May 1975); children—Steven R., Scott Paul; m. Brent John Murray, Aug. 19, 1979. Student Morraine Valley Community Coll., Palos Park, Ill., 1979; A. in Fin., Fin. Inst., Chgo., 1980; lic. in real estate St. Xavier Coll., Chgo., 1985. Adminstrv. asst. Goodwill Industries, Chgo., 1962-67, also tchr. sign lang.; owner Stan's Auto Rebuilders, Oak Lawn, Ill., 1967-73; asst. v.p. Great Am. Fed., Oak Park, Ill., 1975-85; sr. underwriter Draper & Kramer, Chgo., 1985; sr. underwriter Lyons Mortgage Corp., Rolling Meadows, Ill., 1985—. Mem. Soc. Loan Underwriters, Oak Lawn Bus. and Profl. Womens Club (pres. 1986—), Ill. Fedn. Bus. and Profl. Womens Club (state bd.). Club: Leo Parents (bd. dirs. 1982—) (Chgo.). Lodges: Odd Fellows, Rebekahs of Ill. Avocations: scuba diving; crocheting; needlepoint; reading. Home: 2735 W Seipp St Chicago IL 60652 Office: Lyons Mortgage 2 Crossroads of Commerce Rolling Meadows IL 60008

MURRAY, RUTH CLARICE BACCUS, educational administrator; b. Dallas, Mar. 13, 1931; d. Jasper and Edna (Nixon) Baccus; m. Alton Murray, Sept. 4, 1953; 1 dau., Gail Anne. B.A., Dillard U., 1951; M.Ed., Tuskegee Inst., 1962; Doctorate Edn., Nova U., 1982. With Dallas Ind. Sch. Dist., 1951—, tchr. elem. schs., 1951-71, instructional cons., 1971-75, asst. to dep. asst. supt. elem. ops., 1976-78, asst. prin. R.C. Buckner Learning Ctr., 1979—; condr. workshop Assn. Childhood Edn., Dallas, 1983—. Recipient Outstanding Service award for acad. achievement, Classroom Tchrs. Dallas. Mem. Assn. Childhood Edn., NEA, Dallas Sch. Adminstrs. Assn., Dallas Bilingual Assn., Internat. Reading Assn., Nova U. Alumni Assn., Dillard U. Alumni Assn., Phi Delta Kappa. Democrat. Mem. Ch. of Christ. Club: L'Entre Nous Bridge (v.p.) (Dallas). Home: 5816 Shady Crest Trail Dallas TX 75241 Office: R C Buckner Sch Dallas Ind Sch Dist 400 Ella Ave Dallas TX 75217

MURRAY, SHIREY PHILLIPS, personnel consultant; b. Poteet, Tex., Nov. 10, 1943; d. Clyde Hawood and Clara Lee (Wilson) Phillips; m. David A. Murray, Dec. 21, 1962 (div. 1980); children—David II, Toby. B.S. magna cum laude, Tex. A & I U., 1968. Cert. tchr., Tex. Tchr. English lang. Woodsboro Ind. Sch. Dist., Tex., 1969-71; owner, mgr. Murray's Fine Furnishings, Woodsboro and Refugio, Tex., 1971-78; personnel cons. Snelling and Snelling Personnel Cons., Corpus Christi, Tex., 1978-81; founder, owner Anne Wilson Personnel Cons., Corpus Christi, 1981—, Austin, Tex., 1984—; founder, owner, Anne Wilson Temporary Personnel, Corpus Christi, 1982—; expert witness on employment related subjects. Mem. South Tex. Women's Forum, 1980—; com. mem. Employment Devel. Program of Corpus Christi, 1984. Admitted to Golden Honor Circle, Snelling & Snelling, 1979, 80, 81. Mem. Tex. Assn. Personnel Cons., Corpus Christi C. of C., Austin C. of C., Alpha Chi Honor Soc. Republican. Methodist. Home: 309 Southern St Corpus Christi TX 78404 Office: Anne Wilson Personnel Cons PO Box 346 Corpus Christi TX 78403

MURRAY, SHIRLEY MAE, sales consultant; b. Detroit, July 31, 1933; d. Edward Raymond and Loris Corine (Beckemeyer) Hatmaker; m. Thomas Arthur Murray, Feb. 5, 1955; children—Michele Lynn, Victoria Louise, Jacqueline Kay. Student Wayne State U., 1954, U. Minn., 1972. Co-owner Murray and Assocs., Scottsdale, Ariz., 1975-77; mktg. mgr. World of Palm Aire, Inc., Pompano Beach, Fla., 1977-79; sales cons. DVR & W, Inc., Mpls., 1979-82, Facility Systems, Inc., Edina, Minn., 1982—; cons. Women Reentering Bus., Mpls. Recipient Million Dollar award, Facility Systems Inc., 1984, 85; judge Distbv. Ednl. Clubs Am., St. Paul, 1986. Mem. Profl. Sales Assn. (pres. 1985-86, Presdl. award 1986), Nat. Assn. Female Execs. Avocations: symphony chorus; piano; Alpine and cross country skiing; tennis; golf; reading. Home: 5333 Highpointe Dr Bloomington MN 55437 Office: Facility Systems Inc 4100 W 76th St Edina MN 55435

MURRAY, SONIA BENNETT, former real estate executive; b. Norfolk, Eng., May 15, 1936; came to U.S., 1956, naturalized, 1961; d. Marcus Warburton and Ruth Lillian (Clarke) B.; m. Gilbert Lafayette Murray, Jr., June 25, 1955; children—Gilbert L. III, Keith David, Kathryn Sonia. Student U. Miss., 1958-61, Miss. Gulf Coast Jr. Coll., 1982—, U. Ala., 1983—. Mgr. Airway Apts., Biloxi, Miss., 1958-65; owner Airway Apts. and other properties, 1965—. Pres. Friends of Biloxi Libraries, 1979-81. Republican. Humanist. Author: Shell Life and Shell Collecting, 1969; Shell Collectors' Handbook and Identifier, 1974. Address: 1609 Oaklawn Pl Biloxi MS 39530

MURREL, KATHLEEN RICE, computer services company executive; b. Ann Arbor, Mich., Mar. 4, 1953; d. Thomas Russell and Thelma Joyce (Mullreed) Rice; m. Richard Lee Murrel, Sept. 18, 1982. A.B.A., Cleary Coll., Ypsilanti, Mich., 1973, A.B.A. in Data Processing, 1983; B.B.A. in Data Processing, 1986. Sec., Midwest Microwave, Ann Arbor, 1973-75; office asst. Kurkjian-Samborn, Ann Arbor, 1975-76; legal asst. Dever Profl., Ann Arbor, 1977-78; computer installation expeditor Mfg. Data Systems, Ann Arbor, 1979-83; mgr. office automation Anvil Corp., Ann Arbor, 1984—; owner, pres. Kathy's Typing Service, Ann Arbor, 1976—. Mem. Nat. Assn. Female Execs. Avocations: reading; sports. Home: 1517 Jackson Ave Ann Arbor MI 48103 Office: Anvil Corp PO Box 1088 Ann Arbor MI 48106

MURRELL, CASTELLA BURNLEY, educator, biology consultant; b. Nashville, Jan. 26, 1926; d. Stephen Alexander and Maynie (Young) Burnley; m. Irvin Maurice Murrell (dec. 1975); children—Janis, Irvin, Bertrand, Audrey. B.S., U. Louisville, 1948; M.S., U. Ill., Urbana, 1950; postgrad. U. Chgo., summers 1960-65. Microbiologist Provident Hosp., Chgo., 1950-52; research asst. U. Ill.-Chgo., 1952-54; microbiologist U. Chgo., 1954-58; research asst. Armour Research, Chgo., 1959-60; tchr. biology Chgo. Bd. Edn., 1960—, biology cons., 1969-72. Contbr. articles to profl. jours. Recipient Sci. Fair awards Chgo. Area Sci. Tchrs. Assn., 1964, 65, 67, Ill. Outstanding Tchr. award Chgo. Bd. Edn., 1966, Fellowship Honor award, 1967, citation Chgo. Heart Assn., 1967, 68. Mem. Nat. Sci. Tchrs. Assn., Nat. Assn. Female Execs., Ill. Soc. Microbiologists, Ill. Sci. Tchrs. Assn., Chgo. Biology Roundtable, Christian Educators Assn., Alpha Kappa Alpha. Methodist. Avocations: photography; tennis. Home: 9730 S Green St Chicago IL 60643

MURTHY, SUMATHI, physician; b. Bangalore, India, Feb. 13, 1954; d. M.V. and Malathi L. Nagarat; m. C.N. Murthy, Dec. 29, 1977 (dec. 1982); 1 son, Kesav. S.S.L.C., Bharatiya Vidyapeetha, Bangalore, 1970; P.U.C., Nat. Coll., Bangalore, 1971; M.B.B.S., Bangalore Med. Coll., 1977. Intern Victoria Combined Hosps., Bangalore, 1977-78; resident Monmouth Med. Ctr., Long Branch, N.J., 1981-83, St. Luke's-Roosevelt Hosp. Ctr., N.Y.C., 1983—. Mem. Soc. Nuclear Medicine.

MURYS, PATTI DARLENE, nurse; b. Connersville, Ind., Dec. 6, 1934; d. Frederick Jacob and Pattie Bernece (Perry) Quenzer; R.N. (scholar), St. Vincent's Hosp. Sch. Nursing, 1956; R.T., St. John's Hosp. Sch. Radiol. Tech., 1963; B.S.N., Purdue U., 1972; M.A. (grantee), U. Iowa, 1973; m. Donald Frank Murys, Aug. 19, 1973. Staff nurse St. Vincent's Hosp., Indpls., 1956-58; radiol. technologist, head nurse St. John's Hosp., Springfield, Ill., 1963-64; instr. St. Margaret's Hosp. Sch. Nursing, Hammond, Ind., 1965, St. Catherine's Hosp. Sch. Radiol. Tech., 1965; nurse ICU, St. Margaret's Hosp., Hammond, 1965-69; inservice instr. St. Catherines Hosp., East Chicago, Ind., 1969-71, supr., 1971-72; instr. Jackson Meml. Hosp., Miami, Fla., 1973; nurse clinician Parkway Gen. Hosp., Miami, 1974-79; relief supr. acting dir. ednl. services Southeastern Med. Center, Miami, 1979—. Instr., CPR Am. Heart Assn., East Chicago, Ind., Miami; active Girl Scouts U.S.A. Mem. Am. Bus. Woman's Assn., Nat. League Nurses, Nat. Wildlife Fedn., Am. Soc. for Health Care Edn. and Tng., South Fla. Emergency Med. Assn. Office: Southeastern Med Center 1750 NE 167th St Miami FL 33162

MUSE, MARGARET BRADLEY, city official; b. LaGrange, Ga., June 15, 1942; d. Paul Phillip and Myrtle Muriel (Tomlin) James; m. Paul W. Grosch, Apr. 5, 1960 (div. 1966); children—Paul M., Mark W.; m. 2d, Frank Rogers Muse, Apr. 29, 1983. Student El Centro Coll., 1978, Eastfield Coll., 1979, So. Meth. U., 1980-81. Owner dance sch. and real estate agy., Plano, Tex., 1965-69; customer service mgr. Blue Cross-Blue Shield, Dallas, 1969-79; employee benefits adminstr. City of Dallas, 1979—; dir. Sanus Health Plan Tex., 1983—; lectr. Dallas Pub. Library, 1975-79, also profl. groups. Named Employee of Yr., Personnel dept. City of Dallas, 1982; recipient Outstanding Achievement award City of Dallas, 1983. Mem. Internat. Found. Employee Benefits, Pub. Employee Benefit Adminstrs., Am. Mgmt. Assn., Risk Ins. Mgrs. Soc. Office: City of Dallas Employee Benefits 1500 Marilla St 7FS Dallas TX 75201

MUSE, PATRICIA ALICE, writer, educator; b. South Bend, Ind., Nov. 27, 1923; d. Walter L. and Enid (Cockerham) Ashdown; student Columbia U., 1946; B.A., Principia Coll., 1947; postgrad. Seminole Community Coll., 1977, U. Central Fla., 1978, 79, 80, 81, 82; m. Kenneth F. Muse, Dec. 2, 1950; children—Patience Eleanor, Walter Scott. Substitute tchr. public schs., Key West, Fla., also Brunswick, Ga., 1962-68; free lance writer, Casselberry, Fla., 1968—; novels: Sound of Rain, 1971, The Belle Claudine, 1971, paperback, 1973, Eight Candles Glowing, 1976; creative writing instr., Valencia Community Coll., 1974-75; instr. various writers confs. Community resource vol. Orange County (Fla.) Sch. Bd. (cert. of appreciation 1975, 76, 77); tutor Adult Literacy League, 1983—.

MUSE, VONCEIL FOWLER(MRS. BERT C. MUSE), school librarian, educator; b. Tyler, Tex., July 12, 1915; d. Dennis Cleveland and Elva Mary (Wallace) Fowler; m. Bert Cromwell Muse, Dec. 28, 1938 (dec. Jan. 1983). B.A., Tex. Coll., 1936; M.S.L.S., U. So. Calif., 1953; postgrad. NDEA seminars (grantee) Tex. Women's U., 1965. Cert. profl. all levels, Tex. Elem. tchr. Jasper (Tex.) Schs., 1936-37, Trinidad (Tex.) Schs., 1937-39; tchr.-librarian Stanton Rural High Sch., Whitehouse, Tex., 1940-46; co-owner, Tyler (Tex.) Tribune, 1946-49; tchr.-librarian Tyler Schs., 1949-52; sch. librarian Dallas Pub. Schs., 1952-78; past dir. Women's Southwest Fed. Credit Union, Dallas, 1975-80; yearbook chmn. Dallas Sch. Librarians, 1976; mem. social com. Dallas Ret. Tchrs., 1979. Founder, Glenview Neighbors Assn., Dallas, 1980; mem. Mental Health Assn. Dallas County, 1978, Community Connection, Dallas, 1983, South Central Dallas Civic Group, 1984; mem. Maria Morgan br. YWCA, Vis. Nurses Assn. (charter Dallas chpt.), (life), Mus. African Am. Life and Culture, Women's Ctr. of Dallas, Dallas Classroom Tchrs. (bldg. rep. 1969-78), Dallas Ret. Tchrs. Assn., Am. Assn. Ret. Persons (Red Bird chpt. bd. dirs. 1984-85), United Tchrs. Tex. State Tchrs. Assn. (life), NEA (life), Tex. Ret. Tchrs. Assn. (life), Tex. Library Assn., ALA, Tex. and Southwestern Cattle Raisers Assn. (assoc.), Mitchell County Hist. Commn., Tex. Coll. Nat. Alumni, (life), Tex. Coll. Alumni Assn. of Dallas, Alpha Kappa Alpha life). Democrat. Mem. Christian Methodist Episcopal Ch. Lodge: Court of Calanthe.

MUSGRAVE, ANN ROBINSON, interior designer; b. Houston, Apr. 20, 1938; d. Carr and Annie Beth (Towles) Robinson; children—R. Darrell Ford, Charlotte Lee Hayman. Student Rollins Coll., 1956-59, So. Meth. U., 1959-60. Pres., Ann R. Musgrave Interiors Inc., Dallas, 1966—. Bd. dirs., mem. nominating com. Cystic Fibrosis, Dallas, 1981—; bd. dirs., sec., mem. exec. com. Prevent Blindness, Dallas, 1983—. Mem. Interior Bus. Design, Am. Soc. Interior Designers (assoc.). Republican. Episcopalian. Club: University (Dallas). Office: Ann R Musgrave Interiors Inc 2404 Cedar Springs Dallas TX 75201

MUSGRAVE, BELINDA LOUISE, accountant; b. Memphis, Nov. 9, 1955; d. John Davie and Chaney Lee (Chandress) Holland; m. Cleetus Orahl Musgrave, Jan. 25, 1974 (div. Aug. 1982); 1 dau., Natasha Leah. B.B.A., Lamar U., 1976. C.P.A., Tex. Staff acct. Douglas B. Thomson & Assocs., Houston, 1976-77, sr. acct., 1979-80, ptnr. Thomson, Musgrave & Smith, Houston, 1981-83, owner, mgr., 1983—; v.p. Northpoint Computer Services, Inc., 1984—. Mem. N.W. Houston C. of C., Am. Inst. C.P.A.s, Tex. Soc. C.P.A.s, Am. Womens Soc. C.P.A.s, Nat. Assn. Female Execs. Republican.

MUSGRAVE, THEA, composer, conductor; b. Edinburgh, Scotland; ed. Edinburgh U., Paris Conservatory; Mus.B.; hon. doctorate Smith Coll., Old Dominion U.; m. Peter Mark, 1971. Composer: (opera) The Decision (first performed by New Opera Co. at Sadler's Wells, 1967), The Voice of Ariadne (first performed at Aldeburgh Festival 1973; U.S. premiere N.Y.C. Opera 1977), Mary Queen of Scots (first performed by Scottish Opera 1977), A Christmas Carol (first performed by Va. Opera Assn. 1979); Harriet, The Woman Called Moses (first performed by Va. Opera 1985); (ballet) Beauty and the Beast, 1969; The Phoenix and the Turtle and The Five Ages of Man for choir and orch.; Triptych for tenor and orch.; clarinet, horn and viola concertos; Night Music for chamber orch.; chamber concertos 1, 2 and 3; other vocal, chamber and orchestral works. Recipient Koussevitzky award; Guggenheim fellow. Address: care Novello & Co Ltd 8 Lower James St London W1 England

MUSGROVE, JUDY AUTRY, advertising agency executive; b. San Antonio, Tex., Aug. 5, 1946; d. Monte L. and Mary E. (Hohner) Autry; m. 1969 (div. 1974). Student U. Tex., 1964-68. Bus. mgr. Emergency Med. Services, Inc., Houston, 1974-80; mgr. bus. affairs Eisaman, Johns & Laws Advt., Inc., Houston, 1981-83, v.p. bus. affairs, 1984—; guest lectr. Vol., cardiac care program Bellaire Hosp., Houston, 1979-80; com. chmn. Greater Hartford Open Golf Tournament (Conn.), 1970-71. Mem. Nat. Assn. Female Execs., Am. Bus. Women's Assn. (dir. Houston 1980-87, Woman of Yr. award 1984), Fedn. Houston Profl. Women (organizing chmn. 1981, exec. bd. 1982, 83, charter pres. 1982, com. chmn. 1985, 86). Office: Eisaman Johns & Laws Advertising Inc 2121 Sage Rd Suite 145 Houston TX 77056

MUSHEL, MARY FELIX, health care executive, medical technologist; b. Little Falls, Minn., Feb. 11, 1932; d. Felix Thomas and Helen Augustine (Parent) M.; B.A., Coll. St. Catherine, St. Paul, 1956; M.T., St. Mary's Hosp. Madison, Wis., 1957; M.A., U. Iowa, 1972. Joined Franciscan Sisters of Little Falls, 1952. Lab. supr. Our Lady of Mercy Hosp., Alexandria, Minn., 1957-70, asst. adminstr., 1960-69; communications and recruitment St. Francis High Sch., Little Falls, 1972-74; co-adminstr. Our Lady of the Way Hosp., Martin, Ky., 1974-79; chemistry supr. U. Ky. Hosp., Lexington, 1979-80; pres., exec. dir. Franciscan Sisters Health Care, Little Falls, 1980—; cons. med. technologist. St. Michael's Hosp., Sauk Centre, Minn., 1966-69. Com. chmn. League Women Voters, Alexandria, Minn., 1967. Operating grantee Clinic Family Health Ctr., Martin, 1978. Mem. Am. Soc. Med. Technologists (Minn. Med. Technologist of Yr. 1964), Am. Soc. Pub. Health, Nat. Assn. Female Execs., Am. Coll. Hosp. Adminstrs. Roman Catholic. Home: 116 8th Ave SE Little Falls MN 56345 Office: Franciscan Sisters Health Care 116 8th Ave SE Little Falls MN 56345

MUSOLINO, ELLA MARIE, professional tennis executive; b. N.Y.C., Apr. 22, 1942; d. Frank and Eva Patricia (Yarusevich) Grassi; m. Ronald J. Musolino, Oct. 14, 1962 (div. 1978); 1 child, Dennis Alexander. Sec. U.S. AEC, N.Y.C., 1959-61; sales asst. De La Rue Banknote Co., N.Y.C., 1961-66; sales and service rep. U.S. Banknote Corp., N.Y.C., 1966-67; gen. mgr. N.Y. Apples Team Tennis, N.Y.C., 1976-78; pres., founder Sports Etcetera, Inc., N.Y.C., 1978—; tournament mgr. U.S. Open Tennis Championships, 1969-75; tournament dir. Avon Championships, Madison Sq. Garden, 1979-82, Va. Slims Championships, 1983—. Mem. Assn. Tournament Dirs., others. Republican. Roman Catholic. Avocations: tennis; reading. Office: Sports Etcetera Inc 4 Penn Plaza New York NY 10001

MUSSO, JUDY GAIL, word processing service specialist; b. San Diego, Aug. 20, 1938; d. Raymond S. and Ruth M. (Geaslin) Hotchkiss. Student San Diego State U., 1957-59. Sales mgr. Sheraton Inn, Tulsa, 1969-71; owner, real estate agt. Stanley Investments, Tulsa, 1971-72; mktg. cons. Standard & Poors, N.Y.C., 1972-73; word processing service specialist Norrell Services, Dallas, 1982—. Sec.-treas. Apollo Investment Club, San Diego, 1966-68. Mem. Hon. Order Ky. Cols. Republican. Presbyterian. Avocations: oil painting; reading; computers. Home: 2206 Walraven Ln Dallas TX 75235

MUSTONE, AMELIA P., state legislator; b. Salem, Mass., July 16, 1928; d. Udo A. and Alberta (Durand) Poppey; m. John J. Mustone, 1950; children—John, Lisa, Mary Ellen, Anastasia, Jessica. B.A., Goddard Coll., Vt. Pres., Meriden Bd. Edn., Conn., 1974-78; mem. Conn. State Senate from 13th Dist., 1979—, dep. minority leader, 1985. Mem. Nat. Conf. State Legislators, Council on State Govts., Caucus New Eng. State Legislators, Conn. Women's Polit. Caucus, Conn. Student Loan Found.; vice chmn. New Eng. Bd. Higher Edn. Recipient Citizen of Yr. award Civitan Club, 1978. Mem. Meridan LWV, Latin Am. Soc. (hon.), NAACP. Roman Catholic.

MUSUMECI, IRENE CORVA, publishing company executive; b. Bklyn., Feb. 27, 1955; d. Vito Charles and Bessie (Martino) Corva; m. Matthew R. Musumeci, Nov. 24, 1979. Student pub. schs., Bay Shore, N.Y. Personnel asst. Bowe Walsh & Assocs., Melville, N.Y., 1975-80; personnel mgr. CMP Publs., Manhasset, N.Y., 1980—; personnel cons. Robert Wilson, Acct., West Hempstead, N.Y., 1984—; v.p., co-owner Matty's Elec. Contracting Co., Carle Place, N.Y., 1985—. Mem. Nat. Assn. Female Execs., Am. Soc. Personnel Adminstrn. Republican. Lutheran. Avocations: reading; sports activities; interior decorating. Office: CMP Publs Inc 600 Community Dr Manhasset NY 11514

MUTCHLER, JANE FRANCES, acct.; b. Janesville, Wis., Feb. 26, 1941; d. Frederick Gerald and Anne Marie (Healy) M.; B.A. in Edn., U. S. Fla., 1973, B.A. in Acctg., 1976, M.Acctg., 1977; Ph.D., U. Ill., 1983; children—Tami Jeanne, Susan Marie (Parr). Tchr., United Day Care Center, Tampa, Fla., 1971-73; instr. U. South Fla., Tampa, 1976-78; adminstrv. asst. intermediate acctg. program Arthur Andersen & Co., Champaign, Ill., summers 1979-81; grad. research asst., grad. teaching asst. U. Ill., Champaign, 1978-82; asst. prof. acctg. Ohio State U., fall 1983; mgmt. cons., 1977-82. Contbr. articles to Jour. Acctg. Research and Auditing, Jour. Practice and Theory; mem. editorial bd. Auditing: a Jour. Practice and Theory. Am. Soc. Women Accts. Margaret Keldie scholar, 1979-80; Am. Inst. C.P.A.s fellow, 1982; recipient Research Opportunities in Auditing award Peat Marwick, 1983. C.P.A., Fla. Mem. Am. Acctg. Assn., Am. Inst. C.P.A.s, Fla. Inst. C.P.A.s. Office: Faculty of Acctg Ohio State Univ 408 Hagerty Hall 1775 College Rd Columbus OH 43210

MUTO, SUSAN ANNETTE, educator; b. Pitts., Dec. 11, 1942; d. Frank and Helen (Scardamalia) M.; B.A. in Journalism and English, Duquesne U., 1964; M.A., U. Pitts., 1967, Ph.D. in English Lit., 1970. Asst. dir. Inst. of Formative Spirituality, Duquesne U., Pitts., 1965-80, dir., 1980—, faculty coordinator grad. programs in foundational formation, 1979—, prof., 1981—; guest lectr. formative reading various colls. and community orgns., 1970—. Mem. Edith Stein Guild, Epiphany Assn., Phi Kappa Phi. Author: Approaching the Sacred: An Introduction to Spiritual Reading, 1973; Steps Along the Way, 1975; A Practical Guide to Spiritual Reading, 1976; The Journey Homeward: On the Road of Spiritual Reading, 1977; (with Adrian van Kaam) The Emergent Self 1968, The Participant Self, 1969; Tell Me Who I Am, 1977; Celebrating the Single Life, 1982; Blessings That Make Us Be, 1982; Pathways of Spiritual Living, 1984; contbr. articles on spiritual reading to religious and secular publs. Home: 2223 Wenzell Ave Pittsburgh PA 15216 Office: Institute of Formative Spirituality Duquesne U Pittsburgh PA 15282

MUZZY, DIANA LEE, bicycle clothing manufacturing company executive; b. Hanover, Pa., Oct. 28, 1949; d. Leo Esiah and Alice Wilkinson (Rudolph) M. B.S., U. Calif.-Berkeley, 1972. Lic. animal health technician, Calif. Asst., Orinda Vet. Clinic, Calif., 1971-74; animal health technician Wilson Animal Hosp., Concord, Calif., 1974-78; owner, operator Vigorelli, Oakland, 1979—. Cons. Battered Women's Alternatives, Concord, Calif., 1981-84. Mem. Women's Sports Found. Democrat. Avocation: running. Office: Vigorelli 2200 Adeline St Suite 250 Oakland CA 94607

MYATT, SANDRA D., real estate broker; b. Fort Wayne, Ind., May 26, 1943; d. Gaylord Murrey and Marjorie Jean (Anderson) Van Der Veer; m. Jack Lytton Dillard, Feb. 22, 1961 (div. 1965); m. Benjamin F. Myatt, Jr., Jan. 1, 1981; 1 child, Randolph William Dillard. Grad., Fla. Atlantic U., 1974; grad. Realtors Inst. Tenn., 1984. Real estate broker Rose Martin Inc., Realtors, Dickson, Tenn., 1981—. Mem. Nat. Assn. Realtors, Tenn. Assn. Realtors, Dickson County Bd. Realtors (sec. 1984, chmn. grievance com. 1986, Million Dollar Sales Club 1982, 83, 84, 85), Nashville Bd. Realtors, Nat. Rifle Assn., Republican. Club: Ladies Aux. of V.F.W. Lodge: Women of the Moose. Avocation: sport fishing. Office: Rose Martin Inc Realtors 706 E College St PO Box 400 Dickson TN 37055

MYER, NANCI KELLNER, advertising sales representative; b. Phila., Feb. 15, 1944; d. Theodore Robert and Meredith Ruth (Runyan) Kellner; children—Linda, Laura, Brian. R.N., Lankenau Hosp. Sch. Nursing, Phila., 1965. Asst. mgr. Casual Corner, San Jose, Calif., 1978-80; zone mgr. Cole Nat. Co., Cleve., 1980-81; br. mgr. Adia Temporary Services, San Jose, 1981-83; project supr. DMP Publs., San Jose, 1983-85; sr. account exec. San Jose Bus. Jour., 1985—; Herbalife supr., Los Angeles, 1984-86; lectr. on nutrition, various civic and profl. orgns. Counselor Los Gatos Christian Ch., Calif., 1984-86. Mem. Nat. Assn. Female Execs. Republican. Christian. Avocations: tennis; racquetball; swimming; crafts; reading. Office: San Jose Bus Jour 80 S Market St San Jose CA 95113

MYERS, CONNIE LYCANS, laboratory administrator educator; b. Huntington, W.Va., May 18, 1950; d. Billy and Loretta Bea (Bentley) Lycans; B.S., Marshall U., 1972; cert. Cabell Huntington Hosp. Sch. Med. Tech., 1972; m. Terry Lee Myers, June 15, 1971; 1 dau., Leigh Lycans. Med. technologist St. Mary's Hosp., Huntington, 1972, supr. microbiology, 1974-79; dept. supr. Halifax Med. Center, Daytona Beach, Fla., 1973-74; clin. instr. Marshall U., Huntington, 1975-79; clin. lab. supr./edn. coordinator Sch. Med. Tech., Decatur (Ill.) Meml. Hosp., 1979-81, lab. mgr., program dir., 1981—; clin. instr. Western Ill. U., Macomb, 1980—, Eastern Ill. U., Charleston, 1980—, Millikin U., Decatur, 1980—, Ill. State U., Normal, 1980—. Chmn., Decatur Meml. Hosp. Red Cross Blood Drive, 1979-80; solicitor United Way, 1979-853, Am. Cancer Soc., 1982-83. Mem. Am. Soc. Clin. Pathologists, Accreditation and Inspection Team, Vol. Hosp. Am., Inc. (lab. com.), Midwest Assn. Edn. Resource Sharing in Clin. Med. Tech., Clin. Lab. Mgmt. Assn. Home: 1375 W Sunset St Decatur IL 62522 Office: 2300 N Edward St Decatur IL 62526

MYERS, ELLEN HOWELL, educator; b. Bryan, Tex., Feb. 16, 1941; d. Douglas Wister and Ann Olive (Emory) Howell; student Mt. Vernon Jr. Coll., 1959-61, U. Madrid, 1961-62; B.A., Sophie Newcomb Coll. of Tulane U., 1963; M.A., U. Va., 1965, Ph.D., 1970; m. William Allen Myers, Dec. 23, 1967; 1 son, William Webb. Lectr. U. Houston, 1966-67; instr. Okla. State U., Stillwater, 1967-70; asst. prof. San Antonio Coll., 1970-73, assoc. prof., 1973-77, prof. history, 1977—. S.W. Conf. Commn. on Higher Edn. and Campus Ministry Meth. Ch., 1978-81; bd. dirs. Family Service Assn., 1978-85, pres., 1983-84; bd. dirs. San Antonio Area Red Cross, 1979—; bd. dirs. Laurel Heights Weekday Sch., 1980-83, chmn., 1982-83. Mem. Tex. Jr. Coll. Tchrs. Assn., SW Conf. on Latin Am. Studies (exec. com., 1974-75), AAUP (exec. com. San Antonio Coll., 1973-74), Conf. on Latin Am. History, Phi Alpha Theta. Democrat. Methodist. Clubs: Jr. League of San Antonio (bd. dirs., 1977-79), Kappa Alpha Theta. Author student's rev. manuals for The American Nation (J. Garraty), 1975, 77, 79, 83, 87, instrs. manuals, 1977, 79, 81, 83, 85, 87; contbr. articles to publs. in field. Home: 307 Arcadia Pl San Antonio TX 78209 Office: 1300 San Pedro San Antonio TX 78284

MYERS, GWEN MCHANEY, nurse, political worker; b. Dierks, Ark., May 15, 1925; d. Murray and Hattie M. (Ganno) McHaney; B.S. in Psychology, U. Ark., 1945; postgrad. Tenn. Sch. Nursing, 1958; Nursing Home Adminstr., Vanderbilt U., 1971; m. Ralph M. Myers, Jan. 27, 1973 (dec.); children—Jimmy Webster, Patti Vance, Vicki Loree. Dir. of nursing Bristol (Tenn.) Nursing Home, 1960-69; adminstr. Smiths Nursing Home, Johnson City, Tenn., 1971-78; office mgr. Jim Cooper, Morristown, Tenn., 1982—. Cons. various polit. campaigns, 1979—; mem. Democratic State Resolution Com., Nashville, 1982—; del. Dem. Nat. Conv., 1980; chmn. Social Security Task Force. Recipient Nurse of Yr. award Tenn. Nurses Assn., 1962. Mem. Nursing Home Assn., Tenn. Nursing Assn. Baptist. Clubs: DAR (regent), Geneal. Soc., Garden. Columnist: Citizen-Tribune, Morristown; composer numerous songs, 1948—. Home: 4421 Ashford Dr Morristown TN 37814

MYERS, HELEN LORETTA, temporary services manager; b. Hammond, Ind., Sept. 22, 1934; d. Leslie Gilbert and Bessie Vickers (Pollard) Coapstick; m. Ivan Oteen Myers, Dec. 2, 1961 (dec. 1978). Student, St. Joseph's Coll., East Chicago, Ind., 1957-59. Sec., State Farm Ins., Griffith, Ind., 1969; owner, operator Myers' Restaurant, Hartford, Ky., 1969-77, Highland Body Shop, Ind., 1977-84; supr. Kelly Services, Merrillville, Ind., 1984-85, resident br. mgr., Chgo., 1985—; mem. adv. com. Daley Coll., Chgo.; mem. Hyde Park C. of C., Automotive Service Counsils (sec.-treas. 1977-86). Republican. Club: Scherwood Golf (Schererville, Ind.). Lodge: Eastern Star (matron 1967-68, state appts., Grand rep. to Ala. 1974-78). Avocations: golfing; reading; hand crafts. Office: Kelly Services 7601 S Kostner Chicago IL 60652

MYERS, HORTENSE, writer, journalist, educator; b. Indpls., July 15, 1913; d. Walter Joseph and Estella Edith (Smith) Powner; m. Stanley Marvin Myers, Apr. 30, 1947 (dec.); 1 son, Mark Powner Myers. B.S. in Journalism, Butler U., 1953. Reporter, asst. editor Old Trail News, Indpls., 1934-42; statehouse reporter Internat. News Service and merged UPI, Indpls., 1942-81, columnist UPI, 1981—; adj. prof. journalism Ind. U.-Purdue U.-Indpls. Co-author children's books Childhood of Famous Americans series: Carl Ben Eielson, Cecil DeMille, Vilhjalmur Stefansson, Edward R. Murrow, Vincent Lombardi, Joseph Pulitzer; co-author biography: Robert F. Kennedy, the Brother Within, 1962. Mem. Gov.'s Commn. on Individual Privacy, Ind., 1976-77; mem. Muscular Dystrophy Found. Ind., Marion County Council on Aging, Ind. Council Churches interpretation chmn., Ind. Interreligious Commn. on Human Equality, Indpls. Com. on Fgn. Relations. Named Sagamore of the Wabash, 1963, 72, 76, 81; hon. speaker Ind. Ho. of Reps., 1982; Recipient Ind. Journalism award Ball State U., 1982; Outstanding Alumus award in Journalism, Butler U., 1986; named to Ind. Hall of Fame for Journalism, 1977; named hon. sec. of State of Ind., 1986. Mem. Nat. Fedn. Press Women (pres. 1962-65, Woman of Yr 1966), Women in Communication (local pres. 1957-58, (Nat. Headliner 1967), Woman's Press Club Ind. (pres. 1954-55, Kate Milner Rabb award 1965), Indpls. Press Club (pres. 1976-77, Ind. Newsman of Yr. award 1972), Sigma Delta Chi (Ind. chpt. pres. 1973-74). Methodist. Club: Zonta (pres. 1982-83). Home: 7839 W 56th St Indianapolis IN 46254

MYERS, KATHLEEN ANN, financial executive; b. Braddock, Pa., Mar. 7, 1943; d. Charles John and Roseann (Leddon) Myers; m. Richard Ralph Mrazik, Jan. 20, 1962 (div. 1969); children—Karen Ann, Robert Bruce, Rosemary Margaret, Thomas John; m. 2d, Thomas Howard Cobb, Apr. 16, 1976 (dec. 1984). B.A. in Mgmt., Webster U., 1982. Exec. sec. Gen. Dynamics Corp., St. Louis, 1971-75; ins. agt. Bankers Life Nebr., St. Louis, 1975-76; asst. campaign mgr. U.S. Senate campaign, St. Louis, 1976; legal asst. Consol. Grain & Barge Co., St. Louis, 1977-82, officer mgr., 1982-83, dir. banking ops., 1983—; lectr. Webster U., St. Louis, 1981—, St. Louis Community Coll., 1978-81; lectr. St. Louis Assn. Legal Assts., 1978-81. Republican. Roman Catholic. Home: 12907 Nimes Dr Saint Louis MO 63141 Office: Consolidated Grain & Barge Co 5100 Oakland Ave Saint Louis MO 63110

MYERS, MARY ELIZABETH PETERMAN, engineer; b. Jefferson City, Mo., Nov. 12, 1940; d. Russell Sanford and Mildred Irene (Berry) Peterman; m. Lynn Dean Myers, Jan. 8, 1972; children—Andre-Sanford, Timothy Gerrard. B.A., U. Mo.-St. Louis, 1978; postgrad. in bus. adminstrn. Lindenwood Coll. Cert. quality engr., Mo. Quality engr. McDonnell Dow Electric, St. Charles, Mo., 1968-78; Vitek Systems, St. Louis, 1980—. Mem. Am. Soc. Quality Control (program chmn.), Bus. and Profl. Women. Office: Vitek Systems 595 Anglum Dr Hazelwood MO 63042

MYERS, PATRICIA ANN, printing company executive; b. Boston, Jan. 5, 1934; d. Ralph Harding and Lana Ardelle (Wheeler) Holt; m. Raymond E. Myers, Oct. 23, 1954 (dec. May 1977); children—Gary Dixon, Gregory John, Geoffrey Raymond. Grad. high sch., Hingham, Mass. Sec. U.S. Army, Boston, 1951-53; model, Boston, 1953-59; real estate broker Roscoe Real Estate, Huntington, Conn., 1972-74; sec. Remlitho, Inc., Norwalk, Conn., 1973-77, pres., Stratford, Conn., 1977—; dir. Lafayette Bank & Trust, Stratford; bd. dirs. Printing Industry of Conn., 1984—. Pres. Trumbull PTA and Trumbull PTA Council, Conn., 1962-70; den mother Cub Scouts Am., N.Y. State and Trumbull, 1963-73; mem., sec. Republican Town Com., Trumbull., 1975-77; mem. Bd. Edn., Trumbull, 1977-79; mem. Sacred Heart U. Library Bd. Recipient Community Service award Sacred Heart U., Fairfield, Conn., 1983. Mem. Master Printers of Am. (bd. dirs.), Women in Communications (sec. 1985-86), Concerned Women Colleagues (sec. 1983-84), Stratford C. of C., Bridgeport Bus. and Industry Council, Nat. Assn. Printers and Lithographers. Republican. Episcopalian. Avocations: reading; sewing; gardening. Office: Remlitho Inc 20 Hathaway Dr Stratford CT 06497

MYERS, PATRICIA ANN, nurse, educator; b. Houston, May 9, 1950; d. Aljerry and Ethel Lee (Jackson) M. B.S., Prairie View A&M Coll., 1977. R.N., Tex. Nurse, Jefferson Davis Hosp., Houston, 1974-77; asst. head nurse emergency rm. U. Tex. M.D. Anderson Med. Ctr., Houston, 1977—; instr. Houston Community Coll., 1982—; nurse Home Med. Services, Houston, 1983—. Sec., God in Christ Missionary Baptist Ch., Houston, 1978-83. Mem. Houston Oncology Nurse's Soc., Oncology Nurse's Soc., Chi Eta Phi. Democrat. Clubs: Black Tapestry Social Service, Brentwood Civic (Houston).

MYERS, RUTH ANN, immigration and naturalization service administrator; b. Louisville, June 10, 1939; d. David and Eva (Zimmerman) M. Student U. Louisville. Immigration examiner Immigration and Naturalization Service, Los Angeles, 1972-77, asst. dist. dir., Cleve., 1977-78, immigration insp., Washington, 1978-82, dep. dist. dir., Chgo., 1982-84, dist. dir., Phoenix, 1984—. Mem. Assn. Immigration and Naturalization Service Dist. Dirs. (bd. govs. 1982—), Nat. Council Jewish Women. Republican. Jewish. Lodges: Soroptomist (participant 1st women's town hall 1986), Phoenix Charter 100, B'nai Brith. Avocations: reading; jigsaw puzzles; games; walking. Home: 7910 Thomas Rd #109 Scottsdale AZ 85251 Office: Immigration and Naturalization Service 230 N 1st Ave Phoenix AZ 85025

MYERS, SONJA KAY "CASEY", manufacturer's sales agency executive, consultant; b. Quincy, Ill., Aug. 17, 1942; d. Earl Dan and Hazel Louise (Johnson) Reynolds; m. Donald Edward Myers, Feb. 14, 1983; children—Christopher and Carrie Taylor, Catherine Casida. Grad. Wichita Sch. Practical Nursing, 1974; student U. Houston, grad. Hotel Mgmt. Short Course, 1979; student Quincy Coll., Gem City Bus. Coll. With St. Joseph Hosp., 1974-75; acct. exec. KFH/KBRA radio, 1975; sales mgr. Ramada Hotel Corp., 1976; sales dir. Sunbelt Hotels Inc. (Ramada Inn West), Houston, 1979-82; mktg. dir. Nassau Bay Hilton, Houston, 1982-84; v.p. CDM Mfrs. Agts. Inc., Houston, 1984—. Author monthly column "Inside Business", 1984—. Charter mem. Tex. Exec. Women, Houston; producer "Signature Wichita", Kans., 1976; housing chmn. Mo. Jr. Miss Pageant, St. Louis, 1972. Named Disting. Vol. Nat. Found. March of Dimes, 1976. Mem. Nat. Water Well Assn. (chmn. mfrs. rep. com. 1985—), Tex. Water Well Assn. (bd. dirs. 1985—), La. Water Well Assn. (bd. dirs., sec.-treas. 1985—), Tex. Exec. Women (charter mem.), Hotel Sales Mktg. Assn. (sec. Tex. chpt. 1982; historian Houston 1982), Tex. Hotel Sales Mktg. Assn. (pres.-elect 1983), Clear Lake C. of C. Republican. Episcopalian. Avocations: obedience training and showing Dobermans; writing; walking; lifting weights. Office: CDM Mfrs Agts Inc 12430 Hwy 3 B-6 Houston TX 77598

MYERS, URSULA SENNEWALD, social services adminstr.; b. Rochester, N.Y., July 5, 1928; d. Arthur George and Luise (Moeller) Sennewald; student U. Rochester, 1946-48; B.S. in Indsl. and Labor Relations, Cornell U., 1950; M.S.W., U. Wis., Madison, 1970; m. Richard R. Myers, June 12, 1951; children—Lisa, Robin (dec.), Theodore, Bruce. Social worker Rock County Social Services, Janesville, Wis., 1965-70, supr. I, 1970-79, acting dir., 1979, dir., 1979—; chmn. 1984 Wis. Social Services Block Grant Planning Com.; instr. U. Wis., Whitewater, 1978-79. Named Woman of Yr. in Govt. YWCA, 1984. Mem. Acad. Cert. Social Workers, Nat. Assn. Social Workers. Unitarian. Contbg. author: Introduction to Social Welfare Institutions.

MYERSON, ELEANOR, state representative; b. Winthrop, Mass., May 9, 1922; d. Jacob B. and Rebecca Lillian (Cohen) Applebaum; m. Morton Myerson, Dec. 3, 1942; children—Joseph, Ann. B.A. magna cum laude, Smith Coll., 1943. Selectman Town of Brookline, Mass., 1970-82; mem. Mass. Ho. of Reps., 1983—. State sec. Americans for Democratic Action, Boston, 1969; bd. dirs. Mass. Assn. for Blind, Brookline, 1984—, Brookline Com. on the Arts, 1984—. Democrat. Office: State House Boston MA 02133

MYERSON, JEANNE ROBIN, real estate executive; b. Evanston, Ill., Apr. 9, 1953; d. Paul E. and Marilyn (Lapp) M.; B.A., Grinnell Coll., 1975; M.C.R.P., Harvard U., 1978. With employment project Iowa Commn. on Status of Women, Des Moines, 1975-76; with Westat, Inc., Rockville, Md., 1976; mktg. asst. community affairs and mktg. dept. Mass. Bay Transit Authority, Boston, 1977-78; asst. dir. resource devel. Office of Communities and Devel., Commonwealth of Mass., Boston, 1978-80; econ. devel. dir. Riverside-Cambridgeport Community Corp., Cambridge, Mass., 1980-82; sr. project mgr. real estate investments Met. Life Ins. Co., Boston, 1982—; dir. Cybermation, Inc. Bd. dirs. Boston Neighborhood Network, 1980-83, Pvt. Industry Council, Cambridge, 1981-83, Neighborhood Devel. Corp. of Jamaica Plain (Mass.), 1982—; mem. Democratic Ward Com., 1981-85. Mem. Phi Beta Kappa. Democrat. Author articles on community devel. policy.

MYERSON, MARSHA S., personnel representative; b. Chgo., Sept. 18, 1958; d. Bernard and Shirley Elaine (Hart) Myerson. B.S.W., U. Ill.-Urbana, 1980, M.A. in Labor Indsl. Relations, 1982. Exec. compensation intern Wyatt Co., Chgo., summer 1981, personnel rep. corp. staff Northwest Industries, Inc., Chgo., 1982—. Mem Am. Soc. Personnel Adminstrn., Human Resources Mgmt. Assn. (tng. and devel. com. 1984—), U. Ill. Alumni Assn. (fund-raiser alumni affairs, Chgo. rep. 1984—). Home: 2340 N Commonwealth Chicago IL 60614 Office: Northwest Industries Inc 6300 Sears Tower Chicago IL 60606

MYHILL, (LEONA) SUSIE, secretarial service company executive; b. Lynwood, Calif., Jan. 6, 1951; d. Jack Gilbert and (Ozella) Joy (Lucas) Smith;

B.A., So. Calif. Coll., 1972; postgrad. Calif. State U., Fullerton, 1975-76, Orange Coast Coll., 1973-75, Coastline Community Coll., 1980-82; m. Loren Lee Myhill, June 9, 1972; 1 son, Lucas. Office mgr., sec., bookkeeper Household Fin. Corp., Orange, Calif., 1969-72; legal sec. Heinly, Lindley & Thrasher, Santa Ana, Calif., 1972-77; owner, operator Myhill Profl. Services, Newport Beach, Calif., 1977—; wedding coordinator. Supt. Sunday sch., children's ch. leader, Bible study tchr. Mem. Nat. Assn. Female Execs., Christian Bus. and Profl. Women's Club. Republican. Club: After 5 (chmn. 1981-84). Home: 1059 Santa Cruz Circle Costa Mesa CA 92626

MYKYTA, MARY ANN, laboratory executive; b. Dover, Del., Aug. 5, 1937; d. Roland and Anna Elizabeth (King) Walls; R.N., Meml. Hosp., Wilmington, Del., 1958; m. Lubomyr Mykyta, June 20, 1959; children—Maria Lydia, Natalie Vera, John Lubomyr, Laryssa Ann. Med.-surg. charge nurse Meml. Hosp., Wilmington, 1958-60; partner, v.p., sales mgr. Delaware Valley Indsl. X-Ray Co., Springfield, Pa., 1960-65; realtor asso. Gordon A. Weinberg Real Estate, Harrisburg, Pa., 1968-72; partner, v.p., rental properties gen. mgr. Commonwealth Trading & Mortgage Corp., Harrisburg, 1970-72; sales rep. Astrotech, Inc., Harrisburg, 1972-74, sales dir., 1974-75, v.p., gen. mgr., 1975, v.p., dir. regional real estate ops. and investments, 1976—; pres. Allentown Testing Labs., Inc., 1983—; v.p. Cert. Testing Labs., Inc., 1983—. Registered nurse, Del., Pa.; notary public. Mem. Nat. Assn. Female Execs., Am. Mgmt. Assn., Harrisburg Builders Exchange, Am. Assn. Notaries, Pa. Assn. Notaries, Meml. Hosp. Alumni Assn., Sanford Alumni Assn. Republican. Byzantine Catholic. Club: Penn-Garden Civic. Home: 5912 Colwyn Dr Harrisburg PA 17109 Office: PO Box 6159 7801 Allentown Blvd Harrisburg PA 17112

MYLES, ANN ETHEL, financial executive; b. Pennsauken, N.J., July 30, 1927; d. William Joseph and Ethel (Schaffer) M.; student St. Elizabeth's Coll., Acad. Advanced Traffic, St. Joseph's Coll. Indsl. Relations. Asst. mgr., credit rep. Farm Credit Service, Moorestown, N.J., 1963-72, aquatic loan officer, asst. gen. mgr., 1963-76, gen. mgr., 1976-81; pres. Farmers Prodn. Credit Assn., Moorestown, also Fed. Land Bank Assn., Moorestown, 1981—; lectr., workshop coordinator agrl. fin. confs. Mem. N.J. Marine Fishery Council, 1980—. Mem. N.J. Agrl. Soc., N.J. Farm Bur. Roman Catholic. Home: 15 Ambler Rd Cherry Hill NJ 08002 Office: Main St PO Box 226 Rancocas NJ 08073

MYRICK, DEBORAH DIANE, telecommunications systems engineer; b. Ogdensburg, N.Y., Jan. 4, 1951; d. Harold LeRoy Myrick and Alecia Ethel (Chase) Hartt. B.A., U. Conn., 1973; cert. Paralegal Inst., 1973; student Northeastern U. Communications rep. ITT Communications Systems, Boston, 1976-80; sales engr. GTE Bus. Communications Systems, Needham, Mass., 1980-81; product mgr. Wang Labs, Inc., Lowell, Mass., 1981-84; sr. sales engr. SONECOR Systems, Burlington, Mass., 1984—. Chmn. Dem. Election Primary Com., Pelham, N.H., 1984; mem. Town Cable Com., Pelham, 1983. Mem. Inst. Celtic Studies. Democrat. Roman Catholic. Club: Irish Unity Conf. (Boston). Avocations: reading, needlecrafts, gardening. Home: 4 Woodlawn Dr Pelham NH 03076 Office: SONECOR Systems 67 S Bedford St Burlington MA 01803

MYRICK, SUELLEN, advertising agency executive; b. Tiffin, Ohio, Aug. 1, 1941; d. William Henry and Margaret Ellen (Roby) Wilkins; student Heidelberg Coll., 1959-60; m. James E. Forest, May 5, 1962; children—Gregory Allyn, Daniel James; m. 2d, W. Edward Myrick, Jr., Sept. 11, 1977. Exec. sec. to mayor and city mgr. City of Alliance (Ohio), 1962-63; dir. br. office Stark County Ct. of Juvenile and Domestic Relations, Alliance, 1963-65; pres. Myrick Agy., Charlotte, N.C., 1971—; pres. To Market, Inc., Charlotte, 1981—. Mem. adv. bd. Children's Theatre, Charlotte, 1981-84; mem.-at-large Charlotte City Council, 1983-85; mem. adv. bd. Substance Abuse Council, Mental Health Authority, Charlotte; mem. adv. bd. U.s. Small Bus. Adminstrn.; communications chmn. Charlotte Clean City Com.; bd. dirs. Hezikiah Alexander House, Uptown Shelter, Share a Home; chmn. public relations Republican Party, Charlotte. Recipient Woman of Yr. award Harrisonburg, Va., 1968. Mem. LWV, Women's Polit. Caucus, Nat. Assn. Women Execs., C. of C. (vocat. edn. adv. commn. chair small bus. action council). Republican. Methodist. Club: Rep. Women's. Home: 310 W 8th St Charlotte NC 28202 Office: 505 N Poplar St Charlotte NC 28202

MYSLIBORSKI, JUDITH ANN, physician, educator; b. Greenport, N.Y., Apr. 3, 1947; d. Theodore David and Anna Jane (Bialecki) M. B.S., SUNY-Albany, 1969; M.D., Ind. U.-Indpls., 1973. Diplomate Am. Bd. Dermatology. Asst. prof. dept. medicine div. dermatology Albany Med. Coll. (N.Y.), 1977-80, clin. asst. prof., 1980—; asst. attending physician, dermatologist Albany Med. Ctr. Hosp., 1977—; clin. asst. prof. medicine St. Peter Hosp., Albany, 1980—; mem. cons. staff The Child's Hosp., Albany, 1982—. Bd. dirs. U. Albany Fund, 1982-85. Recipient Janet M. Glasgow award of achievement Ind. U., 1973. Fellow Am. Acad. Dermatology; mem. New England Dermatol. Soc., Central N.Y. Dermatol. Soc. (pres. 1983-85), Capital Dist. Dermatology Soc., N.Y. State Soc. Dermatology (dir. 1981-84). Home: 222 Heritage Rd Guilderland NY 12084 Office: Capital Dist Dermatology Assocs PC 22 New Scotland Ave Albany NY 12208

NACK, JULIA RILEY, advocacy and protective services executive; b. Clarksville, Tenn., July 11, 1946; d. Hugh Madison and Marjorie Ellen (Bash) Riley; m. Gary Taylor Nack, Sept. 22, 1979; 1 child, Tiffany Taylor; m. Samuel Lee Hensley, Jan. 1, 1969 (div. Nov. 1974). B.A., Minor State Coll., 1972; M.Ed., Ohio U., 1978. Planning mgr. Ky. Dept. Justice, Frankfort, 1974-76; adminstr. Ctr. for Human devel., Athens, Ohio, 1977-79; program dir. sentinel Services Inc., Columbus, Ohio, 1979-83; program dir. Advocacy and Protective Services, Inc., Columbus, 1983—. Mem. Guardian Law Reform task Force, 1985—; bd dirs. Pommed'Api Bilingual Pre Sch., Columbus, 1983-85. Mem. Nat. Assn. Female Execs., Assn. Retarded Citizens Ohio. Democrat. Mem. United Ch. Christ. Office: Advocacy Protective Services Inc 986 W Goodale Blvd Columbus OH 43212

NACOL, BARBARA LEIGH, health care exec.; b. Charleston, S.C., Feb. 2, 1948; d. Edheworth Blythe and Amelia (Neil) Hunt; B.A., U. Houston, 1973; M.A., Ph.D.; ed. Med. U. Houston, Tex. A&M U., Edison Coll. Mem. Tchr. Corps, Houston, 1973-75; tchr. Magnet program Houston Ind. Sch. Dist., 1975-77; adminstr. Law Office Mae Nacol and Assos., Houston, 1977-79, exec. dir. Hyperbaric Oxygen Med. Center, Houston, 1979—. Dep. constable precinct 1 Harris County, 1980. Mem. Undersea Med. Soc., Am. Judicature Soc., Environ. Edn. Assn. (charter). Presbyterian. Author papers in field. Office: 5220 Travis St Houston TX 77002

NACOL, MAE, lawyer; b. Beaumont, Tex., June 15, 1944; d. William Samuel and Ethel (Bowman) Nacol; B.A. in Behavioral Scis., Rice U., 1965; LL.B., South Tex. Coll. Law, 1969; children—Shawn Alexander, Catherine Regina. Admitted to Tex. Bar, 1969, since practiced in Houston. Diamond cons. for jewelry stores and ins. cos., 1961—. Pres. 240 basic police course Tex. A&M System; chmn. bd. HBO Med. Center Houston. Recipient Mayor's Recognition award Houston, 1972. Ford Found. fellow, 1965. Mem. Am., Tex., Internat., Fed., Houston (chmn. candidates com. 1970, chmn. membership com. 1971, chmn. lawyer's referral com. 1972), bar assns., Tex. Trial Lawyers Assn., Houston Trial Lawyers Assn., Nat. Assn. Women Lawyers, Am. Judicature Soc. Home: 6012 Memorial Dr Houston TX 77007 Office: 500 Jefferson Suite 1915 Houston TX 77002

NADEEM, MICHELE, broadcast journalist; b. Attleboro, Mass., Jan. 7, 1959; d. Anthony George and Jeanette (Glaiel) N. B.A., Boston Coll., 1980; M.S., Boston U., 1982. Prodn. asst. ABC Sports, N.Y.C., 1978; freelance comml. announcer, Boston, Providence, 1979—; prodn., desk asst. WBZ-TV News, Boston, 1980; assoc. producer WCVB-TV, Boston, 1981; news anchor, reporter WARA, Attleboro, 1982; reporter, producer, host United-Artists Columbia Cablevision, North Attleboro, 1983-85; news, feature, fashion reporter Evening Times, Pawtucket, R.I., 1983—; newswriter, assoc. producer WNEV-TV, Boston, 1984—. Pub. relations dir. Attleboro Area Assn. for Retarded Children, 1981-83; chairperson Town of North Attleboro Cable Adv. Commn., 1983—; press sec. com. to elect candidate for Mass. Senate, 1983; participant Chaminade Opera, 1974-76, 81, Boston Coll. Alumni Band, Chestnut Hill, Mass., 1980—. Recipient Merit cert. Town of Plainville, Mass., 1982, United-Artists Columbia Cablevision Producers award, 1983. Mem. Women in Communications, Nat. Acad. TV Arts and Scis., Omicron Delta Epsilon. Roman Catholic. Home: 225 Hoppin Hill Ave North Attleboro MA 02760

NADELMAN, LORRAINE, psychology educator, developmental psychologist; b. N.Y.C.; d. William Nadelman and Sally (Kozlin) Nadelman King; m. Sidney Warschausky; children—Seth, Judith, Carl. B.A., NYU, 1945, Ph.D., 1953. Teaching asst. NYU, N.Y.C., 1945-48, instr. psychology, 1948-51; asst. prof. Mt. Holyoke Coll., South Hadley, Mass., 1951-57; lectr. U. Mich., Ann Arbor, 1962-69, assoc. prof., 1969—, undergrad. chmn., 1985—. Author: Research Manual in Child Development, 1982. Contbr. articles to profl. jours. Trustee, program chmn. Ann Arbor Hands-On Mus., 1978-85. Traveling exhbn. award Internat. Yr. of Child, 1979; research grantee Rackham, 1979-82, Coll. Lit., Sci. and Arts, 1982-83, sci. faculty fellow NSF, Tavistock, London, 1965-66. Mem. Am. Psychol. Assn., Soc. Research in Child Devel., Internat. Soc. for Study of Behavioral Devel., Midwest Psychol. Assn., Phi Beta Kappa, others. Office: U Mich Dept Psychology Ann Arbor MI 48109

NADLER, HEDDA CAROL, public relations firm executive; b. N.Y.C., June 15, 1944; d. Julius Louis and Julia (Nemzer) Cohen; m. David G. Nadler, Oct. 3, 1965 (div. 1979); 1 child, Laura Lee; m. Burton Earl Hurvich, Dec. 8, 1984. B.B.A., CCNY, 1965. Officer, exec. Straus Assocs., N.Y.C., 1965-80; prin., exec. v.p. Mount & Nadler, Inc., N.Y.C., 1980—. Mem. No-Load Mut. Fund Assn. (co-chmn. 1985—). Avocations: antique collecting. Office: Mount and Nadler Inc 509 Madison Ave New York NY 10022

NADZICK, JUDITH ANN, accountant; b. Paterson, N.J., Mar. 6, 1948; d. John and Ethel (McDonald) N.; B.B.A. in Acctg., U. Miami (Fla.), 1971. C.P.A., N.J. Staff accountant, mgr. Ernst & Whinney, C.P.A.s, N.Y.C., 1971-78; asst. treas. Gulf & Western Industries, Inc., N.Y.C., 1979-82, asst. v.p., 1980-82, v.p., 1982-83; v.p., corp. controller United Mchts. and Mfrs. Inc., N.Y.C., 1983-85, sr. v.p., 1985-86, exec. v.p., chief fin. officer, 1986—. Mem. Am. Inst. C.P.A.s, Nat. Assn. Accts., N.Y. State Soc. C.P.A.s, U. Miami Alumni Assn., Delta Delta Delta. Roman Catholic. Home: 2 Lincoln Sq New York NY 10023 Office: 1407 Broadway New York NY 10018

NAGEL, EVELYN, symphony association executive; b. Portland, Oreg., Apr. 8, 1928; d. Aaron and Rose (Freedbaum) Davis; m. Stanley Blair Nagel, Aug. 21, 1949; children—Scott, Robert. Student U. Oreg., 1946-48. Comptroller Fountain Gallery of Art, Portland, 1966—; dir. devel. Oreg. Symphony Assn., Portland, 1973—; bd. dirs., v.p., sec. Oreg. Symphony Assn., 1970-74; mem. founding com. Oreg. Advocates for the Arts, Portland, 1980-81; mem. selection jury for architects Performing Arts Ctr., Portland, 1981-82; advisor to bd. dirs. Pacific Ballet Theatre, Portland, 1984—. Trustee, Congregation Beth Israel, Portland, 1972-84, sec. bd. trustees, 1978-80. Recipient 1st ann. spl. award Past Presidents of Women's Assn. of Oreg. Symphony, 1985. Mem. Am. Symphony Orch. League, Willamette Valley Devel. Officers (co-founder 1977-78). Republican. Jewish. Avocation: music. Office: Oreg Symphony Assn 813 SW Alder St Portland OR 97205

NAGEL, MARY JANE, home entertainment retail company executive; b. New Rochelle, N.Y., July 15, 1952; d. Lawrence William, Jr. and Frances Theresa (Meehan) N.; student public schs., New Rochelle. Mail order div. mgr. Citadel Record Club, Larchmont, N.Y., 1968-71; record store mgr. Longines Symphonette Stereo, Larchmont, 1971-74; divisional mgr. Sam Goody, Inc., Maspeth, N.Y., 1974-78, record/tape buyer, 1978-81, softgoods adminstrn. mgr., Edison, N.J., 1981-83, dir. field merchandising, 1984, field ops. mgr., 1985—. Mem. Nat. Assn. Female Execs. Roman Catholic. Office: Sam Goody Inc 96 Executive Ave Edison NJ 08817

NAGEL-SMITH,, TONI ALEKSANDRA SZAMSKI, clinical social worker; b. Balt., Oct. 9, 1946; d. Edward Joseph and Edith Helen (Yankoski) Szamski; B.A., Muhlenberg Coll., 1968; M.S.W., Adelphi U., 1972; m. Thomas J. Smith; children—Jeffrey Roger Nagel, Christopher Glynn Smith. Grad. teaching fellow Adelphi U., 1968-76; clin. social worker, supr. pediatric project Bellevue Hosp., N.Y.C., 1968-74; social worker Bedford (N.Y.) Central Sch. Dist., 1974—; pvt. practice clin. social worker, 1975—; former adj. prof. Westchester Community Coll.; field supr. Columbia U. Grad. Sch. Social Work. Past mem. adv. bd. Dept. Social Services, Mt. Kisco, Mem. Nat. Assn. Social Workers, Acad. Cert. Social Workers, N.Y. State Sch. Social Workers Assn. Home: West Road Box 101 Pound Ridge NY 10576 Office: Bedford Central School District PO Box 390 Bedford NY 10506

NAGLE, DIANE GULLIKSEN, advertising agency executive, public relations consultant; b. Chgo., Aug. 9, 1942; d. John Raymond and Willamene Veronica (Hegenberger) Gulliksen; m. John Joseph Nagle, June 12, 1965 (div.); children—Shannon Maura, Melinda Lee, John Joseph Jr. Student Barat Coll., 1960-62, Loyola U., Rome, 1962, Chgo., 1962. Dir. mktg. Another Prodn. Co., Denver, 1975-77; dir. spl. events U. Denver, 1977-79; dir. pub. relations Presbyn./St. Luke's Med. Ctr., Denver, 1979-81; mgr. advt. and sales promotion United Banks of Colo., Denver, 1981-83; pres. Nagle Croce Advt., Inc., Denver, 1983—; participant workshops in field. Bd. dirs. Denver YWCA, 1984—. Winner 1st place ann. report, Art Dir.'s Club Denver, 1980, Am. Inst. Graphic Arts, N.Y., 1979; winner 1st place Internat. Pub. Relations Campaign, McEachern Nat. Hosp., 1980; recipient Gold Quill award Internat. Assn. Bus. Communicators, 1983. Mem. Pub. Relations Soc. Am. (recipient Gold Pick award 1980), Denver Advt. Fedn. (recipient Alphie award 1983), Colo. Soc. Hosp. Pub. Relations (pres. 1980-81), Leadership Denver Assn., Denver Art Mus., Mile Hi Republican Women. Clubs: Internat. Athletic, Jr. League (project dir. 1972-80) (Denver). Home: 619 Cook St Denver CO 80206 Office: Nagle Croce Advertising 1620 Market St Suite 400 Denver CO 80202

NAGLE, JEAN SUE, sociologist, psychologist; b. Detroit; d. Peter and Hedy (Grusczynski) Karabacz; student U. Chgo., 1953-55; M.A., N.Mex. Highlands U., 1960, M.S., 1967; Ph.D., Union Grad. Sch., 1977; postgrad. Bryn Mawr Inst. Women in Higher Edn. Adminstrn., 1981, U. Chgo.; m. Robert D. Nagle, Nov. 20, 1956; children—Carl A., Sonya L., Paula E. Diagnostic technician Vocat. Counseling Inst., Detroit, 1952; research technician United Auto Workers-CIO, Detroit, 1958; clin. psychology intern N.Mex. State Hosp., Las Vegas, 1962-63; clin. psychology trainee VA Hosp., Omaha and Lincoln, Nebr., 1963-64; instr. sociology N.W. Mo. State U., Maryville, 1966-70, asst. prof. sociology and psychology, 1971—. Bd. dirs. Inst. Discourse. N.W. Mo. State U. grantee, 1981, 82. Mem. Am. Psychol. Assn., Am. Sociol. Assn., Midwest Sociol. Soc., Psychology/Sociology Club, Mo. Psychol. Assn., World Federalists, Psi Chi, Pi Gamma Mu. Home: 510 W 1st St Maryville MO 64468 Office: Dept Psychology/Sociology NW Mo State U Maryville MO 64468

NAGLE, NANCY ELIZABETH, automotive manufacturing executive; b. Houston, Mar. 27, 1951; d. John Ware and Elizabeth Geraldine (Dawkins) Nagle; m. William Edward Zinsmeister, Oct. 22, 1983. B.F.A., So. Meth. U., 1973; M.B.A., U. Tex., 1977. Creative asst. Clinton Frank Advt., Dallas, 1974-75; teaching asst. U. Tex., Austin, 1976-77; trainee Ford Motor Co., Houston, 1978, zone mgr., 1979-81, dealer leasing and rental mgr., 1982, bus. mgr., 1983-84, car merchandising mgr., 1984; sales devel. mgr., 1985, Ford div. light truck tng. coordinator, 1986—; adj. prof. Coll. of Mainland, 1985. Author: Role Models of Educated Women Regarding Marriage and Career, 1977. Mem. Houston Mus. Fine Arts, Daus. Am. Republic, Daus. Republic Tex., Magna Carta Dames, Tex. Ex-Students Assn., So. Meth. U. Alumni Assn. Episcopalian. Home: 1100 Augusta Dr #21 Houston TX 77057 Office: Ford Motor Co 2110 Governors Circle Houston TX 77092

NAGLEY GREVE, MADOLYN SUE, menswear company executive; b. Columbus, Ohio, July 24, 1952; d. Kenneth Frye and Virginia (McDowell) Nagley; m. Harald Gerhard Greve, Apr. 9, 1983. B.S., Adrian (Mich.) Coll., 1974; guest student Fashion Inst. Tech., N.Y.C., 1973. Asst. buyer Abraham Straus, Bklyn., 1974-75, Lord & Taylor, N.Y.C., 1975-80; mdse. analyst Assoc. Merchandising Corp., N.Y.C., 1980-82; v.p. sales Jonathan Bennett Neckwear, N.Y.C., 1982—. Co-chmn. publicity for fete Womans Aux. of Princeton Med. Ctrs., 1986. Mem. Woman's Network at Fifth Ave. (pres. 1982-83), Women's Assn. Fifth Ave Presbyn. Ch., Phi Gamma Nu, Chi Omega. Republican. Home: 9 Brook Dr W Kingston NJ 08528 Office: Jonathan Bennett Inc 50 W 34th St New York NY 10001

NAGY, RUTH THEODORA, accountant, tax consultant; b. Freeport, N.Y., Feb. 7, 1924; d. John Daniel and Isabel Anna (Kiss) Kormendy; student U. S.C., 1975; m. Gustave Joseph Nagy, May 6, 1945; children—Robert John, Patricia Jean, Gerald Joseph. With J.D. Kormendy, Acct., Freeport, N.Y., 1938-54; jr. acct. Am. Bus. Credit Corp., N.Y.C., 1941-50; payroll cost acct. C.E. Morris Co., Columbus, Ohio, 1964-65; tax cons., public acct., owner and mgr. Accu-Trol Tax Service, Cayce, S.C., 1967—; enrolled agt. IRS, 1979. Mem. Nat. Assn. Pub. Accts., S.C. Assn. Pub. Accts. (pres. Columbia chpt.), S.C. Tax Council (pres. 1985—). Republican. Baptist. Clubs: Columbia Camera, Columbia Gem-Mineral Soc. Home: 513 Shady Ln Cayce SC 29033 Office: 1102 12th St Cayce SC 29033

NAHEMOW, LUCILLE DAVIS, psychologist; b. N.Y.C., July 7, 1933; d. William and Flora (Fisher) Davis; B.S. in Psychology, Bklyn. Coll., 1955, M.A., 1957; Ph.D. in Social Psychology (Univ. fellow, NIMH fellow), Columbia U., 1963; m. Martin David Nahemow, 1952 (div. 1966); children—Katharine, Barbara; m. Stanley Fisher (div.); m. Paul J. Bekowies, Dec. 21, 1985. Teaching fellow, then grad. instr. Bklyn. Coll., 1955-64; research assoc. Ednl. Clinic, Hunter Coll., N.Y.C., 1958-59; sr. scientist biometrics research N.Y. State Dept. Mental Hygiene, 1959-66; dir. research Lincoln Hosp.-Albert Einstein Coll. Medicine, 1967-68; research assoc., mem. doctoral faculty environ. psychology program City U. N.Y., 1968-71; sr. scientist Phila. Geriatric Center, 1971-76; project dir. N.Y. State Health Dept., 1973-76, HEW, 1975-76; mem. grad. faculty Pratt Inst., 1967-68, CUNY Grad. Center, 1968-71, Sarah Lawrence Coll., 1971-72; dir. div. gerontology; psychologist Lincoln Inst. Psychotherapy, 1976-81; clin. psychologist Bellevue Hosp., 1980-81. N.Y.U. Med. Center 1978-81; dir. Gerontology Ctr., W.Va. U., from 1981; now dir. Univ. Campus Traveler's Ctr. on Aging, U. Conn. Editor: Humor and Aging, 1986. Mem. Am. Psychol. Assn., Eastern Psychol. Assn., Gerontol. Soc., N.Y. Soc. Psychol. Study Social Issues, AAAS, Gray Panthers, Sigma Xi, Psi Chi, Alpha Kappa Delta. Author: (with Pousada) Geriatric Diagnostics, 1983. Editor: Methodology for the Evaluation of Residential Environments for the Functionally Handicapped, 1975; (with others) Establishing Geriatric Teaching Programs, 1983. Contbr. articles profl. jours. Address: Gerontology Ctr WVA U Morgantown WV 26506

NAISMITH, LAURIE, state official; b. Norfolk, Va., Apr. 21, 1952; d. George and Mary Helen (Campbell) N. B.A., Old Dominion U., 1975. Legis. staff Nat. Student Lobby, Washington, 1973; legis. asst. Del. Robert E. Washington, Norfolk, Va., 1974-76; cons. Va. Internship Program, Richmond, 1975; field dir. Adm. Elmo R. Zumwalt for U.S. Senate Campaign, 1976; dir. scheduling and advance Robb for Lt. Gov. campaign, 1977, 81; dir. pub. affairs/programs Lt. Gov. Robb, Richmond, 1978-81; transition team Gov.-Elect Robb, Richmond, 1981-82; sec. of state Commonwealth of Va., Richmond, 1982-85; mem. State Agy. Group, Richmond, 1982—; mem. Alcoholic Beverage Control Bd., 1985. Del. Democratic Convs., 1972, 76, 77, 78, 80, 81; hon. sec. Va. Young Dems., Richmond, 1983; bd. mem. Richmond Bi-Centennial Commn., 1982; mem. Commn. on Intergovtl. Cooperation, 1982; bd. mem. Richmond Renaissance Citizens Adv. Commn., 1983; mem. steering com. Gov.'s Awards for Arts, 1984; mem. Leadership Metro Richmond, Richmond Met. C. of C., 1983-84; Va. rep. Nat. Adv. Com. to Eleanor Roosevelt Centennial Commn., 1984; bd. dirs. Richmond Symphony Orch., 1986. Recipient Exec. Dirs. award Nat. Black Assn. for Speech, Lang. and Hearings, 1983; named Fast Track Favorite, Commonwealth Mag., 1983. Mem. Women Execs. in State Govt. (conf. program chair 1984), Nat. Assn. Secs. State (chmn. fin. com., mem. voter edn. com. 1982), Nat. Assn. Extradition Ofcls. Democrat. Presbyterian. Mem. Sigma Alpha (pres. 1975). Office: State Capitol Richmond VA 23219

NAJARIAN, BARBARA, art director; b. N.Y.C., July 24, 1950; d. Edward H. and Ann (Chontorian) N. B.F.A., Art Ctr. Coll. Design, Los Angeles, 1971; U. Calif.-UCLA, 1972; postgrad. Royal Coll. Art, London, 1980. Freelance art dir., Los Angeles, 1973-78; art dir. Young & Rubicam-West, Los Angeles, 1978-80, Gray Advt., Inc., N.Y.C., 1980-81, J. Walter Thompson, Inc., N.Y.C., 1981-83; sr. art dir. Grey Advt., Inc., Mpls., 1983-85; creative supr. Campbell-Mithun Advt., Inc., Mpls., 1985—; creative cons. BTG Prodns., Inc., 1982-83, Janus Fin. Mktg., 1984; graphics cons. and designer. Vol., Hopkins Area Little League, Minn., 1984-86, Sloane Kettering Inst., 1980-82, Neuropsychiat. Inst., UCLA, 1974-78. Recipient Lulu award Women's Advt. Club Los Angeles, 1977; Clio award, 1982. Mem. Nat. Assn. Female Execs., Advt. Club Mpls., Copywriters and Art Dirs. Club Mpls. Avocations: painting; reading; crossword puzzles; golf; travel. Office: Campbell-Mithun 222 S 9th St Minneapolis MN 55403

NAJARIAN, MARY, state senator; b. Aug. 13, 1932. B.S., W.Va. U., 1954. Former mem. Maine Ho. of Reps.; now mem. Maine Senate. Alt. del. Democratic Nat. Conv., 1976, del., 1980. Office: Maine State Capitol Bldg Augusta ME 04333*

NAKACHE, MARGARET ANN, artist; b. Hartford, Conn., Dec. 17, 1932; d. Joseph Charles and Alice Mable (Coyle) Lynch; B.F.A., R.I. Sch. Design, 1954; French cert. L'Ecole Nationale Superieure Des Beaux-Arts, Paris, 1954-56; m. Fernand Robert Nakache, Aug. 17, 1957; children—Catherine, Patricia. Artist, Universal Films, N.Y.C., 1956-57; designer Girl Scouts U.S.A., N.Y.C., 1959-62; one-woman shows: retrospective exhbn. Palos Verdes (Calif.) Gallery, 1971, La Gallerie du Meridien, Paris, 1975, 77, 79, Prince Royal Gallery, Alexandria, Va., 1978, Hunter House, Vienna, Va., 1982, retrospective exhbn. Georgetown U. Hosp., Washington, 1985; group shows include: Art Barn, Washington, 1978, Cape Cod Art Assn., West Barnstable, Mass., 1979, 83, Colvin Mill Run, Va., 1980; represented in permanent collections: L'Ambassade du Liban, Paris, Clinique Adda, Creteil, France, Prince Royal Gallery, Our Lady of Victory Ch., Centerville, Mass., Georgetown U. Hosp., Washington. Mem. Vienna Arts Soc. Roman Catholic. Home: 1448 Woodacre McLean VA 22101

NAKAGAWA, ANN MEGUMI, lawyer; b. Wahiawa, Hawaii, Jan. 8, 1954; d. Kiyoto and Masako (Sato) Nakagawa; m. Ralph Mamoru Migita, July 27, 1980; 1 son, Ryan Yusuke. A.B., U. Calif.-Berkeley, 1976, J.D., Georgetown U., 1979. Bar: Hawaii 1979, U.S. Dist. Ct. Hawaii 1979, U.S. Dist. Ct. (no. dist.) Calif. 1983. Legis. aide Hawaii State Legislature, Honolulu, 1974; law clk. U.S. Dept. Justice, Washington, 1978-79, GSA, Washington, 1978; atty. SBA, San Francisco, 1979—. Mem. Hawaii State Bd. Edn., 1972-74. Recipient Spl. Achievement award, Dist. Employee of Yr. award, Region Disting. Service award, all SBA, 1983. Mem. Hawaii State Bar Assn., ABA. Office: SBA 211 Main St 4th floor San Francisco CA 94105

NAKOS, KATHLEEN BARBARA, association executive; b. Bartow, Fla., Feb. 16, 1949; d. James Nick and Dorothy (Velmer) Pihakis; m. Nolan A. Nakos, Oct. 8, 1967 (div. 1979); children—Alexander E., Spiro N., James N. Student U. Ala.-Birmingham. Asst. pub. relations dir. Carraway Meth. Med. Ctr., Birmingham, 1979-80; met. regional dir. Am. Heart Assn., Ala. affiliate, Birmingham, 1980-82, exec. dir. Nev. affiliate, Reno, 1982-85, council devel. dir. Tex. affiliate, Houston, 1985—. Named Outstanding Regional Dir., Am. Heart Assn., Ala., 1982; Bronze Hope Chest award Nat. Multiple Sclerosis Soc., 1975, also award Central Ala. chpt.; Nat. Soc. Heart Assn. Profls. fellow, 1983-84. Mem. Am. Women in Radio and TV, Reno C. of C. Republican. Greek Orthodox. Clubs: Reno Advt., Soroptimists, Zonta, Birmingham Press, Birminghamm Ballet, Ladies Philanthropic Soc. Home: 6504 Newcastle Bellaire TX 77401 Office: Am Heart Assn Tex Affiliate 1415 La Concha Houston TX 77054

NALLEY, BLANCHE ALMEDIA (MEDA), real estate development executive, property management director; b. Rocky Mount, N.C., June 26, 1939; d. Walter McDonald, Jr., and Ella Blanche (Phelps) Peacock; m. Richard Kingsman Nalley, Jr., Jan. 16, 1960 (div. 1967); children—Michelle, Karen, Natalie. A.A., U. Fla., 1960. Controller, sta. WPGC, Washington, 1965-68, Trans Continental Industries, Washington, 1968-71, Atlantic Elec. and Bldrs. Hardware, Washington, 1971-74, LBG Distrbrs., Washington, 1974-79; dir. property mgmt., devel. and constrn. Ingersoll & Bloch Chartered, Washington, 1979—; renovation cons. Nunnery Assocs., Washington, 1983-85, J.C. Assocs., Washington, 1984—; constrn. cons. P St Assn., Washington, 1985-86; owners rep. 801 Pa. Ave. Assn., Washington, 1985-86. Active design and constrn. hist. structures into office space, 1985-86, renovation hist. landmark bldg., 1985-86. Vol. Alexandria Hosp., Va., 1984; v.p. Elem. Sch. PTA, Hyattsville, Md., 1975, sec. Middle Sch. PTA, 1975. Mem. Property Mgmt. Assn., Apt. Office Bldg. Assn., Multi Housing Assn. Republican. Avocations: Running; aerobics; swimming; indoor gardening; crocheting; cooking. Home: 4540 Garbo Ct Annandale VA 22003 Office: J C Associates 1401 16th St NW Washington DC 20036

NAMM, SUSAN HAMMEL, banker; b. Bklyn., June 28, 1939; d. William J. and Mildred (Henigson) Hammel; B.S. in Mass Communications, Emerson Coll., 1961; children—Adam Edward, Leslie Ellen. Vice pres., mktg. dir. Westchester Community Health Plan, White Plains, N.Y., 1976-78; v.p., exec. dir. So. Conn. Community Health Plan, Stamford, 1978-80; asst. to v.p. devel. Emerson Coll., 1966-76; dir. public relations Burke Rehab. Center, 1968-69;

v.p. Citibank, N.Y.C., 1980—; tchr. Am. Mgmt. Assn., 1977. Active YWCA; tchr. swimming So. Conn. Bus. Assn., 1978-80; bd. dirs. 42d Street Ednl. and Theatrical Ctr.; mem. N.Y. Statue of Liberty Centennial Commn.; founder Westchester Assn. for Gifted and Talented Children, 1974; chmn. Programs of Cultural Enrichment for Children, Richmond, Va., 1967; bd. dirs. YWCA, N.Y.C.; ambassador The Empire State, Statue of Liberty Found. Recipient award City of Richmond, 1968. Mem. Bus. Womens Gold Assn. Club: Sky. Office: Citibank 123 E 86th St New York NY 10028

NANCE, BETTY LOVE, librarian; b. Nashville, Oct. 29, 1923; d. Granville Scott and Clara (Mills) Nance. B.A. magna cum laude in English, Trinity U., 1957; A.M. in Library Sci., U. Mich., 1958. Head dept. acquisitions Stephen F. Austin U. Library, Nacogdoches, Tex., 1958-59; librarian 1st Nat. Bank, Fort Worth, 1959-61; head catalog dept. Trinity U., San Antonio, 1961-63; head tech. processes U. Tex. Law Library, Austin, 1963-66; head catalog dept. Tex. A&M U. Library, College Station, 1966-69; chief bibliographic services Washington U. Library, St. Louis, 1970; head dept. acquisitions Va. Commonwealth U. Library, Richmond, 1971-73; head tech. processes Howard Payne U. Library, Brownwood, Tex., 1974-79; library dir. Edinburg Pub. Library, Tex., 1980—. Mem. ALA, Pub. Library Assn., Tex. Library Assn., Hidalgo County Library Assn. (v.p. 1980-81, pres. 1981-82), Pan Am. Round Table of Edinburg (corr. sec. 1986-87), Edinburg Bus. and Profl. Womens Club (founding bd. dirs., pres. 1986-87), Alpha Lambda Delta, Alpha Chi. Methodist. Club: West Hidalgo Zonta (bd. dirs. 1986—). Home: 1602 John St Apt 4 Edinburg TX 78539 Office: Edinburg Pub Library 401 E Cano St Edinburg TX 78539

NANCE, MARY JOE, educator; b. Carthage, Tex., Aug. 7, 1921; d. F. F. and Mary Elizabeth (Knight) Born; B.B.A., North Tex. State U., 1953; postgrad. Northwestern State U. La., 1974; M.E., Antioch U., 1978; m. Earl C. Nance, July 12, 1946; 1 child, David Earl. Tchr., Port Isabel (Tex.) Integrated Sch. Dist., to 1979; tchr. English, Splendora (Tex.) High Sch., 1979-80, McLeod, Tex., 1980-81, Bremond, Tex., 1981—. Served with USAAF, 1942-45. Recipient Image Maker award Carthage C. of C., 1984; cert. bus. educator. Mem. Nat. Bus. Edn. Assn., NEA, Tex. Tchrs. Assn., Tex. Bus. Tchrs. Assn. (cert. of appreciation 1978), Nat. Women's Army Corps Vets. Assn., Air Force Assn. (life), Assn. Supervision and Curriculum Devel., Council for Basic Edn., Nat. Hist. Soc., Tex. Council English Tchrs. Baptist.

NAPIER, SELONIA ANN, government official; b. Memphis, Sept. 18, 1942; d. Charles O. and Selonia (Haynes) Cox; div.; 1 child, Wendy Ann. Assoc. Bus., Cuyahoga Community Coll., Cleve., 1977; B.Bus., Dyke Coll., 1979. Exec. sec. Pride Inc., Cleve., 1970-71; floor supr. Helix Co., Cleve., 1971-75; media asst. Cuyahoga Community Coll., Cleve., 1976-77; library asst. Dyke Coll., Cleve., 1978-79; supr. mortgage loans HUD, Cleve., 1979—. Recipient Edwin J. Williams award Nat. Assn. Black Accts., Cleve., 1978; Spl. Achievement award HUD, Cleve., 1982; named to Fed. Women's Council Women of Achievement, Cleve., 1982. Mem. Nat. Assn. for Female Execs., Fed. Women's Club. Democrat. Baptist. Lodge: Masons. Avocations: skating, sewing, redecorating. Home: 2197 E 100th St Cleveland OH 44106 Office: HUD 1375 Euclid Ave #420 Cleveland OH 44115

NAPLES, SUSAN LORRAINE, property management company executive; b. Claremont, N.H., May 15, 1949; d. Robert William Gerrie and Margaret Lorraine (Leavitt) Baney; m. Marc Zolla Talisman, Dec. 17, 1976 (div. 1984); 1 child, Clinton Eric. Student pub. schs. Santa Ana. Project dir., personnel dir. Community Devel. Council, Santa Ana, Calif., 1974-76; founder Women's Transitional Living Ctr., Orange, Calif., 1976, exec. dir. 1976-78; sr. account exec. Profl. Community Mgmt., El Toro, Calif., 1978-81; pres. Cardinal Property Mgmt., Inc., Santa Ana, 1981—. Co-author: How to Start a Shelter for Battered Women, 1977. Participant White House Conf. on Domestic Violence, 1977. Mem. NOW (pres. Orange County chpt. 1976, co-coordinator domestic violence task force Calif. chpt. 1977), Orange County Alliance for Survival, Orange County Wheelmen. Democrat. Avocations: cycling, jogging, miniatures. Office: Cardinal Property Mgmt Inc Suite H 1535 E 17th St Santa Ana CA 92701

NAPOLITANO, TONI KARLIN, sales representative; b. Miami Beach, Fla., Mar. 13, 1946; d. Jack David Karlin and Sophie Freida (Eisenstat) Karlin Weinstein; m. Edward A. Napolitano, Mar. 15, 1964 (div. Feb. 1982); children—Edward Vincent, Vincent James, Lori Lee. Master Cosmetologist, North Miami Sch. Cosmetology, Fla., 1963; Realtor, Gold Coast Sch. Real Estate, Ft. Lauderdale, Fla., 1981. Sales and mgmt. positions Sondro Cosmetics, Ft. Lauderdale, 1973-75; market research interviewer Bea Alenik Field Services, Ft. Lauderdale, 1975-79; fine jewelry sales person, gold buyer J.C. Penney Co., Plantation, Fla., 1979-84; sales rep. Tura Optical Co., Broward County, 1984; sales rep. MCI Airsignal, Inc., Ft. Lauderdale, 1984—; cons. Memrionics, Ft. Lauderdale, 1984-85; mktg. cons. Tax Reduction Workshops, Ft. Lauderdale, 1984—. Group facilitator Ctr. for Group Counseling, Faulk Found., Boca Raton, Fla., 1975-79; mem. consumer adv. bd. Pantry Pride Stores, Ft. Lauderdale, 1974-79. Recipient several regional and nat. sales awards MCI Airsignal, Inc., 1984, 85. Mem. Nat. Assn. Female Execs. Republican. Jewish. Avocations: travel, tennis, reading, dancing. Home: 2170 NW 85th Ave Sunrise FL 33322 Office: MCI Airsignal Inc 800 Corporate Dr Suite 320 Fort Lauderdale FL 33334

NARDI, ANNETTE MADELEINE, journalist; b. Bklyn., Dec. 24, 1933; d. John Joseph and Josephine (Alcuri) Tricarico; m. Ralph Francis Nardi, June 28, 1953 (dec.); children—Francis, John, Laurence, Lisa Nardi Girgenti. A.A. in Journalism, Hunter Coll., 1953; B.A. in English, Queens Coll., 1979. Editor Successful Servicing, John F. Rider Pub., N.Y.C., 1950-53; editor Alumni News, pub. info. asst. St. Louis, U., 1953-55; freelance writer Bayside Times (N.Y.), 1979-80; pub. relations coordinator Queensborough Community Coll., Bayside, 1980—. Editor newsletter St. Francis Hosp., Roslyn, N.Y., 1976-77; designer, editor newsletter 11th Dist. Dental Soc. Aux., Jamaica, N.Y., 1978-79. Mem. Women in Communications, Inc., Internat. Women's Writers Guild, Higher Edn. Com. Am. Italian Heritage, Democrat. Roman Catholic. Office: Queensborough Community Coll 56th Ave & Springfield Blvd Bayside NY 11364

NARIN, CAROLE A., real estate broker; b. Chgo., Jan. 8, 1939; d. Robert Lee and Mildred Rose (Myerburg) Shapiro; m. Francis Narin, July 6, 1958; children—Cynthia Narin, Sheri Lynn. A.S., B.A., Edison State Coll. Sales assoc. Century 21 Bleakly Agy., Cherry Hill, N.J., 1974-76, broker assoc., 1976-81, pres., broker, 1981—. Mem. Camden County Bd. Realtors (dir. 1982-85, sec. 1985), Cherry Hill C. of C. Office: Century 21 Bleakly Agy 2075 Route 70 Cherry Hill NJ 08003

NARIN, SANDRA CAROLE GOLDBERG, lawyer; b. Phila., Apr. 2, 1941; d. Woolf and Ida (Moliver) Goldberg; m. Stephen B. Narin, Sept. 29, 1963; children—Howard Glen, Brenda Teri. B.A., Bryn Mawr Coll., 1962; M.A., U. Pa., 1963, Ph.D., 1973; J.D., Villanova U., 1983. Bar: Pa. 1983. Instr. Russian, Haverford (Pa.) Coll., 1965-66; tchr. Russian Central High Sch., Phila., 1965-66; instr. Russian, Ursinus Coll., Collegeville, Pa., 1967-68; assoc. Narin & Chait, Phila., 1983—. Mem. Lower Merion Twp. Intersch. Council, Lower Merion, Pa., 1972—, sec., pres., 1974-76, 76-78; mem. citizen adv. com. Lower Merion (Pa.) Sch. Bd., 1977-79. Mem. ABA, Pa. Bar Assn., Phila. Bar Assn. Democrat. Clubs: Green Valley Country (Lafayette Hill, Pa.); Bryn Mawr Coll. (Phila.). Home: 331 Mallwyd Rd Merion PA 19066 Office: Narin and Chait 1521 Locust St 10th Floor Philadelphia PA 19102

NARISI, STELLA MARIA, heavy equipment mfg. co. exec.; b. Fort Smith, Ark., Oct. 24, 1950; d. Vincent J. and Norma J. Narisi; B.B.A., U. Tex., 1972, J.D., 1975. Admitted to Tex. bar, 1975; staff atty. enforcement div. Tex. State Securities Bd., Houston, 1975-79; corp. sec., in-house counsel Marathon Mfg. Co., Houston, 1979—. Mem. Am. Bar Assn., Tex. Bar Assn., Houston Bar Assn. Club: Houston. Office: 1900 Marathon Bldg 600 Jefferson Houston TX 77002

NARON, CONNIE COX, food company executive; b. Vicksburg, Miss., Oct. 22, 1950; d. Melvin O'Neal and Grace Belinda (Brouilette) Cox Benner; m. James Randolph Naron, June 2, 1966; children—Cyndi, Sonya, Andrew Jon. Student, U. Ark. Sales rep. Cox's Relish Co. Inc., Dermott, Ark., 1977-83, sec.-treas., Daingerfield, Tex., 1983-84, v.p. adminstrn., 1984—. Mem. Nat. Assn. Female Execs., U.S. C. of C., Nat. Food Processors Assn., Dallas C. of C., Tex. Dept. Agr. Avocations: art; poetry; photography; travel. Office: Cox's Relish Co Inc 405 Coffey PO Box 183 Daingerfield TX 75638

NAROV, FRUMA, structural engineer; b. Germany, Oct. 25, 1947; d. Abraham and Paula Arieli; B.S., Technion, Israel Inst. Tech., 1968; m. David Narov, Jan. 25, 1970; children—Hilla, Yoav. Structural engr. Lev Zetlin Assocs., Inc., N.Y.C., 1970-72, sr. structural engr., 1972-76, assoc., 1978-84, v.p., 1984—; project engr. Cannon Design Inc., Buffalo, 1977-78. Served to lt. Israeli Def. Forces, 1968-70. Registered profl. engr., N.Y. Mem. ASCE. Jewish. Office: Lev Zetlin Assocs Inc 641 Ave of Americas New York NY 10001

NARRIN, JANE ANNE, corporate recruiting executive; b. Detroit, Aug. 12, 1945; B.A., Fla. Atlantic U., 1966, M.A., 1970. Cert. social worker. Counselor, Broward County Schs., Fort Lauderdale, Fla., 1970-74; pres. J.A. Narrin and Assocs., Inc., Computer Search Firm, Bloomfield Hills, Mich., 1975—; cons. resource mgmt., mktg., communications, Detroit, 1984—. Pub. Options Newsletter, 1984—. Recipient Leadership award Bus. Assn. Mem. Nat. Wildlife Fedn., Save the Whale Found., Project Hope. Avocations: writing; photography; creative arts; dancing. Office: J A Narrin and Assocs Inc 4036 Telegraph Rd #5 Bloomfield Hills MI 48013

NARROW, NANCY HENTIG, lawyer; b. Chgo., May 16, 1954; d. William Hector and Geneva Jeanette (Hofer) H.; m. Steven Robert Narrow, Apr. 24, 1982; children—Megan Michelle, Timothy Charles. B.A., Salem Coll., 1974; J.D., Washington U., St. Louis, 1981. Bar: Mo. 1981. Asst. pub. defender State Mo., Jackson, 1981-82, pub. defender, Benton, Mo., 1983—. Bd. dirs., program chmn., past chmn. fundraising com. WISER Inc. Women's Ctr. and Safehouse, Cape Girardeau, 1982—. Mem. ABA, Mo. Bar Assn., Mo. Assn. Criminal Def. Lawyers, Scott County Bar Assn., Cape Girardeau County Bar Assn. Phi Delta Phi. Lutheran. Club: Zonta. Home: 2215 Bainbridge Rd Jackson MO 63755 Office: Public Defender 33d Jud Circuit PO Box 429 Benton MO 63736

NARUSIS, REGINA GYTĖ FIRANT, lawyer; b. Kaunas, Lithuania, Oct. 12, 1936; d. Victor and Eugenia S. (Cesnavicius) Firant; brought to U.S., 1949, naturalized, 1955; B.A., U. Ill., 1957, J.D., 1959; m. Bernard V. Narusis, June 19, 1959; children—Victor John, Ellen Marie, Susan Marie. Bar: Ill. 1960. Partner firm Narusis & Narusis, Cary, Ill., 1961—; city atty. City of McHenry (Ill.), 1973—; village atty. Fox River Grove, Ill., 1967-73; asst. state's atty., McHenry County, Ill., 1968-75, head juvenile div., 1968-75. Mem. McHenry County Bd. Health, Woodstock, Ill., 1964-75; mem., pres. Dist. 46 Sch. Bd., McHenry County, 1964-79; mem. McHenry County Welfare Services Com., 1968-75; mem. adminstrv. council, mem. exec. bd. Marian Central Cath. High Sch., 1981—. Mem. Ill. Bar Assn., McHenry County Bar Assn., Women's Bar Assn., Am. Judicature Soc., Nat. Dist. Attys. Assn., Kappa Beta Pi. Address: 213 W Lake Shore Dr Cary IL 60013

NASH, ANN ELIZABETH, educational consultant, researcher, educator, author; b. Winnipeg, Man., Can., Dec. 12, 1928; d. John Wills and Margaret Agnes (Gray) Macleod; m. Richard Earl Bachtel, Dec. 19, 1947; children—Margaret Ann, John Macleod, Bradley Wills; m. 2d, Louis Philip Nash, June 30, 1978. A.B., Occidental Coll., 1947; M.A., Calif. State U.-Los Angeles, 1976. Cert. tchr., adminstr., Calif. Elem. tchr. pub. and pvt. schs. in Calif., 1947-50, 64-77; dir. Emergency Sch. Aid Act program, spl. projects, spl. arts State of Calif., 1977-80; leader, mem. program rev. team Calif. State Dept. Edn., 1981—; cons. Pasadena Unified Sch. Dist., 1981—; teaching asst., adj. prof. U. So. Calif.; cons. sch. dists., state depts. edn.; presenter workshops/seminars; mem. legis. task forces. Mem. resource allocation com. City of Pasadena; mem. Los Angeles World Affairs Council; mem. docent council Pasadena Hist. Soc.; mem. Pasadena Philharm. Com.; mem. women's com. Pasadena Symphony Assn.; chmn. Pasadena-Mishima (Japan) Sister Cities Internat. Com. Emergency Sch. Aid Act grantee, 1977-81. Mem. World Council Gifted and Talented Children, Internat. Soc. Edn. Through Art, Council Exceptional Children, Am. Ednl. Research Assn., Assn. Supervision and Curriculum Devel., Nat. Art Educators Assn., Calif. Art Educators Assn., Calif. Humanities Edn. Assn., AAUW, Phi Delta Kappa, Kappa Delta Pi, Assistance League of Pasadena. Contbr. articles to publs.; writer/editor: Arts for the Gifted and Talented, 1981; author Nat. Directory of Programs for Artistically Gifted and Talented Students, K-12, 1985. Office: 732 Pinehurst Dr Pasadena CA 91106

NASH, CONSTANCE ELLEN, furniture manufacturing company executive; b. Rockville Centre, N.Y., Jan. 21, 1957; d. James Francis and Virginia H. Nash; m. Andrew E. Karsh, Aug. 6, 1982. Vice-pres., sales mgr. San Diego Design Inc., 1979—. Active San Diego Symphony. Named Small Bus. Person of Yr., San Diego, 1985. Mem. San Diego Employers Assn., San Diego C. of C., Santee C. of C., San Diego Entrepreneur Club. Office: San Diego Design Inc 9366 Abraham Way Santee CA 92071

NASH, DONSANELL, mortician; b. Kosciusko, Miss., Jan. 17, 1949; d. Doty Edward Nash and Velma (Lee) Brown; 1 son, Doty Edward Nash II. Student Loop Jr. City Coll., 1968-71; diploma, Worsham Coll. Mortuary Sci., 1972. Lic. mortician. Acctg. clk. Vening Co., Chgo., 1967-68; customer service rep. John M. Smythe Furniture Co., Chgo., 1968-69; auto payment premium clk. CNA Ins. Co., Chgo., 1969-70; bus. mgr. Doty Nash Funeral Home, Ltd., Chgo., 1970—; workshop leader Women in Funeral Service, 1980. Founder, leader Lovely Ladies Widow Group, Chgo., 1979—. Mem. Cook County Assn. Funeral Home Owners (sec. 1980-82), Nat. Funeral Dirs. Assn., Ill. Selected Morticians Assn. (edn. chmn. 1980-83), Nat. Funeral Dirs. and Morticians, Chgo. Assn. Commerce and Industry (mem. youth motivation com. 1981-82), Women in Mgmt., Females in Funeral Service (pres. Chgo. chpt. 1980-83). Baptist. Club: Internat. Toastmistress (Chgo.). Lodge: Order of Eastern Star. Home: 9324 S Avalon St Chicago IL 60619 Office: Doty Nash Funeral Home Ltd 8620 S Stony Island Ave Chicago IL 60617

NASH, ELIZABETH IVES, securities co. exec.; b. West Chazy, N.Y., Aug. 5, 1909; d. Alfred Peabody and Eleanor Collista (Stoughton) Ives; student bus. colls.; m. Maynard Nash, Dec. 7, 1929; 1 son, Paul Ives. Sec., treas., dir. Maynard Nash, Inc., contractor, Stamford, Conn., 1950-68; asst. v.p. Hardy, Hardy & Assos., Sarasota, Fla., 1961-76; stock broker, fin. planning exec. Raymond, James & Assos., Inc., mem. N.Y. Stock Exchange, Sarasota, 1976—. Mem. N.Y., Phila., Balt., Washington stock exchanges. Bd. dirs. First Step. Mem. Mut. Fund Council, Internat. Fin. Planners. Club: Field (Sarasota). Home: 1601 Pelican Point Dr H215 Sarasota FL 33581 Office: 1718 Main St Sarasota FL 33577

NASH, HELEN ELIZABETH, pediatrician; b. Atlanta, Aug. 8, 1921; d. Homer Erwin and Marie (Graves) N.; B.A., Spelman Coll., 1942; M.D., Meharry Med. Coll., 1945; m. James B. Abernathy, Aug. 1, 1964. Intern, resident Homer Phillips Hosp., St. Louis, 1945-49; asso. prof. clin. pediatrics Washington U., St. Louis, 1949—; practice medicine specializing in pediatrics, St. Louis, 1949—; pediatric supr. H.G. Phillips Hosp., 1949-64; mem. staff St. Louis Children's Hosp., St. Luke's Hosp., Jewish Hosp. of St. Louis, St. Louis Maternity Hosp.; mem. Mo. Welfare Commn., 1969-73. Diplomate Am. Bd. Pediatrics. Mem. St. Louis Med. Soc. (Hon. life), Mo. Med. Soc., AMA, Am. Acad. Pediatrics, St. Louis Pediatric Soc. Home: 5783 Lindell Blvd St Louis MO 63112 Office: 1441 N Grand St Saint Louis MO 63106

NASH, JACQUELINE AVANETTE, lawyer; b. Shreveport, La., Feb. 13, 1959; d. Murphy and Idella (Henson) N. B.A., So. U., 1980, J.D., 1983. Bar: La. 1983. Legis. asst. La. Ho. of Reps., Baton Rouge, 1980-83; staff atty. La. Dept. Health and Human Resources, Baton Rouge, 1983—; sole practice, Baton Rouge, 1983—; asst. parish atty. City of Baton Rouge, Parish of East Baton Rouge, 1984—. Mem. ABA, Nat. Bar Assn., La. Trial Lawyers Assn., La. State Bar Assn., Baton Rouge Bar Assn., Southeastern Voters League, LWV, Alpha Kappa Alpha. Democrat. Baptist. Office: 2151 N Foster Dr Baton Rouge LA 70806

NASH, JULIE WATTS, librarian; b. Wichita, Kans., June 28, 1956; d. William Eugene and Patsie Lee (Monson) Watts; m. Larry J. Nash, Feb. 14, 1981. B.G.S., Emporia State U., 1978; M.L.S., Emporia State U., 1982. Head br. librarian Kansas City (Mo.) Pub. Library, 1980-81; acquisitions librarian Park Coll. Library, Parkville, Mo., 1981-82; pub. services librarian Monessen (Pa.) Pub. Library, 1983-84; head br. librarian Lane Rd. Library, Columbus, Ohio, 1984—; research cons. Compucare, Inc., Pitts., 1983. Mem. ALA, Kappa Delta Pi. Republican. Presbyterian. Home: 6447 Cranston Way Dublin OH 43017 Office: 1945 Lane Rd Columbus OH 43220

NASH, MARGRIT WEBER, hotel executive; b. Hamburg, Germany, Sept. 5, 1939; came to U.S., 1967, naturalized, 1975; s. Herbert and Marie (Lensch) Weber; m. John F. Nash, Feb. 11, 1961 (div. Jan. 1981); children—Martin, Helen. B.Sc. in Hotel Mgmt., Hotel Mgmt. Sch., Bad Reichenhall, Fed. Republic Germany, 1959; Assoc. Lang. Degree, Manchester U., Eng., 1960, Brussels U., 1961. Hotel mgmt. trainee Kurhotel, GLotterbad, Fed. Republic Germany, 1959-60; buyer, editor Internat. Bookseller, London, 1962-66; dir. wines European Selected Wines, N.Y.C., 1980-82; guest service dir. Omni Hotel, Atlanta, 1984—; free-lance translator, Atlanta, 1969-79. Compiler, editor: Guide to the International Traveler, 1985. Membership dir. Atlanta LWV, 1975-77, human resources dir., 1978; pres. congregation Unitarian Universalist Ch., Atlanta, 1979-81, pres. S.E. dist. mid-South, 1977-80. Recipient Image Maker award Atlanta Profl. Women's Assn., 1983, 84, Atlanta Woman award Creative Loafing, 1986. Mem. Ga. Hospitality Orgn. Avocations: statite sculpture; gardening; classical music; reading. Home: 3197 Laramie Dr NW Atlanta GA 30339 Office: OMNI Internat Hotel One Omni International Atlanta GA 30335

NASH, MARILYN JEAN, editor, author; b. Houston, Oct. 17, 1950; d. Alfred Leroy and Doris Jean (Anderson) Lewis; B.B.A., U. Houston, 1975; m. Shannon T. Nash, Apr. 11, 1980; 1 dau. by previous marriage, Angela Christine Rittel. Acctg. clk. Fin. Services, Gulf Oil Corp., Houston, 1971-75; mktg. rep. AM Internat., Houston, 1976-80; self-employed copywriter, 1980-86; communications dir. Shaw Systems, 1986—; ; cons. in field. Mem. Phi Gamma Nu Alumni. Contbr. articles, photographs and short stories to various publs.

NASH, RUTH COWAN (MRS. BRADLEY D. NASH), journalist; b. Salt Lake City, Utah; d. William Henry and Ida (Baldwin) Cowan; A.B., U. Tex., 1923; m. Bradley D. Nash, June 30, 1956. Tchr. pub. high sch., San Antonio, 1924-27; reporter San Antonio Evening News, 1928, United Press, 1929; corr. AP, Chgo., 1929-40, Washington, 1940-43, 45-56, war corr., North Africa, Gt. Britain, Europe, 1943-45, retired, 1956; free lance journalist, 1956—; asst. to undersec. of health edn. and welfare, 1958-61; pres. Travelers Service, Inc., Charles Town, W.Va. Cons., pub. relations dir. women's div., Republican Nat. Com., Washington; mem. Def. Adv. Com. on Women in the Services, 1958-61. Clubs: Nat. Press, Washington Press (pres. 1947-48), Overseas Press, Am. Newspaper Women's; Writer and Press (London). Home: High Acres Farm Box 122 Route 3 Harpers Ferry WV 25425

NASH, THERESA IRENE, educator, accountant; b. Kosse, Tex., May 11, 1936; d. Dwain Evans and Adell Irene (Clay) Slaughter; m. Charles Robert Nash, May 11, 1956; children—Kimberly, Kelly, Kara. B.E., S.W. Tex. State U., 1957. Tchr. Texas City Ind. Sch. Dist., Tex., 1968-71, Cy-Fair Ind. Sch. Dist., Houston, 1973—. Mem. Tex. State Tchr's Assn. (rep. 1980). Republican. Baptist. Avocation: reading. Office: Bleyl Jr High Sch 10800 Mills Rd Houston TX 77070

NASH-MORGAN, LEONORA ELIZABETH, physician, surgeon; b. Holyoke, Mass., Aug. 13, 1910; d. George Harlan and Edna Doris (Snell) Nash; B.A., Mt. Holyoke Coll., 1932, M.A., 1933; fellow Harvard U., 1933-34; M.D. (W.K. Kellogg grantee), U. Mich., 1939; m. John Dickinson Morgan, Aug. 27, 1940; children—John Dickinson, Leonora Elizabeth, Harlan Kellogg, Elizabeth Emily. Intern, resident U. Mich., 1938-39; physician Iowa State Coll., Cedar Falls, 1939-40; practice medicine and surgery, Erie, Ill., 1941-54, Moline, Ill., 1954—; chmn. utilization rev. com. Oak Glen Nursing Home, Coal Valley, Ill.; lectr. medicine, childhood, adolescence, marriage; mem. staff Lutheran, Moline Public hosps. Mem. Moline Youth Commn., 1964-68; physician Rock Island County Free Venereal Disease Clinic, 1975-77; mem. Center Study of the Presidency, 1976—, nat. adv. council, N.Y.C., 1979—. Recipient article of recognition Moline Dispatch, 1982. Fellow Am. Acad. Family Physicians; mem. Ill. Acad. Family Physicians (past pres., past dir., past del. Rock Island chpt.), Rock Island County Med. Soc., Ill. Med. Soc., Am. Assn. Physicians and Surgeons, AMA, Internat. Soc. Advanced Edn., Photog. Soc. Am., Alpha Epsilon Iota. Republican. Episcopalian. Clubs: Harvard (Chgo.); Sanderling (Sarasota, Fla.). Research on permeability of capillaries, lymphatic system, tetanus; inventor specialized humidifier, 1975. Office: 1630 5th Ave Moline IL 61265

NASON, F(REDA) LEE, telephone company executive; b. Bridgeport, Conn., July 5, 1944; d. Walter Gustav and Ruth Mathilda (Fohrenbach) Mayer; m. Paul Harris Nason, Jan. 25, 1963 (div.); 1 child, George Harris; m. Donald Joseph Hunt, June 27, 1982. B.S., Northeastern U., 1973; M.Arch., MIT, 1977. Lic. constrn. supr., Mass. Project mgr. real estate ops. New Eng. Tel. & Tel., Boston, 1971-82, dist. mgr. real estate ops., 1982—. Original sponsor Proposition 2-1/2, Mass., 1980; conv. credentials committeeperson Libertarian Nat. Party, 1978-80, chmn. Mass., 1978; treas., newsletter editor Assn. Liberterian Feminists, 1983—. Mem. Nat. Assn. Women in Constrn. (cost effectiveness chmn. 1984—), New Eng. Constrn. Users Council (profl. assn. liaison, 1983—), Mass. Bldg. Council. Lutheran. Office: New England Tel and Tel Room 1101 245 State St Boston MA 02109

NASON, THELMA STEIN, writer, teacher; b. N.Y.C., July 13, 1920; d. Gerson and Bella (Czernitzski) Stein; m. Alvin Nason, Oct. 18, 1944 (dec. Jan., 1978); children—Deborah R., Steffi R., Jean L., Gerson S., Benjamin M. B.A., Bklyn. Coll., 1941; postgrad. U. Chgo., 1941-42; M.A., Johns Hopkins U., 1968. Instr. econs. Williams Coll., Williamstown, Mass., 1942-43; wage and disputes analyst War Labor Bd., Chgo., N.Y.C., 1943-44; labor rep. CIO, N.Y.C., Washington, San Francisco, 1944-47; cons. Md. Planning Commn., 1952-53; instr. writing Johns Hopkins U., Balt., 1969-78; freelance writer, Balt., 1958—; sr. research assoc. sociology Brandeis U., Waltham, Mass., 1980—. Author: A Stranger Here, Myself, 1977, short stories. Contbr. articles to jours., newspapers. Vice pres. PTA, Mt. Washington, Balt., 1956-58; vis. scholar Bunting Inst., Radcliffe Coll., Cambridge, Mass., 1979-80. Fellow MacDowell Colony, Peterborough, N.H., 1973, 74, 76, Va. Ctr. for Creative Arts, Sweetbriar, 1984, 85. Mem. PEN, Poets and Writers Assn., Nat. Writers Union. Avocations: theatre; reading; music; swimming; walking.

NASSIF, JANET ZHUN, health consultant, author; b. Cleve., Dec. 27, 1946; d. Peter W. and Ellen Marie (Stempien) Zhun; m. Frederick Joseph Nassif. B.A., Case Western Res. U., 1968; M.P.H., Columbia U., 1981. Social worker, N.Y.C., 1968-72; mgmt. analyst Human Resources Adminstrn., N.Y.C., 1972-73; coordinator health careers counseling United Hosp. Fund, N.Y.C., 1973-76; coordinator Community Health Promotion, Nat. Health Council, N.Y.C., 1976-80; cons. to various corps. including Nat. Health Council, Nat. Homecaring Council, Holt, Rinehart and Winston, Am. Soc. Allied Health Professions; bd. dirs. New Healthways, Inc., N.Y.C., 1980—. Author: Medicine's New Technology, 1979; Handbook of Health Careers, 1980; Modern Health, 1985; The Home Health Care Solution, 1985. Presenter, planner health care N.Y. State Internat. Women's Year, Albany, 1977. Mem. Am. Sch. Health Assn., Am. Pub. Health Assn., Nat. Ctr. Health Edn. Home: 675 S Gulfview Blvd Clearwater Beach FL 33515

NAST, CAROL ANN, medical laboratory executive; b. Champaign, Ill., Nov. 8, 1945; d. Christian Anthony and Lelia Mae (Glover) Nast; B.S., M.S., Tex. Christian U. Med. technologist Harris Hosp., Ft. Worth, 1967-72; chief med. technologist Presbyn. Hosp., Dallas, 1972-73; mfg. dir. Nuclear Med. Labs., Dallas, 1973-85; ops. mgr. Bio Rad Labs., Richmond, Calif., 1985—; adv. bd. Women in Sci. Program U. Tex., Arlington. Mem. Am. Prodn. and Inventory Control Soc., Am. Soc. Clin. Pathologists (asso. mem., cert. med. technologist), Sierra Club, Mensa. Clubs: Dallas Cross Country, Aerobics Center. Home: 4 Chapparal Ct Novata CA 94947 Office: 2400 Wright Ave Richmond CA 94804

NAST, DIANNE MARTHA, lawyer; b. Moorestown, N.J., Jan. 30, 1946; d. Henry Daniel and Anastasia (Lovenduski) Nast; m. Joseph Francis Roda, Aug. 23, 1980; children—Michael, Daniel, Joseph, Joshua. B.A., Pa. State U., 1965; J.D., Rutgers U., 1976. Bar: Pa. 1976, N.J. 1976. Mem. firm Kohn, Savatt, Klein & Graf, P.C., Phila., 1976—; mem. lawyers adv. com. U.S. Ct. Appeals (3d cir.), 1982-84, chmn., 1983-84, mem. com. on revision jud. conduct rules; mem. U.S. Ct. Appeals Jud. Conf. Permanent Planning Com., 1980—. Active various charitable and fund raising orgns. Mem. Phila. Bar Assn. (chmn. fed. ct. com. 1984—), Pa. Bar Assn. (ho. of dels. 1983—, co-chmn. anti-trust com. litigation sect., chmn. bicentennial com.), ABA, N.J. Bar Assn., Pa. Trial Lawyers Assn., Phila. Trial Lawyers Assn., Am. Judicature Soc., Pa. State U. Alumni Assn., Rutgers Law Sch. Alumni Assn., Pa. Acad. Fine Arts, Pa. Farm Mus. of Landis Valley Assocs., Community Gallery of Lancaster County, Lancaster County Hist. Soc., Ephrata Cloister Assocs., Rockford Found., Phila. Zool. Soc., Nat. Acquatic Soc., Smithsonian Instn., Met. Mus. Art N.Y. Club: Peale (Phila.). Home: 1059 Sylvan Rd Lancaster PA 17601 Office: Kohn Savett Klein & Graf PC 1100 Market St Philadelphia PA 19107

NASTRO-VENTRE, PATRICIA, advertising and publishing executive; b. Bklyn., Aug. 7, 1943; d. Joseph Peter and Helen Mary (Costa) Nastro; m. Albert Ventre, May 13, 1985; 1 child, Jean-Paul. B.F.A., NYU/Parsons Sch. Design, 1965. Ptnr., Periodicals With A Purpose, Port Washington, N.Y., 1977—, Tankoos & Ventre Advt., Port Washington, 1979—. Designer Gaines Dog Chart, 1981 (Printing Industries N.Y. award 1981); photographer Rhapsody in Blue, 1984 (Beneath the Sea award 1984). Mem. Advt. Women N.Y., Am. Inst. Graphic Artists, L.I. Advt. Club, YMHA. Republican. Roman Catholic. Avocations: skiing, scuba diving, underwater photography, ballroom dancing. Office: Tankoos and Ventre Advt 18 Cross St Port Washington NY 11050

NATHAN, GRACE JUNE, sales promotion company executive; b. Chgo., June 1, 1919; d. Joel Charles and Mary Frances (Majewska) Benjamin; 2 yr. diploma Wright Coll., 1938; B.S., U. Chgo., 1940; M.S., U. Ill., 1942; postgrad. U. Tex., 1948-49, Cornell U., 1956-57; m. Edward Reub Nathan, Apr. 5, 1975. Instr., Wright Coll., Chgo., 1943; bacteriologist Chgo. Health Dept., 1944-45; asst. sci. editor World Book Ency., Chgo., 1946-47; chief geology librarian U. Tex., Austin, 1948-49; instr. Texarkana (Tex.) Coll., 1950-52; editor Instrumentation Mag., 1953-55; acct. exec. Fulton Morrissey Advt. Agy., Chgo., 1958-61; v.p. Product Exposure, Inc., Chgo., 1961-73, pres., 1973—; cons. to various marketing firms. Mem. Am. Inst. Econ. Research, Am. Friends Austria, Art Inst. Chgo., Premium Advt. Assn. Am., Chgo. Premium Assn., Assn. TV Merchandisers, Nat. Com. Monetary Reform. Home: 3200 N Lake Shore Dr Chicago IL 60657 Office: 11 E Hubbard St Chicago IL 60611

NATHANSON, A. LYNN, broadcasting company executive; b. Sydney, N.S., Can., Dec. 4, 1955; came to U.S., 1970; d. Norris Lionel and Reva (Brook) N.; m. Mark Joseph Pandiscio, Oct. 8, 1978. A.B. in Music and French, Brown U., 1977. Program mgr., announcer CJCB-FM, Sydney, 1978; floor dir., asst. dir. WJAR-TV, Providence, 1979-80; devel. officer Boston Biomed. Research Inst., 1980-81; concert mgr. Mus. Fine Arts, Boston, 1980-81, mgr. Remis Auditorium, Mus. Fine Arts, 1981-82; sr. v.p. Charles River Broadcasting, Waltham, Mass., 1982—; cons. CJCB-AM, CKPE-FM, Sydney, 1986. Chmn. fundraiser Dana Farber Cancer Inst., Boston, 1986; mem. benefit com. Pro Arte Chamber Orch. Mem. Boston Symphony Assn. Vols., Advt. Club of Boston, Classical Music Broadcasters Assn., Assn. for Classical Music. Jewish. Avocations: piano; skiing; swimming; singing. Home: 241 Perkins St J-202 Boston MA 02130 Office: Charles River Broadcasting WCRB 750 South St Waltham MA 02254

NATHANSON, LINDA SUE, technical writer, industrial trainer; b. Washington, Aug. 11, 1946; d. Nat and Edith (Weinstein) Nathanson. B.S., U. Md., 1969; M.A., UCLA, 1970, Ph.D., 1975. Sr. research scientist, tng. dir. Rockland Research Inst., Orangeburg, N.Y., 1975-77; research fellow Albert Einstein Coll. Medicine, Bronx, N.Y., 1978-79; asst. prof. psychology Coll. Optometry, SUNY, N.Y.C., 1978-79; adj. asst. prof. computer sci. Pace U., 1977-79; adj. asst. prof. psychology Queens Coll., CUNY, Hunter Coll., 1977-78; pres. Cabri Prodns., Inc., Fort Lee, N.J., 1979-81; exec. dir. Ctr. for Applied Behavior Research, Inc., Fort Lee, 1979-83; research supr. D'Arcy-MacManus & Masius, St. Louis, 1981-83; software tng. mgr. On-Line Software Internat., Fort Lee, 1983-85; ind. cons., 1985—. Recipient NIMH Research Service award, 1979; NSF research fellow, 1963, 1965. Mem. Am. Psychol. Assn., Am. Mktg. Assn. Contbr. articles to profl. jours. Home and Office: 1645 Kaufer Ln Fort Lee NJ 07024

NATHANSON, MAUREEN REILLY, manufacturing company executive; b. Lynn, Mass., Aug. 20, 1942; d. Matthew Louis and Kathleen (Coyne) Reilly; children—Robin, Neal, Matthew. Student pub. schs., Lynn. Demonstrator, Polaroid Corp., Cambridge, Mass., 1967-77, mdse. rep., 1977-79. mktg. rep., 1979-82, area mgr., 1982-84, mktg. rep., 1984-85, dist. sales mgr. N.E., 1985—. Mem. Women in Sales. Roman Catholic. Avocations: tennis, reading; nautilus; travel. Home: 25 Nickerson Rd Lexington MA 02173 Office: Polaroid Corp 114 1st Ave Needham MA 02194

NATYSON, FRANCES, psychologist, educator; b. New Haven, Nov. 20, 1923; d. John Harry and Rozalia Natyson; R.N., Yale-New Haven Hosp. Sch. Nursing, 1946; B.A. in Psychology, Hunter Coll., 1969; M.A., New Sch. for Social Research, 1972; Ed.D., Columbia U., 1982. Various nursing positions at hosps. in N.Y.C., including Bellevue Hosp., Presbyn. Hosp., Roosevelt Hosp. and Hosp. For Cancer and Allied Diseases, 1946—; alcoholism counselor Cabrini Med. Center, N.Y.C., 1972—; pvt. practice counseling and psychotherapy. Mem. Mayor's com. on alcohol problems in schs., 1973. Mem. Am. Psychol. Assn., Soc. Behavioral Medicine, Am. Nurses Assn., N.Y. State Nurses Assn., Soc. for Public Health Edn., Inst. of Society, Ethics and Life Scis., N.Y. Fedn. of Alcoholism Counselors, Union Concerned Scientists, Kappa Delta Pi. Contbr. articles in field to profl. jours. Home: 562 West End Ave New York NY 10024

NAUGHTON, JODIE-KAY MARIE, manufacturing company executive; b. Chgo., Sept. 9, 1951; d. Joseph Martin and Evelyn Marie (Milne) N.; A.B.A., Wright City Coll., 1979; B.A., Lakeland Coll., 1984; m. Robert Anthony Memmel, Jr., Nov. 17, 1979. With Western Electric Co., various locations, 1969—, customer service rep., 1979-80, payroll and acctg. specialist, Milw., 1980; now with Ameritech Services, Inc., Arlington Heights, Ill. Bd. dirs. Future Pioneers, 1979, Concerner Consumers League Inc., Milw.; adviser Jr. Achievement, 1974, 75; v.p. Wright Newman Ctr., 1977; creator Weco Wackos, clown troupe, 1978; asst. adminstr. Midwest Region Hunger Project, 1980. Home: 234 Granville Ave Bellwood IL 60104 Office: 3040 W Salt Creek Ln Arlington Heights IL 60005

NAUGHTON, MARIE ANN, corporate manager; b. Boston, Feb. 19, 1954; d. Robert J. and Beatrice T. (McDonald) N.; B.S. in Speech magna cum laude, Emerson Coll., 1976; M.A., Ind. U., 1977. Speech-lang. pathologist Dedham (Mass.) public schs., 1977-79; speech-lang. pathologist Mass. Gen. Hosp., Boston, 1979-81; speech pathologist Mt. Auburn Hosp., Cambridge, Mass., 1982-84; mgr. Curtis-Newton Corp., Spltys. Div., 1984—. Mem. Am. Speech, Lang. and Hearing Assn. (cert. clin. competence), Mass. Speech and Hearing Assn., Zeta Phi Eta. Author: A Coarticulation Manual for the Remediation of /S/, 1979. Home: 77 Circuit Rd Dedham MA 02026 Office: 963 Watertown St West Newton MA 02165

NAUGLE, CHARLOTTE JUNE, educator; b. Long Beach, Calif., June 1, 1938; d. Robert F. and Florence A. (Smith) Ballenger; A.A., San Bernardino Valley Coll., 1959; B.A., Calif. State U., 1966, M.A., 1978; m. John R. Naugle, Jr., June 26, 1965; children—Roberta Lynn, Marina Rae. Tchr., Barstow (Calif.) Sch. Dist., 1966, U.S. Dependent Sch., Kenitra, Morocco, 1967-69; tchr., bilingual coordinator, state demonstration tchr. Colton (Calif.) Sch. Dist., 1970-81, state compensation project dir., 1981-83; prin. Smith Demonstration Sch., Bloomington, Calif., 1984—; ednl. cons.; extension instr. Calif. State U., San Bernardino, 1975-77. Public edn. chmn. San Bernardino-Riverside Counties, Am. Cancer Soc., 1979-81. Recipient, Able Toastmasters award, 1982; Outstanding Tchr. of Writing award Inland Area Writing Project, U. Calif., Riverside, 1980. Mem. Nat. Assn. Exec. Women, Assn. Supervision and Curriculum Devel., Phi Delta Kappa. Republican. Clubs: Writers Circle, Toastmasters (internat. pres. 1980, div. ednl. v.p. 1981). Home: 17358 El Molino St Bloomington CA 92316 Office: 9551 Linden St Bloomington CA 92316

NAUGLE, MARGARET VANCE, communications executive; b. West Point, Miss., Nov. 17, 1946; d. James O'Neil and Allie Laura (Stevens) Vance; B.S., Miss. State Coll. for Women, 1970; M.Ed., Miss. State U., 1977, Ed.D., 1980; m. Andrew Kincannon Naugle, III, Jan. 4, 1979; 1 dau., Laura Natalie Pickens. With admissions office Miss. State Coll. for Women, 1970; tchr. Lowndes County (Miss.) Schs., 1970-73, Hendry County (Fla.) Schs., 1973-74, Pickens County (Ala.) Schs., 1974-75; dir. adult edn. Miss. Band of Choctaw Indians, 1976-80; tng. specialist Daniel Constrn.-Weyerhauser Columbus Project, 1980-82; adj. prof. U. Ala., Tuscaloosa, 1980-81; dir. community relation Golden Triangle Regional Med. Ctr., 1982-84; dir. spl. projects Seminole Mfg. Co., Columbus, 1984—; tech. advisor Fermodyl Labs., Inc.; tchr. Seminole Tribe of Fla., Golden Triangle Vo-Tech Miss. Recipient Gold awards in advt., 4, 1982, 2, 1983. Mem. Am. Soc. Tng. and Devel., Assn. for Supervision and Curriculum Devel., Miss. Assn. for Supervision and Curriculum Devel., Nat. Assn. Public Continuing and Adult Edn. (nat. award for program 1976), Adult Basic Edn. Commn., Miss. Assn. for Public Continuing and Adult Edn., Adult Edn. Assn. U.S.A., Pub. Relations Assn. Miss. (pres., dir.), Golden Triangle Advt. Fedn. (dir.), Am. Advt. Fedn., C. of C., So. Pub. Relations Fedn. (award of merit 1983). Mem. Christian Church (Disciples of Christ). Club: Investment, Toastmasters (pres.). Author: A Comparison of the EDL Learning 100 Program and the Workbook Method of Teaching Reading to Choctaw Adults, 1980; Mill Economics, Parts I and II, 1981; author monthly newsletters; contbr. articles to Indian and profl. publs., 1976-79. Home: PO Box 1152 202 Court St West Point MS 39773 Office: Seminole Mfg Co PO Box 391 Columbus MS 39703

NAUMANN, MARY LYNN, insurance company executive; b. Houston, July 19, 1940; d. James Reuben and Sarah Gladys (Foster) Spaulding; m. Halmude Naumann, Jr., Aug. 29, 1958; children—Dana Lynn, Halmude III. Student St. Louis Inst. Music, 1958, U. Houston, 1959. C.P.C.U., Tex. Real estate broker, Houston, 1962-65; underwriting asst. Royal Globe Ins., Houston, 1965-67; sr. underwriter Indsl. Indemity, Houston, 1967-75; casualty supr. Aetna Ins. Co., Houston, 1975-80; asst. v.p. Emett & Chandler Tex., Houston, 1980-81; S.W. regional mgr. AIG Risk Mgmt., Houston, 1981—; adj. prof. U. Houston, 1975-79, Houston Bapt. U., 1979-82; instr. Houston Sch. Ins., 1975-78. Mem. Houston C.P.C.U. Assn. (pres. 1981-82, dir. 1978—), Nat. Soc. C.P.C.U.s (com. mem.), Houston Casualty Roundtable (v.p. 1975-76). Home: 7343 Birchtree Forest Houston TX 77088 Office: AIG Risk Mgmt 2200 North Loop West Suite 200 Houston TX 77018

NAVAJAS-SOUFFRONT, EMMA DOLORES, lawyer, legal and management consultant; b. Ponce, P.R., Mar. 26, 1947; d. Cesar F. and Emma S. Navajas; m. Arthur J. Rytting (dec.). B.A. magna cum laude, Cath. U. P.R., 1967, J.D. magna cum laude, 1971. Bar: P.R. 1971, U.S. Supreme Ct. 1977, D.C. 1978, U.S. Ct. Appeals (D.C. cir.) 1978, U.S. Ct. Appeals (4th cir.) 1978, U.S. Dist. Ct. P.R. 1979. Asst. prof. history dept. Cath. U. P.R., 1967-68, 69; trial atty. criminal div. U.S. Dept. Justice, Washington, 1971-73; law enforcement program lectr. Harford Community Coll., Athens, Greece, 1973-74; atty. adviser Office of Commonwealth of P.R., Washington, 1977-78, gen. counsel (name changed to P.R. Fed. Affairs Adminstrn.), 1978-79, dep. dir., 1979-82, dir., Washington, 1982-85; founder, pres. Cultural Ctr. of P.R. in Washington; mem. P.R. Interagy. Com. for Devel. of Internat. Commerce, 1982-85; mem. P.R. Open Skies-Sea Task Force, 1978-85. Contbr. writings to publs.; speaker conv. Undergrad. scholar, 1964-67; scholar law studies, 1968-71; named Disting. Alumna, Cath. U. P.R., 1983, Disting. Alumna, Law Sch., Cath. U. P.R., 1983. Mem. ABA, Fed. Bar Assn., Nat. Puerto Rican Coalition, Nat. Conf. Puerto Rican Women, Legal Services Corp. Tng. Task Force, P.R. Legal Def. and Edn. Fund, Puerto Rican Family Inst. (nat. trustee), Eta Gamma Delta (Disting. Mem. award 1983), Phi Alpha Theta, Alpha Mu Gamma (chpt. pres. 1966-67). Home: 8101 Connecticut Ave Apt N 402 Chevy Chase MD 20815

NAVARRO, ANNA MARIA, consultant; b. Havana, Cuba, Mar. 1, 1947; naturalized, 1963; d. Eugene and Maria (Castro) Navarro; m. Robert James Domrese, June 14, 1971 (div. 1978). B.A., New Coll., 1967; M.P.A., Princeton U., 1969. Project dir. Ind. Research Assocs., Washington, 1969-70; dir. opinion research Muskie For Pres., Washington, 1970-72; v.p., ptnr. Fleishman-Hillard, Inc., St. Louis, 1973-76; dir. social responsibility Monsanto Corp., St. Louis, 1976-79; founder Work Transitions, St. Louis, 1979—. Cons. Harriett Woods for U.S. Senate, St. Louis, 1981-82, Harriett Woods-Lt. Gov., St. Louis, 1982—; trustee Tower Grove Park, St. Louis, 1983—; asst. campaign mgr. Congressman John Brademas, South Bend, Ind., 1969, Mayor John Poelker, St. Louis, 1973. Mem. Am. Assn. for Counseling and Devel., Career Planning and Adult Devel. Network. Democrat. Office: Work Transitions 2256 S 39th St Saint Louis MO 63110

NAVE, JEAN RUSSELL, marketing and management training company executive; b. Burbank, Calif., Jan. 18, 1949; d. Gale Paul and Carolyn Margaret (Ludwig) Bartlett; m. Thomas R. Russell, June 18, 1968 (div. 1973); 1 child, Robert Gale; m. 2d, Claude Felix Nave, Aug. 6, 1983. Student Antelope Valley Coll., 1967, also numerous pvt. sales tng. courses. Mktg. rep. Bank of Am., Los Angeles, 1968-73; maj. account rep. Xerox Corp., Los Angeles, 1974-75; advisor, mktg. rep. Service Bur. Co., Los Angeles, 1975-79; field sales rep. Hewlett Packard Co., Santa Ana, Calif., 1979-80; mktg. mgr. Automatic Data Processing, Portland, Oreg., 1980-82; pres. Motivational Dynamics, Inc., Portland, 1981—, also dir.; mktg. cons. J.T. Warren Computer Service, Portland, 1983—; host TV show Traveling the Road of Success; dir. Resource Plus, Portland. Author: (book, tapes) Women ... The World's Greatest Salesmen, 1984, Traveling the road of Success. Active Republican polit. campaigns, Calif. and Oreg., 1970—. Mem. Am. Mktg. Assn., Project Mgmt. Inst. (v.p. 1981), Inst. Profl. and Managerial Women. Baptist. Club: Portland City. Home: 360 SW Breeze Ct Portland OR 97225 Office: Motivational Dynamics Inc PO Box 25104 Portland OR 97225

NAVRATILOVA, MARTINA, professional tennis player; b. Prague, Czechoslovakia, Oct. 18, 1956; came to U.S. 1975, naturalized, 1981; d. Miroslav Navratil and Jana Navratilova; student schs. in Czechoslovakia. Profl. tennis player, 1975—. Winner Czechoslovak Nat. Singles, 1972-74, U.S. Indoor Singles, 1975, Va. Slims Tournament, 1978, 83, Wimbledon Singles Championship, 1978, 79, 82, 83, 84, 85, 86, French Open Singles, 1982, 84, Wimbledon Doubles, 1982, 83, 84, Family Circle Cup, 1982, Fedn. Cup, 1982, U.S. Open Singles and Women's Doubles, 1983, 84, Australian Open, 1983, 85; ITF world champion, 1979, 82, 83, 84, 85. Named hon. citizen Dallas; AP Female Athlete of Yr., 1983. Mem. Women's Tennis Assn. (dir. exec. com.). Office: care US Tennis Assn 51 E 42d St New York NY 10017*

NAY, JOANNE FRYE, industrial engineer; b. Hollywood, Calif., Dec. 2, 1935; s. A. L. and Ruby (Mayer) Frye; m. Paul Dyer Nay, Nov. 27, 1959; children—Kevin, Steve, John. B.S.I.E., Stanford U., 1958; M.B.A., Calif. State U.-Bakersfield, 1984. Jr. indsl. engr. Smith Corona Marchant, Emeryville, Calif., 1959-60; standards analyst Ampex, Redwood City, Calif., 1971-72; indsl. engr. Gen. Dynamics, San Diego, 1972-73; indsl. engr. Jostens, Porterville, Calif., 1974-75, sr. indsl. engr., 1976-77, chief indsl. engr., 1978—. Mem. Status of Women Commn., Tulare County, Calif., 1979-83. Mem. Inst. Indsl. Engring., Soc. Women Engrs, NOW. Avocations: supporting activities that increase the dignity of people; hiking; reading. Home: 441 E Mill Porterville CA 93257 Office: Jostens PO Box 849 Porterville CA 93258

NAYLE, PATRICIA LYNN, state personnel officer; b. Columbus, Ind., Sept. 26, 1951; d. Ray Herman and Mary Lucille (Buckles) Nayle. B.S. in Home Econs., Merchandising, So. La. U., 1974; postgrad. U. Houston, 1976-81. Personnel clk. Tex. Dept. Human Resources, Houston, 1975-76, personnel asst., 1976-80, personnel officer, 1980—. Mem. Nat. Assn. Female Execs., AAUW, Phi Kappa Phi, Alpha Sigma Tau (alumnae chpt. pres. 1977-79, dist. pres. 1980-82, dir. expansion nat. council 1982—). Office: Dept Human Resources PO Box 16017 Houston TX 77022

NAYLOR, PHYLLIS REYNOLDS, author; b. Anderson, Ind., Jan. 4, 1933; d. Eugene Spencer and Lura Mae (Schield) Reynolds; m. Thomas A. Tedesco, Jr., Sept. 9, 1951 (div. 1960); m. Rex V. Naylor, May 26, 1960; children—Jeffrey, Michael. Diploma Joliet Jr. Coll., 1953; B.A., Am. U., Washington, 1963. Clin. sec. Billings Hosp., Chgo., 1953-56; elem. tchr., Hazelcrest, Ill., 1956; asst. exec. sec. Montgomery County Edn. Assn., Md., 1958-59; editorial asst. NEA, Washington, 1959-60; free-lance author, Bethesda, Md., 1960—. Author: 50 books including Crazy Love—an autobiographical account of marriage and madness, 1977; Revelations, 1979; A String of Chances, 1982 (ALA notable book award 1982); The Agony of Alice, 1985. Recipient Golden Kite award Soc. Children's Book Writers, 1978; Child Study award Bank Street Coll., 1983; Edgar Allan Poe award Mystery Writers Am., 1985. Mem. Children's Book Guild of Washington (pres. 1974-75, 83-84), Soc. Children's Book Writers, Authors Guild, PEN, Council for a Livable World, SANE, Physicians for Social Responsibility, Amnesty Internat. Unitarian. Avocations: theater; madrigal singing; swimming. Home and Office: 9910 Holmhurst Rd Bethesda MD 20817

NEAL, ALICE THELMA, former teacher, farmer; b. Knox County, Ind., Oct. 16, 1915; d. James and Allie (Fox) N. Student Vincennes U. (Ind.), 1933-35; B.S., Ind. State U.-Terre Haute, 1948. Tchr. Aliceville Sch., Ragsdale, Ind., 1937-47, 55-61, Bruceville Sch. (Ind.), 1949-55, Shoals Elem. Sch. (Ind.), 1961-69; farmer, Bicknell, Ind. Pres. DelVer Sunday Sch. Class, Vincennes, 1973-74, 76-77. Mem. Knox County Ret. Tchrs. (treas. 1979-80), Ind. Retired Tchrs., DAR (regent 1982-84). Democrat. Home: Rural Route 1 Box 70 Bicknell IN 47512

NEAL, ANNE DEHAYDEN, lawyer; b. Indpls., Mar. 22, 1955; d. James Thomas and Georgianne (Davis) N.; m. Thomas Evert Petri, Mar. 26, 1983. A.B., Harvard U., 1977, J.D., 1980. Bar: N.Y. 1981, U.S. Dist. Ct. (so. dist.) N.Y. 1981, U.S. Dist. Ct. (ea. dist.) N.Y. 1981, U.S. Ct. Claims 1982, U.S. Ct. Appeals (fed. cir.) 1982, D.C. 1984, Wis. 1986. Assoc., Rogers & Wells, N.Y.C., 1980-82; gen. counsel Office of Adminstrn., Exec. Office Pres., Washington, 1982-84; assoc. Wiley & Rein, Washington, 1984—. Docent, lectr. on arts Jr. League of Washington, 1982—; founding mem. Nat. Mus. of Women in Arts, 1984—; chmn. Com. on Nat. Mus. of Women in Arts, 1985—; chmn. New Leadership Fund, 1985—. Pulliam journalism fellow Indpls. News, 1977. Mem. Fed. Communications Bar Assn., ABA, Communications Law Forum. Colonial Dames Am., Phi Beta Kappa. Republican. Methodist. Club: Dramatic (Indpls.). Home: 2918 Olive St NW Washington DC 20007 Office: Wiley & Rein 1776 K St NW Washington DC 20006

NEAL, CHARLOTTE ANNE, educator; b. Hampton, Iowa, May 8, 1937; d. Sebo and Marion Bradford (Boutin-Clock) Reysack; B.A., U. No. Iowa, 1958; M.Ed., DePaul U. (Chgo.), 1966; divorced; children—Rachel Elizabeth, Kory Bradford. Tchr., 4th grade, Des Moines Ind. Sch. Dist., 1958-59; tchr., 3d grade Glenview (Ill.) Pub. Schs., 1959-61, tchr. 3d grade, psychol. ednl. diagnostic Schaumburg Dist. Schs., Hoffman Estates, Ill., 1961-69; supr. learning disabilities and behavior disorders Springfield (Ill.) Pub. Schs., 1969-73; psycho-ednl. diagnostician Barrington (Ill.) Sch. Dist. 220, 1973-77; ednl. strategist Area Edn. Agy. 7, Cedar Falls, Iowa, 1978—; ednl. cons. Spl. Edn. Dist. Lake County, Gurnee, Ill., summer, 1968. Certified K-14 teaching and supervising in guidance, counseling, elementary supervisory K-9, elementary K-9 teaching, spl. K-12 learning disabilities. Mem. NEA, Ill. Edn. Assn. Author: Handbook for Learning Disabilities Tchrs., 1971. Home: 1102 Sunset Dr Parkersburg IA 50665 Office: 3712 Cedar Hts Dr Cedar Falls IA 50613

NEAL, CONSTANCE ANN TRILLICH, lawyer, librarian; b. Chgo., Apr. 16, 1949; d. Lee and Ruth (Goodhue) Trillich; m. Robert Dale Neal, Dec. 25, 1972; 1 son, Adam Danforth. B.A. in French, U. Tenn., 1971, cert. Sorbonne, 1970; M.Ln., Emory U., 1979; J.D., Mercer Law Sch., 1982. Bar: Ga. 1982. Reservationist AAA, Tampa, Fla., 1971-72; library tech. asst. I, Mercer U., Macon, Ga., 1973-74, library tech. asst. II, 1974-78; teaching asst. Mercer Law Sch., Macon, 1981; cataloger Mercer Med. Sch., Macon, 1980-82; sole practice, Macon, 1982—; research asst. Ctr. Constl. Studies, Macon, 1983; instr. bus. Wesleyan Coll., Macon, 1982. Bd. dirs. Macon Council World Affairs, 1981-82; mem. Friends Emory Libraries, Atlanta, 1980—; mem. Friends Eckerd Coll. Library, St. Petersburg, Fla., 1980—. Mem. ABA, Am. Soc. Law and Medicine, Am. Judicature Soc., DAR (Kaskaski chpt.), Macon Mus. Arts and Scis., La Leche League (sec. 1985), Phi Alpha Delta. Republican. Presbyterian.

NEAL, DONNA JEANNE, marketing executive; b. Bridgeport, Conn., Dec. 5, 1953; d. Sydney James and Marion Jeanne (Moran) N. B.A. in Sociology, Middlebury Coll., 1975; M.B.A. in Mgmt. Sci., Pace U., 1983. Researcher Decision Research Corp., Lexington, Mass., 1975-76, field/coding dir./analyst, 1976-78, account exec., analyst, ops. dir., 1978-80; research analyst Gen. Foods Corp., White Plains, N.Y., 1980-81, research supr., 1982-84, category research mgr., 1984—. Mem. N.Y. Zool. Soc., 1981—, Mus. Natural History, N.Y.C., 1982—, Channel 13, N.Y.C., 1981—. Mem. NOW, Am. Mktg. Assn., Inst. Mgmt. Sci. Democrat. Avocations: bridge; swimming; harness race horses. Home: Box 74 North White Plains NY 10603 Office: Gen Foods Corp 250 North St NG-3 White Plains NY 10625

NEAL, KATHY, former city official; b. Los Angeles, Aug. 9, 1949; d. Elvin Vernon and Doris Eva (Golden) N.; m. Elihu M. Harris. student U. So. Calif., 1974-75; B.A., Calif. State U., Los Angeles, 1975; M.P.A., U. San Francisco, 1983; cert. in Spanish, U. Salamanca, 1967. Dir., Little Playmates Childrens Center, Los Angeles, 1971-74; legis. analyst Los Angeles City Council, 1975-84; mng. ptnr. 24K, 1984; fund raising cons.; dir. Builders Mut. Surety Co. Vice pres. bd. govs. Calif. Community Colls., also chmn. legis. and adminstrv. com., 1981—; mem. Calif. Democratic Central Com., 1979—; sponsor, adv. Black Womens Forum, 1979—; bd. dirs. Miss Watts Summer Pageant, 1976—, Westside Women's Clinic, 1985—; chmn. politics com. Coordinating com. Internat. Womens Yr. State Conf., 1977; asst. coordinator telethon United High Blood Pressure Found., 1978; co-founder, chmn. Black Edn. Network, 1985—; chmn. Speaker's Bur., Crenshaw-West Adams-Leimert Consortium, 1985—. Mem. Am. Soc. Public Adminstrs., Alpha Kappa Alpha. Office: 1208 1/2 Washington Blvd Venice CA 90291

NEAL, MARGARET (MRS. PETER S. PATRIQUIN), publishing company executive, editor; b. Springfield, Mass., Aug. 21, 1933; d. Robert Miller and Helen (Smith) N.; ed. Stephens Coll., U. Wis., U. Mo., Tulsa U.; Levintritt fellow in chamber music; student Yale U. Summer Music Sch.; children—Dorcas Alicia Neal, Judith Elaine, Keith Lowell Neal. Profl. musician, 1945-62; advt. copywriter, group head Grey Advt. Inc., 1962-66; freelance advt. copywriter, 1966—, freelance copy editor, 1966-73; asst. v.p. editorial bur. Bus. Practice div. Prentice-Hall, Waterford, Conn., 1973—; mng. editor Fair Employment Practices Guidelines, Exec. Action Series. Past pres. West River Village, Guilford, Conn., 1976-77; past mem. public relations com. Hammonasset Sch. Author: Management and the Metric System, 1975; Executives Desk Guide to Key Legal Problems, 1979, others. Home: 7 Mather Trail Old Lyme CT 06371 Office: 24 Rope Ferry Rd Waterford CT 06386

NEAL, MARTHA WINIFRED, college store administrator; b. San Antonio, June 23, 1938; d. Oscar Arnold and Martha Winifred (Hosack) Trevino; m. Dwight Calvin Neal, Nov. 23, 1956; children—Dwight Alan, Elizabeth Ann. Student Howard Payne Coll., 1956, San Antonio Coll., 1956, U. Mo.-Kansas City, 1975. Clerical worker Nat. Security Agy., Ft. Meade, Md., 1957-60; sec., biller, bookkeeper Armstrong Plumbing Suply Co., San Antonio, 1960-64; clerical worker Russell Stover Candies, Kansas City, Mo., 1964-66; supr. purchasing Nazarene Pub. House, Kansas City, 1966-78; bookstore mgr., dir. purchasing Point Loma Coll., San Diego, 1978—. Mem. Nat. Assn. Ednl. Buyers, Nat. Assn. Female Execs., Nat. Assn. Coll. Stores, So. Calif. Assn. Coll. Stores, Calif. Assn. Coll. Stores (chmn. 1978—, mem. panels for seminars), Point Loma Coll. Women's Aux. (staff rep.). Republican. Mem. Ch. of Nazarene. Avocations: swimming; Sunday sch. teaching; color consulting. Office: Point Loma Coll Bookstore 3900 Lomaland Dr San Diego CA 92106

NEASE, JUDITH ALLGOOD, marriage and family therapist; b. Arlington, Mass., Nov. 15, 1930; d. Dwight Maurice Allgood and Sophie (Wolf) Allgood Morris; student Rockford Coll., 1949-50; B.A., N.Y.U., 1953, M.A., 1954; M.S., Columbia U. Sch. Social Work, 1956; m. Theron Stanford Nease, Sept. 1, 1962; children—Susan Elizabeth, Alison Allgood. Social worker Bellevue Psychiat. Hosp., N.Y.C., 1956-59; psychiat. social worker St. Luke's Hosp., N.Y.C., 1959-62; asst. psychiat. social worker supr. N.J. Neuropsychiat. Inst., Princeton, 1962-64; marriage and family therapist Druid Hills Pastoral Counseling Service, Atlanta, 1973—, asst. dir. social work supr., co-leader group, 1973—; asst. dir., co-leader Pastoral Counseling Service, Columbia Theol. Sem., 1973—; marriage and family therapist Catholic Social Services, Atlanta, 1978—; pvt. practice marriage and family therapy. Mem. Nat. Assn. Social Workers, Acad. Cert. Social Workers, Am. Assn. Marriage and Family Therapy, Am. Group Psychotherapy Assn., Atlanta Group Psychotherapy Assn. Republican. Episcopalian. Home and Office: Cedar Park Way Stone Mountain GA 30083 Office: 680 W Peachtree St NW Atlanta GA 30308

NEASE, VIRGINIA LEE, social worker; b. Toronto, Ont., Can., May 5, 1939; d. Norman Miller and Willie Belle (Terry) Dunn; m. Corley Harrell Nease, Dec. 30, 1967; children—Michael Lovett, Paul Robert. B.A., Fla. State U., 1962; M.S.W., Tulane U., 1966. Social work aide ARC, Charleston, S.C., 1962-64; social work supr., Columbus, Ga., 1966-68; social work supr. Child Guidance Clinic, Savannah, Ga., 1968-71; social work supr. Community Mental Health Center, Savannah, 1971-74; service coordinator Tidelands Community Mental Health Center, Savannah, 1974—; family therapist pvt. practice Savannah, 1979—. Bd. dirs. Hospice, Savannah, 1980-84, sec., 1983-84. Scholarship in her name awarded by Nat. Assn. Social Workers, 1973—. Mem. Aux. Ga. Optometric Assn. (pres. 1972-73), Nat. Assn. Social Workers (pres. S.E. chpt. 1971), Nat. Assn. Social Workers, Acad. Cert. Social Workers. Episcopalian. Home: 4 Margrave Ln Savannah GA 31411 Office: 7203 Hodgson Meml Dr Savannah GA 31406

NEATHERY, ALICIA, sculptress; b. Bogotá, Columbia, Nov. 22, 1915; d. Ramon and Isabel (Reyes) Serrano; came to U.S., 1935, naturalized, 1939; ed. Academia de Bellas Artes, Argentina, 1950-52, Corcoran Sch. Art, Academie de Beaux Arts, Meuron, Switzerland, 1962-64; m. Jack B. Neathery, Apr. 24,

1935; 1 dau., Elizabeth. Owner, dir. Art Sch. and Atelier, Washington, 1956-58; tchr. sculpture and ceramics, Potomac/Darnestown, Md., 1969-70; founder, dir., restorer Centro Internat. de Cultura y Arte Spain, 1972-74; commd. work in sculpture, ceramics, potter's wheel, portraiture, Houston, 1974—; one woman shows: Smithsonian Instn., Washington, 1955, Gallery Chatel, Washington, 1958, Jung Center, Houston, 1976; group shows include: (Mus. Natural History, Washington, 1955-56, Balt. Mus., 1960-61, Mus. Art, Neuchatel, Switerland, 1963; represented in permanent collections: Smithsonian Instn., also pvt. collections; judge Internat. Biennial Exhibit Balt. Mus. Art, 1964, Am. Artists League, 1968. Club: Contemporary Art (Montgomery County, Tex.). Office: PO Box 553 Conroe TX 77301 Home: PO Box 1506 Kennebunkport ME 04046

NEBEL, SUSAN KERWIN, human resources coordinator; b. Jersey City, Dec. 22, 1947; d. Raymond Anthony and Marion R. (Keogh) Kerwin; m. Thomas J. Nebel, July 31, 1982. B.A. in Psychology, Fairleigh Dickinson U., 1973; postgrad. Sch. Bus. Seton Hall U., 1979-81. Personnel rep. Nabisco, Inc., East Hanover, N.J., 1977-79, employment adminstr., 1979-80, employment mgr., 1980-81, coordinator human resource planning programs, Parsippany, N.J., 1983—; staffing coordinator Nabisco Brands USA, East Hanover, 1982-83; dir. personnel Gen. Entertainment Corp., Pine Brooks, N.J., 1981-82. Bd. dirs. Morris County Hotline, Denville, N.J., 1982—. Mem. Employment Mgrs. Assn., Am. Soc. Personnel Adminstrs., Human Resource Planning Soc. Roman Catholic. Home: 28 Snyder Dr Wharton NJ 07885 Office: Nabisco Brands Inc Nabisco Brands Plaza Parsippany NJ 07054

NEBEN, MYRA EDELSTEIN, editor; b. Bklyn., July 23, 1940; d. Louis and Renee (Fine) Edelstein; m. Michael Daniel Neben, Sept. 10, 1960; children—Steven Samuel, Susan Cheryl. B.S.J., Ohio U., 1960. Copygirl Cleve. Press, 1960; reporter Peabody Times, (Mass.), 1968-69; news editor Bowie News (Md.), 1972-76; editor Leisure World News, Laguna Hills, Calif., 1977—. Mem. Women in Communications, Inc., Orange County Press Club (news story award 1979, headline award 1983), Md.-Del.-D.C. Press Assn (news story award 1975). Jewish. Home: 13 Elfin Irvine CA 92714 Office: Leisure World News PO Box 2068 Laguna Hills CA 92654

NEBIL, CORINNE ELIZABETH, artist; b. Varmland, Sweden, Apr. 30, 1918; came to U.S., 1920, naturalized, 1942; d. Eric and Elisabet (Tillstrom) Erickson; student NAD, 1954, Traphagen Sch. Fashion, 1955-56, Art Students League, N.Y.C., 1949-52, Whitney Sch. Art, 1948, U. Bridgeport, 1955; m. Roland Nebil; 1 dau., Ninette. Co-owner The Little Gallery, Bridgeport, Conn., 1954-60; art dir. Kid Stuff mag., 1964; free lance fashion illustrator, 1966-81; one-woman shows: Westport Country Playhouse, 1955, Chappalier Gallery, N.Y.C., 1958, Radio City Music Hall, N.Y.C., 1955, others; group shows: Art-U.S.A., Madison Sq. Garden, N.Y.C., 1948, Pastel Soc. Am., N.Y.C., 1982, Smithsonian Instn., Washington, 1965, Lincoln Ctr., Avery Fischer Hall, 1982, Swedish-Am. Artists travelling show, 1967, also others; represented in numerous pvt. collections; instr. art Famous Artists Schs. Internat., Westport, Conn., 1975-76, Central Fla. Jr. Coll., 1981—, Silvermine Sch. Art, Norwalk, Conn., 1980, Bridgeport Art League and Conn. Classic Arts Workshop, 1981-82. Recipient numerous awards, latest being best portrait award Conn. Show, 1982. Mem. Nat. League Am. Penwomen, Conn. Classic Arts, Pastel Soc. Am. Designer, painter ceiling mural St. Joseph's Ch., Bridgeport, Conn., 1958. Home: 853 NE 10th Ave Ocala FL 32670

NEDDE, JOYCE FERRIS, lawyer; b. Cin., May 7, 1937; d. Ladell H. and Ruth (Clark) Ferris; B.A., Northwestern U., 1958; postgrad. Harvard U. Law Sch., 1958-59; J.D., U. Louisville, 1961; m. Norman Robert Nedde, Aug. 26, 1961; children—Crystal, Susan-Marie. Admitted to Ky. bar, 1961, U.S. Supreme Ct. bar, 1966, Calif. bar, 1967; atty. Corps Engrs., Louisville, 1961-62; atty. Ky. Dept. Hwys., Frankfort, 1963-64; asst. atty. gen., Frankfort, 1964-66; dep. atty. gen., San Francisco, 1966-72; dep. dist. atty., Monterey County (Calif.), 1972-74, Santa Clara County (Calif.), San Jose, 1974—; prof. law Lincoln U., 1984—. Mem. Ky. Gov.'s Commn. on Status Women, 1965-66. Mem. Santa Clara County Bar Assn. (trustee), Santa Clara County Women Lawyers (pres. 1977), Queen's Bench (pres. 1971-72), AAUW, Zeta Tau Alpha. Home: 15996 Grandview Ave Monte Sereno CA 95030 Office: 70 W Hedding St Suite 5W San Jose CA 95110

NEE, LINDA ELIZABETH, social worker; b. Boston, Dec. 29, 1938; d. Thomas Markham and Ellen Thomas (Jamieson) Nee; B.A., Russell Sage Coll., 1961; M.S. in Social Work, Va. Commonwealth U., 1968. Social worker, social service dept., N.Y. Neurol. Inst., Columbia Presbyn. Med. Center, N.Y.C., 1961-66; med. social worker Tb San., Med. Coll. Va., Richmond, summer 1967; clin. social worker social work dept. Clin. Center, NIH, Bethesda, Md., 1968-74, clin. research social worker sect. exptl. therapeutics, lab. clin. sci., NIMH, Bethesda, 1974-84; clin. genetics research assoc. Nat. Inst. Neurol. and Communicative Disorders and Stroke, 1984—; mem. ethics com. Md. State Bd. Social Work Examiners, 1979—. Adv., organizer, bd. dirs. Met. D.C. chpt. Alzheimer's and Related Diseases Assn., 1979—, pres., 1982—. Mem. Nat. Assn. Social Workers (chmn. ethics and grievances 1977-79; pres. Met. Washington 1975-77). Editor: Jour. Social Work Met. Washington, 1975-77; columnist: The Bulletin newsletter Nat. Assn. Social Workers, 1975-77; contbr. articles to profl. jours. Office: Clin Center Nat Inst Neurol and Communicative Disorders and StrokeBethesda MD 20205

NEE, M. COLEMAN, college president; b. Taylor, Pa., Nov. 14, 1917; d. Coleman James and Nora Ann (Hopkins) N.; A.B., Marywood Coll., Scranton, Pa., 1939, M.A., 1943; M.S., U. Notre Dame, 1959; hon. degree, U. Scranton, 1983. Joined Sisters of Immaculate Heart of Mary, Roman Cath. Ch., 1941; high sch. tchr. Scranton Public Schs., 1939-41, Marywood Sem., Scranton, 1943-55; asso. prof. math. Marywood Coll., Scranton, 1959-68, pres., 1970—. Adv. bd. Scranton YWCA, 1978-85, Jr. League of Scranton, 1981—. Named Outstanding Pennsylvanian, 1980. Mem. Pa. Assn. Colls. and Univs. (exec. com.), Commn. Ind. Colls., Am. Assn. Colls., Nat. Assn. Ind. Colls., Assn. Cath. Colls., Scranton C. of C. (bd. dirs. 1981—, sec. bd., 1982—). Address: Marywood Coll Scranton PA 18509

NEEDELMAN, BARBARA, research health scientist; b. Phila., July 23, 1943; d. Alec and Margaret Grace (Pollina) N.; B.A., Beaver Coll., 1965; postgrad. Temple U., 1965-66. With dept. pediatrics Southwestern Med. Sch., Dallas, 1968-71; research technician dept. human genetics U. Pa., Phila., 1971-75; supervisory research health sci. specialist VA Hosp., Phila., 1975—; partner Danielle Hair & Makeup Salon, 1979—. Co-founder Women Organized Against Rape, mem. steering com., sec., 1972-75. Mem. Soc. Research Adminstrs. Home: 538 South St Philadelphia PA 19147 Office: 151E VA Hosp 39th and Woodland Ave Philadelphia PA 19104

NEEDLE, SUSAN JUDITH, business executive; b. Newark, June 18, 1941; d. Joseph J. and Betty (Levinson) N.; m. Robert J. Henderson. B.Ed., U. Miami (Fla.), 1962; M.A. in Human Resources and Psychology, U. Houston, 1980. Tchr. public schs., Fla., 1963-72, Houston, 1973-77; part-time profl. model, 1974-79; sales mgr. ADF Services, Houston, 1975-80; event mgr. Summit Arena, Houston, 1980-83; pres. Colorific, Inc., Houston, 1976—, Can. Am. Energy Corp., 1983—; assoc. prof. Coll. of Mainland, Dickinson, Tex., 1984—; v.p., sec. Total H.E.L.P., Inc., Houston, 1984—; fashion and beauty editor Clear Lake Voice. Named Outstanding Educator in Fla., 1968. Mem. Nat. Assn. Female Execs. (dir.), Exec. Link, Am. Inst. Esthetics, Hotel Sales Mgmt. Assn., Performax, Am. Bus. Women's Assn. (ways and means, hospitality chmn., pres. 1984-85, v.p. 1985-86), Profl. Image Cons. Assn. Internat., Nat. Fashion and Image Cons. Assn. (pres. Bay Area chpt.), Profl. Speakers Internat., Internat. Platform Assn., Assn. Bus. and Profl. Women, Alpha Epsilon Phi, Alpha Kappa Alpha. Democrat. Jewish. Address: 15302 Pleasant Valley Rd Houston TX 77062

NEEL, PEGGY SUE association executive, consultant; b. Kingston, Okla., Dec. 2, 1934; d. Grover Cleveland and Lorene (Findley) Lasiter; m. Johnny J. Easley, Jan. 4, 1954 (div. 1968); 1 child, Kathryn Sue. Student Murry Jr. Coll., 1953-54. Clk.-typist Tinker AFB, Oklahoma City, 1954-60, procurement clk., 1961-63, personnel clk., sec., 1964-69; exec. sec. Larry Jones Evangelical Assn., Oklahoma City, 1970-75; bookkeeper, sec., procurement clk. Ch. of New Life, Oklahoma City, 1976-78; bookkeeper, exec. sec. legal spl. asst. to pres. and adminstrv. v.p. for Larry Jones Internat. Ministeries, Oklahoma City, 1979—; v.p. counseling Women's Aglow, State of Okla., 1976-78, v.p. adminstrn., 1978-80. Author: How To Pray According to God's Will, 1982. Active Chickasaw Indian Tribe. Avocations: oil painting; studying history of American Indians. Home: 507 SW 55th St Oklahoma City OK 73109

NEEL, ALICE, painter; b. Merion Square, Pa., Jan. 28, 1900. Student Phila. Sch. Design for Women, 1921-25; Doctorate (hon.), Moore Coll. Art, 1971. Group shows include: Retrospectives Moore Coll. Art, 1971, Whitney Mus. Art, 1974, 77, 80, 82, Pa. Acad. Fine Arts, 1980, 81, Newport Harbor Art Mus., Newport Beach, Calif., 1981-82, Hirshhorn Mus., Washington, 1982, Met. Mus. N.Y., 1982, Robert Miller Gallery, 1982, Eleanor Ettinger, Inc., N.Y., 1982, Vanderwoude Tananbaum Gallery, 1982; represented in permanent collections Met. Mus. Art, Mus. Modern Art, Whitney Mus. Am. Art, Hirshhorn Mus., Am. Mus. Moscow, others; easel painter Fed. Works Agy., 1933-43; lectr. painting seminar U. Pa. Grad. Sch., 1971-72; lectr. Skowhegan Sch. Painting and Sculpture, summer 1972. Recipient Longview Found. award, 1962; Am. Acad. Arts and Letters award, 1969; Benjamin Altman Figure prize N.A.D., 1971. Mem. Artists Equity Assn. Address: 300 W 107th St Apt 3A New York NY 10025

NEEL, JUDY MURPHY, association executive; b. Rhome, Tex., Sept. 16, 1926; d. James W. and Linna B. (Vess) Neel; m. George E. Tashjian, Dec. 15, 1946 (div.); children—Mary B. Tashjian Schmidt, Janet E. Tashjian Wescott, Susan E. Tashjian Salinas; m. 2d, Ellis F. Murphy, Jr., Dec. 30, 1975. B.S., Northwestern U.-Chgo., 1976; M.B.A., Roosevelt U., 1983. Cert. assn. exec. Vice-pres. Murphy, Tashjian & Assocs., Chgo., 1960-73; exec. dir. Automotive Affiliated Rep. Assn., Chgo., 1973-78; mgr. Automotive Service Ind. Assn., Chgo., 1978-80; exec. dir. Am. Soc. Safety Engrs., Park Ridge, Ill., 1980—. Mem. Chgo. Soc. Assn. Execs. (dir. 1979—, pres. 1985—), Am. Soc. Assn. Execs. (Key award 1986), Council Engring. and Sci. Socs., AAAS. Republican. Office: Am Soc Safety Engrs 850 Busse Hwy Park Ridge IL 60068

NEELEY, KATHLEEN MARJORIE, training consultant; b. Jacksonville, Fla., Dec. 22, 1946; d. Grady Hardin and Marjorie (Brooke) Neeley. B.A. in Modern Langs., U. S.C., 1969, postgrad., 1972-75. Tchr. Sumter Area Schs., Dalzell, S.C., 1969-70; counselor Newberry Tng. Program, Newberry, S.C., 1970-71; counselor coordinator tng. programs City of Columbia (S.C.), 1971-76; comprehensive employment tng. program dir. Midland Tech. Coll., Columbia, 1976-77; area coordinator Manpower Services, State Bd. Tech. and Comprehensive Edn., Columbia, 1977-83, tng. cons. Indsl. and Econ. Devel. Div., 1983—. Named Woman of Yr., Am. Bus. Women, Columbia, S.C., 1976. Mem. S.C. Indsl. Developers Assn., Nat. Female Execs. Assn., Nat. Employment and Tng. Assn., S.C. Tech. Edn. Assn., Carolina Soc. Tng. and Devel., Am. Bus. Women's Assn., Sigma Delta Chi. Democrat. Methodist. Office: SC State Bd for Tech and Comprehensive Edn 111 Executive Center Dr Columbia SC 29210

NEELY, WENDY ELIZABETH, insurance company executive; b. Denver, Dec. 13, 1936; d. Lewis James and Thelma Ruth (Howard) Hanscom; m. Patrick Ranse Neely, June 25, 1955; children—Gregory, Steven, Douglas. A.A., Fullerton Coll., 1978. Lic. fire and casualty ins. agt., Calif. Office mgr. Coll. Protection Ins., Anaheim, Calif., 1978-80; field rep. Balboa Ins., subs. Avco, Irvine, Calif., 1980-84, supr. customer service, 1984-85, mgr. customer service, 1985—. Sec. Orange Sister City Assn., Calif., 1982-85, pres., 1986; sec. So. Calif. chpt. Sister City Internat., 1986. Mem. Nat. Assn. Female Execs. Republican. Avocations: gardening; reading. Home: 4329 Addington Dr Anaheim CA 92807 Office: Balboa Ins 17770 Cartwright Rd 2 Irvine CA 92714

NEESA, FAE SWEET, writer; b. Chgo., July 10, 1948; d. Jason J. and Ione D. Sweet. B.A., U. Ill., 1969. Mem. staff HUD, 1969-71; profl. polit. work, 1971-74; tchr. YMCA, 1974-75; writer, communications work Delta Sky Crains Chgo. Bus., Chgo. Sun Times, Chgo. Tribune, also numerous corps. including U.S. Gypsum, Borg Warner, Allstate, Macarthur Found. Recipient award Internat. Assn. Bus. Communicators. Mem. Am. Soc. Journalists and Authors, Ind. Writers Chgo., Am. Soc. Cybernetics, Assn. for Multi Image (bronze award). Club: Chgo. Press. Office: 1931 N Lincoln Park W Chicago IL 60614*

NEESE, GERTRUDE ELIZABETH FLESH KENNEDY, realty co. exec.; b. N.Y.C., Mar. 9, 1925; d. Bernard William and Dorothy Katherine (Reimund) Flesh; B.A., U. Havana (Cuba), 1944; m. Alonzo Aldrich Neese, Nov. 10, 1978 (dec. Aug. 1981); children—Christopher H. Bohner, Stephen Edward Bohner, Karen Bohner Hyden. Stewardess-purser Pan Am. World Airways, 1945-47; pvt. investments, Rio de Janeiro, Brazil, Coral Gables, Fla. and N.Y.C., 1947-57; pres. Lockhart Realty, Inc., Sewall's Point, Stuart, Fla., 1957—, also dir.; pres., dir. Sewall's Point Estates, Inc., Stuart, Lockhart Sales, Inc., Stuart, Lockhart Devel., Inc., Sewall's Point, Neese Land Co.; v.p., dir. Dunes Club, Hutchinson Island, Stuart, Fla., chmn. Sewall's Point Code Enforcement Bd. Pres. United Fund of Sewall's Point, 1958-70, bd. dirs., 1958—; trustee Martin County (Fla.) Library, Martin County Hist. Soc.; bd. dirs. Am. Cancer Soc. Mem. Nat. Inst. Real Estate Brokers, Am. Inst. Real Estate Appraisers, NAREB, World Wings Internat., Fla. Assn. Realtors. Clubs: Sailfish Point, Yacht and Country (dir.) (Stuart); Sakonnet Golf (Little Compton, R.I.). Home and Office: 2 N Sewall's Point Rd Stuart FL 33494

NEESE, SANDRA ANNE, lawyer; b. Lapel, Ind., Apr. 8, 1936; d. Oral Manfred and Alma Mae (Meeker) Neese. A.B., Ind. U., 1958, J.D., 1961. Bar: Ind. 1961, U.S. Dist. Ct. (so. dist.) Ind. 1961. Dep. atty. gen. State of Ind., Indpls., 1961-63; vol. atty. U.S. Peace Corps, Liberia, 1963-65; field rep., then dir. compliance, acting asst. dir. Mo. Commn. on Human Rights, Jefferson City, 1965-70; regional counsel EEOC, Kansas City, Mo., 1970-72, sr. trial atty., Chgo., 1973-74, supervisory trial atty., 1974-79, regional atty., Milw., 1979—. Mem. ACLU, Milw., 1979; mem. Amnesty Internat., 1981. Recipient Freedom Fund award NAACP, Jefferson City, 1970. Mem. Ind. State Bar Assn., ABA, Fed. Bar Assn., Am. Judicature Soc., Ind. U. Alumni Assn., Wis. Assn. Women Lawyers. Methodist.

NEFF, FRANCINE IRVING, corporate director, former U.S. treasurer; b. Albuquerque, Dec. 6, 1925; d. Edward Hackett and Georga (Henderson) Irving; B.A., U. N.Mex., 1948; D.H.L. (hon.), Mt. St. Mary's Coll., Newburgh, N.Y., 1974; LL.D. (hon.), Am. Internat. Coll., Springfield, Mass., 1975, N.Mex. State U., Las Cruces, 1976; m. Edward John Neff, June 7, 1948; children—Sindle Neff Tomforde, Edward Vann. Thirty Fifth Treas. of U.S. Treasury Dept., 1974-77, also nat. dir. U.S. Savs. Bonds div., 1974-77; v.p. Rio Grande Valley Bank, Albuquerque, 1977-82; dir. Hershey Foods Corp., 1978—, E-Systems, Inc., Dallas, 1978—, La. Pacific Corp., 1984—. Active Republican Party, 1966—; pres. Albuquerque Rep. Federated Women's Club, 1977, Rep. Women's Fed. Forum, 1975; chmn. N.Mex. Women for Nixon Campaign Com., 1968; del. Rep. Nat. Conv., 1968, 72; mem. exec. com. Rep. Nat. Com., 1972-74, nat. committeewoman for N.Mex., 1970-74. Mem. nat. bd. Camp Fire Girls, 1976-78; campaign chmn. profl. div. United Way Greater Albuquerque, 1977, bd. dirs., 1977-79; bd. advs. Lovelace Med. Center, 1979-82; mem. Def. Adv. Com., Women in the Services, 1981-84; trustees Cottey Coll., 1982—; bd. dirs. Horatio Alger Assn. Disting. Ams., 1981-84. Recipient Disting. Alumnae citation Cottey Coll., Nevada, Mo., 1975, Horatio Alger award Am. Schs. and Colls. Assn., 1976, Exceptional Service award Treasury Dept., 1976. Mem. Am. Bankers Assn. (banking adv. 1979-81), PEO (past chpt. pres.), Mortar Board Alumnae (past chpt. pres.), Phi Theta Kappa (Outstanding Nat. Alumni award 1976), Alpha Delta Pi (chpt. Outstanding Alumna award nat. chpt. 1975, past chpt. pres.), Sigma Alpha Iota, Pi Lambda Theta. Episcopalian.

NEGLEY, JULIE CARITHERS, museum director; b. Atlanta, May 18, 1960; d. Edward Ernest and Mary Howard (Watkins) Carithers; B.A., Agnes Scott Coll., 1982; m. Joseph Leslie Negley, Aug. 22, 1981. Research intern Atlanta Hist. Soc., summer 1980, research asst., 1980; archtl. survey project assoc. Atlanta Preservation Center, Atlanta Urban Design Commn., 1981; research cons. Soil Systems, Inc., Marietta, Ga., 1981; rare books asst. U. Ga. Libraries, Athens, 1981-82; mus. dir. Washington-Wilkes Hist. Mus., Washington, Ga., 1982-83; slide librarian High Mus. Art, Atlanta, 1983-84; dir. Roswell Hist. Preservation Commn. (Ga.), 1984—. Mem. Atlanta Hist. Soc., Ga. Trust for Historic Preservation, Madison-Morgan Cultural Ctr., Roswell Hist. Soc., Washington-Wilkes Hist. Found., Agnes Scott Coll. Alumni Assn. Presbyterian. Home: 4894 Hawk Trail Marietta GA 30066 Office: Roswell Hist Preservation Commn 180 Bulloch Ave Roswell GA 30075

NEGLEY, SHIRLEY ANNE, nursing educator; b. Pitts., May 4, 1937; d. Ronald Dickson and Helen (King) N.; B.S.N., U. Pitts., 1960, M.N.Ed., 1966. Staff nurse Allegheny Gen. Hosp., Pitts., 1960, head nurse, 1960-61, mem. faculty Sch. Nursing, 1961-64; instr. obstetric nursing Pa. State U. Sch. Nursing, Pitts., 1966-67; mem. faculty U. Pitts. Sch. Nursing, 1967—, assoc. prof., program dir. family nurse practitioner, 1979—; cons. Pa. Bd. Nurse Examiners, 1981—. Mem. Am. Nurses Assn., Sigma Theta Tau. Home: 216 O'Hara Woods Pittsburgh PA 15238 Office: 426 Victoria Hall Pittsburgh PA 15261

NEIDIGK, DIANNE, image consultant; b. Monette, Ark., June 28, 1945; d. William Thomas and Thelma Elizabeth (Wells) Wilkerson; m. Lester Dale Neidigk, Feb. 28, 1964; children—Tami Elizabeth, Scott Alan, Lance Dale, Byron Ross. Student, Sam Houston State U., 1963-65, U. Houston, 1969-70. Sub. tchr. Tomball Ind. Sch. Dist., Tex., 1970-74; owner Total Image & Assocs., Houston, 1980—; dir. Colorific, Houston, 1983-85; v.p. L.D. Neidigk Inc., Magnolia, 1978—. Author: (newspaper) Total Image, 1984; (home study course) Total Image, 1986. Mem. Nat. Speakers Assn., Nat. Assn. Female Execs., Exec. Women's Network, Houston Speaker Assn., Tomball Bus. and Profl. Women, Beta Sigma Phi. Republican. Club: Study (Tomball). Avocations: private pilot; tennis; sewing; reading. Home: 1543 Virgie Magnolia TX 77355 Office: Total Image & Assocs 28105 Tomball Pkwy Tomball TX 77375

NEIHART, CARLENE ROSE, organist, choral director; b. Girard, Kans., Nov. 11, 1929; s. William Earl and Florene Ella (Morrison) Schifferdecker; m. James Leroy Neihart, 1950; children—Robert Earl, David James, Carl William. B.A. in Music, Pittsburg State U., 1950; M.A. in Music, Kans. U., 1955, postgrad., 1955-65. Mem. faculty Park Coll., Parkville, Mo., U. Mo., Kansas City; organist St. Paul's Episcopal Ch., Kansas City, Kans., 1955-59, St. Andrew's Episcopal Ch., Kansas City, Mo., 1959-76; artist in residence Mid America Nazarene Coll., Olathe, Kans., 1978—; organist, dir. music New Reform Temple, Kansas City, Mo., 1980—, Central Presbyterian Ch., Kansas City, 1976—; presenter of approximately 20 concerts each year on the pipe organ for universities, Am. Guild of Organists chapters, and for dedication of new church organs; presenter of workshops on playing and teaching the pipe organ. NEA grantee 1984. Represented the U.S. in 1982 by appearing in 9 concerts throughout Netherlands in celebration and recognition of 200 years of Dutch-U.S. Relationships; selected by NEA to give organ recitals in the Arts Am. program overseas, 1982. Mem. Am. Guild Organists (Mo. chmn. 1976-84, performer nat. and regional convs.).

NEIL, JESSIE PRUITT, civic worker; b. Pasadena, Calif., Oct 20, 1927; d. Cecil D. and Jessie (Parsons) Pruitt; B.A., U. So. Calif., 1950; m. Edmund R. Neil, Mar. 24, 1956; children—Edmund R. II, Jessica R., Richard William. Dir. design Leland Gardens Bldg. Corp., 1950-56; sales dir. Washington Sq. Bldg. Corp., 1950-1952; pres. Barrett Devel. Corp., 1951-72; sec. Reliance Bldg. Corp., 1951-68; self-employed home designer, 1953; sec., v.p. So. Counties Escrow, 1956-86, mgn. dir. Desert & Delta Safaris (Pty) Lit., 1980-86; pres. Futuramic Homes, Inc., 1956-68. Founder Cardiac League Guild of Huntington Meml. Hosp., 1963, pres., 1966, 67, pres. Women's Council, 1967; v.p. San Marino League, 1968-72; v.p. docent council Pasadena Mus. Modern Art, 1969, pres. docent council, 1971-72, mem. membership council, ex-officio trustee, 1971-72; mem. Assistance League. Asso. U. So. Calif.; mem. women's council KCET/28; patron Pasadena Art. Mus.; hon. life mem. Arcadia Meth. Hosp.; mem. costume council Los Angeles County Mus.; founder Los Angeles Music Center, also mem. blue ribbon 400. Recipient graphics award Pasadena Arts Council, 1968. Mem. Docent League So. Calif., Nine O'Clock Players, AIM (asso.), Opera Assos. of Met. Opera, World Affairs Council, Internat. Platform Assn. Delta Zeta. Home: 301 Hermosa St South Pasadena CA 91030

NEILL, JANE RUTH MIES, telecommunications executive; b. Milw., July 31, 1950; d. Edmund and Ruth Margaret (Dominik) Mies; m. Thomas Edward Neill, Aug. 31, 1985. Student U. Wis.-Milw., 1968-69; A.A., Concordia Coll., Milw., 1971. With Spheeris Mdse. Corp., Milw., 1965-71; bus. rep. Wis. Bell, Inc., Milw., 1971-76, bus. office supr., 1976-81, cutover coordinator, 1981-84, asst. staff mgr. corp. mechanization, 1984—. Writer profl. manuals, ch. programs and presentations. Counselor, Brookfield Lutheran Ch., Wis., 1976-84; mem. Nat. Republican Presdl. Task Force, Washington, 1982-83. Recipient Key Player award Wis. Bell and Ameritech, 1982, Outstanding Performance award Wis. Bell, 1983. Mem. Telecommunications Mgrs. Orgn., Ameritech Regional Mechanized User Groups, Telephone Pioneers, Smithsonian Assocs. Avocations: sailing, biking, tennis, reading, traveling.

NEILL, LAQUITA JOYCE BELL, media educator, home economist, librarian; b. Humphreys County, Miss., Aug. 10, 1930; d. Clarence Marvin and Dorothy (Parker) Bell; m. Robert Wood Neill, Apr. 29, 1956; 1 child, Robert Wood, Jr. B.S. in Home Econs., Delta State U., Cleve., 1952, M.L.S., 1977. Asst. home economist Panola County, Miss. Cooperative Extension Service, Batesville, 1952-54, home economist Carroll County, Carrollton, Miss., 1954-57; bookkeeper, teller Peoples Bank & Trust Co., North Carrollton, 1959-61; instr. home econs. Leflore County, Greenwood, Miss., 1961-62, Carroll County, Carrollton, 1962-77; media dir. Leflore County High Sch., Itta Bena, Miss., 1977-78, Winona Elem. Sch., Miss., 1978-79, J.Z. George Sch., North Carrollton, 1979—; ptnr. Bell Farms, Tchula and Belzoni, Miss.; dir. Neill Forest Products, Inc., Carrollton, Neill Realty, Inc., Carrollton. Trustee, mem. adminstrv. bd. Carrollton United Methodist Ch. Named Regional Star Tchr. Miss. Econ. Council, 1973. Mem. Miss. Library Assn., Miss. Assn. Media Educators, ALA, Miss. Archeol. Assn. (Cottanlandia chpt.), Miss. Assn. Educators, NEA, Delta State Univ. Alumni Assn., UDC (The H. D. Money chpt.), Carroll Soc. for Preservation of Antiquites, Internat. Bell Soc. (bd. govs.), Clan Bell Descendants, Council of Scottish Clan Assns., Zeta State (Alpha Phi chpt.), Delta Kappa Gamma. Club: Cherokee Rose Garden. Home: 204 Washington St Carrollton MS 38917 Office: PO Box 264 Carrollton MS 38917

NEISSER, INGRID, insurance broker; b. Essen, Fed. Republic Germany, Nov. 24, 1953; came to U.S., 1956; d. Helmut Kurt and Rose (Titus) N.; m. Frank J. Pignataro, Feb. 3, 1980; stepchildren—Frank Jr., Robert J., Suzanne G. B.A. in Math., Upsala Coll., 1975. C.L.U. Math. tchr. Clifford Scott High Sch., East Orange, N.J., 1975; adminstrv. asst. W.S. Vogel Agy., East Orange, 1975-77, brokerage mgr., 1977-83; owner, pres. Brokers Services, Inc., N.Y.C., 1983—. Named Prodn. Leader, Columbian Mut. Life Ins. Co., Binghamton, N.Y., 1981, 82, 84. Mem. N.Y. City Life Underwriters, Am. Soc. C.L.U.s. Episcopalian. Avocations: sailing, travel, gardening. Home: 26 Tatum Dr Middletown NJ 07748 Office: Brokers Services Inc 420 Lexington Ave New York NY 10170

NELKIN, DOROTHY, sociologist, educator; b. Boston, July 30, 1933; A.B. in Philosophy, Cornell U., 1954; m. Mark S. Nelkin. Research assoc. Sch. Indsl. and Labor Relations, 1963-69, sr. research assoc. program on sci., tech., society, 1970-72, assoc. prof. program on sci., tech., society and dept. of city and regional planning, 1973-76, prof. sociology, 1977—, also grad. fields of planning, pub. policy, sociology; vis. assoc. in polit. sci. M.I.T., 1975-76; maitre de conference associé U. Paris XII, 1975-76; vis. assoc. resources for future, Washington; maitre de recherche Ecole Polytechnique, Paris, 1980-81; vis. scholar Russell Sage Found., 1983-84; cons. OECD, Paris, 1973-74, 75-76, Ednl. Devel. Center, Cambridge, Mass., 1973-74, Einstein-Montefiore Med. Center, Bronx, 1974-75, Inst. for Environ., Berlin, 1978-79, Pub. TV Sta. KCTS, 1981, ACLU, 1981; panel mem. Nat. Acad. Scis., 1976-78, del. to Internat. Union of History of Philosophy of Sci., 1977. Grantee NSF, 1971-73, 75-77, 76-78, 79-80, German Marshall Fund, 1978-80; Guggenheim fellow, 1984. Fellow Hastings Inst. of Soc., Ethics and Life Scis.; mem. AAAS (dir. 1983—), Internat. Council for Sci. Policy Studies (conf. organizer, 1978), Soc. for History of Tech. (adv. council 1977-81), Soc. for Social Studies of Sci. (exec. council 1976-78, pres. 1978-79), Nat. Council on Health Tech., Medicine in Pub. Interest (dir. 1980—), Council for Advancement of Sci. Writers (dir. 1980—). Author: On the Season: Aspects of the Migrant Labor System, 1970; (with William H. Friedland) Migrant: Farm Workers in America's Northwest, 1971; Nuclear Power and its Critics, The Cayuga Lake Controversy, 1971; The Politics of Housing Innovation: The Fate of the Civilian Industrial Technology Program, 1971; The University and Military Research: Moral Politics at M.I.T., 1972; Methadone Maintenance—A Technological Fix, 1973; Jetport: The Boston Airport Controversy, 1975; Science Textbook Controversies: The Politics of Equal Time, 1977; Technological Decisions and Democracy: European Experiments in Public Participation, 1977; Controversy: Politics of Technical Decisions, 1979; The Atom Besieged: Extra-Parliamentary Dissent in France and Germany, 1981; The Creation Controversy, 1982; Workers at Risk, 1984; Science as Intellectual Property, 1984; contbr. articles, book revs. to profl. publs.; editorial advisor to Social Studies of Sci., 1974—; mem. adv. bds. Sci., Tech. and Human Values, 1976—, Chgo. U. Press book series Science and Its Conceptual Foundations, 1980—; mem. adv. bd. of editors Zeit-schrift für umwelt politik, 1978; mem. editorial bds. Knowledge: Creation, Diffusion Utilization, 1978—, contbr. invited papers to profl. confs. U.S., Can., France,

Scotland, Germany, Yugoslavia, Netherlands, Sweden, Norway. Home: 119 Heights Ct Ithaca NY 14850 Office: 632 Clark Hall Cornell Univ Ithaca NY 14853

NELLI, ELIZABETH ROLFE, univ. dean; b. Toronto, Ont., Can., Feb. 14, 1935; came to U.S., 1956; d. George Millar and Anne Noela (Seaborne) Thomson; B.A., U. Chgo., 1959; M.A., U. Ky., 1974, Ed.D., 1980; m. Bert S. Nelli, Dec. 28, 1961; children—Steven, Christopher, William. Elem. sch. tchr., Toronto, 1955-56, Chgo., 1956-59, Vancouver, B.C., Can., 1959-61; nursery sch. tchr. U. Chgo., 1964-65; kindergarten tchr. Inner City Vol. Programs, Lexington, Ky., 1969-72; research asst./asso. U. Ky., Lexington, 1974-79, asst. to dean, 1979-80, asst. dean Coll. Edn., 1980-84; asst. dir. tchr. edn. and Cert. Ky. Dept. Edn., 1984—; mem. nat. accreditation teams Nat. Council for Accreditation Tchr. Edn., 1980—. Bd. dirs. Ky. Citizens for Child Devel., 1980—. Mem. Assn. Supervision and Curriculum Devel., Assn. Tchr. Educators, Daycare and Child Devel. Council Am., Nat. Assn. Edn. Young Children, Bluegrass Assn. Children under Six, Ky. Citizens for Child Devel., Women's Neighborly Orgn., Phi Delta Kappa. Author: (with Dan Arnold, George Denemark, Andrew Robinson and Edgar Sagan) Quality Control in Teacher Education: Some Policy Issues, 1977; (with G. Denemark) Emerging Patterns of Initial Preparation for Teachers Generic Teaching, 1980; Program Redesign in Teacher Preparation, 1981; Five Myths in Need of Reality, 1981; A Model for Evaluating Teacher Education PRograms, 1984; and other works. Office: Div Tchr Edn and Cert Ky Dept Edn Frankfort KY 40601

NELLIS, MURIEL GOLLON, literary agent, author; b. N.Y.C., Sept. 13, 1931; d. Abraham and Sara (Fried) Gollon; m. Joseph Leon Nellis, Dec. 12, 1964; children—Barbara, David M.; m. Howard S. Pressman, 1950 (div. 1962); children—Adam J., Amy E. Student New Sch. Social Research 1947, Hofstra U., 1948. Continuity dir. WLNA Radio, Peekskill, N.Y., 1949-50; traffic mgr. WGNR Radio, New Rochelle, N.Y., 1950; women's continuity dir. WIP Radio, Phila., 1955-56; traffic/sales dir. WDAS Radio, Phila., 1956-57; pres., pub. Murette/M&N Publishers, Chester, Pa. and N.Y.C., 1960-65; pres., chief exec. officer NRCA Inc., Washington, 1972—; prin. Lit./Creative Artist Agy., Washington, 1982—; author: The Female Fix, 1980; pub., mng. editor Lady's Circle mag., 1963-65; editor, writer Drug Abuse Education, 1972. Contbr. articles to Harper's Bazaar mag., Ms. mag. Bd. dirs. LWV, Washington, 1967; mem. Task Force Drug Abuse in Schs., Washington, 1973; cons. Gov.'s Com. on Substance Abuse, Honolulu, 1977, Senate and Ho. of Reps. coms. on heath and crime, 1974-76. nat. dir. Alliance Regional Coalitions, 1976-78; mem. panel Presdl. Commn. on Mental Health, 1978; designer, mgr. Internat. Conf. Drugs, Alcohol, Womens Health, Washington,/Fla., 1975; cons., editor NIMH, 1972; juror book awards Am. Psychol. Assn., 1981—. Mem. ABA (assoc.), Am. Pub. Health Assn. Lodge: Hadassah (life). Home: 3539 Albemarle St NW Washington DC 20008

NELSCH, CAROLYN DIANE, graphic designer, advertising account executive; B. Oklahoma City, Aug. 1, 1951; d. Raul and Carmen (Diaz) Munoz; children—Laura, Ryan; m. William D. Nelsch, Oct. 8, 1983. B.A. in Art, Central State U., 1972. Layout artist TG&Y, Oklahoma City, 1971-73; typesetter, artist Multicopy Printing, Mount Clemens, Mich., 1973-76; prodn. artist, freelance Industry Media, Denver, 1976-79; art dir. Denver Ctr. for Performing Arts, 1979-81; tech. illustrator Martin Marietta, Littleton, Colo., 1981-82; mgr. Gen. Communications, Denver, 1982-83; art dir. Denver mag., Vail Scene, DSI, Denver Bus. World, Denver, 1982-83; pres. C.Designs, Inc., Denver, 1983—; cons. Stevens Elem., Denver, 1984—, St. John's Episcopal Ch., Denver, 1983—. Vice pres. Women of St. John's, Denver, 1985—. Mem. Denver Advt. Fedn. Avocations: cross country skiing; horseback riding Home: 1254 St Paul Denver CO 80206

NELSEN, BETTY JO, state legislator; b. Boston, Oct. 11, 1935; B.S., Mass. State Coll., 1957; married; 3 children. Mem. Wis. Ho. of Reps., 1979—. Mem. Citizens' Govtl. Research Bur.; former pres. Jr. League Milw.; bd. dirs. Milw. Mgmt. Support Orgn.; mem. North Shore Republican Club; trustee Shorewood Civic Improvement Found.; bd. dirs. United Way of Greater Milw.; mem. Goals for Milw. 2000. Office: Wis Ho of Reps Room 310 W State Capitol Madison WI 53702*

NELSON, AMERICA ELIZABETH, pediatrician; b. Chgo., Apr. 9, 1932; d. Lorenzo Raymond and Blanche Juanita (Crawford) Nelson; A.B. in English, U. Mich., Ann Arbor, 1952, M.S. in Zoology, 1954; postgrad. Tenn. State U., 1952-53, U. Chgo., 1955-56; M.D., Howard U., 1961; M.P.H., U. Ill., 1973. Intern, Hahnemann Med. Sch. and Hosps., Phila., 1961-62; resident pediatrics Michael Reese Hosp., Chgo., 1962-63, U. Mich., Ann Arbor, 1964; practice medicine specializing in pediatric cardiology, Detroit, 1963; with father, practice medicine specializing in pediatrics, Baldwin, Mich., 1964-71, 75—; pediatrician Tice Clinic, U. Ill., Cook County Hosp., 1965, 66; pediatrician Mile's Sq. Health Center, Chgo., 1967; pediatrician Infant Welfare Soc., Chgo., 1968; cons. pediatrician, child devel. Kalamazoo Child Guidance Clinic, 1969-70, coordinator drug abuse program, 1969-70; med. dir. Chgo. Residential Manpower Center, 1971-72; pediatrician, child devel. Dyslexia Meml. Inst., Chgo., 1972—; founder, project dir., med. dir. Deerwood Developmental Ctr. Inc., Cherry Valley Twp., Lake County, Mich., 1981-84; lectr. U. Ill. at Chgo. Circle, 1972-73; clin. instr. U. Ill.-Presbyn.-St. Luke's Hosp., 1965-73; asst. prof. Mental Retardation Inst., N.Y. Med. Coll., 1974; cons. in field. Mem. AAAS, Pi Lambda Theta. Contbr. articles to profl. jours. Home: PO Box 760 Baldwin MI 49304

NELSON, AUDREY ELAINE, nurse educator; b. York, Nebr., Jan. 7, 1949; d. Milton Lars and Audrey Elizabeth (Watson) Nelson. Student U. Nebr., 1967-69; B.S. in Nursing, U. Nebr. Med. Center-Omaha, 1972; M.S. in Nursing, U. Wis., 1974. Registered nurse; CPR cert. Staff nurse York Gen. Hosp., 1972-73; asst. prof. nursing U. Nebr. Coll. Nursing, Omaha, 1974-78, second yr. coordinator, 1978-80, asst. prof., 1980—; part time staff nurse U. Nebr. Hosp., Omaha, 1979—; cons. Community Coll., Wichita, Kans., 1979, others; speaker in field. Mem. ARC, 1972; active York County (Nebr.) 4-H Clubs, 1955-67. March of Dimes Scholar, 1970-72; partipant Maternal-Child Health Service Project U. Wis., 1972-74. Mem. Am. Nurses Assn., Nebr. Nurses Assn. (cabinet mem. nursing practice 1984—, spl. recognition awards 1980, 84, other awards), Nebr. Nurses Assn. Dist. II (pres. 1982-84, profl. achievement award 1981), Nat. League of Nursing, U. Wis. Sch. Nursing Alumni Assn., U. Nebr. Coll. Nursing Alumni Assn. (life), Sigma Theta Tau (charter mem. chpt.), Phi Delta Gamma (pres. chpt. 1984; nat. conv. chmn. 1982, nat. dir. fin. 1984-86), Phi Delta Kappa. Democrat. Lutheran. Club: U. Nebr. Faculty Women's. Office: U Nebr Coll Nursing 4111 Dewey Ave Omaha NE 68105

NELSON, BARBARA ANN BOLTON, organization executive; b. Olean, N.Y., Mar. 2, 1935; d. Carl Newton and Evelyn Marguerite (Eliason) Bolton; R.N., Millard Fillmore Sch. Nursing, 1956; m. Ross W. Nelson, Aug. 5, 1961 (dec.); children—Kimberly, Karl, Kerri. Operating room nurse Millard Fillmore Hosp., 1956-59; emergency room nurse Bradford Hosp., 1959-63; pediatric office nurse, Canandaigua, N.Y., 1964-68; nurse 4-H Camp, Canandaigua, 1969-72; chmn. canteen and disaster ARC, Canandaigua, 1972-76, sec., 1976, exec. dir. West Ontario County chpt., 1977—. Dog obedience coordinator Ontario County 4-H Clubs, 1966—, obedience judge N.Y. State Fair, Syracuse, 1980-85; bd. dirs. Am. Field Service, 1971-75; bd. dirs. Canandaigua Family YMCA, 1975-80, chmn. Ann. Y Auction, 1975; bd. dirs. Ontario County Ambulance and Rescue Assn., 1983—; mem. Canandaigua Safety Council, 1979; chmn. Lengths for Lives, Am. Cancer Soc., 1974-77; mem. Canandaigua Ambulance Squad, 1977—; pres. Canandaigua Emergency Squad, 1980-81, trustee, 1981-84 Cert. advanced first aid instr. Recipient recognition awards from various orgns. including: ARC, 1972, West Ontario County chpt. ARC, 1974, Bus. and Profl. Women's Orgn., 1970; Outstanding Vol. award Vol. Action Center, 1972; 4-H Gold Clover award, 1979; Disting. Community Service award N.Y. State Gas and Electric Co., 1985; registered nurse, N.Y. State; registered emergency med. technician, N.Y. State; cert. cardio-pulmonary resuscitation instr.; cert. high sch. swimming referee, N.Y. Baptist. Clubs: Dog Obedience of Rochester (show trophy chmn. 1976-80), Kanadasaga Kennel (dir. 1977-79, show trophy chmn. 1976—). Lodge: Elks. Home: 29 Dorset Dr Canandaigua NY 14424 Office: West Ontario County Chpt ARC 47 Phelps St Canandaigua NY 14424

NELSON, BARBARA KAY, computer resources company executive; b. Dayton, Ohio, May 20, 1947; d. Orville James and Catherine Ann (Pentenburg) Weber; m. Theodore Joseph Nelson II, Nov. 8, 1969; children—Theodore Joseph III, Jason Michael. B.A., U. Dayton, 1969; M.A., Webster U., 1985. TV co-host Sta. WHIO-TV, Dayton, 1969; dept. mgr. Elder-Beerman, Dayton, 1969-70; customer service rep. Ohio Bell Telephone, Dayton, 1970; adminstrv. coordinator AmeriSource, San Antonio, 1984—. Mem. exec. bd. Oak Grove Elementary Sch. PTA, San Antonio, 1981—; mem. religious edn. com. St. Mark;s Ch., San Antonio, 1983-84; mem. North San Antonio Chamber/Pub. Art, 1984-85. Mem. Nat. Assn. Female Execs. Club: FLW Officers Wives (pres. 1980-81). Avocations: art; jogging; bicycling; racquetball; reading.

NELSON, CAROL ANN, state financial analyst; b. Yakima, Wash., Nov. 11, 1955; d. Robert Leland and Helen R. (Griffith) Blehm; m. Steven Alan Nelson, June 17, 1978. B.A. in Liberal Arts, Calif. State U.-Sacramento, 1978. Cert. elem. educator, Calif. Asst. fin. budget analyst Calif. Dept. Fin., Sacramento, 1980—; budget cons. Calif. State Govt., Sacramento, 1983—. Analyst: Governor's Budget, State of California, 1985, 86. Republican. Avocations: travel; horticulture; architectural design.

NELSON, CLARA SINGLETON, aerospace company executive; b. Union Ridge, Tenn., Apr. 10, 1935; d. Ernest Caldwell and Willie Emma (Hord) Singleton; m. Joe Edward Nelson, July 26, 1953; children—Drexel Edward, Dorissia Lynett. Student Tenn. State U., 1961-62, Middle Tenn. State U., 1984; A.S., Motlow Coll., 1978. Sec., adminstrv. asst. Bedford County Sch., Shelbyville, Tenn., 1957-64; sec., personnel asst. Aro, Inc., Arnold Air Force Sta., Tenn., 1964-71; mem. pub. relations staff, job interviewer Employment Security, Shelbyville, 1971-81; personnel rep. Calspan Corp., Arnold Air Force Sta., 1981—; mem. adv. bd. Tenn. Area Vocat. Sch., Shelbyville, 1979—, Bedford Moore Vocat. Ctr., Shelbyville, 1979—; cons., dir. Career Devel. Workshops, Shelbyville. Chmn. Equal Employment Opportunity Adv. Commn., 1983—, Tullahoma Job Service Improvement Com., Tenn., 1985—; mem. Tenn. Gov.'s Better Schs. Com., 1985—. Recipient cert. of appreciation ARC, 1985. Mem. Highland Rim Personnel Assn. (treas. 1983-84), Nat. Assn. Female Execs. (network dir. 1985), Tenn. State U. Cluster (chmn. com. 1984—), Tenn. Placement Assn. Methodist. Avocations: reading; gardening. Home: 118 Scotland Heights Shelbyville TN 37160 Office: Calspan Corp Mail Stop 430 Arnold Air Force Station TN 37389

NELSON, CONNIE RAE, pharmacy technician, educator, lecturer; b. Lewistown, Mont., Aug. 19, 1950; d. Ward Wallace and Violet May (Charette) Dickson; m. Alan C. Nelson, July 23, 1977; children—Russell Robert, Nicole Elaine. Pharmacy asst. level A degree, Clover Park Vocat. Tech. Inst., Tacoma, 1979; degree in pharmacology Bates Vocat. Tech. Inst., Tacoma, 1982. Lic. pharmacy asst. level A. Druggist clk. Thrifty Drugs, Tacoma, 1972-79; intern in hematology, oncology, pediatrics Madigan Army Med. Ctr., Tacoma, 1979-80; pharmacy asst. A, St. Joseph Hosp., Tacoma, 1979-84; pharmacy instr. Clover Park Vocat. Tech. Inst., Tacoma, 1984—. Archtl. and land developer West Tapps Maintenance Co., Sumner, Wash., 1979—, legal and pub. affairs mem., 1984—, pres., 1985—. Mem. Wash. State Soc. Hosp. Pharmacists (pres. Pharmacy Asst. chpt. 1984—), Wash. State Soc. Pharmacy Assts. (founder, pres. 1985—). Avocations: lecturing; camping; horticulture. Home: 18710 58th St E Sumner WA 98390 Office: Clover Park Vocat Tech Inst 4500 Steilacoom Lakewood Ctr Tacoma WA 98499

NELSON, DEBORAH LYDIA, mortician; b. Winona, Minn., Dec. 30, 1960; d. Lloyd Eldridge and Bernice Helen Hertha (Rumsch) N. Student U. Wis.-LaCrosse, 1979-80, summer 1982, Winona State U., summers 1979-82; B.S. in Mortuary Sci., U. Minn.-Mpls., 1982; cert. in eye enucleation, U. Iowa, 1984. Lic. mortician, Minn., Iowa, Tex.; registered Conf. Funeral Service Exam. Bds. Practicum student Bradshaw-Hauge Funeral Homes, St. Paul, 1982; mortician Dykeman Funeral Services, Waterloo, Iowa, 1982-84, Schumacher Funeral Home, Denver, Iowa, 1982-84, Greenwood/Mt. Olivet Funeral Homes, Ft. Worth, 1984—; organist 1st Baptist Ch., Winona, 1978-80, Community United Methodist Ch., Columbia Heights, Minn., 1980-82. Mem. Nat. Assn. for Female Execs., Phi Kappa Phi. Democrat. Lutheran. Avocations: flying, skiing, bicycling, music, swimming. Office: Greenwood Funeral Home PO Box 9450 3100 White Settlement Rd Fort Worth TX 76107

NELSON, DIANA, former state legislator; b. Berlin, Wis., Oct. 15, 1941; d. Llewellyn James and Virginia Laurel (Shaver) Walker; B.S., U. Wis., 1963; m. Thomas David Nelson, Aug. 22, 1964; children—Stephanie, Brian. Mem. Ill. Ho. of Reps., 1981-85. Congl. candidate Ill. 13th Dist., 1984; candidate Cook County Clk., 1986. Republican. Congregationalist. Home: 5025 Woodland Ave Western Springs IL 60558

NELSON, DONIE ALBERTA, TV and cable production company executive; b. Los Angeles, June 13, 1942; d. Raymond Oscar and Corinne (Valdez) N.; A.A., Santa Monica City Coll., 1972; student U. Calif., Berkeley, 1960-61, UCLA, 1971; m. Foster George Phelps, May 30, 1981; 1 dau., Molly Corinne. Asst. story editor MGM Films, Culver City, Calif., 1972-75, story editor, 1975-77; dir. creative affairs Christiana Prodns., Los Angeles, 1977-79; freelance creative cons., story editor, ind. producer for TV, 1979-82; freelance mag. writer, pub. cons., book editor, Los Angeles, 1979-82; feature writer, asst. to editor Showcase mag., Encino, Calif., 1981-82; dir. devel. feature film, TV and cable Solofilm Co., Los Angeles, 1982; dir. devel. TV and cable Sherwood Prodns. Inc., Culver City, 1982-83; interviewer Natural History of AIDS Research Project, Sch. Pub. Health, UCLA, 1984-85; devel. exec. Procter & Gamble Prodns., Inc., 1985—; guest speaker Los Angeles Career Planning Center, 1979, U. So. Calif. Film Sch., 1980. Vol., Hollygrove Home for Children, 1975-77; sec. Culver City Employees Assn., 1970, Culver City Parks and Recreation Commn., 1969-70. Recipient Service award Los Angeles chpt. Women in Communications, Inc., 1978; Outstanding Journalism Student of Year award Warren High Sch., Downey, Calif., 1960. Mem. Acad. TV Arts and Scis., Women in Communications (past Los Angeles chpt. pres., Woman of Achievement award Far West region 1983), Women in Film, NOW, Am. Film Inst. Asso. producer Like Normal People, 1979.

NELSON, DOROTHY WRIGHT, judge; b. San Pedro, Calif., Sept. 30, 1928; d. Harry Earl and Lorna Amy Wright; B.A., UCLA, 1950, J.D., 1953; LL.M., U. So. Calif., 1956; LL.D., Western State U., 1980, U. So. Calif., 1983; m. James Frank Nelson, Dec. 27, 1950; children—Franklin Wright, Lorna Jean. Admitted to Calif. bar, 1954; pvt. practice law, Los Angeles, from 1954; research asso. fellow U. So. Calif., 1953-56; instr., 1957-58, asst. prof., 1958-61, asso. prof., 1961-67, prof., 1967, asso. dean., 1965-67, dean, 1967-80; judge U.S. Ct. Appeals 9th Circuit, Los Angeles, 1980—; cons. Project STAR, Law Enforcement Assistance Adminstrn.; adv. com. Nat. Jud. Edn. Program to Promote Equality for Women and Men in Cts., 1982—; dir. Farmers Ins. Co. Co-chmn. Confronting Myths in Edn. for Pres. Nixon's White House Conf. on Children. Bd. dirs. Council on Legal Edn. for Profl. Responsibility, 1971—, Constnl. Right Found., 1971—, Los Angeles County Bar Found., 1982—, Am. Nat. Inst. for Social Advancement; adv. bd. Nat. Center for State Cts., 1971-73; co-chair UN Day Calif., 1982; bd. dirs. Dispute Resolution Ctr., Pasadena, Calif., 1982—; mem. adv. com. Guardian Ad Litem Program Superior Ct., Los Angeles, 1982—; mem. reviewing bd. Preventive Law Prize Awards, 1982—. Named Alumnus of Yr., UCLA, 1967, recipient Profl. Achievement award, 1969; named Times Woman of Yr., 1968; recipient U. Judaism Humanitarian award, 1973; AWARE Internat. award, 1970; Ernestine Stalhut Outstanding Woman Lawyer award, 1972; Pax Orbis ex Jure Medallion award World Peace Through Law Center, 1975; Lustman fellow Yale U., 1977; CORO Found. Public Service award, 1978. Fellow Am. Bar Found.; mem. Am. Law Inst., Bar Calif. (bd. dirs. continuing edn. bar commn. 1967-74), Am. Judicature Soc. (exec. com. 1976—, dir. 1972-75, 76—, research adv. com. 1974—, editorial adv. bd. Judicature 1974—, v.p. 1977-79, chmn. bd. 1979-81; award 1985), ABA (sect. on jud. adminstrn.; chmn. com. on edn. in jud. adminstrn. 1972-79), Los Angeles County Bar Found. (bd. dirs. 1982—), Los Angeles World Affairs Council, Town Hall, Phi Beta Kappa, Phi Kappa Phi, Order of Coif (nat. v.p. 1974-76). Baha'i. Author: Judicial Adminstration and The Administration of Justice, 1975. Contbr. articles to profl. jours. Office: US Court House 312 N Spring St Los Angeles CA 90012

NELSON, ELIZABETH, educator; b. Birmingham, Ala.; d. John and Mary (Dunigan) Nelson; B.S., Ala. State Tchrs. Coll., 1939; M.S., Wayne State U., 1948; postgrad. N.Y. U., U. Heidelberg, Mich. State U., U. Md., U. Paris, U. Neuchatel (Switzerland), La Verne Coll., 1975. Tchr., Jefferson County (Ala.) Public Schs., 1939-45; tchr. George Washington Carver Sch., Ferndale, Mich., 1945-55, prin., 1955-58, curriculum coordinator, 1959; tchr. Bad Kreuznach (Germany) Elementary Sch., U.S. Army, 1962; tchr. Vassincourt (France) Am. Elementary Sch. Overseas Dependents Schs., Dept. Def., U.S. Army, 1963-65, Verdun (France) Am. Elementary Sch., 1966; tchr. SHAPE Internat. Elementary Sch., NATO SHAPE Support Groups Sect., SHAPE, Belgium, 1967—, minority studies coordinator Am. sect., 1975—, 1981 & 82. 3d grade chmn. Am. sect., 1978-79. Recipient award for contbns. to edn. and people of Mich., Gov. Mich., 1955. Mem. Nat., Overseas edn. assns., NAACP, League Women Voters, Zeta Phi Beta.

NELSON, ETHELYN BARNETT, civic worker; b. Bessemer, Ala., Jan. 16, 1925; d. Laurence McBride and Ethel Victoria Fortesque (King) Barnett; student Huntingdon Coll., 1943, U. Ala., 1948, George Washington U., 1948-49, 74; m. Stuart David Nelson, May 6, 1949; children—Terryl Lynn, Cynthia Dianne, Jacqueline Margo. Sec., U.S. Air Force, Montgomery, Ala. and Panama Canal Zone, 1944-49; sec. to dep. undersec. U.S. Dept. State, Washington, 1951-53, U.S. Ho. of Reps. and U.S. Senate, 1959-60; adminstrv. asst. editorial div. Nat. Geog. Soc., Washington, 1962-65; rec. sec. Dist. IV, Nat. Capital Area Fedn. Garden Clubs, Inc., Washington, 1981-83. Mem. Women's Com. Nat. Symphony Orch., Vols. for Washington Ballet, Washington Opera Guild. Mem. Salvation Army Aux., Suburban Hosp. Assn. Republican. Clubs: Landon Woods Garden (pres. 1978-80), Congressional Country; Capital Speakers (Washington). Patentee. Home: 6410 Maiden Ln Bethesda MD 20817

NELSON, GAYLE, real estate investor, county official; b. Tallahassee, Fla., Nov. 4, 1938; d. Arthur Leon and Ida (Swatts) N. B.A. in English, Speech, Fla. State U., 1960; postgrad. U. Toronto, 1963. English tchr. Northeast Sr. High Sch., Ft. Lauderdale, Fla., 1960-64; corp. mgr. nat. mktg. services Olivetti Underwood Corp., N.Y.C., 1964-70; nat. tng. dir. L'Eggs Products, Inc., Winston-Salem, N.Y., 1970-76; owner Nelson Properties, Tallahassee, 1976—; county commr. Leon County Bd. of County Commrs., Tallahassee, 1978—. Bd. dirs. State Assn. County Commrs., Fla., 1982—, Fla. History Assocs., Fla. History Mus., Tallahassee, 1984—, Apalachee Regional Planning Council, 1982—, Fla. Regional Planning Councils, 1983—; chmn. Met. Planning Orgn., Tallahassee, 1982-83, Regional Tech. Rev. Com., 1980-84; mem. Gov.'s Task Force on Mental Health, 1983-84; active mem. Tiger Bay, 1978—. Democrat. Episcopalian. Clubs: Gov.'s, Pilot, Econs. (Tallahassee). Avocations: tennis; sailing; skiing; reading. Home: 1718 Pepper Dr Tallahassee FL 32304 Office: Bd of County Commrs County Court House Tallahassee FL 32301

NELSON, HAZEL FOWLER (MRS. BOWEN CRESTON NELSON), writer; b. Mulhall, Okla., May 16, 1905; d. Oscar Frederick and Belle Virginia (Lowe) Fowler; B.A., U. Okla., 1927; postgrad. U. Wis., 1928; m. Bowen Creston Nelson Oct. 26, 1941; 1 dau., Creston Annette. Tchr. journalism, English, sponsor publs. Chickasha (Okla.) High Sch., 1927-30; reporter Norman (Okla.) Transcript, 1930-37; feature writer Oklahoma City Times, 1937-41; mil. editor Miami (Fla.) Herald, 1942-45; officer Nelson Mortgage Co., Inc., Miami, 1941-69, sec., dir., 1942-69; now free-lance writer. Mem. bd. Children's Service Bur., Miami, 1952; v.p. Franklin Bush chpt. U. Miami Women's Cancer Assn., 1961, pres., 1970. Recipient silver award Miami's Fgn. War Brides for assistance through newspaper series, 1946. Mem. Soc. So. Families, Fla. Hist. Assn., Internat. Platform Assn., Women in Communications (pres. U. Okla. chpt. 1927, Miami chpt. 1952-53). Democrat. Mem. Christian Ch. (pres. women's fellowship 1963-64). Home: 10255 SW 53d Ave Miami FL 33156

NELSON, HELEN DALE, foodservice distribution company executive; b. Houston, Sept. 18, 1955; d. Richard and Marjorie S. Nelson. B.A. in Psychology, U. Tex., Austin, 1977; M.Counseling and Personnel Services, U. Mo., 1978. Various student personnel positions U. Mo., Columbia, 1977-78; personnel coordinator Sysco Corp., Houston, 1978—. Chairperson adv. bd. dirs. Women's Ctr., U. Mo., 1977-78, mem. dean's com. for grad. edn., 1977-78; assoc. vestry woman Ch. of St. John the Divine, Houston, 1984-86; mem. Jr. League of Houston, 1980—, Arts Symposium of Houston; bd. dirs. Homeowners Assn., Houston, 1982-85. Mem. Am. Soc. Personnel Adminstrn., Houston Personnel Assn. Office: Sysco Corp 1177 W Loop S Houston TX 77027

NELSON, HELENE MARGARET, state official; b. Madison, Wis., Mar. 4, 1950; d. Earl Warren and Carol (Burnson) N.; m. Douglas R. Campbell, Jan. 27, 1978. B.A. summa cum laude, Oberlin Coll., 1972. Analyst, supr. Legis. Fiscal Bur., Madison, Wis., 1972-75; sr. budget planner U. Wis. System, Madison, 1975-77; dep. sec. Wis. Dept. Transp., Madison, 1977-78, dep. sec. Wis. Dept. Revenue, 1979-81, Wis. Dept. Health and Social Services, 1981-83, Wis. Dept. Industry, Labor and Human Relations, Madison, 1983—. Named Pub. Adminstr. of Yr., Am. Soc. Pub. Adminstrn., 1984. Office: Dept Industry Labor and Human Relations 201 E Washington Ave Madison WI 53702

NELSON, HOLLY JEAN, veterinarian; b. San Francisco, Sept. 30, 1947; d. Harold Raymond and Jean Louise (Whited) N. B.S. in Animal Sci., U. Calif.-Davis, 1970; D.V.M., 1977. Veterinarian Minerva Vet. Clinic (Ohio), 1977-78; founder, veterinarian Middlefield Pet Hosp. (Ohio), 1978-80; veterinarian Cameron Park Vet. Hosp., Shingle Springs, Calif., 1980—; breeder, trainer, exhibiter purebred Dalmatian dogs. Vet. columnist Spots Illustrated, 1979-82; research on health problems in Dalmatians. Mem. AVMA, Sacramento Valley Vet. Med. Assn., Dalmatian Club Am., Dalmatian Club No. Calif. Home: 3880 Lakeview Dr Shingle Springs CA 95682 Office: 3931 Cambridge Rd Shingle Springs CA 95682

NELSON, JANET KATHRYN, broadcast engineer; b. Indpls., Jan. 15, 1954; d. Robert Eddinger and Carol Jean (Nelson) N.; m. Phillip Edward Callighan, Sept. 6, 1975. B.A., North Central Coll., Naperville, Ill., 1975; tech. cert. DeVry Inst. Broadcast personality Sta. WGSB, Geneva, Ill., 1975-79, Sta. WYEN-FM, Des Plaines, Ill., 1977-79; sales rep. MCI Telecommunications, Chgo., 1979-80; asst. engr.-charge WGN-TV, Chgo., 1981—; v.p. Ctr. Communications, Inc., Lombard, Ill., 1985—. Mem. Nat. Acad. TV Arts and Scis. Avocations: music, sports. Home: 6340 Americana Dr Unit 618-A Willowbrook IL 60514 Office: WGN TV 2501 Bradley Pl Chicago IL 60618

NELSON, JANIE RISH, hospital executive; b. Gloster, Miss., Mar. 1, 1941; d. William Hubert and Essie Dell (Davis) Rish; m. John Preston Nelson, Jr., Aug. 19, 1984. Student S.W. Miss. Jr. Coll., 1959-61, Stephens Coll., 1981—. Accredited record technician. Admissions clk. Field Hosp., Centreville, Miss., 1963-68, asst. dir. med. records, 1968-73; dir. med. records West Feliciana Parish Hosp., St. Francisville, La., 1976—. Med. records cons. Beverly Enterprises & Centreville Health Care, 1983-84. Mem. nat. adv. bd. Am. Security Council, 1984-85; mem. U.S. Congl. Adv. Bd. for La., 1985; fund raiser Republican Com., 1984. Mem. Am. Med. Records Assn., La. Med. Records Assn., Nat. Assn. Female Execs., Tumor Registration Assn. La., Miss. Sheriffs Assn. (hon.). Republican. Presbyterian. Club: Civic. Avocations: Reading; public speaking; gardening. Home: PO Box 374 Centreville MS 39631

NELSON, JENNY STEWART, dietitian; b. Caney, Kans., July 6, 1949; d. James Harold and Frances Viola (Rekestraw) Stewart; m. Gary Leroy Nelson, Apr. 26, 1975 (div.). B.A., U. No. Colo., 1971; M.S., Oreg. State U., 1983. Dietetic intern U. Oreg. Med. Sch., Portland, 1971-72; adminstrv. dietitian Meth. Hosp., Indpls., 1972-73; food service supr. Portland State U., 1973; clin. dietitian St. Vincent Hosp., Portland, 1973; food service mgr. U. Oreg. Health Sci. Ctr., Portland, 1973-75; asst. dir. food service Dammasch State Hosp., Wilsonville, Oreg., 1975-83; asst. dir. food and nutrition service U. Chgo. Med. Ctr., 1983-84; asst. dir. food service St. Catherine Hosp., East Chicago, Ind., 1984; chief dietitian U.S. Med. Ctr. for Fed. Prisoners, 1984—; instr. diet tech. program Portland Community Coll., 1978-80, Head Start Program, Greeley, Colo., 1971. Author: Field Feeding for the U.S. Army Reserve, 1981. Active Republican Women's Orgn., 1980. Recipient scholarship for dietetic interns Colo. Dietetic Assn., 1971; Oreg. State U. grantee, 1982; Army commendation medal, 1980, 82; Oreg. Young Dietitian of Yr. award, 1980. Mem. Am. Dietetic Assn., Ill. Dietetic Assn., Am. Soc. Hosp. Food Service Adminstrs., Soc. Advancement Food Service Research, Am. Correctional Food Service Assn., Nat. Assn. Female Execs. Republican. Episcopalian. Home: 2015 S Ciccone Dr Springfield MO 65807 Office: US Med Ctr Fed Prisoners 1900 W Sunshine St Springfield MO 65802

NELSON, JULIE D., lawyer; b. N.Y.C., Sept. 8, 1954; d. John D. and Eileen M. (Canning) Krohn; m. James L. Nelson, Dec. 29, 1973; children—Morgan, Max. B.S., U. Iowa, 1975, J.D., 1978. Bar: D.C., Colo. Law clk. to presiding justice Iowa Supreme Ct., Des Moines, 1978-79; assoc. Sidley & Austin, Washington, 1979-84; atty. AT&T Info. Systems, Denver, 1984—; instr. U. Iowa Sch. Law, summer 1983, U. Phoenix, 1986—. Mem. Order of Coif, Phi Beta Kappa. Democrat. Office: AT&T Info Systems Suite 1181 7979 E Tufts Pkwy Denver CO 80237

NELSON, LAURA KAY, editor; b. Larned, Kans., May 12, 1962; d. Keith Charles and Thelma Wandalee (Wright) N. A.A., Dodge City Community Coll., 1982; B.S., U. Kans., 1984. Reporter Tiller & Toiler, Larned, Kans., 1984; area reporter Tribune, Great Bend, Kans., 1984-85; assoc. editor High Plains Jour., Dodge City, Kans., 1985—. Mem. Nat. Assn. for Female Execs., U. Kans. Alumni Assn. and Journalism Soc. Democrat. Avocations: archeology; frontier history. Home: 100 Plains Apt 15 Dodge City KS 67801 Office: High Plains Jour 1500 E Wyatt Earp Blvd Dodge City KS 67801

NELSON, LAURIE CAROLYN, lawyer; b. N.Y.C., Oct. 13, 1955; d. Daniel Jack and Norma Augusta (Ranard) Nelson. B.A. with distinction, Swarthmore Coll., 1977; J.D., Bklyn. Law Sch., 1982. Bar: N.Y. 1983. Generalist paralegal Mcpl. Employees Legal Services, N.Y.C., 1977-79; assoc. Lewis & Clarkson, N.Y.C., 1982—. Contbr. articles to profl. jours.; editor Bklyn. Law Rev., 1981-82. Recipient Am. Jurisprudence award, 1980, 81. Mem. ABA, N.Y. State Bar Assn., New York County Bar Assn. Democrat. Unitarian. Club: Swarthmore of N.Y. Home: 101 Perry St Apt 2E New York NY 10014 Office: Lewis & Clarkson 99 Wall St New York NY 10005

NELSON, LINDA JANE, health care company marketing executive, consultant; b. St. Louis, Mar. 24, 1959; d. James Benjamin and Betty Jane (Myers) N. B.A. summa cum laude William Woods Coll., 1981; M.A., Webster U., 1982. Radio intern Stas.-KFAL/KKCA, Fulton, Mo., 1981; paralegal Herzog, Kral, Burroughs & Specter, St. Louis, 1981-82; staffing coordinator, then mktg. coordinator Spectrum Emergency Care, St. Louis, 1982-85, mktg. mgr., 1985—. Party chmn. Heart Assn., St. Louis, 1982—. Recipient Flair award Advt. Fedn. St. Louis, 1984, Hosps. award Hagen Mktg. Research and Hospitals mag., 1984; presdl. acad. scholar William Woods Coll., Fulton, 1977-81. Mem. Am. Mktg. Assn., Internat. Assn. Bus. Communicators, Nat. Assn. Female Execs., Alpha Phi Alumnae Assn. (pres. chpt. 1985-87). Republican. Presbyterian. Club: Bon Amis (program com. 1985—) (St. Louis). Avocations: running; travel; sports; French; needlepoint. Home: 12082 Charter House Ln Creve Coeur MO 63146 Office: Spectrum Emergency Care 999 Executive Pkwy Saint Louis MO 63141

NELSON, LINDA KATHERINE SUTTON, theatrical lighting cons.; b. Kankakee, Ill., Nov. 8, 1951; d. Milford E. and Dorothea A. Sutton; B.A., U. Md., 1974; m. John Morgan Nelson, Apr. 9, 1977; 1 son, Damon John. Lighting design cons. Alaska Stagecraft, Inc., Anchorage, 1976-83, corp. v.p., 1979-83, sec.-treas., 1983-84, bus. mgr., 1983-84, pres.-gen. mgr., 1984—; bus. agt. Internat. Alliance of Theatrical Stage Employees and Moving Picture Machine Operators of U.S. and Can., Local 770, Anchorage, 1978-83, pres. local 918, 1983—; master electrician Anchorage Civic Opera, 1978-80, lighting designer, 1980-81; resident lighting designer Anchorage Community Theatre, 1980-82; partner SRO Productions, Anchorage, 1981—. Vol. lighting designer Theatre Guild, Inc., Anchorage, 1976-81, technical instr., 1976-81. Mem. Nat. Assn. Female Execs., Am. Mgmt. Assn., Am. Rental Assn., Central Labor Council, Coalition of Labor Union Women. Democrat. Episcopalian. Office: PO Box 4637 Anchorage AK 99509

NELSON, MARGARET ROSE, lawyer; b. St. George, Utah, May 27, 1952; d. V. Pershing and Hattie (Jones) Nelson. B.A. magna cum laude, Brigham Young U., 1973, J.D., 1976. Bar: Utah, 1977, U.S. Dist. Ct. Utah 1977, U.S. Ct. Appeals (10th cir.) 1977, D.C. 1979, U.S. Supreme Ct. 1980. Cert. secondary tchr., Utah. Assoc. law firm Aldrich & Nelson, Provo, Utah, 1977-80; tchr. law and banking Utah Tech. Coll., 1978, 81; law instr. Utah State Police Acad., Salt Lake City, 1981; mem. Utah State Bd. Edn., Utah State Bd. Vocat. Edn., Salt Lake City, 1983—, also mem. joint liaison com. Utah State Bd. Regents; dep. Utah County atty. County Atty.'s Office, Provo, Utah, 1977—. Trustee Utah Legal Services, Salt Lake City, 1983—, mem. adv. bd., Provo, 1977-78; mem. exec. com. Am. Inn of Ct. I, Provo and Salt Lake City, 1980-83; bd. dirs. Utah State Permanent Community Impact Fund, 1984—; mem. Utah State ad hoc com. to revise Juvenile Ct. rules of practice and procedure, 1981-82; mem. Provo Freedom Festival Children's Parade Com., 1978; mem. Utah State Disaster Relief Bd., 1984—; bd. dirs. Mountainland Head Start, 1984—. Mem. central com. Utah County Republican Party, 1982—, del., 1982; alt. del. Nat. Rep. Conv., 1984; mem. Provo, Sch. Dist. Vocat. Adv. Council, 1982—. Mem. ABA, Nat. Dist. Atty.'s Assn., Central Utah Bar Assn. (sec. treas. 1979) Assn. Trial Lawyers Am., Lawyers of Utah, Utah Statewide Assn. Prosecutors, Utah Trial Lawyers Assn., Am. Judicature Soc., Nat. Assn. State Bds. Edn., Utah County League Women Voters (mem. nominating com. 1983), Provo C. of C. (dir., 1984—), Orem C. of C. (mem. small bus. council 1983—), Phi Kappa Phi. Mormon. Home: 210 West 000 South Orem UT 84058 Office: PO Box 357 Provo UT 84603

NELSON, MARITA LEE, anatomist; b. Torrance, Calif., Aug. 8, 1934; d. Lee George and Marie Blanche (Waples) N.; B.S., UCLA, 1957, M.S., 1959; Ph.D. in Anatomy (Univ. fellow), U. Calif., Berkeley, 1968. Instr., Ill. State U., 1960-64; asso. U. Calif., Berkeley, 1965-68, instr., 1968-69, acting asst. prof., 1969, asst. prof., 1972-74; asst. prof. Georgetown U. Schs. Medicine-Dentistry, 1969-72; asso. prof. anatomy and reproductive biology John A. Burns Sch. Medicine, U. Hawaii, 1974-82, prof., 1982—. Recipient Teaching award Kaiser Found., 1977, Golden Pineapple award John A. Burns Sch. Medicine, 1979, Excellence in Teaching award, 1984; Disting. Teaching award U. Calif.-Berkeley, 1983; Regents medal for Excellence in Teaching, U. Hawaii, 1986. Mem. Am. Assn. Anatomists, Am. Assn. Clin. Anatomists, Soc. Study Reprodn., Endocrine Soc., AAAS, AAUP, Assn. Women in Sci., Hawaiian Assn. Women in Sci., Hawaiian Acad. Sci., Sigma Xi, Pi Lambda Theta. Research on environ. endocrinology and initiation of puberty, effects of high altitude on seasonal changes on maturation and pituitary function. Office: 1960 East-West Rd Honolulu HI 96822

NELSON, MARY CARROLL, artist, author; b. Bryan, Tex., Apr. 24, 1929; d. James Vincent and Mary Elizabeth (Langton) Carroll; B.A. in Fine Arts, Barnard Coll., 1950; M.A., U. N.Mex., 1963; m. Edwin Blakely Nelson, June 27, 1950; children—Patricia Ann, Edwin Blakely. Guest curator Layering: An Art of Time and Space, Albuquerque Mus., 1985; represented in pvt. collections in U.S., Germany, Eng., Australia; American Indian Biography Series, 1971-76; (with Robert E. Wood) Watercolor Workshop, 1974; (with Ramon Kelley) Ramon Kelley Paints Portraits and Figures, 1977; The Legendary Artists of Taos, 1980; Masters of Western Art, 1982; Connecting, the Art of Beth Ames Swartz; (catologues) American Western Art in Beijing, 1981; Layering: An Art of Time and Space, 1985; contbg. editor Am. Artist, 1976—. Mem. Soc. Layerists in Multi-Media (founder, sec. 1982), Albuquerque Mus. Found., N.Mex. Watercolor Soc. Home: 1408 Georgia St NE Albuquerque NM 87110

NELSON, MARY JEAN, real estate broker; b. Hungary, Mar. 5; came to U.S., 1921, naturalized, 1939; d. Alexander and Mary (Cseh) Bartok; ed. public schs.; m. Julius C. Nelson, Oct. 24, 1938; children—Judith Ann, Robert J. Buyer, Edelman Bros. Dept. Store, Lindenhurst, N.Y., 1932-43, Hillman's Shoppe, Bayshore, N.Y., 1943-45; now pres. M.J. Nelson Realty Inc., Active Girls Scouts U.S.A. Recipient Dist. Service award South Shore Suffolk chpt. L.I. Bd. Realtors, 1976, 78. Mem. L.I. Bd. Realtors. Home: 37 Willow Ln Lindenhurst NY 11957 Office: 111 W Sunrise Hwy Lindenhurst NY 11757

NELSON, PAMELA LEIGH, publishing company executive; b. Des Moines, Oct. 18, 1947; d. Clare S. and Eleanor (Greef) Orth; B.S., U. N.Mex., 1969; M.S., U. Kans., 1975. Tchr., Albuquerque Public Schs., 1969-72, Shawnee Mission (Kans.) Public Schs., 1972-76; cons. Macmillan Pub. Co., Kansas City, 1976-79; dir. mktg. services Am. Book Co., N.Y.C., 1979-81; product mgr. D. C. Heath & Co., Lexington, Mass., 1981-82; sr. product mgr. Allyn and Bacon Inc., Newton, Mass., 1982-85; product line mgr. Ginn and Co., 1985—. Mem. Assn. Am. Pubs., Internat. Reading Assn., Nat. Council Social Studies, Nat. Council Tchrs. English, Phi Mu Alumni Assn., Kans. U. Alumni Assn., U. N.Mex. Alumni Assn. AAUW, Jr. League, Women in Communications. Republican. Presbyterian. Club: PEO. Home: 255 Massachusetts Ave Boston MA 02115 Office: 191 Spring St Lexington MA 02179

NELSON, PATRICIA LEE, real estate broker, commercial artist; b. El Paso, Tex., Dec. 3, 1949; d. Edward Adam and Carol Ann (Conlee) Walsh; m. Ben Scott Nelson, June 5, 1971; children—E. Carl, C. Katharine. B.F.A., N.Mex. State U., 1971. Head artist Trend Binder, Bryan, Tex., 1971-72; artist Tex. A&M U. Printing Ctr., College Station, 1972-74; free lance comml. artist, Las Vegas, N.Mex., 1974-83; real estate agt. Realty of Las Vegas, 1980-81; real estate broker Olafson Agy., Las Vegas, 1981—; also photographer. Project leader San Miguel County 4-H, Las Vegas, 1975-83; sec. San Miguel County Fair Assn., 1981-83, pres. 1985. Recipient cert. of appreciation as outstanding project leader N.Mex. State U., 1975-82, Outstanding Leader award for 4-H Photography Project, Eastman Kodak, 1981, photography awards, 1982-83. Mem. Nat. Bd. Realtors, N.Mex. Bd. Realtors, Las Vegas Bd. Realtors (sec. 1981-82), Santa Fe Bd. Realtors, PEO (pres. 1984-85), Zeta Tau Alpha Alumnae. Republican. Methodist. Home: 1201 8th St Las Vegas NM 87701 Office: Century 21 Olafson Agy 834 Grand Ave Las Vegas NM 87701

NELSON, PATRICIA SWEAZEY, international management consultant; b. Seattle, Mar. 5, 1927; d. Manley Earl and F. Pauline (Pickard) S.; m. Russell Paul Nelson; children—Cynthia, Andrea, Barry. B.A. magna cum laude, U. Wash., 1971; postgrad. Whitworth Coll., 1985. Interpreter Italian prisoners of war U.S. Army, Seattle, 1944-45; interpreter, adminstr. trouble-shooter Pomona Valley Community Hosp., 1950-53; lead tchr. of Kindergarten, program developer, co-dir. Alpental Kinderschule, Seattle Day Nursery, 1956-69; export/import mgr. Warn Internat., Seattle, 1971-72; trainer computer transition and corp. hdqrs. mgmt. devel. team Unigard Ins., Seattle, 1972-74; dir. Nelson Internat. Assocs., Seattle, 1974—; researcher/cons. Swissair Transport, 1982—. Author: Guide to Girl Scout Backpacking, 1965. Council cons. in Alpine travel Girl Scouts U.S.A., Seattle, 1960-67, also trainer, leader, explorer advisor; designer, dir. commissary program, bd. dirs. King County Search and Rescue Assn., 1967-74; trainer, trouble shooter Nat. Disaster Team Mgmt., Teton Dam, Idaho; dir. sites, program developer, Lichtenfeld Backpacking Encampment, 1964-67. Mem. Assn. for Tng. and Devel., Soc. for Internat. Edn., Tng. and Research.

NELSON, PHYLLIS, control system engineering executive; b. Abdal, Nebr., Feb. 24, 1920; d. Frank LeRoy and Elsie (Hodges) N. Student Los Angeles State Coll., 1952-57. Registered profl. engr., Calif. With sales dept. Fischer & Porter Co., Los Angeles, 1949-72; co-founder, pres. Flowmetrics Inc., Los Angeles, 1976—. Developer glass tube rotameter, turbine meters. Mem. Instrument Soc. Am., So. Calif. Meter Assn. Avocations: bridge, golf, dancing, music. Office: Flowmetrics Inc 7447 E Slauson St Los Angeles CA 90040

NELSON, REBECCA SUE, mathematics educator; b. Rochester, Ind., July 19, 1944; d. Everett William and Pauline (Ault) Russell; B.S., Ball State U., 1965, M.A., 1967; Ed.D., Ind. U. 1972; 1 son by previous marriage—Timothy Scott. Tchr., Yorktown (Ind.) Elem. Sch., 1967-69; asso. instr. Ind. U., Bloomington, 1969-71; mem. faculty Ball State U., Muncie, Ind., 1971—, asso. prof., 1975-79, prof., 1979—; cons. elem. math, Ind. schs. Recipient Outstanding Young Faculty award Ball State U., 1974. Mem. Nat. Council Tchrs. Math (Central Region rep. 1979-82), Ind. Council Tchrs. Math (nat. del. 1973-78, pres. 1977, adv. council 1978—), Nat. Assn. Suprs. Math, Mich. Council Tchrs. Math, Pi Lambda Theta. Author: Pattern Block Games, 1982; contbr. articles to profl. jours. Home: 5400 W CR 400 N Muncie IN 47304 Office: Dept Math Ball State U Muncie IN 47306

NELSON, ROMAINE WALTINA, auditor, tax consultant; b. Washington, Dec. 31, 1951; d. Walter Wesley Belcher and Betty Jean (Petty) Toye; m. Oliver Elliot Nelson, Nov. 14, 1966; children—Adrienne Olivia, Angela Tina. B.S. in Bus. Mgmt., U. Md., 1984; A.A. in Acctg., Prince Georges Community Coll., 1979. Clk., typist FTC, Washington, 1974, acctg. technician, 1974-77, fiscal asst., 1977-78, acct., 1979-79; auditor Pension Benefit Guaranty Corp., Washington, 1979—. Mem. exec. bd. Woodrow Wilson Sr. High Sch. Home & Sch. Assn./PTA, Washington, 1983; mem. Nat. Assn. Minority Polit. Women, Washington, 1984—. Recipient Chritian Leadership certificate St. Anthony High Sch., Washington, 1982; Outstanding Service Recognition award Woodrow Wilson Sr. High Sch. Home & Sch. Assn./PTA, 1983-84. Mem. Nat. Assn. Female Execs., D.C. State Fedn. Bus. and Profl. Women Inc., Federally Employed Women, Alpha Kappa Alpha. Democrat. Baptist. Avocations: traveling; reading; music appreciation. Office: Pension Benefit Guaranty Corp 2020 K St NW Washington DC 20006

NELSON, RUBY EVERTON, banker; b. Logan, Utah, Feb. 18, 1923; d. John Elva and Lucy (Waldron) Everton; student Utah State Agrl. Coll.; m. Caril G. Nelson, Jan. 1, 1965; children—Sharilyn, Judy, Vicki; stepchildren—Alan, James. Cost acct. Wickes Engring. & Constrn. Co., Logan, Utah, 1943-45; with A.B. Robbs Trust Co., Phoenix, 1950-64, sec.-treas., 1955-64, mgr. mortgage servicing, 1960-64; with Continental Bank, Phoenix, 1964—, asst. v.p., comptroller, 1966-70, v.p., comptroller, 1970-76, sr. v.p., comptroller, 1976—, supr. mortgage servicing dept., 1960—; dir. Continental Service Corp. Mem. Nat. Assn. Bank Women, Ariz. Bankers Assn. Republican. Mormon. Clubs: Kiva, Moon Valley Country. Office: Continental Bank 4000 N Central Ave Phoenix AZ 05012

NELSON, RUTH ARLENE, elementary and special education educator; b. Sac City, Iowa, May 22, 1940; d. Wilbur O. and M. Juanita (Key) N. B.S. in Edn., Abilene Christian U., 1971; M.S. in Curriculum and Instrn., Corpus Christi U., 1984, M.S. in Elem. Edn., 1985. Cert. elem. tchr., Tex. Supr., educator Mexia State Sch., Tex., 1972; educator spl. edn. Tri-County Edn. Coop, Stamford, Tex., 1972-73, Abilene State Sch., Tex., 1973-75; elem. and spl. edn. tchr. Corpus Christi Ind. Sch. Dist., 1975-81; elem. tchr. Tuloso Midway Ind. Sch. Dist., Corpus Christi, 1981-85; instrnl. cons. Region 18 Edn. Service Ctr., Midland, Tex., 1985—. Vol., trainer Am. Cancer Soc., Corpus Christi, 1984-85. Mem. NEA, Tex. Tchrs. Assn. (trainer 1985—), Assn. for Supervision and Curriculum Devel., Tex. Assn. Prins. and Suprs., Nat. Assn. Female Execs., AAUW, Phi Delta Kappa. Republican. Mem. Ch. of Christ. Avocations: horseback riding; reading; travel. Home: 3100 Caldera Blvd Apt 1711 Midland TX 79705 Office: Region 18 Edn Service Ctr 2811 LaForce Blvd Midland TX 79711

NELSON, VALERIE RAE, nurse, naval officer; b. LaCrosse, Wis., Mar. 11, 1955; d. Delbert Arnold and Gloria Mae (Gee) Nelson. B.S. in Nursing, Viterbo Coll., 1981. R.N., Wis. Nursing asst. LaCrosse Luth. Hosp., 1974-75, 77-81, nurse, 1981-82; hosp. corpsman U.S. Naval Hosp., Annapolis, Md., 1975-77; commd. ensign U.S. Navy, 1982; nurse U.S. Naval Hosp., Camp LeJeune, N.C., 1982-85, Craven Community Hosp., 1985—, mem. Navy nursing edn. com., 1982—. Named Reservist of Yr., Greater LaCrosse Area C. of C., 1981. Lutheran. Lodge: Order Eastern Star (officer LaCrosse 1973-81). Address: Route 1 Box 403A Maysville NC 28555

NELSON, VITA JOY, editor, publisher; b. N.Y.C., Dec. 9, 1937; d. Leon Abraham and Bertha (Sher) Reiner; m. Lester Nelson, Aug. 27, 1961; children—Lee Reiner, Clifford Samuel, Cara Ritchie. B.A., Boston U., 1959. Promotion copywriter Street & Smith, N.Y.C., 1958-59; asst. to mng. editor Mademoiselle Mag., N.Y.C., 1959-60; mcpl. bond trader Granger & Co., N.Y.C., 1960-63; editor, publisher Westchester Mag., Mamaroneck, N.Y., 1968-80, L.I. Mag., 1973-78, Moneypaper, Larchmont, N.Y., 1981—. Bd. dirs. Westchester Tourism Council, Westchester County, N.Y., 1974-75, Sackerpath council Girl Scouts U.S.A., White Plains, N.Y., 1976-79; bd. govs. v.p. Am. Jewish Com., Westchester, N.Y., 1979—. Recipient citation Council Arts, 1972; Media award Pub. Relations Soc. Am., 1974. Mem. Women in Communications (Outstanding Communicator award 1983), Sigma Delta Chi. Democrat. Avocations: cooking, remodeling. Home: Pleasant Ridge Rd Harrison NY 10528 Office: Temper of the Times Communications 2 Madison Ave Larchmont NY 10538

NELSON-HERBER, JOAN, teacher educator; b. Bklyn., May 28, 1930; d. William Law and Camille Marie (Morgan) Baumann; B.A., Coll. William and Mary, 1962; M.Ed., U. Pitts., 1966, Ph.D., 1970; m. Harold L. Herber, July 3, 1974; children—Joanne Nelson, Craig Nelson, Mark Nelson. Tchr., Hampton (Va.) Pub. Schs., 1962-65; asst. prof. U. Pitts., 1970-71, dir. reading clinic, 1970-73, assoc. prof., 1971-75, dept. chmn., 1972-74; assoc. prof. SUNY, Binghamton, 1975-78, prof., 1978—, dir. profl. edn., 1979-81, 83-84; pres. TRICA Cons., Inc., 1978—; cons. in edn. Bd. dirs. Cortland Repertory Theatre, 1980-81; asso. dir. Network of Secondary Sch. Demonstration Centers for Teaching Reading in Content Areas, 1980—. Mem. Internat. Reading Assn. (chmn. publs. com.), Am. Ednl. Research Assn., Nat. Council Tchrs. English, Nat. Reading Council, N.Y. Reading Assn., Pi Lambda Theta, Phi Delta Kappa. Republican. Club: Cortland Country. Author: Changing Views, 1980, rev., 1983; Meeting Challenges, 1980, rev., 1986; (with Harold Herber) Reading Across the Curriculum, 1977); contbr. articles to profl. jours. Home: 15 Braeside Dr Homer NY 13077 Office: Div Profl Edn SUNY Binghamton NY 13901

NELSON-HUMPHRIES, TESSA, author, educator; b. Yorkshire, Eng.; came to U.S., 1959; M.A. (AAUW fellow), U. N.C., 1965; Ph.D. (AAUW fellow), U. Liverpool (Eng.), 1973; m. Kenneth Nelson Brown (dec.); m. 2d, Cecil H. Unthank, 1963 (dec. 1979). Head dept. English, Walsall, Eng., 1956-58; dir. English studies Windsor Coll., Buenos Aires, Argentina, 1958-59; instr. U. N.Mex., 1960-63; prof. English lit. Cumberland Coll., Williamsburg, Ky., 1964—; mem. Bread Loaf Writers' Conf., Middlebury, Vt., 1978. Fulbright fellow, 1955-56; Danforth award, 1964; recipient Short Story prize, U.K., 1975; article prize, U.K., 1985; Julia Cairns Silver Trophy for poetry, U.K., 1978, Best Actress award, 1962, 79; Mellon Found. grantee, China, 1981; James Still fellow in humanities U. Ky., 1983. Mem. Mensa, Soc. Women Writers and Journalists U.K., Soc. Authors U.K., Nat. Council Tchrs. English, Laurel County Humane Soc., Vegetarian Soc. U.K. Author children's stories, mag. articles; columnist British Alive!, 1973—; contbr. poetry to Outposts, Confrontations, Blue Unicorn. Home: York Cottage Route 4 Box 944 Williamsburg KY 40769 Office: Dept English Cumberland College Williamsburg KY 40769

NEMCHEK, LEE RACHEL, law librarian; b. Phila., Oct. 27, 1954; d. Philip H. Nemchek and Elaine Harriet (Shapiro) Harrison. B.A. magna cum laude, Loyola U., Chgo., 1976; M.F.A. in Theater, UCLA, 1978; M.S. in Library Sci., U. So. Calif., Los Angeles, 1981. Library asst. II, U. So. Calif. Dental Library, 1979-80; librarian I, Pasadena (Calif.) Pub. Library, 1979-81; asst. law librarian Irell & Manella, Los Angeles, 1981-83; library asst. Cedars-Sinai Med. Ctr., Los Angeles, 1983-84; law librarian Pepper, Hamilton & Scheetz, Los Angeles, 1983-84, Manatt, Phelps, Rothenberg & Tunney, Los Angeles, 1984-85, Morrison & Foerster, Los Angeles, 1985—; cons. Nat. Health Law Program, Los Angeles, 1983, Library Mgmt. Systems, Los Angeles, 1984-85, Hanna & Morton, Los Angeles, 1986—. Contbr. articles to publs. Named outstanding grad. in Theatre, Loyola U. Theater dept., 1976; Schmidt Found. scholar Loyola U., 1976, Wilson Found., U. So. Calif., 1980, Libraria Sodalitas, U. So. Calif., 1981. Mem. Am. Assn. Law Libraries, ALA, Theatre Library Assn., So. Calif. Assn. Law Libraries. Democrat. Home: 1523 S Wooser St #2 Los Angeles CA 90035 Office: Morrison & Foerster 333 S Grand Ave Los Angeles CA 90071

NEMETH, PATTI MARIE, biomedical research scientist, educator; b. Tulsa, Nov. 8, 1946; d. Eugene M. and Juanita V. Cox; 1 child, Tessa Elisabeth. B.S., U. Ariz., 1969; Ph.D. (USPHS fellow 1972-77), UCLA, 1977. Alexander von Humboldt fellow in biomed. research U. Konstanz (W.Ger.), 1977-80, postdoctoral fellow in biomed. research Univ. Coll., London, 1978; asst. prof. neurology, neurosurgery, anatomy, and neurobiology Washington U., St. Louis, 1980-86, assoc. prof., 1986—. NIH, Muscular Dystrophy Assn. grantee. Mem. Biophys. Soc. Am., Soc. Neurosci., Am. Assn. Anatomists, Fedn. European Biochem. Socs. Contbr. articles in field to profl. jours. Office: Washington U Sch Medicine Dept Neurology Saint Louis MO 63110

NEMETZ, ANNETTE MARIE, materials engineer; b. Whitehall, Pa., May 13, 1954; d. Stephen Louis and Anna Julia (Schadl) N. A.A., Lehigh County Community Coll., 1975; B.S., Rensselaer Poly. Inst., 1980. Devel. engr. Combustion Engring., Inc., Windsor, Conn., 1980-82, prin. startup engr., Palo Verde, Ariz., 1982—; co-owner, mgr. The Happy Llama Co., Telluride, Colo., 1985—. Mem. C-E Women's Network (co-founder), Solar Energy Assn. Conn. (bd. dirs. 1980-82), AAUW, Alpha Sigma Mu, Mensa. Roman Catholic. Club: Palo Verde Ski (founder, pres. 1984—). Avocations: skiing; outdoor activities; tennis; art; travel-investments. Home: 2716 W Mercer Ln Phoenix AZ 85029 Office: Combustion Engring Inc PO Box 49 Palo Verde AZ 85343 also 1000 Prospect Hill Rd Windsor CT 06095

NEMIRO, BEVERLY MIRIUM ANDERSON, writer, educator; b. St. Paul, May 29, 1925; d. Martin and Anna Mae (Oshanyk) Anderson; student Reed Coll., 1943-44; B.A., U. Colo., 1947; postgrad. U. Denver; m. Jerome Morton Nemiro, Feb 10, 1951 (div. May 1975); children—Guy Samuel, Lee Anna, Dee Martin. Tchr., Seattle pub. schs., 1945-46; fashion coordinator, dir. Denver Dry Goods Co., 1948-51; free lance fashion model, 1951-58, 78—; fashion dir. Denver Market Week Assn., 1952-53; moderator TV program Your Preschool Child, Denver, 1955-56; free lance writer gen. articles and nonfiction books, 1958—; dir. public relations Fairmont Hotel, Denver, 1979-80; instr. writing and communications U. Colo., Denver Center, 1970—, U. Calif., 1976-78. Active Denver Art Mus., Colo. Opera Guild, Denver Symphony Group, Achievement Rewards for Coll. Scientists, Children's Hosp. Assn.; pres. Denver Jr. Symphony Guild, 1959-60. Recipient Top Hand award Colo. Authors' League, 1969, 72, 79, 80, 81, 82, 100 Best Books of Yr. award N.Y. Times, 1969, 71; named One of Colo.'s Women of Yr., Denver Post, 1964. Mem. Public Relations Soc. Am., Am. Soc. Journalists and Authors, Nat. Writers Club, Colo. Authors League (dir. 1969—), Authors Guild, Authors League Am., U. Denver Woman's Library Assn., Colo. Women's Coll. Library Assn., Soc. Profl. Journalists, Kappa Alpha Theta. Author: The Complete Book of High Altitude Baking, 1961; Colorado a la Carte, 1963; The Lunch Box Cookbook, 1965; Colorado a la Carte, Series II, 1966; Where to Eat in Colorado, 1967; The High Altitude Cookbook, 1969; The Busy People's Cookbook (Better Homes and Gardens Book Club selection 1971), 1971; Single After Fifty, 1978 (paperback edit. 1980); The New High Altitude Cookbook, 1980; contbr. articles to periodicals and newspapers. Home: 420 S Marion Pkwy Apt 1003 Denver CO 80209

NEMKO, BARBARA GAIL, academic coordinator, educational planner; b. Bronx, N.Y., Jan. 24, 1945; d. Herbert and Leona (Beder) Padrid; m. Martin Nathan Nemko, Dec. 26, 1976; 1 child, Amy Helene. B.A., Queens Coll., 1964, M.S., 1972; Ph.D., U. Calif.-Berkeley, 1981. Dir. of evaluation (partnership) U. Calif.-Berkeley, 1978-80; project dir. Calif. State Dept. Edn., U. Calif.-Davis, 1979—; cons. Berkeley Unified Sch. Dist., 1974-75, Sonoma State U., Rohnert Park, Calif., 1983—, Calif. State U.-Sacramento, 1983—, Calif. State U.-Los Angeles, 1985—; mem. regional action team State Dept. Edn., Sacramento, 1984—. Author: Resource Guide for Teachers of Disadvantaged Students in Health Careers Programs, 1983; (with M. Nemko) How to Get Your Child a Private School Education in a Public School, in press. Mem. Calif. Assn. Vocat. Educators, Am. Vocat. Assn. Jewish. Avocations: tennis; theatre; music; reading. Home: 5936 Chabolyn Terr Oakland CA 94618 Office: U Calif Dept Applied Behavioral Scis AOB 4 Davis CA 95616

NENNER, VICTORIA CORICH, nurse; b. Marshall, Tex., Jan. 17, 1945; d. Bernard Paul and Mary DeLayne (Bowen) Corich; B.S. in Nursing (Regents scholar, Krost-Freeman scholar, Mary Gobbs Jones Nursing scholar), Tex. Women's U., 1966; cert. U. Paris, summer 1966; M.S. in Nursing, U. San Diego, 1984; m. Paul Edwin Nenner, Aug. 12, 1970. Mem. nursing staff St. Thomas Hosp., London, 1966-67, Parkland Meml. Hosp., Dallas, 1967-68; coordinator nursing continuing edn. Scripps Meml. Hosp., La Jolla, Calif., 1974-85; v.p. Marvik Ednl. Services, Inc.; mem. part-time faculty U. Calif., San Diego; mem. vis. faculty U. B.C.; mem. Inservice Council San Diego and Imperial Counties, 1974—, pres., 1976-77; mem. San Diego Community Colls. Health Edn. Adv. Bd., 1976—. Served to capt. Nurse Corps, USAF, 1968-73. Named Tex. Student Nurse of Year, 1966. Mem. Am. Soc. Health Edn. and Tng., Nat. League Nursing, Am. Nurses Assn., Nat. Assn. Female Execs., Sigma Theta Tau. Author articles in field; producer oncology nursing ednl. videotapes. Home: 3937 Southview Dr San Diego CA 92117

NESBIT, PHYLLIS SCHNEIDER (MRS. PETER N. NESBIT), district judge; b. New Kirk, Okla., Sept. 21, 1919; d. Vernon Lee and Irma Mae (Biddle) Schneider; B.S. in Chemistry, U. Ala., 1948, LL.B., 1958, J.D., 1969; m. Peter N. Nesbit, Sept. 14, 1939. Draftsman, Drydock & Shipbldg. Co., Mobile, Ala., 1942-45; tech. sec. B. F. Goodrich Co., Tuscaloosa, Ala., 1949-55; sec. Ala. Bus. Research Council, University, 1955-58; admitted to Ala. bar, 1958; partner firm Brantley & Nesbit, and predecessor firm, Robertsdale, Ala., 1958-76; judge Mcpl. Ct., Daphne, Ala., 1964-76, Silverhill, Ala., 1969-76; city atty. City of Loxley (Ala.), 1974-76; dist. judge Baldwin County (Ala.), 1977—. Sec., Daphne Civic Assn., 1962—; treas. Joint Legis. Council Ala., 1972-73. Mem. Ala. State Bar, Baldwin County Bar Assn. (pres. 1967-68), Nat. Assn. Women Lawyers, Ala. Women Lawyers Assn. (pres. 1966-67), Ala. Mcpl. Judges Assn. (pres. 1970-73), Ala. Council Judges of Juvenile Ct. (treas. 1979-81), Ala. Assn. Dist. Judges, Am. Judicature Soc., Bus. and Profl. Women's Club (pres. 1974-75), Gamma Sigma Epsilon. Mem. Order Eastern Star (worthy matron 1963-64). Home: 302 Creek Dr Fairhope AL 36532 Office: 1138 Bay Minette AL 36507

NESBITT, LENORE CARRERO, federal court judge; b. 1932; m. Joseph Nesbitt; children—Sarah, Thomas. A.A., Stephens Coll., 1952; B.S., Northwestern U., 1954; postgrad. U. Fla. Law Sch., 1954-55; LL.B., U. Miami, 1957. Research asst. 1st Dist. Ct. of Appeals, 1957-59; assoc. Nesbitt & Nesbitt, 1960-63; spl. asst. atty. gen., 1961-63; research asst. Dade County Circuit Ct.,

1963-65; assoc. with John R. Terry, 1969-73, Petersen, McGowan & Feder, 1973-75; state judge circuit and appellate divs., 1975-82; judge U.S. Dist. Ct. for So. Fla., Miami, 1983—; Counsel Fla. Bd. Med. Examiners, 1970-71. Office: US Dist Ct PO Box 010669 Flagler Sta Miami FL 38101*

NESBITT, MARGOT LORD (MRS. CHARLES R. NESBITT), fine arts appraiser; b. Tonbridge, Kent, Eng., Feb. 13, 1927; d. Douglas G.R. and Octave (Waghorne) Lord; came to U.S., 1930, naturalized, 1937; B.A. in English Lit., U. Okla., 1950, B.F.A. in Art History, 1970, M.A., 1975; m. Charles R. Nesbitt, June 6, 1948; children—Nancy Margot, Douglas Charles, Carolyn Jane. Appraiser fine arts, Oklahoma City, 1968—; treas. Apollo Oil Corp., 1974—. Mem. Okla. Arts and Humanities Council, 1971-76; mem. women's com. Oklahoma City Symphony, 1964—; life mem. Okla. Art Center, women's bd., 1962-63; chmn. art collection State of Okla., 1975-76; bd. dirs. Okla. Found. for Disabled, 1972-75; bd. advisers Nat. Trust Historic Preservation, 1976-81. Mem. English Speaking Union, Okla. Hist. Soc. (dir. 1975-85), Hist. Preservation Oklahoma City (treas. 1977-80), Am. Soc. Appraisers (sr. mem.; pres. Okla. chpt. 1978-79), Appraisers' Assn. Am., Kappa Alpha Theta (pres. alumni chpt. 1962-64, Okla. chmn. Theta Link 1965-66, treas. corp. bd. 1976-77). Democrat. Episcopalian (treas. assemblies 1971-72, mem. women's bd. 1971-72, treas. altar guild 1972-73, treas. St. Paul's Cathedral 1976-78, mem. vestry 1978-85, jr. warden 1978-82, 84-85). Clubs: Connoisseur (pres. 1956-57); Early American Glass (treas. 1973-75). Address: 1703 N Hudson St Oklahoma City OK 73103

NESBITT, NANCY ANNE, public utility official; b. Fort Worth, Aug. 19, 1937; d. Charles Keith and Naomi Lucille Nesbitt; student North Tex. State U., 1957. Clk. invoice processing Gulf States Utilities, Beaumont, Tex., 1958-78, gen. clk. invoice processing, 1978-79, sect. head invoice processing and materials mgmt., 1979-81, supr. procurement control-materials mgmt., 1981-83, supr. system purchasing services, 1982—. Youth dir. Pine Burr Bapt. Ch. Mem. Nat. Assn. Female Execs., Am. Mgmt. Assn., Am. Security Council (nat. adv. bd.), U.S. Congl. Adv. Bd., Research Inst. Am., North Tex. State U. Alumni Assn., Sabine Neches Purchasing Assn., Beaumont C. of C. (chmn. freight transp. users com.), Beaumont Assn. for Mental Health. Baptist. Clubs: Emeral Century, Order Eastern Star, Live Wires, Bus. and Profl. Men's.

NESBITT, RUTH, social worker, psychotherapist; b. Johnson City, N.Y., Sept. 18, 1936; d. James Roland and Mary Elizabeth (Ward) Flaherty; B.S. in Pharmacy magna cum laude, St. John's U., 1962; postgrad., N.Y.U., 1968-71; m. John W. Nesbitt, Dec. 6, 1974; stepchildren—Mary Terese, Patrick. Dept. dir. pharmacy and outpatient services DePaul Hosp., Norfolk, Va., 1962-68, instr. Sch. Nursing, bd. dirs., 1962-68; supr. childrens services Bklyn. Bur. Community Services, 1971-73; dir. social services Wyoming Conf. Childrens Home, Binghamton, N.Y., 1973-75; psychotherapist Broome Devel. Service, Binghamton, 1976—. Active human devel. service in parish church. Recipient Bristol award, St. John's U., 1962. Lic. psychotherapist, cert. social worker, N.Y. Mem. Nat. Assn. Social Workers, Acad. Cert. Social Workers, Va. Soc. Hosp. Pharmacists (pres. 1965-67). Office: Arch St Johnson City NY 13790

NESS, ANITA KAY, nurse, educator; b. Lexington, Nebr., Aug. 31, 1945; d. Robert Van and Dorothy Louise Whitson; B.S. in Natural Sci., Nebr. Wesleyan U., 1966; R.N., Bryan Meml. Hosp., Lincoln, Nebr., 1966; M.N., Wichita State U., 1981; m. Gary Dale Ness, Nov. 27, 1975; 1 son, Jason Robert. Instr. nursing, acting dir. nursing Butler County Community Coll., El Dorado, Kans., 1969-72; instr. nursing Wichita State U., 1972-75, Ft. Hayes State U., Hayes, Kans., 1975-80; home dialysis supr. clients, Ellis County, Kans., 1978-80; dir. nursing edn. Dodge City (Kans.) Community Coll., 1980—; bd. dirs., dir. vols. Hospice Orgn., Dodge City, 1980—. Mem. Am. Nurses Assn., Am. Heart Assn., Kans. Nurses Assn. Republican. Club: Soroptomists. Office: Dodge City Community Coll Hwy 50 Bypass and 14th St Dodge City KS 67801

NESS, SANDRA MARIE, civic leader; b. Watertown, S.D., Dec. 25, 1937; d. Shebel J. and Etma Meta (Eschbach) Sarkees; m. Clayton A. Ness, Feb. 6, 1960; children—Christopher Allen, Leslie Anne, Mara Marie. Student, Am. Inst. of the Air, 1955-56. Announcer, copy writer KHIL, Brighton, Colo., 1955-59; legal stenographer Dist. Atty., Rapid City, S.D., 1959-67, Sheriff, Rapid City, 1967-69, Everett E. Berry, Stillwater, Okla., 1970-74; 1st dep. Ct. Clk.-Payne County, Stillwater, 1974-79, clk., 1979—. Precinct chmn. Payne County Democratic Party, 1971—, co-chmn., 1985; county conv. sec., Payne County, 1974—; membership chmn., past co-chmn. Stillwater Women's Polit. Caucus, 1982—, chair, 1986—; state recorder Okla. Woman's Polit. Caucus, 1982—. Recipient Community Service award Stillwater Domestic Violence, 1982, Meritorious Service award Okla. Women's Polit. Caucus, 1984. Mem. LWV (chmn. budget com. 1984—), Payne County Legal Secs. (sec. 1974-75, pres. 1975-76, 85—), ACLU, (bd. dirs. 1983—), Common Cause, Payne County Peace Network, Stillwater C. of C. (legis. com. 1983—), Ct. Clks. Assn., Payne County Officers and Deps. Assn. (v.p. 1985—), Nat. Women's Polit. Caucus (budget com. 1985—), State Officers and Deps. Assn. Roman Catholic. Clubs: Toastmasters (pres. 1983-84), Stillwater Sailing. Avocations: reading; sailing

NESTOS, ANGELA, nursing administrator; b. Franklin, Pa., July 12, 1936; d. George and Mary (Cooklis) Nestos; R.N., Presbyn.-Univ. Hosp. Sch. Nursing, 1957. Staff nurse operating room Presbyn.-Univ. Hosp., Pitts., 1957-60, head nurse, 1960-62, asst. supr. operating room, 1962, acting operating room supr., 1962, operating room supr., 1962-66, dir. operating rooms, 1966—; lectr. in field; cons. on operating rooms. Named Outstanding Alumna, Presbyn. U. Hosp. Nurses Alumnae Assn., 1983. Mem. Assn. Operating Room Nurses, Nat. League for Nursing, Presbyn.-Univ. Hosp. Sch. Nursing Alumnae Assn. Episcopalian. Author in field. Home: 262 N Dithridge St Pittsburgh PA 15213 Office: DeSoto at O'Hara St Pittsburgh PA 15213

NESWALD, BARBARA ANNE, retail executive; b. N.Y.C., Jan. 14, 1935; d. Edward and Veronica (Presby) Lutz; m. Ronald Geoffrey, Nov. 15, 1952 (div. Jan. 1957); children—Kurt, Linda, Elizabeth. Regents scholar Hunter Coll., N.Y.C. Media dir. R.M. Klosterman, Inc., Los Angeles, 1960-64; copywriter, Los Angeles, 1964-73; copy chief Broadway Dept. Store, Los Angeles, 1973-76; creative dir. Lucky Stores, Inc., Buena Park, Calif., 1976-79; v.p. advt. Top Value Enterprises, Dayton, Ohio, 1979-82; sales promotion dir. Clover Stores, Phila., 1982—. Mem. adv. bd. Los Angeles Trade Tech. Coll., 1976-77; vol. Coalition of Advs. for the Rights of the Infirm Elderly, Phila., 1982—. Recipient 36 advt. awards. Mem. Women in Communications, Inc., Advt. Club of Phila. (chmn. entertainment com.). Office: Clover Stores 801 Market St Philadelphia PA 19105

NETSCH, DAWN CLARK, state senator, law educator; b. Cin., Sept. 16, 1926; d. William Keith and Hazel Dawn (Harrison) Clark; m. Walter A. Netsch, Oct. 19, 1963. B.A. with distinction, Northwestern U., 1948, J.D. magna cum laude, 1952. Bar: Ill., D.C. Mem. staff LWV of Cook County, Ill., 1949; assoc. Covington & Burling, Washington, 1952-54, Snyder, Chadwell, Keck, Kayser & Ruggles, Chgo., 1957-61; law clk. Judge Julius J. Hoffman, U.S. Dist. Ct. (no. dist.) Ill., 1954-56; adminstrv. and legal aide to Otto Kerner, Gov. of Ill., 1961-65; mem. faculty Northwestern U. Sch. Law, Chgo., 1965—; mem. Ill. Senate, 1972—. Author: (with Daniel R. Mandelker) State and Local Government in a Federal System, 1977, (with Daniel R. Mandelker and Peter Salsich), 2d edit., 1983. Contbr. articles to profl. publs. Mem. staff Vols. for Stevenson, 1952; research asst. Stevenson-Kefauver Campaign, 1956; mem. Ill. Intergovtl. Relations Commn., 1962-65; cons. Nat. Adv. Commn. on Civil Disorders, 1967; bd. dirs. Leadership Council for Met. Open Communities, Near North Community Orgn. Recipient Ethel Parker Best Legislator award Ind. Voters Ill., 1973, 75, 77, 79, 81; Best Legislator award Ill. Edn. Assn., 1973; Golden award Environ. Legislator, Ill. League of Conservation Voters, 1973; Environ. Legislators of Yr. award Ill. Environ. Council, 1975, 77, 79, 81; citation of Appreciation, Fair Employment Practices Commn., 1978; Spl. Recognition award Ill. Alcoholism and Drug Dependence Assn., 1981; cert. of Distinction, Ill. NOW, 1983; Excellence in Enterprise award Chgo. chpt. Nat. Assn. Women Bus. Owners, 1983; Nat. Pub. Service Achievement award Common Cause, 1984; Legis. award Ill. Assn. Sch. Bds., 1984; Legis. Service award Chgo. Lung Assn., 1985, others. Mem. Ill. State Bar Assn., Chgo. Bar Assn. (mem. constl. law com. 1981-82), ACLU (bd. dirs. Ill. div.), AAUP, Ill. Welfare Assn., LWV, Legal Club, Law Club, Met. Housing and Planning Council, Nat. Mcpl. League, Order of Coif, Phi Beta Kappa. Democrat. Avocations: music; baseball. Office: 715 W Armitage Chicago IL 60614

NETTER, EDITH MARGARET, lawyer; b. N.Y.C., Oct. 27, 1949; d. Eric Max and Marion (Rothschild) N. B.A. with honors, Syracuse U., 1970; tchr. cert. Washington U., St. Louis, 1974, M.A., 1975, J.D., 1978. Bar: Ill. 1979, Conn. 1981. Tchr., Middlesex County Ho. of Corrections, Billerica, Mass., 1974; editor, staff atty. Am. Planning Assn., Chgo., 1978-81; assoc. Robinson & Cole, Hartford, Conn., 1981—; adj. prof. U. Ill.-Chgo., 1981, Western New Eng. Coll. Sch. Law, Springfield, Mass., 1978, U. Conn., 1983-84. Co-producer, soundperson film Like a Rose, 1976 (Cine Eagle award); co-editor: A Planner's Guide to Land Use Law, 1983; editor: Land Use Law: Issues for the Eighties, 1982; editor Land Use Law and Zoning Digest, 1978-81. Ford Found. grantee, 1979-80; Law Student Civil Rights Research Council grantee, 1975; recipient Diana Donald award Am. Planning Assn., 1983. Mem. Am. Planning Assn. (dir. 1983—, sec.-treas. 1984-85), Conn. Women in Planning and Devel. (dir. 1983-84), ABA, Conn. Bar Assn., Hartford County Bar Assn., Hartford Assn. Women Attys., Hartford Archtl. Conservancy. Office: Robinson & Cole One Commercial Plaza Hartford CT 06103

NETTER, VIRGINIA THOMPSON, produce company owner; b. Hardyville, Ky., Nov. 2, 1931; d. Duluth Sydnor and Vera (Asbury) Thompson; m. S. Mitchell Netter, Oct. 4, 1947; children—Ronald Lee, Candace Netter Harrison. B.A., U. Louisville, 1982; postgrad. in clin. and counseling psychology Spalding U., 1983—. Owner, Netter Produce Co., Louisville, 1954—, Big Four Farms, Belmont, Ky., 1959—. Named Ky. col., 1982. Mem. Woodcock Soc., Psi Chi, Phi Kappa Phi. Avocations: ballroom dancing, horseback riding, traveling. Home: 1029 Alta Vista Rd Louisville KY 40205 Office: Netter Produce Co 331-335 Produce Plaza Louisville KY 40202

NETTESHEIM, CHRISTINE COOK, judge; b. Oakland, Calif., Aug. 26, 1944; d. Leo Marshall and Carolyn Grant (Odell) C.; m. Paul Henry Nettesheim, Feb. 18, 1978. B.A., Stanford U., 1966; J.D., U. Utah-Salt Lake City, 1969. Bar: Utah 1969, D.C. 1972, Calif. 1982. Trial atty. U.S. Dept. Justice, Washington, 1970-72, FTC, Washington, 1972-74; with litigation div. Hogan & Hartson, Washington, 1974-76; spl. counsel Pension Benefit Guaranty Corp., Washington, 1976-78; dep. gen. counsel U.S. Ry. Assn., Washington, 1978-80; litigation atty. Shack & Kimball, Washington, 1980-83; judge U.S. Ct. Claims, Washington, 1983—. Mem. ABA (tax, pub. contact and jud. adminstrn. div.), State Bar Assn. Calif., Bar Assn. D.C., Utah State Bar Assn., Order of Coif. Republican. Presbyterian. Clubs: City Tavern (Washington). Office: US Claims Ct 717 Madison Pl NW Washington DC 20005

NETTLESHIP, PATRICIA SHARYN, investment group executive; b. Calif.; A.A., Stephens Coll.; A.B., U. Mo.; A.M.P., Harvard U.; children—Stephen, Lisa, Gunnar. Co-founder, sec.-treas. North Pacific Constrn. Co., Yakima, Wash., 1969-72, chmn., pres., chief exec. officer, 1973—; chmn. bd. North Pacific Investment Group; chief exec. officer NPCC CM; dir. Western Bank Commerce, SAPLASA, Sacramento de la plata; chmn. Competitive Enterprise Found. Mem. tax policy subcom. Econ. Council, Republican Nat. Com.; bd. regents Loyola Marymount U.; nat. bd. dirs. Jr. Achievement; chmn. Competitive Enterprise Found.; nat. vice chmn. Bus. for Reagan-Bush; mem. Pres.' Adv. Com. on Women's Bus. Ownership. Mem. Young Pres. Orgn. (rep. to various fgn. countries, chmn. Washington Nat. Conf. 1979, chmn. econ. edn. workshop), Constrn. Mgmt. Assn. Am. (bd. dirs., chmn. 1984 ann. conf.) Episcopalian. Clubs: Seattle Yacht, Harvard Bus. Sch., Wash. Athletic. Office: PO Box 2535 Yakima WA 98907

NEU, IRENE DOROTHY, historian, educator; b. Cin.; d. Frederick Francis and Mary Clara (Holterman) N.; B.A., Marietta Coll., 1944; M.A., Cornell U., 1945, Ph.D., 1950; m. Robert Leslie Jones, Nov. 25, 1976. Fellow, Research Center Entrepreneurial History, Harvard U., 1950-51; instr. Rockford (Ill.) Coll., 1951-52, Conn. Coll., New London, 1953-54; asso. prof. S.E. Mo. State Coll., Cape Girardeau, Mo., 1956-62, prof., 1962-64; asso. prof. Ind. U., Bloomington, 1964-70, prof. history, 1970-86, prof. emeritus history, 1986—. Fulbright fellow Italy, 1954-55; Social Sci. Research Council faculty fellow, 1960-61; Eleutherian Mills Hist. Library sr. fellow, 1970. Mem. Am. Hist. Assn., Orgn. Am. Historians, Econ. History Assn., Bus. History Conf., Ind. Hist. Soc., Phi Beta Kappa. Author: Erastus Corning, Merchant and Financier, 1794-1872, 1960; co-author: The American Railroad Network, 1861-1890, 1956; contbr. articles in field to profl. jours. Home: 206 Brentwood St Marietta OH 45750

NEUBERGER, CARMEN GUEVARA, university dean and administrator; b. Manila, Philippines, Jan. 5, 1935; came to U.S., 1949, naturalized, 1952; d. Santiago Garcia and Carmen (Fernandez) Guevara; B.S., U. Md., 1955; M.Ed., Am. U., 1973, Ed.D., 1977, J.D., 1983; m. Jack Adams Neuberger, June 11, 1955; children—Catherine Adams, Cynthia Ann Neuberger Stayton, Carmen Lea, Christine Jane, Mary Jo. Tchr. pub. schs., Washington, 1969-73; acting asst. dir. Internat. Student and Faculty Ctr., Am. U., Washington, 1974, asst. to dir. acad. adminstrn., 1974-76, asst. to v.p. student life, 1976-77, dean students, 1977—, asst. provost, 1983—, acting vice provost, 1985-86; coordinator for D.C., Am. Council on Edn., Nat. Identification program for Women in Higher Edn. Adminstrn., 1980-82. Mem. Archdiocese of Washington Bd. Edn., 1976-79. Am. U. fellow, 1972-73; recipient St. Ann's medal, Girl Scouts U.S.A., 1974. Mem. Council for Advancement of Standards in Student Devel./Student Personnel, So. Regional Accreditation Assn. (vs. team 1981, 83, 85), Nat. Cath. Edn. Assn. (nat. forum for Cath. parent orgns. 1979-82), Nat. Assn. Women Deans, Adminstrs. and Counselors (nat. treas. 1979-81, nat. pres. 1983-84), Nat. Assn. Student Personnel Adminstrs. (dir. 1972-82), Mortar Bd. (Cap and Gown chpt. citation 1982), Phi Kappa Phi, Omicron Nu. Democrat. Roman Catholic. Club: Mortar Bd. Alumni (pres. 1984-86) (Washington). Contbr. articles to profl. jours. Office: Div Student Life MGC 200 The Am Univ Washington DC 20016

NEUBURGER, VIRGINIA MARIE, financial analyst, consultant; b. Chgo., Mar. 17, 1947; d. Robert Frank and Verne J. (Van Cata) Davis; divorced; children—Jack R. R. Barnette, Christopher D. M. Barnette, David T. J. Neuburger. Student Moorpark Coll., Calif., 1984-86. Ins. lic., Calif.; ordained to ministry Temple of Light, 1977. Sales mgr. Grand Plaza Hotel, Rosemont, Ill., 1975-77; pastor, founder God's House, Evanston, Ill., 1977-80; athletics bus. mgr. Pepperdine U., Malibu, Calif., 1980-82, budget and planning analyst, 1984—; field underwriter N.Y. Life Ins. and Annuity Corp. Cons., Calif., 1982—; mgmt. cons. Checkbook, Thousand Oaks, Calif., 1984; dir., founder Ins.. Seminars, Ventury County, Calif., 1984-85; cons. Farmers Ins., Simi Valley, Calif., 1985-86; dir., lectr. Alternative Med. Treatment, 1977-78. Author: Herbology, 1976. Com. chairperson Ventura council Boy Scouts Am., 1982-84; pres., founder Pepperdine Hiker's Club, 1985-86. Recipient Vol. of Yr. award Boy Scouts Am. Troop 799, 1982-84; State of Ill. scholar, 1965; Swedish Covenant Hosp., 1965. Mem. Nat. Assn. Life Underwriters. Republican. Lodge: Zonta (asst. treas. and budget chairperson local club 1984). Avocations: cross country hiking; herbology; geology. Office: Pepperdine U 24255 Pacific Coast Hwy Malibu CA 90265

NEUER, JUDITH ANN, utility company official; b. Rochester, N.Y., Dec. 4, 1943; d. Edward George and Elizabeth Grace (Specht) N.; B.S. in Biology, Alfred U., 1965. Research assoc. U. Rochester Med. Sch., 1965-68; computer systems analyst Rochester Inst. Tech., 1968-70, now lectr.; systems cons. Sybron Corp., 1970-72, mgr. order processing, 1973-75, distbn. and customer service mgr., 1975-76; mgr. stores and receiving Xerox Corp., Webster, N.Y., 1976-77, mgr. systems and ops. planning, 1977-79, mgr. mfg. ops., 1980-85; quality specialist Fla. Power and Light, Miami, 1985—. Program cons. women in bus. and career devel. Rochester YMCA; founding mem. steering com., bd. dirs. Women's Career Center of Rochester; bd. mgrs. Lost Mountain Manor Condominium Complex. Mem. Am. Prodn. and Inventory Control Soc., AAUW. Republican. Presbyterian. Home: 8800 SW 123 Ct Miami FL 33186 Office: Fla Power & Light PO Box 029100 Miami FL 33102

NEUFELD, ELIZABETH FONDAL, biochemist, educator; b. Paris, Sept. 27, 1928; U.S. citizen; m. 1951; Ph.D., U. Calif., 1956; D.H.C. (hon.), U. Rene Descartes, Paris, 1978; D.Sc. (hon.), Russell Sage Coll., Troy, N.Y., 1981. Asst. research biochemist U. Calif.-Berkeley, 1956-63, Nat. Inst. Arthritis, Metabolism and Digestive Diseases, Bethesda, Md., 1963-73, research biochemist, 1973-79, chief sect. human biochem. genetics, 1979-84, chief genetics and biochem. br., 1980-84; prof. chmn. dept. biol. chemistry UCLA Sch. Medicine, 1984—. USPHS fellow U. Calif., Berkeley, 1957-63. Recipient Dickson prize U. Pitts., 1974, Hillebrand award, 1975, Gairdner Found. award 1982; William Allan award, 1982; Albert Lasker Clin. Med. Research award, 1982; William Allan award, 1982; Elliott Cresson Medal, 1984. Mem. Nat. Acad. Sci., Am. Acad. Arts and Sci., Am. Soc. Human Genetics, Am. Chem. Soc., Am. Soc. Biol. Chemists, Am. Soc. Cell Biology, Am. Soc. Clin. Investigation. Office: Dept Biol Chemistry UCLA Sch Medicine Los Angeles CA 90024

NEUGARTEN, BERNICE LEVIN, social scientist; b. Norfolk, Nebr., Feb. 11, 1916; d. David L. and Sadie (Segall) Levin; m. Fritz Neugarten, July 1, 1940; children—Dail Ann, Jerrold. B.A., U. Chgo., 1936, Ph.D., 1943; D.Sc. (hon.), U. So. Calif., 1980. Research asso. Com. on Human Devel., U. Chgo., 1948-50, asst. prof., 1951-60, asso. prof., 1960-64, prof., 1964-80, chmn., 1969-73; prof. edn. and sociology Northwestern U., 1980—; mem. council U. Chgo. Senate, 1968-71, 72-75, 78-80, chmn. council com. on univ. women, 1969-70. Mem. tech. com. research and demonstration White House Conf. on Aging, 1971; tech. advisory com. on aging research HEW, 1972-73; nat. advisory council Nat. Inst. on Aging, 1975-76, 1978-81, Fed. Council on Aging, 1978-81; dep. chmn. White House Conf. on Aging, 1981; sr. mem. Inst. Medicine of Nat. Acad. Scis. Recipient Am. Psychol. Found. Teaching award, 1975, Disting. Contbn. award, 1980; Disting. Psychologist award Ill. Psychol. Assn., 1979. Fellow AAAS, Am. Psychol. Assn. (council reps. 1967-69, 73-76), Am. Sociol. Assn., Gerontol. Soc. (pres. 1968-69, Kleemeier award for research in aging 1971, Brookdale award 1982); mem. Am. Acad. Arts and Scis., Internat. Assn. Gerontology (governing council 1975-78, chmn. N. Am. exec. com. 1983—), Sigma Xi, Phi Delta Kappa, Pi Lambda Theta. Author: (with R. J. Havighurst) American Indian and White Children: A Social-Psychological Investigation, 1955, Society and Education, 1957, rev., 1974, Personality in Middle and Late Life, 1964; co-author: Adjustment to Retirement, 1969; Social Status in the City, 1971. Editor: Middle Age and Aging, 1968; Age or Need? Public Policies for Older People, 1982. Asso. editor Jour. Gerontology, 1958-61, Human Devel., 1962-68. Contbr. chpts. to books, articles to profl. jours. Office: Northwestern U Evanston IL 60201

NEUHAUS, RUBY, health services administration educator; b. Dec. 23, 1932; s. Coy Elkin and Pauline (Thorn) Hart; m. Sept. 3, 1955; children—Leah, Paul, Rachel. B.A., Bklyn. Coll., 1955; M.S.W., Fordham U., 1957; Ph.D., NYU, 1973. Cert. social worker, N.Y. State. Adminstrv. asst. dir. Lutheran Med. Ctr., 1953-55; unit dir. U. Minn. Hosp. Psychiat. Div., 1957-59; supr. Lutheran Social Services, Mpls., 1959-64; field work preceptor adminstrn. U. Minn., 1960-62; adj. lectr. dept. sociology St. Olaf Coll., 1961; adminstrv. dir. N.Y. Counseling and Consultation Service, 1964-72; dir. fieldwork program Adelphi U., 1972-74, adj. lectr. dept. sociology, 1972; regional dir. Nassau County Mental Health Clinic, 1975-77; asst. prof. pub. adminstrn. SUNY Empire State Coll., 1974-75; assoc. prof. dept. health services Herbert H. Lehman Coll. CUNY, 1977—, chmn. dept., 1980—; adj. lectr. sociology L.I. U., 1972; adj. asst. prof. urban studies SUNY, Old Westbury, 1976. Author: (with other) Family Crises, 1980, Successful Aging, 1983, Interdisciplinary health Team Development, 1983, others. Bd. dirs. Consumer Council, Health Ins. Plan of N.Y. Hicksville Ctr., East Nassau, 1981-82. Recipient Bklyn. Coll. CUNY All Coll. award, 1955; Founders Day award NYU, 1974; fellow Wheatridge Found., 1955-57, NYU, 1970-71, Inst. on Man and Sci., 1983. Mem. Contemporary Authors, Nat. Assn. Social Workers, Am. Sociol. Assn., Am. Soc. Pub. Adminstrn., Am. Acad. Health Adminstrn., Assn. Univ. Programs in Health Adminstrn., Beta Mu (award 1955). Office: Herbert H Lehman Coll CUNY Bedford Park Blvd W Bronx NY 10468

NEUHEISEL, JANE ANN, public relations administrator; b. LaCrosse, Wis., May 11, 1936; d. Tilmer Russell Jackson and Verna May (Morrison) Jackson Hagen; m. Richard Gerald Neuheisel, Sept. 6, 1958; children—Rick, Nancy, Kate, Debbie. B.S., U. Wis., 1958. Pub. relations adminstr. State Hist. Soc. Wis., Madison, 1958-61; spl. asst. to mayor Tempe, Ariz., 1982—. Vice-pres. Faculty Wives Ariz. State U., 1973, Desert Samaritan Hosp. Aux., Tempe, 1978; chmn. Internat. Festival Tempe, 1972, 73; publicity chmn. Tempe Sister City Orgn., 1972—; bd. dirs. Fine Arts Ctr. Tempe, 1983—. Mem. Women in Communications, Inc., Phi Kappa Phi. Republican. Home: 2109 E Balboa Dr Tempe AZ 85282

NEULS-BATES, CAROL, businesswoman, musicologist; b. Bklyn., Dec. 1, 1939; d. Frederick Carl and Edith Tindall Neuls; B.A. cum laude, Wellesley Coll., 1961; Ph.D., Yale U., 1970; postgrad. N.Y.U. Sch. Bus. Adminstrn., 1979; m. William Boulton Bates, Jr., Sept. 1, 1962; 1 dau., Julia Barstow. Mng. editor RILM: Abstracts of Music Lit., Grad. Center City U. N.Y., 1972-75, project dir., co-prin. investigator Women in Am. Music, 1976-79; adj. asst. prof. music Hunter Coll., City U. N.Y., 1973-75; asst. to curator Lincoln Center Library Performing Arts, 1975-76; asst. editor Coll. Music Symposium, 1975-78; asst. prof. music Bklyn. Coll. City U. N.Y., 1978-82; account supr. John O'Donnell Co., N.Y.C., 1982-85, v.p., 1986—. Yale U. fellow, 1962-67; Radcliffe Inst. grantee, 1968-70; research grantee Nat. Endowment Humanities, 1976-79, Ford Found., 1977-79, Nat. Fedn. Music Clubs, 1978. Mem. Coll. Music Soc. (council 1975-78), Am. Musicol. Soc., Sonneck Soc., Inst. Research in History, Nat. Women's Studies Assn., Nat. Soc. Fund Raising Execs., NOW. Author: Women in Music: An Anthology of Source Readings from the Middle Ages to the Present, 1982; Women in American Music: A Bibliography of Music and Literature, 1979; contbr. articles to music jours., 43 articles to New Grove Dictionary of Music in the United States. Home: 145 E 16th St New York NY 10003

NEUMAN, JANET NUSBAUM, retired educator; b. N.Y.C., Oct. 14, 1894; d. David and Hattie (Ballin) Nusbaum; widowed; children—Robert Ballin, Alice. Kindergarten degree, Prat Inst. Normal Sch., Bklyn., 1916. Kindergarten tchr. Pub. Schs., N.Y.C., 1916-17; lectr. various colls. and schs. Author: Today, Tomorrow & Yesterday, 1978, also poetry and articles. Pub. relations chmn. Womens Internat. League for Peace and Freedom, Phila.; one of original group Women Strike for Peace, 1962—; dir. refugee orientation group Washington Hebrew Congregation, 1940; co-founder D.C. Area Gray Panthers; participated early peace demonstrations. Recipient Citation for Outstanding Service to Community Mayor and Community Leaders of Washington, 1981. Mem. SANE. Democrat. Home: 3001 Veazey Terr 1016 Washington DC 20008

NEUMAN, NANCY ADAMS MOSSHAMMER, civic leader; b. Greenwich, Conn., July 24, 1936; d. Alden Smith and Margaret (Mevis) Mosshammer; B.A., Pomona Coll., 1957, LL.D., 1983; M.A., U. Calif. at Berkeley, 1961; m. Mark Donald Neuman, Dec. 23, 1958; children—Deborah Neuman Metzler, Jennifer Fuller, Jeffrey Abbott. Pres., Lewisburg (Pa.) area League Women Voters, 1967-70; bd. dirs. LWV Pa., 1970-77, pres., 1975-77; bd. dirs. LWV U.S., 1977—, 2d v.p., 1978-80, 1st v.p., 1982-84, pres., 1986—; mem. Pa. Gov.'s Commn. on Mortgage and Interest Rates, 1973, Pa. Commonwealth Child Devel. Com., 1974-75; bd. dirs. Housing Assistance Council, Inc., Washington, 1974—, pres., 1978-80; bd. dirs. Nat. Council on Agrl. Life and Labor, 1974-79, Nat. Rural Housing Coalition, 1975—, Pa. Housing Fin. Agy., 1975-80; Disciplinary Bd. Supreme Ct. Pa., 1980-85; mem. Pa. Gov.'s Task Force on Voter Registration, 1975-76, Nat. Task Force for Implementation Equal Rights Amendment, 1975-77; mem. adv. com. Pa. Gov.'s Interdepartmental Council on Seasonal Farmworkers, 1975-77; mem. Appellate Ct. Nominating Commn. Pa., 1976-79; mem. Fed. Jud. Nominating Commn. Pa., 1977-85, chmn., 1978-81, 82-83; mem. Pa. Gov.'s Study Commn. on Pub. Employee Relations, 1976-78; del. Internat. Women's Yr. Conf., 1977; bd. dirs. ERAmerica, Inc., 1st v.p., 1977-79, Nat. Low Income Housing Coalition, 1979-82; Rural Am., 1979-81, Fed. Home Loan Bank Pitts., 1979-82; mem. Nat. Adv. Com. for Women, 1978-79; mem. nat. adv. com. Pa. Neighborhood Preservation Support System, 1976-77; bd. dirs. Pa. Women's Campaign Fund, 1984-86, Rural Coalition, Washington, 1984—; Virginia Travis lectureship Bucknell U., 1982. Recipient Disting. Alumna award MacDuffie Sch. for Girls, 1979; Liberty Bell award Pa. Bar Assn., 1983.Mem. Am. Arbitration Assn. (bd. dirs. 1986—). Home: 132 Verna Rd Lewisburg PA 17837

NEUMAN, STEPHANIE SELLORS, clinical psychologist; b. Pueblo, Colo., Dec. 14, 1945; d. John and Catherine (Swing) Sellors; m. Robert L. Bolton, Sept. 28, 1982; B.A., Miami U., 1967; M.A., Case Western Res. U., 1974, Ph.D., 1976. Social worker, spl. edn. tchr., 1967-72; clin. psychologist, research dir. Mental Devel. Center, Cleve., 1973-77; psychology cons. Cuyahoga County Bd. Mental Retardation, Cleve., 1974-77; research coordinator State of Ohio Dept. Mental Health and Mental Retardation, Cleve., 1977-81; staff psychologist Cleve. Met. Gen. Hosp., 1978-80; asst. clin. prof. dept. psychiatry Sch. Medicine Case Western Res. U., Cleve., 1978-82, asst. clin. prof. dept. pediatrics, 1980-82; cons. psychologist Unit Meth. Children's Home, Berea, Ohio, 1977-81; pvt. practice psychology, 1980—; host Dr. Stephanie Neuman Show, Sta. WERE, 1981-82, Sta. WJW, 1982-83; staff psychologist Sta. WEWS-TV, 1982-83, Sta. WKYC-TV, 1982-83; pres., pub. SNB Pub., Inc., Brecksville, Ohio, 1984—; cons. Hanna Perkins Sch., Lake Ridge Acad., Council Econ. Opportunities, Cleve., 1974-77, Lake County Mental Health Center, 1981-82. Recipient Gold achievement Am. Psychiatric Assn., 1980; Progressive Architecture award, 1983. Mem. Am. Psychol. Assn., Am.

Orthopsychiat. Assn., Ohio Psychol. Assn., Cleve. Psychol. Assn., Nat. Registry Health Service Providers in Psychology. Author: The Home Decorator, 1984; Feelings: Everybody Has Them, 1985; mem. adv. bd. New Cleve. Women Jour., 1983—. Office: 10603 Glen Forest Trail Brecksville OH 44141

NEUMANN, DEBORAH, insurance company executive; b. Glens Falls, N.Y., Feb. 15, 1951; d. John Herman and Florence Mary (LaMarque) N.; student Albany State U., 1969-71. Cert. prof. ins. woman. Accounts receivable clk. Continental Ins. Co., Glens Falls, N.Y., 1971-74; claims adjuster trainee Underwriters Adjustment Co., Malden, Mass., 1974-77, property claims specialist, Boston, 1977-78; property examiner Mass. Fair Plan, Boston, 1978-79, sr. property claims examiner, 1979-80, supr. property claims, 1980-84; supr. property claims Hanover Ins. Co., Waltham, Mass., 1984-85, owner Neumann & Assocs., Ind. Mortgage Brokers and Appraisers, 1985—. Mem. Mass. Assn. Ins. Women, Adjusters Roundtable, Internat. Assn. Arson Investigators, Nat. Assn. Underwater Instrs. Clubs: Aquawoman, N.E. Aquarium Dive, Blue Goose (hon. Mem. Boston chpt.). Office: 400-2 Totten Pond Rd Waltham MA

NEUMEYER, FLORENCE SHIRLEY, political consultant; b. Houston, Dec. 8, 1934; d. Tom R. and Kathren E. (Webster) Jackson; m. Victor Lee Neumeyer, Nov. 26, 1955 (div. July 1976); 1 son, Randall Lee. Cert. in real estate Houston Community Coll., 1977. Polit. cons., various campaigns, Houston, 1972-84; real estate salesperson Gary Green Referrals, Houston, 1979-84; exec. asst. to Mayor of Houston, 1978-82; owner Florence Neumeyer & Assocs., Houston, 1982—. Mem. Vols. in Pub. Schs., Houston Ind. Sch. Dist., 1974-75, room mother, com. mem. PTA, 1964-77; mem. steering com. law enforcement and criminal justice Magnet High Sch., Houston, 1979—; Republican precinct chmn., Harris County, Tex., 1973-84; coordinator Jim McConn for Mayor, Houston, 1977; pub. relations dir. Tex. Fedn. Rep. Women, 1974-76, editor Party Line quar. publ., 1974-76; community relations dir. Gethsemane Lutheran Ch., Houston, 1973-74, youth dir., 1973-76, Sunday Sch. tchr., 1961-76. Recipient cert. appreciation Bd. Edn. Houston Ind. Sch. Dist., 1981; cert. appreciation Houston Park Police and Law Enforcement Students, 1981. Mem. Houston Profl. Women's Rep. Club (pres. 1983-84), Am. Bus. Women's Assn. (v.p. Houston 1980). Home: 2710 Helberg St Houston TX 77092

NEUMILLER, ROSE MARIE, health care executive; b. Wolf Point, Mont., Apr. 26, 1949; d. Jacob and Elizabeth Ann (Heser) N.; student Mont. State U., 1967-68. Med. records clk., then med. records dir. Trinity Hosp., Wolf Point, 1968-76; cons. med. record mgmt., 1974—, rev. coordinator Mont. Found. Med. Care, Helena, 1976-86; mem. subarea council Health Systems Agy., 1980-82; organizer, pres. Wolf Point Diabetes Assn., 1982-84; chmn. Emergency Med. Services Council, 1986—. Chmn. Roosevelt County nursing and health program ARC, 1982—, Roosevelt County Emergency Food and Shelter Bd., 1986—. Accredited records technician. Mem. Mont. Med. Record Assn. (chmn. public relations and recruitment 1981-83). Home: 427 Fallon St Box 505 Wolf Point MT 59201 Office: Trinity Hosp Knapp St Wolf Point MT 59201

NEUNDORFER, MARTHA LU, manufacturing executive; b. Cleve., Sept. 15, 1945; d. William and Evelyn Marie (Rodhe) N.; B.S. in Math., Allegheny Coll., 1966; postgrad. Cleve. State U., 1969-70; exec. M.B.A. program U. Houston, 1981-83; m. Willard T. Dean, Apr. 18, 1970 (div. 1978). Info. retrieval tech. Univ. Hosp. Cleve., 1966-67; ALC programmer NCCS, Cleve., 1967-69; systems programmer Cleve. State U., 1970-71; systems analyst, project leader Celanese Piping Systems, Columbus, 1972-75; mktg. rep. Advanced Systems, Inc., Atlanta, 1975-78; market analyst ASI, Chgo., 1978-79; v.p., sec., dir. Nat. Air Vibrator Co., Houston, 1979-81, trustee pension and profit sharing plans, 1979-81; mgr. travel industry systems Sperry Corp., 1982—; founder, pres. Omni Export, Inc., 1981—. Cert. data processor. Mem. Am. Mgmt. Assn., Data Processing Mgmt. Assn., Ind. Computer Cons. Assn., Nat. Assn. Women Bus. Owners, Women in Data Processing, Arts Symposium Young Women of the Arts, Am. Youth Hostels, Sierra Club, Nature Conservancy, Earthwatch, Exec. Program Assn. (pres. 1983-84). Roman Catholic. Club: Forum (Houston). Home: 701 Elmway Circle Norristown PA 19401 Office: PO Box 500 M5216M Blue Bell PA 19424-0001

NEUSCHELE, SHARON JO, college dean; b. Toledo, Ohio, July 12, 1936; 1 child, Brent Philip. B.E., U. Toledo, 1965, M.Ed., 1969, Ph.D., 1973. Cert. elem., secondary tchr., Ohio. Asst. prof. Ohio Dominican Coll., Columbus, 1970-73, St. Cloud U., Minn., 1973-74; assoc. prof. Ohio State U., Columbus, 1974-79; dean instl. planning Lourdes Coll., Sylvania, Ohio, 1980—; cons. U. Hawaii, 1979, others. Bd. dirs. Trinity-St. Paul Inner City Program, Toledo, 1968; cons. Ohio Civil Rights Commn., 1972; active Democratic campaigns. U. Toledo fellow, 1967-69, recipient Citation, U. Toledo, 1979, Journalistic Excellence award Columbia Press Assn., N.Y.C., 1954. Mem. Am. Council Edn., Ohio Conf. Coll. and Univ. Planning, Soc. Coll. and Univ. Planning (com. 1984-85), Phi Theta Kappa, Phi Kappa Phi (Citation 1973), U. Toledo Alumni Assn., U.S. Coast Guard Aux. Lutheran. Avocations: fossil and mineral collecting; poetry; novel writing; horseback riding. Office: Lourdes College 6832 Convent Blvd Sylvania OH 43560

NEUTZE, LOUISE ELIZABETH, leasing company executive; b. Phila., Feb. 9, 1948; d. Lee Lange and Marion Margaret (Trautman) Zell; m. William C. Neutze, July 16, 1967 (div. 1975); children—Marlee E., Roxanne L. Student U. Balt., 1966-67. Small fleet rep. Comml. Credit, Balt., 1976-79; controller L-J Leasing, Balt., 1979-84; v.p. 1st Eastern Leasing, Balt., 1984—. Pres. Lutherville Timonium Recreation Council, Timonium, Md., 1983-86; Republican candidate Balt. County Council. Mem. Eastern Assn. Equipment Lessors. Episcopalian. Clubs: Soroptimist Internat. (treas. 1985-86), Friendshp (1st v.p. 1985-86) (Balt.). Avocations: bowling; coaching softball and basketball.

NEUWIRTH, GLORIA SALOB, lawyer; b. N.Y.C., Aug. 16, 1934; d. Nathan and Jennie (Leff) Salob; m. Robert S. Neuwirth, June 9, 1957; children—Susan Madeleine, Jessica Anne, Laura Helaine, Michael Jonathan. B.A., Hunter Coll., 1955; J.D., Yale U., 1958. Bar: N.Y. 1959, Fla. 1979. Assoc. dir. Joint Research Project on Ct. Calendar Congestion, Assn. of Bar City N.Y. and Columbia U. Project for Effective Justice, N.Y.C., 1958-61; assoc., then ptnr. Kridel, Slater & Neuwirth, N.Y.C., 1976-82; assoc. Kaye, Scholer, Fierman, Hays & Handler, N.Y.C., from 1982; now mem. firm Graubard, Moskovitz, Dannett, Horowitz & Mollen, N.Y.C., Kridel and Neuwirth, N.Y.C.; trustee Blueberry, Inc., 1962-70. Mem. adv. bd. Spuyten Duyvil Pre-Sch., 1967-71; trustee Riverdale Country Sch., 1981—; trustee Nat. Kidney Found. of N.Y./N.J. Inc., 1980—, Nat. Kidney Found., Inc., 1980—; arbitrator Better Bus. Bur., Network Orgn. Bronx Women, Inc. Mem. Assn. Bar City N.Y., N.Y. State Bar Assn., ABA (com. on tax and estate planning, com. on anatomical gifts), Estate Planning Council N.Y.C., Fla. Bar Assn., Fed. Bar Council, Nat. Health Lawyers Assn. Contbr. articles to profl. jours. Home: 630 W 254th St Riverdale NY 10471 Office: Kridel and Neuwirth 360 Lexington Ave New York NY 10017

NEVELSON, LOUISE, sculptor; b. Kiev, Russia; d. Isaac and Minna Sadie (Smolerank) Berliaswky; studied with Hans Hoffman, Germany, 1931; hon. degrees Hamlin U., Mpls., Sch. Art and Design, Bowdoin Coll., Hobart and William Smith Coll.; m. Charles Nevelson (dec.); 1 son, Myron Nevelson. One-woman shows Janis Gallery, The Bienniel, Venice, Italy, 1963, also in Germany, London, Paris, Documenta III, 1964, Pace galleries, N.Y.C., Columbus, 1969, 71, Museo Civico de Torino, 1969, Gal. Jeanne Bucher, Paris, 1969, Kroller-Muller Mus., Holland, 1969, Akron Art Inst., 1969, Museum Fine Arts, Houston, 1969, U. Tex., 1970, Galerie de France, Rennes, 1981, also numerous others; one-woman retrospective exhbn. Whitney Mus. Am. Art, 1970; represented permanent collections Julliard Sch., Princeton, Whitney Mus. Am. Art, Bklyn. Mus., Neward Mus., Carnegie Inst., Sara Robi Found., Brandeis U., Birmingham Mus., Houston Mus., Riverside Mus., Mus. Modern Art, Met. Mus. Art, N.Y. U. Mus., Nebr. Mus., Guggenheim Mus., N.Y.C., Art Inst. Chgo., Tate Gallery, London, Hirshorn Mus., Washington, Los Angeles County Mus. Art, Musée d'Art Moderne de la Ville de Paris, also numerous pvt. collections. Recipient 1st award United Soc. Artists, 1959; award Chgo. Inst., 1959; Ford Found. gift for Tamarind Workshop, Norfolk Mus., 1963; Brandeis U. Creative Arts award for sculpture 1971; Skowhegan medal for sculpture, 1971; AIA award, 1977; Nat. Medal of Arts, 1985. Mem. Am. Acad. and Inst. Arts and Letters Fedn. Modern Painters and Sculptors (past v.p.), Artists Equity (past pres.), Am. Abstract Artists, Sculptors Guild (exec. bd.). Address: care Pace Gallery 32 E 57th St New York NY 10022*

NEVES, CAROL PATTERSON, security analyst; b. Montclair, N.J.; d. Charles and Agnes (Patterson) Neves. B.A., Trinity Coll., 1954; M.B.A., Harvard U., 1955. Research trainee Merrill Lynch, N.Y.C., 1955-60, security analyst, 1960-68, sr. security analyst, comglomerates, 1968—, v.p., 1974—; mem. All-Am. Research Team Instnl. Investors, 1978-85. Contbr. articles to profl. jours. Trustee Trinity Coll., Washington, 1986—. Mem. Diversified Cos. Analyst Group (founder, pres. 1979-80, treas. 1980-82), N.Y. Soc. Security Analysts; Women's Bond Club N.Y. Clubs: Spring Lake Bath and Tennis, Spring Lake Golf, Harvard. Office: Merrill Lynch 1 Liberty Plaza New York NY 08750

NEVILLE, JANICE NELSON, nutritionist, dietitian; b. Schenectady, Dec. 1, 1930; d. William Anthony and Margaret (Adams) Nelson; B.S., Carnegie Inst. Tech., 1952; M.S. (research fellow 1953), U. Ala., 1953, M.P.H., 1962; D.Sc., U. Pitts., 1964; divorced; children—James Gleeson, Lynn Marie. Clinic dietitian, instr. Univ. Hosps., Birmingham, Ala., 1954, research dietitian alcoholism, obesity, serum lipids and diet Grad. Sch. Public Health, 1956-64, asst. research prof. nutrition, 1965; mem. faculty Case Western Res. U., 1965—, prof. nutrition, 1977—, chmn. dept., 1974-82; trustee, chmn. various coms. N.E. Ohio affiliate Am. Heart Assn., 1975-87, v.p., 1985-86, pres.-elect, 1986-87, trustee, 1975-84; adv. com. FDA, 1977-78; mem. grant and contract rev. com. USPHS, NIH. Recipient Meritorious Service medal N.E. Ohio affiliate Am. Heart Assn. Mem. Am. Dietetic Assn. (chmn. nat. adv. com. Dial-a-Dietitian 1975-78, area coordinator 1978-81, speaker-elect 1982, speaker 1983-84, dir. 1982-86, pres.-elect 1986-87), AAAS, Am. Pub. Health Assn., Soc. Nutrition Edn., Am. Home Econs. Assn., Am. Coll. Nutrition (cons. editor), Dietetic Practice Groups, N.Y. Acad. Scis., Ohio Dietetic Assn. (pres. 1973-75; Pres.'s award 1981), Cleve. Dietetic Assn. (Disting. Service award), Sigma Xi. Author articles in field, chpts. in books. Office: Dept Nutrition Case Western Res U 2121 Abington Rd 312A Cleveland OH 44106

NEVINS, ELEANOR THEADORA, educator, computer researcher; b. Bklyn., Feb. 21, 1930; d. Benjamin and Alice (Rosenblum) Krown; m. Alfred Nevins, Feb. 4, 1951 (div. 1978); children—Sherry Nevins Dudley, Roni Nevins Prescott, Barry Jay, Phyllis. B.A. in Biology and Physiology, Hunter Coll., N.Y.C., 1951; M.S. in Edn., L.I.U., 1977. Cert. tchr., Fla., N.Y. Tchr. Dade County Sch. System, Miami, 1980—; freelance computer programmer, Miami, N.Y.C., 1982-85. Pres. Cancer Care, Inc., Nat. Cancer Found., Baldwin chpt., N.Y., 1973-74, v.p. pub. relations Nassau/Suffolk regional bd., 1974-75, publicity chmn., 1969-73; active Crime Watch, North Miami Beach, Fla., 1982-85. Mem. AAAS, Internat. Soc. Clin. Lab. Technologists, Fla. Soc. Med. Technologists, N.Y. Acad. Sci., NOW, JDL. Democrat. Jewish. Avocations: driving; needlepoint.

NEVINS, SHEILA, television director and producer; b. N.Y.C.; d. Benjamin and Stella N.; B.A., Barnard Coll., 1960; M.F.A. (Three Arts fellow), Yale U., 1963; m. Sidney Koch; 1 son, David Andrew. TV producer Great Am. Dream Machine, NET, 1970-72, The Reasoner Report, ABC, 1973, Feeling Good, Children's TV Workshop, 1975-76, Who's Who, CBS, 1977-78; dir. documentary programming Home Box Office, N.Y.C., 1978-86, v.p. family programming and documentaries, 1986—; pres. Spinning Reels, Inc., 1982-86. Bd. dirs. Women's Action Alliance. Recipient Peabody award, 1986. Mem. Writers Guild Am., Women in Film.

NEWBERG, DOROTHY BECK (MRS. WILLIAM C. NEWBERG), portrait artist; b. Detroit, May 30, 1919; d. Charles William and Mary (Labedz) Beck; student Detroit Conservatory Music, 1938; m. William C. Newberg, Nov. 3, 1939; children—Judith Anne (Mrs. John Robert Bookwalter), Robert Charles, James William, William Charles. Mem. Thomas Hart Benton Assos., Kansas City Art Inst., 1975—. Trustee Detroit Adventure, 1967-71, originator A Drop in Bucket Program for talented inner-city children. Trustee, Franklin-Wright Settlements, 1971-74, Meadowbrook Gallery, Oakland U., 1972-74; bd. dirs. Your Heritage House, 1972-75. Recipient Heart of Gold award, 1969; Mich. vol. leadership award, 1969. Mem. Birmingham Soc. Women Painters, Birmingham-Bloomfield Art Assn. (dir. 1960-62, trustee 1965-67), Sierra Arts Found. Presbyterian. Home: 2000 Dant Blvd Reno NV 89509

NEWBERG, ELLEN JOYCE, library administrator; b. Wellman, Iowa, Sept. 29, 1941; d. Carl Clarence and Elda Grace (White) Herr; m. Alan Keith Newberg, June 11, 1965. B.A., Sioux Falls Coll., 1962; M.L.S., U. Ill., 1963. Asst. dir. library Sioux Falls Coll., S.D., 1963-66; library cataloger U. Wyo., Laramie, 1966-67, U. Oreg., Eugene, 1967-69; asst. library dir. Rocky Mountain Coll., Billings, Mont., 1969-73; head tech. services library Parmly Billings Library, 1973-82, dir., 1982—; Western Library Network retrospective conversion trainer Mont. State Library, 1981-82; OCLC installation trainer Dowling Coll. Library, Oakdale, N.Y., 1978-79. Contbr. articles to profl. jours. Recipient Great Performance in the Library award Exxon, 1985. Mem. Mont. Assn. Female Execs., ALA, Mont. Library Assn. (various offices), Pacific Northwest Library Assn. (Mont. rep. 1980-82, joint planning team 1981-82). Avocations: gourmet cooking; gardening; hiking. Office: Parmly Billings Library 510 N Broadway Billings MT 59101

NEWBERRY, ELIZABETH CARTER, greenhouse executive, florist; b. Blackwell, Tex., Nov. 25, 1921; d. Thaddeus Payton and Bessie Julia (Clark) Carter; m. Weldon Omar Newberry, Sept. 24, 1950 (dec. Nov. 1984); 1 child, Paula Jean Newberry Arnold. Student Hardin Simmons U., 1938-39. Office mgr. F. W. Woolworth, Abilene, Tex., 1939-50; acct. Western Devel. & Investment Corp., Englewood, Colo., 1968-72; owner operator Newberry Bros. Greenhouse, Denver, 1972—; dir. Western Devel. and Investment Corp. Englewood, Colo. Pres. Ellsworth Elem. Sch. PTA, Denver, 1961-62; v.p. Hill Jr. High Sch. PTA, Denver. Republican. Baptist. Home: 201 Monroe Denver CO 80206 Office: Newberry Bros Greenhouse 201 Garfield Denver CO 80206

NEWBY, DOROTHY JANE, electrical manufacturing company executive; b. Waco, Tex., July 23, 1932; d. Everett and Zella Mae (Parrigin) Barton; student bus. U. Houston, 1951; m. Bobby Jerome Newby, Nov. 16, 1974; children by previous marriage—Charmaine Rene Hebert, Marvin Reed Hebert. Sec., Farnsworth & Chambers, Inc., Houston, 1959-60; exec. sec. Butler Drilling Co., Houston, 1960-65, S.I.P., Inc., Houston, 1965-69; adminstrv. mgr. Mensor Corp., Houston, 1969-78; v.p. adminstrn. F.F. Smith & Assos., Inc., Houston, 1979-86, dir., 1986; dir. Mensor Corp., Mem. Am. Mgmt. Assn., Nat. Assn. Female Execs. Baptist. Clubs: Sweet Adelines, Inc., Antique Auto. of Am., Willys Overland Jeepster, Slavonic Benevolent Order Tex. Home: 1622 Tannehill St Houston TX 77008

NEWBY, LUCINDA SUSAN, retired educator; b. Fredericksburg, Ind., Sept. 21, 1915; d. Dawson Patrick and Ola Elsie (Gilham) N. B.S., Butler U., Indpls., 1948, M.S., 1953. Tchr. pub. schs., Fredericksburg, 1939-44, New Albany, Ind., 1944-45, Knightstown, Ind., 1945-80. Bd. dirs. Wapehani council Girl Scouts U.S.A., also chmn. camp; bd. dirs. United Fund, Henry County Cancer Soc. (Ind.). Recipient Thanks Badge Wapehani council Girl Scouts U.S.A., 1960; Tchr. Yr. award Charles Beard Sch., Knightstown, 1980; Citizen of Yr. award Knightstown C. of C., 1979. Mem. DAR (regent 1982-84), Delta Kappa Gamma (pres. 1982-84), Tri Kappa (pres. 1974-75). Democrat. Methodist. Club: Shakespeare (pres.). Lodge: Order Eastern Star. Home: 474 N Jefferson St Knightstown IN 46148

NEWCOMB, CAMERON JANE, banker, mortgage underwriter, consultant; b. Greenwich, Conn., Aug. 1, 1961; d. Robert Cozine and Dorothy Arline (Leith) N. Student U. Conn., Stamford, 1981, SUNY-Purchase, 1982; B.A. in Geology, Mount Holyoke Coll., 1983; postgrad. U. Bridgeport, 1983-84, Pace U., 1985—. Research cons. Am. Mus. Natural History, N.Y.C., 1980—; personal banker Conn. Nat. Bank, Stamford, 1984-86; mortgage underwriter U.S. Money Ctrs., Greenwich, 1986—. Author: (with Guy Musser) Malaysian Murids and The Giant Rat of Sumatra, 1983; Taxonomy of Indochinese Rattus, 1985. Treas. Amnesty Internat., South Hadley, Mass., 1981-83. Recipient Sci. award Greenwich Acad., 1979; Am. Mus. Natural History grand. award, 1982, 83. Mem. Soc. Vertebrate Paleontologists, Paleontol. Soc., Nat. Assn. Female Execs., Nat. Assn. Bank Women. Republican. Avocations: collecting Emperial Chinese ink sticks and antique fans; philately; Chinese brushwork. Home: PO Box 4272 Greenwich CT 06830

NEWCOMB, GLORIA JEAN (KING), printing company executive; Memphis, Aug. 26, 1942; d. Le Roy and Mary Ann (Campbell) King; student public schs., Barlow, Ky.; m. John B. Newcomb, Feb. 14, 1962; children—John Kelly, Paige Lynnette. Copywriter, traffic mgr. Sta. WDXR, Paducah, Ky., 1960-62; copywriter Sta. WOC-TV, Davenport, Iowa, 1962; research asso. Indsl. Research Inc., Beverly Shores, Ind., 1963-67, promotion mgr., 1967-70; originator and hostess daily and weekly talk shows Sta. WIMS, Michigan City, Ind., 1970-71; promotion dir., nat. conf. dir. Dun-Donnelley Pub. Corp., Chgo., 1971-73; v.p. sales Foster Printing Inc., Michigan City, Ind., 1973-76; founder, pres. Newcomb Printing Services, Inc., Michigan City, 1976—; bd. contbrs. News-Dispatch, 1985—. Publicity chmn. Michigan City United Way, 1979, bd. dirs., 1984—; bd. dirs. Michigan City Heart Fund, 1979-82, YMCA, 1982-86; mem. entrepreneurial adv. bd. Michigan City Schs., 1984—; co-chmn. fund raising Michigan City Tower Restoration Com., 1979-80; bd. dirs. Jr. Achievement, 1980-85. Recipient award of Excellence, Artists Guild of Chgo. Design Show, 1978, Potlatch Corp., 1981; cert. of craftsmanship Weyerhaeuser Paper Co., 1978, Champion Papers award Champion Internat. Corp., 1978, cert. of excellence Strathmore Paper Co., 1978; silver award Circulation Direct Mail Folio, 1982, gold award, 1983. Mem. Michiana Advt. Club (co-founder; dir. 1974-82, pres. 1976, Disting. Service award 1976), Chgo. Assn. Direct Mkgt., Chgo. Printing Industries Am., Nat. Assn. Printers and Lithographers, Graphic Arts Tech. Found., Nat. Composition Assn., LaPorte Purchasing Assn., Michigan City Area C. of C. Club: Chgo. Athletic Assn. (communications com. 1986). Home: 2027 E Coolspring Michigan City IN 46360 Office: PO Box 452 605 E Ninth St Michigan City IN 46360

NEWCOMBE, JOANNE PAULINE, educational administrator; b. Chicopee, Mass., July 10, 1947; d. Eugene L. and Veronica Rita Maciolek Galuska; m. Randall William Helweg, Aug. 29, 1970 (div.); m. Edward Jeffrey Newcombe, Oct. 9, 1982. B.A., U. Mass., 1969; M.Ed., U. Lowell, 1975, Ed.D., Northeastern U., 1985. Cert. tchr., adminstr., Mass. Tchr. Ellsworth Sch., Windsor, Conn., 1969-70, Muraco Sch., Winchester, Mass., 1970-75; asst. prin. Londonderry Jr. High Sch., (N.H.), 1975-78; prin. South Sch., Londonderry, 1978-80, Birch Hill Sch., Nashua, N.H., 1980-84; dir. instructional services Ludington Area Schs. (Mich.), 1984-86; supt. schs., Auburn, Mass., 1986—; mem. faculty Lesley Coll., Cambridge, Mass., 1971-74. Speaker nat. convs. on ednl. adminstrn. Mem. Nashua Assn. Sch. Prins. (pres. 1983-84), N.H. Coalition Ednl. Leaders (pres. 1980-82), N.H. Assn. Sch. Prins. (exec. bd. 1982-84, regional v.p. 1978-80, regional pres. 1980-82), Phi Delta Kappa, Kappa Delta Pi, Delta Kappa Gamma. Democrat. Roman Catholic. Home: 216 Tolpa Circle Chicopee MA 01020 Office: Auburn Pub Schs Auburn MA 01501

NEWCORN, CLAUDIA DANA, consumer products company executive, helicopter pilot; b. N.Y.C., Aug. 9, 1958; d. Andrew Robert and Ruth Ann (Duplain) N. B.A., Wellesley Coll., 1981; M.B.A., Northeastern U., 1986. Asst. mgr. internat. mktg. services Polaroid Corp., Cambridge, Mass., 1985; research asst. Harvard Bus. Sch., Boston, 1981-82; dir. mktg. research Gen. Computer Co., Cambridge, Mass., 1982-84; cons., editor Nolan, Norton & Co., Lexington, Mass., 1985-86; asst. product mgr. Silkience Brand, Gillette Corp., Boston, 1986—; writer Children's Inst. Lit., Darien, Conn., 1985—. Author (poems): Tent: Napkin Poems, 1986. Co-author: Tentatively: Bit Parts, 1986. Author numerous poems (named golden Poet 1985, 86). Wellesley Coll. scholar, 1981. Mem. Am. Mktg. Assn., Nat. Assn. Female Execs., Sigma Xi (assoc.), Beta Gamma Sigma, Phi Kappa Phi. Avocations: scuba diving, riding, helicopter flying, rock climbing, chess, poetry, costume design. Home: 503 Beacon St #7 Boston MA 02115

NEWELL, GLADYS ELIZABETH, former educator, civic worker; b. Ticonderoga, N.Y., Aug. 31, 1908; d. Charles R. and Elizabeth (Ives) N.; A.B., SUNY, Albany, 1930, M.A., 1935. Tchr., Corinth (N.Y.) High Sch., 1930-33, Bethlehem Central High Sch., Delmar, N.Y., 1933-45; supr. social studies Bethlehem Central Schs., Delmar, 1946-71; mem. N.Y. State Regents Com. on Exams., 1950-53, N.Y. Social Studies Council Curriculum Com., 1961-63, N.Y. State Mental Health Planning Commn., 1963-64. Bd. dirs., v.p. SUNY, Albany Benevolent Assn.; adv. com. N.Y. delegation White House Conf., 1955. Recipient Bus. and Profl. Women Outstanding Citizen award Tri-Village area, 1953; State Coll. Alumni Bertha E. Brimmer award for outstanding teaching, 1955; Citizenship Conf. Outstanding Tchr. award Syracuse U., 1962; Distinguished Alumnus award State U. at Albany, 1969. Mem. N.Y. State Tchrs. Assn. (dir. 1950-69, pres. 1966-67), Eastern Zone Bethlehem Central (a founder, past pres.), Albany Supervisory Dist. (past pres.) tchrs. assns., NEA (life mem., rep. of N.Y. State Tchrs. Assn. at tchr. edn. and profl. standards meetings), N.Y. State (past pres.), Capital Dist. (past pres.), Nat. councils social studies, LWV (past pres. Albany County), UN Assn. U.S.A. (past chpt. dir.), World Affairs Council (past dir. Albany), AAUW (1st v.p. Essex County br.), Fort Carillon Bus. and Profl. Women's Club, N.Y. State Ret. Tchrs. Assn. (del to Gov.'s Conf. Libraries 1978), N.Y. Ret. Tchrs. Assn., Delta Kappa Gamma, Pi Gamma Mu. Methodist. Club: New Horizons. Contbr. articles to profl. jours. Home: 17 John St Ticonderoga NY 12883

NEWELL, KATHERINE ANN, lawyer; b. Phila., May 5, 1947; m. Francis P. Newell, Aug. 16, 1975. A.B. magna cum laude, Temple U., 1969; J.D. cum laude, Villanova U., 1975; LL.M., Georgetown U., 1979. Bar: Pa. 1975, D.C. 1980. Atty.-advisor Office of Chief Counsel, Dept. Treasury, Washington, 1975-78; assoc. firm Schnader, Harrison, Segal & Lewis, Phila., 1978—; mem. adj. faculty grad. tax program Villanova U. Law Sch., 1983—. Mem. ABA (tax-exempt fin. com. sect. taxation 1982—), Pa. Bar Assn., D.C. Bar Assn., Phila. Bar Assn. Office: Schnader Harrison Segal & Lewis Suite 3600 1600 Market St Philadelphia PA 19103

NEWELL, REBECCA G., psychiatric nurse; b. Savannah, Ga., July 4, 1953; d. Henry Morgan and Julia (Rogers) Grimes; A.A., Armstrong State Coll., 1973, B.S. in Nursing, 1980; postgrad. Sch. Grad. Nursing, Med. Coll. Ga., 1980; m. E. Andrew Newell, June 14, 1980. With Charter Broad Oaks Hosp., Savannah, Ga., 1973—, coordinator utilization rev. and staff devel., 1975-80, asst. dir. nursing, 1980-82, nursing adminstr., 1982—; adj. faculty Armstrong Coll. Sch. Nursing. cons. Council Recruitment and Retention of Nurses, 1978—; profl. staff exchange cons. Recipient Leadership award Vocat. Indsl. Clubs Am., 1971. Mem. Hist. Savannah Found., Am. Nurses Assn., Ga. Nurses Assn., Am. Bus. Womens Assn., Ga. Hosp. Assn. Soc. Nursing Service Adminstrs., Ga. Hosp. Assn. Soc. Utilization Rev. Coordinators. Baptist. Home: 11407 Willis Dr Savannah GA 31404

NEWELL, SALLY OTTAWAY, veterinarian; b. Ypsilanti, Mich., July 2, 1936; d. Henry Jackson and Ruth Marie (Montgomery) Ottaway; B.S., E. Carolina U., 1958; D.V.M., U. Ga., 1970; m. John Richard Newell, June 28, 1958 (div. 1985); children—Deonne Marie, Mary Jo, Penni Sue. Research asst. N.C. State U., Raleigh, 1958-60; research asso. U. Ga., 1970-73; gen. practice vet. medicine, Elberton, Hartwell, and Athens, Ga., 1973-74; coordinator U. Ga. Lab. Animal Care, Athens, 1974—. Mem. Am. Assn. Lab. Animal Sci. (pres. 1982), AVMA, Am. Soc. Primatologists, Am. Soc. Lab. Animal Practitioners, Sigma Xi. Episcopalian. Author articles in field. Home: 184 Highland Park Dr Athens GA 30605 Office: Office of the Vice Pres for Research U Ga Athens GA 30602

NEWELL, VIRGINIA SHAW, retired educator; b. Eau Claire, Wis., Jan. 15, 1901; d. La Forrest and Caroline (Wingen) Newell; student Eau Claire Normal Sch., 1919-21; B.A., U. Wis., Madison, 1924, postgrad., 1964-68; postgrad. Northwestern U., 1941; M.A., Catholic U. Am., 1951. Tchr., Eau Claire Sr. High Sch., 1924-43; tchr., drama dir. Adams-Friendship High Sch., Adams, Wis., 1951-54; tchr. English and speech, drama dir. Westfield (Wis.) High Sch., 1954-55; tchr. English, drama dir. Medford (Wis.) High Sch., 1955-57; tchr. English and speech, drama dir. Marinette, Wis., 1957-63; tchr., dir. forensics, dir. contest plays Adams-Friendship High Sch., 1963-66; tchr. Title I remedial and devel. reading, 1966-70; free-lance writer. Vol. Adams County unit Am. Cancer Soc., 1972-75, crusade chmn., 1975, bd. dirs., 1975-77, recipient Cert. of Merit, 1977; pres. Adams County Assn. Republican Women, 1969-73; publicity chmn. Adams County Rep. Party, 1973-76; vice chairperson, 1976; coordinator congressman's re-election campaign, 1972; sponsor Nat. Rep. Congressional Com., 1984; mem. Winnebago County Rep. Women, Nat. Fedn. Rep. Women, Rep. Nat. Com. Served to lt. Women's Res., USCG, 1943-46. Ann. fellow Intercontinental Biog. Assn.; mem. Res. Officers Assn. U.S. (life), AAUW, Winnebago County Ret. Tchrs. Assn. (life), Wis. Ret. Tchrs. Assn. (life), Winnebago County Ret. Tchrs. Assn., Smithsonian Assocs., Nat. Ret. Tchrs. Assn., Cath. U. Am. Alumni Assn., U.Wis.-Eau Claire Alumni Assn., Paine Art Ctr. and Arboretum, Nat. Travel Club, Delta Kappa Gamma Soc. Internat., Half Century Club of U. Wis.-Eau Claire. Roman Catholic. Club: 20th Century (Oshkosh). Author: (radio play) Charity, Inc., 1941; asst. editor: Stories and Poems from the First Grade through the Eighth, 1924; contbr. articles to profl. jours. Home: 200 Merritt Ave Apt 108 Oshkosh WI 54901

NEWLAND, NANCY J., transportation brokerage company executive; b. Ogden, Utah, June 30, 1954; d. Ellis Walter and Carol Lou (Ogden) Newland;

m. James L. Looney, Oct. 8, 1977; 1 child, Michael R. Student Minot Bus. Sch., 1972-73. Acct., Rice-Lindquist, Minot, N.D. 1973; sec. H.E. Everson Co., Rugby, N.D., 1973-76, Western Brokers, Inc., Denver, 1976-79; pres. Nancy's Brokerage, Inc., Denver, 1979—. Avocations: sewing; needlecraft; bowling; gardening. Home: 15002 E Chenango Ave Aurora CO 80015 Office: Nancy's Brokerage Inc 6100 Smith Rd Suite 205 Denver CO 80216

NEWLIN, MARGARET RUDD, poet, literary critic; b. N.Y.C., Feb. 27, 1925; d. James Harold and Marie (McLaughlin) Rudd; m. Nicholas Newlin, Apr. 2, 1956 (dec. 1976); children—James Rudd, David Shipley, Robert Plunkett, Thomas Sims. B.A., Bryn Mawr Coll., 1947; Ph.D., U. Reading, Eng., 1951; D.Litt. (hon.), Washington Coll., 1980. Various teaching positions, Bryn Mawr Coll., Washington Coll., 1950s; condr. workshops in field. Author: Divided Image, 1953; (lit. criticism) Organiz'd Innocence, 1956; (poetry) The Fragile Immigrants, 1971; Day of Sirens, 1973, The Snow Falls Upward, 1976, The Book of Mourning, 1982, Collected Poems 1963-1984, 1986. Contbr. articles to profl. jours. AAUW fellow, 1948-49, Am. Philos. Soc. fellow, 1950-51. Nat. Endowment for Humanities fellow, 1976-77. Democrat. Avocations: swimming; raising small wild animals and birds. Home: Shipley Farm Secane PA 19018

NEWLON, FELICE DOLORES, medical group administrator; b. Reno, Nev., May 5, 1954; d. Richard and Rita Regina (Munoz) Arriandiaga. B.A., U. Nev., 1976, postgrad. 1976-78. Location supr. Maxicare, Hawthorne, Calif., 1979-80; dir. mem. group relations Unified Med. Groups, Bellflower, Calif., 1980-82; dir. physician recruitment and tng. Health Force Mgmt. Group, Thousand Oaks, Calif., 1982-83; adminstr. Prairie Med. Group-Santa Monica, Calif., 1983—; health care mgmt. cons. Writer tng. manuals for health care groups. Mem. Unified Med. Groups Assn., Med. Group Mgmt. Assn., Nat. Assn. Female Execs., AAUW, Santa Monica C. of C. Club: Marina City (Marina Del Rey, Calif.). Home: Apt 8 20563 S Vermont Ave Torrance CA 90502 Office: Prairie Medical Group 524 Colorado Ave Santa Monica CA 90401

NEWMAN, ANITA NADINE, physician; b. Honolulu, June 13, 1949; d. William Reece Elton and Margie Ruth (Pollard) Newman; m. Frank Ellis Burkett, Dec. 30, 1978; children—Justin Ellis, Chelsea Newman. A.B., Stanford U., 1971; M.D., Dartmouth Coll., 1975. Diplomate Am. Bd. Otolaryngology. Intern, resident in gen. surgery Northwestern Meml. Hosp., Chgo., 1975-77, resident in otolaryngology, 1977-78; resident UCLA Hosp. and Clinics, 1979-82, asst. prof., 1982—; staff surgeon Wadsworth VA Hosp., Los Angeles, 1982-84; research fellow in neurotology UCLA, 1984—. Contbr. articles to med. jours. Mem. alumni admissions support com. Darmouth Med. Sch. Alumni Council, 1983—. Mem. Am. Acad. Otolaryngology, Am. Med. Women's Assn., Los Angeles County Med. Women's Assn., Assn. Research in Otolaryngology, Stanford Women's Honor Soc. Democrat. Office: UCLA Hosp and Clinics Div Head and Neck Surgery Westwood CA 90024

NEWMAN, ANNETTE GOERLICH, shopping center manager; b. Fresno, Calif., Jan. 19, 1940; d. David August and Mary Eloise (Simpson) Goerlich; Pharm.D., U. Calif., San Francisco, 1963; children—Anne Kristen, Mark David, Gregory Hartley. Pharmacist, Village Drug, 1963-69; relief pharmacist, 1969-72; store mgr. The Drug Store of Fig Garden Village, 1972-77; mgr. Fig Garden Village Shopping Center, Fresno, 1977—; dir. Fig Garden Mcht. Assn.; sec. bd. dirs. Fig Garden Village, Inc. Active Fresno Community Analysis Citizens Com., Littlest Angel chpt. Children's Home Soc., Ladies Aid to Retarded Children, Women's Symphony League; bd. dirs. Fresno Arts Center, St. Agnes Med. Found.; mem. council of 100, Fresno Art Ctr. Women's Yr. Nominee, Rosalie M. Stern award, 1971, 72; registered pharmacist, Calif. Mem. Fresno-Madera Pharm. Assn., Pharm. Alumni Assn. U. Calif., Nat. Assn. Female Execs., Jr. League of Fresno, AAUW, Alpha Phi. Club: Soroptimists. Home: 3909 W Fir Ave Fresno CA 93711 Office: 5082 N Palm Ave Suite A Fresno CA 93704

NEWMAN, BARBARA MILLER, psychologist, educator; b. Chgo., Sept. 6, 1944; d. Irving George and Florence (Levy) Miller; student Bryn Mawr Coll.; A.B. with honors in Psychology, U. Mich., 1966, Ph.D. in Devel. Psychology, 1971; m. Philip R. Newman, June 12, 1966; children—Samuel Asher, Abraham Levy, Rachel Florence. Undergrad. research asst. in psychology U. Mich., 1963-64, research asst. in psychology, 1964-69, teaching fellow, 1965-71, asst. project dir. Inst. for Social Research, 1971-72, univ. lectr. in psychology and research assoc., 1971-72; asst. prof. psychology Russell Sage Coll., 1972-76, assoc. prof., 1977-78; assoc. prof. dept. family relations and human devel., chmn. dept. family relations and human devel. Ohio State U., 1978-83, prof., 1983—. Mem. Eastern Psychol. Assn., Soc. Research in Child Devel., AAAS, Am. Psychol. Assn., Nat. Council Family Relations, Groves Conf. on Marriage and Family, N.Y. Acad. Scis., Midwestern Psychol. Assn., Western Psychol. Assn., Am. Home Econs. Assn. Author books including: (with P. Newman) Living: The Process of Adjustment, 1981; Development Through Life, 1987; Understanding Adulthood, 1983; Adolescent Development, 1986; contbr. chpts., articles to profl. publs. Office: Dept Family Relations and Human Devel 1787 Neil Ave Room 315 Columbus OH 43210

NEWMAN, CAROL, editor, marketing executive; b. N.J., Mar. 10, 1947; d. George W. and Virginia (Ransom) Austermuhl; m. Robert F. Newman, Jr., June 23, 1972; children—Luke, Jack. B.S., Temple U., 1969; M.B.A., NYU, 1983. Asst. editor to exec. editor Publishers Services, Inc., Phila., 1970-74; program editor, developer Research for Better Schs., Phila., 1974-76; editor-in-chief Webster div. McGraw-Hill Book Co., N.Y.C., 1977-80, dir. secondary mktg. strategies, 1981—. Author: Your Wedding, Your Way; editor numerous ednl. textbooks and mags., 1970—. Recipient Golden Eagle award McGraw-Hill Book Co., 1982. Mem. Assn. Am. Publishers (program chmn. copyright com. 1980-81). Office: McGraw-Hill Book Co. 1221 Ave of the Americas New York NY 10020

NEWMAN, CAROL LINDA, lawyer; b. Yonkers, N.Y., Aug. 7, 1949; d. Richard Joseph and Pauline Frances (Stoll) N. A.B. summa cum laude, Brown U., 1971, M.A., 1971; postgrad. Harvard Law Sch., 1972-73; J.D. cum laude, George Washington U., 1977. Bar: D.C. 1977, Calif. 1979. Asst. dir. personnel Washington Hilton Hotel, 1973-75; atty. U.S. Dept. Justice Anti-Trust Div., Los Angeles and Washington, 1977-80; assoc. firm Alschuler, Grossman & Pines, Los Angeles, 1980-82, Costello & Walcher, Los Angeles, 1982-85, Rosen, Wachtell & Gilbert, Los Angeles, 1985—; faculty Grad. Sch. Bus. Golden Gate U., Los Angeles, 1982. Gifts fundraiser Brown U., Los Angeles, 1983; Libertarian party candidate Calif. Atty. Gen., 1986. Mem. ABA, Los Angeles County Bar Assn., Order of Coif, Phi Beta Kappa. Libertarian. Home: 7150 Carlson Circle #19 Canoga Park CA 91303 Office: Rosen Wachtell Gilbert 1888 Century Pk E Suite 2100 Los Angeles CA 90067

NEWMAN, CLAIRE POE, business exec.; b. Jacksonville, Fla., Dec. 12, 1926; d. Leslie Ralph and Gertrude (Criswell) Poe; student Fla. State Coll. for Women, 1944-45, Tulane U., 1971-73; m. Robert Jacob Newman, July 3, 1948; children—Leslie Claire, Robert, Christopher David. Co-owner Vineyards in Burgundy, France; v.p., dir. Carrollton Realty Co. of New Orleans, 1956—. Mem. various coms. New Orleans Mus. Art. Mem. Women's com. New Orleans Philharmonic Symphony Assn., 1961—, chmn. orch. relations com., 1961-63; chmn. New Orleans Easter Seal Drive, 1963; La. trustee Nat. Soc. Crippled Children and Adults, 1963-65. Mem. Women's Aux. C. of C., New Orleans Soc. Archeol. Inst. Am. (v.p. 1972-74), Confrérie des Chevaliers du Tastevin, Sigma Kappa. Club: Metairie Country, Kitzbuehel (Austria) Golf, Golden Skibook (Kitzbuehel), Pass Christian (Miss.) Yacht; Ski (Arlberg). Home: 1111 Falcon Rd Metairie LA 70005 Also Tiemberg Kitzbuehel Austria

NEWMAN, COLLEEN ALEXANDER, public relations executive; b. Georgetown, Guyana, Feb. 11, 1942; came to U.S., 1969, naturalized, 1977; d. J.A. and Marian (Griffith) Alexander; B.A., U. West Indies/U. London, 1964; m. Alan Newman, Feb. 7, 1970. UN del., diplomat Govt. of Guyana in Chile and Venezuela, 1966-69; editorial services supr. AT & T, 1969-72; tech. news mgr. Consol. Edison Co. N.Y., Inc., 1972-77, asst. to v.p., 1977-79, asst. v.p., 1979-80, v.p. corp. communications, 1980-86; pres. Newman Assocs., 1986—; chmn. N.Y. Power Pool Public Relations Com., 1978-80; lectr. tech. writing L.I. U., 1977. Adv. bd. Boys Choir of Harlem; adv. com. Phelps-Stokes Ctr. for Human Devel.; mem. Coalition of 100 Black Women; bd. dirs. Associated Black Charities. Recipient Black Achievers in Industry award, 1977, Clarion award Women in Communications, 1984; hon. mem. YWCA Acad. Women Achievers, 1984. Mem. Pub. Relations Soc. Am., Edison Engring. Soc. (pres. 1980-81). Office: 350 1st Ave New York NY 10010

NEWMAN, ELLA TYRAS, financial consultant; b. Hof, W.Ger., Jan. 2, 1948; came to U.S., 1950, naturalized, 1955; d. Leo and Olga (Agatstein) Tyras; B.A. in Econs., CCNY, 1968; M.B.A. Baruch Coll., 1973; m. Ian Frederick Newman, Sept. 7, 1969; children—Jamie Tyras, David Andrew. With Bankers Trust Co., N.Y.C., 1968-78, investment officer personal trust investment dept., 1973-78; ind. fin. cons., 1979-82; exec. recruiter acctg., fin. and banking Westfield Personnel, White Plains, N.Y., 1981-82; exec. recruiter acctg. fin. and banking Velen Assocs. (name formerly Walker Brody Personnel), Stamford, Conn., 1984—; adj. prof. Pace U., 1980—; lectr. Coll. New Rochelle (N.Y.), 1979, 80, 83, 84, Manhattanville Coll., 1984, 86, Dutchess Community Coll., 1978; tchr. Am. Inst. Banking, 1978-79. Bd. dirs. Chappaqua (N.Y.) New Neighbors, 1980-82. Mem. Nat. Assn. Accts. (dir.), Am. Soc. Acctg. Women.

NEWMAN, ELLEN MAGNIN, consultant; b. San Francisco, Apr. 19, 1928; d. Cyril Isaac and Anna Smithline Magnin; student Stanford U., 1945-48; m. Walter Simon Newman, Sr., Oct. 15, 1950; children—Walter Simon, Robert Magnin (dec.), John Donald. With Joseph Magnin Co., San Francisco, 1948-69, women's apparel buyer, 1948-54, developer sales tng., 1954-60, dir. product devel., 1960-64, dir. new products and new brs., 1964-69; spl. asst. to pres. Joseph Magnin, San Francisco, 1969-72; in house cons. consumer affairs Amfac, Honolulu, 1972-74; pres. Ellen Newman Assos., San Francisco, 1974—; dir. Wells Fargo & Co., Wells Fargo Bank, San Francisco, Kaiser Aluminum & Chem. Corp., Oakland, Calif. Mem. Mayor's Fiscal Adv. Com. City San Francisco; v.p. bd. govs. San Francisco Symphony; council mem. SRI Internat.; mem. adv. council Grad. Sch. Bus., Stanford U.; vice chmn. U. Calif. San Francisco Found. Mem. Com. 200, Women's Forum West, San Francisco C. of C. (v.p., bd. dirs.). Club: Metropolitan. Office: 323 Geary St Suite 507 San Francisco CA 94102

NEWMAN, FRANCES MAE, real estate management company executive; b. Elm Grove, Ohio, Dec. 15, 1938; d. Earl E. and Phena (Dunn) Whitworth; student Ohio U., 1960—; asso. degree in acctg. Internat. Accts. Soc., 1969; m. Carson Newman, July 13, 1958; children—Brad, Carmen. Office mgr., credit mgr. Clarence Vallery Sons, Inc., Waverly, Ohio, 1956-74; v.p. RMS Mgmt. Corp., Chillicothe, Ohio, 1974-84; v.p. RMS Properties (merged with RMS Mgmt. Corp.), 1984—; owner, operator Clothes Corral, men and women's apparel, Waverly, 1981-83, Carmen's, 1983—. Instr. cert. apt. mgr. tng. courses. Mem. Waverly Jaycettes (pres. 1970), Chillicothe Bus. and Profl. Womens Club (dist. dir.), Nat. Assn. Female Execs. Home: 90 Prosperity Rd Waverly OH 45690 Office: 126 W 2d St Waverly OH 45690

NEWMAN, JANICE MARIE, municipal official; b. N.Y.C., Aug. 11, 1951; d. Robert and Clara (White) Swindler; m. Roger Kevin Newman, Jan. 20, 1972 (div. July 1980); 1 child, Germaine M. Swindler-Newman (dec.). B.A., Smith Coll., 1973; J.D., Rutgers U., 1980. Bar: N.J. 1983. Adminstrv. asst. Corp. Ann. Reports, N.Y.C., 1972-73; pub. relations asst. Lippincott & Margulies, N.Y.C., 1973; journalist Essex Forum Newspaper, East Orange, N.J., 1973; pub. info. officer City of Newark, 1974-82, asst. communications dir. Mayor's Office, 1982—; producer, host Newark and Reality, 1974-85, Newark Report, 1985—. Contbr. articles to mags., 1975. Recipient Pub. Service award N.J. Voice Newspaper, 1977; Achievement award Minority Contractors and Craftsmen Trade Assn., 1982; named to Outstanding Young Women Am., U.S. Jaycees, 1984. Mem. Nat. Assn. Media Women (rec. sec. 1985-86, Media Woman of Yr. award 1985), N.J. Women Lawyers Assn. (pres. 1986-87), Nat. Council Negro Women, Garden State Bar Assn. (bd. dirs. 1986—). Democrat. Episcopalian. Home: 115 Sunset Ave PO Box 6070 Newark NJ 07106 Office: City of Newark 920 Broad St Newark NJ 07102

NEWMAN, JESSE ANNE CAMP, state official; b. Camden, N.J., Apr. 6, 1951; d. Thomas Bradley and Isabel June (Houston) Camp; m. Gerald Michael Newman, Sept. 1, 1972. B.A., U. Pitts., 1973; M.P.A., Fairleigh Dickinson U., 1982. With purchasing dept. Compuscan, Teterboro, N.J., 1973-77; asst. contract adminstr. CompuScan, Inc., Teterboro, 1977-78, mgr. order info. ctr. CompuScan, Inc., 1978-80; legis. asst. N.Y. State Senate, Albany, 1980-81, research dir., 1981—. Co-chmn. Clarkstown Drug Abuse Prevention Bd., 1981—; mem. The Hunger Project, Rockland County, N.Y., 1983. Home: 4D Church Ln Valley Cottage NY 10989 Office: care State Senator Linda Winikow 706 LOB Albany NY 12247

NEWMAN, LAURA ROBIN, auditor, accountant; b. San Antonio, July 3, 1917; d. Edward Richards and Jennie Gertrude (Schraut) Robin; m. Lloyd George Newman, Aug. 20, 1955 (div.); 1 dau., Elizabeth Lee Newman Easterlin. A.A., San Antonio Coll., 1955; B.S. in Bus. Adminstrn., Our Lady of Lake U., 1979. Acct. VA, San Antonio, 1978-80, auditor office of insp. gen., Atlanta, 1980-82, Dallas, 1982—. Mem. Am. Bus. Women's Assn. (pres. El Camino chpt. San Antonio, 1966-67, Woman of Yr. award 1967, del. to nat. conv. 1967), Assn. Govt. Accts., San Antonio Geneal. and Hist. Soc. Baptist. Lodge: Order Eastern Star. Home: PO Box 201067 Dallas TX 75220 Office: Office of Inspector Gen VA Room 280 2626 W Mockingbird Ln Dallas TX 75235

NEWMAN, LIBBY, painter, printmaker, curator; b. Rockland Del., Nov. 17, 1925; d. Hyman and Dora (Horowitz) Goldberg; children—Don, Andrea Newman Orsher. B.F.A., Phila. Coll. Art; postgrad. U. Pa., Villanova U. Mem. visual arts panel Pa. Council on Arts, 1971-76; artist-in-residence/curator exhbns. University City Sci. Ctr., Phila., 1975—; co-curator sculpture Gov.'s Mansion, Harrisburg, Pa., 1979—; one-man shows Phila. Art Alliance, 1971, 81, Mangel Gallery, Phila., 1972, 75, 78, 84, University City Sci. Ctr. Gallery, Phila.; group shows include Mangel Gallery, 1972-86, Pa. Acad. Fine Arts, Phila., Peale Galleries of Pa. Acad. Fine Arts, Woodmere Art Gallery, Chestnut Hill, Pa., Moore Coll. Art, Phila., Fritz Miller Gallery, N.Y.C., William Penn State Mus., Harrisburg, Pa., Fountain Gallery, Portland, Oreg., Del. Art Mus., Wilmington, Phila. Mus. Art, Circle Gallery, N.Y.C., Chgo., So. Alleghenies Mus. Art, Loretto, Pa., Mus. Phila. Civic Ctr., Moore Coll. Art, Phila., 1982, Sichuan Fine Arts Inst., Changging, People's Republic China, 1985, Tianjin Fine Arts Coll., People's Republic China, 1986, Art in City Hall, Phila., 1986; represented in permanent collections Phila. Mus. Art, Nat. Mus. Belgrade (Yugoslavia), Mus. Modern Art, Buenos Aires, Argentina, U. Pa. Law Sch., Mus. Phila. Civic Ctr., Temple U. Law Sch., Phila., Glassboro State Coll. (N.J.), Free Library Phila., University City Sci. Ctr., Phila., St. Joseph's Coll., Phila., St. Charles Borromeo Sem., Overbrook, Pa., Temple U. Health and Sci. Ctr., Phila., Nationalities Service Ctr., Phila., Phila. Assn. Clin. Trials. Editor: R. Buckminster Fuller Sketchbook, 1981; A City Sketched: A Guide to the Art and History of Philadelphia, 1976. Mem. Mayor's Com. for Sci. and Tech., 1979-82. Recipient Fleischer Art Meml. award; Cheltenham Nat. Graphic award; Best Pictures of the Yr. award Phila. Art Alliance; Carl Zigrosser Nat. Meml. award Am. Color Print Exhbn.; chosen for vis. artist project Brandywine Graphics, 1984; Nat. Endowment grantee, 1973. Mem. Artists Equity Assn. (pres. Phila. chpt. 1969-71), Am. Color Print Assn., Phila. Art Alliance, Phila. Watercolor Club. Home: 327 Meeting House Ln Merion PA 19066 Office: University City Sci Ctr 3624 Market St Philadelphia PA 19104

NEWMAN, MARGARET ANN, nurse; b. Memphis, Oct. 10, 1933; d. Ivo Mathias and Mamie Love (Donald) N.; B.S.H.E., Baylor U., 1954; B.S.N., U. Tenn., Memphis, 1962; M.S., U. Calif., San Francisco, 1964; Ph.D., N.Y.U., 1971. Dir. nursing, asst. prof. nursing Clin. Research Center, U. Tenn., 1964-67; asst. prof. N.Y.U., 1971-75, asso. prof., 1975-77; prof. in charge grad. program and research dept. nursing Pa. State U., 1977-80, prof. nursing, 1977-84; prof. nursing U. Minn., 1984—. Recipient Outstanding Alumnus award U. Tenn. Coll. Nursing, 1975; Disting. Alumnus award NYU Div. Nursing, 1984; Am. Jour. Nursing Scholar, 1979-80. Fellow Am. Acad. Nursing. Author: Theory Development in Nursing, 1979; Health as Expanding Consiousness, 1986; editor: (with others) Source Book of Nursing Research, 1973, 2d edit., 1977. Research on movement, time perception and consciousness as indices of health. Home: 289 E 5th St Saint Paul MN 55101 Office: 6-101 Health Scis Unit F 308 Harvard St Minneapolis MN 55455

NEWMAN, MARY KATHERINE, nurse, administrator; b. Tulsa, July 2, 1931; d. Willie James and Lurenda Marie (Calloway) Saulters; m. Julius A. Newman, Jr., Aug. 31, 1980. B.S.N., Dillard U., 1954; M.Ed., Loyola U., New Orleans, 1974. R.N., La. Staff nurse Charity Hosp., New Orleans, 1954-57; staff nurse VA Hosp., New Orleans, 1957-68, head nurse, 1968-76, nursing adminstr., 1976-80, asst. chief nurse in quality assurance, 1980—; prof. nursing Dillard U., New Orleans, part-time 1978-79. Mem. Urban League, Women in Main Stream, Dillard U. Alumni, Loyola U. Alumni (all New Orleans). Named Fed. Woman of Yr., VA Hosp. New Orleans, 1981. Mem. Nat. Orgn. VA Nurses, Alpha Kappa Alpha, Kappa Delta Pi. Democrat. Baptist.

NEWMAN, MARY TURNER, library media specialist; b. Miami, Fla., Apr. 8, 1935; d. Horace Roger and Mary Elizabeth (Richards) Turner; m. James Lamar Newman, Feb. 2, 1963 (div.); 1 dau., Catherine Elizabeth. B.A., U. Tenn., 1957; M.A., Fla. Atlantic U., 1972. Instr. Journalism Edi on Sr. High Sch., Miami, Fla., 1957-59, 1961-64; with spl. services U.S. Govt., Germany, France, 1959-61; instr. Dade County Bd. Pub. Instrn., Miami, 1967-68, library media specialist, 1969—, instr. travel, guidance, 1976—; tchr. Edn. Ctr. Profl. Resource Advisor Bd. Pub. Instrn., Miami, 1982-83; mem. faculty council Ida M. Fisher Jr. High, Miami Beach, Fla., 1975-78; travel counselor Adult Community Sch., Miami Beach, 1979—; chmn. Joint Book Selection Com. Dade County, 1975-78, 81—; sponsor Drama Club, Chess Club Dade County Schs., 1976-83; sect. editor features, articles Dade County Media Specialists Jour., 1979—. Bd. dirs. Miami Jr. Woman's Club, 1964-75; sec., treas. Women of Ch. Miami Shores Presbyn. Ch., 1964-69; mem. Cancer Assn. U. Miami, 1965-69. Winner 3d prize oil on canvas Dade County Women Artists, 1968. Mem. Am. Bus. Women's Assn., Fla. Assn. Media in Edn. (pres. 1984-85), Am. Assn. Sch. Libraries (regional co-ordinator), ALA, Dade County Media Specialists' Assn. (bd. dirs. 1969-83), Assn. Ednl. Communications and Tech. (com. chmn. 1983—), Fla. Council for Social Studies, Phi Delta Kappa. Democrat. Presbyterian. Office: 800 NE 137th St North Miami FL 33138

NEWMAN, MAXINE PLACKER, insurance consultant; b. Haslem, Tex., Nov. 21, 1922; d. L. H. and Beatrice Rosetta (Stuart) Placker: B.S., Stephen F. Austin State U., 1943; m. Robert Wayne Newman, May 23, 1975; 1 son, Stephen Randall Hillin (by previous marriage). Acct., Lamar U., Beaumont, Tex., 1956-58; office mgr. Williamson Ins. Agy., Beaumont, 1958-72; v.p. Alexander & Alexander, Dallas, 1972-79; cons. Bellefonte Ins. Co., Cin., 1979—; v.p. Ralph K. Kemp & Assocs., Inc. office mgr., treas. Ralph K. Kemp & Assocs., Inc., Dallas, 1979—. . Mem. Am. Bus. Women Assn. (Woman of Yr. 1979), Nat. Assn. Ins. Women, Dallas Assn. Ins. Women, Beta Sigma Phi (Woman of Yr. 1966). Republican. Baptist. Clubs: Trophy, Women's, Trophy Ladies Golf Assn. Address: 114 Carnoustie Dr Roanoke TX 76262

NEWMAN, PAULINE, federal judge; b. N.Y.C., June 20, 1927; d. Maxwell Henry and Rosella Newman. B.A., Vassar Coll., 1947; M.A., Columbia U., 1948; Ph.D. (Henry B. Loomis fellow), Yale U., 1952; LL.B., NYU, 1958. Bar: N.Y. 1958, Pa. 1959, U.S. Supreme Ct. 1972, U.S. Ct. Customs and Patent Appeals, 1978, U.S. Ct. Appeals (3rd cir.) 1981, U.S. Ct. Appeals (Fed. cir.) 1982. Research chemist Am. Cyanamid Co., Bound Brook, N.J., 1951-54; mem. patent staff FMC Corp., N.Y.C., 1954-75, Phila., 1975-84, dir. dept. patent and licensing, 1969-84; judge U.S. Ct. Appeals, Washington, 1984—; dir. Research Corp.; program specialist UNESCO Dept. Natural Scis., Paris, 1961-62; mem. State Dept. Adv. Com. on Internat. Indsl. Property, 1974—; lectr. in field. Contbr. articles to profl. jours. Bd. dirs. Med. Coll. Pa., 1975—, Midgard Found.; trustee Phila. Coll. Pharmacy and Sci. Mem. ABA (council sect. patent trademark and copyright 1982—), Am. Patent Law Assn. (dir. 1981—), U.S. Trademark Assn. (dir. 1975-79, v.p. 1978-79), Am. Chem. Soc. (dir. 1972-81), Am. Inst. Chemists (dir. 1960-66, 70-76), Pacific Indsl. Property Assn. (pres. 1979-80). Clubs: Vassar, Yale; Phila. Racquet. Address: US Ct of Appeals 717 Madison Pl NW Washington DC 20439*

NEWMAN, PHYLLIS, counselor/therapist, hypnotist; b. N.Y.C., Aug. 20, 1933; d. Max and Frieda Yetta (Pechter) Hershkowitz; B.S., Mercy Coll., 1977; M.S., L.I.U., 1979; m. Milton Newman, Dec. 28, 1952; children—Renee Holly, Eileen Sharon, Jeffrey Mark. Pvt. practice hypnosis and therapy, Peekskill, N.Y., 1977—; lectr. in field; lectr. Pepsico Fitness Ctr., Purchase, N.Y., 1984; dir. counseling Hypnosis Group, 1979—. Mem. parents exec. bd. Purdue U., 1978-83, mem. pres.' council, 1983—; mem. Hand to Mouth Players, Garrison, N.Y. Mem. Am. Assn. Counseling and Devel., Am. Mental Health Counselors Assn., N.Y. Soc. Ericksonian Hypnosis, Am. Assn. Profl. Hypnotherapists. Contbr. articles to profl. jours. Address: 2 Gallows Hill Rd RFD Box 2 Peekskill NY 10566

NEWMAN, SHARON ANN, television producer; b. N.Y.C., June 13, 1952; d. Frank Saul and Janis Miriam (Schloss) N.; m. Howard Mark Gluss, Aug. 7, 1983. B.F.A., U. Miami, 1973; M.F.A., U. Utah, 1978. Tchr. nursery sch. Jewish Community Center, 1978-80; library asst. Marriott Library, Salt Lake City, 1976-80, manuscript processor, 1980; youth librarian, creative arts specialist Maricopa County Library, Phoenix, 1980; dir. Young Conservatory, Am. Conservatory Theatre, San Francisco, 1981-83; adminstrv. asst. TV and motion picture syndication Embassy Telecommunications, Los Angeles, 1983-84; asst. producer The Jeffersons, 1984; dir. adminstrn. Home Box Office, Los Angeles, 1984-86, exec. asst. original programming, 1986—. Author: (plays) Once Upon a Chicken, 1976; Rumplestiltskin's Revenge, 1977. Mem. Nat. Assn. Female Execs., Internat. Platform Assn., Press Club San Francisco, Childrens Theatre Assn., Am. Theatre Assn., Internat. Reiki Assn. Jewish. Home: 4112 Madison Ave Culver City CA 90230 Office: Home Box Office 2049 Century Park E Suite 4100 Los Angeles CA 90067

NEWMARK, ANDREA, nutrition consultant and researcher, financial adviser; b. Freeport, N.Y., Dec. 8, 1960; d. Barry Oscar and Phyllis Helena (Schiffer) N. B.S. in Biochemistry, SUNY-Binghamton, 1982. Regional distbr. Munch-A-Bunch, Hicksville, N.Y., 1983-84; pres. ACN Analysis, Levittown, N.Y., 1984—; educator Yours, Ours, Mine Ctr., Levittown, 1983-84; cons. Fantasy Gifts, Levittown, 1985—; lectr., leader workshops in field, N.Y.C. area, 1986—. Author pamphlets in field. Editor A Healthy Outlook, 1986—. Canvasser, N.Y. Pub. Interest Research Group, 1982-83. Mem. Nat. Assn. Female Execs. Avocations: travel; kite flying. Home: 273 N Newbridge Rd Levittown NY 11756

NEWMARK, MARILYN (MRS. LEONARD J. MEISELMAN), sculptor; b. N.Y.C., July 20, 1928; d. Edward Ellis and Mabel (Davies) Newmark; student Adelphi Coll., 1945-47, Alfred U., 1949; m. Leonard J. Meiselman, Mar. 15, 1952. Sculptor, specializing in horses, equestrian figures, dogs in sporting scenes; exhibited in group shows: sculpture exhbn. NAD, Nat. Arts Club, Nat. Art Mus. of Sport (all N.Y.C.), James Ford Bell Mus., Wis., Smithsonian Instn., Washington, Pa. Acad. Natural Scis.; represented in permanent collections at Nat. Mus. Racing, N.Y., Internat. Mus. of Horse Ky., Nat. Art Mus. of Sport, also pvt. collections. Recipient Anna Hyatt Huntington award, 1970-75, 80-83, 86; award Council Am. Artists Socs., 1972, 73, 79, 80; Hudson Valley John Newington award, 1973, 77, gold medal, 1979; NAD Ellin P. Speyer award, 1974, Artist Fund award, 1982. Fellow Nat. Sculpture Soc. (council 1973-75, rec. sec. 1976, sec. 1977-79, council 1981-83, Bronze medal 1986), Am. Artists Profl. League (Gold medal 1974, 77); mem. Allied Artists Am. (gold medal 1981), Pen and Brush Club (gold medal 1977, Solo award 1974, 78, 80), Soc. Animal Artists (jury of admissions 1972-75), Nat. Acad. Equine Artists (founding mem.), Nassau Suffolk Horsemans Assn. (dir., corr. sec. 1969-83). Clubs: Catherine Lorillard Wolfe Art (jury of admissions N.Y.C. 1972-74, Gold medal 1973); Smithtown Hunt, Nat. Steeplechase and Hunt Assn., Past Meadowbrook Hunt (L.I., N.Y.). Address: Woodhollow Rd East Hills NY 11577

NEWMARK, MARIS S., interior designer, consultant; b. Bklyn., May 1, 1943; d. Louis G. and Pauline (Cantor) Levine; m. Alan Robert Newmark, Nov. 23, 1961; children—Jeffrey Todd, Kerri Gay. Student Bklyn. Coll., Moore Coll. Art; cert. Phila. Coll. Art, 1984. Mdse. mgr. J.C. Penney Co., Audubon and Voorhees, N.J., 1973-80; sr. dist. designer Phila. and N.J. dists. Cort Furniture Rental, Maple Shade, N.J., 1980-83; pres. Maris Newmark Interior Design, Inc., Cherry Hill, N.J., 1983—. Vol. charity orgns., Cherry Hill, 1976—; leader Girl Scouts U.S.A., Cherry Hill, 1974-75; pres., founder Deborah Hosp. Charity chpt., Bklyn., 1962-63. Mem. Nat. Home Fashion League, Nat. Assn. Female Execs. Democrat. Jewish. Avocations: travel; yoga; photography; art. Home and Office: 41 Strathmore Dr Cherry Hill NJ 08003

NEWSOM, BARBARA JOAN, association controller, golf club owner; b. Indpls., June 10, 1936; d. Floyd Herbert and Cora Eleanor (Gabel) Dreyer; m. Drextle Lee Newsom, Oct. 15, 1954; children—Diana Lee, Cynthia Lou, John Adam, Patricia Kay. Student pub. schs., Indpls. Clk. typist Allison div. Gen. Motors Co., 1954, 56; bookkeeper Greenfield Country Club Pro Shop (Ind.), 1956-59; mgr., bookkeeper Hazelden Country Club, Brook, Ind., 1959-60; bookkeeper Harrison Lake Country Club Pro Shop, Columbus, Ind., 1960-73; co-owner, Golf Club of Ind., Zionsville, 1973—; bookkeeper nat. hdqrs. Amateur Athletic Union, Indpls., 1974-76, bus. mgr., 1976-81, comptroller, 1981—. Leader 4H Club, 1971-73, 79—; sec. PTA, 1967-69; treas. PTO, 1974-75; deacon, elder Christian Ch. (Disciples of Christ). Home: 8585 N 925 E Brownsburg IN 46112 Office: 3400 86th St W Indianapolis IN 46268

NEWSOM, DOUGLAS ANN JOHNSON, journalist, educator; b. Dallas, Jan. 16, 1934; d. J. Douglas and R. Grace (Dickson) Johnson; B.J. cum laude, U. Tex., 1954, B.F.A. summa cum laude, 1955, M.J., 1956, Ph.D., 1978; m. Mack Newsom, Jr., Oct. 27, 1956 (div. 1980); children—Michael Douglas, Kevin Jackson, Nancy Elizabeth, William Macklemore. Gen. publicity State Fair Tex., 1955; advt. and promotion Newsom's Women's Wear, 1956-57; publicity Auto Market Show, 1961; lab. instr. radio-tv news-writing course U. Tex., 1961-62; local publicist Tex. Boys Choir, 1964-69, nat. publicist, 1967-69; prof. journalism Tex. Christian U., 1969—, chmn. journalism dept., 1979-86; public relations dir. ann. Gt. S.W. Boat Show, 1966-72; public relations cons., writer, 1965—; public relations Horace Ainsworth Co., Dallas, 1971-75; dir. ONEOK, energy co. Mem. Public Relations Found. Tex. (life mem.), Mortar Bd. Alumnae, Women in Communications (nat. public relations dir. 1969-71, rep. to World Press Freedom Com.), Public Relations Soc. Am. (accredited, nat. chmn. edn. sect. 1984), Am. Women in Radio and TV, Assn. for Edn. in Journalism and Mass Communication (past pres. public relations div.; pres. 1984-85), Tex. Public Relations Assn. (dir.), Accrediting Council for Edn. in Journalism and Mass Communications (nat. chmn. accrediting com. 1981-83), Found. for Pub. Relations Research and Edn., Tex. Journalism Edn. Council (pres. 1981), Delta Delta Delta. Episcopalian. Author: This Is PR, 1976, 3d edit., 1984; Writing in Public Relations Practice: Form and Style, 1980, 2d edit., 1986; Media Writing, 1984. Home: 4237 Shannon Dr Fort Worth TX 76116 Office: Dept Journalism Tex Christian U Fort Worth TX 76129

NEWSOM, JAN LYNN REIMANN, lawyer; b. Madison, Wis., Feb. 28, 1947; d. Curtis Whitt and Doris Elizabeth (Jerde) R.; m. Neil Edward Newsom, Apr. 15, 1972; children—Kelly Ann, Loren Elizabeth. B.A., U. Tex.-Austin, 1969; J.D., 1971. Bar: Tex. 1972, U.S. Dist. Ct. (no. dist.) Tex. 1982. Vice-pres. legal Nat. Compliance Cons., Dallas, 1972; corp. legal atty. Blue Cross & Blue Shield Tex., Dallas, 1972—. Bd. dirs., chmn. nominating com. Am. Cancer Soc., Dallas central unit, 1978—; mem. nat. EEO task force Blue Cross and Blue Shield Assn., Chgo., 1979—; mem. Innovators, Dallas Symphony Orch. League, 1983—. Mem. ABA, State Bar Tex., Dallas Bar Assn., Alpha Chi Omega Alumnae. Republican. Methodist. Home: 6040 Preston Haven Dallas TX 75230 Office: Legal Div Blue Cross and Blue Shield Tex PO Box 655730 Dallas TX 75265-5730

NEWSOM, LILA ROGERS, psychol. examiner; b. Pittsboro, Ind., Sept. 14, 1937; d. Alfred O. and Willa Mae (Giffin) Rogers; B.A., Abilene Christian Coll., 1959; M.A. (NDEA fellow), U. Hawaii, 1961; m. Bobby G. Newsom, Sept. 15, 1960; children—Robert Michael, James Eric, Dana Marie, Daniel Edward. Psychol. examiner Bristol Mental Health Clinic, Bristol Tenn.-Va., 1961-65; instr. psychology U. Tenn., Chattanooga, 1973-78; cons., psychol. examiner Hamilton County Juvenile Ct., Chattanooga, 1975-78; psychol. examiner Chattanooga Testing and Counseling, 1978—; cons. psychol. examiner Hamilton County Sch. System, Chattanooga, 1982—; psychol. examiner Team Evaluation Ctr., 1983—. Mem. Am. Psychol. Assn. Republican. Mem. Ch. of Christ. Home: 1312 Scout Rd Hixson TN 37343 Office: Suite 413 Whitehall Med Ctr 960 E 3d St Chattanooga TN 37403

NEWTON, BARBARA ELEANORE, physical therapist; b. Glendale, Calif., Jan. 16, 1951; d. Ernest Welton and Mary Elizabeth (Gurney) Estey; m. Douglas Edward Newton, June 7, 1970 (div. Dec. 1982); children—David Edward, Kristy Anne. Student Pacific Union Coll., 1968-70; B.S., Loma Linda U., 1972. Public health phys. therapist Calif. Children's Services, San Bernardino, 1973-76, phys. therapist, Stockton, Calif., 1982-83; substitute phys. therapist Sch. Dist. Tacoma, 1979-80; cert. phys. therapist Ednl. Services Dist. 101, Spokane, 1983—. Mem. Am. Phys. Therapy Assn., Wash. Phys. Therapy Assn., Loma Linda U. Alumni Assn. Republican. Seventh Day Adventist. Avocations: Snow skiing; horse riding; backpacking. Office: Ednl Service Dist 101 W1025 Indiana Ave Spokane WA 99205

NEWTON, DENISE L., mortgage company account executive, financial consultant; b. Chgo., Apr. 17, 1958; d. Edward R. and Janet (Carey) Muchala; m. Terrance J. Newton, Oct. 28, 1978. Student pub. schs., Chgo. Br. mgr. Gen. Fin. Corp., Chgo., 1977-79; teller 1st Bank and Trust Co., Oldsmar, Fla., 1979-81; closing agt. Chase Manhattan of Fla., Tampa, 1982-83; account exec. Citicorp, Clearwater, Fla., 1981—. Mem. Am. Bus. Women Assn. (pres. chpt. 1985), Fla. Mortgage Broker Assn., Oldsmar C. of C. Republican. Roman Catholic. Lodge: Oldsmar Lioness (pres. 1984-85). Home: 442 Evergreen Dr Oldsmar FL 33557 Office: Citicorp 2561 Countryside Blvd Suites 1-2 Clearwater FL 33519

NEWTON, DOROTHY RUTH ARMSTRONG, principal; b. Dallas, Sept. 8, 1923; d. Albert Frederick and Mayme B. (Miller) Armstrong; B.A., U. Tex., Arlington, 1967, M.A., 1973; adminstr.'s cert. North Tex. State U., 1980; m. James L. Newton, Mar. 27, 1942; children—Diana Jay, Rena Kathleen, Carole Ruth. Sec., Reconstrn. Fin. Corp., CSC, Washington, 1941-42; tchr. Jefferson Middle Sch., Grand Prairie, Tex., 1968-69; tchr. Grand Prairie High Sch., 1969-81, asst. prin., 1981-85, prin. alternative edn. ctr. Grand Prairie Ind. Sch. Dist., 1985—. Served with Women's Res., USMC, 1943-45. Cert. tchr. for life, cert. sch. adminstr., Tex. Mem. Assn. Supervision and Curriculum Devel., Nat. Assn. Secondary Prins., Tex. Assn. Secondary Schs. Prins., Grand Prairie Prins. Assn., Assn. Tex. Profl. Educators (local treas. 1980-81), AAUW, Phi Delta Kappa. Republican. Mem. Christian Ch. (Disciples of Christ). Club: Roadrunners. Office: 101 High School Dr Grand Prairie TX 75050

NEWTON, PATRICIA LEE, lawyer; real estate investor; b. Tulsa, Okla., Jan. 13, 1948; d. Kenneth Ross and Mary Winifred (Rick) N.; m. Stephen J. Rechichae, Jan. 9, 1970 (div.); 1 dau., Rachel; m. 2d, Sabin Rife Thompson, Feb. 10, 1981. B.S., U. Tenn., 1971, J.D., 1975. Bar: Tenn. 1975. Social worker Middle Tenn. Mental Health Ctr., Nashville, 1971-72; assoc. Gilbreath, Carpenter, Knoxville, 1974-76; trial atty. Patricia Newton, Knoxville, 1976-78; sr. trial atty. Pub. Defender's Office, Nashville, 1979-80; assoc. E.E. Edwards & Assocs., Nashville, 1980-81; sr. asst. gen. counsel Tenn. Dept. Health and Environ., Nashville, 1981—; bd. dirs. C&FS Adoption Adv. Bd., Knoxville, 1977-78; instr. Knoxville Women's Ctr., 1977-78. Active Homeowners Assn. Creekside Meadows, Nashville, 1980-81, Univ. Sch. Aux., Nashville, 1981—, Women's Polit. Caucus, Nashville, 1981—, Knox County Democratic Com., 1977-78, Friends of Spencer Acad., Nashville, 1979-81, Friends of Bellevue Library, Nashville, 1984—. Mem. ABA, Tenn. Assn. Criminal Def. Lawyers. Democrat. Roman Catholic. Office: Office of Gen Counsel Dept Health and Environment Cordell Hull Bldg Nashville TN 37219

NEWTON, RENEE DENISE, association executive, consultant; b. Detroit, June 23, 1955; d. John Wilbert and Mary (Butler) N. B.A., Morse Sch. Bus., 1977; student Eastern Conn. State Coll., 1973-74, Morris Brown Coll., 1977-82. Adminstrv. asst. U. Conn., Storrs, 1974-76; pension analyst Aetna Life Ins. Co., Hartford, 1976-77, pension technician, 1979-80; video-journalist Cable News Network, Atlanta, 1980-81; asst. to area councils Atlanta C. of C., 1983—; cons. Commn. on Christian Social Relations, Atlanta, 1982—; spl. cons. Marcus-Diversified Services, Inc., Atlanta, 1982—; mem. support staff Pub. Relations Soc. Am., Atlanta, 1983—. Vol. Chuck Williams Election campaign City Council, Atlanta, 1978, Michael Lomax Re-election County Commn., Atlanta, 1979, Just Us Theatre, Atlanta, 1983, Atlanta Symphony, 1983. Recipient New Membership award Atlanta C. of C., 1983. Mem. Women in Communications, Nat. Exec. Women, Media Women, Univ. Women, Women Entrepreneurs, Phi Beta Lambda. Methodist. Home: 5401 Old National Hwy 209 College Park GA 30349 Office: Atlanta C of C 1300 N Omni Internat Atlanta GA 30303

NICCOLINI, DIANORA, photographer; b. Florence, Italy, Oct. 3, 1936; d. George and Elaine (Augsbury) N.; came to U.S., 1945, naturalized, 1960; student Hunter Coll., 1955-62, Art Students League, 1960, Germain Sch. Photography, 1962. Med. photographer Manhattan Eye, Ear and Throat Hosp., 1963-65; organizer med. photography dept., 1st chief med. photographer Lenox Hill Hosp., 1965-67; organizer, head dept. med. and audio visual edn. St. Clare's Hosp., N.Y.C., 1967-76; mem. Third Eye Gallery, N.Y.C., 1974-76; owner Dianora Niccolini Creations, 1976—; instr. photography Camera Club N.Y., 1978-79, Germaine Sch. Photography, 1978-79, N.Y. Inst. Photography, 1981-83; one woman shows 209 Photo Gallery, Top of the Stairs Gallery, Third Eye Gallery, 1974, 75, 77, West Broadway Gallery, N.Y.C., 1981, Camera Club N.Y., 1982, Photographics Unltd. Gallery, N.Y.C., 1981, Overseas Press Club, N.Y.C., 1983, Impulse Gallery, Provincetown, Mass., 1983; project dir. Photography over 65, N.Y.C., 1978; pub. portfolios. Mem. Women Photographers N.Y. (founder 1974), Biol. Photog. Assn., Assn. Ind. Video and Filmmakers, Internat. Center Photography, Am. Soc. Mag. Photographers, Am. Soc. Picture Profls., Profl. Women Photographers (coordinator), Integral Yoga Inst. Author: Women of Vision, 1982; author/photographer: Men in Focus, 1983; editor: P.W.P. Times, 1981-82; contbr. to photog. books, 1979, 80; contbg. editor Functional Photography, 1979-80, N.Y. Photo Dist. News, 1980. Home: 356 E 78th St New York NY 10021 Office: Dianora Niccolini Creations 2 W 32d St Suite 200 New York NY 10001

NICE-HOOD, BONITA COLLETTE, exercise physiology specialist, dancer, choreographer; b. Aiken, S.C., June 3, 1954; d. Rance and Mary Louise (Aidkens) Nice; m. Dennis Levesque, June 14, 1978 (div. 1978); m. Danny Brice Hood, Dec. 28, 1985. Student St. Johns River Jr. Coll., 1972-78; A.A., Santa Fe Community Coll., 1982; B.S. in Exercise Physiology, U. Fla., 1985. Cert. profl. aerobic instr., CPR, Master Cake Decorator. Exercise instr. Putnam County Sch. Bd., Palatka, Fla., 1972-80; dance tchr. Gail Moore Sch. Dance, Brunswick, Ga., 1978-80; exercise instr. N. Fla. Community Coll., Ocala, 1980-82 prin. jazz tchr. Katherine Knight Sch. Dance, Leesburg, Fla., 1980-82; aerobic instr. Leesburg Health Studio, 1980-82; supr. exercise program N. Fla. Regional Hosp., Gainesville, 1984; tchr. aerobic dance Gainesville Health and Fitness Ctr., 1982—; owner Bodi Techniques Exercise and Dance Studio; pacesetter Shape Mag., N.E. Fla. Area, 1986—; coordinator super class Aerobics and Fitness Assn. Am., Fla., 1986. Choreographer religious play: Because I weep, 1984. Treas. Little Women Palatka, 1971-72; fund raiser Dance for the Heart, Gainesville, 1984, Jazzercise, Gainesville, 1985. Recipient Heroic Hero award, Savant, Leadership Edn. and Resource Network, U. Fla., 1985. Mem. AAHPER Dance, Coll. Sports Medicine, Internat. Dance Educators Assn., Dance Edutors Am.; Delta Psi Kappa, Alpha Xi Delta. Republican. Methodist. Lodge: Order Eastern Star (organist chpt. 33 1984-86). Avocations: running; snow skiing; ceramics; painting; cake decorating. Home: 204 Hargrove St Palatka FL 32077

NICHELSON, CATHY, contract specialist; b. Huntsville, Ala., July 22, 1961; d. William Rosser and Susie Mae (Parks) Nichelson; widowed 1981; children—Barbara, Anthony, Cathy, Debby. B.A., Ala. A&M U., 1984, postgrad. in bus., 1985—. Receptionist, Huntsville Jr. Coll., 1980; sales rep. Avon, Huntsville, 1982-84; contract specialist NASA Marshall Space Flight Ctr., Huntsville, 1980—. Editor: The Winner Poetry, 1983. Mem. nat. Assn. Female Execs., Instrument Soc. Am., Am. Mus. History, Democrat. Seventh-day Adventist. Avocations: weaving; basketmaking; cooking; fishing; classical music. Office: NASA/Marshall Space Flight Ctr AP 48 Marshall Space Flight Ctr AL 35812

NICHOLAS, COLOMBE MARGARET, fashion licensing exec.; b. Larchmont, N.Y., Nov. 6, 1944; d. Dimitri Paul and Colombe Irene Nicholas; student Coll. de Montreaux (Switzerland), 1960; B.A., U. Dayton, 1964; J.D., U. Cin., 1968; m. Leonard Rosenberg. Buyer Macy's 1970-75; buyer, divisional mdse. mgr. Bloomingdale's, 1975-78; v.p., mdse. mgr. Bonwit Teller, 1978-80; pres. Christian Dior N.Y., Inc., N.Y.C., 1980—. Mem. Young Pres.'s Orgn. Office: 104 N 40th St New York NY 10018

NICHOLAS, MAY THERESA, string instrument company executive, b. Phila., Aug. 8, 1944; d. Charles B. and Irene L. N.; B.S. in Applied Music (scholar), Temple U., 1966: cert. Internazionale Sommerakademie des Mozarteums, Salzburg, Austria, 1965; diploma Orff-Institut, Salzburg 1965; diploma M.W. Funk Real Estate Inst., 1984. With House of Primavera, Phila., 1964-79, sec.-treas., 1968-79, dir., 1968-79; sec.-treas. Phila. Sales Co. Inc., div., 1971-79, dir., 1971-79; gen. mgr. RW Service and Supplies div. Italo-Am. String Instrument Co., Inc., Cherry Hill, N.J., 1979-82, also dir.; gen. mgr., chief fin. officer Trial Mus. Supplies, Inc., 1986—; prin. Nicholas Services, property mgmt.; violin maker. Recipient Vira I. Heinz award, 1965; N.J. State scholar, 1962-65. Mem. Violin Soc. Am. (charter), Nat. Assn. Music Mchts., Phila. Direct Mktg. Club. Democrat. Presbyterian. Home: 6338 Irving Ave Pennsauken NJ 08109 Office: PO Box 1002 Merchantville NJ 08109

NICHOLAS, NICKIE LEE, industrial hygienist; b. Lake Charles, La., Jan. 19, 1938; d. Clyde Lee and Jessie Mae (Lyons) N.; B.S., U. Houston, 1960, M.S., 1966. Tchr. sci. Pasadena (Tex.) Ind. Sch. Dist., 1960-61; chemist FDA, Dallas, 1961-62, VA Hosp., Houston, 1962-66; chief biochemist Baylor U. Coll. Medicine, 1966-68; chemist NASA, Johnson Spacecraft Center, 1968-73; analytical chemist TVA, Muscle Shoals, Ala., 1973-75; indsl. hygienist, compliance officer Occupational Safety and Health Adminstrn., Dept. Labor, Houston, 1975-79, area dir., Tulsa, 1979-82, mgr., Austin, 1982—; mem. faculty VA Sch. Med. Tech., Houston, 1963-66. Recipient award for outstanding achievement German embassy, 1958, Suggestion award VA, 1963, Group Achievement award Skylab Med. Team, NASA, 1974; Personal Achievement award Dept. Labor Fed. Women's Program, 1984. Mem. Am. Chem. Soc. (dir. analytical group Southeastern Tex. and Brazosport sects. 1971, chmn. elect 1973), Am. Assn. Clin. Chemists, Am. Harp Soc., Fed. Exec. Assn. (pres. 1984-85), Kappa Epsilon. Home: 1305 Shannon Oaks Austin TX 78746 Office: 611 E 6th St Suite 303 Austin TX 78701

NICHOLAS, RUTH MARIE, travel agent, tour operator; b. Buffalo, N.Y., June 22, 1929; d. Charles Howard and Lorette (Huster) Lovell; m. Donald Joseph Nicholas, Sept. 7, 1961; children—Donald J. Jr., Robert Paul, James Douglas. A.B., Trinity Coll., 1952. Tchr., counselor Jackson Jr. High Sch., Detroit, 1955-76; coordinator sr. citizen program Plainwell Community Edn. Ctr., Mich., 1977-82; owner Shangri La Travel Service, Plainwell, 1982—; agt. Travelers Ins. Co., Hartford, Conn., 1983—. Recipient scholarship Ursuline Acad., 1943, Trinity Coll., 1946; T Pin award Trinity Coll., 1950; NSF fellow, 1956. Mem. Nat. Tour Assn., Nat. Assn. Female Execs., Plainwell C. of C., Kalamazoo C. of C. Republican. Roman Catholic. Club: Lake Doster Tennis (pres. 1982-84). Avocations: tennis; photography; cooking. Home: 366 Shangri La Circle Plainwell MI 49080 Office: Shangri La Travel Service 352 12th St Plainwell MI 49080

NICHOLAS, SUSAN KEHOE, communications and training company executive, consultant; b. Cleve., Dec. 5, 1947; d. John William and Mary Margaret (Swicia) Kehoe; m. Gerald Nicholas, May 15, 1970 (div.); children—Patricia, Mark. B.A., U. Detroit, 1970; M.A., Oakland U., 1980, Ph.D., 1983. Cert. secondary tchr., Mich. Trainer ESL Utica Community Schs., Mich., 1974-78; coordinator program Oakland Univ., Rochester, Mich., 1980-83; adj. prof. mktg. Wayne State Univ., Detroit, 1983-85, U. Mich., Ann Arbor, 1984-85; pres., owner Nicholas & Assocs., Inc., Birmingham, Mich., 1983—; trainer, program designer Gen. Motors, Detroit, 1984—; trainer, cons. Nat. Steel, Ecorse, Mich., 1984—; trainer, speech coach AM Gen., Livonia, Mich., 1984—; presenter Nat. Reading Conf., 1981, 83, Internat. Reading Assn., 1982, Am. Edn. Research Assn., 1982, Conf. on Coll. Composition, 1984. Mem. Am. Soc. for Tng. and Devel., Internat. Assn. Bus. Communicators, Econ. Club Detroit, Pub. Relations Soc. Am. Avocations: reading; travel; dancing. Home and Office: 3858 Lincoln West Birmingham MI 48010

NICHOLS, ALLISON SUE, engineer; b. New Haven, Mar. 15, 1957; d. Philip Paul and Arlene Janice (Lieberman) Donenfeld; m. Malcolm Swift Nichols, Dec. 30, 1979. B.S.C.E., Union Coll., Schenectady, 1977; M.B.A., Golden Gate U., 1981. Intern N.Y. State Energy Office, Albany, N.Y., 1976-77, editor bull., 1976; assoc. resident mgr. Gen. Electric Co., Louisville, 1977-78, resident mgr., Schenectady, 1978-79; project engr. Swinerton & Walberg Co., San Francisco, 1980-81, asst. project mgr., 1981-83, project mgr., 1983-85; project mgr. George Hyman Constrn. Co., Boston, 1985—. Contbr. articles to Seventeen mag., Empire State Energy News. Actress various theatres, including for Danville Old Towne Theater (Calif.), 1982, Eugene O'Neill Soc., Lafayette, Calif., 1983. Mem. ASCE (assoc.; v.p. student chpt. 1976-77), Nat. Assn. Female Execs. Republican. Jewish. Lodge: B'nai B'rith (Danville). Home: Nine Hawthorne Pl Boston MA 02114 Office: George Hyman Constrn Co 410 Boylston St Boston MA 02116

NICHOLS, BARBARA D., marketing executive; b. Boston, Aug. 19, 1947; d. Charles Morris and Jeannette N. B.A., Simmons Coll., 1969; M.S., Cornell U., 1971. Mgr. mktg. services Automated Bldg., Miami, Fla., 1972-76; project mgr. Crown Zellerbach, San Francisco, 1976-78, div. mgr. market research, 1978-80, div. mgr. market devel., San Leandro, 1980-81, mktg. mgr., San Francisco, 1981—; guest lectr. U. Miami, 1971-76; session chair, moderator Constrn. Market Seminars, Chgo., 1971-79. Author: (with others) Guide to Construction Marketing research, 1978. Editor: (with others) Business Info-Source for the Forest Products Industry, 1979. Mem. ARC, Calif., Mothers Against Drunk Drivers, Californians for Nonsmokers Rights, Am. Lung Assn. Recipient service awards San Francisco Jr. C. of C., 1977-79. Mem. Am. Mgmt. Assn. (course instr. 1980-83), Am. Mktg. Assn., Potato Chip/Snack Food Assn. (contbr. annual industry report 1982-84). Clubs: Cornell, Ivy (San Francisco). Office: Crown Zellerbach 1 Bush St Suite 1700 San Francisco CA 94104

NICHOLS, BERNICE PAULINE, civic worker, artist; b. Delta, Colo., Jan. 13, 1932; d. John Obert and Pauline Gertrude (Hockett) Graybeal; m. Darrel Duaine Nichols, Sept. 3, 1950; children—Linda F. Nichols Baker, E. Marlene Nichols DeMarcus, Dennis D. Art student Whitworth Coll. Sales clk. J.C. Penny Co., Spokane, Wash., 1950-51; fashion show dir. Sarah Coventry Jewelry, Ephrata, Wash., 1958-59; welcome hostess Merchants of Ephrata, 1969-71; Artist "Fruit Basket" still life (hon. mention 1983), black and white drawing Fall Art Festival. Jurist Grant County Superior Ct., Ephrata, 1968, Spokane County Superior Ct., Wash., 1978; mem. Spokane County Library Assn., 1980—; pres. Am. Luth. Ch. Women, 1980-81; mem. parents council Pacific Luth. U., Spokane, 1982—. Recipient 6th Flight Runner Up award Lakeview Golf and County Club, 1968. Republican. Club: Compass (Spokane). Lodges: Eagles, Narcisse Grange. Avocations: painting; golf; swimming; walking; singing. Home: 212 W Dawn Spokane WA 99218

NICHOLS, CYNTHIA LEIGH, lawyer; b. Gainesville, Fla., Aug. 3, 1957; d. Donald Gilbert and Betty Catherine (Bullard) Nichols. B.S., Fla. State U., 1978; J.D., Stetson U., 1980. Bar: Fla. 1981. Law clk. Fla. Supreme Ct., Tallahassee, 1981; asst. state atty. State of Fla., Jacksonville, 1981-82; sole practice, Jacksonville, 1982-83; ptnr. Nichols & Nichols, Jacksonville, 1983—. Mem. ABA, Fla. Bar Assn., Jacksonville Bar Assn., Assn. Trial Lawyers Am. Democrat. Baptist. Home: 13936 Mandarin Rd Jacksonville FL 32223 Office: Nichols & Nichols 340-1 E Adams St Jacksonville FL 32202

NICHOLS, EDIE DIANE, real estate executive; b. Grahamstown, Eastern Cape Province, Republic of South Africa, Mar. 28, 1939; came to U.S., 1963; d. Cyril Doughtry and Dorothy Ethel (Nottingham) Tyson; m. John F. Nichols, Dec. 16, 1962; 1 son, Ian Tyson. Adminstrv. asst. Am. Acad. Medicine, N.Y.C., 1963-64, Jack Lenor Larsen, Inc., N.Y.C., 1964-70; v.p. John Scott Fones, Inc., N.Y.C., 1971-76, Howard J. Rubenstein Assocs. Inc., N.Y.C., 1976-80; dir. communications Carl Byoir & Assocs., N.Y.C., 1981-83; account supr. Hill and Knowlton, N.Y.C., 1983-85; with Cross & Brown Co., N.Y.C. Trustee, Central Park Hist. Soc., N.Y.C., 1978-80. Mem. NOW, N.Y. Women in Communications (pub. relations chair 1980-81). Republican. Episcopalian. Club: City (trustee). (N.Y.C.). Home: 16 Stuyvesant Oval New York NY 10009 Office: Cross & Brown Co 63 Wall St New York NY 10005

NICHOLS, ELIZABETH ANN, word processing company executive; b. Springfield, Mass., Dec. 26, 1959; d. Edwin Arthur and Gail Jean (Nagle) N. B.A. cum laude, William Smith Coll., 1980. Office mgr. Pete's Cycles, New Haven, 1976-80; copywriter, office mgr. Craig Altschul Assocs., New Haven, 1980-82; pres. Word Flow, Inc., New Haven, 1982—. Mem. pub. relations com. Women, Business and the Future, New Haven, 1985. Mem. Assn. Info. Systems Profls. Roman Catholic. Avocations: singing; backpacking; gardening. Office: Word Flow Inc 205 Whitney Ave New Haven CT 06511

NICHOLS, GENEVIEVE BOND, compressor manufacturing company executive; b. Martinsville, Va., June 7, 1943; d. Charles Oliver Bond and Myrtle (Ingram) Bond Gollehon; stepdau. Joseph M. Gollehon, Jr. B.S. in Bus. Edn., Radford Coll.-Va. Poly. Inst., 1964; postgrad. in personnel adminstrn. Ala. A&M U., 1983—. Contracts adminstr. Boeing Co., Huntsville, Ala., 1964-73; personnel sec. Wolverine div. Universal Oil Products, Inc., Decatur, Ala., 1976-77; personnel specialist Copeland Corp., Hartselle, Ala., 1977-81, personnel supr., 1981-84, employee relations mgr., Rushville, Ind., 1984—. Named to Saturn/Apollo Roll of Honor, Boeing Co., 1971, 72. Mem. Am. Soc. for Personnel Adminstrn. (chpt. dir. 1984), Decatur Personnel Officers Assn., Community Relations Assn., Bus. and Profl. Women, Hartselle Mgmt. Assn. (sec. 1984), Phi Beta Lambda (state sec. 1963). Episcopalian. Home: 623 N Morgan St Rushville IN 46173 Office: Copeland Corp Conrad C Harcourt Way Rushville IN 46173

NICHOLS, JACQUELINE BRUCE, archeologist; b. Harlan, Ky., Oct. 14, 1941; d. Jack Corum and Martha Jayne (Miracle) Bruce; B.A., Wellesley Coll., 1963; M.A., SUNY, Albany, 1977; m. David Edward Nichols, Mar. 4, 1963; children—Corinna Elizabeth, David Andrew, Patrick Edward. Tchr., Bedford (Eng.) Schs., 1963-64; dir. Archeol. Field Labs., SUNY, Albany, 1976-77, Cath. U., 1978; v.p. Gt. Basin Found. for Archeol. Research, 1979; pres. Atechiston, Inc., Albuquerque, 1980—; co-founder, editor Flintknappers Exchange, 1977; founder, pub. Am. Archeology, 1980—. Wallace Stegner fellow, 1963-64. Mem. AAAS, Soc. Am. Archaeology, Nat. Assn. Women Bus. Owners, Soc. Archeol. Sci., Found. for Desert Archaeology (dir. 1980—). Republican. Home: 81 W Mountain Rd Ridgefield CT 06877 Office: 4426 Constitution NE Albuquerque NM 87110

NICHOLS, JANET ELLEN, educator; b. Rockville Centre, N.Y., Apr. 7, 1950; d. John B. and Virginia Florence (Raupp) Greenhouse; m. John G. Nichols, June 9, 1973; 1 dau., Virginia Anne. B.A., Adelphi U., 1971; M.S., Lehigh U., 1973; postgrad., Colo. State U., 1973-76. Teaching asst. Lehigh U., Bethlehem, Pa., 1971-73, Colo. State U., Ft. Collins, 1973-76; instr. math. U. So. Colo., Pueblo, 1977-79, asst. prof., 1979—. NDEA Title IV fellow, 1971-73. Mem. Am. Math. Soc., Math. Assn. Am., Sigma Xi, Pi Mu Epsilon, Delta Tau Alpha, Delta Phi Alpha. Home: PO Box 214 Canon City CO 81212 Office: Dept Mathematics U So Colo Pueblo CO 81001

NICHOLS, LESLIE JEAN BRASHEAR, farm and vineyard executive; b. Lubbock, Tex., Apr. 3, 1942; d. Cecil I. and Elizabeth (Blain) Brashear; m. Harold Dean Nichols, Dec. 26, 1967; 1 child, Leslie Michelle. B.S. in Edn., Tex. Tech U., 1964, M.Ed., 1973, postgrad., 1976. Cert. tchr., social and rehab. cert. for nursing homes, Tex. Tchr. phys. edn., coach, pub. schs., Crosbyton, Tex., 1964-66; head girls coach, pub. schs., New Home, Tex., 1966-67, Frenship, Tex., 1967-68; ptnr., bus. mgr. Nichols Farms and Vineyard, Idalou, Tex., 1967—; social and rehab. dir. Pkwy Nursing Home, Lubbock, Tex., 1973-77; owner, operator Nicole's Specialities; artist. Pres. Lubbock Osteo. Guild, 1973-77; nat. conv. chmn. Nat. Osteo. Guild Assn., Lubbock, 1977; sec. bd. dirs. Lubbock Garden and Arts Ctr., 1983—, co-chmn. '85 Fiesta, treas., 1985—; pres. Idalou PTA, 1984—; active Lubbock Cultural Affairs, 1985—; fundraising chmn., rep. to bd. dirs. Lubbock Garden and Arts Ctr., Lubbock Art Assn., 1985—. Mem. Am. Alliance Health, Phys. Edn., Recreation and Dance, Tex. Tech Ex-Students, Tau Beta Sigma (Alumni chpt.) (pres. 1976—). Republican. Baptist. Avocations: golf; tennis; basketball; softball; photography. Home and Office: Route 2 Box 169 Idalou TX 79329

NICHOLS, MARGARET ROWELL, social worker; b. Malden, Mass., Aug. 1, 1920; d. John Munn and Edith (Temple) Rowell; m. Paul R. Nichols, June 22, 1941; children—David R., Barbara Nichols Pierimarchi, Carol Nichols Friesen. A.B., Denison U., Granville, Ohio, 1943; M.S.W., Boston U., 1950. Admitting officer, social worker Carney Hosp., Boston, 1948-52; mem. Disability Rev. Team, Boston, 1952-53; social worker Mass. Gen. Hosp., Boston, 1953-55; clin. social worker West Roxbury VA Med. Ctr., Boston, 1955-57; clin. social worker, fieldwork supr. VA, Boston, 1957-64, clin. social worker, student supr. Psychiatry Clinic, 1964—. Recipient Hands and Heart award VA, 1981. Mem. Nat. Assn. Social Workers, Acad. Cert. Social Workers, Boston Gerontologic Psychiatry, Mass. Acad. Psychiat. Social Workers, Nat. Registry Health Care Providers., Baptist Womens Soc. (past pres., deaconess, past chairperson missionary bd. Needham, Mass.). Baptist. Office: VA Boston Psychiatry Clinic 17 Court St Boston MA 02108

NICHOLS, MARTHA MARIE, savings and loan association officer; b. Dallas, Sept. 29, 1956; d. Henry Louis and Elaine Mary (Guentherman) N. B.S. in Polit. Sci., So. Methodist U., Dallas, 1978. Correspondent, Dallas Fed. Savs. & Loan Assn., Dallas, 1978-79, telephone transfer rep., 1979-80, tng. instr., 1980, tng. devel. specialist, 1980-82, br. mgr., asst. v.p., Ft. Worth, 1982-83, br. mgr., asst. v.p., Dallas, from 1983, now v.p.; mem. Inst. Fin. Edn., Dallas, 1981-82. Recipient 1st place Speech Contest Inst. Fin. Edn., 1979. Mem. Nat. Assn. Female Execs., Pi Sigma Alpha, Pi Beta Phi. Republican. Home: 7503 Pebblestone Dr Dallas TX 75230 Office: Dallas Fed Savs & Loan Assn PO Box 12709 8333 Douglas Ave Dallas TX 75225

NICHOLS, MARY PEROT, broadcast executive; b. York, Pa., Oct. 11, 1926; d. Charles Poultney and Dorothy (Leonard) Perot; B.A. in Polit. Sci., Swarthmore Coll., 1948; m. Robert Brayton Nichols, Oct. 11, 1953 (div. 1967); children—Kerstin, Duncan, Eliza. Reporter, polit. columnist Village Voice, N.Y.C., 1958-66, city editor, columnist, 1968-75; dir. public relations N.Y.C.

Parks, Recreation and Cultural Affairs Adminstrn., 1966-68; free-lance journalist, investigative columnist Boston Herald Am., 1975-76; dir. communications Office of Mayor, Boston, 1977-78; dir. Sta. WNYC Radio-TV, N.Y.C.'s Mcpl. Broadcasting System, public broadcasting stas. associated with Nat. Public Radio and Public Broadcasting System, 1978-80, 84—; dir. communications U. Pa., Phila., 1980-83; sec., dir. Eastern Public Radio Network, 1979-80. Trustee Com. for Arts in Pa., Parks Council N.Y.C., 1969-75; bd. dirs. Public Interest Law Center Phila. Recipient Rosebuds award for investigation of organized crime, journalism rev. More, 1973. Mem. Forum Exec. Women (exec. bd.). Democrat. Club: Cosmopolitan of Phila. Contbr. articles to various publs., including Barron's, New Republic. Address: 505 LaGuardia Pl New York NY 10012 Office: WNYC 1 Centre St New York NY 10007

NICHOLS, NANCY, financial consultant; b. Monroe, Mich., Dec. 1, 1939; d. Joseph William and Eva Arlene (Smith) Smith; m. Raymond Arlyn Nichols, Jan. 17, 1959; children—Anita Marie Nichols Baran, Amy Beth Nichols Forrest. Student U. Mich., 1972, Washtenaw Community Coll., 1974, Siena Heights Coll., 1983. Sales staff Glover Real Estate, Adrian, Mich., 1972-75; mgr. Bennett Ambulance, Tecumseh, Mich., 1972-75; acting dir. Lenawee Health Dept., Adrian, 1975-78; owner, capt. Anywhere Sports Fishing, Monroe, 1978-85; assoc., cons. Stauder, Barch & Assoc., Ann Arbor, Mich., 1985—; speaker in seminars concerning pub. health laws and regulations, unification of health systems, county govt., women in decision making roles. Bd. dirs. U. Mich. Sch. Pub. Health, 1980-85, Community Mental Health Bd. Lenawee County, 1975-84; vice-chmn. exec. bd. Tecumseh Housing Commn., 1975—; chmn. exec. com. South Central Substance Abuse Commn., 1976-84; chairperson Human Service Bd., 1976-84, Lenawee County Democratic Party, Adrian, 1985-86, Lewanee County Health Bd., 1976-78, Lenawee County Energy Task Force, 1980-81; candidate for state rep. Lenawee County, 1984; county commnr. Lenawee County, 1974-84; mem. Industry/Edn. Coordinating Council (3 counties), 1983-85, State Health Coordinating Council, 1980-84, Selection com. for State Dir. Pub. Health, 1981, State Mich. com. for Unification of Pub. Mental Health System, 1979, State Mich. Substance Abuse Consolidation Task Force, 1975-76, Mich. Assn. Bds. Health, 1976-84, pres. 1983; bd. dirs. Mich. Mid-South Health Systems Agy., 1976-83, pres. 1981. Named Democrat of Yr. Lenawee Democratic Party, 1985; recipient Mich. Legis. Cert. Tribute for Outstanding Service in Health field, 1983, 85, Mich. Minuteman Citation Honor for Promoting Mich. and community, 1979; Namesake of the Nancy Nichols Award for Outstanding contribution to the Substance Abuse field by the Substance Abuse Program Directors in Calhouns, Hillsdale, Jackson and Lenawee Counties, 1983. Mem. Bus. and Profl. Women. Democrat. Methodist. Clubs: Safari (sec. 1984—) (Tecumseh). Lodge: Order Eastern Star (past matron). Home: 216 North Oneida St Tecumseh MI 49286 Office: Stauder Barch & Assoc 3989 Research Park Ann Arbor MI 48104

NICHOLS, VICKI ANNE, natural resource company executive, consultant; b. Denver, June 10, 1949; d. Glenn Warner and Loretta Irene (Chalender) Adams; m. Robert Howard Nichols, Oct. 28, 1972 (div. Feb. 1981); children—Christopher Travis, Lindsay Meredith. B.A., Colo. Coll., Colorado Springs, 1972; postgrad. U. Denver, 1976-77. Treas., controller, dir. Polaris Resources, Inc., Denver, 1972—; controller, dir. Polaris Oil & Gas Inc., Denver, 1978-84; controller, corp. sec., dir. Polaris Gold Corp., Denver, 1981—; corp. sec., dir. Assoc. Pipe & Supply Co., Golden, Colo., 1982—; v.p., dir. Polaris Crane & Equipment Co., Commerce City, Colo., 1983-84; owner Nichols Bus. Services, Wheat Ridge, Colo., 1976—. Home: 4305 Brentwood St Wheat Ridge CO 80033 Office: Polaris Resources Inc 999 18th St Suite 3270 Denver CO 80202

NICHOLS, VICKI LYNN, business official; b. Cin., July 4, 1955; d. Dale Peter Nichols and Janet Josephine (Nagele) Nichols Mortimer. File clk. Dayco Corp., Cin., 1974-75, order entry processor, 1975-76, br. mgr., sec., 1976-77, personal sec., regional saleswoman, 1977-78, inside sales coordinator, West Chester, Ohio, 1978-80, sr. inside sales coordinator, 1980-82, office mgr., 1982—. Author: Branch Training Manuals, 1980 (cert. of accomplishment 1982). Roman Catholic. Avocations: travel; bowling; reading; collecting Star Trek memorabilia. Home: 6712 Harrison Ave Apt 4 Cincinnati OH 45257 Office: Dayco Corp 7379 Squire Ct West Chester OH 45069

NICHOLS, VIRGINIA V., insurance agent, accountant; b. Monroe County, Mo., Oct. 26, 1928; d. Elmer W. and Frances L. (McKinney) N.; student Belleville (Ill.) Jr. Coll., 1959-60, Rockhurst Coll., 1964-65, Avila Coll., Kansas City, Mo., 1981-82. Sec., Panhandle Eastern Pipeline Co., Kansas City, Mo., 1964-65, St. Louis County Dept. Revenue, 1965-69, Forest Park Community Coll., 1969-71, Nooney Co., St. Louis, 1971-77, J. A. Baer Enterprises, St. Louis, 1979; acct. Panhandle Eastern Pipe Line Co., Kansas City, Mo., 1979-85. Vol., ARC, 1965—. Mem. Am. Soc. Women Accts., Profl. Secs. Internat. (Sec. of Year 1969, sec. Mo. div. 1975-76), Jr. Women's C. of C. (Girl of Year 1975, pres. 1974-75). Republican. Episcopalian. Home: PO Box 5832 Kansas City MO 64111

NICHOLSON, DIANA LONG, lawyer; b. Pittsburgh, Kans., Aug. 18, 1939; d. William Paul and Buenta (Nott) Long; m. Michael Nicholson, June 21, 1964. B.M.E., Northwestern U., 1961; M.M., So. Ill. U., 1963; Ph.D., NYU, 1971; J.D., St. Johns U., 1976. Teaching assoc. So. Ill. U., Carbondale, 1961-63; supr. Livonia Pub. Schs. (Mich.), 1963-64; tchr. Roslyn Pub. Schs. (N.Y.), 1964-67, Northport Pub. Schs. (N.Y.) 1967-77; assoc. Linden & Deutsch, N.Y.C., 1977-78; ptnr. Corner, Finn, Nicholson & Chas, Bklyn., 1978—; vis. assoc. prof. Pratt Inst., Bklyn., 1979—. Recipient Founders Day award NYU, 1971; Outstanding Paper award ASCAP, 1975. Mem. ABA. Home: 35 Hilton Ave Garden City NY 11530 Office: Corner Finn Nicholson & Charles 32 Court St Brooklyn NY 11201

NICHOLSON, EDNA ELIZABETH, retired public health official; b. Redwood Falls, Minn., Dec. 23, 1907; d. Ernest Crawford and Alma (Bordeaux) N.; A.B., U. Mich., 1930, M.S. in Pub. Health, 1931, certificate in social work, 1931. Nat. Tb Assn. fellow in social research, 1930-31; med. social work ARC, U.S. Naval Hosp., Great Lakes, Ill., 1931-33; asst. dir. med. relief service Cook County Bur. Public Welfare, Chgo., 1933-35; instr. social aspects of nursing Cook County Sch. Nursing and asst. dir. social service Cook County Hosp., Chgo., 1935-37; dir. med. relief service Chgo. Relief Adminstrn., 1938-42; vis. lectr. Sch. Hygiene and Pub. Health, U. Mich., 1939; cons. on med. assistance, bur. pub. assistance Fed. Security Agency, 1942-44; dir. Central Service for Chronically Ill, Inst. Medicine, Chgo., 1944-54; exec. dir. Inst. Medicine of Chgo., 1955-64; sr. specialist program ops. and standards Med. Services Adminstrn., HEW, 1964-71; spl. lectr. program in hosp. adminstrn. Northwestern U., 1945-60; tech. adviser Commn. on Chronic Illness, 1949-56. Recipient Cancer Care award Nat. Cancer Found., 1955. Mem. Am. Public Health Assn., Phi Beta Kappa, Delta Omega, Sigma Kappa. Author: Terminal Care for Cancer Patients, 1950; Surveying Community Needs and Resources for Care of the Chronically Ill, 1950; The Nurse and Chronic Illness: Planning New Institutional Facilities for Longterm Care, 1956; A Comprehensive Community Plan for Meeting the Problems of Chronic Illness, 1959. Contbr. to profl. jours. Home: 107 Brewster Ln La Grange Park IL 60525

NICHOLSON, FREDA HYAMS, museum executive, medical educator; b. Asheville, N.C., Sept. 10, 1934; d. John Fred and Thelma (Lewis) Hyams; m. Henry Hale Nicholson, Jr., Sept. 24, 1956; children—Henry Hale III, Miller, J. Christy, Michael, Amanda, Stuart. R.N., St. Joseph's Hosp., 1955; B.S. in Nursing and Biology, Queens Coll., 1959, L.H.D. (hon.), 1982; M.Ed., U. N.C.-Charlotte, 1976. Surg. nurse Ochsner Clinic, New Orleans, 1955-56; nursing adminstr. Presbyn. Hosp., Charlotte, N.C., 1956-59; instr. biology and nursing Central Piedmont Coll., Charlotte, part-time 1965-71; instr. nursing U. N.C., Charlotte, part-time 1976-81; health educator, edn. curator Charlotte Nature Mus., 1971-80; acting dir. Discovery Place, Charlotte, 1981; exec. dir., chief exec. officer Sci. Mus. (Discovery Place Nature Mus.), 1981—; cons. health Health Adventure, Asheville, 1968; mem. mus. planning com. Sci. Mus. Project, Little Rock, 1984; in internat. partnership NEA, Washington, 1983; mem. U.S. Cultural Commn./India, participant in seminar in India, 1984. Bd. dirs. United Way, Charlotte, 1983, March of Dimes, Charlotte, 1978-83, Jr. Achievement, 1983—, Mission Air, 1984—; cons. Gov.'s Com. for Econ. Growth through Edn., 1984; active mem. local, state and nat. med. auxs., 1956—; mem. bd. visitors J.C. Smith U., Charlotte, 1983—. Named Woman of Yr., City of Charlotte, 1982, Nat. Outstanding Alumna Alpha Chi Omega, 1983, Outstanding Alumna Queens Coll., 1982. Mem. Women Execs., Assoc. Sci./Tech. Ctrs. (sec. 1984—), Greater Charlotte C. of C. (advt. com.), Jr. Women, Guild of Nature Mus., AAUW. Office: Sci Mus Charlotte Inc 301 N Tryon St Charlotte NC 29202

NICHOLSON, MYREEN MOORE, researcher, artist; b. Norfolk, Va., June 2, 1940; d. William Chester and Illeen (Fox) Moore, m. Roland Quarles Nicholson, Jan. 9, 1964 (div. 1978); 1 child, Andrea Joy; m. Harold Wellington McKinney, II, Jan. 18, 1981; 1 child, Cara Isadora. B.A., William and Mary Coll., 1962; M.S.L.S., U. N.C., 1971; postgrad. Old Dominion U., 1962-64, 64-68, 75—, The Citadel, 1968-69. English tchr., Chesapeake, Va., 1962-63; dept. head Portsmouth Bus. Coll., Va., 1963-64; tech. writer City Planning/Art Commn., Norfolk, 1964-65; art tchr. Norfolk pub. schs., 1965-67; prof. lit. and art Palmer Jr. Coll., Charleston, S.C., 1968; librarian Charleston Schs., 1968-69; asst. to dir. City Library Norfolk, 1970-72, research librarian, 1972—; dir. W. Ghent Arts Alliance, Norfolk, 1978—. Book reviewer Art Book Revs., Library Jour., 1973-76; editor, illustrator Acquisitions Bibliographies, 1970-76. Active Virginia Beach Arts Ctr., 1978—, Peninsula Art Ctr., 1983—; bd. dirs. W. Ghent Art/Lit. Festival, 1979. Recipient Coll. William and Mary art scholar, 1958; Nat. Endowment Arts grantee, 1975; nominations Gov.'s award for arts. Mem. ALA, Southeastern Library Assn., Poetry Soc. Va., Art Libraries Soc. N.Am., Tidewater Artists Assn., Acad. Am. Poets. Home: 1404 Gates Ave Norfolk VA 23507 Office: Norfolk Pub Library 301 E City Hall Ave Norfolk VA 23510

NICKELL, PATRICIA ANNE, public relations executive, journalist; b. Louisville, May 15, 1947; d. Asa White and Marjorie Anne (Palmgren) Nickell. B.A., U. Ky., 1969, M.A., 1971. Tchr. English and journalism Lafayette High Sch., Lexington, Ky., 1972-79; mag. editor Newcomb Coll., Tulane U., New Orleans, 1979; dir. pub. relations East Jefferson Gen. Hosp., Metairie, La., 1980—. Editor The Examiner mag., 1982 (Pelican award 1982); contbr. articles to profl. jours. Recipient award of excellence Internat. Assn. Bus. Communicators, 1981, award of merit for feature writing Dist. II S.E., 1982; award of merit Pub. Relations Soc. Am., 1983. Mem. Women in Communications (pres. 1982-83), Am. Soc. Hosp. Pub. Relations, La. Soc. Hosp. Pub. Relations (treas. 1982-84), Nat. Fedn. Press Women. Democrat. Roman Catholic. Club: Press (New Orleans). Home: 4332 B Georgia Ave Kenner LA 70065 Office: Public Relations Dept East Jefferson Gen Hosp 4200 Houma Blvd Metairie LA 70011

NICKERSON, JAN, finance executive, accountant; b. Greenwich, Conn., Aug. 4, 1949; d. Robert Edward and Mary Jane (Caldwell) N.; m. John Marks Graham, Oct. 11, 1975. B.S. in Hotel Adminstrn., Cornell U., 1971, M.B.A. in Acctg., 1972. C.P.A., Mass. Sr. acct. Arthur Andersen & Co., Boston, 1972-75; mgr. acctg., dir. internal audit Incoterm Co., Wellesley, Mass., 1975-78; v.p. corp. controller Interactive Data Corp., Waltham, Mass., 1978-85; v.p. fin. Chase Access Services Corp., Waltham, 1985—. Mem. Mass. Soc. Cert. Pub. Accts., Alpha Lambda Delta, Ye Hosts. Avocations: bridge; creative sewing; cooking; home improvements. Office: Chase Access Services Corp 460 Totten Pond Rd Waltham MA 02154

NICKERSON, JENNIE RUTH, sculptor; b. Appleton, Wis., Nov. 23, 1905; d. Robert Wellington and Kate Mary (Ellis) N.; student Detroit Sch. Applied Art, 1924-27, NAD, 1928-32; pupil Ahron Ben-Shmuel; m. Edmund Greacen, Jr., Dec. 30, 1935; children—Elizabeth Ruth, Barbara Eleanor. Sculptor, 1932—; represented in permanent collections at Eden (N.C.) Post Office, New Brunswick (N.J.) Post Office, Cedar Rapids Art Assn., Newark Mus., Montclair Mus., Interchurch Center, N.Y.C., also pvt. collections; tchr. Roerich Mus., N.Y.C., 1933-34, Westchester Art Workshop, 1947-68, Nat. Acad. Sch. Fine Arts, 1979-81. Charter mem. White Plains Civic Art Commn. 1948-60. Recipient Saltus Gold medal, 1935; Am. Artists Profl. League medal, 1936; Montclair Art Mus. medal, 1936. Guggenheim fellow, 1946-47. Fellow Nat. Sculpture Soc. (council 1982-83); mem. NAD (council 1978-81), Audubon Artists N.Y.C., Hudson Valley Art Assn. Republican. Home: 106 Woodcrest Ave White Plains NY 10604

NICKERSON, MARY CARTER, educational administrator; b. Washington, Mar 18, 1945; d. Marshall Sylvester and Preot (Nichols) Carter; B.A., Stanford U., 1968; M.A. in Guidance and Counseling, U. Colo., 1982; children—Erik Carter, Kitren Carter; m. Kent W. Mueller; stepchildren—Kirsten, Lisa, Kurt Mueller. Tchr. English, Public Schs. Palo Alto (Calif.), 1969-71; farmer, horse trainer, riding tchr., Starkville, Miss., 1971-77; dir. women's athletics. asst. dir. admissions Fountain Valley Sch., Colorado Springs, 1977-78, dir. admissions and fin. aid, 1978-81; dir. Ednl. Counseling Offices, Colorado Springs, 1981—; dir. mktg. U.S. Air Force Acad., 1984—; ednl. cons.; mem. long range planning com. Secondary Schs. Admissions Test Bd., 1979-82. Mem. Palmer Drug Abuse Bd., 1982-83, Domestic Violence Adv. Bd., 1983—. Cert. secondary tchr., Calif. Mem. Ind. Ednl. Counselors Assn., Nat. Assn. Coll. Admissions Counselors, Rocky Mountain Assn. Coll. Admissions Counselors, Northend Homeowners Assn., Stanford Alumni Assn. Episcopalian. Club: Whitworth Hunt (dir. 1975-77). Office: 1619 N Tejon St Colorado Springs CO 80907

NICKLAS, DEBORAH ANNSIMON, hospital planning and marketing administrator; b. Washington, Dec. 30, 1955; d. Martin Stanley and Rita Edith (Scheinhorn) S. B.A., Ithaca Coll., 1978; M.P.A. (scholar), U. So. Calif., 1981. Asst. dir. admissions Ithaca Coll. (N.Y.), 1978-79; research analyst Nat. Med. Enterprises, Los Angeles, 1979-80, adminstrv. resident Inter-Community Med. Ctr., Covina, Calif., 1980-81, dir. planning and mktg., 1981-85, v.p. planning and mktg., 1985—; instr. U. So. Calif., 1982, 84, U. La Verne, 1985; mem. Hosp. Council Planning Com., 1983-84; editor Exchanges, So. Calif. Soc. Hosp. Planners, 1983. Mem. community adv. bd. Charter Oak Hosp., Covina, 1981-84; residency adv. com. U. So. Calif., 1981-84; mem. United Way Task Force on Aging. Mem. Women in Health Adminstrn. (area rep. 1982), Am. Mktg. Assn., Soc. Hosp. Planning, Am. Coll. Health Care Execs., Health Care Execs. So. Calif., U. So. Calif. Health Services Adminstrn. Alumni Assn. pres. 1984-85). Office: Inter Community Med Ctr 303 N Third Ave Covina CA 91723

NICKLEN, PEGGY GENE, nurse; b. Omaha, Nebr., Aug. 27, 1952; d. Harold Edward Nicklen and Mary Elizabeth (Davis) Wiese; 1 child, Anthony Cook. B.S. in Nursing and English, Mount Marty Coll., Yankton, S.D., 1980. R.N., Nebr. Psychiat. technician Douglas County Hosp., Omaha, 1970-75; tutor Aid the Vietnamese, Yankton, S.D., 1978-80; psychiat. charge nurse St. Joseph Hosp., Omaha, 1980-82; med. charge nurse Luth. Community Hosp., Norfolk, Nebr., 1982-85; psychiat. nurse Norfolk Regional Ctr., 1985—. Editor mag. Mid Stream, 1976-80. Sec., Young Republicans, Yankton, 1979. Named Outstanding Young Woman Am., 1980. Mem. Am. Nurses Assn., Nat. Nurses Assn. Democrat. Roman Catholic. Avocations: writing nursing articles; crocheting; reading. Home: 108 Elm St Norfolk NE 68701 Office: Norfolk Regional Ctr Norfolk NE 68701

NICKLE-ROYSE, BONNY SYLVIA, university dean; b. Ipswich, Eng., Sept. 17, 1957, came to U.S., 1960; d. Duncan Owen and Irene Sylvia (Amatt) Nickle; m. Steven Blakeney Royse, Oct. 25, 1981. B.F.A., U. Calif.-Irvine, 1978; B.B.A., Nat. U., Irvine, 1982, M.B.A., 1983. Ref. asst. Orange County Pub. Library, Laguna Beach, Calif., 1974-78; office mgr. R.C. Taylor Co. Realtors, Newport Beach, Calif., 1978-81; dir. adminstrn. Re/Max Realtors, Newport Beach, 1981-82; dean continuing edn. for Orange and Los Angeles Counties, Nat. U., Irvine, 1982—; cons. continuing edn. Hughes Aircraft, 1982—, Lockheed Corp., 1982—. Panhellenic sorority scholar, 1975—. Law Sch. scholar, 1983—. Mem. Assn. M.B.A. Execs., Am. Soc. Tng. and Devel., AAUW, Nat. Assn. Female Execs., U. Calif.-Irvine Alumni Assn., Nat. U. Alumni Assn. Democrat. Presbyterian. Clubs: Jacques Doumani; Irvine Clubhouse. Office: National University 2112 Business Center Dr Irvine CA 92715

NICKLES, ELIZABETH ANNE, advertising executive, writer; b. Miami Beach, Fla., May 29, 1949; d. Arnold C. and Audrey (Reid) Nelson. B.S., Northwestern U., 1968; M.A., DePaul U., Chgo., 1970. Successively editorial asst. Scott, Foresman & Co., Glenview, Ill.; creative supr. Esquire Inc., Chgo.; copy supr. Marsteller Inc., Chgo.; assoc. creative dir. J. Walter Thompson, Chgo.; sr. v.p., creative dir. D'Arcy MacManus Masius, Chgo., 1980—; pvt. practice mktg. cons., Chgo., 1981—; founding bd. mem. Internat. Radio Festival, N.Y.C., 1982—; owner nationally-projectable survey Update Women. Author: The Coming Matriarchy, 1982; contbr. articles to mags. Mem. adv. bd. Mid-Am. chpt. ARC, Chgo., 1980-83. Recipient Advt. Women of the Yr. Women's Advt. Club, Chgo., 1982; Outstanding Young Woman Achiever award Nat. Council of Women of U.S., N.Y.C., 1982; named Glamour's Top 10 Working Women for 1982, Glamour's All Time Top 10 Working Women, 1984. Mem. Women's Advt. Club Chgo., The Chgo. Network. Episcopalian. Office: D'Arcy MacManus & Masius 200 E Randolph St Chicago IL 60601

NICKOLS, DIANE MARY, high technology electronics company official; b. Buffalo, Mar. 7, 1948; d. Thomas William Nickols and Norine Olive (Wild) Nickols Knab; 1 dau., Renee Marie. B.A., SUNY-Buffalo, 1971, M.A., 1974, M.S. in Indsl. Engring., 1976. Owner, cons. engr. Am. Research Corp., Estill Springs, Tenn., 1976-78; process control engr. Carrier Corp., McMinville, Tenn., 1976-77; devel. engr. Gen. Electric Co., Evendale, Ohio, 1977-79, mgr. overseas mktg. Europe-Africa-Mideast, 1979-81; mgr. indsl. engring. Sanders & Assocs., Nashua, N.H., 1981-83; sr. task mgr. GTE Sylvania, Needham, Mass., 1983-84; dep. div. mgr. Scientific Systems, Cambridge, Mass., 1984—. Author tech. reports; co-developed ultrasound as means of diagnosing deep dermal burns. Asst. state coordinator Tenn. NOW, Estill Springs, 1976-78. SUNY-Buffalo research fellow, also recipient Chas. and Myra Jacobowitz Fund award for Outstanding Engring. Fellow Inst. Indsl. Engrs., 1973-82, Health Physics Soc., 1976-78; mem. profl. socs. Democrat.

NICOL, MARJORIE CARMICHAEL, research psychologist; b. Orange, N.J., Jan. 6, 1924; d. Norman Carmichael and Ethel Sarah (Siviter) N.; B.A., Upsala Coll.; M.S., 1978; M.Ph. CUNY, 1985, now postgrad. Art dir. Finneran Advt. Co., N.Y.C., 1944-47; mgr. advt. prodn. RCA, Harrison, N.J., 1948-58; advt. mgr., writer NPS Advt., East Orange, N.J., 1960-67; v.p. measurement and evaluation; F.L. Merritt, Inc., Montclair, N.J., 1967—. Officer Rafiki, Essex County, N.J., 1965—; officer Montclair Rehab. Orgn., 1981—; founder Met. Opera at Lincoln Center. Republican. Presbyterian. Author: Nicol Index. Avocation: world-wide eclipse chaser. Home: 89 Linden St Millburn NJ 07041 Office: PO Box 392 Montclair NJ 07042

NICOLL, DEBORAH DAWSON, lawyer; b. Canton, Ohio, Oct. 4, 1950; d. Ronald Cook and Catherine deSales (Ryan) Dawson; m. Stephen Gilbert Truxell, Feb. 14, 1969 (div. July 1974); children—Jennifer Marie, Erin Kate; m. 2d, Robert Joseph Nicoll, Nov. 8, 1980; 1 dau., Courtney Elise. Student Mt. Union Coll., 1968-71; B.S., Kent State U., 1976; J.D., U. Akron, 1981. Bar: Ohio 1981. Jud. clk. Stark County Common Pleas Ct., Canton, 1980-82; sole practice, Alliance, Ohio, 1982—; asst. prosecutor Stark County Civil Div., 1985—; legal advisor Alliance Area Domestic Violence Shelter, 1983-84, chmn. bd., 1985—. Bd. dirs. Stark County Legal Aid Soc., 1985—. Mem. ABA, Ohio Bar Assn., Stark County Bar Assn., Assn. Trial Lawyers Am., Alliance Area C. of C. Democrat. Roman Catholic. Home: 1224 S Union Ave Alliance OH 44601 Office: 27 W Cambridge St Alliance OH 44601

NICOLOSI, DOROTHY EMILY, non-profit organization executive; b. N.Y.C., July 15, 1931; d. Thomas and Aurora (Scoppa) Nicolosi; B.S. in Edn., Fordham U., 1963, cert. Introductory Mgmt. Devel., 1967, cert. Advanced Mgmt. Devel., 1968; M. Public Adminstrn., N.Y. U., 1979. Exec. sec. Arabol Mfg. Co., N.Y.C., 1950-55; research asst. Smith Richardson Found., N.Y.C., 1955-60; cons. Robert A. Taft Meml. Found., Washington, 1960-61; asst. sec., office mgr. United Student Aid Fund, Inc., N.Y.C., 1961-63; sec., treas., exec. adminstr. Nat. Strategy Info. Center, Inc., N.Y.C., 1963-84, v.p., treas., 1984—, dir., 1978—. Mem. Am. Acad. Polit. and Social Sci., Am. Soc. Public Adminstrn., Acad. Polit. Sci. Republican. Roman Catholic. Home: 3103 Fairfield Ave Riverdale NY 10463 Office: 150 E 58th St New York NY 10155

NICOLOSI, SHERILL BOLEY, lawyer; b. East Brunswick, N.J., Dec. 20, 1953; d. Edward Gayle and Sally (Friedlander) Boley; m. Anthony Joseph Nicolosi, Mar. 3, 1979. B.A., Hartwick Coll., 1976; J.D., South Tex. Coll. Law, 1979. Title II testing supr. Houston Ind. Sch. Dist., 1976-77; law clk. Tex. Atty. Gens. Office, Houston, 1977-79; atty. at law Turner & Loiseau Legal Co., Houston, 1979; spl. prosecutor, legal screening officer, Harris County, Tex., 1979-85; mem. bd. B&G Vending Corp., East Brunswick, 1977—. Mem. John Hill for Chief Justice Steering Com., Houston, 1984. Law Enforcement Assistance Adminstrn., grantee, Austin, 1979-83. Mem. ABA, Houston Bar Assn., Tex. Bar Assn., Tex. Young Lawyers Assn., Hartwick Coll. Alumni Assn., South Tex. Coll. Law Alumni Assn., Delta Theta Phi. Democrat. Jewish.

NIDA, JANE BOLSTER, retired librarian; b. Chgo., July 19, 1918; d. Chalmer A. and Elsie Rosalie (Sonderman) Bolster; m. Dow Hughes Nida, Sept. 1, 1946; 1 child, Janice Beth Nida Michaels. B.A., Aurora U., 1942; B.S. in L.S., U. Ill., 1943. Cert. librarian, Va. Asst. to reference dept. head, head of circulation, head reference dept. Aurora Pub. Library, Ill., 1935-46; acquisitions librarian Ohio U., Athens, 1947; research librarian Touche, Bailey, Niven, Detroit, 1950-51; dir. Falls Church Pub. Library, Va., 1951-54; asst. dir. Dept. Libraries, Arlington, Va., 1954-57, dir., 1957-80; staff asst., program dir. ARC, England and Paris, 1944-45; cons. on loan under the Intergovernmental Personnel Act to U.S. AID, Washington and West Africa, 1979-80; mem. Govs. com. Revise State Laws for Libraries, Richmond, Va., 1968-71. Contbr. articles to profl. pubs. Bd. dirs., officer Am. Cancer Soc., No. Va., 1971-84, coordinator Reach to Recovery, Am. Cancer Soc. No. Va., 1973-76. Recipient Meritorius Civilian Service award Pres. Truman, 1946; Outstanding Alumnus award Aurora U., 1979. Mem. ALA, D.C. Library Assn., Va. Library Assn. (hon. life, pres. 1969-70), Arlington Hist. Soc. (charter), AAUW. Avocations: Travel; reading; property management. Home: 4907 29th St N Arlington VA 22207

NIDETCH, JEAN, health service exec.; b. Bklyn., Oct. 12, 1923; d. David and May (Rodin) Slutsky; children—David, Richard. Founding pres. Weight Watchers Internat., Inc., Manhasset, L.I. Cons., N.Y. State Assembly Mental Hygiene Com. 1968; adviser Joint Legis. Com. on Child Care Needs, Legislature N.Y. Pres., Weight Watchers Found. Named Mktg. Woman of Yr.; hon. adm. Gt. Navy Nebr. Woman of Yr., Forest Hills Youth Assn.; recipient Woman of Achievement award, Speakers award Sales Promotion Execs. Assn. Mem. Washington Sq. Bus. and Profl. Womens Club, AFTRA. Author: Jean Nidetch: Weight Watchers Cookbook, 1966; The Story of Weight Watchers, 1970; Program Cookbook. Office: care Weight Watchers International 800 Community Drive Manhasset NY 11030*

NIEDERHAUSER, MARY CHARLOTTE, hospital administrator; b. Bucyrus, Ohio, Aug. 1, 1943; d. Richard Wayne and Mary Maxine (Cammarn) N.; grad. Ohio Valley Hosp. Sch. Nursing, 1964; B.A., Barat Coll., 1978; M.B.A., U. Chgo., 1981. Staff nurse L.A. Weiss Meml. Hosp., Chgo., 1965-68, nursing supr., 1968-76; critical care supr. Skokie Valley Community Hosp., Skokie, Ill., 1976-77; dir. nursing Forkosh Meml. Hosp., Chgo., 1977-79, v.p. patient care services, 1979-84, asst. adminstr., 1984—. guest speaker on critical care nursing mgmt., Kansas City, Apr. 1977, Atlanta, May 1977, Chgo., Oct. 1977; cons. adolescent alcoholism treatment programs, stress mgmt. for women. Mem. Chgo. Health Execs. Forum, Am. Coll. Hosp. Adminstrs., Lincoln Sq. C. of C., No. Bus. and Industry Council of Chgo., U. Chgo. Women's Bus. Club (dir. 1983), Exec. Program Club of U. Chgo. Grad. Sch. Bus., Am. Heart Assn., Ill. Soc. Nurse Adminstrs., U. Chgo. Hosp. Adminstrn. Alumni Assn., Chgo. Area Health Planning Assn., Women's Health Exec. Network, Delta Epsilon Sigma. Home: 2634 W Berwyn St Chicago IL 60625 Office: 2544 W Montrose Ave Chicago IL 60618

NIEDERMEIER, CHRISTINE MARIE, lawyer, state legislator; b. Bridgeport, Conn., Oct. 21, 1951; d. Jerome J. and Marie Perkins N.; A.B. in Govt., Georgetown U., 1973, J.D., 1977. Legis. analyst in housing and urban affairs Library of Congress, Washington, 1973-74; staff asst. to Gov. of Conn., Hartford, 1975; legis. asst. Congressman Christopher J. Dodd of Conn., Washington, 1975-77; assoc. Day, Berry and Howard, Hartford, Conn., summer 1976; schedule and advance aide Nat. Presdl. Campaign of Gov. Edmund G. Brown, Jr., 1976; admitted to Conn. bar, 1977, U.S. Dist. Ct. bar, 1977, D.C. bar, 1979; assoc. firm Trager and Trager, Fairfield, Conn., 1977-81, Winthrop, Stimson, Putnam and Roberts, Stamford, Conn., 1982—; mem. Conn. Ho. of Reps., 1979—, former mem. appropriations com., govt. adminstrn. and elections com., mem. energy and pub. utilities com., ad hoc legis. com. on arts, past chmn., now ranking mem. transp. com., past chmn., now mem. transp. and communications com. Nat. Conf. State Legislators. Lawyers com. rep. United Way Campaign, 1977-79; mem. Fairfield Rep. Town Meeting, 1977-79; mem. Democratic Town Com., Fairfield; bd. dirs. Conn. Audubon Soc.; mem. U. Bridgeport Law Sch. Fund Com., also bd. assocs.; former mem. Fairfield Parking Authority Adv. Com.; mem. Parents and Friends of Retarded Citizens, Inc.; vice chmn. president's council Sacred Heart U.; mem. Fairfield County Heart Assn. Recipient Disting. Service award Georgetown U., 1973. Mem. ABA, Conn. Bar Assn., D.C. Bar Assn., Greater Bridgeport Bar Assn., Fairfield C. of C., Fairfield LWV. Office: State Capitol Hartford CT 06106

NIEDLING, HOPE HOTCHKISS, dietitian; b. Meriden, Ill., Feb. 14, 1922; d. Bert and Myrle Glenn (Vaughn) Hotchkiss; student North Central Coll.,

1939-40; B.S., U. Ill., 1943; M.S. in Food Sci. and Nutrition, U. Wis. 1974; m. Ivan Martin Niedling, June 26, 1948. Teaching dietitian Univ. Hosp., Balt., 1944; dietitian public sch. cafeterias, Balt., 1944-48; dir. admisions Thomas Sch. Retailing, Phila., 1954-55; instr. foods U. Wis., Stevens Point, 1967-68; food service supr., instr. Mid-State, N.Central and Fox Valley Tech. Insts., Wis., 1973-75; cons. dietitian nursing homes in Wis., 1973—. Chmn., Village of Plover Cancer Fund Drive, 1977-78; bd. dirs. Stout Found., U. Wis., 1977—; sec.-treas. Joint Com. Edn. State of Wis., 1978—. Recipient Loyalty award U. Ill., 1978, award of merit U. Ill. Home Econs. Assn., 1979. Mem. Am. (ho. of dels. 1974-77), Wis. dietetic assns., No. Wis. Dietetic Assn. (pres. 1971-73), Soc. Nutrition Edn., Nutrition Today Soc., Nutritionists in Bus., Wis. Assn. Registered Parliamentarians (state corr. sec. 1978-80), Wis. Fedn. Women's Clubs (1st v.p. 1978-80), U. Ill. Home Econs. Alumni Assn. (bd. dirs. 1972-78), Colonial Dames XVII Century, Daus. Am. Colonists, Nat. Assn. Registered Parliamentarians, Wis. Public Health Assn. (mem. aging com. 1974-78), Portage County Humane Soc. (sec. 1973—), Wis. Fedn. Women's Clubs (pres. 1980-82), Gen. Fedn. Women's Clubs (sec.-treas. region 1982-84, chmn. internat. aid div. 1982-84, pres. Gt. Lakes region 1984—), Colonial Dames XVII Century (1st v.p. Wis. 1981-83, pres. 1983—), DAR (Sec. 1977-80, 1st vice regent 1980-83, state regent 1983-86, chpt. regent 1972-77, chpt. registrar 1977—, pres. Wis. state officers club 1976-77, nat. bd. mgmt. 1983—), AAUW (pres. br. 1968-72, state corr. sec. 1970-72), U. Ill. Alumni Assn. (dir. 1973), NCCJ (disting. merit citation 1976; vice chmn. Wis. region 1975—; Portage County chmn. Nat. Brotherhood Week 1972—), Wis. Soc. Children Am. Revolution (sr. state corr. sec. 1984-86, sr. state 1st v.p. 1986—), Wis. Soc. Am. Revolution (state organizing sec.), DAR (nat. chmn. lineage research com.), Wis. Fedn. Republican Women (dist. chmn. 1969-74), Gamma Sigma Delta, Epsilon Sigma Omicron. Methodist. Clubs: Order Eastern Star, Order of Amaranth, Order White Shrine of Jerusalem, Stevens Point Area Woman's (pres. 1972-74, 76-78, Stevens Point Woman's (pres. 1970-72). Address: 1008 3rd St Stevens Point WI 54481

NIEHAUS, SUZANNE MARIE, accountant; b. Quincy, Ill., Aug. 3, 1957; d. Carl Joseph and Winnifred Ruth (Pohlman) N. B.S. in Accountancy, Ill. State U., 1979. Sr. auditor DeKalb Agresearch, Inc., 1979-82; asst. controller Pride Oil Well Service, Houston, 1982—. Mem. Am. Soc. Women Accts.

NIELSEN, GEORGIA HOPE, lawyer; b. Ft. Worth, Jan. 9, 1950; d. William Walter and Patricia J. (Jansen) N. B.A., Tex. Tech. Univ., 1973; J.D., St. Mary's Univ., 1979. Bar: Tex. 1979. With S.W. Bell Telephone Co., Amarillo and Lubbock, Tex., 1968-76; sole practice, Amarillo, 1979—. Treas. Potter-Randall Democratic Women, Amarillo, 1982. Mem. ABA, Tex. Bar Assn., Nat. Assn. Parliamentarians, Tex. Assn. Parliamentarians (pres. Hazel Crawley unit 1982). Phi Alpha Delta. Roman Catholic. Home: 2709 A Curtis Dr Amarillo TX 79109 Office: Hope Nielsen 3014 SW 26th St Suite 3000 Amarillo TX 79109

NIELSEN, LISA TAGE, opinion research company executive; b. Glen Ridge, N.J., June 8, 1946; d. Axel Tage and Winifred Phyllis (Eisenhart) N.; student Skidmore Coll., 1964-65; B.A., U. Miami, 1968, M.B.A., 1973; m. Jeffrey J. Gaydos, Apr. 21, 1978. Circulation trainee Miami Herald Pub. Co. (Fla.), 1972-74, research mgr., 1974-76; research mgr. Gannett Rochester Newspapers (N.Y.), 1976-77; sr. media analyst Market Opinion Research, Detroit, 1977-78, mgr. media div., 1978-81, v.p. media research, 1981-84; owner, pres. Market Link Co., 1984—. Vol., Grosse Pointe (Mich.) Tree Com., 1981—. Mem. Women in Communications (v.p. Detroit chpt. 1981-82), Internat. Newspaper Promotion Assn., Am. Assn. Public Opinion Research. Presbyterian. Clubs: Economic of Detroit. Home: 19961 Norton Ct Grosse Pointe Woods MI 48236 Office: Market Opinion Research 550 Washington Blvd Detroit MI 48226

NIELSEN, MARY ANN, day care operator; b. Portland, Oreg., July 5, 1948; d. John Fredrick and Olga Mae (Bleuler) Schwender; m. James Stuart Nielsen, Oct. 7, 1967; children—Lisa Ann, Christine Ann. Cert. Bassist Fashion and Merchandising Sch., 1967. Clk. fashion Montgomery Ward, Salem, Oreg., 1964-66, Clk., delivery process merchandiser, 1970-79; letter carrier U.S. Postal Service, Portland, 1979-82; owner, dir. Heidi-Ho Rockwood Day Nursery, Portland, 1981—. Mem. Rockwood Mchts. Assn. Club: Royal Oaks Country (Vancouver, Wash.). Avocations: oil painting; hiking. Home: 18331 E Burnside St Portland OR 97233 Office: Heidi-Ho Rockwood Day Nursery 18331 E Burnside St Portland OR 97233

NIELSEN, NANCY ANNE, data processing specialist; b. Salem, Mass., Sept. 12, 1934; d. Frank Ellwood and Myrtle Annie (Peterson) Root; B.A. in Math., U. N.H., 1957; m. Glenn Foster Nielsen, Nov. 27, 1959; children—Peder Root, Edward Stapleford. Programmer Rand Corp., Hanscom Field, Lexington, Mass., Topsham AFS, Maine, 1957-58; sr. programmer analyst System Devel. Corp., Santa Monica, Calif., 1958-60, 1960-62; engring. programmer Litton, Canoga Park, Calif., 1964; programming cons. Am. Inst. for Research, West Los Angeles, 1963-64; sr. programmer analyst System Devel. Corp., Santa Monica, 1965-69, sect. head, 1969-79, computer systems specialist, 1979-84, sr. systems specialist, 1984—; tech. cons. U.S. Air Force. Den leader, troop com. sec. Boy Scouts Am., 1971-75; vestry mem. St. Martin-in-the Fields Episcopal Ch., 1972-74, clk. of the vestry, 1984. Mem. System Devel. Corp. Mgmt. Assn. Club: Canoga Park Jr. Women's. (safety chmn., treas. 1963-65). Home: 5774 Willow View Dr Camarillo CA 93010

NIEMEYER, MAXINE BREWER, ins. exec.; b. Detroit, Jan. 14, 1920; d. Daniel Frederick and Ella (Case) Niemeyer; student Detroit Coll. Bus., 1938-39, Exec. Sec. Assn. (hon.), 1960; grad. Dale Carnegie course, 1946; student Wayne U., 1958, Wayne State and U. Mich. Extension Schs., 1961-64, 65—. Gen. office clk. Hart Sewing Machine Supplies Co., Detroit, 1938-39; cashier, sec. N.Am. Life Assurance Co., Detroit, 1939-41, office mgr., 1942-43; office mgr. L.A. Walden & Co., Detroit, 1943-46; asst. office mgr. Dr. Ralph H. Pino, Ophthalmologist, Detroit, 1946-48; registrar Leadership Tng., Inc., Detroit, 1948-50; sec. to mgr. market analysis and dealer orgn dept. Sales div. Chevrolet Motor Co., Detroit, 1950-56; office mgr., sec. to Walter R. Cavanaugh, C.L.U., 1956—, corp. sec. 1958—, mgr. policyholders service and sales promotion, 1966; agy. mgr. Phoenix Mut. Life, also owner and pres. M.B. Niemeyer CLU & Assos., 1966—; pres. Bus. and Estate Fin. Coordinators Inc.; advanced underwriting cons., agt., surplus lines mgr. Phoenix Cos.; registered rep. Phoenix Equity Planning Corp. Named Detroit Sec. of Yr. Detroit chpt. Nat. Secs. Assn. Internat., 1960, One of Top Ten Working Women Central Bus. Dist. Assn., Detroit, 1965; C.L.U.; chartered fin. counselor; lic. life ins. counselor. Mem. Nat. Secs. Assn. (pres. Detroit chpt. 1962-64), Detroit Assn. Life Underwriters (pres. 1974-75), Am. Soc. C.L.U.s (past regional dir.; pres. Detroit chpt. 1973-74), Am. Coll. C.L.U.s (trustee), Million Dollar Round Table, Fin. and Estate Planning Council Detroit (dir.), Life Ins. Leaders Mich., Mich. Assn. Life Ins. Counselors (dir.), Internat. Assn. Fin. Planners, Alpha Iota Internat. (chpt. pres. 1944). Presbyterian. Club: Soroptimist (pres. 1972—) (Grosse Pointe, Mich.). Home: 1792 Vernier Rd Grosse Pointe Woods MI 48236 Office: 3000 Town Center Suite 202 Southfield MI 48075

NIEMIRA, CAROLINE MARIE, direct marketing company executive; b. Chgo., Nov. 22, 1947; d. Thaddeus Felix and Regina (Penkala) Niemira; B.A. with highest honors and distinction in Linguistics, U. Mich., 1969; M. Mgmt., Northwestern U., 1976. Editorial asst. Edmund A. Smason Public Relations, Chgo., 1969-72; sr. account supr. Jack E. Schlegal Advt., Chgo., 1972-75; gen. corr. Nielsen Communication Team, Dublin, Ireland, 1976; account exec. Communique Public Relations, Dublin, Ireland, 1977-78; account exec., prodn. mgmt. Exec. Mktg. Services, Houston, 1979, asst. nat. accounts mgr., 1981; freelance bus. communicator, Houston, 1980; owner Niemira Direct Communications, Houston, 1982-84, Boston, 1984—; Chgo. corr. Women's Almanac, 1975; corr. Writers' Internat., 1971. Advt., public relations mgr. Alderman Dick Simpson, Chgo., 1972-75. Recipient Matrix award Women in Communications, Inc., 1981, 84; Soc. Tech. Communication award, 1980; Leadership award Direct Mail Mktg. Assn., 1981; cert. of award Houston Advt. Fedn. Grand Prix, 1983. Mem. New England Direct Mktg. Assn., Women's Direct Response Group, Direct Mktg. Creative Guild, Inc., Women in Communications, Inc., Internat. Assn. Bus. Communicators (award of merit 1983) Bus./Profl. Advt. Assn., Iota Sigma Epsilon, Phi Chi Theta, Sigma Kappa. Creator, editor The Executive, 1979-82. Office: PO Box 147 Boston MA 02101

NIERMAN, MARJORY, executive secretary; b. Fairplay, Colo., Aug. 15, 1936; d. Warren Henry and Bernadean (Bailey) Yarroll; m. Leon Keith Nierman, Mar. 18, 1956; children—Sharon RaNae Thompson, Darlene Suzette Beaman, Steve. Student LaSalle U., 1977-79. Teller supr. First Nat. Bank, Arvada, Colo., 1968-71; collections Grant Square Bank, Oklahoma City, 1972-73; sec. to pres. Downers Grove Bank, (Ill.) 1973-75; adminstrv. asst. Houston N.W. Med. Ctr., 1975-77; v.p. Sumed Enterprises, Inc., Houston, 1977-78, pres., 1978-81; now exec. sec. to pres. InterFirst Bank of Tomball, Houston. Vol. Houston N.W. Hosp. Aux., 1983. Republican. Lutheran. Clubs: Angels, Bd. of Fellowship (Houston). Home: 22210 Greenbrook Houston TX 77073

NIES, HELEN WILSON, U.S. circuit judge; b. Birmingham, Ala., Aug. 7, 1925; d. George Earl and Lida Blanche (Erckert) Wilson; B.A., U. Mich., 1946, J.D., 1948; m. John Dirk Nies, July 10, 1948; children—Dirk, Nancy, Eric. Admitted to Mich. bar, 1948, D.C. bar, 1961, U.S. Supreme Ct. bar, 1962; atty. Dept. Justice, Washington, 1948-51, Office Price Stabilization, Washington, 1951-52; asso. firm Pattishall, McAuliffe and Hofstetter, Washington, 1960-66, resident partner, 1966-77; partner firm Howrey & Simon, Washington, 1978-80; judge U.S. Ct. Customs and Patent Appeals, 1980-82; circuit judge U.S. Ct. Appeals for Fed. Circuit, 1982—; mem. public adv. com. trademark affairs Dept. Commerce, 1976-80; mem. adv. bd. BNA's Patent Trademark and Copyright Jour., 1976-78. Bd. vis's. U. Mich. Law Sch., 1975-78. Anne E. Shipman Stevens scholar, 1945-47. Mem. Am. Bar Assn. (chmn. com. 203, 1972-74, com. 504, 1975-76, trademark div. 1977-78), Bar Assn. D.C. (chmn. patent trademark copyright sect. 1975-76, dir. 1976-78), U.S. Trademark Assn. (chmn. lawyers adv. com. 1974-76, dir. 1976-78), Am. Patent Law Assn., Fed. Bar Assn., Nat. Assn. Women Lawyers, Women's Bar Assn. D.C. (Woman Lawyer of Yr. 1980), Order of Coif, Phi Beta Kappa, Phi Kappa Phi. Contbr. articles to legal jours.; lectr. in field.

NIES, LEE MARIA, artist; b. N.Y.C., June 20, 1931; d. Julian Armando and Aida (Estremera) Gonzalez; m. Basil Nicholas Soriano, May 3, 1953 (div. 1975); children—Nicholas, Mark, Lee Ann, Diana; m. William Arthur Nies, Nov. 12, 1977. Student, Art Career Sch., N.Y.C., 1949-50, Workshop of Advt. and Editorial Art, N.Y.C., 1950-51. Designer, Norcross Greetings Co., N.Y.C., 1951-54; art dir. Pollyanna Greetings Co., N.Y.C., 1954-56; freelance artist packaging and illustrations, N.Y.C., 1956-74; multi-color art dir., Clifton, N.J., 1974-79; owner, pres. Notch Studio, Little Falls, N.J., 1974—; artist N.J. Bell, Newark, 1979—. Illustrator children's books: Come to the Circus, 1983; Quietime Book I, 1983; Quietime Book II, 1984. Vol., Passaic Valley Hospice, Wayne, N.J., 1980—. Recipient Advt. Achievement award Electrical Wholesaling, 1980; cert. Wayne Gen. Hospice, 1980. Republican. Avocations: antique glass and bottle collecting; Bible study. Home: 229 Wilmore Rd Little Falls NJ 07424 Office: Notch Studio 229 Wilmore Rd Little Falls NJ 07424

NIEVES, PRISCILLA, commodities trading co. exec.,; b. San Juan, P.R., Dec. 14, 1950; d. Benito and Benita (Nieves-Jimenez) Nieves-Baez; B.A. (Alice Baldwin scholar), Duke U., 1972; M.B.A., U. N.C., 1977; m. Andrew E. Cardwell, July 2, 1981. Part-owner Waste Paper & Equipment, Durham, N.C., 1976-79; asst. brand mgr. Legg's Products div. Hanes Hosiery, Winston-Salem, N.C., 1977-79; asst. brand mgr. Miller Brewing Co., Milw., 1979; brand mgr. Wine Spectrum, Coca-Cola, Atlanta, 1979-82; partner Cardwell Nieves Inc., Atlanta, 1982—. Mem. High Mus. Art, Found. of Truth. Roman Catholic. Address: 15 Parkgate Dr Atlanta GA 30328

NIEZGODSKI-WOLFF, CYNDI LU, fitness center executive; b. Louisville, July 17, 1952; d. James Mark and Kathryn Lucetta (Murphy) Wolff. B.S. in Speech and Theatre, Ball State U., 1974. Merchandiser, SupeRx Drugs, Indpls., 1979-81; group mgr. Zayre Inc., Atlanta, 1981-83; area dir. Living Well Inc., Miami, 1983—. Creator: AquaRobics fitness class. Named Mgr. of Yr., Living Well, 1983, 84, Area Dir. of Yr., 1985. Office: Living Well Inc 370 S State Rd #7 Hollywood FL 33023

NIGHTINGALE, JOANNE CAROL, hospital financial administrator; b. Buffalo, Nov. 20, 1937; d. George J. and Alta M. (Drayer) Young; children—Judi, David. B.S. in Bus. Adminstrn., U. Redlands, 1982. Dir. acctg. Loma Linda U. Ctr. for Dependent Behavior, Calif., 1975-77, dir. budget and acctg. Loma Linda Community Hosp., 1977—. Treas. Redlands Seventh Day Adventist Ch., 1970-75; treas. Health Ministry Found., 1975-80; deaconess Univ. Ch. Seventh Day Adventist, 1980—; bd. dir. Carefree Village Condo Assn., 1986. Mem. Healthcare Fin. Mgmt. Assn., Nat. Assn. Female Execs., Assn. Western Hosps. Club: Toastmasters. Home: PO Box 636 Loma Linda CA 92354

NIGHTINGALE, JULIE, commercial photographer; b. Snoqualmie, Wash., Mar. 11, 1957; d. Robert Charles and Frances (Flaherty) N.; m. Thomas William Curran, June 29, 1984; 1 child, Thomas William III. B.S., Bellevue Community Coll., 1976; B.A., Brooks Inst., Santa Barbara, Calif., 1979. Asst. art dir. Creative Directions, Westport, Conn., 1980-81; owner Stock Shots, Westport, 1981-82; ptnr., photographer Hyon/Nightingale Assocs., Norwalk, Conn., 1982—. Mem. Conn. Art Dirs. Republican. Roman Catholic. Club: Brownson Country (Huntington, Conn.). Office: Nightingale Photography Inc 535 Post Rd E Westport CT 06880

NIGHTMAN, DIANA LEE, hospital executive; b. Latrobe, Pa., Dec. 12, 1956; d. Roy Evan and Vera May (Scherer) Sobinsky; m. Jelette Anthony Nightman, Feb. 14, 1975. B.A. in Journalism and Communications summa cum laude, Point Park Coll., 1981. Reporter, features writer Uniontown Herald-Standard (Pa.), 1981-82, pub. relations coordinator Uniontown Hosp., 1982—. Served with U.S. Army, 1975-78. Scripps-Howard scholar Point Park Coll., 1979-81. Mem. Women in Communications, Pub. Relations Soc. of Health Care Orgns., Laurel Highlands Advt. Assn., Pub. Relations Soc. of Hosp. Assn. Pa., Am. Soc. for Hosp. Pub. Relations. Democrat. Roman Catholic. Office: Uniontown Hospital 500 W Berkeley St Uniontown PA 15401

NIGOGHOSIAN, ALICE MARIE, university press executive, publishing consultant, editor; b. Detroit, Apr. 9, 1939; d. Sam and Agnes O. (Vartanian) N. B.A. in Mass Communications, Wayne State U., Detroit, 1969. Editorial and prodn. sec. Wayne State U. Press., Detroit, 1961-68, asst. prodn. mgr., 1968-69, 70-77, publishing prodn. coordinator, 1977-79, prodn. and design mgr., 1979—, assoc. dir., 1986—; on air promotion supr., writer Sta. WKBD-TV, Southfield, Mich., 1969-70. Editor: On the Urban Scene, 1972; The Professor & the Public, 1972; To Enforce Education, 1974; Detroit and Its Banks, 1974; Forty Years On: A History of Cranbrook School, 1976; Smith, Hinchman & Grylls, 1978, others; publishing cons. various books. Mem. Soc. Scholarly Pub., Founders Soc., Detroit Inst. Arts. Club: Book of Detroit. Home: 2652 Somerset Blvd Troy MI 48084 Office: Wayne State Univ Press 5959 Woodward Ave Detroit MI 48202

NIHILL, KAREN BAILEY, nursing administrator; b. Erie, Pa., Mar. 15, 1947; d. William C. and Eleanor (Danielson) Bailey; R.N., Hamot Med. Center, Erie, 1968; postgrad. U. Pa., 1974—; 1 son, Liam H. Critical care nurse Hamot Med. Ctr., 1968-71, VA Hosp., Phila., 1974-77; dir. nursing Chapel Manor and Nursing Home, Phila., 1977—, also Phila. Protestant Home and Elmira Jeffries Nursing Home. Active Lutheran Ch. Women's Orgn. Served to lt. Nurse Corps, U.S. Navy, 1971-73. VA grantee, 1974. Mem. Am. Assn. Critical Care Nurses, Pa. Nurses Assn. Republican. Home: 172 W Thelma St Philadelphia PA 19140

NIKAZY, DEBRA ECCLES, lawyer; b. Belleville, Ill., Jan. 29, 1953; d. Wayne Allen Eccles and Della Leah Fannin; m. Steven Walter Nikazy, Oct. 10, 1982. B.A. in Mass Communications, Morehead State U., Ky., 1974; J.D., Villanova U., 1982. Bars: Pa. 1982, Tex. 1983, U.S. Dist. Ct. (ea. dist.) Pa. 1983, U.S. Dist. Ct. (we. dist.) Tex. 1984. Announcer, Sta. WMKY, Morehead, Ky., 1970-74, Sta, WIEL, Elizabethtown, Ky., 1974-75; announcer, music dir. Sta. WCSC/WXTC, Charleston, S.C., 1975-76; announcer Sta. KTSA/KTFM, San Antonio, 1976; announcer, news dir. Sta. KSAQ/KZZD, San Antonio, 1976-77; announcer Sta. WZZD/WIBG, Phila., 1977-79, Sta. WFIL/WUSL, Phila., 1979-82; assoc. Law Offices of Victor Toth, Washington, 1982; sole practice, Phila., 1982-83; corp. counsel Valu-Line, Austin, Tex., 1983; staff atty. Pub. Utility Commn. Tex., Austin, 1983-85, Tex. Water Commn., Austin, 1985—. Mem. ABA, Nat. Assn. Female Execs., Austin Writers League. Democrat. Roman Catholic. Avocation: writing. Office: Legal Div Tex Water Commn PO Box 13087 Capitol Sta Austin TX 78711

NIKLAUSKI, MARIANNE NANCY, cytotechnologist; b. Phila., Aug. 19, 1942; d. Edward S. and Pauline S. (Polner) Bay; student Pa. State U., 1960-63; degree in cytotech. U. Pa., 1964; m. Leonard Niklauski, Oct. 27, 1977. Cytotechnologist, Lower Bucks County Hosp., Bristol, Pa., 1964-65; supr. cytology, clin. lab. Walter G. Sawchak, Trenton, N.J., 1965-80; cytotechnologist MDS Labs., Cherry Hill, N.J., 1980-81; supr. cytology Torresdale div. Frankford Hosp., Phila., 1981—. Am. Cancer Soc. grantee, 1963. Mem. Am. Soc. Clin. Pathologists, Del. Valley Soc. Cytotechnologists. Home: 211 Cleveland Ave Edgewater Park NJ 08010 Office: Frankford Hosp Red Lion and Knights Rd Philadelphia PA 19114

NIKO, SHARON MARIE, nurse; b. Easton, Pa., Oct. 26, 1952; d. Louis and Martha Leona (Shaw) N. Diploma, Allentown Hosp. Sch. Nursing, 1973. R.N., Pa.; cert. med.-surg. nurse. Missionary welfare services Ch. Jesus Christ Latter Day Saints, Veracruz-Villahermosa, Mex., 1974-76; staff nurse Garden Nursing Home, Phillipsburg, N.J., 1973-74, Easton Hosp., Pa., 1976—. Mem. Am. Nurses Assn., Pa. Nurses Assn. Democrat. Avocations: reading; needlework. Home: 424 4th St West Easton PA 18042 Office: Easton Hosp 21st and Lehigh Sts Easton PA 18042

NILES, BARBARA JEAN, training coordinator; b. Chgo., Nov. 21, 1930; d. Thomas H. and Florence (Gregory) Slick; m. Olus L. Loftin, 1962 (dec. 1969); m. William L. Niles, Jan. 24, 1970. B.S., U. So. Calif., 1953; M.S., Calif. Luth. Coll., 1979. Tchr., Pasadena City Coll., 1956-58; indsl. nurse Royal Industries, Pasadena, 1959-66; head nurse Xerox Corp., Pasadena, 1966-72; devel. and tng. coordinator 3M, Camarillo, Calif., 1973—. Vice-chmn. Am. Bd. Occupational Health Nursing, N.Y.C., 1977-82; mem. U. So. Calif. Adv. Bd. Community Edn., Camarillo, 1983—. Republican. Office: 3M 300 S Lewis Rd Camarillo CA 93010

NILES, DORIS KILDALE, educator; b. Eureka, Calif., July 26, 1903; d. Alfred Walter and Laura (Peterson) Kildale; m. Arthur D. Niles, Mar. 11, 1938; children—Katey Niles Walker, Malcolm A., Margaret Niles Rice, James Alfred. A.B., Stanford U., 1926; M.A., 1927; Ph.D., 1931; postgrad. Harvard U., 1930. Teaching asst. dept. botany Stanford U., 1927-28, Ariz. State Coll., 1932, Humboldt State Coll., Arcata, Calif., 1928-45, 55-59; assoc. prof. U. Calif. Extension at Davis, 1958—, curator Nat. Histor Museum, Coll. of Redwoods; exec. dir. Nature Discovery Vols. Mem. Calif. Acad. Scis., N.Y. Acad. Scis., Sierra Club, Phi Beta Kappa, Sigma Xi, Sigma Delta Pi, Pi Lambda Theta. Club: Commonwealth Calif. Home: PO Box 307 Loleta CA 95551 Office: U Calif Extension Davis CA 95616

NILLES, KAREN LYNN, nurse; b. Milw., Jan. 8, 1954; d. Enzo and Lydia Ann (Naspini) Fiorelli; m. Mark Anthony Nilles, May 26, 1979; 1 child, Anthony P. B.S. in Nursing, U. Wis.-Milw., 1978. R.N., Wis. Nursing asst. St. Luke's Hosp., Milw., 1974-75, nursing unit sec., 1975-79, staff nurse IV, orthopedics, 1979-85, chmn. unit based quality assurance, 1984—, employee health specialist Samaritan Health Care, Inc., 1985—. Roman Catholic. Avocations: music; art; theater; sports.

NILSEN, BARBARA YVONNE, lawyer, water utility executive; b. Glendale, Calif., Oct. 23, 1941; d. Allen Blair and Ina Lee (Stewart) Scott; A.A., San Jose City Coll., 1972; B.S. in Bus., San Jose State U., 1974; J.D. Lincoln U., 1983; m. William Nilsen, May 15, 1976; children—Tina, Valerie, Jamie Ng, Michael Ng. Dir. personnel, sec. San Jose Water Co., Calif., 1964—. Chmn. allocations panel Santa Clara County United Way, 1983, vice chmn. bd. trustees, 1986; bd. dirs. Central chpt., 1983; pres. League of Friends on Commn. Status of Women, 1984; pres. Seven Trees Village Homeowners Assn., 1974. Named Disting. Citizen of Yr., City of San Jose, 1981. Mem. Am. Water Works Assn. (sec. Calif./Nev. chpt. 1980, dir. 1982, conf. dir. 1986). Democrat. Roman Catholic. Clubs: Fairway Glen Women's Golf, San Jose Quota (pres. 1978-79). Office: 374 W Santa Clara St San Jose CA 95196

NIMS, NIKKI LISÉ, state agency representative; fashion consultant; b. Tallahassee, Fla., Nov. 28, 1946; d. Harry Nick and Nedra (White) N.; 1 child, Nickolas H. Martin. B.S., Fla. A&M U., 1970; cert. Flori Roberts Cosmetics Co., 1969, Sears Tng. Sch. Fashion Coordinators, 1971. Vis. instr. Fla. A&M U., Sch. Social Scis., Tallahassee, 1977-79; freelance fashion coordinator, Tallahassee, 1978—; mktg. rep. Fla. Dept. Agr., Tallahassee, 1979-82; devel. rep. Fla. Film Commn., Tallahassee, 1982—. Cons. Urban League, 1980, Mrs. Am. Pagaent, 1985; active Ebony Fashion Fair, 1980, Fla. Voters League, 1984—, NAACP, 1984-85; judge Fla. Strawberry Festival, 1982-83. Recipient Most Outstanding Student award in fashion merchandising Fla. A&M U., 1970; Am. Bus. Women's Assn. award, 1978. Mem. Assn. Film Commrs., Nat. Assn. Female Execs., Alpha Kappa Alpha (Outstanding Service Award 1978). Democrat. Avocations: reading; creative writing; music; fishing; travel. Home: 502 Bragg Dr Tallahassee FL 32304

NINO, DIANNE DENISE, employment and training executive; b. Trinidad, Colo., Mar. 13, 1949; d. Vincent and Margaret (Romero) Abeyta; m. George Leonard Trancoso, Oct. 11, 1969 (div. Nov. 1976); 1 son, Brian; m. 2d, Daniel P. Nino, Dec. 10, 1983. Student Colo. Women's Coll., clk. U. Colo., 1967-68; A.A., Trinidad State Jr. Coll., 1969. Loan clk. Mattel Credit Union, City of Industry, Calif., 1970-71; asst. office mgr. Power Equipment Co., Baldwin Park, Calif., 1972-73; office mgr. M.R. Schwarts, M.D., El Monte, Calif., 1973-74; personnel counselor SER-Jobs for Progress, Denver, 1974-77; tech. assistance specialist Nat. SER Office, Denver, 1977-80; exec. dir. SER-Jobs for Progress, 1980—; sec.-treas. El Dorado Denver Industries, 1983-85, chmn. bd., 1985—; treas. Denver Central Corp., 1982—. Chmn. bd. Denver Community Devel. Corp., 1981-84; vol. counselor Resource Ctr. for Battered Women, 1979; com. chmn. Hispanic Ann. Salute, Denver, 1980—; vol. campaigns Councilman Sandos and Mayor Pena, 1982-83; mem. Denver Voter Registration and Edn. Project, 1983. Recipient Good Citizen award DAR, Trinidad, 1967; named Nat. SER Dir. of Yr., 1984. Mem. Nat. Assn. Female Execs., Am. G.I. Forum (Mile Hi chpt. chmn. 1979—). Democrat. Roman Catholic. Office: Denver SER-Jobs for Progress 2915 W 7th Ave Denver CO 80204

NIPE, CATHERINE LAYTON, retired librarian, consultant; b. Bridgeton, N.J., Apr. 28, 1921; d. Fletcher Powers and Helen Preston (Sweeten) Layton; m. Harold John Nipe, Sept. 12, 1942; children—John Alvin, Helen Nipe Upperman, Steven P., Warren J. B.S.L.S., Rutgers U., 1942; M.S., Glassboro State U., 1969. Govt. librarian Del. Ordinance Depot, Pedricktown, N.J., 1942-44; librarian, instr. Penns Grove High Sch. (N.J.), 1957-62; library instr. Salem County Tech. Inst., Carneys Point, N.J., 1962-69; circulation librarian Glassboro State Coll. (N.J.), 1969-72; reference librarian Gloucester County Coll., Sewell, N.J., 1972-82. Pres., trustee Pitman Library, 1970-83; chmn. adv. com. Gloucester County Vocat. Sch., 1973-84; sec. bd. Christian edn. First Baptist Ch., Pitman, 1980-82, trustee, 1984—. Mem. Gloucester Librarians Orgn. (pres. 1972, Librarian of Yr. 1981), N.J. Library Assn., ALA, Camden Area Reference Council (chmn. 1980-82). Home: 549 West Ave Pitman NJ 08071 Office: McCowan Meml Library 15 Pitman Ave Pitman NJ 08071

NIRO, CHERYL IPPOLITO, lawyer; b. Paso Robles, Calif., Feb. 19, 1950; d. Samuel James and Nancy (Canezaro) Ippolito; m. William Luciano Niro, July 1, 1979; children—Christopher William, Melissa Leigh. B.S. with highest honors, U. Ill., 1972; J.D. (teaching asst.), No. Ill. U., 1980. Bar: Ill. 1981, U.S. Dist. Ct. (no. dist.) Ill. 1981. Dir., Gifted Program/Learning Resource Ctr., Sch. Dist. 45, Villa Park, Ill., 1973-79; assoc. Pope Ballard Sheppard & Fowle, Chgo., 1980-81, Niro, Scavone, Haller & Niro, Ltd. (and predecessor). Chgo., 1981—; cons. Ill. Office Edn., 1975; exec. dir. Com. to Commemorate U.S. Constitution in Ill., 1985—. Co-editor: Apple Pie, 1975. Mem. Oak Park Women's Connection, 1981—; U. Ill. Speakers Bur.; bd. dirs. U. Chgo. Lying-In Hosp., 1982—. Ill. State scholar, 1968-72. Mem. ABA, Ill. Bar Assn. (standing com. legal-related edn. for pub.) Chgo. Bar Assn., DuPage County Bar Assn., Am. Trial Lawyers Assn., Ill. Trial Lawyers Assn., NEA, Mortar Bd., Phi Kappa Phi, Alpha Lambda Delta, Delta Gamma. Home: 332 N Scoville Ave Oak Park IL 60302 Office: Niro Scavone Haller & Niro Ltd 200 W Madison St Suite 3500 Chicago IL 60606

NISHIO, DENYSE ANN, physician; b. Detroit, Feb. 19, 1951; d. John James and Pauline Marie (Mercier) Fox; m. James Neal Nishio, Dec. 30, 1976. B.S., U. Mich., 1972, M.D., 1976. Intern in ob-gyn U. Mich., 1976-77, intern in internal medicine, 1977-78, resident in internal medicine, 1978-80; practice medicine specializing in internal medicine; dir. acute care clinic U. Calif.-Davis, Sacramento, 1980—. Mem. Am. Med. Women's Assn. Home: 5050 Keane Dr Carmichael CA 95608

NISKA, MARALIN, opera singer; b. San Pedro, Calif.; d. William Albert and Vera Zoe (Stott) Dice; B.A., UCLA, postgrad., 1959-60; postgrad. Music Acad. of West, 1958-60, U. So. Calif., 1958-59, Long Beach State U.; m. William P. Mullen, May 23, 1970. Debut as Manon in Manon, Ebell Theatre, Los Angeles,

1959; with Met. Nat. Co., 1965-67, N.Y.C. Opera, 1967—, Met. Opera, 1972—; debuts include: Los Angeles Opera, 1959, Opera Co. of Boston, Tulsa Opera, San Diego Opera, 1965, Santa Fe Opera, 1968, Miami Opera, Phila. Opera; voice tchr., Santa Fe. Mem. Am. Guild Mus. Artists (gov. 1977-79), Screen Actors Guild. Democrat. Office: care Tony Hartman 250 W 57th St Suite 1128A New York NY 10019

NITSCHKE, IZETTA LOUISE (ZET), artist, researcher; b. Bowling Green, Ohio, July 22, 1943; d. Robert William and Jennie Francis (Goodwin) Eckert; m. Gene Arthur Nitschke, Aug. 29, 1964; children—Daniel R., Nicholas R. Student Art Inst. Chgo., 1962-64, U. Chgo., 1962-64. Engring. auditor 3M Co., St. Paul, 1964-66, artist graphic systems, 1966-69; in charge of raw materials sch. orders Paramount Ceramics, Fairmont, Minn., 1969-71; cadet univ. activities U.S. Air Force R.O.T.C. detachment 780, S.D. State U., Brookings, 1972-75; freelance artist, researcher, Brookings, 1975—. Artist ceramic display Nat. History Mus., Chgo., 1963. Cover designer Univ. Resource Material Bowling Green State U., 1983. Patentee in field. Publicity chmn. Hosp. Aux. Holiday Tour of Homes, Brookings, 1984; vol. Hosp. Blood Bank, Brookings, 1984—; bd. dirs. Brookings PTA, 1985-86. Recipient Outstanding Unit award Air Force ROTC, 1972. Mem. Reading Reform Found., ROTC Angel Flight, Arnold Air Soc., Am. Legion Aux. Independent. Methodist. Avocations: chess; bridge; reading; classical music. Home: 1616 Sioux Trail Brookings SD 57006

NIX, BARBARA LOIS, real estate broker; b. Yakima, Wash., Sept. 25, 1929; d. Martin Clayton and Norma (Gunter) Westfield; A.A., Sierra Coll., 1978; m. B.H. Nix, July 12, 1968; children—William Martin Dahl, Theresa Irene Dahl; step-children—Dennis Leon, Denise Lynn. Bookkeeper, office mgr. Lakeport (Calif.) Tire Service, 1966-69, Dr. K.J. Absher, Grass Valley, Calif., 1972-75; real estate sales and office mgr. Rough and Ready Land Co., Penn Valley, Calif., 1976-77, co-owner, v.p., sec., 1978—, also of Wildwood West Real Estate and Lake of the Pines Sales. Youth and welfare chmn. Yakima Federated Jr. Women's Club, 1957; den mother Cub Scouts, 1959-60; leader Girl Scouts, 1961-62. Recipient Pres.'s award Sierra Coll., 1973; others. Mem. Penn Valley C. of C., Nat. Assn. Female Execs., Antique Soc. Penn Valley (founder, pres. 1978), St. Mary's Coll. Aux., Sierra Nevada Meml. Hosp. Aux., Nevada County Arts Council. Democrat. Roman Catholic. Clubs: Job's Daus. (life), Lady Elks. Home: 18321 Jayhawk Dr Penn Valley CA 95946 Office: PO Box 191 Rough and Ready CA 95975

NIX, LINDA ANNE, television station executive; b. Lynn, Mass., Sept. 20, 1943; d. Norman Arthur and Gladys Mae (Charlton) Bean, Jr.; m. Henry Taylor Betts, Jr., Sept. 5, 1964 (div. 1970); m. John Asa Nix, Nov. 24, 1971. Student Syracuse U., 1961-64; B.A., Scarritt Coll., 1965; postgrad. Middle Tenn. State U., 1971-73. Mobile coordinator Children's Mus., Nashville, 1967-69; promotion dir. Sta. WDCN-TV/8, Nashville, 1969-82; dir. pub. info. Sta. WYES-TV/12, New Orleans, 1982—; mem. pub. info. adv. com. Pub. Broadcasting Service, Washington, 1977-80, chmn. 1979-80. mem. festival task force, 1979-80. Author, editor: (tchr. workbook) Yellow Submarine, 1968. Contbr. articles to profl. jours. Bd. dirs. Nashville League for Hearing Impaired, 1973-77; chmn. membership com. Council of community Services, Nashville, 1978-80; mem. allocation panel United Way Greater Nashville, 1979-81, United Way Greater New Orleans, 1982—. Mem. Pub. Relations Assn. Am. (chmn. accreditation com. 1985), Broadcast Promotion and Mktg. Execs., Inc. (bd. dirs. 1982—, sec. 1985—). Avocations: flying (multi-engine, comml. pilot); sewing. Home: PO Box 6703 Metairie LA 70009 Office: Sta WYES-TV/12 PO Box 24026 New Orleans LA 70184

NIXON, AGNES ECKHARDT, TV writer, producer; b. Chgo., Dec. 10, 1927; d. Harry Joseph and Agnes Patricia (Dalton) Eckhardt; B.S. in Speech, Northwestern U., 1948; m. Robert Henry Adolphus Nixon, Apr. 6, 1951; children—Catherine Agnes, Mary Frances, Robert Henry, Emily Anne. Writer TV programs Studio One, 1950, Hallmark, 1952-53, Robert Montgomery Presents, 1952-54; co-creator with Irna Phillips daytime serial As The World Turns, 1957-59; head writer The Guiding Light, 1959-65, Another World, 1965-67; creator, producer One Life to Live, ABC, 1967—, All My Children, 1970—, The Manions of America, 1982—, Loving, 1983—. Trustee, TV Conf. Found. Inst. Recipient numerous citations for outstanding contbn. to daytime television and public service. Mem. Internat. Radio and TV Soc., Nat. Acad. TV Arts and Scis. (editorial bd. Jour., Trustees award). Roman Catholic. Guest columnist arts and leisure sect. New York Times.

NIXON, TAMARA FRIEDMAN, economist; b. Cleve., June 3, 1938; d. Victor and Eva J. (Osteryoung) Friedman; B.A. with honors in econs. (Wellesley scholar), Wellesley Coll., 1959; M.B.A. (fellow), U. Pitts., 1961; m. Daniel D. Nixon, June 14, 1959; children—Asa Joel, Naomi Devorah, Victoria Eve. Asst. economist Fed. Res. Bank, N.Y.C., 1959-60, 61-62; economist R.P. Wolff Econ. Research, Miami, Fla., 1972-75; econ. cons., Miami, 1975-79; sr. v.p. Washington Savs. & Loan Assn., Miami Beach, Fla., 1979-81; pres. T.F. Nixon Econ. Cons. Inc., 1982—; sr. v.p. CenTrust Savs. Bank, 1984—; real estate feasibility cons.; investment adminstr. Land use chmn. Dade County chpt. LWV, 1975-76. Mem. Econ. Soc. S. Fla. (v.p. programs, dir.), Am. Econ. Assn. Office: 4646 North Bay Rd Miami Beach FL 33140

NIXON, THELMA CATHERINE PATRICIA RYAN (MRS. RICHARD M. NIXON), wife of former Pres. of U.S.; b. Ely, Nev., Mar. 16, 1912; grad. cum laude U. So. Calif., 1937, L.H.D., 1961; m. Richard Milhous Nixon, June 21, 1940; children—Patricia (Mrs. Edward Finch Cox), Julie (Mrs. Dwight David Eisenhower II). X-ray technician, N.Y.C., 1931-33; tchr. high schs., Cal., 1937-41; govt. economist, 1942-45. Promoter of world wide humanitarian service, volunteerism in U.S. Decorated grand cross Order of Sun for relief work at time of massive earthquake, 1971 (Peru); grand cordon Most Venerable Order Knighthood Pioneers (Liberia), 1972; named among most admired women George Gallup polls, 1957, 68, 69, 70, 71. *

NJUGUNA, BEVERLY WOHNER, lawyer; b. Milw., Aug. 18, 1940; d. Joseph C. and Bernice (McCoy) Thomas; m. George M. Njuguna, Apr. 18, 1971 (div. Sept. 1982); 1 child, Mbugua. B.S. in Bus. Adminstrn., Roosevelt U., 1964; M.S.W., U. Wis.-Milw., 1968; J.D., U. Wis., 1979. Bar: Wis. 1980. Tng. coordinator Jane Addams Tng. Center for VISTA, Chgo., 1968-69; sch. social worker Chgo. Bd. Edn., Chgo., 1969-73; dir. social services Martin Center, Inc., Milw., 1974-77; assoc. Miller Law Offices, Milw., 1980—. Mem. City of Milw. MBE Loan Com. bd. dirs. YWCA-Phillips Ctr., 1985—; mem. Task Force on Regulations and Restrictions, Gov.'s Conf. on Small Bus.; pres. Black Women's Network, Inc., 1980-82, 85—; regional coordinator Networking Together, Inc., 1984. Mem. ABA, State Bar Wis., Nat. Assn. Black Women Attys., Delta Sigma Theta. Baptist. Home: 1618 N 24th Pl Milwaukee WI 53205 Office: Miller Law Offices 2303 N 39th St Milwaukee WI 53210

NOBEL, JEAN ANNE, cytotechnologist, histologist; b. N.Y.C., Feb. 28, 1934; d. Robert and Irene May (McCullough) Ritchie; Cert. lab. tech., St. Francis Hosp., Jersey City, 1956; cert. histology East Orange Gen. Hosp., 1960; cert. cytology Presbyterian Hosp., Newark, 1971; m. James L. Nobel, Oct. 30, 1954; 1 dau., Donna Jean Nobel Marsula. Supr. histology Kimball Med. Ctr., Lakewood, N.J., 1965-73, supr. histology and cytology, 1982—; supr. cytology Walson Army Hosp., Ft. Dix., N.J., 1973-75; cytotechnologist Obstet. Assocs., Bricktown, N.J., 1975-82. Leader Monmouth County and Ocean County councils Girl Scouts U.S.A., 1964-70; instr. Spl. Olympics Swimming, Ft. Dix, 1973-75. Mem. Greater N.Y. Assn. Cytotechnologists, N.J. Assn. Cytotechnologists, N.J. Histology Soc. Home: 22 Field St Toms River NJ 08753 Office: Kimball Med Ctr Lakewood NJ 08701

NOBLE, BARBARA ANNETTE, lawyer, rehabilitation counselor for deaf; b. Crownpoint, N.Mex., May 13, 1943; d. Charles Edmund and Annette (King) N.; B.A. in English and Psychology, UCLA, 1965; postgrad. Calif. State U., Los Angeles, 1967-68; cert. in counseling for the deaf, U. Tenn., 1971; J.D., Northrop U., 1977. Disability analyst State of Calif., Los Angeles, 1965-68, rehab. counselor, 1968, rehab. counselor for the deaf and hard of hearing, 1968-78, sr. rehab. counselor for the deaf and hard of hearing, 1976-78; admitted to Calif. bar, 1977; vol. staff atty. So. Calif. Center Law and the Deaf, 1978; dep. atty. gen. State of Calif., 1978—; cons. U.S. Postal Service, 1970-78; cons. Silent Industries. Mem. com. for handicapped Los Angeles City Council, 1979-82; mem. deaf adv. com. El Camino Coll., 1976-78. Cert. rehab. counselor. Mem. Calif. Bar, Women Lawyers Assn. Los Angeles, Northrop U. Alumni Assn., UCLA Alumni Assn. Office: 3580 Wilshire Blvd Suite 800 Los Angeles CA 90010

NOBLE, BARBARA RUTH, nurse; b. Washington, Oct. 2, 1952; d. Franklin Eugene and Mary Ellen (Nash) Smith; m. Clay Alan Noble, Sept. 20, 1975; children—Beverly Ruth, Carol Anne, Craig Alan. B.S.N., Baylor U., 1975; cert. paralegal studies, Southwestern Paralegal Inst., 1978. R.N. Dir. nurses Permian Lodge, Inc., Midland, Tex., 1975-76; charge nurse Meml. Hosp., Seminole, Tex., 1977-78; head nurse, relief supr. Citizens Gen. Hosp., Houston, 1978—; legal asst. ed. malpractice Andrews & Kurth, Houston, 1978-80; legal asst. personal injury Butler & Binion, Houston, 1980-83; owner Noble Services, Houston, 1983—; lectr. in field. Contbg. author: State Bar of Tex. Seminar publication, 1983. Mem. Houston Legal Asst. Assn. (1st v.p. 1981-82, corr. sec. 1985-87, treas. 1980-81), Legal Asst. State Bar Tex., Am. Nurses Assn., Tex. Nurses Assn. Republican. Episcopalian. Office: Noble Services 18303 Oakhampton Dr Houston TX 77084

NOBLE, FRANCES ELIZABETH, educator, author; b. Chgo., Sept. 3, 1903; d. George William and Clara Louise (Lane) N.; B.A. cum laude, Northwestern U., 1924, M.A., 1926, Ph.D., 1945. Mem. faculty Western Mich. U., Kalamazoo, 1931—, prof. French, head dept., 1955-73, prof. emerita, 1973—; French tchr. Fort Lauderdale (Fla.) Public Library, 1978—. Pres., Crippled Children's Guild of Broward County. Decorated palmes academiques, 1945. Mem. Alliance Française (past pres.), Am. Assn. Tchrs. of French, Phi Beta Kappa. Republican. Author: (novel) Destiny's Daughter, 1980; The Political Ideas of Alfred de Musset, 1945; also articles. Home: 2915 NE Center Ave Fort Lauderdale FL 33308

NOBLE, MARION LOUISE, computer company executive; b. Lawrence, Mass., July 5, 1948; d. Walter Norman and Louise Marie (Reis) Armitage; m. Fred Donald, June 20, 1970. B.A. in Journalism, Northeastern U., 1970; M.B.A., Babson Coll., 1977. News reporter Lowell Sun, Mass., 1966-68; pub. relations editor New Eng. Telephone, Boston, 1968-70; recruiter Computer Systems div. RCA, Marlboro, Mass., 1970-71; personnel adminstr. Sanders Assocs., Bedford, Mass., 1971-72; dir. compensation, benefits and human resource info. systems Data Gen., Westboro, Mass., 1972—. Mem. Human Resource Systems Profls., Am. Compensation Assn. Avocations: ice dancing; sailing; biking; real estate. Home: 50 Highcrest Rd North Falmouth MA 02556 Office: Data Gen Corp 4400 Computer Dr Westboro MA 01450

NOBLE, MITZI MCALEXANDER, travel company executive; b. Kingsport, Tenn., Feb. 6, 1941; d. Buren and Ruby Estelle (Hodges) McAlexander; m. Paul Benjamin Noble, June 29, 1957; children—Michael B., James B. Student, Nat. Bus. Coll., 1958-59, U. Mich., 1958, Ind. U., 1963-65; R.B.A., Shepherd Coll., 1985; postgrad. Wesley Theol. Sem., 1985-86. Co-owner, dir. personnel, soloist All-Student Band, Winchester, Va., 1965-69; co-owner, gen. mgr. Ednl. Tour Consultants, Winchester, 1967—, Noble's Travel World, Winchester, 1975—; sales and mktg. rep. Air France, Washington, 1970-75; lectr. Shenandoah Coll. and Conservatory of Mus., Winchester, 1982. Chmn. Downtown Devel. Bd., Winchester, 1977-83; mem. selection and budget com. United Fund, Winchester, 1984—; bd. dirs. Wayside Found. for the Arts, Middletown, Va., 1981-84. Mem. Actor's Equity Assn., Retail Mchts. Assn. (officer, dir. 1970-81), Winchester C. of C. (officer, dir. 1979-83), Sigma Alpha Iota, Tau Beta Sigma. Episcopalian. Club: Quota (exec. bd.) (Winchester). Avocations: music; cantor and soloist; music theatre; church leadership; world travel. Home: Route 4 Box 37 Merriman's Ln Winchester VA 22601 Office: Noble's Travel World 16 N Braddock St Winchester VA 22601

NOBLE, (RUTH) ELAINE, counseling institute executive; B.F.A., Boston U., 1966; M.S., Emerson Coll., 1970; Ed.M., Harvard U., 1974; postgrad. U. Mass., 1983—. Instr. speech Colby Jr. Coll., New London, N.H., 1966-67, North Shore Community Coll., Beverly, Mass., 1967-68; asst. advt. mgr. Sweetheart Plastics, Wilmington, Mass., 1968-70; instr. speech Emerson Coll., Boston, 1970-74; mem. Mass. Ho. of Reps. from 6th Suffolk Dist., 1974-78; spl. asst. to mayor for govtl. relations, Boston, 1979-83; adminstrv. asst. to Speaker of House, Boston, 1983-84; pres. Noble Assocs., Boston, 1984—; pres. Pride Inst., in-patient treatment ctr. for gay men and lesbians; lectr. in field. Bd. dirs. Boston Evening Med. Ctr., 1981—, Mass. Assn. Alcoholism Service, 1983—, Serenity Recovery House, 1984—, Ams. for Democratic Action, 1975—, Mass. Civil Liberties Union, 1975, Vis. Nurses Assn., 1975-79; mem. Ward 5 Com., 1975-78, chmn. Ward 3 Com., 1979-84; chmn. Dem. City Com., 1980-84; mem. adv. bd. Neighborhood Assn. of Back Bay, 1976-78, Newbury St. Crime Com., 1977. Named Outstanding Young Leader Boston C. of C., 1977; Boston U. trustee scholar, 1963-66. Mem. AAUP, Phi Delta Kappa. Office: Pride Inst 14400 Martin Dr Eden Prairie MN 55344

NOBLITT, MARILYN RUTH BARNES, temporary employment service executive; b. Laramie, Wyo., Jan. 8, 1937; d. Frederick Clayton and Sarah Ruth (Brandt) Barnes; m. Jack L. Noblitt, Dec. 27, 1958; children—Alan Lee, Jacqueline Ann, Daniel Jay, Douglas Keith. B.S. with honors, U. Wyo., 1959. Br. mgr. Kelly Services Inc., Cheyenne, Wyo., 1977—. Recipient Gold medal Kelly Services, Detroit, 1979, Outstanding Br. performance award, 1981. Mem. Assn. Records Mgrs. and Adminstrs. (dir. Cheyenne 1982-84), Am. Soc. Personnel Adminstrn. (pres. Cheyenne 1984—), Cheyenne C. of C., Women's Ednl. Service Assn., P.E.O., Kappa Kappa Gamma Alumnae Assn. Republican. Presbyterian. Club: Zonta. Office: Kelly Services Inc 1720 Carey St Suite 600 Cheyenne WY 82001

NOBLITT, NANCY ANNE, aerospace engineer; b. Roanoke, Va., Aug. 14, 1959; d. Jerry Spencer and Mary Louise (Jerrell) N. B.A., Mills Coll., Oakland, Calif., 1982. Aerospace engr. turbine engine div. components br. turbine group aero-propulsion lab. Wright-Patterson AFB, Ohio, 1982-84, engine assessment br. spl. engines group, 1984—. Math and sci. tutor Centerville Sch. Bd., Ohio. Recipient Notable Achievement award U.S. Air Force, 1984. Avocation: book collecting. Home: 2041 Whipp Rd Kettering OH 45440 Office: AFWAL-POTA Bldg 18 Room D 19 Wright Patterson AFB OH 45433

NOBOA, PATRICIA LYNN, printing company executive; b. Cin., Sept. 6, 1947; d. William Emile and Marie Virginia (Ballbach) Hakes; children—Aric Israel, Rene Carlos. Diploma Presbyterian-St. Luke's Sch. Nursing, Chgo., 1967. Patient care supr. Alexandria Hosp., Va., 1976-78; pres. Renaissance Reprographics, Inc., Reston, Va., 1985—; pres. Va. Leasing & Copying Inc., Reston, 1978—. Pres. Reston Bd. Commerce, 1985; v.p. Planned Community Archives, Inc., 1985. Named Reston Citizen of Yr., 1985. Mem. Nat. Assn. Quick Printers (bd. dirs. Captial chpt. 1984-85), Fairfax County C. of C. (bd. dirs. 1985). Episcopalian. Avocations: computers, music. Home: 11617 Newbridge Ct Reston VA 22091 Office: Virginia Leasing & Copying Inc 11800 Sunrise Valley Dr Reston VA 22091

NOCHMAN, LOIS WOOD KIVI (MRS. MARVIN NOCHMAN), educator; b. Detroit, Nov. 5, 1924; d. Peter K. and Annetta Lois (Wood) Kivi; A.B., U. Mich., 1946, A.M., 1949; m. Harold I. Pitchford, Sept. 6, 1944 (div. May 1949); children—Jean Pitchford Horiszny, Joyce Lynn Pitchford McGinnis; m. 2d, Marvin A. Nochman, Aug. 15, 1953; 1 son, Joseph Asa. Tchr. adult edn., Honolulu, 1947, Ypsilanti (Mich.) High Sch., 1951-52; spl. instr. English, Wayne State U., Detroit, 1953, 54; tchr. Highland Park (Mich.) Coll., 1950-51, instr. English, 1954-83. Mem. exec. bd. Highland Park Fedn. Tchrs., 1963, 64, 65, 66, 71, 72, mem. 1st bargaining team, 1965-66, 73, del. to Nat. Conv., 1964, 71, 72, 73, 74, rep. higher edn. to Mich. Fedn. Tchrs. Exec. Com., 1972, 73, 74, 75, 76; mem. faculty adv. com. Gov.'s Commn. on Higher Edn., 1973—. Tchr. Baha'i schs., Davison, Mich., 1954, 55, 58, 59, 63, 64, 65, 66, Beaulac, Que., Can., 1960, Greenacre, Maine, 1965; sec. local spiritual assembly Baha'is, Ann Arbor, 1953, sec., Detroit, 1954, chmn., 1955; mem. nat. com. Baha'is U.S., 1955-68; sec. Davison Bahai Sch. Com. and Council, 1956, 58, 63, 64, 65, 66, 67, 68; Baha'i lectr. Mem. Modern Lang. Assn., Nat. Council Tchrs. English, Mich. Coll. English Assn., Am. Fedn. Tchrs., Nat. Soc. Lit. and Arts, Women's Equity and Action League (sec. Mich. chpt. 1975-79), Alpha Lambda Delta, Alpha Gamma Delta. Contbr. poems to mags. Home: 25227 Parkwood Huntington Woods MI 48070

NOE, CAROLINE HANSHE, hotel executive; b. Hartford, Conn., Jan. 7, 1959; d. William Brenton and Hope Elizabeth (Turner) N. B.A., Columbia U., 1982. Mgmt. trainee Sheraton Corp., Sheraton Carlton, Washington, 1983-84, conf. coordinator Sheraton Plaza, Chgo., 1984-86, Sheraton New Orleans, 1986—. Mem. Barnard alumni Assn. (rep. to Ivy Connection 1983-84), Hotel Sales and Mktg. Assn., Bus. and Profl. Women's Club of New Orleans, Alliance Française. Presbyterian. Club: Ivy Connection (Washington). Avocations: skiing; fencing; squash. Office: Sheraton New Orleans 500 Canal St New Orleans LA 70130

NOE, ELNORA (ELLIE), chem. co. exec.; b. Evansville, Ind., Aug. 23, 1928; d. Thomas and Evelyn (West) Dieter; student Ind. U.-Purdue U., Indpls. Sec., Pitman Moore Co., Indpls., 1946; with Dow Chem. Co., Indpls., 1960—, public relations asst. then mgr. employee communications, 1970—. Mem. public relations com. ARC, Indpls.; mem. steering com. Learn About Bus. Recipient 2 place award as Businesswoman of Yr., Indpls. Bus. and Profl. Women's Assn., 1980. Mem. Am. Bus. Women Assn. (woman of yr. 1965; past pres.), Ind. Assn. Bus. Communicators (communicator of yr. 1977), Women in Communications (Louise Eleanor Kleinhenz award 1984), Nat. Fedn. Press Women, Women's Press Club Ind. (past v.p.). Club: Zonta Internat. (dist. public relations chmn. 1978-80, area dir. 1980-82, pres. Indpls. 1977-79). Office: PO Box 68511 Indianapolis IN 46268

NOE, SALLY (SARA) WOODWORTH, educator, local history researcher; b. Kansas City, Mo., Mar. 18, 1926; d. Hugh Johnson and Katharine (McAntire) Woodworth; m. Robert Clark Noe, Aug. 14, 1945; children—Katharine Merry, Thomas Clark, William Dean. B.A., U. N.Mex., 1969, M.A., 1984. Cert. tchr., N.Mex. Elem. tchr. Morenci Pub. Schs., Ariz., 1946-47; elem. tchr. Gallup-McKinley County Sch. Dist., N.Mex., 1955-56, tchr. Office Navajo Edn. Opportunity, Concentrated Employment Practice, 1968-69, tchr. secondary social studies, 1969—, chmn. dept. social studies, 1977—; social studies evaluator, N.Mex. schs., 1975—; instr. U. N.Mex., Gallup, 1986. Author N.Mex. Council for Social Studies and State N.Mex. Dept. Edn. unit for Native Am. history, 1979; author Gallup centennial calendar, 1981. Head rug clk. InterTribal Indian Ceremonial, Gallup, 1976—; regional dir. N.Mex. History Day; bd. dirs. N.Mex. Law Related Edn. Program; mem. com. Ft. Wingate Preservation Task Force, 1984, Com. on Status of History in N.Mex. Pub. Schs., 1984; bd. dirs. N.Mex. Law Related Edn. Recipient 3d Place award Hist. Soc. div. Kazanjian Found., 1970, Tchr.'s medal Freedom Found. at Valley Forge, 1973, Inst. for Am. Indian History award Newberry Library, 1978, McKinley Area Council Govts. award for hist. preservation, 1985; Ethnic Am. Coe fellow Stanford U., Calif., 1979; SW Inst. Research on Women fellow U. Ariz., 1983; Spl. Programs in Citizenship Edn. fellow Wake Forest U. Sch. Law, 1985. Mem. N.Mex. Council for Social Studies (pres. 1980-81), N.Mex. Hist. Soc. (presenter), Nat. Council Social Studies, N.Mex. Archeol. Soc. (cert. crew mem., presenter), N.Mex. Soc. for Preservation History, Gallup Hist. Soc., Internat. Platform Assn., Delta Kappa Gamma (pres. Gallup chpt. 1979-80), Alpha Delta Pi. Democrat. Episcopalian. Lodges: Order Eastern Star, PEO. Home: PO Box 502 1911 Mark St Gallup NM 87301 Office: Gallup High Sch PO Box 39 Gallup NM 87301

NOELLISTE, GLORIA JEAN, pipeline company executive; b. Detroit, Nov. 1, 1953; d. Clyde Tingle and Ella (Charleston) Taylor; m. Dieumeme Exima Noelliste, May 26, 1979; children—Joseph Daniel, Leila Ann. B.A., Mich. State U., 1975; tchr.'s cert. C. H. Mason Bible Coll., 1976; postgrad. William Tyndale Coll., 1977-79, Moody Bible Inst., 1983, Wheaton Grad. Sch., 1982—. Pub. auditor Arthur Andersen & Co., C.P.A.s, Detroit, 1975-76; internal auditor Am. Natural Resources, Detroit, 1976-77, staff EDP auditor, 1978-79; assoc. auditor Natural Gas Pipeline Co., Chgo., 1979-80, EDP auditor, 1981-82, data adminstr., 1982-85, System analyst, 1986—; fin. sec. C. H. Mason Found., Detroit, 1978-79; tax cons. Nat. Black Evang. Assn., Detroit, 1975-76. Contbr. Beautiful for Him, nat. black christian women's mag. Pres., Pastors' Wives Fellowship, 1982—; pres. Orgn. Haitian Children Edn. Assn., 1979—; vol. Harper Hosp. Rehab. Ctr., Detroit, 1976-79, St. Francis Hosp., Evanston, Ill., 1980; tchr. Quest II, 1980—. Recipient scholarships Cass Tech. High Sch., 1971-75, Gibson Ednl. Found., 1971, Nat. Assn. Black Accts., 1975; named Outstanding Worker, Ch. of God in Christ, Bus. and Profl. Women, 1979. Mem. Exec. Christian Women (contbr. newsletter 1983), Women Econ. Club, Nat. Black Evang. Assn., Nat. Assn. Black Accts. Democrat. Pentecostal. Club: Mich. State U. Alumni.

NOGUEIRAS, MARY, travel agent; b. Havana, July 18, 1929; d. Jose Antonio and Carmen (Carrasco) Gonzalez; m. Humberto Mario Nogueiras, June 28, 1952; children—Diane Michelle, Eileen Lillian, Denise Susan, Brenda Lynn. A.S., Havana Bus. U., 1948; student Sch. Bus. Edn., U. Miami, 1948-52. Bilingual sec. U. Miami forensics dept., Coral Gables, 1949-52; bilingual sec., asst. to mgr. Brown & Bigelow, Mpls., 1952-54; salesperson, various cos., Miami, 1960-75; owner, mgr. Directions in Design, Miami, 1980-83; pres. Bermar Travel Inc., Coral Gables, Fla., 1983—. Bd. dirs. Doctors Hosp. Aux. Coral Gables, 1960-75, Dade County Med. Aux., 1960-66, pres., 1966-67. Mem. Am. Soc. Travel Agts., Meeting Planners Assn., Riviera County Club Womens Golf Assn. (past pres.). Republican. Roman Catholic. Office: Bermar Travel Inc 6851 Yumuri St Miami FL 33146

NOKES, JACKIE, broadcasting company executive; b. Salt Lake City, Feb. 9, 1929; d. James Owen and Edna Amelia (Hansen) White; student UCLA, 1946-49, U. Utah, 1949-50; m. Andrew Grey Nokes (div.); children—Patricia Nokes Kerbs, Laurence Paul, Beau James, Anthony Grey. Broadcaster, KLS Radio and TV, 1961-74; now community edn. liaison KSL-AM-TV, Salt Lake City. Mem. nat. adv. council So. Utah State Coll.; mem. exec. com. Utah Soc. for Prevention of Blindness; bd. dirs. Utah chpt. Freedom Found. at Valley Forge; trustee Cottonwood-Alta View Hosp. Found.; mem. adv. com. on free enterprise/econ. edn. Utah State Bd. Edn.; bd. dirs. Utah Council on Econ. Edn. Recipient Shield award Delta Gamma; award for patriotic programs Freedoms Found.; Carnation Community Service award Vol. Action Center, Salt Lake City; Hon. Alumna award Utah State U., 1979; Person of Vision award; Bus. Person of Yr. award Future Bus. Leaders Am. Mem. Am. Women in Radio and TV (nat. v.p. 1967-69), Salt Lake Area C. of C. Home: 2075 Lincoln Ln Salt Lake City UT 84124 Office: Broadcast House 5 Triad Salt Lake City UT 84180

NOLAN, AGNES FOLK, real estate executive, lawyer; b. N.Y.C., Aug. 6, 1931; d. William James and Agnes (Sikora) Gilligan; B.A., Trinity Coll., 1952; LL.B., Columbia U., 1955; m. Richard Nolan, Jan. 31, 1959; children—Anthony R., Christopher Whitbread, Timothy Robert, Mariana Celeste, Katherine Hope. Admitted to N.Y. bar, 1957, U.S. Supreme Ct. bar, 1965; practice with firm Cadvalader, Wickersham and Taft, N.Y.C., 1955-60; asst. gen. counsel Kaiser-Roth Corp., N.Y.C., 1960-62; pres. Whitbread Nolan Inc., N.Y.C., 1962—, Windham Properties Inc., 1982—. Bd. dirs., pres. Am. Friends of Westminister Cathedral. Mem. Am. Bar Assn., Real Estate Bd. N.Y. Club: Lake George. Home: 271 Central Park West New York NY 10024 Office: 600 Madison Ave New York NY 10022

NOLAN, BILLIE SCHRECKER, lawyer; b. Pitts., Oct. 1, 1957; d. William Charles and Dorothy May (Fransko) Schrecker; m. Kenneth John Nolan, Apr. 7, 1984. B.A., Bethany Coll., 1979; J.D., U. Pitts., 1982. Bar: Pa. 1982, U.S. Dist. Ct. (western dist.) Pa. 1982, U.S. Ct. Appeals (3d circuit) 1984. Law clk. Manifesto, Doherty, Love & Talarico, Pitts., 1980-81, Egler & Reinstadtler, Pitts., 1981-82; assoc. Egler, Anstandig, Garrett & Riley, Pitts., 1982—. Mem. ABA, Pa. Bar Assn., Allegheny County Bar Assn., Lambda Iota Tau, Omicron Delta Epsilon, Phi Delta Epsilon, Phi Alpha Delta, Phi Mu. Republican. Lutheran. Office: Egler Anstandig Garrett & Riley 428 Forbes Ave 2100 Lawyers Bldg P Pittsburgh PA 15219

NOLAN, CAROLE RITA, broadcasting company executive; b. Chgo., Jan. 28, 1932; d. Martin Francis and Caroline Rita (Alton) N.; B.A., De Paul U., 1954, M.A., 1961. Tchr. Chgo. public schs., 1954-61, sci. cons., 1961-66, dir. instructional TV, 1966-71; dir. bur. telecommunications and broadcasting, mgr. Sta. WBEZ-FM, Chgo., 1971—; mem. faculty Northeastern U., 1964-65, De Paul U., 1975—; cons. Comptons Ency., 1964-65, Chgo. Area Sch. TV, 1964-72, Ill. TV Adv. Council, 1969. Bd. dirs. Am. Chamber Symphony, Ella Flagg Young Women Adminstrs., Chicagoland Radio Info. Services. Mem. Nat. Assn. Ednl. Broadcasters, Ill. Assn. Supervision and Curriculum, Chgo. Network, Nat. Pub. Radio, Japan Am. Soc., DePaul Univ. Alumni Assn., Delta Kappa Gamma. Office: 1819 W Pershing Rd Chicago IL 60609

NOLAN, KAREN LORI, advertising agency executive; b. Paterson, N.J., Nov. 18, 1958; d. Martin Alek and Florence (Miller) Rosenthal; m. Timothy Reynolds Nolan, June 24, 1984. B.S., Montclair State Coll., Upper Montclair, N.J., 1981; postgrad. Fairleigh Dickinson U., 1982—. Mktg. asst. Kem Mfg. Co., Inc., Fairlawn, N.J., 1975-80; graphics mgr. The Montclarion Inc., Upper Montclair, N.J., 1978-80; advt. mgr. Meadox Med., Inc., Oakland, N.J., 1980-82; asst. sales dir. Telegraphics Internat., Clifton, N.J., 1983; sales promotion mgr. Rediform Office Products, Clifton, 1983-84; account exec. McGovern Advt., Inc., Red Bank, N.J., 1984-85, Allen Cons., Inc., Holmdel, N.J., 1986—. Mem. Bus./Profl. Advt. Assn. (mem. exec. bd. 1982—), Am. Mktg. Assn., Montclair Athletic Commn. (dir. 1979-80). Democrat. Jewish.

Home: 517 W Front St Red Bank NJ 07701 Office: Allen Cons Inc 51 E Main St Holmdel NJ 07733

NOLAN, LONE KIRSTEN, real estate investment counselor and executive; b. Copenhagen, Oct. 9, 1938; d. Johannes and Elizabeth (Zachariassen) Jansen; came to U.S., 1957, naturalized, 1964; m. Gene Nolan, Mar. 19, 1973; children—Glenn Muller, Erik Muller. Adminstrv. asst. Am. Nat. Bank and Trust, Morristown, N.J., 1967-72; asst. cashier First Nat. Iron Bank, 1972; comptroller and ops. officer Panama City Nat. Bank, 1973-74; asst. v.p. Lee County Bank, Ft. Myers, Fla., 1974-76; customer and IRA investments exec. Priscilla Murphy Realty, Sanibel, Fla., 1976-77; pres. Century 21 Nolan Realty, Ft. Myers, 1977-80; pres. AAIM Realty Group, Ft. Myers, 1980-81; real estate investment counselor Merrill Lynch, Boca Raton, Fla., 1982-85; mgr. Merrill Lynch Realty, Palm Beach, Fla., 1984-85; mgr. Alan Bush Realty, Inc., Boca Raton, 1985—; mem. A.L. Williams Agy. Mem. Internat. Real Estate Fedn., Nat. Assn. Realtors, Realtors Nat. Mktg. Inst., Fla. Real Estate Exchangors. Home: 7129 Promenade Dr Apt A-202 Boca Raton FL 33433 Office: Alan Bush Realty Inc 21301 Powerline Rd Suite 210 Boca Raton FL 33433

NOLAN, LOUISE MARY, serigrapher, superintendent, educator, author; b. Boston, Sept. 28, 1947; d. John Joseph and Helen (Spiers) Nolan; B.A., Regis Coll., 1969; M.Ed., Boston U., 1971 postgrad., 1981-82; postgrad Fitchburg State Coll., 1972-74, Salem State Coll., 1977-79; Ph.D. in Curriculum and Instruction, Boston Coll., 1986. Counselor, Camp Thoreau, Inc., Concord, Mass., 1964-68; tchr., chmn. sci. dept. John F. Kennedy Meml. Jr. High Sch., Woburn, Mass., 1969-86; asst. superintendent for curriculum and instruction Woburn Pub. Schs., 1986—; co-owner Ruth and Louise Silkscreening, Lexington, Mass., Fancypants, Carlisle, Mass.; dir. ecology program Curry Coll., Milton, Mass., summer 1977. Vice chmn. Mass. Sci. Fair Com. NSF grantee, 1972-73, 77-79, 81-82; Boston U. fellow, 1983-84; F.A.C.E. grantee, 1983—. Mem. Mass. Tchrs. Assn., NEA, AAAS, Nat. Assn. Sci. Tchrs., Mass. Assn. Sci. Tchrs., Nat. Assn. Biology Tchrs., Nat. Assn. Research in Sci. Teaching. Sch. Sci. and Math. Assn., Middlesex County Tchrs. Assn., Woburn Tchrs. Assn., Beta Beta Beta, Pi Lambda Theta. Democrat. Roman Catholic. Clubs: Museum Fine Arts, Lit. Guild, Concord Art Assn., Mus. of Sci., Theatre Guild. Author: Y.E.S.—A Comprehensive Guide to Students Educating Youth in Environmental Sciences; Bioluminescence—An Experimental Guide; Marine Plankton; Health Physical Science; Using Computers in Science; Teachers Perceptions of the Quality and Effectiveness of Free and Inexpensive Materials Related to Energy Education. Home: 9 Stevens Rd Lexington MA 02173 Office: Adminstrn Bldg Woburn Pub Schs Woburn MA 01801

NOLAND, KATHRYN CRISP, interior designer, educator; b. Bryson City, N.C., Mar. 10, 1951; d. French Orion and Margaret (Colville) C.; m. David Allen Noland, Feb. 25, 1978. B.S., Western Carolina U., 1973, M.S., 1983. Free-lance designer Interior Design Ctr., Robbinsville, N.C., 1973-75; interior designer Noland Interiors, Inc., Lake Junaluska, N.C., 1975—; part-time instr. Western Carolina U., Cullowhee, N.C., 1981—. Mem. Am. Soc. Interior Designers (cert.). Beta Sigma Phi (pres. 1979-80). Democrat. Presbyterian. Club: Altrusa Internat. Avocations: music (piano), needlepoint. Home: PO Box 249 Balsam View Dr Balsam NC 28707 Office: Noland Interiors Inc Hwy 209 Lake Junaluska NC 28745

NOLAND, PATRICIA HAMPTON, poet, editor, writer; b. New Orleans; d. Leon Maxwell and Clara Hampton (Whittle) Noland; B.A., U. Houston, 1981; Dr. Leadership in Poetry (hon.), Internat. Acad. Leadership, Philippines, 1969; D.L.H. (hon.) Free U. Asia, 1973; Diploma of Merit in Lit., U. Arts, Salsomaggiore Terme, Italy, 1982. Vol., Mental Health Center, St. Joseph's Hosp., Houston, 1970-71; founder, pres., editor monthly newsletter Internat. Poetry Inst., Houston, 1969—. Chmn. music com. 1st Ch. of Christ Scientist, Houston, 1983-86. Named Hon. Internat. Poet Laureate, United Poets Laureate Internat., Manila, 1969. Mem. Am. Hort. Soc., Mus. Fin Arts Houston, Met. Opera Guild, Am. Film Inst., Smithsonian Instn., Nat. Trust Hist. Preservation, Coustean Soc., Mus. for Women in Art, Planetary Soc., Poetry Soc. Tex., Internat. Platform Assn., Mus. of Art of Am. West, Mus. Fine Arts Boston, Isabella Stewart Gardner Mus. Boston, Met. Mus. Art, Norton Gallery and Sch. Art Palm Beach, New Orleans Mus. Art, Chgo. Art Inst., Colonial Williamsburg Found., Alliance Francaise Houston, English-Speaking Union. Democrat. Club: Jr. League Luncheon. Author: Poems, 1960; editor: Whoever Heard a Birdie Cry?, 1970. Home: 2400 Westheimer Rd Apt 215W Houston TX 77098 Office: PO Box 53087 Houston TX 77052

NOLE, ANGELA D., city official; b. Utica, N.Y., June 28, 1931; d. Nicholas and Angela (Graziadei) N.; grad. high sch.; m. James A. DeBella, Sept. 23, 1963; children—Bonnie A. Sardino, Elizabeth, Judiann, Jamie. Sec., Oneida County Dept. Social Services, 1950-63, Gen. Electric Co., 1956-59; admitting clk. St. Elizabeth Hosp., 1968-72; exec. sec. N.Y. State Teamsters, 1972-76; asst. budget dir. City of Utica, from 1978, now office mgr.; exec. sec. Municipal Housing Authority. Active local Democratic politics to elect Judge Harold Hymes, Judge John E. Flemma, Judge Anthony Garramone, Judge John L. Murad, Lawrence T. George for Utica City Judge, John F. Kennedy for pres., Robert F. Kennedy for N.Y. senator; bd. dirs. Notre Dame High Sch. Parents Orgn. Mem. Bus. and Profl. Women's Club, Nat. Assn. Bus. and Profl. Women. Roman Catholic. Home: 448 Elmhurst Rd Utica NY 13502 Office: 1 Kennedy Plaza Utica NY 13502

NOLIN, MARTA VICTORIA, intern psychologist; b. Eastchester, N.Y., May 23, 1952; d. Joseph H. and Victoria B. (Toteff) N.; B.A. magna cum laude, Boston U., 1974; M.A., Assumption Coll., 1977; postgrad. in counseling psychology U. Mo., Columbia. Residence hall dir. Boston U., 1974-75; head of residence U. Mass., Amherst, 1977-78, sr. head of residence, 1978-79; asst. dean for student life Ohio Wesleyan U., Delaware, 1979-83; counselor Project Self Discovery U. Mo.-Columbia, 1983-84, counselor intern Women's Ctr., 1984-85, intern psychologist Univ. Counseling Services, 1985-87. Mem. Am. Coll. Personnel Assn., Am. Assn. Counseling and Devel., Am. Psychol. Assn. Democrat. Office: 220 Parker Hall Counseling Services U Mo-Columbia MO 65211

NOLL, B(EVERLY) GAYLE, college dean; b. Seymour, Tex., Jan. 23, 1942; d. Murrie and Marie Machen; m. Charles Anthony Noll, III, Mar. 27, 1964; children—A'lisa Marie, Charles Anthony, IV. B.A. in Journalism, Tex. Tech U., 1964, M.A. in Communications, 1973, postgrad. in ednl. adminstrn., 1982-85; postgrad. U. Tex.-Permian Basin, 1982-85. Report and edn. editor Lubbock Avalanche-Jour., Tex., 1964-67; dir. student publ. Lubbock High Sch., 1966; copywriter Womack Claypoole Advt., Odessa, Tex., summer 1967; news reporter Odessa Am., 1967-69; instr. journalism, pub. relations dir. Odessa Coll., 1970-71, coll. relations dir., 1970-82, dean of continuing edn., 1982—. Author: Chuck Wagon Gang Story, 1970, Odessa College 25-Year Hostory, 1971. Recipient numerous awards. Mem. Tex. Assn. Community Edn. for Community and Jr. Colls. (sec.-treas. 1984-86), Tex. Assn. Community Service and Continuing Edn. (bd. dirs. 1984-85), Dist. IV Case (bd. dirs., exec. officer 1984-85), Nat. Council Community Relations, Nat. Council Community Services and Continuing Edn., Odessa C. of C., Phi Kappa Phi. Home: 3963 Lakeside Odessa TX 79762 Office: Odessa Coll 201 W University Odessa TX 79764

NOLL, WENDY LANGMAID, advertising company executive; b. N.Y.C., Oct. 1, 1949; d. Anthony Frances and Ann (Linderman) Noll. A.A., Colby Coll. Women, 1969; B.A., Boston U., 1971. Traffic scheduling supr. Young & Rubicam, Inc., N.Y.C., 1974-79, traffic coordination supr., 1979-81, asst. TV comml. producer, 1981-83, TV comml. producer, 1983—. Office: Young & Rubicam Inc 285 Madison Ave New York NY 10017

NOLTE, JUDITH ANN, magazine editor; b. Hampton, Iowa, Sept. 17, 1938; d. Clifford P. and Sigrid M. (Johnson) Nolte; B.S., U. Minn., 1960; M.A., in English, N.Y. U., 1965; m. Randers H. Heimer, May 7, 1971. Tchr. English, Middletown (N.Y.) High Sch., 1960-62, High Sch. of Commerce, N.Y.C., 1962-64; merchandising editor Conde Nast Publs., N.Y.C., 1964-69; editor-in-chief Am. Baby mag., N.Y.C., 1969—, Weight Watchers mag., 1980-83. Mem. Am. Soc. Mag. Editors (pres. 1986—), Mortar Bd., Delta Gamma. Office: 575 Lexington Ave New York NY 10022

NOONAN, PATRICIA SAULNIER, editor, writer; b. Lynn, Mass., Jan. 29, 1945; d. Paul Hypolite and Bernadette Florida (Dion) Saulnier; student Merrimack Coll., 1962-63, Siena Coll., 1970; m. Frank R. Noonan, Aug. 22, 1964; children—Kathleen, Kelly, Kristin. Free-lance writer, reporter Beacon Pub., Acton, Mass., 1978; writer, reporter, clipboard editor Voice Newspapers, Louisville, Ky., 1979, Ky. Bus. Ledger, Louisville, 1979; bus. editor Voice Newspapers, Scripps-Howard Co., Louisville, 1979, exec. editor, 1980-81; copy editor and editor Guy Gannett Newspapers, Portland, Maine, 1981—. Bd. dirs. Portland Concert Assn.; trustee Maine Council Econ. Edn. Mem. Sigma Delta Chi. Republican. Roman Catholic. Home: 10 Ship Channel Rd South Portland ME 04106 Office: Guy Gannett Newspapers 390 Congress St Portland ME 04101

NOONER, MARIANNA REBECCA, fashion executive; b. Corpus Christi, Tex., Sept. 9, 1951; d. R.C. and Evelyn Helen (Habeeb) Nooner; B.S.E., U. Ark., 1973; M.A., U. Tex., 1979. Sales rep. Am. Can. Corp., Dallas, 1973-77, Mobil Chem. Co. div. Mobil Oil Co., Dallas, 1977-80; acct. exec. Calvin Klein Menswear, Dallas, 1980-86, Giorgio Armani Menswear, 1986—. Mem. Women's Com. Dallas Ballet; active Dallas Symphony League Innovators, Dallas Mus. Art. Named Salesman of Yr. Calvin Klein Sportswear, 1982. Mem. NOW, Delta Gamma. Republican. Episcopalian. Club: Cotillion (Dallas). Home: 9612 Glenacre Circle Dallas TX 75243

NORBACK, DIANE HAGEMAN, pathologist; b. Comfrey, Minn., Mar. 22, 1946; d. Evan Herman and Emma Alvina (Meier) Hageman; B.A., Luther Coll., 1966; M.A.T., Northwestern U., 1967; Ph.D., U. Wis., 1973, M.D., 1974; m. John Palmer Norback, Aug. 20, 1966; children—Christopher James, Nathaniel Charles. Asst. prof. dept. pathology U. Wis., Madison, 1975-81, assoc. prof., 1981—, dir. hematology lab. Clin. Sci. Center, 1982—; chief electron microscopy VA Hosp., Madison, 1977-82. Am. Cancer Soc. Jr. Faculty fellow, 1977-80. Mem. Am. Assn. Pathologists, Soc. Toxicology, Internat. Acad. Pathology, Electron Microscopic Soc. Am., Wis. Soc. Pathologists. Home: 2622 Van Hise Ave Madison WI 53705 Office: Dept of Pathology Univ Wisconsin Madison WI 53706

NORBACK, JUDITH CAROL SHAUL, psychologist, educator, author; b. Rochester, N.Y., July 5, 1953; d. John Daley and Barbara (Bark) Shaul; B.A. magna cum laude (fellow), Cornell U., 1975; M.A., Princeton U., 1977, Ph.D., 1979; m. Craig T. Norback, Oct. 12, 1976. Instr. psychology Cornell U., 1973-75, Princeton U., 1976-79, Rutgers U., 1981, 86—; systems programmer McGraw-Hill Co., 1981-83, Princeton U. Computer Ctr., 1983-85. Author: The Alcohol and Drug Abuse Yearbook/Directory, 1979; The Mental Health Yearbook/Directory, 1979; The Sourcebook of Aid for the Mentally and Physically Handicapped, 1983; The Sourcebook of Family Planning and Family Counseling, 1983; The Complete Guide to Computer Careers, 1986. Mem. Am. Psychol. Assn., Mensa. Assn. Princeton Grad. Alumni.

NORCEL, JACQUELINE JOYCE CASALE, educational administrator; b. Bklyn., Nov. 19, 1940; d. Frederick and Josephine Jeanette (Bestafka) Casale; m. Edward John Norcel, Feb. 24, 1962. B.S., Fordham U., 1961; M.S., Bklyn. Coll., 1966; 6th yr. cert. So. Conn. State U., 1980; postgrad. Bridgeport U. Elem. tchr., pub. schs., N.Y.C., 1961-80; prin. Coventry Schs., Conn., 1980-84, Trumbull Schs., Conn., 1984—; guest lectr. So. Conn. State U., 1980—; cons. Monson Schs., Mass., 1984; mem. adj. faculty Sacred Heart U., Fairfield, Conn., 1985—. Editor: Best of the Decade, 1980. Contbr. articles to profl. jours. Chmn. bldg. com. Trumbull Bd. Edn., 1978-80; chmn. Sch. Benefit Com., Trumbull, 1985-86; catechist Bridgeport Diocese, Roman Catholic Ch., Conn., 1975—, youth minister, 1979—, coordinator, evaluator leadership tng. workshops for teens and adults, 1979—. Recipient Town of Trumbull Service award, 1982. Mem. N.E. Regional Elem. Prins. Assn. (rep. 1984-86, sec. 1986-87), Elem. Middle Sch. Prins. Assn. (pres. 1985-86, Pres.'s award 1981-85), Adminstrn. and Supervision Assn. (sec. 1980-81, pres. 1981-82, exec. bd. 1982-83), Hartford Area Prins. and Suprs. Assn. (local pres. 1981-82), Nat. Assn. Elem. Sch. Prins. (del. to gen. assemblies 1984, 85, 86), Assn. Supervision and Curriculum Devel., Conn. Assn. Supervision and Curriculum Devel., Eastern Conn. Council of Internat. Reading Assn., New Eng. Coalition Ednl. Leaders, Associated Tchrs. of Math. in Conn., Phi Delta Kappa, Pi Lambda Theta (Beta Sigma chpt.). Republican. Home: 5240 Madison Ave Trumbull CT 06611 Office: Tashua Sch 401 Stonehouse Rd Trumbull CT 06611

NORCROSS, LOIS MANLEY, professional communicator; b. Orange, Conn.; d. Roy Ellis and Viola Agnes (Ericson) N.; A.A., Centenary Coll. for Women; B.S., Quinnipiac Coll.; M.A., Fairfield U. Dir. public relations Greater New Haven C. of C., 1966-68; acting dir. Better Bus. Bur. Greater New Haven, 1968-69; communications specialist Olin Corp., New Haven, 1969-74; editor employee newsletters, cons. editor employee communications Olin chem. plants in U.S., 1974-78; info. services coordinator Communications Office, Dept. Adminstrv. Services, State of Conn., 1978-81, editor State Scene, 1979-85, info. services officer Personnel Devel. Ctr., 1985—. Cons. publicity adv. bd. Conn. Public TV, 1981-82. Recipient Outstanding Service award Conn. chpt. Internat. Assn. Bus. Communicators, 1980. Mem. Women in Communications, Internat. Assn. Bus. Communicators (chpt. pres.), Conn. State Women in Mgmt. (pres. 1984). Congregationalist. Club: Appalachian Mountain. Office: Personnel Devel Ctr 61 Woodland St Hartford CT 06105

NORDALE, MARY ANITA, lawyer, state official; b. Fairbanks, Alaska, Apr. 8, 1934; d. Alton Gerald and Katherine (Driscoll) Nordale; B.A., Gonzaga U., 1957; J.D., George Washington U., 1966. Bar: D.C. 1967, Alaska 1969. Mem. staff U.S. Senator E.L. Bartlett, Washington, 1960-68; asst. U.S. atty., Fairbanks, 1968-69, asst. dist. atty., 1969-70; br. counsel SBA, Fairbanks, 1970-72; sole practice law, Fairbanks, 1972-83; ptnr. firm Nordale & Cooper, 1983-84; commr. Alaska Dept. Revenue, 1984—. Mem. Central Dist. Dem. Com., Fairbanks, 1973; bd. dirs. Fairbanks Rehab. Assn., Inc., 1970-77, pres., 1971-73; bd. dirs. Compas, Fairbanks, 1971-77, Fairbanks chpt. Alaska Retarded Children's Assn., 1973-75; vice chmn. Alaska Reapportionment Bd., 1983-84. Mem. Fed., Am., D.C., Alaska, Tanana Valley bar assns., Am. Judicature Soc. Office: Pouch S Juneau AK 99811

NORDEEN, PEGGY ANN, advertising executive; b. Muscatine, Iowa, July 27, 1946; d. Gene E. and Marylou Nordeen; B.A. in Journalism and English, U. Iowa, 1968. Gen. assignment news reporter Davenport (Iowa) Times-Democrat, 1966-69; with Sperry-Boon Inc., Chgo., 1970-78, v.p., dir. 1976-78; pres. Starmark, Inc., Chgo., 1978—. Mem. Viking Ship Restoration Com., Chgo., 1979; Iowa Realtors Assn. scholar, 1964. Mem. Am. Mktg. Assn. (v.p. communications Chgo. chpt. 1974), Publicity Club Chgo. (sec., dir. 1973-74), Gamma Phi Beta. Mem. Christian Ch. (Disciples of Christ). Home: Lake Shore Dr Chicago IL 60611 Office: Starmark Bldg 706 N Dearborn St Chicago IL 60610

NORDHAGEN, HALLIE HUERTH, nursing home administrator; b. Sarona, Wis., Apr. 2, 1914; d. Mathias James and Ethel Elizabeth (Fann) Huerth; B.Ed., U. Wis., Superior, 1938, M.A., 1949; m. Carl E. Nordhagen, May 24, 1947; children—Bruce Carl, Brian Keith. Prin., tchr. Wis. Public Schs., 1932-46; supervising tchr. Wis. Community Coll., 1946-48; psychiat. adminstr. Trempealeau County Health Care Center, psychiat. nursing home, Whitehall, Wis., 1959—; mem. Wis. Nursing Home Adminstrs. Examining Bd.; fellow Menninger Clinic, Topeka, 1979-81. Recipient Disting. Service award in edn. and hosp. adminstrn., London, 1967, award for services to human services programs Wis. Assn. Human Services, 1972, award for outstanding services to exceptional children Assn. Retarded Children, 1978, award for accomplishments in human resources Trempealeau County Conservation Service, 1981, Wis. State Senate citation for contbns. to health care, 1983; citation for contbns. Wis. Gov., 1984. Mem. Wis. Assn. County Homes (bd. dirs.), Wis. Edn. Assn., Wis. Assn. Human Services Programs, Am. Lutheran Ch. Women. Clubs: Whitehall Country, Women's. Author: Wisconsin Indians, 1966. Home: 2220 Claire St Whitehall WI 54773

NORDIN, PHYLLIS ECK, sculptor, designer, consultant; b. Chgo. Student Beloit Coll., Wayne State U.; B.S., U. Toledo, 1963, B.A. cum laude, 1972; postgrad. Sch. Design, Toledo Mus. Art. Free-lance design and art cons. various builders, chs., businesses and individuals, 1972—. Prin. works include large bronze sculptures Lucas County Main Library, Toledo, Christ figure St. Joan of Arc Ch., Maumee, Ohio, Ronald McDonald House, Toledo, First English Evangel. Luth. Ch., Grosse Pointe Woods, Mich., Christ Presbyn. Ch., Covenant Presbyn. Ch., Toledo, Toledo Hosp., Reynolds Br. Library, Toledo, stone wall mural Epworth United Methodist Ch., Toledo, Beloit Coll., Wis., bronze fountain U. Toledo, numerous others; exhibited Allied Artists Am., Salmagundi Club, numerous others. Represented by Collectors Corner Toledo Mus. Art, 1970-83. Recipient Alpha award Foothills Art Ctr., 1983, First prize Ann. Nat. Art Exhbn., 1978, also numerous others. Mem. Arts Commn. Greater Toledo, Toledo Design Rev. Bd., Nat. Assn. Women Artists, Interfaith Forum Religion Art Architecture, Ohio Designer Craftsmen, Toledo Modern Art Group (trustee, 1982—). Home and Studio: 4035 Tantara Rd Toledo OH 43623

NORDINE, D. JEANE, nurse; b. Clinton, Ill., June 10, 1935; d. Bronce and Mildred (Bourne) Reynolds; m. Louis R. Nordine, Feb. 26, 1955 (div. 1983); children—Lawrence Douglas, Susan Marie, Louis Eric, Sharon Lee. R.N., St. Joseph's Sch. Nursing, Bloomington, Ill., 1955; student Amarillo Coll., 1985—. R.N., Ill., Colo. Office nurse Durango Med.-Surg. Assocs., Colo., 1978-79; charge nurse Mercy Hosp., Durango, 1976-79; supr. Pikes Peak Manor, Colorado Springs, Colo., 1979-83; staff nurse VA, Amarillo, Tex., 1983—. Mem. Amarillo Women's Network, Federally Employed Women, Arthritis Found. Republican. Lutheran. Avocations: reading; quilting, golfing. Office: VA Med Ctr 6010 Amarillo Blvd W Amarillo TX 79106

NORDSTROM, SUSAN ELLEN, advertising agency executive; b. Tampa, Fla., Nov. 19, 1952; d. Ralph Samuel and Evelyn Seymour (Eynon) Hardman; B.A., Keuka Coll., Keuka Park, N.Y., 1974; m. Thomas J. Nordstrom, June 1, 1974. Br. rep. Household Fin. Corp., Edison, N.J., 1974-75; patient service rep. Rutgers Mental Health Center, Piscataway, N.J., 1975-76; asst. planner Conahay & Lyon Advt., N.Y.C., 1976-79; sr. media planner Foote Cone & Belding Advt., N.Y.C., 1979-82; assoc. media group head Wells Rich Greene Advt., N.Y.C. 1982-84; dir. Media Services Gillespie Advt., Princeton, N.J., 1984—. Mem. Nat. Assn. Female Execs., AMA Aux. Office: Clarkstown Rd Princeton NJ 08540

NORDYKE, ELEANOR COLE, population researcher, public health nurse; b. Los Angeles, June 15, 1927; d. Ralph G. and Louise Noble (Carter) Cole; m. Robert Allan Nordyke, June 18, 1950; children—Mary Ellen, Carolyn, Thomas, Susan, Gretchen. B.S., Stanford U., 1950; P.H.N. accreditation U. Calif.-Berkeley, 1952; M.P.H., U. Hawaii, 1969. Pub. health nurse San Francisco Dept. Health, 1950-52; nurse-tchr. Punahou Sch., Honolulu, 1966-67; clinic coordinator East-West Population Inst., East-West Ctr., Honolulu, 1969-75, population researcher, 1975-82; research fellow, 1982—; cons. Hawaii Commn. on Population, Honolulu, 1970-83; mem. Hawaii Policy Action Group for Family Planning, Honolulu, 1971—, chmn., 1976-77. Author: (with Robert Gardner) The Demographic Situation in Hawaii, 1974; The Peopling of Hawaii, 1977; A Profile of Hawaii's Elderly Population, 1984; mem. editorial bd. Hawaiian Jour. History, 1980—; contbr. articles to profl. jours. Bd. dirs. YMCA Central, Honolulu, 1970—, vice chmn. bd., 1978-79; bd. dirs. Hawaii Planned Parenthood, Honolulu, 1974-78, Friends of Library of Hawaii, 1985—; trustee Hawaiian Hist. Soc., 1978-82; trustee Arcadia Retirement Residence, Honolulu, 1978—. Mem. Population Assn. Am., Population Reference Bur., Hawaii Pub. Health Assn., Am. Statis. Assn., Hawaii Econ. Assn., Phi Beta Kappa. Democrat. Congregationalist. Home: 2013 Kakela Dr Honolulu HI 96822 Office: Population Inst East-West Ctr 1777 East-West Rd Honolulu HI 96848

NOREK, FRANCES THERESE, states attorney; b. Chgo., Mar. 9, 1947; d. Michael S. and Viola C. (Harbecke) N.; m. John E. Flavin, Aug. 31, 1968 (div.); 1 child, John Michael. B.A., Loyola U., Chgo., 1968, J.D., 1973. Bar: Ill. 1973, U.S. Dist. Ct. (no. dist.) Ill. 1973, U.S. Ct. Appeals (7th cir.) 1974. Assoc. Alter, Weiss, Whitesel & Laff, Chgo., 1973-74; asst. states atty. Cook County, Chgo., 1974—; mem. trial practice faculty Loyola U. Sch. Law, Chgo., 1980; judge, evaluator mock trial competitions, Chgo., 1978—; contbr., speaker Inst. Criminal Justice, 1982—; mem. Chgo. and Cook County Criminal Justice Commn., 1978-81; lectr. in field. Recipient Emil Gumpert award Am. Coll. Trial Lawyers, 1982. Mem. ABA, Ill. State Bar Assn., Chgo. Bar Assn. (instr. fed. trial bar adv. program young lawyer's sect. 1983—). Office: Cook County States Attys Office 500 Richard J Daley Ctr Chicago IL 60602

NORELLI, NANCY BLACK, lawyer; b. Charlotte, N.C., Oct. 29, 1949; d. James Hampton and Beulah (Howell) Black; m. Ronald Allen Norelli, Sept. 5, 1971; children—Andrew, Margaret, Lee. B.A. with honors, Wellesley Coll., 1972; J.D., Northeastern U., 1976. Bar: Mass. 1977, N.C. 1977. Spl. asst. atty. gen. Commonwealth of Mass., Boston., 1976-77; assoc. Helms, Mulliss & Johnston, Charlotte, N.C., 1977-83; ptnr. Kennedy Covington, Lobdell & Hickman, 1985—. Bd. dirs. Vol. Lawyers Program, Charlotte, 1982—; chmn. Law Day Com., Charlotte, 1980, 84; adv. bd. Charlotte Mecklenburg Pub. Library System, 1984. Mem. ABA, N.C. Bar Assn. (legal services planning com. 1984-86), Mecklenburg County Bar Assn. (exec. com. Charlotte 1980-83), Charlotte Estate Planning Council. Home: 954 Granville Charlotte NC 28207

NORELLI, PATRICIA ANN, educator; b. McKeesport, Pa., July 13, 1941; d. Patrick and Lillian (Colaizzi) N. B.A., Clark U., 1963, M.A., 1964. Tchr. English, Stoneham High Sch., Mass., 1966—. Mem. Stoneham Tchrs. Assn., Mass. Tchrs. Assn., NEA, Nat. Council Tchrs. English. Roman Catholic. Avocations: Gardening; running. Home: 3 Harrison St Stoneham MA 02180 Office: Stoneham High Sch 149 Franklin St Stoneham MA 02180

NORKIN, CYNTHIA CLAIR, physical therapist; b. Boston, May 6, 1932; d. Miles Nelson and Carolyn (Green) Clair; B.S. in Edn., Tufts U., 1954; cert. phys. therapy Bouve Boston Coll., 1954; M.S., Boston U., 1973, Ed.D., 1983; m. Stanislav A. Norkin, Feb. 19, 1955 (dec. 1970); 1 dau., Alexandra. Instr., Bouve-Boston Coll., 1954-55; staff phys. therapist New Eng. Med. Center, Boston, 1954-55; staff phys. therapist Abington Meml. Hosp., Abington, Pa., 1965-70, Eastern Montgomery County Vis. Nurse Assn., 1970-72; asst. prof. phys. therapy Sargent Coll., Boston U., 1973-83; dir. Sch. Phys. Therapy, Ohio U., Athens, 1983—; cons. Boston Center Ind. Living, Cambridge Vis. Nurse Assn., Mass. Medicaid Cost Effectiveness Project, 1978; sec. Health Planning Council Greater Boston, 1976-78. Trustee Brimmer and May Sch., 1980. Mem. Am., Mass. (chmn. Mass. quality assurance com. 1980—) phys. therapy assns., Am. Public Health Assn., AAAS, Mass. Assn. Mental Health. Episcopalian. Author: (with others) Joint Structure and Function: A Comprehensive Analysis, 1983; Joint Measurement: A Guide to Goniometry, 1984. Office: Sch Phys Therapy Convocation Ctr Ohio U Athens OH 45701

NORMAN, CHARLOTTE RUTH, remedial reading educator; b. Center, Tex., Dec. 17, 1940; d. Weldon Spottswood and Rowena Ruth (Steele) Sanders; m. Marion Henry Norman, Dec. 23, 1965 (dec. 1968). B.S. in Elem. Edn., N. Tex. State U., 1963, M.Ed. in Elem. Edn., 1965; cert. in lang. learning disabilities, Lamar State U., 1972. Tchr. elem. schs. Dallas Ind. Sch. Dist., 1963-65, Deer Park Ind. Sch. Dist. (Tex.), 1965-66, Marine Corps Sch. Quantico, Va., 1966-67, Deer Park Ind. Sch. Dist., 1967—; tchr. English as a Second Lang. Changsha Ry. Inst., People's Republic of China, summer 1980. Faculty rep. Parkwood PTO, Deer Park, 1981—. Mem. Deer Park Assn. Childhood Edn. (pres. 1979), Tex. Assn. Childhood Edn. (v.p. of adolescence in charge of pub. and internat. affairs 1980-82), U.S.-China People's Friendship Assn., Internat. Reading Assn., Assn. Tex. Profl. Educators, Tex. Assn. for Gifted and Talented, Alpha Phi. Democrat. Methodist. Home: 12337 Ashcroft Houston TX 77035

NORMAN, CHERIE SHELTON, lawyer; b. Ft. Collins, Colo., Sept. 25, 1950; d. Willie L. and Doris E. (Hoopes) Shelton; m. J. Thomas Norman, May 27, 1972; children—Elizabeth Ella, Robert Thomas, Victoria Cherie. B.S., U. Wyo., 1973, M.S., 1974, J.D., 1979. Bar: Wyo. 1979. Assoc. John Burk, P.C., Casper, Wyo., 1979-82; sole practice law, Casper, 1982—; U.S. trustee in bankruptcy, Casper, 1982—; pres. Ross Law Forum, Laramie, 1978-79. Dir. Community Recreation, Inc., Casper, 1980-84; 1st v.p. Casper Republican Women, 1984; parliamentarian Wyo. Rep. Women, Casper, 1983—. Mem. ABA, Wyo. State Bar, Assn. Trial Lawyers Am., Wyo. Trial Lawyers, Assn. Bankruptcy Trustees, Bus. and Profl. Women., Sigma Alpha Eta (v.p. Laramie 1972). Episcopalian. Home: 4361 S Ash Casper WY 82601 Office: 311 S Center Casper WY 83601

NORMAN, CORA ELLEN GARNER, state official, b. Columbia County, Ark., Nov. 7, 1926; d. Robert Everett and Jewel Melissa (Beasley) Garner; m. William Harvey Norman, May 28, 1946; children—Robert Henry, Judith Ellen Norman Bratton. B.A., U. Tex.-El Paso, 1949; M.S., U. Miss., 1964, Ph.D., 1975; postgrad. Inst. of Edn. Mgmt. and Inst. Lifelong Mgmt., Harvard U., 1978, 79, U. London, 1985. Tchr., Holly Springs High Sch. (Miss.), 1964-65; sci. tchr. Lafayette County High Sch., Oxford, Miss., 1965-66; adminstrv. asst. to dir. continuing edn. U. Miss., 1966-69; exec. dir. Miss. Com. for Humanities, Jackson, 1972—. Chmn. Miss. Polit. Women's Caucus, 1978; pres. Miss. Women's Cabinet Pub. Affairs; active Virginia Gildersleeve Internat. Fund for Univ. Women, Miss. State Adv. Com. to U.S. Commn. on Civil Rights. Recipient citation for leadership community and social devel. Rust Coll., 1974; Women of Achievement award Oxford, 1982; One of 14 Ole Miss Alumnae cited for success Ole Miss Alumni Rev., 1982. Mem. LWV (chpt. pres. 1971), AAUW (state pres. 1974-76; Coll. Faculty award 1963, v.p. Ednl. Found. 1985—). Democrat. Methodist. Office: Miss Com for Humanities 3825 Ridgewood Rd Room 111 Jackson MS 39211

NORMAN, LAURA GAIL, reflexologist; b. L.I., N.Y., Apr. 17, 1950; d. Steven S. and Irene Mazur; B.S. with distinction, Boston U., 1972; M.S., Adelphi U., 1976; postgrad. Internat. Inst. Reflexology, 1976, Swedish Inst. Med. Massage Therapy, 1981. Tchr., relaxation therapist, reflexologist Maimonides Inst., Far Rockaway, N.Y., 1974-79; pvt. practice reflexology, N.Y.C., 1972—; dir. Laura Norman & Assocs. Mem. Internat. Inst. Reflexology, Med. Massage Therapists Alliance, Am. Massage and Therapy Assn., Inc., Nat. Health Fedn., Am. Fedn. Tchrs. (pres. 1968), Nat. Assn. Female Execs. Club: B'nai B'rith (pres. 1968). Office: 2 E 37th St New York NY 10016

NORMAN, MARILYN FAY, construction company executive; b. Ord, Nebr., July 19, 1958; d. Clayton Leo and Dorothy Maxine (Anderson) Montanye; m. Michael Lee Norman, June 2, 1979; children—Cody Christina, Ciara Cain. A.A.S., Lincoln Sch. Commerce, 1978. Cert., Nat. Secs. Assn. Office mgr. Vance D. Rogers, Republican candidate for Gov., Lincoln, 1977-78; sec.-treas. Peterson Constrn. Co., Lincoln, 1978—. Republican. Roman Catholic. Avocations: Reading; fishing. Home: 2400 N 63d St Lincoln NE 68507 Office: Peterson Constrn Co 4825 S 16th St Lincoln NE 68512

NORMAN, MARSHA, playwright; b. Louisville; d. Billie and Bertha Williams; m. Michael Norman (div.); m. 2d, Dann Byck, 1978. Grad. Agnes Scott Coll., 1969; M.A.T., U. Louisville, 1971. Worker disturbed children Central State Hosp., Louisville; tchr. Ky. Dept. Health, 1969-70, Jefferson County Pub. Schs., Ky., 1970-72; sch. project dir. Ky. Arts Commn., 1972-76; editor young people's column Louisville Times, 1974-79; Author plays: Getting Out, off-Broadway 1979 (Outer Critics Circle award, John Gassner New Playwrights medal), Third and Oak, 'Night, Mother (1983 Pulitzer prize for drama), The Holdup, Traveller in the Dark, 1984. Recipient Susan Smith Blackburn prize for 'Night, Mother, 1983; Nat. Endowment for Arts grantee, 1978-79; Rockefeller playwright-in-residence grantee, 1979-80. Address: care Hill & Wang 19 Union Sq W New York NY 10003*

NORMAN, MARY MARSHALL, college president; b. Auburn, N.Y., Jan. 10, 1937; d. Anthony John and Zita Norman; B.S. cum laude, LeMoyne Coll., 1958; M.A., Marquette, U., 1960; Ed.D., Pa. State U., 1971. Tchr., St. Cecilia's Elem. Sch., Theinsville, Wis., 1959-60; vocat. counselor Marquette U., Milw., 1959-60; dir. testing and counseling U. Rochester (N.Y.), 1960-62; dir. testing and counseling, dean women, asso. dean coll., asst. dean students, dir. student activities, asst. prof. psychology Corning (N.Y.) Community Coll., 1962-68; research asst. Center for Study Higher Edn., Pa. State U., University Park, 1969-71; dean faculty South Campus, Community Coll. Allegheny County, West Mifflin, Pa., 1971-72, exec. dean, coll. v.p., 1972-82; pres. Orange County Community Coll., 1982—; cons. Boricua Coll., N.Y.C., 1976-77; reader NSF, 1977-78; mem. govtl. commn. com. Am. Assn. Community and Jr. Colls., 1976-79, bd. dirs., 1982—; mem. and chmn. various middle state accreditation teams. Bd. dirs. Orange County United Way. Mem. Am. Assn. Higher Edn., Nat. Assn. Women Deans Counselors, Am. Assn. Women in Community and Jr. Colls. (charter, Woman of Yr. 1981), Pa. Assn. Two-Yr. Colls., Pa. Assn. Acad. Deans, Pitts. Council Women Execs. (charter), Am. Council on Edn. (Pa. rep. identification women for adminstrn. 1978—), Pa. Council on Higher Edn., Orange County C. of C., Gamma Pi Epsilon. Contbr. articles to profl. jours. Home: 8 Crabapple Ln Middletown NY 10940 Office: 115 South St Middletown NY 10940

NORMAN, TRUDY, data processing executive; b. Carlinville, Ill., Mar. 12, 1936; d. Ralph Earl and Gladys Mae (Shade) Challans; student James Millikin U., 1968-70; children—Carol Lischalk, James Norman, Cheryl Spencer. Mgr. client services Central Computing Corp., Decatur, Ill., 1968-71; sr. systems analyst STAT:TAB Corp., Chgo., 1971-74; project mgr. Chgo. Bd. Edn., 1974-78; mgr. data services Central Telephone, Chgo., 1978-80; dir. system services, dir. corp. recruitment Advanced System Applications, Inc., Bloomingdale, Ill., 1980—; cons. in field. Active Lakeview Citizens Council, 1979—, Riverview Neighbors, 1981—, Addams Center, 1975-82. Mem. Am. Mgmt. Assn., Fin. Mgrs. Soc., Data Processing Mgmt. Assn., Assn. for Women in Computing (nat. liaison Chgo. chpt. 1985—), Data Processing Mgmt. Assn., Am. Soc. for Personnel Adminstrn., Am. Soc. for Tng. and Devel. Club: BMW Owners Club. Contbr. articles to profl. jours. Home: 3320 N Hamilton Ave Chicago IL 60618

NORMANDIN, MARY ANNE, educational administrator, arts organization consultant; b. Portland, Oreg., Feb. 4, 1928; d. Thomas Eben and Anne Marie (Schmit) Shea; m. Talbot Herbert Normandin, Sept. 24, 1949 (dec.); children—John Louis, Sue Marie, Paul Herbert, Frederick Lyle, Frank Talbot. B.A., Marylhurst Coll., 1949; postgrad. U. Oreg., Oreg. State U., 1965-70, Journalism and pub. relations faculty, dir. pub. info. and publs. Marylhurst Coll., Lake Oswego, Oreg., 1963-70; asst. to dean Northwestern Sch. Law of Lewis and Clark Coll., Portland, Oreg., 1970-71, asst. to pres., 1971—; dir. AMFAC, Inc., Honolulu, 1979—, chmn. audit com., 1983—. Bd. dirs. Roger Bounds Found., Hermiston, Oreg., 1981—; bd. dirs. Oreg. Arts Found., Portland, 1975—, pres., 1977-82; bd. dirs. City Club Found., Portland, 1980-83, St. Andrews Legal Clinic, Portland, 1983—, Contemporary Crafts Assn., Portland, 1978-85; active Oreg. Community Found., Oreg. Hist. Soc., Portland Art Assn., Met. Mus. Art. Mem. Nat. Council Univ. Research Adminstrs. (exec. com. 1977-80), Am. Council on Edn. State of Oreg. Nat. Identification Program (chmn. 1983-86); mem. City of Portland Cable Regulatory Commn., 1984—, Met. Arts Commn., 1985—; mem. adv. com. Portland Performing Arts Ctr., 1984—. Republican. Roman Catholic. Office: Lewis and Clark Coll 0615 SW Palatine Hill Rd Portland OR 97219

NORNESS, PAULA LEE, land surveyor; b. Eugene, Oreg., Sept. 21, 1943; d. Stephen Harold and Hazle Anne (Watkins) Ford; m. KennethMcRight Norness, July 17, 1943; 1 child, KennethMcRight. Grad. high sch., Eugene. Registered profl. land surveyor, Oreg. Draftsman Stephen H. Ford & Assocs., Eugene, 1962-74, surveyor, prin., 1974—; mem. Oreg. Bd. Engring. Examiners, 1982-85. Mem. Am. Congress on Surveying and Mapping, Profl. Land Surveyors of Oreg. (chpt. pres. 1978), Nat. Conf. Engring. Examiners. Republican. Roman Catholic. Lodges: Altrusa (treas. Eugene 1976), Women of Moose. Avocations: writing; drawing; gardening; cooking; sewing. Home: 27116 Crow Rd Eugene OR 97402 Office: Stephen H Ford Inc 795 Willamette St Suite 405 Eugene OR 97401

NORRIS, BARBARA THERESA, financial manager; b. Bklyn., Nov. 20, 1948; d. William Valentine and Stella (Laskowski) N.; diploma L.I. Coll. Hosp. Sch. Nursing, 1968; B.S. with honors, CUNY, 1982. Charge nurse medicine/surgery L.I. Coll. Hosp., Bklyn., 1968-69, asst. head nurse labor/delivery unit, 1969-72, asst. dir. nursing, 1972-74, staff devel. instr., 1974-79, staff cons. materials mgmt. and nursing recruitment, 1979-80, staff cons. materials mgmt., 1980—; pres., mktg. cons. Barbara Norris, Inc., 1980—. Recipient N.Y. State Regents Incentive award, 1966; Nursing Sch. scholar Women's Floral Assn., 1968; lic. nurse, N.Y. Mem. L.I. Coll. Hosp. Sch. Nursing Alumnae Assn., Am. Assn. Critical Care Nurses, N.Y. Heart Assn., Smithsonian Assocs., Nat. Mus. Women in Arts (charter), Arline Shahmanesh Hodgkins Research Orgn. Editor Nursing Communications, 1976-79; contbr. to poetry anthologies. Office: Amvest Inc 224 3d Ave Westwood NJ 07024

NORRIS, CYNTHIA JEANETTE, educator; b. Chattanooga, July 7, 1937; d. David Leigh and Mary Juanita (Morgan) Hudson; m. Joseph Leon Norris, June 2, 1956 (div. Aug. 1984); children—Sherry Lynne Norris Hutsell, Dayna Karen. B.S., Tenn. Wesleyan U., 1967; M.S., U. Tenn., 1975, Ed.D., 1984. Tchr. Chattanooga City Schs., 1969-70; tchr. Athens City Schs., Tenn., 1964-74, spl. edn. dir., 1974-84, prin. Westside Sch., Athens, 1984-86; adj. prof. U. Tenn., Chattanooga, 1982-86; cons. human resource devel. Unique, Athens, 1980-86; cons. effectiveness tng. Thomas Gordon Assocs., Salona Beach, Calif., 1975-86; cons. Tenn. elem. sch. com. So. Assn. Colls. and Schs., 1983-86. Bd. dirs. McMinn Adult Activity Ctr., Athens, 1983-85, Athens Day Care Ctrs., 1980-86. Mem. Tenn. Assn. for Gifted (treas. 1978-80), Assn. for Supervision and Curriculum Devel., Tenn. Assn. Supervision and Curriculum Devel., Am. Soc. for Tng. and Devel., Athens Edn. Assn. (sec. 1968-70), Tenn. Edn. Assn., NEA, Nat. Assn. Elem. Sch. Prins., Phi Delta Kappa (Knoxville chpt. outstanding research award 1984), Phi Kappa Phi, Alpha Chi. Club: Civitan (Athens). Avocations: music; dancing; writing poetry. Office: Univ Houston Dept Ednl Leadership Houston TX 77004

NORRIS, ELIZABETH DOWNE, librarian; b. White Plains, N.Y., Apr. 25, 1914; d. Albro Farwell and Alice Elizabeth (Morse) Downe; B.A., Smith Coll., 1936; M.Div., Yale U., 1939; M.L.S., Columbia U., 1955; 1 son, Donald E. Norris. Asst. residence dir. New Haven YWCA, 1940-42; religious edn. librarian Union Theol. Sem., N.Y.C., 1953-57; librarian NCCJ, N.Y.C., 1957-63; head librarian Nat. Bd. YWCA, N.Y.C., 1963—, dir. Nat. Bd. Archives Project, 1976—, YWCA historian, 1980—. Recipient Henry Foote Lewis prize in religion, 1934. Mem. Spl. Libraries Assn., Soc. Am. Archivists. Mem. United Ch. Christ. Editor: Feminine Figures: Selected Facts about American Women and Girls, 1968-72; Subject Headings on Women, 1973; Recent Trends in Professionalism, 1973; The YWCA Advances Women's Rights, 1855-1983, 1983; Dairy of a Volunteer, 1983; Women and Children First; a Century of YWCA Services to Children, 1984; contbg. librarian Mental Health Book Rev. Index, 1961-72; editor, mem. adv. com. Books for Brotherhood, ann. 1957-76; contbr. articles to jours. Home: 505 La Guardia Pl New York City NY 10012 Office: 726 Broadway New York NY 10003

NORRIS, GRENDA LAVERNE, broadcasting company producer; b. Phenix City, Ala., Sept. 9, 1957; d. Walter Wilson and Lucy (Crowell) N. B.S., Boston U., 1980. Advt. intern Young & Rubicam, Inc., N.Y.C., 1979; teaching asst. Boston U., 1980; writer, asst. editor Sta. WPFW, Washington, 1982, producer, engr., 1983—; radio engr., announcer intern Sta. WINX, Rockville, Md., 1983; ind. TV producer, Washington, 1983—. Mem. Women in Communication, Delta Sigma Theta. Home: Silver Spring MD Office: WPFW Radio 700 H St NW Washington DC 20001

NORRIS, JANE HARTWELL, special education educator; b. Dallas, Apr. 16, 1941; d. J. Frank and Rita (Donaho) N. B.S. in Edn., N. Tex. State U., 1965; M.Ed., Tex. Woman's U., 1972, Ed.D., 1979. Cert. tchr., Tex.; registered profl. diagnostician, Tex. Hosp. recreation therapist Am. Nat. Red Cross, St. Louis, 1965-71; tchr. Denton Ind. Sch. Dist., Tex., 1972-77; teaching asst. Tex. Woman's U., Denton, 1977-79, adj. prof., summer 1980; ednl. diagnostician Plano Ind. Sch. Dist., Tex., 1979-80; asst. prof., coordinator spl. edn. W. Tex. State U., Canyon, 1980—; cons. in field. Tex. Woman's U. fellow, 1977, 78, 79; HEW grantee, 1971-72. Mem. Council for Exceptional Children (faculty advisor W. Tex. State U., 1982—), Assn. for Children and Adults with Learning Disabilities, Tex. Assn. for Improvement in Reading, Nat. Assn. Female Execs., Tex. Assn. for Ednl. Diagnosticians, Pi Lambda Theta (pres. 1973-75, nat. com. 1975-77, sec. and historian 1977-78), Phi Delta Kappa. Club: Sweet Adelines (charter Pride O'Palo Duro chpt.; asst. dir., co-show chmn., co-chmn. ways and means, past bd. dirs. and corr. sec.). Avocations: barbershop quartets; needlework; furniture refinishing; reading; renovating house. Office: West Tex State U PO Box 172 West Tex Sta Canyon TX 79016

NORRIS, JANE PARSONS, banker; b. Lewiston, Maine, July 30, 1924; d. George Francis and Luella Louise (Small) Parsons; m. Leon Manfred Norris, July 22, 1947; 1 child, Linda Ann. B.A., Bates Coll., 1946; cert. Maine N.H. Vt. Sch. Banking, Hanover, N.H., 1971. With Mechanics Savs. Bank, Auburn, Maine, 1956—, exec. v.p., chief exec. officer, 1979-82, pres., chief exec. officer, 1982—, bd. dirs., 1969—. dir. Patrons Oxford Mut. Ins. Co., Auburn, 1978—; chmn. com. Maine-N.H.-Vt. Sch. Savs. Banking, 1984-86. Trustee, exec. com. Bates Coll., Lewiston, 1977—; bd. dir. Central Maine Med. Ctr., 1978—. Mem. Savs. Banks Assn. Maine (exec. com. 1982—), Nat. Assn. Bank Women. Republican. Congregationalist. Avocations: History; archeology; needle work. Office: Mechanics Savs Bank 100 Minot Ave PO Box 239 Auburn ME 04210

NORRIS, JOSEPHINE MIRANDA, banker; b. Havana, Cuba, Oct. 8, 1955; came to U.S., 1957, naturalized, 1963; d. Roberto Miranda and Maruja (Gonzalez) N. B.A., Wellesley Coll., 1977; M.I.A., Columbia U., 1979. Sales asst. ABC-TV Spot Sales, N.Y.C., 1979-81; asst. sec. Mfrs. Hanover Trust Co., N.Y.C., 1981-85; 2d v.p. Chase Manhattan Bank, N.Y.C., 1985—. Home: 69-01 35th Ave Apt 7B Woodside NY 11377 Office: Chase Manhattan Bank New York NY

NORRIS, KATHLEEN ANN, lawyer; b. Kansas City, Mo., Feb. 3, 1943; d. William Wayne and Bernice Irene (Moline) N. B.S.L., Western State U., Fullerton, Calif., 1981, J.D., 1981. Bar: Calif. 1981, U.S. Dist. Ct. (9th dist.) Calif. 1982. Sole practice, Corona del Mar, Calif., 1981-84; cons. Calif. Senate Select Com. on Anat. Transplantation, 1984-85; chief pub. info. office Calif. Dept. Social Services, 1985—. Bd. dirs. Newport Harbor Republican Women, Newport Beach, Calif., 1972-76; active vol. Hoag Hosp. Aux., 1972-75; mem. Nat. Women's Polit. Caucus, 1983; active singing mem. Pacific Chorale, 1974-84; continuance fund chairperson Beacon Bay chpt. Orange County Philharm. Soc., 1973-77; mem. Cabaret chpt. Orange County Performing Arts Ctr. Assn., 1983. Mem. ABA, Calif. Bar. Assn., Calif. Women Lawyers, Orange County Bar Assn., Orange County Women Lawyers, Calif. Women Appointees, Corona del Mar C. of C. (bd. dirs. 1983), Newport Harbor C. of C., DAR. Republican. Clubs: Zonta (Newport Harbor, Calif.) (bd. dirs. 1983), Lincoln. Office: 744 P St 17-16 Sacramento CA 95814

NORRIS, MARUJA MIRANDA, giftware retailer; b. Havana, Cuba, Mar. 19, 1933; came to U.S., 1957; d. José and María (García) González; m. Robert M. Norris, Nov. 18, 1951; children—Robert, Josephine. Grad. Sacred Heart Sch., Havana, 1951; diploma Chgo. Sch. Interior Decoration, 1965. Owner Miranda's, Rockford, Ill., 1984—. Bd. dirs. Spanish Services, Keith County Day Sch., Rockford; vol. County Med. Aux., Rockford, 1961-84. Republican. Roman Catholic. Clubs: Rockford Country, City, Woman's (Rockford). Home: 3510 Val Mark Terr Rockford IL 61107 Office: Miranda's 1641 N Alpine Rd Rockford IL

NORRIS, PATRICIA KILMER, public relations executive; b. New Rochelle, N.Y., Feb. 7, 1933; d. Hugh and Patricia (Polk) Kilmer; student Sweet Briar Coll., 1951-52, Westchester Comml. Sch., 1953-54; m. James Alexander Norris, Feb. 16, 1957; children—Melissa Polk, Benjamin White II. Asst. beauty editor Glamour mag., N.Y.C., 1954-55; sr. exec. sec. McCann-Erickson Inc., N.Y.C., 1955-59; sec. to pres., office mgr. Thomson-Leeds Co., Inc., N.Y.C., 1959-62; dir. pub. relations Glenview (Ill.) Park Dist., 1975-78; freelance writer/pub. relations, Glenview, 1978—. Rec. sec. Glenview Aux., 1968-70, pres., 1970-72, v.p. pres.'s council of all auxs. Skokie Valley Hosp., 1972-73, pres., 1973-74; active Glenview Bi-Centennial Commn., 1976; active Northfield Twp. Republican Women's Club, 1974—, publicity chmn., 1977-79, active 10th Dist. Rep. Women's Club, 1974—; publicity chmn. Glenbrook So. High Sch. Instrumental League, 1978-79, Glenview Area Hist. Soc. Coach House/Library, 1978-79; pres. Grove Heritage Assn., 1979-83, pres.' adviser, 1983-84; founder, rec. sec. Save the Grove Com., 1973-75; mem. Citizens' Adv. Com. for the Grove, 1975-76; bd. dirs. Lawrence Hall Sch. for Boys, v.p., 1986—; publicity chmn., bd. dirs. Episcopal Ch. Women, 1984-86. Recipient Cert. of Merit, Village of Glenview. Mem. Glenview LWV (chmn. local environ. study com. 1983—, bd. dirs. 1984—, observors chmn. 1984-86, sec. 1986—). Episcopalian. Club: North Shore Public Relations. Home: 4121 Kennicott Ln Glenview IL 60025

NORRY, PATRICIA GOODWIN, government official; b. Cin.; d. Robert Clifford and Marion Schmadel Goodwin; A.B., Seton Hill Coll., 1958; postgrad. George Washington U., 1958-61, (Nat. Inst. Pub. Affairs fellow) Stanford U., 1968-69; m. Leonard J. Norry, Dec., 1969; 1 son, Douglas. Staff asst. to chmn. AEC, Washington, 1961-68; spl. asst. to dir. research Nuclear Regulatory Commn., Washington, 1970-78, dep. dir. adminstrn., 1979-82, dir. adminstrn., 1982—. Pres., Bradley Elem. Sch. PTA, 1981-82; bd. dirs. Energy Fed. Credit Union, 1980-82. Mem. Am. Soc. Public Adminstrn. Office: US Nuclear Regulatory Commn 1717 H St NW Washington DC 20555*

NORSTROM, DIANA DARNELL, account executive; b. Houston, May 1, 1956; d. John Fletcher and Betty Jo (Perkins) Darnell; m. Daniel Scott Norstrom, Jan. 8, 1982; 1 stepson, Adrian. A.B. with honors in Anthropology, Vassar Coll., 1978; M.S.M., Houston Baptist U., 1984. Counselor family planning Holyoke Hosp. (Mass.), 1978-79; mgmt. trainer, personnel generalist Rotan Meosle, 1979-82; account exec., 1984—; sales, trainer Paine, Webber, Jackson & Curtis, Houston, 1982-84. Sec. Vassar Alumni Club at Houston, 1980—. Mem. Am. Soc. Tng. and Devel., Houston Securities Dealers Assn., Assn. Bus. Women Am., Women's Profl. Assn. Home: 8522 Hazy Meadow Houston TX 77040 Office: Rotan Mosle Inc 16945 Northchase Dr Suite 100 Houston TX 77210

NORTH, KATHRYN E. KEESEY (MRS. EUGENE C. NORTH), ret. educator; b. Columbia, Pa., Jan. 25, 1916; d. Isaac and Elizabeth (French) Keesey; B.S., Ithaca Coll., 1938; M.A., N.Y. U., 1950; m. Eugene C. North, Aug. 18, 1938. Dir. music Cairo (N.Y.) Central Sch. Dist., 1938; music edn. cons. Argyle (N.Y.) Central Sch. Dist., 1939; dir. gen. music curriculum Hartford (N.Y.) Central Sch. Dist., 1939; mem. staff Del. Dept. Pub. Instrn., Dover, 1943; dir. music edn. Herricks (N.Y.) Pub. Schs., 1944-71; ret., 1971. Vis. lectr. Ithaca Coll., summers 1959, 60, 62-65, Fairleigh-Dickinson U., Rutherford, N.J., summer 1966, Albertus Magnus Coll., New Haven, summer 1968; instr. Adelphi Coll., 1954-55, Sch. Edn., N.Y.U., 1964-65. Mem. Music Educators Nat. Conf., N.E.A., N.Y. State Sch. Music Assn., N.Y. State Tchrs. Assn., Nassau Music Educators Assn. (exec. bd. 1947-58), N.Y. State Council Adminstrs. Music Edn. (chpt. v.p. 1967-68), Herricks Tchrs. Assn. (pres. 1948), Sigma Alpha Iota. Mem. Order Eastern Star. Home: 1645 Calle Camille La Jolla CA 92037

NORTHCROSS, WINIFRED WHEELOCK, city official, elections consultant; b. New Orleans, Apr. 17, 1947; d. Elfred and Rosa Alice (Green) Wheelock; m. Wilson Hill Northcross, Jr., Apr. 9, 1977; children—Jill Inez, Christopher Wilson. B.A., So. U., 1969, M.A., 1972. Research asst. U. Mich., Ann Arbor, 1972; field rep. City of Ann Arbor, Mich., 1972-74, dep. city clerk, 1974-81, city clerk, 1981—, chmn. city election commn., 1981—; elections cons. Ann Arbor Public Schs., 1974—. Del. to Tubingen, Fed. Republic Germany, City of Ann Arbor, 1976; intern Capitol Hill Washington Research Project, 1971. Study grant U. Mich., 1968. Mem. Bus. Profl. Women, Nat. Polit. Congress Black Women, Women in Municipal Govt. (pres. 1984—), Internat. Inst. of Mcpl. Clerks (mem. com. fed. legis. 1983—), Mich. Mcpl. Clerks Assn., Alpha Kappa Alpha. Avocations: theater; hiking; reading. Home: 801 Sunrise Ct Ann Arbor MI 48103 Office: City Clerk's Office 100 N Fifth Ave Ann Arbor MI 48104

NORTHCUTT, JACQUELINE CARLA, school principal; b. Logan, W.Va., Feb. 4, 1943; d. Kenneth Carlton and Willa Rae (Hale) Cook; m. Benjamin Wylie Northcutt, Aug. 11, 1967. A.A., Lee Coll., Cleveland, Tenn., 1963; B.A., Shorter Coll., 1965; M.Ed., W.Ga. Coll., 1975, Ed.S., 1978; Ed.D., U. Ga., 1981. Cert. ednl. adminstr., Ga. Tchr. Cobb County Bd. Edn., Marietta, 1965-77, asst. prin., 1977-81, prin. Oakwood High Sch., 1981—. Contbg. author: Feeling Growth, 1977. Editor: Career Education in the Elementary School, 1975. Coordinator Phenomenal Woman Conf., Kennesaw, Ga., 1984-85. Mem. adv. bd. Ga. Prins.' Inst. Named Tchr. of Yr., Awtrey Middle Sch., Acworth, Ga., 1968. Mem. Nat. Assn. Secondary Prins., Assn. Ga. Prins. (presentor 1982, 83), 7th dist. program chmn. 1983-84), Ga. Assn. Ednl. Leaders, Alliance for Invitational Edn., Assn. Supervision and Curriculum Devel., Phi Delta Kappa (v.p. 1984—). Club: Toastmasters (pres. 1982-83). Avocations: piano, house plants. Home: 311 Rockmoor Trail Marietta GA 30066 Office: Oakwood High Sch 1560 Joyner Ave Marietta GA 30060

NORTHEY, LOIS M., nursing home administrator; b. Mahanoy City, Pa., June 22, 1925; d. George H. and Della M. (Birch) N.; R.N., Episcopal Hosp., Phila., 1945. Dir. patient care service Negley House, Pitts., 1971-74, exec. dir., 1973-78, now adminstr.; cons. Wightman Health Center, Pitts., 1979—; adminstr. Oakmont Residence, 1980— Oakmont Nursing Ctr., 1984—. Mem. Assn. Rehab. Nurses, Am. Acad. Med. Adminstrs., Nat. League Nursing, Am. Coll. Nursing Home Adminstrs., Health Care Facilities Assn. Pa. Republican. Roman Catholic. Address: 11 Kinzua Rd Pittsburgh PA 15239

NORTHRUP, LORI, manufacturing executive; b. Cleve., July 27, 1959; d. Jack Antone and Alice (Werder) Bares; m. George William Northrup, May 6, 1984. B.B.A., St. Bonaventure U., 1982. Founder, pres. Stride Tool, Inc., Ellicottville, N.Y., 1980—. Editor monthly newspaper E'ville Events, 1981—. Avocations: raising and training llamas and Tennessee Walkers. Home: Box 6 Ellicottville NY 14731 Office: Stride Tool Inc 48 Washington St Ellicottville NY 14731

NORTHWAY, WANDA I., Realtor; b. Warrenton, Mo., July 11, 1942; d. Herman W. and Goldie M. (Wood) Proctor; m. Donald H. Northway, June 12, 1965; 1 child, Michelle Dawn. Student U. Mo., 1966; grad. Realtors Inst., 1973. Realtor assoc. Gentry Real Estate, Columbia, Mo., 1970-80; Realtor Griffin Real Estate, Columbia, 1980-81; ptnr. Realtor House of Brokers Realty, Inc., Columbia, 1981—. Contbr. articles to profl. jours. Vol. ARC, Columbia; mem. advisor com. Stephen Coll., Columbia; mem. allocation com. United Way, Columbia, Mem. Nat. Assn. Realtors (cert. residential specialist, nat. dir. 1977), Mo. Assn. Realtors (Realtor Assoc. of Yr. 1978, dir. 1974-77, mem. exec. com. 1977, mem. Million Dollar Club), Columbia Bd. Realtors (pres. 1982, Realtor-Assoc. of Yr. 1974, Realtor of Yr. 1980), Epsilon Sigma Alpha (pres. local chpt., state sec.). Republican. Baptist. Club: Mo. Fedn. Women's (pres. 1980-81). Avocations: collector antiques. Home: 1004 Westport Dr Columbia MO 65203 Office: House of Brokers Realty Inc 2100 I-70 Dr SW Columbia MO 65203

NORTON, DONNA ELITHE, teacher educator; b. Durand, Wis., Oct. 15, 1934; d. Earl William and Elithe Bernice (Longsdorf) Proue; B.S. (Elem. Edn. honors scholar), U. Wis., River Falls, 1956; M.S. in Curriculum and Instrn., U. Wis., Madison, 1973, Ph.D. in Curriculum and Instrn., 1976; m. Verland Wilson Norton, Aug. 9, 1958; children—Bradley Wilson, Saundra Elithe. Tchr., River Falls, 1956-59, Madison, 1959-63; remedial reading tchr., Madison, 1969-72, Title I reading cons., 1974-76; lectr. U. Wis., Madison, 1974-76; asst. prof. ednl. curriculum and instrn. Tex. A&M U., College Station, 1976-80, assoc. prof., 1980-86, prof., 1986—, dir. reading lab., 1977-80, dir. multiethnic/multicultural research, 1984—; cons.; conf. presenter. Treas., PTA, 1970-71, program chmn., 1971-72. Recipient Outstanding Univ. Teaching award Tex. A&M U., 1977, Disting. Achievement award, 1982; Tex. A&M U. research grantee, 1976, 80, 82-84; Conoco grantee, 1982-84; Meadows Found. grantee, 1984, 85, 86; cert. elem. tchr., reading tchr., reading specialist, Wis. Mem. Internat. Reading Assn., Nat. Council Tchrs. of English, Coll. Reading Assn., Assn. Ednl. Biographers, Children's Lit. Assn., AAUW, Phi Delta Kappa, Alpha Delta Kappa. Methodist. Author: The Effective Teaching of Language Arts, 1980, 85; Language Arts Activities for Children, 1980, 85; Through the Eyes of a Child: An Introduction to Children's Literature (1st place award for design and typography Nat. Composition Assn. 1983), 1983; editorial bd. Tex. tech Jour. Edn., 1984; contbr. articles and revs. to profl. jours. Home: 125 Lee Ave College Station TX 77840 Office: Dept of EDCI Texas A&M University College Station TX 77843

NORTON, JANET MCCARTY, lawyer; b. Louisville, Mar. 5, 1956; d. William Jones and Jewell May (Teater) McC. B.A., U. Ky., 1978, J.D., 1981. Bar: Ky. 1981. Research analyst Ky. Devel. Cabinet, Frankfort, 1977-80; cons., Lexington, Ky., 1980-81; staff atty. Ky. Ct. Appeals, Frankfort, 1981-82; atty. Humana Inc., Louisville, 1982—. Active polit. campaign, 1981. Recipient Am. Jurisprudence award, 1979. Mem. Ky. Bar Assn., ABA, Louisville-Jefferson County Women Lawyers Assn., Ky. LWV, Louisville Jaycees, Phi Beta Kappa. Democrat. Roman Catholic. Office: Humana Inc PO Box 1438 Louisville KY 40201

NORTON, KAREN ANN, accounting executive; b. Paynesville, Minn., Nov. 1, 1950; d. Dale Francis and Ruby Grace (Gehlhar) N. B.A., U. Minn., 1972; postgrad. U. Md., 1978; cert. acctg. U.S. Dept. Agr. Grad. Sch., 1978; postgrad. Calif. State Poly.-Pomona, 1984, 86. C.P.A., Md. Securities transactions analyst Bur. of Pub. Debt., Washington, 1972-79, internal auditor, 1979-81; internal auditor IRS, Washington, 1981; sr. acct. World Vision Internat., Monrovia, Calif., 1981-83, acctg. supr., 1983—; cons. (vol.) info. systems John M. Perkins Found., Pasadena, Calif., 1985—. Author (poetry): Ode to Joyce, 1985 (Golden Poet award 1985). Second v.p. chpt. Nat. Treasury Employees Union, Washington, 1978, editor chpt. newsletter; mem. M-2 Prisoners Sponsorship Program, Chino, Calif., 1984—. Recipient Spl. Achievement award Dept. Treasury, 1976, Superior Performance award, 1977-78; Charles and Ellors Alliss scholar, 1968. Mem. Christian Ministries Mgmt. Assn., Nat. Assn. Accts. Mem. Covenant Ch. Avocations: chess; racquetball; mountain climbing; whitewater rafting; sky diving.

NORTON, VIRGINIA SKEEN (MRS. JOHN H. NORTON, JR.), civic worker; b. Atlanta, June 1, 1907; d. Lola Percy and Rebecca (Baldwin) Skeen; A.B., Agnes Scott Coll., 1928; student Columbia U., 1934-35, m. John Hughes Norton, Jr., Dec. 16, 1938; children—Virginia Skeen Norton Kraft, John Hughes III. With personnel dept. Retail Credit Co., Atlanta, 1929-31, sec. to v.p., gen. mgr. Davison-Paxon, Co., Atlanta, 1931-34; with Aluminium Ltd., N.Y.C., 1935-41, sec. to pres., 1937-41; sec. to pres. Colonial Williamsburg, Inc., N.Y.C., 1943-44. Bd. dirs. North Shore Assos. Chgo. Commons, 1951-54, Infant Welfare Soc. Chgo., 1953-54, Catherine Morrill Day Nursery, Portland, Maine, 1956-59. Mem. Central Fla. Civic Theater Guild, Loch Haven Arts Soc., Winter Park Meml. Hosp. Aux., Morse Art Gallery Assocs. (dir.

1982-84), Nat. Soc. Colonial Dames Am. Episcopalian. Address: 700 Melrose Ave Apt A-22 Winter Park FL 32789

NORWOOD, DOROTHY F., Supreme Court deputy clerk; b. Prattville, Ala., July 31, 1943; d. Ralph L. and Gladys (Dawson) Ferrell; m. William R. Norwood, Apr. 2, 1965; children—Jay, Richard. B.S., Auburn U., 1978; J.D., Jones Law Inst., 1981. Steno clk. State Ala., Montgomery, 1961-71; asst. clk. Ala. Supreme Ct., Montgomery, 1971-77, acting dep. clk., 1977-82, acting clk., 1982-83, dep. clk., 1983—. Author Assignment of Cases, 1979, Assistance to Attorneys, 1981. Mem. Ala. State Bar (chmn. com.), Am. Bar Assn., Montgomery County Bar Assn., Nat. Conf. Appellate (sec., treas. 1978-82). Club: Zonta (rec. sec. 1985—). Home: 1310 Magnolia Ave Montgomery AL 36106 Office: Ala Supreme Ct 445 Dexter Ave Montgomery AL 36130

NORWOOD, JANET LIPPE, economist, government official; b. Newark, Dec. 11, 1923; d. M. Turner and Thelma (Levinson) Lippe; B.A., N.J. Coll. Women, 1945; M.A., Fletcher Sch. Law and Diplomacy, 1946, Ph.D., 1949; LL.D. (hon.), Fla. Internat. U., 1979, Carnegie Mellon U., 1984; m. Bernard Norwood, June 25, 1943; children—Stephen Harlan, Peter Carlton. Instr., Wellesley Coll., 1948-49; economist William L. Clayton Center, Fletcher Sch. Law and Diplomacy, 1953-58; with Bur. Labor Stats., Dept. Labor, Washington, 1963—, dep. commr. data analysis, 1973-75, dep. commr. bur., 1975-78, acting commr. bur., 1978-79, commr. labor stats., 1979—; mem. bd. overseers, vis. com., stats. dept. Harvard U., 1976—; mem. visitors com. econ. dept. MIT. Recipient Disting. Achievement award, Sec. Labor, 1972, spl. commendation, 1977; Philip Arnow award Dept. Labor, 1979, Elmer Staats award, 1982 Fellow Am. Stats. Assn. (v.p.), AAAS; mem. Douglass Soc., Am. Econ. Assn. (exec. com.), Indsl. Relations Research Assn., Nat. Assn. Bus. Economists, Women's Caucus in Stats., Nat. Acad. Pub. Adminstrn. (Pub. Service award), Internat. Statis. Assn. (council). Author: (monograph) Labor Law and Practice in the Union of Burma, 1963; collaborator: International Trade Policy Issues, 1963; contbr. articles to profl. publs. Office: 441 G St NW Washington DC 20212

NOTESTINE, JENNINE BERNARD, insurance executive; b. Hartford, Conn., Sept. 27, 1960; d. R. Ron and Terese H. (Hermann) Bernard; m. Kenneth E. Notestine, Sept. 22, 1984. A.S., Quinnipiac Coll., Hamden, Conn., 1980, B.S. in Mktg., 1982. Lic. casualty adjuster, Conn. Fin. analyst The Travelers, Hartford, 1983—. Recipient Pres.'s Scholarship prize Quinnipiac Coll., 1982. Mem. Quinnipiac Coll. Alumni Assn. Republican. Congregationalist. Club: Women's. Avocations: flute, sailing, camping.

NOTHERN, ELLA LOUISE, nurse; b. Salina, Kans., Jan. 30, 1931; d. Herman Herbert and Eva Alice (Beil) Will; m. M. Roland Nothern, Nov. 22, 1950; children—David Will, Matthew Roland, Nathan Jon. B.A., Kans. Wesleyan U., Salina, 1973; Assoc. degree in Nursing, Cloud County Community Coll., Concordia, Kans., 1981. R.N., Kans. Pre-sch. tchr., Glasco, Kans., 1974-75, tchr. Glasco High Sch., 1975-76; clk. bus. office Mitchell County Hosp., Beloit, Kans., 1976-77; activity dir. Nicol Home, Glasco, 1977-79; nurse psychiatric unit St. Joseph's Hosp., Concordia, 1981-84; charge nurse Good Samaritan Ctr., Minneapolis, Kans., 1984—. Mem. exec. com. Central Kans. Library System, Great Bend, 1977-84; bd. dirs. Pawnee Mental Health Ctr., Manhattan, Kans., 1982-84; mem. ambulance crew Glasco Ambulance Service, 1979-84. Mem. ALA (co-chmn. publicity com. trustee div. 1983-84, Kans. Library Assn. (v.p. trustee div. 1982-84), Lutheran Missionary Soc. (pres. 1960-61), Epsilon Sigma Alpha (pres. 1964-65). Republican. Home: Route 1 Salina KS 67401 Office: Good Samaritan Ctr Minneapolis KS

NOTTENKAMPER, MARGO ADKINS, office products company marketing executive; b. Berwyn, Ill., Nov. 28, 1958; d. Lawrence W. and Alice B. (Cooling) Adkins; m. Andrew L. Nottenkamper, June 17, 1984. A.S. in Bus., Elgin Community Coll., 1982. Acctg. clk. Square D Co., Schiller Park, Ill., 1976-77; exec. sec. Green Bay Packaging, Franklin Park, Ill., 1977-78; from exec. sec. to advt. mgr. Fellowes Mfg. Co. (parent co. Bankers Box), Itasca, Ill., 1978-84; advt. and sales promotion mgr. H. S. Crocker Co., Inc., Burlingame, Calif., 1984-86, mktg. mgr., 1986—; advt. cons., meeting planner Am. Office Products Distbrs., Wheaton, Ill., 1984—. Mem. Nat. Assn. Female Execs. Avocations: English horseback riding; cooking. Office: H S Crocker Co Inc 851 Hinckley Rd Burlingame CA 94010

NOTTKE, NANCY JANE, educator; b. Lakewood, Ohio, Mar. 30, 1948; d. Clark DeWitt and Frances (Watterson) Fiscus; B.S. with honors in Elementary Edn., Ohio U., Athens, 1969, M.Ed., 1977; m. Bruce Douglas Nottke; children—Sara Elizabeth, Nathan Douglas. Intern tchr. The Children's House, Pearl City, Hawaii, 1970-71; tchr. sci. St. Anthony's Schs., Kailua, Hawaii, 1971-72; tchr. Holy Family Sch., Honolulu, 1972-73; tchr. kindergarten Trimble Local Schs., Glouster, Ohio, 1973-77, tchr. 2d grade, 1977—. Martha Holden Jennings scholar, 1976-77. Elder, 1st Presbyn. Ch., Athens. Mem. NEA, Trimble Local Tchrs. Assn. (pres. 1976-77, treas. 1985-86), Southeastern Ohio Tchrs. Assn., AAUW (chmn. newsletter 1974-76, rec. sec. 1978-79, edn. founds. 1979-81, legis. chmn. 1981-83), Delta Kappa Gamma. Club: Eastern Star. Cert., Ohio. Home: RD 6 32 Chapel Ln Athens OH 45701 Office: Route 3 Box 447 Trimble Elementary Sch Glouster OH 45732

NOVAK, ALINA SIDNEY, consultant; b. London, Jan. 12, 1947; came to U.S., 1952, naturalized, 1963; d. Jan and Marta (Wendlandt) Nowosielski; B.A., CCNY, 1969. Research analyst Nat. Econs. Research Assos., Inc., N.Y.C., 1969-70, Royal Globe Ins. Co., N.Y.C., 1970-71, Analytical Methods and Applications, Inc., Washington, 1971-72, Scholarship, Edn. and Def. Fund Racial Equality, Inc., N.Y.C., 1972-74; fin. analyst Equitable Life Assurance Soc. U.S., N.Y.C., 1974-84; with Home Box Office, Inc., N.Y.C., 1984, Sundance Software Inc., Armonk, N.Y., 1985—; founder Networks, 1976; pres. Networks Unltd., Inc. Recipient Big Apple award N.Y.C. Jr. C. of C., 1980. Mem. Am. Econs. Assn., Fortune 500 Bus. and Profl. Women's Club, Women in Communications, Assn. for Systems Mgmt. Home: 337 44th St Apt 6 Brooklyn NY 11220 Office: 22 High St Armonk NY 10504

NOVAK, CAROL ANN, multi-company executive; b. Plankington, S.D., Nov. 8, 1925; d. Frederick Laurence and Vera Marie (Lindekugel) Lindekugel; m. Kenneth R. Novak, Feb. 14, 1953 (dec. May 1982); children—Charles Arnold, Tanna Ann Novak Scriven, Nancy Ann. Student, Yankton Coll., 1943-44. Sec. State Auditor, Pierre, S.D., after 1944, U.S. Geol. Survey, Pierre, 1947; cutter, folder Boeing Airplane Co., Seattle, 1949-51; sec. Western Airlines, Seattle, 1951-55; sec.-treas., Novak Homes, Seattle, 1953—; sec. SEA-KOTA, Inc., Seattle, 1955-82, pres., 1983—; sec. Cascade Door Co., Seattle, 1957-83, pres., 1983—; owner, operator Agate & Crescent Beach Park, Port Angeles, Wash., 1962-77, Carols Crescent Beach, 1985—; sec. Agate & Crescent Beach Tree Farm., Port Angeles, 1965—. Home: 3440 Crescent Beach Rd Port Angeles WA 98362 Office: Agate & Crescent Beach 3454 Crescent Beach Rd Port Angeles WA 98362

NOVAK, DIANE MARIE, nurse; b. Chgo., June 7, 1951; d. William Charles and Bertha Marie (Rich) N.; R.N., Augustana Hosp., Chgo., 1971; postgrad. Loop Coll., Chgo., Northeastern Ill. U. Mem. nursing staff Augustana Hosp., 1971-73, 74-86, asst. coordinator med.-surg. unit, 1976-80, staff nurse dept. pediatrics, 1980-86, asst. unit coordinator pediatrics and stroke unit, 1982-83, staff nurse obstetrics, 1983-86; labor and delivery nurse Luth. Gen. Hosp., Park Ridge, Ill., 1986—; staff nurse surg. and burn unit Evanston (Ill.) Hosp., 1973-74; in-service instr., CPR tchr. Mem. Transcultural Nursing Soc. Office: Luth Gen Hosp 1775 Dempster St Park Ridge IL 60068

NOVAK, JO-ANN STOUT, chemical engineer; b. Glen Ridge, N.J., June 25, 1956; d. Herbert Austin and Anna (Messina) Stout; B.Chem. Engring., Ga. Inst. Tech., 1977; M.B.A., Oakland U., 1984; m. John Robert Novak Jr., Oct. 30, 1976. Trainee AC Spark Plug div. Gen. Motors Corp., Flint, Mich., 1977-78, chemist, 1978-79, exptl. chemist, 1979-81, mfg. engr., 1981-84, sr. mfg. engr., 1984—. Cert. engr.-in-tng., Ga. Mem. Am. Electroplaters Soc. (dir. Saginaw Valley br. 1981-83, ednl. chmn. 1984-85, sec.-treas. 1985-86, 2d v.p. 1986-87), Am. Inst. Chem. Engrs., Soc. Mfg. Engrs. Office: AC Spark Plug Div Gen Motors Corp 1300 N Dort Hwy Flint MI 48556

NOVAK, NINA, lawyer; b. Basking Ridge, N.J., Oct. 2, 1952; d. Edward Lawrence and Rita Virginia (Myers) N. B.A., Roanoke Coll., 1974; J.D., U. Richmond, 1976. Bar: Va. 1977, D.C. 1984. Assoc. Taylor, Walker & Adams, Norfolk, Va., 1977-80; asst. resident counsel Va. Hosp. Assn., Richmond, 1980-82; assoc. Miles & Stockridge, Washington, 1982—. Mem. ABA, Va. Bar Assn., Am. Acad. Hosp. Attys., Nat. Health Lawyers Assn., Roanoke Coll. Alumni Assn. (pres. 1981—). Republican. Home: 2873B-2 S Buchanan St Arlington VA 22206 Office: Miles & Stockbridge Suite 500 1701 Pennsylvania Ave NW Washington DC 20006

NOVAK, RENA ANN, travel and restaurant executive; b. Torrance, Calif., Nov. 12, 1951; d. John B. and Mary E. (Olufsen) Depue; m. Robert Paul Novak, Apr. 18, 1970; 1 child, Brenda Suzanne. A.A. in Computer Sci., Control Data Corp., 1971. Travel counselor Flying Tiger Line, Los Angeles, 1973-77, Am. Express, Torrance, Calif., 1977-78; mgr. comml. Thomas Cook Travel, Newport Beach, Calif., 1978-79; pres. Oui Travel, Inc., Medford, Oreg., 1979—; owner Bear Creek Travel, Medford, 1984—, Baccala's Pizza, Medford, 1982—. Vice-pres. pub. relations Medford chpt. Muscular Dystrophy Assn., 1980-81; sec. Medford-Alba Sister City Com.; bd. dirs. Visitors and Conv. Bur.; assoc. bd. dirs. Peter Britt Festival. Mem. Inst. Cert. Travel Agts. (study group leader 1980—), Am. Bus. Women's Assn. (chair coms.). Republican. Roman Catholic. Club: Soroptimists (chair coms.). Avocation: travel. Home: 2533 Southport Way Medford OR 97504 Office: Bear Creek Travel 820 Crater Lake Ave Suite 111 Medford OR 97504

NOVAK, SHIRLEY A., librarian; b. Rochelle, Ill., May 29, 1936; d. Don and Irma (Olson) Archer; B.S. in Elementary Edn., No. Ill. U., Dekalb, 1970. M.S. in Instructional Tech., 1975; cert. media instrn. and supervision; m. Leonard S. Novak; children—Lance Kendall, Pamela Kay. Tchr., Durand (Ill.) Elementary Sch., 1955-56, Pecatonica (Ill.) Elementary Sch., 1957-58, Windsor Sch., Loves Park, Ill., 1959-70, learning center dir., 1970-74, head librarian Harlem High Sch., 1974-84, learning ctr. dir. Harlem Jr. High Sch., 1984—. Vice pres. Rockford area TI Users Group, 1983-85; pres. Friends of the North Suburban Dist. Library, 1984-85. Mem. ALA, Am. Assn. Sch. Librarians, NEA, Ill. Edn. Assn., Harlem Educators Assn. (treas. 1980-81), Ill. Audio-Visual Assn., No. Ill. Media Assn., Am. Bus. Women's Assn. Lutheran. Certified in teaching, media instructiion. Home: 5412 Garden Plain Ave Loves Park IL 61111 Office: 735 Windsor Rd Loves Park IL 61111

NOVAK, VICKIE LYNN, librarian; b. Chgo., Feb. 17, 1952; d. Albert Henry and Elsie Marie (Bortolami) N.; B.A., Quincy Coll., 1973; M.S.L.S., U. Ky., 1974. Adminstrv. librarian Acorn Public Library Dist., Oak Forest, Ill., 1974—, joint cons. bldg., 1975-80; mem. adv. bd. Learning Exchange's Spl. Library Project, 1979-80; mem. Ill. White House Conf. on Library and Info. Services, 1978. Ill. State Library scholar, 1972-73, 73-74; named Outstanding Modern Lang. Student, Quincy Coll., 1974. Mem. ALA (architecture for public libraries com. bldgs. and equipment sect. adminstrn. and mgmt. div. 1981-83, conf. planning com. 1985), Ill. Library Assn. (mem.-at-large dist. library round table 1982, sec. 1983-84), Library Adminstrs. Conf. No. Ill., South Suburban Library Assn. (pres. 1979-80), Oak Forest C. of C., ABU Arabian Horse Club (sec. 1981—, del. 1980), U. Ky. Alumni Club, Friends of Library, Internat. Arabian Horse Assn. (Dressage com.), Am. Horse Shows Assn., U.S. Dressage Fedn., Ill. Dressage Assn., Beta Phi Mu. Roman Catholic. Office: 15624 S Central Ave Oak Forest IL 60452

NOVAKOVICH, NADA, lawyer; b. Feb. 24, 1924; d. Peter and Ljuba (Matyasevich) N.; m. Luke Aluevich, 1961 (dec. 1971). LL.B., George Washington U., 1950. Bar: Nev. 1950, U.S. Dist. Ct. Nev. 1950, U.S. Dist. Ct. D.C. 1950. Sole practice, Reno, 1950—; mem. Gov.'s Adv. Com. Status of Women, 1959. Author: And His Name Was Luke, 1976. Democratic candidate for U.S. Ho. of Reps., 1956; mem. Gov.'s Fulbright Scholarship Com. Mem. Nev. Bar Assn., Washoe County Bar Assn. (sec. 1951-56), ABA, D.C. Bar Assn., Reno C. of C. (dir. 1973-76), Phi Delta Delta. Serbian Orthodox. Club: Soroptimists (Reno). Home: 146 Greenridge Dr Reno NV 89509 Office: 50 W Liberty St Reno NV 89505

NOVAKOWSKI, DEBORAH LEE, telecommunications company executive; b. Chgo., Feb. 22, 1960; d. Eugene John and Jacqueline Marie (Brozek) N. B.A. in Mktg., U. Ill.; M.B.A. in Acctg., Loyola U. of Chgo. Traffic engr. MCI, Chgo., 1981-83, supr. traffic engring., 1983-85, mgr. network mgmt., 1985-86, ops. mgr., 1986—. Named to Pres.'s Club, MCI Midwest, 1985, Director's Club, 1983. Mem. Nat. Assn. Female Execs., Loyola Alumni Assn., U. Ill. Alumni Assn. Office: MCI Telecommunications 205 N Michigan Ave Chicago IL 60601

NOVICK, JUDITH LYNNE, lawyer; b. N.Y.C., Mar. 7, 1943; d. Abraham G. and Matilda (Davidov) Novick. B.A. in Anthropology, Cornell U., 1964; postgrad. U. Pa., 1965-67; J.D. cum laude, Boston Coll., 1979. Bar: Mass. 1979. Tchr. African/Asian studies Berkshire Farm Sch. and Services for Youth, 1967-68, chmn. social studies dept., 1968-71; curriculum cons. Sleighton Sch. for Girls, Darlington, Pa., 1971-73; counsel Halper Investment Trust, Newton, Mass., 1979-81; sole practice law, Stoughton, Mass., 1981—. Mem. Mass. Bar Assn., ABA, Mass. Assn. Women Lawyers. Jewish. Office: 45 Kennedy Rd Stoughton MA 02072

NOVINA, TRUDI (MRS. CHARLES E. COAKLEY), fibers company official; b. Bklyn., Dec. 8; d. Isidor and Lilian (Greenberg) Novina; B.A., Bklyn. Coll., 1950; M.B.A., Fordham U., 1981; m. Leo H. Papazian, June 24, 1956 (dec. 1964); children—Lyssa D., Gregory M.; m. Charles E. Coakley, Apr. 27, 1968. Reporter, N.Y. World Telegram & Sun, N.Y.C., 1950-54, asst. woman's editor, 1954-57, home furnishings editor, 1957-60; free-lance writer, 1960-64; account exec., dir. home fashions publicity Donald Degnan Assos., N.Y.C., 1964-69; mgr. publicity Allied Fibers, Allied-Signal Corp., N.Y.C., 1969—. Mem. Am. Inst. Interior Designers, Nat. Home Fashions League (chpt. v.p. 1972-73), Fashion Group. Club: Overseas Press (N.Y.C.). Editor: House and Garden Decorating Book, 1965. Contbr. articles to various mags. Home: 34 W 89th St New York NY 10024 Office: 1411 Broadway New York NY 10018

NOVITCH, CLARA MARGARET, accountant; b. New Haven, Mar. 30, 1937; d. Albert Walter and Helen M. (Torquato) Gaudette; student Felt & Tarrant Bus. Sch., 1955, IBM Computer Sch., 1956, Asbury Park Bus. Coll., 1969; m. Leonard Novitch, Apr. 2, 1975; children—Henry Chelston, Steven Chelston, Richard Chelston, Daniel Chelston, John Chelston, Joseph Chelston. With Schiffenhaus Bros., Newark, 1955-56, Law Firm Russo & Courtney, Toms River, N.J., 1972-73; legis. aide State Sen. John F. Russo, 1973-74; with Novitronics Data Inc., Point Pleasant, N.J., 1974—; acct., partner L. Novitch & Co., Pt. Pleasant, 1973—. Exec. bd. mem. Emma Havens Young Sch., Brick Town (N.J.) PTA, 1977—, treas. for Williamsburg com., 1979—; Dem. committeewoman Dist. 8, Brick Town, 1977—. Lic. real estate agt., N.J., 1966—; lic. pub. acct., N.J. Mem. Nat. Assn. Pub. Accts., N.J. Assn. Pub. Accts. (state pres. 1986—, pres. Monmouth Ocean chpt. 1982-83, 83-84) Nat. Assn. Women Accts., N.J. Assn. Women Accts., Nat. Assn. Female Execs. Roman Catholic. Club: Network (dir. 1979-80). State editor, Tastic mag., 1977. Home: 64 Havens Dr Brick Town NJ 08723 Office: 600 Arnold Ave Point Pleasant Beach NJ 08742

NOVOGROD, NANCY ELLEN, editor; b. N.Y.C., Jan. 30, 1949; d. Max and Hilda (Kirschbaum) Gerstein; m. John Campner Novogrod, Nov. 7, 1976; children—James Campner, Caroline Anne. A.B., Mt. Holyoke Coll., 1971. Reader The New Yorker, N.Y.C., 1973-76, sec. fiction dept., 1971-73; asst. editor Clarkson N. Potter, Inc., N.Y.C., 1977-78, assoc. editor, 1978-80, editor, 1980-83, sr. editor, 1984—. Office: Clarkson N Potter Inc 225 Park Ave New York NY 10003

NOWAK, EMMY, manufacturing company executive; b. Hamburg, Germany, Nov. 15, 1923; d. Erwin and Elfriede (Mueller) Stamm; m. Joseph E. Gorgens, Dec. 26, 1944 (div. 1960); 1 child, Richard; m. Bernard J. Nowak, Feb. 12, 1966. R.N., Bridgeport Hosp. Sch. Nursing, Conn., 1945. Registered nurse, Conn. With Alloy Engring. Co. Inc., Bridgeport, 1958—, pres., chief exec. officer, 1982—. Recipient Salute to Women award YMCA, Bridgeport, 1982. Mem. Bridgeport C. of C. (exec. bd. dirs. 1982—), Bridgeport Hosp. Alumnae Assn. Republican. Episcopalian. Office: Alloy Engring Co Inc 304 Seaview Ave PO Box 4036 Bridgeport CT 06607

NOWAK, JACQUELYN LOUISE, state official; b. Harrisburg, Pa., Sept. 2, 1937; d. John Henry and Irene Louise (Clark) Snyder; children—Andrew Alfred, IV, Deirdre Anne. Student Pa. State U., 1973-74; B.A., Lycoming Coll., 1975. Editorial writer Patriot News Co., Harrisburg, Pa., 1957-58; dir. West Shore Sr. Citizens Center, New Cumberland, Pa., 1969-72; exec. dir. Cumberland County Office Aging, Carlisle, Pa., 1972-80; dir. Bur. Advocacy, Pa. Dept. Aging, Harrisburg, 1980—. Recorder, Pa. Gov's. Council Aging, Central Region, 1972-74; chmn. pub. relations, 1973-74; mem. state planning com. Pa. State Conf. Aging, 1974, panelist, 1975-78; mem. state bd. Pa. Council Homemakers-Home Health Aide Services, 1972-80, v.p., 1975, chmn. ann. meeting, 1973-75; sr. citizens subcom. chmn. Pa. Atty. Gens. Commn. to Prevent Shoplifting, 1983; mem. adv. com. Tri-County Ret. Sr. Vol. Program, 1972-74; bd. dirs. Council Human Services Cumberland, Dauphin, and Perry Counties, 1973-74; mem. service com. Family and Children's Service Harrisburg, 1970-74, mem. policy com., 1973-74, bd. dirs. Cumberland County unit Am. Cancer Soc., 1964-76, state del., 1964-66, chmn. county pub. relations, 1965-66, cancer crusade chmn., 1964. Recipient Herman Melitzer award, Pa. Conf. Aging, 1978; named Woman of the Year WIOO Radio, Carlisle, Pa., 1979. Mem. Nat. Assn. Area Ags. on Aging (dir. 1975-80, pres. 1976-77; sec. 1978-79), Harrisburg Art Assn., Mechanicsburg Art Center (bd. dirs. 1984—), Gerontol Soc. Am., Am. Trauma Soc. (Pa. div. state bd. 1985—), Older Women's League (founder chpt.). Clubs: Zonta (Harrisburg); Federation of Women's (div. chmn. 1972-76), Torch (2nd v.p. 1985-86). Home: 505 Geary Ave New Cumberland PA 17070 Office: Bur of Advocacy Pa Dept of Aging 231 State St Harrisburg PA 17101

NOWELL, ELIZABETH CAMERON CLEMONS, author; b. Berkeley, Calif.; d. Alfred George and Edith (Catton) Cameron; A.B. San Jose State Coll., 1928; M.A., Stanford U., 1937; m. Wood Clemons, Dec. 22, 1946 (div. Dec. 1958); m. Arthur G. Robinson, May 27, 1961 (dec. Jan. 1967); m. Nelson T. Nowell, Feb. 15, 1969 (dec. Sept. 1973). With edn. dept. San Jose State Coll., 1928-39, in service tng. U. Calif. Extension Div., 1939-42; elem. editor The John C. Winston Co., 1942-43, Silver Burdett Co., 1943-44, D.C. Heath, 1944-46; instr. English dept. U. Minn., 1947; writing, editing publs. services Gen. Mills, 1947-50; freelance writer, 1950—; reading cons. Monterey City Sch., 1959-62, asso. editor Calif. edit. Am. Home Mag., 1965-70; mem. seminar faculty Embroiderers Guild, 1980, Monterey Peninsula Coll., 1978-82; judge needlework Good Samaritan Hosp., Los Angeles, 1977, 79, 83 Montalvo Center for Arts, Saratoga, Calif., 1980, 82, Status Needle Art Show, Burlingame, Calif., 1982, Altrusa Needlework Exhbn., Santa Maria, Calif., 1982, Scripps Meml. Hosp., La Jolla, Calif., 1980, 86, others. Bd. dirs. Community Hosp. Aux.; bd. dirs. Harrison Meml. Library, 1971-76, Monterey Symphony Assn., 1974-75; vestryman St. Dunstan's Episcopal Ch., 1974-77. Mem. Nat. League Am. Pen Women, Authors Guild, LWV, Nat. Embroidery Tchrs. Assn. (nat. dir. 1978—), Embroiderers Guild Am. (nat. dir. 1978-81, nat. fin. com. 1984—; nat. fin. guidelines chmn. 1986, nat. judges cert. com. 1984—, pres. chpt. 1977-78; judge needlework exhbns. 1977—), Kappa Alpha Theta, Pi Lambda Theta, Delta Phi Upsilon, Kappa Delta Pi, Delta Kappa Gamma. Republican. Clubs: Casa Abrego (historian 1979-83), Monterey Peninsula Country, Soroptimist. Author: The Pixie Dictionary, 1953; the Catholic Child's First Dictionary, 1954; The Winston Dictionary for Canadian School Children, 1955; Away I Go, 1956; All About Baby, 1956; I Live on A Farm, 1956; A Wish for Billy, 1956; Wings, Wheels, and Motors, 1957; The Big Book of Real Fire Engines, 1958; The Big Book of Real Trains, 1958; The Big Book of Real Trucks, 1958; Rodeo Days, 1960; Shells Are Where You Find Them, 1960; Rocks and The World Around You, 1960; Big and Little, 1961; Tide Pools and Beaches, 1964; Tides, Waves, and Currents, 1967; Here and There Stories; Now and Then Stories; Near and Far Stories; A Source Book for the Teaching of Literature for Children (all 1967); The Seven Seas, 1971; The Friendly Frog, 1971; What I Like, 1971; also feature articles in nat. mags. Address: PO Box 686 Carmel CA 93921

NOWELL, LUCILLE (LUCY) TERRY, costume designer, educator; b. Leeds, Ala., Sept. 24, 1951; d. Thomas Daniel and Martha Dowdy (Thomason) Terry; B.A., U. Ala., 1972, M.A. (Grad. Council fellow), 1974, M.F.A., U. New Orleans, 1982; m. Thomas Ruffin Nowell, May 4, 1974; 1 dau., Jessica Marian. Guest artist U. Montevallo (Ala.), 1974-76; asst. prof. and coordinator dramatic arts Lynchburg (Va.) Coll., 1976—. Mem. Southeastern Theatre Conf. (adv. bd. dirs. 1981-83), U.S. Inst. for Theatre Tech. (dir. 1982—, chmn. nat. membership com. 1984-86). Mem. Disciples of Christ Ch. Costumer designer for over 35 plays and mus. in ednl. theatre, 1974—. Home: 7108 Richland Dr Lynchburg VA 24502 Office: Dramatic Arts Lynchburg Coll Lynchburg VA 24501

NOWICKI, EDWINA KIM, automatic test equipment manufacturing company executive; b. Trenton, N.J., Sept 18, 1961; d. Edward Peter and Susan (Chasny) N. B.S. in Elec. and Biomed. Engring., Duke U., 1983. Tech. tng. program Genrad Inc., Concord, Mass., 1983-85, tech. support specialist, Waltham, Mass., 1985—. Recipient Employee Recognition awards Genrad Inc., 1985, 86. Mem. Nat. Assn. Female Execs., Kappa Alpha Theta. Lutheran. Club: Duke Alumni (Boston). Avocations: racquetball, squash, travel. Home: 28 Brentwood St Apt 12 Allston MA 02134 Office: Genrad Inc 170 Tracer Ln Waltham MA 02254

NOWIK, DOROTHY ADAM, medical equipment company executive; b. Chgo., July 25, 1944; d. Adam Harry and Helen (Kichkaylo) Wanaski; m. Eugene Nicholas Nowik, Aug. 9, 1978; children—George Eugene, Helen Eugene. A.A., Columbia Coll., Seattle, 1980. Sec., Zenco Engring. Corp., Chgo., 1969-70, adminstrv. asst. to pres., 1970-71; sales rep. MediZenco USA Ltd., Chgo., 1971-73; ptnr. Pacific Med. Systems, Bellevue, Wash., 1973-76, pres., 1976—. Mem. Nat. Assn Female Execs. Mem. Orthodox Ch. in Am. Avocations: cycling, tennis, needlework. Home: 2804 127th Ave NE Bellevue WA 98005 Office: Pacific Med Systems Inc 15055 NE Bel-Rel Road Bellevue WA 98007

NOXON, MARGARET WALTERS, community volunteer; b. Detroit, Dec. 16, 1903; d. George Alexander and Ethelwyn (Taylor) Walters; grad., Liggett Sch. for Girls, Det., 1922; life teaching certificate Wayne State U., 1925; student Columbia Tchrs. Coll., 1939-40; m. Herbert Richards Noxon, July 15, 1926 (dec. Aug. 4, 1971). Bd. dirs. Coll. Club, Detroit, 1925-30; mem. Salvation Army Aux., Detroit, 1926—; mem. Coll. Club, Summit N.J., 1941—; historian D.A.R., N.Y.C., 1943-46, vice regent, 1946-49; dir. New Eng., Women, 1961-64; dir. Woodycrest-Five Points Child Care, 1961-77; bd. dirs. ARC, Summit, N.J., service com. chmn. uniforms and insignias, 1943-45; v.p. N.Y. Infirmary Aux., N.Y.C., 1948-58, bd. dirs., 1959-80. Recipient award for meritorious personal service ARC, 1945. Mem. Nat. Inst. Social Scis., Grand Jury Assn. N.Y. County, D.A.R. (dir. 1950-70), St. David's Soc. State N.Y., English-Speaking Union, Daus. Am. Colonists, AAUW, Southampton Colonial Soc., Nat. Woman's Farm and Garden Assn. (dir. met. br. 1975—, dir. N.Y. State div. 1978-80, mem. nat. council 1978-80), Ch. Women's League for Patriotic Service, Women's Bible Soc. N.Y., Alpha Sigma Tau. Republican. Presbyterian. Clubs: Southampton (N.Y.) Bath and Tennis, City Gardens (dir. 1963-68, mem. adv. com. 1968-74, dir. 1974-80, adv. bd. 1980-83), York (bd. govs. 1965-66, 73-77), Barnard (trustee 1979-81), Sorosis (v.p. 1979-81), Regency (N.Y.C.). Home: 1100 Madison Ave Apt 10C Box 86 New York NY 10028

NOZIGLIA, CARLA MILLER, crime laboratory administrator, medical technologist; b. Erie, Pa., Oct. 11, 1941; d. Earnest Carl John and Eileen Hervie (Murphy) Miller; m. Keith William Noziglia, Nov. 21, 1969; children—Pama Amy, Kathryn Josephine. B.S. in Biology and Chemistry, Villa Maria Coll., 1963; M.S. in Adminstrn., Lindenwood Coll., 1984. Registered med. technologist. Asst. head spl. chemistry Hamot Med. Ctr., Erie, 1965-69; pathologist's assoc. Galion Community Hosp., Ohio, 1969-75; dir. crime lab. Mansfield Police Dept., Ohio, 1975-81; supr. crime lab. St. Louis County Police Dept., St. Louis, 1981-84; dir. crime lab. Las Vegas Met. Police Dept., 1984—; instr., advisor North Central Tech. Coll., Mansfield, 1980-81; instr. St. Louis Police Acad., 1982-84, U. Nev.-Las Vegas, 1985—. Abstracts editor Jour. Police Sci. and Adminstrn., 1983—. Pres. St. Mary Parish Council, 1980; mem. Gov.'s Commn. on Intoxication, Carson City, Nev., 1984—. Recipient Award of Merit, Ohio Ho. of Reps., 1980. Fellow Am. Acad. Forensic Scis. (program chmn. 1986); mem. Am. Soc. Crime Lab. Dirs. (treas. 1981, 82, pres. 1986-87, bd. dirs. 1980-83, 85-87), Am. Soc. Med. Technologists, Midwest Assn. Forensic Scientists (bd. dirs. 1982-84), S.W. Assn. Forensic Scientists, N.W. Assn. Forensic Scientists, Calif. Assn. Criminalists, Calif. Assn. Crime Lab. Dirs., Am. Legion (aux. pres.). Republican. Roman Catholic. Avocations: reading; sewing; knitting; swimming. Home: 1025 Pagosa Way Las Vegas NV 89128 Office: 601 E Fremont Las Vegas NV 89101

NUGENT, CHRISTINE MURPHY, educator; b. Suffern, N.Y., Nov. 30, 1951; d. Thomas William and Kathleen Christina (Connors) Murphy; A.A., Edward Williams Coll., 1975; B.S., Fairleigh Dickinson U., 1978, M.B.A., 1982; m. William R. Nugent, Jan. 30, 1971; 1 dau., Maura Kathleen. Adminstrv. asst. to dir. product mgmt. Thomas J. Lipton, Inc., Englewood Cliffs, N.J., 1972-75, adminstrv. asst. to exec. v.p. mktg., 1975-78, consumer promotions adminstr., 1979, sales promotion analyst, 1979-83; prof. Edward William Coll., Fairleigh Dickinson U., 1983—. Republican. Roman Catholic. Office: Edward Williams Coll 150 Kotte Pl Hackensack NJ 07601

NUGENT, NELLE, theatrical producer; b. Jersey City, May 24, 1939; d. John Patrick and Evelyn Adelaide (Stern) N.; B.S., Skidmore Coll., 1960, L.H.D. (hon.), 1981; m. Jolyon Fox Stern, Apr. 7, 1982. Stage mgr. off-Broadway, N.Y.C., 1960-63, Broadway, 1964-69; v.p. prodn. services Theatre Now, Inc., N.Y.C., 1968-70; assoc. mng. dir. Nederlander Orgn., N.Y.C., 1970-76; chmn. McCann and Nugent Prodns., Inc., N.Y.C., 1976—; pres. Foxboro Prodns. Inc., 1986—; producer Dracula, The Elephant Man, Mornings at Seven, Home, Amadeus, Piaf, Rose, Nicholas Nickleby, The Dresser, Mass Appeal, Pilobolus, All's Well that Ends Well, Good, Total Abandon, Pacific Overtures (revival), Painting Churches, The Glass Menagerie (revival), The Lady and the Clarinet, Cyrano de Bergerac, Much Ado About Nothing, Leader of the Pack; ind. producer TV Spls. Mornings at Seven, Piaf, Pilobolus Ballet Co., CBS Video, film A Fighting Choice (Walt Disney prodns.), 1986. Voting mem. Blue Cross-Blue Shield; bd. visitors Syracuse U.; bd. dirs. League N.Y. Theatres. Recipient Tony awards for Dracula, The Elephant Man, Mornings at Seven, Amadeus, Nicholas Nickleby; N.Y. Drama Critics award for The Elephant Man, Nicholas Nickleby; Drama Desk awards for Amadeus, The Elephant Man, Nicholas Nickleby; obie award Painting Churches; Los Angeles Critics awards; Entrepreneurial Woman of Yr. award, 1981; Woman of Achievement, N.Y. Women's Republican Club, 1986. Office: Foxboro Productions Inc 130 E 67th St New York NY 10021

NUGENT, VERNA LOUISE, utility engineer; b. Dallas, Oct. 4, 1940; d. Cecil Edward and Neva (Snow) Holden; m. Donald Ray Ancelin, Jan. 30, 1959 (div. 1968); children—Brian, Babbette; m. 2d, David Nugent, Jan. 16, 1969; children—Steven, Sharon. B.A. in Polit. Sci., U. Tex., 1980, M.A. in Criminal Justice, 1985. Sec. Tex. Power and Light Co., Dallas, 1958-59; draftsman Southwestern Bell Telephone Co., Mineral Wells, Tex., 1968-69; engr. drafting Plant Service Co., Ft. Worth, 1970-83; engr. Apollo Cable Co., Ft. Worth, 1982-83; utility engr. Plant Service Co. and Tel-Plant Design Co., Ft. Worth, 1982—. Active Boy Scouts Am. Mem. Phi Theta Kappa, Alpha Chi. Republican. Roman Catholic. Club: Arlington Music. Home: 1024 Clemson Dr Arlington TX 76012

NUNEZ, JOSEPHINE OROZCO, college administrator; b. San Antonio, Oct. 29, 1932; d. Joe M. and Juanita (Linares) Orozco; student St. Mary's U., 1969, Dyer Sch. Real Estate, 1969, Our Lady of the Lake U., 1976; m. Ruben R. Nunez, May 13, 1978; children—Pete, Michael Anthony, Mary Elizabeth Mazuca. With A.B. Frank Wholesale, San Antonio, 1951-55; sec. Fireman & Policeman Assn., San Antonio, 1961-62, Teamsters Local 657, San Antonio, 1962-65, Cath. Chancery Office, San Antonio, 1965-68; with St. Mary's U., San Antonio, 1968-71, exec. sec. Office Mex.-Am. Studies, also asst. coordinator new careers program, 1969-70; with Our Lady of the Lake U., San Antonio, 1971—, adminstrv. asst., 1978—; bookkeeper Title XX, Tex. Dept. Human Resources Project, 1978-81, adminstrv. asst., 1982—. Active Democratic Women of Bexar County, 1962-68, Our Lady of Pillar Christian Renewal Center, 1966-70; exec. dir. Addiction Research Commn., Our Lady of Mt. Carmel Hosp., Austin, 1972-73; treas. Archdiocesan Credit Union, 1975-76; bd. dirs. King William Assn., San Antonio, 1978—, treas., 1981—; mem. Our Lady of the Lake U. Non-Acad. Personnel Council, 1977-78, staff orgn., 1971—, Bed and Breakfast of San Antonio, 1983—; Co-chmn. St. Mary's Ch. Tex. Irish Festival, 1985, Chmn., 1986; active United Way. NIH grantee, 1971. Roman Catholic. Home: 325 Madison San Antonio TX 78204 Office: Worden Sch Social Service 411 SW 24th St Worden Sch San Antonio TX 78285

NUNEZ, YOLANDA RULL, accountant; b. Havanna, Cuba, Oct. 6, 1952; came to U.S., 1966, naturalized, 1976; d. Miguel Angel and Yolanda (Suarez) Gonzalez; m. Victor J. Nunez, June 26, 1976; 1 child, Sergio. B.S., U. Ill., 1979. Acct., O.M.A.R., Inc., Chgo., 1977—, full charge bookkeeper, 1971-77, office mgr. supr., 1982—, office mgr., 1981-82; acct. WBBS-TV Sta./Channel 60, Chgo., 1979-83, Hat-Co, Chgo., 1978—; keypuncher/data processing social sci. dept. Northwestern U., Evanston, Ill., 1969; research-field work supr. O.M.A.R., Inc., Chgo., 1968-69, audio technician, 1972-73; asst. radio producer Buenos Dias Chgo. Radio Program WEDC, Chgo., 1969-70; treas. Cuban Am. C. of C. Credit Union, Chgo., 1975-76. Mem. Ctr. for Research and Polit. Leadership, Chgo., 1967-82; mem., bookkeeper Cuban Intellectuals for the Liberty of Cuba, 1979-80. Recipient award H. Whitney MacMillan Co., Chgo., 1983. Roman Catholic. Home: 7657 Long St Skokie IL 60077 Office: OMAR Inc 5525 N Broadway Chicago IL 60640

NUNN, BARBARA ELAINE, educator; b. Washington, Mar. 14, 1947; d. Charles Edward Nunn and Elsie Eunice (Smith) Press. B.A., U. Fla., 1969; M.Ed., U. Miami, 1975. Tchr. math. Miami Sr. High Sch., 1969-76, Coral Springs High Sch., Fla., 1976-82, Taravella High Sch., Coral Springs, 1982-83, Coral Springs High Sch., 1983—; coordinator high sch. summer math inst. Broward County Schs., Ft. Lauderdale, 1984, 85; speaker in field. Named Broward County High Sch. Math. Tchr. of Yr., Broward County Council Tchrs. Math., 1985; state finalist Presdl. award for excellence in math. teaching, 1984, 85. Mem. Fla. Council Tchrs. Math. (pres. 1981), Broward County Council Tchrs. Math. (pres. 1977-78), Nat. Council Tchrs. Math., Delta Kappa Gamma (chpt. pres. 1984-86), Phi Delta Kappa. Democrat. Presbyterian. Home: 8821 Hampshire Dr #204 Coral Springs FL 33065 Office: Coral Springs High Sch 7201 W Sample Rd Coral Springs FL 33065

NURMELA, CATHERINE ANN, nurse; b. Marquette, Mich., July 15, 1953; d. Peter Marcus and Gladys Geraldine (Nopola) N. A.A., Suomi Coll., Hancock, Mich., 1973; B.A., St. Olaf Coll., 1975; B.S.N., Idaho State U., 1980. Charge nurse Bannock Meml. Hosp., Pocatello, Idaho, 1980-81; nurse St. Joseph Hosp., Chgo., 1981-84, nursing quality assurance nurse, 1984-84, diabetic instr., 1984-86; instr. risk factors and heart disease, 1986—, also cardiac rehab. nurse educator. Mem. Am. Nurses Assn., Ill. Nurses Assn., Ill. Assn. Quality Assurance Profls. Democrat. Lutheran. Home: 3621 N Pine Grove Chicago IL 60613 Office: St Joseph Hosp 2900 N Lake Shore Dr Chicago IL 60657

NUSIM, ROBERTA, publisher, educator; b. N.Y.C., Dec. 1, 1943; d. Seymour and Ranna (Weiner) N.; m. Stephen Jablonsky, Aug. 29, 1965. B.A. in English, CCNY, 1964; M.A. in English, CUNY, 1966. Tchr., N.Y.C. Bd. Edn., 1964-73; v.p. program devel. Mind, Inc., Westport, Conn., 1973-76; pres. Mind Media, Westport, 1976-78; founder, pres. Lifetime Learning Systems, Inc., Fairfield, Conn., 1978—. Author audio visual teaching programs. Editor: Let's Talk About Health, 1980. Camp dir. Lake Bryn Mawr Camp, Honesdale, Pa., 1968-71; founder, dir. The Film Study Guild, Fairfield, Conn., 1979—. Mem. Home Econs. in Bus., Am. Film Inst., Women in Communication. Jewish. Avocations: painting; photography; writing. Office: Lifetime Learning Systems Inc 36 Sanford St Fairfield CT 06430

NUSSDORF, GERRIE E., psychologist; b. Bklyn., Feb. 2, 1944; d. Edith Posner and Oscar Nussdorf. Ph.D. in Psychology, Fordham U., 1975; cert. psychoanalysis and psychotherapy Postgrad. Center for Mental Health, 1981. Computer programmer, 1966-69; psychology intern Fairfield Hills Hosp., Newtown, Conn., 1972-73; staff psychologist Nyack (N.Y.) Cons. Center, 1975-78; asso. psychologist Rockland Psychiat. Center, Orangeburg, N.Y., 1978-80; therapist, tng. candidate adult program Postgrad. Center Mental Health, N.Y.C., 1977-81; prin. psychologist Manhattan Psychiat. Center, N.Y.C., 1980—; pvt. practice, N.Y.C., 1981—; adj. instr. psychology Marymount Manhattan Coll., 1974; tri-state coordinator Assn. Women in Psychology, 1975, 76. NDEA Title IV teaching fellow, 1969-72; Regents scholar, 1961-65. Mem. Am. Psychol. Assn., Assn. Women in Psychology, Eastern Psychol. Assn., Postgrad. Center Mental Health Psychoanalytic Soc., Austin Healey Club Am., Sports Car Club Am. Home: 305 W 13th St New York NY 10014 Office: Dept Psychology Manhattan Psychiatric Center Wards Island New York NY 10035

NUTT, ANNE BAILEY, aerospace company community relations executive; b. Los Angeles, Oct. 16, 1940; d. Wilbur and Margaret (Robinson) Bailey; m. Stephen Douglas Nutt, Sept. 1, 1962 (div. Nov. 1982); children—Elizabeth Anne, Kathleen Margaret. B.A. in Polit. Sci., Stanford U., 1962; M.S. in Library Sci., U. So. Calif., 1968. Asst. to office mgr. Forster Gemmill & Farmer, Los Angeles, summers 1959, 60, 65; elem. asst. Agnes Irwin Sch., Rosemont, Pa., 1963-64; research asst. to law librarian Stanford U. Law Sch., Palo Alto, Calif., 1966-67; jr. museum librarian Met. Mus. Art, N.Y.C., 1971-74; intern in pub. affairs Coro Found., Orange County, Calif., 1979; mgr. community relations Northrop Corp., Anaheim, Calif., 1982—. Bd. dirs. Jr. League, N.Y.C., 1974-76, chairperson provisional tng., 1974-76, bd. dirs., Newport Harbor, Calif., 1976-82, rec. sec., 1978-79, pres., 1981-82; mem. Area VI council Assn. Jr. Leagues, 1980-81, editor child advocacy programs, 1980-81; v.p. devel. Orange County Arts Alliance, 1982-84, v.p. planning and bus. affairs, 1984-86; mem. agy. relations com. United Way Orange County, 1982—, chairperson info. and referral task force, 1983—; v.p. bd. dirs. New Directions for Women, Inc., Costa Mesa, Calif., 1982-85; mem. women's exec. cabinet Orange County chpt. March of Dimes, 1982—; chairperson adv. council for furniture and equipment for non-profits Vol. Ctrs. Orange County, 1983-86; bd. dirs. Performing Arts Assn. Orange County, 1983—, now v.p. nominating com.; mem. adv. com. Tech. Exchange Ctr., 1984—; mem. adv. bd. North Orange County YWCA, 1984-86; mem. Orange County Needs Assessment Adv. Com., 1984—; mem. mktg. com. Exploratory Learning Ctr., Santa Ana, Calif., 1983-86, mem. adv. com., 1986—; pres. Red Ribbon 100 chpt. ARC, 1985-86; chair silver medallion recognition YWCA, 1985-86. Recipient cert. appreciation and recognition N.Y. State Dept. Correction, 1975, cert. merit Orange County Bd. Suprs., 1982, Outstanding Service award Orange County Arts Alliance, 1983. Mem. Orange County C. of C. (bd. dirs. 1985—), Orange County Community Relations Council (pres. 1985-86), Corp. Vol. Council Los Angeles/Orange County, ALA. Republican. Presbyterian. Office: Northrop Corp ElectroMech Div 500 E Orangethorpe Anaheim CA 92801

NYCUM, SUSAN HUBBELL, lawyer; B.A., Ohio Wesleyan U., 1956; J.D., Duquesne U., 1960. Admitted to Pa. bar, 1962, Calif. bar, 1974, U.S. Supreme Ct. bar, 1967; individual practice law, Pitts., 1962-65; dir. computerized research systems for lawyers U. Pitts./Aspen Systems Corp., Pitts., 1965-68; mgr. ops. and user services Carnegie Mellon U. Computer Cr., 1968-69; dir. Stanford U. Computer Cr., 1969-72; law and computer fellow Stanford U. Law Sch., 1972-73; cons. computers and law, San Francisco, 1973-74; assoc. firm MacLeod Fuller Muir & Godwin, Los Altos, Calif., 1974-75; partner firm Chickering & Gregory, practicing gen. bus. law with emphasis on computers, San Francisco, 1975-80; partner firm Gaston Snow & Ely Bartlett, Boston, Palo Alto, Miami, N.Y.C. and Washington, 1980—; co-prin. investigator study on computer abuse NSF, 1972—; mem. adv. bd. for math. and computer sci. NSF; area dir. all law related session Nat. Computer Confs., 1975, 78, 80, 81; lectr. Practising Law Inst., 1975—; mem. panel on transborder data flow Am. Fedn. Info. Processing Socs., 1979-80; chmn. Office Tech. Assessment Task Force on Nat. Info. Systems, 1979-80. Chmn. evening div. Jr. League Palo Alto (Calif.), 1975-76; mem. Town of Portola Valley (Calif.) Open Space Acquisition Com., 1977. Mem. Am. Bar Assn. (chmn. sect. sci. and tech. 1979-80), Internat. Bar Assn., Assn. Computing Machinery (chmn. standing com. legal issues 1975—, mem.-at-large council 1976—, nat. lectr. 1977—), Computer law Assn. (dir. 1975—, v.p. 1984, pres. 1985-86), Calif. State Bar Assn. (chmn. com. law and computers 1977-78, founder and 1st chmn. sect. econs. of law 1978-79), EDUCOM (trustee 1978—), Nat. Conf. Lawyers and Scientists, Peninsula Profl. Women's Network, DAR, Mortar Bd., Phi Beta Kappa, Delta Sigma Rho, Pi Sigma Alpha, Pi Delta Epsilon. Author: Your Computer and the Law, 1975; Protection of Proprietary Interests in Computer Software, 1981; contbr. articles to profl. jours. Office: 660 Hansen Way Palo Alto CA 94304

NYE, MIRIAM MAURINE BAKER, writer; b. Castana, Iowa, June 14, 1918; d. Horace Boies and Hazel Dean (Waples) Hawthorn; B.A., Morningside Coll., 1939, postgrad., 1957-58; postgrad. U. Ariz., 1973, U. S.D., 1975-77, New Coll., U. Edinburgh (Scotland), 1974; m. Carl E. Baker, June 21, 1941 (dec. 1970); children—Kent Alfred, Dale Hawthorn; m. 2d, John Arthur Nye, Dec. 25, 1973. Tchr. jr. high sch., Rock Falls, Ill., 1939-41, Moville (Iowa) Community Sch., 1957-62, Woodbury Central Community Sch., Climbing Hill, Iowa, 1962-64; homemaking columnist Sioux City (Iowa) Jour.'s Farm Weekly, 1953-81; author: Recipes and Ideas From the Kitchen Window, 1973; But I Never Thought He'd Die: Practical Help for Widows, 1978; speaker, Iowa, Nebr., Minn., S.D. Counselor, Iowa State U., 1972—; county adv. Iowa Children's and Family Services, 1980-84; mem. public relations com. Farm Bur., Woodbury County, 1980-82; lay del. Iowa United Meth. Conf., 1981-83. Recipient Alumni award Morningside Coll., 1969, Service award Woodbury County Fair, 1969, Friend of Extension award Iowa State U., 1981. Mem. AAUW, Iowa Fedn. Women's Clubs (dist. creative writing chmn. 1978-80), Common Cause, Alpha Kappa Delta, Sigma Tau Delta. Methodist. Home and Office: Box 193 Route 2 Moville IA 51039

NYE, SANDRA GAYLE, lawyer, psychiatric social worker, consultant; b. Chgo., Jan. 12, 1935; d. Harry A. and Mildred (Blumenthal) Iseberg; children—Elizabeth Robin, Jonathan Douglas. J.D., DePaul U., 1962; M.S.W., Loyola U.-Chgo., 1974. Bar: Ill. 1963, U.S. Dist. Ct. (no. dist.) Ill. 1966, U.S. Supreme Ct. 1967. Ptnr., Nye and Nye, Chgo., 1962-74; dir. child and family law and psychiatry Inst. Juvenile Research, Chgo., 1974-78; dir. legal services Jewish Family and Community Services, Chgo., 1978-80; dir. Ill. Guardianship and Advocacy Commn., 1979-82; pres. Nye, Brent & Shoenberger, Ltd., Chgo., 1982-85, Sandra G. Nye & Assocs., Chgo., 1985—; asst. prof. psychiatry Abraham Lincoln Sch. Medicine, U. Ill., Chgo., 1978—; mem. faculty Inst. for Family Studies, Northwestern U. Sch. Medicine. Mem. com. on confidentiality Ill. Gov.'s Commn. to Revise the Mental Health Code, 1976-77; mem. Ill. Commn. on Children-Com. on Youth and the Law, 1975-79; mem. Oak Park (Ill.) Beautification Commn., 1969-73. Mem. ABA (chmn. mental health law com., family law sect.), Ill. State Bar Assn., Chgo. Bar Assn. (chmn. juvenile law com.), Women's Bar Assn., Am. Soc. Law and Medicine, Am. Orthopsychiat. Assn., Am. Assn. Psychiat. Services for Children. Home: 1150 N Lake Shore Dr Chicago IL 60611 Office: 180 N Michigan Ave Suite 1605 Chicago IL 60601

NYEPAH, SHIRLEY IRVING THIGPEN, financial executive; b. Tuskegee, Ala., Apr. 18, 1946; d. Victor W. and Mary Magdeline (Ashford) Irving; children—Arenza Thigpen, Jr., Mary Victoria Irving. B.A., U. Ala.-Tuscaloosa, 1979; M.Ed., Tuskegee U., 1985. Journalist, columnist NNPA, Washington, 1979—; pianist/recording artists, various cities, 1979—; profl. sec. various instns., Tuskegee, Washington, 1962—; pres., founder Sound of Tuskegee, Inc., Ala., 1984—, Fin. Aid Resources, Tuskegee, 1980—; fin. aid cons.; sec. Serenity Services, Tuskegee, 1985—; staff writer Tuskegee News, 1985—. Contbg. editor Core mag., 1974, 83. Contbr. articles to profl. jours. Charter mem. Republican Presdl. Task Force, Washington, 1984—, Presdl. Commn., 1986; mem. Nat. Conservative Polit. Action Com., Alexandria, Va., 1985—, Am. Inst. Cancer Research, Washington, 1984—, Africare steering com., 1976. Mem. Nat. Assn. Female Execs., Kappa Delta Pi. Baptist. Home: 1602 Notasulga Rd Tuskegee AL 36083 Office: Office of Financial Aid Old Administration Bldg Tuskegee Univ Tuskegee AL 36088

NYGAARD, LINDA ANN, nursing administrator; b. Minot, N.D., Nov. 8, 1948; d. Clayton M. Fjeld and Tillie (Geiser) Fjeld Ringdahl; m. Tyrone Keith Nygaard, July 12, 1969; children—Christopher, Adam. Diploma in Nursing with honors, Sisters St. Francis, 1969; B.A. in Nursing summa cum laude, Jamestown Coll., 1984. Staff nurse cardiac care unit St. Joseph's Hosp., Minot, N.D., 1969-71; charge nurse intensive care unit and cardiac care unit Air Force Regional Hosp., Minot, 1971-73; dir. nursing Dunseith Nursing Home, N.D., 1973-75; asst. dir. nursing Chem. Dependency Unit, N.D. State Hosp., Jamestown, 1975—. Tchr. Trinity Lutheran Ch., Jamestown, 1982, 85, edn. com., 1985; speaker's bur. Jamestown C. of C., 1985. Recipient Student Nurse of Yr. award Mouse River Dist. Student Nurses Assn., 1969. Mem. N.D. Nurses Assn. (fin. com. 1979), AAUW, N.D. Pub. Employees Assn. Avocations: reading; camping; racquetball; fishing. Home: 421 6th St SE Jamestown ND 58401

NYLEN, MARIE USSING, government health research administrator; b. Copenhagen, Apr. 13, 1924; m. 1956; 3 children. D.D.S., Royal Dental Coll. Denmark, 1947, D.Odontologiae honoris causa, 1973. Individual practice dentistry, 1947-48; instr. ops. Royal Dental Coll., 1948-49, asst. prof. oral diagnosis, 1951-55; guest worker dental histology Nat. Inst. Dental Research, 1949-50, vis. assoc. biophysics, 1955-60, biologist, 1960-65; acting chief Lab. Histology and Pathology, 1965-69, chief Lab. Biol. Structure HEW, 1969-76, assoc. dir. intramural research, from 1976, now assoc. dir. extramural research. Recipient Superior Service Honor award HEW, 1969, Fed. Womans award HEW, 1975. Fellow AAAS, Am. Coll. Dentists; mem. Electron Microscopy Soc., Am. Dental Assn., Internat. Assn. Dental Research (pres. Washington sect. 1971-72, mem. exhibits com. 1971—, mem. sr. fgn. dental scientist com. 1972—, (chmn. local arrangements com. 1972-73), Internat. Assn. Dental Research (chmn. ad hoc com. consideration tooth designation 1972-73, research award 1970), Danish Dental Assn. Nordic Odontologic Assn., Fedn. Dentaire Internat., Washington Soc. Electron Microscopy (sec. treas. 1962-65), Am. Soc. Cell Biology, Am. Assn. Anatomists, Scandinavian Soc. Forensic Odontology, Am. Soc. Forensic Odontology, D.D. Ash Pathology Club (hon.). Office: Nat Inst Dental Research 9000 Rockville Pike Bethesda MD 20892

NYQUIST, IRENE MAE, patent information specialist; b. Washington, Feb. 18, 1931; d. Leo Wilfred and Susan (Cox) Cote; m. Richard Allen Nyquist, Jan. 28, 1956; children—Richard H., Jean, Kathryn, Robert. B.S., St. John's U., N.Y., 1952; M.S., U. Minn., 1955; M.A., Central Mich. U., 1974. Chemist, Dow Chem. Co., Midland, Mich., 1955-57, office supr. legal dept., 1975-80, patent info. specialist, 1980—. Mem. curriculum council Midland Pub. Schs., 1973-77, sec., 1974-76; mem. Midland Community Relations Commn., 1977-83. Fulbright scholar U. Reading, Eng., 1953-54. Mem. Saginaw Valley Patent Law Assn., Am. Chem. Soc., Sigma Xi. Democrat. Lutheran. Avocations: travel; photography; philately. Home: 3707 Westbrier Terr Midland MI 48640 Office: Dow Chem Co Patent Dept 1776 Bldg Midland MI 48640

OAKAR, MARY ROSE, congresswoman; b. Cleve., Mar. 5, 1940; d. Joseph and Margaret Oakar; B.A. in English, Speech and Drama, Ursuline Coll., Cleve., 1962; M.A. in English, John Carroll U., Cleve., 1966; postgrad. Royal Acad. Dramatic Arts, London, Eng., Westham Adult Coll., Warwickshire, Eng., Columbia U.; L.H.D. (hon.), Ursuline Coll., LL.D. (hon.), Ashland Coll. Instr. English and drama Lourdes Acad., Cleve., 1963-70; asst. prof. English, speech and drama Cuyahoga Community Coll., Cleve., 1968-75; mem. 95th-99th Congresses from 20th Ohio Dist., mem. Banking, Fin. and Urban Affairs Com., Select Com. on Aging, Post Office and Civil Service Com., House Adminstrn. Com.; co-chmn. Task Force Employment and Tng., Northeast-Midwest Congl. Coalition; mem. Nat. Commn. on Unemployment Compensation. City councilwoman, Cleve., 1973-76; Democratic state central committeewoman 20th Dist., 1974-76; trustee Fedn. for Community Planning, Health and Planning Commn., Community Info. Service, Soc. for Crippled Children, YWCA, Cuyahoga Community Coll., Cleve. Ballet; adv. Com. Mothers Against Drunk Drivers, Sr. Citizens Resources Inc., Overseas Edn. Fund. Recipient Outstanding Service award OEO, 1973-75, Community Service awards Am. Indian Center, 1973, Nationalities Services Center, 1974, Club San Lorenzo, 1976; named Ursuline Coll. Alumni of Yr., 1977, Cuyahoga County Dem. Woman of Yr., 1977, knight Order St. Ladislaus, 1980, One of Ten Best Legislators, 50+ Mag.; Woman of Yr., Cuyahoga County Women's Polit. Caucus, 1983. Office: 2436 Rayburn House Office Bldg Washington DC 20515

OAKLEY, DEBORAH JANE, researcher, educator; b. Detroit, Jan. 31, 1937; d. George F. and Kathryn (Willson) Hacker; B.A., Swarthmore Coll., 1958; M.A., Brown U., 1960; M.P.H., U. Mich., 1969, Ph.D., 1977; m. Bruce Oakley, June 16, 1958; children—Ingrid Andrea, Brian Benjamin. Dir. teenage and adult programs YWCA, Providence, 1959-63; editorial asst. Stockholm U., 1963-64; research investigator, lectr. dept. population planning U. Mich., 1971-77; asst. prof. community health programs U. Mich., Ann Arbor, 1977-79, asst. prof. nursing research, 1979-81, asso. prof., 1981—. Trustee, Womens Health Research Inst., 1981—. Recipient Margaret Sanger award Washtenaw County Planned Parenthood, 1975; Outstanding Young Woman of Ann Arbor award Jaycees, 1970. Mem. Am. Public Health Assn. (chmn. population sect. council), Internat. Union Sci. Study Population, Midwest Nursing Research Soc., Population Assn. Am., Delta Omega. Democrat. Author: (with Leslie Corsa) Population Planning, 1979; contbr. articles to profl. jours. Home: 5200 S Lake Rd Chelsea MI 48118 Office: Sch Nursing U Mich Ann Arbor MI 48109

OAKLEY, MARY ANN BRYANT, lawyer; b. Buckhannon, W.Va., June 22, 1940; d. Hubert Herndon and Mary F. (Deeds) Bryant; m. Godfrey P. Oakley, Jr., Sept. 2, 1961; children—Martha, Susan, Robert. A.B., Duke U., 1962; M.A., Emory U., 1970, J.D., 1974. Tchr., Winston-Salem/Forsyth County Schs., N.C., 1961-65; assoc. Margie Pitts Hames, Atlanta, 1974-80; ptnr. Stagg Hoy & Oakley, Atlanta, 1980-83, Oakley & Bonner, Atlanta, 1984—. Contbr. articles to law jours. Notes and Comments editor Emory Law Jour., 1973-74. Author: Elizabeth Cady Stanton, 1972; Bd. dirs. Atlanta Met. YWCA, 1975-79, 1st v.p., 1976-77; mem. Leadership Atlanta, 1979; bd. dirs. Ga. chpt. ACLU, 1981-83; trustee Unitarian Universalist Congregation Atlanta, 1977-80, pres., 1979-80, mem. Unitarian Universalist Commn. Appraisal, 1980-85; bd. dirs. Unitarian Universalist Service Com., 1984—. Nat. Merit scholar, 1958. Mem. ABA, Am. Judicature Soc., State Bar Ga. (chmn. individual rights sect. 1979-81, chmn. bench and bar com. 1984—), Atlanta Bar Assn., Lawyers Club Atlanta, No. Dist. Bar Council, Ga. Assn. Women Lawyers, Ga. State Bar Disciplinary Bd., Ga. Women's Polit. Caucus, LWV, Phi Beta Kappa, Order of Coif. Home: 897 Barton Woods Rd NE Atlanta GA 30307 Office: 133 Carnegie Way Suite 508 Atlanta GA 30303

OATES, JOYCE CAROL, author; b. Lockport, N.Y., June 16, 1938; d. Frederic James and Caroline (Bush) Oates; B.A., Syracuse U., 1960; M.A., U. Wis., 1961; m. Raymond Joseph Smith, Jan. 23, 1961. Prof. English, U. Detroit, 1961-67, U. Windsor (Ont., Can.), from 1967; vis. prof. English, Princeton U., 1978—. Mem. Am. Acad. and Inst. Arts and Letters. Recipient O. Henry Prize Story award, 1967-68. Guggenheim fellow, 1967-68. Author: (stories) By The North Gate, 1963; (play) The Sweet Enemy, 1965; (novel) With Shuddering Fall, 1965; (stories) Upon the Sweeping Flood, 1966; (novel) A Garden of Earthly Delights, 1967; (poems) Women in Love, 1968; Expensive People, 1968; Them, 1969; (poems) Anonymous Sins, 1969; (stories) The Wheel of Love, 1970; (poems) Love and its Derangements, 1970; (novel) Wonderland, 1971; (essays) The Edge of Impossibility, 1971; (stories) Marriages and Infidelities, 1972; (poems) Angel Fire, 1973; (novel) Do With Me What You Will, 1973; (play) Sunday Dinner, produced at Am. Place Theatre, 1970; (essays) The Hostile Sun; The Poetry of D.H. Lawrence, 1973; (poems) Dreaming America, 1973; (stories) The Hungry Ghosts, 1974; (stories) The Goddess and other Women, 1974; (essays) New Heaven, New Earth, 1974; (play) Miracle Play, 1974; (stories) Where Are You Going, Where Have You Been, 1974; (stories) The Poisoned Kiss and Other Portuguese Stories, 1975; (stories) The Seduction and Other Stories, 1975; (novel) The Assassins, 1975; (stories) Crossing the Border, 1976; (novels) Childwold, 1976, The Triumph of the Spider Monkey, 1977; (stories) Night-Side, 1977; (novel) Son of the Morning, 1978; Unholy Loves, 1979; Bellefleur, 1980; (play) Daisy (prod. Cubiculo Theatre N.Y.C.) 1980; A Sentimental Education, 1981; Contraries: Essays, 1981; (novels) Angel of Light, 1981, A Bloodsmoor Romance, 1982; Mysteries of Winterthurn, 1984, Last Days, 1984, Solstice, 1985, Marya: A Life, 1986; editor: Scenes from American Life, 1973, Ont. Rev.; The Best American Short Stories, 1979; also fiction in nat. mags. Recipient Nat. Book award for Them, 1970. Mem. Phi Beta Kappa. Office: Princeton U Creative Writing Program 185 Nassau St Princeton NJ 08540*

OATES, LOUISE ELIZABETH, lawyer; b. Lake Charles, La., Aug. 16, 1945; d. Lewis and Elizabeth (Baker) Conn; m. Gary David Oates, Dec. 4, 1980; Traci Yvonne Conn, Jeffrey David, Jacque. B. Law, Lincoln U., 1978. Bar: Calif. 1978. Sec. UTC, Sunnyvale, Calif., 1966-75; legal sec. Grogan, Vogelgesang & von Dioszeghy, Campbell, Calif., 1975-76; paralegal Berliner, Cohen & Biagini, San Jose, Calif., 1976-78, assoc., 1978-79; sole practice, Los Gatos, Calif., 1979—. Mem. ABA, Santa Clara County Bar Assn., West Valley Bar Assn. Club: Los Gatos Yacht (treas. 1983-84). Office: 20S Santa Cruz Ave Suite 102 Los Gatos CA 95030

OATES, VIRGINIA, educator; b. Shelby, N.C., Nov. 28, 1946; d. Charles Melawyer and Lucy (Hunter) O. B.S., A&T State U.-Greensboro, N.C.; M.Ed., Temple U.; Ph.D., U. Conn., 1979. Adminstrv. asst. Univ. Hosp., Phila., 1966-68; tng. specialist Temple U. Health Scis. Ctr., Phila., 1968-73; Ednl. Profs., Devel. fellow U. Conn., Storrs, 1973-74, 75-76, profl. asst. to v.p. student affairs, 1978; staff asst. to vice chancellor acad. affairs Mass. State Bd. Edn., Boston, 1976-77; assoc. dir. and cons. dept. social adminstrn. Temple U.,

Phila., 1980-82; prof. Massasoit Community Coll., Brockton, Mass., 1982-84; chief asst. to pres. for instl. aid programs Johnson C. Smith Univ., Charlotte, N.C., 1984—; cons. Rafkin & Keels, Phila., Chmn., Jimmy Carter 53.8% Com., Brockton, 1978; mem. Brockton Health Council, 1978; mem. Democratic Women's Assn.; founder Garden of Eden Bus. Enterprises. Recipient Four Chaplains Legion of Honor award, Phila., 1983. Mem. Am. Pub. Health Assn., Am. Assn. Higher Edn., Am. Vocat. Assn., Am. Coll. Health Assn., Brockton C. of C. Club: Pinochle Bridge and Tennis. Home: 825 N Morgan St Shelby NC 28150 Office: Johnson C Smith Univ Charlotte NC 28216

OATEY, JENNIFER SUE, recreational sports adminstr.; b. Rochester, Minn., Aug. 30, 1949; d. Elwyn Brown and Phyllis Eileen (Quammen) Larson. B.S., N. Mex. State U., 1971, M.A.T., 1973; Ph.D. in Edn., U. Minn., 1981. Asst. dir. recreational sports U. Mich., Ann Arbor, 1976-77; intramural supr. Stephen Austin State U., Nacogdoches, Tex., 1975-76; campus center coordinator Brainerd (Minn.) Community Coll., 1974-75; phys. edn. instr., asst. intramural dir. N.Mex. State U., Las Cruces, 1973-74; assoc. dir. recreational sports U. Minn., Mpls., 1977—. Bd. dirs. Univ. YWCA, 1981-83, Minn. Council on Health, 1983—; mem. Minn. Gov.'s Council in Health Promotion and Wellness, 1982-83. Mem. Nat. Intramural-Recreational Sports Assn. (dir. Minn. 1977-81, mem. editorial bd. Jour., 1981—), Can. Intramural Recreation Assn., Sons of Norway, U. Minn. Alumni Assn., Phi Theta Kappa. Lutheran. Home: 333 Oak Grove Apt 308 Minneapolis MN 55403 Office: 108 Cooke Hall U Minn Minneapolis MN 55455

O'BANNION, MINDY MARTHA MARTIN, nurse; b. Cushing, Okla., Aug. 19, 1953; d. John William and Martha Florence (Vineyard) Martin; student Okla. State U., 1971-73, Oscar Rose Jr. Coll., 1973; grad. St. Anthony Sch. Nursing, 1975; m. William Neal O'Bannion, Oct. 9, 1976; children—Mindi Martha Mae, William Neale Aaron. Nursing asst. Cushing Mcpl. Hosp., 1973-75, head nurse surg. floor, 1975-76, charge nurse med. unit, 1978-79, 82-83; staff nurse Met. Hosp., Dallas, 1985; staff nurse med. unit Mesquite Community Hosp., Tex., 1985—. Mem. social com. Royal Haven Bapt. Ch. Women's Missionary Union, Dallas, 1977-78; mem. extension dept. nursery First Bapt. Ch., Cushing, 1979-82, extension dept. presch., 1982—; treas., mem. nominating com. Joyce Harms group Women's Missionary Union. Mem. Am., Tex., Okla. State nurses assns., St. Anthony Hosp. Sch. Nursing Alumnae, Alpha Xi Delta (corr. sec. 1973), Tau Beta Sigma. Baptist. Home: 2939 Oxfordshire Ln Farmers Branch TX 75234

O'BANNON, DONNA M. EDWARDS, lawyer; b. N.Y.C., June 26, 1957; d. Theodore U. and Ione Louise (Dunkley) Edwards; m. Don T. O'Bannon, Jr., Dec. 11, 1982. B.A. in Econs., Wellesley Coll., 1979; J.D., U. Va., 1982. Bar: Tex. 1982. Tax atty. Exxon Co., Houston, 1982—. Contbr. article to law jour. Bd. dirs. Parents Anonymous of Houston, 1984—. Mem. Tex. Bar Assn., Houston Bar Assn., Houston Lawyers Assn., Houston Barristers Wives Assn. Office: Exxon Co PO Box 392 Houston TX 77001

OBARA, PATRICIA EVELYN, banker, lawyer; b. Springfield, Mass., Sept. 26, 1952; d. Adam John and Evelyn Victoria (Pazik) O.; m. Walter W. Wronka, Jr., Oct. 8, 1977; children—Matthew Obara, Marissa Obara. B.A., Colgate U., 1974; J.D., Rutgers U., 1977. Bar: N.J. 1977. Vice-pres., asst. counsel, asst. sec. United Jersey Banks, Princeton, N.J., 1979—. Mem. ABA, N.J. Bar Assn., Somerset County Bar Assn., Princeton Bar Assn., Corp. Counsel Assn., Bank Counsel Group N.J., N.J. Bankers Assn. Roman Catholic. Office: United Jersey Banks PO Box 2066 Princeton NJ 08540

OBAYASHI, PATRICIA ANNE CHOW, dietitian; b. Los Angeles, Jan. 15, 1953; d. George Kazuo and Clara Hisae (Tsuchiyama) Obayashi; m. Patrick H.Y. Chow, Oct. 15, 1983. B.S., Calif. Poly. State U., 1975; M.S., U. Ariz., 1977; cert. in graphic design, U. Santa Cruz, 1984. Registered dietitian. Clin. dietitian Stanford U. Hosp., Calif., 1977—, chairperson edn. com., dept. dietetics, 1979-81. Mem. Calif. Dietetic Assn. (pub. chairperson 1982, resource panel 1985-86), Am. Dietetic Assn. (speaker, com. co-chairperson 1983; Recognized Young Dietitian of Yr. 1983), Am. Soc. Parenteral and Enteral Nutrition, Phi Upsilon Omicron. Avocations: cooking, travel, skiing, gardening, ballroom dancing. Office: Dept Dietetics C108 Stanford U Hosp Pasteur Dr Stanford CA 94305

OBENZA, LESLIE JARON, pediatrician; b. Camotes, Cebu, Philippines, Mar. 3, 1943; came to U.S., 1972, naturalized, 1980; d. Juan P. and Antonina Obenza. Student U. Visayas, Cebu City, Philippines, 1958 61; M.D., Cebu Inst. Tech. Coll. Medicine, 1966. Practice medicine, Philippines, 1966-72; house physician Hope Haven Children's Hosp., Jacksonville, Fla., 1973; rotating intern French Polyclinic Hosp., N.Y.C., 1973-74; rehab. medicine resident King's County Hosp., Bklyn., 1974-75; resident pediatrics U. Hosp. of Jacksonville, Fla., 1975-77; pediatrician March AFB, Riverside, Calif., 1977-80, Hillsborough County Health Dept., Tampa, Fla., 1981, N.Y.C. Health Dept., 1981—. Served to maj. M.C., USAF, 1977-80, Res., 1982—. Mem. Cebu Inst. Medicine Alumni Assn. Ea. U.S. Home: 250 Hampton Green Staten Island NY 10312 Office: City NY Dept Health 303 9th Ave New York NY 10001

OBERHAUSEN, JOYCE ANN, aircraft company executive; b. Plain Dealing, La., Nov. 12, 1941; d. George Dewey and Jettie Cleo (Farrington) Wynn; m. James J. Oberhausen, Oct. 15, 1966; 1 dau., Georgann; m. Dale Estein, Sept. 15, 1968 (div. 1960); children—Darla Renee Estein Oberhausen Minor, Dale Henry Estein Oberhausen. Student Ayers Bus. Sch., Shreveport, 1962-63, U. Ala., 1964-65. Stenographer, sec. Lincoln Nat. Life Co., Shreveport, 1965-66; sec. Baifield Industries, Shreveport, 1975-86; art tchr., Huntsville, Ala., 1974—; v.p. Precision Splty. Co., Huntsville, 1966—, Mil. Aircraft, Huntsville, 1979—; pres. Wynnson Enterprises, Huntsville, 1983—. Mgr. basketball team Meridianville, 1985-86. Mem. Internat. Porcelain Guild, Nat. Assn. Female Execs., People to People, porcelain Portrait Soc. Avocations; oil painting; antiques; handcrafts; gourmet cooking; horseback riding. Home: 156 Spencer Dr Meridianville AL 35759 Office: Precision Splty Corp 150 Wells Rd Meridianville AL 35759

OBERHOLTZER, CAROLE ANNE, sales engineer; b. Norristown, Pa., May 26, 1951; d. Michael Andrew Anthony Piekarski and Rita Felica (Szczesny) Hart; m. Gary Lee Oberholtzer, Aug. 29, 1970. Student Montgomery County Community Coll., BLue Bell, Pa., 1969-70, 76-78. Staff mem. Kelly Advtg. Co., Lancaster, Pa., 1973-75; bldg. mgr. and supr. Robertshaw Controls Co., King of Prussia, Pa., 1976-79, service and constrn. coordinator, 1979-81, sales engr., Norristown, Pa., 1981-85, sr. sales engr., 1985—; cons. State of Pa. energy grant applications, 1985—. Mem. Am. Inst. Plant Engrs. (bd. dirs. 1983—, treas. 1985-86, membership chmn. 1983—; cert. of appreciation 1984), Inst. Engrs., (Friends of Phila. Mus. Art). Republican. Roman Catholic. Avocations: golf; tennis; racquet ball; gourmet cooking. Home: 2276 Mulberry Ln Lafayette Hill PA 19444 Office: Robertshaw Controls Co 705 General Washington Ave Suite 210 Norristown PA 19406

OBERNDORFER, JANET, home economist; b. Flushing, N.Y., Jan. 6, 1941; d. Colonel Abbott and Molly Boone (Spencer) Oberndorfer. B.S. in Home Econs., U. R.I., 1963. Home Econs. tchr. Cen. Islip Sr. High Sch. (N.Y.), 1963-65; home economist Borden, Inc., N.Y.C., 1966-69; home economist Wheat Flour Inst., Chgo., 1970-72; mgr. home economics Sharp Electronics, Paramus, N.J., 1973; asst. to circulation dir. market letter Merrill Lynch et al, N.Y.C., 1974-80; pres. Lady Resourceful, Inc., Garden City, N.Y., 1980—. Mem. Garden City Hist. Soc. (N.Y.), 1982—; mem. Nat. Trust for Hist. Preservation, Washington, 1983—; mem. Met. Mus. Art, N.Y.C., 1983—; mem. North Shore Preservation Soc. Oyster Bay, N.Y., 1981-84. Named Honors Grad. Advt. Mktg. Edn. Advt. Club N.Y., 1970; appointee to advisory council Coll. Human Sci. Services U. R.I., Kingston, 1982. Mem. Home Economists in Bus., Am. Home Econs. Assn., N.Y. State Home Econs. Assn., Soc. for Nutrition Edn., Women in Communications. Club: Appalachian Mountain. (N.Y. Chpt.). Contbr. articles to mags. Office: Lady Resourceful Inc PO Box 7241 Garden City NY 11530

OBLINGER, JOSEPHINE KNEIDL HARRINGTON (MRS. WALTER L. OBLINGER), state agency administrator, former state legislator; b. Chgo., Feb. 14, 1913; d. Thomas William and Margaret (Kneidl) Harrington; B.S., U. Ill., 1933; LL.B., U. Detroit, 1943, J.D., 1977; L.H.D., Sioux Empire Coll., 1966; m. Walter L. Oblinger, Apr. 27, 1940; 1 son, Carl D. Tchr. Lanphier High Sch., Springfield, Ill., 1951-62; clk. Sangamon County, assessor Capital Twp., Springfield, 1962-69; asst. dir. Ill. Dept. Registration and Edn., Springfield, 1970—; mem. Ill. Ho. of Reps., 1978-85; dir. Gov.'s Office of Sr. Involvement, 1985—; exec. dir. Gov.'s Office of Vol. Action, 1970-73; asst. to pres. Lincoln Land Community Coll., 1973-77; dir. Ill. Dept. on Aging, 1977-78; adj. prof. gerontology Sangamon State U.; mem. Ill. Council on Aging; rep. nat. bd. Nat. Assn. State Units on Aging, HEW. Sec. Springfield and Sangamon County Community Action, 1965-70, pres., 1970-75, treas., 1975—; mem. fin. com. Child and Family Service, Springfield, 1965-71; mem. Sangamon County planning com. United Community Services, 1971—; mem. Urban League, 1955—, Nat. Com. for Day Care of Children, 1960—; bd. dirs. Nat. Center for Voluntary Action, 1971-77, RSVP (Ret. Sr. Vol. Program), Sangamon County Salvation Army, Ill. Council Continuing Higher Edn.; officer, Republican Women's Luncheon Club, 1959—, pres., 1963—; chmn. Sangamon County Rep. com., 1965—; 1st v.p. Ill. Fedn. Rep. Women, 1972, pres., 1974-76; del. Rep. Nat. Conv., 1972; del., chmn. older women's concerns com. White House Conf. on Aging, 1981—; mem. Fed. Council on Aging, 1981; bd. dirs., pres. Sangamon County Council on Alcoholism and Drugs, 1973-74; pres. Planning Consortium for Services to Children in Ill. Continuing Higher Edn., 1978; pres. Ill. State Enforcement Agys. to Recover Children, 1985—; mem. Ill. Nutrition Adv. Council, Sangamon County Mental Health Bd; chmn. Sangamon County March of Dimes, 1981; mem. Ill. interagy. coordinating com. Ill. Employment and Tng. Council; mem. Sangamon County Mental Health Bd.; hon. mem. bd. Sojourn House bd. dirs. Ill. YWCA, 1986. Mem. Ill. Assn. County Clks. and Recorders (pres.), Am. Bus. Women's Assn., Ill., Sangamon County bar assns., NAACP (exec. bd.), U. Ill. Alumni Assn., Nat. Assn. Counties, Nat. Assn. Recorders and Clks., Ill. Fedn. Tchrs. (pres. 1959-63, parliamentarian, 1963—), Conf. Women Legislators, Sangamon County Hist. Soc., P.E.O., Am. Assn. Vol. Services Coordinators (chmn. public policy com., 1st v.p. 1975), Ill. Assn. Sr. Centers, Bus. and Profl. Women's Club, Kappa Delta Pi, Sigma Delta Pi, Delta Delta Delta. Clubs: Springfield Altrusa (pres. 1967-68, legal advisor, dir. 1981—) (Springfield). Office: Stratton Bldg Springfield IL

OBLINGER, NANCY LEE, communications exec.; b. Fort Sill, Okla., May 18, 1945; d. Richard Lee and Jane Catherine (Fleig) O.; student U. Calif., Santa Barbara, 1963-64, Kent State U., 1964-65. Adminstrv. asst. VanBarneveld & Ellis Public Relations, Los Angeles, 1965-67, Md. Casualty Co., Los Angeles, 1968-72; asst. v.p. Foremark Corp., Swett & Crawford Group, Los Angeles, 1972—, asst. v.p., mgr. corp. communications, 1976—. Recipient awards Am. Inst. Graphic Arts Show, 1978, Communication Arts Soc. Show, 1979. Mem. Internat. Assn. Bus. Communicators, Ins. Advt. Conf. (award of excellence 1980), Insurers Public Relations Council, So. Calif. Bus. Communicators (award of excellence 1978). Republican. Episcopalian. Club: Toastmasters. Office: Foremark Corp 4201 Wilshire Blvd Los Angeles CA 90010

O'BOYLE, SHEILA MARY, lawyer, accountant; b. San Francisco, Aug. 28, 1956; d. Frank Vincent and Eleanor Kathryn (Rodenhausen) O'B.; m. Moshe Litman, Sept. 9, 1978; 1 child, Marissa Michelle. B.S. in Bus. Adminstrn., Calif. State U.-Northridge, 1978; J.D., U. West Los Angeles, 1982. Bar: Calif. 1982. Auditor, corp. examiner Calif. Dept. Corps., Los Angeles, 1978; acct. Transam. Ins. Services, Los Angeles, 1979; sole practice, Simi Valley, Calif., 1982—. Vice pres. Simi Republican Women; mem. Ventura County Rep. Central Com. Recipient John Gorfinkel award U. West Los Angeles, 1980; Am. Jurisprudence award Bancroft Whitney Pub. Co., San Francisco, 1981. Mem. State Bar Calif., ABA, Ventura County Bar Assn., U. West Los Angeles Alumni Assn., AAUW (treas. chpt.), Simi Valley C. of C. Home and Office: 2333 E Birchfield St Simi Valley CA 93065

OBRENTZ, PAULINE TROPP, interior designer, consultant; b. New Haven, June 10, 1908; d. Samuel and Tillie (Werebitzik) Tropp; m. Abraham Irving Obrentz, Feb. 22, 1931 (dec. Jan. 1980); children—Hugh Leonard (dec.), Bruce Everett. Student Yale U. Sch. Art, 1925; grad. Conn. State Tchrs. Coll., 1926. Head design dept. Mallary Furniture, White Plains, N.Y., 1939-55; owner Pauline Obrentz Interiors Inc., Belleair, Fla., 1968—; tchr. interior design N.Y. Inst. Tech., 1966, St. Petersburg Jr. Coll., Clearwater, Fla., 1970. Works include: Shannon Airport Hotel, Ireland; Pepsi Cola offices, Rome; VA Hosp., Westchester County, N.Y.; Cardinal McCluskey Home for Catholic Children, White Plains, Temple Israel, White Plains, Polish Heritage Room, Tampa U., Hebrew Nat. Orphan Home, Yonkers, N.Y., Library at Hebrew Inst., White Plains, numerous others. Mem. Nat. Home Fashion League, Am. Soc. Interior Designers, Antique Club Am., Bus. and Profl. Assn. Belleair, AAUP, Nat. Council Jewish Women. Club: Hadassah. Home: 1741 Golf View Dr Belleair FL 33516 Office: Pauline Obrentz Interiors Inc PO Box 1363 Largo FL 33540

O'BRIEN, ANN BROZOVICH, county recorder; b. Dawson, N.Mex., July 27, 1920; d. Paul and Katarina (Malovich) Brozovich; divorced; children Douglas R., David L.; m. John Bene, Dec. 15, 1977. Student Henager Bus. Coll., 1938-40. County recorder Carbon County, Price, Utah, 1963—. Sec., treas. Carbon County Democratic Party, 1970—. Methodist. Lodge: Order Eastern Star (treas. 1977, Worthy Matron 1984). Home: Route 3 Box 134 Price UT 84501 Office: Carbon County Courthouse Bldg Price UT 84501

O'BRIEN, ANNA BELLE CLEMENT, state senator; b. Scottsville, Ky.; married; 3 stepchildren. Student McMurray Coll. Mem. Tenn. Senate. Active Am. Legion Aux., Cumberland County Mental Health Assn., DAR, Cumberland County Beautiful Assn., Hosp. Aux.; adv. council Maccasin Bend Psychiat. Hosp., Chattanooga; bd. dirs. Plateau Mental Health Ctr., Cookeville, Tenn.; bd. dirs. Wharton Nursing Home, Cumberland County, Crossville C. of C. Mem. Bus. and Profl. Women's Club, Democratic Women's Club. Clubs: Top Town Garden, Marie Ervin Home Demonstration, Lake Tansi Village Women's. Office: Tenn Senate State Capitol Nashville TN 37219*

O'BRIEN, CATHERINE LOUISE, museum administrator; b. N.Y.C., July 21, 1930; d. Edward Denmark and Catherine Louise (Browne) O'B.; m. Philip R. James, Sept. 9, 1950 (div. 1955); m. Sterling Noel, Apr. 14, 1955 (div. 1960). B.A., Finch Coll., N.Y.C., 1950; postgrad. Williams Coll., Williamstown, Mass., 1956-57, Sarah Lawrence Coll., 1986-87. Reprodn. mgr. Met. Mus. Art, N.Y.C., 1975—. Exhibited in group shows at Parrish Art Mus., Southampton, N.Y., 1965-70, Met. Mus. Art, N.Y.C., 1975-85, Guild Hall Exhibit, East Hampton, N.Y., 1965-85. Mem. aux. Southampton Hosp., 1970-85; founder East Hampton Horse Show, Ladies Village Improvement Soc., East Hampton, 1970—; mem. fair coms. St. James Ch., N.Y.C., St. Luke's Ch., East Hampton, 1970-85; mem. alumnae adv. bd. Marymount Coll., N.Y.C., 1984-86. Mem. DAR (vice regent East Hampton chpt. 1974-85), Colonial Dames Am. (archives com. 1980-85), Daus. Brit. Empire (historian 1978-85), United Daus. Confederacy (state historian 1970-85), Daus. Colonial Wars (corr. sec. 1983-85), Sons and Daus. of the Pilgrims (corr. sec. 1983-85), Victorian Soc., Soc. Mayflower Descs. (life), English Speaking Union, New Eng. Soc. (mem. ball com. 1983-86), Daus. of Cin. (historian 1979-85). Republican. Episcopalian. Clubs: Devon Yacht, Maidstone (East Hampton, N.Y.); Southampton Yacht (N.Y.); Metropolitan (N.Y.C.) (women's com., chmn. debutante ball 1980-84); Reciprocal/India House, St. Anthony Union League (N.Y.C.). Avocations: show horses; dogs. Home: 605 Park Ave New York NY 10021 Office: Met Mus Art Fifth Ave New York NY 10028

O'BRIEN, DEANA MICHAEL, semiconductor manufacturing executive; b. Mt. Shasta, Calif., Dec. 14, 1951; d. Arthur Junior and Lola Dell (Weiss) Michael; m. Forrest James O'Brien, Feb. 7, 1971; children—Shannon Renee, Michael James. A.A., Bryant & Stratton Coll. Commerce, San Jose, Calif., 1972. Mktg. sec. Am. Microsystems, Inc., Santa Clara, Calif., 1973-74, adminstrv. asst., 1974-76, program adminstr., 1976-80; mktg. adminstr. Calif. Devices, Inc., San Jose, 1981-83, product mktg. mgr., 1983-85; tactical mktg. mgr. Monolithic Memories, Inc., Santa Clara, 1985—; ptnr. Forrest O'Brien Engring., Inc., automotive repair and after market turbocharging, Santa Clara, 1976—. Mem. Nat. Assn. for Female Execs. Avocations: traveling; boating; camping; jeeping; antiques. Office: Monolithic Memories Inc 2175 Mission College Blvd MS Bldg 10 Santa Clara CA 95054

O'BRIEN, GEORGIA ANNE, gourmet catering executive; b. Florence, Mass., Feb. 24, 1939; d. Edward Paul and Mildred Elizabeth (Sylvester) Hannigan; m. Henry J. North, June 21, 1958 (div. Nov. 1978); children—Nicholas, Lawrence, Sue-Georgia; m. James Edward O'Brien, July 25, 1982. Diploma Hopkins Acad., Hadley, Mass., 1956; student Baypath Jr. Coll., Longmeadow, Mass., 1980-81, Springfield Tech. Community Coll., 1984. Legal sec. Park & Dee, Attys., Springfield, Mass., 1975-78; sales rep. Assoc. Air Freight, Windsor Locks, Conn., 1978-80, Pilot Air Freight, Windsor Locks, 1980-82; account exec. Flying Tigers, Los Angeles, 1982-84; pres. G.A. Gourmet Caterers, Longmeadow, 1984—. Bd. govs. Berkshire County Traffic Club, Pittsfield, Mass., 1981-83; vol. arbitrator Better Bus. Burs. Nat. Consumer Arbitration, Springfield, 1984—. Mem. Nat. Assn. Profl. Saleswomen (pres. 1982-84, founder chpt. 1982). Republican. Congregationalist. Clubs: Community Women's (pres. 1974-75), Longmeadow Maternal Assn. (corr. sec. 1985-86). Avocations: boating, fishing, gardening.

O'BRIEN, GRACE WILHELMINA EHLIG, psychologist, retired educational administrator, writer, lectr.; b. Los Angeles, Aug. 27, 1922; d. Max Carl and Janette (Rentchler) Ehlig; A.A., Pasadena City Coll., 1942; A.B., UCLA, 1944, postgrad., 1944-46; postgrad. Riverside City Coll., 1946; postgrad. Calif. State Coll. at Los Angeles, 1954-66, 68-78, M.A. in Guidance, 1964; m. Louis J. O'Brien, Nov. 8, 1947; children—Carol Jean, Lawrence John, Perry Lewis. Tchr., Perris (Calif.) Union High Sch., 1945-46; tchr., counselor, psychometrist Los Angeles City Schs., 1946-66, cons. counselor, sch. psychologist Elem. Secondary Edn. Act, Edn. and Guidance program, 1966-68; head counselor, asst. prin. Garden Gate Opportunity Sch., 1968-73; vice prin. Markham Jr. High Sch., 1973, Belvedere Jr. High Sch., 1974; asst. prin. Garfield High Sch., 1974-75, Mt. Vernon Jr. High Sch., Los Angeles, 1975-76; prin. Garden Gate High Sch., 1977-80, Johnson High Sch., 1980-84. Den mother chmn. Cub Scouts, 1964-66. Recipient spl. service award Boy Scouts, 1964. Mem. UCLA Alumni Assn., Sr. High Prins. Assn., Los Angeles Assn. Sch. Adminstrs., Calif. Assn. Sch. Adminstrs., DAR, Phi Delta Kappa, Pi Lambda Theta, Chi Delta Phi. Presbyterian (supt. Sunday sch. 1953-54). Home: 3880 Shadow Grove Rd Pasadena CA 91107 Office: 900 E 42d St Los Angeles CA 90011

O'BRIEN, JANET ALISSA, lawyer; b. Providence, Jan. 3, 1942; d. Patrick Daniel and Elsie Bloom (Newton) O'Brien; m. Robert John Lascola, June 19, 1965 (div. 1983); children—Robert John, Christopher David, Kara Michelle. B.Ed., R.I. Coll., 1963; M.S., SUNY-Buffalo, 1971, J.D., 1981. Bar: Ill. 1981. Tchr., U.S. Peace Corps, Liberia, W. Africa, 1963-64, Babcock Jr. High Sch., Westerly, R.I., 1964-65, Cantalician Ctr. for Learning, Buffalo, 1971; staff atty. U.S. Ct. Appeals, 7th Cir., Chgo., 1981-83; assoc. law firm Altheimer & Gray, Chgo., 1983—. Editor, contbr. articles Buffalo Law Rev., 1979-81. Mem. ABA, Ill. State Bar Assn., Chgo. Bar Assn. Office: Altheimer & Gray 333 W Wacker Dr Chicago IL 60606

O'BRIEN, JUDITH ANN, insurance company manager, consultant; b. Milw., Aug. 22, 1946; d. Edward Andrew and Charlotte Isabelle (Miller) Tomic; m. John E. O'Brien, Jr., Mar. 21, 1970 (div. Jan. 1973); 1 child, Bridget M. B.S. in Pharmacy, U. Wis.-Madison, 1970; M.B.A., Oakland U., Rochester, Mich., 1981. Registered pharmacist, Oreg., Mich. Dir. pharmacy Cascade Health Care, Portland, 1972-74; dir. spl. projects Am. Pharm. Assn., Washington, 1974-76; dir. drug reimbursement programs Nat. Assn. Chain Drug Stores, Arlington, Va., 1976; sr. policy analyst Blue Cross and Blue Shield of Mich., Detroit, 1977-80, coordinator, 1980-83, mgr. divisional projects., 1983—; instr. Portland State U., 1970-74; cons. HEW, Rockville, Md., 1973-78. Editor: Pharmaceutical Services in the Long Term Care Facility, 1974. Vol., Outside-in Socio-Med. Aid Clinic, Portland, 1970-73; bd. dirs. Family Players, West Bloomfield, Mich., 1978-81. Mem. Am. Mgmt. Assn., Am. Pharm. Assn., Mich. Pharmacists Assn., Nat. Assn. Female Execs. Republican. Roman Catholic. Avocations: theatre, gourmet cooking; Aztec culture. Home: 1266 Henrietta St Birmingham MI 48009 Office: Blue Cross and Blue Shield of Mich 600 Lafayette E Detroit MI 48226

O'BRIEN, LIBBY ATKINS, public relations exec.; b. N.Y.C., Mar. 17, 1913; d. Richard Travis and Alice Gordon (Quigley) Atkins; grad. Kendall Hall, 1931; m. Richard Thomas O'Brien, June 25, 1935 (dec.); children—Francis DeSales, Sarah Jane O'Brien Prezalor. Car rep. Brady Stannard Motors, Brewster, N.Y., Blanchard Motors, Greenwich, Conn., and Tolm Motors, Darren, Conn., 1940-46; producer TV show Libby O'Brien's Table Toppers, 1946-48; commentator, dir. women's programs WLAD, Danbury, Conn., 1948-51, WSTC, Stamford, Conn., 1951-53; asst. dir. public relations Save the Children Fedn., 1954-55; advt. mgr. Roux Distbg. Corp., 1956-57; public relations mgr. Lily Tulip Cup Corp., 1957-64; owner, mgr. Libby O'Brien Enterprises, Inc., 1964-69; owner, breeder, exporter O'Brien Donkey Farm, promoter of tourism in Kenmare, Ireland, 1969-76; book collaborator; active Utilizing Sr. Energy, Know Your Body-Am. Health Orgn.; publicity chmn. Greenwich Meals on Wheels. Collector, seller old N.Y.C. st. signs. Mem. Am. Women in Radio and TV, Public Relations Assn., Public Relations Inst. U.K. Republican. Home: 44 Arcadia Rd Old Greenwich CT 06870

O'BRIEN, LORETTA SULLIVAN, lawyer; b. Boston, June 13, 1930; d. Franklin James and Frances (Sullivan) O;B.; m. William P. Shields, Aug. 27, 1949 (div. May 6, 1971); children—Candice P., Leslie A. A.D., U. Mass., 1969; cert. Simmons Sch. Social Work, 1973; J.D., New Eng. Sch. Law, Boston, 1977. Bar: Mass. 1977. Sr. social worker Mass. Dept. Pub. Welfare, Norwood, 1972-78; founder, owner, Norwood Legal Ctr., 1978—. Mem. ABA, Western Norfolk County Bar Assn. (pres. 1985—), NOW, LWV (pres.). Club: Appalachian Mountain (chmn. com. 1981—). Home: 150 S Walpole St Sharon MA 02067 Office: Norwood Legal Ctr 648 Washington St Suite 12 Norwood MA 02062

O'BRIEN, MARY DEVON, communications company executive, strategic planning-consultant; b. Buenos Aires, Argentina, Feb. 13, 1944; came to U.S., 1949, naturalized, 1962; d. George Earle and Margaret Frances (Richards) Owen; m. Gordon Covert O'Brien, Feb. 16, 1962 (div. Aug. 1982); children—Christopher Covert, Devon Elizabeth; m. Christopher Gerard Smith, May 28, 1983. B.S., Rutgers U., 1975, M.B.A., 1976. Controller manpower Def. Communications div. ITT, Nutley, N.J., 1977-80, adminstr. program, 1977-78, mgr. cost, schedule control, 1978-79, mgr. spl. project, 1979-80; mgr. project Avionics div. ITT, Nutley, 1970-81, sr. mgr. project, 1981—; cons. strategic planning, N.J., 1983—; lectr. in field, 1977—. Author: Pace: System Manual, 1979, Voices, 1982. Chmn. Citizens Budget Adv. Com., Maplewood, N.J., 1981-82, chmn. recreation, library, pub. services, 1982-83, chmn. pub. safety, emergency services, 1983-84, chmn. schs. and edn., 1984-85; bd. dirs., officer Civic Assn., Maplewood, 1984—; mem. Maplewood Zoning Bd., 1983—; officer, mem. exec. bd. N.J. Project Mgmt. Inst., 1985-86, 86-87; chmn. Project Mgmt. Assn. Charter Com. Recipient Anti-Shoplifting Program award Distributive Edn. Club Am., 1981, N.J. Fedn. of Women's Clubs, 1981, 82, Retail Mchts. Assn., 1981, 82; Commendation and Merit awards Air Force Inst. Tech., 1981; Pres.'s Safety award ITT, 1983; State award N.J. Fedn. of Women's Clubs Garden Show, 1982; Cert. Spl. Merit award N.J. Fedn. of Women's Clubs, 1982. Mem. Assn. M.B.A. Execs., Grand Jury Assn., Nat. Security Indsl. Assn., Assn. for Info. and Image Mgmt., ITT Mgmt. Assn., LWV. Mem. Christian Ch. Club: Maplewood Women's (pres. 1980-82). Home: 594 Valley St Maplewood NJ 07040 Office: ITT Avionics 390 Washington Ave Nutley NJ 07110

O'BRIEN, MAURA ANN, ethicist; b. Bronx, N.Y., Aug. 3, 1959; B.A., Duke U., 1981; M.A., Georgetown U., 1985, postgrad., 1985—. Congl. legis. aide, Washington, 1982; mng. editor Jour. Medicine and Philosophy, Washington, 1983, 85; research assoc. Masi Research Cons., Inc., Washington, 1983-85; fellow Kennedy Inst. Ethics, Georgetown U., Washington, 1983-86; assoc. for ethics N.Y. State Task Force on Life and Law, N.Y.C., 1985—. NEH fellow, 1984-85; Inst. for Humane Studies fellow, 1985; Fulbright fellow, 1987-88. mem. Philos. Soc. Washington, Am. Soc. Law and Medicine. Clubs: Washington Philosophy, Duke of Washington. Office: NY State Task Force on Life and Law 33 W 34th St 3d Floor New York NY 10001-3071

O'BRIEN, PATRICIA FLORENCE, former real estate and appraisal company executive, educator; b. Truro, N.S., Can., Sept. 15, 1914; d. Clarence Osborne and Florence Isabel (Ripley) Davidson; B.S., Marquette U., Milw., 1958, M.A. in Spanish, 1961; M.A. in English Lit., U. Alta., 1966; m. Cyril Cornelius O'Brien, July 27, 1957; stepchildren—Maureen Louise, Terry Michael, Christopher Joseph. Social worker, Halifax, N.S., 1933-42; public sch. tchr., 1942-52; chmn. dept. English English Cath. Coll., La Paz, Bolivia, 1952-56; instr. Spanish Carroll Coll., Waukesha, Wis., 1959-60, Mt. Mary Coll., Milw., 1960-62; tchr. math. and Spanish Solomon Juneau High Sch., Milw., 1962-63; instr. English U. Alta., Edmonton, 1965-70; sec.-treas. Adan Research Co. Ltd., Edmonton, 1969—; pres. Patra Real Estate and Appraisal Co. Ltd., 1975-82; instr. art Lakeland Coll., Vermilion, Alta.; sec. Prince of Peace Research Inst., Mundare, Alta., 1980—. Decorated lady Equestrian Order Holy Sepulchre Jerusalem, 1979, lady comdr. Lady Magistral Grace Mil. Order Most Holy Savior and St. Bridget of Sweden, 1982, lady grand oficier, 1986. Mem. Assn. Pontifical Knights, Royal Soc. Arts, Marquette U. Faculty Wives Assn. (past dir.), Phi Delta Gamma (pres. 1960-62), Sigma Delta Pi (sec. 1960-61), Pi Mu Epsilon, Phi Delta Phi, Alpha Mu Gamma. Club: Laura Reid Art (pres. 1976-78) (Vegreville, Alta.). Author papers in field, also poetry.

Address: PO Box 503 Clandonald County of Vermilion River AB T0B 0X0 Canada

O'BRIEN, SANDRA ROUSSEL, early childhood educator; b. New Orleans, Oct. 8, 1955; d. Daniel Keller and Theresa (Louque) Roussel; m. Matthew Stephen O'Brien, Dec. 16, 1977; children—Erin Anne, Kathleen Margery (Kati). B.A. in Edn., Nicholls State U., 1978. Tchr. Sacred Heart Elem. Sch., Norco, La., 1978-80, St. Charles Borromeo, Destrehan, La., 1980-81; dir. Montessori tchr. Ormond Coll. d'Enfants, Destrehan, 1981—. Mem. La. Assn. Edn. Young Children. Democrat. Roman Catholic. Avocations: flower and interior designing; make-up consultant; tennis; aerobics. Home: 384 Hester Dr LaPlace LA 70068 Office: Ormond Coll 13 Storehouse Ln Destrehan LA 70047

O'BRIEN-MOLINA, MARGARET ANNE, video production executive; b. Trieste, Italy, Apr. 22, 1949; came to U.S., 1952; d. Walter Joseph and Elena Amelia (Rova) O'Brien; m. Kenneth W. Hoagland, Jr., Mar. 16, 1974 (div. 1978); m. Juan-Carlos Molina, May 2, 1981. B.A., U. Houston, 1978. Info. specialist U.S. Army, Fort Ord, Calif., 1973-76; researcher Houston Post, 1978-79; reporter Metro News, Inc., Houston, 1980; mng. editor Sta. KTRK-TV, Houston, 1980-84; pres. WIN Video Prodns., Inc., Houston, 1984—. Mem. capital fundraising com. Houston Area Women's Ctr., 1985. Served with U.S. Army, 1973-76. Named KTRK-TV Woman of Yr., 1983. Mem. Leadership Tex., Houston C. of C., Am. Quarter Horse Assn., Tex. Amateur Quarter Horse Assn. Democrat. Roman Catholic. Avocation: horseback riding. Home: 4110 Norfolk Houston TX 77027 Office: WIN Prodns 1738 Westheimer Houston TX 77098

O'BYRNE, NATALIE KWASNESKI, adult and child psychiatrist; b. Bklyn., Nov. 29, 1933; d. Julian Leon and Jeannette Pauline (Kowalski) Kwasneski; B.S. in Chemistry cum laude, St. John's U., 1955; M.D., State U. N.Y., Bklyn., 1959; m. William O'Byrne, June 13, 1959; children—Cecily, Matthew, Stephanie, Gabrielle, Luke. Intern, Kings County Hosp., N.Y.C., 1960-61; resident in pediatrics Children's Hosp., San Francisco, 1962-63, adolescent medicine fellow, 1963-64; resident in adult psychiatry St. Mary's Hosp., San Francisco, 1964-66, in child psychiatry, 1966-68; practice medicine specializing in adult, child and adolescent psychiatry, Green Brae, Calif., 1968—; assoc. clin. prof. U. Calif. (San Francisco); sr. supervising psychiatrist Langley-Porter Children's Service. Diplomate Am. Bd. Psychiatry and Neurology. Fellow Am. Psychiat. Assn., Am. Acad. Child Psychiatry; mem. AMA, Calif. Med. Assn., Marin, San Francisco med. socs., No. Calif. Psychiat. Assn., Regional Orgn. Child-Adolescent Psychiatry, Nat. Guild Cath. Psychiatrists (dir.). Roman Catholic. Home: 715 Butterfield Rd San Anselmo CA 94960 Office: 481 Via Hidalgo Suite 220 Greenbrae CA 94904

O'CALLAGHAN, LINDA KATHERINE BOURGAULT, educational administration, consultant, editorial assistant; b. Laconia, N.H., Sept. 21, 1946; d. William A. and Helen Doris (Morrison) Bourgault; m. Ronald J. O'Callaghan, Aug. 31, 1985. A.S., Fisher Jr. Coll., 1966; B.G.S., Plymouth State Coll., 1981. Receptionist Normandin, Cheney & O'Neil, Laconia, N.H., 1973-74; mem. customer service dept. Tram/Diamond Corp., Winnisquam, N.H., 1974-76; alumni sec. Plymouth State Coll., N.H., 1976-78, acting dir., 1978-80, dir. alumni relations, 1980—; cons. Lyndon State Coll., Lyndonville, Vt., 1981-84, North Adams State, Mass., 1982—; editorial asst. Oriental Rug Review, Meredith, N.H., 1985—. Campaign worker McCarthy Campaign Hdqrs., Staten Island, N.Y., 1968, McGovern Campaign Hdqrs., Laconia, 1972; vol. Domestic Violence Task Force, Plymouth, 1982. Mem. Profl., Adminstrv. and Tech. Senate Plymouth State Coll., N.H. Women in Higher Edn. Adminstrn., N.H. Council Fund Raising Execs., Council for Advancement and Support of Edn., Phi Kappa Phi. Avocations: oriental rugs, art appreciation, architecture, antiques, skiing. Home: Beech Hill Rd Meredith NH 03253 Office: Plymouth State Coll Russell House Plymouth NH 03264

OCAMPO, BLANCA-LEONOR, real estate sales executive; b. San Diego, Sept. 6, 1938; d. Rafael Daniel and Josefina-Leonor (Rojas) Ocampo; m. Jan. 31, 1966 (div. Dec. 1980); children—Shelley Zisman, Adrian Brooke Zisman. B.A., Colo. Womens Coll., 1971; M.P.A., U. Kans., 1984; postgrad. Washburn Sch. Law, 1984—. Mgr. comml. sales and fin. Raffee's Carpets, San Diego, 1960-66; office mgr., paralegal Sanford Zisman, P.C., Denver, 1966-74; v.p. Colo. Econ. Devel. Assn., Denver, 1974-76; grad. program coordinator U. Kans., Topeka, 1983-84; br. mgr. sales Dennis Eskie & Assocs., Topeka, 1985—. Vice pres. LWV, Topeka, 1984—; mem. Shawnee County Zoning Commn., Topeka, 1983—; bilingual docent Denver Art Mus., 1969-78; pres. Library Assocs., Denver, 1973-75. Mem. Assn. for Action. Republican. Roman Catholic. Avocations: Writing poetry; reading; walking; golf; art. Home: 1500 SW 24th St Topeka KS 66611 Office: Dennis Eskie & Assocs 6261 SW 9th St Topeka KS 66615

O'CARROLL, ANITA LOUISE, legal editor, lawyer; b. Jersey City, Nov. 19, 1953; d. Henry Patrick and Anita (Babikian) O'C. Student Pa. State U., 1971-72; B.A., Rutgers U., 1975; J.D., N.Y. Law Sch., 1978. Bar: N.J. 1983, Pa. 1983. Legal asst. Manhattan Dist. Atty., N.Y.C., 1977, Bergen County Counsel, Hackensack, N.J., 1977; jud. clk. Judge James I. Toscano, Hackensack, 1978-79, Judge J. Emmet Cassidy, Hackensack, 1979; legal editor West Pub. Co., Mineola, N.Y., 1980-85; staff atty. Office of Hearings and Appeals Social Security Adminstrn., Newark, 1985—. Author: A Synthesis of New York Case Law on the Bill of Particulars and Pretrial Discovery, 1977; editor Legal Ency. Guide to American Law, 1981. PTA scholar, 1971. Mem. ABA, N.J. Bar Assn., Pa. Bar Assn., Assn. Trial Lawyers Am., Bergen County Bar Assn., Nat. Assn. Female Execs. Republican. Home: 264 De Soto Pl Fairview NJ 07022 Office: Office Hearings and Appeals Social Security Adminstrn 60 Park Pl 5th Floor Newark NJ 07102

OCASIO, JOSEFA, nurse; b. Mayaguez, P.R., Nov. 4, 1940; came to U.S., 1949; d. Jose Ocasio and Josefina (Jorge) O.; L.P.N., Bellavista Hosp., 1964; R.N., Manhattan Community Coll., City U. N.Y., 1978; B.A. in Hosp. Adminstrn., CCNY, 1981; cert. in childbirth Council Childbirth Educators, 1978; M.P.H., Columbia U., 1984; divorced; children—Brenda, Joey. Office nurse, 1964-66; mem. nursing staff Columbia-Presbyn. Med. Center, N.Y.C., 1966—; parent educator Lamaze Inst., Lenox Hill Hosp., 1980-81; Lamaze instr., 1978—; public health nurse N.Y.C. Bur. Child Welfare, 1980-81; founder, 1976, since dir., tchr. pregnancy prevention Washington Heights Youth Outreach Program; bd. dirs. East Harlem Health Council, 1980—; sec. gen. Hispanic Health Congress No. Manhattan, 1980—; mem. program planning and facilities com. Presbyn. Hosp. Community Health Council, 1979—. Mem. Am. Nurses Assn., Nat. Assn. Female Execs., Women's Health Network, Internat. Childbirth Assn., Am. Pub. Health Assn., N.Y. State Nurses Assn., Met. Childbirth Assn. N.Y.C., Nat. Astrological Soc., Internat. Coll. Astrology. Address: 600 W 178th St New York NY 10033

OCCHIUZZO, LUCIA RAJSZEL, restaurant executive; b. Casablanca, Morocco, Nov. 5, 1951; came to U.S., 1958, naturalized, 1973; d. Tadeusz Joseph and Irmina Elizabeth (Wacholska) Rajszel; m. Joel Occhiuzzo, Dec. 9, 1976. B.A., Montclair U., 1974. Owner, pres. Mr. O's, Dallas, 1977-83, L n J's Restaurant & Club, Richardson, Tex., 1984—. Guest star Sta. Telecable TV, 1985. Contbr. articles to newspapers. Recipient Restaurant of Month award Dallas Times Herald, 1978. Mem. Richardson C. of C., ASCAP. Republican. Roman Catholic. Avocations: music; photography; writing. Home: 156 Hidden Circle Richardson TX 75080 Office: L n J's Restaurant & Club 2475 Promenade Ctr Richardson TX 75080

OCHAL, BETHANY JACQUITA, library director; b. Flint, Mich., Dec. 2, 1917; d. Llewellyn Lane and Idah B. (Stewart) Ziegler; A.B., Wayne State U., 1944, J.D., 1945; m. Edward Louis Ochal, July 1, 1944; children—Myrna Irene, Edward Llewellyn. Admitted to Mich. bar, 1945; practiced in Detroit, 1945-52; reference librarian Detroit Bar Assn. Library, 1952-60, librarian, 1960-61; law librarian Wayne State U. Law Sch. Library, Detroit, 1961-72; dir. Orange County (Calif.) Law Library, Santa Ana, 1972—; mem. faculty rotating insts. Am. Assn. Law Libraries, 1972, 73, 75, 79. Mem. State Bar Mich. (chmn. legal publs. com. 1968-70), Women Lawyers Assn. Mich. (pres. 1966-67), Am. Assn. Law Libraries (chmn. membership com. 1965-67, chmn. chpts. com. 1968-70, chmn. audiovisual com. 1970-71, 81-82), Ohio Regional Assn. Law Libraries (pres. 1969-70), Internat. Assn. Law Libraries, Assn. for Info. and Image Mgmt. Democrat. Club: Soroptimist. Contbr. to Law Library Jour. Home: 2541 N Alona Santa Ana CA 92706 Office: 515 N Flower Santa Ana CA 92703

OCHMAN, B. L., public relations executive, writer; b. N.Y.C., Mar. 13, 1948; d. Reuben and Dorothy (Bussel) Friedman. B.A. in Journalism, U. Bridgeport (Conn.), 1967. Account exec. Leo Miller Assocs., Westport, Conn., 1967-74; pub. relations dir. M. Hohner Inc., L.I., N.Y., 1974-76; editorial dir. Ruder & Finn Pub. Relations, N.Y.C., 1976-78; account supr. Ben Kubasik Pub. Relations, N.Y.C., 1978-79; pres., chief kvetch Rent-A-Kvetch, Inc., N.Y.C., 1979—; pres. B.L. Ochman Pub. Relations, N.Y.C., 1979—. Mem. Publicity Club N.Y., Am. Women Entrepeneurs, N.Y. Assn. Women Bus. Owners. Democrat. Office: BL Ochman Pub Relations 10 E 21st St New York NY 10010

O'CHUK, GRAYCE XENIA, school nurse; b. Zion, Ill., Oct. 21, 1919; d. Vasily Titus and Xenia (Solunanchuk) Omelianchuk; m. Jacob Stipanuk, Dec. 2, 1944 (div. Dec. 1980); children—James Jacob, Jane Paula, Jeane Grayce, Timothy Peter. R.N., St. Luke's Hosp., 1944; B.S.A., Ariz. State U., 1970; M.A., U. LaVerne, 1980. Indsl. nurse Am. Motors, Kenosha, Wis., 1945-46, 53-54; charge nurse Kenosha (Wis.) Meml. Hosp., 1952-53, 55-57; indsl. nurse Internat. Metals, Phoenix, 1958-59; inservice dir. Tempe (Ariz.) Community Hosp., 1959-62; sch. nurse Scottsdale (Ariz.) Schs., 1962-70, Los Angeles County Supt. Schs., Div. Spl. Edn., Downey, Calif., 1970—; sub-chmn. health edn. com. Scottsdale Schs., 1967-69; instigated 1st orthopedically handicapped pub. edn. in Scottsdale Schs., 1965. Author: Nursing Procedures-Tempe Community Hospital, 1961; High School Health Assistant Procedures, 1964; Operational Methods of Screening the Visual Acuity of Multi-Handicapped Students, 1984-85; Lay Inservice on Vision/Vision Problems; author tape/slides: A Box ZPC Memories, 1983. Bd. dirs. San Gabriel Valley Regional Ctr., State Calif., 1978-82; ad hoc chmn. Med. Delivery System, San Francisco State U. grad. fellow, 1970; Calif. del. White House Conf. Physically Handicapped, 1977. Mem. Am. Sch. Health Assn., Council Exceptional Children, Nat. Assn. Autistic Children, Calif. Assn. Physically Handicapped, Calif. Sch. Nurses Assn. Democrat. Home: 4348 Toyon Circle LaVerne CA 91750 Office: E San Gabriel Valley Sch 4400 N Roxburgh St Covina CA 91722

O'CONNELL, AMY ALEXANDRE, educator; b. Oak Park, Ill., May 15, 1936; m. William J. O'Connell, Aug. 4, 1962 (div. July 1980); children—Amy Elizabeth, William Joseph, Barrett Thomas. B.S. in Edn., Eastern Ill. U., Charleston, 1958; cert. travel agt., Roberta Fisher Travel Sch., Arlington Heights, Ill., 1978; M.A. in Spl. Edn., Northeastern Ill. U., Chgo., 1983; doctoral student No. Ill. U., 1984—. Speech therapist pub. schs., Springfield, Ill., 1958-60; speech and hearing therapist Sch. Dist. 67, Morton Grove, Ill., 1960-63; co-author Speechmaster series Go-Mo Publications, Cedar Rapids, Iowa, 1965-80; travel agt. Robert Fisher Travel, 1977-78; speech and lang. therapist Sch. Dist. 15, Palatine, Ill., 1981—; travel agt. outside sales Cove Travel; 1983—. Bd. dirs. Prizel Academic Inst., Arlington Heights, 1983—. Mem. Jung Inst., Cousteau Soc., Internat. Platform Assn., Nat. Alliance for Mentally Ill., Ill. Edn. Assn., NEA, Smithsonian Instn., Am. Mus. Natural History, Art Inst. Chgo., Ill. Council on Understanding Learning Disabilities, Am. Council on Learning Disabilities, Northwest Speech Assn. Home: 708 E Lynden Ln Arlington Heights IL 60005

O'CONNELL, AMY PERKINS, advertising agency executive; b. Washington, Feb. 22, 1959; d. Raymond Lamont and Margaret (Johnson) Perkins; m. Michael Francis O'Connell, June 5, 1982. B.A., U. Md., 1980; M.A. SUNY-Albany, 1981. Research asst. Vietnam Veterans Am., Albany, N.Y., 1980-81; grad. teaching asst. SUNY-Albany, 1980-81; assoc. mktg. firm Porter, Novelli & Assocs., Washington, 1981-83; v.p., research dir. J. Walter Thompson, Washington, 1983—; guest lectr. George Washington U., 1982; mem. panel U. Md. Career Day, 1983; pres. Employee Interest Group, Porter, Novelli & Assocs., Washington, 1983. SUNY-Albany Scholarship awardee, 1980-81. Mem. Am. Mktg. Assn., Speech Communication Assn., Redland Crossing Homeowners Assn., U. Md. Alumni Assn., Sigma Kappa Alumni Assn. Democrat. Methodist. Home: 15918 Indian Hills Terrace Derwood MD 20855 Office: J Walter Thompson 1156 15th St NW Washington DC 20005

O'CONNELL, ANNA PORRECA, biologist; b. Phila., Apr. 26, 1937; d. Francis Paul and Anna Agnes (Donatucci) Porreca; A.B., Temple U., 1959. Mem. staff Inst. Cancer Research, Phila., 1959—, research asso., 1972-81, sr. research assoc., 1981—. Mem. Am. Soc. Microbiology, Pa. Soc. Microbiology, N.Y. Acad. Scis. Author papers in field. Office: 7701 Burholme Ave Philadelphia PA 19111

O'CONNELL, JEANNE, insurance underwriting specialist, potter; b. Stoneham, Mass., Dec. 9, 1951; d. Kenneth Edward and Frances Evelyn (Matulewicz) O'C. Student U. Oreg., 1971-72; B.F.A. cum laude, U. Mass.-Amherst, 1974; U. Calif.-Sacramento, summer 1973; postgrad. Northeastern U., 1975; Exec. M.B.A., Suffolk U., M.B.A., 1984. C.P.C.U.; cert. profl. ins. woman. Ins. clk. S.B. Swaim & Co., Boston, part time 1969-72, Hollis Perrin & Co., Boston, 1972; underwriting asst. Pub. Service Mut. Ins. Co., Newton, Mass., 1974-77; personal lines analyst Comml. Union Ins. Co., Boston, 1977-80, sr. personal lines analyst, 1980-83, tech. specialist, 1983—; founder, dir. Red Dragon Arts Coop., Boston, 1983; potter, artist Radcliffe Pottery Studio, 1980-84; potter, Boston. Mem. exec. student adv. bd. Suffolk U., 1982-83, student liaison mem. between Exec. M.B.A. Program and regular M.B.A. Program and dean's adv. bd., coordinator Exec. M.B.A. Program Policy Seminar Weekend, 1983. Mem. Nat. Assn. Female Execs., Nat. Assn. Ins. Women, Mass. Assn. Ins. Women (fin. and scholarship coms., leader edn. seminars Boston), Assn. Casualty and Property Underwriters, Soc. C.P.C.U.s, Delta Mu Delta. Home: 41 Atkins St Brighton MA 02135 Office: Commercial Union Ins Cos One Beacon St Boston MA 02108

O'CONNELL, KARON KEESEE, nurse; b. Memphis, Tenn., Nov. 18, 1955; d. Wilson Doggett and Dorothy Vivian (Whitworth) Keesee; m. John Francis O'Connell, Jan. 28, 1978. B.S. in Nursing, U. Tenn., 1977. R.N., Tenn. Nurse, Methodist Hosp., Memphis, 1977-78; concurrent rev. mgr. Mid-South Found. Med. Care, Memphis, 1978-80; dir. nursing services Upjohn Health Care, Memphis, 1980—. Recipient Outstanding Young Woman of Am. award, 1982. Mem. We Care Home Care (bd. dirs.). Republican. Roman Catholic. Avocation: skiing. Office: Upjohn Health Care Services PO Box 17725 Memphis TN 38117

O'CONNELL, LINDA LOU, construction company executive; b. Amherst, Ohio, Jan. 12, 1952; d. Robert Michael and Betty Louise (Fitzgerald) Benoit; m. James Edward Schuman, June 22, 1974 (div. Aug. 1976); m. James Douglas O'Connell, Nov. 19, 1977. Cert., Lorain Bus. Coll., 1969, Bee County Coll., 1981. Keypunch operator Luxaire Westinghouse, Elyria, Ohio, 1970-74; title clk. Lakeway Ford Sales, Mathis, Tex., 1974-75; bookkeeper Mathis Ind. Sch., Tex., 1975-79, sec. to supt., 1979-82; pres. J.D. Constrn. Inc., Ingleside, Tex., 1979—; asst. Charm and Modeling by Gladys Ruth, Corpus Christi, 1984—; cert. cons. BeautiControl Cosmetics, Dallas, 1985—. Mem. Nat. Assn. Female Execs., Ingleside C. of C. (treas., bd. dirs. 1986). Roman Catholic. Clubs: Garden (corr. sec. 1986—), Christian Womens. Avocations: water skiing; dancing; oil painting; boating; reading; modeling. Home: 110 Sunset Dr Mathis TX 78368 Office: J D Constrn Inc PO Box 328 Ingleside TX 78362

O'CONNELL, MARY ANN, state senator; b. Albuquerque, Aug. 3, 1934; d. James Aubrey and Dorothy Nell (Batsel) Gray; m. Robert Emmett O'Connell, Feb. 21, 1977; children—Ervin Jeffery, Aubrey Gray. Grad. high sch. Albuquerque. Exec. dir. Blvd. Shopping Ctr., Las Vegas, Nev., 1968-76, Citizen Pvt. Enterprise, Las Vegas, 1976; media supr. Southwest Advt., Las Vegas, 1977—; owner, operator Confort Inn, Las Vegas, 1985—; mem. Nev. Senate, 1984—. Pres. Citizen Pvt. Enterprise, Las Vegas, 1982-84, Secret Witness, Las Vegas, 1981-82; vice chmn. Gov.'s Mental Health-Mental Retardation, Nev., 1983—. Recipient Silver Beaver award Boy Scouts Am., 1980, Outstanding Citizenship award Bd. Realtors, 1975, Commendation award Mayor O. Grayson, Las Vegas, 1975. Republican. Office: 525 Bonanza Rd Las Vegas NV

O'CONNELL, MARY ELLEN, consulting firm executive; b. Plainfield, N.J., Nov. 3, 1956; d. John Forster and Regina Anne (McCarthy) O'Connell. B.S. in Early Childhoold Edn., Trenton State Coll., 1978. Pub. sch. tchr. Head Start, Somerville, N.J., 1978-79; account exec. Mgmt. Recruiters, Union, N.J., 1979-82; owner, search cons. Priority Search, Inc., Hillside, N.J., 1982—. Recipient Top 10 Account Execs. East Coast award Mgmt. Recruiters, 1981. Mem. N.J. Assn. Personnel Cons. Office: Priority Search Inc 1351 Liberty Ave Hillside NJ 07205

O'CONNELL-EARLEY, ELEANOR MAE, data processing consultant; b. Boston, Nov. 24, 1938; d. Arthur H. and Cecelia J. (Kelleher) O'Connell; m. Michael F. Earley, Nov. 3, 1965 (div. May 1975); children—Cecelia, Barbara. B.S. in Math., Emmanuel Coll., Boston, 1960. Systems engr. IBM, N.Y.C., 1960-67; data processing mgr. Brookhaven Textiles, N.Y.C., 1968-80; cons. Vantage Computers, Hartford, Conn., 1980-83, Comp Data, Hartford, 1983-85; prin. EDR Cons., Hartford, 1985—, Tampa Fla., 1985—. Mem. Eastern Small Bus. Fedn., Ind. Computer Cons. Assn., Nat. Assn. Female Execs. Democrat. Roman Catholic. Avocations: sailing; dancing. Home and Office: 1480 Gulf Blvd Clearwater FL 33515

O'CONNOR, ADA ELBERTA, business executive; b. Beaumont, Tex., Nov. 5, 1951; d. Elbert Harry and Jennea Isabelle (McCormick) Eubanks; m. Curtis Lee Wilkinson, May 19, 1970 (div. 1976); 1 son, Christoper Lance; m. 2d, Patrick Meyer O'Connor, June 4, 1982. Student Houston Community Coll., 1982—. Sec. to exec. v.p. Geoscis. Internat. Inc., Houston, 1976-77; sec.-receptionist Bland Devel. Corp., Houston, 1978-79; sec. to pres. Telecommunications Specialists, Inc. Houston, 1979-80, order to billing coordinator, 1980-81, order to billing supr., 1981-82, credit mgr., 1982—. Charter mem. Statue of Liberty Ellis Island Found., N.Y.C., 1983-84; supporter Greenpeace, Washington, 1983, Planned Parenthood Assn., N.Y.C., 1983. Mem. Houston Assn. Credit Mgmt., Nat. Assn. Female Execs., Am. Mgmt. Assn., Houston Zool. Soc. Office: Telecommunications Specialists Inc 8901 Knight Rd Houston TX 77054

O'CONNOR, CONNIE COLLEEN, data processing executive; b. Oklahoma City, July 13, 1946; d. William Leon and Evelyn Colleen (Hodam) O'Connor. B.S. in Math., Purdue U., 1969. Sr. system analyst City of Houston, 1971-75; bus. system analyst Turner, Collie & Braden, Houston, 1975-79; system analyst Tex. Eastern Transmission, Houston, 1979-80; supr. fin. systems Joy Petroleum, Houston, 1980-81; mgr. product devel. Hydril Co., Houston, 1981-83; owner Datum Systems, Houston, 1982—, dir., 1985—; lectr. computers U. Houston Downtown Coll., 1974-75. Mem. Houston Area League IBM Personal Computer Users. Home: 23303 Bright Star Spring TX 77373 Office: Datum Systems Inc 16800 Imperial Valley Dr Suite 130 Houston TX 77060

O'CONNOR, CONSTANCE, publisher; b. N.Y.C.; d. Thomas J. and Constance D. (Egan) Reilly; B.S., Fordham U., 1948; m. James T. Sutter, 1944 (div. 1963); children—Valerie Sutter-Remy, Meredith McGraw, John W. Sutter, Russell J. Sutter; m. 2d, John J. O'Connor, 1968. Editor Spectator, house organ Standard & Poor's, N.Y.C., 1948; owner Sutter Agy., public relations, Mt. Vernon, N.Y., 1963-66; asst. dir. pub. relations Community Hosp. Green Cove; dir. publicity N.Y. State Pavilion, Worlds Fair, N.Y.C., 1964-66; founder, editor Yankee Trader, Port Jefferson, N.Y., 1966—; pres. Osprey Publs. Inc., 1966—, Yankee Ad-Pak Corp., 1981—, For Singles Only Mag., 1984—; pub. Harbor Chronicle Weekly News, 1980—, The Trumpeteer, Osprey Graphics, Inc. Mem. Brookhaven Small Bus. Adv. Council. bd. dirs. Postal Customers Club L.I. Served with WAC. Mem. N.Y. State Advt. Pubs. Assn., L.I. Pubs. Assn., L.I. Advt. Club, Amiral de Grasse Soc., Decisions, Women in Commerce (bd. dirs.), Nat. Assn. Advt. Newspapers, Am. Legion, Stony Brook Found., Internat. Platform Assn., L.I. Assn. Roman Catholic. Clubs: Overseas Press (N.Y.C.); L.I. Press, Old Field. Author: Le Heros Forgotten. Contbr. articles to profl. publs. Home: 153 Quaker Path Setauket NY 11733 Office: 1110 Route 25A Port Jefferson Station NY 11776

O'CONNOR, COURTNAY PATRICIA (ALICE ROSEMARY), nurse, educator, researcher; b. Ajo, Ariz., Oct. 21, 1942; d. Daniel John and Susan Ellen (Breen) O'Connor; student U. Ariz., 1967-68; B.S.N., Incarnate Word Coll., San Antonio, 1964; m. John David Stricklin, May 31, 1964 (div.); children—John Eric, Michael Morrow. Mem. surg. cardio-vascular research team SW Research Inst., San Antonio, 1962-64; nurse Highsmith-Rainey Hosp., Fayetteville, N.C., 1964-65; operating room supr. New Cornelia Hosp., Ajo, 1966-69, asst. dir. nurses, 1968-69; with Hillcrest Gen. Hosp., Silver City, N.Mex., 1969-81, supervisory nurse, 1969-81, asst. chmn. nursing div., 1979-81, dir. in-service edn., 1979-81; ind. nursing research, writer, lectr., 1978—; instr. advanced cardiac life support; cons., lectr. in field. Chmn. Grant County chpt. Am. Heart Assn.; concert chmn. Grant County Choral Union; coordinator, resource person Medic Alert Program, 1976-79. Mem. Assn. Critical Care Nurses. Republican. Roman Catholic. Contbr. articles to profl. jours. Home: 44100 Blackhawk Silver City NM 88061

O'CONNOR, DORIS JULIA, oil company foundation executive; b. N.Y.C. Apr. 30, 1930; d. Joseph D. and Mary (Longinotti) Bisagni; m. Gerard T. O'Connor, Oct. 8, 1950 (div. Dec. 1972); 1 dau., Kim C. B.A. cum laude in Econs., U. Houston, 1975. Adminstrv. asst. Shell Cos. Found., Inc., N.Y.C., 1966-71, asst. sec., Houston, 1971-73, sec., 1973-76, sr. v.p., dir., mem. exec. com., 1976—. Corp. assoc. United Way of Am., Washington, 1976—; corp. advisor Bus. Com. of Arts, N.Y.C., 1976—; del. Bus. Com. of Arts, Houston, 1982—; dir. Ind. Sector, Washington, 1981-83, vice chmn., 1983—; mem. contbns. council Conf. Bd., N.Y.C., 1976—; advisor Council of Better Bus. Burs., Washington, 1975—. Mem. Omicron Delta Epsilon.

O'CONNOR, FRANCINE MARIE, magazine executive; b. Springfield, Mass., Apr. 8, 1930; d. Wallace Harold and Celestine Margaret (Morrison) Provost; m. John Francis O'Connor, Dec. 29, 1951; children—Margaret Anne, Kathryn Mary O'Connor Boswell, Timothy John. Grad. high sch., Springfield. Freelance writer, St. Louis, 1969-75; freelance book reviewer St. Louis Post Dispatch, 1970-73; editorial asst. Liguorian Mag., Liguori, Mo., 1975-76, mng. editor, 1976—. Author: (bull. series) Explaining God's Word, 1977-85, Exploring Our Faith, 1982—; (sacrament series) First Communion-First Penance, 1985; (ABC's of Faith series) 1977—; (catechism) Jesus Loves You, 1983; ABC's of the Rosary, 1984. Mem. Catholic Press Assn. Roman Catholic. Avocations: fishing; bird watching; travelling. Office: Liguori Pubs 1 Liguori Dr Liguori MO 63057

O'CONNOR, JEAN SMITH, poet, author; b. nr. Hamlin, W.Va.; d. Oscar French and Florence (Adkins) Smith; grad. W.Va. Bus. Coll.; m. Gerald Francis O'Connor, Aug. 3, 1929; children—Joan Florence (Mrs. Alfred James Dickerson, Jr.), Peggy Frances (Mrs. Lanny J. Pixley), Geraldine Phyllis (Mrs. Philip James Barrons). Mem. editorial staff Echoes of W.Va., Charleston, 1952-56; v.p., sec.-treas. Line Creek Coal Corp., Charleston, 1962-66. Mem. W.Va. Poetry Soc. (organizer Charleston chpt. 1968, state pres. 1968-69), Acad. Am. Poets (affiliate), Nat. League Am. Pen Women (state pres. 1964-66, organizer Huntington br. 1966, nat. poetry chmn. 1970-72, W.Va. letters chmn. 1980-82), Cath. Daus. Am., Huntington Poetry Guild. Democrat. Roman Catholic. Club: St. Agnes Garden. Author: The Quiet Hills, 1963. Editor: Poets' Crossroads, 1953-76. Home: Apt 4K Plaza East 4300 N Ocean Blvd Fort Lauderdale FL 33308

O'CONNOR, JOYCE MARIE, artist, educator; b. Oklahoma City, Apr. 1, 1934; d. Neal William and Oleighla Julia (Osborne) Taylor; B.S. in Bus. Adminstrn., Calif. State U., Sacramento, 1982; m. Kelly J. O'Connor, Aug. 29, 1953; children—Dana Price, Mary Kellyeen O'Connor Davis. Bookkeeper First Nat. Bank, Burns, Oreg., 1956-57; with Peoples Nat. Bank of Moses Lake (Wash.), 1958-59; legal stenographer to judge, Stigler, Okla., 1960-62; loan counselor United Credit Union, Misawa, Japan, 1967-68; cashier McClellan Non-Commd. Officers Club, McClellan AFB, Sacramento, 1969-70; fine and applied arts tchr. adult edn. Grant Sch. Dist., Sacramento, 1977—; tchr. N. Highlands Dist., various orgns. Mem. Soc. Western Artists, Calif. Arts League, Highlands Artists Guild, Pastel Soc. West Coast. Democrat. Methodist. Clubs: Non-Commd. Officers Wives (past officer AFB bases). Home and Office: 3564 Sun Maiden Way North Highlands CA 95660

O'CONNOR, KATHLEEN MAUREEN, association executive; b. Cleve., Oct. 22, 1946; d. Jack Lawrence and Cathryn Marie (Taylor) Connor. B.A., Assumption Coll., 1973; M.A., Clark U., 1976, M.B.A., 1980. Mgr. product devel. and mktg. St. Cyr Cosmetics, Worcester, Mass., 1975-76; tng. specialist Chess King, Worcester, 1976-77, assoc. mgr. store communications, N.Y.C., 1978-80; co-founder, pres. Kaci Cosmetics, N.Y.C., 1980-83; dir. mem. services Nat. Retail Mchts. Assn., N.Y.C., 1983—; cons. in retail mktg./promotion. Writer/speaker audio and video tapes. Mem. Am. Mktg. Assn., The Fashion Group, Am. Soc. Assn. Execs., Direct Mktg. Assn., Retail Advt. Conf. Office: Nat Retail Merchants Assn 100 W 31st St New York NY 10001

O'CONNOR, MICHOL, lawyer; b. Houston, Nov. 30, 1942; d. Charles Cary O'Connor and Ida Mae (Mueller) Baird; B.A., U. Tex.-Austin, 1966; J.D., U. Houston, 1973; 1 son, Baird James Craft. Admitted to Tex. bar, 1973; law clk. 1st Ct. Civil Appeals, Houston, 1974-75; asst. dist. atty. Harris County Dist. Attys. Office, Houston, 1975-76; assoc. firm Kronzer, Abraham & Watkins, Houston, 1976-78; asst. U.S. atty. U.S. Atty.'s Office, So. Dist. Tex., Houston, 1978-81; corp. counsel Century Devel. Corp., 1981-82. Democratic nominee 1st

Ct. Appeals of Tex., 1984; of counsel Haight, Gardner, Poor & Havens, 1985—. Recipient award for jour. article Tex. Bar Found., 1978. Mem. ABA, Tex. Bar Assn. (chmn. adminstrn. justice com.), Houston Bar Assn. (dir. 1977-79), Houston Young Lawyers (dir. 1975-76, Outstanding Contbn. award 1975), Order of Barons. Contbr. articles to profl. and polit. jours. Office: 3900 Texas Commerce Tower Houston TX 77002

O'CONNOR, NINA LOUISE, nurse; b. Long Beach, Calif., Mar. 10, 1934; d. Quincy Arthur and Evie Lorraine (Boykin) Roberts; A.A., R.N., Pasadena City Coll., 1976; children—Dennis E., Michael H., Patricia S. Nurse surg. service Meth. Hosp. of So. Calif., Arcadia, 1976, staff nurse surg. ICU, 1977-79, head nurse surg. ICU, 1979-80; rev. mgr. PSRO, 1980-81, dir. profl. services, 1981-82, exec. dir., 1982-84; with Los Angeles dist. ops./rev. Calif. Med. Rev., Inc., 1984—; lectr., author. Youth coordinator Pasadena (Calif.) council Girl Scouts U.S.A., 1964-74; mem. Pasadena Election Bd., 1964—. youth leader Congl. Ch., 1964-74. Cert. advanced life support in CPR, critical care R.N. Mem. Assn. Critical Care Nurses, Nat. Critical Care Inst., Alpha Gamma Sigma, Delta Gamma Omega, Sigma Phi Nu. Congregationalist. Home: 3870 Mayfair Dr Pasadena CA 91107

O'CONNOR, PATRICIA VINCENT, advertising executive; b. Oak Park, Ill., Apr. 30, 1945; d. Charles Ray and Mary du Bois (Starr) V.; m. Michael William O'Connor, Oct. 9, 1970; children—Eric Vincent, Kyle Stewart, Lindsay Erin. B.A. in Polit. Sci., U. Colo.-Boulder, 1967; postgrad. advanced advt. Northwestern U., 1972. Vice pres., group account, media dir. J. Walter Thompson, Chgo., 1969—; cons. Harvey Scholnick & Assoc., Chgo., 1983—. Recipient Leadership award Chgo. YWCA, 1982. Episcopalian.

O'CONNOR, PEGGY LEE, computer company manager; b. Chgo., Apr. 20, 1953; d. William Stanley and Eleanor Sopie (Levandowski) Czaska; m. Charles B. O'Connor, III, Feb. 14, 1978. B.S. in Biology, Northeastern Ill. U., 1982; M.B.A., No. Ill. U., 1985. Emergency med. technologist, 1976-82; instr. Chgo. City Wide Colls., 1976-81; program dir. U. Ill. Hosp. 1979-81; program dir. Fermilab, Roselle, 1978-82; dist. adminstrv. mgr. Decision Data Services, Schaumburg, Ill., 1981—. Recipient Phoenix award Decision Data Services, 1983. Mem. Nat. Assn. Female Execs., Women in Info. Processing, Women in Bus. Avocation: computers. Office: Decision Data Services Inc 300 N Martingale Rd Schaumburg Il 60194

O'CONNOR, PETRIE CATHERINE, personnel executive; b. Mahopac, N.Y., Jan. 8, 1947; d. Louis Alphonso and Catherine Theresa (Sammartino) Freda; children—Matthew O'Connor, Jared Petrie. Student St. Joseph's U., 1967-68. Mgr. personnel adminstrn. Itel Corp., San Francisco, 1973-78; dir. word processing services, 1978-79; dir. human recources ADP, Inc., Hayward, Calif., 1979—; advisor Hayward Unified Sch. Dist. B.E.S.T. Program, Hayward, Calif., 1982-83. Mem. Internat. Assn. Personnel Women, Am. Soc. Personnel Adminstrn., Am. Soc. Profl. and Exec. Women, No. Calif. Human Resources Council, Nat. Assn. Female Execs., Bay Area Personnel Assn. Office: ADP Inc 2380 W Winton Ave Hayward CA 94545

O'CONNOR, SALLY ANNE, bank official; b. Newton, Mass., Mar. 12, 1942; d. Frank Martin and Mary O'Connor; student Newton Coll., 1960-62; A.S. with honors, Garland Coll., 1964. Vice pres., gen. mgr. Hampshire House, Boston, 1971-79; dir. mktg. Coopers of Boston, 1980-81; mgr., spl. events mgr. Bank of Boston, 1981—. Bd. dirs. Public Action for Arts, Jr. Council of the Symphony, Mus. Fine Arts Council. Mem. Jr. League Boston. Republican. Home: 1284 Beacon St Brookline MA 02146 Office: 100 Federal St HO-17 Boston MA 02110

O'CONNOR, SANDRA DAY, U.S. Supreme Court justice; b. El Paso, Tex., Mar. 26, 1930; d. Harry A. and Ada Mae (Wilkey) Day; B.A., Stanford U., 1950, LL.B. (bd. editors Law Rev.), 1952; m. John Jay O'Connor, III, Dec. 1952; children—Scott, Brian, Jay. Admitted to Calif. bar, 1952, Ariz. bar, 1957; dep. county atty., San Mateo, Calif., 1952-53; civil atty. Q.M. Market Center, Frankfurt/Main, W.Ger., 1954-57; pvt. practice law, Phoenix, 1959-65; individual practice, Maryvale, Ariz., 1959-60; asst. atty. gen., Ariz., 1965-69; mem. Ariz. Senate, 1969-75, Majortity leader, 1973-74; judge Superior Ct., Maricopa County, Ariz., 1974-79, Ariz. Ct. Appeals, Phoenix, 1979-81, assoc. justice Supreme Ct. U.S., 1981—; juvenile ct. referee, 1962-64; chmn. vis. bd. Maricopa County Juvenile Detention Home, 1963-64; chmn. com. to reorganize lower cts. Ariz. Supreme Ct., 1974-75; mem. Anglo-Am. Legal Exchange, 1980; chairperson judges tng. and edn. com. Maricopa County Supreme Ct.; faculty Robert A. Taft Inst. Govt.; vice chmn. Select Law Enforcement Rev. Commn., 1979-80. Past Rep. dist. chmn.; mem. Maricopa County Bd. Adjustments and Appeals, 1963-64, Ariz. Personnel Commn., 1968-69. Nat. Def. Adv. Com. Women in Services, 1974-76. Mem. nat. bd. Smithsonian Assocs., 1981—; Ariz. State Personnel Commn., 1967-69; trustee Stanford U., 1976-80; bd. dirs. Ariz. Acad.; pres. Heard Mus., 1980-81; bd. dirs. Phoenix Hist. Soc., 1974-77; adv. bd. Salvation Army, 1975-19; Named Phoenix Woman of Year, Advt. Club, 1972; recipient award NCCJ, 1975, Disting. Achievement award Ariz. State U., 1980. Mem. ABA, State Bar Ariz. Office: Supreme Ct of US 1 1st St NE Washington DC 20543

O'CONNOR, SARA RAE, office supplies and printing sales representative; b. Highland Park, Ill., Oct. 20, 1951; d. Raymond Owen and Georganna Sara (Shrosbree) O'C.; m. Patrick Dennis Bogengberger, Aug. 23, 1969 (div. 1975); children—Rachel Ann, Kari Elizabeth. Student Los Angeles City Coll., 1970-72. With printing order desk Economy Office Supply, Los Angeles, 1979-80, printing supr., 1980-81, printing sales rep., 1981-84, office supplies and printing outside sales rep., 1984—. Active Wilton Pl. Sch. PTA, 1975-82, pres. 1976-77, 77-78; mem. Immaculate Heart High Sch. Parents Council, 1983-82, St. Gregory's Parent Club, 1985-86. Mem. Nat. Assn. Female Execs., Wilshire C. of C. Democrat. Roman Catholic. Club: Democratic (Beverly Hills). Avocations: Ice skating; swimming; horseback riding; tennis. Office: Economy Office Supply 1342 S LaBrea Ave Los Angeles CA 99019

O'CONNOR, TERESA FRANCES, English educator, author; b. London, June 17, 1943; came to U.S., 1950, naturalized, 1959; d. James Patrick and Gladys Irene (Kersey) O'Connor; m. Hirotsugu Aoki, Jan. 25, 1972; 1 child, Owen O'Connor-Aoki. B.A., CUNY, 1963; M.Philosophy, NYU, 1980, Ph.D., 1985; Prof. (hon.), Hebei U., Baoding, China, 1985. Assoc. prof. Coll. S.I., N.Y.C., 1968—; vis. prof. Hebei Tchrs. U., China, 1980; dir. Chinese-Am. Ednl. Exchange, N.Y.C., 1980—. Translator: Celebration of Life, 1972. Contbr. articles to profl. publs. Mem. CUNY Women's Coalition (founding mem). Office: Coll SI English Dept 715 Ocean Terr Staten Island NY 10301

O'CONNOR, TERRI TYLER, public relations specialist; b. Los Angeles, Mar. 7, 1946; d. Alan Dexter and Mae (Littleton) Tyler; m. Timothy James O'Connor, May 10, 1971 (div. 1981); children—Timothy, Christine, Jason. B.S. magna cum laude, North Tex. State U., 1979. Feature editor Conroe Courier, Tex., 1968-70; advt. salesperson News-Texans, Inc., Irving, 1971-73; pub. relations asst. State Fair of Tex., Dallas, 1978-79; TV producer Belo Bradcasting, Dallas, 1980-81; owner Syncon Producers, Inc., Dallas, 1981-82; pub. info. dir. Brookhaven Coll., Dallas, 1983-85, instr., 1984-85. Field producer Entertainment Tonight, 1982; assoc. dir. TV program Miss USA Tex. Pageant, 1982; producer TV program Richard Hogue Weekdays, 1982. Bd. dirs. Miss Dallas Scholarship Pageant, 1982. Mem. Nat. Council Community Relations (bd. dirs. 1983-84), Council Advancement and Support of Edn., Farmers Branch C. of C. Republican. Roman Catholic. Home: 1805 Southstone Irving TX 75060

ODA, LOIS SHAFFER, clothing manufacturing company executive; b. Lynn, Mass., Oct. 15, 1946; d. Roy Alan and Frances Anne (Oremland) Shaffer; m. Stephen Roy Oda, Aug. 14, 1976; 1 child, Mark Roy. Student U. N.Mex., 1964-68. Publs. asst. Ampex, 1970-71; adminstrv. asst. Tishman Constrn., Los Angeles, 1971-73, Blackfield Hawaii, 1973-75; regional coordinator Century 21 Real Estate, Honolulu, 1974-75; asst. office adminstrv. mgr. Pacific Ins., 1975-82; owner, pres. BabyMark Hawaii, Kaneohe, 1982—, Avocations: reading; designing. Office: 46-188 Lilpuna Rd Kaneohe HI 96744

ODDO, LUCIA CADENHEAD, marketing research executive; b. Austin, Tex., Nov. 11, 1952; d. Charles P. and Eleanor A. (Edwards) Cadenhead; b. Thomas Joseph Oddo, Mar. 24, 1979. Student Bradley U., 1970-72; B.S., U. Ill., Champaign, 1974; M.S. in Mgmt., Northwestern U., 1983. Supr. A.C. Nielsen Co., Mason City, Iowa, 1974-76, project dir., Northbrook, Ill., 1976-77, mgr., 1977-81, v.p., 1981, assoc. dir. research, 1984—. Mem. com. Am. Cancer Soc., 1983. Mem. Am. Mgmt. Assn., Am. Mktg. Assn., Am. Soc. Quality Control, Women in Mgmt. (chpt. pres. 1983-84, exec. bd. 1983-85). Republican. Office: AC Nielsen Co Nielsen Plaza Northbrook IL 60062

O'DEA, CONSTANCE LOUISE, public finance credit analyst, former state official, educator; b. N.Y.C., June 27, 1948; d. John W. J. and Valerie C. O'Dea; B.A. (Durant scholar), Wellesley Coll., 1968; M.A. (Grad. Prize fellow), Harvard U., 1973. Asst. coordinator systems analysis group Inst. Space Research, Nat. Research Council of Brazil, Sao Paulo, 1973-74; vis. prof. Tech. Inst. Aeros., Sao Paulo, 1974; instr. Am. Sch., Rio de Janeiro, Brazil, 1975-77, coordinator research and devel. planning N.J. Dept. Edn., Trenton, 1978-83, project mgr., 1983-85; credit analyst Moody's Investors Service, 1985—; cons. in field. Rep. for Rio de Janeiro-Belo Horizonte to Wellesley (Mass.) Coll., 1976-77. Ford Found. fellow Harvard U., 1969-73; Fanny Bullock Workman fellow Wellesley Coll., 1969-70. Mem. Phi Beta Kappa. Clubs: N.Y. Wellesley, St. Bartholomew Community. Editor, collaborator: The Social Economy of the Future, 1979. Home: 63 W 85th St New York NY 10024 Office: 99 Church St New York NY 10007

O'DELL, JOAN ELIZABETH, business executive, lawyer; b. East Dubuque, Ill., May 3, 1932; d. Peter Emerson and Olive (Bonnet) O'dell; children—Dominique R., Nicole L. B.A. cum laude, U. Miami, 1956, J.D., 1958. Bar: Fla. 1958, D.C. 1974, Ill. 1978; lic. real estate broker. Trial atty. U.S. SEC, Washington, 1959-60; asst. state atty. Office State Atty., Miami, Fla., 1960-64, Dade County Atty.'s Office, Miami, 1964-70; county atty. Palm Beach County Atty.'s Office, West Palm Beach, Fla., 1970-71; regional gen. counsel. U.S. EPA, Region IV, Atlanta, 1971-73, assoc. gen. counsel, Washington, 1973-77; sr. counsel Nalco Chem. Co., Oakbrook, Ill., 1977-78; v.p. Angel Mining, Tenn., 1979—; pres. South West Land Investments, Miami, Fla., 1979—. Bd. dirs. Tucson Women's Found., 1982-84, U. Ariz. Bus. and Profl. Women's Club, Tucson, 1981-85; bd. dirs. LWV Tucson, 1981-85, pres., 1984-86; bd. dirs. LWV Ariz., 1985-86, chmn. nat. security study; mem. AAUW, Tucson; mem. Exec. Women's Council, Tucson, 1982-85. Mem. ABA, Fed. Bar Assn., Fla. Bar Assn., D.C. Bar Assn., Dade County Bar Assn., Pima County Bar Assn. (assoc.), Ariz. Women Lawyers Assn. (assoc.), Tucson Bd. Realtors, Tucson C. of C. (state govt. com. 1982-85). Office: 720 NE 69th St Suite 4B Miami FL 33138 also 17 E 80th St #1 New York NY 10021

O'DELL, KAROL JOANNE, experimental prototype company executive; b. Lafayette, Colo., Jan. 4, 1936; d. Clarence Willis and Thelma (Stoner) O'D. Student Wayne State U., 1953-56, U. Detroit, 1956-57. Sec. IBM, Detroit, 1957-59; from bookkeeper to office mgr. Jo-Ad Industries, Inc., 1959-84, v.p., 1984—. Treas. Detroit Puppeteers Guild, 1983—; active Salvation Army. Mem. Nat. Assn. Female Execs. Avocations: puppetry; religious education; reading.

O'DELL, KIM MARIE, environmentalist; b. Westerly, R.I., Aug. 22, 1957; d. James A. and Dorothy (Gulluscio) Sposato; m. Michael P. O'Dell, Jan. 5, 1980. B.A., U. R.I., 1979; postgrad. Fla. Atlantic U., 1984. Chem. lab. technician So. Fla. Water Mgmt. Dist., West Palm Beach, Fla., 1980-84, environmentalist, 1984—. Contbr. articles to profl. jours. Mem. Fla. Acad. Sci., Am. Soc. Limnology and Oceanography. Roman Catholic. Avocations: sewing; tennis; golf. Home: 13095 Bel Haven Ct West Palm Beach FL 33414 Office: South Fla Water Mgmt Dist 3301 Gun Club Rd West Palm Beach FL 33406

O'DELL, LYNN MARIE LUEGGE, librarian; b. Berwyn, Ill. Feb. 24, 1938; d. George Emil and Helen Marie (Pesek) Luegge; student Lyons Twp. Jr. Coll., La Grange, Ill., 1957; student N. Ill. U., Elgin Community Coll., U. Ill.; m. Norman D. O'Dell, Dec. 14, 1957; children—Jeffrey, Jerry. Sec. Martin Co., Chgo., 1957-59; librarian, Carol Stream (Ill.) Public Library, 1964—; exec. com. Du Page County Library System, 1967, 68, 71—, pres. automation governing com., 1981-85, pres. adminstrv. librarians adv. com., 1985-86. Active Carol Stream unit Central DuPage Hosp. Aux.; sec. Carol Stream Bicentennial Commn. Named Woman of Year, Wheaton Bus. and Profl. Woman's Club, 1968. Mem. ALA, Ill. Library Assn., Library Adminstrs. Conf. No. Ill., Carol Stream Hist. Soc. (1st v.p.). Club: Carol Stream Woman's (sec. 1968, 1st v.p. 1969). Lutheran (organist). Home: 182 Yuma Ln Carol Stream IL 60188 Office: 616 Hiawatha Dr Carol Stream IL 60188

ODELL, MARY JANE, state official; b. Algona, Iowa, July 28, 1923; d. Eugene and Madge (Lewis) Neville; m. Gary Chinn (dec. 1966); children—Brad, Chris; m. John J.P. Odell (dec. 1984). B.A., U. Iowa, 1945; D. (hon.), Simpson Coll., Indianola, Iowa, 1982. Hostess pub. affairs TV and radio programs, Des Moines and Chgo.; sec. state State of Iowa, Des Moines. Mem. Iowa ERA Com., 1979-80; chmn. Iowa Easter Seal Soc., 1979-83. Recipient Emmy awards, 1972, 75; George Washington Carver Meritorious Service award for Community Race Relations, Simpson Coll., 1978, Iowa Women's Hall of Fame award Commn. on Status of Women, 1979. Republican. Club: Iowa Women's Polit. Caucus.

ODEM, LAURA JUANITA BURTON, personnel executive; b. Newark, Jan. 21, 1947; d. Herman L. and Iola (Brantley) Burton; B.A., Spelman Coll., 1968; postgrad. Control Data Inst., 1970; m. Jerry Odem, Sept. 4, 1970; 1 dau., Veronica Michelle. Social worker Los Angeles County Public Social Services, 1968-70; chief personnel tng., 1970-72, personnel analyst with personnel dept., 1972-74, team leader, 1974-77, community devel. analyst, 1974-77, now personnel mgmt. specialist. Past pres. Black Women's Network; mem. Inter-Alumni Council United Negro Coll. Fund. Mem. So. Calif. Personnel Mgmt. Assn. Club: Jack and Jill of Am. Presbyterian. Home: 1222 S Alvira St Los Angeles CA 90035 Office: 222 N Grand Ave Los Angeles CA 90012

ODEN, FRAN, commercial interior designer; b. Duncan, Okla., Apr. 29, 1946; d. Elbert Gates and Loretta (Prater) McPhail; m. David B. Oden, May 23, 1980; children—Shanon Anne, Dana MacKensie, David Gates. B.A., U. Okla., 1968. Designer, Frankfurt-Short-Bruza, Oklahoma City, 1969-75; dir. design The Benham Group, Oklahoma City, 1975-77; design coordinator Scott Rice, Oklahoma City, 1977-79; prin. Fran Oden Assocs., Oklahoma City, 1979—; cons. The Benhan Group, 1979-80, Frankfurt-Short-Bruza, 1977-81. Design and space planning for TG&Y Corp. Hdqrs., Oklahoma City, Okla. Gas & Electric, Los Alamos Sci. Lab. Support Facility, Hertz Corp. Reservation and Data Ctrs., Mobile Oil Corp., Bapt. Med. Ctr., Am. Airlines Exec. Offices, others. Mem. Am. Soc. Interior Designers, Nat. Assn. Female Execs. Republican. Baptist. Avocation: triathlete. Home: 8012 Wilshire Hills Dr Oklahoma City OK 73132 Office: Fran Oden Assocs 6414 C North Santa Fe Oklahoma City OK 73116

ODIORNE, ALICE SOULEK, lawyer; b. Newport News, Va., Apr. 27, 1953; d. Dale Sinclair and Lucy (Bishop) Soulek; B.A. with honors, Baylor U., 1975, J.D., 1978; m. James T. Odiorne, Apr. 26, 1980; children—James Michael, Raymond Andrew; 1 son by previous marriage, Toby Aaron Quinn. Admitted to Tex. bar, 1979; ptnr. firm James T. Odiorne, Bastrop, Tex., 1978-84; regional child welfare atty. Tex. Dept. Human Resources, 1984-86, asst. regional atty., 1986—. Bd. dirs. Bastrop Opera House, 1979-80, Austin dist. United Meth. Ch. Mem. Bastrop County Bar Assn. (pres. 1980-81), ABA, Tex. State Bar (family law sect.), Tex. Young Lawyers Assn. Democrat. Methodist. Office: PO Box 15995 Austin TX 78761

ODLE, LYDIA ANN, real estate company executive; b. N.Y.C., May 4, 1945; d. John and Caroline (Allis) Karpinol; m. Robert C. Odle, Jr., Aug. 2, 1969. B.S., Mich. State U., 1967. Lic. real estate broker, Va. Instr. Alexandria pub. schs., Va., 1969-73; broker Golubin & Warwick, Inc., Alexandria, 1973-76; pres. Manarin & Odle, Inc., Alexandria, 1976—. Republican. Roman Catholic. Home: 219 S Lee St Alexandria VA 22314 Office: Manarin & Odle Realtors 400 S Washington St Alexandria VA 22314

ODOARDI, ANTOINETTE MARIE, pharmacologist; b. Pietranico, Italy, Apr. 19, 1952; d. Vincent and Lucy (Colucci) O.; came to U.S., 1955, naturalized, 1961; B.S. (Scholar 1970-74), Coll. White Plains, 1974; M.S. (teaching asst. 1975-76), Fordham U., 1977, postgrad N.Y. Med. Coll., 1978-81; M.B.A. candidate U. Conn., 1984—. Clin. data analyst Revlon Health Care Group, Tuckahoe, N.Y., 1976-83; quality assurance assoc. Ayerst Labs., N.Y.C., 1983-85; project adminstr. Miles Pharms., West Haven, Conn., 1985—. Mem. N.Y. Acad. Sci., Sigma Xi. Home: 91 Strawberry Hill Ave Unit 230 Stamford CT 06902 Office: 400 Morgan Ln West Haven CT 06516

O'DOHERTY, KATHLEEN MARIE, librarian; b. Woburn, Mass., May 25, 1950; d. Thomas and Elizabeth Theresa (Keleher) O'D. B.A., Northeastern U., 1973; M.S., Simmons Coll., 1979. Asst. reference librarian, asst. cataloguer Woburn Pub. Library, 1977-79; cataloguer Bradford Coll. (Mass.), 1979-81, library dir., 1981-83; library dir. Brooks Sch., North Andover, Mass., 1983—; pres. Merrimack InterLibrary Coop., North Andover, 1983—. Bd. dirs. Children and Family Aid Soc., Haverhill, Mass., 1984—. Mem. Mass. Assn. Ednl. Media, ALA. Home: 1 Carleton Sq Bradford MA 01830 Office: Brooks Sch 1160 Great Pond Rd North Andover MA 01845

ODOM, CAROLYN, publishing company executive; b. Augusta, Ga.; d. Plannie C. and Marjorie (Waldo) Odom. B.A., Spelman Coll., 1966; M.A., Am. U., 1970. Dep. dir. N.Y.C. Health and Hosp. Adminstrn., 1972-76; communications coordinator Nat. Health Council, N.Y.C., 1976-77; dir. pub. affairs Earl G. Graves Ltd., N.Y.C., 1977-83, v.p. corp. communications, 1983—. Contbr. articles to profl. jours. Mem. Women in Communications, The EDGES Group. Office: Earl G Graves Ltd 130 Fifth Ave New York NY 10011

O'DONNELL, ALICE LOUISE, government official; b. Stanwood, Wash.; d. John James and Jeannette May (Anderson) O'Donnell. Student U. Wash., 1932, U. So. Calif., 1943-44; student George Washington U, 1940-42, J.D., 1954. Bars: U.S. Dist. Ct. D.C., U.S. Supreme Ct., U.S. Ct. of Appeals (D.C. cir.). With staff Atty. Gen. U.S., 1945-49; mem. staff Justice Clark, Supreme Ct. of U.S., Washington, 1949-67; lawyer Fed. Jud. Center, Washington, 1968—, dir. div. inter-jud. affairs and info. services, 1971—; sec.-treas. Nat. Center for State Cts., 1971-81. Vice-chmn. bd. dirs. Potomac Law Sch., Washington, 1975-79. Fellow Inst. Jud. Adminstrn. (pres.-elect 1985); mem. ABA (mem. div. jud. adminstrn., chmn. 1973-74), Fed. Bar Assn., Am. Judicature Soc., Nat. Lawyers Club Washington (bd. govs.), Supreme Ct. Hist. Soc. (v.p.), Thomas More Soc. Am., Phi Alpha Delta. Roman Catholic. Home: The Towers 4201 Cathedral Ave NW Washington DC 20016 Office: Dolley Madison House 1520 H St NW Washington DC 20005

O'DONNELL, ELIZABETH MARY, sport training for handicapped association executive; b. Buffalo, Sept. 30, 1953; d. Francis William and Eileen Marie (Sager) O'D. Grad., Holy Angels Acad., 1971. Competitive ice skater, 1958-71; performer Ice Capades, 1971-73; dir. recreational skating, power skating and figure skating, mgr. pro shop, coach and trainer hockey teams at 5 arenas, Western N.Y., 1973-77; pres., founder Skating Assn. for the Blind and Handicapped, Inc., Buffalo, 1976—; producer ice shows at local arenas, 1974—; producer Ice Extravaganzas at Buffalo Meml. Auditorium with nat. skaters, Buffalo Sabres, Buffalo Bills, media stars and numerous handicapped skaters, 1979—; speaker throughout U.S.; seminar speaker on motivation, leadership, volunteerism and sensory awareness; U.S. rep. World Profl. Figure Skating Championships, Jaca, Spain, 1978. Author: Teaching the Handicapped Through Ice Skating, 1977; co-author: Special Olympics Skating Manual, 1983; writer song Dream Your Dream, 1984. Coordinator winter activities events Women for Downtown Buffalo; trainer on pub. speaking Jr. League, Buffalo; bd.-dirs.-at-large Boys and Girls Clubs, Erie County, N.Y., 1986-89. Recipient numerous freestyle club and interclub skating titles Buffalo Skating Club competitions and other regional competitions, 1958-71; Humanitarian of Yr. award Am. Vets. Assn., 1981; Leader of Yr. award Jr. C. of C., 1983; local and tri-state regional Service to Mankind awards Sertoma, 1984; Citizen of Yr. award Buffalo News, 1985. Mem. U.S. Figure Skating Assn. (Gold Dance award, Figure Skating award). Avocations: Cecchetti and Russian ballet; tap dancing; sports; sewing and designing; reading. Home: 218 Carolina St Buffalo NY 14201 Office: Skating Assn for Blind and Handicapped 3236 Main St Buffalo NY 14214

O'DONNELL, HILARY CAMP, construction company executive; b. Arlington, Va., Apr. 22, 1961; d. William Edward III and Virginia Marie (O'Donnell) Camp; m. Michael Sean O'Donnell, Aug. 10, 1985. Student U. Oslo Internat. Summer Sch., 1981; B.A. in Polit. Sci. magna cum laude, Mt. St. Mary's Coll., Emmitsburg, Md., 1983. Supr., workflow analyst Claims Adminstrs. Corp., Rockville, Md., 1983-86; with Acacia Constrn. Corp., Gaithersburg, Md., 1982—, exec. v.p., 1986—. Mem. Nat. Assn. for Female Execs., Gaithersburg C. of C., Pi Sigma Alpha. Republican. Roman Catholic. Avocations: jogging, racquetball, volleyball, tutoring. Home: 19936 Stoney Point Way Germantown MD 20874 Office Acacia Constrn Corp 7609 Airpark Rd Bay J Gaithersburg MD 20879

O'DONNELL, RUTH MAYS, hospital administrator; b. Hillsboro, Oreg., Oct. 18, 1954; d. Elmer Cypher and Harriet Ruth (Martin) Mays. B.S. in Polit. Sci., Oreg. State U., 1976; M.P.A., Pa. State U., 1977. Personnel analyst Pa. Liquor Control Bd., Harrisburg, 1977; asst. dir. personnel Eagleville (Pa.) Hosp., 1978-79, dir. personnel, 1979-83, dir. human resources, 1983-84, assoc. adminstr., 1984—. Mem. Am. Soc. for Personnel Adminstrn., Am. Mgmt. Assn., Suburban Phila. Hosp. Personnel Soc. Republican. Presbyterian. Home: 1027 Valley Forge Rd 195 Devon PA 19333 Office: Eagleville Hosp 100 Eagleville Rd Eagleville PA 19408

O'DRISCOLL, MARGARET MILLAR (PEGGY), real estate broker; b. Hollywood, Calif., Aug. 2, 1925; d. Russell Hartney and Marion Scott (Macarthur) Millar; m. William Harrington Walker, Jan. 10, 1949 (dec. Dec. 22, 1968); children—William Russell Walker, Elizabeth Howland, Hiram Scott Walker; m. 2d, James O'Driscoll, Oct. 17, 1970. Student UCLA, 1942-44. Lic. ins. solicitor, real estate broker, Calif. Salesman, Carol Smart Real Estate, Del Mar, Calif., 1966-68, Bernard & Assocs., Solana Beach, Calif., 1968-70; owner Town and Country Real Estate, Rancho Santa Fe, Calif., 1970—; pres. Peggy O'Driscoll Enterprises, Inc. Mem. publicity com. Rancho Santa Fe Republican Women, 1950-58; mem. San Dieguito Citizens Planning Group, 1977-78; mem. vestry St. Peter's Episcopal Ch., Del Mar, 1976-78; bd. dirs. Rancho Santa Fe Community Services Dist., 1982-85, chmn., 1985, mem., 1986—. Mem. San Dieguito Bd Realtors (v.p. 1980-82, pres. 1983-84), Calif. Assn. Realtors (bd. dirs. 1981-86, ins. trustee 1982-86, regional v.p. dist. 29 1986), Rancho Sante Fe Hist. Soc. (bd. dirs. 1985-86), San Diego County Council Real Estate Bds. Clubs: Rancho Santa Fe Garden (publicity chmn. 1965-74), Rancho Santa Fe Women's Golf (founding mem.). Home: PO Box 457 Rancho Santa Fe CA 92067 Office: PO Box 44 Rancho Santa Fe CA 92067

OEHLERT, ALICE GREENE, civic worker; b. Munson, Pa., May 17, 1912; d. Hugh R. and Elva (Howe) Greene; grad. Thomas W. Evans Dental Inst., U. Pa., 1931; m. Benjamin H. Oehlert, Mar. 27, 1937; children—Benjamin H. III, Wendy Howe. Bd. dirs. Henry St. Settlement, N.Y.C., 1956-68, Browse Gallery of Atlanta Art Assn., 1959-61, Palm Beach (Fla.) Community Chest, 1971-73; sec. Bargain Box, Inc., N.Y.C., 1956-69; trustee Atlanta Art Assn., 1966-67; mem. adv. council Young Women's Community Club, Orlando, Fla., 1963-64; bd. dirs. Orange County chpt. Nat. Found., 1962-64; mem. women's aux. Piedmont Hosp., Atlanta, 1965-67; mem. adv. bd. jr. adv. com. High Mus. Art, Atlanta, 1965-67; v.p. Loch Haven Art Center of Orlando Art Assn., 1963-64, trustee, 1964-65; chmn. cultural affairs Greater Orlando C. of C., 1964-65; hon. pres. Am. Women's Club, Islamabad, Pakistan, 1967-69; chmn. 1st Designer Showcase, Islamabad, 1967-69; Am. dir. to all Pakistan Women's Club, Islamabad, 1967-69; bd. dirs. picture program Good Samaritan Hosp., West Palm Beach, Fla., 1969-70, mem. adv. bd. fund raising com. for women's aux., 1970-73, chmn. Ball Jour., 1978-82; hon. patron ARC, chmn. Palm Beach ARC Designers Showcase, 1976. Recipient commendation ARC, 1976, Palm Beach Garden Club Showcase, 1973. Mem. DAR. Republican. Presbyterian.

OELKERS, CAROL LYNN, statistics educator, consultant; b. Montreal, Que., Can., Aug. 7, 1941; d. Orwill Ernest and Evelyn Ester (Hall) Marchant; m. Herbert H. Oelkers, May 29, 1971; children—Keith Ross, Scott Carl. B.Sc., McGill U., Montreal, 1962, M.Sc., 1968; B.A., Sir George Williams Coll., 1965. Statistician, Imperial Tobacco Ltd., Montreal, 1962-68; prof. stats. Dawson Coll., Montreal, 1969-71; stats. cons. Carol Marchant, Montreal, 1968-71; spl. lectr. in econs. St. John Fisher Coll., Rochester, N.Y., 1972—; ptnr. in statis. cons. C & H Assoc., Rochester, 1983—. Mem. Rochester Women Network. Presbyterian. Avocations: tennis, needlework, volunteer at school. Home: 107 Longsworth Dr Rochester NY 14625 Office: St John Fisher Coll East Ave Rochester NY 14623 also C & H Assocs 107 Longsworth Dr Rochester NY 14625

OFARIM, DIANE, psychotherapist; b. Chgo., Feb. 25, 1944; d. Gustave and Freidella (Reiff) Platt; M.A. in Clin. Psychology, Pepperdine Coll., 1966; postgrad. U. So. Calif., 1966-71; 1 dau., Monica. With various social service agys. including juvenile probation, family and group therapy Los Angeles Dept. Public Aid, 1962-70, Cook County Juvenile Ct., Chgo., 1970-75, pvt. practice psychotherapy, specializing in psychoanalytically oriented, interpersonal relationships, individuals, couples and group therapy, Evanston, Ill.,

1975—; Mem. Assn. for Humanistic Psychology, Am. Psychol. Assn., Am. Personnel and Guidance Assn., Psi Chi. Office: 1603 Orrington Suite 1044 Evanston IL 60201

O'FARRELL, LUCY SHELTON, real estate company executive; Warrenton, Ga., Dec. 25, 1918; d. Bennett Gordon and Mary VanDella (Dye) Shelton; student Ga. State Women's Coll., 1936-37, Hurst Bus. Coll., 1937-38; m. Oscar Cameron O'Farrell, July 21, 1941; 1 dau., Carol Lynn. Cert. real estate broker. Sec., Lockhart Ins. & Realty Co., Atlanta, 1939-41; sec., rater, office mgr., agent Gen. Ins. Merritt & McKenzie, Atlanta, 1941-71; sales asso. Clover Realty Co., Atlanta, 1971-75, br. mgr., v.p., 1975-81; with Spratlin-Clover, Realtors, Atlanta. Mem. Nat. Assn. Realtors, Ga. Assn. Realtors, Atlanta Bd. Realtors, Womens Council Realtors, Sales Mgrs. Club, Ga. Assn. Parliamentarians, Nat. Assn. Parliamentarians, Atlanta Ins. Women. Democrat. Baptist. Club: Toastmasters. Home: 7264 Selkirk Dr NW Atlanta GA 30328 Office: Clover Realty Realtors 4511 Chamblee Dunwoody Rd NE Atlanta GA 30338

OFFERMAN, CHRISTIANE TOENNE, marketing consultant; b. Hannover, Germany, Apr. 30, 1947; came to U.s., 1977; d. Adolf and Eva (Kretzschmar) Toenne; m. Louis Offerman, May 15, 1983; 1 child, Anna. M.B.A., U. Hamburg, Fed. Republic Germany, 1972; postgrad. Clark U., 1977-78. Project dir. GFM, Hamburg, 1973-74, Makrotest, Dusseldorf, Fed. Republic Germany, 1974-75, Delphi Marktforschung, Dusseldorf, 1975-80; ptnr. Delphi Sales Cons., Inc., Lexington, Mass. and Chatham, N.J., 1980-84, Oasis, Inc., N.Y.C., 1984—. Pub. relations coordinator Amnesty Internat., Dusseldorf, 1975-77, group leader, Worcester, Mass., 1977-78. Mem. Smaller Bus. Assn., Nat. Assn. Female Execs. Lutheran. Office: Oasis Cons Inc 32 Broadway New York NY 10004

OFFHOUSE, CHARLOTTE DOROTHY, wholistic health educator, nurse; b. Paterson, N.J., May 5, 1941; d. Charles D. and Marguerite (Beutenmuller) O. R.N., St. Luke's Hosp., N.Y.C., 1962; B.S., Columbia U., 1966; M.A. in Edn., Holy Names Coll., Oakland, Calif., 1973; Ph.D., Calif. Inst. Integral Studies, San Francisco, 1985; C.M.T., Acupressure Workshop, Berkeley, Calif., 1985. R.N., Calif., N.Y. Pvt. duty nurse, N.Y.C., 1962-66; med. office coordinator, San Francisco, 1966-67; patient care coordinator Pacific Heights Convalescent Hosp., San Francisco, 1967-71; assoc. coordinator Regional Med. Programs, San Francisco, 1971-74; adminstr. The Living Centers, Vallejo, Calif., 1974-77, dir. staff devel., 1977-85; pvt. practice, 1986—; bd. dirs. Min-An Health Ctr., San Francisco, 1983—; assoc. clin. prof. U. Calif.-San Francisco, 1974—; cons. Longevity Scis. Research Ctr., Hangzhou, China, 1984—; v.p. Hospice Services of Solano County, 1977-80. Author: Extended Care, 1973. Contbr. articles to profl. jour. Mem. Soc. for Wholistic Nursing, Nursing Edn. Alumnae Assn. Columbia U., East-West Acad. of Healing Arts. Avocations: driving; play Tai Ji Quan; practice Chinese yoga. Home: 40 Scenic Way San Francisco CA 94121 Office: The Living Centers PO Box 5028 Vallejo CA 94591

OFFNER, MARY ELLEN, financial manager; b. St. Louis, Aug. 10, 1954; d. Lawrence Joseph and Audre June (Cooper) O. B.S. summa cum laude, in Biology, Maryville Coll., St. Louis, 1976. Research asst. Washington U. Sch. Med., 1976-77; salesperson Creativity Unltd., St. Louis, 1977-78; fin. analyst McDonnell Douglas Corp., St. Louis, 1978-83; dir./fin. mgr. W.A.R.M., Inc., Detroit, 1983—; fin. cons. S/W Detroit Constrn. Co., 1983—. Vol. instr. Archdiocese of St. Louis, 1981-83; active Big Bros./Big Sisters, 1981-83; fin. adv. Jr. Achievement, 1980-83. Recipient cert. of achievement Archdiocese of St. Louis, 1982. Mem. Nat. Assn. Female Execs., St. Louis Women's Polit. Caucus, St. Louis Women's Commerce Assn., Delta Epsilon Sigma. Republican. Roman Catholic. Club: Toastmasters. Avocations: gardening; bicycling. Office: WARM Inc 4835 Michigan Ave Detroit MI 48210

OFTEDAHL, LAURA RUTH, public relations executive; b. Libertyville, Ill., June 28, 1952; d. Everett John and Elaine Doris (Van Horn) O. B.S., U. Ill., 1974. Air personality Sta. WGMW, Riviera Beach, Fla., 1974-75, Sta. WRKR, Racine, Wis., 1975; pub. service dir. Sta. WGEZ, Beloit, Wis., 1975-77; sales mgr. Frostee Foam Co., Antioch, Ill., 1977-79; field services rep. Lions of Ill. Found., Oak Park, 1979-81; dir. pub. affairs Am. Council of Blind, Washington, 1981—; advisor Endependence Ctr., Arlington, Va., 1982—. Editor Old Dominion Council of Blind newsletter, 1981-85, Blind Student Advocate, 1982—; contbr. articles on recreation for blind persons for profl. jours. Bd. dirs., v.p. Old Dominion Council of Blind, 1981-85; bd. dirs., v.p. Nat. Capital Citizens with Low Vision, Washington, 1982-85, pres., 1985—; bd. dirs. Ski for Light, Inc., Mpls., 1983—. Recipient gold medal silver medal Nat. Championships-Skiing-U.S. Assn. Blind Athletes, 1982, gold medals, 1983, gold medals, 1985; silver medal World Olympics for Disabled, Innsbruck, Austria, 1984; Media award for radio presentation Pres.'s Com. on Employment of Handicapped, 1985. Mem. U.S. Assn. Blind Athletes, Women in Communications, Pub. Relations Soc. Am. Lutheran. Clubs: Ski, Potomac Pedalers Touring, Potomac Appalachian Trail (Washington); Am. Blind Bowling Assn. (Louisville). Lodge: Sons of Norway (Washington). Home: 5406 Roanoke Ave Apt 51 Alexandria VA 22311 Office: Am Council of the Blind 1010 Vermont Ave NW Suite 1100 Washington DC 20005

OGAN, ANNE PETERSON, stockbroker; b. Balt., Apr. 28, 1947; d. Harold Leon Peterson and Grace Legate (Olmsted) Potts Burge; m. Nicholas Ogan, Aug. 26, 1967; 1 son, Alexander Peterson. B.A., Radcliffe Coll., 1969. Security analyst Union Commerce Bank, Cleve., 1969-71, Ball Burget Kraus, Cleve., 1971-73; asst. to pres. Technicare Corp., Cleve., 1973-74; security analyst McDonald & Co., Cleve., 1974-77; equity salesman Salomon Bros., Cleve., 1977-79, First Boston Corp., Cleve., 1979—. Mem. Cleve. Soc. Security Analysts (sec. 1981-82). Club: Harvard U. (treas. 1982-84) (Cleve.). Office: First Boston Corp 100 Erieview Plaza Cleveland OH 44114

O'GARA, BARBARA ANN, soap company executive; b. Newark, Aug. 8, 1953; d. Frank Percy and Rose (Giordano) Stevens; m. Michael Larry O'Gara, Mar. 21, 1981; 1 stepchild, Jennifer Kelly. A.A., Keystone Jr. Coll., 1973; B.A., U. Ariz., 1976. Media buyer Wells, Rich, Green/Townsend, Irvine, Calif., 1977-80; dist. sales mgr. Armour-Dial, Phoenix, 1980-82; regional sales mgr. Guest Supply, Inc., North Brunswick, N.J., 1982-85; dir. hotel sales Neutrogena Corp., Los Angeles, 1985—. Keystone Jr. Coll. scholar, 1972, Morris County scholar, 1971; recipient Outstanding Sales Accomplishment award Armour-Dial, 1981. Mem. Nat. Assn. Female Execs. Republican. Roman Catholic. Avocations: tennis; jogging; golf. Home: 41 Carriage Hill Ln Laguna Hills CA 92653 Office: Neutrogena Corp 5755 W 96th St Los Angeles CA 90045

OGDEN, GERALDINE SAVARY, computer company and landscaping company executive, researcher and developer, inventor; b. Brooksville, Fla., Sept. 22, 1929; d. Norman Pinkney and Maude (Bullard) Savary; m. Robert Thomas Ogden, Aug. 12, 1950; children—Robert Thomas, Jr., Donna Lee Bonomi. Profl. tng. in horticulture, research and writing, nursing. Pres. Sign of the Time, Selden, N.Y., 1970-74, B.G. Micro-Purchasing, Inc., Scottsdale, Ariz., 1979—; owner, author, pub. Ogden Advt. & Research, Floral City, Fla., 1975-78; owner, mgr. Ogden Nursery Products, Inverness, Fla., 1974-79, Dove Systems, Scottsdale, 1980—, LAW Ins. Co., Scottsdale, 1985—; owner Dove Landscaping and Citrus Nursery, Floral City, Fla., 1986—; v.p. sales Computer Clinic, Mesa, Ariz., 1982-84; researcher Geri-Health of Fla., 1984-85. Author: Inverness and Citrus County Mapping Guide; What Florida Residents Should Know About Taxes; A Touch of Soul, 1983; (poetry) From A Liberated Mind, 1972; Favorite Recipes of 40 U.S. Presidents, 1985. Contbr. articles to profl. jours. and popular mags.; designer white dove symbol for women's liberation movement, 1970. Democrat. Home: 8968 Marvin Ave Floral City FL 32636 Office: Law Insurance Co 8483 E Chaparral Rd Scottsdale AZ 85251

OGDEN, TINA LOUISE, state public relations administrator; b. N.Y.C., Aug. 4, 1959. B.S., Cornell U., 1980; postgrad. Brown U., 1980. Engr. Norman Porter Assocs., N.Y.C., 1981; researcher Rockwell Internat., Thousand Oaks, Calif., 1981-82; research staff assoc. pub. info. N.Y. Power Authority Indian Point 3 Nuclear Plant, Buchanan, 1984—. Amateur radio communicator Westchester Emergency Communication Assn., White Plains, N.Y., 1986. Brown U. research grantee, 1980. Mem. Pub. Relations Soc. Am., Soc. Women Engrs., Women In Communications, Cornell U. Alumni Assn. (chpt. v.p. 1985-87). Republican. Office: NY Power Authority Indian Point 3 Nuclear Plant PO Box 215 Buchanan NY 10511

OGI, IRENE AYAKO, lawyer; b. San Jose, Calif., May 10, 1948; d. Irving Toshiro and Gladys Yukiko (Nakashima) Ogi. Student, U. Calif.-Davis, 1966-68, Internat. Christian U., Tokyo, 1968-69; B.A., U. Calif.-Berkeley, 1970; J.D., U. Calif.-Davis, 1975. Bar: Calif. 1981. Discovery coordinator Homestake Mining Co., San Francisco, 1977-81; assoc. Skjerven, Morrill, San Francisco, 1981-83; sole practice, Oakland, Calif., 1983—; judge protem Santa Clara County Superior Ct., San Jose, 1984—; guest lectr. labor law J.F.K. U., Orinda, Calif., 1984—; mem. adv. bd. U. San Francisco Coll. Profl. Studies, 1984—. Mem. Japanese Am. Citizens League, Oakland, 1984—; v.p. adv. bd. R.S.V.P. (Ret. Srs. Vol. Program), Oakland, 1984—. Mem. San Francisco Trial Lawyers Assn., San Francisco Bar Assn., Alameda County Bar Assn. Republican. Buddhist. Club: Barracuda (pres. Oakland-San Francisco 1984). Office: 848 Cleveland St Oakland CA 94606

OGILVIE, MARGARET PRUETT, counselor; b. McKinney, Tex., Jan. 8, 1922; d. William Walter and Ida Mae (Houk) Pruett; B.A., Baylor U., 1943; M.Ed., Hardin Simmons U., 1968; m. Frederick Henry Ogilvie, May 13, 1943; children—Ida Margaret, James William. Tchr. pub. and pvt. schs., Tex., Calif., Alaska, W.Ger., 1944, 53-65; guidance counselor Dentsville High Sch., Columbia, S.C., 1968-69, Northwest H.S., Clarksville, Tenn., 1970-72; personal and marital counselor, Fairfield Glade, Tenn., 1972—; co-owner F & M Gems & Jewelry. Treas. Officers' Wives Club, Ft. Irwin, Calif.; chmn. vols. ARC, Ft. Irwin, 1965; pres. Women's Golf Assn., Ft. Irwin, 1965-66; v.p. Ch. Women United, Crossville, Tenn., 1972-74; bd. dirs. Cumberland County Mental Health Assn., 1975—; mem. legis. com. and pub. affairs com. Tenn. Mental Health Assn., 1976—, mem. exec. bd., 1977—; vol. Christian Service Corps, Home Mission Bd. of So. Bapt. Conv., 1985-86; mem. Middle Tenn. com. Internat. Women's Yr., 1975; bd. dirs. Battered Women, Inc., Crossville, 1984-85. Mem. Am. Personnel and Guidance Assn., Nat. Ret. Tchrs. Assn., Bus. and Profl. Women's Club (chmn. 1973-75), DAR (parliamentarian Crab Orchard chpt. 1981), Pi Gamma Mu. Democrat. Baptist (choir dir., organist 1972—). Clubs: Fairfield Glade Women's (parliamentarian 1974-77), Fairfield Glade Women's Golf Assn. (pres. 1973, 2d v.p. 1986), Fairfield Glade Sq. Dance; Order Eastern Star (Amanda chpt. IV). Home: 240 Snead Dr PO Box 1522 Fairfield Glade TN 38555

OGLE, PEGGY ANN, human services consultant; b. Washington, Feb. 3, 1950; d. William Paul and Lurlene (Lazenby) Ogle. A.A., Miami Dade Coll., 1969; B.S., Fla. State U., 1972, M.S., 1976. Spl. educator Jackson County Schs., Marianna, Fla., 1972-73; edn. dir. Sunland-Tallahassee, Fla., 1974-76; program supr. BARA, Tallahassee, 1976-77; program examiner Dept. of H.R.S., Tallahassee, 1977-79; program adminstr. Dept. of H.R.S.-V., St. Petersburg, Fla., 1979; dir. client services PARC Ctr., St. Petersburg, 1979-82; pres. Program Design Ltd., St. Petersburg, 1982—; strategic planning cons. Ann Storck Ctr., Ft. Lauderdale, Fla., 1982-86; cons. State of Fla., Tallahassee, 1982-86; staff trainer, cons. ARA DevCon, Tallahassee, 1984-86; researcher, cons. L.R. O'Neall & Assocs., Tallahassee, 1984-86. Author: Being Human, 1983. Editor: Developmental Nursing, 1985. Contbr. articles to profl. jours. Chmn. Pinellas County Housing Coalition, St. Petersburg, 1982-83. State of Fla. grad. fellow, 1975; recipient Citizenship award, D.A.R., 1972. Mem. Am. Assn. Mental Deficiencies (gen. div. chmn. S.E. affiliate), Assn. for Severly Handicapped, Life Concepts, Inc. Avocations: tennis; swimming; skiing. Office: Program Design Ltd 600 43d Ave NE Saint Petersburg FL 33703

OGLESBY, JUDITH SMITH, advertising and public relations executive; b. Dallas, Oct. 26, 1947; d. John Stanton and Marie Lowetta (Mullins) Smith; m. Ronald T. Oglesby, June 1, 1968 (div. 1978); children—Sharon Elizabeth, Stephen Wofford. B.A. in English and Journalism, So. Meth. U., 1980; student Baylor U., 1966-67. Freelance writer, advt. and pub. relations cons., Dallas, 1978—; with Mitchell & Co. Advt., Dallas, 1980-81; account exec. TCUL Services, Inc., Dallas, 1981-83; dir. pub. relations Case and Assocs., Dallas, 1983-85; pres. Oglesby Communications, 1985—. Vice pres., founder Ellis County Republican Women's Club, Ennis, Tex., 1973; mem. Downtown Rep. Women's Club, Dallas, 1980—; mem. coms. and bds. Grace Union Presbytery, Dallas, 1973—; tchr. Highland Park Presbyn. Ch., 1979—. Mem. By Invitation Only (founder, v.p., dir.), Women in Communication, Dallas Ad League, Pub. Relations Soc. Am., DAR.

OGLETREE, SUSAN LIPFORD, educator; b. Atlanta, Aug. 7, 1953; d. Elbert Augustus and Roxie (Prince) Lipford; m. Thomas Howell Ogletree, Mar. 13, 1976; children—August Elena, Tee Howell; Mus.B., West Ga. Coll., 1973, M.Elem. Edn., 1974, Ed.S., 1985. Teaching cert. music edn. K-12, Ga.; teaching cert. elem. edn. 1-8, Ga.; teaching cert. adminstr. supervision 1-12, Ga. Asst. prin., band dir., tchr. Temple Elem./High Sch., Temple, Ga., 1973-78; headmistress Oak Mountain Acad., Carrollton, Ga., 1978—; bd. dirs. Georgian Country Day Sch., Carrollton, Ga., 1984-85; dir. Children's Theatre, Carrollton, 1980—. Mem. Phi Delta Kappa, Sigma Alpha Iota. Republican. Methodist. Avocations: skiing. Home: 1042 Old Newnan Rd Carrollton GA 30117 Office: 1575 S Hwy 16 Carrollton GA 30117

OGLETREE-BROWN, YVONNE THERESA, graphic designer; b. Chgo., Feb. 1, 1955; d. Lewis W. and Betty Lucille (Brown) Ogletree. A.A. in Graphic Design, Kennedy-King Coll., 1975; B.F.A., Ind. State U., 1979. Asst. art dir. Proctor & Gardner Advt., Inc., Chgo., 1979-82; prodn. artist Sharp Hartwig Advt., Inc., Seattle, 1982-86; freelance designer, Seattle, 1982—. Mem. Soc. Typographic Artists.

O'GORMAN, PATRICIA ALICE, psychologist; b. N.Y.C., May 27, 1946; d. Patrick M. and Mary L. (Kohut) O'G.; B.A., CCNY, 1968, M.S., 1970; Ph.D., Fordham U., 1975; m. Robert Allen Ross, Aug. 12, 1979. Clin. Asst. dept. sch. psychology Bklyn. Coll., 1973-74, adj. lectr., 1974; dir. dept. prevention and edn. Nat. Council on Alcoholism, N.Y.C., 1974-79; clin. instr. dept. psychiatry N.Y.U., N.Y.C., 1976-79; dir. div. prevention Nat. Inst. Alcohol Abuse, Rockville, Md., 1979-81; chief psychologist Berkshire Farm Ctr. and Services for Youth, Canaan, N.Y., 1981-84; pvt. practice psychology East Greenbush, N.Y., 1981—; nat. and internat. lectr. on alcoholism prevention; also spokesperson on radio, TV and press; cons. VA Hosp., Albany, N.Y., 1978-79, SUNY, Albany, 1979, 81, N.Y. Council on Children and Families, Albany, 1979, Ministry Labour and Social Affairs, Israel, 1981, 84; mem. grad. edn. nat. adv. com. project Physician Requirements for 1990's, 1982. Mem. Pres. Carter's Transition Task Force on Health, 1976; mem. N.Y. Gov.'s Transition Task Force on Alcohol and Substance Abuse, also chmn. com. on prevention, 1976; mem. adv. bd. Info. Exchange on the Young Adult Chronics; mem. adv. subcom. on alcoholism N.Y. State Senate, 1977-79; mem. alcohol and drug work group for promoting health and preventing disease Objectives for Nation, 1979; nat. adv. bd. Women in Crisis Conf., 1981-82. Mem. Am. Psychol. Assn., Am. Pub. Health Assn., Research Soc. on Alcoholism, Nat. Assn. Children of Alcoholics (founding exec. com.), Psychol. Assn. N.E. N.Y. (treas.). Democrat. Author: (with P. Finn) Teaching About Alcohol, 1981; also articles. Editorial bd. Focus on Women: Jour. of Addiction and Health, 1981-82. Home: Rural Delivery Box 300 East Chatham NY 12060 Office: 568 Columbia Turnpike East Greenbush NY 12061

O'GRADY, ELINOR M., secretarial service owner; b. Chgo.; d. Arthur O. and Anna L. (Miller) Atkins; m. Norman Hohnstock, Oct. 12, 1940 (div. 1945); 1 child, Judith A.; m. Michael A. O'Grady, Jr., Dec. 16, 1950; 1 child, Michael A. Office mgr. N. Soifer, M.D. & Assocs., Dayton, Ohio, 1950-79; pres. Park Ave. Secretarial Service, Dayton, 1980—. Mem. Tri-City Bus. and Profl. Women (sec. 1983-84), Profl. Secs. Internat., Am. Bus. Women Assn. Club: Pilot (pres. 1984-85) (Kettering, Ohio). Avocations: golf; landscape gardening; boating; sailing; crocheting. Home: 2513 Hackney Dr Kettering OH 45420 Office: 53 Park Ave Dayton OH 45419

OGRINZ, CORDELIA ELAINE, banker; b. Balt., Oct. 30, 1947; d. Alexander John, Jr., and Camilla Victoria (VonDracek) Ogrinz. B.Mus., Bucknell U., 1969; grad. Sch. Bank Mgmt., U. Va., 1976; M.B.A., Loyola Coll.-Balt., 1981. Mgmt. trainee Md. Nat. Bank, Balt., 1969-70, asst. mgr., 1971-72, mgr., officer, 1973-75, asst. v.p. mktg., 1976-78, asst. v.p. advt., 1979-81, v.p. mktg. communications, 1982—; dir. William T. Walters Assocs., Walter's Art Gallery, Balt., 1979-82; pub. sector rep., cons. advt. com. Dept. Econ. Devel., State of Md., 1982. Charter mem. Exec. Women's Council Balt., 1978—; treas. profl. div. Women's Assn. Balt. Symphony Orch., 1972-75; mem. nominating com. Ind. Republican Coalition Balt.; campaign vol. Balt. Rep. Club. Recipient awards for advt. campaigns including Bank Mktg. Assn. Best of TV award, 1980, Effie award, 1981, FAE award, 1981, Best of Print Addy award, 1985. Mem. Nat. Assn. Bank Women, Advt. Assn. Balt., Am. Mktg. Assn., Bank Mktg. Assn. (Best of Print award 1982, 83), Mu Phi Epsilon. Club: Jr. League Balt. Office: Md Nat Bank 225 N Calvert St Baltimore MD 21202

O'HAIRE, BETTY NEWELL, lawyer; b. Laurenburg, N.C., Feb. 21, 1936; d. Ernest F. Newell and Laura E. (McCraney) Newell Culver; m. James P. Cash, June 12, 1964 (dec. Oct. 1969); m. 2d Joseph W. O'Haire, June 19, 1970. Student U. Ga., 1967-69, U. Fla., Daytona Beach, 1970-72; J.D. magna cum laude, John Marshall Law Sch., Atlanta, 1979. Bar: Ga. 1979. Mgr., Credit Bur. Thomasville (Ga.), 1960-61; owner-mgr. Credit Bur. Jesup (Ga.), 1961-68; owner-mgr. Ga. So. Credit, Inc., Jesup, 1973-83, legal cons., 1983—; sec.-treas. Atlantic American, Inc., Jesup, 1970—; sole practice law, Jesup, 1979—; mem. nat. com. Assoc. Credit Burs., Inc., Houston, 1979-85; dir. Assoc. Credit Burs. Ga., Inc., 1960-67, 73-85, chmn., 1984-85. Recipient Ednl. award Assn. Credit Burs. S.E., 1964; Credit Reporting award Assn. Credit Burs. Am., 1964. Mem. Jesup Bar Assn. (sec.-treas. 1980-81, pres. 1982-83), Wayne County C. of C. (ednl. chmn. 1978-79, pres. 1981-82). Episcopalian. Address: PO Box 431 Jesup GA 31545

O'HALLORAN, (LAVERNE M.) KATHLEEN (MRS. JOHN R. O'HALLORAN, JR.), realtor; b. Laurium, Mich., Nov. 15, 1921; d. Joseph Wilfred and Della K. (Gervais) Shaffer; student Fond Du Lac Comml. Coll., 1938-40, Fresno City Coll., 1965-66; m. John Richard O'Halloran, Jr., July 15, 1942; children—Sheila Ann O'Halloran Stoll, Gregory, Michael, Maureen O'Halloran Benelli, Sean, Margaret O'Halloran Johnson. Co-owner Hamlin Hotel, San Francisco, 1946-48, Lazy F Guest Ranch, Ellensburg, Wash., 1948-50; real estate broker, Fresno, 1965—. Charter mem. Infant of Prague Adoption Agy. Aux., 1954—, sec., 1955; mem. Mayor's Com. Community Devel., 1963-64; pres. Sacred Heart Mothers Club, 1959; pres. Calif. Citizens for Decent Lit., 1961-63, Central Calif. Citizens for Decent Lit., 1959-64; sec. Sacred Heart Altar Soc., 1976-78; precinct chmn. Goldwater campaign, 1964; chmn. Fresno County United Republicans Calif., 1962; area coordinator Clean Campaign Ballot Initiative, 1966; candidate Fresno City Council, 1961. Mem. Fresno Bd. Realtors, Nat. Assn. Real Estate Bds., Women's League, Fresno Art Ctr., St. Agnes Service Guild. Roman Catholic. Home: 3503 N Bond St Fresno CA 93726

OHANESSIAN, JENNIFER ANNE MONAHAN, advertising and public relations agency executive; b. Tacoma, Wash., Oct. 19, 1953; d. Gerald Lawrence and Marie Cecile (Hazen) Monahan; m. Krikor Aram Ohanessian, May 16, 1981; children—Gregory Maknos Elliott, Justin Aram Monahan. B.A. in Communications, Wash. State U., 1975. Adminstrv. asst. to acct. exec., acct. supr., v.p. Claire Harrison Assocs., San Francisco, 1975—. Recipient Medallion award No. Calif. chapt. Pub. Relations Soc. Am., 1981, Merit award, 1985, Lulu award Los Angeles Women Advt., 1985. Mem. Heritage, Wash. State U. Alumni Assn., San Francisco Bay Area Publicity Club, Alpha Delta Pi. Republican. Episcopalian. Avocations: interior decorating; travel. Home: 1423 37th Ave San Francisco CA 94122 Office: Claire Harrison Assocs Inc 54 Mint St 5th Floor San Francisco CA 94103

O'HANLON, MAUREEN ANNE, hotel executive; b. Omaha, Aug. 12, 1950; d. Robert Edward and Janet Marie (Foley) O'Hanlon. Student, U. Bordeaux (France), 1970-71; B.A., U. Colo., 1972. Sales mgr. Loews Hotels, N.Y.C., 1974-78; nat. dir. sales Princess Hotels, N.Y.C., 1978-80; dir. sales Trusthouse Forte Hotels, N.Y.C., 1980-81; dir. sales Meridien Hotels, N.Y.C., 1981-84; nat. dir. sales Radisson Hotel Corp., N.Y.C., 1984—. Mem. Hotel Sales Mgmt. Assn. (dir. 1983-85), Meeting Planners Internat., Soc. Incentive Travel Execs. Office: Radisson Hotels Inc 875 Ave of Americas New York NY 10001

O'HARA, KATHY MARLEEN, physician; b. Bridgeport, Conn., Feb. 22, 1951; d. Walter Edgar and Grace Dorothy (Potter) Magill; B.S. cum laude in Biology, Oral Roberts U., Tulsa, 1973; D.O., Coll. Osteo. Medicine and Surgery, Des Moines, 1977. Intern, Des Moines Gen. Hosp., 1977-78; emergency room physician Salem County Meml. Hosp., Salem, N.J., 1981—; guest speaker. Served with USN, 1978-80. Mem. Am. Osteo. Assn., Am. Med. Women's Assn., Christian Med. Soc., Assn. Mil. Osteo. Physicians and Surgeons, AAUW, Sigma Sigma Phi. Republican. Mem. Assembly of God. Home: RD #1 Box 341 Salem NJ 08079 Office: Salem County Memorial Hospital Salem NJ 08079

O'HARA, PHYLLIS JEAN, administrator, former state official; b. Des Moines, May 2, 1945; d. Ronald Earl Slaymaker and Helen Agnes (Ware) Wetteland; m. James Michael Trombley, June 21, 1980; children—James Brian, Michael Patrick, Erica Megan. Student U. Nebr., 1971-74. Exec. dir. Nebr. Commn. on Status of Women, Lincoln, 1974-85; exec. dir. Alternatives to Family Violence, 1985—; organizational effectiveness trainer Nat. Assn. Commns. on Women, 1983; coordinator Exec. Dirs. Exchange, 1981-83; mem. exec. com. Colo. Domestic Violence Coalition; mem. Nebr. Vocational Edn. Task Force on Sex Equity; coordinator Nebr. Legislative Network; mem. Ctr. for Co-Equal Edn. Adv. Com.; mem. Nebr. Displaced Homemakers Planning Com.; past mem. Nebr. Balance of State CETA Adv. Com.; bd. dirs. Alcohol Counselors Tng. Inst. Nebr.; former chair Legis. Com. Revising Divorce Laws; past mem. Nebr. Task Force Women Alcohol and Drugs, Nebr. Task Force on Domestic Violence, Nebr. Ad Hoc Affirmative Action Com., Legis. Com. to Revise Nebr. Laws to Eliminate Discrimination. Contbg. author: Organizational Handbook for Commissions on Women, 1983. Bd. dirs. Lincoln Council on Alcoholism and Drugs, 1984—; pub. edn. com. chair Gov.'s Task Force on Sexual Assault, Lincoln, 1981—; mem. Nebr. Coalition for Women, Lincoln, 1980—; former chair Older Women's League, Lincoln, 1981-85. Mem. Nat. Assn. Commns. on Women (v.p.), United Way Assn. Agy. Execs. Democrat. Unitarian. Home: 10226 E Fair Pl Englewood CO 80111 Office: PO Box 385 Commerce City CO 80037

OHARENKO, MARIA T., public relations official; b. Louvain, Belgium, Dec. 25, 1950; came to U.S., 1951; d. Vladimir and Lubomyra (Kotz) O. B.S., Northwestern U., 1972, M.S., 1973. Pub. info. officer U.S. AEC, ERDA, Dept. Energy, Argonne and Chgo., Ill., 1973-79; pub. info. and news media advance officer U.S. Dept. Energy, Washington, 1980-81; corp. press. relations mgr. Northrop Corp., Los Angeles, 1981—. Mem. Aviation/Space Writers Assn., Women in Communications, Sigma Delta Chi. Ukrainian Catholic. Office: Northrop Corp 1840 Century Park E Los Angeles CA 90067

O'HEAR, MARION KAYE, business manager; b. Akron, Ohio, Mar. 16, 1939; d. George Kenneth and Ruth Evelyn (Klingstedt) Sues; B.Ed., Kent (Ohio) State U., 1962; paralegal student Hammel Bus. Coll., Akron, 1979; divorced; children—Tod J., Timothy J., Thomas B. Sec., Akron, 1960-77; paralegal sec. firm Segedy & Umbaugh, Akron, 1977-82; bus. mgr. Substation Maintenance, Inc., 1982—. Mem. exec. bd. WITAN women's orgn., 1963, treas., 1973; fund raiser Akron Center Drug Abuse. Mem. Am. Assn. Exec. Bus. Women, Nat. Assn. Legal Secs., Akron Assn. Paralegals, Beta Sigma Phi (past pres.). Republican. Home: 3301 Boyne Rd Copley Twp Norton OH 44203 Office: 577 Kennedy Rd Akron OH 44305

OHLENFORST, CYNTHIA MORGAN, lawyer; b. Dallas, May 17, 1949; d. Robert Ernest and Alice Helen (Ingels) Morgan; m. Patrick Michael Ohlenforst, June 12, 1971; children—Kristen Michelle, Lauren Jennifer, Megan Kathryn. B.A., Loyola U.-New Orleans, 1970; M.A., U. Dallas, 1974; J.D. magna cum laude, So. Meth. U., 1980. Bar: Tex. 1980. Tchr., Bishop Lynch High Sch., Dallas, 1971-74, Mt. Carmel High Sch., Houston, 1974-76, Jesuit Coll. Preparatory, Dallas, 1976-77; assoc. Hughes & Luce, Dallas, 1980—. Active Leadership Tex., 1984; Dean Search Com. So. Meth. U. Sch. Law, 1978-80; bd. dirs. Lone Star Council Camp Fire; corp. council Shakespeare Festival of Dallas. Recipient Outstanding Secondary Tchr. Am. award, 1975-76. Mem. Dallas Bar Assn., ABA, State Bar Tex. (com. legis. devel.), Tex. Young Lawyers Assn. Republican. Roman Catholic. Office: Hughes & Luce 1000 Dallas Bldg Dallas TX 75201

OJANLATVA, ANSA TERTTU TELLERVO, lecturer; b. Piippola, Finland, Mar. 19, 1948; came to US, 1973; s. Leevi Johannes and Kerttu (Helmi) O.; M.S., U. Ill., 1975; Ph.D. (teaching asst.), So. Ill. U., 1977; grad. U. Jyvaskyla (Finland), 1971. Lectr. San Francisco State U., 1977-78; asst. prof. U. Houston, 1978-81; lectr. Calif. State Coll., San Bernardino, 1981-84; asst. prof., coordinator health sci. program La. State U., 1984—; cons. family life edn. San Diego State U., 1981; chmn. health edn. profl. edn. sect. Tex. Assn. Health, Phys. Edn. and Recreation, 1981; mem. Houston steering com. Internat. Yr. of Disabled Persons, 1981. Am.-Scandinavian Found. grantee, 1976-77; cert. sex educator. Mem. Am. Assn. Sex Educators, Counselors and Therapists (continuing edn. com. 1982—), Nat. Rehab. Counseling Assn. (task force sexuality and disability 1982—), Internat. Union Health Edn. (publs. com.), Nat. Assn. Female Execs., Eta Sigma Gamma, Phi Delta Kappa. Editor audiovisual revs. column Hygie, 1986—. Contbr. articles to profl. jours. Office: Sch HPERD La State U Baton Rouge LA 70803

OKA, YASU, physician; b. Japan, June 6, 1930; came to U.S., 1956; d. Kozo and Yoshi Shimada; m. Masamichi Oka, Mar. 17, 1956; children—Marie, Lisa. Intern St. Joseph Hosp., Denver, 1956; intern Bronx Mcpl. Hosp. Ctr., N.Y.C., 1957; resident in anesthesiology Albert Einstein Coll. Medicine, N.Y.C., 1959, prof., 1981—. Mem. Am. Assn. Anesthesiologists, Internat. Anesthesiologist Research Soc., N.Y. State Assn. Anesthesiologists, N.Y. Acad. Medicine, Soc. Cardiovascular Anesthesiology, N.Y. Soc. Thoracic Surgery, Am. Heart Assn. Home: 5 Crossway Scarsdale NY 10583 Office: Albert Einstein Coll Medicine Bronx NY 10461

O'KEEFE, KATHLEEN MARY, state government official; b. Butte, Mont., Mar. 25, 1933; d. Hugh I. and Kathleen Mary (Harris) O'Keefe; B.A. in Communications, St. Mary Coll., Xavier, Kans., 1954; m. Nick B. Baker, Sept. 18, 1954 (div. 1970); children—Patrick, Susan, Michael, Cynthia, Hugh, Mardeen. Profl. singer, mem. Kathie Baker Quartet, 1962-72; research cons. Wash. Ho. of Reps., Olympia, 1972-73; info. officer Wash. Employment Security Commn., Seattle, 1973-81, dir. public affairs, 1981—; freelance writer, composer, producer, 1973—. Founder, pres. bd. Eden, Inc., visual and performing arts, 1975—; public relations chmn. Nat. Women's Democratic Conv., Seattle, 1979, Wash. Dem. Women, 1976—; bd. dirs., public relations chmn. Eastside Mental Health Center, Bellevue, Wash., 1979-81; Dem. candidate Wash. State Senate, 1968. Recipient Black Community award for composition The Beaufort County Jail, Seattle, 1975, Silver medal Seattle Creative Awards Show for composing, directing and producing Rent A Kid, TV public service spot, 1979. Mem. Wash. Press Women. Democrat. Roman Catholic. Author handbook on TV prodn., guide to coping with unemployment; composer numerous songs, also producer Job Service spots. Home: 14480 NE 31st St J-204 Bellevue WA 98007 Office: 212 Maple Park Olympia WA 98504

OKELL, JOBYNA LOUISE, public health administrator, accountant; b. Miami, Fla., Nov. 21, 1937; d. George Shaffer and Evelyn Maude (Pottmyer) O. B.B.A., U. Miami-Fla., 1961; postgrad. U. Miami, 1962, Nova U., 1976—. Acct. Crippled Children's Soc., Miami, Fla., 1964-65, Am. Coll. Found., Miami, 1965-66; owner Jobyna's Miniatures, Coral Gables, Fla., 1978—; exec. dir./adminstr., corp. dir. Fla. Health Profl. Services, Inc., Coral Gables, 1967—; dir., treas. Fla. Health Nursing Service, Inc., 1985-86. Dist. chmn. Young Democrats Dade County and Fla., 1956-68; vice regent DAR, Coral Gables chpt., 1968-86, active Irish Georgian Soc., English Speaking Union; treas., dir. Merrick Manor Found., 1974-75; active Friends of Library, U. Miami, 1974-83; adv. bd. channeling project Miami Jewish Home and Hosp. for Aged, 1982-83. Recipient Outstanding County Young Democrat award Young Dems. Fla., 1964; Truman award Outstanding Young Dem. Young Dems. Dade County, 1965; Outstanding Jr. DAR, 1972. Mem. Am. Pub. Health Assn., Nat. League Nursing, Am. Soc. Pub. Adminstrn., Dade/Monroe Assn. Home Health Agys. (pres./dir. 1974-76), Health Planning Council South Fla., Health Systems Agy. South Fla., Fla. Assn. Home Health Agys., South Fla. In-Home Services (pres. 1985-86), Red-Sunset Merchants Assn., Nat. Assn. Miniature Enthusiasts, Internat. Guild Miniature Artisans, Gamma Alpha Chi, Alpha Delta Pi. Republican. Episcopalian. Home: 715 Palermo Ave Coral Gables FL 33134 Office: Fla Health Profl Services Inc 1510 Venera Ave Coral Gables FL 33146

OKER, JUANITA ANN, electronics company executive; b. Mpls., Mar. 25, 1940; d. Robert Joseph and Arlene (Karon) Hokanson Roy; m. Thomas Fredrick Roddy, May 29, 1982; children—Catherine, Robert, Caron, Clay, Jill. Ed. vocat. sch., Mpls. With Dahlberg Hearing Aid Co., 1973-74, Starkey's Labs., Mpls., 1974-81; founder, owner, pres. Thunderbird Electronics, Golden Valley, Minn., 1981—. Featured in Nat. Geog. film on American Indians, 1985. Named Minority Mfr. of Yr., Chgo. regional office Minority Bus. Devel. Agy., 1984. Mem. Nat. Contract Mgmt. Assn., Minn. Indian Contractors Assn., Minn. Chippewa Tribe. Office: Thunderbird Electronics 925 Winnetka Ave N Golden Valley MN 55427

OKINAGA, GENEVIEVE TAKEMOTO, state official; b. Hilo, Hawaii, Nov. 18, 1927; d. Nobuji and Kay (Takemoto) Tokushiro; m. Sam N. Okinaga, Aug. 20, 1949; children—Carner, Mia. B.A., U. Hawaii, 1945; M.Ed., 1967. Tchr., field supr. undergrads. Hawaii State Dept. Edn., Honolulu, 1958-64; grad. studies intern, center supr. U. Hawaii, Honolulu, 1964-68; program designer Neighborhood Youth Corps, Honolulu, 1967-68; sch. adminstr. Hawaii State Dept. Edn., Honolulu, 1968-69; state program specialist in early childhood edn., 1969-76; dir. Gov.'s Office Children and Youth, Honolulu, 1976—; mem. nat. bd. Fed. Adv. Bd. on Child Abuse and Neglect, Washington, 1979-81; project dir. Hawaii Internat. Yr. of the Child, Honolulu, 1979, Gov.'s White House Conf. on Children and Youth, Honolulu, 1981. Author: A Model of a Proposal for a Federal Grant, 1979; A Curriculum Guide for Early Childhood Education, 1972; Experimental Remedial Reading Program, 1966. Mem. Nat. Assn. State Dirs. Child Devel. (sec.-treas. 1982-84, pres. 1984-86), Hawaii Assn. Edn. Young Children, Hawaii Assn. Student Teaching, Hawaii Edn. Assn., Pi Lambda Theta, Delta Kappa Gamma. Office: Office of the Gov Office of Children and Youth PO Box 3044 Honolulu HI 96802

OKOSHI, EUGENIA SUMIYE, artist; b. Seattle; d. Masanari and Riyoko (Fukoda) Ushiyama; student Seattle U., 1954-57, Henry Fry Mus. Modern Art, Seattle, 1957-59; m. George Mukai, Mar. 21, 1976. One-woman shows Gallery Internat., N.Y.C., 1970, Miami Mus. Modern Art, 1970, Westbeth Courtyard Gallery, N.Y.C., 1972, Galerie Salson, Tokyo, 1982; exhibited in group shows Met. Mus. Art, N.Y.C., 1977, World Trade Center, N.Y.C., 1979, Tokyo Nat. Mus., 1979, Pace U. Gallery, Briarcliff, N.Y., 1981, Joslyn Center Arts, Torrance, Calif., Newark Mus., 1983, Bergen Mus. Art and Scis., 1983, Am. Acad. Arts and Scis., 1984, Nassau Community Coll., 1985-86, Port Washington Pub. Library, L.I., N.Y., 1985, Hudson River Mus., 1985; represented in permanent collectiosn at Miami Mus. Modern Art, Low Gallery, U. Maimi, Nat. Women's Edn. Center, Japan. Mem. Burr Artists, Hudson River Artists Assn., Japanese Artists Assn. N.Y. Episcopalian. Address: 155 Bank St New York NY 10014

OKPALOBI, MARTIS JONES, executive development consultant; b. Dayton, Ohio; d. Henry and Martha Rosetta (Fields) Jones; children—Ucheamaka, Chukwuemeka. B.S., Miami U., Oxford, Ohio, 1969; M.A., SUNY-Albany, 1971; Ph.D., Vanderbilt U., 1977. Sr. planner N.Y. State Dept. Edn., Albany, N.Y., 1971-74; research specialist Tenn. Dept. Edn., Nashville, 1974-77; pres. Results Unltd., Assocs., Dallas, 1977—; cons., lectr. mgmt. devel. Trustee Goals for Dallas, OIC's of Am. program chmn.; active March of Dimes; 1st v.p. Republican Council of Dallas County, 1980-82; presdl. appointee fellowship bd. Nat. Grad. Fellows Program, 1985. Recipient Leon H. Sullivan award for outstanding leadership, 1981; Businesswoman of Yr., Iota Phi Lambda, 1979. Mem. Am. Psychol. Assn., Am. Soc. Tng. and Devel., Leadership Dallas, Opportunity Dallas, Exec. Women of Dallas, Leadership Tex., Bus. and Profl. Women. Republican. Club: Toastmasters. Contbr. articles to profl. jours. Office: PO Box 64917 Dallas TX 75206

OLAH, JUDITH AGNES, chemist; b. Budapest, Jan. 21, 1929; came to U.S., 1964, naturalized, 1969; d. Janos and Magaret (Kraus) Lengyel; M.S. in Chemistry, Tech. U. Budapest, 1955; m. George A. Olah, July 9, 1949; children—George John, Ronald Peter. Research chemist Central Research Inst., Hungarian Acad. Scis., 1955-56; research asso. Case Western Res. U., Cleve., 1966-77; adj. asst. prof. chemistry U. So. Calif., 1977-79, adj. asso. prof., 1979—. Mem. Iota Sigma Pi. Contbr. articles on organic chemistry to profl. jours., chpts. in books. Home: 2252 Gloaming Way Beverly Hills CA 90210 Office: Dept of Chemistry University of Southern California University Park Los Angeles CA 90007

OLAH, SUSAN ROSE, artist; b. Budapest, Hungary, June 14, 1947; d. Joseph and Emma (Hupcsak) Olah; came to Can., 1957, naturalized, 1962; student Art Instrn. Sch., Mpls., 1966-69. Tchr. art Wascana Hosp., Regina, Sask., Can., 1969-72, art cons., talent evaluator, 1970-72; exhibited in one woman shows at Gallery of Roof, Regina, 1973, Galerie Mouffe, Paris, 1977, Galerie Vallombreuse, Blarritz, France, 1977. Recipient awards Regina Exhbn., 1960, Mpls. award for painting, 1967, cert. of attainment Art Instrn., Sch., Mpls., 1969, gold medal in art Accademia Italia Belle Arti e del Lavoro, 1979; diploma of merit Università delle Arti, Parma, Italy, 1982; Golden Centaur, Accademia Italia, 1982; gold medal Internat. Parliament for Peace and Safety, 1983; honor award Centro Studi e Richerche delle Nazioni (Italy), 1984; Oscar d' Italia, Accademia Italia, 1985; European Banner of the Arts, Accademia Europea, 1985. Mem. Internat. Order Vols. for Peace (Italy). Home: 37 Haultain Crescent Regina SK S4S 4B4 Canada

OLASOV, EVE FRANCES, television station executive; b. Charleston, S.C., Jan. 7, 1951; d. Bernard J. and Harriet Jean (Tigher) O.; m. Cyrus E. Newitt, Oct. 31, 1976 (div. 1979); m. William M. Haynes, Jan. 16, 1986. A.A., Bradford Coll., 1971, B.A., U. Wis., 1975. Air switcher Sta. WCSC-TV, Charleston, 1975-76, promotion dir., 1976-83, program dir., 1983-84, v.p., program dir., 1984—. Chmn. TV com. Trident United Way, Charleston, 1985. Mem. Nat. Assn. TV Program Execs., Advt. Fedn. Democrat. Jewish. Home: 29-B Brockman Dr Charleston SC 29412 Office: Sta WCSC-TV 485 E Bay St Charleston SC 29402

O'LAUGHLIN, SISTER JEANNE, university administrator. Pres., Barry U., Miami Shores, Fla. Office: Barry U 11300 NE 2d Ave Miami Shores FL 33161*

OLCHAK, RHODA PEARL, market research agency executive; b. N.Y.C., Jan. 17, 1931; d. Aaron and Dora (Stern) Machlin; m. Seymour Olchak, Nov. 4, 1950; children—Robert G., Lawrence S., David A. Student CCNY. Owner, Olchak Market Research Co., Bowie, Md., 1970-77; v.p. CTIS, Crofton, Md., 1981-82; pres. Olchak Market Research Co. Inc., Greenbelt, Md., 1983—. Recipient award of Excellence Nat. Analysts, 1979. Mem. Mktg. Research Assn. (pres. 1982-83, Presdl. award 1983, Testimonial-founder award; Mid-Atlantic chpt.), Am. Mktg. Assn., Women in Advt. and Mktg. Jewish. Home: 12410 Madeley Ln Bowie MD 20715 Office: Olchak Market Research Inc 6194 Greenbelt Rd Greenbelt MD 20770

OLCOTT, JOANNE ELIZABETH, naval officer; b. Portland, Oreg., May 12, 1958; d. Richard Hutton and Eleanor (Looker) O. B.S., Oreg. State U., 1980. Commd. ensign U.S. Navy, 1980, advanced through grades to lt., 1985; oceanographic watch officer, Guam, 1981-82, Antigua, W.I., 1982-84; adminstrv. officer, Antigua, 1983-84; ops. officer, Salt Lake City, 1984-85, chief testing mgmt. sect., 1985—. Mem. Nat. Assn. Female Execs., Kappa Delta. Republican. Episcopalian. Avocations: athletics; reading. Home: 1010 S 400 E Salt Lake City UT 84111 Office: Mil Entrance Processing Sta Bldg 106 Soldiers Circle Fort Douglas UT 84113

OLDEN, ANNA BEATRICE, educator; b. Pinehurst, N.C., Mar. 15, 1931; d. Allen and Anna (Wallace) Bethea; B.A., Bennett Coll., 1952; postgrad. Bank Street Coll., N.Y.C., Am. U., Mary Wood Coll.; m. Simon J. Olden, June 12, 1953 (div.); children—Darryl Craig, Pamela Lynette, Brian Kevin. Tchr. Kannapolis (N.C.) Public Schs., 1952-53, Carousel Sch., Jamaica Estates, N.Y. and Headstart tchr., curriculum coordinator, supr., St. Albans, N.Y., 1955-69; tchr. Cecil County (Md.) Public Schs., 1969—. Mem. NEA, Md. Tchrs. Assn., Cecil County Tchrs. Assn., Internat. Reading Assn. Methodist. Home: 1 Bristal Way New Castle DE 19720

OLDFATHER, PAULA MARIE, computer company executive; b. Rosenberg, Tex., Aug. 3, 1940; d. Theron Andrew and Pansy Blossom (Carpenter) O.; B.S. with honors in Math., UCLA, 1966. Mem. tech. staff RAND Corp., Santa Monica, Calif., 1964-67; analyst, programmer Auerbach Assos., Phila., 1967-69; mgr. systems and programming CARA Corp., Phila., 1969-71, v.p., 1975-82; pres. Belmont & Oldfather, Inc., Glen Mills, Pa., 1982—; tchr. SIMSCRIPT programming USAF, 1965-67. Mem. Assn. Computing Machinery, Data Entry Mgmt. Assn., Soc. Ambulatory Med. Systems, Nat. Assn. Female Execs. Author computer materials. Home: 21 Winding Way RD 5 Glen Mills PA 19342 Office: Baltimore Pike and Cheyney Rd Concord Village Shops Glen Mills PA 19342

OLDHAM, ELAINE DOROTHEA, educator; b. Coalinga, Calif., June 29, 1931; d. Claude Smith Oldham and Dorothy Elaine (Hill) Wilkens. A.B. in History, U. Calif.-Berkeley, 1953; M.S. in Sch. Adminstrn., Calif. State U.-Hayward, 1976; postgrad. U. Calif.-Berkeley, Harvard U., Mills Coll. Tchr. Piedmont Unified Sch. Dist., Calif., 1956—. Pres., bd. dirs. Camron Stanford House Preservaiton Assn., 1979-86, adminstrv. v.p., bd. dirs., 1976-79, mem. various civic and community support groups; bd. dirs. Anne Martin Children's Ctr. Mem. Am. Assn. Museums, Am. Assn. Mus. Trustees, Internat. Council Museums, Am. Assn. State and Local History, DAR (Outstanding Tchr. Am. History award), Colonial Dames Am., Magna Charta Dames, Hugeunot Soc., Plantagenent Soc., Order of Washington, Order St. George and Descs. of Knights of Garter, U. Calif. Alumni Assn. (co-chmn. and chmn. of 10th and 25th yr. class reunions), Prytanean Alumnae Assn. (bd. dirs.), Phi Delta Kappa, Delta Kappa Gamma. Republican. Episcopalian. Club: Women's Athletic of Alameda County. Office: Magnolia Ave Piedmont CA 94611

OLDHAM, MAXINE JERNIGAN, real estate broker; b. Whittier, Calif., Oct. 13, 1923; d. John K. and Lela Hessie (Mears) Jernigan; m. Laurance Montgomery Oldham, Oct. 28, 1941; 1 child, John Laurence. A.A., San Diego City Coll., 1973; student Western State U. Law, San Diego, 1976-77, LaSalle U., 1977-78; grad. Realtors Inst., Sacramento, 1978. Mgr. Edin Harig Realty, LaMesa, Calif., 1966-70; tchr. Bd. Edn., San Diego, 1959-66; mgr. Julia Cave Real Estate, San Diego, 1970-73; salesman Computer Realty, San Diego, 1973-74; owner Shelter Island Realty, San Diego, 1974—; owner Shelter Island Realty, San Diego, 1980-86. Author: Jernigan History, 1982, Mears Geneology, 1985. Mem. Civil Service Commn., San Diego, 1957-58. Mem. Nat. Assn. Realtors, Calif. Assn. Realtors, San Diego Bd. Realtors, San Diego Apt. Assn., DAR, Colonial Dames 17th Century, Internat. Fedn. Univ. Women. Republican. Roman Catholic. Avocations: music; theater; painting; geneology; continuing edn. Home: 3348 Lowell St San Diego CA 92106 Office: Shelter Island Realty 2810 Lytton St San Diego CA 92110

OLDHAM, PHYLLIS VIRGINIA KIDD, librarian; b. Lafayette, Ind., Mar. 19, 1926; d. Hulbert Haven and Grace Ellene (Doup) Kidd; B.S., Purdue U., 1948, M.S., Butler U., 1966; children—Stephen Kidd. Tchr. English, Jefferson High Sch., Lafayette, 1950; tchr., librarian Tudor Hall Sch., Indpls., 1954-70; librarian Park Tudor Sch., 1970—; mem. exec. bd. Central Ind. Area Library Services Authority, sec., 1983-85. Active People-to-People Internat.; dist. dir. People-to-People Student Ambassador Program, 1970-80; chmn. bd. Central Christian Ch., Indpls., 1979-81; mem. adv. bd. Indpls. Zool. Soc. Mem. ALA, Marion County Librarians Assn. (pres. 1969-72), Ind. Media Educators, Kappa Delta Pi, Delta Kappa Gamma (treas. Alpha Eta chpt. 1974-80), Pi Beta Phi. Club: La Sertoma (dist. gov. 1969-70) (Indpls.). Home: 7015 Warwick Rd Indianapolis IN 46220 Office: 7200 N College St Indianapolis IN 46240

OLDING, DOROTHY (MCKEOWN), lit. agt.; b. N.Y.C., Apr. 12, 1910; d. Addington Eric and Seraphine (Theodor) O.; student Columbia U., 1927-29; m. Edward V. McKeown, Aug. 14, 1946 (dec. 1951). Asst. fiction editor Am. mag., N.Y.C., 1929-38; with Harold Ober Assocs. Inc., lit. agy., N.Y.C., 1938—, partner, then exec. v.p., 1949-72, pres., 1972—. Home: 447 E 57th St New York NY 10022 Office: 40 E 49th St New York NY 10017

OLDS, SHARRON LEE, leasing company executive; b. Highland Park, Mich., Nov. 3, 1939; d. Emil and Sally (DiBlasi) O. Departmental sec. Wayne State U. Libraries, Detroit, 1958-76; mng. coordinator Jack Barnes Dance Centers, West Bloomfield, Mich., 1976-80; br. office mgr. Corp. Funding, Inc., Birmingham, Mich., 1980-84; v.p. Corp. Resources, Inc., Birmingham, 1984—. Mem. Am. Assn. Individual Investors, Nat. Assn. Female Execs. Republican. Avocations: dance; flying; table tennis. Office: Corp Resources Inc 16231 W 14 Mile Rd Birmingham MI 48009

OLDS, TRACY FREEMAN, programmer, analyst; b. Philippi, W.Va., July 17, 1956; d. Billie Dennis and Pauline (Hotsinpiller) Freeman; m. Daniel Ray Olds, Oct. 14, 1978; children—Tasha Marie, Kendyl Lane. A.A., Potomac State Coll., 1976; postgrad. W. Va. U., 1978-80; B.S., U. Houston, 1985. Programmer, Columbia Gas Transmission Co., Charleston, W.Va., 1976-77, sr. programmer, 1977; sr. programmer W.Va. U. Hosp., Morgantown, 1977-79, systems analyst, 1979-81; sr. programmer analyst Igloo Corp., Houston, 1981-82, Raymond Internat., Houston, 1982-85, GC Services, 1985—. Chmn. pool com., bd. dirs. Parkridge Community Improvement Assn., Houston, 1983. Mem. Golden Key, Phi Kappa Phi, Beta Gamma Sigma. Republican. Methodist. Home: 3803 Kingston Vale Houston TX 77082 Office: GC Services 6330 Gulfton Houston TX 77081

O'LEARY, ALICE, advertising agency executive; b. Medford, Mass., Jan. 24, 1932; d. Arthur J. O'Leary and Alice T. (Dyer) O'Leary O'Brien. Studied voice and piano, pvt. music schs., Boston and N.Y.C., 1950-54. Profl. singer, 1950-54; v.p. Joseph Mack Assocs., N.Y.C., 1960-70; pres. Syndicated Airtime, N.Y.C., 1970-75; sr. v.p. Hartel, Cataland & Gornick, N.Y.C., 1975-76, Altschiller, Reitzfeld & Jackson, N.Y.C., 1976-78; pres. Kaprielian O'Leary Advt., Inc., N.Y.C., 1981—. Co-developer, producer cassettes Cook Along with James Beard, 1974. Mem. Am. Assn. Advt. Agys. (bd. dirs. N.Y. council 1984), Advt. Women N.Y., Advt. Agy. Found. Avocations: tennis, skiing. Office: Kaprielian O'Leary Advt Inc 1995 Broadway New York NY 10023

O'LEARY, DIANE ELIZABETH, clinical psychologist; b. Palo Alto, Calif., Sept. 12, 1943; d. Ralph Francis and Margaret (Kroener) Huntsberger; m. Michael Robert O'Leary, June 8, 1973; children—Aileen, Maureen. B.A., Stanford U., 1967; Ph.D., U. Wash., 1977. Research asst. Inst. for Study of Human Problems Stanford U., 1965-69; teaching asst. U. Wash., 1969-72, research asst., 1978-79; predoctoral intern Seattle VA Med. Ctr., 1972-73, Highline-West Seattle Community Mental Health Ctr., Burien, Wash., 1973-74; staff psychologist, 1974-75; pvt. practice clin. psychology, Seattle, 1979-80; lectr. PLU, Tacoma, 1978-79; pvt. practice clin. psychology Kitsap Psychiat. Assocs., Bremerton, Wash., 1978-82, O'Leary & O'Leary, Inc. P.S., 1982—. Rose Marie Stern scholar, 1966-67; USPHS fellow, 1969-70. Contbr. articles to profl. jours. Mem. Am. Psychol Assn., Wash. State Psychol. Assn., Assn. Advancement Psychology. Home: PO Box 4745 Rolling Bay WA 98061 Office: O'Leary & O'Leary Inc PS 2500 Cherry Ave Suite 201 Bremerton WA 98310

O'LEARY, SISTER MICHELE, health system administrator; b. Pitts., Apr. 11, 1935; d. Jeremiah Thomas and Mary Agnes (Mobrey) O'L.; B.S., Carlow Coll., 1960; M.Ed., Duquesne U., 1970; M.P.H., U. Pitts., 1978. Joined Sisters of Mercy, Roman Catholic Ch., 1955; elem. sch. tchr. Cath. Schs. Office, Diocese of Pitts., 1960-66; adminstr. St. Regis Elem. Sch., Pitts., 1966-74; sch. supr. Pitts. Diocese Schs. Office, 1974-77; asso. dir. Health Systems Agy. S.W. Pa., Pitts., 1978-82; dir. Health Edn. Ctr., 1982-83; pres. Pitts. Mercy Health Coop., 1984—. Mem. Center for Edn. Action-U. Pitts. Task Force on Ednl. Issues, 1970-71; chmn. Interfaith Drug Prevention Agy., 1970-71; mem. City of Pitts. Model City Commn., 1970-74, City Pitts. Gov's Study Commn., 1973-75; chmn. Allegheny City Drug and Alcohol Bd., 1978-80, Women's Polit. Caucus of Allegheny County; bd. dirs. Pub. Leadership Bd., 1980—, Cancer Guidance Inst., 1980—, Cath. Charities-Diocese of Pitts., 1981—, St. Joseph's Hosp., Atlanta, 1984—. Mem. Am. Public Health Assn., Am. Health Planning Assn., Am. Hosp. Assn., Cath. Health Assn., Pa. Elected Women's Assn. Office: 3333 5th Ave Pittsburgh PA 15213

O'LEARY, PATRICIA ANN, nurse, educator; b. Steubenville, Ohio, May 15, 1949; d. John Paul and Rita Catherine (Andrews) O'L. L.P.N., Bellaire Sch. Practical Nursing (Ohio), 1969; R.N., Mercy Hosp. Sch. Nursing, Pitts., 1973; B.S.N., West Liberty State Coll., 1978; M.S.N., Vanderbilt U. 1980; postgrad. W.Va. U., 1981-83. L.P.N., Ohio Valley Hosp., Steubenville, 1969-73; staff nurse Cleve. Clinic, 1973-75, Ohio Valley Hosp., 1975-79; nursing supr. Royal Pavilion Extended Care Facility, Steubenville, 1979; instr. nursing West Liberty State Coll. (W.Va.), 1980-84; asst. prof. East Carolina U. Sch. Nursing, Greenville, N.C., 1984—. Bueleh Boyd scholar AAUW, 1979. Mem. Am. Nurses Assn., West Liberty State Coll. Alumni Assn., Vanderbilt U. Alumni Assn., Vanderbilt U. Nurses Alumni Assn. Democrat. Roman Catholic. Clubs: Brenda Lee Fan. Contbr.: Adult Health Nursing Examination Review Book, 1984. Home: 1149 Mulberry Ln #35C Greenville NC 27834 Office: East Carolina U Sch Nursing Greenville NC 27834

OLESKER, SARA LOIS, interior designer, merchandising firm executive; b. Chgo., Oct. 3, 1942; d. Irving and Libby (Rubenstein) Schwartz; m. Thomas Olesker, Jr., July 19, 1964; children—Elizabeth, Peter. B.F.A., Ind. U., 1964; postgrad. Ill. Inst. Tech., 1965-67, Chgo. Art Inst., 1967. Tchr. art pub. schs., Chgo., 1964-68; v.p. Childs-Dreyfus Group, Chgo., 1975-84; pres. Sara Olesker, Ltd., Chgo., 1983—, OSA, Inc., Chgo., 1984—; mem. faculty Inst. Residential Mktg., Roosevelt U., Chgo., 1984—; speaker, instr. at meetings. Contbr. articles to trade publs. Treas. Mother's Aid, Chgo. Lying In Hosp., 1981-82; bd. dirs. Chgo. Chamber Music Soc., 1982-83, pres., 1983-84. Mem. Greater Chgo. Home Builders Assn., Nat. Assn. Home Builders, Urban Land Inst., Inst. Residential Mktg. Office: Sara Olesker Ltd 444 W Webster Ave Chicago IL 60614

OLIAN, JOANNE CONSTANCE, curator, art historian; b. N.Y.C.; d. Richard Edward and Dorothy (Singer) Wahrman; m. Howard Olian, Sept. 7, 1947; children—Jane Wendy (Mrs. Thomas Mooney), Patricia Ann. Student, Syracuse U.; B.A., Hofstra U., 1969; M.A., NYU, 1972. Grad. internship Met. Mus., N.Y.C., 1973; asst. curator Mus. of City of N.Y., 1974, curator costume collection, 1975—; vis. lectr. Parsons Sch. Design, Musée des Arts Decoratifs, Paris, summer 1983, 84, 85. Author: The House of Worth: The Gilded Age, 1860-1918, 1982; contbr. articles to profl. jours., chpts. to books. Mem. Centre Internat. d'Etude des Textiles Anciens, Internat. Council Mus., (costume com.), Costume Soc. Am. (dir. 1976-79, 83-86), Fashion Group (dir. 1985-86). Club: Cosmopolitan (N.Y.C.). Home: Shepherds Ln Sands Point NY 11050 Office: Mus of City of New York 1220 Fifth Ave New York NY 10029

OLIN, FERRIS, art librarian, art historian; b. Trenton, N.J., June 27, 1948; d. Harry William and Naomi (Hanft) O.; m. Mitchell Adley Leon, Nov. 23, 1972; 1 dau., Anya Louise Olin Leon. B.A., Douglass Coll., 1970; M.L.S., Rutgers U., 1972, M.A., 1975. Reference librarian Finkelstein Library, Spring Valley, N.Y., 1972-74; cons., librarian Consortium for Ednl. Equity, Rutgers U., New Brunswick, N.J., 1975-76, assoc. prof., art librarian, 1976—, cons. Consortium Ednl. Equity, 1977-78; cons. N.Y. Feminist Art Inst., N.Y.C., 1978, N.J. Dept. Ednl.-EEO Div., Trenton, N.J., 1979; mem. adv. bd. Lexicon Iconographicum Mythologicae Classicae, New Brunswick, N.J., 1983—; mem. Research Libraries Group, Art and Architecture Program, Com., Palo Alto, Calif., 1979—; curator exhibitions art, architecture and material culture, 1976—. Author: Fair Play I, 1976; contbr. Biographic Dictionary of Women Artists, 1985; co-editor Libraries, 1980; editor Books and Beyond, 1980-82; column editor Art Documentation, 1980—. Guest co-curator Middlesex County Cultural and Heritage Commn., North Brunswick, N.J., 1982-84, others; coordinator Women in the Community project Mary Jacobs Meml. Library, Rocky Hill, N.J., 1981-83 others. Grantee, Nat. Endowment for Humanities, NEH Pub. Library/Radcliffe Coll., Cambridge, Mass., 1981-83, N.J. Com. for Humanities, 1983, N.J. Hist. Commn., 1983. Mem. ALA, Art Libraries Soc. N.Am. (mem. exec. bd. N.J. chpt. 1977-81), Assn. Coll. and Research Libraries, Coll. Art Assn., Nat. Women's Studies Assn. (chmn. art exhibition com. for 1984 nat. conf.), Soc. Archtl. Historians (mem. exec. bd. N.J. chpt. 1978-81), Women Library Workers, Women's Caucus for Art (adv. bd. N.J. chpt. 1982—), N.J. Library Assn. Office: Art Library Voorhees Hall Rutgers U Hamilton St New Brunswick NJ 08903

OLINCY, MARGARET MARY, trade pub. co. exec.; b. Chgo., July 19, 1947; d. Walter Haworth, Jr. and Mary Louise (Richards) Faget; B.A., Mich. State U., 1969; M.A., 1970, M.B.A., 1974; m. Stephen Robert Olincy, Nov. 26, 1977; children—Mary Elizabeth, Daniel Stan. Sales rep. Scott Periodicals, Elmhurst, Ill., 1975—, sec., dir., 1976—; sec. Constrn. Industry Press, 1976—. Mem. Women's Aux. of Misericordia. Mem. Nat. Assn. Female Execs. Home: 355 Oakdale Ave Lake Forest IL 60045 Office: 135 Addison St Elmhurst IL 60126

OLINDER, PATRICIA JANE, nurse anesthetist; b. Schenectady, N.Y., Apr. 15, 1926; d. John and Bessie V. (Petroski) Olinder. R.N., Russell Sage Coll., 1947, B.S., 1950; postgrad. U. Rochester, 1948-49; Cert. Nurse Anesthetist, Duke U. 1958. Nurse anesthetist, Tex., N.Y. Clin. instr. Ellis Hosp., Schenectady, N.Y., 1950-51; office nurse Louis P. Tischler, M.D., Schenectady, N.Y., 1951-57; staff nurse anesthetist, clin. instr. Robert B. Green Hosp., San Antonio, 1958-60, Bridgeport Hosp. (Conn.), 1960-61, Robert B. Green Hosp.-U. Tex. Health Scis. Ctr., San Antonio, 1961-77, chief nurse anesthetist, 1977—; cons. anesthesia State Chest Hosp., San Antonio, 1977—; hon. cons., mem. affiliate teaching faculty Nurse Anesthesia Residency Program, Med. Exec. Com., Wilford Hall U.S. Air Force Med. Ctr., Lackland AFB, Tex. Research, publs. on anesthetic drugs. Kellas scholar Russell Sage Coll., 1950. Mem. Am. Assn. Nurse Anesthetists, Tex. Assn. Nurse Anesthetists. Roman Catholic. Office: U Tex Health Sci Ctr 7703 Floyd Curl Dr San Antonio TX 78284

OLINGER, CARLA DRAGAN, medical advertising executive; b. Cin., Oct. 8, 1947; d. Carl Edward and Selene Ethel (Neal) Dragan; m. Chauncey Greene Olinger, Jr., May 30, 1981. B.A., Douglass Coll., 1975. Mgr. info. retrieval services Frank J. Corbett, Inc., N.Y.C., 1976-77; editor, proofreader, prodn. asst. Rolf W. Rosenthal, Inc., N.Y.C., 1977-78, copywriter, 1978-80, copy supr., 1980-82, v.p. copy dept., 1982-83; v.p., group copy supr., adminstrv. copy supr. Rolf W. Rosenthal, Inc., div. Ogilvy & Mather, 1984—. Editor: Antimicrobial Prescribing (Harold Neu), 1979. Mem. Am. Med. Writers Assn. Office: Rolf W Rosenthal Inc 41 Madison Ave New York NY 10010

OLINGER, MARY ANN, public television station executive; b. Shelbyville, Ind., May 19, 1944; d. Cecil Franklin and Virginia M. (Williams) Fisher; m. O. Oren Olinger, Aug. 22, 1964; children—Ann Lynnette, Beth Ann. B.S., Ind. U., 1967; M.A., Ball State U., 1974. Tchr. Muncie Community Schs., 1967-70; devel. dir. PBS Sta. WIPB-TV, Muncie, 1979—; pub. info. dir. Emens Auditorium, Muncie, 1981-85. Legis. key person Ind. Optometric Assn., Indpls., 1976-79; div. chmn. United Way campaign, Muncie, 1979; mem. planning com. Muncie Community Schs., 1985; bd. dirs. United Day Care Ctr., Muncie, 1979-84, Muncie Children's Mus., 1986—. Mem. Pi Beta Phi (state and nat. officer 1972-80), Psi Iota Xi. Club: Delaware Country (bd. dirs. 1983—) (Muncie). Office: WIPB-TV 620 W Minnetrista Blvd Muncie IN 47303

OLIPHANT, ERNIE L., safety educator, public relations executive, consultant; b. Richmond, Ind., Oct. 25, 1934; d. Ernest E. and Beulah A. (Jones) Reid; m. George B. Oliphant, Sept. 25, 1955; children—David, Wendell, Rebecca. Student, Earlham Coll., 1953-55, Ariz. State U., 1974, Phoenix Coll., 1974-78. Planner, organizer, moderator confs., programs for various women's clubs, safety assns., 1971—; assoc. dir. Operation Lifesaver Nat. Safety Council, Phoenix, 1978—; cons. Fed. R.R. Adminstrn.; Tustin Enterprises, Richards and Assocs; lectr. in field.; adviser Am. Ry. Engring. Assn., Calif. Assn. Women Hwy. Safety Leaders, numerous others. Mem. R.R./Hwy. grade crossing com. Ariz. Corp. Commn.; mem. transp. and system com. Ariz. Gov.'s Commn. on Environment; mem. Ariz. Gov.'s Council Women for Hwy. Safety; mem. motor vehicle traffic safety at hwy.-r.r. grade crossings com., roadway environment com., women's div. com. Nat. Safety Council; mem. Phoenix Traffic Accident Reduction Program; task force mem. U.S. Dept. Transp. on Grade Crossing Safety. Recipient Safety award SW Safety Congress, 1973; citation of Merit Adv. Commn. on Ariz. Environment, 1974; Gov.'s award for hwy. safety, 1978; Gov.'s Merit of Recognition Outstanding Service in Hwy. Safety, 1980. Mem. Assn. R.R. Editors, Nat. Assn. Female Execs., Inc., Pub. Relations Soc. Am., R.R. Pub. Relations Assn., Nat. Acad. Scis. (dir. transp. research, planning, adminstrn. of transp. safety com., r.r.-hwy. grade crossing safety com.), Women's Transp. Seminar, Ariz. Fedn. Women's Clubs (named pres. of yr. 1968), Ariz. Safety Assn. (safety recognition award 1975), Gen. Fedn. Women's Clubs (internat. bd. dirs.), Nat. Assn. Women Hwy. Safety Leaders (pres.), Phi Theta Kappa. Republican. Quaker. Author of tech. publs.

OLIVA, GERALDINE E., pediatrician, administrator; b. N.Y.C., Nov. 7, 1943; d. Peter Henry and Juliet (Piscopo) Oliva; m. Edward Solomon Kersh, Sept. 12, 1975; children—Dylan, Eli. B.A., Conn. Coll., 1965; M.D., Boston U., 1968; M.P.H., U. Calif., Berkeley, 1973. Diplomate Am. Bd. Pediatrics. Intern, Boston City Hosp.; resident Charity Hosp.-Tulane Div., New Orleans, and Montefiore Hosp., Bronx, N.Y.; mem. child devel. staff Children's Hosp., Oakland, Calif., 1973-75, dir. teen clinics, 1973-76, now mem. staff; med. dir. Planned Parenthood, San Francisco, 1975-82; pediatrician Rainbow Pediatrics, Richmond, Calif., 1983-84; dir. maternal and child health San Francisco County Health Dept., 1984—; mem., cons. Center for Health Tng., San Francisco, 1982-83, Calif. Office Family Planning, Sacramento, 1981-83, San Francisco Health Dept., 1983. Contbr. articles to various publs. Mem. Berkeley Womens Health Collective, Berkeley, Calif., 1973-76; mem. Des Action, San Francisco, 1976-80; bd. dirs. Coalition for the Med. Rights of Women, San Francisco, 1982-84. Radcliff scholar, 1966-67. Fellow Am. Acad. Pediatrics; mem. Am. Pub. Health Assn., Soc. Adolescent Medicine, Assn. Planned Parenthood Profls., Calif. Am. Women's Med. Assn. Democrat. Home: 25 Manor Dr Piedmont CA 94611

OLIVA, VIVIEN ALICE, bilingual/bicultural counselor; b. Tampa, Fla., Mar. 1, 1946; d. Martin Ernest and Alice Amparo (Rivero) Oliva. B.A., Fla. State U., 1967, M.A., 1969; M.Ed. in Guidance and Counseling, Loyola U., New Orleans, 1976; postgrad. U. New Orleans, 1982—. Cert. nat. counselor. Tchr. Spanish, Riverdale High Sch. and Grace King High Sch., Metairie, La., 1967, 69-78; guidance counselor West Jefferson High Sch. and Bonnabel High Sch., Harvey and Metairie, La., 1978-79, 80-83, bilingual/bicultural counselor, 1984—. Recipient Outstanding Counselor in Spl. Counseling Program award Loyola U., New Orleans, 1986. Mem. Am. Personnel and Guidance Assn., Am. Assn. Multicultural Counseling Devel., Jefferson Parish Guidance Assn. (pres. 1982-83). Democrat. Roman Catholic. Office: 501 Manhattan Blvd Harvey LA 70058

OLIVARIUS, ANN MARIE, municipal finance officer; b. Bklyn., Feb. 23, 1932; d. Edward Joseph and Mary Teresa (Adams) Beckley; m. Kenneth William Olivarius, Dec. 26, 1953; children—Ann Marie, Mary Pat, Noël, Christine, Kathi. B.S. in Math., St. John's U., N.Y., 1953; M.A.T. in Math. cum laude, Fairleigh Dickinson U., 1972. Cert. tax collector, cert. mcpl. fin. officer, N.J. Actuarial asst. Met. Life Ins. Co., N.Y.C., 1953-54; tchr. Park Ridge High Sch., N.J., 1968-71; reporter Local Rev., Park Ridge, 1975-80; also real estate broker, office mgr. Terr. Realty, Montvale, N.J., 1975-80; chief fin. officer Twp. River Vale, N.J., 1980—. Chairperson Fish Orgn. No. Bergen County, N.J., 1973-74; trustee Park Ridge Bd. Edn., 1972-74. Mem. Am. Soc. Profl. Adminstrs., N.J. Mcpl. Fin. Officers Assn., N.J. Tax Collectors and Treas. Episcopalian. Avocations: bridge; backgammon; bowling; dancing. Home: 15 Burkhardt Ln Harrington Park NJ 07640 Office: Municipal Bldg 5800 Riverdale Rd River Vale NJ 07675

OLIVARIUS-IMLAH, MARYPAT, advertising/marketing executive; b. Bklyn., Oct. 25, 1957; d. Kenneth William Joseph and Ann Marie (Beckley) Olivarius; m. Craig Alexander Olivarius-Imlah, Sept. 18, 1982. B.S. in Mktg. and Communications, Ramapo State Coll. N.J., 1979; M.B.A. in Mktg. and Mgmt., Fairleigh Dickinson U., 1985. Researcher, pub. relations McNeil/Lehrer Report, WNET-TV, N.Y.C., 1977; salesperson Terrace Realty, Montvale, N.J., 1977-79; direct mail advt. copywriter Prentice-Hall, Inc., Englewood Cliffs, N.J., 1979-81; editor, promotional designer Beauty & Barber Supply Inst., Englewood, N.J., 1981-83; nat. dir. advt. and pub. relations Emerson Radio Corp., North Bergen, N.J., 1983-85; founder, pres. Imagery Advt., Upper Saddle River, N.J., 1985—; cons. to small businesses, 1983—. Mem. Nat. Assn. Female Execs. Democrat. Roman Catholic. Home and Office: Beecher Hill Rd Hinesburg VT 05461

OLIVE, SUSAN FREYA, lawyer; b. Durham, N.C., June 26, 1952; d. B.B. and Denyse L.A. (Edwards) O.; m. Richard Anthony Rall, June 28, 1980; children—Erin Alyssa, Park Anthony. A.B. in Med.-Legal Interface, Brown U., 1974; J.D. with distinction, Duke U., 1977. Bar: N.C. 1976, U.S. Ct. Mil. Appeals 1976, U.S. Dist. Ct. (ea. and we. dists.) N.C. 1977. Sole practice, Durham, N.C., 1976-77, 79; spl. counsel 9th Jud. Dist., Butner, N.C., 1977-79; ptnr. Olive, Faust & Olive, Durham, N.C., 1979-80, Olive & Olive, Durham, 1980—; regional chmn. nat. alumni schs. program for central N.C., Brown U., 1977—; guest lectr. trial advocacy clinic Duke U. Sch. Law, Durham, N.C., 1982—, supervising atty. trial advocacy clinic outplacement, 1982-83; participant supervising atty. Duke U., Durham, N.C., 1982—; guest lectr. N.C. Sch. Sci. and Math., Durham, 1983—; lectr. continuing legal edn. program N.C. Bar Found, Raleigh, 1983; mem. N.C. Fed. Bar Adv. Council, 1984—; mem. merit selection panel U.S. Dist. Ct. (mid. dist.) N.C., 1984, mem. atty. qualifications rev. com., 1984—. Author: (booklet) Mental Illness and the Criminal Defendant: Incapacity to Stand Trial and the Insanity Defense, 1983. Editor, The Durham Docket newsletter, 1977-83; (handbook) Reference Guide for Area Mental Health, Mental Retardation & Substance Abuse Board Members in North Carolina, 1980. Bd. dirs. Mental Health Assn. in Durham County, N.C., 1979-83, chmn. legis. com., 1980-82; bd. dirs. N.C. Prisoners' Legal Services, Inc., Raleigh, 1980—; fin. dir. Knox 1984 Gubernatorial Campaign, Durham County, N.C., 1984. Recipient membership N.C. Coll. Advocacy, N.C. Bar Found., 1983—; recipient scholarships Brown U., 1970-74. Mem. Durham County Bar Assn. (sec. 1981-82, 1st v.p. 1982-83, pres. 1983-84), Fourteenth Jud. Dist. Bar (sec. 1981-82, 1st v.p. 1982-83, pres. 1983-84), N.C. Bar Assn. (rep. to Dorothea Dix Hosp. med./legal adv. com. 1980—, chmn. com. on mental health law 1982-84, nominations com. 1983-84, assoc. patent, trademark and copyright law com. 1983-84, chmn. patent, trademark and copyright law com. 1984—), N.C. State Bar, Carolina Patent, Trademark and Copyright Law Assn., N.C. Acad. Trial Lawyers (lectr. continuing legal edn. program 1983), N.C. Assn. Women Attys., ABA, Am. Soc. Law and Medicine, Assn. Trial Lawyers Am. Democrat. Episcopalian. Office: Olive & Olive 500 Memorial St PO Box 2049 Durham NC 27702*

OLIVER, BONNIE BONDURANT, educational telecommunications company executive, consultant; b. St. Louis, Jan. 25, 1933; d. Benjamin Burns and Florence Mary (Spencer) Bondurant; m. Donald Edgar Wiese, June 19, 1954 (div. 1972); children—Kurt Rowland, Martha Jill Wiese Reid; m. Raymond Elliott Oliver, Dec. 8, 1972. B.A., Monmouth Coll., Ill., 1954; M.A., U. Mo., 1957; postgrad. U. Calif.-Irvine, 1963-65. Lic. tchr., Calif.; lic. in ednl. adminstrn. Sci. TV tchr. Santa Ana Schs., Calif., 1966-70; dir. media Santa Ana Unified Schs., 1970-72; adminstr. Regional Ednl. TV, Downey, Calif., 1973-78; mgr. edn. tech. unit Calif. Dept. Edn., Sacramento, 1978-81; dep. dir. Calif. Pub. Broadcasting Commn., Sacramento, 1981-83; pres. Oliver and Co., Newport Beach, Calif., 1983—; project dir. Sta. KCET-TV, Los Angeles; dir. Pub. Service Satellite Consort, Washington; cons. Calif. Dept. Edn., Sacramento, Ky. Ednl. TV, Lexington. Contbr. articles to popular mags. Mem. friends com. Orange Commn. on Status of Women, Santa Ana, 1976; chmn. adv. com. Internat. Childrens TV, Washington, 1979; trustee Stanford Home for Children, Sacramento, 1980-84. C-Span Cable Network fellow, Washington, 1980. Mem. Acad. TV Arts and Sci., Calif. Media Library Edn. Assn., Am. Mgmt. Assn., Friends of Coro Found. Republican. Avocation: running. Home: 1309 W Bay Ave Newport Beach CA 92661 Office: Oliver and Co PO Box 1213 Newport Beach CA 92663

OLIVER, CHERYL SUZANNE, personnel manager; b. Alton, Ill., Nov. 18, 1947; d. William Edward and Freda Mae (Harner) Gillespie; m. Thomas Stevens Oliver, Jr., Feb. 5, 1972; children—Thomas Stevens, Elizabeth Loreen, John Vincent. B.A., Western Ill. U., 1969. Personnel mgr. People, Inc., Buffalo, 1974—; speaker various colls., Buffalo. Served to 1st lt. USMC, 1969-72; served to capt. Army N.G., 1978-83. Recipient various awards N.Y. Army N.G., 1979. Republican. Roman Catholic. Avocations: travel; camping; sailing. Home: 156 Amsterdam St Tonawanda NY 14150 Office: People Inc 320 Central Park Plaza Buffalo NY 14214

OLIVER, DOROTHY BILLUPS, accountant; b. Elmore, Ala., Sept. 20, 1935; d. Jim Billups and Fannie L. (Harris) Billups Dumas; m. Henry Oliver Jr., Aug. 16, 1959; children—Sherryl Denise Oliver Taylor, Stephen Darnell, David-Henry. B.S., Hampton Inst., 1959; M.B.A., Fairleigh Dickinson U., 1975; student Am. Internat. Coll., 1953-54. Acct., Brock & Co., Phila., 1959-60; research acct., asst. to controller Einstein Med. Center, Phila., 1960-65; acct., analyst Interpace, Parsippany, N.J., 1966-67; agt. IRS, Newark, 1967-80; mem. mgmt. cadre U.S. Treasury Dept., exam. group mgr. exam. div. IRS, Newark, 1980—. First v.p. LWV Montclair-Glen Ridge, N.J., 1981—; bd. dirs. LWV Phila.-Spartansburg; mem. Byram Twp. Bd. Edn., 1970-71; treas. Sussex County Council of Chs.; bd. dirs. YWCA Montclair North Essex; pres. PTA Byram Twp. Recipient Spl. Achievement award IRS, 1978; Disting. Achievement award Montclair Bd. Edn., 1985. Mem. Nat. Assn. Female Execs., AAUW, Assn. Improvement Minorities Newark, Hampton Alumni Assn. (pres. North Jersey 1982—), Alpha Kappa Alpha. Methodist.

OLIVER, GLORIA NUNN, consultant, trainer, educator; b. Atlanta, Oct. 10, 1922; d. Inman Fuller and Willie Lou (Post) Nunn; m. Alfred Bruce Oliver, Apr. 9, 1944 (dec. May 1973); children—Leslie Ann, Lori Lee. A.A., Pasadena Jr. Coll., 1943; B.S., Calif. State Coll.-Hayward, 1967; M.A. in Supervision/Adminstrn., Montclair State Coll., 1985. Owner, operator A.B. Oliver Co., San Leandro, Calif., 1945-77; acctg. supr. Hayward Area Recreation Dist., 1950-70; supr. accts. receivable Singer Bus. Machines (became subs. TRW 1976), San Leandro, 1970-75, mgr. accounts receivable customer service div., Fairfield, N.J., 1975-78; mgr. accounts receivable customer service div. TRW, Fairfield, 1976-78, mgr. analytical services customer service div., 1978-80, tng. mgr. fin. dept. customer service div., 1980-83, fin. analyst customer service div., 1983-86; adj. mem. faculty Passaic County Community Coll., Paterson, N.J., 1982—. Mem. Am. Soc. Tng. and Devel., Nat. Assn. Female Execs., Phi Kappa Phi. Republican. Christian Scientist. Home: 100 Pierson Miller Dr Apt C-52 Pompton Lakes NJ 07442

OLIVER, HEATHER JULIE, health care systems analyst; b. Port-of-Spain, Trinidad, Feb. 16, 1960; came to U.S. 1972, naturalized 1972; d. Wally Peter and Sybil Dolores (Benjamin) Oliver. B.S./B.A., Quinnipiac Coll., 1982; M.P.H., Yale U., 1985. Intern St. Raphael Hosp., New Haven, 1980-81, cons., 1982-83, pulmonary tech., 1983-84; researcher Yale New Haven Hosp., 1984, Conn. Food Bank, New Haven, 1984; health care analyst N.Y. Hosp. Corp., N.Y.C., 1985—. Mem. Nat. Assn. Female Execs., Am. Coll. Hosp. Adminstrs., Am. Pub. Health Adminstrn. Club: Yale. Avocations: singing; acting. Office: NY City Health & Hosp Corp 230 W 41 St New York NY 10036

OLIVER, KAREN LOUISE, cosmetics company executive, editor; b. Oakland, Calif., May 30, 1948; d. Bernard Joseph Lozares and Billie Louise (Moore) Lozares Musante; m. Jerry H. Tokofsky, Oct. 4, 1982. A.A., Foothill Coll., 1968; B.A., Calif. State U.-Hayward, 1974; M.B.A., U. Calif.-Irvine. Asst. buyer cosmetics Magnin & Co., San Francisco, 1974-75; regional tng. dir. Lancome Cosmetics, San Francisco, 1975-81; nat. tng. dir. Airline Services Unltd., San Francisco, 1981-82; regional tng. dir. Shiseido Cosmetics, Los Angeles, 1983—; beauty editor Hollywood Reporter, Los Angeles, 1985—. Fund raiser Democratic Party, San Francisco, 1980-82. Recipient Cons. of Yr. award Lancome Cosmetics, 1980; High Achiever award Shiseido Cosmetics, 1985. Democrat. Episcopalian. Office: Shiseido Cosmetics Am 900 3d Ave New York NY 10022

OLIVER, LINDA BITHELL, lawyer; b. Portsmouth, Va., May 14, 1944; d. Walter Charles and Nondus (Hoge) Bithell; m. David Rogers Oliver, Jr., July 3, 1965; children—David Rogers, Morgan Bithell. Student U. Idaho, 1962-65; A.B. in Am. History, Conn. Coll., 1969; J.D., U. San Diego, 1979. Bar: Calif. 1980, Wash., 1981, Idaho 1980, Hawaii 1981. Law clk. Marinos, Styn & Studebaker, San Diego, 1978-79; law clk. Calif. Ct. of Appeals, San Diego, 1979; assoc. Bishop, Cunningham & Hartman, Bremerton, Wash., 1980-81; assoc. Stirling & Kleintop, Honolulu, 1982-83; lectr. Central Tex. Coll., Yokosuka, Japan, 1983; tax cons. Price-Waterhouse, Tokyo, 1983—; chmn. Bar Mil. Affairs Com., Bremerton, 1981; mem. family law com. Hawaii Circuit Ct., Honolulu, 1982-83. Guest lectr. Punahoe Sch., Honolulu, 1982-83, Kaelepulu Sch. Gifted Children, Honolulu, 1983; expert witness Honolulu Sch. Bd., 1983, House Senate Legis. Coms., Honolulu, 1983; mediator Neighborhood Justice Ctr., Honolulu, 1983. Recipient Richardson award U. San Diego, 1979. Mem. ABA (family law sect. 1980—), Assn. Trial Lawyers Am., Calif. Women Lawyers' Assn., Wash. Women Lawyers Assn., Hawaii Women Lawyers Assn. (bd. dirs. 1982-83, bd. dirs. found. 1982-83), Kitsap County Bar Assn. (chmn. mil. affairs com. 1981), Navy League Republican. Mormon. Club: Yo Kosuka Officers' Wives. Home: ComSubGru Seven Box 50 Seattle WA 98762

OLIVER, LYDA MONTES DE OCA, research biochemist; b. Cali, Valle, Colombia, July 31, 1945; came to U.S., 1973; d. Ricardo Montes de Oca, and Aura Renteria; m. George Edward Oliver, Jan. 4, 1973. Med. technologist, U. del Valle, Cali, Colombia, 1967; M.Mgmt., Northwestern U., 1985. Med. technologist Pub. Health Dept., Cali, 1968-73; med. technologist Northwestern U., Chgo., 1974-75, research technologist, 1975-78, sr. research technologist, 1978—, mgr. urology lab., 1983-85; founder Oliver Imports & Exports, Inc.; exec. v.p. Am. Gaskets Corp., 1986—. Contbr. articles to sci. jours. Vol., 48th ward Republican orgn., 1982-83, elections judge, 1982—. Mem. Northwestern U. Profl. Women's Assn. Roman Catholic. Clubs: Northwestern Mgmt., Chgo. Mgmt. Avocations: jogging; bicycling; reading. Home: 6033 N Sheridan Rd 29 E Chicago IL 60660 Office: 9375 W Chestnut Ave Franklin Park IL 60131

OLIVER, MARGARETTE GENEVA, special educator; b. Menifee, Ark., July 21, 1934; d. Alonzo M. Watson and Gertha Lee (Birts) Oliver; m. Jesse Manuel Oliver, Oct. 20, 1973 (div. July 1981). B.A., Philander Smith Coll., 1975; postgrad. U. Central Ark., 1976-79, 80, 82, 85. Cert. tchr., Ark. 4H program asst. U. Ark., Little Rock, 1973-75; instr. Conway Human Devel. Ctr., Ark., 1975—; vol. info. coordinator Conway County, 1981-83. Program chmn. Women's Civic League, Menifee, 1986; chmn. calendar bd. Conway County Arts Council, 1986. Recipient cert. of recognition State of Ark., 1982; others. Mem. NAACP (chpt. sec. 1986), Am. Assn. Mental Deficiency, Ark. State Employees Assn. (dir., v.p. 1978-82), Smithsonian Instn., Nat. Assn. Female Execs., Bus. and Profl. Women Conway, Concerned Citizens of Faulkner County. Lodge: Order Eastern Star (youth dir. 1984—). Home: Woodland-Gen Delivery Menifee AR 72107 Office: Conway Human Devel Ctr Seibenmorgan Rd Conway AR 72032

OLIVER, MARLYS MAE, editor, writer; b. St. Paul, Mar. 23, 1930; d. Earle R. and Margaret A. (Parrott) Benner; m. Alfred Leo Oliver, Apr. 28, 1951; children—Stephanie Margaret, David Earle. A.A., Lakewood Community Coll., 1970; student Metro State U., 1976-77. Graphic artist Lakewood Community Coll., White Bear Lake, Minn., 1968-70; corr. Women Sports mag., N.Y.C., 1973-77; editor Press Publs., White Bear Lake, 1972-76; mng. editor Frogtown Forum, St. Paul, 1976-77; mayor City of Birchwood (Minn.), 1977-83; editor Press Publs., White Bear Lake, 1982—; pres., dir. Cable Access Corp. Mem. White Bear Lake Arts Council, dir., 1975; bd. dirs. Lakeshore Players, 1984-85. Recipient numerous awards in journalism. Mem. Minn. Newspaper Assn., Nat. Newspaper Assn., Minn. Press Women (past treas.), Suburban Newspaper Assn., Midwest Writers Conf (com.) Mem. Democratic Farm Labor Party. Lodge: Job's Daus. (Queen 1949). Contbr. numerous articles and poems to popular mags. Home: 139 Birchwood Ave Birchwood Village MN 55110 Office: Press Publications 4779 Bloom Ave White Bear Lake MN 55110

OLIVER, MARY, poet; b. Maple Heights, Ohio, Sept. 10, 1935; d. Edward William and Helen Mary (Vlasak) O. Student, Ohio State U., 1955-56, Vassar Coll., 1956-57. Chmn. writing dept. Fine Arts Work Center, Provincetown, 1972, 73, mem. writing com., 1984, 85, 86; Mather vis. prof. Case-Western Res. U., 1980, 82; poet in residence Bucknell U., 1985; Elliston poet in residence U. Cin., 1986. Author: No Voyage and Other Poems, 1963, enlarged edit., 1965, The River Styx, Ohio, 1972, The Night Traveler, 1978, Twelve Moons, 1979, American Primitive, 1983; Dream Work, 1986; contbr.: others. Yale Rev. Recipient Shelley Meml. award, 1970, Alice Fay di Castagnola award, 1973; Cleve. Arts prize for lit., 1979; Achievement award Am. Acad. and Inst. Arts and Letters, 1983; Pulitzer prize for poetry, 1984; Nat. Endowment fellow, 1972-73; Guggenheim fellow, 1980-81. Mem. Poetry Soc. Am., PEN. Address: care Molly Malone Cook Box 338 Provincetown MA 02657

OLIVER, MARY ANN URSO, lawyer; b. Tampa, Fla., Aug. 25, 1948; d. Philip and Mary (Frisco) Urso; B.A. magna cum laude, U. Mass., 1970; J.D., Boston Coll., 1973; m. Richard Allen Oliver, May 23, 1972; children—Edward Raymond, Robert Philip. Admitted to D.C. bar, 1973, Va. bar, 1975, U.S. Supreme Ct. bar, 1980; atty. electric and telephone div. U.S. Dept. Agr., Washington, 1973-77; atty. SEC, Washington, 1977-80, dep. asst. dir. div. corp. regulation, 1980-84; ptnr. Oliver & Oliver, P.C., Washington, 1984—. Mem. Am. Bar Assn., D.C. Bar Assn., Boston Coll. Alumni Assn., Phi Beta Kappa, Phi Kappa Phi. Office: 1511 K St NW Suite 1100 Washington DC 20005

OLIVER, MARY WILHELMINA, law librarian, educator; b. Cumberland, Md., May 4, 1919; d. John Arlington and Sophia (Lear) Oliver; A.B., Western Md. Coll., 1940; B.S. L.S., Drexel Inst. Tech., 1943; J.D., U. N.C., 1951. Asst. circulation librarian N.J. Coll. Women, 1943-45; asst. in law library U. Va., 1945-47; asst. reference, social sci. librarian Drake U., 1947-49; research asst. Inst. Govt., U. N.C., 1951-52, asst. law librarian, 1952-55, asst. prof. law, law librarian, 1955-59, asso. prof. law, law librarian, 1959-69, prof. law, law librarian, 1969-84, prof. law, law librarian emeritus, 1984—; admitted to N.C. bar, 1951. Mem. Internat. Assn. Law Libraries, Am. Assn. Law Libraries (pres.) Spl. Libraries Assn., Am., Bar Assn., N.C. Bar Assn., Assn. Am. Law Schs. (exec. com. 1979-81), Am. Soc. Legal History, Law Alumni Assn. U. N.C., Seldon Soc., Order of Coif. Home: Box 733 Chapel Hill NC 27514 Office: U NC Law Library Chapel Hill NC 27514

OLIVER, PHYLLIS RYBINSKI, contract specialist; b. Lakeland, Fla., Sept. 3, 1953; d. Marion Michael and Estelle Barbara (Ogorzelec) Rybinski; B.A. in Internat. Affairs, Fla. State U., 1975; M.P.A., U. West Fla., 1986. Mem. adminstrv. staff Ga. Inst. Tech., Atlanta, 1975-82, contracting officer, 1979-81, asst. to dir. Sch. Chemistry, 1981-82; sr. contract adminstr. Metric Systems Corp., Fort Walton Beach, Fla., 1982—. Asst. leader NW Fla. Council Girl Scouts U.S. Mem. AAUW, Atlanta Friendship Force Club, Nat. Contract Mgmt. Assn. Republican. Roman Catholic. Home: 129 Newcastle Circle Fort Walton Beach FL 32548 Office: 736 N Beal St Fort Walton Beach FL 32548

OLIVERI, MADELINE ROSE, newspaper editor; b. Bklyn., Dec. 2, 1924; d. Attilio Michael and Carmela Louise (Falcone) Ippolito; m. John Frank Oliveri, Jan. 4, 1947; children—Constance Rose Wendlek, Lydia Jean Fichtman. Student Colby Coll., 1941-42, Hunter Coll., 1942-43; N.Y. Stock Exchange Inst., 1945-46. Registered rep. N.Y. Stock Exchange, 1947. Lab. technician Sherman Labs., Bklyn., 1942; exec. asst. to pres. DeNobili Cigar Co., N.Y.C., 1944-52; order room asst. E.F. Hutton & Co., N.Y.C., 1944-47; registered rep. N.Y. Stock Exchange H. Hentz & Co., N.Y.C., 1947-52; newspaper editor Rev. Newspapers, Ronkonkoma, N.Y., 1959-77; mng. editor Rev. Graphics, Ronkonkoma, 1977-84; cons., 1984—; TV commentator, interviewer Suffolk Cablevision, Central Islip, N.Y., 1974-76; pres. TS Graphics, Ronkonkoma, 1978-79. Sec. PTA, St. Joseph's Sch., Kings Park, N.Y., 1957-58; active Commack Aux., Cerebral Palsy Assn. Republican. Roman Catholic. Clubs: Sons of Italy, United Music Sponsors (sec. 1970-71). Home: 22 Cottonwood Dr Commack NY 11725 also 1261 Gillespie Dr Palm Harbor FL 33563

OLIVETI, SUSAN GAIL, association official; b. Bklyn., Nov. 1, 1938; d. Peter and Nancy Jane (Wolk) Randolph; m. Fosco Anthony Oliveti, Sept. 18, 1970; children by previous marriage—Lois, Peter, Elizabeth Ruben. Student CCNY, 1956-58, NYU, 1967-68; R.N., Jewish Hosp. Sch. Nursing, 1958. Adminstrv. asst. Ogilvy & Mather, N.Y.C., 1966-68; TV rep. Adam Young, Inc., N.Y.C., 1968-69; exec. asst. Paramount Pictures, N.Y.C., 1969-80; mgr. convs. and media events Warner Amex Satellite Enterprise Co., N.Y.C., 1980-83; exhibits specialist Siemens Med. Systems, Iselin, N.J., 1984-85; meetings mgr. U.S. Trademark Assn., N.Y.C., 1985—. Recipient spl. honors United Airlines, 1978. Mem. Meeting Planners Internat. (reception com., edn. com.), Women in Cable, Nat. Cable TV Assn. (meeting planner 1980-83), N.J. Travel and Conf. Mgrs. Assn. Office: US Trademark Assn 6 E 45th St New York NY 10017

OLKEN, DEBORAH JEANNE, client service representative; b. Lynn, Mass., May 21, 1953; d. Harry G. and Ruth E. (Kaufman) Olken. A.B., U. Pa., 1976; M.B.A., Babson Coll., Mass., 1983. Group ops. agt. Crimson Travel Service, Cambridge, Mass., 1977-79; research assoc. Inst. Cert. Travel Agts., Wellesley, Mass., 1979-80; sr. fin. analyst Bank of Am., San Francisco, 1984-85, fin. cons., 1985-86; client service rep. IRI, San Francisco, 1986—. Mem. World Affairs Council No. Calif. Club: Commonwealth (San Francisco). Avocations: sailing; photography.

OLLIS, HESTER GREY, insurance executive; b. Eldorado, Okla., Mar. 19, 1914; d. Embry G. and Gladys Gertrude (Wood) West; m. Lawrence Woodbridge Ollis, Oct. 21, 1934; children—Ronald Arkwright, Hester Elizabeth Ollis Massey. Partner, sec. Ollis and Co., Springfield, Mo., 1955-60, v.p., 1960-70, pres., 1970-72, v.p., dir., 1972—, semi-ret. Treas. steering com. Goals for Springfield, 1972-73; membership chmn. Community Concert Assn., 1970-71; pres. St. Anne's Guild, St. John's Episcopal Ch., Drury Coll. Aux. Mem. Springfield Assn. Ind. Ins. Agts (sec. treas.), P.E.O. (treas. chpt.), Drury Coll. Women's Aux. (pres.). Republican. Clubs: Soroptimists, Harriet E. Shepard Saturday (pres.). Home: 3745 E Monroe St Springfield MO 65804 Office: 2274 E Sunshine St Springfield MO 65804

OLMAN, MARYELLEN, human resources administrator; b. Grand Rapids, Mich., Dec. 24, 1946; d. Norman Adolph and Mary Irene (McCarthy) Olman; m. Richard Isaac Fine, Nov. 25, 1982. B.A. in Community Service, Mich. State U., 1968. Legis. researcher Hon. Gerald R. Ford, U.S. Ho. of Reps., 1969-71; spl. asst. Hon. Jack F. Kemp, U.S. Ho. of Reps., 1971-74; personnel analyst Los Angeles City Housing Authority, 1975-78; profl. placement rep. Gen. Telephone of Calif., Santa Monica, 1978-81, mgmt. staffing adminstr., 1981—. Mem. Los Angeles Internat. Visitors Assn., 1982—; mem. founders circle Los Angeles Music Ctr. Mem. Am. Soc. Personnel Adminstrs., Coll. Placement Council, Western Coll. Placement Assn., Personnel and Indsl. Relations Assn. Republican. Home: 5331 Horizon Dr Malibu CA 90265

OLMEDO-BORECKY, STEPHANIE KATHRYN, air force officer; b. Denver, Jan. 16, 1950; d. Lloyd and Juanita (Morales) Olmedo Putnam; m. Steven John Borecky, Sept. 23, 1978; 1 child, Kittrick John. M.A., U. No. Colo., 1979. Tchr. of deaf Amoskeege Sc. Dist., Claremont, N.H., 1973, Gov. Baxter Sch. for Deaf, Falmouth, Maine, 1973-74, Pueblo Sch. Dist., Colo., 1975-77; commd. 2d lt. U.S. Air Force, 1981, advanced through grades to capt., 1985; exec. support officer Ellsworth AFB, S.D., 1981-85, Dyess AFB, Tex., 1985—. Decorated Colo. Air N.G. Outstanding Airman of Year, 1975, Res. Forces Meritorious Service medal, 1977, USAF commendation medal, 1985. Mem. Air Force Assn., Nat. Assn. Exec. Females. Roman Catholic. Home:

2957 Stonecrest Dr Abilene TX 79606 Office: 96 Combat Support Group Dyess AFB TX 79607

OLMSTEAD, KAREN JO, nurse; b. Port Angeles, Wash., Jan. 4, 1951; d. George Herman Jr. and Joanna (Jordan) Schoenfeldt; b. Cecil Wayne Olmstead, Dec. 20, 1967; children—Wayne Thomas, Justina Jo. B.A. in Edn., Peinisula Coll., 1969, A.A., 1981, A.A.S., 1982, R.N., 1982. Group counselor Family Resource Ctr., Port Angeles, 1975-80; nurse aide Olympic Meml. Hosp., Port Angeles, 1980-81, L.P.N., 1981-82, R.N., 1982—, charge nurse psychiat. detox unit, 1984—. Parent aide Exchange Club Ctr. for Prevention of Child Abuse, Port Angeles; active Wash. Assn. County Child Abuse Councils, Seattle; founder, pres. Clallam County Parent Adv. Council for Learning Disabilities, 1984. Recipient Most Improved Family in Entire Western Region award Exchange Club Ctr. Prevention Child Abuse, 1985. Mem. Wash. Nurses Assn., Am. Nurses Assn. Avocations: raising and riding horses; reading; crocheting; aerobics. Home: 915 Scrivner Rd Port Angeles WA 98362 Office: Olympic Meml Hosp 939 Caroline St Port Angeles WA 98362

OLMSTED, MARY SEYMOUR, foreign service officer; b. Duluth, Minn., Sept. 28, 1919; d. George Chauncey and Zadia Sarah (McDonald) O.; A.B., Mt. Holyoke Coll., South Hadley, Mass., 1941; M.A., Columbia U., 1945; postgrad. Fletcher Sch. Law and Diplomacy, Medford, Mass., 1955-56. Fgn. service officer U.S. Dept. State, 1945-79, dep. dir. personnel, Washington, 1971-74, ambassador, Port Moresby, Papua, New Guinea, 1975-79; dir. 3900 Watson Coop., Washington, 1984—. Co-author: (research pamphlet) Women At State, 1984. Recipient Harter award U.S. Dept. State, 1972, Superior Honor award, 1973. Mem. Soc. Women Geographers, Exec. Seminar Alumni Assn. (treas. 1983-84). Democrat. Episcopalian. Club: Woman's Nat. Democratic.

OLMSTED, PATRICIA PALMER, educational researcher; b. Chgo., Sept. 19, 1940; d. Richard O. and Marion E. (Huffman) Palmer; B.A. in Psychology, Mich. State U., 1962; postgrad. Stanford U., 1962-63; M.A., Columbia U., 1965; Ph.D., U. Fla., 1977. Grad. research asst. Columbia U., N.Y.C., 1964, public health trainee in psychopathology, 1964-65; assoc. research scientist dept. med. genetics Psychiatric Inst., N.Y.C., 1965-66; asst. research coordinator Merrill-Palmer Inst., Detroit, 1966-68, instr., 1966-69, research coordinator, 1966-69; instr. Coll. Edn., U. Fla., Gainesville, 1969-71, asst. in edn., 1971-73, assoc. in edn., 1973-77; clin. asst. prof. Sch. Edn., U. N.C., Chapel Hill, 1977-82, clin. assoc. prof., 1982—, dir. parent edn. follow through program, 1977—; cons. various public schs., 1969—. Dept. of Edn. grantee, 1977-84. Mem. Am. Psychol. Assn., Soc. for Research in Child Devel., Am. Ednl. Research Assn., Nat. Assn. for Edn. of Young Children, Phi Delta Kappa. Contbr. articles on research in edn. to profl. publs.; contbr. chpts. to books on edn. Home: 49 Cedar Terrace Rd Chapel Hill NC 27514 Office: High/Scope Ednl Research Found 600 N River St Ypsilanti MI 48198

OLMSTED, SHIRLEY, fertilizer and seed company account executive; b. Marysville, Ohio, Oct. 28, 1939; d. Clarence Conrad and Hattie Marie (Wallace) Dunn; m. Thomas Lake Mullaney, Apr. 27, 1958 (dec. May 1958); children—Tami Sue, Tomi Sue; m. Michael Olmsted, Feb. 21, 1960 (div. Apr. 1968); 1 child, R. Todd. Student pub. schs., Raymond, Ohio. Field sales adminstrv. sec. O.M. Scott & Sons, Marysville, Ohio, 1969-72, sec. Scotts Tng. Inst., 1972-76, customer service rep., 1976-81, customer service adminstrv. coordinator, 1981-82, Burpee sales rep., 1982-83, account exec., 1983—. Editor customer service operaint manual, 1981. Speaker Chatham Village of Memphis, Tenn., 1985. Named to 100% Club O.M. Scott & Sons, 1984, 85, other awards, 1984, 85. Mem. Nat. Assn. Female Execs., Nat. Assn. Profl. Saleswomen. Republican. Club: Positive Christian Singles (Memphis). Avocations: reading; water skiing; travel; country music; piano. Office: O M Scott & Sons 14111 Scottslawn Rd Marysville OH 43040

O'LOUGHLIN, CYNTHIA ANNE, geophysical technician; b. Bartlesville, Okla., Oct. 1, 1947; d. Joseph Michael Cheront and Dorothy Marie (Vaden) O'L. Student Lindonwood Coll., St. Charles, Mo., 1965-66, Central State Coll., Edmond, Okla., 1970; B.A., Loretto Heights Coll., 1970. Clerical positions John A. Brown Co., Oklahoma City, 1970-71; divisional mgr. Sakowitz, Houston, 1972-79; sr. geophys. technician Gulf Oil Exploration and Prodn. Co., Houston, 1980—. Contbr. article to Denver Post. Mem. Save the Whales Found., Save the Porpoise Found., Jacques Cousteau Found., Direct Mail Mktg. Assn., NOW, others. Republican. Roman Catholic. Office: Gulf Oil Exploration and Prodn Co 11111 S Wilcrest St Room 2309 Houston TX 77099

OLSEN, DAGNE BORG, state legislator; b. Dalton, Minn., Mar. 19, 1933; d. Glenn F. and Esther J. (Stortroen) Borg; m. Duane D. Olsen, June 25, 1955; children—Deanna, Douglas, Dick. B.S., U. N.D., 1955. Tchr., Gilby and Midway Schs., Gilby, N.D., 1955-57, 60-62; ptnr. Cottonwood Farm, Manvel, N.D., 1955—; mem. N.D. Ho. of Reps., 1980—; attended White House Briefing, Washington, 1984; mem. White House Conf. on Natural Beauty, Washington, 1965; mem. exec. com. N.D. Council on Devel. Disabilities, Bismarck, 1982—; vol. mgr. 2 businesses Assn. Retarded Citizens, Grand Forks, N.D., 1970—, pres., 1966, 84, dir., 1966—. Editor: Manvel Centennial History Book, 1982; editor From Trails to Tribute, 1964; Valley Key, 1976-80; Profile Potpourri, 1976-80. Pres., Grand Forks County Spl. Edn. Bd., 1971-80; past pres., bd. dirs. Agassiz Enterprises, 1972—; mem. Mayor's Com. on Employment of Handicapped, 1982—; mem. governing bd. United Hosp., Grand Forks; past pres., vol. United Hosp. Aux.; precinct committeeman, dist. 19 vice-chmn. Republican Party, 1974-80, state conv. del., 1976, 78, 80, 82, 84, state platform com., 1980; mem. adv. com. Turtle River State Park; mem. Gov.'s Com. on Community Betterment, 1960-66, Gov.'s. Econ. Devel. Conf., 1981, Ednl. Tech. Conf., 1983, Agrl. Conf., 1984, Indsl. Climate Conf., 1984, Gov.'s Adv. Council on Volunteerism, 1984. Recipient Outstanding Leadership award Gov. State N.D., 1964; Outstanding Vol. Service award Gov. State N.D., 1979; Manvel, Grand Prize award N.D. Community Betterment, 1962; named 4-H Blue Ribbon Club Leader, 1967-71; Grand Forks Woman of Yr., 1978; Outstanding Farm, Soil Conservation Dist., 1980; Outstanding Parent, Assn. Retarded Citizens, 1977, Mem. of Yr., 1981, U.S.-North Central region Mem. of Yr., 1982. Mem. Pi Lambda Theta, Delta Phi Delta, Delta Zeta. Republican. Lutheran. Club: Manvel Woman's (pres. 4 times). Home: Rural Route 1 Manuel ND 58256 Office: State Capitol Bldg Bismarck ND 58505

OLSEN, INGER ANNA, psychologist; b. Copper Mountain, B.C, Can., Dec. 25, 1926; d. Arthur I.J. and Dagmar O.; B.S., Wash. State U., 1954, M.S., 1956, Ph.D., 1962. Psychiat. nurse Provincial Mental Health Services B.C., 1947-51, psychologist, 1956-58; psychologist Vancouver (B.C.) City Met. Health Services, 1958-60, Wash. State U. Student Counseling Center, Pullman, 1960-62; sr. psychologist Met. Health Services, Vancouver, 1962-66; instr. psychology Vancouver Community Coll., 1966—; docent Vancouver Aquarium Assn. Bd. dirs. Second Mile Soc., 1975—. Mem. Assn. Childhood Edn. Internat., Am. Psychol. Assn., B.C. Psychol. Assn., Gerontol. Soc., Can. Assn. Gerontology, B.C. Assn. Gerontology, Phi Beta Kappa, Sigma Xi, Alpha Kappa Delta. Contbr. articles to profl. jours. Home: 1255 Bidwell St Apt 1910 Vancouver BC V6G 2K8 Canada Office: 100 W 49th Ave Vancouver BC V5Y 2Z6 Canada

OLSEN, KARIN LYNN, editor; b. Dallas, Oct. 15, 1959; d. Kenneth Bruce and Marilyn (Jennings) O. grad. Okla. State U., 1981. Editor, sales rep. Country Club Publs., Oklahoma City, 1981. Contbr. articles to profl. jours. Big Sister, Big Bros./Big Sisters, Oklahoma City, 1984-85; mem. Citizens Adv. Council, Am. Inst. Cancer Research, Washington, 1984. Mem. Women in Communications (pres. 1980-81), Sigma Delta Chi, Pi Beta Phi. Republican. Episcopalian. Home: 11550 N May Apt 107 Oklahoma City OK 73120 Office: Country Club Publs 6531 Classen Blvd Oklahoma City OK 73116

OLSEN, KIRSTEN, broker; b. Copenhagen, Nov. 5, 1942; came to U.S., 1948, naturalized, 1956; d. Jens Peder and Else Emilie (Jorgensen) Jensen; student Coll. San Mateo, 1964; grad. Stanford U. Exec. Inst., 1976; m. Thomas Allen Skornia, May 22, 1976; 1 child, Erika Skornia-Olsen. Asst. to pres. Drexler Tech., Palo Alto, Calif., from 1968, mgr. public relations, to 1973; investment broker Merrill Lynch, San Jose, Calif., 1973, Palo Alto, to 1977, Paine Webber Jackson & Curtis, Palo Alto, 1977-80, Smith Barney Harris Upham, Menlo Park, Calif., 1980-82; pres. Kirsten Olsen & Co., Inc., Investment Brokers, 1982—; ptnr. Triangle Ventures.; dir. NCA Corp. trustee San Jose-Cleve. Ballet; Democratic Party nominee U.S. Congress, 1978-80. Mem. Calif. Elected Women. Lutheran. Club: Peninsula Stock and Bond (past pres.) (Palo Alto). Home: 1601 Stone Pine Ln Atherton CA 94025 Office: 2035 Landings Dr Mountain View CA 94043

OLSEN, LINDA, interactive video manager; b. Nashua, N.H., May 6, 1956; d. Zenny and Doris (Smith) O. B.S., So. Conn. U., 1978, M.S., 1979. Sales rep. Video Edn. Co. Am., Boston, 1979-81, Climson Group, Cambridge, Mass., 1981-83, Digital Equipment Corp., Atlanta, 1983-86; sales exec. Tech. Industries of Ga., Atlanta, 1986—. Scholar for health studies, So. Conn. U., Mex., 1978. Mem. Internat. Interactive Communication Soc., Internat. TV Assn., Am. Multi-Image Assn. Office: Technical Industries of Ga 6000 Peachtree Rd NE Atlanta GA 30341

OLSEN, LINDA ELAINE, clin. psychologist; b. Oregon City, Oreg., Jan. 16, 1947; d. Clarence A. and Marilyn M. (Roppell) O.; B.A., Vassar Coll., 1968; Ph.D. (Margaret Floy Washburn fellow 1968), U. Chgo., 1975. Psychologist, Chgo. Counseling and Psychotherapy Center, 1968-73, Calif. Sch. Profl. Psychology, Los Angeles, 1973-76; clin. psychologist Los Angeles Family Inst., 1975—; asst. clin. prof. psychiatry UCLA, 1981—. USPHS trainee, 1970-71. Mem. Am. Psychol. Assn. (editorial bd. Jour. Psychotherapy 1973-76), Calif. State Psychol. Assn., Am. Family Therapy Assn. (charter). Author workbook and cassette tapes: Experiential Focusing Training Program, 1975.

OLSEN, MARGARET ANN, numismatist, retail exec.; b. Chgo., July 22, 1944; d. Carl Johan and Ruth Vera Olsen; R.N., Swedish Covenant Hosp., Chgo., 1965; B.S., No. Ill. U., 1968. Mem. nursing staff hosps. in Ill. and Colo., 1962-74; cons. Adams County Mental Health Center, Commerce City, Colo., 1973-74; fin. dir., instr. Rocky Mountain Transactional Analysis Inst., Littleton, Colo., 1974-76; cons. Rimel Assos. in Psychiatry, P.C., Denver, 1974-75; therapist Profl. Counseling Assos., Littleton, Colo., 1974-77; instr. Profl. Tng. Center, Littleton, 1975-77; therapist Denver Mental Health Group, 1977-80; pres. Westminster Coin & Jewelry, Ltd., also mgr., v.p., pres. Westminster Coin Co. (Colo.), 1974—. Bd. govs. Adelphi U., Garden City, N.J., 1982—. Mem. Inst. Numismatic and Philatelic Studies, Internat. Trasactional Analysis Assn. (dir. Rocky Mountain chpt.), Am. Nurses Assn., Am. Numismatic Assn., Am. Soc. Appraisers; Industry Council for Tangible Assets, Nat. Assn. Coin and Precious Metals Dealers, Nat. Assn. Female Execs., Fla. United Numismatists Inc., Internat. Soc. Appraisers, Token and Medal Soc., Soc. Paper Money Collectors, Facts Trading Info. System, Colo. Wyo. Numismatic Assn., Colo. Ednl. Numismatic Assn. Office: 3489 W 72d Ave Suite 100 Westminster CO 80030

OLSEN, MARTHA BROWN, state official; b. Cookeville, Tenn., June 6, 1948; d. Raymond and Mary Elizabeth Brown; B.S., Tenn. Technol. U., 1970; postgrad. U. Western Australia, 1970-71, Tenn. State U., 1977-78, Harvard U., 1979; m. Robert J. Olsen, Sept. 15, 1972. Asst. commr. revenue Tenn. Dept. Revenue, Nashville, 1979-80, commr., 1980-84; commr. personnel State of Tenn., 1984—, sr. v.p., corporate personnel adminstr. First Am. Corp., 1986—; exec. asst. to chancellor U. Tenn., Nashville, 1975-79, dir. devel. and alumni relations, 1974-75. Republican. Mem. Christian Ch. Office: Dept Personnel James K Polk Bldg Suite 200 Nashville TN 37219

OLSEN, SUZANNE, operations research engineer, mathematics educator; b. Olean, N.Y., Nov. 6, 1940; d. Francis Martin and Theodoshia Theresa (Oslowski) Wroblewski; m. William Ray Olsen, Mar. 5, 1960 (div. 1972); children—Laura Elizabeth, Kristen Suzanne; m. Max Finkle, Jr., Aug. 7, 1982; stepchildren—David Eldridge, John Joseph, Christopher Alan. B.A. in Math., SUNY-Buffalo, 1968, M.Ed., in Math., 1972, M.S. in Indsl. Engring., 1980. Cert. tchr. math., N.Y. Math. tchr. West Seneca Schs., N.Y., 1968-80, dept. head, 1976-80; engr. ANR Pipeline Co., Detroit, 1980-84; sr. engr. Gen. Motors, Warren, Mich., 1984—; adj. faculty Walsh Coll., Troy, Mich., 1985—. Mem. Ops. Research Soc. Am. (regional v.p. 1985-87), Tech. Inst. Mgmt. (regional v.p. 1985-87). Club: Women's Economic (Detroit, chmn. conf. 1986). Home: 2774 Orchard Trail Troy MI 48098 Office: General Motors 30400 Mound Rd Warren MI 48090

OLSEN, THEODORA EGBERT PECK (MRS. SEVERT ANDREW OLSEN), artist; b. Union, N.J., Sept. 6, 1909; d. Edward Egbert and Theodorea G. (Tucker) Peck; student N.Y. Sch. Design, 1928-29, Pratt-Phoenix Sch. Design, N.Y.C., 1929-32, Coll. City N.Y., 1955, Wagner Coll., summer 1965; m. Ray Sheldon Wilbur, Sept. 8, 1933 (dec. 1966); 1 dau., Margaret Anne (Mrs. Prudhomme); m. 2d, Severt Andrew Olsen, July 17, 1967 (dec. Feb. 1975); stepchildren Arlene Christine, Severt Eugene (dec.). Exhibited at Contemporary Gallery, Newark, 1932, S.I. Mus., 1947-65, N.Y.C. Fedn. Women's Clubs exhibit, 1961, Island Art Center Gallery, New Dorp, S.I., 1961, 33d N.J. Exhbn., Montclair Art Mus., 1964, Summit (N.J.) Art Center, 1965; outdoor shows at Sailors Snug Harbour, S.I., 1956-63, Greenwich Village, N.Y.C., 1961-64, Southhampton and Westhampton (L.I.) Beach, 1964, Summit Art Center, N.J., 1967, Spring Festival Arts, Staten Island, 1968; represented in permanent collection at Wagner Coll., S.I., S.I. Mus.; prin. works include View From Guild Hall, Show Case, Variation on Theme VIII, Long Island Expressway, Seed Pods, Emergence from Chrysalis. Cons., lectr., pvt. tchr., 1934—; tchr. painting YWCA, S.I., 1968-72. Active fund-raising Richmond Mem. Hosp., 1946-54, com. to beautify halls Tottenville (S.I.) High Sch., 1958-60. Recipient S.I. Mus.-Wagner Coll. Purchase award, 1958—; Julius Weisglass award S.I. Mus., 2d prize, 1960, 1st prize, 1965; 1st prize and Honorable mention N.Y.C. Fedn. Women's Clubs competition, 1961. Founder, hon. life mem. South Shore Artists Group (pres. 1946-47, 49-61, 2d v.p. 1965-66); mem. S.I. Hist. Soc. Women's Aux., S.I. Hist. Soc., Nat. Assn. Mil. Widows, Pratt-Phoenix Sch. Design Alumni (jury awards 1949), Epsilon Nu Sigma. Clubs: Prince Bay Women's (pres. 1969-71); Coast Guard Officer's Wives. Home: 72 Bayview Ave Prince Bay Staten Island NY 10309

OLSEN, VIRGINIA DAYE, real estate broker; b. Kansas City, Mo., Aug. 13, 1953; d. Ray and Earlyne Virginia (Stanfield) Sims. B.S. cum laude in Animal Sci. and Industries, Kans. State U., 1974. Lic. real estate salesman, Kans., real estate broker, Mo. Salesperson Wilson Foods, Oklahoma City, 1975-77; mgr. Kans. Beef Council div. Kans. Livestock Assn., Topeka, 1977-78; asst. to editor Kans. Stockman mag., Topeka, 1977-78; sales assoc. Kroh Bros. Realty, Kansas City, Mo., 1979-80, broker-mgr., 1980—. Little Am. Royal scholar, 1973. Mem. Gamma Sigma Delta (life), Alpha Zeta (life), Phi Kappa Phi, Beta Sigma Phi (charter). Home: 7921 Belleview Kansas City MO 64114 Office: Kroh Bros Realty 13005 State Line Kansas City MO 64145

OLSON, BONNIE WAGGONER BRETERNITZ, civic worker; b. North Platte, Nebr., May 30, 1916; d. Floyd Emil and Edith (Waggoner) Breternitz; A.B., U. Chgo., 1947; m. O. Donald Olson, May 17, 1944; children—Pamela Lynne, Douglas Donald. Dep. clk. Dist. Ct., Lincoln County, Nebr., 1940-42; advt. researcher Burke & Assos., Chgo., 1942; contbg. newspaper columnist Chgo. Herald-Am., 1943; social worker ARC, Chgo., 1942-44; exec. sec. Econometrica, Cowles Commn. for Research in Econs., Chgo., 1945-47. Active Chgo. Maternity Center Fund Drive, 1953; mem. Colo. Springs Community Council, 1956-58, chmn. children's div., 1956-58, mem. exec. bd., 1956-58, mem. budget com., 1957-58; mem. Colorado Springs Charter Assn., 1956-60, mem. exec. bd., 1957-59, sec., 1958; chmn. El Paso County PTA, Protective Services for Children, 1959-61; chmn. women's div. fund drive ARC, 1961; mem. LWV, 1957—, mem. state children's law com., 1961-63; chmn. ad hoc com. El Paso County Citizens Com. for Nat. Probation and Parole Survey, Juvenile Ct. Procedures and Detention, 1957-61; mem. children's adv. com. Colo. Child Welfare Dept., 1959-63, chmn., 1961; del. White House Conf. on Children and Youth, 1960, 70; sec. Citizens Ad Hoc Com. for Comprehensive Mental Health Clinic for Pikes Peak Region, 1966—; mem. Colorado Springs Human Relations Commn., 1968-71; sustaining mem. Symphony Guild, 1970-72, Fine Arts Center, 1957—; bd. dirs. Pikes Peak Mental Health Center, 1964-67; del. Colo. Gov.'s Conf. on Aging, 1980; observer White House Conf. on Aging, 1981. Recipient Lane Bryant Ann. Nat. Awards citation, 1961; alumni citation for public service U. Chgo., 1961. Mem. Am. Acad. Polit. and Social Sci., Council on Religion and Internat. Affairs. Episcopalian. Clubs: Quadranglar, University (Chgo.); Garden of the Gods, ENT Officers Wives (hon.) (Colorado Springs). Home: 2110 Hercules Dr Colorado Springs CO 80906

OLSON, CHARLOTTE GRETHEL ELKINS, medical records administrator; b. Gilbert, W.Va., Sept. 14, 1922; d. Rush and Mary Ellen (White) Elkins; B.A., Goddard Coll., 1968; grad. Sch. for Med. Record Adminstrs., USPHS Hosp., 1969. Chief med. info. sect. VA Hosps. at Martinsburg, W.Va., 1970-71, West Side Chgo., 1971-72, Durham, N.C., 1972-74, Bay Pines, Fla., 1975-76, Martinsburg, W.Va., 1976-80, Mountain Home, Tenn., 1981—; with Project Hope Agencia, Brazil, S.Am., 1974; vol. Sage Meml. Hosp., Ganado, Ariz., 1971. Recipient Cert. of Appreciation, Project Hope. Mem. Am. Med. Record Assn., Tenn. Med. Record Assn., W.Va. Med. Record Assn. (pres.-elect 1980-81), AAUW (treas. Chgo. br. 1972). Republican. Presbyterian. Club: Order Eastern Star. Home: Route 5 PO Box 2535 Elizabethtown TN 37643

OLSON, CHRISTINA LYNNE, journalist; b. Honolulu, Aug. 19, 1947; d. Walter Lewis and Jessica Rose (Schneck) Olson; m. Stanley Wills Cloud, Jan. 5, 1980; 1 dau., Caroline Wills. B.A., U. Ariz., 1969. Reporter, editor A.P., Salt Lake City, 1970-72, San Francisco, 1972, nat. feature writer, 1972-73, fgn. desk editor, 1973-74, fgn. corr., Moscow, USSR, 1974-76, polit. reporter, Washington, 1976-77; White House corr. Balt. Sun, Washington, 1977-79, polit. writer, 1979-81; freelance mng. writer, Los Angeles, 1982—; sr. lectr. Sch. Journalism, U. So. Calif., Los Angeles, 1983—. Contbr. articles to mags. Mem. Women in Communications, Phi Beta Kappa, Phi Kappa Phi. Democrat. Roman Catholic.

OLSON, DEBRA ANN, lawyer; b. Clarksdale, Miss., Mar. 5, 1952; d. Marvin Jerome and Norma Sarah (Pries) Bacharach; m. Edward Clinton Olson, Aug. 15, 1976. B.A. with high honors, U. Tex.-Austin, 1973; J.D. cum laude, So. Meth. U., 1977. Bar: Tex. 1977, Calif. 1984. Summer clk. firm Baker & Botts, Houston, 1976; assoc. firm Coke & Coke, Dallas, 1977-81; atty. InterFirst Corp., Dallas, 1981-83. Contbr. articles to Southwestern Law Jour., notes and comments editor, 1976-77. Mem. The 500, Inc., Dallas, 1980-83; mem. Innovators of Dallas Symphony Orch. League, 1980-83. Mem. ABA, State Bar Calif., State Bar Tex., Order of Coif, Alpha Lambda Delta, Phi Beta Kappa, Phi Kappa Phi. Address: Menlo Park CA

OLSON, DIANE FAYNE, psychologist; b. Mpls.; d. Douglas Donald and Mabel Dorothey (Hagen) Christensen; m. Timothy M. Olson, Sept. 21, 1968 (div. 1978); 1 child, Emily S. L. B.A. in Psychology magna cum laude, U. Minn., 1968, Ph.D., 1972. Lic. consulting psychologist. Sr. clin. psychologist Hennepin County Gen. Hosp., Mpls., 1971-73; dir. partial hospitalization unit U. Minn., 1977—; sr. clin. psychologist Pilot City Mental Health Ctr., Mpls., 1975-78; ptnr., exec. v.p. dor and associates, inc., Mpls., 1978-83; pres. Affiliated Psychol. Services, Inc., Mpls., 1983—. Bd. dirs. United Neighborhood Ctrs. Am., 1977—; pres. bd. dirs. Northside Settlement Services, Inc., 1980-82, 1st v.p. 1978-80, v.p. program and planning, 1977-78; treas., bd. dirs. Pillsbury United Neighborhood Ctr., 1983—; chmn. allocation panel United Way of Mpls., 1979—; bd. dirs. Jr. Achievement of Twin Cities, Mchts. of Old St. Anthony, Harriet Tubman Womens' Shelter; pres. Assn. Labor-Mgmt., Cons. on Alcoholism, Inc., Minn. 1980-83. Contbr. articles to profl. jours. Recipient Bronze leadership award Jr. Achievement, 1983, Gold medal award Legal Aid Soc., 1980, Disting. Service award Northside Neighborhood Services, 1979. Mem. Am. Psychol. Assn., Assn. Labor, Mgmt., Cons. on Alcoholism Inc., Mental Health Assn., Minn. Psychol. Assn., Am. Mgmt. Assn., Mchts. of Old St. Anthony, Minn. Women's Econ. Roundtable, Horizon 100. Democrat. Lutheran. Home: 169 Seymour Ave SE Minneapolis MN 55414 Office: Affiliated Psychol Services 1400 Internat Centre 900 S 2d Ave Minneapolis MN 55402

OLSON, DONNA RAE, medical technologist; b. St. Louis, Oct. 20, 1947; d. Roy William and Ann Elizabeth (O'Donnell) O. B.A. in Biology, Cath. U. Am., 1964, B.S. in Med. Tech., 1966, M.A. in Ednl. Tech., 1973, Ed.D. in Ednl. Tech., 1985; M.A. in Health Care Mgmt. and Supervision, Central Mich. U., 1981. Clin. chemistry supr. Washington Hosp. Center, 1965-69, teaching coordinator Sch. Med. Tech., 1969-72; clin. chemistry technologist NIH, Bethesda, Md., 1972—. Recipient various govt. awards. Mem. Am. Soc. Clin. Pathologists (affiliate), Am. Soc. Med. Technologists, Am. Mgmt. Assn., Clin. Lab. Mgmt. Assn., D.C. Soc. Med. Tech. (ednl. coordinator 1979-81), Va. Soc. Med. Tech. Home: 6001 Landon Ln Bethesda MD 20817 Office: Clin Chem Service NIH Bethesda MD 20814

OLSON, DORISE EVELYN (MRS. RAUL J. MINA-MORA), artist; b. N.Y.C., June 8, 1932; d. Athur C. and Anna (Carlson) Olson; student Art Student's League, L.I. Art League, Woodstock, N.Y., Traphagen Sch. Design, N.Y.; m. Raul J. Mina-Mora, Oct. 27, 1967. One-man shows at Caravan House Galleries, Lord & Taylor's Galleries, Different Drummer Gallery, 1976, Nat. Art League, Wickford Art Gallery, W. Ris Galleries, N.J., Rosequist Gallery, Ariz.; exhibited in group shows at Bklyn. Mus., Nat. Arts Club, Nat. Acad., Nat. Acad. Fine Arts, Met. Mus. Arts, Community Gallery with Burr Artists, 1977, Goldsboro (N.C.) Art Mus., 1977, Parrish Art Mus., 1970, 72, Springfield (Mass.) Art Mus., Stony Brook U., Cork Gallery, Avery Fisher Hall, Lincoln Center, 1980, others; represented in pvt. collections; tchr. painting Islip Art Mus. Demonstrator watercolor for various schs. and pvt. clubs. Recipient award Bus. and Profl. Women's Club, N.Y.C., 1967; gold medal Knickerbocker Artists, 1968; Hydenryk award Catherine Lorillard Wolfe Art Club, 1969; 1st place award in watercolor Bklyn. Mus. competition, 1966, 67, 69, Windsor and Newton award, Nat. Arts League Gold medal, 70, Grumbacher award 1971, 1st prize for watercolor Malverne Artists, 1973, best watercolor award Burr Artists, 1974, Forbes award, 1981, Newman award Nat. Soc. Painters in Casein and Acrylic, 1981, others. Mem. Am. Artists Profl. League (award 1979), Allied Artists Am., Catherine Lorillard Wolfe Art Club, Nat. Soc. Painters in Casein and Acrylic, Knickerbocker Artists (award 1979), Nat. Arts Club, Audubon Artists. Address: 87 Central Blvd Box 256 Oakdale NY 11769

OLSON, ENID CLARA THALMAN, social service administrator, educator; b. Richfield, Utah, Mar. 10, 1923; d. John Earl and Ida Arelia (Hansen) Thalman; m. Arnold Olson, Apr. 23, 1942 (div.); 1 son, Steven Arnold. B.S. in Psychology, U. Ariz., 1971, M.S. in Child Devel. and Family Relations, 1972. Cert. community coll. instr., Ariz.; cert. educator, counselor, supr., adminstrv. officer Calif. Extension agt. Coop. Extension Service, Tucson, 1975-76; health services surveyor II Ariz. Dept. Health Services, Phoenix, 1977-79; supr. counselling and case mgmt. City of Phoenix, 1980-82; state coordinator Expanded Food and Nutrition Edn. Program, Coop. Extension Service, U. Hawaii, 1982-84; social service supr. West Hawaii unit Dept. Social Service and Housing. Chmn. grant rev. Santa Cruz County (Ariz.) Comprehensive Health Planning Council, 1972-74; co-chmn. Ariz. Human Resource Commn., 1977. Mem. Hawaii Nutrition Council, Hawaii UN Assn. (exec. bd.), Hawaii Home Econs. Assn., Psi Chi, Phi Theta Kappa, Kappa Delta Pi. Democrat. Unitarian Universalist. Club: Altrusa (pres., dir. Ambos Nogales, pres. Phoenix 1981-82, pres. Honolulu 1984-85).

OLSON, EVELYN MAR, furniture sales company executive, marketing and advertising consultant; b. Akron, Ohio, Nov. 10, 1950; d. Myrle Mylo Olson and Luz (Talaña) Schwartz. B.A. in Mass Media Communication, U. Akron, 1980. Sec., Goodyear Tire & Rubber Co., Akron, 1968-73, adminstrv. asst. to gen. mgr. chem. div., 1973-75, visual merchandiser advt., 1975-77, display coordinator advt., 1977-79, advt. mgr. Central and S.W. regions, Dallas, 1979-83; mktg. dir., dir., sec. to bd. Budji Corp., Los Angeles, 1983—. Choreographer, actress, dancer, singer musicals including Carnival, Guys and Dolls, Fiorello, Jacques Brel, Apple Tree, HMS Pinafore, Fantasticks, South Pacific, Pippin, Dames at Sea, The King and I, Can-Can and Black Comedy; pres. Goodyear Community Theatre, Akron, 1977-80; dir. Dallas Repertory Theatre, 1981-83; entertainment chmn. 500, Inc. Artfest, Dallas, 1983; county rep. United Way, 1970. Mem. Women in Communications, Actors Equity Assn. Democrat. Roman Catholic. Club: Toastmasters (Best Speaker award 1972). Home: 11951 Clonlee Ave Granada Hills CA 91344 Office: Budji Corp 8844 Beverly Blvd Los Angeles CA 90048

OLSON, GLORIA ELLAINE, retail executive; b. Luck, Wis., Jan. 21, 1935; d. Lewis John and Stella (Larson) Jensen; m. Dale LeRoy Olson, Mar. 5, 1953; children—William, Debra, Scott, Kari, Beth. Women's editor ABC Newspapers, Anoka, Minn., 1968-76, editor, 1976-84, asst. mng. editor, 1976-84; owner, operator GloriAnne's, Inc., Ham Lake, Minn., 1984—. With pub. info. dept. Am. Cancer Soc., Anoka County; pub. info. chmn. Star Cities Com., Ham Lake, 1983-84; mem. adv. council Assn. Retarded Citizens, Anoka County, 1983-84. Recipient Woman of Achievement award North Metro Bus. and Profl. Women, 1980-81. Mem. Press Women of Minn., Minn. Press Women (pres. 1979-81), Nat. Press Women. Democrat. Lutheran. Home: 3527 InterLachen Dr Ham Lake MN 55304 Office: 320 Crosstown Mall 17565 Central Ave NE Ham Lake MN 55304

OLSON, JULIE ANN, systems consultant, educator; b. Oklahoma City, May 14, 1957; d. Willard Alton and Ruth Harriet (Ehlers) O.; m. Kevin Peter McAuliffe, Oct. 12, 1985. B.A. in History, Augustana Coll., 1979; postgrad. Keller Grad. Sch. Mgmt., Chgo. Systems analyst Continental Bank, Chgo., 1979-82; systems cons. Computer Ptnrs., Oakbrook, Ill., 1982—; instr. data processing Oakton Community Coll., Des Plaines, 1983—. Exec. dir., chmn.

scholarship Miss Northwest Communities Inc., Des Plaines, 1984—. Mem. Data Processing Mgmt. Assn. (asst. faculty coordinator Student chpt. 1985—), Nat. Assn. Female Execs. Lutheran. Avocations: classical pianist; reading; flamenco dancing; snow skiing; cross stitch. Home: 167 Village Ct Des Plaines IL 60016 Office: Computer Ptnrs 122 W 22d St Oakbrook IL 60521

OLSON, KATHRYN ADELE, lawyer; b. Bemidji, Minn., Aug. 5, 1946; d. Herbert Earl and Vivian Adele (Brink) Olson. B.A., U. Colo., 1968; J.D. cum laude, Yeshiva U., 1982. Bar: N.Y. 1983. Law clk. firm Weitzner, Levine & Louis, N.Y.C., 1981-82; assoc. firm Shea & Gould, N.Y.C., 1982—. Adminstrv. asst. Democratic Nat. Com., N.Y.C., 1976; chmn. women's com. Learning to Read through Arts, Guggenheim Mus., N.Y.C., 1976—; active Union Settlement House, N.Y.C., 1982—. Mem. ABA, New York County Bar Assn. Lutheran. Office: Shea & Gould 330 Madison Ave New York NY 10017

OLSON, KATHY RAE, special education instructor; b. Bismarck, N.D., Oct. 24, 1950; d. Raymond Charles and Virginia Ann (Mason) Lynch; m. Barth Eugene Olson, Aug. 11, 1973; 1 son, William Raymond. B.S., U. N.D., 1972. Cert. elem. tchr. with spl. edn. credential, N.D. Instr., Grafton State Sch., N.D., 1972-74; tchr. spl. edn. Grand Forks Sch. Dist., N.D., 1974—; dir. Agassiz Enterprises. Bd. dirs. Assn. Retarded Citizens; dir. spl. needs recreation program Grand Forks Park Bd., 1973-76; mem. Spl. Olympics Mgmt. Team, 1984-85. Named N.D. Tchr. of Yr., Council of Chief State Sch. Officers, 1981. Mem. AAUW, Delta Kappa Gamma (sec. 1984-86), Alpha Phi (alumni pres. 1984-86). Republican. Roman Catholic. Avocations: sporting events; civic work; cross stitch; outdoor activity. Home: 3208 Walnut St Grand Forks ND 58201

OLSON, LINDA SUE, radiologic technologist; b. Bklyn., July 26, 1954; d. Burton T. and Mary J. (Cosgrove) Stesen; m. Randal Lee Olson, May 4, 1984. Radiologic technician Fla. Hosp., Orlando, 1974. Cert. radiologic technologist, Calif. Staff radiologic technologist Fla. Hosp., Orlando, 1972-78, Beverly Hosp., Montebello, Calif., 1978-82; radiologic tech. supr. Kaiser Permanente, Bellflower, Calif., 1982—. Mem. Nat. Assn. Female Execs., Calif. Soc. Radiologic Technologists. Republican. Club: Keeshond of Am. Avocations: showing and training showdogs; bowling. Home: 444-A S San Jose Ave Covina CA 91723

OLSON, MARIAN EDNA, nurse, social pschologist; b. Newman Grove, Nebr., July 20, 1923; d. Edwrd and Ethel Thelma (Hougland) Olson; diploma U. Nebr., 1944, B.S.N., 1953; M.A., State U. Iowa, 1961, M.A. in Psychology, 1962; Ph.D. in Psychology, UCLA, 1966. Staff nurse, supr. U. Tex. Med. Br., Galveston, 1944-49; with U. Iowa, Iowa City, 1949-59, supr. 1953-55, asst. dir. 1955-59; asst. prof. nursing UCLA, 1965-67; prof. nursing U. Hawaii, 1967-70, 78-82; dir. nursing Wilcox Hosp. and Health Center, Lihue, 1970-77; chmn. Hawaii Bd. Nursing, 1974-80; prof. nursing No. Mich. U., 1984—. Mem. Am. Nurses Assn. (mem. nat. accreditation bd. continuing edn. 1975-78), Nat. League Nursing, Am. Hosp. Assn., Am. Public Health Assn., LWV. Democrat. Roman Catholic. Home and office: 6223 County 513T Rd Rapid River MI 49878

OLSON, MARIAN KATHERINE, publisher; b. Tulsa, Oct. 15, 1933; d. Sherwood Joseph and Katherine M. (Miller) Lahman; B.A. in Polit. Sci., U. Colo., 1954, M.A. in Elem. Edn., 1962; Ed.D. in Ednl. Adminstrsn., U. Tulsa, 1969; m. Ronald Keith Olson, Oct. 27, 1956. Tchr. public schs., Wyo., Colo., Mont., 1958-67; teaching fellow, adj. instr. edn. U. Tulsa, 1968-69; asst. prof. edn. Eastern Mont. State Coll., 1970; program asso. research adminstrn. Mont. State U., 1970-75; on leave with Energy Policy Office of White House, then with Fed. Energy Adminstrn., 1973-74; with Dept. Energy, and predecessor, 1975—, program analyst, 1975-79, chief planning and environ. compliance br., 1979-83; pres. LNG Resources, Bannack Pub. Co., Lawyers Research. Grantee Okla. Consortium Higher Edn., 1969, NIMH, 1974. Mem. Am. Assn. Budget and Program Analysis, Internat. Assn. Ind. Pubs., Women in Energy, Kappa Delta Pi, Phi Alpha Theta, Kappa Alpha Theta. Republican. Author articles in field. Office: 707 Poppy Dr Brighton CO 80601

OLSON, MELODIE ANN, nursing educator; b. Chicago Heights, Ill., Dec. 5, 1941; d. Melvin Richard and Gwenyth (Hills) Olson. Diploma in nursing, Ill. Masonic Hosp., 1963; B.S.N., U. Ill.-Chgo., 1966; M.S. N., DePaul U., 1970; Ph.D., U. Tex., 1982. R.N., Ill. Staff nurse Ill. Masonic Hosp., Chgo., 1963-65, instr., 1965-69; staff nurse VA Research Hosp., Chgo., 1965-66; nursing educator Luth. Sch. Nursing, Madang, Papua-New Guinea, 1969-75; assoc. prof. nursing San Antonio Coll., 1975-83; assoc. prof. nursing Med. U. S.C., Charleston, 1983—. Contbr. chpts. to books. Coordinator inservice edn. for home health Aides Sr. Citizens Ctr., 1984—; sec. Shemwood II Neighborhood Assn., 1985-86; mem. Palmetto-Low County Health Systems Agy., 1985—. Mem. Am. Nurses Assn., S.C. Nurses Assn. (chmn. council continuing edn. 1986), Sigma Theta Tau (research com. chpt. 1982-83). Lutheran. Office: Med U of SC Grad Program Coll Nursing Charleston SC 29425

OLSON, SONA MAHAKIAN, real estate company executive; B. New Haven, June 4, 1939; d. Hagop and Hasmig (Kazanjian) Mahakian; m. Edwin Walter Olson, Aug. 14, 1984; children—Julio Cesar Caro, Marcos Esteban Caro. Student U. Mich., 1956-58, So. Conn. State Coll., 1958-59. Instr., Instituto Dominico-Americano, Santo Domingo, Dominican Republic, 1963-65; research asst. in sociology, Yale U., New Haven, 1966-69, adminstrv. asst. Trumbull Coll., 1969-72, asst. mgr. custodial services, 1972-75, mgr. custodial housing, 1975-81; assoc. dir. bldgs. and grounds Columbia U., N.Y.C., 1981-84; asst. v.p. ops. The Mendik Realty Co., Inc., N.Y.C., 1984-85; v.p. ops. Mendik Realty Co., Inc., N.Y.C., 1986—; cons. Task Forces Mgmt. Com., City of New Haven, 1978. Research asst. book: Migrant in the City (Lloyd H. Rogler), 1970. Campaign mgr. Republican state senator, Hamden, Conn., 1980. Recipient Women in Leadership award YWCA New Haven, 1977; fellow Morse Coll., Yale U. Mem. Bldg. Owners Mgmt. Assn. Club: Mory's Assn. (New Haven). Home: 21 Claremont Ave Apt 42 New York NY 10027 Office: Mendik Realty Co Inc 330 Madison Ave New York NY 10017

OLSON, THERESE MARIE, real estate broker; b. Boston, Nov. 10, 1950; d. Chester S. and Therese K. (Carey) Kirylo; m. John Edward Olson, Nov. 28, 1981; stepchildren—Tamela, E. Scott. B.S. in Bus., Dickinson State Coll., 1973; postgrad. Boston State Coll. U. N.D., N.D. State U., 1977-80. Adminstrv. asst. N.D. Council for Humanities, Dickinson, 1973-77; dir. Cooperative Edn., Dickinson State Coll., 1977, coordinator Youth Employment Programs, 1978-79; sales agt. Price Real Estate Agy., Dickinson, 1979-82; broker assoc. Joe LaDuke Real Estate Inc. Dickinson, 1982—. Active NOW, Jerry Waldera for Senate Campaign, N.D., 1982; chmn. adv. bd. Dickinson Day Care Ctr., 1977-79; mem. The Learning Tree; chmn., Big Bros. and Big Sisters, 1977-80; mem. N.D. Humanities Council, 1985-89. Mem. Badland Bd. Realtors (com. chmn. 1979-81), N.D. Assn. Realtors (com. chmn., 1979-81), Nat. Assn. Realtors, AAUW (chmn. local and state coms. 1973—). Democrat. Roman Catholic. Home: 964 Sims St Dickinson ND 58601 Office: Joe LaDuke Real Estate Inc 667 East Villard St PO Box 607 Dickinson ND 58601

OLSON-HELLERUD, LINDA KATHRYN, educator; b. Wisconsin Rapids, Wis., Aug. 26, 1947; d. Samuel Ellsworth and Lillian (Dvorak) Olson; B.S., U. Wis.-Stevens Point, 1969, teaching cert., 1970, M.S.T., 1972; postgrad. U. Wis. at Madison, 1969-70; M.S., U. Wis. at Whitewater, 1975; Ed.S., U. Wis.-Stout, 1978. Clk., Univ. Counseling Center, U. Wis., Stevens Point, 1965-69; elementary sch. tchr., Wisconsin Rapids, 1970-76, sch. counselor, 1976-79, dist. elem. guidance dir., after 1979, now elem. instr., cons. Active Wisconsin Rapids Hosp. Aux. Mem. NEA, Wisconsin Rapids Edn. Assn., Am. Personnel and Guidance Assn., Am. Sch. Counselor Assn., Wis. Sch. Counselor Assn., Assn. for Measurement and Evaluation in Guidance, Internat. Reading Assn., Wis. Reading Assn., AAUW, Community Career Edn. Assn. Mem. Moravian Ch. Club: Hosp. Aux. Women's. Home: 120 11th St N Wisconsin Rapids WI 54494 Office: Mead Elem Sch Wisconsin Rapids WI 54494

OLSZEWSKI, AGNES PAULINE, marketing educator, consultant; B. Lodz, Poland, Jan. 25, 1947; came to U.S. 1976; d. Alexander and Eleanore (Majewicz) Olszewski; m. Tad Kondratowicz, Apr. 29, 1971; 1 son, Matthew. M.D. in Social Psychology, U. Warsaw, Poland, 1974, Ph.D. in Indsl. and Social Psychology, 1974; M.B.A., in Marketing, Fordham U. 1980. Cert. African Studies, 1974. Asst. prof. social, indsl. psychology, U. Warsaw, 1970-74, assoc. prof., 1974-76, 80-81; adj. prof. Seton Hall U., W. Paul Stillman Sch. Bus., S. Orange, N.J. 1980, 81, asst. prof. marketing, 1980-81; adv. Marketing Club, student counselor; vis. prof. Fairleigh Dickinson U. Sch. Bus., Teaneck, N.J., 1980-81; coordinator, cons. Inst. Home Market Trade, Warsaw, 1974-76; cons. marketing to various bus. cos., Berger County, N.J., 1982—. Author: (with Prof. S. Mika) Studies on Attitudes, 1977; Youth Market, Its Objectives, Mechanisms & Perspectives, 1980; reviewer Dryden Press; Holt, Reinhart add Winston Publ. Corp.; contbr. articles in field to both Poland, U.S. publs. Mem. Am. Marketing Assn. (lectr. 1983, dir. collegiate activities N.J. chpt. 1982—), Am. Acad. Marketing Sci. Office: Seton Hall U Sch Bus S Orange NJ 07079

OLTARZ-SCHWARTZ, SARA, lawyer; b. Ostrow, Poland, May 5, 1945; came to U.S., 1950, naturalized 1956; d. Simon and Mindy (Salzburg) Oltarz; m. Michael Alan Schwartz, Dec. 8, 1973; children—Carl, Justin. B.A., NYU, 1969; J.D., N.Y. Law Sch., 1972. Bar: N.Y. 1973, Mich. 1980, U.S. Dist. Ct. (so. and ea. dists.) 1974, U.S. Ct. Appeals (2d cir.) 1975, U.S. Ct. Mil. Appeals 1976, U.S. Ct. Appeals (6th cir.) 1983, U.S. Supreme Ct. 1976. Asst. dist. atty. Kings County, Bklyn., 1972-77; adj. prof. N.Y. Law Sch., 1978-79; of counsel David F. DuMouchel, P.C., Detroit, 1982-83; sole practice, Detroit, 1983—. Recipient Am. Jurisprudence award for N.Y. practice Lawyers Coop. Pub. Co., 1972. Mem. ABA, State Bar Mich., Oakland County Bar Assn., Internat. Assn. Jewish Lawyers and Jurists. Office: 1930 Buhl Bldg Detroit MI 48226

OLYMPIA, JOSIE LIM, psychiatrist; b. Or. Mindoro, Philippines, Feb. 9, 1944; came to U.S., 1967; B.S., U. Philippines, 1962, M.D., 1967. Rotating intern Mt. Sinai Hosp., Milw., 1968; resident in psychiatry Buffalo Psychiat. Center, 1968-71, psychiatrist I, II, III, 1971-77, dir. med. edn., 1977—; asst. chief psychiatry service Buffalo VA Med. Center, 1981—; assoc. clin. prof. psychiatry SUNY, Buffalo; cons. Niagara Falls Meml. Med. Center, N.Y. Bur. of Disability. Served to lt. comdr. USAR. NEH grantee, 1979. Fellow Am. Psychiat. Assn., Am. Orthopsychiat. Assn. Roman Catholic. Office: VA Med Center 2495 Bailey Ave Buffalo NY 14215

OLZENDAM, HARRIETT STEELE, retired lawyer; b. Dover, N.H., Aug. 5, 1914; d. Enoch Ned and Lena Marion (Steele) Olzendam; B.A., Wellesley Coll., 1936; M.A., Trinity Coll., 1942; J.D. with distinction, U. Conn., 1946. Admitted to Conn. bar, 1946, Fed. Dist. bar, 1948; with The Travelers Ins. Co., Hartford, Conn., 1937-79, chief contract underwriter, 1951-61, asst. sec., 1961-69, sec., 1969-79. Mem. residence com. YWCA, Hartford, Conn., 1964-79, dir., 1971-77, sec., 1972-74, v.p., 1974-75, pres., 1975-77, mem. fin. com., 1975-79, personnel com., 1979—. Mem. Am., Hartford County bar assns., Am. Judicature Soc., Mental Health Assn. Conn. (nominating com. 1976-78, trustee 1979—), Conn. Ins. Assn. (group com.), Conn. Health Reins. Assn. (chmn. forms com.), Soc. Group Contract Analysts, Wellesley Coll. Alumnae Assn., U. Conn. Sch. Law, Trinity Coll. alumni assns., Mark Twain Meml., Wadsworth Atheneum, Antiquarian and Landmarks Soc. Conn., Nat. Audubon Soc., Nat. Wildlife Fedn., Smithsonian Assos., Hartford Easter Seal Rehab. Center. Republican. Conglist. Clubs: Wellesley (fin. chmn. 1975-77, 1st v.p. 1977-79), Quota (corr. sec. Hartford 1970-78, 1st v.p. 1978—), Town and County (gov. 1978-82, rec. sec. 1979-80, personnel com. 1978-82, chmn. personnel com. 1980-82, fin. com. 1979-82, exec. com. 1979—). Address: 2012 Blvd West Hartford CT 06107

O'MALEY, KIMBERLEE, sports marketing consultant, talent agent; b. Richmond, Ind., Apr. 4, 1957; d. Robert L. and Dorothy (Steinwedel) O'M. B.A. with highest honors, U. Va., 1979; M.S in Internat. Polit. Econs., U. Calif.-Berkeley, 1980. With Crocker Nat. Bank, San Francisco, 1980-81; fgn. currency trader Citibank, San Francisco, 1981-82; aerobics tchr., sports mktg. cons., Hawaii, 1982-83; spl. asst. to pres. ProServ, Washington, 1983-84; pres. KO & Assocs., Los Angeles and N.Y.C., 1984-85; v.p. creative services Garvey Mktg. Group, San Diego, 1985—. Fundraiser, Camp Rainbow for terminally ill children, Malibu, 1985-86, Big Bros., 1985; mem. com. San Diego League, 1985—. U.S. State Dept. fellow, 1979-80; UN intern, 1980; Calif. State legis. fellow, 1980-81. Mem. Am. Mktg. Assn., Nat. Assn. Female Execs., Raven Soc. Republican. Lutheran. Avocations: swimming; skydiving; aerobics; skiing; tennis. Office: Garvey Mktg Group 4320 La Jolla Village Dr San Diego CA 92122

O'MALLEY, PATRICIA ELLEN, industrial chemicals company executive; b. Scranton, Pa., May 10, 1935; d. Stanley Francis and Clare Helen (Fadden) Coar; m. Frank Jerome O'Malley, Oct. 6, 1953; children—F. Jerome, Brian, Ellen, Kevin, Karen, Timothy, Sean, Christopher, Kathleen. B.A., Rosemont Coll., Pa., 1954. Model, Pa. and Ct., 1960-67; office mgr. pvt. med. office, Westport, Conn., 1965-67; bus. mgr. Norwalk Periodontics, 1967-75; adminstrv. dir. New Eng. Found. Allergic Diseases, Norwalk, 1975-81; asst. to pres., dir. resources Berol Chems. Inc., Westport, Conn., 1981—. Mem. Nat. Assn. Female Execs., Smithsonian Instn. Roman Catholic. Clubs: U.S. Figure Skating Assn.; Weston Racquet, Women's Guild-St. Francis Assissi. Avocations: figure skating; windsurfing; modern dance; singing. Home: 38 Tobacco Rd Weston CT 06883

O'MARA MCMAHON, PEGGY NOREEN, editor, publisher; b. Kenosha, Wis., May 14, 1947; d. Oliver Edward and Ruth Helen (Slater) O'Mara; m. John William McMahon, May 27, 1973; children—Lally, Finnie, Bram, Nora. B.S., U. Wis.-Milw., 1970. Tchr. high sch. Alamogordo High Sch., N.Mex., 1971-72; tchr. spl. edn. Zia Sch., Alamogordo, 1972-73; M.B.A. coordinator U. Utah, Holloman AFB, N.Mex., 1973; freelance writer, 1973-77; assoc. editor Mothering Mag., Albuquerque, 1978-80, editor, pub., Santa Fe, 1980—; leader La Leche League, Franklin Park, Ill., 1975—. Editor: Mother Poet, 1983. Bd. dirs. Midwifery Tng. Inst., Albuquerque, 1983—, N.Mex. State Midwifery Adv. Bd., Santa Fe, 1984—. Mem. Midwives Alliance N.Am., Internat. Childbirth Edn. Assn., Nat. Fedn. Press Women (1st place award 1984), Nat. Assn. Safe Alternatives in Birth, N.Mex. Press Women (1st place awards 1984), N.Mex. Press Assn. Avocations: herb gardening; ornithology; alternative health. Home: Route 7 Box 124K Santa Fe NM 87501 Office: Mothering Publs PO Box 8410 Santa Fe NM 87504

O'MEARA, VICKI ANN, lawyer, army officer; b. Mpls., May 13, 1957; d. James Michael and Joan Kathleen (Schepers) O'Meara; A.B., Cornell U., 1979; J.D., Northwestern U., 1982; postgrad. George Washington U., 1983—. Intern police instr. Mpls. Police Dept., 1975-76; legal intern Office of Hennepin County Atty., Mpls., 1977; joined ROTC, 1975, advanced through grades to capt. U.S. Army, 1982; asst. gen. counsel Sec. of Army, Pentagon, Washington, 1982—; lectr. environ. law at confs. and schs. throughout U.S., 1982—, high sch. civil rights programs, Washington, 1982; hon. faculty mem. Army Logistics Mgmt. Ctr.Editor Northwestern Law Rev., 1981-82; contbr. articles to legal and govtl. lit. Foster parent Christian Children's Fund, 1983—. Nat. scholar, Coll. scholar, Women's scholar Cornell U., 1975-79; recipient Outstanding Sr. award Cornell U., 1979, Disting. Mil. Grad. award, 1979, Army Achievement medal, 1984, Litigation award and Atty. Gen. commendation Dept. Justice. Mem. ABA, Minn. Bar Assn., D.C. Bar Assn., Fed. Bar Assn., Washington Humane Soc. (vol.), Soc. for Prevention Cruelty to Animals. Roman Catholic. Clubs: Cornell (Washington), Athletic (Pentagon). Home: 15 Gessford Ct SE Washington DC 20003 Office: Office of Gen Counsel Sec of Army Pentagon Room 2E727 Washington DC 20310

OMELTCHENKO, ALEXIS, film company executive; b. Yonkers, N.Y., Dec. 6, 1957; d. Stephen William and Maria (Oliver) O. B.S., Georgetown U., 1979. Am. films acquisitions staff Leon Films, Madrid, Spain, 1979-80; prodn. coordinator D.P. Films, Barcelona, Spain, 1980-81; producer M.E. Prodns., Los Angeles, 1981-82; pres., exec. producer Pendulum Prodns., Los Angeles, 1982—. Recipient Cine Golden Eagle for He Believes short, 1982. Mem. Music Video Producers Assn. (officer 1984—). Democrat. Office: Pendulum Productions Inc 7351 Sunset Blvd Los Angeles CA 90046

OMOHUNDRO, DELIGHT DIXON, publishing company executive, lecturer, writer; b. Fairfield, Conn.; d. DeLoss F. and Virginia L. Dixon; B.A. (nat. scholar), Cornell U.; M.S., U. Bridgeport, 1979; m. William A. Omohundro, July 27, 1957; children—William, Jeffrey, Robert. Dir. advt. Warnaco, Bridgeport, Conn., 1960-68; pres. Delight Dixon Assos., Westport, Conn., 1968-78; syndicated columnist Chgo. Tribune, 1974; v.p. Carthage Community Press, Inc. (N.Y.), 1982—; lectr. Syracuse U.; mktg. cons. U.S. and Can. cos. Recipient Andy award N.Y. Advt. Club, 1967, 69. Mem. Fashion Group, Am. Mktg. Assn., Am. Women in Radio and TV. Author: The Consumer Goes to Market, 1973; How to Win the Grocery Game, 1974; cost of Living Cookbook, 1974.

OMOIELE, MARNA TAMBURA, sociologist, radio station moderator; b. Dayton, Ohio, May 6, 1948; d. Morgan and Mary Louise (Marshall) Revere; m. Robert Alexander Turner Jr., Apr. 30, 1983 (div. 1984); children—Nyota Binta Ain Omoiele, Robert Alexander Turner III, Christopher Turner, Yemane Turner. B.A. in Sociology, Wright State U., 1974, postgrad. in liberal arts, 1978-79; M.S. in Corrections, Xavier U., Cin., 1976. Cert. secondary edn. tchr., Ohio; lic. cosmetologist. Pre-sentence investigator Montgomery County Adult Probation Dept., Dayton, 1973-75; social counselor Hamilton County Adult Parole, Cin., 1975-77; tchr. Huber Heights Sch., Dayton, 1979; mem. exec. bd., treas. West Montgomery County Food Program, Dayton, 1979—. Chmn. internat. div. Nat. Council of Negro Women, N.Y., 1979—; mem. Dayton Urban League, 1982—; mem. adv. bd. Montgomery County Animal Shelter, 1986—. Recipient Employee of Yr. award City of Dayton 1981. Mem. Dayton and Montgomery County Black Mgr. Assn., Democratic Voters League, Nat. Black Ind. Polit. Party, Nat. Assn. Blacks in Criminal Justice (charter), Am. Soc. Criminology, Fedn. of Dayton/N.Y. Bus. and Profl. Women, Inc. (chmn. ways and means 1982-84), Jack and Jill Am. Baptist. Home: 334 Kenwood Ave Dayton OH 45405 Office: City of Dayton 702 Salem Ave Dayton OH 45406

OMOTO, REBECCA SARAH, advertising agency executive; b. Chgo., Aug. 12, 1947; d. John Gabriel and Agnes Margaret (Sargis) Israel; m. Thomas Paul Omoto, Jan. 19, 1966; 1 child, Mark. Student Met. State U., Denver, 1973-75. Mgr., Elizabeth Israel Advt., Littleton, Colo., 1981-83; owner, mgr. Omoto Advt., Englewood, Colo., 1983—. Avocations: writing poetry; reading. Office: Omoto Advt 4086 S Federal Blvd Englewood CO 80110

O'NAN, PATSY ANN, campsite owner-operator; b. Adrian, Mich., Mar. 15, 1937; d. Ray E. and Phyllis M. (Knoblauch) Wilt; m. Willim A. McCarty, June 6, 1966 (div. June 1968); children—Vincent, Victor; m. James P. O'Nan, Nov. 27, 1971; children—Michael, Dawn, Ellen, Robin. A.A., Monreo County Community Coll., Mich., 1977; Cert., Sch. Gerontology, U. Mich., 1971. Nursing supr. Ypsilanti State Psychiat. Hosp., Mich., 1965-75; owner-operator Smokerise Campsites, Calhoun, Ga., 1978—. Sec., Gordon County 4-H Leaders, Calhoun, 1984-85. Mem. N.W. Ga. Travel Assn. (dir. 1981—), Gordon County C. of C. (tourism com. 1985—). Lutheran. Avocations: reading; travel. Office: Smokerise Campsites Rt 5 Calhoun GA 30701

ONASSIS, JACQUELINE BOUVIER KENNEDY, editor, widow of 35th Pres. of U.S.;, b. Southhampton, L.I. N.Y., July 28, 1929; d. John Vernou III and Janet (Lee) Bouvier; grad. Miss Porter's Sch., Farmington, Conn., 1947; student Vassar Coll., 1947-48; The Sorbonne, Paris, France, 1949; B.A., George Washington U., 1951; m. John Fitzgerald Kennedy, Sept. 12, 1953 (35th Pres. U.S.A.) (dec. Nov. 22, 1963); children—Caroline Bouvier, John Fitzgerald, Patrick Bouvier (dec.); m. 2d, Aristotle Onassis, Oct. 20, 1968 (dec. Mar. 1975). Inquiring photographer Washington Times-Herald (now Washington Post and Times Herald). 1952; cons. editor Viking Press, 1975-77; assoc. editor Doubleday & Co., 1978-82, editor, 1982—. Planned and conducted restoration decor of White House, 1961-63. Trustee Whitney Mus. Am. Art. Recipient Prix de Paris, Vogue mag., 1951; TV Emmy award for pub. service 1962. Office: care Doubleday Pub Co 245 Park Ave New York NY 10167*

ONDEK, VIOLET CECILIA HUGHES, insurance and investment company executive; b. Phila.; d. Lewis Rhodes and Cecilia Regina (Gerhard) Winnemore; student pub. schs., Colwyn-Darby, Pa.; m. Steve Michael Ondek, June 29, 1963; children—Joan Elaine Hughes Wolfe, George Blaine Hughes. Corr. Phila., Bull., 1949-51, Upper Darby News, 1948-51; mem. advt. dept. Gettysburg (Pa.) Times and News, 1951-53; owner, operator V.C. Hughes Co., residential constrn., Biglerville, Pa., 1953-72; co-founder, sec.-treas., dir. Corporate Investment Co., Biglerville, 1970-84; sec.-treas., dir. Corporate Life Ins. Co., Corporate Land Investment Co. Mem. adv. council U.S. SBA, 1976—; appointee Gov. Thornburgh's Council for Small Bus., Pa.; mem. Republican Council Women. Mem. Adams County Home Builders Assn. (charter), Adams County Hist. Soc., Music Box Soc. Internat., Biglerville Hist. and Preservation Soc. (bd. dirs.). Presbyterian. Clubs: Woman's of Colwyn, Woman's of Gettysburg. Home: Guernsey Rd Rural Delivery 2 Biglerville PA 17307

ONDO, JANICE LUCILLE, apparel company executive; b. Belen, N.Mex., Feb. 8, 1949; d. James Oakley and Anna Lee (Burson) Hughes; m. James M. Ondo, Feb. 29, 1980; 1 child, Crystal M. Import traffic mgr. Hurley & Co., Bellevue, Wash., 1972; v.p. adminstrn. Lance Imports, Inc., Seattle, 1973-77; import specialist Contact Lumber Co., Portland, Oreg., 1978; v.p. Rainier Imports, Inc., Bellevue, 1979-84; pres. Kesa Corp., Bellevue, 1984—. Office: Kesa Corp 1750 112th Ave NE Suite B-220 Bellevue WA 98004

ONDRASIK, ALLISON PARISH, librarian; b. Havre de Grace, Md., Aug. 17, 1953; d. Edward John and Barbara Allen (Parish) Ondrasik. B.A., Western Md. Coll., 1975; M.L.S., U. Md., 1976; postgrad. Va. Poly. Inst., 1979, Pepperdine U., 1981. Asst. librarian Emory (Va.) and Henry Coll., 1977-78; instrn. librarian Radford (Va.) U., 1978-79, user services librarian 1979-80; social scis. librarian Old Dominion U., Norfolk, Va., 1980-82; program asst. U. Wash., Seattle, 1982; info. scientist Franklin Research Ctr., Silver Spring, Md., 1982-84, project dir., 1984—; library research asst. Montgomery County Pub. Schs., Rockville, Md., 1982; indexer/editor Info. Mgmt. Services, Bethesda, 1977. Co-author: DataMap edits., 1983—; Bibliography in Policy Studies Jour., 1980. Alumni sec. Western Md. Coll., 1977—; leader Girl Scouts U.S.A., Emory, 1977-78. Inst. Am. Studies fellow, 1981. Mem. ALA, Am. Soc. Info. Sci., Am. Soc. Indexers, Phi Kappa Phi, Beta Phi Mu, Pi Gamma Mu, AAUW. Democrat. Episcopalian. Home: 12608 Grace-Max St Rockville MD 20853 Office: Franklin Research Ctr 1320 Fenwick Ln Silver Spring MD 20910

O'NEAL, BARBARA LYNNE, administrator; b. Washington, May 4, 1939; d. Orton Thomas and Edna Earle (Ryals) Campbell; B.A., Baylor U., 1973; children—Kai Lynne, Carlton Clay, John F. Legal sec. Carlton Smith, Waco, Tex., 1960-62, John F. O'Neal, Hamilton, Tex., 1962-66; tchr. Waco Ind. Sch. Dist., 1973-83; dir. field ops. Bob Krueger U.S. Senate Campaign, 1983-84; dir. personnel Tex. Comptroller of Pub. Accounts, Austin, 1984—. Sec. McLennan County Dem. Conv., 1978; del. Dem. Nat. Conv., 1980. Named outstanding tchr. of Tex., 1975. Mem. NEA, Tex. State Tchrs. Assn. (pres. 1982-83), Waco Classroom Tchrs. Assn. (pres. 1977-78), Alpha Delta Kappa. Baptist. Home: 1106 San Augustine Dr Austin TX 78733 Office: LBJ Bldg 111 E 17th St Room 124 Austin TX 78774

O'NEAL, DOROTHY DECKER, fabric sales company executive; b. Akron, Ohio, Dec. 8, 1923; d. Clyde Earl and Mary Iva (King) Decker; m. Robert Frank O'Neal, Dec. 4, 1943; 1 child, Aileen Adele. Purchasing agt. Firestone Tire and Rubber Co., Akron, 1941-43; free lance fashion model, Little Rock, 1944-46; freelance fashion cons., Akron, 1947-52; owner, mgr. Canal Shop, Peninsula, Ohio, 1953-60, Fashion With Fabrics, Sierra Vista, Ariz., 1979—. Editor: Bi-Centennial Cook Book, 1976; Yule in the Mules Cook Book, 1977. Chmn. Goldwater for Pres. Com., Battle Creek, Mich., 1963-64. Mem. Greater Fedn. Women's Clubs, Am. Assn. Hosp. Auxs. Republican. Unitarian. Avocations: sewing; cooking; fashion shows; travel; career seminars; Home: 4391 Plaza Oro Loma Sierra Vista AZ 85635 Office: Fashion with Fabrics 1502 E Fry Blvd Sierra Vista AZ 85635

O'NEAL, MARGARET FUNDERBURK, consulting and purchasing firm owner; b. LaGrange, Ga., Jan. 12, 1949; d. George William and Margaret Cleaveland (Dodd) Funderburk; m. William Ennis O'Neal, Aug. 30, 1969. B.A., Agnes Scott Coll., 1971. Mgr. The Frog Pond, Inc., Atlanta, 1976-79; project mgr. ADM Assocs. Inc., Atlanta, 1979-82; pres., owner Focus Interior Contracting, Inc., Atlanta, 1982—. Methodist. Club: Women Bus. Owners (Atlanta). Avocation: reading. Office: Focus Interior Contracting 1900 Emery St Suite 450 Atlanta GA 30318

O'NEAL, PEGGY ANN, lawyer; b. Houston, Aug. 31, 1952; d. J.W. and Mary Beth (Garnett) O. Student, So. Meth. U., 1970-71; B.A., U. Ark., 1974, J.D., 1976. Bar: Ark. 1976, U.S. Dist. Ct. (we. dist.) Ark. 1976. Asst. atty. gen. State of Ark., Little Rock, 1977-79, state purchasing dir., Little Rock, 1979-81; sole practice, Fort Smith, Ark., 1981-83; assoc. Dorsey Ryan, Fort Smith, 1983-85, Hardin & Grace, Little Rock, 1985 . Vice pres., sec. Community Band of Western Ark., Fort Smith, 1981-84; pres. Crossover Sch., Fort Smith, 1981, Comprehensive Juvenile Services, Fort Smith, Sebastian County Young Democrats, Fort Smith; vol. United Way, Fort Smith, 1984; mem. Jr. League of Little Rock, Jr. Civic League, Fort Smith, Ark. Regional Minority Purchasing Council, Sebastian County Democratic Com., Ark. Dem. Com.; mem. adv. bd. trustees Sparks Regional Med. Ctr., Fort Smith; nat. committeewoman Ark. Young Dems. named Outstanding Young Woman of Am., 1984. Mem. ABA (chmn. Ark. pub. contract law sect. 1981-84), Sebastian County Bar Assn. (sec.-treas. 1982-83), Pulaski County Bar Assn., Nat. Assn. State Purchasing Officials, Fort Smith Assn. Petroleum Landmen, Phi Alpha

Delta (vice justice 1974-75), Alpha Delta Pi. Methodist. Lodge: Zonta (corresponding sec. 1983-84). Home: 1315 Kavanaugh Apt 1 Little Rock AR 72205 Office: Hardin & Grace Suite 200 Union Station Sq Little Rock AR 72201

O'NEIL, BARBARA NEWSOM, advertising executive, media consultant; b. Bethlehem, Pa., Mar. 31, 1940; d. John Tettemer and M. Katherine (McCloskey) O'Neil. A.B., U. N.C., 1962; M.B.A., Northwestern U., 1969. Media supr. Leo Burnett Co., Inc., Chgo., 1964-66; asst. mgr. mktg. services Time, Inc., Chgo., 1967-69; asst. media dir. Tatham-Laird & Kudner, Chgo., 1970-72; asst. dir. media services Coca Cola Foods-Houston, 1977-78; media dir. Schey Advt., Houston, 1979-80; pres. O'Neil Advt., Houston, 1981—. Author: Art Deco in Houston, 1983. Bd. dirs. Soc. for Performing Arts, Houston, 1975-85, chmn. assocs., 1980-85; bd. dirs. Theatre Under the Stars, Houston, 1982-85; trustee Houston Grand Opera, 1985—; mem. Houston Ballet Guild, Rice Design Alliance, Houston, Houston Symphony Soc., 1974-76, Houston Mus. Fine Arts. Mem. Houston Advt. Fedn., (assoc.), Am. Mktg. Assn., Chgo. Advt. Club. Republican. Episcopalian. Home: 3006 Virginia St Houston TX 77098

O'NEIL, GERALDINE BAYNARD, real estate management company executive; b. Brevard, N.C., Sept. 7, 1945; d. Lyda Clint and Gertrude Mary (Nesbitt) B.; m. Billy Gordon O'Neil, June 25, 1970 (div. Oct. 1978); 1 child, Laura Beth. Student DeKalb Jr. Coll., 1970, Atlanta Inst. Real Estate, 1979. Cert. Realtor, broker. Office mgr. Fibreboard Corp., San Francisco, 1971-76; property mgr. G&M Mgmt. Corp., Atlanta, 1976-80; asst. controller Bridan Industries, Atlanta, 1980-81; asst. dir. property mgmt. Broadmoor Group St. Louis, 1981-83; property mgr. Krupp Realty, Boston, 1983-84; exec. v.p. Bayshore Mgmt. Co., Atlanta, 1984—. Mem. Nat. Bd. Realtors, Ga. Bd. Realtors, Atlanta Bd. Realtors, Apt. Owners and Mgrs. Assn., Builders Owners and Mgrs. Assn. Republican. Clubs: Nat. Assn. Female Execs. (network dir.), Atlanta Network Exec. Women. Avocations: creative writing; reading; dancing; bowling; sewing. Home: 747 Willow Creek Dr NE Atlanta GA 30238 Office: Bayshore Mgmt Co 325 Hammond Dr NE Suite 300 Atlanta GA 30328

O'NEIL, KATHERINE BRENNAN, educator; b. Phila.; d. Robert and Katherine (McGuigan) Brennan; A.B. summa cum laude, Mundelein Coll., 1934; A.M., Loyola U., Chgo., 1936; postgrad. U. N.C., 1968, Villanova U., 1963; m. Charles Joseph O'Neil, Dec. 28, 1935; children—Rickard, Stephen, Mary O'Neil Gericke (dec.), Maureen. Tchr. pvt. schs., Ill., Wis., 1947-61; adminstrv. asst. Loyola U., Chgo., 1944-46; exec. sec. Nat. Home and Sch. Service, Washington, 1961-64; prof. behavioral scis. Harcum Jr. Coll., Bryn Mawr, Pa., 1964—. chmn. dept., 1967—; Wis. del. White House Conf. on Children and Youth, 1960; mem. task force on health and welfare Pres.'s Commn. on Status of Women, 1966-67. Mem. round table Nat. Orgns. for Better Schs., 1960-68; mem. Shorewood Civic Study Group and Neighborhood Council, 1956-60; internat. expert Internat. Lay Congress, Rome, 1967; cons. home and sch. Nat. Council Cath. Women, 1964-66. Recipient Mundelein coll. Achievement award, Mt. Carmel award; Philip Klein Meml. award Harcum Jr. Coll., 1984. Mem. Common Cause, AAUP, Am., Am. Cath. hist. assns., Nat. Council Family Relations, Am. Sociol. Assn., Am. Acad. Polit. and Social Sci., Assn. Women in Community and Jr. Colls., Easter Community Coll. Social Sci. Assn., Community Coll. Humanities Assn., Mundelein Coll. Alumnae (past pres.). Democrat. Roman Catholic. Home: 17 S Roberts St Bryn Mawr PA 19010 Office: Harcum Jr Coll Bryn Mawr PA 19010

O'NEILL, MARGARET, psychological counselor; b. Youngstown, Ohio, Jan. 23, 1935; d. Julius and Anna (Zakel) Huegel; m. Thomas B. O'Neill, Oct. 21, 1971 (div. 1979); children by previous marriage—Paul McCann, Kathleen McCann, Kevin McCann. B.S. in Nursing, UCLA, 1961, M.S. in Nursing, 1963; M.A. in Counseling, Calif. Luth. Coll., Thousand Oaks, 1974; Ph.D. in Psychology, U.S. Internat. U., San Diego, 1986. Cert. hypnotherapist, Calif. Instr. Ventura Coll., Calif., 1965-69, dept. chair, 1969-74, coordinator Women's Ctr., 1974-79, counselor, 1979—; marriage, family and child therapist, cons., Ventura, 1981—; trainer, cons. County of Ventura, 1984—. Mem. Am. Assn. Holistic Health, Am. Assn. Humanistic Psychology, Nat. Assn. Female Execs., Calif. Tchr.'s Assn., Calif. Assn. Marriage Family Therapists. Republican. Unitarian Universalist. Avocations: reading; dancing; hiking; walking. Office: 2590 E Main St Suite 202 Ventura CA 93003

O'NEILL, MARY JANE, health agency executive; b. Detroit, Feb. 24, 1923; d. Frank Roger and Kathryn (Rice) Kilcoyne; Ph.B. summa cum laude, U. Detroit, 1944; postgrad. U. Wis., 1949-50; m. Michael James O'Neill, May 31, 1948; children—Michael, Maureen, Kevin, John, Kathryn. Editor, East Side Shopper, Detroit, 1939-45; club editor Detroit Free Press, 1945-48; reporter UP, Milw. and Madison, Wis., 1949; dir. public relations Fairfax-Falls Church (Va.) Community Chest, 1955-60; copy editor Falls Ch. Sun-Echo, 1958-60; free-lance writer, Washington, 1960-63; asso. editor Med. World News, Washington, 1963-66; dir. public relations Westchester Lighthouse, N.Y. Assn. for Blind, 1967-71; dir. public edn. The Lighthouse, N.Y.C., 1971-73, dir. public relations, 1973-80; exec. dir. Eye-Bank for Sight Restoration, Inc., 1980—. Mem. Women in Communications (pres. N.Y. chpt. 1980-81, Matrix award Westchester chpt. 1984), Eye-Bank Assn. Am. (lay adv. bd. 1981-83, dir. 1983-86), Public Relations Soc. Am., Publicity Club, Women Execs. in Pub. Relations (dir. 1982—, pres. 1986-87). Club: Cosmopolitan. Office: 210 E 64 St New York NY 10021

O'NEILL, MAUREEN ANNE, arts adminstrator, city administrator; b. Seattle, Nov. 11, 1948; d. Robert P. and Barbara F. (Pettinger) O'N. B.A. in Sociology cum laude, Wash. State U., 1971; M.A., Bowling Green U., 1972. Grad. asst. dept. coll. student personnel Bowling Green (Ohio) U., 1971-72; asst. coordinator coll. activities SUNY-Geneseo, 1972-75, acting coordinator coll. activities, 1975-76; regional mgr. northeast Kazuko Hillyer Internat. Agy., N.Y.C., 1976-77; mgr. pub. performing arts U. Wash., Seattle, 1977-81; mgr. performing and visual arts Parks and Recreation, City of Seattle, 1981-83, recreation dist. mgr., 1983—; cons. Nat. Endowment for Arts, 1980, 81; mem. edn. com. Seattle Art Mus., 1981—. Bd. dirs. Bumbershoot-Seattle Arts Festival, 1979, 80; bd. dirs. Folklife Festival, 1982—, treas., 1985—; cantor Sacred Heart Ch., Seattle, 1982—. Mem. Nat. Entertainment and Campus Activities Assn. (dir. 1969-72, Cert. of Appreciation 1975), Western Alliance Arts Adminstrs. (v.p. 1978-80), Arts Alliance Wash. State, Allied Arts Seattle, Seattle Folklore Soc., Wash. Recreation and Parks Assn., Nat. Recreation and Parks Assn., Phi Beta Kappa, Mu Phi Epsilon, Alpha Delta Pi. Roman Catholic. Home: PO Box 19278 Seattle WA 98109 Office: 100 Dexter Ave N Seattle WA 98109

ONG, LAUREEN E., television executive; b. N.Y.C., Sept. 24, 1952; d. Douglas and Marion (Chin) Ong; m. Frank A. Fadil, Nov. 26, 1976 (div. 1985). B.A., Montclair State Coll., 1974; M.A., Columbia U., 1977. Traffic coordinator TVS TV Network, N.Y.C., 1974-77; v.p. Sports Syndication Co., N.Y.C., 1977-74; Program dir. CBS Sports Div., N.Y.C., 1979-81; v.p. broadcasting Chgo. White Sox, 1981—; v.p. programming, adminstrn. Sportsvision of Chgo., 1981—. Bd. dirs. Big Bros./Big Sisters of Chgo., 1983. Mem. Nat. Cable TV Assn., Woman in Cable, Women in Communications, Cable TV Adminstrv. and Mktg. execs. Lutheran. Home: 210 E Pearson Chicago IL 60611 Office: Sportsvision of Chicago 980 N Michigan Ave Chicago IL 60611

ONLEY, SISTER FRANCESCA, college president; b. Phila., Mar. 4, 1933; d. Edward Patrick and Marie (Rice) O. B.A., Holy Family Coll., 1959; M.S., Marywood Coll., 1966; Ph.D., So. Ill. U., 1985. Cert. secondary counselor, Penn. Tchr. Nazareth Acad. Grade Sch., Phila., 1952-64; tchr. Nazareth Acad., Phila., 1964-67, vice prin., counselor, 1967-72, prin., 1972-80; pres. Holy Family Coll., Phila., 1980—bd. dirs. Comcast, Phila., 1983—. Bd. officer, sec. N.E. br. ARC, Phila., 1984—, bd. dirs., 1983—. Recipient Alumni award Holy Family Coll. Alumni 1982. Mem. Middle State Assn. Schs. and Colls., Assn. Governing Bds., Council Ind. Colls., Northeast C. of C. (bd. dirs. 1983—). Democrat. Roman Catholic. Office: Holy Family Coll Grant and Frankford Aves Philadelphia PA 19114

ONO, YOKO, conceptual artist, singer; b. Tokyo, Japan, Feb. 18, 1933; U.S. citizen; m. John Lennon, 1969 (dec.); 1 child, Sean; 1 child by previous marriage, Kyoko. Student Peers' Sch., Gakushuin U., Tokyo, Sarah Lawrence Coll., Harvard U. One person shows, Alchemical Wedding, Albert Hall, London, 1967, Evening with Yoko Ono, Birmingham, 1968, Event, U. Wales, 1969, Everson Mus., Syracuse, N.Y., 1971, others; exhibited Fluxshoe, Sch. Art, Falmouth, Cornwall, Eng., 1972; recorded albums (with John Lennon): Double Fantasy, 1980, Milk and Honey, 1984; solo albums include Starpeace, 1985. Author six film scripts, Tokyo, 1964, thirteen film score scores, London, 1967, John & Yoko Calendar, 1970, Grapefruit, London, 1970, A Hole to See the Sky Through, N.Y., 1971. Address: care Polygram Classics Inc 810 7th Ave New York NY 10019

ONOFREY, JANE ELIZABETH, systems engineer; b. Derby, Conn., Sept. 4, 1931; d. Frank Ralph and Mary Onofrey. B.S., Tex. Woman's U., 1953; M.B.A., So. Meth. U., 1971. Systems engr. IBM, Dallas, 1954—. Office: IBM 8435 N Stemmons Freeway Dallas TX 75247

ONOUE, AMY NAGAYAMA, former sales executive; b. Lanai City, Lanai, Hawaii, June 2, 1937; d. William Tokuichi and Setsuyo (Imamura) Nagayama; grad. Hilo Comml. Coll., 1957; m. George Toshimi Onoue, June 1, 1957; children—Steven, Lynn, Mavis, Glenn, Gail. Sec. to mgr. Von Hamm Young Drug Wholesale, 1957; Golden Galaxy mgr. Tupperware Home Parties, 1961-75; exec. sr. state area mgr. Jewels by Parklane, 1975-76; area mgr. Hawaii, Celebrity Jewels, 1976-77; corp. pres. Toriam, Inc., Honolulu, 1977-82; regional mgr. Cher Beli Creations, 1982-83; furniture cons. J.C. Penney, Pearlridge, 1984—. Bd. dirs. Family Community Leadership Project, 1981-84, sec., 1981-82; cultural arts chmn., Univ. Extension, pres. Univ. Extension West Council, 1979-80, state historian, 1981-83, chmn. public realtions-community outreach, 1981-83, Outstanding Woman of Yr., 1977. Mem. Hawaii Extension Homemakers Council (conv. chmn. 1985). Home: 1836 Ala Noe Pl Honolulu HI 96819

ONSKT, NANCY RAE, systems engineer; b. Findlay, Ohio, Apr. 17, 1939; d. Raymond E. and Bonita M. (Leary) O. Student U. Toledo, 1966, Owens Tech. Coll., 1972. Order entry supr. Four-Phase, Cupertino, Calif., 1974-76; mgr. mktg. systems, Fairchild, San Jose, Calif., 1976-81; sr. product mgr. Savin, Sunnyvale, Calif., 1981-82; MIS mgr. Inmac Corp., Santa Clara, Calif., 1982-85; system engr. Hewlett-Packard, Santa Clara, 1985—; systems cons. System Application Computer Services, Santa Clara, 1976—. Mem. NOW, Assn. System Mgmt., Summit Orgn., Women's Found., Women's Entrepreneur Assn. Democrat. Roman Catholic. Home: 2404 Golf Links Circle Santa Clara CA 95050

ONYEALI, BARBARA ANN, educator; b. Chgo., Mar. 8, 1935; d. Elmer and Maude Mary (Elder) Page; B.Ed., Chgo. Tchrs. Coll., 1963; M.E., Erikson Inst. for Early Childhood Edn., Loyola U., Chgo., 1973; children—Amaechi Samuel, Elkanah Okwudili. Dictaphone operator, mental health centers, Chgo., 1953-60; tchr. kindergarten Medill Primary Sch., Chgo., 1963-69, Head Start tchr., 1972-75; parent resource tchr. Cockrell Child Parent Center, Chgo., 1975—; also tchr. dance, dir. day camp, workshop leader, instr. jr. coll., supr. Sunday sch. Sec., Tchrs. div. Operation P.U.S.H., Chgo., 1970-72; leader Cub Scout program, Chgo., 1977-80, com. chmn., 1981-82. HEW Head Start Leadership Tng. grantee, 1971-73. Mem. Am. Fedn. Tchrs., Nat. Assn. Edn. Young Children, Field Museum Natural History. Club: Chgo. Health and Racquetball. Office: 30 E 61st St Chicago IL 60637

OPALKA, JOYCE ANNE, retail exec.; b. Phila., June 9, 1947; d. John Joseph and Josephine (Wielehowski) Tomczyszyn; cert. bus. mgmt. Am. Mgmt. Assn., 1978; corr. student Pa. State U., 1974-77; m. John Opalka, Sept. 14, 1968. Sec., U.S. Food Equipment Co., Phila., 1965-66; sec. Acme Markets, Inc., Phila., 1966-73, adminstrv. asst. data processing, 1973-79, supr. data processing adminstrv. services, 1979-81, M.I.S. adminstr., 1981—. Mem. Nat. Assn. Female Execs., Am. Mgmt. Assn., Am. Soc. Profl. and Exec. Women, Am. Soc. for Tng. and Devel., Am. Assn. Individual Investors, Am. Biog. Inst. Home 542 7th Ave Warminster PA 18974 Office: 124 N 15th St Philadelphia PA 19101

OPAR, PATRICIA ANN, guidance counselor; b. Troy, N.Y., June 3, 1938; d. Paul and Martha Theresa (Kawola) Opar; B.A., Coll. St. Rose, 1960, M.A., 1963; M.S. in Edn., Siena Coll., 1965; postgrad. (NDEA grantee) Western Mich. U., 1965, N. Adams State Coll., SUNY, Albany, Russell Sage Coll. Nat. cert. counselor and career counselor; cert. guidance counselor, sch. dist. adminstr., elem. and secondary tchr., N.Y. State. Tchr., S. Colonie Central Sch. Dist., Albany, N.Y., 1960-63, guidance counselor, 1965—, mem. curriculum rev. bd., 1979-82, coordinator continuing edn., 1980-81; summer youth counselor div. employment N.Y. State Dept. of Labor, 1969. Bd. dirs. Colonie Youth Centers, Albany, 1979-81. Mem. Am. Assn. Counseling and Devel., (dir. Senate), Am. Sch. Counselor Assn., Nat. Career Devel. Assn., N.Y. State Assn. Counseling Devel. (sec., chmn. by-laws rev. com., exec. council, senate), Capital Dist. Counseling Assn. (pres., sec., chmn. program and in-service edn. com., trustee), N.Y. State United Tchrs., Delta Epsilon Sigma. Ukrainian Catholic. Home: 3 Kerry Ln Albany NY 12211 Office: Sand Creek Middle Sch 329 Sand Creek Rd Albany NY 12205

OPARENOVICH, SANDRA, property tax research company executive; b. Galveston, Tex., Jan. 29, 1952; d. Steve and Rosemary (Burkham) Oparenovich; m. Max A. Harris, Sept. 9, 1972 (div. Nov. 1980). B.A., U. Houston, 1978. Sec., Best Uniform Supply Co., Houston, 1972-77, St. John the Divine, Houston, 1978-79; v.p., ptnr. Dual H Enterprises, Inc., Houston, 1979—. Sustaining mem. Republican Nat. Com., Washington, 1982. Mem. Tex. Assn. Assessing Officers (assoc.), Tex. Assn. Appraisal Dists., Lambda Chi Alpha (mem. crescents).

OPENSHAW, LINDA LEEK, social worker; b. Provo, Utah, Oct. 30, 1948; d. Kenneth Frank and Della Mae (Williams) Leek; B.A. in English, U. Utah, 1971, M.S.W., 1974, D.S.W., 1981; m. David Byron Openshaw, July 10, 1975; children—Amy Elizabeth, Alison Rebecca, Lauren Jane, Patrick David. Tchr. English, Strategakis Sch., Athens, Greece, 1972; psychiat. social worker Stanislaus Mental Health, Brief Treatment Program, Modesto, Calif., 1974-76; instr. Chapman Coll., Merced, Calif., 1975; psychiat. social worker Weber Mental Health, Intake Team, Ogden, Utah, 1976-77; women's group coordinator YWCA, Ogden, 1976-77; juvenile ct. alcohol sch. instr., Salt Lake City, 1978-80; sch. social worker East High Sch., Salt Lake Sch. Dist., Salt Lake City, 1977-80, Highland High Sch., 1983—; contract clinician Latter-Day Saints Social Services, Salt Lake City, 1984-85; trainer for tchrs. Salt Lake Sch. Dist., 1979-80, Utah Div. Alcohol and Drugs, 1982-84. Del., Utah Democratic Conv., 1974. Lic. clin. and cert. social worker, Utah. Mem. Utah Council Sch. Social Workers (pres. 1979-80), Nat. Assn. Social Workers (chmn. chpt. nominating com. 1982-83, com. inquiry 1984-86), Acad. Cert. Social Workers, Phi Kappa Phi, Alumni Bd. U. Utah Sch. Social Work (sec. 1983). Democrat. Mem. Ch. of Jesus Christ of Latter-day Saints. Home: 2214 Whitaker Dr Salt Lake City UT 84118

OPITZ, KAREN LEE, printing company executive; b. Milw., Dec. 9, 1941; d. George Charles and Lillian Amanda (Benson) West; m. Charles John Opitz, Oct. 24, 1964; children—Michael, Daniel. B.S., U. Wis. Milw., 1963; M.S., 1968. Tchr., elem. sch., Brown Deer, Wis., 1963-67, River Hills, Wis., 1967-68; dir., prin. Creative Playcare Ctr., Brookfield, Wis., 1975-77; pres. First Impressions Printing Inc., Ocala, Fla., 1980—; dir. Action Packets, Inc., Ocala. Mem. Indsl. Devel. Council Ocala, 1978—. Mem. C. of C. Ocala (bd. dirs. 1984—; small bus. person of yr. 1984), Advt. Fedn. (treas. 1983-84, Addy's 1981-85), Fla. Pub. Relations Assn. Republican. Lutheran. Club: ALtrusa (v.p. 1985-86). Avocations: Travel; primitive art. Home: 2471 SW 37th St Ocala FL 32674 Office: First Impressions Printing Inc 1517 SW 27th Ave Ocala FL 32674

OPPENHEIM, JEAN REEVE, educator; b. Cohoes, N.Y., Mar. 5, 1931; d. Charles Thomas and Velma (Bowden) Reeve; B.A., Cornell U., 1952; M.A., Wesleyan U., 1981; postgrad. Tchrs. Coll., Columbia U., 1978—; children—Naomi Stern, Charles Bruce. Asst. chemistry lab. Cornell U., Ithaca, N.Y., 1952-53; lab. asst. in chemistry N.Y.U., Belleview Med. Center, N.Y.C., 1953-57; math. tchr. Henley Sch., Nightingale-Banford Sch., Bentley Sch., 1958-61; math. coordinator Calhoun Sch., N.Y.C., 1963-80; chmn. math. dept. Friends Sem., N.Y.C., 1980—; condr. workshops, speaker in field. Mem. Assn. Tchrs. in Ind. Schs. N.Y.C. and Vicinity (exec. bd., 1975—, pres., 1979—), Nat. Council Tchrs. of Math., Assn. Supervision and Curriculum Devel., Kappa Delta Pi. Editor, author math. textbooks and tests, 1974-77; co-author chem. papers, 1953-58. Office: 222 E 16th St New York NY 10003

OPPENHEIM, MARTHA KUNKEL, pianist; b. Port Arthur, Tex., June 25, 1935; d. Samuel Adam and Grace (Moncure) Kunkel; m. Russell Edward Oppenheim, June 18, 1960; children—Lauren Susan, Kristin Lee Oppenheim Mortenson. B.Mus. with honors, U. Tex., 1957; M.Mus., U. Tex., 1959; diploma in piano Juilliard Sch. Music, 1960; student Am. Conservatory, Fontainebleau, France, 1956, 58. Soloist with Amarillo Symphony, Austin Symphony, U. Tex. Orch., San Antonio Symphony, Dallas Symphony, Heilbronner Kammer Orch., Heilbron, Germany; solo and chamber music recitals in Tex., N.Y., France; mem. Halcyon Trio, 1974-77; teaching asst. U. Tex., 1957-59, 68-69; pvt. piano tchr., San Antonio, 1962—. Recipient First Place award Internat. Piano Recording Festival, Nat. Guild Piano Tchrs., 1956, 57; First Place award Tuesday Mus. Club Young Artist Competition, 1956; First Place award Young Artist Competition, Amarillo Symphony, 1959; First Place award G. B. Dealey Competition, Dallas Symphony and Dallas Morning News, 1959; Scholarships, U. Tex. and Juilliard Sch. Music. Mem. Music Tchrs. Nat. Assn., Tex. Music Tchrs. Assn., San Antonio Music Tchrs. Assn., Sigma Alpha Iota, Pi Kappa Lambda. Presbyterian. Club: Tuesday Musical (bd. dirs.) (San Antonio). Home: 9118 E Valley View Ln San Antonio TX 78217

OPPENHEIMER, JANE MARION, biologist, historian, educator; b. Phila., Sept. 19, 1911; d. James Harry and Sylvia (Stern) O. B.A., Bryn Mawr Coll., 1932; Ph.D., Yale, 1935, postgrad. (Sterling fellow), 1935-36, Am. Assn. U. Women fellow, 1936-37; Sc.D. (hon.), Brown U., 1976. Research fellow embryology U. Rochester, 1937-38; faculty Bryn Mawr (Pa.) Coll., 1938—, prof., 1953-80, prof. emeritus, 1980—, acting dean grad. sch., 2d semester, 1946-47; Vis. prof. biology Johns Hopkins, 1966-67; exchange prof. U. Paris, 1969. Author: New Aspects of John and William Hunter, 1946, Essays in History of Embryology and Biology, 1967; Co-editor: Founds. Exptl. Embryology, 1964; editor 2d edit., 1974; asso. editor: Jour. Morphology, 1956-58, Quar. Rev. Biol, 1963-64; mem. editorial bd.: Am. Zoologist, 1965-70, Jour. History Biology, 1967-75, Quar. Rev. Biology, 1968-75; sect. editor developmental biology; Biol. Abstracts, 1970-73. Mem. history life scis. study sect. NIH, 1966-70. Recipient Lucius Wilbur Cross medal Yale Grad. Alumni Assn., 1971; Guggenheim Meml. Found. fellow, 1942-43, 52-53; Rockefeller Found. fellow, 1950-51; NSF postdoctoral fellow, 1959-60. Fellow AAAS (sec. sect. L 1955-58, council del. sect. G 1980-83, com. on council affairs 1981-82), Phila. Coll. Physicians (hon.); mem. Am. Soc. Zoologists (treas. 1957-59, chmn. div. devel. biology 1967, pres. 1973), Am. Assn. Anatomists, History of Sci. Soc. (mem. council 1975-77), Am. Assn. History Medicine (mem. council 1971-74), Am. Soc. Naturalists, Soc. for Developmental Biology, Internat. Soc. for Developmental Biology, Am. Inst. Biol. Scis. (mem. at large governing bd. 1974-77), Internat. Soc. History Medicine, Internat. Acad. History of Sci. (Paris) (corr.), Internat. Acad. History Medicine (Paris), Am. Philos. Soc. (mem. council 1982-85, exec. com. 1984—). Office: Biology Bldg Bryn Mawr Coll Bryn Mawr PA 19010

OPPENHEIMER, MILDRED MARCUIS, corporation executive; b. Waco, Tex., Dec. 11, 1929; d. Jacob and Mary (Goldberg) Marcuis; children—Jay William, Barrie Rose. Student So. Meth. U., 1964-66, U. Pa., Wharton Sch. Fin., 1977. Pres. Weight Watchers of Ft. Worth, Arlington, Tex., 1967—. Mem. Weight Watchers Franchise Assn. (dir. 1978-82, v.p. 1984-86). Address: Weight Watchers of Fort Worth Inc 404 N Collins Arlington TX 76011

OPPENHEIMER, SELMA LEVY (MRS. REUBEN OPPENHEIMER), artist; b. Balt.; d. William and Beatrice (Stern) Levy; A.B., Goucher Coll., 1919; student Md. Inst., 1920-22; m. Reuben Oppenheimer, June 26, 1922; children—Martin J., Joan (Mrs. Stanley Weiss). One-man show Har Sinai Synagogue, 1977, McDonough Sch., Balt., 1978; exhibited in group shows at Balt. Mus. Art, 1935-61, also invitational exhbn., 1968, Peale Mus., 1938-66, Phila. Art Alliance, 1940, So. State, 1947, Hagerstown Mus. Fine Arts, Pa. Acad., 1938, Chgo. Art Inst., 1952, Phillips Meml. Gallery, 1938, Corcoran Gallery, 1941-47, 51, 56, 57, 60, Va. Mus. Fine Arts, 1938, Ringling Mus. Art, 1960, Calif. Palace Legion Honor, San Francisco, 1938, Mus. Modern Art, N.Y.C., 1933, Smithsonian Instn., 1956, N.A.D., N.Y.C., 1938-66, Royal Acad. Galleries, Edinburgh, Scotland, 1963, Royal Birmingham (Eng.) Soc. Artists Galleries, 1963, Johns Hopkins Med. Residence Hall, 1961, Goucher Coll., 1965, 76, Jewish Community Center Retrospective Exhibit, 1967; with traveling exhbn. U.S., 1963-65, Scotland (Edinburg), 1964, France, 1965; represented in permanent collection Balt. Pub. Schs., U. Md., Loyola Coll. Chmn. art com. Jewish Community Center, Balt., 1958-65, bd. dirs., 1958-64; corr. sec. Balt. br. Council Jewish Women; publicity chmn. Md. Fedn. Women's Clubs; sec.-treas. Balt. Art Festival; vice chmn. artists com. Balt. Mus. Art, 1950, artists com., trustee, 1961-72, chmn. classical arts accessions com., 1969—. Recipient medal Md. Inst., 1933, Balt. Mus. Art, 1935, 38, Balt. Water Color Club, 1939, award oil painting Nat. Assn. Women Artists, 1957, 60, 65, purchase award Loyola Coll., 1967. Mem. Nat. Assn. Women Artists, Artists Equity Assn. (past pres. Md. chpt.), Am. Fedn. Arts, Balt. Watercolor Club. Clubs: Hamilton Street (Balt.); Suburban (Pikesville, Md.). Address: 7121 Park Heights Ave Baltimore MD 21215

OPPENHEIMER, SUZI, state senator; m. Martin J. Oppenheimer; children—Marcy, Evan, Josh, Alexandra. B.A. in Econs., Conn. Coll. for Women; M.B.A., Columbia U. Former security analyst various brokerage houses, N.Y.C.; mayor City of Mamaroneck, N.Y., 1977; mem. N.Y. State Senate, 1984—, mem. edn., commerce, econ. devel. and small bus., child care, consumer protection, transp. coms. Former pres. Mamaroneck LWV, Westchester County Village Ofcls. Assn., Westchester Mcpl. Planning Fedn. Democrat. Office: NY State Capitol Bldg Albany NY 12224*

O'QUINN, APRIL GALE, physician, educator; b. Columbia, Miss., Apr. 21, 1936; d. R.V. and Anna Pauline (Cook) O'Q.; diploma Scott and White Hosp. Sch. Nursing, 1965; A.A., Temple Jr. Coll., 1965; B.S. with honors, Baylor U., 1968; M.D., U. Tex. Med. Br., 1971. Intern, U. Tex. Med. Br., Galveston, 1971-72, resident ob-gyn., 1972-75; fellow in oncology M.D. Anderson Hosp., Houston, Tex., 1976-78; practice medicine specializing in ob-gyn., Galveston, 1978-81; asst. prof. dept. ob-gyn. U. Tex. Med. Br., Galveston, 1975-81; practice medicine specializing in ob-gyn, New Orleans, 1981—; mem. staff John Sealy Hosp., St. Mary's Hosp., Galveston, Tulane Med. Center, New Orleans Charity Hosp., So. Baptist Hosp. and Touro Infirmary, New Orleans; assoc. prof., dir. div. gynecol. oncology dept. ob-gyn Tulane U. Sch. Medicine, New Orleans, 1981—. Diplomate Am. Bd. Ob-Gyn. Fellow Willard R. Cooke Obstetrical and Gynecologic Soc., Am. Coll. Ob-Gyn.; mem. Soc. Gynecologic Oncologists, Western Assn. Gynecol. Oncologists, Tex. Assn. Obstetricians and Gynecologists, Houston Gynecol. and Obstetrical Soc., Tex. Med. Assn., Galveston County Med. Soc., Felix Rutledge Soc. Republican. Baptist. Home: 6249 Carlson Dr New Orleans LA 70122 Office: Dept Ob-Gyn Tulane U Sch Medicine New Orleans LA 70112

ORAV, HELLE REISSAR, retired dentist; b. Tartu, Estonia, July 10, 1925; came to U.S., 1949, naturalized, 1954; d. Johan and Adele Johanna (Minski) Reissar; m. Arnold Orav, May 30, 1952; children—Ilmar Erik, Hillar Thomas. Student Friedrich Alexander U., Erlangen, West Germany, 1946-49; D.D.S., NYU, 1952. Practice dentistry, N.Y.C., 1952, 60, 62, 68, Valencia, Venezuela, 1953-68. Counselor, Red Cross, Valencia, 1954-55; past mem. Rotary Ladies Republican. Lutheran. Clubs: Country of Maracaibo (Venezuela); Palm Beach Polo and Country (Fla.); Korp Filiae Patriae (N.Y.C.). Avocations: Pre-Colombian art; bridge; travel; swimming; reading. Home: 44 Cocoanut Row Palm Beach FL 33480

ORCHARD, DONNA LEE, box company executive; b. Kansas City, Mo., Dec. 27, 1931; d. Max Edward and Ruth Louise (Kerst) Arenson; m. Edgar L. Orchard, Feb. 5, 1957; children—Laura Ellen Orchard Massie, Barri Louise Orchard Sapp, Caroline Courtney. Student Washington U., St. Louis, 1950, U. Mo.-Kansas City, 1952. Office mgr. Gentry & Voskamp Architects, Kansas City, 1953-57; sec., synopsis editor for publ. release Sovereign TV Prodn. (Gen. Electric, Dupont Theaters), Hollywood, Calif., 1951-52; pres., owner Orchard Box Co., St. Louis, 1979—; v.p. Orco Sales Co. Patentee in field. Pres., Washington U. Women's Soc., St. Louis, 1982-84; bd. mem. Temple Israel, St. Louis, 1982—; sec. Gateway Theater, St. Louis; life mem., v.p. Primitive Arts Soc., St. Louis Art Mus., 1980-81; bd. dirs. St. Louis Opera Guild, founder womens com. 1960-63; bd. dirs., life mem. Jewish Hosp. Aux., Brandeis U.; bd. dirs. St. Louis Symphony Womens Soc., St. Louis Zoo Assn., League of Women Voters, 1958-59; life mem. Hilton Theater, Webster Coll. Mem. Nat. Assn. Women Bus. Owners, Kansas City C. of C. (wage and hour com. 1955-57). Republican. Jewish. Club: Whittemore House. Avocations: collector of art, gardening, raising of Koi, research of art and oriental porcelains. Home: One Robindale Dr Saint Louis MO 63124 Office: Orchard Box Co 1326 Baur Blvd Saint Louis MO 63132

ORCUTT, BEN AVIS, social work educator; b. Falco, Ala., Oct. 17, 1914; d. Benjamin A. and Emily Olive Adams; A.B., U. Ala., 1936; M.A., Tulane U., 1939, M.S.W., 1942; D.S.W., Columbia U., 1962. Social worker, acting field dir. ARC, LaGarde Gen. Hosp., New Orleans, Fort Benning (Ga.) Regional Hosp., 1942-46; chief social work service VA regional office, Phoenix, 1946-51, chief social work service unit outpatient office, Birmingham, Ala., 1954-57, 58; research asst. Research Center Sch. Social Work, Columbia U., N.Y.C., 1960-62, field adv. social work, 1962, asso. prof. social work, 1965-76; asso. prof. social work La. State U., Baton Rouge, 1962-65; prof. social work, dir. doctoral program U. Ala., University, 1976-84; research cons. Tavistock Centre, London, 1972. Mem. alumni bd. Sch. Social Work, Columbia U., 1985—. NIMH fellow, 1957-60. Mem. Council Social Work Edn., Nat. Assn. Social Workers, Am. Assn. Orthopsychiatry, Found. Thanatology, N.Y. Acad. Scis., Ala. Conf. Social Welfare, Group for Advancement Doctoral Edn. (steering com., editor newsletter 1980-83). Episcopalian. Club: Zonta. Author: (with Harry P. Orcutt) America's Riding Horses, 1958; (with Elizabeth R. Prichard, Jean Collard, Austin H. Kutscher, Irene Seeland, Nathan Lefkowitz) Social Work with the Dying Patient and the Family, 1977; (with others) Social Work and Thanatology, 1980; editor: Poverty and Social Casework Services, 1974; editorial bd. Jour. Social Work, 1982-84; contbr. articles to profl. books and jours. Home: 222 Fox Run Tuscaloosa AL 35406 Office: PO Box 1935 University AL 35486

ORDOWER, MYRNA E., insurance broker; b. Chgo., Oct. 8; d. Abe Herman and Gussie (Rubinsky) Berliner; m. Sidney L. Ordower, Mar. 4, 1961; children—Cheryl, Karyn, Steven. Student, U. Ill., Northwestern U. Underwriter, Bergman & Lefkow Ins., Chgo., 1952-61; unit mgr. Near North Ins., Chgo., 1974-82; owner, pres. Myrna Ordower Enterprises, Chgo., 1982—; v.p., stockholder Rockwood Co., 1982—. Founder, Women's Exec. Network, Chgo., 1983—; co-founder Corp. Connections, Chgo., 1985. Bd. dirs. Little City Found. for Mentally Retarded Children, Women's bd. Chgo. Urban League; fund raiser Muscular Dystrophy, Chgo.; del. White House Conf. Small Bus., 1986. Mem. Nat. Assn. Women Bus. Owners (bd. dirs.), Nat. Assn. Ins. Women. Home: 5502 S Harper Ave Chicago IL 60637 Office: Myrna Ordower Enterprises 20 N Wacker Dr Chicago IL 60606

O'REILLY, PATRICIA POYNTER, public utility manager; b. Terre Haute, Ind., Sept. 5, 1947; d. Robert Lee and Betty Jean (Yohe) Poynter; m. Timothy David Wilson, Feb. 4, 1967 (div. 1969); children—Kimberly Susan, Timothy David Jr.; m. Robert William O'Reilly, Sept. 27, 1974 (div. 1986). A.A., Purdue U., 1981; A.G.S., Ind. U., 1984. Exec. sec. GTE, Ft. Wayne, Ind., 1972-73, sales rep., 1973-78, staffing asst., 1978-79, supr., 1979-82, coordinator spl. projects, 1982, mgr. billing & collections, 1982—; pres. Bob's Militaria, Ft. Wayne, 1983-86; sec. Waves Unlimited, Pompano, Fla., 1984—; pres. Waves Unlimited of Fla., Pompano, 1985—. Vol. United Way., 1981—, Spl. Olympics, 1982—. Mem. Nat. Assn. Female Execs., Credit Women Internat., Purdue Alumni Assn., Ind. Alumni Assn., Fort Wayne C. of C. (pres. club 1983—, Safety award 1981), Phi Theta Kappa. Episcopalian. Avocations; Deep sea fishing; painting. Home: 7619 Clover Meadow Dr Fort Wayne IN 46815 Office: GTE 3301 Wayne Trace PO Box 270 Fort Wayne IN 46801-2300

ORITO, MARY ALICE, fashion designer; b. Kansas City, Kans., July 10, 1941; d. John and Alice McNamara; student Emporia State Tchrs. Coll., Sch. Visual Arts, Parsons Sch. Design, New Sch. Social Research; m. Hiroshi Orito, Aug. 1963 (div. 1972). Designer, Aileen Girl, 1964, Petite Leigue, 1965-67, Jack Winter, 1968-71, Hang Ups Sportswear, 1971-74; exec. design dir. Clyde Sportswear, 1975-78; designer/cons. Bagatelle Internat. Ltd., N.Y.C., 1978-81; costume designer Search for Tomorrow, CBS-TV, N.Y.C., 1981-84; design cons., 1984—; costume designer for theater, TV and music videos. Merit scholar, 1961-64. Mem. United Scenic Artists, Nat. Acad. TV Arts and Scis. Democrat. Mem. Unity Ch.

ORJIAS, BETTY KYZAR, banker; b. Tallulah, La., Aug. 27, 1935; d. Autie James and Annie Marjorie (Mills) Kyzar; student pub. schs., Tallulah; m. Theodor Orjias, Jan. 15, 1956; children—Autie Theodor, Arthur Christian, Susan Stephanie. Operator South Central Bell Tel. Co., Tallulah, 1955, New Orleans, 1956, service asst., directory clerk, operator-supr. tng., 1959; teller So. Nat. Bank, Tallulah, 1970-75, head teller, 1975-76, asst. cashier, 1976-83, asst. v.p., 1983—. Den mother Cub Scouts; adviser 4-H Club, tchr.; treas. Tallulah High Sch. Band Boosters, 1969—; active Tallulah Acad. Parents Club, 1970-81; treas. March of Dimes, 1977-80; scorekeeper Little League Baseball, 1965-68. Republican. Baptist. Club: Madison Parish Home Demonstration. Home: 910 Madison St Tallulah LA 71282 Office: 500 Askew St Tallulah LA 71282

ORLAN, ALICE MARY, designer, researcher, travel consultant; b. Richmond Hill, N.Y., Mar. 12, 1927; d. John Joseph and Eugenia (Cisyk) O.; m. John Berwecky, May 30, 1948; children—Kenneth, Patricia and Elizabeth (twins). Student N.Y. Phoenix Sch. Design, N.Y.C., 1945-51; diploma custom millinery Traphagen Sch. of Fashion, 1961. Internat. travel cons. AAA of N.Y., N.Y.C., 1945-52; freelance designer Originals by Ayobee, N.J., 1952-69; buyer, mgr. interior designer L. Bambergers, N.J., 1969-80; internat. tour escort, east coat rep. Shipka Travel, Cleve., 1967-70; internat. tour operator Halychanka Heritage Tours, Pa., 1970—; interior designer, buyer, mgr. antiques and gift shops, dir. restoration Buck Hill Inn, Buck Hill Falls, Pa., 1985—. Nat. cultural dir. League Ukrainian Catholics, 1972-81; pres. Pius X council, Warrington, Pa., 1975-83. Mem. Ukrainian Nat. Assn. (regional organizer 1983-84), Ukrainian Nat. Women's League (pres. br. 112, 1978-84, pub. relations dir. N.Y.C. and Phila. regional councils 1963—, 78). Republican. Club: Nat. Fedn. Women's. Avocations: iconography; illustration; needlepoint; tchr. Ukrainian embroidery; evolution of historic stitches. Home: 99 Ferndale NY 12734

ORLANDO, JOYCE RYAN, public relations director; b. Steubenville, Ohio, Aug. 9, 1942; d. Orel B. and Alice (Mountford) Ryan; m. Joseph M. Orlando, Sept. 1, 1962 (div. Feb. 1976); children—Suzanne Elizabeth, Melissa Ann. Student U. Steubenville, 1981—. Mktg. dir. Fort Steuben Mall, Steubenville, 1974-81; asst. dir. pub. relations U. Steubenville, 1981-83, dir. pub. relations, 1983—. Bd. dirs. Jeffco Workshop, Steubenville, 1982—; chmn. Jefferson County Leukemia Soc., 1980—; mem. Steubenville Fiesta Com., 1984; past bd. dirs. Nat. Found. Birth Defects, United Way. Author/editor: A Guide to Steubenville for the Handicapped, 1974. Democrat. Episcopalian. Avocations: skiing; racquetball. Home: 136 Meadow Rd Wintersville OH 43952 Office: U Steubenville Franciscan Way Steubenville OH 43952

ORLEBEKE, HANNAH LEWIN, foundation public affairs executive; b. Malden, Mass., Oct. 22, 1937; d. Henry and Eva (Litchman) Lewin; m. Alan Paul Orlebeke, May 11, 1984; children by previous marriage—Philip Gottlieb, Sharon Gottlieb, Billy Gottlieb. B.S. in Bus. Adminstrn., Simmons Coll., 1958; cert. in edn. Simmons Coll., 1958. Tchr. Malden High Sch., 1958-59; mktg. staff Schultz Donahoe, N.Y.C., 1975-78; pub. relations positions Am. Health Found., N.Y.C., 1979-82, mgr. pub. affairs, 1982—; mem. adv. bd. Vis. Nurse Service, Westchester County, N.Y., 1984—; mem. Blue Cross adv. council Blue Cross/Blue Shield, N.Y.C., 1984—; mem. roundtable on health White Plains C. of C., N.Y., 1984—. Author: Overview, Secretaries, 1981. Mem. Adminstrv. Mgmt. Soc., Westchester County C. of C., Women in Communications. Avocations: music; golf. Office: Am Health Found Dana Rd Valhalla NY 10595

ORLING, ANNE, art consultant, appraiser; b. N.Y.C.; d. Joseph and Bertha (Elsner) Acks; B.S., in Art Adminstrn., SUNY, Old Westbury, 1977; art student Art Students League, also studied art with pvt. tchrs.; m. Michael Orling; children—Merry, Jeffrey, Alan. One-woman shows include: Silvermine Guild, Lafayette (Ind.) Art Center, U. Ariz., Tucson, Pa. State U., Hazleton, Baldwin Wallace Coll., Berea, Ohio, U. Idaho, Moscow, U. Fla., Gainesville; group shows include: Hofstra U., Hempstead, N.Y., L.I.U., Bklyn., N.Y. World's Fair Fine Arts Pavilion, Silvermine Guild, New Canaan, Conn., N.Y.C. Center, Provincetown Art Assn., NAD, Hofstra U., Heckscher Mus., Adelphi U., Fordham U., Bklyn. Coll., UN Plaza, Royal Acad., Stockholm; represented in permanent collections UN, C.W. Post Coll., many pvt. collections; former mem. staff North Shore Community Arts Center. Founder, v.p. bd. trustees Fine Arts Mus. L.I., Hempstead, N.Y. Recipient 1st prize Hofstra U., 1960, Heckscher Mus., 1960; award Silvermine Guild, 1960, East Hampton Guild, 1960, Winners Show at Hofstra U., 1964, 65; 2d prize Lincoln House, 1965. Mem. Appraisers Assn. Am., Profl. Artists Guild (pres.). Home: 69 Shelter Ln Roslyn Heights NY 11577

ORMAN, BETTY, social worker, administrator; b. Detroit, Nov. 24, 1928; d. Robert Israel and Lillian (Aberson) Fleiss; B.A., Wayne State U., 1950; M.S.W. Ariz. State U., 1973; m. Bernie Orman, Oct. 22, 1950; children—Rodger, Marc. With State of Mich., 1952-56; caseworker Jewish Family Service, Tucson, 1961-71, social worker, 1973-79, asst. exec. dir., 1979-83, dir. counseling services, 1983—; asso. prof. Pima Community Coll., 1979—; mem. field faculty Ariz. State U., 1977-79, 83—. Mem. Family and Social Service Task Force, City of Tucson, 1975-77. Mem. Nat. Assn. Social Workers (chairperson div. II 1982-84), Acad. Cert. Social Workers, Am. Acad. Family Mediators, Nat. Registry Clin. Social Workers. Home: 7358 E Kenyon Dr Tucson AZ 85710 Office: 102 N Plumer St Tucson AZ 85719

ORMISTON, HELEN MAINE, manufacturing company official; b. Potsdam, N.Y., Apr. 3, 1931; d. Leon Eugene and Anne (Chase) Maine; m. Ray L. Ormiston, Nov. 20, 1949 (dec. Jan. 1970); children—Kathleen, Linda, Randy, Roger. Keypunch operator Climax Mfg. Co., Castorland, N.Y., 1963-72, asst. data processing mgr., 1972-77, credit mgr., 1977-81, credit/office mgr., 1981—, treas. Fed. Credit Union, 1973—. Mem. Nat. Assn. Credit Mgrs. Republican. Methodist. Home: 7 N Main St Carthage NY 13619 Office: Climax Mfg Co Climax St Castorland NY 13620

ORMOND, CYNTHIA LYNN, construction company executive; b. Houston, July 1, 1954; d. Charles William and Dolores (Woods) Ormond. Student U. Tex., 1973, Sam Houston State U., 1974-77. Vice-pres. Ormco Drywall, Houston, 1978—. Mem. Drywall and Interior Systems Contractors Assn. of Houston (dir. 1983—), Assn. Wall and Ceiling Industries Internat. (vice chmn. resdl. and light comml. com. 1984-85). Republican. Baptist. Office: Ormco Drywall & Insulating Co 8133 Jackrabbit Rd Houston TX 77095

ORMSBY, MARGARET ANCHORETTA, historian; b. Quesnel, B.C., Can., June 7, 1909; d. George Lewis and Margaret Turner (McArthur) O. B.A., U. B.C., 1929, M.A., 1931, D.Lit., 1974; Ph.D., Bryn Mawr Coll., 1937; LL.D. (hon.), U. Man., 1964, U. Notre Dame, Nelson, B.C., 1968, Simon Fraser U., 1971, U. Victoria, 1976. Head of history Sarah Dix Hamlin Sch., San Francisco, 1937-40; spl. lectr. in history McMaster U., 1940-43; lectr. in history U. B.C., Vancouver, 1943, asst. prof., 1946, assoc. prof., 1949, prof., 1955, head history dept., 1965-74, vis. prof. history, 1974-75; vis. prof. U. Western Ont., 1977, U. Toronto, 1978. Author: British Columbia: A History, 1958, rev. edit., 1971; A Pioneer Gentlewoman in British Columbia: The Recollections of Susan Allison, 1976. Contbr. intro. Fort Victoria Letters 1946-51, 1979; contbr. Dictionary Can. Biography, vols. IX, X, XI. Mem. B.C. Heritage Adv. Bd., 1971-83; mem. Hist. Sites and Monuments Bd. Can., 1960-68, Sir John A. Mcdonald Prize Com. in Can. History, 1977-79. Recipient Merit award Am. State and Local History Soc., 1959, 75, Regional History award Can. Hist. Assn., 1983; Centennial medal, 1967. Mem. Can. Hist. Assn. (pres. 1965-66), Okanagan Hist. Soc. Fellow Royal Soc. Can. Anglican. Avocation: fruit growing. Office: 12407 Coldstream Creek Rd Vernon BC V1B 1G2 Canada

OROPILLA, TERESITA BACANI, psychiatrist; b. Naga City, Philippines, Mar. 17, 1929; came to U.S., 1973, naturalized, 1979; d. Gerardo Bacani and Policarpia Ruivivar; A.A., U. Santo Tomas, Manila, 1950, M.D. cum laude, 1956; m. Ricardo Oropilla, Oct. 29, 1960; children—Joseph Marius, Teresa Ann. Intern, U. Santo Tomas, 1955-56; rotating intern U. Louisville, 1956-57, resident in pediatrics, 1957-58, resident in psychiatry, 1976-79, asst. prof., 1980—; practice medicine specializing in pediatrics, Philippines, 1959-73; staff physician Children's Treatment Service, Louisville, 1973-78; mem. psychiat. staff, charge mental hygiene clinic VA Med. Center, 1980—; vol. med. missions, Guatemala, 1976. Diplomate Am. Bd. Psychiatry and Neurology. Mem. Jefferson County Med. Soc., Ky. Med. Assn., Filipino-Am. Soc., Philippine Med. Assn. Ky. (treas.). Roman Catholic. Home: 2517 Stonehurst Dr Louisville KY 40222 Office: 800 Zorn Ave Louisville KY 40202

OROSZ, JUDY INEZ, pediatrician; b. Woodbury, Ga., July 16, 1945; d. Joseph Michael and Ruby Inez (Brown) Orosz; student U. Ga., 1963-64; B.S. in Biology, Ga. State U., 1967; M.D., Med. Coll. Ga., 1971. Intern, Baroness Erlanger Hosp., Chattanooga, Tenn., 1971-72; resident T.C. Thompson Children's Hosp., Chattanooga, 1972-74, chief resident, 1973-74; pvt. practice medicine specializing in pediatrics, Cartersville, Ga., 1974-79; mem. staff Gracewood (Ga.) State Sch. and Hosp., 1979-81; asst. prof. pediatrics Med. Coll. Ga., Augusta, 1980—, dir. ambulatory pediatrics, 1980—; pres. med. staff Sam Howell Meml. Hosp., 1977,78. Mem. adv. bd. Bartow County Tng. Center, 1974-76; active Nat. Found. March of Dimes, 1976-77; v.p. bd. dirs. Augusta Child Advocacy Ctr., 1986. Named Dept. Pediatrics Tchr. of Yr., Med. Coll. Ga., 1981; Ann. Social Work award Univ. Hosp., 1985. Mem. Richmond County Med. Soc., Med. Assn. Ga., AMA, Am. Acad. Pediatrics, Bapt. Med.-Dental Fellowship (fin. chmn. 1983-85, v.p. Ga. chpt. 1985-86, pres. 1986-87), Nat. Perinatal Assn., Med. Coll. Ga. Alumni Assn. (treas. women physician's council 1983-84). Baptist. Contbr. articles to profl. jours. Home: 4451 Forrest Dr Martinez GA 30907 Office: 1350 Walton Way Augusta GA 30910

OROSZ, JULIA ELIZABETH, nurse, educator, consultant; b. Alliance, Ohio, Nov. 5, 1948; d. William and Rachel (Doss) O.; m. Gerald Rogers Coker, July 5, 1976 (div. 1980). Nursing diploma Lutheran Hosp. Sch. Nursing, Cleve., 1970; B.S. in Nursing, U. Cin., 1973; M.S. in Nursing, U. Ala.-Birmingham, 1975. R.N., Ohio, Tex. Staff nurse Children's Hosp. Akron, Ohio, 1970-71, 75-77; health clinic nurse U. Cin., 1972-73; asst. prof. Maryville Coll. St. Louis, 1977-80, U. Tex. Health Sci. Ctr., San Antonio, 1980-84; clin. specialist Barberton Citizen's Hosp., Ohio, 1984-85; regional perinatal edn. coordinator Children's Med. Ctr., Akron, 1985—; health care assoc. Sch. Medicine, Washington U., St. Louis, 1978-79; cons. health care services Lutheran Ch. Mo. Synod: Internat. Youth Gathering, 1983. Editor NeoGram, 1985—; contbg. editor Northeast Ohio Perinatal Newsletter, 1985—. Vol. ARC, San Antonio, Akron, 1970—; speaker San Antonio Coalition for Children, Youth and Families, 1980-84, Children's Med. Ctr., Akron, 1985—; vol. Carter Presdl. Campaign, Akron, 1976. Named to Outstanding Young Women Am., U.S. Jaycees, 1981, 83; Klaus Meml. scholar Luth. Hosp. Sch. Nursing, 1970; grad. fellow U. Ala.-Birmingham, 1973. Mem. Am. Nurses Assn. (council perinatal nurses 1985), Tex. Nurses Assn. (chmn. dist. social com. 1982-84), Ohio Perinatal Assn. (bd. dirs. 1986), U. Cin. Alumni Assn. (life), Sigma Theta Tau. Avocations: counted cross stitch; piano; pipe organ; cooking; painting. Home: 2115 Braewick Circle Apt 3 Akron OH 44313 Office: Children's Med Ctr of Akron Newborn Office 281 Locust St Akron OH 44308

O'ROURKE, ALICE ANNA, historian; b. Downs, Ill., Aug. 25, 1923; d. Martin and Mary (Hickey) O'R.; B.A., Rosary Coll., 1949; M.A., U. Notre Dame, 1958; Ph.D., U. Calif., Berkeley, 1963. Joined Sinsinawa Dominican Religious Congregation, Roman Catholic Ch.; tchr., high schs., 1951-57; instr. history Rosary Coll., 1957-60, asst. prof., assoc. prof., 1963-67, prof., 1973-77; assoc. prof. Saginaw Valley Coll., 1969-73; pres. Edgewood Coll. Madison, Wis., 1977-83. Author: Good Work Begun: Centennial History of Peoria Diocese, 1977; Sown on Good Ground, 1984; Let Us Set Out: Sinsinawa Dominicans, 1949-1985, 1986. Home: Rosary Coll River Forest IL 60305

O'ROURKE, MARGARET MARY, government official; b. East Chicago, Ind., Nov. 2, 1945; d. Edward J. and Helen M. (Saprony) Savage; B.A., Marygrove Coll., Detroit, 1967; M.P.A., George Washington U., Washington, 1980; grad. Nat. War Coll., 1986; m. John E. O'Rourke, May 16, 1969. Import specialist U.S. Customs Service, Detroit, 1967-71, systems analyst, Washington, 1971-76, chief mgmt. info. br., 1976-77, spl. asst. to commr. data processing, 1977-79, dir. office mgmt. insp., 1979-82, dir. office trade ops., 1982—. Recipient Outstanding Performance award U.S. Customs Service, 1977, Sr. Exec. Bonus award, 1985. Mem. Sr. Exec. Assn., Am. Soc. Public Adminstrn. Roman Catholic. Home: 1211 Tulane Dr Alexandria VA 22307 Office: 1301 Constitution Ave NW Washington DC 20229

O'ROURKE, MARGUERITE PATRICIA, insurance company official; b. N.Y.C., May 10, 1950; d. William Lawrence and Olive Rose (Ponte) O'R.; B.A. in Polit. Sci. (Ednl. Opportunity grantee, N.J. State scholar), Am. U., 1972. Adminstrn. asst. Asso. Merchandising Corp., Washington, 1972-73; various positions Savage/Fogarty Co., Inc., Alexandria, Va., 1973-79; property mgr. Community Mgmt. Corp., Reston, Va., 1979-80; property mgr. Braedon Cos., Washington, 1980-81, dir. property mgmt., 1981-82; v.p. bldgs. adminstrn. Smithy Braedon Property Co., Washington, 1982-83; sr. real estate officer-asset mgmt. Northwestern Mut. Life Real Estate Div., 1983—; corp. sec. Savage/Fogarty Co., Inc., 1978-79. Intern Senator Claiborne Pell, R.I., 1971. Mem. Inst. Real Estate Mgrs., Property Mgrs. Assn., Washington Bd. Realtors, Save The Bay, Environ. Def. Fund, Union Concerned Scientists, Cousteau Soc., Nat. Trust for Historic Preservation, Smithsonian Instn., Am. Film Inst. Office: 1133 20th St Washington DC 20036

O'ROURKE, MARSHA CAROLYN, surgeon; b. Jacksonville, Fla., Mar. 10, 1949; d. Gerald G. and Willie O. (Martin) O'R.; m. Vincent J. Schafmeister, III, 1970 (div. 1978). B.A., Wheaton Coll., 1970; M.D., Free U. Brussels, 1977. Diplomate Am. Bd. Surgery, 1983; lic., N.Y. 1978, Calif. 1983. Intern, Albany (N.Y.) Med. Ctr. Hosp., 1977-78, resident, 1977-81, chief resident, 1981-82; gen. surgeon Community Health Plan, Latham, N.Y., 1982-85; practice gen. surgery, Augusta, Maine, 1985—; acting supt. Tintswalo Hosp., Acornhoek, South Africa, 1983. Active Women Overseas for Equality, Physicians for Social Responsibility, Physicians for Abortion Rights. Fellow ACS; mem. AMA, Sierra Club. Home: Route 1 Box 3405 Wayne ME 04284 Office: 89 Hospital St Augusta ME 04350

ORR, DONNA MARIE BRONSON, distribution company executive; b. Little Falls, N.Y., Oct. 12, 1943; d. Cecil Carl and Mary Jane (Adamko) Bronson; m. Jack Richard Glover, June 17, 1967 (div. Dec. 1976); 1 child, James Patrick (dec.); m. George Joseph Orr, Feb. 2, 1978. A.A.S., SUNY-Cobleskill, 1963; B.S., Rochester Inst. Tech., 1966; M.A., NYU, 1977. Registered dietitian. Dietitian in-service edn. St. Vincent's Med. Ctr., S.I., N.Y., 1967-68; nutrition clinic dietitian Evanston Hosp., Ill., 1968-70; asst. adminstrv. dietitian S.I. Hosp., 1970-74; chief clin. dietitian St. Vincent's Med. Ctr., S.I., 1975-76; nutritionist, instr. Temple U. Dental Sch., Phila., 1977-78; mfrs. rep. Orr Assocs., Spring House, Pa., 1978-80; pres. Edgewater Distbrs., Burlington, N.J., 1981—; vis. lectr. Community Coll. Phila., 1978, 81, 85, Immaculata Coll., Pa., 1979, 81, 85. Author bus. manuals. Mem. N.J. Assn. Women Bus. Owners (chpt. by-laws chmn. 1983, chpt. membership chmn. 1984, chpt. pres. 1985), Am. Dietetic Assn. (mem. ann. meeting com. 1981-82), N.J. Dietetic Assn., Phila. Dietetic Assn. (food adminstrn. co-chmn. 1978-79, nutrition time chmn. 1980-81), Nutrition Today Soc., Divorced, Separated and Remarried Catholics Burlington County, Phi Theta Kappa, Omicron Nu. Roman Catholic. Avocations: gardening; crafts. Office: Edgewater Distbrs Inc 1130 US Route 130 N Burlington NJ 08016

ORR, ELAINE LOUISE, government official; b. Washington, Aug. 14, 1951; d. Miles D. and H. Rita (Rooney) O. B.A., U. Dayton, 1972; M.A., Am. U., 1974. Evaluator, GAO, Washington, 1974-78, spl. asst. to asst. comptroller gen., 1979-80, dir. internat. liaison, 1980—. Editor, Internat. Jour. Govt. Auditing, 1983—, Nat. Young Profls. Forum News, 1982-83. Elected gov. D.C. Girls State, DAR, 1969. Mem. Am. Consortium Internat. Public Adminstrn. (v.p., 1985—, past bd. dirs.), Am. Soc. Public Adminstrn. (life, bd. dirs. women in public adminsrn. sect. 1984-85), Assn. Govt. Accts. (com. mem. 1982—). Democrat. Club: Beth Racquet and Health (Md.). Avocations: Gardening; music; reading; theater. Office: GAO 441 G St NW Room 7131 Washington DC 20548

ORR, KARIN KATHLEEN, columnist; b. Grand Rapids, Mich., Sept. 27, 1942; d. Ray Wilson and Joan (Bosworth) McClow; B.A., Albion Coll., 1964; M.A., Wayne State U., 1966, Ph.D., 1976; m. Vance Womack Orr, Mar. 29, 1965; children—Deirdre Ellen, Caitlin Elizabeth, Maurya Kathleen, Vance W. III. Legal sec. James Knopper, atty., Grandville, Mich., 1961; artists' model Albion (Mich.) Coll., 1963-64; asst. Wayne State U., Detroit, 1964-68; instr. English, Grand Rapids (Mich.) Jr. Coll., 1968-81; dir. drama, 1969-81, sec. faculty council, 1978-81; instr. drama Aquinas Coll., 1979-81; acting instr. Grand Rapids Civic Theatre; columnist Grand Rapids Press, Wonderland mag. Mem. Arts Cooking with Karin, Council Greater Grand Rapids, 1970-80; chmn. Festival '75, Jr. Arts Council, 1975-79; co-chmn. Springfest benefit auction for art mus., 1978; bd. dirs. Opera Assn. Western Mich., 1972-81, Grand Rapids Civic Theatre, 1976-80; mem. exec. bd., chmn. public affairs, 1st v.p. Jr. League of Grand Rapids, pres., 1981-82; mem. Area IV nominating com. Assn. Jr. Leagues, 1982-84 co-chmn. auction Channel 35, Public TV, 1981; mem. adv. bd. Performing Arts Center, Grand Valley State Colls., 1976-79; trustee Grand Valley State Colls.; membership chmn., exec. com. Grand Rapids Art Mus., 1983-85; mem. 5th dist. Women's adv. com. U.S. Senator Paul Henry. Recipient certificate merit for service Grand Rapids Art Council, 1975; Vol. of Yr. award YWCA, 1984. Mem. Alpha Xi Delta. Home: 1841 Buttrick St Ada MI 49301 Office: 1841 Buttrick Ada MI 49309

ORR, KAY A., state official; b. Burlington, Iowa, Jan. 2, 1939; d. Ralph Robert and Sadie Lucille (Skoglund) Stark; m. William Dayton Orr, Sept. 26, 1957; children—John William, Suzanne. Student U. Iowa, 1956-57. Exec. asst. to gov. State Nebr., Lincoln, 1979-81, apptd. state treas., 1981-83, elected, 1982—. Rep. nominee for gov. of Nebr., 1986. Co-chmn. Republican Nat. Platform Com., 1984; apptd. to USDA Users Adv. Bd., 1985—; trustee Hastings Coll., Nebr., 1985—. Office: Nebr State Treasurer Room 2003 State Capitol Lincoln NE 68509

ORR, MARLENE B., editor, consultant; b. Wichita, June 28, 1939; d. Bediah Esper and Victoria N. (Farha) Samra; m. Kenneth Thomas Orr, Dec. 28, 1963; children—Kathryn Elisabeth, Paige Marlene. B.A. cum laude, U. Wichita, 1961; postgrad. in English (grad. assistantship) U. Nebr., 1961. Copy editor Jour. Am. Med. Assn., Chgo., 1961-63; textbook editor Henry Regnery Co., Chgo., 1963-64; manuscript editor U. Chgo. Press, 1964-68; editorial dir. Langston, Kitch & Assoc., Topeka, 1977-80; cons., asst. treas. Ken Orr & Assocs., Inc., Topeka, 1980—; editorial cons., Topeka, 1971-77. Editor: The Kansas Legislature, 1974; Recollections of an Herpetologist, 1975; Structured Systems Design, 1978; Structured Requirements Definition, 1979. Vice-pres. Dance Arts of Topeka, 1982-83; sec. PTA, Topeka, 1975-76; newsletter author Topeka Assn. Gifted, 1973. Mem. Women in Communications, Inc. (membership rev. com. 1982), Gamma Phi Beta. Democrat. Home: 104 Woodlawn Topeka KS 66606 Office: Ken Orr & Assocs Inc 1725 Gage Topeka KS 66604

ORR, N'OMI, computer graphics consulting executive; b. Atlantic City, Feb. 13, 1938; d. Walter Corson and Mary Ethel (Strockbine) Smith; m. Joel Nathanael Orr; children—David, Anne, John, Thomas, Stephen, Sharon. Pres., Orr Assocs., Inc., Washington and Danbury, Conn., 1979—, Naomi Orr Agy., 1980—; dir. The CADD/CAM Inst., Washington, 1982—; asst. dir. Computer Graphics Inst. Am.; pub. Honeycomb Library, 1982—. Author: A Cure for Cancer, 1984; The Common Cold: Cause and Cure, 1983; editor: The Computer Graphics Newsletter, 1976-78; The Computer Graphics Extravaganza, 1977; How to Implement CADD, 1981; The Top Ten Multistation CADD Systems, 1982; The Low Cost CADD Systems, 1983. Mem. Nat. Computer Graphics Assn. Office: Orr Associates Inc 9029 Weant Great Falls VA 22066

ORR, PEARL LEE, emergency management city-county executive; b. Henderson, N.C., Oct. 27, 1931; d. William Edgar Woodlief and Reba Colon (Lee) Marshall; m. Elmer Roscoe Orr, Aug. 24, 1949; children—Susan Lee Orr Rexrode, William Roscoe. Diploma, Henderson Bus. Coll., 1950. Bookkeeper, Roth-Stewart Co., Henderson, 1961-62; legal sec. Gholson & Gholson, Henderson, 1962-66; sec. Henderson-Vance Co. CD, Henderson, 1966-78, coordinator Henderson-Vance Co., emergency mgmt., 1978—. Officer, chmn. Jr. Woman's Club, Henderson, 1957-66; ex-officio mem. adv. council Region K, Emergency Med. Services, 1985—. Named Woman of Yr., Henderson Jr. Woman's Club, 1960. Mem. N.C. Emergency Mgmt. Assn. (Gen. Edward Foster Griffin award 1984; pres. 1983-84, state rep. 1984-85), Nat. Coordinating Council on Emergency Mgmt. Democrat. Baptist. Avocations; travel; reading. Home: 115 Zollicoffer Ave Henderson NC 17536 Office: Henderson-Vance Co Emergency Mgmt PO Box 1094 Henderson NC 27536

ORSHER, SUSAN BURNS, trade association executive; b. Phila., Oct. 27, 1952; d. Henry E. and Selma R. (Windermann) Burns; m. Thomas E. Wilcher, Oct. 12, 1983. B.A., Lafayette Coll., 1974; J.D., NYU, 1977. Bar: N.Y. 1978. Counsel Ind. Ins. Agts. Am., Inc., N.Y.C., 1977-79, asst. gen. counsel, 1979-83, v.p., corp. sec., 1983—; counsel Ind. Ins. Agts. Am. Ednl. Found., N.Y.C., 1983—; chmn. Legal Com. Future One, N.Y.C., 1982—. Founder Nat. Agents Polit. Action Commn., Washington, 1983. Mem. ABA, N.Y. County Lawyers Assn., Phi Beta Kappa. Contbr. articles to profl. jours.

ORSINI, BETTE SWENSON, reporter; Reporter, St. Petersburg Times, Fla. Co-recipient Pulitzer Prize for nat. reporting, 1980. Office: St Petersburg Times Times Pub Co PO Box 1121 Saint Petersburg FL 33731*

ORSINI, MERRILY ANN, personal service company executive; b. Little Rock, Mar. 16, 1947; d. Edmund Nicholas Orsini and Dorothy Angeline (May) Orsini Jones; m. Donald Wayne Coaplen, Sept. 12, 1970 (div. Apr. 1985);

children—Joshua Philip Orsini Coaplen, Caleb Armstrong Orsini Coaplen. B.A., U. Ky., 1969; M.S.S.W., U. Louisville, 1977. Systems analyst Cybernetics & Systems, Louisville, 1969-71; ednl. coordinator Bur. for Social Services, Louisville, 1971-78; pres. Home Mgmt. Service, Louisville, 1981—. Bd. dirs. Mus. History and Sci., Louisville, 1982-85, Ky. Contemporary Theatre, 1985—. Mem. Entrepreneur Soc. Home: 2433 Hawthorne Ave Louisville KY 40205 Office: Home Mgmt Service 2005 Longest Ave Louisville KY 40204

ORTEGA, KATHERINE D., treasurer of U.S.; b. Tularosa, N.Mex., July 16, 1934. B.A., Eastern N.Mex. U., 1957. Tax supr. Peat, Marwick, Mitchell & Co., 1969-72; v.p., cashier Pan Am. Nat. Bank, 1972-75; pres., dir. Santa Ana State Bank, 1975-77; cons. Otero Savs. & Loan Assn.; commr. Copyright Royalty Tribunal, 1982-83; treas. of U.S., Washington, 1983—; Keynote speaker Rep. Nat. Conv., 1984. Address: Office of Treas of US 15th and Pennsylvania Aves Washington DC 20220*

ORTH, ARDEAN SYLVIA, nurse; b. Racine, Wis., Oct. 5, 1947; d. Alfons and Evelyn Florence (Hahnefeld) O.; R.N., Deaconess Hosp., Milw., 1968; B.S., Evangel Coll., Springfield, Mo., 1973; M.S., U. Wis., Milw., 1980. Staff nurse, then head nurse Milw. County Mental Health Center, 1968-72, 76-77; head nurse Lutheran Hosp., Milw., 1973-75; dir. Community Mental Health Nursing, Waukesha, Wis., 1977—; ednl. cons., lectr. Waukesha County Tech. Inst., 1985, 86; workshop leader, 1979—; adv. com. Mental Health Assn. Waukesha County, 1979—. Mem. Nat. League Nursing, Evangel Coll. Alumni Assn. Republican. Baptist. Home: 8510-8 W Waterford Ave Greenfield WI 53228 Office: 25042 W Northview Rd Waukesha WI 53186

ORTIZ, IRMA, university adminstrator, interpreter; b. Calexico, Calif., May 28, 1922; d. Camilo Enrique and Emelina (Trujillo) O.; 1 adopted child, Kumari Mary Ruth Danda. A.A., Imperial Valley Coll., 1942; B.B.A., Academia Coss y Leon, 1942. Cert. profl. sec., 1966. Stenographer U. Calif. Agrl. Extension, El Centro, 1942, sec., 1943-64; adminstrv. sec. U. Calif. Coop. Extension, El Centro, 1965-79, adminstrv. asst., 1980—; speaker various high schs. and colls. Dir. Salvation Army, El Centro, 1968-79; chmn. Imperial Valley Coll. Community review com., Calif., 1977-78; pres. Imperial Valley Community Concert Assn., 1983—. Recipient Red Feather award Community Chest, El Centro, 1953; named Employee of Yr. Imperial County, 1969. Mem. Pilot Club (sec. western region 1968-69, 1st v.p. El Centro chpt. 1969-70), Beta Sigma Phi. Republican. Roman Catholic. Club: Euterpe (Mex.) (pres. 1945. Avocations: Travel; reading; music; silvercraft; painting.

ORTIZ, MARIA ELENA, banker; b. Havana, Cuba, May 14, 1950; came to U.S. 1969, naturalized 1979; d. Roberto and Gladys M. (Fajin) Ortiz. Grad. diploma, Electronic Computer Programming Inst., 1974; student Upsala Coll., 1981. With City Nat. Bank, Newark, 1972-75, asst. cashier, 1975-78, ops. officer, 1978—; notary public. CPR cert. ARC, 1985. Recipient award for recognition of profl. achievement City Nat. Bank, 1985; Presdl. Achievement award Republican Nat. Com., 1984. Mem. Am. Mgmt. Assn., Am. Inst. Banking, Am. Chartered Inst. of Fin. Comtrollers, Am. Soc. Notaries, U.S. Olympic Soc., Nat. Assn. Female Execs. Republican. Roman Catholic. Club: Ju-Jitsu. Avocations: travel; photography; martial arts. Office: City Nat Bank of NJ 900 Broad St Newark NJ 07102

ORTIZ, MARIA ELENA, educator; b. Cuidad Acuna, Coahuila, Mex. (parents Am. citizens); d. Isaias and Margaret (Muro) Ortiz; A.S., San Antonio Coll., 1966; B.S., S.W. Tex. State U., 1968, M.A., 1970; Ph.D., Tex. Woman's U., 1973. Lab. instr. S.W. Tex. State U., San Marcos, 1966-70, Tex. Woman's U., Denton, 1970-72; prof. biology Calif. Poly. State U., San Luis Obispo, 1972—; research participant Argonne Nat. Lab., summer 1975, Oak Ridge Nat. Lab., summer 1976, Battelle N.W. Lab., 1977 Lab. Biomed. and Environ. Scis., UCLA, summer 1981. NSF summer research trainee, 1971. Mem. AAAS, Am. Soc. Zoologists, Nat. Geog. Soc., Sigma Tau Sigma, Kappa Delta Pi, Beta Beta Beta. Office: Biol Scis Calif Poly State U San Luis Obispo CA 93407

ORTLUND, (ELIZABETH) ANNE, writer, musician; b. Wichita, Kans., Dec. 3, 1923; d. Joseph Burton and Mary Elizabeth (Weible) Sweet; m. Raymond Carl Ortlund, Apr. 27, 1946; children—Sherrill Anne, Margot Jeanne, Raymond Carl, Nels Robert. Student Am. U., 1941-43; B.Music, U. Redlands, Calif., 1945; Assoc. Degree, Am. Guild of Organists, 1944. Organist, Old-Fashioned Revival Hour and Joyful Sound, Radio World-Wide, 1960-75; composer hymns, anthems, N.Y.C., 1963-77; worldwide speaker to pastors, missionaries, chs. Orgn. Renewal Ministries, Newport Beach, Calif., 1980—; composer 250 anthems for hymnals including Macedonia (theme hymn Billy Graham and Christianity Today's Congress on Evangelism, Berlin, 1966); books include: Up with Worship, 1975; Disciplines of the Beautiful Woman, 1977; (with Raymond Carl Ortlund) The Best Half of Life, 1976; Discipling One Another, 1979; Children Are Wet Cement (Christie award Christian Booksellers Assn. 1982), 1981; Joanna: A Story of Renewal, 1982; Build a Great Marriage, 1984; (with Raymond C. Ortlund) Staying Power, 1986. Named Profl. Woman of Yr., Pasadena Bus. and Profl. Women, 1975; recipient SESAC award Gospel Musicians, 1978. Home: 32 Whitewater Dr Corona Del Mar CA 92625 Office: Renewal Ministries 4500 Campus Dr Suite 662 Newport Beach CA 92660

ORTOLEVA, LAURA LYNN, marketing communications executive; b. Chgo., Apr. 27, 1956; d. Salvatore Henry and Loretta Elvira (Kosiba) Ortoleva. A.A., Harper Jr. Coll., 1975; B.A., U. Ill., 1977, M.S. in Advt., 1979. Instr. bus. writing U. Ill.-Champaign, 1979-80; asst. promotion dept. The News-Gazette, Champaign, 1979-80; copywriter Abelson-Frankel, Chgo., 1980-82; mktg. cons. Flair Communications, Chgo., 1982-83; copy dir. Lee Hill, Inc., Chgo., 1983-84; account mgr. Storandt, Kay & Pann, Chgo., 1984-86; advt. supr. NEC Home Electronics, Woodale, 1986—; mktg. cons., Chgo., 1982—. Youth leader St. Francis Borgia Teen Club, Chgo., 1982; tutor Cycle Program: Project Teens, coll. bound, Chgo., 1983. Campaign winner Ill. Dept. Transp., 1979, Champaign Advt. Club, 1980; Home: 3550 N Lake Shore Dr Chicago IL 60657

ORULLIAN, B. LARAE, banker; b. Salt Lake City, May 15, 1933; d. Alma and Bessie (Bacon) O.; cert. Am. Inst. Banking, 1961, 63, 67; grad. Nat. Real Estate Banking Sch., Ohio State U., 1969-71. With Tracy Collins Trust Co., Salt Lake City, 1951-54; sec. to exec. sec. Union Nat. Bank, Denver, 1954-57; exec. sec. Guaranty Bank, Denver, 1957-64, asst. cashier, 1964-67, asst. v.p., 1967-70, v.p., 1970-75, exec. v.p., 1975-77, also dir.; pres., chief exec. officer, dir. The Women's Bank N.A., Denver, 1977—, Equitable Bankshares of Colo., 1980—; dir. Equitable Bank Littleton; adv. bd., dir. Colo. Blue Cross/Blue Shield, lectr. Nat. treas. Girl Scouts U.S.A., 1981. Mem. Bus. and Profl. Women Colo. (3d Century award 1977), Denver C. of C. (chair govtl. affairs bd.), Am. Inst. Banking, Nat. Assn. Bank Women, Women in Bus. Assn., Women's Forum, Com. of 200, Denver Partnership,Colo. Bankers Assn. (bd. dirs.). Republican. Mormon. Clubs: Zonta, Soroptimist, Denver. Home: 10 S Ammons St Lakewood CO 80226

OSBORN, CATHARINA LOUISE, radion station executive; b. Sneek, Friesland, The Netherlands, July 31, 1955; came to U.S., 1962; naturalized, 1967; d. Sietze Nmn and Ban Nio (Lee) Veldhuis; m. John Douglas Osborn, Nov. 20, 1976 (div. Apr. 1981); 1 child, Ryan Douglas. Student Chico State U., Calif., 1973-75. Account exec. Sta. KFYE, Fresno, Calif., 1979-80, Sta. KOSO, Inc., Modesto, Calif., 1980-83; gen. sales mgr. Sta. KBEE/KHYV Modesto Broadcasting Inc., 1983-84, sta. mgr., 1984-86; gen. sales mgr. Sta. KDJK, Goldrush Broadcasting Inc., Oakdale, Calif., 1986—. Calif. State scholar, 1973. Mem. Soroptomist Internat. Republican. Methodist. Home: 2420 Killarney Modesto CA 95355 Office: KBEE/KHYV Modesto Broadcasting Inc 1581 Cummins Dr 135 Modesto CA 95355

OSBORN, DAISY MARIE, missionary organization executive; b. Merced, Calif., Sept. 23, 1924; d. Christopher Columbus and Clara Irene (Otis) Washburn; student public schs., Merced; L.H.D. (hon.), Bethel Christian Coll., Riverside, Calif., 1983; D.Div. (hon.), Zoe Coll., Jacksonville, Fla., 1983; m. T.L. Osborn, Apr. 5, 1942; children—Marie L. (dec.), T.L. (dec.), LaDonna C. Osborn Nickerson, Mary E. (dec.). Co-founder, exec. adminstr., pres. Osborn Found., Tulsa, 1947—. Editor: Faith Digest Mag., 1956—; author numerous articles, tng. cassettes; cinematographer 9 feature-length color documentary films. Home: PO Box 4598 Winter Park FL 32793 Office: PO Box 707572 Tulsa OK 74170

OSBORN, MARY JANE MERTEN, biochemist, educator; b. Colorado Springs, Colo., Sept. 24, 1927; d. Arthur John and Vivien Naomi (Morgan) Merten; B.A., U. Calif., Berkeley, 1948; Ph.D., U. Wash., 1958; m. Ralph Kenneth Osborn, Oct. 26, 1950. Postdoctoral fellow N.Y.U. Med. Sch., 1959-61, instr., then asst. prof., 1961-63; asst. prof., then asso. prof. Albert Einstein Coll. Medicine, Bronx, N.Y., 1963-68; prof. microbiology U. Conn. Health Center, Farmington, 1968—, chairperson, 1980—; mem. bd. sci. counselors Nat. Heart, Lung and Blood Inst., 1975-79; mem. Nat. Sci. Bd., 1980—; mem. adv. council Nat. Inst. Gen. Med. Sci., 1983—. NIH fellow, 1959-61, grantee, 1962—; grantee NSF, 1965-68, Am. Heart Assn., 1968-71. Fellow Am. Acad. Arts and Scis., Nat. Acad. Scis.; mem. Am. Chem. Soc. (chmn. div. biol. chemistry 1975-76), Am. Soc. Biol. Chemists (pres. 1981-82), Am. Soc. Microbiologists. Democrat. Asso. editor Jour. Biol. Chemistry, 1978-80; contbr. articles profl. jours. Office: Dept Microbiology Univ Conn Health Center Farmington CT 06032

OSBORN, RUTH KESNER, businesswoman, nurse; b. Lewiston, Maine, June 12, 1935; d. I. Louis and Ella Elizabeth (Gaudu) Kesner; m. Robert E. Pitts, Dec. 3, 1963 (div. 1973), m. Paul Robinson Osborn, Sept. 28, 1980; 1 child, Karen. B.S. NYU. R.N., Fla., Ariz., Ohio, N.Y. Supr., Jackson Meml. Hosp., Miami, Fla. 1957-60; detective City of Miami Police, 1960-72; owner Ariz. Forest Supply, Inc., Flagstaff, 1975-81, cons., 1981-83; trauma specialist COCONINO County Jail, Flagstaff, Ariz., 1983—; pres. Shimá Trading Co., Inc.; owner Wana Oneida Ltd., Flagstaff. Patentee woodburning stove, 1978. Bus. adv. bd. Native Ams. for Community Action, Flagstaff, Ariz., 1982—. Republican. Office: Wana Oneida Ltd 2160A N 4th St Flagstaff AZ 86001

OSBORN, SUSAN ELAINE BENIOFF, business opportunity broker; b. Los Angeles, June 28, 1944; d. Dave Benioff and Florence (Cohen) Benioff Werner; m. John Dean Osborn, Aug. 29, 1969 (div. 1979). Student Calif. State U.-Los Angeles, 1962-64; grad. Realtors Inst., Los Angeles, 1980. Lic. real estate broker, cert. residential specialist. Ops. teller Union Bank, Los Angeles and Pasadena, Calif., 1964-69; assoc. broker Century 21-Surf Realty, Huntington Beach, Calif., 1973-80; v.p., broker Calif. Practice Sales, brokerage specializing in dental practices, Anaheim, Calif., 1984—; owner, pres. The Coach Works, Huntington Beach, 1980—. Writer pamphlet on winemaking; inventor sole grippers. Mem. Huntington Beach-Fountain Valley Bd. Realtors (Realtor of Yr. 1976, pres. 1978, state bd. dirs. 1975-80), Calif. Assn. Realtors (state chmn. 1979-80), Huntington Beach C. of C. (bd. dirs. 1978-85, ambassador 1983-84), Women's Active 20/30 Club Orange County (2d v.p. 1982—, pres. 1984). Club: Soroptimist Internat. (pres. 1976) (Huntington Beach). Republican. Mem. Ch. of Religious Sci. Avocations: setting up fund-raisers, theme parties, reading, foreign travel. Office: Calif Practice Sales 1730 S Douglass Rd Anaheim CA 92806

OSBORNE, CAROL ANN, lawyer; b. Erie, Pa., Aug. 26, 1938; d. Clarence Henry and Grace Louise Bronson; LL.B., Western State U., 1977, J.D., 1978; m. Dwight E. Osborne, Jr., Jan. 1, 1965; children—Dwight E., Joy Louise. Bar: Calif. 1978. Legal sec., Orange County, Calif., 1967-78; individual practice, Orange, Calif., 1978-83; assoc. with Maxine L. Lazzara, Downey, Calif., 1983-85; sole practice, Downey, Calif., 1985—. Active PTA Kraemer Jr. High Sch. and Van Buren Elem. Sch.; treas. Kraemer Parent Booster Club, 1979-80; mem. Valencia High Sch. PTA, others. Mem. ABA, Calif. Bar Assn., Orange County Bar Assn., Calif. Trial Lawyers Assn., Orange County Trial Lawyers Assn., Southeast Bar Assn., Am. Bus. Women's Assn. (chpt. officer), Western State U. Alumni Assn., Nu Beta Epsilon. Republican. Office: 8221 3d St #201 Downey CA 90241

OSBORNE, MAGGIE (MARGARET ELLEN), novelist; b. Hollywood, Calif., June 10, 1941; d. William Edward and Zelma Lucille (King) Prather; m. Charles Ralph Carter, Dec. 26, 1966; 1 child, Zane Earl; m. 2d, George Muncy Osborne II, Apr. 22, 1972. Flight attendant United Air Lines, Denver, 1963-67; owner Hospitality House, Denver, 1968-72; freelance writer, 1979—. Author: Alexa, 1980; Salem's Daughter, 1981; Portrait in Passion, 1981; Yankee Princess, 1982; Rage to Love, 1983; Flight to Fancy, 1984; Winter Magic, 1986; Castles and Fairy Tales, 1986. Mem. Romance Writers Am. (sec. 1983-84, nat. dir. 1983-84, pres. 1984-85, 85-86, named Denver chpt. Writer of Yr. 1984), Rocky Mountain Writers Guild (resident writer 1982-84, named Writer of Yr. 1981), Colo. Authors League, Mensa. Methodist. Club: Denver Women's Press. Home: PO Box F Dillon CO 80435

OSBORNE, POLLY ENZOR, real estate broker; b. Nichols, S.C., Sept. 28; d. Quittie Montro and Leona Harrington (Joyner) Enzor; m. Chester Floyd, Sept. 19, 1941 (dec. 1975); children—Austin E. Floyd, Rachel Floyd Harjes. Student Grad. Realtors Inst., So. Coll., Columbia, S.C., 1976-78. Owner, mgr. Floyd's, Nichols, S.C., 1943-63; with Market Restaurant, Columbia, S.C., 1963-70; Food service staff Ramada Inn, Columbia, 1970-75; part owner Rigbys, Columbia, 1975-77; real estate broker Bob Capes Realty, Columbia, 1976—. Named to Two Million Dollar Club, Columbia Bd. Realtors, 1985; recipient Disting. Sales award Columbia Sales and Mktg., 1983, 84, 85. Republican. Presbyterian. Avocation: gardening. Home: 302 S Waccamaw St Columbia SC 29205 Office: Bob Capes Realty 3105 Devine St Columbia SC 29205

OSCHER, MARILYN JAVELIN, manufacturing company executive; b. N.Y.C., Oct. 16, 1928; d. Isaac and Rose (Sigar) Smith; m. Robert Lawrence Oscher, May 3, 1958 (dec. 1980); children—Robin, Ivy Oscher Giller, Todd, Eric. B.A., Bklyn. Coll., 1949. Assoc. Riverside Industries, Bettendorf, Iowa, 1970-76; ptnr. Alloys & Exothermics, Davenport, Iowa, 1984—. Home: 2751 S Ocean Dr Hollywood FL 33019

OSGUTHORPE, SUSAN GALE LIKINS, nursing administrator, consultant; b. Salt Lake City, July 8, 1948; d. Corwin Hale and Virginia Louise (Snyder) Likins; m. Steven Garn Osguthorpe, Jan. 29, 1983. B.S. cum laude in Nursing, U. Utah, 1971, M.S. in Nursing, 1981. Staff nurse Holy Cross Hosp., Salt Lake City, 1971-73, 74-75, supr., 1974-81, critical care nurse clinician, 1981-82, clin. dir. critical care services, 1982-84; clin. dir. Cardiovascular Nursing Virginia Mason, Seattle, 1984—; staff nurse Sisters of Mercy Hosp., Buffalo, 1973, St. Joseph's Hosp., Syracuse, N.Y., 1973-74; mem. clin. faculty Weber State Coll., 1980-84, U. Utah, 1982-84, U. Wash., 1986—; instr., trainer Utah Heart Assn.; teaching cons. Hewlett Packard & Sorenson Research Co., Salt Lake Fire Dept.; lectr. in field. Editorial rev. bd. FOCUS mag. Mem. nursing edn. com. Utah Heart Assn., Am. Heart Assn; mem. healthsite com. Wash. Heart Assn. Mem. Am. Assn. for Critical Care Nurses (mem. mgmt. spl. interest group com.), Mortar Bd., Sigma Theta Tau (Gamma Rho chpt., research award). Alpha Lambda Delta. Republican. Congregationalist. Home: 5805 E Mercer Way Mercer Island WA 98040

O'SHEA, ALICE TUOHY, child advocate attorney; b. Washington, Mar. 6, 1919; d. Thomas Bernard and Edna (Doyle) Tuohy; m. John J. O'Shea, May 31, 1947; children—Sean, Timothy, Kathleen, Patrick. J.D., Cath. U. Am., 1936, postgrad. in speech and drama, 1942; grad. Nat. Jud. Coll., 1978. Bar: Pa. 1974, U.S. Dist. Ct. (ea. dist.) Pa. 1974, U.S. Supreme Ct. 1978. Staff, Ho. of Reps., Washington, 1936-46; assoc. devel. dir. Med. Mission Sisters, Fox Chase, Pa., 1967-70; faculty dept. theology, Gwynedd-Mercy Coll., Gwynedd, Valley, Pa., 1966-67; co-founder, original assoc. dir. community service Cardinal's Commn. on Human Relations, 1964-66; staff atty. Defender Assn. Phila., 1974-76, founder, chief legal officer, adminstr. child advocacy unit, 1976-81, defender child advocate, 1981—; lectr. in field. Mem. forensic sect. Hahnemann Med. Coll. and Hosp., 1979—; mem. Joint Council on Criminal Justice System of Pa. Commonwealth, 1979-80; adv. bd. Big Sisters, 1977—; mem. Gov.'s Commn. on Status of Women, 1967-73; chmn. bd. adv. council St. Mar's Home for Children, 1958-64; bd. dirs., exec. com., v.p. Parents Anonymous, 1980—; mem. Middle Atlantic Partnership for Children and Youth, 1982—; bd. dirs. St. Thomas Moore Soc., No. Home for Children; bd. dirs., exec. com. The Bridge, 1978—. Mem. Phila. Bar Assn., ABA, Pa. Bar Assn., Brehon Legal Soc., Nat. Assn. Women Lawyers, Am. Psychology Law Soc., Am. Arbitration Assn. Home: 602 Washington Square S Philadelphia PA 19106 Office: Defender Assn Philadelphia 121 N Broad St 9th Floor Philadelphia PA 19106

OSINSKI, (BONNIE) ELIZABETH, fund raiser; b. Buffalo, Apr. 19, 1941; d. Henry J. and Antoinette R. (Lopian) O.; B.A., Mercyhurst Coll., 1962; M.P.A., N.Y. U., 1981. Social worker Cath. Charities of Buffalo, 1962-64; media analyst A.C. Nielsen Co., N.Y.C., 1964-66, WNEW-TV, N.Y.C., 1966-68, WOR-TV, N.Y.C., 1968-70, The Marschalk Co., N.Y.C., 1970-73, Ted Bates Advt., N.Y.C., 1973-75; program officer, cons. N.Y. region ACTION, 1975-77; owner, pres. Project Planning Perspectives, N.Y.C., 1979-82; lectr. Grad. Sch. Public Adminstrn., N.Y. U., 1979—; trainer Center Mgmt. Devel. and Orgn. Research, Baruch Coll., 1980—; dir. grant resources Am. Lung Assn., N.Y.C., 1982-84; dir. devel. ICIS/The Door, N.Y.C., 1984—. Mem. Grad. Sch. Public Adminstrn. Alumni Assn. (dir. 1981—), Am. Soc. Public Adminstrn., Nat. Soc. Fund Raising Execs. (dir. 1986—). Club: Appalachian Mountain.

OSKEY, D. BETH, banker; b. Red Wing, Minn., Dec. 23, 1921; d. Alvin E. and Effie O. (Thompson) Feldman; student U. Wis., River Falls, 1939-41; B.A., Met. State U., Minn., 1975; grad. degree in banking, U. Wis., 1973, postgrad. in banking, 1977; student in interior decorating LaSalle Extension U., Chgo., 1970; m. Warren B. Oskey, Sept. 27, 1941; children—Jo Cheryl, Warren A., Peter (dec.), Jeffrey L. Officer, Hiawatha Nat. Bank, Hager City, Wis., 1959—, cashier, 1978-79, pres., 1979, exec. v.p., dir., sec. bd. dirs., 1959—, now also chmn. bd., sec., mem. discount com.; with First Nat. Bank of Glenwood, Glenwood City, Wis., 1965— pres., exec. v.p., 1979—, dir., sec. bd., 1965—, sec., mem. discount com.; v.p. bd. dirs. speaker on women in banking. Banking com. Vo-Tech Sch., Red Wing, Minn.; former officer civic orgns. Mem. Ind. Bankers Am., Wis. Bankers Assn., Am. Bankers Assn. Republican. Lutheran. Club: Minn. Fedn. Women's Clubs (treas., pres. dist. III, 1978—, v.p. Minn.). Home: 1022 Hallstrom Dr Red Wing MN 55066 also 1561 Leisure World Mesa AZ 85206 Office: Hiawatha National Bank Hager City WI 54014

OSLER, DOROTHY K., state legislator; b. Dayton, Ohio, Aug. 19, 1923; d. Carl M. and Pearl A. (Tobias) Karstaedt; B.S. cum laude in Bus. Adminstrn., Miami U., Oxford, Ohio, 1945; m. David K. Osler, Oct. 26, 1946; children—Scott C., David D. Mem. Conn. Ho. of Reps., 1973—. Mem. Greenwich (Conn.) Rep. Town Meeting, 1968—, Eastern Greenwich Women's Rep. Club, 1970—; sec. Conn. Student Loan Found., 1973-83, v.p., 1983-84; mem. Spl. Edn. Cost Commn., 1976-77, Sch. Fin. Adv. Panel, 1977-78, Edn. Equity Study Com., 1980-81, Commn. on Goals for U. Conn. Health Center, 1975-76, Commn. Conn.'s Future, 1985—; bd. dirs. ARC, 1975. Mem. Conn. Order of Women Legislators (sec. 1983-84, pres. 1985-86), LWV (pres. Greenwich chpt. 1965-67, sec. Conn. chpt. 1967-72), AAUW (dir. 1971-73), Mortar Board, Phi Beta Kappa, Alpha Omicron Pi. Republican. Christian Scientist. Bi-weekly columnist local newspaper, 1973—.

OSLER, JULIE, public relations executive; b. N.Y.C., Feb. 11, 1947; d. David Saul Osler and Grace Rose (Brown) Osler Sonenblick; m. Jonathan Dolger, Oct. 6, 1974 (div. 1983). B.A., George Washington U., 1968; M.A., Columbia U., 1969. Tchr. Lexington Sch. for Deaf, N.Y.C., 1969-73; editorial coordinator New Ingenue Mag., 1973-75; assoc. dir. pub. relations PBS, 1975-80; dir. pub. relations Showtime, 1980-81; v.p. pub. relations The Entertainment Channel, 1981-83; pres. Julie Osler Pub. Relations, 1983—. U.S. Office Edn. fellow 1968-69. Mem. Am. Women in Radio and TV, Internat. Radio and TV Soc., Women in Communication, Broadcast Promotion Assn., Women in Cable, Pub. Relations Soc. Am., Women Execs. in Pub. Relations, Women's Media Group. Office: Julie Osler Pub Relations 515 Madison Ave Suite 700 New York NY 10022

OSMAN, MARY ELLA WILLIAMS, journal editor; b. Honea Path, S.C.; d. Humphrey Bates and Jennie Louise (Williams) Williams; student Coll. William and Mary, Ga. State Coll. for Women; A.B., Presbyn. Coll., 1939; B.S. in L.S., U. N.C., 1944; m. John Osman, Oct. 22, 1936. Asst. librarian Presbyn. Coll., Clinton, S.C., 1936-38, Union Theol. Sem., Richmond, Va., 1938-44; sr. cataloger, asst. librarian Southwestern Coll., Memphis, 1944-52; asst. test cities project Ford Found. Fund for Adult Edn., N.Y.C., 1952-57, assoc. dir. office of info., 1957-61, exec. asst. to pres., sec. to bd. dirs., 1960-61; asst. librarian AIA, Washington, 1962-68, asst. editor AIA Jour., 1969-72, assoc. editor, 1972-77, sr. editor, 1978—. Mem. AIA (hon.), Chi Delta Phi, Kappa Delta. Presbyn. Contbr. to various mags. Home: 415 Harden St Columbia SC 29205 Office: AIA 1735 New York Ave Washington DC 20006

OSMOND, LYNN JOYCE, symphony orchestra manager; b. St. Catherines, Ont., Can., Mar. 31, 1957; d. George Osmond and Joyce Edith Stanton. B.Music with honors, Queens U., 1980; numerous courses and seminars in field, Adminstrv. asst. Assn. of Can. Orchs., Ont. Fedn. of Symphony Orchs., Toronto, 1980-81; exec. dir. Mississauga Symphonic Assn., Ont., 1981-83; youth orch. coordinator for Ont., Ont. Fedn. Symphony Orchs., Toronto, 1981-84; festival co ordinator Ont. Youth Orch. Festival, 1983-83, gen. mgr. Thunder Bay Symphony Orch., Ont., 1983-85, Orch. London Ont., Can., 1985—; dir. Can. Assn. Youth Orchs., Banff, Alta.; mem. adv. bd. Performing Arts Mgmt. Confedn. Coll., Thunder Bay, 1984—; bd. dirs. performing Arts Ctr. for Tomorrow (PACT). Arts Mgmt. Tng. grantee Can. Council, 1984. Mem. Thunder Bay Regional Arts Council (pres.), Thunder Bay Press Club, Thunder Bay Women's Network, Thunder Bay Toastmaster's Internat., Ont. Fedn. Symphony Orchestras (dir. dirs.), London C. of C., Dirs. Club of London, Am. Symphony Orch. League (bd. dirs. youth orch.), Queen's U. Alumni Assn. (class agt.). Conservative. Anglican. Avocations: music, sports. Home: 5-234 Central Ave London ON N6A 1M8 Canada

OSMUN, ELAINE, racquetball and fitness facility executive; b. Houston, Feb. 19, 1957; d. Dean Warren and Mary Virginia (Mathews) O. B.S. in Edn., Stephen F. Austin State U., 1979, M.Ed., 1982. Tchr., coach Sabine Ind. Sch. Dist., Gladewater, Tex., 1979-81; grad. asst. Stephen F. Austin State U., Nacogdoches, Tex., 1981-82; owner, gen. mgr. The Court Club, Nacogdoches, 1983—. Mem. Internat. Racquet Sports Assn., Am. Amateur Racquetball Assn. East Tex.-North La. Racquetball Club Assn., Nacogdoches County C. of C. Republican Episcopalian. Avocations; racquetball; camping; backpacking. Office: The Court Club 4822 N University Dr Nacogdoches TX 75961

OSSENBERG, HELLA SVETLANA, psychoanalyst; b. Kiev, Russia, June 10, 1930; came to U.S., 1957, naturalized, 1964; d. Anatole E. and Tatiana N. (Dombrovski) Donath; diploma langs. and psychology, U. Heidelberg (W. Ger.), 1953; M.S., Columbia U., 1968; cert. Nat. Psychol. Assn. Psychoanalysis, 1977; m. Carl H. Ossenberg, June 7, 1958. Sr. psychiat. social worker VA Mental Hygiene Clinic, N.Y.C., 1968-80, pvt. practice psychoanalysis, N.Y.C., 1975—; mem. Theodor Reik Cons. Center, 1978—; field instr. Columbia U., Fordham U. schs. social work. Mem. Nat. Assn. Social Workers, Acad. Cert. Social Workers, Nat. Psychol. Assn. Psychoanalysis, Nat. Assn. Advancement Phychoanalysis (Am. Bds. Accreditation and Certification), Council Psychoanalytic Psychotherapists. Home: 820 West End Ave New York NY 10025 Office: 345 W 58th St New York NY 10019

OSSOFSKY, HELEN JOHNS (MRS. ELI OSSOFSKY), physician; b. Phila., Dec. 7, 1921; d. William Calloway and Gertrude (Schindele) Johns; A.B., Mt. Holyoke Coll., 1943; student Women's Med. Coll. Pa., 1950-52; M.D., Johns Hopkins U., 1954; m. Eli Ossofsky, Aug. 8, 1950, (dec. Oct. 1950). Intern Oslev Med. Service, Johns Hopkins, 1954-55, resident Pediatrics Cornell U., N.Y. Hosp., 1955-56, Pediatrics Johns Hopkins, 1956-57; research assoc. Johns Hopkins Sch. Hygiene and Pub. Health, 1957-59; asst. prof. Georgetown U. Sch. Medicine, 1959-66, asso. prof. pediatrics, 1966-79; supervisory med. officer D.C. Dept. Pub. Health, 1959-62, med. cons. div. mental retardation, 1967-69; child psychiatry consultation practice, McLean, Va., 1966—. Cons., Inst. Child Health and Human Devel., NIH, Bethesda, Md., 1962-63; cons. in med. tng. div. chronic diseases USPHS, 1964-65; cons. Va. Assn. Children with Learning Disabilities, Psychiatric Inst. Washington, 1972—fellow Am. Acad. Pediatrics, 1975; lectr. Cath. U. Sch. Cardiovascular Nursing, 1959-79; mem. advisory council Cybernetic Research Inst. Mem. Fairfax County Med. Soc., AMA, Washington Psychiat. Soc., Am. Psychiat. Assn., Johns Hopkins Med. and Surg. Assn., Phi Beta Kappa. Author: Tumors of the Eye and Adnexa in Infancy and Childhood, 1962; also articles in profl. jours. Address: 1333 Merrie Ridge Rd McLean VA 22101

OSTAP, MARTINE ELIZABETH, educator; b. New Brunswick, N.J., Mar. 31, 1959; d. Helen M. O.; B.A. with honors, in English, with honors in Am. Studies, U. Wyo., 1981, M.A. in Am. Studies, 1984; M.A. in English, U. Tex., El Paso, 1983; postgrad. in English U. N. Mex. Instr. English U. Tex., El Paso, 1981-83, research asst. English composition, 1982; Teaching assoc. English, U. N. Mex. Contbr. to Jack London Newsletter. William Robertson Coe fellow, 1984. Mem. Omicron Delta Kappa. Home: 1271 N 17th St Laramie WY 82070 Office: Dept of English Humanities Bldg Room 264 U N Mex Albuquerque N Mex 87131

OSTER, ROSE MARIE GUNHILD, university administrator; b. Stockholm, Feb. 26, 1934; d. Herbert Jonas and Emma Wilhelmina (Johnson) Hagetorn; came to U.S., 1958; Fil. mag., U. Stockholm, 1956; D. Phil., Kiel (Germany) U., 1958; m. Ludwig F. Oster, May 17, 1956; children—Ulrika, Mattias.

Postdoctoral research fellow linguistics Yale U., 1958-60, research fellow Germanic langs., 1960-64, lectr. Swedish, 1964-66; mem. faculty U. Colo., Boulder, 1966-80, assoc. prof. Germanic langs. and lits., 1970-77, prof., 1977-80, chmn. dept., 1972-75, assoc. dean Grad. Sch., 1975-79, assoc. vice chancellor for grad. affairs, 1979-80; dean for grad. studies and research U. Md., College Park, 1980-83, prof. Germanic langs. and lits., 1980—. Mem. Fulbright Nat. Screening Com. Scandinavia, 1973, 83-86; mem. selection com. for Scandinavia, Council for Internat. Exchange of Scholars, 1983-87; cons. panelist Nat. Endowment for Humanities, 1975—, mem. bd. cons., 1980—; state coordinator Am. Council on Edn., Colo., 1978-80, Md., 1981-83; mem. exec. com. Assn. Grad. Schs., 1980-83; mem. deans exec. com. African-Am. Inst., 1981—; cons. in field. Carnegie fellow, 1974; grantee Swedish Govt., Am. Scandinavian Found. Mem. Soc. Advancement Scandinavian Studies (pres. 1979-80), Am. Scandinavian Assn. Nat. Capital Area (pres. 1983—), MLA, Am.-Scandinavian Found., Am. Assn. Higher Edn., AAUP, NOW. Contbr. articles and revs. to profl. publs. Home: 8315 North Brook Ln #303 Bethesda MD 20814 Office: Jimenez Bldg U Md College Park MD 20742

OSTERBERG, CHERYL LYNN, lawyer; b. Redbank, N.J., June 18, 1951; d. Wesley Harold and Mary Warburton (Norman) Osterberg. B.A., U. Colo., 1976; J.D., So. Tex. Coll. Law, 1982. Bar: Tex. 1983. Mem. sr. faculty Am. Coll. Real Estate, Houston, 1982—; sole practice, Conroe, Tex., 1983—; vol. lawyer Tex. Farm Crisis Hotline, Tex. Dept. Agr. Vol. John Hill Statewide Steering Com., Austin, Tex., 1984. Mem. ABA, Tex. Bar Assn., Montgomery County Bar Assn., So. Tex. Coll. Law Alumni Assn. Office: 603 N San Jacinto Conroe TX 77301

OSTERMAN, CAROL ANN, sales representative; b. Detroit, Dec. 25, 1954; d. Charles Thomas and Betty Louise (Bryant) Little; m. Daniel Robert Osterman, Aug. 19, 1973; children—Brandon Todd, Adam Brent. Student Oakland Community Coll., 1975-77; B.A., Birmingham Conservatory, Mich., 1972. Salesperson, Gantos Inc., Novi, Mich., 1978-79; supr., dept. mgr. K-Mart Corp., Plymouth, Mich., 1979-81; sales assoc. Real Estate One, Farmington Hills, Mich., 1982—; sales merchandiser Lipton/Lawry's Inc., Englewood Cliffs, N.J., 1983-84; sales rep., shelf mgmt. The Pfeister Co., Livonia, Mich., 1984—; cons. We Shop-You Stop, Inc., Canton, Mich., 1985-86; mktg. cons. Electrogas Service Co., Southfield, Mich., 1983-86. Mem. Mich. Citizens Lobby, Lansing, 1982; bd. dirs. Jaycees, Canton, Mich., 1986; mem. Smithsonian Assocs., Washington, 1986; others. Recipient Sales recognition award Treesweet Products, 1986, Pillsbury Products, 1985, Tyson Products, 1985, Welch's products, 1985. Mem. Nat. Assn. Female Execs., Aircraft Owners and Pilots Assn. Avocations: pilot; fitness; sailing; camping; photography. Home: 42788 Saltz Rd Canton MI 48187 Office: The Pfeister Co 36300 Schoolcraft Livonia MI 48187

OSTOYICH, SANDRA MARIE, librarian; b. N.Y.C., Jan. 5, 1939; d. Joseph F. and Theresa L. (Troglio) Bonesio; m. Matthew John Ostoyich, Aug. 1, 1965; children—Joseph Allen, Thomas James. B.A., Antioch Coll., 1960; M.L.S., SUNY-Albany, 1971. Editorial asst. Magnum Publs., N.Y.C., 1960-63; tchr. Boiceville pub. schs. (N.Y.), 1963-65; reference librarian, Kingston Library (N.Y.), 1971-73; media specialist Saugerties Pub. Schs. (N.Y.), 1974—, mem. computer task force, 1982. Active LWV, Saugerties Citizens Advocating Responsible Edn. Mem. ALA, N.Y. Library Assn., Sch. Library Media Specialists of Southeastern N.Y., Middle States Assn. Schs. and Colls. (vis. com.), Beta Phi Mu. Roman Catholic. Home: 2076 2 Sila Dr Saugerties NY 12477 Office: Saugerties High Sch Washington Ave Extension Saugerties NY 12477

OSTRAGER, PAMELA GOODMAN, lawyer; b. N.Y.C., Dec. 7, 1949; d. Morton and Marilyn Goodman; m. Barry R. Ostrager, Apr. 8, 1972; 1 dau., Ann-Elizabeth. B.A., CCNY, 1970; J.D., N.Y. Law Sch., 1973. Bar: N.Y. 1974. Law clk. to judge U.S. Dist. Ct. (so. dist.) N.Y. 1973-75; assoc., then ptnr. firm Coudert Bros., N.Y.C., 1975—. Mem. Assn. Bar City of New York (mem. copyright com.), Fed. Bar Council (fed. bar com.). Home: 930 Fifth Ave New York NY Office: Coudert Bros 200 Park Ave New York NY 10017

OSTRANDER, JOYCE MARY, temporary personnel services provider, motivational speaker; b. Buffalo, Dec. 25, 1949; d. Mary Dorothy (Rybczynski) Landwehr; m. Randolph M. Ulm, Sept. 7, 1968 (div. 1978); m. Timothy Herbert Ostrander, Oct. 23, 1983; children—Scott, Tracey. Student SUNY-Buffalo, 1968-69, Bryant and Stratton U. Sales rep. Victor Temporary Services, Buffalo, 1970-79; gen. mgr. Marcott Assoc. Temporaries, Buffalo, 1980-82; owner, gen. mgr. Temp Careers, Inc., Buffalo, and Bradenton, Fla., 1982—; speaker to profl. groups and in-service seminars. Active Boys Clubs of Manatee, Fla.; bd. dirs. Everywoman Opportunity Ctr. Mem. Nat. Assn. Female Execs. (network dir.), Nat. Assn. Temporary Services, Buffalo Assn. Temporary Services, Buffalo C. of C., Sarasota C. of C. (com. of 100). Republican. Avocations: skiing; travel; piano; church-related activities. Home: 19 Devereaux Ave Buffalo NY 14214 Office: Temp Careers Inc 547 Franklin St Buffalo NY 14202

OSTROM, JACQUELYN RENEE, public relations executive; b. Lockport, N.Y., Dec. 14, 1950; d. Elmer Van and Helen Louise (Cain) Ostrom; B.A., Ohio State U., 1973; postgrad. U. Fla., 1978; m. Theodore P. Remley, Jr., Dec. 30, 1977 (div. Apr. 1982). Congressional intern Rep. Henry P. Smith, III, Washington, 1970; floor dir. Sta. WLWC-TV, Columbus, Ohio, 1973; reporter/producer Sta. WSVA-TV-AM, Harrisonburg, Va., 1973-75; reporter/anchor Sta. WDBJ-TV, Roanoke, Va., 1975-76; public relations adminstr. and tng. asst. Dominion Bankshares Corp., Roanoke, 1976-77; writer/producer Health Ctr. Communications Office, U. Fla., Gainesville, 1978; asso. dir. media edn. and producer U.S. C. of C., Washington, 1978-79; dir. pub. relations Nat. Health Agys. for Combined Fed. Campaign, Alexandria, Va., 1979-83; pub. relations and broadcast cons., 1983—; cons., lectr. Pres. bd. dirs. Arlington Homeowners Assn., 1981-83; chmn. Arlington Archtl. Control Com., 1980-81; sec. bd. dirs. First United Meth. Ch., Salem, Va., 1976-77; mem. Annandale United Meth. Ch., 1981—. Mem. Women in Communications, Ohio State U. Alumni Assn., Sigma Delta Chi. Club: Washington Ski. Contbr. articles to profl. jours. Home: 2737-D S Walter Reed Dr Arlington VA 22206 Office: PO Box 6450 Arlington VA 22206

OSTWALD, SHARON KAY, public health educator, nursing consultant; b. Gary, Ind., Jan. 4, 1941; d. James William and Vera Ellen (Seneff) Mills; m. Melvin George Ostwald, Oct. 8, 1966; children—James Melvin, Tanya Kay. Nursing Diploma, West Suburban Hosp., 1962; B.S., Wheaton Coll., 1964; M.S., U. Minn., 1976, Ph.D., 1986; postgrad. Tex. A&M U., 1979. Cert. pub. health nurse, adult nurse practitioner. Instr., Swedish Hosp., Mpls., 1964-69, Luth. Deaconess Hosp., Mpls., 1971-74; asst. prof. U. Minn., Mpls., 1974—; cons. VA Med. Ctr., St. Cloud, Minn., 1980—; pres. Ostwald Assocs., Inc., Excelsior, Minn., 1983—; clin. cons. Minn. Hosp. Assn., St. Paul, 1975-76; research cons. The Press, Inc., Chanhassen, Minn., 1984-85; primary health cons. Struve Clinic, Inc., Mpls., 1979—, nursing cons. Mt. Olivet Homes, Inc., Mpls., 1974-84. Author audio-visual programs. Contbr. articles to profl. jours. Grantee Northwest Area Found., 1984, Sigma Alpha Epsilon Nat. Leadership Found., 1983. Mem. Am. Pub. Health Assn., Gerontol. Soc. Am., Minn. Pub. Health Assn., Sigma Theta Tau, Phi Delta Kappa. Lutheran. Club: Campus U. Minn. Office: Univ Minn SPH 420 Delaware St SE (Mayo 197) Minneapolis MN 55455

O'SULLIVAN, LYNDA TROUTMAN, lawyer; b. Oil City, Pa., Aug. 30, 1952; d. Perry John and Vivian Dorothy (Schreffler) Troutman; m. P. Kevin O'Sullivan, Dec. 15, 1979. B.A., Am. U., 1974; J.D., Georgetown U., 1978, postgrad; Bar: D.C. 1978; assoc. firm Chapman, Duff & Paul, Washington, 1978-82, Gadsby & Hannah, Washington, 1983-85, Perkins Coie, Washington, 1985—; lectr. Contbr. articles to profl. jours. Mem. ABA (vice chmn. com. on acctg. and cost pricing sect. pub. contract law), D.C. Bar Assn., Women's Bar Assn. of D.C. Office: Perkins Coie 1110 Vermont Ave NW Washington DC 20005

OSVATH, MARIA BUJTAS, wholesale gem stones company executive; b. Pasadena, Calif., Feb. 10, 1962; d. Csaba and Kornelia Osvath. B.A., U. Pacific, 1984. Mgr. Smart Gems, Visalia, Calif., 1984; pres. The World of Gems, Visalia, 1985—. Voter registor Republican Party, Fresno, 1984. Roman Catholic. Avocations: tennis; horses. Office: The World of Gems PO Box 4155 Visalia CA 93277

OSVATH, SUSAN MARGARET, school librarian, educator; b. Holyoke, Mass., July 11, 1944; d. John Herbert Friedhaber and Anne Mary (Pruzinsky) Friedhaber Hard; m. Robert Osvath, Feb. 17, 1973; 1 dau., Rebecca Jeanne. B.A., Daemen Coll., 1967; M.L.S., State U. Coll.-Geneseo, 1974. Tchr. English, French, DeSales High Sch., Columbus, Ohio, 1967-68; housemother St. Vincent's Orphanage, Columbus, 1968; tchr. English, French, Mater Dei High Sch., New Monmouth, N.J., 1968-69; records librarian Children's Aid Soc., Buffalo, 1970; tchr. English, French, religion, library Archbishop Carroll High Sch., Buffalo, 1970-74; librarian asst. Arcade Free Library (N.Y.), 1975-81; sch. librarian Pioneer High Sch., Yorkshire, N.Y., 1981—; council mem. Cattaraugus-Allegany Sch. Library System, 1986—. Mem. Citizens' Activist Group to fight zoning change, Arcade, N.Y., 1982-83; tchr. St. Mary's Ch., East Arcade, N.Y., 1977-84, lector, 1980-84. Mem. ALA, N.Y. Library Assn., Sch. Library Assn. Western N.Y. Roman Catholic. Home: 2269 Sullivan Rd East Arcade NY 14009 Office: Pioneer High Sch Library PO Box 579 Yorkshire NY 14173

OTI, MARIA MILAGROSA, magazine executive; b. Yaguajay, Las Villas, Cuba, Dec. 8, 1955; came to U.S., 1961, naturalized, 1970; d. Enrique Alberto and Maria Milagros (Celaya) Oti; m. Michael Christopher Howell, Dec. 30, 1977 (div. 1980). B.B.A., Fla. Internat. U., 1983. Salesperson, French Rooms Ltd., Kansas City, Mo., 1976, Styx, Baer & Fuller, Overland Park, Kans., 1976; orthodontic asst. Dr. David Parrish, Overland Park, 1976-77; casualty underwriting corr. Wausau Ins., Overland Park, Kans., 1978-80; mgr. mktg. The Excel Group, Miami, 1982-83; circulation mgr. Miami-South Fla. Mag., Miami, 1983—, South Fla. Home & Garden, 1984—. Participant, Leadership Miami, 1984. Mem. Miami Design Preservation League, Tropical Audubon Soc., Fla. Zool. Soc., Am. Mktg. Assn. (v.p. pub. relations Fla. Internat. U. chpt. 1982, pres. chpt. 1982-83). Office: Miami-South Fla Mag 75 SW 15 Rd Miami FL 33129

OTSTOTT, GRETA VIRGINIA, interior designer, artist; b. Dallas, July 22, 1933; d. Ramon E. and Virginia H. (Anderson) Espinosa; m. Daniel Dushane Otstott, Jan. 7, 1955; children—Dana D. Otstott Shear, Cheryl Lynn. A.A., El Centro Coll., 1975; B.A., So. Meth. U., 1954. Artist, Fenne-Vaughn Co., Dallas, 1954-55, Dallas Times Herald, 1955-57, Edward Fields Inc., Dallas, 1973-74; head design ctr. Standard Fixture Co., Dallas, 1976-81; art dir. Hancock Ltd., Dallas, 1981-82; owner, mgr. Go Enterprises, Dallas, 1982—. Pres. Richardson Unitarian Ch., Dallas, 1976-77; leader troop Girl Scouts U.S.A., 1964-69, also tchr. Explore Group, Dallas, 1968-74. Mem. Am. Soc. Interior Designers (cert. 1980), Am. Inst. Bus. Designers, Am. Needlework Craft Guild, Dallas Needlework and Textile Guild (sec. 1986-87), Fiber Artists of Dallas (sec.). Author: Bride of the 50's, Woman of the 80's, 1983.

OTT, ELIZABETH KARG, psychologist; b. Akron, Ohio, Aug. 11, 1929; d. Bert George and Mary Magdelen (Sadler) Karg; B.A., Western State Coll. Colo., 1969; M.A., U. Akron, 1971, Ph.D., 1974. children—Christine, Mary Catherine. Tchr. elem. schs., Akron, 1958-65; coordinator tng. profl. staff State of Ohio, Columbus, 1974; asst. prof. psychology Marywood Coll., Scranton, Pa., 1974-77; clin. dir. psychology internship tng. program N.E. Ohio U. Coll. Medicine, Cuyahoga Falls, 1977—, asst. prof., 1981—; pvt. practice, Cuyahoga Falls, 1974—; dir. psychology Fallsview Psychiat. Hosp. Mem. Am. Psychol. Assn., Ohio Psychol. Assn., Cleve. Psychol. Assn., State Assn. Psychologists and Psychol. Assts., Soc. Clin. and Exptl. Hypnosis. Roman Catholic. Home: 1340 Weathervane Ln Akron OH 44313 Office: 2125 Front St Cuyahoga Falls OH 44221

OTT, LAURIE ANN, nurse; b. Chester, Pa., Aug. 28, 1959; d. Ellwood Eugene and Phyllis (Frazier) O. B.S. in Nursing, Thomas Jefferson U., 1981; M.S. in Nursing, Va. Commonwealth U., 1984, Clin. Nurse Specialist, 1984. Nurse intern Cedars of Lebanon Hosp., Miami, Fla., 1979-80, Met. Hosp., Phila., 1980-81, Childrens Hosp. Phila., 1981; head nurse Summit Camp, Honesdale, Pa., summer 1983; nurse Cumberland Hosp., New Kent, Va., 1983—; nurse, clinician Med. Coll. Va., Richmond, 1981—. Advisor med. explorers Robert E. Lee council Boy Scouts Am., Richmond, 1981-82; instr. ARC, Richmond, 1981—; cons. Sudden Infant Death Syndrome Guild, Richmond, 1981—; asst. coach Spl. Olympics, Richmond, 1982, 83. Fellow Nat. Assn. Pediatric Nurse Assocs. and Practitioners; mem. Infant Mental Health Assn., Nat. Nurses Assn., Va. Nurses Assn., Va. Perinatal Nurses Assn., Sigma Theta Tau. Republican. Home: 5810 D Westower Dr Richmond VA 23225 Office: Medical Coll of Va Marshall St Richmond VA 23225

OTT, PAULINE ROXANN, nurse; b. Balt., Mar. 25, 1955; d. Thurston Roosevelt and Helen Lydia (Boyer) Glass; m. Michael James Dean Ott, July 22, 1983; 1 child, Matthew Earl. A.A., Los Angeles City Coll., 1975, A.Nursing, 1982; B.A. in Social Welfare, San Francisco State U., 1977. R.N., Calif. Nurse, St. Joseph Med. Ctr., Burbank, Calif., 1982—. Caravan dir. summer camps for youth Wilshire YMCA, Los Angeles, 1975-81. Office: St Joseph Med Ctr Buena Vista/Alameda Burbank CA 91505

OTTE, LAURA JEAN, county health department adminstrator; b. Concordia, Kans., July 4, 1949; d. Irwin Edgar Johnson and Carol Lee (Stanton) Williams; m. Melvin Alfred Otte, Dec. 17, 1971; children—Brenda Sue, Matthew Lee, Jason Andrew. Grad. Asbury Hosp. Sch. Nursing, Salina, Kans., 1970; part-time student Kans. State U., 1975-82. Charge nurse Morton County Hosp., Elkhart, Kans., 1970-71; ICU, emergency rm., Med. charge nurse Mitchell County Hosp., Beloit, Kans., 1971-76; adminstr. Mitchell County Health Dept., North Central Kans. Home Health, Beloit, 1977—; sch. nurse St. John Grad Sch., Beloit, St. John High Sch., Beloit, St. Boniface High Sch., Tipton, Kans., 1977—; bd. dirs., nurse, sec. Solomon Valley Hospice, Inc., Beloit, 1982—; Bloodmobile vol. nurse ARC, Beloit, 1975—; vol. nurse Am. Heart Assn., Beloit, 1978-83; publicity dir., cons. Beloit Cancer Soc. State and fed. health grantee. Mem. Am. Nurses Assn., Kans. Pub. Health Assn., Kans. Assn. Local Health Depts., Kans. State Nurses Assn. (dist. bd. dirs. 1979-80), Kans. Assn. Home Health Agys., Kans. Pub. Health Assn. Republican. Lutheran. Clubs: Andromeda, Willow Springs Players (Beloit) (sec. 1985—). Home: 414 E Court St Beloit KS 67420 Office: Box 217 400 W 8th St Beloit KS 67420

OTTO, DIANE LYNN, lawyer; b. St. Louis, May 7, 1958; d. Loten Thomas and Wilma May (Wilson) Baskin; m. Scott William Otto, June 17, 1978. B.A., Oakland U., 1979; J.D., U. Detroit, 1982. Bar: Mich. 1982. Law clk., atty. Mich. Nat. Bank, Troy, Mich., 1980-82; assoc. law firm Lapham & Doyle, Farmington, Mich., 1982-83; atty. Co-op Services Credit Union, Dearborn, Mich., 1983-84; legal cons. to pres., atty. Citizens Comml. & Savs. Bank, Flint, 1984—. Contbr. articles to profl. jours. Sec., Sugden Lake Civic Assn., 1982-84. U.S. Govt. law sch. tuition grantee, 1979, 80. Mem. ABA, Mich. State Bar Assn., Women Lawyers Assn., Oakland County Bar Assn., Genesee County Bar Assn. Lutheran.

OTTO, JOAN RAE, educational diagnostician; b. Galveston, Tex., Aug. 15, 1948; d. Robert Lloyal and Marjory Lucille (Waterman) Yelderman; m. Clarence McKay Otto, Jr., July 15, 1972; children—Kathryn Jaquelene, Michelle McKay. B.S., U. Tex., 1970; M.Ed., San Houston State U., 1975. Cert. profl. ednl. diagnostician. Tchr. elem. schs. Cypress-Fairbanks Ind. Sch. Dist., Houston, 1971-73, Lamar Ind. Sch. Dist., Rosenberg, Tex., 1973-76; real estate broker Century 21 McKay Otto, Rosenberg, 1976-82; ednl. diagnostician Fort Bend Ind. Sch. Dist., Stafford, Tex., 1982-83, Austin Ind. Sch. Dist. (Tex.), 1983-84. Mem. Council Exceptional Children, Tex. Classroom Tchrs. Assn., Hou-Met Chpt. Tex. Ednl. Diagnosticians, DAR (registrar 1977-79). Club: New Century Garden (v.p., founder). Author: Teague-Waddel Home (Tex. Hist. Marker award) 1977. Home: 1803 Bay Hill Dr Austin TX 78746

OTTO, MARGARET AMELIA, librarian; b. Boston, Oct. 22, 1937; d. Henry Earlen and Mary (McLennan) O.; children—Christopher, Peter. A.B., Boston U., 1960; M.S., Simmons Coll., 1963, M.A., 1970; M.A. (hon.), Dartmouth Coll., 1981. Asst. sci. librarian M.I.T., Cambridge, 1963, Lindgren librarian, 1964-67, acting sci. librarian, 1967-69, asst. dir., 1969-75, asso. dir., 1976-79; librarian of coll. Dartmouth Coll., Hanover, N.H., 1979—; pres., chmn. bd. Universal Serials and Book Exchange, Inc., 1980-81. Council on Library Resources fellow, 1974; elected to Collegium of Disting. Alumnus Boston U., 1980. Mem. ALA. Home: 16 Dresden Rd Hanover NH 03755 Office: 115 Baker Library Dartmouth Coll Hanover NH 03755

OTTO, SARA VIRGINIA, molluscan histopathologist; b. Pitts., Sept. 2, 1942; d. Oscar Francis and Helen Virginia (Shook) O.; A.B., MacMurray Coll., 1964. Histotechnician, chemistry lab. technician Biol. Lab., Dept. of Interior, Oxford, Md., 1964-65; charge project lab. dept. pathobiology, tissue culture technician Johns Hopkins U., 1965-66; leader marine animal disease investigations Tidewater Adminstrn. Lab. Unit. Md. Dept. Natural Resources, Annapolis, 1967—; cons.; guest lectr. zoology U. Md. Former pres. Talbot Little Theatre. Mem. AAAS, Crustacean Soc., N.Y. Acad. Scis., Alliance Francaise, Sigma Xi. Club: Eastern Star (past matron). Editor Jour. Nat. Shellfisheries Assn., 1973-74; contbr. articles to profl. jours. Office: Maryland Dept Natural Resources Tawes State Office Bldg C 2 Annapolis MD 21401

OUBRE, JENNIFER VAL BOORMAN, business executive, accountant; b. South Bend, Ind., Feb. 14, 1951; d. Raymond D'Classe and Arlene Hazel (Brittian) Boorman; m. Mickey Lee Estep, Dec. 10, 1970 (div. 1971); m. Noah Joseph Oubre, Apr. 12, 1974; 1 child, Dawn Jayelyn. Student Ind. U. Fort Wayne Art Inst., 1969-71, Delgado Coll., Algiers, La., 1981-85. Artist The Rope Walk, Key West, Fla., 1970-72; mgr. Oakwood Villager Apts., Gretna, La., 1972-74; asst. mgr. Garden Oaks Apts., Algiers, 1974-75; corp. sec., controller Surplus Tires of La. Inc. and Gen. Indsl. Tire Supply, Harvey, La., 1977-86; controller Telex communications Western Union, New Orleans, 1984—; comml. artist, recruiting artwork U.S. Navy, New Orleans, 1972. Mem. Nat. Assn. Female Execs., Biloxi Miss. Art Assn. Avocations: oil and watercolor painting; graphic design. Home: 220 Brett Dr Gretna LA 70056 Office: PO Box 908 1444 Manhattan Blvd Harvey LA 70059

OUDENNE, MICHELE MARIE, state official, real estate salesperson; b. Trenton, N.J., Feb. 1, 1959; d. Dominick Anthony and Stella Madeline (Patermo) Iorio; m. Edward Harold Oudenne, May 31, 1986. Student U. Hartford, 1977-78; B.A. in Sociology, Rider Coll., 1981. Lic. in real estate, N.J. Ops. analyst N.J. Dept. Human Services, Trenton, 1982-84, sr. ops. analyst, 1984—; sales assoc. Krol Realty, Trenton, 1983—. Mem. Mercer County Realtor Assocs., Nat. Assn. Female Execs. Roman Catholic. Home: 25 Hemlock Ct Hamilton NJ 08619

OUELLETTE, ELAINE BRENDA, nurse, physician's assistant; b. Hamlin Plantation, Maine, June 20, 1955; d. Gerald Reginald and Constance B. (Duperry) Lapierre; m. Vernon Rodney Ouellette, June 1, 1977; 1 dau., Jennifer Lee. B.S.N. with honors, U. So. Maine, 1977; cert. physician's asst., Van Buren Hosp. (Maine), 1981. R.N., Maine. Staff nurse Van Buren Hosp., 1977-78, emergency and operating supr., 1978-85; instr. adult edn., 1980—, staff edn. instr., 1981—; instr. No. Maine Vocat. Tech. Inst., Presque Isle, Maine, 1983—; physician's asst. Dr. William Chan, Van Buren, 1982—; inservice coordinator Borderview Manor Nursing Home, 1984—; instr. pharmacology Personal Care Homes Assn., 1986—; instr. CPR, Advanced Cardiac Life Support; diabetes cons., educator. Mem. Centennial Com., Van Buren, 1982; sec. Reunion Com. Class of '73, Van Buren, 1983. Recipient Recognition award Van Buren Ambulance Service, 1982. Mem. Assn. Operating Room Nurses, Down East Assn. Physicians Assts., Am. Diabetes Assn., Diabetes Support Group, No. Maine Gymnastics Judges Assn. Democrat. Roman Catholic. Clubs: Van Buren Fire Dept. Women's Aux. (pres. 1982-83, v.p. 1983-84), Van Buren Hosp. Aux. Home: 21 Lynne St Van Buren ME 04785 Office: Van Buren Hosp 2 Main St Van Buren ME 04785

OUELLETTE, JANE LEE YOUNG, biology educator; b. Charlotte, N.C., Dec. 29, 1929; d. James Thomas and Nancy Isabel (Yarbrough) Young; m. Armand Roland Ouellette, Aug. 3, 1951 (dec. Oct. 1984); children—Elizabeth Anne, James Young, Emily Jane, Frances Lee. B.A., Winthrop Coll., 1950; M.A., Oberlin Coll., 1952; postgrad. Coll. Medicine, Baylor U., 1974, U. Tex.-Houston, 1976-83, Tex. Woman's U., 1980-82. Lic. tchr., Tex. Tchr. Marina Regina High Sch., Hartsdale, N.Y., 1969-70, Spring Ind. Sch. System, Tex., 1972-78; instr. biology North Harris County Coll., Houston, 1979—. Mem. Internat. Assn. for Study of Pain, N.Y. Acad. Sci., AAAS, Internat. Chronobiol. Soc., People to People Internat. Democrat. Home: 1619 Big Horn St Houston TX 77090 Office: North Harris County Coll 2700 W W Thorne Dr Houston TX 77073

OUTERBRIDGE, CHERYL ARLENE, lawyer; b. Monte Vista, Colo., July 11, 1943; d. George Herbert and Gladys Mae (Walker) Hazard; m. J. Robert Outerbridge June 4, 1961 (div.); 1 child, Grant Hazard; m. Carl F. Nagy, Nov. 16, 1985. B.A., U. Denver, 1968; J.D., U. Colo., 1975. Bar: Colo. 1975. Assoc., Gorsuch, Kirgis, Campbell, Walker & Grover, Denver, 1975-79; staff atty. Amax Inc., Golden, Colo., 1979-81, sr. atty., 1985—; editor Am. Law of Mining (2d edit.), Rocky Mt. Mineral Law Found., Denver, 1981-85. Contbr. articles to profl. jours. Mem. ABA, Colo. Bar Assn., Denver Bar Assn., Women in Mining (chmn. bylaws 1980), Order of Coif, Phi Beta Kappa. Office: 1707 Cole Blvd Golden CO 80401

OUTHWAITE, LUCILLE CONRAD, ballerina, educator; b. Peoria, Ill., Feb. 26, 1909; d. Frederick Albert and Della (Cornett) Conrad; m. Leonard Outhwaite, Mar. 1, 1936 (dec. 1978); children—Ann Outhwaite Maurer, Lynn Outhwaite Pulsifer. Student, U. Nebr., 1928-30, Mills Coll., 1931-32; student piano, Paris, 1933-35, Legat Sch., London, 1934, N.Y.C. Ballet, N.Y.C., 1936-41, Royal Ballet Sch., London, 1957-59. Tchr. ballet Perry Mansfield, Steamboat Springs, Colo., 1932, Cape Playhouse, Dennis, Mass., 1937-41, Jr. League, N.Y.C., 1937-41, King Coit Sch., N.Y.C., 1937-41; toured with Am. Ambassador Ballet, Europe and S. Am., 1933-35; owner, tchr. dance sch., Oyster Bay, N.Y., 1949-57. Producer, choreographer ballets Alice in Wonderland, 1951, Pied Piper of Hamlin, 1952. Author: Birds in Flight, 1984. Mem. English Speaking Union, Preservation Soc., Alliance Française, Delta Gamma. Republican. Episcopalian. Club: Mills. Coll., Spouting Rock Beach, Clambake (Newport, R.I.). Office: Beachmound Bellevue Ave Newport RI 02840

OUTTZ, JANICE HAMILTON, demographic researcher; b. Monroe, La., June 18, 1951; d. O'sha James and Virgie Mae (Richmond) Hamilton; m. James Lawrence Outtz, June 3, 1972; children—Jabari Hamilton, Hasina Hamilton. B.A., Howard U., 1972, M.A., 1976; postgrad. U. Md. Counselor, D.C. Juvenile Ct., 1970; research asst. Washington Ctr. Metro. Studies, 1971-76; instr. Montgomery Coll., Takoma Park, Md., 1975; program analyst Nat. Adv. Council, Washington, 1976; ednl. researcher Howard U., Washington, 1976-79; research assoc. Greater Washington Research Ctr., Washington, 1979—; survey researcher cons. Howard U., 1978, Hutchinson Family Service (Kans.), 1979, Community Found., Washington, 1980; analyst poverty data United Planning Orgn., Washington, 1981. Contbr. research articles to profl. jours. 1st v.p. Nat. Council Negro Women, Washington, 1984-86; mem. Prince George County LWV (Md.); newsletter editor Nat. Council Negro Women, 1980, 83-84; bd. dirs. Nat. Capital Area LWV, 1985-87. Howard U. fellow, 1973; named to Dean's Honor Roll, Howard U., 1971; recipient Mary McLeod Bethune award Nat. Council Negro Women, 1981. Mem. Assn. Pub. Policy Analysis, Govt. Research Assn., Am. Statis. Assn. Democrat. Roman Catholic. Home: 7208 Martin's Ct Lanham MD 20706 Office: Greater Washington Research Ctr 1717 Massachusetts Ave NW Washington DC 20036

OVERCASH-ANTHONY, CHERYL ANN, investment analyst; b. Abington, Pa., Feb. 12, 1955; d. Clifton Odel and Christine Ruth (von Brauchitsch) Overcash; m. David Banks Anthony, Jr., Aug. 29, 1981. B.A., Hollins Coll., 1977; M.B.A. Tex. Christian U., 1979. Acctg. mgr. Sanger Harris Co., Dallas, 1979-81; bus./market analyst Xerox Corp., Dallas, 1981-83; investment analyst Inter First Investment Mgmt., Dallas, 1983-85; investment analyst, portfolio mgr. Baulder Asset Mgmt., Denver, 1985—. Office: 5331 Mercedes Ave Dallas TX 75206

OVERCAST, SHERYL MEAKIN, advertising executive; b. Lynwood, Calif., May 31, 1956; d. Lawrence Neil and Bonnie Jean (Ritter) Meakin; m. Steven E. Overcast, Feb. 29, 1980. B.A., Calif. State U., 1979. Community relations dir. The Sawyer Schs., Westwood, Calif., 1979-81; account exec. Jaffe/Murr Advt., Inc., Anaheim, Calif., 1981-82; owner, mgr. Overcast Advt., Inc., Orange County, Calif., 1982—. Home: 21062 Shepherd Ln Huntington Beach CA 92646 Office: Overcast Advt 1301 Pacifico Anaheim CA 92802

OVERLAND, WANDA IDELLE, university administrator; b. Harvey, N.D., Sept. 15, 1953; d. Ingwald T. and Edna M. Overland; B.S., N.D. State U., 1975, M.S., 1982. Tchr. home econs. N.H. high schs., 1975-78; head resident residential life/housing N.D. State U., 1978-81, adminstrv. asst. Coll. Home Econs., 1978-81; exec. dir. YMCA at N.D. State U., 1981-84, student affairs officer, 1984—; tchr. adult edn. courses; speaker, cons., workshop leader in field. Chmn. N.D. State U. Campus Equity, 1982. Christine Finlayson scholar, 1978-80; Elsie Stark Martin scholar, 1974; named Hillsboro Outstanding Young Educator, 1978. Mem. Am. Personnel and Guidance Assn., Am. Home Econs. Assn., Kappa Delta Pi, Phi Upsilon Omicron. Republican. Lutheran.

Club: N.D. State U. Women's. Office: ND State U Memorial Union Fargo ND 58105

OVERMYER, ELIZABETH CLARK, television executive; b. Toledo, Ohio, July 1, 1957; d. Daniel Harrison and Shirley Ann (Clark) O. B.A., U. Denver, 1979. Assoc. producer ABC Sports Inc., N.Y.C., 1980-82; prodn. mgr. ABC Sports 1984 Olympic Unit, N.Y.C., 1983-84; prodn. mgr. Ohlmeyer Communications Cos., N.Y.C., 1985—; sr. prodn. mgr. ABC Sports 1988 Olympic Games, Calgary, 1986. Recipient Emmy award for TV series American Sportsman, 1981. Mem. Women in Communications, Inc. Republican. Episcopalian.

OVERSTREET, KATHLEEN, journalist; b. Savannah, Ga., July 19, 1951; d. Edward Kinchley and Evelyn (Griner) O.; student Wesleyan Coll., 1969-71; B.A. in Speech/Journalism, Ga. Southern Coll., 1973. Library asst. San Antonio Light, 1973-74, staff writer, 1974-81, asst. editor —Slot—, 1981-82, TV editor, 1982—. Founder Bexar County Women's Center, 1977, sec. bd. dirs., 1977-78, 82—, chmn. bd. dirs., 1978-80. Recipient Feature Writing award UPI, 1980, 1978. Mem. Women in Communications (dir.), San Antonio Press Club (dir.), Tex. Press Women, Local 25 Newspaper Guild, Sigma Delta Chi. Democrat. Office: PO Box 161 San Antonio TX 78291

OVERTON, HELEN PARKER (MRS. SAMUEL WATKINS OVERTON), Realtor; b. Memphis, Dec. 30, 1920; d. William and Pearl (Pinkston) Parker; m. Samuel Watkins Overton, Sept. 3, 1952; children—Helen Parker (Mrs. William Barron Brown), Napoleon Hill. Exec. sec. Memphis State U., 1941-43, Chgo. and So. Air Lines, 1943-46, Memphis Bd. Edn., 1948-50; dir. women's programs Sta. WHBQ-TV, Memphis, 1950-52. Pres., Beethoven Club, 1960-66, 72-78, Mid-South Opera Guild, 1967-85; dir. auditions Mid-South region Met. Opera, 1960-71, mem. nat. council, 1960-71; chmn. Tenn. Arts Commn., 1968-70; bd. dirs. Opera Memphis, 1956—, Arts Appreciation, 1960—, Tenn. Arts Commn., 1967-74. Mem. Sigma Alpha Iota, Alpha Gamma Delta. Clubs: Memphis Country (Memphis). Home: 5476 Collingwood Cove Memphis TN 38119

OVERTON, MEREDITH ANN, educator; b. Kansas City, Mo., Jan. 4, 1947; d. James Howard and Viola May (Moats) Holloway. B.S. in Home Econs., Kans. State U., 1969; M.S., U. Kans., 1973; postgrad. U. Mo., 1974-75. Dietetic intern Houston VA Hosp., 1969-70; adminstrv./clin. dietitian Mpls. VA Hosp., 1970-71; dietitian coordinator for nutrition edn. med. students U. Kans. Med. Center, 1972-74, clin. dietitian, instr., 1973-74; clin. dietitian/trainee counselor Good Samaritan Hosp. and Med. Center, Portland, Oreg., 1975-76; sales rep. nutritional div. Mead Johnson, Portland, 1976-78; asst. prof., dir. dietetic internship Oreg. Health Scis. U., Portland, 1978—; mem. faculty Clackamas Community Coll., 1976-78, Portland State U., 1978-81; mem. dietetic adv. council Oreg. State U. Active March of Dimes, Hawaii Dietetic Assn., Multiple Sclerosis. AAUW scholar, 1966-67; Midwest Fish & Frozen Seafood scholar, 1967-68; Martha S. Pittman scholar, 1968-69; Bessie Brooks West scholar, 1968-69. Mem. Am. Dietetic Assn., Oreg. Dietetic Assn., Portland Dietetic Assn., Am. Council Sci. and Health, Western Region Coll. and Univ. Tchrs. of Foods and Nutrition, Soc. Nutrition Edn., Oreg. Nutrition Council, Am. Diabetes Assn., Am. Home Econs. Assn., Phi Kappa Phi, Omicron Nu, Phi Upsilon Omicron, Alpha Lambda Delta. Methodist. Author: (with B. P. Lukert) Clinical Nutrition-A Physiologic Approach, 1977; (with A.L. Fortuna) 1981 Dietetic Internship Funding Survey, 1982; contbr. to The Taste of Success: Dysphagia Intervention for the Adult, 1983. Home and Office: 7835 SW Raintree Dr Beaverton OR 97005

OVERTON, NANCY JANE, stockbroker; b. Pikeville, N.C., July 17, 1940; d. James H. and Ola (Morris) O. B.A., Duke U., 1962. Research analyst N.Y. Life Ins. Co., N.Y.C., 1962-63; asst. to office mgr. Nat. Ind. Conf. Bd., N.Y.C., 1963-66; sec. to commn. on computer center Harvard U., Boston, 1966-67; adminstrv. asst., institutional trading dept. Paine Webber Jackson & Curtis, Boston, 1967-70, sales asst. Reynolds Securities, Jacksonville, Fla., 1970-75; stockbroker Dean Witter Reynolds Inc., Jacksonville, 1975-83, assoc. v.p. investments, 1983-85; investment officer Johnson, Lane, Space, Smith & Co., Inc., 1985—. Bd. dirs. N. Fla. Campfire Girls, 1976-79, Riverside Avondale Preservation, 1976-77. Nat. Methodist scholar, 1958 59. Mem. Jacksonville Stock & Bond Club, Jacksonville Women's Network, Jacksonville C. of C. (com. of 100, 1983). Republican. Episcopalian. Clubs: University, Big Tree Racquet. Home: 1846 Margaret St Unit 9 D Jacksonville FL 32204

OVERTON, ROSILYN GAY HOFFMAN, economist, insurance company executive; b. Corsicana, Tex., July 10, 1942; d. Billy Clarence and Ima Elise (Gay) Hoffman; B.S. in Math., Wright State U., Dayton, Ohio, 1972, M.S. in Applied Econs. (fellow), 1973; postgrad. N.Y. U. Grad. Sch. Bus., 1974—; m. Aaron Lewis Overton, Jr., July 2, 1960 (div. Mar. 1975); children—Aaron Lewis III, Adam Jerome. Research analyst Nat. Security Agy., Dept. Def., 1962-67; bus. reporter Dayton Jour.-Herald, 1973-74; economist First Nat. City Bank, N.Y.C., 1974, A.T. & T. Co., 1974-75; broker Merrill Lynch, N.Y.C., 1975-80; asst. v.p. E.F. Hutton & Co., N.Y.C., 1980-84; nat. mktg. dir. investment products Manhattan Life ins. co., 1984—; v.p. Manhattan Capital Mgmt. Inc., N.Y.C., 1985—. Friend, N.Y.C. Mayor's Commn. on Status of Women. Named Businesswoman of Yr., N.Y.C., 1976. Mem. Nat., N.Y. assns. bus. economists, Nat. Fedn. Bus. and Profl. Women, Women's Econ. Roundtable, Gotham Bus. and Profl. Womens Club, Wright State U. Alumni Assn. (dir.), Mensa. Methodist. Club: Zonta (pres.). Author: (with John Treacy) Measuring Externalities of Strip Coal Mining via Property Tax Assessment, 1973; editor: Monthly Economic Letter, First Nat. City Bank, 1974. Office: Manhattan Capital Mgmt Inc 111 W 57th St New York NY 10019

OVIATT, ROBERTA OPAL, real estate broker, researcher, volunteer; b. Ririe, Idaho, Jan. 5, 1932; d. Robert Randolph and Lena Opal (Traughber) Fleming; m. Jack R. Van Noy, Aug. 12, 1948 (div. June 1971); children—John R., Kurt L., Albert E.; m. 2d, LeRoy Ellsworth Oviatt, July 15, 1972. Student Brigham Young U., 1948-50, U. Tacoma, 1963-64, Centralia Coll., 1968-71. With Rochester Realty, Wash., 1977—, broker, 1963—. Vol. Community Action, Rochester, 1982—; treas. Citizens Group, Rochester, 1982—. Mem. Rochester C. of C. (sec. treas. 1982-83, pres., 1983—), Grand Mound Lutheran. Avocations: reading; travel; golf; swimming; needle point. Home: 21644 Old Hwy 99 SW Centralia WA 98531 Office: Rochester Realty 10139 Hwy 12 Box 45 Rochester WA 98579

OWEN, ADRIENNE ELIZABETH, manufacturing company executive; b. Chgo., July 15, 1950; d. Edward Joseph and Jeannette Wanda (Kida) Czekaj; 1 child, Edward Tillman Owen. B.A., U. Tex.-Arlington, 1971, M.B.A., 1980. Tchr., Nolan High Sch., Fort Worth, 1972-73; adminstrv. asst. AMX Co., Arlington, 1973-77, Docutel, Dallas, 1977-78; adminstrv. asst. The Drawing Board, Dallas, 1978-80, sales researcher, Dallas, 1978-81; creative coordinator D.B.G.C.I., Dallas, 1981-82; nat. sales support mgr. MSD Systems, Dallas, 1983—. Mem. Am. Mktg. Assn. (Metroplex Marketer editor 1981-84, publicity dir. 1981), Sigma Delta Pi. Office: MSD Systems Inc 10031 Monroe 206 Dallas TX 75229

OWEN, CHERI AVERY, public mental health administrator; b. Clay Center, Kans., Nov. 13, 1946; d. Albion John and Grace Elverra (Myers) Avery. B.S. in Home Econs. in Journalism, Kans. State U., 1968; M.A. in Mental Health Communication, Syracuse U., 1970. Dir. info. North Central Kans. Guidance Ctr., Manhattan, 1969-70; health edn. and tng. specialist Office Mental Health and Mental Retardation, Phila., 1970-74, dir. tng., info., edn. and com. participation, 1975-82, human resource devel. specialist, 1982-85, dep. dir. mental health div., 1985—; sec., treas. Mgmt. Internat. and Tng. Corp.; editor, publs. evaluator, mem. adv. council Mental Health Materials Ctr., N.Y.C., 1975-85; charter assoc. mem., corr. nat. mag. Nat. Ctr. for Health Edn., N.Y.C., 1984—; 1st v.p. Nat. Com. for Mental Health Edn., 1980-81; cons. Asian Am. Women's Assn., 1985—, Phila. Self-Help Clearinghouse, 1983-84, Nat. Assn. Continuing Edn. Dirs. Conf., Phila., 1984, Region III Consortium of Consultation and Edn. Providers, N.Y. and N.J., 1978-79, ann. plan-writing editing United Hosps., Phila., 1984; chair com. teenage pregnancy prevention Phila. Youth Services Coordinating Office, 1983-85; state mental health del. to nat. project Council on Social Work Edn., N.Y.C., 1976; cons. on domestic violence Phila. Mayor's Commn. for Women, 1983—; del. from Phila. Commn. for Women and African Am. Inst. to UN non.-govt. orgn. Forum, Nairobi, Kenya, 1985; spl. corr. for Phila. Tribune to UN Decade for Women World Conf., 1985; advisor, cons. Coalition SE Asian Mutual assistance assns., Phila., 1984—; mem. Women's Way legis. lobbying group, 1985—. Contbr. numerous articles to newsletters and newspapers, also chpt. to book. Producer videotape on refugee women in Phila., 1985; prodn. supr. film Give Us a Chance, 1979 (Nat. Assn. Mental Health Info. Officers award 1980). NIMH fellow and intern Syracuse U., 1968-70; Title XX Social Service trainee Pa. Office Mental Health, 1977-78; recipient top award Nat. Presswomen's Assn., Kans., 1969, Accomplishment cert. City Employees Combined Campaign, 1985; named Internat. Ambassador of Good Will, Mayor Phila., 1985. Mem. Nat. Women's Health Network. Avocations: travel; international networking and project development; development of videotape library on women and minorities; African martial arts. Office: Office Mental Health 1101 Market St 7th Floor Philadelphia PA 19107

OWEN, DEBBIE ANNE, nursing home administrator; b. Galesburg, Ill., Aug. 12, 1955; d. John Herbert Hillman and Jean (Lindquist) Hillman Rude; m. Donald Dean Owen, Oct. 7, 1976 (div. 1983). Grad. Meth. Med. Ctr., Peoria, Ill., 1976. R.N., Ill. Charge nurse Cottage Hosp., Galesburg, 1976-77; administr. Abingdon Nursing Home, Ill., 1977-81; owner, pres. Owen Nursing Ctrs., Springfield, Ill., 1981—. Named Young Career Woman of Yr., Bus. and Profl. Women's Club, Galesburg, 1980, Abingdon Boss of Yr., 1983. Mem. Ill. Health Care Assn. (bd. dirs. 1984—). Republican. Avocations: building restoration; boating. Office: Owen Nursing Ctrs 3009 S 6th St Springfield IL 62704

OWEN, SUE ANN, poet; b. Clarinda, Iowa, Sept. 5, 1942; d. Theodore Reynold and Elizabeth (Roderick) Matthews; m. Thomas Charles Owen, Aug. 29, 1964; B.A. in English, U. Wis., 1964; M.F.A. in Writing, Goddard Coll., 1978. Poet in schs. Arts and Humanities Council, Baton Rouge, 1980-81, vis. artist, 1982—; participant writing confs. Author: Nursery Rhymes for the Dead, 1980; contbr. poems to mags., anthologies, including Harvard Mag., Iowa Rev., The Nation, Poetry, Ploughshares, So. Rev., Horisont, BLM, others; readings in Boston, N.Y.C., Washington, San Francisco, New Orleans. Mem. Poetry Soc. Am., Associated Writing Programs, Poets and Writers, Arts and Humanities Council (Baton Rouge). Home: 2015 General Cleburne Baton Rouge LA 70810

OWEN, SUZANNE, savings and loan executive; b. Lincoln, Nebr., Oct. 6, 1926; d. Arthur C. and Hazel E. (Edwards) O.; B.S. in Bus. Adminstrn., U. Nebr., Lincoln, 1948. With G.F. Lessenhop & Sons, Inc., Lincoln, 1948-57; with First Fed. Lincoln, 1963—, v.p., dir. personnel, 1975-81, 1st v.p., 1981—. Mem. Adminstrv. Mgmt. Soc. (past dir. local chpt.), Lincoln Personnel Mgmt. Assn., Phi Chi Theta. Republican. Christian Scientist. Clubs: Altrusa, Wooden Spoon (past treas.), Twig Daniels Network, Exec. Women's Breakfast Group, Pi Beta Phi Alumnae, Order of Eastern Star (Lincoln). Office: First Fed Lincoln 13th and N Sts Lincoln NE 68508

OWEN, SYLVIA, financial collection company executive; b. Peoria, Ill., June 3, 1951; d. Robert William Peterson and Leona Roberta (Filkins) P. Student U. Ill.-Chgo. Sales mgr. Am. Copy and Equipment Sales Co., Northbrook, Ill., 1976-78; asst. v.p., regional sales supr. Fin. Collection Agys., Chgo., 1978—. Mem. Ill. Assn. of Student Fin. Aid Adminstrs. (cert. recognition 1984), Nat. Assn. Coll. and Univ. Bus. Officers, Nat. Assn. Female Execs. Democrat. Avocations: reading; theatre; aerobics; bicycling. Office: Fin Collection Agys 500 N Michigan Ave Suite 2230 Chicago IL 60611

OWENS, BARBARA ANN, computer trainer and analyst, training consultant; b. East Gulf, W.Va., Mar. 20, 1948; d. Robert Odell and Oretha (Winston) Gibson. B.S. in Bus. Adminstrn., Bluefield State Coll., 1966-69; postgrad. NYU, 1976-77; grad. computer sci. program Baruch Coll., CCNY, 1982-83. Adminstrv. editorial asst. CCNY, 1972-76; asst. mgr. IEEE, N.Y.C., 1976-78, Wang tech. analyst Equitable Life Assurance, N.Y.C., 1979-83; computer trainer/analyst Fried, Frank, Harris, Shriver, N.Y.C. and Washington, 1983—; cons. computer vendor software tng. Holtzman, Wise, Shepard, N.Y.C., 1985—, Custom Word Processing, N.Y.C., 1985—, Solo Temporary Agy., N.Y.C., 1985—. Home: 8-10 27th Ave Astoria NY 11102 Office: Fried Frank Harris Shriver One New York Plaza New York NY 10004

OWENS, BARBARA ANN, telecommunications company manager; b. Memphis, Sept. 1, 1948; d. Harwood Casey and Anna Lou (Webb) Owens; m. Carroll Lynn Hughes, Feb. 24, 1978; 1 child, Kimberlyn Casey. B.S.Ed. summa cum laude, U. Tenn.-Knoxville, 1970; M.S. in Social Work, U. Tenn., 1975. Caseworker, supr. Tenn. Dept. Human Services, Knoxville, 1970-75; dir. social services ARC, Knoxville, 1975-77; bus. office supr. South Central Bell Tel. Co., Knoxville and Maryville, 1977-80; phone ctr. supr. South Central Bell, Maryville, Tenn., 1980-82; asst. staff mgr. Bell South Services, Birmingham, Ala., 1983—. Mem. Nat. Assn. Female Execs., Future Telephone Pioneers. Methodist. Clubs: Birmingham Big Orange, Network Birmingham. Avocations: personal computers; basketball; spectator sports. Home: 6574 Quail Run Dr Helena AL 35080 Office: Bell South Services 505 N 20th St Suite 500 Birmingham AL 35283

OWENS, BRENDA JOYCE, nursing educator; b. Lafayette, La., Nov. 28, 1949; d. Felton and Melba Marie (Wiltz) Hypolite; m. John Cleveland Owens, June 23, 1973; children—Kya Nischelle, Tiffany Danielle. B.S. in Nursing, Dillard U., New Orleans, 1971; M.S. in Nursing, Cath. U. Am., 1978. Staff nurse Michael Reese Hosp., Chgo., 1971-73; asst. head nurse, staff nurse D.C. Gen. Hosp., Washington, 1973-75; staff nurse Children's Hosp., Washington, 1976-78; instr. to asst. prof. nursing La. State U., New Orleans, 1978—, also staff nurse Mercy Hosp., New Orleans, 1983—. Dillard U. scholar, 1967; trainee Cath. U. Am., 1977. Mem. Nat. Black Nurses Assn. (dir. New Orleans chpt.), Am. Nurses Assn., La. Nurses Assn., Am. Assn. Critical Care Nurses (cert.), Nat. League Nursing (accreditation site visitor), Sigma Theta Tau. Democrat. Roman Catholic. Club: St. Leo the Great Sch. Parents. Home: 7650 Dune Dr New Orleans LA 70128

OWENS, CAROLYN LOUISE, psychologist; b. Memphis, Oct. 20, 1947; d. Doris Louise Brown White; m. William Charles Owens, Aug. 29, 1966; children—William Charles, Robert Channing, Veronica Nicole. B.A. in Psychology, U. Ill.-Chgo., 1965; M.A. Sch. Psychometry, Ind. State U., 1970; Advanced Cert. Adminstrn., Chgo. State U., 1979; Psy.D. in Psychology, Ill. Sch. Profl. Psychology, 1984. Spl. edn. tchr. Chgo. Bd. Edn., 1970-73, sch. psychologist, 1973-82, research psychologist, 1982—. Mem. Chgo. Assn. Sch. Psychologists, Nat. Assn. Sch. Psychologists, Phi Delta Kappa. Democrat. Lutheran. Avocation: art. Office: Chicago Bd Edn BCS 6th Floor Center 1819 W Pershing Rd Chicago IL 60609

OWENS, DONNA, mayor of Toledo; b. Toledo, Aug. 24, 1936; 3 children. Student Stautzenberger Bus. Coll., Toledo. Former mem. Toledo City Council; mayor City of Toledo, 1983—. Mem. Toledo-Lucas County Council for Human Services, Internat. Inst. Greater Toledo, Lucas County Improvement Corp., Toledo Area Employment and Tng. Consortium, Assn. of Two Toledos, Toledo Econ. Planning Council, Criminal Justice Coordinating Council, Ohio Sch. Bd. Assn., Career Edn. Adv. Com., St. Vincent Hosp. and Med. Guild; mem. exec. com. Toledo Met. Area Council Govts.; vice chmn. SSS No. Dist. 564 Appeal Bd., Fed. Jud. Dist. Ohio; mem. adv. bd. U.S. Conf. Mayors; chmn. fin., adminstrn. and inter-govtl. relations policy com. Nat League Cities; chmn. adv. bd. on missing children Justice Dept.; bd. dirs. YMCA, Toledo-Lucas County Conv. and Visitors Bur., Pub. Broadcasting-WGTE-TV, West Toledo Sr. Ctr, Substance Abuse Service, Inc.; bd. mgrs. West Toledo YMCA. Recipient Community Service award VFW, Legion of Leaders award YMCA, 1976, 1st Student Govt. Politics and Govt. award U. Toledo, 1982. Mem. Toledo Mus. Art, Fourth Ward Old Timers Assn., Old Newsboys (4th v.p.). Office: Office of Mayor One Government Ctr Suite 2200 Toledo OH 43604*

OWENS, EVALYN BERGSTRAND, former educator; b. Danville, Ill., Sept. 9, 1907; d. John Ivard and Esther (Jernberg) Bergstrand; B.S., U. Minn., 1928, postgrad., 1939-41; M.S., Iowa State Coll., 1936; m. Emery E. Owens, Dec. 1948 (dec. 1978). Nutritionist, Nassau County (L.I.) Com. Tb and Public Health, 1928-29, Freeport (L.I.) public schs., 1929-30; tchr. home econs., Frederic, Wis. 1930-32, Waupaca (Wis.) High Sch., 1932-35; teaching grad. asst. home econs. Iowa State Coll., 1935-36; instr. home mgmt., child devel. Mich. State Coll., 1936-39, asst. prof., 1941-42; instr. home econs. U. Minn., 1939-40; dean home econs. U. Conn., 1942-49; instr. home mgmt., child devel. Iowa State Coll. summer 1937, acting head home mgmt. dept., summer 1938, 39. Exec. com. Family Service Agy. Waukesha County; mem. Waukesha County Council Child Welfare, Social Agys. Council; mem. bd. vistors U. Wis., 1950-60; mem. research adv. com. U.S. Dept. Agr., 1954-60. Recipient outstanding achievement award, U. Minn., 1956. Mem. Am. (treas. 1952-54), Tex. home econs. assns., Omicron Nu, Phi Upsilon Omicron, Pi Lambda Theta, Iota Sigma Pi, Kappa Alpha Theta. Republican. Lutheran. Address: 212 N 40th St McAllen TX 78501 also 5300 Vernon Ave Apt 313 Mineapolis MN 55436

OWENS, JOAN D., writer, producer; b. Los Angeles, June 2, 1942; d. Albert Lazar and Esther (Lipson) Kaplan; B.A. in History, U. Calif.-Berkeley, 1964, postgrad., 1965; postgrad. Sorbonne, Cours de Civilisation Français, 1964. Assoc. producer public affairs KHJ-TV, Los Angeles, 1965-66; assoc. producer, producer, writer David L. Wolper Prodns., Metromedia Producers Corp., Alan Landsburg Prodns., Alan Sloan Prodns. and CRM Prodns., Los Angeles, 1969-75; writer CBS and ABC network children's programming, Hollywood, Calif., 1976-77; exec. producer KOCE-TV, 1982-85. Recipient Gold medal Internat. Film and TV Festival N.Y., 1975; Chris Bronze plaque Columbus Film Festival, 1975; Bronze medal V.I. Internat. Film Festival, 1975; award for creative excellence U.S. Internat. Film Festival, 1975. Mem. Women in Film (dir. 1976-78), Writers Guild Am.-West. Writer, producer numerous television documentaries and ednl. films including Say Goodbye (asso. producer), 1971; It Takes a Lot of Love, 1972; The Explorers, 1973; CBS pilots, 1977, French nat. TV spls., 1979-80, Disney Telecommunications, 1981, Painting with Elke Sommer, 1984, Filmation Studios, 1985.

OWENS, JOANNA MAIDEN, local health director; b. Saltville, Va., June 24, 1929; d. Hobart McKinley and Jamie Lake (Crenshaw) Maiden; m. Russell U. Owens, Aug. 14, 1976; stepchildren—Sharon Owens Leonard, Dennis Owens, Janet Owens Taylor. A.A., Va. Intermont Coll., 1948; B.S., Westhampton Coll., U. Richmond, 1950; M.D., Med. Coll. Pa., 1955; M.P.H., Johns Hopkins U., 1967. Med. missionary So. Baptist Conv., Joinkrama, Nigeria, 1958-66; med. cons. Floyd County Health Service, Prestonsburg, Ky., 1967-69; local health dist. dir. Va. Dept. Health, Wise, 1969-74, Abingdon, 1974-79, Saluda, 1979—. Named Alumna of Yr., Va. Intermont Coll., 1962; Outstanding Citizen of Yr., Va. Council in Social Welfare, 1983-84. Mem. AMA, Am. Pub. Health Assn., Am. Med. Women's Assn., Am. Coll. Preventive Medicine, Phi Beta Kappa. Office: Middle Peninsula Health Dist Box 415 Saluda VA 23149

OWENS, LESSIE VIOLA, librarian; b. Bucksport, S.C., Aug. 9, 1945; d. Zack and Frances (Mishoe) O. B.S., Howard U., 1967; M.Library and Info. Sci., U. Md., 1972. Children's librarian D.C. Pub. Library, Washington, 1967-69, asst. br. librarian, 1969-74, head br. librarian, 1975—; mem. coll. youth motivation task force Nat. Alliance for Bus., 1983-84. Coordinator, grant writer Young Voices, New Drums, 1980; editor: (with William Hardin) Emminent Black Leaders in Librarianship. Sec., bd. dirs. Friendship Community Settlement House, Washington, 1972—; mem. Southwest Neighborhood Assembly, Washington, 1978-83; mem. Southwest Community Scholarship Com., Washington, 1977—; mem. Southwest Festival of the Arts Com., Washington, 1978-83; bd. dirs., big sister Juvenile Justice Project, Washington, 1973-75. Mem. ALA, Pub. Library Assn. Baptist. Home: 804 Geranium St NW Washington DC 20012 Office: Watha T Daniel Br DC Pub Library 8th and Rhode Island Ave NW Washington DC 20012

OWENS, LORRAINE LUCILLE, handwriting analyst, cons.; b. Pettus, Tex., Sept. 19, 1927; d. Bernard Phillip and Lucille Lillian (Newman) Hopkins; B.A. in Psychology, Ottawa (Kans.) U., 1977; m. George Erwin Owens, Feb. 5, 1947; children—Janet Lucille, George Erwin, David M., Lynn L. Partner, Allen and Owens, Kansas City, Mo., 1970-80; pres. Kaleidoscope Corp., Kansas City, Mo., 1980—; lectr., seminar speaker; psychology instr. Graphoanalysis Congress, Chgo., 1978-81; cons. with psychologist Lansing State Prison, Marillac Sch. Bd. dirs. Marillac Sch., Kansas City, Mo., 1977-82; troop, troop organizer Mid Continent council Girl Scouts U.S.A., 1962-72. Mem. Internat. Graphoanalysis Soc. (certificate of merit, 1979). Republican. Unity Ch. Author: Different Ways to Describe Traits, 1976; Handwriting Analysis Dictionary, 1981. Home: 6300 Verona Shawnee Mission KS 66208 Office: 1524 Crystal Kansas City MO 64126

OWENS, MARGARET ALMA, educational administrator; b. Houston, Mar. 10, 1938; d. Leon Edgar and Velma Rotha (Miller) Owen; m. Robert Harvey Owens, May 28, 1958 (div. 1975); children—Robert Stephen, Keith Randall. B.S., Mary-Hardin Baylor U., 1960; M.Ed., Tex. Woman's U., 1972; supervision cert., 1975; postgrad., 1979-82. Cert. mid-mgmt. adminstr. Tex. Vocat. home economist Tex. A & M U., Bryan, Tex., 1960-64, substitute tchr. Dallas Ind. Sch. Dist., 1965-67, permanent substitute tchr. in home econs. and sci., 1968-69, tchr. spl. edn., 1969-71; jr. acct. Burgess Manning Co., Dallas, 1967-68; asst. dir. Camp Nerby, Oak Cliff YMCA, Dallas, 1968; tchr. spl. edn. Austin Ind. Sch. Dist., Tex., 1971-74, supr. secondary spl. edn., 1974 ; adminstrv. intern Southwest Tex. State U., San Marcos, 1973; cons. San Marcos Bapt. Acad., Tex., 1976; mem. student tchr. adv. com. U. Tex., Austin, 1984—; citizen ambassador of edn. to China, 1986. Author, editor, advisor various profl. tng. materials. Active various Tex. councils Boy Scouts Am., 1968—. Recipient The Golden Measure Achievement award Grand Prairie YMCA, 1968; Outstanding Leadership award Boy Scouts Am., 1971; Fed. edn. grantee, 1971-72. Mem. Council for Exceptional Children (v.p. 1971), Austin Assn. Pub. Sch. Adminstrs. (chmn. task force), Alpha Delta Kappa (former officer), Pi Lambda Theta. Baptist. Clubs: Paramont Theatre, World-Wide Vacation, Hyde Park Singles. Lodge: Demolay (pres. Mother's Aux. 1977-78). Avocations: reading, travel; art collections; theatre; gourmet cooking. Home: 1777 Cricket Hollow Dr Austin TX 78758 Office: Austin Independent Sch Dist 6016 Dillard Circle Austin TX 78752

OWENS, PAMELA ANN, accountant, interior designer; b. Cleve., May 29, 1956; d. James Calvin and Hattie Mae (Stanley) O. B.A., Shaw U., 1977. Dental asst., Raleigh, N.C., 1976-77, Cleve., 1977-78; continuity dir. United Broadcasting Co., Cleve., 1978-80; sales rep. Midland Ins. Co., Cleve., 1980-81; jr. acct. Polytech, Inc., Cleve., 1981—; propr. Signature Interiors, Cleve., 1984—. Author: On the Yard. Mem. Nat. Assn. Female Execs., Working Women's Assn., Black Profls. Assn. Democrat. Baptist. Avocations: writing; photography; sewing. Office: Polytech Inc 1744 Payne Ave Cleveland OH 44112

OWENS, RUTH ANN, hotel clerk and auditor; b. West Frankfort, Ill., Oct. 2, 1943; d. Oscar Dean and Mary Belle (Dorris) West; m. William Kelly Owens, Sept. 4, 1964; children—William Joseph, John Dean. Office sec. Gibbs Inc. Co., Benton, Ill., 1961-64, Pekin Ins. Co., Ill., 1965-66, Valu Fair Dept. Store, Oceanside, Calif., 1969-71; auditor, hostess, desk clk. Holiday Inn, Benton, 1968-69, 71-73; desk clk. Super 8 Motel, Mt. Vernon, Ill., 1985—. Pres. Sesser Woman's Club, Ill., 1977-78, founder crime prevention program; den mother Boy Scouts Am., 1976-77, 80; former pres. Benton Woman's Club; treas. Franklin County Woman's Club, Ill.; apptd. mem. Benton Youth Bd., 1980—; mem. Rep. Nat. Com.; tchr. Sunday Sch., past pres. Women's Missionary program North Benton Bapt. Ch. Mem. Benton Garden Club (past pres.), Beta Sigma Phi (new chpt. sponsor, numerous offices, Girl of Yr. 1977, 82, 84). Avocations: flower gardening; baking. Home: 1201 E Anna St Benton IL 62812

OWENS, SHELBY JEAN, electrologist; b. Flintville, Tenn., Dec. 18, 1936; d. Harvey Chrethton and Emma Lucille (McDonald) Langford; m. David Randall Owens, Mar. 12, 1953 (div. Feb. 1970); children—Karen, Kristie, Kaylon; m. Richard Allen Brewer, May 26, 1977. Diploma Hoffman Electrolysis Inst., N.Y.C., 1968, postgrad. cert., 1972. Cert. clin. electrologist. Tech. typist Thiokol Chem. Corp., Huntsville, Ala., 1957-60; exec. sec. CFW Constrn. Co., Fayetteville, Tenn., 1961-65; pvt. practice electrolysis, Winchester, Tenn., 1968-70, Huntsville, 1970-77, Pensacola, Fla., 1975—. Recipient Pres.'s award Am. Electrolysis Assn., 1984. Mem. Soc. Clin. and Med. Electrologists, Electrolysis Soc. Fla. (lobbyist 1979-86, pres. 1982—), Am. Bus. Women's Assn. (Pensacola charter chpt.) (past pres., Woman of Yr. award 1984). Democrat. Avocations: sewing; writing. Home: 3801 N 12th Ave Pensacola FL 32503 Office: Shelby Owens Electrologist 5113 N Davis Suite 8 Pensacola FL 32503

OWENS, SUSAN S., real estate executive; b. Flint, Mich., Mar. 10, 1953; d. Erney B. and Margaret (Sperla) Jablonski; M. David G. Owens, Aug. 10, 1974. B.B.A., U. Mich., 1975; postgrad. Harvard Summer Coll., 1976; M.B.A., Keller Grad. Sch. Mgmt., 1983. Lic. stockbroker, real estate broker. Dir. admissions Fisher Coll. evening div., Boston, 1975-76; acct. exec. The Revlon Corp., N.Y.C., 1976-81; mem. investment group Grubb & Ellis, Chgo., 1984; v.p. The Related Cos., Chgo., N.Y.C., 1984—; dir., officer Strategy Ptnrs., Chgo., 1985; cons. Revlon, Chgo., 1981-83. Author Revlon Reflexion newsletter, 1975-81; author, editor Happenings newsletter, 1984-85. Mem. Chgo. Council on Fgn. Relations, 1983—, Chgo. Art Inst., 1983—. Recipient Best Mktg. Presentation award Revlon, 1977; named Marketer of Yr., E.F. Hutton, 1984. Mem. Nat. Assn. Female Execs., Nat. Assn. Security Dealers, Young Exec. Club, Chi

Omega. Club: U. Mich. (Chgo.). Avocations: skiing; traveling; racketball; diving. Home: 155 N Harbor Dr #5112 Chicago IL 60601

OWENS, TERESA F(AY), marketing/sales executive; b. Cheoah, N.C., May 18, 1954; d. Clarence Edward and Doris Pauline (Quilliams) O. B.A., Mars Hill Coll., 1975; postgrad. U. Louisville, 1975-76. Social worker Sheltered Workshop, Louisville, 1976-77, River Region Mental Health Bd., Louisville, 1977-78; dist. sales rep. Chromalloy Photographics, Louisville, 1978; mktg. rep. McDonnell Douglas Automation, St. Louis, 1978-81, account mgr., Altanta, 1981-84; account mgr. Info. Sci., 1984-85; mktg. mgr. Mgmt. Sci. Am., 1985; mktg. mgr. HBO & Co., 1986—. Mars Hill Coll. Pres.'s scholar, 1972. Mem. Nat. Assn. Female Execs., Atlanta Women's Network, Ga. Women's Polit. Caucus, LWV, High Mus. Art. Home: 7120 Stonington Dr NE Atlanta GA 30328

OWENS-POTE, KAREN ASKEY, nutrition consultant; b. Indiana, Pa., Dec. 3, 1945; d. William Anthony and Cleo Margaret (Lyons) Askey; B.S. in Home Econs., Indiana U. of Pa., 1967; M.S. in Food and Nutrition, Va. Poly. Inst. and State U., 1970; postgrad. in bus. mgmt. Pepperdine U., 1979-80; m. Wilfred D. Pote, Feb. 14, 1981. Dir. dietetics and food service Somerset (Pa.) Community Hosp., 1970; food mgr. supr. Restaurant-Hotel div. Stouffer Food Corp., Cleve., 1967-68; allied health nutritionist, sr. dietitian City of Hope Nat. Med. Center, Duarte, Calif., 1970-71; chief nutritionist U. Calif. Med. Center-Irvine, Orange, Calif., 1971-74; prin. K.A. Owens Assos., Sierra Madre, Calif., 1972-80; pres. K.A. Owens & Assos., Inc., St. Paul and San Diego, 1981—; health editor Copley Radio Network, 1986—; mgr. nutritional affairs Gen. Foods Corp., White Plains, N.Y., 1980-81; instr. public health nutrition U. Minn., Mpls., 1981—; chmn., asst. prof. home econs. and dietetics Pepperdine U., Malibu, Calif., 1974-80; adj. prof. social ecology U. Calif., Irvine, 1972-74; lectr., researcher in human nutrition Va. Poly. Inst. and State U., Blacksburg, 1968-70; condr. ednl. seminars in field, Calif., Idaho, Minn.; cons. Henkel U.S.A., Bozell & Jacobs, Manning Selvage & Lee, Schwan's Sales Enterprises, Kane-Miller Corp., Anderson-Hendrickson & Co., Van de Kamp Frozen Foods, Pillsbury Co., Robert Marston and Assocs., Inc., Hunt-Wesson Foods, Inc., Dinah's Place, NBC-TV, Longevity Centers, Inc., Glass Packaging Inst., Home Savs. and Loan Assn., various public relations and advt. agencies, profl. assns. and firms, utilities, hosps., govt. and civic groups. Vol. and fundraising U. Minn.; active fundraising for community projects. Registered dietitian. Mem. Am. Dietetic Assn., Am. Fedn. TV and Radio Artists, Phi Tau Sigma, Kappa Omicron Phi. Republican. Methodist. Office: 4416 Topa Topa Dr Suite 300 La Mesa CA 92041

OWNBEY, VIRGINIA KAY, architect; b. Miami, June 2, 1946; d. Hal Norwood and Mary Virginia (Williams) Buchanan; B.Arch., Okla. State U., 1970; m. Charles Lewis Ownbey, Aug. 11, 1974; children—Christine Vanessa, Wade Preston. Archtl. draftsperson Frank L. Hope & Assos., Santa Ana, Calif., 1970-73, Am. Devel., Torrance, Calif., 1973-74, J. Ward Dawson, Architect, Tustin, Calif., 1975-76; architect Archi & Tekton, Newport Beach, Calif., 1977-79; individual practice, Tustin, 1979-83, Manitou Springs, Colo., 1983—. Nat. Endowment Arts grantee, 1969. Mem. Women's Archtl. League. Methodist. Address: 810 Crystal Park Rd Manitou Springs CO 80829

OXENBERG, DEBI LYNN, nurse, nurse oncologist; b. Flint, Mich., May 28, 1953; d. Marvin Hugh and Rhoda (Schneider) Gottlieb; m. Allen George Smith, III, Aug. 9, 1973 (div. 1979); m. Larry Dennis Oxenberg, June 20, 1982; 1 child, Stefanie Caryn. A.A., Eastern Mich. U., 1973; postgrad. Mott Community Coll., 1979-80; R.N., Hurley Sch. Nursing, 1982. R.N., Mich., Ohio. Salesman, bookkeeper Blossom Shoppe, Flint, 1975-77, 79-82; oncology nurse, staff nurse Hurley Med. Ctr., Flint, 1982; oncology nurse, staff nurse Grant Med. Ctr., Columbus, Ohio, 1983-85, nurse oncologist, 1985—. Mem. Oncology Nurse Soc., Am. Nurses Soc. Jewish. Avocations: biking; reading; needle point; gardening.

OXLEY, ANN, TV exec.; b. Canton, Ohio, Aug. 3, 1924; d. Edward and Dorothy (Duffy) Adang; B.A. with distinction, Ind. U., 1974, M.P.A., 1982; m. Jack Raymond Oxley, Aug. 10, 1946; children—Kathleen Oxley Wiggins, Maureen Oxley Gaff, Joseph, Jeffrey, Christeen Oxley Rhodes, Daniel, Julianne, Jamie, Kevin, Valerie, Amy. Advt. account salesperson Ft. Wayne (Ind.) Jour. Gazette, 1945-47; office mgr. Ind. Equestrian Assn., Ft. Wayne, 1971-73; research dir. Taxpayers Research Assn., Ft. Wayne, 1974-76; exec. dir. Ft. Wayne Pub. TV Inc., 1976—. Active Bicentennial Com., 1976; adviser Media Arts Panel Ind. Arts Commn. Mem. AAUW, Internat. Assn. Bus. Communicators, Women in Communications, Ind. Pub. Broadcasters Soc. (dir.), Mensa Internat., C. of C. (cultural com.), Phi Alpha Alpha. Roman Catholic. Home: 4305 Arlington St Fort Wayne IN 46807 Office: 227 E Washington Blvd Fort Wayne IN 46802

OXLEY, GERALDINE MOTTA, life insurance executive; b. Hoboken, N.J., June 25, 1930; d. Edward Joseph and Mary Ellen (Green) Motta; B.S. in Math., Coll. Mt. St. Vincent, 1951; postgrad. NYU, 1955-59; m. John Edward Oxley, Sept. 19, 1953. Mem. coll. trainee program N.Y. Life Ins. Co., N.Y.C., 1951-54, data processing programmer, 1954-59, mgr. systems programming, 1959-68, dir. electronics research, 1968-73, asst. v.p., 1973-75, 2d v.p., 1975-78, v.p., 1978—. Trustee, Manhattan Coll., 1982—. Mem. Assn. Computer Machinery, Coll. Mt. St. Vincent Alumnae Assn. (pres. 1969-71, fund dir. 1975-76). Office: NY Life Ins Co 51 Madison Ave New York NY 10010

OXLEY, JEAN ELIZABETH, county official; b. Center Point, Iowa, Nov. 26, 1925; d. Carl E. and Edna (Smiley) Liabo; m. Myron B. Oxley, Feb. 16, 1957; children—JoAnne, Ralph. Student Luther Coll., Iowa, 1943-45; B.A., U Iowa, 1947; postgrad U. Wis., summer 1948. Tchr. high sch., Belle Plaine, Iowa, 1947-49, Clinton, Iowa, 1949-50; with YWCA, Cedar Rapids Iowa, 1951-55, Dayton, Ohio, 1956-57; tchr. LaSalle High Sch., Cedar Rapids, 1966-71; mem. Linn County Bd. Suprs., Cedar Rapids, 1973—. Mem. Supreme Ct. Adv. Law Libraries, 1985, State Adv. Juvenile Justice, 1984; bd. dirs. Project Independence, 1984-85; chmn. Linn County Democratic Central Com., 1971-73. Mem. Bus. and Profl. Women (pres 1984-85), 6th Dist. County Officers (pres. 1983-85), East Central Council of Govts. (chmn. 1983-85). Methodist. Club: Quota (gov. 1985-86). Home:2266 Oxley Rd Marion IA 52302 Office: Linn County Bd Suprs 930 1st St SW Cedar Rapids IA 52404

OYLER, SUSAN DEBORAH, microbiologist; b. Roanoke, Va., Apr. 21, 1950; d. Dalton Oliver and Margaret Clay (Waldron) O.; B.A. in Biology, U. Va., 1972; Med. Technologist, Duke U., 1973; M.S. in Microbiology (A.D. Williams fellow 1973-74, NIH grantee 1974-76), Med. Coll. Va., 1976. Mgr. lab. Family Med. Center, Richmond, Va., 1975-76; gen. lab. supr. Physicians Clin. Labs., Richmond, 1976-78; supr. biol. formulation Technicon Corp., Middletown, Va., 1978-80; specialist fermentation tech. support Abbott Labs., N. Chicago, Ill., 1980—; mem. faculty J. Sargeant Reynolds Community Coll., Richmond, 1976-77. Regional rep. Va. Democratic Conv., 1976. Mem. Am. Soc. Clin. Pathologists, Soc. Ind. Microbiologists, Am. Soc. Microbiologists, Am. Mgmt. Assn., Nat. Assn. Female Execs. Home: 6029 Village Ln Roanoke VA 24019

OZAN, MARILYN FRANCES RALEY, mailing service executive; b. Memphis, Jan. 31, 1946; d. Claude Mason and Mary Reba (Pruett) Raley; m. Richard Vance Ozan, June 29, 1968; 1 child, Melynda Ellen. B.A., Baylor U., 1968. Cert. secondary tchr. Advtg. dir. Baylor Bookstore, Waco, Tex., 1965-68; substitute tchr. Orange County Ind. Sch. Dist., Orlando, Fla., 1969; tchr. San Antonio Ind. Sch. Dist., 1971-77; owner, pres. The Mailing Service, Greensboro, N.C., 1978—; bd. dirs. Spl. Events TV Network, Greensboro, 1984—; sec. Ozan Communications, Greensboro, 1983—. Stage mgr. City Stage, United Arts Council, Greensboro, 1984-85; active local Girl Scouts U.S. Recipient cert. appreciation Lowell Jr. High Sch. PTA, San Antonio, 1975. Mem. Piedmont Triad Advt. Fedn. (mailing coordinator), Greensboro Area C. of C. Republican. Avocations: spiritual exploration, metaphysical awareness, photography, reading, writing poetry. Home: 106 E Brentwood St Greensboro NC 27403 Office: The Mailing Service PO Box 20064 Greensboro NC 27420

OZER, LISA GOLDBERG, lawyer; b. Killeen, Tex., Feb. 14, 1954; d. Nathaniel and Renee (Slutzky) Goldberg; m. Robert Howard Ozer, May 13, 1979. B.A. summa cum laude, Tufts U., 1976; J.D., U. Pa., 1979. Bar: N.Y. 1980, N.J. 1985. Assoc. Kronish, Lieb, Weiner & Hellman, N.Y.C., 1979-85. Mem. ABA, Phi Beta Kappa. Home: 187 Great Hills Dr South Orange NJ 07079

OZICK, CYNTHIA, author; b. N.Y.C., Apr. 17, 1928; d. William and Celia (Regelson) Ozick; m. Bernard Hallote, Sept. 7, 1952; 1 dau., Rachel Sarah. B.A. cum laude with honors in English, NYU, 1949; M.A., Ohio State U., 1950; hon. degrees Yeshiva U., 1984, Hebrew Union Coll., 1984, Williams Coll., 1986. Author: Trust, 1966; The Pagan Rabbi and Other Stories, 1971; Bloodshed and Three Novellas, 1976; Levitation: Five Fictions, 1982; Art and Ardor: Essays, 1983; The Cannibal Galaxy, 1983; fiction, poetry, criticism, revs., translations, 100 essays in numerous periodicals and anthologies. Recipient Mildred and Harold Strauss Livings award Am. Acad. Arts and Letters, 1983, Rea award for short story, 1986; Guggenheim fellow, 1982. Fellow Am. Acad. Arts and Scis.; mem. Phi Beta Kappa. Office: care Alfred A Knopf Inc 201 E 50th St New York NY 10022

OZOLS, LIA, medical technologist; b. Riga, Latvia, Jan. 4, 1929; came to U.S., 1950, naturalized, 1959; d. Karlis and Olga Rozenfelds; B.S., U. Minn., 1957; postgrad. Metro State U., Minn., 1980; m. Laimons Ozols, Mar. 19, 1956; children—Ingemars, Arnis. Med. technologist U. Minn. Hosps., 1957-61; chief adminstrv. technologist Abbott Hosp., Mpls., 1957-77; administrv. lab. dir. Abbott-Northwestern Hosp., 1977-79; dir. Les Soeurs Orgn., Mpls., 1979—. Chair adv. bd. City of Richfield (Minn.) Dept. Health; bd. dirs. South Hennepin Human Services Council, Minn., 1986. Recipient Key to City, Richfield, 1985. Mem. Am. Soc. Clin. Pathologists, Am. Soc. Med. Technology, Minn. Microbiologists, Minn. Soc. Med. Technology, Minn. LWV, Women's Equity Action League (v.p. 1981-82), Women's Consortium, Minn. Women's Network, Exec. Females. Club: Selga (pres. 1981-82). Home: 2012 W 68th St Minneapolis MN 55423

PAAL, KATHERINE BAYS, educator, consultant; b. Shreveport, La., Dec. 31, 1953; d. Robert Payne and Lilburn (Sandoz) Bays; m. Rutland Beard Paal, June 28, 1975; children—Rutland Beard, Jr., Ryan Collinson. B.A., Roanoke Coll., 1975; M.B.A., Loyola Coll., Balt., 1978. Sr. mktg. research analyst First Nat. Bank of Md., Balt., 1975-78; asst. prof. Towson State U., Md., 1978—; asst. prof. dept. bus. adminstrn. Coll. of Notre Dame, Balt., 1984—; cons. Carey Communications, Towson, 1981-84; ptnr. Career Concepts, Balt., Mktg. Assocs., Balt., 1985—. Mktg. chmn. Jr. League of Balt., 1984—. Home: 6765 N Charles St Baltimore MD 21204 Office: Coll of Notre Dame 4701 N Charles St Baltimore MD 21210

PAARFUS, BARBARA DIANE LEIDHOLDT, psychologist; b. Hartford, Conn., Apr. 29, 1936; d. Louis Frederick and Helen Gladys Christine (Christensen) Leidholdt. B.A., Gettysburg Coll., 1957; M.A., Temple U., 1959. Lic. psychologist, Va. Tchr., Overbrook Sch. for the Blind, Phila., 1958-60; guidance counselor Henrico County Sch. Bd., Richmond, Va., 1960-61; psychologist and instr. psychiatry dept. Med. Coll. Va., Richmond, 1961-73; sch. psychologist Richmond Pub. Schs., 1973-79; psychologist, psychology asst. Westbrook Psychiat. Hosp., Richmond, 1982-83; psychologist Mecklenburg County Sch. Bd., Boydton, Va., 1984—; cons. Fredericksburg Mental Hygiene Clinic, 1966, Multiple Handicapped Program Richmond Pub. Schs., 1981. Vol., Solo/Discovery Singles Orgn.; active Parents Without Parents, Off Broad St. Players Drama Group, ch. activities. Recipient Phi Delta Gamma award, Temple U., 1959; Cert. of Appreciation, Rehab. Action Program, Richmond, 1976. Mem. Am. Psychol. Assn., Va. Psychol. Assn., Va. Assn. Sch. Psychologists, Gettysburg Coll. Alumni Assn., Chi Omega. Home: 4610 Bromley Ln Richmond VA 23226

PACE, CAROLINA JOLLIFF, educational communications consultant; b. Dallas, Apr. 12, 1938; d. Lindsay Gafford and Carolina (Juden) Jolliff; student Holton-Arms Sch., 1956-57; B.A. in Comparative Lit., So. Meth. U., 1960; m. John McIver Pace, Oct. 7, 1961. Dir. corp. fund raising Dallas Theatre Center, 1960-61; exec. sec. Dallas Book and Author Luncheon, 1959-63; promotional and instnl. cons. Henry Regnery-Reilly & Lee Pub. Co., Chgo., 1962-65; pub. trade rep. various companies, institutional rep. Don R. Phillips Co., Southeastern area, 1965-67; Southwestern rep. Ednl. Reading Service Inc.-Troll Assos., Mahwah, N.J., 1967-72; v.p., dir. multimedia div. Melton Book Co., Inc., Dallas, 1972-79; v.p. mktg. Webster's Internat., Inc., Nashville, 1980-82; pres. Carolina Pace, Inc., 1982—; cons. U.S. Dept. HHS, 1982—, U.S. Dept. Edn., 1977—; speaker Nat. Center for Severely Handicapped, Peabody Coll., Nashville. Bd. dirs., v.p., asso. in spl. edn. tech. ASET; nat. advisory bd. Nat. Info. Center for Spl. Edn. Materials; bd. dirs. Corpus; mem. adv. bd. Grad. Sch. Info. and Communication, U. Tex., Austin. Mem. ALA, Womens Nat. Book Assn., Women in Communications, Friends of Highland Park Library, DAR, Dallas Civic Opera Assn., Nat. Audio-Visual Assn. (speaker 1979 conf.), Assn. Ednl. and Communications Tech., Council Exceptional Children (publicity chmn. 1979 internat. conf.), Dallas Chamber Music Soc., Pub. Relations Soc. Am., Tex. Library Assn., Internat. Communications Industry Assn., Friends Dallas Pub. Library, Downtown Dallas Central Bus. Dist. Assn., Dallas West End Assn., So. Meml., Press Club Dallas, Dallas Zool. Soc. Dallas Art Assn., Alpha Delta Pi. Presbyterian. Home: 4524 Lorraine Ave Dallas TX 75205

PACE, NORMA, association executive, economist; grad. Hunter Coll., 1941; grad. study Columbia U.; Ph.D. (hon.), Mich. Technol. U., Poly. Inst. N.Y., Cedar Crest Coll., Grove City Coll., CUNY, Staff, Econometric Inst.; with U.S. Economics Corp., bus. adv. cons. service, 1944-71, pres., dir., dir. research, 1969-71; v.p., dir. indsl. econs. Lionel D. Edie & Co., N.Y.C., 1971-73; sr. v.p. Am. Paper Inst.; asst. devel. visual aids for teaching econs. Columbia Visual Lab.; dir. Sears, Roebuck & Co., Sperry Corp., Minn. Mining and Mfg. Co., Milton Bradley Co., Vulcan Materials Co., A.O. Smith. Adv. bd. Columbia U. Grad. Sch. Bus.; trustee Com. for Econ. Devel.; mem. Nat. Commn. for Employment Policy. Named to Hunter Coll. Hall of Fame, 1973, recipient Outstanding Achievement award. Mem. U.S. C. of C. (bd. dirs.). Address: Am Paper Inst 260 Madison Ave New York NY 10016

PACE, SHIRLEY LOVON, educational administrator; b. Madison County, Tex.; d. Henry and Lillie Mae (Brown) Nealey; M.A., Southwestern U., 1974; m. Roy Pace, May 2, 1970; children—Julia, Sheretta. Pres., La Rochelle Acads., Houston, 1971—; exec. dir. Larochelle Community Devel. Inc., Houston, 1973—, La Rochelle Community Devel. Inc., Houston, 1980—; cons. bus. Mem. Civic Com., Houston, pres., 1979-80; chmn. home econ. edn. adv. council, pres. adv. bd. Houston Ind. Sch. Dist. Named Outstanding Employer, 1980, 81. Mem. Nat. Assn. Female Execs., Tex. Lic. Child Care. Mem. Ch. of Christ. Club: Meadows Garden. Office: 2600 S Loop W Suite 250 Houston TX 77054

PACELLA, MARGARET ANN, data processing manager; b. Phila., July 18, 1954; d. Anthony Phillip and Margaret T. (McManus) P. Cert. in Data Processing. Computer Edn. Inst., 1972. Data controller Edwards Shoes, Phila., 1973-74; programmer McGee Ins., Phila., 1975-80; mgr. data processing Telco, Phila., 1980-85; dir. Mgmt. info. services Agusta Aviation, Trevose, Pa., 1985—; cons. Fishman & Tobin, Phila., 1982-83. Mem. Data Processing Mgmt. Assn., Assn. Inst. Certification Computer Profls., Bus. and Profl. Women Club (treas. 1985-86). Democrat. Roman Catholic. Avocations: music. Office: Agusta Aviation Corp 2 Neshaminy Interplex Ct Trevose PA 19047

PACELLA, PATRICIA ANN, food service company executive; b. Chgo., Apr. 19, 1951; d. Ralph Theodore and Edith Elaine (Telfer) Pyle; m. Richard Dirk Pacella, Dec. 22, 1979; 1 child, Richard Eliot. Student public schs. Bethel Park, Pa. With CODE, Inc., Pitts., 1970—, mktg. coorinator, 1978-80, dir. mktg., 1980—. Recipient Innovative Merit award ID Mag., 1981; Pacesetter award for outstanding woman in category of distbn. Roundtable for Women in Food Service, 1986. Mem. Internat. Food Service Mfrs. Assn. Republican. Clubs: Pennsbury Racquet, Greentree Racquet. Avocations: Tennis; dancing; knitting; crocheting. Home: 694 Carriage Circle Pittsburgh PA 15205 Office: CODE Inc 1910 Cochran Rd Manor Oak Bldg 2 Suite 480 Pittsburgh PA 15220

PACE-OWENS, SYLVIA, nurse practitioner, clinical administrator; b. St. Joseph, Mo., Oct. 16, 1936; children—Laura, Sara, Alan. B.S. in Nursing, U. Tex.-Galveston, 1960. R.N.; lic. ob-gyn nurse practitioner. Ob-gyn nurse practitioner Harris County Health Dept., Houston, 1975-78, Planned Parenthood, Houston, 1978-79; ob-gyn nurse practitioner Reproductive Services, Houston, 1979-80, clinic dir., 1980-82; clin. coordinator in vitro fertilization/embryo transfer program U. Tex. Med. Sch., Houston, 1982-84; IVF/G.I.F.T. nurse coordinator The Woman's Hosp. Tex., 1984—. Contbr. chpt. to Human In Vitro Fertilization and Embryo Transfer (Quigley and Wolfe), 1984; also articles on in vitro fertilization and embryo transfer program. Named Hon. Faculty Assoc., U. Texas Sch. Nursing, Houston, 1982—. Mem. Americ Fertility Soc., Am. Nurses Assn., Tex. Nurses Assn., Nurses Assn. of Am. Coll. Ob-Gyn. (cert. Ob-gyn nurse practitioner 1981), Primary Council of Nurse Practitioners, Hockaday Alumnae Assn., Kappa Kappa Gamma Alumnae. Episcopalian. Office: Woman's Hosp of Tex 7600 Fannin Houston TX 77054

PACHOLSKI, AUDREY PHYLLIS, university official, consultant; b. Concord, Mass., May 16, 1961; d. Stanislaus Stephen and Audrey Phyllis (Paulhus) P. B.S., Mankato State U., 1983. Publicist Mankato State U., Minn., 1983-85, ann. fund officer, 1985—; cons. pub. relations. Bd. dirs. fund raising council Mankato Area Coalition for Affordable Housing, 1985—; big sister YMCA program. Mem. Nat. Soc. Fund Raising Execs., Nat. Assn. Female Execs., Mankato Area C. of C. (ACT 2000 arts adv. com. 1985-86). Democrat. Roman Catholic. Lodges: Toastmasters, Zonta (jr. bd. 1985-86). Avocations: acting; singing; writing; painting. Home: 609 S 4th St Mankato MN 56001 Office: Mankato State U PO Box 101 Mankato MN 56001

PACK, PHOEBE KATHERINE FINLEY, civic worker; b. Portland, Oreg., Feb. 2, 1907; d. William Lovell and Irene (Barnhart) Finley; student U. Calif., Berkeley, 1926-27; B.A., U. Oreg., 1930; m. Arthur Newton Pack, June 11, 1936; children—Charles Lathrop, Phoebe Irene. Layman referee Pima County Juvenile Ct., Tucson, 1958-71; patron Menninger Found., Topeka; mem. Alcoholism Council So. Ariz., 1960—; bd. dirs. Kress Nursing Sch., Tucson, 1957-67, Pima County Assn. for Mental Health, 1958—, Ariz. Assn. for Mental Health, Phoenix, 1963—, U. Ariz. Found., Casa de los Niños Crisis Nursery; co-founder Ariz.-Sonora Desert Mus., Tucson, 1975—, Ghost Ranch Found., N.Mex.; bd. dirs. St. Mary's Hosp., Tucson, Tucson Urban League, Tucson YMCA Youth Found. Mem. Mt. Vernon Ladies Assn. Union (state vice regent, 1962-84),Mt. Vernon One Hundred (founder), Nature Conservancy (life), Alpha Phi. Home: Villa Compana Apt 415K 6651 E Carondelet Tucson AZ 85710

PACKARD, BARBARA BAUGH, physician, scientist administrator, physiologist; b. Uniontown, Pa., Mar. 10, 1938; d. Walter Ray and Yolanda (Ciarlo) Baugh; m. Lawrence Arthur Krames, Nov. 24, 1963 (div. 1970); m. 2d John E. Packard III, July 14, 1979. B.S., Waynesburg Coll., 1960; M.S., W. Va. U., 1961, Ph.D., 1964; M.D., U. Ala.-Birmingham, 1974. Physiologist myocardial infraction br. Nat. Heart Inst., Bethesda, Md., 1967-71; research assoc. U. Ala.-Birmingham, 1971-74; med. intern Johns Hopkins Hosp., Balt., 1974-75; sr. med. scientist adminstr. cardiac disease br. div. heart and vascular disease Nat. Heart, Lung, and Blood Inst., Bethesda, Md., 1975-79, assoc. dir. cardiology, 1979-80, dir. div. heart and vascular diseases, 1980-86, dir. office of Program Planning and Evaluation, assoc. dir. for sci. ops., 1986—. Mem. editorial bd.: Jour. Soviet Research in Cardiovascular Diseases, 1980-82. Served with USPHS, 1975—. Recipient Commendation medal USPHS, 1978. Fellow Am. Coll. Cardiology; mem. Am. Physiol Soc., Am. Heart Assn., Johns Hopkins Med. and Surgical Soc., Sigma Xi. Home: 10401 Grosvenor Pl Rockville MD 20852 Office: Nat Heart Lung and Blood Inst Bethesda MD 20892

PACKARD, KATRINA BERNIECE DANNHAUS, planner; b. Freeport, Tex., Feb. 2, 1953; d. Harvey Dean Walter Henry and Wilma Berniece (Adams) Dannhaus; m. Steven DeWitt Packard, Aug. 7, 1971 (div. Dec. 1979); 1 son, Jason DeWitt. A.A. with honors, Coll. of Mainland, Texas City, Tex., 1979; B.A. cum laude, U. Houston, 1982; student law South Tex. Coll. Law, Houston, 1982—. Cert. peer counselor, alcoholism counselor. Legal sec. Dist. Atty., Huntsville, Tex., 1971-72; adminstrv. sec. Sam Houston State U., Huntsville, 1972-74, Pierce, Goodwin, Flanaga, Houston, 1974-75; legal sec. Vinson & Elkins, Houston, 1975-77; exec. dir. Bay Area Commn. Drugs and Alcohol, Houston, 1977-79; planner Houston-Galveston Area Council, Houston, 1979—. Del. White House Conf. on Children, 1970, White House Conf. on Youth, 1971; com. chmn. Tex. White House Conf., Austin, 1970; v.p. Tex. Youth Conf., Austin, 1968-71, state counselor, 1969; mem. Leadership Inst. Tex.; bd. dirs. Recovery Ctr., Inc., 1978-80, Clear Lake Social Service Ctr., 1980, U. Houston/Clear Lake Cultural Ctr., 1980, Tex. Community Services, 1978, Four C's Clinic, LaMarque, Tex., 1979-80, Women's Ctr., Coll. of Mainland, 1980; mem. Children's Council Tex., 1978-80, Assn. Vol. Coordinators, 1978-80, Galveston County Assn. Social Service Dirs., 1978-80. Mem. Golden Key, Phi Theta Kappa, Phi Delta Phi. Home: 13262 Trailhollow St Houston TX 77079

PACKARD, RUTH MCCREA, retired social worker; b. Cashmere, Wash., May 3, 1920; d. Donald Preston and Maude Maggie Adelaide (Richardson) McCrea; B.A. magna cum laude, U. Puget Sound, 1942; M.S.W., U. Wash., 1964; m. Gail Vernard Packard, Aug. 8, 1944; children—Margaret, Mary, Martha, Melinda. Sr. social worker Long Beach (Calif.) Gen. Hosp., 1964-68, supr. M.S.W., 1970-81; supervising med. social worker Ranchos Los Amigos Hosp., Downey, Calif., 1968-69; supr. M.S.W. program, U. Oreg. Med. Sch., Portland, 1969-70; dir. Clin. Social Work div. Los Angeles County, Calif. Children Services, 1981-85; field instr. social work UCLA, 1972-73, U. So. Calif., 1973-74, Calif. State U., Long Beach, 1971-81. Lic. clin. social worker, Calif. Mem. Nat. Assn. Social Workers, Acad. Cert. Social Workers. Mem. Ch. of Religious Sci. (lic. sci. of mind practitioner).

PACKER, KATHERINE HELEN, librarian, educational administrator; b. Toronto, Ont., Can., Mar. 20, 1918; d. Cleve Alexander and Rosa Ruel (Dibblee) Smith; m. William A. Packer, Sept. 27, 1941; 1 dau., Marianne Katherine. B.A., U. Toronto, 1941; A.M.L.S., U. Mich., 1953; Ph.D., U. Md., 1975. Cataloguer William L. Clements Library, U. Mich., 1953-55, U. Man. Library, Winnipeg, Can., 1956-59; cataloguer U. Toronto Library, 1959-63, asst. prof. Faculty Library Sci., 1967-75, asso. prof., 1975-78, prof., dean, 1979—; head cataloguer York U. Library, Toronto, 1963-64; chief librarian Ont. Coll. Edn., Toronto, 1964-67; Can. Council Library Schs. rep. to Adv. Bd. on Sci. and Tech. Info., NRC Can., 1976-78. Author: Early American School Books, 1954. Recipient Disting. Alumnus award U. Mich., 1981. Mem. Am. Assn. Library Schs., ALA, Am. Soc. Info. Sci., Can. Library Assn. (Howard Phalin award 1972), Internat. Fedn. Library Assns., Phi Kappa Phi. Home: 53 Gormley Ave Toronto ON M4V 1Y9 Canada Office: Faculty Library and Info Sci U Toronto 140 Saint George St Toronto ON M5S 1A1 Canada

PACKER, MARQUERITE JUNE, assn. exec.; b. Seattle, Mar. 30, 1929; d. Frank Elizah and Susan Veronica (Grue) Thomas; student public schs., Seattle; m. George Albany Packer, Feb. 15, 1969; children—Edward Thomas Jones, Blake Reid Jones. Clk., Columbia br. Seattle Public Library, 1943-45, main br., 1946-54, in charge delinquent dept., 1950-54; clk., asst. librarian Puyallup (Wash.) Public Library, 1962-67; photo librarian Am. Plywood Assn., Tacoma, 1967-68, supr. central files, 1968-69, co-mgr. Records Center, 1969-74, records mgr., 1974—. Mem. edn. com., bd. dirs. Westop Credit Union, Tacoma, 1975—; active edn. groups United Meth. Ch., Puyallup, 1974—. Recipient Golden Acorn award PTA, 1969. Democrat. Club: Elks. Home: 15409 100th Ave E Puyallup WA 98373 Office: 7011 S 19th PO Box 11700 Tacoma WA 98411

PADBERG, HELEN SWAN, violinist; b. Shawnee, Okla., May 3, 1919; d. Frank Pusey and Birdie B. (Rudell) Swan; A.A., Stephens Coll., 1938; Mus.B., U. Okla., 1940; Mus.M., Northwestern U., 1941; student Jacques Gordon; m. Frank Padberg, Feb. 6, 1943; children—Frank, Kristen. Solo performances and concerts, 1932—; mem. faculty string quartet and symphony soloist Stephens Coll., 1937-38; violinist Oklahoma City Symphony Summer Concerts, 1940; soloist Northwestern U. Symphony, 1941; USO performer, 1941-44; violinist Nat. Orchestral Assn. and Am. Youth Orch., N.Y.C., 1944-46; tchr. strings Public Schs. Maywood (Ill.), 1946-47; asst. concertmaster West Suburban Symphony, Chgo., 1947-48; mem. Chgo. Women's Symphony, Chgo. Civic Orch. and chamber music groups, 1947-51; violinist Ark. String Trio, 1952-58; concertmaster Ark. Symphony and Little Rock Philharmonic, 1953-57, Marjorie Lawrence TV Series, Ark., 1953-54; pvt. tchr. violin, Little Rock, 1953-66; accompanist and performer on piano, harp. Co-founder Little Rock Chamber Music Soc., 1954; pres. Ark. Med. Soc. Aux., 1962-63, historian, 1963—; pres. bd. dirs. Vis. Nurse Assn. of Pulaski County (Ark.), 1967-69. Mem. Am. Harp Soc., Chgo. Harp Soc. (sec. 1979 84), Am. Fedn. Musicians, Am. Opera Soc. of Chgo. (v.p. and program chmn. 1981-82, pres. 1984—), Pi Kappa Lambda, Mu Phi Epsilon, Pi Beta Phi (pres. Little Rock Alumnae Club). Presbyterian. Clubs: Aesthetic (pres. Little Rock); Woman's Athletic of Chgo. Home: 175 E Delaware Pl Chicago IL 60611

PADEN, BETTY BURNS, lawyer, educator; b. Evanston, Ill., July 9, 1937; d. Joseph Ferdinand and Estelle (Taggart) Burns; m. Alvin Robert Paden, Aug. 18, 1962; children—Renee Lynn, Tina Jo. A.A., Kendall Coll., 1958; B.A., Roosevelt U., 1961, M.A., 1963, postgrad., 1966-67; Ed.D., Loyola U., Chgo.,

1970; J.D., No. Ill. U., 1979. Bar: Ill. 1980. Tchr., Chgo. Bd. Edn., 1961-67; author, cons. various pub. cos., 1967—; editor, writer Scott Foresman & Co., Glenview, Ill., 1967-68; instr. edn. Loyola U., Chgo., 1968-70; sole practice law, Evanston, Ill., 1980—; prof. edn. Northeastern Ill. U., Chgo., 1970—; cons. Silver Burdett Pub. Co., Morristown, N.J., 1981; reader, evaluator Ill. Supt. Pub. Instrn., 1974-82; core advisor Union Grad. Sch., Yellow Springs, Ohio, 1974-78; cons. Chgo. Consortium of Colls. and U. Chgo., 1974-75, Chgo. Bd. Edn., 1974-76. Author, editor: More Power, 1968; Moving Ahead, 1968; co-author: What Are They Up To, 1971; What Does It Take?, 1971; author: Truth is Stranger than Fiction, 1982; also short stories. Mem. Evanston (Ill.) Zoning Bd. Appeals, 1982—; bd. dirs. Evanston Community Devel. Corp., 1982—; officer Evanston PTA, 1970—. Kalm scholar, 1957-58; Com. Organized Research grantee, 1974-75; Kellogg fellow, 1984; UNI Found. fellow, 1984; named Woman of Year for Outstanding Service to Community, NAACP, 1983. Mem. AAUP (pres.-elect 1976-77), Internat. Reading Assn., Assn. Supervision and Curriculum Devel., Assn. Tchrs. Edn. (field rep.), ABA, Ill. Bar Assn., Chgo. Bar Assn. Democrat. Methodist. Office: Northeastern Ill U 5500 N Saint Louis Ave Chicago IL 60625

PADESKY, CHRISTINE ANNE, psychologist, educator; b. La Crosse, Wis., Mar. 6, 1953; d. Robert Charles and Phyllis Anne (Jankowski) P. B.A., Yale U., 1974; M.A., UCLA, 1975, Ph.D., 1981. Lic. psychologist, Calif. Lectr. Calif. State U.-Fullerton, 1978-80; assoc. dir. Y.S.P., Inc., Costa Mesa, Calif., 1979-82; instr. Calif. Sch. Profl. Psychology, Los Angeles, 1980-83; pvt. practice psychology, Newport Beach, Calif., 1982—; vis. lectr. U. Calif.-Irvine, 1984, now mem. adv. com. for extension mental health programs; dir. Ctr. for Cognitive Therapy, Newport Beach, Calif., 1983—; cons. Mesa Vista Psychiat. Hosp., San Diego, 1984—; lectr. in field. Editor Internat. Cognitive Therapy Newsletter, 1985—. Contbr. articles to profl. jours. Bd. mem. Orange County Criminal Justice Adv. Group, Calif., 1980-82, Parents United of Orange County, 1980-82; mem. adv. bd. Human Services Agy. Orange County, 1981; bd. dirs. Family Service Assn., Orange County, 1982—. Pres.'s Australian Sci. scholar, 1970. Mem. Am. Psychol. Assn., Assn. Advancement Behavior Therapy, Nat. Registry Health Providers in Psychology, Calif. Psychol. Assn., Orange County Psychol. Assn., Orange County Mental Health Assn., Yale U. Alumni Assn. (alumni schs. com. Orange county chpt. 1983—), UCLA Alumni Assn. (life mem.), NOW. Office: Ctr for Cognitive Therapy 1101 Dove St Suite 228 Newport Beach CA 92660

PADILLA, LISAAYN, computer company communications specialist; b. Manhattan, N.Y., Dec. 25, 1962; d. William James and Elaine Sue (Wanerman) P. B.A. in Psychology, Boston U., 1983; student Rockland Community Coll., 1979-80, SUNY-Syracuse, 1979-80; postgrad. Suffolk U. Law Sch., 1985—. Asst. to dir. NIMH Life Skills Rockland community Coll., Suffern, N.Y., 1982; student worker comptroller's office, Boston U., 1981-82; assoc. programmer IBM, Purchase, N.Y., 1983-85, sr. communications support specialist, Boston, 1985—. Co-chmn. student concerns com. Boston U., 1980-82; instr. CPR/first aid ARC, White Plains, N.Y. 1976—. Mem. Student Bar Assn. (rep. 1985-86), Rockland County Women's Network. Democrat.

PADILLA, OLGA ILAGAN, nurse; b. Bongabon, Philippines, Jan. 24, 1947; came to U.S., 1969; naturalized, 1976; d. Azarias David and Consolacion (Ilagan) P. B.S. in Nursing, U. Santo Tomas, Manila, 1967; Med. Nurse Practitioner Roosevelt Meml. Hosp., Chgo., 1976. R.N., Ill., Ohio. Head nurse Roosevelt Meml. Hosp., Chgo., 1972-75, adult nurse practitioner, 1975-78; dir. nurse practitioners Chgo. Ctr. Hosp., 1978-84; dir. nurse practitioners, 3 clinics, Chgo., 1980-84; dir. utilization rev. dept., Chgo. HMO, 1984—; med. paralegal cons., 1984—. Mem. Am. Nurses Assn., Ill. Nurses Assn., Nurse Practitioners Assn., Continuing Edn. Assn. Republican. Home: 5445 N Sheridan St Chicago IL 60640 Office: Chgo HMO 540 N LaSalle St Chicago IL 60610

PADNOS, DONNA MOTEL, healthcare administrator; b. Chgo., Oct. 12, 1941; d. Sidney Benjamin and Beatrice (Sachs) Motel; B.S., U. Ill., 1962, M.S., 1978; M.B.A., U. Chgo., 1982; m. Richard D. Padnos, Aug. 27, 1961; children—Stephen, Beth, Gerald. Teaching asst., research asst. U. Ill., Chgo., 1973-77; pediatric research technician Michael Reese Hosp. and Med. Center, Chgo., 1977-80, adminstrv. asst., anesthesiology, 1980-83, project coordinator, medicine, 1983-84; bus. mgr. Greenberg Radiology Clinic, 1984-85; adminstrv. asst. Glen Ellyn Profl. Assocs., Ill., 1985—. Membership chmn. LWV, Chgo., 1969-70, land use chmn., 1971-73, health care com. mem., 1978-82. Mem. Chgo. Health Execs. Forum, Ill. Soc. Anesthesiologists (exec. sec. 1981-83), Women's Health Exec. Network. (bull. editor 1982-83, treas. 1983-84), Assn. Adminstrs. Ambulatory services, Soc. for Hosp. Planning and Mktg., Med. Group Mgmt. Assn., Nat. Assn. for Female Execs. Contbr. articles to profl. jours. Home: 1459 W Byron St Chicago IL 60613 Office: 454 Pennsylvania Ave Glen Ellyn IL 60137

PADRO, CARMEN AWILDA, ednl. adminstr.; b. Mayaguez, P.R., Feb. 2, 1944; d. Angel Padro and Carmen Teresa Velez; B.A., Inter Am. U., 1967, M.A., 1974; postgrad. N.Y. U., 1976-81. Tchr. secondary sch., Mayaguez, 1967-70; sch. and community relations coordinator Mayaguez Sch. Dist., 1970-76; sch. and community relations gen. supr. Mayaguez Region Dept. Edn., 1976-80; exec. dir. fine arts project Dept. Edn., Ramey Base, Mayaguez, 1981—, gen. supr. Sch. adminstrn., 1981-85. Bd. dirs. Project Hope for Ages. Recipient Leaderships award Am. Legion, 1963, Bus. and Profl. Women, 1976. Mem. Assn. Supervision and Curriculum Devel., P.R. Educators in Action Orgn., Bus. and Profl. Women's Club. Office: Oficina Regional Centro Gubernamental Mayaguez PR 00708

PADUANO, DORIS JEAN, general contractor, compliance consultant; b. Seattle Oct. 28, 1929; d. Helmer Edward Trettevik and Margaret (Estella) Warren; m. Frank Paduano, May 27, 1972 (dec. 1979); children—Gery Pierpont Williams, Galye Lee Williams, Lorna Jean Williams. Student Seattle Community Coll., 1965-66. With Boeing Co., Seattle, 1953-78; office mgr. Frank Paduano Co., Seattle, 1970-75, pres., 1975—. Mem. Assoc. Women Contractors (charter mem., sec. 1980-82, com. mem.), Assoc. Gen. Contractors (mem. com.), Wash. Dump Truck Assn. (sec. 1984—, bd. dirs.), Women Construction Council (sec., treas. 1980—), Puget Sound Mycology Soc. (fellow 1971-77, sec. 1974-75). Democrat. Lutheran. Clubs: Supreme Emblem of U.S., Lake City Emblem, Lodges: Women of Moose, Elks. Avocations: fishing; mycology; gardening; sports Home: 6756 7th Ave NW Seattle WA 98117 Office: 3A Industries Frank Paduano Co 706 Union St Seattle WA 98117

PADULA, MARY L., state legislator. Mem. Mass. Senate, 1983—. Republican. Office: Mass Senate State Capitol Boston MA 02133*

PADZENSKY, ROCHELLE G., bookkeeping service executive; b. Chgo., July 4, 1936; d. Edward H. and Mary B. (Battock) Kreisman; m. Herbert R. Padzensky, June 17, 1956; children—Leslie Jay, Lori Beth. Bookkeeper, Lincoln Finance Co., Denver, 1955-56; teller Colo. Indsl. Bank, Denver, 1956-57, Peoples Bank, Cedar Rapids, Iowa, 1957-58; supr. mktg. research surveys Frank Magid Assocs., Denver, 1969-72; savs. supr. Colo. Fed. Savs., Denver, 1973-78; sec. Perkin-Elmer Data Systems, Denver, 1978-79; v.p. KHL Corp., Denver, 1979-85; owner, pres. Books Plus, 1985—. Named Outstanding Student, Savs. and Loan League, Denver, 1976, 77. Mem. Nat. Assn. Female Execs. Democrat. Jewish. Home: 3792 S Sebring Ct Denver CO 80237

PAGANO-JOANNIDES, DONNA LEE, corporate executive; b. Portland, Oreg., Aug. 10, 1948; d. Don Samuel and Lelia Ann (Galano) Pagano; m. Dennis Nicholas Joannides, Apr. 17, 1982. Student U. of the Ams., Mexico City, 1967; B.S., Oreg. State U., 1970, M.Ed., 1974; postgrad. Portland State U., 1980. Cert. tchr., adminstr. Curriculum instr., Corvallis Schs., Oreg., 1970-76, acting vice prin. 1975—; chmn. dept. Beaverton Schs., Oreg., 1976-79, curriculum asst., 1979-80, staff devel., 1980-82; pres. Nat. Bus. Execs., Denver, 1982—; cons. in field. Author: (curriculum devel.) State of Oreg., 1974-77; (handbook) NBE Network Aerobics, 1984. Contbr. articles to profl. jours. Mem. Bus. and Profl. Women, Am. Mgmt. Assn., Nat. Assn. Female Execs., Internat. Network Social Network Analysis, Kappa Kappa Gamma. Republican. Roman Catholic. Clubs: Rocky Mountain, Spaniel (Denver, field trial sec.). Avocations: traveling; camping; hiking; archery; needlework; writing. Office: Nat Bus Execs 1873 S Bellaire #702 Denver CO 80222

PAGE, CAROL DEAN, county official; b. Kaysville, Utah, Apr. 22, 1934; d. Joseph Melvin and Cora Pearl (Flint) Hill; m. Wayne Stoker Page, July 24, 1952; children—Kent H., Thomas H., Curtis W., Tyler R. Student Weber State Coll. Title abstracter Security Title Co., Farmington, Utah, 1957-79; county recorder Davis County, Farmington, 1979—; mem. Utah Plat Standards Commn. Dist. vice chmn. Republican Orgn., Layton, Utah, 1983, dist. chmn., 1984. Recipient Pursuit of Excellence award Ch. of Jesus Christ of Latterday Saints, 1983. Mem. Internat. Assn. Clks., Recorders and Treas. (bd. dirs. 1982—), Utah Assn. Counties (2d v.p. 1983-84), Utah Assn. County Recorders (pres. 1984—), Davis County Golf Assn. (pres. 1982). Avocations: skiing; volleyball racket ball; golf; knitting. Home: 881 E 225 N Layton UT 84041 Office: PO Box 618 Farmington UT 84025

PAGE, DOROTHY JEAN, personnel executive; b. Phila., Oct. 11, 1951; d. Alfred H. and Dorothy (Marvin) Cotton; m. Michael Robert Page, Oct. 31, 1951. B.A., Juniata Coll., 1973. Mgmt. trainee J. C. Penney Co., Upper Darby, Pa., 1972-75, personnel mgr., 1975-78; corp. affirmative action officer ARA Services, Phila., 1978-79, corp. EEO projects mgr., 1979-80; v.p. personnel ARA Instl. Services, Chgo., 1980-82; v.p. personnel ARA Hosp. Food Mgmt., Phila., 1982—. Co. rep. March of Dimes, Phila., 1983-84. Mem. Am. Soc. Personnel Adminstrn. Home: 24 Pugh Rd Wayne PA 19087 Office: ARA Hosp Food Mgmt 6th and Walnut Sts Philadelphia PA 19106

PAGE, DOZZIE LYONS, educator; b. Tiptonville, Tenn., Apr. 13, 1921; d. Lessie LeRoy and Carrie (Oldham) Lyons; B.S.Ed., Chgo. Tchrs. Coll., 1968; M.S.Ed., Chgo. State U., 1976; M.A. in Bus. Edn., Govs. State U., 1979; children—Rita, Gerald. Cashier receptionist Unity Mut. Life Ins. Co., Chgo., 1939-47; sec. United Transport Service Employees Union, Chgo., 1947-51; sec. to dir. West Side YMCA, Chgo., 1951-53; sec., office mgr. Joint Council Dining Car Employees AFL CIO, Chgo., 1957-59; sr. stenographer Chgo. Police Dept., 1962-65; tchr. office practice Manpower Devel. Tng. Act, Chgo. Bd. Edn., 1965-67; tchr., coordinator distributive edn. Dunbar Vocat. High Sch., Chgo., 1968—. Mem. Office Edn. Assn., Distributive Edn. Clubs Am., Chgo. Urban League, Chgo. Bus. Edn. Assn. (exec. bd. 1983—), Ill., Am. personnel and guidance assns., Am. Vocat. Assn., Nat., Ill. bus. edn. assns., Chgo. State U. Alumni Assn., Governor's State U. Alumni Assn., Phi Delta Kappa. Home: 6127 Justine St S Chicago IL 60636 Office: 3000 ML King Dr Chicago IL 60616

PAGE, EDDEE ELIZABETH, banker; b. Salisbury, N.C., Dec. 8, 1942; d. James Richard and Aline (Houston) Giles; m. Russell M. Page, Oct. 2, 1961 (dec. May 1980); children—Judith, Russell M., Nathan, James. A.S. in Gen. Bus. with honors, Norwalk Community Coll., 1985; student U. Conn. From teller to head teller State Nat. Bank, Darien, Conn., 1969-75, adminstrv. asst., 1975-79; asst. br. mgr. Citytrust Bank, Bridgeport, Conn., 1979-81, loan workout officer, 1981-83, asst. v.p., corp. fin. services sales officer, 1983—; fin. sec. Conn. Minority Bankers, New Haven, 1980-82. Treas. St. Joseph's Home/Sch. Assn., Norwalk, Conn., 1978-82; trustee Faith Tabernacle Ch., Stamford, Conn., 1979-86, mem. credit com. Faith Tabernacle Fed. Credit Union, 1981-85. Democrat. Baptist. Home: 71 Marlin Dr Norwalk CT 06854 Office: Citytrust Bank 961 Main St Bridgeport CT 06601

PAGE, JANET LOUISE, accountant; b. Monterey Park, Calif., Feb. 4, 1944; d. John Lester and Maxine (Clift) P.; B.S., Brigham Young U., 1966. Auditor, Peat, Marwick, Mitchell & Co., Los Angeles, 1966-71; controller H.F. Ahmanson & Co., Los Angeles, 1971-74, dir. internal audit, 1974-81, v.p., controller, 1981—. C.P.A., Calif. Mem. Am. Inst. C.P.A.s, Am. Mgmt. Assn., Fin. Execs. Inst., Calif. Soc. C.P.A.s. Republican. Mormon. Office: 3731 Wilshire Blvd Suite 500 Los Angeles CA 90010

PAGE, KAREN ANN, publisher; b. Warren, Mich., May 8, 1962; d. George L. and Joan (Banaszewski) P. B.A., Northwestern U., 1983. Researcher, Com. of 200, Chgo., 1981; founder, pres. Cakes Unlimited, Evanston, Ill., 1980-83; corp. analyst Shearson Lehman Brothers, N.Y.C., 1983-85; mag. devel. staff Time Inc., N.Y.C., 1985; mgr. FDP Assocs., N.Y.C., 1985-86; Pub., editor in chief N.Y. Women's Jour., N.Y.C., 1986—. Freelance writer Working Woman mag., 1986; mem. career mktg. bd. Mademoiselle Mag., 1983—. Fundraiser Mondale/Ferraro, 1984. grantee NEH, 1981. Mem. Nat. Assn. Young Profl. Women (nat. pres., bd. dirs., founder 1984—), Women's Econ. Round Table.

PAGE, LINDA KAY, state official; b. Wadsworth, Ohio, Oct. 4, 1943; s. Frederick Meredith and Martha Irene (Vance) P. Student Franklin U., 1970-75, Sch. Banking, Ohio U., 1976-77; cert. Nat. Personnel Sch., U. Md.-Am. Bankers Assn., 1981; grad. banking program U. Wis.-Madison, 1982-84. Asst. v.p., gen. mgr. Bancohio Corp., Columbus, Ohio, 1975-78, v.p., dist. mgr., 1979-80, v.p., mgr. employee relations, 1980-81, v.p., div. mgr., 1982-83; commr. of banks State of Ohio, Columbus, 1983—; guest speaker, lectr. various banking groups. Bd. dirs. Clark County Mental Health Bd., Springfield, Ohio, 1982-83, Springfield Met. Housing, 1982-83; bd. advisers Orgn. Indsl. Standards, Springfield, 1982-83. Recipient Leadership Columbus award Sta. WTVN and Columbus Leadership Program, 1975, 82, Outstanding Service award Clark County Mental Health Bd., 1983. Mem. Nat. Assn. Bank Women (pres. 1980-81), Bus. and Profl. Women's Club, LWV, Conf. State Bank Suprs. (bd. dirs. 1984-85), dist. chmn. 1984-85), Ohio Bankers Assn. (bd. dirs. 1982-83). Lodge: Zonta. Avocations: tennis; animal protection; matchbook collecting. Home: 1330 Erickson Ave Columbus OH 43227 Office: Dept Commerce Div of Banks 2 Nationwide Plaza Columbus OH 43215

PAGE, MARJORIE EILEEN, county officia; b. Stratton, Nebr., July 21, 1920; d. Coral and Ruby Eleanor (Clark) Brouse; m. Harold Ray Page, May 18, 1947; 1 child, James Edward. Student pub. schs., Littleton, Colo. Clk. Clerk & Recorder's Office, Littleton, Colo., 1941-48, dep. clk., 1948-56, clk., recorder, 1956—. Bd. dirs. Met. Mental Health Assn., Arapahoe chpt., 1963-65; active various fund raising orgns.; mem. Sewell Found. Aux. Named Woman of Yr., Englewood Bus. and Profl. Women's Club, 1962-63; Disting. Service award, Nat. Assn. Counties, 1982; Clk. of Yr., Nat. Assn. County Recorders and Clks., 1982, others. Mem. Colo. Assn. County Clks. and Recorders (sec.-treas.), Nat. Assn. County Recorders and Clks. (pres. 1974-75), Nat. Assn. Counties (dir. 1985-86), Englewood Bus. and Profl. Women's Club, Centennial C. of C. Lutheran. Republican. Club: Zonta. Avocations: hiking; cooking; collecting antiques. Home: 5 Robincrest Ln Littleton CO 80123 Office: Arapahoe County Clerk and Recorder 5334 S Prince St Littleton CO 80166

PAGE, RUTH, dancer; b. Indpls.; d. Lafayette and Marian (Heinly) Page; student Tudor Hall, Indpls., N.Y.C. L.H.D., DePaul U., 1980, Ind. U., 1981, Lincoln Coll., Ill., 1985; m. Thomas Hart Fisher, Feb. 8, 1925 (dec.). Dancer with Pavlowa at age of 15; performed in leading role of J. Alden Carpenter's The Birthday of the Infanta, produced by Chgo. Opera Co., 1919, later in N.Y.C.; toured U.S. as prin. dancer with Adolph Bolm's Ballet, later appeared in London with Mr. Bolm; premiere danseuse 2d Music Box Revue, N.Y.C., 1921-23, Chgo. Allied Arts performances, 1924, 25, 26; studied under Enrico Cecchetti at Monte Carlo, 1925; premiere danseuse Mcpl. Opera Co., Buenos Aires, Ravinia Opera Co., 1926-31; guest soloist with Met. Opera Co., 1926-28; guest artist at enthronement ceremonies for Emperor Hirohito, Japan, 1928; performed series of Am. dances before Sophil Soc., Moscow, 1930; ballet dir. Chgo. Opera, 1934-37, 42-43, 45; dir. Fed. Theatre Dance Project, Chgo., 1938-39; S. Am. tour with first dance group as co-dir. Page-Stone Ballet, 1940; guest choreographer with Bentley Stone, dancer Frankie and Johnny for Ballet Russe de Monte Carlo, 1945; guest choreographer, dancer The Bells for Ballet Russe de Monte Carlo, 1946, Billy Sunday, 1948; Impromptu au Bois, and Revanche, Les Ballets des Champs-Elysees, 1951, Royal Festival Ballet, Vilia, 1953; co-dir. Les Ballets Americains, Theatre des Champs Elysees, Paris, 1950; ballet mistress Chgo. Lyric Opera, 1954-69; choreographer, dir. Ruth Page's Chgo. Opera Ballet, 1956-66, Ruth Page's Internat. Ballet, 1966-70; choreographer Merry Widow Ballet, 1956, Susanna and the Barber, 1957, Salome, 1957, Triumph of Chastity, 1958, El Amor Brujo, 1958, Camille, 1958, Carmen, 1959, Fledermaus, 1960, Concertino, 1961, Mefistofela, 1962, Bullets or Bon-Bons, 1965, Nutcracker, 1965-81, Carmina Burana, 1966, Bolero, 1967, Dancer's Ritual, 1968, Alice in the Garden, 1970, also Alice in Wonderland and Alice Through the Looking Glass at Pitts. Ballet Theatre, 1971, Catulli Carmina, 1973, Chain of Fools, 1973, Alice in Wonderland, 1978, Frankie and Johnny (produced by Dance Theater of Harlem), Covent Garden, 1981, New York, 1982; lectr. tour Ruth Page's Invitation to the Dance, 1971-72. Recipient award Adult Council Greater Chgo., 1963; citation outstanding service Ballet Guild Chgo. Mem. Chgo. Nat. Assn. Dance Masters (hon.). Clubs: Arts, Friday, Racquet (Chgo.). Contbr. to mags. Address: Ruth Page Found Sch Dance 1016 N Dearborn St Chicago IL 60610

PAGE, SALLY JACQUELYN, univ. adminstr.; b. Saginaw, Mich., July 8, 1943; d. William Henry and Doris Effie (Knippel) P.; B.A., U. Iowa, 1965; M.B.A., So. Ill. U., 1973. Copy editor, C.V. Mosby Co., St. Louis, 1965-69; editorial cons. Editorial Assos., Edwardsville, Ill., 1969-70; research adminstr. So. Ill. U., 1970-74, asst. to pres., affirmative action officer, 1974-77; civil rights officer U. N.D., Grand Forks, 1977—, lectr. mgmt., 1978—, mem. women's equity com., 1980—, handicapped facilities com., 1981—; mem. Grand Forks Mayor's Com. on Employment of Handicapped, 1984—, vice chair, 1986—; polit. commentator Sta. KFJM, 1981—. Pres., Pine to Prairie council Girl Scouts U.S.A., 1980-85; mem. Grand Forks Civil Service Task Force; mem. Grand Forks Civil Service Commn., 1983, chmn., 1984, 86; mem. employment com. Ill. Commn. on Status of Women, 1976-77; mem. Bicentennial Com. Edwardsville, 1976, Bikeway Task Force Edwardsville, 1975-77. Mem. AAUW (dir. Ill. 1975-77), Am. Assn. Affirmative Action, Soc. Research Adminstrs., M.B.A. Assn. Republican. Presbyterian. Home: 3121 Cherry St Grand Forks ND 58201 Office: Univ ND Grand Forks ND 58202

PAGE, SARA MARIE, social worker; b. Wheeling, W.Va., Oct. 25, 1940; d. Dominic R. and Josephine L. (Giardino) Page; B.A. cum laude, Muskingum Coll., 1963; M.S.W., Case Western Res. U., 1965; 1 dau., Eve Marie. Sr. psychiat. social worker Akron (Ohio) Child Guidance Center, 1965-71; chief social worker, children's unit Ga. Mental Health Inst., Atlanta, 1972-75, program dir., children's unit, 1975-77; pvt. practice psychiat. social work, Atlanta; field instr. grad. social work Western Res. U., U. Ga. Mem. Nat. Assn. Social Workers, Acad. Cert. Social Workers, Atlanta Mental Health Assn. Home: 5465 Mt Vernon Pkwy NW Atlanta GA 30327 Office: 6111 Peachtree Dunwoody Rd Suite F-103 Atlanta GA 30328

PAGEL, DEBORAH JOANNE, health physicist, biologist; b. Chgo., Apr. 25, 1955; d. Raymond Frank and Amelia Emelda (Suchecki) Heppeler; m. Richard Arlin Pagel, Aug. 4, 1979. B.S. in Biology, Elmhurst Coll., 1981. Sr. health physics technician Argonne Nat. Lab. (Ill.), 1977-81; gen. health physicist Commonwealth Edison Dresden Nuclear Sta., Morris, Ill., 1981-85; lead health physicist Prodn. Tng. Ctr., Commonwealth Edison, Wilmington, Ill., 1985—. Contbr. articles to profl. jours. Fund solicitor Crusade of Mercy/United Fund, 1981—. Mem. Health Physics Soc., Am. Nuclear Soc., Nat. Am. Nuclear Soc., Assn. Women in Sci., Argonne Lab. Equal Opportunity Assn. Republican. Roman Catholic. Office: Commonwealth Edison PTC RR 2 Box 120 Essex Rd Wilmington IL 60481

PAGELS, ELAINE HIESEY, historian of religion, educator; b. Palo Alto, Calif., Feb. 13, 1943; d. William McKinley and Louise Sophia (Boogaert) Hiesey; B.A., Stanford, 1964, M.A., 1965; Ph.D., Harvard, 1970; m. Heinz R. Pagels, June 7, 1969. Asst. prof. history of religion Barnard Coll., Columbia, 1970-74, from asso. prof. to prof., chairperson dept. religion, 1974-82; Harrington Spear Paine prof. religion Princeton U., 1982—. Nat. Endowment Humanities grantee, 1973; Mellon fellow Aspen Inst. Humanistic Studies, 1974, Hazen fellow, 1975; Rockefeller fellow, 1978-79; Guggenheim fellow, 1979—; MacArthur prize fellow, 1981—. Mem. Soc. Bibl. Lit., Am. Acad. Religion. Episcopalian. Club: Bibl. Theologians. Author: The Johannine Gospel in Gnostic Exegesis, 1973; The Gnostic Paul, 1975; The Gnostic Gospels, 1979.

PAGLIARO, TRUDY STEINBRECHER, health industry executive; b. Phila., Nov. 11, 1939; d. Henry Nicholas and Martha Gertrude (Arnold) Steinbrecher; m. Dominic A. Pagliaro, Mar. 11, 1960 (div. 1984); children—Andre, Pamela, Brenda, Gina. B.A. in History and Econs., Georgian Ct., 1976, cert. edn., 1978; postgrad. Rutgers U., 1981-84. Cert. tchr. kindergarten through 12th grade, N.J. With sales and customer service dept. Tenco, Inc., Linden, N.J., 1978-80; med. sales rep. Maj. Med. Supply Co., Middletown, N.J., 1980-81; sales rep. Thermascan Inc., N.Y.C., 1982-83; regional sales mgr. Team, Inc., South Plainfield, N.J., 1983-85; dir. sales Biopharm Inc., N.Y.C., 1985—; cons. Litton Microwave, Union, N.J., 1980—. Vol. Battered Wives Support Group, N.J., 1982-83; panelist Georgian Ct. Coll. Workshops/Women in Sales, N.J., 1982—. Mem. Health Industry Distbg. Assn., Nat. Assn. Profl. Saleswomen, Georgian Ct. Coll. Alumni. Republican. Lutheran. Avocations: sketching; sculpture; music; sailing; golf. Home: 1 Madison Gardens Old Bridge NJ 08857 Office: Biopharm Inc 521 Fifth Ave 22d Floor New York NY 10111

PAGTAKHAN-SO, LEONOR, pediatrician, allergist; b. Philippines, June 28, 1941; d. Bartolome Reyes Pagtakhan and Rosario Salamanca; M.D., Manila Central U., 1965; m. Ojien Hwat So; children—Rosalina Ann, Robert Emerson. Intern, Springfield (Mass.) Hosp., 1971, resident, 1972-73; house physician Northampton (Mass.) State Hosp., 1968-70; fellow in pediatrics St. Clare's Hosp., Schenectady, 1974-75, practice medicine specializing in pediatrics and allergy, Pikeville, Ky., 1975—. Diplomate Am. Bd. Pediatrics. Fellow Am. Acad. Pediatrics; mem. AMA, Am. Coll. Allergists, Am. Acad. Allergy and Immunology, Pike County Med. Soc., Ky. Med. Assn. Democrat. Roman Catholic. Address: Island Creek Med Bldg Box 2229 Pikeville KY 41501

PAIGE, CANDACE DERI, lawyer; b. Bridgeport, Conn., Feb. 22, 1956; d. Anthony and Rose D. (Deri) P.; m. Paul M. Mandeville, May 14, 1983. B.A. summa cum laude, Fairfield U., 1978, J.D., Western New Eng. Sch. Law, Springfield, Mass., 1981. Bar: Conn. 1982. Law clk. Trager & Trager, Fairfield, Conn., 1979, Owens & Schine, Bridgeport, Conn., 1980; assoc. Law Offices James Miller, Jr., Westport, Conn., 1981-82, Law Offices Colin Gunn, Westport, 1982—; legis. asst. Office of Hon. Stewart B. McKinney, Washington, 1977. Mem. Conn. Bar Assn., ABA, Westport Bar Assn., Greater Bridgeport Bar Assn., Westport Women's Bar Assn. Home: 372 Knapps Hwy Fairfield CT 06430 Office: Law Offices of Colin Gunn 35 Church Ln Westport CT 06880

PAIGE, RUTH ULLMANN, psychologist; b. Germany, May 4; came to U.S., 1938, naturalized, 1946; d. Adolf and Else (Heumann-Abraham) Ullmann; B.A., Bklyn. Coll., 1956; M.S. (scholar), CUNY, 1957; postgrad. U. Kans., Lawrence, 1957-60; Ph.D., U. Oreg., Eugene, 1978; m. Albert B. Paige, Mar. 20, 1954; children—David, Elizabeth, Rebekah. Teaching and research asst. counseling psychology U. Kans., 1957-58; sch. psychologist, Shawnee, Kans., 1958-59; remedial reading instr., also pvt. practice, Lawrence, 1957-63; psychologist Lawrence-Douglas County Mental Health Clinic, 1959-63; psychology research asst. Menninger Clinic, Topeka, 1963; psychology research asst. VA Hosp., Leavenworth, Kans., 1964-65; counselor Group Processes, Inc., Seattle, 1969-72; psychologist intern Snohomish County Mental Health Clinic, Everett, Wash., 1973-74, Highline-West Seattle Mental Health Center, 1974-75; dir. Counseling Center programs North Seattle Community Coll., 1979-86; pvt. practice clin. psychology, Seattle, 1985—; cons. family mediation King County Family Ct., 1978—; instr. Lane Community coll., 1972-73; vol. instr. U. Oreg., 1972-73. Mem. Am. Psychol. Assn., Western Psychol. Assn., Wash. State Psychol. Assn. (pres. 1985), Assn. Women in Psychology, Counseling and Guidance Dirs. Assn. Wash. Community Colls. (pres. 1981-82), N.W. Family Therapy Inst. Contbr. articles to profl. jours. Home: 13436 NE 47th St Bellevue WA 98005 Office: 3216 NE 45th Pl Suite 303 Seattle WA 98105

PAINE, JACQUELYN LOU, candy company executive; b. Bedford, Ohio, July 28, 1945; d. Jay Allen and Luella (Majernik) P.; m. Robert Gordon Barr, Sept. 17, 1983. B.S., Ohio U., 1968; M.A., Ohio State U., 1973; M.B.A., Case Western Res. U., 1981. Exec. asst., chief exec. officer C. & O. Ry., Cleve., 1968-70; instr. Inst. Montana, Zug, Switzerland, 1973-75; corp. planner Firestone Tire Co., Akron, Ohio, 1978-79; mgr. fin. and adminstrn. Central Nat. Bank, Cleve., 1979-82; pres. Haribo of Am., Balt., 1982—. Mem. Exec. and Profl. Women's Network, Nat. Candy Wholesalers Assn., Nat. Confectioners Assn., Nat. Candy Brokers Assn., Nat. Assn. Splty. Food Trade. Avocations: photography; travel; skiing. Home: 807 S Charles St Baltimore MD 21230

PAINE, SALLY JANE, computer asisted telecommunications company executive; b. Haverhill, England, Apr. 4, 1938; came to U.S., 1974, naturalized, 1983; d. William Vinter Gurteen and Mary Cooper; m. G. Eustis Paine, Sept. 13, 1975. Owner, Boutique, England, 1962-65; pres. Anchor Foods, Virgin Islands, 1977-81; corp. sec. The Wine Exchange Ltd., Phila., 1984—. Republican. Mem. Ch. of England. Office: The Wine Exchange Ltd 1811 Chestnut St Philadelphia PA 19103 also Wex France 1 Av de Verdun 33500 Libourne France also Wine Exchange UK Ltd Asphalte House Palace St London SW1 E5HS England

PAINTER, JUDY ANN, advertising company executive; b. Huntington, N.Y., July 23, 1952; d. Joseph Albert and Shirley Arlene (Stephens) P. B.A. in English, SUNY, 1981. Adminstrv. asst. Marsteller, N.Y.C., 1981-82; copywriter Arrow Electronics, Melville, N.Y., 1982-83; Kopf & Isaacson, Melville, 1983-84; copywriter/contact Foote, Cone & Belding, N.Y.C., 1984—. Mem. L.I. Advt. Club (bd. dirs. 1986—, named Best on L.I. 1984). Republican. Home: 276 Morches Rd St James NY 11780 Office: Foote Cone & Belding Advt 101 Park Ave New York NY 10178

PAINTER, SUSAN MADELINE HAWKINS, state official; b. Nashville, July 10, 1949; d. Charles Clarence and Helen Katherine (Dickerson) H.; m. William Paul Painter, Jan. 2, 1971. B.S., Auburn U., 1971, M.Ed., 1972; postgrad. in pub. adminstrn. U. Colo., 1983—. Cert. rehab. counselor. Rehab. counselor State La., Shreveport, 1971-73; rehab. counselor State of Colo., Denver, 1978-80, supervising counselor, 1980-81, program supr., 1982—, mem. facilities and grant review com., 1984—; owner Words at Work Cons.; treas., bd. mem. Computer Tng. for Severely Handicapped, Denver, 1984—; bd. dirs. Arapahoe Private Industry Council, Englewood, Colo., 1983-84. Co-author of forms for Colo. Div. Rehab., 1984 (recognized by Fed. Rehab. Services Adminstrn. 1984), co-author of job-share policy, proposal, 1985. Bd. dirs. Lake Arbor-Homeowner's Assn., Arvada, Colo., 1979-81, newsletter author, editor; mem. Nat. Women's Polit. Caucus, Denver, 1981—, Nat. Abortion Rights Action League, Denver, 1980—. Recipient McCorry award for Outstanding Supr., Colo. Dept. Social Services, Denver, 1984. Mem. Colo. Rehab. Assn. (bd. dirs., treas. 1980—), Am. Soc. Pub. Adminstrn., Nat. Rehab Adminstrn. Assn. Democrat. Episcopalian. Avocations: writing; travel. Office: Colo Div Rehab 1435 Grove St Denver CO 80204

PAIR, BRENDA BENNETT, insurance executive; b. Aug. 26, 1940; d. Robert Joseph and Clarissa M. (Weekes) Bennett; m. James H. Pair Jr., Apr. 4, 1969; children—Richard Steven, Randall Joseph, Ronald Gregory. Student De Kalb Coll., 1971. Lic. property and casualty agt., surplus lines agt. Ga. Underwriter W.K. Stringer Co., Atlanta, 1961-65, Tharpe & Assocs., Atlanta, 1965-68; sr. v.p. Alexander & Howden, Atlanta, 1968-82; exec. v.p., ptnr. Assocs. Pair Ins. Inc., Atlanta, 1982—; pres. Pair Underwriting Mgrs., Inc.; v.p. Paramount Claims Inc.; dir., v.p. Chandler Ins. Co. Ltd. Mem. Atlanta Assn. Ins. Women (exec. bd. 1977-80, Davisons adv. bd. 1978-79, pres. 1978-79, Ins. Woman of Yr. 1979-80), Profl. Ins. Agts. Ga., Nat. Assn. Female Execs. Republican. Episcopalian. Home: 202 Brandywine Circle Dunwoody GA 30338 also 5550 Spring Valley Dallas TX 75240 Office: 1155 Hammond Dr Atlanta GA 30328 also 15301 Dallas Pkwy Dallas TX 75248

PAIS, CLAUDETTE RACHEL, horse-racing consultant; b. Timmins, Ont., Can., Aug. 11, 1941; came to U.S., 1962, naturalized, 1975; d. Patrick Xavier and Jeannette Marie (Labelle) Bigras; student U. Toronto, 1959-61, extension courses UCLA, 1981; m. Alfred Frank Pais, May 5, 1965; children—Louise, Frank. Co-owner Pais Properties, Santa Monica, Calif., 1965—; founding pres. Golden Bear Raceway, Sacramento, 1975-76, Standardbred Owners Calif., Santa Monica, 1977-78; organizer stockholder relations Hollywood Park, Inc., Inglewood, Calif., 1978-82; mem. Calif. Horse Racing Bd. Com. and Subcom. Off-Track Wagering Calif., 1975—; adv. com. Sch. Racing, U.Ariz. Mem. citizens adv. com. City Santa Monica, 1976; commr. Parks and Recreation, City Santa Monica, 1977-79; dir., sec. Girls Club Santa Monica Bay Area, Inc., 1978-80; assoc. Pepperdine U., 1980—. Recipient award City of Santa Monica, 1977, 79; named Ky. Col. Mem. Nat. Cowboy Hall Fame. Home: 1115 14th St Suite 306 Santa Monica CA 90403 Office: 1400 California Ave Santa Monica CA 90403

PAISS, DORIS BELL, educational and psychological consultant, lecturer, educator; b. Phila., Nov. 19, 1929; d. Simon and Sarah (Freedman) Cohen; m. Lee Paiss, July 26, 1953; children—Jana, Michael. B.F.A., Barnard Coll., 1954; postgrad. Los Angeles City Coll., 1962-63; M.A., Columbia U., 1963, Ph.D. in Philosophy of Ancient Civilizations, 1976, degree in Geriatrics in Abnormal Psychology, 1978. Active Jewish education, 1963-86; ednl. dir. M.D. Hoffman Regional Hebrew High Sch., Phila., 1973-83; coordinator Daroff Campus of Sr. Adult Studies, Raymond and Miriam Klein br. Jewish Community Ctr., Phila., 1982-85, mem. faculty Daroff Campus Adult Studies, 1978-85; cons., lectr. on stress, memory, time mgmt., devel. human potential, Phila., 1976-86, guest lectr. Columbia U., U. Wis., U. Calif.-Santa Barbara, Oberlin Coll., Rochester Inst. Tech., Rutgers U., U. Tampa, Coalition for Jewish Edn., writers' confs., community service orgns., indsl. seminars; mem. faculty Inst. Awareness, 1980-83, Satinsky Inst. for Blind, 1980-85; free-lance writer and producer comml., indsl. and ednl. films, 1950-70. Recipient numerous awards. Mem. Nat. Assn. Female Execs., Am. Film Inst. Democrat. Jewish. Avocations: research on memory; show music.

PAJAK, CHRISTINE DIANE, computer programmer; b. Great Lakes, Ill., Mar. 19, 1962; d. Michael Anthony and Alda Marie (Ashcroft) Colonna; m. Jeffrey Scott Pajak, Oct. 18, 1980. A.A.S. with honors in Data Processing, Clark County Coll., 1985. Lead checker Vegas Village, Las Vegas, 1978-79; salesperson Sears, Roebuck & Co., Las Vegas, 1979, Broadway Southwest, Las Vegas, 1979; clk. III and teller First Interstate Bank, Las Vegas, 1979-85; computer programmer Golden Nugget Hotel/Casino, Las Vegas, 1985—. Mem. campaign staffs Democratic candidates in Nev., 1978, 82. Mem. Nat. Assn. Female Execs. Roman Catholic. Avocations: snow skiing; water skiing; hiking; bowling; swimming.

PALADINO, JEANNETTE E., advt./pub. relations exec.; b. Bklyn.; d. Albert E. and Jennie Paladino; B.A., Hofstra U., 1962; m. Charles Antin, June 5, 1976. Reporter, L.I. Comml. Rev., 1961-63; pub. relations account supr. Batten, Barton, Durstine & Osborn, Inc., 1963-68; pub. relations dir./advt. account exec. Warwick, Advt., 1968-72; pub. relations officer Econ. Devel. Adminstrn. Commonwealth P.R., N.Y.C., 1972-76; pub. relations mgr. Anaconda Co., N.Y.C., 1976-78; sr. v.p. corp. communications Marsh & McLennan, Inc., N.Y.C., 1978-83; sr. v.p., dir. communications Bowery Savs. Bank, N.Y.C., 1984—. Recipient Matrix award N.Y. Women in Communications, 1982. Mem. Women's Forum, N.Y. Women in Communications, Pub. Relations Soc. Am. Office: 110 E 42d St New York NY 10017

PALAGONIA, GRACE STUCKE, lab. technologist; b. Freedom, Pa., Mar. 26, 1907; d. Elias Edward and Margaret Grace (Whipple) Stucke; student Garfield Coll., 1922-23, Pitts. Homeopathic Hosp. Sch. Nursing, 1926-28, Coll. of Wooster (Ohio), 1928-29, N.Y.U., 1943-52, N.Y.U. Med. Center Hosp., 1955-56; m. Charles A. Crandell, July 17, 1929; children—Peggy Crandell Gordon, Susan Crandell Flego; m. 2d, G.J. Palagonia, Mar. 8, 1946. Sec., Townsend Co., Fallston, Pa., 1923-25; gen. mgr. Hill Sanitatium, Wooster, Ohio, 1928-30; health, safety, personnel dir. Hardy Plastics and Chem. Corp., Bklyn., 1942-52; pvt. practice safety cons., lectr., 1952-56; EEG technologist Morristown (N.J.) Meml. Hosp., 1956-68; instr. EEG tech. Univ. Hosp., N.Y.U., 1961-64; EEG technologist Neurol. Assocs., Huntington, N.Y., 1970—; instr. ARC, N.J., N.Y., 1940-56; del. Pres. Eisenhower's Occupational Safety Conf., 1954. Mem. exec. bd. City of N.Y. Health Dept., 1944-47. Cert. med. EEG technologist. Mem. Am. Soc. Safety Engrs. (emeritus), Am. Soc. EEG Technicians (charter), Eastern Soc. EEG Technicians, Met. EEG Soc., Clin. EEG Technicians and Tecnologists, Vets. of Safety Internat., N.J. Fedn. Women's Clubs (art chmn.), N.Y.U. Center for Safety Alumni, Greater N.Y. Safety Council (plant lectr., conv. exhibit com. 1947-71), N.Y. Plastics Industry Safety Council (adv. com. 1945-50). Lectr., demonstrator accident prevention. Home: 31 Doris Ave Northport NY 11768 Office: 164 E Main St Huntington NY 11743

PALANCA, TERILYN, information management consultant; b. Chicago Heights, Ill., Aug. 15, 1957; d. Raymond Anthony and Barbara Jean (Schweizer) P. B.A., Coll. William and Mary, 1979; M.B.A., Rutgers U., 1983. Chief auditor, mgr. Williamsburg Hilton, Va., 1979-81; corp. auditor RCA Corp., Princeton, N.J., 1982-83; EDP cons. Price Waterhouse & Co., N.Y.C., 1983-84; data base adminstr. Chubb & Son, Inc., Warren, N.J., 1984-85; cons., tech. mgr. Applied Data Research, Inc., Paramus, N.J., 1985—. Campaigner, Women for Reagan, Madison, N.J., 1984. Mem. Assn. of Inst. for Cert. Computer Profls. (cert. in data processing), Am. Mgmt. Assn., Nat. Assn. Female Execs. Republican. Avocations: Masterwork Chorus; pianist; literature; hiking; animal aid. Office: Applied Data Research Inc 95 Route 17 S Paramus NJ 07652

PALERMO, CHERYL GWENDOLYN, computer programmer, administrative secretary; b. Blythe, Calif., July 19, 1948; d. Philip Gabriel and Dorothy Juanita (Nelson) P. Student Palo Verde Coll., Cerritos Coll., Coll. of Desert, 1973—. Lic. X-ray tech., Calif. Dental asst./office mgr. Bill T. Utley DDS, Downey Calif., 1970-73; sec./acct. Glen Organ Ford, Compton, Calif., 1973-74; sec. Security Pacific Nat. Bank, Blythe and Indio, Calif. 1974-78; escrow officer, office mgr. D. Gulbrandsen, DDS, Palm Springs, Calif., 1978-82; programmer/adminstrv. sec. U.S. Elevator Corp., Los Angeles, 1982—. Vol. Nat. M/S Found., 1980-82. Mem. Nat. Banking Women's Assn., 1978. Office: JS Elevator Corp 7711 S Paramount Blvd Pico Rivera CA 90660

PALEY, GRACE, author; b. N.Y.C., Dec. 11, 1922; d. Isaac and Mary (Ridnyik) Goodside; ed. Hunder Coll., NYU; m. Jess Paley, June 20, 1942; children—Nora, Dan; m. 2d, Robert Nichols. Formerly tchr. Columbia Syracuse U.; now mem. lit. faculty Sarah Lawrence Coll., CUNY. Sec., N.Y. Greenwich Village Peace Center. Recipient Lit. award for short story writing Nat. Inst. Arts and Letters, 1970; Guggenheim fellow. Mem. Am. Acad. and Inst. Arts and Letters. Author short stories: The Little Disturbances of Man, 1959; Enormous Changes at the Last Minute, 1975; Later the Same Day, 1985; stories pub. in Atlantic, Esquire, Ikon, Genesis West, Accent, New Yorker, others. Home: 126 W 11th St New York NY 10011 Office: Sarah Lawrence Coll Bronxville NY 10708

PALLADINO-KING, TERRI, lawyer; b. Bklyn., June 21, 1948; d. Frank Anthony and Phyllis (Aquila) Palladino; m. William E. King, Jr., Feb. 15, 1981; 1 son, Nicholas. B.A. in Edn., SUNY-Fredonia, 1970, M.S. in Edn., 1972; J.D., San Francisco Law Sch., 1981. Bar: Calif. 1982. Legal asst. Bunch & White, San Francisco, 1976-80, Leslie S. Patrick, Inc., San Francisco, 1980-83; sole practice, Santa Rosa, Calif., 1983—; dir., legal counsel, chmn. fund raising com. Calif. Parenting Inst., Santa Rosa, 1983—. Active Rohnert Park Women's Assn., 1983, 84. Recipient Am. Jurisprudence award, 1978; San Francisco Lawyers Club scholar, 1979. Mem. ABA, Calif. Bar Assn., Sonoma County Bar Assn. (steering com., women-in-law com.), Sonoma County Legal Services Found., Assn. Trial Lawyers Am., Queens Bench San Francisco, Calif. Women Lawyers, Santa Rosa C. of C., Rohnert Park C. of C., Women in Networking for Growth and Success, Windsor C. of C. Club: Soroptimist. Home: 6015 Elsa Ave Rohnert Park CA 94928 Office: 405 Chinn St Santa Rosa CA 95404

PALLANSCH, THEALOY, physical therapist; b. Veblen, S.D., Jan. 5, 1955; d. Kenneth Eugene and Ellen Lorraine (Rinas) Skarnagel; m. John Edward Pallansch, Sept. 8, 1979; 1 child, Karie Marie. Student S.D. State U., 1973-76; B.S. cum laude, U. N.D., 1978. Lic. phys. therapist, Minn., N.D., S.D. Staff phys. therapist Whetstone Valley Home, Milbank, S.D., 1978-79; chief phys. therapist Madison Hosp., Minn., 1978-79, Ortonville Hosp., Minn., 1978-79; dir. phys. therapy Lake Area Hosp., Webster, S.D., 1979—, Veblen Rural Phys. Therapy Clinic, 1984—; cons. Bethesda Home, Webster, S.D. Mem. Am. Phys. Therapy Assn., S.D. Phys. Therapy Assn., Pi Gamma Mu. Republican. Lutheran. Avocations: singing; horseback riding, hiking, gardening, hunting, piano. Home: Rural Route 1 Box 101 Veblen SD 57270 Office: North City Limits Lake Area Hosp Webster SD

PALLASCH, MAGDALENA HELENA (MRS. BERNHARD MICHAEL PALLASCH), artist; b. Chgo., Sept. 6; d. Frank and Anna (Meier) Fixari; student Chgo. Acad. Fine Arts, 1922-26, Am. Acad. Fine Arts, 1926-30, U. Chgo., 1960, Art Inst. Chgo.; pvt. study with Joseph Allworthy, 1935-38; m. Bernhard Pallasch, Nov. 26, 1931; children—Bernhard Michael, Diana Pallasch Miller. Contbr. two murals and ten life size figures for Century of Progress Exhbn., Chgo., 1933-34; free-lance portrait artist, Chgo., 1958—; represented in permanent collections Loyola U., Chgo., Barat Coll., Lake Forest, Ill., Internat. Coll. Surgeons, Chgo., Columbus Hosp. Med. Library, Chgo. Roman Cath. Archdiocese Office, Cardinal Newman Coll., St. Louis. Mem. Presentation Ball Aux.; mem. President's Club, Loyola U., also mem. women's bd., permanent mem. bd. dirs. Parents Assn. Recipient first award for still life, Arts Club, N.Y.C., 1960; First award, Washington, D.C. Nat. League of Am. Pen Women, 1972; 1st place and best of show State Exhibit, Springfield, Ill., 1973; 1st award Chgo. Womans Club, 1978. Mem. Nat. League of Am. Pen Women (v.p. Chgo. branch 1966-68, art chmn. 1978-80, Margaret Dingle Meml. award 1979), Friends of Austria, Friends of D'Arcy Gallery of Medieval and Renaissance Art, Am. Soc. Arts and Letters, Cenacle. Clubs: Illinois Club for Cath. Women (gov. 1979—), Cuneo Meml. Hosp. Aux. (bd. mem.), Fidelitas (bd. mem.). Home and studio: 723 Junior Terr Chicago IL 60613

PALLENIK, JANICE LYNN, greeting card company manager; b. Toledo, Ohio, Jan. 22, 1947; d. Lawrence A. and Lois (Hines) Jewett; m. David John Pallenik, Aug. 8, 1970; 1 child, Gregory. B.S. in Edn., Ohio U., 1969; postgrad. U. Md., 1971. Programmer, Jobbers Supply, Cleve., 1974-78; supr. Acme Cleve., 1978-80, mgr., 1980-83; mgr. Am. Greetings, Cleve., 1983—; cons. Basic Computer Workshops, North Ridgeville, Ohio, 1981—; presenter in field. Bd. dirs. Corn Festival, North Ridgeville, 1985. Mem. Cleve. Quality Assurance Assn. (treas. 1986—). Republican. Methodist. Avocations: financial investments; reading; travel. Home: 21939 Shagbark Trail Strongsville OH 44136 Office: Am Greetings Corp 10500 American Rd Cleveland OH 44144

PALM, NANCY CLEONE, medical center administrator, radiography technologist; b. Portland, Oreg., July 8, 1939; d. Oscar Emanuel and Hallie Vernice (Thurber) Palm. Student U. Oreg. Sch. Radiology, 1957; grad. Hosp. Corpswave, Hosp. Corps Sch., Great Lakes (Ill. Naval Base), 1958; grad. X-ray Tech., Sch. Radiology, Bremerton, Wash. Naval Base, 1961. Lic. radiography technologist, Oreg. Chief radiography technologist New Lincoln Hosp., Toledo, Oreg., 1961-63; sr. radiography technologist Gresham (Oreg.) Gen. Hosp., 1963-64; chief radiography technologist Neurol. Clinic, Portland, Oreg., 1965-79; head bookkeeper Rinehart Clinic, Wheeler, Oreg., 1979-80; owner, gen. mgr. San Dune Motel, Manzanita, Oreg., 1971-83; bus. agt. Rinehart Found., Inc., Manzanita, 1983—; owner Sears & Roebuck Catalog Store, Nehalem, Oreg., 1979-81; adminstr. mgr. Rinehart Found., Inc. (Nehalem Bay Med. Ctr.), Manzanita and Garibaldi, Oreg., 1980—. Sponsor Willamette council Campfire Girls, Inc., 1982—. Served with USN, 1958-61. Fellow Nat. Coll. Radiography Technologists; mem. Oreg. Med. Group Mgmt. Assn., Nat. Assn. Female Execs., Am. Registry Clin. Radiography Technologists (nat. dir. 1970-76, trustee 1972-74, sec. 71-72, pres. 72-74; Citation award 1970, Disting. Service award 1971, 73, Order of Golden Ray 1974, founder Margaret Harris Award Competition 1973). Republican. Presbyterian. Home: 423 Dorcas Lane PO Box 262 Manzanita OR 97130 Office: Hwy 101 Manzanita OR 97130

PALM, PHYLLIS WALD, child evaluation center administrator; b. Newark, July 9, 1938; d. Max and Fanny (Werner) Wald; m. Gilbert R. Palm, June 22, 1958 (div. 1973); children—Steven, Linda, Ted. B.A., Douglass Coll., 1959; M.A., Montclair State Coll., 1973; Ph.D., NYU, 1983. Cert. in learning disabilities, N.J.; lic. psychologist, N.Y. Tchr. elem. schs., Newark and Florham Park, N.J., 1965-67; learning cons. Bd. Edn., Glen Ridge, N.J., 1972-75; primary therapist Jersey City Med. Ctr., 1975-78; adminstrv. dir., pres. Summit Child Evaluation Ctr. Inc., Jersey City, 1978—; vice chmn. Children's Adv. Council, Jersey City, 1976—; mem. program com. Head Start, Jersey City, 1984—; bd. dirs. Child Devel. Ctr., Jersey City, 1984—. Mem. Assn. Learning Cons., Council for Children with Learning Disabilities, N.Y.-N.J. Brain Injured Assn. Avocation: aerobic exercise. Home: 9 Tulip Ct Livingston NJ 07039 Office: Summit Child Evaluation Ctr Inc St Francis Hosp 25 McWilliams Pl Jersey City NY 07302

PALMA, JANIS, translator, court interpreter; b. N.Y.C., Nov. 27, 1954; d. Edward W. and Nilda H. (de Jesus) P.; m. Hector Fernando Garza-Trejo, Nov. 22, 1978; children—Luis Garza-y-Palma, Melody Garza-y-Palma (dec. 1986). Student Universidad de Puerto Rico, Rio Piedras, 1972-73; B.A., U. Tex., 1977; postgrad. Instituto Tecnologico y de Estudios Superiores des Monterrey, Mex., 1981-82, Pan Am. U., 1985. Cert. English-Spanish ct. interpreter Adminstrv. Office U.S. Cts., 1981; accredited transl. Am. Translators Assn., 1986. Ind. interpreter-translator, Miami, Fla., 1979-81; adj. prof. Instituto Tecnologico y de Estudios Superiores de Monterrey, Queretaro, Mex., 1981-82; offcl. ct. interpreter U.S. Dist. Ct. (so. dist.) Tex., 1982-83; contractor, owner Palma & Assocs., Brownsville, Tex., 1983-85; ind. contractor English-Spanish judiciary interpreter and translator U.S. Dist. Cts., N.Y., 1986—; cons. com. on ct. interpreters Tex. Bar Assn., 1983-85; trainer Interpreters Inst. La Jolla, Calif., 1984—; author Tex. Ct. Interpreters Act bill introduced by Senator Rene Olivera, 1985. Editor Fed. Ct. Interpreters' Newsletter, 1982-83, Citations newsletter/jour., 1983—; compiler Federal Court Terminology, English-Spanish glossary, 1983. Mem. steering com. Austin Arts Council, Tex., 1977-78. Mem. Ct. Interpreters and Translators Assn. (pres. southwest chpt. 1983-85), Am. Translators Assn. (chmn. publs. com., tng. and edn.). Avocations: painting; drawing. Home: 815 E 14th St Apt 6B Brooklyn NY 11230

PALMER, ADA MARGARET, computer executive; b. Arkansas City, Kans., Feb. 8, 1940; d. Mark Lloyd Palmer and Eunice Elizabeth (Thompson) Palmer Schnitzer; A.A., Colo. Woman's Coll., 1960; B.A., George Washington, U., 1962. Adv. sr. programmer Merrill Lynch, N.Y.C., 1969-72; systems analyst Tchrs. Ins. & Annuity, N.Y.C., 1972-77; systems specialist N.Y. Times, N.Y.C., 1977-81; mktg. dir. Applied Systems Resources, Inc., N.Y.C., 1981-82; asst. mgr. Mfrs. Hanover Trust, N.Y.C., 1982—. Republican. Methodist. Home: 201 W 85th St Apt 11 A New York NY 10024 Office: 40 Wall St New York NY 10005

PALMER, DAISY ANN, marketing coordinator; b. Burkburnett, Tex.; d. Leroy Evans and Christine Cleo (Givens) Walker; children—Christy Ann Guyn, Cyndi Ann Thompson. Cert. in Human Relations, Oreg. Coll. Edn., 1976, B.A. cum laude in Liberal Studies, Edwards U., Tex., 1983. Cert. interpreter for hearing impaired, Tex. Mgr., R.R. Realty/Ins., Wichita Falls, Tex., 1973-75; cons. state agys., 1975—; asst. coordinator Travis County Services for Deaf, Austin, 1979-81; adminstr. Tex. Assn. Deaf, Austin, 1981-85; promotion dir. McGregor Studios, Austin, 1981—; mktg. coordinator Tex. Mcpl. League, Austin, 1985—. Editor: Tex. Assn. Deaf Directory of Services, 1984; researcher and author of statis. studies. Chmn. Gov.'s Communication Barriers Council, 1984; vice chair Austin St. Sch. Adv. Council, 1984-86. Recipient Golden Hand award Nat. Assn. Deaf. Mem. Nat. Registry Interpreters, Tex. Assn. Deaf (award for legis. activities 1983), Austin Bus. League. Home: 1824 S IH 35 Suite 253 Austin TX 78704 Office: Tex Mcpl League 211 E 7th Suite 1020 Austin TX 78701

PALMER, DOREEN PAMELA, internist, gastroenterologist, consultant; b. Kingston, Jamaica, West Indies, June 1, 1949; came to U.S., 1967; d. Granville and Icilda (Dunbar) P. B.A., Herbert Lehman Coll., 1972; M.D., Downstate Med. Ctr., 1976. Diplomate Am. Bd. Internal Medicine. Med. intern Downstate Med. Ctr., Bklyn., 1976-77, med. resident, 1977-79; fellow gastroenterology Balt. City-Johns Hopkins, 1979-81; asst. prof. medicine N.Y. Med. Coll., N.Y.C., 1981—; asst. chief gastroenterology div. Met. Hosp. Ctr., N.Y.C., 1981-82, chief, 1982—; mem. med. sch. admission com. N.Y. Med. Coll., N.Y.C., 1983—; pvt. practice internal medicine and gastroenterology, N.Y.C.; med. cons. Abbott Lab., Inc., Chgo., 1983-84, cons., Detroit, 1983. Contbr. articles to profl. jours. Fellow Westchester County Med. Soc.; mem. Provident Clin. Soc., Women in Medicine, Coalition of 100 Black Women. Episcopalian. Home: PO Box 571 White Plains NY 10602 Office: 133 E 73d St New York NY

PALMER, ELEASE DENISE GLAUDE, banker; b. Conway, S.C., June 19, 1953; d. George and Arviller (Livingstone) Palmer; m. Eric G. Glaude, Aug. 29, 1981. B.A., Herbert Leham Coll., 1975; M.A., NYU, 1978; Bus. cert. L.I. U., 1982. Adminstrv. asst. LeMans Haberdashers, N.Y.C., 1975-77; tchr. N.Y.C. Bd. Edn., 1977-79; career edn. coordinator Econ. Devel. Corp., N.Y.C. Bd. Edn., 1979-80; sr. contract mgr. Pvt. Industry Council, N.Y.C., 1980-84; tng. analyst Bankers Trust Co., N.Y.C., 1984—. Editor: Newsletter Friendship Times, 1983. Pres. Nat. Council Negro Women, N.Y.C., 1982-84. Mem. Am. Soc. Tng. and Devel., Wall Street Adv. Council, Nat. Assn. Female Execs., Nat. Council Negro Women. Home: 25 W 132d St #11 New York NY 10037

PALMER, ELIZABETH ANN, lawyer; b. Hartford, Conn., Aug. 19, 1956; d. Kalman Poliner and Helen (Pious) Palmer. B.A. cum laude, Wesleyan U., Middletown, Conn., 1978; J.D., Boston U., 1981, LL.M., 1984. Bar: Conn. 1981, Mass. 1982, U.S. Dist. Ct. Conn. 1982, U.S. Dist. Ct. Mass. 1984. Spl. dep. asst. state's atty. Office Chief State's Atty., Wallingford, Conn., 1981-82; tax examiner Mass. Dept. Revenue, Boston, 1984; staff tax acct. Peat Marwick Mitchell & Co., Hartford, 1985; assoc. tax counsel Beneficial Mgmt. Corp., Peapack, N.J., 1985—. Alumni admissions interviewer Wesleyan U., 1978—; mem. Wesleyan Alumni Fund, 1982—. Johnston Trust scholar Wesleyan U., 1974-76. Mem. ABA. Home: 134 Clover St Middletown CT 06457

PALMER, EMILY MILLS, city administrator; b. Lexington, Ky., June 4, 1934; d. Leonard Daniel and Sallye Belle (Rowe) Mills; m. Frank Palmer, Jr., Dec. 11, 1952 (div. Apr. 1973); children—Frankye Alaine, Gregory Timothy, Tracey Victoria; m. Michael D. Gresham, Apr. 17, 1973 (div. Dec. 1979). Student Ky. State Coll., Frankfort, 1951-53; B.A. in Behavioral Sci., U. Ky.-Lexington, 1953-55; postgrad. George Williams Coll., Chgo., Harper Jr. Coll., Palatine, Ill., Ball State U., Muncie, Ind. Tchr., City of Lexington Schs., 1956-60; dir. women's and girl's activities Recreation dept. City of Evanston (Ill.), 1961-67, also dir. Foster Community Ctr., supr. youth activities and spl. events, 1970-73, supr. cultural arts and spl. events, 1973—; pres. Mitchell & Palmer Pub. Relations, 1982—; tchr. Howardton Day Sch., Chgo., 1967-69; spl. edn. counselor Evanston Twp. High Sch., 1968-70; pub. relations dir. State of Ill. Community Edn., 1979-80; dir. Nichols Lighted Sch. and Drop-In Ctr., Evanston, 1973—. Mem. Women in Mgmt., Nat. Black Readers and Lang. Educators (chairperson for spl. events 1980—), Nat. Assn. TV and Radio Announcers (sec. 1973-75). Home: 5455 N Sheridan Rd Apt 3811 Chicago IL 60640

PALMER, HEATHER, radiation therapy technologist, administrator; b. Erie, Pa., July 28, 1947; d. Robert E. and Iris J. (Harridine) Wheeler. Grad. Radiology Sch., Hamot Med. Ctr., Erie, Pa., 1965-67, grad. Radiation Therapy Sch., 1971-72; cert. in allied health/dosimetry U. Kans.-Kansas City, 1978-79; B.A. in Allied Health/Mgmt., Nat. Coll. Edn., 1984. Staff x-ray technologist Hamot Med. Ctr., 1967-69, staff radiation therapy technologist, 1969-74; asst. chief radiation therapy tech., instr. U. Kans., 1974-78; dosimetrist St. Joseph Hosp., Elgin, Ill., 1979-81, chief technologist, program dir. Radiation Therapy Sch., 1981—. Mem. adv. com. for Col. Palmer House Crystal Lake (Ill.) City Council, 1980. Mem. Am. Assn. Med. Dosimetrists (charter), Am. Registry Radiologic Technologists, Am. Assn. Physicists in Medicine, Ill. Soc. Radiation Therapy Technologists. Author articles. Home: 820 Broadway Ave Crystal Lake IL 60014 Office: 77 N Airlite St Elgin IL 60120

PALMER, JANICE MASON, special education educator; b. Chgo., Mar. 10, 1942; d. Arthur John and Sarah Crawford (Forsyth) Blaha; m. Carl Massa, Aug. 29, 1964 (div. 1979); children—Heather Ellen, David Carl; m. Jeffrey Todd Palmer, Apr. 3, 1981. B.A., Northeastern Ill. U., 1975, M.A. in Spl. Edn., 1979. Cert. sch. adminstr., Ill. Clin. diagnostician Sch. Dist. U-46, Elgin, Ill., 1980-83; chmn. spl. edn. Clovis High Sch., Calif., 1983; cons. Sch. Dist. U-46, Elgin, 1984—, various psychiat. Hosps., Ill., 1984—; sr. cons. Mason Palmer & Assocs., Schaumburg, Ill., 1984—; instr. spl. edn. Northeastern Ill. U. Grad. Coll., Chgo., 1984—. cons. Inst. Child Neurology, Arlington Heights, Ill., 1979—. Office: Mason Palmer & Assoc 125 Mendon Ln Schaumburg IL 60193

PALMER, JUDITH LYNN, oil company managerial secretary, civic worker; b. Friona, Tex., Apr. 2, 1947; d. Vance DeKater and Allie Blanche (Graham) Crume; m. William Glen Nelson, Jr., Aug. 24, 1964 (div. Oct. 1978); 1 child, Michael Dobbin; m. Ronald Douglas Palmer, June 5, 1979; 1 child, Brian Jason. Student West Tex. State U., 1972; Midland Coll., 1980-81, Permian Basin Grad. Ctr., Midland, Tex., 1981-83. Long distance operator Southwestern Bell, Amarillo, Tex., 1965-68; sec. FDIC, Saguache, Colo., 1968-70; bookkeeper Affiliated Mfg. Co., Tulia, Tex., 1970-72; office mgr., bookkeeper South Plains Council Boy Scouts Am., Lubbock, Tex., 1972-80; managerial sec. Cities Service Oil and Gas Corp., Midland, 1980—. Trainer, South Plains Council Boy Scouts Am., Lubbock, 1973-80, Buffalo Trail council Boy Scouts Am., Midland, 1983—; chmn. Cities Service Blood Bank, Midland, 1984—; pres. Petro-Plains Council Camp Fire, Inc., Midland, 1984—; coordinator, sec. Cities Golf Tournament, 1983—; community service trainee Leadership Midland, 1985; loaned exec. Midland United Way (Named Vol. of Yr. 1985). Mem. Midland Desk and Derrick, Profl. Sec. Internat. Republican. Methodist. Lodge: Lioness Internat. (charter mem. 1985). Avocations: tennis, skiing, backpacking, camping. Office: Cities Service Oil & Gas Corp PO Box 1919 Midland TX 79702

PALMER, LINDA CONNER, telecommunications manufacturer's sales representative; b. Lexington, Ky., Aug. 5, 1949; d. Walter Thomas and Anna Mark (Hendrix) Conner; m. Jeffrey Taylor Palmer, June 20, 1981. B.S. in Edn., No. Ill. U., 1971; student Morton Jr. Coll., 1967-69. Substitute tchr. Pub. Schs., DuPage County, Ill., 1971-72; asst. office mgr. B.A.M. Agy., Chgo., 1972-73; adminstrv. asst. Budget Rent-A-Car, Chgo., 1973-76, Mesirow & Co., Chgo., 1976-77; account mgr. Tellabs, Inc., Lisle, Ill., 1977-81, Oakland, Calif., 1981—; ptnr. Palmer & Assocs., mktg., 1984—. Republican. Roman Catholic.

PALMER, MARGARET FRANCES, petroleum company executive; b. Kaufman, Tex., Oct. 11, 1926; d. Roy Lee and Raychel Frances (Bell) Palmer; B.A., magna cum laude, Tex. Woman's U., Denton, 1947; postgrad. So. Methodist U. Translator, sec. fgn. dept. Eugene B. Smith & Co., cotton mchts., Dallas, 1948-53, DeGoiyer and MacNaughton, petroleum cons., Dallas,

1953-58; asst. corp. sec., sec. to pres. Dorchester Gas Corp., and predecessor, Dallas, 1958-77, corp. sec. charge stockholder relations, 1977-84, co. acquired by Damson Oil Corp., 1984, asst. sec., 1984—. Mem. Am. Soc. Corp. Secs., Desk and Derrick Club Dallas, Epsilon Sigma Alpha. Republican. Episcopalian. Office: 5439 Anita Dallas TX 75206

PALMER, MARILYN JOAN, educator; b. Mahoning County, Ohio, Mar. 3, 1933; d. Rudolph George and Marian Eleanor Wynn; phys. therapy cert. UCLA, 1954, B.S., 1955; M.A. in Philosophy, Ohio State U., 1969; postgrad. U. Okla., 1981—; m. Richard Palmer, Nov. 10, 1956 (div. 1972); children—Ricky, Larry, Kevin. Phys. therapist Neil Ave. Sch. for Handicapped, Columbus, Ohio, 1968-69; instr. philosophy Ohio State U., Columbus, 1969; instr. English, Youngstown (Ohio) State U., 1970-71; writer, editor The Economy Co., ednl. publs., Oklahoma City, 1977-81; grad. asst. in English, U. Okla., Norman, 1981—; free-lance editing and cons. Fund-raiser Easter Seal Soc., 1965-68; den mother coordinator Boy Scouts Am., 1966, 67. Dept. Energy grantee, 1976. Mem. AAUP, Am. Phys. Therapy Assn., Soc. for Women in Philosophy, Alpha Xi Delta (nat. editor Quill 1984-86). Editor: Kindergarten Keys Teacher's Guidebook, 1982, author parochial supplement, 1982. Office: 760 Van Fleet Oval Norman OK 73069

PALMER, MARY LEE, psychotherapist; b. Passaic, N.J., Dec. 20, 1946; d. George Nicholson and Clydie Kyle (Ellis) Brunt; m. Russell Francis Palmer, Nov. 29, 1968 (div. 1972); 1 child: Nicole Lee Palmer. Diploma, St. Pius High Sch., Atlanta, 1964; B.A., Oglethorpe U., Atlanta, 1964-68; M.S.W., U. Ga., 1974. Cert. social worker Ga. Protective services caseworker Gordon County Dept. Family & Child Services, Calhoun, Ga., 1969-72; outpatient therapist Drug Program, Escambia County Mental Health Clinic, Pensacola, Fla., 1974-76; group and family therapist Peachford Hosp., Atlanta, 1976-83; psychotherapist Atlanta Ctr. for Psychotherapy, Atlanta, 1983-86; co-owner, pres. Atlanta Area Clin. Services, 1986—; cons. Nanny-Pop Ins. Inc., Atlanta, 1984-86, bd. dirs., 1985-86. Writer: (local mental health newsletter) Up-Date, 1983—; speaker numerous seminars; interviewed for TV shows on health care. Trainer, supr. Crisis Hot Line, Pensacola, 1974-76; mem. Ga. Coalition on Health Care, Atlanta, 1984-86, Atlanta Coalition on Health Care, 1984-86; group leader Women's Awareness Group, Atlanta, 1986. Ford Found. Program fellow, 1972-73. Mem. Nat. Assn. Social Workers, Acad. Cert. Social Workers, Ga. Council on Social Welfare, So. Regional Inst. Democrat. Unitarian-Universalist. Club: Atlanta Ski. Avocations: Pottery; racquetball; sailing; bridge; scrabble; horse-back riding; skiing. Home: 2707 Huntington Chase Dunwoody GA 30338 Office: Atlanta Area Clin Services 8097 Roswell Rd Suite A-102 Atlanta GA 30338

PALMER, MICHELE DELORIS, lawyer; b. Oberlin, Ohio, Aug. 12, 1954; d. Luther Robert and Katherine Estelle (Peterson) P. B.A., Oakwood Coll., Huntsville, Ala., 1975; J.D., Howard U., 1978. Bar: Wis. 1978. Staff atty. juvenile div. Legal Aid Soc. of Milw., 1978-79; staff atty. juvenile div. Office of State Pub. Defender, Milw., 1979-80; atty. office of dist. counsel IRS, Los Angeles, 1980-83, atty. office of chief counsel, criminal tax div., Washington, 1983—. Mem. ABA, Nat. Bar Assn., State Bar Wis., Phi Alpha Delta. Adventist. Home: 9785 Early Spring Way Columbia MD 21046 Office: Office of Chief Counsel Internal Revenue Service 1111 Constitution Ave NW Room 4607 Washington DC 20224

PALMER, PATRICIA MARIE, market supervisor; b. Savannah, Ga., Mar. 12, 1949; d. Harry Parsons and Frances (deBorde) P. B.Edn., U. Fla., 1972. Traffic/sales sec. WGGG Radio, Gainesville, Fla., 1973-74, sales rep., 1974-76, sales mgr., 1976-78; sales rep. WDAE/WJYW Radio, Tampa, Fla., 1978-79; field sales rep. 3M Nat., Tampa, 1979-85, market supr., 1985—. Bd. dirs. Tampa Advt. Fedn., 1983—, Hillsborough County Suicide and Crisis Ctr., Tampa, 1985—. Democrat. Roman Catholic. Office: 3M Nat Advt 6904 Cypress Park Dr Tampa FL 33623

PALMER, PATRICIA TEXTER, language educator; b. Detroit, June 10, 1932; d. Elmer Clinton and Helen (Rotchford) Texter; B.A., U. Mich., 1953; M.Ed., Nat. Coll. Edn., 1958; M.A., San Francisco State U., 1966; postgrad. Stanford U., 1968, Hayward State U., 1968-69; m. David Jean Palmer, June 4, 1955. Chmn. speech dept. Grosse Pointe (Mich.) Univ. Sch., 1953-55; tchr. South Margarita Sch., Panama, C.Z., 1955-56, Kipling Sch., Deerfield, Ill., 1956-57; chmn. Rio San Gabriel Sch., Downey, Calif., 1957-59; tchr. devel. reading, journalism advisor Roosevelt High Sch., Honolulu, 1959-62; tchr. English, speech, journalism advisor El Camino High Sch., South San Francisco, Calif., 1962-68; tchr., chmn. ESL dept. South San Francisco Unified Sch. Dist., 1968-81; dir. ESL Inst., Millbrae, Calif., 1978—; adj. faculty mem. New Coll. Calif., 1982—; master tchr. for Calif. in ESL, Calif. Council Adult Edn., 1979-81. Precinct chmn. North San Mateo (Calif.) Republican Com., 1963-64, asst. div. chmn., 1963-64; mem. San Mateo County Aviation Com. Recipient Concours de Francais prix, 1947; Jeannette M. Liggett Meml. award for excellence in history, 1949; commendation for journalism Hawaii State Legislature, 1962. Mem. TESOL, Calif. Council Adult Edn., Calif. Tchrs. Assn., NEA, Internat. Platform Assn., U. Mich. Alumnae Assn., Nat. Coll. Edn. Alumnae Assn., Chi Omega. Republican. Roman Catholic. Home: 2917 Franciscan Ct San Carlos CA 94070 Office: 450 Chadbourne Ave Millbrae CA 94030

PALMER, SUSAN LOUISE, aviation quality control supervisor, convention services consultant; b. Chgo., Feb. 22, 1950; d. Victor Elwyn and Marian Dorothea (Karlstrom) Palmer. B.A., Beloit Coll., 1972. Asst. curator Logan Mus., Beloit, Wis., 1972-73; program coordinator DUO Internat., Los Angeles, Miami, Fla., London, 1973-79; ptnr., agt. Rental and Relocation Services, Miami, 1979; chief insp. quality control Design Engring. Corp. Am., Miami, 1979—; conv. services cons., Miami, Fla., 1982-84. Contbr. articles to profl. jours. Mem. Am. Anthropol. Assn., Nat. Assn. Female Exec., Phi Beta Kappa, Theta Pi Gamma (sec. 1970-72). Club: Palm Coast Association (activities coordinator 1980-84) (Miami). Home: 1050 Wren Ave Miami Springs FL 33166

PALMER, SUZANNE MARIE, financial planner; b. Flint, Mich., Mar. 23, 1938; d. Lowell M. and Monta R. (Wascher) Hill; m. John D. Palmer, Aug. 25, 1962 (div. Jan. 1976); children—Geoffrey D., Joshua R. B.A., U. Miami, 1960. Cert. fin. planner; registered investment advisor. Tchr. Edmonds Sch. Dist., Wash., 1971-79; registered rep. KMS Fin. Services Inc., Seattle, 1979—; cert. fin. planner Suzanne Palmer & Assocs., Mukilteo, Wash., 1980—, registered investment advisor, 1984—. Mem. Internat. Assn. Fin. Planners, Snohomish County Women Bus. Owners (treas. 1985). Avocations: tennis, jogging. Office: Suzanne M Palmer & Assocs 7702 Speedway A PO Box 470 Mukilteo WA 98275

PALMER-LITCHFIELD, BARBARA, counseling services adminstr.; b. Bklyn., Aug. 31, 1938; s. Harold Palmer and Elsie E. (De Peyster) Palmer Hatton; B.A., Bklyn. Coll., 1962; postgrad. Rutgers U., 1975; M.A., Goddard-Cambridge Inst., 1980; m. Joseph L. Litchfield, Apr. 18, 1975. Dir., Family Life Service Center, Bklyn., 1965-70; coordinator staff inservice Bklyn. Devel. Services, 1970-71, community services specialist, 1971-73; cons. John C. Corrigan Mental Health Center, Fall River, Mass., 1973-74; dir. Driving While Intoxicated Program, Cape Cod, Mass. and Islands, 1974-75; pvt. practice counseling, 1974—; founder, pres. The Cape Shelter, Hyannis, Mass., 1976-79, Network of Women of Color in Therapeutic Community, 1981—; clin. dir. I Can Network, Attleboro, Mass. and Providence, 1980—; forensic psychotherapist Mass. correctional instns., 1984—; cons. to govt. agys., various bus. firms, 1976—. Bd. dirs. Third World Coalition, 1975—. Cert. Alcohol counselor, Mass.; lic. pvt. tchr., N.Y. Mem. Am. Personnel and Guidance Assn., Assn. Women in Psychology, Am. Black Psychologists Assn., Nat. Assn. Female Execs., Assn. Black Profls. Forensic Services, AAU. Buddhist. Club: Hyannis Community. Home: 2 Adams Rd West Yarmouth MA 02673 also 249 Union Ave Providence RI 02909 Office: 575 Washington St Attleboro MA also 1055 N Main St Providence RI 02904

PALMER-MALLEY, JANIS V., educational administrator; b. Ft. Mitchell, Ky., Sept. 20, 1950; d. Charles B. and Ethel V. (Voss) Palmer; m. Alfred Dever Malley, Mar. 20, 1983. B.S. in Sociology, No. Ky. U., 1972, cert. in teaching, 1973. Tchr. social studies Erlanger Bd. Edn., Ky., 1973-75; founder, dir., owner Little Red Sch. House, Erlanger, 1975—. Officer Humane Edn. Auxillary, Ft. Mitchell, 1983—. Mem. Ky. Assn. Sch. Adminstrs., Big Sisters Am., Friends Animals, People for Ethical Treatment of Animals. Republican. Lutheran. Avocations: animal welfare work; tennis; swimming; children's welfare. Office: Little Red Sch House 4104 Dixie Hwy Erlanger KY 41018

PALMER-ROGERS, ERIKA GISELA, lawyer; b. N.Y.C., Nov. 28, 1942; d. Erik Schojth and Gisela Elizabeth (Svika) Palmer; m. Richard Harold Beckman, Sept. 12, 1963 (div. 1977); children—Timothy, Angela, Christopher, Benjamin; m. 2d Leo Abbott Rogers, Aug. 2, 1980; stepchildren—Keith, Rayna, Arlin, Brian. B.A., U. Fla.-Gainesville, 1962; M.A., Ariz. State U., 1964; J.D., John Marshall Law Sch., Chgo., 1980, LL.M., 1985. Bar: Ill. 1980, Nev. 1981. Tchr. elem. sch. Robbins AFB Sch. Dist., Warner Robbins, Ga., 1965-68; tchr. elem. and jr. high sch. Torrance (Calif.) Unified Sch. Dist., 1968-74; owner, mgr. hog farm, Capron, Ill., 1974-78; law clk. Wittenberg Tyson & Hardy, Chgo., 1977-80, U.S. Bankruptcy Ct., Las Vegas, 1981-82; atty. Office of U.S. Trustee, Chgo., 1982-83; atty. Arthur Andersen & Co., Chgo., 1983-85; sole practice, 1985—. Mem. ABA (mem. bus./bankruptcy com., comml. fin. service com.), Ill. Bar Assn., Women's Bar Assn. Ill., Comml. Law League, Chgo. Bar Assn. (mem. bankruptcy and reorganization com.). Home: 1901 S Prospect St Park Ridge IL 60068 Office: 33 N Dearborn St Suite 1030 Chicago IL 60602

PALMORE, MARY KATE, obstetrician and gynecologist; b. Chgo., July 24, 1952; d. Richard Eugene and Mary Kate (Mann) P.; B.A. in Biology, Hampton Inst., 1974; M.D., Rush Med. Coll., 1978. Community rep. Chgo. Dept. Human Resources, summers 1976, 76; resident in ob-gyn Presbyn.-St. Luke's Med. Center, Chgo., 1978-82, also adj. attending staff, instr. Rush Med. Coll., 1981-82; obstetrician and gynecologist Kaiser Permanente of Tex., Dallas, 1982—. Bd. dirs., v.p. community affairs and pub. relations Girls Clubs of Dallas, 1984—. Mem. Am. Med. Women's Assn., AMA, Nat. Med. Assn. Democrat. United Methodist. Office: 7777 Forest Ln Suite 2-333 Dallas TX 75230

PALUZZI, JEANNE GERRITSEN, public relations counselor; b. Zeeland, Mich., Sept. 18, 1934; d. Gerrit John and Mary (Staal) Gerritsen; student Calvin Coll., Grand Rapids, Mich., 1952-53, Wayne State U., 1970-76; m. Rocco Paluzzi, Apr. 7, 1956 (div. Apr. 8, 1971); children—Jeanna Marie, Nicholas, Paul, Karen Adele. Asst. to dir. public affairs Smith Hinchman & Grylls, Inc., Detroit, 1972-73; co-mgr. public relations Albert Kahn Asso., Detroit, 1973-74; owner Jeanne Paluzzi & Co., Detroit, 1974-76; public relations exec. Young & Rubicam, Inc., Detroit, 1976-79; pres. JGP Public Relations, Inc., Livonia, Mich., 1979-84; pres. JGP Mktg. Group Internat., Inc., 1984—; mem. Livonia Indsl. Devel. Commns., 1981-83, Livonia Cable TV Adv. Com., 1981. Bd. dirs. Met. Detroit YWCA; mem. Wayne 2d Dist. Republican Exec. Com., 1981-83; bd. dirs. Rep. Women's Task Force, 1982-84; mem. nat. adv. council SBA, 1982—; del. White House Conf. on Small Bus., 1986. Recipient Demmy award, 1976; United Found. award, 1977; Region V SBA Women in Bus. Adv. of Yr. award, 1981; Vanguard award, 1984. Mem. Public Relations Soc. Am. (accredited), Women In Communications (program chmn. nat. conv. 1978, chmn. fin. com. 1977-78, 1st v.p. Detroit chpt. 1978-79, v.p. chpt. public relations 1980-82), Small Bus. Assn. Mich. (v.p. polit. action com. 1984—), Small Bus. United (bd. dirs. 1983-84), Nat. Assn. Women Bus. Owners (v.p. public relations Mich. chpt. 1980-82, pres. elect 1981, pres. 1982, nat. pub. relations chair 1983 nat. sec. 1984), Bus./Profl. Advt. Assn., Livonia C. of C. (dir. 1980-83, bus. and econ. devel. council), Mich. C. of C., Greater Detroit C. of C., World Trade Council. Clubs: Renaissance, Detroit Press, Econ. of Detroit, Women's Econ. of Detroit. Home: 17315 Rougeway St Livonia MI 48152 Office: 34935 Schoolcraft Ste 206 Livonia MI 48150-1317

PALZER, DORIS MAWHINNEY, home economist; b. Phila., May 17, 1925; d. John A. and Anne Evelyn (Gledhill) Mawhinney; B.S., Pa. State U., 1947; M.S., Cornell U., 1955; Ed.D., Temple U., 1978; m. E. Watson, Palzer, Apr. 27, 1957; children—Ellen Ann, Jeffrey Eric. Tchr. home econs. public schs., Phila., 1947-50, Neshaminy Sch. Dist., 1952-54, Pennsbury Sch. Dist., 1966-70, 73-74, Hopewell Valley Sch. Dist., Pennington, N.J., 1975-76; mem. faculty Glassboro (N.J.) State Coll., 1976—, chmn. dept. home econs., 1977—; chemist Kessler Chem. Co., Phila., 1950-51. Zeta Tau Alpha grantee, 1974-75; Glassboro State Coll. grantee. Mem. AAUW (rep., state parliamentarian Pa., pres. br., scholarship grant named in her honor), Am. Home Econs. Assn., N.J. Home Econs. Assn., Am. Vocat. Assn., N.J. Vocat. Edn. Assn., Nat. Council Adminstrs. Home Econs., Nat Assn. Parliamentarians, Pa. State U. Alumni Assn., Cornell U. Alumni Assn., Phi Delta Kappa, Kappa Omicron Phi, Zeta Tau Alpha. Home: 2104 Acqueduct Ln Cherry Hill NJ 08003 Office: Dept Home Econs Glassboro State Coll Glassboro NJ 08028

PAN, LORETTA REN-QIU, educator; b. Changchow, China, Oct. 1, 1917, came to U.S., 1951, naturalized, 1965; d. Ke-jun and Mei-ying (Hsüeh) P.; B.A. in English Lit., Ginling Coll., 1940; cert. English Lit., Mt. Holyoke Coll., 1952. Instr. English, Nanking U., 1940-41; instr. English and Chinese, St. Mary's Girls Sch., Shanghai, 1941-44; instr. English, Ginling Coll., 1944-45; sr. translator info. dept. Brit. Embassy, Shanghai, 1945-48; Chinese editor U.S. Consulate Gen., Hong Kong, 1949-51; researcher, editorial asst. modern China project Columbia U., 1955-60, lectr. Chinese, 1960-67, sr. lectr., 1968—. Methodist. Contbr. to various profl. publs. Home: 600 W 111th St New York NY 10025 Office: Dept East Asian Langs and Cultures Columbia U New York NY 10027

PANCOAST, JUDITH C., publishing company executive; b. Camden, N.J., July 12, 1949; d. Robert A. and Marie Pancoast. B.A., U. Maine, 1971; M.B.A., U. Pa., 1979. Underwriter, asst. sec. Cameron & Colby Co., Boston, 1972-77, bus. analyst Pepsi Co., Purchase, N.Y., 1979-81; sr. planning analyst Macmillan, Inc., N.Y.C., 1981-82, mgr. devel. info. service group, 1983-85, mgr. ops. Macmillan Directory div., 1985—. Methodist. Office: Nat Register Pub Co 3004 Glenview Rd Wilmette IL 60091

PANDICK, MARGARET LEAL, election commissioner; b. Delhi, N.Y., Feb. 20, 1912; d. Ernest Albert and Margaret (Simon) Leal; m. Andrew Lawrence Pandick, May 30, 1936 (dec. Mar. 1963); children—Linda Pandick Franzese, Thomas O. Dep. commr. Delaware County Bd. Elections, Delhi, 1958-75, commr., 1975—. Vice-chmn. Delaware County Democratic Com., 1960—. Named Democratic Women of Yr., Delaware County, 1969. Mem. N.Y. State Assn. Election Commrs. (sec., treas. 1968—). Presbyterian. Avocations: needle point; gardening. Home: 4 Delview Terr Delhi NY 13753 Office: Delaware County Bd Elections Gallant Ave Delhi NY 13753

PANEK, JERI HERNDON, computer/public relations exec.; b. Salt Lake City, June 15, 1939; d. Norman C. and Geraldine E. (Griffin) Herndon; ed. U. Utah; m. Larry H. Panek, Sept. 20, 1958 (div.); 1 son, Brad. Public relations asst. Univac, Salt Lake City, 1961-69; dir. communications U. Utah, Salt Lake City, 1969-73; coordinator communications Sperry-Univac, Salt Lake City, 1973-74; electronic data processing communications coordinator Singer Bus. Machines Internat. Div., Brussels, Belgium, 1974-76; public relations and corp. planning mgr. Beehive Internat., Salt Lake City, 1977-80; program mgr., sales rep. Digistar computer graphics Evans & Sutherland Computer Corp., Salt Lake City, 1980—. Mem. Public Relations Soc. Am. (chmn. membership com., editor newsletter, chpt. treas. 1968—, v.p., immediate pas pres.), Assn. Computing Machinery (mem. conf. and symposia com. 1972-74), Internat. Planetarium Soc., Planetarium Assn. Can., C. of C. (aviation com.). Home: 1754 So Oak Springs Dr Salt Lake City UT 84108 Office: 580 Arapeen Dr Salt Lake City UT 84108

PANELA, DEBRA LYNNE, interior and fashion designer, business management consultant; b. Honolulu, July 28, 1961; d. Sixto Quindag and Emilia Morales (Tehero) P. B.S. in Dance Choreography, Brigham Young U. Office mgr. David G. Stringer AIA and Assocs., Ltd., Honolulu, 1982; office mgr., paralegal Gima & Harrison, Honolulu, 1982-84; owner, fashion and interior designer, mgmt. cons. The Tangy Mango, Honolulu, 1980—; mktg. and pub. affairs dir. d'Image Internat. of Hawaii, Honolulu, 1985—; adminstrv. asst. to house counsel Gentry Cos., Honolulu, 1986—. Choreographer numerous mini-musicals, opers "The Magic Flute"; instr. aerobics and exercise. Pres. Young Women's Orgn., Ch. of Jesus Christ of Latterday Saints, Honolulu, 1981-82. Named 1st Princess, Miss Filipinas Hawaii Am. 1986. Mem. Nat. Assn. Female Execs., Am. Bus. Women's Assn. Democrat. Mormon. Avocations: dance; music; theatre; fine arts; fitness.

PANERO, ROXANNE JEANNE, advertising agency executive, educator; b. Bronx, N.Y., Mar. 8, 1944; d. Carl Sylvius Panero and Jeanne (Kenyon) DeSonie. B.F.A., Barry Coll. Cert. tchr., Fla. Co-propr., Miami Studios (Fla.), 1965-71; mem. faculty Barry Coll., Miami, Miami-Dade Jr. Coll., 1971-72; propr. Grafis Studio, Bloomington, Ind., 1972-75; creative dir. R.L. Silver Assocs., N.Y.C., 1975-80, v.p., 1980—; mem. faculty Fashion Inst., N.Y.C., 1980—, Manhattan Community Coll., N.Y.C., 1979-80; exhibitor Hortt Meml., Ft. Lauderdale, Fla., 1971, Eleven Eleven, Miami, 1971. Designer manuals and books; panelist on cable television program, Bloomington, Ind., 1974. Creative dir. Chelsea Coalition on Housing, N.Y.C., 1976—; treas. 301 W. 17 St. Tenants Assn., N.Y.C., 1976—; designer 301 W. 17 St. Block Assn., N.Y.C., 1976—. Recipient award of Excellence, Potlach, 1980; cert. of excellence Graphics Gallery, N.Y.C., 1981; Spl. Merit award Printing Industry Metro N.Y., 1980, 81, 83. Mem. Art Dirs. Club N.Y., Graphic Artists Guild N.Y., Barry Coll. Alumni Assn. Office: RL Silver Assocs 527 Madison Ave New York NY 10022

PANFIL, ANNE TREVASKIS, lawyer; b. Phila., May 7, 1948; d. John Pellow Gregory and Anne (Keller) Trevaskis; m. Allen Carl Panfil, Apr. 8, 1972. B.A., U. R.I., 1970; M.Ed., Villanova U., 1975; J.D., Temple U., 1978. Bar: Pa. 1979, U.S. Dist. Ct. (ea. dist.) Pa. Tchr. psychology Swarthmore-Rutledge Union Sch. Dist., Swarthmore, Pa., 1970-71; owner swimming pool mgmt. service Lansdale, Pa., 1970-75; assoc. Mattioni, Mattioni & Mattioni, Phila., 1978-79, John P. Trevaskis, Jr., P.C., Media, Pa., 1979-80; staff counsel Pa. Supreme Ct. Criminal Procedural Rules Com., Phila., 1980—. Contbr. articles to profl. jours. Vol. legal counsel Lansdale Performing Arts Ctr., Pa., 1983—. Decorated Legion of Honor, Chapel of Four Chaplains, Phila., 1984. Mem. Bar of U.S. Supreme Ct., Pa. Bar Assn., ABA, Kappa Delta Pi, Phi Alpha Delta. Democrat. Club: Leeds & Northrup Ski (pres. 1979-80). Office: Supreme Ct of Pa Criminal Procedural Rules Com Temple Law Sch 1719 N Broad St Philadelphia PA 19122

PANG, MAY FUNG YEE, actress; b. N.Y.C., Oct. 24, 1950; d. Jack Fee and Linda (Lim) Pang. Student pub. schs., N.Y.C. Asst. to John Lennon and Yoko Ono, 1970-76; asst. Island Records, N.Y.C., 1977-78; music pub. United Artists Music, N.Y.C., 1981-83; appeared in films Hot Shot, Heartburn; TV roles in The Equalizer, Our Family Honor, Choices; appeared in music videos: Fashion (David Bowie), Satisfaction Guaranteed (The Firm), Oh Yeah (Bill Withers. Author: Loving John, 1983. Mem. Screen Actors Guild, AFTRA, Musicians Union Local 47. Roman Catholic. Avocations: photography; travel.

PANICCIA, PATRICIA LYNN, television news reporter and anchorwoman, lawyer; b. Glendale, Calif., Sept. 19, 1952; d. Valentino and Mary (Napoleon) P.; m. Jeffrey McDowell Mailes, Oct. 5, 1985. B.A. in Communication, U. Hawaii-Honolulu, 1977; J.D., Pepperdine U. Law Sch., Malibu, Calif., 1981. Bar: Hawaii 1981, Calif. 1982. Law clk. Hon. Samuel P. King U. S. Dist. Ct., Honolulu, 1980; newswriter Sta. KTLA-TV, Los Angeles, 1981-83; reporter, anchor woman Sta. KEYT-TV, Santa Barbara, Calif., 1983-84; reporter Sta. KCOP-TV, Los Angeles, 1984—; profl. surfer, 1977-81. Mem. Calif. State Bar (mem. com. on fair trial and free press 1983-84, pub. affairs com. 1985-86), Hawaii Bar Assn., Los Angeles County Bar Assn., ABA, Phi Delta Phi (historian 1980-81). Office: Channel 13 News 915 N La Brea Ave Los Angeles CA 90038

PANOS SCHMITT, A(THANASIA) NANCY, marketing educator; b. Great Falls, Mont., Oct. 2, 1951; d. Alexander H. and Katherine (Papadrikopoulos) Panos; m. Gary Allen Schmitt, June 14, 1974; 1 son, Kyle Christopher. B.S., U. Utah, 1974, M.B.A., 1979; M.S., Va. Tech., 1976. Research specialist U. Utah, Salt Lake City, 1977-78; market adminstr. Mountain Bell Telephone Co., Salt Lake City, 1979-80; asst. prof., chairperson mktg. dept. Westminster Coll., Salt Lake City, 1980—, owner, pres. Mktg./Mgmt. Inc., Salt Lake City, 1982—. Mem. Am. Mktg. Assn., Western Mktg. Assn., Salt Lake C. of C., Phi Beta Lambda, Phi Eta Sigma, Phi Sigma. Democrat. Greek Orthodox. Club: Zonta. Office: Westminster Coll Sch Bus 1840 S 1300 East Salt Lake City UT 84105

PANOZZO, DIANE JEAN, business executive; b. Chgo., Dec. 16, 1937; d. Anthony Muffy and Genevieve Phyllis (Coffero) P.; B.A., Coll. St. Francis, Joliet, Ill., 1959. Mgr., Variety Personnel Service, Chgo., 1959-71; adminstrv. asst. Finn. Industries div. Potlatch Forests, Inc., Chgo., 1971-72; exec. asst. to chmn., pres. Chemetron Corp., Chgo., 1972-79; adminstrv. asst. Price Waterhouse & Co., Chgo., 1979-80; adminstrv. sec. Chgo. Sch. Fin. Authority, 1980-81; exec. asst. to chmn. Telemedia, Inc., Chgo., 1981—; v.p. fin. Jonpir, Inc., Hinsdale, Ill., 1981-86. Home: 1455 Sandburg Terr #1602 Chicago IL 60610 Office: 310 S Michigan Ave Chicago IL 60604

PANT, LAURIE W., educator; b. Rochester, N.Y., July 19, 1944; d. Howard William and Mary Doris (Lyons) Waldorf; m. Ramesh Prasad, July 16, 1966; 1 child, Casey Rohini. B.A., Coll. New Rochelle, 1966; M.Ed., Emory U., 1969; M.B.A., Boston U., 1978, postgrad., 1983—. Tchr. secondary schs., N.Y., Ohio, Ga., 1966-75; office mgr., acct. Am. Institional Textile Inc., Hartford, Conn., 1975-77; fin. analyst Gillette Co., Boston, 1978-79; instr. Bentley Coll., Waltham, Mass., 1979-84, Boston Coll., Chestnut Hill, 1984—. Author: (with Elliott Levy) Lecture Guide to Accompany Fundamental Accounting Principles, 1984. Mem. Am. Acctg. Assn. Mailing Address: 1 Sunset Rock Rd Andover MA 01810 Address: Boston College Chestnut Hill MA 02167

PANTANO, LYNN THERESA, clinical psychologist; b. Detroit, Sept. 1, 1949; d. Guy Dewey and Lois Ulin (Buchanan) Pantano; B.A. in Psychology with honors, Wayne State U., 1971, M.A. (grad. scholar), 1975, Ph.D. in Clin. Psychology, 1979; m. Kenneth Andrew Skuzenski, July 20, 1979. Neuropsychology clin. asst. Harper Hosp., Detroit, 1971-72, neuropsychology intern, 1975-76; psychology clin. asst. Lafayette Clinic, Detroit, 1972-74, psychology intern, 1974-75; psychologist, unit coordinator Northeast and Northwest Centers, Detroit Psychiat. Inst., 1976-79, Northwest Center, Northville Regional Psychiat. Hosp., Detroit, 1979-81; psychologist Alt. Living Service, Southgate (Mich.) Regional Center, 1981-82; dir. psychology Kingswood Hosp., Ferndale, Mich., 1982—; clin. psychologist E. Pointe Mental Health Assn., Harper Woods, Mich., 1981—; asst. adj. prof. dept. psychiatry Coll. Osteo. Medicine, Mich. State U., Lansing., 1982—. NSF grantee, 1970, USPHS grantee, 1971-72. Mem. Am., Midwestern, Eastern, Mich. psychol. assns., Mich. Soc. Clin. Psychologists, Internat. Neuropsychology Soc., Gerontol. Soc. Am., Phi Beta Kappa, Psi Chi. Roman Catholic. Contbr. articles in field to profl. publs. Home: 19228 Linville Ave Grosse Pointe Woods MI 48236 Office: 10300 W Eight Mile St Ferndale MI 48220

PANZA, GEORGENE ANGELA, insurance company executive; b. Bklyn., Mar. 9, 1950; d. Ben and Marian Delores (Boccio) Sfraga; m. James Panza, July 1, 1984; 1 child, Andrea L. Cardamone. B.A. in Psychology, Hofstra U., 1971. Diplomate Internat. Claims Assn. Claims/sr. claims examiner N.Y. Life Ins., N.Y.C., 1971-76, 78-79, claims/sr. claims analyst, 1979-81, mgr., 1981—, exec. asst., 1981-82, asst. v.p., 1982-84, corp. v.p., 1984—, service product dir., 1985-86. Trustee, Washington Green Assn., 1985—. Hofstra U. scholar, 1967-71. Mem. Am. Mgmt. Assn., Nat. Assn. Female Execs., Life Office Mgmt. Assn. (chmn. ordinary ins. services com.). Avocations: tennis; horseback riding; dancing. Office: NY Life Ins Co 51 Madison Ave New York NY 10010

PAOLINI, SHIRLEY JOAN, humanities educator; b. Cleve.; d. James and Anne D. (Jurist) Burke; B.A., Mount St. Mary's Coll., Los Angeles; postgrad. (Swiss Govt. fellow), U. Lausanne; M.A., Calif. State U., Fullerton, 1966; Ph.D., U. Calif., Irvine, 1973; m. Maurizio Paolini; children—Kenneth, Marco, Angela, Laura. Tchr., Whittier (Calif.) High Sch., 1966-67; asst. dir. edn. Nat. Systems Corp., Newport Beach, Calif., 1971-73; asst. prof. English, asst. specialist U. Hawaii, Honolulu, 1973-75; dir. planning Chaminade U., Honolulu, 1975-78; art-reach dir. Anchorage Arts Council, 1978-79; assoc. prof. humanities, dean univ. affairs Alaska Pacific U., Anchorage, 1979-85, prof. humanities, 1985—; ednl. cons., Hawaii, Alaska, 1973—; co-mgr. CHEL Alaska Region, 1985—. Project dir. Nat. Endowment for Humanities Grants, 1977-82, Strengthening Developing Instns. grant coordinator, 1975-81. Recipient Los Angeles Consulate award French Govt. Mem. MLA, Am. Comparative Lit. Assn., Internat. Am. Comparative Lit. Assn., Am. Assn. Italian Studies, Internat. Platform Assn. Pacific Philol. Assn., Council for Advancement Exptl. Learning (asso.), World Affairs Council (Anchorage). Democrat. Roman Catholic. Author: Confessions of Sin and Love in the Middle Ages - Dante's Commedia and St. Augustine's Confessions, 1982. Editor: Hawaii Open Program Courses, 1974-75. Contbr. poems, monographs, articles. Home: 1242 St Gotthard Ave Anchorage AK 99508 Office: Communication Arts Dept Alaska Pacific U Anchorage AK 99508

PAOLUCCI, ANNE ATTURA, English language educator, author; b. Rome; d. Joseph and Lucy (Guidoni) Attura; B.A., Barnard Coll.; M.A., Columbia U.; Ph.D.; Fulbright scholar U. Rome; m. Henry Paolucci. Mem. faculty Brearley Sch., N.Y.C., CCNY; univ. research prof. St. John's U., Jamaica,

N.Y., 1969-77, prof. English, 1977—, acting head dept. English lit., 1974, chmn. dept. English, 1982—, dir. Dr. Arts degree program in English, 1983—; Fulbright lectr. Am. drama U. Naples, 1965-67; spl. lectr. Renaissance Inst., Ashland, Oreg., 1973, 74; founder, editor Rev. Nat. Lits., 1970—; founder, exec. dir. Council Nat. Lits., 1974—; founder, pres. Columbus: Countdown 1992, 1985—; writer in residence Yaddo, 1965; vis. fellow Humanities Research Center, Australian Nat. U., Canberra, 1979; U.S. rep. Internat. Poetry Festival, Struga, Yugoslavia, 1981; mem. Am. adv. bd. Australian-Am. Bicentennial Found.; 1983—; mem. N.Am. adv. bd. Shakespeare Globe Project, 1983—; dir. Shakespeare and The World series of bilingual dramatic readings, summer 1981; author: Cipango! (A One-Act Play About Christopher Columbus), 1985; Pirandello's Theater: The Recovery of the Modern Stage for Dramatic Art, 1974; From Tension to Tonic: The Plays of Edward Albee, 1972; Hegel on Tragedy, 1962; Machiavelli's Mandragola, 1962; Poems Written for Sbek's Mummies, Marie Menken and Other Important People, Places and Things, 1977; Eight Short Stories 1977; (one-act play) Minions of the Race, 1978; (poems) Riding the Mast Where It Swings, 1980; Sepia Tones: Seven Short Stories, 1985, 2d edit., 1986. Mem. Nat. Grad. Fellows Bd. Garibaldi scholar 1948-50; grantee Columbia U. 1963, 64, 65; Woodbridge fellow 1961-62; recipient Drama award Medieval and Renaissance Inst. 1972; named Disting. Alumna in News Barnard Coll. mag. 1973; Woman of Yr., Dr. Herman Henry Scholarship Found., 1973; Women of Yr., AMITA, 1970; Elena Cornaro award N.Y. State OSIA, 1980; Educator's award Bklyn. Coll., 1982, City-Wide Italian Heritage Week award, 1982, other citations and awards. Mem. Dante Soc. Am., Pirandello Soc. Am. (pres. 1979—), World Centre Shakespeare Studies, Conf. Editors Learned Jours., Nat. Soc. Lit. and Arts, Internat. Shakespeare Assn., Shakespeare Assn. Am., Renaissance Soc. Am., Renaissance Inst. Japan, Internat. Comparative Lit. Assn., Am. Comparative lit. Assn., Am. Byron Soc., Internat. Byron Soc., PEN. Office: St John's University Jamaica NY 11439

PAPA, PHYLLIS MARYANN, ballet dancer and director, choreographer, educator; b. Trenton, N.J., Jan. 30, 1950; d. Armando Carmen and Mary (Grace) P.; student ballet Royal Ballet Centre, 1955-62, Am. Ballet Center, N.Y.C., 1962-65, Harkness House for Ballet Arts, N.Y.C., 1965-68; m. Thomas E. de Ment, Jr., Sept. 2, 1979; children—Janelle and Tamara (twins). Dancer, Princeton (N.J.) Ballet Co., 1963-68, Harkness Youth Co., N.Y.C., 1965-68, Am. Ballet Theatre, N.Y.C., 1968-70, Royal Danish Ballet, Copenhagen, 1970-72; founder Mercer Ballet (formerly W. Jersey Ballet Co.), Mooretown, N.J., 1972—, artistic dir., 1972—; founder, artistic dir., Ballet Concertante, chamber ballet, Mooretown, 1975—; artistic dir., ballet mistress, prin. dancer Stars of Am. Ballet, N.Y.C.; prin. dancer Atlanta Ballet Co., 1978—; tchr. Royal Dance Centre, Royal Ballet Centre, Mercer County Community Coll.; founder Am. Internat. Ballet, Inc., N.Y.C., 1979—, choreographer, prin. dancer S.E. Asia tour, 1980; prin. dancer, ballet mistress Ballets Elan, 1980; artistic dir. Atlantic City Ballet, 1981—; founding dir. Atlantic Contemporary Ballet Theatre cons. in field; choreographer over 20 ballets for regional and profl. cos. Grantee N.J. State Council of Arts and Nat. Endowment on Arts, 1975-76, 82.

PAPA-LEWIS, ROSEMARY, educator; b. Los Angeles, Dec. 12, 1950; d. Ralph Michael and Josephine (Sirchia) Papa; m. William Ernest Lewis, Aug. 2, 1975; children—Jessica, Giselle, Sofia. A.A., Pasadena City Coll., 1970; B.A., Calif. State U.-Los Angeles, 1972; M.A., Calif. State U.-Northridge, 1977; Ed.D., U. Nebr.-Lincoln, 1983. Lic. tchr., Calif., Nev., Nebr.; counselors lic. K-12, Calif., Nev., Nebr.; adminstr.'s lic. K-12, Calif., Nev., Nebr. Tchr., Nativity Sch., El Monte, Calif., 1972-73, Cortez Elem. Sch., West Covina, Calif., 1973-74, Hollenbeck Jr. High Sch., West Covina, 1974-75; activity dir., tchr. Sierra Vista Jr. High Sch., Saugus, Calif. 1975-78; prin. K-8, St. Mary's Sch., Bellevue, Nebr., 1979-84; chief adminstr. K-12, Holy Name Sch., Omaha, 1984-85; vis. asst. prof. dept. ednl. leadership and founds. U. New Orleans, 1985—. Mem. Nat. Elem. Prins. Assn., Am. Ednl. Research Assn., Am. Soc. Curriculum Devel., Nebr. Council Sch. Adminstrs., Met. Omaha Elem. Prins., Phi Delta Kappa, Delta Kappa Gamma. Democrat. Roman Catholic. Avocations: scuba diving; skiing; sewing. Home: 100 Windward Passage Slidell LA 70458 Office: U New Orleans Dept Ednl Leadership and Founds Lakefront New Orleans LA 70148

PAPALIA, DIANE ELLEN, educator; b. Englewood, N.J., Apr. 26, 1947; d. Edward Peter and Madeline (Borrin) Papalia; A.B., Vassar Coll., 1968; M.S., W.Va. U., 1970, Ph.D. (NSF fellow), 1971; m. Jonathan Finlay, June 19, 1976. Asst. prof. child and family studies U. Wis., Madison, 1971-75, assoc. prof., 1975-78, prof., 1978—, assoc. dean grad. studies and research Sch. Family Resources and Consumer Scis., 1982-83. Am. Council Edn. fellow, 1979-80; U. Wis. grantee. Fellow Gerontol. Soc.; mem. Am. Psychol. Assn., Soc. Research in Child Devel., Nat. Council Family Relations, Psi Chi. Author: (with Sally W. Olds) A Child's World: Infancy through Adolescence, 1975, 79, 82; Human Development, 1978, 81, 86; Psychology, 1985; contbr. articles to profl. jours. Home: 606 Blue Ridge Pkwy Madison WI 53705 Office: 1430 Linden Dr Madison WI 53706

PAPARELLO, ANNETTE GRACE, educator, consultant; b. Bklyn.; d. Joseph John and Constance K. (Libasci) P. M.A.L.S., SUNY-Stony Brook, 1974; Ed.M., Tchr.'s Coll., N.Y.C., 1981; systems analyst cert. Grumman Data Systems, Woodbury, N.Y., 1981. Cert. tchr., N.Y. Bilingual tchr. Pub. Sch. 116, Bklyn., 1972-74; tchr. ESL, Spanish, Little Flower United Free Sch. Dist., Wading River, N.Y., 1973-79; tchr. ESL, Shoreham-Wading River Sch. Dist., Shoreham, N.Y., 1980—, microcomputer cons., 1982—; mem. faculty dept. Puerto Rican studies SUNY-Stony Brook, 1974-75; instr. data processing Suffolk Community Coll., Selden, N.Y., 1983-84; speaker at profl. confs.; cons. AT&T, Morriston, N.J., 1985; cons. ednl. computers. Telephone hotline responder Response, Suffolk County, N.Y., 1974-76; bd. dirs. Theatre Three, Port Jefferson, N.Y., 1975-80. Recipient cert. of commendation Nat. Found. Cancer Research, 1984. Mem. TESOL, Statue of Liberty Found. (charter), Kappa Delta Pi. Home: 27 Cedar Ave Miller Place NY 11764 Office: Shoreham-Wading River Sch Dist Route 25A Shoreham NY 11786

PAPAZIAN, RITA MALLETT, journalist, freelance writer, photographer; b. Yonkers, N.Y., Jan. 6, 1940; d. Vincent Stephen and Aida (Schini) Mallett; m. Norman Gabriel Papaziana, June 2, 1962 (div. 1982); children—Maria, Norman, Jr., Ellen. B.A., Hofstra U., 1962, M.S., 1966. Tchr. English, W. Trespar Clarke High Sch., Westbury, N.Y., 1962-65; library aide Fairfield (Conn.) Pub. Schs., 1973-75; reporter Fairfield (Conn.) Citizen, 1975-80; editor Norwalk (Conn.) News, 1980—; freelance writer various newspapers, mags., 1977—. Recipient Matrix award Women in Communications, 1982; Best Editorial award New Eng. Press, Boston, 1982. Mem. Women in Communications. Home: 334 Rowland Rd Fairfield CT 06430 Office: Norwalk News 133 Washington St Norwalk CT 06854

PAPE, BARBARA HARRIS, lawyer; b. Casper, Wyo., Aug. 12, 1936; d. Herbert Garfield and Leah Jean (Case) Harris; m. William Martin Pape, June 28, 1969; children—Kyri Dannan, Kirsten Tara. A.A. in Theatre, Stephens Coll., 1956; B.J., B.A., U. Mo., 1960, M.A., 1966, B.S. in Edn., 1968, Ph.D., J.D., 1980. Bar: Mo. 1981, U.S. Dist. Ct. (we. dist.) Mo. 1981. Mem. faculty U. Mo., Columbia, 1966-74; daily TV show hostess Triton Prodns., Inc., Columbia, 1973-76; realtor Tara Realty, Columbia, 1977-81; sole practice, Columbia, 1981-82; ptnr. Cronan, Robinson, Lampton & Pape, Columbia, 1982-85; sole practice law, Columbia, 1986—. Assoc. editor Litigation mag., 1983—. Contbr. articles to mags. Bd. dirs. Columbia Resource Ctr., Inc., 1981—; pres. adv. bd. YWCA, YMCA, Columbia, 1977-78; trustee Coll. Arts and Scis., U. Mo., 1983—. Recipient Roscoe Anderson award for outstanding oral advocacy, 1981. Mem. ABA, Mo. Bar Assn., Boone County Bar Assn., Assn. Trial Lawyers Am. (nat. vice chmn. publs. 1986—), Mo. Assn. Trial Lawyers, Mo. Criminal Def. Lawyers, Stephens Coll. Alumni Assn. (bd. dirs. 1977-80), Internat. Order Barristers, Kappa Tau Alpha, Delta Theta Phi. Democrat. Home: 3301 Westcreek Circle Columbia MO 65203 Office: Cronan Robinson et al 1200 Rogers Suite 200 Columbia MO 65201

PAPEN-DANIEL, MICHELE, counselor educator, psychotherapist; b. El Paso, Tex., Dec. 6, 1943; d. Frank O. and Julia (Stevenson) Papen; children—David Thomas, Julie Daniel, Ralph Daniel. B.A. in Secondary Edn. with honors, U. N.Mex., 1970; M.A. in Edn., Ariz. State U., 1971, M.Counseling, 1972, Ph.D., 1985. Lic. marriage, family and child counselor, Calif. Staff psychologist, North Mountain Behavioral Inst., Phoenix, 1972-74; vis. prof. dept. psychology, Mesa (Ariz.) Community Coll., 1974-76, psychol. cons., dept. spl. services, 1974-76; grad. teaching assoc., instr. dept. secondary edn. Ariz. State U., Tempe, 1974-77; counselor, instr. dept. counseling Chaffey Coll., Alta Loma, Calif., 1977-78, dir. counseling, 1978-79, counseling and testing supr., 1980-81; marriage, family and child counselor Alta Loma Family and Psychol. Services, 1979; vis. lectr. European Grad. Ctr., U. So. Calif., 1979-80; lectr. Calif. State Coll., Fullerton, 1980-81; asst. prof. psychology U. La Verne (Calif.), 1981—, also program specialist; exec. dir. Calif. Psychoednl. Systems, Inc., 1982-85; asst. prof. counselor edn. Calif. State Coll., Bakersfield, 1985—. pvt. practice marriage, family and child counseling; condr. tng. workshops in field, U.S., Holland, Belgium, Eng., P.R., Germany; also lectr.; dir. First Nat. Bank of Dona Ana County, Las Cruces, N.Mex. Trustee Claremont Collegiate Sch., 1978-80; Mem. Am. Assn. Counseling and Devel., Am. Psychol. Assn., Calif. Assn. Counseling and Devel., Western Psychol. Assn., Pi Lambda Theta, Phi Kappa Phi. Contbr. writings to profl. publs. in field; author fed. grant projects.

PAPP, MAUREEN WILLIAMS, village manager; b. Harrisburg, Pa., July 31, 1948; d. Francis Joseph and Marie Kathryn (Flanagan) Williams; m. Robert Allan Papp, Oct. 27, 1978; stepchildren—Michael Allan, Susan Elizabeth. B.A. in History, Pa. State U., 1970. Cert. secondary tchr., Pa. Tchrs. aide Lower Dauphin High Sch., Hummelstown, Pa., 1970-71; sec. Translation House, Washington, 1971, Sanders Assocs., Washington, 1971-73, Golden Bear, Inc., North Palm Beach, Fla., 1973; office mgr. Bertram Yacht Brokerage, North Palm Beach, 1973-74; realtor St. Andrews Club, Delray Beach, Fla., 1975; mgrs. asst. Lost Tree Club, Inc., North Palm Beach, 1975-78, village mgr., 1978—. Democrat. Roman Catholic. Avocations: Swimming; biking; reading; bridge; exercising. Office: Lost Tree Village Property Owners Assn Inc PO Box 14338 North Palm Beach FL 33408

PAPPAS, DESPINA K., restaurateur; b. Patmos, Greece, Apr. 21, 1932; came to U.S., 1935, naturalized, 1953; d. John Nick and Margaret (Miaoulis) Kleoudis; m. John Dan Pappas, Sept. 25, 1955 (dec. Apr. 1978); children—Viki Joan Pappas Moustoukas, Margaret Denise Pappas Minetos, Dennis John. Grad. high sch. Office sec. Straus-Frank Co., Houston, 1950-56; sec. City of Houston, 1956-60; owner-mgr. Rustic Oak Restaurant, Hempstead, Tex., 1978—. Mem. Bus. and Profl. Women Hempstead, Nat. Restaurant Assn., Tex. Restaurant Assn., Houston C. of C., Philoptohos Soc. Lodge: Daus. of Penelope (sec. 1976-78, dir. 1981-83). Home: 2018 Greengrass St Houston TX 77008 Office: Rustic Oak Restaurant 735 10th St Hempstead TX 77445

PAPPAS, HAZEL LORENE, retired accountant; b. West Blocton, Ala., Apr. 16, 1921; d. Lewis Foster and Annie Elizabeth (Tatum) Weaver; m. Christos S. Pappas, June 12, 1961. C.P.A., Ala. Record keeper Lee's Grill, Montgomery, Ala., 1942; bookkeeper Ala. Machinery, Montgomery, 1942-62, Duke Ins. Agy., Montgomery, 1962-83, Ricks, Lind, Davis Real Estate, Montgomery, 1962—. Vol. driver Am. Cancer Soc., Montgomery, 1984—; aux. vol. Baptist Hosp., Montgomery, 1984—. Mem. Ins. Women Montgomery (pres. 1981-82). Democrat. Home: 1069 Druid Hills Dr Montgomery AL 36111

PAPPAS, NANCY LEE, restauranteur; b. Youngstown, Ohio, July 20, 1949; d. Paul and Harriet (George) Pappas; m. George Maranos, Apr. 1, 1977; children—Nicolette, Alexandra. B.A. cum laude in English, Youngstown State U., 1971; M.A. in Diagnostic and Remedial Edn., Miami U., Ohio, 1975. Cert. tchr. K-12, reading supr., Ohio; lic. real estate salesman, Tex. Tchr. English, Ashtabula County Schs. (Ohio), 1971-73, Great Oaks Sch. Dist., Cin., 1973-75; remedial reading specialist Dayton Pub. Sch. (Ohio), 1975-78; software coordinator Fisk Telephone Systems, Houston, 1978-80; v.p. Maranos Inc., Houston, 1982—; sec. Pamar Inc., 1983—. Mem. NOW, Nat. Abortion Rights Action League, Tex. Abortion Rights Action League. Democrat. Greek Orthodox.

PAQUETTE, LEOTA ROSE, association executive; b. Clay Center, Kans., Mar. 24, 1944; d. Leonard Lewis and Hedwig Pauline (Fox) Paquette. B.S., East Tenn. State U., 1980. Admissions and records clk. Kans. State U., Manhattan, 1964-67; field mktg. asst. Eastman Chem. Products div. Eastman Kodak, Chgo., Kansas City and Kingsport, Tenn., 1967-81; advt. sales mgr. Christian Booksellers Assn., Colorado Springs, Colo., 1981—. Mem. Sigma Delta Chi. Democrat. Home: 1411 Territory Trail Colorado Springs CO 80919 Office: Christian Booksellers Assn PO Box 200 Colorado Springs CO 80901

PARADISE, RAMONA ELIZABETH, lawyer; b. Cleve., Dec. 23, 1952; d. Anthony Lewis and Constance Isabelle (Saye) Paradise; m. James Albert Hill, Nov. 23, 1976; 1 son, Geoffrey Thomas. B.A., Case Western Res. U., 1974; J.D., Cleveland Marshall Coll. of Law, 1978. Bar: Ohio 1979, U.S. Dist. Ct. (no dist.) Ohio 1979, U.S. Ct. Appeals (6th cir.) 1982. Counsel, Regional Income Tax Agy., Brecksville, Ohio, 1979-82; sole practice, Cleve., 1979—. Mem. ABA, Ohio State Bar Assn., Citizens League of Greater Cleve., Delta Theta Phi. Republican. Office: City of Cleveland Heights 2953 Mayfield Rd Cleveland Heights OH 44118

PARAMOURE, IRENE MARZELLA, mathematics educator; b. Ocala. Fla., Oct. 21, 1940; d. Marvin Leon Williams and Narlie (Doyle) Williams Campbell; m. Clifford G. Paramoure, Jr., June 9, 1959 (div. 1968); children—Michelle, Reginald G. B.S., Trenton State Coll., 1974, M.Ed., 1976, postgrad., 1976-78. Cert. elem. tchr., N.J. Basic skills math. tchr. Trenton Bd. Edn., N.J., 1973—, mem. curriculum com., 1984—; day care supr., summer camp dir. East Trenton Day Care and Community Ctr., 1975-85; math. tutor Mercer County Community Coll., Trenton, 1983-84. Acting sec. Community Ednl. Adv. Council, Hamilton Twp., N.J., 1982—; clk. Gen. Election Bd., Mercer County, N.J., 1983—; mem. Exec. Plus Women's Orgn., Trenton, 1985—. Mem. N.J. Ednl. Assn., Tchrs. Ednl. Assn., NEA, Nat. Assn. Female Execs., Zeta Phi Beta (chpt. parliamentarian 1978—). Democrat. Methodist. Avocations: reading; travel; aerobics. Home: 47 N Johnston Ave Trenton NJ 08609

PARCHEM, DOROTHY VAN NEST, city government housing official; b. Detroit, June 18, 1922; d. Alfred Earl and Helen Cecelia (O'Neil) Van Nest; m. John Anthony Parchem, June 23, 1944 (dec. Oct. 1958); children—Johanna Marie Parchem Welty, Ann Christine. B.S. in Spl. Edn., Eastern Mich. U., 1944; M.A. in Latin Am. Studies, U. of Ams., 1966. Cert. tchr., Mich., Ind. Tchr., cons. South Bend Sch. System, Inc., 1967-69; tchr. Spanish, Latin Am. history St. Mary's Acad., South Bend, 1960-62; dir. Project Star, Nat. Urban League, South Bend, 1969-74; supr. citizens services Housing Allowance Office, Rand Corp., South Bend, 1974-85; dir. sect. 8 programs Dallas Housing Authority, 1985—, dir. occupancy for resident services, 1985—. Active Urban Coalition, South Bend, 1968-75, South Bend YMCA, 1983-85, Boys' Clubs Am., South Bend, 1980-84; ethnic festival co-chmn. City-County South Bend and St. Joseph County, 1976-80. Recipient Outstanding Service award Urban League, 1973; Spl. Recognition award South Bend Housing Allowance Office, 1985. Mem. Kappa Delta Pi. Republican. Roman Catholic. Club: Notre Dame Alumni. Avocations: golf; swimming; reading. Home: 7867 Meadow Park Dr Dallas TX 75230 Office: Dallas Housing Authority 2525 Lucas Dr Dallas TX 75219

PARDEE, MARGARET ROSS, violinist, violist, educator; b. Valdosta, Ga., May 10, 1920; d. William Augustus and Frances Ross (Burton) P.; diploma Inst. Mus. Art, Juilliard Sch. Music, 1940, grad. diploma, 1942, diploma Juilliard Grad. Sch., 1945; m. Daniel Rogers Butterly, July 5, 1944. Instr. violin and viola Manhattanville Coll. Sacred Heart, N.Y.C., 1942-54, Juilliard Sch., N.Y.C., 1942—, Meadowmount Sch. Music, Westport, N.Y., 1956-84; faculty Estherwood Sch. and Summer Festival, 1984—; concert master Great Neck (L.I.) Symphony, 1954-85; adj. assoc. prof. music Queens Coll., Flushing, N.Y., 1978—; adj. asso. prof. Adelphi U., Garden City, N.Y., 1979-83; adj. prof. SUNY, Purchase, 1980—debut N.Y. Town Hall, 1952; toured U.S. as soloist and in chamber music groups; soloed with symphony orchs. in Miss., N.J., D.C. and N.Y.; mem. jury for internat. competitions. Bd. dirs. Meadowmount Sch. Music. Mem. Soc. for Strings (dir. 1965-86), Associated Music Tchrs. League N.Y. (cert.), N.Y. State Music Tchrs. Assn. (cert.), Music Tchrs. Nat. Assn., Am. Fedn. Musicians, Viola Research Soc. Office: care Juilliard Sch Lincoln Center Plaza New York NY 10023

PARDO, MARIAN URSULA, investment management company executive; b. Rockville Centre, N.Y., Sept. 23, 1946; d. Francis V. and Dorothy E. (Bellidora) P.; B.A., Barnard Coll., 1968; m. Michael S. Toonkel. With Morgan Guaranty Trust Co. N.Y., N.Y.C., 1968-84, v.p. investment div., 1978-84; with J.P. Morgan Investment Inc., 1984—. Chmn. bd. dirs. Opportunity Resources for Arts. Mem. Robert Morris Assocs. (gov. N.Y. chpt. 1977-79), Bank and Fin. Analysts Assn. Office: Morgan Guaranty Trust Co NY 9 W 57th St New York NY 10019

PARDUE, ROBERTA DARLENE, television executive, writer; b. Chickasha, Okla., Aug. 6, 1931; d. Robert Lee and Mary Gem (Price) Dennis; m. Oliver Lee Pearson, Sept. 7, 1950 (div. 1968); children—Lee, Pamela, Jane; m. 2d, Fred Mac Pardue, Feb. 14, 1970. Student Navarro Jr. Coll., 1948-49; B.A., North Tex. State U., 1951. Writer for radio sta., Vernon, Tex., 1940-48; producer, writer Sta. KAND, Corsicana, Tex., 1948-50, Sta. KTRK-TV-AM-FM, Houston, 1950-61; free-lance writer, Los Angeles, 1961-66, Houston, 1970-74; account exec., writer daily radio editorial commentary Nahas-Blumberg, Houston, 1967-70; ops. mgr. Sta. KXTX-TV, Dallas, 1974-86, retired; free-lance writer/producer; cons. on operation radio and TV stas., Tex., Mass., Ala., 1974—; writer, producer Mus. Fine Arts, Houston and Dallas, Goals for Dallas; judge Lincoln awards and Gov.'s Commn. on Handicapped, Dallas and Ft. Worth, 1983. Author: Texas Justice, 1953; writer TV scripts. Announcer, commentator Houston Republican Com., 1963; poll judge, Dallas; speaker for EEOC; pres. PTA, Calif. and Tex., 1961, 64, Jr. League, Calif., 1961, Young Reps., Calif., Tex., Kans., 1955-65. Mem. Am. Women in Radio and TV (sr. v.p. 1958-59), Sigma Delta Chi.

PARENTEAU, IRENE FORCIER, controller; b. Coventry, R.I., Dec. 23, 1933; d. Regis and Evelyn (Levesque) P.; A.S., Leiscester Jr. Coll., 1953; student U. R.I., 1978-80, Bryant Coll., 1981-82; 1 dau., Renee Edith. Acct., Carley & Nardella, West Warwick, R.I., 1962-65, Golden Lantern, Warwick, R.I., 1966-67; controller Coventry Narrow Fabrics, Inc., Coventry, 1967—. Mem. Am. Inst. Corp. Controllers. Roman Catholic. Office: Coventry Narrow Fabrics Inc 624 Washington St Coventry RI 02816

PARENTI, LINDA SUZANNE, investment firm consultant; b. Dayton, Ohio, July 13, 1960; d. Frank V. and Adele M. (Cekun) P. B.S. in Bus. Adminstrn. cum laude, U. Dayton, 1982, postgrad.; 1985—. Asst. to pres. James Investment Research, Inc., Alpha, Ohio, 1982-86; fin. cons. Shearson Lehman Bros., Inc., N.Y.C., 1986—; treas., corp. sec. PAK Software Systems, Inc., Alpha, 1984-85. Active Hipple Labs. Cancer Research, Dayton, Ohio, 1983—, Citizen's Choice, Washington, 1984—, Montgomery County Young Republican Club, Ohio, 1985—. Recipient award of outstanding service U. Dayton, 1982. Mem. U. Dayton Alumni Assn. (Dayton chpt.), Nat. Right to Life, Alpha Xi (life mem.). Roman Catholic. Office: Shearson Lehman Bros Inc 300 Gem Plaza 3d and Main Sts Dayton OH 45402

PARHAM, RUBY INEZ MYERS, civic worker, former educator; b. Tamaha, Okla., Nov. 4, 1914; d. Ola T. and Bursha Bell (Culver) Myers; B.S. in Edn., Northeastern State Coll., 1940, M.Teaching, 1955; m. Rufus K. McCollum, Dec. 31, 1937 (dec. Oct. 1966); m. Jewell A. Parham, June 10, 1973; stepchildren—Bill, Donal E., Ann (Mrs. Everett George), Garry. Tchr. rural schs., Haskell County, Stigler, Okla., 1934-38, Adair County, Stilwell, Okla., 1946-50, Cherokee County, Tahlequah, Okla., 1939-46, 50-66; tchr. Westville (Okla.) Jr. High Sch., 1966-77, ret., 1977. Vol., pres. Tahlequah City Hosp. Aux., 1982-83, 84-85, 85-86; vice chmn. Bapt. Women's Missionary Union, also past pres.; chmn. Nutrition Site Council, Tahlequah; mem. project council Cookson Hills Community Action Found., Inc.; adv. com. Helping Hands; precinct worker Republican party Recipient Oklahoma Bankers award, 1965. Mem. Nat., Okla. edn. assns., Sr. Citizens, Nat. Ret. Tchrs. Assn., Okla. Ret. Tchrs. Assn., Am. Assn. Ret. Persons, Am. Legion Aux., Northeastern State U. Alumni Assn. (life), Nat. Wildlife Assn., sr. Citizens Tahlequah, Kappa Kappa Iota (royal high lady Tahlequah, Okla., 1953-55), Delta Kappa Gamma. Clubs: Rebekah (noble grand 1959-60, jr. noble grand 1960-61, lodge dep. 1961-63, musician), Order Eastern Star (worthy matron 1979, organist, chmn. edn. com.). Home: 215 S College St Tahlequah OK 74464

PARISE, SANDRA KATHLEEN RADER, lawyer; b. Charleston, W.Va., Jan. 29, 1954; d. Clarence Warren and Betty Jane (Booth) Rader; m. Patrick Michael Parise, Mar. 25, 1978. B.S. in Bus. Adminstrn. U. S.C., 1975; J.D., 1981. Bar: S.C. 1981. Ptnr. Fairey & Parise, Columbia, S.C., 1981—. Mem. S.C. Bar Assn., ABA, Nat. Assn. Criminal Def. Lawyers, 1st Amendment Lawyers Assn, Greater Columbia C. of C. (chairperson adopt-a-sch. program) 1983-84. Methodist. Home: Fairey & Parise PO Box 8443 Columbia SC 29202 Office: Fairey & Parise PO Box 8443 1720 Main St Suite 103 Columbia SC 29202

PARISH, MARION ROBBINS, speech-language pathologist; b. Houston, Feb. 2, 1944; d. Walter Alvis and Maude Marion (Robbins) P.; B.A., U. Tex., Austin, 1966; M.A., Our Lady of Lake Coll., 1967. Speech pathologist Corpus Christi (Tex.) Speech and Hearing Center, 1966; instr., supr. undergrads. Our Lady of Lake Coll., San Antonio, 1967-72; dir./owner Speech Pathology Assocs., Houston, 1972—; founder, dir. Parish Children's Sch., 1982—; cons. in field. Active, Jr. League Houston. Mem. Houston Area Assn. Communication Disorders, Am. Speech-Lang.-Hearing Assn., Tex. Speech-Lang.-Hearing Assn. (pres.), Council for Exceptional Children, Orton Soc. Office: 11059 Timberline Houston TX 77043

PARISH, SHIRLEY RAE, nurse; b. Great Bend, Kans., Aug. 29, 1956; d. Lee Allen and Edna Mae (Nusser) P. A.S., Seward County Community Jr. Coll., 1976; B.S. in Nursing, W. Tex. State U., 1978; M.Nursing, Wichita State U., 1984. R.N. Staff nurse, Tex. Tech. U. Health Scis. Ctr., Lubbock, 1978-79, St. Francis Hosp., Wichita, Kans., 1979-80, Wesley Med. Ctr., Wichita, 1980-84, City of Faith Med. and Research Ctr., Tulsa, 1984—. Grad. nurse fellow, Wesley Med. Ctr.-Wichita State U., 1983. Mem. Am. Nurses Assn., Oncology Nursing Soc. (com. chmn. Wichita Area Chpt. 1982-84). Baptist. Home: PO Box 702211 Tulsa OK 74170 Office: 8181 S Lewis Tulsa OK 74136

PARISI, BONNIE LEE, clinical social worker; b. Columbia, S.C., July 1, 1946; d. Dominick George and Barbara Pauline Parisi; B.A. in Psychology, Sacred Heart Coll., Belmont, N.C., 1970; M.S.W., U. S.C., 1978. Social worker Guilford County Mental Health Center, Greensboro, N.C., 1970-74; clin. social worker Upper Savannah Health Dept., Greenwood, S.C., 1978-79; outreach services coordinator, vol. services coordinator. Tri-County Mental Health Center, Dillon, S.C., 1979—; trainer, group facilitator Partners-In-Parenting, Greenwood, 1978-79; mem. steering com., conf. group facilitator White House Conf. on Families, 1980. Registered social worker. Mem. Nat. Assn. Social Workers, Acad. Cert. Social Workers, S.C. Assn. Social Workers (com. on inquiry), S.C. Social Welfare Forum, S.C. Soc. Clin. Social Workers. Club: Dillon Pilot (chaplain 1981-92, v.p. 1982-83). Home: PO Box 350 Dillon SC 29536 Office: PO Box 929 Dillon SC 29536

PARK, DOROTHY GOODWIN DENT (MRS. ROY HAMPTON PARK), broadcasting, newspaper exec.; b. Raleigh, N.C.; d. Walter Reed and Mildred (Goodwin) Dent; student Peace Jr. Coll., 1925-33; A.B., Meredith Coll., 1936; m. Roy Hampton Park, Oct. 3, 1936; children—Roy Hampton, Adelaide Hinton. Sec., dir. RHP, Inc., Ithaca, N.Y., 1945—, Park Communications, Inc., Ithaca, N.Y., 1983—, Roy H. Park Broadcasting of Va., Inc., Sta. WTVR-TV-AM-FM, Richmond, 1965—, Roy H. Park Broadcasting of Tri-Cities, Inc., Sta. WJHL-TV, Johnson City, Tenn., 1964—, Roy H. Park Broadcasting of Tenn., Inc., Sta. WDEF-TV-AM-FM, Chattanooga, 1963—, Park Broadcasting, Inc., Ithaca, 1942—, Roy H. Park Broadcasting, Inc., Sta. WNCT-TV-FM, Greenville, N.C., 1962—, Roy H. Park Radio, Inc., Sta. WNCT-AM, Greenville, 1963—, Park Found., Inc., Greenville, 1966—, Cobb House of Rock Hill, S.C. Inc., 1967—, Roy H. Park Broadcasting of Midwest, Inc., Sta. WNAX-AM, Yankton, S.D., 1968—, Roy H. Park Broadcasting of Roanoke, Inc., Sta. WSLS-TV, 1969—, Roy H. Park Broadcasting of Utica-Rome, N.Y., Inc., Sta. WUTR-TV, 1969—, Park Newspapers, Inc., Ithaca, 1972—, Park Outdoor Advt. of Scranton-Wilkes-Barre, Inc., Park Newspapers of Ga., Inc., 1972—, KWJJ-AM, Portland, Ore., 1973—, RHP Newspapers, Inc., Ithaca, 1973—, Roy H. Park Broadcasting of Birmingham (Ala.), Inc., 1973—, Park Newspapers of Va., Inc., 1973—, Birmingham TV Corp., Sta. WBMG-TV, 1973—, Lockport Publs., Inc., Ithaca, 1973—, Lockport (N.Y.) Union Sun & Jour. Inc., 1973—, Prince William Pub. Co., Inc., Manassas, Va., 1973—, Roy H. Park Broadcasting of Lake County, Inc., Sta. KJJO, St. Louis Park, Minn., 1974—, Roy H. Park Broadcasting of Minn., Inc., Sta. KRSI-AM, St. Louis Park, 1974—, Contemporary FM, Inc., Sta. KJIB-FM, Portland, 1974—, Roy H. Park Broadcasting of Syracuse, Inc., 1976—, Roy H. Park Broadcasting of Wash., Inc., Sta. KEZX-FM, Portland, 1975—, Park Newspapers of Neb., Inc., Ithaca, 1975—, Press Printing Co., Nebraska City, Neb., 1975—, Park Newspapers of Fla., Inc., Brooksville, 1975—Roy H. Park Broadcasting of Syracuse, Inc., WHEN-AM, 1976—; Roy H. Park Broadcasting of Finger Lakes, Inc., WRRB-FM, 1977—, Park Newspapers of St. Lawrence, Inc., Ithaca, 1975—, Northern. N.Y. Pub. Co., Odensburg, 1975—, Courier-Freman, Inc., Potsdam, N.Y., 1975—, Massena (N.Y.) Observer Pub. Co., 1975—, St. Lawrence Plaindealer, Inc., Canton, N.Y., 1975—, Park Newspapers of Ill., Inc., 1979—, State & Aurora, Inc.,

Broken Arrow, Okla., 1979—, Southside Publs., Inc., 1979—, WND, Inc., Sapulpa, Okla., 1979—, Park Newspapers of Newton, Inc., 1979—, Park Newspapers of Morganton, Inc., 1979—, Park Newspapers of Statesville, Inc., 1979—, Park Newspapers of Concord, Inc., 1980—, Park Newspapers of Perry, Ga., Inc., 1980—, Park Newspapers of Michigan, Inc., 1980, Park Newspapers of Ark., Inc., 1981, Park Newspapers of Lumberton, N.C., 1982, Park Newspapers of Moore County, N.C., Inc., 1982, Park Newspapers of Devils Lake, N.D., Inc., 1982, Park Newspapers of Marion, N.C. Inc., 1982, Park Newspapers of Waynesboro, Va., Inc., 1983, Park Newspapers of Medina, N.Y., 1984. Bd. visitors Peace Coll., Raleigh, 1968—. Mem. DAR (1st vice regent 1955-57), Daus. Am. Colonists, Nat. Soc. Magna Charta Dames, Sovereign Colonial Soc. Ams. Royal Descent, Descs. Knights of Garter, Colonial Order of Crown, Service League Ithaca, LWV. Presbyterian. Clubs: Garden (Ithaca), Ithaca Woman's. Home: 205 Devon Rd Ithaca NY 14850 Office: Terrace Hill PO Box 550 Ithaca NY 14850

PARK, GLADYS JAYNAR, health planner, consultant; b. Waialua, Hawaii, Apr. 17, 1931; d. Joseph Ponciano and Alice Cruz (Sales) J.; m. David Tai Young, Dec. 12, 1953; children—Sandra Eai Lan, Lawrence J. B.S. in Nursing, U. Hawaii, 1960, M.P.H., 1973. Staff nurse The Queen's Hosp., Honolulu, 1953-54; pvt. duty nurse, Honolulu, 1954-55; staff pub. health nurse State Dept. Health, Honolulu, 1955-64, supr. chest clinic, 1964-66, project supr., 1966-68, pub. health nursing supr., 1968-73, comprehensive health planning coordinator I, 1973-77, comprehensive health planning officer, 1977—. Sec., Palolo Community Council, Honolulu, 1966-68; mem., chmn. Palolo Community Action Program, Honolulu, 1966-68; mem. State Sr. Ctr. Med. Adv. Com., Honolulu, 1975-77; mem. Honolulu Home Care Adv. Com., 1975-77; mem. State Bd. Audiology and Speech Pathology, Honolulu, 1979-82; trustee Palama Settlement, Honolulu, 1974-82; mem. interim adv. bd. Western Ctr. for Health Planning, San Francisco, 1975-76. Mem. Am. Pub. Health Assn., Hawaii Pub. Health Assn. (pres. 1981), Hawaii Nurses Assn. (membership chmn. 1966-68), Phi Kappa Phi. Clubs: Gen. Fedn. Women's Clubs (corr. sec. 1979); Waialua (sec.) (Honolulu). Office: State Health Planning and Devel Agy PO Box 3378 Honolulu HI 96801

PARK, JOAN ANNETTE, laboratory equipment manufacturing company executive; b. Appleton City, Mo., Nov. 24, 1956; d. Edwin Nathaniel and Julie Joan (Pavlik) Park. B.S. in Bus. Adminstrn., S.W. Mo. State U., 1979; postgrad. in bus. adminstrn. Rockhurst Coll., 1984. Personnel asst. Labconco Corp., Kansas City, Mo., 1979-81, personnel specialist, 1981, personnel mgr., 1981—. Internal coordinator United Way, Kansas City, Mo., 1981—, account coordinator, 1982-83; chmn. Dodson Indsl. Group, Kansas City, Mo., 1983—; bd. dirs. Marlborough Neighborhood Assn., Kansas City, Mo., 1982. Mem. Personnel Mgmt. Assn. Kansas City (mem. various coms.), Am. Soc. for Personnel Adminstrn. Office: Labconco Corp 8811 Prospect St Kansas City MO 64132

PARKAS, IVA RICHEY, educator, historian, curator, paralegal; b. Comanche County, Tex., June 28, 1907; d. Andrew Jackson and Pearl Lucretia (Kennedy) Richey; grad. Wayland Coll., 1927; B.A., Tex. Tech. U., 1935; M.Litt., U. Pitts., 1950; postgrad. UCLA, 1960, Pa. State U., 1961, U. Calif., Berkeley, 1962, Duquesne U., 1963, Carnegie-Mellon U., 1968; m. George Eduardo Parkas, May 5, 1945. Curator, historian Fort Pitt Blockhouse, Pitts., 1946-52, asst. curator-historian, 1964-84; tchr. U.S. history Pitts. sr. high schs., 1953-72; paralegal Allegheny County (Pa.) Law Dept., 1977-82. Del., White House Conf. on Children and Youth, Washington, 1960, 70, World Food Conf., Rome, 1974; U.S. Congl. Sr. Citizens intern, Washington, 1984. Named Disting. Alumnae, U. Pitts., 1978; recipient Valley Forge Classroom Tchr.'s medal, 1960. Henry Clay Frick Ednl. fellow; NDEA grantee; Greater Pitts. Air Force Squadron scholar, Pitts. Press scholar, 1960. Mem. NEA (life), AAUW (pres. Pitts. br. 1974-76), Hist. Soc. Western Pa., Western Pa. Council Social Studies (pres. 1969-71,), DAR (regent Pitts. chpt. 1987-89), U. Pitts. Alumnae Assn. (bd. dirs. 1978—, v.p. 1984), Pa. Retired Pub. Sch. Employees Assn. (chairperson Am. revolution bicentennial), Western Pa. Hist. Soc., Delta Kappa Gamma, Phi Alpha Theta. Editor: So Your Children Can Tell Their Children, 1976. Contbr. articles on hist. subjects to newspapers, mags. Home: 5520 Fifth Ave Pittsburgh PA 15232

PARKE, JANET DIANE, interior designer; b. Winnemucca, Nev., Aug. 20, 1930; d. Willard Virdell and Lois (Carlson) Booth; m. Jack Evan Parke, June 11, 1950; children—Deborah Diane Parke Smith, Cary Evan, James Robert. B.A., Brigham Young U., 1950. Interior designer Brunson Homes, Reno, Nev., 1972-74, Bakers Interiors, Reno, 1976-81, Tristan Parke Interiors, Reno, 1981—. Designer showcase homes. Bd. dirs. Nev. Jr. Miss, 1969-79; hostes Miss Nev., Reno, 1974-77; com. mem. Congressman Jim Santini, Reno. Mem. AIA (assoc.), Nev. Home Builders Assn. (assoc.), Sigma Nu (pres. White Rose chpt. 1952-53). Democrat. Mormon. Lodges: Order Ea. Star, Daus. of Nile. Office: Tristan Parke Interiors 26 Hillcrest Dr Reno NV 89509

PARKE, PRISCILLA ANN, financial consultant; b. Uniontown, Pa., Sept. 25, 1950; d. Allen Jones and Auberta Ann (Crawford) P.; 1 dau., Danielle Colette Parke Betancourt. B.F.A., Pratt Inst., 1972. Asst. buyer Abraham & Straus, Bklyn., 1972-73, dept. mgr., Huntington, N.Y., 1973-75; salesperson Burlington Industries, N.Y.C., 1975-77, sales mgr., 1977-81; merchandising mgr. Espresso div. Chestnut Ridge Industries, N.Y.C., 1981-83; fin. cons. Shearson/Lehman Bros., N.Y.C., 1983—; bus. cons. clothing mfrs. Research on finishes for rainwear. Home: 184 73d St Brooklyn NY 11209 Office: 1 Penn Plaza New York NY 10119

PARKER, AMY ANGELA, fabric designer; b. Waynesville, N.C., Sept. 25, 1962; d. Wiley Wilburn and Charlotte Jean (Smith) P. B.S., Western Carolina U., 1984. Designer C&A Mastercraft, Spindale, N.C., 1984—; adviser Explorer Scouts, Boy Scouts Am., Spindale, N.C., 1985—. Mem. Nat. Assn. Female Execs. Home: Route 2 Box 929A Forest City NC 28043 Office: C&A Mastercraft 210 Park St Spindale NC 28160

PARKER, BEATRICE GRADY, stock brokerage executive; b. Detroit, July 27, 1951; m. Gregory Parker, June 7, 1980. B.A., Ohio U., 1973. Sales rep. Nat. Cash Register, Detroit, 1977-80; account exec. Merrill Lynch, Westfield, N.J., 1980-85, asst. v.p., 1985—. Mem. Phi Chi Theta. Avocations: bike riding; aerobics; travel. Office: Merrill Lynch 195 Elm St Westfield NJ 07090

PARKER, BOOTS FARTHING, management consultant, public relations executive; b. Boone, N.C., Dec. 25, 1929; d. Joseph Edward and Polly Ida (Harmon) Farthing; student Ohio State U., 1948; m. Paul Hixson, Dec. 31, 1949 (dec. 1968); m. 2d, W. Dale Parker, Sept. 13, 1968; 1 adopted dau., Jacquelyn Susan. With Greenpark Hotel, Blowing Rock, N.C., and Sea Ranch Hotel, Ft. Lauderdale, Fla., 1947-48, O'Neil Co., Akron, Ohio, 1948-67; chief Firestone's United Trading Co., also ofcl. hostess, chief of protocol Firestone Internat., Monrovia, Liberia, 1958-61; with Holiday Inns. Am., F.W. Woolworth, Fla., 1967-72; pres. Multiple Services, Titusville, Fla., 1972—; art collector. Former mem. Democratic Exec. Com. Recipient Internat. Humanitarian award, London, 1972, Disting. Service award Fla. Sheriff's Assn., 1976; hon. col. Ala. State Militia; named hon. navy recruiter U.S. Navy Dept., 1977. Mem. N.Y. Vets. Police Assn., Va. Sheriffs Assn. Clubs: Royal Oak Golf and Country, Order of Does, Fla. Fraternal Order Police. Home: PO Box 246 Deck Hill Boone NC 28607 Office: PO Box 1441 Titusville FL 32781

PARKER, CYNTHIA VICTORIA, marketing analyst; b. Baton Rouge, La., May 21, 1956; d. Sidney B. and Bernice (Martin) P. B.A. in Math, U. Fla., 1978; postgrad. U. Pitts., 1984. With Westinghouse Electric Co., 1979—, planning analyst constrn. div., Pitts., 1984, mktg. rep., analyst transmission and distbn. components div., Bloomington, Ind., 1984-85, customer service supr., Chgo., 1985—. Adviser Pitts. Urban Youth Action Career Counseling, 1982-84; mem. task force on minority-women's career programming, WOED Pub. TV, Pitts., 1983. Mem. Nat. Tech. Assn. (pres. chpt. 1983-84), Toastmasters Internat., Alpha Kappa Alpha. Republican. Episcopalian. Home: 149 Thomas Rd Bolingbrook IL 60439

PARKER, EDNA G., judge; b. Johnston County, N.C., 1930; 1 son, Douglas Benjamin. Student N.J. Coll. for Women (now Douglass Coll.); B.A. with honors, U. Ariz., 1953; postgrad. U. Ariz. Law Sch.; LL.B., George Washington U., 1957. Law clk. to judges U.S. Ct. Claims, 1957-59; atty./advisor Office of Gen. Counsel, Dept. Navy, 1959-60; trial atty. civil and tax div. Dept. Justice, 1960-69; adminstrv. judge Contract Appeals Bd., Dept. Transp., 1969-77; spl. trial judge U.S. Tax Ct., 1980—. Mem. ABA, Fed. Bar Assn., D.C. Bar, D.C. Bar Assn., Women's Bar Assn. D.C., Nat. Assn. Women Lawyers, Nat. Assn. Women Judges. Office: US Tax Ct 400 2d St NW Washington DC 20217*

PARKER, ELINOR MILNOR, editor; b. Jersey City, Mar. 20, 1906; d. Charles Wolcott and Emily (Fuller) P.; A.B., Bryn Mawr Coll., 1927. Gen. asst. The Bookshop, Morristown, N.J., 1928-38; head children's books, then asst. mgr. Scribner Book Store, N.Y.C., 1938-53; editor trade books Charles Scribner's Sons, 1953-79, dir., 1966-79, asst. sec., 1970-79, v.p., 1973-79, editorial cons., 1979—. Mem. Nat. Soc. Colonial Dames. Episcopalian. Club: Cosmopolitan (N.Y.C.). Author: Cooking for One, 1949; Some Dogs, 1950; Entertaining Singlehanded, 1952; Most Gracious Majesty, 1953. Compiler: A Birthday Garland, 1949; 100 Story Poems, 1951; 100 Poems About People, 1955; I Was Just Thinking, 1959; 100 More Story Poems, 1960; The Singing and the Gold, 1962; Poems of William Wordsworth, 1964; Here and There, 1967; Four Seasons Five Senses, 1974; Poets and the English Scene, 1975; Echoes of the Sea, 1977; Letters and Numbers for Needlepoint, 1978. Home: 30 E 72d St New York NY 10021

PARKER, ELIZABETH ANN, city festival executive; b. Worcester, Mass., Oct. 31, 1952; d. Patrick Alfred and Mae Elizabeth (Mathieu) Germain; m. James Phillips parker, Sept. 16, 1978; children—Amanda Duff, Nickolas patrick. B.A., Case Western Res. U., 1974. Box office mgr., Tower Theatre, Houston, 1979-81; dir. ticketing service Majestic Performing Arts Ctr., San Antonio, 1981-83, asst. dir., 1983-84; mng. dir. Berkshire Ballet, Pittsfield, Mass., 1984-85; dir. ticket services San Antonio Festival, 1985—. Mem. AAUW, Box Office Mgrs. Internat., Nat. Assn. Female Execs. Democrat. Roman Catholic. Avocations: camping; hiking; gardening; sewing; old films. Office: San Antonio Festival 339 S Presa St San Antonio TX 78205

PARKER, HARRIET MASHBURN, university administrator; b. Jackson County, N.C., June 26, 1935; d. Avery Richard and Lydia (Higdon) Mashburn; B.S.Ed., Western Carolina U., 1957; m. Grady C. Parker, Sept. 3, 1955; children—Greg, Doug, Tony. Asst. registrar Western Carolina U., 1957-69, registrar, 1970—. Named Boss of Yr., Western Carolina chpt. N.C. Assn. Ednl. Office Personnel, 1979, Dist. Boss of Yr., 1980; cert. tchr. bus., health and phys.edn., N.C. Mem. Am. Assn. Collegiate Registrars and Admissions Officers, So. Assn. Collegiate Registrars and Admissions Officers, Carolinas Assn. Collegiate Registrars and Admissions Officer, N.C. State Employees Assn., AAUW (pres. 1982-86), Jackson County C. of C., Jackson County Bus. and Profl. Women (pres. 1982-83), Camp Lab Parent-Tchr. Orgn. Baptist. Club: Order Eastern Star (past matron, dist. dep.). Home: Route 66 Box 40 Cullowhee NC 28723 Office: 201 Robinson Adminstrn Bldg Western Carolina U Cullowhee NC 28723

PARKER, JANEL LESLIE, nursing administrator; b. Ft. Wayne, Ind., July 13, 1952; d. Kenneth Joseph and Margaret Ellen (Wittmer) Dager; m. David E. Parker, May 18, 1979; 1 child, Jonathan David. A.Nursing Sci., Purdue U., 1973; B.S.N., Ind. Central U., 1982; M.S.N., 1983. Staff nurse Ind. U. Med. Ctr., Indpls., 1973-77; head nurse Methodist Hosp., Indpls., 1977-79; nursing supr. Rush Presbyn. St. Luke Med. Ctr., Chgo., 1979-80; dir. nursing Dialysis Inst. Ind., Indpls., 1982-83; clin. nursing supr. Northwestern Meml. Hosp., Chgo., 1983—; dir. Nurse Fellowship Program Am. Med. Products, Freehold, N.J., 1983—; ind. cons. Editor, 2d author: Principles of Hemodialysis, 1984. Guest editor Profl. Jour. Dialysis and Transplant, 1985. Contbr. articles to profl. jours. Mem. disaster program ARC, Indpls., 1978-80. Robert Wood Johnson Found. scholar, 1982. Mem. Am. Nurses Assn. (cert.), Council of Nephrology Nurses and Techs., Nat. Kidney Found., Am. Nephrology Nurses Assn. (chpt. pres. 1978-79, pres. 1985—). Republican. Episcopalian. Avocations: golf, jogging, skiing. Office: Northwestern Meml Hosp Superior St and Fairbanks Ct Chgo IL 60611

PARKER, JERI, educator, writer, consultant; b. Rexburg, Idaho, Oct. 28, 1939; d. Elbert and Shirley (Stoddard) P.; B.A., Brigham Young U., 1957; M.A., U. Utah, 1970, Ph.D. (Pres. Research fellow), 1973; postgrad. Am. U., Beirut, summer 1962, U. Grenoble, summer 1963, U. Cambridge U., 1983. Dir. Women's Center, Westminster Coll., Salt Lake City, 1975-79; dir. Summer Writing Workshop, U. Utah, Salt Lake City, 1980-81, instr. English, 1979-83; tech. writing cons. Exxon, Chevron, Shell Oil, U.S. Navy, NASA, others; mem. bd. advs. Network Publs., Odyssey House, 1979. Mem. Delta Kappa Gamma. Mormon. Club: Literary. Author: Uneasy Survivors: Five Women Writers, 1975, also tech. writing manuals for engrs.; contbr. theatre revs., poems, short stories to various publs. Home and office: 936 Browning Ave Salt Lake City UT 84105

PARKER, JOAN MARY, real estate broker; b. Passaic, N.J., May 25, 1939; d. John and Mary (Baumann) Schablik; m. Edward James Parker, Sep. 30, 1961 children—David, Lauren, Renee. B.A., Coll. St. Elizabeth, 1961. Engring. asst. Exxon Co., Florham park, N.J., 1961-62; real estate agt. Masters Realty, Wayne, N.J., 1973-78; real estate broker, sales assoc. Century 21 Casey Realty Inc., Wayne, N.J., 1978-85, Schlott Realtors, Inc., Wayne, 1986—. Mem. N.J. Assn. Realtors (million dollar sales award 1984), Passaic County Bd. Realtors. Roman Catholic. Home: 6 Reed Ct Wayne NJ 07470 Office: Schlott Realtors Inc 1094 Hamburg Turnpike Wayne NJ 07470

PARKER, JUDITH, wholesale jewelry company executive; b. St. Louis, Aug. 31, 1930; d. John Isbel and Ruth (Backof) Parker; m. William C. Brown, Mar. 27, 1954 (div. Dec. 1966); children—Stacy, Mark; m. 2d Robert F. Nennert, June 3, 1967 (div. 1974); 1 son, Peter; m. 3d Ronald Elmer Parker, Nov. 20, 1981. Student Milliken U., 1948-50, U. Mo., 1950-51, Washington U., St. Louis, 1951. Receptionist Arnold Research Orgn., St. Louis, 1951-52; asst. tooth dept. Midvale Dental Supply, St. Louis, 1952-54; salesman Parker Jewelry Co., Inc., St. Louis, 1963-76, pres., 1976—. Mem. Arcade Bldg. Assn. (pres. 1974-76), Downtown Women of St. Louis. Republican. Methodist. Home: 10 York Hills St Louis MO 63114 Office: Parker Jewelry Co Inc 915 Olive Suite 219 C St Louis MO 63101

PARKER, JUDITH ANN, nurse; b. Butler, Pa., June 10, 1952; d. Edward Joseph Parker and Bette Ellen (Irwin) Parker Hillard. Diploma in Nursing, St. Francis Gen. Hosp., Pitts., 1978. R.N., Fla., Pa. Acting head nurse St. Francis Gen. Hosp., 1978-79; team leader Coral Reef Hosp., Miami, 1980-83; charge nurse Highland Park Hosp., Miami, 1983-85, program coordinator adolescent psychiat. unit, 1985—. Republican. Presbyterian. Avocations: dancing, reading, boating, needlework. Home: 9375 Fontainebleau Blvd #L428 Miami FL 33172 Office: Highland Park Gen Hosp 1660 NW 7th Ct Miami FL 33136

PARKER, JUDITH KOEHLER, science educator; b. Dalhart, Tex., May 12, 1940; d. James Albert and Mildred Zimlich K.; B.S., St. Louis U., 1962; M.A., Washington U., 1979; m. Gerald E. Parker, Dec. 30, 1964; children—James E., G. Michael. Head bacteriologist St. Louis U. Hosp., 1962-63; bacteriologist N.Mex. Pub. Health Dept., 1963-64; instr., head bacteriologist St. Louis U. Hosp., 1964-66; med. technologist S.W. Med. Center, St. Louis County, Mo., 1966-72; adj. instr. Maryville Coll., Sunset Hills, Mo., 1981-83, mgr. sci. lab., 1983—; propr. Splty. Retail Shop, 1981-84. Bd. dirs. Spl. Sch. St. Louis County, 1982-88, pres., 1983-87; Bonhomme Democratic committeewoman, 1979-86; mem. Mo. State Dem. Com., 1980—; del. Nat. Dem. Conv., 1980. Mo. State Conv., 1980, 84. Mem. Am. Soc. Clin. Pathologists (affiliate), Mo. Assn. Children with Learning Disabilities, Gamma Pi Epsilon, Pi Lambda Theta. Roman Catholic. Home: 116 Hollywood Kirkwood MO 63122

PARKER, KATHLEEN, media entrepreneur, journalist; b. Ortonville, Minn., May 23, 1948; d. L.R. and Barbara (Bruskin) Severin; m. John B. Parker, May 19, 1973. B.A., Barnard Coll., 1970; M.S., Columbia U., 1973. Writer, AP, N.Y.C., 1973-74; journalist CBS Network News, Los Angeles, 1974; reporter, anchor woman Sta. KFMB-TV, San Diego, 1975-79; pres. Pacific Communications, South Lake Tahoe, Calif., 1979—; owner, operator Sta. KOWL-AM, Inc., South Lake Tahoe, 1979-83, Sta. KIKI-AM and KAMI-FM, Honolulu, 1980—, Sta. KIKI Licensing Corp., Toykyo, 1981—, Parker Communications Sta. KTCZ-FM and KTCJ-AM, Mpsl., 1984—, Desert Communications Sta. KXTZ-FM, Las Vegas, Nev., 1984—. Mem. Twin City Broadcasting Assn. (sec. 1984-85), Nat. Assn. Broadcasters. Clubs: Soroptimist Internat. Avocations: bird watching, art collecting, mystery reading, jogging. Office: Parker Cos 2826 IDS Ctr Minneapolis MN 55402

PARKER, LAURA LEE, graphic designer, marketing communications executive; b. Denver, Feb. 2, 1947; d. Harry Arthur and Sarah Geneva (Jones) Steinbach; b. John Whiteman Parker, Aug. 10, 1971 (div. 1975). Student Colo. Inst. Art, 1966-68, San Francisco Acad. Art, 1968-70, San Francisco Art Inst., 1971. Graphic designer Wells Fargo Bank, San Francisco, 1971-76; ptnr. Ariel, San Francisco, 1977-82; prin., designer Laura Parker Design, San Francisco, 1982—. Editor, Vermissa Herald, 1982-84. Mem. pub. relations com. Resource Found., 1983. Recipient 1st place prize Nat. Assn. Fund Raising Counsel, 1984; award of excellence Nat. Assn. Art Dirs. and Designers, 1986. Mem. San Francisco Art Dirs. Club (bd. dirs.), Am. Inst. Graphic Artists. Clubs: Adventuresses of Sherlock Holmes (N.Y.C.) (Hon. Miss Miles); Scowers and Molly Maguires (San Francisco) (editor Stanger). Home: 3150 Franklin St #11 San Francisco CA 94123 Office: Laura Parker Design 110 S Park Ave San Francisco CA 94107

PARKER, LENORE, organization executive; b. Rome, N.Y., Mar. 21, 1933; d. Anthony and Ena (Rizzuto) La Gatta; m. James F. Parker, Jan. 25, 1957 (dec. 1985); 1 son, Donald. B.S., Fordham U., 1955. Dir. pub. relations Am. Med. Ctr. of Denver, 1963-67; exec. dir. Am. Council for Emigres in Professions, N.Y.C., 1967-78; exec. dir. YWCA of City N.Y., 1978—. Contbr. chpts. to books, articles to profl. jours. Bd. dirs. Am. Immigration and Citizen Conf., N.Y.C.; chmn. Women Execs. in Human Services, N.Y.C., Community Council Greater N.Y.; treas. Pvt. Industry Council, N.Y.C., 1984—.

PARKER, LINDA MARIAN BATES, university administrator; b. Cin., Feb. 23, 1944; d. Ernest Louis and Mary Elizabeth Bates; m. Breland Kennedy Parker, Nov. 24, 1946; children—Robbin, Brandon. B.S., U. Dayton, 1965; M.A., U. Cin., 1970. Market researcher Proctor & Gamble Co., Cin., 1965-66; tng. coordinator Shillito's Dept. Store, Cin., 1966-70; head resident counselor U. Cin., 1971-75, assoc. dir. career planning and placement, 1975-76, assoc. vice provost study affairs, 1981—. Pres., Black Career Women, Inc., Cin., 1977—; bd. dirs. Cin. Local Devel. Co., 1983—; trustee Black Career Women's Resource Center, Inc., Cin., 1982—, WCET Pub. TV, Cin., 1974-75; pres. Jr. Alliance for Social and Civic Action, Cin., 1974; bd. dirs. Charter Com., 1979. Named Woman of Yr., Cin. Enquirer, 1983; Career Woman of Achievement, YWCA, 1982; recipient Unsung Heroine award Nat. Women's Conf. NAACP, 1982; Advocate award Women in Communications, 1982. Mem. Midwest Coll. Placement Assn. (chmn. ann meeting 1979). Roman Catholic. Office: Black Career Women Inc 2015 Madison Rd Cincinnati OH 45208

PARKER, LUCY T., psychologist, academy director; b. Vienna, Austria, Jan. 21, 1933; came to U.S., 1939, naturalized, 1945; d. Joseph and Maria (Tauber) Thimann; B.S., Boston U., 1958, Ed.M., 1965, Ed.D., 1974; Ph.D., Heed U., 1973; m. Robert Alan Parker, Feb. 1, 1980; children: Karen Sue, Janet Lee, Geoffrey Samuel, Linda Ann. Elem. tchr. Bellingham (Mass.) Public Schs., 1958-59; tchr. jr. high sch. Temple Shalom, Newton, Mass., 1962-64; sch. adjustment counselor Needham (Mass.) Public Schs., 1964-67; pvt. practice psychotherapy, crisis intervention, Waban, Mass., 1965-72; counseling psychologist Leslie B. Cutler Child Guidance Clinic, Norwood, Mass., 1967-70, Walker Home for Children, Needham, 1968-72; clin. dir. Chestnut Hill (Mass.) Psychotherapy Assocs., 1970-85; v.p. Universal Freedom, Inc., 1970-85; sr. cons. Parker Assocs., 1977-85; dir. Parker Acad., 1985—; lectr. in psychology Northeastern U. Grad. Sch. Edn., 1966-67; asst. prof. edn. Lesley Coll., 1967-72; assoc. prof. psychology and edn., New Eng. coordinator, Heed U., 1972-74, prof., 1972-78; assoc. prof. edn. Newton Coll., 1972-75; guest lectr. colls., univs., 1966-78; research assoc. in behavioral scis. Mass. Coll. Optometry, 1973-75; sensitivity group trainer, cons. human relations Nat. Tng. Labs., 1968-80; cons., condr. seminars and workshops in field. Bd. dirs. Washingtonian Hosp., Jamaica Plain, Mass., 1967-77. Lic. psychologist, cert. elem. tchr., guidance counselor, dir. guidance, sch. adjustment counselor, Mass.; diplomate Am. Acad. Behavioral Medicine, Internat. Assn. Profl. Counseling and Psychotherapy. Fellow Am. Acad. Optometry, Internat. Council Sex Edn. and Parenthood; mem. Am. Psychol. Assn., AAUP, Am. Soc. Clin. Hypnosis, Am. Assn. Sex Educators and Counselors, Am. Assn. Marriage and Family Therapists, Am. Personnel and Guidance Assn., Mass. Psychol. Assn. Research, publs. in field. Address: The Parker Acad 248 Concord Rd Sudbury MA 01776

PARKER, LYNDA MICHELE, psychiatrist; b. Phila., Sept. 28, 1947; d. Albert Francis and Dorothy Thomasinia (Herriott) P.; B.A., C. W. Post Coll., 1968; M.A. (Martin Luther King Jr. scholar 1968-70), N.Y.U., 1970; M.D., Cornell U., 1974; postgrad. N.Y. Psychoanalytic Inst., 1977-82. Intern, N.Y. Hosp., N.Y.C., 1975; resident in psychiatry Payne Whitney Clinic, N.Y.C., 1975-78; psychiatrist in charge day program Cabrini Med. Center, N.Y.C., 1978-79, attending psychiatrist, 1978—; admitting psychiatrist inpatient psychiat. treatment Payne Whitney Clinic, N.Y.C., 1978—, supr. psychiatry residents, 1978—, supr. long-term psychotherapy, 1980-82; attending psychiatrist N.Y. Hosp., Cornell Med. Center, 1979—; practice medicine specializing in psychiatry, N.Y.C., 1979—; instr. psychiatry Cornell U. Med. Coll., 1979-86, asst. prof., 1986—; instr. psychiatry, N.Y. Med. Coll., 1978—; psychiat. cons. Bldg. Service 32BJ Health Fund, 1983—, Inwood House, N.Y.C., 1983—, Time-Life Inc., 1986. Mem. Am. Psychiat. Assn., Am. Womens Med. Assn. Episcopalian. Office: 4 E 89th St New York NY 10028

PARKER, MARGERY ELEANOR, sales representative; b. Scranton, Pa., Sept. 24, 1946; d. Roswell James and Margery Elizabeth (Thomas) Parker; B.S. in Med. Tech., Temple U., 1968. Research technologist Temple U. Sch. Medicine, Phila., 1968-76; instr. Coulter Electronics, Islamorada, Fla., 1976-77, sales rep. Curtin Matheson Sci., Allentown, Pa., 1977-80, Calbiochem-Behring Corp., Allentown, Pa. 1980-83, Rupp and Bowman, 1983-84, The Jobst Inst., 1984—. Mem. Am. Soc. Clin. Pathologists, Allentown Art Mus. Assn., Cetronia Ambulance Corps. Republican. Presbyterian.

PARKER, MARILYN MORRIS, business executive; b. St. Louis, Jan. 2, 1935; d. Walter Louis and R. Viola (Morris) Priebe; B.B.A., Washington U., 1954, M.B.A., 1955; m. H. Virgil Parker, Mar. 11, 1971. With IBM Corp., various locations, 1957—, mgr. IBM Aids, Los Angeles, 1971-75, mgr. performance evaluation, San Jose, Calif., 1976-79, tech. asst. to mgr. performance and tech., 1979-80, mgr. IBM Los Angeles Sci. Center, 1981—; v.p. Cherokee Creek Enterprises, Los Angeles and San Jose, 1973—. Co-founder, pres. Am. Indian Scholarship Fund, 1971-76, No. Calif. regional dir., 1977-80, exec. dir., 1981—; mem. Santa Clara County Alcoholism Adv. Bd., 1977; bd. dirs. Try Found., 1977-78. Named KNX Newsradio Citizen of the Week, Feb. 1974; recipient City of Los Angeles Cert. of Merit, 1976, others. Mem. Cherokee Confederacy, Am. Indian Edn. Assn., Washington U. Alumni Council, Am. Harp Soc. Lutheran. Office: 11601 Wilshire Blvd Los Angeles CA 90025

PARKER, MARION DEAN HUGHES, home care service executive; b. Greenwich, Conn., July 21, 1911; d. Walter A. and Marion K. (Dean) Hughes; B.A., UCLA, 1932; m. Conkey P. Whitehead, Nov. 14, 1929 (div. Aug. 1933); m. Andrew Granville Pierce III, Oct. 21, 1933; m. Willard Parker, Oct. 5, 1939 (div. 1951); 1 child, Walter van Eps. Actress appearing in Broadway prodns. New Faces, Three Waltzes, I Must Love Someone, on tour in The Women, The Man Who Came to Dinner, Lady in the Dark; various night club engagements; appeared in motion picture All About Eve; TV appearances; owner, mgr. Marion Parker's Guys & Dolls, Scottsdale, Ariz., 1951-59; mng. dir., purchasing agt. shipboard gift and accessory shops Am. Export Lines, 1960-64; dir. spl. events ITT, N.Y.C., 1965-66; exec. dir. Assn. Operating Room Nurses, N.Y.C., 1966-68; pres. Home Care-Ring Service, N.Y.C., 1968—; staff Park East Real Estate; asst. to v.p. in charge devel. Bennett Coll., Millbrook, N.Y., 1970; pub. relations cons., 1970—. Mem. Women's Nat. Republican Club, N.Y.C., Manhattan East Rep. Club, N.Y.C.; sustaining mem. Rep. Nat. Com., 1981—. Mem. Screen Actors Guild, Actors Equity. Address: 301 E 78th St New York NY 10021

PARKER, MARY EVELYN DICKERSON (MRS. W. BRYANT PARKER), state official; b. Fullerton, La., Nov. 8, 1920; d. Racia E. and Addie (Graham) Dickerson; B.A., Northwestern State Coll., 1941; diploma of social welfare, La. State U., 1943; m. W. Bryant Parker, Oct. 31, 1954 (dec. May 1965); children—Mary Bryant, Ann Graham. Social worker, Allen Parish, La., 1941-42; personnel adminstr. War Dept., Camp Claiborne, La., 1943-47; editor Oakdale (La.) Jour., 1947-48; exec. dir. La. Dept. of Commerce and Industry, Baton Rouge, 1948-52; with Mut. of N.Y., Baton Rouge, 1952-56; chmn. State Bd. of Pub. Welfare, Baton Rouge, 1950-51; commr. La. Dept. of Pub. Welfare, Baton Rouge, 1956-63; commr. Div. of Adminstrn., State of La., Baton Rouge, 1964-67; treas. State of La., Baton Rouge, 1968—. Chmn. White House Conf. on Children and Youth, 1960; pres. La. Conf. of Social Welfare, 1959-61; nat. Democratic Committeewoman, 1948-52; bd. dirs. Womans Hosp., Baton Rouge; trustee Episcopal High Sch., Baton Rouge, Baton Rouge Gen. Hosp.

Found.; mem. adv. council Coll. Bus., Tulane U., New Orleans. Named Baton Rouge Woman of Yr., 1976. Baptist. Office: PO Box 44154 Capitol Sta Baton Rouge LA 70804

PARKER, PATRICIA ANN, guidance counselor; b. Atlanta, Feb. 6, 1943; d. Willie Lee and Ella M. (Branch) P. B.A., Glassboro State Coll., 1965, M.A. in Student Personnel, 1976, M.A. in Pub. Sch. Adminstrn., 1985. Elem. tchr., Hammonton, N.J., 1965-78; elem. counselor Magnolia Sch. Dist., N.J., 1978-83; jr. high sch. counselor Lower Camden County Regional High Dist. 1, Atco, N.J., 1983-85, dir. pupil personnel services Kingsway Regional High Sch., 1985—, chair Intro to Vocations Adv. Council, 1984—; mem. Winslow Twp. Desegregation Commn., 1984—. Mem. Community Mothers, Atco, 1984. Recipient Outstanding Citizen award Community Mothers, 1983; Citizens award N.J. Assn. Colored Women's Clubs, 1983. Mem. NAACP, Am. Assn. Counseling and Dvel., NEA, N.J. Edn. Assn., Camden County Edn. Assn. Democrat. Baptist. Home: 144 Arbor Meadow Dr Sicklerville NJ 08081 Office: Kingsway Regional High Sch King's Hwy Swedesboro NJ 08085

PARKER, RUBY BRASTOW, telecommunications executive; b. Boston, June 11, 1947; d. Richard Brastow and Ruby (Stoddard) P. B.A., U. Mass., 1969; M.S., Central Conn. Coll., 1973. Tchr. Hartford Pub. Sch., Conn., 1969-74; counselor Haverhill Pub. Sch., Mass., 1974-81; with computer prodn. support dept. Honeywell, Waltham, Mass., 1981-83, telecommunications project analyst, 1983—. Fellow NOW. Home: 10 Washington Ave Billerica MA 01821 Office: Honeywell 200 Smith St Waltham MA 02154

PARKER, SUSAN ANN, law office manager; b. Marblehead, Mass., May 29, 1951; d. Thomas Edward and Elizabeth Rose (Wheeler) Flaherty; m. Michael McMillan Parker, July 31, 1976 (div. 1985. A.S. with honors, Marian Ct. Jr. Coll., Swampscott, Mass., 1972; student in bus. adminstrn. Northeastern U., 1980—. Lic. real estate broker; notary public. Exec. sec. R.M. Bradley & Co., Inc., Boston, 1972-78; adminstrv. asst. to treas. Boston Mortgage Co., 1978-79; office mgr. MB Mgmt. Corp., Boston, 1979-81; founder Parker Assocs., Boston, 1981—; law office mgr. Goodwin, Procter & Hoar, Boston, 1982—. Bd. dirs., clk. 1070 Beacon St. Tenants' Coop. Corp., Brookline, Mass., 1982-84, 86-87; mktg. researcher Com. to Elect William B. Golden State Senator, 1984; mem. Friends of Hall Pond, Inc., Brookline. Mem. Am. Mgmt. Assn., Greater Boston C. of C., Marian Ct. Jr. Coll. Alumnae Assn. Democrat. Roman Catholic. Avocations: sailing; skiing; collecting antiques; ballet. Home: 1070 Beacon St Brookline MA 02146 Office: Goodwin Procter & Hoar Exchange Pl Boston MA 02109

PARKER, TERRY MARIE, lawyer, city official; b. Higginsville, Mo., Apr. 16, 1948; d. Elvis Wyatt and Lola Mae (Jennings) P.; B.A., U. Mo., Kansas City, 1970; J.D., U. Kans., 1973; M.P.A., Ariz. State U., 1984; m. Robert David Sparks, Jan. 3, 1980. Admitted to Kans. bar, 1973; staff atty. Ariz. Legis. Council, Phoenix, 1973-78; mgmt. asst., mgmt. and budget dept. City of Phoenix, 1978-80, cable communications officer Office Cable Communications, 1980—. Mem. Am. Bar Assn., Internat. Soc. Pub. Telecommunications Profls. (pres.), Kans. Bar Assn., Internat. City Mgmt. Assn., Ariz. Mcpl. Mgmt. Assts. Assn., Am. Soc. Public Adminstrn., Nat. Assn. Telecommunications Officers and Advisors (exec. com.), Women in Cable (dir. Ariz. chpt.). Club: Soroptomists Internat. Office: 620 W Washington 4th Floor Phoenix AZ 85003

PARKER, TREELA M(AY), army non-commissioned officer; b. Wise County, Va., Aug. 21, 1954; d. James Hobert and Bonnie F. (Begley) P. A.A., Cecil Community Coll., 1974; B.S. in Social Psychology with distinction, Park Coll., Parksville, Mo., 1983; postgrad. in behavioral scis. Catholic U. Am., 1985—. Enlisted as pvt. 1st class U.S. Army, 1975, advanced through grades to sgt. 1st class, 1984; legal clk. Hdqrs. 1st Maintenance Bn., Ludwigsburg, W. Ger., 1976-78; ops. specialist 235th Signal Detachment, Fort Monmouth, N.J., 1978-79; asst. noncommissioned officer-in-charge 209th Mil. Intelligence Bn., Yong San Seoul, Korea, 1979-80, Army community services Hdqrs. Installation Support Activity, Fort Monmouth, 1980-81; adminstrv. asst. to dir. of personal info. systems directorate Mil. Personnel Ctr., Alexandria, Va., 1981-83; chief top secret repository NATO Subregistry Army Materiel Command, Alexandria, 1983—, also asst. instr. for phys. fitness test, 1984-86; mem. promotion selection bds., 1984-86, Soldier of Yr./Quarter Bds., 1984-86. Author NATO Subregistry Newsletter, 1984-86. Decorated Army Commendation medals. Mem. Women's Army Corps Vet. Assn., Phi Theta Kappa. Avocations: horseback riding; reading; writing prose and poetry; dancing; theatre. Office: Hdqrs Army Materiel Command Attn: AMCPE-AR 50001 Eisenhower Ave Alexandria VA 22333

PARKER, VIRGINIA ANNE, ranch administrator; b. Brockton, Mass., Apr. 24, 1918; d. John and Jennie (Krusas) Salus; student Bryant Stratton Coll., Boston, 1938, Columbia U., 1941; m. John Glendon Parker, Feb. 1942 (div. 1952); one dau., Deborah Anne. Sales supr. Reuben H. Donnelley Corp., N.Y.C., 1944-46; traveling sales rep. Elizabeth Arden Inc., N.Y.C., 1946-47; advt. salesperson Park East Pub. Co., N.Y.C., 1947-48; point of sale display work Parker Kleinhans Assos. and V.A. Parker Co., N.Y.C., 1950-55; merchandising coordinator WGBS Radio Sta., Miami, 1957-59; lighting cons. Verd-A-Ray Corp., Miami, 1960-63; string writer, advt. salesperson Palm Beach Post Times, Fla., 1963-65; advt. salesperson Avon Park Sun, Fla., and Sebring News, Fla., 1965-67; sales mgr. radio sta. WJCM, Sebring, and advt. salesperson radio sta. WIPC, Lake Wales, Fla., 1967-69; office mgr., trustee asst., exec. sec. Griffith Ranch Inc., Okeechobee, Fla., 1969-80, semi-ret., 1980, now vol. worker with retarded and handicapped, also with ret. vol. sr. programs Nu-Hope. Mem. Bus. and Profl. Women Miami (2d v.p., rec. sec. 1958-60, state award for nat. security 1960), Parents Without Ptnrs. Fla. (news editor 1962-63). Club: Advt. Miami. Address: 415 Mat-Lo Ave PO Box 1112 Sebring FL 33870

PARKER-JOHNSON, PATRICIA EVANS, software and consulting company executive; b. Atlanta, June 25, 1954; d. Robert Carlton and Martha Elizabeth (Leyhew) Evans; student Vol. State Community Coll., Belmont Coll., 1972-74; m. James F. Parker, Jr., Sept. 5, 1975; 1 dau., Angela Beth; m. Donald R. Johnson, Dec. 24, 1985. Acctg. clk. Jenkins & Tallent, Nashville; exec. v.p., sec.-treas., gen. mgr. Bus. Machines, Inc., Nashville; now controller, mktg. dir. Creative Synergy Corp., Atlanta. Mem. Exec. Women Internat., Beta Sigma Phi. Baptist. Home: 1929 Hunter's Bend Ct Mariettad GA 30062 Office: 2839 Paces Ferry Rd Suite 320 Atlanta GA 30339

PARKERSON, MICHELLE DENISE, film production company executive; b. Washington, Jan. 11, 1953. B.A. in TV-Film Prodn., Temple U., 1974. TV engr. WRC-TV NBC, Washington, 1975, WTTG-TV Metromedia Inc., Washington, 1976-83; dir., producer Eye of the Storm Prodns. Inc., Washington, 1982—; vis. instr. U. Del., 1985; asst. prof. Temple U., 1986; lectr., seminars in field. Dir., producer films Sojourn, 1973 (Judges prize Am. Women in Radio and TV 1975), But Then, She's Betty Carter, 1980. Producer video: Gotta Make This Journey, 1983 (Leigh Whipper award Phila. Internat. Film Festival 1985). Contbr. essays, rev., poetry and fiction to profl. publs.G Grantee D.C. Commn. on Arts and Humanities, 1980-81, 84-85, Corp. for Pub. Broadcasting, 1983, Gay Edn. Fund, 1983; NEA fellow, 1980; Robert Flaherty Film Seminar, Cornell U., 1984; recipient Grand prize N.Y. Black Film Festival, 1976, Edith Blum Lecture Performance Series award Washington Women's Arts Ctr., 1983, ENIK Arts Soc. award, 1984, Community Recognition award U. D.C., 1984, Jerry Heil Meml. award Gertrude Stein Democratic Club, 1985. Mem. Am. Film Inst., Assn. Ind. Video and Filmmakers. Home: 1716 Florida Ave NW #2 Washington DC 20009

PARKES, SUSAN CAROL, lawyer; b. Nashville, July 9, 1955; d. Thomas Theodore and Peggy Ann (Taylor) P. B.A. in Polit. Sci., Miss. U. for Women, 1977; J.D., U. Tenn., 1980. Bar: Tenn. 1980. Assoc. firm Ahles & Kinnard, Lebanon, Tenn., 1980-83; sole practice law, Lebanon, 1983—; counsel Inter-Agy. Youth Council, Lebanon, 1983—. Chmn. Lebanon chpt. March of Dimes, 1982. Mem. ABA, Tenn. Bar Assn., Wilson County Bar Assn., Nashville Women's Bar Assn., Phi Delta Phi. Methodist. Home: 1425 Alhambra Dr Lebanon TN 37087 Office: 202 E Gay St Lebanon TN 37087

PARKIN, SHARON KAYE, bookkeeper; b. Portland, Oreg., Nov. 21, 1940; d. Charles Edward and Beulah Elizabeth (Foraker) King; m. Russell Jerome Gartrell, Aug. 5, 1960 (div. Dec. 1971); children—Mark Russell, William Edward; m. Jack Edgar Parkin, Feb. 21, 1975. Student, Portland State U., 1959-60. Timekeeper, Sears, Roebuck & Co., Redmond, Wash., 1971-77; bookkeeper, acct. Bristol Bay Area Health Corp., Dillingham, Alaska, Mental Health Corp., Bellingham, Wash., 1982; bookkeeper Whatcom Counseling, 1978-80, Charlie's Marine, Juneau, Alaska, 1980-81, L & M Supplies, Dillingham, 1983—; owner, pres. Parkin Bookkeeping, 1984—; notary public State of Alaska, 1983—. Democrat. Mem. Christian Ch. Avocations: boating; fishing; hunting; traceling; crochet. Home: PO Box 10196 Dillingham AK 99576 Office: L & M Supplies PO Box 10196 Dillingham AK 99576

PARKMAN, MARJORIE FRANCES, restaurant chain executive; b. Dover-Foxcroft, Maine, Dec. 1, 1946; d. Gordon R. Parkman and Ruth E. (Bean) Jenkins. 1 son, Thomas Michael. Student pub. schs. Manchester, Conn. Sec., bookkeeper Agy. Service Assn., Manchester, Conn., 1965-70; bookkeeping supr. Congen Adminstrv. Services, Manchester, 1970-73; bookkeeper, asst. office mgr. The Steak Club Inc., Manchester, 1973-77, office mgr., controller, 1977-80, treas., 1980—, also dir. Treas., dir. Millbridge Hollow Condo Assn. Inc., Manchester, 1980-83. Republican. Methodist. Home: 10 Greenhill St Manchester CT 06040 Office: The Steak Club Inc 60 Hilliard St Manchester CT 06040

PARKS, BONNIE RAYE, cosmetic company account manager; b. Chesapeake, Va., June 26, 1957; d. Ray William and Bonnie (Jones) P. Student Craven Community Coll., 1980-81, Tidewater Community Coll., 1981-82. Beauty advisor, Belk Dept. Store, Newbern, N.C., 1977-83, Leggett Store, Virginia Beach Va., 1982-83; sales counselor Empress Spa, Virginia Beach, 1983-84; sales cons. Revlon, Inc., N.Y.C., 1984-85, regional tng. mgr., Virginia Beach, 1985-86, account mgr., sales, Birmingham, Ala., 1986—. Recipient Cert. of Merit, Belk Dept. Store, 1980. Mem. Nat. Assn. Female Execs. Home: 214 Morning Sun Dr Birmingham AL 35243

PARKS, JANET ELAINE, pharmacist; b. Watertown, S.D., Oct. 20, 1946; d. Dale O. and Della E. (Horn) P. B.S., S.D. State U., 1970; M.B.A., U. Minn., 1981. Registered pharmacist, Minn., Iowa, Wis. Staff pharmacist St. Luke's Hosp., Duluth, Minn., 1970-81; fin. cons. Parks & Parks, Marshall, Minn., 1981-82; pharmacy cons. J. Parks, Mason City, Iowa, 1982-85; night pharmacist St. Joseph Mercy Hosp., Mason City, 1982-85; dir. pharmacy Tomah Meml. Hosp., Wis., 1985—; pharmacy cons. Tomah Care Ctr., 1985—; fin. cons. Methodist chs. Mem. AAUW, Am. Soc. Hosp. Pharmacists (region sec. 1975), Nat. Assn. Future Women (photographer 1984), Nat. Assn. Female Execs., Phi Kappa Phi, Rho Chi. Methodist. Avocations: nature photography; needlecraft; cross-country skiing; bicycling; personal computers. Home: 1209 Butts Ave Tomah WI 54660 Office: Tomah Meml Hosp 321 Butts Ave Tomah WI 54660

PARKS, JANICE JEAN, technical recruiter; b. Washington, Jan. 22, 1957; d. Francis Anthony and Estelle Delores (Sutter) Avallone; m. Gary Wray Parks, Oct. 14, 1978 (div. 1979). Student, Strayer Coll., Montgomery Coll. Tech. recruiter Dunhill of Rockville, Md., 1976-77, PRG Inc., Rockville, 1977-79; tech. recruiter Office Search, Rockville, 1979-82, Elm Assocs., Rockville, 1982-83; corp. tech. recruiter Comp-U-Staff, Towson, Md., 1983; v.p., owner, tech. recruiter Park-Douglas & Assocs., Rockville, 1984—. Mem. Nat. Assn. Female Execs. Avocations: camping; gardening; fishing; needlepoint; cooking. Office: Park-Douglas & Assocs Inc 6110 Executive Blvd Rockville MD 20852

PARKS, JULIA ETTA, educator; b. Kansas City, Kans., Apr. 5, 1923; d. Hays and Idella Long; B.Ed., Washburn U., 1959, M.Ed., 1965; Ed.D., U. Kans., 1980; m. James A. Parks, Aug. 10, 1941; 1 son, James Hays. Tchr., Lowman Hill Elem. Sch., 1959-64; faculty Washburn U., Topeka, Kans., 1964—, asso. prof. edn. 1981—, mem. pres.'s adv. council, 1981—, chair edn., phys. edn., health and recreation div.; mem. vis. teams Nat. Council for Accreditation of Tchr. Edn., 1974—. Bd. dirs. Children's Hour, 1981—, Mulvane Art Center, 1974-78. Recipient Alumni award for Teaching Excellence, Washburn U., 1983. Mem. Internat. Reading Assn., Kans. Reading Assn., Kans. Reading Profls. Higher Edn., Delta Kappa Gamma, Phi Delta Kappa. Methodist. Club: Links (pres.). Office: Washburn U Dept Edn 1700 College Ave Topeka KS 66621

PARKS, MARY ANGELA, law clerk; d. Fred Lea and Georgene Louise (Capiross) P. Cert. du BANF, Université Laval, Que., Can., 1979; B.A. in French, Allegheny Coll., 1980; cert. paralegal, Pa. State U., 1983. Corp. legal asst. Rothman, Gordon, Foreman & Groudine, Pitts., 1980-83, Farella, Braun & Martel, San Francisco, 1983-84, Brobeck, Phleger & Harrison, San Francisco, 1984-86; law clk. Reed, Smith, Shaw & McClay, Pitts., 1986—. Vol. Calif. Republican Party, San Francisco, 1985—. Mem. San Francisco Assn. Legal Assts. (membership dir. 1985), Nat. Assn. Legal Assts., Nat. Fedn. Paralegal Assns. (real estate practice sect.), Women in Brokerage, AAUW, Nat. Soc. DAR, United Daus. of Confederacy, World Affairs Council of No. Calif. Presbyterian. Avocations: needlework; bicycling; hiking; cooking.

PARKS, NANCY G., public relations and advertising executive; b. St. Paul, Dec. 21, 1939; d. Gordon L. and Ethelmae (Severson) Gilmore; m. Arthur A. Parks, Aug. 5, 1961; 1 child, Robin G. B.A., Goucher Coll., 1961. Tchr. Roland Park Country Sch., Balt., 1961-67, Nat. Cathedral Sch., Washington, 1967-68; asst. editor children's books Cowles Communications, Inc., 1968-70; free lance writer, stringer, Kansas City, Mo., 1970-77; prin., co-owner Parks/Parks & Co., Kansas City, 1977—. Author: Getting It Together In Kansas City, 1975. Mem. Clean City Commn., Kansas City, 1981-84; bd. dirs. Coterie Children's Theatre, Kansas City, 1983—, Multiple Sclerosis Soc., 1984—; mem. spl. pub. relations com. Am. Cancer Soc., Kansas City, 1984—. Mem. Kansas City Advt. Club (awards of merit). Episcopalian. Homestead Country (Shawnee Mission, Kans.). Office: Parks/Parks & Co 420 W 42d St Kansas City MO 64113

PARKS, SUE ANN, residential care center administrator; b. Dayton, Ohio, Oct. 7, 1947; d. Bob Donald and Lucille (Kem) Fogle; m. Leslie Dean Parks, Mar. 15, 1968; children—Amy Sue, Sarah Ann. Student, U. Cin., 1971, Anderson Coll., 1982. Supr., Winegardner & Hammons, Cin., 1971-73; bus. asst. Russell M. Ruetz, D.D.S., Racine, Wis., 1973-74; returns clk. First Piedmont Bank, Greenville, S.C., 1974-75; computer operator Williams Acctg., Anderson, S.C., 1975-76; exec. dir. Anderson County Arts Council, 1976-81; asst. adminstr. Seneca Residential Care Ctr., S.C., 1981—. Bd. dirs. Community Arts S.C. Arts Commn., Columbia, 1980-81, Anderson Heritage and Hist. Soc., Anderson, 1984-85, Anderson Jr. Assembly, 1985-86. Club: Anderson Jr. Woman's (bd. dirs. 1983-84, pres. 1985-86). Avocations: tennis, skiing, sailing, horseback riding. Home: 2901 Rambling Path Anderson SC 29621 Office: Seneca Residential Care Ctr Route 6 Box 302 Seneca SC 29678

PARKS, SUZANNE LOWRY, psychiatric nurse, educator; b. Columbus, Ohio, Feb. 29, 1936; d. Frank Carson and Mabel (Brown) Lowry Morris; B.S., Emory U., 1958; M.S., U. Md., 1959; postgrad. U. Hawaii, 1983—; children—Jennifer, Kristin, Greg. Asst. prof. psychiat. nursing U. Va., 1959-61, U. N.C., Chapel Hill, 1961-63, grad. faculty, 1975-81; asst. prof., dir. div. psychiat. nursing Duke U., 1964-67; clin. instr. psychiatry Sch. Medicine, Emory U., Atlanta, 1968-71; asst. prof., nursing coordinator Appalachian Area Nursing Inservice project Clemson (S.C.) U., 1973-75; clin. staff Northside Mental Health Center, 1975-81; dir. staff devel. Hawaii State Hosp., Kaneoke, 1981-83; nurse Lainolu Retirement Center, Wakakii, 1983-85; asst. prof. Hawaii Loa Coll., Kaweohe, 1985—. Mem. Am., Hawaii nurses assns., Am. Guild of Hypnotherapists, Assn. Research and Enlightenment, Friends and Families of Schizophrenics, Mental Health Assn. Home: 2345 Ali Wai Blvd #1004 Honolulu HI 96815

PARLATO, LINDA GAE, painter; b. Aurora, Ill., Dec. 20, 1939; d. Gaylord Major and Sophie Lucille (Baskovich) Renz; B.A., Milw. Downer Coll., 1960; postgrad. Drury Coll., 1972; M.F.A., SUNY-Buffalo, 1985; m. George S. Parlato, June 25, 1960; children—Marcella, Salvatore, Gae Lynn, Gina Lee. One-woman show: Gallery Upstairs, Orchard Park, N.Y., 1976, Patterson Gallery, Westfield, N.Y., 1984, Buscaglia-Castellani Gallery, Niagara Falls, N.Y., 1985; group shows include: Mid-South Exhibit, Memphis, 1971, 72, Watercolor U.S.A., Springfield, Mo., 1973, St. Louis Art Mus., 1974, Mid-Am. V Nelson Gallery Kansas City, 1974, Am. Watercolor Soc., 1976, NAD, 1977, AAO Gallery, Buffalo, 1980, 81, Hallwalls Mems. Show, 1984, 86; represented in permanent collections: Lawrence U., Spiva Art Center of So. Mo. Coll., Sch. of Ozarks; co-owner Park Central Art Gallery, Springfield, Mo., 1972-75, instr., 1974-82. Mem. Am. Watercolor Soc. (asso.), Women's Caucus for Art. Republican. Roman Catholic. Home and Studio: 3 Red Brick Rd Orchard Park NY 14127

PARMESE, BARBARA JEAN, physician peer review organization executive, consultant; b. Hackensack, N.J., Sept. 21, 1954; d. Jack and Rose (Lodato) Insinga; m. Vincent James Parmese, Oct. 6, 1984. B.S., Trenton State Coll., 1976; postgrad. William Paterson Coll., 1979-80. Health record analyst Hackensack Med. Ctr., 1976-79; quality assurance analyst Englewood Hosp., N.J., 1979-80; quality rev. mgr. Assn. Profl. Health Care Rev., Saddle Brook, N.J., 1980-82, asst. dir., 1982-83, exec. dir., 1983-85; assoc. exec. dir. North Jersey Physicians Rev., Saddle Brook, 1985—; mem. reimbursement adv. com. N.J. Dept. Health, Trenton, 1986. Mem. Am. Mgmt. Assn. Home: 487 Kaplan Ave Hackensack NJ 07601 Office: North Jersey Physicians Rev 299 Market St Saddle Brook NJ 07662

PARNELL, DIANA DEANGELIS, dermatologist; b. Tacoma, Wash., May 18, 1940; d. Fulvio Garibaldi and Ruth Margaret (Nordlund) DeAngelis; m. Francis W. Parnell, Feb. 27, 1965; children—Cheryl Lynn, John Francis, Kathleen Diana, Alison Anne, Thomas William. B.S., Pa. State U., 1961; M.D., Georgetown U., 1965. Diplomate Nat. Bd. Examiners, Am. Bd. Dermatology. Intern, Univ. Hosps., U. Wis., Madison, 1965-66, resident in dermatology, 1966-69; dermatologist Univ. Health Service, U. Wis., Madison, 1969-70; practice medicine specializing in dermatology, Greenbrae, Calif., 1970-76, 78—, Ridgewood, N.J., 1976-78; corp. med. cons. indsl. dermatology, 1976—; v.p. Parnell Med. Corp., Greenbrae, 1980—; pres. Parnell Pharms., San Rafael, Calif.; clins. instr. medicine U. Wis. Sch. Medicine, Madison, 1969-70; clin. instr. dermatology U. Calif. Sch. Medicine, San Francisco, 1970-76; mem. staff Marin Gen. Hosp., Greenbrae, 1970—, Ross Gen. Hosp. (Calif.), 1970-75, 78-84, Valley Hosp. Ridgewood, N.J., 1976-78. Fellow Am. Acad. Dermatology; mem. Pacific Dermatol. Assn., San Francisco Dermatol. Soc., Am. Soc. Dermatol. Surgery, Nat. Women's Polit. Caucus, Delta Delta Delta. Republican. Roman Catholic. Home: PO Box 1383 Ross CA 94957 Office: 599 Sir Francis Drake Blvd Greenbrae CA 94904

PARNELL, SHEILA RAE, trade association executive; b. Danville, Va., Dec. 14, 1943; d. James Clarence and Neva (Neel) Catlett; children—John J. Parnell, Cara Beth Parnell. Student pub. schs., Callands, Va. Adminstrv. asst. Area Health Edn. Ctr., Wilmington, N.C., 1973-79; asst. v.p. Houston Apt. Assn., 1981—. Adviser explorer scouts Cape Fear council Boy Scouts Am., Wilmington, 1974-79. Recipient Dist. Award of Merit, Boy Scouts Am., 1978, Leadership award, 1979. Mem. Nat. Assn. Female Execs., Am. Soc. Assn. Execs., Houston Soc. Assn. Execs. Avocations: shell craft, needlework beachcombing.

PAROLLA, HELEN RAINEY, women's association public affairs and public policy executive, writer; b. Eugene, Oreg., Jan. 15, 1925; d. Homer Price and Mildred (Collins) Rainey; m. Curry William Gillmore, Sept. 15, 1945 (div. 1968); children—Homer Rainey Gillmore, Daniel Scott Gillmore, Todd Harrison Gillmore; m. Otmar Beatus Parolla, June 27, 1970. Student Oberlin Coll., 1942-43; B.A., U. Tex., 1946, M.A., 1947; postgrad. McCoy Coll., Johns Hopkins U., 1950-51. Speaker, organizer Homer Rainey's gubernatorial campaign, Austin, Tex., 1946; instr. English, U. Tex., Austin, 1946-47; asst. dir. pub. affairs, nat. bd. YWCA, N.Y.C., 1947-49, program cons., 1975-76, coordinator pub. affairs and pub. policy, 1976—; mgmt. aide Housing Authority, Balt., 1950-52; tchr. English, Holy Name of Mary Sch., Croton-on-Hudson, N.Y., 1971-72; writer, researcher, analyst C. W. Wittman, Inc., Mount Kisco, N.Y., 1972-74; portraitist; pub. speaker. Author: (novel) The Gates of Strength, 1947; (newsletter) Public Policy Bull., 1976-86; also numerous articles in YWCA Interchange, 1976-86. Editor: Public Policy, a Continuing YWCA Program, 1976-86. Past pres., bd. dirs. Religious Coalition for Abortion Rights, Washington, 1976-86; mem. unit com. div. ch. and society Nat. Council Chs., N.Y.C., 1976-86; supt., tchr. ch. sch. Scarborough Presbyterian Ch., N.Y., 1956-86; elder Presbyn. Ch., U.S.A., 1960—; promoter, organizer Interfaith Adult Edn. Seminars, 1966, 68; del. Synod of N.E., N.Y.C., 1978; mem. council on women and the ch. Presbytery of Hudson River, 1979-86; pres. Handel Choir of Balt., 1950-56; bd. dirs. Ossining Choral Soc., N.Y., 1964-68, Human SERVE, 1970—, Religious Network for Equality for Women, N.Y.C., 1976-86, Mem. ACLU, Union Concerned Scientists, Nat. Com. on Pay Equity, Women's Vote Project, Save our Security Coalition, Full Employment Action Council, Phi Beta Kappa. Democrat. Avocations: singing in choral groups; reading; interpretive dance.

PARR, DORIS ANN, financial institution executive, consultant; b. Fergus Falls, Minn., July 10, 1933; d. Henry Fritzolf and Esther Marie (Ahlgren) Peterson; m. Mark Hoffman, 1949 (div. 1960); children—Cynthia Lee Davis, David Alan Hoffman; m. 2d, Harold R. Parr, 1961 (div. 1974). Student Am. Savs. and Loan Inst., 1965-66, Pioneer Nat. Title Ins. Co., 1969, Menlo Coll. Sch. Bus. Adminstrn., 1975. Comml. loan officer Savbank Service Corp., Seattle, 1975-77; exec. v.p., mgr. Sound Savs. & Loan, Seattle, 1976-78; v.p. Queen City Savs. & Loan, Seattle, 1978-82; v.p., mgr. State Savs. & Loan Assn., Dallas, 1983-84; pres. Nat. Real Estate Mortgage Services, Inc., Dallas, 1984—; instr. real estate law San Francisco City Coll., 1975. Recipient 1st Place Speech trophy Am. Savs. & Loan Inst., 1964. Mem. Assn. Profl. Mortgage Women (program chmn. Seattle 1969-70, San Jose 1973-74, pres. 1975-76, Woman of Yr. award 1979), U.S. Savs. & Loan League (consumer affairs and secondary market com.), Nat. Assn. Female Execs., Fed. Home Loan Bank Bd. (maj. comml. loan underwriter). Organized and managed 1st U.S. minority savs. and loan assn. Home: 5981 Arapaho Rd Dallas TX 75248 Office: Nat Real Estate Mortgage Services Inc 5025 Arapaho Rd Suite 220 Palmer Ctr Dallas TX 75248

PARR, SHERRIE LYNN, childbirth educator, speech pathologist, realtor; b. Hammond, Ind., Oct. 20, 1948; d. John Bernard Boersma and Jean Helen (Klooster) DeYoung; m. Gerhardt Vander Wal, Mar. 20, 1970 (div. 1973); m. John Eugene Parr, Nov. 27, 1974; children—Jayme Renee, John William. B.S., No. Ill. U., 1971; Lic. speech pathologist, Ill.; lic. real estate salesperson, Ill.; cert. childbirth instr. Speech therapist Sch. Dist. 151, South Holland, Ill., 1971-81, workshop dir., 1974-81; real estate salesperson Ridge Realty, Lansing, Ill., 1978—; childbirth educator Office of Dr. C.M. Rawlins, Munster, Ind., 1981—, breastfeeding counselor, 1980-84. Mem. residency program Free Street Theater, Chgo., 1974, 75; Coordinator McGovern for Pres. campaign, Lansing, 1972; dir. Pre-Sch. Story Hour, Munster, 1982-83. Mem. Ill. Speech, Hearing and Lang. Assn., Internat. Childbirth Edn. Assn., Childbirth Educator Tng. Assn. (cert.), NEA (South Cook County rep. 1973-79). Mem. Christian Reformed Ch. Avocations: politics; reading history. Home: 118 Beverly Pl Munster IN 46321 Office: Childbirth Educators 7550 Hohman Ave Munster IN 46321

PARR, SUSAN ELIZABETH, nursing administrator; b. Balt., Sept. 2, 1935; d. David L. and Mary E. (Connolly) P. Student Community Coll. Balt., 1954-56; B.A. in Gen. Studies, U. Balt., 1984; student U. Md., 1966; R.N., Md. Gen. Hosp., 1956. Cert. in nursing adminstrn. Am. Nurses Assn. Staff nurse Md. Gen. Hosp., 1956-60, head nurse, 1960-63; instr. nursing Balt. Bd. Edn., 1963-66; supr. nursing Sinai Hosp., Inc., Balt., 1966-80; asst. dir. Levindale Geriatric, Balt., 1980-82, Pimlico Manor Nursing Home, Balt., 1982-83; coordinator Lafayette Square Nursing Center, Balt., 1983-84; asst. dir. nursing Eastpoint Nursing Home, Balt., 1984—; mem. audit com., procedure com. Levindale Geriatric Hosp. Past chmn. ARC blood drive Sinai Hosp. Jewish. Home: 3209 Brendan Ave Baltimore MD 21213

PARRIS, CAROLYN P., county council clerk; b. Spartanburg, S.C., Sept. 10, 1943; d. Robert Lester and Bernice (Godfrey) Padgett; m. Wyman J. Parris, Dec. 21, 1963; children—Cynthia, Audra. Grad. Robinsons Bus. Coll., 1962. Clk. Hyatt, Depass & Ramen Attys., Spartanburg, 1962-68; clk. to council Spartanburg County, 1968—. Mem. S.C. Women in Govt., 1985—. Mem. S.C. Clks. to Council Assn., S.C. Assn. of Counties, Bus. and Profl. Women's Club. Home: 801 Holly Springs Rd Lyman SC 29365 Office: Spartanburg County Council Box 5666 Spartanburg SC 29304

PARRIS, NINA GUMPERT, curator, writer, researcher; b. Berlin, Ger., Sept. 11, 1927; came to U.S., 1937, naturalized, 1944; d. Martin and Charlotte (Blaschko) Gumpert; m. Arthur Parris, Feb. 13, 1949 (div. 1974); children—Carl Joseph, Thomas Martin. B.A., Bryn Mawr Coll., 1968; M.A., U. Pa., 1969, Ph.D., 1979. Teaching fellow U. Mich., Ann Arbor, 1969-70; lectr. Phila. Coll. Art, 1970-71; research asst. Phila. Mus. Art, 1970-71; curator, lectr. U. Vt. Robert Hall Fleming Mus., Burlington, 1971-79; chief curator Columbia Mus., S.C., 1979—. Author Prints, Paintings and Drawings in Collection of Robert Hall Fleming Mus., 1979, collection catalogue S.C. Collection Columbia Mus., 1985. Author exhibition catalogue Through a Master Printer, 1985. Columnist, State newspaper, Columbia, 1984—. Bd. dirs. Photography Cooperative,

Montpelier, Vt., 1977-79, Chittenden Arts Council, Burlington, Vt., 1976-78. Woodrow Wilson fellow, 1968, Univ. fellow Ford Found., 1968-72; grantee NEA, NEH, S.C. Com. Humanities, Vt. Council Arts. Mem. Am. Assn. Museums (pres. curator's com. 1985—, v.p. 1983-85), Art Mus. Com. Internat. Council Mus., New Eng. Assn. Mus., Southeastern Mus. Assn. Office: Columbia Mus 1112 Bull St Columbia SC 29201

PARRIS, SHARON M(AE), cosmetics company executive; b. Buffalo, Mar. 5, 1939; d. Edward Vernon and Margaret (Wragge) Morley; m. Robert Eugene Parris, June 9, 1957; children—Larry Allan, Mark Edward, Ronald Scott, Robert Andrew. Student Brevard Jr. Coll., 1956-57. Clk.-typist, Sears & Roebuck, West Palm Beach, Fla., 1968; sec. Central Supply, West Palm Beach, 1969; corp. sec. S.E. Indsl. Tool, Palm Beach Gardens, Fla., 1969-70, Tool Sales, Riviera Beach, Fla., 1971-72; profl. beauty cons. Mary Kay Cosmetics, Dallas, 1970-72, dir., 1972-73, sr. dir., 1973-81, nat. sales dir., 1982—. Home: 7137 St Andrews Lake Worth FL 33463

PARRISH, CYNTHIA JOYCE, accounting executive; b. Rock Hill, S.C., Nov. 26, 1955; d. William Kelly and Margaret Elizabeth (Robinson) P.; m. Michael Eugene Ritcher, Aug. 21, 1977 (div. Dec. 1983). B.S., Winthrop Coll., 1976; M.B.A., U. Mo., 1983. Auditor, Monsanto Co., St. Louis, 1976-78; area acctg. supr., 1978-81, acctg. supervision, 1981-84, acctg. supt. 1984—. Hotline counselor, treas. advocates bd. Women's Self Help Ctr., St. Louis, 1984—. Mem. Nat. Assn. Accts. Episcopalian. Home: 651 Lewiston Dr St Louis MO 63122 Office: Monsanto Co 500 Monsanto Ave Sauget IL 62205

PARRISH, DIANE SCHMIDT, lawyer; b. Sedalia, Mo., Mar. 1, 1952; d. Richard R. and Vivian J. (McAtee) Schmidt; m. Steven C. Parrish, Jan. 16, 1982; 1 dau., Amanda; m. Ken D. Percy, June 1, 1974 (div. 1980). A.A., Johnson County (Kans.) Community Coll., 1972; B.S. in Dental Hygiene, U. Mo.-Kansas City, 1974; J.D., U. Kans.-Lawrence, 1979. Bar: Mo. 1979, U.S. Dist. Ct. Mo. 1979, U.S. Ct. Appeals (8th cir.) 1983. Assoc., Shook, Hardy & Bacon, Kansas City, Mo., 1979-83; sole practice, from 1983. Editor Kans. Law Rev., 1978-79. Mem. Central Exchange, Kansas City, Mo.; mem. Leawood Plan Commn.; preschool coordinator Country Club Christian Ch. Mem. ABA, Kansas City (Mo.) Bar Assn., Lawyers Assn. Kansas City, Assn. Women Lawyers, Mo. Bar Assn., Order of Coif. Democrat. Mem. Disciples of Christ.

PARRISH, LAURA ALMA, lawyer; b. Takoma Park, Md., Nov. 12, 1951; d. Stanley Earl and Enid Walter (Bean) P. B.S., U. Oreg., 1973, J.D., 1976. Bar: Oreg. 1976, U.S. Dist. Ct. Oreg. 1977. Assoc., Luvaas, Cobb, Richards, Eugene, Oreg., 1977-79, ptnr., 1979-83; mcpl. ct. judge pro tem City of Eugene, 1981-85; ptnr. Hutchinson, Anderson Cox & Teising P.C., Eugene, 1983—. Campaigner United Way of Lane County, Eugene, 1979, 81, 82; bd. dirs. Lane County Legal Aid, Eugene, 1981-84; bd. dirs. Oreg. State Bd. Psychologist Examiners, Salem, 1982—, vice chmn., 1985-86. Mem. Oreg. State Bar, Lane County Bar Assn. (dir. 1981-83, sec. treas. 1983-84, pres. 1985-86), U.S. Dist. Ct. Bar, Oreg. Trial Lawyers Assn. Republican. Methodist. Office: Hutchinson Anderson Cox & Teising PC 777 High St #200 Eugene OR 97401

PARRISH, MARY ANNE, advertising executive; b. Virginia Beach, Va., Jan. 21, 1953; d. Elijah and Maria Upchurch (Roberson) Parrish; m. Philip Michael Hadfield Semsch, May 21, 1981 (div.). A.A. in Bus. Adminstrn., Palm Beach Jr. Coll., 1973; B.A. in Journalism, U. Md., 1978. Asst. to v.p. Richard A. Viguerie Co., Falls Church, Va., 1978-79; asst. fundraising dir. Connally for Pres., Arlington, Va., 1979-80; cons. CBS, Rockville, Md., 1980-82; pres. Zeta Media Systems Corp./Copyworks div., Falls Church, 1982—; dir. Listworks, Inc., Fairfax, Va., 1981; chmn. bd. S. Tigre & Assocs., Washington, 1982—. Mem. Direct Mail Mktg. Assn., Capitol Flyers (sec. 1982—). Address: PO Box 17289 Washington DC 20041

PARRISH, MICKEY JOYCE, oil company executive, accountant; b.Koscuisko, Miss., Dec. 6, 1945; d. Hosea Holcomb and Lavada (Ferguson) Lewis; children—Randall, Matthew; m. D. Russell Parrish, June 28, 1975. B.S., La. Tech. U., 1979. Exec. dir. Sherer, Underwood, Mayhall, Jasper, Ala., 1972-75; exec. asst. Richard Rubin, M.D., P.A., Decatur, Ala., 1975-76; acct. La. Tech. U., Ruston, La., 1979-80, owner, prin. Mickey J. Parrish & Assocs., Ruston, 1982—; gen. mgr. Big State Ranch-Baron Oil, Ruston, 1980—; lectr. in field. Mem. troop leadership council Boy Scouts Am., 1980—; chmn. steering com. La. Dept. Edn., 1984—; mem. Mayor's Commn. for Women, Ruston, La., 1985—. Mem. Nat. Assn. Female Execs. (network dir.), Nat. Assn. Accts., Petroleum Accts. Soc. Dallas, Am. Mgmt. Assn., Nat. Fedn. Ind. Bus. Owners, Am. Bus. Women's Assn. (1 of Top Ten Bus. Women 1984, dist II v.p. 1985—). Baptist. Office: Big State Ranch-Baron Oil 101 Reynolds Dr PO Box 1992 Ruston LA 71270

PARRISH, NANCY ELAINE, state senator; b. Cedar Vale, Kans., Nov. 9, 1948; d. Julian Milton and Vergie (Bryant) Buchele; m. Jim Parrish, 1970; children—Leslie Elgin, Tyler Jonathan. B.S., Kans. State U., 1970; M.S., U. Kans., 1974. Mem. Kans. Senate, 1980—, chmn. adv. commn. on juvenile offender programs. Mem. edn. task force Midwestern Conf. Council State Govts., 1981—; chmn. Shawnee County Legis. Del.; pres. Council for Exceptional Children, Topeka, 1978-79; active Boys' Club of Topeka; bd. dirs. Mental Health Assn.; bd. advisors Sch. of Future, 1980—. Mem. LWV, Foster Parent Assn., Phi Kappa Phi, Kappa Kappa Gamma. Democrat. Office: Kans State Capitol Bldg Topeka KS 66612*

PARRISH, SHAREN DENISE, civil engineer; b. Opa Locka, Fla., Aug. 17, 1959; d. Frank Junior and Alice Lee (Baldwin) Brown; m. Anthony Parrish, Aug. 20, 1983; 1 child, Anthony. A.A. in Bus. Adminstrn., Fla. State U., 1978; B.S. in Civil Engrng., U. Fla., 1982. Lic. engr. intern. Civil engr. Post, Buckley, Schuh & Ternigan, Cons. Engrs., Miami, Fla., 1982; profl. engrng. intern Dept. Transp. Fla., Miami, 1982; service planner engr., Fla. Power and Light, Miami, 1983—. Mem. Harris Chapel Methodist Ch., Ft. Lauderdale, Engrng. Leadership Circle, U. Fla., Gainesville, 1981—. Mem. Nat. Tech. Assn. (founding pres. S. Fla. 1984-85, treas. 1985—, leadership award 1985), Fla. Engrng. Soc., ASCE, Fla. Blue Key, Alpha Kappa Alpha (Soror of Yr. 1982). Democrat. Baptist. Club: Silhouette. Avocations: jogging; swimming; dancing. Home: 3345 NW 23rd Ct Lauderdale Lakes FL 33312

PARRISH, SHARON LEE, lawyer; b. Wray, Colo., Sept. 7, 1956; d. William Sims and Alice Louise (Berg) Parrish. B.B.A. in Acctg., Colo. State U., 1979; J.D., U. Houston, 1985. Bar: Tex. 1985; C.P.A., Tex. Acct., Shell Oil Co., Houston, 1979-81, tax acct., 1981-84; assoc. Chamberlain, Hrdlicka, White, Johnson & Williams, 1985—. Mem. disaster relief team ARC, Houston, 1981. Mem. Am. Inst. C.P.A.s, Tex. Soc. C.P.A.s (Houston chpt.), Tex. Bar Assn., ABA. Republican. Methodist. Lodge: Order Eastern Star. Home: 9110 Goodmeadow Dr Houston TX 77064 Office: Chamberlain Hrdlicka White Johnson & Williams 1400 Citicorp Ctr 1200 Smith St Houston TX 77002

PARRISH, SUSAN HANSELL, public relations executive; b. Toronto, Ont., Can., Dec. 29, 1937; came to U.S., 1941; d. Howard F. and Isabel (Johnson) Hansell; m. T. Kirk Parrish, Jan. 9, 1960 (div. 1979); children—Linn C., Wayne E., S. Scott; m. 2d Lawrence A. Bianchi, Aug. 26, 1983. Student Manhattanville Coll., Purchase, N.Y., 1955-58, NYU, 1975-76. Researcher, Time, Inc., N.Y.C., 1959-68; tchr. Met. Mus. Art, N.Y.C., 1972-75; pub. relations exec. N.W. Ayer, N.Y.C., 1976-77; pub. relations exec. Hill, Holliday, Connors, Cosmopulos, Boston, 1977—, v.p., dir. pub. relations, 1979—. Executor, Pub. Info. Campaign on Hazardous Waste Disposal, 1981, recipient Bell Ringer award, 1982; cons. Wang Ctr. Performing Arts, Vis. Nurse Assn. Mem. Ad Club Greater Boston (cons. 1979-82), New Eng. Broadcasters Assn., Fashion Group. Home: 29A Chestnut St Boston MA 02108 Office: Hill Holliday Connors Cosmopulos 200 Clarendon St Boston MA 02116

PARRIS-MILLER, JUNE HAZEL FRANCES, counselor; b. Golden Grove, Guyana, June 12, 1954; came to U.S., 1973; d. Carmel St. John and Leila Winifred (Parris) Miller; A.A., Finch Coll., 1975; B.A., Marymount Manhattan Coll., 1977; M.A., Columbia U. Tchrs. Coll., 1978, Ed.M., 1979; postgrad. Inst. for Moral Edn., Harvard U., summer 1980. Dir. guidance St. Mark's Day Sch., sch. for immigrant students, Bklyn., 1979-81; counselor higher edn. opportunity program Le Moyne Coll., 1981—. Editor, compiler: On the Move: A Career Handbook for Higher Education Opportunity Program Students, 1984; compiler: Financial Aid Sources for Foreign Students: A Selected Listing, 1984; contbr. writer Heritage mag., 1984—. Recipient cert. of appreciation Project Double Discovery, Columbia U., 1979, Across Culture Caribbean Am., 1978; Woodrow Wilson Nat. Fellowship Found. adminstrv. and program fellow, 1984. Lic. guidance counselor, N.Y. State. Mem. World Council for Curriculum and Instrn., AAUW, Am. Assn. for Counseling and Devel., Nat. Assn. Women Deans, Adminstrs. and Counselors. Mem. Moravian Ch. Office: Le Moyne Coll Le Moyne Heights Syracuse NY 13214

PARROTT, BARBARA ANN, publishing company manager; b. Bronx, N.Y., Nov. 8, 1950; d. Robert and Celia (Stevenson) P. B.B.A., Baruch Coll., CUNY, 1982. Editorial asst. Ziff-Davis Pub. Co., N.Y.C., 1970-73, adminstrv. asst., 1973-75, mktg. asst., 1975-78, asst. bus. mgr., 1978-81; distbn. mgr. Dell Pub. Co., N.Y.C., 1981—. Mem. Am. Soc. Profl. and Exec. Women, Nat. Assn. Female Execs. Democrat. Avocations: reading; crafts; theater; bicycle riding. Office: Dell Pub Co One Dag Hammarsjolkd Plaza New York NY 10017

PARRY, CAROL JACQUELINE, banker; b. Chgo., Apr. 12, 1941; d. Ralph Geoffrey and Estelle (Hoffman) Newman; student UCLA, 1959-61; B.A., Tufts U., 1964; M.S.W. (NSF fellow), U. Conn., 1969. Dir. program planning N.Y.C. Agy. Child Devel., 1971-72; assoc. McKinsey & Co., N.Y.C., 1972-74; asst. commr. City N.Y. Dept. Social Services, 1974-77; sr. v.p., div. head Chem. Bank, N.Y.C., 1978—. Mem. bd. advs. Sta. WNET, N.Y.C., 1979—; bd. dirs. N.Y. Urban Coalition, N.Y.C., N.Y. Landmarks Conservancy; treas. Nat. Child Labor Com. Office: 277 Park Ave New York NY 10017

PARRY, CYNTHIA KAY, oil company financial analyst; b. Bayshore, N.Y., Mar. 8, 1947; d. Sidney Wildred and Wanda Kay (Wilson) Parry. B.A., Hartwick Coll., 1969; J.D., Syracuse U., 1972, M.S. in Acctg., 1973. Bar: D.C. 1975, N.Y. 1976. Sr. auditor Ernst & Ernst, N.Y.C., 1973-75; auditor Price Waterhouse & Co., Paris, 1975-78; mgr. internal audit Met. Mus. Art, N.Y.C., 1978-80; auditor Exxon Corp., Florham Park, N.J., 1980-83, fin. analyst, acctg. research, N.Y.C., 1983—. Bd. dirs. Artists' Choice Mus., N.Y.C., 1982—. Mem. Vol. Lawyers for Arts, ABA. Home: 330 W 56th St Apt 3N New York NY 10019 Office: Exxon Corp 1251 Ave of Americas New York NY 10020

PARRY, FRANCES ELLEN COLEY, librarian, consultant; b. Welch, W.Va., May 11, 1932; d. William Fred and Frances (Gilkeson) Coley; m. Thomas H. Parry, Aug. 15, 1956; children—Virginia Gilkeson (dec.), William Thomas, Robert Brinsmead. B.A., Agnes Scott Coll., Decatur, Ga., 1953; M.Ed., U. Va., 1958; M.S.L.S., U. S.C., 1985. Tchr., Petersburg pub. schs., Va., 1953-55, Broward County pub. schs., Ft. Lauderdale, Fla., 1956-58; librarian Waynesboro pub. schs., Va., 1955-56, 63-67, tchr., 1962-63; librarian Pickens County pub. schs., S.C., 1971—. Sec., Clemson Republican Precint, S.C., 1980-82; del. County and State Rep. Conv., Pickens and Columbia, S.C., 1982; chmn. S.C. Children's Book Award Com., 1985-86. Mem. NEA, S.C. Edn. Assn., S.C. Library Assn., Pickens County Edn. Assn., S.C. Assn. Sch. Librarians (exec. bd. 1985-86), Phi Delta Kappa, Kappa Delta Phi. Presbyterian. Avocations: needlework, gardening, reading, entertaining. Home: 113 E Brookwood Dr Clemson SC 29631 Office: Liberty Elem Sch N Hillcrest St Liberty SC 29631

PARRY, NANCY, physician, surgeon; b. Salt Lake City, Dec. 20, 1940; d. Nathaniel Edmunds and Dortha Nell (Harris) P.; B.S., U. Utah, 1963; M.D., U. Calif., Irvine, 1967. Intern, Latter-Day Saints Hosp., Salt Lake City, 1967-68; gen. practice medicine and surgery, Anaheim, Calif., 1969—; mem. staff Martin Luther Hosp., Anaheim, Anaheim Meml. Hosp., West Anaheim Community Hosp.; originator, developer, pres. Parry Devel. Co., Sun Valley, Idaho, Maui, Hawaii, Lancaster, Anaheim and Carlsbad, Calif., Salt Lake City, 1973—; developer, mng. gen. partner Med. Arts East, Anaheim, 1974—; developer Parry Profl. Bldg.; pres. Breast Inst.; pres. Profl. Edn. Services, Anaheim, 1975—; mem. gen. practice com. Martin Luther Hosp. Bd. dirs. Martin Luther Hosp. Found., 1982—. Orange County Med. Assn. Found. Diplomate Am. Bd. Family Practice. Fellow Acad. Family Physicians; mem. Am. Coll. Emergency Physicians, AMA, Am. Women Med. Assn., Orange County Women in Bus. (dir.), Calif. Med. Assn., Orange County Med. Assn. Address: 1801 W Romneya Dr #601 Anaheim CA 92801

PARRY, RANDINE ELIZABETH, psychologist; b. Hartford, Conn., Sept. 6, 1947; d. William Brown and Mary Elizabeth (Caton) P.; m. Stanley A. Cruwys; children—Robert W. Parry-Cruwys, Brendon C. Parry-Cruwys. A.B., Mt. Holyoke Coll., 1968; Ph.D. (USPHS fellow, 1968-72), U. Chgo., 1977. Staff psychologist behavior analysis research lab., dept. psychiatry, U. Chgo., 1971-74, dir. fluency clinic, 1974-77; dir. psychology Walter Fernald State Sch., Waltham, Mass., 1977-80, chief psychologist, 1980—; lic. psychologist SE Counseling Assocs., Norwood, Mass., 1980-82; vis. asst. prof. Northeastern U., Boston, 1977-80; cons. Human Resource Inst. of Franklin, Mass., 1979-81. Contbr. papers to profl. confs. Active NOW, 1974—, chmn. ERA com., Chgo. chpt., 1974-77; mem. Women's Polit. Caucus, 1977—, ACLU, 1978—, Nat. Abortion Rights Action League, 1977—, Friends of Family Planning, 1981—, Belmont Day Sch. Parents Assn., Friends of Sturbridge Village, 1981—, N.E. Aquarium, Mus. Fine Arts, Mus. Sci., Boston, 1979—; bd. dirs. Waverley Oaks Child Devel. Center, 1984—. Mem. Am. Psychol. Assn., Eastern Psychol. Assn., New Eng. Psychol. Assn., Mass. Psychol. Assn., Assn. for Applied Behavior Analysis, Assn. for Advancement of Behavior Therapy, Assn. for Advancement of Psychology, Assn. for Women in Psychology, Boston Behavior Therapy Interest Group. Home: 15 Cherry Oca Ln Framingham MA 01701 Office: Dept Psychology Walter Fernald State Sch 200 Trapelo Rd Waltham MA 02154

PARSEGHIAN, LAURA MARIA, wine and distilled spirits company executive; b. Kearny, N.J., Apr. 25, 1957; d. Louis and June E. (Aromando) Picillo; m. Donald R. Parseghian, Sept. 10, 1983. Student N.J. Inst. Tech., 1977; B.S. in Acctg., Montclair State Coll., 1980. Gas station auditor Amerada Hess Corp., Woodbridge, N.J., 1980, corp. staff auditor, 1981-82; auditor Joseph E. Seagram's Sons, N.Y.C., 1982-83, audit supr., 1983, mgr. adminstrn., 1983-86, budget mgr. MIS, 1986—; sales rep. Schlott Realtors, Matawan, N.J. Mem. Nat. Assn. Female Execs., N.J. Bd. Realtors. Democrat. Roman Catholic. Office: Joseph E Seagram & Sons Inc 800 3d Ave New York NY 10022

PARSONS, GAIL, accountant; b. Salt Lake City, Mar. 12, 1946; d. Paul Eugene and Virginia (Jarvis) P.; B.S. in Acctg., U. Utah, 1969; m. Carl Andersen Heyes, July 25, 1975. Staff acct. Hansen, Barnett & Maxwell, C.P.A.'s, Salt Lake City, 1969-75; controller Timberhaus Ski Shops, Inc., Park City and Snowbird, Utah, 1975-76; pvt. practice as cert. public accountant, Salt Lake City, 1976—. C.P.A., Utah, Mem. Am. Inst. C.P.A.'s, Am. Woman's Soc. C.P.A.'s, Utah Assn. C.P.A.'s. Home and office: 5641 Oakdale Dr Salt Lake City UT 84121

PARSONS, LEONA MAE, hospital administrator; b. Newark, Ohio, Sept. 13, 1932; d. Enos Andrew and Emma Mae (Simmers) Chew; R.N., Andrews U., 1960; B.S. in Nursing, So. Missionary Coll., 1980; m. David J. Parsons, June 14, 1953; children—Davona Joy, Cynthia Carol, David J. Operating room supr. Bongo Hosp., Angola, Africa, 1961-68; dir. nurses Bongo Mission Hosp., Angola, 1968-75; nurse in charge refugee camps S. African Govt., Windhoek, S.W. Africa, 1975-76; matron, dir. nurses Windhoek (S.W. Africa) State Hosp., 1976-79; asst. v.p. Fla. Hosp., Orlando, 1980—. Mem. adv. bd. Seminole Community Coll., 1981—; adv. com. Seminole Community Coll. co-op., Seminole County Child Abuse Prevention. Mem. Assn. Seventh-day Adventist Nurses (bd. dirs. 1981—), Nat. League Nurses, Fla. League Nurses, Fla. Nurses Assn., Coalition Childbirth Educators (bd. dirs.), Fla. Hosp. Assn., Fla. Orgn. Nurse Execs., Nat. Perinatal Assn., Fla. Perinatal Assn., Loma Linda Med. Soc. Aux., Fla. Med. Soc. Aux., Am. Soc. Psychoprophylaxis in Obstetrics, Fla. Soc. Hosp. Nursing Service Adminstrs., Nat. Assn. Female Execs., S. African Nurses Assn., Orange County Med. Soc. Aux. (bd. dirs.), Am. Med. Assn. Aux.

PARSONS, PATRICIA ANN HUDSON, educator; b. Byron, Mich., Jan. 17, 1951; d. Donald Robert and K. Lucille (Wakeman) Hudson; B.A., Spring Arbor Coll., 1973; M.A., Central Mich. U., 1983; m. J. Mark Parsons, Oct. 14, 1972; children—Caleb Joseph, Jordan Donald. Tchr., Evart (Mich.) High Sch., 1974-75; media specialist Evart Public Schs., 1975-81, elem. sch. tchr., 1981-82, K-12 media specialist, 1982—. Mem. Evart Edn. Assn., Mich. Edn. Assn., NEA, Mich. Assn. Media In Edn. (regional chmn. 1985-86), FCO Media Selection Com., Mich. Cheerleading Coaches Assn. (dir. 1978-80, v.p. 1980-81, 82-83, state championship com. mem. 1979-83), Evart Profl. and Bus. Women. Methodist. Club: Evart Sports Boosters. Contbr. articles to profl. publs. Home: 624 N Main St Evart MI 49631 Office: Evart Public Sch 515 N Cedar St Evart MI 49631

PARSONS, PATTY LEIGH, labor union lawyer; b. Pocomoke City, Md., Feb. 20, 1954; d. E. Carmel Wilson (stepfather) and Evelyn Gay (Carter) Parsons-Wilson; m. Harry Dorman McKnett, May 24, 1980. B.A. in Psychology, U. Md., Balt., 1976; J.D., U. Balt., 1979. Bar: Md. 1981, U.S. Ct. Appeals (4th cir.) 1984. Residential counselor U. Md., Balt., 1973-76; adminstr. Juvenile Law Clinic, Balt., 1979-80; legal asst. Edelman & Rubenstein P.A., Balt., 1979-81; labor atty. Edelman & Rubenstein, P.A., Balt., 1981-85; labor atty. Abato, Rubenstein and Abato, P.A., Balt., 1985—; Drug counselor Open Arms Community Counseling Ctr., Balt., 1972-73. Recipient Md. Poetry Soc. award, 1972; Outstanding Adv. award, U. Balt., 1977-78. Mem. Md. State Bar Assn. (adv. bd. labor sect.), ABA, Balt. City Bar Assn., Indsl. Relations Research Assn., Coalition of Labor Union Women. Democrat. Home: 4 Deauville Ct Baltimore MD 21208 Office: Abato Rubenstein and Abato 2360 W Joppa Rd Lutherville MD 21093

PARTAIN, JEAN ELLEN, marketing and public relations consultant; b. Orange, N.J., Aug. 12, 1949; d.James Kenneth and Elizabeth (Gillilan) Britton; m. Paul Alan Partain, May 7, 1976. Prodn. head Westport News, Conn., 1965-67; account exec. Fred Thompson Co., Westport, Conn., 1967-69; freelance worker in area of advt. and bus. services, Weston, Conn., 1969-74; adminstrv. asst. Gary, Thomasson, Hall & Marks, Corpus Christi, Tex., 1974-75; contract worker Assured Temporary Service, Austin, Tex., 1976-77; mgr. word processing ctr., 1977-78; self-employed, Austin, 1978-79; legal asst. State Bar of Tex., Austin, 1979-81; owner, pres. bsi/LDI, Austin, 1981—. Contbr. articles to tech. and profl. jours. Bd.dirs. Austin Area Urban League, 1984—, Austin Community Gardens, 1986; mem. pub. relations task force Gov.'s Commn. for Women, 1985, Austin Commn. for Women, 1985-86. Recipient cert. of appreciation Austin Area Urban League, 1984, Chairman's award Austin Area Urban League, 1985. Mem. Am. Bus. Women's Assn., Am. Consultant's League, Am. Mgmt. Assn., Austin Women's Bus.League, Nat. Assn. Female Execs. Episcopalian. Home: 10902 Meadgreen Ct Auston TX 78758 Office: bsi/LSI 3930 Bee Cave Rd Suite I Austin TX 78746

PARTON, DOLLY REBECCA, singer, actress; b. nr. Sevierville, Tenn., Jan. 19, 1946; d. Robert Lee and Avie Lee (Owens) Parton; grad. high sch.; m. Carl Dean, May 30, 1966. Country music singer, composer, radio and TV personality; entertainer, Las Vegas; radio appearances include Grand Ole Opry, WSM Radio, Nashville, Cass Walker program, Knoxville; TV appearance include Porter Wagoner Show, from 1967, Cass Walker program, Bill Anderson Show, Wilburn Bros. Show; Tonight Show, Merv Griffin Show, Mike Douglas show, Acad. Awards Telecast; film actress Nine to Five, 1980, Best Little Whorehouse in Texas, 1982, Rhinestone, 1984; rec. artist Mercury, Monument, RCA record cos.; developer Dollywood theme park, Tenn. Recipient (with Porter Wagoner) Vocal Group of Year award 1968, Vocal Duo of Year award, all Country Music Assn., 1970, 71; Dolly Parton Day, Sevier County, Tenn., designated Oct. 7, 1967; Nashville Metronome award, 1979; Grammy award, 1979, 81; named Female Vocalist of Yr., Country Mus. Assn., 1976, 77; Country and Western Star of Yr., 1977, Entertainer of Yr., Acad. Country Mus., 1978; Am. Music award, 1984. Recordings include Dumb Blonde, Something Fishy, I Couldn't Wait Forever, Daddy Was an Old Time Preacher Man, Joshua, Jolene, Here You Come Again, New Harvest, First Gathering (Am. Music award 1977), It's All Wrong, But It's Alright, Best of Dolly Parton, Heartbreaker, Dolly, Dolly, Dolly Real Love. Composer: Dumb Blonde, Something Fishy; (with others) I'm in No Condition, Ol' Handy Man, Friends Tell Me, Put It Off Until Tomorrow, The Company You Keep, You Know How to Hurt A Guy, Two Doors Down, 9 to 5, Heartbreak Express, Do I Ever Cross Your Mind?, Hollywood Potters, Act Like a Fool, My Blue Ridge Mountain Boy, As Much as Ever, Prime of Our Love, Barbara on Your Mind, numerous others. Address: care Creative Artists Agy Inc 1888 Century Park E Suite 1400 Los Angeles CA 90067

PARTRIDGE, JOY, financial services executive; b. Los Angeles, Oct. 19, 1948; d. Richard Leroy Stanton and Phyllis Maud (Cunningham) Stanton Higginbotham; m. Steven R. Partridge, Sept. 27, 1970. B.A. in Anthropology, Ariz. State U., 1970, B.S. in Acctg., 1973. Vice pres. Garland Enterprises, Phoenix, 1970-76; pres. Bus. World Acctg. Systems, Phoenix, 1976-85, Bus. World Fin. Services, Phoenix, 1985—, Higginbotham & Partridge Real Estate, Phoenix, 1984—, dir. Western Security Bank, Phoenix, Republic Nat. Bank, Phoenix. Founder, Businessmen for Free Enterprises, Phoenix, 1978—; prin. violist Scottsdale Symphony Orch., 1980-85, bd. dirs. orch., 1975—. Republican. Office: Business World 2110 N 24th St Phoenix AZ 85008

PARTRIDGE, MARIKA DENHAM, broadcaster; b. Newport, R.I., Aug. 7, 1955; d. Benjamin Waring and Cora Carter (Cheney) P. Student, Am. Coll. in Paris, France, 1972-73, New Eng. Coll., Sussex, Eng., 1973-74; B.A. in Canadian Studies and Geography, U. Vt., 1976. Vol. programmer Sta. KT00-FM, Juneau, Alaska, 1976, mus. dir., 1976-78; pres. bd. Sta. KCAW-FM, Sitka, Alaska, 1979-81, program dir., 1981-86; founder Raven Radio Found., Sitka, 1979-81. Cartographer: Crown of the World, 1980. Photographer: Profiles from the Past, 1979. Organizer, 1st Alaska Radio Conf., Sitka, 1980. Avocation: music. Home: 2901 18th St NW 504 Washington DC 20009 Office: Raven Radio Found PO Box 520 Sitka AK 99835

PARTRITZ, JOAN ELIZABETH, lawyer, educator; b. Chgo., July 16, 1931; d. Norman John and Florence Mae (Russell) Partritz. A.B., Ball State U., Muncie, Ind., 1953; M.A., Whittier Coll., 1963; J.D., Loyola U., Los Angeles, 1977. Bar: Calif. 1977, U.S. Dist. Ct. (cen. dist.) Calif. 1981. Copywriter Nelson Advt. Service, Los Angeles, 1952-53; speech, hearing therapist Port Hueneme (Calif.) Sch. Dist., 1953-54; tchr. math. Montebellow (Calif.) Sch. Dist., 1954-77; assoc. Parker & Dally, Pomona, Calif., 1977—; prof. Calif. State U., Los Angeles, 1978—; cons. Foxtail Publs., Los Angeles, 1978—; dir. ins. law seminars, Pomona, Calif., 1979—; comedy writer Foster Prodns., Los Angeles, 1980-83; Co-author California Modern Mathematics, 1960. Vol. atty. ACLU; mem. speakers bur. NOW, Women's Polit. Caucus. Grantee NSF, 1965, 66, 69. Mem. ABA (tort com. 1978-80, ins. com. 1978—, nat. jurisprudence award 1976), Calif. Bar Assn., Women Trial Lawyers Assn., Los Angeles Bar Assn., Bus. Law Assn., Calif. Tchrs. Assn. (key note speaker 1979, state salary com. 1970-71), La Habra Art Assn. (contbr., distbr.), AAUW. Home: 10515 S Portada Dr Whittier CA 90603 Office: Parker and Dally 281 S Thomas 5th Floor Pomona CA 91766

PARZYCH, CYNTHIA MARY, book publisher; b. New Britain, Conn., Sept. 30, 1951; d. Stanley Frank and Dorothy Clara (Sobieraj) Parzych. B.A. in Fine Arts, Trinity Coll., 1973. Asst. to chmn. Abbeville Press, Inc., N.Y.C., 1976-79; assoc. pub. Rutledge Books, Inc., N.Y.C., 1980-81; pub. Rutledge Press, N.Y.C., 1981-82; pres. Mandarin Offset, Inc., N.Y.C., 1982-86, Cynthia Parzych Pub., N.Y.C., 1982—; chmn. bd. Reading Rainbow Gazette, N.Y.C., 1983—; cons. Am. Circle Book Club, 1981-82, The Image Bank, 1982-84. Producer: American Folk Art of the 20th Century, 1984 (English Speaking Union Ambassador award 1984). Democrat. Roman Catholic. Home: 64 W 82d St New York NY 10024

PASAKARNIS, PAMELA ANN, worldwide diagnostics company executive; b. Pittsfield, Mass., May 11, 1949; d. Richard W. and Regina (Piskorski) Turner; m. Donald L. Pasakarnis, May 25, 1974; children—Seth M., Casey. B.A., Northeastern U., 1972; M.T., New Eng. Deaconess Hosp., Boston, 1973. Staff med. technologist New Eng. Deaconess Hosp., 1972-75, supr. clin. chemistry, 1975-77; tech. product supr. Corning Med. Co., Medfield, Mass., 1977-83, product mgr. clin. instrumentation, 1983-85; mgr. mktg. communications CIBA Corning Diagnostics Corp., Medfield, 1985—. Mem. Am. Assn. Clin. Chemists, Clin. Lab. Mgrs. Assn., Biomed. Mktg. Assn., Am. Mgmt. Assn. Republican. Avocations: winemaking; fashion design; interior decorating; needlework. Home: 3 Partridge Ln Walpole MA 02081

PASCHAL, ANNE BALES, educator; b. Runnels County, Tex., Oct. 10, 1929; d. Wirt Samuel and Lora Louise (Corum) Bales; B.S. Angelo State U., 1970, M. Sch. Adminstrn., 1983; m. Bill Paschal, Dec. 16, 1946; children—William Douglas, Susan Louise Paschal Spates, Paul Neal. Tchr. math. Central High Sch., San Angelo, Tex., 1970—; workshop presenter; dir. Concho Educators Fed. Credit Union, 1975-80, pres. bd., 1979-80. Recipient Leadership and Scholarship award Angelo State U., 1970. Acad. Excellence awards, 1968, 69, Leadership and Achievement award Angelo U., 1969, 70; named Outstanding Tchr., Central High Sch., 1977, Tchr. of Yr., 1978. Mem. Nat. Council Tchrs. of Math., San Angelo Council Tchrs. of Math (v.p. 1975), NEA, Tex. Tchrs. Assn., (local treas. 1978-79), Tex. State Classroom Tchrs. Assn. (treas. 1978-79), Kappa Delta Pi, Delta Kappa Gamma, Pi Mu Epsilon, Sigma Tau

Delta, Alpha Chi, Phi Delta Kappa. Republican. Home: 801 W Ave D San Angelo TX 76901 Office: 100 Cottonwood St San Angelo TX 76901

PASCHAL, L. TERESA, univ. dean; b. Langdale, Ala., Aug. 30, 1952; d. Thomas W. and Sara (Crutchfield) P.; B.S., Auburn U., 1974; M.Ed. in Student Personnel in Higher Edn., U. Ga., 1979. Tchr. vocat. home econs., LaGrange, Ga., 1974-75, Hamilton, Ga., 1976-77; edn. coordinator Up With People, Tucson, 1975-76; grad. supr. U. Ga., 1977-79; program adviser Ill. State U., Normal, 1979-80; asst. dean student life Clemson (S.C.) U., 1980—. Mem. Oconee Community Theatre, Anderson Community Theatre Episcopal Ch. choir. Mem. Nat. Panhellenic Council, Nat. Assn. Women Deans, Adminstrs. and Counselors, So. Assn. Coll. Personnel Adminstrs., U. Ga. Alumnae Assn., Auburn Alumnae Assn., Alpha Lambda Delta, Kappa Delta Pi, Phi Delta Kappa, Delta Gamma.

PASCHALL, AMY KING, state official; b. Atlanta, Feb. 9, 1951; d. Walter Goode and Eliza (King) P.; B.A. in Communications, Grinnell Coll., 1973. With Ga. Dept. Labor, Atlanta, 1973—, public relations and info. specialist, 1974—; mem. Gov.'s Council on Deaf, 1978—; cons.; freelance writer, photographer, 1975—; co-chmn. publicity com. Metro Atlanta Task Com. on Handicapped, 1981, chmn., 1982; leader pub. relations sect. 14th Southeastern Regional Inst. on Deafness, 1984; cons. 5th ann. Ga. Inst. on Deafness, 1984. Named Handicapped Profl. Woman of Yr., Decatur (Ga.) Pilot Club, 1981. Mem. Internat. Assn. Personnel Employment Security (recipient writing awards, com. chmn. 1973—, mem. handicapped services com. 1984), Women in Communications, Inc. Office: Room 658 State Labor Bldg Atlanta GA 30334

PASCHALL, ERNESTINE HORTON, educational administrator; b. Lenoir, N.C., June 7; d. Thomas Solomon and Dorothy Inez (Patterson) Horton; m. James Arthur Paschall, Sept. 9, (div.); 1 dau., Pamela Inez. B.A., Bennett Coll.; M.A., U. So. Calif., Los Angeles, 1956. Cert. tchr., N.C., Calif. Tchr. elem. sch., Henderson, N.C., 1948-49, Morganton, N.C., Sparta, N.C., Los Angeles, 1956-71; adminstr. Children's Ctrs., Los Angeles, 1971—, staff services coordinator, 1983—; librarian Los Angeles Schs., 1957-59, playground dir., 1965, tng. tchr., 1969-70. Contbr. articles to profl. jours. Mem. Women in Edn. Leadership, Los Angeles, 1984. Interchange for Community Action, Los Angeles, 1984; rep. United Way, Los Angeles, 1978-79. Recipient life membership plaque Parent Adv. Com., 1978; plaque Educare, U. So. Calif., 1980; cert. of appreciation Friends of Multi-Learning, 1981. Mem. Bus. and Profl. Women's Club, Assn. Calif. Sch. Adminstrs., Council Black Adminstrs., Bennett Coll. Alumnae (v.p., pres.), Delta Sigma Theta, Phi Delta Kappa (cert. of merit 1976). Methodist. Office: Child Devel Div 1360 W Temple St Los Angeles CA 90026

PASCHALL, PAMELA GENELLE, financial analyst; b. Pasadena, Calif., June 18, 1949; d. James Edward and Mary Anita (Butler) P.; B.S., U. So. Calif., 1976. Asst. dir. fiscal services Pasadena (Calif.) Unified Sch. Dist., 1972-78; staff acct. George C. Troutman, C.P.A., Louisville, 1978-80; sr. staff acct. Celanese Water Soluble Polymers Co., Louisville, 1980-82; supr. gen. acctg. Celanese Splty. Resins Co., 1983; sr. fin. analyst Celanese Internat. Co., N.Y.C., 1984—. Mem. Ky. Soc. C.P.A.s, Nat. Acctg. Assn., Am. Inst. C.P.A.s. Home: 42 Ralph St Stamford CT 06902 Office: 1211 Ave of Americas New York NY 10036

PASCHKE, KAREN ANNE, journalist, author, public relations executive; b. Pitts., Mar. 7, 1948; d. Frederick John, Jr., and Gladys Mary (Steinhardt) Killmeyer; m. Robert Michael Paschke, Aug. 29, 1970 (div. Nov. 1983); children—Jesse Frank, Joshua Kane. Student speech and drama Penn Hall Jr. Coll., 1966-67; B.A. in Broadcast and Sociology, Marquette U., 1970. Assoc. editor Nat. Safety Council, Chgo., 1970-72; editor, research asst. U.S. Savs. and Loan League, Chgo., 1972; editor, dir. pub. relations Nat. Eye Research Found., Chgo., 1972-73; editorial dir. Red Bud Publs., Columbus, Ohio, 1974-76; pres., creative dir. Pace Media, Columbus, 1976-83; dir. communications Price Waterhouse, Columbus, 1983-85; dir. pub. relations Med. Ctr. Hosp., Chillicothe, Ohio, 1985—; cons.; freelance writer, contbr. trade and comml. publs.; books include: Construction: Principles, Materials and Methods, 1972; City Slicker's Guide to Self Sufficiency, 1981-82; Heavenly Herbs, 1982; Borden: A Price Waterhouse Perspective, 1984; also novels, 1979-80. Recipient Communicators award Gt. Lakes Regional Com., 1983. Mem. Nat. Assn. Female Execs., Pub. Relations Soc. Am., Women in Communications, Internat. Assn. Bus. Communicators, Ohio Hosp. Assn., Hosp. Assn. Central Ohio, Zeta Phi Eta. Clubs: Penn Hall Alumni, Marquette U. Alumni. Office: Med Ctr Hosp 272 Hospital Rd Chillicothe OH 45601

PASCHKES, MITZI ELLEN, cataloger, librarian; b. Newark, Sept. 15, 1953; d. Harold and Carole (Weiss) Binder; m. Mark J. Paschkes, Jan. 29, 1984. B.A., Rutgers U., 1975; M.L.S., U. Tenn., 1976; A.A.S., Houston Community Coll., 1982. Temporary asst. reference librarian Fairleigh Dickinson U., Rutherford, N.J., 1977-78; sr. reference librarian Ridgewood Pub. Library (N.J.), 1978-80; from asst. librarian to librarian Bernard Johnson Inc., Houston, 1980-81; from cataloging asst. to asst. cataloger Harris County Pub. Library, Houston, 1982—. Author: Catalogue to the Lawson D. Franklin Manuscript Collection, 1976. Mem. N.J. Library Assn., Spl. Libraries Assn., Nat. Assn. Female Execs. Office: Harris County Pub Library 49 San Jacinto 200 Houston TX 77002

PASCOCELLO, CAROL, public relations consultant; b. N.Y.C., Nov. 17, 1952; d. William Charles and Gloria (Digilio) P. B.A., Lehman Coll., 1975; postgrad. NYU, 1981. Community relations dir. N.Y. Ctr. Community Affairs, N.Y.C., 1978-80; pres. Carol Pasco Assocs., Inc., N.Y.C., 1980—. Editor Byline Bull., 1982-83, SEBCO Newsletter, 1980—, Union Hosp. Newsletter, 1984—. Recipient Outstanding Contbn. and Dedicated Service award State N.Y., Bronx, 1980, Recognition for Devel. Youth Programs, N.Y.C. Police Dept., Bronx, 1980, Flying Col. award Delta Air Lines, N.Y.C., 1984. Mem. Nat. Orgn. Italian Am. Women (v.p. 1980, editor newsletter 1980-85), N.Y. Press Club, N.Y. Publicity Club, N.Y. Ctr. Community Affairs, Bronx C. of C. Office: Carol Pasco Assocs Inc 1938 Williamsbridge Rd Bronx NY 10461

PASCUAL, MARGARITA FRANCISCA CANDIDO, internist, cardiologist; b. Manila, Sept. 17, 1938; came to U.S., 1964, naturalized, 1977; d. Manuel and Carmen (Galvez) Candido; A.A., U. San Tomas, 1956, M.D., 1961; m. Dominador Pascual, June 21, 1964; children—Christine, Susan, David, Catherine, Daniel, Darren, Dominador III. Rotating intern U. Santo Tomas Affiliated Hosps., 1960-61; resident in ob-gyn, internal medicine, surgery and pediatrics St. Anne's Hosp., Manila, 1961-64; rotating intern N.Y. Polyclinic Hosp., N.Y.C., 1964-65; resident in internal medicine Bklyn. Jewish Hosp., 1965-66, Lincoln-Albert Einstein Coll. Medicine, N.Y.C., 1966-68; fellow in cardiology Bklyn. Jewish Hosp., 1968-69; fellow in cardiology Beth Israel Med. Center, Manhattan, 1969-70, cardiopulmonary fellow, 1970-71; cardiopulmonary fellow Kings County (N.Y.) Downstate Med. Center, 1971-72; practice medicine specializing in internal medicine and cardiology, N.Y.C., 1972-73, Brentwood and Lake Ronkonkoma, N.Y., 1973—; mem. staffs Southside, Good Samaritan, Smithtown Gen. hosps., St. James Plaza, St. James Nursing Home, Sunrise Manor Nursing Home, Berkshire Nursing Center; sch. physician Half Hollow Hills Sch. Dist. Mem. Suffolk, N.Y. State med. socs., Am. Soc. Internal Medicine, Suffolk, N.Y. heart assns. Office: 16 Washington Ave Brentwood NY 11717 also 210 Ronkonkoma Ave Lake Ronkonkoma NY 11779

PASKAWICZ, JEANNE FRANCES, psychiatric physician assistant; b. Phila., Mar. 3, 1944; d. Alex and Lillian P.; B.Sc., Phila. Coll. Pharmacy, 1965; M.A., Villanova U., 1972; M.S., St. Joseph U., 1979; B.Sc., Hahnemann U., 1984. Lab. technician Episcopal Hosp., Phila., 1966; now psychiat. physician asst. J.F.K. Mental Health/Mental Retardation Ctr., Phila.; tchr. St. Hubert High Sch., Phila., 1968-82; lectr. Holy Family Coll., Phila., 1972—. Mem. corp. bd. Phila. Coll. Pharmacy, 1970-82; mem. biology curriculum com. Archdiocese of Phila., 1981-83. Recipient Geneol. award Phila. Coll. Pharmacy, 1962. Mem. Am. Inst. Biol. Scis., Nat. Assn. Biology Tchrs., Am. Acad. Physician Assts., Pa. Soc. Physician Assts., Nat. Sci. Tchrs. Assn., Lambda Kappa Sigma. Republican. Roman Catholic. Assoc. editor Biol. Abstracts, Phila., 1967—. Home: PO Box 11595 Philadelphia PA 11595 Office: Hahnemann U 230 N Broad St Philadelphia PA

PASQUARIELLA, SUSAN KINGSLEY, librarian; b. Newark, Feb. 11, 1944; d. William and Gertrude (Kruessel) Kingsley; m. Bernard Guy Pasquariella, Sept. 29, 1973. B.A., Skidmore Coll., 1966; M.S., Columbia U., 1972, D.L.S., 1981. Research asst. Sloan Kettering Inst., N.Y.C., 1967-70, Cornell Med. Ctr., N.Y.C., 1970-71; indexer, reference librarian Columbia U., N.Y.C., 1972-75, sr. librarian, 1975-79, head librarian, 1979—, dir. info. services Ctr. Population and Family Health, 1979—; cons. Recipient George Virgil Fuller award Columbia U., 1978. Mem. Assn. Population/Family Planning Libraries and Info. Ctrs. (officer 1976—), UN Population Info. Network, ALA, Spl. Libraries Assn., Med. Library Assn. (cert. 1974, 83). Contbr. articles to profl. jours. Home: 200 Cabrini Blvd New York NY 10033 Office: Center Population and Family Health Columbia U 60 Haven Ave New York NY 10032

PASS, CAROLYN JOAN, dermatologist; b. Balt., May 14, 1941; d. Isidore Earl and Rhea (Koplowitz) P.; B.S., U. Md., 1962, M.D., 1966; m. Richard Malcolm Susel, June 23, 1963; children—Steven, Gary. Rotating intern USPHS Hosp., Balt., 1966-67; med. resident St. Agnes Hosp., Balt., 1967-71; dermatology resident and fellow U. Md. Sch. Medicine Hosps., 1971—; pvt. practice specializing in dermatology, Balt. and Ellicott City, Md., 1971—; mem. staff James Lawrence Kernan, St. Agnes, South Balt. Gen. and Bon Secours hosps.; vol. dermatology clinics U. Md., St. Agnes hosps.; asst. prof. medicine U. Md. Sch. Medicine, 1971—; mem. exec. com. adv. bd. Nat. Program in Dermatology, 1975. Diplomate Am. Bd. Dermatology. Mem. AMA, Med. and Chirurg. Faculty Md., Balt. City Med. Soc. (del. 1974), Am. Women's Med. Assn., Am. Acad. Dermatology (award exhibit 1970), Soc. Investigative Dermatology, Md. Dermatology Soc. (sec.-treas. 1974-76, pres. 1976-77), Dermatology Found., Soc. Contemporary Medicine and Surgery, Cowpet Bay Gourmet Soc. Jewish. Clubs: Suburban Country (Balt.); Country Garden, Gourmet-SSS. Contbr. articles to profl. jours. Home: Timberlane 8410 Park Heights Ave Pikesville MD 21208 Office: Suite 301 Pine Heights Med Center 1001 Pine Heights Ave Baltimore MD 21229 also Howard County Med Center Chevrolet Dr and Saint John's Ln Ellicott City MD 21043

PASS, DELORES MERCER, business executive; b. Jacksonville, Fla., Sept. 20, 1940; d. S. Sherman and Margaret (Mixon) Mercer; m. Orien L. Pass, Feb. 14, 1965; children—Mark Gregory, Deborah Suzanne. Student Jacksonville U., 1961-63. Sec., A&P Co., Jacksonville, 1958-60; adminstrv. asst. Internat. Harvester, Inc., Jacksonville, 1961-69; gen. mgr. Underhill Agy., Inc., Jacksonville, 1969-77; pres. Conval-Aide Med. Staffing, Inc., 1977—, Associated Temp. Staffing, Inc., Jacksonville, 1978—, Associated Dental Temps., Jacksonville, 1983—; mem. Nat. Assn. Temp. Services (membership chmn. 1983-84, sec. 1986), Jacksonville C. of C. (v.p. 1985, treas. 1986), Salvation Army (bd. dir.), Com. of 200, Jacksonville Women's Network; recipient Eve award Fla. Pub. Co., Jacksonville, 1983, Top Mgmt. award Sales and Mktg. Execs. Jacksonville. Mem. N.E. Fla. Assn. Women Bus. Owners. Democrat. Methodist. Office: Associated Temporary Staffing Inc 3850 Beach Blvd Jacksonville FL 32207

PASSAFIUME, JANET LOUISE, telecommunications systems engineer; b. Evergreen Park, Ill., July 14, 1954; d. William Mathias and Ada (Ferguson) Schroeder. Student pub. schs. Casualty claims mgr. Cragin & Pike, Inc., Las Vegas, Nev., 1975-77; clerical supr. Capital Credit Corp., Miami, Fla., 1977-78; telecommunications analyst Ryder System Inc., Miami, 1978-81; purchasing asst. Gen. Foods Corp., White Plains, N.Y., 1981-82; sr. engr. No. Telecom Inc., N.Y.C., 1982-84; supr. engring. Sonecor Systems, N.Y.C., 1984—. Assoc. Consumers Union, N.Y.C., 1984—; mem. Greenpeace, Calif., 1984—. Mem. Nat. Assn. Female Execs. Democrat. Avocations: writing; handcrafts; sewing; aerobics; dancing. Home: RFD 2 Box 19 Adair Rd Peekskill NY 10566 Office: Sonecor Systems 140 E 45th St New York NY 10017

PASSAMANECK, RANDI LEA, medical technologist; b. Richmond, Va., May 18, 1942; d. Yale and Ann (Berman) P.; B.S. in Med. Tech., U. N.C., 1964; postgrad. Johns Hopkins Hosp., 1972-73. Research technologist USPHS Hosp., Balt., 1964-65; lab. scientist U. Md. Hosp., Balt., 1965-72, tech. and adminstrv. specialist, 1973-74; lab. assoc. Johns Hopkins Hosp., Balt., 1972-73; dir. tech. services ARC Blood Services, Chesapeake region, Balt., 1974-85; tech. services specialist ARC, Washington, 1985—. Bd. dirs. Mid-Atlantic Assn. Blood Banks, 1976-81, pres., 1979-80; mem. tech. workshop com. Am. Assn. Blood Banks, 1976-78; v.p. Washington-Balt. Blood Study Group, 1975-76; mem. tech. adv. com. ARC, 1982-84. Mem. Am. Soc. Clin. Pathologists, Am. Soc. Med. Tech., Internat. Soc. Blood Transfusion, Md. Soc. Med. Tech., Pa. Assn. Blood Banks, Regulatory Affairs Profls. Soc. Democrat. Jewish. Office: ARC 17th and D Sts NW Washington DC 20006

PASSARO, MARIA CONCETTA PASTORE, lecturer, translator; b. Brienza, Potenza, Basilicata, Italy, Oct. 2, 1943; came to U.S., 1958, naturalized, 1962; d. Pasqualino and Carmela (Viscardi) Pastore; m. Vincent J. Passaro, May 16, 1965; children—Maria Antonietta, Susette Lucia. B.A. cum laude, Lehman Coll., 1974; M.A., Hunter Coll., 1980; postgrad. in Comparative Lit., CUNY, 1982—. Cert. secondary and elem. tchr., N.Y., Instr. The Masters High Sch., Dobbs Ferry, N.Y., 1976-77; curriculum specialist Mamaroneck Schs., N.Y., 1978-81; adj. lectr. Fordham U., Bronx, N.Y., 1981-83, 85—, H. Lehman Coll., Bronx, 1981—, Hunter Coll., N.Y.C., 1985; cons. White Plains Schs., Westchester, N.Y., 1978-81. Author: The Bilingual Play: Pinocchio, 1981, (plays) G. Garibaldi, 1982, Francis of Assisi, 1982, Il Cinque Maggio, 1985. Translator: Gente Mia and Other Poems (Joseph Tusiani), 1982, Michael Angelo, 1986. Recipient Lang. award Martini and Rossi, 1974; Cert. of Initiative, Fordham U., 1976; Fulbright scholar U.S. Tchrs. Exchange Program, 1981. Mem. AAUP, Am. Assn. Tchrs. Italian, MLA, Can. Soc. Italian Studies. Roman Catholic. Home: 26 Soundview Ave Yonkers NY 10704 Office: Herbert H Lehman Coll Bedford Park Blvd West Bronx NY 10468

PASSMORE, PATRICIA V., management consultant; b. Bryn Mawr, Pa., Oct. 4, 1950; d. Lincoln Alan and Helen (Vrooman) Passmore; B.A., Skidmore Coll., 1972; M.B.A., Golden Gate U., 1976. Research asst. Bur. Econ. Geology, Austin, Tex., 1972-73; cons. human relations Gilroy Foods, Inc. (Calif.), 1976; operational bus. planner Gen. Electric Co., Burlington, Vt., 1977-79; mgr. mktg. planning and adminstrn. Simmonds Precision Products, Inc., Vergennes, Vt., 1979-80; mem. faculty dept. bus. and econs. Trinity Coll., Burlington, Vt., 1980-82; prin. Vt. Cons. Group, Burlington, 1982—; assoc. Innovation Assocs., Inc., Framingham, Mass., 1983—; v.p. operations Techtron R & D, Inc., 1986—. Trustee, v.p. Williston Federated Ch., 1978-79, 84—, Heppe Meml. Fund., 1972—, Vt. Symphony Orch., 1980—; bd. dirs., v.p. Babcf Ctr. for Children and Families, 1983-86. Mem. AAUW, Women Bus. Owners of Vt., Skidmore Coll. Alumni Assn. (dir. 1980-83), Am. Mgmt. Assn., Nat. Assn. Female Execs., Am. Soc. Profl. and Exec. Women, Lake Champlain Regional C. of C. (dir. 1983—). Address: Techtron R & D Inc One Mill St Burlington VT 05401

PASSO, JANICE MARLENE, government official, lawyer; b. Washington, Feb. 2, 1955; d. Hyman and Charlotte Tobey (Footer) Passo; m. Paul Augustus Lawhorne, Jr., May 20, 1984. B.A. in Govt. and Politics, U. Md., 1977, postgrad., 1981—; J.D., George Washington U., 1980. Bar: D.C. 1980, Md. 1981. Legal intern U.S. Labor Dept., Washington, 1978, Consumer Product Safety Commn., Washington, 1978-80; grants mgmt. specialist D.C. Dept. Employment Services, Washington, 1980-81; contract negotiator Naval Surface Weapons Ctr., White Oaks, Md., 1981-83; contract specialist Naval Sea Systems Command, Washington, 1983—. Recipient sustained superior performance award Naval Surface Weapons Ctr., 1982. Mem. Md. Bar Assn., D.C. Bar Assn., ABA, Women's Bar Assn. D.C., Phi Beta Kappa. Democrat. Jewish. Home: 1330 New Hampshire Ave NW #805 Washington DC 20036 Office: Naval Sea Systems Command Washington DC 20362

PASSOFF, MICHELLE, public relations consultant; b. Neptune, N.J., June 3, 1953; d. Daniel and Diane B. (Hansom) P. B.S., Syracuse U., 1975. Copy editor Syracuse Post Standard (N.Y.), 1974-75; assoc. editor publs. Coca Cola Co. U.S.A., Atlanta, 1975-76; asst. to bur. chief NBC Network News, Atlanta, 1976-77; account supr. Rowland Co., N.Y.C., 1977-80; owner, mgr. Michelle Passoff Publicity, N.Y.C., 1980-83; v.p. S3C Communications div. Gerard Souham Group Communications Cos., Inc., N.Y.C. and Paris, 1983—. Mem. Nat. Assn. Female Execs. Home: 305 E 40 St New York NY 10016 Office: S3C Communications Co 500 Fifth Ave New York NY 10036

PASTEN, LAURA JEAN, veterinarian; b. Tacoma, May 25, 1949; d. Frank Larry and Jean Mary (Slavich) Brajkovich; student Stanford U., 1970; B.A. in Physiology, U. Calif., Davis, 1970, D.V.M. (regents scholar), 1974; postgrad. Cornell U., 1975. Veterinarian, Nevada County Vet. Hosp., Grass Valley Calif., 1975-80; pvt. practice vet. medicine, owner Mother Lode Vet. Hosp., Grass Valley, 1980—; affiliate staff Sierra Nevada Meml. Hosp.; lectr. in field. Bd. dirs. Sierra Services for Blind. Recipient Internat. award Vet. Econs., 1982. Mem. AVMA, Calif. Vet. Med. Assn. (ethics com.), Mother Lode Vet. Assn., Am. Animal Hosp. Assn. (Mother Lode Vet. Hosp. cited for excellence), Nat. Ophthal. Soc., Nat. Pygmy Goat Assn., Nat. Appaloosa Soc., Nat. Assn. Underwater Instrs., Sacramento Valley Vet. Assn. (exec. com. officer), Denver Area Med. Soc., Internat. Vet. Assn. Am., Endurance Riding Soc. Republican. Lutheran. Club: Grass Valley Bus. Women. Author: (with Dr. Muller) Canine Dermatology, 1970; contbr. articles to profl. jours. Home: 15978 Shebley Rd Grass Valley CA 95945 Office: 11509 La Barr Meadows Rd Grass Valley CA 95949

PASTERNACK, MARCIA ANNE, librarian; b. Buffalo, Jan. 27, 1945; d. Sidney Charles and Sylvia Rochelle (Bornstein) Pasternack. Student, SUNY-Geneseo, 1963-65; B.A., Daemen Coll., 1967; M.L.S., SUNY-Buffalo, 1970. Catalog librarian Kent State U. (Ohio), 1970-71; asst. librarian N.Y. State Library, Albany, 1973—. Co-founder Fund for a Democratic Majority, Washington, 1983; mem. So. Poverty Law Ctr., Montgomery, Ala., 1984, Infant Formula Action Coalition, Mpls., 1983, Impact, Washington, 1984, Statue of Liberty/Ellis Island Found., 1983—, ACLU, People for the Am. Way, Nat. Planned Parenthood Assn., N.Y. Easter Seal Soc., Freedom to Read Found. Mem. No. Ohio Tech. Services Librarians, N.Y. Library Assn., ALA. Democrat. Jewish. Club: Library Sch. Alumni Assn. Office: NY State Library Empire State Plaza Albany NY 12230

PASTERNAK, EUGENIA, instn. adminstr.; b. Ukraine, Jan. 8, 1919; d. Mychail and Maria (Okonska) Nowakiwsky; student philosophy Goethe U., Germany, 1945-47; cert. Shaw Bus. Coll., Toronto, Ont., Can., 1956; diploma McMaster U., 1971; m. Eugene Pasternak, July 19, 1944. Came to Can., 1948, naturalized, 1955. Tchr., prin. jr. coll., Galitzia, Ukraina, 1939-42; exec. relief coms., also ARC during and after World War II; exec. Multiblitz Photog., Toronto, 1955-57; acct. Legal Humeniuk and Romanko, Toronto, 1958-63; pres. Ukrainian Home for Aged, Toronto, 1961-73; dir., adminstr. Ivan Frankso Home, Toronto, 1964—. Mem. Ont. Internal Group Com.; commr. for taking affidavits Province Ont. Recipient medal and scroll Ukrainian Can. Com., 1962, Free Cossacs of Ukraine, 1978; citation and medal Union for Freedom of Ukraine in Australia, 1977. Mem. Internat. Platform Assn., Gerontol. Soc., Can. Assn. Gerontology. Clubs: Ukrainian Pensioners (pres.), Ukrainian Arts, Crafts and Hobbies. Address: 767 Royal York Rd Toronto ON M8Y 2T3 Canada

PASTOR, MILLIE A., interior designer; b. Wayne County, Mich.; d. Martin Joseph and Bessie B. Kloka; student U. Detroit, 1947-48; B.S.N.E., R.N., Mercy Coll., 1951; m. Robert Henry Pastor, Sept. 29, 1951; children—Robert Henry, George H., Patricia C., Karen M. Founder pres. Pastor Interiors, Inc., Bloomfield Hills, Mich., 1965—; cons. URI, Nashville; cons., speaker, mem. nat. women's bd. Northwood Inst. Pres., Project Hope, 1973-75; commr. Mich. Am. Revolution Bicentennial, 1972-78; mem. exec. bd. March of Dimes; bd. dirs. Christ Child Soc., 1960-68, Mich. Artrain; pres. Am. Lung Assn. Southeastern Mich.; bd. dirs. March of Dimes, 1980-82, Women's Com. of Detroit Symphony Orch.; active Boys and Girls Club Met. Detroit. Recipient Outstanding Contbn. award March of Dimes, 1977-79; Outstanding Fund Raising Vol. award Nat. Soc. Fund Raising Execs., 1982; named Women of Yr., Boys Town of Italy, 1980. Mem. Nat. Home Fashions League (Image Maker award Mich. chpt. 1979, v.p.), Am. Soc. Interior Designers, Design Lighting Inst., Detroit Zool. Soc., Orch. Hall Assn., Am. Art Founders Soc., Mich. Cancer Soc. Republican. Club: Women's Econ. Studio: Grand Traverse Br 6110 Valleyway Dr Grand Traverse Village MI 49610

PASTORIUS, CAROLEE GANS, musician, educator; b. Phila., Aug. 5, 1945; d. William Thomas and Nancy McFarlin (Warren) Gans; m. Gary Francis Pastorius, July 18, 1970; children—Francis Christian, Erich Andrew. B.Mus., Westminster Choir Coll., 1967; postgrad. New Eng. Conservatory, 1967-68, West Chester State U., 1970-71, Pa. State U., 1971-72. Organist, choirmaster Trinity Episcopal Ch., Washington, 1977-78; instr. music Monte Cassino Sch., Tulsa, 1979-80; assoc. conductor Arts Musicale, Tulsa, 1978-79; musician in residence St. Paul's Episcopal Ch., Pitts., 1980-84; organist, choirmaster Ch. of the Advent, Pitts., 1984—; pvt. piano and voice tchr., University Park, Pa., also Pitts., 1974—; grad. asst. Pa. State U., University Park, 1971-72. Recital organist, Tulsa, Pitts., 1979, 80; singer Arts Musicale, Paul Hill Chorale, recitals, Phila., Tulsa, Pitts, 1969, 72-73, 80; chamber music coordinator and performer, Pitts., 1983-84. Recipient Presser award Theodore Presser Music Co., 1965, 66. Mem. Am. Guild Organists, Pitts. Piano Tchrs. Assn. Democrat. Episcopalian. Avocation: tennis.

PASTUSZEK, LYDIA MARIA, energy planner; b. Chester, Pa., Mar. 6, 1954; d. William John and Theodozia (Kiziuk) B.; m. Brian James Monahan, July 23, 1977. B.A. cum laude, Clark U., 1975; M.C.R.P., Harvard U., 1977. Real estate broker cert. Energy analyst New Eng. Regional Commn., Boston, 1977-79; sr. econ. analyst Mass. Energy Facilities Siting Council, Boston, 1979-81; mgr. load and revenue forecasting New Eng. Power Service Co., Westboro, Mass., 1981-85, dir. demand planning, 1985—; dir. New Eng. Econ. Project, Boston, 1982—. Mem. Internat. Assn. Energy Econs., Phi Beta Kappa. Home: 128 Madison Ave Watertown MA 02172 Office: New Eng Power Service Co 25 Research Dr Westboro MA 01582

PATAK, STACY RUTH, insurance company sales representative; b. Passaic, N.J., Sept. 12, 1959; d. Frederick Anton and Marjorie Jean (Barrall) P. B.A. in English Lit., Hiram Coll., 1981; postgrad. Montclair State Coll., 1982. Customer service mgr. J. Arthur Moore Co., South Hackensack, N.J., 1982-83; ins. sales rep. Nat. Office Supply, South Hackensack, 1983-84; sales rep. Arvine Union, Passaic, 1984-85, Met. Life Ins. Co., Secaucus, N.J., 1985—. Author: Spring Rain, Smile, 1982. Recipient Vachael Lindsay Meml. Poetry prize Hiram Coll., 1981. Mem. Nat. Assn. for Rights of Animals, Assn. Ethical Treatment Animals, Nat. Assn. Female Execs., Nat. Assn. Securities Dealers (registered rep.), Nat. Assn. Life Underwriters. Home: 234 Roosevelt Ave Apt G Lodi NJ 07644 Office: Met Life Ins Co 1 Harmon Plaza 4th Floor Meadowlands Pkwy Secaucus NJ 07094

PATAKY, MARIE ANN, accountant; b. Wilkensburg, Pa.; d. John Andrew and Elizabeth Ann (Koczka) P.; B.S. in B.A., Robert Morris Coll., 1974; A.S. in Data Processing, Community Coll. Allegheny County, Pitts., 1970. Auditor, Peat, Marwick, Mitchell & Co., Pitts., 1974-76; tax acct. G.L. Roteman & Assos., Pitts., 1976-77; acctg. cons. Career & Life Planning Inst., Pitts., 1977-78; tax acct. Westinghouse Electric, Pitts., 1978-80; internal auditor Johnson & Johnson, New Brunswick, N.J., 1980-81; tax supr. Interpublic Group of Cos., Inc., N.Y.C., 1981—; fin. cons., dir. Contrarian Investment Inst., Princeton, N.J., 1981—. Treas., Children's Hosp. Fund., 1979-80. C.P.A., Pa., cert. fin. planner, Pa.; Robert Morris scholar, 1972-74. Mem. Am. Inst. C.P.A.s, Pa. Inst. C.P.A.s, Nat. Assn. Accts., Assn. M.B.A. Execs., Am. Women's Soc. C.P.A.s, Inst. Cert. Fin. Planners, Internat. Inst. Fin. Planning. Club: Toastmistress (treas. 1979-80). Address: Box 1442 Palmer Sq Princeton NJ 08540

PATANE, PATTI, computer company executive; b. Palm Springs, Calif., Oct. 30, 1944; d. Alfred Francis and Jean Sybilla (Campbell) Patane; m. Stephen Martine Sherer, June 28, 1983. Grad. high sch., Palm Springs. Owner publishing co., Palm Springs, 1964-82; reporter, anchorperson, producer various comml. TV stas., Tex. and Ohio, 1968-80; writer, producer ednl. TV series devel., 1980—; ptnr., chief exec. officer The Logic Group, computer software and hardware prodn., mortgage banking, lending, Rancho Mirage, Calif., 1983—. Avocations: flying, scuba diving. Home: 71-519 Biskra Rd Rancho Mirage CA 92270

PATCH, LORRAINE MARIE, investment systems manager; b. Revere, Mass., Feb. 21, 1947; d. William Albert and Mary Rita (Gelardi) P.; B.A. magna cum laude in Mgmt. (Coll. Profl. Studies prize 1978), U. Mass., Boston, 1978; M.B.A., Suffolk U., 1981; Ed.M., Harvard U., 1986; 1 son, Derek Scott Burke. Benefits coordinator, money market bookkeeper State St. Bank and Trust Co., Boston, 1968-76; freshmen adv. U. Mass., Boston, 1976-77; customer service rep. First Nat. Bank Boston, 1977-78; analyst investment systems group TMI Systems Corp. (now SEI Corp.), Lexington, Mass., 1980-81, staff cons., sect. mgr., 1981-82, mgr. investment mgmt. dept., 1983—. Mem. search com. for chancellor U. Mass., 1979; coordinator Spl. Edn. Parents Adv. Council of Natick. Mem. Female Execs. Assn., Assn. Women in Computing, Am. Mgmt. Assn., Women in Mgmt. Network Assn. (co-founder 1981, treas. 1981-83), AAUW, U. Mass. Alumni Assn. Suffolk U. Alumni Assn., NOW. Home: 30 Bradford Rd Natick MA 01760 Office: 101 Main St Cambridge MA 02142

PATCHETT, ISABEL STEDMAN, marketing consultant, marketing educator; b. Hartford, Conn., July 2, 1924; d. Lewis Hosmer and Margaret Lorimer (Wilson) Stedman; m. Edward Heber Patchett, June 14, 1947; 1 child, Lewis Heber. B.S., U. Conn., 1951; M.B.A., U. Hartford, 1965. Supr. group dept. The Travelers, Hartford, Conn., 1952-65; analyst mktg. research Royal Typewriter, Hartford, 1965-68; asst. mktg. research mgr. Scovill Inc., Waterbury, Conn., 1968-85; v.p. Profl. Mgmt. Inst., Rocky Hill, Conn., 1974—. Author: Statis. Techniques for Mgrs. and Adminstrs., 1982. Vol. ARC, Farmington, Conn., 1980—; mgr. Republican candidate from 6th Congl. Dist., Farmington, 1970. Mem. Am. Mktg. Assn. (treas. 1965-68), Am. Statis. Assn. Congregationalist. Lodge: Masons. Avocation: golf. Home: 146 W Avon Rd Unionville CT Office: 37 Danforth Ln Rocky Hill Ct

PATE, DEBORAH DAVIDSON, electrical engineer; b. Nashville, Mar. 23, 1951; d. Tuyl Kenneth and Therese (Hanley) Davidson; m. Gerald Michael Ground, July 14, 1969 (div. 1976); m. Bobby Glenn Pate, Aug. 7, 1978; foster children—Lorie Ellen Lewis, Randy James Lewis. B.S. in Engring., U. Tenn., 1981. Registered profl. engr., Tenn. Audit cler, Tenn. Dept. Rev., Nashville, 1974-75; account clk. Blair, Follen, Allen, & Walker, Nashville, 1975-76; freelance wallpaper hanger, decorator, Nashville, 1976-81; materials engr. Nashville Electric Service, 1982—. Recipient Andrew Holt scholarship U. Tenn. Alumnae, 1976-81. Mem. Internat. Assn. Quality Circle, (leader). Republican. Roman Catholic. Club: Toastmasters Internat. Avocations: horticulture; needlework; bluegrass music. Home: 1317 Stratford Ave Nashville TN 37216 Office: Nashville Electric Service 1214 Church St Nashville TN 37203

PATE, JACQUELINE HAIL, facilities adminstr.; b. Amarillo, Tex., Apr. 7, 1930; d. Ewen and Virginia Smith (Crosland) Hail; student Southwestern U., Georgetown, Tex., 1947-48; children—Charles (dec.), John Durst, Virginia Pate Edgecomb, Christopher. Exec. sec. Western Gear Corp., Houston, 1974-76; adminstr., treas., dir. Aberrant Behavior Center, also dir. Personality Profiles, Inc., Corp. Procedures, Inc., Dallas, 1976-79; facilities mgr. Digital Equipment Corp., Dallas, 1979—. Active PTA, Dallas, 1958-73. Internat. Facility Mgmt. Assn., Mem. Farmers Branch Bus. C. of C., Daus. Republic of Tex. Methodist. Club: Metrocrest. Home: 3519 Casa Verde Apt 268 Dallas TX 75234 Office: 12100 Ford Rd Suite 200 Dallas TX 75234

PATE, JANET MARIE, oil company supervisor, professional dancer; b. El Paso, Tex., Aug. 18, 1954; d. Henry Douglas and Ava Juanita (Langston) Brown; m. George Dewey Pate, III, Jan. 19, 1979; 1 son, Zachary Michael. Lease analysts Tex. Oil & Gas Corp., Dallas, 1973-78; lease records supr. Lear Petroleum Corp., Dallas, 1978-83, O.I.L. Energy, Inc., Dallas, 1983, AA Energy Corp., Dallas, 1983—; dance tchr. Mountain View Coll., Dallas, 1980, Rockwall Health Spa (Tex.), 1980; pvt. tchr., 1981; cons. Lear Petroleum Corp., Dallas, 1983. Author, editor: Lease Record Training Manual, 1983. Sponsor charity benefit Foster Parents Assn., Dallas, 1980. Mem. Dallas Assn. Petroleum Landmen. Office: AA Energy 1500 Fidelity Union Tower Dallas TX 75201

PATE, JOAN SEITZ, judge; b. Islip, N.Y.; d. Anthony and Frances Kowalski; m. Raymond Seitz (div.); children—Laura, Cherryl; m. Howard M. Pate, Dec. 9, 1961; stepchildren—Patricia, Barbara, Marsha, Peggy. B.S., Ariz. State U.; J.D., U. Ariz., 1974. Bar: Ariz. 1974, D.C. 1976, Ky. 1978. Pvt. practice acctg., Phoenix, 1956-69; trial atty. U.S. Dept. Justice, Washington, 1974-78; ptnr. Goldberg & Simpson, Louisville, 1978-83; spl. trial judge U.S. Tax Ct., Washington, 1983—. Contbr. articles to legal jours. Recipient award Ariz. Soc. C.P.A.s, 1954. Mem. Fed. Bar Assn. (dir. 1983—), ABA, Nat. Assn. Accts., Ky., Ariz., D.C. bar assns., Order of Coif. Home: 1325 18th St NW Apt 304 Washington DC 20036 Office: US Tax Ct 400 2d St NW Washington DC 20217

PATE-COMBS, PAULETTE MICHELLE, technical equipment illustrator; b. Dayton, Ohio, Jan. 30, 1957; d. Benny Lawson and Sylvia Jeanne (Christian) Pate; m. Keith Erick Combs, July 17, 1985; 1 child, Corrahn LaMarr Pate. Tech. illustration assoc., Sinclair Community Coll., 1985. Parish sec. officer adminstr., Westwood Luth. Ch., Dayton, 1978-81; receptionist United Health Services, Dayton, 1981; clk. typist Mil. Personnel, Wright-Patterson AFB, Ohio, 1981, editorial asst. Mil. Specifications and Standards div., 1981-83, tech. illustrator aide, 1983-84, tech. equipment illustrator, 1984—, co-chmn. EEO com. Directorate of Support Systems Engring., 1983-84, chmn., 1984-86, dep. for engring., 1985—; freelance graphic artist, Dayton, 1978—. Del. Nat. Blacks in Govt. Assembly, Washington, 1984, 85; hospitality com. chmn. Greater Dayton chpt. Blacks in Govt., Dayton, 1985; newsletter artist, 1985; dir. Parish Emergency Food Service, Westwood Luth. Ch., 1979-81; kickoff runner Combined Fed. Campaign, Wright-Patterson AFB, 1982, 83, 84. Recipient various award Wright-Patterson AFB, 1983-85. Mem. Greater Dayton chpt. of Blacks in Govt. (panel mem. tips on rising to the top 1984, corr. sec. 1986). Democrat. Lutheran. Club: Sashay Prodn. Modeling Co. (model 1985—) (Dayton). Avocations: graphic designing; painting; flower arranging; camping; bowling. Office: Specifications and Standards Div ASD/ENES Wright-Patterson AFB OH 45433

PATEL, MARILYN HALL, judge; b. Amsterdam, N.Y., Sept. 2, 1938; d. Lloyd Manning and Nina J. (Thorpe) Hall; m. Magan C. Patel, Sept. 2, 1966; 1 child, Gian. B.A., Wheaton Coll., N.Y., 1959; J.D., Fordham Law Sch., 1963. Bar: N.Y. 1963, Calif. 1970. Mng. atty. Benson & Morris, N.Y.C., 1963-65; sole practice, N.Y.C., 1965-67, San Francisco, 1971-76; atty. U.S. Dept. Justice, San Francisco, 1967-71; judge Mcpl. Ct. Alameda County, Oakland, Calif., 1976-80, U.S. Dist. Ct. (no. dist.) Calif., San Francisco, 1980—; adj. profl. law Hastings Coll. Law, San Francisco, 1974-76. Author: Immigration and Nationality Law, 1974. Contbr. articles to profl. publs. Mem. Am. Judicature Soc. (bd. dirs.), ACLU (bd. dirs.), Now (mem. legal defense and edn. fund), ABA (litigation sect.), Calif. Conf. Judges, Nat. Assn. Women Judges, Advocates for Women (co-founder). Democrat. Avocations: piano; travel. Office: US Dist Ct 450 Golden Gate Ave San Francisco CA 94102

PATEL, THELMA GRAFSTEIN, lawyer, educator; b. N.Y.C., Mar. 14, 1922; d. George and Anna (Silver) Grafstein; m. Sam Patel, Feb. 2, 1946; children—Daniel, Andrew. B.A., Bklyn. Coll., 1946; M.A., Queens Coll., 1965; J.D., Hofstra Univ., 1980. Bar: N.Y. 1980. Tchr. Hewlett-Woodmere Schs. (N.Y.), 1957-77; sole practice, Woodmere, 1980-81; atty. DC 37 Mcpl. Employees Legal Services, N.Y.C., 1981-84; cons. Am. Film Inst., 1969-75; lectr. New Sch. Social Research, N.Y.C., 1969-72, Ctr. Understanding, N.Y.C., 1969-74; lectr.-demonstrator N.Y. State Communication Assn., 1969-71. Dir. record Folkways Call of Freedom, 1962; dir. films, 1962-77; editor booklets, children's stories, poems. Vol. YMCA, Lawrence, N.Y., 1954-55, Temple Beth El Nursery Sch., Cedarhurst, N.Y., 1956-57; negotiator Union Contracts, N.Y.C., 1940-75. Recipient N.Y. State Tchr. of Yr. award N.Y. State Dept. Edn. and Bd. Regents, 1973; Nat. Tchr. of Yr. Honor Roll award, 1973; Resolutions of Congratulation award N.Y. Senate/Assembly, 1974. Mem. Hewlett-Woodmere Faculty Assn. (pres. 1969-72), ABA, N.Y. State Bar Assn., Nassau County Bar Assn. Democrat. Jewish. Home and Office: 113 Longworth Ave Box 142 Woodmere NY 11598

PATERNO, DOROTHY JEANNE, soprano; b. Clifton Forge, Va., Apr. 17, 1934; d. Earl Lee and Lena (Wilmoth) Van Lear; m. Joseph Paterno, Aug. 4, 1956; children—Anthony J., Joseph Martin. Student pub. schs., Fairmont Sr. High Sch., W.Va. Dancer, tchr. numerous recitals, 1944-54; choreographer George M., Finian's Rainbow, West Side Story, Chorus Line; producer An Evening with Cole Porter; mem. Performing Arts Group of Greater Miami, 1976-84; singer numerous churches; appeared in Camelot, Brigadoon, South Pacific, My Fair Lady, Fiddler on the Roof and The Mikado, 1977-81; singer appearing at numerous state fairs. Home: 6475 Allison Rd Miami Beach FL 33141

PATERSON, NANCY MARIE, nursing administrator; b. Bklyn., Sept. 8, 1945; d. John Francis and Margaret C. (Stenman) P. Diploma Central Islip Sch. Nursing, N.Y., 1966; B.S., L.I. U., 1968; M.S., Adelphi U., 1973. Nurse clinician Bellevue Hosp., N.Y.C., 1968-71; clin. specialist, assoc. dir. Westchester div. N.Y. Cornell Med. Ctr., White Plains, 1973-80; assoc. dir., dep. dir. nursing City Hosp. Ctr. at Elmhurst, Queens, N.Y., 1980—. Pres. River Hill Condominium Assn., Yonkers, 1982-84. Nurses tng. grantee U.S. Govt., 1968, 1971-73. Mem. N.Y. State Nurses Assn. Avocations: sailing; cross-country skiing.

PATERSON, SHEENA, editor; b. Scotland, May 8, 1942; emigrated to Can., 1966, came to U.S., 1966; d. James and Jean (Kelly) Michie; A.L.C.M., London Coll. Speech and Music, 1959; m. Robert M. Paterson, Aug. 19, 1961 (div. Feb. 1984); children—Karen, Paul. Reporter, Scottish Daily Record, Glasgow. 1959-66; Toronto editor Weekend mag., 1969-73, mng. editor mag., 1973-74, editor-in-chief, 1974-76; Insight editor Toronto Star, 1977-78, Saturday editor, 1978-81, asst. mng. editor, 1981-82; assoc. editor Los Angeles Herald Examiner, 1982—. EEC scholar, 1981; recipient Woman of Merit award YWCA, 1975. Mem. Am. Assn. Sunday and Feature Editors (past pres.), Am. Soc. Newspaper Editors. Office: 1111 S Broadway Los Angeles CA 90015

PATKOWSKI, IRENE, registered nurse; b. Cleve., Dec. 5, 1956; d. Jerzy and Regina (Kuligowski) P. B.S.N., Ursuline Coll., Ohio, 1983. R.N., Ohio. Psychiat. staff nurse Met. Gen. Hosp., Cleve., 1983-85; fitness technician One Fitness Ctr., Cleve., 1985; surg. staff nurse Mt. Sinai Hosp., Cleve., 1985—; lectr. in field. Mem. Nat. Assn. Female Execs., Aerobic Way Cert. Agy., Ursuline Coll. Nursing Honors Soc., Reebok Profl. Instr. Alliance. Republican. Roman Catholic. Avocations: raising plants; collecting antiques; bicycling; yoga; swimming. Home: 12700 Lake Ave #1909 Lakewood OH 44107

PATMAN, JEAN ELIZABETH, journalist; b. Lincolnshire, Eng., Dec. 12, 1946; came to U.S., 1955, naturalized, 1967; d. Donald Geoffrey and Regina (Iwanir) P.; m. Lou Schwartz. B.A. in English, City Coll. N.Y., 1967. Stringer, Newsweek, N.Y.C., 1966-67; copygirl, then asst. to entertainment editor N.Y. Post, 1964-70; successively copy editor, spl. sects. editor, night city editor Reporter-Dispatch, White Plains, N.Y., 1970-74; asso. editor United Feature Syndicate, N.Y.C., 1974-75; successively copy editor, asst. news editor, news editor, Sunday editor Newsday, Long Island, N.Y., 1975-80, exec. news editor, 1980-83, fgn. editor, 1984—. Mem. Sigma Delta Chi. Club: Newswomen's (N.Y.C.). Office: Newsday Long Island NY 11747

PATON, MARY MARGARET, business executive; b. St. Louis, Feb. 18, 1918; d. William L. and Margaret (Brown) Paton; student pub. schs. Clk. typist Dun & Bradstreet, St. Louis, 1935-36; clk. typist, sec. Wm. A. Straub, Inc., Clayton, Mo., 1936-44, sec. to pres., 1947-53, corp. sec., 1950—, buyer, 1963—, supr. restaurant ops., 1953-72; with U.S. Civil Service, Army Air Base, Tonopah, Nev., 1944-46; sec. Parkside Realty Co., Clayton, 1950—; pres. Pro-Mir Garments, Ltd., St. Louis, 1971—. Presbyterian. Home: 8845 Burton Ave Saint Louis MO 63114 Office: 8282 Forsyth Blvd Clayton MO 63105

PATRICK, ELIZABETH LEAHY, personnel search company executive; b. Kingston, N.Y., Dec. 2, 1952; d. Thomas F. and Lucy G. (Dunn) Leahy; B.A. cum laude in Psychology, Marist Coll., 1974. Prin. dancer, instr. Deborah Vinton Sch. Ballet, New Paltz, N.Y., 1974-78; tech. placement cons. Perry-White Assocs., San Francisco, 1978-79; pres. cert. employment specialist, software engring. placement Heuristics Search, Inc., personnel service, Santa Clara, Calif., 1980—. Mem. Nat. Assn. Female Execs., Nat. Assn. Personnel Cons., Calif. Assn. Personnel Cons. (dir.), Women in Electronics, Entrepreneurs Alliance, Women in Info. Processing, Am. Assn. Individual Investors. Republican. Office: Heuristics Search Inc 4633 Old Ironsides Dr Suite 300 Santa Clara CA 95050 Home: San Jose CA

PATRICK, GAIL DENISE, lawyer; b. Columbus, Ohio, July 24, 1954; d. David Bruce and Florence Marie (Ramsey) Patrick. A.B., Wellesley Coll. (Mass.), 1976; J.D., Capital U., 1979. Bar: Ohio 1979. Law clk. Franklin County Mcpl. Ct., Columbus, Ohio, 1978-79; tax auditor IRS, Detroit, 1979-80; staff atty. SEOLS, St. Clairsville, Ohio, 1980-82; staff atty. Legal Aid Soc. of Columbus, 1982—. Vice pres. Capital U. Law Sch. Student Govt., Columbus, 1978-79. Nat. Merit Scholar, 1971. Mem. Assn. Trial Lawyers Am., Ohio State Bar Assn., Columbus Bar Assn., ABA, ACLU of Central Ohio (bd. dirs. 1983, 84). Club: Wellesley (Columbus; sec. 1982-84, pres. 1984-86). Home: 1313 Watkins Rd Columbus OH 43207 Office: Legal Aid Soc of Columbus 40 W Gay St Columbus OH 43215

PATRICK, GEORGIA O'BRIEN LAKAYTIS, communications executive; b. Dallas, July 2, 1945; d. Jack Dallas and Jane (Childs) O'Brien; B.J., U. Mo., 1967; m. Thomas Donald Patrick, Oct. 23, 1981. Tech. writer Mo. Regional Med. Programs, Columbia and Kansas City, 1967-69; public relations dir. Center for Student Life, U. Mo., Columbia, 1969-76; communications dir. Am. Home Econs. Assn., Washington, 1976-81; exec. v.p. The Communicators, Inc., Washington, 1981—. Mem. Am. Soc. Assn. Execs., Internat. Assn. Bus. Communicators, Pub. Relations Soc. Am., Counselors Acad., Washington Bus. Communicators (v.p. 1981-82), Council of Communications Mgmt. Contbr. articles to profl. jours. Home: Blue Ridge Acres Box 11 Harpers Ferry WV 25425 Office: 966 Hungerford Dr Suite 14 Rockville MD 20850

PATRICK, GRACIE MAE, nurse; b. Jones County, Miss., Sept. 15, 1933; d. Richard Franklin and Margaret Corinne (Upchurch) Bonner; diploma South Miss. Charity Hosp., 1956; B.S.N., William Cary Coll., 1982; m. Joe Neil Patrick, Dec. 27, 1952; children—Joe Neil, Debra Elaine. Nurse, various hosps., U.S., 1956-65; nurse VA Hosp., Biloxi, Miss., 1965—, head nurse, 1970-85; nurse recruiter VAMC, APD coordinator nursing service. Mem. Am., Miss. nurses assns., Internat. Urol. Scis. Inc. Home: 224 Holly Hills Dr Biloxi MS 39532 Office: VA Hosp Biloxi MS

PATRICK, IRENE FAY, county commissioner, auto parts company executive; b. Erlanger, Ky., Aug. 7, 1929; d. Darlton Martin and Nora Colston; m. Charles Abrahm Patrick, July 2, 1949; children—Charlene Tipton, Tracy Sam Beck. Student Chgo. Sch. Interior Design, 1967. Vice pres., co-owner Patrick Auto Parts & Sales, Inc., Hebron, Ky., 1952—; county commr. Boone County, Ky., 1977—; mem. Ky. Port Authority, Wilder and Newport, Ky., 1981—. Pres. PTA, Hebron, 1972-73, Homemakers, Hebron, 1972; vice chmn. Boone County Democrat Exec. Bd., 1973-74. Recipient Gold Bracelet award Vice Pres. Humphrey, 1969, 73, Ky. Col. awards Ford-Brethitt, 1973; named Outstanding Dem. Ky., 1985. Mem. Nat. Assn. Counties (vice chmn. waterways 1984-85), Ky. Women Democrats (treas. No. Ky. 1973-77, bd. dirs. 1973-77, bd. dirs. Community Action Commn. (bd. dirs. 1985), DAR. Mem. Ch. of Christ. Avocations: helping senior citizens; antiques; art; walking; community activities. Home: 2420 Petersburg Rd Hebron KY 41048

PATRICK, JANET CLINE, medical society administrator; b. San Francisco, June 30, 1934; d. John Wesley and Edith Bertha (Corde) Cline; m. Robert John Patrick Jr., June 13, 1959; children—John McKinnon, Stewart McLellan, William Robert. B.A., Stanford U., 1955; postgrad. U. Calif.-Berkeley, 1957, George Washington U., 1978-82. English tchr. George Washington High Sch., San Francisco, 1957, K.D. Burke Sch., San Francisco, 1957-59, Berkeley Inst., Bklyn., 1959-63; placement counselor Washington Sch. Secs., Washington, 1976-78, asst. dir. placement, 1978-81; mgr. med. personnel service Med. Soc. D.C., 1981—. Chmn. area 2 planning com. Montgomery County Pub. Schs. (Md.), 1974-75; mem. vestry, corr. sec., Christ Ch., Kensington, Md., 1982-84, vestry, sr. warden, 1984-85. Mem. Employment Mgmt. Assn., Met. D.C. Med. Group Mgmt. Assn., Phi Beta Kappa. Republican. Episcopalian. Club: Jr. League (Washington). Home: 3 Washington Circle NW 804 Washington DC 20037 Office: Med Soc DC 2007 Eye St NW Washington DC 20006

PATRIE, CHERYL CHRISTINE, teacher; b. Dobbs Ferry, N.Y., June 8, 1947; d. Edward F. and Antoinette C. (Patrie) P. B.A. in Edn., U. Fla., 1969; M.S. in Edn., U. Miami, 1979. Tchr., Marion County Sch. Bd., Ocala, Fla., 1970, Dade County Sch. Bd., Miami, Fla., 1974—; bldg. union steward United Tchrs. Dade, 1979—; faculty council Lorah Park Elem. Sch., Miami, 1979-85, dropout prevention com., 1985, career lab. cons., 1983-85, Human Growth and Devel. cons., 1983-85, comprehensive plan com., 1984—, phys. fitness co-chmn., 1984—. Mem. Crisis in Inner City task force United Tchrs. Dade, Miami, 1984-85. Named Tchr. of Yr., Lorah Park Elem. Sch., 1986. Mem. United Tchrs. Dade. (Disting. Service award 1984). Home: 1127 Robin Ave Miami Springs FL 33166 Office: Lorah Park Elem 5160 NW 31st Ave Miami FL 33142

PATRON, JUNE EILEEN, govt. ofcl.; b. N.Y.C., May 15; d. Irving B. and Mollie Patron; A.B. in Govt. with honors, Clark U., Worcester, Mass., 1965; M.A., Am. U., 1967. With U.S. Dept. of Labor, 1966—, head Black Lung benefits program, 1976-79, asst. adminstr. pension and welfare benefit programs, 1979—; mem. Sr. Exec. Service. Recipient various awards Dept. Labor. Office: 200 Constitution Ave NW Washington DC 20210

PATRYN, ELAINE LILLIAN, real estate broker, life and health insurance salesperson; b. Phila., Sept. 14, 1937; d. Frank and Lillian Helen (Genga) Borgioni; div.; 1 child, Steven James. B.S., Chestnut Hill Coll., 1959; postgrad. in acctg. and bus. law St. Joseph's Coll., Phila., 1960-61, Coll. for Fin. Planning, Denver, 1986. Engring. asst. Gen. Electric Co., Phila., 1959-61, math. technician, Santa Barbara, Calif., 1961-62, Reseda, Calif., 1964-65, King of Prussia, Pa., 1966-67; math. technician Space Tech. Lab., Redondo Beach, Calif., 1962-64; real estate broker Patryn Realty Corp., Ocala, Fla., 1980—; instr. Gold Coast Sch. Real Estate, Ocala, 1983-84. Mem. AAUW (treas. 1980-81), Nat. Assn. Female Execs. (network dir. 1985-86), Internat. Assn. Fin. Planners. Republican. Roman Catholic. Home: 525 Emerald Rd Ocala FL 32672 Office: Patryn Realty Corp 6661 SE Maricamp Rd Ocala FL 32672

PATT, RUTH MARCUS, author, archivist; b. New Brunswick, N.J., Sept. 29, 1919; d. Joseph David and Bessie Sarah (Laurie) Marcus; m. Milton S. Patt, Mar. 22, 1942; children—Richard A., Steven L. B.A., Douglass Coll., Rutgers U., 1940. Psychiat. social worker Marlboro State Hosp., N.J., 1940-42. Author: The Jewish Scene in N.J.'s Raritan Valley: 1698-1948, 1977. Editor, author: Tercentennial Lectures, 1982. Mem. community adv. bd. U. Medicine and Dentistry N.J.-Robert Wood Johnson Med. Sch., 1980—; tercentennial gen. chmn. City of New Brunswick, N.J., 1979-82; N.B. Tercentennial chmn., Middlesex County, N.J., 1983. Recipient Lehman award Israel Bond Com., Raritan Valley, N.J., 1970, medal Rutgers U., 1980, Woman of Yr. award Jewish Fedn., Raritan Valley, 1980, award of recognition N.J. Hist. Commn., 1980. Mem. Jewish Hist. Soc. Central Jersey (founder, pres. 1977-85), Douglass Alumnae Assn. Club: Hadassah (New Brunswick, N.J.) (pres. 1952-56). Avocations: researching Jewish community history; tennis; golf. Home: 1050 George St Apt 9-L New Brunswick NJ 08901

PATTELENA, VICKI RAE, vocal recording artist; b. Detroit, Sept. 8, 1953; d. Raymond Harry and Theresa (LeFevre) Carter; m. Daniel Joseph Pattelena, Oct. 14, 1983. Student Farmington Music Acad., 1972-73, Wayne State U., 1980. Artist/vocalist Contemporary Christian Music, 1984, 86. Mem. Nat. Assn. Female Execs., Houston Symphony Chorale. Republican. Roman Catholic. Avocations: writing books; music; piano; theatre. Home: PO Box 323 Barker TX 77413

PATTEN, BEBE HARRISON, clergywoman, college president, chancellor; b. Waverly, Tenn., Sept. 3, 1913; d. Newton Felix and Mattie Priscilla (Whitson) Harrison; D.D., McKinley-Roosevelt Coll., 1941; D.Litt., Temple Hall Coll. and Sem., 1943; m. Carl Thomas Patten, Oct. 23, 1935 (dec. 1958); children—Bebe Rebecca and Priscilla Carla (twins), Carl Thomas. Ordained to ministry Ministerial Assn. of Evangelism, 1935; evangelist in nationwide campaigns, 1933-50; founder, pres. Christian Evang. Chs. of Am., Oakland, Calif., 1944—; founder, pres. Patten Bible Coll., Oakland, 1945-83, chancellor, 1983—; founder program daily nation-wide radio ministry The Shepherd Hour, 1934—, daily TV telecast, 1976—, nat telecast, 1979—; founder, pres. Acad. Christian Edn., 1944—; pastor Christian Cathedral, Oakland, 1950—; mem. Am. Israel Pub. Affairs Com., Washington, 1983. Recipient numerous awards including medallion for religious affairs Israeli Fgn. Ministry, 1969, medal Govt. Press Office, Jerusalem, 1971, Gentile honoree Jewish Nat. Fund, 1975, Hidden Heroine award San Francisco Bay council Girl Scouts U.S.A., 1976, medallion Ben Gurion Research Inst., 1977, resolution of commendation Calif. Senate Rules Com., 1978; hon. fellow Bar-Ilan U., Israel. Mem. Am. Assn. Pres. Ind. Colls. and Univs., Zionist Orgn. Am., Am. Jewish Hist. Soc., Am. Acad. Religion, Soc. Bibl. Lit., Am. Assn. Higher Edn., Religious Edn. Assn., Bar-Ilan U. Assn. (exec. bd.). Author: Give Me Back My Soul (in English, Japanese, Spanish and Chinese), 1973; editor-in-chief The Trumpet Call, 1953—; composer 20 Gospel Songs, 1945; chair in social action established in her name at Bar-Ilan U., 1981. Address: 2433 Coolidge Ave Oakland CA 94601

PATTEN, FLORENCE WOODWORTH, cytotechnologist; b. Albany, Oreg., Jan. 27, 1935; d. Marshall Melvin and Grace Janet (Chalmers) Woodworth; B.S., U. Oreg., 1957, postgrad., 1958, 59; cert. sCUBAdiver Nat. Assn. SCUBA Diving Schs., 1982; m. Stanley Fletcher Patten, Jr., Oct. 20, 1979. Chief cytotechnologist U. Wash., Seattle, 1959-65; cytology supr. U. Oreg. Med. Sch., Portland, 1966-70; chief cytotechnologist and ednl. coordinator U. Rochester (N.Y.) Med. Center, 1970-80, asst. prof. pathology, 1977-80, clin. asst. prof. pathology and sr. tech. assoc. obstetrics/gynecology, 1980-83, asst. prof. ob gyn, 1983—; mem. faculty-tutorials in clin. cytology Internat. Acad. Cytology and U. Chgo., 1971—. Recipient Internat. Acad. Cytology Cytotechnologist award, 1977; Am. Soc. Cytology Cytotechnologist of the Yr. award 1979, Cert. of Merit, 1980. Mem. Am. Soc. Cytology, Am. Soc. Clin. Pathologists, Internat. Acad. Cytology, Am. Soc. Cytotechnology, Phi Beta Kappa, Alpha Chi Omega. Club: P.E.O. Editor, The Cytotechnologist Bull., 1973-80; asst. editor Acta Cytologica, 1982—. Office: PO Box 668 601 Elmwood Ave Rochester NY 14642

PATTEN, LINDA FRANK, banker; b. Chgo., Sept. 5, 1949; d. Eugene T. and Annette (Fell) Frank; B.A., St. Olaf Coll., 1971; M.B.A., So. Meth. U., 1977; m. Clark W. Patten, May 17, 1975; 1 child, Jennifer Lin. Successively computer programmer, mgr. adminstrn., personnel cons., mgr. staffing Res. Life Ins. Co., Dallas, 1975-77; compensation analyst-internat., Bank of Am., San Francisco, 1977-78, tng. officer South, Los Angeles, 1979-80; head mgmt. tng., 1980-81, asst. v.p., head tng. dept., 1981-82, v.p. human resource planning and adminstrn., San Francisco, 1982-83; v.p., mgr. personal banking div. tng. Crocker Bank, San Francisco, 1983—. Served with U.S. Army, 1970-74. Decorated Army Commendation medal with oak leaf cluster. Mem. Am. Soc. for Tng. and Devel., Internat. Assn. Personnel Women, Am. Compensation Assn., Nat. Assn. Female Execs. Republican. Lutheran. Home: 3545 Perada Dr Walnut Creek CA 94598 Office: 74 New Montgomery (7) San Francisco CA 94105

PATTEN-SEWARD, PATRICIA, human service organization administrator; b. Newton, Mass., Mar. 6, 1945; d. Robert Ross and Jean Barnes (Smith) Patten; m. Thomas Philip Seward, III, Oct. 2, 1965; children—Amy Elizabeth, William Ross. Diploma in Nursing New Eng. Bapt. Hosp. Sch. Nursing, 1965; B.S. in Psychology, SUNY, 1979; M.S. in Edn., Elmira Coll., 1981; M.S. in Human Services, Cornell U., 1983, Ph.D. in Human Services, 1983. Registered nurse, N.Y., Mass. Staff nurse New Eng. Bapt. Hosp., Boston, 1965-66, 1970-71; nurse. tchr. health Post Sch. Dist., Corning, N.Y., 1973-79; project coordinator Steuben-Alleg BOCES Painted Post, N.Y., 1979-81; teaching asst., lectr. Cornell U., Ithaca, N.Y., 1981-83; exec. dir. ARC, Elmira, N.Y., 1983—; cons. N.Y. State Edn. Dept., Albany, 1983, Corning-Painted Post Sch. Dist., Corning, 1981-82. Author: Me, My Baby and Blubber, 1980; A Teacher's Guide to Divorce, 1981. Sec., N.Y. State div. Am. Cancer Soc., 1982, chmn. pub. edn., 1983—. Mem. N.Y. State Fedn. Profl. Health Educators (pres. 1983). Home: Yorktown 3B Corning NY 14830 Office: Chemung County Chpt ARC 462 W Church St Elmira NY 14901

PATTERSON, BARBARA RUTH, marketing company executive; b. Milw., Nov. 21, 1932; d. Charles Ray and Esther Anna (Vahsholtz) Walters; m. Morris Donald Patterson, Aug. 17, 1972; m. Kenneth Walter Hoxie, Sept. 19, 1953 (div. Oct. 1970); children—Kenneth J., Kelly G., Kathleen A., Kevin R. B.S. in Bus. Adminstrn., Waynesburg Coll., 1976. Exec. recruiter Cook Assocs., Chgo., 1977-78; recruiter Casey Services, Inc., Arlington Heights, Ill., 1978-80; v.p. fin. MGAI Inc., Wheeling, Ill., 1980-83, pres., chief operating officer, 1983—; dir. Network, Inc., Wheeling, MGAI Trading Co.; pres. Chgo. Sales & Mktg., Wheeling, 1984—. Mem. Women in Mgmt. (bd. dirs., treas. 1982-83), Nat. Assn. Women Bus. Owners, Am. Mgmt. Assn. Republican. Lutheran. Avocations: sailing; gardening; car racing spectator. Home: 447 Partridge Ln Deerfield IL 60015 Office: MGAI Inc 1400 S Wolf Rd Wheeling IL 60015

PATTERSON, CLEMENTINE, educator; b. Houston, Feb. 27, 1943; d. Emmett and Gladys (Rideaux) Riggs; m. Leonard Curtiss Patterson, Aug. 18, 1961; children—Toni Yvette, Thaddeus Wayne. B.S. in Home Econs., Tex. So. U., 1973. Long distance operator Southwestern Bell Telephone Co., Houston, 1967-72; real estate salesman Williams Realty Co., Houston, 1968-70; tchr. home econs. Houston Ind. Sch. Dist., 1974—; advisor Future Homemakers Am., Houston, 1974—. Co-author: Home Economics Cooperative Education Curriculum Guides I and II, 1983. Mem. NEA, Houston Fedn. Tchrs. Democrat. Roman Catholic. Home: 6714 Foster St Houston TX 77021

PATTERSON, DEBORAH LYNN, research geologist; b. San Francisco, Sept. 6, 1951; d. Raymond John and Donna Lucille (Davey) P. B.A., U. Calif.-Santa Barbara, 1973, M.A., 1978, Ph.D., 1983. Research asst. U. Calif.-Santa Barbara, various times, 1974-81; research micropaleontologist Union Oil Research, Brea, Calif., 1976; field geologist Exxon Minerals U.S.A., Casper, Wyo., 1977; research geologist Exxon Prodn. Research, Houston, 1981—. Contbg. author: The Geology of Baja, Calif., 1984; speaker nat. meetings Geol. Soc. Am., 1979 (nomination best paper). Individual research grantee Union Oil Found., Calif., 1977, Penrose Com. Geol. Soc. Am., 1980, Chevron, Exxon, Gulf, Mobil, Amoco, U. Calif.-Santa Barbara; only woman to conduct field program in Baja, 1974-81. Mem. Am. Assn. Petroleum Geologists (research grantee 1979), Soc. Econ. Paleontologists and Mineralogists, Sigma Xi. Home: 6103 Ludington #939 Houston TX 77035 Office: Exxon Prodn Research Co PO Box 2189 Houston TX 77035

PATTERSON, ELIZABETH JOHNSTON, state senator; b. Columbia, S.C., Nov. 18, 1939; d. Olin DeWitt and Gladys (Atkinson) Johnston; B.A., Columbia Coll., 1961; postgrad. in polit. sci. U. S.C., 1961, 62, 64; m. Dwight Fleming Patterson, Jr., Apr. 15, 1967; children—Dwight Fleming, Olin DeWitt, Catherine Leigh. Pub. affairs officer Peace Corps, Washington, 1962-64; recruiter VISTA, OEO, Washington, 1965-66; state coordinator Head Start and VISTA, OEO, Columbia, 1966-67; tri-county dir. Head Start, Piedmont Community Actions, Spartanburg, S.C., 1967-68; adminstrv. asst. Congressman James R. Mann, Spartanburg, 1969-70; mem. Spartanburg County Council, 1975-76; mem. S.C. State Senate, 1979—. Trustee, Wofford Coll.; bd. dirs. Charles Lea Center, Spartanburg Council on Aging; pres. Spartanburg Democratic Women, 1968; v.p. Spartanburg County Dem. party, 1968-70, sec., 1970-75. Mem. Bus. and Profl. Women's Club, Alpha Kappa Gamma. Methodist. Home: 1275 Partridge Rd Spartanburg SC 29302 Office: 508 Gressette Bldg Columbia SC 29202

PATTERSON, JANET DOERR, banker; b. Rochester, Minn., Oct. 7, 1941; d. Rudy Ernest and Mary Leone (Wilkes) Doerr; student U. Iowa, 1959-61; m. Walter Patterson, Apr. 22, 1978. Dir. mktg. The Drovers Nat. Bank of Chgo., 1976-78; dir. mktg. Lawndale Trust and Savs. Bank, Chgo., 1978, v.p. comml. banking group, 1978-79, pres., chief exec. officer, 1979-83; pres., chief exec. officer Bank of Chgo., 1983—. Episcopalian. Club: Econ. of Chgo. Home: 2819 35th St Oak Brook IL 60521 Office: 1050 W Wilson Ave Chicago IL 60640

PATTERSON, JENNIFER AVRIL KINMOND, dermatologist, researcher, educator; b. Edinburgh, Scotland, Apr. 17, 1952; came to U.S., 1978; d. John Armorer and Marjorie Jane Stephenson (Kinmond) P.; m. Howard Stringer, July 29, 1978. B.Sc. with honors in Physiology, Middlesex Hosp. Med. Sch. U. London, 1972, M.B. B.S., 1975. Diplomate Am. Bd. Dermatology, Am. Bd. Dermatopathology. Intern in medicine, Middlesex Hosp., London, intern in surgery, Cheltenham Gen. Hosp., Eng., 1976-77; resident in medicine Northwick Park Hosp., Harrow, Eng., 1977-78; fellow in dermatopathology, NYU Med. Ctr., 1978-79, teaching asst. in pathology, 1979-80; resident in dermatology, Columbia Presbyn. Med. Ctr., N.Y.C., 1980-82, instr. dermatology, 1982-84, asst. prof. dermatology, 1984—; guest lectr. symposia, hosps., profl. confs. U.S., Eng. Contbr. articles to profl. publs. Mem. Royal Coll. Physicians (lic.), Royal Coll. Surgeons, N.Y. State Med. Soc., N.Y. Acad. Scis., Soc. for Investigative Dermatology. Mem. Ch. of England. Office: Columbia Presbyn Med Assocs 38 E 61st St New York NY 10024

PATTERSON, JOAN ELLEN, educator; b. N.Y.C., May 7, 1950; d. Dennis E. and Josepine H. (Bakszanska) McGlynn; m. Russell A. Patterson, Dec. 20, 1975; children—Thomas Russell, Edward Joseph. A.A., Kingsborough Community Coll., CUNY, 1970, B.A. in Cultural Anthropology, Richmond Coll., 1972; M.S. in Spl. Edn., Adelphi U., 1975. Cert. spl. educator, cert. early childhood educator N.Y. Stte. Head tchr. Hammels-Arverne Day Care, Rockaway Beach, N.Y., 1973-75; therapeutic tchr. Kennedy Child Care Ctr., N.Y.C., 1975-78; ednl. dir. Tot Lot, Inc., New Hyde Park, N.Y., 1984-85; head tchr. Assn. for Children with Down Syndrome, Bellmore, N.Y., 1985—; cons. in spl. edn., early childhood edn.; coordinator program St. Joseph's Religious Edn. Ctr., Babylon, N.Y., 1984—, also lectr. women's studies; tchr., organizer presch. CCD program St. Camillus Ch., Rockaway Beach, 1972-76. Dist. rep. St. Joseph's Parish Council, Babylon, 1980-81; organizer Talking Over Understanding Children with Handicaps, St. Joseph's Ch., 1981, coordinator parish blood driv, 1981. Mem. Early Childhood Edn. Council Suffolk/Nassau County, Nat. Assn. Edn. of Young Children, Nat. Assn. Female Execs. Democrat. Roman Catholic. Avocations: needlecrafts; hiking; beachcombing. Home: 16 Barberry Rd West Islip NY 11795 Office: 2616 Martin Ave Bellmore NY 11710

PATTERSON, JUDITH ELAINE BONDS, mfg. co. personnel exec.; b. Columbia, S.C., Oct. 17, 1952; d. Edgar and Mary Evelyn (Heath) Bonds; grad. Aiken County Sch. Nursing, 1972; student Aiken Tech. Coll., 1976-78, U. S.C., Aiken, 1981—; m. William Kim Patterson, Sept. 21, 1975; children—William Richard Holley II, Amber Elizabeth Leigh. Operating room nurse Aiken County Hosp., Aiken, S.C., 1972-74; indsl. nurse Harvey Hubbell, Inc., Aiken, 1974-78; personnel adminstr. Beecham Products, Aiken, 1978—. Mem. budget and evaluation com. United Way Aiken County, 1981-82, in-plant chmn., 1976, 77, 79, 80, 81; chmn. public edn. Aiken County chpt. Am. Cancer Soc., 1975. Aiken Bus. and Profl. Women's Club ednl. grantee, 1971. Mem. Am. Soc. Personnel Adminstrs., Nat. Assn. Female Execs., Beta Sigma Phi (Girl of Yr. 1979). Baptist. Office: Beecham Products 65 Windham Blvd Aiken SC 29801

PATTERSON, KATHERINE HULEN, pharmacist; b. Caracas, Venezuela, Dec. 21, 1947; d. Joseph T. and Antoinette (deLarroque) H.; m. Gary Wayne Patterson, May 31, 1969; children—Katherine Denise, Gary Wayne. B.F.A., U. Miss., 1969; B.S., U. Houston, 1980. Pharmacist, mgr. Superex Drugs, Houston, 1980-81, Walgreen Drugs, Houston, 1981-84, Gordon Drugs, Houston, 1984—. Mem. Spring Branch PTA, Houston, 1974—; sec. Spring Shadows Women's Club, 1973-74; rep. Spring Shadows Civic Assn., 1976-77. Mem. Am. Pharm. Assn., Tex. Pharm. Assn., Harris County Pharm. Assn. (bd. councillors 1984-86), Alpha Delta Pi. Republican. Roman Catholic. Clubs: U. Miss., Real Estate Investment (Houston). Avocations: swimming; tennis; reading; cooking. Home: 2819 Shadowdale Dr Houston TX 77043

PATTERSON, LUCY PHELPS, educator; b. Dallas, Tex., June 21, 1931; d. John C. and Florence L. (Harllee) Phelps; A.B., Howard U., 1950; M.S.W., U. Denver, 1963; m. Albert S. Patterson, Nov. 25, 1950; 1 son, Albert Harllee. Tabulating machine operator supr. Dept. Commerce, Bur. Census, Washington, 1950-52, Dept. Navy, Bur. of Ships, Washington, 1952-54; caseworker dept. public welfare Dallas, 1954-61, casework supr., 1963-68; dir. Interagy. Project, Dallas, 1968-71; exec. dir. Dallas County Child Care Council, 1971-73; planning dir. Community Council of Greater Dallas, 1973-74; asst. prof. and field work coordinator N. Tex. State U., 1974-78; Ethel Carter Branham prof. Bishop Coll., Dallas, 1978—, dir. social work, 1978—; cons. to Creative Learning Center, Rhodes Terrace Pre-sch., Head Start Consultation Register, Inst. Urban Studies, So. Meth. U. Councilwoman, City of Dallas, 1973-80. Recipient Outstanding Woman award Women's Center of Dallas, 1978, Public Service award Elite Newspaper, 1978; named Mother of Yr., 1979. Mem. Nat. Assn. Social Workers, Acad. Cert. Social Workers, Council on Social Work Edn., Tex. Assn. Coll. Tchrs., Nat. Assn. Black Social Workers, Dallas County Mental Health Assn., NOW, Tex. Black Polit. Caucus, Tex. Assn. of Women Elected Ofcls., Women's Council of Dallas County, LWV, Nat. Council of Negro Women, Council on Consumer Edn., Alpha Kappa Alpha. Republican. Methodist. Club: Altrusa. Weekly columnist Post Tribune, 1973-80, The Dallas Weekly, 1973-80. Home: 2779 Almeda Dr Dallas TX 75216 Office: 3837 Simpson Stuart Rd Dallas TX 75241

PATTERSON, MARGARET JEAN, lawyer; b. Casper, Wyo, July 9, 1933; d. Roy Gilbert Currie and Clara Charlotte (Stevenson) Bartshe; m. Burwell Spotswood Patterson, Jan. 1, 1958 (dec. 1975); 1 son, Bruce Burwell. B.S. in Law, U. Wyo., Laramie, 1955, J.D., 1973. Bar: Wyo. 1974, Okla. 1974, D.C. Staff mem U.S. Senator Frank A Barrett, Washington, 1957-58; legal aid Dawson, Nagel, Sherman & Howard, Denver, 1958-60; first dep. clk. Natrona County Dist. Ct. (Wyo.), Casper, 1963-71; mgr. collection div., atty. credit card ctr. Phillips Petroleum Co., Bartlesville, Okla., 1975—. Mem. Desk and Derrick, Jane Phillips Sorority, AAUW, ABA. Home: 4812 Brookline Dr Bartlesville OK 74006 Office: Phillips Petroleum Co 5th & Keeler Sts Bartlesville OK 74005

PATTERSON, MARILYN JEAN, petroleum services company executive; b. Dallas, Nov. 2, 1943; d. J.D. and Mary Lois (Powell) Williams; m. Richard Lester Patterson, Aug. 19, 1967 (div. 1979); 1 child, Corbett Layne Patterson. B.S. in Edn., Abilene Christian U., 1966. Tchr. sch. systems, Abilene and Dallas, 1966-70; polit. liason customer relations R.S. Tapp & Co., Lubbock, Tex., 1976-80; exec. v.p. Increased Energy Corp., Coleman, Tex., 1981-83; pres. Increased Resources Corp., Abilene, 1983-84, PetroScis. Internat. Inc., Abilene, 1984—; cons. in field. Contbr. articles to profl. jours., lectr. profl. confs. Mem. spl. task force Disabled Children Christian Homes, Abilene, 1985—; chmn. capital campaign Abilene Christian Schs., 1985—, exec. bd. trustees, 1985—; adminstrv. bd. Christian Homes of Abilene, 1985—. Named in Portrait in Oil, Abilene Reporter News, 1985. Mem. Nat. Assn. Female Execs., Tex. Found. Women's Resources (Leadership Tex. 1986). Clubs: Women's, Women for Abilene, Desk and Derrick, Republican Women; South Plains Republican (founder); Christian University (Abilene). Avocation: cooking. Home: 2 Hilliard Cir Abilene TX 79601 Office: PetroScis Internat Inc 514 Petroleum Ctr Abilene TX 79601

PATTERSON, MARJORIE SCOTT SELLERS, librarian; b. Decatur, Ala., Apr. 18, 1925; d. Clyde R. and Eula W. (Lewis) Scott; student Kansas City Met. Jr. Coll., Park Coll.; m. Leonard S. Sellers, Nov. 25, 1943 (div.); children—Carol, Steve, Mark; m. Thomas W. Patterson, 1983. Substitute and library asst. Oak Park Sr. High Sch., North Kansas City, Mo., 1968-71; periodicals bank coordinator Kansas City Regional Council for Higher Edn., 1971-74; co-founder, dir. Mid-Am. inter-library services, interlibrary loans librarian Park Coll., Parkville, Mo., 1974-81; founder Access to Info. Services Assos., 1981—; owner, operator Bell Rd. Barn Book, rare and out-of-print books, 1981—; mem. N. Central Evaluation Com. Mem. ALA, Mo. Library Assn., Kans. Library Assn., Mo. Assn. Coll. and Research Libraries, Mountain Plains Library Assn., Am. Assn. for Higher Edn., Oral History Assn., Kansas City Women's C. of C. Methodist. Editor: The Loaner newsletter, 1974-80, Mid Am. Shelflist newsletter, 1981—. Address: care Gen Delivery Sewanee TN 37375

PATTERSON, PAMELA DOROTHY MESSMORE, pension fund administrator; b. N.Y.C., Dec. 24, 1946; d. Francis B. and Dorothy R. Weeks (Heckle) Messmore; B.A. in Econs. summa cum laude, Fordham U., 1976, M.B.A. in Mgmt. Acctg., 1978; div. Fin. analyst Eastern Air Lines, Inc., Miami, Fla., 1979-81; asst. mgr. pension fund trusts and investments ITT Corp., N.Y.C., 1977-79, mgr. pension trusts, 1983—; v.p. Messmore & Damon, Inc., N.Y.C., 1981-83. Mem. Fordham U. Alumni Assn., DAR, Japan Soc. Republican. Office: 320 Park Ave New York NY 10022

PATTERSON, PATRICIA DUNN, electronics corporation executive; b. Dallas, Aug. 28, 1946. B.A. in Communications cum laude, U. Tex.-Dallas, 1981; A.A., Eastfield Coll., Dallas, 1978; postgrad. So. Meth. U., 1981-85. Editor, Geophys. Service Inc., Tex. Instruments, Dallas, 1980-83, mktg. communications adminstr. equipment group, 1983—; community access producer Warner-Amex Qube Cable, Dallas, 1983—. Contbr. poetry, short story to lit. mags. Univ. scholar U. Tex.-Dallas, 1979-80. Mem. Women in Communications, U.S.A. Film Festival, Third Coast Screenwriters (pres. 1983—). Home: 4725 Oakwood St Garland TX 75043 Office: Texas Instruments/Equipment Group 8505 Forest Ln PO Box 660246 MS 3127 Dallas TX 75266

PATTERSON, PEGGY JEAN, real estate broker; b. Macon County, N.C., Nov. 10, 1940; d. Jay B. and Agnes Aletha (Saunders) Moore; student Southwestern Tech. Coll., 1974; m. Morris Patterson, Aug. 23, 1970; children—Kenneth Douglas, Aletha Darlene. Sec., John Phelan Real Estate, Highlands, N.C., 1973-74; broker Jones Real Estate, Franklin, N.C., 1974-75; owner, pres., sec. Patterson Realty, Inc., Franklin, 1977—. Mem. adv. com. South Western Tech. Coll. Recipient Membership award Franklin Area C. of C., 1980; Beautification award Franklin Garden Club, 1980. Mem. C. of C. (dir. 1980), Better Bus. Bur., N.C. Assn. Realtors (dir. 1981—), Franklin Bd. Realtors (sec. 1979, pres. 1981), Nat. Assn. Female Execs., Nat. Assn. Realtors. Republican. Baptist. Clubs: Merchants Assn., Bus. and Profl. Women's. Home: Route 1 Box 76 Otto NC 28763 Office: 146 Palmer St Franklin NC 28734

PATTERSON, PEGGY PRACHT, science laboratory administrator; b. Oakland, Calif., Dec. 23, 1947; d. Loren Eugene and Frankie Ethelene (Dupree) P.; B.A. in Music, Calif. State U., Hayward, 1970, student in Bus. Adminstrn.; 1 son, John Thomas Yeandle. Computer operator Haskins & Sells, C.P.A.s, San Francisco, 1974-75; staff asst. to dir. Lawrence Berkeley Lab., 1976—. Mem. Nat. Assn. Female Execs., Nat. Notary Assn. Office: Lawrence Berkeley Lab Calif 1 Cyclotron Rd Berkeley CA 94720

PATTERSON, POLLY REILLY (MRS. W. RAY PATTERSON), ret. communications co. exec., civic worker; b. Wilkinsburg, Pa.; d. Thomas L. and Margaret (Coughey) Reilly; student U. Pitts.; m. W. Ray Patterson, Sept. 2, 1943. With Bell Telephone Co. of Pa., Pitts., 1925-71, beginning as clk., successively various mgmt. positions, 1935-64, staff asso. pub. relations staff, 1965-71; dir. Chatham Village Homes, Inc., 1973-76. Asst. treas. Allegheny County Soc. for Crippled Children, 1962-66, v.p., 1966-70; bd. dirs. Jr. Achievement, Inc. of S.W. Pa., 1950-71, Pitts. YWCA, 1964-72, Pa. Soc. Crippled Children and Adults, 1960-68; mem. nat. ho. of dels. Nat. Soc. for Crippled Children and Adults, 1965-67; ann. mem. United Way Allegheny County, 1972—. Named One of Pitts.'s Ten Outstanding Women, Pitts. Sun Telegraph, 1959, Pitts. Advt. Woman of Yr., 1958; recipient Crystal Prism award Am. Advt. Fedn., 1972, 75. Mem. Assn. Pitts. Clubs (dir. 1946-81, pres. 1953), Altrusa Internat. (pres. Pitts. club 1950-51), Pitts. Advt. Club (v.p., sec. 1929-69), Bus. and Profl. Women's Club Pitts., Telephone Pioneers. Home: 402 Olympia Rd Pittsburgh PA 15211

PATTERSON, REBECCA GAIL, public relations executive; b. Little Rock, Mar. 9, 1952; d. Alexander and Wanza Louise (Hoover) Humphrey; m. William R. Kennan, Mar. 24, 1976 (div. Sept. 1982); children—Jeffrey Maitland, Matthew Alexander; m. Ronny Patrick Patterson, July 23, 1983. B.A. in Speech Communications, U. Ark., 1974, M.A. in Speech, 1975; postgrad. Tex. Tech. U., 1980, West Tex. State U., 1981-82. Tchr. Rogers Pub. Schs., Ark., 1975-76, Moore Pub. Schs., Okla., 1977-79; recruiter Tex. State Tech. Inst., Amarillo, 1981-82, dir. pub. info. and news, 1982—; chmn. Tex. State Tech. Inst. Tex. Ind. Assn., Amarillo, 1984-86. Mem. Nat. Assn. Vocat. Tech. Edn. Communicators (sec.-treas. 1984-85, conf. coordinator 1986; award of merit 1984), Nat. Sch. Pub. Relations Assn., Internat. Assn. Bus. Communicators, Tex. Sch. Pub. Relations Assn., Amarillo C. of C., Amarillo Women's Network. Mem. Ch. of Christ. Home: 5703 Winkler Amarillo TX 79109 Office: Tex State Tech Inst Pub Info PO Box 11035 Amarillo TX 79111

PATTERSON, VALERIE LYLES, systems analyst; b. Miami, Fla., Oct. 27, 1955; d. Benny Lee Lyles and Shirley Agatha (Jones) Lyles McLean; m. Abdullah Jabril Abdul-Hakeem, Oct. 27, 1976; children—Yaasmeen Ruqqya, Emahn Jamillah. A.A., Miami-Dade Coll., 1977; B.S. in Health Services Adminstrn., Fla. Internat. U., 1981. Pharmacy clerk Grand Drugs Store, Miami, Fla., 1972-76; pharmacy technician Bapt. Hosp., Miami, 1976-78, Cedars Med. Ctr., Miami, 1979-82; tng. instr. Cedars Med. Ctr., Miami. Community CPR instr. Am. Heart Assn., Miami, 1983-84; loaned exec. United Way Dade County, Miami, 1983, panel mem., 1984-85; sec. Miami Black Arts Council, 1974; bd. dirs. Cedars Credit Union. Mem. Fla. Soc. Hosp. Pharmacists (state supportive personnel com. 1980-81), Nat. Assn. Female Execs., Am. Soc. Tng. and Devel., Fla. Internat. U. Alumni Assn., Am. Coll. Hosp. Adminstrs., AAUW. Democrat. Moslem. Office: Cedars Med Ctr 1400 NW 12th Ave Miami FL 33136

PATTERSON, VIRGINIA CATHARINE, religious organization executive; b. N.Mex., Jan. 23, 1931; d. Edward Cecil and Edith Elizabeth (Roweton) P. B.A., U. Tulsa, 1953; M.A. Bible/Missions, Columbia Bible Coll. (S.C.), 1956; M.S. Elem. Ed., Okla. State U., 1963; Ed.D., No. Ill. U., DeKalb, 1978. Tchr., recreation dir. Girls Indsl. Sch., Columbia, S.C., 1954-57; tchr., asst. prin., Kent Acad., Nigeria, 1958-68; publ. dir. Pioneer Girls, Inc., Wheaton, Ill., 1969-70; pres. Pioneer Ministries, Inc., Wheaton, Ill., 1970—; adj. prof. Wheaton Coll. Grad. Sch. (Ill.), 1979—. Author: A Touch of God, 1979. Presbyterian. Office: Pioneer Ministries 27W130 St Charles Rd Wheaton IL 60187

PATTERSON, VIRGINIA GOODWIN, social worker; b. Nashville, Feb. 21, 1917; d. Marsh and Lena Grace (Givens) Goodwin; B.S., Peabody Coll., 1968; M.S.W., U. Tenn., 1970; lic. pvt. social work practitioner; lic. social worker; m. Fletcher Woodall Patterson, June 17, 1940; 1 dau., Judith Ellen Patterson Various secretarial positions, 1934-43; dir. day camp Cumberland Valley Girl Scout council, Nashville, summers 1953-62; sec. Centenary Methodist Community Center, Nashville, 1961-64; dir. resident camp Sycamore Hills, Ashland City, Tenn., summers 1963-65; case worker United Methodist Community Center, 1970-71; social case worker, dir. day care for elderly Sr. Citizens, Inc., Nashville, 1971—; v.p. Cumberland Valley Girl Scout council, 1963-64; youth tchr., counselor Dalewood Meth. Ch., 1950—, pres. Women's Soc. Christian Service. Pres. Isaac Litton High Sch. PTA, Nashville, 1959-61. Recipient Thanks badge Girl Scouts, 1961. Mem. Nat. Assn. Social Workers (past chpt. registrar, corr. sec.), Tenn. Fedn. Aging (pres. 1982-84, sec. 1984-86), Nat. Council Aging, Pi Gamma Mu (past chpt. sec.). Republican. Lodges: Soroptimists of Nashville (pres. 1986), Civitan. Contbr. articles to profl. jours. Home: 1709 Sherwood Ln Nashville TN 37216 Office: 1801 Broadway Nashville TN 37203

PATTERSON, VIRGINIA LOUISE, diversified business equipment company executive; b. Chgo., Jan. 31, 1945; d. Paul E. and Alice (Gumbrell) P. B.S., U. Ill.-Urbana, 1967. Systems engr. IBM, Palo Alto, Calif., 1971-74, mktg. support rep., San Francisco, 1974-76, Atlanta, 1976-78, systems engring. mgr., Lubbock, Tex., 1978-81, mgr. VM products support, Irving, Tex., 1981-82, mgr. nat. customer assistance ctr., 1983—. Artist, fine art batik, 1978-83. Advisor, San Francisco Jr. Achievement, 1974-76. Republican.

PATTERSON, VIVIAN ROGERS, banker; b. Wake County, N.C., June 2, 1924; d. Lattie Raymond and Dala Earnal (Prince) Rogers; B.S.C., N.C. Coll., 1951, M.S.C., 1961; postgrad. Stonier Grad. Sch. Banking, Rutgers U., 1978, Cannon's Trust Sch., U. N.C., 1981; m. Cecil L. Patterson, Apr. 1, 1956. With Mechanics and Farmers Bank, Durham, N.C., 1944—, asst. v.p., 1967-68, v.p., 1968—, corp. sec., 1979—, trust officer, 1980—; mem. adv. council Sch. Bus., N.C. Central U., Durham; dir. REMCA, Inc. Past mem. fin. com. Harriet Tubman br. YWCA, Durham; past sec., 1st v.p. Durham chpt. Am. Cancer Soc.; past unit leader Durham United Fund; pres. bd. dirs. Durham YWCA, ARC; mem. vestry St. Titus Episcopal Ch., Durham; active Durham chpt. ARC; Ch. Women del. Gen. Conv., Episcopal Ch., 1973, lay del., 1982. Mem. Am Inst. Banking, Nat. Assn. Bank Women, Durham Council Estate Planning, Durham Bus. and Profl. Women's Club, NAACP, N.C. Central U. Alumni Assn., Delta Sigma Theta. Clubs: Lawson St. Community, Downtown. Home: 409 Lawson St Durham NC 27707 Office: PO Box 1932 Durham NC 27702

PATTERSON, ZELLA JUSTINA BLACK, home economist, historian; b. Coyle, Okla., May 20, 1909; d. Thomas and Mary Elizabeth (Horst) Black; B.S. in Home Econs. Edn., Langston (Okla.) U., 1937; M.S., Colo. State U., Ft. Collins, 1941; postgrad. U. Calif.-Berkeley, Okla. State U.; m. George W. Patterson, Dec. 24, 1946 (dec.). Elem. sch. tchr., 1931-34; extension worker, 1934-36; vocat. home econs. tchr., supervising tchr., 1937-60; mem. faculty Langston U., 1937-46, 60-72, prof. home econs. and home econs. edn., 1965-72, chmn. dept., 1965-72; family living specialist coop. extension Okla. State U.-U.S. Dept. Agr., 1972-74; mem. Langston Community Edn. Adv. Com.; bd. dirs. Logan County Hist. Soc.; mem. Diamond Jubilee Commn. Okla. Author: Langston University: A History, 1979, A Garden of Poems, 1978; also family histories. Recipient Honor Alumna award Colo. State U., 1976, Outstanding Woman award Langston U., 1979; named ambassador of Good Will; named to Hall of Fame, Nat. Langston U. Alumni Assn., 1983. Mem. Okla. Edn. Assn. (Outstanding Educator Recognition award 1973), Am. Home Econs. Assn., Okla. Home Econs. Assn., Okla. Ret. Soc., Nat. Ret. Tchrs. Assn., Guthrie Arts and Humanities Council, Okla. Hist. Soc. (bd. dirs. historic preservation com. 1984—, bd. dirs., chmn. Black heritage com.), Alpha Kappa Alpha. Republican. Baptist. Clubs: Langston Beautiful, Order Eastern Star, Langston-Coyle Bus. and Profl. Women's. Author: Churches of Langston. Contbr. poem to anthology. Address: PO Box 96 Langston OK 73050

PATTISON, BRENDA LEONE, social worker; b. Converse, La.; d. William Wilson and Nellie (Ebarb) Leone; m. Guffey Lynn Pattison, June 20, 1981 (div. 1985). B.S., Northwestern State U., 1980. Dental asst., Many, La., 1970-76, med. sec., 1976-81; social worker, program specialist Sabine Assn. for Retarded Citizens, Many, 1981—. Named Miss La. V.F.W., 1970-71. Mem. Am. Assn. Mental Deficiency, La. Assn. Retarded Citizens, Nat. Assn. for Retarded Citizens. Avocations: aerobics; dancing; horseback riding; swimming; skiing. Home: Route 1 Box 1W Zwolle LA 71486 Office: Sabine Assn for Retarded Citizens 545 W San Antonio Ave Many LA 71449

PATTISON-LEHNING, BARBARA JEANNE, educational ombudsman, marketing consultant; b. Tacoma, Wash., Jan. 2, 1936; d. Richard Stanley and Elizabeth June (Miller) Bennatts; m. Thomas Wesley Lehning, Aug. 26, 1983; children—Mark, Scott, Kimberly, Trishawn. B.A. in Communications, U. Wash., 1972; M. Bus., City U., Seattle, 1979. Promotion dir. Sta. KIRO-TV, Seattle, 1960-67; editor TV Guide, Seattle, 1967-73; legis. asst. Seattle councilman, 1973-76; chmn. internat. conf. Assn. for Children with Learning Disabilities, Seattle, 1976; ombudsman Wash. State Parent Community Relations Project, Seattle, 1976—; cons. Rising Star Enterprise, Seattle, 1983—; co-owner, Cheese Factory Stores, Tacoma, Wash., 1984—. Author, producer various video tapes and brochures. Strategist, Re-elect Councilwoman V. Galle, Seattle, 1984, Re-elect Councilwoman J. William, 1984; county coordinator Re-elect State Supt., King County, 1984. Recipient Award of Merit, Wash. State Spl. Edn., 1983; named Outstanding Citizen, Wash. Assn. Children, 1982. Mem. Wash. Press Assn. (sec. 1982-83, pres. 1983-84, cons., Woman of Achievement award 1984), Wash. Soc. for Intelligence Tng. (fund-raiser 1986, cons.), Wash. Generals, Gov.'s Com. Employment (chmn. pub. relations and edn. coms. 1982-85), Women of Variety (sec., v.p. 1982—), Seattle C. of C. (small bus. com. 1986, activist 1984—). Democrat. Avocations: biking; reading. Home: 9319 42d Ave NE Seattle WA 98115

PATTON, CONNIE GARCIA, educator; b. Luarca, Spain, Nov. 7, 1941; d. Antonio Garcia and Palmira Garcia (Lavin) Mendez; B.A., U. N.Mex., 1964, M.A., 1966; doctoral candidate U. Kans., 1984; m. Michael G. Patton, July 5, 1970; children—Michael Anthony, Ryan Blake. Instr., Peace Corps, 1964-66; asso. prof. fgn. lang. Emporia (Kans.) State U., 1966—; court translator Lyon County Courthouse, 1974—. Bd. dirs. Sexual Offense Services, 1974-78; v.p. Big Bro.-Big Sister, 1977-79. Ford Found. grad. fellow, 1963-66; NEH grantee, 1976, 78; recipient Xi Phi Outstanding Faculty award, 1976, 77; named Outstanding Young Kansan, Jaycees, 1977. Mem. Am. Assn. Tchrs. Spanish and Portuguese, MLA, AAUP, Sigma Delta Pi. Author: Spanish Vocabulary Units, 1975; Castles in Spain, 1984. Home: 2919 Monterey Dr Emporia KS 66801 Office: 1200 Commercial St Emporia KS 66801

PATTON, JESSICA, designer; b. N.Y.C., July 13, 1920; d. Frederick Henry and Jessie Davis (Woolley) P.; A.B., Stephens Coll., 1939; B.A., Mich. State U., 1941; postgrad. Am. Acad. Dramatic Art, 1941-42; m. George Barkentin, Apr. 21, 1942; children—Perii Alexandra, Pamela Meredith. Fashion model, 1942-47; fashion cons. for films Stage Door Canteen, 1943, Cover Girl, 1944; fashion editor Jr. Bazaar, 1947-48, Good Housekeeping, 1949-51; fashion cons. Mademoiselle mag., 1947-53; prodn. designer for advt. and indsl. films, 1951-61; partner Van Glintenkamp Enterprises, prods. docu-dramas and indsl. films, N.Y.C., 1961—; v.p. White O'Morn Film Corp., 1977—. Recipient Silver Phoenix for film Zebra, Atlanta Film Festival, 1975, Gold medal for Nanette: An Aside, V.I. Internat. Film Festival, 1978. Mem. Am. Soc. Mag. Photographers, Salmagundi Club, Nat. Arts Club. Office: 5 E 16th St New York NY 10003

PATTON, JOANNA, advertising agency executive; b. Quincy, Ill., Dec. 20, 1946; d. John H. and Jane Vandike P.; student Stetson U., 1964-66, Fla. State U., 1966-67. Para legal, Miami, Fla., 1968-74; exec. asst. Louis Nizer, Atty., N.Y.C., 1974-77; adminstrv. asst. to pres. Cosmair, N.Y.C., 1977-78, mgr. public relations, 1978, dir. public relations, 1978-79, mktg. dir., 1980-81; owner Joanna Patton Advt., N.Y.C., 1982-83; ptnr. Levinger & Patton, N.Y.C., 1983—; ptnr. Cotas Minard Patton McIver, Inc. 1986—. Mem. Fashion Group, Advt. Women N.Y. Office: 405 Lexington Ave New York NY 10174

PATTON, LORRAINE ANN, nurse, cosmetics consultant; b. Douglas, W.Va., Feb. 1, 1944; d. Willard A. and Ethel Mae (Reel) Day; m. John William Shields, Feb. 19, 1964 (div. Mar. 1978); children—John David, Richard William, Vivian Ann; m. Robert Lee Patton, May 12, 1983. Assoc. Nursing, Fairmont State Coll., 1981. Med. asst. Dr. Gene Harlow, Grafton, W.Va., 1972-77; ins. clk. Fairmont Gen., W.Va., 1977-78; truck loader United Parcel Service, Fairmont, 1978; switch board operator Fairmont Gen., 1978-81, nurse, 1981—. Avocations: fishing; camping; sewing; knitting; crocheting; traveling. Home: 1014 Fay St Fairmont WV 26554 Office: Fairmont Gen Hosp 1325 Locust Ave Fairmont WV 26554

PATTON, MARGARET ELIZABETH, banker; b. Galax, Va., Mar. 20, 1946; d. Carl Theile and Mary Alice (Williams) Meyertons; m. Howard R. Patton, Jan. 20, 1968 (div. Dec. 1982). B.S., La. State U., 1968; grad. diploma Am. Savs. and Loan Inst., 1973. Tchr., Houston Ind. Sch. Dist., 1968-69; installment loan officer Houston First Savs. Assn., 1969-74; v.p., mgr. First City Nat. Bank, Houston, 1974—. Chmn. bd. Delia Stewart Jazz Dance Co., Houston, 1982-85; bus. vol. for arts C. of C., Houston, 1982—. Mem. Am. Savs. and Loan Inst. (adv. gov. 1973), Houston Savs. and Loan Inst. (2d v.p. 1973, program chmn. mkg. info. group 1985-86), Tex. Mariners Cruising Assn. Republican. Episcopalian. Clubs: Seabrook Sailing (sec. 1976-77), Houston Ctr. (Houston). Home: Mariner Village No 51 4747 Nasa Rd Seabrook TX 77586 Office: First City Nat Bank 1001 Main St Houston TX 77002

PATTON, ROSEMARY, property management company executive; b. Dallas, Nov. 4, 1939; d. Homer and Effie Lorene (Jones) Platt; m. James Doyle Patton, May 27, 1979 (div. July 1983). Student pub. schs. Asst. v.p. Lincoln Property Co., Dallas, 1974-85; v.p., chief operating officer Dalcor Property Mgmt., 1985—. Republican. Home: 3535 Webb Chapel 1404 Dallas TX 75220

PAUL, ALIDA RUTH, arts and crafts educator; b. San Antonio, May 30, 1953; d. Richard Irving and Anne Louise (Holman) Paul. B.S. in Edn., Southwest Tex. State U., 1975; M.Ed., U. Houston, 1984. Cert. tchr., Tex. Tchr. art and crafts Houston Ind. Sch. Dist., 1975—. Mem. Am. Assn. Counseling and Devel., Tex. Assn. Counseling and Devel. Republican. Episcopalian. Home: 17727 Wolfhollow St Houston TX 77084

PAUL, EVE W., lawyer; b. N.Y.C., June 16, 1930; d. Leo and Tamara (Sogolow) Weinschenker; A.B., Cornell U., 1950; J.D., Columbia U., 1952; m. Robert D. Paul, Apr. 9, 1952; children—Jeremy Ralph, Sarah Elizabeth. N.Y. 1952, Conn. 1960. Asso., Botein, Hays, Sklar & Herzberg, N.Y.C., 1952-54, Bernard D. Cahn, N.Y.C., 1954-56; pvt. practice law, Stamford, Conn., 1960-70; staff atty. Legal Aid Soc., N.Y.C., 1970-71; assoc. Greenbaum, Wolff & Ernst, N.Y.C., 1972-78; gen. counsel Conn. Women's Bank, Greenwich, 1974-77; v.p. legal affairs Planned Parenthood Fedn. of Am., N.Y.C., 1979—; lectr. in field. Trustee, Cornell U., 1979-84; mem. Stamford Planning Bd., 1967-70. Mem. N.Y.C. Bar Assn., ABA, Conn. Bar Assn., Stamford Bar Assn., N.Y. County Lawyers Assn., Nat. Assn. Women Lawyers, U.S. Trademark Assn. Contbr. articles to profl. jours. Office: 810 7th Ave New York NY 10019

PAUL, GRACE, retired medical technologist, author; b. Liberal, Kans., Mar. 12, 1908; d. David and Myrtle Helen (Brewer) P.; student Tulsa U., 1930-36, Auburn U., 1948, Columbia U., 1949-51. Med. technologist St. Johns Hosp., Tulsa, 1930-36, VA Hosp., Wadsworth, Kans., 1947-48; plant quarantine insp. U.S. Dept. Agr., N.Y.C., 1948-51; claims examiner Social Security Adminstrn., Balt., 1956-71; market research interviewer Response Analysis, Princeton, N.J., 1973-76. Vol. worker United Way of Temple (Tex.), 1974—, Cultural Activities Center, Youth Services Bur., Ret. Sr. Vol. Program; active CAC Humanities Council of Temple, 1972-84. Served with WAC, 1944-46. Recipient Central Tex. Jefferson award, 1983; named Outstanding Ch. Vol. of Temple, 1986. Mem. Am. Soc. Med. Technologists, Entomol. Soc. Am., Internat. Platform Assn. Presbyn. Club: Business and Professional Women's. Author: Your Future in Medical Technology, 1962; A Short Course in Skilled Supervision, 1965, contbr. to Environ. Engr.'s Handbook, vol. III, 1975. Address: 705 N Main St Temple TX 76501

PAUL, JOYCE WERTHMAN, management consultant; b. Detroit, Oct. 31, 1941; d. Alfred J. and Mary L. (Janssen) Werthman; student public schs., Warren, Mich.; m. Robert A. Paul, Sept. 23, 1961; children—Kathleen, Carol, Brian. Sales mgr. Tupperware Home Parties, Detroit, 1964-71; distbr. Act II Jewelry Co., Orlando, Fla., 1974-76; sales mgr. Deco Plants Co., Detroit, 1976-79, nat. sales counselor, St. Louis, 1979-81; mgmt. cons. The Joyce Paul Co., Rochester, Mich., 1981—; motivational speaking specialist. Vol., Mich. Spl. Olympics, 1978-82. Mem. The Direct Selling Assn. Author: The Unit Leaders Growing Guide, 1980, others. Address: 5953 Barbara Circle Roanoke VA 24018

PAULEY, JANE, TV journalist; b. Indpls., Oct. 31, 1950; m. Garry Trudeau, 1980; children—Ross and Rachel (twins). B.A. in Polit. Sci., Ind. U., 1971; D. Journalism (hon.), DePauw U., 1978. Reporter, WISH-TV, Indpls., co-anchor mid-day news reports and anchor weekend news reports; co-anchor nightly news WMAQ-TV, Chgo., 1975-76; on-air staff The Today Show, 1976—; a prin. newscaster NBC News Update, 1977—; co-anchor Early Today (NBC News); prepares and delivers Money Matters (NBC); Monday-Friday anchor NYT News, NBC Radio Network. Office: care NBC News Today 30 Rockefeller Plaza New York NY 10020*

PAULI, LYDIA LYGIA BOKS (MRS. BENNO PAULI), retired physician; b. Vladivostok, Russia; d. Alois and Tatiana (Sapilov) Boks; m. Benno Pauli, Oct. 11, 1952. B.S., Gymnasium, Czechoslovakia; M.D., U. Graz, Austria, 1950. Rotating intern St. Johns Episcopal Hosp., N.Y.C., 1950-51; pediatric intern Johns Hopkins Hosp., Balt., 1951-53, asst. resident, 1953-54, fellow in pediatrics, 1954-57, assoc. Epilepsy Clinic, 1955-57, assoc. dir., 1957-73, cons. convulsive disorders for comprehensive health care, 1967-70; instr. pediatrics Johns Hopkins Sch. Medicine, Balt., 1957-63, asst. prof., 1963—, assoc. dir. Samuel Livingston Epilepsy Diagnostic and Treatment Center, 1973-75; cons. on convulsive disorders Md. Dept. Health, 1957—; cons. Md. Dept. Vocat. Rehab., 1957-77. Contbg. author: Comprehensive Textbook of Psychiatry, 1967, 3d rev. edit., 1980. Bd. dirs. Chesapeake Assn. for Epilepsy. Recipient 1st prize of exhibit Am. Acad. Neurology, 1962, Gold award Am. Psychiat. Assn., 1967 Citation for outstanding service Gov. Md., 1981. Mem. AMA, N.Y. Acad. Scis., Am. Epilepsy Soc., Md. Soc for Research, Balt. Med. and Chirurg. Soc.; asso. Am. Acad. Neurology, Am. Acad. Pediatrics, Balt. Neurol. Soc. Research and publs. on exptl. anti-convulsive drugs, heredity in epilepsy, socio-econ. aspects and employment in epilepsy. Home: 6651 Loch Hill Rd Baltimore MD 21239

PAULIN, ANNE MEREDITH, medical salesman; b. Richmond, Va., Dec. 15, 1954; d. Lehan Bernard and Thelma Monroe (Sutton) Paulin. B.A. in Polit. Sci., Agnes Scott Coll., 1977. Territory mgr. Kendall Co. div. Colgate Palmolive, Atlanta, 1979-81; cardiopulmonary system specialist Baxter Travenol Labs, Atlanta, 1981-83; terr. mgr. Deseret div. Warner Lambert, Atlanta, 1983—; pres., owner Hermelon, Atlanta, 1982—. Contbr. articles to profl. jours. Mem. Atlanta Ballet, Soc., 1983—, Atlanta Ballet Guild, 1982—; mem. Jr. Com. Atlanta Symphony Orch., 1980—; bd. dirs. Terpsichore, 1983; bd. dirs., v.p. City Ctr. Dance Theatre, 1981-83; mem. High Mus. Art, 1973—, High Mus. Art Young Careers, 1983—, King and Queen County Hist. Soc., 1971—; charter mem. New High Mus. Art, 1982—; mem. jr. com. Shepherd Spinal Ctr., 1983—. Named Charles A. Dana Found. scholar, 1976. Mem. Nat. Assn. Female Execs., Atlanta Hist. Soc., Current Historians, Ga. Trust for Historic Preservation, Arts Festival Soc., High Mus., Alpha Sigma Beta. (pres. 1976—). Roman Catholic. Home: Atlanta GA 30327

PAULK, LOIS JEAN, statistical analyst, business manager; b. Abbottstown, Pa., Aug. 24, 1931; d. Stewart Philip and Florence Kathryn (Mummert) Ruth; m. George Thomas Paulk, Sept. 6, 1969. B.A., Pa. State U., 1953. Engring. expeditor AMP Inc., Harrisburg, Pa., 1953-56, statis. analyst, 1956-59, head statis. analysis, 1959-73, systems procedures coordinator, 1957-73, mem. divisional cost improvement com., 1966-73, sales stats. tng. coordinator, 1963-73; v.p., asst. sec. Mobile Home Brokers Inc., Hanover, Pa., 1973-83; v.p., treas. GTP Enterprises, Inc., Gettysburg, Pa. Chmn. legis. task force Pa. Mfg. Housing Assn., Harrisburg, Pa., 1979-80. Mem. Gov.'s Com. for Constl. Rev., State of Pa., 1963-66; chmn. Parks and Recreation Commn., 1966-72; sec. Zoning Hearing Bd., 1972-79; mem. Zoning Revision Com., Boro of New Cumberland, Pa., 1977-79; mem. exec. bd., chmn. personnel YWCA, Gettysburg, 1980-83; mem. Indoor Sports Complex Fund Commn., 1978-81; active Coll. Liberal Arts Endowment Fund; mem. alumni council Pa. State U., 1984—. Mem. AAUW (bd. dirs. 1954-56), Coll. of Liberal Arts Alumni Soc. (pres. 1982-84), Phi Mu. Republican. Methodist. Club: Pennsylvania Fedn. Women's Clubs (pres., chmn. legis. com.) (New Cumberland, Pa.). Home: 841 Hancock Dr Lake Heritage Gettysburg PA 17325

PAULSEN, JOANN RUTH, fashion accessory business executive; b. San Francisco, Aug. 13, 1941; d. James Steven and Ruth Elizabeth (Harmon) Paulsen; m. Armando Ernesto Damy, July 28, 1966 (div. 1970). A.A., Santa Rosa Jr. Coll., 1961; B.F.A., Inst. Allende, San Miguel de Allende, Mex., 1975. Freelance artist and photographer, Mexico City, 1963-73; owner, designer Frajo, San Miguel Allende, 1975—; pres. Frajo, Ltd., La Mesa, Calif., 1982—. Exhibited paintings and photography in one-woman shows, Mexico City, 1961-80. Recipient Grand Cross of Colors, Rainbow Girls, 1959; Excelsior trophy Excelsior Newspaper, 1969. Mem. Nat. Assn. Women Bus. Owners, La Mesa C. of C., U.S. C. of C., Grow. Address: PO Box 3839 La Mesa CA 92041 Office: Frajo Ltd 8140 Commercial St La Mesa CA 92041

PAULSON, CAROL ALICE, accounting firm administrator; b. Ambrose, N.D., Apr. 5, 1930; d. Louis J. and Mathilda J. (Anderson) P. Exec. dir. Rexall Drug Co., Los Angeles, 1948-69; adminstrv. mgr. Peat, Marwick, Mitchell & Co., Los Angeles, 1970—. Organist Hollywood Lutheran Ch., Los Angeles, 1956-86. Recipient Woman of Yr. award YWCA, Los Angeles, 1983. Republican. Avocations: music; reading; traveling. Home: 7736 Via Napoli Burbank CA 91504 Office: Peat, Marwick Mitchell & Co 725 S Figueroa St Los Angeles CA 90017

PAULSON, LYNDA ROSE, tng. specialist; b. Indpls., Oct. 18, 1939; d. Alfred E. and Mary Louis (Gladden) Fitch; B.A., Ind. U., 1961; children—Phillip Todd, Paige Anne Paulson. Mgr., Margie's Bridal Salon, Melrose Park, Ill., 1967-68; account exec. Sheraton Hotel, Oak Brook, Ill., 1968-70; regional sales mgr. Dale Carnegie Inst., Westchester, Ill., 1970-79; pres., founder Success Strategies, Inc., Clarendon Hills, Ill., 1979—; developer retail sales and people mgmt. seminars; designer Exec. Speaking Seminars; speech coach; instr. Am. Mgmt. Assn., Dale Carnegie courses. Recipient awards for prodn. Dale Carnegie Inst., 1976-79, awards for profl. instrn., 1977-79; named Entrepreneur of Yr., Women in Mgmt., 1981, Who to Look for in '81, Entree mag., 1981. Mem. Nat. Assn. Women Bus. Owners, Women in Mgmt., Am. Mgmt. Assn., Young Pres. Orgn., Internat. Speakers Assn. Republican. Clubs: Executives, Chgo. Health (Chgo); Willowbrook Racquet, Oak Brook Racquet, Sports Fitness Inst. Home and Office: 921 Marina Dr Napa CA 94558

PAULSON, SANDRA L., real estate executive; b. Helena, Mont., May 14, 1946; d. Jack and Lucille A. (Tooker) Stambaugh Bourquin; m. Wallace Paulson, Aug. 31, 1961 (div. 1977); 1 child, Jacquie. B.S., U. Mont., 1973. Data processor Am. State Bank, Williston, S.D., 1965-67; clk. Williams County Ct., Williston, 1967-69; tchr. Sch. Dist. #1, Missoula, Mont., 1974-75; salesperson Lambros Realty, Missoula, 1976-84, gen. mgr., 1984—; pres. Hartman Investments, Missoula, 1976—. Contbr. article to profl. jour. Named Miss Williston, Bus. Profl. Women, 1968. Mem. Nat. Assn. Female Execs (network dir. 1984-86), Nat. Assn. Realtors, Missoula County Realtors (com. 1986), Mont. Assn. Realtors (state and county dir. 1980-81, v.p. 1980-81). Avocations: piano; guitar; skiing; backpacking. Home: 400 Connell Missoula MT 59801 Office: Lambros Realty 1001 S Higgins Missoula MT 59801

PAULSTON, CHRISTINA BRATT, educator; b. Stockholm, Dec. 30, 1932; came to U.S., 1951, naturalized, 1960; d. Lennart and Elsa (Facht) B.; B.A., Carleton Coll., 1953; M.A., U. Minn., 1955; Ed.D., Columbia U., 1966; m. Rolland Paulston, July 26, 1963; children—Christopher, Ian. Tchr. Clara City and Pine Island (Minn.) High Schs., 1955-60, Am. Sch. Tangier (Morocco), 1960-62, Katrineholm Allmanna Laroverk, Katrineholm, Sweden, 1962-63; circulation librarian East Asian Library, Columbia U., 1963-64, asst. instr. Tchrs. Coll., 1964-66; prof. Pontificia Universidad Catolica del Peru, Lima, 1966-67; cons. Instituto Linguistico de Verano, Lima, 1967-68; asst. dir. English Lang. Inst., U. Pitts., 1969-70, dir., 1970—, prof. linguistics, 1969—, acting chmn. dept. gen. linguistics, 1974-75, chmn., 1975—. Recipient Research award Am. Ednl. Research Assn., 1980. Democrat. Episcopalian. Contbr. articles to profl. jours.; author books. Office: Linguistics CL 2801 U Pitts Pittsburgh PA 15260

PAULU, FRANCES BROWN, international center administrator; b. Hastings, Minn., June 22, 1920; d. Thomas Andrew and Florence Ida (Tuttle) Brown; B.A. magna cum laude, U. Minn., 1940, postgrad. Sch. Social Work, 1942-44; m. Burton Paulu, June 29, 1942; children—Sarah Leith Paulu Boittin, Nancy Jean Paulu Hyde, Thomas Scott. Case worker Family Welfare Assn. Mpls., 1943-45; interviewer Community Health and Welfare Council, Mpls., 1963; sch. social worker Project Head Start, Mpls., 1966; program dir. Minn. Internat. Center, Mpls., 1970-72, exec. dir., 1972-84; exec. dir. Minn. Internat. Ctr./World Affairs Ctr., 1984—. Pres. UN Rally, 1970-72; chmn. Mpls. Charter Commn., 1972-74; bd. dirs. Urban Coalition of Mpls., 1967-70, Minn. World Affairs Center, 1972-84; mem. tourism adv. com. City of Mpls., 1976-83; dir. Minn. World Trade Week, 1977-81; adv. council Minn. World Trade Ctr., 1984-86; mem. mgmt. team Minn. Awareness Project, 1982—. DeWitt Jennings Payne scholar, 1939-40. Mem. Nat. Council for Internat. Visitors (officer and/or exec. com. mem. 1975-81), Nat. Assn. for Fgn. Student Affairs, LWV (pres. Mpls. 1967-69), UN Assn. Minn. (adv. council 1979—), Mpls.-St. Paul Com. on Fgn. Relations, Phi Beta Kappa, Alpha Omicron Pi, Lambda Alpha Psi. Home: 5005 Wentworth Ave Minneapolis MN 55419 Office: Minn Internat Center 711 East River Rd Minneapolis MN 55455

PAULU, NANCY JEAN, journalist; b. Mpls., Nov. 21, 1949; d. Burton and Frances Tuttle (Brown) P.; B.A., Lawrence U., 1971; Ed.M., Harvard U., 1980. Sec., Mpls. Star and Tribune Co., Mpls., 1971-72, news asst., 1972-73, reporter, 1973—, edn. reporter, 1977—. Commentator, interviewer KTCA Public TV, St. Paul, 1979—; guest lectr. U. Minn., 1976—. Contbr. articles to Edn. Week. Bd. dirs. Big Sisters Assn., Mpls., 1981-84. Recipient writing awards Minn. Edn. Assn., 1979-82, Nat. Sch. Bds. Assn., 1980, 82; Bush Found. fellow, 1979-80. Mem. Edn. Writers Assn., Phi Delta Kappa. Home: 3 Francis St #2 Milton MA 02186

PAULUS, NORMA JEAN PETERSEN, lawyer; b. Belgrade, Nebr., Mar. 13, 1933; d. Paul Emil and Ella Marie (Hellbusch) Petersen; LL.B., Willamette Law Sch., 1962; LL.D., Linfield Coll., 1985; m. William G. Paulus, Aug. 16, 1958; children—Elizabeth, William Frederick. Sec. to Harney County Dist. Atty., 1950-53; legal sec., Salem, Oreg., 1953-55; sec. to chief justice Oreg. Supreme Ct., 1955-61; admitted to Oreg. bar, 1962; of counsel Paulus and Callaghan, Salem, mem. Oreg. Ho. of Reps., 1971-77; sec. state of Oreg., Salem, 1977-85; of cousel firm Paulus, Rhoten & Lien, 1985-86; dir. Pacific Northwest Bell; adj. prof. Willamette U. Coll. Law, 1985. Fellow Eagleton Inst. Politics, 1971; trustee Willamette U., 1978—; bd. dirs. Benedictine Found. of Oreg., 1980—, Oreg. Grade. Ctr., 1985—, Mid Willamette Valley council Camp Fire Girls, 1985—, Oreg. Innovation Network, 1985—; overseer Whitman Coll., 1985—; bd. cons. Goodwill Industries of Oreg.; mem. Salem Human Relations Commn., 1967-70, Marion-Polk Boundary Commn., 1970-71; mem. Presdl. Commn. to Monitor Philippines Election, 1986. Recipient Distinguished Service award City of Salem, 1971; Path Breaker award Oreg. Women's Polit. Caucus, 1976; named One of 10 Women of Future, Ladies Home Jour., 1979. Woman of Yr., Oreg. Inst Managerial and Profl. Women, 1982, Oreg. Women Lawyers, 1982, Woman who Made a Difference award Nat. Women's Forum, 1985. Mem. Nat. Soc. State Legislators (dir. 1971-72), Oreg. State Bar, Nat. Order Women Legislators, Women Execs. in State Govt., Women's Polit. Caucus Bus. and Profl. Women's Club (Golden Torch award 1971), Zonta Internat., Delta Kappa Gamma. Office: 750 Front St NE Salem OR 97301

PAUSHTER, JANIS LYNN, educational administrator; b. Springfield, Mass., Oct. 17, 1947; d. Matthew Harry and Anne Diatlove (Lutz) P.; m. Neil Robert Eisner, Feb. 8, 1981. B.A., Syracuse U., 1969; M.A., Columbia U., 1971, Ed.M., 1975, Ed.D., 1976. Tchr., N.Y.C. pub. schs., 1971-73; instr. William Paterson Coll., Wayne, N.J., 1973-74; project assoc. Nat. Assn. State Dirs. Spl. Edn., Washington, 1976-77; program and services specialist Fairfax County pub. schs., Va., 1977-79, coordinator due process, 1979-85, dir. adminstrv. services, 1985—. Instr., U. Va., Falls Church, 1978—, George Mason U., Fairfax, Va., 1979—; cons. Nat. Assn. State Dirs. Spl. Edn., 1985—, CPR Pub., 1985—. Pres., Hillside Ridge Community Assn., 1983-84; chmn. archlt. controls com., 1984-85, chmn. maintenance com., 1985-86. Fellow Inst. Ednl. Leadership, 1984-85. Mem. Nat. Assn. State Dirs. Spl. Edn., Council Exceptional Children, Phi Delta Kappa. Democrat. Jewish. Avocations: mysteries. Office: Fairfax County Public Schs 10310 Layton Hall Dr Fairfax VA 22030

PAUTH, PATRICIA RUTH, librarian; b. Rochester, N.Y., Feb. 14, 1936; d. Frank Alvin and Ruth Rose (Vose) P.; student Wittenberg U., Springfield, Ohio, 1953-56. Library asst. periodicals dept. Rush Rhees Library, U. Rochester (N.Y.), 1956-59; with Price Waterhouse & Co., N.Y.C., 1959—, purchasing asst., 1959-63, reference librarian, 1963-72, asst. librarian, 1972-74, head librarian, 1974—, mgr. info. services, 1985—. Mem. Spl. Libraries Assn., Am. Soc. for Info. Sci., DAR, Union Street Gardens Assn. (past treas., pres.). Home: 376 Union St Brooklyn NY 11231 Office: 153 E 53d St New York NY 10022

PAUTSCH, DELORES ALMA, business executive; b. Fond du Lac, Wis., Oct. 30, 1928; d. William Frederick and Alma Pauline (Schmidt) Mielke; student Fond du Lac Bus. Coll., 1945-46; m. Milton Gustave Pautsch, Nov. 5, 1949; children—Floyd A., Joy Faye, Bonnie Mae and Betsy Mae (dec.)(twins). With Nat. Rivet Co., 1946-47, Johnson Truck Service, 1947-49, Milt's Service Sta., 1949-52, Nash Waupun, 1952-57, Peters Oil Co., 1957-62; self-employed floral designer, 1963-75; owner, pres. Pautsch Distbg. Co., Waupun, Wis., 1975-85; with Scientia, Houston, 1985—. Home: 734 S Madison St Waupun WI 53963

PAVEL, LINDA JOYCE, medical technologist, epidemiology coordinator; b. Pickstown, S.D., July 18, 1951; d. Rudolph John and Helen (Fuchs) P.; m. Glenn Willian Custard, 1973 (div. 1974). B.S. in Biology and Chemistry, U. S.D., 1973. With U.S. Govt. Indian Health Service, 1976—, staff med. technologist, Wagner, S.D., 1976, Chinle, Ariz., 1976-79, asst. lab. supr., Pine Ridge, S.D., 1979-81, supervisory med. technologist, Eagle Butte, S.D., 1981-83, Poplar, Mont., 1983—, epidemiology coordinator, Fort Peck Indian Reservation, Poplar, 1985—, condr. mgmt. course, 1986, condr. hematology course, 1979, cons. tchr., Eagle Butte and Poplar, 1981—; substitute instr. in bacteriology Navajo Community Coll., Tsaile, Ariz., 1978. Tchr., Ch. of Christ Mission, Many Farms, Ariz., 1977-78; co-founder Roosevelt County Epidemiology Team, Mont., 1986; mem. Wagner Indian Health Service Com. on Alcoholism, 1976. Recipient various awards Indian Health Service. Mem. Am. Soc. Clin. Pathologists, Nat. Assn. Female Execs. Avocations: reading; gardening; writing. Home: 504 Roosevelt Poplar MT 59255 Office: Verne Gibbs Health Center 107 H St Poplar MT 59255

PAVELKA, ELAINE BLANCHE, mathematics educator; b. Chgo.; d. Frank Joseph and Mildred Bohumila (Seidl) P.; B.A., M.S., Northwestern U.; Ph.D., U. Ill. With Northwestern U. Aerial Measurements Lab., Evanston, Ill.; tchr. Leyden Community High Sch., Franklin Park, Ill.; prof. math. Morton Coll., Cicero, Ill.; speaker 3d Internat. Congress Math. Edn., Karlsruhe, Germany, 1976. Recipient sci. talent award Westinghouse Elec. Co. Mem. Am. Edn. Research Assn., Am. Math. Assn. 2-Year Colls., Am. Math. Soc., Assn. Women in Math., Can. Soc. History and Philosophy of Math., Ill. Council Tchr. of Math., Ill. Math. Assn. Community Colls., Math. Assn. Am., Math. Action Group, Ga. Center Study and Teaching and Learning Math., Nat. Council Tchrs. of Math., Sch. Sci. and Math. Assn., Soc. Indsl. and Applied Math., Northwestern U. Alumni Assn., U. Ill. Alumni Assn., Am. Mensa Ltd., Intertel, Sigma Delta Epsilon, Pi Mu Epsilon. Home: 1900 Euclid Ave Berwyn IL 60402 Office: 3801 S Central Ave Cicero IL 60650

PAVETTO, CHRISTINA MARIE, economist, educator; b. Syracuse, N.Y., Feb. 25, 1960; d. John Carl and Shirley (Browne) P. B.S., SUNY-Oswego, 1982, postgrad., 1985—; postgrad. Marymount Coll., 1979, Syracuse U., 1986. Med. Service rep. Bristol Labs. div. Bristol-Meyers Co., Syracuse, 1982-85; prof. econs. Central City Bus. Inst., Syracuse, 1985—. Mem. Am. Mktg. Assn. Republican. Roman Catholic. Office: 953 James St Syracuse NY 13203

PAVLOV, HELENE, physician, educator; b. Phila., Aug. 1, 1946; d. Al and Sylvia Pavlov; m. Harvey Zeichner, Sept. 4, 1983. A.B., Temple U., Phila., 1968, M.D., 1972. Diplomate Am. Bd. Radiology. Intern, Lenox Hill Hosp., N.Y.C., 1972-73; resident in radiology Germantown Hosp., Phila., 1973-76; fellow Hosp. for Spl. Surgery, N.Y.C., 1976-77, attending radiologist, 1983—; asst. prof. Cornell U., N.Y.C., 1977-83, assoc. prof. radiology, 1983—; asst. attending N.Y. Hosp., N.Y.C., 1977-83, assoc. attending, 1983—. Author: Atlas of Knee Menisci, 1983; mem. editorial bd. Contemporary Orthopaedics; bimonthly columnist Contemporary Orthopaedics; reviewer sci. jour.; contbr. chpts. and articles in radiology, orthopedic surgery and sports medicine to profl. publs. Mem. Radiol. Soc. N.Am., Internat. Skeltal Soc., Am. Roentgen Ray Soc., Am. Coll. Radiology (alt. del. to N.Y. state chpt.), Am. Assn. Women Radiologists, N.Y. Roentgen Ray Soc. Office: Hosp for Spl Surgery 535 E 70th St New York NY 10021

PAWLIW, OKSANNA BOHDANNA, editor, drilling industry data service executive; b. Cohoes, N.Y., Oct. 6, 1951; d. Mykola and Olha (Makohin) Pawliw. Student U. de Dijon (France), 1971-72; B.A., Coll. St. Rose, Albany, N.Y., 1973; postgrad. U. St. Clement, Rome, 1974; M.A., SUNY-Albany, 1975. Lic. ins. broker, N.Y. Ins. agt. State Farm Ins., Cohoes, N.Y., 1976; translator Acad. of Langs., Houston, 1978-79; editor, pub. relations Kaneb Services, Inc., Houston, 1980-84; with Offshore Data Services, Inc., 1984—; freelance translator, Houston, 1979—. Recipient Excellence in French award Alliance Francaise, 1973, Lang. Dept. Coll. St. Rose, 1973; Outstanding Progress in Spanish award Coll. St. Rose, 1973; Bus. Woman of the Month award Times Union newspaper, Albany, 1976. Mem. Alliance Francaise de Houston, Ukrainian Nat. Women's League Am. (sec. 1982-84), Soc. Profl. Journalists. Roman Catholic. Club: Ukrainian Cultural (Houston). Home: 3907 Echo Grove Ln Houston TX 77043 Office: 3346 Walnut Rd Houston TX 77042

PAWLOWSKI, KATHLEEN MARY, nurse, administrator; b. Amsterdam, N.Y., Feb. 23, 1947; d. Joseph Thomas and Catherine (Boggie) Ciskanow; m. Robert George Pawlowski, Oct. 17, 1970; children—John Robert, Christine Marie. R.N., Albany Med. Ctr., (N.Y.), 1967. Staff nurse St. Mary's Hosp., Amsterdam, 1967-71, 74-78; health service nurse SUNY, Cobleskill, N.Y., 1971; staff nurse Meontgomery County Nursing Service, Fonda, N.Y., 1978-82; nursing dir. Quality Care, Fultonville, N.Y., 1983—. Mem. com. OFA Older Am. Health Fair, Amsterdam, 1983—; bd. dirs. Community Health Ctr., Amsterdam, 1984—; bd. dirs., vol. adv. bd. Touch-Cancer Support Group, Amsterdam, 1984—. Mem. Albany Med. Ctr. Sch. Nursing Alumni Assn. Roman Catholic. Avocations: reading; cooking; sewing; swimming. Office: Quality Care 67 Division St Amsterdam NY 12010

PAWLUC, SONIA M., lawyer; b. Miami, Fla., June 25, 1957; d. Casimer and Genevieve A (Pawelczyk) Pawluc. B.A. magna cum laude, U. Miami, 1977, J.D. magna cum laude, 1981. Bar: Fla. 1981, N.C. 1986, D.C. 1986, U.S. Dist. Ct. (so. dist.) Fla. (gen.) 1981, (trial) 1983, U.S. Ct. Appeals (11th cir.) 1981, U.S. Dist. Ct. (mid. dist.) Fla. 1985, U.S. Ct. Appeals (D.C. cir.) 1986, U.S. Supreme Ct. 1986. Assoc. Holland & Knight, Miami, 1981-83, Morgan, Lewis & Bockius, Miami, 1983—. Mem. ABA, Dade County Bar Assn., Acad. Fla. Trial Lawyers, Assn. Trial Lawyers Am., Soc. Profl. Journalists, Soc. Wig and Robe, Phi Kappa Phi, Kappa Tau Alpha, Delta Theta Mu. Democrat. Roman Catholic. Contbr. articles to profl. jours.; bd. editors so. Dist. Digest, 1981-82. Home: 6441 SW 36th St Miami FL 33155 Office: Morgan Lewis & Bockius 3200 Miami Center 100 Chopin Plaza Miami FL 33131

PAXTON, ALICE ADAMS, artist, designer; b. Hagerstown, Md., May 19, 1914; d. William Albert and Josephine (Adams) Rosenberger; student Peabody Inst. Music, Balt., 1937-38; grad. Parson's Sch. Design, N.Y., 1940; studied portrait painting with J. Laurie Wallace, 1944-46; studied with Augustus

Dunbier, 1947-48, Sylvia Curtis, 1949, Milton Wolsky, 1950, Frank Sapousek, 1951; m. James Love Paxton, Jr., June 26, 1942 (div.); 1 son, William Allen III. Free-lance work archtl. renderings and interior design for various N.Y. interior decorators, 1937-40; interior designer, spl. furnishings designer and muralist Orchard and Wilhelm, furniture store, Omaha, 1940-42; designer interior Chapel Boys' Town, Nebr., 1942; tchr. art classes Alice Paxton Studio, Omaha, 1957-64; dir. Paxton-Mitchell Co., Omaha; tchr. mech. drawing, archtl. rendering, mech. perspective Parson's Sch. Design, N.Y., 1937-40; one-man show of archtl. renderings, Washington County Mus. Fine Arts, Hagerstown, 1944; exhibited group shows at Joslyn Mus., Omaha, 1943, 44, Ann. Exhbn. Cumberland Valley Artists, Hagerstown, Md., 1945; represented permanent collections at No. Natural Gas Co. Bldg., Omaha, Swanson Found., Omaha, also pvt. collections. Vol. designer, decorator recreation room Omaha Blood Bank, A.R.C., 1943, recreation room Creighton U., 1943, lounge psychiat. ward Lincoln (Nebr.) Army Hosp., 1944; planner color coordinator Children's Hosp., Omaha, 1947, painted murals, 1948, decorated dental room, 1950; also numerous other vol. profl. activities for civic orgns., hosps., clubs, chs., also community playhouse. Co-chmn. camp and hosp. coms. A.R.C., 1943-45, county com. select and send gifts servicemen, 1943-46; mem. Ak-Sar-Ben Ball com., Omaha, 1946-48; judge select Easter Seal design, Joslyn Mus., 1946; mem. council Girl Scouts U.S.A., Omaha, 1943-47; spl. drs. chmn. Jr. League, Omaha, 1947-48, chmn. Jr. League Red Cross, fund dr., 1947-48; bd. drs., vol. worker Creche, Omaha, 1954-56; chmn. Jr. League Community Chest Fund Dr., 1948-50; co-chmn. Infantile Paralysis Appeal, 1944; establishing wildlife sanctuary. Recipient three teaching scholarships Parson's Sch. Design, 1937-40; presdl. citation A.R.C. activities, 1946; 1st prize Ann. Midwest Show Joslyn Mus., 1943; painted and decorated straw elephant bag which was presented to Mrs. Richard Nixon, 1960. Contbr. articles and photographs Popular Home mag., 1958. Mem. Asso. Artists Omaha (charter), Jr. League Omaha, Am. Security Council (nat. adv. bd.), Internat. Platform Assn., U.S. Hist. Soc. Republican. Episcopalian. Club: Fountain Head Country. Home: 300 Meadowbrook Rd Hagerstown MD 21740

PAXTON, CAROL JEANNE, environmental engineer; b. Richmond, Ind., May 5, 1928; d. Elbert Raymond and Lenora Ione (Watkins) Belcher; B.S. in Mech. Engring., Trinity U., San Antonio, 1948; M.B.A., Iowa State U., 1975; student environ. mgmt. and engring. U. Va., 1975; m. William Clark Paxton, Sept. 1, 1946; children—James, Joan, Sandra, Patricia, Dale, Mark, Dana. Mgr. fin. planning and contracts Aerojet-Gen. Corp., 1949-63; owner Carol's Engring. Cons., Huntington Beach, Calif., 1965-68; lab. supr. Mason & Hangar-Silas Mason Co., Inc., Burlington, Iowa, 1968-77; engring. scientist, OSHA compliance officer State of N.Mex., 1977; environ. engring. supr. Zia Co., Los Alamos, 1977-84; with Mason & Hanger-Silas Mason Co., Inc., Amarillo, Tex., 1984—; cons., lectr. in field. Pres., Mediapolis (Iowa) United Way, 1970-72; chmn. Mediapolis Mothers March of Dimes, 1972-73; v.p. Mediapolis Mchts. Assn., 1973-74; pres. bd. dirs., treas., project coordinator N.Mex. State Employees Commuters Assn., Inc., 1977—; nat. membership chmn. Am. Rideshaing Profls., 1981. Recipient Sec. Def. award, 1976. Mem. Soc. Women Engrs., N.Mex. Network Women in Sci. and Engring., LWV, Women's Polit. Caucus. Democrat. Methodist. Office: Mason & Hanger-Silas Mason Co Inc PO Box 30020 Amarillo TX 79177

PAXTON, DORIS HALL, real estate executive; b. Ft. Worth, June 23, 1931; d. Allon Killough and Ruth Augusta (McRae) Hall; m. James Robert Paxton, Aug. 14, 1954; children—Mary McRae, Ruth Hall, Martha Ellen Paxton Lemons, Jane Stratton Paxton Bonnet, Sarah Elizabeth, Rebecca Lee. B.S., U. Tex., 1952. Field rep. Am. Cancer Soc., Austin, Tex., 1953-54; broker, owner First Realty, Palestine, Tex., 1975—; owner Diet Ctr. of Palestine. Founder, Wesley Communicty Ch. Mem. Palestine Bd. Realtors (dir. 1981-84), Phi Beta Kappa. Mem. Wesley Community Ch. Clubs: Harvey Woman's, Lit. Forum (v.p. 1970-71, pres. 1971-72) (Palestine). Home: 126 Meadowbrook Dr Palestine TX 75801 Office: First Realty 1000 N Church Palestine TX 75801

PAYAD, AURORA TORRES, management services executive; b. Cavite, Philippines, Jan. 12, 1938; came to U.S., 1978; d. Isidro Paglinawan and Felicidad (Torres) P. LL.B., Lyceum of the Philippines, 1959; M.P.A., U. Philippines, 1967; M.P.A., Ph.D. in Pub. Adminstrn., U. So. Calif., 1975. Admitted to Philippine bar, 1960. Tng. specialist and professorial lectr. Local Govt. Center, Manila, Philippines, 1975-76; asst. prof. U. Philippines, Manila, 1976-78; Pepperdine U., Los Angeles, 1979-81; lectr. U. So. Calif., Los Angeles, 1978-81; assoc. prof. Calif. State Coll., San Bernardino, 1981-85; owner D'Avon Gift Ctr., 1986—; dir. Techo-Indsl. Mgmt. Services, 1986—. Author, co-author short stories, research papers, jour. article. Club advisor Pub. Adminstrn. Club, San Bernardino, 1983; v.p., treas. Jr. Women's Club, San Bernardino, 1983. Grad. fellow U. Philippines, 1965-67; U.S. AID-Nat. Econ. Council grantee, 1970-72; Ford Found. dissertation grantee, Bangkok, Thailand, 1973-74. Mem. Am. Soc. Pub. Adminstrn. (exec. com. sect. on profl. and organizational devel.), Acad. Polit. Sci., Calif. State Assocs.

PAYNE, AMILEE WENDT, securities broker, designer; b. Houston, Dec. 27, 1948; d. B. Jack and Billie Amilee (Harris) Wendt; m. Richard Thames Lamkin, Sept. 19, 1969 (div. June 1975); 1 child, Richard Harris; m. Francis Cameron Payne, Jr., Nov. 26, 1982. Student So. Methodist U., 1967-69. Contract paralegal various firms, Houston, 1972—; pvt. practice contract interior design, Houston, 1975—; ptnr. EAJL Wendt Farms, Houston, 1975—; drilling fund mgr. Tangent Oil & Gas, Houston, 1981; broker Cameron Payne Securities Corp., Houston, 1986—; corporate sec. Cameron Payne & Co., Inc., Houston, 1982—. Presentation chmn. Children's Mus. of Houston Guild Bd., 1984-85, spl. events chmn., 1985-86; docent Houston Ballet, 1984-85; vol. Houston Ballet Market, 1984-86; spl. events chmn. steering com. Boy Scouts Am., 1984-85, rep. at large, 1985-86; mem. assoc. bd. Stages Repertory Theatre, 1986—. Mem. Nat. Assn. Female Execs. Republican. Episcopalian. Club: The Houstonian. Home: 2307 Locke Ln Houston TX 77019 Office: Cameron Payne Securities Corp 1000 Louisiana St Suite 4490 Houston TX 77002

PAYNE, BARBARA CASTEEL, lawyer; b. Houston, Jan. 23, 1940; d. Bryon Wharton Casteel and Sydell Louise (Sterling) Dodson; m. Thomas Nelson Payne, Oct. 5, 1957; children—Gary Allen, Melanie Rhea, Dina Dae, Deidre Dee. B.A. summa cum laude in Psychology, U. Bridgeport (Conn.), 1979; J.D., Hofstra U., 1981. Bar: Conn. 1983, U.S. Tax Ct., U.S. Dist. Ct. Conn. Sole practice, Wilton, Conn., 1983-84, Stamford, Conn., 1986—; atty. ITT, Tempe, Ariz., 1984-85; assoc. Law Offices of David Wallman, 1985-86; sole practice, 1986—; legis. cons., Phoenix, 1984. Dana scholar, 1979. Mem. ABA, Conn. Attys. Title Ins. Co., Assn. Trial Lawyers Am., Conn. Bar Assn. (lawyers and community sect.), Toastmasters (ednl. v.p.). Democrat. Methodist. Home: 35 W Brother Dr Greenwich CT 06830 Office: Barbara C Payne Atty at Law 133 Summer St Stamford Ct 06901

PAYNE, DORIS NELL, nurse medical supervisor; b. Atlanta, Aug. 20, 1934; d. Nolan Grady and Katherine Lucile (Sentel) Hughes Gardner; m. James Willard Payne, Sept. 15, 1956 (div. 1979); children—Michael Steven, James Mark. R.N., Emory U., 1956. Surg. nurse Cary Meml. Hosp., Caribou, Maine, 1956-57; head nurse Crawford W. Long Hosp., Atlanta, 1958-60; nurse supr. Indsl. Clinic, Atlanta, 1961-63; office nurse obs.-gyn, Atlanta, 1964-68; indsl. nurse Sears-Roebuck, Atlanta, 1969-71; med. supr. Dekalb County Sheriff's Dept., Decatur, Ga., 1974—, instr. inservice, 1978-83; instr. State Ga., Ga. Peace Officers Standard and Tng. Council, 1981-83. Student instr. U.S. Dept. Justice Human Relations, Decatur, Ga., 1981. Named Family of Yr., Jr. Woman's Club of Lithonia (Ga.), 1972; recipient 2d prize Shell-Gen. Fedn. Women's Club Environ. Conservation Program, 1973. Mem. Am. Correctional Health Service Assn. Lutheran. Clubs: Jr. Woman's (pres. 1972-73), Women's Soc. Christian Service (Lithonia, Ga.). Home: 6143 Queen Anne Ct Norcross GA 30093 Office: Dekalb County Sheriff's Dept 3630 Camp Circle Decatur GA 30032

PAYNE, EUGENIA COLLETTE, computer programmer; b. Harlan, Ky., Sept. 20, 1961; d. Victor Claude and Lois Annette (Barnes) P. B.S. in Bus. Adminstrn., Ohio State U., 1983. Assoc. programmer Marathon Oil Co., Findlay, Ohio, 1984-85; computer programmer EDP Temps, Southfield, Mich., 1985-86; Systems and programmer analyst Chrysler Corp., Highland Park, Mich., 1986—. Mem. Black Data Processing Assocs., Ohio State U. Alumni Assn., Alpha Kappa Alpha. Methodist. Club: United Methodist Women.

PAYNE, GAIL ANN CURTIS, radio sta. exec.; b. Stonewall, Okla., July 3, 1940; d. William Raymond and Thelma May (Schwandt) Curtis; B.A. in English Edn., Central State U., Edmond, Okla., 1963; m. William Haydon Payne, July 3, 1960; children—Anne M., Kelly Gail, Haydon Michelle, William Haydon II. With Sta. KWHP, Edmond, 1962-79, news reporter, 1962-72, pub. relations dir., corp. sec., 1972-79; v.p. Central Broadcast Co., Inc., Tulsa, 1977-82; real estate sales asso. Bob Turner and Assos., Edmond, 1977-81; part-time sec. Louis Holshouser Advt., Edmond, 1979-81; pres. Payne Radio Properties, 1982—. Chmn. Cerebral Palsey, Edmond. Mem. Nat. Assn. Broadcasters, Greater Oklahoma City FM Broadcasters, Edmond Bd. Realtors, Okla. Bd. Realtors, Edmond C. of C., Town and Country Homemakers Extension Group (past pres.). Democrat. Club: Merry Modern Mother's (sec.). Office: 3405 E Louisville St Broken Arrow OK 74012

PAYNE, JANICE HONEYCUTT, real estate executive; b. Fisher, La., Apr. 5; d. William C. and Lillie Belle (Carpenter) Honeycutt; m. Thomas Bruce Payne, July 22, 1936; children—Mary Jan Payne Winston, Thomas Bruce Jr. Student La. State U., 1934-40; grad. Realtors Inst., 1972. Staff bus. office La. State U., Baton Rouge, 1938-40; sales agt. Bernette Hennington, Jackson, Miss., 1958-59; sales mgr. J.E. Carter Co., Jackson, 1959-60; owner, mng. broker Payne Realty, Jackson, 1960—; bd. dirs. Multiple Listing Service, Jackson, 1967, 76-77, 81-82, sec.-treas., 1976-77, v.p., 1985-86, pres., 1986—. Active Woman's Soc. Christian Service, Broadmeadow Methodist Ch., Jackson, 1950—; recipient Life Membership pen, 1960. Mem. Nat. Bd. Realtors, Miss. Bd. Realtors, Jackson Bd. Realtors (Realtor of Yr. 1984), Women's Council Realtors (sec. 1985, mem. profl. standards com.), Jackson C. of C. (bd. dirs. 1975). Club: Concordia (past v.p., pres.) (Jackson). Lodge: Soroptimist. Avocations: reading, gardening, flower arranging, knitting, travel. Home: 4407 Northover Dr Jackson MS 39211 Office: Payne Realty 6265 Pear Orchard Rd Jackson MS 39211

PAYNE, JANIE LEAH, banker; b. Pampa, Tex., July 18, 1954; d. Phillip Paul and Betty Lou (Scott) P. B.S., McMurry Coll., Abilene, Tex., 1977. Acct., Nueve Operating Co., Abilene, 1977-80, Westwood Energy, Abilene, 1981-82; trust employee benefits adminstr. Merc. Nat. Bank, Dallas, 1982—. Mem. Am. Bus. Women's Assn. (pres. 1980-82), West Central Tex. Oil and Gas Assn. (sec. 1980-82), Am. Inst. Banking. Republican. Baptist. Home: 4214 Esters Rd Apt 114C Irving TX 75038

PAYNE, JILL VIRGINIA, printing company executive; b. Wichita, Kans., Nov. 14, 1948; d. Richard and Macel Flora (Kidson) K.; m. Haskel Landis Payne, Aug. 21, 1937 (div. Dec. 1984); children—Amber, Tia, Asa. Operator S.W. Bell, Dallas, 1967-68; copy ctr. operator Trailways, Dallas, 1976-78; duplicating mgr. NCG Copy Ctr., Dallas, 1978-83; ptnr. Action Copy, Dallas, 1983—; facilities mgr. U.S. EPA, Dallas, 1978-82. Named Outstanding Community Contbr. Oak Lawn Today, 1983. Mem. Nat. Assn. Quick Printer, Printing Industries Am., Dallas Chamber Women's Network (bd. dirs. 1982-84), Dallas Bus. League. Avocations: aerobic dance; painting; weaving; Texas history. Office: Action Copy PO Box 7191 Dallas TX 75209

PAYNE, JUNE PATRICIA, editor; b. Albuquerque, May 20, 1930; d. Stanley Thomas and Effie (Pierce) P. B.A., Ariz. State U., 1952. Assoc. editor Ariz. Beverage Jour., Phoenix, 1952-64; asst. editor state desk Ariz. Republic, Phoenix, 1964; editorial asst., editor Bur. Publs., Ariz. State U., 1964-81, editor community relations, 1981-85, asst. dir. univ. publs., 1982-85. Editor newspaper ASU Insight, 1983-85; mem. editorial bd. Jour. of American Indian Edn., 1976-81. Mem. Photographic Soc. Am., Ariz. Press Women, Women in Communications Inc. Club: Phoenix Press. Home: 4733 E Cambridge St Phoenix AZ 85008 Office: Publs Dept Ariz State U Matthews Hall 102 Tempe AZ 85287

PAYNE, KATRINA ANNE, accounting consultant; b. Elkhart, Ind., Feb. 4, 1950; d. Kenneth Dean and Alpha-Jean (Harthill) Brouse; m. William Howard Payne, Mar. 17, 1979; 1 stepchild, Kristina Suzanne. Student North Park Coll., Chgo., 1967-69; B.A., Calif. State U.-Los Angeles, 1973. Lab. technician Solid State Dielectrics, Sun Valley, Calif., 1971-74, lab. supr., 1974-76, lab. mgr., 1976-79, spl. projects mgr., 1979-82; ind. cons. for small bus. acctg., Sunland, Calif., 1982—. Mem. Republican Senatorial Inner Circle, Washington, 1984-85. Mem. Am. Ceramic Soc. (treas. So. Calif. sect. 1981, sec. 1982, chmn. 1984). Baptist. Avocations: playing piano, alpine skiing, swimming, sailing. Home: 9856 Sunland Blvd Sunland CA 91040

PAYNE, MARTHA LEE HARVEY, interior designer; b. Oakland, Calif., Sept. 29, 1944; d. Ira Omar and Dorothy (Page) Harvey; B.A., So. Meth. U., 1966; postgrad. UCLA, 1975; children—Gregory Thomas, Alysha Carol, David Lee Harvey. Retail trainee Neiman-Marcus, Dallas, 1964-65; interior designer Jan Grierson, Austin, Tex., 1970; owner, operator Inside-Out Interior Design, Pacific Palisades, Calif., 1974-81; fabric buyer, furniture designer Elite Upholstery Co., City of Industry, Calif., 1975; West coast area mgr. decorative fabrics Milliken & Co., Los Angeles, 1976-78; Calif. ter. mgr. Design Resources, Los Angeles, 1978-80; account exec. Pindler & Pindler, Los Angeles, 1980-81; nat. account mgr. Coral of Chgo., 1981-82; West Coast regional mgr. Computer Roomers, Dallas, 1982-84; exec. v.p. mktg., owner Highland Three, Inc., 1984-85; owner Contract Connection, Dallas, 1985—. Chmn. fund-raising com. YMCA, 1975-76, football coach YMCA, 1975-79. Mem. Am. Soc. Interior Designers (West Coast nat. v.p. 1976), S.W. Furniture Mfrs. Assn., So. Meth. U. Alumni Assn. Republican.

PAYNE, MILDRED LYNETTE, educator; b. Houston, Oct. 14, 1945; d. Norman Emory and Clara LaVerne (Nunalee) Payne. B.A., Baylor U., 1967; postgrad. Sam Houston State U., 1968-70; M.Ed., U. Houston, 1974, postgrad., 1978-80. Lic. ednl. diagnostician, tchr., Tex. Tchr., North Forest Ind. Sch. Dist., Houston, 1967-76, ednl. diagnostician, 1976-78, dir. spl. edn., 1978-81; project dir. Harris County Dept., Houston, 1981-83; agt. State Farm Ins., Houston, 1983-84; counselor Woodland Hills Elem. Sch., Humble Ind. Sch. Dist. (Tex.), 1984—. Author: Zingo, Creative Reading Activities, Book 1, 1976; Zingo, Creative Reading Activities, Book 2, 1976. Mem. Council for Exceptional Children (pres. 1981-83), Tex. Adminstrn. Spl. Edn. (regional coordinator 1978-81), Gulf Coast Adminstrn. Spl. Edn. (sec. 1979-80), Delta Kappa Gamma. Democrat. Mem. Unity Ch. Christianity. Home: 5738 D Easthampton Houston TX 77039 Office: State Farm Ins Agy 1730 W Mt Houston Rd Houston TX 77038

PAYNE, ROSLYN BRAEMAN, government official; b. Kansas City, Mo., Apr. 30, 1946; d. Aaron and Sophie (Pincus) Braeman; m. Lisle Warren Payne, Dec. 27, 1973; children—Matthew, Andrew. B.B.A., U. Mich.; M.B.A., Harvard Bus. Sch. Intern, 1st National Bank of Chgo., 1968, Coopers & Lybrand, N.Y.C., 1969; v.p., prin. Eastdil Realty, N.Y.C., San Francisco, 1970-81; group v.p., gen. mgr. Genstar Corp., San Francisco, 1981-85; pres., chief exec. officer Fed. Asset Disposition Assn., San Francisco, 1986—; dir. Fin. Center Bank, San Francisco, First Am. Title Guaranty Co., Oakland, Calif., 1978—. Mem. Bay Area Mortgage Assn. (pres. 1981-82), Women's Forum West (dir., treas. 1981-83), Real Estate Research Council, Urban Land Inst., Lambda Alpha (dir.). Clubs: Peninsula Golf and Tennis, Menlo Circus. Office: Federal Asset Disposition Assn 433 California St #400 San Francisco CA 94108

PEABODY, CECELIA MARY, advertising company executive; b. Fordham, Eng., May 7, 1946; came to U.S., 1947; d. Walter Francis and Mary (Kimmons) P.; m. Ralph Patrick Yannarelli, June 15, 1968 (div. Mar. 1984); 1 child, Patrick Charles. B.A., Western Coll., Oxford, Ohio, 1968; M.A.T., Montclair State U., N.J., 1971. Tchr. English, Mt. St. Dominic Sch., Caldwell, N.J., 1968-70; tchr. English head dept. Lacordaire Acad., Upper Montclair, N.J., 1970-72; campaign asst. Am. ORT Fedn., N.Y.C., 1980-81; regional mgr. Walt Peabody Advt., Inc., Ft. Lauderdale, 1981-84, v.p., 1984—. Mem. Met. Bowling Writers Assn., Nat. Assn. Female Execs. Republican. Presbyterian. Home: 106 Cecelia Ave Cliffside Park NJ 07010 Office: Walt Peabody Advt Service Inc 1160 NE 24th Ct Fort Lauderdale FL 33305

PEABODY, PENELOPE ANN, business association executive, consultant; b. Billings, Mont., Feb. 4, 1939; d. Claire Austin and Pauline (Quarles) Wagner; m. Wayne L. Wilson, Sept. 4, 1964 (div. June 1970); m. 2d, Gerald A. Peabody, Jr., Nov. 24, 1976; children—Victoria, Mary Jane. B.A. in Journalism, U. Mont., 1961, M.A., 1967. Mgr. community relations Metro, Seattle, 1971-75, spl. asst. to exec. dir., 1975-77, acting exec. dir., 1977, dir. pub. services, 1978-80; cons. Peabody & Assocs., Seattle, 1980-85; exec. dir. Seattle/King County Econ. Devel. Council, Seattle, 1985—; vis. lectr. Sch. Communications, U. Wash., Seattle, 1981. Contbg. author: A Century of Montana Journalism, 1967. Bd. dirs. Bellevue Community Coll. Found., Wash., 1982—, mem. adv. bd. Womens Ctr., 1983—; pres. Eastside Mcpl. League, King County, Wash., 1984-85. Mem. Econ. Devel. Execs. Wash., Community Devel. Roundtable. Congregationalist. Clubs: Bellevue Athletic; Rainier, City, Wash. Athletic (Seattle). Avocations: fishing; boating; writing; hiking; traveling. Office: Seattle/King County Econ Devel Council 1520 One Union Square Seattle WA 98101

PEACE, BETH ANGELA, lawyer; b. Magnolia, Ark., June 7, 1956; d. William Dwight and Patsy Ruth (Temple) P. Student So. Ark. U., Magnolia, 1974-75; B.A., La. State U., Baton Rouge, 1977; J.D., U. Ark.-Fayetteville, 1980. Bar: Ark. 1980. Ptnr., Huffman & Peace, Rogers, Ark., 1980-81; sole practice, Fayetteville, 1980-83. Contbr. poetry. Mem. ABA, Ark. Bar Assn. Home: Route 2 Box 309 A Lincoln AR 72744

PEACE, LISA BURK, systems programmer; b. San Diego, Jan. 31, 1960; d. Curtis R. and Karen (Schwab) Burk; m. Robert Dale Peace, June 1, 1985. A.A., Chipola Jr. Coll., Fla., 1980; B.S., U. West Fla., 1982. Computer systems analyst I, State of Fla., Tallahassee, 1982-83, II, 1983-84; programmer/analyst R.J. Kelly & Assocs., Tallahassee, 1985; systems programmer N.W. Regional Data Ctr., Tallahassee, 1985—. Editor bull. Capital Chatter, 1985-86. Vol., Leon County Humane Soc., 1985. Mem. Am. Bus. Women's Assn. (bull. chmn. 1985—), Nat. Assn. Female Execs. Democrat. Avocations: sewing; knitting; jogging. Office: 2048 E Paul Dirac Dr Tallahassee FL 32304

PEACE, MIRIAM SISKIN, cytotechnologist, lawyer; b. Winnipeg, Man., Can., Feb. 13, 1931; d. David L. and Rissa (Ghitter) Siskin; cert. Sch. of Cytology, Med. Coll. of Ga., 1951; L.L.B., John Marshall Sch. Law, 1972; children—Brian Smiley, Carl Smiley, Janice Smiley Hazlehurst, Vickie Smiley Sholes, Rissa Peace. Cytologist Med. Coll. of Ga., Augusta, 1951-52, Grady Hosp., Atlanta, 1956-57; supr. St. Joseph's Infirmary, Atlanta, 1957-62, Peace Labs., Atlanta, 1962-69; cytotechnologist Peachtree Lab., Atlanta, 1969—; supr. Piedmont Hosp., Atlanta, 1979—; admitted to Ga. bar, 1973; individual practice law, Atlanta, 1974-75. Precinct co-chmn. Andrew Young campaign for Congress, 1970, 72. Mem. Am. Soc. Clin. Pathologists (registered cytotechnologist, charter mem.), Am. Soc. for Cytotechnology, State Bar of Ga. Democrat. Jewish. Home: 4717 Roswell Rd NE Apt D7 Atlanta GA 30342 Office: 1968 Peachtree Rd NW Atlanta GA 30309

PEACOCK, LARITA WILLIAMS, information systems specialist; b. Madisonville, Ky., Mar. 24, 1954; d. Charles Eugene and Clara Bell (Smith) Williams; B.A. in Math., Princeton U., 1973; M.B.A., Stanford U., 1975; m. Hubert Leonard Peacock, Jr., Aug. 30, 1980; 1 child, William Swinson. Systems analyst Exxon Corp., Florham Park, N.J., 1976-77, Exxon Chem. Co. U.S.A., Houston, 1977-79; project mgr. info. systems dept. Marriott Corp., Bethesda, Md., 1980-82, mgr. systems devel. Roy Rogers div., 1982-84, mgr. MIS info. systems dept., 1984—. Mem. Nat. Assn. Female Execs., AAUW. Address: 20634 Neerwinder St Germantown MD 20874

PEACOCK, MOLLY, poet, English educator; b. Buffalo, June 30, 1947; d. Edward Frank and Pauline Ruth (Wright) P. B.A. magna cum laude, Harpur Coll., Binghamton, N.Y., 1969; M.A. with honors, Johns Hopkins U., 1977. Adminstr., lectr. in English, SUNY-Binghamton, 1970-76; lectr. Johns Hopkins U., Balt., 1977-78; poet-in-residence Del. Arts Council, Wilminton, 1978-81; instr. English, Friends Sem., N.Y.C., 1981—; lectr. various colls. and univs.; vis. poet N.Y. State Poets-in-Schs. Program, 1973-76; dir. Wilminton Writing Workshops. Author: And Live Apart, 1980; Raw Heaven, 1984. Danforth Found. fellow, 1976; Yaddo fellow, 1980, 82, Ingram Merrill Found., 1981, New Va. Rev., 1983; grantee Creative Artists Pub. Service Program, 1977, N.Y. Found. for Arts, 1985. Mem. Poetry Soc. Am. (governing bd. 1984—), MacDowell Colony (fellows com. 1982—, v.p. 1985), PEN. Home: 321 E 71 St Apt 5F New York NY 10021 Office: Friends Sem 222 E 16th St New York NY 10003

PEACOCK, WANDA MAUREEN, financial executive; b. Cleve., Nov. 27, 1944; d. Claude Daniel and Louise Irene (Browder) P.; m. Arthur Joseph Owens, Aug. 19, 1962 (div. 1969); children—Aurelia, Arthur. A.A., Cuyahoga Coll., Cleve., 1974; B.S., Dyke Coll., Cleve., 1976; postgrad. in banking and fin. Golden Gate U., Los Angeles, 1981-82. Income tax auditor IRS, Cleve., 1975-77; adminstrv. asst. Cleve. Job Corps Ctr., 1977-80; credit asst. Crocker Nat. Bank, Los Angeles, 1980-81, adminstr., 1981-83; cost analyst Aerojet ElectroSystems, Azusa, Calif., 1985—; income tax cons. Beneficial Tax Ctr., Pomona, Calif., 1980—, fin. planner, 1983—. Sunday sch. tchr. Temple Baptist Ch., Cleve., 1977-80; youth counselor Mt. Moriah Bapt. Ch., Los Angeles, 1981-82; counselor Praise Chapel, Ontario, Calif., 1984—. Mem. Nat. Soc. Pub. Adminstrs., Nat. Assn. Female Execs., Afro-Am. Soc. Democrat. Home: 8470 Kirkwood St Rancho Cucamonga CA 91730 Office: Aerojet ElectroSystems 1100 Hollyvale St Azusa CA 91702

PEAK, LORI MARIE, travel agency executive; b. Alliance, Ohio, Feb. 8, 1953; d. Frank Nick and Violet Richie (Polidan) Salaski; children—Anthony, Jessica. A.A., Mott Community Coll., Flint, Mich., 1973; Religious tng. permit Diocese of Lansing, Mich., 1973; A.A., Henry Ford Community Coll., 1979; B.S. in Elem. Edn./Spl. Edn., Wayne State U., 1982. Dental technician pvt. dental office, Flint, 1969-73; Out-patient clk. St. Joseph Hosp., Flint, 1973-75; sales distr. Tiara Exclusives, Dunkirk, Ind., 1978-79; dist. sales mgr. Wright Air Lines, Cleve., 1982-85; pres., owner Peak Travel Industries, 1984—. Served with USN, 1975-77. Mem. Nat. Assn. Female Execs., Dist. Area Sales Mgr. Assn., Detroit Women in Travel Assn., Detroit Passenger and Traffic Orgn., Detroit/Windsor Interline Club, Pi Lambda Theta. Home: 109 Fisher Ct Clawson MI 48017

PEALER-WENZEL, DEANNA RUTH, lawyer; b. Danville, Pa., Oct. 9, 1952; d. Harlan Dean and Ruth (Appleman) Pealer; m. Francis G. Wenzel, Jr., Aug. 30, 1980. B.A., Mansfield U., 1974; J.D., Dickinson Sch. Law, 1977. Bar: Pa. 1977. Claims atty. Nationwide Ins. Co., Harrisburg, Pa., 1977-79; sole practice, Bloomsburg, Pa., 1979—; spl. master Columbia County Ct., Bloomsburg, 1982—. Chmn., Columbia County Heart Fund Drive, Bloomsburg, 1980; bd. dirs. North Central Pa. chpt., Am. Heart Assn., Williamsport, 1980-83; mem. adv. bd. Children and Youth Services Agy., Columbia County, Pa., 1981-82; bd. dirs. Columbia County YMCA, Bloomsburg, 1983; co-chmn. publicity Bloomsburg Hosp. Aux., Bloomin Follies, Bloomsburg, 1984; crusade chmn. Am. Cancer Soc., 1985. Mem. ABA, Pa. Bar Assn., Columbia-Montour Bar Assn. (law day chmn. 1981-83, treas. 1984-85). Democrat. Methodist. Home: 455 Market St Bloomsburg PA 17815 Office: 455 Market St Bloomsburg PA 17815

PEARCE, BETTY MCMURRAY, engineering executive; b. Hastings, Nebr., Oct. 11, 1926; d. Frank Madry and Scereta (Mudd) McMurray; B.S. in Aerospace, U. Tex., Austin, 1949; 1 dau., Karen A. Harsley. Draftsman, Koch & Fowler, Civil Engrs., Dallas, 1945-47; with Vought Corp., Dallas, 1949—, project engr., 1955-77, engring project mgr., 1977-82; dir. LTV Fed. Credit Union, 1981-85; dir. A-T Engring. Club; cons. Pres., St. Andrews Catholic Ch. Council, Fort Worth, 1977-78; mem. Bishop's Adv. Council Fort Worth Diocese, 1980—, chmn. service com., 1980—, pres., 1981—. Mem. AIAA, Tech. Mktg. Soc. Am., St. Joseph's Hosp. Aux. Home: 4205 Galway Ave Fort Worth TX 76109 Office: PO Box 225907 Dallas TX 75265

PEARCE, DOROTHY ANDREE DE LORENZO, civic worker; b. N.Y.C., Mar. 22, 1927; d. Andrew John and Margaret Florence (Robilotti) De Lorenzo; m. Charles Wellington Pearce, Apr. 2, 1955 (div. Dec. 1983); children—John Y., Charles Wellington, Andrew F., Margaret E. B.A. in Sci., Barnard Coll., Columbia U., 1947. Research asst. cardiac catheterization lab. Bellevue Hosp., N.Y.C., 1948-50; research asst. Cornell U. Med. Coll., N.Y.C., 1950-55; exec. research librarian Shell Chem. Co., Houston, 1955-56, N.Y.C., 1956-57; bd. dirs. Greenwich House Settlement House, N.Y.C., 1946-47; Social hostess Young Women's Republican Club N.Y., Inc., 1946-54; thrift shop rep. Soc. N.Y. Hosp. Women's Aux., 1959-60; active New Orleans Opera House Assn. Women's Guild, 1964-73, bd. govs., 1965-73; bd. dirs. Sara Mayo Hosp. Guild, 1964—, chmn. hospitality com., 1967-72; active Crippled Children's Hosp. Guild, 1965—; active DePaul Hosp. Women's Aux., 1968-85, bd. dirs., 1985—, Valencia Mother's Aux., 1971-79, New Orleans Mus. Art, 1972—, Sophia Gumbel Women's Guild, 1972—, Friends of the Zoo, 1982—, Lighthouse for Blind Women's Guild, 1983—, St. Elizabeth's Home for Infants, 1984—; mem. Gallier Hall Women's Com., 1967-71; bd. dirs. Mercy Hosp. Women's Aux., 1965-72, pres., 1970; mem. fund raising com. Hotel Dieu Women's Aux., 1968;

bd. dirs., chmn. edn. and research fund com. Orleans Parish Med. Soc. Women's Aux., 1969-71; bd. dirs. Vis. Nurses Assns., 1971. Mem. New Orleans Spring Fiesta Assn., New Orleans Opera House Assn., New Orleans Garden Soc. (chmn. Christmas decorations 1969-70), Fgn. Relations Assn., AAUW, La. Landmark Soc., Roman Catholic. Avocations: music; travel; fine arts.

PEARCE, JANE, psychiatrist; b. Austin, Tex., Jan. 13, 1914; d. James Edward and Belinda (Doppelmayer) P.; student Radcliffe Coll., 1931-32; B.A. cum laude, U. Tex., Austin, 1934; M.D., U. Chgo., 1941, Ph.D., 1941; student Washington Sch. Psychiatry, 1947-48; grad. William A. White Inst., N.Y.C., 1944-49; student Inst. Individual Psychology, Chgo., 1936-41; children from previous marriage—Sarah, Robert, Paul, Christopher. Intern, Harriet Lane Hosp., Balt., 1942, Albany (N.Y.) Hosp., 1942-43, resident in psychiatry, 1943; resident N.Y. State Psychiat. Inst., N.Y.C., 1943-44, 48-49; pvt. practice psychoanalysis, N.Y.C., 1944—; tng. analyst William Alanson White Inst., 1946-57, faculty, 1950-57; co-founder, asst. dir., research dir., supr. Sullivan Inst. Research in Psychoanalysis, N.Y.C., 1957-77; mem. faculty N.Y. U., 1951-53; co-founder, clin. dir. North Side Center, N.Y.C., 1945-46. Diplomate Am. Bd. Psychiatry and Neurology. Fellow Am. Assn. Social Psychiatry; mem. AMA, Am. Psychiat. Assn., Physicians for Social Responsibility, Phi Beta Kappa, Sigma Xi, Kappa Kappa Gamma. Democrat. Author: (with Saul Newton) The Conditions of Human Growth, 1963; contbr. articles to profl. jours. Home: 332 W 77th St New York NY 10024 Office: 332 W 77th St New York NY 10024

PEARCE, JOAN DELAP, research company executive; b. Oakland, Calif., June 13, 1930; d. Robert Jerome and Wilhelmina (Reaume) DeLap; m. Gerald Allan Pearce, June 18, 1953; 1 child, Scott Ford. Student, U. Oreg., 1948-55. Research assoc. deForest Research, Los Angeles, 1966-78; dir. research Walt Disney Prodns., Burbank, Calif., 1978; assoc. dir. deForest Research, Los Angeles, 1978—; lighting dir. Wilcoxen Players, Beverly Hills, Calif., 1955-60, Theatre 40, Los Angeles, 1960-66. Bd. advisors Living History Ctr., Marin County, Calif., 1982—. Mem. Am. Film Inst. Democrat. Avocations: photography; travel; theater; swimming. Home: 2621 Rutherford Dr Los Angeles CA 90068 Office: deForest Research Service 780 N Gower St Los Angeles CA 90038

PEARCE, MARTHA VIRGINIA, educator; b. Wilmington, Del., Sept. 26, 1929; d. Alva Elmer and Mary Rickards (Clark) P.; B.S., Columbia U., 1958; M.S., Boston U., 1965; Ed.D., Ariz. State U., 1980. Faculty asso. Ariz. State U., Tempe, 1977-81, asst. prof. aero. tech., 1981—. Served with Nurses Corps, USN, 1954-75. Mem. Nat. Assn. Flight Instrs., Soaring Soc. Am., Ninety-Nines, Inc., Ariz. Adult Edn. Assn., Pi Lambda Theta, Alpha Eta Rho. Home: 2331 E Aspen Dr Tempe AZ 85282 Office: Ariz State U Tempe AZ 85287

PEARCE, MARY MCCALLUM (MRS. CLARENCE A PEARCE), artist; b. Hesperia, Mich., Feb. 17, 1906; d. Archibald and Mabel (McNeil) McCallum; A.B., Oberlin Coll., 1927; student John Huntington Inst., 1929-34, Cleve. Inst. Art, 1935-37, 54, Dayton Art Inst., 1946-49; m. Clarence A. Pearce, June 30, 1928 (dec.); children—Mary Martha (Mrs. William B. Robinson), Thomas McCallum. One man shows at Cleve. Women's City Club, 1959, 69, Cleve. Orch., 1967, Cleve. Playhouse Gallery, 1968, 71, 76, Van Wezel Hall, 1979, Sarasota (Fla.) Library, 1979, Hilton Leech Gallery, Sarasota, 1979, 80, 81, 86 Fed. Bank, Sarasota, 1980; exhibited in group shows at Oberlin Art Mus., Akron Art Inst., Grand Rapids (Mich.) Art Gallery, Dayton (Ohio) Art Inst., Smithsonian Inst., Birmingham Mus. of Art, Am. Watercolor Soc., Cleve. Mus. Art, Foster Harmon Galleries, 1986, many others: represented in pvt. collections: tchr. art, supr. pub. schs., Mayfield Heights, Ohio, 1927-28, Maple Heights, Ohio, 1928-30, Chagrin Falls, Ohio, 1938-39. Named best woman artist Ohio Watercolor Soc., 1955; recipient Bush Meml. award Columbus Gallery Fine Arts, 1962; nat. 1st prize for drawing Nat. League Am. Penwomen, 1966, 68; Littlehouse award Ala. Watercolor Soc., 1967; Wolfe award Columbus Gallery Fine Arts, 1971; awards Longboat Key Art Center, 1973, 75, 79-86; award Southeastern Art Soc., 1975; Merit award Art League Manatee County, 1977, 78, 3d prize, 1985; 3d prize Sarasota Art Assn., 1977, 78, Merit award, 1981, 85; 1st prize Venice (Fla.) Art League, 1979, 81, 82, 83, 86, 2d prize, 1979, 80, 81, 3d prize, 1978, merit award, 1985; 1st prize Hilton Leech Gallery, 1981, 85, numerous others. Mem. Nat. League Am. Pen Women (treas. 1962), Am. (assoc.), Ala., Fla. watercolor socs. Republican. Congregationalist. Home: 5400 Ocean Blvd Apt 1401 Sarasota FL 33581

PEARCY, CYNTHIA ANN, nurse; b. Providence, May 31, 1946; d. William Frances and Marcella Rose Ferris; R.N., Grace Hosp., Detroit, 1967; divorced; children—Shawn Michael, Ryan Robert. Staff nurse Grace Hosp., 1967-68; head nurse ICU, Martin Place Hosp., Warren, Mich., 1968-69; charge nurse intensive cardiac care S. Macomb Hosp., Warren, 1971-73; head nurse intensive care stepdown St. Joseph Hosp., Mt. Clemens, Mich., 1975-80, edn. coordinator critical care services, 1980—, also instr. coronary care. Mem. Nat. Assn. Female Execs., Internat. Platform Assn., Am. Heart Assn. (1st v.p. Macomb County div.), Am. Assn. Critical Care Nurses. Roman Catholic. Home: 37342 Glenbrook Mount Clemens MI 48043 Office: 215 North Ave Mount Clemens MI 48043

PEARLMAN, FLORENCE SADOFF, social worker; b. N.Y.C., Dec. 26, 1928; d. Sam and Eva (Brunstein) Sadoff; B.A., Barnard Coll., 1950; M.S.W., Wurzweiler Sch. Social Work, 1971; m. Donald Pearlman, June 22, 1947 (div. Feb. 1971); children—David J., Erica Lee (dec.). Editorial staff profl. jours., 1951-54; alumnae sec. Briarcliff Coll., Briarcliff Manor, N.Y., 1966-67; psychiat. social worker Westchester County (N.Y.) Mental Health Clinics, 1971; supr. Alcoholism Clinic, Yonkers, 1974-75, sr. social worker, 1986—. Mem. coms. Planned Parenthood-World Population, 1965-75, bd. dirs., 1966-72; active Planned Parenthood Westchester, 1962-80; bd. dirs. Assoc. Alumnae of Barnard Coll., 1975-78. Mem. Acad. Cert. Social Workers, Nat. Assn. Social Workers, Assn. Amateur Chamber Music Soc., Am. Orthopsychiat. Assn. Democrat. Jewish. Club: The Bohemians. Home: 17 Cedar Road S Katonah NY 10536

PEARLMAN, MARION OLA, educational administrator, actress, consultant; b. Mechanicsville, N.Y., Dec. 24, 1920; d. Charles Forrest and Minnie (Mayhew) McBride; m. Albert M. Pearlman, June 9, 1963 (dec. Jan. 1985); 1 son, Michael Edward. B.S., SUNY-Buffalo, 1951; M.Ed., U. Ariz., 1959. Tchr., Pierce Creek Sch., Binghamton, N.Y., 1940-42; tchr. Skaneateles, N.Y., 1942-43; vacation relief agt., reservation clk., ticket agt., auditor, supr. sales control Am. Airlines, Buffalo, 1943-48; ins. analyst Aetna Casualty and Surety Co., Buffalo, 1948-49; tchr., Lancaster, N.Y., 1949-51, University Heights, Tucson, Ariz., 1951-59; Livingston, Calif., 1959-60; cons. elem. edn. County Office Edn., Napa, Calif., supr. Alum Rock Sch. Dist., San Jose, Calif., 1961-62; supr. schs. Nogales, Ariz., 1962-63; tch. Gump Sch. for retarded, blind, emotionally handicapped, deaf, trainable and educable retarded, 1964-78; prin. Valencia Sch., Sunnyside Unified Sch. Dist. #12, Tucson, 1978-83; pvt. cons., 1983—; actress Sunset Years, Access TV, 1984—; lectr. Kans. State Tchrs. Coll., Emporia. Mem. exec. com. Tucson House for Retarded; bd. dirs. Beacon Found. for Mentally Retarded; active PTA, PTO; del. to Ariz. State Assembly. Cert. elem. tchr. Democrat. Jewish. Mem. NEA, Ariz. Edn. Assn., Tucson Edn. Assn., Sunnyside Adminstrs. Assn., AAUW (membership com., del. to nat. conv.), Phi Delta Kappa, Pi Lambda Theta.

PEARLMAN, NANCY SPARKS, business entrepreneur; b. Sheffield, Ala., Jan. 31, 1940; d. Robert Roy and Sybil Laverne (Cox) Sparks; m. Jerome Pearlman, May 30, 1970. B.A., Ga. State U., 1967; M.A., William Patterson State U., 1972. Dir. bus. affairs SUNY-N.Y.C., 1968-76; pres. Double Eagle Equipment Co., Inc., Dayton, N.J., 1977—. Home: 47 Patton Dr East Brunswick NJ 08816 Office: Double Eagle Equipment Co Inc 285 Dayton-Jamesburg Rd Dayton NJ 08810

PEARRIE, PATRICIA MAE, accountant; b. Detroit, Nov. 19, 1956; d. Odis and Verdie Lee (Braden) P. B.B.A., Eastern Mich. U., 1981. Acct., Colwell Mortgage Corp., Houston, 1983—, Exec. Mgmt. Internat., Houston, 1981-83; jr. acct. Eastern Mich. U., Ypsilanti, 1979-81. Active Big Sisters Program, Ypsilanti, 1980-81; mem. State Gospel Choir, Detroit, 1973, Satori Theatre Group, Detroit, 1973. Mem. Alpha Kappa Alpha (dean of pledges 1976). Democrat. Baptist. Office: Colwell Mortgage Corp 5177 Richmond Ave Houston TX 77056

PEARSALL, PENNY LEA, cosmetics sales executive; b. Fayetteville, N.C., Jan. 14, 1942; d. Arthur H. and Ruby Mae P.; A.A., Lees-McRae Coll., 1962; student med. record library sci. N.C. Baptist Hosp., Winston-Salem, N.C., 1963. Med. record adminstr. Med. Coll. Va. Hosp., 1963-65; dir. med. records Westbrook Psychiat. Hosp., Richmond, Va., 1965-70; dir. med. record consulting Am. Health Services, Richmond, 1970-72; dir. med. records Henrico Doctor's Hosp., Richmond, 1976-81; exec. sr. dir. Mary Kay Cosmetics, Glen Allen, Va., 1975-86; cons. to nursing home facilities. Recipient 3 Cadillacs, Mary Kay Cosmetics, 1980—, named to 350,000 Club, 1982, 500,000 Club, 1982, 600,000 Club, 1983; Sammy award, Richmond, 1982. Mem. Am., Va. med. record assns., Richmond Area Women Bus. Owners. Home and Office: 8652 Rio Grande Rd Richmond VA 23229

PEARSON, ANN CHAMPAGNE, economic/tax advantage company salesperson; b. Orlando, Fla., July 9, 1953; d. Edward David and Mary Ruth (Hoffpauier) Champagne; m. Paul E. Pearson, Mar. 31, 1972 (div. Feb. 1984); children—Eric, Brandon. Student U. South. La., 1970-74, La. State U., 1979-81. Jr. acct., Employers Inc., Dallas, 1975-79; office mgr. GEO'je's, Baton Rouge, 1979-81; owner, pres. Office Mgr. Inc., Baton Rouge, 1981-82; sales asst. Equitvest, Baton Rouge, 1982-84; mktg. dir. Hall Fin., Dallas and Houston, 1984-86, direct sales rep. C, Newport Beach, Calif., 1986—. Chmn. com. Re-elect Mayor Whitmire, Houston, 1985. Mem. Newport Beach C. of C., NABC Writers Assn., Nat. Assn. Female Execs. Republican. Lutheran. Avocations: tennis; racquetball; jogging; jazzercize. Office Hall Fin Group 610 Newport Ctr Dr #830 Newport Beach CA 92660

PEARSON, ANTONIA GRACE, social worker; b. N.Y.C., June 10, 1955; d. Nellie Lisby Pearson; 1 son, James Arthur Epps III. Student Howard U., 1975-78; B.S., Herbert H. Lehman Coll., 1982; B.R.E., Abundant Life Tabernacle Bible Inst., Bronx, 1984; postgrad. Columbia U., 1986—. Sec., Abundant Life Tabernacle, Bronx, 1982-83; computer operator Mass. Mut. Ins. Co., N.Y.C., 1982-83; social worker Edwin Gould Services for Children, N.Y.C., 1983—. Mgr. book store Abundant Life Tabernacle, Bronx, 1985—, coordinator social events, 1984—, youth coordinator, 1985—. Democrat. Avocations: volleyball; running; theatre. Mailing Address: 285 E 156th St Bronx NY 10451 Office: Care Abundant Life Tabernacle 2692 3d Ave Bronx NY 10452

PEARSON, BELINDA KEMP, economist, consultant; b. Kansas City, Mo., Apr. 14, 1931; d. William Ewing and Margaret Norton (Johnson) Kemp; m. Carl Erik Pearson, Sept. 15, 1953; children—Erik, Frederick, Margaret. B.A., Wellesley Coll., 1952; M.A., Tufts U., 1954, Ph.D., 1958. Research asst. Harvard U., Cambridge, Mass., 1954-55; instr. econs. Suffolk U., Boston, 1956-59; lectr. econs. Wellesley Coll., Mass., 1964-65; econ. analyst, asst. economist Seafirst Bank, Seattle, 1966-79, v.p., 1974-85, chief economist, 1979-85; dir., treas. Lektor Inc., Bellevue, Wash., 1984—; mem. Wash. Gov.'s Council Econ. Advisors, Olympia, 1979—; dir. Pacific N.W. Regional Econ. Conf., 1979—; mem. econ. devel./edn. council Assn. Wash. Bus., Olympia, 1983—. Mem. Wash. State Library Commn., Olympia, 1976-84, vice chmn., 1983-84; bd. regents Wash. State U., Pullman, 1985—. Fulbright scholar London Sch. Econs., 1952-53. Mem. Am. Econ. Assn., Nat. Assn. Bus. Economists (chmn. arrangements ann. meeting 1982), Seattle Economists Club (pres. 1973-74), LWV, Mcpl. League Seattle. Office: Lektor Inc 305 108th Ave NE Suite 100 Bellevue WA 98004

PEARSON, BETSY JOANNE, medical technologist; b. Chester County, S.C., June 28, 1949; d. J.O. and Eloise Bobbie Jean (Reese) Pearson. B.S. in Biology, Tuskegee Inst., 1971; cert. in med. tech. Maharry Med. Coll., Nashville, 1972. Staff med. technologist Mound Bayou Community Health Ctr. and Hosp. (Miss.), 1973; staff med. technologist, then supr. microbiology lab., Chester, S.C., 1973-78, asst. chief med. tech., 1976-78; instr. lab. and nursing service Chester County Hosp. (S.C.), 1973-78, chemistry and blood bank med. technologist, 1978—, Musician, Chester County Bapt. Women's Conv., 1978—. Mem. Am. Soc. Clin. Pathologists, Am. Soc. Med. Tech., Nat. Cert. Agy. Med. Lab. Personnel, S.C. Emergency Med. Services Assn., S.C. Soc. Med. Tech., Women's Unltd. Profl. Orgn., Delta Sigma Theta (chpt. journalist). Established and endowed Betsy Pearson ann. award, Meharry Med. Coll. Home: 72 By-Pass Box 42 Chester SC 29706 Office: 1000 Blythe Blvd Charlotte NC 28232

PEARSON, CAROL ANN, air force officer; b. Van Nuys, Calif., May 21, 1954; d. Ralph M. and Florence Ilma (Faber) Tyler; m. Clinton Charles Pearson, July 14, 1978. A.A.S. in Gen. Bus. Mgmt., U. Alaska, 1981; B.A.S. in Personnel Mgmt. and Labor Relations, U. Md., 1983; A.A.S. in Resource Mgmt., Air Force Community Coll., 1984. Diet therapist aide Calabassass Hosp., Calif., 1972; enlisted U.S. Air Force, 1973, advanced through grades to 1st lt., 1986; diet specialist, Tex., Alaska, 1973-75; med. adminstrv. specialist, Alaska, Md., 1976-84, contract mgmt. officer, Loring AFB, Maine, 1984—. Mem. Alaska Prospector's Soc. (pres. 1979), Spinner's and Weaver's Guild. Republican. Home: PO Box 566 Loring AFB ME 04751 Office: 42 BMW/LGC Loring AFB ME 04751

PEARSON, DOROTHY MARIE, social worker, educator; b. Darbun, Miss., June 22, 1937; d. Wallace and Annie Bell (Stovall) P.; B.A. magna cum laude (La. Legis. scholar), So. U., 1958; M.S., U. Wis., 1960, Ph.D., 1973; cert. grad. program in mgmt. Simmons Coll., 1979. Psychiat. social worker Milw. County (Wis.) Mental Health Center, 1960-64; asst. prof. Sch. Social Welfare, U. Wis., Milw., 1964-70; pres. Urban Resources, Inc., Milw., 1970-73; asst. prof. Sch. Medicine, U. Miami (Fla.), 1973-75; adj. prof. Sch. Social Work, Barry Coll., Miami, 1973-75; asso. dean, prof. Sch. Social Work, Howard U., Washington, 1975—, founding dir. doctoral program, 1976, chmn. Conf. on Women, 1979; co-founder Bogalusa (La.) Tng. Center, 1954, Wis. Assn. Black Social Workers, 1972; charter mem. Wis. Assn. Social Workers for the Retarded, 1966; treas. Wis. Rehab. Assn., 1971-72; cons. Jewish Vocat. Service, Milw., 1966-73, Opportunities Industrialization Center, Milw., 1968-70; advisor Nat. Study of Black Americans, Mich., 1978, Women in Crisis Conf., N.Y., 1980; evaluator Middle States Assn. Secondary Schs. and Colls., 1981. Recipient service awards Bogalusa Tng. Center, 1955, Barry Coll. Assn. Black Student Social Workers, 1973; NIMH trainee, 1970-73, tng. grantee, 1976-80. Mem. Council on Social Work Edn. (chmn. Black Caucus, commr. on edn. planning), Nat. Assn. Social Workers (v.p. Met. D.C. chpt., chmn. labor task force), Am. Orthopsychiat. Assn., Acad. Certified Social Workers, Alpha Kappa Mu. Club: Black Women's Agenda. Contbr. sect. to publ. in field. Office: School Social Work Howard Univ 2400-6th St NW Washington DC 20059

PEARSON, FAITH WAYNE, management information systems executive; b. Monroeville, Ind., Oct. 24, 1921; d. Joshua Paul and Roxie Etta (Faith) Wayne; m. Alphonsus Dubocq, Sept. 6, 1942 (div. Jan. 1950); children—Lance McDonald Croxall, Hal Wayne Croxall; m. Robert Justin Pearson, Aug. 16, 1958. B.S., Purdue U., 1942. Analytical engr. Hamilton Stand div. UTC, East Hartford, Conn., 1942-47; corp. sec., v.p., treas., dir. divs. United Steel of Am., N.Y.C., 1950-62; program supr. Conn. Gen. Life Ins. Co., Hartford, 1962-67; dir. info. systems Town of Wethersfield, Conn., 1972-81; pres., chmn. Mgmt. Info. Systems & Tng., Inc., Farmington, Conn., 1978—; tchr. Inst. Pub. Service, U. Conn., 1977, Yale U., 1978; speaker various assns., agys. Co-author: monograph Low Cost Data Management Tools for Municipalities, 1976; Computers Without Programmers, 1981. Mem. Farmington Republican Town Com., 1982-83. Recipient Outstanding Contbn. award Am. Soc. for Pub. Adminstrn., 1975. Mem. Govt. Mgmt. Info. Scis. (Outstanding Service award 1980-81, nat. pres. 1981), Data Processing Mgmt. Assn., Alpha Xi Omega. Home: 77 Ely Rd Farmington CT 06032 Office: Mgmt Info Systems & Tng Inc 1 Monteith Dr Farmington CT 06032

PEARSON, LOUISE MARY, manufacturing company executive; b. Inverness, Scotland, Dec. 14, 1919 (parents Am. citizens); d. Louis Houston and Jessie M. (McKenzie) Lenox; grad. high sch.; m. Nels Kenneth Pearson, June 28, 1941; children—Lorine Pearson Walters, Karla. Dir. Wauconda Tool & Engring. Co., Inc., Algonquin, Ill., 1950-86; reporter Oak Leaflet, Crystal Lake, Ill., 1944-47, Sidelights, Wilmette, Ill., 1969-72, 79-82. Active Girl Scouts U.S.A., 1955-65. Recipient award for appreciation work with Girl Scouts, 1965. Clubs: Antique Automobile of Am. (Hershey, Pa.); Veteran Motor Car (Boston); Classic Car of Am. (Madison, N.J.). Home: 125 Dole Ave Crystal Lake IL 60014

PEARSON, MARILYN BIRCH, lawyer; b. Anderson, Ind., Sept. 8, 1937; d. Charles Eugene and Frances Elizabeth (Barnett) Birch; m. Gary Bruce Pearson, Mar. 22, 1957; children—Eric John, Amy Lynn, Jill Ann, Mary Jo. B.S., Mich. State U., 1959; M.S. in Adminstrn., Central Mich. U., 1980; J.D., Thomas M. Cooley Law Sch., 1980. Bar: Mich. 1981. Research technician Mich. State U., East Lansing, 1959-60; founder, organizer, dir. Midland County Vols. in Probation (Mich.), 1972-76; staff intern Ho. of Reps., Lansing, Mich., 1977-78; law clk./intern Legal Aid, Lansing, Mich., 1978-80; sole practice, Lansing, 1981-85; staff atty. UAW-GM Legal Services, 1985—. Editor HELPS (booklet), 1972; VIP Handbook, 1974. Leader Mitten Bay Council Girl Scouts U.S. 1966-73; bd. dirs. Mich. Vols. in Corrections, 1976; founder Pro Bono Lawyers Service, Lansing, Mich., 1982, bd. dirs., 1983-85; mem. citizens adv. com. for Vols. in Probation, Lansing, Mich., 1983-85. Recipient Liberty Bell award Midland County Bar Assn., 1974. Mem. Women Lawyers Assn. Mich. (v.p. Mid-Mich. region 1982-83, pres. Mid-Mich. region 1983-84, co-chmn., bd. dirs. state legis. com. 1984—), AAUW (chmn. various coms. 1966-77), Mich. Bar Assn., ABA, Am. Trial Lawyers Assn., Ingham County Bar Assn. Baptist. Office: 3801 W Boulevard Dr Flint MI 48501

PEARSON, MARJORIE, architectural historian; b. St. Paul, Oct. 26, 1948; d. Edwin Leonard and Gladys Mildred (Troolin) P. B.A., U. Chgo., 1970, M.A., 1972; M.Phil., CUNY, 1984. Research asst. Ill. Hist. Structures Survey, Chgo., 1971-72; researcher Landmarks Preservation Commn., N.Y.C., 1973-76, dep. dir. research, 1976-78, dir. research, 1978—. Contbr. articles to profl. jours. Mem. Soc. Archtl. Historians, Coll. Art Assn., Nat. Trust Hist. Preservation. Democrat. Home: 850 E 23rd St Brooklyn NY 11210 Office: Landmarks Preservation Commn 20 Vesey St New York NY 10007

PEARSON, MARY LYNN, medical technologist; b. Milw., Dec. 13, 1944; d. Arvid Robert and Mary (Haven) Pearson; B.S., U. Wis., Madison, 1967. Med. technologist St. Michael Hosp., Milw., 1970-73, 74, Comprehensive Drug Program of Dade County, Miami, Fla., 1973; supr. clin. toxicology, dept. pathology Milw. County Med. Complex, 1974—. Mem. Am. Soc. Clin. Pathologists, Am. Soc. Med. Technologists, Madison-Chgo.-Milw. Mass Spectrometry Discussion Group. Lutheran. Contbr. articles to profl. jours. Office: 8700 W Wisconsin Ave Milwaukee WI 53226

PEARSON, PATRICIA HARE, psychotherapist; b. Dallas, July 30, 1950; d. Winston Hare and Phyllis Muriel (Skogan) P. B.A., So. Methodist U., 1972; M.S.W., U. Tex. Arlington, 1976. Counselor supr. Salvation Army, Dallas, 1974-75; psychotherapist, Dallas, 1975—; pres. Making Contact Seminars, Dallas, 1974—; cons. in field. Bd. dirs. Turtle Creek Manor, Inc., 1982-84; mem. speakers bur. Dallas Women's Found., 1985; adviser pub. awareness State of Tex. 1986; mem. Women's Ctr. Dallas, 1986, Susan G. Komen Found., Dallas, 1986. Named A Woman of 1985, Two Byrds Pub. Co., 1985. Mem. Dallas Soc. for Bioenergetic Analysis (bd. dirs.), Am. Group Psychotherapy, Nat. Assn. Social Workers, Internat. Inst. Bioenergetic Analysis. Mem. United Ch. of Christ. Avocations: scuba diving; walking; reading; sailing. Home: 9328 Chiswell Dallas TX 75238 Office: 8350 Meadow Rd Suite 284 Dallas TX 75231

PEARSON, SUSAN WINIFRED, educational administrator; b. Wasco, Calif., Oct. 8, 1941; d. Gerald Thomas and Maxine (Jensen) P.; B.S., Tex. Christian U., 1963, M.Ed., 1971; Ed.D., U. Houston, 1982. Tchr. history, chmn. dept. Spring Branch Ind. Sch. Dist., Houston, 1963-68; personnel asst. Tenneco Inc., Houston, 1969-70; grad. asst. Tex. Christian U., 1970-71; dir. student activities Navarro Jr. Coll., Corsicana, Tex., 1972-73; dir. counseling services North Harris County Coll., Houston, 1973-84, div. head bus., communications and fine arts, developmental studies and counseling, 1984-86, dean instrn./student services, 1986—. Mem. Am. Personnel and Guidance Assn., Am. Coll. Personnel Assn., Nat. Assn. Women Deans, Adminstrs. and Counselors, So. Coll. Personnel Assn., Tex. Assn. Women Deans, Adminstrs. and Counselors, Tex. Assn. Coll. and Univ. Student Personnel Adminstrs., Phi Kappa Phi, Delta Gamma. Presbyterian. Author articles in field. Office: 20000 Kingwood Dr Kingwood TX 77339

PEASE, CAROL HELENE, physical oceanographer, polar meteorologist; b. Bay City, Mich., Dec. 29, 1949; d. George Olson and Mernabelle Hattie (Laabs) P.; m. Alexander Jeffrey Chester, June 16, 1974 (div. May 1978). Student U. Mich., 1968-71; B.S. in Math., U. Miami, 1972; M.S. in Phys. Oceanography, U. Wash., 1975, M.S. in Meteorology, 1981, Ph.C. in Meteorology, 1985. Research asst. Arctic ice dynamics joint expt. U. Wash., Seattle, 1972-75; oceanographer Pacific Marine Environ. Lab.-NOAA, Seattle, 1975-78, sea ice project leader, 1978—; session chmn. Symposium on Meteorology and Oceanography of N.Am. High Latitudes, 1984. Mem. Assn. Women in Sci., Am. Geophys. Union, Am. Meteorol. Soc., AAAS, Standing Com. on Polar Meteorology and Oceanography, Arboretum Found., Seattle Art Mus., Nat. Women's Polit. Caucus. Club: Corinthian Yacht (Seattle). Lodge: Daughters of Norway (sec. 1978-81). Avocations: race keelboats; gardening. Office: Pacific Marine Environ Lab 7600 Sand Point Way NE Seattle WA 98115

PEASE, ELEANOR THOMPSON (MRS. DONALD CARGILL PEASE), lawyer; b. Bucyrus, Ohio, Mar. 28, 1923; s. Edgar William and Mary (Biss) Thompson; m. Donald Cargill Pease, Sept. 9, 1949; 1 child, William Thompson. B.A., Vassar Coll., 1944; J.D., Yale U., 1946. Bar: U.S. Dist. Ct. D.C., U.S. Ct. Appeals (D.C. cir.) 1947. Corp. lawyer E.I. Dupont Co., 1947-49. By-laws chmn. Jr. League, Wilmington, Del., 1951-53, bd. dirs., 1951-53, mag. chmn., 1959-60, edn. com., 1961-62; pres. Jr. League of Wilmington Sustainers Garden Club, 1969-70; by-laws chmn., bd. dirs. Del. Soc. Prevention Cruelty to Animals, 1950-52; day chmn. Winterthur Mus. Jr. League docents, 1955-61; del., class rep. Vassar Alumnae Council, 1954; parliamentarian Girl Scouts, Wilmington, 1957, 59; pres. Del. Vassar Club, 1960-62; area chmn. United Fund, 1960-62; exec. com. Women's Coll. Info. Program, 1961; docent Del. Art Mus., 1961-63; mem. Cts. Task Force Del. Agy. to Reduce Crime, 1968-71. Bd. dirs. Vol. bur. Del. Welfare Council, 1950-52, Friends of John Dickinson Mansion, 1979-80. Mem. Del. Hist. Soc., Nat. Trust for Hist. Preservation, Nat. Soc. Colonial Dames Am. (bd. mgrs. 1973-79, pres. Del. chpt. 1976-79), Roger Williams Family Assn. Republican. Presbyterian. (deacon). Home: 804 Princeton Rd Westover Hills Wilmington DE 19807

PEASLEE, CATHERINE GOREY, publisher; b. Joliet, Ill., Nov. 17, 1922; d. Thomas Vincent and Rose Veronica (Bolger) Gorey; m. Alexander L. Peaslee, Dec. 2, 1944; children—Sarah E., Ann L., Margaret N., Elizabeth R. S. B.A., Miami U., Oxford, Ohio, 1944; M.A., George Washington U., Washington, 1963. Pres., Charlottesville Observer, Inc., Va., 1978—; pub., editor Charlottesville-Albemarle Observer. Pres. Meml. Planning Soc. of the Piedmont, Charlottesville, 1973-74, 1983—; vice chmn. Pvt. Industry Council. Mem. LWV. Home: 305-D 2d St Charlottesville VA 22901 Office: Charlottesville Albemarle Observer 100 South St Charlottesville VA 22901-0617

PEASLEE, MARY ELLEN, computer executive; b. Calais, Maine, Oct. 24, 1933; d. Herbert and Minnie (McDowell) Hold; m. Garfield Peaslee, July 2, 1928; children—Jennifer, Beverley. Student pub. schs., Maine. Dir. customer services First of Boston Computersities, 1969-75; mgmt. analyst Bur. Budget, Maine, 1975-77; dir. central licensing Bus. Regulation (now computer Services) State of Maine, Augusta, 1977—. Mem. and sec. Windsor Planning Bd., 1979—; mem. Republican Town Com., 1983—. Recipient Cert., Kiwanis, Augusta, Maine, 1965; Appreciation award, Mid-State Coll., 1985. Mem. Clearinghouse on Licensure Enforcement and Registration, Ins. Women of Central Maine (pres. 1965-66). Lodge: Grange. Avocations: swimming; camping; sewing; writing. Home: RFD 6 Box 723 Augusta ME 04330 Office: Dept Bus OCC and Prof Reg Computer Services State House Station #35 Augusta ME 04333

PEAVEY, MELIA MCRAE, electronics company executive; b. Meridian, Miss., Aug. 18, 1954; d. John L. McRae, Jr. and Doris (Hagwood) Goodman; m. Hartley D. Peavey, Nov. 18, 1977; children—Joseph Thomas, Marcus Clinton. Vice pres. Peavey Electronics Corp., Meridian, Miss., 1980—; pres. Audio Media Research, Meridian, 1980—, PV Fin., Meridian, 1984—; dir. First United Bank, Meridian, 1982—. Bd. dirs. Jr. Achievement, Meridian, 1983, Blood Services, Meridian, 1984—. Republican. Baptist. Office: Peavey Electronics Corp 711 A St Meridian MS 39301

PECARICH, PAMELA JAE, accountant; b. Grand Island, Nebr., Nov. 11, 1943; d. A.J. and Lorraine Hanway; student U. Calif.-Berkeley, 1961-62; B.S. with honors, Calif. State U., 1969; postgrad. in acctg. U. Wash., 1971-72; m. Frank J. Pecarich, Apr. 13, 1965; 1 son, Jason Dean. C.P.A. Sr. cons. revenue and taxation com. Calif. State Assembly, 1969-74; cons. U.S. Adminstrv. Conf., Washington, 1974-75; dir. Office Policy and Planning, Commodity Futures Trading Commn., 1975-77; staff dir. subcom. on oversight U.S. Ho. of Reps. Ways and Means Com., 1977-81, chief tax policy analyst, 1981-84; ptnr. nat. tax directorate Coopers & Lybrand, Washington, 1984—. Mem. Am. Soc. Pub. Adminstrn., Beta Alpha Psi, Beta Gamma Sigma, Phi Kappa Phi. Office: 1800 M St NW Washington DC 20036

PECK, DIANNE KAWECKI, architect; b. Jersey City, June 13, 1945; d. Thaddeus Walter and Harriet Ann (Zlotkowski) Kawecki; B.A. in Arch., Carnegie Mellon U., 1968; m. Gerald Paul Peck, Sept. 1, 1968; children—Samantha Gillian, Alexis Hilary. Architect, P.O.D. Research & Devel., 1968, Kohler-Daniels & Assos., Vienna, Va., 1969-71, Beery-Rio & Assos., Annandale, Va., 1971-73; partner Peck & Peck Architects, Occoquan, Va., 1973-74, Peck, Peck & Williams, Occoquan, 1974-81; corp. officer Peck Peck & Assos., Inc., Woodbridge, Va., 1981—. Work pub. in Am. Architecture, 1985. Vice pres. Vocat. Edn. Found., 1976; chairwoman architects and engrs. United Way; mem. Health Systems Agy. of No. Va., commendations, 1977; mem. Washington Profl. Women's Coop.; chairwoman Indsl. Devel. Authority of Prince William, 1976, vice chair, 1977, mem., 1975-79. Recipient commendation Prince William Bd. Suprs., 1976, State of Art award for Control Hdqrs. design, 1985. Mem. Prince William C. of C. (dir.). Republican. Roman Catholic. Club: Soroptimist. Research on inner-city rehab. Office: 1924 Opitz Blvd Woodbridge VA 22191

PECK, ELLIE ENRIQUEZ, state official; b. Sacramento, Oct. 21, 1934; d. Rafael Enriquez and Eloisa Garcia Rivera; m. Raymond Charles Peck, Sept. 5, 1957; children—Reginaldo, Enrico, Francisca Guerrero, Teresa, Linda, Margaret, Raymond Charles, Christina. Student polit. sci. Sacramento State U., 1974. Tng. services coordinator Calif. Div. Hwys., Sacramento, 1963-67; tech. and mgmt. cons., Sacramento, 1968-78; expert examiner Calif. Personnel Bd., 1976-78; tng. cons. Calif. Personnel Devel. Center, Sacramento, 1978; spl. cons. Calif. Commn. on Fair Employment and Housing, 1978; community services rep. U.S. Bur. of Census, No. Calif. counties, 1978-80; spl. cons. Calif. Dept. Consumer Affairs, Sacramento, 1980-83, project dir. Golden State Sr. Discount Program, 1980-83; asst. chief of staff and dir. spl. programs for Calif. Lt. Gov., 1983—; chairperson Calif. Suprs.' Forum, 1966. Trustee, Stanford Settlement, Inc., Sacramento, 1975-79, hon. life trustee, 1979—; bd. dirs. Sacramento Emergency Housing Center, 1974-77; del. Democratic Nat. Conv., 1976; co-chairperson rules com., mem. exec. bd. Calif. Dem. Central Com. Recipient numerous awards, including Outstanding Community Service award Comuicaciones Unidos de Norte Atzlan, 1975, 77, Outstanding Service award, Chicano/Hispanic Dem. Caucus, 1979, Vol. Service award Calif. Human Devel. Corp., 1981. Mem. NAACP, Nat. Women's Polit. Caucus, Comision Femenil Mexicana Nacional Inc. (nat. exec. bd. 1979-81, chpt. pres. 1981-83). Club: Hispanic Dem. Sacramento County (v.p. 1982-83). Author U.S. Office Consumer Edn. publ., 1982, Calif. Dept. Consumer Affairs publ., 1981. Home: 2667 Coleman Way Sacramento CA 95818

PECK, GAYLE LOUISE, med. technologist; b. Yonkers, N.Y., Mar. 14, 1948; d. Joseph John and Jean Elizabeth Canepi; B.S., Quinnipiac Coll., Hamden, Conn., 1970; diploma in med. tech. Hosp. of St. Raphael, New Haven, 1970; m. Laurance Edward Peck, Oct. 13, 1973. Supr. chemistry Mt. Sinai Hosp., Hartford, Conn., 1971-72; mem. lab. staff VA Med. Center, Palo Alto, Calif., 1972—, asst. supr. blood bank, 1976—; instr. Sch. Med. Tech., San Francisco State U., 1979—. Mem. Am. Soc. Clin. Pathologists (asso.), South Bay Immunology Club (pres. 1979). Office: VA Med Center 3801 Miranda Ave Palo Alto CA 94304

PECK, NANCY DILLMAN, lawyer; b. St. Louis, July 24, 1935; d. Kennett Wade and Dorothy Horton (Pershall) Dillman; m. Robert Arnold Feldman, Jan. 2, 1982; children by previous marriage—Kate Peck Volta, Edward P. Peck, David N. Peck. Student Wellesley Coll., 1953-56; B.A., U. Rochester, 1970; LL.D., SUNY-Amherst, 1979. Bar: N.Y. 1980. Adminstrv. asst. Harvard U. Sch. Medicine, Boston, 1957-60; adminstr. Clin. Research Ctr., Washington U. Sch. Medicine, St. Louis, 1960-63; human resources dir. Neighborhood Health Ctrs., Rochester, N.Y., 1970-73; exec. dir. Rochester Area Found., 1973-76; assoc. firm Antell & Harris, Rochester, 1979-83, ptnr., 1983—. Bd. dirs. City-County Youth Bur., Rochester, 1971-76, Urban League, Rochester, 1975, ARC, Rochester, 1973-76, Bucket Dance Theater, Rochester, 1983-84; bd. dirs., chmn. Project Unique, Rochester, 1970-75; mem., chmn. various coms. Jr. League of Am. Mem. Monroe County Bar Assn. (exec. com. family law sect.), N.Y. State Bar Assn., ABA, Greater Rochester Assn. Women Lawyers. Democrat. Home: 1438 East Ave Rochester NY 14610

PECK, SHEILA, portfolio manager, securities analyst; b. Grosse Pointe, Mich., Oct. 9, 1957; d. Rankin Philip and Elaine (Zimmerman) P.; B.A. in Bus. Adminstrn., Rollins Coll., 1979. Securities analyst, office equipment industry Standard & Poor's Corp., N.Y.C., 1979-82; asst. v.p. investments The Savs. Banks Retirement System, N.Y.C., 1983-84; v.p. Carret and Co., Inc., N.Y.C., 1984—. Mem. N.Y. Soc. Security Analysts, N.Y. Jr. League, Sigma Gamma Assn., Kappa Kappa Gamma. Republican. Roman Catholic. Club: Apple Platform Tennis. Home: 123 Harbor Dr Stamford CT 06902 Office: 122 E 42d St New York NY 10168

PEDERSEN, AMANDA B., lawyer; b. New Haven, Conn., Sept. 20, 1944; d. Gerald P. Norton, Sept. 25, 1971; children—Jeremy, Elizabeth, Adam. A.B., Vassar Coll., 1966; J.D., George Washington U., 1972. Bar: D.C. Asst. gen. counsel Cost of Living Council, Washington, 1974; assoc. Bergson Borkland Margolis & Adler, Washington, 1975-78, ptnr., 1979-81; dep. dir. Bur. Consumer Protection, FTC, Washington, 1982-85, acting dir., 1985—; mem. hearing com. Bd. Profl. Responsibility, D.C. Ct. Appeals, 1978-83. Mem. Adminstrv. Conf. U.S., ABA. Office: Fed Trade Commn 7th St and Pennsylvania Ave Washington DC 20580

PEDERSEN, JACQUE BECK, talent manager, consultant; b. Houston, Mar. 1, 1951; d. Henry Edward Bates and Edna Louise (Branham) Bates Malloy; m. Tommy Lee Beck, Jan. 27, 1970 (div. Jan. 1974); 1 son, Tommy Lee; m. Palle W. Pedersen, June 9, 1981; 1 dau., Erika Nicole. Acct. Porter Paint, Louisville, 1974-77, Coca-Cola, Memphis, 1977-79; export mgr. I.W.P., Memphis, 1979-82; dir. shareholder relations Aquanautics, Tacoma, Wash., 1982-83; owner, mgr. Portfolio, Mission Viejo, Calif., 1983—; cons. in field. Author: Models, Actresses and Other Crazies, 1983. Mem. Nat. Assn. Female Execs., South Sound Women's Network, World Modeling Assn. (Outstanding Sch. award 1983), NOW, LWV. Democrat. Episcopalian. Home: 29802 Andrea Way Laguna Niguel CA 92677

PEDERSEN, JOANNE VIRGINIA, interior designer, contractor; b. Atlanta, Dec. 13; d. Warren W. and Virginia M. Stautz; m. Gene F. Pedersen, Aug. 29, 1943; children—Lief G., Dean J., Kristin Joanne Pedersen Wright. Freelance interior designer, 1963—; prin. Mark V. Design Internat., La Jolla, Calif., 1971—; prin., treas. All Seasons Travel; prin. Porcher/West Imports; prin. J.V. Petersen, Gen. Contracting. . Bd. dirs. North County Coll., San Diego Opera Guild, La Jolla, 1963, chmn.-pres. La Jolla Unit; Door of Hope Chmn. Salvation Army, 1962; vol. aid Scripps Meml. Hosp., 1963. Recipient Design of Merit award Ceramic Tile & Marble Inst. of San Diego, 1982. Mem. Am. Soc. Interior Designers (v.p.), San Diego C. of C., La Jolla C. of C./Town Council. Contbr. articles on interior design to mags. Office: 5440 Morehouse Dr San Diego CA

PEDERSON, DEE ANN, veterinarian; Bellville, Ill., Oct. 15, 1943; d. Alvin Reece Phillips and Bobby Lynn (Robinson) Dragon; m. Jack R. Roscher, June 13, 1959 (div. 1972); children—Matthew J., Leigh Ann; m. Eddie Glen Pederson, Mar. 13, 1974. Veterinarian, owner Animal Clinic, Waco, Tex., 1974—; vice chmn. Animal Control Adv. Bd., 1981-82. Mem., sec. Central Tex. Zool. Soc., Waco, 1977-83; mem. adv. bd. Tex. State Tech. U., Waco, 1979-82. Mem. N. Central Tex. Vet. Med. Assn. (pres. 1980-82) Tex. Vet. Med. Assn., AVMA. Republican. Club: Altrusa (Waco) Home: 1013 Cindy Circle Waco TX 76710 Office: Animal Clinic 6201 New McGregor Hwy Waco TX 76710

PEDEVILLANO, MARY THERESA, human resources manager; b. Ridgewood, N.J., May 16, 1953; d. John Robert and Gloria Marie (Casey) Pedevillano; m. Philip Stanley Borba, Dec. 22, 1979. B.S. in Bus. Adminstrn., U. Md., 1976; M.Indsl. and Labor Relations, Cornell U., 1978. Teaching asst. Cornell U., Ithaca, N.Y., 1977-78; employee relations assoc. Am. Can Co., Greenwich, Conn., 1978-79, coordinator employee relations, Green Bay, Wis., 1979-80; supr. employment affirmative action Clairol, Inc., N.Y.C., 1980-82, mgr. human resources and EEO, Saddle Brook, N.J., 1982—. Adult advisor Jr. Achievement, Green Bay, 1979-80; chmn. United Way plant campaign, Am. Can Co., 1979. Mem. Am. Soc. Personnel Adminstrs., N.J. Employers Assn., Indsl. Relations Research Assn., Cornell L.R. Alumni Assn. Office: Clairol Inc 141 N Fifth St Saddle Brook NJ 07630

PEDIGO, SKIP MARCHEL, public relations exec.; b. Sharon, Tenn., May 30, 1933; d. Ocie D. and Nellie Lee (Garrett) Cooley; B.A., Calif. State U., 1970; m. Jerry L. Pedigo, Dec. 10, 1977; 1 dau., Alison. Copywriter/account supr. Chris Art Studio, Costa Mesa, Calif., 1971-73; mktg. dir. Pacific City Bank, Huntington Beach, Calif., 1973; promotion/mktg. dir. for Westminster (Calif.) Mall, Homart Devel. Co., 1974-76; editor Orange Coast mag., Newport Beach, 1976-78, Sr. Life mag., Newport Beach, 1978, HomeBuyer's Guide, Newport Beach, 1979; pres. Pedigo Public Relations, Newport Beach, 1979-80; owner/partner Coombe & Pedigo Public Relations, Newport Beach, 1980—; owner Pedigo Pub., Huntington Beach, 1985—; lectr. in field. Bd. dirs. The Rap Center, Tustin, Calif., 1973-74; mem. spl. events bd. City of Huntington Beach, 1979. Mem. C. of C., Nat. Council Shopping Centers, Women Can Win, Nat. Assn. Female Execs., Orange County Coast Assn., Am. Soc. Profl. and Exec. Women, AAUW. Contbr. articles to profl. jours. and consumer publs. Home: 6652 Luciento Dr Huntington Beach CA 92647 Office: 359 San Miguel Dr Suite 110 Newport Beach CA 92660

PEEBLES, KAY EUVONNE, nurse; b. Aiken, S.C., Aug. 17, 1949; d. Vernon Lewis and Merle Euvonne (Leaphart) Rhoden; m. Phillip R. McElhaney, May 26, 1968 (div. 1979); children—Laura Lynn, Jonathan Pierce; m. R.A. Peebles, June 2, 1983. A.S. in Nursing, U. S.C.-Aiken, 1977. R.N., Fla., Ga., S.C. Staff nurse Hosp. Corp. Am., Aiken, 1976-77, head nurse, Largo, Fla., 1978-81; staff nurse Med. Coll. Ga., Augusta, 1981-85; head nurse S.C. Dept. Corrections, Columbia, 1983—. Instr. Am. Heart Assn., Augusta, Columbia, 1981-85; vol. Coalition Assist Abused Persons, Aiken, 1984. Recipient Betty Crocker award Gen. Mills, Inc., 1964. Mem. Am. Nurses Assn., S.C. State Employees Assn., S.C. Nurses Assn., S.C. Law Enforcement Officers Assn., Am. Correctional Assn., Am. Correctional Health Services Assn. (state treas. 1986-87), Nat. Assn. Female Execs., Omicron Theta Alpha, Beta Club. Republican. Baptist. Club: Toastmasters. Avocation: sewing. Home: 907 Creekside Pl Columbia SC 29210 Office: S C Dept Corrections 4546 Broad River Rd Columbia SC 29210

PEELER, CAROL CUENOD, investment company executive; b. Houston, Mar. 7, 1955; d. Emile Marc and Martha (Moore) Cuenod; m. Charles Lee Peeler, Jr. Feb. 7, 1981; 1 dau., Christie Ann. B.A. in Math., U. Tex.-Austin, 1977. Money market specialist First Internat. Investment Mgmt., Dallas, 1977-78, fixed income portfolio mgr., 1978-80; trust investment officer Preston State Bank, Dallas, 1980-81; v.p. Hillcrest Equities, Inc., Dallas, 1981—; pres. Hillcrest Securities Corp., Inc., Dallas, 1981—; sec.-treas., dir. Systems Holding Co., Dallas, 1983—; organizer, dir. Preston North Nat. Bank, Dallas. Sunday sch. tchr. Ch. of Incarnation, Dallas, 1978-79; vol. Ronald McDonald House, Dallas, 1981-82, Bill Clements Campaign for Gov., Dallas, 1982, Soc. for Prevention of Cruelty to Animals, Dallas, 1982-83. Natural Scis. Honor scholar U, Tex.-Austin, 1977. Mem. Inst. Chartered Fin. Analysts, Fin. Analysts Fedn., Phi Beta Kappa, Kappa Kappa Gamma. Republican. Episcopalian. Club: Dallas Jr. League Office: Hillcrest Equities Inc 2501 Cedar Springs Suite 500 Dallas TX 75201

PEGUES, JOHNNIE FRANCES, broadcast sales manager; b. Alto, Tex., Apr. 19, 1946; d. John L. and Addie P. (Mayhar) P.; m. Phillip David Morgan, Mar. 22, 1969 (div. Sept. 1973); 1 child, Keith Edward Pegues. A.A., Jacksonville Coll., 1966; B.A., Stephen F. Austin State Coll., 1969. Ops. mgr. Sta. KFWD-FM, Dallas, 1973-75; local sales rep. Sta. KAFM-FM, Dallas, 1975-77, KSCS-FM, Dallas, 1977; regional salesperson Riley Reps., Dallas, 1978; v.p. sunbelt div. Jack Masla & Co., Dallas, 1979—. Author: Central High: The Story, 1984. Mem. Irving PTA, Tex., 1977—. Recipient profl. awards. Mem. Am. Women in Radio and TV (dir. 1985-86, pres. 1984-85), S.W. Broadcast Reps. Assn. (pres. 1981-83). Democrat. Avocations: reading; fishing; basketball; landscaping; genealogy. Home: 2504 Edinburgh St Irving TX 75062 Office: 1720 Regal Row #212 Dallas TX 75235

PEGUES, KATHLEEN GARCIA, educator; b. Gainesville, Fla., Apr. 4, 1949; d. Robert C. Garcia and Joy (Stevens) Garcia Wood; m. John K. Pegues IV, Aug. 13, 1977; children—Emily, Adam. B.A., Sweet Briar Coll., Va., 1971; M. Ed., U. Va., 1974. English instr. Fauquier County Pub. Schs., Warrenton, Va., 1974—. Bd. dirs. Fauquier Soc. Prevention Cruelty to Animals, 1976—; deacon Warrenton Presbyterian Ch., Va., 1980-83; coordinator Ch. World Service Crop Hunger Walk, Warrenton, 1983-86. recipient Fauquier County Excellence in Edn. fellowship 1984. Club: Laff-A-Lot Clown Alley. Avocations: make stained glass windows; work to reduce world hunger. Home: 22 Hillcrest Ln Jeffersonton VA 22724 Office: Fauquier High Sch Waterloo Rd Warrentown VA 22186

PEIRCE, CAROL MARSHALL, English language educator; b. Columbia, Mo., Feb. 1, 1922; d. Charles Hamilton and Helen Emily (Davault) Williams; A.B., Fla. State U., 1942; M.A. (McGregor fellow, DuPont fellow), U. Va., 1943; Ph.D. (Harvard tutor, Anne Radcliffe traveling fellow), Radcliffe Coll./Harvard U., 1951; m. Brooke Peirce, July 12, 1952. Head English dept. Fairfax Hall, Waynesboro, Va., 1943-44; instr. English Cedar Crest Coll., Allentown, Pa., 1944-46; instr. English, Harvard U., 1952-53; asst. dean instrn. Radcliffe Coll., Cambridge, 1950-53; head English extension homestudy U. Va., Charlottesville, 1953-54; asst. dir. admissions Goucher Coll., Towson, Md., 1956-62; prof. and chmn. English, U. Balt., 1968—, holder Disting. Teaching chair Coll. Liberal Arts, 1981-82, chmn. humanities div., 1972-80; chmn. bd. New Poets Series, 1975-80; vis. scholar Lucy Cavendish Coll., U. Cambridge (Eng.), 1977-78. Mem. Edgar Allen Poe Soc. (dir. 1973—), Lawrence Durrell Soc. (nat. pres. 1980-82), MLA, Md. Assn. English Depts., Chi Delta Phi, Phi Alpha Theta, Phi Kappa Phi, Phi Beta Kappa. Author: (with Brooke Peirce) A Study of Literary Types and An Introduction to English Literature from Chaucer to the Eighteenth Century, 1954, A Study of Literary Types and An Introduction to English Literature from the Eighteenth Century to the Present, 1954; contbr. chpts. to books, articles to profl. jours. Office: Dept English U Balt Baltimore MD 21201

PEIRCE, ELLEN RUST, legal educator; b. Washington, May 5, 1947; d. Wentworth W. and Ethel M. (Byrne) P.; m. Daniel A. Graham, June 10, 1978; 1 child, William. B.A., Bryn Mawr Coll., 1971; J.D., Duke U., 1976. Bar: N.Y. 1977, D.C. 1977, N.C. 1979. Assoc., Mudge Rose Guthrie & Alexander, N.Y.C., 1976-78, Powe Porter Alphin & Whichard, Durham, N.C., 1978-80; asst. prof. law U. N.C. Sch. Bus. Adminstrn., Chapel Hill, 1980-85, assoc. prof., 1986—; legal cons. IBM, 1983-84, various software cos., N.C.; counsel SSI, Durham, 1978—. Contbr. articles and chpts. to legal jours.; editor Duke Legal Research and Writing, 1975-76; reviewer legal pub. cos. Mem. ABA, N.Y. State Bar Assn., D.C. Bar Assn., N.C. Bar Assn., Am. Bus. Law Assn., Southeastern Regional Bus. Law Assn. (sec. 1981-82, v.p. 1982-83, pres.-elect 1983-84). Episcopalian. Home: Route 1 Box 178 Hillsborough NC 27278 Office: U NC Sch Bus Adminstrn Carroll Hall Chapel Hill NC 27278

PEKAR, CATHERINE DUSEK, nurse; b. Chgo., Aug. 4, 1951; d. Anton J. and Rose Mary (Zielonka) Dusek; B.S. in Nursing, St. Xavier Coll., Chgo., 1973; M.S.N., Loyola U., Chgo., 1978; R.N.; m. Dennis J. Pekar, May 28, 1978. Staff nurse birth unit and women's ambulatory care clinic Rush-Presbyn.-St. Luke's Med. Center, Chgo., 1973-75; maternal/child health instr. Meml. Hosp. DuPage County, Elmhurst, Ill., 1975-77; head nurse, clin. nursing instr. U. Chgo. Med. Center, 1977-80; adminstrv. dir. maternal/child nursing St. Joseph Hosp., Chgo., 1980—, also mem. adv. bd. for women's health; instr. LaMaze childbirth edn., 1980—; CPR instr. Am. Heart Assn., 1980—. Mem. Internat. Childbirth Edn. Assn., Am. Nurses Assn., Nurses Assn. of Am. Coll. Ob-Gyn, Parent and Child Edn. Soc., Midwest Parentcraft Center, Ill. Soc. Nurse Adminstrs., Ill. Nurses Assn. (dist. program chmn. 1976-77), Sigma Theta Tau. Roman Catholic. Office: 2900 N Lake Shore Dr Chicago IL 60657

PELC-GRANT, BARBARA LEE, hotel company executive, consultant; b. Charleroi, Pa., Mar. 20, 1950; d. Charles Joseph and Eleanor P. (Gricas) Krupensky; m. James R. Grant, Sept. 28, 1985. B.A. in English and Edn., Alliance Coll., 1972. Cert. tchr., Conn. Tchr. English, Enfield Sch. Systems, Conn., 1972-73; adminstrv. asst. Conn. Yankee Motor Inn, Niantic, 1973-77; asst. to v.p. Will County Foods, Joliet, Ill., 1978-79; dir. sales Metro Mamada, Jackson, Miss., 1979, gen. mgr., 1979-81; gen. mgr. Ramada Inn, Bennington, Vt., 1981—; cons. Nat. Hospitality Corp., Melville, N.Y., 1984—. Mem. Hotel Sales and Mktg. Assn. Internat., Nat. Assn. Female Execs., Vt. Lodging and Restaurant Assn. (pres. 1986—, legis. chmn. 1985-86, bd. dirs. 1982—), Polish Nat. Alliance. Avocations: Alpine skiing; snorkeling; travel. Home: 128 Greenleaf Dr Latham NY 12110 Office: Ramada Inn Route 7 and Kocher Dr Bennington VT 05201

PELIO, LENA, ballet educator; b. Akron, Ohio, June 11, 1918; d. Isador and Anna (Rujila) Stein; m. Andrew Pelio, Mar. 1, 1941 (dec. 1985); children—Luana Pelio Hansen, Lisa Pelio Whittaker. Cert. tchr. Cecchetti Method of Ballet. Founder, tchr. Lena Pelio Sch. of Dance, Flint, 1937—; founder, dir. Flint Ballet Theatre, 1960—. Bd. dirs. March of Dimes, Flint, 1975—; tchr. Mott Found. Dance Program, Flint, 1938-50; choreographer Flint Light Opera Co., 1938-41, Fine Arts Festival Program, Flint, 1972-78, Musical Performing Arts Assn., Flint, 1970-75, various Flint community players musicals, high sch. musicals, civic affairs, fashion shows. Recipient plaques of appreciation March of Dimes 1970, 72, 76, 80, Flint Ballet Theatre, 1970; Silver Tray award Flint Ballet Theatre, 1965; Pewter Ballerina award Flint Ballet Theatre, 1985. Mem. Cecchetti Council Am. (bd. dirs. 1972—), Dance Educators Am. Republican. Episcopalian. Avocations: reading; concerts; plays; lectures; musicals. Home and Studio: 6255 Torrey Rd Flint MI 48507

PELL, MARY CHASE (CHASEY), civic worker; b. Binghamton, N.Y., May 23, 1915; d. Charles Orlando and Mary (Lane) Chase; m. Wilbur F. Pell, Jr., Sept. 14, 1940; children—Wilbur F., Charles Chase. B.A., Smith Coll., 1937. Case worker Binghamton State Hosp., 1937; sociology tchr. Charles W. Wilson Meml. Hosp., Johnson City, N.Y., 1938; commentator travel and industry, sta. WSVL, Shelbyville, Ind., 1962-67. Contbr. articles to publs. Chmn. Ind. Fund Raising Com. for Smith Coll., Indpls., 1961; bd. dirs. Nat. Mental Health Assn., 1961-79, pres. 1976-77; pres. Ind. Mental Health Meml. Found., Indpls., 1964-65, Mental Health Assn. Ind., Indpls., 1962-63; commr. Ind. Mental Health Planning Commn., Indpls., 1964-65; mem. Central Ind. Task Force on Mental Health Planning, 1965-66; mem. Ind. Com. on Nursing, Indpls., 1965-66, Central Ind. Regional Mental Health Planning Com., 1968; chmn. Manpower Conf. on Mental Health, Washington, 1969; del. Ind. Republican Conv., 1951; vice chmn. Shelbyville Rep. Com., 1951; sec. Ind. Com. for Rockefeller, 1969-70; pres. Indpls. Smith Coll. Club, 1969-70; participant Nat. Health Forum of Nat. Health Council, N.Y.C., 1971; pres. Mental Health Assn. Ill., Springfield, 1975; mem. Gov.'s Commn. for Revision of Mental Health Code Ill., 1975-76; v.p. for N.Am., World Fedn. for Mental Health, 1977-79; bd. dirs. Vis. Nurse Assn. Evanston (Ill.), 1975, v.p. 1981—; community mental health adviser Jr. League of Chgo., 1979-83; mem. Ill. Guardianship and Advocacy Commn., 1978-86, chmn., 1981; mem. adv. com. to sect. on psychiatry and the law, Rush-Presbyn.-St. Luke's Med. Ctr., Chgo., 1978—; mem. home health adv. com. to Dept. Pub. Health, State of Ill., 1982—; pres. Mental Health Assn. Chgo., 1983-84; pres. Smith Coll. Alumnae of Chgo., 1984-86; mem. Women's Bd. Northwestern U., Aux. of Evanston and Glenbrook Hosps., University Guild of Evanston, Jr. League Evanston, pres. Ind. Lawyers' Wives, Indpls., 1959-60; treas. Nat. Lawyers' Wives, 1961-62. Recipient Outstanding Citizen award Shelby County C. of C., 1959-60, Outstanding Vol. of Yr. award Indpls. Jr. League, 1962, Leadership award Mental Health Assn. Ind., 1971, Arts and Humanities award, Shelbyville Rotary Club, 1981; named One of Ten Most Newsworthy Women In Ind., Indpls. News, 1962, Disting. Leader in Vol. Mental Health Movement, Ill. Ho. of Reps., 1976, Miss. Coll., 1976, Ala. Lt. Gov., 1980. Presbyterian. Clubs: Fortnightly (Chgo.); Garden of Evanston. Home: 1427 Hinman Ave Evanston IL 60201

PELL, PYRMA DAPHNE TILTON, civic worker; b. N.Y.C., Feb. 5, 1909; d. Newell Whiting and Mildred Olive (Bigelow) Tilton; student Queens Coll., London, 1921-26, Kunst Akademie, Vennia, Austria, 1927-28; m. John Howland Gibbs Pell, Sept. 3, 1929; children—Sarah Gibbs, John Bigelow. Active in preservation and restoration Fort Ticonderoga, N.Y., 1950—, also coordinator spl. events, 1950—; treas. Friends of Chung Ang U., Korea, 1965-71, recipient spl. award, 1971. Recipient First award Historic Preservation, Garden Club Am., 1973. Mem. Am. Acad. Poets (co-founder), Colonial Dames Am., Assn. Churchill Fellows of Westminster Coll., Alpha Xi Delta. Christian Scientist. Club: Colony. Home: 870 Fifth Ave New York NY 10021 also The Pavilion Fort Ticonderoga NY 12883 also Pelican Pl Bellevue Ave Newport RI 02840

PELLERIN, BEVERLY JEAN, product manager; b. Meriden, Conn., Nov. 2, 1951; d. George William and Dorothy Marie (Wayland) P. B.S.Ed., U. Conn., 1973. Band tchr. Valley Regional High Sch., Deep River, Conn., 1973-75; office mgr. Consol. Cigar Co., Glastonbury, Conn., 1975-80; foreman I and II, 1980-82; product mgr. Marshall Industries, Wallingford, Conn., 1983—. Mem. Nat. Assn. Female Execs. Roman Catholic. Club: Goebel Collectors. Avocations: horseback riding; aerobics; reading. Home: 532 Main St Portland CT 06480

PELLERIN, DEBORAH CATHERINE, television executive; b. Worcester, Mass., June 12, 1953; d. Vincent Thomas and Maria Josephine (Caramelle) Dagnostine; m. Gordon Robert Pellerin, June 7, 1975; 1 child, Adam. Traffic and bus. assoc. Sta. WSMW-TV, Worcester, 1971-75; acctg. asst. Newman and Brier, C.P.A.s, Pawtucket, R.I., 1975-77; radio traffic mgr. Sta. WJAR, Providence, 1977-79; traffic assoc. Sta. WJAR-TV, Providence, 1982-83; dir. traffic and data services Sta. WXNE-TV, Needham, Mass., 1983—. Mem. Nat. Assn. Female Execs. Avocations: reading; needlework; bike riding. Home: 12 Richardson Ave Norton MA 02766

PELLICANO, DONNA JOANNE, information company executive; b. Newark, Sept. 12, 1945; d. Amel Romeo and Antoinette Marie (Maglione) Petronella; m. Joseph F. Pellicano, Aug. 24, 1969 (div. 1982); children—Dana Joanne, Carla Maria. B.A. in Math., Rutgers U., 1967, M.B.A., 1985. Sci. computer programmer Bell Telephone Labs., Whippany, N.J., 1967-69; tech. support rep. Rapidata, Inc., Fairfield, N.J., 1969-71; applications devel. rep., 1971-73, mgr. software services, 1973-75, mgr. documentation and tng., 1975-78; systems cons. Global Health Found., Rockville, Md., 1978-80; asst. v.p. United Hosp. Med. Ctr., Newark, 1980-85; dir. systems Info. Resources, Fairfield, 1985—. Recipient Award of Excellence, Soc. Tech. Communications, 1977, cert. merit, 1977. Mem. Asst. Hosp. Dirs. Assn., Data Processing Mgmt. Assn., Assn. Exec. M.B.A.s, Beta Gamma Sigma. Roman Catholic. Avocations: Bridge; Racketball. Home: 20 Cambridge Rd Bloomfield NJ 07003 Office: Info Resources 1260 Bloomfield Ave Fairfield NJ 07006

PELLMAN, RENEE GREENBERG, psychotherapist; b. N.Y.C., May 12, 1936; d. Irving and Dorothy (Sherman) Greenberg; B.A., Brandeis U., 1954; M.A., Columbia U., 1958; Ph.D., Rutgers U., 1980; children—Amy, David. Pvt. practice psychotherapy, sex therapy, N.Y.C., 1965—; sr. psychotherapist Bronx-Lebanon Hosp. Center, Dept. Psychiatry, N.Y.C., 1966-69; clin. supr., asst. dir. Big Brothers Residence, N.Y.C., 1969-71; cons. Office of Child Devel., U.S. Govt., 1969-73; clin. supr. Youth Services, Jewish Family Service, N.Y.C., 1971-76; sr. family therapist Family Mental Health Clinic, Jewish Family Service, N.Y.C., 1971-76; lectr. and cons. in field. Fellow Am. Orthopsychiatry, Acad. Cert. Social Workers, N.Y. State Soc. Clin. Social Work; mem. Am. Group Psychotherapy Assn., Eastern Assn. Sex Therapists, Eastern Group Psychotherapy Assn. Contbr. articles to profl. publs. Office: 111 E 80th St Apt 7B New York NY 10014

PELOSI, LORRAINE MARY, educational administrator; b. N.Y.C., Apr. 8, 1941; d. Joshua and Elizabeth Orgel (Deming) Esposito; B.S., Pace Coll., 1971; m. William Demarest, Jan. 13, 1962 (dec. 1969); children—William, Susan, Robert; m. 2d, Andrew Pelosi, Apr. 7, 1971; children—Gina, Nicole. Pvt. tutor, Thornwood, N.Y., 1969; nursery sch. asst. Pace Little Sch./Pace Cottage, Pleasantville, N.Y., 1970; tchr. emotionally disturbed Pleasantville (N.Y.) Cottage Sch., 1970-73; founder, dir., tchr. Gingerbread Nursery Sch., St. Petersburg, Fla., 1972—; founder, dir. Wellington Sch., St. Petersburg, 1974; founder, pres. Gingerbread Nursery Sch., Seminole, Fla., 1978—; pres. Gingerbread-Wellington Schs., St. Petersburg, 1975—; founder Gingerbread Nursery Sch. Azalea, St. Petersburg, 1982; pres. Gingerbread Sch. NE, Inc.; founder Gingerbread-Wellington Sch.-Bardmoor, Seminole, 1983. Lectr., cons. Mem. So. Assn. Children Under Six Pinellas Assn. Children Under Six, Pinellas Assn. Acad. Non-Public Schs., Women's Forum. Lutheran. Home: 931 79 St S Saint Petersburg FL 33707 Office: 4355 Central Ave Saint Petersburg FL 33713

PELTIER, LINDA JEANNE, legal educator; b. St. Louis, Nov. 29, 1948; d. Louis Cook and Louisa Harriet (Russell) Peltier; m. James Edward Britain, June 23, 1979. B.A. in Polit. Sci., Bucknell U., 1970; J.D., George Washington U., 1973. Bar: D.C. 1973, U.S. Ct. Claims 1974, Pa. 1975. Assoc., Fried, Frank, Harris et al, Washington, 1973-74; staff atty. Susquehanna Legal Services, Williamsport, Pa., 1974-77; asst. prof. law U. Ky., Lexington, 1977-79; asst., then assoc. prof. law New Eng. Sch. Law, Boston, 1979-82; assoc. prof. law, U. Cin., 1982—, chmn. univ. jud.'council, 1983—; mem. support group Ctr. for Law and Human Values, N.Y.C., 1983—; coordinator, creator Hunger and Law Conf., Cin., 1983; others. Contbr. articles to profl. jours. Editor-in-chief Vol. 41, George Washington U. Law Rev., 1972-73. Ending Hunger briefing leader The Hunger Project, San Francisco, 1984; mem. mental health/mental retardation adv. bd. Union-Snyder Community Counseling Service, Lewisburg, Pa., 1975-77; adviser Law Explorer Posts 100/830, Williamsport Pa. and Lexington, Ky., 1975-79. Jr. Year Abroad grantee Inst. Am. Univs., France, 1968-69. Mem. ABA. Democrat. Episcopalian. Home: 37 Forest Ave Cincinnati OH 45215 Office: Univ Cin College of Law Cincinnati OH 45221-0040

PELTON, CAROL ANN, hospital administrator; b. Toledo, Ohio, Oct. 24, 1947; d. Olin LeRoy and Mary Magdalene (Sexton) Pelton; m. Ronald J. Schmitt, 1966 (div. 1978); children—Tammy, Lorrie, A.S. in Comml. Studies, U. Toledo, 1967; B.S. in Pub. Health, U. N.C., 1981; M.S. in Health Adminstrn., St. Thomas of Villanova U., 1986. Cert. profl. in quality assurance. Asst. mgr. Hickory Farms Ohio, West Palm Beach, Fla., 1967-72, owner, mgr., Tampa, Fla., 1976-79, gen. mgr., Ft. Lauderdale, Fla., 1981-84; asst. dir. unit mgmt. St. Mary's Hosp., West Palm Beach, 1972-75; adminstrv. resident Southeastern Gen. Hosp., Lumberton, N.C., 1980; quality assurance dir. Humana Cypress, Pompano Beach, Fla., 1984—. Counselor Sexual Assault Treatment Ctr., Ft. Lauderdale, 1984-85; counselor, program chmn. Orange County Rape Crisis Ctr., Chapel Hill, N.C., 1980-81; EMT, dispatcher Inter-City Rescue Squad, Lake Park, Fla., 1974-75. Recipient Best New Mktg. Idea award Hickory Farms Ohio, 1982, Work Recognition for State Referendum, Gov. of Ohio, 1966. Mem. Broward Assn. Quality Assurance Profls. (pres. 1985—), Fla. Assn. Quality Assurance Profls. (del. 1985—), So. Fla. Diag. Related Groups Mgmt. Assn., Nat. Assn. Quality Assurance Profls., Phi Theta Kappa, Tau Rho Alpha (co-founder 1966-67), Beta Sigma Phi. Republican. Roman Catholic. Office: Humana Hosp Cypress 600 SW 3rd St Pompano Beach FL 33060

PELTON, SANDRA ANN ZIRKELBACH, physical therapist, health care administrator; b. Erie, Pa., Nov. 11, 1955; d. Robert Eugene Zirkelbach and Lois Marie (Weber) Calhoun; 1 dau., Tiffany Louise. B.S. in Phys. Therapy, U. Tex. Med. Br., Galveston, 1977. Lic. phys. therapist Tex. Bd. Phys. Therapy Examiners. Phys. therapist Rutherford Gen. Hosp., Mesquite, Tex., 1977-78; dir. phys. therapy Fairfield (Tex.) Meml. Hosp., 1978-79; regional dir. phys. therapy TPT, Inc., Houston, 1979-81, v.p. phys. therapy, 1981-82, exec. v.p., Sugar Land, Tex., 1983-84, pres., 1984-85, owner, pres. RCSA, 1985—; mem. adv. com. Houston Community Coll., 1982-85. Mem. Am. Phys. Therapy Assn., Tex. Phys. Therapy Assn., Nat. Assn. Female Execs., U. Tex. Med. Br. Alumni Assn., Mothers Against Drunk Drivers. Republican. Roman Catholic. Home: 1622 Plantation Richmond TX 77469 Office: RCSA 1305 FM 359 Suite H Richmond TX 77469

PELUSO, CAROL ANN, broadcasting executive; b. Auburn, N.Y., Feb. 28, 1941; d. Joseph N., Sr., and Georgianna (Wood) Peluso; student Auburn public schs. Clk.-typist, receptionist McCulley Adjustment Co., Shreveport, La., 1962-65; office mgr. KJOE Radio, Shreveport, 1965-70; adminstrv. asst. Dynamic Broadcasting, Austin, Tex., 1970-72; ops. mgr. KTRM AM-FM, Beaumont, Tex., 1972-74; gen. mgr. KJOE Radio, Shreveport, 1974-75; v.p., sta. mgr. KRBE Radio, Houston, 1975—. Served with USAF, 1959-62. Mem. Nat. Assn. Female Execs., Houston Assn. Credit Mgrs. Roman Catholic. Home: 2131 Linea del Pino Houston TX 77077 Office: 9801 Westheimer Rd Houston TX 77042

PELUSO, SUSAN LINDA, research chemist, educator; b. N.Y.C., Jan. 15, 1952; d. Patrick James and Ida Angela (Vitarelli) P.; B.A. in Chemistry and Biology, Hofstra U., Hempstead, N.Y., 1975, Ph.D. in Chemistry (teaching asst. 1975, fellow 1976-79), Brown U., 1980. Research chemist E.I. du Pont de Nemours & Co., Inc., Wilmington, Del., 1979-84; adj. faculty Pa. State U., Delaware County, 1984—; asst. prof. U. Del., Newark, 1984—. Tchr. Christian doctrine Immaculate Heart of Mary Roman Catholic Ch., Wilmington, 1981-82, oblate of St. Benedict, 1983—. Mem. Am. Chem. Soc., AAAS, Soc. for Applied Spectroscopy, Am. Inst. Chem. Engrs., Sigma Xi. Contbr. articles to profl. jours. Home: 814 Bezel Rd Wilmington DE 19803 Office: Chem Dept U Del Newark DE 19716

PELZ, CAROLINE DUNCOMBE, educational administrator; b. White Plains, N.Y.; d. David Sanford and Helena (Ebert) Duncombe; A.B., Barnard Coll., 1940; m. Edward Joseph Pelz, July 11, 1942; children—Caroline Pelz Elbow, Margaret L. (dec.), Patricia Pelz Hart, Sanford M. Adjustments supr. R.H. Macy & Co., N.Y.C., 1940-42; admissions interviewer Barnard Coll., 1960-63; alumni sec. Allen-Stevenson Sch., N.Y.C., 1967-70, admissions asst., 1969-70; adminstrv. asst. Ednl. Records Bur., N.Y.C., 1970-72; dir. admissions Grace Church Sch., N.Y.C., 1972—. Trustee Barnard Coll., 1963-67. Mem. Barnard Coll. Alumnae Assn. (pres. 1963-66), Woman's Nat. Farm and Garden Assn. (scholarship chmn. N.Y.C. met. br. 1981—), English-Speaking Union. Republican. Episcopalian. Home: 55 E 87th St New York NY 10128 Office: 86 4th Ave New York City NY 10003

PEMBERTON, JANETTE MATTHEW, educator; b. Trinidad, W.I.; came to U.S., 1961, naturalized, 1974; d. Cecil E. and A. Elaine Matthew; B.A., Howard U., 1965, M.A., 1967; Arts D., Catholic U. Am., 1978; m. Sandi Macpherson Pemberton. Asst. instr. Howard U., 1967; instr. Bowie State Coll., 1968; asst. prof. Prince George's Community Coll., 1968-71, assoc. prof. dept. English, 1971-82, prof., 1982—, mem. acad. standards and regulations com., 1979, chmn. Afro-Am. studies com., 1976-78, mem. affirmative action com., 1973-74; guest instr. Cath. U., 1975-78. Nat. Teaching fellow, 1968; recipient Teaching award Cath. U. Am., 1975; Community Leadership award, 1976; Disting. Women's award, 1980; Outstanding Service and Achievement award, 1981; named to Hall of Fame for contbns. to edn., 1985. Mem. Washington Soc. Performing Arts, Nat. Symphony Orch., Internat. Platform Assn., Nat. Council Tchrs. English, Edn. Writers Assn., MLA, Am. Assn. Advancement of Humanities, AAUP, Nat. Soc. Lit. and Arts. Seventh-day Adventist. Author: Transcendatalism and the Promise of Educational Reform, 1980; The Teaching of Afro-American Poetry: An Aesthetic Approach, 1978; Discussions on Aristotle's Ethics: Implications for Teachers and Administrators, 1980. Office: 301 Largo Rd Largo MD 20870

PENA, ANTONIA MURILLO, physician, radiologist; b. San Diego, July 18, 1946; d. Blas and Elvira (Murillo) Pena. B.A., Loma Linda U., Riverside, Calif., 1968; M.D., 1973. Diplomate Nat. Bd. Radiology. Intern, White Meml. Med. Ctr., Los Angeles, 1973-74, resident, 1974-77; radiologist Paradise Valley Hosp., National City, Calif., 1978-79; neuroradiology fellow Los Angeles County-U.So. Calif. Med. Ctr., 1977-78, 79-80; radiologist Arlington Radiology Med. Group, Riverside, Calif., 1980—; attending staff Riverside Gen. Hosp. U. Med. Ctr., 1980—; assoc. staff Parkview Community Hosp., 1980—; cons. radiologist Computerized Diagnostic Med. Group of Riverside, 1980—; cons. Veitch Student Health Ctr., Riverside, 1980—. Mem. Radiol. Soc. N.Am., Am. Coll. Radiology, Calif. Radiol. Soc., AMA, Calif. Med. Assn., Am. Assn. Women Radiologists, Inland Radiology Soc., Am. Soc. Neuroradiology (sr.), Riverside County Med. Soc. Republican. Seventh-Day Adventist. Office: 9851 Magnolia Ave Riverside CA

PEÑA, MICHI E., systems engineer; b. Chgo., July 16, 1955; d. Severo George and Mildred M. (Salmeron) P.; B.A., North Park Coll., 1975; M.B.A., Roosevelt U., 1978; postgrad. Northwestern U., 1981—. Office mgr., bookkeeper Airways Broadcasting Sales, Niles, Ill., 1974-76; systems engr. IBM, Chgo., 1977-82; sr. systems engr. Paradyne Corp., Des Plaines, Ill., 1982—. Mem. Data Processing Mgmt. Assn., Nat. Assn. Female Execs., NOW, ACLU, Sierra Club. Home: 1106 S Elmwood St Oak Park IL 60304 Office: 200 W Madison St Suite 3230 Chicago IL 60606

PENCE, JUDITH ANN, oboist; b. Springfield, Ohio, Apr. 1, 1933; d. Lowell David and Thelma Marcellite (Kelsey) Isenbarger; B.M., Butler U., 1955; M.A., Ball State U., 1966; m. Homer Charles Pence, July 16, 1955; children—Terry Alan, Kristin Ilona. Oboist, Indpls. Symphony Orch., 1955-56, 71-85, soloist, 1972; instr. music Ball State U., 1958-70, Butler U., 1972-78; oboist Musical Arts Quintet, 1960-70, Sebago Long Lake Region Chamber Music, summers 1972—; recitalist Carnegie Hall, 1963, 66; rec. artist Musical Arts Quintet, Indpls. Symphony Orch. Mem. Internat. Conf. Symphony and Opera Musicians.

PENCE, MARY LOU, author, journalist, historian; b. Big Timber, Mont., Nov. 8, 1906; d. John Christopher and Hattie Violet (Overholtz) Stone; m. Alfred M. Pence, June 1, 1932 (dec. 1980). Cert. U. Wyo., 1930; student Eastern Mont. U., 1931-32, John Robert Powers Finishing Sch., 1962; hon. degree Am. Coll. Quill, 1933, U. Wyo. Pres.'s Council, 1981. Woman's page editor, feature writer Laramie Boomerang, Wyo., 1946-52; editor Petticoat Politics, 1953-54; spl. feature writer, news stories writer Denver Post, 1951-56. Author: The Ghost Towns of Wyoming (award of merit 1957), 1957; The Laramie Story (awards), 1968; Anthologies in Tales and Legends of the Old West, 1962; Water Trails West, 1980; Women Who Made the West, 1982; Boswell, the Story of a Frontier Lawman (Nat. Fedn. Press Women award), 1978; contbr. articles to profl. jours. Founder Police Athletic Club for Young Boys, 1952-58; pres. U. Wyo. Panhellenic Council, 1960-74; publicity dir. Am. Legion Aux., 1949-52; chmn. Albany County United Fund Drive, 1953. Recipient Nat. Fedn. Press Women top award; Feature Story Empire Mag. award, Denver, 1951; News Story award Denver Post, 1952; Woman of Achievement award Wyo. Press Women, 1983. Mem. Nat. Fedn. Press Women (regional v.p. 1951-53, bd. dirs. 1953-58, life mem.), Western Writers Am. (nat. publicity dir. 1978-81), Wyo. Press Women, Nat. Outlaw and Lawman Authors, Nat. Hist. Preservation, Wyo. Hist. Soc. (charter mem.). Westerners Laramie Corral. Republican. Episcopalian.

PENCE, VIRGINIA ROSALIE (JEAN), real estate company executive; b. Chgo., July 12, 1925; d. William R. and Sophie (Kumlacky) Cottrell; m. Robert A. Pence, June 14, 1947; children—Marjorie Pence Tuinstra, Robert J. Cert. in Real Estate, Central YMCA Coll., Chgo., 1976. Real estate sales assoc. William Knight Realtors, LaGrange, Ill., 1962-70, sales mgr., 1970-76; pres. Pence & Co., Realtors, LaGrange, 1977—. Chmn., LaGrange Go-Getters Com. Channel 11 WTTW, Chgo., 1973-74. Mem. Nat. Assn. Realtors, Ill. Assn. Realtors, LaGrange Bd. Realtors (chmn. profl. standards com. 1985-86), LaGrange Bd. Realtors (sec.-treas. 1973-75, dir. Multiple Listing Service 1978), DuPage Bd. Realtors, Women's Council Realtors (pres. West Suburban chpt. 1979-81),, DAR. Congregationalist. Clubs: LaGrange Park Woman's (sec. 1967-68); Coterie (Western Springs, Ill.) (pres. 1982-83). Office: Pence & Co Realtors 42 S LaGrange Rd LaGrange IL 60525

PENCSAK, NANCY MUMFORD, information systems administrator; b. Raleigh, N.C., Nov. 4, 1937; d. Carey Gardner and Cleone (Cooper) Mumford; m. Raymond J. Pencsak, June 10, 1961 (div.); children—David Charles, Patricia Susanne, John Stephen. B.S. in Engring. Math., N.C. State Coll., 1959; postgrad. U. Dallas, 1980. Programmer analyst IBM, Omaha, 1959-62; systems engr. Electronic Data Systems, Dallas, 1977-79, U.S. Life Systems, Dallas, 1979-81; product devel. mgr. Intrans, Inc., Shreveport, La., 1981-82; project mgr. U.S. Telephone, Inc., Dallas, 1982-83; project coordinator Hogan Systems, Inc., Dallas, 1983-84, mgr. corp. systems, 1984—; curriculum adv. com. Richland Coll., Dallas, 1983—. Mem. Women in Computing (founder, treas. 1980, 81, 83—, co-chmn. seminar 1984), Am. Mgmt. Assn., Nat. Assn. Female Execs. Club: Austin Newcomers (v.p. 1972-73, membership chmn. 1970-72). Home: 7620 Indian Springs Rd Dallas TX 75248 Office: Hogan Systems Inc 5080 Spectrum Dr Dallas TX 75248

PENDLETON, CAROLYN M., banker; b. Park City, Utah, May 17, 1941; d. Charles Henry and Sarah Madge (Petersen) John; children—Rick L. Dowden, Randy S. Dowden. Student U. So. Calif., UCLA, El Camino Coll. With Crocker Bank, Los Angeles, 1966-72, br. mgr., 1972-75, ops. officer, 1975-79, asst. v.p., account officer, 1979-81; asst. v.p. product devel. First Interstate Bank, Los Angeles, 1981-83; v.p., mgr. Calif. Fed. Savs. & Loan, Los Angeles, 1983—; banking advisor So. Calif. Regional Occupational Ctr., Torrance, Calif., 1973-81; instr. Jr. Achievement, Los Angeles, 1981-83; bd. govs. AIB, Los Angeles, 1971-75. Recipient Leadership award, YWCA, 1980. Mem. Nat. Assn. Female Execs, Nat. Assn. Bank Women, Big Sisters of Los Angeles. Republican. Mem. Ch. of Jesus Christ of Latter day Saints. Club: Los Angeles Athletic. Avocation: running. Home: 424 Kelton Ave #402 Los Angeles CA 90024 Office: Calif Federal Savs & Loan 5670 Wilshire Blvd Suite 1849 Los Angeles CA 90036

PENDLETON, ELISABETH MORGAN, lawyer; b. N.Y.C., Oct. 14, 1941; d. Aubrey Niel and Constance Cutter (Morrow) Morgan; m. Miles S. Pendleton, Jr., Aug. 13, 1967; children—Constance M., Nathaniel P. B.A., Smith Coll., 1962; J.D., Harvard U., 1967. Bar: D.C. 1968, U.S. Supreme Ct. 1980. Editorial asst. Look Mag., N.Y.C., 1963-64; tchr. Am. Internat. Sch., Tel Aviv, Israel, 1968-70; prof. Université Officielle, Bujumbura, Burundi, 1970-72; assoc. law firm Arent, Fox, Kintner, Plotkin & Kahn, Washington, 1967-68, 73-74; office mgr. Los Angeles Times, Brussels, 1978-79; assoc. law firm Shaw, Pittman, Potts & Trowbridge, Washington, 1974-76, 79—. Mem. Friends of Smith Coll. Library, 1973-76; trustee Milton (Mass.) Acad., 1980—. Mem. ABA (sect. internat. law), D.C. Bar Assn., Alumnae Assn. Smith Coll., Phi Beta Kappa. Club: Cosmopolitan. Office: Shaw Pittman Potts & Trowbridge 1800 M St NW Washington DC 20036

PENDLETON, THELMA BROWN, physical therapist, health service administrator; b. Rome, Ga., Jan. 30, 1911; d. John O. and Alma (Ingram) Brown; diploma Provident Hosp. Sch. Nursing, 1931; cert. Loyola U., 1942, Northwestern U., 1946; m. George W. Pendleton, Mar. 2, 1946; 1 son, George William. Pediatric nurse Rosenwald Found., Chgo., 1931-32; staff nurse Vis. Nurse Assn., Chgo., 1932-45; chief phys. therapy Provident Hosp., Chgo., 1946-55; phys. therapy cons. Parents Assn., Inc., Chgo., 1956-60; cons. United Cerebral Palsy of Greater Chgo.'s Pipers Portal Schs., 1961-63, dir., 1963-64; dir. phys. therapy services LaRabida Children's Hosp. and Research Center, Chgo., 1964-75; mem. nat. com. Joint Orthopedic Nursing Adv. Services, 1947-55; clin. supr., instr. programs in phys. therapy Northwestern U. Med. Sch., Chgo., 1947-55, 64-75; cons. United Cerebral Palsy, 1970-75; lectr. Japanese service com. on Cerebral Palsy, 1970; mem. Ill. Phys. Therapy Exam. Com., 1952-62. Recipient cert. of commendation CSC Cook County (Ill.), 1961, Citation of Merit, Wands Cerebral Palsy Unit, 1961. Mem. Am., Ill. phys. therapy assns., Provident Hosp. Nurses Alumni Assn. Democrat. Clubs: Tu-Fours Bolivia. Author: Low Budget Gourmet, 1977; (booklet) Patient Positioning, 1981; contbr. articles on phys. therapy to profl. jours.; contbr. to Am. Poetry Anthology. Address: 2631 S Indiana Ave Chicago IL 60616

PENEDO, ROSEANNE IRENE, financial analyst; b. Danbury, Conn., Feb. 9, 1952; d. Jose Augusto and Rosa (Machado) P.; B.A., Vassar Coll., 1973; M.A. Middlebury Coll., 1974; M.B.A., in Fin., The Am. U., 1983. Tchr. Danbury Bd. Edn., Conn., 1975-81; fin. analyst Malarkey-Taylor Assoc., Washington D.C., 1983—. Mem. Danbury Conservation Commn., 1981. Mem. Am. Women in Radio and Television, Women in Cable. Democrat. Roman Catholic. Office: Malarkey-Taylor Assoc Inc 1301 Pennsylvania Ave Suite 200 Washington DC 20004

PENFOLD, DAWN MARIE, tourism consultant, conference planner; b. Buffalo, July 3, 1955; d. Daniel and Doris Marie (Brown) P. B.A. in Modern Langs., St. Bonaventure U., 1977. Mktg. coordinator Massy Papiers Peint, Paris, 1974-75; fundraising coordinator Nat. Multiple Sclerosis Soc., Buffalo, 1978-79; asst. dir. admissions Daemen Coll., Buffalo, 1979-81; prin. owner DMP Assocs., N.Y.C., 1981—; conf. planner Am. Inst. C.P.A.s, 1984—; cons. Holland Am. Cruise Lines, N.Y.C., 1982, Hilton Internat., N.Y.C., 1982, Westin Hotels, N.Y.C., 1982, Am. Soc. Pub. Adminstrs., N.Y.C., 1983, Julien J. Studley, Inc., N.Y.C., 1983; dir. tourism Bklyn. Bridge Centennial Commn. Chmn. tourism com. 1989 N.Y. World's Fair, 1981—; mem. spl. events com. N.Y. State Statue of Liberty Centennial, 1983—. Mem. Travel and Tourism Research Assn. (chmn. 1982-83), Women Execs. in Tourism, Hotel, Sales Mgmt. Assn., Meeting Planners Internat., Pi Delta Phi. Roman Catholic.

PENICK, LINDA SUE BOBBITT, city social services administrator; b. Lynchburg, Va., Sept. 25, 1950; d. James Randolph and Edith Juanita (Layne) Bobbitt; m. William Frank Penick, Feb. 8, 1971. B.A., Longwood Coll., 1980, postgrad., fall 1984. Sec., bookkeeper Hub Dept. Stores, Farmville, Va., 1972-77; sec., treas. Cam Auto Truck Parts, Inc., Bills Auto Body Repair, Cam Road Runner Service, Farmville, 1977-85; clk. Lynchburg Div. Social Services, 1985—. Mem. Nat. Assn. Female Execs. Episcopalian. Club: Home Demonstration. Avocations: piano; sewing; cooking; gardening; needlework. Mailing Address: Route 2 PO Box 94 Lynchburg VA 24501

PENINGER, PATRICIA ANN, building contractor; b. Cross Plains, Tex., Oct. 15, 1931; d. C.L. and Mildred E. (Walker) Browning; m. Donald M. Peninger, Feb. 11, 1949; children—Debra, Marsha, Eric. Student Weatherford Jr. Coll., 1961-62. Chief dep. County Tax Office, Weatherford, Tex., 1969-75; pres., gen. ptnr., bookkeeper Penco Builders, Inc., Millsap, Tex., 1977—. Democrat. Baptist. Avocations: interior decorating, sewing. Address: Route 1 Box 164 Millsap TX 76066

PENLAND, EULA EILEEN, personnel executive; b. St. Louis, Nov. 3, 1931; d. William and Eula Aura (Covington) Mummert; m. Robert Samuel Penland, Feb. 19, 1983; children by previous marriage—Ralph E., Frances Eileen, Pamela Darlene. Student Del Mar Coll., 1949, Victoria Coll., 1969, U. N.Mex., 1972. Bookkeeper, Tarrant Wholesale Distbrs., Corpus Christi, Tex., 1963, Zarsky Lumber Co., Corpus Christi, 1963-64; with Tex. Employers Ins. Co., Corpus Christi, 1965; with E. I. DuPont De Nemours & Co., Inc., Victoria, Tex., 1965-71; exec. sec. The Heil Co., Huntsville, Tex., 1977-78; personnel dir. Continental Savings Assn., Angleton, Tex., 1978—; cons. in field. Editor newsletter Continental Express, 1980-84; contbr. articles to profl. jours. Volunteer, Sheriff's Campaign, Angleton, 1980, United Way, 1982—; leader Camp Fire Girls, 1961-62; den mother Boy Scouts Am., Houston, 1958-59. Nat. Honor Soc. scholar, 1948. Mem. Am. Soc. Personnel Assn., Inst. Fin. Edn., others. Democrat. Methodist. Office: Continental Savings Assn 4500 Bissonnet Bellaire TX 77401

PENN, MARY MCNAMARA, dentist; b. Chgo., Dec. 6, 1946; d. George Arthur and Mary Margaret (Ammond) McNamara; m. Richard Knight Penn, Oct. 6, 1968 (div. 1979); 1 child, John Andrew; m. John Bailey Ross, Dec. 31, 1982; 1 child, John Bailey Ross. B.A., U. Miami, Oxford, Ohio, 1968; D.D.S., UCLA, 1980. Pvt. practice dentistry, Los Angeles, 1980—. Author: Glickman's Clinical Periodontology, 1979; also articles. Active Physicians for Social Responsibility, Los Angeles, 1983—, NOW, Los Angeles, 1984—, Freeze Phase II, San Fernando Valley, Calif., 1984—. Mem. Am. Assn. Women Dentists, Women in Health, Am. Soc. Clin. Hypnosis (ethics com. 1984-86). Home: 11359 Darby Ave Northridge CA 91326 Office: 11600 Wilshire Blvd Suite 300 Los Angeles CA 90025

PENN, MELINDA HISCOX CARTER, lawyer; b. Atlanta, Apr. 18, 1941; d. Harold William Hiscox and Freda Elizabeth (Meyer) Hiscox Teague; m. Walter Lee Penn, Apr. 23, 1983; children by previous marriage—Pannill Carter, Coates Carter. B.A., Goucher Coll., 1963; M.F.A., U. N.C.-Greensboro, 1968; J.D., Stetson Coll. Law, 1979. Bar: Fla. 1979, Va. 1980. Tchr. English, Martinsville High Sch. (Va.), 1965-66; librarian Carlisle Sch., Martinsville, 1968-70; tchr. English, Hillsborough Community Coll., Tampa, Fla., 1974-76; pvt. practice law, Martinsville, 1981-82; atty., ptnr., Smith & Penn, Martinsville, 1982—; asst. commonwealth atty. City of Martinsville, 1982—. Pres., Am. Cancer Soc., Martinsville, 1983—; bd. dirs. W. C. Ham Learning Ctr., 1982—, Patrick Henry Drug and Alcohol Council, 1982—, Stoneleigh Council. Mem. Women Attys. Va. (dir.), ABA, Va. Bar Assn., Martinsville Bar Assn., Va. Trial Lawyers Assn., Peidmont Arts Assn. (dir.), Phi Delta Phi. Republican. Episcopalian. Club: Chatmoss Country. Home: 1107 Knollwood Pl Martinsville VA 24112 Office: Smith and Penn PC PO Box 1311 26 W Church St Martinsville VA 24114

PENN, PATSY SHARON, construction company executive, federal contract administrator; b. Clinton, Ind.; d. B. Franklin and Edith May (Hutson) Market; m. Robert Eugene Penn, Jan. 18, 1964; 1 child, Brookelyn Shane. M. Cosmetology, Smart Appearance Beauty Acad., Terre Haute, Ind., 1967. Owner, mgr. stylist Hair Fashions by Patsy, Rockville, Ind., 1969-79; contract adminstr. Penn & Penn Gen. Contractors, Rockville, 1977-79; owner, operator Midway Construction Co., Rockville, 1981—; organizer, project estimator, Midway Construction Co., Rockville, 1981—, contract adminstr., 1981—, sec., bookkeeper, 1981—, legal council Dept. of Interior Contract Appeals, 1983-84. Monitering of legis. request Pres. of the U.S., Washington, 1984. Home: Rural Route 4 US 36 W Rockville IN 47872 Office: Midway Construction Co Rural Route 4 US 36 W Rockville IN 47872

PENNDORF, DORIS MARIE, nurse anesthetist; b. Elizabeth, N.J., Dec. 15, 1946; d. John Sebastian and Harriet Adele (Clarke) P. R.N., Stormont Vail Sch. Nursing, 1969; cert. registered nurse anesthetist, Hosp. St. Raphael Sch. Nurse Anesthesia, 1975. Staff cert. registered nurse anesthetist, instr. Anesthesia Assocs. New Haven, P.C., 1975-76; staff cert. registered nurse anesthetist Med. Anesthesiology Assocs., Fairfield, Conn., 1976-78, Mt. Sinai Hosp. and Med. Ctr., Hartford, Conn., 1978-80, Woodland Anesthesiology Assocs., P.C., Hartford, 1980—. Mem. Am. Assn. Nurse Anesthetists (mem. ad hoc com. on chem. dependency 1985—), New Eng. Assembly Nurse Anesthetists (mem. exec. bd. 1979-80), Conn. Nurses' Assn. (peer assistance edn. com. chairperson 1985—), Conn. Assn. Nurse Anesthetists (trustee, sec., chairperson ad hoc com. on chem. dependency 1985-86, chmn. well-being com. 1986—), Am. Nurses' Assn. Democrat. Jewish. Avocations: geneology; landscaping. Home: 484 Fern St West Hartford CT 06107

PENNELL, FRANCES, management consultant; b. Boston, Aug. 6, 1951; d. Walter Francis and Helen (Redmond) P.; B.S., Simmons Coll., 1973; M.P.H. in Health Adminstrn., Columbia U., 1978; M.B.A. in Fin., N.Y.U., 1983. Emergency room med. technologist Martha's Vineyard Hosp., Mass., 1973; med. technologist, ednl. in-service coordinator Park Med. Lab., Brookline, Mass., 1974-76; mgmt. cons. Macro Systems, Inc., Silver Spring, Md., 1977; program and fin. analyst N.Y.C., Health and Hosp.'s Corp., 1978-80; mgr. Coopers & Lybrand, N.Y.C., 1980-84, dir., 1985—; sr. v.p. Comprehensive Cancer Care Corp., 1984-85. Mem. Hosp. Fin. Mgmt. Assn., Am. Soc. Clin. Pathologists (registered med. technologist). Contbr. articles on health care industry to profl. jours. Home: 105 W 70th St Apt 5R New York NY 10023 Office: 1251 Ave of the Americas New York NY 10020

PENNEY, SHERI LAYNE, diversified company official; b. Logan, Utah, July 24, 1943; d. Darwin Reuben and Billie Bryan (Perry) P.; B.A., U. Utah, 1966. Tech. writer Computer Sci. Corp., El Segundo, Calif., 1969-70, customer systems rep., 1970-71; programmer/analyst Wm. O'Neil & Co., Westwood, Calif., 1971-73; tech. rep. Nat. CSS, Los Angeles, 1976-79, sales rep., 1979; users' group analyst Xerox Corp., El Segundo, 1973-75, sales promotions mgr., 1979—. Mem. Nat. Assn. Female Execs. Democrat. Club: Beach Cities Ski. Editor: Exchange User's News, 1973-75, Weekly Briefing, 1974-75, Output, 1979-80, Insider, 1982, Xerox tradeshows, brochures and films. Office: 101 Continental Blvd C4-47 El Segundo CA 90245

PENNFIELD, LINDA SHARPE, personnel executive, b. Roscrea, Ireland; came to U.S., 1970; d. Michael Joseph and Mary (Byrne) Sharpe; m. Edward Bruce Pennfield, Aug. 22, 1974. B.A., U. London, 1969. Personnel mgr. United Media Enterprises, N.Y.C., 1975—. Mem. Am. Soc. Personnel Adminstrn. (bd. dirs. 1984, chairperson accreditation com. 1981), Newspaper Personnel Relations Assn., N.Y. Personnel Mgmt. Assn. (chmn. compensation com. 1984-85, bd. dirs. 1985-86). Home: 401 E 74th St New York NY 10021

PENNICK, LORAINE ANNE, accountant; b. New Haven, Mar. 18, 1954; d. Rocco W. Sr. and Mary C. (Cassella) Gargano; m. Edward David Pennick, July 12, 1980. B.S., summa cum laude, U. New Haven, 1976; A.S., Southern Conn. State U., 1974. C.P.A., Conn. Lic. real estate broker, Conn. Property mgr. Crestwood Mgmt., West Haven, Conn., 1973-78; sr. tax acct. Deloitte Haskins & Sells, New Haven, 1978-84; tax planning So. New Eng. Telephone Co., New Haven, 1984; tax mgr. LIGHTNET, New Haven, 1984—; instr. Becker C.P.A. rev. course, Fairfield, Conn., 1982-86. Treas., RESPOND, New Haven, 1982-85; commr. West Haven Fair Rent Commn., 1982-84. Mem. Conn. Soc. C.P.A.s, Am. Inst. C.P.A.s, Conn. Estate and Tax Planning Council, Greater New Haven Jaycees (controler 1983-84, treas. 1985-86). Roman Catholic. Home: 430 Barton Dr Orange CT 06477 Office: LIGHTNET 195 Church St New Haven CT 06510

PENNINGTON, CARYLON M., educator; b. Florence, Ala., Nov. 30, 1944; d. Herschel J. and Inas (Austin) Pennington. B.S.W., Eastern Tenn. State U., 1971, M.Ed., 1979. With Colony Sq. Hotel, Atlanta, 1975-77; tchr. Fulton County Bd. Edn., Atlanta, 1979-81; with Rivera Hyatt-Hotal, Atlanta, 1981-82; tchr. Fulton County Bd. Edn., Atlanta, 1983—. Mem. Save the Fox Theater, Atlanta Arts Festival, High Mus. Atlanta. Mem. Nat. Tchrs. Assn., Fulton County Assn. of Edn., Internat. Reading Assn., Ga. Conf. Internat. Reading Assn., Chpt. I Evaluation Com. Republican. Roman Catholic. Clubs: Rosary Soc. Lodge: Rosicrucian. Avocations: photography; camping; classical music; jazz; antiques. Home: 808 Greenwood Ave Apt 2

Atlanta GA 30306 Office: S M Avery Elementary Sch 2110 W John Wesley Ave College Park GA 30337

PENNINGTON, DORIS ETHEL, association executive; b. Gibson County, Tenn., Aug. 15, 1933; d. Jesse Curn and Wreatha Sedoris (Malugen) Buckingham; student Wesley Theol. Sem., 1969-71, George Washington U., 1981—; m. Philip Wayne Pennington, Nov. 29, 1951; children—Philip Michael, Richard Wayne. Clk., FBI, Washington, St. Louis, 1951-52, 53-55; adminstrv. asst. Foundry United Meth. Ch., 1965-70; sec./office mgr. Hughes and McCloskey Law Offices, Washington, 1971-75; sales asso. Routh Robbins Realtors, Alexandria, Va., 1975-78; adminstrv. asst. to pres. Computer and Bus. Equipment Mfrs. Assn., Washington, 1977; dir. personnel/asst. sec. Electronic Industries Assn., Washington, 1977—; realtor asso. Laughlin Realtors, McLean, Va., 1979—. Mem. Am. Soc. Assn. Execs., Exec. Female, Am. Soc. Personnel Adminstrs., Nat. Assn. Realtors, No. Va. Bd. Realtors. Democrat. Lodge: Order Eastern Star. Home: 6656 Madison of McLean McLean VA 22101 Office: 2001 Eye St NW Washington DC 20006

PENNINGTON, INEZ SCOTT, photography executive; b. Nashville, Mar. 22, 1958; d. Thomas Guv and Phyllis (Thorp) P. B.A. with honors, Vassar Coll., 1980; student Barbieri Ctr., Rome, 1979. Photographer, owner Pennington Galleries, Nashville, 1981—; owner, mgr. New Focus, Nashville, 1986—; ofcl. photographer Am. Grand Prix Assn., Cleve., 1983—, U.S. Equestrian Team, South Hamilton, Mass., 1985—. Photographer for numerous horse show catalogues and posters, also books and mags. in field. Mem. Nikon Profl. Services, Associated Photographers Internat., Nat. Equine Photographic Soc., Am. Soc. Mag. Photography. Office: 631 4th Ave S Nashville TN 37210

PENNINGTON, JANIS OPHELIA, educator, linguistic specialist; b. Akron, Ohio, Apr. 15, 1951; d. William Thomas and Rebecca (Russell) P. B.A., San Jose State U., 1973; M.A., U. San Francisco, 1980. Claims rep. Social Security Commn., Los Angeles, 1973-75, 76-78; educator Los Angeles Unified Schs., 1978—, grade coordinator, 1983—, master tchr. coordinator, 1984—, faculty chmn. 1982, mentor tchr., 1985-86. Co-author: It's Urgent, 1976. Co-editor: Friendship Speaks, 1981. Leader Girl Scouts U.S.A., Los Angeles, 1980-83. Recipient Ill. Youth Orch. Sesquicentennial Com. medal, 1968; Environ. Agy. grantee, 1976. Mem. Sigma Gamma Rho (co-founder Epsilon Omicron chpt. sec. 1973). Democrat. Home: 7634 9th St Apt C Buena Park CA 90621

PENNINGTON, MARY ANNE, art museum director art educator; b. Franklin, Va., Apr. 12, 1943; d. James Clifton and Martha Julia (Futrell) P.; m. Walter Joseph Shackelford, Nov. 26, 1981. Student East Carolina U., 1962; B.F.A., Va. Commonwealth U., 1965, M.F.A., 1966; postgrad. Cameron U., 1970, East Carolina U., 1972, U. N.C., Chapel Hill, 1980. Instr. art Presbyterian Coll., Clinton, S.C., 1966-69; tchr. art in Pitt County, 1970-71, Greenville City Sch. Systems (N.C.), 1971-73; instr. art Pitt Community Coll., 1972-73; coordinator visual arts and humanities program, Ludwigsberg, W.Ger., 1974-76; vis. artist-in-residence Salt Pond Art Ctr., Blacksburg, Va., summer, 1978; asst. prof. art Pembroke State U. (N.C.), 1976-80; exec. dir. Greenville Mus. Art, 1980—; judge art competition, 1967—; speaker N.C. Dept. Corrections, 1980—; guest lectr. art Converse Coll., Spartanburg, S.C., summer, 1966. Author: Application of Industrial Sand Casting to Sculpture, 1966; also articles. Bd. dirs. Pitt-Greenville Arts Council; program coordinator Pitt-Greenville Leadership Inst., 1982—. Recipient Vol. award N.C. Gov., 1981; N.C. Disting. Women award, 1986. Mem. Am. Assn. Mus., Southeastern Mus. Conf., Inc., N.C. Mus. Council. Office: Greenville Mus Art 802 S Evans St Greenville NC 27834

PENNISI, MARY EVELYN, color consultant; b. Long Beach, N.Y., Aug. 12, 1946; d. William Maddox and Agnes Elizabeth (Sweeney) O'Brien; m. Peter Pennisi, Feb. 3, 1968; 1 child, Mark Edward. Student Fashion Inst. Tech., N.Y.C., 1964-65, student Brown's Bus. Sch., Rockville Center, N.Y., 1965-66, Parsons Sch. Design, White Plains, N.Y., 1975. Rep., Color Me Beautiful, Tex., 1979-83; owner, operator The Color Studio, Richardson, Tex., 1983—; prin. Communicative Seminars, Inc., Richardson, 1984—, The Color Studio Eyewear, Richardson, 1983—. Author tng. manual. Mem. Am. Bus. Women's Assn., Richardson C. of C., Dallas C. of C., Dallas Better Bus. Bur. Avocations: skiing, walking, designing clothing. Home: 1202 Eton Dr Richardson TX 75080 Office: Color Studio 1703 Windsong Terr Richardson TX 75081

PENNY, JOSEPHINE B., retired banker; b. N.Y.C., July 7, 1925; d. Charles and Delia (Fahey) Booy; student Columbia U., Am. Inst. Banking; grad. Sch. Bank Adminstrn. U. Wis., 1975; m. John T. Penny, July 15, 1950 (div.); children—John T., Charleen Penny DeMauro, Patricia Penny Paras. With Prentice-Hall, N.Y.C., 1942-43; with Trade Bank & Trust Co., 1943-52, 61-70; with Nat. Westminster Bank U.S.A., 1970-85, v.p., dep. auditor, 1978-85. Mem. Bank Adminstrn. Inst. (chpt. dir.), Nat. Assn. Bank Women (chpt. chmn. 1980-81). Home: 131 Sawyer Ave Staten Island NY 10314

PENNY, LINDA LEA, social work administrator; b. Big Spring, Tex., Aug. 6, 1943; d. Charlie Nichol and Bonnie Wayne (Tartt) Farrar; m. Larry Lee Penny, Oct. 27, 1967; 1 child, Larry Lee II. B.S.W., Tex. Woman's U., 1975, M.A. in Sociology, 1977; diploma Inst. for English Speaking Students, Internat. Grad. Sch., U. Stockholm, 1978. Cert. social worker. Coordinator human resources Catholic Charities, Fort Worth, 1975-76; program specialist Tex. Dept. Human Resources, Austin, 1977; program specialist/ombudsman Tex. Gov.'s Com. on Aging, Austin, 1978-80; project dir., tng. dir. Ctr. for Pub. Interest, Dallas, 1980-82; dir. social work dept. Presbyn. Hosp., Dallas, 1982-84, Meml. Hosp., Cleburne, Tex., 1984—; pvt. cons./trainer, Cleburne, 1980—; ptnr., cons. Gormet Basket, Cleburne, 1985-86. Bd. dirs. Johnson County Family Crisis Ctr., Cleburne, 1985-86. Samuel E. Ziegler Found. fellow, Dallas, 1976-77. Mem. Tex. Soc. Hosp. Social Work Dirs., Am. Bus. Women's Assn., Nat. Assn. Female Execs., Assn. Ind. Real Estate Owners, Am. Mensa. Democrat. Lutheran. Avocations: real estate investments; refinishing antiques; collecting glassware. Home: Route 2 Box 139 Godley TX 76044 Office: Meml Hosp 1600 N Main St Cleburne TX 76031

PENNYCUFF, LOUISE A., health agency executive; b. Robbins, Tenn., Oct. 9, 1944; d. Ervin and Grace (Young) Silcox; children—Nella, Connie. L.P.N., Livingston Vocat. Sch., 1970; student St. Joseph's Coll., 1983-84; A.Respiratory Sci., Roane State Coll., 1982. Cert. respiratory therapist. With Jamestown Shirt Factory, Tenn., 1963-68; dietary asst. Fentress County Hosp., Jamestown, 1968-70, practical nurse, 1970-80, respiratory therapist, 1980-83; clin. dir. Buckeye Quality Home Health Agy., Jamestown, 1983—; respiratory therapy cons. Vol., ARC Blood Mobile, Jamestown, 1983—. Fellow Am. Nurses Assn.; mem. Am. Respiratory Therapy Assn., Nat. Assn. Female Execs., Tenn. Nurses Assn. Baptist. Avocations: crafts; sewing; reading; horse back riding; tennis. Home: PO Box 912 Jamestown TN 38556 Office: Buckeye Quality Home Health Agy PO Box 1197 Jamestown TN 38556

PENROSE, CYNTHIA C., administrator, consultant; b. Manila, Philippines, Nov. 24, 1939; came to U.S., 1940; d. Douglas Lee Lipscomb Cordiner and Jane (Sturgeon) Edises; m. Douglas Francis Penrose, July 11, 1959 (div. 1981); children—Vicki Lynn, Lee Douglas; m. Alan Harrison Magazine, Aug. 30, 1984. B.A., U. Calif.-Berkeley, 1963; M.B.A., U. Santa Clara, 1977. Cert. social services. Vice pres and dir. employment Resource Ctr. for Women, Palo Alto, Calif., 1973-78; bus. planner Raychem Corp., Menlo Park, Calif., 1979; adminstrv. mgr. Electric Power Research Inst., Palo Alto, 1979-83; dir. ops. Utility Data Inst., Washington, 1984-85; dir. ops. Randmark, Inc., 1986—; sr. ptnr. MB Assocs., Washington, 1983—; bd. dirs. and treas. Unique Enterprises, Washington, 1985—. Bd. dirs., v.p. LWV, Berkeley and Palo Alto, 1966-73; chmn. program adv. council Resource Ctr. for Women, Palo Alto, 1980-83; mem. Affirmative Action Adv. Com. Palo Alto, 1975-76. Mem. Exec. Women's Roundtable (Washington, founder), Peninsula Profl. Women's Network (v.p. 1981-82), Women in Energy, Am. Soc. Assn. Execs., Wed. Group, AAUW, LWV. Democrat. Episcopalian. Avocations: swimming; nutrition and health; reading. Home: 7430 Fountainhead Dr Annandale VA 22003 Office: Randmark Inc 2100 M St NW Washington DC 20037

PENSO, ALESA MARIE SMITH, writer, educator; b. Carmel, Calif., July 29, 1952; d. Hugh Everett and Gyla M. (Marmont) Smith; m. Patrick M. Penso, Apr. 5, 1975; children—Marc, Neil. B.A. with honors, U. Calif.-Santa Cruz, 1974; M.A., U. Wash., 1985. Tchr., Girls' Town, Kingston, Jamaica, 1975-76, Wolmer's Girls Sch., Kingston, 1974-75, Upward Bound, Coll. of Virgin Islands, 1977-78; dir. Udhailiyah Preschool, Saudi Arabia, 1980-82. Contbr. stories to children's mags., also articles to mags. Sec. V.I. Archeol. Soc., 1977-79; bd. dirs. Udhailiyah Preschool, 1980-82. Mem. Soc. Children's Bookwriters. Avocations: anthropology; innovative travel; jogging; tennis. Home: 16013 SE 31st St Bellevue WA 98008

PENTA, IRENE PLATT, nurse, club woman; b. Concord, N.H., Jan. 2, 1920; d. Frank Bishop and Ida Louisa (Cable) Platt; student Portland Jr. Coll., 1939; R.N., Dr. Drummond's Hosp. Nursing Sch., Portland, Maine, 1942; m. Walter E. Penta, Sept. 25, 1943; 1 son, Donald Platt. Nurse, Maine Med. Center, Portland, 1942-43, Mercy Hosp., Portland, 1943, Boston City Hosp., 1943-44, Beth Israel Hosp., Boston, 1944, Mass. Gen. Hosp., Boston, 1944, Deaconess Hosp., Boston, 1943, Meth. Hosp., Dallas, 1944-45, Med. Arts, Dallas, 1944-45, So. Bapt. Hosp., Dallas, 1944-45. Sec., Woman's Aux. Maine Med. Assn., Portland, 1955-56, v.p., 1956-57, pres.-elect, 1957-58, pres., 1958-59, bd. dirs., 1955—, chmn. internat. health-womans aux. 1967—; v.p. Ladies of Kiwanis, Portland, 1958, pres., 1959, bd. dirs., 1957—; active aux. Maine Med. Center; mem. organizational com. Tri-State Health Careers Research Group, Portland, 1960-61; rural health chmn. region one, Woman's Aux. to AMA, 1960-65, Maine internat. health chmn. Mem. Maine Nurses Assn., Dr. Drummonds Hosp. Alumni Assn. (pres. 1964-66, 82—), Maine Hist. Soc., Internat. Platform Assn., Wives Wing of Aerospace Med. Assn., Nat. Soc. Daus. of Founders and Patriots Am., Nat. Soc. Women Descs. Ancient and Honorable Arty. Co. (v.p. Maine chpt. assts. 1972—). Congregationalist (pres. Jr. Guild 1956). Club: Woodfords (Portland). Home: 316 Woodford St Portland ME 04103

PENTLAND, DAME SUE-BYRD, ballerina; b. Sioux City, Iowa, Mar. 25, 1928; d. Edgar O. and Mabel (French) Hill; student Ark. U., 1943; m. Ernest Edward Roberts, June 10, 1944 (dec. Sept. 1960); 1 son, William-Hill; m. 2d, Robert Pentland, Jr., Jan. 25, 1963 (dec. July 1979). Formerly prima ballerina Miami Ballet; tchr. acad. classical ballet technique St. Stephen's Episcopal Day Sch., Coconut Grove, Fla., 1959-62. Active USO; prin. dancer, soloist The Iham Follies for crippled children, 1953-61; mem. Debutante Com., Opera Guild Greater Miami. Recipient gold medal U.S.O.; Queen of Hearts award Variety Internat. Club, 1971, Great Gal award, 1972, Angel award, 1980, 1st Golden Harvest Queen, 1984, Lady of Justice, St. John of Jerusalem, Knights of Malta Mem. U.D.C., Dance Masters Am., Internat. Platform Assn., Soc. Univ. Founders. So. Republican. Episcopalian. Clubs: Miami Woman's (perpetual mem., chmn. ballet, drama and music div. fine arts dept., 1958-60, 61-62), Hibiscus Garden; U. Miami Woman's; Indian Creek Country, Surf; Golden Hills Turf and Golf Country (Ocala, Fla.); Brookfield West, Country (Roswell, Ga.). Home: Quarter-Mile Farms Fairfield FL 32634 also 12173 Mountain Laurel Dr Brookfield West Roswell GA 30075 also Pentland-Court 2813 N Surf Rd Hollywood Beach FL 33019

PENTZ-MCBRIDE, JANA MIA, radio station manager; b. Beatrice, Nebr., May 30, 1955; d. Gordon Charles Bud and Maxine (Duis) Pentz; m. Bryce E. McBride, June 18, 1977; 1 child, Andrew Ryan. B.A. in Broadcast Journalism, U. Nebr., 1977. Acct., v.p. Mia Enterprises, Inc., Beatrice, Nebr., 1977-78; office mgr. Winner, Nichols & Meister, Scottsbluff, Nebr., 1979-80; adminstrv. asst. Mia Enterprises, Inc., Beatrice, 1980-83, gen. mgr., v.p., 1983—. Co-producer: Vietnamese Americans, 1976. Mem. Bd. Pub. Works, 1983—; bd. dirs., pres. YWCA, Beatrice, 1981—; capt. Gage County United Way, Beatrice, 1983—; mem. Nebr. Commn. on Status of Women, Lincoln, 1984-85; treas. Gage County Task Force on Domestic Violence, Beatrice, 1981-82; Vol. Domestic Abuse; bd. dirs. Domestic Abuse Prevention Line Vols., Crete, Nebr., 1980-82; mem. Jud. Nominating Commn. 18th Dist. Nebr., 1985—, Nebr. Council Pub. Relations for Agr., 1985—. Recipient Cert. of Service City of Beatrice, 1983; named Businesswoman of Yr., Women's div. C. of C., Beatrice, 1984. Mem. Am. Women in Radio/TV, Nebr. Broadcasters Assn. (bd. mem. 1983—), Nebr. Coalition for Women, Victim Support, Inc. (v.p. 1984—). Republican. Methodist. Avocations: biking; swimming; reading. Office: KWBE/KMAZ 200 Sherman St Beatrice NE 68310

PENWELL, JOANNE ALBERTA MARGARET, educator; b. Pitts., Apr. 7; d. Henry J. and Alberta May (Ing) Reis; m. Stanley Curtiss Campbell, Dec. 27, 1955 (dec. 1956); 1 son, Scott Jeffrey; m. Richard McMaster Penwell, Oct. 31, 1959; children—Steven Richard, Shawn Michael. B.S.N., M.S.N., U. Pitts.; M.Ed., John Carroll U., 1983. R.N., Pa., Ohio. Operating rm. nurse Presbyn. Hosp., Pitts.; faculty Presbyn. Univ. Hosp., Pitts., U. Pitts., 1958-61, Central Sch. Practical Nursing, Cleve., 1973; asst. prof. nursing Lakeland Community Coll., Cleve./Mentor, Ohio, 1973—; cons. Geauga Community Hosp., 1976-79, Madison Hosp., 1980; dir. Home Health Care, Inc., Mentor, 1983. Mem. Am. Nurses Assn., Nat. League Nursing, Geauga Nurses Assn. (treas. 1970-73), Sigma Tau Delta. Republican. Episcopalian. Clubs: Russell Women's, Chagrin Jr. Women's, Episcopal Ch. Women. Office: Lakeland Community Coll Rt 306 Mentor OH 44060

PEPE, LENNA GRACE (PENNY), nurse; b. Woonsocket, R.I., Jan. 5, 1933; d. Marcus Clinton and Marjorie Luella (Atwell) Shurtleff; m. William Lawrence Elston, Feb. 13, 1954 (div. Feb. 23, 1983); children—William L., Robin W., Jeffrey D., David W.; m. Charles Louis Pepe, July 27, 1985. R.N., Youngstown Hosp. Sch. Nursing, Ohio, 1953. R.N., Conn., Ohio, N.Y., Fla. Surg. nurse Mahoning Valley Hosp., Warren, Ohio, 1954-55; supr. Eastland Orthopedic Assocs., Inc., Warren, 1970-82; dir. nursing Golfcrest Nursing Ctr., Hollywood, Fla., 1983—. Avocations: swimming, reading, coin collecting. Office: Golfcrest Nursing Ctr 600 N 17th Ave Hollywood FL 33020

PEPIN, BEVERLY K., entrepreneur, model, actress; b. Hamilton, Ont., Can., Apr. 26, 1942; came to U.S. 1943; d. James Hill and Martha Esther (Evert) Kay; children—Robert, Deborah, Danielle. Student Eastern Conn. State U., Weist Baron Acting Sch., Hanover Sch. Modeling. Sales tng. dir. Holiday Magic, 1971-73; owner, dir. Hanover Models, Inc., Hartford, Conn., 1973-85; owner Today's Total Woman, Hartford, 1986—; talk show guest and co-producer WFSB-TV3, Hartford, 1974-78; co-host Easter Seals Telethon, WTNH, New Haven, 1978-83, Weekly Conn. State Lottery Show, Hartford, 1981-84; guest appearances on various talk shows; model television commls. Exec. bd. Greater Hartford Conv., Visitors Bur., Hartford, 1978-84; adv. bd. Miss Universe Pageant, Hartford, 1977-81. Named Mrs. Conn. USA, 1979; recipient TM Award for Community Service, 1983. Mem. Advt. Club Greater Hartford, Sales and Mktg. Execs. (treas. 1975-77), Hartford C. of C. Democrat. Christian Ch. Avocations: hang gliding. Address: 30 Stoney Brook Dr Glastonbury CT 06033

PEPPER, KATHLEEN RAE, real estate broker associate; b. Webster, City, Iowa, Feb. 21, 1953; d. Eldon Leonard and Donna Mae (Anderson) Moats; m. William Russell Pepper, Oct. 3, 1977. Student Iowa State U., 1971-73, Jones Real Estate Coll., 1981. Lic. broker, Colo. Personnel counselor Better Bus. Personnel, Colorado Springs, Colo., 1978-80; agt. Ken Reyhons Realtors, Pueblo, Colo., 1982-83; agt. Eagle Real Estate Assocs., Pueblo, 1983-85, broker assoc., 1985—. Mem. Pueblo Bd. Realtors, Nat. Assn. Realtors. Office: Eagle Real Estate Assocs Inc 3606 C Morris Ave Pueblo CO 81008

PERCER, PEGGY STEADMAN, weight control/fitness company executive; b. Kingsport, Tenn., June 22, 1941; d. Frank and Mary Elizabeth (Hartgrove) Crawford; m. Chammie Howard Percer, Jr., May 14, 1982; children by previous marriage—Scott Lynn, Angela Michelle. Student pub. schs., Kingsport, Tenn. Mgr. Dollar Discount Store, Kingsport, Tenn., 1966-72; substitute tchr. Sullvan County Schs., Kingsport, 1972-77; div. mgr. Cosmopolitan Spa, Inc., Kingsport, 1977-81; dir., pres. Women's Weight Loss Clinics, Inc., Norton, Va., 1981-83; rep. Women's Weight Loss Clinics of Am., Canton, Ohio, 1982-83; pres., dir. Fitness/Weight Control, Inc., Kingsport, 1981—; sec. Women's Fitness Ctr., Inc., 1982. Chmn., Cystic Fibrosis Found., Kingsport, 1983-85; sponsor presentation The Changing Woman Seminar, Kingsport, 1983. Named Employee of the Year, Cosmopolitan Spa, Inc., Kingsport, 1978, Salesperson of Yr., 1978. Republican. Baptist. Club: Altrusa (corr. sec.). Avocations: piano; reading; golf; swimming; exercise. Home: 4027 Potato Hill Rd Kingsport TN 37660 Office: Women's Fitness Weight Control Center 1944 Brookside Dr Kingsport TN 37660

PEREGOY, PHYLLIS JONES, real estate broker; b. Spotsylvania, Va., Apr. 5, 1942; d. Richie Marshall Jones and Louise Emma (Sutherland) Dickerson; m. Charles K. Dempsey, Aug. 6, 1959 (div. 1965); 1 child, Cheryl Lynn; m. Nelson Gray, Aug. 19, 1968. Student Jefferson Sch. of Commerce, 1960-62. Cert. residential broker; G.R.I. Owner Heritage Realtors, Lawton, Okla., 1977—; pres. Heritage Mortgage, Inc., Lawton, 1984—, Peregoy Enterprises, Inc., Lawton, 1985—. Mem. Nat. Assn. Realtors, Grad. Realtors Inst., Realtors Nat. Mktg. Inst. (cert.), Lawton Bd. Realtors (bd. dirs. 1983-85 pres. 1986). Methodist. Office: Heritage Realtors 44 Cache Rd Sq Lawton OK 73505

PEREIRA, CORNELIA KARIN, editor, communications director; b. Hamburg, Germany, July 20, 1952; came to U.S., 1954; d. Fritz Felix Arthur and Ellen Helga (Thrun) Buchholz; m. Richard Louis Pereira, Aug. 30, 1980. B.S. in Journalism, U. Fla., 1979; hon. cert. in German, Goethe Inst. (Germany), 1974. Tchr. English Berlitz Sch., Düsseldorf, Germany, 1975-76; receptionist Frankfurt Sheraton Hotel (Germany), 1976-77; community editor Houston Community News, 1980-82; mng. editor, 1982-83; editor pub. affairs Nat. Found. Advancement Arts, Miami, Fla., 1983—, also dir. communications; trend editorial asst. Conroe Courier (Tex.), 1982; Author: Growing Up with Jennifer (feature writing award 1982), 1982; author/editor Area Air Crash Preparedness (news service award 1982), 1982. Recipient Jr. Olympic medals, 1963. Mem. Women in Communications, Inc., Photogroup, Inc., Ctr. for Fine Arts. Roman Catholic. Office: Nat Found Advancement Arts 100 N Biscayne Blvd Miami FL 33132

PEREIRA, JORGINA ANTUNES, technical specialist; b. Rio De Janeiro, Brazil, Aug. 12, 1944; came to U.S., 1974; d. Rafael and Maria Dolores Antunes Pereira; B.A., Social Service Sch. Rio De Janeiro, 1970; B.G.S. with emphasis in Computer Sci., Roosevelt U., 1978, M.S. in Info. Systems, 1985; m. Mark Louis Branham, Dec. 31, 1980. Head social work programs Paroquia Santa Cruz De Copacabana, Rio De Janeiro, 1971-73; mem. council of internat. program Jane Addams Grad. Sch. Social Work, U. Ill., Chgo., 1974-75; trainee No. Trust Bank, Chgo., 1977-78, programmer, 1978-79, sr. programmer, 1979-80, tech. analyst, 1980-82, systems analyst, 1982-84; sr. systems analyst Montgomery Ward, 1984-86, assoc. tech. specialist, 1986—. Bd. dirs. Council of Internat. Program for Social Workers, Chgo., 1979-81, 85—. Mem. Library Computer and Info. Scis., Data Processing Mgmt. Assn., Franklin Honor Soc. Home: 665 W Roscoe Chicago IL 60657 Office: 1 Montgomery Ward Plaza Chicago IL 60671

PERELLA, SUSANNE B., librarian; b. Providence, R.I., Mar. 19, 1936; d. Laurence J. and Harriet (Delaplane) Brennan; B.A., U. Conn., 1960; M.L.S., U. Mich., 1967. Head, MBA Library, U. Conn., Hartford, 1964-66; sr. asst. librarian Grad. Sch. Bus., Public Adminstrn., Cornell U., 1967-72; chief readers' services FTC, Washington, 1972-79, library dir., 1979—; vice chmn. Fed. Library and Info. Network, 1985—. Mem. Law Librarians Soc. (dir. 1980-81), Spl. Libraries Assn. (bd. dirs. Washington chpt. 1983-85), Am. Assn. Law Libraries, Beta Phi Mu. Office: FTC 6th and Pennsylvania Aves NW Washington DC 20580

PERENCHIO, LISA MARIE, advertising executive; b. San Mateo, Calif., Sept. 28, 1957; d. Fred August and Shirley Ann (Ingalls) DeLucchi; m. John Gardner Perenchio, Sept. 12, 1981. B.A., U. Calif.-San Diego, 1979; M.B.A., San Diego State U., 1981. Asst. to pres. South Coast Equities, San Diego, 1979-81; research analyst Ogilvy and Mather, Los Angeles, 1981-83; asst. v.p. Security Pacific Bank, Los Angeles, 1983-84; account exec. Foote, Cone & Belding, Los Angeles, 1984—. Mem. Pacific Palisades Residents Assn., 1983. Mem. Am. Mktg. Assn. (dir. 1983—). Office: Foote Cone & Belding 11601 Wilshire Blvd Los Angeles CA 90025

PEREZ, EDITH ADALJISA, physician; b. Humacao, P.R., Apr. 30, 1956; d. Ruben and Edith (Maldonado) Perez; B.S. magna cum laude, U. P.R., 1975, M.D., 1979. Diplomate Nat. Bd. Med. Examiners, Am. Bd. Internal Medicine. Resident in internal medicine Loma Linda U., 1979-82; physician Nat. Health Service Corps, 1982-84; fellow in hematology-oncology U. Calif.-Davis program Martinez VA Hosp., 1984—. Mosby scholar, 1975. Mem. AMA, ACP.

PEREZ, JOSEPHINE, psychiatrist, marital and family therapist, educator; b. Tijuana, Mex., Feb. 10, 1941, naturalized, 1968. B.S. in Biology, U. Santiago de Compostela, Spain, 1971; M.D., 1975. Clerkships in internal medicine, gen. surgery, otorhinolaryngology, dermatology and venereology Gen. Hosp. of Galicia (Spain), 1972-75; resident in gen. psychiatry U. Miami (Fla.), Jackson Meml. Hosp. and VA Hosp., Miami, 1976-78; practice medicine specializing in psychiatry, marital and family therapy, individual psychotherapy, Miami, Fla., 1979—; nuclear medicine technician, EEG technician, supr. Electrographic Labs., Encino, Calif., 1963-71; emergency room physician Miami Dade Hosp., 1975; attending psychiatrist Jackson Meml. Hosp., 1979—, asst. dir. adolescent psychiat. unit, 1979-83; mem. clin. faculty U. Miami Sch. Medicine, 1979—, clin. instr. psychiatry, 1979—. Mem. AMA (Physicians' Recognition award 1980, 83, 86), Am. Assn. for Marital and Family Therapy (cert. clin. mem., treas. 1982-84, pres.-elect 1985—), Am. Psychiat. Assn., South Fla. Psychiat. Soc., Am. Med. Women's Assn. Office: 921 SW 27th Ave Suite 2A Miami FL 33135

PEREZ, KATHLEEN KAILEY, electro-optics company executive; b. Los Angeles, Mar. 27, 1950; d. Orin Eugene and Amy Ruth (Munsell) Kailey; m. Rafael Enrique Perez, Apr. 17, 1976; 1 child, David Andrew. B.S. in Bus. Adminstrn., U. So. Calif., Los Angeles, 1976; M.B.A., Calif. State U.-Los Angeles, 1985. Sr. zone acct. So. Pacific Transp. Co., Los Angeles, 1969-80; sr. acct. C.F. Braun Co., Alhambra, Calif., 1980-84; sr. fin. adminstr. Loral Electro-Optical Systems, Pasadena, Calif., 1984—. Site council mem. San Gabriel Sch. Dist., Calif., 1985—; bd. dirs. San Gabriel Edn. Found., 1986; mem. fin. com. First United Methodist Ch., San Gabriel, 1986—. Mem. Nat. Assn. Female Execs, Tech. Mktg. Soc. Am., Nat. Mgmt. Assn. Democrat. Home: 1224 S California St San Gabriel CA 91776 Office: Loral Electro-Optical Systems 300 N Halstead St Pasadena CA 91109

PEREZ, MARIA ESTELLA, lawyer; b. Harlingen, Tex., Oct. 7, 1949; d. Cesario Renteria and Socorro (Gutierrez) P. B.A., Pan Am. U., 1969; J.D., U. Houston, 1974. Bar: Tex. 1974, U.S. Supreme Ct. 1982, U.S. Dist. Ct. (so. dist.) Tex. 1976. Social worker Rio Grande State Ctr. Mental Health and Mental Retardation, Edinburg, Tex., 1969-71; legal research analyst Chicano Tng. Ctr., Houston, 1974; ptnr. Vela, Vela & Perez, Harlingen, 1974-76; adj. prof. Pan Am U., Edinburg, 1975; city atty. Lyford (Tex.), 1975-78; ptnr. Malant & Perez, Brownsville, Tex., 1976; judge Mcpl. Ct. Primera (Tex.), 1976-78; sole practice, Brownsville, 1976—. Bd. dirs. Contractors Indsl. Assn., 1975-77; mem. adv. bd. Tropical Tex. Ctr. Mental Health/Mental Retardation Drug Abuse Program, McAllen, Edinburg and Brownsville, 1976-77; mem. pub. relations com., bd. dirs. Rio Grande State Ctr. Mental Health and Mental Retardation, Harlingen and Brownsville, 1976—; founder, v.p., pres., bd. dirs. Harlingen Mexican-Am. C. of C., 1976-82; bd. dirs. Lower Rio Grande Valley Devel. Council, 1976-78, Cameron & Willacy Counties Community Projects Head Start Policy Council, 1976-77, Brownsville ARC, 1978-80, Brownsville Women's Polit. Caucus, 1977-79, Tex. Instn. Ednl. Devel., San Antonio, 1978-81; bd. dirs., parliamentarian U.S. Hispanic C. of C., 1980-82, Tex. Assn. Mexican-Am. C. of C., 1977-79, 81-82; founder and mem. Commn. on Status of Women Cameron County, 1977-79; founder, bd. dirs. Su Clinica Familiar, 1978-80; bd. dirs., pres. Southmost Bus. and Profl. Women's Club, 1977-79, 81-82; founder, v.p., mem. Tex. Women's Polit. Caucus. Mem. Tex. Bar Assn., ABA, Cameron County Bar Assn. (dir. 1978-80), Tex. Criminal Trial Lawyers Assn., Nat. Assn. Immigration and Nationality Lawyers, Tex. Assn. Immigration and Nationality Lawyers, Alumni Assn. Pan Am. U. (charter; dir. 1978-82), Phi Alpha Delta. Democrat. Roman Catholic. Home: 1315 E Taylor Harlingen TX 78550 Office: PO Box 2065 1238 E Madison Brownsville TX 78520

PEREZ, NADIA ESTHER, physician; b. N.Y.C., Dec. 10, 1950; d. Sixto Mercado and Secundina (Couvertier) Ortiz; m. Luis Agosto Perez, July 7, 1970; children—Joaquin, Cristina, Julio. M.D., Columbia U., N.Y.C., 1979. Diplomate Nat. Bd. Med. Examiners. Intern, St. Lukes Hosp., N.Y.C., 1979-80; med. dir. Harlem Hosp., N.Y.C., 1980-82; family practitioner Margaretville Meml. Hosp. (N.Y.), 1982-83, East Harlem Council for Human Services, N.Y.C., 1983-84; emergency room physician No. Dutchess Hosp., Rhinebeck, N.Y., 1984—. Mem. N.Y. State Med. Soc. Democrat. Roman Catholic. Home: Barrytown NY 12507 Office: PO Box 692 Rhinebeck NY 12572

PEREZ-GERDES, MARTA RITA, advertising account executive; b. Matanzas, Cuba, Aug. 24, 1957; came to U.S., Feb. 3, 1966; d. Jose Herminio and Marta (Gonzalez) Perez; m. Paul William Gerdes, Sept. 3, 1983. B.S.E., Northwestern U., 1979; M.A. Communications, U. Ill.-Chgo., 1983. Research asst. O.M.A.R., Inc., Chgo., 1979-80, account exec., 1980-82, acct. supr., 1982-85; account supr. Hispanial J. Walter Thompson, 1985—. Mem. Nat. Assn. Female Execs.

PERFALL, ALISON ELLEN, advertising sales executive; b. New Hyde Park, N.Y., July 26, 1956; d. Arthur G. Perfall and Beryl Shiela (Howell) Ahrens;

B.B.A., U. Wis.-Whitewater, 1978; M.B.A., Hofstra U., 1984. Classified telephone sales rep. Newsday, Inc., Melville, N.Y., 1978-80, classified spl. projects telephone sales rep., 1980-82, coop. advt. telephone sales rep., 1982, classified-automotive advt. sales rep., 1982-83, coop. advt. sales rep., 1983-84; nat. advt. account exec. Times Mirror Nat. Mktg., N.Y.C., 1984-86, account exec. classified-recruitment advt., Los Angeles, 1986—. Mem. Advt. Women N.Y., Newspaper Advt. Sales Assn., Nat. Assn. Female Execs., Alpha Sigma. Episcopalian. Office: Times Mirror Nat Mktg 11601 Wilshire Blvd Los Angeles CA 90025

PERGERICHT, FRANCES LEE, lawyer; b. Cleve., June 4, 1952; d. Joseph and Ann Pergericht; m. Roman G. Kuperman, Feb. 24, 1982. B.A. magna cum laude, Case Western Res. U., 1974; J.D., Washington U., St. Louis, 1978. Bar: Ill. 1981, N.H. 1979. Law clk. presiding justice U.S. Dist. Ct. No. Dist. Ill., Chgo., 1979-81; assoc. Jenner & Block, Chgo., 1981-83; asst. regional atty Dept. Health and Human Services, Chgo., 1983—. Topics editor Washington U. Law Quar., 1977-78. Mem. Chgo. Bar Assn., Chgo. Council Lawyers, Phi Beta Kappa. Office: Dept Health and Human Services 300 S Wacker Dr Chicago IL 60606

PERINBAM, BARBARA MARIE, history educator; b. Kingston, Jamaica, W.I.; came to U.S., 1964, naturalized, 1978; d. Eugene Hawthorne and Isoline Isabel (DaCosta) DaCosta. B.A. with honors, London Sch. Econs., 1955; M.A., U. Toronto (Can.), 1959; Ph.D., Georgetown U., 1969. Instr. dept. history U. Md., College Park, 1968-69, asst. prof., 1969-76, assoc. prof., 1976—; lectr., cons. Fgn. Service Inst., U.S. Dept. State, Washington, 1973-83; vis. prof. Sch. Advanced Internat. Studies, Washington, 1978, 84—. Author: Holy Violence: The Revolutionary Thought of Frantz Fanon, 1983; also articles. Recipient research awards U. Md., Am. Philos. Soc., 1969-83; Hoover Inst. War, Revolution and Peace fellow, 1971-72; Fulbright Rev. Bd. award, 1982-83. Mem. African Studies Assn. (nominating com. 1973-75, bd. dirs. 1976-78), Can. Assn. African Studies, Am. Hist. Assn. (mem. women's com. 1975-77), Middle East Studies Assn. Democrat. Avocations: music; ballet; theatre; travel; museums; art galleries. Office: Dept History U Md College Park MD 20742

PERINE, MAXINE HARRIET, educator; b. Worth County, Mo., May 11, 1918; d. Robert Rozwell and Della Dale (Martin) P.; B.S. in Edn., Central Mo. State U., 1944; M.A., Columbia U., 1954, profl. diploma, 1960, Ed.D., 1977. Tchr., Worth County schs., 1935-44, Kansas City (Mo.) public schs., 1944-59; reading cons. Kansas City (Mo.) public schs., 1959-64; editor Holt, Rinehart, Winston, N.Y.C., 1964; mem. faculty U. Mich., Flint, 1964—, prof. specializing in reading, dept. edn., 1972—; vis. scholar Columbia U., 1978; chair World Congress of Reading, Dublin, 1982; speaker. Mem. Internat. Reading Assn., AAUP, Kappa Delta Pi (chpt. founding counselor 1980—, internat. com. constn. and bylaws 1982-84), Delta Kappa Gamma (named Woman of Distinction 1972). Presbyterian. Author, editor in field. Office: 1321 E Court St Flint MI 48503

PERKINS, ANNIE JONES, classroom educator; b. High Point, N.C., May 7, 1932; d. Hose and Odessa (Rucker) Jones; m. Joseph Perkins, Aug. 26, 1962 (div. 1984); 1 child, Ozzie. B.S., W.Va. State U., 1951; M.S., Columbia U., 1959. Tchr., coach Swift Meml. Jr. Coll., Rogersville, Tenn., 1952-53, Spencer Sr. High Sch., Columbus, Ga., 1953-55, Saulsbury High Sch., Md., 1955-57; prof. phys. edn. Prairie View A&W Coll., Tex., 1957-63, N.C. A&T Coll., Greensboro, 1963-64; classroom tchr. Orange County Sch. Bd., Orlando, Fla., 1964—. Recipient Appreciation award Walker Jr. High Sch., Orlando, 1973, Appreciation award Westridge Jr. High Sch., Orlando, 1980. Mem. Orange County Classroom Tchrs. Assn., Fla. Teaching Profession, NEA, Alpha Kappa Alpha (voter registrar 1982). Democrat. Roman Catholic.

PERKINS, (DARRYL) JOY, personnel service executive; b. Batesville, Ark., June 14, 1949; d. Richard Long and Royce June (Jeffery) Dunn; m. Van Ray Perkins, Sept. 4, 1970. B.A. in History and English, U. Tex.-Arlington, 1973. Cert. personnel cons. Cons., Adminstrv. Support Group, Inc., Dallas, 1973-74, cons., 1974-77, office mgr., 1977-84, v.p., 1984, pres., 1984-85; v.p. Diversified Human Relations Group, Inc. (merger), 1985—. Mem. Tex. Assn. Personnel Consultants (dir. 1982-85, pres. 1985-86), Metroplex Assn. Personnel Consultants (dir. 1980-81, pres. 1982-83). Republican. Office: Adminstrv Support Group Inc 15400 Knoll Trail 212 Dallas TX 75248

PERKINS, DEBORAH HOWARD, nurse; b. Richmond, Va., Mar. 19, 1958; d. Adrian Leo and Rose Marie (Falls) Howard; m. Russell Wayne Perkins, Dec. 27, 1977; children—Russell Wayne, Jr., William Henry, B.S. in Nursing Duke U., 1979. Staff nurse II, nurse preceptor Charlotte Meml. Hosp. and Med. Ctr., Charlotte, N.C., 1979-83; part time staff nurse Henrico Doctors Hosp., Richmond, Va., 1984—. Pres. Baptist Young Women's Orgn., Second Bapt. Ch., Richmond, 1984—. Recipient Outstanding Young Women Am. award, 1983; Sidney Aaronsen scholar, 1979. Mem. Am. Nurses Assn., Va. Nurses Assn., Sigma Theta Tau, Phi Eta Sigma. Republican. Avocations: Needlework; volunteer activities.

PERKINS, ESTHER ROBERTA, literary agent; b. Elkton, Md., May 10, 1927, d. Clarence Roberts and Esther Crouch (Terrell) P.; student West Chester State Tchrs. Coll., 1945-47, U. Del. Acct., E. I. duPont de Nemours & Co., Inc., Wilmington, Del., 1947-65; records specialist U. Del., 1966-78; partner Holly Press, Hockessin, Del., 1977-83; owner Esther R. Perkins Lit. Agy., Childs, Md., 1979—; author's agt. Mem. adv. com. Cecil County Arts Council. Mem. Authors Guild, Nat. Assn. Female Execs., Nat. Writer's Club, DAR. Republican. Methodist. Author: Backroading Through Cecil County Maryland, 1978; Things I Wish I'd Said, 1979; Canal Town, Historic Chesapeake City, Maryland, 1983. Home and office: PO Box 48 Childs MD 21916

PERKINS, MARIAN EMILY, lawyer; b. Chgo., Aug. 8, 1959; d. Toussaint and Thelma (Tillman) P. B.B.A., Howard U., 1981, J.D., 1985. Bar: Ill. Law clk. FAA, Washington, 1980, NAACP Legal Def. Fund, Washington, 1982, Office of D.C.Bar Counsel, 1983; legis. intern Office of City of Chgo., Washington, 1984; atty. Chgo. Transit Authority law dept., 1985—. Vol. polit. campaigns, 1981—. Mem. Delta Sigma Theta. Democrat. Unitarian-Universalist. Avocations: playing the violin; tennis; reading; jogging. Home: 3648 S Rhodes Ave Chicago IL 60653

PERKINS, MARIETTA L., trust examiner; b. Sioux Falls, S.D., Sept. 11, 1955; d. James Russell and Shirley Mae (Lemonds) Perkins. B.A., Concordia Coll., Minn., 1976; M.B.A., U. S.D., 1980. Asst. nat. trust examiner Comptroller of Examiner of the Currency, Kansas City, Mo., 1978-81; sub-regional supr. NTE, Austin, Tex., 1981-83; nat. trust examiner Comptroller of the Currency, Washington, 1983—. Mem. Women in Housing and Fin., Nat. Assn. Female Execs. Democrat. Avocations: tennis; photography; biking. Home: 2546E S Arlington Mill Dr Arlington VA 22206 Office: Comptroller of the Currency L'Enfant Plaza Washington DC 20219

PERKINS, MARTHA LOUISE, banker; b. Elkton, Ky., Aug. 24, 1915; d. Sterling and Sallie (Chesnut) P.; student public schs., Elkton. With Elkton Bank & Trust Co., 1937—, past pres., now chmn. bd., dir. Mem. adminstrv. bd. Petrie Meml. Methodist Episcopal Ch.; treas. City of Elkton, 17 yrs.; treas. Todd County Bd. Edn., 25 yrs. Address: Elkton Bank Trust Co Public Sq Elkton KY 42220

PERKINS, NANCY JANE, industrial designer; b. Phila., Nov. 5, 1949; d. Gordon Osborne and Martha Elizabeth (Keichline) P.; student Ohio U., 1967-68; B.F.A. in Indsl. Design, U. Ill., Champaign, 1972. Indsl. designer Peterson Bednar Assos., Evanston, Ill., 1972-74, Deschamps Mills Assos., Bartlett, Ill., 1974-75; dir. graphic design Cameo Container Corp., Chgo., 1975-76; indsl. design cons. Sears Roebuck & Co., Chgo., 1977—; founder Perkins Design Ltd., indsl. design cons. co., 1979—; asst. prof. grad. design Seminar U. Ill. at Chgo., 1982, instr. undergrad. design, 1984; keynote speaker Soc. Automotive Engrs., 1980, Women in Design, 1982, 84, Meadow Club, 1983, U. Ill. Disting. Alumni Lecture Series, 1983. Contbr. to profl. publs. Co-leader Cadette troop DuPage County council Girl Scouts U.S.A., 1978-79. Recipient Outstanding Alumni award U. Ill. Alumni Jour., 1981. Mem. Indsl. Designers Soc. Am. (treas. Chgo. chpt. 1977-79, vice chmn. 1979-80, chmn. 1981, dist. membership 1982, ann. conf. com. 1983, publs. com. 1985-86). Patentee marine, automotive and consumer products. Home: 1926 Prairie Square 227 Schaumburg IL 60195 Office: BSC 23-23 D/817 Sears Tower Chicago IL 60684

PERKINS, VICTORIA JANE, lawyer; b. Morristown, N.J., Aug. 15, 1945; d. John Edward and Marion Roberta (Deats) P.; m. Roger Alan Hess; 1 dau., Sarah Alison Perkins Hess. B.A. with honors, Douglass Coll., 1967; M.A.T. magna cum laude, Monmouth Coll., 1973; J.D. cum laude, Harvard U., 1976. Bar: D.C. 1976. Tchr. English, South River (N.J.) High Sch., 1967-69, Ocean Twp. (N.J.) High Sch., 1969-71; underwriter Prudential Ins. Co., Newark, 1971-73; assoc. Shaw, Pittman, Potts & Trowbridge, Washington, 1976-83, ptnr., 1984—. Mem. D.C. Bar Assn., ABA, Phi Beta Kappa. Presbyterian. Office: Shaw Pittman Potts & Trowbridge 1800 M St NW Washington DC 20036

PERKINS-CARPENTER, BETTY LOU, business executive; b. Rochester N.Y., Jan. 22, 1931; d. Edward C. and Bertha M. (Loeser) Kalmn; m. Floyd F. Perkins, Jan. 31, 1951 (div. 1979); children—Cheryl Lee, F. Scott; m. Marcellus Chipman Carpenter, Oct. 10, 1981. B.S. in Phys. Edn. Adminstrn., Empire State Coll., N.Y., 1979; M.S. in Early Childhood Edn. Adminstrn., Nova U., 1983. Tchr.-coach Rochester YWCA, 1954-59, Perkins Swimming Sch., Penfield, N.Y., 1959-64; pres. Perkins Swim Club, Inc., Rochester, 1964—, Perkins Fit By Five, Inc., Rochester, 1969—, Child Fitness Prodns., Inc., Rochester, 1983—, Fit By Five Franchise Corp., Rochester, 1984—; diving coach Olympic Games, Montreal, 1976; mem. adv. com. N.Y. State Task Force Phys. Fitness and Sports, 1978-82; bd. dirs. U.S. Olympic Diving Com., 1976-80; cons. European sports facilities, 1969-83, Pres.'s Council on Phys. Fitness and Sports, 1986; mem. adv. com. Community Savs. Bank, Rochester, 1976-79. Am. editor: Teaching Babies to Swim, 1979. Contbr. articles to profl. jours. Exec. producer audio-visual instructional materials. Served with USAF, 1948-51. Recipient Gold medal Inst. Achievement of Human Potential, Brazil, 1973; Mike Malone Meml. Diving award, 1977; Cady Diving award, 1977; named to Monroe County Athletes Hall of Fame, Rochester, 1979; named Sports Woman of Yr., U.S. Olympic Diving Commn., 1979. Mem. U.S. Diving Assn. (life, numerous offices), Rochester Assn. Edn. of Young Children, Nova U. Alumnae Assn., Genesee Valley Sports Medicine Council, AAUW. Republican. Club: Oak Hill Country (Rochester). Lodge: Order Eastern Star (life). Avocations: swimming; cross-country skiing; reading; travel. Office: Perkins Swim Club 1606 Penfield Rd Rochester NY 14625

PERKINSON, DIANA AGNES, rug import company executive; b. Prostejov, Czechoslovakia, June 27, 1941; came to U.S., 1962; d. John Charles and Agnes Diana (Sincl) Zouzelka; m. David Francis Perkinson, Mar. 6, 1965; children—Dana Leissa, David. B.A., U. Lausanne (Switzerland), 1960; M.A., U. Madrid, 1961; M.B.A., Case Western Res. U., 1963; cert. internat. mktg. Oxford (Eng.) U., 1962. Assoc. Allen Hartman & Schreiber, Cleve., 1963-64; interpreter Tower Internat. Inc., Cleve., 1964-66; pres. Oriental Rug Importers Ltd., Cleve., 1979—; treas. Oriental Rug Designers, Inc., Cleve., 1980—; sec., treas. Oriental Rug Cons., Inc., Cleve., 1980—; chmn. Foxworthy's Inc. subs. Oriental Rug Importers Ft. Myers, Naples, Sanibel, Fla.; dir. Beckwith & Assocs., Inc., Cleve., Dix-Bur Investments, Ltd. Trustee, Cleve. Ballet, 1979, exec. com., 1981; mem. Cleve. Mayor's Adv. Com.; trustee Diabetes Assn. Greater Cleve.; chmn. grantsmanship Jr. League of Cleve., 1982; mem. mem. Cleve. Found.-Women in Philanthropy, 1982; trustee Diabetes Assn. Greater Cleve. Mem. Women Bus. Owners Assn., Oriental Rug Retailers Am. (dir. 1983). Republican. Roman Catholic. Clubs: Cleve. Racquet, Recreation League (Cleve.). Home: Ravencrest 14400 County Line Rd Cleveland OH 44022 also Stratford at Pelican Bay Crayton Rd Naples FL 33940 Office: Oriental Rug Importers Ltd Inc 23533 Mercantile Rd Beachwood OH 44122

PERKS, BARBARA ANN MARCUS, psychologist; b. Wilson, Pa., July 1, 1937; d. Alfred M. and Lillian (Reibman) Marcus; B.S., Pa. State U., 1959; M.A., Columbia U., 1963; cert. in ednl. psychology Oxford (Eng.) U., 1965; postgrad. U. Oreg., U.S. Internat. U.; Ed.D., U. B.C., 1984; m. Anthony Manning Perks, Sept. 9, 1963. Tchr. gifted Hamden (Conn.) Sch. Dist., 1959-62; reading cons. Oxfordshire County, Littlemore, Eng., 1964-65; sch. psychologist Vancouver (B.C., Can.) Sch. Bd., 1972-76; supr. student tchrs. U. B.C., Vancouver, 1977-78, cons. Research Center, 1978-79, ednl. psychologist, child and family unit child psychiatry Health Scis. Centre Hosp., 1979-81, lectr., 1977—; instr. psychology Langara Coll., 1985; pvt. practice counseling and teaching, Burnaby, B.C., 1985-86. Recipient Can. Daus. League award; Provincial Council of B.C. award, 1981, U. B.C. awards, 1980, Jonathan Rogers award, 1984; Univ. fellow, Dr. MacKenzie Am. Alumni scholar U. B.C., 1976; U. B.C. summer scholar, 1982; cert. psychologist, B.C. Mem. Am. Psychol. Assn., B.C. Psychol. Assn., Assn. Humanistic Psychology, Nat. Assn. Sch. Psychology, Am. Ednl. Research, N.Am. Soc. Adlerian Psychology, Am. Orthopsychiat. Assn., Mortar Bd., Pi Sigma Alpha, Pi Lambda Theta, Kappa Delta Pi. Clubs: Figure Skating (Vancouver, B.C., New Haven, Conn., Allentown, Pa.). Author research papers. Home: 4570 Glenwood Ave North Vancouver BC V7R 4G5 Canada Office: U BC Dept Ednl Psychology Faculty of Edn 2125 Main Mall U BC Vancouver BC V6T 1Z5 Canada

PERLESS, ELLEN, advertising executive; b. N.Y.C., Sept. 9, 1941; d. Joseph B. and Bertha (Messenger) Kaplan; m. Robert Perless, July 2, 1965. Student Smith Coll., 1958-59, Bard Coll., 1959-62. Copywriter, Doyle Dane Bernbach, N.Y.C., 1964-70; copywriter Young & Rubicam, N.Y.C., 1970-74, v.p., creative supr., 1974-78, sr. v.p., assoc. creative dir., 1978-84; v.p., assoc. creative dir. Leber Katz Ptnrs., N.Y.C., 1984-85, sr. v.p., creative dir., 1986—. Recipient various awards including Merit awards Art Dirs. Club, Clio awards. Mem. One Club for Art & Copy. Club: Northeast Harbor Fleet (Maine). Office Leber Katz Partners 767 Fifth Ave New York NY 10153

PERLMAN, CINDY LOU, chinaware company executive; b. N.Y.C., Jan. 30, 1957; d. Harold H. Perlman and Joanne Betty Perlman Schwartz; m. Peter Lothar Kleinschmidt, July 20, 1986. A.A.S., Fashion Inst. Tech., 1976, student, 1982-83; student Mudelein Coll., 1979-81; cert. Dale Carnegie, Chgo., 1980. Facility supr. J&P Hayman's, N.Y.C., 1976-78; mgr. Midwest dist. Omniform div. John Meyer, Norwich, Conn., 1978-81; br. mgr. Nutri/System, N.Y.C., 1982-83; designer liaison Rego Internat., N.Y.C., 1984—. Active Deborah Heart Fund, N.Y.C., 1970—; vol. worker with deaf. Mem. Inst. Bus. Designers, Am. Soc. Interior Designers, Resources Council, Nat. Assn. Female Execs. Avocations: horses; computers.

PERLMAN, EILEEN ELEANOR, civic worker, former restaurant chain executive; b. Chgo., Oct. 31, 1935; d. Bennett Viggo and Eleanor Lucille Christensen; m. Clifford Seely Perlman, July 30, 1959 (div. 1969); children—Jason, Clayton, Ivy. Student Northwestern U., nights 1954, Patricia Stevens Modeling Sch., 1955, Liberty Baptist Coll., 1977-79. Co-founder, Lum's, Inc., Miami Beach, Fla., 1958; fin. sec., treas. Christian Womens Club, South Fla., 1973-75; visitation chmn. Granada Presbyn. Ch., 1973-75, circle chmn., 1978; active Protect Our Children, anti-ERA campaign, ARC, Women for Responsible Legis. and Polit. Action (dir., corr. sec. 1979-80), Floridians Against Casino Takeover, Christian Broadcasting Network, Inc., 700 Club, Old Time Gospel Hour, Faith Partners, Moral Majority; mem. transp. com., scholarship fund com. Westminster Christian Sch.; com. mem. Jews for Jesus; nat. adv. com. Am. Security Council; prayer chmn. Fla. So. dist. Concerned Women for Am., 1980—; sustaining mem. Republican Party; sponsor Rep. Victory Fund, 1980. Mem. U.S. Lawn Tennis Assn., U.S. Figure Skating Assn. (dir. Miami chpt.), Interfaith Comm. Against Blasphemy, Am. Bridge Club, Internat. Platform Assn., Nat. Fedn. Rep. Women. Republican. Presbyterian. Clubs: Century (Miami Christian U.); California (N. Miami). Home: 13217 Whistler Ave Granada Hills CA 91344

PERLMAN, RHEA, actress; b. Bklyn., Mar. 31; m. Danny DeVito; children—Lucy Chet, Gracie Fan. Grad. Hunter Coll. Appearances various off-Broadway plays; co-founder Colonnades Theatre Lab., N.Y.; roles various movies made for TV, The Ratings Game, 1984, for cable TV; appearances on TV series Taxi, Series Cheers, 1982—(Emmy nomination). Recipient Emmy award 1984 for outstanding supporting actress in a comedy series. Address: care NBC press Dept 30 Rockefeller Plaza New York NY 10020*

PERLMAN, SUSAN GAIL, organization executive; b. N.Y.C., Dec. 29, 1950; d. Philip and Pearl Perlman; ed. Hunter Coll., N.Y.C., 1967-71. Copywriter, Blaine Thompson Advt., N.Y.C., 1968-71; copywriter J.C. Penney Co., N.Y.C., 1971-72; exec. info. officer Jews for Jesus, San Francisco, 1972—, bd. dirs., also editor Issues mag.; speaker, cons. in field; asst. coordinator Lausanne Consultation on Jewish Evangelism; mem. Internat. Council Bibl. Inerrancy, Congress on Bible Com.; del. Conservative Baptist Assn. Am.; mem. Lausanne Com. for World Evangelization. Democrat. Baptist. Editorial adviser: Mishkan; author articles in field. Office: 60 Haight St San Francisco CA 94102

PERLMUTTER, DONNA, newspaper music and dance critic; b. Phila.; d. Myer and Bessie (Krasno) Stein; m. Jona Perlmutter, Mar. 21, 1964; children—Aaron, Matthew. B.A., Pa. State U., 1958; M.S., Yeshiva U., 1959. Music and dance critic Los Angeles Herald Examiner, 1975-84, Los Angeles Times, 1984—; dance critic Dance Mag., N.Y.C., 1980—; music critic Opera News, N.Y.C., 1981—, Ovation Mag., N.Y.C., 1983—; panelist, speaker various music and dance orgns. Mem. Music Critics Assn. Home: 10507 Le Conte Ave Los Angeles CA 90024

PERLOFF, JEAN MARCOSSON, lawyer; b. Lakewood, Ohio, June 25, 1942; d. John Solomon and Marcella Catherine (Borngen) Marcosson; m. William H. Perloff, Dec. 26, 1968. B.A. magna cum laude, Lake Erie Coll., 1965; M.A., UCLA, 1967; J.D. magna cum laude, Ventura Coll. Law, 1976. Bar: Calif. 1976. Assoc. in Italian, U. Calif.-Santa Barbara, 1966-70; law clk. paralegal Ventura County Pub. Defender's Office, 1975; sole practice law, Ventura, Calif., 1977-78; co-prin. firm Clabaugh & Perloff, P.C., Ventura, 1979-82; instr. Ventura Coll. Law and Santa Barbara Law Inst., 1976-79; sr. jud. atty. to presiding justice 6th Div., 2d Dist. Ct. Appeals, Ventura, 1982—. Bd. dirs. Santa Barbara Zool. Gardens, 1983—. Chancellor's teaching fellow in Italian, UCLA, 1965. Mem. Calif. State Bar, ABA, Calif. Women Lawyers, Ventura County Bar Assn., Women Lawyers of Ventura County (dir. 1981-82), Ventura County Criminal Def. Bar Assn. (pres. 1979), Mar Vista Bus. and Profl. Women's Assn., Kappa Alpha Sigma. Home: 1384 Plaza Pacifica Santa Barbara CA 93108 Office: 2d Dist Ct Appeals 1280 S Victoria Ave Ventura CA 93003

PERLOV, DADIE, association executive; b. N.Y.C., June 8, 1929; d. Aaron and Anna Heitman; B.A., NYU, 1950; m. Norman Perlov, May 29, 1950; children—Nancy, Jane, Amy. Exec. dir. Operation Open City, N.Y.C., 1962-64; dir. field services Nat. Council Jewish Women, Inc., N.Y.C., 1968-74, exec. dir., 1981—; exec. dir. N.Y. Library Assn., 1974-81. Writer, speaker on assn. mgmt. Mem. panel Sch. Bd. Dist. 26, 1967; bd. visitors Pratt U. Cert. assn. exec., 1978; mem. adv. bd. Nat. Inst. Against Prejudice and Violence, 1985; bd. dirs. Global Perspectives in Edn.; mem. Chancellor Task Force on Sex Equity. Recipient Recognition award N.Y. Library Assn., 1978. Mem. N.Y. Soc. Assn. Execs. (dir. 1980-82, pres. 1985-86; Exec. of Yr. 1980), Internat. Platform Assn., Am. Soc. Assn. Execs. (assn. evaluator; award of excellence 1983), Internat. Council Library Assn. Execs. (v.p. 1979-81), Nat. Jewish Community Relations Council and Conf. of Pres., LWV (chpt. pres. 1960-62). Office: Nat Council Jewish Women 15 E 26th St New York NY 10010

PERLSTEIN, BRENDA, real estate broker; b. Barnegat, N.J., Mar. 8, 1942; d. Bruno and Nellie (Taylor) Agnoli; m. Harry Perlstein (dec. 1970); children—Diana, Lisa, Sari. Student Real Estate Sch., Atlantic City, 1962. Real estate broker, N.J. Pres., Pearl Realty, Bradley Beach, N.J., 1980—. Mem. N.J. Bd. Realtors, Monmouth County Bd. Realtors, Nat. Bd. Realtors. Republican. Office: 608 Main St Bradley Beach NJ 07720 also 704 Main St Asbury Park NJ 07712

PERNICK, SANDRA ROSE, business executive; b. Chgo., Oct. 7, 1944; d. Karl and Diana (Matlin) Witt; m. Steven L. Pernick, Oct. 11, 1964; children—Kevin Michael, Kelly Andrew. B.A., Roosevelt U., Chgo., 1964. Corr. Time, Inc., 1964-66; tchr. emotionally handicapped children Chgo. Pub. Schs., 1966-68; pres. bd. dirs. Orchard Village, Skokie, Ill., 1976—; pres. Direct Response Corp., Des Plaines, Ill., 1981—. Advisor Assn. Spl. Edn., Skokie, Ill.; mem. mental health com. Nat. Council Jewish Women. Mem. Nat. Assn. Retarded Citizens, Ill. Assn. Retarded Citizens. Home: 2936 Greenleaf Wilmette IL 60091 Office: 1865 Miner St Des Plaines IL 60016

PERNICONE, MARGARET MARY, advt. agy. exec.; b. Omaha, Jan. 10, 1951; d. I.J. and Marian (Bergman) P.; student Ariz. State U., 1969-71. Copywriter/producer Bozell & Jacobs, Inc., Omaha, 1972-76; freelance copywriter/producer, Omaha, 1976-77; sr. copywriter/producer Bernstein/Rein, Kansas City, Mo., 1977-78; sr. copywriter/broadcaster prodn. mgr. Barrett-Yehle, Kansas City, 1978-81; v.p., creative dir. Smith & Yehle, Inc., Kansas City, 1981—; tchr. advt. Nettleton Bus. Coll., Omaha, 1975-76. Recipient numerous advt. awards. Mem. Nat. Assn. Female Execs. Office: Smith & Yehle Inc 3217 Broadway Kansas City MO 64111

PERNSTEINER, CAROL ANN, hotel executive; d. Alvin Anton and Lillian Therese (Spreen) P. B.A., Marquette U., 1969. With The Sheraton Corp., 1971—, front office mgr. Sheraton Washington, D.C., 1979-81, resident mgr. Sheraton St. Louis Hotel, 1981—. Capt. Operation Brightside, St. Louis, 1984-86. Recipient Pres.'s award The Sheraton Corp., Washington, 1979. Mem. Adminstrv. Mgmt. Soc., Am. Hotel and Motel Assn. Republican. Avocations: violin; piano. Home and Office: Sheraton Saint Louis Hotel 910 N 7th St Saint Louis MO 63101

PERO, VICTORIA HODGES, lawyer; b. Daytona, Fla., July 19, 1955; d. Thomas Clifton and Margaret Mary (Kelly) Hodges; m. David Francis Pero, June 23, 1979; 1 child, Joshua David. B.A., U. Fla., 1976, J.D., 1979. Bar: Fla. 1980. Asst. state atty. 6th Jud. Cir., Clearwater, Fla., 1979—; cons. Child Protection Team, Clearwater, 1983-84. Mem. ABA, Fla. Bar Assn. Democrat. Presbyterian. Office: State Attorney's Office PO Box 5028 Clearwater FL 33518

PEROTTI, ROSE NORMA, lawyer; b. St. Louis, Aug. 10, 1930; d. Joseph and Dorothy Mary (Roleski) Perotti. B.A., Fontbonne Coll., St. Louis, 1952; J.D., St. Louis U., 1957. Bar: Mo. 1958. Trademark atty. Sutherland, Polster & Taylor, St. Louis, 1958-63, Sutherland Law Office, 1964-70; trademark atty. Monsanto Co., St. Louis, 1971-85, sr. trademark atty., 1985—. Honored with dedication of faculty office in her name, St. Louis U. Sch. Law, 1980. Mem. Mo. Bar Assn., Bar Assn. Met. St. Louis, ABA, Am. Judicature Soc., Smithsonian Assocs., Friends St. Louis Art Museum, Mo. Bot. Garden. Office: Monsanto Co 800 N Lindbergh Blvd Saint Louis MO 63167

PERRAULT, PATSY ANN, advertising agency executive; b. Darrouzett, Tex., Mar. 30, 1939; d. Carson Lee and Mamie (Allen) Altmiller; m. Ronald Ray Weaver, Sept. 3, 1960 (div. July 1979); children—Leanne Weaver, Douglas Weaver; m. Thomas Burt Perrault, July 25, 1981. B.S., West Tex. State U., 1961, M.A., 1964. Program dir. Sta. KFMK, Houston, 1971-74; media buyer McCann-Erickson, Houston, 1974-77; media planner Smith, Smith, Baldwin & Carlberg, Houston, 1977-78; media supr. Rives Smith, Baldwin & Carlberg, Houston, 1978-80; media mgr. Houston Coca-Cola Bottling, 1980-81; v.p., media dir. W. B. Doner, Houston, 1981-83; ptnr., exec. v.p. Taylor Brown & Barnhill, Houston, 1983—; v.p., owner Media Source. Tchr., group leader Calvary Ch. at Mary Bates, Houston, 1981-83; mem. Sharpstown Civic Assn. Mem. Alpha Delta Pi. Republican. Mem. Assembly of God Ch. Club: Sharpstown High Booster (Houston).

PERREAULT, CONSTANCE FLORENCE, college administrator; b. Providence, Sept. 9, 1927; d. Alphonse and Malvina Ida (Chevalier) P. B.A., Rivier Coll., 1959; M.Ed., R.I. Coll., 1972. Joined Sisters of the Presentation, Roman Cath. Ch., 1945. Tchr., St. Regis Acad., Berlin, N.H., 1948-52, Guardian Angel Sch., Berlin, 1952-59; tchr., prin. St. Albert Sch., West Stewartstown, N.H., 1959-67; prin. St. Marie's Elem. Sch., Manchester, N.H., 1967-70, Monsignor Vincent Sch., West Warwick, R.I., 1970-73; alumni dir. Rivier Coll., Nashua, N.H., 1973—; superior Sisters of the Presentation, Nashua, 1984—. Bd. dirs. Big Bros.-Big Sisters of Greater Nashua, 1980-84; mem. pastoral team Rivier Charismatic Prayer Community, 1973—. Mem. Council for Support and Advancement Edn. Democrat. Avocations: sewing, needlecraft, swimming. Home: 429 S Main St Nashua NH 03060 Office: Rivier Coll 429 S Main St Nashua NH 03060

PERREAULT, SISTER JEANNE, college administrator. Pres., Rivier Coll., Nashua, N.H. Office: Rivier Coll 410 Main St Nashua NH 03060*

PERRETTI, SERENA, fed. magistrate; b. Passaic, N.J., Oct. 3, 1928; d. Peter N. and Jessie (Ingram) P.; A.B., Vassar Coll., 1948; J.D. with honors, Rutgers U., 1954; postgrad. dept. religious studies Seton Hall U., 1982; m. Richard S. Benson, Mar. 27, 1962; children—Thane, Serena, Peter. Admitted to N.J. bar, 1955; individual practice law, Passaic, 1955-76; U.S. magistrate, Newark, 1976—; panelist, participant seminars. Sec., Passaic County Ethics Com., 1969, mem., 1969-71, 75-76; mem. Passaic Bd. Edn., 1956-59. Mem. Passaic County Bar Assn. (sec. 1976, trustee 1973-76), Assn. Fed. Bar N.J., Nat. Assn. Women Judges. Republican. Mem. United Ch. of Christ. Mng. editor Rutgers Law

Rev., 1953, editor-in-chief, 1954; contbr. articles to profl. publs. Office: US Court House and Post Office Newark NJ 07101

PERRI, AUDREY ANN, lawyer; b. Oxnard, Calif., Feb. 2, 1936; d. Zafon Audry and Francis May (Sandblom) Hartman; m. Frank Perri, Aug. 10, 1958; children—Michael, Michelle. B.A., U. Redlands, 1958; J.D., LaVerne Coll., 1976. Cert. family law specialist State Bar Calif. Tchr. English as fgn. lang., Reykjavic and Akureyre, Iceland, 1962-63; tchr. English and govt. various high schs., Calif., Ill., 1958-76; dep. dist. atty. San Bernardino County, 1976-80; ptnr. law firm Covington & Crowe, Ontario, Calif., 1980—. Articles editor: Jour. Juvenile Justice Law Rev., 1975-76. Mem., host, chmn. Internat. Exchange Program, 1965-84; com. mem. Upland (Calif.) City Council, 1970; mem. Dem. State Central Com., 1981-82; bd. dirs. NCCJ, 1977-82. Mem. Inland Counties Women at Law (founding pres. 1980-81), Calif. Women Lawyers (dir. 1980-84, 1st v.p. 1984), San Bernardino County Bar Assn. (mem. com. 1977-84, dir. 1981-83, 84—), ABA, Calif. State Bar (conf. del. 1977-86, exec. com. 1985—), AAUW (pres. Ontario-Upland br. 1969-70). Home: 8373 Camino Sur Cucamonga CA 91730 Office: Covington & Crowe PO Box 1515 Ontario CA 91762

PERRI, GENEVIEVE BEATRIX, landscape contracting company executive, consultant; b. Ramsey, N.J., Dec. 24, 1915; d. Michael S. and Elvira Catherine (Romano) Perri. Student, Goucher Coll., 1933-34; A.B., Barnard Coll., 1937; postgrad. Columbia U. Grad. Sch., 1938-40; cert. in botany N.Y. Bot. Garden, 1963; postgrad. Westchester Community Coll. Cert. in comml. pesticide application in ornamental horticulture, N.Y. Sec. Roman Landscape Contracting Co., Inc., Mt. Vernon, N.Y., 1941-45, purchasing agt., 1945-59, v.p., 1959-72, pres., 1972—; mem. Landscape Materials Info. Service, Callicoon, N.Y., 1959-83. Tutor in English Vietnamese refugees. Recipient Nat. Plant Am. award Am. Assn. Nurserymen, Inc., 1958, 62, certs. Merit, 1969, 74, 77, cert. Appreciation, 1974, Accident Control Engring. awards State Ins. Fund of N.Y., 1964, 65. Republican. Roman Catholic. Avocations: travel; swimming; needlepoint. Office: Roman Landscape Contracting Co Inc 35 Colonial Pl Mount Vernon NY 10550

PERRIN, ELIZABETH ANN, university program administrator; b. Cleve., Apr. 16, 1951; d. Alfred Emerson and Monzell (Moore) Jackson; m. David T. P. Perrin, Aug. 25, 1973; children—Caleb, Quianee. Grad. cum laude Point Park Coll., Pitts., 1975; postgrad. in orgnl. communications Howard U. Account rep. Gen. Electric Co., Boston, 1975-77; career counselor/coordinator programs Tom Skinner Assos., Howard U., Washington, 1978-80; dir. career counseling and placement Engine Co. No. 2, an ednl. orgn., Washington, 1980-81; minority and women program specialist Corning Glass Works (N.Y.), 1981-83; placement and alumni affairs officer Howard U. Sch. Law, 1984—. Adviser NAACP Youth Group, Elmira, N.Y.; chairperson com. for social justice Friendship Baptist Ch., Corning. Recipient Cleve. Scholarship award, 1969. Mem. Soc. Black Profls. (mem. com. profl. image), Black Career Women, Soc. Women Engrs. (asso.), Am. Personnel and Guidance Assn., Am. Soc. Personnel Adminstrn., Am. Soc. Tng. and Devel., Nat. Assn. Female Execs. Office: Alumni Affairs Office Howard U Washington DC

PERRIN, ELLEN HAYS, university dean; b. Buckhannon, W.Va.; d. Charles Gilbert and Geraldine Sexton (Hays) P.; B.S. in Music Edn., Duquesne U., 1946; M.Edn., U. Pitts., 1952, Ph.D., 1974. Tchr. music West Mifflin (Pa.) Dist. Schs., 1947-61, counselor, 1961-64; dean women Slippery Rock (Pa.) U., 1965-70, asst. to v.p. for student affairs, 1970-72, dir. counseling and career services, 1972-74, assoc. prof. counseling and ednl. psychology, 1980—, dean students, 1974-85; mem. supts. adv. com. West Mifflin Dist. Schs., 1955-60. Mem. steering com. Pitts. Fgn. Affairs Forum, 1959-60; mem. com. on edn. Pa. Gov.'s Commn. on Status of Women, 1965-66; mem. Pitts. Bicentennial Assembly, 1958-59. Mem. NEA, Pa. Edn. Assn. (pres. West Mifflin br. 1962-64, exec. com. west region 1963-64, v.p. assn. ind. sch. dists. Allegheny County 1963-64), AAUW (pres. Pitts. br. 1958-62, Pa. div. chmn. status of women 1962-63, chmn. cultural interests 1963-64, area rep. for edn. 1964-66, chmn. edn. projects for state div., chmn. topic of study 1967-69, fellowship award named in her honor 1970), Nat. (parliamentarian 1975-76, 77-78, nat. treas. 1981-83), Pa. (parliamentarian 1969-72, 2d v.p. 1972-74, legis. chmn. 1976-78, pres. 1979-81), Western Pa. (sec. 1970-71) assns. women deans, adminstrs. and counselors, DAR (conservation chmn. local chpt. 1959-62, chpt. chaplain 1963-65), Nat. Soc. U.S. Daus. of 1812, Nat. soc. Dames of Ct. of Honor (state pres. 1985-87), Hereditary Order of First families of Mass. (charter mem. 1985), Nat. Soc. Daus. Colonial Wars (state registrar 1985-88), Daus. Am. Colonists, Nat. Soc. Women Descs. of Ancient and Hon. Arty. Co., (state pres. 1985-88), Colonial Dames XVII Century (bylaws chmn. local chpt. 1978-80, parliamentarian chpt. 1980-82, state corr. sec. 1981-83, 1st v.p. chpt. 1983-85, state pres. 1983-85), Nat., Pa. (membership chmn. 1972) assns. student personnel adminstrs., Doctoral Assn. U. Pitts., Phi Delta Kappa. Presbyterian. Clubs: South Hills Coll. (Pitts.); Women's (chmn. edn. com. 1970-72) (Slippery Rock); Zonta Internat. (organizing pres. Slippery Rock-New Wilmington-Grove City area 1980-81, parliamentarian dist. IV 1974-76); Order Eastern Star (Grove City, Pa.). Home: 140 Longue Vue Dr Mt Lebanon Pittsburgh PA 15228 Office: Slippery Rock U Slippery Rock PA 16057

PERRIN, SARAH ANN, lawyer; b. Neoga, Ill., Dec. 13, 1904; d. James Lee and Bertha Frances (Baker) Figenbaum; LL.B., George Washington U., 1941, J.D., 1964; m. James Frank Perrin, Dec. 24, 1926. Bar: D.C. 1942. Assoc. atty. Mabel Walker Willebrandt, law office, Washington, 1941-42; atty. various fed. housing agys., 1942-69, asst. gen. counsel FHA, Washington, 1959-60, asst. gen. counsel HUD, Washington, 1960-69; sec. Nat. Housing Conf., Washington, 1970-80; research cons. housing and urban devel., Palmyra, Va., 1970—; acting sec. Nat. Housing Research Council, Washington, 1973-80; bd. dirs. Nat. Housing Conf., 1972—. Trustee Found. for Coop. Housing, 1975—; mem. Blue Ridge Presbytery Div. Mission, Presbyterian Ch., 1979-80. Mem. ABA Fed. Bar Assn., Women's Bar Assn. D.C. (pres. 1959-60), Charlottesville Area Women's Bar Assn., Fluvanna County Bar Assn., Nat. Assn. Women Lawyers, George Washington Law Assn., Phi Alpha Delta (internat. pres. 1955-57), Fluvanna County Hist. Soc. (pres. 1973-75). Club: Order Eastern Star. Home: Solitude Plantation Palmyra VA 22963

PERRONE, GINA FERNOW, hearing instrument specialist; b. Phila., Aug. 29, 1947; d. Ralph Edward and Katherine (Fernow) Gordy; m. Preston I. Perrone, Dec. 19, 1969; children—Carl, Scott. Student U. Miami, 1966-68, Katharine Gibbs Sch., 1968, NYU, 1968. Adminstrv. analyst IBM Corp., 1970-79; office mgr. Greiner Engring., Orlando, 1979-81; sales mgr. The Colony Beach & Tennis Resort, Longboat Key, Fla., 1982-83; sales ops. mgr. Electone, Inc., Orlando, 1983-85; telemktg. mgr. Omni Bus. Systems, Inc., Melbourne, Fla., 1985-86; specialist Gulf Atlantic Hearing Aid Ctrs. Inc., Melbourne, 1986—. Langston-Hughes Poetry scholar, 1968. Mem. Am. Mgmt. Assn., Am. Soc. Profls. and Exec. Women, Fla. Hearing Aid Soc., Telemktg. Mgrs. Assn. Home: 345 Cathedral Oak Dr Vero Beach FL 32963 Office: Gulf Atlantic Hearing Aid Ctrs 1700 W New Haven Ave Melbourne FL 32904

PERRY, ANNE MARIE LITCHFIELD, educator; b. LaJunta, Colo., May 20, 1943; d. Robert Silas and Anne (Kennedy) Hovey; B.S. in Edn., Drake U., 1966; M.A., U. Tex., Austin, 1969; Ph.D., Tex. A&M U., 1977; m. Franklin Haile Perry, Dec. 21, 1968; children—Kristina Marie, Tad Kennedy. Grade sch. tchr., San Antonio, 1966-67, Austin, 1967-68; research asso. Research and Devel. Center, U. Tex., Austin, 1968; grad. asst., instr. Tex. A&M U., 1969-70; kindergarten tchr., 1970-72; instr. U. St. Thomas, 1973-74; spl. edn. tchr., supr. Cypress-Fairbanks Ind. Sch. Dist., Houston, 1974-77, supr. gifted/talented, bilingual, English lang. devel. programs, 1977-80; mem. adj. grad. faculty U. Houston, 1979-80; lower sch. dir. curriculum and ednl. resources Kinkaid Sch., Houston, 1980—, dir. young writers workshops, 1985-86; cons. gifted/talented edn., 1978—; cons. teaching of writing, 1985—. Author and photographer: Riders Ready, 1985. Named Tchr. of Yr., Hancock Elem. Sch., 1975. Mem. Nat. Assn. Gifted Children, Tex. Assn. for Gifted and Talented, Assn. Supervision and Curriculum Devel. Presbyterian.

PERRY, BLANCHE BELLE, physical therapist; b. New Bedford, Mass., Sept. 2, 1929; d. Joseph Rudolph and Beatrice (Faria) Andrews; B.S., Ithaca (N.Y.) Coll., 1951; M.A., Assumption Coll., Worcester, Mass., 1978; m. Louis Perry, Nov. 26, 1953; (dec. 1980); children—Marcia, Susan, Tracey, Evelyn. Office and hosp. phys. therapist, Mass. and N.Y., 1961-65; dir. rehab. services St. Luke's Hosp., New Bedford, 1967—; chmn. public edn. Greater New Bedford area chpt. Am. Cancer Soc., 1980; profl. adv. com. Vis. Nurse Assn. Wareham, 1980; corporator New Bedford Five Cents Savs. Bank./Chmn. Mattapoisett Sch. Com., 1970; vice chmn. Mass. Sch. Commn. Area IV, 1972-75; sec. Old Colony Regional Vocat. Sch. Com., 1973—; trustee Abner Pease Scholarship Found.; bd. dirs. New Bedford YWCA. Grantee Elks Nat. Found., 1965. Mem. Am. Phys. Therapy Assn., Nat. Rehab. Adminstrs. Assn., Wareham Bus. and Profl. Women's Club, Delta Kappa Gamma. Republican. Club: Mattapoisett Women's. Home: 41 Aucoot Rd Mattapoisett MA 02739 Office: 101 Page St New Bedford MA 02740

PERRY, CAROLE JOAN, educator, manufacturing executive; b. Bklyn., Aug. 12, 1942; d. Allen and Ruth (Dworkin) Marcus; B.A., Bklyn. Coll., 1964; M.S., Richmond Coll., 1974; m. Lawrence Perry, Aug. 29, 1966; children—Jeffrey, Lori. Tchr., Public Sch. 244, Bklyn., 1954, Gladstone St. Sch., Azusa, Calif., 1966-68, sci. enrichment tchr., 1967-68; tchr. Public Sch. 22, S.I., N.Y., 1972; v.p. Avant-Guard Devices, Bklyn., 1972—, Rapidcircuit, Inc., 1972—, also dir. product mktg.; v.p., sec. Designalarm, Inc., 1982—; sec. Microtech Industries, Bklyn., 1982—; electronics tchr. S.I. Public Schs., 1982—. Leader, Brownies, S.I., 1976-77. Mem. Am. Radio Relay League. Club: S.I. Tennis. Author tech. articles on energy saving devices, also articles on teaching radio in pub. schs. Home: 10 Berglund Ave Staten Island NY 10314 Office: Intermediate Sch 72 33 Ferndale Ave Staten Island NY 10314

PERRY, CATHERINE EASON, county official; b. Elizabeth City, N.C., Feb. 2, 1946; d. Earl Lee and Lydia Irene (Key) Eason; m. Roy Williams Perry, Jan. 21, 1968; stepchildren—Vicky, Jennean, Gay, Jimmy, Andy, Michael, Mitzi. Student Carolina Coll. Commerce, 1965-67. Sales clk. Chesson's, Elizabeth City, 1960-65; bank teller Peoples Bank Elizabeth City, 1965-67; owner, operator The Malt Shop, Elizabeth City, 1969-71; bookkeeper, receptionist Dr. L. E. Sawyer, Elizabeth City, 1972-80; supr. of elections Pasquotank County, N.C., 1982—. Treas. Albemarle Hopeline, Elizabeth City, 1982—; past pres. Elizabeth City Jr. Woman's Club; pres., Elizabeth City Woman's Club, 1983—; treas. Crimes Against Women Task Force, Elizabeth City, 1982—; sec. Elizabeth City Girls Club, 1981—; 1st v.p. N.C. Fedn. Women's Clubs dist. 16, 1981—, protocol/hospitality chmn. Named Hon. Life Mem. N.C. Fedn. Womens Clubs; Jr. Clubwoman of Yr. N.C. Fedn. Women's Clubs, 1982; Woman of Yr. Elizabeth City Jaycettes, 1979; Jr. Clubwoman N.C. Fedn. Women Clubs dist 16, 1975, 82. Mem. N.C. Suprs. of Elections. Democrat. Methodist. Avocations: needlecrafts, sewing; gardening; walking. Home: 301 Hastings Ln Elizabeth City NC 27909 Office: Supr Elections Bd Pasquotank County Seat Courthouse Annex-Box 28 Elizabeth City NC 27909

PERRY, DOROTHEA MAY (WOODS), real estate executive; b. Boston, June 3, 1926; d. Cecil Woods and Lillian Hattie (Hogan) Stevens; m. Loyd Wayne Perry, Dec. 23, 1951; 1 child, Diane Lilyan Perry Martin. Student Arlington Acad. Music (Mass.), 1943-44, Danville Jr. Coll., 1973-74. Lic. real estate agt., Ill. Band singer, part-time, 1943—; with sales and mgmt. various cosmetics and advt. firms, 1958-74; leasing and promotion Knollwood-on-the-Lake Apts., Danville, Ill., 1974-75, Am. Homestead Corp., Quincy, Ill., 1975-76; broker Ill. and Ind. Isaacson Real Estate and Century 21 Real Estate, Danville, 1976-78; owner, broker Dorothea Perry Real Estate, Danville, 1978—. Democratic candidate for county treas. Vermilion County (Ill.), 1982; chmn. Human Resources Commn., Danville, 1979-84; coordinator Litchfield Centennial Choir (Ill.), 1953; active Red Mask Players, Sweet Adelines; mem. Vermilion County Opportunity Industrialization Ctr.; bd. dirs., state sec. Ill. council Opportunity Industrialization Ctrs. Am., 1984—. Recipient Katy award Red Mask Players, 1966, 67. Mem. Nat. Assn. Realtors, Ill. Assn. Realtors, Danville Area Bd. Realtors (legis. chmn. 1985), Multiple Listing Service, Bus. Women Am., Bus. and Profl. Women, Toastmasters Internat. (Outstanding Toastmaster 1984, 85, contest winner 1984, 85, pres. Uncle Joe Cannon club 1986—, coordinator seminar 1985-86). Baptist. Club: Zonta. Home: 1606 N Gilbert St Danville IL 61832 Office: Dorothea Perry Real Estate 903 N Walnut St Danville IL 61832

PERRY, ELYCE DORATHY, medical technologist; b. Chgo., Oct. 18, 1945; d. Roy Earl and Dorathy Mary (Ziegler) Hall; B.S., Coll. St. Francis, Joliet, Ill., 1967; m. Allan E. Perry, Nov. 21, 1970; children—Mara Élan, Max Joshua. Bench technologist St. James Hosp., Chicago Heights, Ill., 1967-69; mem. staff St. Francis Hosp., Blue Island, Ill., 1968—, chem. supr., 1972-73, tech. supr., 1973—; saleswoman McNulty Real Estate, 1979-83; dir. SuPer Industries, Inc., 1983—; tchr. immunology, 1971-72, 73-77. Mem. Am. Soc. Clin. Pathologists. Roman Catholic. Home: 2505 Burr Oak St Blue Island IL 60406 Office: 12935 Gregory St Blue Island IL 60406

PERRY, EVELYN REIS, sound communications company executive, consultant; b. N.Y.C., Mar. 9; d. Lou L. and Bertl (Wolf) Reis; m. Charles G. Perry III, Jan. 7, 1968; children—Charles G. IV, David Reis. B.A., Univ. Wis., 1963; student Am. Acad. Dramatic Arts, 1958-59, Univ. N.Mex., 1963-64, Lic. real estate broker, N.C. Vol. ETV project Peace Corps, 1963-65, program officer-radio/tv Peace Corps, Washington, 1965-68; dir. Vols. in Service to Am. (VISTA), Raleigh, N.C., 1977-80; exec. dir. CETA Program for Displaced Homemakers, Raleigh, 1980-81; cons. exec. dir. to Recycle Raleigh for Food and Fuel, Theater in the Park, 1981-83, Artspace, Inc., Raleigh, 1983-84; pres., gen. mgr. Carolina Sound Communications, Muzak, Charleston, S.C., 1984—; pub. relations account exec. various cos., Washington, Syracuse, N.Y., 1969-71; cons. pub. relations and orgn. Olympic Organizing Com., Mexico City, 1968; cons. pub. relations, fundraising, arts mgmt. pub. speaking, Ill., Pa., N.C., 1971-77; organizational and pub. speaking cons. Perry & Assocs., Raleigh, 1980—. Mem. adv. bd. Gov.'s Office Citizen Affairs, Raleigh, 1981-85; mem. Involvement Council of Wake County, N.C., Raleigh, 1981-84; mem. Adv. Council to Vols. in Service to Am., Raleigh, 1980-84; mem. Pres.'s adv. bd. Peace Corps, Washington, 1980-82; bd. dirs. Voluntary Action Center, Raleigh, 1980-84. Mem. N.C. Council of Women's Orgns. (pres., v.p. 1982-84), Charleston Hotel and Motel Assn., N.C. Assn. Vol. Adminstrs. (bd. dirs. 1980-84), Internat. Planned Music Assn., Am. Assn. Female Execs., Nat. Fedn. Independent Businesses, Charleston Assn. Female Execs. Office: Carolina Sound Communications Inc 1023 Wappoo Rd Suite B-27 Charleston SC 29407

PERRY, JEAN LOUISE, educator; b. Richland, Wash., May 13, 1950; d. Russell S. and Sue W. Perry; B.S., Miami U., Oxford, Ohio, 1972; M.S., U. Ill., Urbana, 1973, Ph.D., 1976. Cons. ednl. placement office U. Ill., 1973-75, adminstrv. intern Coll. Applied Life Studies, 1975-76, asst. dean, 1976-77, assoc. dean, 1978-81; asst. prof. dept. phys. edn., 1976-81; assoc. prof. phys. edn. San Francisco State U., 1981-84, prof., 1984—, chmn. dept., 1981—. Named to excellent tchr. list U. Ill., 1973-79. Mem. AAHPERD (fellow research consortium), Am. Assn. Higher Edn., Am. Ednl. Research Assn., Nat. Assn. Phys. Edn. in Higher Edn., Nat. Assn. Girls and Women in Sports (guide coordinator, pres.), Delta Psi Kappa, Phi Delta Kappa. Home 3216 Sun Valley Ave Walnut Creek CA 94596

PERRY, KATHARINE BROWNE, agricultural meteorologist; b. Washington, Mar. 19, 1952; d. Arthur Vincent and Mary Elizabeth (King) Browne; B.S., Pa. State U., 1974, M.S., 1976, Ph.D., 1979; m. Steven Gerard Perry, Oct. 2, 1976; children—Matthew Thomas, James Arthur, Kathleen Elizabeth. Research asst. Pa. State U., State College, 1979-80; extension specialist N.C. State U., Raleigh, 1980-81, asst. prof., 1982-86, assoc. prof., 1986—. Mem. Am. Meteorol. Soc., Am. Soc. Hort. Sci., Sigma Xi, Alpha Zeta, Gamma Sigma Delta. Home: 1226 Kilmory Dr Cary NC 27511 Office: Box 7609 Raleigh NC 27695

PERRY, KATHRYN MARGARET, security executive; b. Milw., Aug. 15, 1950; d. Lewis Gordon and Margaret Joyce (Bryner) P.; B.A., U. Wis., Green Bay, 1976; M.A., Pepperdine U., 1979. Commd. 2d lt. U.S. Army, 1968, advanced through grades to capt., 1980; platoon leader 511th Mil. Police Corps, Ft. Dix, N.J., 1976-77; exec. comdr. 532d Mil. Police Corps, Ft. Dix, 1977-78; detachment comdr. 759th Mil. Police Corps, Ft. Dix, 1978-79; capt. USAR; supr. security Spin Physics div. Kodak Co., San Diego, 1979—. Mem. Republican Presdl. Task Force; chartered mem. Rep. Senatorial Inner Circle; mem. U.S. Senatorial Club. Decorated Army Commendation medal with 2 oak leaf clusters, Army Achievement medal, 1984. Cert. protection profl. Am. Soc. Indsl. Security. Mem. Nat. Inst. Law Enforcement and Criminal Justice. Home: 7582 Angola Circle San Diego CA 92126 Office: 3099 Science Park Rd San Diego CA 92121

PERRY, MARGARET, librarian, writer; b. Cin., Nov. 15, 1933; d. Rufus Patterson and Elizabeth Munford (Anthony) P.; A.B., Western Mich. U., 1954; M.S.L.S., Cath. U. Am., 1959. Reference librarian N.Y. Pub. Library, 1954-55, 57-58; U.S. Army librarian, Europe, 1959-63, 64-67; circulation librarian U.S. Mil. Acad., 1967-70; Asst. dir. libraries for reader services U. Rochester (N.Y.), 1975-82, edn. librarian, 1970-75, asst. prof. English, 1972-75, assoc. prof., 1975-82; dir. libraries Valparaiso U. (Ind.), 1982—; speaker profl. meetings; books include: A Bio-Bibliography of Countee P. Cullen 1903-1946, 1971; Silence to the Drums: A Survey of the Literature of the Harlem Renaissance, 1976; The Harlem Renaissance, an Annotated Bibliography and Commentary, 1982; assoc. editor U. Rochester Library Bull., 1970-73; contbg. editor: Afro-Americans in New York Life and History, 1978; contbr. to What Black Librarians Are Saying, 1973; contbr. articles, stories and revs. to lit. and library jours., lit. jours. Former bd. dirs. Urban League Rochester. Recipient 1st prize Armed Forces Writers League Short Story Contest, 1965; 2d prize Frances Steloff Fiction Prize, 1968. Mem. ALA, Delta Kappa Gamma. Democrat. Roman Catholic. Home: 1200 Wood St Valparaiso IN 46383 Office: 219 Moellering Library Valparaiso University Valparaiso IN 46383

PERRY, NANCY ESTELLE, psychologist; b. Pitts., Oct. 30, 1934; d. Simon Warren and Estelle Cecelia (Zaluski) Reichard; B.S., Ohio State U., 1956, M.A. in Psychology, 1969, Ph.D. in Psychology (EPDA fellow), 1973; m. John Cleveland; children—Scott, Karen, Elaine. Nurse, various locations, 1956-63; sch. psychologist Public Schs. Columbus (Ohio), 1970-72; human devel. specialist Madison County (Ohio) Schs., 1972-75; pvt. practice clin. psychology, cons. psychology, Worthington, Ohio, 1975-80; tchr. U. Wis. Sch. Nursing, Milw., 1980-83, Milw. Devel. Center, 1980-83; pvt. practice Assoc. Mental Health Services, 1983—. Ohio Dept. Edn. grantee, 1973-76. Mem. Am. Nurses Assn., Wis. Nurses Assn., Am. Psychol. Assn., Ohio Psychol. Assn., Orgnl. Devel. Network, Internat. Assn. Applied Social Scientists, Am. Assn. Marriage and Family Counselors. Home: 2210 Charter Mall Mequon WI 53092 Office: 6310 N Port Washing Rd Milwaukee WI 53211

PERRY, NANCY JO, investment company executive; b. Olean, N.Y., Dec. 12, 1931; d. Thomas Bronson and Doris Marjory (Bacon) White; student Gustavus Adolphus Coll.; grad. Bethesda Hosp. Sch. Nursing, St. Paul, 1952; m. Charles Robert Perry, Apr. 9, 1955; children—Elizabeth Perry Sewell, Charles Thomas, Nancy Marie. Asst. head nurse U. Colo. Gen. Hosp., 1953-55; co-owner, dir. Perry Gas Co., Perry Energy Co., Odessa, Tex., 1967-82; v.p. Perry Investments, Perry Found., 1982—; past sec.-treas. Perry Energy Co., Perry Gas Processors, Perry Gas Transmissions, Inc., PGP Gas Products, Inc., Rockies Oil and Gas Corp. Bd. dirs. Odessa Council on Alcoholism, Task Force on Women; bd. dirs. Our New Beginnings, halfway house for recovering alcoholic women, sec., 1982-86; pres. bd. dirs. West Tex. Pastoral Counseling Center; gov.'s appointee Tex. Commn. on Alcohol and Drug Abuse, 1985—. Presbyterian (elder). Home: 9 San Miguel Sq Odessa TX 79762 Office: 621 State National Plaza Odessa TX 79762

PERRY, PRISCILLA ROSENFELD, community, political and media relations consultant; b. Brockton, Mass., July 2, 1932; d. Michael Louis and Lena Sylvia (Altman) Rosenfeld; m. Morton L. Perry, Apr. 6, 1958 (div. June 1974); children—Pamela, Aaron; m. 2d, Eugene H. Man, Sept. 15, 1976. B.Ed., U. Miami, 1955, M.A., 1971. Assoc. dir. Anti-Defamation League, B'nai B'rith Fla. Regional Office, Miami, 1954-58; coordinator urban affairs project U. Miami, Coral Gables, Fla., 1968-71, instr. dept. human relations, 1968-70, assoc. dir. Ctr. for Urban and Regional Studies, 1971-73, dir. ctr., 1973-75, founder and dir. Inst. for Study Aging, 1975-80; cons. community, polit. and media relations, South Miami, Fla., 1980—. Editor, Miami Interaction, 1968-75; contbr. articles to prof. jours. Founder, League of Working Mothers, Miami-Dade County, Fla., 1972; chmn. health planning council Environ. Health Planning Com., Miami, 1978; dir. Sta.-WLRN-TV, Miami-Dade County, 1979—. Bd. dirs. Greater Miami C. of C. New World Com., 1983; charter bd. dirs. Area Agy. on Aging/United Way Dade County, 1980—; mem. Miami Mayor's Com. on Budget; mem. Ade County Commn. on Status of Women. Recipient Women in Bus. and Industry award YWCA, 1983; Adminstrn. on Aging grantee U. Miami, 1976-79, 77. Mem. Fla. Council on Aging (trustee 1979), So. Gerontol. Soc. (v.p. 1979-80; founding mem.), Council Univ. Insts. for Urban Affairs, Am. Soc. Pub. Adminstrn., Am. Inst. Planners, Gerontol. Soc. Democrat. Jewish. Home and Office: Priscilla R Perry and AssocsInc 5740 SW 64th Pl South Miami FL 33143

PERRY, SUSAN N., communications executive; b. Redwood City, Calif., Dec. 1, 1953; d. Archibald Alexander and Anne Louise (White) Chaney; m. William Alan Perry, Oct. 6, 1983. Grad. high sch. Ballard High, Seattle, 1971. Sec. King County, Seattle, 1974-76; asst. William Perry & Assocs., Seattle, 1976-81; pres. Resource Systems, Inc., now First Class Communications, Inc., Seattle, 1981—. Mem. Direct Mktg. Assn., Seattle C. of C. Avocations: white water rafting; motor sports racing.

PERRYMAN, POLLY, technical writing company executive; b. Hammond, Ind., Feb. 15, 1947; d. Joseph Robert Altenbach and Bertha Helen (Specht) Gephart; m. Lawrence A. Perryman, June 12, 1965 (div. 1974); children—Curtis, Leiha, Candice, Corey. Student Gov.'s State U., 1979; Assoc. Applied Sci., Joliet Jr. Coll., 1978. Computer operator Valley View Sch. Dist., Romeoville, Ill., 1978-80; mgr. data processing Village Communications, Romeoville, 1980-81; tech. writer Profl. Computer Resources, Oak Brook, Ill., 1981-82; owner, pres. Documentation Services, Inc., Romeoville, 1982—; dir. Indoco, Inc., Joliet. Contbr. articles to profl. jours. Precinct committeeman Republican Party, DuPage Twp., 1982—; mem. zoning bd. Village of Romeoville, 1978-82; bd. trustees Joliet Jr. Coll., 1977-78. Guest speaker Software Expo '84 Hitchcock Publishers, 1984. Mem. IEEE (working group for end-user manual standards 1984—), Ill. Software Assn. and Ctr., Am. Bus. Women's Assn. (program chmn. 1982). Presbyterian. Avocations: collector clowns, swimming, football. Home: 797 Farragut Ave Romeoville IL 60441 Office: Documentation Services Inc PO Box 474R Romeoville IL 60441

PERSELL, CAROLINE HODGES, sociologist, educator, author, researcher, consultant; b. Fort Wayne, Ind., Jan. 16, 1941; d. Albert Randolph and Katherine (Rogers) Hodges; m. Charles Bowen Persell, III, June 17, 1967; children—Patricia Emily, Stephen David. B.A., Swarthmore Coll., 1962; M.A., Columbia U., 1967, Ph.D., 1971. Nat. coordinator Nat. Scholarship Service and Fund for Negro Students, N.Y.C., 1962-66; project dir. Bur. Applied Social Research, N.Y.C., 1968-71; asst. prof. NYU, 1971-76, assoc. prof., 1976—, dir. grad. studies dept. sociology, 1984—. Author: Education & Inequality, 1977, Understanding Society, 1984; (with Cookson) Preparing for Power, 1985. Assoc. editor: Teaching Sociology, 1983-85. Contbr. articles to profl. jours. Fund raiser St. Luke's Sch., 1983-84, Stuyvesant High Sch., N.Y.C., 1985. Recipient Faculty Devel. award NSF, 1978-79, Women Educators' Research award, 1978; grantee Nat. Inst. Edn., 1983-84, Elm Trust of Great Britain, 1984, Tel Aviv U., 1985. Mem. AAAS, Am. Sociol. Assn. (chair sec. 1983-84), Am. Ednl. Research Assn. (chmn. book award com. 1985), Author's Guild, Eastern Sociol. Assn., Internat. Sociol. Assn., Sociologists for Women in Soc. (chmn. fin. com. 1983-85). Avocations: Violin; gardening; opera; sports. Office: Dept Sociology NYU 269 Mercer St New York NY 10003

PERSILY, NANCY ALFRED, business executive; b. Albany, N.Y., July 24, 1943; d. Nathan Charles and Shirley (Jasper) Alfred; m. Andrew A. Persily, June 9, 1968 (dec.); children—Nathaniel Alfred, Meredith Mallis. B.S., Cornell U., 1964; M.P.H., Yale U., 1966. Resident, Montefiore Hosp., Bronx, N.Y., 1965-66; spl. asst. to pres. Mt. Sinai Med. Center N.Y.C., 1966-70; prof. Fla. Internat. U., Miami, 1973-77; dir. planning and mktg. Mt. Sinai Med. Ctr., Miami Beach, Fla., 1977-82; pres. Persily Assocs., Miami, 1982—; adj. prof. Bernard Baruch Coll., N.Y.C., 1970-72; ad. assoc. prof. Sch. Medicine U. Miami, 1979—. Author, editor: Hospitals and the Aged, 1983; contbr. articles to publs. Pres., Agys. Concerned with the Elderly, Miami, 1978—; chmn. health council South Fla. Tech. Adv. Com. on Rehab., Miami, 1983. USPHS trainee, Yale U., 1964, faculty trainee, UCLA, 1967. Fellow Am. Pub. Health Assn. (sect. council 1980-84); mem. Soc. for Hosp. Planners (edn. com. 1982-84), Gerontol. Soc. Am., Am. Hosp. Assn. Democrat. Jewish. Home: 7600 SW 125th St Miami FL 33156 Office: Persily Assocs 1450 Madruga Ave Suite 304 Coral Gables FL 33146

PERSING, JENNIFER IRENE, visual director; b. Topeka, Kans., June 22, 1961; d. Morris Elwood and Melba Irene (Cunning) Persing. Student Platt Coll., 1981, Mo. Western State Coll., 1981. Textile mgr. Frenn's Fabric, Topeka, Kans., 1978-80; design cons. Furniture City, St. Joseph, Mo., 1980-81; fashion cons., visual dir. J.C. Penney Co., Kansas City, Mo., 1981-84; visual dir. Finbenders, Inc., St. Joseph, Mo., 1984—; fashion cons. Visual Novations, Kansas City, 1983-86, free-lance design cons., 1984—, interior designer, 1984—; producer bridal showsings, J.C. Penney Co., 1982-84; model various civic-benefit events. Mem. Nat. Assn. Female Execs., Nat. Assn. Display Industries. Christian Ch. Office: Visual Novations 6735 Holmes Kansas City MO 64131

PERSKY, MARLA SUSAN, lawyer; b. Pitts., Feb. 15, 1956; d. Bernard and Elaine (Matus) Persky; m. Craig Heberton IV, May 20, 1984. B.S., Northwestern U., 1977; J.D., Washington U., 1982. Bar: Ill. 1982. Asst. dir. med. records Chgo. Lake Shore Hosp., 1978; sales/mktg. rep. Colgate-Palmolive Co., Chgo., 1978-79; mem. firm Lurie Sklar & Simon, Chgo., 1982-86; corp. counsel Travenol Labs., Inc., 1986—. Sr. editor Urban Law Ann., 1981-82; contbr. articles to profl. jours. Mem. Chgo. Bar Assn., Ill. Bar Assn. (writing contest award 1983), ABA (vice chmn. medicine and law com.), Am. Soc. Law and Medicine, Am. Acad. Hosp. Attys. Democrat. Office: Travenol Labs Inc One Baxter Pkwy IL 60015

PERSON, DOROTHY EVELYN, genealogy educator; b. Battle Ground, Wash., Mar. 19, 1924; d. Ivan Llewelyn and Claire Inez (Spencer) Wooldridge; m. Vernon Lyle Person, Nov. 26, 1944; children—Pamela Rae, Renee Arlene, Timothy Ivan. A.A., Clark Coll., 1960; B.A., U. Portland, 1963, M.A., 1968. Cert. tchr., Wash. Elem., jr. high tchr. Hockinson Sch., Brush Prairie, Wash., 1961-81, retired; tchr. lacemaking, Vancouver, Wash., 1982; tchr. genealogy Clark Coll., Vancouver, 1983—. Author: From a Forest Clearing, 1978; Leaves From Family Tree, 1978; Spencer Citings, 1986. Pres. PTA, Battle Gound, 1962; judge Clark County Fair, 1973-85, Wash. County Fair, Oreg., Skamania Fair, Wash. Scholar Vancouver PTA, 1960. Mem. Ft. Vancouver Hist. Soc. (mem. com. 1965-66,85), Clark County Geneal. Soc. (lectr. 1980—), DAR, Daughters of Pioneers (pres., sec. 1972-80). Clubs: Clark County Quilters (v.p. 1982-83), Volcano Lacemakers (pres., sec. 1981—)(Vancouver); Columbia Stitchery Guild. Republican. Avocations: history and genealogy; needlework; lacemaking; quilting; sewing. Home: 12336 NE 299th St Battle Ground WA 98604

PERSONETTE, EDITH DOLORES, advertising agency executive; b. N.Y.C., Apr. 8, 1933; d. Thomas William and Mary Margaret (Rielly) Trimble; m. Alan Jay Personette, June 6, 1953; children—Alan J., Jr., Laura Ann Personette Null, Nancy Lee. With Schey Advt., Houston, 1971—, asst. to pres., 1971-72, acct. exec., 1973-74, v.p., 1975-80, ptnr., 1979-80, pres., 1980—; adj. prof. bus. and econs. Houston Bapt. Coll., 1973-74; guest lectr. Tex. A & M U., College Station, 1979, U. Houston, 1980, Houston Bapt. Coll., 1983, Houston Community Coll., 1983. Mem. Sales and Marketing Council, Houston Advt. Fedn., Houston C. of C. Republican. Roman Catholic. Home: 7547 Maple Tree Dr Houston TX 77088 Office: Schey Advertising 5 Greenway Plaza Suite 610 Houston TX 77046

PESIKOFF, BETTE S., lawyer; b. N.Y.C., Oct. 9, 1942; d. Stephen and Ethel (Barrett) Schein; m. Richard B. Pesikoff, June 7, 1964; children—David, Joshua, Daniel. B.S., NYU, 1963, M.A., 1964; J.D., U. Houston, 1974. Bar: Tex. 1974. Tchr. pub. schs., N.Y.C., 1964-68; sole practice law, Houston, 1977—; lectr. various profl. groups. Mem. ABA (sec. family law sect. 1985-86), State Bar Tex., Houston Bar Assn. (exec. com. family law sect. 1980-81), Nat. Council Jewish Women. Democrat. Jewish. Clubs: Forum, Baylor Faculty Wives. Office: 3816 W Alabama Suite 200 Houston TX 77027

PETER, LILY, plantation operator, writer; b. Marvell, Ark.; d. William Oliver and Florence (Mobrey) P.; B.S., Memphis State U., 1927; M.A., Vanderbilt U., 1938; postgrad. U. Chgo., 1930, Columbia U., 1935-36; L.H.D. (hon.), Moravian Coll., Bethlehem, Pa., 1965, Hendrix Coll., Conway, Ark., 1983; LL.D. (hon.), U. Ark., 1975. Owner, operator plantations, Marvell and Ratio, Ark.; writer poetry, feature articles pub. in SW Quar., Am. poetry Mag., Etude, Silhouettes, Am. Weave, others; mem. staff Southwest Writers Conf., Corpus Christi, Tex., 1954—, sponsor Ark. Writers' Conf. Chmn. Poetry Day in Ark., 1953—; state coordinator Ark. Bicentennial Music, 1975-76. Hon. trustee Moravian Music Found.; mem. nat. council Met. Opera Assn., N.Y.C.; bd. dirs. So. Ginners Assn., Nat. River Acad., Helena, Ark., Ark. State Festival Arts, Ark. Symphony Orch., Ark. Opera Theatre; mem. Circle of 15, Sigma Alpha Iota, 1974. Recipient Moramus award, Friends of Moravian Music, 1964; Distinguished Alumni award Vanderbilt U., 1964; named Ark. Democrat Woman of Year, 1971; Liberty Bell award Phillips County Bar Assn., 1971; Kenneth Beaudoin Gemstone award, 1967; named poet laureate of Ark., 1971, Ark. Conservationist of Year, 1975, highest honor in conservation Nat. Wildlife Fedn., 1976; Phillips County C. of C. Citizen of Year award, 1983, Ark. Community Devel. Program award, 1985. Mem DAR (hon. state regent), Nat. League Am. Pen Women, Ark. Authors and Composers Soc. (Gold Cup of Achievement 1965), Poets' Roundtable Ark. (C.C. Allard award 1962), Nat. Fedn. Music Clubs (Ark. state chmn. bicentennial 1973-75), Poetry socs. of Tenn., Tex., Ga., Okla. (Gold Cup 1967), Big Creek Protective Assn. (chmn. 1974—), Sigma Alpha Iota. Democrat. Episcopalian. Clubs: Pacaha (Helena, Ark.); Woman's City (Little Rock, Ark.). Author: The Green Linen of Summer, 1964; The Great Riding, 1966; The Sea Dream of the Mississippi, 1973; In the Beginning, 1983. Home: Route 2 Box 69 Marvell AR 72366

PETERING, JANICE FAYE, hotel executive; b. Covington, Ky., Feb. 10, 1950; d. Edward Charles Petering and Shirley Ellen (McKenzie) Petering Brancucci. Student Eastern Ky. U., 1969. Night auditor Caesars Palace Hotel, Las Vegas, 1970-80; accounts receivable supr. Tropicana Hotel & Country Club, Las Vegas, 1980-82, casino comptroller, 1982-83, ops. comptroller, 1983-85, hotel mgr., 1985—. Recipient Completion award Ramada Mgmt. Inst., 1982. Mem. Greater Las Vegas C. of C., Internat. Assn. Hospitality Accts., Hotel-Motel Assn. Roman Catholic. Avocations: skiing, bowling, golf, softball, reading. Office: Tropicana Hotel & Country Club 3801 Las Vegas Blvd S Las Vegas NV 89109

PETERMAN, DONNA COLE, corporate communications executive; b. St. Louis, Nov. 9, 1947; d. William H. and Helen Cole; B.J., U. Mo., 1969; M.B.A., U. Chgo., 1984; m. John Andre Peterman, Feb. 7, 1970. Editor, employee publs. Edison Bros. Stores, Inc., St. Louis, 1969-72; dir. public relations Ron Katz & Assocs., St. Louis 1972-73; editor St. Louis Realty & Investment, 1973-74; chmn. statewide polit. campaign Citizens for Ashcroft, Mo., 1974; asst. media dir. DeKalb County, Ga., 1975; writer Atlanta Mag., 1975; dir. internal communications, exec. speechwriter Sears Roebuck and Co., Atlanta, 1976-80; dir. public affairs Seraco Group-Homart Devel. Co., Chgo., 1980-82; dir. corp. editorial services Sears Roebuck and Co., Chgo., 1982-83, dir. corp. communications, 1983-85; first v.p., dir. corp. communications Dean Witter Fin. Services Group, N.Y.C., 1985-86, sr. v.p., dir. corp. communications, 1986—. Bd. dirs. Trust Inc. Mem. Internat. Assn. Bus. Communicators, Public Relations Soc. Am., Nat. Assn. Corp. Real Estate Execs., Kappa Tau Alpha, Alpha Chi Omega. Republican. Roman Catholic. Clubs: Hugenot Yacht, City Midday, Columbia Yacht. Office: Dean Witter Fin Services 101 Barclay 22d Floor New York NY 10007

PETERS, ALVERA CALLAHAN, educator; b. Covington, La., Feb. 3, 1934; d. Coleman and Gladys James (Barnes) Callahan; m. Robert E. Peters, Sr., Jan. 3, 1957 (div. 1977); children—Dee Anne, Robert, Jr., Darlynne. B.S., Grambling State U., 1956; M.S., Chgo. State U., 1983. Tchr. English, McCullough Sch., Monticello, Miss., 1956-58, Sherman Hills High Sch., Forest, Miss., 1960-62, Wendell Phillips High Sch., Chgo., 1962-76, Corliss High Sch., Chgo., 1977—; social worker Dept. Pub. Aid, Chgo., 1963-64; tchr.-coordinator Urban Skills Inst., Chgo., 1984— Mem. Operation Push, Chgo., 1979; sec., treas. West Pullman Community Orgn., Chgo., 1973; dir. Baptist Tng. Union, New Friendship Bapt. Ch., Chgo., 1984—. Mem. NAACP, Ill. Inst. Tech. Parent Alumni, Nat. Council Tchrs. English, Am. Fedn. Tchrs., Ill. Adult and Continuing Edn. Assn., Nat. Council Negro Women, Alpha Kappa Alpha (dean pledges 1954-55). Democrat. Club: Coasters (pres., founder 1981) (Chgo.). Home: 456 W 118th St Chicago IL 60628

PETERS, AULANA LOUISE, government commissioner; b. Shreveport, La., Nov. 30, 1941; d. Clyde A. and Eula Mae Pharis; m. Bruce F. Peters, Oct. 7, 1967; B.A. in Philosophy, Coll. of New Rochelle, 1963; J.D., U. So. Calif., 1973. Bar: Calif. 1974. Sec., English corr. Publimondial, Spa, Milan, Italy, 1963, Fibramianto, Spa, Milan, 1964; Turkish del. to OECD, Paris, 1965; adminstrv. asst., 1966-67; assoc. Gibson, Dunn and Crutcher, Los Angeles, 1973-80, ptnr., 1980-84; commr. U.S. SEC, Washington, 1984—; lectr. Rutger Group, Los Angeles Supreme Ct., 1981; mem. civil litigation cons. group. State Bar of Calif., Los Angeles, 1983-84; panelist Assn. Bus. Trial Lawyers, Los Angeles, 1982. Recipient Disting. Alumna award Ebonics Club So. Calif., 1984; U. So. Calif. scholar, 1970-73. Mem. Los Angeles County Bar Assn., ABA, Women Lawyers Assn. So. Calif., Black Women Lawyers Assn. Los Angeles, Women's Forum. Democrat. Roman Catholic. Office: US SEC 450 5th St NW Stop 6-7 Washington DC 20549

PETERS, B. JEANNE, business executive; b. Chgo., May 26, 1940; d. James William and Evelyn (Short) Hill; B.A., No. Ill. U., 1962; postgrad. U. Ill., Northwestern U.; children—Lisa L., Krylyn G. Tchr., ednl. writer suburban sch. dists., Ill., 1962-74; pres. Affirmative Action Cons., Wheeling, Ill., 1974-77; employee relations adminstr. Motorola, Inc., 1978-79, corporate dir. affirmative action and compliance, 1979-84, dir. sector tng. and devel., Phoenix, 1984-85; pres. Cons. Consortium, Phoenix, 1985—; tech. adv. mem. U.S. Employer Del. ILO, 1981, 82, 83, 86. Recipient award YWCA, 1978. Mem. Am. Soc. Personnel Adminstrs., Am. Soc. Tng. and Devel. Unitarian. Home: 7811 E Beryl St Scottsdale AZ 85258 Office: 500 E Thomas Phoenix AZ 85012

PETERS, BARBARA ANN, obstetrician and gynecologist; b. Chapel Hill, N.C., Sept. 3, 1954; d. Richard Morse and Ann Wilson (DeHuff) P. B.A. in Human Biology, Stanford U., 1975; M.D. cum laude, Yale U., 1979. Resident in ob-gyn, Stanford U. (Calif.), 1980-83; practice medicine specializing in ob-gyn, Palo Alto, Calif., 1983—; vol. clin. faculty Sch. Medicine Stanford U., 1983—; Ob-Gyn cons. Our Health Ctr., Palo Alto, 1981-83. Active NOW. Recipient award Contbn. to Curriculum Planning, Upjohn Co., 1979; named outstanding resident instr., Stanford U. Med. Students, 1981, 82. Mem. Alpha Omega Alpha. Democrat. Office: 880 Middlefield Rd Palo Alto CA 94301

PETERS, BERNADETTE (BERNADETTE LAZZARA), actress; b. Queens, N.Y., Feb. 28, 1948; d. Peter and Marguerite (Maltese) Lazzara; student Quintano Sch. Young Profls., N.Y.C. Regular on TV series All's Fair, 1976-77; frequent guest appearances on TV; films include: The Longest Yard, 1974, Silent Movie, 1976, Vigilante Force, 1976, W.C. Fields and Me, 1976, The Jerk, 1979, Pennies From Heaven, 1981, Heart Beeps, 1981, Tulips, 1981, Annie, 1982; stage appearances include: The Most Happy Fella, 1959, Gypsy, 1961, This is Google, 1962, Riverwind, 1966, The Penny Friend, 1966, Curly McDimple, 1966, Johnny No-Trump, 1967, George M!, 1968, Dames at Sea, 1968, La Strada, 1969, W.C., 1971, On the Town, 1971, Tartuffe, 1972, Mack and Mabel, 1974; Sally and Marsha, 1982, Sunday in the Park with George, 1984; Song and Dance, 1985; nightclub singer, rec. artist MCA Records. Recipient Drama Desk award for Dames at Sea, 1968; Tony nominations for On the Town, 1971, Mack and Mable, 1974, Sunday in the Park with George, 1984; Tony award, Drama Desk award, Drama League award for Song and Dance, 1986. Office: care Richard Grant & Assocs 8500 Wilshire Blvd Suite 520 Beverly Hills CA 90211

PETERS, CAROL ANN HOPPES, nurse; b. Coaldale, Pa., May 14, 1960; d. Ernest Earl and Florence Eileen (Boyer) Hoppes; m. James Elliot Peters. Diploma St. Luke's Sch. Nursing, 1980; B.S. with distinction in Nursing, U. Va., 1983. Registered nurse, Va., Pa. Staff nurse U. Va., Charlottesville, 1980-83, clinician, 1983-84; staff nurse, oncology specialist Presbyterian-U. Pa. Med. Ctr., Phila., 1984-85; asst. head nurse oncology research unit Hosp. of U. Pa., 1985—. Vol., Am. Cancer Soc., Carbon County 1970-80, Phila., 1985—, Ronald MacDonald House, Phila., 1985—. Mem. Am. Assn. Critical Care Nurses, Oncology Nurses Soc., DAR. Republican. Avocations: Hiking; photography; knitting; needlepoint; reading.

PETERS, CAROL BEATTIE TAYLOR, mathematician; b. Washington, May 10, 1932; d. Edwin Lucius and Lois (Beattie) Taylor; B.S., U. Md., 1954, M.A., 1958; m. Frank Albert Peters, Feb. 26, 1955; children—Thomas, June, Erick, Victor. Group mgr. Tech. Operations, Inc., Arlington, Va., 1957-62, sr. staff scientist, 1964-66; supervisory analyst Datatrol Corp., Silver Spring, Md., 1962; project dir. Computer Concepts, Inc., Silver Spring, 1963-64; mem. tech. staff Informatics Inc., Bethesda, Md., 1966-67, tech. dir. advanced tech., 1967-76; sr. tech. dir. Ocean Data Systems, Rockville, Md., 1976-83; dir. Informatics Gen. Corp., Rockville, Md., 1983—. Mem. Assn. Computing Machinery, IEEE Computer Group. Home: 12321 Glen Mill Rd Potomac MD 20854 Office: 6011 Executive Blvd Rockville MD 20852

PETERS, DIANNE KAY, property management company official; b. Plainwell, Mich., Nov. 26, 1953; d. Clarence J. and Evelyn Jean (Hadaway) Wesseling; m. David Richard Peters, Aug. 11, 1978; children—David M., Kelly Jean. Cosmetologist, State Coll. Beauty, 1972. Cosmetologist, Loraine's Beauty Shop, Plainwell, 1972-74; asst. adminstr. Monarch Mgmt. Co., Newport Beach, Calif., 1974-78; adminstr. Paul Ash Investment, Tucson, 1978-79, Summit Mgmt., Kalamazoo, 1979-81; adminstr. acctg. U. Tex. Med. Br., Galveston, 1981-82; adminstr. Con Am Mgmt. Corp., San Diego, 1982—. Active McCarthy Presdl. Campaign, Mich., 1971-72. Rotary Club scholar, 1971. Mem. Nat. Assn. Female Execs., Mus. Natural History, Smithsonian Inst. Republican. Mem. Ch. of God. Office: Continental American Mgmt Corp 1764 San Diego Ave San Diego CA 92110

PETERS, DOROTHY MARIE, educator; b. Sutton, Nebr., Oct. 23, 1913; d. Sylvester and Anna (Olander) Peters; A.B. with high distinction, Nebr. Wesleyan U., 1941; M.A., Northwestern U., 1957; Ed.D., Ind. U., 1968. Tchr. Nebr. pub. schs., 1931-38; caseworker Douglas County Assistance Bur., Omaha, 1941; hosp. field dir., gen. field rep. ARC, 1941-50; social worker Urban League, Meth. Ch., Washington, 1951-53; asst. prin., dir. guidance, Manlius (Ill.) Community High Sch., 1953-58; dean of girls, guidance dir. Woodruff High Sch., Peoria, Ill., 1958-66; vis. prof. edn. Bradley U., Peoria, 1959-77; coordinator, dir. Title I programs Peoria Public Sch. System, 1966-68, dir. pupil services, 1968-72; dir. counseling and evaluation Title I Programs, 1972-73; vol. dir. youth service programs, vol. program cons. Central Ill. chpt. and Heart of Ill. div. ARC, Peoria, 1973-77; owner, operator Ability-Achievement Unlimited Cons. Services, Saratoga Springs, N.Y., 1978-81; spl. cons. Courage Center, Golden Valley, Minn., 1981—; mem. sr. adv. bd. F&M Marquette Nat. Bank, 1981—. Bd. dirs. home service com. disaster com. Peoria chpt. ARC, 1958-73; pres., bd. dirs. Ct. Counselor Program; mem. Mayor's Human Resources Council, City of Peoria; chmn. met. adv. com. transp. for handicapped; ednl. dir., prin., bd. dirs. Catalyst High Sch., 1975-77; hon. life bd. mem. Am. Nat. Red Cross; mem. Saratoga Springs Hosp. Bldg. Rehab. Com.; founder, steering com. Open Sesame, Saratoga Springs, 1978-81; appointee N.Y. State Employment and Tng. Council, 1979-81, Saratoga County Employment and Tng. Com., 1979-81; bd. dirs. Unlimited Potential, 1979-81; mem. Metro Mobility Adv. Task Force, Mpls., 1981—, mem. policy com., 1984—; mem. vol. action com. United Way, Mpls., 1982—. Mem. Peoria Edn. Assn. (v.p. 1962-64), Ill. Guidance and Personnel Assn. (v.p. Area 8, 1963-64), NEA, Ill. Edn. Assn. (del. 1962-64), Am. Personnel and Guidance Assn., Am. Sch. Counselors Assn., Nat. Assn. Women Deans and Counselors (K-12 task force chmn. 1974—, editorial bd. Jour.), Ill. Vocat. Guidance Assn. (dir.), Ill. Assn. Women Deans and Counselors, Phi Kappa Phi, Psi Chi, Pi Gamma Mu, Pi Lambda Theta, Delta Kappa Gamma, Alpha Gamma Delta. Address: 2523 Portland Ave S Apt 1501 Minneapolis MN 55404

PETERS, ELIZABETH ANNE, educator; b. Hebron, Ill., June 9, 1940; d. Tibbets E. and Ruby Marie (Giddens) Rolls; B.S., U. Ill., 1962, M.S., 1967; postgrad. U. Ill., 1970-74, Iowa State U., 1974, Northwestern U., 1980; div. Tchr., Bremen High Sch., Midlothian, Ill., 1962-65, Waller High Sch., Chgo., 1965-67, Evanston (Ill.) High Sch., 1967-70; instr., coordinator food service adminstrn. and hotel mgmt. Coll. DuPage, Glen Ellyn, Ill., 1970-75; clin. dietitian U. Chgo. Hosps. and Clinics, 1975; asst. restaurant mgr. Hyatt Regency, Chgo., summer 1980; prof., coordinator hospitality mgmt. program Chicago City-Wide Coll., 1976—; cons. bds. health, colls. Mem. adv. com. No. Ill. U.; judge various food contests; mem. Chgo. Council on Fgn. Relations; v.p. Near North chpt. Lyric Opera Guild; trustee Three Arts Club Chgo. Recipient Nat. Restaurant Assn. Fellowship award, 1980; Master Tchrs. Seminar Fellowship award, 1974; Nat. Leadership Devel. Fellowship award, 1975. Registered Dietitan. Mem. Nat. Restaurant Assn., Ill. Restaurant Assn., Chgo. Restaurant Assn., Am. Dietetic Assn., Ill. Dietetic Assn., Chgo. Nutrition Assn., Ill Nutrition Com., Chgo. Dietetic Assn. (dir.), Soc. Nutrition Edn., Inst. Food Technologists, Restaurant Women's Club Chgo. (dir.), Council on Hotel-Restaurant Edn. Clubs: Flossmoor Country, Lake Geneva Yacht, Canyon. Home: 215 E Chestnut St Chicago IL 60611 Office: 30 E Lake St Chicago IL 60601

PETERS, ELLEN ASH, state Supreme Court justice; b. Berlin, Mar. 21, 1930; naturalized citizen U.S.; B.A. cum laude, Swarthmore Coll., 1951; LL.B. cum laude, Yale U., 1954, M.A. (hon.), 1964, LL.D., 1984; LL.D. (hon.), U. Hartford, 1983, Swarthmore Coll., 1983, Georgetown U., 1984, Conn. Coll., 1984, N.Y. Law Sch., 1984, Colgate U., 1986, St. Joseph Coll., 1986. Law clk. to U.S. Circuit Ct. Judge Charles E. Clark, 1954-55; assoc. in law U. Calif., Berkeley, 1955-56; faculty Yale U. Sch. Law, New Haven, 1956—, adj. prof., 1978-84; assoc. justice Supreme Ct. Conn., 1978-84, chief justice, 1984—; mem. Conn. Law Revision Commn., 1978-84. Trustee, Yale U., 1986—. Author: Commercial Transaction, Cases, Text and Problems, 1971; A Negotiable Instruments Primer, 1974; contbr. numerous articles to legal jours. Office: Supreme Court Bldg Drawer N Station A 231 Capitol Ave Hartford CT 06106

PETERS, EUNICE SARAH BATES LOWERY, artist; b. Chelsea, Mass., Oct. 18, 1906; d. William Edgar and Eunice Hall (Fergusson) Lowery; grad. Famous Artists Sch., Mind Psi-Genics; M. Psycho-Cybernetics, Am. Inst. Motivational Sci.; m. William J. Peters, June 3, 1927 (dec. June 1967); children—Eunice L. Peters Harrington, William J. Exhibited in one-woman shows at Alhambra Library, Calif., 1976; group shows: Pasadena Soc. Artists, San Gabriel Soc. Arts; sec., dir. Trail Chem. Corp., El Monte, Calif., 1947. Mem. Pasadena Arts Council, Pasadena Artists Assn., San Gabriel Fine Arts and Culture Assn., Pasadena Artists, Nat. League Am. Pen Women (pres. Pasadena br. 1972-74, historian and achievement chmn. 1984-86), Composers and Artists (Pasadena br.). Home: 1315 Monterey Pl San Marino CA 91108 Office: 9904 Gidley St El Monte CA 91731

PETERS, FRANCES BARBARA, textile researcher; b. Lowell, Mass., Nov. 8, 1936; d. Teotonio Medina and Barbara (Sperling) Davis; m. Frank Charles Peters, Jan. 6, 1964; children—Charles Frank, Deborah Lee. B.S. in Textile Chemistry, Lowell Technol. Inst., 1961; postgrad. U. Mo., 1974-75; M.S. in Plastics, U. Lowell, 1978. Tech. dir. U. Lowell Research Found., 1974-79, vis. lectr. U. Lowell, 1978-79; mgr. fabrics lab. NIKE, Inc., Exeter, N.H., 1979-81; research textile technologist U.S. Army Research and Devel. Labs., Natick, Mass., 1981-85; dir. finishes, fiber and fabrics Foss Mfg. Co., Haverhill, Mass., 1985—. Contbr. articles to profl. jours. Assoc. The Textile Inst., Manchester, Eng., 1982. Mem. Am. Assn. Textile Chemists and Colorists (corp. rep. 1977-79), ASTM, TAPPI, Am. Assn. Textile Tech. (mem. exec. council 1980—, sec., 1982-84, chmn. 1984-86). Roman Catholic. Clubs: Toastmasters (sgt. at arms 1985), Colonial Treasure Hunters (editor 1983—). Avocations: metal detecting; archaeology; museums; traveling. Home: 12 Blodgett St Lowell MA 01851 Office: Foss Mfg Co Inc 1 Whitney Ave Haverhill MA 01830

PETERS, JANET J., textile manufacturing company executive; b. Reading, Pa., Oct. 6, 1930; d. James Hubert and Dorothy Mary (Knoblanch) McElfatrich; m. Henry A. Peters; 1 child, Lisa Renee. Student June McAdam Coll. Vice pres. Vanity Fair Mills, Wyomissing, Pa., 19 - ; v.p. VF Corp., Wyomissing, 19 —. Chmn. Mother's Day Luncheon Mother's Day Council Am., N.Y.C., 1980—; bd. dirs., fundraiser Reading Community Coll., 1983—; active Factory for Sr. Citizens, Fleetwood, Pa., 1983—. Office: VF Corp Park Rd Wyomissing PA 19610

PETERS, JEANNE CRIDER, petroleum company official; b. Thicket, Tex., July 7, 1945; d. Labern Thomas and Margaret Bonita (Kelly) Crider. B.A., U. Houston, 1967, postgrad., 1967-68; postgrad. U. So. Utah, 1967, Sam Houston State U., 1969. Tchr., Royal Ind. Sch. Dist., Brookshire, Tex., 1967-69, Columbus Ind. Sch. Dist. (Tex.), 1969-74; asst. dir. admissions St. Luke's/Tex. Children's Hosp., Houston, 1974; sec. Practice Mgmt., Houston, 1975; adminstrv. sec. IBM Corp., Houston, 1975-77; sr. sec. II, Tenn. Gas Pipeline, Houston, 1979—; guest lectr. U. Tex. Petroleum Extension Service, 1981-84, Colo. Northwestern Community Coll., Rangely, 1982—. Mem. ednl. adv. bd. Colo. Northwestern Community Coll., 1982—. Recipient Outstanding Contbn. to Bus. and Office Edn. award Colo. Northwestern Community Coll., 1983. Mem. Gamma Sigma Sigma (life). Methodist. Home: 6000 Sun Forest Apt 1902 Houston TX 77092 Office: Tenn Gas Pipeline Co PO Box 2511 Houston TX 77001

PETERS, JUDITH ROCHELLE, educator, administrator; b. Phila., July 16, 1951; d. John Bernard and Priscilla Jo (Johnson) P.; B.S. (Senatorial scholar), Pa. State U., 1973; postgrad. Temple U. Sch. Pharmacy, 1975-77; M.B.A., H.H.S.A., Cornell U., 1977. Supr., lifeguard Phila. Dept. Recreation, 1971-74; pharmacy intern Needle & Boonin, Zachian Bros. and Bell Family Pharmacies, Phila., 1976-79; mgr., partner Adero Pharmacy, Phila., 1980-83; sci. specialist Phila. Bd. Edn.; exec. dir. Urban Health Network Inc., 1984, YMCA of West Phila., 1985—. Vol., Big Sisters Am., ARC, Phila.; elder Lombard Central United Presbyterian Ch., Phila. Mem. Nat. Assn. Health Services Execs., Am. Public Health Assn., Internat. City Mgmt. Assn., United Presbyn. Women. Club: United Soul Ensemble. Office: 8120 Chestnut St Philadelphia PA 19139

PETERS, JUDY GALE, manufacturing company official, educator; b. Matoaka, W.Va., Dec. 13, 1941; d. Thomas Delbert and Vicie Clarice (Mundy) Hankins; m. Jesse Everitt Lobdell, Jr., Dec. 2, 1963 (div. Jan. 1975); 1 child, Jesse Everitt III; m. Kenneth Rae Peters, June 6, 1975 (div. Dec. 1984) 1 child, Kenneth Phillip. B.S., Radford Coll., 1964. Tchr. county schs., Licking County, Ohio, 1964-73; with Hydrostrut Co., Newark, Ohio, 1974-76; buyer Anchor Coupling Co., Hebron, Ohio, 1976-78; expeditor Diebold Inc., Hebron, 1978-80, buyer, 1980—. Advisor 4-H Club Band, Licking County, 1965-67. Named Tchr. of Yr., Northridge Local Schs., 1972. Mem. Am. Choral Dirs., Diebold Mgmt. Club, Nat. Assn. Female Execs. Club: Utica Music Boosters (Ohio). Lodge: Phythias. Avocations: reading; writing; dancing; bowling. Home: 3525 Johnstown Utica Rd Utica OH 43080

PETERS, LIBBY ANN, city official; b. Cleve., Feb. 9, 1931; d. Joseph and Bertha (Hajek) Montvicka; m. Howard Henry Peters, Aug. 25, 1951 (div. 1976); children—Bruce A., Laureen D. Clk.-typist Dale Black and Co. CPA, Cleve., 1961-66; mgr. Dairy Queen, Richfield, Ohio, 1966-71; clk. of council Richfield Village, Ohio, 1971-72, dir. fin., 1972—. Treas. Richfield Civic. Assn., 1969, Richfield Toll Free Service Assn., 1970, PTA, Horse Show, Art Show, others, 1960-70; sec. Planning Commn. and Bd. Zoning Appeals, Richfield, 1968-71. Mem. Nat. Mcpl. Treas. Assn., Ohio Mcpl. Treas. Assn., Ohio Mcpl. Fin. Officers Assn., (northeast Ohio chpt. pres., v.p. sec., treas. 1977-80), Ohio Assn. Tax Adminstrs. (pres. 1973-76). Avocations: fishing; gardening; camping. Home: 3018 Farnham Rd Richfield OH 44286 Office: Village of Richfield 4410 W Streetsboro Rd Richfield OH 44286

PETERS, MERCEDES, psychoanalyst; b. N.Y.C.; B.S., L.I. U., 1945; postgrad. Columbia U., 1944-45; M.S., U Conn., 1953; tng. in psychotherapy Am. Inst. Psychotherapy and Psychoanalysis, 1960-70; grad. Postgrad. Center Mental Health; doctoral candidate Union Grad. Sch. Social worker various agys., pub. instns., 1945-63; staff affiliate, sr. psychotherapist Community Guidance Service, 1960-75; affiliate Postgrad. Center for Mental Health, 1974-76; pvt. practice psychotherapy, Bklyn., 1961—. Certified psychoanalyst Am. Examining Bd. Psychoanalysis; certified mental health cons. Fellow Am. Orthopsychiat. Assn.; mem. Nat. Assn. Social Workers, Nat. Assn. for Advancement Psychoanalysis, LWV, NAACP, Brooklyn Heights Mus. Soc. Office: 142 Joralemon Brooklyn NY 11201

PETERS, PATRICIA ELAINE, bank mgr.; b. Chgo., Oct. 14, 1941; d. Lawrence and Kathlee R. (Lyons) P.; B.A., Marycrest Coll., Davenport, Iowa, 1963; m. James Richard Carter, Jan. 1, 1982. With Morgan Guaranty Trust Co., N.Y.C., 1969—, mgr. N.Am. research unit, 1978-81, instl. portfolio mgr., 1981—. Mem. Fin. Women's Assn., N.Y. Soc. Security Analysts. Office: 9 W 57th St New York NY 10019

PETERS, ROBERTA, soprano; b. N.Y.C., May 4, 1930; d. Sol and Ruth (Hirsch) Peters; ed. privately; Litt.D. Elmira Coll., 1967; Mus. D., Ithaca Coll., 1968, Colby Coll., 1980; L.H.D., Westminster Coll., 1974, Lehigh U., 1977; m. Bertram Fields, Apr. 10, 1955; children—Paul, Bruce. Met. Opera debut as Zerlina in Don Giovanni, 1950, also appeared in Rigoletto, The Magic Flute, The Barber of Seville, The Marriage of Figaro, Lucia di Lammermoor, Die Fledermaus, Don Pasquale, L'Elisir d'Amore, Lakme, Cosi fan Tutte, La Sonnambula, Martha, Richard Strauss' Ariadne auf Naxos; recorded numerous operas; appeared motion pictures Tonight We Sing; frequent appearances radio and TV; sang at Royal Opera House, Covent Garden, London, Eng., summers 1951-60, Cin. Opera, summers 1952-53, 58, Vienna State Opera, 1963, Salzburg Festival, 1963, 64; debuts at festival in Vienna and Munich, 1963, 64; concert tours in U.S., Soviet Union, Scandinavian countries, Isreal; debut Kirov Opera, Leningrad, USSR, 1972, Bolshoi Opera, Moscow, 1972. Named Women of Yr., Fedn. Women's Clubs, 1964; 1st Am. to receive Bolshoi medal. Author: Debut at the Met. Office: ICM Artists Ltd 40 W 57th St New York NY 10019 also care Herbert H Breslin Inc 119 W 57th St New York NY 10019

PETERS, SHIRLEY RUTH, interior designer; b. Saint Joseph, Mo., June 12, 1939; d. Lowell Wayne and Ruth Fern (Miller) Parkhurst; m. Jerry LeRoy Peters, Sr., Dec. 31, 1954; children—Brenda Kay, Jerry L., Jr., Kerri Kay. Housewife, Saint Joseph, Mo., 1954-67; various sales and mktg., Kansas City,

Mo., 1967-78; residential and commercial design and decorating, Kansas City, 1978—; design cons. Shirley's Decorating Spltys. (now Inc.), Kansas City, 1978—; speaker. Mem. PTA, Saint Joseph, pres., 1963-64, mem. Women's Traffic Club, Kansas City, 1967-72, pres., 1970-71. Home: 5611 NW Oakridge Ct Kansas City MO 64151 Office: 6900 NW 83d St Kansas City MO 64152

PETERS, VERA CONSTANCE ASTER HESS, real estate exec.; b. Bklyn., Apr. 3, 1945; d. Charles H. and Erna Anna (Schoen) Aster; student Latter-day Saints Bus. Coll., 1958, U. Utah, 1961; m. Ted Peters, Nov. 23, 1980; children by previous marriage—Troy Dee, Tyrone Chad. Legal sec., office mgr. Gordon I. Hyde, Salt Lake City, 1969-71; adminstrv. asst. Flying Diamond Oil Corp., Salt Lake City, 1971-74, also exec. sec. to chmn. bd.; sec. treas. Shuhart Industries, Inc., Salt Lake City, 1974-77; Realtor, 1977-80; broker, 1980—; owner, pres. Market Realty, Inc., 1980-85; pres. Peters & Co., 1985—. Mem. Nat. Assn. Realtors, Salt Lake Bd. Realtors, Women's Council Realtors, LWV. Lutheran. Home: 1120 E 400 N Bountiful UT 84010

PETERSEN, DEBRA ANN, human resources executive; b. Evergreen Park, Ill., Nov. 25, 1956; d. Thomas William and Celeste Marie (Kuczora) Moran; m. Norman Robert Petersen, Jr., Apr. 1, 1978. A.A., Scottsdale Community Coll., 1975; B.S., Ariz. State U., 1977. Sec., S.W. Savs. & Loan Assn., Phoenix, 1978-79, personnel asst., 1979-81, asst. dir. human resources, 1981—, asst. v.p., 1982—, asst. dir. human resources, 1983—. Mem. S.W. Savs. Polit. Action Com., Phoenix, 1983—. Mem. Phoenix Personnel Mgmt. Assn. (co-chmn. compensation com.), Am. Soc. Personnel Adminstrn., Fin. Affirmative Action Assn., Am. Compensation Assn. Republican. Roman Catholic. Home: 3876 W Chicago St Chandler AZ 85226 Office: SW Savings and Loan Assn 3101 N Central Ave Phoenix AZ 85012

PETERSEN, HELEN EVELYN, wholesale tobacco company executive; b. Everett, Wash., Apr. 23, 1913; d. Mathew Thomas and Amanda Margaret (Heffernan); m. Leo Petersen, Dec. 31, 1936 (dec. Mar. 1969); children—Ronald Carl, Gregary Thomas. Grad. Everett High Sch., 1931. Owner, Northwest Distributors Inc., Everett, 1948—, Petersen Vendors Inc., Everett, 1960—. Mem. Nat. Candy Wholesalers Assn. (Candy Distributor of Yr. 1976), Nat. Assn. Tobacco Distributors. Methodist. Club: Soroptimist (pres. 1958). Home: Box 1235 Mukilteo WA 98275 Office: Northwest Distributors Inc 2500 Hewitt Ave Everett WA 98201 also Petersen Vendors 2110 37th St Everett WA 98201

PETERSEN, MARGARET HASBROUCK, painter, sculptor, fashion and accessory designer, ceramics artist; b. Yakima, Wash., Oct. 11, 1940; d. Ralph Louis and Evelyn Mae (Williams) Johnson; m. Orval L. Petersen, Feb. 9, 1979; children by previous marriage—Tracy Fredrick Kemp, Dana Kenneth Price. Student U. Colo., Foothills Coll., Yavapai Coll.; also various profl. workshops, seminars. Owner, operator Hasbrouck Petersen Inc.—Fine Arts Plus, Sedona, Ariz., 1965—; guest speaker in field, Eng., Germany, U.S. One-woman show Ratliff-Williams Gallery, Sedona, 1986; group shows include Sedona Art Ctr., Tulac Ctr. for Arts, No. Ariz. U.; represented in permanent collections Sedona Art Ctr.; also pvt. collections U.S. and abroad. Recipient numerous art awards and honors, including award of excellence AWA Exhibit, No. Ariz. U., 1985; 1st place in Watercolor Sedona Art Ctr., 1985. Mem. Ariz. Watercolor Assn., Sedona Art Galleries and Assocs., Sedona Art Ctr. Artists and Craftsmen's Guild (past pres.).

PETERSEN, TONI, library administrator, information specialist; b. N.Y.C., May 13, 1933; s. Joseph John and Julia (Fiore) De Rosa; m. Norman Richard Petersen, Jan. 28, 1956; children—Kristen, Mark, Joanna. B.A., Bklyn. Coll., 1956; M.L.S., Simmons Coll., 1963. Exec. editor Internat. Repertory of Lit. of Art, Williamstown, Mass., 1972-80; dir. Bennington Coll. Library, Vt., 1980-86; dir. Art and Architecture Thesaurus, J. Paul Getty Art History Info. Program, Los Angeles, 1983—; adv. bd. mem. George Eastman House, Rochester, N.Y., 1982-83; reviewer NEH, Washington, 1985—. Contbr. articles to profl. jours. Mem. Art Libraries Soc. N.Am. (chmn. 1985-86), Vt. Library Assn., Am. Numismatics Soc. (adv. bd. 1983—). Office: Bennington Coll Library Bennington VT 05201

PETERSEN, MRS. WILLIAM J. (BESSIE RASMUS PETERSEN), orgn. exec., club woman; b. Cherokee, Iowa, June 30, 1902; d. Andrew John and Singni (Nystedt) Rasmus; B.A., State U. Iowa, 1926, M.A., 1930; m. William John Petersen, Sept. 25, 1937. Speech pathologist Rockefeller Found. Mental Hygiene Clinic for Iowa, Iowa City, 1926-28; instr. speech, phonetics U. Iowa, 1928-37; organizer, dir. U. Iowa, Articulatory Speech Clinic, 1928-37; lectr., speech pathology U. Nebr., summers 1931, 37, 38, 39, 40, 41; lectr. Butler U., summer 1937; cons. spl. edn. Iowa Dept. Pub. Edn., 1948-50; asst. dir. Iowa State Hist. Soc. Tours, 1948—. Mem. com. White House Conf. on Spl. Edn., 1929. Mem. Girl Scout Council, 1938-41. Mem. Needlework Guild of Am. (pres. 1939), AAUW (pres. 1940), Iowa Speech and Hearing Assn., Iowa Bus. and Profl. Women's Club, Iowa State Hist. Soc., League Women Voters Iowa Fedn. Women's Clubs, Sigma Xi, Chi Omega. Mem. Order Eastern Star. Club: University. Home: 329 Ellis Ave Iowa City IA 52240

PETERSON, ANNE CECELIA, lodging industry executive; b. Sacramento, Aug. 7, 1943; d. John Nelson and Anna Rae (Andersen) Hathaway; m. Paul Eugene Peterson, Aug. 29, 1972. B.A., San Francisco State Coll., 1965. Sales asst. Am. Can Co., San Francisco, 1966-71; research mgr. Clorox, Oakland, Calif., 1971-85; research mgr. Westin Hotel Co., Seattle, 1986—. Mem. Am. Mktg. Assn. Avocations: hiking; stitchery; bird and whale watching; reading. Home: 1547C Santa Clara St Alameda CA 94501

PETERSON, ARLENE JULIETTE, constrn. co. exec.; b. Winner, S.D., Apr. 27, 1936; d. Elwood Lloyd and Geneva Carolyn (Mayes) Miller; B.S., Black Hills State Coll., 1968; children—Richard Allen, Dean Allen. Tchr. pub. schs., Meade County, S.D., 1959-60; spl. edn. tchr. Title I Program, New Underwood, S.D., 1960-72; office mgr. Overhead Dr. Co., Rapid City, S.D., 1972-75; office mgr. Dean Kurtz Constrn. Co., Rapid City, 1975—, sec.-treas., 1976—, dir., 1979—. Mem. Asso. Gen. Contractors Am., Women in Constrn. Republican. Lutheran. Home: 2110 6th Ave Rapid City SD 57701 Office: PO Box 1917 Rand Rd Rapid City SD 57709

PETERSON, AULI IRENE, translator-interpreter; b. Lahti, Finland, Jan. 23, 1937; came to U.S., 1981; d. Valo and Irene (Niinikoski) Ahonen; m. Charles H. Peterson; children—Mika Rytokoski, Katja Rytokoski. B.A., Helsinki U., Finland, 1961, M.A., 1963. Cert. translator Ministry of Justice, Finland. Lectr. English, Lahti Inst. Tech., 1963-82; translator-interpreter, Bethesda, Md., 1982—; profl. fgn. lang. specialist Dept. State, Washington, 1981—; translator Joint Publs. Research Service, Arlington, Va., 1985—. Author: (with Peter Dodds and Satu Ilaja) Engineering English, 1979. Bd. dirs. League Finnish-Am. Socs., Helsinki, 1973-81; chmn. Finnish-Am. Soc., Lahti, 1980-81. Grantee Adminstrn. for Vocat. Edn., Helsinki, in Washington, 1974. Mem. Modern Lang. Assn., Phi Sigma Iota. Home: 9512 Brooke Dr Bethesda MD 20817

PETERSON, BARBARA JOYCE, artist, doll artist and designer; b. Lewiston, Idaho, Oct. 17, 1943; d. Clarence Vard and Emma (McGarrah) Jackson; m. James John Peterson, June 4, 1965 (div. 1980); children—Sandra Renae, Jason John; m. James William Comley, Oct. 9, 1981. Artist, designer Keepsake Originals, Springdale, Ark., 1976—. Original porcelain doll designer: The Farmer, 1978 (award 1978), Grandmother, 1979 (award 1979), Albert and Emma, Bundle of Joey, 1985. Mem. United Fedn. Doll Clubs (awards 1978, 79, 85). Club: N.W. Ark. Heirloom Doll. Avocations: photography. Home: 103 Lakeview Dr Springdale AR 72764 Office: Keepsake Originals PO Box 784 418 E Emma St Springdale AR 72765

PETERSON, DONNA C., state senator. B.A. in Anthropology, U. Minn.; married; 2 children. Mem. Minn. Senate, 1982—. Mem. Democratic-Farmer-Labor Party. Office: Minn State Capitol Bldg Saint Paul MN 55155*

PETERSON, DOROTHY FAYE, accountant; b. Lake Preston, S.D., Oct. 29, 1921; d. John Howard and Bertha Faye (Holm) Payne; student Merritt Bus. Coll., 1939; secretarial cert. Healds Bus. Coll., 1944; m. Lennard Martin Peterson, Apr. 15, 1950; children—Cristine Ann, Scott Martin. Analyst, U.S. Govt. Air Transport Command, Alameda, Calif., 1943-47; exec. sec., investigator Montgomery Ward, Oakland, Calif., 1947-50; tax acct. Watkins & Klee, Mendocino, Calif., 1951-61; pvt. practice tax acctg. and enrolled agt., Mendocino, Calif., 1961—. Sec. Mendocino-Little River Cemetery Dist., 1964—; fin. officer Mendocino City Community Services Dist., 1974—; trustee Mendocino Sch. Dist., 1958-61; commr. Mendocino County Civil Service Commn., 1962-65; trustee Mendocino Presbyn. Ch., 1970-74. Mem. Nat. Enrolled Agts. Assn., Nat. Soc. Accts., Calif. Enrolled Agts. Assn., Mendocino Bus. and Profl. Council (treas. 1976-80), Soroptomists Internat. of Ft. Bragg. Democrat. Presbyterian. Office: 10540 Lansing St Mendocino CA 95460

PETERSON, ESTHER EGGERTSEN, consumer advocate; b. Provo, Utah, Dec. 9, 1906; d. Lars E. and Annie (Nielson) Eggertsen; children—Karen Wilken, Iver Peterson, Eric Peterson, Lars Peterson. A.B., Brigham Young U., 1927; M.A., Columbia U., 1931. Dir. Women's Bur., Labor Dept., Washington, 1961, asst. sec. of labor for labor stds., 1961-69, exec. vice chmn. Pres.'s Commn. on Status of Women, 1961-63; spl. asst. to Pres. for Consumer Affairs, Washington, 1964-67, 76-80, chmn. Pres.'s Com. on Consumer Interests, 1964-67; chmn. Consumer Affairs Council, Washington, 1976-80; rep. Internat. Orgn. Consumers Unions, 1986—; v.p. consumer programs and consumer advisor to pres. Giant Food Corp., 1970-77; asst. dir. edn. Amalgamated Clothing Workers, 1939-44, legis. rep., 1945-48; legis. rep. indsl. union dept. AFL-CIO, 1957-61; faculty Branch Agrl. Coll., Utah, 1927-29, Winsor-Sch., Boston, 1930-35, Bryn Mawr Summer Sch. for Women Workers in Industry, 1935-38. Recipient Medal of Freedom, 1979, Food Mktg. Inst. Industry Statesmanship award, 1977; Trumpeter award, Nat. Consumers League, 1981; elected to State of Utah's Beehive Hall of Fame. Address: 7714 13th St NW Washington DC 20012

PETERSON, GEORGIANA (TOMAS), music educator, composer; b. Chgo., Feb. 19, 1925; d. Julius Tomas and Josephine (Hrbek) P.; student Northwestern U., 1947, Roosevelt U., 1947-48; B.M. cum laude, Am. Conservatory Chgo., 1949, M.M.E. magna cum laude, 1964; postgrad. N.Y. U., 1976; m. Robert G. Peterson, Sept. 8, 1949 (div. 1972); children—Kent Alan, Kevin Scott. Free-lance model, Chgo., 1940's; singer Sta. WENR, Chgo., 1962-65; coordinator music-arts Westmont (Ill.) Public Sch. Dist., 1965-67; cons., instr. N. Central Coll., Naperville, Ill., 1965-67; chmn. music Villa Park (Ill.) Sch. Dist. 45, 1965-67; asst. prof. music, pub. relations, music dept. Trenton (N.J.) State Coll.; publicity writer, coordinator Summit (N.J.) Art Center, 1979-80. Mem. Music Educators Nat. Conf., N.J. Music Educators Assn., Music Industry Council, Fla. Music Educators, AAUP, Delta Omicron. Author: Music Dynamics, 1965; Getting to Know Music, 1965, books IV, V, 1966, book VI, 1967, books, I, III, rev., 1974, book IV, 1975; Movable Do, 1972; New Dimensions of Music; contbr. articles to profl. jours.; composer; (musical compositions for children) Night, If, First Bell Song, Happy Thoughts, Little Boy Blue, Riddle, Where Go The Boats, Whisky Frisky, New Song About Jonathing Bing, Of the Bells. Home: 195 N Mayflower Way Jamesburg NJ 08831 Office: Trenton State Coll Dept Music Trenton NJ 08625

PETERSON, HAZEL AGNES, consulting petroleum geologist; b. Houston; d. Howard Lynn, Sr., and Carrie Rice (Brown) P.; B.A. in Geology, N.Y. U., 1939; M.A. in Geology, U. Tex., 1942; postgrad. various univs. Jr. subsurface geologist Shell Oil Co., Houston, 1942; subsurface geologist Texaco, Houston and Tulsa, 1942-44, Sun Oil Co., Dallas and Corpus Christi, Tex., 1944-52; supervising geologist Seaboard Oil Co. of Del., Dallas, 1952-54; pvt. practice cons. petroleum geologist, Dallas, Commerce and Denton, Tex., 1952—; asst. prof. E.Tex. State U., Commerce, 1958-78; former water resources adv. City of Commerce. Mem. City of Commerce Planning and Zoning Commn., 1977-82. Research grantee, U.S. Nat. Park Service, 1959-61; faculty research grantee E.Tex. State U., 1960s. Mem. Am. Assn. Petroleum Geologists (cert. petroleum geologist), Dallas Geol. Soc., Dallas Geneal. Soc., Sigma Xi (hon.). Methodist. Clubs: DAR (vice regent Benjamin Lyon chpt., 1955-57, acting regent 1956-57, regent 1983-85, vice-chmn. 93d Continental Congress Spl. Services Com.), Soc. New Eng. Women (rec. sec. Tex. Colony), Tex. State Soc. DAR, Huguenot Soc. of Founders of Manakin (Tex. Br.), Ariel, Denton Panhellenic, Delta Zeta. Condr. research profl. fields and local history; contbr. articles to various publs. Home and Office: 820 Hillcrest Denton TX 76201

PETERSON, JANIS ELLEN, publishing company executive; b. Lansing, Ill., Mar. 26, 1950; d. William H. and Mildred (Freytag) Woods Peterson. Student Columbia U., Chgo., 1974-77, Loyola U., 1979. Sec., Atlantic Richfield/Sinclair Co., Chgo., 1969-71; sec. Playboy Mag., Chgo., 1971-80, asst. promotion mgr., 1980-82, nat. promotion mgr., 1982—. Mem. Nat. Assn. Female Execs. Democrat. Office: Playboy Mag 919 N Michigan Ave Chicago IL 60611

PETERSON, JEANNE LOUISE, lawyer; b. Washington, Apr. 21, 1945; d. Carl W. and Olive M. (Foerster) Tiller; m. John E. Peterson, Sept. 14, 1968 (div. Apr. 1983); children—Kristin, Ian, Karin. B.A. in History, Kalamazoo Coll., 1966; M.A. in African History, U. Edinburgh (Scotland), 1967; J.D. cum laude, Mich. State U., 1980. Bar: Mich. 1980. Acting head history dept. Milton Margai Tchrs. Coll., Freetown, Sierra Leone, 1971-73; lectr. history dept. U. Sierra Leone, Freetown, 1973-75; cons., tchr. Dickinson-Iron Counties Head Start Program, Iron Mountain, Mich., 1975-76; atty. Mich. State Housing Devel. Authority, Lansing, 1980—. Trustee Grand Ledge Bd. Edn. (Mich.), 1982-83, v.p., 1983-84, pres., 1984-85. Mem. ABA, Mich. Bar Assn., Women Lawyers Assn. Mich. Democrat. Home: 6627 Mt Hope Hwy Grand Ledge MI 48837 Office: Mich State Housing Devel Authority 401 S Washington Sq Lansing MI 48933

PETERSON, JEANNIE ELLEN, association executive; b. Traverse City, Mich., Feb. 18, 1940; d. Paulus E. Peterson and Ellen Rebecca (Glommen) Peterson Johnson; B.S. in Journalism, Northwestern U.-Ill., 1962, M.S. in Journalism, 1963. Freelance travel writer, 1963-71; asst. editor Ambio, Internat. Environ. Jour., Royal Swedish Acad. Scis., Stockholm, 1972-77, editor-in-chief, 1978-81; dep. chief info. and external relations UN Fund for Population, N.Y.C., 1981-85, sr. info. policy officer Fund Population Activities, 1985-86, dep. rep., sr. adviser population, Manila, 1986—; dir. pub. info. Ctr. Consequences of Nuclear War, Washington, 1984—; mem. adv. com. U.S. Nat. Acad. Scis. Inst. Medicine Cont. Med. Implications of Nuclear War, 1985. Editor: The Aftermath: The Human and Ecological Consequences of Nuclear War, 1983. Recipient awards San Francisco Advt. Art Dirs. Club Show, 1968, Los Angeles Advt. Art Dirs. Club Show, 1968, Am. Advt. Fedn. Competition, 1969. Mem. Swedish Assn. Sci. Journalism (chmn. organizing com. 1980). Home: 333 E 49th St Apt 10-L New York NY 10017

PETERSON, JIMMIE RUTH, savs. and loan exec.; b. Tenaha, Tex., Jan. 7, 1922; d. Fred Sue and Jimmie Jewell (Currie) Stillwell; student Garner Bus. Sch. and Inst. Fin. Edn., New Orleans, 1974-75; m. Oscar Isidore Peterson, Dec. 15, 1941; 1 son, Fred Stillwell. With Central Savs. and Loan Assn., New Orleans, 1950—, loan clk., cashier, 1950-66, asst. v.p., 1966-71, v.p., 1971-73, exec. v.p., 1973-74, pres., 1974-78, dir., 1971—, chmn. bd. dirs., 1978-81, cons., 1981—. Tchr., St. Bernard United Meth. Ch., 1955-75; cubs den mother Pack 277 New Orleans Area council Boy Scouts Am., Chalmette, La., 1960-69; mem. Urban League Task Force, New Orleans. Mem. Home Builders Assn. Greater New Orleans (dir., 1978-81; dir. Ladies Aux. 1979; recipient Spike award 1979, 80, Spikette award 1979), New Orleans Realtors (dir. Women's Council 1979), Internat. House (World Trade Center, New Orleans), U.S. League of Savs. and Loan Assns., La. State League Savs. Assns., League of Savs. and Loan-Homestead Assn. Met. New Orleans, Greater New Orleans Exec. Assn., Inst. Fin. Edn. Democrat. Clubs: Carolyn Park Garden (Chalmette), Pandora Carnival (New Orleans), Order Eastern Star, Daus. of Desert, Daus. of Nile, Jerusalem Temple Clownettes. First woman to serve on bd. dirs. Central Savs. and Loan Assn. and on bd. of Home Builders Assn. Greater New Orleans; winner nat. and local flower shows. Office: 710 Canal St New Orleans LA 70130

PETERSON, JOANNA BRISTOL, cookie company executive; b. Long Beach, Calif., Oct. 4, 1946; d. Charles David and Marilyn (Foster) Bristol; m. Richard L. Peterson, Jan. 2, 1976 (div. Oct. 1983). A.A., Foothill Jr. Coll., 1968, Probate paralegal Hutchinson, Black, Boulder, Colo., 1970-73; real state broker Peterson Real Estate, Vail, Colo., 1978—; pres., owner Cookies Unltd., Denver, 1978 . Mem. adv. bd. Old Town Square, Fort Collins, Colo., 1985—; vol. Vail Ski Museum, 1977, Eagle Valley Arts Council, Vail, 1977. Home and Office: 500 Monroe St Denver CO 80206

PETERSON, JUDITH ELIZABETH, educator, mgmt. cons.; b. White Plains, N.Y., Mar. 25, 1946; d. Leroy and Etta (Tate) Peterson; B.A., Utica Coll., Syracuse U., 1968; M.Ed., U. Mass., 1972, postgrad., 1972-76. Tchr. French, Whitesboro Jr. High Sch., Whitesboro, N.Y., 1968-71; exec. sec. Five Coll. Black Studies Exec. Com., Amherst, Mass., 1974-76; cons. Aetna Life and Casualty, Hartford, Conn., 1977-78, sr. cons., 1978-80, adminstr., 1980; 2d v.p. Chase Manhattan Bank, N.Y.C., 1980—; youth motivation task force cons. Nat. Alliance Bus., 1980—. First v.p. NAACP, Amherst, 1976. W. K. Kellogg Found. fellow, 1973-74; Ford Exec. Leadership Program, fellow, 1972-73; Nat. Fellowships Fund fellow, 1973-74. Mem. AAUW, Am. Soc. Tng. and Devel., Human Resources Planning Soc., Nat. Assn. Female Execs. (network dir.), Urban League. Home: 60 Lawn Ave #40 Stamford CT 06902 Office: 80 Pine St 20th Floor New York NY 10081

PETERSON, KIMBERLY ANN, service organization communications executive; b. Chgo., Apr. 10, 1959; d. John Lowell and Carol Celene (Hajicek) Bender; m. Douglas Richard Peterson, Nov. 28, 1981. B.A. in Communications, Wartburg Coll., 1981; student U. No. Iowa, 1986—. Reporter, editor sta. KIMT-TV, Mason City, Iowa, 1981; anchor, reporter sta. KXEL/KOKZ, Waterloo, Iowa, 1981-83; dir. office of info. Hawkeye Region-Hawkeye chpt. ARC, Waterloo, 1983—, author-editor-graphics ann. report, 1984-85. Editor, graphic designer: AIDS edn. package Understanding Our Fears, 1985. Vol. pub. relations Family Service League, other non-profit agys., Waterloo, 1983—; vol. fundraising sta. KUNI-KHKE, NPR affiliate, Cedar Falls, Iowa, 1984—. Recipient 1st Place award ARC, 1985 2d Place award, 1986. Mem. Nat. Assn. Female Execs., Soc. Collegiate Journalists, Networkers-Waterloo Women's Group, Women in Communications. Republican. Avocations: horseback riding, freelance writing, dancing, photography, audio/visual prodns. Home: 404 Randall Waterloo IA 50701 Office: Blood Services Dept Hawkeye Region Chpt ARC 2530 University Ave Waterloo IA 50701

PETERSON, LESLIE ANN, lawyer; b. St. Louis, July 20, 1957; d. Harold August and Mary Estelle (Shelton) Peterson. B.A. summa cum laude, St. Louis U., 1978, M.A. in Pub. Adminstrn., 1983, J.D., 1982. Bar: Mo. 1982, Ill. 1983, U.S. Dist. Ct. (we. dist.) Mo. 1982, U.S. Dist. Ct. (no. dist.) Ill. 1983. Leasing agt. Lindell Towers, St. Louis, 1980-81; asst. to solicitor Dunn & Baker Law Firm, Devon, Exeter, Eng., 1981; adminstrv. aide to city mgr. Govt. of University City (Mo.), 1982; atty. Thomas C. O'Brien, Ltd., Chgo., 1983-84, Leake, Esposito & Heuel, Chgo., 1984—; research asst. St. Louis U. Law Sch., 1981. St. Louis U. Academic scholar, 1978. Mem. ABA, Ill. State Bar Assn., Mo. State Bar Assn., Chgo. Bar Assn., Bar Assn. Met. St. Louis, Phi Beta Kappa, Alpha Sigma Nu Jesuit, Pi Sigma Alpha, Phi Alpha Theta (vice justice 1981-82). Roman Catholic. Clubs: Student Government Association (pre-law rep. 1977-78) (St. Louis). Home: 151 N Michigan Ave Apt 2319 Chicago IL 60601 Office: 79 W Monroe Suite 1010 Chicago IL 60603

PETERSON, LISA JESSICA, human resources executive; b. Chgo., Nov. 24, 1959; d. Roman Kolkowicz and Helene (Can) Molstad; m. Daniel James Peterson, May 5, 1985. B.A. in Polit. Sci., UCLA, 1981; M.Sc. in Personnel Mgmt., London Sch. Econs., 1983. Personnel asst. E.B.I., Santa Monica, Calif., 1977-81; tng. dir. Bullocks Dept. Stores, Los Angeles, 1981-82; human resources adminstr. Commuter Transp. Services, Los Angeles, 1984-85; human resources mgr. SONY Corp. Am., Compton, Calif., 1985—. Mem. Am. Soc. Personnel Adminstrs., ASTD, Am. Compensation Assn., Internat. Assn. Personnel Women. Democrat. Jewish. Clubs: Am. Friends of L.S.E., Brentwood-Palisades Chorale. Avocation: tennis. Office: SONY Corp of Am 700 W Artesia Blvd Compton CA 90220

PETERSON, LOIS IRENE, transportation company executive; b. Falun, Kans., Mar. 25, 1935; d. Robert Theodore and M. LaVerne (Oleen) Dauer; m. Gerald L. Peterson, Mar. 13, 1955 (dec. May 1971); children—Dennis G., Linda Diane Peterson Johnson, Barbara Lynn Peterson Denny. Pub. Acct., Bell & Howell Internat. Acctg., Chgo., 1974; student Brown-Mackie Coll., Salina, Kans., 1983. Co-owner, Gerald's IGA Store, Falun, Kans., 1960-66, Gerald's Trucking Service, Falun, 1966-71; pres., 1972—; sec., treas. Wheat State Carriers Inc., Salina, Kans., 1985—; asst. office mgr. Eldon's IGA Stores, Inc., McPherson, Kans., 1966-71; asst. office mgr. Smoky Hill Feedlot, Inc., Falun, 1971—; speaker in field. Treas., Rural Water Dist. #1, Kans., 1972-75; bd. dirs. Falun Drainage Assn., 1979. Mem. Kans. Motor Carriers Assn. (dir. 1979-82, 84—, Safety awards 1977, 78, 79, 80, 82, 83, 84), Am. Trucking Assn. (state del. 1980-82). Avocations: photography, travel, reading, sewing. Home: Box 8 Falun KS 67442 Office: Gerald's Trucking Service Falun KS 67442

PETERSON, MARCIA WRAITH, nursing adminstr.; b. Robinson, Ill., Aug. 5, 1953; d. George Bernard and Helen (Wheeler) Wraith; R.N., Harris Coll. Nursing, 1977; B.S.N., Tex. Chrisitan U., 1977; m. Timothy Alan Peterson, July 6, 1975; children—Mindy Anne, Shawn Michael. Staff nurse labor and delivery Harris Hosp. Meth., Fort Worth, 1977-78; dir. med. services Lena Pope Home, Fort Worth, 1978; coordinator maternity edn. Harris Hosp. Meth., Fort Worth, 1978-80; nurse adminstr. Edna Gladney Home, Fort Worth, 1980—. CPR instr. trainer Am. Heart Assn.; first aid instr. ARC. Mem. Nurses Assn. of Am. Coll. Ob-Gyn., Tex. Hosp. Assn., Tex. Soc. Hosp. Nursing Service Adminstrs., Tex. Soaring Assn., Soaring Soc. Am. Office: Edna Gladney Home 2308 Hemphill St Fort Worth TX 76110

PETERSON, MARGARET MARY, radiation therapist, consultant; b. Newark, July 25, 1948; d. Andrew Joseph and Margaret Mary P.; student in X-ray tech. USPHS Hosp., S.I., N.Y., 1966-68; student in radiation tech. Los Angeles County/U.So. Calif. Med. Center, 1969-70; A.A. in Bus. Adminstrn., San Mateo City Coll., 1978, U. Phoenix, 1982. Staff technician, dosimetrist Los Angeles County/U. So. Calif. Med. Center, 1969-71; dosimetrist City of Hope Nat. Med. Center, Duarte, Calif., 1971-74; radiation therapy technologist So. Bay Hosp., Redondo Beach, Calif., 1974-76; dept. mgr., dosimetrist Peninsula Hosp. and Med. Center, Burlingame, Calif., 1976-81; clin. cons. ATC Med. Technology, Sunnyvale, Calif., 1981-82; locum tenens technologist, 1982-86; intern Hayward Edn. Fund, 1986; cons. in field. Supervisory com. Peninsula Hosp. Credit Union, 1979-83, mgmt. steering com., 1980-81, vice chmn., 1981. Grantee, State of Calif., 1980-83; lic., cert. radiology and radiation therapy. Mem. Am. Assn. Med. Dosimetrists (pres., 1979-81), Assn. Univ. Radiol. Technologists, Am. Soc. Radiol. Technologists, Calif. Soc. Radiol. Technologists (joint rev. com. therapeutic radiologists com. on tech. and edn. com. Am. Assn. Med. Dosimetrists), No. Calif. Soc. Radiation Therapy Technologists (pres.). Home: 645 Topaz St Redwood City CA 94061

PETERSON, MARJORIE ANN, communications consultant; educator; b. Sioux Falls, S.D., Aug. 10, 1940; d. Charles Henry and Marion Mattie (Duis) Brother; m. Wayne Roger Erickson, Nov. 1960 (div.); 1 son, David Charles; m. 2d, David Glenn Peterson, Aug. 6, 1977. B.A. in Speech Communication, Bethel Coll., 1970; postgrad. in pub. adminstrn., U. Okla., 1981—. Instr. speech and debate Bethel Coll., St. Paul, 1970-72; freelance cons., writer, audio-visual producer, St. Paul, 1972-80; tchr. adult edn. Temple U., European div., 1981-83; organizational devel. cons. U.S. Army, Ansbach, W.Ger., 1983; master tchr. Big Bend Community Coll., European div., 1983-84; conf. planner, publs. editor Nat. Assn. Alcoholism and Drug Abuse Counselors, 1984—; tech. writer, editor Jaycor, 1985—. Bd. dirs., treas. Employment Support Ctr., Washington, 1984—. Author: How to Finish Your Own Home, 1979; contbr. articles to profl. jours. Dir., sec. People Inc., St. Paul, 1974-80; commr., task force chmn. Planning Commn., Arden Hills, Minn., 1976-80; chmn. Bd. Appeals, Arden Hills, 1974-76; active Park and Recreation Com., Arden Hills, 1974-76; elder Central Presbyn. Ch., St. Paul, 1975-79, New York Ave Presbyn. Ch., Washington, 1986—; gov., speaker, discussion group chmn. Am. Women's Activities, Germany, 1982-84, area conf. planner, 1982-84. Recipient Ansbach Mil. Community Exceptional Service award, 1984. Mem. Women in Communications, Inc. (chmn. audio-visual seminar 1978), Am. Soc. Pub. Adminstrs., Pi Kappa Delta (spl. distinction 1970). Republican. Presbyterian. Address: 943A S Rolfe Arlington VA 22204

PETERSON, MARY LOUISE, trucking company executive; b. New Orleans, Dec. 20, 1940; d. Edmond Adam's and Dorethea (Fletcher) Peterson; children—DeVon Daniel, Danita Daniel, Michelle Johnson, Mitchel Johnson. Owner, mgr. Agee's 24 Hour Moving & Storage Co., Los Angeles, also All Day All Night Moving & Storage Inc. Home: 1837 S Bronson St Los Angeles CA 90019 Office: Agee's 24 Hour Moving & Storage Co 806 W 47th St Los Angeles CA 90037

PETERSON, MILDRED OTHMER, lecturer, photographer, writer, librarian, civic leader, world traveller; b. Omaha, Oct. 19, 1902; d. Frederick George and Freda Darling (Snyder) Othmer; student U. Nebr., U. Iowa, U. Chgo., Northwestern U., Am. U. Switzerland, 1985; m. Howard R. Peterson, Aug. 25, 1923 (dec. Feb. 1970). Asst., Central High Sch. Library, Omaha, 1915-19, Tech. High Sch. Library, 1919-20, U. Nebr. Library, 1921-23; dir. public relations and gen. asst. Des Moines Public Library, 1928-35; broadcaster weekly book programs WHO and other Iowa radio stas.; columnist, writer Mid-West News Syndicate, Des Moines Register and Tribune, editor Book Marks, 1929-35; editor Adelphean of Alpha Delta Pi, 1938-39; writer and spl. asst. ALA, 1935—, Chgo. Tribune, 1941—; lectr. on travel, fgn. jewelry and internat. relations, 1940—; lectr. S.S. Rotterdam of Holland Am. Line, 1971, Illini Girls State, 1975; del. 1st Assembly Librarians of Americas, Washington, 1947; lectr. throughout U.S. Exec. Services Corp. Chgo., 1983. Chgo. chmn. India Famine Relief, 1943; a founder, pres. Pan. Am. Bd. Edn., 1955-58; founder, pres. Internat. Visitors Center, 1954-58, life bd. dirs., 1986; Chgo. rep. State Dept. Founding Conf. on Community Services to Fgn. Visitors, Washington, 1957; mem. Mayor's Com. on Chgo. Beautiful, cited by Chgo. Sun and Ill. Adult Edn. Council; bd. dirs. YWCA; mem. 75th, 100th and 110th anniversary coms. Hyde Park Union Ch., also mem. mission bd., council; bd. dirs. Friends of Channel 11, PBS, 1982—. Recipient world understanding merit award Chgo. Council Fgn. Relations, 1955; named Woman of Yr. for U.S. and Can., Alpha Delta Pi, 1955; Disting. Service award Pan-Am Bd. Edn., 1966, also founders award, 1968; Uruguayan medal, 1952; Internat. Eloy Alfaro medal, 1952, medal Order of Carlos Manuel de Cespedes, 1956 (Cuba); medal Order of Vasco Nunez de Balboa (Panama), 1956; Internat. Friendship award Girl Scouts of Philippines, 1971; Simon Bolivar trophy Fedn. Latin Am. Orgns., 1976; Outstanding Service award Nat. Council for Community Service to Internat. Visitors, 1977; named Woman of Yr., Friends Chgo. Sch. and Workshop for the Retarded, 1975; Disting. Service award U. Nebr., 1955; named disting. alumnae U. Nebr., 1983. Fellow Am. Internat. Acad. (life); mem. Nat. Council Women U.S., Pan-Am Bd. Edn., U.S. Capitol, Ill., Nebr., Chgo., Hyde Park hist. socs., Chgo. Natural History Mus., Citizenship Council Met. Chgo., Oriental Inst., Chgo. Mus. Sci. and Industry, Am. Heritage Council, ALA, Ill. Library Assn., Friends Chgo. Public Library, Chgo. Opera Guild, Chgo. Hort. Soc., Am. Security Council, Lincoln Park Zool. Soc., Mus. Contemporary Art, Crossroads Student Center, Hyde Park-Kenwood Community Conf., Internat. House Assn. (dir., v.p.), Japan-Am. Soc., Soc. Woman Geographers (chpt. pres.; nat. v.p.), Ill. Partners of Ams. (gov.'s com. Sao Paulo, Brazil), Council Fgn. Relations (speakers bur.), Pan Am. Council (a founder, disting. service award 1966, v.p. 1984), Library Internat. Relations (consular ball com. 18 yrs.), U. Nebr. Alumni Assn. (past pres. local chpts., Disting. Achievement award), U. Nebr. Found., Chgo. Symphony Orch. Soc., Chgo. Art Inst. (Disting. Service award 1979), U. Chgo. Service League (dir.), Am. Legion Aux. (state bds. Iowa and Ill.), AAUW, LWV, Children's Benefit League, United Negro Coll. Fund Bd., Renaissance Soc., Peruvian Arts Soc., U.S.-China People's Friendship Assn., Hispanic Soc. Chgo., Chgo. Acad. Scis. (woman's bd.) Chgo. Chamber Orch. Assn., John G. Shedd Soc., Internat. Platform Assn., Friends of Parks, Chgo. Lung Assn. (bd. dirs. 1986), Internat. Platform Assn., Cook County Hosp. Aux., Grant Park Concert Soc., English Speaking Union, Internat. Fedn. Library Assns. (mem. local com. for Chgo. meeting 1985), Alpha Delta Pi (past pres. local alumnae chpts., nat. bd. dirs.), Xi Delta. Clubs: Order Eastern Star, College, Quadrangle, Ill. Athletic, U. Chgo. Dames, Iowa Authors, Lakeside Lawn Bowling, Hyde Park Neighborhood, Travelers' Century. Contbr. articles to newspapers, periodicals, encys. and yearbooks. Visited and photographed over 230 fng. countries; travels and lectures on fgn. countries; unofcl. attendant numerous internat. confs. Address: 5834 Stony Island Ave Chicago IL 60637

PETERSON, NANCY ANN, real estate broker; b. Fargo, N.D., Sept. 18, 1947; d. Simar Kristian and Rhoda Alice (Anderson) Nelson; m. John William Peterson, Oct. 20, 1967 (dec. Aug. 1979); 1 child, Dauvin John. B.S., Moorhead State U., 1979; student Real Conservatorio, Madrid, Spain, 1981. Cert. comml. investment mgr. Nat. Bd. Realtors. Owner, pres. Circle Realtors Inc., Fargo, 1971—. Bd. dirs. Plains Art Mus., Moorhead, Minn., 1983—; treas. O'Rourke-Plains Mus., Moorhead, 1984-85. Mem. Nat. Assn. Realtors, Fargo-Moorhead Bd. Realtors, Women's Council Realtors (pres. 1977), Fargo-Moorhead Home Builders, Linden Assoc. Lodge: Zonta. Avocations: classical guitar; fishing; scuba diving; skiing. Office: Circle Realtors Inc 1220 Main Ave Fargo ND 58103

PETERSON, NANCY SANDERS, special tool manufacturing company executive; b. Nashville, July 2; d. Theodore Roosevelt and Alice Gray (Batey) Sanders; m. John Louis Peterson, Oct. 24, 1953 (dec. Sept. 1979); children—Christine P. Mitchell, Diane P. Edwards, John L., Jr., Angela P. Graham, Gretchen P. Herbert, Linda Elaine. Student Siena Coll. Vice pres. Peterson Tool Co., Inc., Nashville, 1969-79, pres., 1979—; dir., v.p. Sanders Transfer Storage Co., Inc., Nashville, 1970—. Chmn. Mayoral Task Force, Nashville, 1983—; bd. dirs. Operation Chem. Awareness in Nashville, 1983—, APTA Bellemeade Mansion, 1985—, Mid-Tenn. chpt. Nat. Kidney Found., 1985—. Named Career Woman of Yr., Germaine Monteil/Castner Knott Co., Nashville, 1984. Mem. Women in Bus. Inc. (mem. adv. bd. 1984), Pvt. Industry Council (bd. dirs. 1984—; mem. exec. com. 1985—), Nashville Area C. of C., Nashville Symphony Guild, Friends of Cheekwood. Republican. Roman Catholic. Clubs: Cedar Creek (Mount Juliet, Tenn.) (bd. mem. 1979-83); Nashville Yacht (commodore 1981-82), 100 (bd. dirs. 1980—), Nat. Commodore (capt. 1981—) (Nashville). Avocations: dancing; boating; spectator sports. Office: Peterson Tool Co Inc PO Box 100830 739 Fesslers Ln Nashville TN 37210

PETERSON, PEGGY ELIZABETH, educational consultant; b. Dayton, Ohio, Sept. 24, 1935; d. Reginald Curp and Ila Gussie (Roush) Curp Costello, m. Guy F. Hostetler, Mar. 3, 1957 (div. Feb. 1970); children—Keely, Todd; m. James H. Peterson, Aug. 6, 1974; children—Brownie, Michael, Ginger. B.A., Ariz. State U., 1965; M.A., 1969; Ed.D. in Ednl. Leadership, Nova U., 1985. Dir. Montessori Schs., Anchorage, 1961-66; elem. childhood liaison Ariz. Dept. Edn. and Edn. Commn. of the States, Colo., 1971-73; elem. childhood dir. Nueva Learning Ctr., Hillsborough, Calif., 1973-74; pres. Expanding Devel., Inc., Evergreen, Colo., 1975—; pvt. ednl. cons., 40 states and 7 countries, 1974—; lead ednl. cons. Sci. Research Assocs./IBM, Western states, 1974-82; fed. project dir. Title 3 on 7 Indian Reservations, Ariz., 1969-72. Author: Modern Montessori, 1975 (Design award 1975), Staff Development, 1983, The Teacher Is Not a Myth, 1984; co-author lang. program Inupiaq for NW Alaska Arctic Sch., 1980-81. Mem. Assn. Curriculum Dirs., Assn. Sch. Adminstrs., NEA, Ariz. Edn. Assn., Classroom Tchrs. Assn. (pres. 1969-70). Democrat. Roman Catholic. Home: PO Box 4185 Cave Creek AZ 85321 Office: Expanding Devel Inc PO Box 2226 Evergreen CO 80439

PETERSON, PRISCILLA JEAN RUNNELS, company executive, employment and corporate recruiter; b. Manchester, N.H., Oct. 25, 1940; d. Larned Ernest and Josephine W. (Mills) Runnels; m. Gideon A. Robarge, Feb. 11, 1958 (div. 1964); children—Ronald Gideon, Anne Carin; m. John Arthur Peterson, Apr. 3, 1964; children—Amy Dawn, John Arthur, II. Student Mich. State U., 1960-73. Adminstrn. asst. Mgmt. Recruiters, Lansing, Mich., 1974-75; mgr. OfficeMates 5, Lansing, 1975-77; gen. mgr. Mgmt. Recruiters-OfficeMates, Lansing, 1977-78, owner, pres., 1978—; pres. Ronnoco Assocs., Inc., Lansing, 1978—; mem. State Mich. Bd. Licensing and Regulations, Lansing, 1981—. Pres. bd. dirs. Jr. Achievement, Lansing, 1984; div. chmn. Capital Area United Way, Lansing, 1985; mem. corp. gift com. Lansing Gen. Hosp., 1984; precinct capt. Ingham County Republicans, Lansing, 1977-78. Recipient Citation award Lansing Police Dept., 1969; Leadership award Nat. Bus. Leadership Conf., 1985. Mem. Nat. Assn. Career Women (founder 1979, Career Woman Yr. award 1985, pres. Lansing chpt. 1979-81, pres. nat. bd. 1983—), Adminstrv. Mgmt. Soc. (v.p. 1976-79), Mich. Assn. Personnel Cons.s (ethics com. 1977-80), Lansing C. of C. (com. chmn. 1975-85). Republican. Avocations: golf; traveling; writing. Home: 1971 Heatherton Dr Holt MI 48842 Office: Mgmt Recruiters-Officemates 5 920 Long Blvd Suite 15 Lansing MI 48910

PETERSON, SARAH JEAN, mfg. co. employee benefits mgr.; b. Lamberton, Pa., Nov. 21, 1926; d. Harry Franklin and Ethel (Hails) Momeyer; student Drake Bus. Sch., 1944-46; m. Richard J. Peterson, Dec. 7, 1979; children by previous marriage—Andrew John, Francis John, Mary John. Sec., John & John, Uniontown, Pa., 1944-49, Mut. of N.Y., Plainfield, N.J., 1957-59; sec. Mack Trucks, Inc., Plainfield and Bridgewater, N.J., 1960-73, supr. personnel services, Bridgewater, 1973-77, mgr. personnel, Allentown, 1977-79, corp. mgr. employee benefits, 1979—. Industry rep. Somerset County (N.J.) Adv. Council, 1966-67; mem. Employer's Adv. Council, Allentown, Pa., 1977-79; mem. Lehigh Valley (Pa.) Manpower Assn., 1977-79; mem. Mayor's Council for Employment of Youth, Allentown, 1977-79; bd. dirs. Women's Correctional Inst., Clinton, N.J., 1974-77; loaned exec. United Way of Somerset Valley, 1975; bd. dirs. Sheltered Workshops, 1975-79, Valley Youth House, Bethlehem, Pa., 1979—. Mem. Community Indsl. Relations Orgn., Allentown C. of C. Personnel Forum. Clubs: Suburban Women's, Beaver Brook Country, Arrowhead Lake Country. Office: Mack Trucks Inc 2100 Mack Blvd Allentown PA 18105

PETERSON, SHARON LEE, school psychologist, consultant; b. Durand, Wis., July 26, 1946; d. George T. and Bonnie Mae (Rooney) Hall; m. John D. Stauffacher, Nov. 26, 1966 (div. Feb. 1977); children—Megan Anne, Alison Hall; m. Steven J. Peterson, Feb. 8, 1979 (dec. Dec. 1981). B..A., U. Wis.-Eau Claire, 1972, M.S. Edn., 1976; Ph.D., U. Iowa, 1986. Cert. sch. psychologist, Wis., Iowa, N.J., Pa. Sch. Psychologist Coop. Edn. Service Agy. 3, Gillett, Wis., 1975-76, Keystone Area Edn. Agy., Dubuque, Iowa, 1976-84, Haddonfield Sch., N.J., 1985—; freelance cons., Mt. Laurel, N.J., 1985—. Sec. bd. dirs. Dubuque Art Assn., 1983-85; cons. Battered Women's Program, Dubuque, 1983-85. Mem. Am. Psychol. Assn., Nat. Assn. Sch. Psychologists, Iowa Sch. Psychologists Assn., Iowa Assn. Alternative Schs., N.J. Assn. Sch. Psychologists, Nat. Assn. Exec. Women, Phi Delta Kappa. Avocations: reading, swimming, skiing. Home: 101 Holly Pkwy Williamstown NJ 08094 Office: Haddonfield Sch Dist Kings Hwy Haddonfield NJ 08054

PETERSON, SHIRLEY VIOLET, state agency administrator; b. Edgeley, N.D., June 16, 1936; d. Carl E. and Dorothy (Schnell) Fischer; m. Curt Peterson; children—Shane, Chad. B.S. in Elem. Edn., Jamestown Coll. (N.D.), 1956; M.S. in Edn. Adminstrn. and Communications, Moorhead State U. (Minn.), 1965. Dir. gifted and talented Fargo Sch. Dist. (N.D.), 1974-77; pub. affairs dir. Greater N.D. Assn., Fargo, 1977-81; dir. bus. challenge Dickinson State Coll. (N.D.), 1977-80; exec. dir. Job Service N.D., Bismarck, 1981—; vice chairperson Interstate Conf. of Employment Security Agys. Data Processing Com., Washington, 1983—; mem. Def. Adv. Com. on Women in Services, Washington, 1983—. State chmn. Internat. Women's Yr., 1975; chmn. N.D. Women's Employment Conf. Recipient Woman of the Yr. award Fargo YWCA, 1981; Disting. Alumni award Moorhead State U., 1981; Women in Govt. award U.S. Jaycee Women, 1983. Republican. Lutheran. Office: Job Service North Dakota 1000 E Divide Ave Bismarck ND 58502

PETERSON, STEPHANIE CRAIG MCGINNIS, nurse, nursing educational administrator; b. Topeka, Dec. 30, 1945; d. Joseph Edward and Marjean Elaine (Meyer) McGinnis; m. Donald Stowe Peterson, Oct. 1, 1966 (div.). Diploma Stormont-Vail Sch. Nursing, 1966; B.S. in Health Arts, Coll. St. Francis, 1982. R.N., Kans., Mo. Instr. med. and surg. nursing Stormont Vail Sch. Nursing, Topeka, 1967-70; supr. surg. nursing Newman Meml. Hosp., Emporia, Kans., 1970-73; staff nurse Meml. Hosp., Topeka, 1966-67, inservice instr., 1976-77, spl. projects coordinator, 1977-78, asst. supt. nurses, 1973-75; asst. dir. edn. Spelman Meml. Hosp., Smithville, Mo., 1979, staff nurse operating room, 1984-85; nurse emergency dept. Allentown Osteo. Med. Ctr., Pa., 1985—. Lectr., cons. in field. Mem. Am. Nurses Assn., Nat. League for Nursing, Am. Assn. Critical Care Nurses, Kans. State Nurses Assn., Am. Soc. Healthcare Educators and Trainers. Home: RD 2 Box 2058A Bangor PA 18013 Office: Allentown Osteo Med Ctr 1736 Hamilton Allentown PA

PETERSON, SUSAN ANN, film producer, media trainer, public relations consultant; b. Rhinelander, Wis., Aug. 21, 1945; d. Harold Carl and Violet Anna Maria (Engstrom) P. B.A., Denison U. Reporter Sta. WCCO-TV, Mpls., 1968-70, Sta. WRC-TV, Washington, 1970-79; fgn. corr. CBS News, London, 1979-80; on air corr. NBC News, Washington, 1980-83; owner, pres. Susan Peterson Prodns., Washington, 1983—. Recipient Excellence in Journalism award Nat. Assn. for Home Care, 1982. Mem. Am. Women in Radio and TV, Women in Communications, Women in Film. Office: 1825 K St NW Washington DC 20006

PETERSON, VICKI JENKINS, clinical social worker; b. Wichita, Kans., Feb. 22, 1949; d. William Harvard and Emelyne Bess (Gumm) Jenkins; m. Richard Herbert Peterson, Oct. 4, 1980; children—Erin, Michael, Chris. B.A., Duke U., 1971; M.S.W., U. N.C., 1980. Clin. social worker Western Carolina Ctr., Morganton, N.C., 1975-80, coordinator child and family services, 1980-83; exec. dir. Hospice Burke County, Morganton, 1983-84; dir. mktg. Mountain MicroSystems, Morganton, 1984—; instr. Western Piedmont Community Coll., 1985—; cons. Morganton Area Psychologists and Attys., 1982-84. Steering com. Burke Soup Kitchen, Morganton, 1985—; pres. bd. dirs. 1st Presbyn. Preschool Program, Morganton, 1985—; pres. Durham Rape Crisis Ctr., N.C., 1975; lay reader St. Marys Episc. Ch., Morganton, 1983—. Named Outstanding Young Woman in Am. 1981, Outstanding Staff Mem. Western Carolina Ctr. 1982. Mem. Nat. Assn. Social Workers, Am. Assn. Mental Deficiency, N.C. Assn. Social Workers Mental Health, Assn. Retarded Citizens. Democrat. Episcopalian. Avocations: pastry chef; reading; travel; radio broadcasting. Home: 112 Holly Pl Morganton NC 28655 Office: Mountain Micro Systems 407 E Union St Morganton NC 28655

PETERSON, YVONNE ADAMS, educator; b. Logansport, La., Nov. 6, 1949; d. Less Lee and Beatrice (Johnson) Adams; m. Riley Peterson, Jr., July 27, 1974; 1 child, Rashida Shani. B.S., Grambling State U., 1971; M.Ed., Tex. So. U., 1978; B. Mission Edn., Inter-Baptist Sem., 1981, M. Mission Edn., 1983, D. Mission Edn., 1984. Tchr. spl. edn. N. Forest Ind. Sch. Dist., Houston, 1971-77; homebound tchr. N. Forest Ind. Sch. Dist., 1978—; tchr. English, Inter-Bapt. Sem., Houston, 1980—; supr. YMCA, Houston, 1979-80; dir. Vocat. Bible Sch., Houston, 1982—. Active Friends of the Downtown Conv. Center, Houston, 1983, PTA, Houston, 1977—. Mem. NAACP, Sigma Gamma Rho. Democrat. Baptist. Address: 9610 Bean St Houston TX 77078

PETERSON-VITA, ELIZABETH ANN, psychologist; b. N.Y.C., Apr. 16, 1955; d. Donald Arthur and Adelphine Rose (Lippman) Peterson; m. James Paul Vita, June 10, 1978. B.A., NYU, 1975; M.A., L.I. U., 1977, Ph.D., 1984. Lic. psychologist, N.Y. Psychology intern Northport VA Med. Ctr., N.Y., 1978-79; clin. psychologist L.I. Cons. Ctr., Rego Park, N.Y., 1979-85; clin. psychologist J.F.K. Med. Ctr., Edison, N.J., 1980, Northport VA Med. Ctr., 1980-85; instr. in clin. psychiatry SUNY-Stony Brook, 1985—; staff psychologist South Oaks Hosp., Amityville, N.Y., 1985—; dir. internship tng. South Oaks Hosp., 1985—; cons. to psychology service Northport VA Med. Ctr., 1985—; pvt. practice psychology, Amityville and West Islip, N.Y., 1985—. Mem. Am. Psychol. Assn., N.Y. Neuropsychology Group, N.Y. Acad. Sci., N.Y. Soc. Clin. Psychologists, Nat. Register of Health Service Providers in Psychology. Presbyterian. Avocations: theatre; film arts; art history; creative writing. Home: 182-25 Wexford Terr Jamaica Estates NY 11432 Office: 400 Sunrise Hwy Amityville NY 11701 also 735 B Montauk Hwy West Islip NY 11795

PETILLO, LUCILLE KERSMARKI, musical instrument company executive, consultant; b. Neptune, N.J.; d. Charles George and Phyllis L. (Vecchione) Kersmarki; m. Phillip Joseph Petillo, June 21, 1971; children—Phillip, Stephen, Michael, David, Timothy. A.A., Monmouth U., W. Long Beach, N.J., 1966, B.S., 1968, M.S., 1970. Cert. tchr. 5th grade tchr. Woodmere Sch., Eatontown, N.J., 1968-76; exec. Phil-Lu Inc., Ocean, N.J., 1976-80, pres., 1980—; promoter, mgr. Phillip Petillo-Luthier, Ocean, 1976—; press agt. Petillo Guitar, Ocean, 1976—; cons. med., ednl. Phil-Lu Inc., Ocean, 1976—. Editor photographer Guitar Making, Guitar Player Mag., 1976—, Wood Binding, Music Trades, 1978-80, Neck Repairs, Musical Merchandise Review, 1978-80. Participant Little League, Ocean, St. Mary's Basketball, Ocean; Mem. Concerned Parents, N.Y. Zoological Soc., Mus. Nat. History. Mem. Monmouth Alumni Assn. Avocations: profl. singer, performer. Home and Office: Phil Lu Inc 1206 Herbert Ave Ocean NJ 07712

PETILLO, M. JOANN, analytical chemist, researcher; b. Balt., May 30, 1959; d. Frank and Carmen Marta (Fimiani) P. B.S. in Biology, Loyola Coll., Balt., 1981; postgrad. U. Balt. Analytical chemist Ecol. Analysts, Sparks, Md., 1982-83, Martin Marietta Corp., Balt., 1983-84; lab. mgr. Arundel Corp., Towson, Md., 1984—. Mem. Am. Concrete Inst., Soc. Applied Spectroscopy, Materials Research Soc., ASTM, Smithsonian Assocs., Nat. Assn. Female Execs. Democrat. Roman Catholic. Lodge: Sons of Italy. Avocations: jogging; raquetball; bicycling; piano. Home: 1541 Pickett Rd Lutherville MD 21093 Office: The Arundel Corp 6806 Greenspring Ave Baltimore MD 21209

PETKASH, RITA MARIE, county official; b. Binghamton, N.Y., Apr. 15, 1947; d. George Louis and Regina Marie (Stolarcyk) P.; m. Stuart Harmon Traub, Aug. 16, 1975 (div. Oct. 1981); 1 child, Tanna Nicole. B.S. in Edn., SUNY-Cortland, 1975. Asst. budget officer County of Cortland, N.Y., 1975-79, budget officer, 1979-80; fin. and devel. cons. Spencer-Fitts, Inc., Belchertown, Mass., 1980-82; dir. devel. Rehab. Services, Inc., Binghamton, N.Y., 1982-85; sr. planner for facilities and design County of Broome, N.Y., 1985—; home constrn./design cons., 1981—; fund raising cons. 1890 House, Cortland, 1981; adminstrv. asst. fund raising Broome Legal Assistance Corp., Binghamton, 1982-83. Democrat. Roman Catholic. Avocations: reading; home renovations; gardening; outdoor sports. Home: RD 1 Box 8A Harpursville NY 13787 Office: Broome County Planning Dept PO Box 1766 Binghamton NY 13902

PETKOFF, RUTH LINKSMAN, educator; b. Bklyn., Nov. 27, 1924; d. Morris and Miriam (Schiff) Linksman; B.A., L.I.U., 1946; M.A. in Ednl. Adminstrn., Fed. City Coll., Washington, 1975; Ed.D. in Ednl. Adminstrn., Va. Poly. Inst. and State U., 1984; m. Leonard Petkoff, Apr. 20, 1969; children—Marcy, Carrie. Contract adminstr. Linochine Products Co., N.Y.C., 1949-59; v.p. Boraca Corp., P.R., 1959-69; instr. lang. and culture, Seoul, Korea, 1969-71; cons. continuing edn. women Fed. City Coll., also U. Va., Falls Church, 1973-74; career counselor Washington Opportunities Women, 1973-75; career devel. coordinator Arlington (Va.) Career Center, 1974-76; supr. CETA Tng. Center, Arlington, 1975—; co-dir. Career Edn. Project Handicapped, 1975-76; lectr. vocat. rehab. Trinity Coll., Washington, 1978—; mem. Arlington Coalition Career Edn., 1979—; also Title IX Coordinating Com.; mem. vocat. com. Va. Mental Health and Mental Retardation Services Bd.; cons. in field Mem. Am. Vocat. Assn., Nat. Skill Center Adminstrs. Assn., Adult Edn. Assn., Nat. Assn. Female Execs., Nat. Employment and Tng. Assn., Va. Employment and Tng. Assn. (pres. 1981), Va. Vocat. Assn. (v.p. 1981), Arlington Bus. and Profl. Women, Women's Am. ORT. Author curriculum materials, papers in field. 22101 Office: 818 S Walter Reed Dr Arlington VA 22204

PETRANEK, BARBARA SUE, public relations exec.; b. Rochester, N.Y., Mar. 26, 1944; d. Milton and Thelma (Baker) Ergas; student U. Buffalo, 1963-64, U. Rochester, 1974-75; children—Lisa Faye, Erin Gayle, Jennifer Anne. Asst. dir. public relations Rochester/Monroe County chpt. ARC, Rochester, 1977-78, dir. public relations nat. capital div., Washington, 1978-80; mgr. press and publicity WRC-TV, NBC, Washington, 1980—. Mem. Women in Communications. Office: 4001 Nebraska Ave Washington DC 20016

PETRAS, CAROL-LYNN MARIE, insurance agent; b. St. Louis, May 30, 1951; d. Charles Joseph Howard and Rosella (Klein) Howard Mertz; m. Joseph William Petras, July 10, 1976; children—Joseph William, Caroline Joelle. B.A. in Psychology, St. Louis U., 1972, agy. mgmt. tng. cert. Tchr., Lindburgh Sch. Dist., St. Louis, 1972-77, Brentwood Sch. Dist., St. Louis, 1979-80; life underwriter Penn Mut., Phila., 1980-85; mgmt. assoc. Penn Mut., St. Louis, 1981-85; apptd. supr. Monarch St. Louis Agy., 1985, gen. agt., 1986—. Fund raiser Easter Seals Campaign, Mo. Assn. Life Underwriters for Old News Boys Local Charities, 1982; active Lindburgh Sch. Dist. Mothers Club and PTO, Regional Commerce and Growth Assn. Recipient Penn Mut. Pres.'s Club, Royal Blue, Top Club awards; award St. Louis Gen. Agts. and Mgrs. Assn., 1981. Mem. Nat. Assn. Life Underwriters, Mo. Life Underwriters, Monarch Key Club. Office: 1807 Park Suite 318 Saint Louis MO 63146

PETRAS, KATHLEEN ANN, emergency medical technician; b. Middletown, Conn., Mar. 17, 1958; d. Alois Francis and Arlene Gladys (Barrett) P. B.A., York Coll. Pa., 1980; student Greater Hartford Community Coll., 1985—. EMT, adminstr. Hunter's Meriden Ambulance Service, Conn., 1980-83; EMT/intermediate New Britain Emergency Med. Services, Inc., Conn., 1983—. Senatorial intern, Capitol Hill, Washington, 1975; vol. Middlesex Assn. Retarded Citizens, 1980—. Fellow Am. Heart Assn.; mem. Nat. Assn. Female Execs. Democrat. Methodist. Home: 33 Virginia Dr Middletown CT 06457 Office: New Britain Emergency Med Services 153 Arch St New Britain C0T 06051

PETRAS, KATHLEEN MARY SHAFER, surgical supply company executive; b. Chgo., Dec. 29, 1948; d. James Albert and Irene Jeanne (Yurcega) Shafer; m. Kenneth Allan Petras, Sept. 24, 1983. B.S. in Speech Edn., Northwestern U., 1970. Benefits counselor Hosp. Service Corp., Chgo., 1970-73; personnel rep. Am. V. Mueller div. Am. Hosp. Supply Corp., Chgo., 1973-74, inventory coordinator, 1974-77, product mgr., 1977-82, sr. product mgr. urology, 1982-83, market mgr.-cardiovascular, 1984—. Roman Catholic. Home: 6151 N Drake St Chicago IL 60659 Office: American V Mueller Div Baxter-Travenol Corp 6600 W Touhy Chicago IL 60648

PETREA, MARTA LYNNE MURRAY, industrial laboratory technician; b. Seminole, Okla., Nov. 21, 1953; d. Herbert Leroy and Mary Elizabeth (Wham) Murray; m. Robert Edward Petrea, May 8, 1971 (div. May 1976); 1 child, Micah Murray. Student Parkland Jr. Coll., 1976-77; B.S. in Biology, U. Houston, 1980. Sr. lab. technician Shell Devel. Co., Houston, 1980—. Republican. Presbyterian. Home: 15770 Bellaire St Apt 1110 Houston TX 77083 Office: Shell Devel Co Westhollow Research Center 3333 Hwy 6 S Houston TX 77082

PETRINI, MARCIA AGNES, nurse, educator; b. Sharon, Pa., Oct. 21, 1941; d. Victor Leo and Patricia Agnes (Biggins) P.; children—Colleen, Theresa, Moira. B.S. in Nursing, Cath. U. Am., 1963; M.S. (USPHS Title II grantee, 1964-65), U. Calif., San Francisco, 1965; Ph.D., SUNY, Buffalo, 1977; M.P.A., Harvard U., 1985. Faculty St. Joseph's Coll., Emmittsburg, Md., 1963-64, SUNY, Buffalo, 1965-77, Cath. U. Am., Washington, 1977-79; grad. faculty, chmn. dept. parent child nursing, U. Cin., 1979-82; prof., dir. nursing program Thiel Coll., Greenville, Pa., 1981-84. Contbg. author article to profl. publ. Allocation Bd., United Way, 1975-77; mem. Chgo. Mus. HHS grantee, 1980-82, Area Health Edn. Council grantee, 1979-80, 81-83. Mem. Am. Nursing Assn., Nat. League for Nursing (grantee, 1974), Assn. for Supervision and Curriculum Devel., Hastings Center, Smithsoniam Instn., Alumnae Assn., Assn. for the Care of Children's Health, Nat. Assn. for the Edn. of Young Children, Day Care Council of Am., Nat. Assoc. of Pediatric Nurse Associates/Practitioners. Clubs: Suburban Study (pres., 1973-74), Garden. Home: 16110 Avenido Venusto #7 San Diego CA 92128 Office: Home Homeside Care Group San Diego CA 92128 also Nat U San Diego CA 92108

PETRINOVIC, RUTH CHAVES, ballet teacher, choreographer; b. Great Neck, N.Y., Jan. 29, 1931; d. Alvaro da Silva Ferreira and Mildred (Byron) Chaves; m. Frano John Petrinovic, May 15, 1953 (div. 1980); children—Robert Francis, Alexis Alvaro. B.A., The Principia, Elsah, Ill., 1952. Dir. Imperial Studios, Ft. Lauderdale, Fla., 1963-73; founder, dir. Atlantic Found. for Performing Arts, Ft. Lauderdale, 1973-82; dir. ballet Greater Miami Opera, Fla., 1978-82; asst. dir. research and tng. Harkness House for Ballet Arts, N.Y.C., 1966-68, dir. research and tng., 1968-70; com. dir. Marin Ballet, San Rafael, Calif., 1983—; mem., master tchr. Fla. State Dance Assn., 1980-82. Choreographer: (ballets) 14 one-act ballets including Romeo and Juliet, Carmina Burana, 1974—; 3 full-length ballets including Nutcracker, Cinderella, 1974-81; ballet for opera including Adriana Lecouvreur, Turandot, 1978-82. Mem. Pacific Regional Ballet Assn. (pres. 1983, bd. dirs. 1984—). Avocations; travel; theatre; music. Office: Marin Ballet 100 Elm St San Rafael CA 94901

PETRO, VIVIAN HAZEL, wallcovering sales company executive; b. Plainfield, N.J., Nov. 13, 1921; d. Victor and Hazel (Vaughn) Petersen; student Pasadena Bus. Coll., 1943-44, Middlesex County Coll., 1972-73; m. Albert R. Petro, Aug. 3, 1947; children—Robert, Edward, Donna. Office mgr. Central Cutter Corp., Somerset, N.J., 1965-73; head dept. teller tng. Franklin State Bank, 1973-78; pres. Wallpaper Factory, Point Pleasant, N.J., 1978—; instr. banking to Spanish-speaking class Union County Coll., 1977. State Commr. N.J. Bd. Pharmacy, 1973-78; pres. scholarship com. Assn. PTAs of Edison, 1965-68; pres. Edison (N.J.) Republican Club, 1967-68; pres. PTA, Stelton Sch., Thomas Jefferson Jr. High Sch., Edison; pres. Edison Council PTA, 1968-69. Club: Midstreams Women's (sec.). Office: 2700 Bridge Ave Point Pleasant NJ 08742

PETRONE, AUGUSTA HENDERSON, educator, political volunteer; b. Cambridge, Mass., Mar. 10, 1937; d. Ernest and Mary (Stephens) Henderson; m. Joseph Carlton Petrone, June 23, 1958. B.A., Smith Coll., 1958; diplome, Sorbonne, Paris, 1962. English tchr. Seminary High Sch., Alexandria, Va., 1964-65, Kyunghi High Sch., Seoul, Korea, 1965-66, Sudo Women's Tchrs. Coll., Seoul, 1965-66; French tchr. Marshalltown Community Coll., Iowa, 1973-74; Reagan spokesman TV round-table, Geneva, Switzerland, 1976; Reagan chmn. Marshall County, Iowa, 1975-76, 79-80; Reagan-Bush co-chmn. State Iowa, Des Moines, 1983-84; coordinator Dutch's Dollies (161 costumed supporters of "Dutch" Reagan). Contbg. author The Feel of Korea, 1966. Weekly columnist Korea Times, 1966. Troop leader North Atlantic council Am. Girl Scouts, Fontainebleau, France, 1960; social welfare aide ARC, Fort Hood, Tex., 1962-63; adult advisor Young Republicans, Marshalltown, 1972-80; nat. com. woman Iowa Young Reps., 1974-75. Mem. Capitol Hill Club, Women's Nat. Rep. Club. Episcopalian. Home: 1608 W Main St Marshalltown IA 50158

PETROS, SOPHIE KARIPIDES, home economist, director public relations; b. Canton, Ohio, Nov. 4, 1932; d. Constantine N. and Martha (Sideropoulos) Karipides; student Ohio State U., 1950-52; B.S. in Journalism, Northwestern U., 1954; m. Thomas S. Petros, Jan. 10, 1960; 1 son, Dean. Tchr. home econs. St. Charles Borromeo Environ. House, Chgo., 1958; publicity-promotion asst. Toni Co., Chgo., 1954-55; TV account exec. Yardis Advt. Co., Phila., 1955-56; TV writer, demonstrator Crestline Co., Chgo., 1957; home service rep. Peoples Gas Light & Coke Co., Chgo., 1957-62; dir. pub. relations and advt., sec. Dial On Corp., Milw., 1962—; condr. gourmet cooking show Sta. WISN-TV, Milw., 1971—, cooking feature Sta. WCPX, Orlando, Fla., 1984; owner-mgr. Sophie Kay's Restaurant, 1980, Sophie Kay's Fine Dining, Hales Corners, Wis., 1980-84, Sophie Kay's Top of Daytona Restaurant, 1984; free-lance food demonstrator; free-lance TV commls., 1956—. Chmn., Hope for Hope Fund, Canton, 1954. Recipient debate award Nat. Forensic League, 1950. Mem. AFTRA, Am. Home Econs. Assn., Home Econs. in Bus., Northwestern U. Alumni Assn., Theta Sigma Phi, Alpha Xi Delta. Greek Orthodox. Club: Annunciation Women's. Author: Sophie Kay's Step-by-Step Cook Book, 1972; Sophie Kay's Family Cookbook, 1975; Jr. Chef Cookbook, 1977; Sophie Kay's Yogurt Cookery, 1978; Sophie Kay's Pasta Cookery, 1979; The Chicken Cookbook, 1981; One Dish Meals, 1982; Microwave Cooking, 1983. Home: 2615 S Atlantic Ave Daytona Beach Shores FL 32018

PETROSHIUS, SUSAN MARIE, marketing educator; b. Waukegan, Ill., Oct. 23, 1952; d. Lawrence Joseph and Hazel Florence (Ward) Petroshius; m. Kenneth Evan Crocker, Aug. 23, 1980. A.B., Syracuse U., 1973; M.S. in Bus. Adminstrn., U. Mass., 1978; Ph.D., Va. Poly. Inst. and State U., 1983. Service rep. Ill. Bell Telephone Co., Highland Park, 1974-76; instr. mktg. Va. Poly. Inst. and State U., Blacksburg, 1979-81; asst. prof. mktg. Bowling Green State U. (Ohio), 1981—. Contbr. articles to various publs. Mem. Am. Mktg. Assn., Assn. for Consumer Research, Am. Psychol. Assn., Acad. Mktg. Sci., Nat. Assn. Female Execs., NOW, Alpha Kappa Psi, Beta Gamma Sigma, Phi Kappa Phi. Home: 560 Candyce Ct Perrysburg OH 43403 Office: Bowling Green State U Dept of Mktg Bowling Green OH 43401

PETROVICH, SUSAN FRANCES, lawyer; b. Washington, July 6, 1947; d. George C. and Frances Lillian (Swift) Dewey; m. James Petrovich, Aug. 18, 1979. B.A., U. Calif.-Santa Barbara, 1969; J.D., Hastings Coll. Law, 1975. Bar: Calif. 1975. Mem. firm Hatch & Parent, Santa Barbara, Calif., 1975—. Mem. ABA, Santa Barbara County Bar Assn., Am. Trial Lawyers Assn., Calif. Trial Lawyers Assn., Santa Barbara County Barristers Club. Address: Hatch and Parent 21 E Carrillo St Santa Barbara CA 93101

PETSCO, EILEEN MARIE, real estate broker, land developer; b. N.Y.C., May 14, 1939; d. William and Rosemary (Murray) Sullivan; m. Feb. 8, 1959; children—Rosemary, John Kerry. A.A., Suffolk Community Coll., 1974. Sales assoc. Janette Drexler Real Estate, 1970-77; broker, owner Cornell Petsco, Real Estate, Port Jefferson, N.Y., 1977—. Mem. L.I. Bd. Realtors, Three Village C. of C., Port Jefferson C. of C. Avocations: tennis; gardening; sailing. Home: 117 Old Field Rd Setauket NY 11733 Office: Cornell Petsco 140 E Main St Port Jefferson NY 11777

PETTAWAY, I. M., writer; b. Los Angeles, May 28, 1959; d. David and Gertrude V. (Tucker) P. A.A., Santa Monica Coll., 1982; postgrad. U. Calif.-Santa Barbara, UCLA. Assoc. producer Shakespeare Soc., Hollywood, 1977-83; asst. to Abigail Van Buren, Hollywood, 1982-85, Dyer/Kahn, Los Angeles, 1983-84, Andary Prodns., Hollywood, 1977-86; adminstrv. sec. to March Fong Eu, Los Angeles, 1986—; Author: Renting an Apartment in Los Angeles, 1984. Sec., North Venice Community Group, 1979; charter mem. Contemporary Mus., Los Angeles. Mem. Shakespeare Soc. Am. (life; angel), Nat. Assn. Female Execs. Republican. Avocations: chess; skating; sailing; travel; creating. Office: PO Box 480882 Los Angeles CA 90404

PETTEBONE-LONG, KATHLEEN, editor, publisher; b. Louisville, Apr. 28, 1945; d. John Elliott II and Elsie Mae (Gyles) Pettebone; m. 2d, R. Eugene Long, Jr., June 29, 1974. Student Meredith Coll., 1963-65; B.A., U. Md., 1967; postgrad. Radcliffe Coll., 1970, Harvard U., 1972-73; postgrad. U. Pa. Wharton Sch., 1977-78. Asst. editor Naval Inst., 1968-70; asst. dir. pub. relations, instr. Anne Arundel Community Coll., Arnold, Md., 1970-71; asst. editor Nutrition Today, 1973-74; sr. book editor Robert J. Brady Pub. Co., a Prentice-Hall Co., 1974-77, acting mng. editor, 1975-76; pres., chief exec. officer KPL & Assocs., Annapolis, Md., 1976-83; dir. pub. activities Nat. Inst. Child Support Enforcement, Univ. Research Corp., Washington, 1979-81; mng. editor, pub. BioSci. mag. Am. Inst. Biol. Scis., Arlington, Va., 1981-84; exec. editor, pub. Computer Graphics News mag. Scherago Assocs. Pub., Inc., N.Y.C., 1984—; guest lectr. publs. specialist program George Washington U., 1977-82; cons. publs. Author: The History and Fundamentals of Child Support Enforcement, 1980; Paternity Establishment: Who Does It Benefit, 1981; author filmstrip: (with P. Semler-Carlson) Child Support Enforcement; Program Basics, 1980; contbr. articles to jours.; editor numerous books, including: Junks and Sampans of the Yangtze (Assn. Am. Univ. Press award 1971), 1971; Rape: Victims of Crisis, 1974; Current Medical Abbreviations, 1977; The Madness in Sports, 1977; author teaching aids for Nutrition Today. Mem. Soc. Scholarly Pub. Council Biology Editors (chmn. com. on pub. policy 1984—), Am. Soc. Tng. and Devel., Washington Book Pubs., The Word Guild, Balt. Pubs. Assn., AAUW, NOW, Meredith Coll. Alumni Assn. Democrat. Methodist. Clubs: Chesapeake Bay Yacht Racing Assn., Indian Landing Boat, Jr. League of Balt. Lodge: DAR. Office: Computer Graphics News 1090 Generalis Hwy Crownsville MD 21032 also 1515 Broadway 10th Floor New York NY 10036

PETTERSON, SYLVIA ROYSENE, radiologist; b. Worcester, Mass., Aug. 21, 1944; d. Roy Gustav Adolphus and Miriam Sylvia (Anderson) Petterson; B.S. with honors, Fla. So. Coll., 1966; M.D., U. Miami (Fla.), 1970. Intern in surgery St. Vincent Hosp., Worcester, Mass., 1970-71, resident in pathology, 1971-72, radiology, 1972-75, chief resident, 1974-75; staff. radiologist Indian River Meml. Hosp., Vero Beach, Fla., 1976-79, Sebastian River Med. Center, Sebastian, Fla., 1976-79, Fla. Med. Center, Ft. Lauderdale, Fla., 1979-80, St. Francis Hosp., Miami Beach, Fla., 1979-80, Broward Med. Center, Ft. Lauderdale, 1980—, Imperial Point Hosp., Ft. Lauderdale, 1980—, North Broward Hosp., Ft. Lauderdale, 1980—; partner W.W. McCorkle M.D. and W. B. Whittiker, M.D., Vero Beach, 1976-79, Cunningham and Rasken, M.D., P.A., Tamarac, Fla., 1979-80; asso. North Broward Radiologists, Ft. Lauderdale, 1981—; advisor Radiol. Technologist tng. program Indian River Community Coll., Ft. Pierce, 1976—, Broward Community Coll., Fort Lauderdale, 1980—. Named Young Alumnus of the Year, Fla. So. Coll., 1973. Mem. AMA (Physician Recognition award, 1973, 76, 79, 82), Fla. Med. Assn., Broward County Med. Assn., New Eng. Roentgen Ray Soc., Am. Med. Women's Assn., Radiology Soc. N. Am., Am. Assn. Women Radiologists. Republican. Methodist. Contbr. articles to med. jours. Home: 350 NE 24th Ct Boca Raton FL 33432 Office: Broward Gen Med Center 1600 S Andrews Ave Fort Lauderdale FL 33316

PETTIETTE, ALISON YVONNE, lawyer; b. Brockton, Mass., Aug. 16, 1952; d. David and Loretta (LeClair) Waters; Student Sorbonne, Paris, 1971-72; B.A., Sophie Newcomb Coll., 1972; M.A., Rice U., 1974; J.D., Bates Coll., 1978. Bar: Tex. 1979, U.S. Dist. Ct. (so. dist.) Tex. 1979, U.S. Ct. Appeals (5th cir.) 1980. Ptnr. Harvill & Hardy, Houston, 1979-83; sole practice, Houston, 1983-84; assoc. O'Quinn & Hagans, Houston, 1984—; editor Houston Law Rev. U. Houston, 1976-78. Exercise instr. YWCA, Houston, 1976-81, U. St. Thomas, Houston, 1982—. NDEA fellow Rice U., Houston, 1972-74; Woodrow Wilson scholar, Tulane U., New Orleans, 1972. Mem. ABA, Assn. Trial Lawyers Am., Tex. Trial Lawyers Assn., Houston Trial Lawyers Assn., Phi Delta Phi, Phi Beta Kappa. Office: O'Quinn & Hagans 3200 Tx Commerce Twr Houston TX 77002

PETTIGREW, KAREN BETH, lawyer; b. Lubbock, Tex., July 28, 1948; d. Jim Moore and Wanda Beth (Chastain) Pettigrew. B.A. with honors, Tex. Tech. U., 1970; J.D., So. Meth. U., 1974. Bar: Tex. 1974, U.S. Tax Ct., U.S. Dist. Ct. (so. and no. dists.) Tex. Staff mem. U.S. Senator John G. Tower, Dallas, 1970-71; law clk. U.S. Dept. Justice, Tax Div., Dallas, 1973-74; atty. Andrews & Kurth, Houston, 1974-80, Wyckoff, Russell, Dunn & Frazier, Houston, 1980-82, Morris, Tinsley & Snowden, Houston, 1982-84, Thelen, Marrin, Johnson & Bridges, Houston, 1984—; mem. steering com. A. J. Thomas Found., Dallas, 1983—; bd. dirs. Magna Marine Services, Inc., Houston, 1983—. Bd. dirs. Tex. Tech. U. Century Club, Houston, 1982—, Bellaire Christian Ch., Houston, 1983; bd. dirs. Houston Red Raider Club, 1983, v.p., 1984—; mem. group ticket sales com. Houston Livestock Show and Rodeo, Houston, 1983—; bd. visitors So. Meth. U. Law Sch., 1980-83. Acad. scholar Tex. Tech. U., 1966-70, So. Meth. U. Sch. Law, 1971-74. Mem. Houston Bar Assn., Tex. Bar Assn., ABA, Phi Delta Phi, Phi Kappa Phi, Alpha Lambda Delta, Phi Alpha Theta, Phi Sigma Alpha. Republican (del. state conv. 1984). Mem. Disciples of Christ. Home: 3650 Glen Haven Houston TX 77025 Office: Thelen Marrin Johnson & Bridges 1300 Texas American Bank Bldg Houston TX 77002

PETTIJOHN, JOYCE LORRAINE, pharmacist; b. Portland, Oreg., Jan. 7, 1955; d. Elzo Irving and Verona Muriel (McKittrick) Pettijohn; B.S. with honors in Pharmacy, Oreg. State U., 1978; postgrad. in bus. adminstrn. U. Puget Sound, 1980-81. Pharmacy extern St. Vincent's Hosp., Portland, 1977; pharmacy intern Lakeshore Clinic Pharmacy, Kirkland, Wash., 1978; staff pharmacist Evergreen Pharm. Services, Kirkland, 1979-80, sr. staff pharmacist, 1981—; dir. Health Products, Inc., Kirkland, 1981-85. Lic. pharmacist, Wash., Calif., Oreg. Mem. Am., Wash. State pharm. assns. Office: 200 Kirkwood Mall Kirkland WA 98033

PETTIS, JOAN NANCY, dietitian; b. N.Y.C., Apr. 26, 1948; d. Moe and Susan Tabachnick) Weinstein; m. William J. Pettis, Aug. 11, 1983; stepchildren —Mathew, Lisa. B.S. in Nutrition, Cornell U., 1969; M.S. in Nutrition, Case Western Res. U., 1974. Registered dietitian. Asst. food editor Good Housekeeping Inst., N.Y.C., 1969-70; therapeutic dietitian Genesee Hosp., Rochester, N.Y., 1970-73; nutrition services cons. N.Y. State Dept. Health, Rochester, 1974-75; adminstrv. dietitian Highland Hosp., Rochester, 1975-80; asst. dir. dietetics Strong Meml. Hosp., Rochester, 1980-82, dir. dietetics, 1982—; cons. dietitian Anthony Jordan Health Ctr., Rochester, 1977-78; cons. nutritionist Wegman's Food Markets, Rochester, 1980-81. Asst. editor: Good Housekeeping's Timesaver Cookbook, 1970. Mem. adv. com. food adminstrn. Monroe Community Coll., 1983—; bd. dirs. Jewish Home Rochester, 1980—. Mem. Am. Dietetic Assn., Genesee Dietetic Assn., Nutrition Today Soc., Soc. for Nutrition Edn. Democrat. Jewish. Avocations: dancing, crocheting, guitar playing. Office: Dietetics Dept Strong Meml Hosp Box 613 601 Elmwood Ave Rochester NY 14642

PETTIS, SHIRLEY NEIL, business executive, former congresswoman; b. Mountain View, Calif.; d. Harold Oliver and Dorothy Susan (O'Neil) McCumber; m. Jerry Pettis, (dec. 1975); children—Peter Dwight, Deborah Neil. Student Andrews U., U. Calif.-Berkeley. Co-founder, mgr. Magnetic Tape Duplicator, Hollywood, Calif., 1951-64; Audio-Digest Found., Glendale, Calif., 1951-55; sec., treas. Pettis, Inc., Hollywood, 1958-64; mem. 94-95th Congresses from Calif. 37th Dist.; dir. corp. bds. Kemper Group, 1979—. Mem. Pres.'s Arms Commn. Control and Disarmament Commn., 1981-83; trustee U. Redlands, 1979-82; v.p., pres. Women's Research and Edn. Inst., Washington, 1979-82. Mem. DAR. Republican. Clubs: Congressional, Capitol Hill, Pauma Valley Country. Home: 12315 Ridge Circle Los Angeles CA 90049

PETTIT, MARGARET ESTA, broadcasting executive; b. Provo, Utah, July 22, 1926; d. Howard Hammil and Edith Susan (Cummins) Cain; student public schs.; m. Claud Martin Pettit, July 30, 1948; children—Ruth Elaine, Paul Martin. Co-owner, office supr. Sta. KEOS, Flagstaff, Ariz., 1960-61; co-owner, bookkeeper Sta. KWIV, Douglas, Wyo., 1965-74; co-owner, bookkeeper, program dir., office supr. Sta. KCMP, Brush Colo., 1976-82; dir. Custom Broadcasting Co., Denver; sec.-treas., dir. Ranchland Broadcasting Co.; dir., v.p. Better Day, Inc., Arvada, Colo. Bd. dirs. Jefferson Park Community Activity Assn., Denver, 1981-84, North Fed. Recreation, Denver, 1984—. Mem. Model T Ford Club. Baptist. Home and Office: 8320 W 66th Ave Arvada CO 80004

PETTIT, WENDY JEAN, advertising agency executive; b. Gary, Ind., Oct. 6, 1945; d. Wendell E. and Ethel (Binkley) Pettit. B.A., MacMurray Coll., 1967; M.S.B.A., Ind. U., 1978. Acctg. clk. J. Walter Thompson USA, Chgo., 1967-68, adminstrv. asst., 1968-72, personnel asst., 1973-74, fin. analyst, 1974-78, office services asst., 1978-79, acctg. dept. mgr., 1979—. Bd. dirs. Miller Citizens Corp., Gary, 1979—. Named Career Woman of the Year, Bus. and Profl. Women, Gary, 1967. Mem. Nat. Assn. Female Execs., LWV. Methodist. Avocations: singing; piano; cooking. Home: 8000 Oak Ave Gary IN 46403 Office: J Walter Thompson USA Inc 875 N Michigan Ave Chicago IL 60611

PETTY, PEGGY JOYCE, hospital administrator; b. Ft. Worth, Nov. 20, 1932; d. Julius Marcellus and Ruby Ozell (Quinn) Hirth; m. Glenn Royce Petty, Sept. 10, 1954; children—Glenn, Jr., Kirk, Robert, Steven. Diploma, Parkland Hosp. Sch. Nursing, Dallas, 1953; B.S. in Health Care Adminstrn., East Tex. State U., 1982. Lic. R.N., Tex. Supr. operating room Good Shepherd Hosp., Longview, Tex., 1960-61; head nurse labor and delivery The Methodist Hosp., Houston, 1968-73, supr. ob-gyn, 1978-81; dir. nursing Odessa Women's and Children's Hosp., Tex., 1975-77; chief operating officer Fort Bend Community Hosp., Missouri City, Tex., 1983—; nursing cons. Southwestern Gen. Hosp., El Paso, Tex., 1982-83. Pres., bd. dirs. Ft. Bend unit Am. Cancer Soc., Missouri City, 1984—; bd. dirs. Tex. for War on Drugs, Ft. Bend, 1985—; Ft. Bend County Women's Refuge Ctr., 1984—. Pres.'s scholar, 1981. Mem. Tex. Soc. Hosp. Nursing Service Adminstrs. Assn. Houston Area Nursing Service Adminstrs. (sec. 1985—), Nat. Assn. Nurse Execs., Sigma Theta Tau. Republican. Baptist. Avocations: oil painting; golfing; tennis; aerobics. Home: 2710 Meadow Creek Dr Missouri City TX 77459 Office: Fort Bend Community Hosp 3803 FM1092 Missouri City TX 77459

PETTY, PRISCILLA HAYES, writer, newspaper columnist, consultant; b. Nashville, Aug. 22, 1940; d. Anderson Boyd and Margaret Louise (Lauper) Hayes; m. Gene Paul Petty, Jan. 10, 1961; children—Eric, Damon, Boyd. B.A. in English, Vanderbilt U., 1962; student Russian Inst., Dartmouth Coll., 1965. Cert. tchr., Ohio. Tchr. English, Cin. Suburban Pub. Schs., 1962-65, head dept. English, tchr., 1971-79; newspaper columnist Cin. Enquirer, 1978—, also syndicated newspaper columnist Gannett News Service, Washngton, 1982—; cons. Arthur Andersen & Co., 1981-82; writer United Western Corp., 1982. Author: History of a Boardsman (oral history), 1979. Mem. Cin. Council World Affairs; chmn. Cin. Media-Bus. Exchange, 1983; founder, pres. bd. trustees Cin. Oral History Found., 1984—. Named Outstanding Tchr., Project Teach, Ohio Edn. Assn., 1978. Mem. Women in Communications (Outstanding Communicator of Yr. 1985), Oral History Assn., Sigma Delta Chi. Club: Woman's City (Cin.). Home: 229 Oliver Rd Cincinnati OH 45215

PETTYJOHN, CAROL LAVONNE, genetic engineering company executive, controller; b. Maple Creek, Sask., Can., May 13, 1940; came to U.S., 1948, naturalized, 1986; d. Glenn C. Pettyjohn and Ruth I. (Cox) Pettyjohn Savchenko; m. Thomas Edward Hatfield, June 13, 1958 (div. 1964); 1 child, Tamra R.; m. Dan Franklin Black, Oct. 1, 1964 (div. 1971); children—Kelley S., Anthony G. Student Memphis State U., 1958-59, San Diego State U., 1960, Bapt. Meml. Hosp. Sch. Nursing, 1957-59, Atlanta Law Sch., 1963, U. Maine, 1976, Coll. DuPage, 1984. Staff nurse Erlanger Hosp., Chattanooga, 1961-62, DeKalb Gen. Hosp., Decatur, Ga., 1962-63; med. cons. Prudential Ins. Co., Atlanta, 1964-67, employment interviewer, 1967-71; personnel mgr. Montgomery Wards, Jacksonville, Fla., 1972-75; office mgr. Drs. Wildstein, Kaiser, Schlemann, Springvale, Maine, 1975-78; pres., owner Options Agy., Sanford, Maine, 1978-81; controller, product mgr., div. mgr. Immuno Genetics, Inc., Eldora, Iowa and Vineland, N.J., 1981—; bus. cons. Sanford Fire Dept., 1979-81, Drs. Harrigan, Pollard, Peterlein, Schlemann, Kaiser, Buell, Bellevaun, 1978-81. Area coordinator NOW, Jacksonville, Fla., 1974-75, Portland, Maine, 1975-79; softball coach Little League, Sanford, 1977-82; mem. LWV, Sanford, 1978-79; bd. dirs. Big Bros./Big Sisters, Biddeford, Maine, 1979-80. Mem. Nat. Assn. Female Execs. (network dir. 1985—), Nat. Agrl. Mktg. Assn., Livestock Conservation Inst. Democrat. Avocations: reading; softball; chess; music; fishing; camping. Office: Immuno Genetics Inc/IBS PO Box 496 Airport Rd Eldora IA 50627

PETZEL, FLORENCE ELOISE, educator; b. Crosbyton, Tex., Apr. 1, 1911; d. William D. and A. Eloise (Punchard) P.; Ph.B., U. Chgo., 1931, A.M., 1934; Ph.D., U. Minn., 1954. Instr., Judson Coll., 1936-38; vis. instr. Tex. State Coll. for Women, 1937; asst. prof. textiles Ohio State U., 1938-48; asso. prof. U. Ala., 1950-54; prof. Oreg. State U., 1954-61, 67-75, 77, prof. emeritus, 1975—, dept. head, 1954-61, 67-75; prof., div. head U. Tex., 1961-63; prof. Tex. Tech. U., 1963-67; vis. prof. Wash. State U., 1967. Effie I. Raitt fellow, 1949-50. Mem. Portland Art Assn., Seattle Art Mus., Textile Mus., San Francisco Opera Assn., Portland Opera Assn., Sigma Xi, Phi Kappa Phi, Omicron Nu, Iota Sigma Pi, Sigma Delta Epsilon, Am. Assn. Ret. Persons. Author articles in field. Home: 730 NW 35th St Corvallis OR 97330

PEUGH, SARAH LOUISE PEARSON (MRS. WALTER STEPHEN PEUGH, SR.), freelance writer; b. Houston, Miss., Oct. 4, 1924; d. Edd Monroe (dec.) and Mattie (Shivers) (dec.) Pearson; student Trevecca Coll., 1941-43, Miss. state Extension, 1964, Auburn U., 1970, student Itawamba Jr. Coll., 1970; m. Walter Stephen Peugh, Sr., Dec. 20, 1947; children—Sarah Peugh Franks, Mary Jo Peugh Ayres, Steve, Bob. Clk., teller First Nat. Bank, Phila. and San Diego, 1944; owner Town House Restaurant, Aberdeen, Miss., 1952-62; owner, grad., bridal cons. Wedding Services, Aberdeen, 1969-76; columnist Aberdeen Examiner, 1970-74, 77; Aberdeen News Herald, 1974-75. Exec. sec. ARC, Aberdeen, 1972-73, bd. dirs. 1973-77; bd. dirs. Miss. YMCA, 1974-78, Miss. for Ednl. TV, 1978-80; chmn. Council Clubs and City Beautiful Commn., 1974-76; area rep. Keep Miss. Beautiful, 1974-76; initiator Butterfly scholarship Miss. Fedn. Women's Clubs, 1978, Amblin scholarship, 1976, organizer 1st Juniorette Club, 1974. Miss. YMCA, Youth Gov. scholarship, 1977. Named Most Outstanding Woman, Jr. Aux. Charity Ball, Aberdeen, 1972. Mem. Aberdeen C. of C., Miss. Press Women, Miss. Fedn. Women's Clubs (Outstanding Woman of Yr. 1981), Nat. Fedn. Press Women, Miss. Poetry Soc. (organizer North Branch, Miss. chpt. 1979), Public Relations Assn. of Miss., N.E. Miss. Tourism Council, Am. Legion Aux. Clubs: Woman's (pres. 1973-74), Home and Garden, Gourmet (founder), Miss. Fashion Women (founder, exec. dir.). Editor: The Glencoe Story, 1967, Clubwoman Mag., The Miss. Clubwoman, 1984—; mem. editorial bd. Lyric Miss., 50th anthology; contbr. poetry to various publs. Address: 205 Hillcrest St Aberdeen MS 39730

PEVELER, SARAH KATHRYN FESSLER, personnel official; b. Mt. Vernon, Ill., Feb. 21, 1947; d. Floyd Roscoe and Mildred Faye (Carson) Fessler; B.A., Emory U., 1969; postgrad. U. South Sch. Theology, 1980-84; m. R. David Peveler, June 14, 1969 (div. Aug. 1981). Tng. dir. Ill. Shore council Girl Scout U.S.A., Wilmette, Ill., 1970-73, Abnaki council, Brewer, Maine, 1973-75, tng. dir., dir. field services Shawnee council, Martinsburg, W.Va., 1976-77; personnel dir. Seamen's Ch. Inst. N.Y. and N.J., N.Y.C., 1978-80; personnel dir. Trinity Ch., N.Y.C., 1980—; owner, propr. The Uncommon Resume, cons. firm. Personnel com. Greater N.Y. council Girl Scouts U.S.A.; mem. Episcopal Women's Caucus; mem. clergy compensation com. Episcopal Diocese of N.Y. Mem. Am. Soc. Personnel Adminstrn., N.Y. Personnel Mgmt. Assn., Phi Mu. Club: St. Bartholomew's City. Office: 74 Trinity Pl New York NY 10006

PEVEN, DOROTHY ESTELLE SPINKA, psychiatric social worker; b. Chgo.; grad. with highest honors, Roosevelt U., Chgo., 1969; M.S.W. (NIMH grantee), Jane Addams Sch. Social Work, U. Ill., Chgo., 1969; cert. in psychotherapy Alfred Adler Inst., Chgo., 1972. Psychotherapist in group pvt. practice, Chgo., 1969—; mem. faculty, tng. therapist Alfred Adler Inst., Chgo.; allied health profl. St. Joseph Hosp., Chgo., also cons. In-Patient Service Community Mental Health, 1972—; condr. seminars, workshops, lectr. women's issues; cons., lectr. Alfred Adler Insts., St. Louis, Vancouver, B.C., Cleve., Toronto; lectr. N. Am. Soc. Adlerian Psychology, N.Y.C., Congress of Internat. Assn. Individual Psychology, Zurich, Switzerland, Vienna Austria, Amsterdam, Netherlands. Mem. Acad. Cert. Social Workers, Nat. Assn. Social Workers, N. Am. Soc. Adlerian Psychology (officer), Am. Assn. Marriage and Family Therapy, Internat. Assn. Individual Psychology (council). Contbr. (I. Kutash, ed.) Psychotherapist's Casebook, articles to profl. jours. Home: 6033 N Sheridan Rd 42D Chicago IL 60660 Office: 400 Lake-Cook Rd Deerfield IL 60015 and 2800 N Sheridan Rd Chicago IL 60657

PEWITT, EDITH MARIE, educational administrator; b. Greenville, Tex., Feb. 27, 1926; d. Charles Ambrose, Jr. and Beulah Edna (King) Hendrix; m. Edgar Lee Pewitt, Feb. 23, 1945; children—Edith Pamela Pewitt Chatagnier, Robert Lewis, II, Edgar Lee. B.S., Tex. Women's U., 1961; M.Ed., N. Tex. State U., 1964, Ed.D., 1967. Supr. sch. lunches to tchr. Grapevine Ind. Sch. Dist., Tex., 1958-66; research asst., lab. instr. to asst. prof. edn. N. Tex. State U., 1966-68; coordinator curriculum Edn. Service Ctr., Region XI, Ft. Worth, 1968-70; cons. Novato Unified Sch. Dist., Calif., 1970-71, adminstrv. asst., 1971-72; staff devel. coordinator Ptnrs. in Career Edn., Arlington, Tex., 1972-74; tchr. high sch. sci., instructional leader, coordinator Career Planning Acad., Ft. Worth Ind. Sch. Dist., 1974—; cons. in field. Mem. NEA, Adminstrv. Women in Edn. (membership chmn. 1980-81), Assn. Supervision and Curriculum Devel., Soc. Study Edn., Nat. Aci. Tchrs. Assn., Tex. Tchrs. Assn., Tex. Assn. Supervision and Curriculum Devel., Ft. Worth Public Schs. Adminstrs. Assn., LWV, Kappa Delta Pi (past chpt. pres.), Phi Delta Kappa. Methodist. Home: 303 Ridge Rd Grapevine TX 76051 Office: 3813 Valentine St Fort Worth TX 76107

PEYTON, JUDITH SAGER, advertising agency executive; b. Boston, May 20, 1948; d. William Frederick and Marilyn (Williams) Sager; m. Stephen Charles Peyton, June 14, 1969 (div. Sept. 1984). B.S. in Math., U. Ill., 1969. Programmer-analyst Computer Gains, Arlington Heights, Ill., 1969-70; sr. systems analyst Survey Research Lab., U. Ill.-Chgo., 1970-76; mgr. statis. services Britt & Frerichs, Inc., Chgo., 1976-78; assoc. research dir. Leo Burnett Co., Inc., Chgo., 1978—; lectr. basic and advanced stats.; mktg. cons. Environ. chmn. West Jackson Blvd. Historic Preservation Dist., Chgo., 1979-81, area devel. chmn., 1981-83, pres., 1983-84. Mem. Am. Mktg. Assn. Clubs: Fortnightly, Burnett Running (Chgo.). Avocations: historic renovation; music; gardening. Home: 1501 W Jackson Blvd Chicago IL 60607 Office: Leo Burnett Co Inc Prudential Plaza Chicago IL 60601

PFAELZER, MARIANA R., federal judge; b. 1926; A.B., U. Calif.-Santa Barbara; LL.B., UCLA Sch. Law, 1957. Admitted to bar, 1958; mem. firm Bautzer, Rothman & Kuchler, Los Angeles, 1957-78, ptnr., 1969-78; judge U.S. Dist. Ct. for Dist. Central Calif., 1978—. Mem. Am. Bar Assn. Office: US Dist Ct 312 N Spring St Los Angeles CA 90012*

PFAFFENROTH, SARA BEEKEY, educator; b. Reading, Pa., Dec. 2, 1941; d. Cyrus Ezra and Viola Bessie (Sweigart) Beekey; A.B., Bryn Mawr Coll., 1963; M.A., Ind. U., 1964; m. Peter Albert Pfaffenroth, June 26, 1966; children—Elizabeth Kilmer, Peter Cyrus, Catherine Genevieve. Instr. English, Northwestern Mich. Coll., Traverse City, 1964-66, Middlesex County Coll., Edison, N.J., 1966-68; prof. English, County Coll. of Morris, Randolph, N.J., 1968—; grants cons., 1979-82. Recipient poetry award Bryn Mawr Arts Council, 1963, Gertrude Saucier Hist. Poetry award, 1970; mid-career fellow Princeton U., 1983-84. Mem. N.J. Poetry Soc. (trustee), MLA, Coll. English Assn., Jane Austen Soc. N.Am. Lutheran. Editor anthologies: Beyond Tether, 1975; A Palette of Poets, 1976; Endless Waters Welling Up, 1977; From Rim to Rim, 1978; Crystal Cadences, 1980. Home: Box 429 Chester NJ 07930 Office: County College of Morris Randolph NJ 07801

PFEIFFER, JANE CAHILL, former broadcasting co. executive, consultant; b. Washington, Sept. 29, 1932; d. John Joseph and Helen (Reilly) Cahill; B.A., U. Md., 1954; m. Ralph A. Pfeiffer, Jr., June 3, 1975. With IBM Corp., Armonk, N.Y., 1955-76, sec. mgmt. rev. com., 1970, dir. communications, 1971, v.p. communications and govt. relations, 1972-76, bus. cons., 1976-78; chmn. NBC, Inc., N.Y.C., 1978-81; bus. cons., 1981—; dir. Ashland Oil Co., Chesebrough-Ponds, Inc., Internat. Paper Co., J.C. Penney Co., Ashland Oil Co. Participant, White House Fellows program, 1966; mem. Council on Fgn. Relations, Overseas Devel. Council, Pres.'s Commn. Mil. Compensation, 1978-79, Pres.'s Commn. White House Fellows, 1976-81. Trustee, Rockefeller Found., 1973-85, U. Notre Dame, Carnegie Hall; chmn. bd. trustees U. Md. Found. Office: Field Point Circle Greenwich CT 06830

PFEIFFER, JOAN CROCKER, broadcasting executive; b. Providence; d. Harry Lewis and Irene Juliette (Vallez) Crocker; children—Steven Harry, Richard Alan; m. Peter W. Pfeiffer, Jr., Nov. 11, 1972. Student U. R. I., R.I. Jr. Coll., Rutgers U.; cert. Katherine Gibbs Sch., 1967. Advt. asst. Career Counseling, Providence, 1973; asst. to gen. mgr., producer Sta. WJAR-TV, Providence, 1973-74; air personality, producer Sta. WJAR-AM, Providence, 1974-77; morning personality, prodn. pub. service dir. Sta. WNRI-AM, Woonsocket, R.I., 1977-80; air personality Sta. WPRO-AM, Providence, 1980; morning personality Sta. WMYS-FM, New Bedford, Mass., 1980—, program dir., ops. mgr., 1981—; appearances include seminars, TV programs Bd. Dirs. Escape Hatch, Englewood, N.J., 1968-70. Recipient Tribute to Women YWCA, 1984. Mem. AFTRA, DAR. Avocations: gardening; reading; theatre. Home: Tingley Dr Cumberland RI 02864 Office: WMYS FM 737 County St New Bedford MA 02741

PFEIFFER, MARGARET ANNE, tax analyst; b. Terre Haute, Ind., Feb. 18, 1948; d. Albert and Lena Leah (Osmon) Kasubjak; m. William Joseph Pfeiffer, Sr., July 30, 1965; 1 child, William Joseph, Jr. Cert. mgmt. with honors, Lake

Forest Sch. Mgmt., 1983. Tax clk. City Products Corp., Des Plaines, Ill., 1976-80; accountemps mgr. Robert Half of Chgo., Schaumburg, Ill., 1980; asst. controller Builders Plumbing Supply, Northbrook, Ill., 1980-81; tax analyst UNOCAL, Schaumburg, 1981—. Pres-sch. gym tchr. Northwest Suburban YMCA, Des Plaines, 1975-76. Mem. Nat. Assn. Accts. (bd. dirs. 1981-83, v.p. membership 1984, v.p. adminstrn., 1985; pres. local chpt. 1986—), Desk and Derrick Club (pres. local chpt. 1985—, bd. dirs. 1983, 84), DAR. Avocations: miniature doll houses; sewing; camping. Home: 7500 N Elmhurst Rd #108 Des Plaines IL 60018

PFEIFFER, MARGUERITE WESSELS, state agency official; b. Tyler, Tex., Mar. 16, 1933; d. George Bernard and Anita (Ledbetter) Wessels; m. David Graham Pfeiffer, June 25, 1955 (div. 1980); children—Clifford George, Katherine Graham, Carol Graham. Student Gulf Park Coll., 1950-51; B.F.A. in Music, U. Tex., 1955; postgrad. Northeastern U., 1972-73; M.P.A., Suffolk U., 1977. Adminstrv. asst. to treas. All Saint's Episcopal Ch., Brookline, Mass., 1973-75; adminstrv. asst. proposed faculty union Northeastern U., Boston, 1975; research cons. Worcester Area Transitional Housing, Boston, 1977-79; procedures clk. Trial Ct. of Mass., Brookline, 1980-85, account clk., 1985—; mem. host com. for Eastern Regional Child Support Conf., Trial Ct. Mass., Boston, 1983. Contbr. and research cons. to publs. Treas., mem. exec. bd. Brookline Citizens for Participation in Politics, 1974—; coordinator vol. program Runkle Sch. Brookline PTO, 1974, 75; adv. bd. Calvary St. Andrews Episcopal Ch., Rochester, N.Y., 1969-70; human services com. Brookline Ct. Centennial Commn., 1982. Mem. Office and Profl. Workers Union, Nat. Assn. Female Execs., Eastern Regional Conf. on Uniform Reciprocal Enforcement Support Act, Boston Intercollegiate Alumnae Assn. (chmn. philanthropy 1984—). NOW, Pi Alpha Alpha. Democrat. Episcopalian. Avocations: Piano; gardening; concerts, art films, exhibits; cooking; woodworking; travel. Home: 17 Corey Rd Brookline MA 02146 Office: Brookline Dist Court 360 Washington St Brookline MA 02146

PFEIFFER, PHYLLIS KRAMER, publisher; b. N.Y.C., Feb. 11, 1949; d. Jacob N. and Estelle G. Rosenbaum-Pfeiffer; student Harvard U., 1967, N.Y.U., 1968, 72, Ithaca Coll., 1969; B.S., Cornell U., 1970; postgrad. U. San Diego, 1976-78; m. Stephen M. Pfeiffer, Dec. 21, 1969; 1 son, Andrew Kramer. Instr., Miss Porter's Sch., Farmington, Conn., 1970; tchr. N.Y.C. Bd. Edn., Dewey Jr. High Sch., 1970-73; research Hunter Coll., N.Y., 1971-72; account exec. La Jolla (Calif.) Light, 1973-75, advt. dir., 1975-77, gen. mgr., 1977-78, pub., 1978—; exec. v.p. Harte Hanks So. Calif. Newspapers, 1985—; dir. communications center San Diego State U., 1980—. Bd. dirs. La Jolla Cancer Research Found., 1979-82; bd. dirs. Alvarado Hosp., 1981—, chmn. fin. com., 1986, sec. bd., 1986; co-chmn. Operation USS La Jolla, U.S. Navy, 1980—; mem. mktg. com. United Way, 1979-81; bd. dirs. YMCA, San Diego Ballet, 1980; trustee La Jollan's Inc., 1975-78; mem. Conv. and Visitors Bur. Blue Ribbon Com. on Future, 1983, resource panel Child Abuse Prevention Found., 1983—; chmn. mktg. com. United Way, 1983. N.Y. Bd. Edn. grantee, 1971-72. Mem. Am. Newspaper Pubs. Assn., Calif. Newspaper Pubs. Assn. (bd. dirs., exec. com.), Women in Communications, Chancellor's Assn. U. Calif.-San Diego, Calif. Newspaper Advt. Execs. Assn. Club: La Jolla Beach and Tennis. Home: 6024 Avenida Cresta La Jolla CA 92037 Office: PO Box 1927 450 Pearl St La Jolla CA 92038

PFEIFFER, SOPHIA DOUGLASS, lawyer; b. N.Y.C., Aug. 10, 1918; d. Franklin Chamberlin and Sophie Douglass (White) Wells; m. Timothy Adams Pfeiffer, June 7, 1941; children—Timothy Franklin, Penelope Mersereau Keenan, Sophie Douglass. A.B., Vassar Coll., 1939; J.D., Northeastern U., 1975. Bar: R.I. 1975, U.S. Ct. Apls. (1st cir.) 1980, U.S. Supreme Ct. 1979. Editorial researcher Time, Inc., N.Y.C., 1940-41; writer Office War Info., Washington, 1941-43, N.Y.C., 1943-45; editorial staff Nat. Geog. Mag., Washington, 1958-59, 68-70; editor Turkish Jour. Pediatrics, Ankara, 1961-63; staff atty. R.I. Supreme Ct., Providence, 1975-76, chief staff atty., 1977-86. Contbr. in field. Pres., Karachi Am. Sch. (Pakistan), 1955-56. Mem. ABA, R.I. Bar Assn. (ho. of dels. 1979-81), R.I. Women Lawyers, ACLU, NOW.

PFEIFFER, TERESA CRIBB, tobacco company official; b. Nashville, Ga., Mar. 12, 1957; d. Clyde and Dorothy Lee (Dykes) Cribb; m. John William Pfeiffer, Oct. 20, 1984. B.A., St. Norbert Coll., 1979. Supr., A.C. Nielsen, Green Bay, Wis., 1979-80; with Lorillard, Inc., 1980—, sales rep., Green Bay, 1980-81, asst. div. mgr., Springfield, Ill., 1981-82, div. mgr., Milw., 1982-84, mgr. chain accounts, Milw., 1984-85, Jacksonville, Fla., 1985—, bd. mem. No. Contractors, Inc., Milw., 1984-85; mktg. cons. Williams Energy Systems, Milw., 1983. Active Planned Parenthood Am. Mem. Nat. Assn. Female Execs., Tobacco Action Network, Home Improvement Council (Milw.), Alumni Assn. St. Norbert Coll. Republican. Avocations: Photography; painting; aerobics; dog training. Office: Lorillard Inc 1100 Cesery Blvd Jacksonville FL 32211

PFLAGER, RUTH WOOD, communications coordinator; b. Springfield Mass., Mar. 3, 1917; d. Walter Guy and Mabel (Munson) Wood; B.S., U. Mass., 1938; postgrad. Northwestern U., 1939-40; m. Miller S. Pflager, Aug. 31, 1940; children—Sandra P. Wischmeyer, Charlene P. Balistrere, William Wood, Jessie Pflager Avery. Program chmn., v.p. Radio and TV Council Greater Cleve., Inc., 1973-75, pres., 1975-77, exec. dir., 1977-79. Mem. Communications Commn., Greater Cleve. Interchurch Council, 1972—, vice chmn. 1981-82, chmn., 1983—; chmn. Community Mental Health Inst., 1981-82; communications coordinator Ch. Women United in Cleve., 1974-82, bull. editor, 1974-78, honor award, 1980; chmn. media concerns Ch. Women United in Ohio, 1979-81; chmn. TV Tune-In, 1981—. Recipient Outstanding Service award Radio-TV Council, 1977. Mem. AAUW (br. pres. 1977-79, com. on women Ohio div. 1979-81, chmn. media concerns task force), Am. Council Better Broadcasts (life mem., sec. 1979-80 v.p. 1980—), Nat. Assn. Better Broadcasting, Nat. Citizens Com. for Broadcasting, Orange Hist. Soc. Methodist. Club: Women's City (mem. mental health com. 1974—) (Cleve.). Home: 4349 S Hilltop Dr Chagrin Falls OH 44022 Office: 2230 Euclid Ave Cleveland OH 44115

PHARES, MARGUERITE LINTON, ballet teacher, artistic director; b. Columbus, Ohio, Mar. 4, 1917; d. Henry Jehu and Viola Alice (Carmean) Linton; m. Hugh Kinzel Phares, Jr., June 6, 1941; children—Hugh III, Lisa Elaine. B.S. in Music Edn., Ohio State U., 1939. Profl. dancer, N.Y.C., 1939-41; ballet tchr. various schs. Glendale, Calif., 1941-43, Mt. Vernon, N.Y., 1944-47; prin. Marguerite Phares Sch. of Dance, Sacramento, Calif., 1947—; artistic dir. Theatre Ballet of Sacramento, 1967—; choreographer ballets: Cinderella, 1977, 78; Sleeping Beauty, 1980, 85; Romeo and Juliet, 1984; regional dir. Internat. Ballet Competition, Jackson, Miss., 1981, regional field judge, Sacramento, 1982-83. Recipient Outstanding Tchr. Plaudit award Nat. Dance Assn., 1978. Mem. Pacific Regional Ballet Assn. (sec. 1977-79, pres. 1980-81), Delta Zeta (pres. 1954-55). Republican. Office: Marguerite Phares Sch Dance 4430 Marconi Ave Sacramento CA 95821

PHARIS, RUTH MCCALISTER, banker; b. San Diego, Feb. 13, 1934; d. William L. and Mary E. (Beuk) McC.; grad. Del Mar Coll., Corpus Christi, Tex., 1975-79; m. E. Edwin Pharis, Mar. 14, 1953; children—Beth, Tracey, Todd. Asst. cashier Parkdale State Bank, Corpus Christi, 1970-72, asst. v.p., 1972-76, v.p., 1976-79; v.p. Cullen Center Bank & Trust, Houston, 1979-81, sr. v.p., 1982—; instr. Am. Inst. Banking, 1977-79. Mem. adv. council Houston Community Colls. Mem. Am. Soc. Personnel Adminstrs., Bank Adminstrn. Inst. (v.p. Coastal Bend chpt. 1979), Nat. Assn. Bank Women (ednl. chmn. Coastal Bend group), Am. Inst. Banking (rep.), Tex. Bankers Assn. (council 1983-84), Coastal Bend Personnel Soc. (v.p.), Houston Personnel Assn., Corpus Christi C. of C. (mem. women's com. 1976-79). Republican. Baptist. Club: Order Eastern Star. Home: 5102 Wightman Ct Houston TX 77069 Office: 600 Jefferson St Houston TX 77001

PHEASANT-ANGELO, MICHELLE, interior designer; b. Los Angeles, Dec. 23, 1946; d. Homer Chilvers and Mary Evelyn (Pugh) Pheasant; m. John Anthony Angelo, Apr. 6, 1974; children—Mary Alexis, John Timothy. B.F.A., U. So. Calif., 1969. Designer Roger Wood Design, Los Angeles, 1968-71; prin. Michelle Pheasant Design, Los Angeles, 1971-74, Michelle Pheasant Design, Inc., Monterey, Calif., 1974—. Mem. Inst. Bus. Designers (bd. dirs. 1983-85), Monterey Peninsula Leadership Program. Democrat. Avocations: horseback riding, skiing, dancing. Office: Michelle Pheasant Design Inc 419 Webster St Monterey CA 93940

PHELAN, F. ADELE, foundation executive; b. Denver, Nov. 15, 1935; d. Frank Adam and Della Catherine (Pigotti) Muto; B.A. in English, Webster Coll., 1959; M.A. in English (Woodrow Wilson fellow), St. Louis U., 1962; M.A. in Ednl. Psychology (NDEA Inst. fellow), U. Minn., 1974; m. Gerry Phelan, Oct. 9, 1971. Chmn. English dept. Machebeuf High Sch., Denver, 1961-67; mem. faculty English dept. Loretto Heights Coll., Denver, 1967-68, dir. counseling, 1968-70, dean of students, 1970-74, pres., 1975-83; dir. programs Piton Found., 1983-85; pres. Clayton Found., 1985—; asst. to dean of students U. Denver, 1974-75; dir. 1st Interstate Bank of Denver. Mem. Colo. Bd. Ethics; mem. council Public TV-Channel 6; trustee Kent Denver Country Day Sch.; bd. dirs. Mile Hi council Girl Scouts U.S.; mem. Women's Forum Colo. Recipient Ann. Salute to Women award, 1982. Office: 511 16th St Denver CO 80202

PHELAN, JANE CHESTER, technical writer; b. Hartford, Conn., May 4, 1945; d. Ebbe Carl and Ruth Emma (Chester) Blomstrand; m. Clifford James Phelan, Sept. 4, 1965. B.A., Central Conn. State U., 1972. Child care worker Child & Family Services, Hartford, Conn., 1966-69; dir. Home Care Services, 1973; with Travelers Ins. Co., 1973—, sr. tech. writer, 1982—. Mem. Women in Communications, Soc. Tech. Communications. Office: Travelers Ins Co 1 Tower Sq Hartford CT 06115

PHELPS, ANN FAMBROUGH, contractor; b. Gadsden Ala., May 24, 1933; d. Floyd J. and Jewel C. (Underwood) Fambrough; m. Frederick Allen Bennett, Sept. 6, 1952 (div. Nov. 1966); 1 child, Sharon Ann Bennett Metzner; m. Alvin Jr. Phelps, Apr. 6, 1985. Student U. Calif. San Diego, 1954, U. N.C.-Fayetteville, 1956—. Mgr. motel, Balt., 1964-77; v.p., treas. A.J. Phelps Land Clearing, Inc., Jessup, Md., 1980—. State sec. United Cerebral Palsy, 1963-64. Democrat. Lodges: Order Eastern Star; Moose (jr. regent 1963-64). Home: PO Box 107 Jessup MD 20794 Office: PO Box 85 Jessup MD 20794

PHELPS, BETTY JEANE POTTENGER, peace activist; b. Warsaw, Ind., Oct. 20, 1921; d. Royal and Erba Ermal (Hinkson) Pottenger; A.B., Manchester Coll., 1943; registered Occupational Therapist, Washington U., St. Louis, 1952; m. Charles Puterbaugh Phelps, June 5, 1955 (dec. 1969); children—Carl James, Rebecca Susan. Tchr., Richland Center Sch., Rochester, Ind., 1943-44, Lakeview Sch., Tulia, Tex., 1944-45; staff therapist, student supr. Indpls. Gen. Hosp., 1953; dir. occupational therapy James O. Parramore Hosp., Crown Point, Ind., 1954-55; cons. occupational therapy Miller's Merry Manor, Peru, Ind. Vol. worker Meals-on-Wheels, 1972-86; mem. polit. action com. Campaign for UN Reform; local contact person Hoosiers for Equal Rights Amendment; active Common Cause, Nat. Audubon Soc.; vol. Leukemia Soc. Mem. Universal Esperanto Assn. (del.), World Federalists (v.p. Ind., nat. bd. dirs.), Internat. Platform Assn., Wilderness Soc., Women's Internat. League for Peace and Freedom. Democrat. Presbyterian. Home: 18 E 2d St Peru IN 46970

PHELPS, CARLENE SALTER, publishing executive, entrepreneur; b. Thomaston, Ga., Mar. 24, 1942; d. Raymond Elmo and Nellie Ruth (Dickerson) Salter; m. Joe Mitchell Phelps, Mar. 3, 1963; children—John Mitchell, Raymond Kell. A.S., Abraham Baldwin Coll., 1962. Sales mgr. Coffee County Broadcasters, Inc., Douglas, Ga., 1971-79; owner, entrepreneur The Douglas Shopper, 1980—, Advertising Mart, Inc., Douglas, 1983—; owner, pub. The Coffee Cup, Douglas, 1985—; cons. CJ Enterprises, Douglas, 1982—. Editor, pub. The Douglas Shopper (1st place for Gen. Excellence, Southeast Advt. Pub. Assn. 1983). Chmn. Coffee County Blood-mobile, 1976. Recipient 2nd place award in Southeast region for printed advt. Gen. Motors Advt. Awards, 1982, 83. Mem. Southeast Advt. Pub. Assn. (Best self-promotion advt. campaign 1983), Ind. Free Publ. of Am., Coffee County Jaycettes (pres. 1975), Ga. Jaycettes (mental health chmn. 1976), Douglas C. of C. (Christmas parade chmn. 1979), South Ga. Shoppers Assn. (co-founder 1986—). Baptist. Avocations: church activities; travel. Office: Advertising Mart Inc 313 N Peterson Ave Douglas GA 31533

PHELPS, CONNIE LEA, educator; b. Sioux City, Iowa, Aug. 4, 1953; d. Robert William and Carol Lea (Yeager) Rice; m. Ronald Wayne Phelps, May 31, 1975. Diploma fgn. missions with honors Moody Bible Inst., 1977; B.S. in Bibl. Studies, Dallas Bible Coll., 1981; M.Ed., East Tex. State U., 1982; postgrad. U. Ark., 1985—. Publs. asst. Epsilon Sigma Alpha Internat., Loveland, Colo., 1972-74; sec. receptionist Am. Graphics Press, Dallas, 1978-79; tchr. Pleasant Wood Christian Sch., Dallas, 1979-82, Beverly Hills Christian Sch., Dallas, 1982-83; tchr., elem. coordinator Three Lakes Christian Sch., Troy, Mont., 1983-85; grad. asst. U. Ark., 1985—; advisor Educators Mus. Adv. Council, Dallas, 1981-83. Contbr. articles to profl. jours. Mem. Friends of 7 Pub. TV, Spokane, Wash., 1983, KPBX Spokane Pub. Radio, 1983, Dallas Mus. Fine Arts, 1980-82. Mem. Tex. State Tchrs. Assn., Poets Roundtable Ark., Mont. Assn. Tchrs. of English and Lang. Arts, Phi Delta Kappa. Republican. Home: 709 Maple Dr Springdale AR 72764 Office: U Ark Grad Edn Bldg 219 Fayetteville AR 72701

PHELPS, DIANA JAYNE, nurse; b. Louisville, Sept. 25, 1941; d. James Windsor and Victoria Burt (Sappio) Deeble; R.N., St. Mary's Sch. Nursing, 1962; m. Marshall Lyons Phelps, Jan. 25, 1963; children—Peter Marshall, Deborah Lynn, Sarah Victoria, Rebecca Lynn. Charge nurse pediatrics Meml. Hosp., Worcester, Mass., 1964-66; nursery and pediatric nurse Grossmont Hosp., La Mesa, Calif., 1968-72; water safety instr. San Diego and Tustin, Calif., 1974-77; exec. dir. Orange County Apple Sch., Costa Mesa, Calif., 1977-80; child birth educator Shaw Health Center, Los Angeles, 1980—; lectr. in field. Chmn. bd. dirs. Orange County Apple Sch., 1977-80; adv. Com. on Pub. Health and Safety, 1981; vol. aide program Elem. Sch. Reading, La Mesa, 1972-73; pres. San Diego chpt. Children's Asthma Research Inst. & Hosp., 1970-72; ordained minister Ch. of Scientology. Recipient Pub. Service award Am. Acad. Husband-Coached Childbirth, 1976. Mem. Am. Cultural Assn. (v.p. 1980-81), Internat. Profl. Assn. (pres. 1979), La Leche League Internat., Internat. Childbirth Educators Assn., Soc. for Protection of Unborn Through Nutrition, Nat. Assn. Parents and Profls. for Safe Alternative in Childbirth. Author: How Natural Childbirth Can Protect You and Your Baby, 1979; producer: Welcome to Our World, movie, 1976. Address: 1401 Bryan Ave Tustin CA 92680

PHELPS, VADA JO, town official; b. Laramie, Wyo., Aug. 30, 1943; d. Joseph Marion and Zula Alsetta (Curtis) Thronebury; m. Bobby Eugene Andrews, Feb. 11, 1962 (dec. Feb. 1976); children—Terri Lynelle, Joel Douglas; m. Robert Lee Phelps, Sept. 20, 1979. Student U. Denver, 1982-86. Office mgr. Prudential Nat. Co., Denver, 1961-64; policy clk. Conn. Mut. Life Ins. Co., Denver, 1964-68; computer operator Genuine Auto Parts Co., Denver, 1969-70; bookkeeper Summit County Schs., Frisco, Colo., 1970-71; office mgr. B.D.F. Constrn. Co., Frisco, 1972-76, town clk.-treas. Town of Frisco, 1976—. Mem. accountability com. Summit Schs., Frisco, 1973-75. Mem. Internat. Inst. Mcpl. Clks. (cert. mcpl. clk.), Colo. City Clks., Colo. Mcpl. Fin. Officers Assn., Mcpl. Treas. Assn., Epsilon Sigma Alpha Internat. (Woman of Yr. award 1980). Republican. Mem. Church of Christ. Club: TOPS (Frisco). Avocations: traveling; reading; school. Home: 334 Emily Ln PO Box 313 Frisco CO 80443 Office: Town of Frisco 1 Main St Box 370 Frisco CO 80443

PHILBRICK, MARGARET ELDER, artist; b. Northampton, Mass., July 4, 1914; d. David and Mildred (Pattison) Elder; m. Otis A. Philbrick, May 24, 1941 (dec. Apr. 1973); 1 son, Otis. Grad. Mass. Sch. Art, Boston, 1937; postgrad. De Cordova Mus., Lincoln, Mass., 1964-65. One women shows: retrospective Ainsworth Gallery, 1972, Westwood Gallery (Mass.), 1977, retrospective Westenhook Gallery, Sheffield, Mass., 1977; group shows include: Boston Printmakers, 1948—, Soc. Am. Graphic Artists, 1954—, Nat. Acad., annually 1970-81, New Eng. Watercolor Soc., 1956—; 50 yr. retrospective exhbn., Westenhook Gallery, Sheffield, Mass., 1985; represented in permanent collections: Library of Congress, New Britain Mus., Addison Gallery, 1st Nat. Bank, Dallas and Boston, Met. Mus., Phila. Mus., Boston Pub. Library, Phila. Mus.; illustrator books: On Gardening, 1964, In Praise of Vegetables, 1966, Natural Flower Arrangements, 1972, Sheffield Frontier Town, 1976. Recipient Presentation print Albany Print Club (N.Y.), 1981; Best in Show award So. Berkshires Arts Council, Great Barrington, Mass., 1981; 1st prize watercolor Pittsfield Art Leage (Mass.), 1981. Mem. Soc. Am. Graphic Artists (Alice Standish Buel Purchase award 1971), Boston Printmakers (mem. exec. bd. 1950—), New Eng. Watercolor Soc. (mem. exec. bd. 1974-76, Hatfield award 1962), Academic Artists (1st Graphics award 1957, 86). Office: Westenhook Gallery Sheffield MA 01257

PHILLIPS, ALMA FAYE, lawyer; b. Pitts., Aug. 31, 1925; d. Alexander Harvey and Jean (Ginsberg) Weinberger; m. Leonard Phillips, Mar. 24, 1946; children—Robin, Susan, Nancy. B.A., U. Calif.-Berkeley, 1972; J.D., San Francisco Law Sch., 1977. Bar: Calif. 1979. Sole practice, Oakland, Calif., 1979—; pro tem judge Alameda County Mcpl. Ct., Oakland-Piedmont-Emeryville Jud. Dist. (Calif.), 1983—; mem. Voluntary Legal Services Program. Past pres., life mem. PTA, Oakland. Mem. Alameda County Bar Assn. (client's relation com., fee arbitration com.), San Francisco Lawyers Club, Calif. Bar Assn., San Francisco Bar Assn. Club: Highlands Country (pres., dir. 1983) (Oakland). Office: 1 Kaiser Plaza Suite 1135 Oakland CA 94612

PHILLIPS, BESSIE GERTRUDE WRIGHT, educator; b. Erie, Pa.; d. Charles Clayton and Mary Gertrude (Allen) Wright; m. Stephen Phillips, Oct. 2, 1942 (dec. Jan. 1971); children—Jane Appleton, Margaret Duncan (Mrs. Robert Cummings), Ann Willard (Mrs. Kevin Waters). A.B., Fla. State Coll. Women, Tallahassee, 1930; M.A., Mount Holyoke Coll. 1933. Sec. internat. hdqrs. World YMCA, Geneva, Switzerland, 1933-34; math. tchr. Washington Sem., Pa., 1930-32; acad. head, math tchr. Milw.-Downer Sem., Wis., 1934-37; trustee New Eng. Coll., Henniker, N.H., 1952-61, Orme Sch., Mayer, Ariz. 1962—, Peabody Mus., Salem, Mass., 1971—; bd. advisers Council for Advancement Small Colls., Washington, 1959-69; vis. com. for edn. Peabody Mus., 1983—; ednl. cons. in field. Bd. dirs. Salem Female Charitable Soc., 1943—, Mack Indsl. Sch., Salem, 1943—. Mem. Nat. Soc. Colonial Dames, Bostonian Soc., Cum Laude Soc. Republican. Presbyterian. Clubs: Chilton, Union, Eastern Yacht. Home: 30 Chestnut St Salem MA 01970

PHILLIPS, COLETTE ALICE-MAUDE, public relations consultant, educator; b. St. Johns, Antigua, W.I., Sept. 20, 1954; d. Douglas Alfred Richard and Ione Alice-Maude (Francis) P. A.S., Grahm Jr. Coll., Boston, 1974; B.S. summa cum laude, Emerson Coll., Boston, 1976, M.S., 1979. Editor in chief Govt. of Antigua, St. John's, 1976-78; TV talk show host Antigua Broadcasting Service, St. Johns, 1977-78; pub. relations dir. Patriot's Trail council Girl Scouts U.S.A., Boston, 1980-84; pub. relations mgr. Cablevision of Boston, 1984—; instr. Stone Hill Coll., North Easton, Mass., 1982—, Emerson Coll., 1984—. Dir. Urban League Eastern Mass., 1980—, Metro Council Ednl. Opportunity, Boston, 1981—; pub. info. com. Am. Cancer Soc., Boston, 1978—; cabinet mem. Finnegan for Boston Com., Boston, 1983. Recipient Outstanding Alumni award Emerson Coll., 1983, Internat. Student award Grahm Jr. Coll., 1974, Am. Cancer Soc. Intern award, 1976; United Way Agy. award for outstanding achievement in communication, 1981. Mem. Pub. Relations Soc. Am., Women in Communication (bd. dirs. 1984-85), Mass. Assn. Mental Health (bd. dirs. 1984—), Soc. Advancement Mgmt. Methodist. Home: 41 Colborne Rd Brighton MA 02135 Office: Cablevision of Boston 28 Travis St Boston MA 02134

PHILLIPS, DARLENE ANN, nurse epidemiologist, consultant; b. Springfield, Mass., July 24, 1951; d. Walter Theodore and Ann Christine (Morris) Kurman; m. George Stanley Phillips, Oct. 23, 1943. B.S.N., St. Anselm Coll., 1973; grad. course in surveillance, prevention and control of nosocomial infections U. Iowa, 1981; M.S. in Health Sci., Quinnipiac Coll., 1984. R.N., Conn. Staff nurse gynecology Yale New Haven Hosp., 1974-75, staff nurse ambulatory surgery, 1977-80, staff nurse recovery, 1975-81, infection control coordinator, 1981-83; nurse eipdemiologist Holyoke Hosp., Mass., 1983—. Recipient Otis Clapp award Am. Assn. Occupational Health Nursing, 1985. Mem. Assn. Practitioners Infection Control (New Eng. preceptor 1986-87), Area Health Edn. Ctr. Pioneer Valley, Nat. Assn. Female Execs., Sigma Theta Tau. Roman Catholic. Avocations: needlework; landscaping. Home: 158 Edgewood Rd West Springfield MA 01089 Office: Holyoke Hosp Inc 575 Beech St Holyoke MA 01040

PHILLIPS, DEBORAH LYNNE, telecommunications executive; b. Key West, Fla., Jan. 12, 1951; d. Melvin and Margaret Janet (Paul) P.; m. Mark David Bechtold, Dec. 24, 1974 (div. Nov. 1983). A.A., Pensacola Jr. Coll., 1971; student U. Md. Adminstrv. asst. J.A. Overton & Co., Coronado, Calif., 1971-73; communication dispatcher Police Dept., Imperial Beach, Calif., 1973-75; adminstrv. asst. Grace Bros. Ltd., Waipahu, Hawaii, 1976-77, Shah Assocs., Leonardtown, Md., 1979-80; telecommunication mgr. Tracor, Inc., California, Md., 1980—. Mem. Margaret Brent Bus. and Profl. Women's Club (chair young careerist 1982-83, chair by-laws 1982—, nat. bus. women's chair 1983—), Alpha Sigma Lambda. Office: Tracor Inc Star Route Box 302 California MD 20619

PHILLIPS, DOROTHY KAY, lawyer; b. Camden, N.J., Nov. 2, 1945; d. Benjamin L. and Sadye (Levinsky) Phillips; m. Manny D. Pokotilow; children—Bethann P., David M. Schaffzin. B.S. magna cum laude in English Lit., U. Pa., 1964; M.A. in Human Sexuality, Family Life and Marriage Counseling and Edn., NYU, 1975; J.D., Villanova U., 1978. Bar: Pa., N.J., U.S. Dist. Ct. N.J., U.S. Dist. Ct. (ea. dist.) Pa., U.S. Ct. Appeals (3d cir.), U.S. Supreme Ct. Tchr., Haddon Twp. High Sch. (N.J.), and Haddon Heights High Sch. (N.J.), 1964-70; lectr., counselor Marriage Council of Phila., marriage and family life counselor Marriage and Family Life Assocs., Willingboro, N.J., lectr. U. Pa. and Hahnemann Med. Schs., profl. cons., lectr. Lankenau Hosp., Phila., 1970-75; atty. Adler, Barish, Daniels, Levin & Creskoff, Phila., 1978-79, Astor, Weiss & Newman, Phila., 1979-80; ptnr. Romisher & Phillips, P.C., Phila., 1981-86; sole practice, 1986—; guest speaker radio and TV shows; featured in newspaper and mag. articles. Author: (with Gerald Gingrich) A Layman's Introductory Bibliographical Guide on Family Living and Sex Education, 1973. Mem. Rosenbach Found., Art Alliance, Phila.; bd. dirs. Philadanco; mem. Bus. and Profl. Women's Coalition of Fedn. Jewish Agys. Greater Phila. Mem. ABA, Assn. Trial Lawyers Am., Pa. Trial Lawyers Assn., Pa. Bar Assn., N.J. Bar Assn., Phila. Bar Assn. (chmn. early settlement program 1983-84, mem. rules drafting com. custody rules), Phila. Trial Lawyers Assn., Montgomery County Bar Assn., Camden County Bar Assn., Bus. Women's Network, Tau Epsilon Rho Law Soc., Kappa Delta Epsilon, Mensa. Club: Lawyers. Office: 220 S 16th St Suite 600 Philadelphia PA 19102

PHILLIPS, DOROTHY REID, library technician; b. Hingham, Mass., Apr. 21, 1924; d. James Henry and Emma Louise (Davis) Reid; m. Earl Wendell Phillips, Apr. 22, 1944; children—Earl W., Jr., Betty Herrera, Carol Coe. Cert., Durham Vocat. Sch., 1952; B.S. in Comml. Edn., N.C. Central U., 1959; postgrad. U. Colo., 1969; M.Human Relations, Webster Coll., 1979; postgrad. Grad. Sch. Library Sci., U. Denver, 1983. Vocat. nurse Meml. Hosp., U. N.C., Chapel Hill, 1955-59; vol. work, Cairo, Egypt, 1965-67; library technician Base Library, Lowry AFB, Colo., 1960-65, Fitzsimons Med. Library, Aurora, Colo., 1976—. Recipient Sustained Superior Performance award Med. tech. Library, Fitzsimons Army Med. Center, 1982, 83. Mem. AAUW (chpt. community rep. 1982-83, state chmn. edn. found. 1982-84, pres. Denver br. 1984-86), Altrusa Internat. (corr. sec. Denver 1982-83, bd. dirs. 1984-85), Delta Sigma Theta (corr. sec. Denver 1964-66). Democrat. Presbyterian. Home: 3085 Fairfax St Denver CO 80207 Office: Medical Technical Library Fitzsimons Army Med Center Aurora CO 80045

PHILLIPS, EDITH BELLE, library science educator; b. Shelby, Mich., Mar. 24, 1921; d. Boyd Earl and Jessie Beatrice (Rankin) Crowl; m. Clarence Albert Phillips, June 19, 1943 (dec. 1981); children—Jonathan Kirk, Sara Grace (dec.). B.A., Eastern Mich. U., 1942; postgrad. Wayne State U., 1942-45, U. Chgo., 1945; M.L.S., U. Mich., 1949. Jr. librarian U. Mich., Ann Arbor, 1945-49; librarian Chgo. Jewish Acad., 1951-52; cataloger and asst. dir. Kent County Library, Grand Rapids, Mich., 1953-55; asst. sch. librarian Mich. Pub. Schs., Grandville, 1958-62; head catalog and book selection coordinator Library of Mich., Lansing, 1962-68; assoc. prof. library sci., 1968-83, acad. program coordinator, 1983—; del. Mich. White House Conf., Lansing, 1979; tchr. A-J Seminar, Southfield, Mich., 1981; cons. City of Detroit, 1982, Gale Research Co., Detroit, 1982-83; mem. adv. com. Oakland Community Coll., Farmington Hills, Mich., 1983—. Author: (with others) Managment and Use of State Documents in Indiana, 1970. Editor: (with others) Background Reading in Building Library Collection, 1979. Mem. Friends of Detroit Pub. Library, 1970—, Founders' Soc., Inst. of Arts, Detroit, 1977—; Mem. AAUP, Assn. for Library and Info. sci. Edn. (liaison rep. 1979—), ALA, Mich. Library Assn. (chmn. library edn. caucus 1982-84), Women's Nat. Book Assn. (pres., bd. dirs. Detroit), LWV (bd. dirs. Southfield 1981—), ACLU (bd. dirs. Detroit 1981—), Kappa Delta Pi, Pi Gamma Mu. Avocations: reading; theatre; hiking; swimming. Office: 315 Kresge Library Library Sci Program Wayne State U Detroit MI 48202

PHILLIPS, ELIZABETH JOAN, advertising company executive; b. Cleve., July 8, 1938; d. Joseph and Helen (Walter) Tinl; m. Erwin Phillips, June 1956 (div. 1960); 1 son, Michael A. B.A., Fordham U., 1980. Account exec., David Cogan Mgmt., N.Y.C., 1969-70; account exec. N.F.L. Films, N.Y.C., 1977-78; mgr. sports programs Avon Products, N.Y.C., 1978-84; v.p. Needham, Harper & Steers, N.Y.C., 1984—. Mem. exec. com. Vanderbilt YMCA, N.Y.C.,

1976-84; ofcl. 1984 Olympic Games, Los Angeles, 1984; referee Women's Olympic Marathon, Los Angeles, 1984; pres. Met. Athletics Congress, N.Y.C., 1980-83. Club: N.Y. Road Runners (v.p., mem. exec. com. 1976-84). Office: Needham Harper & Steers 909 3d Ave New York NY 10022

PHILLIPS, ELIZABETH LOUISE (BETTY LOU), author; b. Cleve.; d. Michael N. and Elizabeth D. (Materna) Suvak; m. John S. Phillips, Jan. 27, 1963 (div. Jan. 1981); children—Bruce, Bryce, Brian; m. 2d, John D.C. Roach, Aug. 28, 1982. B.S., Syracuse U., 1960; postgrad. in English, Case Western Res. U., 1963-64. Cert. elem. and spl. edn. tchr., N.Y. Tchr. pub. schs., Shaker Heights, Ohio, 1960-66; sportswriter Cleve. Press, 1976-77; spl. features editor Pro Quarterback Mag., N.Y.C., 1976-79; freelance writer specializing in books for young people, 1976—. Author: Chris Evert: First Lady of Tennis, 1977; Picture Story of Dorothy Hamill (ALA Booklist selection), 1978; American Quarter Horse, 1979; Earl Campbell: Houston Oiler Superstar, 1979; Picture Story of Nancy Lopez, (ALA Notable book), 1980; Go! Fight! Win! The NCA Guide for Cheerleaders (ALA Booklist), 1981; Something for Nothing, 1981; Brush Up on Your Hair (ALA Booklist), 1981; contbr. feature on hair New Book of Knowledge; included in de Grummond Collection, U. So. Miss.; also contbr. articles to young adult and sports mags. Mem. Soc. Children's Book Writers, Internat. Platform Assn., Delta Delta Delta. Republican. Roman Catholic. Home: 1923 Olympia Dr Houston TX 77019

PHILLIPS, FRANCES ISABELLE, former educational administrator; b. Newark, Feb. 5, 1912; d. William Webster and Susan Isabelle (Snyder) P.; diploma Newark State Coll., 1933; B.Ed., Rutgers U., 1938, M.Ed., 1949. Tchr., N.J. elem. schs., 1933-48; tchr. of deaf, Newark, 1948-57; chmn. dept. edn. Gallaudet Coll., Washington, 1959-65; dir. spl. edn. West Essex Area Schs., Essex County, N.J., 1965-67; assoc. prof. Paterson State Coll., 1967-68; coordinator programs for deaf and hearing impaired, Hackensack, N.J., 1968-73, Bergen County Spl. Services Sch. Dist., 1973-74; mem. Gov.'s Ad Hoc Com. on Deaf Edn., 1968-74; adv. bd. N.J. Assn. Children with Hearing Impairment. Recipient Outstanding Alumni award Kean Coll., 1970. Mem. AAUW, Am. Assn. for Mental Deficiency, Conf. Ednl. Adminstrs. Serving the Deaf (hon.), Conv. Am. Instrs. of the Deaf, N.J. Speech and Hearing Assn., Assn. for Supervision and Curriculum Devel., Kappa Delta Pi. Club: Montclair (N.J.) Music. Home: 97 Haddon Pl Upper Montclair NJ 07043

PHILLIPS, GAYLE SARRATT, county official; b. Gaffney, S.C., June 26, 1939; d. Garland and Ethel (Wood) Sarratt; m. Dennis Lane Phillips, Aug. 30, 1958; children—Dennis Lane, Gregory Alan. Student Limestone Coll., 1985—. Clk. to county auditor Cherokee County, Gaffney, S.C., 1962-66, dep. auditor 1966-79, county assessor, 1979-85, county auditor, 1985—. Capt. United Way, Gaffney, 1984; del. S.C. Democratic Com., 1982, 1984; chmn. Cherokee County Dem. Com., 1984—; organist, music dir. New Heights Bapt. Ch., Gaffney, 1977—. Named Career Woman of Yr., Bus. and Profl. Women Assn., 1985. Mem. S.C. Assn. Assessing Ofcls. (treas. 1982—), S.C. Auditors and Treas. Assn. Avocations: softball; music. Home: Route 1 Box 408 Gaffney SC 29340 Office: PO Box 32 Gaffney SC 29342

PHILLIPS, GENEVA FICKER, editor; b. Staunton, Ill., Aug. 1, 1920; d. Arthur Edwin and Lillian Agnes (Woods) Ficker; m. James Emerson Phillips, Jr., June 6, 1955 (dec. 1979). B.S. in Journalism, U. Ill., 1942; M.A. in English Lit., UCLA, 1953. Copy desk Chgo. Jour. Commerce, 1942-43; editorial asst. patents Radio Research Lab., Harvard U., Cambridge, Mass., 1943-45; asst. editor adminstrv. publs. U. Ill., Urbana, 1946-47; editorial asst. Quar. of Film, Radio and TV, UCLA, 1952-53; mng. editor The Works of John Dryden, Dept. English, UCLA, 1964—. Bd. dirs. Univ. Religious Conf., Los Angeles, 1979—. UCLA teaching fellow, 1950-53, grad. fellow 1954-55. Mem. Assn. Acad. Women UCLA, Friends of Huntington Library, Friends of UCLA Library, Renaissance Soc. So. Calif., Conf. Christianity and Lit., Soc. Mayflower Descs. Lutheran. Home: 213 First Anita Dr Los Angeles CA 90049 Office: Dept English UCLA 2225 Rolfe Hall Los Angeles CA 90024

PHILLIPS, GWENDOLYN LORRAINE, chemical company executive, consultant; b. Washington, N.J., Sept. 20, 1946; d. Harold Winfield and Fredra Mary (Williams) Jackson; m. Tony Phillips, Nov. 11, 1982 (div. Nov. 1983). B.S. in Math., Morgan State U., 1968; M.S., N.J. Inst. Tech., 1978; cert. Wharton Sch., U. Pa., 1980. Cert. Lit. Tng. Inst. Analyst Sandoz Pharms., East Hanover, N.J., 1978, coordinator, 1980-82; rep. Dorsey Labs., Lincoln, Nebr., 1978-79; adminstr. Sandoz Corp., Wasco, Calif., 1979-80; supr. Sandoz Chems., Fairlawn, N.J., 1982-83, mgr., 1983—; cons., 1985-86. Mem. Nat. Fire Protection Inst., Nat. Assn. Female Execs., Chem. Personnel Assn., Delta Sigma Theta. Democrat. Mem. Islam. Club: Toastmasters. Avocations: photography; video technology; writing. Home: 60 Bergen St Garfield NJ 07026 Office: Sandoz Chems Fairlawn Ave and 3d St Fairlawn Nj 07410

PHILLIPS, JANA LAIRD, utility company program development specialist; b. Dallas, Mar. 8, 1958; d. Paul Craig and Naomi Jane (Affholder) Laird; m. David Watkins Phillips, Apr. 2, 1983. B.B.A., Baylor U., 1980. Market researcher Southwest Research, Dallas, 1978-79; staff writer Office of Pub. Affairs Baylor U., 1979; regulatory staff asst. Tex. Power & Light Co., Dallas, 1981; procedure writing analyst Tex. Utilities Services Co., Dallas, 1981-82; program devel. specialist Tex. Power & Light Co., Dallas, 1983—. Author: (short story) Missing in Israel, 1973. Mem. Dallas County Republican Assembly, 1980—; mem. asst. social chmn. Dallas County Young Republicans, 1980-83; mem. 500, Inc., Dallas, 1983-84. Mem. Press Club Dallas, Alpha Kappa Psi (sec. 1979), Sigma Delta Chi, Kappa Alpha Theta (asst. social chmn. 1979-80). Office: Tex Power & Light Co PO Box 660268 Dallas TX 75266

PHILLIPS, JAYNE ANNE, writer; b. Buckhannon, W. Va., July 19, 1952; d. Russell Randolph and Martha Jane (Thornhill) Phillips; m. Mark Brian Stockman, May 26; 1 son, Theo Thornhill; stepsons—Ben, Noah. B.A. in English, W.Va., U., 1974; M.F.A., U. Iowa, 1978. Teaching fellow M.F.A. Program U. Iowa, Iowa City, 1977-78; lectr. Humboldt State U., Arcata, Calif., 1978-79; fellow Fine Arts Work Ctr., Provincetown, Mass., 1979-80, Bunting Inst., Radcliffe Coll., Cambridge, Mass., 1980-81; asst. prof. English, Boston U., 1982-83. Author: Machine Dreams, 1984; (short stories) Black Tickets, 1979; limited edits. Fast Lanes, 1984; How Mickey Made It, 1981; Counting, 1978; Sweethearts, 1976. Recipient Sue Kaufman award Am. Acad. and Inst. Arts and Letters, 1980; fellow Nat. Endowment for Arts, 1978, 85. Mem. Authors Guild, PEN. Democrat. Office: care E P Dutton 2 Park Ave New York NY

PHILLIPS, JEAN BROWN, public relations consultant; b. Phila.; d. Harold T. and Elizabeth (Ulrich) Brown; m. John Tudor Phillips (dec.); 1 child, Barbara Jean. B.S., Drexel U. Producer, broadcaster Sta. WTVT-TV, Tampa, Fla., 1962-64; pub. relations exec. Frank Shattuck Co., N.Y.C., 1964-68, Creamer Dickson Basford, N.Y.C., 1968-72; editor Good Food mag., N.Y.C., 1972-75; pres. Phillips Communications, N.Y.C., 1976—; producer TV program Our Turn, 1982—. Cons., Displaced Homemaker Program, N.Y.C., 1982—, Midlife Inst., Marymont Manhattan Coll., N.Y.C., 1982—; founder, pres. Manhattan Older Women's League, N.Y.C., 1981. Mem. Am. Women in Radio and TV, Am. Home Econs. Assn. (N.Y. State Spotlight award 1982), Pub. Relations Soc. Am. Club: Overseas Press (N.Y.C.). Home: 360 W 22d St Apt 2E New York NY 10011

PHILLIPS, JOAN RYAN, florist; b. Louisville, May 9, 1941; d. John Lawrence and Lucile Graham (Wymond) Ryan; m. Richard Blankinship, Apr. 10, 1960 (div. 1974); m. Robert Edward Phillips, Oct. 26, 1974; children—Kimberly Graham, Jacquelin Ryan. Student Christian Coll., Columbia, Mo., 1959-61, St. Petersburg Jr. Coll., Fla., 1965-66. Owner, mgr. Northeast Florist, St. Petersburg, 1967-75, Maas Bros. Florist, St. Petersburg, 1975—, Clearwater, Fla., 1978-82. Bd. advisers St. Petersburg Vocat. Tech. Inst., 1984—. Recipient Golden Circle award Florist Transworld Delivery, 1984—. Home: 405 18th Ave NE Saint Petersburg FL 33704 Office: Maas Bros Florists 124 2d St N Saint Petersburg FL 33701

PHILLIPS, JUDITH INEZ, medical-legal consultant, nurse; b. Des Moines, Aug. 21, 1935; d. James S. and Catherine (Moore) Woodman; m. Weldon Bruce Phillips, May 24, 1958; 1 child, Gary Edwin; stepchildren—Cathey M. Brady, Weldon B., David Layne. B.S. in Nursing, Tex. Christian U., 1958; R.N., Harris Coll. Nursing, 1958; postgrad. Tex. Woman's U., 1967. Instr. N.W. Tex. Hosp. Sch. Nursing, Amarillo, 1958-59, St. Anthony Hosp. Sch. Nursing, Amarillo, 1959-60; staff nurse, evening supr. VA Hosp., Amarillo, 1960-68; clin. dir. rehab. High Plains Baptist Hosp., Amarillo, 1968-84; ptnr., cons. Inter-Profl. Cons., Canyon, Tex., 1983—; asst. instr., cons. West Tex. State U., 1968-78; cons. in-services Amarillo nursing homes, 1968-84; advisor health edn. programs Amarillo Pub. Schs., 1979-84. Columnist Fort Worth Star-Telegram, 1954-57. Contbr., mem. editorial bd. High Plains Highlights, 1968-84. Mem. Amarillo Women's Network, Amarillo C. of C., Tex. Nurses Assn. Republican. Baptist. Avocations: camping; travel; hand work; grandchildren. Home: 2522 12th Ave Canyon TX 79015 Office: Inter-Profl Cons PO Box 450 Canyon TX 79015

PHILLIPS, JUDITH PARKER, interior designer; b. Guantanamo Bay, Cuba, Sept. 16, 1954; d. John Adams and Frances Adeline (Zaino) Parker; B.S., U. Conn., 1976; m. Nicholas William Phillips, III, Apr. 14, 1978; 1 child, Kirsten Marie. Designer, Clark Contract Interiors, Hartford, Conn., 1976-78; project designer Contract Interiors, Detroit, 1978-79, Silvers, Inc., Detroit, 1980; sr. project designer Interiors Internat., Inc., Grand Rapids, Mich., 1980-81, design mgr., 1982-84, mgr. corporate showroom design, 1984-85; designer, Space planner Allied Office Interiors, 1985—; works include: sports complexes, schs. and housing in Saudi Arabia, Gen. Motors; freelance designer pvt. residences. Worthy advisor Rainbow Girls, Order Eastern Star, 1976—, recipient Grand Cross of Color; organizer glass recycling center, 1972. Recipient 1st prize student competition Inst. Bus. Designers, 1976. Mem. Inst. Bus. Designers (affiliate), Profl. Women's Network, Mgrs. and Suprs. Am. Seating Club, Blodgett Area Neighborhood Assn. Republican. Congregationalist. Home: 546 Maple Hill Lansing MI 48910 Office: 1048 Pierpont Suite 10 Lansing MI

PHILLIPS, KAREN BORLAUG, staff U.S. senate; b. Long Beach, Calif., Oct. 1, 1956; d. Paul Vincent and Wilma (Tish) Borlaug. Student Cath. U. P.R., 1973-74; B.A., U. N.D., 1977, B.S., 1977; postgrad. George Washington U., 1978-80. Research asst. research and spl. programs adminstrn. U.S. Dept. Transp., Washington, 1977-78, economist, office of sec., Washington, 1978-82; profl. staff mem. (majority) Com. Commerce, Sci., Transp., U.S. Senate, Washington, 1982-85; tax economist Com. on Fin., U.S. Senate, Washington, 1985—. Contbg. author studies, publs. in field. Recipient award for Meritorious Achievement, Sec. Transp., 1980, Spl. Achievement awards, 1978, 80, Outstanding Performance awards, 1978, 80, 81. Mem. Am. Econ. Assn., Women's Transp. Seminar, Transp. Research Forum, Blue Key, Phi Beta Kappa, Omicron Delta Epsilon. Republican. Lutheran. Office: 508 Dirksen Senate Office Bldg Washington DC 20510

PHILLIPS, LINDA JANE, software engineer; b. Pitts., Mar. 12, 1948; d. Henry Albert and Frances Helen (Moore) P.; B.S. in Math, U. Mass., Amherst, 1971; postgrad. Rensselaer Poly. Inst. Tchr. Stoneleigh-Burnham Sch., Greenfield, Mass., 1971-73, Assabet Valley Regional Vocat. High Sch., Marlborough, Mass., 1973; supr. software devel. Gerber Sci. Instruments, South Windsor, Conn., 1974-78; mgr. design software Gerber Systems Tech., Inc., South Windsor, 1979-80; dir. software engring. Nova Robotics, East Hartford, Conn., 1981-84; supr. CAD/CAM tech. Pratt and Whitney, East Hartford, Conn., 1984—. Gerber rep. to working com. Initial Graphics Exchange Specification, Nat. Bur. Standards, Gaithersburg, Md., 1980. NSF grantee, 1979. Mem. Nat. Assn. Female Execs., Computer and Automated Systems Assn. (sr.), Soc. Mfg. Engrs./CASA (sr.), The Computer Mus. (Boston) (founding), Alpha Gamma Delta. Office: 400 Main St 105-18 East Hartford CT 06108

PHILLIPS, LINDA LOU, pharmacist; b. Mason City, Iowa, Sept. 3, 1952; d. Reece Webster and Bettye Frances (Martin) Phillips. B.S. in Polit. Sci., So. Meth. U., 1974; B.S. in Pharmacy, U. Ark., 1976; M.S. in Pharmacy, U. Houston, 1980. Registered pharmacist, Tex. Pharmacy intern Palace Drug Store, Forrest City, Ark., 1976-77; pharmacy resident Hermann Hosp., Houston, 1978-79; dir. pharmacy Alvin Community Hosp., (Tex.), 1979-80; relief pharmacist Twelve Oaks Hosp., Houston, 1980; cons. pharmacist Health Facilities, Inc., Houston, 1980-81; pharmacy supr. Meth. Hosp., Houston, 1981—. Mem. Am. Pharm. Assn., Am. Soc. Hosp. Pharmacists, So. Meth. U. Alumni Assn., Ark. Alumni Assn., Arts Symposium of Houston, Am. Cancer Soc., Young Republicans, Rho Chi, Pi Sigma Alpha. Republican. Methodist. Club: Girls' Cotillion (bd. dirs. 1983-85). Home: 7400 Bellerive #403 Houston TX 77036 Office: Meth Hosp Pharmacy 6565 Fannin Houston TX 77030

PHILLIPS, LOIS BRINEN, university administrator; b. Bklyn., Mar. 1, 1940; d. Joseph and Stella Gloria (Gaffin) Brinen; children—Tracy Ann, Craig Gary. B.A., Queens Coll., 1961; Ed.M., U. Mass., 1973; Ph.D., U. Calif.-Santa Barbara, 1986. Speech tchr. Richmond Hill High Sch., Queens, N.Y., 1961-63; program dir. continuing edn. U. Mass., Amherst, 1971-72; univ. programmer, instr. U. Calif.-Santa Barbara, 1974-76; assoc. dean Antioch U., Santa Barbara, 1977—; cons. (feminist in residence) Loyola of Concordia, Montreal, Que., Can., 1976; producer Pacific Coast Community TV, Santa Barbara, 1974-76. Contbr. articles to profl. jours. Named Outstanding Woman, Santa Barbara County Commn. on Women, 1985. Mem. Research on Women and Communication, South Coast Bus. Network. Democrat. Jewish. Avocations: art; design activities; exercising; film studies. Office: Antioch U 914 Santa Barbara St Santa Barbara CA 93101

PHILLIPS, LOIS GAIL, exotic bird breeder; b. Detroit, June 21, 1939; d. John Patrick and Leona Victoria (Wagner) P.; B.S. in Chemistry, Fresno (Calif.) State Coll., 1962. Radiol. chemist Nat. Canners Assn., Berkeley, Calif., 1963-64; tchr. Progress Sch., Long Beach, Calif., 1966-67; vol. Peace Corps tchr., Nepal, 1967-69; univ. extension tchr. Nepal tng. programs, Davis, Calif., 1969-71; nursery employee Valley Gardens, Woodland, Calif., 1971-74, Farrell's Garden Center, Sonoma, Calif., 1974-75; mgr. 7-Eleven Store, Petaluma, Calif., 1977-85; environ. chemist Empire Environ., Santa Rosa, Calif., 1985—; owner Bodega Birds. Bd. dirs. Sonoma County People Econ. Opportunity, 1978-81, sec. to bd., 1978-79. Mem. ACLU, Am. Fedn. Aviculture, Nat. Audubon Soc., Sierra Club. Home: 1821 Lakeville St Apt 55 Petaluma CA 94952 Office: 3400 Standish Ave Santa Rosa CA 95407

PHILLIPS, LOIS PLOWDEN, travel agency owner; b. Ft. Gaines, Ga., Dec. 30, 1927; d. Leonard Dale and Helen (Lindsay) Plowden; m. James Henry Phillips, Aug. 25, 1956 (div. Feb. 1959); 1 child, Jaye Dale. Student Ga. State Coll. for Women, 1946-48. Adminstrv. asst. U.S. Air Force, Warner Robins, Ga., 1950-56; asst. buyer Mut. Buying Syndicate, N.Y.C., 1957-59; owner, operator Junior Vogue, Macon, Ga., 1960-69; mgr. Lee-Roi, Atlanta and Highland, N.C., 1971-73; mgr., buyer Isakson's, Atlanta, 1974-76; owner, mgr., pres., Mercury Travel, Inc., Atlanta and Marietta, Ga., 1977—. Mem. Am. Soc. Travel, Prost Exec. Women. Republican. Clubs: Idle Hour (Macon, Ga.). Avocations: travel; gardening. Home: 250 Halah Circle Atlanta GA 30328 Office: Mercury Travel Service Inc 1325 Johnson Ferry Rd Marietta GA 30067

PHILLIPS, MARGARITA GÓMEZ, microbiologist; b. Jerez, Zacatecas, Mex., July 20, 1942; came to U.S., 1964, naturalized, 1972; d. José Gómez and Guadalupe Lamas (de la Torre) Lozano; diploma Adult Tech. Sch., 1967; B.A. in Microbiology, U. S. Fla., 1972; m. Perry Lineal Phillips, Jan. 13, 1962; 1 son, José. Med. lab. technician Manatee Meml. Hosp., Bradenton, Fla., 1967-68; med. technologist Community Hosp., New Port Richey, Fla., 1973-74, head microbiology, 1974-75, asst. to mgr., 1975-80; microbiologist Smith Kline Clin. Labs., Tampa, Fla., 1980-82; chief technologist, mgr. Internat. Clin. Labs., Inc., New Port Richey, 1982—. Mem. Am. Soc. Clin. Pathologists, Am. Soc. Microbiology, Am. Soc. Med. Technology, Soc. Applied Anthropology, Nat. Cert. Agy. Lab. Personnel, Fla. Assn. Blood Banks, U. South Fla. Alumni Assn. Democrat. Roman Catholic. Home: 912 Linwood Terr Lutz FL 33549 Office: Colonial Med Center 151 Sunset Blvd Suite 6 New Port Richey FL 33552

PHILLIPS, MARILYN CHENAULT, legal administrator; b. Mt. Vernon, Ill., Oct. 21, 1949; d. Nathan Bullock and Marguerite (Woodberry) Chenault; m. Tom Dee McFall, Aug. 29, 1969; children—Shannon, Nathan; m. 2d, Troy David Phillips, Aug. 14, 1981; stepchildren—Todd, Brittany. B.S. with honors, Okla. State U., 1970. Adminstrv. asst. Opticks, Inc. div. G. D. Searle, Dallas, 1977-78; office adminstr. Baker, Glast, Riddle, Tuttle & Elliott, Dallas, 1978-81; dir. adminstrn. Haynes and Boone, Dallas, 1981—; lectr. instr. So. Meth. U. Sch. Law, Dallas, 1981—, paralegal program, 1981—. Lou Wentz scholar Coll. Bus., Okla. State U., Stillwater, 1969-70, also C.V. Richardson scholar, 1969-70; named Outstanding Office Mgmt. Grad., 1970. Mem. Nat. Assn. Legal Adminstrs. (bd. dirs. of adminstrn. sect. 1979-85, large firm adminstrn. sect. 1985—, instr. law office adminstrn. course 1984, pres. Dallas chpt. 1985-86), VS Legal Users Group (v.p.1985—), Wang Legal Adv. Council. Methodist. Home: 7038 Midbury St Dallas TX 75230 Office: Haynes and Boone Law Firm 3100 InterFirst Plaza Dallas TX 75202

PHILLIPS, MARION GRUMMAN, author, civic worker; b. N.Y.C., Feb. 11, 1922; d. Leroy Randle and Rose Marion (Werther) Grumman; student Mt. Holyoke Coll., 1940-42; B.A., Adelphi U., 1981; m. Ellis Laurimore Phillips, Jr., June 13, 1942; children—Valerie Rose (Mrs. Adrian Parsegian), Elise Marion (Mrs. Edward E. Watts III), Ellis Laurimore III, Kathryn Noel (Mrs. Philip Zimmermann), Cynthia Louise. Civic vol. Mary C. Wheeler Sch., 1964-68, Historic Ithaca, Inc., 1972-76; vol. Ellis L. Phillips Found., 1960—, now v.p.; bd. dirs. North Shore Jr. League, 1960-61, 64-65, 68-69, Family Service Assn. Nassau County, 1963-69, Homemaker Service Assn. Nassau County, 1959-61; writer; books include: (light verse) A Foot in the Door, 1965; The Whale-Going, Going, Gone, 1977; Doctors Make Me Sick (So I Cured Myself of Arthritis); Richard and Rhoda, Letters from the Civil War, 1982; A B-Tour of Britain, 1986; editor Jr. League Shore Lines, 1960-61; contbr. articles on fund raising to mags. Episcopalian. Clubs: Creek, Mt. Holyoke of N.Y., PEO Sisterhood, Hanover Garden. Home: Point of View Rural Route 1 Box 274 Sharon VT 05065

PHILLIPS, MELISSA JANE, physician, naval officer; b. Newport, Tenn., June 21, 1954; d. James Monroe and Lillian Jane (Ford) Phillips. B.S., Carson-Newman Coll., 1976; M.D., U. Tenn., 1980. Diplomate Am. Bd. Family Practice. Commd. officer U.S. Navy, 1977, advanced through grades to lt. comdr., 1984; resident Eastern Tenn. State U. Coll. Medicine, Kinsport, 1980-83; staff physician Navy Hosp.-Marine Combat Ctr., Twentynine Palms, Calif., 1983-85, quality assurance dir., 1983-85; staff physician Navy Hosp., Memphis, 1985—. Active Women's Missionary Union, Kingsport, 1980-83; tchr. Baptist Acteens, Kingsport, 1982-83; singer Kingsport Choral Soc., 1981. Fellow Am. Assn. Family Practice; mem. AMA (Physician's Recognition award 1983), Am. Assn. Family Practice. Baptist. Office: Navy Hosp NAS Memphis Memphis TN 38054

PHILLIPS, MIRIAM ERNESTINE, civic worker; b. Haverhill, Mass., Mar. 11, 1918; d. William B. and Ermina Floride (Coburn) Faulcon; m. Oscar George Dudley Phillips, Dec. 19, 1954; children—Peter Joshua, Miriam Elaine. B.A., U. Mass.-Boston, 1985. Adminstrv. asst. Am. Bapt. Chs. of Mass., Boston, 1948-58. Contbr. articles to religious publs. Nat. denominational v.p. Church Women United, 1974-77, Northeast regional v.p., 1977-80, other nat. and state offices; mem.-at-large Gen. Council, Am. Bapt. Chs. USA, 1969-71, rep. to gen. bd., 1971-78, Participant study tour to People's Republic of China, 1978; mem. exec. com. Bd. Nat. Ministries; rep. to Nat. Council Chs., 1969-72, del. to World Council Chs., 1968; v.p. Am. Bapt. Chs. Mass., 1972, 73, mem. personnel com., mem. communications com.; nat. chmn. communications Am. Bapt. Women USA, 1964-68; trustee Mass. Bible Soc.; trustee Andover Newton Theol. Sch., 1969—, sec. bd. dirs., mem. coms.; commr. Medford Housing Authority, Mass., 1972—, chmn., 1974-75; co-founder Medford br. NAACP, chmn. press and publicity; bd. dirs. Middlesex-Cambridge Lung Assn., Family Service Assn. of Greater Boston, Resthaven Home; missionary Am. Bapt. Mission, Hong Kong, and Japan. Recipient Valiant Woman award Ch. Women United, 1979. Avocation; travel. Home: 94 Monument St Medford MA 02155

PHILLIPS, NANCY CHAMBERS, social worker; b. Danville, Ky., Oct. 11, 1941; d. Alvia Jackson and Virginia Oradell Chambers; B.A., Georgetown Coll., 1962; M.S.W., U. Denver, 1968; postgrad. Tulane U., 1981—; m. Eldon Franklin Phillips, Nov. 27, 1968 (div. 1984). Tchr., Hazard (Ky.) High Sch., 1962; social worker Ky. Dept. Econ. Security, 1964-71; rehab. counselor Ky. Bur. Vocat. Rehab., 1971-72; team leader Cath. Social Services, Bureau, Ky., 1972-74; instr. U. Cin., 1972-77; vis. asst. prof. Fla. Internat. U., 1977-79; asst. prof. social work Idaho State U., Pocatello, 1979-81; research asst. Child Welfare Tng. Center Region VI, Tulane U., New Orleans, 1981-83; village mgr. Countryside Village, Belle Chasse State Sch., New Orleans, 1983-85; asst. supr. case mgmt. services Office Mental Retardation/Developmental Disabilities, Dept. Health and Human Resources, Belle Chasse Regional Service Ctr., 1985-86; now social worker Depelchin Children's Ctr., Houston, 1986—; former mem. profl. adv. bd. Fla. Soc. Autistic Children, South Fla. Soc. Autistic Children, Ohio State U. Community Edn. Unit Adv. Council. Formerly active children's subcom. Dade and Monroe Counties Mental Health Bd., United Family and Children's Services, Family and Child Advocacy in Action Group. Recipient ednl. stipend Ky. Dept. Econ. Security, 1966-68; named Ky. col. Mem. Nat. Assn. Social Workers, Council Social Work Edn., South Fla. Soc. Autistic Children (hon., nat. cert. of recognition 1979, Disting. Service award 1979). Home: 3821 Byron Houston TX 77005 Office: Depelchin Children's Ctr 100 Sandman Houston TX 77007

PHILLIPS, NORMAN JEAN, association executive; b. Denver, Mar. 17, 1938; d. Norman Clyde and Mary Asunda (Fantoni) Collins; m. Harold Ray Phillips, Sept. 30; children—Harold Ray, Allen, Dean Robert (dec.); m. Eugene Pfeiffer (div.). With Bank of Am., Escondido, Calif., 1956-65; receptionist, bookkeeper graybill Med. Clinic, Escondido, 1965-69; sec. treas. Harold Phillips Corp., Escondido, Calif., 1969—. Pres., Mothers Against Drunk Driving San Diego County, 1982—, Nat. Mothers Against Drunk Driving, 1985—, MADD/Nat. Council for Chpt. Affairs, 1985—; numerous TV and radio appearances, 1982—; mem. Presdl. Commn. on Drunk Driving, 1986, Nat. Commn. Against Drunk Driving, 1986. Recipient Outstanding Safety Vol. award Safety Engrs. San Diego, 1985, One of Outstanding Women San Diego County, ARC Orgn., 1985, One of San Diegans to Watch in '86, San Diego Mag., 1986. Club: Country Friends (Rancho Sante Fe).

PHILLIPS, PRISCILLA MOULTON, business educator; b. Lewiston, Maine, Nov. 6, 1918; d. Clement Richmond and Myrtle (Marston) Moulton; student Auburn (Maine) Sch. Commerce, 1939-42; B.S., Boston U., 1947, M.S., 1948, certificate Advanced Grad. Study, 1962, Ed.D., 1965; m. Warren Davis Phillips, June 20, 1964. Tchr. bus. dept. Edward Little High Sch., Auburn, 1942-47; summer demonstration tchr. Sch. Edn. Boston U., 1948, Tchrs. Coll., Columbia, 1949; supr. secretarial studies Bryant Coll., Smithfield, R.I., 1948-65, asst. dean secretarial sci. dept., bus. tchr. edn. dept., 1965-68, chmn. edn. dept., 1968-83; adv. bd. Citizens Bank R.I. Mem. corp. St. Mary's Home for Children, North Providence, R.I., St. Elizabeth Home, Providence; jr. warden vestry, clk. of vestry, pres. Episc. Ch. Women, St. Stephen's Episcopal Ch., also former trustee Nashotah (Wis.) House, Episcopal Sem., 1974-82; bd. dirs. Red Bridge Council Republican Women, 1983—, pres., 1985—; bd. dirs. Greater R.I. chpt. ARC, 1983—. Mem. Eastern Bus. Edn. Assn., New Eng. Bus. Educators Assn. (past pres.), Eastern States Assn. Tchr. Edn. (past pres.), Pottery and Porcelain (past pres.), Travelers Aid Soc. R.I. (past pres.), Pi Lambda Theta, Delta Pi Epsilon. Clubs: Agawam Hunt; Colonial Dames R.I. (historian), Soc. Mayflower Descendent, Providence Art, Providence County Garden. Contbg. editor: The Shorthand Corner in Business Education World, 1962-64, co-author column The Chalkboard, 1969-77. Contbr. articles to profl. mags.

PHILLIPS, ROSE MARY DEROSA (MRS. EMIL R. PHILLIPS), banker, retired city official; b. New Rochelle, N.Y., Feb. 18, 1918; d. Carl and Lucy (Cioffari) DeRosa; student Syracuse U., 1968-69; m. Emil Ralph Phillips, Sept. 28, 1941; children—Emil Ralph, Barbara Jean Phillips Pope, John R., Catherine Gulati. Employed with City of New Rochelle, 1935-74, city clk., 1964-74; former asst. cashier and exec. sec. to pres. Key Biscayne Bank (Fla.), now ret.; real estate broker, operator agy. Past trustee Police Pension Fund, City of New Rochelle, 1964-74, trustee Fire Pension Fund, 1964-74. Mem. N.Y. State Assn. City and Village Clks. (hon. life; sec. 1973—), Internat. Assn. Republican. Club: Soroptimist (pres. 1958-60) (New Rochelle). Home: 27 Beattie Ln New Rochelle NY 10805

PHILLIPS, SANDRA ADELE, physical education teacher; b. Cleve., Dec. 28, 1948; d. Eugene E. and Eva M. (Foster) Curtain; m. William K. Phillips, July 19, 1969 (div. 1981); children—Kimberly Adele, Kyllan Adele. B.S. in Edn., Cleve. State Coll., 1975, M.A. in Edn., 1984. Physical edn. tchr. Warrensville (Ohio) Heights High Sch., 1975—, dept. chmn., boys and girls track coach, 1983—. Active youth counseling East Mount Zion Bapt. Chr., 1978—. Martha Holden Jennings scholar, 1981-82. Democrat. Home: 2975 Becket Rd Cleveland OH 44120 Office: Warrensville Heights High School 4270 Northfield Rd Warrensville OH 44120

PHILLIPS, SUSAN MEREDITH, government economist; b. Richmond, Va., Dec. 23, 1944; G.A., Agnes Scott Coll., 1967; M.S., La. State U., 1971, Ph.D., 1973. Asst. prof. fin. La. State U., 1973-74; asst. prof. fin. U. Iowa, 1974-78, assoc. prof., 1978-82, interim asst. v.p. fin. and univ. services, 1979-80, assoc. v.p. fin. and univ. services, 1980-82; fellow in econ. policy Brookings Inst., 1976-77; econ. fellow SEC, 1977-78, dir. econ. and policy research; commr.

Commodity Futures Trading Commn., Washington, 1982-83, chmn., 1983—. Office: 2033 K St NW Washington DC 20581*

PHILLIPS, WILMA FRANCES, educational psychologist; b. St. Louis, May 2, 1927; d. Albert James and Anna Viola (Worstell) Fox; B.S. with highest honors, U. So. Miss., 1963; M.A.E., Ball State U., Muncie, Ind., 1972, Ed.D. (doctoral fellow), 1975; postdoctoral student U. Calif., Irvine and Loma Linda U., Riverside, Calif.; m. Doyle C. Phillips, Feb. 11, 1946; children—Lyndon C., Devaron Phillips Otis, Clayton C.; m. 2d, Bernard G. Dyer. Classroom tchr. Richmond (Ind.) Community Schs., 1969-73; assoc. prof. curriculum instrn. Loma Linda U., 1975-80; sch. psychologist Moreno Valley Sch. Dist., Sunnymead, Calif., 1980—; chmn. liaison com. early childhood edn. Calif. Articulation Conf.; mem. Riverside County Spl. Edn. Adv. Com., 1981-82; rep. task force on spl. edn. Gen. Conf. Seventh-day Adventist Pvt. Sch. System; chmn. early childhood edn. nat. com. Gen. Conf. Seventh-day Adventists. Cert. tchr., adminstr., spl. edn. tchr., reading specialist, early childhood edn. specialist, pupil personnel services, sch. psychologist, Calif. Mem. Nat. Assn. Sch. Psychologists, Calif. Assn. Sch. Psychologists, Southeast Counties Sch. Psychologists Assn. (pres. 1984); Council Exceptional Children, Internat. Reading Soc., Nat. Assn. Edn. of Young Children, Calif. Profs. Early Childhood Edn., Orgn. Mondiale pour l'Education, Prescolaire World Orgn. for Early Childhood Edn., Pi Lambda Theta, Phi Delta Kappa, Kappa Delta Phi. Republican. Cons. The Ladder of Life: Early Childhood Edn. Series, 1977—. Office: 13911 Perris Blvd Sunnymead CA 92388

PHILLIPS-GROENDYKE, VIRGINIA GAIL, oil co. exec.; b. Phillipsburg, Kans., Feb. 1, 1952; d. Boyd D. and JoAnn (Larimore) Phillips; B.A. in Polit. Sci., Okla. State U., 1974; M.B.A., Phillips U., 1978; m. John D. Groendyke, Aug. 17, 1985. Social worker HEW, Enid (Okla.) State Sch., 1975-76, coordinator vol. services, 1976; office mgr. Phillips Oil Operating Co., Enid, 1976—; pres. Ra-Gale Ltd. Petroleum Investment Co., Enid, 1976—; asst. to pres. and v.p. Eagle Petroleum Corp., Oklahoma City, 1978; title analyst Grace Petroleum Corp., Oklahoma City, 1979; co-owner Ra-Gale Trucking, 1981—. Contact worker Christian Telephone Ministry, Enid, 1975; worker United Fund Dr., Enid, 1975; mem. aquatics com. YMCA, Enid, 1976; bd. dirs. YWCA, 1981—. Selected as overseas student in Sweden, Phillips U., 1974, 1st female grad. of M.B.A. program, 1978; Mem. Nat. Polit. Sci. Orgn., Desk and Derrick Nat. Women's Petroleum Industry Assn. (Enid chpt. membership chmn. 1978), Phillips U. Geol. Soc., Phillips U. Masters of Bus. Assn., Alpha Phi (v.p. 1972). Club: Altrusa (Mem. of Year 1982). Author: Requirements for Small Business Policy manual, 1978. Office: PO Box 1728 Enid OK 73701

PHINIZY, YVONNE SHIRLEY, social worker; b. Bklyn., Dec. 11, 1946; d. Shirley La Mont and Rose Mae (Scott) Smith; children—Suzette, Mark. A.A., SUNY-Farmingdale, 1974; B.A., SUNY-Stony Brook, 1976, M.S.W., 1979. Therapist counseling service YMCA Outreach, Centereach, N.Y., 1979-84; social worker Wyandanch Schs., N.Y., 1980-86; therapist counseling service Babylon Drug and Alcohol Clinic, N.Y., 1984—; social worker Martin Luther King Health Clinic, Wyandanch, 1986—. Active Good Samaritan Hosp. Women's Guild, Wyandanch, 1985—, Women's Republican Club, Babylon. Mem. Nat. Assn. Social Workers, Nat. Assn. Black Social Workers (local treas. 1978-79, chpt. Outstanding Service award 1979). Avocations: reading; singing; piano. Office: Martin Luther King Clinic Straight Path Wyandanch NY 11798

PIACENTINI, PATRICIA RUTH YOUNG, sch. psychologist; b. Glen Ridge, N.J., Oct. 25, 1950; d. William Vernon and Elaine (Engelbrecht) Young; B.A., U. Va., 1972; M.A., Seton Hall U., 1975; m. Michael J. Piacentini, Nov. 27, 1976; children—Michael, Timothy, Matthew. Sch. psychologist Point Pleasant Beach (N.J.) Public Schs., 1976-78; dir.-psychologist Stafford Twp. Project, 1975-79; sch. psychologist Manchester Twp., N.J., 1977—, also Ridgeway Sch., Lakehurst, N.J.: cons. psychologist Project Gain, Tuckerton Pre-Sch. for Handicapped, 1979-80. Mem. exec. bd. Ocean County Unit for Retarded Citizens, 1975-77. Mem. N.J. Psychol. Assn., Ocean County Coalition for Pre-Sch. Edn., Nat. Assn. Sch. Psychologists, Am. Psychol. Assn., Monmouth County Med. Aux., Ocean County Med. Aux., N.J. Assn. Sch. Psychologists, Freehold Area Drs. Wives Assn. Presbyterian. Club: Manasquan River Yacht. Home: 810 Schoolhouse Rd Brielle NJ 08730 Office: Ridgeway Sch Route 571 Lakehurst NJ 08759

PIANETTI, CATHERINE NATALIE, occupational therapist; b. Rock Spring, Wyo., June 4, 1909; d. Anthony and Anna Mary (Plecco) P., diploma Seattle Pacific Coll., 1932; B.A. in Edn., Central Wash. U., 1938; postgrad. U. Wash., 1940; cert. of proficiency in occupational therapy Mills Coll., 1945. Tchr., Wash. Public Schs., 1936-45; chief occupational therapist Marion (Ind.) VA Hosp., 1948-50, 54-69; head occupational therapist NP sect. Walter Reed Army Hosp., 1950, Valley Forge Army Hsop., 1952-53; chief occupational therapist Downey (Ill.) VA Hosp., 1953-54; ret., 1969; lectr. Ball State U., Purdue U., Marion and Anderson colls. Bd. dirs., sec., v.p. Family Service Orgn.; bd. dirs., treas., v.p. Grant County Mental Health Assn.; bd. dirs. Blind Assn., Retarded Children Assn. Served from 1st lt. to capt., Womens Med. Specialists Corps., U.S. Army, 1950-53. Recipient Excellence in Communications with Pub. award, 1969, Mgrs. commendation on retirement, 1969. Mem. Am., Ind. occupational therapy assns., Am. Legion Aux. (1st and 2d vice comdr. Rainier Valley Post 139, 1971-72, comdr. 1976, comdr. Service Girls Post 1977, comdr. 1st Seattle Dist. 1978-79), 20 and 4, 8 and 40 (pres. 1976, chmn. 1979—), Pioneers of Columbia, Nat. Assn. Fed. Employees. Roman Catholic. Clubs: Seattle Womens Century (publicity chmn. rec. sec. Past Pres.'s Assembly 1974-75, treas. 1975-77, v.p. 1976-78, pres. 1979-81), DAV, Gen. Fedn. Womens' Clubs. Contbr. articles to profl. jours. Home: 4221 47th Ave S Seattle WA 98118

PIANTADOSI, JEANETTE KEMCHICK, educational consultant; b. Point Pleasant, N.J., Sept. 2, 1954; d. Patrick John and Gloria Edith (Stensland) Kmiechick; B.A. magna cum laude in Sociology, Am. U., 1977, M.Ed. in Student Devel., 1979; postgrad. (Charles Revson fellow) George Washington U., 1981; m. William Jay Collard, Mar. 12, 1982. Dir., Office of Fin. Aid Am. U., Washington, 1977-81; legis. aide (as Charles Revson fellow) Rep. Patricia Schroeder, Washington, 1981-82; dir. fed. and state relations Systems Research Inc., Washington, 1981-82; v.p. mktg. Sigma Systems Inc., 1982-84; v.p. The Wyndgate Group Ltd., 1984—; lectr., cons. Asst. cheerleading coach Spring Lake Elem. Sch., 1971-72; cheerleading coach St. Dominic's Elem. Sch., 1972-75, Catholic Youth Orgn., 1972-75; Mem. Del. Assn. Student Fin. Aid Adminstrs., D.C. Assn. Student Fin. Aid Adminstrs., Md. Assn. Student Fin. Adminstrs., NE Assn. Student Employment Adminstrs (sec. 1981-82), Eastern Assn. Student Fin. Aid Adminstrs. (exec. council, ex-officio mem. 1980-81) rep. to exec. bd. Washington 1978-81, pres. Washington 1980-81), Nat. Assn. Student Fin. Aid Adminstrs., Nat. Assn. Women Deans, Adminstrs. and Counselors, Fedn. Orgns. Profl. Women (liaison 1981-82), NOW, AAUW, Nat. Assn. Coll. Admissions Counselors, Phi Theta Kappa, Phi Kappa Phi. Democrat. Roman Catholic. Home: 11421 Sutter's Mill Circle Gold River CA 95670 Office: 9310 Tech Center Dr Suite 230 Sacramento CA 95826

PIAZZA, DEBRA JEAN, banker; b. Mineola, N.Y., Apr. 14, 1955; d. Frank V. Tobia and Euphemia A. Stepelton; A.S. in Bus. Adminstrn., SUNY, 1980; postgrad. Adelphi U., 1980; m. John Piazza, Aug. 31, 1974. Sec., Franklin Nat. and European Am. Bank, Westbury, N.Y., 1973-79; asst. sec. European Am. Bank, Westbury, 1979-80; v.p. Marine Midland Bank, N.Y.C., 1980—; speaker various cash mgmt. related confs., 1981—. Bd. dirs. N.Y. Diabetes Assn., 1977—, sec. bd., 1977-78, chmn. membership, 1981. Mem. Nat. Assn. Female Execs., Nat. Corporate Cash Mgmt. Assn., Cash Mgmt. Inst. Office: 140 Broadway New York NY 10015

PIAZZA, MARGUERITE, opera singer, actress, supper club entertainer; b. New Orleans, May 6, 1926; d. Albert William and Michaela (Piazza) Luft; Mus.B., Loyola U. of South; Mus.M., La. State U.; D.Mus. (hon.), Christian Bros. Coll., Memphis, 1973; L.H.D. honoris causa, Loyola U. at Chgo., 1975; m. William J. Condon, July 15, 1953 (dec. Mar. 1968); children—Gregory, James (dec. Oct. 1975), Shirley, William J., Marguerite P., Anna Becky; m. Francis Harrison Bergtholdt, Nov. 8, 1970. Soprano, N.Y.C. Center Opera, 1948, Met. Opera Co., 1950; TV artist Show of Shows, NBC, 1950-54; founder Marguerite Piazza Thanksgiving Gala for the benefit of St. Jude's Hosp., 1976. Dir. Cemrel, Inc. Bd. dirs. St. Jude Found., Found. World Literacy, NCCJ, Memphis Symphony Orch. Nat. chmn. Soc. for Cure Epilepsy; nat. crusade chmn. Am. Cancer Soc., 1971. Recipient Sesquicentennial medal for Carnegie Hall Concert, 1952; service award Chgo. Heart Assn., 1956, Fedn. Jewish Philanthropies of N.Y., 1956; named Queen of Memphi, Memphis Cotton Carnival, 1973, Person of the Year Louisianna Council for Performing Arts, 1975. Mem. Woman's Exchange, Beta Sigma Omicron, Phi Beta. Roman Catholic. Clubs: Memphis Country, Memphis Hunt and Polo, New Orleans Country. Home: 6018 River Oaks Rd Memphis TN 38119

PICACHE, JOSEFINA REYES, travel service company executive, marriage counselor; b. Bulacan, Philippines, June 19, 1945; came to U.S., 1970; d. Cesar Garcia and Leona (Pilao) Delos Reyes; m. Danilo Sabal Picache, Oct. 20, 1968; children—Beverly Reyes, Abigail Reyes. B.S. in Edn.-Guidance and Counseling, U. Philippines/East, 1967; M.S. in Edn. Adminstrn./Supervision, Old Dominion U., 1980. Guidance counselor Torres High Sch., Manila, 1967; asst. dir. Philippine Soc. for Prevention of Cruelty to Animals, Manila, 1968; adminstrv. asst. to alumni dir. Old Dominion U., Norfolk, Va., 1976-83; pres./owner Luna Internat. Travel, Virginia Beach, Va., 1983—. Recipient Achievement award Atlantic Filipino News, Norfolk, 1980, Recognition award Old Dominion U. Alumni Assn., Norfolk, 1984. Fellow Nat. Assn. Female Execs., Better Bus. Bur., Hampton Road C. of C., Womens' Network Tidewater, Holland Plaza Phase I and II Assn. Avocations: tennis; basketball; reading; traveling. Home: 5224 Hancock Ct Virginia Beach VA 23464 Office: Luna Internat Travel Service 4350 Holland Plaza Virginia Beach VA 23452

PICARDI, SHIRLEY MAE, university administrator; b. Margaretville, N.Y., Feb. 20, 1948; d. Clifford Daniel and Edna Rose (Moore) Ives; A.B. summa cum laude in chemistry, Radcliffe Coll., 1970; S.M., M.I.T., 1972, Ph.D. in Food Sci., 1976, S.M. in Mgmt., 1981; m. Anthony Charles Picardi, Sept. 4, 1970. Indsl. liaison officer M.I.T., Cambridge, 1976-79, asst. dir. Indsl. Liaison Program, 1979-80, spl. asst. to v.p. for resource devel., 1981, sec. Alumni Assn. 1981-85, bursar, 1985—; lectr. in field. NSF grad. fellow, 1970-73; Nestle Co. fellow, 1973-74; Nutrition Found. fellow, 1974-75; Alfred P. Sloan fellow, 1980-81. Mem. Inst. Food Technologists, Phi Beta Kappa, Sigma Xi. Contbr. articles to profl. jours. Office: Bursar's Office MIT Room E19-215 Cambridge MA 02139

PICCIANO, JACQUELINE LUCILLE, medical librarian; b. Los Angeles, July 19, 1928; d. Frank Booth and Margaret Mary (Metzler) Chambers; m. Eugene Michael Picciano, Dec. 31, 1955; children—Louis, Eugene, Stephen, Michael. B.A., Trinity Coll., Washington, 1946-50; M.S. in L.S., Cath. U., Washington, 1952; M.B.A., Rutgers U., 1986. Reference librarian Nat. Library Medicine, Washington, 1951-56; librarian of sci. library Hoffmann LaRoche Inc., Nutley, N.J., 1956-57; librarian Acad. Medicine N.J., Bloomfield, 1960-71; librarian Am. Jour. Nursing Co., N.Y.C., 1971-81; library systems coordinator Read More Publs., N.Y.C., 1982-84; assoc. librarian for document delivery Cornell U. Med. Coll., N.Y.C., 1984—; editor Internat. Nursing Index, N.Y.C., 1971-81; mem. Interagy. Council on Library Resources for Nursing, 1969-81, 84—, chmn. pro tem, 1983, pres., 1985-86; hosp. library cons., 1964—; mem. adv. com. N.Y./N.J. Regional Med. Library, N.Y.C., 1971-81, chmn., 1974-75, chmn.-elect governance council, 1977-78. Contbr. articles to profl. jours. Trinity Coll. scholar, 1946; fellow Cath. U., 1950. Mem. Med. Library Assn. (nat. by-laws chmn. 1979-82, nominating com. 1978, 83; pres. N.Y./N.J. chpt. 1974-75, chmn. program com. 1972-73, 82-84), AAUW (1st v.p. Bloomfield br. 1983-84, 86—), ALA (dir. div. 1968-71, by-laws chmn. 1972-73), Am. Soc. Info. Sci. (chmn. hospitality com. ann. meeting 1980, program com. 1984—). Roman Catholic. Home: 380 Essex Ave Bloomfield NJ 07003 Office: Cornell U Med Coll Library 1300 York Ave New York NY 10021

PICKEL, JOYCE KILEY, psychologist; b. Boston, Dec. 20, 1939; B.S. in Edn., Boston State Coll., 1961; M.Ed. (NDEA fellow 1967), R.I. Coll., 1968; M.A. (NDEA fellow 1967-68), Mich. State U., 1969; doctoral candidate No. Ill. U., 1982; m. Edward McDonald, Aug. 24, 1960 (div. Mar. 77); children—Catherine, Maureen, Edward; m. Mark Pickel, Apr. 6, 1982. Tchr. schs. in Mass. and R.I., 1962-66; guidance counselor Grand Ledge (Mich.) schs., 1966-67; diagnostician Eaton County Intermediate Sch. Dist., Charlotte, Mich., 1968-69; psychometrist, Hammond, Ind., 1969-70; coordinator programs emotionally disturbed and learning disabled, sch. psychometrist N.W. Ind. Spl. Edn. Coop., Highland 1970-72; instr. Ind. U., Northwest campus, Gary, 1970-72; program dir. Trade Winds Rehab. Center, Gary, Ind., 1972-73; supervising sch. psychologist Thornton Fractional Twp. High Sch. 215, Calumet City, Ill., 1973—. Vice pres. Wilbur Wright Middle Sch. PTA, Munster, Ind., 1975-76; mem. planning bd. Lake Area United Way, 1973—; 1st v.p. Greater Hammond Community Council, 1974-76. Recipient award Hammond Community Council, 1974, 75, 76, Community Service award Greater Hammond Community Council, 1975. Mem. Nat. Assn. Sch. Psychologists, Council Exceptional Children, Am. Fedn. Tchrs., Ill. Psychol. Assn., Ill. Sch. Psychol. Assn., Assn. Supervision and Curriculum Devel., South Met. Assn. Sch. Psychologists (pres. 1983-84, bd. dirs. 1985-86), Phi Delta Kappa. Office: 1601 Wentworth Ave Calumet City IL 60409

PICKENS, EVA HALL, writer, editor; b. Lafayette, La., Jan. 4, 1956; d. David Lee and Beulah (Kimble) Hall; m. Arthur Pickens, Jr., Aug. 9, 1980. B.A. in Journalism, So. U., Baton Rouge, 1977; M.A. in Telecommunications, Tex. So. U., 1986; postgrad. La. State U., 1980. Reporter, Opelousas Daily World, La., 1977-82; copywriter M. David Lowe Personnel Services, Houston, 1982-83; adminstrv. asst. Network Design Services, Houston, 1983—; freelance writer-photographer, Houston, 1980—. Publicity chmn. United Way of Greater Opelousas, 1977-82; mem. Houston Visitors Council, 1985-86. Recipient UPI Writers award for feature writing, 1980; named Most Supportive Staff, Univ. Program Council, 1984-85; Council for Advance and Support Edn. scholar, 1985. Mem. Nat. Assn. Female Execs., AAUW, Romeos (advisor 1985-86), Houston Area Urban League, Sigma Delta Chi, Sigma Gamma Rho (advisor 1985-86). Baptist. Avocations: writing; photography; bowling; playing cards. Home: 15918 Kenbrook Houston TX 77489

PICKENS, ZELDA JO, county official; b. Amarillo, Tex., Jan. 21, 1947; d. Mansel and Freddie B. (Burrows) Roach; m. Ronnie Kenneth Pickens, May 30, 1964; children—Ronald Douglas, Steven Graham. Student Amarillo Coll., 1976, Frank Phillips Coll., 1985. Cert. assessor, Tex.; registered profl. appraiser, tax assessor collector. Dep. Sherman County Tax Office, Stratford, Tex., 1974-76, chief dep., 1976-80, tax assessor collector, 1981—; mem. Bd. Tax Profl. Examiners. Chmn. com. 4-H Parent-Leaders Assn., 1981—; active Big Blue Band Boosters Assn., Stratford, 1981-85. Named Woman of Yr., Young Homemakers, Sherman County, 1971; hon. chpt. farmer, Future Farmers Am., Stratford, 1983-84. Mem. Stratford C. of C. (bd. dirs., 1982-85), Panhandle Tax Assessor Collectors (pres. 1982-84), Tax Assessor Collectors Assn. Tex. (bd. dirs. 1985—), Tex. Assn. Assessing Officers, Inst. Cert. Tex. Assessors. Democrat. Methodist. Clubs: Young Homemakers Sherman County (pres. 1969-72). Avocations: painting; needlepoint; camping. Office: Sherman County Tax Office Courthouse 701 N 3d St PO Box 1229 Stratford TX 79084

PICKETT, BARBARA ANN, tourism industry planning executive, consultant; b. Peterborough, Ont., Can., July 26, 1949; d. John Harris and Alice Mary (Perry) P.; m. Warren Bruce Adamson, Dec. 27, 1980. B.B.A., U. New Brunswick, Fredericton, 1971. Research officer Tourism New Brunswick, Fredericton, 1972-75; recreation & tourism planner Hunter and Assocs., Toronto, 1975-78; cons. Frank Wolman & Assoc., Toronto, 1978-79; prin. Pannell Kerr Forster, Toronto, 1979—; dir. Tourism and Travel Research Assn., Can.; Adv. bd. Pyerson Poly. Inst., Toronto, 1983—. Contbr. articles to profl. publs. Mem. Tourism and Travel Research Assn. (dir. 1983—), Am. Mktg. Assn., Accomodation Motel Ont. Assn. Progressive Conservative. Anglican. Club: Cobblestone. Avocations: sewing, gardening. Home: 1396 Glenwood Dr Port Credit ON L5G 2X1 Canada Office: Pannell Kerr Forster 55 University Ave Suite 800 Toronto Ont M5J 2K4 Canada

PICKETT, BETTY RUTH HORENSTEIN, psychologist; b. Providence, Feb. 15, 1926; d. Isadore S. and Etta (Morrison) Horenstein; A.B., Pembroke Coll., Brown U., 1945; M.S., Brown U., 1947, Ph.D., 1949; m. James McPherson Pickett, Mar. 10, 1952. Asst. prof. psychology U. Minn., Duluth Br., 1949-51, U. Nebr., 1951; lectr. psychology U. Conn., 1952; profl. asso. Bio-Scis. Info. Exchange, Smithsonian Instn., Washington, 1953-58; exec. sec. behavioral scis. study sect., div. research grants NIH, Bethesda, 1958-59, exec. sec. expt. psychology study sect., 1959-61; cons. NIMH Research Grants, HEW, region 1, Boston, 1962-63; exec. sec. research career program NIMH, Bethesda, 1963-66, chief cognition and learning sect., behavioral scis. research br., 1966-68, dep. dir. div. extramural research programs, 1968-74, dir. div. spl. mental health programs, 1974-75, acting dir. div. extramural research program, 1975-77; asso. dir. extra mural and collaborative research program Nat. Inst. Aging, 1977-79; dep. dir. Nat. Inst. Child Health and Human Devel., Rockville, 1979-81, acting dir., 1981-82, dir. div. research resources, 1982—. Mem. Am., Eastern psychol. assns., Psychonomic Soc., Assn. Women in Sci., Phi Beta Kappa, Sigma Xi. Contbr. articles to profl. jours. Home: 2561 Waterside Dr NW Washington DC 20008 Office: Div Research Resources Bldg 31 Rm 5B-03 Bethesda MD 20892

PICKETT, ELISABETH PAULINE, urological surgeon; b. Dallas, Feb. 18, 1918; d. John Charles and Emma Corinne Pickett. A.B., U. Colo., 1941, M.D., 1944. Diplomate Am. Bd. Surgery, Am. Bd. Urology. Intern, King's County Hosp., Bklyn., 1944-46; postgrad. in surgery N.Y. Med. Coll., 1946-47; resident in surgery N.Y. Infirmary, 1948-50, Meml.-Sloan Kettering Med. Ctr., N.Y.C., 1951-54; resident in urology N.Y. Hosp. Cornell U., 1954-55; fellow in urology Meml.-Sloan Kettering Med. Ctr., 1955-56; sect. head urology N.Y. Infirmary, 1956-75; attending urologist Meml. Sloan Kettering, 1956-79; sect. head urology Castle Point VA Med. Ctr. (N.Y.), 1976—. Mem. Pan Pacific Surg. Soc., Surg. Oncol. Soc. Home: 201 C Commons Way Fishkill NY 12524 Office: Castle Point VA Med Ctr Castle Point NY 12511

PICKFORD, LINDA ANN, shipping equipment and postage meter company executive, educator; b. Springfield, Mass., Mar. 19, 1959; d. Robert Cameron and Elizabeth Ann (Gross) P. B.A., Gettysburg, Coll., 1981; M.Ed., Rutgers U., 1985. Cert. reading specialist, elem. tchr., N.J. Supr. recreation facility Morris County Park Commn., Morristown, N.J., 1977-83; elem. tchr. Chester Twp. Pub. Schs., N.J., 1981-83; area sales rep. Pitney Bowes Inc., Cedar Knolls, N.J., 1983—; adj. faculty instr. Montclair State Coll., Upper Montclair, N.J., 1985—. Morris County committeewoman Republican party, Randolph, N.J., 1983—; vol. swimming instr. ARC, Morristown, 1975—. Recipient Excellence award Pitney Bowes Inc., 1983-84. Mem. Nat. Assn. Female Execs., NEA, Delta Gamma. Presbyterian. Avocations: snow skiing; aerobic dancing; scuba diving; swimming. Office: Pitney Bowes Inc 16 Wing Dr Cedar Knolls NJ 07927

PICKFORD, SHIRLEY ROBERTA CLAY, computer and financial consultant; b. London, Aug. 17, 1949; d. Thomas R. and Maisey D. (Clay) P.; children—Clay, Christina. B.A. cum laude, Boston U., 1969; M.A., Brandeis U., 1972; Ph.D., Tex. A&M U., 1977. C.P.A., Fla.; lic. Realtor, Fla. Owner, fin. cons. Fin. Planning for Women, Inc., Orlando, Fla., 1977-86; asst. prof. acctg. U. Central Fla., Orlando, 1977-81; assoc. prof. Fla. Atlantic U., Boca Raton, 1982-85; owner, computer cons. COMPSOL, Inc., Orlando, 1982—, also dir.; cons. Fla. Dept. Law Enforcement, 1978-80. Author: Accounting Principles, 1980-82. Fla. Dept. Law Enforcement grantee, 1980, 81. Mem. Am. Inst. C.P.A.s, Am. Acctg. Assn., Electronic Data Processing Assn., Phi Kappa Phi, Beta Gamma Sigma, Alpha Beta Sigma, Fla. Exec. Women (founder, pres. 1980-81). Avocations: running; reading; music.

PICONE, EDITH, real estate company executive; b. Bklyn., Jan. 24, 1917; d. Amedeo and Domenica (Smilari) Moretti; m. John Picone, Jan. 24, 1952 (dec.); children—John Jr., Peter, Elisa. Grad. high sch., Bklyn. Buyer, Goldsmith Bros., N.Y.C., 1934-51; mgr. Bellmore Liquor Co., Greenwich, Conn., 1951-72; pres. John and John, Inc., Greenwich, 1972-77; gen. ptnr. PIC Assocs., Greenwich, 1977—. Republican. Roman Catholic. Lodge: Order Eastern Star (Matron 1949-52). Avocations: travel; cooking; philately.

PICOTTE, SUSAN CARROLL, lawyer; b. Brighton, Mass., Sept. 2, 1954; d. John Dennis, Jr., and Patricia (Curran) Carroll; m. William Burgess Picotte, Aug. 12, 1978; 1 son, David Hunter. B.A. in Econs. magna cum laude, Russell Sage Coll., 1976; J.D., Union U., Albany, N.Y., 1979. Bar: N.Y. 1980, U.S. Dist. Ct. (no. dist.) N.Y. 1980. Legal clk. O'Connell & Aronowitz, P.C., Albany, 1978-79; assoc. firm Cooper, Erving & Savage, Albany, 1979-82, ptnr., 1983—. Bd. dirs., 1st v.p. Council Community Services N.E. N.Y., Albany, 1980-86; trustee Shaker Heritage Soc., 1983-86; mem. Jr. League Troy, Inc., 1981—. Mem. ABA, N.Y. State Bar Assn., Albany County Bar Assn. (dir.), N.Y. State Women's Bar Assn., Emma Willard Sch. Alumnae Assn. (dir. 1982—). Club: Hudson River (Albany). Office: Cooper Erving & Savage 35 State St Albany NY 12207

PIEL, ELEANOR JACKSON, lawyer; b. Santa Monica, Calif., Sept. 22, 1920; d. Louis Harris and Blanche Mellicent (Virden) Jackson; student U. Calif. at Los Angeles, 1936-39; B.A., U. Calif.-Berkeley, 1940, LL.B., 1943, postgrad. U. So. Calif., 1940-41; m. Gerard Piel, June 24, 1955; 1 dau., Eleanor Jackson. Bar: Calif. 1943, N.Y. 1957. Law clk. U.S. Dist. Ct., San Francisco, 1939, 44; dep. atty. gen. State of Calif., 1944, clk. U.S. Senate Civil Service Com., 1945; legal adviser Supreme Command Allied Powers, Japan, 1945-48; practice law, Los Angeles, 1948-55; atty. Legal Aid. Soc., N.Y.C., 1957-58; practice in N.Y.C., 1957—. Trustee, NYU, Med. Center, 1967—. Fellow ABA, Com. Public Justice; mem. Assn. Bar. City N.Y. (mem. spl. com. to revise criminal code 1970—, com. on penology 1971—, grievance com. 1973—, vice chmn.). Clubs: Cosmopolitan, Women's City (counsel). Home: 320 Central Park W New York NY 10025 Office: 36 W 44th St New York NY 10036

PIEL, JUDITH LOTT, nurse; b. Sumrall, Miss., Jan. 16, 1943; d. William Pearce and Barbara (Howard) Lott; m. J. Richard Piel, Aug. 2, 1971; children Christopher Blake, Matthis W. A.S.N., Troy State U., 1982. Registered nurse, Ala. Cardiac care nurse Bapt. Med. Center, Montgomery, Ala., 1982 . Democrat. Baptist. Clubs: Montgomery Toastmistresses, Montgomery Jaycettes.

PIEPENBRINK, NANCY LEA, nurse; b. Morrison, Ill., Nov. 4, 1948; d. Albert L. and Arlene E. (Montgomery) Benedict; B.S. Nursing, Ill. Wesleyan U., 1970; M.A., Central Mich. U., 1984; m. Harold C. Piepenbrink, Aug. 4, 1972; 1 dau., Alison Lea. Cert. mental health adminstr. Nurse, Ill. Dept. Med. Health, Chgo., 1970-73; head nurse VA Research Hosp., Chgo., 1973-75, VA Hosp., Bklyn., 1975-76, Ohio State Univ. Hosp., Columbus, 1976-77; nurse cons. on accrediation Ohio Dept. Mental Health, Columbus, 1977-78; dir. nursing Longview State Hosp., Cin., 1978—. Mem. Am. Nurses Assn. (cert. nurse adminstr.), Ohio Nurses Assn., Dirs. of Nursing of Ohio Mental Health, Dirs. of Nursing of Greater Cin. Area, Assn. Mental Health Adminstrs. (cert. mental health adminstr.). Home: 9499 Mapleknoll Cincinnati OH 45239

PIEPER, JANET LEAH, university administrator; b. Norfolk, Nebr., Feb. 12, 1932; d. Walter Arthur Arnold and Alma Eulalia (Heintzelman) Steffen; B.Sc., U. Nebr., 1954; postgrad. Omaha U., 1957-58, Butler U., 1965-66; M.A., U. Nebr., 1969, Ph.D., 1976; m. Donald R. Pieper, June 20, 1954; children—David Richard, James Steffen, Steven Donald. Math., English and journalism tchr. Stanton (Nebr.) High Sch., 1954-56; instr. English, Omaha U., 1956-58; asst. dir., editor Study Commn. Undergrad. Edn., U. Nebr., Lincoln, 1972-75, adminstrv. asst. to dean, 1976-78; dir. dept. personnel State Nebr., Lincoln, 1978-83; dir. personnel and employee relations Calif. Poly. State U., San Luis Obispo, 1984—. Chmn., Savs. Bond Dr. State Employees, 1978-81. AAUW Edn. Found. Project grantee, 1979-80, AAUW individual project grantee, 1973-74, Johnson fellow, 1971-72. Mem. AAUW (edn. chmn. state div. 1968-79), Nat. Assn. State Personnel Execs., Internat. Personnel Mgmt. Assn., Mortar Bd. Alumni Assn. (pres. 1978-79), Phi Beta Kappa, Pi Lambda Theta, Pi Mu Epsilon, Delta Phi Alpha, Gamma Phi Beta, PEO. Club: Sweet Adelines. Home: PO Box 730 Avila Beach CA 93424 Office: Administration Bldg Calif Poly State U San Luis Obispo CA 93407

PIEPER, PATRICIA R., artist, photographer; b. Paterson, N.J., Jan. 28, 1923; d. Francis William and Barbara Margareth (Ludwig) Farabaugh; student Baron von Palm, 1937-39, Deal (N.J.) Conservatory, summers 1939, 40, Utah State U., 1950-52; m. George F. Pieper, July 1, 1941 (dec. May 3, 1981); 1 dau., Patricia Lynn. One-woman shows: Charles Russell Mus., Great Falls, Mont., 1955, Fisher Gallery, Washington, 1966, Tampa City Library, 1977, 78, 79, 80, 81, 83, 84, Center Place Art Ctr., Brandon, Fla., 1985; exhibited in group shows: Davidson Art Gallery, Middletown, Conn., 1968, Helena (Mont.) Hist. Mus., 1955, Dept. Commerce Alaska Statehood Show, 1959, Joslyn Mus., Omaha, 1961, Denver Mus. Natural History, 1955, St. Joseph's Hosp. Gallery, 1980, 82; represented in pvt. collections. Pres., Bell Lake Assn., 1976-78, 79. Winner photog. competition Gen. Telephone Co. of Fla., 1979. Mem. Pasco County (Fla.) Water Adv. Council, 1978—, chmn., 1979-82, 83-84, 86; gov.'s appointee to SW Fla. Water Mgmt. Dist., Hillsboro River Basin Bd., 1981-82, 84—; active Save Our Rivers program, 1982-84, 85-86, chmn., 1986; adv. bd. Tampa YMCA, 1979-80. Mem. Nat. League Am. Pen Women (v.p. Tampa 1976-78, Woman of Yr. award 1977-78), Tampa Art Mus., Land O' Lakes C. of C. (dir. 1981-82, outstanding service award 1980), Fla. Geneal. Soc., West State Archaeol. Soc. Clubs: Lutz, Land O' Lakes Women's. Home and Studio: PO Box 15 Land O' Lakes FL 33539

PIEPERGERDES, LADON JOY, city health administrator, nurse; b. St. Joseph, Mo., Feb. 7, 1944; d. Donald Wilford and Beulah Louise (Powell) P. B.S.N., U. Mo., 1969; M.P.H., Johns Hopkins U., 1978. R.N., Mo.; cert. pediatric nurse practitioner, Ariz. Staff nurse U. Mo. Med. Ctr., Columbia, 1965-68, supr., 1966-67, charge nurse pediatric outpatient dept., 1969-72; pub. health nurse Columbia Health Dept., 1969; preceptor div. nursing Graceland Coll., Independence, Mo., 1973, instr., 1975-77; pediatric nurse practitioner Community Health of South Dade, Inc., Homestead, Fla., 1974; asst. prof. nursing Humboldt State U., Arcada, Calif., 1978-79; nursing supr. Independence Health Dept. Home Health Agy., 1979-85, asst. to health dir., 1985—; health team mem., expatriate nurse, Haiti, W.I., 1970-82; bd. dirs. Missions Health Found., Independence, 1980—; mem. Health Ministries Commn., Independence, 1982—. Scholar Am. Cancer Soc., 1965, Am. Bus. Women's Assn., 1978; USPHS trainee, 1968, 78. Mem. Kansas City Regional Home Health Assn. (v.p. 1983-84), Am. Pub. Health Assn., Am. Nurses Assn., Mo. Nurses Assn., Latter-day Saints Profl. Nurses Assn. (chmn. camp nursing 1975-77). Office: Independence Health Dept Home Health Agy 223 N Memorial Dr Independence MO 64050

PIEPER-JONES, ALEXANDRA, communications specialist; b. Norristown, Pa., Nov. 3, 1955; d. Harry Joseph and Regina Delores (Turner) Pieper; m. Ray N. Jones, Nov. 29, 1980; 1 child, Anne-Marie Jones. Student Flagler Coll., St. Augustine, Fla., 1973-74; B.A., U. Ga., 1978; postgrad. Ga. State U., Atlanta, 1981-85. Pub. relations dir. Ga. Lung Assn., Atlanta, 1978-82; editor publs. Days Inns of Am., Atlanta, 1982-83, editor Sept. Days mag., 1982-83, Days World newsletter, 1982-83; dir. communications Brawner Psychiat. Inst., Atlanta, 1983-85. Pub. relations vol. Ga. Lung Assn., 1983—; coach church high sch. girls basketball, 1979—. Athletic scholar, 1973. Mem. Internat. Assn. Bus. Communicators (communications awards 1983, 84), Pub. Relations Soc. Am., Women in Communication (v.p. fin. Ga. chpt. 1981-83), Atlanta Press Club. Democrat. Home: 57 Rolling Hills Ct Valdosta GA 31602

PIEPHO, SUSAN BRAND, chemist; b. Pound Ridge, N.Y., Apr. 28, 1942; d. Byron Alexander and Katherine F. (Brammer) Brand; B.A. summa cum laude with honors in Chemistry, Smith Coll., 1964; M.A. in Sci. Edn., Columbia U., 1965; Ph.D. in Phys. Chemistry (NDEA fellow 1968-70, A.T. Gwathmey Meml. award 1970), U.Va., 1970; m. Edward Lee Piepho, June 13, 1964. Secondary sch. tchr., N.Y.C. and Charlottesville, Va.,1965-67; asst. prof. chemistry Sweet Briar (Va.) Coll., 1971-73; postdoctoral research asso. U. Va., 1973-75; NATO postdoctoral fellow Oxford (Eng.) U., 1975-76; postdoctoral fellow U.So. Calif., 1976; asst. prof., then asso. prof. chemistry Randolph-Macon Woman's Coll., Lynchburg, Va., 1977-81; assoc. prof. chemistry Sweet Briar Coll., 1981-84, prof., 1984—, chmn. chemistry dept., 1982-86. NSF grantee, 1979, 82, 83, 86. Mem. Am. Chem. Soc., Am. Phys. Soc., AAAS, AAUP, ACLU (chmn. Lynchburg chpt. 1977-81), Common Cause (coordinator Amherst County, Va. 1979-82), Phi Beta Kappa, Sigma Xi. Democrat. Episcopalian. Club: Village Garden (treas. 1980-82, v.p. 1986-87). Author (with Paul N. Schatz) Group Theory in Spectroscopy: With Applications to Magnetic Circular Dichroism, 1983, also papers in field. Home: Box AM Briarhurst Dr Sweet Briar VA 24595 Office: Dept Chemistry Sweet Briar Coll Sweet Briar VA 24595

PIER, BETTY LAWWILL, farmer; b. Lexington, Ky., Jan. 7, 1940; d. James William and Nettie Cleveland (Wills) Lawwill; children—Andrea, Antony, Hunter, Jason, Errin. Secretarial diploma, W. Va. Career Coll., 1974; B.S. cum laude, Fairmont State Coll., 1982; postgrad. W.Va. Coll. Grad. Studies. Cert. counselor in service W.Va. Assn. Alcohol and Drug Abuse Counselors. Vol. coordinator Domestic Violence Shelter, Clarksburg, W. Va., 1981-82; adminstrv. aide Fairmont Emergency Hosp., W. Va., 1982-83; substance abuse counselor Appalachian Mental Health, Elkins, W. Va., 1983—; cons. Detoxification Unit Broaddus Hosp., Philippi, W.Va., 1983—; county coordinator Chem. People, Philippi, 1984—. Pres. Rachel Community Improvement Assn., W.Va., 1979-83; co-founder, publicity chmn. Soup Opera, Fairmont, 1982-83; bd. dirs. Country Living Farms Inc., Philippi, 1984—. Recipient Achievement Recognition and Monetary award Soroptimist Internat. 1979. Mem. W.Va. Assn. Alcohol and Drug Abuse Counselors, Bus. and Profl. Women, Swine Growers Assn. Avocations: swine growing; antique restoration; reading. Home: Rt 1 Box 203B Volga WV 26238 Office: Appalachian Mental Health Ctr 209 S Main St Philippi WV 26416

PIERCE, ADA CHRISTINE, medical technologist; b. Pampa, Tex., May 15, 1936; d. Lillard Garland and Laura Lorine (Brummett) P.; m. Alan Arthur Abraham, July 25, 1964 (div. Oct. 1980); children—Kevin, Kathleen, Kimberly, Kelly. B.S., Tex. Christian U., 1958. Cert. med. technologist Am. Soc. Clin. Pathologists. Med. technologist Worley Hosp., Pampa, 1958-60, Parkland Hosp., Dallas, 1961; med. technologist M.D. Anderson Hosp., Houston, 1978—, asst. chief, 1984—. Active membership League Women Voters, Eldorado, Ark., 1968-72; chmn. membership PTA, Houston, 1975, sec., 1976; pres. Christian Women's Fellowship, El Dorado, 1970-71, pres., 1972-73; elder Heights Christian Ch., Houston, 1978-83. Democrat. Home: 1450 Martin St Houston TX 77018

PIERCE, ANITA MAE, business executive; b. Johnson City, Tenn., June 21, 1946; d. Robert Bruce and Kathryn Ina (Heaton) P. m. Arthur Steve Fair, Feb. 20, 1965 (div. Apr. 1969); m. 2d, John Randolph Maher, Nov. 26, 1974 (div. Jan. 1984). Student East Tenn. State U., 1964-67. Sec. Tenn. Eastman Co. div. Kodak, Kingsport, 1964-65, 66-67; purchasing adminstrv. asst. solar aircraft div. Internat. Harvester Co., Inc., San Diego, 1965-66; with IBM Corp., Raleigh, N.C., Kingsport, Tenn., Cin., Armonk, N.Y., White Plains, N.Y., Atlanta, 1967—, mgr. central employment office, infor systems group, S.W. mktg. div., Atlanta, 1978—. Presbyterian. Home: 58 Middleton Ct Smyrna GA 30080 Office: 5775-C Glenridge Dr Atlanta GA 30328

PIERCE, CAROL ANN SMITH, psychologist; b. New Braunfels, Tex., Oct. 5, 1945; d. Charlie Robert and Pearly Joyce (Koch) Smith; B.S. in Edn., S.W. Tex. State U., 1969; M.A. in Psychology and Counseling, East Tex. State U., 1975, Ph.D. in Psychology, 1979; m. Max Pierce, June 20, 1979; children—Scott Orin, Zachary Ivan. Middle sch. tchr. Springfield Ind. Sch. Dist., 1969-73; mem. faculty East Tex. State U., 1975-79; staff psychologist East Tex. Mental Health/Mental Retardation Center, 1979-80; dir. Grayson County Guidance Clinic, Denison, Tex., 1980-82; pvt. practice psychology Sherman Psychol. Services (Tex.), 1982—; cons. in field; instr. continuing edn. Sherman Ind. Sch. Dist. Adv. bds. spl. edn. Sherman and Denison Ind. Sch. Dists. Mem. Am. Psychol. Assn., Southwestern Psychol. Assn., Tex. Psychol. Assn., Texoma Psychol. Assn. (pres.), Grayson County Social Services Assn. Episcopalian. Office: 2511 N Travis St Sherman TX 75090

PIERCE, CHARLOTTE, real estate broker; b. Paris, Ark., Nov. 28, 1937; d. Charles N. and Ruth McCormick; m. James B. Pierce, Jan. 1, 1956; 1 child, Elizabeth. Student N.Mex. State U., 1956-57, Eastern N.Mex. U., 1959-66, Norris Sch. Real Estate, 1983, Amarillo Coll., 1985. Real estate broker, N.Mex. Sec. to v.p. fin. N.Mex. State U., Las Cruces, 1956-58; legal sec. Smith & Smith, Clovis, N.Mex., 1959-66; legal sec., Aldridge, Aldridge & Harding, Farwell, Tex., 1966-76, office mgr., escrow mgr., 1976-83; owner, broker Pierce Real Estate, Texico, N.Mex., 1983—. Real estate loan packager USDA Farmers Home Adminstrn., Curry County, N.Mex., 1984—. Sec., Democratic Com. 2d Precinct, Texico, 1959-69; del. platform conv. N.Mex. Dem. Conv., 1968. Mem. Clovis Bd. Realtors, Realtors Assn. N.Mex., Nat. Assn. Realtors, Texico C. of C. (bd. dirs. 1985). Baptist. Avocations: travel; fishing; bird watching. Home: 400 Craig St Texico NM 88135

PIERCE, DELILA FRANCES, judge; b. St. Cloud, Minn., Jan. 21, 1934; d. Lawrence August and Alvina Elizabeth (Hechtel) Pierskalla. B.S., U. Minn.-Mpls., 1957, J.D. cum laude, 1958. Bar: Minn. 1958. Assoc. Robert L. Ehlers, St. Paul, Minn., 1958-59; ptnr. Mitchell & Pierce, Mpls., 1959-65; sole practice, Mpls., 1966-73; referee Family Ct., Dist. Ct., Hennepin County, Minn., Mpls., 1973-74; judge Hennepin County Mcpl. Ct., Mpls., 1974-83, Dist. Ct. Minn. (4th jud. dist.), 1983—; mem. adv. bd. Genesis II, Mpls., 1975-76. Fellow Am. Acad. Matrimonial Lawyers; mem. Am. Judges Assn., Nat. Assn. Women Judges, ABA, Am. Judicature Soc., Minn. State Bar Assn., Hennepin County Bar Assn., Minn. Dist. Judges Assn., Minnesota County Judges Assn. (bd. dirs. 1984—), Hennepin Hist. Soc., Mpls. Soc. Fine Arts. Office: Dist Ct Minn 4th Jud Dist Hennepin County Govt Ctr Minneapolis MN 55487

PIERCE, ELIZABETH GAY, club woman; b. N.Y.C., Mar. 26, 1907; d. Martin and Julia DeWitt (Stone) Gay; m. William Curtis Pierce, June 19, 1929; children—Martin Gay, William Curtis (dec.), Elizabeth Gay, Josiah. B.A., Barnard Coll., 1929. Vol. worker Boston City Hosp., 1929-30, Community Service Soc., 1931-32; mem. dependent children's sect. Welfare Council, N.Y.C., 1939-40; bd. dirs. Half Orphan Home (now Windham House), 1939-40; chmn. house com. North Shore Holiday House, Huntington, N.Y., 1944, pres., 1945; co-chmn. thrift shop com. Knickerbocker Hosp., N.Y.C., 1957-64; mem. exec. com. of women's com. Legal Aid Soc., N.Y.C., 1958; mem. exec. com. Women's Aux. Knickerbocker Hosp., 1960-64; bd. mgrs. Nat. Soc. Colonial Dames in State N.Y., 1962-67, corr. sec., 1965-67, pres., 1967-70; nat. pres. Nat. Soc. Colonial Dames Am., 1972-76, hon. pres., 1976—; trustee Jone Gallery Mus., Sebago, Maine, 1985—. Mem. Soc. Mayflower Descs. in State N.Y. (bd. assts., chmn. house com.), Nat. Soc. Daus. Founders and Patriots, Soc. Preservation New Eng. Antiquities (Maine council 1976—, mem., past chmn. Marrett House com.), Maine Citizens for Historic Preservation (adv. council 1983—), Grange. Episcopalian. Club: Colony. Home: Box 352 Route 1 West Baldwin ME 04091

PIERCE, GRACE WAGNER, environmentalist; b. Coatesville, Pa., May 9, 1926; d. Jacob and Grace Anne (Wallace) Wagner; student Goldey Coll., 1944, Wesley Jr. Coll., 1970, 73; pupil art Howard Schroder, Loren Kohut, Lon Fluman; m. W. Lemar Pierce, Dec. 15, 1945 (dec.); children—Linda Pierce Dolan, Barry Wallace Clark Pierce, Susan Pierce Gottfried. Owner, Pierce's Pharmacy, Inc., Dover, Del., 1962—; issues specialist Wilderness Soc., Washington, 1975-78; chmn. Watch Our Waterways, 1978-80; nat. environ. dir. Nat. Unity Campaign for John Anderson, 1980; nat. vice chmn. Nat. Unity Party, 1983—, acting chmn., 1985. Republican committeewoman 29th dist. Kent County, Del., 1966-69; chmn. vols. Kent County Rep. campaign, 1968; del. Rep. Nat. Conv., 1968; program chmn. Del. Fedn. Rep. Women, 1968-69; vice chmn. Kent County Rep. Com., 1969-72, vice chmn. edn. com., 1973—; pres. Fedn. Rep. Women Del., 1970-72; Rep. committeewoman 31st dist. Kent County, 1973—; chmn. Kent County campaign Gov. R.W. Peterson, 1972; candidate Del. Ho. of Reps., 1974. Pres. jr. bd. Kent Gen. Hosp., 1960-62; work with presch. children Capitol Green Community Center, 1970-71; chmn. East Coast Environ. Leadership Conf., 1974; mem. women's study com. Del. Tech. and Community Coll. Bd. dirs. Kent Gen. Hosp., 1971-76, Delawareans for Orderly Devel.; mem. Del. Water Quality Awareness Com., 1975-80, Del. Task Force on Low Level Radioactive Waste, 1984—; bd. dirs. Del. Audubon Soc., 1981—, pres., 1984—; treas. City Council of Slaughter Beach, 1981-83, sec., 1983—; mem. Citizens' Adv. Com. on Hazardous Waste of Delaware City, 1985—. Mem. Rehoboth Art League. Home: 1403 Shallcross Ave Wilmington DE 19806 Office: Del Audubon Soc Box 1713 Wilmington DE 19801

PIERCE, JANIS VAUGHN, insurance executive, consultant; b. Memphis, Dec. 23, 1934; d. Jesse Wynne and Dorothy Arnette (Lloyd) Vaughn; B.A. (univ. scholar), U. Miss., 1956, M.A., 1964; m. Gerald Swetnam Pierce, May 27, 1956; children—Ann Elizabeth Swetnam, John Willard. High sch. tchr., 1957-58; mem. faculty Memphis Univ. Sch., 1964-66, Memphis State U., 1968-75; agt. Aetna Life Ins. Co., Memphis, 1977-80, career supr., 1980—, mgr., 1983, supr. prime/career, 1984, chmn. Aetna Women's Task Force, 1980-85; agy. tng. Specialist Union Central Life Ins. Co., Memphis, 1985—; v.p., dir. Consultants System, Inc., bus. cons., 1975-84, pres., 1984—. Pres., Women's Resources Center, Memphis, 1974-77; sec. Tenn. chpt. Women's Polit. Caucus, 1975-76; bd. dirs., treas., mem. exec. com. Memphis YWCA, 1979—; mem. Memphis Area Transit Authority, 1982—, chmn. fin. and adminstrn. com., 1983—; bd. dirs. The Support Ctr.; mem. Tenn. adv. com. U.S. Civil Rights Commn., 1980—, steering com. Big Break, 1978; mem. adv. bd. Porterheath Children's Ctr., 1984—. Named Aetna Regionnaire, 1977-82, First Year Top Achiever, 1977; mem. Leadership Memphis, 1981. C.L.U. Mem. Million Dollar Roundtable, 1978, 79, Women Leaders Roundtable, 1978—. CLU. Mem. Nat. Assn. Life Underwriters, Tenn. Life Underwriters Assn., Am. Pub. Transp. Assn. (governing bds. com. 1985—), Women's Life Underwriters Conf. (bd. dirs., pres. 1985), Memphis Life Underwriters Assn. (bd. dirs. 1982, edn. chmn. 1982, pub. service com. 1983, law and legis. chmn. 1984, pres. 1986), Memphis PTA (council 1971-72), Memphis Soc. CLUs, LWV, AAUW, Mortar Bd. (regional coordinator 1972-78), Memphis C.L.U. Assn., C. of C. (ambassador 1980), Alpha Lambda Delta, Sigma Delta Pi. Republican. Episcopalian. Club: Le Bonheur (dir.), Memphis State U. Women's (pres. 1978). Home: 4743 Park Ave Memphis TN 38117 Office: Cons System Inc 5394 Estate Office Dr #1 Memphis TN38119

PIERCE, JOANN LEA, direct mail advertising consultant; b. Des Moines, Oct. 7, 1957; d. Richard Eugene and L. Ann (O'Bleanus) P. B.S., MacMurray Coll., 1978; M.A., Sangamon State U., 1979. Reporter, Record-Herald, Indianola, Iowa, 1979-80; asst. pres. sec. NOW, Springfield, Ill., 1980; copywriter Scott, Foresman & Co., Glenview, Ill., 1981-82; sr. copywriter Bradford Exchange, Niles, Ill., 1982-84; v.p., creative dir. PDM, Inc., Northfield, Ill., 1984-85; founder, owner Lea Pierce & Assocs., direct mktg. cons., 1986—; co-founder, prin. Sisters of Cinema, TV and film Scriptwriting, 1985—; creative cons. L.E. Kelley Mktg., Bloomington, Minn., 1983—. Mem. Nat. Assn. Female Execs., Chgo. Women in Advt., Chgo. Assn. Direct Mktg., NOW (founder South Lake chpt. 1981, pres. North Lake chpt. 1981-82, fundraising cons. Ill. 1982-85, Ill. polit. action com. 1983-85). Democrat. Home and Office: PO Box 326 Lake Bluff IL 60044

PIERCE, LISA, international management consulting company executive; b. Reading, Pa., Aug. 5, 1948; d. Charles S. and Emma Louise (Yost) P.; m. Mark L. Rutledge, Jan. 1, 1983. B.A., Hood Coll., 1970; postgrad. George Washington U. Grad. Sch. Bus., 1974-75. Program specialist Concentrated Employment Program, Pitts., 1970-73; economist, trade specialist U.S. Dep. Commerce, Washington, 1973-75; v.p. George A. Suter Assocs., Inc., Pitts., 1975-81, pres. Pierce Suter Assocs., Inc., Pitts., 1981—; dir. Labomet Inc., Pitts., Supermarket Systems, Inc., Chgo., GAM Lab. Fittings, Inc., Saxonburg, Pa. Bd. dirs. Grandview Tower Assn., Pitts., 1985. Republican. Club: Rolling Rock. (Ligonier, Pa.). Avocations: Fly fishing; hunting; scuba diving. Home: 1700 Grandview Ave Pittsburgh PA 15211 Office: Pierce Suter Assocs 711 Penn Ave Pittsburgh PA 15222

PIERCE, LOIS IRENE, office manager, horticulturist; b. Livingston, Mont., Apr. 14, 1919; d. Arthur L. and Iona L. (Park) Bruner; m. Augustus Edward Olson, Apr. 1, 1941 (div. 1954); 1 child, Neal W.; m. William Leroy Pierce, July 10, 1954; children—Deborah A., Richard L., Judith I. Grad. high sch. Propr. Olson Photog. Studio, Chelan, Wash., 1944-47; acct. Eddie's Flying Service, Chelan, 1942-51; bus driver, dispatcher Anchorage City Transit, 1951-55; office mgr., ptnr. Allied Builders, Spenard, Alaska, 1961-71; office mgr., ptnr. Pierce Holly Farms, Mulino, Oreg., 1971—; sec.-treas. Arctic Utilities, Inc., Spenard, 1961-71. Painter; poet. Republican. Baptist. Avocation: horticulture. Home and Office: 28404 S Hwy 213 Mulino OR 97042

PIERCE, MARY LOU, real estate investment firm executive; b. Mayodan, N.C., Dec. 19, 1937; d. Charles Howard and Dovie Ruth (Staples) Carter; m. Carl Edward Sauls, Nov. 11, 1955 (div. 1965); children—Carl Edward III, Teresa Sauls Frick; m. Al Stephen Pierce, July 2, 1965; children—Charles Vann, Candace Anjanette; 1 stepchild, Guy Stephen. Student pub. schs., Pomona, N.C., and Greensboro, N.C. Sec. Am. Discount, Greensboro, 1956-60, Black-Cad-Olds, Greensboro, 1960-62; bookkeeper Am. Discount, Greensboro, 1962-63; sec. Capitol Radio & TV, Nashville, 1963-65; ptnr., comptroller A. Steve Pierce & Assocs., Kernersville, N.C., 1965—. Recipient Exec.'s Wife/Husband award N.C. Assn. Long Term Care Facilities, 1981. Democrat. Home: 8921 Goodwill Church Rd Kernersville NC 27285 Office: A Steve Pierce & Assocs PO Box 1487 Kernersville NC 27285

PIERCE, MILDRED LOUISE, librarian; b. Fulton County, Ga., Nov. 30, 1928; d. John Oliver Pierce and Florence Idella (Carr) Sansted; m. Harry Eugene Springer, Oct. 17, 1967; 1 son, Jesse Ladd. B.S. in Edn., SUNY-Geneseo, 1951; M.A. in Librarianship, U. Denver, 1955. Library asst. SUNY-New Paltz, 1951; elem. librarian Hastings Pub. Schs., Hastings-on-the Hudson, N.Y., 1951; library grad. student aide Denver Pub. Library, 1954-55; children's bookmobile librarian Alexander Mitchell Pub. Library, Aberdeen, S.D., 1955-56; librarian Mineral County Sch. Dist., Hawthorne, Nev., 1956-64; adult edn. tchr. Clark County Sch. Dist., Las Vegas, 1964-65; tech. librarian RADSAFE, Reynolds Elec. and Engrng. Co., Mercury, Nev., 1965-67; reference cons. Mother Lode Library System, Auburn, Calif., 1967-68; dir. Tech. Info. Service, Hawthorne, 1976—. Author: Nevada Rockfinder, 1970; columnist An Ounce of Prevention, 1973-75; editor Wordwebs, 1979-81. Founder, trustee Walker-Wassuk Arts Alliance, Hawthorne, 1977; founder trustee Preservation Mineral County Courthouse and Flag Chowder and Marching Soc., 1982; candidate Nev. Senate, 1976, Nev. Assembly, 1978, 80. Mem. ALA, NEA, Nev. State Tchrs. Assn., Mineral County Tchrs. Assn., Mineral County Council on Alcohol and Drug Abuse, Mountain Plains Library Assn., Nev. Alliance for the Arts, Kappa Delta Pi. Republican. Episcopalian. Home: 674 I St PO Box 1721 Hawthorne NV 89415 Office: Tech Info Service PO Box 1721 500 E Fifth St Hawthorne NV 89415

PIERCE, SYLVIA YELLIN, social work administrator; b. Bklyn., May 31, 1926; d. Nathan and Tillie Spector; B.S.W., Adelphi U., 1974, M.S.W., 1975; children—Marion Yellin Bilich, Ronnie Yellin Charme. Staff social worker Glen Cove (N.Y.) Hosp., 1976-78; dir. social work dept. Community Hosp. Glen Cove, 1978—; pvt. practice marital and bereavement counseling Floral Park, N.Y., 1978—. Recipient Public Service award Anti-Defamation League, 1964. Mem. Glen Cove Inter-Agy. Council, Nat. Assn. Social Workers, Hosp. Dirs. Social Work, Soc. Clin. Social Work Psychotherapists, Acad. Cert. Social Workers, Nassau County Dirs. Hosp. Social Work, Nat. Assn. Social Workers. Home: 269-28 N Grand Central Pkwy Floral Park NY 11005 Office: Community Hosp at Glen Cove Saint Andrews Ln Glen Cove NY 11542

PIERCE-MEARNS, PENELOPE RUTH, marketing communications administrator, graphic designer; b. Newark, N.Y., June 13, 1947; d. Harold Austin and Annie Winefred (Schiltz) Pierce; m. Guy Earnst Martin, May 25, 1968 (div. July 1976); children—Timothy Guy, Rebecca Ann; m. James William Mearns, July 15, 1979. A.A.S., State Univ. Agr. and Tech. Col.-Farmingdale, N.Y. 1967. Retail art dir. Hutchins/Y & R, Rochester, N.Y., 1968-69; freelance graphic artist, Rochester, 1969-74; asst. art dir. Baldwin Advt., Rochester, 1974-78; art dir. Bausch & Lomb, Rochester, 1978-83; mktg. communications mgr., 1982-85; advt. mgr. Nagle Co. div. Sybron Corp., Rochester, 1985—. Vol. Sta. WXXI-Pub. Broadcasting System, Rochester, 1985-86. Mem. Rochester Women's Roundtable, Mktg. Communicators of Rochester, Rochester Soc. Communicating Arts. Avocations: sailing; traveling. Home: 131 Wintergreen Way Rochester NY 14618 Office: Nagle Co Div Sybron Corp 75 Panorama Creek Dr Rochester NY 14602

PIERPONT, GLENNA GAIL, energy/gas pipe line co. exec.; b. Bellville, Tex., Mar. 21, 1950; d. Steve A and Eunice S. Gindorf; B.S., Stephen F. Austin State U., 1972; m. William G. Pierpont, June 25, 1972. With, Transco Energy Co., 1973—, mgr. employee relations and personnel adminstrn., Houston, Tex., 1983—. Mem. Houston Personnel Assn., Sigma Kappa (nat. officer). Republican. Presbyterian. Home: 4206 Southwestern St Houston TX 77005 Office: Transco Energy Co PO Box 1396 Houston TX 77251

PIERSANTE, DENISE, public relations executive; b. Detroit, Jan. 9, 1954; d. Joseph Gordon and Virginia (Grunwald) P.; m. Wilfred Lewis Was II, June 7, 1975 (div. 1981). B.A. in Communications, Mich. State U., 1978. Tchr. Northwestern Ohio Community Action Commn., Defiance, 1979-80, counselor, 1980-82, job developer, 1982-83; job developer Pvt. Industry Council, Defiance, 1983, job developer coordinator, 1983-84, dir. pub. relations and job devel., 1984—; cons. Small Bus. Mgmt., Archbold, Ohio, 1985—; promotion dir. Miss Northwest Ohio Pageant, Defiance, 1985—; pub. relations coordinator Defiance County Social Service Agys., 1981—; author of various grants. Editor Job Tng. Partnership Act newsletter, 1984—, Defiance County Social Service Agys. newsletter, 1981—. Organizer, Auglaize River Race, Defiance, 1985. Nat. Merit scholar, 1972; recipient Am. Legion Citizenship award, 1969, 72. Mem. Pub. Relations Soc. Am., Nat. Assn. Female Execs., Jaycees (Jaycee of Month 1985). Club: Bus. and Profl. Women (Defiance). Home: 344 Rosewood Apt 37 Defiance OH 43512 Office: Pvt Industry Council 1933 E 2d St Defiance OH 43512

PIERSON, BONNIE COLLINS, school counselor; b. Corsicana, Tex., Nov. 4, 1943; d. Bill and Reba (Edmundson) Collins; B.A., Sam Houston State U., 1965; M.Ed., U. Houston, 1968; m. E. Benjamin Pierson, Nov. 27, 1970; stepchildren—Ben, Kitty, Richard, Greg, Luke, Lindsey. Tchr. English and French, Cy-Fair High Sch., Cypress-Fairbanks Ind. Sch. Dist., Houston, 1965-68, counselor Dean Jr. High Sch., 1968-70; counselor Del Valle (Tex.) Mid-Sch., 1970—. Recipient award for APGA, 1982, Disting. Legis. Ser. Award, APGA senator, 1982-85. Mem. Am. Assn. Retarded Citizens, NEA, Tex. Tchrs. Assn., Am. Assn. Counseling and Devel., Tex. Assn. Counseling and Devel. (lobbyist 1977—, pres. 1980-81), Am. Sch. Counselors Assn., Tex. Sch. Counselors Assn. (pres. 1978-79), Tex. Career Guidance Assn., Tex. Assn. Non-White Concerns, Nat. Vocat. Guidance Assn., Am. Assn. Mental Health Counselors, Tex. Mental Health Counselors Assn., Kappa Delta Pi, Alpha Chi Omega (TACD Rhosine Fleming Outstanding Counselor award 1985). Democrat. Presbyterian. Home: 10916 River Terr Austin TX 78733 Office: Del Valle Mid-School Del Valle TX 78617

PIERSON, KATHLEEN MARY, child care administrator, consultant; b. Detroit, Apr. 17, 1949; d. Peter and Elsa (Stanke) Kornberger; m. David Alan Pierson, Aug. 23, 1980 (div. Nov. 1981). A.S., Macomb Coll., Mich., 1974; B.S., Central U. Mich., 1976. Model, Detroit, 1970-74, also piano player, lounges; horse jockey, Detroit, 1974-78; recreation therapist Rehab. Inst., Detroit, 1978-81; exec. dir. Kreative Korners, Warren, Mich., 1981—; cons. low income child care centers Mich., 1986—. Bd. dirs. Macomb Coll., Warren, Mich., 1984—. Guest of Honor, Mich. Opportunity Soc., 1985, Easter Seal Soc., 1976. Mem. South Warren Community Orgn., Nat. Exec. Female Assn. Lutheran. Avocations: Doberman breeding; playing classical music; horseback riding. Home: 34160 Ryan Rd Sterling Heights MI 48077 Office: Kreative Korners Inc 22021 Memphis St Warren MI 48091

PIERSON, LOWANDA, nurse; b. Berkeley, Calif., Dec. 8, 1952; d. Frank Paul and Lela (Huggins) Smith; B.S. in Nursing, San Jose State U., 1975; m. Willie C. Pierson, June 22, 1974; children—Rukiya J., Anesah Naemah; 1 stepson, Micheal Sheldon. Profl. interviewer Field Research, San Francisco, 1973; staff nurse Choppe Hosp., San Mateo, Calif., 1975-76; staff nurse, asst. head nurse Children's Hosp. Med. Center, Oakland, Calif., 1976-78; head nurse O'Connor Hosp., San Jose; Calif., 1980; staff nurse med. ICU, Valley Med. Center, San Jose, 1981—. Mem. Calif. Nurses Assn., Critical Care Nurses Assn., Registered Nurses Profl. Assn. Democrat. Home: 3491 Tally Rd San Jose CA 95148

PIETRO, DEBORAH LOIS, data processing co. exec. b. Worcester, Mass., Nov. 9, 1950; d. Lawrence Foss and Ellen (Syrene) Seal; B.A. in Edn., Worcester State Coll., 1972; M.Natural Sci., Worcester Poly. Inst., 1978. Tchr. biology Kennedy Jr. High Sch., Natick, Mass., 1972-78; coordinator info. support services Mid-Coast Tchr. Center, Rockport, Maine, 1979-80; mgr. edn. services group, dir. sch. practices info. network Bibliog. Retrieval Services, div. Indian Head Co., Latham, N.Y., 1980—; cons. in field. Recipient various certs. appreciation. Democrat. Designer computer programs. Office: BRS 1200 Route 7 Latham NY 12110

PIETROCOLA, DONNA MARIE, surgeon; b. N.Y.C., Nov. 20, 1950; d. Joseph and Katherine (DiGeorgio) P.; m. Steven Pinheiro, July 16, 1976; children—Christopher John, Katherine Marie. B.S. in Biology, Wagner Coll., 1971; M.D., Albany Med. Coll., 1975. Diplomate Am. Bd. Surgery. Resident in gen. surgery Albany Med. Ctr. Hosp. (N.Y.), 1975-79, fellow renal transplantation, 1979-80, attending surgeon, 1980—; staff surgeon Albany VA Med Ctr., 1984—; asst. prof. surgery Albany Med. Coll., 1980—; courtesy staff Glens Falls Hosp., 1983, St. Mary's Hosp., 1983; instr. advanced cardiac life support Am. Heart Assn., 1982. Contbr. articles to profl. jours. Fellow ACS; mem. Assn. Acad. Surgeons, N.Y. Transplant Soc. Home: 9 Pepper Ln Loudonville NY 12211 Office: Albany VA Med Ctr Holland Ave Albany NY 12208

PIETTE, MICHELLE ELLEN, educator; b. Appleton, Wis., July 10, 1952; d. Norbert L. and Rosemarie P.; B.S., U. Wis., LaCrosse, 1975, M.S., 1980. Phys. edn. instr., Dodgeville, Wis., 1976-79; grad. asst. U. Wis., LaCrosse, 1979-80; asst. prof., athletic tng. program dir. Ariz. State U., Tempe, 1980—. Mem. Nat. Athletic Trainers Assn., Ariz. Athletic Trainers Assn. (chmn. profl. edn. com.), Ariz. Assn. Health, Phys. Edn., Recreation and Dance. Office: PEBE 146 Ariz State U Tempe AZ 85287

PIFALO, THERESA ANN, business executive; b. June 28, 1949; d. Joseph and Josephine (Polefrone) Picadio; m. William Joseph Pifalo. B.S.J.E., W.Va. U., 1970; M.S., California State Coll. (Pa.), 1974. Cert. tchr. journalism, English, Pa. Tchr. remedial reading Salisbury Elk-Lick Sch. Dist. (Pa.), 1970-71, tchr. accelerated classes, 1975-79; reading supr. Berlin-Brothers Valley Sch. Dist., Berlin, Pa., 1971-75; v.p. Pifalo Co., Inc., Cumberland, Md., 1979—; office mgr. B & B Masonry Contractors, Cumberland, 1979—; pres.

Art-To-Wear, Markleton, Pa., 1983—. Roman Catholic. Home: RD 1 Box 37A Markleton PA 15551 Office: Art-To-Wear RD 1 Box 37A Markleton PA 15551

PIGOTT, HANNE MARIA ALICE, property management company executive; b. Rothenburg, Ger., Feb. 3, 1948; came to U.S., 1973; d. Heinz Willy and Marianne (Weismann) Ahl; m. Joel Edward Pigott, Dec. 30, 1971 (div. 1978). M.S., U. Hamburg, 1971. Acquisition specialist Pump Sportshoe Factory, Herzogenaurach, Ger., 1971-73; v.p. L.C.H. Properties, Killeen, Tex., 1975-77; property mgr. Sanders Campbell, Dallas, 1977-79; dir. facilities mgmt. Dallas County Mental Health/Mental Retardation, Dallas, 1980-82; v.p. Joe Foster Mgmt., Dallas, 1982—. Mem. Bell County Apt. Assn. (pres. 1975-77), Tex. Apt. Assn. (dir. 1976), Bldg. Owners and Mgrs. Assn., Nat. Fire Protection Assn. Lutheran. Address: 7011 Stefani St Dallas TX 75225

PIGOTT, IRINA VSEVOLODOVNA, educational administrator; b. Blagoveschensk, Russia, Dec. 4, 1917; came to U.S., 1939, naturalized, 1947; d. Vsevolod V. and Sophia (Reprev) Obolianinoff; m. Nicholas Prischepenko, Feb. 1945 (dec. Nov. 1964); children—George, Helen. Grad. YMCA Jr. Coll., Manchuria, 1937; B.A., Mills Coll., 1942; cert. social work U. Calif.-Berkeley, 1944; M.A. in Early Childhood Edn., NYU, 1951. Dir.-owner Parsons Nursery, Flushing, N.Y., 1951-59; dir. Montessori Sch., N.Y.C., 1966-67; dir., tchr. Day Care Ctr., Harlem, 1967-68; dir.-owner East Manhattan Sch. for Bright and Gifted, N.Y.C., 1968—; organizer, pres., exec. dir. Non-Profl. Children's Performing Arts Guild, Inc., N.Y.C., 1961-65. Organizer Back Yard Theatre, Bayside, N.Y., 1959-61. Democrat. Greek Orthodox. Avocations: music; dance; theatre; art; sports. Office: East Manhattan School 208-210 E 18th St New York NY 10003

PIJOT, BARBARA LEIGH, advertising executive; b. Memphis, Mar. 13, 1952; d. Joseph David and Betty Lou (Roberts) Pijot; m. William Ray Logan, May 25, 1975 (div. 1979); m. 2d, James Gregory Natherson, Mar. 20, 1982. B.S., U. Fla., 1974. Asst. buyer, dept. mgr. Davison's, Atlanta, 1974-75; exec. trainee Joel Reedy, Inc., Tampa, Fla., 1975-78; media dir. Denton & French, Tampa, 1978-79; media dir., account supr., sr. v.p. Rafshoon Advt., Atlanta, 1979-82; advt. cons., Atlanta, 1982-83; account supr. Goodwin, Dannenbaum, Littman & Wingfield, Houston, 1983—. Mem. Mensa, Alpha Delta Pi. Republican. Presbyterian. Office: Goodwin Dannenbaum Littman & Wingfield 7676 Woodway Houston TX 77063

PIKE, DIANE KENNEDY (MARIANNE PAULUS), author, teacher-group facilitator; b. Norfolk, Nebr., Jan. 24, 1938; d. George Edward and Arlene Alice (Wyant) Kennedy; m. James Albert Pike, Dec. 20, 1968 (dec.). B.A., Stanford U., 1959; M.A., Columbia U., 1964. Missionary, tchr. United Methodist Ch., Montevideo, Uruguay, 1959-62; tchr. Unified Sch. Dist., San Jose, Calif., 1964-65; dir. youth-children's work First United Meth. Ch., Palo Alto, Calif., 1965-67; exec. dir. New Focus, Found., Santa Barbara, Calif., 1967-69; pres. Bishop Pike Found., Santa Barbara, 1969-72, The Love Project, San Diego, Calif., 1972—. Author: Search, 1970, Cosmic Unfoldment: the Individualizing Process as Mirrored in the Life of Jesus, 1976, Life is Victorious! How to Grow Through Grief, 1976, My Journey into Self, Phase One, 1979, The Process of Awakening: An Overview, 1985, (pamphlet) The Exodus Pattern: A Myth for our Time, 1974; (with others) (book) The Other Side, 1968, The Wilderness Revolt, 1972, Channeling Love Energy, 1974, The Love Project Way, 1980, (phamphlet) When We Love You, 1976. Co-editor: (mag.) The Seeker Mag., 1972—. Contbr. articles to popular mags. Democrat. Office: The Love Project PO Box 7601 San Diego CA 92107

PIKE, NANCY BROOKS, med. technologist; b. McComb, Miss., Oct. 22, 1952; d. James Hilton and Maxine (Arnold) Brooks; B.S., La. State U., 1975; m. Michael Alan Pike, Apr. 6, 1974; 1 son, Nathan Alan. Staff technologist Our Lady of the Lake Med. Center, Baton Rouge, La., 1975-76, Texoma Med. Center, Denison, Tex., 1976-80, asso. dir. labs., 1980—; med. lab. technician clin. coordinator Grayson County Coll. and various hosp. coms.; lectr. in field. Vol. worker Cystic Fibrosis, Multiple Sclerosis, March of Dimes; Acteen leader First Baptist Ch. Mem. Am. Soc. Clin. Pathologists (cert. med. technologist, specialist in hematology), Phi Mu, Beta Sigma Phi, Lambda Tau. Democrat. Club: Denison Rod & Gun. Office: Texoma Med Center 1000 Memorial St Denison TX 75020

PIKE, PRISCILLA RAE, court reporting services executive; b. Los Angeles, Dec. 7, 1930; d. Raymond Bruce and Amy Elizabeth (Dunaway) Linganfield; student schs. Glendale, Calif.; m. William F. Pike, Aug. 7, 1949; children—Pamela R. Pike Plowman, Lauri E. Pike Miller, Gary W., Thomas C. Various positions Ventura County (Calif.) dist. atty's office, superior ct.; county clk. Ventura County Bd. Suprs., 1970-75; hearing reporter Calif. Coastal Commn., Ventura, 1977—; founder Priscilla Pike Hearing Reporter Services, Ventura, 1978—; ct. reporter coordinator Pacific Career Coll., West Los Angeles, Calif.; conf. planner, author; participant confs. U.S., Can. Bd. dirs. Friends of Commn. for Women Ventura County. Mem. Nat. Ct. Reporters Assn., Calif. Ct. Reporters Assn., Nat. Assn. Female Execs. Christian Scientist. Republican. Office: 3639 E Harbor Blvd Suite 203-A Ventura CA 93001

PILAND, JULIA CASSIN, media executive; b. Columbia, Mo., Nov. 13, 1950; d. Eugene Paul and Reba Mae (Nelson) Cassin, m. Philip James Piland, May 18, 1974; children—Katherine Julia, Andrew Nelson, Sara Ann. Student U. Mo.-Columbia, 1968-70, So. Meth. U., 1971-74. Media asst. Tracy-Locke, Inc., Dallas, 1970-74, assoc. media dir., 1984—; media dir. Popejoy & Fischel Advt., Dallas, 1974-79; media supr. Bozell & Jacobs, Inc., Dallas, 1979-81; advt. mgr. Curtis Mathes Corp., Dallas, 1981-84. Mem. Dallas Mus. of Art, Dallas Advt. League, Assn. Broadcasting Execs. Tex. Republican. Episcopalian. Home: 1908 Royalwood Arlington TX 76006 Office: Tracy-Locke Inc PO Box 50129 Dallas TX 75250

PILAO, LEONORA CARRIAGA, nurse; b. Lucena City, Philippines, Feb. 20, 1951; came to U.S., 1973, naturalized, 1981; d. Norberto Pamposa and Natalia Laloon (Carriaga) P.; B.S. in Nursing, U. of the Philippines, 1972; postgrad. in gerontology Rutgers U., 1976, U. Pa., 1980; postgrad. in philosophy Manhattan Sch. Practical Philosophy and Econs., 1984—. Head nurse Senator Convalescent Center, Atlantic City, 1973-74; nursing supr. Senator Manor Nursing Home, Atlantic City, 1974-75; dir. in-service edn. Shore Manor Nursing Home, Atlantic City, 1975-76, asst. dir. nursing, 1976-77; dir. nursing services SCA Intermediate Care Facility, Atlantic City, 1977—, alternate adminstr., 1979—; mgmt. cons. Golden Crest Convalescent Center, Atlantic City, 1978-80, 85—; chmn. com. investigating impact of casino industry to health care delivery Atlantic County, 1980; participant Kellogg Found. nursing adminstrn. tng. program U. Pa., 1982, Soviet-Am. Gerontol. Nursing Study Tour, 1982; guest speaker civic orgn. Mem. Am. Nurses Assn., N.J. Assn. In-Service Edn. and Tng., N.J. League of Nursing, Nat. Assn. Female Execs. Condr. research on efficacy of influenza vaccine among elderly, 1980. Home: Somers Point NJ 08244 Office: 166 S South Carolina Ave Atlantic City NJ 08401

PILE, MARY PAULINE, psychotherapist; b. Oceanside, Calif., Sept. 16, 1954; d. Thomas North and Kathryn Mae Pile; B.S. with honors, Western Ill. U., 1975; M.A., Ball State U., 1977; postgrad. Fielding Inst., 1984—. Staff psychologist Youth Care, Inc., Greensboro, N.C., 1977-84; psychotherapist, Greensboro, N.C., 1983—; adj. instr. Guilford Tech. Community Coll., Jamestown, N.C., 1985—. Mem. women's adv. com. Humana Hosp., Greensboro, 1985—; bd. dirs. Family Life Council, 1984—, Crisis Control Ctr., Greensboro, 1984—; mem. Commn. on Status of Women, 1980—, Task Force on Battered Women, 1977-79. Named Rookie of Yr., Greensboro Jaycettes, 1980. Mem. Womens Profl. Forum, Am. Assn. Marriage and Family Therapists, Guilford Psychol. Soc. (sec. 1980-81), Assn. for Anorexia Nervosa and Assoc. Disorders, PEO (chpt. officer 1982), Young Womens Bus. and Profl. Club (program chmn.), Sigma Xi, Psi Chi, Alpha Lambda Delta. Democrat. Presbyterian. Club: Zonta. Avocations: travel; reading; swimming. Office: Ctr for Psychotherapy 912 N Elm St Greensboro NC 27401

PILIERE, DIANE FRANCINE, business executive; b. Camden, N.J., July 21, 1940; d. John and Mary (DiSalvio) P. B.S. in Social Sci., St. Joseph's U., 1970; M.S. in Bus. and Psychology, Miami U., 1973; doctoral candidate Pace U. Adminstr., RCA Corp., Camden, N.J., 1958-72; mgmt. devel. specialist Gen. Dynamics, Groton, Conn., 1973-77; mgr. Singer-Kearfott, Little Falls, N.J., 1977—. Bd. dirs. John C. Crystal Ctr., N.Y.C., 1982—, CETA Industry Council, Paterson, N.J., 1981-82. Recipient Tribute to Women in Industry award YWCA Ridgewood (N.J.), 1982. Mem. Am. Soc. Tng. and Devel., Am. Mgmt. Assn. Home: 180 Montclair Ave Upper Montclair NJ 07043 ... Office: Singer-Kearfott Div 1150 McBride Ave Little Falls NJ 07424

PILL, CYNTHIA JOAN, social worker; b. N.Y.C., Mar. 30, 1939; d. Alfred and Edna (Strauss) Fruchtman; B.S. cum laude, Jackson Coll., Tufts U., 1961; M.S., Sch. Social Work, Simmons Coll. 1963; m. Robert Pill, July 29, 1961; children—Laura, Daniel, Karen. Clin. social worker Concord (Mass.) Family Service, 1965-78; coordinator family life edn. Family Counseling Service, Newton, Mass., 1979-83; pvt. practice clin. social work, Newton, Mass., 1979—; co-founder, clin. social worker Remarriage Counseling Collaborative, Newton, Mass., 1981—; cons. Hospice of the Good Shepherd Inc., 1979-84. Lic. ind. clin. social worker. Mem. Mass. Acad. Psychiat. Social Work, Nat. Assn. Social Workers, Soc. Family Therapy and Research, Nat. Assn. Social Workers, Register Clin. Social Workers. Contbr. to profl. publs. Address: 14 Mason Rd Newton Center MA 02159

PILLING, JANET KAVANAUGH, lawyer; b. Akron, Ohio, Sept. 5, 1951; d. Paul and Marjorie (Logue) Kavanaugh. B.A., Ohio Wesleyan U., 1973; J.D., U. Mo., 1975; LL.M., Villanova U., 1985. Bar: Pa. 1976, U.S. Tax Ct. 1976, U.S. Dist. Ct. (ea. dist.) Pa. 1976. Atty., Schnader, Harrison, Segal & Lewis, Phila., 1976-83; gen. counsel Kistler-Tiffany Cos., Wayne, Pa., 1983—. Mem. ABA, Phila. Bar Assn., Pa. Bar Assn., Montgomery County Estate Planning Council, Chester County Estate Planning Council, Phi Beta Kappa, Phi Delta Phi. Office: Kistler Tiffany Cos Suite 706 987 Old Eagle School Rd Wayne PA 19087

PILLON, SHARON THERESA, nurse, hospital administrator; b. Ont., Can., Mar. 8, 1949; came to U.S., 1973; d. Joseph Adolph and Marion Elizabeth (Bondy) Pillon; R.N. diploma, Hotel Dieu Hosp. Sch. Nursing, Windsor, Ont., 1970; B.S. in Mgmt., Pacific Christian Coll., 1980; M.B.A., Calif. State U., 1984. Pres., Calif. Med. Careers, Inc., Redondo Beach, 1978-79; dir. edn. La Mirada (Calif.) Community Hosp., 1978-80, Westside Hosp.-Am. Med. Internat., Inc., Los Angeles, 1980—; dir. nursing Meml. Hosp., Hawthorne, Calif., 1981—; dir. nursing AMI South Bay Hosp., Redondo Beach, Calif., 1984—; instr. basic cardiac life support Am. Heart Assn.; mem. Nursing Adminstrs. Council, Los Angeles; active Health Fair Expo. Mem. Nat. Assn. Female Execs. Roman Catholic. Office: 514 N Prospect Ave Redondo Beach CA 90277

PILOUS, BETTY SCHEIBEL, nurse; b. Cleve., July 30, 1948; d. Raymond W. and Dorothy E. (Groth) S.; m. Lee Alan Pilous, Sept. 11, 1970; 1 child. Diploma in nursing Huron Rd. Hosp., Cleve., 1970. R.N., Ohio; cert. med.-surg. nurse, nursing adminstr. Nurse, Huron Rd. Hosp., Cleve., 1970-71, Hillcrest Hosp., Cleve., 1974-77; head nurse, relief supr. Oak Park Hosp., Oakwood, Ohio, 1977-81; head nurse med.-surg. Bedford Hosp., Ohio, 1981—; instr. ARC, Am. Heart Assn. Mem. health and safety com. Twinsburg Schs., Ohio, 1984—, mem. curriculum com., 1981-83; counselor jr. high youth 1st Congl. Ch., Twinsburg. Mem. Ohio Jaycee Women (past dist. coordinator, treas.). Lodge: Order Eastern Star. Avocations: aerobics; hiking. Office: Bedford Hosp 44 Blaine St Bedford OH 44146

PILZER, CECILY RUTH, children's librarian; b. Boston, Feb. 4, 1947; d. Howard Tasker and Eloise (Humez) Evans; m. Charles Leo Pilzer, Sept. 10, 1979; 1 dau., Sarah Jean. A.B., Wilmington Coll., 1970; M.L.S., Cath. U. Am., 1977. Library technician Nat. Bur. Standards, Gaithersburg, Md., 1970-71; library asst. Montgomery County Pub. Libraries, Rockville, Md., 1971-77, librarian, 1977-79, children's librarian, 1979—. Mem. ALA. Democrat. Jewish.

PINCH, PATRICIA ANN, medical technologist; b. Port Hueneme, Calif., Oct. 8, 1947; d. William Claude and Lois (Monroe) Pinch; m. Vincent J. Lupo, Apr. 6, 1973 (dec. 1975). B.S. in Med. Tech., Med. Coll. Va., 1969. Human cytogenetic researcher Bklyn. Hosp., 1970-72; animal genetic researcher Mt. Sinai Hosp., N.Y.C., 1972-74; med. tech. supr., owner Vee-Jay Clin. Labs., Bklyn., 1974—. Mem. Am. Soc. Clin. Pathologists. Roman Catholic. Office: 2834 Coney Island Ave Brooklyn NY 11235

PINEDA, MARIANNA, sculptor, educator; b. Evanston, Ill., May 10, 1925; d. George and Marinna (Dickinson) Packard; m. Harold Tovish, Jan. 14, 1946; children—Margo, Aaron, Nina. Student Cranbrook Acad. Art, summer 1942, Bennington Coll., 1942-43, U. Calif.-Berkeley, 1943-45, Columbia U., 1945-46, Ossip Zadkaine Sch. Drawing and Sculpture, Paris, 1949-50. Instr. sculpture Newton Coll. Sacred Heart, 1972-75, Boston Coll., 1975-77; vis. assoc. prof. Boston U., 1974, 78, 83, 84; one-woman shows include: Walker Art Ctr., Mpls., 1952; exhibitions include: Currier Gallery, Vt., 1954, De Cordove Mus., Lincoln, Mass., Premier Gallery, Mpls., 1963, Swetzoff Gallery, Boston, 1953, 64, Honolulu Acad. Art, 1970, Alpha Gallery, Boston, 1972, Newton Coll. (Mass.), Bumpus Gallery, Duxbury, Mass., Contemporary Art Ctr., Honolulu, 1982-83, Pine Manor Coll. (Mass.), 1984; group shows include: Galerie 8 Paris, 1950, Met. Mus. Art, N.Y.C., 1951, Whitney Mus. Am. Art, N.Y.C., 1953, 55, 57, Mus. Modern Art, N.Y.C., 1960, Art Inst. Chgo., 1959, 61, DeCordove Mus., 1975, Boston Arts Festival, 1985, Boston Visual Artists Union, 1986, Artists of Bunting Inst., Cambridge, Mass., 1986; represented permanent collections: Walker Art Ctr., Mus. Fine Arts, Boston, Williams Coll. (Mass.), Dartmouth Coll., Hanover N.H., Addison Gallery, Andover, Mass., Munson-Williams-Proctor Inst., Ithaca, N.Y., Fogg Art Mus., Cambridge, Mass., Radcliffe Coll., Boston Pub. Library, State of Hawaii; commd. work: Twirling, Bronze figure group, East Boston Housing for Elderly, The Spirit of Lili'uokalani bronze, Hawaii State Capitol. Office: 46 Porter Rd Cambridge MA 02140*

PINELLI, PATRICIA RUTH, real estate executive; b. Chgo., Feb. 28, 1929; d. Roland Beyer and Agnes Ann (Doolan) Lally; m. Henry Andrew Pinelli, Jan. 20, 1951; children—Kathleen Pinelli McAfee, Maureen Pinelli Jones, Dana, Charles. Student, Wright Jr. Coll., 1945-47, Ft. Lauderdale Coll., 1974. Sec. sales promotion Cadillac Motor Car Div., Chgo., 1949-54; realtor assoc. Glenview Realty, Ill., 1969-72, Cummings & Cohen Real Estate, Ft. Lauderdale, 1974-78, Cummings Realty, Ft. Lauderdale, 1978-79, Home Mktg. of Fla., Ft. Lauderdale, 1979-81, Cummings & Cohen Real Estate, Inc., Lauderdale-By-The-Sea, Fla., 1981—. Area chmn. North Shore Mental Health Assn., Glenview, 1962; treas. Democratic Club of Galt Ocean Mile, Ft. Lauderdale, 1980. Named to Million Dollar Club, Am. Invesco, Chgo., 1980. Mem. Ft. Lauderdale Bd. Realtors (com. mem. 1978-82), Nat. Assn. Realtors, Fla. Real Estate Exchangors, Nat. Assn. Female Execs., Ft. Lauderdale Investment Div., Nat. Right to Life. Roman Catholic. Clubs: Suburban, Orchesis, Valley-Lo Sports. Avocations: swimming; golf; aerobics; bowling; travel. Office: Cummings & Cohen Real Estate Inc 227 Commercial Blvd Lauderdale-By-The-Sea FL 33308

PINGREE, DIANNE, publisher, video producer; b. Dallas, B.F.A. magna cum laude, So. Meth. U., 1976; A.A. summa cum laude, Richland Coll., 1974; m. Harlan Pingree. Freelance journalist, 1974-76; editor, pub. Tex. Woman Mag., Dallas, 1977-80; pres. Tex. Woman, Inc., Dallas, 1980-85; owner, operator Dianne Pingree & Assocs., Dallas, 1985—. Recipient Women Helping Women award Women's Center Dallas, 1980. Mem. Women in Communications (Matrix award 1979), Exec. Women Dallas (sec., bd. mem. 1981, v.p. 1982, pres. 1983-84), Dallas Communications Council, Dallas Press Club (Gridiron Show award 1982), Tex. Hist. Assn., Dallas Hist. Assn., AAUW, Sigma Delta Chi. Office: 5551 Yale Blvd Dallas TX 75206

PINHEIRO, MARIA-ODETTE, B.N., physician; b. Cape Verde Islands, Sept. 5, 1943; came to U.S., 1974; d. Armando and Julieta B. (Neves) Pinheiro. M. Divinity, Nazarene Theol. Sem., 1978; M.D., U. Coimbra, Portugal, 1968. Cert. clin. pathologist, Portugal. Asst. med. biochemistry U. Coimbra, Portugal, 1969-74; resident ob/gyn Truman Med. Ctr., U. Mo., Kansas City, 1979-80, Boston City Hosp., 1980-82; practice medicine specializing in ob/gyn, Brockton, Mass., 1982—; mem. staff Brockton Hosp., 1982. Fellow Am. Coll. ob/gyn. Mem. Ch. of Nazarene. Office: 235 Quincy St Brockton MA 02402

PINKAVA, JUDITH ALICE, nurse, CPR instructor; b. Weymouth, Mass., May 20, 1961; d. Roy Victor and Dorothy Eleanor (Ericson) Nelson; m. Christopher Francis Pinkava, June 30, 1984. Student Mass. Bay Community Coll., 1978, Wesleyan U., 1979-80; Diploma in Nursing New England Baptist Hosp., 1983. R.N., Mass. Nursing asst. Colonial Nursing Home, Weymouth, 1980-81, Braintree Manor, Mass., 1981-82, New Eng. Bapt. Hosp., Boston, 1982-83, South Shore Hosp., Weymouth, 1982-83; nurse Faulkner Hosp., Boston, 1983-85, Anodyne Agy., 1985, Med. Temporaries, 1985-86; CPR instr., 1981-84. Sec., treas. United Ch. of Christ Youth Group, 1979. Mem. Diploma Nurses Assn. (assoc., student rep, 1982-83). Republican. Avocations: Skiing; cycling; swimming; collector.

PINKE, JUDITH ANN, metropolitan official; b. Ft. Snelling, Minn., Oct. 16, 1944; d. August Henry and Dorothy E. (Bartelt) Hinrichs; m. Kurt G.O. Pinke, June 29, 1974. B.A. cum laude, St. Olaf Coll., 1966; postgrad. Kennedy Sch. Govt., Harvard U., 1980. Supr., tchr. Mpls. Pub. Schs., 1966-71; writer/editor U. Minn., Mpls., 1971-72; counselor Secretarial Placement, Edina, Minn., 1972-73; asst. to commr. Minn. Dept. Labor and Industry, St. Paul, 1973-76; mgr. info. resources Minn. Dept. Adminstrn., St. Paul, 1976-77; asst. commr. for fin. and adminstrn. Minn. Dept. Transp., St. Paul, 1977-85; dir. met. systems dept. Met. Council Twin Cities Area, 1985—; reader advanced placement exams. Ednl. Testing Service, Princeton, N.J., 1968-71; mem. steering com. Minn. Revenue Recapture Project, St. Paul, 1981. Producer televideo conf. presentation The Productive Office, 1984. Mem. Minn. Info. Policy Council 1979-85 chmn., 1982-85; co-founder Women in State Employment, 1976—; adv. bd. Mem. Loft, Women Execs. in State Govt. (founding), Horizon 100, LWV. Office: Met Council 300 Med Sq Bldg Saint Paul MN 55101

PINKERTON, HELEN JEANETTE, health care executive; b. Chattanooga, Mar. 17, 1956; D. Jesse Robert and Irene Louise (Boyd) Pinkerton. B.S., U. Tenn.-Knoxville, 1979, M.P.H., 1980. Intern, Southeast Regional Health Dept., Chattanooga, 1979, Alex B. Shipley Health Dept., Knoxville, 1980; coordinator hypertension Alton Park Health Ctr., Chattanooga, 1981—; council mem. Task Force on Prevention of Handicapping Conditions, Chattanooga, 1984—. Contbr. to Tenn. Hypertension Control Manual, 1984. Chaplain Joyful Noise, Chattanooga, 1974—; mem. Bapt. Student Union. Doak scholar, 1977. Mem. Tenn. Soc. Pub. Health, Nat. Assn. Female Execs., Women Network Inc., Hypertension Coalition (chmn. 1984—), Alton Park C. of C. (council mem. 1982—), Alpha Kappa Alpha, Gamma Sigma Sigma. Democrat. Baptist. Avocations: walking; reading; singing; jogging. Home: 4103 Dayton Blvd Chattanooga TN 37415 Office: Alton Park Health Center 100 E 37th St Chattanooga TN 37410

PINKERTON, MARJORIE JEAN, librarian, library science educator; b. Chgo., June 15, 1934; d. Robert Rex and Evelyn Isabel (Scott) Glass; m. James Ronald Pinkerton, June 29, 1957; children—Steven James, Kathryn Lynn. B.A. in Spanish and History, Carroll Coll., 1956; M.A. in Spanish, U. Wis.-Madison, 1964; M.A. in Library Sci., U. Mo., 1973. Tchr. high sch., Pardeeville, Wis., 1956-57, Preble, Wis., 1958-59; library asst. Meml. Library, U. Wis., Madison, 1959-64; substitute tchr., librarian Columbia Pub. Schs., Mo., 1965-73; ednl. materials librarian, asst. prof. William Woods Coll., Fulton, Mo., 1973-81, assoc. prof., 1985—, dir. Dulany Library, 1981—. Co-author: Outdoor Recreation and Leisure, 1969. Contbr. articles to profl. jours. Mem. Bd. Adjustment, City of Columbia, 1971-75, chmn., 1973-74; dir. Nat. Ghost Ranch Found., United Presbyterian Ch., Santa Fe, N.Mex., 1981-84; mem. Columbia Safety Council, 1967—, pres., 1969-70. Recipient award for community service New Democratic Coalition, Columbia, 1976. Mem. ALA, Mo. Assn. Coll. and Research Libraries (chmn. 1984-85), Mo. Library Assn. (com. chmn. 1978-79), Mid-Mo. Associated Colls. and Univs. (chmn. library com. 1984-85), League Women Voters (v.p. 1967-68), Beta Phi Mu (pres. 1974-76, 85-86). Presbyterian. Clubs: UN (pres. 1970—), Friends of the Library (Columbia) (sec.-treas. 1977-78). Avocations: genealogy; reading; travel; walking; aerobics. Home: 1014 Westport Dr Columbia MO 65203 Office: William Woods Coll Dulany Library Fulton MO 65251

PINKHAM, ELEANOR HUMPHREY, university librarian; b. Chgo., May 7, 1926; d. Edward Lemuel and Grace Eleanor (Cushing) Humphrey; A.B., Kalamazoo Coll., 1948; M.S. in Library Sci. (Alice Louise LeFevre scholar), Western Mich. U., 1967; m. James Hansen Pinkham, July 10, 1948; children—Laurie Sue, Carol Lynn. Public services librarian Kalamazoo Coll., 1967-68, asst. librarian, 1960-70, library dir., 1971—; vis. lectr. Western Mich. U. Sch. Librarianship, 1970-84; mem. adv. bd., 1977-81, also adv. bd. Inst. Cistercian Studies library, 1975-80. Mem. ALA, Mich. Library Assn. (pres. 1983-84, chmn. acad. div. 1977-78), Mich. Library Consortium (exec. council 1974-82, chmn. 1977-78), AAUP, OCLC Users Council, Beta Phi Mu. Home: 2319 Glenwood Dr Kalamazoo MI 49008 Office: 1200 Academy St Kalamazoo MI 49007

PINKHAM, ROBIN REMICK, financial executive; b. Bridgeport, Conn., May 5, 1944; d. Irving Grant and Theresa Helena (Busci) Pinkham; A.B. in English, Conn. Coll. Women, 1965; postgrad. N.Y. Inst. Fin., 1965-66. With Paine, Webber, N.Y.C., 1965-68, Scudder, Stevens & Clark, N.Y.C., 1969-72, Wood Walker, N.Y.C., 1972-73; pension fund investment mgr. Nat. Forge Co., N.Y.C., from 1973, now asst. treas. Vol., Lighthouse for the Blind, 1966-68. Registered investment counsellor. Mem. N.Y. Soc. Security Analysts, Fin. Analysts Fedn. Republican. Home: 245 E 63d St Apt 1127 New York NY 10021 Office: 780 3d Ave Suite 2401 New York NY 10017

PINNEY, EVELYN JONES, micro computer company executive; b. Albuquerque, Sept. 18, 1955; d. Kenneth Raymond and Midori (Kawano) Jones; m. Charles Porter Pinney, May 27, 1979. B.A. cum laude, Lewis and Clark Coll., 1977; cert. Computer Careers Inst., Portland, 1982. Mgr. Cedar Pacific Properties, Portland, 1980-82; micro computer salesman IBM Corp., Portland, 1982-83; micro computer specialist Harsh Investments, Portland, 1983-84; N.W. regional mgr. Applied Computer Cons., Portland, 1984-85; pres. Mktg. N.W., Inc., Lake Oswego, Oreg., 1980-85, Advanced Micro Solutions, Portland, 1985—; cons. Columbia Edgewater Country Club, Portland, 1984-85, IBM Product Ctr., Portland, 1985. Tech. editor Lotus 123 Home and Office Companion, 1984. Mem. Data Processing Mgrs. Assn., Nat. Assn. Female Execs., AAUW, Lewis and Clark Alumni Assn., Portland PC Users Group. Republican. Club: Columbia Edgewater Country (Portland). Avocations: skiing; swimming; classical piano; photography. Office: Advanced Micro Solutions Inc 1001 SW 5th St Suite 1000 Portland OR 97204

PINO, LITA VAZQUEZ, marketing consultant; b. Havana, Cuba, Jan. 1, 1951; came to U.S., 1960; d. Eugenio A. and Maria Teresa (Garcia-Montes) Vazquez; m. J. Pino, 1969 (div. 1981); children—George, Lianne. B.B.A. with honors, U. Miami, 1972, postgrad., 1980. Project specialist U. Miami (Fla.), Coral Gables, 1977-80; coordinator copywriting Cons. Pharm. Advt., Key Biscayne, Fla., 1980-81; mng. cons. M.E.T.A., Pub. Relations Cons., Miami, Fla., 1981-82; mktg. project mgr. Paramount Internat. Coin Corp., Miami, 1982-83; mktg. mgr. Interval Internat., South Miami, 1983-84; with Mgmt. Consultants of South Fla., 1984—. Mem. Am. Mktg. Assn., Nat. Assn. Female Execs., Am. Mgmt. Assn. Republican. Roman Catholic. Home: 11400 SW 94th Ave Miami FL 33176 Office: Mgmt Consultants of South Fla 9951 SW 108th St Miami FL 33176

PINO, VICTORIA RAMONA, digital equipment manufacturing executive; b. Magdalena, N.Mex., Apr. 15, 1950; d. Benses Trujillo and Mary Sostena (Sanchez) P. Grad. high sch., Albuquerque. Quality analyst Digital Equipment Corp., Albuquerque, 1976-77, product safety engr., 1977-78, assoc. quality engr., 1977-79, quality control supr., 1979-81, prodn. supr., 1981—, insp. cons., 1976—, Quality Circles facilitator, 1984—. Recipient Plaque for pilot programs Digital Equipment Corp., 1985. Sketcher for Rio Grande Audubon Soc., Albuquerque, 1980. Democrat. Roman Catholic. Avocations: drawing, fishing, camping, collecting butterflies and thimbles. Home: 536 La Vega Rd SW Albuquerque NM 87105 Office: Digital Equipment Corp 5600 Kircher Blvd NE Albuquerque NM 87108

PINSON, MARGUERITE LORETTA, ednl. cons.; b. Willard, N.Mex., May 25, 1912; d. Ephriam Eastlan and Lucy Ethlyn (Angle) Berry; B.S. in Edn., Ark. State Coll., Conway, 1948; M.S., U. Ark., Fayetteville, 1951; children—Ralph Young, Sue Young Wilson. Tchr., Little Rock Schs., 1943-53; tchr. Anaheim (Calif.) Elem. Sch., 1953-57; dir. elem. edn. Chapman Coll., Orange, Calif., 1957-59; cons. Orange County (Calif.) Dept. Edn., Santa Ana, 1959-77; program rev. cons. Calif. State Dept. Edn., 1977-82; mem. adv. panel Nat. Affiliation for Literacy Advance, 1980—. Mem. NEA, Calif. Tchrs. Assn., Fgn. Lang. Assn., Phi Theta Kappa, Alpha Chi, Kappa Delta Pi, Delta Kappa Gamma. Democrat. Methodist. Home: 2744 Lorenzo Ave Costa Mesa CA 92626

PINTA, WANDA BOHAN (MRS. R. JACK PINTA), home economist; b. Greenfield, Iowa, Sept. 11, 1918; d. Edward Philip and Stella (Plymesser) Bohan; B.S., Iowa State U., 1943; postgrad. Calif. State U., Los Angeles,

1956-59; m. R. Jack Pinta, Apr. 17, 1948 (dec. Sept. 1982). Tech. writer, editor Gen. Motors Corp., Milford, Mich., 1943-45; sr. home economist Los Angeles Dept. Water and Power, 1956-61, dir. consumer services, 1961—, supr. ednl. services, 1981—. Pub. relations dir. LWV, Des Moines, 1953-55; sec. Assn. for UN, Des Moines, 1953-55. Recipient Laura McCall Home Service Achievement award, 1960, Alma award Assn. Home Appliance Mfrs., 1971, 73. Mem. Am. (mem. consumer interests com. 1968-70), Calif. (pres. Los Angeles 1966-67) home econs. assns., Los Angeles Home Economist in Bus., Internat. Fedn. Home Economists, Elec. Women's Round Table (nat. dir., nat. pres. 1978-80), Soc. Consumer Affairs Profls. (sec. So. Calif. chpt. 1978-79), Los Angeles City/County Energy Edn. Council (newsletter editor 1981—, pres. 1983-84), Calif. Energy Edn. Forum, Iowa State U. Alumni Assn., Los Angeles World Affairs Council, Town Hall. Episcopalian. Mem. Order Eastern Star. Club: Pilot (pres. Van Nuys 1962-63). Home: 5744 Vantage Ave North Hollywood CA 91607 Office: 111 N Hope St Los Angeles CA 90012

PINTEN, MARLENE JUNE, educator, association administrator; b. Ashland, Wis., July 29, 1932; d. Arthur Emery and Monica Gertrude (Fromholz) P. B.A., Coll. St. Scholastica, 1954; M.A., U. Minn., 1965. Tchr., Pulaski High Sch. (Wis.), 1954-55, Stanbrook Hall, Duluth, Minn., 1955-59, Acad. Holy Angels, Richfield, Minn., 1959-61; social worker Cath. Welfare Services, Mpls., 1961-64; sch. counselor Burnsville High Sch. (Minn.), 1964-66, Lincoln Sr. High Sch., Bloomington, Minn., 1966-74, dir. guidance, 1975-82; pres. Am. Sch. Counselor Assn., Alexandria, Va., 1982-83, cons., 1983-84; counselor Jefferson Sr. High Sch., Bloomington, Minn., 1984—; adv. bd. Campus Access for Disabled Student-Closer Look, Washington, 1983—; bd. dirs. Higher Edn. and the Handicapped, Washington, 1981-83; adv. bd., trustee Citizens Scholarship Found. Am., Concord, N.H., 1983—. Contbr. articles to profl. jours. and newsletters. Chmn. Bloomington Youth Commn. City Council (Minn.), 1971; treas., bd. dirs. Family Edn. Ctr., Edina, Minn., 1973-75; bd. dirs. Bloomington Scholarship Found., 1974-76, Citizens Scholarship Found.-Midwest, St. Peter, Minn., 1976-80. Recipient Outstanding Community Service award Lions Club, Bloomington, 1974; Leadership and Service award Bloomington Counselors Assn., 1980; Marjorie Quandr award Coll. St. Scholastica, 1982; Outstanding Service award City of Bloomington, 1975. Mem. Am. Assn. Counseling and Guidance (senate 1982, 84 bd. dirs. 1982-83, service award 1983), Am. Sch. Counselor Assn. (governing bd. 1981-84, leadership award 1983), Minn. Sch. Counselor Assn. (bd. dirs 1971-81, pres. 1978-80, disting. service award 1976-78, leadership award 1980), Minn. Personnel and Guidance Assn. (bd. dirs. 1976-80), AAUW, World Future Soc., Delta Kappa Gamma. Democrat. Roman Catholic. Office: Jefferson Sr High Sch 4001 W 102d St Bloomington MN 55431

PIO COSTA, ROSALIND, real estate developer; b. Caldwell, N.J., May 9, 1920; d. Alfred and Violet Petrulio; widowed Aug. 1974; children—Anthony III, Robin Ann Lahue. B.A., Upsala Coll., 1940. Owner boutique Chez Mam'selle, Caldwell, 1941-49; owner, v.p. Pio Costa Enterprises, Fairfield, N.J., 1950—; pres. Boonton Enterprises. Mem. Women's aux. Columbus Hosp., Newark, N.J. Mem. N.J. Profl. Women. Republican. Roman Catholic. Avocations: golf; music; swimming; theater. Office: 1275 Bloomfield Ave Fairfield NJ 07006

PIOMELLI, MARIA-ROSARIA, architect; b. Naples, Italy, Oct. 24, 1937; d. Alberto and Giuseppina (Trapanese) Angrisano; came to U.S., 1957; B.Arch., M.I.T., 1960; M.Art Accademia d'Arte, Naples, 1955; m. Sergio Piomelli, M.D., Apr. 25, 1956; children—Ascanio Alberto, Fosca Francesca. Designer, Warner Burns Toan & Lunde, Architects, N.Y.C., 1963-69; asso. architect E.H. Grosmann Architect, Rotterdam, Netherlands, 1969-70; project architect I.M. Pei & Partners, N.Y.C., 1971-74; prin. Rosaria Piomelli, Architect, N.Y.C., 1971—; tchr. design and bldg. systems tech. Pratt Inst., CCNY, 1971-76, chmn. faculty Pratt Inst. Sch. Architecture, Bklyn., 1975-79; dean Sch. Architecture, CCNY, 1980-83; disting. prof. U. Calif.-Berkeley Sch. Architecture, 1984; organizer exhibit Women in Architecture, 1974. Chmn., N.Y.C./AIA Equal Opportunity Com., 1973-75. Recipient HEW design award for Brown U. Sci. Library, 1966; Mudd Found. design award for Oberlin Coll. Learning Center, 1973. Mem. AIA (dir. exec. com. N.Y. chpt. 1977-79). Home: 390 W Broadway New York NY 10012

PIORE, NORA, university administrator; b. N.Y.C., Nov. 28, 1912; m. 1931; 3 children. A.B., U. Wis., 1933, M.A., 1934. Economist, Com. Labor and Pub. Welfare, U.S. Senate, 1950-53; program analyst Interdept. Com. on Low Incomes, N.Y., 1956-57; spl. asst. to commr. Dept. Health N.Y.C., 1962-68; vis. scientist, dir. Hosp. Out-Patient Studies Program, Assn. for Aid to Crippled Children, N.Y., 1968-71; assoc. dir. Ctr. Community Health Systems, Columbia U., N.Y.C., 1972—; adj. prof. urban studies Hunter Coll., 1962-71; cons. Carnegie Corp., R.W. Johnson Found., HEW, 1965—; vis. fellow Ctr. Health Care Studies, United Hosp. Found., 1978—; program health adminstr. and economist Sch. Pub. Health, Columbia U., 1972—; apptd. mem. Nat. Health Adv. Council, USPHS, HEW, 1964-69, N.Y. State Rev. and Planning Council, 1975—, U.S. Nat. Commn. Vital and Health Stats., 1978—; mem. nat. council Alan Guttmacher Inst., 1974—; mem. tech. bd. Milbank Meml. Fund., 1976-78. Mem. Inst. Medicine-Nat. Acad. Sci.; assoc. fellow N.Y. Acad. Sci.; fellow Am. Pub. Health Assn., Indsl. Relations Research Assn., Am. Econ. Assn. Address: United Hosp Fund 3 E 54th St New York NY 10022*

PIOTROWSKA, BARBARA BEATA, architect; b. Poland, Oct. 26, 1938; came to U.S., 1968; d. Jan and Zofia (Debski) P.; m. Zdravko M. Maljkovic, Sept. 27, 1974 (div.). M.Arch., Warsaw Poly. Inst. (Poland), 1962. Chief engr. K.B.M., Warsaw, Poland, 1962-64; architect, Paris, 1964-68; archtl. designer, N.J., 1968-76; owner, architect B. Piotrowska R.A., Upper Montclair, N.J., 1976—. Designer and contractor residences, office bldgs., apts. Home and Office: 5 Rutgers Pl Upper Montclair NJ 07043

PIPER, KATHRYN THOMAS, advertising agency executive; b. Denver; d. Ernest and Thelma (Wall) Thomas; m. James Piper (div.); children—James B., Jerrold S., Gwendolyn S. Piper Shakespeare. B.A., Loretto Heights Coll., 1972. Owner, pres. Piper & Assocs., Denver, 1965—; v.p. Yuan Chinese Restaurant, Denver, 1978—, Pacific Internat. Trade, Denver, 1981—. Editor, Denver Social Register, 1967—. Dir. protocol Denver Bal de Ballet, 1968; mem. bd. N.Y. Debutante Ball, N.Y.C., 1968; mem. am. com. Vienna Debutante Ball, Austria, 1970. Named Colo. Woman of Achievement, Colo. Press Women, 1977. Mem. Nat. Fedn. Press Women (Woman of Achievement 1978), Denver Press Women, Colo. Press Women, Catalyst Corp. Bd. Resource. Clubs: Garden of Gods (Colorado Springs, Colo.); Metropolitan (Denver). Avocations: bridge; backgammon; collecting oriental art; travel; charity and social work. Home: 120 S Marion Pkwy Denver CO 80209 Office: Piper & Assocs Ltd 1805 S Bellaire St Suite 215 Denver CO 80222

PIPITONE, PHYLLIS LUIS, psychologist; b. Chgo.; d. Max and Antoinette Walkey; student Chgo. Conservatory Music, 1941-44, Peabody Conservatory Music, 1945, Chgo. Tchrs. Coll., 1946-47, So. Meth. U., 1951-52; M.A., U. Akron, 1967; Ph.D. (NIMH grantee, HEW Child Devel. fellow), Kent State U., 1974; m. S. Joseph Pipitone, Aug. 28, 1948 (dec.); children—Guy, Daniel, Paul; m. 2d, Thomas A. Cox, Jan. 3, 1980. With B.S. & H. Advt. Agy., Chgo., 1941-43; instr. piano and theory Music Acad. Chgo.; psychologist, instr. U. Akron and Kent State U., 1970-79; pvt. practice psychology, Akron, Ohio, 1967—; lectr. Served with WAC, AUS, 1944-46. Mem. Am. Psychol. Assn., Nat. Assn. Sch. Psychologists, Mensa, Council Exceptional Children, Am. Hypnosis Soc., Psi Research Group. Clubs: Tuesday Musical, Weathervane Theatre, Akron Women's City, Wadsworth Women's. Home: 224 Pheasant Run Wadsworth OH 44281

PIPKIN, DOLORES LOUISE, accountant; b. Granite City, Ill., May 19, 1933; d. George Edward and Maude Leona (Lewis) Robinson; m. James Lewis Pipkin, Aug. 16, 1957 (div.); children—Sandra Louise, Cynthia LaDele. A.A. in Edn., A.S. in Acctg., A.S. in Bus. Mgmt., Napa Coll., 1978. Bookkeeper Nesco, Ill., telephone co., Seattle, 1951-54; sales mgr. Avon products, Stanley Home products Dutchmaid clothing, 1956-66; interior decorater Macy's Co., Concord, Calif., 1966-69; office mgr. Spanish Flat Resort, Lake Berreyessa, Calif., 1969-75; acct. Appco Mfg. Co., Chula Vista, Calif., 1975-77; staff acct. John Fulkerson, C.P.A., Napa, Calif., 1977-78; pres. DLS Systems, Inc., Napa, 1978-84, ASAP Acctg. Services, 1984—. Mem. adv. com. Napa Coll., 1980-81. Mem. Nat. Assn. Accts. Mem. Assemblies of God Ch. CA Office: ASAP Acctg Services 5 Financial Plaza Napa CA 94558

PIPKIN, EDITH VINCENT, nurse, administrator; b. Middleton, Tenn., Nov. 12, 1932; d. Thomas Aubrey and Alma Octavia (Pirtle) Vincent; m. Homer Lee Pipkin, May 14, 1952; children—Barbara Pipkin Baker, Betsy Pipkin Hillsman, Amelia. A.S. in Nursing, Union U., 1979; student St. Joseph's Coll., 1985—. Lic. practical nurse, Tenn.; registered nurse, Tenn. Physician asst., Bolivar, Tenn., 1974-75; aide Ripley Hosp., Ms., 1972-74, Bolivar Hosp., 1975-76; practical nurse Care Inn, Bolivar, 1975-78, asst. dir., 1979-80; practical nurse Jackson Hosp., Tenn., 1978-79; supr. Western Institute, Tenn., 1980-84, dir. nursing Nat. T. Winston Devel., 1984—. Campaign asst. Hardeman County Democrats, 1982. Fellow Assn. for Retarded Citizens; mem. Nat. T. Winston Infection Control (pres. 1984-85). Mem. Ch. of Christ. Club: Woman's (pres. 1955-56). Lodge: Woodmen of World. Avocations: swimming; walking; bicycling. Home: 439 N Main St Middleton TN 38052

PIPPINS, LOIS AILEEN, county official; b. Bertrand, Mo., Aug. 9, 1929; d. Winfred Lee and Gladys Lucille (Farier) Mellen; m. Harold C. Pippins, Aug. 4, 1948; children—Harold Clifford Jr., Randy Lee. Grad. high sch., Warsaw, Mo. Sales clk. Vaughn Dry Goods, Weaubleau, Mo., 1965-70; mgr. F.M. Store, Bolivar, Mo., 1970-72; dep. circuit clk. Hickory County, Mo., 1973-74, collection office clk., 1974, dep. county clk., 1975-78, circuit clk., ex-officio recorder, 1979—. Republican. Baptist. Home: Route 1 Box 517 Flemington MO 65650 Office: Clk Circuit Ct Hickory county Seat County Courthouse Hermitage MO 65668

PIRKLE, NITA, real estate appraiser and broker; b. Port Arthur, Tex., May 7, 1935; d. Kenneth A. and Johnnie (Garner) Alloway; m. John Thomas Pirkle, July 31, 1970; children—Cynthia Diane, Donna Kay, Carol Anita, Shannon Dale. Student Massey Bus. Coll., 1970; broker Ahrens Sch. Real Estate, 1972; M.Residential Appraising, M.Farm and Land Appraising, M.Sr. Appraising, Lincoln Inst., 1983. Cert. real estate appraiser; cert. broker. Legal sec. Pratt & Gardner, Houston, 1963-67, Watts & Patterson, Houston, 1967-70; real estate salesperson John T. Pirkle Real Estate, Houston, 1970-72; broker Pirkle Real Estate, Houston, 1972-83, appraiser, 1983—, also owner/pres. Mem. Houston Bd. Realtors, Tex. Assn. Realtors, Nat. Assn. Realtors, Nat. Assn. Master Appraisers. Republican. Office: Pirkle Real Estate 721 E 11th St Houston TX 77008

PIRSCH, CAROL MCBRIDE, telephone company community relations supervisor, state senator; b. Omaha, Dec. 27, 1936; d. Lyle Erwin and Hilfrie Louise (Lebeck) McBride; student U. Miami, Oxford, Ohio, U. Nebr., Omaha; m. Allen I. Pirsch, Mar. 28, 1954; children—Pennie Elizabeth, Pamela Elaine, Patrice Eileen, Phyllis Erika, Peter Allen, Perry Andrew. Former mem. data processing staff Omaha Public Schs.; former mem. wage practices dept. Western Electric Co., Omaha; former legal sec., Omaha; former office mgr. Pirsch Food Brokerage Co., Inc., Omaha; former employment supr. Northwestern Bell Telephone Co., Omaha, now supr. community relations; mem. Nebr. Senate, 1978—. Bd. dirs. U. Nebr. at Omaha Parents Assn., Nebr. Developmental Disabilities Council; pres. Nebr. Coalition for Victims of Crime. Recipient Golden Elephant award; Outstanding Legis. Leadership award Nat. Orgn. Victim Assistance. Mem. Orgn. Women Legislators, Tangier Women's Aux., Mgmt. Women's Assn. Clubs: Pilot, Omaha Women's, N.W. Civic, Benson Republican Women's. Office: State Capitol Lincoln NE 68509*

PIRT, NANCY EILEEN, lawyer; b. Pitts., Apr. 6, 1952; d. John Joseph and Helen Marie (Giza) P. B.A. cum laude in Speech and Hearing Therapy, U. Pitts., 1974; J.D., Duquesne U., 1979; M.P.H., Harvard U., 1986. Bar: Pa. 1979. Law clk. Office of Public Defender, Pitts., 1976-77; sr. law clk. Superior Ct. Pa., Pitts., 1977-83; sole practice, Pitts., 1979—; mem. bd. arbitrators Allegheny County, Pitts., 1981-84; mem. Com. for More Women Judges, Pitts., 1984; mem. Gov.'s/MBA Commn. on the Unmet Legal Needs of Children, 1986. Mem. editorial staff Duquesne Law Rev. U. Pitts. scholar, 1970-71; Pa. Higher Edn. Assistance Agy. scholar, 1970-71. Mem. ABA, Allegheny County Bar Assn. Home: 2358 Eldridge St Pittsburgh PA 15217

PIRTLE, IVYL LEORA FLEMING (MRS. J. MAX PIRTLE), librarian; b. nr. Ottumwa, Iowa, Jan. 11, 1906; d. Barton Earl and Lillie (Roberts) Fleming; student Iowa State Coll., 1931; B.A., U. Fla., 1944; M.A., Fla. State U., 1951; m. J. Max Pirtle, Sept. 17, 1938. Tchr. elementary schs., Iowa, 1924-39; tchr. Grace Stern Pvt. Sch., Miami Beach, Fla., 1939-40; tchr. elementary schs., Indiantown, 1940-43; tchr. primary grades, Stuart, 1943-50; demonstration tchr. Fla. State U., Tallahassee, summer 1949; tchr. Palmetto Sch., West Palm Beach, 1950-55; supr. elementary edn. Palm Beach County, 1955-65, dir. library services, 1965-70; mem. Fla. steering com. NDEA, 1958-68. Trustee Jr. Mus. Palm Beach County, 1960-63. Recipient certificate of appreciation Fla. Dept. Edn., 1969. Mem. Assn. Childhood Edn. Internat. (br. pres. 1953-55, primary edn. com. 1954-56), Fla. Assn. Sch. Librarians (area chmn. 1959-62), NEA, Fla. Edn. Assn. (state chmn. dept. suprs. 1959-60, dept. suprs. citation for meritorious service 1968), Assn. Supervision and Curriculum Devel., Delta Kappa Gamma (chpt. pres. 1955-59), Kappa Delta Pi, Phi Kappa Phi. Club: Zonta. Contbr. articles to profl. jours. Home: 340 Nottingham Blvd West Palm Beach FL 33405

PITCHER, VIRGINIA LEA, association executive; b. Marshalltown, Iowa, July 16, 1947; d. Milo Shields and Elsie Fredricka (Zelle) P.; B.S. in Edn., Drake U., Des Moines, 1969; M.A. in Guidance and Counseling, U. Iowa, 1972. Secondary sch. math. tchr. Midland Community Schs., Wyoming, Iowa, 1969-72; social security disability examiner State of Tenn., 1973-74; legis. asst. Health Ins. Assn. Am., Washington, 1974-76; staff asst. Met. Life Ins. Co., Washington, 1976-79; Washington asst. ACS, 1979-85; dir. Washington Office, Am. Coll. Emergency Physicians, 1985—. Mem. Women in Govt. Relations, Am. Soc. Assn. Execs., Health on Wednesday, Founders Park Community Assn., Alpha Lambda Delta, Pi Omega Pi. Republican. Methodist. Club: Capitol Hill. Home: 111 Quay St Alexandria VA 22314 Office: 2000 L St NW Suite 200 Washington DC 20036

PITCOCK, SALLY LYNN, marina executive; b. Fresno, Calif., Nov. 15, 1954; d. Lenford and Bonnie Lee (Hancock) Brigance; m. Jimmy Darrell Pitcock, Sept. 20, 1980. A.A. in Gen. Edn., Merced Jr. Coll., Calif., 1975. Owner, operator Sally's Pet Shop, Chowchilla, Calif., 1975-76; bakery mgr. Perry's Food Store, Chowchilla, 1976-78; elegibility worker Madera County Welfare, Calif., 1978-79; hardware clk. Coast to Coast, Chowchilla, 1979-80; day care facility Pitcock Family DC, Merced, 1980-81; marina owner, operator Woodward Marina, Oakdale, Calif., 1981—. Republican. Avocations: hunting; fishing; traveling; dreaming. Home and Office: 14536 26 Mile Rd Oakdale CA 95361

PITKIN, PATRICIA A., library administrator; b. Rochester, N.Y., Oct. 6, 1951; d. Patrick and Marie (Perrotta) Albanese. B.A. in Philosophy, SUNY-Geneseo, 1973, M.L.S., 1974. Database mgr., original cataloger Rochester Inst. Tech., 1974-75, head systems dept., 1975-79, head automated and tech. services, 1979-81, acting dir. Wallace Meml. Library, 1981-83, dir. libraries, 1983—; mem. adv. bd. Rochester Regional Research Council, 1981—. Mem. Dataphase Users Group (pres. 1984—). Office: Rochester Inst Tech Wallace Meml Library 1 Lomb Memorial Dr Rochester NY 14623

PITMAN, JUDITH LYNNE, educational marketing executive; b. Pueblo, Colo., Jan. 30. 1945; d. Leonard Lynn and Maxine Ruth Pitman; B.S., U. Ariz., 1967; M.B.A., Pepperdine U., Malibu, Calif., 1977. Med. technologist supr. Mills Hosp., San Mateo, Calif., 1966-69; mgr. San Diego Analytical Labs., 1969-74; mgr. Immunodiagostics, San Diego, 1974-76; mktg. planning mgr. Beckman Instruments, Inc., 1976-78; mktg. dir. Central Fed. Savs. & Loan Assn., 1978-81; pres., owner Wheaton Communications San Diego, 1981—. Mem. Savs. Instns. Mktg. Soc., Bank Mktg. Assn., Internat. Assn. Fin. Planners. Club: Entrepreneur. Office: 2732 5th Ave San Diego CA 92103

PITONE, LOUISE KATHERINE, personnel executive; b. Bklyn., Nov. 18, 1938; d. Salvatore and Dorothy Louise (Madebach) Grande; m. Fred Pitone, Jan. 23, 1960; children—Daniel, Barbara, Christopher. B.A., Bklyn. Coll., 1962. Group ins. underwriter Guardian Life Ins., N.Y.C., 1956-61; comml. actor Procter & Gamble, N.Y.C., 1971; personnel specialist J.C. Penney, DeWitt, N.Y., 1974-78; personnel mgr. Blue Cross & Blue Shield, Syracuse, 1978-81; mgmt. cons., Syracuse, 1981—; personnel dir. Syracuse Research Corp., 1982—. Mem. Am. Soc. Tng. and Devel. (asst. regional dir. 1982-83, trainer of yr. region 2, 1983, outstanding communications award 1981), Am. Soc. Personnel Adminstrs. (sec. 1983-84), Am. Compensation Assn., Coll. Placement Council. Republican. Club: Jr. League (sec. admissions 1975-78). Home: 103 Dewittshire Rd Dewitt NY 13214 Office: Syracuse Research Corp Merrill Ln Syracuse NY 13210

PITOU, PENNY, travel agency owner, professional skier; b. Bayside, L.I., N.Y., Oct. 8, 1938; d. Augustus and Eualie (Schaefer) Pitou; m. Egon Norbert Zimmermann, Feb. 19, 1961; children—Christian Egon, Kim Erik; m. Milo L. Pike, Sept. 1, 1981. Student Middlebury Coll., 1957. Certified profl. skier instr., 1965. Operator, co-dir. Penny Pitou Ski Sch., Gunstock, N.H., 1961-68. Blue Hills, Mass., 1963-68; ski fashion cons. White Stag, 1960-70; coach girl's ski team Laconia High Sch., N.H., 1965-66; owner Penny Pitou Travel, Inc., Laconia, N.H., 1974—, Concord, N.H., 1979—, Plymouth, N.H., 1985—, Wolfeboro, N.H., 1985—; dir. Laconia People's Nat. Bank, 1967-68. Appeared various TV programs including What's My Line, To Tell the Truth, The Today Show; appeared numerous mag. covers; speaker various orgns. Chmn. bd. advisors Wildcat Winners Circle, U. N.H., 1981—. Recipient numerous awards including two silver medals Winter Olympics, Squaw Valley, Calif., 1960; New Eng. Council award, 1960; Nat. Ski Hall of Fame award, 1961. Named Women of Yr., Mademoiselle Mag., 1965; rep. Pres. Gerald Ford as head of presl. del. at Olympics, Innsbruck, Austria, 1976. Home: RFD #7 Box 94 Gilford NH 03246 Office: Penny Pitou Travel Inc 55 Canal St Laconia NH 03246

PITRE, JANICE L., enterostomal therapist; b. Cambria, N.Y., Mar. 27, 1936; d. Clarence Henry and Magdelina Elizabeth (Strothman) Stoelting; m. Woodrow Lee Pitre, June 7, 1963; children—Eric Lee, Virginia Elizabeth. Nursing diploma Genesse Hosp. Sch. Nursing, Rochester, N.Y., 1956; enterostomal therapist cert., Roswell Park Inst., Buffalo, 1980; B.S., Coll. St. Francis, Joliet, Ill., 1984. Staff nurse Athens-Limestone Hosp., Ala., 1967-68, Holzer Med. Ctr., Gallipolis, Ohio, 1970, Robinson Meml. Hosp., Ravenna, Ohio, 1970-72, Union Hosp., Terre Haute, Ind., 1972-75; enterostomal therapist Winona Meml. Hosp., Indlps., 1975—, instr. Reach to Recovery, Indpls., 1975—, Indpls. Rehab. Nurses, 1975—. Tchr., Prince of Peace Lutheran Sunday Sch., Indpls., 1975—. Served to 1st lt. USAF, 1958-61, PTO. Roswell Park Meml. Inst. grantee 1980. Mem. United Ostomy Assn., Internat. Assn. Enterostomal Therapists, Am. Cancer Soc., Ann. Rehab. Nurses. Club: Indpls. Zoo. Avocations: gardening; caring for sick animals. Office: Winona Meml Hosp 3232 N Meridian St Indianapolis IN 46222

PITRE, VIRGINIA MARY, educator; b. N.Y.C., Sept. 5, 1926; d. Francis M. and Mary Catherine (Boyce) Hackett; m. Victor H. Pitre, June 26, 1954 (div. 1974). B.B.A., St. John's U., 1954; postgrad. NYU, 1964-67. Field rep. Social Security, Bronx, N.Y., 1961-67, ops. supr., 1967-72; adminstrv. asst., 1972-73; asst. mgr. Social Security Adminstrn., White Plains, N.Y., 1973-84; tchr. St. John Vianney, Bronx, N.Y., 1984—. Pres. Olinville Taxpayers Assn., Bronx; 1984—; personnel sgt. Aux. Police, Bronx, 1970-72; leader Boy Scouts Am., Bronx, 1978. Recipient Presidential Achievement award Republican party, Washington, 1982. Fellow Am. Soc. Pub. Adminstrn., Federally Employed Women, Social Security Mgmt. Assn., St. John's Alumni Assn. Republican.

PITTARI, LINDA, brokerage firm executive; b. Bklyn., Nov. 22, 1944; d. Edward and Grace Pittari; B. Profl. Studies with distinction, Pace U., 1978; M.S. in Human Resource Mgmt., New Sch. Social Research, 1982. Sec., Merrill Lynch, N.Y.C., 1962-72, exec. sec., 1972-76, tng. adminstr., 1976-78, adminstrv. mgr., 1978-80, asst. v.p., mgr. mgmt. resources, 1980-82, v.p., mgr. manpower resources, 1982-83, v.p., mgr. mgmt. resources and devel., 1985—. Cert. profile assessment center adminstr. Devel. Dimension Internat. Mem. Career Planning and Adult Devel. Network, Am. Soc. Tng. and Devel. Office: 800 Scudders Mill Rd Plainsboro NJ 08536

PITTMAN, BRENDA JOYCE, nurse; b. Houston, Dec. 15, 1949; d. Freddie Lee and Lee Artie (Criswell) Pittman; m. Jan. 28, 1972 (div. 1974). B.S. in Nursing, Prairie View A&M U., 1972. R.N., Tex.; cert. phlebotomist. Staff nurse Tb unit Jefferson Davis Hosp., also charge nurse gynecology unit St. Luke's Hosp., 1970-77; substitute tchr. Houston Ind. Sch. Dist., 1976-77; asst. to immunization supr. immunization and communicable disease dept. Houston Health Dept., 1977-78, asst. charge nurse Riverside Health Ctr., 1978-79, charge nurse teen clinic, 1979-82; staff nurse hosp. base home care VA Hosp., Houston, 1982-85; staff nurse Mainland Home Health and Pvt. Duty Services, League City, Tex., 1985—. Author of nursing manual used as standard for teen clinic; Patient and Caregiver's Handbook to Hospital Base Home Care, 1984. U. Houston fellow, 1977-84. Mem. Am. Nurses Assn., Tex. Nurses Assn., Tex. Pub. Health Assn., Nat. Nurses Assn., Nurses Orgn. of VA. Democrat. Baptist. Home: 12215 Woodcliff Dr Houston TX 77013

PITTMAN, SANZEE GLEE, nurse, educator; b. Shattuck, Okla., Feb. 15, 1948; d. Loyd Edwin and Jacquiline Genevieve (Woods) Wanger; m. Harry Lee Pittman, Feb. 21, 1970 (div. Feb. 1983); children—Eric Loyd, Zaneta Zoe, Jarrod Heath, Damara Grace. R.N., Mercy Hosp. Sch. Nursing, Oklahoma City, 1969; student Central Okla. State U., 1983—. Staff nurse Mercy Hosp., Oklahoma City, 1969-70, Mercy Hosp., San Diego, 1970, Newman Meml. Hosp., Shattuck, Okla., 1971-73; clk.-typist Army-Air Force Exchange Hdqrs., Camp Mercy, Okinawa, 1973; staff nurse Spohn Hosp., Corpus Christi, Tex., 1975-78, Bay Gen. Hosp., Chula Vista, Calif., 1979-82; instr. High Plains Area Vo Tech Sch. of Practical Nursing, Woodward, Okla., 1983—; asst. supr. Newman Meml. Hosp., Shattuck, Okla., 1971-73; asst. head nurse Spohn Hosp., Corpus Christi, Tex., 1976-78. Navy family ombudsman USS Belleau Wood LHA3, San Diego, 1979-82; mem. Sur Pac Ombudsman, San Diego, 1979-82; mem. worship com., ch. pianist Fargo (Okla.) United Meth. Ch., 1982—. Mem. Am. Vocat. Assn., Health Occupations Edn., Am. Nurses Assn., Okla. Nurses Assn., Okla. Vocat. Assn. Republican. Methodist. Home: Box 274 Fargo OK 73840 Office: High Plains Area Vocational Tech 3921 34th St Woodward OK 73801

PITTMAN, VIDA JONES, administrative writer; b. Dallas, July 14, 1939; d. William Sanford and Djelma (Harper) Jones; m. Billy Edward Pittman, Nov. 22, 1968; children—Rebecca Diane, Pamela Carol. A.A., Grayson County Coll., 1975; B.A., U. Tex.-Dallas, 1984. Publs. specialist Tex. Instruments, Inc., Dallas, 1962-69; software writer Sci. Control, Carrollton, Tex., 1969-71; lead editor Fishbach & Moore, Dallas, 1971-73; sr. writer Rockwell Internat., Dallas, 1973-75, mktg. info. analyst, 1975-77; sr. writer, 1977—; cons. City of Sherman (Tex.), 1976-77, Western Electric Co., Winston-Salem, N.C., 1975-76, Scan Marine div. Pratt & Whitney, Montreal, Que., Can., 1982. Mem. arts and humanities bd. City of Sherman, 1976-77; leader 4-H Club Grayson County, Van Alstyne, Tex., 1980-84. Recipient Incentive award Tex. Instruments, 1968; 1st place award for painting State Fair Tex., 1983. Mem. Women in Communications, Grayson County Geneal. Soc. (v.p. 1980), Sherman Art League (Best of Show award 1982), DAR, Young Women's Orgn. (pres. Sherman 1984), Internat. Platform Assn. Republican. Mormon. Home: Route 1 Box 516 Van Alstyne TX 75095 Office: Rockwell Internat Corp 3200 E Renner Richardson TX 75081

PITTS, DARLENE ANNIS, educator; b. Ft. Worth, Oct. 2, 1943; d. Thomas Malcolm and Vilma Frances (Grizzle) Pitts. B.Ed., U. Miami, 1967; M.A., Tex. Woman's U., 1982. Tchr., Dade County Schs., Miami, Fla., 1967-68, Dallas Sch. Dist., 1968-71, Irving (Tex.) Sch. Dist., 1972-77; tchr., instructional specialist Dallas Sch. Dist., 1981—; presentor, cons. Tex. Edn. Agy. Workshops, Austin, 1982-83, Tex. Assn. Health, Phys. Edn. and Recreation, Dallas, 1981-83. Author family seminars, 1981-82; appeared in nat. film for Am. Heart Assn. You Are the Heart of Our Association, 1983. Chmn. Dallas County youth edn. Am. Heart Assn., 1982-84, mem. com. for state textbook and curriculum rev., 1982-84. Republican. Methodist.

PITTS, ELAINE RUTH HALLEAD (MRS. PAUL ELBERT PITTS), co. exec.; b. Chgo., June 20, 1917; d. Harry Albert and Ethel Mae (Waring) Hallead; student Ill. Inst. Tech., 1948-49, Art Inst. Chgo., 1947-48, N.Y.U., 1976-78; m. Paul Elbert Pitts., Aug. 25, 1945. Packaging engr. Aldens, Inc., Chgo., 1943-46; sr. packaging engr. Spiegel, Inc., Chgo., 1946-52; mgr. package engring. Sperry & Hutchinson Co., Chgo., 1953-59, mgr. consumer relations, N.Y.C., 1959-70, dir. consumer affairs, N.Y.C., 1970, v.p. corp. relations, 1970-79; partner Dalton/Pitts Assos., San Mateo, Calif., 1979—; lectr. M I T, U. Wis., Purdue U., UCLA, Ill. Inst. Tech., U. Ill. Nat. adv. bd. Distributive Edn. Clubs Am., 1962—, vice chmn., 1964, chmn., 1965; bd. dirs. S and H Found., 1974-79; mem. Ariz. State U. packaging adv. bd. Mem. Secs. Guild Chgo. Boys' Clubs (pres. 1963), Bus. and Profl. Women's Club, Soc. Packaging and Handling Engrs. (chpt. pres. 1957, nat. chmn. bd. 1966-67), Office Edn. Assn. (dir.), Soc. Women Engrs. (exec. com. 1968-69, 77-80, trustee 1982—), Am. Women in Radio and TV (v.p. 1969-70, pres. 1973-74, bd. dirs. Found. 1982—), Public Relations Soc. Am. (chmn. pub. affairs sect. 1985, bd. dirs. 1986—), U.S. C. of C. (consumer affairs com. 1975-79). Home: 1081 Beach Park Blvd Apt. 214 Foster City CA 94404 Office: 307 S B St San Mateo CA 94401

PITTS, MARGARET JANE, chemist; b. Spokane, Wash., Aug. 10, 1923; d. Herbert Ryder and Gladys (Burchett) P. B.S. in Chemistry, Wash. State U., 1946. Chemist, Electrometall. Co., Spokane, 1943-44, div. indsl. research Wash. State U., Pullman, 1945-46, Hayne Stellite Co., Kokomo, Ind., 1946-51, Pacific NW Alloys, Spokane, 1951-53, Pitts. Testing Labs., Portland, 1954-56, Boeing Co., Seattle, 1956-60, U. Wash., Seattle, 1960-63, Comml. Chems., Inc., Seattle, 1964-66, Puget Sound Naval Shipyard, Bremerton, Wash., 1966-77, Naval Undersea Warfare Engring. Station, Keyport, Wash., 1977—. Mem. Am. Chem. Soc., ASTM, Soc. for Applied Spectroscopy, AAUW, Federally Employed Women, Iota Sigma Pi, Alpha Delta Pi. Republican. Club: Bus. and Profl. Women. Home: 1717 E 16th St Apt 105 Bremerton WA 98310 Office: Code 312 Naval Undersea Warfare Engring Station Keyport WA 98345

PIVA, LILLY BELLE, former county and city labor union official; b. Gatesville, Tex., Aug. 11, 1918; d. William Wesley and Lillie Emaline (Lawrence) Payne; m. Francis Peter Piva, Jan. 21, 1937; children—Francis Anthony, Robert Lewis, Nicholas Dean. Student Tacoma Community Coll., 1968. Riveter Boeing Aircraft, Tacoma, 1942-43; cook mgr. Tacoma Sch. Dist., 1950-59; staff rep. Am. Fedn. State, County and Mcpl. Employees Council II, Seattle, 1962-78, staff rep. local 120, 1962-78; v.p. Central Labor Council, Tacoma, 1976-78. Bd. dirs. United Way Pierce County, Tacoma, 1967-72; commr. Tacoma Housing Authority, 1978-82; union counsellor Community Services AFL-CIO, Tacoma, 1967; committeeperson Democratic party, Tacoma, 1985. Recipient Certs. of Appreciation, Supt. Pub. Instrn., State Wash., 1985, Dem. Nat. Com., Washington, 1982. Democrat. Methodist. Clubs: 1918 Club, Candidates Forum (vice-chmn.) (Tacoma). Avocations: bowling. Home: 2410 N Stevens St Tacoma WA 98406

PIXLEY, MARY ELLEN, insurance company executive;; b. Wabash County, Ill., Apr. 24, 1924; d. Walter Mack and Cora May (Schnitz) P. Diploma, Lockyear's Bus. Coll., 1943. Sec., office mgr. Am. Surety Co., Evansville, Ind., 1943-46; adminstrv. asst. Mfrs. Casualty Co., Indpls., 1946-51; office mgr. O.K. Mannan & Co., Indpls., 1951-56; v.p./treas. Alexander & Alexander of Ind., Inc., Indpls., 1956—. Author, editor: From Pothooks to Pots and Pans with the Pixleys, 1969; Casseroles and Stuff, 1983, contbr. articles to profl. jours. Bd. dirs. Mut. Service Found., Indpls., 1980—. Recipient Sec. of Yr. award Profl. Sec.'s Assn., 1956, 65, Ins. Woman of Yr. award, 1958, 76, Woman of Yr. award, 1978. Mem. Profl. Secs. Internat., Indpls. Assn. Ins. Women (employment chmn. 1965—, edn. chmn. 1982—), Adminstrv. Mgmt. Soc. (merit award chmn. 1983—, area 9 sec./treas. 1982—, program coordinator 1982-84), Am. Soc. Personnel Assn., Nat. Assn. Ins. Women (region IV edn. adv. com. 1982—, individual edn. award 1982), Indpls. Zool. Soc., Connor Prairie Farms, Indpls. Mus. Art, Women in Networking. Republican. Methodist. Home: 2505 DePauw Rd Indianapolis IN 46227 Office: Alexander & Alexander of Ind Inc 25 Monument Circle PO Box 7019 Indianapolis IN 46207

PIZZOLATO, MARY ANN ROSE, chemical engineer; b. Newark, Apr. 23, 1953; d. Benjamin and Jennie (Lombardino) P.; B.S.Ch.E., Rutgers U., 1976. Process engr. FMC Corp., Carteret, N.J., 1976, asst. area supr., 1977-78; chem. engr. Gulf Oil Co.-U.S.A., Phila., 1978-80, sr. refining analyst, Houston, 1980-84, feedstock coordinator, 1984-85; part-owner Scarlett O's doll shop, Humble, Tex., 1985—. George Auchter scholar, 1974-76; Ross scholar, 1974-76. Mem. Am. Inst. Chem. Engrs., Rutgers Alumni Assn., Rutgers Engring. Soc., Nat. Assn. Female Execs., Soc. Women Engrs. Roman Catholic. Home: 7503 Live Oak Dr Humble TX 77396 Office: 9634 FM 1960 By-Pass Humble TX 77338

PLACEK-ZIMMERMAN, ELLYN CLARE, educator, consultant; b. Chgo., Sept. 3, 1951; d. Clarence Joseph and Jerrine LaMarr (Ruhlow) Placek; m. Allan John Zimmerman, Aug. 10, 1974; 1 child, Alissa Jan. B.S., No. Ill., 1973, M.S., 1977, C.A.S., 1978, Ed.D., 1982. Tchr. Arlington Heights Pub. Sch., Ill., 1973-75, 75-76, dir. library and learning ctr., 1976-81, tchr. lang. arts and reading jr. high sch., 1981-84, tchr. kindergarten, 1984—; mem. part-time faculty Coll. of Edn., Roosevelt U., Chgo., 1983-84; cons. in field; mem. steering com. Curriculum'90 Conf., De Kalb, Ill., 1985; lectr. in field. Contbg. author: Feeling Good About Food. Sec. Scarsdale Estates Homeowners Assn., Arlington Heights, 1983; hon. life mem. PTA. Mem. Ill. Assn. for Supervision and Curriculum Devel., Ill. Assn. Tchrs. of English (cons., speaker conf. 1984), Ill. Women Adminstrs. (publicity com. conf. 1985). Avocation: playing guitar. Home: 402 E Orchard Arlington Heights IL 60005 Office: Arlington Heights Pub Sch Dist 25 301 W South St Arlington Heights IL 60005

PLAGGE, CHERYL LYNN, executive recruiting company executive; b. Hampton, Iowa, Sept. 20, 1954; d. Merlin Dale and Shirley Jean (Olson) P. B.A., Iowa State U., 1976, also postgrad. in psychology. Therapist, psychiat. technician Mercy Hosp., Mason City, Iowa, 1976-79; exec. recruiter, asst. mgr. Mgmt. Recruiters and Office Mates 5, Mason City, 1979-81, owner, mgr., 1981—. Mem. Iowa Assn. Personnel Cons, Nat. Assn. Personnel Cons. Office: Mgmt Recruiters and Office Mates 5 520 S Pierce Ave Suite 226 Mason City IA 50401

PLANA, CHARLOTTE DUNLOP, communications research company official; b. Berwyn, Ill., Nov. 4, 1942; d. James Thomas and Violet Mary (Bartik) Dunlop; 1 son, Theodore J. B.L.A., Mundelein Coll., 1981. Sec., Western Electric Co., Chgo., 1960-76, personnel investigator, 1976-78, sect. chief, 1978-81, Springfield, N.J., 1981-83; tech. mgr., tech. systems Bell Communications Research, Morristown, N.J., 1983—. Mem. AAUW. Club: Summit Coll. Office: Bell Communications Research 445 South St Morristown NJ 07960

PLANAS, ZOILA GARCIA, educator, translator; b. Cruces, Cuba, Mar. 10, 1921; came to U.S., 1965; d. Pedro Luis and Zoila Rosa (Quintero) Garcia; 1 son, Osvaldo Luis B., Cienfuegos Coll. (Cuba), 1945; M., Havana Coll. (Cuba), 1949; postgrad. Tex. Woman's U., Denton, 1975-79. Cert. elem., bilingual and kindergarten tchr. Tchr., Havana Sch. Dist., 1945-64, Dallas Sch. Dist., 1975—. Named Tchr. of Yr., Dallas Assn. Bilingual Edn., 1982-83. Mem. NEA, Dallas Classroom Tchrs., Tex. State Tchrs. Assn. Republican. Baptist. Home: 2307 S Vernon St #215 Dallas TX 75224 Office: Lorenzo de Zavala Sch 3214 Winnetka St Dallas TX 75211

PLANCK-KUPFERER, LYNNETTE, office consultant; b. Dallas, Feb. 29, 1948; d. Paul Grayson and Marilyn Lois (Schmidt) Planck; student Colo. State U., 1965-66, Colo. U., Denver, 1968—; m. Marvin Theodore Kupferer, Jr., Oct. 4, 1980; children—Chantel Planck, Frederick Marshall Kupferer. Profl. model, Denver, 1966-75; store model, fashion coordinator Neusteters Dept. Store, Denver, 1969-72; office mgr. George Epcar Co., Denver, 1972-75; adminstrv. asst. Cryovac div. W.R. Grace & Co., Lakewood, Colo., 1975-79; office cons., 1980-85; spl. events mgr. Denver Dept. Store, 1979-80; modeling tchr., asst. to dir. J. F. Images, Inc., Englewood, Colo., 1970. Mem. Nat. Assn. Female Execs. Episcopalian. Club: Secretary (Denver).

PLANTHOLD, MILDRED ANN, association executive, mayor; b. St. Louis, Mar. 3, 1913; d. Frederick F. and Amanda-Marie Ann (Rook) P.; student N.Y. U., 1935-36, Washington U., St. Louis, 1936-37; m. Louis Cardinal Michie, Apr. 23, 1955 (dec.). Instr. speech Chautauqua (N.Y.) Summer Schs., 1937-38; speech instr. Notre Dame Acad., Quincy, Ill. and Belleville, Ill., also women's editor St. Louis Register, 1940-41; ch. editor St. Louis Globe-Democrat, 1941-43, women's editor, fashion and food editor, 1941-56; exec. sec. Allied Florists of Greater St. Louis, 1956-78; exec. sec. Profl. Florists of Mississippi Valley, 1978-83. Mem. adv. com. hort. div. East Central Coll., Union, Mo., 1976—; mayor Town of Piney Park (Mo.), 1954-58, 79-83; bd. trustees Scenic Regional Library System, 1971-73. Named St. Louis Woman of Achievement, 1948; recipient award Am. Meat Inst., 1950; Sterling trophy Netherlands Flower-Bulb Inst., 1965; John Walker award Soc. Am. Florists, 1982. Mem. Nat. Fedn. Press Women (life, pres. 1969-71), Mo. Press Women (life, pres. 1975-77), Women in Communications (30 yr. commendation 1980), Soc. Am. Florists Assn. Execs. Div. (chmn. 1966-70). Author, dir. documentary film on convent life, 1953. Home: Rural Route 1 Box 175 Saint Clair MO 63077

PLATH, CHARLOTTE MULLER, travel consultant; b. Mount Kisco, N.Y., Dec. 1, 1938; d. John Blair and Henrietta Spencer (Sterling) Muller; m. Richard Leroy Plath, Jan. 28, 1957; children—Janet Marie, Judith Ruth. Student U. Vt., 1956-58. Travel cons. Tri-Boro Travel Service, Kinnelon, N.J., 1973-84, owner, 1984—. Mem. Am. Soc. Travel Agts., Caribbean Tourist Assn., Cruise Lines Internat. Assn., Internat. Air Transport Assn., Airline Reporting Corp. Republican. Episcopalian. Home: 25 Dogwood Trail Kinnelon NJ 07405 Office: Tri-Boro Travel Service Route 23 Kinnelon NJ 07405

PLATT, JAN KAMINIS county official; b. St. Petersburg, Fla., Sept. 27, 1936; d. Peter Clifton and Adele (Diamond) Kaminis; m. William R. Platt, Feb. 8, 1963; 1 son, Kevin Peter. B.S., Fla. State U., 1958; postgrad. U. Fla. Law Sch., 1958-59, U. Va., 1962, Vanderbilt U., 1964. Pub. sch. tchr. Hillsborough County, Tampa, Fla., 1959-60; field dir. Girl Scouts U.S.A., Tampa, 1960-62; city councilman Tampa City Council, 1974-78; county commr. Hillsborough County, 1979—; chmn. Hillsborough County Bd. County commrs., 1980-81, 83-84; chmn. Tampa Bay Regional Planning Council, 1982; chmn. West Coast Regional Water Supply Authority, Tampa, 1985; chmn. Hillsborough County Council of Govts., 1976, 79; chmn. Sunshine Amendment Drive 7th Congrl. Dist., Tampa, 1976; chmn. Community Action Agy., Tampa, 1980-81, 83-84; chmn. Tampa Charter Revision Commn., 1975; chmn. Prison Sitting Task Force, Tampa, 1983, Tampa Housing Study Com., 1983, Met. Planning Orgn., Tampa, 1984, Bd. Tax Adjustment, Tampa, 1984; appointee Constitution Revision Commn., Fla., 1977, HRS Dist. IV Adv. Council, Fla.; mem. Hillsborough County Expressway Authority, Taxicab Commn., Tampa; mem. steering com. Nat. Assn. Counties Environ. Task Force, U.S. Bd. dirs. March of Dimes, Tampa, The Fla. Orchestra, Tampa; trustee Hillsborough County Hosp. Authority, Tampa, 1984-85; pres. Suncoast Girl Scout Council, Citizens Alert, Tampa, Bay View Garden Club; v.p. Hillsborough County Bar Aux.; mem. adv. bd. Northside Community Mental Health Ctr.: Access House, Tampa; active mem. Arts Council of Tampa-Hillsborough County, 1983-85, Drug Abuse Coordinating Council Orgn., Tampa, Bd. Criminal Justice, Tampa, Fla. Council on Aging, Inebriate Task Force, Tampa, Tampa Downtown Devel. Authority Task Force, Tampa Sports Authority, Tampa Area Mental Health Bd., Children's Study Commn., Manahill Area Agy. on Aging, Tampa, Athena Soc., Tampa Area Com. on Foreign Affairs, League of Women Voters. Recipient Outstanding Community Athena Soc. Service award, 1976, First Annual Humanitarian award Nat. Orgn. for Prevention of Animal Suffering, 1981, Spessard Holland Meml. award Tampa Bay Com. for Good Govt., 1979, First Lady of Yr. award Beta Sigma Phi, 1980, Women Helping Women award Soroptimist Internat. Tampa, 1983, Eliza Wolff award Tampa United Methodist Ctrs., 1982, Good Govt. award Tampa Jaycees, 1983, Good Govt. award League of Women Voters, 1983. Mem. Am. Judicature Soc., State Assn. County Commrs. Fla. (at-large dir.), AAUW (bd. dirs.), Mortar Bd., Garnet Key, Phi Beta Kappa, Phi Kappa Phi. Democrat. Episcopalian. Home: 4606 Beach Park Dr Tampa FL 33609 Office: Hillsborough County Commn PO Box 1110 Tampa FL 33601

PLATUS, LIBBY, artist, sculptor; b. Los Angeles, Aug. 18, 1939; d. Benjamin Lyon and Gertrude Goldman; children—Julie Linda, Diana Lisa. B.A., UCLA, 1961. Group shows include Richmond (Calif.) Designer Craftsmen, 1971, E. B. Crocker Gallery, Sacramento, 1973, Comsky Gallery, Beverly Hills, Calif., 1973, Galeria del Sol, Santa Barbara, Calif., 1973, Laguna Beach (Calif.) Mus. Art, 1973, Riverside (Calif.) Art Center, 1974, Calif. State U. Northridge, Los Angeles, 1974, Calif. State U., Fullerton, 1974, Calif. Design '76, Los Angeles, 1976, Cleve. Mus. Art, 1977; represented in collections: Tex. Christian U., Faberge Hdqrs., N.Y.C., numerous other public and pvt. collections; commd. works: Big Canyon Country Club, Newport Beach, Calif., Carolando Hyatt Hotel, Orlando, Fla., Mc Culloch's Silver Lakes Resort Hotel, Victorville, Calif., Blue Cross So. Calif., Los Angeles; lectr., condr. workshops numerous internat., nat., regional and state meetings, including World Craft Conf., Kyoto, Japan, 1978, Vienna, Austria, 1980, Glasgow (Scotland) Sch. Art, 1980, 84, Loughborough Coll. Art, Eng., 1980, 84, Konstfackskolan, Sweden, 1984, Goldsmith's Coll., Eng., 1984; Taideteo Ilinen Korkeakoulo, Finland, 1984; juror regional exhbn. Fairbanks Art Assn., Alaska, 1984; mem. Los Angeles Olympics 1984 Cultural and Fine Arts Commn., 1980-84, Los Angeles Olympics 1984 Citizens Adv. Commn. 1980-84; mem. Los Angeles County Museum Art Costume Council, adv. bd. Crafts Report Edn. Fund; mem. Craft and Folk Art Mus. Contemporary Craft Council. Recipient Graphic Achievement award Fox River Paper Corp., 1974; winner Tex. Christian U. Nat. Invitational Fiberwork Competition, 1977. Mem. Artists Equity (adv. bd. Los Angeles chpt. 1981—), Women In Bus., Am. Crafts Council, Handweavers Guild Am., Women's Caucus for Art. Home and Office: PO Box 64610 Los Angeles CA 90064

PLAYER, GERALDINE (JERI), small business executive; b. Cleve., Mar. 26, 1952; d. Cornelius Millsape and Ola Mae (Maxle) Fisher; m. Van O. Player, Aug. 27, 1970 (dec. Mar. 1975); children—Ricardo T., Van O., Michelle. Student Sawyer Coll. Bus., Mayfield, Ohio, Virginia Marti Sch. Design, Lakewood, Ohio, Inst. Children's Lit., Conn. Owner, Jeri's Designs, Inc., Cleve., 1970—, Success Writers, Cleve., 1986—; fashion cons. Active adoptive parenting orgn. Mem. Nat. Assn. Female Execs. Club: Back Wall (Beachwood, Ohio). Lodge: Brotherhood (Bklyn.). Avocations: aerobics; photography; theatre; speech. Home and office: 14217 Scioto Ave East Cleveland OH 44112

PLAYER, THELMA B., librarian; b. Owosso, Mich.; d. Walter B. and Grace (Willoughby) Player; B.A., Western Mich. U., 1954. Reference asst. USAF Aero. Chart and Info. Center, Washington, 1954-57; reference librarian U.S. Navy Hydrographic Office, Suitland, Md., 1957-58; asst. librarian, 1958-59; tech. library br. head U.S. Navy Spl. Project Office, Washington, 1959-68, Strategic Systems Project Office, 1969-76. Mem. Spl. Libraries Assn., D.C. Library Assn., AAUW, English-Speaking Union, Nat. Geneal. Soc., Internat. Soc. Brit. Genealogy and Family History, Ohio Geneal. Soc., Royal Oak Found., Friends Folger Library. Episcopalian. Home: 730 24th St NW Washington DC 20037

PLEMING, LAURA CHALKER, educator; b. Sheridan, Wyo., May 25, 1913; d. Sidney Thomas and Florence Theresa (Woodbury) Chalker; B.A., Long Beach State Coll. (now Calif. State U., Long Beach), 1953, M.A. in Speech and Drama, 1954; postgrad. U. So. Calif., 1960-63; Rel.D., Sch. Theology, Claremont, Calif., 1968; m. Edward Kibbler Pleming, Aug. 25, 1938; children—Edward Kibbler, Rowena Pleming Chamberlin, Sidney Thomas. Profl. Bible tchr., 1953—; lectr. Calif. State U., Long Beach, 1960-66, U. So. Calif., 1963-65; Bible scholar for teaching Scriptures Program, First Ch. of Christ Scientist, Boston, 1970-75; freelance Bible lectr., tchr., resource person for adult seminars, 1954—; active in summer teaching for young people, 1963-68; tchr. adult edn. Principia Coll., summers 1969-71; tour lectr. to Middle East, yearly, 1974—; mem. archaeol. team, Negev, Israel. Mem. Am. Acad. Religion, AAUP, Soc. Bibl. Lit. and Exegesis, Am. Schs. Oriental Research, Inst. Mediterranean Studies, Religious Edn. Assn., Internat. Congress Septuagint and Cognate Studies, Gamma Theta Upsilon, Zeta Tau Alpha, Phi Beta. Republican. Christian Scientist. Author: Triumph of Job, 1979; editor Bibleletter, 1968, 76, 82-86. Home: 2999 E Ocean Blvd Apt 2020 Long Beach CA 90803

PLESHETTE, SUZANNE, actress; b. N.Y.C., Jan 31; d. Eugene Pleshette and Geraldine Pleshette Rivers; student Syracuse (N.Y.) U., Finch Coll., N.Y.C.; m. Thomas Joseph Gallagher, III, Mar. 16, 1968. Star in Broadway prodns. Compulsion, Cold Wind and The Warm, The Golden Fleecing, Two for the Sea-Saw, The Miracle Worker, Special Occasions; star numerous TV prodns. including: Bob Newhart Show, 1972-78, CBS-TV series Suzanne Pleshette Is Maggie Briggs, 1983, CBS-TV limited series of 6 episodes Bridges to Cross, 1986; star 30 feature films including: (debut film) Geisha Boy, The Birds, If It's Tuesday This Must Be Belgium, Nevada Smith, Suppose They Gave a War and Nobody Came, Support Your Local Gunfighter, Hot Stuff, Oh God! Book II; TV movies include: Flesh and Blood, If Things Were Different, The Starmaker, Fantasies, Help Wanted: Male, Dixie, Changing Habits, One Cooks, the Other Doesn't, various others.

PLETCHER, PAT, mental health administrator; b. Rensselaer, Ind., May 11, 1948; d. Acy and Eva (May) McCarty; m. Mike Pletcher, Aug. 8, 1970; children—Troy, Kelli. Student Portsmouth Interstate Coll. Bus., 1967, Ohio U., 1985—. Acct. Ohio U. Bookstores, Athens, 1967-71; teller People's Credit Union, Middletown, R.I., 1971-73; data control coordinator Boston U., 1973-74; adminstrv. asst. Southeastern Ohio Regional Council on Alcoholism, Athens, 1975-76, chmn., 1981, 82; dir. planning and fin. Athens Hocking Vinton Community Mental Health Bd., 1976—; mem. Ohio Medicaid Task Force. Coordinator Chem. People, 1983; chmn. community issues com. Athens County, 1984, 85; treas. My Sister's Place, 1978; chmn. Alexander Jr. High Sch. Bldg. Steering Com., Albany, Ohio, 1985. Recipient Elizabeth Mills Obleness award Ohio U., 1984. Mem. Assn. Mental Health Adminstrn., Ohio Budget Coalition, Ohio Coalition for Homeless. Democrat. Club: Athens Civitan (charter). Avocations: politics; reading; public education projects. Home: Route 1 Box 267A Albany OH 45710 Office: Athens Hocking Vinton Community Mental Health Bd PO Box 130 Athens OH 45701

PLEWINSKI, TERESA MARIA SAUER, physician; b. Poland; d. Gustav and Jadwiga (Bedynski) Sauer; naturalized, 1974; M.D., Wroclaw and Warsaw Med. Sch., 1951, Ph.D., 1966; m. Gustav L. Plewinski, Apr. 5, 1949; children—Magdalena, Michael. Intern, resident in internal medicine Columbus Hosp., N.Y.C., 1969-73; dep. surgeon-in-chief Children's Hosp., Warsaw, Poland, 1958-67; pediatric surgeon-in-chief Regional Hosp., Ho, Ghana, 1968; attending physician Cabrini Med. Center, N.Y.C., 1973—. Recipient Physician's Recognition award AMA, 1972, 75, 78. Fellow A.C.P., Am. Acad. Family Practice; mem. N.Y. Acad. Scis., Polish Inst. Arts and Scis. in Am. Research and publs. in med. field. Home: 10 Waterside Plaza New York NY 10010 Office: 242 E 19th St New York NY 10003

PLEXICO, ANDREA LYNN, systems engineer; b. Kansas City, Mo., Dec. 14, 1962; d. Gene and Kathryn Leora (Lewellen) Plexico. A.S., Mo. Inst. Tech., 1983; B.S., DeVry Inst. Tech., 1984. Computer operator Compton/Sysco, Independence, Mo., 1983-84; systems engr. Electronic Data Systems, Dallas, 1984—. Bus. Women of Am. scholar, 1981; Mutual Farmers Assn. scholar, 1981; Honor award DeVry Inst. Tech., 1984, Mo. Inst. Tech., 1983. Mem. Nat. Assn. Female Execs., Data Processing Mgmt. Assn., Am. Film Inst. Republican. Methodist. Avocations: piano; aerobics; camping; cycling. Office: Electronic Data Systems 3260 Big Beaver Rd Troy MI 48084

PLIMPTON, PAULINE AMES, civic worker; b. North Easton, Mass., Oct. 22, 1901; d. Oakes and Blanche Ames; B.A., Smith Coll., 1922; m. Francis T.P. Plimpton, June 4, 1926; children—George Ames, Francis T.P., Oakes Ames, Sarah Gay. Pres., House of Industry, 1940-48; bd. dirs. Inst. World Affairs, 1940-74, Pub. Edn. Assn., 1933-44; chmn. United Campaign Fund for Planned Parenthood of Manhattan and Bronx, 1946-49; chmn. Planned Parenthood Fedn. Am. campaign, 1959-60, bd. dirs. 1959-67, 70-73; chmn. United Campaign, 1964; bd. dirs. Planned Parenthood of N.Y.C., 1965-74; rep. Western Hemisphere region Internat. Planned Parenthood Fedn., 1970-73; fund raiser Ladies' Aux. Philharmonic Symphony Soc. N.Y., N.Y. Legal Aid Soc., ARC; mem. adv. council Friends of columbia Libraries, 1986—. Recipient Planned Parenthood award for devoted service, 1969. Republican. Unitarian. Clubs: Cosmopolitan, River (N.Y.C.); Piping Rock (Locust Valley, N.Y.); Ausable (Adirondacks). Contbr. author, editor, compiler Orchids at Christmas, 1975; The Ancestry of Blanche Butler Ames and Adelbert Ames, 1977; Oakes Ames—Jottings of a Harvard Botanist, 1979; Orchids in Bronze, Am. Orchid Soc. Bull., Sept. 1983; The Plimpton Papers-Law and Diplomacy, 1985. Home: 131 E 66th St New York NY 10021 also 168 Chichester Rd West Hills Huntington NY 11743

PLITT, JEANNE GIVEN, librarian; b. Whitehall, N.Y., Aug. 27, 1927; s. Charles Russell and Anna Marie (Noyes) Given; student St. Lawrence U., 1945-47; A.B., U. Md., 1940; postgrad. Am. U., 1960-61; M.L.S., Cath. U. Am., 1968; m. Ferdinand Charles Plitt, Jr., Jan. 19, 1952; children—Christine, Marie, Charles Randolph. Library asst. Spl. Services div. U.S. Army, 1949-51; tchr. secondary schs., Md. and Va.; reference librarian Alexandria (Va.) Library, 1967-68, asst. dir., 1968-70, dir., 1970—; chmn. librarians' tech. com. Council Govts., Washington, 1971-72, 80-81; chmn. No. Va. Library Networking Com. Active Little Theatre Group, Alexandria. Recipient Alexandria Pub. Service award, 1964, 74. Mem. ALA, Va. Library Assn., Manuscript Soc., PTA, U. Md., Cath. U. alumni assns., Alexandria Assn., Urban League, Alexandria Hist. Soc. (dir. 1974—). Roman Catholic. Club: Zonta (sec. chpt. 1972-73, dir. 1973-74). Office: Alexandria Library 717 Queen St Alexandria VA 22314

PLODZIEN, CAROL ANNA, educator; b. Chgo., Oct. 7, 1948; d. Joseph Thomas and Elizabeth Ann (Hempel) P. B.S., No. Ill. U., 1971; M.S., George Williams Coll., 1979. Tchr. phys. edn. William Fremd High Sch., Palatine, Ill., 1971—. Author: (with June E. Meyer) Thinking Straight, 1983. Named Coach of Yr., Mid-Suburban League North, 1983-84. Mem. Ill. Girls Basketball Assn. (pres. 1979-80), Ill. Coaches Assn. for Girls' and Women's Sports, Nat. Wildlife Fedn. Roman Catholic. Office: William Fremd High Sch 1000 S Quentin Rd Palatine IL 60067

PLONA, MARY FEBRONIA, nun, administrator home for aged; b. Gardner, Mass., Oct. 2, 1912; d. Alexander and Alexandra (Wiski) Plona. R.N., St. Catherine's Hosp. Sch. Nursing, Bklyn., 1944; B.S. in Nursing, St. Joseph Coll., West Hartford, Conn., 1959. Joined Daus. of Mary of Immaculate Conception, Roman Catholic Ch., 1936. Nurse, New Britain Meml. Hosp. (Conn.), 1944-54; adminstr. Our Lady of Rose Hill Home, New Britain, 1961-62, St. Lucian's Home for Aged, New Britain, 1965—. Bd. dirs. Sancta Maria Hosp., Cambridge, Mass., 1973-76, Monsignor Bojnowski Manor, New Britain, 1974—. Mem. Con. Soc. Gerontology, Conn. Assn. for Non Profit Facilities for Aging (bd. dirs. 1967-74, 76—), Cath. Hosp. Assn. (New Eng. Conf.), Cath. Nurses (bd. dirs. Hartford chpt. 1960), New Britain Council Cath. Nurses (bd. dirs. 1960), St. Catherine's Hosp. Nurses Alumnae Assn., Nat. Geriatric Soc., Nat. Council on Aging, New Britain Area Conf. of Chs. Address: 532 Burritt St New Britain CT 06053

PLOPA, PATRICIA ANN, clinical psychologist; b. Detroit, Jan. 9, 1949; d. John and Jane (Miarecki) Gorski; m. Jeffrey David Plopa, Aug. 24, 1973; 1 dau., Lisa Michelle. B.A., Mich. State U., 1971; M.A., U. Detroit, 1976, Ph.D., 1977. Instr., U. Detroit, 1971-73, psychol. examiner, therapist Adult Psychiat. Clinic, Detroit, 1972-74; psychol. intern Children's Ctr. of Wayne County, Detroit, 1973-74, Sinai Hosp., Detroit, 1974-75; therapist, research asst. U. Detroit Psychology Clinic, 1972-77; therapist Project Headline: Family Counseling Ctr., Eastwood Clinic, Detroit, 1976-77; clin. psychologist Adult/Youth Devel. Services, Farmington, Mich., 1977-83; pvt. practice Maple Clinic, Birmingham, Mich., 1977-83, Northland Clinic, Southfield, Mich., 1980—; cons. Marriage Growth Ctr., 1983—; adj. faculty dept. psychology U. Detroit, 1986—. Mich. State Trustees scholar, 1967-71; U. Detroit teaching fellow, 1971-73. Mem. Mich. Soc. Clin. Psychologists (exec. com. council 1981-83, directory editor 1981-83), Mich. Psychol. Assn. (continuing edn. com. 1981-85), Mich. Soc. Psychoanalytic Psychology (program planning com. 1981-82), Am. Psychol. Assn., Nat. Register Health Service Providers in Psychology, Friends of Mich. Psychoanalytic Soc. (program planning com. 1981-83), Phi Beta Kappa. Home: 4655 Pickering Rd Birmingham MI 48010 Office: 17117 W Nine Mile Rd Suite 1221 Southfield MI 48075

PLOTT, ELIZABETH ANN, graphic arts studio executive, typographer; b. Mocksville, N.C., Sept. 18, 1948; d. Milton Artis and Annie Lee (Speaks) P.; m. James Norman Galliher, Apr. 8, 1978. Student Brevard Coll., 1966-68; B.A. in Behavioral Sci., Scarritt Coll., 1970; postgrad. Tenn. State U., 1972. Typesetter, Computer Composition, Nashville, 1970-75; mgr. Cumberland Graphics, Nashville, 1975-76; salesperson Yaeger Typesetting, Columbus, Ohio, 1977-78; owner Graphic Directions, Columbus, 1978—. Mem. Printing Industry of Central Ohio, Columbus Soc. Communication Arts. Democrat. Methodist. Avocations: skin-diving; hiking; traveling; reading; cooking. Home: 97 Kinder Pl Gahanna OH 43230 Office: L & J Graphic Directions 324 Agler Rd Gahanna OH 43230

PLOTZ, JUDITH LYNN, insurance broker; b. Cleve., Nov. 15, 1950; d. Charles D. and Pauline F. (McMillan) P.; m. Gregory E. Policastro, May 21, 1983; 1 son, William Charles. Student Lakeland Coll., 1973-75, Scarritt Coll., 1975-76, Bankers Inst. Sch., 1977-79, Case Western Res. Law Sch. Buyer, Higbee Dept. Stores, Mentor, Ohio, 1968-71; dist. mgr. Res. Life Ins. Co., Panama City, Fla., 1975-79; sales mgr. Prudential Ins. Co., Tampa, 1979-82; account mgr. Rollins, Brudick Hunter, Cleve., 1982-83; asst. v.p. Frank B. Hall Cons. Co., Cleve., 1983—; pres. J.L. Plotz, Inc., 1984—; lectr. in field. Recipient award Marjory Wetzel Found., 1970; Nat. Quality award Nat. Assn. Life Underwriters, 1980-82. Mem. Life Underwriters Assn., Midwest Pension Orgn., Assn. Profl. Bus. Women (Top Achiever 1980). Office: J L Plotz & Co Inc One Erieview Plaza Suite 900 Cleveland OH 44114

PLUMB, PAMELA PELTON, former mayor, councilwoman; b. St. Louis, Oct. 26, 1943; d. Frank E. and Dorothey-Lee (Culver) Pelton; B.A., Smith Coll., 1965; M.A., N.Y. U., 1967; m. Peter Scott Plumb, June 11, 1966; children—Jessica Culver, David Scott. Tchr., Master's Sch., Dobbs Ferry, N.Y., 1967-69; exec. dir. Greater Portland (Maine) Landmarks, 1969-71; engaged in civic and vol. work, 1971-79; mem. Portland City Council, 1979—, mayor, 1981-82; vice chmn. Peoples Heritage Savs. Bank. Bd. dirs. Maine Devel. Found.; bd. dirs. Nat. League Cities, 1983—, 2d v.p., 1985-86. Recipient Doric Dames's Bullfinch award for preservation, 1979; Greater Portland Landmark's Preservation award, 1980; Deborah Morton award Westbrook Coll., Portland, 1982; Neal W. Allen award Greater Portland C. of C., 1982;

named Portland and Maine Outstanding Young Woman, Jaycees, 1979. Democrat. Office: City Hall 389 Congress St Portland ME 04101

PLUMER, REBECCA LANEY, physician; b. Kingman, Ariz., Jan. 6, 1947; d. Samuel Keith and Sandra Helen (Samsel) Laney; m. Robert I. Plumer, June 12, 1965; children—Kimberly (stepdau.), Brian Lewis. B.S., Loma Linda U., 1976; M.D., U. Calif.-Irvine, 1980, specialty degree Phys. Medicine, Rehab., 1983. Diplomate Am. Bd. Phys. Medicine and Rehab. Intern, U. Calif.-Irvine, 1980-81; rotating resident U. Calif.-Irvine Med. Ctr./Long Beach VA Hosp., 1980-83; chief resident U. Calif.-Irvine Med. Ctr. dept. phys. medicine and rehab., Orange, 1982-83; med. dir. rehab. services Saddleback Hosp., Laguna Hills, Calif., 1983—; dir. South Coast Multisplty. Group, Long Beach, Calif., 1983-84; dir. Saddleback Rehab. Med. Assocs., 1986—; physician assoc. Rehab. Assocs., Long Beach and Laguna Hills, 1983—. Researcher, inventor: intra-oral device for Sleep apnea, 1979; researcher electromyographic technique, 1980. Recipient Med. Rehab. award U. Calif., Irvine, 1980; Sandoz award Sandoz Pharms. U. Calif., Irvine, 1980. Fellow Am. Acad. Phys. Medicine and Rehab. Republican. Office: Rehab Assocs 23561 Paseo de Valencia Laguna Hills CA 92653

PLUMMER, AGNES FOLEY, small business owner; b. St. Augustine, Tex., Nov. 16, 1909; d. Hugh and Mary Willie (Sims) Foley; m. Weley F. Plummer, Mar. 24, 1934; children—Beverly Anne, Frances Plummer Crozier, Carolynn Agnes Plummer Willson, Wesley F., Mary Sandra Plummer McCoy, Patrick Foley. Owner, Beaumont Printing and Lithographing Co., Tex., since 1935—. Active Cancer Crusade, 1969-70, also Beaumont Civic Opera; pres. Am. Little League Aux., 1952-54; bd. dirs. Better Bus. Bur., 1971-75, Program for Human Services Graphic Arts Sch., 1984-86; council St. Anne's Ch., Beaumont, 1985—; mem. prin.'s club Kelly High Sch. Recipient Bishop's award Diocese of Beaumont, 1972. Mem. Sabine Area Advt. Fedn., C. of C. (ambassador), Houston Litho Club, BPM Club. Clubs: Winnow Creek Country, Soroptimists (past club pres.). Home: 204 E Circuit Dr Beaumont TX 77706 Office: 3015 College St Beaumont TX 77701

PLUMMER, EDNA MAE, business woman; b. Conrad, Iowa, May 29, 1921; d. Elmer Leonard and Fern (Haggin) Schultz; diploma in bus. Spencerian Coll., Louisville, 1942; m. Kenneth (dec.); 1 son, Jerald D. Plummer. Stenographer, Monarch Equipment Co., Louisville, 1942-45; sec. Army Air Forces, Louisville, 1945-46, L&N R.R., Louisville, 1946; with Chevrolet Motor div. Gen. Motors Corp., Louisville, 1946—, cashier, sec., 1974—. Mem. nat. bd. advisors Am. Biog. Inst. Mem. Am. Bus. Women's Assn. (Woman of Yr. 1979-80, corr. sec. River City chpt. 1976, sec. 1977, v.p. 1978, pres. 1979), Ky. Women's C. of C. (mem. legis. com. 1979-80, exec. bd. 1980—, sec. 1981-82, pres. 1983-84). Democrat. Mem. Christian Ch. Club: Woodson Bend Resort. Office: 4501 Indian Trail Louisville KY 40313

PLUMMER, ELIZABETH MARY, nurse educator; b. Waterbury, Conn., Aug. 3, 1921; d. Thomas F. and Josephine M. (McCarthy) P.; B.A., Hunter Coll., 1944; M.N., Yale U. Sch. Nursing, 1946; M.A., Columbia U., 1959. Staff nurse Bklyn. Vis. Nurses Assn., 1946-47; sr. dept. head Conn. State Dept. Vocat. Edn., New Haven, 1947-58; field instr. nursing Tchr.'s Coll., Columbia U., N.Y.C., 1959-60; asst. prof. Grad. Sch. Nursing, N.Y. Med. Coll., 1960-62; asst. prof. L.I. U., 1962-64; asso. prof. med. surg. nursing Grad. Sch. Nursing, N.Y. Med. Coll., 1964-65, prof., 1966-73; prof. nursing Grad. Sch. of Nursing, Pace U., Pleasantville, N.Y., 1973—, asst. to dean for clin. affiliations, 1978—, asst. to dean for clin. affairs Sch. Nursing; mem. N.Y.C. Comprehensive Health Planning Com., 1971-74; cons. rehab. nursing Montrose VA Hosp., 1972-73. Mem. Right to Life Com., 1976—, East Harlem Community Health Council, 1970-73. Recipient Outstanding Tchr. award Keenan Trust Fund, 1976; Outstanding Alumna award Yale U. Sch. Nursing, 1982. Mem. Nat. League for Nursing, Soc. Nursing Profls. Am. Pub. Health Assn., Am. Nurses Assn. (cert. in gerontol. nursing, 25-yr. honor), Nursing Intragy. Orgn. Geriatric Nursing, Am. Heart Assn., N.Y. Acad. Sci., Yale U. Sch. Nursing Alumnae Assn. (chmn. N.Y. regional group), Pi Lambda Theta, Kappa Delta Pi, Sigma Theta Tau (charter mem.). Roman Catholic. Contbr. articles on nursing to profl. publs. Home: 317 96th St Brooklyn NY 11209 Office: Pace Univ Elm Rd Briarcliff NY 10510

PLUMMER, ORA BEATRICE, nursing consultant; b. Mexia, Tex., May 25, 1940; d. Macie Idella (Echols); B.S. in Nursing, U. N.Mex., 1961; M.S. in Nursing Edn., UCLA, 1966; children—Kimberly, Kevin, Cheryl. Nurses aide Bataan Meml. Meth. Hosp., Albuquerque, 1958-60, staff nurse, 1961-62, 67-68; staff nurse, charge nurse, relief supr. Hollywood (Calif.) Community Hosp., 1962-64; instr. U. N.Mex. Coll. of Nursing, Albuquerque, 1968-69; sr. instr. U. Colo. Sch. Nursing, Denver, 1971-74; asst. prof. U. Colo. Sch. Nursing, Denver, 1974-76; staff asso. III Western Interstate Commn. for Higher Edn., Boulder, Colo., 1976-78; dir. nursing Garden Manor Nursing Home, Lakewood, Colo., 1978-79; nursing cons. Colo. Dept. Health, Denver, 1979—. Active Colo. Cluster of Schs.-faculty devel.; mem. adv. bd. Affiliated Children's and Family Services, 1977; mem. state instl. child abuse and neglect adv. com., 1984—; mem. planning com. State Wide Conf. on Black Health Concerns, 1977; mem. staff devel. com. Western Interstate Commn. for Higher Edn., 1978, minority affairs com., 1978, coordinating com. for baccalaureate program, 1971-76; active minority affairs U. Colo. Med. Center, 1971-72; mem. ednl. resources com. public relations com., rev. com. for reappointment, promotion, and tenure U. Colo. Sch. Nursing, 1971-76. Mem. Am. Nurses Assn., Colo. Nurses Assn. (affirmative action comm. 1977, 78, 79), Phi Delta Kappa. Contbr. articles in field to profl. jours. Office: 4210 E 11th Ave Denver CO 80013

PLUNKETT, ANNE MARIE CECILIA, banker; b. Rochester, Minn., July 15, 1932; d. Eugene and Anna (Regan) Leddy; B.A., Manhattanville Coll., Purchase, N.Y., 1953; postgrad. Fordham U., 1953-54; m. Richard Harding Plunkett, July 12, 1958; children—Pamela, Patricia, Richard Harding, Julianne, Maureen. Instr. socio-econ. problems St. Marys Sch. Nursing, Rochester, 1957-58, 65-66; chmn. bd. Rochester Bank & Trust Co., 1973-82; v.p., sec. Midwest Video Electronics, Inc., Rhinelander, Wis., 1972-79; dir. Medelco, Inc., 1973-78. Pres., Olmsted County Lawyers Wives, 1959-60; leader Girl Scouts U.S.A., 1969-72; vol. tchr. St. Johns Religious Edn., 1972-75; founder Southeastern Minn. Regional Arts Council, 1973; chmn. Minn. Arts Bd., 1974-75; co-chairperson Minn. Bicentennial Commn., 1975-76; v.p., mem. finance com. United Way, Olmsted County, 1978, bd. dirs., 1976-78; chmn. subcom. on elementary edn. Rochester Sch. Dist. 535 Citizens Adv. Com. on Ednl. Facilities, 1976-77; coordinator Minn. Aesthetic Environment Program for Olmsted County, 1977; co-founder condrs. com. Rochester Symphony Orch., 1977; mem. Pres.'s Forum, Minn. Bible Coll., Rochester, 1977-79; mem. exec. com. Rochester Pres.'s Council, Coll. St. Teresa, Winona, Minn., 1977-78; adv. com. Agrl. Interpretative Center, Fairmont, Minn., 1979; 1st Dist. coordinator vol. activities Vice Pres. Walter F. Mondale, 1968; del. State Conv. from Olmsted County, Minn. Democratic party, 1974, 76, 78; nat. treas. U.S. Sen. Wendell R. Anderson Vol. Com., 1977-83; bd. dirs. AAU Rochester Swim Club, Family Consultation Center, Rochester YWCA, 1969-70, Lourdes High Sch. Devel. Fund; vol. Mondale for Pres. campaign, 1984; mem. Gov.'s Task Force Women's History Interperative Ctr., 1985—. Recipient Outstanding Vol. medal St. Marys Hosp., 1967, plaque of appreciation Olmsted County Bicentennial Commn., 1976, medallion and cert. of recognition Minn. Bicentennial Commn., 1976, cert. of appreciation Gov.'s Aesthetic Environ. Program, 1977. AAUW Ednl. Found. grantee, 1976. Mem. AAUW (founder Dayton Benefit for Scholarships 1955, dir. Rochester br. 1955-56, 75-77), Hospitality Inst. Tech. and Mgmt. (bd. dirs.), Rochester Banks Clearing House Assn. (chairperson 1977-78), Audubon Soc. (bd. dirs. Zumbro Valley chpt. 1986—), Needlework Guild (v.p. 1986—). Home: 2918 SW 15th Ave Rochester MN 55902 Office: Rochester Bank & Trust Co Box 6478 Rochester MN 55903

PLUNKETT, LINDA WILKINS, nurse clinical educator; b. Bennettsville, S.C., Oct. 2, 1947; d. Robert Emmett and Nelle (Hamer) Wilkins; m. Walter Carroll Plunkett, Apr. 2, 1983; children—Emily Nelle, Walter Carroll IV. A.D. in Nursing, Central Piedmont Community Coll., 1967; B.S. in Nursing, U. N.C., 1972; M.S. in Nursing, U. Ala.-Birmingham, 1978. Cert. cardiovascular nurse clinician, U. N.C. Staff nurse Charlotte Meml. Hosp. (N.C.), 1967-70; staff nurse N.C. Meml. Hosp., Chapel Hill, 1972-74, head nurse, 1974-77; clin. nursing specialist, clin. nursing instr. U. Ala., Birmingham, 1978-83; staff nurse Audie Murphy VA Hosp., San Antonio, 1983-84; vol. nurse World Missions Bd. of Presbyn. Ch., Chunju, Korea, summer 1968; mem. faculty organizational panel Ala. State Hypertension Conf., 1978-83. Contbr. articles to profl. jours. Vol. nurse ARC, Charlotte and Birmingham, 1969, 82; vol. local and state level Am. Heart Assn., Birmingham, 1978-83. Mem. Am. Assn. Critical Care Nurses, U. N.C. Alumni Assn. (sec./treas. 1979-81), U. Ala. Birmingham Alumni Assn., Sigma Theta Tau. Presbyterian. Home: PO Box 402 Lewisburg WV 24901

PLUNKETT, MELBA KATHLEEN, mfg. co. exec.; b. Marietta, Ill., Mar. 20, 1929; d. Lester George and Florence Marie (Hutchins) Bonnett; student public schs.; m. James P. Plunkett, Aug. 18, 1951; children—Julie Marie Plunkett Hayden, Gregory James. Co-founder, 1961, since sec.-treas., dir. Coils, Inc., Huntley, Ill. Mem. U.S. C. of C., Ill. Mfg. Assn., Ill. C. of C., Ill. Notary Assn. Roman Catholic. Home: Route 1 Sleepy Hollow Rd West Dundee IL 60118 Office: 11716 Algonquin Rd Huntley IL 60142

PLYLER, MARY DODSON, social services administrator; b. Norfolk, Va., Aug. 30, 1920; d. James Robert and Lizzie Eleanor (Gillette) Dodson; m. Conrad Norfleet Plyler, Feb. 19, 1944; children—Conrad Norfleet, R. Hardy, Elizabeth K. B.S., Longwood Coll., 1942; postgrad. Va. Commonwealth U., 1970-71. Social worker Norfolk Dept. Social Services, 1942-44; social worker Gatesville Dept. Social Services, N.C., 1962-70, dir., 1970—; chmn. Albermarle Regional Devel. Health Com., 1974; mem. Home Health Adv. Com., Hertford-Gates Counties, 1976-78. Mem. Gatesville Town Council, 1954-64, vice mayor, 1960-64; mem. Gates County Status of Women Council, 1983-84. Mem. N.C. Dirs. Assn. (services, income maintenance, fiscal coms. 1978-83), N.C. Social Services Assn., Gatesville Women's Club (pres. 1952), Gatesville United Methodist Women (pres. 1953), Colonial Dames, Soc. Mayflower Desc. Democrat. Avocations: reading; bridge; knitting. Home: PO Box 32 Gatesville NC 27938 Office: Dept Social Services PO Box 185 Gatesville NC 27938

POAGE, JANET ROY, environmentalist; b. Agujita, Mexico, Nov. 5, 1919 (father Am. citizen); d. William Allen and Katherine Lee (Yelvington) Roy; m. Oren James Poage, Aug. 17, 1949; children—Jane, James, Nancy, Carolyn, Gatrel. B.A. in Fgn. Langs., U. Tex., 1946. Reporter, editor NIH, Bethesda, Md., 1946-48, program analyst, 1948-50; vol. exec. dir. Wild Basin Wilderness, Austin, Tex., also pres. bd. dirs., 1981-84, emeritus, 1984—. Creator: Money Management for Low Income Families, 1976-78; author, editor: Wild Basin Wilderness slide show, 1980. Bd. dirs. Golden Opportunity Ctr., Dover, Del., 1961-64; vol. Dover chpt. ARC, Bermuda chpt., Austin, 1961—; chmn. Com. for Environmental Integrity, West Lake Hills, Austin, 1967, Zoning and Planning Commn., City of West Lake Hills, 1968-71; awards chmn. com. Com. on Energy and Environ. Edn., Tex. Edn. Agy., Austin, 1980-82. Recipient Citizenship award AIA, 1978, Banner award Women in Communications, 1982. Mem. Austin C. of C. (quality of life com. 1985—), Audubon Soc., Austin Natural Sci. Assn. (bd. dirs., pub. relations chmn. 1979-80), Phi Beta Kappa. Democrat. Episcopalian. Clubs: Sierra (Austin), WLH Garden (Austin) (program chmn., 2d v.p. 1976-77). Avocations: swimming; snorkeling; nature programs. Home: 509 Laurel Valley Rd Austin TX 78746

POBANZ, RITA BERNADETTE, nurse; b. Bklyn., Oct. 16, 1941; d. John Daniel and Mary Robert (Simpson) Grady; A.D.N. with honors, Eastern N.Mex. U., 1974; m. Kenneth Walter Pobanz, June 5, 1960; children—Karen, Stephen. Staff nurse Gerald Champion Hosp., Alamogordo, N.Mex., 1974; critical care staff, charge nurse, intensive care instr. Hampton (Va.) Gen. Hosp., 1974-79, patient edn. coordinator, 1978-79, critical care coordinator, 1980-82; critical care supr. Holy Cross Hosp., Austin, Tex., 1979-80; asst. dir. nursing Coliseum Park Nursing Home, Hampton, 1982-85; head nurse, trauma and plastic surgery U. Cin. Hosp., 1985—. Office chmn. Family Services, USAF, 1961-62, publicity chmn., 1962-64; hosp. vol. ARC, 1967-70; den leader Cub Scouts Am., 1970, C.P.R. instr. Am. Heart Assn., 1979-81. Mem. Am. Assn. Critical Care Nurses (sec. Tidewater chpt. 1981, pres.-elect. Tidewater chpt. 1982), Nat. League Nursing, Carolina-Va. Soc. Critical Care Medicine, Phi Theta Kappa. Home: 3152 Shorewalk Rd Maineville OH 45039 Office: U Cin Hosp Mail Drop 725 5 S East St Cincinnati OH 45267

POCOCK, JENNIE ANN, artist; b. Tokyo, Dec. 1, 1950; came to U.S., 1958; d. Donald Allen and Namiko (Endo) Pocock; ed. U. Mich., 1969-73. Archtl. sec., word-processing operator Ayres, Lewis, Norris & May, Ann Arbor, Mich., 1972-76; archtl. sec., word processor Prentice & Chan, Ohlhausen, Architects and Planners, N.Y.C., 1976-84; adminstrv. sec. Beyer Blinder Belle, Architects and Planners, 1984—; exhibited works group shows, 1977-81; works represented permanent collections. Office: 112 W 14th St New York NY 10012

PODGOR, ELLEN SUE, lawyer; b. Bklyn., Jan. 30, 1952; d. Benjamin and Yetta (Shilensky) Podgor. B.S. magna cum laude, Syracuse U., 1973; J.D., Ind. Sch. Law-Indpls., 1976. Bar: Ind. 1976, N.Y. 1984. Instr., Ind. U.-Purdue U.-Indpls., 1975-76; law clk. Kroger, Gardis & Regas, Indpls., 1975-76; dep. prosecutor Lake County Prosecutor's Office, Crown Point, Ind., 1976-78, asst. county atty., 1981-83; ptnr. Nicholls & Podgor, Crown Point, Ind., 1978—. Assoc. editor: Ind. Law Rev., 1975-76; contbr. articles to legal jours. Del., Ind. Democratic State Conv., 1982; bd. dirs. Lake County chpt. Am. Cancer Soc., 1982-83. Mem. ABA, Ind. Bar Assn., Lake County Bar Assn., AAUW, Nat. Assn. Criminal Def. Lawyers, Women Lawyers Assn. Lake and Porter County (past pres.), Lakeshore Bus. and Profl. Women's Club. Democrat. Jewish. Home: 9724 Johnson St Crown Point IN 46307

PODGORSKI, TERESA MARIE, college administrator; b. Hamburg, Germany, June 24, 1949; came to U.S., 1951, naturalized, 1970; d. Tadeusz John and Irene (Wojcik) Podgorski; A.A.S., Essex County Coll., 1970; B.A., Montclair State Coll., 1972; Ed.M., U. Buffalo, 1977. Bookkeeper, sec. Archdiocese of Newark, 1966-73; instr. St. Thomas Aquinas High Sch., Edison, N.J., 1972-76; assoc. dean Bryant and Stratton Bus. Inst., Clarence, N.Y., 1977-80, acad. dean Cleve. br., 1980—, ednl. policy devel. com., writer curriculum, 1980; textbook reviewer, cons. Mem. Nat. Bus. Edn. Assn., Assn. Info. Systems Profls., Ohio Bus. Tchrs. Assn., Assn. Supervision and Curriculum Devel., Am. Vocat. Assn., Nat. Assn. Female Execs. Roman Catholic. Office: 26700 Brookpark Rd Extension North Olmsted OH 44070

PODLES, ELEANOR PAULINE, state senator; b. Dudley, Mass., June 6, 1920; d. Francis and Pauline Magiera; student U. N.H.; m. Francis J. Podles, June 28, 1941; children—L. Patricia Podles Barrett, Elizabeth Lee Podles Keegan. Mem. N.H. Ho. of Reps., 1976-80; selectman City of Manchester, 1976-81; mem. N.H. Senate, 1980—, asst. majority whip, mem. fin. com., chmn. public affairs com., public instns. health and welfare com. Del., N.H. Republican Conv., 1976, 78, N.H. Constl. Conv., 1984; pres. Manchester Rep. Women's Club, 1979-80; bd. dirs. St. Joseph's Community Service; state chmn. Am. Legis. Exchange Council. Mem. Am. Legis. Exchange Council, Orgn. Women Legislators. Club: Manchester Country. Address: 185 Walnut Hill Ave Manchester NH 03104

PODOLAK, AUDREY REGINA, accountant, translator; b. Cairo, Egypt, Oct. 10, 1928; came to U.S., 1953; d. Antonio and Vilma (Botta) Maieroni; m. Devere Anthony Campbell, Sept. 12, 1954 (div. 1971); 1 child, Miranda Liala; m. Edwin Michael Podolak, Jan. 24, 1972. B.A. in Acctg. and Fgn. Langs., ed. in Egypt and Eng., 1951. Acct. ABC Jalousies Inc., Miami, Fla., 1953-55; Lehigh Constrn. Co., Glen Burnie, Md., 1955-57; sr. bookkeeper Vis. Nurse Assn., Los Angeles, 1964-67, comptroller, Easter Union County, N.J., 1967-69, Home Health Service, Passaic City, N.J., 1969-72; comptroller Hadley Realty and Law Offices, Hadley, Mass., 1972—. Designer acctg. form for Medicare/Medicaid services, 1966. Vol. Republican candidates for Senate, Glen Burnie, Md., 1956, Brit. Red Cross, London, 1948-52, Women's Vol. Service, London, 1950-52, ARC, Balt. and Miami, Fla. Recipient cert. of Appreciation, Cooperative Edn. Programs, Passaic City. Roman Catholic. Avocations: classical theatre; travel; building restoration. Home: 5 North Ln Hadley MA 01035 Office: Hadley Realty and Law Offices 116 Russell St Hadley MA 01035

PODURI, KANAKADURGA RAO, physician; b. Attili, Andhra, India, Jan. 21, 1944; came to U.S., 1970; d. Sri Ramarao and Sita (Pusuluri) Ayyagari; m. S.R.S. Rao Poduri, Aug. 22, 1970; children—Annapurna, Purna, S. Ramgopal. Student Andhra U., Waltair, India, 1961; M.B.B.S., Karnatak U., Hubli, India, 1970; M.D., SUNY, 1984. Diplomate Am. Bd. Phys. Medicine and Rehab. Extern St. Mary's Hosp., Rochester, N.Y., 1971-72, intern, 1972-73, resident in phys. medicine and rehab. Strong Meml. Hosp., Rochester, 1976-80; clin. instr., asst. physician U. Rochester Med. Ctr., 1981—; clin. faculty Strong Meml. Hosp., Rochester, 1981—; clin. faculty rehab. unit area hosps., Rochester, 1981—, cons., 1981—. Mem. AMA (clin. instr. 1981—, physician's recognition award 1980, 83), Med. Women's Assn. Rochester, Am. Acad. Phys. Medicine and Rehab. Hindu. Home: 66 Irving Rd Rochester NY 14618 Office: Strong Meml Hosp Box 644 601 Elmwood Ave Rochester NY 14642

POE, JUDITH REBECCA, restoration company executive, juvenile official; b. Wynne, Ark., Aug. 8, 1951; d. Terrell Brooks and Fanning (Virginia) Hewlett; m. Ronald B. Upton, July 7, 1969 (div. Aug. 1982); children—Cynthia Renee, Ronald Bruce Jr.; m. Marvin Dale Poe, Jan. 7, 1983; children—Anthony, Bryan. Student Ark. State U. Owner, pres. Mobile Home Mfrs., Forrest City, Ark., 1971-73; owner Newport Housing, 1974-78; owner, pres. J&M Enterprises, Newport, 1982—, Instant Shade, 1984—; juvenile ofcl. City of Newport, 1984—; dir., vol. coordinator Juvenile Cts., Newport, 1981—. Chairperson, Planning Comm., Newport, 1983—. Recipient Gov.'s Excellent award Gov. of Ark., 1982, 83. Mem. Bus. Profl. Women's Orgn. (fellow), Ark. Law Enforcement Orgn., Newport C. of C. Democrat. Presbyterian. Avocations: golfing; painting; baseball coaching; scuba diving; singing. Office: J&M Enterprises Hwy 67 N Newport AR 72112

POE, MERRY REX, insurance agency executive; insurance agent; b. Geneva, Ohio, Oct. 8, 1957; d. Glenn George and Ethel (Horvath) Rex; m. Gregory Scott Poe, July 25, 1981. B.S., Miami U., Oxford, Ohio, 1980. Lic. property, casualty, life, accident and health agt., Ohio; lic., registered rep. Nat. Assn. Securities Dealers. Underwriter trainee Shelby Mut., Ohio, 1980-81; adminstrv. agt. Johnson & Higgins, Cleve., 1981-82; agt. Planned Ins. Counseling, Inc., Chesterland, Ohio, 1982—, v.p., 1982—; ind. ins. agt. Vol. Am. Cancer Soc., Novelty, 1985. Mem. Profl. Ins. Agts. Assn. Republican. Presbyterian. Office: Planned Ins Counseling Inc 12200 Sperry Rd Chesterland OH 44026

POETHIG, EUNICE BLANCHARD, clergy; b. Hempstead, N.Y., Jan. 16, 1930; d. Werner J. and Juliet (Stroh) Blanchard; m. Richard Paul Poethig, June 7, 1952; children—Richard Scott, Kathryn Aileen, Johanna Klare, Margaret Juliet, Erika Christy. B.A., De Pauw U., 1951; M.A., Union Theol. Seminary, 1952; M.Div., McCormick Theol. Sem., 1975, S.T.M., 1977; Ph.D., Union Theol. Seminary, 1985. Ordained to ministry Presbyterian Ch., 1979; missionary United Presbyn. Ch. USA to United Ch. of Christ in Philippines, 1956-72; mem. faculty Ellinwood Coll. Christian Edn., Manila, 1957-61; mem. faculty, campus ministry Philippine Women's U., Manila, 1962-68; editor New Day Pubs., Manila, 1969-72; curriculum editor Nat. Council Chs., Manila, 1962-72; assoc. exec. Presbytery Chgo., 1979-85; exec. Presbytery of Western N.Y., 1986—; speaker United Presbyn. Women, 1973, 76, 79, 81, 85; mem. Council Execs., Ill. Council Chs., 1980-85. Author: Bible Studies in Concern, Response, A.D., 1975. Editor Hymn book-series: Everybody, I Love You, 1971-72, 150 Plus Tomorrow, 1982, 85. Mem. organizing bd. Asian Center Theology and Strategy, Chgo., 1974; bd. dirs. Ch. Women United, Chgo., 1974-79; trustee McCormick Theol. Sem., Chgo., 1974-75. Recipient Walker Cup, DePauw U., 1951. Nettie F. McCormick fellow in Old Testament Hebrew, McCormick Sem., Chgo., 1975. Mem. Soc. Bibl. Lit., Soc. Ethnomusicology, Am. Schs. Oriental Research, Witherspoon Soc. Office: Presbytery of Western NY 2450 Main St Buffalo NY 14214

POETTER, MABLE REECE, nurse; b. Ellijay, Ga., Jan. 11, 1920; d. George W. and Neatie (West) Reece; diploma Sch. Nursing Ga. Baptist Hosp., 1943; Dr. Human Services (hon.), Tift Coll., 1984; m. Louis J. Poetter, Dec. 17, 1943; children—Marcia Ann Poetter Pedigo, Rita Lynn Poetter Evans, Dana Faye. Asst. to dir. nursing Ga. Bapt. Hosp., Atlanta; evening supr., surg. supr., obstet. supr., instr. nursing Mercer (Ga.) U.; co founder with husband Anneewakee Found. and Treatment Center, Douglasville, Ga., also dir. nursing services, trustee; pres. Anneewakee Estates Inc.; caterer, wedding cons. Girl Scout leader, also camp nurse; class sponsor Future Nurses Assn.; mem. coms., tchr. Sunday Sch., 1st Bapt. Ch., Douglasville. Mem. Ga. Bapt. Hosp. Alumnae Assn. (Edna Earle Teal award 1984), Emergency Dept. Nurses Assn., Nursing Assn. Ga., 5th Dist. Nurses Assn. Ga., Am., Ga. State nurses assns., Savannah Assn. Garden Clubs, Douglas County Social Services Council. Home: 1946 Tara Circle Douglasville GA 30135 Office: 4771 Anneewakee Rd Douglasville GA 30135

POFF, PAMELA SUE, lawyer, state agency administrator; b. Hoboken, N.J., July 22, 1951; d. Carl Arthur and May Carolyn (Kane) Anderson; 1 dau., Cori Meredith. B.A., Upsala Coll., East Orange, N.J., 1973; J.D., Seton Hall U., 1976; cert. EEO studies Cornell U. Law clk., Greenberg, Margolis & Ziegler, East Orange, 1974-76; jud. sec. Superior Ct., Elizabeth, N.J., 1976-77; corp. EEO mgr. Mut. Benefit Life Ins. Co., Newark, 1977-80; dep. dir. Div. Civil Rights State of N.J., Newark and Trenton, 1980-82, dir., 1982—; mem. adj. faculty Rutgers U., New Brunswick, 1981—, Am. Inst. Banking, 1981—; cons. to pvt. industry. Editor: N.J. Employers Guide, 1984; contbr. articles to profl. jours. Mem. Concerned Persons for Adoption, Whippany, N.J., 1979; post advisor Boy Scouts Am., Newark, 1979-80; mem. council Upsala Planned Giving Council, East Orange, 1983-84; bd. dirs. Salvation Army, Newark, 1984; mem. Gov.'s Task Force on New Horizons in Housing, Gov.'s Task Force on Equitable Compensation. Recipient Disting. Alumni award Upsala Coll., 1983, Seton Hall U., 1984. Mem. Equal Opportunity Compliance Assn. (founder, pres. 1978-80), N.J. Human and Civil Rights Assn., N.J. Bar Assn. Republican. Lutheran. Club: Toastmasters (v.p. 1978-79). Lodge: Vasa Order Am. Office: NJ Div on Civil Rights 1100 Raymond Blvd Newark NJ 07102*

POGGIOLI, FRANCES CONSOLO MOSTEL, educator, rehabilitation therapist; b. N.Y.C., Apr. 30, 1930; d. Anthony and Mary (Iannuzzi) Consolo; m. Irving Mostel, June 26, 1954 (dec. Aug. 1969); m. Lester John Poggioli, Oct. 27, 1974. B.B.A., St. John's U., Bklyn., 1952; M.S., L.I. U., 1959; postgrad. Buffalo U., U. Siena, 1973, Bklyn. Coll., 1974; doctoral equivalency, CUNY, 1974. Therapist VA Hosp., Bklyn., 1953-54; dir. N.Y. Sch. Industry, N.Y.C., 1954-57; lectr. L.I. U., Bklyn., 1959-62; bus. educator Heffley & Brown, Bklyn., 1963-65; prof. bus. and secretarial option Kingsborough Community Coll. of CUNY, Bklyn., 1965—, recruiter-advisor, 1973—, med. coordinator, 1972—; mem. employment com. bd. higher edn., CUNY, 1983, coordinator employment in med. field, Bklyn. and N.Y.C., 1971—. lectr. U. Siena, summer 1974. Author: (texts) Pitman Medical Shorthand Outlines, 1980; Gregg Medical Shorthand Outlines, 1980; Century 21 Medical Shorthand Outlines, 1981; Word Information Processing-Medical Projects, 1981, 84; also articles in med. and ednl. jours. Mem. Italian-Am. Adv. Com., Bklyn., 1983—. Fellow CUNY Bd. Higher Edn., 1983-84. Fellow Am. Assn. Rehab. Therapy (cert. rehab. therapist); mem. Eastern Bus. Edn. Assn. (conf. chmn. 1983). Roman Catholic (eucharistic minister). Avocations: research; writing; travel; languages; handcrafts. Office: Kingsborough Community Coll CUNY 2301 Oriental Blvd Brooklyn NY 11235

POGO, BEATRIZ, cell biologist and virologist; b. Buenos Aires, Argentina, Dec. 24, 1932; d. Dario and Maria Teresa (Vergnory) Garcia-Tunon; came to U.S., 1964, naturalized, 1976; B.S., Lycee No. 1, Buenos Aires, 1950; M.D., Sch. Medicine, Buenos Aires, 1956; D.M.Sci., 1961; m. Angel Oscar Pogo, Jan. 13, 1956; children—Gustavo, Gabriela. Asst. prof. cell biology Inst. Cell Biology, Cordoba U., Argentina, 1962-64; research asso. Rockefeller U., N.Y.C., 1964-67; asst. Public Health Research Inst., N.Y.C., 1967-69, asso., 1969-73, asso. mem., 1973-78; prof. exptl. cell biology and microbiology Mt. Sinai Sch. Medicine, City U. N.Y., N.Y.C., 1978—. Damon Runyon Fund fellow, 1964-65; Am. Cancer Soc. grantee, 1970-73, research devel. award, 1984; NIH grantee, 1975—. Mem. AAAS, Am. Assn. Cancer Research, Am. Soc. Cell Biology, Harvey Soc., Assn. Women in Sci. (v.p. 1981-83, pres. Met. N.Y., 1983-85, pres. 1984, Disting. Woman in Scis. award 1984), Am. Microbiol. Soc., Am. Soc. for Virology, N.Y. Acad. Scis., Friend Commn. on Status of Women N.Y.C. Contbr. articles to profl. jours. Office: Mt Sinai Sch Medicine 1 Gustave Levy Pl New York NY 10029

POGODIN, ARLYNE, construction company executive; b. Chgo., Jan. 21, 1947; d. Arnold M. and Bertha (Erkes) P.; B.A., DePaul U., 1980. Timekeeper Morris Handler Co., Chgo., 1964-70; comptroller, v.p. Lazar & Assocs. of Ill., Chgo., 1970-77; corp. sec., comptroller Interior Alterations, Inc., Chgo., 1977—; pres. Rly and Assos. Inc., ins. agts. and cons., Chgo. Clubs: Mt. Sinai Hosp. Service, De Paul Century. Office: 550 W Jackson Blvd Chicago IL 60606

POGUE, J. MARIE, food corporation marketing manager; b. Galveston, Tex., July 23, 1951; d. John Henry and Anne (Cartwright) Biggers; m. D. Eric Pogue, Aug. 21, 1982. B.S. in Biology, U. Houston, 1974. Chemist, Dow Chem. Co., Freeport, Tex., 1974-81, sales rep., Dallas, 1981-82; promotion mgr., 1982-83; promotion mgr. Norcliff Thayer, Tarrytown, N.Y., 1983-84, Nestle Foods Corp., White Plains, N.Y., 1984—. Mem. Promotion Mktg. Assn. Am. (Outstanding Promotion of the Yr. award 1986), NAACP, Nat. Assn. Female Execs. Democrat. Home: 8 Myrtledale Rd Scarsdale NY 10583 Office: Nestle Foods Corp 100 Bloomingdale Rd White Plains NY 10605

POGUE, MARY ELLEN, civic worker; b. Fremont, Nebr., Oct. 27, 1904; d. Frank E. and Mary (Coe) Edgerton; B.F.A., U. Nebr., 1926; studied violin with Harrison Keller, Boston, 1926-28, Kemp Stillings Master Class, N.Y.C., 1939-40; m. L. Welch Pogue, Sept. 8, 1926; children—Richard Welch, William Lloyd, John Marshall. Mem. Potomac String Ensemble, 1947-80. Vice chmn. Montgomery County (Md.) Victory Garden Center, 1946-47; pres. Bethesda Community Garden Club, 1946-48; mem. bd. Montgomery County YWCA, 1946-50, 52-55; bd. govs., historian Gov. William Bradford Compact, 1966—; bd. dirs. Ind. Agy. Women, 1983—. Mem. Mayflower Soc. (dir. D.C. 1955—), Nat. Geneal. Soc., Nat. Soc. Women Descs. Ancient and Hon. Arty. Co. (Va. Ct.), Columbia Hist. Soc., Art Group (chmn. 1977-78), Capital Speaker's, PEO (pres. D.C. chpt. 1957-59), Mortar Bd. (pres. D.C. alumni 1966-67), Delta Omicron Music. Methodist. Editor: Favorite Menus and Recipes of Mary Edgerton of Aurora, Nebr. (cookbook), 1963; Edgerton-Coe History, 1965. Home: 5204 Kenwood Ave Chevy Chase MD 20815

POHL, GAIL PIERCE, association executive, writer; b. Stigler, Okla., Nov. 18, 1938; d. William James and Kathleen Louise (McConnell) Pierce; B.A., U. Okla., 1960; m. Lee W. Pohl, July 7, 1962; 1 dau., Leslie Kathleen. Reporter, Okla. Bus. News, Oklahoma City, 1960-65, news editor, 1966-72; pub. relations assoc. Am. Mut. Ins. Alliance, Chgo., 1972; editor Jour. Am. Ins., 1973-76; dir. publs. Alliance Am. Insurers, Chgo., 1976-78, dir. policy communications, 1978-79; exec. dir. Nat. Self-Service Storage Assn., Eureka Springs, Ark., 1981—. Pres., trustee 1st Montessori Sch. Atlanta Parents Assn., 1980-81. Mem. Women in Communications, Mut. Ins. Communicators (1st place award for editorial excellence 1977, 78), Chgo. Assn. Bus. Communicators (awards for bus. news writing 1978, mag. editing 1978, feature writing 1978; competition judge mag. editing 1979), Ins. Distaff Execs. Assn. Chgo. (legis. com. 1977-78, pub. relations com. 1976-78, exec. bd. 1978-79), Nat. Assn. Ins. Women (ethics com. 1977-79), Soc. Consumer Affairs Profls. in Bus., Bus. and Profl. Women (chpt. pres. 1985-86), Am. Soc. Assn. Execs. Home: 270 Spring St Eureka Springs AR 72632

POHLY, SHEILA RIMLAND, educational psychologist; b. N.Y.C., Oct. 10, 1946; d. Selig and Anne (Liberman) Rimland; student Russell Sage Coll., 1963-65; B.S. with distinction, Cornell U., 1967, M.S., 1968; permanent cert. sch. psychologist N.Y. State, Columbia U. Tchrs. Coll., 1971; Ph.D. in Psychology, SUNY, Stony Brook, 1979; m. Lawrence M. Pohly, Aug. 20, 1967; children—Michael Brian, Robert Scott. Instr. SUNY, Stony Brook, 1978-79; adj. faculty C.W. Post Coll., L.I. U., 1980—; sch. psychologist, gifted and talented program Northport-East Northport (N.Y.) Union Free Sch. Dist., 1980—; pvt. practice psychology, 1983—; cons. sch. dists. Active Citizens-Profl. Adv. Com. on Gifted Edn., Roslyn Pub. Schs., 1981-83; mem. alumni interviewing com. Cornell U., 1981—; mem. sch. bd. local Temple Sch., 1980-84. Mem. Am. Psychol. Assn., Nassau County Psychol. Assn., Nat. Assn. Gifted Children, Orton Soc., Cornell U. Alumni Assn., Phi Kappa Phi, Omicron Nu. Contbg. author writings to profl. publs., papers to profl. confs. Home: 3 Meadow Rd Old Westbury NY 11568 Office: 110 Elwood Rd Northport NY 11768

POINSETT, LINDA KAY, real estate executive; b. Cape Girardeau, Mo., July 12, 1950; d. Loren A. and Lois Marie (Morrison) Huffman; m. Michael Poinsett, Sept. 3, 1970 (div. Feb. 1974); m. Ronald Howard Silverman, Oct. 3, 1983. B.S., U. So. Mo., 1970. Real estate broker Murdoch & Coll. Inc., St. Louis, 1981—. Mem. beautification com. Downtown St. Louis, 1985, 86 (Better Downtown award 1985). Mem. Regional Commerce and Growth Assn., Comml. Real Estate Women (sec. 1981), Ambassadors of St. Louis, Nat. Assn. Female Execs., Nat. Assn. Indsl. and Office Park Developers. Avocations: reading; movies; travel. Office: Murdoch & Coll Inc 314 N Broadway Saint Louis MO 63102

POINTER, JEAN MARIE, educational administrator, educator; b. Clatskanie, Oreg., Feb. 6, 1927; d. William Alexander and Mary Sylvia (Steele) Godwin; m. Ramon Harvey Pointer, Mar. 6, 1946 (dec. 1980); children—Pamela Jean, Ramon William, Debra Marie. B.S., Whitman Coll., 1959; M.L.S., U. Oreg., 1966, U. So. Calif., 1966; Ph.D., U.S. Internat. U., San Diego, 1979. Cert. tchr., adminstr., librarian, Calif. Tchr. Umapine High Sch., Oreg., 1959-60, Morrison Elem. Sch., Norwalk, Calif., 1960-61; librarian Lakewood Jr. High Sch., Little Lake, Calif., 1961-62; dist. librarian Buena Park Sch. Dist., Calif., 1962-66; adminstr. instructional support systems Norwalk-La Mirada Unified Sch. Dist., 1966—; lectr. Calif. State U.-Long Beach, part-time 1970—, mem. adv. bd. instructional media dept., 1975—; mem. recognition of merit com. Claremont Reading Conf., Calif., 1970—. Editor Norwalk-La Mirada Student Author Project, 1979—. Recipient Disting. Service award Calif. State U.-Long Beach, 1977. Mem. Calif. Media and Library Educators Assn. (pres. so. sect. 1983), Assn. Calif. Sch. Adminstrs., ALA, Internat. Reading Assn. (pres. Rio Hondo council 1984), PTA (hon. life mem. Norwalk). Club: Toastmasters (treas. 1983-84) (Norwalk). Lodge: Soroptimists. Home: 6535 Circulo Dali Anaheim CA 92807 Office: Norwalk-La Mirada Unified Sch Dist 12820 S Pioneer St Norwalk CA 90650

POJAWA, KATHERINE MARY, insurance company executive; b. Jersey City, June 18, 1947; d. Ben Joseph and Frances Mary (Drabik) P. B.A., Coll. of St. Elizabeth, 1969; M.A., Jersey City State Coll., 1973. Tng. supr. Prudential Ins. Co., Newark, 1969-72, mgr. skills tng. Prudential Property & Casualty Ins. Co., Holmdel, N.J., 1972-76, personnel mgr., 1976-78, mgr. field services, Newark, 1978-79, dir. field services, 1979-83, dir. personnel relations, 1983—. Mem. Am. Soc. Personnel Adminstrs. Democrat. Roman Catholic. Office: Prudential Ins Co 745 Broad St 17 Plaza Newark NJ 07101

POKORNY, NANCY GORDON, school principal; b. Stephenville, Nfld., Can., May 12, 1942 (parents Am. citizens); d. Harold Leo and Irmstraud Hildegard (Weyrich) Gordon; m. Larry Jon Matthews, May 31, 1964 (div. 1971); 1 child, Jennifer Marie; m. Jerry James Pokorny, Nov. 12, 1971. B.A. in Edn., U. Mich., 1964; M.A. in Sch. Adminstrn., U. Denver, 1978; Ph.D. in Sch. Adminstrn., U. Colo., 1985. Tchr., Ann Arbor Pub. Schs., Mich., 1964-68, Albuquerque Pub. Schs., 1965-66, Laramie Pub. Schs., Wyo., 1970-71; tchr. Aurora Hills Middle Sch., Colo., 1973-77, learning coordinator, 1977-81; prin. West Middle Sch., Aurora, 1981—; cons. Aurora Pub. Schs., 1977—, mem. adminstrv. council, 1984—; vis. team chmn. North Central Assn., Greeley, Colo., 1983—. Contbr. articles on travel to jours. Mem. Nat. Assn. Secondary Sch. Prins., Colo. Assn. Sch. Execs., Nat. Middle Sch. Assn., Sch. Execs. of Aurora (treas. 1978-79), Club Aquarius, Am. Mensa Ltd., U.S. Ski Assn. (sec. Ski Country Ski Council, 1971-73, mem. U.S. Citizen Alpine Ski Team, 1975), Profl. Assn. Dive Instrs. (divemaster 1984—), U. Mich. Alumni Assn., Pi Beta Phi. Avocations: travel; scuba diving (archeological and search-rescue); writing; off-road motorcycling. Home: 5976 S Kenton St Englewood CO 80111 Office: West Middle Sch 10100 E 13th Ave Aurora CO 80010

POLAN, NANCY MOORE, artist; b. Newark, Ohio; d. William Tracy and Francis (Flesher) Moore; A.B., Marshall U., 1936; m. Lincoln Milton Polan, Mar. 28, 1934; children—Charles Edwin, William Joseph Marion. One-man shows Charleston Art Gallery, 1961, 67, 73, Greenbrier, 1963, Huntington Galleries, 1963, 66, 71, N.Y. World's Fair, 1965, W.Va. U., 1966, Carroll Reese Mus., 1967; exhibited in group shows Am. Watercolor Soc., Allied Artists of Am., Nat. Arts Club, 1968-74, 76-77, Pa. Acad. Fine Arts, Opening of Creative Arts Center W.Va. U., 1969, Internat. Platform Assn. Art Exhibit, 1968-69, 72, 73, 74, 79, Allied Artists W.Va., 1968-69, Joan Miro Graphic Exhbn., Barcelona, Spain, 1970, XXI Exhibit Contemporary Art, La Scala, Florence, Italy, 1971, Rassegna Internazionale d'Arte Grafica, Siena, Italy, 1973, 79, 82, Opening of Parkersburg (W.Va.) Art Center, 1975, Internat. Platform Assn. Ann. Exhbn., 1979, others. Hon. v.p. Centro Studi e Scambi Internazionale, Rome, Italy, 1977. Recipient Acad. of Italy with Gold medal, 1979; recipient Norton Meml. award 3d Nat. Jury Show Am. Art, Chautauqua, N.Y., 1960; Purchase prize, Jurors award, Watercolor award Huntington Galleries, 1960, 61; Nat. Arts Club for watercolor, 1969; Gold medal Masters of Modern Art exhbn., La Scala Gallery, Florence, 1975, Gold medal Accademia Italia delle Arti, Parma, Italy, 1984, 85, many others. Mem. DAR, Allied Artists W.Va., Internat. Platform Assn. (3d award-painting in ann. art exhbn. 1977), Allied Artists Am. (asso.), Huntington Galleries, Tri-State Arts Assn. (Equal Merit award 1978), Sunrise Found., Pen and Brush (Grumbacher award 1978), Am. Watercolor Soc. (assoc.), Am. Fedn. Arts, Nat. Arts Club, Leonardo da Vinci Acad. (Rome), Vero Beach Art Club, W.Va. Watercolor Soc., Sigma Kappa. Episcopalian. Address: 2 Prospect Dr Huntington WV 25701 also 2106 Club Dr Vero Beach FL 32963

POLAND, SUSAN LEE, lawyer; b. Washington, June 8, 1955; d. Sherman Swett and Nancy Ann (Leland) Poland. B.A., Sarah Lawrence Coll., 1977; B.A. in Law, Cambridge U. (Eng.), 1979; LL.M., N.Y.U., 1981. Bar: N.Y. 1982. Assoc., Weil, Gotshal & Manges, N.Y.C., 1981—. Mem. ABA. Democrat. Episcopalian. Home: 200 E 82d St Apt 14J New York NY 10028 Office: Weil Gotshal & Manges 767 Fifth Ave New York NY 10153

POLASCIK, MARY ANN, ophthalmologist; b. Elkhorn, W.Va., Dec. 28, 1940; d. Michael and Elizabeth (Halko) Polascik; B.A., Rutgers U., 1967; M.D., Pritzker Sch. Medicine, 1971; m. Joseph Elie, Oct. 2, 1973; 1 dau., Laura Elizabeth Polascik. Jr. pharmacologist Ciba Pharm. Co., Summit, N.J., 1961-67; intern Billings Hosp., Chgo., 1971-72; resident in ophthalmology U. Chgo. Hosp., 1972-75; practice medicine specializing in ophthalmology, Dixon, Ill., 1975—; pres. McNichols Clinic, Ltd.; cons. ophthalmology, Dixon Devel. Center; mem. staff Katherine Shaw Bethea Hosp., Dixon, Dixon Developmental Center Hosp. Bd. dirs. Sinissippi Mental Health Center, 1976-81, Winnebago Center for Blind. Mem. AMA, Ill. Med. Soc., Ill., Am. assns. ophthalmology, Alpha Sigma Lambda. Roman Catholic. Clubs: Galena Territory, Dixon Country. Office: 120 S Hennepin Dixon IL 61021

POLCAR, GERTRUDE ELIZABETH, judge; b. Cleve., Oct. 10, 1916; d. Martin and Gertrude M. (Jirele) Polcar; student Leland Stanford Jr. U., 1934-36; A.B. in Law, U. Chgo., 1938, J.D., 1940. Admitted to Ohio bar, 1941, U.S. Supreme Ct. bar, 1981; individual practice law, Parma, 1942-44, 50-56, 60-71; asst. atty. gen. of Ohio, 1945-49, 57-59; councilman City of Parma, 1960-68; mem. Ohio Ho. of Reps. from Dist. 51, 1969-71; judge Parma Mcpl. Ct., 1972—, presiding and adminstrv. judge, 1976-77, 82-83; v.p.-at-large Greater Cleve. Safety Council. Mem. Republican State Central Com. from 20th Dist., 1954-64; mem. South Ridge Civic Assn.; dir.-at-large Friends of Parma Libraries, 1981—. Recipient superior jud. service awards Supreme Ct. Ohio, 1975-86. Mem. Ohio, Cuyahoga County, Parma bar assns., Bar Assn. Greater Cleve., Cleve. Women Lawyers' Assn., Ohio Mcpl. Judges Assn. (trustee), Greater Cleve. Mcpl. Judges Assn. (pres. 1982), Ohio Jud. Conf., Am. Judges Assn., Parma Area Hist. Soc. Clubs: Order Eastern Star, Ladies Oriental Shrine N.Am. Home: 7060 Ridge Rd Parma OH 44129 Office: 5750 W 54th St Parma OH 44129

POLCHA, SHARON ANN, service company executive; b. Queens, N.Y., Mar. 3, 1953; d. Francis Xavier and Mary Patricia (Melenchek) Clark. m. Joseph John Polcha III, Apr. 12, 1980. B.S., Bloomsburg U., 1975; M.A., U. Scranton, 1985. With RCA Service Co., Drums, Pa., 1977—, mgr. enrollee support, 1983-85, mgr. adminstrn. and support, 1985—, corp. compliance reviewer, Cherry Hill, N.J., 1986—. Named Nat. Mgr. of Yr., RCA Job Corps Program, Cherry Hill, 1984; Mgr. of Yr., Keystone Job Corps Ctr., 1984, 85. Mem. Nat. Assn. Female Execs. Sec., Keystone Job Corps Ctr. Greater Hazleton Community Relations Council, 1983—, Wiles Barre Community Relations Council, 1984—. Democrat. Roman Catholic. Home: RD 3 Box 95 Drums PA 18222 Office: RCA Service Co Box 37 Foothills Dr Drums PA 18222

POLEMITOU, OLGA ANDREA, accountant; b. Nicosia, Cyprus, June 28, 1950; d. Takis and Georgia (Nicolaou) Chrysanthou. B.A. with honors, U. London, 1971; Ph.D., Ind. U.-Bloomington, 1981. C.P.A., Ind. Asst. productivity officer Internat. Labor Office/Cyprus Productivity Ctr., Nicosia, 1971-74; cons. Arthur Young & Co., N.Y.C., 1981; mgr. Coopers & Lybrand, Newark, 1981-83; mgr. Bell Atlantic, Phila., 1983—. Contbr. articles to profl. jours. Bus. cons. project bus. Jr. Achievement, Indpls., 1984-85; mem. adv. council Community Edn., West Windsor, Plainsboro, N.J., 1986. Mem. Nat. Assn. Female Execs., Nat. Trust for Hist. Preservation, Am. Inst. C.P.A.s. Avocations: water skiing; tennis. Home: PO Box 401 Princeton Junction NJ 08550 Office: Bell Atlantic 1600 Market St Philadelphia PA 19103

POLEVOY, NANCY TALLY, lawyer, social worker; b. N.Y.C., May 27, 1944; d. Charles H. and Bernice M. (Gang) Tally; student Mt. Holyoke Coll., 1962-64; B.A., Barnard Coll., 1966; M.S. (NIMH scholar), Columbia U. Sch. Social Work, 1968, J.D., Columbia U. Sch. Law, 1986; m. Martin D. Polevoy, Mar. 19, 1967; children—Jason Tally, John Gerald. Caseworker, unmarried mothers' service Louise Wise Services, N.Y.C., 1967, caseworker, adoption dept., 1969-71; caseworker Youth Consultation Service, N.Y.C., 1968-69; asst. research scientist, psychiat. social worker, dept. child psychiatry N.Y.U. Med. Center, N.Y.C., 1973-81; adv. ct. appointed spl. advs. Manhattan Family Ct., N.Y.C., 1981-82; social work cons., 1981—. Recipient French Govt. prize, 1963. Mem. Nat. Assn. Social Workers, Acad. Cert. Social Workers, Alumni Assn. Columbia U. Sch. Social Work. Contbr. articles on early infantile autism to profl. jours. Home: 1155 Park Ave New York NY 10128 Office: 1155 Park Ave New York NY 10128

POLINSKY, JANET NABOICHECK, state legislator; b. Hartford, Conn., Dec. 6, 1930; d. Louis H. and Lillian S. Naboicheck; B.A., U. Conn., 1953; postgrad. Harvard U. Bus. Sch., 1954; m. Hubert N. Polinsky, Sept. 21, 1958; children—Gerald, David, Beth. Mem. Waterford 2d Charter Commn. (Conn.), 1967-68, Waterford Conservation Commn., 1968-69; Waterford rep. Town Meeting, 1969-71, S.E. Conn. Regional Planning Agy., 1971-73; mem. Waterford Planning and Zoning Commn., 1970-76, chmn., 1973-76; mem. Waterford Democratic Town Com., 1976—, del. State Dem. Conv., 1976, 78, 80, 82, 84, 86; mem. Conn. Ho. of Reps. from 38th Dist., 1977—, asst. majority leader, 1981-83, chmn. appropriations com., 1983-84, ranking mem., 19875-86, minority whip, 1985-86. Trustee Eugene O'Neill Meml. Theatre Center, 1973-76, 81—; mem. New Eng. Bd. Higher Edn., 1981-83; mem. fiscal affairs com. Eastern Conf. Council of State Govts., 1983—. Named Woman of Yr., Waterford Jr. Women's Club, 1977, Nehantic Women's Bus. and Profl. Club, 1979, Legislator of Yr., Conn. Library Assn., 1980. Mem. Order Women Legislators, Delta Kappa Gamma (hon.). Home: 19 E Neck Rd Waterford CT 06385 Office: State Capitol Hartford CT 06106

POLITE, EDMONIA ALLEN, consultant; b. Washington, June 22, 1922; d. Thomas Samuel and Narcissus Bertha (Porter) Allen-Sylvester; m. George Frederick Polite, Jan. 5, 1941; 1 child, Frederick Gartrell. B.A., Roosevelt U., 1958; M.Ed., Loyola U., Chgo., 1966; Ph.D. in Adminstrn. and Supervision, Purdue U., 1973; D.Div., Eastern U., Tampa, Fla., 1971, D.Edn. Psychology, 1972. Dir. Media Ctr., City of Chgo., 1958-69, 73-81; instr. media scis. Purdue U., West Lafayette, Ind., 1969-73; pres. Cons. Inc., Chgo. and Orlando, Fla., 1974—; dir. Community Tutoring Ctr., Chgo., 1974-80; cons. Lake Region Conf., Detroit, 1966, Librarians, Inc., Chgo., 1970-71. Author: In Passing, 1970; People Who Help Us, 1982. Founder South End Parents Council, Chgo., 1960, Humanitarian Profls., Chgo., 1974, Orlando, 1983—; bd. dirs. Salem House, Chgo., 1980—. Recipient Outstanding Service award Lions Club, Chgo., 1975, Outstanding Educator award Fla. A&M U. Alumni Assn. Mem. Nat. Assn. Club Women (archives dir. 1980—), Ill. Audio Visual Assn., Phi Delta Kappa. Club: Successful Progressors (Orlando) (pres. 1983—). Avocations: writing; community service; counselling. Home: PO Box 150459 Orlando FL 32858

POLK, EDWINA ROWAND, engineer, surveyor; b. Lakeland, Fla., Jan. 30, 1921; d. Charles Adrian and Edith Ruth (Gramling) Rowand; m. Virgil Isaac Polk, Jan. 2, 1949; 1 child, Edith. B.S. in Math., Fla. So. Coll., 1942; postgrad. The Citadel, 1943. Registered land surveyor, Fla. Draftsman U.S. Navy, Charleston, S.C., 1942-45; tchr. math. Brandon High Sch., Fla., 1945-46; draftsman Food Machinery, Lakeland, 1946-49; draftsman designer, 1949-63; designer Polk County, Bartow, Fla., 1963-76, asst. county engr., 1976—; tchr., mem. tech. com. Polk Community Coll., Winter Haven, Fla., 1966-69. Mem. Fla. Soc. Profl. Land Surveyors. Democrat. Baptist. Avocations: history; antiques; cooking. Home: 302 Ariana St Lakeland FL 33803 Office: Polk County Engring 168 W Main St Bartow FL 33830

POLK, MARY JO MCCRACKEN, state official; b. Quitaque, Tex.; d. Leon and Lockwood McCracken; B.B.A., U. Tex., El Paso, 1967; m. D. Wade Polk, May 15, 1948; children—Linda, Paul, Laura. Elem. and kindergarten tchr., 1967-78; mem. Tex. Ho. of Reps., 1979-84, mem. energy com., jud. affairs com., urban needs com., steering com., mem. ways and means com., chmn. human services com., chmn. select com. on teenage pregnancy; exec. asst. to commr. Tex. Dept. Human Services, 1984—. Bd. dirs. Runaway Center and Sch. for Teen-Age Parents. Mem. Nat. Conf. State Legislatures (human resources com.), Tex. Tchrs. Assn. (life), Tex. Elected Women. Democrat. Methodist. Home: 2409 Versailles Cedar Park TX 78613 Office: 701 W 51st St Austin TX 78769

POLK, MELANIE ROSA, engineering scheduler; b. Houston, Sept. 13, 1955; d. John H. and Ramona (Smith) P. Student Pearl River Jr. Coll., Poplarville, Miss., 1973-74, Jackson County Jr. Coll., Pascagoula, Miss., 1974-75, U. Houston, 1979-82. Prodn. control scheduler Ingalls Shipyard, Pascagoula, 1976-78; sr. engring. scheduler Brown & Root, Houston, 1978-84; sr. engring. scheduler Litton Data Systems, Pascagoula, 1984-85, sr. engring. scheduler, New Orleans, 1985-86; sr. research and devel. scheduler Litton Guidance and Control, Woodland Hills, Calif., 1986—. Contbr. to Best Loved American Poems, 1979, 80. Mem. Assn. Profl. Planners and Schedulers (treas. 1979-80), Nat. Assn. Female Execs. Avocations: scuba diving; sky diving; modeling; acting; traveling. Office: Litton Guidence and Control 5500 Canoga Ave Woodland Hills CA 91367

POLKOW, LINDA ROSE, rehabilitation services administrator, occupational therapist; b. N.Y.C., Apr. 8, 1953; d. John Hans and Leonore (Hamburger) Schiff; m. Melvin Samuel Polkow, June 22, 1975; 1 child, Eric Daniel. B.S., NYU, 1975, postgrad. in pub. adminstrn., 1981—. Lic. occupational therapist. Dir. occupational therapy Burke Rehab. Ctr., White Plains, N.Y., 1975-84; rehab. services coordinator Barnert Meml. Hosp. Ctr., Paterson, N.J., 1984—; vis. guest lectr. various colls. and univs. Contbr. articles to profl. publs. Mem. Jewish Community Ctr., Paramus, N.J., 1982—, parent group Child Care Learning Ctr., Hackensack, N.J., 1982—; utilization reviewer Vis. Nurses Assn. Westchester, White Plains, N.Y., 1980-84. Democrat. Avocations: tennis; biking; camping; travel; reading.

POLLACK, CAROL LOUGH, nurse, photojournalist; b. Wheeling, W.Va., Dec. 25, 1924; d. John J. and Mabel L. (Dague) Lough; R.N., Ohio Valley Gen. Hosp., 1945; B.S., Western Res. U., 1955; postgrad. Johns Hopkins U., 1962-63, Catholic U., 1965-66, N.Y. U., 1949-50; m. Ronald Paul Pollack, Jan. 26, 1956; 1 son, John Ronald. Adminstr. charge nursing service Mt. Sinai Hosp., Cleve., 1953-57; instr. public health City of Cleve., 1957-59; instr. surgery Sinai Hosp., Balt., 1961-63; sch. nurse Franklin Sr. High Sch., Reisterstown, Md., 1964—; polit. reporter Times Newspapers, Baltimore County, Md., 1964-71; editor Northwest County News, 1971-75; editor Tribune, Reisterstown, 1976-77; photojournalist, feature writer Community Times, Randallstown News, Reisterstown, 1978—. Sec. Reisterstown Community Corp.; v.p. Historic Reisterstown; chmn. Reisterstown Historic Room; mem. Baltimore County Gen. Hosp. Found. Bd.; mem. exec. bd. Humane Soc., Reisterstown; tchr. Sunday sch. Trinity Lutheran Ch., Reisterstown; mem. Baltimore County Landmarks Preservation Commn., 1982—; hon. mem. Reisterstown Vol. Fire Co., Glyndon Vol. Fire Co. Recipient Meritorious Service award Nat. Hdqrs. CAP, 1979; named Woman of Year, Woman's Club Reisterstown, 1979; Outstanding Vol. Service award Baltimore County Public Library, 1982. Mem. Bus. and Profl. Women, Delmarva Press Club, Am. Nurses Assn., Md. State Nurses Assn. Club: Federated Woman's of Glyndon. Author: Reisterstown, 1966, 8th rev. edit., 1976. Home: 303 Cherry Hill Rd Reisterstown MD 21136 Office: PO Box 247 Reisterstown MD 21136

POLLACK, EVE REBECCA, fashion marketing educator, consultant; b. N.Y.C., Oct. 27, 1933; d. Meyer and Frieda P. B.A., NYU, 1950, M.S. in Bus. and Retailing, 1954; postgrad. in Bus. and Law, Baruch Coll., 1966-67, in Edn. and Bus., CCNY, 1967-69, Coll. Ins., 1972-76. Asst. buyer Franklin Simon, N.Y.C., 1954-57; apparel buyer Chernoff Herman, N.Y.C., 1957-63; jr. dress buyer Popular Merchandising, 1963-65; apparel buyer Bramson's, Chgo., 1965-67, Tailored Woman, N.Y.C., 1967-70; pension cons. Conn. Mut. Life, N.Y.C., 1970-77; mktg. dir. Golden Step Footwear, N.Y.C., 1977-78; asst. prof. mktg. Passaic County Coll., Paterson, N.J., 1979-80; acad. dean Tobe-Coburn Sch. Fashion and Merchandising, N.Y.C., 1980-81; instr. Fashion Inst. Tech., N.Y.C., 1981—; cons. Am. Women's Econ. Devel. Corp., N.Y.C., 1979-80; fashion cons. Guy LaRoche, N.A., Inc., N.Y.C., 1983. Vol. United Hosp. Fund, NYU Hosp., 1978. Recipient vol. service award NYU Hosp.; honorarium Purude U., 1973. Mem. Fashion Group. Democrat. Jewish. Club: Zonta. Home: 301 E 21st St New York NY 10010 Office: Fashion Inst Tech 227 W 27th St New York NY 10001

POLLACK, FLORENCE ZAKS, executive relocation and conference management company executive; b. Washington, Pa., May 17, 1938; d. Charles and Ruth (Isaacson) Zaks; m. Richard Harlan Pollack, Feb. 3, 1963; children—Melissa, Stephanie. B.A., Flora Stone Mather Coll., Western Res. U., 1961. Pres., treas. Exec. Arrangements, Inc., Cleve., 1978—. Lobbyist Ohio Citizens Com. for Arts, Columbus, 1975-83; mem. Leadership Cleve., 1978-79; trustee Jr. Com., Cleve. Orch., Cleve. Ballet, Jr. Com. of No. Ohio Opera Assn., Cleve. Opera, Shakers Lakes Regional Nature Ctr., Cleve. Music Sch. Settlement, Playhouse Sq. Cabinet, Cleve. Conv. and Visitors Bur., Cleve. Modern Dance Assn. Named Idea Woman of Yr., Cleve. Plain Dealer, 1975; named to Au Courrant list Cleve. Mag., 1979, named to Cleve.'s 100 Most Influential Women, 1985. Mem. Cleve. Area Meeting Planning. Independent. Clubs: Skating, University, Women's City, Playhouse. Avocations: travel; reading. Office: Exec Arrangements Inc 13221 Shaker Sq Cleveland OH 44120

POLLACK, LANA, state senator; b. Ludington, Mich., Oct. 11, 1942; d. Abbie and Genevieve (Siegel) Schoenberger; m. Henry Pollack, 1963; children—Sara (dec.), John. B.A., U. Mich., 1965, M.A., 1970; postgrad. Am. Acad. Performing Arts, 1976, Am. U. Instr. Washtenaw Community Coll., 1975-81; sr. adminstr. John Howard Compound Sch., Zambia, 1970-71; chmn. Ann Arbor Democratic Party (Mich.), 1975-77; mgr. campaign for State Senate, 1978, campaign for 2d Congl. Dist., 1980; regional coordinator gubernatorial campaign, 1981; mem. Mich. State Senate, 1983—. Trustee, Ann Arbor Bd. Edn., 1979-82. Democrat. Office: 465 Farnum Bldg Lansing MI 48909

POLLACK, MARY LOUISE, hotel executive; b. Phila., Nov. 15, 1949; d. Edward Latshaw and Mary Louise (Dempsey) Gruber; m. Stephen J. Pollack, May 15, 1977 (div. 1981). B.A. in English, Duke U., 1971; postgrad. Hotel Sch., Cornell U. Cert. tchr., Pa. Travel agt. G & O Travel, N.Y.C., 1977-80; sales mgr. Halloran House, N.Y.C., 1980-81; regional dir. Halloran Hotels, N.Y.C., 1981-83, nat. dir. sales, 1983-84; assoc. dir. mktg. Treadway Hotels and Resorts, Saddle Brook, N.J., 1984-85, dir. mktg., 1985—; dir. Somerset Hotels, N.J. Mem. Hotel Sales Mgrs. Assn. Internat., U.S. Tour Operators Assn., Am. Bus Assn., Meeting Planners Internat., Nat. Passenger Traffic Assn., Am. Soc. Travel Agts., Travel Industry Assn. Am. (planning com. 1983-84), Nat. Tour Assn. (conv. com. 1982-84, membership com. 1984, cert. com. 1986), Pa. Travel Council (program chmn. for 1st Gov.'s Conf. on Travel 1983, mem. mktg. com. 1983). Republican. Lutheran. Clubs: Elmwood Park Athletic (N.J.); Brookside Country (Pottstown, Pa.). Avocations: golf; tennis; culinary arts; real estate. Home: 519 River Renaissance East Rutherford NJ 07073

POLLAK, FRANCES ANDERSON, manufacturing company executive; b. N.Y.C., June 8, 1949; d. Bernard E. and Brenda (Anderson) P.; student Sorbonne, U. Paris, 1969-70; B.A., Hollins Coll., 1971; M.Regulatory Policy, George Washington U., 1983. Staff office standards and regulations EPA, Washington, 1971-72; staff Commerce Com. subcom. on aviation U.S. Senate, Washington, 1972-75; asst. dir. govt. relations dept. Nat. Cable TV Assn., Washington, 1975-76; Washington rep. Goodyear Tire & Rubber Co., 1977-81; dep. dir. public affairs Union Camp Corp., 1981—. Mem. Washington Com. for CARE. Mem. Women in Govt. Relations (chmn. regulatory relations com. 1979-80, chmn. congressional relations com. 1980-81, dir. 1980-82, chmn. task force on state chpts. 1981-82), Nat. Council Career Women (dir. 1979-82, chmn. state chpt. com. Women in Govt. Relations 1982-83), Am. League Lobbyists (dir. 1985—), Women in Housing and Fin., Nat. Energy Resources Orgn., Women's Econ. Roundtable, Washington Area State Relations Group, Am. Mgmt. Assn., Indsl. Energy Users Forum, Am. Paper Inst. (govt. relations com.), Nat. Assn. Female Execs., Washington Area State Relations Group, Women in Transp. Clubs: Capital Hill, Nat. Democratic, Republican Women's, City Tavern, Georgetown. Office: 1850 K St NW Suite 390 Washington DC 20006

POLLAN, CAROLYN JOAN, state legislator; b. Houston, July 12, 1937; d. Rex and Faith (Basye) Clark; B.S. in Radio and TV, John Brown U., 1959; postgrad. NYU, 1959; m. George A. Pollan, Jan. 6, 1962; children—Cee Cee, Todd (dec.), Robert. Mem. Ark. Ho. of Reps., 1974—, now sr. Republican mem.; del. Am. Soviet Seminar, Am. Council Young Polit. Leaders, Exeter, N.H., 1976. Vice chmn. Ark. Rep. Com., 1972-76; del. Rep. Nat. Conv., 1976; bd. dirs. Ark. Cancer Soc., Ark. Easter Seals Soc.; bd. dirs. Greg Kistler Treatment Center for Physically Handicapped, Ark. Found. Assoc. Colls., 4-H Found. for Sebastian County; trustee John Brown U.; mem. legis. adv. com. So. Regional Edn. Bd. Recipient Conservation Legislator of Yr. award Ark. Wildlife Fedn., Nat. Wildlife Fedn., Sears Roebuck & Co., 1976, Outstanding

State Legislator of Yr. award Ark. Pub. Employees Assn., 1979; named 1 of 10 Outstanding Legislators, Assembly of Govtl. Employees, 1980, Legislator of Yr., Ark. Human Service Providers Assn., 1982; voted 1 of Ft. Smith's 10 Most Influential Citizens, S.W. Times Record Readers, 1979. Mem. Ft. Smith Car Restoration Assn. Baptist. Office: 400 N 8th St Fort Smith AR 72901

POLLARD, BOBBIE JEAN, librarian, educator; b. Anguilla, Miss., June 16, 1942; d. J.D. and Delia (Washington) Thornton; m. Wilbert B. Pollard, Apr. 27, 1974; 1 dau., Abiola. B.A. in English Lit., Jackson (Miss.) State U., 1964; M.L.S., Atlanta U., 1965; M.A. in Edn., NYU, 1974. Librarian, acting br. librarian Bklyn. Pub. Library, 1965-70; asst. prof. library sci. Baruch Coll., N.Y.C., 1970-78, 79—; sr. librarian U. Benin, Benin City, Nigeria, 1968. Rockefeller Found. scholar, 1965-66; Profl. Staff Congress grantee, CUNY, 1983-84. Mem. ALA, Assn. Coll. and Research Libraries (chmn. N.Y.C. area 1983-84), Library Assn. CUNY (chmn. Inst.) 1976, Nat. Assn. Female Execs., Beta Phi Mu, Alpha Kappa Mu. Democrat. Baptist. Home: 382 Central Park W New York NY 10025 Office: Baruch College Library 156 25th St New York NY 10025

POLLARD, DARLENE DAVENPORT, data processing co. sales ofcl.; b. Washington, Feb. 23, 1949; d. Bennett Gibson and Margaret Theresa (Schemmer) Davenport; B.A. in English Lit., Clemson U., 1972; diploma S.C. Bankers Sch., 1979. Teller, First Citizens Bank & Trust, Columbia, S.C., 1972-73, Barnett Bank of Fla., Deland, 1973; utility teller C&S Nat. Bank, Columbia, 1974-75, teller tng. officer, 1975-78, corr. banking asst. ops. officer, 1978-80, ops. officer and corr. banking data processing coordinator, 1980-82; sales rep. Gate City Data Processors Inc., Greensboro, N.C., 1982—. Mem. Am. Inst. Banking, Nat. Assn. Bank Women. Republican. Methodist. Clubs: Civitan (sec. Dutch Fork of Columbia 1980-81, pres.-elect 1981-82, pres. 1982—, named Civitan of Year 1980-81). Office: Gate City Data Processors Inc 311 Pomona Dr PO Box 8149 Greensboro NC 27419

POLLARD, FRANCES MARGUERITE, librarian; b. Florence, Ala., Oct. 7, 1920; d. Lorenzo Marquis and Carrie (Mayfield) Pollard; Jr. Coll. diploma, Selma U., 1938; B.S., Ala. State Coll., 1941; M.S. in L.S., Western Res. U., 1949, Ph.D., 1963; postgrad. Columbia, 1952-54. Tchr. elem. sch., Waterloo, Ala., 1938-39, Marengo County Tng. Sch., Thomaston, Ala., 1941-42, Sterling High Sch., Sheffield, Ala., 1942-43; library asst. Enlisted Men's Library 2, Fort McClellan, Ala., 1943-46, Ala. State Coll., Montgomery, 1946-48; student aide children' room Sterling br. Cleve. Public Library, 1948-49; asst. librarian Ala. State Coll., 1949-61, head librarian, 1961-63; adminstrv. asst. Booth Library, Eastern Ill. U., Charleston, 1963-70, prof. library sci., head library sci. dept., 1970-79, exec. asst. for library services, 1979—; mem. Ill. State Library Adv. Com., 1967-73, subcom. LSCA Title I and Title II, 1967-77. Mem. ALA, Ill. Library Assn., Am. Acad. Polit. and Social Sci., Soc. Applied Anthropology, Am. Sociol. Assn. (assoc.), AAUP, AAUW, Alpha Kappa Alpha, Delta Kappa Gamma. Author: (with others) Major Problems in Education of Librarians, 1954, Illinois Literary Reflections of the Bicentennial Year. Editor: Procs. of Personnel Evaluation Inst., 1975. Home: 1330 A St Charleston IL 61920

POLLARD, HINDA GREYSER, management educator, lawyer; b. Boston, Sept. 2, 1937; d. Morris and Gladys (Koven) Greyser; m. Alan Payson Pollard, Sept. 5, 1960; children—Daniel Lincoln, John Franklin. A.B. magna cum laude, Tufts U., 1959; J.D. Boalt Hall Sch. Law, U. Calif.-Berkeley, 1964; student (sponsored State Dept.) Helsinki, Finland, 1964-65, Moscow, USSR, 1965-66. Bar: R.I. 1978, U.S. Dist. Ct. 1978. Teaching assoc. Harvard Bus. Sch., Boston, 1959-60; instr. Fisher Jr. Coll., Attleboro, Mass., 1976-79; asst. prof. mgmt. dept. Bryant Coll., Smithfield, R.I., 1979-83, assoc. prof., 1983—, chmn. dept., 1981—, coordinator internship program, 1981—, Small Bus. Inst. coordinator, 1983—; mem. Small Bus. Inst. Dirs.' Assn., 1982—; sole practice law, Providence, 1978—. Author articles in field; contbr. to profl. report. Divisional Keyperson, United Way, Smithfield, 1983. Boalt Hall scholar, 1961-62. Mem. ABA (labor and employment sect.), Acad. of Mgmt., AAUW (Bryant Coll. instl. rep. 1981—), Nat. Soc. for Internships and Experiential Edn., Indsl. Relations Research Assn., Phi Beta Kappa. Home: 567 Wayland Ave Providence RI 02906 Office: Bryant Coll Smithfield RI 02917

POLLARD, MARY ELIZABETH, convalescent hospital administrator; b. New London, Conn., May 25, 1911; d. Daniel Joseph and Ella Mary (Donaghue) Moran; m. Leo Pollard, Oct. 13, 1962. Student Joseph Lawrence Sch. Nursing, 1933-36; cert. Northeastern U., 1962. Nurse, Dr. Lena's Surg. Hosp., New London, Conn., 1936-49; owner, adminstr. Mary Elizabeth Convalescent Home, Mystic, Conn., 1949-59, pres., 1960-65; adminstr., pres. Beechwood Manor Convalescent Hosp., New London, 1956-79, pres., 1979—. Mem. fin. com., parish council St. Mary's Star of the Sea Ch., New London. Fellow Am. Coll. Health Care Adminstrs.; mem. Conn. Assn. Extended Health Care Facilities (1st v.p. 1968-69), Alumni Assn. Joseph Lawrence Sch. Nursing, Cath. Nurses Assn. Republican. Roman Catholic. Avocations: archtl. designing; dressmaking. Office: Beechwood Manor Inc 31 Vauxhall St New London CT 06320

POLLATSEK, MOLLY, art company executive; b. N.Y.C., Oct. 16, 1911; d. Jacob and Diana (Schachter) Seltzer; m. Solomon Haas, Sept. 10, 1939 (dec. Aug. 1954); 1 child, Jill; m. Sidney Pollatsek, Feb. 27, 1973; 1 child, Michael. Grad., Eastern Dist. High Sch., N.Y.C. Sec., Walter P Chrysler, N.Y.C., 1930-42; exec. asst. A.J. Schneierson, 1955-72; pres. Idea Art Corp., N.Y.C., 1983—. Office: Idea Art Corp 799 Broadway New York NY 10003

POLLITT, GERTRUDE STEIN, psychotherapist, clinical social worker; came to U.S., 1949, naturalized, 1951; b. Vienna, Austria; d. Julius and Sidoni (Brauch) Stein; Social Service course Brit. Council, London, 1943-44; B.A., Roosevelt U., 1954; M.A., U. Chgo., 1956; cert. Chgo. Inst. Psychoanalysis, 1963; m. Erwin P. Pollitt, Jan. 13, 1951 (dec. Aug. 1977). Resident social worker Anna Freud Residential Nursery Sch., Essex, Eng., 1944-45; dep. dir. UN, U.S. Zone, Germany, 1945-48; psychiat. social worker Jewish Children's Bur., Chgo., 1955-63; pvt. practice as psychotherapist and/or clin. social worker, Glencoe, Ill., 1961—; cons. Winnetka Community Nursery Sch., 1962-63, North Shore Congregation Israel Nursery Sch., 1966-69, Oakwood Home for Aged, Highland Park High Sch., 1979-80; instr. profl. devel. programs Chgo. Inst. for Psychoanalysis, 1982, Sch. Social Service Adminstrn., U. Chgo.; mem. faculty profl. devel. program Sch. Social Service Adminstrn., U. Chgo. Bd. dirs. Glencoe Youth Service, Menninger Found. Fellow Am. Orthopsychiat. Assn.; mem. Nat. Assn. Social Workers (chmn. pvt. practice com. 1965-70), Ill. Soc. Clin. Social Workers (bd. dirs.), Acad. Cert. Social Workers, Nat. Registry Health Care Providers in Clin. Social Work. Contbr. articles to profl. jours. Home and office: 481 Oakdale Ave Glencoe IL 60022

POLLOCK, ANN DELPHINE, real estate executive; b. Flagstaff, Ariz., Dec. 15, 1946; d. Thomas Elmer and Dorothy Oldham (Peach) P.; m. Nick Charles King, Aug. 31, 1968 (div.); children—Nick Charles, Justin Keith. Student U. Ariz., 1963-65; B.S. in Mktg., No. Ariz. U., 1968. Lic. real estate broker, Ariz. Adminstrv. sec. Coldwell Banker & Co., Phoenix, 1969-76; office mgr. Rierson, Ledbetter & Assocs., Phoenix, 1976-79; asst. v.p. Community Devel. Corp., Scottsdale, Ariz., 1979-80; sales assoc. No. Ariz. Realty, Flagstaff, 1980-82; broker, ptnr. Kinsey-Pollock, Inc., Flagstaff, 1982—. Mem. ann. fundraising com. No. Ariz. U., Flagstaff, 1981—, mem. pres.'s screening com. for dean, 1982; mem. steering com. R. Kimball for Cong. Commr., Flagstaff, 1982; bd. dirs. Flagstaff Pine Country Pro-Rodeo, Inc.; mem. adv. bd. Salvation Army, Flagstaff Corps. Mem. Flagstaff C. of C. (dir. 1980-86). Republican. Episcopalian. Home: 2001 N Navajo Dr Flagstaff AZ 86001 Office: Kinsey-Pollock Inc PO Box 1835 Flagstaff AZ 86002

POLLOCK, LOUISE, financial planner; b. Pitts., Apr. 2, 1919; d. Walter Edward and Anna Katherine (Schoenberger) Brickman; student U. Tex., 1936-37; grad. Coll. Fin. Planning, 1975-77; m. Robert Thomas Pollock, Mar. 10, 1968 (dec.); children—John W. Carlisle, Jr., Noel Griffin, Carol Klippenstein. Branch mgr. Fort Worth (Tex.) Savs. and Loan Assn., 1954-63, Trevost Savs. & Loan Assn., Phila., 1963-68; estate planning specialist Ralph S. Wilford Co., La Mesa, Calif., 1970-77; pres., cert. fin. planner Sentra Securities Corp.; instr. diversified investments div. adult edn. San Diego Community Coll. Mem. Internat. Assn. Fin. Planners, Inst. Cert. Fin. Planners, Nat. Alumni Assn. Coll. of Fin. Planning., Women's Service, Bus. and Profl. Clubs of San Diego (life mem. pres.'s council), Women in Bus. Coll. of the Emeriti (former pres. aux. council), Registry Fin. Planning Practioners Republican. Swedenborgian. Club: Altrusa (past pres.). Home: 10803 Escobar Dr San Diego CA 92124 Office: 2820 Camino del Rio Suite 300 San Diego CA 92108

POLLOWY, ANNE-MARIE, systems planning educator, consultant; b. Budapest, Hungary, July 14, 1938; came to U.S., 1975; d. Tibor and Margaret (Ebensparger) Balazs; m. George Pollowy, Dec. 28, 1964 (div. Dec. 1975); children—Richard, Nissa. B.Arch., McGill U., Montreal, Que., 1960; M. Mgmt., U. Montreal, 1969; Ph.D. in Mgmt., Union Experimenting Coll. and Univs., Cin., 1979. Asst. prof. planning and architecture U. Montreal, 1968-78; v.p. Social Systems Mgmt. Cons. Inc., Balt., 1981—; prof. systems planning Morgan State U., Balt., 1979—; cons. Sojourner-Douglass Coll., Balt., 1983—; treas., ptnr. Chipt Devel. Corp., Balt., 1984—. Author: The Urban Nest, 1977, Elements of Change: Policies to Projects, 1984-85. Mem. Am. Soc. Cybernetics, Soc. Gen. Systems Research, Am. Planning Assn. Avocation: travel. Office: Morgan State U Baltimore MD 21239

POLLREIS, PATTY LEWIS, communications company executive; b. Omaha, Oct. 1, 1952; d. Harlan Gale and Mildred Olive (Noyes) Lewis; m. James Morgan Holden, Apr. 15, 1974 (div. 1977); m. Leonard Val Pollreis, Dec. 8, 1978. B.A. in Psychology, Bellevue Coll., 1984. Sales rep. Northwestern Bell Telephone Co., Omaha, 1976-78, account exec. industry cons., 1978-82, 84-85, mgr. real estate design and constrn., 1985—; account exec. industry cons. AT&T Info. Systems, Omaha, 1982-83. Trustee Sanitary Improvement Dist. 1, Union Nebr., 1984—. Mem. Nat. Assn. Female Execs. Republican. Mem. Christian Ch. (Disciples of Christ). Avocations: skiing; water skiing; snowmobiling; reading. Office: Northwestern Bell 100 S 19th-Izard Omaha NE 60005

POLO, GINIE RUTH MORRIS, author, speaker; b. Big Spring, Tex., June 13, 1944; d. T. R. and Vera Lucille Morris; m. Kenneth Ray Polo, July 18, 1966 (div. June 1968); 1 child, Audrei V. Kae. B.A., Angelo State U., 1969. Cert. tchr., Tex. With pub. relations Houston Grand Opera, 1973-74; tchr. English and speech Conroe Ind. Sch. Dist., Tex., 1974-78, Forson Ind. Sch. Dist., Tex., 1978-80; stockbroker E. F. Hutton & Co., Inc., West Tex. offices, 1981-82; Kahn & Co., Dallas, 1983-84; pres. Ginie Polo & Assocs., Inc., Dallas, 1985—; with Christian radio, Lubbock, Tex., 1981-82; pub. speaker Fun-Ed, Dallas, 1985—. Author: How to WIN Pageants, 1985. Contbr. articles to Lifestyle Dallas mag., 1985. Vol. ARC, Big Spring, Tex., 1978; active Women Aglow, Big Spring, v.p., 1978; mem. exec. com. Dallas County Democrats Kennedy Meml., Dallas, 1983. Named Tchr. of Yr., Mark Twin Jr. High Sch. student body, 1971. Episcopalian. Home: 15221 Preston Rd Apt 2089 Dallas TX 75240 Office: Ginie Polo & Assocs Inc 14902 Preston Rd Suite 212-206 Dallas TX 75240

POLOMSKY, SHIRLEY REIKO, air force officer; b. Honolulu, Nov. 11, 1943; d. Satoshi and Yukimi (Sawamoto) Kodani; 1 dau., Kimberly Mariko. B.A., Wash. State U., 1965; M.A., U. No. Colo., 1977. Tchr. speech and English Mt. Tahoma High Sch., Tacoma, 1965-67; commd. 2d lt. U.S. Air Force, 1967, advanced through grades to lt. col., 1984; personnel officer Otis AFB, Falmouth, Mass., 1967-69, Hickam AFB, Honolulu, 1969-71, Udorn Royal Thai Air Base, 1971-72; personnel officer Kelly AFB, San Antonio 1972-74, info. officer 1974-76; pub. affairs officer, briefing officer Wright-Patterson AFB, Dayton, Ohio, 1976-79; chief pub. affairs Yokota Air Base, Tokyo, 1979-82; chief internal info. and community relations div. Andrews AFB, Camp Springs, Md., 1982-86; dep. pub. affairs officer U.S. Forces Korea, Yongsan Army Garrison, Seoul, 1986—. Decorated Air Force Commendation medal with 2 oak leaf clusters, Meritorious Service medal. Mem. AAUW (past program v.p., membership v.p. 1984-86), Women in Communications, Inc., Ben Franklin Club (charter pres. 1978-79), Air Force Assn. Home: Officer's Housing Yongsan ArmyGarrison Seoul Korea Office: Hdqrs Air Force Systems Command Andrews AFB MD 20334

POLON, LINDA BETH, educator, writer, illustrator; b. Balt., Oct. 7, 1943; d. Harold Bernard and Edith Judith Wolff; m. Marty I. Polon, Dec. 18, 1966 (div. Aug. 1983); m. Robert Dorsey, Apr. 13, 1986. B.A. in History, UCLA, 1966. Elem. tchr. Los Angeles Bd. Edn., 1967—; writer-illustrator Scott Foresman Pub. Co., Glenview, Ill., 1979—, Frank Schaffer Pub. Co., Torrance, Calif., 1981-82, Learning Works, Santa Barbara, Calif., 1981-82; editorial reviewer Prentice Hall Pub. Co., Santa Monica, Calif., 1982-83. Author: (juvenile books) Creative Teaching Games, 1974; Teaching Games for Fun, 1976; Making Kids Click, 1979; Write up a Storm, 1979; Stir Up a Story, 1981; Paragraph Production, 1981; Using Words Correctly, 3d-4th grades, 1981, 5th-6th grades, 1981; Whole Earth Holiday Book, 1983; Writing Whirlwind, 1986; Magic Story Starters, 1986. Mem. Soc. Children's Book Writers. Democrat. Home: 1515 Manning Ave Apt 3 Los Angeles CA 90024 Office: Los Angeles Bd of Edn Hobart Blvd Sch 980 S Hobart Blvd Los Angeles CA 90006

POLOVY, MARIAN, lawyer; b. N.Y.C., May 8, 1952; d. Nicholas and Mary (Maksymorch) Polovy; B.A. in English (scholar), Marymount Coll., 1974; J.D., Southwestern U., 1979. U.S. Senate intern, Senator James Buckley, Washington, 1974; bar: N.Y. 1980, U.S. Dist. Ct. (so. dist.) N.Y. 1980, U.S. Supreme Ct. 1984; atty. U.S. Dept. Energy, N.Y.C., 1979-80; assoc. firm Martin, Clearwater & Bell, N.Y.C., 1980-81, firm Evans, Orr, Pacelli, Norton & Laffan, N.Y.C., 1981-83; sole practice, 1983—. Farmer's Ins. Group scholar, 1975; Mabel Wilson Richards scholar, 1978. Mem. N.Y. State Bar Assn., N.Y. Trial Lawyers Assn., N.Y. State Women's Bar Assn., N.Y. C. of C. Internat. Union Advocats, N.Y. County Bar Assn., Cath. Lawyers Guild (fin. sec. 1980—). Mem. Law Rev.; contbr. articles to profl. jours. Home: 2017 Coleman St Brooklyn NY 11234 Office: 461 Park Ave S New York NY 10016

POLSKY, CYNTHIA HAZEN, artist, art administrator, publisher; b. N.Y.C., Feb. 28, 1939; d. Joseph and Lita Hazen; student Art Students League and New Sch. Social Research, 1957-60; B.A. in Psychology cum laude, Marymount Manhattan Coll., 1977; M.B.A., Fordham U., 1981; m. Leon B. Polsky, Apr. 19, 1957; children—Alexander M., Nicholas W. Works exhibited in mus. Los Angeles, Houston, East Hampton, N.Y., St. Mary's City, Md., Wichita, Kans., and N.Y.C., 1968-77; represented in public collections: Corcoran Mus., Washington, Herbert F. Johnson Mus., Cornell U., Allentown (Pa.) Mus. Art, Fogg Mus., Cambridge, Mass., Guild Hall, East Hampton, Rockefeller U., 1st Women's Bank N.Y., Storm King Art Center, Mountainville, N.Y., Israel Mus., Jerusalem; pres. Octagon Communications Internat., N.Y.C.; mem. adv. com. Columbia U.; v.p., trustee Storm King Art Center. Mem. vis. com. dept. Far Eastern art, dept. 20th Century art Met. Mus.

POLVAY, JEANNE DONOGHUE, modeling company executive; b. Stamford, Conn., May 9, 1941; d. George Edward and Irene Rene (Albert) Donoghue; student Marymount Jr. Coll., 1959, U. Conn., 1972; m. Jerome I. Polvay, July 19, 1981; children by previous marriage—George Gregory, Timothy Joseph. With Conn. Modeling Agy., Stamford, 1960-65; partner Charming Way Boutique, Stamford, 1965-68; tchr. YWCA, Stamford, 1965-73; regional mgr. Community Ambassador, Ridgefield, Conn., 1973-74; instr., dir. admissions Barbizon Schs., Stamford, 1973-75, pres., 1975—, also pres. Barbizon Sch. of Westchester, White Plains, N.Y. Mem. citizens cons. com. J.M. Wright Tech. Sch., Stamford, 1978—. Mem. Better Bus. Bur. (dir. 1979-80). Republican. Roman Catholic. Club: Landmark. Home: 316 Talmadge Hill Rd New Canaan CT 06840 Office: 26 6th St Stamford CT 06905 also 190 E Post Rd White Plains NY 10601

POLVAY, MARINA SCHERBATOFF, food consultant; b. Krasnojars, USSR, July 24, 1928; came to U.S., 1952, naturalized, 1955; d. Konstantine Scherbatoff and Eugenia Szenutovits-Berezsni; B.S., Innsbruck (Austria) U., 1949; m. Murray Polvay, Feb. 26, 1960. Exec. v.p. Slenderella Internat., 1952-60; owner Marina Polvay Assos. Inc., food cons. and public relations, North Miami, Fla., 1968—, Culinary Communications Inc., Miami Shores, Fla.; author for mags., cookbooks, 1962—; host radio and TV talk shows. Past pres. Miami Ballet Soc., Theatre Arts League, Pearl S Buck Found. Mem. Sommelier Guild, Confrerie de la Chaine des Rotisseurs. Writers Guild and League, Writers Club, Fashion Group, Internat. Assn. Cooking Schs. Republican. Mem. Russian Orthodox Ch. Author: Marina Polvay's Best International Recipies, 1972; Florida Heritage Cookbook, 1976; The Dracula Cookbook, 1978; All Along the Danube, 1979; The Energy Saver's Cookbook, 1980; Slimming and Healthy Cooking of Italy, 1981. Home: 9250 NE 10th Ct Miami Shores FL 33138 Office: 9315 Park Dr Suite A1 Miami Shores FL 33138

POLVOGT, ALENE, accountant; b. Dallas, Oct. 5, 1923; d. Carl W. and Bennie (Lowry) P.; B.B.A., So. Meth. U., 1976. Pvt. practice acctg., Dallas, 1974—; mem. faculty U. Tex., Dallas, 1980—. Mem. Am. Inst. C.P.A.s, Tex. Soc. C.P.A.s, Petroleum Accts. Soc. Dallas. Republican. Presbyterian. Home: 5841-A Sandhurst St Dallas TX 75218 Office: 2060 N Collins Suite 100 Richardson TX 75080

POMPARELLI, JOANNE MARIE, communications company executive; b. San Francisco, Mar. 4, 1923; d. Leonard Ross and Veronica Margaret (Dervin) Blodgett; m. Arthur H. Bowen, Apr. 18, 1942 (div. 1967); children—Jane, Lyn, Denise, Diane; m. Joseph J. Pomparelli, May 1, 1968; children—Gregory, Barbara. B.E., U. Calif.-Berkeley, 1942. Former tchr. various pub. schs., Calif. and N.J.; pvt. practice interior design, Cherry Hill, N.J., 1969-72; founder, chief exec. officer Radio Page Communications, Cherry Hill, 1973—. Mem. Cherry Hill C. of C., South Jersey C. of C. Republican. Roman Catholic. Club: Atlantic City Country. Home: 2 Pendleton Dr Cherry Hill NJ 08003 Office: Radio Page Communications Old Marlton Pike W Cherry Hill NJ 08003

POND, PHYLLIS JOAN, state legislator; b. Warren, Ind., Oct. 25, 1930; d. Clifford E. and Rosa E. (Hunnicutt) Ruble; B.S., Ball State U., Muncie, Ind., 1951; M.S., Ind. U., 1963; m. George W. Pond, June 10, 1951; children—William, Douglas, Jean Ann. Tchr. home econs., 1951-54; kindergarten tchr., 1961—; mem. Ind. Ho. of Reps. from 15th Dist., 1978-82, from 20th Dist., 1982—, majority asst. caucus chmn. Del. Ind. Republican Conv., 1976, 80; alt. del. Rep. Nat. Conv., 1980. Mem. AAUW. Lutheran. Club: New Haven Woman's.

PONDER, CATHERINE, clergywoman; b. Hartsville, S.C., Feb. 14, 1927; d. Roy Charles and Kathleen (Parrish) Cook; student U. N.C. Extension, 1946, Worth Bus. Coll., 1948; B.S. in Edn., Unity Ministerial Sch., 1956; D.D. (hon.), Assn. Unity Chs., 1976; m. Robert Stearns, June 19, 1970; 1 son by previous marriage, Richard. Ordained to ministry Unity Sch. Christianity, 1958; minister Unity Ch., Birmingham, Ala., 1956-61; founder, minister Unity Ch., Austin, Tex., 1961-69, San Antonio, 1969-73, Palm Desert, Calif., 1973—. Mem. Assn. Unity Chs., Inc., Internat. New Thought Alliance, Internat. Platform Assn. Clubs: Bermuda Dunes Country, Racquet (Palm Springs, Calif.); Los Angeles. Author: The Dynamic Laws of Prosperity, 1962; The Prosperity Secret of the Ages, 1964; The Dynamic Laws of Healing, 1966; The Healing Secret of the Ages, 1967; Pray and Grow Rich, 1968; The Millionaires of Genesis, 1976; The Millionaire Moses, 1977; The Millionaire Joshua, 1978; The Millionaire from Nazareth, 1979; Secret of Unlimited Prosperity, 1980; Open Your Mind to Receive, 1983; Dare to Prosper!, 1983; The Prospering Power of Prayer, 1983; Open Your Mind to Prosperity, 1984; The Prospering Power of Love, 1984. Office: 73-669 Hwy 111 Palm Desert CA 92260

PONDER, MARIAN RUTH, educator; b. Waterloo, Iowa, July 12, 1932; d. Lee Roland and Leone Hyacinth (Holdiman) Rigdon; B.A. (Purple and Gold math. scholar), U. No. Iowa, 1952; M.S.E., Drake U., 1960; postgrad. U. Wis., 1961-62, San Diego State U., 1980-81, Carleton Coll., 1980-81, U. No. Ia., 1961-66, Drake U., 1971-75; m. Joseph Glen Ponder, June 28, 1953; children—Dwight Lee, David Glen, Dean Joseph. Tchr. math., sci. Anamosa, Iowa, 1952-53, Monroe, Iowa, 1953-56, Newton, Iowa, 1956-64, 66—, head dept. math. Newton Schs., 1978—. Ch. treas. Community Heights Alliance Ch., 1980-82, 83—, Sunday sch. secretariat, 1966-82. Maytag scholar, 1960; Maytag Corp. grantee, 1962; Delta Kappa Gamma scholar, 1960, 81. Mem. Nat. Council Tchrs. Math., NEA, Iowa Edn. Assn., Newton Community Edn. Assn. (chief negotiator 1985-87, pres. 1985-87), Iowa Council Tchrs. Math., Jasper County Hist. Soc., Delta Kappa Gamma (state treas. 1978—), Kappa Mu Epsilon, Kappa Delta Pi, Lambda Delta Lambda. Republican. Mem. Christian and Missionary Alliance Ch. Home: 620 E 17 St N Newton IA 50208 Office: E 4th St S Newton IA 50208

PONTIUS, GERALDINE CAROL, architect; b. Greensburg, Pa., Jan. 24, 1947; d. Paul Edward and Doris (Hesselmeyer) Pontius; A.B., Barnard Coll., 1968; postgrad. N.Y. Studio Sch. Drawing and Painting, 1968; M.Arch, Columbia U., 1974. Design architect Urban Deadline Architects, John Young Architect, N.Y.C., 1976-77, I. M.Pei and Partners, Architects, N.Y.C., 1977-82, Kohn, Pedersen, Fox, Assos., P.C., Architects, N.Y.C., 1982—; vis. faculty Columbia U., summers 1981-86; faculty Parsons Sch. Design, 1980-83; visual artist, 1964—; numerous exhbns., 1964—. Recipient Grand prize AIA Jour. Drawing Contest, 1982. Lic. architect, N.Y. State. Studio: 30 W 26th St New York NY 10010 Office: Kohn Pedersen Fox Assocs 111 W 57th St 16th Fl New York NY 10019

PONTON, LISA S., lawyer; b. Jacksonville, Fla., Feb. 21, 1953; d. Roger Melvin and Mary (Tate) Stamper; m. Paul Sherman Ponton, Apr. 22, 1978. B.A., Spelman Coll., 1974; M.S.W., U. Pitts., 1976, J.D., 1981. Bar: Pa. 1981. Social worker Child Welfare Services, Pitts., 1976-78; counselor U. Pitts., 1978-81; legal intern Neighborhood Legal Services, Pitts., 1979-81, atty., 1981; supr. employment practices U.S. Steel Corp., Pitts., 1981—. Mem. Pa. Coalition, 1983. Mem. Pa. Bar Assn., Am. Trial Lawyers Assn., ABA, Nat. Bar Assn., Alpha Kappa Alpha. Home: 372 Willow Hedge Dr Monroeville PA 15146 Office: US Steel Homestead Works Homestead PA 15120

POOL, DEANNA, educator, satellite engineering group comptroller; b. Rabat, Morocco, North Africa, Apr. 21, 1942; came to U.S., 1975; d. Joseph and Perla (Dery) Amar; m. David Lynn Pool, Oct. 5, 1964; children—Nathaniel Dan, Michael Messod, Joel Eli. Student Universite de Rabat, 1960-61; diploma in Hispanic culture Centro Cultural Espanol, Madrid, Spain, 1964. Chief comml. liaisons and fgn. markets dept. Ministry of Commerce, Industry, Mines & Merchant Marine, Rabat, 1961-62; asst. to dir. fin. Caisse de Depot, 1962-64; co-owner, Marshall Tool and Die, Kansas City, Mo., 1975-77, Bio-Safe, Kansas City, 1977-80; co-owner, comptroller Satellite Engring. Group, Kansas City, 1980—; lectr. in Morocco, Honduras, Philippines, 1960-75; guest lectr., U. Mo.-Kansas City, 1984—; lectr. in field. Mem. Mo. Conservation Soc., Soc. Prevention Cruelty to Animals. Jewish. Avocations: Antiques; embroidery; reading. Home: 114 Hackberry Lee's Summit MO 64063 Office: Satellite Engring Group 3127 Belmont St Kansas City MO 64129

POOL, MARY KATHERINE, healthcare official; b. Port Huron, Mich., May 17, 1956; d. Eugene Edward and Bernadette Margret (Donnette) P. A.B., St. Clair County Community Coll., Port Huron; B.B.A. magna cum laude, Northwood Inst., Midland, Mich. Med. sec. Port Huron Hosp., 1976-77, health record analyst, 1977-80, quality assurance coordinator, 1980-81, quality assurance supr., 1981—; pres. Port Huron Hosp. Employees Fed. Credit Union, 1982—, dir., 1979-82. Contbr. articles to profl. jours. Bd. dirs. Vis. Nurses Assn. St. Clair County, 1984. Recipient Job Application award Office Edn. Assn., 1975. Mem. Nat. Assn. Quality Assurance Profls., Mich. Assn. Quality Assurance Profls. Republican. Lutheran. Club: Port Huron Hosp. Fellowship (treas.). Home: 2911 Omar St Port Huron MI 48060 Office: Port Huron Hospital 1001 Kearney St Port Huron MI 48060

POOLE, GERTRUDE MARGARET, accounting and finance educator; b. N.Y.C., Oct. 26, 1939; d. Robert John and Gertrude Amelia (Toulman) P.; B.B.A., Pace U., 1974; M.B.A., Rutgers U., 1982. Mgr. mdse. acctg. Reader's Digest, N.Y.C., 1965-74; staff acct. Coopers & Lybrand, N.Y.C., 1974-75; sr. acct. SS&O C.P.A.s, Perth Amboy, N.J., 1975-77; tax and internal audit sr. Church & Dwight, Piscataway, N.J., 1977-78; chief acctg. and control div. Fed. Res. Employee Benefits System, N.Y.C., 1978-82; asst. prof. Sch. Bus. Adminstrn., Monmouth Coll., West Long Branch, N.J., 1982—. C.P.A., N.Y., N.J. Mem. NOW (chmn. speaker's bur. Monmouth chpt. 1974-75), N.J. Soc. C.P.A.s, Am. Inst. C.P.A.s, Nat. Assn. Female Execs., LINK, Am. Soc. Women Accts. Roman Catholic. Home: 2006 F St South Belmar NJ 07719 Office: Monmouth Coll Sch Bus Adminstrn West Long Branch NJ 07764

POOLE, JODI ANNE, publisher, record company executive; b. N.Y.C., June 17, 1949; d. Paul and Antonina Nancy (Menegio) Manata; m. Edward F. Poole, Sept. 9, 1972. Student in music appreciation, U. Hawaii, 1967-68, in music theory, NYU, 1969-72, in engring., Recording Inst., 1977-78; hon. programer degree Program Inst., 1968-69. Adminstrv. asst. BMI, N.Y.C., 1968-72; profl. mgr. Screen Gems, N.Y.C., 1972-77, CBS Songs, N.Y.C., 1977-79; creative mgr. RBR Communications, N.Y.C., 1979-81; pres. Major Music Corp., N.Y.C., 1981—, chmn. bd.; pres. Word of Mouth Music, Dirty Poole Music, RKD Records; cons. Young Music Pub., 1977—, Women in Music Corp., 1981—, Women in Music Coalition, 1982—. Democrat. Roman Catholic. Home: 8502 Newkirk Ave North Bergen NJ 07047

POOR, ANNE, painter; b. N.Y.C., Jan. 2, 1918; d. Henry Varnum and Bessie (Breuer) P.; student Bennington Coll., 1936, 38, Art Students League, 1935. Works exhibited Am. Brit. Art Center, 1944, 45, 48, Maynard Walker Gallery, 1950, Graham Gallery, 1957-59, 62, 68-71; executed murals P.O., Gleason, Tenn., DePew, N.Y.; South Solon (Maine) Free Meeting House, 1957, others; represented permanent collections Whitney Mus., Bklyn. Mus., Wichita Mus., Art Inst. Chgo.; mem. faculty Skowhegan Sch. Painting and Sculpture,

1947-61. Artist corr. WAC, 1943-45. Edwin Austin Abbey Meml. fellow, 1948; grantee Nat. Inst. Arts and Letters, 1957; recipient Benjamin Altman 1st prize landscape painting N.A.D., 1971. Mem. Artists Equity Assn. Illustrator: Greece, 1964. Office: Graham Gallery 1014 Madison Ave New York NY 10021*

POOR, SUZANNE DONALDSON, advertising and public relations executive; b. Somers Point, N.J., Oct. 6, 1933; d. James Watt and Roberta (Radford) Donaldson; m. Richard Sumner Poor, Mar. 19, 1955 (div. Sept. 1984); children—Jonathan Scott, Jeffrey Sumner, Sara Suzanne. A.B., Mt. Holyoke Coll., 1955; M.A., Montclair State Coll., 1975; postgrad NYU, 1977—; photography student New Sch. Social Research, 1979. Reporter, copy writer WFLB, WFLB-TV, Fayetteville, NC., 1955-56; dir. public relations Montclair YMCA, N.J., 1965-69; dir. public relations Girl Scouts Greater Essex County, Montclair, 1969-74; assoc. pub. relations dept. Nat. League Nursing, N.Y.C., 1974; freelance public relations, photography, Montclair, 1974-76; dir. communications Insts. Religion and Health, N.Y.C., 1976-78; ptnr., pres. Miller/Poor Assocs., Verona, N.J., 1978—. Pres. bd. trustees Doubletree Gallery, Montclair, 1977-79; trustee Friends of N.J. Network. Mem. Am. Soc. Mag. Photographers, Am. Woman's Econ. Devel. Corp., Nat. Assn. Female Execs., Exec. Women N.J. (bd. dirs. 1980-83), Ad Club NJ (bd. govs. 1983—, editor Ad Talk, 1982—. Democrat. Episcopalian. Club: Bradford Bath and Tennis. Avocations: bicycling; swimming; tennis; furniture restoration. Home: 30 Plymouth St Montclair NJ 07042 Office: Miller/Poor Assocs 280 Bloomfield Ave Verona NJ 07044

POOS, DENISE MARIE, electric utility engineer; b. Arlington, Va., Dec. 18, 1958; d. Frank William and Catherine Jeannette (Kolakoski) P. B.S. in Mech. Engring., Ga. Inst. Tech., 1982. Mech. design engr. trainee Nottingham & Assocs., McLean, Va., 1977-81; fuels engr. West Tex. Utilities Co., Abilene, 1982—. Sci. fair judge Jr. League of Abilene, 1985, 86. Mem. Tex. Soc. Profl. Engrs. (bd. dirs. Abilene chpt. 1986—), Soc. Women Engrs., ASME. Republican. Roman Catholic. Avocations: swimming; softball; reading. Home: 1601 S Palm St Abilene TX 79602 Office: West Tex Utilities Co 1026 N 3rd St Box 841 Abilene TX 79604

POPE, CATHERINE LEE, mental health center administrator; b. Lubbock, Tex., Jan. 1, 1949; d. Norbert Dean Emery and Cozzette (Allison) Emery Roberts; 1 child, Dustin Michael. B.A., Tex. Tech U., 1972, M.A., 1977. Mental health program dir. Lubbock Mental Health/Mental Retardation Ctr., 1978—; co-exec. dir. Eagle's Wing Inc. Correction's Halfway House, 1981—; cons. Tex. Dept. Mental Health/Mental Retardation, 1983—. Democrat. Avocations: skiing; rafting. Office: Lubbock Regional Mental Health/Mental Retardation Ctr 1210 Texas St Lubbock TX 79401

POPE, DONNA, government official; b. Cleve., Oct. 15, 1931; d. John Emil and Marie Josephine (Thiel) Kolnik; m. Raymond Pope, Oct. 21, 1951; children—Candace Pope Wooley, Cheryl Ann. Student public schs. Supr. election ofcls. dept. Cuyahoga County Bd. Elections, Cleve., 1965-68; mem. Ohio Ho. of Reps., 1972-81, minority whip; dir. U.S. Mint, Washington, 1981—. Vice chmn. Cuyahoga County Republican Exec. Com.; mem. Greater Cleve. Citizens League. Mem. Bus and Profl. Women's Club. Roman Catholic. Office: US Mint Office of Dir 633 3d St NW Washington DC 20020

POPE, MARGARET ALSTON, office manager, real estate broker; b. Catherine, Ala., June 14, 1921; d. Nathaniel Lowry and Willie (Henderson) Alston; m. Leslie E. Pope, Aug. 1, 1940. Student Ala. Sch. Real Estate, 1969, Hobson Tech. Coll., 1974-75, Ala. Licensing Sch., 1981. Licensed real estate broker. Clerk County Govt. Barbour County, Clayton, Ala., 1943; bookkeeper Bank of Thomasville, Ala., 1944-45; buyer-mgr. Pope Enterprises, Thomasville, 1955—; licensed agt. Independent Ins. Agy., Thomasville, 1971—; broker, office mgr. Pope's Real Estate, Thomasville, 1970—. Com. mem. Clarke County Mental Health, Grove Hill, Ala., 1963—; bd. dirs. Fed. Emergency Mgmt. Assn., 1984—; organizer, bd. dirs. Civic Club of Teenagers, 1962, local Jr. Service Club, 1965; S.S. tchr., church clerk, mem. ch. choir; officer 4th dist. Ala. Fed. Women's Clubs, 1980-82; chmn. Democratic Women for Wallace, Clarke County, 1974, 82, Leukemia Dr., Thomasville, Ala., 1966; mem. planning com. city semi-sesquicentennial, Thomasville, 1963; mem. city beautification com., Thomasville, 1965, 85, Clarke County Bd. Pensions and Security, 1964—, Ala. Health Coordination Council, 1983—, Ala. Health Planning Devel. Com., 1983—. Mem. V.F.W. Aux. (pres. 1958-59), Thomasville C. of C. Democrat. Baptist. Club: Worthwhile (pres. 1962-64, 78-80) (Thomasville). Lodge: Order Eastern Star. Home: Hwy #5 North Thomasville AL 36784 Office: Pope's Real Estate PO Box 576 Thomasville AL 36784

POPE, REBECCA, special education educator; b. Lexington, Ky., Aug. 7, 1948; d. Charles B. and Vela (Moran) Reid; m. W. David Pope, Aug. 16, 1969 (div. Feb. 1981); children—Mark Andrew David, Michael Charles. B.A., Asbury Coll., 1969; cert. supr. East Tex. U., 1984; M.Ed., Western Ky. U., 1978. Cert. tchr. elem. edn., Ky. Tchr. music elem. sch. Fayette County Ind. Sch. Dist., Lexington, 1969-70, tchr. elem. sch., 1970-72; clin. diagnostician Western Ky. U., Bowling Green, 1977-78, spl. edn. for most handicapping conditions-coordinator Richardson Ind. Sch. Dist. (Tex.), 1978-81, spl. edn. tchr. emotionally disturbed, 1981—, cons., 1980; lectr. in field. Group leader Mental Health-Mental Retardation, Austin, Tex., 1976-77; in-hospl program for new parents of handicapped children, Austin, 1976-77. Recipient Outstanding Achievement in Spl. Edn. tchr. award Richardson Ind. Sch. Dist., 1983. Mem. NEA, Tex. Edn. Assn., Council for Exceptional Children (state student rep. 1977-78), Council for Children with Behavior Disorders, Internat. Platform Assn., Phi Delta Kappa. Democrat. Methodist. Club: Asbury Coll. Fine Arts (v.p. 1967-68, pres. 1968-69). Home: 14240 Haymeadow St Apt 1019 Dallas TX 75240 Office: RISD-Spring Creek Elem Sch 7667 Roundrock Rd Dallas TX 75248

POPE, SUZETTE STANLEY, accountant; b. Florala, Ala., Sept. 15, 1925; d. Raymond T. and Vashti Viola (Williams) Stanley; m. W. Norelle Pope, June 22, 1947; children—Stephanie Suzanne, Brently Preston. A.S., Miami-Dade Community Coll., 1967; B.B.A., U. Miami, 1969, M.B.A., 1971; Ed.S., U. Fla., 1976. Staff acct. Stuzin C.P.A.s; supr. acctg. staff Dade County Pub. Schs., Miami, Fla., 1969-75, chief acct. acctg. div., 1976-83, accounts payable div., 1983—. Contbr. articles to profl. publs. Bd. dirs. United Manpower Service, Inc., Miami, 1976—; trustee Bay Oaks Home, 1981—. Named Outstanding Adminstr., Dade County Pub. Schs., 1982. Mem. Assn. Sch. Bus. Officials, Fla. Support Adminstr. Assn., Fla. Sch. Fin. Council, Soroptimist Internat. (chmn. tng. awards sect. 1982-84, del. So. region, 1981—), Am. Soc. Women Accts. (v.p. 1982-83), Assn. Sch. Bus. Ofcls., AAUW, Coral Gables Bus. and Profl. Womens Club (v.p. 1984-85). Democrat. Baptist. Home: 3925 NW 4th Terrace Miami FL 33126 Office: Dade County Pub Schs Room 602 1450 NE 2d Ave Miami FL 33132

POPEL, JUDITH JEPSEN, educational administrator, educator; b. Kankakee, Ill., Sept. 3, 1940; d. Joseph Louis and Hilda Marie (Bourgeois) Jepsen; m. Gary A. Popel, Sept. 2, 1961; children—Anne Popel Leonard, Therese Popel Wyman, Margaret. A.B. in Elem. Edn., Ga. State U., 1973; M.Ed., U. Ill., 1976, adminstrv. cert., 1985. Advt. rep. Paxton Record, Ill., 1969-70; tchr. 1st grade Tolono Primary Sch., Ill., 1974-77; tchr. 4th grade St. Malachy Sch., Rantoul, Ill., 1977-79, tchr. 2d grade, 1979-81; chpt. 1 reading tchr. Ludlow Community Consol. Dist. 142, Ill., 1981—, prin., 1985—. Pres. Paxton Unit 2 Schs. Bd. Edn., 1979—; sec. East Central Ill. Ednl. Service Ctr. Regional Governing Bd., 1985—; mem. zoning bd. City of Paxton, 1977-81; past pres., bd. dirs. Paxton Day Care Ctr., Paxton Hosp. Aux., 1965—, St.' Mary Council Cath. Women; founder, co-ordinator Paxton Meals on Wheels, 1981—; sec. regional governing bd. East Central Ill. Ednl. Service Ctr., 1985—. Named Woman of Yr., Council Cath. Women, 1967, Those Who Excel, Ill. State Bd. Edn., 1983. Mem. Ludlow Edn. Assn. (pres. 1981—), AAUW (legis. chair 1978—), Mortar Bd., Phi Delta Kappa, Kappa Delta Epsilon, Kappa Delta Pi, Delta Kappa Gamma, Beta Sigma Phi (officer 1962—). Club: Paxton Woman's (v.p. 1984—). Home: 358 W Pells St Paxton IL 60957 Office: PO Box 156 Ludlow IL 60949

POPPER, MERNA SALLOP, publisher; b. N.Y.C.; d. Herbert Arthur and Helen Irene (Koss) Sallop; m. John Edward Popper, Mar. 3, 1961; children; Robert Arthur, Juliet Ellen. B.A., Sarah Lawrence Coll. Pres., Popper-Strong Communications, pub. Women's News, bus. and profl. women's newspaper, and New Men's News, Mamaroneck, N.Y. Office: Women's News 154 E Boston Post Rd Box 396 Mamaroneck NY 10543

POPPER, PAMELA ANNE, investment banker; b. Columbus, Ohio, Oct. 24, 1956; d. Edwin D. and Eleanor Ida P. Student Ohio State U. Assoc. dir. Conservatory of Piano, Columbus, 1974-79; v.p. The Window Man, Columbus, 1979-81; chmn. bd. Nat. Veg Tec, Columbus, 1985—; pres. Popper Brace Scott, Columbus, 1981—; v.p., dir. Hamilton Fin. Co., Columbus, 1983—; pres., dir. Keystone Nat. Devel. Corp.; dir. Shelter One Group Corp. Chmn. bd. Neoteric Dance Theatre, Columbus, 1985—, Netcare Found., Columbus, 1985—; bd. dirs. Treemar Retreat, South Webster, Ohio, 1986—, Ballet Met., Columbus, 1976-79. Recipient Vol. award Netcare Corp., 1984; profl. sales awards. Mem. Columbus Life Underwriters, Columbus Area Leadership Program, Nat. Assn. Profl. Saleswomen. Republican. Home: 3346 Mansion Way Upper Arlington OH 43221 Office: 1001 Eastwind Dr #305 Westerville OH 43081

POPRICK, MARY ANN, psychologist; b. Chgo., June 25, 1939; d. Michael and Mary (Mihalcik) Poprick; B.A., De Paul U., 1960, M.A., 1964; Ph.D., Loyola U., Chgo., 1968. Intern in psychology Elgin (Ill.) State Hosp., 1961-62; staff psychologist, 1962; staff psychologist Ill. State Tng. Sch. for Girls, Geneva, 1962-63, Mt. Sinai Hosp., Chgo., 1963-64; lectr. psychology Loyola U. at Chgo., 1964-67; asst. prof. Lewis U., Lockport, 1967-70, assoc. prof., 1970-75, chmn. dept., 1968-72 (on leave 1972-73); postdoctoral intern in clin. psychology Ill. State Psychiat. Inst., Chgo., 1972-73; pvt. clin. practice David Psychiat. Clinic, Ltd., South Holland Ill., 1973—; assoc. sci. staff Riveredge Hosp., Forest Park, Ill., 1975-76; mem. sci. staff dept. psychiatry Christ Hosp., Oak Lawn, Ill., 1983—. Co-chmn. commn. on personal growth and devel. Congregation of 3d Order St. Francis of Mary Immaculate, Joliet, 1970-71; clin. resource person Cath. Archdiocese of Chgo., 1977—. Mem. Am. Psychol. Assn. (rep. from Ill. 1985—), Calif., Ill. (sec.-treas. acad. sect. 1975-77, mem. student devel. com. 1975-77, chmn. acad. sect. 1977-78, 78-79, mem. program com. 1977-78, sec. 1979-81, pres.-elect 1981-82, pres. 1982-83, past pres. 1983-84, chmn. program com. 1981-82, awards com. 1983-86), Midwestern psychol. assn., Soc. for Sci. Study Religion, AAAS, Chgo. Assn. Psychoanalytical Psychology, Kappa Gamma Pi, Psi Chi (sec. 1964-65, pres. 1965-66). Home: 547 Marquette Ave Calumet City IL 60409 Office: 645 E 170th St South Holland IL 60473

POQUETTE, NELL FARNHAM, food brokerage executive; b. DeFuniak Springs, Fla., Jan. 16, 1932; d. Thomas D. and Mary Katherine (Mixon) Farnham; m. Vernon Lyle Lipp, May 19, 1951 (div. Jan. 1964); children—Angela Yvette Lipp Hunt, Desiree Renee Lipp Wiltsey, V. Lyle Lipp II; m. Harold Francis Poquette, Sept. 9, 1978. Student Rollins Coll. Various real estate positions, Orlando, Fla., 1968-75; v.p. Comml. Food Brokers Inc., Clearwater, Fla., 1977—. Democrat. Mormon. Avocations: biking, walking, cooking, handcrafts. Home: 595 N Bayshore Dr Safety Harbor FL 33572 Office: Comml Food Brokers Inc 2596 Nursery Rd Clearwater FL 33546

PORADA, EDITH, educator, archeologist; b. Vienna, Austria, Aug. 22, 1912; Ph.D., U. Vienna, 1935. Mem. faculty Queens Coll., 1950-58; mem faculty Columbia U., 1958—, prof. art history and archaeology, 1964-83, emeritus sr. lectr., 1983—; hon. curator seals and tablets Pierpont Morgan Library, 1956—. Recipient award for disting. achievement Archaeol. Inst. Am., 1977. Fellow Am. Acad. Arts and Scis., Brit. Acad. (corr.), Austrian Acad.; mem. Am. Philos. Soc. Author: Alt Iran, 1963; The Art of Ancient Iran, 1965; also monographs, articles. Office: 815 Dept Art History Columbia U Schermerhorn Hall New York NY 10027*

PORITSKY, SUSAN, psychiatrist; b. Phila., Apr. 2, 1950; d. Albert L. and Blanche E. (Schwartz) Poritsky; B.A. magna cum laude, U. Pa., 1971; M.D., Hahnemann Med. Coll., 1978. Intern, Pa. Hosp., 1978-79; resident in psychiatry, Inst. Pa. Hosp., Phila., 1979-82; psychology research asst. Am. Inst. Research, 1970; assoc. behavioral analyst The Boeing Co., 1971; employment counselor/employment interviewer Pa. Bur. Employment Security, 1971-74; emergency service psychiatrist N.W. Center Community Mental Health Center, 1979-80; med. staff Northwestern Inst. Psychiatry, 1980; emergency service psychiatrist West Phila. Community Mental Health Consortium, 1980; mgmt. physician Haverford State Hosp., 1980-82; practice medicine specializing in psychiatry, Phila., 1982—; med. staff Eagleville Hosp. and Rehab. Center, 1980-82; instr. in psychiatry U. Pa. Med. Sch., Phila., 1979—; med. staff Inst. of Pa. Hosp., 1982—, Pa. Hosp., 1982—. NIMH med. student fellow, 1976; diplomate Am. Bd. Psychiatry and Neurology, Nat. Bd. Med. Examiners. Mem. AMA, Am. Med. Women's Assn., Pa. Psychiat. Assn., Am. Psychiat. Assn., Phila. Psychiat. Soc. (council mem.), Phila. Soc. Adolescent Psychiatry, Del. Valley Group Psychotherapy Soc. Contbr. articles to profl. jours. Office: 111 N 49th St Philadelphia PA 19139

PORTER, CHRISTINE RUTH, locksmith; b. Miami, Fla., June 28, 1939; d. Harley E. Wilkinson and Christina J. (Godwin) Barry; m. Clarence M. Porter, Nov. 25, 1957 (dec. Feb. 1985); children—Grant Scott, Tina Lori. Co-owner Amoco Sta., Miami, 1957-71; co-owner Porter's Locksmith, Miami, 1971-80, owner, pres., Opalocka, Fla., 1980—. Mem. Assoc. Locksmiths Am. (tchr. 1975; cert. of appreciation 1978), So. Fla. Locksmith Assn. (Locksmith of Yr. 1979; sec. 1976-78), Southeastern Regional Locksmith Assn. (tchr. 1977-79), Fla. Bd. Locksmiths. Republican. Baptist. Avocation: reading. Office: Porter's Locksmith 13801 NW 27 Ave Opalocka FL 33054

PORTER, CLARA LOU, management consultant; b. Tonopah, Nev., Feb. 13, 1940; d. Ernest Clarence and Lois Gail (Titus) Hildebrand; student U. Nev., 1976-77, Clark County Community Coll., 1981—; m. Jimmy O'Neal Porter, Nov. 15, 1957 (div. 1979); children—James Douglas, John Barrett, Barbara Dianne, Robyn Louise, Jeffrey O'Neal. Machine bookkeeper First Nat. Bank, Las Vegas, 1957-58, 63-65; supr. machine bookkeepers Alaska Nat. Bank, Fairbanks, 1960-61; asst. dir. personnel So. Nev. Meml. Hosp., Las Vegas, 1966-77; bus. mgr. Emergency Assocs., Las Vegas, 1978-82; prin. C. Porter Med. Mgmt. Cons., Inc., Las Vegas, 1982—; sole owner Secretarial Support Services Nev., 1983—; dir. Exec. Suites of Am. Democrat. Baptist. Home: 127 Victory Rd Henderson NV 89015 Office: 2810 W Charleston Blvd F-62 Las Vegas NV 89102

PORTER, DIANNA MARIE, gerontologist; b. Butte, Mont., July 31, 1942; d. Harold Coleman and Josephine Veronica (Sullivan) P. B.A., St. Mary Coll., Xavier, Kans., 1964; M.A., North Tex. State U., 1977. Social worker Cath. Charities, Helena, Mont., 1966-69, Family Services, Butte, Mont., 1970-73; cons. U.S. Senate, Washington, 1977-78; coordinator Mont. State U., Bozeman, 1978; coordinator U. Tex. Med. Sch., Houston, 1978-80, dir. edn., 1980-83; cons. Sheltering Arms, Houston, 1983. Editor: Introduction to Gerontology and Geriatrics, 1984; mng. editor Gerontology and Geriatrics Edn., 1980-83; contbr. articles on geriatric edn. to profl. jours. Co-founder local chpt. NOW, Butte, Mont., 1971, Women's Polit. Caucus, Butte, 1972, Older Women's League, Houston, 1983; ac hoc advisor 1981 White House Conf. on Aging, Washington, 1980. Mem. ABA, Older Women's League, Gray Panthers, S.W. Soc. on Aging, Western Gerontol. Soc. Democrat.

PORTER, DIXIE LEE, corporate executive; b. Bountiful, Utah, June 7, 1931; d. John Lloyd and Ida May (Robinson) Mathis; B.S., U. Calif.-Berkeley, 1956, M.B.A., 1957. Personnel aide City of Berkeley, 1957-59; employment supr. Kaiser Health Found., Los Angeles, 1959-60; personnel analyst UCLA, 1961-63; personnel mgr. Reuben H. Donnelley, Santa Monica, Calif., 1963-64, Good Samaritan Hosp., San Jose, Calif., 1965-67; fgn. service officer AID, Saigon, Vietnam, 1967-71; gen. agt. Charter Security Life Ins. Co., Jacksonville, Fla., 1972-82; gen. agt. Kennesaw Life Ins. Co., Atlanta, 1978—, Phila. Life Ins. Co., Phila., 1978—; pres. Women's Ins. Enterprises, Ltd., San Jose, 1979—; sec.-treas. RWJ Investment Corp.; cons. in field; dir. Aegis Health Corp. Co-chairperson Comprehensive Health Planning Commn. Santa Clara County, Calif., 1973-76; bd. dirs. U. Calif. Sch. Bus. Adminstrn., Berkeley, 1974-76; mem. Christian Children's Found.; mem. task force on equal access to econ. power U.S. Nat. Women's Agenda, 1977—. Served with USMC, 1950-52. C.L.U. Mem. C.L.U. Soc., U. Calif. Alumni Assn., U. Calif. Sch. Bus. Adminstrn. Alumni Assn., U. Calif. Campanile Assn., AAUW, World Wildlife Fund, Prytanean Alumni, Beta Gamma Sigma. Republican. Episcopalian. Office: PO Box 64 Los Gatos CA 95031

PORTER, DONNA JUNE, interior designer; b. Alva, Okla., June 24, 1937; d. Floyd Robert and Elsie Martha (Schick) Paris; b. Max. E. Walters, Aug., 1959 (div. 1981); m. Jerry R. Porter, Sept. 21, 1983; children—Terri Sue, Bradford Paris. B.S., Okla. State U., 1959; postgrad., 1970; Kansas City Art Inst., 1979. Tchr., Jefferson County Schs., Denver, 1962-64, Shawnee Mission Schs., Kans., 1964-66; dir. restaurant design Frontier Foods, Stillwater, Okla., 1967-72; dir. design Great Am. Restaurant Co., Kansas City, Mo., 1972-80; owner, designer D.J. Interior Design, Kansas City, 1980—. Bd. dirs. Kansas City Conv. and Vis. Bur., 1975-78, Kansas City Met. Parents Anonymous, 1984—. Recipient Key to City Mayor Cin., 1976. Mem. Interior Design Excellence Com., Nat. Assn. Women Bus. Owners, Friends of Art, Profl. Sources Greater Kansas City, Historic Kansas City Soc., Chi Omega (Outstanding Chi Omega, Okla. 1974, Chi Omega of Yr. 1981) Nat. Dir. extension 1979-82, PEO (chaplain 1979-81). Democrat. Mem. Disciples of Christ Ch. Clubs: Carriage (exec. com.), Chi O Mothers (pres.) (Kansas City). Avocation: tennis. Home and Office: 812 W 59th Terr Kansas City MO 64113

PORTER, ELISABETH SCOTT LEEZEE, furniture leasing executive; b. Richmond, Va., Mar. 23, 1942; d. Buford and Mary (Nixon) S.; m. William Lane Porter, Jr., Aug. 23, 1963 (div. 1971); 1 dau., Erin. Student Sweet Briar Coll., 1961-62, Pan. Am. Bus. Sch., 1963. Pres., The Porter Group Inc., Washington, 1971-81, Antique and Contemporary Leasing, Inc., Washington, 1974—; founder, dir. The Women's Nat. Bank, Washington, 1976-83; dir. 1st Women's Nat. Bank Corp., Washington, 1980-84. Mem. fin. com. Episcopal Diocese Washington; mem. adv. bd. WAMU-FM, Washington; founder, mem. Inst. Bus. Designers, Washington; mem. Allied Bd. Trade; Democratic co-chmn. The Women's Campaign Fund, Washington; mem. Democratic Women's Council; bd. dirs. Women's Campaign Research Fund; mem. Democratic Nat. Com.; mem. vestry Grace Episcopal Ch., Georgetown; mem. adv. bd. Washington Opera; mem. Georgetown Citizen's Assn.; mem. adv. bd. Elk Hill Farm (Va.). Mem. Nat. Assn. Women Bus. Owners, Georgetown Bus. and Profl. Orgn., Washington C. of C. Democrat. Episcopalian. Clubs: The Colony (N.Y.C.); Pisces (Washington). Office: Antique and Contemporary Leasing Inc 3401 K St NW Washington DC 20007

PORTER, ELIZABETH ANN, security guard company executive; b. Durham, N.C., Jan. 13, 1961; d. Robert Jared and Ella Mae (Meador) P. B.S. in Acctg. with honors, U.S.C., 1982. Staff acct. Cooper and Lybrand, C.P.A.s, Charlotte, N.C., 1982-83; owner, operator Security Guards, Inc., Louisville, 1983—. Mem. Am. Mgmt. Soc. Baptist. Office: Security Guards Inc 1313 Lyndon Ln Suite 210 Louisville KY 40222

PORTER, HELEN VINEY, lawyer; b. Logansport, Ind., Sept. 7, 1935; s. Charles Lowry and Florence Helen (Kunkel) V.; m. Lewis Morgan Porter, Jr., Dec. 26, 1966; children—Alicia Michelle, Andrew Morgan. A.B., Ind. U., 1957; J.D., U. Louisville, 1961. Bar: Ind. and Ill. 1961, U.S. Supreme Ct. 1971. Atty. office chief counsel Midwest regional office IRS, Chgo., 1961-73; assoc. regional atty. litigation center Equal Employment Opportunity Commn., Chgo., 1973-74; practice in, Northbrook, Ill., 1974-79, 80—; ptnr. Porter & Andersen, Chgo., 1979-80; lectr. Law in Am. Found., Chgo., summer, 1973, 74; assoc. prof. No. Ill. Coll. Law (formerly Lewis U. Coll. Law), Glen Ellyn, Ill., 1975-79. Lectr. women's rights and fed. taxation to bar assns., civic groups. Fellow Am. Bar Found., Ill. State Bar Found.; mem. Women's Bar Assn. Ill. (pres. 1972-73), ABA (chmn. standing com. gavel awards 1983-85, bd. editors jour. 1984—), Fed. Bar Assn. (pres. Chgo. chpt. 1974-75), Ill. Bar Assn. (del. 1972-78), Nat. Assn. Women Lawyers (pres. 1973-74). Home and Office: 225 Maple Row Northbrook IL 60062

PORTER, MARY FAITH, security administrator; b. Muskegon, Mich., May 13, 1958; d. Maurice Raymond and LaVeryl Cornelia (Wade) P. B.A., Mich. State U., 1980; A.A., Muskegon Community Coll., 1978. Cert. security trainer. Ops. mgr. security dept. The Methodist Hosp., Houston, 1981—, chairperson mktg. com., 1983-84. Instr. trainer defensive driving Tex. Safety Assn., Austin, 1982; instr. trainer CPR, Am. Heart Assn., Houston, 1982; mem. Methodist Hosp. com. of United Way, Houston, 1983. Recipient Scholarship, State Mich., Lansing, 1976. Mem. Am. Soc. Indsl. Security (edn. com. 1983-84), Am. Acad. Security Educators and Trainers, Texas Gulf Coast Crime Prevention Assn., NOW, Alpha Phi Sigma. Office: Methodist Hosp 6565 Fannin St Houston TX 77030

PORTER, MAXIENE HELEN GREVE, civic worker; b. Los Angeles; d. Henry Chris and Meyerl (Dixon) Greve; student U. So. Calif., 1928; m. Wellington Denny Palmer, Nov. 18, 1929 (dec. Mar. 1933); children—Virginia Palmer Stanhagen, Wellington Denny; m. 2d, Dalc R. Porter, May 17, 1941. Accounting clk. Inglewood (Calif.) Sch. System, 1948-51, dep. tax collector City of San Luis Obispo (Calif.), 1963-65; acctg. clk. San Luis Obispo County Schs., 1965-66; asst. innkeeper Holiday Inn, Darien, Conn., 1967, Alexandria, Va.; innkeeper Holiday Inn, Falls Church, Va., 1973—; asst. gen. mgr. Darien Motor Lodge Assos.; sec.-asst. treas. Seven Fountains Corp., tax cons. H & R Block, 1975-79, office mgr., 1976; acctg. and sales rep. Frankie Welch of Va. and Am., 1979-81. Officer, Native Daus. Golden West, 1953—, state pres., 1959-60; chmn. various coms. Calif. Fedn. Womens Clubs, 1960-63; v.p. Bus. and Profl. Women, 1936-37; sec. Inglewood Coordinating Council, 1945-47, pres., 1947-48; pres., various other offices West Ebell Club, Los Angeles, 1947, 60-63; mem. public relations com. YWCA, Fairfax County, Va., 1967-68, Fairfax Hosp. Aux., 1967-68, spl. pub. com. Smithsonian Assn., 1967-68; sec.-treas. Pinecrest Citizens Assn., 1968, v.p., 1974; chmn. finance com. Va. Commn. Status of Women, 1973-75; docent vol. chmn. Green Spring Farm Park, Fairfax County, 1979-80; treas. Greater Falls Church Republican Womens Club, 1968-70, v.p., 1973-74, pres., 1975-76; treas. Va. Fedn. Rep. Women, 1968—, parliamentarian, 1976-80; vice-chmn. Va. Nixon Inaugural Com., 1968-69; treas. Va. Women for Nixon, 1968; mem. Fairfax County Nixon for Pres. Com., co-chmn. Fairfax County Ladies for Lin—Gov.'s Campaign, 1969; mem. Fairfax County Rep. Com., 1968—, dist. chmn., 1974—, sec., 1975-76. Mem. Fairfax County C. of C. (legis., edn., polit. activities coms. 1973-74), Nat. Trust for Historic Preservation, Nat. Hist. Soc., Va., Metro (mem. program com., v.p. 1972-73) motel assns., Am. Mgmt. Assn., Fairfax Cultural Assn. (membership com. mem. 1969—). Clubs: Toastmistress (treas. No. Va. 1975, organizer, charter pres. Falls Church 1977-78, pres., 1983-84 council extension chmn. 1977-78, council treas. 1979-80, council sec. 1980-81, council v.p. 1981-82, council pres. 1982-83, parliamentarian 1983-84 editor council newsletter 1978-79, regional awards chmn. 1983-85), Annandale Women's, No. Va. Fedn. Women's (registration chmn. 1980, conservation and energy com., scholarship com. 1982-84, pub. affairs chmn. 1984-86), Nat Genealogy Soc., Maine Hist. Soc., Maine Geneal. Soc., Piebscot Hist. Soc., Kittery Hist. Soc. Lutheran. Home: PO Box 11464 Alexandria VA 22312 also Orr's Island ME

PORTER, NADINE SUMPTER, science educator; b. Mt. Pleasant, Pa., May 27, 1944; d. A. Guy and Lois (Messner) Nicholls; m. James Robert Sumpter, May 7, 1966 (div. 1978); children—Kristin Joy, Kerry Susanne; m. Verleon H. Porter, Mar. 15, 1980. B.S., Pa. State U., 1965; M.S., Tex. A&M U., 1969; Ed.D., U. Houston, 1980. Cert. tchr., Tex. Research asst. Parke Davis & Co., Ann Arbor, Mich., 1966-67; research asst. Tex. A&M U., College Station, 1969-70; biology instr. Coll. DuPage, Glen Ellyn, Ill., 1971-72; instr. Houston Community Coll., 1973-77; teaching fellow U. Houston, 1977-79; tchr. chemistry Kinkaid Sch., Houston 1979—; tech. writer New Sci. Prospects, Houston, 1981—; v.p. Vapor Recovery & Compression Equipment, Inc., 1984—; lectr. in field. Contbg. editor Enhanced Energy Recovery newsletter, 1982; contbr. articles to profl. jours. Zone chmn. March of Dimes, Houston, 1982-84. Mem. Nat. Sci. Tchrs. Assn. Met. Houston Chem. Tchrs. Assn. (sec. 1982-84, safety chmn. 1985-86), Am. Chem. Soc., Associated Chemistry Tchrs. Tex., Houston Assn. Biology Tchrs. (chmn. 1985-86), Iota Sigma Pi. Home: 2818 Kismet St Houston TX 77043 Office: Kinkaid Sch 201 Kinkaid Sch Dr Houston TX 77024

PORTER, SELMA BUYER, adult education administrator; b. Paterson, N.J., Mar. 5, 1929; d. Jacob and Ida (Friedman) Buyer; m. Allen Norman Porter, Sept. 16, 1951; 1 child, Michelle Jane. B.A., Smith Coll., 1950; M.A., Kean Coll., 1978. Sec., translator Societe Generale, N.Y.C., 1951-53; owner, operator Grand Motel, Columbia, S.C., 1953-57; sr. sec. IBM, Newark, 1957-61; tchr. adult edn. Newark Bd. Edn., 1968-74; head tchr. Adult Learning Ctr., Newark, 1974-77, dir., 1977—; chairperson GED commencement com. Newark Bd. Edn., 1974-78, mem. textbook eval. com., 1975-81, chmn. 1982—, mem. Eng. as Second Lang. Com., 1981-82. Mem. exec. bd. Hadassah, Springfield, N.J., 1965-72, Thelma A. Sandmeier Sch., PTA, Springfield, 1967-71. Mem. N.J. Assn. Lifelong Learning, Kappa Delta Pi. Jewish. Avocations: Gourmet cooking; collecting antique Belleek, Limoges, Tiffany. Office: Adult Learning Ctr 380 Broad St Newark NJ 07104

PORTER, SYLVIA F(IELD), financial writer; b. Patchogue, N.Y., June 18, 1913; d. Louis and Rose (Maisel) Feldman; B.A. magna cum laude, Hunter Coll., 1932; postgrad. Grad. Sch. Bus. Adminstrn., NYU; 15 hon. degrees; m. Reed R. Porter, 1931 (div.); 1 child, Chris Sarah; m. 2d, Sumner Collins, 1943;

1 stepson, Sumner Campbell; m. 3d, James F. Fox, 1979. Founder weekly news letter Reporting on Govts.; asso. N.Y. Post, 1935-77; syndicated financial columnist Daily News, 1978—; editor-in-chief Sylvia Porter's Personal Finance mag. Mem. Phi Beta Kappa. Author: How to Make Money in Government Bonds; If War Comes to the American Home; Sylvia Porter's Annual Income Tax Guide; Sylvia Porter's Money Book; Sylvia Porter's New Money Book for the 1980's, 1979; Your Own Money, 1982; Love and Money, 1985. Recipient Centennial Medal Hunter Coll., 1970; Disting. Service in Journalism award U. Mo., 1975; William Allen White award, 1978. Mem. Phi Beta Kappa. Home: 2 Fifth Ave New York NY 10011 Office: care Universal Press Syndicate 4400 Johnson Dr Fairway KS 66205

PORTER, VERNA LOUISE, lawyer; b. Los Angeles, May 31, 1941. B.A., Calif. State U., 1963; J.D., Southwestern U., 1977. Bar: Calif. 1977, U.S. Dist. Ct. (cen. dist.) Calif. 1978, U.S. Ct. Appeals (9th cir.) 1978. Ptnr. Eisler & Porter, Los Angeles, 1978-79, mng. ptnr., 1979—; speaker on landlord-tenant law to real estate profls., including San Fernando Bd. Realtors. Editorial asst., contbr. Apt. Owner Builder; contbr. to Apt. Bus. Outlook, Real Property News, Apt. Age. Mem. ABA, Calif. State Bar (real property law sect., subcom. on landlord tenant law, panelist conv. 1983), Los Angeles County Bar Assn., Los Angeles Trial Lawyers Assn., Landlord Trial Lawyers Assn. (founding mem., pres.), da Camera Soc. Republican. Office: 500 S Virgil Ave Suite 360 Los Angeles CA 90020

PORTER, VIVIAN SMITHERS, hospital administrator, educational administrator; b. Davy, W.Va., Nov. 8, 1930; d. Ay and Elsie (McKeenan) Smithers; M. Thomas H. Martin, Apr. 7, 1951 (div. Jan. 1974); children—Pamela S. Martin Hanaburgh, Geary T.; m. George W. Porter, June 28, 1974. B.S., Empire State Coll., 1972; M.B.A., Pacific Coast U., 1985, Ph.D., 1986. Registered electro-encephalographic technologist. EKG-EEG technologist Norfolk Gen. Hosp. (Va.), 1964-69; EKG-EEG supr. Vassar Bros. Hosp., Poughkeepsie, N.Y., 1969-74; program dir. Sch. EEG Tech., dir. EEG dept. St. Joseph's Hosp., Tampa, Fla., 1974—; lectr. in field. Author profl. papers. Mem. Am. Soc. EEG Technologists (trustee 1980-82), So. Soc. EEG Technologists (dir. 1978-79), Fla. Soc. EEG Tech. (pres. 1977-79), Internat. Platform Assn., Nat. Assn. Female Execs., Beta Sigma (pres. 1953—), Alpha Nu (life mem., preceptor). Democrat. Club: Tiger-Bay of Tampa. Office: St Joseph's Hosp 3001 W Buffalo Ave Tampa FL 33607

PORTNOY, BARBARA MAE, health care executive; b. St. Louis, May 28, 1949; d. Stanwood Robert and Dorothy (Demba) P. B.A., U. Minn., 1970, M.S. in Hosp. and Health Care Adminstrn., 1980. Cert. advanced credential long term care adminstrn., Minn. Dir. St. Paul Model Cities Sr. Citizen Ctr., 1971-75; exec. adminstr. Willows Convalescent Ctr., Inc., Mpls., 1975-83; dir. ops. Hillhaven Corp., Houston, 1983—; dir. Health Care Group, Inc., Mpls., 1982-83. Contbr. chpt. in Fiscal Leadership, 1983. Named One of Successful Women Under Thirty, Mpls. Sun Newspaper. Fellow Am. Coll. Long Term Care Adminstrs.; mem. Minn. Assn. Health Care Facilities (dir.-at-large 1981, treas. 1982-83, exec. council 1982-83, named Mem. of Yr. 1982, recipient Better Life award for edn. 1982). Office: Hillhaven Corp 6633 Hillcroft Houston TX 77081

PORTNOY, KATHY LYNNE, lawyer; b. St. Louis, June 19, 1953; d. Stanwood Robert and Dorothy (Demba) Portnoy; m. Bruce Warren Callner, Mar. 9, 1983. B.A., SUNY-Stony Brook, 1975; J.D. with distinction, Emory U., 1978. Bar: Ga. 1979, U.S. Ct. Appeals 1978, U.S. Dist. Ct. (11th cir.) 1978. Law clk. State of Ga. Ct. of Appeals, Atlanta, 1978-80; assoc. Alembik, Fine & Callner, P.A., Atlanta, 1980—; assoc. legal counsel Ga. ERA, Atlanta, 1981-83; cons. Ga. State Legislature, Atlanta, 1981—. Contbg. editor Family Law Journal, 1982-83. Vol. lawyer Atlanta Legal Aid Soc., 1980—, Ga. Vol. Lawyers for Arts, Atlanta, 1980—. Mem. ABA, Atlanta Bar Assn., Ga. Bar Assn., Order of Coif. Democrat. Jewish. Club: Atlanta Women's Literary Group (pres. 1983—). Office: Alembik Fine & Callner PA Suite 300 225 Peachtree St NE Atlanta GA 30303

PORUCZNIK, MARY ANN, writer, advertising and public relations consultant; b. Chgo., May 4, 1948; d. John Charles and Anna J. (Malec) P. B.A., St. Xavier Coll., Chgo., 1970; postgrad. Northwestern U., 1971-73, Triton Coll., 1981-82. Editor publs. CAC Ins. Co., Chgo., 1972-75, asst. dir. advt. and sales, 1975; advt. and sales promotion CNA Ins. Co., Chgo., 1975-77; dir. mktg. services N.Am. Co. Life and Health Ins., Chgo., 1977-81; gen. ptnr. Taurus Communications, Oak Park, Ill., 1981-86; profl. writer, Oak Park, 1986—. Mem. Ind. Writers Chgo. (bd. dirs. 1986), Nat. Assn. Female Execs., Direct Mktg. Assn., VFW Aux., NOW (newsletter editor 1985-86), Avocations: filet crochet; camping; cooking; bridge; music. Address: 133 LeMoyne Pkwy Oak Park IL 60302

POSCHMANN, ROBINA CHATALIAN, nurse, guidance counselor, tennis player; b. Providence, Dec. 24, 1916; d. Sarkis and Marina (Davidian) Chatalian; m. George Poschmann, 1940; children—Paul, Ingrid, Christina. R.N. diploma Manhattan State Hosp., 1939; B.S. in Nursing, St. Johns. U., 1958, M.Edn., 1962; student Harvard U., 1960. R.N., N.Y.; cert. guidance counselor, N.Y. Psychiat. nurse N.Y. State Psychiat. Inst., N.Y.C., 1940-43; pediatric-obstet: nurse Glen Cove Community Hosp., N.Y., 1952-55; pub. health nurse Nassau County Dept. Health, Garden City, N.Y., 1955-58; sch. nurse, tchr. Middle Sch., Glen Cove, N.Y., 1958-62; guidance counselor Bethpage High Sch., N.Y., 1962-77. Organist, St. Gertrude's Roman Cath. Ch., Bayville, N.Y., 1962-77; organist, music dir. Holy Family Cath. Ch., Hilton Head, S.C., 1977—. Ranked #1 in age group for state of S.C., S.C. Tennis Assn., 1985; ranked 19th nationally in women's 60 singles, 1985. Mem. Am. Guild Organists, Am. Nurses Assn., U.S. Tennis Assn. (ranked 16th in nation in sr. singles category 1983). Republican. Roman Catholic. Club: Royal Racquet (bd. dirs. Hilton Head, S.C.). Avocation: travel; renaissance and baroque music; tennis. Home: 65 Planters Row Hilton Head SC 29928

POSEY, ELSA, dance educator, artistic director; b. Huntington, N.Y., June 27, 1938; d. Jack Moody and Martha Edna (Kimmick) P.; children—Theo A. D. Novak, Thayer A. C. Novak. Student, Met. Opera Ballet Sch., N.Y.C., 1952-54, Ballet Russe de Monte Carlo, N.Y.C., 1954-56, Sch. Am. Ballet, N.Y.C., 1955-60, Am. Ballet Theatre Sch., N.Y.C., 1954-60, Dance Dept. 92d St., N.Y.C., 1952-58, Dance Notation Bur., N.Y.C., 1966. Co-dir. All About Dance Co., Huntington, N.Y., 1969-76; dir. Posey Dance Co., Huntington, 1976-79, artistic dir., 1980—; artistic dir. L.I. Ballet, Northport, N.Y., 1979-80; pres. Posey Sch. of Dance, Inc., Northport, 1953-85, also dir.; dir. Am. Dance Guild, Inc., N.Y.C., Cultural Arts Inst., Balt. Author: At Ease with Dance, 1979. Mem. Am. Dance Guild (founding mem., pres. 1983-84), Am. Dance Therapy Assn., Council on Research in Dance, Dance Critics Assn., Dance History Scholars, NEA (dance movement specialist). Avocation: sailing. Office: Posey Sch Dance PO Box 254 Northport NY 11768

POSNER, MARY MCCLEARY, public relations executive; b. Kansas City, Mo., Mar. 21, 1939; d. Glenn Avann and Julia Porter (Quinby) McCleary; student Ohio Wesleyan U., 1957-59; A.B., U. Mo., 1961; M.A., Ind. U., 1962; postgrad. N.Y.U., 1967-69; m. Alan Kent Posner, Dec. 27, 1965. Public relations supr. AT&T, N.Y.C., 1962-68; sr. v.p. Harshe-Rotman & Druck, Inc., N.Y.C., 1968-79; pres., owner Posner McCleary Inc., Armonk, N.Y., 1979—. Charles Waldo Haskins assoc. N.Y.U. Sch. Bus. and Pub. Adminstrn. Bd. dirs. Ind. Coll. Fund N.Y., Inc., Westchester County chpt. ARC, 1986—; trustee Ohio Wesleyan U., 1973—, mem. exec. com., 1980—, mem. orgn. com., 1980—. chmn. student affairs com., 1981—; mem. N.Y. Dist. Council, U.S. SBA, 1972-76; mem. N.J. Dist. Export Council, 1980-81; mem. fundraising com. U. Mo. Law Sch. Found., Columbia; mem. regional panel Pres.'s Commn. on White House Fellowships, 1985—. Mem. Internat. Public Relations Assn., Assn. Pvt. Enterprise Edn. Republican. Methodist. Office: PO Box 690 Armonk NY 10504

POSNICK, SUSAN ELAINE, makeup artist; b. Springfield, Mass., Dec. 31, 1951; d. Simon and Florence (Adler) Posnick. B.S. in Edn., Boston U., 1973. Elem. tchr., St. Croix Schs., V.I., 1973-75; makeup cons. Elizabeth Arden, 1975-76; freelance makeup artist, Dallas, 1976-83; owner, makeup artist Surface Ltd., Irving, Tex., 1983—, Dallas, 1984—; cons. in field. Film credits include: The Texas Picture, When She Says No, Face of Rage, Cowboy, All Am. Beauty, Me & Mr. Stenner, He's Not Your Son, Intent to Kill, McMahon Variety Show, NFL Today, many comml. credits. Mem. Dallas Mus. Fine Arts, Tex. Film and Tape Assn., Women in Film. Jewish. Office: Surface Ltd 6309 N O'Connor Irving TX 75039

POST, EDITH, sch. counselor; b. N.Y.C., Mar. 22, 1920; d. Samuel and Sarah (Bucholtz) Dolitzky; B.S., Boston U., 1941, M.S.W., 1943; m. Milton Macy Post, Sept. 8, 1946; chidlren—Andrea Post Rae, Judith Post Yudkoff. Sch. adjustment counselor South Hadley Public Schs., 1966-72; coordintor community-family resources Mt. Holyoke Coll. Learning Devel. Center, 1972-77; counselor Holyoke (Mass.) Public Schs., 1977-81, tchr. support team, 1981-82; pvt. practice counseling, 1982—; cons. Incorporator, Holyoke Vis. Nurse Assn., 1962—; bd dirs. Pioneer Devel. Center, 1978-82; mem. Sch. Improvement Council, Holyoke Pub. Schs., 1985—. Lic. ind. clin. social worker, Mass. Mem. Holyoke Tchrs. Club, Mass. Tchrs. Club, NEA, Nat. Assn. Social Workers, Acad. Cert. Social Workers, Mass. Acad. Psychiat. Social Workers, Delta Kappa Gamma. Home: 1319 Northampton St Holyoke MA 01040

POST, JACKIE EDITH, business executive; b. Lakewood, Ohio, Nov. 17, 1928; d. Sidney Walter and Della N. (Korver) Jackson; B.S. cum laude, Miami U., Oxford, Ohio, 1950; 1 dau., Deborah Downs Cottingham Dryer. Sec. (to Henry Laribee), Laribee & Cooper, Lawyers, Medina, Ohio, 1955-69, (to Baya M. Harrison), Harrison, Greene, Mann, Davenport, et al, Lawyers, St. Petersburg, Fla., 1970-72; corp. sec., sec. to chmn. bd. Jack Eckerd Corp., Clearwater, Fla., 1972—. Mem. Beta Gamma Sigma. Republican. Home: 12666 137th Ln N Largo FL 33544 Office: PO Box 4689 Clearwater FL 33518

POST, MARGARET MOORE, journalist; b. Plainfield, Ind., Aug. 16, 1909; d. Robert Wans and Sara Virginia (Rupe) Stephenson; A.B., La. State U., 1930; L.H.D. (hon.), Franklin (Ind.) Coll., 1973; m. Everett L. Moore, Dec. 4, 1932 (dec. Mar. 1952); children—Jo Ann Moore Long, Sue Ellen Moore Walker; m. H. J. Post, 1970 (div. 1977). Reporter, then city editor Logansport (Ind.) Press, 1930-32; editor Mooresville (Ind.) Times, 1933-38; columnist Indpls. Star, 1932-42; head journalism dept. Franklin Coll., 1942-51; copy editor Indpls. News, 1952-53, with public relations dept. Indpls. Star, also Indpls. News, 1953-68, polit. and feature writer Indpls. News, 1968-84; tchr. journalism Ind. U., Indpls., also Def. Info. Center, Ft. Harrison, Indpls., 1954-56; mem. faculty Sch. Police Adminstrn., U. Louisville, 1973-75; editorial adv. bd. Franklin Coll. Mem. Ind. Criminal Justice Commn., 1969-84, Ind. Juvenile Justice and Deliquency Adv. Bd., 1979-84; mem. crime control panel U.S. C. of C., 1959-74; co-chmn. Ind. 1st Child Abuse Conf., 1977; coordinator Indpls. Anti-Crime Crusade, also Women Against Rape, 1962-75; mem. Presdl. Crime Prevention Commn., 1972; bd. dirs. United Cerebral Palsy Indpls.; founding mem. Ind. Assn. Prevention Blindness, Big Sisters Indpls. Recipient Nat. Recognition award Freedoms Found. at Valley Forge, 1968; 1st pl. award Gen. Fedn. Women's Club-Sears Roebuck Found., 1968; award Ind. Council Juvenile Judges, 1980; Casper Community Services award, 1956, 62, 65, 68, 72, 76, 76; name Sagamore of Wabash, 1970, 78, Ind. Mother of Yr., 1965. Mem. Women in Communications (nat. v.p. 1946-52; Headliner award 1968, Clarion award 1975, 75), Nat. Fedn. Press Women, Women's Press Club Ind., Ind. Acad., Gen. Fedn. Women's Clubs, AAUW, Am. Mothers' Com., Ind. Forum, Delta Gamma Mothers' Club. Republican. Quaker. Author: Wives of Indiana Governors, 1982; Plainfield, Indiana, A Pictorial History, 1986; co-author: The Lawbreakers, 1968. Home: 2805 Barbary Ln Apt E Indianapolis IN 46205 Office: 307 N Pennsylvania St Indianapolis IN 46206

POSTELL, ANNE JOHNSON, educational consultant; b. Willacoochee, Ga., Jan. 28, 1923; d. Edward Wesley and Alma (Phillips) Johnson; m. Winton Postell, June 22, 1943; children—Wynefred Landis, Ida Jeanne, Paula Retta. B.S. cum laude, Savannah State Coll., 1957; M.Ed., N.C. State U., 1968. Tchr. pub. schs., Alma, Ga., 1947-48, Ocilla, Ga., 1948-49; home demonstration agy. Ga. Coop. Extension Service, Washington County, 1957-60, area supr. Negro Home Agy., Savannah State Coll., 1960-65, extension home economist, Athens, 1965-69; home econ. and 4-H leader V.I. Extension Service, St. Croix, 1969-77; cons. Ga. Dept. Edn., Atlanta, 1977—; nutrition cons. Action/Region IV, Atlanta, 1977-78; adminstrv. nutrition specialist Coastal Area Planning and Devel. Com., Brunswick, Ga., 1978-80. Vol. Library for Blind, Athens, 1983-84. Kelloggs Found. fellow, 1967-68; recipient Woman of Achievement award V.I. Bus. and Profl. Woman Club, 1976. Mem. Ga. Sch. Food Service Assn. (dist. adviser 1980—), Am. Sch. Food Service Assn., Ga. Nutrition Council, Eta Phi Beta, Epsilon Sigma Phi. Democrat. Methodist. Lodge: Order Eastern Star. Avocations: macrame; ceramics; sewing; furniture refinishing; hiking. Home: 153 Cole Manor Dr Athens GA 30606

POSTGATE, MARY JAUNITA, medical group administrator; b. Grand Junction, Colo., May 19, 1939; d. Eli Richard and Doris Mae (Davis) Joe; m. John W. Postgate Jr., Sept. 27, 1969; children—John W. III, Jennifer L., Mark S., Julie Ruth, William Skylor, Beverly Jeannine; m. Donald L. Reed (div. 1969); 1 son, Donald Lavern. Student Santa Barbara Bus. Coll., 1961, U. Md., Okinawa, 1973, Bakersfield Coll., 1976-82. Asst. bus. office mgr. Bakersfield Meml. Hosp. (Calif.), 1975-78; account receivable mgr. Mercy Hosp., Bakersfield, 1978-80; credit mgr. Navy Oil Co., Bakersfield, 1981-83; adminstr. Pacific Orthopedic Med. Group, Bakersfield, 1983—; Kern County Imaging, 1984—. Chmn., ARC, Okinawa, 1972. Mem. Am. Soc. Women Accts., Nat. Assn. Accts., Greater Bakersfield C. of C., Women's C. of C. Home: 5737 E Brundage Ln Bakersfield CA 93307

POSTON, ERSA HINES, management consultant; b. Paducah, Ky., May 3, 1921; d. Robert S. and Adele (Johnson) Hines; A.B., Ky. State Coll., 1942; M.S.W., Atlanta U., 1946; LL.D., Union Coll., 1971, Fordham U., 1978; D.H.L., Mercy Coll., 1980. Community orgn. sec. Hartford (Conn.) Tb and Health Assn., 1946-47; teen-age program dir. W. side br. YWCA, N.Y.C., 1947-48, adult dir., 1948-49; asst. dir. Clinton Community Center, N.Y.C., 1949-50; dir., 1950-53; field sec. N.Y.C. Welfare and Health Council, 1953-55; field project supr. N.Y.C. Youth Bd., 1955, asst. dir. program rev., 1955-57; area dir. N.Y. State Div. for Youth, 1957-62, youth work coordinator, 1962-64; confidential asst. to Gov. Rockefeller, 1964; dir. N.Y. State Office Econ. Opportunity, 1964-67; pres. N.Y. State CSC, 1967-75, commr., 1975-77; commr. U.S. CSC, 1977-79; vice-chmn. U.S. Merit Systems Protection Bd., 1979-83; pres. Poston Pub. Personnel Mgmt. Cons., McLean, Va., 1983—; former mem. Internat. CSC; mem. adv. council Federally Employed Women. Former mem. Nat. Commn. to Study goals for State Colls. and Univs.; chmn. Pres.'s Adv. Council Intergovtl. Personnel Policy; v.p. Nat. Urban League; U.S. del. UN Gen. Assembly, 1976; vice presiding officer U.S. Commn. on Observance of Internat. Woman's Yr. Bd. govs. Albany Med. Center Hosp.; bd. dirs. Whitney M. Young Meml. Found. Recipient Achievement awards Bklyn. club Nat. Assn. Negro Bus. and Profl. Women's Clubs; Dutchess of Paducah award; Dau. of Paducah plaque; named Ky. col.; Distinguished Alumni award Ky. State Coll.; Distinguished Service award Greater N.Y. chpt. Links; Woman of Year award Central Jersey club Nat. Assn. Negro Bus. and Profl. Women's Clubs; Achievement award Phi Delta Kappa; Populus Dei award Mercy Coll.; Woman of Year award Utility Club; Outstanding Woman of Year award Iota Phi Lambda; Nat. Achievement award Nat. Assn. Negro BPW Clubs, 1967; Outstanding Service award 26th A.D. Rep. Orgn. Queens County; Trail Blazer award Jamaica Club Nat. Assn. Negro BPW Clubs; Benjamin Potoker Brotherhood award, 1970; named 1970 Woman of Year, BPW Club Albany; Equal Opportunity Day award Nat. Urban League, 1976; Spl. award Psi Nu chpt. Omega Psi Phi, 1977; Disting. Public Servant award Capital Press Club, 1978; Founders' Day award Alpha Kappa Alpha, 1978; First award Nat. Black Personnel Assn., 1978; named to N.Y. State Women's Hall of Fame, 1980; many others. Mem. Nat. Assn. Social Workers, Acad. Cert. Social Workers, Nat. Acad. Public Adminstrn., Am. Soc. Public Adminstrn., Internat. Personnel Mgmt. Assn. (Exec. Bd. award Nat. Capital area 1979, hon. life mem.), Nat. Council Negro Women, Links, Nat. Bus. and Profl. Women, Girlfriends, Inc., Lambda Kappa Mu (hon.; Achievement award Nu chpt.), Alpha Kappa Alpha (outstanding awards Bklyn. chpt. 1960, 65). Club- Zonta. Office: 6709 Melrose Dr McLean VA 22101

POSTON, JO ANN DUDLEY, educator; b. Bloomington, Ill., Apr. 24, 1947; d. Oswald Augustus and Syrene (Dow) Dudley; B.Mus. Edn., Madison Coll., 1968; M.Mus., U. N.C., Greensboro, 1977; postgrad. 1982—; postgrad. Westminster Choir Coll., 1969, 83 m. Paul Wade Poston, Jr., June 22, 1968; 1 dau., Lisa Dow. Choral dir. Lexington (N.C.) City Schs., 1968-70; accompanist N.C. Sch. Arts, Winston-Salem, 1970-71; pvt. paino tchr., Lexington, N.C., 1970—; dir. youth choirs First Presbyn. Ch., Lexington, 1977—; head music div., instr. Davidson County Community Coll., Lexington, 1973—; founder, co-dir. Lexington Women's Choral Soc., 1972—; counselor Jr. Music Club, 1970—; guest condr. Davidson County Chorus/Orch. Mem. exec. bd. Council Creative Arts, 1978-80; bd. dirs. Community Concert Assn. Lexington, 1981—. Grantee Arts Council Davidson County, Council Creative Arts, 1979-82. Mem. Am. Women Composers (state chmn. 1974-77), Nat. Fedn. Music Clubs (life), Nat. Guild Piano Tchrs., Am. Coll. Musicians, Am. Choral Dirs. Assn. (state chmn. two-year and community colls. com., state newsletter editor), Community Coll. Humanities Assn., Lexington Music Study Club (pres. 1972-74), Sigma Alpha Iota, Pi Lambda Kappa. Presbyterian. Clubs: Twin City Track. Home: 900 Nottingham Dr Lexington NC 27292 Office: Davidson County Community Coll Box 1287 Lexington NC 27292

POSZE, MARY ELLEN GENS, travel agency executive; b. Lorain, Ohio, Oct. 25, 1935; d. George F. and Mabel (Strehle) Gens; m. Alex Richard Posze, Aug. 22, 1953 (div. Dec. 1980); children—Jennifer Lynn, Vanessa Elizabeth. Student Baldwin-Wallace Coll., 1965, Miami U., Oxford, Ohio, 1961-63, Kans. State U., 1960. Student Union acct. Kans. State U., Manhattan, 1960; office mgr., asst. to nat. adminstr. Phi Kappa Tau, Oxford, Ohio, 1960-63; Realtor, Taft-Hossfeld, Inc., Berea, Ohio, 1965-75; pres., chief exec. officer Village Sq. Travel, Cleve., 1975—; mem. U.S. Congl. Adv. Bd., Washington, 1985. Mem. Greater Balt. Com., Inc., 1983—. Mem. Am. Soc. Travel Agts., Cleve. Advt. Club, Soc. Travel Agts. in Govt., Assn. Retail Travel Agts., Ohio Bd. Realtors, Cleve. Area Bd. Realtors (trustee), Council Smaller Enterprises, Sales and Mktg. Execs. Cleve., Women's City Club, Greater Cleve. Growth Assn., Berea C. of C. (trustee 1977—), Jacksonville C. of C. Home: 249 Stanford Rd Berea OH 44017 Office: Village Sq Travel Inc 433 W Bagley Rd Berea OH 40417

POTAK, NANCY JEAN, adolescent education administrator, educator; b. Denver, Feb. 2, 1941; d. Paul Joseph and Kathryn Eleanor (Lewis) Foehl; m. David Lee Potak, July 27, 1963; children—Stephen, Katherine, Julie. B.A. in English, Colo. State U., 1963; M.A. in East Asian Studies, Sophia U., Tokyo, 1979. Cert. tchr. N.C. Adult, youth activities dir. YWCA, Raleigh, N.C., 1979-81; br. dir. YWCA of Wake County, Raleigh, 1981-82; health fair project dir. Nat. Health Screening Council, Washington, 1982-84; devel. dir. N.C. Soc. to Prevent Blindness, Raleigh, 1984-85; adolescent edn. supr. Charter Northridge Hosp., Raleigh, 1985—. Program dir. Unitarian Fellowship, Raleigh, 1982-83; state lobbyist League of Women Voters of N.C., Durham, 1979-80; bd. dirs. Planned Parenthood, Raleigh, 1980-81. Mem. Community Edn. Network, LWV. Democrat. Club: Dickens' Disciples. Avocations: tennis, reading, camping, home decorating. Home: 2725 Rosedale Ave Raleigh NC 27607 Office: Charter Northridge Hosp 400 Newton Rd Raleigh NC 27609

POTASH, MARLIN SUE, psychologist; b. Paterson, N.J., Oct. 23, 1951; d. Monroe and Perle (Cohen) P.; B.S. magna cum laude, Tufts U., 1973; M.Ed., Boston U., 1975, Ed.D., 1977; m. Frederick H. Fruitman, Dec. 21, 1981; 1 child, Laura Potash Fruitman. Research assoc. Center for Study of Edn., Yale U., 1976; vis. lectr. Tufts U., 1975-76; instr. Emmanuel Coll., 1975-79; dir. clin. services, resocialization treatment coordinator Columbus Nursing Home, East Boston, 1975-76; asst. prof. behavioral sci., dept. public health and community dentistry Boston U. Sch. Grad. Dentistry, 1977-81, asst. clin. prof., 1981-85; instr. Lesley Coll., 1982-85; adj. asst. prof. Fordham U., 1985—; instr. Radcliffe Seminars, Radcliffe Coll., 1983—, Am. Women's Econ. Devel. Corp., 1985—; pvt. practice psychotherapy, 1979—; assoc. Levinson Inst., Cambridge, Mass. 1980-83; psychol. cons. Middlesex Family and Probate Ct., 1980—, Children's All Day Sch., 1985—. regular guest WCVB-TV Good Day TV program. Trustee, Boston Ballet Soc., 1981-83; commr. human relations Youth Resources Commn. Brookline, chairperson budget com., 1982-84. Diplomate Internat. Acad. Profl. Counseling and Psychotherapy. Fellow Mass. Psychol. Assn. (bd. profl. affairs 1979-82), mem. Am. Psychol. Assn., Am. Orthopsychiat. Assn., Acad. Family Psychology. Club: Boston Luncheon (bd. dirs. 1982-84). Contbr. chpt. to book, articles to profl. jours. Home: 1133 Park Ave New York NY 10128

POTENZA, DAISY MCKASKLE, newspaper executive; b. Houston, Mar. 5, 1906; d. George Washington and Dora Amy (Crump) McKaskle; student Sinclair Bus. Coll., 1925, Massey's Bus. Coll., 1924-26, U. Houston; m. Julius Orian Potenza, Sept. 26, 1928; 1 dau., Marjorie Ann (Mrs. William L. Hale) (dec.). With Houston Chronicle, 1926—, adminstrv. asst. to editor-in-chief, 1930—. Exec. sec. Houston Endowment, Inc., 1968-69; bd. dirs. Pin Oak Charity Horse Show, 1978, 79, 80, 81, 82, 83, 84. Recipient award United Fund, 1967—; tribute for exec. service to Chronicle, 1983; outstanding ticket sales awardee Pin Oak Charity Horse Show, Tex. Children's Hosp., 1975-83. Mem. Nat., Tex. press women, Women in Communications, Press Club Houston (hon. life). Methodist. Club: Farm and Ranch. Home: 2405 San Felipe Rd Houston TX 77019 Office: 801 Texas Ave Houston TX 77002

POTOCZAK, PAULA MARY, lawyer; b. Passaic, N.J., Mar. 31, 1951; d. Francis John and Sophia Dorothea (Siemaszko) P. B.A., Wake Forest U., 1973, J.D., 1976. Bar: D.C. 1977, N.C. 1977, U.S. Supreme Ct. 1981, Va. 1983. Atty., Office Regulations and Rulings, U.S. Dept. Treasury, U.S. Customs Service, Washington, 1976-78; trial atty. Civil Div., U.S. Dept. Justice, Washington, 1978-82, asst. U.S. atty., U.S. Atty.'s Office, Alexandria, Va., 1983—; lectr., inst. Atty. Gen. Advocacy Inst., U.S. Dept. Justice, 1980-81. Holy Trinity Roman Catholic Ch. choir, 1981, 82-84; mem. lawyer alumni exec. com. Wake Forest Sch. Law, 1981-84. Republican. Clubs: Sailing Club of Washington, Sea Robins (Fairfax, Va.). Home: 1401 S Barton St Arlington VA 22204 Office: US Attys Office 701 Prince St Alexandria VA 22314

POTTER, DIANE SUE, social worker; b. Pontiac, Ill., Feb. 17, 1944; d. Claire Snyder and Gladys Frances (Ahrends) P.; B.A., Eureka (Ill.) Coll., 1966; M.S.W., W.Va. U., 1971. Tchr. English, Fairbury (Ill.)-Cropsey High Sch., 1966-67; social worker Lincoln (Ill.) State Sch., 1968-69; adoption social worker The Baby Fold, Normal, Ill., 1971-73; social worker Norwalk (Conn.) Hosp., 1973-77; pediatric social work specialist U. Iowa Hosps. and Clinics, Iowa City, 1977—. Mem. Assn. Care of Children in Hosps., Internat. Assn. Pediatric Social Services (charter). Mem. Disciples of Christ Ch. Home: 1004 Oakwood Coralville IA 52241 Office: Dept Social Service U of Iowa Hosps and Clinics Iowa City IA 52240

POTTER, ELAINE CLARKE, sociology and social science educator; b. Warren, Ohio, Jan. 31, 1935; d. Scot Butler Clarke and Lucy Jean (Spiers) Kellers; m. Ralph Miles, Potter, July 13, 1957; 1 child, Russell Alan. B.A. magna cum laude, Case Western Res. U., 1970; M.A., Kent State U., 1972. Office mgr. McGovern/Shriver Hdqrs., Euclid, Ohio, 1972; instr. sociology Ursuline Coll. for Women, Pepper Pike, Ohio, 1973-74; instr. sociology and soc. sci. Cuyahoga Community Coll., Parma, Ohio, 1975—. Mem. Am. Sociol. Assn., AAUP, North Central Sociol. Assn., Sociologists for Women in Soc., ACLU, NOW, Women's Internat. League for Peace and Freedom (pres. Cleve. chpt. 1975-76), Women Space (v.p. 1980), Phi Beta Kappa, Tri Beta. Democrat. Unitarian. Club: Sierra. Avocations: hiking; reading. Home: 2618 Brainard Rd Pepper Pike OH 44124 Office: Cuyahoga Community Coll West Campus 11000 Pleasant Valley Parma OH 44130

POTTER, ELOISE LILLIAN, editor; b. Norfolk, Va., Feb. 17, 1931; d. James B. and Lillian Doreatha (Rackley) Fretz; m. James McConnell Potter, Jr., June 12, 1950 (div. 1976); children—James Brian, David Theodore, Crystal Lillian Potter Horsley, Patricia Eileen Potter Morgan. Student Meredith Coll., 1949-50. Dir. publs. N.C. State Mus. Natural History, 1985—. Editor The Chat, Raleigh, N.C., 1963—, N.C. Biol. Survey, Raleigh, 1981—. Prin. author: Birds of the Carolinas, 1980; sr. author Rackley: A Southern Colonial Family, 1984. Contbr. numerous ornithol. papers and articles to profl. jours. Pres. Little River Hist. Soc., Zebulon, N.C., 1981; mem. Sampson County Hist. Soc., Clinton, N.C. Mem. Am. Ornithologist Union (life), Northeastern Bird-Banding Assn. (life), Carolina Bird Club. Democrat. Methodist. Home: Route 3 Box 114AA Zebulon NC 27597 Office: NC State Mus Natural History PO Box 27647 Raleigh NC 27611

POTTER, EMMA JOSEPHINE HILL, foreign language educator; b. Hackensack, N.J., July 18, 1921; d. James Silas and Martha Loretta (Pyle) Hill; A.B. cum laude with honors, in Classics, Alfred (N.Y.) U., 1943; A.M., Johns Hopkins U., 1946; m. James H. Potter, Mar. 26, 1949. Tchr. Latin, Baltimore County Public Schs., 1943-44; instr. French and Spanish, Balt. Poly. Inst., 1950-83, trustee James Harry Potter Gold medal; instr. Spanish adult edn. classes, 1946-48; sec.-treas. Bruno-Potter Inc., accts., 1980—. Mem. NEA. Md. Edn. Assn., Johns Hopkins U. Alumni Assn., Alfred U. Alumni Assn. Democrat. Roman Catholic. Club: Johns Hopkins U. Faculty.

POTTER, EVELYN GOODWIN, executive recruiter; b. Dumont, N.J.; d. Russell M. and Marie (Hermida) Goodwin; B.A., U. Mich., 1949; m. Neil Potter, June 30, 1950; children—Eugene, Jill. Exec. sec. Office Bd. Trustees, SUNY, N.Y.C., 1950-52; asst. to dir. Profl. Exam. Service, Am. Public Health Assn., 1953-54; dir. public relations SUNY Downstate Med. Center, Bklyn., 1954-75, asst. to pres., 1967-75; v.p. univ. relations Clark U., Worcester, Mass.,

1975-77; v.p. The Cantor Concern, N.Y.C., 1977—; cons. health careers N.Y.C. Bd. Edn., 1963-69; mem. com. on health careers Empire State Health Council, 1964—; public relations com. Council Higher Ednl. Instns. in N.Y.C., 1961-69; bd. dirs. N.Y.C. Health Planning Agy., 1974-75, West Midwood Assn., 1964-65. Recipient certificate of merit Acad. Hosp. Public Relations, 1972, Award Community Agys. Public Relations Assn., 1975. Mem. Assn. Am. Med. Colls., Nat. Assn. Sci. Writers, Am. Coll. Pub. Relations Assn. (citation of merit 1959, 72), Met. Coll. Pub. Relations Assn., Health and Welfare Pub. Relations Soc. (charter mem., dir., chmn. publs. com.), Nat. Assn. Corp. and Profl. Recruiters, Council Advancement and Support Edn. Club: Boston Press. Author: Medical Education in Brooklyn-The First 100 Years, 1960. Home: Westbourne Alger Ct Bronxville NY 10708 Office: The Cantor Concern 171 Madison Ave New York NY

POTTER, JANET LOUISE, librarian; b. Oneonta, N.Y., Oct. 24, 1947; d. R. Waldo and Emily G. (Bain) P. B.A., SUNY-Albany, 1969, M.L.S., 1973; M.A. in History, SUNY-Binghamton, 1979. Reference librarian SUNY-Oneonta, 1973—. Bd. dirs. SUCO Children's Ctr., 1983—. Mem. ALA, N.Y. Librarians Assn., United Univ. Professions (chpt. v.p., negotiations team 1981—), SUNY Librarians Assn. (treas. 1979-81). Office: Milne Library SUNY Oneonta NY 13820

POTTER, NANCY DUTTON, psychologist; b. St. Joseph, Mo., Jan. 16, 1946; d. Paul Vernon and Rosa Lee (Hatfield) Dutton; B.A., Pitzer Coll., 1968; M.A., U. Kans., 1971; Ph.D., U. Mo., 1974; postgrad. Georgetown U., 1977-79; 1 dau., Blakeslee Ann. Chief clin. psychology Keesler AFB Med. Center, Miss., 1976-77; clin. psychologist Malcolm Grow Med. Center, Andrews AFB, Md., 1977-78; asso. dir. Georgetown U. Counseling Center, 1978-79, acting dir., 1979-80, dir. internship tng., 1978-81; pvt. practice psychology, Va. and Md., 1978—. Bd. dirs. Family Counseling Agy., Biloxi, Miss. Served to maj. USAF, 1974—. Lic. psychologist, D.C., Md., Va. Mem. Am. Psychol. Assn., Am. Personnel and Guidance Assn., No. Va. Soc. Clin. Pathologists (v.p. 1984—). Home: 7400 Carath Ct Springfield VA 22153 Office: 5206-B Rolling Rd Burke VA 22015

POTTER, PAMELA LYNNE, veterinarian; b. New Orleans, Dec. 7, 1954; d. George Edward and Betty (Sievers) Potter. D.V.M., La. State U., 1978; student Okla. State U., 1972-74. Zookeeper, Audubon Park Zoo, New Orleans, 1975; fellow in lab. animal medicine U. Mo., 1976; preceptorship St. Louis Zoo, 1977; companion animal, exotic and avian practitioner E. Orleans Vet. Hosp., New Orleans, 1978-80; owner Aark Animal Hosp., Slidell, La., 1980—. Mem. AVMA, Assn. Veterinarians for Animal Rights (dir.), Greenpeace Internat. Home: 120 Rue de la Paix Slidell LA 70461 Office: Aark Animal Hosp 2103 Gause Blvd Slidell LA 70461

POTTER, SHARON MARIE, journalist, editor; b. Sioux City, Iowa, Mar. 7, 1952; d. John Wesley and Elaine Blanche (Tozier) Servine; m. Richard Ora Potter III, Sept. 12, 1975; children—Ryan Matthew, Jeffrey John. Student U. Nebr., 1970-73, U. Mont., 1985—. Pub. info. specialist State of Nebr., Lincoln, 1972-76; manuals editor Hy-Gain Electronics, Lincoln, 1976-77; news editor Sun Newspapers, Lincoln, 1977-80; advt. exec. News-Record, Gillette, Wyo., 1980-81, living editor, 1982-84, spl. feature writer, 1984-85; student writing judge Wyo. Press Women's Assn., Gillette, 1983, 84. Organizer, Campbell County PTO, Gillette, 1983; mem. parents adv. council Sunflower Elem. Sch., Gillette, 1984; mem. Russell Elem. PTA, Missoula. Mem. NOW, Wyo. Press Assn., Women's Internat. Bowling Congress. Republican. Lutheran.

POTTORF, COILA MAE, genealogist, researcher; b. Woodston, Kans., Dec. 11, 1907; d. Will and Cora Maude (Darrow) Richards; children—Bill Roy, Cora Ann Pottorf Skitt. Cert. in Music Edn., Ft. Hays State U., 1927; B.A., U. Denver, 1967, M.A., 1970; postgrad. U. Colo., 1970. Music instr. Consol. Schs., Hygiene, Colo., 1928-32; sr. library asst. Colo. State Library, Denver, 1962-67, jr. librarian Library for Blind, 1968-69, librarian, documentarian, 1970-76; self-employed researcher, genealogist, Denver, 1976—. Author: Historical Notes: Maidu and Cochiti Indian Tribes, 1965; Sigillography, 1964. Vol. for aging, Denver, 1932—; vol. ch. activities, Woodston, Kans. and Denver, 1920 . Recipient commendations Colo. Gov. J. VanDerhoof, 1974, State Dept. Edn., 1976, cert. of merit Colo. State Bd. Edn., 1975; proclamation Colo. Gov. Richard D. Lamm, 1976; Colo. State Library grantee, Denver, 1967-69; Denver U. Library Sch. scholar, 1968. Mem. Internat. Platform Assn., Western Hist. Assn., Archives Assoc., Nat. Geneal. Soc. Club: Eagles (Orange Grove, Calif.). Lodges: Order Eastern Star. Office: Coila M Pottorf Research Cons 2710 S High St Denver CO 80210

POTTS, BARBARA JOYCE, mayor, radiology technician; b. Los Angeles, Feb. 18, 1932; d. Theodore Thomas and Helen Mae (Kelley) Elledge; m. Donald A. Potts, Dec. 27, 1953; children—Tedd, Douglas, Dwight, Laura Potts Ahrenholtz. A.A., Graceland Coll., 1951; cert. Radiol. Tech. Sch., 1953. Radiol. technician Independence Sanitarium and Hosp., Mo., 1953, 58-59, St. Mary's Hosp., Balt., 1954-55; city council mem.-at-large City of Independence, 1978-82, mayor, 1982—; bd. dirs. Mo. Mcpl. League, Jefferson City, 1982—; chmn. Mid.-Am. Regional Council, Kansas City, Mo., 1984-85. Pres., Child Placement Services, Independence, 1972—; mem. Mo. Gov.'s Conf. on Edn., 1976; mem. Independence Charter Rev. Bd., 1977; bd. dirs. Hope House Shelter for Abused Women, Independence, 1982—; trustee Independence Sanitarium and Hosp., 1982—; chmn. Mo. Commn. Local Govt. Cooperation, 1985-88. Recipient Woman of Achievement award Mid-Continent Council Girl Scouts U.S.A., 1983, Jane Adams award Hope House Shelter for Battered Women, 1984, Community Leadership award Comprehensive Mental Health Services, Inc., 1984. Mem. Nat. Women's Polit. Caucus, LWV. Mem. Reorganized Ch. of Jesus Christ of Latter-day Saints. Home: 18508 E 30th Terr Independence MO 64057 Office: City of Independence City Hall 111 E Maple Independence MO 64050

POTTS, CALLIE ANN, postal executive; b. Lexington, Ky., Apr. 24, 1945; d. Edward E. and Frances (Logdon) Roberts; student Ind. U.; m. James L. Potts, June 2, 1973; children—Robert Sparks, Paul Sparks, Mark Sparks. With U.S. Postal Service, Louisville, 1969—, opns. analyst, 1978-81, dir. mail processing, 1981—. Recipient Equal Opportunity award U.S. Postal Service, 1978, Meritorious Service citation, 1980. Mem. Nat. Assn. Female Execs., Fed. Employeed Women. Home: Route 3 Box 156J Floyds Knobs IN 47119 Office: 1420 Gardiner Ln Louisville KY 40231

POTTS, LINDA FRANCES, lawyer; b. Mayfield, Ky., Oct. 3, 1947; d. George Harold and Annabele Frances (Stamps) Potts. Student, So. Mct. U., 1972-73; B.S., U. Tenn.-Knoxville, 1967, J.D., 1970; LL.M., London U., 1971; Cert. Internat. Law, City of London Coll., 1969. Bar: D.C. 1980, Fla. 1981, U.S. Ct. Appeals, 1981, Ct. Internat. Trade 1984. Lectr./instr. So. Meth. U. Law Sch., Dallas, 1972-73; asst. dir. Office Tariff Affairs, U.S. Dept. Treasury, Washington, 1979; dir. Office of Policy, ITA, U.S. Dept. Commerce, Washington, 1981-82; pvt. practice law, Washington, 1983-84; now ptnr. Potts & Kalik, Washington. Contbr. articles to profl. jours. Cox scholar, 1967-68; Green scholar, 1968-69. Fellow So. Meth. U. Law Sch., 1972-73. Mem. ABA, Am. Soc. Internat. Law, Phi Kappa Phi, Alpha Omicron Pi. Episcopalian. Office: Potts & Kalik 1725 K St NW Washington DC 20006

POTTS, TONI S., artist, actress; b. Big Spring, Tex., June 11, 1953; d. Winifred Berl and Violet B. (Nelms) Potts. Grad. Tex. Tech U., 1973. Piping designer Ortloff Corp., Midland, Tex., 1973-76; owner Texstar Prodns., Houston, 1976—; comedy actress Comedy Workshop, Houston, 1980-83; Tech. designer Taylor & Assocs., Houston, 1982-83; artist Houston Comical, 1983—; writer, actress Sta. KUHT-TV, Houston, 1983—. Mem. Nacho Revue Bd. Democrat. Author: P.I.G.S. (Purely Imaginary Graphics of Swine), 1980. Writer, Actress (film) Happy Birthday Vacation, 1980.

POTTSDAMER, JESSIE DREW, educational administrator; b. Tallahassee, Oct. 15; d. Clarence and Rachel (Messer) Drew; m. Vinzant Augustus Pottsdamer; children—Gina Maria, Vinita Denise. B.S. cum laude, Fla. A&M U., 1965; M.S. in Library Sci., Atlanta U., 1971, Ed.S., 1976; postgrad. W. Ga. Coll.; Ed.L., Ga. State U. Itinerant librarian Leon County Schs., Tallahassee, 1965-66; reference librarian Fla. A&M U., Tallahassee, 1966-68; media specialist, Fulton County Schs., Atlanta, 1966-82, prin., 1982—; cons. Fla. A&M U., 1975, Cobb County Schs., So. Assn. Colls. and Schs., Atlanta, 1980—, Cath. Diocese Atlanta, 1981. Author: An Evaluation of the Learning Media Services, 1975; (booklet) How to Work as an Aide, 1967; (handbook) World Media Manual, 1972. Active, United Negro Coll. Fund, High Mus. Art, Nat. PTA, Greater Tri Cities Task Force; supr. task force Goals and Objectives for Fulton County Schs. Mem. ALA, NAACP, Friends of Atlanta Pub. Library, Fulton County Assn. Educators, Ga. Assn. Educators, NEA, Ga. Assn. Elem. Sch. Prins., Nat. Assn. Elem. Sch. Prins. (program presenter 1983), Fulton County Elem. Prins. Assn. (v.p.), Am. Assn. Curriculum Leaders, Fla. A&M Alumni Assn., Atlanta Urban League, Nat. Council Negro Women, Delta Sigma Theta, Beta Phi Mu. Democrat. Episcopalian. Club: Atlanta Chums (pres.). Home: PO Box 42798 Atlanta GA 30311 Office: Love T Nolan Elementary Sch 2725 Creel Rd College Park GA 30349

POULOS, CLARA JEAN, nutritionist, biologist; b. Los Angeles, Jan. 1, 1941; d. James P. and Clara Georgie (Creighton) Hill; Ph.D. in Biology, Fla. State Christian U., 1974; Ph.D. in Nutrition, Donsbach U., 1979; m. Themis Poulos, Jan. 31, 1960. Dir. research Leapou Lab., Aptos, Calif., 1973-76, Monterey Bay Research Inst., Santa Cruz, Calif., 1976—; nutrition specialist, Santa Cruz, 1975—, dir. nutrition-health enhancement and lifestyle planning systems; instr. Santa Cruz Extention U. Calif. and Stoddard Assos. Seminars; cons. Biol-Med. Lab., Chgo., Nutra-Med Research Corp., N.Y., Akorn-Miller Pharmacal, Chgo., Monterey Bay Aquaculture Farms. Recipient Najulander Internat. Research award, 1971, Wainwright Found. award., 1979, various state and local awards. Fellow Internat. Coll. Applied Nutrition, Am. Nutritionist Assn., Internat. Acad. Nutritional Consultants; mem. Am. Diabetes Assn. (profl., pres. chpt.), AAAS, Internat. Platform Soc., Am. Public Health Assn., Calif. Acad. Sci., Internat. Fishery Assn. (health asct.), Club: Toastmistress. Author: Alcoholism—Stress—Hypoglycemia, 1976; The Relationship of Stress to Alcoholism and Hypoglycemia, 1979; contbr. articles to profl. jours. Office: 1595 Soquel Dr Suite 222 Santa Cruz CA 95065

POULTON, ROBERTA DORIS, nurse; consultant; b. Balt., Oct. 19, 1943; d. Charles Robert and Mary Doris (Guercio) P. Nursing diploma Md. Gen. Hosp., 1964. Staff nurse Md. Gen. Hosp., Balt., 1964-67, Project Hope, Columbia, 1967, Tunisia, 1969-70; staff nurse St. Agnes Hosp., Balt., 1968-69, team leader, 1972-83, staff nurse-preceptor, 1983—; cons., Girl Scouts U.S.A., Balt., 1972—, Bapt. Conv. Md., 1963—. Vol. CPR instr. ARC, Balt., 1972—. Mem. Am. Nurses Assn., Md. Nurses Assn., Am. Assn. Critical Care Nurses, Appalachian Trial Conf. Democrat. Baptist.

POUNCY, MATTIE HUNTER, elementary educator; b. Sardis, Ala., July 20, 1924; d. Thomas and Margaret (Jordan) Hunter; m. Hillard Warren Pouncy, Jr., Oct. 12, 1947; 1 child, Hillard Warren III. B.S., Tuskegee Inst., 1948; cert. behavioral disorders in handicapped people, 1961; cert. in value clarification Rutgers U., 1964; handicapped cert. Newark State U., 1968; M.A., Trenton State U., 1977; cert. computer programming Inst. for Profl. Devel., Princeton, 1983. Cert. tchr., N.J., Ala., Ind. Elem. sch. tchr., Union Springs, Ala., 1952-55, New Brunswick, N.J., 1962-67, Plainfield, N.J., 1974—; tchr. handicapped, Gary, Ind., 1959-61, Franklin Twp., N.J., 1967-73; co-founder Princeton Diagnostic Learning Ctr., N.J., 1973-74; lectr. in Black history and civil rights movement, Princeton, 1985—. Author: Reach A Little Deeper, 1985; In Search of Self, 1987. Mem. N.J. Republican State Com., Trenton, N.J., 1984—, Rep. Presdl. Task Force, Washington, 1984—; bd. dirs. Somerset County Assn. for Retarded People, 1970-74. Fed. Title I grantee, 1968, N.J. Title IV grantee, 1983. Mem. Tuskegee Alumni Assn. (Outstanding Service cert. of Honor 1985), African-Am. Women Writers in N.J., Trenton State Coll. Alumni Assn., Nat. Hist. Soc., NEA, N.J. Edn. Assn., Exec. Female, Kappa Delta Pi. Mem. Assembly of God Ch. Avocations: travel; softball; writing; board games. Home: 157 Mansgrove Rd Princeton NJ 08540

POUNDS, JANET LYNN, chemist; b. Dallas, Nov. 29, 1944; d. Truman Edward and Marilynn (Carlton) P.; B.A. in Chemistry, La. State U., 1966, M.S. in Organic Chemistry, 1969; m. Richard Miles Bowen, July 19, 1980; 1 dau., Kristina. Grad. teaching asst. La. State U., 1966-69; tchr. sci. Baker (La.) Jr. High Sch., 1969-70; instr. chemistry So. U., Baton Rouge, 1972-77; research chemist PPG Industries, Corpus Christi, Tex., 1977-80, research chemist, Barberton, Ohio, 1980-85, sr. research chemist, Barberton, 1985—. NIH fellow, 1978. Mem. NOW (La. legis. coordinator 1973-74, ERA coordinator 1974-75), Am. Chem. Soc. Episcopalian. Clubs: Akron All-Breed Dog, Akron Ski. Home: 3097 Baughman Rd Clinton OH 44216 Office: PO Box 31 Barberton OH 44203

POUPORE, NORMA CAREY, former motel executive; b. Burke, N.Y., Sept. 14, 1929; d. Matthew Gabriel and Laura Anna (Moore) Carey; m. Bernard Charles Poupore, Feb. 16, 1952; children—Kevin, Barry, Casey, Michael. Grad. Adirondack Bus. Sch., 1946. With Marine Midland Banks, Malone and Syracuse, N.Y., 1946-53, legal stenographer local attys. and Office Ct. Adminstrn., State of N.Y., 1954-80; owner, operator Gateway Motel, Malone, 1962-86. Mem. Farm Bur. Extension Service (bd. dirs.), Grange, Malone C. of C., Hotel-Motel Assn., Catholic Daus. Am. Republican. Roman Catholic. Club: Malone Golf and Country (bd. dirs.). Lodge: Elks. Avocations: golf; bowling; reading. Home: Whippleville Rd Malone NY 12953

POVLSEN, SHIRLEY, county official; b. Idaho Falls, Idaho, Feb. 26, 1927; d. Rulon Ira Stoker and Louise (Ellsworth) Stoker Brown; m. Walter C. Povlsen, Nov. 23, 1947; children—Catherine J. Povlsen Harwood, Robert R., John W., Eric T., Lori Povlsen Kunz. Student Woodbury Coll., 1945-46. With Agrl. Stblzn. and Conservation Service, U.S. Dept. Agr., Burley, Idaho, 1965-68; treas. Cassia County, Idaho, 1968—. State committeewoman Cassia County Republican Central Com., 1976-83, sec.-treas., 1969. Mem. Idaho Assn. County Treas. (pres. 1974-75), Idaho Assn. Counties (bd. dirs. 1980—), Nat. Assn. County Treas. and Fin. Officers (bd. dirs. 1983—), Burley C. of C. (pres. 1976). Mormon. Lodge: Soroptimist Internat. (pres. Burley 1975-76, gov. Rocky Mountain region 1984-86). Avocations: golfing; snow skiing; camping.

POWELL, ANICE CARPENTER, librarian; b. Moorhead, Miss., Dec. 2, 1928; d. Horace Aubrey and Celeste (Brian) Carpenter; student Sunflower Jr. Coll., 1945-47, Miss. State Coll. Women, 1947-48; B.S., Delta State Coll., 1961, M.L.S., 1974; m. Robert Wainwright Powell, July 19, 1948; children—Penelope Elizabeth, Deborah Alma. Librarian, Sunflower (Miss.) Pub. Library, 1958-61; tchr. English, Isola (Miss.) High Sch., 1961-62; dir. Sunflower County Library, Indianola, Miss., 1962—; mem. adv. council State Instl. Library Services, 1967-71; mem. adv. bd. library services and constrn. act com. Miss. Library Commn., 1978-80. Mem. ALA, Miss. Library Assn. (exec. dir. Nat. Library Week 1975, steering com. 1976, chmn. right to read com. 1976, chmn. legis. com. 1979, chmn. intellectual freedom com. 1975, 80, mem. legis. com. 1973-86, chmn. membership com. 1982, pres. 1984, chmn. nominating com. 1986; Peggy May award 1981), Sunflower County Hist. Soc. (pres. 1983-86), Miss. Literacy Assn., Delta Council, Sunflower County Literacy Council (treas.). Methodist. Home: Box 310 Sunflower MS 38778 Office: Sunflower County Library 201 Cypress Dr Indianola MS 38751

POWELL, BARBARA, clinical psychologist; b. Dexter, Mo., Apr. 25, 1929; d. Clarence Albert and Ethel (Mohrstadt) P.; B.A., Wellesley Coll., 1950; M.A., Columbia U., 1967; Ph.D., Fordham U., 1975; m. Richard W. O'Neill, Jan. 3, 1953 (div. 1966); children—Richard W., Susan P., Jennifer A., Julia K.; m. 2d, Charles J. McCarthy, May 13, 1967 (div. 1978); m. 3d, David S. Burt, June 16, 1983. Copywriter, Parade mag., 1951-52, McCall's, 1952-53; publicity dir. Silvermine Guild Art, New Canaan, Conn., 1964-66; reporter Bridgeport (Conn.) Post, 1964-69; psychologist Dunlap & Assos., Darien, Conn., 1966-67; dir. Guidance Center for Women, U. Conn., 1968-69; intern N.Y. Hosp., Westchester, 1972-73; psychologist St. Mary's in-the-field, Valhalla, N.Y., 1973-77, Behavior Therapy Inst., White Plains, N.Y., 1975-78; pvt. practice clin. psychology, Rowayton, Conn., 1976—; lectr. U. Conn., 1976-77; co-founder, assertive tng. leader Woman's Place, Darien. USPH grantee, 1970-71. Mem. Am. Psychol. Assn., Am. Assn. Marriage and Family Therapists, Am. Assn. Advancement Behavior Therapy, Soc. Clin. and Exptl. Hypnosis, Phi Beta Kappa, Sigma Xi. Author: Careers for Women after Marriage and Children, 1965; How to Raise a Successful Daughter, 1979; Overcoming Shyness, 1979; The Complete Guide to Your Child's Emotional Health, 1984; Alone, Alive and Well, 1985; Good Relationships Are Good Medicine, 1987. Address: 20 Covewood Dr Rowayton CT 06853

POWELL, CHARLENE LITTLEJOHN, educational administrator; b. Marshall County, Ky., June 5, 1911; d. Charles Clyde and Ila Gertrude (Chumbler) Littlejohn; B.S., Murray State U., 1936, M.A., 1960, postgrad., 1961; m. Harry Elmore Powell (dec. 1967). Tchr. pub. schs. Calvert City, Ky., 1932-35, Gilbertsville, Ky., 1939-43; chemist Ky. Ordnance Works, Paducah, 1943-46; prin. Farley Elem. Sch., Paducah, 1947-76; supr. Adult Basic Edn. Program, Night Sch., Paducah, 1967-76. Treas., Reidland Farley Vol. Fire Assn., 1955. Recipient Service award Boy Scouts Am., 1966, Honor award Soil Conservation Dist. Bd. Suprs., 1974, McCrocken County Fiscal Ct. award, 1976, resolution of appreciation McCrocken County Bd. Edn., 1976. Named Citizen of Year, Southside Kiwanis Club, Paducah, 1969, Duchess of Paducah, City of Paducah, 1970, Ky. col., 1976. Mem. McCrocken County Tchrs. Credit Union (clk. 1962—), Murray Alumni Assn. (life), PTA (life), Am. Assn. Ret. Persons (pres. chpt. 1983-84), Nat., Ky., McCrocken (past pres.) edn. assns., Ky., Western Ky. suprs. assns., First Dist. Ret. Tchrs. Assn. (sec. 1979-80, treas.-elect 1979-80), Paducah-McCrocken County Ret. Tchrs. Assn. (pres.-elect 1979-80, pres. 1980-81, v.p. 1985-86). Democrat. Baptist. Home: Route 13 Box 432 Paducah KY 42001

POWELL, DIANA KEARNY, lawyer, poet; b. Washington, Apr. 15, 1910; d. William Glasgow and Alice Van Voorhees (Joline) P.; LL.B., Columbus U., 1940, LL.M., 1942; A.A., George Washington U., 1945; postgrad. Law Sch. Georgetown U., 1957. Admitted to D.C. bar, 1940, U.S. Supreme Ct. bar, 1959; practice law, Washington; contbr. poetry to various mags., 1930—; poetry recitations. Precinct chmn. Republican Party, 1965-68, co-chmn., 1972-75; mem. various campaign coms.; sec. Sodality Holy Name Soc. of St. Matthew's Cathedral, 1978-81, chmn. workshop com., 1975—, pres., 1981-83; mem. Republican Presdl. Task Force, 1982. Recipient various local and nat. poetry awards Nat. League Am. Pen Women; cert. of appreciation Anchor Mental Health Assn., 1975. Mem. ABA, Nat. Assn. Women Lawyers, Internat. Platform Assn, Saintpaulia Internat. Roman Catholic. Author: Poems by Powell, 1986. Asso. editor: Washington Vistas, 1953. Office: 1500 Massachusetts Ave NW Washington DC 20005

POWELL, DORIS B., sales representative; b. Aberdeen, Miss., Oct. 15, 1951; d. Titus Theopolis and Josephine (Cockerham) P. B.S., So. Ill. U. Tchr. Chgo. Bd. Edn., 1975-80; health claims adjuster Kemper Ins., Long Grove, Ill., 1980-82; sales cons. ITT Edn. Services, Chgo., 1982—. Voters registration vol. Chgo., 1984; coordinator Walk Am. Am. Cancer Soc., Chgo. and DuPage County, 1982, 83; bike rider Sickle Cell Anemia Midwest Assn., Chgo., 1977, 81, 83; community action vol. PanHellenic Community Action Council, Chgo., 1983; bd. dirs. Community Health Program, 1984-85. Named Employee of Month ITT Edn. Services, Mem. Nat. Assn. Female Execs., Toastmasters (parliamentarian 1985—, edn. v.p. 1986, Best Speaker award 1985). Democrat. Presbyterian. Avocations: gourmet cooking; reading; swimming; traveling.

POWELL, DOROTHY JEAN, banker; b. Nocona, Tex., Nov. 15, 1927; d. Arthur William and Bertie Belle (McMurtry) McNabb; student Kilgore Coll., 1945-46, Joliet Jr. Coll., 1965-68, Lewis U., 1969-71; m. Robert E. Powell, Apr. 16, 1948; children—Elizabeth Joyce, Patrick Vernon. Clk., First Nat. Bank, Longview, Tex., 1946-47; teller, bookkeeper Cleveland Nat. Bank (Tenn.), 1947-49; sec. to dean students Lewis U., Lockport, Ill., 1965-67; v.p., cashier Heritage First Nat. Bank, Lockport, 1967-82, pres., 1982—, dir., 1978—. Mem. Nat. Assn. Bank Women (state chmn. Ill. group 1976-77), Zonta Internat., Am. Soc. Profl. and Exec. Women, Lockport Bus. and Profl. Women's Club (pres. 1976-77). Home: 706 State St Lemont IL 60439 Office: 800 State St Lockport IL 60441

POWELL, ELINOR VAN DYKE, business executive, nurse, educator; b. Sedalia, Mo., Mar. 20, 1937; d. Frank B. and Mary Irene (Sims) Van Dyke; B.S. in Nursing, U. Mo., 1960, B.S. in Music Edn., 1973, M.Ed., 1978; m. Ira C. Powell, Dec. 31, 1974; children—Stephen, Michelle, Matthew Gaunt. Tchr. public schs., Columbia, Mo., 1974-78; co-founder, co-owner, dir. Galaxy Games, Inc., 1977—, now v.p.; co-owner Galaxy Assocs.; mem. faculty Stephens Coll.; nurse U. Mo.-Columbia Med. Center. Dir. children's choir United Meth. Ch., Columbia, 1964-74; pres. Boone County Assn. Mental Health; pres. Columbia Panhellenic Council; steward Mo. United Meth. Ch. Mem. Am. Choral Dirs. Assn., Mo. Music Educators Assn., Music Educators Nat. Conf., AAUW, U. Mo. Nursing Alumni Assn. (past pres.), Central Mo. Mortarboard Alumni Assn. (pres.), Delta Delta Delta. Republican. Office: PO Box 1802 Columbia MO 65201

POWELL, ERNESTINE BREISCH, lawyer; b. Moundsville, W.Va., Feb. 16, 1906; d. Ernest Elmer and Belle (Wal-lace) Breisch; student Dayton YMCA Law Sch., 1929; m. Roger K. Powell, Nov. 15, 1935; children—R. Keith (dec.), Diane L.D., Bruce W. Admitted to Ohio bar, 1929; tax analyst tax dept. Wall, Cassell & Groneweg, Dayton, Ohio, 1929-31; pvt. practice law, 1931-40, gen. counsel for Dayton Jobbers amd Mfrs. Assn., 1931-41; mem. firm Powell and Powell, Columbus, Ohio, 1944—. Ohio chmn. Nat. Woman's Party, Washington, 1950-51, nat. chmn., 1953-54, hon. nat. chmn. Pres. vol. activities com. Columbus State Sch., 1960-61, trustee, 1957-59. Mem. Nat. Assn. Women Lawyers, Am., Ohio, Columbus bar assns., Nat. Soc. Arts and Letters (pres. Columbus chpt. 1963-64), Nat. Lawyers Club (charter mem.). Co-author: Tax Ideas, 1955; Estate Tax Techniques, 3 vols., 1955-84. Editor-in-chief: Women Lawyers Jour., 1943-45. Office: 1382 Neil Ave Columbus OH 43201

POWELL, GLADYS LUCRECIA, corporate secretary; b. Beacon, N.Y., Jan. 9, 1951; d. Jack L. and Lucrecia (Cambrelen) Cooper; m. July 6, 1969 (div. 1979); children—Andrea Enid, Curtis S. A.A.S. with honors, Dutchess Community Coll., Poughkeepsie, N.Y., 1975; B.S. cum laude in Bus. Administrn., Marist Coll., Poughkeepsie, 1977. Jr. auditor, Central Hudson Gas & Electric Corp., Poughkeepsie, 1977-78, jr. personnel asst., 1978-81, info. specialist, 1981-82, news dir., 1982-83, asst. sec., 1983-84, corp. sec., 1984—; mem. bus. adv. com. Dutchess Community Coll., 1985—; mem. Vassar Bros. Hosp. Assn., 1985—. Bd. dirs. Dutchess County Community Action Agy., Millbrook, N.Y., 1983 , YWCA of Dutchess Co., Poughkeepsie, 1983—; chmn. employee campaign United Way, 1985, mem. central allocations div., Poughkeepsie, 1985—. Mem. Am. Soc. Corp. Secs., Nat. Assn. Female Execs., Zeta Phi Beta. Avocations: horseback riding; golf; spectator sports. Office: Central Hudson Gas & Electric Corp 284 South Ave Poughkeepsie NY 12601

POWELL, JENNY LYNN, newsletter editor; b. Atlanta, Aug. 14, 1960; d. John Robert and Betty Joyce (Brown) Powell. B.A. in Journalism, Ga. State U., 1982. Newsletter editor Crawford Long Hosp., Atlanta, 1981—. Recipient Am. Legion cert. of Disting. Achievement, 1978. Mem. Soc. Profl. Journalists, Women in Communications, Inc. Republican. Baptist.

POWELL, JOY LEE (LEE, BOK SIN), antique dealer, importer; b. Pyong-Yang, Korea, Jan. 29, 1936; came to U.S., 1956, naturalized, 1962; d. Yong Joon and Chn Jai Lee; m. Jimmy Wayne Powell, Sept. 24, 1960 (div. June 1976); children—Chn Jai Lee, Miran Victoria. Student McMurry Coll., Abilene, Tex., 1956-58; B.A., Wayland Baptist U., Plainview, Tex., 1966; postgrad. Central State Coll., Okla., 1967-68. Cert. antique appraiser and consultant. Nurse, Rok Med. Sch. Korea, Pusan, 1950-53; news announcer Pusan Radio Sta., Korea, 1953; tchr. Oklahoma City Sch. Systems, 1968-70; antique dealer, importer Fairfax, Va., 1973—. Contbr. (poetry) New Voices in American Poetry, 1978. Contbr. poems and essays to Korean periodicals. Mem. Nat. Bus. Assn., World Affairs Council Washington, Nat. Assn. Female Execs., Internat. Student House. Avocations: art; painting; music; writing; swimming. Home: 4302 Silas Hutchinson Dr Chantilly VA 22021 Office: PO Box 185 Chantilly VA 22021

POWELL, LOUISA ROSE, psychologist; b. Highland Park, Mich., Oct. 10, 1942; d. Albert and Mildred Loraine (Bos) Feldman; B.S., Roosevelt U., 1966; M.S., U. Chgo., 1969, Ph.D., 1973; m. Philip Melancthon Powell, Dec. 29, 1962; children—David, Aaron, Robert. Intern in psychology VA Hosp., Newington, Conn., 1973-75; instr. So. Conn. State Coll., New Haven, 1975-76; psychologist Austin (Tex.) Evaluation Center, 1979-80, 81-82; dep. dir. gen. clin. services Austin Child Guidance and Evaluation Center, 1982-86; sch. psychologist San Rafael (Calif.) Schs., 1980-81; instr. S.W. Tex. State U., San Marcos, 1978-79; adj. prof. dept. psychology U. Tex., Austin, 1984—, cons. Learning Disabilities Ctr., 1986—; pvt. practice psychology. Chmn. Cub Scouts Pack No. 54, 1977-78; bd. dirs. Capital Area Mental Health Ctr., 1985-86; cellist Austin Community Orch. Lic. psychologist, health services provider, Tex. Mem. Am. Psychol. Assn., Southwestern Psychol. Assn., Tex. Psychol. Assn., Capital Area Psychol. Assn. (sec. 1985-86), Am. Assn. Marital and Family Therapy (assoc.), Soc. Research in Child Devel., Central Tex. Assn. Gifted Children (co-v.p. 1984-85), Am. Orthopsychiat. Assn. Democrat. Home: 3724 Jefferson St Suite 209 Austin TX 78731 Office: 612 W 6th St Austin TX 78701

POWELL, MARCIA L., communications consultant, television personality, author; b. Opelika, Ala., Apr. 19; d. Clyde L. and Leonora (Stowe) P.; m. George Winship, May 21, 1963 (div. 1967); m. 2d John J. Gallagher, Apr. 27, 1969 (div. 1971). A.B. in Journalism, U. Ga., 1962; postgrad. N.Y. Sch. Interior Design, 1968-69, New Sch. Social Research, 1970, NYU, 1979. Club editor

Phoenix Gazette, 1962-64; asst. account exec. Edward Gottlieb & Assocs., N.Y.C., 1964-65; pub. relations specialist Parsons-Jurden Corp., N.Y.C., 1965-66; Eastern editor Housewares Buyer Mag., N.Y.C., 1966-67; home editor Electricity on the Farm, N.Y.C., 1967-73; owner Marcia Powell Enterprises, N.Y.C., 1973—; founding ptnr. RTI Communications, N.Y.C., 1979—; communications dir. J.O.S. Enterprises Inc., Des Moines, 1981—. Co-author: The Honeymoon Handbook, 1980; Beauty Is My Business, 1982; The Look of Success, 1982; The Real You, 1987. Bd. dirs. Found. for Facially Disfigured, Des Moines, 1981—. Recipient Feature Writing award Ariz. Press Women, 1963, Hist. Feature award, 1964; Editorial Excellence award Am. Assn. Home Appliance Mfrs., 1972, 73. Mem. Am. Soc. Journalists and Authors, Women in Communications, Inc. (N.Y. pres. 1969-70), Nat. Acad. TV Arts and Scis., Am. Women in Radio and TV, Authors Guild, Authors League of Am., Cosmetic Exec. Women, Publicity Club N.Y., Fashion Group, Women Bus. Owners N.Y., Am. Home Econs. Assn., Home Economists in Bus., Soc. Profl. Journalists, Alpha Xi Delta (N.Y. pres. 1967-68, 75th ann. cons. 1968, pub. relations circle 1965-67).

POWELL, MARY ALICE, real estate and appliance company executive; b. LaGrange, Tex., June 27, 1942; d. Charles James and Rosalyn (Boelsche) Marik; m. Dudley C. Powell, Aug. 9, 1967; children—Mark Charles, Anna Elisa. B.S., Our Lady of Lake U., 1963, postgrad., 1976-80; postgrad. U. Houston, 1966. Extension home economist Tex. Agrl. Extension Service, Floresville, 1963-65; tchr. Harlandale Ind. Sch. Dist., San Antonio, 1967-68; co-owner Powell Appliance Ctr., 1968-82, House of Vacuums, 1980-82; pres. Powell Realty Devel. Corp., 1973—; v.p. Powell Appliance Ctrs., Inc., 1982—. Sec. Alamo service delivery area Pvt. Industry Council, San Antonio, 1983—; mem. devel. bd. St. Francis Acad. Mem. Am. Mktg. Assn., Appliance Assn. San Antonio, S.E. Bus. and Profl. Womens Club (pres.-elect 1985-86), Southside C. of C., Greater San Antonio C. of C., San Antonio Mus. Assn., Our Lady of Lake U. Alumni Assn. Roman Catholic. Home: 7150 Symphony Ln San Antonio TX 78214 Office: Powell Appliance Ctr 1340 SW Military Dr San Antonio TX 78221

POWELL, MARY LOUISE WELLS, psychologist, educator; b. Asheville, N.C., July 7, 1935; d. John Kendall and Beatrice (Rice) Wells; A.B., U. N.C., 1957, M.S., 1964, Ph.D., 1976; m. Elton George Powell, June 21, 1969. Tchr., Myers Park High Sch., Charlotte, N.C., 1957-58; editorial research asst. Time, Inc., N.Y.C., 1959-60; recreation and program dir. Spl. Services U.S. Forces Europe, Germany and France, 1960-62; resident adviser undergrad. women U. N.C., Chapel Hill, 1963-64, research asso. and asst. to project coordinator State/Fed. Inst. for Profl. Devel., 1964-66; prof. organizational indsl. personnel psychology Appalachian State U., Boone, N.C., 1967—. NDEA fellow, 1966; NASA fellow, 1981. Mem. Am. Psychol. Assn., Southeastern Psychol. Assn., N.C. Assn. Counseling and Devel., So. Mgmt. Assn., N.C. Coll. Personnel Assn., N.C. Vocat. Guidance Assn., Am. Soc. Personnel Adminstrn. (accredited personnel diplomate, tng. and devel.), Am. Soc. Tng. and Devel., Organizational Behavior Teaching Soc., Acad. of Mgmt., AAUW, Pi Delta Phi. Home: 200 Anne Marie Dr Boone NC 28607 Office: 112-A Smith Wright Hall Appalachian State University Boone NC 28608

POWELL, ROSALIE, home economist; b. Milw., Oct. 24, 1947; d. William and Daisy P.; B.S., U. Wis., Stout, 1969, M.S. in Home Econs. Edn., 1974. Extension home economist U. Wis. Extension, Langlade County, 1969-74; Waukesha County, 1976—; instr. U. Wis.-Stout, Menomonie, 1975-76; asst. prof. dept. family devel. U. Wis. Extension, 1976-81, asso. prof., 1981—, chmn. family devel. dept., 1984—. Mem. Am. Home Econs. Assn., Wis. Home Econs. Assn., Nat. Assn. Extension Home Economists, Wis. Assn. Extension Home Economists, Soc. Nutrition Edn., Wis. Consumers League, Bus. and Profl. Women (chpt. pres. 1970-74), Am. Council on Consumer Interests, Gamma Sigma Sigma (nat. pres. 1975-77), Epsilon Sigma Phi. Club: Waukesha Altrusa. Home: 403 Sheffield Rd Waukesha WI 53186 Office: 500 Riverview Ave Waukesha WI 53188

POWELL, SANDRA THERESA, timber company executive; b. Orofino, Idaho, Jan. 9, 1944; s. Harold L. and Margaret E. (Thompson) P. B.S. in Acctg., U. Idaho, 1966. C.P.A., Idaho. Acct., Weyerhaeuser Co., Tacoma, Wash., 1966-67; with Potlatch Corp., 1967—, asst. sec., San Francisco, 1981, sec., asst. treas., 1981—. Mem. Am. Inst. C.P.A.s, Idaho State Bd. Accountancy, Idaho Soc. C.P.A.s, Am. Soc. Corp. Secs. Inc. Office: Potlatch Corp PO Box 3591 San Francisco CA 94119

POWELL, SARA JORDAN, musician, religious worker; b. Waller, Tex., Oct. 6, 1938; d. Samuel Arthur and Mable Ruth (Ponder) Jordan; m. John Atkins Powell, June 24, 1967; 1 child, Mary Benet. B.A., Tex. So. U., 1960; M.R.E., U. St. Thomas, Houston, 1979. Tchr., Chgo. Bd. Edn., 1961-68, Houston Ind. Sch. Dist., 1968-73; youth dir. Gospel Music Workshop Am., Detroit, 1972-76; dir. talent and fine arts Ch. of God in Christ, Memphis, 1974—, dir., cons. ch. hist. mus. and fine arts center, 1980—; mem. nat. reference com. One Nation Under God, Virginia Beach, Va., 1979—; regional sponsor Yr. of the Bible, Washington, 1983; soloist Savoy Record Co., 1972-79. Bd. dirs. talent coordinator Charles Harrison Mason Edn. Found., 1975—; bd. dirs. James Oglethorpe Patterson Fine Arts Scholarships, 1974—; music and talent dir. Juneteenth U.S.A., 1985—. Recipient 1st Pl. award Record Album, Savoy Record Co., 1972. Best Female Vocalist, Gospel Music Workshop Am., 1973, 74, 75, Gold record, 1978; letter of appeciation Cook County Dept. Corrections, Chgo., 1978; Silver Plate award Assembly of God Ch., Calcutta, India, 1978; letter of appreciation for White House performance, Washington, 1979. Mem. Houston PTA, Houston Peoples Workshop (dir. 1981—), Women in Leadership (adv. bd. 1985—). Home: 9203 McAvoy Dr Houston TX 77074

POWER-BARNES, MARIE RUTH, public relations and marketing executive, photographer; b. Trenton, N.J., Jan. 30, 1958; d. Robert Bruce and Mai Norma (Ulesoo) Power; m. Kenneth George Barnes, Aug. 5, 1978. B.A. in Journalism summa cum laude, Rider Coll., 1980. Campaign assoc. Delaware Valley United Way, Lawrenceville, N.J., 1980-82; dir. pub. relations and mktg. Hamilton Hosp., N.J., 1982—. Contbr. articles, cover feature story to profl. jours. and mags.; author, editor, graphic designer. Mem. Am. Soc. Hosp. Pub. Relations, N.J. Hosp. Pub. Relations Assn. (regional coordinator, Percy award 1983, 84, 85), Nat. Assn. Female Execs., Am. Coll. Healthcare Mktg., Am. Mktg. Assn., Sigma Delta Chi, Phi Beta Kappa, Alpha Epsilon Zeta. Lutheran. Office: Hamilton Hosp Whitehorse-Hamilton Square Rd Hamilton NJ 08690

POWERS, CHRISTINE ELIZABETH, pharmaceutical company executive; b. Greenfield, Mass., Dec. 25, 1953; d. Richard Frederic and Jeanne Elizabeth (Day) Powers; B.S. in Chem. Engring., Worcester, Poly. Inst., 1975; postgrad. No. Ill. U. Process engr. Clairol, Inc., Stamford, Conn., 1975-77, prodn. planner, 1977; process engr. Armour-Dial Co., Montgomery, Ill., 1977-78; project engr. Baxter Travenol Labs., Inc., Deerfield, Ill., 1978-81, prodn. supr., 1981-83, process engr., 1983—. Mktg. adviser Jr. Achievement Stamford, 1976-77. Mem. Am. Inst. Chem. Engrs., Soc. Women Engrs., Am. MBA Execs. Republican. Unitarian. Home: 703 Drae Ct Wheeling IL 60090 Office: Travenol Labs Inc PO Box 490 Round Lake IL 60073

POWERS, DONNA MARIE, pizza marketing executive; b. Roslyn, N.Y., Dec. 27, 1957; d. Richard Hal and Joan Marie (Langford) Powers. B.B.A. in Mktg., Auburn U., 1981. With Fulton Nat. Bank, Atlanta, 1978-79; bookkeeper Hart & Assocs., Chamblee, Ga., 1979-80; regional mktg. mgr. Domino's Pizza, Inc., Atlanta, 1982-83, regional mktg. dir., 1983—. Mem. Am. Mktg. Assn., Delta Gamma. Baptist. Club: Auburn (Atlanta). Home: 1103 Treehouse Pkwy Norcross GA 30093 Office: Domino's Pizza Inc 3146B NE Expressway Atlanta GA 30341

POWERS, ELAINE ANN, medical technician, laboratory researcher; b. Peoria, Ill., July 19, 1958; d. Norman Emory and Gladys Elsie (Crofts) P. B.A. in Music Performance, Fla. State U., 1979, B.A. in Biology, 1979; M.S., U. West Fla., 1982. Environ. awareness coordinator Youth Conservation Corps, U.S. Fish and Wildlife Service, 1978, 79; immunology teaching asst. U. West Fla., Pensacola, 1980; biol. technician U.S. EPA, Pensacola, 1980; grad. research asst. U. West Fla., Pensacola, 1980-82; research asst. II, M.D. Anderson Hosp., Houston, 1982-83; med. technician III, lab. supr. bone marrow transplantation, 1983—; vocal soloist Sr. Summer Band Tour Gt. Brit., Peoria, Ill., 1976. Mem. Peoria Civic Opera, 1975; asst. scuba instr. Nat. Assn. Underwater Instrs., Tallahassee, 1976; cardiopulmonary resuscitation instr. Am. Heart Assn. Fla., 1977; mem. Houston Symphony Chorale, 1983. Mem. AAAS, Am. Soc. Zoologists, Sigma Xi. Presbyterian.

POWERS, EVA AGOSTON, clinical psychologist; b. Budapest, Hungary, Mar. 30, 1938; came to U.S., 1940, naturalized, 1945; d. Tibor and Jeanne Iseult (Watson) Agoston; A.B., Smith Coll., 1960; M.A., Boston U., 1962; Ph.D., 1969; m. James F. Powers, July 4, 1960; children—Wayne, Glenn. Psychologist, Childrens' Hosp. Med. Center Boston, 1964-69, Newton (Mass.) Sch. System, 1969-71, Conway (N.H.) Sch. System, 1972-78; dir. child and youth services Seacoast Regional Counseling Center, Portsmouth, N.H., 1979-80; pvt. practice psychol. counseling, Portsmouth, 1980—; cons. to Maine Sch. System, 1978, Center of Hope, Conway, N.H., 1971-73; supr. tng. program N.H. Dept. Edn., Concord, 1972-74. NIMH grantee, 1961, 62; S. Burt Wolbach Research Fund grantee, 1968. Mem. Am. Psychol. Assn., Maine Psychol. Assn., N.H. Psychol. Orgn., N.H. Soc. Psychologists, Mass. Psychol. Assn., Nat. Assn. Psychologists, Am. Orthopsychiat. Assn., Sigma Xi, Phi Beta Kappa. Contbr. articles to profl. publs. Home: Gerrish Island ME Office: Box 4385 Portsmouth NH 03801

POWERS, NANCY MARIE, distribution company executive; b. Mpls., Dec. 21, 1959; d. Warren Paul and Joanne C. (Davis) Powers. A.A., Fla. Jr. Coll., 1980; B.A., U. South Fla., 1982; postgrad. mktg. and mgmt. Jacksonville U. (Fla.), 1983—. Account adminstr. Unit Distbn. Co., Jacksonville, 1976-77; commn. salesman J.C. Penney Co., Jacksonville, 1978-80, Tampa, Fla., 1980-81; supr. Unit Distbn. Co., Jacksonville, 1982, Unit Import/Export Co., Jacksonville, 1982-83; project mgr. Associated Unit Cos., Jacksonville, 1983—. Mem. Am. Mktg. Assn., Warehousing Edn. Resource Com. Roman Catholic. Office: Associated Unit Cos 2001 N Ellis Jacksonville FL 32205

POWERS, NONA, custom framing company executive; b. St. Anthony, Idaho, Feb. 24, 1942; d. Russell H. and Della S. (Mathis) Smith; m. Joe M. Powers, Jan. 2, 1963; children—Kira L., Joe Marvin. A.A. in Art, San Diego City Coll., 1973; B.A. cum laude in Art, San Diego State U., 1976, M.A. in Art, 1978. Instr. San Diego State U., 1976-77; custom framer Potpurri, San Diego, 1978-81; owner, mgr. Monterey Custom Framing, San Diego, 1981—; lectr. in field; color cons. Bainbridge, London, Can. and Am. Br., 1984. Featured in art and decorating mags. Pres. Edison Elem. Sch. PTA, 1975; trustee Religious Sci. Ch. Ctr., San Diego, 1980. Mem. Profl. Picture Framers Assn. of San Diego (numerous awards), Profl. Picture Framers Assn. Guild, La Mesa C. of C., Women's Bus. Owners Assn., Soroptimist Internat. Avocation: writing on color theory and design for framers. Office: Monterey Custom Framing 4703 Spring St La Mesa CA 92041

POWERS, RITA VIRGINIA, conglomerate executive; b. Port Chester, N.Y., Sept. 29, 1922; d. William and Mary Powers. Asst. sec. Homelite div. Textron, Greenwich, Conn., 1954-70, sec., 1970-74; asst. sec. Textron, Inc., Providence, 1974-78, corp. sec., 1978-82, v.p., sec., 1982—. Mem. adv. council Johnson and Wales Coll., 1978-84. Mem. Am. Soc. Corp. Secs. (pres. Boston chpt. 1981-82, adv. com. 1982-85). Roman Catholic. Club: Turks Head (Providence). Home: 140 Blueberry Dr East Greenwich RI 02818 Office: Textron Inc 40 Westminster St Providence RI 02903

POWLEY, ANN MARIE, manufacturing company executive; b. Los Angeles, Dec. 20, 1945; d. Leo Joseph and Ethel Louise (Fitzgerald) Greenhalgh; student Santa Monica (Calif.) Coll., UCLA. Field support officer C.O.R.D.S. program AID mission to Vietnam, 1968-71; adminstrv. asst. Manzuno & Assocs., Inc., Malibu, Calif., 1972-75; supr. sales adminstrn. TRW Datacom Internat., Inc., Los Angeles, 1975-77; nat. logistics mgr. Computer Communications, Inc., Torrance, Calif., 1978-80; materiel mgr. data systems services div. Eaton Corp., Los Angeles, 1981-84; dir. Homestead Enterprises Inc., Los Angeles, 1985—. Mem. Assn. Field Service Mgrs., Nat. Assn. Purchasing Mgrs. (cert. purchasing mgr.), Am. Mgmt. Assn. Home: 2613 Patricia Ave Los Angeles CA 90064

POYER, LISA MARIE, theater administrator; b. Bronx, N.Y., Sept. 4, 1957; d. Newton McLaughlin and Lucia Cecile (Bauduit) P. A.B. cum laude in Government, Harvard Coll., 1977; J.D., Harvard U., 1980. Bar: N.Y. 1981. Asst. dir. Ctr. for Law and Health Care Policy, Bklyn., 1980-81; asst. gen. mgr. Shubert Theatre, Chgo., 1981—. Bd. advisor Opera for a Small Space, Chgo., 1984. Recipient Summer award, Kennedy Inst. Politics, Cambridge, 1976. Democrat. Club: Harvard (N.Y.C., Boston, Chgo.).

POYNTER, MARION KNAUSS, journalist; b. Poughkeepsie, N.Y., Apr. 17, 1926; d. Louis Eugene and Rose Alvina (Arndt) Knauss; A.B., Vassar Coll., 1946; postgrad. Fla. State U., 1950, Am. U., 1960, U. South Fla., 1971; m. Nelson Paul Poynter, May 4, 1970. Advt. sales rep. R.H. Donnelley Corp., 1946-47; researcher Time-Life, Inc., N.Y.C., 1948-49; researcher CIA, Washington, 1952-60; editorial writer, researcher St. Petersburg (Fla.) Times, 1961-70; dir. Times Pub. Co., Semit Corp. Bd. dirs. Poynter Inst. for Media Studies. Mem. Women in Communication, Internat. Press Inst. Address: 629 —A— St SE Washington DC 20003

PRACHT, IRENA, manufacturing company executive; b. Council Grove, Kans., Dec. 24, 1927; d. Berend Hiram and Amanda (Anderson) Bicker; student Kans. Agrl. Coll., 1945-46; B.S., Kans. State Coll., Emporia, 1949; m. Harold Ray Pracht, Oct. 23, 1948; children—Rae Ann Pracht Lowery, Gregory Ray, Rena Rochelle Pracht Coby, Glen Frederick. Bookkeeper, Eby Constrn. Co., Wichita, 1951-52; partner Bell Sewing Centers, Tex., N.Mex., 1954-62, Tri State Sewing Machine Distbrs., Council Grove, Kans., 1962-68; staff acct. Mize, House & Reed C.P.A.s, Topeka, 1968-69; staff acct., gen. ledger supr., controller Farah Mfg. Co., Inc., El Paso, 1969—; partner Pracht Enterprises, El Paso, 1975—; sec. treas. Vernon Investment Corp., El Paso, 1971—; v.p., dir. Tex. Pure Products, El Paso, 1981—. C.P.A., Tex. Mem. Tex. Soc. C.P.A.s, Theta Sigma Upsilon, Xi Phi. Home: 364 McCune Rd El Paso TX 79915 Office: 8889 Gateway West El Paso TX 79925

PRADIA, ALICE EMERY, small business owner; b. Paris, Tex., Mar. 23, 1932; d. Boliver and Dovie Lee (Connally) Emery; m. Andrew Joseph Pradia, Jan. 3, 1959 (div. Nov. 1981). B.S., Tex. So. U., Houston, 1955, M.Ed., 1965, M.Elem. Adminstrn., 1974. Tchr., Bur. Indian Schs., Gallup, N.Mex., 1956-58; tchr. Houston Ind. Sch. Dist., 1959-74, asst. prin., 1974-76, curriculum coordinator, 1976-79; sales mgr. World Book Ency., Houston, 1979—; owner Alice's Boutique, Houston, 1981—. Sec., Civic Club Houston, 1970-75; pres. Rufus Cage Elem. Sch. PTA, Houston, 1971-74. Mem. Tex. So. U. Ex-Student Assn. (sec. 1973-79), Top Ladies of Distinction, Inc., Sigma Gamma Rho. Club: Maroon and Gray. Democrat. Roman Catholic. Home: 5014 Mayflower Houston TX 77023

PRAEGER, HELENE CAROL, lawyer; b. N.Y.C., Sept. 6, 1944; d. Irving and Ruth (Rosenblum) Schechtman; m. Donald Lewis Praeger, June 1, 1976 (div.; 1 child, Denton. A.B., Queens Coll., CUNY, 1966; J.D., N.Y. Law Sch., 1970. Bar: N.Y. 1971, U.S. Dist. Ct. (so. and ea. dists.) N.Y. 1974, U.S. Ct. Appeals, 2d cir.) 1975. Assoc. Family Ct. br. Legal Aid Soc. Bklyn., 1970-72; assoc. litigation dept. Finley, Kumble, Heine, Underberg & Grutman, N.Y.C., 1972-74, Emil, Kobrin, Klein & Garbus, N.Y.C., 1974-76; sole practice law, Poughkeepsie, N.Y., 1976-85, N.Y.C., 1986—. Bd. dirs. Mill St. Loft. Mem. ABA, N.Y. State Bar Assn., N.Y.C. Bar Assn., Mid-Hudson Women's Bar Assn.

PRAGER, CLAIRE JEAN, marketing educator, consultant; b. Bklyn., Aug. 26, 1941; d. Jacob and Gertrude Beatrice (Slote) P.; m. James E. Greeley, 1974. B.A., U. Md., 1963; M.S., NYU, 1964. Dept. mgr. Saks Fifth Ave., Chevy Chase, Md., 1970-73; buyer Woodward & Lothrop, Washington, 1972-76; adj. prof. lectr. Georgetown U., Washington, 1981, George Washington U., Washington, 1981; asst. to fin. dir. Robb for Gov., McLean, Va., 1981; vis. asst. prof. George Washington U. Sch. Govt. and Bus. Adminstrn., Washington, 1982—; founding ptnr. Georgetown Mktg. Inst., Washington, 1980—. Mem. Democratic Nat. Com. Alumni Council, Washington, 1983. Mem. Am. Mktg. Assn. (dir. 1982-83), Washington Fashion Group (treas. 1980-83). Home: 2939 Van Ness St NW Washington DC 20008 Office: George Washington U Sch Govt and Bus Adminstrn Washington DC 20052

PRÄGER-BENETT, NANCY ANN, artist; b. N.Y.C., Mar. 17, 1943; d. Sigmund Godfrey and Eleanor Pauline Prager; student M.A. program Syracuse U., 1961-62; B.F.A., Accademia de Belle Arte, Florence, Italy, 1965; B.A., Cooper Union Coll., 1968; m. Barry Lawrence Benett, June 19, 1966; children—Lara Christina, Andrew Bernard, Ariane Alison. Work exhibited in pvt. individual shows, also mus. and univ. group shows, U.S., Italy, France, Can., Turkey, Am. embassy, Turkish Mission to UN; represented pvt. and corp. collections, U.S., Italy, Eng., Turkey, France, Can.; tchr. Black Emergency Cultural Coalition, Met. Mus., N.Y. prison systems. Mem. Bd. TV Arts and Scis.; chmn. bd. Mannes Coll. Music. Recipient Prix de Paris, 1975, Grand Prix Humanitaire de France, 1976. Mem. Am.-Scandinavian Found., Les Surindependants Societaire, Graphic Art Assn., Smithsonian Assos., Met. Mus., Am.-Italian Found. for Cancer Research. Presbyterian. Club: Saltaire Yacht (dir. 1972-80, gov.). Work noted in Artist USA Bicentennial, N.Y. Art Yearbook, Nouvelle Littaire, Art News Mag., Arts Mag. Home: New York NY 10021 Office: 1400 Broadway New York NY 10018

PRAHL, MARGARET MARSHALL, lawyer; b. Lincoln, Nebr., Nov. 28, 1938; d. Walter E. and Lucy (Heim) Marshall; m. Jerry C. Prahl, Aug. 21, 1960; children—Paula Jean, Jay Marshall, David Andrew. B.A., U. Nebr., 1960; J.D. with honors, U. S.D., 1981. Bar: Iowa 1981, S.D., 1982, U.S. Dist. Ct. (no. and so. dists.) Tchr. Iowa, 1981. English, Lincoln Pub. Schs. (Nebr.), 1960-62; course writer U. Nebr., Lincoln, 1962; copywriter Griffith Advt., Sioux City, Iowa, 1972-73; cons. prin. clients Briar Cliff Coll., Sioux City, 1978, Rosetti Archtl. Assocs., Detroit, 1979; ptnr. Gleysteen, Harper, Eidsmoe, Heidman & Redmond, Attys., Sioux City, 1981—. Editor-in-chief S.D. Law Rev., 1980-81. Mem. Sioux City City Council, 1973-77; pres. Sioux City LWV, 1968-70, bd. dirs., 1968-71; bd. dirs. LWV of Iowa, 1971-73; organizer, bd. dirs. Sioux City Vol. Bur., 1970-73, Siouxland Ctr. for Women, Sioux City, 1974—; bd. dirs. Siouxland Community Blood Bank, Sioux City, 1978—, Woodbury County Tax Research Conf., Sioux City, 1978—, Sanford Community Ctr., Sioux City, 1979—, Marian Health Ctr., Sioux City, 1981—. Named Woman of Yr., Sta.-KMEG-TV, Sioux City, 1973, Woman of Excellence, 1985. Mem. Woodbury County Bar Assn., Iowa Bar Assn., S.D. Bar Assn., ABA, Siouxland Assn. Bus. and Industry (bd. dirs. 1985—). Club: Jr. League (bd. dirs. 1969-71) (Sioux City). Office: Gleysteen Harper Eidsmoe Heidman & Redmond Attys PO Box 3086 Sioux City IA 51102

PRALLE, ELAINE-ANNE JOHNSON, personnel executive; b. Jacksonville, Fla., Dec. 24, 1955; d. Paul E. and Rose (George) Johnson. B.A., U. South Fla., 1979; M.B.A., U. North Fla., 1982. Adminstrv. analyst Blue Cross/Blue Shield, Jacksonville, Fla., 1973-77; tng. coordinator First Fla. Banks, Tampa, 1980-81; dir. personnel Suddath Van Lines, Inc., Jacksonville, 1982—. Mem. employer adv. group, Blue Cross/Shields, Jacksonville, 1984—. Mem. Am. Soc. Personnel Adminstrn., AAUW, Phi Kappa Phi, Beta Gamma Sigma. Democrat. Presbyterian. Office: Suddath Van Lines Inc 5266 Highway Ave Jacksonville FL 32205

PRATCHER, ANN PERRY, administrator; b. Knoxville, Tenn., Feb. 13, 1950; d. Thomas Gilbert and Henri T. (Henderson) Perry; m. Thornton Pratcher, July 20, 1973. A.B. in Philosophy/Religion, Maryville Coll. (Tenn.), 1971; M.S. in Edn., U. Tenn.-Knoxville, 1973; M.B.A., Columbus Coll. (Ga.), 1982 Cert. tchr. spl. edn., Ala., Ky. Tchr. various schs., 1972-75; tchr. adult edn. , Dept. Def., W.Ger., 1975-76; master tchr. Big Bend Community Coll., Moses Lake, Wash., 1977; high sch. EMR cons. Russell County Schs., Ala., 1977-79; non-nurse educator W.Ga. Med. Ctr., LaGrange, 1980-83; dir. child services U.S. Army (Germany), 1983-85; community activities officer Hdqrs. Grafenwoehr Trg. Area, 1985—. Mem. ASTD, Assn. Young Children in Europe, Nat. Assn. Edn. Young children. Office: Commander GTA Attn. AETTG-CA APO New York NY 09114

PRATHER, LENORE LOVING, state supreme court justice; b. West Point, Miss., Sept. 17, 1931; d. Byron Herald and Hattie Hearn (Morris) Loving; m. Robert Brooks Prather, May 30, 1957; children—Pamela, Valerie Jo, Malinda Wayne. B.S., Miss. Coll. for Women, Columbus, 1953; LL.B., U. Miss., 1955. Bar: Miss. 1955. Practiced with B.H. Loving, 1955-60, R.B. Prather, 1962-65; sole practice, West Point, 1965-71; mcpl. judge City of West Point, 1965-71; judge Chancery Ct. 14th Dist. State Miss., Columbus, 1971-82, justice Supreme Ct., Jackson, 1982—. Bd. dirs. Prairie council Girl Scouts U.S.A., 1970; del. Dem. Nat. Conv., West Point, 1962. Mem. Miss. State Bar Assn., Miss. Conf. Judges, Clay County Bar Assn. (sec. 1956-71), DAR Episcopalian. Club: Pilot. Office: Supreme Ct Miss Gartin Bldg PO Box 117 Jackson MS 39205

PRATT, ALICE REYNOLDS, educational administrator; b. Marietta, Ohio, Oct. 5, 1922; d. Thurman J. and Vera L. (Holdren) Reynolds. B.A., U. Okla., 1943. Reporter, high sch. tchr., 1944-50; asst. dir. Houston office Inst. Internat. Edn., 1952-58, dir. office, 1958—, v.p., 1976—. Founding bd. govs. Houston Forum; mem. Houston Com. Fgn. Relations; v.p. Houston World Trade Assn., 1979—; founding mem. Japan Am. Soc. Houston; v.p., bd. dirs., founding mem. Korea-Houston Soc., 1983—; founding mem. Houston-Taipei Soc., Stavanger Sister City Assn.; past nat. bd. dirs. Sister Cities Internat., Nat. Council Internat. Visitors. Decorated Palmes Academiques (France), 1966; Order of Merit (W.Ger.), 1972; knight Order of Leopold II (Belgium), 1973; named Woman of Yr., Houston Bus. and Profl. Women, 1958; recipient Matrix award Theta Sigma Phi, 1961; Nat. Carnation award Gamma Phi Beta, 1976. Republican. Episcopalian.

PRATT, CYNTHIA ANNE, dentist; b. Washington, Dec. 21, 1950; d. William Leonadas and Catherine Louise (Lane) Pratt. B.A., Calif. Western U., 1973; D.D.S., Georgetown U., 1981. Nursing asst. Suburban Hosp., Bethesda, Md., 1973; phlebotomist Suburban Hosp., Bethesda, Md., 1973-75, Mt. Sinai Hosp., N.Y.C., 1975, Sibley Hosp., Washington, 1976, 77, Georgetown U. Hosp., Washington, 1978; emergency room technician Georgetown U. Hosp., Washington, 1978-79; gen. practice dentistry, Washington, 1981-83; practice dentistry specializing in gen. and cosmetic dentistry and temporomandibular joint disorders, Rockville, Md., 1983-85; assoc. dir. Temporomandibular Joint and Facial Pain Treatment Ctr., Bethesda, Clinton, Towson, Md., Washington, 1983-84. Mem. ADA, D.C. Dental Soc., Psi Omega (pres. 1980-81). Episcopalian. Avocations: painting; sailing. Home: 1350 Beverly Rd McLean VA 22101

PRATT, DEBRA KAY, commercial development company executive; b. Bakersfield, Calif., July 29, 1955; d. Richard Eugene and Cleta Rose (Salyards) Bird; m. Geoffrey Baron Pratt, Jan. 29, 1977 (div. 1978). R.N., Bakersfield Jr. Coll., 1974; student Long Beach State U., 1974-75, U. So. Calif., 1976. Sales agt. Fireside Realty, Bakersfield, 1977-78, Contempo Realty, Cupertino, Calif., 1979-80; broker Re/Max Realtors, Los Gatos, Calif., 1980-81; owner, pres. R.B. Malcolm Co., Los Gatos, 1981-83, Lazarion, Inc., Scottsdale, Ariz., 1983—; investment cons. Tower Corp., Grand Cayman, B.W.I., 1980-83, Cayman Mgmt. Co., 1980-83; prodn. coordinator West Heuco Corp., El Paso, Tex., 1982-83. Author poems. Mem. Scottsdale Spl. Olympics program, 1984-85. Mem. Calif. Assn. Realtors, Internat. Real Estate Exchangors, Scottsdale C. of C. Republican. Episcopalian. Avocations: water skiing; sailing; travel; reading; writing. Office: Lazarion Inc 4300 N Miller St #133 Scottsdale AZ 85251

PRATT, ELIZABETH STRATTON, ski resort executive; b. Greenwich, Conn., Mar. 12, 1928; d. John McKee and June (Love) Stratton; m. Truxton Bancroft Pratt, Jr., Oct. 2, 1954 (dec. 1975); children—Polly, Amanda, Elizabeth, Truxton III. B.A., Vassar Coll., 1950. With Time Inc., 1950-51, Ford Found., 1951-57; pres. Mad River Corp., Waitsfield, Vt., to present. Bd. dirs. YMCA, Greenwich, 1985, Stowe Sch., Vt., 1985. Clubs: Round Hill (Greenwich); Amateur Ski (N.Y.C.). Avocations: golf; skiing; gardening. Home: 45 Close Rd Greenwich CT 06830 Office: Mad River Corp Waitsfield VT 05673

PRATT, E(LLEN) MARCELLA MORIN, designer; b. Trail, B.C., Can. (parents Am. citizens); d. Francis George and Rose Delima (Bousquet) Morin; student extension courses Wash. State Coll.; grad. Normal Coll., Victoria, B.C.; m. George Collins Pratt, Sept. 22, 1946. With art dept. Universal Internat. Pictures 1935-46; now home designer and decorator, Calif., Wash. Mem. Assistance League So. Calif. (life), Canadian Red Cross (life), Navy League of the U.S. (life), Mary and Joseph League (life), Eisenhower Med. Aux. (founder, life mem.), Palm Desert, Calif. (life, founder), Desert Mus. Republican. Home: Box 427 Cathedral City CA 92234

PRATT, MARGARET WADE, information science corporation executive; b. Kansas City, Mo., Apr. 5, 1925; d. Walter Wesley and Leone (Smith) P.; B.A., Washburn U., 1945. Dir. maternal and child health studies George Washington U., Washington, 1962-73; dir. maternal and child health studies project Minn. Systems Research, Inc., Washington, 1974-75; pres., project dir. Info. Sciences Research Inst., Washington, 1976—. Mem. Am. Pub. Health Assn., Assn. MCH and CCS Program Dirs. Office: 8027 Leesburg Pike Suite 102 Vienna VA 22180

PRATT, MARTHA LEE, nurse; b. Chattanooga, Tenn., Mar. 25, 1957; d. Joseph Hilliard and Thelma (Lee) Anders; m. Frank Martin Pratt, Jr., Dec. 9, 1977; 1 child, Jessica Kristin. B.S. in Nursing, U. Ala.-Birmingham, 1979. Nurse's aide Univ. Hosp., Birmingham, 1977-79, staff nurse, 1979-80, charge nurse of burn dressing team, 1980—, speaker Burn Ctr., 1980—; researcher Robert Wood Johnson Found., Birmingham, 1985—. Tchr. Valley Creek Baptist Ch., Hueytown, Ala., 1984-85. Mem. Am. Burn Assn., Nat. Burn Prevention Com. Democrat. Avocations: horseback riding; boating; camping; reading. Home: 149 Greenridge Rd Hueytown AL 35023 Office: University Hosp 619 S 19th St JT Room 1114 Birmingham AL 35233

PRATT, MARY DOYLE, nurse; b. Foley, Ala., Oct. 1, 1915; d. Dennis F. and Mary (Brannan) Doyle; m. James T. Ailor, Dec. 12, 1942 (dec. Apr., 1945); m. 2d, Dallas N. Pratt, Sept. 16, 1953; 1 step-son, James Dallas Pratt. Student, South Ga. Tchrs. Coll., 1932-34; R.N., U. Ga. Sch. Nursing, 1941. Asst. chief nurse VA Hosp., Richmond, 1946-48; nurse, supr. laundry service clinic Crib Diaper Service, Washington, 1953-64; charge nurse Miami Heart Hosp. and Hileah Hosp., 1966-70; nurse, night supr. Oakview Care Ctr., Williston, Fla., 1980—. Served to capt. Nurses Corps, AUS, 1942-45. Mem. Am. Nurses Assn. Republican. Episcopalian. Club: Rainbow Springs Country. Address: PO Box 849 Dunnellon FL 32630

PRATT, MILDRED INEZ, educator; b. Henderson, Tex., Oct. 15, 1928; d. R. P. and Eula (Thirkill) Sirls; B.A., Jarvis Coll., 1951; M.A., Butler U., 1952; M.A., Ind. U., 1955; Ph.D., U. Pitts., 1969; m. Theodore A. E.C. Pratt, Nov. 24, 1964; children—Awadagin, Menah. Program dir. All Nations Found., Los Angeles, 1956-59, Rouge Ecorse United Center, Ecorse, Mich., 1959-63; asst. prof. U. Pitts., 1963-69; prof. social work Ill. State U., Normal, 1969—; faculty Cath. U., Rio de Janeiro, Brazil, 1972-73, Fed. U., Rio de Janerio, 1972-73. Mem. Council on Social Work Edn. Contbr. articles to profl. jours. Home: 1405 W Hovey Ave Normal IL 61761 Office: Dept of Sociology and Anthropology Ill State U Normal IL 61761

PRATT, ROSALIE REBOLLO, harpist, educator; b. N.Y.C., Dec. 4, 1933; d. Antonio Ernesto and Eleanor Gertrude (Gibney) Rebollo; Mus.B., Manhattanville Coll., 1954; Mus.M., Pius XII Inst. Fine Arts, Florence, Italy, 1955; Ed.D., Columbia U., 1976; m. Samuel Orson Pratt, Aug. 11, 1964; children—Francesca Christina Pratt Ferguson, Alessandra Maria Pratt Jones. Prin. harpist N.J. Symphony Orch., 1963-65; soloist Mozart Haydn Festival, Avery Fisher Hall, N.Y.C., 1968; tchr. music public schs., Bloomfield and Montclair, N.J., 1962-73; mem. faculty Montclair State Coll., 1973-79; prof., Coordinator grad. studies Brigham Young U., Provo, Utah, 1979-84, prof., 1984—. Fulbright grantee, 1979; Myron Taylor scholar, 1954. Mem. Am. Harp Soc. (Outstanding Service award 1973), AAUP (co-chmn. legis. relations com. N.J. 1978-79), Music Edn. for Handicapped (co-founder, co-chmn., exec. dir.), Coll. Music Soc., Music Educators Nat. Conf., Internat. Soc. Mus. Edn. Commn. Music Therapy in Spl. Edn., Am. Assn. History Medicine, Internationale Gesellschaff für Musik in der Medizin, Phi Kappa Phi, Sigma Alpha Iota. Co-author: Elementary Music for All Learners, 1980; contbr. articles to Music Educators Jour., Am. Harp Jour., others. Editor procs. 2d and 3d Internat. Symposium, Music Edn. for Handicapped, 1982, 85; editor MEH Bull. Office: Harris Fine Arts Center Brigham Young U Provo UT 84602

PRATT, SUZANNE GARRETT, physician; b. Ga., Mar. 9, 1948; d. Roswell and Susie (Keller) Garrett; m. Frank Graham Pratt, III, Sept. 18, 1971; children—Frank Graham, Edward Garrett. B.S. summa cum laude, U. Ga., 1970; M.D., Med. Coll. Ga., 1973. Diplomate Am. Bd. Ob-Gyn. Resident Med. Coll. Ga., Augusta, 1973-77; physician D.D. Eisenhower Army Med. Ctr., Ft. Gordon, Ga., 1977-79; practice medicine specializing in ob-gyn, Rome, Ga., 1980—; coordinator ob-gyn family practice residency program Floyd Med. Ctr., Rome, 1983-84. Nat. Merit scholar U. Ga. Found., 1966-70. Fellow Am. Coll. Obstetricians and Gynecologists; mem. Floyd-Polk-Chattooga Med. Soc. (sec. 1982-84), AMA, Ga. Soc. Obstetricians and Gynecologists, Med. Assn. Ga., Zodiac, Phi Beta Kappa, Phi Kappa Phi. Home: 3 Hill Dale Ln SW Rome GA 30161 Office: Three Rivers Ob-Gyn 909 N 5th Ave Rome GA 30161

PRATTER, MARIANNE BUNZL (MRS. PAUL J. PRATTER), chemical company executive; b. Vienna, Austria, Dec. 21, 1938; d. Izidor and Cerest (Bleier) Bunzl; came to U.S., 1960, naturalized, 1967; B.S. in Chemistry, Budapest U., Hungary, 1957; M.S. in Chemistry, U. Calif. at Los Angeles, 1962; m. Paul J. Pratter, Dec. 13, 1962; children—Joshua E., Adam S. With Research Organic/Inorganic Chems. Corp., Belleville, N.J., 1963—, adminstrv. dir., 1965-68, pres., 1968—; pres. Western div. Research Organic/Inorganic Chems. Corp., Sun Valley, Calif., 1968—. Mem. Am. Chem. Soc. Home: 50 Rock Spring Rd West Orange NJ 07052 Office: 507-519 Main St Belleville NJ 07109

PREBBLE, BARBARA WHALEN, convention manager; b. Cynthiana, Ky., Apr. 4, 1942; d. Ransom and Addie Mae (Laytart) Whalen; m. Billy Reese Prebble, Jan. 26, 1962; children—Carrie Todd, Piper Ellen. B.A., U. Denver, 1981, M.A., 1983. Mktg. asst. Industry Media, Inc., Denver, 1983-84; meeting planner Integrated Resources, Denver, 1984; conv. mgr. Telectronics, Englewood, Colo., 1984—. Trustee Pitkin County Library, Aspen, Colo., 1977-79. Mem. Meeting Planners Internat. (bd. dirs. 1985-86), Health Care Exhibitors Assn., U. Ky. Alumni Assn. (dir. 1977—). Democrat. Avocations: writing; reading. Home: 631 S Monroe Way Denver CO 80209 Office: Telectronics 7400 S Tucson Way Englewood CO 80112

PRECUP, ALICEMARIE VERONICA, editor; b. N.Y.C., Apr. 28, 1945; d. C. Benedict and Alice Isabelle (Fanelli) Mauro; B.A., George Washington U., 1967; m. Ronald G. Precup, Dec. 19, 1964; children—Ronald G., Elizabeth Anne, Margaret Joy. Secondary sch. tchr. D.C. Pub. Sch., 1967-68; references editor Ralph Nader Congress Project, Washington, 1972; prodn. editor Am. Personnel & Guidance Assn., Washington, 1972-75, Am. Inst. Biol. Scis., Washington, 1975-81; editorial cons. Am. Inst. Biol. Scis., Nat. Acad. Scis., Smithsonian Instn. Press, 1982-84; publs. mgr. Nat.-Am. Wholesale Grocers Assn., 1983; mng. editor pub. services U.S. Pharmacopeia, 1983—. Mem. St. Agnes Choir, 1972—, Arlington (Va.) Met. Chorus, 1973—; cantor St. Agnes Parish, 1978—. Mem. Council Biology Editors, Smithsonian Assocs., Soc. for Scholarly Pub., Nat. Assn. Female Execs., NOW. Democrat. Roman Catholic. Contbr. articles to profl. jours. Address: 4123 N Richmond St Arlington VA 22207

PREECE, CHARLOTTE PHILLIPS, foreign affairs and defense analyst, consultant; b. Reading, Pa., Dec. 15, 1953; d. J. Reed and Ruth Augustine (Gensemer) Phillips; m. Rex Richard Matheson Preece, May 31, 1981; children—Ian Phillips, Reed Matheson. B.A. summa cum laude, Pa. State U., 1974; M.A., Fletcher Sch. Law and Diplomacy, 1976; diploma Nat. War Coll., 1983. Analyst in European affairs Congl. Research Service, Washington, 1976-82, specialist in European affairs, 1982—. Contbr. articles to profl. jours. Mem. Nat. War Coll. Alumni Assn., Pa. State U. Alumni Assn., Phi Beta Kappa, Pi Sigma Alpha. Avocations: piano; singing; softball; squash; gardening. Home: 521 Norton Ln Arnold MD 21012 Office: Fgn Affairs and Nat Defense Div Congl Research Service 101 Independence Ave SE Washington DC 20540

PREISKEL, BARBARA SCOTT, lawyer, association executive; b. Washington, July 6, 1924; d. James and B. Beatrix Scott; B.A., Wellesley Coll., 1945; LL.B., Yale U., 1947; m. Robert H. Preiskel, Oct. 28, 1950; children—John S., Richard A. Bar: D.C. 1948, N.Y. 1948, U.S. Supreme Ct. 1960. Law clk. U.S. Dist. Ct., Boston, 1948-49; assoc. firm Poletti, Diamond, Roosevelt, Freidin & Mackay, N.Y.C., 1949-50; assoc. firm Dwight, Royall, Harris, Koegel & Caskey, N.Y.C., 1950-54, cons., N.Y.C., 1954-59; cons. Ford Found. Fund for the Republic, N.Y.C., 1954; dep. atty. Motion Picture Assn. Am., Inc., N.Y.C., 1959-71, v.p., legis. counsel, 1971-77, sr. v.p., gen. atty., 1977-83; dir. Textron Inc., Gen. Electric Co., Mass. Mut. Life Ins. Co., R.H. Macy Corp., Am. Stores Co., Washington Post Co. Mem. Pres.'s. Commn. on Obscenity and Pornography, 1968-70; bd. dirs. Citizens Com. for Children, 1966-72, Child Adoption Service of State Charities Aid Assn., 1961-68, Hillcrest Ctr. for Children, 1958-61, Fedn. of Protestant Welfare Agys., 1959-61, 64—, N.Y. Philharm. Soc., 1971—; bd. dirs. Wiltwyck Sch., 1950-80, chmn. bd., 1969-78; mem. N.Y.C. Bd. Ethics, 1976—; successor trustee Yale Corp., 1977—; trustee Ford Found.; bd. dirs. Med. Edn. for South African Blacks, Inc., 1985—; mem. council of advisors Hunter Coll. Sch. Social Work, 1985—; mem. distbn. com. N.Y. Community Trust, 1978—; mem. operating corp. N.Y. Conv. Center, 1980-83, Mem. Am. Bar Assn., Bar Assn. City of N.Y. (exec. com. 1972-76), ACLU (dir. 1971-79, nat. adv. council 1984—, exec. com. 1973-79), Am. Arbitration Assn., Am. Women's Econ. Devel. Corp. Home: 300 West End Ave New York NY 10023 Office: 36 W 44th St New York NY 10036

PREISLER, RENEE, foundation administrator, professional fundraiser; b. Cleve., Oct. 4, 1936; d. Edwin Donald and Seema D. (Epstein) P.; m. George Lease, Sept. 9, 1956 (div. 1965); children—James J., Tammy R., Brian. J. m. Donald Glickson, Oct. 4, 1968 (div. Nov. 1980). Student U. Miami, 1954-55, Western Res. U., 1955-56, 56-57. Dir. spl. events and pub. relations Sta. KQED/Channel 9, San Francisco, 1978-81; dir. women's div. Jewish Community Fedn., San Francisco, 1981-85; dir. devel. Arthritis Found. of N.E. Ohio, Cleve., 1985—. Mem. Women's Way Resource Ctr., San Francisco, 1980-81. Recipient Pub. TV promotion award Pub. Broadcasting System, 1981. Mem. Ohio Council Fund Raising Execs., Nat. Assn. Fund Raising Execs., Nat. Assn. Female Execs., Assn. Jewish Communal Orgn. Personnel, North Bay Communications Assn. (founding mem., sec. 1979-81). Democrat. Jewish. Avocations: painting; writing; tennis. Office: Arthritis Found NE Ohio 11416 Bellflower Rd Cleveland OH 44106

PRENTICE, ANN ETHELYND, library administrator; b. Grafton, Vt., July 19, 1933; d. Homer Orville and Helen (Cooke) Hurlbut; (div.) children—David, Melody, Holly, Wayne. A.B., U. Rochester, 1954; M.L.S., SUNY, Albany, 1964; D.L.S., Columbia U., 1972; Litt.D. (hon.), Keuka Coll., 1979. Lectr. sch. library and info. sci. SUNY, Albany, 1971-72, asst. prof., 1972-78; dir. grad. sch. library and info. sci. U. Tenn., Knoxville, 1978—. Author: Strategies for Survival, Library Financial Management Today, 1979, The Library Trustee, 1973, Public Library Finance, 1977, Financial Planning for Libraries, 1983; editor: Public Library Quar, 1978-81. Cons. Longrange planning and personnel Knoxville City County Library, 1980, Richland County, S.C. Library System, 1981; Trustee Hyde Park (N.Y.) Free Library, treas., 1973-75, pres., 1976; trustee Mid-Hudson Library System, Poughkeepsie, N.Y., 1975-78. Mem. ALA, Am. Mgmt. Assn., Am. Soc. Info. Sci., AAUP, Assn. Info. Mgrs., Assn. Am. Library Schs., Am. Printing History Assn. Home: 11516 Foxford Dr Knoxville TN 37922 Office: 804 Volunteer Blvd Knoxville TN 37996

PRENTICE, MARY LEA, media ednl. adminstr.; b. Plymouth, Ill., May 16, 1930; d. Clyde J. and Mary R. (Huddleston) Ware; B.S., Western Ill. U., 1958; NDEA scholar Purdue U., summer 1966; M.S. (Delta Kappa Gamma scholar), Ill. State U., 1974; postgrad. U. Mo., 1982; postgrad. (scholar) Photographer's Edn. Workshop, St. Cloud State U., summer 1982; m. Richmond Ellis Prentice, Aug. 4, 1950; children—Rodney Ellis, Gina Luan. Tchr. elem. sch., Hancock County, Ill., 1950-55; library asst. Streator (Ill.) Elem. Schs., 1956-57; media supr. Pikeland Community Unit No. 10 Schs., Pittsfield, Ill., 1961—; mem. North Central Accreditation Visitation Teams, 1965—; cons. Library Book Selection Service, Inc., 1977—. Bd. dirs. Pittsfield Public Library, 1975—; bd. dirs. West Central Ill. area Gt. River Library System, 1982—, v.p., 1986—. Mem. NEA, Ill. Assn. Media Educators, Western Ill. Audiovisual Assn., Div. Sch. Media Specialists, Assn. Ednl. Communications and Tech., Ill. Assn. Edn. Communications and Tech. (treas. 1982—), Delta Kappa Gamma. Methodist. Contbr. articles to profl. jours. Office: Pittsfield High Sch Pittsfield IL 62363

PRESCOTT, EILEEN, marketing executive, writer; b. N.Y.C., June 22, 1949; d. Ray and Kathryn (MacGuire) P.; m. Thomas Michael Drape, Apr. 27, 1985. B.A., Hunter Coll., 1971. Pub. relations dir. Stern & Day, N.Y.C., 1975-77; pres. Eileen Prescott Co., Inc., N.Y.C., 1977-85, Prescott Speaker Mgmt., N.Y.C., 1981-85; v.p., group mgr. Marketshare/Doremus, 1985—; guest tchr. Radcliffe Coll., Boston, 1982, 83, NYU, 1983, George Washington U., Washington, 1983; assoc. Wellesley Coll. Ctr. for Research on Women, Mass., 1984—. Mem. Women in Communications, Pub. Relations Soc. Am., Pubs. Publicity Assn. (Jean Ennis scholar 1976), Am. Mktg. Assn., Women Bus. Owners Assn., LWV. Office: Marketshare/Doremus 41 Madison Ave New York NY 10010

PRESCOTT, ETHELIND SOUTHERLAND, educator; b. Arcadia, Fla., Sept. 22, 1930; d. Frederick and Clara (Warlick) Southerland; B.S. in Edn. magna cum laude, Fla. So. Coll., 1969; m. Bedford Prescott, Mar. 18, 1951; children—Donald B., Linda Gail. Tchr., Zolfo Elem. Sch., Zolfo Springs, Fla., 1969-71, migrant child reading tchr., 1971-73, classroom tchr., 1973-74; migrant child lang. arts tchr. Hardee County, Fla., 1974—. Organist, New Hope Bapt. Ch., Wauchula, Fla., 1973—; mem. youth devel. com., Wauchula, 1974. Mem. Hardee County Edn. Assn., Fla. Edn. Assn. Baptist. Clubs: Wauchula Jr. Woman's (sec. 1956-58). Address: PO Box 52 Wauchula FL 33873

PRESCOTT, LINDA LOU, television station sales executive; b. Huntington, W.Va., June 8, 1942; d. Paul and Christine (Wilburn) Rose; m. James Earl Clay, Mar. 29, 1960 (div. June 1979); children—Donald Earl, Christy Lynn, Paul Louis; m. Roy J. Prescott, Mar. 27, 1981. Student Hillsborough Community Coll., 1971; student in sales tng. TV Bur. Advt., 1983, in mgmt., 1984. Accounts payable clk. Gunter Dunn Stores, Enterprise, Ala., 1977-79; account exec. Sta.-WDHN-TV, Dothan, Ala., 1979-80, Sta.-WKMX, Enterprise, 1980-81; local sales mgr. Sta.-WDHN-TV, Dothan, 1981, gen. sales mgr., 1981—. Author sales, video, radio and TV commls. TV hostess shows Dialing For Dollars, 1979-80, Silver Screen 18, 1980, Happy Half Hour With Linda, 1980, Claybank Jamboree Arts and Crafts Jamboree, 1980, 81-82. TV hostess Cerebral Palsy Telethon, Dothan, 1980; publicity worker S.E. Regional Chili Cook-Off, March of Dimes, 1981, Centennial Retail Com., Dothan, 1985, Jaycees Crippled Children's Golf and Tennis Classic, Dothan, 1985. Mem. TV Bur. Advt., Dothan Advt. Fedn., Dothan C. of C. (media promoter, 1985), Dothan Advt. Fedn. (treas. 1984). Republican. Baptist. Home: 2902 Evans Dr Dothan AL 36303 Office: STa-WDHN PO Box 6237 Dothan AL 36302

PRESCOTT, RITA ELIZABETH, judge; b. North Tonawanda, N.Y., June 6, 1921; d. William Waldo and Marie Eleanore (Dreyer) P.; B.S., U. Pa., 1943, M.S., 1944; LL.B., Temple U., 1949. Tchr. comml. subjects Prospect Park (Pa.) High Sch., 1945-51; admitted to Pa. bar, 1952; individual practice law, 1952-75; law clk. to James C. Crumlish, Sr., Phila., 1951-58, to Judges Sweeney and Diggins, Ct. Common Pleas Delaware County, Media, Pa., 1958-60; ct. adminstr. County of Delaware, Media, 1961-75; judge Ct. Common Pleas, 32nd Jud. Dist. Commonwealth Pa., 1976—, adminstrv. judge civil div., 1980-84. Bd. overseers Del. Law Sch., Widener U., Brandywine, 1982—. Mem. Am. Bar Assn., Pa. Bar Assn., Deleware County Bar Assn., Phila. Bar Assn., Am. Judicature Soc., Inst. Jud. Adminstrs., Nat. Assn. Women Lawyers, Nat. Assn. Trial Ct. Adminstrs., Nat. Fedn. Bus. and Profl. Women, Mortar Bd., Pi Lambda Theta, Alpha Xi Delta. Office: Courthouse Media PA 19063

PRESHAW, PRISCILLA GAY, real estate investor, publicist; b. Mesa, Ariz., Jan. 9, 1948; d. Arthur Dwight and Nina Jean (Gross) Childress; m. Stephen Robert Leathers, Dec. 29, 1967 (div. 1980); children—Robert Wesley, Katherine Gay; m. Ralph Sherwood Preshaw, Oct. 3, 1980; stepchildren—Catherine Jean, Ralph Steven, Karl Richard, Robert Jameson. B.A., Ariz. State U., 1969; postgrad., 1980. Cert. assoc. realtor, Ariz. Feature writer Mesa Tribune, 1968-69, asst. women's editor, 1969, women's editor, 1969-70; copy editor Ariz. Republic, Phoenix, 1970-71; co-owner Leathers Enterprises, Mesa, 1972-80; real estate investor, Mesa, 1980—; publicist Mesa Mus., 1984—. Contbr. numerous articles and photographs to newspapers and mags. Recipient awards Ariz. Press Women, 1969. Mem. Nat. Assn. Realtors, Ariz. Assn. Realtors, Mesa-Chandler Tempe Bd. Realtors, Ariz. Fedn. Press Women, Nat. Fedn. Press Women (Excellence award 1969). Republican. Methodist. Avocations: writing; reading; fishing; hiking; racquetball. Home: 1843 E Gary St Mesa AZ 85203 Office: Mesa Mus 53 N Macdonald St Mesa AZ 85201

PRESKA, MARGARET LOUISE ROBINSON, university president; b. Parma, N.Y., Jan. 23, 1938; d. Ralph Craven and Ellen Elvira (Niemi) Robinson; B.S. summa cum laude, SUNY, Brockport, 1957; M.A., Pa. State U., 1961; Ph.D., Claremont (Calif.) Grad. Sch., 1969; postgrad. Manchester Coll., Oxford (Eng.) U., summer 1973; m. Daniel C. Preska, Jan. 24, 1959; children—Robert, William, Ellen. From instr. to assoc. prof. history and govt. U. LaVerne (Calif.), 1968-75, acad. dean, 1972-75; instr. Starr King Sch. Ministry, Berkeley, Calif., summer 1975; v.p. acad. affair, EEO officer Mankato (Minn.) State U., 1975-79, pres., 1979—; chmn. Fielding Inst.; bd. dirs. Minn. Council Econ. Edn.; mem. commn. govtl. relations Am. Council Edn.; dir. No. State Power Co., Inc., Norwest Bank of Mankato. Sec., Pomona Sign Study Commn., 1965-66; pres. Pomona Valley (Calif.) chpt. UN Assn., 1968-69, Unitarian Soc. Pomona Valley, 1968-69, Pomona (Calif.) chpt. LWV, 1972-74, Lincoln Elem. Sch. PTA, Pomona, 1973-74; mem. Pomona City Charter Revision Commn., 1972; exec. bd. Twin Valley council Boy Scouts Am., 1978; bd. dirs. Mankato Salvation Army, 1979—, Farm Am., Minn. Wellspring; nat. bd. dirs. Elderhostel, Camp Fire, Inc.; chmn. Gov.'s Council on Youth; mem. Mpls.-St. Paul Com. on Fgn. Relations. Named Outstanding Alumna, Claremont Grad. Sch., 1979, Disting. Educator, 1980; grantee Carnegie Found., 1974. Mem. Am. Assn. Univ. Adminstrs. (dir. found.), Am. Assn. State Colls. and Univs., AAUW, Women's Equity Action League, Mankato C. of C. (dir.), P.E.O., Minn. Women's Econ. Roundtable, Delta Sigma Pi, Phi Kappa Phi, Pi Lambda Theta, Delta Kappa Gamma, Kappa Delta Pi. Mem. Democratic-Farmer-Labor Party. Club: Benedicts Dance. Office: Box 24 Mankato State U South Rd and Ellis Ave Mankato MN 56001*

PRESLAR, DOROTHY LYNNE BRADDOCK, corporate transitions consultant; b. Bristol, Tenn., Mar. 2, 1938; d. Roy Lynn and Beulah Elizabeth (Powell) Braddock; m. Lloyd Thomas Preslar, 1958 (div. 1976); children—Lyle Thomas, Anna Reshard. B.A., Wake Forest Coll., 1958; postgrad. Georgetown U., 1974-75, George Washington U., 1976, Am. U., 1981-82. Various positions in pub. relations and law, Winston Salem, N.C. and Washington, 1958-79; legal asst. Arent, Fox, Kintner, Plotkin & Kahn, Washington, 1976-79; sr. legal asst. Wiley & Rein, and predecessor firm, Washington, 1979-83; exec. asst. to pres., corp. sec. Scott Labs., Inc., West Warwick, R.I., 1983-85; mgr. spl. communications Textron Inc., Providence, 1985; pres. POSIT, Providence, 1985—. Mem. com. Adv. Commn. on Women, Providence, 1985-86. Mem. Internat. Assn. Bus. Communicators, Nat. Assn. Female Execs., Phi Beta Kappa. Avocations: painting; song writing. Home: 410 Benefit St Providence RI 02903 Office: POSIT PO Box 3078 Providence RI 02906

PRESLEY, DELIA ANN, public relations executive; b. Paul's Valley, Okla., Aug. 18, 1957; d. Don Featherstone and Betty Anne (McCulley) P. B.A., S.W. Tex. State U., 1979. Field rep. Am. Cancer Soc., Bryan, Tex., 1979-80, dist. exec. dir., Midland, Tex., 1980-82, area pub. info. dir., Midland, 1981-82, area dir. pub. info. and crusade, Dallas, 1982-85; freelance pub. relations cons., 1985—; cons. Fairhill Pvt. Sch., 1983. Artfest vol. 500, Inc., 1983; mem. Community Gold II, Midland, 1981; vol. United Way, Dallas, 1982, employee campaign coordinator, 1983; judge Golden Herald awards Dallas Times Herald, 1984. Recipient awards Am. Cancer Soc. Tex. Div., Inc., 1981-84. Mem. Sigma Delta Chi. Republican. Presbyterian. Home and Office: 6673 Santa Anita St Dallas TX 75214

PRESLEY, NANCY MILLER, truck broker; b. Memphis, May 23, 1934; d. Hart D. and Dorothy (Callaway) Miller; m. W.A. Renfro, Sept. 1, 1961 (div. 1967); children—David Andrew, Lisa Clair; m. Flavis M. Presley, June 15, 1969; 1 child, Kristin Laine. Student U. Tenn., 1959. Dispatcher, Memphis Trucking Co., 1957-61, So. Cargo, Inc., Memphis, 1961-73; pres. Tenn. Truck Brokerage Co., Brownsville, 1974—; transp. cons. U. Miss., Oxford, 1980. Republican. Mem. Ch. of Christ. Avocations: organic gardening; natural health. Office: PO Box 254 Brownsville TN 38012

PRESS, LINDA JEANNE, coffee company executive; b. Rockville Centre, N.Y., Nov. 19, 1953; d. James W. and Virginia (Oxenchuk) P. Student Nassau Community Coll., SUNY-Farmingdale, C.W. Post Coll. Gen. mgr. Controlled Sheet Music Service Inc., Copiague, N.Y., 1974-80; sales adminstr. Modern Main Food Products, Garden City, N.Y., 1980-83; mktg. mgr. DCA, N.Y.C., 1983; v.p. Richheimer Coffee subs. Wechsler Coffee Co., Moonachie, N.J., 1984—; bd. dirs. Music Jobbers Assn., 1979-80. Mem. Nat. Assn. Female Execs. Avocations: skiing; bicycling. Office: Wechsler Coffee Co 10 Empire Blvd Moonachie NJ 07074

PRESSLEY, BETTY M., bond company official; b. St. Stephen, S.C., Mar. 23, 1948; d. Francena (Mack) Green; m. Isaac Pressley; children—Spencer, Tammy. B.S. in Bus. Adminstrn., Fordham U., 1984. Sales asst. Bankers Trust Co., N.Y.C., 1972-84; sales rep. Roosevelt & Cross, N.Y.C., 1984—. Mem. Mcpl. Bond Women Club N.Y., Alpha Sigma Lambda. Avocations: handball; basketball; softball. Home: 880 Boynton Ave Apt 85 Bronx NY 10473 Office: 20 Exchange Pl New York NY 10005

PRESSLEY, JOYCE CAROLYN, clinical research analyst; b. Edneyville, N.C., Jan. 11, 1953; d. Merrimon Lewis and Barbara Lee (Gilliam) P. A.B. in Chemistry, Psychology, U. N.C., 1975; M.P.H. in Health Adminstrn., U. S.C., 1980. Asst. dir. emergency med. service Centralina Council of Govts., Charlotte, N.C., 1976-78; dir. emergency med. services Area IV EMS Program, Research Triangle, N.C., 1980-81; clin. research analyst Duke U., Durham, N.C., 1981—. Author abstracts. Contbr. articles to profl. jours. Docent N.C. Mus. Art, Raleigh, 1984-85; del. N.C. Rep. Party, Chapel Hill, 1976-78. Acad. trainee HEW, 1978-80. Mem. Am. Heart Assn., S.C. Student Pub. Health Assn. (pres. 1978-79), N.C. Art Soc., Duke Faculty Club. Avocations: tennis; art. Home: 1016 Minerva Ave Durham NC 27701 Office: Duke U Box 3860 Durham NC 27710

PRESTAGE, JEWEL LIMAR, political science educator; b. Hutton, La., Aug. 12, 1931; d. Brudis L. and Sallie Bell (Johnson) Limar; B.A., So. U., Baton Rouge, 1951; M.A., U. Iowa, 1952, Ph.D., 1954; m. James J. Prestage, Aug. 12, 1953; children—Terri, James, Eric, Karen, Jay. Asso. prof. polit. sci. Prairie View (Tex.) Coll., 1954-55, 56; asso. prof. polit. sci. So. U., Baton Rouge, 1956-57, 58-62, prof., 1962—, chairperson dept., 1965-83, dean Sch. Pub. Policy and Urban Affairs, 1983—. Chairperson, La. State adv. com. U.S. Commn. on Civil Rights, 1975-82 mem. Nat. Adv. Council on Women's Ednl. Programs, 1980, chairperson, 1981-82. Rockefeller fellow, 1951-52; NSF fellow, 1964; Ford Found. postdoctoral fellow, 1969-70. Mem. Am. (v.p. 1974-75), So. (pres. 1975-76), La. (pres. 1983-84) polit. sci. assns., Southwestern Social Sci. Assn. (pres. 1973-74), Nat. Conf. Black Polit. Scientists (pres. 1976-77), Alpha Kappa Alpha. Author: (with M. Githens) A Portrait of Marginality: Political Behavior of the American Woman, 1976; also articles. Home: 2145-77th Ave Baton Rouge LA 70807 Office: Box 9222 Southern U Baton Rouge LA 70813

PRESTHUS, TONIA LYNN, marketing executive; b. Chgo., Apr. 24, 1949; d. Robert Vance and Anita (Larsen) P. B.A. cum laude, UCLA, 1971; M.A., Calif. State U., 1975; Ph.D., Claremont Coll., 1980. With Pro-Max Engring. Corp., Carson, Calif., 1970-78; nat. sales mgr. ACS Communications, Santa Monica, Calif., 1978; dir. mktg. Analyticum, South Bay, 1979-81; spl. projects dir. Nat. Wallace-Berrie, Los Angeles, 1981-82; dir. mktg. and sales Metro, Inc., Los Angeles, 1982—; cons. Patentee in field. Mem. Am. Mgmt. Assn., Sales and Mktg. Execs., Calif. Med. Records Assn., AAUW. Democrat. Lutheran. Club: Euro-American (v.p. 1978-80). Home: 18-20th Ave Suite A Marina Del Rey CA 90291 Office: Metro Inc 1340 6th St Los Angeles CA 90021

PRESTON, ELAINE VICTORIA, lawyer; b. Erie, Pa., July 1, 1949; d. Joseph Henry and Celia (Tatara) Prezwicki; m. Kenneth Isaacson, Sept. 29, 1979; 1 dau., Mariel Preston. B.A. in English, Villa Maria Coll., 1971; M.Ed., Edinboro U., 1972; J.D., Duquesne U., 1979. Bar: Pa. 1979, U.S. Supreme Ct. 1983. Continuity asst. WSEE-TV, Channel 35, Erie, Pa., 1970-71; pub. relations asst. Model Cities Program, Erie, 1971; tchr. McDowell Sr. High Sch., Millcreek, Pa., 1972-76; residential/comml. real estate salesperson Stevens & Co., Realtors, Erie, 1976; law clk. Watzman & Elovitz, Pitts., 1978; law clk. U.S. Dist. Ct. (we. dist.) Pa., 1978-79; pvt. practice law, Pitts., 1979—. Dir. debate team, theatre club, McDowell Sr. High Sch., Erie, 1973-76; mem. philosophy com. Millcreek Long Range Planning Bd., Erie, 1975-76; mem. Legal Rights of Women, Pitts., 1979—. Mem. ABA, Pa. Bar Assn., Pa. Trial Lawyers Assn., Allegheny County Bar Assn., Assn. Trial Lawyers Am., Duquesne Women Law Students Assn., Alice Maynell Lit. Soc., Order Barristers, Pi Alpha Delta, Kappa Gamma Pi. Democrat. Office: 1512 Frick Bldg Pittsburgh PA 15219

PRESTON, ELIZABETH, veterinarian; b. West Chester, Pa., Sept. 30, 1952; d. Forest and Cheslye Ann (Larrimer) Preston; m. Thomas Woodrow Engle, July 22, 1978. B.S., Pa. State U., 1974; V.M.D., U. Pa., 1978. Veterinarian, Hopewell Vet. Service, Stewartstown, Pa., 1978-83; veterinarian, partner Hopewell Vet. Service, 1983—. Mem. AVMA, Pa. Vet. Med. Assn., Am. Assn. Bovine Practitioners, D.C. Acad. Vet. Medicine. Republican. Mem. Soc. of Friends. Home: RD 3 PO Box 406 Stewartstown PA 17363 Office: Hopewell Vet Service RD 1 PO Box 1005 Stewartstown PA 17363

PRESTON, JENNIFER MCKINNON, employee relations executive; b. St. Joseph, Mo., May 13, 1954; d. Jack L. and Audrey June (Blakley) McKinnon; m. Robert Alan Preston, July 7, 1983. B.A., Mo. Western State Coll., 1978; postgrad. U. Mo.-Kansas City, 1982—. Sec., Dan Garvin M.F.A. Ins. Agy., St. Joseph, Mo., 1972-75; personnel supr. Montgomery Ward, St. Joseph,

1975-79, personnel mgr., 1979-81; personnel mgr. Versatile Farm Equipment Corp., Kansas City, 1981-84; employee relations mgr. Western Auto Supply Co., Kansas City, 1984-85, dir. employee relations, 1985—. Mem. Am. Soc. Personnel Adminstrn., Personnel Mgmt. Assn. Greater Kansas City. Republican. Methodist. Home: 3914 Woodridge St Lee's Summit MO 64063 Office: Western Auto Supply Co 2107 Grand St Kansas City MO 64108

PRESTON, MARY LEE, educator; b. New Willard, Tex., Nov. 20, 1931; d. Damon and Angeline Fletcher Hunter; B.S., Tex. So. U., 1972, M.A.Ed., 1981; m. Foster Preston, Dec. 5, 1950; children—Angie, Alfred, Annie, Foster, Rosemary, Ava, Sherry, Michael, Mona. Clk., Community Chapel Pre-Need Funeral Plans, Houston, 1966-81; instructional coordinator Dunbar Elem. Sch., Houston, 1978-80; 4th grade tchr. and chairperson Anson Jones Sch., Houston Ind. Sch. Dist., 1980—; tchr. vol. Adult Basic Edn. and Gen. Edn. Diploma, 1980-82; edn. cons. Martin Luther King Jr. Community Center, 1979-82, treas. bd. dirs., 1980-81. Pres., Dunbar Alliance Parents, Tchr. Assos. and Patrons, 1975-81; chmn. bd. Purpose, Inc., 1970-74; supr. Shaklee Corp. Named Tchr. of Yr., Anson Jones Sch., 1982, 83. Mem. NEA, Nat. Assn. Female Execs., Tex. State Tchrs. Assn., Houston Tchrs. Assn., Tex. So. Reading Club. Baptist. Lodges: Order Eastern Star (sec.). Home: 3401 Oakdale St Houston TX 77004

PRESTON, SUSAN BETH, insurance broker; b. Sparta, Wis., Jan. 9, 1953; d. David Clayton and Mary Douglas (Wade) Hinshaw; m. Alan Robert Preston, May 18, 1974. Student Mich. State U., 1971-73. Personal line broker's asst. CSE Ins. Co., San Francisco, 1976-77; comml. broker's asst. A. Mason Blodgett & Assocs., San Francisco, 1977-79, ins. broker, life agt., 1979—. Bd. dirs. Camp Fire, Inc., San Francisco, 1980-85, chmn. nominating com., 1982-85; mem. Prison Law Office Bd. of San Quentin, 1984-85. Mem. Profl. Ins. Agts., San Francisco Ins. Women. Methodist. Home: 305 Sylvia Way San Rafael CA 94903 Office: A Mason Blodgett & Assocs 1625 Van Ness St San Francisco CA 94109

PRESTON, VERA ALMA, educator; b. Oklahoma City, May 30, 1942; d. Joe Lafayette and Liberty (Bennett) P.; B.S., Okla. State U., 1962; M.A. (grad. asst.), U. Maine, 1969; m. Norman Bruce Callahan, Oct. 14, 1964 (div. 1976); children—Melissa, Mark. Vol., Peace Corps, Banos, Tungarahua, Ecuador, 1962-64; tchr. Gaithersburg (Md.) High Sch., 1964-65, Edgewood (Md.) High Sch., 1965; instr. math. West Chester (Pa.) State Coll., 1967; part-time math. instr. Berkshire Community Coll., 1973-76; tchr. Zebulon (N.C.) High Sch., 1978-81; tchr. math. Red Rock (Okla.) Pub. Sch., 1982-84, Central Jr. High Sch., Bartlesville, Okla., 1984—; del. Equity Conf., Albuquerque, 1982. Tchr., Sunday sch. Unity Ch., 1978-81; organizer, lst pres. Family Centered Parents, Inc., Wilmington, Del., 1970; organizer Literacy Vols. Am., Pittsfield, Mass., 1976. Mem. Nat. Council Tchrs. of Math., Okla. Council Tchrs. of Math. (dir. 1982-85), Women and Math. Edn. (bd. dirs. 1986—, pres.-elect 1986), Assn. Supervision and Curriculum Devel., Kappa Delta Pi. Republican. Home: 1201 Saddle Lane Bartlesville OK 74006 Office: Central Jr High School 8th & Cherokee Bartlesville OK 74003

PRESTON-COOPER, DOLORES, lawyer; b. Chgo., Oct. 25, 1932; d. Eugene Preston and Lillie (Freeman) Preston Young; m. Clifton J. Cooper, Mar. 2, 1962 (div.); children—Deborah Patillo, Lynnette Love, Esther Cooper, Stephen. B.S., Wayne State U., 1955, M.Ed., 1970, D.Ednl. Sociology, 1975, J.D., 1981. Bar: Mich. 1982. Tchr., Sumpter Twp., Belleville, Mich., 1955-57, Chgo. Bd. Edn., 1958-62; tchr./supervising tchr., black history cons. Detroit Bd. Edn., 1962-70; team leader tchr. corps Wayne State U., Detroit Bd. Edn., 1971; curriculum coordinator Detroit Bd. Edn., 1971-76, tchr. supr., 1976-83; labor negotiator, atty. Detroit Bd. Edn., 1983—; tchr. adult edn. Chgo. Bd. Edn., 1961; adj. instr. Wayne County Community Coll., Detroit, 1976-80. Recipient Fulbright-Hays award Mich. State/Wayne State U., 1982. Mem. State Bar Mich., ABA, NAACP, Mich. Council English Tchrs., Met. Detroit Reading Council (exec. dir., sec. 1982-83), Indsl. Research Assn. Club: Just Us Ladies Bridge (pres. 1980-82, sec. 1982-83, fin. sec. 1984—). Office: Detroit Bd Edn 5057 Woodward Ave Detroit MI 48221

PRETLOW, CAROL JOCELYN, fashion consultant; b. Salisbury, Md., Nov. 9, 1946; d. Kenneth H. and Vivian Virginia (Hughes) P. B.A., Fisk U., 1976; M.A., Norfolk State U., 1982; postgrad. Antioch Law Sch., 1984-85. Fashion columnist The Smithfield Times (Va.), 1977-80; talk show hostess Sta. WAVY-TV, 1978-81; fashion editor Tidewater Life Mag., 1979; reporter, asst. news dir. Sta. WNSB News, Norfolk, Va., 1980-81; press sec. Com. to Elect Fred D. Thompson Jr. Treas. Isle of Wight County, 1981; ind. fashion cons., Smithfield, Va., 1982—; adj. prof. communication Paul D. Camp Community Coll., Franklin, Va. Coordinator Sesquitricentennial Celebration, Isle of Wight County, 1984. Home: RR3 Box 697 Smithfield VA 23430

PREVAUX, CAROL ANN, human resource development executive, consultant; b. Detroit, Apr. 11, 1941; d. Michael and Olisha Katherine (Petryk) Soviak; children—Janine Carole, Steven David, Lorain Carole. Student Henry Ford Coll., Dearborn, Mich., 1959-60, U. Mich.-Ann Arbor, 1960-61; B.A. with high distinction, U. Mich.-Dearborn, 1972. Cert. tchr., Mich., Fla. Resource specialist, Hillsborough County Bd. Edn., Tampa, Fla., 1973-75; dir. Personal Enrichment Resources, St. Petersburg Beach, Fla., 1975-77; mgmt. cons. New View, Inc., Clearwater, Fla., 1977-79; mgmt. devel. specialist Fla. Power Corp., St. Petersburg, 1979-80, supr. mgmt. devel., 1980-82, mgr. human resource devel., 1982-83, dir. human resource devel., 1983—; mem. career planning com. Edison Electric Inst., Washington, 1981-83; chmn. pub. utility mgmt. course planning com. Southeastern Electric Exchange, Atlanta, 1982-85. Columnist: Dearborn Guide, 1958-59. Mem. adv. bd. Eckerd Coll. Mgmt. Devel. Inst., St. Petersburg, 1983—. Recipient Women in Mgmt. award Mid-Day Bus. and Profl. Women's Assn., 1983. Mem. ASTD (pres. 1978-79, 84—), Nat. Assn. Female Execs., U. Mich. Alumni Assn. (bd. dirs. 1986). Avocations: photography; music; swimming. Home: 3280-B 37th Way S Saint Petersburg FL 33711 Office: Fla Power Corp 3201 34th St S Saint Petersburg FL 33711

PREVOST, MARY LYNN, lawyer, executive policy analyst; b. Decatur, Ill.; d. Raymond Lynn and Edith Lydia (Munro) Braden; children—Denise, Nancy, Jeffrey. B.A., Evergreen State Coll., 1979; J.D., U. Puget Sound, 1982. Bar: Wash. 1982. Legal intern Owens, Weaver, Davies & Dominick, Olympia, Wash., 1981; mgmt. analyst State of Wash., Olympia, 1982; staff cons. Office Fin. Mgmt., State of Wash., Olympia, 1982-85, exec. policy analyst, 1985—, on spl. assignment for comparable worth study Office of Gov., 1985—; mem. adv. com. Highline Community Coll. Legal Asst. Program, Midway, Wash., 1977-78; student coordinator Wash. Bar Assn. Conf. on Adoption Legislation, Tacoma, 1981. Program coordinator Rotary Internat. Dist. Conf., Olympia, 1980. Evergreen Found. scholar, 1979. Mem. Wash. Bar Assn., ABA, Governmental Lawyers (pres. 1986—), Wash. Women Lawyers. Methodist. Office: Office of Financial Mgmt Insurance Bldg MS AQ-44 Olympia WA 98504

PREZIOSO, LISA ANN, promotion specialist, journalist; b. Elizabeth, N.J., Aug. 23, 1958; d. Anthony J. and Dorothy J. (Madonia) P. B.A. in Journalism and Urban Communication, Rutgers U., 1980; postgrad. Seton Hall U., 1984—. Advt. sales, staff writer The Chronicle, Fairfield, N.J., 1979; corr. The Star Ledger, Newark, 1979; staff writer The Daily Jour., Elizabeth, 1980-83; promotion specialist Dun & Bradstreet Credit Services, N.J., 1983—; intern U.S. Senator Bill Bradley, 1979. Co-host TV program N.J. Press Conference, 1981. Vol. The Lighthouse, N.Y. Assn. Blind, N.Y.C., 1981-84. Mem. Internat. Assn. Bus. Communicators (Iris award of merit in video tape), N.J. Press Women, Kean Coll. Profl. Women's Assn. Roman Catholic.

PRICE, ALICE L., literary agency executive, writer, consultant; b. Charlottesville, Va., Feb. 3, 1949; d. Robert Huntington and Alice Isabel (Valle) Knight; m. Paul Anthony Price, Oct. 25, 1972 (div. May 1981); 1 child, Rita Michael. B.A., UCLA, 1982, M.B.A., 1982. Owner, mgr. Rocky Mt. Housing, Denver, 1972-74; organizational cons., Los Angeles, 1977-82; organizational cons. Don't Ask Computer Software, Inc., Los Angeles, 1982-83, lit. agt. Peter Livingston Assocs., Boulder, Colo., 1983—; cons. ABC TV, Los Angeles, 1978—, Lorimar Prodns., Los Angeles, 1977-79, Foote, Cone & Belding/Honig, Los Angeles, 1980, Microsystems Cons. Group, Los Angeles, 1980-82. Contbg. author: The World's Great Contemporary Poems, 1981. Contbg. author and editor: How to Get a Man to Make a Commitment, 1985. Editor: Gray Eagles, 1986; Rebecca Wood's Encyclopedia of Whole Foods, 1986. Del. Democratic Party, Colo., 1972, 76, mem. Pres.'s Club, 1979; vol. writing tchr. Boulder County Pub. Schs., 1984—; invited lectr. Colo. Lang. Arts Soc., 1986. Mem. Ind. Lit. Agts. Assn., Inc., Am. Film Inst., Sierra Club, Phi Beta Kappa, Psi Chi, Pi Gamma Mu. Avocations: riding; sailing; swimming; travel. Home: 3150 29th St Boulder CO 80301 Office: Peter Livingston Assocs Inc 947 Walnut St Suite 800 Boulder CO 80302

PRICE, BARBARA JONES, insurance company executive; b. Hammond, La., Oct. 20, 1941; d. Lloyd Lamar and Nell (White) Jones; m. Henry Lewis Price, Jan. 29, 1961 (div.); children—Donald W., Henry L., Elizabeth L., Margaret N. Student, La. State U., 1959-61; B.A., Southeastern La. U., 1971. Vol. service coordinator Hammond State Schs., 1966-69; tchr. Tangipahoa Parish Sch. Bd., Amite, La., 1972; dep. registrar voters Tangipahoa Parish, 1973-74; agt., owner Jones-Hinson Ins. Agy., Inc., Hammond, 1975—. Pres. Tangipahoa Parish PTA, 1972; mem. council La Tangi Bapt. Assn., Hammond, 1985; mem. Gen. Accident La. Producers Adv. Council, New Orleans, 1984—. Named Outstanding Woman of Yr., Bus. and Profl. Women of Hammond, 1969. Mem. Ind. Ins. Agts. Tangipahoa (pres. 1981, bd. dirs. 1985), Soc. Cert. Ins. Counselors. Club: Altrusa (Hammond) (v.p. 1984-86, pres 1986—). Avocation: La. Bapt. Conv. mission volunteer. Home: 625 Rue St Martin Hammond LA 70401 Office: Jones-Hinson Ins Agy Inc Commerce St Hammond LA 70403

PRICE, CAROL-ANN, data processing center executive; b. West Orange, N.J., Apr. 10, 1936; d. Clifford Harold and Helen Anna (Hollum) Minier; m. Thomas J. Price, Sr., Apr. 17, 1955; children—Thomas J. Jr., Robert Alan. B.A. in Bus. Adminstrn., Bellevue Coll., 1975; postgrad. in exec. bus. adminstrn. Creighton U., 1982-83, U. Nebr., 1985—. Cert. Nat. Assn. Coll. and Univ. Bus. Officers. Bus. mgr. Nebr. Coll. Bus., Omaha, 1975-79; controller Bellevue Coll., Nebr., 1979-80, bus. mgr. 1980-81; seminar speaker, panelist, 1982—; mgr. adminstrv. services Land Bank Nat. Data Processing Ctr., Omaha, 1981-84, dir. mgmt. services, 1984—. Coordinator USAF Family Services Orgn., Madrid, Spain, 1958-63; bd. dirs. Am. Kindergarten, Madrid, 1963; team leader United Way Midlands, Omaha, 1973, 74, Bellevue Coll. alumni fund raiser, 1982-86; chmn. bd. dirs. San. Improvement Dist. No. 5, 1985—. Mem. Adminstrv. Mgmt. Soc. (cert. adminstr. mgr., local pres. 1980-81, area asst. dir. 1982-83, internat. bd. dirs. 1983-85, internat. v.p. 1985—, Merit Scroll award 1982, Diamond Merit award 1984). Republican. Episcopalian. Club: Bay Hills Golf (bd. dirs. 1985—, sec./treas. golf course) (Plattsmouth, Nebr.). Avocations: opera; symphony; theatre; travel; golf. Home: Rural Route 2 Buccaneer Bay Plattsmouth NE 68048 Office: Land Bank Nat Data Processing Ctr 7300 Woolworth Ave Omaha NE 68124

PRICE, CHARLOTTE EMOJEAN, police officer; b. Verdun, France, Oct. 29, 1958; d. James Walter and Edith Irene (Barnes) P. Student Nashville State Tech. Inst., 1979-79. Sgt. Capitol Police, State of Tenn., Nashville, 1978—. Mem. Nat. Assn. Female Execs. Democrat. Baptist. Home: 6700 Cabot Dr Apt H8 Nashville TN 37209 Office: Capitol Police Cordell Hull Bldg C3 306 5th Ave N Nashville TN 37219

PRICE, CHERYL AVIS, librarian; b. Oak Park, Ill., Mar. 14, 1944; d. Minor Carr and Malvina D. P.; B.S., Mo. Valley Coll., 1966; M.A., No. Ill. U., 1971; M.A.L.S., Rosary Coll., 1977. Jud. liaison specialist DuPage County Govt., Wheaton, Ill., 1971-73, county law librarian, 1973-79; polit. sci./law librarian No. Ill. U., DeKalb, 1979-81, internat. documents and law librarian, 1981-83, gen. reference librarian, 1983-85. Bibl. Inst. coordinator Ill. Inst. Tech., Chgo., 1986—. Mem. AAUW, ALA, Am. Law Librarians Assn. Office: Founders Library No Ill U DeKalb IL 60115

PRICE, CONNIE R., accountant; author; b. Chgo., Sept. 24, 1954; d. Henry W. and Dorothy M. (McLucas) Price, Jr. B.S. in Bus. Adminstrn., Chgo. State U., 1976. Clerical cashier Marianne Shop, Chgo., 1971-77; plant acct. DeSota Chem. Co., Des Plaines, Ill., 1977-79, fed. tax acct., 1979-80; fed. tax acct. Maremont Corp., Chgo., 1980-83; tax acct. Ill. Tool Works Inc., Chgo., 1983—. Author book of poetry: Those Simple Feelings of Life, 1980; (play) God's Judgement, 1983; author various short stories. Democratic poll watcher, 1982, 83; choir mem. Nat. Bapt. Congress Musical, Chgo., 1983. Recipient Ill. State Monetary award Ill. State Scholarship Commn., 1972. Mem. Chgo. Tax Club, Nat. Assn. Female Execs. Democrat. Baptist. Office: Ill Tool Works Inc 8501 W Higgins Rd Chicago IL 60615

PRICE, CORA LEE BEERS, educator; b. Janesville, Wis., Nov. 28, 1908; d. Clarence Palmer and Cora Bertha (Griffith) Beers; B.A., Beloit Coll., 1932; M.A., Claremont Coll., 1933; Ph.D., Stanford U., 1940; m. Griffith Baley Price, June 18, 1940; children—Cora Lee, Griffith Baley, Lucy Jean, Edwina Clare, Sallie Diane, Doris Joanne. Instr. English, Beloit (Wis.) Coll., 1933-34; asst. in English, Stanford (Calif.) U., 1934-36; instr. English, Cath. U. Am., summer, 1935; tchr. Latin and English, Tulare (Calif.) High Sch., 1936-38; instr. English, Wilson Coll., Chambersburg, Pa., 1938-40; instr. English, U. Kans., Lawrence, 1945-46, 61-65, instr. classics, 1962-67, lectr. classics, 1967-73, asst. prof. classics, 1973-79, emerita, 1979—; asst. prof. English, Baker U., Baldwin, Kans., 1980; organist Bapt. Ch., Janesville, Wis., 1925-34, Lawrence, 1957-59, 61-62. Sec., City Council PTA, Lawrence; bd. dirs. Am. Bapt. Student Center, U. Kans., 1967-72, Lawrence Civic Choir, 1973-74. Claremont Coll. grad. fellow, 1932-33. Mem. Nat. Council Tchrs. English, Am. Classical League, Classical Assn. Middle East and South, AAUW. Baptist. Clubs: Lawrence Music (pres. 1945-47), Kans. U. Women's, Zodiac. Contbr. articles to profl. jours. Home: 1520 Barker Ave Lawrence KS 66044 Office: Classics Dept U of Kans Lawrence KS 66044

PRICE, FAYE HUGHES, mental health adminstr.; b. Indpls.; d. Twidell W. and Lillian Gladys (Hazlewood) Hughes; A.B. with honors (scholar 1939-43), W.Va. State Coll., 1943; postgrad. social work (scholar) Ind. U., 1943-44; M.S.W., Jane Addams Sch., U. Ill., 1951; student summer insts. U. Chgo. 1960-65; m. Frank Price, Jr., June 16, 1945; 1 dau., Faye Michele. Supr. youth activities Flanner House, Indpls., 1945-47; program dir. Parkway Community House, Chgo., 1947-56, dir., 1957-58; dir. social services mental health div. Chgo. Dept. Health, 1958-61, dir. community services, 1961-65, asso. dir. planning and devel., 1965-69, regional program dir., 1969-75, asst. dir. mental health, 1975, acting dir., 1976, asst. dir. bur. mental health, 1976—; cons. various health, welfare and youth agencies; field instr. U. Ill., U. Chgo., Atlanta U., George Williams U.; lectr. Chgo. State U., U. Ill., other profl. workshops, seminars and confs. Active mem. Art Inst. Chgo., Bravo chpt. Chgo. Lyric Opera, Chgo. Urban League, Southside Community Art Center, Chgo., Chgo. YWCA, 9800 Parnell Ave. Block Club, Chgo., DuSable Mus., Chgo. Recipient scholarship Mt. Zion Baptist Ch., 1938-39, Fisk U., 1943; Mother-of-Year award Chgo. State Women's Club, 1975. Mem. Nat. Assn. Social Work, Acad. Certified Social Workers, Ill. Welfare Assn., Ill. Group Psychotherapy Soc., Nat. Conf. on Social Welfare, Council on Social Work Edn., Center for Continuing Edn. of Ill. Mental Health Insts., Nat. Assn. Parliamentarians, Alpha Gamma Pi, Alpha Kappa Alpha, NAACP, U. Ill. Alumni Assn., Nat. Council Negro Women, Urban League, Municipal Employees Soc. Chgo. Episcopalian. Clubs: Jack and Jill of Am. Assos., Links, Inc. (nat. dir. trends and services) (Chgo.), Les Cameos Social, Chums. Address: 9815 S Parnell Ave Chicago IL 60628

PRICE, HOLLISTER ANNE CAWEIN, airline administrator, interior design consultant; b. Memphis, Feb. 11, 1954; d. Madison Albert Cawein and Billie Jeanne (Roberts) Stewart; m. James H. Price, Jr., Oct. 21, 1978 (div. 1985). Student Memphis State U., 1972-75. Office mgr. Bruce Motor Co., Memphis, 1975-76; br. mgr. Central States Agy., Memphis, 1976-78; facility coordinator Fed. Express Corp., Memphis, 1978—; design cons. Smart Shoppes, Inc., Hardy and Trumann, Ark., 1985. Dept. leader Ch. Sch. Edn. Program, Central Ch., 1984-85. Mem. Nat. Assn. Female Execs., Delta Gamma Alumnae. Republican. Episcopalian. Avocations: scuba diving, horseback riding, biking, antique collecting. Office: Fed Express Corp Dept 2660 PO Box 727 Memphis TN 38194

PRICE, JEANNINE ALLEENICA, clinical psychologist; b. Cleve., Oct. 29, 1949; d. Q. Q. and Lisa Denise (Wilson) Ewing; m. T. R. Price, Sept. 2, 1976. B.S., Western Res. U., 1969; M.S., Vanderbilt U., 1974; M.B.A., Stanford U., 1985. Cert. alcoholism counselor, Calif. Health Service coordinator Am. Profile, Nashville, 1970-72; exec. dir. Awareness Concept, San Jose, Calif., 1977-80; mgr. employee assistance program Nat. Semiconductor, Santa Clara, Calif., 1980-81; v.p. AMP, Houston, 1984—; mgmt. cons. employee assistant programs. Author: Smile a Little, Cry a Lot; Gifts of Love; Reflection in the Mirror; Rose Garden Book of Love Poems. Mem. Gov.'s Adv. Council Child Devel. Programs. Mem. Am. Bus. Women's Assn., Nat. Assn. Female Execs., AAUW, Coalition Labor Women, Calif. Assn. Alcohol Counselors, Almaca. Office: 728 N 1st St San Jose CA 95112

PRICE, JOANN, physical education educator; b. Youngstown, Ohio, Oct. 12, 1928; d. Norman Ray and Edith (White) P. B.S. in Edn., Youngstown State U., 1950; M.S., U. Wis., 1955; Ed.D., Ind. U., 1969. Tchr. Canfield Jr. Sr. High Sch., Ohio, 1959-52; instr. Bryn Mawr Coll., Pa., 1952-55; instr. phys. edn. Purdue U., West Lafayette, Ind., 1955-60, asst. prof., 1960-73, assoc. prof., 1973—; cons. Nat. Golf Found., West Palm Beach, Fla., 1966-73; evaluator North Central Assn. Secondary Schs. and Colls., Indpls., Beech Grove, Lagrange, Ind., 1967-83. Contbr. articles to profl. jours. Campaigner YWCA, Lafayette, 1974, 84; hon. rules chmn. Ind. High Sch. Athletic Assn., Lebanon, 1971. Recipient Outstanding Woman in Sports award Lafayette and Purdue Women's Caucus, 1976; named to Athletic Hall of Fame, City of Fort Wayne, Ind., 1975. Mem. Assn. Tchr. Educators, Ind. Assn. for Tchr. Educators, Midwest Assn. Health, Phys. Edn., Recreation and Dance, Nat. Assn. Phys. Edn. in Higher Edn., Ind. Assn. Health, Phys. Edn., Recreation and Dance (treas. 1978-81), Midwest Assn. Coll. Women for Phys. Edn. (v.p. 1970-72), AAHPERD. Republican. Methodist. Ind. women's state golf amateur champion, 1973, 74, 79, 83; Ind. women's state sr. golf champion, 1981, 83. Avocations: golf; gardening; watching most sports. Home: 2224 Huron Rd West Lafayette IN 47906 Office: Purdue Univ Lambert Gym West Lafayette IN 47907

PRICE, JULIE MARIE, public relations executive; b. Tampa, Fla., Mar. 1, 1956; d. Lewis Temple and Charlene Marie (Johnson) Price. B.A., Baylor U., 1978; postgrad. NYU Sch. Continuing Edn. Editorial asst. Vought Corp. (LTV subs.), Dallas, 1978-80; writer, researcher LTV Corp., Dallas, 1980-81, editor employee publs., 1981-82, asst. dir. external communications, 1982-84, supr. fin. communications, 1984—; free-lance writer, Dallas. Contbr. articles to mags. Vol., DART (Dallas Area Rapid Transit), 1983, Dallas Ballet, 1981, KERA-pub. TV fund raising, Dallas, 1982; active The 500 Inc., Big Bros. and Sisters of Met. Dallas; tchr., mem. coms. Wilshire Baptist Ch., Dallas, 1982. Mem. Internat. Assn. Bus. Communicators, Pub. Relations Soc. Am. Democrat. Office: LTV Corp 1525 Elm St Dallas TX 75201

PRICE, LUCILE BRICKNER BROWN, civic worker; b. Decorah, Iowa, May 31, 1902; d. Sidney Eugene and Cora (Drake) Brickner; B.S., Iowa State U., 1925; M.A., Northwestern U., 1940; m. Maynard Wilson Brown, July 2, 1928 (dec. Apr. 1937); m. 2d, Charles Edward Price, Jan. 14, 1961 (dec. Dec. 1983). Asst. dean women Kans. State U., Manhattan, 1925-28; mem. bd. student personnel adminstrn. Northwestern U., 1937-41; personnel research Sears Roebuck & Co., Chgo., 1941-42, overseas club dir. ARC, Eng., Africa, Italy, 1942-45; dir. Child Edn. Found., N.Y.C., 1946-56. Participant 1st and 2d Iowa Humanists Summer Symposiums, 1974, 75. Del. Mid Century White House Conf. on Children and Youth, 1950; mem. com. on program and research of Children's Internat. summer villages, 1952-53; mem. bd. N.E. Iowa Mental Health Center, 1959-62, pres. bd., 1960-61; mem. Iowa State Extension Adv. Com., 1973-75; project chmn. Decorah Hist. Dist. (listed Nat. Register Historic Places); trustee Porter House Mus., Decorah, 1966-78, emeritus bd. dirs., 1982—; participant N. Central Regional Workshop Am. Assn. State and Local History, Mpls., 1975, Midwest Workshop Historic Preservation and Conservation, Iowa State U., 1976, 77; mem. Winneshiek County (Iowa) Civil Service Commn., 1978—. Recipient Alumni Merit award Iowa State U., 1975. Mem. Am. Coll. Personnel Assn., (life), Am. Overseas Assn. (nat. bd.; life), AAUW (life mem., mem. bd. Decorah; recipient Named Gift award 1977), Nat. Assn. Mental Health (del. nat. conf. 1958), Norwegian-Am. Mus. (life, Vesterheim fellow), Winneshiek County Hist. Soc. (life, cert. of appreciation 1984), DAR, Pi Lambda Theta, Chi Omega. Designer, builder house for retirement living. Home: 508 W Broadway Decorah IA 52101

PRICE, MARILYN JEANNE, fund raising consultant; b. N.Y.C., Jan. 24, 1948; d. George Franklin and Mary Anastasia (Barnishin) Lawrence; student Temple Bus. Sch., 1964-66; student U. Md., 1973-74; children—Kimberly Jean. Asst. to sr. printing and paper buyer ARC, Washington 1965-67; conf. planner for classified mil. confs. Nat. Security Indsl. Assn., Washington, 1967-69; fund devel. office asst. Nat. Urban Coalition, Washington, 1970; direct mail/membership coordinator Common Cause, Washington, 1970-72; mgr. direct mail fund raising Epilepsy Found. of Am., Washington, 1973-76; exec. v.p. Bruce W. Eberle & Assocs., Vienna, Va., 1977-81; pres. Response Dynamics, Inc., Vienna, Va., 1981-83; v.p. The Best Lists, Inc., Vienna, 1981-83, also dir.; pres. The Creative Advantage, Inc., Fairfax, Va., 1983—; cons. in field. Asst. to Young Citizens for Johnson, 1964; vol. George McGovern campaign, 1972; Hubert Humphrey campaign, 1968. Recipient Silver Echo award, Direct Mail/Mktg. Assn. Internat. competition for mktg. excellence, 1980. Mem. Nat. Soc. Fund Raisers, Direct Mail Mktg. Assn., Direct Mktg. Club. Home: 9614 Lindenbrook St Fairfax VA 22031 Office: 9401 Lee Hwy Suite 205 Fairfax VA 22031

PRICE, MAUREEN ELIZABETH, hospital pharmacy administrator, editor; b. Fullerton, Calif., Sept. 19, 1944; d. Frank Reed Whitelam and Normajean (Roe) Whitelam Price; m. Donald Claire Kenniston, Jan. 9, 1967 (div. Feb. 1968). B.S., Purdue U., 1972, M.S., 1974. Registered pharmacist Vocat. Rx Service, New Albany, Ind., 1972-73; pharmacy supr. Cook County Hosp., Chgo., 1973-75; clin. pharmacist VA Med. Ctr., Houston, 1975-79; asst. prof. U. Houston, 1975-79; pharmacist-in-charge Eckerd Drug Corp., Houston, 1977-83; assoc. dir. pharmacy East Jefferson Gen. Hosp., Metairie, La., 1983—; cons., Houston, 1975-83; instr. Tex. Woman's U. Sch. Nursing, Houston, 1975-77, lectr. Grad. Sch., 1977-78; lectr. U. Tex. Grad. Sch. Biomed. Sci., Houston, 1978-79. Assoc. editor Infusion, 1977-86; contbr. articles to profl. jours. Regional Judge, Sci. and Engring. Fair, Houston, 1977-83, internat. judge, 1982; CPR instr. Am. Heart Assn., Houston, 1975-82. Served with USN, 1965-68. Scholar, Mesa Coll., 1962, U. Colo., 1963, Purdue U, 1969. Mem. Am. Soc. Hosp. Pharmacists, Am. Soc. Cons. Pharmacists, Am. Soc. Parenteral and Enteral Nutrition, Am. Med. Writers Assn., Rho Chi. Office: E Jefferson Gen Hosp Dept Pharmacy Services 4200 Houma Blvd Metairie LA 70011

PRICE, REINE IRENE, educational administrator; b. Natchitoches, La., Sept. 6, 1950; d. Robert Lee and Neva Lucille (Uhl) Merriam; m. Michael Clinton Price, Aug. 11, 1973; children—Autumn Irene, Gabriel Clinton. B.S. in Edn., Bowling Green State U., 1971; M.S. in Edn., U. Central Ark., 1982; postgrad. in gifted edn. U. Ark., 1984—. Cert. elem. tchr., Ark., cert. biology, gifted and reading specialist. Tchr. Oregon Pub. Schs., Ohio, 1971-72, Immaculate Comception Sch., North Little Rock, Ark., 1974-77; dir. plan edn. North Little Rock Br., 1973-74; reading specialist U. Central Ark., Conway, 1982-83; reading specialist Dardanelle Pub. Schs., Ark., 1983-84, coordinator spl. services, 1984-85; prin. East End Elem. Sch., Bigelow, Ark., 1985—; tutor, Mayflower, Ark., 1981-83; cons. in field. Program developer, coordinator Spl. services 1st Gifted Preschool tied to pub. sch. in Ark., 1984-85. Ch. organist Brumley Baptist Ch., Conway, Ark., 1976-81, youth dir., 1977-80. Mem. Internat. Reading Assn., North Central Reading Assn. Council (sec. 1985-86), Agate Council Educators, Ark. Assn. Ednl. Adminstrs., Ark. Gifted and Talented Edn., Assn. Supervision and Curriculum Devel., Women's Missionary Union (pres. 1978-79, sec. 1979-80), Kappa Delta Pi, Phi Delta Kappa. Democrat. Lodge: Order Eastern Star. Avocations: sewing; needlework; crafts; boating; reading. Home: RR 1 Box 167 Houston AR 72070 Office: East End Elem Sch Bigelow AR 72016

PRICE, ROSALIE PETTUS, artist; b. Birmingham, Ala.; d. Erle and Ellelee (Chapman) Pettus; A.B., Birmingham-So. Coll., 1935; M.A., U. Ala., Tuscaloosa, 1967; m. William Archer Price, Oct. 3, 1936. Painter in watercolors, casein, oil and acrylic; one man shows include: Samford U., 1964, Birmingham Mus. of Art, 1966, 73, 82, Town Hall Gallery, 1968, 75, South Central Bell, 1977; instr. Birmingham (Ala.) Mus. Art, 1967-70, Samford U., 1969-70. Bd. dirs. Birmingham Mus. of Art, 1950-54, vice chmn., 1950-51; bd. trustees Birmingham Music Club, 1956-66, rec. sec., 1958-62. Recipient purchase award Watercolor U.S.A., 1972. Mem. Nat. Watercolor Soc., Nat. Soc. Painters in Casein and Acrylic (W. Alden Brown Meml. award 1970, Joseph A. Cain Meml. award 1983), Birmingham Art Assn. (pres. 1947-49, Little House on Linden purchase award 1968), So. Watercolor Soc., Watercolor Soc. Ala. (sec. 1948-49), La. Watercolor Soc., Pi Beta Phi. Episcopalian. Clubs: Jr. League of Birmingham (chmn. art com. 1947-50), Window Box Garden. Home: 300 Windsor Dr Birmingham AL 35209 Office: 2132 20th Ave S Birmingham AL 35223

PRICE, RUTH ELLEN, med. technologist, lab. adminstr.; b. Chgo., May 19, 1931; d. Stanley and Kathryn Ellen (Carpenter) P.; B.A. in Biology, Willamette

U., 1953; cert. in med. tech. Northwestern, 1954; M.A. in Mgmt., Central Mich. U., 1977. Med. technologist St. Catherine's Hosp., Kenosha, Wis., 1955—, clin. lab. supr., 1966—; product evaluator E. I. DuPont de Nemours, Wilmington, Del. Active Friends of the Museum, Kenosha. Mem. Am. Soc. Clin. Pathology (asso. mem., cert. med. technologist), Nature Conservancy, Am. Soc. Med. Tech., AAUW, Clin. Lab. Mgmt. Assn., Am. Mgmt. Assn., PEO, Chi Omega. Episcopalian. Home: 4510 18th St Kenosha WI 53142 Office: St Catherine's Hosp 3556 7th Ave Kenosha WI 53140

PRICE, SAMMIE LEE, banker; b. Athens, Tex., May 14, 1943; d. Porter S. and Minnie (Evans) Lee; grad. Durhams Bus. Coll., 1963; 1 son, Thomas Lee. With First Nat. Bank, Athens, Tex., 1963-68, People's Nat. Bank, Tyler, Tex., 1968-69, Parkdale State Bank, Corpus Christi, 1969-70; with First Bank, Edna, Tex., 1970—, asst. cashier, 1976-79, cashier, 1979-82, v.p., cashier, 1982—. Treas. Jackson County Unit Salvation Army; co-chmn. Miss Jackson County Scholarship Pageant. Mem. Nat. Assn. Bank Women (sec. Mid-Coastal Group, treas. Crossroads group), Am. Bus. Women's Assn. Club: Pilot (Jackson County) (past treas., dir.). Home: PO Box 697 Edna TX 77957 Office: Box 310 Edna TX 77957

PRICE, THELMA THOMAS, lawyer; b. Summerfield, La., Nov. 24, 1952; d. Robert Charles and Elsie Mae (Trimble) Thomas; m. Lowellton Price, Nov. 29, 1980. B.A., Grambling State U., 1973; J.D., Ohio State U.-Columbus, 1976. Bar: Ohio 1976. Tax atty. SCOA Industries, Inc., Columbus, Ohio, 1976-80, mgr. tax research, 1980—; mem. tax com. Am. Retail Fedn., Washington, 1980—; mem. tax. com. Nat. Retail Merchants Assn., N.Y.C., 1979—; participant Tax Execs. Inst., Cin., 1976—. Chmn. scholarship com. Robert B. Elliott Law Club, 1978—. Mem. Nat. Conf. Black Lawyers, Columbus Bar Assn., Ohio State Bar Assn., ABA, Franklin County Women Lawyers Assn. Democrat. Office: SCOA Industries Inc 33 N High St Columbus OH 43215

PRICE, VICTORIA STONE, advertising and design firm executive, engineering consulting firm marketing executive; b. Washington, Jan. 7, 1952; d. Lloyd Winfree and Patti Jordan (Nentwig) Stone; m. Robert John Howarth, Nov. 11, 1971 (div. Sept. 1983); m. Mark James Price, Aug. 24, 1985. B.A. in Polit. Sci., Va. Poly. Inst. and State U., 1973, M.A. in Polit. Sci., 1975. Vis. lectr. in polit. sci. Radford U., Va., 1975-76; vis. lectr. in polit. sci. Va. Poly. Inst. and State U., Blacksburg, 1976-77, instr. instl. research, 1977-78; prin., owner, founder Advantage Advt. & Design, Blacksburg, 1978—; mktg. dir. Profl. Highrise Services, Inc., Blacksburg, 1985—, also treas., dir. Editor Sea Grant Today, 1978-82. Contbr. articles to various publs. Vice pres., head pub. relations com. Big Bros./Big Sisters of New River Valley, Radford, 1983-86; chairperson pub. edn. com. New River chpt. Am. Cancer Soc., Christiansburg, Va., 1986—. Recipient 1st Place for page make-up Va. Press Women and Nat. Fedn. Press Women, 1980, First Place Feature photo award and First Place photo essay award Va. Press Women and Nat. Fedn. Press Women Communication Contest, 1985. Mem. Va. Press Women (First Place award interview category 1979, Second Place award feature articles 1979, Second Place award publs. regularly edited 1980), Nat. Fedn. Press Women, Va. Artists (Blacksburg chpt.), Pi Sigma Alpha. Episcopalian. Avocations: painting; flying; travel. Home: Route 4 Box 323 Christiansburg VA 24060 Office: Advantage Advt & Design 316 N Main PO Box 886 Blacksburg VA 24060 also Profl Highrise Services 316 N Main St PO Box 758 Blacksburg VA 24060

PRICE-LEE FATT, PATRICIA ANN, automobile leasing consultant; b. Danville, Va., June 19, 1954; d. William Oliver and Bessie Carolyn (Keene) P. Cert. data entry Braxton Bus. Sch., Richmond, Va., 1973; cert. computer ops. data analysis Mgmt. Info. Systems Office, San Antonio, 1980. Ordained to ministry Ch. Gospel Ministry, 1986. With data entry dept. Va. Dept. Taxation, Richmond, 1985; telephone surveyor Stan Parris Campaign for Gov., Richmond, 1985; telephone sec. Sleepy Time & Wakeup, Richmond, 1984; writer, salesman, pres. Sister Starfire & Co., Richmond, 1982—; automobile leasing cons. Trans Leasing, Richmond, 1986—; beauty cons. Avon, Richmond, 1981; distbr. Amway, Richmond, 1980-83; radio/telephone operator FCC, Richmond, 1983—. Contbr. to World of Poetry, 1985 (Golden Poet award), American Poetry Anthology, 1986. Fund raiser Crop Walk for Hunger, Richmond, 1982, Elks Lodge 15, 1985; mem. Crusade for Voters, Richmond, 1982, voters registrant Office of City Registrar, Richmond, 1983; mem. Republican Presdl. Task Force, 1985—. Served with U.S. Army, 1979-81. Recipient Unsung Hero award Met. Bus. Shoppers Guide, Richmond, 1985. Mem. Nat. Assn. Female Execs. (network dir. 1985), Liberian Aux. Assn. (hon. internat. hostess 1983—), NAACP (vets. affairs and armed forces com. 1982), Nat. Com. to Preserve Social Security and Medicare, Smithsonian Assocs., Songwriters of Am. (life). Republican. Buddhist. Avocations: photogrpahy; theater; aerobics; reading; stamp collecting. Home: 225 Laurel Fork Dr Richmond VA 23225

PRICHARD, ELIZABETH ROBINSON, social worker, civic worker; b. N.Y.C., Oct. 20, 1915; d. Harold Grant and Kathryn Virginia (Robinson) P.; B.A., Adelphi U., 1943; M.S., Columbia U. Sch. Social Work, 1947. Home service worker ARC, Bklyn. and N.Y.C., 1943-45, 47-48; social worker N.Y. U., Bellevue Pilot Home Care Project, N.Y.C., 1948-49; asst. dir. social service Columbia-Presbyn. Med. Center, N.Y.C., 1949-54, dir. social services, 1954-81; asst. prof. clin. social work Coll. Physicians and Surgeons, Columbia U., 1957-81; mem. profl. adv. bd. for social work Found. Thanatology, 1970—, mem. exec. com., 1974—. Trustee, Empire State chpt. Myasthenia Gravis Found., 1981—, nat. bd. dirs., 1986—; participant seminar on death Columbia U.; lectr. Brookdale Inst. Aging, Columbia U. Ret. Faculty Projet; mem. New York County Democratic Com. Mem. Nat. Assn. Social Workers, Acad. Cert. Social Workers, Nat. Conf. Social Welfare, Internat. Conf. Social Welfare, Am. Pub. Health Assn., AAAS, N.Y. Acad. Scis., Columbia U. Sch. Social Work Alumni Assn. (bd. dirs. 1984-87). Clubs: Women's City (health and mental health coms. 1981—), City. Editor 2 books on death and dying; contbr. articles on social work and care of terminally ill to profl. publs. Address: 510 E 86th St New York NY 10028

PRICKETT, MARGARET LENORA, manufacturing company executive; b. Council Bluffs, Iowa, Apr. 15, 1940; d. Paul Emmit and Pauline Irene (Pierson) Prickett; student pub. schs., El Monte, Calif.; children—Deborah Ann and Sharon Pauline (twins). With Fenton Industries, Inc., Los Angeles, 1960—, exec. v.p., treas., 1974-85, pres., 1985—; owner A to Z Bookkeeping Services, Sylmar, Calif., 1980—. Mem. pres. adv. bd. World Opportunities Inc., 1981—; adv. bd. Santa Clarita Valley Battered Women's Assn., 1982—. Served with USAF, 1958-59. Named Woman of Achievement, Newhall-Saugus Bus. and Profl. Women's Orgn., 1985-86. Democrat. Baptist. Club: Bus. and Profl. Women's (1st v.p.), Profl. Investment (pres.). Home: 13790 Oro Grande St Sylmar CA 91342 Office: 5801 S Central Ave Los Angeles CA 90011

PRICOLO, EDITH MARIE, integrated circuit mask design engineer; b. Merced, Calif., Nov. 8, 1936; d. Tony and Edith Cecelia (Silva) Azevedo; m. Danhy Ralph Pricolo, Feb. 19, 1955; children—Dennis, Dina, Danette, Damien. Student San Jose State U., 1953-54. Sales clk. J.J. Newberry store, San Jose, 1967; integrated circuit fabrication worker Fairchild Semicondr., Mountain View, Calif., 1967-68, integrated circuit mask designer, 1969-73; integrated circuit mask designer Advanced Microdevices, Sunnyvale, Calif., 1973-84, integrated circuit mask design engr., 1984—. Steering com. mem. Fleming Ave Homeowners Assn., San Jose, 1979-81; funding chmn., counselor Contact 24 hour crisis hotline, San Jose, 1985; tchr. Confrat. of Christian Doctrine, 1973-74. Avocations: refinishing furniture, dancing, photography, sewing. Home: 168 Clareview Ave San Jose CA 95127 Office: Advanced MicroDevices (Semicondr) 901 Thompson Pl Sunnyvale CA 94088

PRIDDY, KATHRYN ANN, retailing executive; b. Dallas, Oct. 15, 1956; d. Ashley Horne and Kathryn Virginia (Amsler) Priddy. B.S. in Edn., U. Tex., 1977; postgrad. in bus. So. Meth. U., 1978-79. Math. tchr. Episcopal Sch. Dallas, 1981-82; owner, pres. Kathryn Ann Priddy, Inc., Dallas, 1983—. Founder, co-chmn. Debutantes' Charity Ball, Dallas, 1982, chmn., 1983; vol. Bill Clements for Gov. Tex., 1978, 82. Mem. Dallas Mus. Fine Arts. Republican. Episcopalian. Clubs: Dallas Jr. League, Slipper (Dallas). Office: 4350 Louvers Ln Dallas TX 75225

PRIDGEN, MICHELLE LYNN, educator; b. St. Louis, July 31, 1954; d. Edward and Doris Jean (Fleming) Stewart; m. Kivy Leon Pridgen, Aug. 26, 1974 (div. May 1982); children—Kivy Leon II, Janee Danese-Michelle. B.S.A., St. Louis U., 1977; student Washington U. St. Louis, 1982; cert. Internat. Air Acad., St. Louis, 1985. Substitute tchr., schs., Fla. and Ill., 1977-80; med. officer mgmt. staff, med. asst. Sunbay Med. Office Bldg. Humana Corp., St. Petersburg, Fla., 1980-82; tchr. Cahokia Sch. Dist., Ill., 1982-86; ednl. coordinator Alpine Investment Group, 1986—; airlines reservations operator Internat. Airline Acad., St. Louis, 1985. Founder, group leader Centreville Young Astronauts Program, 1986. Nat. Merit scholar, 1972. Mem. Nat. Assn. Female Execs. Democrat. Avocations: Travel; poetry; writing; cooking; miniaturist; music. Office: 975 Gardenview Office Pkwy Creve Coeur MO 63121

PRIEL, DAFNA, real estate executive, producer; b. Tel-Aviv, Israel, June 8, 1948; came to U.S. May 1, 1967; naturalized 1976; d. Henry Priel and Jannette (Stepanski) Dankner. Student Tel-Aviv U., 1961-67, Hunter Coll., 1968-70. Personnel mgr. Entertainers, N.Y.C., 1967-69; designer, fine jewelry mfg. Speechles Presents, Inc., N.Y.C., 1969-72; real estate broker Priel Realty, N.Y.C., 1973—; talent coordinator, owner W.W.W. Supper Club, N.Y.C., 1976-79; producer of plays and benefits, N.Y.C., 1984—. Producer Stonewall Meml., Washington Square Park, N.Y., 1973; vol. Elizabeth Holtzman, Bklyn., 1983—, Carol Bellamy, N.Y.C., 1985—, Child Abuse, N.Y.C., 1984—. Served to sgt. Israeli Army, 1965-67. Democrat. Jewish. Office: Priel Realty Corp 442 Amsterdam Ave New York NY 10024

PRIESAND, SALLY JANE, rabbi; b. Cleve., June 27, 1946; d. Irving T. and Rose E. Priesand; B.A. in English, U. Cin., 1968; B. in Hebrew Letters, Hebrew Union Coll., Jewish Inst. Religion, 1971; M.A.H.L., 1972; D.H.L. (hon.), Fla. Internat. U., 1973. Ordained rabbi, 1972; asst. rabbi Stephen Wise Free Synagogue, N.Y.C., 1972-77; asso. rabbi 1977-79; rabbi Temple Beth El, Elizabeth, N.J., 1979-81, Monmouth Reform Temple, Tinton, Falls, N.J., 1981—. Trustee, chmn. religious affairs com. Planned Parenthood Monmouth County; trustee Monmouth Campaign for Nuclear Disarmament; adv. bd. Brookdale Center for Holocaust Studies, 1984. Named Outstanding Young Woman of Yr. of Ohio, 1972; recipient World Gratitude Day award; Eleanor Roosevelt Humanities award State of Israel, 1980. Mem. Am. Jewish Com., Am. Jewish Congress, Central Conf. Am. Rabbis, Assn. Reform Zionists Am. (founding mem., admissions com.), NOW, Religious Leaders for a Free Choice, Shore Area Bd. Rabbis. Clubs: B'nai B'rith, Hadassah. Author: Judaism and the New Woman, 1975; contbr. articles on Judaism to profl. jours. Home: 10 Wedgewood Circle Eatontown NJ 07724 Office: 332 Hance Ave Tinton Falls NJ 07724

PRIESTLEY, LEE SHORE, writer, secondary school educator; b. Iola, Kans., Aug. 30, 1904; d. Edmond and Bess (Dorsa) Shore; m. Orville E. Priestley, June 14, 1926; children—Joseph Shore, Orville Eugene, Jr. Student U. Okla., 1923-25; B.A., N.M. State U., 1952. Cert. secondary tchr., Okla., La. Tchr., Drumright Schs., Okla., 1923-28, Crowley Schs., La., 1943-45, U. Okla., 1960, 74, N.M. State U., Las Cruces, 1976; freelance writer, Las Cruces, 1945. Author: Murder Takes the Baths, 1952; Rocket to the Stars, 1959; A Teacher for Libby, 1960; Rocket Mouse, 1961; A Second Look for Avis, 1961; Believe in Spring, 1964; Now for Nola, 1970; Sound of Always, 1975; Because of Rainbows, 1977; America's Space Shuttle, 1978; various others. Chmn., Drug and Crime Commn., Las Cruces, 1970-72; chmn. bd. trustees Branigan Library, Las Cruces, 1970—; bd. dirs. Good Samaritan Retirement Village, Las Cruces, 1980—, Friends of the Library, Las Cruces, 1975-85; trustee N.M. Library Assn., Santa Fe, 1970-80; mem. City Planning commn., Las Cruces, 1982-85. Named Citizen of the Year Las Cruces Realtors, 1982, N.M. Realtors, 1983, Writer of the Year U. Okla. Sch. Journalism, 1980. Mem. N.M. Press Women (recipient Zia award 1969, 71), Phi Kappa Phi, Delta Kappa Gamma. Democrat. Methodist. Clubs: Altrusa (pres. 1975), Wednesday Lit. (pres. 1975) (Las Cruces), Phi Mu. Lodge: P.E.O. (pres. 1960, 70). Avocations: historical research; drama; music. Home: 426 N Miranda Las Cruces NM 88005

PRIGGE, LILA LOU, business educator; b. Drayton, N.D., June 17, 1941; d. Larus and Petrina A. (Magnusson) Thomasson; m. Glenn Russell Prigge, June 6, 1959; children—G. Randall, Traci Kay. A.A., U. N.D., 1962, B.S. in Edn., 1967, Ph.D., 1971. Sec., U. N.D., Grand Forks, 1962-63, assoc. prof., 1978—; instr. Bottineau Br. N.D. State U., 1968-69; lead instr. 916 Area Vocat. Tech. Inst., White Bear Lake, Minn., 1971-74, instr., East Grand Forks, Minn., 1974-78. Author: (with others) This Business of Metrics, 1978. Editor: The Metric System in Business Education, 1979. Contbr. articles to profl. jours. Sec. PTA, Bottineau, 1967-68, den mother No. Lights Council Boy Scouts Am., 1966-69; leader No. Lights council Brownies, Girl Scouts U.S., 1971-72; Sunday sch. tchr. Am. Lutheran Ch., Bottineau, and North St. Paul, Minn., 1966-69, 71-73. N.D. Bd. Higher Edn. scholar, 1969-71. Mem. AAUW (v.p. 1978-80, pres. 1980-82, counselor 1982-84), N.D. Bus. and Office Edn. Assn. (sec. 1984—), Nat. Bus. Edn. Assn., Am. Vocat. Assn., N.D. Vocational Assn., Phi Beta Lambda (hon. mem.), Phi Delta Kappa (pres. 1981-82, counselor 1982-83), Pi Lambda Theta, Delta Kappa Gamma, Delta Pi Epsilon (v.p. 1976-77, pres. 1985-86), Pi Omega Pi. Office: U ND Box 8236 University Station Grand Forks ND 58202

PRIME, EUGENIE ELSA, librarian; b. Trinidad, W.Indies; came to U.S., 1972; d. Harold John and Millicent L. Prime; B.A. with honors, U. W.Indies, 1966; M.A. in History, Andrews U., Berrien Springs, Mich., 1974; M.S. in L.S., Drexel U., Phila., 1976; M.B.A., UCLA, 1982. Postgrad. research fellow history U. W.Indies, 1966-69; head dept. history Naparima Girls High Sch., Trinidad, 1969-72; psychiat. social worker N.Y. State Dept. Mental Hygiene, 1974; med. librarian Glendale (Calif.) Adventist Med. Center, 1976—; pres. Cinahl Corp., 1981—. Mem. Med. Library Assn., Am. Soc. Indexers, Nat. Assn. Female Execs., Med. Library Group So. Calif. and Ariz., Assn. Info. Mgrs. Seventh-day Adventist. Home: 1727 Holly Dr Apt 301 Glendale CA 91206 Office: 1509 E Wilson Terr Glendale CA 91206

PRIMO, MARIE NASH, shopping centers official; b. Clarksburg, W.Va., Dec. 10, 1928; d. Frank and Josephine (DiMaria) Nash; student pub. schs. Clarksburg; m. Joseph C. Primo, Sept. 27, 1953; 1 dau., Joan E. Sec., Nat. Bank Detroit, 1945-46; exec. sec. Cutting Tool Mfrs. Assn., Detroit, 1946-50; adminstrv. asst. Irwin I. Cohn atty., Detroit, 1950-84; mgr. Bloomfield Shopping Plaza, Birmingham, Mich., 1959—; North Hill Center, Avon Twp., Mich., 1957—; Drayton Plains Shopping Center (Mich.), 1958-84; South Allen Shopping Center, Allen Park, Mich., 1953-77, Huron-Tel Corner, Pontiac, Mich., 1977—; officer, dir., numerous privately held corps. Mem. steering com., treas. Univ. Liggett Antiques Show, 1971-76, advisory com., 1977-80; mem. parents' com. Wellesley Coll., 1979-1981. Mem. Founders Soc. Detroit Inst. Arts, Women's Econ. Club, Mich. Humane Soc., Detroit Sci. Center, Detroit Zool. Soc., Smithsonian Assos., Hist. Soc. Mich., Grosse Pointe War Meml. Assn., Grosse Pointe Pub. Library Assn., Detroit Grand Opera Assn. Roman Catholic. Home: 1341 N Renaud Rd Grosse Pointe Woods MI 48236 Office: 1631 1st National Bldg Detroit MI 48226

PRIMUS, MARY JANE DAVIS, social worker; b. Marion, Iowa, May 31, 1924; d. Lawrence Henry and Verna Leona (Suman) Davis; B.S., Iowa State U., 1950; m. Paul C. Primus, Aug. 23, 1955; children—Kenneth Roy, Donald Karl. Asst. cashier First State Bank, Greene, Iowa, 1942-46; tchr. Oskaloosa (Iowa) public schs., 1950-52; extension home economist Iowa State U., Oskaloosa-Eldora, 1952-57; homemaker, dist. supr. Iowa Dept. Social Service, Webster City, 1970-77; substitute tchr. Eldora Pub. Schs., 1966-68; homemaker health aide supr. Mid-Iowa Community Action OEO, Iowa Dept. Social Service, 1968-69; pres., ptnr. L'Mas, Herbs & Spices Unltd., 1984-86; corr. 4 area newspapers. Den mother Boy Scouts Am., Steamboat Rock, Iowa, 1966-71; leader Girl Scouts Am., Steamboat Rock, 1969-72; mem. Iowa State U. Extension Family Living Council, Hardin County, 1961-65, 83-86, chmn., 1985-86; outreach chmn. Iowa Family and Children Services, 1966-72; field days women's program chmn. Iowa Soil Conservation, 1968. Mem. Am. Home Econs. Assn., Nat. Council Homemaker-Home Health Aide Services, Nat. League Am. Pen Women, Nat. Soc. Lit. and the Arts, Soil Conservation Soc. Am., Am. Legion, Internat. Platform Assn., PEO, Herb Soc. Am. Mem. United Ch. of Christ (pres. 1963-65). Mem. Order Eastern Star. Club: Federated Women's (Steamboat Rock). Author: Through the Window, 1973; Through the Window Twice, 1974; Tracery Windows, 1975; Shuttered Windows, 1977; Wings, 1979; outdoor cooking editor Iowa Wildlife Fedn., 1980; research editor L'Mas Cuisine Cookbook; contbr. poems to various publs.; artist; exhibited in group shows; murals executed in various bus. Office: Steamboat Rock IA 50672

PRINCE, FRANCES ANNE KIELY, civic worker; b. Toledo, Dec. 20, 1923; d. John Thomas and Frances (Pusteoska) Kiely; student U. Louisville, 1947-49; A.B., Berea Coll., 1951; postgrad. Kent Sch. Social Work, 1951, Creighton U., 1969; M.P.A., U. Nebr., Omaha, 1978; m. Richard Edward Prince, Jr., Aug. 17, 1951; children—Anne, Richard III. Instr. flower arranging Western Wyo. Jr. Coll., 1965, 66; editor Nebr. Garden News, 1983—. Chmn., Lone Troop council Girl Scouts U.S.A., 1954-57, trainer leaders, 1954-68, mem. state camping com., 1959-61, bd. mem. Wyo. state council, 1966-69; chmn. Community Improvement, Green River, Wyo., 1959, 63-65, Wyo. Fedn. Women's Clubs State Library Services, 1966-69; mem. Wyo. State Adv. Bd. on Library Inter-Co-op., 1965-69; bd. mem. Sweetwater County Library System, 1962—, pres. bd., 1967-68; adv. council Sch. Dist. 66, 1970—; bd. dirs. Opera Angels, 1971, fund raising chmn., 1971-72, v.p., 1974—; bd. dirs. Morning Musicale, 1971—; bazaar com. Children's Hosp., 1970-75; docent Joslyn Art Mus., 1970—; mem. Nebr. Forestry Adv. Bd., 1976—; citizens adv. bd. Met. Area Planning Agy., 1979—; mem. Nebr. Tree-Planting Commn., 1980—. Recipient Library Service award Sweetwater County Library, 1968; Girl Scout Services award, 1967; Conservation award U.S. Forest Service, 1981; Plant Two Trees award, 1981; Nat. Arbor Day award, 1982. Mem. AAUW, New Neighbors League (dir. 1969-71), Ikebana Internat., Symphony Guild, Omaha Playhouse Guild, ALA, Nebr. Library Assn., Omaha Council Garden Clubs (1st v.p. 1972, pres. 1973-75), Internat. Platform Assn., Nat. Trust for Hist. Preservation, Nebr. Flower Show Judges Council, Nat. Council State Garden Clubs (chmn. arboriculture 1985—), Nebr. Fedn. Garden Clubs (pres. 1978-81). Mem. United Ch. of Christ. Clubs: Intermountain (dir. 1963-69), Garden (dir. 1970-72, pres. 1972-75). Author poetry. Editor Nebr. Garden News, 1983—. Home: 8909 Broadmoor Dr Omaha NE 68114

PRINCE, JACQUELYNNE BOLANDER, nurse, consultant; b. Norfolk, Va., July 4, 1955; d. Jack C. Bolander and Particia (Loud) Bolander Melvin; m. John Martine Prince, Jr., Oct. 1, 1977; children—Emily Alene, John Ryland. B.S., Med. Coll. of Va., 1978; M.S., Tex. Woman's U., 1985. Registered critical care nurse. Staff nurse Med. Coll. of Va., Richmond, 1978-80; asst. nurse coordinator Parkland Hosp., Dallas, 1980-82, supr., 1982-83; head nurse N.C. Meml. Hosp., Chapel Hill, 1983-85; coordinator critical care edn. Wise Appalachian Regional Hosp., Wise, Va., 1985—; cons. in field. Contbr. articles to profl. publs. CPR instr. Am. Heart Assn., Dallas, Chapel Hill, N.C., 1980—. Mem. Assn. Critical Care Nurses, Am. Nurses Assn., North Atlantic Nursing Diagnosis Assn., N.C. Meml. Collaborator Practice com. Baptist. Club: Porkand Woman's (project service chmn. 1980-83). Avocations: skiing, quilting, reading, running. Home: 704 Ridge Ave Norton VA 24273 Office: Wise Appalachian Regional Hosp Wise VA 24293

PRINCE, MARY RUTH, librarian; b. Edwards, Miss., Feb. 22, 1928; d. James Albert and Sarah (Henderson) Brown; A.B., Tougaloo Coll., 1951; M.A., Central Mich. U., 1969; m. James Richard Prince, Apr. 4, 1964; 1 child, Eldred Rene. Librarian, Lawrence (Miss.) High Sch., 1951-52, Boler High Sch., Decatur, Miss., 1953-59, Rosa A. Temple High Sch., Vicksburg, Miss., 1959-64, Stone St. Elem. Sch., Greenwood, Miss., 1964-66, Vicksburg High Sch., 1966-68; asst. prof. Mississippi Valley State U., Itta Bena, Miss., 1968—. Mem. ALA, NAACP, Internat. Platform Assn., Miss. Library Assn., Southeastern Library Assn. Baptist. Home: Route 5 Box 265 Vicksburg MS 39180 Office: Mississippi Valley State Univ Box 38 Itta Bena MS 38941

PRINCE, RUTH WHITE, religious organization consultant; b. Whiteville, N.C., July 16, 1921; d. Lloyd McCoy and Emma Elneta (Ward) White; m. Harry Hymrick Prince, Oct. 18, 1941; children—Harry H., Stephen White. Diploma Wilmington Coll. Cosmetology, N.C., 1941; student So. Bapt. Sem., 1970, 75. Cosmetologist, Tabor City, N.C. 1941-42; sec., Galveston Dry Docks, Tex., 1943-44; florist Clarton Ron Ru, N.C., 1951-58; dir. missions Bladen Bapt. Assn., Elizabethtown, N.C., 1966-80; growth cons. N.C. Bapt. State Conv., Raleigh, 1981—. Trustee, Campbell U., 1978-80; pres. Clarkton PTA, 1969-70. Mem. Am. Bible Soc. (regional coordinator), N.C. Religious Edn. Assn., Dorothea Dix Vol. Guild, Dirs. of Missions (pres. 1975-76). Democrat. Baptist. Avocation: Art; music. Home: PO Box 765 Clarkton NC 28433 Office: NC Bapt Conv PO Box 26508 Raleigh NC 27611

PRINCE, VIVIEN JANE SCHAPIRA, craft import company executive, author: b. Nairobi, Kenya, Nov. 10, 1946; came to U.S., 1977; d. Norbert Nathan Schapira and Doris (Wareham) Bolton; m. William Kenneth Plenderleith, Mar. 1969 (div. Mar. 1974); 1 child, Bruce William; m. Allan Fredrick Prince, Feb. 11, 1976; 1 child, Fiona Claudine. Student Kianda Coll., Newspaper Inst. of N.Y., Inst. Children's Lit. Sec., dep. prin. Univ. Coll., Nairobi, 1963-66, Daly & Figgis, Advocates, Nairobi, 1966-70, instr., owner Riding Establishment, Nairobi, 1967; sec. Archer & Wilcock, Advocates, Nairobi, 1972-74, Hamilton Harrison & Mathews, Advocates, Nairobi, 1974; exec. asst., sec. Wilkinson Sword, Nairobi, 1975-76; owner, mgr. Kenyan Craft Importing and Mgmt., Roxbury, Conn., 1983; lectr. in field; pvt. trainer, 1970-73; lady jockey, Nairobi, Gt. Britain, 1969-74, 84. Author: Kenya: The Years of Change, 1986. Organizer Kenya Fund, Roxbury, 1982—. Named 1st hon. treas. Lady Jockeys' Assn. of Gt. Britain, 1972. Mem. Nat. Assn. Female Execs., Newspaper Inst. Am. Mem. Ch. of Eng. Avocation: breeder Pembroke Welsh Corgi dogs. Home: 193 Apple Ln Roxbury CT 06783

PRINCETON, JEANNE KAY, insurance and investments sales executive; b. Taft, Calif., Dec. 21, 1946; d. Eugene R. Princeton and Dorothy (Johnson) Princeton Frybarger; m. John Morrison Burton, July 30, 1977; stepchildren—Cynthia, Amy. B.A., U. So. Calif., 1969. Sales, Dun & Bradstreet, Inc., Los Angeles, Boston, 1969-76; founder, ptnr. Princeton & Burton, Springfield, N.J., 1976—. Named 1st women salesperson Dun & Bradstreet, Inc., 1969-76, One of Top 10 Women Agts. for Northwestern Mut., 1982—. Mem. Million Dollar Round Table, Women's Life Underwriters Assn., Sales Execs. Club N.Y. Republican. Methodist. Avocation: golf. Home: Mail Pouch Farm Mountainville NJ 08833

PRINCIPAL, VICTORIA, actress; b. Fukuoka, Japan, Jan. 3; d. Victor and Ree (Veal) P.; m. Harry Glassman. Attended Miami-Dade Community Coll. Studied acting with Max Croft, Al Sacks and Estelle Harman. Worked as model; including TV comml. appearances; film debut in The Life and Times of Judge Roy Bean, 1972; other movie appearances include: Earthquake, 1974, Vigilante Force, 1976, I Will I Will...For Now, 1976; TV films include: Last Hours Before Morning, 1975, The Night They Stole Miss Beautiful, 1977, Pleasure Palace, 1980; became theatrical agt., 1975; TV series Dallas, 1978—; other TV appearances include Sixty Years of Seduction, Fantasy Island. Author: The Body Principal. Office: care Lorimar TV Pub Relations 3970 Overland Ave Culver City CA 90230

PRINCIPE, DOLLY AILEEN, publisher, editor, realtor; b. Dearborn, Mich., June 25, 1946; d. Norman Joseph and Delores Julia (Sochor) Murtha; m. Richard B. Principe, Dec. 15, 1962 (div. Feb. 1979); 1 son, Tony Scott. Student pub. schs., Reseda, Calif. Lic. realtor, Calif. Owner Westoaks Realtors, Westlake, Calif., 1965-80; realtor Brown Realty, Westlake, 1981-83; bldg. mgr. Toulon, Inc., Los Angeles, 1983; regional mgr. Mgmt., USA, Century City, Calif., 1983-84; pub., editor-in-chief Comml. Properties Mag., Newport Beach, Calif., 1985—. Treas., Westlake Island Bd. Dirs., 1981; corp. sec. Westlake Lake Mgmt., 1981-83; chmn. fund-raising golf tournament Children's Village, Westlake, 1982. Recipient Cert. of Recognition, Conejo Valley United Sch. Dist., Westlake, 1979; Cert. of Achievement, Los Angeles Pilot's Assn., Van Nuys, Calif., 1983. Mem. Nat. Assn. Female Execs. Republican. Mem. Ch. of Religious Sci. Club: Toastmistress (Westlake) (speaker 1981-82). Avocations: flying airplanes; sailing; golf; horseback riding. Home: Newport Beach CA Office: Comml Properties Mag 177 Riverside Dr Newport Beach CA 92663

PRINCIPE, DOROTHY LOUISE AUGENSTEIN, tool and die manufacturing company executive; b. Newark, July 27, 1938; d. Emil and Louise Regina (Gilbert) Augenstein; m. Louis M. Principe, Nov. 22, 1958 (div.); children—Deborah Principe Arnold, Robin. Student Centenary Coll. Women, Hackettstown, N.J., 1956-58. Asst. mgr., owner laundromats, asst. mgr., part owner drive-in theaters, 1966-76; pres. Universal Tools & Mfg. Co., Springfield, N.J., 1982—. Leader in establishing swimming competition in Carribean. Recipient St. Croix Sports award, 1973-74. Mem. Nat. Assn. Female Execs., N.J. Tool and Die Assn., Nat. Tool and Die Assn. Avocations: hiking, biking, aerobics, crafts. Office: Universal Tools and Mfg Co 115 Victory Rd Springfield NJ 07081

PRINE, HELEN FRANCES, newspaper publisher; b. Calhoun County, Mich., Nov. 13, 1936; d. Henry Woodside and Mildred Martha (Meyer) Hyatt; student Springport (Mich.) public schs.; m. Wesley S. Prine, Aug. 11, 1979; children—Joel, Jeffrey, Anita. Apprentice, Springport Signal, 1953-59, owner, operator, 1977—; linotype and teletype puncher Jackson (Mich.) Citizen Patriot, 1959-67; teletype puncher, layout Lansing (Mich.) State Jour., 1967-77; owner, operator Elegenté Junque and Antiques Mall, Springport. Vice pres. Springport Bus. Assn.; bd. dirs. Irish Hills council Girl Scouts U.S.A., 1985-86.

Recipient Public Service awards 4-H, Boy Scouts Am. Mem. Mich. Press Assn. Home: 11640 Prine Rd Springport MI 49284 Office: 104 Maple St Springport MI 49284

PRINGLE, MARJORIE ANN, transportation company executive; b. Rouleau, Sask., Can., Mar. 25, 1923; d. John George and Agatha (Rabel) Torski; m. Roy Harold Phillips, June 1, 1946 (div. May 1953); children—Roberta Annette, Shirley Kay Phillips Stransky; m. Hobart L. Pringle, Mar. 1, 1975 (dec. Jan. 19 1984). Student pub. schs. Owner, mgr. Central Employment Service, Mansfield, Ohio, 1951-75, Kissell Real Estate Co., Mansfield, 1951-52, Continental Mortgage Co., Mansfield, 1951-52; asst. mgr., mgr. Kelly Services, Mansfield, 1959—; pres. Galion & Mansfield Transit Co., Inc., Mansfield, 1975—; mgr., tour coordinator Pringle Tours, Mansfield, 1975—. Pres., Mansfield Area Transit System, 1977-79; charter mem. Ohio Republican Presdl. Task Force, 1982—. Mem. Bus. and Profl. Women's Club Mansfield (pres. 1962-63, Woman of Yr. 1969). Methodist. Club: Soroptimist Internat. (pres. Mansfield 1963-64, dist. IV dir. 1970-72). Lodge: Moose. Avocations: sewing; crocheting; reading; golfing; bowling. Home: 2075 Willowood Dr S Mansfield OH 44906 Office: Galion & Mansfield Transit Co Inc 1271 Bowman St Mansfield OH 44905

PRIOLEAU, ELIZABETH STEVENS, writer, educator, public affairs executive; b. Richmond, Va., Nov. 14, 1942; d. Hugo Osterhaus and Adeline (Howle) Stevens; A.A., Bennett Coll., Millbrook, N.Y., 1962; B.S., U. Va., Charlottesville, 1966, M.A., 1972; Ph.D., Duke U., 1980; m. Philip Gendron Prioleau, Apr. 3, 1972. Asst. feature editor Charlottesville Daily Progress, 1963-64; instr. English, Fairleigh Dickinson U., 1980; lit. cons. Am. Jour. Dermatopathology, 1980—, John Barnes Prodns., 1980-81; public affairs dir. Marcel Breuer Assocs., N.Y.C., 1981-83; vis. scholar Inst. Research in History, 1981. Recipient Jean Besselievre Boley prize for fiction, 1963. Mem. MLA, Victorian Soc. Am., Lychnos Hon. Soc. Author: Circle of Eros, 1983. Contbr. articles to profl. jours. Home and Office: 1230 Park Ave New York NY 10028

PRISK, PATRICIA, registered nurse, computer programmer; b. Troy, N.Y., Nov. 6, 1944; d. Harold George and Mary Alice (Murphy) Connor; student Hudson Valley Community Coll., 1962; R.N., Samaritan Hosp. Sch. Nursing, 1965; m. William Prisk; children—William, Sandra, Kimberly, Rebecca, Sharon. Staff nurse Samaritan Hosp., 1965, Mt. Sinai Hosp., Hartford, Conn., 1966-69, Johnson Meml. Hosp., Stafford Springs, Conn., 1972-74; supr. Riverside Health Care Center, 1974-76; dir. nursing Middletown (Conn.) Health Care Center, 1976-81, staff nurse, 1981-82; staff nurse Lorraine Manor, Hartford, 1981-83; computer programmer Aetna Life and Casualty Co., Hartford, 1982-83; programmer analyst Hartford Ins. Co., 1983—; lectr., cons. in field. Mem. Conn. Assn. Health Care Facilities. Office: 1 Hartford Plaza Hartford CT

PRISM, CAROLE RHONA, management consultant; b. Balt., Jan. 15, 1944; d. Nathan Klein and Florence (Levine) Klein Romolt; m. Jerome Alan Zeldes, Dec. 8, 1963 (div. May 1969); children—Helen Irene, Sandra Elaine; m. Barton Michael Marymee, June 6, 1980; B.A., Calif. State U.-Northridge, 1973; M.A., Calif. State Coll.-San Bernardino, 1978. Asst. tchr. Dubnoff Sch., North Hollywood, Calif., 1971-72; mental health worker Mental Health Unit, San Bernardino, Calif., 1974-75, adminstr., 1976-77; cons. mgmt., organizational devel., tng., research, Concord, Calif., 1979—; mental health cons. Occupational Health Cons., Oakland, Calif., 1980; pres. Positive Collaborations, Inc., Concord, 1983; dir. Positive Options, Martinez, Calif., 1983-84; program mgr. Comprehensive Care Corp., 1984—. gen. mgr. Ground Zero, Berkeley, Calif. 1983; founder Peer Cons. Group, Walnut Creek, Calif., 1982; resource person various orgns., San Francisco area. Mem. Nat. Assn. Female Execs. Office: Marshale Hale Meml Hosp Adolescent Care Unit 3773 Sacramento St San Francisco CA 94118

PRITCHARD, JAN MARIE, lawyer; b. Dayton, Ohio, July 6, 1954; d. Robert Virgil and Barbara Christine (Vollmer) Hemm; m. Daniel Pence Pritchard, May 31, 1975; children—Douglas Pence, Aidan Christine. B.A., U. Mo.-Columbia, 1975, J.D., 1981. Bank teller First Bank of Commerce, Columbia, Mo., 1974-76; clk. Dillards Dept. Store, Oklahoma City, 1976; teller Shepherd Mall Bank, Oklahoma City, 1976-77; computer operator Fed. Res. Bank, Oklahoma City, 1977-79; hearing officer Mo. State Tax Commn., Jefferson City, 1982—. Bd. advocates U. Mo. Sch. Law, Columbia, 1980, 81. Mem. Mo. Bar Assn., ABA, Internat. Assn. Assessing Officers, Order of Barrister. Republican. Roman Catholic. Office: Mo State Tax Commn 623 E Capitol Ave Jefferson City MO 65101

PRITCHARD, SUSAN MCCOO, office automation company official; b. Astoria, N.Y., Apr. 30, 1951; d. Edward McCoo and Shirley Loretta (Gagnon) DiSabatino; m. John Paul Pritchard, June 12, 1976; 1 son, John Scott. B.A. in Psychology and Sociology, U. Del., 1973. Sales rep. 3-M Bus. Products, Wilmington, Del., 1973-78; sales rep. Raytheon Data Systems, Phila., 1978-80, sales team mgr., 1980-81, br. mgr., 1981-82; mgr. major accounts NBI, Inc., Irvine, Calif., 1982-83, br. mgr., San Bernardino, Calif., 1983—. Active Big Bros./Big Sisters Del., Wilmington, 1973-76. Mem. Assn. Info. Processing Profls., Internat. Word Processing Assn., Nat. Assn. Female Execs. Republican. Roman Catholic. Office: NBI Inc 412 W Hospitality Ln San Bernardino CA 92408

PRITCHARD, YVONNE TUDOR, city official; b. Calif., Aug. 28, 1953; d. Martin and Barbara L. Tudor; B.A., Calif. State Poly. U., 1976; M.P.A., U. So. Calif., 1979. Personnel analyst County of San Bernardino (Calif.), 1976-79; sr. compensation analyst UCLA, 1979, personnel cons., 1980; personnel analyst City of San Bernardino, 1980—. Mem. San Bernardino Commn. on Status of Women. Mem. Internat. Personnel Mgmt. Assn., Nat. Pub. Employee Relations Assn., Am. Soc. Pub. Adminstrn., Inland Area Personnel Mgmt. Assn. (treas. 1981-83, pres.-elect 1983-84). Home: PO Box 702 Crestline CA 92325 Office: Dept Personnel City Hall 300 North D St San Bernardino CA 92418

PRITT, MARILYN HARKINS, mortgage loan executive; b. Cleve., July 27, 1953; d. Wayne George and Ruth Naomi (Thiel) Harkins; m. James Bruce Pritt, May 28, 1972; children—Amy Lynn, Sara Beth. Student, Davis & Elkins Coll., 1971-72, Glenville State Coll., 1973-75. Lic. real estate agent, W.Va. Sec., W. Va. Bd. Regents, Charleston, 1978-79; computer operator McDonough-Caperton, Charleston, 1979-80; mortgage loan officer Home Mortgages, Inc., Charleston, 1980-82, mortgage br. mgr. 1982-83; mortgage loan officer Reliable Mortgage Co., Charleston, 1983-85; mortgage loan originator Magnet Mortgages, Inc., 1985—; fin. con. Area Real Estate Firms, Charleston, 1980—. Named to Million Dollar Club Home Mortgages, Inc., 1982-83, Best Loan Originator, Reliable Mortgage Co., 1983-84, 22 Million Dollar Loan Originator Reliable Mortgage Co., 1984-85. Mem. Women's Council of Realtors, Kanawha Valley Bd. Realtors. Republican. Avocations: aerobics; walking; cooking. Home: 122 Timberlake Circle Scott Depot WV 25560 Office: Magnet Mortgages Inc PO Box 167 Scott Depot WV 26650

PRIVETT, AUDREY R., city official; b. Cin., Sept. 29, 1936; d. Edward S. and Marcy C. (Moehring) Robb; m. Boyce D. Privett, Oct. 30, 1953; children—Boyce, Jr., Linda Privett Patterson, Laura Privett Hayslett. B.S. in Bus. Adminstrn., U. Cin., 1983. City editor Suburban Press, Cin., 1969-77; parks and recreation dir. City of Sharonville, Ohio, 1977-84, community services dir., 1984—; pres. Privett Inspection, Sharonville, 1984—. Author: (weekly newspaper article) Audrey's Analysis, 1969-77; (guest columnist) Cin. Enquirer, 1971. Mem. Princeton Bd. Edn., Ohio, 1974-76, pres., 1977; bd. dirs. ARC, Cin., 1981-84; bd. dirs. Sharonville Christmas Fund, chmn. ways and means com., 1985. Mem. Am. Mgmt. Assn., Soc. Profl. Journalists, Am. Pub. Works Assn., Ohio Parks and Recreation Assn., AAUW. Club: Sharonville Republican. Avocations: skating; skiing; writing. Office: City of Sharonville 10900 Reading Rd Sharonville OH 45241

PROBASCO, DONNA ALEEN, sales and marketing executive, b. Hammond, Ind., Aug. 24, 1947; d. Alex Paul and Dortha Lena (Roach) Richwalski; m. Christopher Garret Probasco, Feb. 24, 1973; children—Christopher Brett, Brittany Dunn. B.A., Ind. U., 1969. Account exec. Chgo. Tribune, 1969-70; dist. sales mgr., account exec. nat. and local sales, asst. to gen. mgr. Reuben N. Donnelley Co., Chgo., 1970-78; account exec. K. Promotions, Chgo., 1979-80, Paramount Mktg., Chgo., 1980-82; pres. Mid-Am. Mktg. Inc., Benton Harbor, Mich., 1982—. Chmn., Lake Mich. Catholic Long Range Planning Commn., St. Joseph, Mich., 1985. Mem. Advt. Specialty Inst., Specialty Advt. Assn. Internat. Avocations: tennis; reading; crafts. Home: 122 Higman Park Benton Harbor MI 49022

PROBERT, CANDY WILSON, home economist; b. Inglewood, Calif., Sept. 13, 1952; d. Richard W. and Dorothy Elaine (Page) Wilson; B.S. in Child Devel. cum laude, U. Utah, 1974, B.S. in Psychology cum laude, 1974; m. Ronald L. Probert, July 10, 1981; 1 dau., Erin McCall. Tchr., Jewish Community Center, Salt Lake City, 1974-75; ballet instr. community edn. Highland High Sch., Salt Lake City, 1970-75; home economist Harmon's Supermarket, Midvale, Utah, 1975—; editor, corr. sec. Food Mktg. Consumer Advs., 1975-76. Apptd. assoc. mem. Kearns (Utah) Town Council, 1982. Recipient Mathew Baird award CIA, Washington, 1973; Ednl. Aid Fund scholar, 1970-73. Mem. Home Economists in Bus., Am. Home Econs. Assn., Food Mktg. Inst., Utah Home Econs. Assn. (co-chmn. spring conv. 1980). Home: 4404 Twilight Dr Kearns UT 84118 Office: 980 E 7200 S Midvale UT 84047

PROCHOTSKY, IRENA, ballet educator; b. Klagenfurt, Austria, Aug. 22, 1941; came to U.S., 1969; d. Elizabeth (Firley) Pepichova; m. Karol Prochotsky, Sept. 22, 1962; 1 child, Andrea. B.A., State Conservatory, Czechoslovakia. Classical ballet dancer; soloist Czechoslovakian Nat. Theatre, Bratislava, 1960-69; tchr. Prochotsky Ballet Ctr., Bethesda, Md., 1970—, also dir.; dir. Bethesda-Chevy Chase Civic Ballet, 1971—. Republican. Office: Prochotsky Ballet Ctr 7939 Norfolk Ave Bethesda MD 20814

PROCOPE, ERNESTA GERTRUDE, insurance broker; b. Bklyn., Feb. 9; d. Clarence and Elvira Forster; m. John L. Procope, July 3, 1954. Student Bklyn. Coll., Coll. Ins., Pohs Inst. Ins.; hon. degrees Morgan State U., 1978, Adelphi U., 1978. Pres., E.G. Bowman Co. Inc., N.Y.C., 1953—, also chief exec. officer; dir. Avon Products, Inc., Chubb Corp., Columbia Gas Systems Inc.; panelist corp. governance and advancement of women Women's Bur., U.S. Dept. Labor, 1981; ambassador 10th Anniversary Independence Celebration, Republic of Gambia, 1975. Trustee N.Y. Zool. Soc., Cornell U., Bklyn. Botanic Gardens; bd. dirs. Salvation Army Greater N.Y., Urban Nat. Corp.; mem. adv. council Gov.'s office Mgmt. and Productivity, 1984—, Bus. Adv. Bd., 1984—. Recipient achievement award Thelma T. Johnson Meml. Scholarship Fund, 1972; bus. achievement award Interracial Council for Bus. Opportunity, 1973; Community Service award F & M Schaefer Brewing Co., 1974; Sojourner Truth award Negro Bus. and Profl. Women's Club, Inc., 1974; Bus. Achievement award Nat. Bus. League, 1976; Catalyst award Women Dirs. of Corps., 1977; honored as disting. black woman in corp. role Nat. Council Negro Women, Inc., 1981, also others. Mem. Nat. Assn. Ins. Brokers, Nat. Assn. Ins. Women, Women's Forum, Alpha Kappa Alpha (hon.). Presbyterian. Club: Cosmopolitan. Office: EG Bowman Co Inc 97 Wall St New York NY

PROCTER, CAROL ANN, cellist; b. Oklahoma City, June 26, 1941; d. Leland Herrick and Alice (McElroy) P.; student Eastman Sch. Music, 1958-60; B.Mus., New Eng. Conservatory of Music, 1963, M.Mus., 1965; Fromm fellow Tanglewood Music Center, Lenox, Mass., 1965. Cellist, Springfield (Mass.) Symphony Orch., 1961-65, Cambridge (Mass.) Festival Orch., 1961-65, Boston Symphony Orch. and Boston Pops, 1965—; mem. New Eng. Harp Trio; viola da gambist Curtisville Consortium; soloist viola da gamba Boston Symphony Orch., 1976, 81, 85, cello Boston Pops, 1980. Recipient Fulbright award, 1965. Mem. Mu Phi Epsilon. Office: Boston Symphony Orchestra Symphony Hall Boston MA 02115

PROCTOR, BARBARA GARDNER, advt. agy. exec., writer; b. Asheville, N.C.; d. William and Bernice (Baxter) Gardner; B.A. Talladega Coll., 1954; m. Carl L. Proctor, July 20, 1961 (div. Nov. 1963); 1 son, Morgan Eugene. Music critic, contbg. editor Down Beat Mag., Chgo., from 1958; internat. dir. Vee Jay Records, Chgo., 1961-64; copy supr. Post-Keyes-Gardner Advt., Inc., 1965-68, Gene Taylor Assos., 1968-69, North Advt. Agy., 1969-70; contbr. to gen. periodicals, from 1952; founder Proctor & Gardner Advt., Chgo., 1970—, now pres., chief exec. officer. Mem. Chgo. Urban League, Chgo. Econ. Devel. Corp. Bd. dirs. People United to Save Humanity, Better Bus. Bur. Cons. pub. relations and promotion, record industry. Recipient Armstrong Creative Writing award, 1954; awards Chgo. Fedn. Advt. Clubs, N.Y. Art Dirs. Club. Woman's Day; Frederick Douglas Humanitarian award, 1975; named Chgo. Advt. Woman of Year, 1974. Mem. Chgo. Media Women, Nat. Assn. Radio Arts and Sci., Women's Advt. Club, Cosmopolitan C. of C. (dir.), Female Execs. Assn., Internat. Platform Assn., Smithsonian Instn. Assos. Author TV documentary Blues for a Gardenia, 1963. Office: Proctor and Gardner Advt 111 E Wacker Dr Chicago IL 60601*

PROCTOR, JEANETTA STARR, educational adminstrator; b. Winnsboro, Tex.; d. Robert Dorman Proctor and Jeanetta Beth (Ingram) Henrix. B.S. cum laude, Tex. Woman's U., 1979. Art dir. Oak Cliff Tribune, Dallas, 1964-68; continuity dir., producer, promotion mgr. KDTV-Channel 39, Dallas, 1968-73; owner Arabian Horse Farm, Susarr Farm, Lewisville, Tex., 1977-81; transp. supr. Lewisville Ind. Sch. Dist., 1981—. Mem. Tex. State Tchrs. Assn., Alpha Chi, Alpha Kappa Delta. Democrat. Club: Humane Soc. (Lewisville). Avocations: building raquetball; tennis; animal rights. Home: 207 Garth Ln Hickory Creek TX 75065

PROCTOR, MARGARET SELFRIDGE, lawyer; b. Wilmington, Del., May 12, 1954; d. David Creighton and Lydia (Richards) Boyer; m. Vernon R. Proctor, May 27, 1978; 1 son, Edward Ford. A.B., Smith Coll., 1976; J.D., Harvard U., 1979. Bar: Del. 1980, U.S. Dist. Ct. Del. 1980, U.S. Ct. Appeals (3d cir.) 1983. Assoc., Potter Anderson & Corroon, Wilmington, Del., 1979-83; dep. atty. gen. Dept. Justice, Wilmington, 1984—. Bd. dirs. The Children's Home, Inc., Claymont, Del., 1980—, sec., 1983—. Mem. ABA, Del. State Bar Assn. (com. sect. on litigation and young lawyers com. 1982—), Wilmington Women in Bus. Republican. Episcopalian. Club: Vicmead Hunt (Greenville, Del.). Office: Dept Justice 820 N French St Wilmington DE 19801

PRODOEHL, PATRICIA ANN, nurse, bus. exec.; b. Oak Park, Ill., Mar. 16, 1938; d. Carl Olaf and Elizabeth Mable (Maas) Larson; R.N., Swedish Am. Hosp., Rockford, Ill., 1959; m. Henry William Prodoehl, June 3, 1961; children—James Carl, Judith Ann; step-children—Lawrence Paul, R. Theresa. Nurse, Swedish Am. Hosp., Rockford, Ill., 1959-60, Johns Hopkins Hosp., Balt., 1960-61, Lutheran Hosp., Balt., 1961-62; sec.-treas. Free State Adjusters, Inc., Balt., 1978—; pres. Office E-Z Move, Balt., 1981—; real estate agt., 1984—. Active Camp Fire Girls, Inc., 1971-81, recipient numerous awards; active Boy Scouts Am., recipient Merit award, 1974; tchr. Sunday Sch., 1968-71, 80-82, supt., 1981—. Recipient Book of Golden Deeds award Exchange Club of Randallstown (Md.). Mem. Am. Mgmt. Assn., Nat. Fedn. Ind. Bus. Lutheran. Club: Woman's (pres. Randallstown 1980-82). Office: 9621 Reistertown Rd Box 5705 Baltimore MD 21208

PROEFROCK, VICKI GAITHER, psychometrist; b. Bloomington, Ill., Sept. 18, 1947; d. Harold Victor and Grace Lucille (Phelps) Gaither; m. David Wayne Proefrock, June 20, 1970; children—Amy, Benjamin. Student Western Ill. U., 1965-66, Memphis State U., 1976-78; B.A., Augusta Coll., 1982. Med. technician Mercy Hosp., Urbana, Ill., 1967-72; med. technician Med. Coll. Ga., Augusta, 1972-74, psychometrist, 1980—; research chemist U. Tenn. Ctr. Health Scis., Memphis, 1975-80. Contbr. articles to profl. jours. Vice pres. Augusta Coll. Women, 1983-84; mem. ways and means com. Assn. Parents of Gifted, Columbia County, Ga., 1983-84; chmn. Friends of Ezekiel Harris; mem. Columbia County Democratic Com., 1982—; mem. Ga. Dem. Com., 1982—; mem. adv. bd. ga. Regional Hosp., Augusta, 1984—; mem. Community Leadership Program, Columbia, 1986—. Recipient de Treville award for hist. article Richmond County Hist. Soc., 1982; named to Outstanding Young Women Am., U.S. Jaycees, 1983, 84; nat. merit scholar Western Ill. U., 1965. Mem. Augusta Area Psychol. Assn. (assoc.), Hist. Augusta, Augusta Coll. Alumni Assn. (bd. dirs. 1983—). Unitarian. Avocations: aerobic dancing; baking; historical research. Home: 4684 Oakley Pirkle Rd Martinez GA 30907 Office: Med Coll Ga Dept Pediatrics BIW 848 Augusta GA 30912

PROFFITT, MARTHA ANNE SOUTHWICK, corporation official, educator; b. Garber, Okla., Apr. 22, 1943; d. Harlow J. and Anna (Pope) Southwick; m. A. James Proffitt, Feb. 19, 1975; children—Suzanne, Melissa. B.A. in Social Ecology, U. Calif.-Irvine, 1975; M.A. in Human Resources Mgmt., U. Redlands (Calif.), 1982. Lic. life and disability agt.; cert. tchr., Calif.; cert. profl. ins. woman. Adminstr. personnel Electronic Data Systems, San Francisco, 1969-71; supr. group ins. McDonnell Douglas Co., Santa Monica, Calif., 1973-75; mgr. benefit payment div. Assn. Adminstrs., Irvine, Calif., 1975-79, v.p. benefits and adminstrn., 1979-81; dir. employee benefits Advanced Health Systems, Irvine, 1981-82, corp. mgr. employee benefits Purex Industries Inc., Lakewood, Calif., 1982—; instr. employee benefits Orange Coast Coll., Costa Mesa, Calif., 1980-81; instr. group ins. Rancho Santiago Sch. Dist., Santa Ana, Calif., 1982-84; cons., instr. Self Funded Adminstrs., Orange County, Calif., 1983; mem. adv. bd. Orange County Family Counseling Service, 1984, bd. dirs., 1980-83. Mem. Parks and Recreation Commn., City of Fountain Valley (Calif.), 1979-83, vice-chmn., 1981-83; chmn. Cultural Arts Com. Fountain Valley, 1981-83, chmn. beautification com., 1979-80. Mem. Los Angeles Employers Health Care Coalition (utilization rev. com. 1983, chmn. alt. del. sys. 1984), Orange County Employers Health Care Coalition (chmn. benefit design 1984, provider liaison 1983-84), Long Beach Chamber, Health Resources Council (chmn. legis. com. 1983, 84), Risk Ins. Mgmt. Soc., Nat. Mgmt. Assn. Club: OMNI Business (Fountain Valley) (charter). Office: Purex Industries Inc 5101 N Clark Ave Lakewood CA 90712

PROFFITT, WANDA JUNE, real estate company executive; b. Burnsville, N.C., May 1, 1942; d. Gudger and Mae (Wyatt) Robinson; m. Bobby Lee Proffitt, July 11, 1958; children—Robert, Amy P. Proffitt Troutman. Student Md. Tech. Coll., 1972; grad. Realtors Inst., Chapel Hill, N.C., 1975. Sec. Robinson Dairy, 1964-72; sec., broker Cy Jordan Realty, Inc., Burnsville, 1972-76, v.p., 1976-81; pres. Realty World Carolina Mountain Realty, Burnsville, 1981—; chmn. Yancey-County Econ. Devel. Com., Burnsville, 1981—; vice chmn. Econ. Devel. Assn. Western N.C., Asheville, 1984—; dir. Mayland Tech. Found., Spruce Pine; dir. N.C. Real Estate Ednl. Found., Chapel Hill, assoc. dean Realtor's Inst., 1977-81; sec. Realty World, Dixie Region, Charlotte, N.C., 1984—; trustee N.C. Realtors Polit. Action Com., Greensboro, 1982—. Bd. dirs. Avery Mitchell Yancey Regional Library, Spruce Pine; treas. Higgins Meml. United Meth. Ch., Burnsville, 1977—. Recipient Vol. award Gov. N.C., 1983, Farm-City Week-Bus. award Yancey County Extension Service, 1982. Mem. Yancey County C. of C. (bd. dirs. 1981-83), N.C. Assn. of Realtors (regional v.p. 1982-84, edn. chmn. 1981, Regional Service award 1979), N.C. Indsl. Assn., N.C. Cert. Residential Specialist Chpt. (sec. 1982-83), Nat. Assn. Realtors, Yancey-Mitchell Bd. Realtors (founding pres.). Democrat. Avocations: reading; hiking; sewing. Home: 411 East By Pass Burnsville NC 28714 Office: Realty World Carolina Mountain Realty Inc 51 West Blvd Burnsville NC 28714

PROFIT, LORETHA SPURS, educator; b. Monroe, La., Aug. 15, 1947; d. James and Willie Mae (Kiper) Spurs; B.A., N.E. La. U., 1976; m. Simon Profit, Jr., June 6, 1966; children—Anthony Simeon, Adriane Sirena, Simon, III. Asst. mgr. Nelsons Drive In and Motel, Monroe, 1966-68, mgr., 1970-73, co-owner, 1980-84; substitute tchr., vol. tutor Ouachita Prish Sch. Bd., Monroe, 1968-69; paraprofl. Swayze Elem. Sch., Monroe, 1973-76; tchr. 2d grade Woodlawn Elem. Sch., W. Monroe, 1976—. Mem. NEA, La. Assn. Educators, Ouachita Assn. Educators (faculty rep.), Assn. Supervision and Curriculum Devel., Northeast La. Reading Assn., Classroom Tchrs. Assn., Internat. Platform Assn. Club: Order Eastern Star. Home: 4005 Gaston St Monroe LA 71203 Office: Route 3 Box 126-C West Monroe LA 71291

PROKOP, RUTH TIMBERLAKE, lawyer; b. San Saba, Tex., May 30, 1939; d. Harry Carver and Anna Grace (Winslow) Timberlake; m. John Andrew Prokop, Aug. 29, 1962 (div.); 1 dau., Kristina Elizabeth. B.A., George Washington U., 1961, J.D., 1965. Staff to Vice Pres. Lyndon B. Johnson, Washington, 1961-62; legis. asst. Pres.'s Commn. on Status of Women, Washington, 1962-64; legis. counsel Pres.'s Com. on Consumer Affairs, Washington, 1964-66; spl. asst. to sec. HUD, Washington, 1966-69; mem. law firm Brownstein, Ziedman & Schomer, Washington, 1970-72; sr. counsel Gen. Telephone Electronics Corp., Washington, 1972-77; gen. counsel HUD, 1977-79; chmn. U.S. Merit Systems Protection Bd., 1979-81; ptnr. Curtis, Mallet-Prevost, Colt & Mosle, Washington, 1981—; dir. McLachlen Nat. Bank, 1982—; bd. dirs. Fed. Nat. Mortgage Assn., 1977-79; mem. Administrv. Conf. U.S., Washington, 1977-80. Co-author: Survey of Laws Relating to Investment of Private Trust Funds & State Retirement Funds in Mortgage Notes, 1969. Mem. ABA (Council on Sci. Tech. 1976, chmn. Com. on Privacy, 1976), D.C. Bar Assn., Assn. Trial Lawyers Am. Episcopalian.

PROLER, LYNETTE GLENYS, antique jewelry company executive; b. Perth, Western Australia, Australia, Oct. 8, 1943; came to U.S., 1961, naturalized, 1965; d. Henry and Hope (Foox) Brown; children—Marcus J., Shayn A. Pres. Lynette Proler Antique Jewellers, Houston, 1976—, also galleries in London and Paris; lectr. gemstones, history of jewelry, Fabergé, and related topics. Sec. Houston Ballet Found., 1971, v.p., 1972; bd. dirs., mem. exec. com. Soc. for Performing Arts, Houston, 1972—; bd. dirs. various cultural orgns., 1972—. Awarded lifetime membership Houston Grand Opera, 1984; named Bus. Woman of Yr., Cerebral Palsy Found., Houston, 1985. Republican. Avocations: travel; antique collecting; renovating old homes. Office: Lynette Proler Antique Jewellers 5015 Westheimer Suite 2155 Houston TX 77056

PROPP, GAIL DANEGOMBERG, computer consultant; b. N.Y.C., Mar. 22, 1946; d. Oscar and Goody (Rosenburgh) Dane; m. Ephraim Propp; B.A. in Econs., Barnard Coll., 1965; children—Eric Wesley, David Marc, Anna Michelle. Instr., programmer IBM Corp., N.Y.C., 1965-66; systems and programmer analyst R.S. Topas Co., N.Y.C., 1966-67; dir. systems and programming Abercrombie & Fitch Co., N.Y.C., 1967-69; dir. corp. data processing and MIS, 1969-77; founder, 1977, since pres. Met Data Systems, Inc., N.Y.C., 1977—; founder, pres. Datatype Internat. Inc. subs. Met Data Systems, 1982—; assoc. dir. Burns Archive of Hist. Med. Photographs, N.Y.C., 1979—. Mem. Am. bd. overseers Bar-Ilan U. Mem. Internat. Council Computers in Edn., Women in Info. Processing, Assn. Systems Mgmt., Data Processing Mgmt. Assn., Photog. History Soc. Am., Photog. Historic Soc. N.Y. Author articles in field. Office: 919 3d Ave New York NY 10022

PROST, MARY ROSE, law enforcement officer, lawyer; b. Detroit, June 11, 1947; d. John Peter and Aileen Theresa (Moroney) McGuinness; m. Patrick Francis Prost, Oct. 16, 1969 (div. Jan. 1986); 1 dau., Megan. B.A., Duquesne U., 1969; J.D., U. Detroit, 1980. Bar: Mich. 1981, U.S. Ct. Appeals (6th cir.) 1983. Police officer Detroit Police Dept., 1971-83, 3d dep. chief, 1983—. Bd. dirs. Federated Council Domestic Violence Programs, Hazel Park, Mich., 1982. Mem. ABA, Assn. Trial Lawyers Am., Mich. Trial Lawyers Assn., Mich. Assn. Chiefs of Police. Office: Detroit Police Dept 1300 Beaubien St Detroit MI 48226

PROTERO, DODI, soprano; b. Toronto, Can., Mar. 13, 1935; came to U.S., 1965; d. Stewart and Dorothy (Flaherty) McIlraith; ed. in Europe. Soprano with Vienna State Opera, Salzburg Festival, Glyndebourne Festival, Rome Opera, San Carlo Opera, Can. Opera, Vancouver Opera, San Antonio Opera, Pitts. Opera Co.; prof. voice U. Ill., Urbana, 1976—; tchr. pvt. voice students, N.Y.C., 1975—; prof. voice Banff (Alta.) Sch. Fine Arts. Can. Council fellow, 1965, 69, 73. Mem. Nat. Assn. Tchrs. of Singing, Equity, AFTRA, Am. Guild Musical Artists, Screen Actors Guild, Ill. State Music Tchrs. Assn. Recorded for Phillips Records on Epic Label; appeared in movie, Vienna City of My Dream, 1958. Home: 1809D Valley Rd Champaign IL 61820 Office: 257 Central Park W Apt 12H New York NY 10024

PROUNIS, LILA DOROTHEA, political scientist, radio producer; b. N.Y.C.; d. Nicholas and Stella (Lambrakis) Gentilini; m. Theodore Othon Prounis, Feb. 22, 1956; children—Othon, Amelia. B.A., Hunter Coll., 1948; M.A., Columbia U., 1950, postgrad. Radio producer Voice of America, N.Y.C. and Washington, 1952-56; non-govtl. orgn. rep. UN, N.Y.C., 1975—, rapporteur, exec. com. 1984-85. Treas., Women's Nat. Philiptochos Greek Orthodox Ch., N.Y.C., 1965-73; mem. Greek Orthodox Archidiocesan Council, N.Y.C., 1975-82; mem. women's com. Am. Cancer Soc., N.Y.C., 1975—; mem. adv. council N.Y. State Div. Human Rights, 1976-78. Recipient Excellence in Radio award Ohio State U., 1956. Clubs: Women's Nat. Republican, Friends of City Ctr (exec. bd. dirs. 1972-75) (N.Y.C.). Avocations: opera; ballet; theater; travel.

PROVENCHER RYDER, FRANCES NORMA, public relations executive; b. Exeter, N.H., Apr. 22, 1947; d. Roger Arthur and Josette Marguerite (Camus) Provencher; m. Benjamin C. Ryder, Apr. 12, 1969 (div. Mar. 1979); 1 child, Tiffany Nicholas. B.A., U. N.H., 1969. Clk. typist, editorial asst. U.S. Embassy, Moscow, 1964-65; asst. editor Durham (N.H.) Advertiser, 1965-69; assoc. editor Kaman Aerospace Corp., Bloomfield, Conn., 1970-71; publs. editor The Hartford Ins. Group (Conn.), 1974-76; pub. relations cons. Fran Ryder Assocs., Farmington, Conn., 1976-78; pub. relations account exec. Shailer Davidoff Rogers, Inc., Fairfield, Conn., 1978-80; sr. account exec. Creamer Dickson Basford, Inc., Hartford, Conn., 1980-83; account group mgr., account exec. Spiro & Assocs., Phila., 1983-84, v.p., assoc. pub. relations dir., 1984-85; sr. v.p. pub. relations Lessner Slossberg Gahl and Ptnrs., Inc., Avon,

Conn., 1985—. Translator: The Cogito in Edmund Husserl's Phenomenology, 1969. Founder, The Art Guild, 1975; bd. dirs. Parent's Assn., Hartford Sch. Ballet, 1982, 83. Recipient Gold Quill awards Internat. Assn. Bus. Communicators, 1974. Mem. Pub. Relations Soc. Am. (accredited; bd. dirs. 1980-84, mem. Counselors Acad. 1982—, spl. commendation 1985), Nat. Assn. Female Execs., Women in Communications, Inc. Republican. Congregationalist. Home: 37 Tunxis Village Farmington CT 06032 Office: Lessner Slossberg Gahl and Ptnrs Inc 17 W Main St Avon CT 06001

PROVENZANO, SANDRA, pilot; b. Tulsa, Jan. 8, 1938; d. Mansford Allen and Mary Elizabeth (Barnes) Hulme; children—Ross Anthony, David Allen, Mark Andrew. With Cruse Aviation, Inc., Houston, 1970-83, chief pilot, chief flight instr., dir. ops., 1979-83; owner, operator Aviation Tng. Consultants, 1983—; pilot examiner, accident prevention counselor FAA, Houston, 1977—; mem. adv. council Houston Aviation, 1980—. Roman Catholic. Mem. Greater Houston Assn. Flight Instrs. (pres. 1982). Club: Bergstrom Aero (chief pilot 1979, mgr. 1979). Contbr. articles to tng. catalogs. Home: 18105 Heritage Ln Nassau Bay TX 77058 Office: 8922 Randolph-Hobby Airport Houston TX 77061

PROVIS, DOROTHY L., artist, sculptor; b. Chgo., Apr. 26, 1926; d. George Kenneth Smith and Ann Hart (Day) Smith Guest; m. William H. Provis, Sr., July 28, 1945; children—Timothy A., William H., Jr. Student Sch. Art Inst., Chgo., 1953-56, U. Wis.-Milw., 1967-68, 69-70. Sculptor, Port Washington, Wis., 1963—; pres. bd. dirs. West Bend Gallery of Fine Arts, Wis., 1984-86, also dir.; speaker in field. Author, lobbyist Wis. Consignment Bill, Madison, 1979; panelist Women's Caucus for Art Conf., Phila., 1983. Wis. Arts Bd. designer-craftsmen grantee, NEA, 1981. Mem. Coalition of Women's Art Orgns. (del. to continuing com. Nat. Women's Conf. 1979, panelist conf. 1981, v.p. for membership/nominations, pres. 1982-85, 1981-85, nat. pres. 1985-87), Wis. Painters and Sculptors (pres. 1982-84, editor newsletter 1982-85), Wis. Women in Arts (legis. liaison 1978-80). Artists for Ednl. Action (corr. 1979—), Wis. Designer Craftsmen, Women's Caucus for Art, Chgo. Artists Coalition, Internat. Sculpture Ctr. Home and Studio: 123 E Beutel Rd Port Washington WI 53074

PROVOST, PHYLLIS EVELYN, lawyer; b. Springfield, Mass., May 7, 1955; d. John Robert and Evelyn Ruth (Parks) Provost; m. Scott Alexander McNeil, Oct. 22, 1983. B.A., U. Notre Dame, 1977, J.D., 1983. Bar: Pa. 1983. Protocol, visitor liaison officer to comdr.-in-chief U.S. Naval Forces in Europe, London, 1977-79; coll. programs mgr. Navy Recruiting Dist., Washington, 1979-80; exec. officer res. component U.S. Naval Weapons Sta., Concord, Calif., 1980; atty. Fed. Govt., Washington, 1984—. Mem. editorial bd. Notre Dame Law Sch. Jour. Legislation. Instr. CCD Catholic Ch., Coll. Park, Md., 1979-80. Served with USN, 1977-80, to lt. USNR. Mem. ABA, Pa. Bar Assn., Allegheny County Bar Assn., Phi Alpha Delta, Royal Naval Club of Mayfair, Internat. Law Soc., Nat. Librarians Assn.

PROVOST, RHONDA MARIE, nurse anesthetist; b. Qunicy, Mass., Sept. 13, 1948; d. John Stanley and Roberta Adelaide (Tangstrom) P. R.N., Qunicy City Hosp. Sch. Nursing, 1969, Nurse Anesthetist, 1971; B.S., George Washington U., 1982. Cert. registered nurse anesthetist. Staff anesthetist, instr. Children's Hosp. Med. Ctr., Boston, 1971-77, staff anesthetist George Washington U. Med. Ctr., Washington, 1977-78; dir. Sch. of Anesthesia, New Eng. Med. Ctr. Hosp., Boston, 1978-79; staff anesthetist Kaiser-Permanente Med. Group, Redwood City, Calif., 1979—; freelance anesthetist Pregnancy Counseling Ctr., San Jose, Calif., 1983-84, Plastic Reconstructive Ambulatory Ctr., Los Altos, Calif., 1984-85. Co-author: Indoor Exercise Book, 1981; Advanced Indoor Exercise Book, 1982; Feeling Fit in Your Forties, 1986; also articles. Sec. bd. dirs. Grant Ave. Condominium Owners Assn., Palo Alto, Calif., 1984, v.p. bd. dirs., 1985. Mem. Am. Assn. Nurse Anesthetists, Calif. Assn. Nurse Anesthetists. Roman Catholic. Avocations: triathletics; piano; snow skiing; water skiing; horseback riding. Home: 107 Lilac Ln Saint Helena CA 94574 Office: Kaiser-Permanente Hosp 1110 Veteran's Blvd Redwood City CA 94063

PROVUS, BARBARA LEE, management consultant; b. Washington, Nov. 20, 1949; d. Severn and Birdell (Eck) P.; m. Fred W. Wackerle. Student N.Y. U., 1969-70; B.A., Russell Sage Coll., 1971; postgrad. Smith Coll., 1971; M.S.I.R., Loyola U., Chgo., 1979. Cons. exec. search and corp. mgmt. devel. Booz, Allen & Hamilton, Inc., Chgo., 1973-80; mgr. mgmt. devel. Federated Dept. Stores, Inc., Cin., 1980-82, v.p. Lamalie Assos., Inc., Chgo., 1982—. Mem. Human Resources Planning Soc. Home: 3750 N Lake Shore Dr Chicago IL 60613 Office: 120 S Riverside Plaza Chicago IL 60606

PROZAN, SYLVIA SIMMONS, lawyer, television newscaster; b. Cleve., Apr. 10, 1933; d. James M. and Dora (Shuman) Simmons; m. George B. Prozan, June 24, 1956; children—Michael, Lawrence, Anne, Rebecca. B.A., Barnard Coll., 1955; M.A., Case Western Reserve U., 1959; J.D., U. Calif.-Berkeley, 1975. Bar: Calif. 1976, U.S. Supreme Ct. 1980. Television prodn. staff NBC, N.Y.C.; pub. affairs staff sta. KQED, KPIX, San Francisco, 1963-65; television newscaster, investigative reporter sta. KNTV, San Jose, Calif., 1968-72; adj. prof. J. F. Kennedy Law Sch., Orinda, Calif., 1979-82; sole practice, Burlingame, Calif., 1976—. Mem. State Bar Calif., Calif. Trial Lawyers Assn., Bar of San Francisco, San Mateo County Bar Assn., Union Internationale des Avocats, AAUW. Democrat. Jewish. Home: 2180 Forest View Ave Hillsborough CA 94010

PRUETT, BARBARA ANN, nurse; b. Ft. Benning, Ga., Feb. 9, 1942; d. Frank Lewis and Margaret Lavata (Lane) Macomber; m. James Curtis Ammerman, Feb. 29, 1962 (div. 1964); m. 2d, John Kenneth Pruett, Sept. 3, 1965; children—Thomas Alan, Afton Elizabeth, Patrick Macomber. Diploma, J.F. Drake State Tech. Coll., Huntsville, Ala., 1979; A.S. Nursing, Calhoun Coll., 1982. R.N. Staff nurse Quality Care Nursing Service, Huntsville, Ala., 1979-81, Big Spring Manor, Huntsville, 1981-82, Kimberly Nursing Home, Huntsville, 1983-86, Bagwell Chiropractic Clinic, Huntsville, 1986—. Vol. worker Am. Cancer Telethon, Huntsville, 1965; vol. nurse Hospice Huntsville, 1979-81, Choose Life, 1985—; dir. nursing service ARC, Huntsville, 1979-83; dir. Women's Missionary Union, Southside Baptist Ch., 1985-86. Clubs: Mended Hearts, Touch (Huntsville). Democrat. Home: 1008 Edgewood Ave Huntsville AL 35801 Office: Bagwell Chiropractic Clinic 600 St Clair Bldg No 3 Huntsville AL 35801

PRUETT, BARBARA JEAN, librarian; b. Madison, Ind., May 8, 1942; d. Fred Phillip and Dorothy Jean (Keel) P. B.S., Ind. U., 1966; M.A. in Librarianship, Calif. State U.-San Jose, 1971. Head librarian LaGrange High Sch. (Ind.), 1966-68, Santa Clara Planning Dept., San Jose, Calif., 1969-71; head research info. ctr. United Farm Workers, Keene, Calif., 1973-75; head social sci. library Catholic U., Washington, 1975-79; head tech. services Internat. Trade Commn., Washington, 1979-83, library dir., 1983—. Author country music articles; pub. Clouds Hill Publs. Mem. ALA (council 1979—), Country Music Assn., Acad. Country Music, D.C. Library Assn., Assn. Recorded Sound Collections, D.C. Library Assn., Fed. Library Com. (exec. adv. com. 1984—). Office: US ITC 701 E St NW Washington DC 20436

PRUETT, SHARON HENSON, petroleum landman; b. Houston, Jan. 8, 1941; d. V. Earl and Foy Lorene (Morton) Henson; diploma, Durham Bus. Coll., 1965; B.S. with honors, East Tex. State U., 1977, now postgrad.; children—Kevin Wayne, Nancy Caroline, Donna Lorene. Sec., Tex. Dept. Human Resources, Pittsburg, 1972-74; med. eligibility worker Tex. Dept. Human Resources, Quitman, 1974-79, proposal devel. specialist, regional planner, dir. data sect. Paris, 1979-80; ind. petroleum land rep., Tyler, Tex., 1980—; cons. Tex. Child Welfare Bds., 1980, Study of Child Welfare Staffing Issues, 1980—. Wood County Rep. Gov.'s Com. on Aging, 1974; sec. ARC, 1973; active PTA. Mem. East Tex. Assn. Petroleum Landmen, Am. Soc. for Public Adminstrn., Nat. Assn. Female Execs., Acad. Polit. Sci., NOW, East Houston Athletic Assn., Pi Sigma Alpha. Contbr. articles to profl. jours. Address: PO Box 764 Quitman TX 75783

PRUITT, ANNE LORING SMITH, university administrator; b. Bainbridge, Ga.; d. Loring Alphonzo and Anne Lee (Ward) Smith; B.S. cum laude, Howard U., 1949; M.A., Columbia U., 1950, Ed.D., 1964; D.H. (hon.), Central State U., Ohio, 1982; m. Ralph L. Pruitt (dec.); 1 dau., Leslie Anne; stepchildren—Dianne, Pamela, Sharon, Ralph L. Counselor, Howard U., Washington, 1950-52; dir. guidance Hutto High Sch., Bainbridge, 1952-55; dean of students Albany (Ga.) State Coll., 1955-59, Fisk U., Nashville, 1959-61; prof. edn. Case Western Res. U., Cleve., 1963-79; prof. edn., assoc. dean Grad. Sch., Ohio State U., Columbus, 1979-84, assoc. provost Office Acad. Affairs, 1984—; cons. So. Regional Edn. Bd., So. Edn. Found.; cons. Cuyahoga Community Coll. Mem. Pres. Johnson's War on Poverty Com., Women's Job Corp.; chmn. com. edn. and youth incentives bd. dirs. Cleve. Urban League, 1965-71; chmn. Street Acad.; mem. Com. Fair Housing; vice chmn. bd. dirs. Central State U.; gen. bd. dirs. Cleve. chpt. ARC, 1978-79; adv. com. USCG Acad. 1980-83. ACE fellow, 1977-78; EPDA Tng. grantee, 1974-76; Grad. and Profl. Opportunity Program grantee, 1980-85; grantee Plans for Progress, So. Edn. Found.; named Alumna of Yr., Howard U., 1975. Mem. Am. Assn. Higher Edn., AAUP, Am. Assn. for Counseling and Devel., Am. Coll. Personnel Assn. (sec. 1972-73, pres. 1976-77), Nat. Vocat. Guidance Assn., Pi Lambda Theta, Kappa Delta Pi, Psi Chi, Alpha Kappa Alpha. Congregationalist. Club: Links. Editorial bd. Jour. Coll. Student Personnel, 1971-72, 76-77; contbr. articles to profl. jours., also chpts. in books. Office: 203 Bricker Hall 190 N Oval Mall Ohio State U Columbus OH 43210

PRUITT, DOROTHY J. GOOCH, educational administrator; b. Granville County, N.C., June 10, 1935; d. Edgar N. and Lorine (Henley) Gooch; m. William Leonard Pruitt, July 22, 1958. B.S., East Carolina U., 1956; M.Ed., U. N.C.-Chapel Hill, 1971; sixth yr. cert. Nova U., 1984, Ed.D., 1985. Home econs. tcr. Granville County Schs., Oxford, N.C., 1956-69; cons. State Dept. Pub. Instrn., Raleigh, N.C., 1972-82; prin. Granville County Schs., 1982—. Bd. dirs. N.C. Sch. Bd. Assn., Raleigh, 1980-82; chmn. Granville County Bd. Edn., 1979-82; v.p. Jr. Woman's Club, Oxford, 1965-66 (named Club Woman of Yr. 1965). Mem. N.C. Assn. Sch. Adminstrs., Am. Sch. Curriculum Devel. Assn., Am. Sch. Curriculum Assn., Am. Ednl. Research Assn., N.C. Future Homakers of Am. (hon.), Alpha Delta Kappa (corr. sec. 1970). Baptist. Home: 106 Country Club Dr Oxford NC 27565 Office: Granville County Schs 223 College St Oxford NC 27565

PRUITT, JANA LEE, lawyer; b. Spokane, Wash., Oct. 6, 1955; d. Ben Marvin and Opal Ellen (McGuire) P. B.A. in Polit. Sci., U. Ky., 1977; J.D., U. Louisville, 1980. Bar: Ky. 1981. Assoc. firm Hardy, Logan & Priddy, Louisville, 1979-81; atty. Am. Ins. Assn., N.Y.C., 1982-85; atty. Health Ins. Assn. Am., Washington, 1985—. Mem. ABA, Ky. Bar Assn., Republican. Methodist. Club: Kentuckians of N.Y. Home: 4100 Massachusetts Ave NW Apt LT06 Washington DC 20016 Office: Health Ins Assn Am 1025 Connecticut Ave NW Suite 1200 Washington DC 20036

PRUNEAU, SANDRA LEE, marketing and advertising company executive; b. Concord, N.H., June 7, 1943; d. Lewis Nathaniel and Arlene Elizabeth (Noyes) Wheeler; m. Richard Edward Pruneau, July 29, 1961; 1 child, Cheryl Renee. With Mktg. Communication, Inc., Wakefield, Mass., 1965—, pres., owner, 1975—; cons., speaker in field. Contbr. articles to profl. publs. Editor: Communicator Extraordinaire. Recipient Achievement award Boston chpt. Soc. for Tech. Communication, 1980, 82, 84; Creative Honors, Art Dirs. Club, numerous photog. awards. Mem. New Eng. Advt. Club, Advt. Club of Greater Boston, Andona Soc. Roman Catholic. Avocations: travel; reading; gourmet cooking. Home: 12 College Circle Andover MA 01810 Office: Mktg Communication Inc 4 Lakeside Office Park Wakefield MA 01880

PRUNIER, JOSEPHINE MARIE RUSSO, nursery school director; b. Boston, Aug. 21, 1947; d. Alfio and Ida Helen Russo; B.A. in English, Merrimack Coll., North Andover, Mass., 1969; m. Gary George Prunier, Apr. 4, 1971; children—Kathryn Rebecca, Matthew Ryan, Elizabeth Rene. Elementary and jr. high sch. tchr., Mass. and Maine, 1969-76; dir. Living and Learning Ctr., Methuen, Mass., Mary Moppetts Sch., Phoenix, 1978-79; dir., owner Rockinghorse Pre-Sch., Phoenix, 1979—. Mem. Ariz. Assn. Child Devel. and Edn. (publicity chmn., membership chmn. 1980-81), NOW, Women Emerging., Am. Astrol. Assn. Republican. Roman Catholic. Author: (novel) Door Knobs. Office: Rockinghorse Pre-sch 1601 E Maryland Ave Phoenix AZ 85016

PRYOR, ANNIE RUTH, nurse, real estate broker; b. Ariton, Ala., Oct. 25, 1936; d. Homer and Fannie (Kelley) Pryor. A.A., Wilson Coll., 1954; R.N., Grant Hosp. Sch. Nursing, 1957; continuing edn. U. Chgo., 1960, West Valley Coll., 1981. Operating room nurse U. Chgo. Hosp., 1957-65, head nurse, 1965-66, supr. clin. instrn., 1966-67; operating room nurse Sequoia Hosp., Redwood City, Calif., 1967-68; office nurse, asst. to pvt. physician, Carmel, Calif., 1968-69; operating room nurse Los Gatos Community Hosp., Calif., Good Samaritan Hosp., San Jose, Calif., 1968-75; owner, broker Vasona Properties & Investments, Campbell, Calif., 1982—. Mem. O'Connor Hosp. Aux., San Jose, 1973—; sponsor Explorer project Post 850, Boy Scouts Am., 1983—; mem. adv. council Sta. KRON-TV, San Francisco. Mem. Nat. Assn. Realtors, Calif. Assn. Realtors, Calif. Assn. Operating Room Nurses, Nat. Assn. Operating Room Nurses. Republican. Baptist. Avocations: painting; tennis; knitting. Home and Office: Vasona Properties & Investments 671 Division St Campbell CA 95008

PRYOR, VIKKI LYNN, lawyer; b. Great Lakes, Ill., Aug. 22, 1953; d. Karl Eugene and Mary Dorothy (Nesbitt) Pryor. B.A. magna cum laude, SUNY-Buffalo, 1975, J.D., 1978. C.P.A. Sec. Bonwit Teller, N.Y.C., 1972-73; office mgr. Ops. Mgmt., Buffalo, 1973-75; law clk. Corp. Counsel, Buffalo, 1976-78; sr. trial atty. Office of Chief Counsel, IRS, Chgo., 1978—. Mem. ABA, Cook County Bar Assn., Erie County Bar Assn., Chgo. Bar Assn., Federally Employed Women (sec. 1980—), Minn. Legal Edn. Resources (dir. 1980-82), Women's Bar Assn. Ill., Women in Mgmt., League Black Women. Home: 605 S Grove Ave Oak Park IL 60304

PRZYBORSKI, JUDY LYNN, lawyer; b. Houston, Oct. 24, 1958; d. Rudolph I. and Lillie (Novak) Kaderka; m. Michael Joseph Przyborski, May 19, 1984. B.A., U. St. Thomas, Houston, 1981; J.D., U. Houston, 1983. Bar: Tex. 1984. Personnel clk. Montgomery Ward & Co., Houston, 1974-83; law clk. firm Ron Hayes, Houston, 1983-84; assoc. law firm Cammack and Welscher, Houston, 1984—; judge U. Houston Moot Ct. Competition, 1983. Mem. ABA, Tex. Bar Assn., Delta Epsilon. Roman Catholic. Home: 700 Dunson Glen #506 Houston TX 77090

PUCHALIK, PATRICIA ANN, nursing administrator; b. Newark, Jan. 28, 1944; d. Arthur Philip and Olwyn Doris (Davies) Corbley; m. Joseph Paul Puchalik, Oct. 16, 1971; children—Joanne, Joseph, Robert. Diploma in nursing, Johns Hopkins Hosp., 1964; B.S.N., Rutgers U., 1969; M.S.N., Seton Hall U., 1979. Staff nurse Johns Hopkins Hosps., Balt., 1964-65; office nurse Summit Med. Group, N.J., 1965-66; supr. Valley Hosp., Ridgewood, N.J., 1971-77, inservice educator, 1977-79, hospice coordinator, 1979-84; dir. med. nursing St. Joseph's Hosp., Paterson, N.J., 1984—; lectr. in field. Mem. N.J. Nurses Assn. (sec. 1975-77, treas. 1978-80, v.p. 1980-82, pres. 1982—; Nurse of Yr. award 1982). Democrat. Roman Catholic. Avocations: home canning; gardening. Home: 677 Meisten St Westwood NJ 07675

PUCKETT, HELEN LOUISE, tax cons. co. exec.; b. Ripley, Ohio, Oct. 29, 1934; d. Joseph and Gladys Muriel (Madden) Haney; student Columbus Bus. U., 1971; m. Marvin R. Puckett, May 29, 1953 (dec.); children—Steven W., Thomas J. Office mgr. Al-Win Tng., Inc., West Jefferson, Ohio, 1971—, sec.-treas., 1971—, agt., 1977-79; notary public, 1975—. Sunday Sch. tchr. London (Ohio) Ch. of Christ, 1975—, pres. Women's Fellowship, 1979-81. Mem. London Bus. and Profl. Women (rec. sec. 1984-85). Home: 130 Columbia Ave London OH 43140 Office: 485 Glade Run Rd West Jefferson OH 43162

PUDVIN, SUZANNE CAROL, advertising executive; b. Bethlehem, Pa., Nov. 10, 1952; d. John Francis and Ruth Harriet (McLernon) P. B.A. in Sociology, Cornell U., 1973, M.A.T., 1975. Home econs. tchr. Webster Central Schs. (N.Y.), 1975-77; account rep. J. Walter Thompson, Atlanta, 1978-79; account exec. Stockton West Burkhart, Dallas, 1979-81, Arnold Harwell McClain, Dallas, 1981-82; account supr. McCann-Erickson, Dallas, 1982—. Vol., Presbyterian Hosp., Dallas, 1982—. Recipient Prominent Women in Advt. award McMillan & Co., 1983. Office: McCann-Erickson 10830 North Central Expwy #246 Dallas TX 75231

PUETT, SAMMIE LYNN, state official, journalism educator; b. Knoxville, Tenn., Sept. 7, 1936; d. Samuel H. and Edith L. (Burkhart) Scandlyn; m. Eugene Puett, Nov. 24, 1968. B.S., U. Tenn., 1958, M.S., 1966. Accredited pub. relations counselor. Sales corr. Plasti-Line, Inc., Knoxville, 1958-60; pub. relations cons. Mcpl. Tech. Adv. Service, U. Tenn., Knoxville, 1960-68, asst. prof. journalism, 1968-73, exec. asst. to chancellor, 1973-78; commr. gen. services State of Tenn., Knoxville, 1979-80, commr. human services, Nashville, 1980-85; assoc. v.p. U. Tenn.-Knoxville, 1985—; mem. State Publs. Com., 1979-80, State Bd. Standards, 1979-80, Medicaid Med. Adv. Com., 1980-85, Commn. on Aging, 1980-85, Gov.'s Task Force on Prevention of Mental Retardation, 1980-83, Gov.'s Task Force on Healthy Children, 1983-85, Gov.'s Task Force on Youth, Alcohol and Drug Abuse, 1984-85; chair Cabinet Council on Social Services, 1983-85; pub. relations cons., 1966- 78; speaker, lectr. Author: 101 Winning Ways to Better Municipal Public Relations, 1967; also articles. Columnist Nation's Cities mag., 1965-73. Mem. editorial bd. Pub. Relations Jour., 1978-80. Bd. dirs. Dogwood Arts Festival, 1976-78, Jr. Achievement, 1975, 76; former chpt. pub. edn. chair Am. Cancer Soc.; former pres. Knoxville City Panhellenic; former sec. Knoxville dist. bd. adminstrn. and missions United Meth. Ch.; mem. adv. bd. dept. home econs. Middle Tenn. State U., 1983-84; del.-at-large Republican Nat. Conv., 1984; mem. Commn. Presdl. Scholars, 1984—; mem. regional selection panel White House Fellows Program, 1985. Recipient Chancellor's citation U. Tenn., 1979; Woman of Achievement award U. Tenn. Commn. on Women, 1980, 83. Mem. Pub. Relations Soc. Am. (Silver Anvil 1975), Nat. Council State Welfare Commrs. (rep. 1984), Pub. Relations Soc. Am. (Silver Anvil 1975; chpt. pres. 1973-74, chair nat. ednl. adv. council 1975, dir. nat. case study competition 1973-76, chair S.E. dist. 1977-78, nat. dir. 1979-80), Sigma Delta Chi (nat. campus affairs com., chpt. dir.). Avocations: roses; music; reading; bridge. Home: 5113 Catalina Dr Knoxville TN 37918 Office: 467 Commn Bldg Knoxville TN 37919

PUFF, JEAN ELLINGWOOD, civic worker; b. Evanston, Ill., July 25, 1924; d. Lloyd and Margaret (Brown) Ellingwood; B.S. in Nursing, Northwestern U., 1947; m. Henry B. Puff, June 10, 1950; children—James Raymond, Margaret Elizabeth. Nurse, student health service, Northwestern U., Evanston, Ill., 1947-48; Pres. Gov. Wentworth Arts Council, N.H., 1973—; bd. dirs. Wolfeboro (N.H.) Playhouse, 1975—; vol. Delta Gamma vision screening, Buffalo, 1960-65, Buffalo Philharmonic, 1959-69; mem. Republican Women's Club., Huggins Hosp. Aid (Wolfeboro). Mem. Evanston Hosp. Alumni Assn., Northwestern U. Alumni Assn., Republican Women's Fedn., Delta Gamma. Presbyterian. Clubs: Lakes Region Tennis. Home: Box 743 Springfield Point Wolfeboro NH 03894

PUGH, MARTHA GREENEWALD, lawyer; b. Washington, Feb. 1, 1913; d. Eugene Ludwig and Mary Martha (Curtis) Greenewald; m. Wallace R. Pugh, Aug. 29, 1935 (div. 1945); children—John Clifford, William Wallace; m. 2d, Wallace R. Pugh, Aug. 29, 1975. B.A. in Physics, U. Colo., 1934; M.S. in Physics, U. Mich., 1936; J.D., Seton Hall U., 1961. Bar: D.C. 1964, U.S. Ct. Appeals (D.C. cir.) 1964, N.J. 1965, U.S. Dist. Ct. N.J. 1965, U.S. Ct. Customs and Patent Appeals 1966, U.S. Ct. Appeals (3d cir.) 1966, U.S. Supreme Ct. 1977, U.S. Patent Office 1947. Instr. physics NYU, N.Y.C., 1941-43; mem. patent staff Bell Telephone Labs., Murray Hill, N.J., 1943-67; patent agt. Gulton Industries, Metuchen, N.J., 1957-58; patent agt., Summit, N.J., 1958-64; sole practice, Summit, 1964-81; ptnr. Mathews, Woodbridge, Goebel, Pugh & Collins, Morristown, N.J., 1981—. Author article Jour. Patent Office Soc. Mem. Coalition for Nuclear Freeze, 1983—. Mem. N.J. Bar Assn. (chmn. patent sect. 1976-77), Union County Bar assn. (trustee 1976-78), ABA, N.J. Patent Law Assn. (2d v.p. 1984, treas. 1985, sec. 1986), Am. Patent Law Assn., Nat. Assn. Women Lawyers, Women Lawyers of Union County, Nat. Soc. Inventors (council), Mortar Bd., Sigma Pi Sigma, Kappa Beta Pi, Pi Beta Phi. Democrat. Unitarian. Club: Green Mountain. Office: Mathews Woodbridge Goebel Pugh & Collins 22 Park Pl PO Box 112M Morristown NJ 07960

PUGH, VALERIE NOVY, psychotherapist, retail executive; b. Austin, Tex., Nov. 21, 1951; d. Sam and Gertrude (Needleman) Novy; m. Michael Lee Pugh, Aug. 13, 1973; children—Bree Novy, Ashley Novy. B.S., U. Tex., 1973; M.S.W., U. Houston, 1978. Pres., Houston Psychotherapy Assocs., 1979—; owner Valerie Designer Lingerie, Houston, 1983—; mem. profl. adv. bd. Parents of Prematures, Houston, 1981-83; cons. Baylor Coll. Medicine, Houston, 1980, Mental Health Assn., Houston, 1979, Houston Orgn. Parent Edn., 1979. Vol., Houston Ind. Sch. Dist., 1979, Beehive Sch., 1979. Mem. Nat. Assn. Social Workers. Jewish. Office: Houston Psychotherapy Assocs 7580 Fannin St Houston TX 77054

PUGLIESE, BARBARA WIERCIOCH, research and analysis co. exec.; b. Lowicz, Poland, Apr. 1, 1941; came to U.S., 1949; naturalized, 1959; d. Henryk and Ludwika (Gostkiewicz) Wiercioch; B.A. cum laude in Math., Conn. Coll. for Women, 1963; m. William Pugliese, Aug. 13, 1973. Programer, mathematician Naval Underwater Systems Center, New London, Conn., 1959-63, ops. research analyst, 1963-67; sr. systems analyst (sonar-tactics) Marine Research Lab., Raytheon Corp., New London, 1967-69; sr. v.p., mgr. effectiveness analysis dept., plant owner Analysis and Tech., Inc., North Stonington, Conn., 1969-81; pres. BWP Cons., 1981—; cons., instr., lectr. on mil. ops. research, navy tactics, tactical and strategic measures of effectiveness and performance exercise/operational design and analysis. NSF grantee, 1962-63. Mem. Mil. Ops. Research Soc., Am. Def. Preparedness Assn., Nat. Security Indsl. Assn., U.S. Naval Inst., Am. Mgmt. Assn. Republican. Contbr. articles on naval ops. to profl. jours.

PUGLISI, ANGELA AURORA, educational consultant, artist; b. Messina, Italy, Jan. 28, 1949; came to U.S., 1954, naturalized, 1980; d. Vittorio and Carmela (Alizzi) P. B.A. cum laude, Dunbarton Coll., 1972; M.F.A., Cath. U., 1974, M.A. in Art History, 1976, M.A. in Modern Langs and Lit., 1977, Ph.D. in Comparative Lit., 1983. Art instr. Cath. U., Washington, 1974-84, lectr. modern langs., 1984-85; cons., writer U.S. Dept. Edn., Washington, 1983-85; faculty fine arts Georgetown U. Sch. Continuing Edn., Washington; various exhbns. of works, 1972-84. Author poetry: Nature's Canvas, 1984, Homage, 1984, Sonnet I, 1985, Primavera, 1986. Founding mem. Italian Cultural Ctr., Washington; bd. dirs. Edn. Enterprises, Children's Internat. Mem. Washington's Women's Art Ctr., Nat. Assn. Female Execs., Corcoran Gallery Art Assocs. Republican. Roman Catholic. Avocation: writing; sculpting.

PUHL, DIANA LYNN, communications company executive; b. Twentynine Palms, Calif., Apr. 11, 1961; d. Harry James and Mary Elaine (Maddox) Ancelet; m. John Thomas Puhl, Sept. 15, 1984; 1 child, Christopher Jon. Student Lee Coll., 1981-83, Rollins Coll., 1983-84. Bookkeeper, Joe D. Hughes, Inc., Houston, 1979-81; programmer Exxon Chem. Co., Mont Belvieu, Tex., 1981-83, AT&T Info. Systems, Maitland, Fla., 1983—. Recipient Spl. Merit award AT&T Info Systems, 1984. Mem. Nat. Assn. Female Execs. Republican. Lutheran. Avocations: tennis; bowling; scuba diving; swimming. Home: 1943 Long Pond Dr Longwood FL 32779 Office: AT&T Info Systems 850 Trafalgar Ct Maitland FL 32751

PUIG, AMELITA UBALDE, medical technologist; b. Philippines, Apr. 20; came to U.S., 1969, naturalized, 1978; d. Francisco Busil and Angeles (Ubalde) P.; B.S. in Med. Tech., U. San Agustin, Philippines, 1966; curso de lengua y cultura Universidad de Salamanca, 1979. Asst. supr. chemistry Yale New Haven Med. Center, 1970-73; sr. technologist hematology dept. Columbia Presbyn. Hosp., N.Y.C., 1973-74; sr. technologist chemistry dept. N.Y.U. Med. Center, 1974—. Mem. Am. Soc. Clin. Pathologists (affiliate mem.), Am. Soc. Clin. Pathologists, U. San Agustin Alumni assn. (fin. com. Northeast chpt. 1985—), Pototan Circle (sec. Eastern Seaboard 1986—), Kahirup U.S.A. (dir. 1974-81, exec. sec. 1981-83). Address: 525 E 14th St Apt 12E New York NY 10009

PUKL, BARBARA JANE SIMEONE, city official; b. Uniontown, Pa., Dec. 28, 1946; d. Alfonso and Annabelle Dora (Galderise) Simeone; m. Frank Joseph Pukl, Aug. 5, 1967; (dec.). Student Pa. State U., Fayette, 1965-67, Gettysburg Coll., 1968-69, Allegheny Community Coll. South Campus, 1975, Fayette Area Vocat.-Tech. Sch., 1974, 81, H & R Block, Tax Preparation, 1982. Notary public, Pa. Sales, unit buying control, PBX Sears Roebuck Co., Uniontown, Pa., 1964-67; floral designer Flowers by Mr. Wayne, Gettysburg, Pa., 1967-68; research librarian asst. Gettysburg Coll. Library, 1968-69; sec. to asst. minister Trinity Presbyn. Ch., Uniontown, 1969-70; bank teller, lottery sales supr. Gallatin Nat. Bank, Uniontown, 1970-72; hard and software lines buyer Mini Mart Furniture, Uniontown, 1973-76; dep. treas., bookkeeper City Treas.'s Office, Uniontown, 1972—; owner, mgr. Pukl Apts., Uniontown, 1972—; tax preparer, tax acct. Sahady Tax and Acctg. Service, Republic, Pa., 1984-85. Mem. adv. council Women's Resource Center, Uniontown, 1979-81; mem. small bus. mgmt. support group Women's Opportunities for Re-tng. Ctr., 1979-81; mem. promotions com. Uniontown Main St. Project, 1984. Mem. Uniontown Council of Republican Women. Mem. Nat. Fedn. Bus. and Profl. Women's Clubs, Uniontown Bus. and Profl. Women (Young Careerist chairperson 1985-86), Am. Fedn. State, County and Municipal Employees (v.p. 1986), Beta Sigma Phi (pres. Delta Chi chpt. 1983-84), Beta Sigma Phi-Uniontown Council Sororities (pres. 1984-85). Episcopalian. Club: Uniontown

Art. Home: 1 W Berkeley St Uniontown PA 15401 Office: 20 N Gallatin Ave Uniontown PA 15401

PULITANO, CONCETTA NORIGENNA, word processor; b. Sicily, Italy, June 16, 1941; came to U.S., 1947, naturalized, 1948; d. Umberto and Benedetta (Triassi) Norigenna; student public schs., North Miami, Fla.; m. Francis Joseph Pulitano, Dec. 29, 1962; children—Maria Anne, Margaret Theresa, Angela Marie. Sec., Ka-Line Pool Products, Hialeah, Fla., 1959-61, Westinghouse, Balt., 1961, Bendix Communications, Balt., 1961-63; student council moderator, sec., learning center coordinator Cathedral Sch., Balt., 1974-83; sec., word processor operator Md. Agy., Balt., 1983-85; exec. sec. Comp-u-Staff, Inc., Towson, Md., 1985—. Democrat. Roman Catholic. Club: Valley Country. Office: Comp-u-Staff Inc Towson MD 21204

PULITZER, EMILY S. RAUH, former museum curator; b. Cin., July 23, 1933; d. Frederick and Harriet (Frank) Rauh; A.B., Bryn Mawr Coll., 1955; student Ecole du Louvre, Paris, France, 1955-56; M.A., Harvard U., 1963. Mem. staff Cin. Art Mus., 1956-57; asst. curator drawings Fogg Art Mus., Harvard, 1957-64, asst. to dir., 1962-63; curator City Art Mus., St. Louis, 1964-73; mem. painting and sculpture com. Mus. Modern Art, 1975—; chmn. visual arts com. Mo. Arts Council, 1976-81; co-chmn. fellows Fogg Art Mus.; mem. bd. Inst. Mus. Services, 1979-83; commr. St. Louis Art Mus., 1981—; bd. dirs. 1st St. Forum, St. Louis, 1980—, Mark Rothko Found., 1976—. Mem. Am. Fedn. Arts (dir. 1976—), Art Mus. Assn. Am. (bd. dirs. 1986—). Home: 4903 Pershing Pl Saint Louis MO 63108

PULLEN, PENNY LYNNE, state legislator; b. Buffalo, Mar. 2, 1947; d. John William and Alice Nettie (McConkey) P.; B.A. in Speech, U. Ill., 1969. TV technician Office Instructional Resources, U. Ill., 1966-68; community newspaper reporter Des Plaines (Ill.) Pub. Co., 1967-72; legislative asst. to Ill. legislators, 1968-77; mem. Ill. Ho. of Reps., 1977—, chmn. ho. exec. com., 1981-82, minority whip, 1983—; mem. Republican Nat. Com., 1984—. Del., Atlantic Alliance Young Polit. Leaders, Brussels, 1977; active Maine Twp. Mental Health Assn.; mem. Nat. Council Ednl. Research, 1983—. Recipient George Washington Honor medal Freedoms Found., 1978, Dwight Eisenhower Freedom medal Chgo. Captive Nations Com., 1977, Outstanding Legislator awards Ill. Press Assn., Ill. Podiatry Soc., Ill. Coroners Assn., Ill. County Clks. Assn., Ill. Hosp. Assn., Ill. Health Care Assn.; named Ill. Young Republican, 1968, Outstanding Young Person, Park Ridge Jaycees, 1981, One of 10 Outstanding Young Persons, Ill. Jaycees, 1981. Mem. Am. Legis. Exchange Council (dir. 1977—, exec. com. 1978-83, 2d vice chmn. 1980-83), DAR. Home: 2604 W Sibley St Park Ridge IL 60068 Office: 22 Main St Park Ridge IL 60068

PULLEY, KATHERINE GALVIN, nurse; b. Monteray, Calif., Sept. 28, 1959; d. Bernard James and Elizabeth Ann (Hayes) Galvin; m. George Robert Pulley, Jr., Aug. 18, 1984. A.S., Patrick Henry Community Coll., 1980; diploma in nursing Roanoke Meml. Hosp., 1983. R.N., Va. Nurse's aide Martinsville-Henry County Hosp., Martinsville, Va., 1978-80; nursing asst. Roanoke Meml. Hosp., Va., 1980-83, R.N., 1983—. Vol. ARC, 1983. Recipient VA Gen. Assembly scholarship, 1980-81, 81-82; Roanoke Meml. Hosp. scholarship, 1980-81; Am. Legion scholarship, 1980-83; Roanoke Acad. Medicine Aux. scholarship, 1981-82, 82-83. Mem. Roanoke Meml. Hosp. Alumni. Roman Catholic. Avocations: traveling; sailing; cross stitching. Office: Roanoke Meml Hosp Bellview at Jefferson Sts Roanoke VA 24033

PULLIAM, JANET LYNN, lawyer; b. Little Rock, June 7, 1946; d. James M. and Lottie M. (Schonert) P. B.A., U. Ark., 1969, postgrad. Law Sch., 1976-78; J.D., U. Ark.-Little Rock, 1979. Bar: Ark. 1976, U.S. Ct. Appeals (8th cir.) 1979, U.S. Dist. Ct. (we. dist.) Tenn 1981, U.S. Supreme Ct. 1982. Adminstrv. asst. City of Little Rock, 1969-70, tng. dir., 1970-73, dir. mgmt. and program analysis, 1973-74; cons. City of Leavenworth (Kans.), 1974-76, City of Wilmington (N.C.), 1975, Pritchett, Ala., 1975-76; cons. nat. tng. and devel. service, Washington, 1974-75; cons. Sch. Medicine, U. Ark.-Little Rock, 1976; counsel, ACLU, Little Rock, 1979-81; cooperating atty. NAACP Legal Def. Fund, N.Y.C., 1979-84; sole practice law, Little Rock. Author: Job Analysis in the Public Sector, 1976 (NSF award). Drafter legislation Women's Polit. Caucus, Little Rock, 1981; chmn. Ark. Women's Polit. Caucus, 1984-85; bd. dirs. Ark. Women's Rights, 1982-84. Recipient Stern award U. Chgo., 1979. Mem. ABA (com. mem. labor and employment sect. 1982-83), Ark. Bar Assn. (com. mem. sect. for deaf 1980-83), Pulaski County Bar, Am. Soc. Pub. Adminstrs. Home: 1001 N McKinley Little Rock AR 72207 Office: Pulliam Law Offices Suite 350 Gazette Bldg 112 W 3d St Little Rock AR 72201

PULLUM, LAURA LANNETTE, industrial engineer; b. Oak Ridge, Oct. 21, 1960; d. Lanis Verble and Deloris Lillian (Tate) Pullum. A.S., Walters State Community Coll., Tenn., 1980; B.S. in Math., U. Ala., 1982, M.S. in Ops. Research, 1986. Systems analyst SRS Techs., Huntsville, Ala., 1982-84, sr. engr., 1984—. Author: Como III Earth Curvature Analysis, 1983; Test Methods and Procedures, 1984; Missile Optimization Program Users' Guide, 1985; Parametric Kickstage Analysis, 1985. Mem. Inst. Indsl. Engrs. Methodist. Avocations: poetry; dancing; basketball; softball. Home: 4952 Seven Pine Circle Huntsville AL 35816 Office: SRS Technologies 555 Sparkman Dr Suite 1406 Huntsville AL 35816

PUMMILL, CAROL SUE, business official, author; b. Springfield, Ohio, Feb. 25, 1950; d. Earl Virgil and Jacqueline Ann (Thurman) P. B.S. in Bus., Wright State U., 1975, M.B.A., 1978. Mgr. Kroger Co., Troy, Ohio, 1976-77; mktg. analyst NCR Corp., Dayton, Ohio, 1978-81, cons. relations specialist, 1981, product mgr., 1981-85, program mgr., 1985—; career bd. rep. Mademoiselle mag., N.Y.C., 1980—. Author essays, poems, newspaper articles. Active Young Democrats, Springfield, Ohio, 1984; canvasser Democratic Party, 1976. Recipient Grad. assistantship Wright State U., 1977. Mem. Recognition Techs. Users Assn., Am. Mktg. Assn., Nat. Assn. Female Execs. Roman Catholic. Office: NCR Corp 1700 S Patterson Blvd Dayton OH 45479

PUMPHREY, JANET KAY, editor; b. Balt., June 18, 1946; d. John Henry and Elsie May (Keefer) P. A.A. in Secondary Edn., Anne Arundel Community Coll., Md., 1967, A.A. in Bus. and Pub. Adminstrn., 1976. Office mgr. Anne Arundel Community Coll., Arnold, Md., 1964—; mng. editor Am. Polygraph Assn., Severna Park, Md., 1973—, archives researcher, 1973—. Editor: (with Albert D. Snyder) Ten Years of Polygraph, 1984; (with Norman Ansley) Justice and the Polygraph, 1985. Mem. Am. Polygraph Assn. (affiliate), Md. Polygraph Assn. (affiliate), Nat. Assn. Female Execs., Anne Arundel County Hist. Soc., Alumni Assn. Anne Arundel Community Coll. Republican. Methodist. Avocations: travel, poetry, gardening. Home: 3 Kimberly Ct Severna Park MD 21146 Office: Am Polygraph Assn PO Box 1061 Severna Park MD 21146

PUNCH, BARBARA JEAN, educator; b. Wharton, Tex., Apr. 3, 1945; d. Gus and Polie (Quinan) Thompson; m. Larry Ted Punch, Dec. 22, 1959 (div. 1979); children—Danny Tyrone, Rita LaNell. Cert. Adminstrn., U. Houston; B.S. in Bus., Tex. So. U., 1960; M.A., 1962. Student tchr. Wheatley High Sch., Houston, 1958-59; instr. Internat. Bus. Coll., Houston, 1960-62; postal clk. U.S. Post Office, Houston, 1958-62; tchr. Isaacs Elementary Sch., Houston, 1960-68, summer 1968; tchr. 3d grade Anson Jones Elementary Sch., Houston, 1968-70, tchr. 1st and 2d grade, 1971-72; reading specialist Houston Ind. Sch. Dist., 1972-73, curriculum coordinator, 1974-75; asst. prin. Alcott Elementary Sch., Houston, 1975-83, S. Mayd Elementary Sch., Houston, 1983-84; curriculum writer Houston Ind. Sch. Dist., 1973-74; supr. Essa Parent Learning Ctr., Pugh Elementary Sch., Houston, 1974; assoc. Robert Ellis Real Estate, Houston, 1981-84; founder, chmn. bd. Concepts Glass and Mirror Corp., Houston, 1984—. Sec., MacGregor Pl. Civic Club, Houston, 1979; campaign leader Com. to Elect Judge Jim Muldrow, Houston, 1981; campaign mem. Com. to Elect Jimmy Carter for Pres., Com. to Elect Mayor Kathryn Whitmire, Houston, 1981, 83. Recipient Profl. Growth award Houston Ind. Sch. Dist., 1965; Disting. Service award Houston Tchrs. Assn., 1963-67; Desegration Sensitivity award U. Tex., Austin, 1969; curriculum writer award Houston Ind. Sch. Dist., 1972-73. Mem. Houston Profl. Adminstrs. (hopitality com. 1980-82), Tex. Elem. Prin. Assn., Houston Bd. Realtors, Zeta Phi Beta, Eta Phi Beta. Democrat. Baptist. Club: Jet Setters Duplicate Bridge (sec. 1973-84). Address: 5131 Stuyvesant Ln Houston TX 77021

PUNCSAK-DUNN, SANDRA, metal and chem. co. exec.; b. Melbourne, Australia, May 28, 1946; came to U.S., 1946, naturalized, 1960; d. Frank and Thelma May Elizabeth (Maher) Puncsak; A.B., U. Calif., Berkeley, 1968; M.A., San Francisco State U., 1970; M.A. in Counseling and Guidance, Lewis and Clark Coll., 1974; postgrad. Pepperdine U., 1970-73. Edn. therapist schs. in Fullerton, Calif. and Beaverton, Oreg., 1973-76; student coordinator Community Experiences for Career Edn., Tigard (Oreg.) Sch. Dist. 233, 1976-78; dep. center dir. Portland (Oreg.) Job Corps Center, 1978; mktg. mgr. Singer Edn. Div., Santa Clara, Calif., 1978-81; mgr. corp. contbns. and social investment Kaiser Aluminum and Chem. Corp., Oakland, Calif., 1981—; cons. in field; lectr. in field. Mem. Peninsula Republican Women's Task Force, 1980-83, mgr. pub. affairs, 1983—. Recipient Tribute to Women in Internat. Mgmt., YWCA, 1983. Phi Beta Kappa Grad. Sch. fellow, 1969-70. Mem. Am. Mgmt. Assn., Bay Area Exec. Women's Forum West, Bay Area Profl. Women's Network, East Bay Women's Polit. Action Com., Phi Beta Kappa. Republican. Roman Catholic. Club: Commonwealth. Profiled in Professional Women and their Mentors, 1982. Home: 12 Hillcrest Ct Oakland CA 94619 Office: 300 Lakeside Dr Oakland CA 94643

PUNDT, COLLEEN LAVONNE, real estate executive; b. Denver, Nov. 21, 1930; d. Ralph LaVerne Massey and Beaulah Merle (Bradley) Herlocker; m. Raymond Edward Stumberg, Oct. 15, 1948 (div. 1961); m. Harry Louis Pundt, Apr. 20, 1964; children—Michelle Lavonne Cole, Roxanne Rae Mayer. Cert., Real Estate Prep. Sch., Denver, 1977. Cert. real estate broker, Colo. Fashion model VA-JA Agy., Denver, 1947-50; property mgr., bookkeeper Kawa & Assocs., Denver, 1969-74, mgr. investment property, 1970-74; bookkeeper Cornell Pharm. Co., Denver, 1974-77; assoc. broker Century 21-Caranna & Fairbanks, Denver, 1977-83; owner, broker Silver Spruce Realty Co., Denver, 1981—. Vol., USO, 1945-47, Republican party, 1970; coordinator Easter Seal Telethon, 1979. Mem. Denver Bd. Realtors, Nat. Assn. Realtors, Colo. Assn. Realtors, Denver C. of C., Denver Real Estate Exchangers. Republican. Episcopalian. Home: 615 S Eliot St Denver CO 80219 Office: Silver Spruce Realty 495 S Federal Blvd #3 Denver CO 80219

PURCELL, ANN MARIE C., medical industrial company product manager; b. Harvey, Ill., Feb. 20, 1957; d. Carlo Leo and Lucille Lillian (Colletti) Allegro; m. Fredrick William Purcell, June 29, 1980; 1 child, Carly Allegro. B.S., Loyola U. Chgo., 1979; postgrad. Keller Grad. Sch. Mgmt., 1981—. Lab. instr. Loyola U. Chgo., 1977-79; research technician Travenol Labs., Inc., Morton Grove, Ill., 1979-80, research asst., 1980, research assoc., 1980-81; product specialist Fenwal Labs. div. Travenol Labs., Inc., Deerfield, Ill., 1981-85, product mgr., 1985—. Mem. Women's Aux. to Dental Soc. Loyola U. Dental Sch., Nat. Assn. Female Execs., Phi Kappa Omega Alumnae (a founder), Tri Beta. Roman Catholic. Home: 3252 Sanders #9A Northbrook IL 60062

PURCELL, JOYCE M., scientific organization administrator; b. Las Vegas, N. Mex., Apr. 20, 1949; d. John Donald and Helen Marie (Griffin) P.; B.A., U. N.Mex., 1975, M.A., 1977; 1 son, W. Daniel Schneider. Staff asst. Coll. Pharmacy, U. N.Mex., 1970-71; authorizations analyst VA, 1971-73; claims analyst Social Security Adminstrn., 1974-75; staff asst. VA Hosp., Albuquerque, 1977-78; cons. Los Alamos Pub. Schs., 1977-78; natural resources and space and sci. analyst Senate Budget Com., Washington, 1977-83; sr. staff officer Space Sci. Bd., Nat. Acad. Scis., 1983—. Mem. Am. Communication Assn., Am. Soc. Tng. and Devel., Am. Geophys. Union, Women in Aerospace. Office: 2100 Pennsylvania Ave NW Room 828 Washington DC 20418

PURCELL, MARY HAMILTON, educator; b. Ft. Worth; d. Joseph Hants and Letha (Gibson) Hamilton; B.A., Mary Hardin-Baylor Coll., 1947; M.A., La. State U., 1948; m. William Paxson Purcell, Jr., Dec. 28, 1950; children—William Paxson III, David Hamilton. Instr., dept. speech and dramatic arts Temple U., Phila., 1948-53, 60-61; part-time instr. speech Cushing Jr. Coll., Bryn Mawr, Pa., 1966-78. Pres., Pa. Program for Women and Girl Offenders, 1968-73; pres. Nether Providence Parent Tchr. Orgn., 1975-76; treas. Virginia Gildersleeve Internat. Fund Univ. Women, 1975-81; bd. dirs. Citizens Crime Commn. of Phila., 1976—; mem. Wallingford-Swarthmore Dist. Sch. Bd., 1977-83; bd. dirs. Nat. Peace Inst. Found., 1983-86, Big Bros./Big Sisters of Am., 1985-87, Pa. Women's Campaign Fund, 1985-88; bd. dirs. Ministers and Missionaries Fund, Am. Bapt. Conv., 1986-88. Named Outstanding Alumna Mary Hardin-Baylor Coll., 1972, Disting. Dau. Pa., 1982; recipient Zeta Phi Eta award excellence in communications, 1983. Mem. AAUW (Pa. div. pres. 1968-70, v.p. middle Atlantic region 1973-77 program v.p. 1979-81 pres. 1981-85), Internat. Fedn. Univ. Women (2d v.p. 1983—), Speech Assn. Am., Pi Kappa Delta, Pi Gamma Mu, Delta Sigma Rho, Alpha Psi Omega, Alpha Chi. Democrat. Baptist. Home: 9 Oak Knoll Dr Wallingford PA 19086

PURCELL, MARY LOUISE GERLINGER, educator; b. Thief River Falls, Minn., July 17, 1923; d. Charles and Lajla (Dale) Gerlinger; student Yankton Coll., 1941-45, Yale Div. Sch., 1949-50, N.Y. U., summer 1949; M.A. (alumni fellow), Tchrs. Coll. Columbia, 1959, Ed.D., 1963; m. Walter A. Kuyawski, June 9, 1950 (dec. July 1954); children—Amelia Allerton, Jon Allerton; m. Dale Purcell, Aug. 26, 1962. Teen-age program dir., YWCA, New Haven, 1945-52; dir. program in family relations, asst. prof. sociology and psychology Earlham Coll., Richmond, Ind., 1959-62, conf. co-ordinator undergrad. edn. for women, 1962; chmn. div. home and community Stephens Coll., Columbia, Mo., 1962-73, chmn. family and community studies, 1962-78, dir. Learning Unltd., continuing edn. for women, 1974-78, developer course The Contemporary Am. Woman, 1962, cons., 1962; prof. family and child devel. Auburn (Ala.) U., 1978—, head dept., 1978-84, spl. Asst. to v.p. acad. affairs, 1985—; vis. prof. Ind. U. Summer Sch., 1970. Cons. student personnel services, Trenton (N.J.) State Coll., 1958-59, 61. Recipient Alumni Achievement award Yankton Coll., 1975. Mem. Am. Home Econs. Assn. (chmn. family relations child devel. sect. 1967-69, 86-88, bd. dirs.), Nat. Council Family Relations (dir., chmn. elect affiliated councils, 1981-82, chmn., 1982-83, nat. program chmn. 1977, chmn. film awards com., chmn. spl. emphases sect., bd. dirs., Ernest G. Osborne award for excellence in teaching 1979), Kappa Delta Pi, Pi Lambda Theta. Presbyterian. Contbr. articles to coll. bulls, jours.

PURCELL, PATRICIA HAWKINS, pediatrician; b. Henderson, N.C., July 4, 1944; d. Frederick Douglas and Mabel Lee (Young) Hawkins; m. Garnell Roscoe Purcell, Jr., Aug. 29, 1970; 1 child, Patrell Young. B.S. in Chemistry, N.C. Central U., 1966; M.D., Hahnemann U., Phila., 1974. Diplomate Am. Bd. Pediatrics. Chemist, E.I. DuPont de Nemours, Wilmington, Del., 1966-70; pediatric resident The Med. Ctr. of Del., 1974-77; pvt. practice pediatrician, Wilmington, 1978—. Med. radio host Sta. WILM, Doctor's House Call, Wilmington, 1984—. Mem. found. bd. N.C. Central U., Durham, 1983—; bd. dirs. YMCA, Wilmington, 1983—, United Way, Wilmington, 1984—, Del. Adolescent Program, Inc., Wilmington, 1982—. Recipient Dedicated Service award Friends of Wilmington, 1982, Recognition-World of Well Being award Girl Scouts U.S., 1983, Outstanding Achiever award Brandywine Profl. Assn., 1985; named Citizen of Yr. Omega Psi Phi, 1984. Fellow Am. Acad. Pediatrics; mem. New Castle County Med. Soc., AMA, Del. State Med. Soc., Nat. Med. Soc., AAUW (Woman of Yr. 1982), Delta Sigma Theta (pres. 1968-70). Democrat. Episcopalian. Club: Jack and Jill. Avocation: antique collecting. Home: 1721 Gunning Dr Forest Hills Park Wilmington DE 19803 Office: Patricia H Purcell MD PA 1508 Pennsylvania Ave Suite 2-C Wilmington DE 19806

PURCELL, PATRICIA PARNIE, orchesta administrator, fundraiser; b. Detroit, Oct. 16, 1944; d. Alexander David and Elaine (Helmer) Parnie; children—Elizabeth, Hugh. B.A., Wells Coll., 1966; M.Ed., Boston U., 1967. Dir. devel. Wells Coll., Aurora, N.Y., 1974-77, v.p. devel., 1976-77; v.p. devel., pub. relations Goucher Coll., Towson, Md., 1977-81; pres. U. Md. Found., Adelphi, 1981-83; exec. dir. Office Instl. Advancement, U. Md. at Balt., 1983-85, dir. devel. Balt. Symphony Orch., 1986—; Md. del. Am. Council Edn. Nat. Identification Program; cons. Council Advancement and Support Edn., Washington, 1983—; mem. Greater Balt. com. the Leadership. Contbr. chpt. to book University Related Foundations, 1984; contbr. articles, book revs. to profl. jours. Mem. Balt. County-wide Sch. Closing Com., Towson, 1979-81. Mem. Council Advancement and Support of Edn. (program chair nat. assembly). Democrat. Presbyterian. Home: 7115 York Rd Baltimore MD 21212 Office: Balt Symphony Orch 1212 Cathedral St Baltimore MD 21201

PURDIN-HORNER, RUTH MARGENE, banker; b. Russellville, Ohio, July 27, 1925; d. George H. and Grace (Baird) Miller; m. Collins Horner, May 19, 1984; children by previous marriage—Nick Purdine, Suzanne Purdin Watson. Student U. Cin., 1970-75. Pres., The Bank of Russellville, Ohio, 1943—. Mem. Russellville Council, 1955-65. Mem. Brown County Bankers Assn. (v.p. 1970-75). Republican. Methodist. Club: Russellville Women's (1st pres. 1950-55). Home: 11 Mohican Cove E Sardinia OH 45171 Office: The Bank of Russellville Columbus and Main Russellville OH 45168

PURDY, CLAIRE JESSICA, insurance company underwriter; b. Denver, Dec. 7, 1933; d. Jesse Edward and Lenna Louise (Ewing) Purdy. Student U. No. Colo. Sec., St. Luke's Hosp., Denver, 1956-63, State Farm Ins. Co., Denver, 1963-69, underwriter, Greeley, Colo., 1969-83, sr. underwriter, 1983—; lectr. Western Ins. Info. Service, 1972-83; ednl. cons. State Farm Ins. Cos., 1983-84, chmn. auto fraud com., 1983-84. Mem. fin. com. Weld County Democrats, Greeley, Colo., 1983-84; chmn. art show reception Greeley Creative Arts Ctr., 1983-84; instr. defensive driving course Nat. Safety Council Chgo., 1973-83. Mem. Ins. Women Greeley (pres. 1979-80), Greeley Audubon Soc. (sec.-treas.). Democrat. Methodist. Home: 2210 28th Ave Greeley CO 80631 Office: State Farm Ins Cos 3001 8th Ave Greeley CO 80631

PURDY, HELEN CARMICHAEL, librarian; b. Miami, Jan. 17, 1920; d. James B. and Alice Cornelia (Brown) C.; m. Joseph Lynn Purdy, Feb. 12, 1946 (div. Aug. 1971). A.B., U. Miami-Coral Gables, 1943; M.S., Fla. State U.-Tallahassee, 1957. Asst. dept. head U.S. Censorship, Miami, 1944-45; library asst. catalog dept. U. Miami, Coral Gales, 1946-56, cataloger, 1957-60, Fla. cataloger, 1961-77/78, head archive and spl. collections dept., 1978, 79—, senator Faculty Senate, 1967-71, mem. council, 1969-71; mem. Women's Adv. Com. on Acad. Affairs, Coral Gables, 1972-81. Mem. Citizens Crime Watch, Miami, 1980—; mem. Republican Nat. Com., Washington, 1981—; mem. Republican Party of Fla., Tallahassee, 1983—. Mem. ALA, Southeastern Library Assn., Fla. Library Assn. (div. vice chmn. 1958-59, chmn. 1959-60), Beta Phi Mu. Episcopalian. Home: 5824 SW 50th St Miami FL 33155 Office: Univ Miami Library Coral Gables FL 33124

PURICELLI, MARJORIE GIBSON, government official; b. Opelika, Ala., Jan. 11, 1923; d. Frederick Meyer and Lottie Belle (Hearn) Gibson; student U. Ala., 1965, 66, Macon Jr. Coll., 1968-71; m. Russell Antonio Puricelli, May 17, 1984; children by previous marriage—William Guy Walter, Ralph Gibson Walter. Contract negotiator trainee Robins AFB, Ga., 1966-68, contract negotiator, 1968-71; fin. analyst HUD, Birmingham and Washington, 1971-75; contract price analyst U.S. Army, Washington, 1976-77; contract price analyst U.S. Marine Corps, Albany, Ga., 1977-80, head contracts support br., contracts div. Marine Corps Logistics Base, Albany, Ga., 1980-84, br. head value analysis engring. data mgmt. br., office competition advocate, 1984—; ptnr. Amare Stained Glass Co. Vice pres. Woman's Caucus, HUD, 1975. Recipient Sustained Superior Performance award U.S. Marine Corps, 1978. Mem. Nat. Contract Mgmt. Assn., Fed. Mgrs. Assn. Home: 466 Church St NE Dawson GA 31742

PURKEY, RUTH ELANE, insurance agency executive; b. Upper Sandusky, Ohio, Apr. 4, 1936; d. Charles William Henry and Avah Alice (Wilson) Butcher; m. Wallace D. Purkey, Jr., Apr. 17, 1955; children—Robin Sue Purkey VanGorder, Justin Neal. Grad. high sch., Millbury, Ohio. Ins. agt. Purkey Ins. Agy., Northwood, Ohio, 1967—, v.p., sec., treas., 1976—; speaker on youth substance abuse to various groups and orgns. Mem., v.p. PTA Genoa Schs., Ohio, 1968-70; club adviser 4-H Clubs Am., Ottawa County, Ohio, 1968-73; bd. dirs., treas. Friends of Library of Genoa, 1972-75; chmn. Village Bikeway Com., Genoa, 1972-76; facilitator Parents Helping Parents, Inc., Toledo, 1985—, mem. exec. bd., 1986; cons. Wood County Juvenile Ct. Adv. Bd., 1985—; mem. Nat. Fedn. Parents for Drug-Free Youth, 1983—. Mem. Profl. Ins. Agts., Nat. Assn. Female Execs., Fedn. Women's Clubs (bd. dirs. Genoa 1973-76). Club: Belle Ami (Genoa) (sec. 1969-70, v.p. 1972-73). Avocations: distance swimming; cross-country skiing; American Indian pottery. Home: 1524 Red Bud Dr Northwood OH 43619 Office: Purkey Ins Agy Inc 3040 Woodville Rd Northwood OH 43619

PURNELL, CAROLYN JEAN, lawyer; b. Memphis, Aug. 16, 1939; d. James Clarence and Mardine (Taylor) P.; B.A., U. Wash., Seattle, 1961, J.D., 1971; divorced; children—Mardine, Monica. Admitted to Wash. bar, 1972; dep. pros. atty. King County, Seattle, 1972-74; legal counsel to mayor of Seattle, 1974-77; atty. Weyerhaeuser Co., Tacoma, 1977—, dir. purchasing, 1981—, legal officer Weyerhaeuser Found.; del. Am. Assembly Law, Palo Alto, Calif., 1981. Vice pres. Housing Devel. Corp., 1977—; loaned exec. Wash. Roundtable and Pacific Celebration '89, 1986—. Mem. Wash. Bar Assn., Seattle-King County Bar Assn., Delta Sigma Theta. Home: 3415 E Denny St Seattle WA 98122 Office: Weyerhaeuser Co Tacoma WA 98477

PURSCH, SUSAN MARIE, religious organization administrator; b. Mpls., Jan. 8, 1948; d. Delroy Paridan and Janice Marie (Johnson) P.; m. Russell Motter Long, Apr. 25, 1981; stepchildren—Christopher, Jonathan. A.A., Waldorf Coll., 1968; B.A., Augsburg Coll., Mpls., 1970. Keypunch and computer operator Fairview Hosp., Mpls., 1968-70; youth and Christian edn. dir. 1st Lutheran Ch., Litchfield, Minn., 1970-73; dir. Christian edn. Gloria Dei Lutheran Ch., Huntingdon Valley, Pa., 1973-74; sec. for youth Global Hunger Concers, Div. for Parish Services Luth. Ch. in Am., Phila., 1974—. Mem. Nat. Assn. Female Execs. Democrat. Lutheran. Avocations: Downhill skiing; travel. Home: 387 E Gowen Ave Philadelphia PA 19119 Office: Div Parish Services 2900 Queen Ln Philadelphia PA 19129

PURSELL, JULIE CROW, corporate communications administrator, media consultant, journalist; b. Nashville, Feb. 26, 1936; d. William Russell and Eleanor Farrell (Weber) Crow; m. William Whitney Pursell, Apr. 26, 1965; children—Ellen Pursell Spicer, Margaret, Laura, Bill, 1 stepchild, Sharon. Student Vanderbilt U., 1953-55, Peabody Coll., 1958-60, U. Tenn., 1961-62. Reporter, feature writer, The Tennessean, Nashville, 1958-65; freelance writer, Nashville, 1965-73; art-home editor Nashville Banner, 1973-80; asst. to mayor City of Nashville, 1980-84; asst. to chmn. Earl Swensson Assocs., Nashville, 1984—. Editor: Symphony Guild newsletter, 1966-68; contbg. editor Tenn. Architect, 1985—. Dir. publicity Vietnam Veterans Day Salute, Nashville, 1981; mem. adv. bd. Nashville Pub. TV, 1981—; dir. publicity Metro Courthouse Day, Nashville, 1982; mem. adv. bd. Belmont Coll. Dept. Communications Arts, Nashville, 1983—; co-dir. grand opening Riverfront Park, Nashville, 1983. Mem. Nashville C. of C. (mem. cultural affairs com. 1984-86), Pub. Relations Soc. Am. (bd. dirs. 1984, 86), Tenn. State Mus. Assn. Inc., AIA (affiliate mem.), Kappa Delta. Roman Catholic. Club: Savage of London (affiliate). Avocations: art; historic preservation; urban planning; travel; history. Home: 895 S Curtiswood Ln Nashville TN 37204 Office: Earl Swensson Assocs Inc 2100 W End Ave Nashville TN 37203

PURTLE, CAROL JEAN, art historian, educator; b. St. Louis, Feb. 20, 1939; d. Clarence Philipp and Rose Bertha (Kloeppel) P.; B.A. magna cum laude, Maryville Coll., St. Louis, 1960; M.A., Manhattanville Coll., Purchase, N.Y., 1966; Ph.D. (NDEA fellow), Washington U., St. Louis, 1976. Joined Religious of Sacred Heart, Roman Catholic Ch., 1963; tchr. Acad. Sacred Heart, St. Charles, Mo., 1964-66, Grand Coteau, La., 1966-68; lectr. art history Maryville Coll., St. Louis, part-time 1969-75; instr. art history Washington U., part-time 1970-76; asst. prof. art and coordinator art history Memphis State U., 1977-82, assoc. prof., 1982—; coordinator nat. symposium 600 Years Netherlandish Art, Memphis, 1982; project dir. Internat. Research Conf. on Tradition and Innovation in Study No. European Art, U. Pitts., 1985. Bd. dirs. Acad. Sacred Heart, New Orleans, 1971-73; trustee Acad. Sacred Heart, Grand Coteau, La., 1982-85. Recipient M. Spalding Young award Maryville Coll., 1960, Ann. Scholarship award 1960; Advanced Research fellow Belgian-Am. Endl. Found., 1974-75; Faculty Devel. award Memphis State U., 1980, 85-86; NDEA fellow, 1968-71; Nat. Endowment for Humanities fellow, 1982; Danforth Assoc., 1979—; faculty research grantee Memphis State U., 1983; Coolidge research fellow, 1985. Mem. Coll. Art Assn. Am., Southeastern Coll. Art Conf., Mid-West Art History Soc., Historians of Netherlandish Art (pres. 1983-85), Assocs. for Religion and Intellectual Life, Delta Epsilon Sigma. Author: The Marian Paintings of Jan van Eyck, 1982, also articles. Home: 767 Mount Moriah Apt 32 Memphis TN 38117 Office: Dept Art Jones Hall Memphis State U Memphis TN 38152

PURUCKER, MARY IRENE, educator; b. Lynn, Mass., Feb. 12, 1934; d. Frederick George and Mary Agnes (Sweeney) Mahoney; m. Frederick J. Purucker Jr., June 23, 1955, children—Katherine Ann, John David. A.A., Boston Coll., 1955; A.B. in English, UCLA, 1963, M.L.S., 1964. Librarian, Los Angeles Pub. Library, 1964-65; librarian, media specialist Santa Monica/Malibu United Sch. Dist., Malibu, Calif., 1965-83, tchr. English, John Adams Jr. High Sch., Santa Monica, 1983-85; librarian Lincoln Jr. High Sch., Santa Monica, 1985—; lectr. UCLA Grad. Sch. Library Info Sci., Los Angeles, 1981—; lectr. Loyola-Marymount, Los Angeles, 1984—. Mem. Mariposa County Fish Camp Town Planning Adv. Council (Calif.), 1978-83. Michael J. Harding scholar Boston Coll., 1952. Mem. ALA, Nat. Council Tchrs. English, Calif. Library Assn., Calif. Media Library Educators Assn., Children's Lit.

Assn. Roman Catholic. Office: Lincoln Jr High Sch Library 1501 California Ave Santa Monica CA 90403

PURVIS, HELEN LOUISE, city clerk and treasurer; b. West Lafayette, Ind., May 16, 1925; d. Herbert Ray and Clara Belle (Venus) Jones; m. Charles Grant Purvis, Aug. 11, 1946 (dec. 1970); children—Patti Jane Schiebel, James Kevin, Kathleen Ann Scherer. Billing clk. Telephone Co., Lafayette, 1942-43; sec. naval tng. dept. Purdue U., West Lafayette, 1943-46; owner Purvis Drug Store, New Haven, Ind., 1947-69; dep. clk., treas. City New Haven, 1975-77, city clk., treas., 1977—; dist. dir. Ind. Mcpl. Clk./Treas., 1984—. Organized New Haven Devel. Corp., 1983; mem. New Haven Republican Central Com., 1975—; vol. Allen-Wells chpt. ARC, Fort Wayne, Ind., 1970—. Mem. Am. Bus. Women's Assn. (Woman of Yr. 1985), New Haven C. of C. (bd. dirs.). Lutheran. Club: New Haven Women's (charter mem. 1955—, membership chmn. 1960-61). Avocations: sports; bridge. Home: 1115 Elm St New Haven IN 46774 Office: City New Haven PO Box 570 New Haven IN 46774

PURVIS, JEAN BURCHINAL, architectural/engineering company executive; b. Washington, Pa., Jan. 28; d. Warren Sturgis and Florence Eleanore (Iseman) Burchinal; m. Joseph Dixon Purvis, Jr., June 24, 1944; children—Joseph Dixon III, William W., Robert D., Sarah J. Purvis Recio, Thomas W. B.A., Chatham Coll., 1942; M.Ed., Slippery Rock U., 1977. Asst. merchandising mgr. E.R. Squibb & Sons, N.Y.C., 1943-45; pub. relations assoc. Alan Imhoff Advt., Butler, Pa., 1965-68; mktg. rep. Burt Hill Kosar Rittelmann Assocs., Butler, 1976-78, dir. communications, 1978—. Author: (with Stephen M. Pozar) A Pictorial History of Butler, 1980. Bd. dirs. Butler Area Sch. Dist., 1965-77; vice chmn. State Adv. Council for Vocat. Edn., 1973-75, mem., 1974, chmn., 1975-77; chmn. pub. relations, mem. program com. Exec. Women's Council, Pitts., 1983—; fin. com. St. Peter's Episcopal Ch. Recipient Disting. Service award Butler JayCees, 1975; Woman of Yr. award Jr. Woman's Club of Butler, 1973. Mem. Soc. for Mktg. Profl. Services, Women in Communications, Butler Area C. of C. (bd. dirs. 1977-80), Greater Pitts. C. of C., Internat. Mgmt. Council. Clubs: Rivers (Pitts.); Butler Country. Avocation: golf. Home: 1211 West Dr Butler PA 16001 Office: Burt Hill Kosar Rittelmann Assocs 400 Morgan Ctr Butler PA 16001

PUSEY, ELLEN PRATT, home economist; b. Milford, Del., Aug. 27, 1928; d. Algeo Newell and Ruby Newton (Boorman) Pratt; B.S., U. Md., 1950, M.S., 1951; m. William W. Pusey, June 12, 1950; children—William W., Patricia A., Cynthia L., Daniel N. Camp dietitian N.Y. Herald Tribune Fresh Air Fund Camps, 1947; supr. cafeteria Roosevelt Hosp., N.Y.C., 1948; supt. sch. cafeterias, Seaford, Del., 1964; field faculty home economist Md. Coop. Ext. Service, Wicomico County, Md., 1967—. Chmn. lower shore council Am. Lung Assn., Md., 1978-79. Mem. Am. Home Econs. Assn., Md. Home Econs. Assn., Nat. Assn. Extension Home Economists, Md. Assn. Extension Home Economists, Tri-County Home Econs. Assn., U. Md. Coll. Home Econs. Alumni Assn. (dir.), Nutrition Jour. Club of Eastern Shore, Phi Kappa Phi, Alpha Xi Delta. Methodist. Club. Soroptimists (pres. 1978) (Salisbury, Md.). Home: 301 W Federal St Snow Hill MD 21863 Office: PO Box 1836 Salisbury MD 21801

PUSEY, MARY HOPE SMITH, farmer; b. Munday, Tex., Sept. 28, 1914; d. John Robert and Maggie Vernon (Benedict) Smith; B.S., U. San Antonio, 1935; M.S., Columbia U. Tchrs. Coll., 1939; m. William Webb Pusey, III, June 18, 1940; children—Mary Faith Pusey Pankin, Diana Enid Pusey Pickral. Engaged in farming, West Tex., 1931—; vol. worker, 1940—; pres. Rockbridge Mental Health Assn., 1966-68, 70-72; bd. dirs. Va. Assn. Mental Health, 1970-76, regional v.p., 1974-76; chmn. adv. bd. Rockbridge Mental Health Clinic, 1970-74; co-chmn. Va. Commn. Study Mental Health and Mental Retardation, 1962-64; hon. mem. Rockbridge Assn. Retarded Citizens, 1970—; mem. bd. Valley Workshop, 1970-78. Recipient Disting. Service award Va. Assn. Mental Health, 1970, Outstanding Service award, 1973, cert. commendation, 1974; numerous certs. recognition. Mem. Grain Sorghum Producers Assn., Am. Agr. Movement. Presbyterian. Clubs: Garden of Va. (conservation chmn. 1954-56, admissions chmn. 1956-58); Blue Ridge Garden (Lexington). Address: 618 Marshall St Lexington VA 24450

PUTCAMP, LUISE, JR., editor, writer; b. San Diego, Mar. 9, 1924; d. William J. and Luise (Zimmermann) P.; student Phoenix Jr. Coll., 1942-43, So. Meth. U., 1946-47, U. Utah, 1955-56; m. Robert H. Johnson, Feb. 24, 1945; children—Robert II., III, Luise Robin, Jan Leah, Stephanie Neale, Jennifer Anne. Reporter, feature writer Anniston (Ala.) Times, 1939-40; Ariz. Republic, Phoenix, 1941-43; asst. news editor Ariz. Network, Phoenix, 1943-44; night news editor Radio Sta WINX, Washington, 1945; telegraph editor Miami Beach Sun-Tropics, 1944, 46; copy editor Dallas News, 1946-51; book page editor Dallas Times Herald, 1951-52; freelance writer, 1953-59; columnist, feature writer Indpls. News, 1961-62; vol. publicist, 1963-66; book page editor Dallas Times Herald, 1968-69; freelance writer, 1973-75; editor, writer The Advocate, Stamford, Conn., 1976-84; freelance writer, Albuquerque, N.Mex., 1984—. Recipient Kaleidograph Press award for Sonnets for the Survivors, 1951; Christopher award for short story in Good Housekeeping, 1955. Mem. Nat. Fedn. Press Women (1st pl. award for personal columns 1980) Tex. Inst. Letters, N.Mex. Press Women, S.W. Writers Workshop. Author: Sonnets for the Survivors, 1952; The Christmas Carol Miracle, 1971; The Night of the Child, 1972. Home and Office: PO Box 877 Placitas NM 87043

PUTNAM, BARBARA DEYO, nurse; b. Brattleboro, Vt., Oct. 28, 1926; d. Harold E. and Grace B. (Thomas) Deyo; m. Richard B. Putnam, Jr., Dec. 11, 1949; children—Richard B., III, Alan E., Jeffrey S. Nurse Springfield Hosp. Tng. Sch. for Nurses, 1945-48. Operating rm. staff nurse Brattleboro (Vt.) Meml. Hosp., 1948-51, asst. night supr., 1961-68, coordinator discharge planning, 1980—; office nurse ob-gyn, 1968-72; pub. health nurse Brattleboro Pub. Health Nursing, 1973-78. Staff vol. ARC, nurse, 1985—; den mother Boy Scouts Am.; pres. PTA, Academy Sch., Brattleboro, 1960; co-organizer Brattleboro chpt. United Ostomy Assn., Inc. Mem. Vt. State Nurses Assn., Nat. Rifle Assn., Brattleboro Sportsmen, Am. Assn.j Ret. Persons.

PUTNAM, BONNIE BEAN, marketing executive; b. Rockville Centre, N.Y., Dec. 20, 1955; d. David Charles and Betty Lou (Simonin) Bean; m. William Shields Putnam, Oct. 29, 1978. A.B. in Can. Studies, Duke U., 1978, A.B. in Econs., 1978, M.B.A., 1983. Material and acctg. mgmt. assoc. Western Elec. Co., Winston-Salem, N.C., 1978-79, material planning specialist, Greensboro, N.C., 1979-80; rate design adminstr. GTE of S.E., Durham, N.C., 1980-83; market research analyst No. Research Triangle Park, N.C., 1983, product mgr., 1983-84, mgr. market research and bus. planning, 1984-85, mgr. contract services, San Ramon, Calif., 1985—. Author research papers. Bd. dirs. Fuqua Sch. Bd., Durham, 1985—. Exec. scholar GTE of S.E., 1981—. Mem. Am. Mktg. Assn., Women in Telecommunications, NOW. Republican. Avocations: cooking, alpine skiing, interior design. Home: 118 Milton Street San Francisco CA 94112 Office: Northern Telecom Dept 7203-2305 Camino Ramon Blvd San Ramon CA 94583

PUTNAM, CAROLINE JENKINS, civic worker; b. Glymont, Md., Nov. 16, 1892; d. Thomas Canfield and Eleanor (Compton) Jenkins; student Mt. St. Agnes Acad., 1905-07; LL.D., Newton Coll. Sacred Heart, 1967, St. Mary's Coll., 1959, Regis Coll., 1952, St. Michael's Coll., 1956; L.H.D., Am. Internat. Coll., 1950, Manhattanville Coll., 1959; L.H.D. (hon.), Duquesne U., 1969; m. Roger Lowell Putnam Oct. 9, 1919; children—Caroline Canfield, Roger Lowell, William Lowell, Anna Lowell (Mrs. Everett P. Tomlinson), Mary Compton (Mrs. Charles W. Chatfield), Michael Courtney Jenkins. Mem. Springfield (Mass.) Housing Authority, 1952-62; mem. adv. bd. Mass. Commn. Against Discrimination, Springfield, 1949—; mem. Commn. for Study of De Facto Segregation Public Schs. of Mass., 1964-65; mem. Mass. sub-com. under Nat. Commn. on Civil Rights, 1959-64; pres. Catholic Scholarships for Negroes, Inc., 1946—. Recipient Jefferson award, 1982. Mem. Kappa Gamma Phi (hon.). Democrat. Roman Catholic. Home: 101 Mulberry St Springfield MA 01105

PUTNAM, FRANCES ISENBERGER, educator, computer school administrator; b. Hilight, Wyo., July 10, 1924; d. Claude Francis and Helen Isabele (Sinclair) Isenberger; m. Harry Gordon Putnam, Feb. 14, 1942; children—Frances Teckla, Barbara Lynne Heffelfinger, Harry Putnam III, Kathleen Doris. B.E., San Diego State U., 1961, M.A., 1965. Life cert. elem. tchr., life cert. guidance and counseling, Calif. Tchr. Campbelland Converse County Schs., Wyo., 1941-54, Las Vegas Pub. Schs., 1955-59; tchr. Chula Vista City Schs., Calif., 1960-68, resource tchr. for gifted, 1968-78, head tchr. for gifted, 1978-84, cons. gifted program and computer sci., 1984—; owner, operator Computer Scholar of Chula Vista, 1984—. Author ednl. materials and computer programs. Recipient Am. Freedom Found. award, 1965. Mem. Chula Vista Assn. Gifted Children (auditor 1982—, Honored Tchr. 1982), Computer Using Educators of Calif., Computer Using Educators of San Diego County, South Bay Ret. Tchrs. Assn., MENSA, Delta Kappa Gamma. Democrat. Presbyterian. Avocations: travel; reading; computer science. Home: 764 Brightwood Ave Chula Vista CA 92010 Office: Computer Scholar of Chula Vista 659 3d Ave Suite B Chula Vista CA 92010

PUTNEY, MARY ENGLER, accountant; b. Overland, Mo., May 1, 1933; d. Bernard Joseph and Marie Theresa (Kunkler) Engler; student Fontbonne Coll., 1951-52; A.A., Sacramento City Coll., 1975; B.S. in Bus. Adminstrn., Calif. State U., 1981; C.P.A., Calif.; m. Patrick J. Putney, Oct. 25, 1952; children—Glennon (dec.), Denise, Patrick M., Michelle. Asst. to acct. Mo. Research Labs., Inc., St. Louis, 1953-55, sec. to controller, 1955-56, adminstrv. asst. to pres., 1958-60; sec. to mgr. Western region fin. Gen. Electric Co., St. Louis, 1960-62; sec. to regional v.p. agrl. loans Crocker Nat. Bank, Sacramento, 1962-67, asst. credit analyst No. region, 1967, sec. to v.p. and mgr. capital office, Sacramento, 1967-72; student tchr. Sacramento County Dept. Edn., after 1979; acctg. technician East Yolo Community Services Dist., 1983; mgmt. specialist USAF Logistics Command, 1984; staff auditor office Insp. Gen., U.S. Dept. Transp., 1984—. Mem. Sacramento Community Commn. for Women, 1978—, rec. sec., 1980-81, bd. dirs., 1980—; mem. planning bd. Golden Empire Health Systems Agy. Mem. Nat. Assn. Accts. (dir., newsletter editor), Fontbonne Coll. Alumni Assn., AAUW (fin. officer 1983—), Assn. Govt. Accts., Am. Soc. Women Accts., Beta Gamma Sigma, Beta Alpha Psi. Roman Catholic. Club: Arden Hills Swim and Tennis. Home: 2616 Point Reyes Way Sacramento CA 95826

PUTTA, BARBARA JEAN, lawyer; b. Elgin, Ill., Nov. 22, 1946; d. John G. and Ruth (Johnson) P.; m. Kenneth H. Mularski, July 24, 1972; children—Jedrek Mularski Bretton Mularski. B.A., U. Ill., 1968; M.A., Columbia U., 1969; J.D., Northwestern U., 1975. Bar: Ill. 1975. Assoc. atty. Mayer Brown & Platt, Chgo., 1975-79, assoc. atty. Butler Rubin Newcomer Saltarelli & Boyd, Chgo., 1980-83, ptnr., 1984—. Vice pres., dirs., Chiaravalle Montessori Sch., Evanston, Ill., 1984—. Mem. ABA, Women's Bar Assn., Ill. State Bar Assn., Chgo. Bar Assn. (chmn. parents seminar 1984). Home: 634 Sheridan Rd Evanston IL 60202 Office: Butler Rubin Newcomer Saltarelli & Boyd 3 First Nat Plaza Chicago IL 60602

PUTZ, CHRISTINE, financial executive, accountant; b. Palmer, Mass., Feb. 4, 1950; d. Anthony Charles and Stephanie Veronica (Niemiec) P. Student Salem State Coll.; Springfield Tech. Coll.; B.S. in Bus. Adminstrn., Western New Eng. Coll., 1979. Chief acct. Wing Meml. Hosp., Palmer, 1969-79; field acct. Hillhaven Corp., Lexington, Mass., 1979-83; fin. dir. Bus. Mgmt., Malden, Mass., 1983—; cons. Melrose VNS, Mass., 1983—. Mem. Nat. Assn. Female Execs. Roman Catholic. Avocations: outdoor activities; sports reading; work. Office: Bus Mgmt Consortium for VNA's of Malden, Medford and Middlesex East 21 Ferry St Malden MA 02148

PYETT, BONNIE LEE, civilian naval official; b. Phila., Aug. 17, 1950; d. Kaiser and Emer Lee (Flemming) P. B.S. in French, Cheyney State Coll., 1972; postgrad. St. Joseph's U., Phila., 1982-84. Inventory mgmt. specialist Aviation Supply Office, U.S. Navy, Phila., 1972-78, team leader, 1978-82, div. dir. support services, 1982-84, supply systems analyst Naval Air Systems Command, Washington, 1984-85, competition advocate, 1985—. Counselor Crime Prevention Assn. Phila., 1966-71; big sister Big Sisters Phila., 1977-80. Sec. of Navy fellow St. Joseph's U., 1982-83; recipient Student Teaching award Cheyney State Coll., 1972. Mem. Nat. Assn. Female Execs., Navy Aviation Exec. Inst. Democrat. Baptist. Avocations: track and field; reading; singing. Home: 7220 Fordson Rd Apt 102 Alexandria VA 22306 Office: Naval Air Systems Command Washington DC 20361

PYLE, BEATRICE ALZIRA, educator; b. West Chester, Pa., May 21, 1922; d. Norman James and Audrey (Dilks) Pyle; B.S., Gettysburg Coll., 1944; M.S. in Hygiene and Phys. Edn., Wellesley Coll., 1946; certificate U. Oslo, 1960. Instr. Gettysburg Coll., 1938-40, Vassar Coll., 1946-52; tchr. pub. schs., Winnetka, Ill., 1952-57; asso. prof. phys. and health edn. Miami U., Oxford, Ohio, 1957—. Mem. Am. Pub. Health Assn., Royal Soc. Health Can. and Eng., Nat., Ohio edn. assns., AAHPER (coordinator aquatic insts. for aquatic council), Ohio Coll. Assn., Am. Camping Assn., AAUW, Ohio, Midwest assns. health, phys. edn. and recreation. Author: Small Craft: An Instructional Textbook for Teachers; Anatomy Handbook; Kinesiology Laboratory Manual. Home: 119 N Campus Ave Oxford OH 45056

PYLE, BOBBIE JO, electronic engineer; b. Duluth, Minn., Oct. 23, 1956; d. Clayton Clifford and Betty Mae (Vogt) P. B.S. in Electronic Engring. Tech., Mankato State U., 1979. Electronic engr. McDonnell Douglas Corp., St. Louis, 1980-84; test support engr. Control Data Corp., Mpls., 1984—. Mem. Nat. Assn. Female Execs. Home: 3512 Baillif Pl Bloomington MN 55431 Office: Control Data Corp 3101 E 80th St Bloomington MN 55420

PYNES, NINA, restaurant executive; b. Syracuse, N.Y., June 25, 1936; d. Samuel and Palma (Quinto) Collette; student Syracuse U., 1955-60; grad. Sch. Arts and Crafts, 1984; m. Buddy Pynes, Nov. 9, 1967; children—Patricia, Mitchell. Owner, operator Big M Supermarket, Weedsport, N.Y., 1962-65; owner, pres., acct. Soo Lin Restaurant, Inc., DeWitt, N.Y., 1967—. Mem. N.Y. State Restaurant Assn., N.Y. State Sheriffs Assn., N.Y. State Chiefs of Police Assn., Foodservice Cert. Soc., Everson Mus., Central N.Y. Tavern Keepers. Office: Soo Lin Restaurant Erie Blvd E DeWitt NY 13214

PYSZ, JEAN ANN, personnel executive; b. Taunton, Mass., May 1, 1947; d. Paul J. and Adela (Baran) Ladebauche; student Fisher Jr. Coll., 1982-83, Stonehill Coll., 1984; 1 son, Mark Richard. Ballet instr., 1963-65; sec. to dist. mgr. Prudential Ins. Co., Taunton, 1965-66; sec. to personnel mgr. Raytheon Co., North Dighton, Mass., 1967-75; exec. sec. to mgr. corporate audit Motorola Inc., Phoenix, 1977-79; asst. to corporate dir. employee relations Robertson Factories, Inc., Taunton, 1979-82, now dir. personnel. Team capt. United Way, 1982; co-dir. Miss Taunton Scholarship Pageant, 1980; chmn. Jobs for Bay State Grads., 1984-85. Mem. Taunton Area C. of C. (v.p. personnel com. 1983-84, chmn. 1984-85), Nat. Assn. Female Execs., Taunton Mgmt. Club (1st v.p. 1985-86).

QUACKENBUSH, MARSHA CLAIRE, librarian; b. Plainfield, N.J., Sept. 23, 1953; d. Marshall Eaton and Marion Baldwin (Hingle) Prindle; children—Susan Carrie, Laura Gene. B.A., Rocky Mt. Coll., 1975; M.L.S., Rutgers U., 1984. Asst. librarian Kelley, Drye & Warren, N.Y.C., 1975-76; tchr. Piscataway High Sch. (N.J.), 1976-77; asst. librarian Somerville Pub. Library (N.J.), 1978-82; tchr. Greenbrook High Sch. (N.J.), 1983-84; reference librarian North Edison Pub. Library, 1984; children's librarian woodbridge Pub. Library, 1984—. N.J. Library Assn. scholar, 1982-83. Mem. N.J. Library Assn., ALA. Democrat. Methodist. Club: Am. Legion. Home: 164 Geary Dr South Plainfield NJ 07080

QUACKENBUSH, RITA JEAN, temporary help computer services executive; b. Edinburg, Tex., Feb. 13, 1947; d. Chalmers Stanford and Deliah May (Mugrdechian) Stromberg; m. Charles W. Quackenbush, Dec. 16, 1978; 1 child, Carrey Colleen. Student U. Minn., 1966; cert. stock broker N.Y. Inst. Fin. Sales rep. Norrell Temporary Services, Inc., Orlando, Fla., 1970-71; br. mgr. Staff Builders Internat., Miami and Orlando, 1971-74; area mgr. CDI Temporary Services, Atlanta, 1976-79; founder, pres. Q TECH, Santa Clara, Calif., 1979—, QBit, Santa Clara, 1983—. Featured in Life mag., 1982. Mem. United Republican Fin. Com., Santa Clara County, 1980—; bd. dirs. Santa Clara County council Girl Scouts U.S.A., 1985—. Mem. Silicon Valley Roundtable, Profl. Women's Roundtable, Am. Electronics Assn. (exec. com. 1985—). Avocations: piloting; water skiing; snow skiing. Office: Q TECH 4701 Patrick Henry Dr Bldg 1 Santa Clara CA 95054

QUADE, SUSAN JOANN, bank executive; b. Detroit, Oct. 9, 1948; d. Donald August and Leona Marie (Pelletier) Stockel. B.S. in Bus. Adminstrn., Upsala Coll., 1977; postgrad. Fairleigh Dickinson U., 1982-84. Profl. banking cert. Am. Inst. Banking. Learning Ctr. mgr., regional tng. coordinator Control Data Corp., N.Y.C., 1973-80, facilitator regional tng. meeting, Phila., 1979; computer-based edn. specialist Butler Service Group at AT&T, Piscataway, N.J., 1980; mgr. tax processing ctr. Norstar Bank of Upstate N.Y., N.Y.C., 1981—, tng. cons., Albany, 1985—. Mem. Essex County Democratic Women's League, 1978, 79; del. N.J. State C. of C. Coll. Bus. Symposium, Morristown, 1976. Mem. Nat. Orgn. Female Execs., Phi Chi Theta. Avocations: writing; reading; travel; photography; Am. history. Home: 42 Charles St Bloomfield NJ 07003

QUAIL, BEVERLY JO, lawyer; b. Glendale, Calif., June 19, 1949; d. John Henry and Dorothy Marie (Sanblom) Q.; m. Timothy D. Roble; children—Benjamin W., Elizabeth L. B.A., U. So. Calif., 1971; J.D., U. Denver, 1974. Bar: Colo. 1974. Assoc., Conover, McClearn & Heppenstall, P.C., Denver, 1974-75; ptnr. Welborn, Dufford & Brown, Denver, 1975—; broker Colo. Assn. Realtors, 1982-84. Mem. Mortar Bd., Denver Bar Assn. (com. 1981-84), ABA (chmn. real property litigation com.), Am. Coll. Real Estate Lawyers, Colo. Real Estate Council. Clubs: Denver (coms.), Cherry Hills Country (Denver). Editor newsletter The Colo. Lawyer, 1983-84; contbr. articles to profl. jours. Home: 19 Random Rd Englewood CO 80110 Office: Welborn Dufford et al 1700 Broadway #1100 Denver CO 80290

QUALLS, CORETHIA, archaeologist; b. Sparta, Tenn., Jan. 17, 1948; d. Malcolm Talmadge and Lucille (Jackson) Qualls. B.A., Marlboro Coll., 1970; M.Phil., Columbia U., 1980, Ph.D., 1981. Exec. curator Mus. of Archaeology of Staten Island, 1981; asst. prof. St. John's U., S.I., 1981-82; cons. curator Queens Mus., N.Y., 1982-83; cons. curator Kuwait Nat. Mus., 1984—; archaeologist Columbia U., 1970-74, NYU Inst. Fine Arts, 1972-73, 84, Johns Hopkins U., 1974; Fulbright prof. archaeology, 1985-86; dir. excavations at Hamad Town, Bahrain for Bahrain Dept. Archaeology, 1985-86. Editor: Seals of the Marcopali Collection, vol. 1, 1984; contbr. articles to profl. jours. Columbia U. fellow, 1970-74; Am. Schs. Oriental Research fellow, 1973-74. Mem. Am. Inst. Archaeology, Am. Oriental Soc., Am. Sch. Oriental Research, Inst. Nautical Archaeology, Brit. Sch. Archaeol. in Iraq, Oriental Club of N.Y.C., Egypt Exploration Soc. Roman Catholic.

QUALLS-SULKOWSKI, SUSAN JANE, athletic educator; b. Detroit, Nov. 20, 1954; d. Roy A. and Mary Susanne (Comer) McLalin; m. 2d Mard Edward Sulkowski, Feb. 18, 1984; m. Cecil O. Qualls, Apr. 23, 1977 (div.). B.S. in Social Sci., Eastern Mich. U., 1976, B.S. in Phys. Edn., 1976; M.S. in Athletic Adminstrn., Mich. State U., 1983. Cert. tchr., Mich. Teller, Mfrs. Bank, Detroit, 1973-76; coach, tchr. Flushing High Sch. (Mich.), 1976-78; coach, tchr. Detroit County Day Sch., Birmingham, Mich., 1978—, athletic dir., 1979—. Active Easter Seals, March of Dimes. Mem. Detroit Field Hockey Assn. (pres. 1981-83), Met. Conf. Athletic League (sec. Birmingham 1979-83), Nat. Volleyball Assn., Mich. High Sch. Athletic Assn. (ski com. 1983—), Delta Psi Kappa (treas. 1974-76). Home: 26150 W 12 Mile Rd Apt 59B Southfield MI 48034

QUAN, ALICE BROWNE, civic worker, clubwoman; b. Fort Worth, Apr. 4, 1908; d. Virgil and Maimee Lee (Robinson) Browne; m. Frank James Quan, Feb. 22, 1966; 1 son, Floyd Davis Raupe. Student Christian Coll., Columbia, Mo., 1925-26; grad. Miss Mason's Sch., Tarrytown, N.Y., 1928; A.B., Okla. U., 1930, M.A. in History, life tchr.'s cert., 1939. Substitute tchr. history jr. and sr. high schs., Oklahoma City, 1941-45; Okla. state pres. Children Am. Revolution, 1941-45, hon. pres., 1945, nat. v.p., 1945-47, nat. librarian, curator 1947-51, editor 1st and 2d state yearbooks, 1941-47; mem. council Girl Scouts U.S.A., Oklahoma City, 1941-43; organizing regent, hon. regent DAR, Paul's Valley, Okla., 1947, Okla. state chmn. bldg. fund, 1950-52, Okla. state membership chmn., 1946-50, rec. sec. Okla. state officers club, 1960; Okla. state women's com. chmn. savs. bond div. U.S. Treasury Dept., 1950-64; docent Bklyn. Children's Mus., 1940-41; mem. pres.'s council Sch. of Ozarks, Mo., 1973—chmn. UN Day, Oklahoma City, 1981; co-chmn. 3d Ann. Heart Ball, 1978; bd. dirs. Oklahoma City Heritage Assn., 1982-83, 86—; pres.'s council Oklahoma City U., 1974-79, mem. bishop's council, 1980—, mem. exec. bd. Library Soc., chmn. benefit for scholarships, 1984, opera exec. bd., 1985—; charter mem. women's com. Okla. Symphony Soc., fund raising chmn., 1950-52; life mem., mem. bd., past v.p. Okla. Art Center, mem. liaison bd., 1973-85; decoration chmn. Beaux Arts Ball, 1958; organizing chmn. Musicade, Okla. Fedn. Music Clubs, 1960; hospitality chmn. Town Hall, Oklahoma City, 1967-70; bd. dirs., v.p. Civic Music Assn., 1974-75, 76-82; adv. com. Oklahoma City Sch. Music, 1975-79; asso. mem. nat. council Met. Opera, 1975-79, patron, 1979—, chmn. Phoebe Circle, 1st Presbyterian Ch., 1976-77, Priscilla Circle, 1977-78, program chmn. women's assn., 1979-81, bd. dirs. Oklahoma City Opera, Met. Opera Southwestern Hospitality; dir. Glencoe Vacherie Plantation, Franklin, La., 1963—, sec.-treas., 1980—; mem. liaison bd. Art League, 1973-86, dir. Ardmore Coca Cola Bottling Co., Ardmore, Okla., 1976-79. Recipient Outstanding Service award U.S. Treasury Dept. 1962; Spl. Service cert. ARC, 1942-46; life teaching cert. in jr. and sr. high sch. history, Okla. Mem. Okla. Soc. Mayflower Descs. (life), Nat. Soc. Old Plymouth Colony Descs. (life), Jr. League Oklahoma City (sustaining), Okla. Sci. and Arts Found. (life), Sovereign Colonial Soc. Ams. Royal Descent (life), Order of Washington (life), Nat. Soc. Descs. Ancient and Honorable Arty. Co., Plantagenet Soc. (life), Soc. Descs. Knights Most Noble Order Garter (life), English Speaking Union (travel chmn. 1974-76, membership chmn. 1976-78, program chmn. 1979-81), Colonial Order of Crown (life), Okla. Assn. Women Hwy. Leaders, Okla. Zool. Soc. (life), Magna Carta Dames (life, state regent 1981-84), Okla. Art League (pres. 1968-69, program chmn. 1981-82), Reviewers Clique (pres. 1978-79), Okla. Opera and Musical Theatre Soc., Gamma Phi Beta (Golden 50 Crescent award 1979), Alpha Tau Omega (state wives and mothers club pres. 1953-54). Clubs: Ladies Music (life, v.p. 1957-64), Redbud Women's (pres. 1968-69, dir. 1969—), Oklahoma City Golf and Country, The Beacon, Lotus, Mayfair, Wednesday Rev. (pres. 1984-86), Embassy, Seventy Five, Eagle Nest, Colonial Bridge (trophy 1935). Alice Quan Wing at Sch. of Ozarks dedicated in her honor, 1980. Address: 1304 Huntington Ave Oklahoma City OK 73116

QUAN, LYNDA MARYE, psychiatric social worker; b. New Orleans, July 9, 1945; d. William Evans and Mary (Hom) Q.; B.A., U. Colo., Boulder, 1966; M.A., U. Mo., Columbia, 1971, M.S.W., 1975. Mem. Peace Corps, Brazil, 1967-69; grad. teaching asst. U. Mo., Columbia, 1969-71; substitute tchr. Columbia Public Schs., 1971; psychiat. social worker Fulton (Mo.) State Hosp., 1971-76; dep. juvenile officer St. Louis County Juvenile Ct., 1975; with Farmington (Mo.) State Hosp., 1976—, supr. psychiat. social work, 1981—; cons., speaker in field. Mem. Nat. Assn. Social Workers (chmn. nomination and leadership com. Mo. chpt. 1981-82, chmn. Southeast unit 1982-84, exec. com. Mo. chpt. 1983, del. assembly 1981, 84, sec. 1984—), Acad. Cert. Social Workers, Bus. and Profl. Women (legis. chmn. 1983), Women's Sports Found., U. Mo. Alumni Assn. (life). Home: Route 2 609 Hillsboro Rd Farmington MO 63640 Office: Farmington State Hosp Farmington MO 63640

QUANTIUS, SUSAN ELIZABETH, government official; b. Milw., Apr. 7, 1957; d. Kent Martin and Barbara Joan (Wackman) Quantius. A.B., Smith Coll., 1979; M.Sc., London Sch. Econs., 1980; M.P.P., Harvard U., 1982. Budget examiner Office Mgmt. and Budget, Washington, 1982—. Truman Found. scholar, 1977; Smith Coll. scholar, 1979. Mem. Phi Beta Kappa. Presbyterian. Office: Office Mgmt and Budget New Exec Office Bldg Room 7026 Washington DC 20503

QUANTRELL-MULLINS, BIANCA RODERT, interior architect; b. Koln, W. Ger., Aug. 4, 1937; came to U.S., 1959, naturalized, 1960; d. Josef Karl and Elsa (Corsi) Rodert; m. Carlisle A. Quantrell, Jr., 1959 (div. 1973); 1 child, Gilonne Corsi Quantrell; m. Henry Foster Mullins, Jr., June 22, 1974. Student World Congress Inst., Atlanta, 1984, London Sch. Econs., 1984. Interior archtl. designer Jova/Daniels/Busby, Atlanta, 1971-72, interior archtl. design project mgr., 1972-74; pres., chief exec. officer, chief operating officer Quantrell Mullins & Assocs., Inc., Atlanta, 1974—; mem. bd. govs. World Trade Club, Atlanta, 1983—. Interior architect Lloyds Bank Internat. Ltd., 1981, Life Ins. Co. Ga., 1985; Dean Witter Reynolds, 1985, Nat. Westminster Bank, 1985, MCI Telecommunications, Ogilvy & Mather, 1985, IBM, 1985. Mem. Central Atlanta Progress, 1985. Named an Interior Design Giant, Interior Design Mag., 1984, 85. Mem. Soc. Internat. Bus. Fellows, AIA (profl. affiliate), Midtown Bus. Assn., German-Am. C. of C. (bd. dirs. 1983), Atlanta C. of C. (mem. internat. task force 1984—), British-Am. Bus. Group (bd. dirs. 1985), Belgian-Am. C. of C. Roman Catholic. Avocations: travel, the arts. Office: 11 17th St NE Atlanta GA 30309

QUARLES, HOLLACE ELLEN HENKEL, businesswoman; b. Cleve., June 4, 1945; d. Charles Edward and Betty Jane (Bowman) Henkel; B.A., U. Ky., 1967; M.L.S., U. Pitts., 1968; m. Frederick Hundley Quarles III, Apr. 12, 1969; children—Ashley Louise, Ellen Michelle. Mem. faculty, dir. computer systems Med. Sch. Library U. Va., Charlottesville, 1968-70; pres. Eastern Mdse. Corp.,

Charlottesville, 1970-74; owner Holly's Glass Studio, 1975-85; dir. pub. relations MooneyMite Aircraft Corp., Charlottesville, 1969—; pres. Commonwealth Capital Corp., Charlottesville, 1978—; Reference Librarian Claude Moore Health Scis. Library, 1985; audio tape librarian Trinity Presbyn. Ch., 1984—. Malloch scholar Med. Library Assn., 1967. Mem. Nat. Assn. Women Bus. Owners. Presbyterian. Office: 141 Ednam Dr Charlottesville VA 22901

QUARTUCCIO, FRANKLYNNE XAVIER, restaurant owner; b. Rockville Center, N.Y., Jan. 1, 1945; d. Frank Antonio and Virginia Caroline (McNally) LaRocca; asso. degree with distinction, Suffolk County Community Coll., 1979; student SUNY, Stony Brook, 1979-81, St. Joseph's Coll., Patchogue, N.Y., 1981—; m. John Quartuccio, Mar. 20, 1962; children—John, Christopher. Adminstrv. asst. Suffolk Community Coll., Selden, N.Y., 1977-79; sr. adminstrn. analyst Equitable Life Assurance Soc. U.S., 1980-83; dep. dir. L.I. Preparation Recruitment Program Inc., 1983-84; co-owner Quartuccio's Restaurant, Ozone Park, N.Y., 1984—. Democratic candidate for town clk. Town of Islip, 1981; dep. zone leader Suffolk County Dem. party, 1982-83; mem. Suffolk County Dem. Com., 1981—; del. Dem. Nat. Conv., 1984; Suffolk County chmn. Women's Equal Opportunity Council, 1980—; mem. adv. bd. Paumanok Algonquin Found., 1978—; bd. dirs. Community Programs Center, 1981-82, L.I. Affirmative Action Program Inc., 1981—. NSF Grantee, 1979-80. Mem. Women's Equal Rights Congress, Equitable Networks, L.I. Women's Coalition (dir.), NOW, Wider Opportunities For Women. Home: 79 Harp Ln Sayville NY 11782

QUARTUCCIO, MARIA BARO, nurse; b. San Luis Obispo, Calif., Oct. 16, 1933; d. David Lopez and Reynalda (Velarde) Baro; m. Anthony Angelo Quartuccio, May 20, 1978. R.N., O'Connor Hosp. Sch. Nursing, 1956; A.A. in Nursing, West Valley Coll., 1972; B.S. in Nursing, San Jose State U., 1977, B.S. in Sociology-Family Counseling, 1977. Nurse O'Connor Hosp., San Jose, Calif., 1953-56; staff nurse, supr. Atascadero Gen. Hosp. (Calif.), 1957-62; nurse, coordinator, supr. Health Dept., San Luis Obispo, Calif., 1962-67; recovery nurse Santa Clara Valley Med. Hosp., San Jose, 1967—. Author: Nursing Manual Procedure, 1966; Visiting Nurse Manual, 1966. Active St. Francis Cabrini Ch., San Jose, 1967—. Mem. Registered Nurse Profl. Assn., Recovery Nurse Assn., Calif. Nurse Assn., Santa Clara Med. Assn. (ednl. and adv. com. 1980—, profl. performance com. 1983). Democrat. Roman Catholic. Home: 4819 Kingdale Dr San Jose CA 95124

QUASS, MARY KATHRYN, radio station executive; b. Fairfield, Iowa, Jan. 29, 1950; d. John Michael Wenke and Genevieve (Seaver) Wenke Cooley; m. Jon Donald Quass, Aug. 12, 1972. B.A., U. No. Iowa, 1972. Cert. radio mktg. cons. Account exec. Stoner Broadcasting Co., Cedar Rapids, Iowa, 1977-79, gen. sales mgr., 1979-82, gen. sales mgr., Des Moines, 1982, v.p. and gen. mgr., 1982—. Trustee Kirkwood Community Coll., Cedar Rapids, 1984—; bd. dirs. Pub. Concerns Inst., Cedar Rapids, 1985. Mem. Profl. Women's Network (bd. dirs. 1978-79). Avocations: reading; painting. Office: Sta KHAK-AM/FM 100 1st Ave NE Suite 9 Cedar Rapids IA 52401

QUATTLEBAUM, DOROTHY EVELYN CLEWIS (MRS. WALTER EMMETT QUATTLEBAUM, JR.), investment co. exec.; b. Unadilla, Ga., Nov. 1, 1924; d. Otis Clyde and Mabel (DuPree) Clewis; student Puttman Bus. Sch., 1953, Chipola Jr. Coll., 1962-64; m. Walter Emmett Quattlebaum, Jr., Oct. 19, 1946; children—Walter Emmett III, Amalia Ann. Sec.-treas. Sneads Telephone Co., 1948-55, Cottondale Telephone Co., 1954-55, Grand Ridge Telephone Co., 1954-55; sec.-treas., dir. Tri-County Telephone Co., Inc., Bonifay, Fla., 1955-62; asst. to stock analyst Quattlebaum Investments, Bonifay, 1962—. Methodist (pres. Wesleyan service guild 1957, 58). Address: PO Box 36 Bonifay FL 32425

QUATTLEBAUM, LUCILLE SCONYERS, hospital administrator; b. Cottondale, Fla., Apr. 9, 1930; d. John Grady and Ida Mae (Roberts) Sconyers; m. Houston J. Quattlebaum, Aug. 2, 1947; children—Wayne, Fred, Tom, Michael. Grad. Campbell's Bus. Coll.; grad. Sch. Allied Health Services Adminstrn. U. Ala. Sec. to adminstr. S.E. Ala. Med. Center, Dothan, 1956-60, exec. sec., 1960-70, adminstrv. asst. to adminstrn., 1970-80, adminstrv. asst., 1980-84, asst. adminstr., 1984—. Mem. edn. com. C. of C., Dothan, Ala.; mem. arts and mus. bd. City of Dothan. Recipient awards for outstanding service S.E. Ala. Med. Center, 1981, 82. Mem. Nat. Assn. Female Execs., Ala. Hosp. Assn., Zonta Internat. (treas.), Dothan C. of C. Baptist.

QUEIOR, VIRGINIA MARY, paving company executive; b. Saranac Lake, N.Y., Aug. 13, 1928; s. George William and Stella (Zustavna) Riebel; m. Oliver Joseph Queior Jr., Aug. 31, 1949 (dec. 1982); children—Timothy Lance, Virginia Lee. Grad. North Country Community Coll. Telephone operator, trainee instr. N.Y. Bell Telephone Co., Saranac Lake, 1946-49, 63-80, Schenectady, 1980, Glen Falls, 1981; pres. Queior Paving Inc., Ray Brook, N.Y., 1982—. Recipient Edward Glannon Art award North Country Community Coll., Saranac Lake, 1985. Home and Office: Queior Paving Inc Box 41 Saranac Lake NY 12983

QUICK, MARGARET ANN, lawyer, tax consultant; b. Erie, Pa., June 13, 1955; d. Charles Edward and Josephine Patricia (Sandphillip) Quick; m. Michael Phillip Maines, Aug. 14, 1983. B.A., Mercyhurst Coll., 1977; J.D., Pepperdine U. Sch. of Law, 1980. Bar: Pa., 1982, U.S. Tax Ct., 1983. Comml. teller Security Peoples Trust Co., Erie, Pa., 1973-77; law clk. Morgan, Wenzel & McNicholas, Los Angeles, 1978-80; tax atty., cons. Touche Ross & Co., Los Angeles, 1982-84; tax atty., Pitts., 1984—. Vice chmn. Young Republicans, Pepperdine U., Malibu, Calif., 1979. Mem. Am. Inst. C.P.A.s, Pa. Bar Assn., ABA. Roman Catholic.

QUICK, SHARON WELLS, real estate agency executive; b. Bethesda, Md., Apr. 13, 1945; d. John Ashley and Alicia (Kenyon) Wells; m. Michael K. Mann, Sept. 6, 1966 (div. July 1971); 1 child, Amy C.; m. Winston C. Fulton, Sept. 3, 1984. B.A., U. Wis.-Madison, 1965; postgrad. Oxford U., Eng., 1965-67, Purdue U., 1974-77. Pres. Shaman & Assocs. Ltd., London, 1967-71; vis. lectr. U. Aberystwyth, Wales, 1971-73; sales assoc. Livesay Realty, Lafayette, Ind., 1977-79; owner, pres. The Wells Agy., Lafayette, 1979—; investment cons. Mem. Realtors Polit. Action Com., 1980—. Mem. Internat. Council Shopping Ctrs., Women in Bus., Midwest Real Estate Exchangors, Nat. Assn. Female Execs., Farm and Land Inst., Internat. Exchangors, Nat. Bd. Realtors, Smithsonian Instn., Nat. Fedn. Independent Bus., C. of C. Lafayette. Republican. Presbyterian. Avocations: music; reading; traveling; cooking; knitting. Home: 1512 Summit Dr West Lafayette IN 47906 Office: The Wells Agy 200 Ferry St Suite C Lafayette IN 47901

QUIGLEY, BEHNAZ ZOLGHADR, educator; b. Tehran, Iran, Nov. 17, 1944; came to U.S., 1968, naturalized, 1978; d. Hamid and Behjat (Shoaibi) Zolghadr; diploma in edn. Tchrs. Tng. Coll., Tehran, 1964; B.A., (scholar), U. Tehran, 1968; M.B.A., U. D.C., 1975; doctoral candidate U. Md.; m. Herbert Gerald Quigley, Aug. 24, 1974; children—Narda, Paran. Tchr. secondary sch. Ministry of Edn., Tehran, 1964-68; instr. in bus. Strayer Coll., Washington, 1975-76, U. D.C., 1975-76, Prince George's Community Coll., Largo, Md., 1976-77; asst. prof. bus. adminstrn. Mt. Vernon Coll., Washington, 1976—, chmn. dept., 1978-79, 82-84; aide to chief economist Iranian Econ. Mission, 1974; freelance cons. World Trade Assos., summer 1975, Distbn. Systems, summer 1979; co-owner, freelance cons. Univ. Systems Assos., 1978—; instr., curriculum developer Middle East Inst., summers 1976—. Mt. Vernon Coll. faculty devel. grantee, George Washington U., summers 1978, 79; Mt. Vernon Coll. ednl. travel grantee, 1978, 79, 80; grantee Middle East Inst., 1977. Mem. Nat. Assn. Female Execs. (dir. Washington area), Assn. M.B.A. Execs., Am. Acctg. Assn., Acad. Mgmt., U. D.C. Alumni Assn. Democrat. Author several books; co-editor: Management Systems: Contemporary Perspectives, 1982; contbr. articles to profl. jours; author bus. book revs. Home: 5 Canfield Ct Potomac MD 20854 Office: 2100 Foxhall Rd Washington DC 20007

QUIGLEY-WOLF, ANNA MARIE HELEN, organizational development consultant; b. Phila., Aug. 15, 1950; d. William Joseph, Jr. and Elizabeth (Harkins) Ailes; B.A., Point Park Coll., Pitts., 1972; postgrad. Temple U., Phila.; M.A., Antioch U., Phila., 1984. Ednl. resource specialist Community Coll. Phila., 1972-74; edn. coordinator Penn Mut. Life Ins. Co., Phila., 1974-76, human resource cons., 1976-81; adminstr. orgn. devel. RCA Service Co., Cherry Hill, N.J., 1981-85; mgr. orgn. devel. Lehigh Press, Inc., Pennsauken, N.J., 1985—; chmn. Women's Resource Group, Phila., 1980-81; speaker in field. Mem. Orgn. Devel. Network, Am. Soc. Tng. and Devel., Nat. Assn Female Execs., Human Resource Planning Soc. Office: Cooper Pkwy Bldg W North Park Dr and Airport Hwy Pennsauken NJ 08109

QUIJAS, JEANENE GAYLE, laboratory equipment and supplies company official; b. Lynnville, Ind., June 14, 1950; d. Homer and Martha Louise (Leonhardt) Ellerbrook; m. Louis Francis Quijas, May 9, 1970 (div. Oct. 1974); 1 child, Loretta Susan. Student med. tech. Career Acad., 1968; student Stephens Coll., 1984-85. Regional supr. Med. Ins. Service, St. Louis, 1968-70; med. technician Blue Ridge Med. Lab., Kansas City, Mo., 1970-76; store mgr. Shelly's Tall Girl Shop, Kansas City, 1976-77; inside sales rep. Fisher Sci. Co., St. Louis, 1977, sales rep., Columbia, Mo., 1978—; div. v.p. Med. Info. Service, Denver, 1977-78. Mem. Orgn. Female Execs. Democrat. Lutheran. Avocations: macrame; decorating; fashion and make-up; old movies. Home: 4609 Knox Dr Columbia MO 65203 Office: Fisher Sci Co 1241 Ambassador Blvd Box 14989 Saint Louis MO 63178

QUILICI, JANET MAUREEN, consultant, marketing director; b. Santa Monica, Calif., June 8, 1944; d. Kyle Edgar and Clarice Viola (Fox) Kolhoff; m. Lawrence John Quilici, Nov. 26, 1966; 1 child, James Lawrence. B.A., Santa Clara U., 1966, Teaching credential, Calif. Pension underwriter Occidental Life Ins., Los Angeles, 1971-77; pension cons. Robert Haber, Inc., San Francisco, 1977-78, Wyatt Co., San Francisco, 1978-81; fin. planner Equity Engring., Inc., Santa Clara, Calif., 1981-82; pension cons., mktg. dir. Plan Design Cons., Inc., San Mateo, Calif., 1983—, Odis, Inc., San Mateo, 1983—; dir. Fin. Planning Forum, Mem. Small Plans Pension Conf. (arrangements com. 1983—), Western Pension Conf., Nat. Assn. Profl. Women. Democrat. Office: Plan Design Cons Inc 1510 W Cape Dr Suite 202 San Mateo CA 94404

QUIMBY, SALLY CROSBY, nursing adminstr.; b. Washington, Nov. 19, 1946; d. Lowell Horace and Millicent Winn (Childs) Quimby. B.S. in Nursing, La. State U., 1975; M.S. in Nursing, Med. Coll. Ga., 1980. Asst. head nurse E. Jefferson Hosp., Metairie, La., 1976; head CCU St. Joseph Hosp., Savannah, Ga., 1977-78, asst. supr. CCU, 1978-80, supr., 1980; dept. head ICU El Camino Hosp., Mountain View, Calif., 1980—; planner CCU for computer monitoring system, 1978-79; instr. CPR, 1978-80. Task force organizer Save Our Satellite, 1977. Named outstanding Graduating Nursing Student, La. State U., 1975. Mem. Am. Nurses Assn., Am. Assn. Critical Care Nurses, Calif. Soc. Nursing Service Adminstrs. (program com. 1985-86), AAUW. Sigma Theta Tau. Democrat. Methodist. Home: 725 Mariposa #305 Mountain View CA 94041 Office: 2500 Grant Rd Mountain View CA 94042

QUINLAN, LIZ (ISADORA) W., public relations executive; b. N.Y.C., Dec. 30, 1937; d. A. Ralph and Mary Ella (Darbee) Wexler; m. Robert J. Quinlan, Aug. 6, 1966. A.B., Vassar Coll., 1959. Assoc. editor Macmillan Pubs., N.Y.C., 1962-65, Reader's Digest Almanac, N.Y.C., 1965-67; publs. editor Assn. of Jr. Leagues, N.Y.C., 1966-72, 76-80, dir. communications, 1980—; cons. pub. relations, N.Y.C., 1972-80; mem. rev. com. Ind. Sector/Ad Council Nat. Voluntarism Ad Campaign, 1982-83; rep. to subcom. of Presdl. Task Force for Pvt. Sector Initiatives, 1982. Contbr. articles to mags., and assn. jours. Mem. governing com. Off-the-Record Series, Fgn. Policy Assn., N.Y.C., 1977-85. Recipient cert. of merit Art Dirs.' Club, 1970. Pub. Relations Soc. Am., Mem. Women in Communications, Alumnae/Alumni of Vassar Coll. (dir. 1982-86, pres. 1986—). Episcopalian. Club: Vassar of N.Y. (dir. 1972-79, pres. 1976-79). Home: 200 East End Ave New York NY 10128 Office: Assn of Jr Leagues Inc 825 3d Ave New York NY 10022

QUINN, BARBARA ANN, athletic administrator; b. Freehold, N.J., Jan. 13, 1933; d. Walter Stanley and Mary (Craig) Harris; B.S. in Health and Phys. Edn., Ursinus Coll., 1955; M.A., Trenton State Coll., 1968. Dir. phys. edn. for girls Charles Ellis Sch., Newtown Square, Pa., 1956-60; instr. phys. edn. Pennsbury Schs., Yardley, Pa., 1960-63, Exeter Twp. High Sch., Reading, Pa., 1963-66, Hartwick Coll., Oneonta, N.Y., 1966-68; asst. prof. phys. and health edn. Madison Coll., Harrisonburg, Va., 1968-71; instr. phys. edn. Whitemarsh Jr. High Sch., Plymouth Meeting, Pa., 1971-74; dir. women's intercollegiate athletics U. Nev., Las Vegas, 1974-76; dir. women's intercollegiate athletics Simpson Coll., Indianola, Iowa, 1977-78; dir. women's athletics U. N.C., Asheville, 1978-81; dir. women's intercoll. athletics SUNY, Cortland, 1981-84; fitness dir. St. Joseph's Hosp., Asheville, N.C., 1985—; site dir. Western Region, Women's U.S. Olympic Basketball Trials, Las Vegas, 1976, U.S. Volleyball Assn. Coaches Clinic, Simpson Coll., 1977; chmn. selection com. Va. State Lacrosse Tournament, 1970-71; mem. selection com. So. Dist. Lacrosse Tournament, 1970-71; coach So. dist. team U.S. Women's Lacrosse Assn. Nat. Tournament, 1971; mem. women's soccer com. Nat. Collegiate Athletic Assn. 1982-84, chmn. NE region; participant 5th Nat. Inst. Girls' Sports Advanced Basketball Coaching, 1969. Mem. AAHPER (sec. coll. div. N.Y. State chpt. 1967), Va. Women's Lacrosse Assn. (chmn. nominations com. 1970-71), Nat. Assn. Coll. Athletic Dirs., N.Y. Assn. Intercollegiate Athletics for Women (chair ethics and eligibility com. 1982). Address: RD 3 Box 238 Bear Branch Rd Mars Hill NC 28754

QUINN, BETTY NYE, educator; b. Buffalo, Mar. 22, 1921; d. Fritz Arthur and Alma (Svenson) Hedberg; A.B., Mt. Holyoke Coll., 1941; A.M., Bryn Mawr Coll., 1942, Ph.D., 1944; m. John F. Quinn, Sept. 21, 1950. Analyst, U.S. Army, 1944-46, CIA, 1947; instr., asst. prof. Vassar Coll., Poughkeepsie, N.Y., 1948-59, dir. pub. relations, 1952-59, assoc. prof., 1959-68; prof. classics Mt. Holyoke Coll., South Hadley, Mass., 1968—. Am. Acad. Rome fellow, 1942-43; Am. Philos. Soc. grantee, 1952. Mem. Am. Philos. Assn., Mediaeval Acad. Am., Classics Assn. New Eng. (pres. 1970-71) Vergilian Soc. Am. Republican. Lutheran. Home: 27 W Parkview Dr South Hadley MA 01075 Office: Mount Holyoke Coll South Hadley MA 01075

QUINN, BEVERLY ANN, organization executive, counselor; b. Indpls., Jan. 4, 1946; d. William Houston and Mary (Boozer) Clark; m. Wilbert Quinn, Feb. 22, 1969 (div.); children—Cory J., Shaunah M. B.S., Austin Peay U., 1972; M.S., U. Tenn., 1983. Sr. social counselor Dept. Human Services, Clarksville, Tenn., 1973-83; program dir. YWCA, Clarksville, 1984—. Mem. Nat. Women's Polit. Caucus, Community Service Orgn. (v.p. 1984-85), Nashville C. of C., Nat. Assn. Career Women (v.p. 1984-85). Democrat. Roman Catholic. Avocations: needle crafts; sports; reading; self-improvement. Home: PO Box 261 Clarksville TN 37040

QUINN, CENTA THERESA, county official; b. Port Jervis, N.Y., Aug. 23, 1930; d. Merritt A. and Centa (Bunk) Q. Student pub. schs., Milford, Pa. Clk. Pa. Dept. Transp., Milford, 1949-55; commr.'s clk. County of Pike, Milford, 1955—. Crusade chmn. Pike County Cancer Soc., 1982, 83. Republican. Avocations: reading; bowling.

QUINN, CHRISTINE AGNES, radiologist; b. Cleve., Sept. 23, 1946; d. Paul Leo and Estelle Christine Q.; B.A., Marquette U., 1967; M.D., Med. Coll. Pa., 1971; m. Paul C. Janicki, July 11, 1970; children—Sarah Christine, Megan Alexandra. Intern, St. Luke's Hosp., Cleve., 1971-72; resident in diagnostic radiology Cleve. Clinic Found., 1972-75, radiologist, 1975-81; radiologist Marymount Hosp., Cleve., 1981—. Diplomate Am. Bd. Radiology. Mem. Radiol. Soc. N. Am., Am. Coll. Radiology, Soc. Nuclear Medicine, Ohio, Cuyahoga County med. socs., AMA. Contbr. to CRC Handbook Series, Vol. II, 1977; contbr. articles to profl. jours. Home: 2781 Sherbrooke Rd Shaker Heights OH 44122 Office: 12300 McCracken Rd Cleveland OH 44125

QUINN, JANE BRYANT, journalist; b. Niagara Falls, N.Y., Feb. 5, 1939; d. Frank Leonard and Ada (Laurie) Bryant; B.A. magna cum laude, Middlebury Coll., 1960; m. David Conrad Quinn, June 10, 1967; children—Matthew Alexander, Justin Bryant. Assoc. editor Insiders Newsletter, N.Y.C., 1962-65, co-editor, 1966-67; sr. editor Cowles Book Co., N.Y.C., 1968; editor-in-chief Bus. Week Letter, N.Y.C., 1969-73, gen. mgr., 1973-74; syndicated fin. columnist Washington Post Writers Group, 1974—; contbr. fin. column Women's Day mag., 1974—; contbr. NBC News and Info. Service, 1976-77; columnist Newsweek, 1978—; bus. corr. WCBS-TV News, 1980-81; spl. corr. CBS-TV Morning News, 1981-84, CBS-TV Evening News, 1984—. Mem. Phi Beta Kappa. Author: Everyone's Money Book, 1978; Updated Everyone's Money Book, 1980. Office: Newsweek 444 Madison Ave New York NY 10022

QUINN, JOANNE, nurse; b. S.I., N.Y., June 18, 1956; d. Joseph Paul and Josephine (Amodeo) Q. Diploma in nursing Bayonne Hosp. Sch. Nursing, N.J., 1980; B.S. in Nursing, Jersey City State Coll., 1984. Staff nurse med. surg. unit Doctor's Hosp., S.I., 1980-81, asst. head nurse, 1982-84, asst. head nurse emergency dept., 1984—. Mem. Sigma Theta Tau. Roman Catholic. Home: 480 Tysens Ln Staten Island NY 10306

QUINN, JULIA PROVINCE, civic worker; b. Franklin, Ind., Feb. 23; d. Oran Arnold and Lillian (Ditmars) Province; B.A., Franklin Coll., 1937; M.S., Smith Coll. Sch. Social Work, 1939; m. Robert William Quinn, Jan. 21, 1942; children—Robert Sean, Judith Ditmars. Caseworker, student supr. Community Service Soc., N.Y.C., 1939-44; caseworker community research Family Service Soc., New Haven, 1946; social worker in research, dept. preventive medicine Yale U. Sch. Medicine, New Haven, 1946-49; research asst. dept. preventive medicine Vanderbilt U. Sch. Medicine, Nashville, 1969-70. Bd. dirs. Tenn. Bot. Gardens and Fine Arts Center, 1976-81, Friends of J. F. Kennedy Center, 1976-81, Family and Children's Service, Nashville, 1977-83, Friends of Cheekwood, 1966-81, Nashville Symphony Assn., 1978-85, Tenn. Performing Arts Found., 1979—; bd. dirs. Nashville Opera Assn., 1983—, chmn. pub. relations, 1985—; chmn. public relations Friends of Cheekwood, 1966-68, 72-74, 76-78, Tenn. Performing Arts Found., 1978-85, Family and Children's Service, 1978-83; mem. adv. bd. Vanderbilt Center for Fertility and Reproductive Research, 1981-85. Recipient Nashville Vol. Activist award Cain-Sloan and Germaine Monteil, 1979. Mem. Nat. Assn. Social Workers, Acad. Cert. Social Workers, Ladies Hermitage Assn., Vanderbilt Med. Center Aux., Nashville Area C. of C. (cultural affairs com. 1979-85). Democrat. Presbyterian. Clubs: Smith Coll., Centennial (Nashville); Vanderbilt Garden, Vanderbilt Woman's. Contbr. articles to social work and med. jours. Home: 508 Park Center Dr Nashville TN 37205

QUINN, LOIS MARIE, health services administrator; b. Boston, Sept. 8, 1933; d. Charles Edward and Grace Marie (Lowder) Seabrook; R.N., Boston City Hosp., 1954; B.A., Glassboro State Coll., 1977; M.A., Central Mich. U., 1982; m. Richard Edward Quinn, Feb. 2, 1955; children—Deborah Marie, Christopher Edward, Erin Elizabeth, Patrick Richard. Pediatric staff nurse Boston City Hosp., 1954-56; staff nurse, coronary care nurse, supr., patient edn. coordinator, dir. nursing service Rancocas Valley Hosp., Willingboro, N.J., 1967-78; nursing mgmt. cons. Am. Medicorp., Bala Cynwyd, Pa., 1977-78; asst. adminstr. Washington Meml. Hosp., Turnersville, N.J., 1978-80; pres. Lois Quinn Assocs., Nursing Mgmt. Cons., Willingboro, N.J., 1980-83; mgr. nursing services Universal Health Services, Inc., King of Prussia, Pa., 1983-84, dir. mgmt. services, 1984—. Cert. nursing adminstr. Mem. Common Cause, Am. Nurses Assn., N.J. Nurses Assn. (coordinator So. N.J. nursing adminstrs. and educators 1975-77), Am. Heart Assn., ARC, Sigma Iota Epsilon. Roman Catholic. Featured in newspaper articles. Address: 360 Old Forge Crossing Devon PA 19333

QUINN, MAUREEN LORETTA, human resources administrator; b. Bklyn., July 11, 1932; d. Peter and Margaret (Betts) Butawice; m. Thomas Quinn, Apr. 10, 1963 (div. 1968); 1 child, Megan. B.A., NYU, 1960. Dept. head G.B. Buck Actuary, N.Y., 1949-55; office mgr. Film Creation, N.Y., 1955-57; adminstrv. asst. NYU, 1957-61, Cox & Co. Engring., N.Y., 1962-64; admissions coordinator Polytech. Inst. Bklyn., N.Y., 1966-69; nursing recruiter The Bklyn. Hosp., 1969-71; mng. dir. overseas operations Starr Internat., London, 1971-72; asst. to personnel dir. Vis. Nurse Service of N.Y., 1973-75, asst. dir. personnel, 1975, dir. personnel, 1975-84, chief human resources officer, 1984—. Bd. dirs. U.S. Com. for UNICEF, 1983—, Family Care Services, 1984—. Mem. Am. Soc. Personnel Adminstrs., Am. Mgmt. Assn., N.Y.C. of C., Assn. Hosp. Personnel Adminstrs., Am. Hosp. Assn., Nat. Home Care Assn. Roman Catholic. Avocations: reading, interior decorating, jogging. Home: 274 1st Ave New York NY 10009 Office: Vis Nurse Service of NY 107 E 70th St New York NY 10021

QUINN, PHYLLIS MARY, association information services executive; b. Garfield Heights, Ohio, Mar. 18, 1952; d. George M. and Helen K. (Morrissey) Q. B.A., St. Mary's Coll., Notre Dame, Ind., 1974; M.Ed., Am. U., 1976. Cert. Nat. Archives-Modern Archives Inst. Sr. library asst. Georgetown U. Med. Library, Washington, 1974-76; reading specialist Immaculate Conception Acad., Washington, 1976-77; tchr.-reading specialist St. Mark's Sch., Hyattsville, Md., 1977-78; coordinator info. Am. Phys. Therapy Assn., Washington and Alexandria, Va., 1978—, archivist, 1980—; treas. coordinator Rehab. Info. Round Table, 1983-85. Author: Back Care Educational Resource Guide, 1983; author Am. Phys. Therapy Calendar, 1983, Holistic Health Educational Resource Guide, 1983. Elk's scholar, 1970. Mem. Soc. Am. Archivists, Med. Library Assn., D.C. Health Sci. Network, Mid-Atlantic Regional Archives Conf. Home: 8719 Burning Tree Rd Bethesda MD 20817 Office: Am Phys Therapy Assn 1111 N Fairfax St Alexandria VA 22314

QUIRK, DONNA HAWKINS, financial analyst; b. Chgo., Sept. 29, 1955; d. Martin Francis and Monica Mae (Hesslau) Hawkins; m. John James Quirk, Dec. 5, 1981. B.S. in Commerce, DePaul U., Chgo., 1977, M.B.A., 1982. With Jewel Food Stores, Melrose Park, Ill., 1977—, acctg. mgr., 1980-85, fin. analyst, 1985—. Mem. Assn. M.B.A. Execs., Nat. Assn. Female Execs., Beta Gamma Sigma, Delta Mu Delta. Roman Catholic. Avocations: reading; ceramics; sports. Home: 5046 N Mason Ave Chicago IL 60630 Office: Jewel Food Stores 1955 W North Ave Melrose Park IL 60160

QUISENBERRY, SHARRON SUE, entomologist, educator; b. Kirksville, Mo., Apr. 19, 1945; d. Thomas Leonard and Bonnie P. (Hays) Grogan; B.S. (NSF and Regents scholar), N.E. Mo. State U., 1966; postgrad. Thiel Coll. (NSF scholar), 1972; M.A., Hood Coll., 1975; M.S., U. Mo., 1977, Ph.D., 1980; m. Larry D. Quisenberry, Oct. 10, 1965. Tchr. sci. high schs. Lewis County, Mo., 1966-67, Macon County, Mo., 1968-69, Prince George's County, Md., 1969-74; devel. specialist Research and Devel. Center for Cognitive Learning, U. Wis., Madison, 1974-75; asst. prof. entomology Iowa State U., Ames, 1980-82; asst. prof. entomology La. State U., Baton Rouge, 1982-85, assoc. prof., 1985—. Recipient Leonard Haseman Recognition award U. Mo., 1979. Mem. Am. Registry Profl. Entomols., Entomol. Soc. Am., AAAS, Sigma Xi, Delta Sigma Gamma. Subject editor: Jour. Entomol. Soc. Contbr. articles to entomol. jours. Office: Dept of Entymology 418 Life Science Bldg 70803 Louisiana State Univ Baton Rouge LA 70803

RABB, ALLYN THOMAS, nurse; b. Birmingham, Ala., July 1, 1951; d. Joseph Hugh and Barbara Eileen (Dorough) Thomas; m. Neven Rabb, Sept. 18, 1982. A.A. in Nursing, Jefferson State Coll., Birmingham, 1981; B.S. in Psychology cum laude, Birmingham-So. Coll., 1985, postgrad., 1985—. R.N., Ala. Nurse Brookwood Med. Ctr., Birmingham, 1982-83, 83-84, Bapt. Med. Ctr.-Montclair, Birmingham, 1984—; nurse Children's Hosp., Birmingham, 1983, research asst., 1985—. Mem. Psi Chi. Democrat. Episcopalian. Avocations: horseback riding; photography; writing. Home: 131 E Hawthorne Rd Birmingham AL 35209 Office: Bapt Med Ctr-Montclair 800 Montclair Rd Birmingham AL 35213

RABENOLD, KATHRYN TUTTLE, missionary, pianist, public accountant; b. Burlington Boro, Pa., Apr. 21, 1907; d. Clay F. and Mae Elsie (Beach) Tuttle; student public schs., Sayre, Pa., courses Internat. Accts. Soc., Pa. State U.; m. LeRoy M. Cook, Dec. 26, 1929 (dec. June 1953); children—Doris Anne (Mrs. Thomas P. Knapp), William LeRoy; m. 2d, Clarence R. Rabenold, Sept. 19, 1959 (dec. June 1971). Bookkeeper, Merritt Plumbing Shop, Waverly, N.Y., 1923-26; clk.-stenographer Ingersoll-Rand Co., Athens, Pa., 1926-29; payroll clk. Perfection Laundry, Sayre, 1930; partner with husband in acctg. office, Athens, 1937-53; owner, operator Cook Acctg. Service, Athens, 1953-69; public acct. with H. E. Weller, Athens, 1969-77; pianist with Patsy Prescott, gospel singer, 1977—. Telephone counselor Trinity Broadcasting Assn., Phoenix. Enrolled to practice before IRS. Mem. Nat., Pa. socs. public accts., Nat. Soc. Tax Cons. (life). Mem. Assembly of God Ch. Home: 6500 W Glendale Ave Sp 49 Glendale AZ 85301

RABINOVICH, MARCELLE, consulting speech pathologist/audiologist; b. N.Y.C., Aug. 21, 1927; d. David and Berthe (Laber) Michaelson; m. Lester Schuster, Mar. 16, 1951 (div. Feb. 1978); children—Jamie, Adrienne, Matthew, Daniel; m. Joseph Rabinovich, Mar. 2, 1978. Premed. student NYU, 1944-48; B.A. in Acting/Theatre, Adelphi U., 1969; M.S. in speech and Hearing, L.I. U., 1973. Educator, speech pathologist VA, Northport, N.Y., 1969-73; tchr. Nassau County Jail, East Meadow, N.Y., 1967-73; speech pathologist Mt. Sinai Hosp., N.Y.C., 1970-80; tchr. N.Y.C. Pub. Schs., 1980—; cons. speech pathology, N.Y.C., 1980—. Author: Sharpen Your Tongue, 1982, Cooking, 1985. Mem. Aux. Police-Mounted, Manhattan, 1976-78; tchr. CAP, 1941-42, U.S. Army Anti-Aircraft Command, N.Y.C., 1943-45. Mem. Nat. Assn. Female Execs., Nat. Bd. Movie Rev., Internat. Acad. Preventive Medicine. Republican. Jewish. Club: Turf and Field (Jamaic, N.Y.). Avocations: tennis; singing; dancing; horses; painting; sculpture.

RABINOWITZ, AIJA SOLVEIGA GABLIKS, association executive; b. Newark, Nov. 7, 1958; d. Maigonis and Ausma Velta (Oss) Gabliks; m. Stuart Alan Rabinowitz, Oct. 12, 1980; children—Aaron, Adam, Amanda. B.S.M.E., Tufts U., 1980; M.B.A., Georgetown U., 1986. Engring. asst. U.S. Army C.E., Waltham, Mass., 1977-79; mech. engr. Raytheon Co., Bedford, Mass., 1979, design and devel. engr., Wayland, Mass., 1982-84; task mgr. systems div. AVCO, Wilmington, Mass., 1980-82; asst. to mktg. dir. ARC, Washington, 1985—. Mem. ASME (chmn. women and minorities com. 1983-84, Outstanding Accomplishments award 1980), AIAA (bd. dirs. New Eng. sect. 1982-84, sect. chmn. career environment com. 1983-84, sect. co-chmn. program 1982-83, Service Excellence award 1980), Nat. Assn. Female Execs., Assn. M.B.A. Execs. Lutheran. Avocations: gourmet cooking; reading; athletics. Home: 5820 Osceola Rd Bethesda MD 20816 Office: ARC Hdqrs 1750 E St NW Washington DC 20006

RABINOWITZ, REBECCA SUSAN, psychotherapist; b. N.Y.C., Jan. 19, 1953; d. Bernard and Ann Hoch (Kubie) R.; A.B. in Sociology, Washington U., St. Louis, 1975, M.S.W. (Comprehensive Care Corp. fellow), George Warren Brown Sch. Social Work, 1977; cert. Rutgers U. Summer Sch. Alcohol Studies, 1979; m. Frank M. Calabrese, June 7, 1981. Chief psychiat. social worker alcohol treatment program Inst. Psychiatry, Northwestern Meml. Hosp., Chgo., 1977-78; exec. adminstr., spl. health cons. Atlantic Chem. Corp., Nutley, N.J., 1978-79; asst. to dir. Madeleine Borg Counseling Services, N.Y.C., 1980-81; chief therapist/asst. program coordinator CAREUNIT, Buena Park, Calif., 1981-82; pvt. practice psychotherapy, cons. alcohol, Montclair, N.J., 1979—; exec. dir. N.J. Alcoholism Assn., 1982—; dir. pub. relations Jersey City Med. Center, 1983—; social work instr. Northwestern U. Med. Sch., 1978; condr. alcoholism in-service workshops. Active in numerous polit. campaigns, local, and nat.; active in local N.J. tenants rights movements. Cert. social worker, Ill. Mem. Nat. Assn. Social Workers, Acad. Cert. Social Workers, Am. Soc. Hosp. Pub. Relations, N.J. Hosp. Pub. Relations Assn., Hudson County C. of C., Am. Soc. Profl. and Exec. Women, Am. Public Health Assn., Alumni-Parents Assn. Washington U. (local coordinator).

RABURN, JOSEPHINE, librarian, educator; b. Norman, Okla., Dec. 6, 1929; d. Albert E. and Josephine D. (Hudson) Riling; m. James Winston Raburn, Sept. 29, 1950; children—Catherine Anne Heller, Dora Lynn Greenleaf. B.S., U. Okla., 1950, M.L.S., 1964, Ph.D., 1981. Library asst. Spl. Services, Ft. Sill, Okla., 1962-63, reference, adminstrv. librarian, 1964-66; reference and circulation librarian Morris Sweatt Tech. Library, 1966-67; spl. instr. U. Okla. Sch. Library Sci., 1966-67; reference librarian Cameron A&M Jr. Coll., 1967-68; instr. Cameron U., Lawton, Okla., 1968-72, asst. prof., 1972-81, assoc. prof., 1981-85, prof., 1985—, dept. chmn., 1982-83, head lang. arts div., 1983—; trustee Lawton Pub. Library, pres. bd., 1973-76, also systems analyst; adv. com. library tech. asst. program Rose State Coll., Oklahoma City, 1986-88; cons. in field. Mem. mammography bd. Meml. Hosp., 1979-81, sec., 1979-80. Recipient Disting. Faculty award Cameron U., 1976; Helen Olander scholar, 1979. Mem. ALA, Okla. Library Assn. (sec. Sequoyah Children's Book award com. 1985-86), Okla. Orgn. Ednl. Tech., Assn. Ednl. Communications and Tech., Adolescent Lit. Assn., AAUW, Friends of Library, Beta Phi Mu (pres. Lambda chpt. 1973), Phi Kappa Phi, Delta Kappa Gamma (pres. Xi chpt. 1986-88), Alpha Delta Kappa. Democrat. Methodist. Contbr. articles to profl. jours., chpts. to books, presentations in library sci. Home: 511 NW 40th St Lawton OK 73505 Office: Cameron U Lawton OK 73505

RABY, PATSY SHARP, educator; b. Huntsville, Ala., Apr. 3, 1942; d. Hearvie Lee and Edna Lynette (League) Sharp; m. Tommy Mirrel Raby, Apr. 28, 1961; 1 child, Tommy Mirrel. B.S.E., Athens Coll., Ala., 1967; M.A., Ala. A&M Coll., 1975. Tchr., instructional leader Madison County Bd. Edn., Huntsville, 1962-85, Harvest Sch., Ala., 1985—. Mem. Madison County Edn. Assn. (bd. dirs. 1977-82), Ala. Edn. Assn., NEA, Madison County Prins. Assn., Assn. Supervision and Curriculum Devel. Democrat. Baptist. Avocations: traveling; hiking; farming. Home: McKee Rd Route 2 Box 338 Toney AL 35773 Office: Harvest Sch Harvest AL 35749

RACE, CHARLEEN HEINISCH, biology educator, computer science educator; b. Lakewood, Ohio, Nov. 3, 1949; d. Charles Frank and Evelyn M. (Bufe) Heinisch; m. Norman Glenn Adams, July 27, 1974 (div. June 1980); 1 child, Julie.; m. John Merton Race, Sept. 12, 1980; 1 child, Cory. B.S. in Secondary Edn., Kent State U., 1972. Cert. tchr. biol. scis. Tchr., Akron Schs., Ohio, 1973-83, Kent City Schs., Ohio, 1984—; community educator Townhall II Helpline, Kent, 1983-84. Producer, dir. Miss Portage County Scholarship pageant, Miss Am., 1978; state judge Miss Ohio local pageants, 1976; advisor United Youth Fellowship United Ch. of Christ, Kent, 1984, tchr. confirmation class, 1985; leader Brownie Troop, Kent council Girl Scouts U.S., 1982; advisor Booster Club Kent, 1984—; group leader Community Intervention, Kent., 1983—. Named Miss Ohio World Pageant Orgn., 1970. Mem. Kent Edn. Sddn., Kent Tchrs. Assn., Kent Community Intervention, Alpha Gamma Delta (v.p. 1969-71). Democrat. Avocations: bird watching; downhill skiing. Home: 6262 Martency Ave Kent OH 44240 Office: Kent City Schs 1400 N Mantua Kent OH 44240

RACHELS, PATRICIA PRITCHETT, museum administrator; b. Fort Benning, Ga., Aug. 14, 1924; d. Clifton Augustine and Elsie May (Freedenburg) Pritchett; m. Thomas Blackstone Rachels, Jr., Aug. 1, 1953 (div.); children—Mallory Anne, Leslie Pritchett. B.A. in Math., Vassar Coll., 1945. Ballistician, Nat. Bur. Standards, Washington, 1945-47; statis. analyst Hawaiian Econ. Found., Honolulu, 1948-50; sec. Sec. Air. Force, Pentagon, Washington, 1950-54; tchr. math. Riverview and PREW Schs., Sarasota, Fla., 1969-73; prodn. mgr. Siesta Key Pelican, Sarasota, 1976-78; gen. mgr. Fla. West Coast Symphony, Sarasota, 1978-79; mus. dir. Selby Bot. Gardens, Sarasota, 1983—. Camping and crafts instr. Gulf Coast council Girl Scouts U.S., 1970-73; water safety instr. ARC, Sarasota, 1969-79; vol. Ringling Mus. Children's Carnival, Sarasota, 1967-74; bd. dirs. Fla. Ballet Co., Sarasota, 1980—. Acad. and Fine Arts scholar, 1942-45. Mem. S.E. Museums Conf., Ringling Museums, AAUW. Avocations: water sports; tennis; travel; reading.

RACICOT, JANETTE MARIE, digital equipment company executive; b. Cambridge, Mass., Apr. 17, 1953; d. Albert Joseph and Marie Irnee (Villirilli) Racicot Monahan; m. Robert Todd Buerschaper, Nov. 1, 1981. B.S., Boston Coll., 1975, M.B.A, 1979. Customer account rep. Interactive Scis., Braintree, Mass., 1975-77; research analyst Boston Coll., Chestnut Hill, Mass., 1977-79; cons. H & P Assocs., Chestnut Hill, 1977-79; mgmt. cons. Digital Equipment Corp., Maynard, Mass., 1979-81, mgr. mgmt. scis., Stow, Mass., 1981-83, mktg. scis. mgr., Marlboro, Mass., 1983—; mem. mktg. faculty Boston Coll. Evening Coll., 1979-81. Mem. Am. Mktg. Assn. Democrat. Roman Catholic. Avocation: piano; aerobics; cycling; cooking; reading. Home: 10 Eliot Rd Belmont MA 02178 Office: Digital Equipment Corp Iron Way Marlboro MA 01752

RACITI, DOMENICA GRACE, publishing company executive; b. N.Y.C., June 2, 1928; d. Joseph and Marie (DiBiase) Raciti. B.Ed., SUNY-New Paltz, 1948; M.Ed., Columbia U., 1953, profl. diploma, 1956. Tchr. 1st grade, White Plains, N.Y., 1948-53; remedial reading tchr., Bogota, N.J., 1953-55; reading specialist Bd. Coop. Ednl. Services, White Plains, 1955-63; lang. arts cons. Northeastern U.S., 1963-65; nat. curriculum coordinator Am. Book Co., 1965-68, dir. mktg. services, N.Y.C., 1968-70, exec. editor lang. arts, 1970-73, v.p., dir. mktg., 1973-75; v.p., gen. mgr. for reading and lang. arts Houghton Mifflin Co., Boston, 1975-81, v.p., editorial dir. langs., 1981—. Mem. Internat. Reading Assn., Nat. Council Tchrs. English. Office: Houghton-Mifflin Co 1 Beacon St Boston MA 02108

RACY, JANET LOUISE, retail fashion executive; b. Bklyn., Jan. 3, 1952; d. Albert John and Louise Elsie (Bressmer) R. A.A.S., Fashion Inst. Tech., 1973; B.A., Queens Coll., 1977; M.A., NYU, 1978. Designer Rivets, N.Y.C., 1973-74, Goulder Co., N.Y.C., 1974-75; free-lance designer, cons. fashion, N.Y.C., 1973-82; fashion coordinator Assoc. Dry Goods, N.Y.C., 1978-82, fashion dir., 1982—; mktg. dir. Gear Inc., N.Y.C., 1982; cons. NYU, 1977—, lectr. fashion merchandising and design, 1977—, adj. prof. fashion merchandising, 1978—. Recipient Community Service award NYU, 1978, Spl. Recognition award Distributive Edn. Clubs Am., 1983; Tobé scholar Inst. Retail Mgmt., NYU, 1977. Mem. Fashion Group, Fashion Rountable, Met. Mus. Art. Contbg. editor Textile Fabrics and their Selection. Office: Assoc Dry Goods 417 Fifth Ave New York NY 10016

RAD, RITA MARIA, counties administrator, consultant; b. Havana, Cuba, Nov. 27, 1949; d. Severo Jose and Hilda Margarita (Hernandez) Chica; m. Jesus Salomon Rad, Sept. 14, 1974; children—Stephanie Anne, Andrea Victoria. Cert. achievement Fla. Computer Coll., 1970; A.A., Miami Dade Community Coll., 1972; B.A. in Psychology, Fla. Internat. U., 1974, M.P.A., 1982. Screening specialist Dade County Pub. Schs., Miami, Fla., 1974-76; tchr. Francisco Baldor Sch., Miami, 1976-77; social service worker State of Fla., Miami, 1977-79, counselor, 1979-80, mental health cons., 1980-82; fiscal dir. Dade-Monroe Mental Health Bd., Miami, 1982-83; rehab. cons. Conservco, Ft. Lauderdale, Fla., 1984—. Mem. Fla. Internat. U. Student Alumni Assn., Hist. Mus. So. Fla., Nat. Assn. Female Execs. Zool. Soc. Fla. Republican. Roman Catholic. Office: Conservco 150 S Pine Island Rd Plantation FL 33324

RADER, DEBORAH EARLY, nurse, educator, consultant; b. Morristown, Tenn., Sept. 1, 1952; d. James W. and Aileen (Courtney) Early; m. Francis Howard Rader, Aug. 22, 1981. B.S.N., East Tenn. State U., 1974; M.S.N., U. Tenn., 1981. Nurse, Doctors Hosp., Morristown, Tenn., 1974-76; family nurse practioner Bogard Primary Clinic, Cosby, Tenn., 1977-79; nursing instr. Walters State Community Coll., Morristown, 1980—; emergency room nursing cons., 1983—; expert witness Tenn. Senate subcom. on nurse practioners, 1978. Mem. Tenn. Primary Care Assn., Phi Kappa Phi, Sigma Theta Tau. Republican. Baptist. Office: Walters State Community Coll Morristown TN 37814

RADFORD, NANCY ARSENAUX, steel equipment company executive; b. Smyrna, Ga., Feb. 12, 1946; d. Nolan J. and Lois A. Arsenaux; m. Edward W. Radford, Sept. 7, 1968; children—Tracey A., Shannon A. B.S., Ga. Coll., 1968. Vice-pres., saleswoman South-Radford, Newnan, Ga., 1981-82; v.p. Radford Equipment Co., Lilburn, Ga., 1982—. Club: Buford Woman's (pres. 1980-81, 84-85), Ga. Fedn. Women's Clubs (safety chmn. 1984-86). Office: Radford Equipment Co 449 Pleasant Hill Rd Lilburn GA 30247

RADFORD, NANCY GREER, drug abuse treatment center executive; b. Asheville, N.C., July 14, 1953; d. Plato Whittington and Zella (Graham) Greer. B.A., Appalachian State U., 1975; M.Criminal Justice, U. S.C., 1978. Grad. asst. Appalachian State U., Boone, N.C., 1974, coordinator, 1975-76; grad. asst. U. S.C., Columbia, 1976-77; rehab. assoc. S.C. Dept. Corrections, Columbia, 1979-81; residential dir. River Region Human Services, Jacksonville, Fla., 1982-85, clin. dir., 1985—; cons. in field; com. mem. Acad. of Criminal Justice Scis., Columbia, 1976-77. Com. mem. Duval County Sch. Bd. Jacksonville, 1985—, chmn. com., 1985—. Mem. Nat. Assn. Female Execs., Am. Correctional Assn., Fla. Alcohol and Drug Abuse Assn. (bd. dirs.). Democrat. Baptist. Club: Upbeat. Avocations: singing; reading; horticulture; photography. Home: 931 LaSalle St Jacksonville FL 32207 Office: River Region Human Services Inc 1045 Riverside Ave #300 Jacksonville FL 32204

RADICE, ANNE IMELDA, museum director; b. Buffalo, Feb. 29, 1948; d. Lawrence J. and Anne Imelda (Marino) R. A.B., Wheaton Coll., 1969; M.A., Villa Schi Fanoia, Florence, Italy, 1972; Ph.D., U. N.C., 1976; M.B.A., Am. U., 1984. Asst. curator, staff lectr. Nat. Gallery Art, Washington, 1972-76; archtl. historian U.S. Capitol, Washington, 1976-80, curator, 1980-85; dir. Nat. Mus. Women in Arts, Washington, 1985—. Office: Nat Mus Women in the Arts 4590 Mac Arthur Blvd NW Washington DC 20007

RADIN, LAURA LEVINE, state official; b. N.Y.C., Aug. 24, 1944; d. Samuel Archie and Ray (Tessler) L; m. Kalman David Radin, June 15, 1965 (div. 1972). B.S., CCNY, 1965; M.A., Columbia U., 1978. Employment interviewer N.Y. State Dept. Labor, N.Y.C., 1965-67, vocat. counselor, 1967-70, supervising interviewer, 1970-76, employement security mgr., 1976-80; environ. programs specialist Port Authority of N.Y. and N.J., Weehawken, N.J., 1984, hazardous materials specialist, 1984, asst. mgr. Lincoln Tunnel, 1984—. Co-author: Creativity: A Human Resource, 1984. Mem. Women's Equity-Port Authority N.Y. and N.J., Women's Transp. Sem., City Coll. Alumni Assn. Bronx High Sch. Sci. Alumni Assn. Democrat. Jewish. Avocations: piano playing; tennis; skiing; travel. Office: Port Authority NY and NJ Lincoln Tunnel Off 500 JF Kennedy Blvd East Weehawken NJ 07087

RADLAUER, PATRICIA THOMASINE, designer; b. N.Y.C., Feb. 15, 1940; d. John Joseph and Lucinda Mary (Hinphy) McLoughlin; m. David Max Radlauer, Oct. 6, 1959; children—Mark Alfred, Daniel John. Student Plaza Bus. Sch., 1956-57, New Sch. Social Research, 1957, Palau Studios, 1968-70, Suffolk Community Coll., 1970-72. Legal sec. Giamo & Nicolossi, N.Y.C., 1958, exec. sec. World Wide Auto Corp., N.Y.C., 1956-59; advt. and display Sterns, N.Y.C., 1959-62; pres. Interiors by Patricia, Greenlawn, N.Y., 1967—; designer Designers Showcase, Nassau County, 1981-82. Committeeman Suffolk County Liberal Party, 1975. Mem. Am. Soc. Interior Designers (assoc.), Nat. Assn. Women in Constrn. Office: Interiors by Patricia 52 Broadway Greenlawn NY 11740

RADLEY, VIRGINIA LOUISE, educational administrator; b. Marion, N.Y., Aug. 12, 1927; d. Howard James and Lula (Ferris) R. B.A., Russell Sage Coll., 1949, L.H.D., 1981; M.A., U. Rochester, 1952; M.S., Syracuse U., 1957, Ph.D., 1958. Instr. English Chatham (Va.) Hall, 1952-55; asst. dean students, asst. prof. English Goucher Coll., 1957-59; dean freshmen, asst. prof. English Russell Sage Coll., 1959-60, assoc. dean, assoc. prof. English, 1960-61, prof. chmn. dept., 1961-69; dean coll., prof. English Nazareth Coll., Rochester, N.Y., 1969-73; provost for undergrad. edn., central adminstrn. State U. N.Y., Albany, 1973-74; exec. v.p., provost Coll. Arts and Scis., State U. N.Y., Oswego, 1974-76, acting pres., 1976-78, pres., 1978—; vis. prof. Syracuse U., summer 1957-59, Nazareth Coll., summer 1965; cons. N.Y. State Dept. Edn.; Chmn. commn. on women Am. Council on Edn., 1978-81; mem. commn. on higher edn. Middle States Assn., 1979—. Author: Samuel Taylor Coleridge, 1966, Elizabeth Barrett Browning, 1972, also articles. Mem. MLA (chmn. regional sect. Romanticisn 1969), English Inst., Pi Lambda Theta. Republican. Home: Shady Shore SUNY Oswego NY 13126

RADLO, MARJORIE RUTH, software company executive; b. Boston, Aug. 16, 1956; d. Jason Lester and Irene (Frank) Radlo; m. Behrouz S. Zandi, Sept. 1, 1985. B.A., U. Vt., 1978; M.B.A., Northeastern U., 1983. Sales rep. Metromedia, N.Y.C., 1980-81; internat. sales rep. Data Gen., Westboro, Mass., 1983-84; sales, computer staff A.B. Dick Co., Santa Clara, Calif., 1984-85; regional sales mgr. Marc Software Internat., Palo Alto, Calif., 1985—. Contbr. article to profl. jour. Mem. Assn. Exec. Saleswomen, Am. Mktg. Assn., Assn. M.B.A. Execs., Am. Mgmt. Assn., Sunnyvale C. of C., Sunnyvale Women in Bus. Jewish. Club: Sales Strategy and Mgmt. Group (San Jose). Avocations: Swimming; sailing; reading; films; travel. Home: 7439 Stanford Pl Cupertino CA 95014 Office: Marc Software Internat 260 Sheridan Ave Palo Alto CA 94306

RADMACHER, CAMILLE J., librarian; b. Monmouth, Ill., Apr. 14, 1917; d. Harry M. and Esther (Greenleaf) R.; student Monmouth Coll., 1935-37. With adult dept. Warren County Library, Monmouth, 1937-48, head county librarian, 1948—, exec. dir. Western Ill. Library System, 1965-82; exec. dir. Nat. Library Week in State of Ill., 1959. Mem. Monmouth Coll. Community Concert Lecture Bd., 1967-72; mem. adv. com. Ill. State Library, 1962-72. Mem. Ill. Library Assn. (Ill. Librarian Citation award 1967), Women's Nat. Book Assn., DAR. Methodist. Clubs: Order Eastern Star, Altrusa (treas. 1968-69, dir. 1978-80). Office: 60-62 Public Sq Monmouth IL 61462

RADS, DEBRA ANN, insurance agency executive; b. Berwyn, Ill., May 19, 1957; d. Raymond E. and Eleanore M. (Gersch) R. Student MacCormac Coll., 1975; Assoc. in Underwriting, Ins. Sch. of Chgo., 1981. Ins. rater INA, Chgo., 1976-78, underwriter trainee, 1978-79; underwriter AIG, Chgo., 1979-81; sr. underwriter Royal Ins. Co., Chgo., 1981-83; spl. ins. programs mgr. Frank A. Cramsie, Oak Brook Terrace, Ill., 1983—; instr. Chgo. Bd. Underwriters, 1981-85. Vol. Westchester Park Dist., Ill., 1983-84; income devel. chmn. Am. Cancer Soc., Westchester, 1980—. Mem. Nat. Assn. Ins. Women (edn. chmn. 1984-85, cert. 1985), Nat. Assn. Female Execs. Republican. Roman Catholic. Avocations: needlework; dance; reading; collecting miniatures. Home: 1933 Burns Westchester IL 60153

RAE, SALLY ANN, educational administrator; b. Long Beach, Calif., Feb. 25, 1958; d. Clayton Carol and Ann Carol (Giorlando) Fullenwider; m. Scott Bothic Rae, May 6, 1984. B.A. in Communications, Pepperdine U., 1980. Asst. dir. admissions Pepperdine U., 1980-83, assoc. dir. admissions, 1983—, chairperson academic scholarship com., 1980—. Mem. Pepperdine Univ. Alumni Bd., Malibu, Calif., 1982—; chairperson Pepperdine Univ. Young Alumni, Malibu, 1983—; mem. Fedn. Republican Women, Los Angeles, 1984. Mem. Tex. Assn. Coll. Admissions Counselors, Western Assn. Coll. Admissions Counselors. Republican. Home: 19241 Weymouth Ln Huntington Beach CA 92646 Office: Pepperdine University Admissions Office 24255 Pacific Coast Hwy Malibu CA 90265

RAEBER, SANDI L., financial executive; b. St. Louis, July 24, 1949; d. George Leslie and Arline Erna (Hoffman) Hartupee; m. John Arthur Raeber, Aug. 16, 1969. A.A., Jefferson Coll., 1969; A.B., Washington U., St. Louis, 1975, M.B.A. with honors, 1980. Sec. market research Doane Agrl. Service, St. Louis, 1969-70; sec. Washington U. Sch. Law, St. Louis, 1970-75, registrar, 1975-79; fin. mgr. Pacific Fruit Express, San Francisco, 1981-83; fin. mgr. John A. Raeber, AIA, CSI, San Francisco, 1983—; conf. lectr. Design Build Automation, Los Angeles, 1983-84. Mem. Phi Theta Kappa, Beta Gamma Sigma. Home: 428 43d Ave San Francisco CA 94121 Office: John A Raeber AIA CSI 519 Teresita Blvd San Francisco CA 94127

RAEDER, MYRNA SHARON, law educator, lawyer; b. N.Y.C., Feb. 4, 1947; d. Samuel and Estelle (Auslander) R.; m. Terry Oliver Kelly, July 13, 1975; 1 child, Thomas Oliver. B.A., Hunter Coll., 1968; J.D., NYU, 1971; LL.M., Georgetown U., 1975. Bar: N.Y. 1972, D.C. 1972, Calif. 1972. Spl. asst. U.S. atty. U.S. Atty.'s Office, Washington, 1972-73; asst. prof. U. San Francisco Sch. Law, 1973-75; assoc. O'Melveny & Myers, Los Angeles, 1975-79; assoc. prof. Southwestern U. Sch. Law, Los Angeles, 1979-82, prof., 1983—. Prettyman fellow Georgetown Law Ctr., Washington, 1971-73. Mem. ABA, Assn. Am. Law Schs. (com. on sects. 1984—, chairperson women in legal edn. sect. 1982), Order of Coif, Phi Beta Kappa. Office: Southwestern U Sch Law 675 S Westmoreland Los Angeles CA 90005

RAEFSKY, BARBARA LYONS, librarian; b. Phila., Nov. 27; d. Morris T. and Ethel (Belostosky) Lyons; m. Manuel Raefsky, Sept. 7, 1958; children—Lisa Marta, Jessica Hope. A.B. with honors, U. Pa., 1957; M.S.L.S., Drexel U., 1958. Librarian, Bushrod Library, Phila., 1958-59; jr. reference librarian Temple U., Phila., 1959-60; substitute tchr. Cherry Hill, (N.J.) Pub. Schs., 1975-79, 80-81; librarian Heritage Jr. High Sch., 1979-80; librarian Doane Acad., Saint Mary's Hall, Burlington N.J., 1981-82, dir. library services, 1982—. Active Cherry Hill PTA, 1966-81, Brownies, Girl Scouts U.S.A., 1972-78. Mem. ALA, Am. Assn. Sch. Librarians, N.J. Library Assn. (publs. com.), AAUW, LWV (publs. chmn. br. 1977-79), Am. Assn. Sch. Librarians. Home: 2 Cherry Tree Ln Cherry Hill NJ 08002 Office: St Mary's Hall/Doane Acad Riverbank St Burlington NJ 08016

RAFAELS, DIANE, marketing director; b. Kingsport, Tenn., Aug. 7, 1940; d. John Claude and Sarah Katherine (Piety) Catron; m. David Michael Deans, Oct. 25, 1957 (div. Sept. 1975) children—Juliana Susan, Leslie Gloria; m. Umberto Rafaels, July 6, 1985. A.A., Sullins Coll., Bristol, Va., 1959. Cert. mktg. dir. Assoc. account exec. Ehrich-Manes Advt., Bethesda, Md., 1974-76; asst. mall mgr. Kettler Bros., Gaithersburg, Md., 1976-79; mktg. dir. Farber Co., Pompano Beach, Fla., 1979-80, Springfield Mall, Va., 1980-83; communications mgr. MD-IPA, Rockville, Md., 1983; dir. mktg. Chas. E. Smith Cos., Arlington, Va., 1983—; mem. adv. bd., dir. MD-IPA, Rockville; cons., Publicity & Media Resources, Falls Church, Va. Contbr. articles to profl. jours. and mags. Chmn. communications com. Fairfax County Arts Council, Va., 1982-83; publicity com. Internat. Children's Festival-Wolftrap, Vienna, Va., 1982-83. Recipient Vol. Recognition awards Fairfax County Fire Dept., 1983, N. Va. Lung Assn., 1983, United Way, 1982-83. Mem. Internat. Council Shopping Ctrs., Women in Advt. and Mktg., Washington Ad Club, Fairfax County C. of C. (communications com. 1981-84), Arlington County C. of C. (communications com. 1984-85), Montgomery County C. of C. (communications com. 1983). Democrat. Methodist. Clubs: Jr. Women's of Rockville (pres. 1972-73), Jr. Clubs (Md. state dir. 1974-76), Contemporary (v.p. 1984—). Avocations: tennis; reading; needlework; health club. Office: Chas E Smith Cos 1735 Jeff Davis Hwy Arlington VA 22202

RAFFERTY, GENEVIEVE KENNEDY, social service agy. adminstr.; b. Davenport, Iowa, Jan. 21, 1922; d. Thomas Cyril and Mabel Veronica (Finefield) Kennedy; B.A., St. Ambrose Coll., 1942; postgrad. U. Iowa, 1972; m. Daniel J. Rafferty, Aug. 22, 1942; children—Daniel D., Michele M., Genevieve, Thomas K., Eileen M., Margaret M., Sheila M. Real estate saleswoman Manhard Realty, Moline, Ill., 1950-59; substitute tchr., Rock Island, Ill., 1963-67; head start tchr. Rock Island-Scott County Dept. Social Services, 1966; public welfare worker Scott County Dept. Social Services, Davenport, Iowa, 1967-72, exec. dir. Info., Referral and Assistance Service, Rock Island, 1972—; chair Rock Island Housing Authority; mem. Quad-City Council on Crime and Delinquency, 1977-80; mem. Rock Island County Council on Alcoholism, 1976-82; chairperson CETA Adv. Bd., 1982—; bd. dirs. Quint-City Drug Abuse. Named Social Worker of Yr. Quad-City, Nat Assn. Social Workers, 1973. Mem. Nat. Assn. Social Workers, Iowa Council Info. and Referral Providers, Nat. Conf. Social Welfare, Ill. Welfare Assn., NOW, Ill. Alliance Info. and Referral Services (dir.). Republican. Roman Catholic. Office: 2002 3d Ave Rock Island IL 61201

RAGAN, BARBARA MARY, television and theatre producer, financial management and real estate company executive; b. Toledo, Ohio, Feb. 27, 1949; d. Robert Charles and Edith Lucy (Mahoney) R. B.A., Cath. U. Am., 1971; M.B.A., NYU, 1986. Producer, assoc. producer Broadway/Regional Theatre, 1974-77; asst. gen. mgr. Alexander H. Cohen Prodns., N.Y., 1977-79, acct. pub. Livingston Wachtell & Co., C.P.A.'s, N.Y., 1979-82; mgr. theatre programming RCTV-Entertainment Channel, N.Y., 1982-83; controller Ornstein Orgn., N.Y., 1983-85; v.p., exec. producer Candico Prodns., Inc. N.Y.C., 19—; adv. bd. Actors Studio, N.Y.; controller N.Y. Women in Film, N.Y., 1984—; cons. Cable TV Studies, 1976—. Contbr. articles to profl. jours. Intern U.S. House Reps., Washington, 1967-68; conferee White House Conf. on Conservation and Natural Beauty, Washington, 1967; mem. U.S. State Dept. Tour of Europe, 1970-71. Recipient Ohio Conservationist award Ohio Forestry Assn., 1967. Nat. Merit Found. scholar 1967-71. Mem. Dramatists Guild, N.Y. Acad. TV Arts and Scis. Avocation: music. Home: 60 E 9 St New York NY 10003

RAGAN, ELIZABETH HOFFMAN, retired business executive; b. Albemarle, N.C., Nov. 11, 1916; d. Joseph Filson and Lilly Bassett (Carter) Hoffman; cert. bus. adminstrn. High Point Coll., 1937; m. Herbert Tomlinson Ragan, Oct. 14, 1939; 1 son, Herbert Tomlinson. Head bond dept. Sunflower Ordnance Works, Hercules Powder Co., DeSota, Kans., 1942-45; sec.-treas. Ragan-Carmichael, Inc., High Point, N.C., 1956-74, Staple Products, Inc., High Point, 1956-74, R & C Holding Co., Inc., High Point, 1956-74, sec. Ragan Hardware Co., Inc. (merger), High Point, 1974-82; trustee Ragan-Hardware, Inc., Profit Sharing Trust and Pension Trust, 1974-82. Cellist, N.C. Symphony, 1932-35. Mem. adv. bd. Maryfield Nursing Home, 1975-79; bd. visitors High Point Coll., 1979-82; mem. exec. bd. Friends of Guilford Coll. Library, 1980-82. Democrat. Mem. Soc. of Friends (organist, choir dir.), High Point Hist. Soc. (dir. 1977-81, pres. 1979-80). Author, compiler: The Lineage of the Amos Ragan Family, 1976. Home: 201 Lake Drive East Thomasville NC 27360

RAGLAND, ALWINE MULHEARN, lawyer, judge; b. Monroe, La., July 28, 1913; d. Peter Sherlock and Alwine Louise Johanna (Peters) Mulhearn; A.A., Principia Coll., 1932; J.D., Tulane U., 1935; m. LeRoy Smith, 1947 (dec. 1971); children—LeRoy, Caroline Smith Christman; m. 2d, L. Percy Ragland. Admitted to La. bar, 1935; individual practice law, Tallulah, La., 1935-72; partner firm Mulhearn & Smith, Tallulah, 1972-74; spl. asst. atty. gen. La., 1954; atty. for inheritance tax Coll. La., 1965-73; town atty., Delta, La., 1973-74; judge 16th Jud. Dist., Lake Providence, La., 1974—, 2d Circuit Ct. Appeals, Shreveport, 1976; former pres. Smith Abstract Co., Inc. Active Silver Waters council Girl Scouts U.S.A., 1938-64, dist. dir., 1964; den mother Cub Scouts Am., 1956-57; pres. Band Boosters, 1964-65, PTA, 1965-66; mem. jud. bd. Delta Christian Sch., 1967-74. Mem. Am. Bar Assn., 6th Jud. Dist. Bar Assn. (pres. 1945), La. Bar Assn., Am. Judicature Soc., Am. Judges Assn., La. Judges Assn., Nat. Council Juvenile Ct. Judges, La. Council Juvenile Ct. Judges, So. Juvenile Ct. Judges, Assn. Trial Lawyers Am., La. Trial Lawyers Assn., Family Conciliation Cts. and Services, Nat. Juvenile Ct. Service Assn., La. Conf. Social Welfare, Practicing Law Inst. Methodist. Clubs: Lake Providence Ladies Golf and Tennis, Madison Parish Book. Index editor Tulane Law Rev. Bd., 1932-35. Home: PO Box 392 Lake Providence LA 71254 Office: Court House Bldg PO Box 392 Lake Providence LA 71254

RAGNO, NANCY LOUISE NICKELL, educational writer; b. Phila., Sept. 2, 1938; d. Paul Eugene and Sara Jane (Mensch) Nickell; m. Joseph D. Ragno, Aug. 25, 1960; 1 dau., Michelle. B.A., Lebanon Valley Coll., 1960; M.A., NYU, 1968. Cert. tchr., N.J. Editor, writer Harcourt Brace, N.Y.C., 1968-70;

free-lance ednl. writer, Millington, N.J., 1970-72; sr. editor Silver Burdett Co., Morristown, N.J., 1972-76; editor/writer Houghton Mifflin, Boston, 1976-77; sr. editor J. B. Lippincott Co., Phila., 1977-79; free-lance ednl. writer, Westfield, N.J., 1979—. Author films: The City and the Modern Writer, 1970; Hear It and Write, 1971; Buying on the Installment Plan, 1974; author textbook series: Silver Burdett English, 1984. Bassoonist Harrisburg Symphony Orch. (Pa.), 1959, Plainfield Symphony Orch. (N.J.), 1976, Somerset County Symphony Orch., Somerset, N.J., 1984—, Colonia Woodwind Quintet (N.J.), 1984—. Mem. Nat. Council Tchrs. English, Internat. Reading Assn., Assn. Supervision and Curriculum Devel., Network of Writing-Across-the-Curriculum Program. Democrat. Congregationalist. Home: 36 Dunbar Dr Robbinsville NJ 08691

RAGNONI, MARY CATHERINE, nurse; b. West Hartford, Conn., May 24, 1962; d. Daniel Frank and Eileen Marie (Sheehy) R. B.S., U. Conn., 1984. R. N., Conn. Nurse Hartford Hosp., Conn., 1984—. Mem. council Jimmy Fund Council, Conn. chpt., 1984-85. Mem. Oncology Nursing Soc., Sigma Theta Tau, Phi Kappa Phi, Alpha Lambda Delta. Republican. Roman Catholic.

RAGSDALE, SUSAN ELLEN HOPKIN, lawyer; b. N.Y.C., Sept. 22, 1947; d. Timothy Main and Mary Ann (Menucci) Hopkin; m. James Alan Ragsdale, June 12, 1976. B.A. with high honors Fla. Internat. U., 1976; J.D., U. Colo., 1980. Bar: Colo. 1980. Law clk. to judge U.S. Bankruptcy Ct., Denver, 1980-81; assoc. Gorsuch, Kirgis, Campbell, Walker & Grover, Denver, 1981-83, Davis Graham & Stubbs, Denver, 1983—. Mem. ABA (bus. bankruptcy com. 1983-84), Colo. Bar Assn., Denver Bar Assn. Democrat. Roman Catholic. Home: 3165 Endicott Dr Boulder CO 80303 Office: Davis Graham & Stubbs 370 17th St Suite 4700 PO Box 185 Denver CO 80201

RAGUSA, JOAN, compensation excutive; b. Paterson, N.J., Apr. 28, 1953; d. Joseph and Lucy (LaMacchia) R.; m. John Francis Naudts, Mar. 28, 1980. B.Communications, William Paterson Coll., 1974, M.Counseling, 1980; cert. in indsl./organizational psychology Bloomfield Coll., 1984. Customer service rep. Beattie Mfg., Little Falls, N.J., 1976-78; employment asst. S. B. Thomas, Inc., Totowa, N.J., 1978-80, supr. personnel adminstrn., 1980-82, mgr. recruiting, 1982-85, compensation adminstr., 1985—; cons. Hubschmitt Assocs./Indsl. Psychologists, Totowa, N.J., 1982-85; assoc., Bus. and Profl. Services/Writing Service, Franklin Lakes, N.J., 1982—; lectr. Passaic County Coll. Career Series, Paterson, N.J., 1981-82; workshop leader Montclair State Coll. Community Services, Montclair, N.J., 1981. Telephone counselor William Paterson Coll. Helpline, Wayne, N.J., 1974-79. Mem. Am. Soc. Personnel Adminstrs., Am. Compensation Assn. Office: SB Thomas Inc 930 N Riverview Dr Totowa NJ 07512

RAHBAR, ZITA INA, health insurance executive; b. Kaunas, Lithuania, Mar. 15, 1937; came to U.S. 1949; d. Stasys and Ona (Eitkeviciute) Carneckas; m. Vytautas Dudenas, June 20, 1960 (div. 1965); m. 2d, Darius Rahbar, Mar. 26, 1970. B.A. St. Xavier Coll., Chgo., 1957; postgrad. in physiology U. Chgo., 1957-59, M.B.A., 1978. Mng. editor Lyons & Carnahan div. Meredith Corp., Chgo., 1960-68, mgr. program planning, 1968-73; exec. cons. George S. May Co., Chgo., 1973-75; sr. cons. planning Blue Shield Assn., Chgo., 1975-76, dir. corp. planning Blue Shield/Blue Cross Assn., 1976-78, sr. dir. program devel. and implementation, 1978-81, v.p. mktg. Blue Cross Calif., Los Angeles and Oakland, Calif., 1981—. Bd. dirs. Bethune Ballet, Los Angeles, 1982—; mem. com. Orgn. Women Execs., Los Angeles, 1982—; co-founder Women in Pub., Chgo., 1965; mem. NOW, Town Hall Calif., Chgo. Council Fgn. Relations, World Affairs Council Los Angeles. Fellow U. Chgo., 1957-58. Mem. Am. Mgmt. Assn., Am. Mktg. Assn., AAAS, Republican. Roman Catholic. Home: 912 Blue Spring Dr Westlake Village CA 91361

RAHDERT, ELIZABETH ROSE QUANZ, clinical pharmacist, clin. psychologist; b. Evanston, Ill., May 13, 1935; d. Carl Peter and Josephine Anne (Kirk) Quanz; student Albert Ludwigs Universitat, Freiburg, W.Ger., 1955-56; B.S. in pharmacy, Purdue U., 1958, M.S. in Psychology, 1975, Ph.D. in Psychology (David Ross fellow), 1980; m. June 7, 1958 (div. 1982); children—David A., Diana M. Research pharmacologist asst. in biomed. research Dow Chem. Co., Indpls., 1959-61; asst. dir. spl. edn. Greater Lafayette (Ind.) Area Spl. Services, 1976-77; psychology intern VA Hosp., Danville, Ill., 1979-80; asst. prof. clin. pharmacy Purdue U., 1980—; clin. psychopharmacologist treatment research br. Div. Clin. Research, Nat. Inst. Drug Abuse, Rockville, Md., 1985—. Bd. dirs. Family Service Agy., Tippecanoe County, Ind., 1971-75; bd. dirs. Tippecanoe County Youth Services Bur., 1973-76, pres. bd., 1974-76. Mem. Am. Psychol. Assn., Ind. Psychol. Assn., Am. Pharm. Assn., Ind. Pharmacists Assn., Am. Soc. Hosp. Pharmacists, Ind. Soc. Hosp. Pharmacists, Am. Assn. Colls. Pharmacy, AAUW, Kappa Epsilon. Office: Div Clin Research Nat Inst on Drug Abuse 5600 Fishers Ln Rockville MD 20857

RAHEEL, MASTURA, textile scientist, educator; b. Lahore, Pakistan, Mar. 1, 1938; d. Sultan Mohamad and Firdous Dean; M.S., Punjab U., 1959, Okla. State U., 1962; Ph.D., U. Minn., 1971; m. Akbar Javed Raheel, Jan. 25, 1959; children—Seemal, Salman. Asst. prof., head dept. textiles and clothing Home Econs. Coll., Lahore, Pakistan, 1960-77; lectr. textiles and clothing U. Minn., 1977-78; vis. prof. Ind. U., Bloomington, 1978; asst. prof. textile sci. U. Ill., Urbana, 1978-84, assoc. prof., 1984—. Ford. Found. fellow, 1960-62, 68-71, research award grantee, 1979—. Mem. Am. Coll. Profs. Textiles and Clothing, Am. Assn. Textile Chemists and Colorists, Am. Home Econs. Assn., Coll. International de L'enseignement Textile, Omicron Nu, Sigma Xi. Contbr. research articles to profl. and tech. jours. Home: 1904 S Vine St Urbana IL 61801 Office: 239 Bevier Hall U Ill Urbana IL 61801

RAHM, KAREN ELIZABETH LANE, business executive; b. Bklyn., Apr. 21, 1944; d. Gilbert H. and Joan Elizabeth (Dean) Lane, Jr.; A.A., Packer Collegiate Inst., 1962; B.A. magna cum laude, Allegheny Coll., 1964; M.A., Ind. U., 1966; m. Carl Michael Rahm, Feb. 3, 1968; 1 son, Christopher Michael. Economist, Fed. Res. Bank of N.Y., 1966-70; planning devel. officer Econ. Devel. Adminstrn., Seattle, 1970-71; successively urban economist, asst. dir. econ. devel., dir. econ. devel. Seattle Dept. Community Devel., 1971-77; mgr. planning div. King County, Seattle, 1977-81; dir. Wash. State Planning and Community Affairs Agy., Olympia, 1981-83; sec. Wash. State Dept. Social and Health Services, 1983-85; sr. dir. portfolio devel. Glacier Park Co. subs. Burlington No., Inc., Seattle, 1986—; mem. Wash. Corrections Standards Bd., 1981-83; mem. Wash. State Housing Fin. Commn., 1983, Wash. State Adv. Commn. on Intergovtl. Relations, 1982-84. Mem. Seattle Bd. Freeholders, 1974-75, Wash. Commn. Constl. Alternatives, 1976; chmn. Nat. Leadership Conf. Women Execs. in State Govt., 1985. Mem. Council State Community Affairs Agys. (sec. 1983), LWV, Lambda Alpha. Office: 1011 Western Ave Seattle WA 98104

RAHMING, ANN SMITH, insurance company executive; b. Lawrence, Mass., Oct. 16, 1936; d. Harold and Myrtle Florence (Kidd) Smith; m. John Christopher Rahming, June 12, 1959 (div. 1974); children—Charles W., Jennifer A.; m. Thomas A. Greene, Aug. 11, 1984. B.S. in Edn., Mass. Coll. Art, 1958. Cert. tchr., Mass., Calif. Supr., Athol-Royalston Regional Sch., Athol, Mass., 1958-59; tchr. various schs., San Diego, London, Quincy, Mass., Buenos Aires, Argentina, 1961-74; sales rep. Loyal Protective, Boston, 1974-76; sales rep. Sun Life of Can., Boston, 1976-78; dir. State Mut. of Am., Worcester, Mass., 1978—. Exhibited tapestry designs Art Show, Lowell U., 1977. Mem. New Eng. Tng. Dirs. Assn. (pres.), Nat. Assn. Ins. Women, Worcester Life Underwriters Assn., Nat. Assn. Exec. Females, Am. Bus. Women's Assn. Home: 220 Nesmith St Lowell MA 01852 Office: State Mut of Am 440 Lincoln St Worcester MA 01605

RAICHE, DOROTHY MARGARET WILLCUTT, educator; b. Springfield, Mass., Nov. 19, 1948; d. Leonard Royal and Dorothy Margaret (Bradley) Willcutt; m. Donald Philippe Raiche, July 14, 1973. B.S. in Edn., Westfield State Coll., 1970, M. Edn., 1983. Cert. adminstr., spl. edn., elem. tchr., prin., tchr. children with moderate spl. needs. Tchr. spl. edn. Monson Pub. Schs., Mass., 1970-78; ednl. adminstr. Avalon Schs., Inc., Lenox, Mass., 1978-85; dir. edn. Hillcrest Ednl. Ctrs., Inc., Lenox, 1985; spl. edn. tchr. Berkshire Children's Community, Great Barrington, Mass., 1985—. Mem. Nat. Assn. Female Execs., Inc., Mass. Elem. Sch. Prins. Assn., Nat. Assn. Elem. Prins., Council for Exceptional Children, Berkshire County Bd. Realtors, Mass. Assn. Realtors, Nat. Assn. Realtors, Nat. Soc. Children and Adults with Autism. Roman Catholic. Avocations: travel, cooking. Home: PO Box 791 Lenox MA 01240-0791 Office: Berkshire Children's Community Learning Ctr 465 S Main St Great Barrington MA 01230

RAIDY, CHERIE SPENCE, lawyer; b. Kansas City, Mo., June 10, 1956; d. Emil Gene and Carol (Austin) Rigg; m. John Edmond Raidy, Oct. 17, 1981. A.B. in Polit. Sci. magna cum laude, U. So. Calif., 1978; J.D., Southwestern U. Law, Los Angeles, 1981. Bar: Calif. 1981, U.S. Dist. Ct. (cen. dist.) Calif. 1982. Sole practice, Pasadena, Calif., 1981-82; corp. counsel Transam. Fin. Corp., Los Angeles, 1982—. Mem. Southwestern Affiliates, Los Angeles County Bar Assn. (co-chmn. Pasadena Law Day 1982—), ABA, Women Lawyers Los Angeles, Jr. Trojan Aux., Themis Soc. Office: Transamerica Financial Corp 1150 S Olive St Suite 2033 Los Angeles CA 90015

RAIMONDO, BEVERLY NICKELL, data processing company executive; b. Lexington, Ky., Feb. 24, 1946; d. William Rice and Frances Louise (Jinkins) Nickell; m. Anthony Neal Raimondo, Apr. 24, 1976; 1 child, Christa Nickell. B.A. in Edn., U. Ky., 1968, M.S.L.S., 1969; postgrad. Xavier U., 1974-78. Librarian, IBM Corp., Lexington, 1969-75, edn. coordinator, 1975-79, mgr., 1979-81, project mgr., 1982-84, adminstrv. asst., 1984—; seminar instr. U. Ky. Community Edn., Lexington, 1981-83. Co-chmn., March of Dimes Mother's March, Lexington, 1984; mem. Fayette County Schs. task force for excellence in edn., 1984-85; mem. Blue Grass Trust for Historic Preservation, 1981—, Leadership Lexington, 1983-84; bd. dirs. Lexington Children's Theatre, 1985—. Recipient IBM IPD Achievement award, 1982. Mem. Profl. Women's Forum, Ky. Library Assn., U. Ky. Alumni Assn., Beta Phi Mu (pres. 1974). Republican. Christian Science. Clubs: Cotillion, Spindletop Hall. Avocations: boating; reading; spectator sports. Home: 1327 Strawberry Ln Lexington KY 40502

RAINE, SUE ANN STROMBOE, management and bank training consulting firm executive; b. New Orleans, Sept. 20, 1940; d. Frances Albert and Nicolina (Nicola) Stromboe; m. Thomas Randolph Raine, July 20, 1968 (div. Feb. 1985); children—Deanne Marie, Robyn Aleen. Student pub. schs., San Antonio. Sec. Frost Nat. Bank, San Antonio, 1957-60, sec., adviser, 1961-66, tng. coordinator, 1966-69, tng. coordinator S.W. Bancshares, Houston, 1970-72; tng. dir. Federated Capital Corp., Houston, 1973-75; cons., pres. Raine Cons., Woodlands, Tex., and Austin, Tex., 1976—. Developer numerous tng. programs. Contbr. numerous articles to profl. jours. Mem. Am. Soc. Tng. and Devel. (pres. Houston chpt. 1975-76, chpt. Excellence award 1975, nat. Highest Membership award 1975, nat. Torch award 1975), Internat. Transactional Analysis Assn. Republican. Roman Catholic.

RAINES, JOAN BINDER, literary agent; b. N.Y.C., July 25, 1931; d. Samuel Lawrence and Shirley (Cooper) Binder; student Columbia U.; m. Theron Raines, July 29, 1971; 1 son, Keith B. Korman. Office mgr. Raines Agy., N.Y.C., 1968, agt., 1969—, ptnr., 1974—. Contbr. articles to N.Y. Daily News Sunday Mag., St. Anthony Messenger. Mem. Soc. Authors' Reps., Authors Guild (assoc.). Jewish. Office: 71 Park Ave New York NY 10016

RAINES, JO-ANN RYAN, real estate salesperson, management consultant; b. N.Y.C., June 4, 1948; d. James Henry Ryan and Vevette Yvonne (Morales) Ryan Lewis; m. Rudolf Lawrence Raines, June 14, 1980; children—Aisha, Dana, Felicia. B.A. in Social Scis., St. John's U., Jamaica, N.Y., 1969; M.A. in Adult Edn. Columbia, U., 1976; cert. in mktg. and mgmt. Trenton State Coll., 1984. Lic. in real estate sales, N.J. Ednl. cons. N.Y. Telephone, N.Y.C., 1969-76; staff mgr. AT&T, Bedminster, N.J., 1976-84; real estate salesperson Bea M. Scott Realty, East Orange, N.J., 1985—; career cons., South Orange, N.J., 1985—. Mem. South Orange/Maplewood Awareness Council, 1982—; bd. dirs. Gardens Nursery Sch., N.Y.C., 1978-81, Assn. Retarded Citizens for Essex County, N.J., 1983—. Mem. Nat. Assn. Female Execs., Nat. Assn. Realtors, Phi Delta Kappa, Sigma Delta Pi, Delta Sigma Theta (v.p. chpt. 1968-69). Democrat. Roman Catholic. Avocations: reading; aerobics; travel. Home: 357 Irving Ave South Orange NJ 07079 Office: Bea M Scott Realty Inc 617A Central Ave East Orange NJ 07017

RAINEY, HELEN KAY, city official; b. Ft. Worth, Jan. 18, 1946; d. Paschal Lee and Ester Katherine (Williams) Godbey; m. Billy King Rainey, Nov. 29, 1975; children—Tammy Denise Black, Shelly Rae Ramos. A.S. in Applied Sci., Tarrant County Jr. Coll., 1985; student North Tex. State U., 1986—. Cert. mcpl. clk., Tex. peace officer. Ct. clk. City of Ft. Worth, 1966-68; transcriber for ct. reporters, Dallas and Tarrant Counties, 1970-75; sec. City of Euless Police Dept., Tex., 1975-81; city sec. Euless, 1981—; speaker, instr. police report writing Tex. A&M U., Tarrant County Jr. Coll. Police Acad., 1979-81; speaker IBM, various computer groups, Tex., Calif., 1983—, N. Tex. State U. Ctr. for Community Services, Denton, 1984—. Recipient Disting. Service awards Euless Police Dept., 1976, 79. Mem. Internat. Inst. Mcpl. Clks. Advanced Acad. (com. on technol. devel. 1984-86), Assn. City Secs. and Clks. Tex., N. Tex. City Secs. Assn. (pres. 1986). Methodist. Avocations: reading; hiking. Home: 21 Stonegate Dr Bedford TX 76022 Office: Euless City Hall 210 N Ector Dr Euless TX 76039-3595

RAINEY, PATRICIA ANN, counselor, writer; b. Dover, N.H., Oct. 14, 1937; d. Wilbur Robert and Helen Mary (Keddy) R.; B.A., U. N.H., 1960, M.Ed., 1967, C.A.G.S., 1976; postgrad. U. Maine, 1967, George Peabody Coll., 1968. Grad. asst., Ford Found. grantee U. N.H., Dover, 1960-61, lecture asst., 1973-74, writer, also Centrex office, 1974—; counselor Renew Counseling Center, Rye, N.H., 1977-82; co-founder, clin. dir. Green Pastures Counseling Assocs., 1982—; tchr. social studies Colebrook (N.H.) Acad., 1961-65; counselor Exeter (N.H.) High Sch., 1965-66, Newport (N.H.) High Sch., 1966-68; asst. prof. psychology Cleveland (Tenn.) State Community Coll., 1968-72. Recipient creative teaching award A.B. Dick Co., 1970. Author: Illusions: A Journey into Perception, 1973; contbr. articles to profl. publs. Home: 173 Mount Vernon St Dover NH 03820

RAINS, MARY JO, banker; b. Konawa, Okla., Oct. 27, 1935; d. Albert Wood and Mary Leona (Winfield) Starns; student Okla. Sch. Banking, 1969, Seminole Jr. Coll., 1970-72, E. Central State U., 1978-79; diploma Am. Inst. Banking, 1981, 83; m. Billy Z. Rains, June 17, 1956; 1 son, Nicky Z. Accounting div. Universal C.I.T., Oklahoma City, 1953-56; cashier Okla. State Bank, Konawa, 1957—, now sr. v.p. Sec., 1st Baptist Ch., Konawa, 1969-79, mem. budgeting com., 1982—. Mem. Okla. Bankers Assn. (dir. women's div. 1974-76), Konawa C. of C., Am. Legion. Club: Order Eastern Star. Home: Route 2 Box 26 Konawa OK 74849 Office: PO Box 156 Konawa OK 74849

RAINS, PATRICIA JANE, learning handicapped educator; b. Portland, Oreg., Mar. 26, 1934; d. Lawrence Marion and Mary Leticia (Roberts) R. A.B. in Edn., Cascade Coll., 1960; B.A. in Elem. Edn., Portland State U., 1962. Cert. tchr. Tchr. Lynch Sch. Dist. 28, Portland, Oreg., 1960-70; tchr. high sch. learning ctr. Tillamook Edn. Service Dist., Oreg., 1970-79, Nehalem Learning Ctr., 1979—, teaching asst. physically handicapped breathing exercises sch. dist. 56, Nehalem, 1983-86; vol. adult tutor Portland Community Coll., 1969-70. Author: Land Series Program, 1957-86. Active Sweet Adelines; pres. Wesleyan Fellowship, Tillamook. Summer sch. scholar, Tillamook Ednl. Service and Oreg. State Dept., 1971. Mem. NEA, Tillamook Edn. Tchrs. Assn. (del., pres. 1970-86), Oreg. Ednl. Assn. (del. 1960-86), Council of Exceptional Children, Nat. Assn. Female Execs., Oreg. Sheriff's Assn. (hon.). Republican. Club: Internat. Tng. in Communication (pres. council 2, 1979). Avocations: travel; bowling; handicrafts; singing; teaching Sunday Sch. kindergarten. Home: PO Box 122 Netarts OR 97143 Office: Nehalem Lower Elementary Sch PO Box 190 Nehalem OR 97131

RAJAGOPAL, SHAKUNTALA, pathologist; b. Kerala, India, Oct. 1, 1940; d. K.V. and Retnamma (Pillai) Sivaraam; grad. Womens Coll., Trivandrum, Kerala, 1956; M.B., B.S., Med. Coll., Trivandrum, 1963; m. K.G. Rajagopal, Jan. 21, 1963; children—Devi, Nimmi, Molly. Resident in pathology West Suburban Hosp., Oak Park, Ill., 1964-69; pathologist, dir. labs., Westlake Community Hosp., Melrose Park, Ill., 1970—; demonstrator in pathology Northwestern U. Med. Sch., Chgo., 1967-75; med. dir. Triton Coll., 1972—; mem. AIDS task force Met. Health Care Council Chgo. Troup leader Girl Scouts U.S.A., 1978-79. Fellow Coll. Am. Pathologists, Am. Soc. Clin. Pathologists (continuing med. edn. award); mem. AMA, Chgo. Med. Soc. (continuing med. edn. com. 1986—), Am. Assn. Blood Banks, Am. Cancer Soc., Kerala Assn. Chgo. (pres. women's aux. 1977-79; v.p. 1980-81, sec. 1984). Hindu. Clubs: The Right; Woodfield Racquet. Home: 1868 Prestwick Dr Palatine IL 60067 Office: 1225 Superior St Melrose Park IL 60160

RAJDEO, HEENA PRANLAL, surgeon; b. Bombay, India, Aug. 16, 1947; came to U.S., 1976; d. Pranlal Vithal das Rajdev and Sushila Shivlal Gosalia. M.B., B.S., U. Bombay, 1969, M.Surgery, 1972. Diplomate Am. Bd. Surgery. Resident gen., plastic, thoracic and orthopedic surgery K.E.M. Hosp., Bombay, 1969-74, tutor in surgery, 1974-75, asst. prof. surgery, 1975-77; resident surgery N.Y. Med. Coll., Valhalla, N.Y., 1978-82, spl. trainee gastrointestinal endoscopy Lincoln Hosp.-N.Y. Med. Coll., 1982; instr. surgery N.Y. Med. Coll., 1982, asst. prof., 1984; asst. attending surgeon Westchester County Med. Center, Valhalla, 1982—, cons. surgeon, surg. clinic, correctional health services, 1983—; asst. attending surgeon Met. Hosp. Center, N.Y.C., 1982—, Lincoln Hosp. Med. Center, 1982—. Contbr. articles to med. jours. Univ. Merit scholar U. Bombay, 1969-70. Fellow Royal Coll. Surgeons Can., A.C.S.; mem. Surg. Soc. of N.Y. Med. Coll., Westchester County Med. Soc., N.Y. State Med. Soc., Soc. Am. Gastrointestinal Endoscopic Surgeons, Assn. Surgeons Indian Origin, Am. Soc. Gastrointestinal Endoscopy. Home: 21 Powder Horn Way Tarrytown NY 10591 Office: Faculty Practice Munger Pavillion Westchester County Med Center Valhalla NY 10595

RAJPAL, KAVITA ASHOK, emergency trauma physician, educator; b. Bombay, India, July 25, 1945; came to U.S., 1974; d. Sunderlal Harcharandas and Satyavati (Sunderlal) Puri; m. Ashok Jaikishen Rajpal, June 6, 1974; children—Ayesha, Nikhil. Student, Jaihind Coll., Bombay, 1962-64; B. Medicine and Surgery, Seth G. Med. Coll., Bombay, 1968; M. in Gen. Surgery, 1973; diploma in surgery, Strong Meml. Hosp., Rochester, N.Y., 1977. Resident in surgery to tutor in pediatric surgery K.E.M. Hosp., Bombay, 1968-74; sr. resident R2 level Strong Meml. Hosp., Rochester, 1975-77; emergency trauma physician, assoc. attending faculty mem. Rochester Gen. Hosp., 1977—. Contbr. articles to med. jours. Participant Indian Assn. of Rochester, Assn. of Indians in Am., India Community Center. Mem. Am. Contemporary Soc. Medicine and Surgery (assoc.), Royal Soc. Medicine London (affiliate). Hindu. Office: Rochester Gen Hosp 1425 Portland Ave Rochester NY 14621

RAKAY, DONNA JANE, musician; b. Delray, Mich., Mar. 16, 1943; d. Louis and Delilah Ann (Leadingham) R.; B.Mus.Edn., Eastern Mich. U., Ypsilanti, Mich., 1965, M.A., 1969. Mem. faculty Lincoln Park (Mich.) schs., 1965—, band dir., Lincoln Park High Sch. bands. Recipient various service awards. Mem. NEA, Mich. Edn. Assn., Mich. Parents, Tchrs. and Students Assn., Nat. Assn. Female Execs., AAUW, Mu Phi Epsilon. Home: 2958 Fort Park St Lincoln Park MI 48146 Office: 1701 Champaign St Lincoln Park MI 48146

RAKESTRAW, REBECCA JONES, clinical social worker; b. Greenville, S.C., Sept. 18, 1943; d. Joseph Clyde and Mildred Idel (Smith) Jones; children—Bryan Robert, Paige Allison, Brooke Lauren. B.A., Mercer U., 1979; M.S.W., U. Ga., 1981. Flight attendant Eastern Airlines, Boston, Atlanta, 1963-65, cons., 1982-83; social worker Ga. Regional Hosp., Atlanta, 1979-80; social worker South DeKalb Mental Health Ctr., Atlanta, 1980-81; therapist Peachtree Parkwood Hosp., Atlanta, 1981-82, aftercare coordinator, 1982-83; family program coordinator Substance Abuse Free Existence, Atlanta, 1983-84, program dir., 1984-85; pvt. practice clin. social work, Atlanta, 1985—; cons. City of Atlanta, Republic Airlines, 1983. Mem. Nat. Assn. Social Workers, Nat. Assn. Clin. Social Workers. Home: 2659 Smoketree Way NE Atlanta GA 30345 Office: 5825 Glenridge Dr Atlanta GA 30328

RAKHMAN, SUSAN ANN SMALL, surgical sciences educator, health facility administrator; b. Wilmington, Del., Apr. 30, 1949; d. Claude Wilbur and Judith Ann (Kolodzjiej) Small; m. Jacob J. Rakhman, May 3, 1981; children—Joshua Josef, Benjamin Baron. Diploma, St. Elizabeth's Hosp. Sch. of Nursing, Brighton, Mass., 1970. R.N.; cert. operating room nurse. Intensive care staff St. Elizabeth's Hosp., Brighton, 1970-71; staff nurse operating room Mass. Eye and Ear Infirmary, Boston, 1970-71; sr. staff nurse operating room, specialized in cardiovascular NYU Med. Ctr., N.Y.C., 1972-77; operating room supr. N.Y. Infirmary, N.Y.C., 1977-79; instr. surg. scis., operating room supr. N.Y. Coll. of Podiatric Medicine (affiliated with Foot Clinics N.Y.), N.Y.C.; lectr., cons. Am. Podiatry Assn. Clin. Conf., N.Y.C., 1984; Podiatric Research Ctr. and Skills Lab.; cons. on office procedures to podiatrists in pvt. practice; lectr. on laser safety in surgery N.Y. Coll. Podiatric Medicine. Contbr. articles to profl. jours.; contbr. Am. Poetry Anthology. Mem. Assn. Operating Rm. Nurses (voting del. ann. congress 4 yrs.), Am. Soc. Lasers in Medicine and Surgery. Democrat. Jewish. Home: 4901 Henry Hudson Pkwy Apt 5H Riverdale NY 10471 Office: N Y Coll Podiatric Medicine 53 E 124th St New York NY 10035

RAKOV, BARBARA STREEM, marketing executive; b. Bklyn., Jan. 4, 1946; d. Harold B. and Claire (Colbert) Streem; m. Harris J. Rakov, Nov. 20, 1970 (div. Mar. 1972). B.S., Boston U., 1967; postgrad. NYU, 1972-74. Market research analyst, product mgr., mktg. mgr. J.B. Williams, N.Y.C., 1967-77; mktg. mgr. Del Labs., Farmingdale, N.Y., 1977-78; product mgr., asst. to office of pres., dir. mktg. and sales Benelux countries, v.p., group mktg. dir. Joseph E. Seagram & Sons, N.Y.C., 1978—. Mem. L'Ordre des Coteaux de Champagne, Les Gastronomesde la Mer, Am. Mgmt. Assn. Avocations: tennis; skiing; squash; reading; water skiing. Home: 376 Shady Rest Dr Noyac NY 11963 Office: Seagram Distillers 375 Park Ave New York NY 10152

RAKOWSKI, BARBARA ANN, educator; b. Flint, Mich., Jan. 24, 1948; d. Casimir Anthony and Harriet Ann (Craft) R.; B.S., Central Mich. U., 1971, M.S., 1978. Tchr. langs. and scis. Sts. Peter and Paul Area High Sch., Saginaw, Mich., 1971-79, chmn. dept. fgn. langs., 1974-79; instr. high sch. program field studies Central Mich. U., Beaver Island, Mich., 1973-81; prin., tchr. Beaver Island Community Schs., 1979-84, also career edn. coordinator. Mem. Nat. Assn. Biology Tchrs., Mich. Elem. and Middle Sch. Prins. Assn., Mich. Assn. Secondary Adminstrs. mem. Byzantine Catholic Ch. Home: 1510 J Portabella Mount Pleasant MI 48858 Office: Sacred Heart Acad 316 E Michigan Mount Pleasant MI 48858

RAKOWSKI, FRANCES ELIZABETH, medical technologist; b. Plymouth, Pa., Apr. 24, 1932; d. Frank Albert and Mary Margaret (Rago) Rakowski. B.S. in Chemistry, Coll. Misericordia, Dallas, Pa., 1953; diploma in med. tech. Robert Packer Hosp., Sayre, Pa., 1954; M.B.A., Nat. U., 1980. Med. technologist hosps. in Pa. and Calif., 1954-61; materials engr. Convair/Astronautics, San Diego, 1961-62; chief med. technologist Coronado Hosp. (Calif.), 1962—; dir. ancillary services Copronado Hosp., Calif., 1984-86; mem. Calif. Clin. Lab. Tech. Adv. Com., 1986-89. Recipient Tribute to Women in Industry award YWCA, 1983. Mem. Am. Soc. Med. Tech., Am. Soc. Clin. Pathologists (assoc.), Calif. Assn. Med. Lab. Tech. (pres. 1972-73), Clin. Lab. Mgmt. Assn. Club: Soroptimist. Home: 5845 Friars Rd #1405 San Diego CA 92108 Office: Coronado Hosp Lab 250 Prospect Pl Coronado CA 92118

RAKOWSKI, SHARON SUSAN, hospital administrator, management educator; b. Chgo., Mar. 31, 1948; d. Stanley S. and Cecilia T. (Svientek) Rakowski; m. Michael A. Kozlowski, Apr. 12, 1975; 1 son, Kevin. B.A., DePaul U., Chgo., 1970, M.B.A., 1980; M.A., Northeastern Ill. U., Chgo., 1975. Accredited human resources profl. Personnel Accreditation Inst. Personnel generalist Am. Hosp. Supply, Evanston, Ill., 1973-76; wage and benefit mgr. St. Anne's Hosp., Chgo., 1976-80; personnel dir. Forkosh Meml. Hosp., Chgo., 1980-85; personnel dir. Mut. Trust Life Ins. Co., 1985—. Mem. DuPage Personnel Assn. (pres. 1979-81), Chgo. Hosp. Personnel Assn. (pres. 1983-84). Office: Mut Trust Life Ins Co 1200 Jorie Blvd Oak Brook IL 60521

RALSTON, CLARICE MCDUFFIE, nurse; b. Tampa, Fla., Feb. 11, 1932; d. Welbourne Clifton and Louise Teresa (Sellers) McDuffie; R.N. diploma Gordon Keller Sch. Nursing, 1953; m. William Kent Ralston, Mar. 12, 1954; children—Diana Lynn (dec.), Stephen Kent. Staff nurse Jackson Meml. Hosp., Miami, Fla., 1953-54, New Braunfels (Tex.) Gen. Hosp., 1954-55; nurse supr. Wichita Falls (Tex.) State Hosp., 1971—. Mem. Am. Nurses Assn. (cert. gerontol. nurse), Tex. Nurses Assn. (charter mem. continuing edn. program), Fla. State Student Nurses Assn. (charter), Tex. Pub. Employees Assn., Air Force Sgts. Assn. Aux. Am. Legion Aux. Democrat. Methodist. Club: Order Eastern Star. Research on hygiene for elderly patients. Home: 815 Preston St Burkburnett TX 76354 Office: Wichita Falls State Hosp PO Box 300 Wichita Falls TX 76307

RALSTON, JOANNE SMOOT, public relations counseling firm executive; b. Phoenix, May 13, 1939; d. A. Glen and Virginia Lee (Smoot); m. Joseph P. Ralston, May 13, 1972 (dec. June 1982). B.A. in Journalism, Ariz. State U., 1960. Reporter, The Ariz. Republic, Phoenix, 1960-62; co-owner, pub. relations dir. The Patton Agy., Phoenix, 1962-71; founder, pres., owner Joanne Ralston & Assocs., Inc., Phoenix, 1971—. Contbr. articles to profl. jours. Bd. dirs. Ariz. Parklands Found., 1984—, Gov.'s Council on Health, Phys. Fitness and Sports, 1984—; task force mem. Water and Natural Resources Council, Phoenix, 1984—; mem. issues com. Ariz. Republican Caucus, 1984—, others.

Recipient Lulu' awards, Los Angeles Advt. Women, 1964—; Gold Quill (2), Internat. Assn. Bus. Communicators, 1985; excellence awards Fin. World mag., 1982-84, others. Mem. Pub. Relations Soc. Am. (counselor sect.), Internat. Assn. Bus. Communicators, Phoenix Press Club (pres. bd.), Investor Relations Inst., Phoenix Met. C. of C. (bd. dirs. 1977-84, 85—). Republican. Clubs: Phoenix Country, Kiva, Phoenix City. Avocations: horses. Home: 8102 N 18th Way Phoenix AZ 85020 Office: Joanne Ralston & Assocs Inc 3003 N Central Ave Suite 1800 Phoenix AZ 85012

RAMANATHAN, ROHINI BALAKRISHNAN, banker; b. New Delhi, India, Nov. 4, 1952; came to U.S., 1972, naturalized, 1984; d. Mayuram Srinivasa Venkata and Gnanam (Sundaresan) Subramanian; m. Balakrishnan Ramanathan, July 4, 1977; children—Karthik, Shankar, Ashwin Kalyan. B.A. with honors, Jesus and Mary Coll., New Delhi, 1972; M.S., Federal City Coll., 1974; Ed.D., Boston U., 1979. Sr. media intern Federal City Coll., Washington, 1973-75; media specialist Fashion Inst. Tech., N.Y.C., 1979-80; sr. mgmt. cons. N.Y.C. Health and Hosps., 1981-82; mgr. computer based tng. Chem. Bank, N.Y.C., 1983—. Contbr. articles to profl. jours. Editor, broadcaster news programs. Bd. dirs. ethnic fellowships Queens Coll. Grad. Library Sch., N.Y., 1980-83. Trustee Carnatic Music Acad. of N.A., N.Y.C., 1979-80. Mem. Asian Indian Women in Am. (founder 1981, editor News 1981-83), Fedn. Indian Assns. (chmn. publicity 1980-82, v.p. N.Y.C. 1986-87), Bharathi Soc. (sec. 1979-80), Avocations: Vocal South Indian classical and other Indian light music; writing; sports. Home: 171 Harris Dr Oceanside NY 11572 Office: Chemical Bank 55 Water St Room 1130 New York NY 10041

RAMBO, SYLVIA H., federal judge; b. Royersford, Pa., Apr. 17, 1936; d. Granville and Hilda (Leonhardt) R.; A.B., Dickinson Coll., 1958; J.D., Dickinson Sch. Law, 1962; LL.D. (hon.), Wilson Coll., 1981; m. George F. Douglas, Jr., Aug. 1, 1970. With trust dept. Bank of Del., Wilmington, 1962-63; admitted to Pa. bar, 1963; pvt. practice law, Carlisle, Pa., 1963-76; pub. defender, Carlisle, 1974-76, chief pub. defender, 1976; judge Ct. Common Pleas, Carlisle, 1976-78; judge U.S. Dist. Ct. Middle Dist. Pa., Harrisburg, 1979—; asst. prof. law Dickinson Sch. Law, 1973-77. Named Alumnus of Yr., Dickinson Sch. Law, 1981. Mem. ABA, Pa. Bar Assn., Nat. Assn. Women Judges, Am. Judicature Soc., Phi Alpha Delta. Democrat. Presbyterian. Home: 399 Barnstable Rd Carlisle PA 17013 Office: PO Box 868 Federal Bldg Walnut St Harrisburg PA 17108

RAMELL, GUNILLA CHRISTINA, energy policy analyst; b. Gothenburg, Sweden, Apr. 23, 1946; came to U.S., 1966, naturalized, 1978; d. Victor K. A. and Alice Linnea (Hornberg) Ramell; B.A. summa cum laude, UCLA, 1970; M.A., Harvard U., 1974. Govt. relations analyst Atlantic Richfield Co., Los Angeles, 1974-77; communications program mgr. Internat. Paper Co., N.Y.C., 1977-78; public affairs specialist Indsl. Indemnity Co., San Francisco, 1978-80; sr. analyst Wholesale Rate Dept., Pacific Gas & Electric Co., San Francisco, 1980—; teaching fellow Harvard U., 1971-74. Mem. platform com. No. Calif. Democratic Party, 1981; United Way sponsored exec., 1982. Alfred P. Sloan Found. fellow, 1972; Washington internship fellow office of Sen. Charles E. Goodell. Mem. Calif. Soc. Mcpl. Fin. Officers, San Francisco Mcpl. Forum, Issues Mgmt. Assn. (founding), Swedish Women's Ednl. Assn. (bd. dirs. 1983-85). Republican. Club: Harvard of San Francisco (bd. dirs. 1982—), Harvard of N.Y.C. Home: 2323 Larkin St San Francisco CA 94109 Office: Pacific Gas and Electric 77 Beale St Room 1530 San Francisco CA 94106

RAMER, GLENNA MAE, lawyer; b. Nappanee, Ind., May 22, 1954; d. Nathan and Emma (Martin) Ramer. B.A., Eastern Mennonite Coll., 1977; J.D., Ind. U., 1980. Bar: Ind. 1980, Tenn. 1981, U.S. Dist. Ct. (ea. dist.) Tenn. 1981. Staff atty. S.E. Tenn. Legal Services, Cleveland, 1980-84; atty. Weill, Ellis, Weems & Copeland, Chattanooga, 1984—, Ellis, Copeland & Ramer, Chattanooga, 1984—; part-time instr. Cleveland (Tenn.) State Community Coll., 1982—. Mem. ABA, Tenn. Bar Assn., Am. Judicature Soc., Chattanooga Bar Assn., Bus. and Profl. Women's Orgn., Bradley County Bar Assn. Democrat. Mennonite. Home: 6302 Hixson Pike C 144 Hixson TN 37343 Office: Ellis Copeland & Ramer 3475 Brainerd Rd 11th Floor Chattanooga TN 37411

RAMEY, AVA LORRAINE, policewoman, detective; b. Northumberland County, Va., Mar. 21, 1951; d. Homer Albert and Marilyn Orenette (Corbin) Campbell; m. Kenneth Lee Howard, Apr. 5, 1972 (div. Mar. 1981); m. Randall Russell Ramey, Aug. 6, 1981; children—Ryan Randall, Robert Ryan. Student Radford Women's Coll., 1969-70, D.C. U., 1970-72, U. Md., 1974-76. Tour guide Landmark Services, Washington, 1970-71; store detective Hecht Co., Washington, 1971-72; policewoman, detective Washington Met. Police Dept., 1972—; owner, dir. Lord Mayor Acad., Capital Children's Mus., Washington, 1984—; owner Mattapony Video, specializing in children's videos, Md., 1986—. Author: (children's book) Tarsha, 1975. Served with USAR, 1977-80. Named among Top Ten Coll. Girls in Am., Glamour mag., 1969. Mem. Exec. Female, Black Women in Law Enforcement, Com. Police Parents (pres. 1983-84). Avocation: white water rafting. Office: Lord Mayor Acad 800 3d St NE Washington DC 20002

RAMEY, EVELYN ROSE, personnel director; b. Selma, N.C., Dec. 30, 1922; d. Needham Henry and Drucilla (Broadwell) Rose; m. Kenneth Franklin Ramey, Feb. 25, 1950; children—John Lanneau, Druscilla Elizabeth, Joseph Clayborn. A.A.S., Kings Bus. Coll., 1940; student U. Tenn., 1950-51, U. N.C., 1951-52, N.C. State U., 1955-56. Woman's editor Carolina Cooperator, Raleigh, 1960-61; editor Cary News (N.C.), 1967-68; writer Sta. WPTF, Raleigh, 1968-73, asst. program dir., 1973-80; mgr. office services Durham Life Broadcasting, 1980-81, personnel dir., 1981—. Mem. career planning and placement com. Coll.-Industry Cluster, St. Augustines Coll., 1982—, chmn. pub. relations com., 1983—; sec. Cary Arts Council, 1967-68; pres. Cary Woman's Club, 1967-68, Women of Ch., Cary Presbyn. Ch., 1960-62; sec. Capital Grange, Raleigh, 1953-54. Mem. Am. Soc. Personnel Adminstrs., Am. Women in Radio and TV (sec. 1976-78). Club: Cary Garden (pres.). Democrat. Presbyterian. Home: 622 Griffis St Cary NC 27511 Office: Durham Life Broadcasting Inc 410 S Salisbury St Raleigh NC 27602

RAMIRES, MANUELA FRANTISCA, recreation equipment manufacturing company executive; b. Chgo., Sept. 4, 1922; d. William Brown and Virgie Frantisca Juanita (Harmon) Jackson; m. Albert Arnell, Oct. 14, 1945 (div. 1960); children—Zachary, Lantz, Nicole; m. 2d John Martinez Ramires, 1963 (div. 1970); 1 son, Michael. M.S. in Mgmt., Lake Forest Advanced Mgmt. Inst., 1979. Sec. to pool supr. Brunswick Corp., Chgo., 1961-66, Compensation services supr., 1966-70, personnel supr., Oak Brook, Ill., 1970-71, mgr. employment, Skokie, Ill., 1971-73, dir. indsl. relations, 1973-79, dir. corp. affairs, 1979—. Bd. dirs. Ill. State Community Coll., 1984. Mem. Women in Govt. Relations (pres. 1984—), Assoc. Employers of Ill. (dir. 1979—), Bus. and Industry Fedn. Econ. Concern, Corp. Responsibility Group, Am. Soc. Personnel Adminstrs., Chgo. Area Pub. Affairs Group, Skokie C. of C., Chgo. C. of C., Ill. C. of C., U.S. C. of C. Independent. Unitarian. Office: Brunswick Corp One Brunswick Plaza Skokie IL 60077

RAMIREZ, AMALIA LOPEZ, employment security planner; b. Brownsville, Tex., May 2, 1943; d. Guadalupe and Domitila (Martinez) Lopez; children—Jessica Ann, Max Allen. Student Del Mar Coll., Corpus Christi, Tex., Tex. Southmost Coll., Brownsville. Exec. sec. Tex. Dem. Exec. Com., Austin, 1968-71; supr. unemployment ins. field services Tex. Employment Commn., Corpus Christi, 1971—. Mem. Internat. Assn. Personnel in Employment Security, Nat. Assn. Female Execs., Mex.-Am. Democrats, LWV, Interfaith. Roman Catholic. Home: 724B Simonetti St Austin TX 78748 Office: Tex Employment Commn TEC Bldg Austin TX 78778

RAMO, VIRGINIA M. SMITH, civic worker; b. Yonkers, N.Y.; d. Abraham Harold and Freda (Kasnetz) Smith; B.S. in Edn., U. So. Calif., D.H.L. (hon.), 1978; m. Simon Ramo; children—James Brian, Alan Martin. Nat. co-chmn. ann. giving U. So. Calif., 1968-70, vice chmn., trustee, 1971—, co-chmn. bd. councilors Sch. Performing Arts, 1975-76, co-chmn. bd. councilors Schs. Med. and Engring.; vice-chmn. bd. overseers Hebrew Union Coll., 1972-75; bd. dirs. The Muses of Calif. Mus. Sci. and industry, UCLA Affiliates, Estelle Doheny Eye Found., U. So. Calif. Sch. Medicine; adv. council Los Angeles County Heart Assn., chmn. com. to endow Chair in cardiology at U. So. Calif.; vice-chmn., bd. dirs. Friends of Library U. So. Calif.; bd. dirs., nat. pres. Achievement Rewards for Coll. Scientists Found., 1975-77; bd. dirs. Les Dames Los Angeles, Community TV So. Calif.; bd. dirs., v.p. Founders Los Angeles Music Center; v.p. Los Angeles Music Center Opera Assn.; v.p. corp. bd. United Way; v.p. Blue Ribbon-400 Performing Arts Council; chmn. com. to endow chair in gerontology U. So. Calif.; vice chmn. campaign Doheny Eye Inst., 1986. Recipient Service award Friends of Libraries, 1974; Nat. Community Service award Alpha Epsilon Phi, 1975; Disting. Service award Am. Heart Assn. 1978; Service award U. So. Calif.; Spl. award U. So. Calif. Music Alumni Assn., 1979; Life Achievement award Mannequins of Los Angeles Assistance League, 1979; Woman of Yr. award PanHellenic Assn., 1981; Disting. Service award U. So. Calif. Sch. Medicine, 1981; U. So. Calif. Town and Gown Recognition award, 1986; Asa V. Call Achievement award U. So. Calif., 1986; Phi Kappa Phi scholarship award U. So. Calif., 1986. Mem. UCLA Med. Aux., U. So. Calif. Pres.'s Circle, Commerce Assos. U. So. Calif., Cedars of Lebanon Hosp. Women's Guild (dir. 1967-68).

RAMON, SHARON JOSEPHINE, personnel management executive; b. Chgo., Nov. 8, 1947; d. Edward Albert and Helen Josephine (Tomasziewski) Mazur; m. Kevin John Ramon, Aug. 4, 1979. B.A., U. Ill.-Chicago, 1969. Caseworker, ct. aide Social Service Dept. of Cir. Ct. Cook County, Chgo., 1969-71; investigator aide U.S. Civil Service Commn., Chgo., 1971-72, personnel staffing specialist, 1972-74, personnel mgmt. specialist, 1974-80; mgmt. cons. U.S. Office Personnel Mgmt., Chgo., 1980-82, personnel mgmt. specialist, 1982-83, personnel staffing specialist, 1983—. Recipient Certs. of Spl. Achievement, U.S. Office Personnel Mgmt., 1980, Cert. of Appreciation, 1981. Mem. Nat. Assn. Female Execs., AAUW. Roman Catholic. Office: US Office Personnel Mgmt 230 S Dearborn Chicago IL 60604

RAMOS, MARY LUZ, army officer; b. Humacao, P.R., Nov. 22, 1952; came to U.S., 1953; d. Victoriano and Andrea (Diaz) Ramos. B.A., Iona Coll., 1975.; M.Adminstrn., Central Mich. U., 1986. Social work aide McMahon Sheltr, N.Y.C., 1975-76; commd. pvt. U.S. Army, 1978, advanced through grades to capt., 1983; personnel mgr., phys. security asst. Fort Meade, Md., 1980-84; company comdr., Fort Lee, Va., 1984-86; chief personnel Kenner Army Community Hosp., Fort Lee, 1986—. Avocations: Drawing; painting; singing.

RAMSBURG, HELEN HARRIS, microbiologist; b. Miami, Fla., Oct. 29, 1925; d. William Henry and Naomi Catharine (Shafer) Harris; A.B. in Biology, Hood Coll., 1947. M.A. in Environ. Biology, 1982; postgrad. U. Md., 1956-60; m. Staley William Ramsburg, Sept. 7, 1946; 1 dau. Cassandra Lee Duncan; foster dau., Angela Andrea Fry. Lab. technician Frederick (Md.) Meml. Hosp., 1947-48; biol. aide NIH, Bethesda, Md., 1948-50; med. biology technician med. unit., Ft. Detrick, Frederick, Md., 1957-59; bacteriologist U.S. Army Research Inst. Infectious Diseases, Ft. Detrick, 1959-62, microbiologist, 1962—. Recipient Spl. Act and Service award, 1964. Lutheran. Co-author profl. articles. Home: 9201 Dublin Rd Walkersville MD 21793 Office: Virology Div US Army Research Inst Infectious Diseases Fort Detrick Frederick MD 21701

RAMSEY, CAROL A., roofing executive; b. Oceanside, N.Y., Nov. 6, 1942; d. Harry P. and Florence L. (Pollard) Trevithick; m. Edward J. Burke, Dec. 23, 1962 (div. 1972); children—Deborah A., Diane C.; m. 2nd Glenn H. Ramsey, June 28, 1985. Student Eastland Vocat., 1986. Sec. Chase Manhattan Bank, N.Y.C., 1960-63; warranty adminstr. Dynamit Nobel Am., Rockleigh, N.J., 1973-85; sec./treas. Ramsey & Assocs., Gahanna, Ohio, 1985—. Registrar Bergen County Council Girl Scouts U.S., Harrington Park, N.J., 1973-74, leader, 1974-77. Avocations: winter skiing; aerobics; gardening. Home and Office: 591 Knights Ave Gahanna OH 43230

RAMSEY, DONNA MOORE, med. technologist, educator; b. Toledo, Jan. 13, 1941; d. Wendle Adolphus and Thelma Grace (Wilson) Moore; B.S. in Zoology, Ohio U., Athens, 1962; diploma med. tech., Mercy Hosp., Toledo, 1963; M.Ed. in Supervision/Coordination Vocat. and Tech. Edn., Rutgers U., 1976; m. James Albert Ramsey, Feb. 9, 1963; children—James Albert, Wendle Scott. Med. technologist, instr. Mercy Hosp., 1963-65, Mt. Carmel Hosp., Columbus, Ohio, 1965-69; med. technologist Doctor's Hosp., Columbus, 1970-71; instr. med. lab. tech. Columbus Tech. Inst., 1972-73; instr. vocat. and tech. edn. Middlesex County (N.J.) Bd. Edn., 1974; med. tech. coordinator Rutgers U. Med. Sch., 1974-75; supr. med. lab. Douglass Coll., Rutgers U., 1976; asst. prof. med. tech. Cuyahoga Community Coll., Cleve., 1976-81, program dir. med. assisting/med. lab. tech., 1981-84, div. head math. and techs., 1984—; panelist med. assisting edn. Ohio Acad. Family Physicians; critiquer, surveyor Nat. Accrediting Agy. for Clin. Lab. Scis. Fipse grantee, 1983. Mem. Am. Soc. Clin. Pathologists, Am. Assn. Med. Assts., Am. Soc. Med. Technologists, Am. Vocat. Assn., Ohio U. Alumni and Friends (sec. arts and scis.), Minorities and Women Higher Edn. (state adv. bd.), Leaders For 80's, Kappa Delta Pi. Office: 11000 Pleasant Valley Rd Parma OH 44130

RAMSEY, JOANNE MARIE, data processing executive; b. Long Branch, N.J., Oct. 13, 1945; d. Erwin P. and Erna M. (Green) Forrest; B.S., Monmouth Coll., 1967; M.S., Stevens Inst. Tech., 1971; 1 dau., Cheryl. Mem. tech. staff Bell Telephone Labs., Holmdel, N.J., 1967-71; programmer analyst Cooper Electric Supply Co., Middletown, N.J., 1971-73; sr. programmer Insco Systems Corp., Neptune, N.J., 1973-78; programmer analyst Internat. Flavors & Fragrances, Hazlet, N.J., 1978-80; project mgr. E.R. Squibb & Sons, Inc., East Brunswick, N.J., 1980—. Mem. Am. Prodn. and Inventory Control Soc., Assn. for Women in Computing. Home: 424 F Highland Ave Atlantic Highlands NJ 07716 Office: 25 Kennedy Blvd East Brunswick NJ 08816

RAMSEY, KEITHA YEULANDA, librarian; b. Bronx, N.Y., July 9, 1958; d. Charles and Jeanette G. M. (Brewster) R. B.S., John Jay Coll. Criminal Justice, N.Y.C., 1980; M.L.S., Pratt Inst., 1986. With John Jay Coll. Criminal Justice Library, 1978—, adj. lectr., 1985-86, higher edn. officer-aide, 1986—. Active women's force Kingsbridge Heights Neighborhood Improvement Assn., Bronx, 1985—. Mem. N.Y. Tech. Services Librarians, Med. Library Assn., Nat. Assn. Female Execs., Am. Mus. Natural History (assoc.). Democrat. Roman Catholic. Avocations: reading; bicycling. Office: John Jay Coll Criminal Justice Library 445 W 59th St New York NY 10019

RAMSEY, LEE ADAMS, artist, educator; b. Clifton, N.J., Dec. 7, 1908; d. James Adams and Daretta (Wagner) Adams; m. Bill Joseph Ramsey, Dec. 21, 1934. R.N., Fifth Ave Hosp., N.Y.C., 1928; student Domestic Art of Porcelain, Newark, 1936-41, Nat. Acad. Design, N.Y.C., 1954-67. R.N., N.Y., N.J. Surgeon's asst., nurse, N.Y.C., 1928-33; supr. sch. nursing, Clifton, 1933-48; tchr. art in oil, pastel and porcelain, Bedminster, N.J., 1955—; painter portraits in oil, pastel and procelain by commn, recipient Bronze medal Nat. Acad., 1967; demonstrator porcelain painting, N.J. and Pa., 1981-82. Mem. Nat. Soc. Arts and Letters (pres. 1959-61), Mid-Atlantic Porcelain Art Tchrs. (pres.), Internat. Porcelain Art Tchrs. (coordinator N.J.), Am. Artists Profl. League, Porcelain Portrait Soc., Nat. Arts Club, Pen and Brush, Inc., Am. Portrait Soc., Federated Art Assn. N.J., Defenders of Wildlife. Republican (exec. com. 1976). Home: Old Farm Rd Bedminster NJ 07921

RAMSEY, SALLY ANN SEITZ, state official; b. Columbus, Ohio, Feb. 15, 1931; d. Albert Blazier and Mildred (Dodson) Seitz; m. Edward Lewis Ramsey, Apr. 11, 1953 (div. 1962); children—Edward Lewis, Sylvia Ann Mitchell. B.A., Ohio State U., 1952, M.A., 1955, postgrad., 1963-66; postgrad. St. Mary Coll.-Xavier, Kans., 1962. Research engr., then sr. research engr. N.Am. Aviation, Inc., Columbus, Ohio, and Downey, Calif., 1962-67; legis. intern State of Ohio, 1964-65; research and info. officer Ohio Dept. Urban Affairs, Columbus, 1967-68; adminstrv. specialist Ohio Dept. Devel., Columbus, 1968; assoc. planner, then sr. planner Div. State Planning, Fla. Dept. Adminstrn., Tallahassee, 1968-76; econ. analysis supr. Fla. Dept. Commerce, 1976—; congl. campaign cons., 1966. U.S. Econ. Devel. Adminstrn. fellow, 1978-79. Mem. Fla. Econs. Club, Kappa Kappa Gamma, Pi Sigma Alpha. Home: 2429 Merrigan Pl Tallahassee FL 32308 Office: Fla Dept Commerce 107 W Gaines St Tallahassee FL 32301

RAMSHAW-REED, JANE, group health insurance broker; b. Albuquerque, Mar. 31, 1949; d. William George and Jean Ramshaw; grad. Trans-World Airlines Flight Hostess Sch., 1969; student U. N.Mex., 1967-71. Sales rep. Clinton P. Anderson, Albuquerque, 1973-74; sales rep. Blue Cross-Blue Shield, Rochester, N.Y., 1974-75; regional dir. mktg. Calif. Pacific Ins. Services, San Diego, 1976-80; owner, pres. Jane Ramshaw-Reed Enterprises, Inc., San Diego, 1980—; speaker profl. meetings. Mem. San Diego Assn. Life Underwriters (pres. 1981, nat. com. 1984-85), Calif. Assn. Life Underwriters (state health ins. chmn. 1980-81), Nat. Assn. Health Underwriters (registered health and disability underwriter), Nat. Assn. Life Underwriters (vice chmn. health com. 1982-84), Employee Benefit Council, North County Assn. Life Underwriters (dir.), Group Health Assn. Am. Republican. Clubs: Charter 100, Soroptimists of Rancho Bernardo, Toastmasters. Home: 3940 Gresham St Apt 142 San Diego CA 92109 Office: 2615 Camino del Rio S Suite 403 San Diego CA 92108

RANALLI, JULIE ANNE, child development center administrator; b. Chgo., Apr. 18, 1957; d. Edwin Joseph and Helen Marie (Kelleher) Orr; m. Donald Michael Ranalli, May 16, 1982. B.A., Rosary Coll., River Forest, Ill., 1979. Tchr. Rosary Coll. Jr. Citizen Ctr., River Forest, 1976-77, asst. dir., 1977-78, student supr., 1978-79, dir., 1979-83; owner, dir. Kaleidoscope Child Devel. Ctr., Oak Park, Ill., 1983—. Mem. Chgo. Assn. for Edn. Young Children, Nat. Assn. for Edn. Young Children, Day Care Action Council, Pre Sch. Owners Assn., Oak Park C. of C., Big Sisters Chgo. Democrat. Roman Catholic. Home: 1127 Woodbine Ave Oak Park IL 60302 Office: Kaleidoscope Child Devel Ctr 7059 W North Ave Oak Park IL 60302

RANARD, JOANN ELLIS, insurance company executive, consultant; b. Phila., Nov. 26, 1946; d. Alfred Horace and Josephine Margaret (Arnesen) Ellis; m. Robert Allan Ranard, Jan. 10, 1981 (div. July 1983); children by previous marriage—Bruce Andrew Hauman III, Christopher Bradley Hauman. B.S. in Edn., Millersville State U., 19—. Pres. Resource Service Ctr., Guilford, Conn., 1973; sr. sales rep. Western Union, Upper Saddle River, N.J., 1977; agt. Aetna Life & Casualty Hartford, Conn., 1981-84; dir. life div. Hannon Agy., East Hartford, Conn., 1984-86; mng. gen. agt. John Alden Ins. Miami, Fla., 1984—; pres. Engring. Health Concepts, Essex, Conn., 1986—. Mem. Nat. Assn. Life Underwriters, Nat. Assn. Security Dealers (lic.), Nat. Assn. Female Execs. Avocations: writing; racquetball; sailing; tennis; riding; swimming; flying; antiques. Home: 95 Book Hill Rd Essex CT 06426 Office: Engring Health Concepts 95 Book Hill Rd Essex CT 06426

RANCK, SHIRLEY ANN, clergywoman, psychologist; b. Jersey City, Oct. 22, 1930; d. Gilbert Holmes and Ann (West) Bush; B.A., Montclair State Coll., 1953; M. Religious Edn., Drew U., 1958; M.A., CCNY, 1964; Ph.D., Fordham U., 1976; M.Div., Starr King U., 1978; children—Scott Holmes Page, James Philip Page, Christina Ann Ranck, Laura Nelle Ranck. Ordained to ministry Unitarian Universalist Ch., 1980; psychologist public schs., Livingston, N.J., 1968-75; clin. psychologist Greystone Park (N.J.) Hosp., 1976; research assoc. Grad. Theol. Union, Berkeley, Calif., 1978-79; minister Starr King Unitarian Ch., Hayward, Calif., 1980, No. Hills Fellowship, Cin., 1980-82; psychologist Counseling Center, U. Cin., 1982-83; pvt. practice psychology, San Francisco, 1983—. Mem. Am. Psychol. Assn., Unitarian Universalist Ministers Assn. Contbr. articles in field to profl. publs. Office: 1507 Masonic San Francisco CA 94117

RANCOUR, JOANN SUE, registered nurse; b. Elyria, Ohio, Nov. 10, 1939; d. Joseph and Ann (Donich) Sokol; diploma M.B. Johnson Sch. Nursing, 1960; B.S. in Profl. Arts, St. Josephs Coll., N. Windham, Maine, 1981; student in psychology Alfred Adler Inst., Chgo., 1976—, Lorain County Community Coll., 1973-75, Ursuline Coll., Cleve., 1976, Baldwin Wallace Coll., 1982; m. Richard Lee Rancour, July 29, 1961; children—Kathleen Ann, Donna Marie. Staff nurse Elyria Meml. Hosp., 1960-62, 72-75, head nurse psychiat. unit, 1975-79; sec.-treas. Alfred Adler Inst. Cleve., 1978-79; nurse Lorain County Juvenile Detention Home, Elyria, 1980; nurse VA Med. Center, Brecksville, Ohio, 1981—. Active PTA, yearbook com., 1969-70, co-chmn. ways and means, 1971; Democratic poll worker, 1971-72; sec. St. Mary's Confrat. Christian Doctrine Program, 1970-71. Mem. Am. Nurses Assn. (cert. generalist practitioner psychiat. and mental health nursing practice), Ohio Nurses Assn., N.Am. Soc. Adlerian Psychology. Roman Catholic. Home: 205 Denison Ave Elyria OH 44035

RAND, HELEN PIERCE (MRS. ROBERT W. RAND), civic worker, artist; b. Coldwater, Mich., Jan. 31, 1926; d. L. Earl and Marjorie (Treacher) Pierce; A.B., U. Mich., 1949; m. Robert W. Rand, Dec. 17, 1949; children—Carl Wheeler II, Richard Pierce. Instr. dentistry U. Mich., 1948-50, translator of Russian, 1951; one-woman show: Gallery 8, Pasadena, Calif., 1980; group shows: Tower Gallery, Hollywood Park, 1965, Pasadena (Calif.) Pub. Library, 1965, Los Angeles City Hall, 1966, Pacific Art Guild Gallery, Westchester, Calif., 1966, Brand Library Gallery, Glendale, 1966, Occidental Bldg., Los Angeles, 1968, Westwood Art Assn., Los Angeles, 1965-67. Rec. sec. Jr. Philharmonic Com., Los Angeles, 1966—, fund drive chair, 1986—, 1st v.p., liaison rep. to Women for Music Ctr., 1971-72; mem. patroness com. of Hollywood Bowl, 1985—; rec. sec. Coll. Alumnae Aux. Assistance League, Los Angeles, 1959—. Mem. Women's Aux. Los Angeles County Med. Assn., UCLA Med. Faculty Wives (dir., chmn. ways and means 1967-68), Jr. Women Assocs. U. Religious Conf., Mother's Club Harvard Sch. (bd. dirs. 1971-72), Town Hall, Blue Ribbon 400, Nat. Art Assn. Home: 521 N Bristol Ave Los Angeles CA 90049

RANDALL, ANN KNIGHT, librarian; b. N.Y.C., Oct. 19, 1942; d. Robert and Ruth (Bayton) Knight; m. Julius Thomas Randall, Nov. 8, 1963; 1 dau., Christine Renee. B.A., Barnard Coll., 1963; M.L.S., Columbia U., 1967, D.L.S., 1977. Instr. Queens Coll. Library, Flushing, N.Y., 1967-69; lectr. Columbia U., N.Y.C., 1970-73; asst. prof. Bklyn. Coll. Library, 1973-76; asst. univ. librarian Brown U., Providence, 1977-82; prof., chief librarian City Coll. Library, N.Y.C., 1982—; rev. panelist Nat. Endowment Humanities, Washington, 1980; cons. New Eng. Regional Med. Library Service, Boston, 1979-80, Dept. State Library Service, Providence, 1980; book cons. RR Bowker, N.Y.C., 1973-75. Essayist: Special Collections, 1982, Ethnic Collections in Libraries, 1983. Advisor Concord Bapt. Ch. Day Care, Bklyn., 1977, Gov.'s Task Force on Libraries, Providence, 1981; com. chmn. YWCA, Bklyn., 1976; mgmt. cons. Assn. Research Libraries, Washington, 1982. Fellow U.S. NDEA, 1969; UCLA sr. fellow Council Library Resources, 1982. Mem. ALA (councilor 1980-84), Assn. Coll. and Research Libraries (chmn. edn. and behavioral scis. sect. 1981-82), Research Libraries Group (rep. 1980-82), N. Atlantic Health Sci. Libraries (regional chmn. 1980-81). Club: Sankore Soc. (Providence) (v.p. 1978-80). Office: City Coll CUNY 5-333 N Acad Center New York NY 10031

RANDALL, CAROL JEAN, customs broker; b. Manlius, Ill., Nov. 12, 1941; d. Harlan K. Black and Nina L. (Heward) Kuriyama; m. Francis David Limoges, Jr., Oct. 15, 1957 (div. 1961); children—David Larry, Dale James; m. Bruce James Randall, Jr., Aug. 2, 1969. Grad. high sch. Med. asst., Redondo Beach, Calif., 1961-63; model, Los Angeles, 1963-64; bookkeeper/hostess Carribean Corp., Los Angeles, 1964-66; import mgr. James G. Wiley, Los Angeles, 1966-74, Internat. Customs Services, Los Angeles, 1974-82, Norman Krieger, Los Angeles, 1983—. Mem. Md. Geneal. Soc., Augustan Soc., S.W. Pa. Geneal. Soc., Eastern Nebr. Geneal. Soc., Democrat. Baptist. Avocations: genealogy; photography; antiques; travel; spectator sports. Home: 19425 Sturgess Dr Torrance CA 90503 Office: Norman Krieger Customs Brokers 5716 W Imperial Hwy Los Angeles CA 90045

RANDALL, CAROLYN DINEEN, U.S. judge; b. Syracuse, N.Y., Jan. 30, 1938; d. Robert E. and Carolyn E. (Bareham) Dineen; A.B. summa cum laude, Smith Coll., 1959; LL.B., Yale U., 1962; m. James D. Randall, Sept. 9, 1961; children—James, Philip, Stephen. Admitted to D.C. bar, 1962, Tex. bar, 1963; individual practice law, Houston, 1962-79; circuit judge U.S. Ct. Appeals 5th Circuit, Houston, 1979—. Trustee, mem. exec. com., treas. Houston Ballet Found., 1967-70; mem. Houston dist. adv. council SBA, 1972-76; mem. Dallas regional panel Pres.' Commn. White House Fellowships, 1972-76, mem. commn., 1977; bd. dirs. Houston chpt. Am. Heart Assn., 1978-79; nat. trustee Palmer Drug Abuse Program, 1978-79; trustee, chmn. audit com. United Way Tex. Gulf Coast, from 1979. Mem. ABA, Fed. Bar Assn., State Bar Tex., Houston Bar Assn., Phi Beta Kappa. Roman Catholic. Office: US Courthouse 515 Rusk St Houston TX 77002•

RANDALL, LAURA JEAN, television news producer; b. Karamursel, Turkey, Jan. 9, 1960; came to U.S., 1963; d. Allan General and Ruby Maxine (Bell) R. B.S. in Broadcast Journalism, Boston U., 1981. News writer, producer Sta. WCVB-TV, Boston, 1980-82; news producer WTN Corp., Washington, 1982—. Mem. Nat. Acad. TV Arts and Scis., Soc. Profl. Journalists, Women in Communications. Republican. Methodist. Home: 2800 Quebec St NW #946 Washington DC 20008 Office: WTN Corp 1705 DeSales St NW Washington DC 20036

RANDALL, LINDA L., nurse; b. Williamson, W.Va., Nov. 5, 1945; d. Opal Ferne (Chapman) C.; diploma St. Mary's Hosp. Sch. Nursing, Huntington, W.Va., 1966; postgrad. W.Va. U., 1969, Marshall U., 1971, St. Joseph's Coll., North Windham, Maine, 1978, U. Central Fla., 1982—; cert. emergency nurse; m. Steven Edward Randall, Oct. 12, 1974. Charge nurse ICU and CCU, St. Mary's Hosp., Huntington, 1966-68; supr. ICU and CCU, Drs. Meml. Hosp., Huntington, 1968-73; team leader CCU, Community Hosp., Springfield, Ohio, 1973-74; charge nurse Urbana (Ohio) Care Center, 1974, dir. nursing services, 1974-78; dir. nursing services The Palms Health Care Center, Sebring, Fla.,

1978-79; asst. head nurse, emergency and employee health services Ringling Bros., Barnum & Bailey Circus World, Orlando, Fla., 1979-80; asst. charge nurse emergency dept. Halifax Hosp. Med. Center, Daytona Beach, Fla., 1980-82; supr. operating room and post anesthesia Daytona Beach (Fla.) Gen. Hosp., 1982—; head nurse emergency dept. Community Hosp. of Bunnell (Fla.), 1983-84; charge nurse emergency dept. Fla. Hosp. Med. Ctr., Orlando, 1984-86; occupational health nurse Repco Inc., Orlando, 1986—; mem. med. staff Daytona Beach Internat. Speedway, 1981—. Bd. dirs. Ohio Hi-Point Joint Vocat. Sch. Allied Health Fields. Mem. Nat. League Nursing, Am., Fla. nurses assns., Emergency Dept. Nurses Assn., Am. Heart Assn. (basic life support instr. 1981, advanced cardiac life support 1982), Am. Assn. Critical Care Nurses, Defenders of Wildlife, Nat. Audubon Soc., Nat. Wildlife Found., Fund for Animals, Cousteau Soc. Republican. Methodist. Home: 3059 Anastasia Ct Apoka FL 32703

RANDALL, LOLLY (PRISCILLA), manufacturers' representative; b. Boston, Aug. 15, 1952; d. Raymond Victor and Priscilla (Richmond) R.; m. Harold Glen Middleton, Dec. 7, 1983; 1 child, Priscilla Eva. B.Arts and Scis., U. Colo., 1973. Asst. to dir. pub. relations Pepsi Cola Co., Mpls., 1975; sales rep. DiCosta Knits, Ltd., San Francisco, 1975-76, Lilli Ann Corp., San Francisco, 1976-78; owner Lolly & Co., Seattle, 1978—; dir. 6100 Bldg. Assn., Seattle, 1981. Mem. Pacific N.W. Toy Assn. (pub. relations officer 1981-82, founding mem. 1981). Republican. Episcopalian. Avocations: volunteer work in field of recovering alcoholics, skiing. Home: 418 SW 189th St Seattle WA 98166 Office: Lolly & Co 6100 4th Ave S #355 Seattle WA 98108

RANDALL, LYNN ELLEN, librarian; b. Chgo., Oct. 10, 1946; d. Ward W. and Hazel A. (Nettles) R. B.A., King's Coll., 1970; M.A., Seton Hall U., 1973; M.L.S., Rutgers U., 1978. Librarian, N.J. Inst. Tech., Newark, 1970-75; library dir. N.E. Bible Coll., Essex Fells, N.J., 1975-81; reference librarian Seton Hall U., South Orange, N.J., 1983-85; dir. library services Berkeley Sch., Little Falls, N.J., 1985—; instr. Morris (N.J.) County Coll., 1981-83. Mem. Union County (N.J.) Heritage Commn., 1975-76. Mem. Middle States Assn. Bible Colls., Am. Assn. Bible Colls. (evaluator 1977, 79, 84), ALA, N.J. Library Assn. (chair automated library services com. 1986—), Assn. Coll. and Research Libraries (com.). Co-author: N.J. Online Directory, 1983. Editor N.J. Libraries, fall 1984, spring 1986. Home: 173 Ridge Rd Apt #-7 Cedar Grove NJ 07009

RANDALL, MARION STANTON, motel executive; b. Ogden, Utah; d. Charles Benjamin and Marian (Savyer) Stanton; m. Edmund W. Baker, Aug. 21, 1948 (div. 1976); children—Jeffrey Alan, Roger Edmund, Laurel Terese, Lisa Diane Baker Barbeau and Maureen Louise (dec.) (triplets), Douglas Owen; m. 2d Raymond L. Randall, June 20, 1981. A.B. in Psychology, Marygrove Coll., Detroit, 1943. Adminstrv. sec., sec. to labor mgmt. bd. Ohio Employment Services, Akron, 1943-45; exec. sec. asst. to exec. tech. editor Govt. Labs., Akron, 1945-48; exec. sec.-adminstrv. asst. Eastman Kodak, Chgo., 1948-49; exec. sec. to exec. dir. in-patient psychiatry U. Minn. Hosps., Mpls., 1949-50; exec. sec. in personnel and field support systems Hughes Aircraft, Culver City, Calif., 1950-55; owner, operator Surfside Motel, Port Hueneme, Calif., 1974-84; legal cons. motels. Exec. sec. Minor League Baseball, West Covina, Calif., 1967. Mem. AAUW (editor chpt. bull. 1968-70, chpt. v.p. programs 1971-72), So. Calif. Psychial. Research. Club: Mary and Joseph League (Los Angeles). Office: PO Box 51 Port Hueneme CA 93041

RANDALL, PATRICIA LORENE, clinical social worker; b. Springfield, Mo., Nov. 14, 1942; d. James Joseph and Bertha (Sperandio) R.; B.A. in Sociology, Mt. St. Scholastica Coll., 1964; M.S.W., St. Louis U., 1966. Staff mem., clin. social worker Family and Children's Service of Greater St. Louis, 1966-80, dir. Clayton (Mo.) dist. office, 1981—. Del. gov.'s adv. bd. Mo. White House Conf. on Families, 1979-80; chmn. St. Louis County Schs. Agys. Com. on Youth, 1969-71; mem. Block Partnership, 1971-72, mem. St. Francis Xavier Parish Council, 1982-83; bd. dirs. New Life Styles Orgn., 1981-84; mem. Children's Mental Health Services Council, 1981—. Cert. Acad. Cert. Social Workers. Mem. Nat. Assn. Social Workers (del. state bd. 1977-79), Am. Assn. Marriage and Family Therapy, Am. Group Psychotherapy Assn., Mo. Assn. Social Welfare, New Life Styles Orgn. Roman Catholic. Clubs: Christian Life Community, Soroptimist Internat. Home: 728 Lilac Ave Webster Groves MO 63119 Office: 107 S Meramec St Clayton MO 63105

RANDALL, RUTH EVELYN, state official; b. Underwood, Iowa, Mar. 4, 1929; d. Oluf and Lillie Martha (Bondo) Larsen; m. Robert Dale Randall, June 17 (dec.); children—Robert, Mark, Diane. Teaching cert. Dana Coll., 1949; B.S., U. Omaha, 1961; M.S., U. Nebr., 1968, Ed.S., 1972, Ed.D. in Edn. Adminstrn., 1976. Asst. prin. Horace Mann pub. schs., Omaha, 1976-78; asst. supt. ISD 196, Rosemount, Minn., 1978-81, dep. supt., 1981, supt., 1981-83; commr. edn. State of Minn., St. Paul, 1983—; chmn. Gov.'s Subcabinet on Edn. and Cultural Affairs; sec. State Bd. Edn.; mem. edn. com. Midwestern Govs. Assn.; mem. Edn. Commn. of the States; chmn. sex equity com. Council Chief State Sch. Officers; mem. edn. com. Nat. Govs. Assn.; mem. policies and priorities com. Council of the Chief State Sch. Officers. Contbr. articles to profl. jours. and mags. Active The Lutheran Women's Caucus, Citizens League, Sci. Mus. Minn., Sta. KTCA. Recipient Disting. Alumnus award Dana Coll., 1984; award of appreciation Apple Valley C. of C., 1983; Woman of Yr. award Minn. Valley Bus. and Profl. Women, 1982; Human Relations award Omaha Edn. Assn., 1978. Mem. Minn. Valley Bus. and Profl. Women's Club, Minn. Assn. for Supervision and Curriculum Devel., Minn. Assn. Sch. Adminstrs., Minn. Council for Gifted and Talented, Adminstrv. Women in Edn. Minn., AAUW, Minn. Soc. Fine Arts, Women Execs. in State Govt. (founding mem.), Nat. Council Adminstrv. Women in Edn., Nat. Congress of Parents and Teachers (life), Am. Edn. Research Assn., Am. Assn. Sch. Adminstrs., Assn. for Supervision and Curriculum Devel., U. Nebr. Omaha Alumni Assn., U. Nebr. Alumni Assn. (life), Dana Coll. Alumni Assn., Phi Delta Kappa, Delta Kappa Gamma. Democrat. Lutheran. Home: 339 Summit Ave Saint Paul MN 55102 Office: Dept Edn 712 Capitol Square Bldg 550 Cedar St Saint Paul MN 55101

RANDALL, SARAH HAMPTON, auditor; b. Rockingham, N.C., Feb. 22, 1925; d. Booker T. Dogherty and Nezzie A. (Pierce) R.; A.S. (Math. Div. scholar, Atlantic City and County Bd. Realtors scholar), Atlantic Community Coll., 1979; student acctg., Stockton State Coll., 1979—. Bill adjustment clk. John Wanamaker's, Phila., 1967-71; asst. to sales mgr. Consol. Laundries, Atlantic City, 1971-72; ins. clk. Equitable Assurance Soc. U.S., Atlantic City, 1972-76; head night auditor Penthouse Boardwalk Hotel, Atlantic City, 1974—; instr. Atlantic Community Coll., 1980—. Mem. curriculum adv. bd. Hospitality Mgmt. div. Atlantic Community Coll., 1978-80; active NOW. Mem. Phi Theta Kappa. Home: 1921 Blaine Ave PO Box 401 Atlantic City NJ 08401 Office: Penthouse Boardwalk Hotel Atlantic City NJ 08404

RANDALL, THELMA MAYE, educator; b. Malakoff, Tex., Dec. 6, 1936; d. Melvin and Clara (Thompson) Langley; B.S., Prairie View A.&M. U., 1956; M.A., Cath. U. Am., 1971; M.A.T., Trinity Coll., 1974; m. Ferrell Baysing Randall, Dec. 29, 1956; children—Roderick Daryl, Alan Wayne. Editorial clk. U.S. Dept. Agr., Forest Service, Washington, 1958-64; travel audit clk. Walter Reed Army Med. Center, Washington, summer 1966; curriculum writer Office of Supervising Dir., Bus. and Office Edn., D.C. Pub. Schs., 1972, 79; tchr. bus. and office edn. Pub. Schs. of D.C., Washington, 1964-79, 80—, chmn. dept. bus. and office edn., 1970-73, guidance counselor, 1979-80; coordinator Cooperative Office Edn. Program, Cardozo Sr. High Sch., 1970-74. Sec., Brightwood Civic Assn., 1968. Mgmt. of Ednl. Change program fellow, 1973-74. Mem. Am. Bus. Women's Assn., Eastern Bus. Edn. Assn., Nat. Bus. Edn. Assn., Am. Personnel and Guidance Assn., Nat. Vocational Guidance Assn., Prairie View A.&M. U. Alumni Club (Washington chpt.), Delta Sigma Theta. Democrat. Roman Catholic. Address: 6658 13th St NW Washington DC 20012

RANDAZZO, PATRICIA ROSE, antiquarian horse books dealer; b. Passaic, N.J., Oct. 17, 1939; d. Anton Philip and Margaret (Healey) Gannon Randazzo; m. Dante R. Greco, June 24, 1964 (div. 1978); children—Tara Romei, Dante Peter. B.A., Trinity Coll., Washington, 1961; M.A.T, Fairleigh Dickinson U., 1971; postgrad. McGill U. Med. Sch., 1961-62, Columbia Sch. Gen. Studies, 1962-63. Biologist, Hoffman-La Roche, Nutley, N.J., 1963; tchr. biology Acad. Holy Angels, Fort Lee, N.J., 1963-64, St. Joseph's Acad., Montvale, N.J., 1969-70; apprentice Peter Tumarkin Fine Books, Inc., N.Y.C., 1979-82; propr. Bucephalus Horse Books, N.Y.C., 1982—; co-op barn mgr. Lindeman Farm, New Vernon, N.J., 1976-79; pres. Riding Club, Trinity Coll., Washington, 1960-61, sr. advisor, 1960-61. Home: PO Box 380 Long Valley NJ 07853 Office: Bucephalus Horse Books 332 W 22d St New York NY 10011

RANDISI, ELAINE MARIE, garment manufacturing company executive; b. Racine, Wis., Dec. 19, 1926; d. John Dewey and Alveta Irene (Raffety) Fehd; A.A., Pasadena Jr. Coll., 1946; B.S. cum laude (Giannini scholar), Golden Gate U., 1978; m. John Paul Randisi, Oct. 12, 1946 (div. July 1972); children—Jeanine Randisi Manson, Martha Randisi Cheney, Joseph, Paula Randisi Small, Catherine Randisi Tateo, George, Anthony. With Raymond Kaiser Engrs., Inc., Oakland, Calif., 1969-75, 77-86, corp. acct., 1978-79, sr. corp. acct., 1979-82, sr. payroll acct., 1983-86; corp. buyer Kaiser Industries Corp., Oakland, 1975-77; with Lilli Ann Corp., San Francisco 1986—; lectr. on astrology Theosophical Soc., San Francisco, 1979—; mem. faculty Am. Fedn. Astrologers Internat. Conv., Chgo., 1982, 84, Los Angeles, 1986. Mem. Speakers Bur., Calif. Assn. for Neurologically Handicapped Children, 1964-70, v.p., 1969; bd. dirs. Ravenwood Homeowners Assn., 1979-82, v.p., 1979-80, sec., 1980-81; mem. organizing com. Minority Bus. Fair, San Francisco, 1976; pres. bd. dirs. Lakewood Condominium Assn. Mem. Am. Fedn. Astrologers, Calif. Scholarship Fedn. (life), Alpha Gamma Sigma (life). Mem. Ch. of Religious Science. Initiated Minority Vendor Purchasing Program for Kaiser Engrs., Inc., 1975-76. Home: 742 Wesley Way Apt 1-C Oakland CA 94610 Office: 2701 16th St San Francisco CA 94103

RANDL, MARY ANNE ELIZA, singer, actress, writer; b. Abington, Pa., Dec. 17, 1949; d. Edwin Kellogg and Marjorie Cromwell (Haupt) Lucas. B.A. in English, Webster Coll., 1971. Cert. tchr. ESL, Calif. Voice-over specialist Sound Film, GmbH, Munich, W.Ger., 1975-77; tech. cons. Rand Corp., Santa Monica, Calif., 1977; nutritional cons. Gt. Earth Vitamins, Los Angeles, 1980-84; tchr. ESL, Los Angeles Unified Schs., 1982—; mem., contbr., actress Los Angeles Performance Workshops, 1977—; cabaret act, 1983—; participant 20th Century Fox Repertory Co., Los Angeles, 1984—. Contbr. poetry to publs. Mem. Women's Research Group Los Angeles. Democrat. Mem. Self-Realization Fellowship. Club: Ambassador Health (Los Angeles). Home: 941 S Lucerne Blvd Los Angeles CA 90019

RANDO, RAE, manager; b. Paterson, N.J., Apr. 12, 1956; d. Frank J. and Rachel R. (Turpstra) R.; m. Dimitri Voicechovski, Nov. 6, 1976. B.S.B.A. candidate Thomas A. Edison State Coll., 1985—; cert. Katharine Gibbs Sch., 1974-76. Tenant/landlord adminstr. Claridge House, Verona, N.J., 1976-79, Paragon Enterprises, West Orange, N.J., 1979-81; account rep. Sci. Mgmt., Parsippany, N.J., 1981-82, mgr. temporary services, 1982-86, mgr. major accounts, 1986—. Canvas vol. Greenpeace, 1980—; trustee North Jersey Psychotherapeutic Inst., 1983—, treas., 1984-85. Avocations: astronomy; skiing; reading. Roman Catholic. Home: Jennings Rd Milton NJ 07438 Office: Sci Mgmt Corp 2001 Rt 46 Waterview Plaza Parsippany NJ 07054

RANDOLPH, ELIZABETH GARLAND SCHMOKE (MRS. JOHN DANIEL RANDOLPH), former ednl. adminstr.; b. Farmville, N.C.; d. John Hagans and Pearl (Johnson) Schmoke; A.B., Shaw U., 1936, H.H.D. (hon.), 1979; M.A., U. Mich., 1945; postgrad. U. N.C., 1964; m. John Daniel Randolph, June 7, 1950 (dec. Dec. 1963). Tchr., English and French, New Hope High Sch., Rutherfordton, N.C., 1936-37; tchr. librarian DuBois High Sch., Wake Forest, N.C., 1937-43, Jordan Sellars High Sch., Burlington, N.C., 1943-44; tchr. English, adminstrv. asst. W. Charlotte (N.C.) High Sch., 1944-58; prin. University Park Elem. Sch., Charlotte, 1958-68; dir. ESEA activities Charlotte-Mecklenburg Schs., 1968-73, adminstrv. asst. for sch. ops., 1973-76, asst. supt., 1976-77, asso. supt., 1977-82. Mem. Charlotte Hosp. Authority, Charlotte-Mecklenburg Arts and Scis. Council, Charlotte-Mecklenburg Public Library; bd. mgrs. Charlotte Meml. Hosp.; trustee Shaw U., N.C. Agrl. and Tech. State U. Mem. AAUW, NEA (life), Assn. Supervision and Curriculum Devel. (pres. 1977-78), Nat. Assn. Adminstrv. Women in Edn., Nat. Council Negro Women, Links, NAACP, Phi Delta Kappa, Delta Kappa Gamma, Alpha Kappa Alpha (Mid-Atlantic regional dir. 1964-68, chmn. standards com., nat. parliamentarian 1974—). Home: 1616 Patton Ave Charlotte NC 28216

RANDOLPH, JOY WHITE, risk management company executive, occupational therapy, rehabilitation, safety and insurance consultant; b. Lebanon, Tenn., July 2, 1953; d. Robert Edgar and Mildred (LeCornu) White; m. John Harvey Randolph, Oct. 9, 1977. B.A., U. Tenn., 1974; M. Occupational Therapy, Tex. Woman's U., 1978. Lic. occupational therapist; cert. ins. rehab. specialist, vocat. evaluator and work adjustment specialist. Admissions social worker Eastern State Psychiat. Hosp., Knoxville, 1974-75; occupational therapist Baylor U. Hosp., Dallas, 1977-79; occupational therapy cons. Regional Edn. Service Ctr., Richardson, Tex., 1979-81; occupational therapy/Back Sch. dir. N. Tex. Bank Inst., Plano, 1981-83; v.p. Back Systems, Inc., Plano, 1983—; cons. Home Health Care of Dallas, 1979-83, N. Tex. Home Health Care, 1979-82, Appletree Home Health Care, 1981-83; profl. adv. com. Tex. Vis. Nurses Assn.; co-dir. Aerobicise for Back Care, 1983; speaker. Mem. Workers Compensation Research Inst., Nat. Rehab. Assn., Nat. Assn. Rehab. Profls. in Pvt. Sector, Tex. Assn. Rehab. Profls. in Pvt. Sector, Am. Occupational Therapy Assn., Tex. Occupational Therapy Assn., World Fedn. Occupational Therapists, Tex. Rehab. Assn. Home: 16701 Rustic Meadows Dallas TX 75248 Office: Back Systems Inc 5495 Beltline Rd Suite 390 Dallas TX 75240

RANDOLPH, SHERYL NORMAN, communications specialist; b. Toledo, Sept. 1, 1955; d. Albert and Elinor Mae (Garwick) Norman; m. Kevin Howard Randolph, May 28, 1977. B.S. in Journalism cum laude, Bowling Green State U., 1977. Dir. corp. sales Commodore Perry Hotel, Toledo, 1977; account rep. United Communications, Southfield, Mich., 1978-79; account exec. Nichols-Bonnell, Detroit, 1979-82; freelance writer, 1982—; corp. communications editor Florists' Transworld Delivery Assn. (FTD), Southfield, 1982—, liaison FTD Pres.'s Council on Govt. and Industry Affairs, 1983—, liaison FTD 75th anniversary com., 1983-85. Jr. Achievement N.W. Ohio scholar, 1973. Mem. Women in Communications, Direct Mktg. Assn. Detroit (bd. dirs.), Adcraft Club Detroit. Republican. Methodist. Office: FTD 29200 Northwestern Southfield MI 48037

RANDOLPH, WILLENE JOYCE, computer specialist; b. Lebanon, Ill., Feb. 7, 1935; d. Rudolph Mitchell and Cleo (Gant) Davis; m. Scott Roosevelt Randolph, Feb. 2, 1952; children—Craig, Teresa, Keith and Kathy (twins). B.A., Stephens Coll., 1985. Sec., USAF, Scott AFB, Ill., 1958-63, computer programmer, 1963-69; computer specialist U.S. Army, St. Louis, 1969-72; data processing instr. State Community Coll., East St. Louis, Ill., dir. computer services/plan and research 1976-81, mem. Ford Found. Adv. Bd., 1984—. Pres., Jack and Jill Am., East St. Louis, 1979; editor newsletter St. Paul Bapt. Ch., East St. Louis, 1982—; precinct committeewoman East St. Louis Precinct 33, 1983. Recipient Outstanding Performance award USAF, 1963; Fed. Women's Program Mgr. of Year award, 1984; Spl. Act award U.S. Army, 1982-84; award of Merit Top Ladies of Distinction, 1984. Mem. Blacks in Govt. (v.p. 1984-85), Federally Employed Women (workshop presenter), Data Processing Mgrs. Assn., Ill. Bus. Edn. Assn., St. Louis Fed. Women's Program Council. Republican. Avocations: travel, reading. Home: 490 N 33d St East Saint Louis IL 62205 Office: US Army ALMSA 210 N Tucker Blvd Saint Louis MO 63188

RANFT, LISA MARIE, computer company executive; b. Queens, N.Y., Mar. 8, 1960; d. Francis Edward and Teresa Veronica (McGrath) R.; m. Robert Lawton Shimer, July 21, 1984. B.A. in Econs., Columbia U., 1983. Fin. analyst IBM, Princeton, N.J., 1983, sr. planner, 1984, product adminstr., Montvale, N.J., 1984-85, mktg. rep., West Orange, N.J., 1985—. Recipient Outstanding Achievement awards IBM, 1984-85. Mem. Nat. Assn. Female Execs., Barnard Coll. Alumni Assn., Peddie Sch. Alumni Assn. Club: Toastmasters. Avocations: tennis; travel; reading. Office: IBM 300 Executive Dr West Orange NJ 07052

RANGE, MARTHA ANN, educator, editor; b. Tucson; d. Ira McKinley and Ruth (Wiley) Ward; Mus. B., U. Ariz., 1962; M.A., U. Mo., 1969; m. Rex McKenzie Range, Aug. 9, 1971; 1 dau., Lori Soprano, Baden Stadttheater, Vienna Volksoper, Radio Vienna, 1963-66; dir. opera theater Tex. A. and I.U., Kingsville, 1970-71; instr. voice North Tex. State U., Denton, 1974-77, U. Tex. at Dallas, Richardson, 1977-80; music and lit. editor RILM, CUNY, Mesquite Arts Rev.; participant IV Internat. Tchaikowsky competition, USSR, 1970. Recipient Met. Opera Assistance award, 1963. Mem. Am. Lit. Translators Assn., Nat. Assn. Tchrs. Singing, Music Tchrs. Nat. Assn., Tex. Music Tchrs. Assn. Author: Russian Diction Manual for Singers. Home and Office: 1021 Lakeshore Dr Mesquite TX 75149

RANGELL, SYDELLE RAY, TV producer; b. Bklyn., July 25, 1931; d. Morris and Pauline (Kaiser) R.; M.A. magna cum laude, Bklyn. Coll., 1954. Former producer Jack Tinker & Ptnrs., Tinker Dodge Delano; v.p., exec. producer Needham Harper & Steers Inc., N.Y.C., 1971-83; exec. TV producer Dancer, Fitzgerald, Sample, N.Y.C., 1983—. Recipient numerous awards. Office: 405 Lexington Ave New York NY 10174

RANGILA, NANCY ARNEVNA, investment counselor; b. Petrozavodsk, Russia, Mar. 28, 1936 (parents Am. citizens); d. Arne and Myrtle Marie (Jacobson) Kujala; B.A., U. S.C., 1958, M.A., 1964; M.B.A., U. So. Calif., 1973; student Reed Coll., 1953-54, Portland State U., 1954-57. Employment counselor Nancy Nolan Agy., Los Angeles, 1960; sec., adminstrv. asst. Bekins Bus. Records Center, Los Angeles, 1961-64; sec., statistician, securities analyst Capital Research & Mgmt. Co., 1964-73; portolio mgr., v.p. Capital Cons., Inc., Portland, Oreg., 1973-82; pres., mgr. Franklin Securities, subs. Benjamin Franklin Fed. Savs. and Loan Assn., Portland. Pres. Planned Parenthood Assn., Portland, 1979-81, dir., 1976-82; bd. dirs. Portland Hosp. Facilities Authority, 1979—; bd. dirs. Portland Civic Theatre, 1977-79, Delaunay Mental Health Clinic, 1979-81. Chartered fin. analyst; cert. employee benefit specialist. Mem. Fin. Analyst Fedn., Western Pension Conf., Internat. Assn. Cert. Employee Benefit Specialists, Portland Soc. Fin. Analysts (past pres., dir.). Republican. Clubs: City of Portland, Multnomah Athletic. Home: 2221 SW 1st Ave 1625 Portland OR 97201

RANHEIM, JOANNA LYNN, nurse; b. Milw., May 10, 1961; d. John William and Judith Bernice (Hanson) R. B.S. in Nursing with honors, UCLA, 1983, postgrad., 1985—. R.N., Calif.; pub. health cert., Calif. Med. unit clerk Santa Clara County Med. Ctr., Campbell, Calif., 1980; nursing service vol. UCLA Med. Ctr., 1980-83, sr. nursing aide, 1982-83, clin. nurse III, 1983—; mem. Nursing Models Com., Los Angeles, 1983—, Clin. Nurses Forum, Los Angeles, 1984—. Author: Orientation Manual, 1984. Mem. Career Group Calvary Ch., 1983—. Recipient Outstanding Nurse award UCLA Med. Ctr., 1984, Incentive award, 1984. Mem. Calif. Nurses Assn., UCLA Sch. Nursing Alumni Assn. Avocations: backpacking; aerobics; travel; reading. Home: 4071 McLaughlin Ave #5 Los Angeles CA 90066 Office: UCLA Med Ctr 10833 LeConte Ave Los Angeles CA 90024

RANKIN, DIANNE MARY, financial planner; b. Mineola, N.Y.; d. David Jay and Rose Mary (Ruggerio) Keller; B.A., U. Louisville (Deans scholar), 1969, postgrad., 1976—; m. Eric Lynn Rankin, Nov. 18, 1972. Stewardess, Pan Am. Airways, 1969-72; material controller RCA, Somerville, N.J., 1972-75; pvt. practice acctg., Flemington, N.J., 1975—; investment adv. SEC, 1982; instr. tax preparation, Flemington, 1976-78. Mem. Delaware Twp. Mcpl. Utilities Authority, 1979—, Delaware Twp. Bd. Adjustment, 1986—. C.P.A., N.J.; cert. fin. planner; registered investment adviser. Mem. Nat. Soc. Public Accts., Nat. Tax Tng. Inst. Address: RD 2 Ferry Rd Flemington NJ 08822

RANKIN, GERALDINE ANN, nursing home administrator, nursing executive; b. Pittston, Maine, Dec. 21, 1933; d. Milton L. and Josephine (Harwood) Merrill; m. Wayne E. Rankin, Dec. 27, 1952; children—Cathy Ann Rankin Connaughton, Wayde A. A.B., Forsyth/Dental Hygiene, 1957; A.B., Greenfield Coll., 1967; B.S., St. Joseph's Coll., 1980. Dir. nursing Merrill Meml. Manor, Gardiner, Maine, 1967-76, Colonial House, Waterville, Maine, 1976-82; resident service dir., 1976—, in-service dir., 1983-85; adminstr. Fieldcrest Manor, Waldoboro, Maine, 1982-83; cons. Merrill Meml. Manor, 1976-83, Country Manor, Coopers Mills, Maine, 1976-79; dir. nursing Service Colonial House, 1976—, Fieldcrest Manor, 1976—. Treas. 'Run for Your Life', Manchester, Maine, 1978-84. Mem. Am. Coll. Health Care Adminstrs., Am. Nurses Assn., Am. Health Care Assn., Forsyth Alumni Assn., Maine Council Nursing Service Adminstrs. Republican. Episcopalian. Avocations: tennis; golf; jogging. Home: Box 119 Manchester ME 04351 Office: Colonial House 110 College Ave Waterville ME 04901

RANKIN, HELEN CROSS, cattle rancher, guest ranch executive; b. Mojave, Calif; d. John Whisman and Cleo Rebecca (Tilley) Cross; m. Leroy Rankin, Jan. 4, 1936 (dec. 1954); children—Julia Jane Shaar, Patricia Helen Denvir, William John. A.B., Calif. State U.-Fresno, 1935. Owner, operator Rankin Cattle Ranch, Caliente, Calif., 1954—; founder, pres. Rank Ranch, Inc., Guest Ranch, 1965—; mem. sect. 15, U.S. Bur. Land Mgmt.; mem. U.S. Food and Agrl. Leaders Tour China, 1983, Australia and N.Z., 1985; dir. U.S. Bur. Land Mgmt. sect. 15. Pres., Children's Home Soc. Calif., 1945. Recipient award Calif. Hist. Soc., 1983, Kern River Valley Hist. Soc., 1983. Mem. Am. Nat. Cattlemen's Assn., Calif. Cattlemen's Assn., Kern County Cattlemen's Assn., Kern County Cowbelles (pres. 1949), Calif. Cowbelles, Nat. Cowbelles. Republican. Baptist. Club: Bakersfield Country. Lodge: Bakersfield Raquet. Office: Rankin Ranch Caliente CA 93518

RANKIN, JUDITH TORLUEMKE, profl. golfer; b. St. Louis, Feb. 18, 1945; d. Paul W. and Waneta (Clifton) Torluemke; student public schs., Eureka, Mo.; m. Walter Rankin, June 12, 1967; 1 son, Walter. Profl. golfer; pres. Ladies Profl. Golfers Assn., 1976-77. Recipient Vare trophy for lowest scoring average, 1973-76; Victor award for Female golfer, 1976; leading money winner, 1976-77; first woman to win more than $100,000 in one year, 1976. Author: Natural Way to Golf Power. Address: 2405 Culpepper Midland TX 79701

RANKIN, MARLENE OWENS, personnel executive, clinical social worker; b. Cleve., Apr. 19, 1939; d. James Cleveland (Jesse) and Minnie Ruth (Solomon) Owens; m. Stuart McLean Rankin, Nov. 19, 1961; 1 son, Stuart Owen. B.S. in Social Welfare, Ohio State U., 1961; A.M. (M.S.W.), U. Chgo., 1978. Cert. social worker; cert. in alcoholism. Caseworker, Cook County Dept. Pub. Aid, Chgo., 1961-66; social worker Project Learn, Chgo., 1968-69; social service planner Chgo. Com. Urban Opportunity, OEO, Chgo., 1969-72, planning coordinator, Model Cities, 1972-74; social service planner Gov.'s Office Human Relations Chgo., 1974-75; therapist United Charities Chgo., 1978-81; dir. personnel, 1981—. Bd. dirs. Hyde Park Neighborhood Club, Chgo., 1982—; mem. Personnel Dir. Group United Way, Chgo., 1982—. Mem. Acad. Cert. Social Workers. Democrat. Methodist. Office: United Charities of Chgo 14 E Jackson Blvd Chicago IL 60604

RANKIN, PEGE BETTY, educator; b. Twin Falls, Idaho, July 23, 1919; d. Marion P. and Margaret (Conway) Betty; B.A., U. Calif.-Berkeley, 1941; postgrad. U. Calif.-Berkeley, Calif. State Coll., Savannah State Coll., San Francisco State Coll.; M.Ed., U. San Francisco, 1976; m. Herbert E. Rankin, June 5, 1941; children—Greg Robert, Todd Conway. Tchr. contract bridge San Francisco Bay area, 1950-69; pres., officer Oakland Pub. Schs. (Calif.), 1967—; tchr. journalism Skyline High Sch., Oakland, 1967—; tchr. guide European coll. tours, summers 1970—. Chmn. div. fund Am. Cancer Soc., 1958; organizer, condr. Mental Health Bridge Charity, 1961; mem. Friends of Herrick Hosp., Friends of Berkeley Library, Wall Street Jour.; mem. adv. bd. Invest in America. Named Outstanding Tchr. Journalism, Calif. PTA; Newspaper Fund fellow, 1969. Mem. AAUW, Am. Contract Bridge League, Oakland Press Honor Assn., Women in Communications (scholarship chmn. 1973), Columbia Scholastic Press Assn., Journalism Educators No. Calif. (v.p. 1980), San Francisco Opera Guild, Calif. Acad. Sci., M.H. de Young Meml. Mus., Smithsonian Assocs., Alpha Chi Alpha. Republican. Methodist. Club: Fannie Hill Ski (San Francisco). Home: 752 Cragmont Ave Berkeley CA 94708 Office: 12250 Skyline Blvd Oakland CA 94619

RANKIN, RACHEL ANN, media specialist; b. High Point, N.C., Mar. 8, 1937; d. Benjamin Carl and Anne Jane (Robinson) Mixson; m. Thomas M. Rankin, July 30, 1961; 1 dau., Roxanne. A.A., Mars Hill Coll., 1957; B.A., Wake Forest U., 1959; M.L.S., U. S.C., 1977. Caseworker, Rockingham County Welfare, Reidsville, N.C., 1959-61; tchr. Reidsville & Rockingham County Schs., Reidsville, Wentworth, 1961-65, Berlin Am. Sch. (W.Ger.), 1967-69, Albemarle County Schs., Charlottesville, Va., 1970-72, Lexington County Schs., Ballentine, S.C., 1973-76; teaching asst., student tchr. supr. Sch. Edn., U. S.C., Columbia, 1976-77; sch. media specialist Montgomery County Schs., Rockville, Md., 1977—. Vice-pres. Berlin Am. PTA, 1967-68; del. European Conf. PTA's, Garmisch, West Germany, 1968; mem. planning com. N.C. Cherry Blossom Ball, Ct., Washington, 1983. Named Most Outstanding Tchr., Jackson Burley Sch., Charlottesville, Va., 1972; ofcl. citation Ho. of Dels., Md. Gen. Assembly, 1983. Mem. NEA (life), Internat. Assn. Sch. Librarians (del. 1983), Am. Assn. Sch. Librarians (del. Montgomery County 1982), ALA, Md. Ednl. Media Orgn., Montgomery County Ednl. Media Specialists Assn. (treas. 1981-82, newsletter editor 1979-80), Montgomery County Edn. Assn., Montgomery County Ednl. Media Specialists Assn. (pres. 1983-84), N.C. State Soc. of Washington (bd. govs. 1984-86), Internat.

Platform Assn., Delta Kappa Gamma. Democrat. Presbyterian. Club: N.C. Soc. (Washington). Home: 2912 Bluff Point Ln Silver Spring MD 20906 Office: Springbrook High Sch 201 Valleybrook Dr Silver Spring MD 20908

RANNEY, HELEN MARGARET, physician; b. Summer Hill, N.Y., Apr. 12, 1920; d. Arthur C. and Alesia (Toolan) R.; A.B., Barnard Coll., 1941; M.D., Columbia U., 1947; Sc.D. (hon.), U. So. Calif., 1979. Intern, Presbyn. Hosp., N.Y.C., 1947-48, resident, 1948-50; practice medicine, specializing in internal medicine, hematology, N.Y.C., 1954-70; asst. physician Presbyn. Hosp., 1954-60; instr. Coll. Physicians and Surgeons, Columbia U., 1954-60; assoc. prof. medicine Albert Einstein Coll. Medicine, 1960-64, prof. medicine, 1965-70; prof. medicine SUNY-Buffalo, 1970-73; prof. medicine U. Calif., San Diego, 1973—, chmn. dept., 1973-86. Mem. Am. Soc. Clin. Investigation, Am. Soc. Hematology, Harvey Soc., Am. Assn. Physicians, Nat. Acad. Sci., Inst. Medicine, Am. Acad. Arts and Scis., Phi Beta Kappa, Sigma Xi, Alpha Omega Alpha. Home: 6229 La Jolla Mesa Dr La Jolla CA 92037

RANSOHOFF, PRISCILLA BURNETT, psychologist, educator; b. Pitts., June 16, 1912; d. Levi Herr and Clara Amelia (Brown) Burnett; B.S., U. Pitts., 1941; M.A., Columbia U., 1952, Ed.D., 1954; m. James Hampton Johnston, Aug. 4, 1934; 1 dau., Priscilla Burnett; m. 2d, Nicholas Sigmund Ransohoff, Nov. 27, 1947. Dir. rehab. Monmouth Med. Center, Long Branch, N.J., 1944-54; pres. Cons. Assocs., Inc., Long Branch, 1954-64; v.p. Dale-Elliot Mgmt. Cons., N.Y.C., 1958-60; edn. adviser U.S. Army Electronics Command, Ft. Monmouth, N.J., 1964-78; organizational effectiveness staff officer U.S. Army Communications Materiel Readiness Command, Ft. Monmouth, 1978—; co-adj. prof. Ocean County Community Coll., Toms River, N.J.; coadj. instr. Monmouth Coll., West Long Branch, N.J., Brookdale Community Coll., Lincroft, N.J. Founder, pres., chmn. bd. Monmouth Rehab. Workshop, Red Bank, N.J., 1954-58; vice chmn. N.J. del. Women's Conf., Houston, 1977 Recipient CECOM Comdr.'s Internat., 1982; Woman of Yr. award Zonta, 1984; cert. practitioner neuro linguistic programming. Mem. Orgn. Devel. Network, Internat. Platform Assn., Federally Employed Women (pres. 1973, 74, chpt. pres. 1984-86), Assn. U.S. Army (chpt. bd. dirs., adv. com. to nat. bd. dirs.), Def. Preparedness Assn., Assn. U.S. Army (sec.), Pi Lambda Theta, Kappa Delta Pi, Delta Zeta. Clubs: Toastmistress, Zonta (sec., bd. dirs. Monmouth chpt.), Order Eastern Star. Home: 13 River Ave Monmouth Beach NJ 07750 Office: Aviation Research and Devel Activity Fort Monmouth NJ 07703

RANSOM, MARGARET PRISCILLA, government official; b. Jackson, N.C., Sept. 17, 1947; d. Lister and Argentina (Lockhart) R.; B.S., N.C. A&T State U., 1969; M.A., Central Mich. U., 1981. With IRS, various locations, 1969—, exempt orgns. analyst, Washington, 1976-82, group mgr., Balt., 1982—. Recipient Communications and Services to Public award IRS, 1971, Disting. performance award, 1982, 85, group award for program accomplishments, 1983. Mem. Nat. Assn. Female Execs., Assn. Improvement of Minorities in Internal Revenue Service, Federally Employed Women, Profl. Mgrs. Assn., Delta Sigma Theta. Office: 31 Hopkins Plaza Baltimore MD 21203

RANZMAN, SUSAN, educational administrator; b. N.Y.C., Feb. 1, 1944; d. Samuel and Estelle (Rodolfsky) Weiner; m. Steven Michael Ranzman, Apr. 2, 1966; 1 son, Scott Michael. B.S., LIU, 1966; M.A., NYU, 1976; postgrad. Seton Hall U., 1981—. Instr., The Berkeley-Claremont Sch., N.Y.C., 1966-76; acad. dean The Berkeley Sch., Little Falls, N.J., 1976-82, acting pres., 1982—. Mem. Nat. Bus. Edn. Assn., N.J. Bus. Edn. Assn., Nat. Assn. Female Execs., NOW, Delta Pi Epsilon. Democrat. Jewish.

RAPP, DORRIE LOUISE, clinical psychologist; b. Chgo., Sept. 14, 1949; d. Edward Thomas and Louise Kathryn (Leisten) Tholke; B.A., U. Ill., Chgo., 1970; Ph.D., Cambridge U., Eng., 1977, diploma in clin. psychology, 1981. Psychologist, Spastics Soc., London, 1976-79; asst. dir. psychol. services Moss Rehab. Hosp., Phila., 1981-83; pvt. practice, 1983—; neuropsychologist Drucker Brain Injury Ctr., 1984-85. Lic. psychologist, Pa. Fellow Am. Acad. Cerebral Palsy and Devel. Medicine (Richmond Cerebral Palsy Center award 1980); mem. Am. Psychol. Assn., Pa. Psychol. Assn., Phila. Soc. Clin. Psychologists, Brit. Psychol. Soc., Nat. Acad. Neuropsychologists, Nat. Head Injury Found., Phila. Clin. Neuropsychology Group, Internat. Neuropsychology Group. Inventor drool control electronic device, 1979; author: Brain Injury Casebook, 1986; contbr. articles in field to profl. publs.

RAPP, MARJORIE LENORE (GREEN), financial manager; b. Elmhurst, Ill., June 5, 1932; d. DeWitt Clinton and Ruth Marion (Mueller) Green; B.A. with honors, U. Chgo., 1951, M.A. with honors, 1954; postgrad. U. Colo.; m. Alan Dean Rapp, June 14, 1953; children—Jeffrey Clinton, Martha Coralynne, David Cyril. Gen. mgr. Sark Aviation, Colorado Springs, Colo., 1961-64; North Union Devel. Co., also LaSalle Devel. Co., Colorado Springs, 1964-76; v.p., chief fin. officer Janus Corp., Colorado Springs, 1964-70; v.p., treas. Med. and Data Services, Inc., Colorado Springs, 1977-78; founder, 1978, owner Pandora Enterprises, Colorado Springs, 1978—; mng. gen. ptnr. Soda Creek Land Co., 1983—; gen. ptnr. RMD Enterprises, 1985—, R&N Enterprises, 1985— (all Colorado Springs); seminar tchr., 1975—. Dir. Candy-Stripe program St. Francis Hosp., Colorado Springs, 1967-68; asst. to minister music First Presbyn. Ch., Colorado Springs, 1967-73, genealogy research librarian Penrose Public Library, Colorado Springs, 1971-73; pres. guild Colorado Springs Choral Soc., 1962-63; treas., bd. dirs. Colo. Opera Festival, 1978-81. Mem. Earthwatch, Nat. Trust Historic Preservation, Nat. Geneal. Soc. New Eng. Hist. and Geneal. Soc., Soc. Preservation New Eng. Antiquities, Colo. Geneal Soc., Pikes Peak Geneal. Soc., Colorado Springs Fine Arts Ctr., Friends of the Pikes Peak Library Dist., Friends of the Pioneers Mus., Friends of White House Ranch, Opera Council of 500, Arthritis Found., Cheyenne Mountain Zoo Vol. Assn., Smithsonian Assocs., Am. Assn. Ret. Persons, AAUW, DAR, Mayflower Soc., Meml. Hosp. Aux. (life), Quadrangler Alumni Assn. (life), El Paso County Med. Aux., Phi Beta Kappa. Republican. Clubs: Colorado Springs Country, Plaza (founder). Address: 4807 Avondale Circle Colorado Springs CO 80917

RAPPAPORT, BARBARA HARRIET, telecommunications company executive; b. Newark, July 14, 1948; d. Arthur Oscar and Selma (Sklaw) R. B.A., Douglass Coll., 1970; M.B.A., Fairleigh Dickenson U., 1979; basic data cert. Pace U., 1983. Sr. sales cons. Coradian Corp., N.Y.C., 1980-82; sr. telecommunications analyst Mfrs. Hanover Trust Co., N.Y.C., 1982-83; govt. mktg. specialist Tel Plus Mid Atlantic, Somerset, N.J., 1984—. Co-chairperson N.J. ERA Campaign, Union, 1974; mem. Union County Democratic Platform Com., N.J., 1973; v.p. Union County Women's Polit. Caucus, 1975; columnist Young Democrats Middlesex County, N.J., 1976. Mem. Nat. Assn. Female Execs., AAUW (chpt. publicity chairperson 1985-86), Women in Telecommunications. Jewish. Avocations: travel; exercise; theater; concerts; reading.

RAPPAPORT, ELAINE, financial analyst; b. Copiague, N.Y., Dec. 10, 1953; d. William and Hannah (Soskin) R.; m. Albert Phaneuf, May 25, 1975 (div. 1979). A.A.S. in Computer Sci., NYU, 1978, B.A. in Fin., 1984. Adminstrv. asst. Citibank, N.A., N.Y.C., 1972-81, fin. analyst, 1981—. Schoemkin scholar NYU, 1979. Mem. Nat. Assn. Bank Cost Analyst, Nat. Assn. Female Execs., TCAPS Users Group. Democrat. Jewish. Avocations: traveling; tennis; swimming. Office: Citibank NA 153 E 53d St New York NY 10043

RAPPAPORT, ELIZABETH APPEL, banker; b. N.Y.C., June 17, 1950; d. Sydney Charles and Rosalind (Appel) R. B.A., Finch Coll., 1972; M.S., Columbia U., 1974; M.B.A., Fordham U., 1980. Asst. sec. Mfrs. Hanover Trust, N.Y.C., 1976-81; asst. v.p. Barclays Bank Internat., N.Y.C., 1981-82, Bank Hapoalim, N.Y.C., 1983; v.p., team leader Creditanstalt-Bankverein, N.Y.C., 1984—. Bd. dirs. Council for a Beautiful Israel, N.Y.C., 1984. Mem. Nat. Assn. Female Execs. Democrat. Jewish. Club: Columbia (N.Y.C.). Office: Creditanstalt-Bankverein 717 Fifth Ave New York NY 10022

RAPPAPORT, MARGARET M., psychologist, consultant, author; b. Buffalo, Nov., 16, 1941; d. Leo J. and Marie L. (Fischle) W.; m. Herbert Rappaport, Oct. 21, 1967; children—Amanda, Alexander. B.A., U. Buffalo, 1967; M.A., SUNY, 1969; Ph.D., U Colo., 1971. Adj. faculty Temple U., Phila., 1974-1984; dir. Inst. for Parent/Child Services, Phila., 1978—; pvt. practice clinician Rappaport Assocs., Phila., 1974— prof., researcher Univ. Dar es Salaam, Tanzania, 1970-74; program dir. Frontrunners, 1978—; child care/devel. cons. to media especialy TV, 1984—. Author books, articles on psychology, parenting, child devel., existential psychology. Mem. NOW, AAUP, NAEYC, DVAEYC. Republican. Club: Phila. Cricket (Pa.). Home: 509 E Sedgwick St Philadelphia PA 19119 Office: Inst for Parent/Child Services Philadelphia PA 19119

RAPPAPORT, YVONNE KINDINGER, educator, lectr.; b. Crestline, Ohio, Feb. 15, 1928; d. Paul Theodore and Florence Iona (Cover) Kindinger; B.S. summa cum laude, Northwestern U., 1949; M.A., Va. Poly. Inst. and State U., 1973, Ph.D., 1980; m. Norman Lewis Rappaport; children—Michael, Laura, Hilary, Stephen, Jocelyn. Personnel officer, then cons. and mgmt. analyst USAF, 1953-63; cons. mgmt. analysis, personnel and public relations, 1963-67; cons. program devel., instr. U. Va., 1967-70, dir. continuing edn. for women, 1970-75, dir. and faculty continuing edn. for adult, 1975—; dir., performer theatre, children's theatre, radio and TV, 1953—; bd. dirs. Coalition Adult Edn. Orgns. U.S., 1979—, sec.-treas., 1981-83, v.p., 1983-84, pres.-elect 1984-85; U.S. rep. UNESCO conf., 1983; cons. in field. Mem. Va. Legis. Adv. Com. Continuing Edn., 1970-71, No. Va. Adv. Com. Ednl. Telecommunications, 1971—; bd. dirs. Home and Sch. Inst., Washington, 1971—; adv. bd. Service League Va., 1976-78. Recipient Meritorious Service award USAF, 1959; Career Devel. award ASTD/TOC, 1980. Mem. Nat. Assn. Women Deans, Adminstrs. and Counselors (S.E. regional coordinator 1973-76), adult edn. assns. U.S. (Nat. Leadership award 1973, 74, 76, 78, 79, 82, 83; v.p. 1978-79; chmn. commn. status women in edn. 1972-74, dir. 1973-83, chmn. council affiliate orgns. 1974-75, chmn. pub. affairs 1975-78), Va. (pres. 1971-73; Recognition of Merit award 1971-73), LWV (state dir. 1968-73, nat. public relations com. 1970-75), AAUW, PTA, Am. Personnel and Guidance Assn., Nat. Univ. Extension Assn., Assn. Continuing Higher Edn., Am. Bus. Women Assn. (award 1960), Phi Delta Kappa. Club; Order Eastern Star. Author handbooks and work books, also radio, TV scripts. Home: 3225 Atlanta St Fairfax VA 22030 Office: Sch Continuing Edn Univ Va Charlottesville VA 22903

RAPPAPORT-MUSSON, JUDITH BARBARA, advertising agency executive; b. N.Y.C., Dec. 16, 1942; d. Norman and Helen (Neuman) Rappaport; m. John Sydney Musson, Nov. 28, 1978; children—Derek, Kimberlee. Student, U. N.C.-Asheville, 1961. Media clk. Burke Dowling Adams, Atlanta, 1962-63; media dir. Marshall Simmons Advt., Miami, 1965-76; sales mgr. WQAM Radio, Miami, 1978-79, WVCG/WYOR Radio, Coral Gables, Fla., 1979-80; ptnr. Britain & Rappaport, Miami, 1983—; Media & Mktg. Specialists, Inc., Miami, 1980—; advt. cons. WLRN-TV, Miami, 1982—, Children's Home Soc., Miami, 1984. Vol. counselor The Starting Place Crisis Ctr., Hollywood, Fla., 1973; vol. Variety Children's Hosp., Miami, 1964; bd. dirs., Jr. Achievement Greater Miami. Mem. Am. Mktg. Assn., Econ. Soc. South Fla. Democrat. Jewish. Office: Britain & Rappaport Inc 10661 N Kendall Dr Suite 113 Miami FL 33176

RAPPLEYEA, TOMI JEAN, financial analyst; b. Peoria, Ill., Nov. 14, 1941; d. Donald Denver and Nadine Alice (Burns) Wilkey; B.S. in Quantitative Methods, U. Ill., 1978; M.B.A., U. Chgo., 1979; m. Frederick Arthur Rappleyea, Nov. 9, 1968; children—Christopher David, Catherine Lynn, Frederick Arthur, Jr. Treas. Cougar, Inc., Bensenville, Ill., 1970-76; sr. systems analyst Exxon, U.S.A., Houston, 1979-80; sr. fin. analyst Exxon USA, Houston, 1980-81, refining analyst, Baytown, Tex., 1981-82, sr. fin. specialist Hdqrs. Computing Services, Houston, 1982—. Head Coach Schiller (Ill.) Park Youth Assn., 1968-74; active Park Ridge Citizens Party, Park Ridge, Ill., 1976-79; dir., treas. Park Ridge Swim Club, 1977-78. C.P.A., Ill., Tex. Mem. Am. Inst. C.P.A.s, Tex. Soc. C.P.A.s (Houston chpt.), AAU, Am. Contract Bridge League, U.S. Masters Swimming Club, Phi Kappa Phi, Beta Gamma Sigma. Home: 8806 Cedarbrake St Houston TX 77055 Office: PO Box 2180 Houston TX 77001

RAPPS, RHONDA WILKINSON, psychologist; b. Baytown, Tex., Aug. 28, 1947; d. John Meier and Helen Alice (Powers) Wilkinson; B.A. with high honors in Psychology, U. Ark., 1969; M.A. (teaching fellow), cert. sch. psychology, Fairleigh Dickinson U., 1973; Psy.D. (teaching fellow) Rutgers U., 1975; m. Paul E. Rapps, Sept. 11, 1975; 1 child, Jennifer Leigh. Sch. psychologist Newark Public Schs., 1972-73, Westfield (N.J.) Public Schs., 1975-81; pvt. practice psychology Human Potential Inst., Warren, N.J., 1978—; cons. mental health agy., nursing home, sch. emotionally disturbed children, Hunterdon Med. Center, tchr. Middlesex County Coll., Fairleigh Dickinson U., Hackensack Hosp. Profl. adv. com. Somerset County Assn. Retarded Citizens. Lic. psychologist, N.J.; cert. sch. psychologist, dir. student personnel services, N.J.; instr. parent effectiveness tng. Mem. Am. Psychol. Assn., Nat. Assn. Sch. Psychologists, Alpha Epsilon Delta, Psi Chi, Kappa Delta Pi, Alpha Chi Omega. Home and Office: 45 Washington Valley Rd Warren NJ 07060

RAPS-BECKERMAN, HELENE IVY, government bond trader; b. Bklyn., Jan. 14, 1954; d. David and Mildred (Mayo) Raps; m. Mitchell Bruce Beckerman, Oct. 12, 1975. B.S. in Mgmt., SUNY-Binghamton, 1975; M.B.A. in Fin. and Econs., Adelphi U., Garden City, N.Y., 1986. Cert. Securities and Exchange Commn., Chgo. Bd. Trade. Bond clk. Dean Witter Reynolds, Inc., N.Y.C., 1975-76, retail bond trader, 1976-78, instl. bond trades, 1978-81, v.p. govt. bond trading, 1981—. Contbg. author: Creating a Management Information System for Medicaid/Medicare, 1976. Pres. Forest Hills Tenants Assn. (N.Y.), 1976-82. Mem. Women's Bond Club N.Y. Office: Dean Witter Reynolds Inc Govt Dept 130 Liberty St New York NY 10006

RARRICK, BEVERLY JOANN, embroidery company executive; b. Junction City, Kans., Dec. 16, 1932; d. Harry E. and Viola B. (Hartman) Smith; m. Walter Rarrick, Feb. 2, 1949 (dic. Sept. 1969); 2 children—Michael R., Marlin J. Grad. high sch., Junction City. Buyer, mgr. Dryer Shoe, Springfield, Mo., 1966-68; book-keeper Zale Corp., 1968-69; credit mgr. Hess & Culbertson, Jewelers, 1969-71; owner, pres. Bev's Embroidery Inc., Springfield, 1970—. Author children's stories. Worker, Civil Def., Springfield, 1970-73; officer React Internat. cancer drive, 1978-80; chmn., sec. Heart Fund; judge beauty contest Dallas County Alumni, Buffalo, Mo., 1980, 82, 85. Named Outstanding Young Woman Am., NCO Wives, 1965. Republican. Baptist. Avocations: crochet; carving; beadwork; oil painting; golfing. Home: 730 W Broadmoor St Springfield MO 56807 Office: Bev's Embroidery 2500 S Holland St Springfield MO 65807

RASBERRY, SHAROL BARTA, accountant, management company executive; b. Red Cloud, Nebr., Oct. 15, 1947; d. Allen James and Orfa Irene (Copley) Barta; B.B.A., U. Nebr., 1969; m. Robert E. Rasberry, Dec. 29, 1968; children—Kimberly, Robert E. Tax prin. Arthur Young & Co., Wichita, Kans., 1969-79; dir. taxes CWG Enterprises, Wichita, Kans., 1979-80; exec. v.p. fin. Capital Management Co., Wichita, 1980—. Bd. dirs. YWCA, 1978, Accent on Kids, 1983—. C.P.A. Mem., Wichita Jr. League, Am. Inst. C.P.A.s, Kans. Soc. C.P.A.s. Republican. Home: 220 Post Oak Wichita KS 67206 Office: 300 N Main St Suite 200 Wichita KS 67201

RASDALL, JOYCE OLIVER, home economist, educator; b. Simpson County, Ky., Dec. 10, 1944; d. Thomas Franklin and Ruth A. (Heard) Oliver; B.S., Western Ky. U., 1965; M.S., U. N.C., Greensboro, 1968; Ph.D., Ohio State U., 1973; m. L. D. Rasdall, Jr., Aug. 15, 1965; children—L. Dow, Rebecca Ruth. Consumer service specialist Warren Rural Electric Coop. Corp., Bowling Green, Ky., 1966-68; research asso. Ohio State U., Columbus, 1970-71; instr., then asst. prof. dept. home econs. Western Ky. U., Bowling Green, 1968-78, assoc. prof. interior design, housing and household equipment, 1978-83, prof., 1983—, sabbatical leave, 1982; TV program Women, Yes, 1966-68; radio program House Call, 1967-68; also lectr. workshops. Trustee, Warren Assn. Bapt. Properties, 1978-82; trustee Campbellsville Coll., 1983-87, mem. exec. com., 1984-86; mem. North Warren Bicentennial Events Com., 1976; assn. dir. Ky. Bapt. Young Women, 1978-84; participant Ky. to Kenya Partnership, 1985; founding benefactor, College Heights Found., Pres.' Club of Western Ky. U., Pres.' Club of Campbellsville Coll.; v.p., then pres. N.Warren PTA, 1978-80; cons. and judge electricity projects 4-H Club. Recipient research award Am. Council on Consumer Interests, 1974, outstanding mem. service award Nat. Rural Electric Coops., 1968, R.C.P. Thomas award Western Ky. U., 1965; faculty research grantee, 1979, 83; faculty devel. grantee, 1983, 85; Am. Home Econs. Assn. fellow Ohio State U., 1970-71. Mem. Am. Home Econs. Assn., Am. Assn. Housing Educators, Ky. Home Econs. Assn. (various coms.), Elec. Women's Roundtable (nat. chmn. Julia Kiene grad. fellowship and Lyle Marner grad. scholarship), ASTM (affiliate, standards devel. com.), Ky. Elec. Women's Round Table (officer, v.p., sec.), Coll. Educators in Home Equipment (pres. elect, pres., chmn. ann. meeting, research award 1985), Internat. Microwave Power Inst., Ky. Youth Electric Adv. Council, Nat. Trust Hist. Preservation, Phi Upsilon Omicron (sponsor univ. chpt., Outstanding Alumnus award Western Ky. U. 1983), Omicron Nu. Clubs: Smiths Grove Woman's (pres.), Ky. Fedn. Women's Clubs (coms.). Author: Information on Consumer Products: A Study of Factors Affecting its Use by Consumers, 1974; Product Information as a Resource: Factors Affecting its Usefulness to Consumers, 1974; The Utility of Product Information as a Resource for Consumer Use, 1977; Consumer Competencies in Household Equipment, 1975; Plan the Light in Your Home, 1970; (with others) Microwave Ovens, 1972; The Energy Dilemma: Some Choices Confronting the American Family, 1978; Energy Productivity and Creativity in the Household (series of slides sets and scripts), 1982; Funds and Instrumentation for Conducting Research with Limited Funds and Heavy Teaching Assignments, 1983; Black Women in Kenya: Roles and Resources, 1986, others. Contbr. articles to profl. jours. Home: PO Box 206 Smiths Grove KY 42171 Office: Dept Home Economics and Family Living Western Ky U Bowling Green KY 42101

RASK, PAMELA ANN, lawyer; b. Boston, Aug. 7, 1948; d. Kenneth Harold and Lorraine (Crehan) R. Student Ruhr U., Bochum, W.Ger., 1969-70; B.A., U. Minn., 1971; M.A., Cornell U., 1974; J.D., N.Y. U., 1981. Bar: D.C. 1982. Bookseller, Kiepert KG, Berlin, 1974-76; atty. U.S. Patent & Trademark Office, Washington, 1981-82; assoc. Brownstein Zeidman & Schomer, Washington, 1983—. Asst. editor: Law and Television of the 80's, 1983. Fulbright fellow, U. Heidelberg, 1973-74. Mem. D.C. Bar Assn., ABA, U.S. Trademark Assn. Office: Brownstein Zeidman & Schomer 1025 Connecticut Ave NW Washington DC 20036

RASKASY, KAREN TONI, information systems executive; b. Trenton, N.J., Sept. 1, 1946; d. Earl Francis and Elizabeth (Trunko) Kamanski; m. Albert Louis Raskasky, Nov. 11, 1978; children—Louis, Michael. B.A., Rutgers U., 1968. Software cons., systems analyst John Licht Assocs., Middletown, N.J., and Ednl. Testing Service, Princeton, N.J., 1970-73; sect. leader, project mgr. Electronics Assocs. Inc., West Long Branch, 1973-75; systems program mgr. Talstar, Princeton, 1977; software cons. Electronic Assocs. Inc., West Long Branch, N.J., and Delta Data Systems Co., Cornell Heights, Pa., 1975-78; mgr. research systems and program Ortho Pharm. Corp., Raritan, N.J., 1980-84, dir. research systems and program, 1984—; mem. com. utilization of computers in research and devel. Johnson & Johnson, New Brunswick, N.J., 1983—, chmn. com. research security white paper, Raritan, 1984-85; mem. research computer validation com. Pharm. Mfrs. Assn., Washington, 1985—. Author and presentor tech. papers. Leader explorer post Boy Scouts Am., Raritan, 1984-85. Named Outstanding Woman in Bus. and Industry, Somerset County C. of C., N.J., 1984. Mem. Assn. Computing Machinery, Drug Info. Assn., Nat. Assn. Female Execs. Avocations: swimming; photography. Home: 156 Cannon Rd Freehold NJ 07728 Office: Ortho Pharm Corp Rt 202 PO Box 300 Raritan NJ 08869-0602

RASMUSSEN, CAREN NANCY, hospital executive; b. Fort Riley, Kans., July 7, 1950; d. Stanley Junior and Katherina Wilhelmina (Wagner) R. A.A.S., Grand Rapids Jr. Coll., 1970; B.S., U. Md., 1977. Med. sec., Walter Reed Army Med. Ctr., Washington, 1970-73, sec. procurement, 1972-76, contract specialist, 1976-79, 81-84; contract specialist Kadena Air Base, Okinawa, 1979-81; procurement analyst Walter Reed Med. ctr., 1984—. Fellow Nat. Assn. Female Execs. Democrat. Avocations: photography; stamp collecting; gardening; travel. Home: 17514 Longview Ln Olney MD 20832 Office: Contracting Div Walter Reed Army Med Ctr Washington DC 20307

RASMUSSEN, LOUISE GARNET, newspaper publisher, editor; b. Roundup, Mont., Aug. 27, 1914; d. Alfred William and Rachel Victoria (Johnston) Eiselein; m. Kenneth P. Rasmussen, Nov. 4, 1944; children—Polly Louise, Eric Neil. B.A. in Journalism, U. Mont., 1937. Reporter, Roundup Record-Tribune, Mont., 1931-37, 52—, editor, 1959—, pub., 1962—; editor/publisher Winnett Times, Roundup, 1975—. Recipient Community Service plaque C. of C., 1980; Outstanding Service award to 4-H, 1983. Mem. Mont. Press Assn. (dir. 1967-69, 75-81, pres. 1979-80), Mont. Advt. Service (pres. 1967-68), Musselshell Valley C. of C. (dir. 1971-80). Republican. Episcopalian. Lodge: P.E.O. (pres. 1980-81). Avocations: gardening; reading; fishing. Home: 324 4th St W PO Box 747 Roundup MT 59072 Office: Roundup Record-Tribune 24 Main St Box 747 Roundup MT 59072

RASMUSSEN, PAULA ANNE, environmental engineer; b. Gardena, Calif., July 7, 1954; d. James Dale and Patricia (Boute) Rasmussen. B.S. in Biology, U. So. Calif., 1976, M.S. in Environmental Engring., 1978. Environ. engr. EPA, San Francisco, 1978-81; san. engr. Calif. Dept. Health, Sanitary Engring. Br., Los Angeles, 1981-83; environ. engr. Calif. Dept. Health, Toxic Substances Control Div., Los Angeles, 1983—, program mgr. storage and treatment permits unit. State scholar Calif., 1974-76; Univ. scholar, U. So. Calif., 1974-76. Mem. Am. Water Works Assn., Calif. Water Pollution Control Assn. Club: Family Fitness (Los Angeles). Home: 205 E Maple Ave El Segundo CA 90245 Office: Dept of Health Toxic Substances Control Div 107 S Broadway Room 7128 Los Angeles CA 90012

RASMUSSEN, SUSAN JEAN, industrial relations manager; b. Lynchburg, Va., Oct. 15, 1953; d. Keith George and Mary Jean (Detamore) R.; m. Anthony Deckard, May 1, 1982. B.A. in Urban Studies, Wright State U., 1974. Human resources trainee Mead Corp., Dayton, Ohio, 1975-76; hourly employment mgr. Mead Packaging, Atlanta, 1976-77, employee relations rep., 1977-79, employee relations supr., 1979-81, mgr. indsl. relations, 1981—. Active NOW. Mem. Am. Soc. Personnel Adminstrn. Presbyterian. Home: 329 Coventry Rd Decatur GA 30030 Office: Mead Packaging 1040 W Marietta St NW Atlanta GA 30318

RASMUSSON, PATRICIA BAILEY, county official; b. Mpls., Apr. 5, 1938; d. Joseph Eaton and Francess Irene (Beck) Bailey; m. Gary Norville Rasmusson, June 30, 1956; children—Katherine Janese Rasmusson Brady, Kelly Judeen Rasmusson Jacobus, Kenton Shane. Student U. Minn., 1963. Registered abstracter. Beautician Pat's Beauty Bar, Elk River, Minn., 1958-62; escrow agent Minn. Title Ins., Mpls., 1962-67; dep. clk. of ct. Sherburne County, Minn., 1967-72, dep. county recorder, 1972-78, county recorder, 1978—; pres. Sherburne County Abstract and Title Co., Elk River, 1978—; tchr. rec. standards to fellow recorders, 1983—, to new county commrs., 1984—. Treas. ARC, Elk River, 1976-79; bd. dirs. Masonic Cancer Hosp. U. Minn., Mpls., 1983-86, Minn. Masonic Home and Care Ctr., Mpls., 1983, 85—; mem. adv. com. Mayor's Council, Elk River, 1982. Mem. Minn. County Recorders Assn. (pres. 1982-83 Recorder of Yr. 1983), Minn. Land Title Assn., Am. Land Title Assn., Minn. County Officers Assn. (pres. 1983-84), Elk River C. of C. (chmn. govt. affairs 1985—, bd. dirs. 1985—). Republican. Mem. United Ch. of Christ. Lodge. Eastern Star (Worthy Grand Matron 1983-84, Worthy Grand Martha 1985—). Avocations: needlepoint; handwork; skiing; swimming; biking. Home: 631 Upland Ave Elk River MN 55330 Office: Sherburne County Abstract and Title Co 327 King Ave Elk River MN 55330

RATCLIFFE, SHIRLEY PENDLETON, real estate broker, cellular telephone executive; b. Blountville, Tenn., Mar. 30, 1932; d. Paris Lee and Elizabeth Armetia (Gammon) Pendleton; m. Robert Issac Ratcliffe, Jan. 26, 1952 (div. Apr. 1970); children—Paula, Louise, Darby. Student U. Ky., 1952, East Tenn. U., 1962-63; grad. Grad. Realtors Inst. Lic. broker, Tenn., Va., N.C. Broker, Pendleton Real Estate, Blountville, 1970—; v.p. Mount Empire Devel. Co., Kingsport, Tenn., 1971-74, Pendleton Land Co., Blountville, 1975—; pres. Tenn. Radio Telephone, Kingsport, 1982—, Cell-Tel of Knoxville, Kingsport, 1985—; chmn. Cellular One, Tri-Cities, Washington, 1984-85; pres. Ragtime Investments, Kingsport, 1978—. Vol. Contact Concern, Kingsport, 1978—; mem. Sullivan County Republican Exec. Bd., Tenn.; bd. dirs. Sullivan County LWV. Methodist. Clubs: Ridgefields Country, Ridgefield Garden. Lodge: Order Eastern Star. Avocations: golf; tennis; bridge. Home: 536-B Fleetwood Ct Kingsport TN 37660 Office: Pendleton Real Estate PO Box 253 Main St Blountville TN 37617

RATH, MARY LOU, county official; b. Buffalo, June 17; d. George Lewis and Margaret M. Whetzle; m. Edward A. Rath, Jan. 10, 1959; children—Allison, Melinda, Edward A., III. B.S., Buffalo State U., 1956; Ins. Broker's lic., U. Buffalo, 1965. Home service rep. Nat. Fuel Gas, Buffalo, 1958-61; communications affiliate Communications Affiliates of N.Y.C., 1961-67; legislator, Erie County, N.Y., 1978—, chmn. Community Sentencing Task Force, 1982, Buffalo Better Bus. Found. Bur., 1983—, various other legis. coms. 1979—. Vice pres. Research and Planning Council, Buffalo and Erie County, 1973-74; pres. Jr. League, 1973-74, mem. admissions com., 1974-78; chmn. Theodore Roosevelt Inaugural Site Restoration com., 1974-78; vol. WBEN "Call for Action", 1974-78; moderator candidates night Coalition for Better Edn., community adv. council SUNY-Buffalo, 1974—, arts adviser, 1981—; mem. Regan Dinner com., 1975; appointed Republican com. woman 8th Dist., Town of Amherst, N.Y., 1979—; trustee Buffalo Sem., 1975-79; bd. dirs. United Way of Buffalo and Erie County, 1977-78; pres. Landmark Soc. of Niagara Frontier, 1977-78; trustee, mem. vestry Calvary Episcopal Ch., Williamsville, N.Y., 1975-78; founding mem. Amherst "Lunch and Issues" program, 1980; bd. dirs. Daemen Coll. Assocs., 1980-81, Buffalo Better Bus. Bur., 1981—, Buffalo Soc. Natural Scis, 1984—; mem. commn. adv. com. State U. of N.Y. at Buffalo, 1985. Recipient Disting. Community Service award Crisis Services, 1984; named Pub. Servant of Yr., Erie County Fedn. Sportsmen's Clubs, 1981, Outstanding Women in Western N.Y., SUNY, 1984; Participant Am. Gas Assn. Lab. Tour, Cleve., 1982 (one of 8 persons invited-nationwide). Mem. Buffalo Philharm. Orchestra Soc., Buffalo Zool. Soc., Erie County Hist. Soc., Landmark Soc. Miagara Frontier, Williamsville Hist. Soc., Amherst C. of C., Buffalo C. of C., Alpha Hon. Soc. Home: 125 S Cayuga Rd Williamsville NY 14221 Office: Erie County Legislature 25 Delaware Ave Buffalo NY 14202

RATHCKE, DOROTHY ANNE, nursing adminstr., consultant; b. Napa, Calif., Mar. 19, 1922; d. Clifford Clark Harris and Florence Emily (Baldwin) Goodman; B.S. in Nursing, U. Calif., Berkeley, 1944; m. George L. Rathcke, Nov. 12, 1955; children—Karen Anne Boren, Clark Harold Kujawka, Karl Lewis. Staff nurse Napa State Hosp., Imola, Calif., 1951-52, psychiat. nursing edn., 1952-63, supt. nursing, 1963-71, nursing cons. office of program rev., 1971-77, coordinator nursing services, 1977-83; mem. task force to develop staffing standards for state hosps. Calif. Dept. Health, 1972-74. Mem. adv. bd. psychiat. technician and asso. degree nursing programs, Napa Coll.; mem. adv. bd. Regional Occupational Program, Napa Unified Sch. Dist.; mem. Com. on Continuing Edn. for Health Occupations, Napa County, 1975-83; bd. dirs. Napa chpt. Am. Heart Assn., 1975-81, v.p., 1976; mem. manpower adv. panel Dept. Mental Health State of Calif., 1981-83. NIMH grantee, 1964-72. Mem. Nat. League Nursing, Calif. League Nursing-Adminstrn., Napa County Mental Health Assn. Democrat. Office: 1912 Sierra Ave Napa CA 94558

RATHE, JUANITA (NITA), secretarial service educator; b. Ionia, Mich., Sept. 10, 1928; d. Wayne and Ernestine (Green) Bradley; m. Lowell R. Rathe, July 2, 1984; children by previous marriages—Suzanne L. Foster, Edward A. Ogden, Dawne Marie Ogden. Student Yuba Jr. Coll., 1957-58. Exec. sec. I.V. Title Co., Modesto, Calif., 1963-66, Gallo Winery, 1966-68; office mgr. R.L. Smith Acctg., Modesto, 1969-75; owner Sec. Service of Stan, Modesto, 1972—; owner, pres. Mid-State College, Inc., Modesto, 1974—. Mem. Nat. Republican Com., 1984. Mem. Calif. Assn. Health Career Educators, Nat. Assn. Health Career Schs., Better Bus. Bur., Nat. Fedn. Ind. Bus., Sonora Bus. and Profl. Women (v.p. 1972-73). Avocations: reading; writing; travel; bicycling; hiking. Office: Mid State College Inc 1314 H St Modesto CA 95354

RATHER, LUCIA JOHNSON, librarian; b. Durham, N.C., Sept. 12, 1934; d. Cecil Slayton and Lucia (Porcher) Johnson; A.B., U. N.C., 1955, M.S. in Library Sci., 1957; m. John Carson Rather, July 11, 1964; children—Susan Wright, Bruce Carson. Mem. staff Library of Congress, 1957—, asst. chief MARC devel. office, 1973-76, dir. cataloging, 1976—. Mem. ALA (Margaret Mann citation 1985), Internat. Fedn. Library Assns. and Instns. (chmn. working group corp. headings 1977-79, chmn. standing com. cataloging 1978-81, chmn. internat. standard bibliog. description rev. com. 1981—), Phi Beta Kappa. Democrat. Co-author: The MARC II Format, 1968. Office: Library of Congress Washington DC 20540

RATHGEB, NANCY ANN, college administrator; b. New Rochelle, N.Y., Apr. 27, 1958; d. Conrad John and Marilyn Kathryn (Mulrein) Rathgeb. B.S., Mercy Coll., N.Y., 1980; postgrad. Long Island U., 1984—. Adminstrv. asst. Mercy Coll., Dobbs Ferry, N.Y., 1980-82, staff acct., 1982-85, asst. controller, 1985—. Mem. Phelps Meml. Hosp. Assn., Nat. Assn. Female Execs., Mercy Coll. Alumni Assn., Delta Mu Delta, Alpha Chi. Democrat. Roman Catholic. Avocations: reading; craftwork. Office: Mercy Coll 555 Broadway Dobbs Ferry NY 10594

RATHORE, UMA PANDEY, utilities executive; b. Unnao, India, Mar. 5, 1950; came to U.S., 1978; d. O Nath and R Devi Pandey; m. Ram N.S. Rathore, Dec. 18, 1978; children—Dinesh, Rana. B.S., Kanpur U., 1965, M.S., 1969. Adviser, Consul Gen. of Iceland to India, 1976-85; v.p. Nevalid Cons., 1974-82; with North Jersey Utilities, Mount Freedom, N.J., 1983—, pres., 1986—. Membership chmn. LWV, 1979-81. Fellow N.J. Women's Network. Avocations: reading; jogging; hiking; mountaineering. Home: 3 Hickory Pl Randolph NJ 07869 Office: North Jersey Utilities PO Box 494 Mount Freedom NJ 07970

RATHVON, LOIS HANSON, dance educator; b. Tacoma, Aug. 24, 1925; d. Carl Arthur and Signe Cedilia (Fries) Hanson; m. Hal Campbell Rathvon, Jan. 22, 1945 (dec. 1978); children—Katherine Rathvon Deitz, Hal Campbell, Richard, William; m. Robert G. McCarter, June 10, 1982. Student Central Wash. State U., 1944-45, Eastern Wash. State U., 1968-69, SUNY-Buffalo, 1972; UCLA, 1972-73; B.F.A. in Dance, Cornish Inst., 1977. Owner, dir. Rathvon Sch. Dance, Richland, Wash., 1950-71, Rathvon Concert Dancers, Richland, 1950-71; dance instr. Co. of Man., Buffalo, 1972; choreographer, lectr. Everett Community Coll., Bellevue Civic Ballet, Richland Allied Arts, Buffalo U. Opera Co., 1972-77; dance instr. Black Arts West, Ewajo, Seattle, 1973; arts cons. King County Arts Commn., Seattle, 1974-75; dir. Hearing Impaired Arts Program, Seattle, 1975-79; dance instr. Cornish Inst., Seattle, 1978-84, recruiting officer, 1978-79, chmn. dance dept., 1979—; co-dir. Cornish Dance Theater, 1981—. Choreographer Nutcracker Suite, 1969-70, Concert Waltz, 1969, Carnival of Animals, 1967, 83, Alone/Together, 1981, Slippery When Wet, 1982, Love is the Thing, 1984; author: (dance study guide) Chronology of Dance Development in the United States, 1975. Mem. King County Arts Commn. Seattle, 1978-81; dance advisor Wash. State Cultural Enrichment Program, 1969-72; bd. dirs. N.W. Sch. Arts, Humanities and Environ., Seattle, 1979-81. Recipient Cultural Achievment award Seattle Music and Arts Found., 1977; Cultural Achiement award Altrusa Club, 1970; Wash. State Arts Commn. grantee, 1969-70. Mem. Conf. on Research in Dance, Dance Notation Bur. (profl. adv. com. 1980-84), Am. Coll. Dance Festival Assn. (bd. dirs. 1985), PEO. Lodge: Soroptimists. Office: Dance Dept Cornish Inst 710 E Roy St Seattle WA 98102

RATKIN, MARILYN LEE, health care coordinator; b. St. Louis, Mo., Jan. 21, 1944; d. Samuel Louis and Mamie (Bachman) Lewin; m. Gary Alan Ratkin, June 12, 1966; children—Kimberlee Jill, Stephani Lyn. Student Northwestern U., 1962-64; B.A. with honors, Washington U., 1966; M.B.A., U. Mo., 1980. Cert. tchr., real estate agt. Elem. tchr. Flynn Park Sch., St. Louis, 1966-67; elem. tchr. Hebron Sch., Pitts., 1967-68; travel agt. Frosch Travel, Houston, 1975; real estate agt. Ira E. Berry, St. Louis, 1981-82; health care coordinator Health Fair, St. Louis, 1982-85. Editor: (cookbook) Life-Saving Recipes, 1970; coordinator, author: Office Personnel Manual, 1981, also brochure. Bd. dirs., mem. div. pub. edn. com. Am. Cancer Soc., St. Louis, 1981—; bd. dirs. Council of Community Orgns., St. Louis, 1981-85; mem. alumni council Northwestern U., 1985—. Recipient Leadership award Jewish Community Ctr., San Antonio, 1973. Mem. Am. Mktg. Assn., Women's Commerce Assn., Beta Gamma Sigma. Jewish.

RATKOVICH, CYNTHIA, lawyer; b. Chgo., May 22, 1957; d. Steve and Mildred (Evans) Ratkovich. B.S., Purdue U., 1979; J.D., U. Iowa, 1982. Bar: Ill. 1982. Paralegal, sec. Sonnenschein, Carlin, Nath & Rosenthal, Chgo., summer 1978; filing clk. Norus Property Co., Chgo., summer 1979, law clk., summer 1980; sec., asst. mgr. L.J. Sheridan & Co., Chgo., summer 1981; in-house counsel Thomas F. Seay, Chgo., summer 1982, 83, ltd. repr., prin., 1982—; counsel CNA Ins. Co., Chgo., 1983—. Mem. ABA, Ill. State Bar Assn., Chgo. Bar Assn., Alpha Lambda Delta, Phi Kappa Phi, Beta Gamma Sigma, Purdue U. Alumni Assn. Serbian Orthodox. Office: CNA Ins Cos CNA Plaza Law Dept 42S Chicago IL 60685

RATLIFF, LEIGH ANN, pharmacist; b. Long Beach, Calif., May 20, 1961; d. Harry Warren and Verna Lee (Zwink) R. D.Pharmacy, U. Pacific, 1984. Registered pharamcist, Calif. Nev. Pharmacist intern Green Bros. Inc., Stockton, Calif., 1982-84, staff pharmacist Thrifty Corp., Long Beach, Calif., 1984-85, head pharmacist, 1986—. Mem. Nat. Assn. Female Execs., Am. Pharm. Assn., Am. Inst. History Pharmacy, Calif. Pharmacist Assn., Lambda Kappa Sigma. Republican. Methodist. Avocations: creative writing; horseback riding; fishing; house plants; painting; drawing. Home: 8100 Park Plaza Apt 224 Stanton CA 90680 Office: Thrifty Drug Store No 299 3300 E Anaheim St Long Beach CA 90804

RATNER, HILDA, physician; b. N.Y.C., Oct. 22, 1911; d. Solomon Philip and Leah Tamar (Altschule) R.; m. Isidor Dressler, July 5, 1938 (dec.); children—Robert E., Martha B. Sultan. B.S., NYU, 1931; M.D., Boston U., 1934. Intern, resident Montefiore Hosp., N.Y.C., 1934-36, N.Y. Infirmary, 1936-37; practice internal medicine, N.Y.C., 1937-79; physician Dept. Health City of N.Y., 1937-49; attending physician N.Y. Infirmary, 1937-77, emeritus, 1977-84; physician advisor PSRO, Queens, 1977-84; instr. family practice Jamaica Hosp.; mem. med. adv. bd. Vis. Nurses of N.Y. Mem. N.Y. Med. Soc., Queens County Med. Soc., Women's Med. Soc. N.Y. Home: 166-25 Powell's Cove Blvd Beechhurst NY 11357

RATNER, LILLIAN GROSS, psychiatrist; b. N.Y.C., Aug. 18, 1932; d. Herman and Sarah (Widelitz) Gross; B.A., Barnard Coll., 1953; postgrad. U. Lausanne (Switzerland), 1954-56; M.D., Duke U., 1959; m. Harold Ratner, Feb. 4, 1961; children—Sanford Miles, Marcia Ellen. Intern, Kings County Hosp., Bklyn., 1959-60, resident, 1967-70, fellow in child psychiatry, 1969-70, psychiatrist devel. evaluation clinic, 1970-72; resident Jewish Hosp. Bklyn., 1960-62, fellow in pediatric psychiatry, 1962-63; physician in charge pediatric psychiat. clinic Greenpoint (N.Y.) Hosp., 1964-67; pvt. practice psychiatry, Great Neck, N.Y., 1970—; clin. instr. psychiatry Downstate Med. Center, Bklyn., 1970-74, clin. asst. prof., 1974—; lectr. in psychiatry Columbia U., 1974—; psychiat. cons. N.Y.C. Bd. Edn., 1972-75, Queens Children's Hosp., 1975—; mem. med. bd. Camp Sussex (N.J.), 1963—, Saras Center, Great Neck, N.Y., 1977—. Diplomate Am. Bd. Pediatrics, Am. Bd. Psychiatry and Neurology, Am. Bd. Child Psychiatry. Fellow Am. Acad. Pediatrics, Am. Acad. Psychiatry, Am. Acad. Child Psychiatry; mem. Am., Nassau, Bklyn. psychiat. assns., Bklyn. (sr. mem.), Nassau pediatric socs., Soc. Adolescent Psychiatry, N.Y. Council Child Psychiatry, Soc. Clin. and Exptl. Hypnosis, Am. Med. Women's Assn. (pres.-elect Nassau), AMA, N.Y., Kings County med. socs., Am. Soc. Clin. Hypnosis, N.Y. Soc. Clin. Hypnosis. Home and Office: 55 Bluebird Dr Great Neck NY 11023

RATNOFF, MARIAN FOREMAN, lawyer, retailing executive; b. Balt.; d. William Elihu and Sophia (Kuff) Foreman; m. Oscar Davis Ratnoff, Mar. 31, 1945; children—William Davis, Martha. Student, Goucher Coll., 1941-43; B.A. in Sociology, U. Chgo., 1946; M.A. in Edn., Western Res. U., 1959; J.D., Case Western Res. U., 1967. Bar: Ohio 1967. Tchr., Balt. Sch. System, 1946-50, Shaker Heights Sch. System, 1950-51; program coordinator Western Res. U., Cleve., 1960-62; assoc. law firm, Cleve., 1967-71; atty. The Higbee Co., Cleve., 1971—, asst. corp. sec., 1974—, v.p., 1981—. Contbr. articles to legal jours. Mem. many civic coms., Cleve. area, 1967—. Mem. ABA, Bar Assn. Greater Cleve., Ohio Bar Assn. Office: The Higbee Co 100 Public Sq Cleveland OH 44113

RATTA, JANICE ANN, nursing care adminstrator, researcher; b. Bklyn., June 16, 1960; d. Joseph Rudolph and Millicent (Mesi) R. A.A.S. in Nursing, Pace U., 1980, postgrad. Staff nurse N.Y. Infirmary-Beekman Hosp., N.Y.C., 1980-83, asst. nursing care coordinator, 1983-84, nursing care coordinator, 1984—. Mem. Am. Nurses Assn., Am. Assn. Critical Care Nurses, Nat. Assn. Female Execs. Democrat. Roman Catholic. Avocations: swimming; gymnastics. Office: New York Infirmary-Beekman Hosp 170 William St New York NY 10038

RATTAN, JOANNE ROBINSON, social worker; b. Beverly, Mass., July 26, 1926; d. Harry George and Kathleen Anderson (Raymond) Robinson; B.S., Mass. Coll. Art, 1948; postgrad U. Wis. Parkside, 1971-73; M.S.W., U. Wis. Milw., 1976; m. Walter Rattan June 8, 1948; children—Neil Whitney, Eric Norman, Mark Walter, Martha Kathleen. Tchr. public schs., Detroit, 1948-49, Kenosha (Wis.) Mus. Art, 1960-61, Kenosha Public Schs., 1965-68; psychiat. social worker Family Counseling Center, Kenosha, 1975-77; psychiat. social worker, owner Kenosha Counseling and Psychiat. Clinic, 1977—; co-founder Women's Horizons, 1976, pres. bd. dirs. 1976-78, staff counseling cons., 1977—; bd. dirs. Childrens Service Soc. Wis., 1960-64, Family Counseling Center, 1964-68, Kenosha Homemakers, 1972-74; v.p. bd. dirs. Planned Parenthood Kenosha, 1977—, Kenosha and Racine ACLU, 1964—, treas. bd. dirs. Wis. ACLU, 1973-77. Mem. Nat. Assn. Social Workers, NOW, Kenosha Art Assn., Kenosha Symphony League Aux., Friends of the Library, Friends of the Mus. Home: 114 68th Pl Kenosha WI 53140 Office: 5910 39th Ave Kenosha WI 53142

RATTRAY, HELEN SELDON, newspaper editor, publisher; b. Bayonne, N.J., Sept. 29, 1934; d. Abraham Harry and Yetta (Spivack) Seldon; B., Douglass Coll., 1956; postgrad. Columbia U., 1958-60; Litt.D. (hon.), L.I.U., 1986. m. Everett T. Rattray, July 22, 1960 (dec.); children—David E., Daniel S., Bess E. Editor, Pub., columnist East Hampton (N.Y.) Star, 1960—; dir., sec.-treas. Graphics of Peconic, Peconic Pioneers. Former treas., bd. trustees Hampton Day Sch., 1969-73. Home: 17 Edwards Ln East Hampton NY 11937 Office: 153 Main St East Hampton NY 11937

RATZENBERGER, SHEILA KRAUS, lawyer; b. Springfield, Mass., Jan. 27, 1955; d. John Stanley and Charlotte Barbara (Krupa) Kraus; m. James Clark Ratzenberger, June 10, 1982; 1 child, Emily Kraus. B.A., Mt. Holyoke Coll., 1976; J.D., Georgetown U., 1979. Bar: D.C. 1979. Atty., Office Gen. Counsel, GAO, Washington, 1979—. Foster parent Christian Children's Fund, 1982—. Mem. ABA, Fed. Bar Assn., D.C. Bar Assn., Phi Beta Kappa, Sigma Xi, Phi Delta Phi.

RATZLAFF, SHERRY ANN, graphic designer, illustrator, educator; b. Chgo., Oct. 22, 1942; d. Carl Frederick and Ruth Irene (Scherry) Grether; 1 child, Jonathan Ratzlaff. B.F.A. cum laude, Syracuse U., 1964; student Art Inst. Chgo., 1953-60, Acad. Fine Arts, Florence, Italy, 1962. Tchr. art Central Sq. Central Sch. Dist., N.Y., 1964-65; asst. art dir. D.J. Moore Advt., Albany, N.Y., 1965-66; art dir. Stationers Corp. & Sch. Clippings, Los Angeles, 1967, Julie Finger Design Studio, Los Angeles, 1967-70; v.p., art dir. Robert Wendell & Assocs., Los Angeles, 1970-72; instr. Merced Coll., Coll. for Kids., Merced, Calif., 1978; developer, coordinator Community and Schs. Arts Programming, Merced, 1977-80, Sonora, Calif., 1980-85; graphic designer, illustrator, freelance, 1959—; cons., lectr. in field; grantswriter, 1981—. Author/illustrator: Inside-Out: Using the Arts to Communicate, 1985, Let's Go to the Farm, 1978; designer, builder agrl. displays, 1979-81. Center coordinator Mother Lode Women's Crisis Ctr., Sonora, 1985—; workshop presenter Sierra Conservation Ctr., Jamestown, Calif., 1985; acad. task force dir. Calif. Women for Agr., 1978-80; founding mem., consumer edn. chmn. Calif. Women for Agr., Merced, 1976-80. Fair-Arts-In-Action grantee, 1983; Calif. Arts Council grantee, 1981, 82; Artists-in-the Schs. grantee, 1977. Avocations: piano; photography; printmaking; travel. Address: 16884 American River Dr W Sonora CA 95370

RAU, CALISTA JANE, librarian; b. Ft. Edward, N.Y., Aug. 14, 1910; d. Edgar Lewis and Lulu Violet (McCarg) Haff; m. Stanley Cortlandt Rau, Aug. 5, 1938; children—Alan Spalding, Lois Spalding Rau Thomae, Kathleen Spalding, Ames Spalding. Mus.B., Syracuse U., 1933; M.L.S., LIU, 1973. Music tchr. pub. schs., East Greenbush, N.Y., 1934-35, Copiague, N.Y., 1935-36, Tarrytown, N.Y., 1937-38; vol. West Islip Pub. Library (N.Y.), 1973-76; reference librarian Copiague Meml. Pub. Library, 1976—. Recipient Lucille Calvert Pallen award LIU, 1973. Mem. Center for Study Democratic Instns., ALA, AAUW, DAR, Mary P. Myton Lit. Soc. Republican. Club: Amityville Woman's (N.Y.). Lodge: Order Eastern Star (chpt. matron 1963). Home: 30 Richmond Ave Amityville NY 11701

RAUCH, KATHLEEN, senior programmer analyst; b. Franklin Square, N.Y., Oct. 30, 1951; d. William C. and Marian (Shull) R.; B.A., U. Rochester, 1973; M.A. in L.S., U. Mich., 1974; postgrad. N.Y. U., 1981-82. Media specialist Sutton (Mass.) Sch., 1974-76; program cons. Advanced Mgmt. Research Internat., N.Y.C., 1976-79; pub. relations cons., N.Y.C., 1979; pres. N.Y. chpt. NOW, N.Y.C., 1979-80; computer programmer Blue Cross/Blue Shield of Greater N.Y., N.Y.C., 1981-83; computer programmer analyst Federal Reserve Bank of N.Y., 1983-84; systems officer Citibank, N.A., 1984-85; sr. programmer analyst Fed. Res. Bank of N.Y., 1986—. Mem. Assn. for Women in Computing (v.p. membership, exec. v.p. treasurer), Data Processing Mgrs. Assn., Assn. for Computing Machinery, Women's Sports Found., NOW (dir. pub. relations N.Y.C. chpt. 1978, v.p. programs 1978, chmn. bd. 1981, founding mem., sec. Service Fund, N.Y.C. chpt. 1981), Caths. for a Free Choice, Greenpeace. Office: Fed Res Bank of NY 59 Maiden Ln 26th Floor New York NY 10045

RAUENHORST, LAURIE FAY, city official; b. Belmond, Iowa, July 6, 1957; d. Loran Keith and Juanita (Reim) Greenfield; m. Henry Theodore Rauenhorst III, Sept. 3, 1983. A.A., North Iowa Area Community Coll., 1977; B.A. in Econs. and Women Studies, Mankato State U., Minn., 1985. Cert. Mcpl. clk. Dep. city clk. City of Mankato, 1978-79, city clk., 1979-82; city clk. City of North Mankato, Minn., 1982—. County del. Democrat-Farmer Labor Party, Blue Earth County, Minn. 1984; sec. regional advisor Planned Parenthood, Mankato, 1982—; county rep. Health systems Agy. 6, Redwood Falls, Minn., 1983-84; mem. Minn. Sec. of State's Election Adv. Com. Mem. LWV (pres. 1985—, editor, 1st v.p. 1980-85), Minn. Clks. and Fin. Officers Assn. (regional v.p. 1982-83), Internat. Inst. Mcpl. Clks. (state membership chmn. 1982-84), League Minn. Cities (services com. 1984-85), Women's Studies Assn. Lutheran. Avocations: reading; crafts; piano and guitar; women's research and issues. Home: 801 Sherman St North Mankato MN 56001 Office: City of North Mankato 1001 Belgrade St North Mankato MN 56001

RAULERSON, LOTTIE E., retired educator; b. Brooker, Fla., June 14, 1907; d. Homer Perry and Nancy (Crosby) Gainey; m. Arthur Franklin Raulerson, Nov. 26, 1924 (dec. Oct. 1977); children—Austin, Earl, Helen, Ted. B.S., Fla. So. Coll., 1950. Tchr., pub. schs., Brooker, Fla., 1921-23, 30-31, Okeechobee, Fla., 1924-30, 32-68. Chmn. OKeechobee County Council on Aging, Fla., 1974-81, Okeechobee Rehab. Facility, 1972—, Okeechobee Residential Facility, 1979—; bd. dirs. Gulfstream Areawide Agy. on Aging, West Palm Beach area, 1975—; mem. adv. bd. Mental Health Assn. Okeechobee, 1984-85. Mem. Fla. Farm Bur. (sec. 1960—), Fla. and Okeechobee County Ret. Tchrs. Assn. (officer 1968-78). Democrat. Baptist. Avocations: crafts. Home: 3896 NW 144th Dr Okeechobee FL 33472

RAUNER, THERESE MADELINE, sch. psychologist; b. N.Y.C., Sept. 18, 1925; d. Andrew Joseph and Anna (Kelly) R.; B.A., Trinity Coll., Washington, 1946; M.S., Fordham U., 1951, Ph.D., 1959. Tchr., Moravian Sem., Bethlehem, Pa., 1951-52, Highland Falls (N.Y.) Central Sch., 1952-55; asst. dir. guidance Ladycliff Coll., Highland Falls, N.Y., 1956-58, dir. guidance, 1959-65; dean of students Elizabeth Seton Coll., Yonkers, N.Y., 1965-67; sch. psychologist West Point (N.Y.) Elem. Sch., 1968—. Mem. Am. Psychol. Assn., Eastern Psychol. Assn. Republican. Roman Catholic. Home: Fort Montgomery NY 10922 Office: West Point Elem Sch West Point NY 10996

RAUTIO, JOYCEANNA "JA", real estate broker; businesswoman, writer; b. Astoria, Oreg., Feb. 29, 1948; d. Arni Theodore and Julie Kathryn (Kendziersk̈i) Rautio; m. Timothy Clay Mitchell, Aug. 30, 1980; stepchildren—Timothy Clay, Glenn Christopher, Heidi Laura Nicole. A.A., Clatsop Community Coll., 1968; B.A. in Polit. Sci., U. Oreg., 1970; M.A. in Internat. Affairs (Scottish Rite Found. fellow), George Washington U., 1975. Congl. asst. U.S. Ho. of Reps., Washington and Lexington, Ky., 1971-77; cons. immigration law, Lexington, 1977-80; sr. adminstrv. aide Commr. Public Works Lexington-Fayette Urban County Govt., 1978-80; realtor-asso. Century 21 Golden Shores Realty, Naples, Fla., 1981-83; realtor ERA Properties of Naples, Inc., 1984; pres. Rautio Communications, 1982—; free-lance writer, Naples, 1980—; notary pub., Fla. Legis. liaison Naples chpt. NOW, 1982-83; sec. Willoughby Acres Homeowners Assn., Naples, 1982-83, pres., 1983-84; mem. Collier County Water Pollution Control Adv. Com., 1985-86. Recipient Pres.'s Cup, Clatsop Community Coll., 1967, Realtors Active in Politics award, 1983. Mem. Naples Area Bd. Realtors (legis. com. 1983-85), Fla. Assn. Realtors, Nat. Assn. Realtors, Women's Council Realtors (v.p. chpt. 1983), LWV (dir. 1983-84), Naples Profl. Women's Network, Nat. Assn. Notaries, Fla. Freelance Writers Assn., Feb. 29th Soc. (founder 1984), Phi Theta Kappa. Roman Catholic. Clubs: Fla. Extension Homemakers, North Naples, Exec. 100 Research on divorced fathers and stepmothers. Home: 10261 Windsor Way Naples FL 33942 Office: PO Box 506 Naples FL 33939

RAVEN, PATRICIA ELAINE (PENNY), real estate broker, fuel alcohol distillery executive columnist; b. Oakland, Calif., Apr. 27, 1943; d. Allen James and Patricia Elaine (McClure) Nichelini; student U. So. Calif., 1961-62, U. Calif., Fresno, 1962-63, Fresno City Coll., 1973; m. Larry Joseph Raven, June 15, 1963; children—Laurence Tagge Allen, Corbyn Lance. Model, Fresno, Calif., 1960—; owner, operator Del Mar Motel and apts., Fresno, 1963-64; owner R Pantry Markets, 1965-72, v.p., 1968—; owner Holy Cow Meat Markets, Fresno, 1965-72; real estate salesman and developer, 1973; real estate broker, owner Raven Co., Fresno, 1974—; v.p. Raven Devel., Inc., 1980—; owner Raven Alcohol Distillery, 1979—; pres. Am. Gasohol, Inc., 1980—; columnist Party Line, Fresno Bee, 1978—. Democratic candidate for lt. gov. Calif., 1978; Fresno County Dem. central com. alt., 1977; pres. Fresno Cancer League, 1972-73, Jackson Sch. PTA, 1980-82; bd. dirs. Women's Symphony League, 1973-74; hon. mem. Fresno Zool. Soc. Named Nat. Betty Crocker Homemaker of Tomorrow, 1961; recipient Mayor's award, 1976; Hon. Service award Jackson Sch. PTA, 1982; Appreciation award United Cerebral Palsy Assn., 1982-86, Calif. Solid Waste Mgmt. Bd., 1982, Fresno Zool. Soc., 1982, Calif. State Senate, 1983, San Joaquin chpt. Assn. Gen. Contractors, 1983, Holland Sch., 1984, Huntington Blvd. Neighbors, 1985; proclamation in her honor City of Fresno, 1985, others. Roman Catholic. Co-author: National Handbook on Toll Roads, 1977. Home: 3504 E Huntington Blvd Fresno CA 93702

RAVIOLA, D'ELIA GIUSEPPINA, anatomist, physician, educator; b. Arona, Italy, Aug. 30, 1935; came to U.S., 1970; d. Giovanni and Milena (Di Toma) d'Elia; M.D. summa cum laude, U. Pavia (Italy), 1959; Ph.D. in Anatomy, 1968; m. Elio Raviola, Mar. 24, 1960; 1 child, Giuseppe James. Resident in oncology U. Pavia, 1964-68, asst. prof., 1960-70; asst. in opthalmology Harvard U. Med. Sch., Cambridge, Mass., 1970-71, lectr. opthalmology, 1978—; assoc. prof. anatomy Boston U. Med. Sch., 1972-78, prof., 1979-85; research prof. physiology, 1985—. Fulbright scholar, 1964; recipient award New Eng. Ophthololmological Soc. Mem. Am. Soc. Cell Biology, Am. Assn. Anatomists, Assn. Research in Vision and Opthalmology, Internat. Soc. Eye Research. Club: Harvard. Office: Dept Anatomy Boston Univ Med Sch Boston MA 02118

RAVITCH, DIANE SILVERS, historian, educator, author; b. Houston, July 1, 1938; d. Walter Cracker and Ann Celia (Katz) Silvers; m. Richard Ravitch, June 26, 1960; children—Joseph, Steven (dec.), Michael. B.A., Wellesley Coll., 1960; Ph.D., Columbia U., 1975; L.H.D. (hon.), Williams Coll., 1984, Reed Coll., 1985. Adj. asst. prof. Teachers Coll., Columbia U., N.Y.C., 1975-78, assoc. prof., 1978-83, adj. prof., 1983—; dir. Ency. Britannica Corp. Author: The Great School Wars, 1974; The Revisionists Revised, 1977; The Troubled Crusade, 1983; The Schools We Deserve, 1985. Trustee N.Y. Pub. Library, N.Y.C., 1981—. Mem. Nat. Acad. Edn., Am. Acad. Arts and Scis., Soc. Am. Historians. Office: Teachers Coll Columbia U Box 177 New York NY 10027

RAWLINGS, MARY, escrow company executive; b. Lansing, Mich., Nov. 17, 1936; d. Frederick Thomas and Anna (Bondy) Belbeck; m. Richard M. Rawlings, Feb. 11, 1967 (div. 1985); children—Bonita Rawlings Walker, Mary Rawlings Rios, R. Patrick. Student, So. Calif. Sch. Escrows, Los Angeles, 1956-57, Pierce Coll., Woodland Hills, Calif., 1959-60. Vice pres., gen. mgr. Manhattan Mortgage Co., North Hollywood, Calif., 1962-66; mgr. San Fernando Valley Escrow Co., Calif., 1966-67; v.p., mgr. Golden West Escrow Co., Panorama City, Calif., 1967-77; pres. The Escrow Office, Inc., Woodland Hills, 1977—; chmn. bd. Escrow Agt.'s Fidelity Corp., Newport Beach, Calif., 1983—; instr. Pierce Coll., 1978-80. Mem. 99's Inc. (Women Pilot of Yr. 1984), Calif. Escrow Assn. (bd. dirs. 1977—), San Fernando Valley Escrow Assn. (pres. 1977). Avocations: flying; air racing. Office: The Escrow Office Inc 21228 Ventura Woodland Hills CA 91364

RAWLINGS, PATTY LOU, dietitian, consultant; b. San Angelo, Tex., Nov. 7, 1951; d. Joe Dalton and Patricia Lucille (Pope) R. B.S., Tex. Woman's U., 1974; M.S., N. Tex. State U., 1979. Dietetic intern Baylor U. Med. Ctr., Dallas, 1975. Clin. dietitian Meth. Hosps. Dallas, 1975-80; adminstrv. dietitian, 1980-82; dir. food service Autum Leaves Retirement Home, Telesis Co., Dallas, 1982—; dietetic cons. Telesis Co., Dallas, 1983—, Gen. Hosp. Lakewood, Dallas, 1981-82. Borden Co. Found. scholar Tex. Woman's U., 1973. Mem. Am. Dietetic Assn., Nat. Assn. Female Execs., Am. Pub. Health Assn., Am. Soc. Hosp. Food Service Adminstrs., Tex. Dietetic Assn., Dallas Dietetic Assn., Phi Upsilon Omicron.

RAWSON, LINDA KENNETT, lawyer; b. N.Y.C., Oct. 31, 1954; d. Kennett Longley and Eleanor S. R.; B.A. cum laude, Harvard U., 1976; J.D., N.Y. Law Sch., 1979; m. Charles Maxwell Harrison, Aug. 28, 1982. Asst. N.Y.C. Law Dept., 1977-78; asst. to gen. counsel Harper & Row Pubs., Inc., N.Y.C., 1980—. Capt. Women's A Squash Team, 1985-86. Recipient cert. for service to law dept. Mayor of N.Y.C., 1978. Mem. N.Y. Women's Bar Assn., Nat.

Acad. TV Arts and Scis., Women in Communications. Clubs: Harvard, Radcliffe (bd. govs. 1980-82), Met. Squash Racquets Assn. (N.Y.C.); Appalachian Mountain. Contbr. chpt. to The Business of Book Pub., 1985. Office: 10 E 53d St 9th Floor New York NY 10022

RAY, CAROLYN, manufacturing company executive; b. West Point, N.Y., Apr. 4, 1948; d. John and Tova Florence (Schwartz) R. B.S., Skidmore Coll., 1970; M.F.A., Tyler Sch. Art, 1972. Artist-adminstr. Prints in Progress, Phila., 1972-75; artist-in-residence U. Mass., Amherst, 1975-77; co-founder and master printer The Fabric Workshop, Phila., 1977; founder, designer Carolyn Ray, Art by the Yard, Phila., 1977—; pres. Carolyn Ray, Inc., Yonkers, 1982—; panelist Pace U., White Plains, N.Y., 1983; artist-in-residence Artpark, Lewiston, N.Y., 1978. Designer Fabrics/series of collections, 1977—; painter paintings and environ. works, 1982—. Artist-adminstr. VISTA, Phila., 1972; sponsor internships R.I. Sch. Design, 1982, 84, Manhattanville Coll., 1981, Coll. New Rochelle, 1983. Recipient Roscoe award for handpainted fabric, Resources Council, 1981, Commendation for Contemporary Printed Fabric, 1983, Roscoe award for handpainted fabric, 1984, for contemporary printed fabric, 1984. Office: Carolyn Ray Inc 578 Nepperhan Ave Yonkers NY 10701

RAY, CHARLOTTE KIDD, banker, lawyer; b. Baton Rouge, Dec. 20, 1954; d. James Marion and Germaine Elizabeth (Hunt) Kidd; m. Ronald Phillip Ray, Mar. 17, 1979; children—Robert Patrick, Robyn Germaine. B.S., La. State U., 1976, J.D., 1978; grad. Nat. Trust Sch., Evanston, Ill., 1983. Bar: La. 1979. Trust adminstr. Fidelity Nat. Bank, Baton Rouge, 1980-81, trust officer, 1981-82, asst. v.p., trust officer, 1982-83, v.p., trust officer, 1983—. Mem. ABA, La. Bar Assn. Republican. Episcopalian. Home: 4160 Palm St Baton Rouge LA 70808 Office: Fidelity National Bank of Baton Rouge PO Drawer 3597 Baton Rouge LA 70821

RAY, CHERYL ANN, computer software executive; b. Des Moines, Aug. 1, 1947; d. George Harper and Clarice Maybelle (Van Patten) Ray Fry; m. David Charles Joss, Apr. 6, 1974 (div. Nov. 1978). B.A., Drake U., 1970, M.A., 1972; postgrad. U. Colo.-Boulder and Colorado Springs part time 1978-84. Tchr. English, Franklin Jr. High Sch., Des Moines, 1970-71, Bondurant Farrar High Sch., Bondurant, Iowa, 1972-74; reading tchr. Heritage High Sch., Littleton, Colo., 1974-76; tchr. gen studies Colo. Tech. Coll., Colorado Springs Colo., 1976-78; tchr. reading Manitou Springs High Sch., Colo., 1978-84; quality control trainer Logical Systems Inc., Colorado Springs, Colo., 1984-85; dir. tng. support and customer relations Summit Med. Systems Inc. and Logical Systems Inc., Colorado Springs, 1985—. Part time instr. Pikes Peak Community Coll., Colo. Tech. Coll., Blair Jr. Coll., 1976-84. Mem. Nat. Assn. Exec. Females, Pikes Peak Humane Soc., Greenpeace. Democrat. Methodist. Avocations: dance; backpacking; cross countryskiing; softball; drama. Home: PO Box 2057 Woodland Park CO 80866 Office: Summit Med Systems Inc 6295 Lehman Dr Suite B-100 Colorado Springs CO 80918

RAY, DORATHEA HAMMERS, retail needlework executive; b. Diboll, Tex., Apr. 28, 1917; d. James Franklin and Maude Augusta (Baines) H.; m. Walter Emery Ray, July 12, 1940; children—Dorathea Bryan Ray Lyons, James Clayton. Student Tex. Woman's U., 1935-38. Analyst, Dupont, Orange, Tex., 1948-82; sales rep. Branson Spl. Advt., Beaumont, Tex., 1982—; owner, sales mgr. Stamps Plus, Orange, 1977—; owner, mgr. The Skein, Orange, 1983—, also designer. Columnist, Opportunity Valley News, 1984—. Chmn. nominating com. Southeast Tex. Women's Commn., Beaumont, 1985; mem. Orange County Sesquicentennial Commn., 1984—; coordinator disaster vols. Orange County chpt. ARC, 1985—. Mem. Nat. Needle Work Assn., Tex. Fedn. Bus. and Profl. Women's Clubs (best dist. dir. 1972), Greater Orange Area C. of C. (bd. dirs. 1983—, chmn. beautification com. 1983—). Democrat. Baptist. Avocations: knitting; reading; crafts. Home: 1213 W Wrenway St Orange TX 77630 Office: The Skein 1213 W Wrenway Orange TX

RAY, HOPE WALKER, b. McConnelsville, Ohio, Oct. 11, 1906; d. S. Carlton and Grace (Wells) Walker; student Malta Normal Sch., 1924-25, Ohio U., 1940-41; B.A. in Edn., George Washington U., 1958; m. Kenneth C. Ray, June 24, 1931; children—John Walker, Beverly Ann Ray Klincko. Tchr., Morgan County (Ohio) Schs., 1925-31. Mem. DAR (past regent), Daus. Colonial Wars, Columbian Women George Washington U., Pi Lambda Theta. Republican, Methodist. Lodge: Order Eastern Star. Author: (elementary grade workbooks) Number Trails, 1938. Address: 1135H Brandywine Blvd Zanesville OH 43701

RAY, JANICE ELAINE, marketing consultant; b. Dallas, Sept. 30, 1946; d. Fletcher and Ella Marie (Newhouse) R.; m. Arthur D. Smith, Jan. 9, 1966 (div. Dec. 1975); children—Jeralyn E. Smith-Ballard, Adrian D. Smith. Student Bishop Coll., Mountainview Coll., Pres. Ebonay Internat., Inc., Dallas, 1980-82, Jewelry By Janice, Dallas; cons. Jase Enterprise, Dallas, 1982—; dir. War-On-Wac (Drugs), Dallas. Candidate Tex. Ho. of Reps., Austin, 1986; mem. Black Republican Council, Dallas, 1986, Rep. Nat. Com., Washington, 1986, Nat. POlit. Council of Black Women, Dallas, 1986. Mem. Nat. Assn. for Female Execs. Republican. Mem. Ch. of God in Christ. Avocations: swimming; reading. Office: Jase Enterprise PO Box 15532 Dallas TX 75215 also Jewelry By Janice 6440 N Central Expressway Dallas TX 75228

RAY, JEAN POORE, farm administrator, government clerk; b. Cassville, Tenn., Dec. 12, 1927; d. Luther James and Vada (Hutchings) Poore; m. Harvey James Wyrick, Nov. 15, 1947 (div. Jan. 1948); m. William Howard Ray, July 2, 1954 (dec. 1976); 1 child, Lawrence Howard. B.A., U. No. Iowa, 1952, grad. student, 1966. Clk., Oak Ridge Nat. Lab., 1946-48; sr. high sch. tchr. Oelwein High Sch., Iowa, 1952-53, Independence High Sch., Iowa, 1953-54; adminstrv. clk. NIH, Bethesda, Md., 1962-64; farm mgr., Waverly, Iowa, 1976—; support clk. IRS, Waterloo, Iowa, 1978—; lectr. N.Y., Iowa. Author: The Diary of a Dead Man, 1972, 2d edit., 1976. Mem. Phi Sigma Phi. Presbyterian. Home: Rural Route 4 c/o The Elms Box 253 Waverly IA 50677 Office: IRS 110 Plaza Circle Waterloo IA 50701

RAY, JEANNE CULLINAN, lawyer, insurance company executive; b. N.Y.C., May 5, 1943; d. Thomas Patrick and Agnes Joan (Buckley) C.; m. John Joseph Ray, Jan. 20, 1968; children—Christopher Lawrence, Douglas James. Student Univ. Coll., Dublin, Ireland, 1963; A.B., Coll. Mt. St. Vincent, Riverdale, N.Y., 1964; LL.B., Fordham U., 1967. Bar: N.Y. 1967. Atty., Mut. Life Ins. Co. N.Y. (MONY), N.Y.C., 1967-68, asst. counsel, 1969-72, assoc. counsel, 1972-73, counsel, 1974-75, asst. gen. counsel, 1976-80, assoc. gen counsel, 1981-83, v.p. pension counsel, 1984-85, v.p. area counsel group and pension ops., 1985—; v.p. law, sec. MONY Securities Corp., N.Y.C., 1980-85; v.p. law, sec. MONY Advisers, Inc., N.Y.C., 1980—; sec. MONYCO, Inc., N.Y.C., 1980-85; v.p., counsel MONY Series Fund, Inc., Balt., 1984—. Contbr. articles to legal jours. Cubmaster, Greater N.Y. council Boy Scouts Am., N.Y.C., 1978-84, mem. bd. rev. and scouting com., 1985—. Mem. ABA (chmn employee benefits com. Tort and Ins. Practice sect. 1981-82, v.p. legislation 1983—), Assn. Life Ins. Counsel (chmn. policyholders tax com. Tax sect. 1982—). Office: MONY 1740 Broadway St New York NY 10019

RAY, JUDITH DIANA, physical education educator; b. St. Louis, Sept. 14, 1946; d. Arthur Charles and Pauline (Malloyd) R.; A.B. in Edn., Harris Tchrs. Coll., 1968; M.A. in Edn., Washington U., St. Louis, 1972; M.S., Wash. State U., 1979. Tchr., St. Louis Bd. Edn., 1968-72; teaching asst. Washington U., 1970-72; lectr. phys. edn. York Coll., CUNY, 1972-75; teaching and research asst Sch. Vet. Medicine, Wash. State U., 1975-78; asst. prof. phys. edn. West Chester (Pa.) State U. 1978—; reflexologist; dance tchr.; equine researcher Wash. State U., 1975-80; mem. Earthwatch team, archaeol. dig, eura de Vetalla, Italy, 1982. Vol. participant 1984 Olympics. Mem. AAHPER, ASTM, Internat. Soc. Biomechanics, Am. Soc. Biomechanics, AAUP, U.S. Fencing Assn., U.S. Fencing Coaches Assn., Internat. Soc. Biomechanics, U.S. Tennis Assn., Alpha Kappa Alpha, Phi Delta Kappa. Office: 7SC West Chester Univ West Chester PA 19380

RAY, PATRICIA COOPER, manufacturing executive, office automation consultant; b. Prattsville, Ark., Mar. 19, 1932; s. Joseph Elwood and Agnes Mildred (Keesee) Cooper; m. Gene Thomas Ray, Feb. 6, 1959; children—Reynaldo, Kimberley (Mrs. Andre Landon). B.A. in Music, Tex. Woman's U., 1953, M.A., 1954. Tchr., Dallas Ind. Sch. Dist., 1954-59; landman S.W. Prodn. Co., Dallas, 1959-65; adminstrv. asst. Johnson Investment Corp., Austin, Tex., 1965-72; mgr. adminstrv. services Victor Equipment Co., Denton, Tex., 1972—; owner, operator Office Systems Cons. Mem. LWV, AAUW. Mem. Am. Mgmt. Assn., Assn. Records Mgrs. and Adminstrs., Assn. Info. System Profls., Assn. Info. and Image Mgmt., Office Tech. Mgmt. Assn., Am. Soc. Composers, Authors, Pubs. Office: PO Drawer 1007 Denton TX 76202

RAY, PATRICIA SILVER, ednl. adminstr.; b. Sacramento, Calif., June 3, 1946; d. John Merlin and Hannah Mary (Silver) Porter; B.A., Coll. Notre Dame, Belmont, Calif., 1968; M.A., Calif. Poly. State U., 1978; Ed.D., Brigham Young U., 1983. Tchr., Oakgrove Sch. Dist., San Jose, Calif., 1968; dept. chmn. Lucia Mar Unified Sch. Dist., Arroyo Grande, Calif., 1970-76, orientation tchr., vice-prin. high sch., 1979-81, vice prin., dir. activities, 1981—. Mem. Commn. on Status of Women, 1978—. Mem. AAUW, Am. Home Econs. Assn., Assn. Calif. Sch. Adminstrs., Calif. Tchrs Assn., Calif. Assn. Dir. Activities, Phi Delta Kappa (3d v.p. 1981-82). Democrat. Roman Catholic. Club: Women's (v.p. 1977-79) (Arroyo Grande, Calif.). Office Lucia Mar Unified Sch 495 Valley Rd Arroyo Grande CA 93420

RAYBURN, CATHERINE MARGARET, medical researcher; b. N.Y.C., July 28, 1945; d. Frederic Courtney and Elaine (Murray) Stone; m. Robert Louis Rayburn, June 10, 1972 (div. 1984); children—David Courtney, Susan Elizabeth, Lara Elaine. B.S., U. Fla., 1967; M.A., U. Mass., 1969. Faculty, U. Fla., Gainesville, 1968-72, lab. technologist, 1973-76; lab. technologist Baylor U., Houston, 1972-73; research technician U. Utah, Salt Lake City, 1980-82, 84—. Contbr. articles to profl. jours. Mem. Women in Math. and Sci. Republican. Episcopalian. Home: 495 N Hills Dr Salt Lake City UT 84103 Office: VA Med Ctr Code 155 Salt Lake City UT 84148

RAYBURN, GEORGINA HANSON, retail executive; b. New Sweden, Maine, Mar. 27, 1920; d. Eric Wilhelm and Naemi Victoria (Rodin) Hanson; physical therapist, Boston Evening Clinic, 1939; med. technologist, Wilson Sch., 1941; B.S., Donsback U., 1978; m. J. Gurney Doore, Oct. 1940; 1 son, James Hanson; m. 2d, George B. Rayburn, Oct. 17, 1950; 1 son, Eric Edward. Floor supr., Boston Evening Clinic; supr. photo shop Coop Drug, Fairbanks, Alaska, 1947-49; clk. Alaska Communication System, Fairbanks, 1949-52; pres., mgr. Gina's Corner Health Food Store, Fairbanks, 1970—, chief exec. officer, 1976. Mem. C. of C. Republican. Lutheran. Clubs: Pioneers of Alaska (pres. 1968, trustee 1972-76), Order Eastern Star (past matron). Home: PO Box 1450 Fairbanks AK 99707 Office: 406 12th Ave Fairbanks AK 99707

RAYMOND, MARGARET PEAKE, social worker; b. Tahlequah, Okla., June 22, 1941; d. Jesse J. and Mary Louise (Breuninger) P.; B.S. in Edn., Northeastern Okla. State U., 1963; M.S.W. (Cherokee Nation of Okla. grantee 1972-74, David Logan fellow 1973-74), U. Okla., Norman, 1974; m. Elgie Victor Raymond, Dec. 30, 1977; children—Reid Scott, Gary Drew, Lisa LaDawn, Victor Jason. Tchr. elem. public schs., Gallup, N.Mex., O'Falon, Mo., Bristow, Okla., 1960-69; dir. talent search Oklahomans for Indian Opportunity, Norman, 1974-75; spl. asst. to dir. Minn. Alcohol and Drug Authority, St. Paul, 1975-78; tribal planner Cherokee Nation of Okla., Tahlequah, 1978; dir. planning and program devel. 1st Phoenix Am. Corp., Mpls., 1978-84, v.p., 1981-84; dir. Minn. Indian Women's Resource Ctr., 1984—; mem. Nat. Indian Bd. on Alcohol and Drug Abuse, 1975-81; mem. community services rev. com. Nat. Inst. on Alcohol Abuse and Alcoholism, 1979-81; mem. Nat. Adv. Council on Drug Abuse, 1981-83. Mem. United Indian Planners Assn., Nat. Congress Am. Indians. Research in field. Home: 2649 Longfellow Ave Minneapolis MN 55407 Office: 2400 Blaisdelle Ave S Minneapolis MN 55407

RAYMOND, RITA, adult education educator; b. Indpls., Feb. 24, 1940; d. William Henry and Mary Marie (Kegrice) Sutt; m. David Adamson Raymond, June 26, 1971. B.A., Manhattan Bible Coll., 1961; M.Div., Christian Theol. Sem., 1964; M.Ed., Ind. U., 1984. Ordained to ministry Christian Ch. (Disciples of Christ), 1966; cert. secondary tchr., Ind. Pastor Christian Ch., Kans., 1959-61; staff Ind. Migrant Ministry, 1961-66; counselor-minister edn. Salvation Army Men's Social Service Ctr., Indpls., 1966-67; Community Action Against Poverty, U.S. Govt., Indpls., 1967-68; social service dir., chaplain Park Dept. Turtle Creek, Indpls., 1968-71; counselor Ind. Women's Prison, 1970-71; tchr. weekday religious edn., Indpls., 1971-75; minister to aging, shut-ins Westminster Presbyterian Ch., Indpls., 1975-80; tchr. adult edn. Indpls. Pub. Schs., 1980—; del. Ind. Literacy, Indpls., 1983-84. Contbg. author: Bright Ideals, 1983; Branching Out, 1984. Chaplain Civil Air Patrol, Indpls., 1971. Recipient Cert. of Appreciation Adult Edn. Indpls., 1984. Mem. Am. Assn. Adult Edn., Ind. Assn. Adult Edn., Disciples Chaplain Assn. CAP (disting. service plaque 1972), Disciples Congress, Internat. Assn. Women Ministers, Christian Theol. Sem. Alumni Assn., Ind. U. Alumni Assn. Republican. Lodge: Woodmen of World. Home: 4643 San Diego Dr Indianapolis IN 46241 Office: Adult Edn Indpls 120 East Walnut St #601 Indianapolis IN 46241

RAY-MORRIS, JACQUELINE, business and management consultant; b. Chester, Pa., Dec. 24, 1952; d. Haywood Filmore and Evelyn Thaw (Humphrey) Ray; m. Alton Pavaughn Morris, Aug. 22, 1981. A.A., Gloucaster County Coll., Sewell, N.J., 1973; B.S., Hampton Inst., Va., 1976. Store asst. mgr., Bambergers, Deptford, N.J., 1976-77; hosp. asst. mgr. Service Master Mgmt., Harrisburg, Pa., 1977-78, coordinating mgr., Harrisburg, 1978-79, Alexandria, Va., 1979-82, dir. edn., Balt., 1982-84; program coordinator, tng. cons. Inst. for Type Devel., Silver Springs, Md., 1985—; pres. Ray-Morris Assocs., Ft. Washington, Md., 1985—; cons. Control Data Bus. Advisors, Inc., Columbia, Md., 1984—. Bd. dirs. Old Towne Child Devel. Ctr., Alexandria, 1984—, Campfire Girls Inc., Columbia, Md., 1985—; chmn. Orgn. Devel. Cons Unlimited, Washington, 1985—; chmn. Youth for Christ, Inc., Washington, 1984—. Mem. Orgn. Devel. Network, Nat. Assn. Exec. Females, Nat. Soc. Notaries. Democrat. Apostolic. Avocations: designing and sewing; tennis; reading; swimming; interior decorating. Home: 2112 Old Fort Hills Ct Fort Washington MD 20744 Office: 6200 Annapolis Rd Suite 422 Landover Hills MD 20784

RAYNOLDS, ELEANOR HURRY, management consultant; b. N.Y.C., Aug. 20, 1937; d. Renwick Washington Hurry and Anna Bailey (Stoddard) Hurry Frame; m. John F. Raynolds III, Jan. 9, 1982; children—Jay C., Jennifer S. Kuhn. A.A., Bennett Coll., 1957. Coordinator coll. relations Squibb Corp., N.Y.C., 1967-68; asst. to owner Meadow Stable, 1973-77; v.p. MSL Internat. Cons., Ltd. (Hay Group), N.Y.C., 1977-81; v.p., mgr. PA Exec. Search Inc., Stamford, Conn., 1981-82; sr. v.p. Boyden Assocs., Inc., 1982-85; ptnr. Ward Howell, N.Y.C., 1985—. Adv. bd. Outward Bound. Decorated comdr. Brit. Empire. Mem. Internat. Assn. Personnel Women (adv. bd. 1979-83), Brit. Am. C. of C. (chmn. activities com., dir., pres. 1983-85, chmn. nominating com. 1985—). Congregationalist. Clubs: Greenwich Field, Mayflower Soc. Home: 202 June Rd Stamford CT 06903 Office: 99 Park Ave New York NY 10016

RAZZAK, MONA ALI, economist, educator, consultant; b. Cairo, Egypt, May 22, 1947; d. Ali Mohamed and Soraya (Abou El Fetouh) Zaky; m. Ibrahim A. Razzak, Aug. 3, 1967; children—Amr, Mostafa. B.A. in Econs., Towson State U., 1981; M.S. in Econ. Edn., Johns Hopkins, 1983. Adminstrv. asst. Council Econ. Edn., Balt., 1982-83, edn. asst., 1983-84, field dir., 1984—; adj. asst. prof. econs. Towson State U. Author: (with George Gergiou) Curriculum Guide Cecil County Economic Elective, 1984, Curriculum Guide Cecil County to Understanding Economics, 1985. Sec. Egyptian Am. Soc. Md., Balt., 1976-78, pres., 1980-81; pres. Arabic Cultural Ctr., Balt., 1979—. Mem. Nat. Assn. Econ. Educators. Republican. Moslem. Home: 12 Fox Knoll Ct Timonium MD 21093 Office: Council Econ Edn Towson State U Towson MD 21204

RDUCH, EVITA JOANNE, lawyer; b. Nurenberg, W. Ger., Dec. 9, 1952; came to U.S., 1958; d. Adolf Victor and Lucie (Schroeder) R. B.A., Blackburn Coll., 1974; J.D., John Marshall Law Sch., 1979. Bar: Tex. 1979, U.S. Supreme Ct. 1982, U.S. Ct. Customs and Patents 1982, U.S. Tax Ct. 1982, U.S. Dist. Ct. (no. dist.) Tex. 1982, U.S. Dist. Ct. (so. dist.) Tex. 1980, U.S. Ct. Appeals (3d, 5th, 7th, 9th, 10th and 11th cirs.). Labor relations rep. Employers' Assn. Greater Chgo., 1976-78; pres. Rduch & Whyburn, Inc., Humble, Tex., 1979-81; sole practice, Humble, 1981-83; sr. ptnr. Rduch & Rowney, Humble, 1983-85; pres. Rduch & Rowney, P.C., 1986—; guest lectr. U. Houston, 1979-81. Bd. dirs., asst. sec. Water Control Improvement Dist. 136, Spring, Tex., 1982-85, v.p., 1986—; textbook adv. com. Spring Ind. Sch. Dist., 1981—; pres., bd. dirs. Birnamwood-Fairfax Homeowners' Assn., Spring, 1980-82; mem. fin. com. St. James Ch., Spring., 1980—; mem. community bd. Mercer Arboretum Adv. Com., 1981-83. Mem. Assn. Trial Lawyers Am., ABA, Houston Bar Assn. (family law sect. 1983-84). Office: Rduch & Rowney PC 20713 Aldine-Westfield Humble TX 77338

REA, HAZEL WHITE, government research administrator; b. Van Buren, Ark., Feb. 2, 1911; d. James Bernard and Massie (Bedford) White; m. Courts D. Rea, Jan. 7, 1938 (dec.); 1 dau., Ruth Rea Hilken. Adminstrv. asst. intramural research program NIMH, Bethesda, Md., 1949-57, adminstrv officer, 1957-75, asso. dir. program mgmt., intramural research program, 1975-83, dep. dir., 1983—; mem. employee adv. com. on group life ins. U.S. Civil Service Commn., 1971-74. Recipient Superior Service award HEW, 1970; Adminstr.'s award Alcohol, Drug Abuse and Mental Health Adminstrn., 1979; Disting. Service award Dept. HHS, 1983. Mem. League Fed. Recreation Assns. (pres. 1961, 62, 64), Found. for Advanced Edn. in Scis. Home: 6700 Melody Ln Bethesda MD 20817 Office: NIH 9000 Rockville Pike Bldg 10 Room 4N-224 Bethesda MD 20205

READ, DOROTHY PATRICIA, nursing educator; b. Sharpsville, Pa.; d. Paul Thomas and Teresa (Silvaggi) Diana; m. John Lewis Read, Feb. 8, 1946 (div. 1976); children—Dana Teresa, John Lewis, Mary Elizabeth, Lance Alexander. R.N., Sharon Gen. Hosp. (Pa.), 1942; B.S. in Nursing magna cum laude, Angelo State U., 1981; M.S. in Nursing, U. Tex.-El Paso, 1982. R.N.; cert. nurse clinician. Nursing lab. coordinator, Angelo State U., San Angelo, Tex., 1973-81, asst. instr. 1981-82, instr., 1982-83, asst. prof., 1983—. Bd. dirs. pres. San Angelo Symphony, 1961; mem. Symphony Guild; county chmn. Republican Party, San Angelo, 1961-63; sec., v.p. Angelo Civic Theatre, 1965-71, Med. Aux., San Angelo, 1963-64. Served to lt. USN. Mem. Am. Nurses Assn., Tex. Nurses Assn., Am. Heart Assn., Tex. Tchrs. Assn., Alpha Chi. Roman Catholic. Club: 48. Home: 2622 Oxford San Angelo TX 76904 Office: Angelo State U W Avenue N San Angelo TX 76904

READ, M. MARGARET, speech pathologist; b. New Castle, Ind., May 31, 1936; d. William Patrick and Mildred Margaret (Parsons) Wallace; B.S., Western Mich. U., 1958; M.S., U. Wis., 1961; postgrad. Northeastern U.; children—Jennifer Parsons, Laurie Alden. Speech therapist Lakeview-Springfield public schs., Battle Creek, Mich., 1958-60; instr. speech Tufts U., 1962-63; cons. speech and lang. therapist Cushing Hosp., Framingham, Mass., 1963-64; dir. Speech and Hearing Clinic, Kennedy Meml. Hosp., 1964-66; dir., co-owner Brockton (Mass.) Speech and Hearing Clinic, 1966-70; clin. instr. Boston U., 1966-73, 73-74; dir. Daniels Speech and Lang. Clinic, Univ. Hosp., Boston, 1966-73; instr. Boston State Coll., 1974; asst. prof. communication disorders Worcester (Mass.) State Coll., 1974-82, co-dir. Collaborative Preschool, 1975-82, dir. Communication Disorders Clinic, 1975-82; pvt. practice speech pathology, 1982—; cons. Lahey Clinic, 1983—; instr. human services program Boston U. Overseas, Ansbach, Ger., 1977; lectr. in field. Mem. Am. Speech-Lang.-Hearing Assn. (cert. clin. competence; legis. council 1980—), Mass. Speech-Lang.-Hearing Assn. (pres.-elect 1980-81). Democrat. Contbr. chpts. to books, articles to profl. jours. Address: 139 Day St Auburndale MA 02166

READEY, LINDA GOLD, city official; b. Cleve., Mar. 9, 1945; d. Gerhard Henry and Margaret Elizabeth (Smith) Gold; m. James August Readey, June 29, 1968; children—Jay Scott, Jonathan Eric. B.A., Wittenberg U., 1967. U.S. Guide at Expo '67 U.S. Dept. State, Montreal, Que., Can., 1967; tchr. English, Columbus Pub. Schs., Ohio, 1968-70; supr. edn. Ohio Hist. Soc., Columbus, 1970-72; survey coordinator Am. Research Bur., Beltsville, Md., 1976-78; staff asst. Ohio Dept. Ins., Columbus, 1981-82; adminstrv. asst. to city mgr. City of Upper Arlington, Ohio, 1984—. Contbr. hist. articles to profl. jours. Trustee, chmn. auxs. Children's Hosp., Columbus, 1984-85; gen. chmn., publicity chmn., vol. chmn. Meml. Golf Tournament, Dublin, Ohio, 1979-82; bd. dirs. Upper Arlington Civic Assn., 1981-83, Childhood League Ctr., Columbus, 1985-86, Children's Mental Health Ctrs., 1985—. Named N.W. Woman of Yr., Upper Arlington Rotary Club, 1983. Mem. Jr. League Columbus, Columbus Bar Assn. Aux. (pres. 1975-81). Avocations: gardening; children's activities and schools. Home: 1695 Roxbury Rd Upper Arlington OH 43212 Office: City of Upper Arlington 3600 Tremont Rd Upper Arlington OH 43221

READO, GERALDINE GLOVER, chemist; b. Houston, Dec. 14, 1948; d. Willard Eugene and Annie Lee (Warren) Glover. B.A. in Chemistry, Dillard U., 1970. Chemist B.F. Goodrich Co., Port Neches, Tex., 1970-74; sr. research chemist Dow Chem. U.S.A., Midland, Mich., 1974-79, devel. supr., 1979-80, product sales mgr., 1980-84, research leader, 1984—. Pres. Career Women in Industry, 1977-78. Recipient cert. of appreciation Dale Carnegie Assn., 1979, Outstanding Grad. Asst. award, 1979. Mem. Nat. Assn. Female Execs., Alpha Kappa Alpha (v.p. Mu Alpha Omega chpt. 1984-86, grad. advisor 1983—, Service award 1982). Baptist. Avocations: owl collector; golfing; dancing; traveling.

READOUT, ROSALEE JOYCE, educator; b. Urbana, Ohio, Nov. 24, 1936; d. Floyd Emerson and Naomi Helen (Hartzler) King; B.Ed., Colo. State U., 1979; Cert. in Fashion Merchandising, Parks Bus. Sch., 1971; A.A., Aims Community Coll., 1977, 78; M.Secondary Edn., Central State U., 1986; m. David Earl Readout, Oct. 29, 1976; children by previous marriage—Judy Allene Stehman Ziller, Jerry Allen Stehman, Kathy Lynn Stehman Potts. Bookkeeper, Shamrock Truck Stop, Greeley, Colo., 1960-63; underwriting asst. State Farm Ins. Co., Greeley, 1964-66; office mgr. Stehman Distbg. Co., Greeley, 1966-70; buyer, asst. bridal cons. Joslins Dept. Store, Denver, 1971-73, buyer, bridal/fashion cons., dept. mgr. Greeley, 1973-77; office mgr., bus. cons. Montey Roofing Co., Loveland, Colo., 1978-80; adult edn. instr. small bus. mgmt. Larimer County Vocat.-Tech. Center, Ft. Collins, Colo., 1978-82, post-secondary instr. clk.-typist program, 1979-82; instr. bus. and office dept. Eastern Okla. County Area Vocat. Center, Choctaw, Okla., 1982—; lectr. in field; corp. sec. Stehman Distributing Co., 1968-73. Mem. bus. women's panel, Job Opportunities Week, 1981—. Mem. Nat. Assn. Female Execs., Nat. Bus. Edn. Assn., Am. Vocat. Assn., Colo. Vocat. Assn., Okla. Vocat. Assn., Okla. Bus. Edn. Assn., Alpha Delta Epsilon. Republican. Home: 2700 SE 27th St Ct Choctaw OK 73020 Office: 4601 N Choctaw Rd Choctaw OK 73020

READ-WHARTON, BETTY ANN, nurse; b. Oklahoma City, June 16, 1953; d. Charles Harold and Mary Ann (Clayton) Bond; m. David Fredrick Wharton, Mar. 9, 1984; 1 child, Christopher. Assoc. Degree, Eastern Okla. State Coll., 1973; B.S., East Central U., 1975; M.S., U. Okla., 1981; Registered nurse, emergency med. technician. Staff nurse McCurtain Meml. Hosp., Idabel, Okla., 1971-73; critical care nurse Valley View Hosp., Ada, Okla., 1973-75, house supr., 1976-82, supr., staff devel. coordinator, 1982—, also mem. numerous community services and edn. programs, 1981—, active fund drive 1983—; dialysis nurse Greater Southeast Gen. Hosp., Washington, 1975-76; vis. prof. East Central U., Ada, 1982; cons. in field; co-founder, flight nurse Aerolife, Ada, 1981—; cons. Okla. Teleconf. Network, Ada; lectr. workshops and seminars. Emergency services coordinator Dist. 5 Spl. Olympics, Ada., 1985. Mem. Emergency Nurses Assn., Okla. Emergency Med. Technicians Assn., Am. Fedn. Nursing, Okla. Nursing Network. Republican. Mem. Ch. of Christ. Avocations: golf, fishing, camping. Office: Valley View Hosp 1300 E 6th Ada OK 74820

REAGAN, NANCY DAVIS (ANNE FRANCIS ROBBINS), wife of President U.S.; b. N.Y.C., July 6, 1923; d. Kenneth and Edith (Luckett) Robbins; adopted dau. Loyal Davis; B.A., Smith Coll.; LL.D. (hon.), Pepperdine U., 1983; m. Ronald Reagan, Mar. 4, 1952; children—Patricia Ann, Ronald Prescott; stepchildren—Maureen, Michael. Contract actress MGM, 1949-56; films include: The Next Voice You Hear, 1950, Donovan's Brain, 1953, Hellcats of the Navy, 1957; civic worker; visited wounded Viet Nam vets., sr. citizens, hosps. and schs. for physically and emotionally handicapped children; active in furthering foster grandparents for handicapped children program, fighting drug and alcohol abuse; hon. nat. chmn. Aid to Adoption of Spl. Kids, 1977; host Nancy Reagan Battles Drug Abuse radio series for WBN, 1984. hon. chmn. U. So. Calif. Panhellenic Council, 46 others; Named one of Ten Most Admired Am. Women, Good Housekeeping mag., 1977, 82, 83, Gallup Poll, 1981, 82, 83; Woman of Yr., Los Angeles Times, 1977; One of 10 Most Influential Women, 1981; One of 10 Most Influential Women, Harper's Bazaar, 1983. permanent mem. Hall of Fame of Ten Best Dressed Women in U.S.; USO Woman of Year, 1982; Presdl. Citation award Rotary Internat., 1984; Humanitarian award Lions Club Internat., 1984; Humanitarian award House Ear Inst., 1984; Woman of Achievement award Girls Club N.Y., 1984. Author: Nancy, 1980; To Love a Child, 1982; formerly author syndicated column on prisoner-of-war and missing-in-action soldiers and their families. Address: care White House 1600 Pennsylvania Ave Washington DC 20500

REAM, CAROLYN, job placement specialist, consultant; b. Tulsa, Feb. 17, 1920; d. John Clarence and Zelma Constance (Garner) Ghormley; m. Errol Jefferson, Feb. 15, 1951; 1 son, Eric Jeffrey. Student Okla. Sch. Bus., Accountancy, Law and Fin., 1937-38, U. Nev.-Las Vegas, 1968-69, Sacramento State U., 1974, San Diego State U., 1975. Cert. rehab. specialist. Personnel asst.

U. Nev., Las Vegas, 1966-70; job devel. specialist Employment Security Dept., Las Vegas, 1970-74, State Bur. Vocat. Rehab., Las Vegas, 1974-76; counselor Nev. Indsl. Commn., Las Vegas, 1976-77, job placement specialist and pub. relations coordinator Jean Hanna Clark Rehab. Center (State Indsl. Ins. System, formerly Nev. Indsl. Commn.), 1977-84; pvt. practice cons. labor market access determinations, career devel., discriminatory employment practices against disabled, Las Vegas, 1983—; oral exam. bd. mem. State of Nev. Personnel Div., Las Vegas, 1967-84; cons., lectr. career orientation Clark County Sch. Dist., Las Vegas, 1971-73; cons., lectr. So. Nev. Meml. Hosp., Las Vegas, 1974-84; cons., advisor vocat. rehab., Tex. Inst. Rehab. and Research, Houston, 1975; cons., trainer Nev. Commn. on Equal Rights of Citizens, Las Vegas, 1975-76; cons., workshop coordinator Ohio Rehab. Services Commn., Columbus, 1978; cons., advisor Valley Hosp., Las Vegas, 1982; cons. accreditation William A. Callahan Rehab. Center, Wilsonville, Oreg., 1982; cons. accessibility for handicapped sta. KVBC-TV, Las Vegas, 1982. Writer, producer shows: Jobortunity, sta. KLAS-TV, 1973; contbr. articles to mag.; author booklets in field. Chmn., Econ. Opportunity Bd. Clark County Adv. Bd. on Transp. for Handicapped and Srs., Las Vegas, 1975—; bd. dirs., sec. United Way So. Nev., 1975—, chmn. budget com.; vice chmn. So. Nev. Com. on Employment of Handicapped, 1977-83, chmn., 1984-85; mem. Winchester Town Adv. Bd., 1978—; mem. adv. bd. Nev. Assn. Handicapped/Ctr. for Ind. Living, 1985—. Recipient cert. of merit, Employment Security Dept., Las Vegas, 1973, cert. of appreciation Nev. Spl. Olympics, 1973-74, Am. Lung Assn. Nev., 1982-83, Multiple Sclerosis Soc., 1982. Mem. Nat. Rehab. Assn. (Margaret Fairbairn award job placement div. 1975, Pacific region rep. 1984—), So. Nev. Personnel Assn. (dir. 1980), Phi Mu Alumnae (coll. advisor Las Vegas 1971, treas. 1972). Democrat. Congregationalist. Home: 400 Greenbriar Townhouse Way Las Vegas NV 89121

REAMS, DENISE MAURTEAL MCCARTY, animator, graphic artist; b. Niagara Falls, N.Y., Aug. 14, 1955; d. Louis Mayo and Georgia Maurteal (Speaks) McCarty; m. Wallace Lynn Reams, Apr. 10, 1981. B.S. in Advt., U. Tex., 1976. Advt. rep. Daily Texan, Austin, 1975-76, Express News, San Antonio, 1977-78; media dir. Alamo Ad Ctr., San Antonio, 1978; broadcast coordinator Anderson Advt., San Antonio, 1978-80; creative dir. Mark VII Prodns., San Antonio, 1980; pres., creative dir. Willming Reams Animation, San Antonio, 1980—. Active San Antonio Jr. League, Jr. Com. San Antonio Symphony, 1981—, S.W. Research Found. Forum, San Antonio, 1982—; vol. Am. Cancer Soc., San Antonio, 1983, Soc. Performing Arts, San Antonio; vol. ann. fund dr. San Antonio Mus. Assn., 1983; mem. steering com. Cattle Baron's Gala, 1983; publicity chmn. Designer Showcase 82, 83, patron party chmn. Designer Showcase 84; bd. dirs./publicity S.W. Found. Forum Gala, 1983, bd. dirs./invitation and program design, 1984. bd. dirs./prizes and poster cycle for Symphony Bike-a-thon; bd. dirs./design and invitation Designer Attic Sale, 1984; bd. dirs. Chgo. Symphony Performance to benefit San Antonio Symphony, 1983. Mem. San Antonio Advt. Fedn. (Addy award 1979, 80, 81), Women in Communications (v.p. pub. relations 1982-83), Alpha Phi. Republican. Episcopalian. Office: Willming Reams Animation Inc 520 N Medina San Antonio TX 78207

REAMS, ELINOR PAYNE (MRS. ARTHUR A. REAMS), international educational specialist, retired government official; b. Dothan, Ala., Apr. 17, 1914; d. Alvin A. and Gladys Wise (Fritter) Payne; A.B. cum laude, Fla. State U., 1935; postgrad. George Washington U., 1940; m. Arthur Arnold Reams, Jan. 11, 1941; 1 dau., Anne Emily Reams Rapoport. Newspaper work, Panama City, Fla., 1935; mgr. Clements Ins. Agy., Miami, Fla., 1935-39; head dept. English, Redland High Sch., Dade County, Fla., 1936-40; writer confidential reports Bur. Contract Information, 1940-41; editorial asst. War Dept., 1941; personnel asst. Co-ordinator Information, 1941-42; personnel officer FSA, 1942-43; mgmt. planning analyst O.W.I., 1945; mgmt. planning officer Dept. State, 1945-48, chief deptl. staff U.S. Adv. Commn. Ednl. Exchange, 1948-52, cons. internat. information adminstrn., 1952-53, Bur. Internat. Sci. and Tech. Affairs, Dept. State, 1973-75; ind. cons. U.S. govt., also pvt. orgns., 1975—; cons. Am. Council Edn., 1955-56, spl. asso. and cons. commn. edn. and internat. affairs, 1956-61, also liaison officer with UNESCO relation staff Dept. State; sr. personnel mgmt. officer Dept. State, 1961-62, chief program planning and mgmt. staff, 1962-63; fgn. affairs officer Policy Review and Research Staff, Bur. Ednl. and Cultural Affairs, Dept. State, 1963-65, asst. dir. policy review and coordination staff, 1965-67, sr. policy officer and asst. exec. dir. council on internat. ednl. and cultural affairs, 1967-70; ind. research cons., 1970—; mem. asst. sec. states com. reorgn., 1946; mem. survey mission rev. ednl. exchange activities in Europe and Near East, Dept. State, 1949; Am. Council Edn. rep. 3d gen. conf. Internat. Assn. Univs., 1960; trustee Jr. Mus. Bay County, Inc., 1976-77; pres. Friends of Bay County Pub. Libraries, Inc., 1977-78. Recipient Meritorious Service award Dept. State, 1964, Superior Service award, 1966, Superior Service Honor award, 1970. Mem. DAR, Delta Delta Delta, Phi Kappa Phi, Beta Pi Theta. Democrat. Presbyn. Clubs: Washington Golf and Country, St. Andrews Bay Yacht, Diplomatic and Consular Officers (pub. affairs and program coms.), Hidden Creek Country. Author report profl. jour. Home: 1434 Woodacre Dr McLean VA 22101

REAMS BUCK, JACQUELINE LOUISE, science and social science educator, consultant; b. Des Moines, Apr. 7, 1927; d. Florence Elizabeth (Brewer) Robinson; m. Edward Eugene Buck; children—Philip, Michael, Riena, Suzanne, Lloyd, Guy. B.A., Calif. State U.-Fullerton; M. Ed., Whittier Coll. With sci. dept. La Habra City Schs., Calif., 1962-68, social science dept., 1968-76, science dept., 1976-82; social science dept. Washington Jr. High, La Habra, 1982—; cons., dir. Orange County Schs. Exhibit, 1966-72, Orange County Service Ctr. Publicity Orgn., 1979-80; v.p. Orange County Service Council, 1975-77. Cons. Universal Studios, MacMillan Pub. and religious films. Publicity chmn. LaHabra Childrens Mus. and Camp, 1978-79; pres. La Habra Bus. and Profl. Women's Club, 1975-76, La Habra Edn. Assn., 1975-76, Imperial Jr. High PTA, La Habra 1978-79, 1981-82. Mem. NEA (nat. del. 1970-78), NAT. Sci. Assn., Nat. Social Sci. Assn., Calif. Social Sci. Assn., Orange County Social Sci. Assn., Calif. Tchrs. Assn. (del. 1969-79), AAUW, Mensa. Office: La Habra City Schs 500 N Walnut La Habra CA 90631

REAMY, MADELINE L., association executive; b. Atlanta, Oct. 4, 1953; d. A. Judson and Eleanor (McMichael) Reamy. Student Phila. Coll. Art, 1971-73; B.F.A., Schiller Coll., Paris, 1975; M.F.A., Syracuse U., 1978. Registrar, Everson Mus. Art, Syracuse, N.Y., 1977-78; mus. educator High Mus. Art, Atlanta, 1978-80; curator of edn. Atlanta Hist. Soc., 1979-84; exec. dir. Joel Chandler Harris Assn., Atlanta, 1984—. Contbr. articles to profl. jours. Mem. steering com. Cornerstone: Historic House Protectors, Atlanta Preservation Ctr., 1985. Recipient Participation award Seminar for Hist. Adminstrn., 1983. Mem. Margaret Mitchell Mus. Assn. (bd. dirs. 1985—), Am. Assn. for State and Local History (mus. edn. cons.), Am. Assn. Museums, Ga. Assn. Museums and Galleries (bd. dirs. 1983—, pres. 1984—). Office: Wrens Nest 1050 Gordon St SW Atlanta GA 30310

REAMY-STEPHENSON, MICHAELIN, marriage and family therapist, educator, consultant; b. N.Y.C., Feb. 20, 1938; d. Judson Reamy and Eleanor Stevens (McMichael) R.; m. James Donald Cowie, Aug. 29, 1959; children—Jennifer D., James J., David K., Laura S.; m. Richard Ward Stephenson, Aug. 31, 1979. B.S. with Distinction in Human Ecology, Cornell U., 1960; M.S.W., U. Ga., 1979. Tchr. swimming, Conn., E. Africa, Lebanon, 1968-75; social work intern, grad. asst., Atlanta, 1978-79; dir. social services, assoc. dir. and coordinator family therapy adult treatment program Brawner Psychiat. Inst., Atlanta, 1980-82; dir. extramural tng., marriage and family therapist Atlanta Inst. Family Studies, 1982—. Mem. Atlanta Com. Children, 1983—; instr. Water Safety ARC, 1957—. Recipient DAR Citizen award, 1956; YMCA award for Disting. Service, White Plains, N.Y., 1958. Mem. Nat. Assn. Social Workers, Am. Assn. Marriage and Family Therapists, Ga. Assn. Marriage and Family Therapists, Cornell U. Human Ecology Alumni Assn., Internat. Platform Assn., Mortar Bd., Omicron Nu, Phi Kappa Phi. Contbr. articles to profl. jours. Home: 1733 Kellogg Springs Dr Dunwoody GA 30338 Office: Atlanta Inst Family Studies 61 8th St Atlanta GA 30309

REARDON, BARBARA DONAHUE, printing brokerage firm executive; b. Methuen, Mass., July 19, 1959; d. Bernard Emerson and Eileen Rita (Riordan) Donahue; m. William Steven White (div. Apr. 1979); 1 child, Christy Ann; m. Thomas John Reardon, Apr. 3, 1982; children—Ryan Thomas, Sean Patrick. Student Tomlinson Coll., 1978-79; Assoc. Sci. in Mktg., Assoc. in Sic. Bus. Adminstrn., St. Petersburg Jr. Coll., 1983. Account rep. St. Petersburg Times, Fla., 1978; prodn. coordinator Modern Graphic Arts, St. Petersburg, 1978-81, sales coordinator, 1981-82; sales rep. Blakes Printing, St. Petersburg, 1982-84; pres. B.D. Reardon & Assocs., Inc., St. Petersburg, 1984—; advisor Alt. Human Services, St. Petersburg, 1983. Actress: Love Takes a Chance, 1985, Summer Rental, 1985, On Assigment with Indy, 1985; model, 1977—. Circuit marshall St. Petersburg Grand Prix, 1985; mem. St. Anthony's Hosp. Guild, 1984-86. Abilities Rehab. Ctr. Guild, 1982-85; supporter Congl. re-election campaign, 1984. Mem. Graphic Artists Guild Central Fla., Tampa Advt. Fedn., Nat. Assn. Female Execs., Bay Area Advt. Fedn. 2 (pub. service chmn. 1983-84, nat. 2d place award 1984). Republican. Roman Catholic. Home: 1935 Montana Ave NE Saint Petersburg FL 33703

REARDON, MAUREEN CAROL, real estate management executive; b. Detroit, Dec. 17, 1948; d. Maurice Martin and Lucille Ann (Cobb) R. Grad. high sch., Birmingham, Mich. Lic. real estate broker; cert. property mgr. Vice pres. Dynamic Mgmt. Inc., Clearwater, Fla., 1977-83; dir. ops. First Columbia Mgmt., Clearwater, 1983; pres. Progressive Mgmt., Inc., Clearwater, 1983—. Mem. C. of C. of U.S., Community Assns. Inst. (bd. dirs. Suncoast chpt. 1983-85), Inst. Real Estate Mgmt. (bd. dirs. West Coast chpt. 1983-84). Roman Catholic. Avocations: sewing; macrame; cooking; swimming. Office: Progressive Mgmt Inc 611 Druid Rd E Suite 709 Clearwater FL 33516

REASER, GAIL G., real estate broker; b. Victoria, Tex., Nov. 27, 1948; d. Minesteu Eugene and Priscilla (Duderstadt) Garner; m. Vernon Neal Reaser, Jr., Mar. 14, 1970; 1 son, Clayton Neal. Student, U. Houston, 1967-70. Lic. real estate broker. Legal sec. Reaser & Wall, Attys., Victoria, Tex., 1970-72; real estate broker Redding-Fitzgerald, Victoria, Tex., 1971-80; real estate broker, owner Re/Max Central, Victoria, Tex., 1980—. Vice-pres. Area Agy. on Aging Nutrition Program, 1982-83; bd. dirs. Victoria Pub. Library; sec.-treas. Victoria Zool. Soc., 1977-80, dir. publicity, 1978-81, bd. dirs., 1977-80. Mem. Victoria C. of C., Victoria Bd. Realtors (sec.-treas. 1983—, pres.-elect 1984—, dir., 1983—), Nat. Assn. Realtors, Tex. Assn. Realtors, Women's Council Realtors, Victoria Bldrs. Assn., Sales and Mktg. Council of Victoria. Democrat. Lutheran. Club: Victoria Law Wives (past sec.-treas., pres.). Office: Re/Max Realtors of Victoria Central Ltd 2210 N Navarro St Victoria TX 77901

REASONS, DIANE, business executive; b. Eldorado, Ill., May 7, 1941; d. John Henry and Oberene (Ratley) Hafford; m. Gary Ronald Reasons, Dec. 30, 1958; children—Cheri Reasons Brown, Karen, Nicole, Michael. Student pub. schs., Eldorado. Vice pres., co-owner Reasons & Assocs., Inc., Franklin, Tenn., 1980—; v.p. G & D Devel., Inc., Franklin, 1980—; founder, owner, operator Custom Color Cons., Franklin, 1983—; motivational speaker, lectr. worldwide. Pub.: America's Handbook for Success, 1982. Founding mem. Citizens Trust, Washington, 1981; mem. invitations com. Washington Charity Dinner, 1981, mem. steering com., 1982; regional chmn. Christian Liberties Rally, Nashville, 1983; sec. Lord's Chapel Christian Acad. Sch. Bd., Brentwood, Tenn., 1983-85. Home: 1402 Devens Dr Brentwood TN 37027 Office: Reasons & Assocs Inc 1710 General George Patton Rd Suite 103 Franklin TN 37064

REAVES, CYNTHIA PATRICE, financial analyst, investment partner; b. Dallas, May 14, 1959; d. Benjamin Earl and Alice Margaret Louise (Luttring) R. B.B.A. in Acctg., N. Tex. State U., 1980. Acctg. trainee ARCO Oil and Gas Co., Lafayette, La., 1980-81, assoc. computer analyst, Dallas, 1981-82, budget analyst ARCO Exploration Co., Dallas, 1982-84, fin. analyst, sr. leasehold acct., 1984—. Advisor Jr. Achievement, Dallas, 1982—; active Noon Forum Com. ARCO Civic Action Program, 1981—, exec. com., 1984—; vol. and mem. Dallas County Hist. Soc., 1980—. Named Outstanding CAP mem. ARCO Civic Action Program, 1982-83. Mem. Wynnewood Bus. and Profl. Women (pres. 1982-83, Young Careerist, 1983), Alpha Xi Delta Alumnae Assn. Office: ARCO Oil and Gas Co PO Box 2819 Suite 11-062C DAB Dallas TX 75221

REAVES, GLORIA ELAINE, computer analyst; b. Passaic, N.J., May 5, 1954; d. Victor Livingston and Marion Lee (Ridley) Connell; m. Terry Maynard Reaves, Oct. 12, 1974 (div. Sept. 1984); 1 child, Christopher James. Student Livington Coll., Univ. Coll., New Brunswick, N.J. Lead programmer, programmer trainee AT&T, Piscataway, N.J., 1975-83, programmer analyst installation support group, 1984—. Democrat. Episcopalian. Clubs: Ricochet Health and Racquet (sec.-treas. 1979-83) (Piscataway); Jersey Ski (Newark). Avocations: racquetball; tennis; skiing; martial arts (Brown Belt); Ninga Isshinru. Home: 121 N Randolphville Rd Piscataway NJ 08854 Office: AT&T Communications Room C85-10-D04 100 Naricon Pl East Brunswick NJ 08816

REAVIS, VIOLA LEA SCHUBERT, educator; b. Miami, Okla., July 11, 1927; d. Joe and Rose Lea (Van Horn) Schubert; m. Robert E. Reavis, Sept. 27, 1946; children—Edwin R., Loretta J., Kieran, Robert II. A.A., Okla. Northeastern A&M Coll., 1973; B.S., Pittsburgh State U., Kans., 1975, M.S., 1961. Sec. Miami Pub. Schs., Okla., 1968-69, tchr., 1979—; tchr. Wyandotte Pub. Schs., Okla., 1977-79. Treas. Republican Women, 1975. Mem. NEA, Okla. Edn. Assn., Miami Classroom Tchrs. Assn., AAUW, Delta Kappa Gamma (scholarship 1985, 86), Beta Sigma Phi, Epsilon Sigma Alpha. Roman Catholic. Avocations: needlepoint; sewing.

REBELSKY, FREDA ETHEL GOULD, psychologist; b. N.Y.C., Mar. 11, 1931; d. William and Sarah (Kaplan) Gould; B.A., U. Chgo., 1950, M.A., 1954; Ph.D., Radcliffe Coll., 1961; m. William Rebelsky, Jan. 1, 1956 (dec. 1979); 1 son, Samuel. Counselor, U. Chgo. Orthogenic Sch., 1952-55; research asst. Kenyon & Eckhart, Inc., 1956-58; research asst. lab. human devel. Harvard U., 1959-60, teaching asst. psychology, then instr. edn., 1960-61; research asso. Speech research lab. Children's Hosp., Boston, 1960-61, M.I.T., 1961-62; mem. faculty Boston U., 1962—, prof. psychology, 1972—, dir. doctoral program in devel. psychology, 1969-74; vis. lectr. U. Utrecht (Netherlands), 1965-67; Froman prof. Russell Sage Coll., Troy, N.Y., 1972. Grantee U.S. Office Edn., 1964-65, Boston U. Grad. Sch., 1967-70, OEO, 1967-69. NIMH, 1974-76; Bunting fellow Radcliffe Coll., 1985-86; recipient Distinguished Tchr. Psychology award Am. Psychol. Found., 1970; Harbison award excellence teaching Danforth Found., 1971; Metcalf award Boston U., 1978; Disting. Career in Psychology award Mass. Psychol. Assn., 1982. Mem. AAAS, Soc. Research Child Devel. (sec. Boston 1963-65), AAUP (sec. Boston U. 1964-65, pres. 1984-85), Am., Eastern, Mass. (chmn. program com. 1962-64) psychol. assns., Mass. Children's Lobby (pres. 1977-81), Sigma Xi, Psi Chi. Author: Child Behavior and Development: A Reader, 1969; Child Behavior and Development, 2d edit., 1973: Life: The Continuous Process, 1975; Growing Children, 1976. Address: 1 Billings Park Newton MA 02158 Office: 64 Cummington St Boston MA 02215

REBENTISCH, SUSAN WEBSTER, radio management consultant; b. Los Angeles, Apr. 24, 1943; d. Maurie E. and Judy A. (Peairs) Webster; m. Edward H. Rebentisch, Dec. 4, 1974. A.A., Parsons Sch. Design, 1965; cert. N.Y. Inst. Photography, 1982; student Mercy Coll., 1986—. Office mgr. Travelworld Inc., N.Y.C., 1970-73; sales rep. Brit. Caledonia Airways, N.Y.C., 1973-74; mgr. Egyptian tours Lindblad Travel Inc., N.Y.C., 1975—; v.p., adminstrv. mgr. The Webster Group, N.Y.C., 1977—. Co-author: St. Luke's Church Sesquicentennial Celebration 1935-85, 1985. 4-H program asst. Coop. Extension 4-H, Mahopac, N.Y., 1984; sr. warden St. Luke's Ch., 1986. Recipient Outstanding Leader award Kodak, 1982. Mem. Southeast Hist. Soc., Photog. Soc. Am. Avocations: photography; gardening.

REBHUN, PEARL G., artist; b. N.Y.C., Feb. 20, 1925; d. Emanuel and Bertha (Pessel) Greenblatt; m. Lionel Earl Rebhun; children—Laurence, Andrew, Donald. Lectr. Nat. Galleries, N.Y.C., 1975—; free-lance artist, Great Neck, N.Y., 1985—. Paintings exhibited worldwide. Vice pres. Lake Success Civic Assn., Great Neck. Recipient Chase Manhattan Bank purchase award, 1985. Mem. Artists Involvement in Art, Nat. Assn. Women Artists (exec. bd., jurist, Grumbacher gold medal 1983, Francis Leiber Meml. award, Elizabeth Erlanger merit award). Avocations: golf; tennis; skiing; swimming. Home and studio: 25 Meadow Woods Rd Great Neck NY 10020

RECANATI, DINA, sculptor; b. Cairo, Egypt, Jan. 15, 1928; d. Albert and Suzanne (Iskandari) Hettena; came to U.S., 1948; student Art Students League, N.Y.C., 1959-62; m. Raphael Recanati, Oct. 8, 1946; children—Oudi, Michael. Exhbns. include Nat. Arts Club, N.Y.C., 1961, 62, Jersey City Mus., 1963, Gordon Gallery, Tel Aviv, 1970-75, Jewish Mus., N.Y.C., 1975, 84, Danforth Mus., Boston, Padua (Italy) Biennale, 1977, Gurewitsch Gallery, N.Y.C., 1978, Silvermine Guild Artists, 1962-65, Claude Bernard Gallery, Paris, 1966, 67, Queens County (N.Y.) Art Cultural Center, 1973, Delson Richter Galleries under auspices Washington Art Fair, 1977, Gray Gallery at N.Y. U., 1978, Julie M. Gallery, Tel-Aviv, 1981, 84; rep. permanent collections Israeli Mus., Jerusalem, Tel Aviv Mus., Ben Gurion Airport, Tel Aviv, President's Garden Collection, Jerusalem, Bet Ariella, Tel-Aviv; executed spl. bronze edit. Gates, Am.-Israel Cultural Found., 1976. Recipient Knickerbocker award Nat. Arts Club, 1961, King Solomon award Am.-Israel Cultural Found., 1977, Louise Waterman Wise award Am. Jewish Congress, 1976. Home: 944 Fifth Ave New York NY 10021 Office: 136 Grand St New York NY 10013

RECH, CLARICE VALGENE, nursing administrator; b. Rhinelander, Wis., Dec. 10, 1933; d. Clarence Rudolph and Anna Valgene (Okerstrom) Olson; m. Jack William Rech, Sept. 25, 1954 (div. Feb. 1982); children—Scott William, Cynthia Marie. R.N., Augustana Sch. Nursing, Chgo., 1954; B.S., Coll. St. Francis, Joliet, Ill., 1981; M.P.A., Roosevelt U., 1986. Staff, head nurse Augustana Hosp., Chgo., 1954-58, dir. inservice edn., 1958-59; ICU nurse Ravenswood Hosp., Chgo., 1964-66, Northwest Community Hosp., Arlington Heights, Ill., 1975-80, supr. Treatment Ctr., 1980—. Trustee, Village Buffalo Grove, 1973-79, plan commr., 1972-73; chmn. various commns. Buffalo Grove, 1973-79. Recipient Josephine De Leonardo Community Service Amvets awards, Ill., 1973; appreciation garden established in her name Buffalo Grove Park Dist., 1980; recipient Status of Women award AAUW, 1978. Lutheran. Avocations: skiing; swimming; quilting. Home: 1233 Franklin Ln Buffalo Grove IL 60089 Office: Northwest Community Treatment Ctr 15 S McHenry Rd Buffalo Grove IL 60090

RECH, LINDA GWYNNE, oil company executive, rancher; b. Madera, Calif., Aug. 23, 1948; d. Ernest P. Anderson and Louella (Dillingham) Anderson Porter; m. Leslie Joe Blythe, Aug. 5, 1967 (div. June 1975); children—Corey Shawn, Cary Shane; m. Stanley L. Rech, Mar. 20, 1976. Grad. high sch., Arvada, Colo. Office sec. Sun Life Assurance Co., Denver, 1966-67; owner Har-Ken Answering Service, Brighton, Colo., 1972-76, P.J.'s Western Wear, Fort Lupton, Colo., 1976-78; co-owner 31 Disposal, Fort Lupton, 1976—, Rech Limousine, Crawford, Colo., 1979—; co-owner, operator Rech Limousin Ranch, Crawford, 1981—. Leader 4-H Club, Crawford, 1984—; v.p. Black Mesa Cowbelles, Crawford, 1984—; chmn. Pioneer Days, Crawford, 1985; sec. Fruitland Mesa, 1984—. Baptist. Address: 3701 A-75 Rd Crawford CO 81415

RECHT, NADYNE MARCEILLE, realtor; b. Ft. Wayne, Ind., Sept. 9, 1921; d. Donald Joseph and Gladys Marie (Bisson) Tierney; student Ind. U., Purdue, 1965-66; m. Ervin John Recht, Nov. 20, 1941; children—Diane Recht Langin, Douglas, Jeannine Recht Wells, Mark, Cynthia, Michael. Saleswoman, Daymude Albersmeyer Butler, Ft. Wayne, 1966-68; broker, supr. Daymude, Albersmeyer Brokers, Ft. Wayne, 1968-70; ptnr. Daymude & Co., 1970-73; broker, ptnr. Recht & Recht, Ft. Wayne, 1973—; treas. Multiple Listing Service, 1983-84; former chmn. Ft. Wayne Bd. Realtors. Active Amnesty Internat.; pres. Maplewood Community Assn. Mem. Civic Theater Guild, Mus. Art, Mental Health Assn., St. Francis Guild. Democrat. Roman Catholic. Club: Jefferson (v.p. 1964). Home: 6853 Woodcrest St Fort Wayne IN 46815 Office: 3330 S Calhoun St Fort Wayne IN 46807

RECORD, MELANIE ANNE, printing shop official, freelance artist; b. Bryan, Tex., Mar. 10, 1957; d. Ralph Vernon and Martha (Baxter) Record. Student Tex. A&M U., 1975-78. With Faubion Printing, Bryan, Tex., 1974-76; artist II, Tex. A&M U. Printing Ctr., College Station, 1976-78, artist typographer, 1978-83, supr. art dept., 1983—. Charter mem. Republican Presdl. Task Force, Washington, 1984—. Mem. Internat. Assn. Bus. Communicators, Univ. and Coll. Designers Assn. Methodist. Avocations: calligraphy; pottery. Home: 107 Helena St Bryan TX 77801 Office: Tex A&M Univ Printing Ctr Ireland St College Station TX 77843

RECTOR, JUSTINE JOYCE, professor, association executive; b. Phila., Feb. 13, 1927; d. Wesley Jackson and Elizabeth (Neal) Jackson Robinson; children—Joyce, Marsha, Renee. B.A. in History, U. Pa., 1970; M.S. in Journalism, Columbia U., 1972; postgrad. U. Pa., 1974, Howard U., 1980, Union Grad. Sch., 1984. Dir. U. Pa., Phila., 1972-76; instr. Temple U., Phila., 1976-78; assoc. prof. Howard U., Washington, 1978—; journalist cons. Pacifica, Washington, 1980—; founder, dir. Nat. Afro-Am. Male Resource Ctr., Washington, 1978—; cons. Pacifica News, Washington, 1980—. Co-author: Issues and Trends in Afro-Am. Journalism, 1980; contbr. articles to profl. jours. Vol. Pacifica News Anchor, Washington, 1980—; staff, editor Area Wide Council N. Phila., 1968-73; Africa panel Am. Friends Service Com., Phila., 1975-78; bd. adoptions Women's Christian Alliance, Phila., 1972-76; vol. recruiter U. Pa., provost's com. affirmative action; active NAACP, Congress African People, Youth Conservation Service, Phila., Women's Soc. Christian Service, Phila. Sch. Dist. Home and Sch. Assn., Congress Racial Equality, Black Power Conf.; leader Girl Scouts U.S.A.; exec. com., v.p. Young Republicans, Phila.; bd. dirs. N. Central Seasoned Citizens Ctr., Phila. Knight Found. grantee, 1971; Fund Investigative Journalism grantee, 1981; recipient Outstanding Leadership award Women in Communication, 1981. Mem. Women in Communications, Inc. (faculty advisor 1978—), Radio/TV News Dirs. Assn., Washington Assn. Black Journalists, Assn. Edn. Journalism, African Heritage Studies. Baptist. Office: Dept Journalism Howard U Washington DC 20059

REDD, J. DIANE, university fund raising and grants management executive; b. Beckley, W.Va., Apr. 10, 1945; d. Robert Fountain and Lillian (Fitts) Redd. B.S., W.Va. State Coll., 1967. Instr. bus. subjects Paterson (N.J.) Bus. Edn., 1967-68; with U. Medicine and Dentistry N.J., Newark, 1968—, adminstrv. asst. research and sponsored programs, 1968-73, asst. dir. health edn., 1973-76, sr. devel. officer, 1976-79, asst. dir. devel., 1979-83, chief devel. and alumni affairs, 1983—. Mem. priorities com., devel. com. United Way of Essex and West Hudson, Newark, 1983-85; chmn. human resources com. Community Adv. Bd., U. Medicine and Dentistry N.J., Newark, 1978-82. Recipient Recognition of Achievement award Young Women of America, Inc., Montgomery, Ala., 1979. Mem. Council Advancement and Support of Edn., Nat. Soc. Fund Raising Execs. Inc., Assn. Am. Med. Colls., Exec. Women N.J., N.J. Soc. Fund Raisers. Democrat. Office: Univ Medicine and Dentistry of New Jersey 100 Bergen St Newark NJ 07103

REDD, JANET FAITH, librarian; b. Albany, Calif., May 24, 1945; d. Joseph Patrick and Faith Pauline (Schoen) R. B.A., U. Calif.-Berkeley, 1967, M.L.S., 1968; M.A., San Jose State U., 1974; Ph.D., Stanford U., 1980, postdoctoral scholar, 1984—. Standard services credential, supervision-library services, Calif. Reference evening librarian asst. cataloger De Anza Coll., Cupertino, Calif., 1968-70, circulation librarian, 1970-77, acquisitions and periodicals librarian, 1978—, pres. faculty senate, 1984-85. Contbr. articles to various publs. Calif. State Scholarships fellow, 1963-68; U. Calif.-Berkeley scholar, 1963-67. Mem. ALA, Calif. Library Assn., Calif. Assn. Research Libraries, Am. Assn. Higher Edn., Assn. Coll. and Research Libraries, Am. Ednl. Research Assn., Wildlife Rescue Assn., Campanile Club, Tower and Flame, Phi Beta Kappa, Beta Phi Mu. Home: 21995 Via Regina Saratoga CA 95070 Office: De Anza Coll Learning Ctr 21250 Stevens Creek Blvd Cupertino CA 95070

REDD, JUDITH BLUITT, personnel director; b. Dallas, May 26, 1949; d. Herbert, Jr. and Doris (Washington) Bluitt; m. Charles B. Redd, Jr., Dec. 26, 1981. B.S., Howard U., 1971; M.S., North Tex. State U., 1984. Editorial asst. McGraw Hill Co., Washington, 1971-73; program asst. Curber Assocs., Washington, 1973-74; agt., mgr. Beeson Travel Bur., Washington, 1974-76; employment specialist Children's Med. Ctr., Dallas, 1977-79; personnel dir. Timberlawn Psychiat. Hosp., Dallas, 1979—. Chmn. vocat. office edn. adv. com. Dallas Ind. Schs., 1983-84. Mem. Tex. Soc. Hosp. Personnel Adminstrn. (pres. 1982-83), Am. Soc. Personnel Adminstrn. Democrat. Home: 201 Rustic Ridge Garland TX 75040 Office: Timberlawn Psychiat Hosp PO Box 11288 Dallas TX 75223

REDDEN, LINDA JOYCE, engineering, architecture and planning company executive; b. Nashville, Feb. 5, 1950; d. Joseph Edward and Bessie Mai (Carr) R. B.A. in History, Tenn. Tech. U., 1972; M.S. in Communications, U. Tenn., 1975. Photographer, Tenn. Tech. U., Cookeville, 1972-73; editor Hendersonville Star News, Tenn., 1975-76; editor, sales promotion exec. Am. Gen. Life and Accident Ins. Co., Nashville, 1975-85; communications coordinator Barge, Waggoner, Sumner & Cannon, Nashville, 1985—. Editor: The Shield, 1980 (award Nat. Fedn. Press Women 1980). Bd. dirs. Mur-Ci Homes for Retarded, Nashville, 1984—; mem. Nashville Symphony Guild, 1985—. Mem. Pub. Relations Soc. Am., Internat. Assn. Bus. Communicators (sec. 1982), Tenn. Women's Press and Authors Club (treas. 1983—), Phi Kappa Phi, Kappa Tau Alpha, Phi Alpha Theta. Avocations: reading; photography; cooking; swimming; travel. Home: 599 Hidden Acres Dr Madison TN 37115 Office: Barge Waggoner Sumner & Cannon 162 3d Ave N Nashville TN 37201

REDDICK, RHODA ANNE, medical microbiologist; b. Waynesboro, Ga., Nov. 2, 1937; d. Loy Winfred and Eileen Elizabeth (Rhodes) R.; A.B., Ga.

Coll., 1958; M.T., Emory U., 1959; M.S., Med. Coll. Ga., 1965, Ph.D., 1968; m. Robert D. Mitchum, June 20, 1970. Med. technologist Emory U. Hosp., Atlanta, 1959-61, Med. Coll. Ga., Augusta, 1961-64; postdoctoral fellow med. microbiology Centers for Disease Control, Atlanta, 1968-70; dir. diagnostic microbiology S.C. Dept. Health and Environ. Control Bur. Labs, Columbia, 1970-75, dir. Div. Lab. Improvement, 1975-82, dir. Div. Clin. Labs., 1982—; clin. asst. prof. microbiology U.S.C. Sch. Medicine, Columbia, 1976—; adj. asst. prof. lab. medicine Med. U.S.C., Charleston, 1977—; specialist Nat. Registry of Microbiology, 1971—. Named Outstanding Microbiologist in S.C., 1983. Diplomate Am. Bd. Med. Microbiology. Fellow Am. Acad. Microbiology; mem. Am. Soc. Microbiology, Am. Soc. Clin. Pathologists, Am. Public Health Assn., Conf. Public Health Lab. Dirs., Southeastern Assn. Clin. Microbiologists, S.C. Public Health Assn. Methodist. Office: PO Box 2202 Columbia SC 29202

REDDING, BARBARA ANN, nurse; b. Gettysburg Pa., Aug. 30, 1939; d. Leonard Francis and Helen Margaret (Yohe) Redding. B.S., St. Joseph Coll., 1961; M.S. in Nursing, U. Pa., 1964; Ed.D., U. Fla., 1982. Staff nurse Grad. Hosp., U. Pa., Phila., 1961-62, instr. practical nursing, 1962-63; instr. nursing St. Joseph Coll., Emmitsburg, Md., 1964-68, asst. prof., 1968-69; asst. prof. U. Mass., Amherst, 1969-73; assoc. prof. Holyoke Community Coll. (Mass.), 1973-75; asst. prof. U. South Fla., Tampa, 1975-78, assoc. prof., 1978—. Mem. Fla. Nurses Assn., Fla. League for Nursing, Assn. Care of Children's Health, Phi Delta Kappa, Kappa Delta Pi, Sigma Theta Tau. Roman Catholic. Home: 8621 Cattail Dr Tampa FL 33617 Office: 12901 N 30th St Tampa FL 33612

REDDY, MARGARET ENAIRE, army officer; b. Boston, Apr. 25, 1956; d. William John and Elizabeth Ann (Enaine) R. B.S. in Health Care Mgmt., U. Ala., 1979. Commd. 2d lt. U.S. Army, 1979, advanced through grades to capt., 1983; med. platoon leader 194th Armored Brigade, Ft. Knox, Ky., 1979-81; ambulance platoon leader 172d Support Bn., Ft. Richardson, Alaska, 1981, officer-in-charge clearing sta., 1981-83, personnel mgr., 1983-84; student Co. A, 1st Bn., Acad. Health Scis., Ft. Sam Houston, Tex., 1984—; assigned comdr., student and med. holding cos. Fitzsimon Army Med. Ctr., Aurora, Colo. Mem. Women of 1st/60 Inf. Bn., Women of 172d Support Bn. Epsicopalian. Home: 2441 NE Loop 410 Apt 109 San Antonio TX 78217 Office: Co A 1st Bn Acad Health Scis Fort Sam Houston TX 78234

REDDY, MARY LUCINDA, public relations executive; b. South Bend, Ind., Nov. 10, 1949; d. Charles Sheridan and Hannah Louise (Moran) R. B.A., Nazareth Coll., 1971; M.A., Ball State U., 1979. Tchr. St. Joseph Sch., Battle Creek, Mich., 1971-72, Powers High Sch., Flint, Mich., 1972-74; dir. communications Nazareth Coll., Kalamazoo, Mich., 1974-77, asst. to pres., 1979-83; dir. pub. relations and devel. Sisters of St. Joseph, Kalamazoo, 1983—. Editor newsletter Ball State U., promoter, 1978-79. Author, designer Can I Not Do, 1978. Editor Grapevine, 1982—. Contbr. articles to profl. jours. Chmn., United Way drive Nazareth Coll., 1974-77, 79-83; active Diocese Kalamazoo Communications Adv. Bd., 1981—, Nazareth Coll. Alumni Bd., 1984—. Recipient Leadership award United Way, Kalamazoo, 1979-83. Mem. Women in Communication, Inc. (scholarship com. 1984-85, workshop presenter 1982—), Fund Raising Inst., Sisters of St. Joseph, AAUW. Roman Catholic. Home: 5229 Amarillo Parchment MI 49004 Office: Sisters of St Joseph Gull Rd Nazareth MI 49074

REDENBARGER, JANICE JEANNE, educator, counselor; b. Brazil, Ind., May 29, 1942; d. Stanley Matthew and Jewell Irene (Jester) Cobley; m. Daniel Joseph Redenbarger, Sept. 6, 1963; children—Susan, Sally, Jennifer. B.A., Ind. State U., 1964, M.S., 1967, postgrad., 1967-77. Office worker, writer Ind. State U. News Bur., Terre Haute, 1960-63; newsroom staff Sta. WTHI-TV, Terre Haute, 1963-64; newspaper reporter Brazil Times (Ind.), 1970—; tchr., counselor Clay City High Sch. (Ind.), 1965—. Chairperson, Sycamore Coordinating Council, Terre Haute, 1975-77, bd. dirs., 1973-79; del. Nat. Forum on Excellence in Edn., Indpls., 1983; reviewer Ind. Gov.'s Textbook Adoption Com., 1983. Mem. Ind. Council Tchrs. English, NEA, Ind. State Tchrs. Assn. (dir. 1978-79, bd. dirs. in service corp. 1985—), Delta Kappa Gamma (pres. chpt. 1982-84), Pi Lambda Theta Iota. Republican. Lodge: Job's Daus. (hon. queen 1961). Home: Rural Route 11 Box 106 Brazil IN 47834 Office: Clay City High Sch 601 Lankford St Clay City IN 47841

REDEWILL, JOYCE CAROL, cosmetic manufacturing executive, consultant, lecturer; b. Bklyn., Oct. 7, 1945; d. Harold Arthur and Alice (Newton) Fliegner; m. Leslie Turner Redewell, May 21, 1977; children—Justin, Andrea, 1 son by previous marriage, Theodore K. Green; 1 stepson, Leslie T. Redewill. B.S., Calif. State U.-Long Beach, 1968; M.B.A., Pepperdine U., 1978. Interplanetary quarantine microbiologist Jet Propulsion Lab., Pasadena, Calif., 1968-69; staff research assoc. UCLA, 1969-75; pres. Caresse, Inc., Santa Monica, Calif., 1972-75, Au Naturel, Inc., Monterey Park, Calif., 1976-84; owner Au Naturel Cosmetics, Venice Beach, Calif., 1984—, De Nouveau Cos., The Nail Polish Factory, Los Angeles, 1985—; founder Cosmetic Research Inst., Los Angeles, 1986—. Inventor nail enamel without formaldehyde resins, nail care natural skin care products. Mem. Friends of Whittier Library. Mem. Fedn. Coatings Tech., Cosmetic Chemist Soc., Beauty and Barber Supply Inst., Nat. Health Food Assn., Nat. Assn. Female Execs. Republican. Club: Women's (Whittier). Avocations: painting; sculpture; horeback riding. Office: Nail Polish Factory 8231 Allport Ave Santa Fe Springs CA 90670

REDGRAVE, VANESSA, actress; b. London, Jan. 30, 1937; d. Michael and Rachel (Kempson) R.; student Central Sch. Speech and Drama, London, 1955-57; m. Tony Richardson, Apr. 28, 1962 (div.); children—Natasha Jane, Joely Kim. Prin. theatrical roles include: Helena in Midsummer Night's Dream, 1959, Stella in The Tiger and the Horse, 1960, Katerina in The Taming of the Shrew, 1961, Rosaline in As You Like It, 1961, Imogene in Cymbeline, 1962, Nina in The Seagull, 1964, Miss Brodie in The Prime of Miss Jean Brodie, 1966; other plays include: Cato Street, 1971, Threepenny Opera, 1972, Twelfth Night, 1972, Anthony and Cleopatra, 1973, Design for Living, 1973, Macbeth, 1975, Lady from the Sea, 1976, 78, 79; The Aspera Papers, Theatre Royal Haymarket, 1984, The Seagull (London Standard Drama award), 1985; film roles include: Leonie in Morgan-A Suitable Case for Treatment (Best Actress award Cannes Film Festival 1966), 1965, Sheila in Sailor from Gibraltar, 1965, Anne-Marie in La Musica, 1965, Jane in Blow Up, 1967, Guinevere in Camelot, 1967, Isadora in Isadora Duncan (Best Actress award Cannes Film Festival), 1968, Cosima in Wagner, 1982. other films include: The Charge of The Light Brigade, 1968, The Seagull, 1968, A Quiet Place in the Country, 1968, Daniel Deronda, 1969, Dropout, 1969, The Trojan Women, 1970, The Devils, 1970, The Holiday, 1971, Mary Queen of Scots, 1971, Murder on the Orient Express, 1974, Winter Rates, 1974, 7% solution, 1975, Julia, 1977, Agatha, 1978, Yanks, 1978, Bear Island, 1979, Playing for Time, 1980; My Body My Child, 1981; Wagner, 1982; The Bostonians (Nat. Soc. Film Critics award), 1985, Wetherby (Nat. Soc. Film Critics award 1986), 1985; also TV appearances. Bd. govs. Central Sch. Speech and Drama, 1963—. Decorated comdr. Order Brit. Empire; recipient Drama award Evening Standard, 1961, Best Actress award Variety Club Gt. Brit., 1961, 66, Brit. Guild TV Producers and Dirs., 1966; Golden Globe award, 1978, Acad. award for best supporting actress, 1977; Emmy award for Playing for Time, 1980-81. Author: Pussies and Tigers, 1964.

REDIGER, LINDA MARY (BRAY), lawyer; b. Flint, Mich., Dec. 31, 1954; d. Rodney Duval and Elizabeth Ann (Moore) Bray; m. David Delbert Rediger, Dec. 30, 1983. B.A., Rutgers U., 1976; postgrad., U. Paris, Sorbonne, 1978; M.A., Mich. State U., 1982; J.D., Thomas M. Cooley Law Sch., Lansing, Mich., 1982. Bar: Mich. 1982, Colo. 1982. Assoc. editor Ingham County News Briefs, Lansing, 1980; law clk. Mich. Atty. Gen., Lansing, 1981-82, Edn. Commn. States, Denver, 1982; atty., adviser U.S. Dept. Def., OCHAMPUS, Appeals and Hearings, Aurora, Colo., 1982-85. Mem. People's Fair Exhibitor Com., Denver, 1983-84; del. 1st Amendment Congress Colo., Denver, 1984. Recipient Outstanding Performance award Dept. Def., 1982-83, 83-84. Mem. ABA, Am. Judicature Soc., Fed. Bar Assn., Denver Bar Assn. (publs. com. 1983-84), Sigma Delta Chi. Republican. Presbyterian. Club: Internat. Athletic (Denver). Office: 1614 Gaylord St Denver CO 80206

REDING, DIANA LEE, nurse, educator; b. Dunkirk, N.Y., Sept. 30, 1942; d. Edward Stanley and Patricia Jewel (Whitaker) Dolski; m. Dwight Courtney Reding, Dec. 2, 1967; children—Dwight C., Christopher Scott. B.S., Hartwick Coll., 1965; M.S., East Tex. State U., 1975. Head nurse Pediatric Outpatient Clinic, Los Angeles County Gen. Hosp., 1965-67; office nurse for pediatrician, Dallas, 1967-68; instr. nursing Dallas County Community Coll. Dist., Dallas, 1968—; cons. dist. stress/burnout workshops Dallas County Community Coll., 1980—; instr. Am. Heart Assn., Dallas, 1980—. Counselor youth Methodist Ch., Irving, Tex., 1980-82. Mem. Dallas County Community Coll. Dist. Faculty Orgn. Avocations: reading; traveling; crocheting. Home: 1321 Lindhurst St Irving TX 75061 Office: Brookhaven Coll 3939 Valley View Farmers Branch TX 75234

REDLER, SHERRY PRESS, audiologist; b. N.Y.C.; d. Martin M. and Elsie (Opin) Press; B.A., Adelphi U., 1954; M.S., So. Conn. State Coll., 1971, postgrad., 1976-79; children—Michael, Steven, Lynda. Speech pathologist Roslyn (N.Y.) Public Schs., 1954-56; tchr. drama Rollins Coll., Winter Park, Fla., 1961-63; personnel counselor Internat. Bus. Assn., Pitts., 1965; speech pathologist Fairfield (Conn.) Public Schs., 1968-75, ednl. audiologist, 1976—; clin. audiologist Rehab. Center, Bridgeport, Conn., 1975-76; sign lang. instr. Bridgeport Rehab. Center, 1976-78, Staples High Sch., Westport, Conn.; instr. So. Conn. State Coll., New Haven, 1976—; lectr., cons. in field; ind. evaluator of programs for hearing impaired; author, project dir. Title IV Fed. Grant, Conn., 1976-80; mem. Conn. State Task Force to assess services provided to mentally retarded, 1981—; author, project dir. sch. audiology program, Conn., 1981. Trustee Congregation B'Nai Israel, 1985—. Mem. Conn. Speech and Hearing Assn. (co-chmn. com. on edn. hearing impaired 1976—), NEA, Conn. Edn. Assn., Fairfield Edn. Assn., Am. Speech and Hearing Assn., Am. Ednl. Audiology Assn. (1st v.p. 1986—). Home: 28 Lockwood Circle Fairfield CT 06430 Office: 60 Thompson St Fairfield CT 06430

REDMOND, BARBARA ANN, art and movement psychotherapist, consultant; b. Bklyn.; d. William and Lisette (Muller) Franklin. B.F.A., Pratt Inst., Bklyn.; M.S., Pace U., 1971; Ed.D., Tchrs. Coll. Columbia U., 1978. Cert. tchr., art therapist, N.Y. Asst. prof. edn. and spl. edn. Bklyn. Coll., 1972-78, adj. asst. prof., 1982—; asst. dir. adult edn. Baruch Coll., CUNY, N.Y.C., 1980-81; pvt. practice psychotherapy, Bklyn., 1978—; prin. Creative Dynamics, Cons., N.Y.C., 1981—; adj. asst. prof. Kingsborough Community Coll., 1982—, Mercy Coll., 1982—; cons., writer Ednl. Film Ctr. Ltd., London, 1973, Interland Film Corp., N.Y.C., 1974; editor, reviewer Prentice-Hall Pubs., 1980. Mem. Nat. Assn. Female Execs., Sales Exec. Club N.Y., Art Therapists Assn. Am., Assn. Humanistic Psychology, Allied Bd. Trade. Club: Montauk (Bklyn.). Avocations: writing; drawing; traveling. Office: 207 E 16h St New York NY

REDMOND, COLLEEN ANNE, magazine publisher; b. Chgo., Apr. 28, 1953; d. William Aloysius and Rita Marie (Riordan) Redmond. M.B.A., Rosary Coll., 1986. Features editor Press Publs., Elmhurst, Ill., 1976-77; publs. specialist Ill. Credit Union League, Oak Brook, Ill., 1977-81; employee publs. mgr. Loyola U. Med. Center, Maywood, Ill., 1981-84; editor Real Estate Bus. mag. Realtors Nat. Mktg. Inst., Chgo., 1984—; dir., chmn. supervisory com. Loyola U. Employees Fed. Credit Union, Maywood, 1982-85. Mem. Internat. Assn. Bus. Communicators, Women in Communications, Friends Channel 11. Home: 239 Mill Rd Apt 407A Addison IL 60601 Office: Realtors Nat Mktg Inst 430 N Michigan Ave Chicago IL 60611

REDMOND, GAIL ELIZABETH, petroleum company executive; b. Milw., July 28, 1946; d. George Foote and Doris Ruth (Roethke) R.; m. John Thomas Happ. Student Coll. St. Catherine, 1964-66; B.S. magna cum laude, Utah State U., 1968. Tchr. public schs., Milw., 1968-70; staff coordinator Med. Personnel Pool, Milw., 1973-76; corp. manpower devel. mgr. Clark Oil & Refining Corp., Milw., 1976-80; sr. advisor communications, employee benefits Conoco, Inc., Ponca City, Okla., 1980-81, coordinator profl. recruiting, 1981-82, coordinator benefit communications, 1982-84; asst. mgr. phase II job evaluation, 1985—, coordinator job evaluation, 1986—. Serving with USNR. Mem. AAUW (editor br. newsletter), Phi Kappa Phi. Office: Conoco Inc PO Box 1267 Ponca City OK 74603

REDMOND, GLORIA HERNANDEZ, genealogical, patriotic and historical organizational worker; b. New Iberia, La.; d. David and Agnes (Hernandez) Redmond. Diploma Henry W. Allen Bus. Sch., 1936. Author: Reminiscences Chalmette Chapter United States Daughters of 1812, 1893-1985, 1985. Reigned as Queen Caliphs of Cairo and Dorians Balls, 1940; Maid in Carnival Balls - Athenians, Nereus, Osiris, Prophets of Persia, New Orleans Floral Trail Ct., 1940. Mem. La. Cols. (pres. Founders chpt. 1978-80), DAR (regent Robert Harvey chpt. 1978-80, pres. regents' council dist. IV La. Soc. 1981-82), U.S. Daus. of 1812 (parliamentarian 1977-80, pres. Chalmette chpt. 1982-85), La. Council for Vieux Carre (v.p. 1982—), Alumnae Bd. of Acad. of Sacred Heart (2d v.p. 1981—), Chalmette Nat. Hist. Park Assn. (sec. 1983—), United Daus. of Confederacy (custodian of Flags Stonewall Jackson chpt. 1985—). Democrat. Roman Catholic. Clubs: New Orleans Country, Debutante of New Orleans (sec. 1941-42). Avocations: oil painting, designing, working needlepoint, collecting antique fans. Home: No 10 Trianon Plaza New Orleans LA 70125

REDMOND, JEAN HELEN, public relations executive; b. Detroit, Apr. 6, 1931; d. Charles Alexander and Helen Isabel (West) Collins; m. Garey Miles Redmond, Sept. 16, 1949; children—Linda Marie Wark, Debra Jeanne Roorda, Steven Gary Redmond. Student So. Ill. U., 1960-62. Pub. relations dir. Shagbark council Girl Scouts U.S.A., Herrin, Ill., 1961-73; exec. dir. Bisbee C. of C., Ariz., 1980-85; propr. Assistance Unltd., pub. relations, 1986—; advisor Ariz. C. of C., Phoenix, 1983—; dir. Econ. Devel. Team, Bisbee, 1981—, Advisor Community Devel. Commn., Bisbee, 1980-83; mem. Bisbee Planning and Zoning Commn.; Bisbee rep. to Cochise County Econ. Devel. Bd. Named Citizen of Yr., Bisbee C. of C., 1981. Mem. Ariz. Assn. Indsl. Devel. (bd. dirs. 1984—), Ariz. Chamber Execs. (dir. 1982-85), Bus. and Profl. Womens Club. (v.p. 1964-66). Home and Office: 116 Clawson Ave PO Box 1115 Bisbee AZ 85603

REDO, MARIA ELAINE, gerontologist, educator; b. N.Y.C., Jan. 12, 1925; d. Ernest and Mary C. Lappano; B.S. in Edn., Fordham U., 1945; cert. in gerontology, Brookdale Sch. Social Sci., 1979; m. S. Frank Redo, June 27, 1948; children—Philip L., Martha Maria. Tchr. pvt. sch., N.Y.C., 1946-56; dir. Child Service League, Queens, N.Y., 1949-57; founder, dir. Community Concern for Sr. Citizens, Inc., N.Y.C. Dept. for the Aging, 1971-85; dir. N.Y.C. Silver Pages Directory, Silver Savers' Passport. Bd. dirs. Escort Service of Yorkville (N.Y.), 1977—, Sr. Citizen Outreach Program for Elderly, N.Y.C., 1970—; mem. Community Planning Bd., N.Y.C., 1970-77; del. Nat. Republican Conv., N.Y.C., 1976, N.Y. State White House Conf. on Aging, 1981, Nat. White House Conf. on Aging, N.Y.C., 1981; del. N.Y. State Conf. on Mid-Life and Older Women, 1983. Recipient Mayor's Cert. of Appreciation N.Y.C., 1975; Hon. Sec. of State of Mont., 1975; Franny award WPIX-TV, 1974. Mem. LWV, Roman Catholic. Club: Met. Rep. (pres. 1975-77). Contbr. tng. manuals, brochures for dept. on aging., 1973-85. Home: 435 E 70th St New York NY 10021 Office: 91 Fifth Ave 5th Floor New York NY 10003

REDRUELLO, ROSA INCHAUSTEGUI, utilities company executive; b. Havana, Cuba, Dec. 6, 1951; came to U.S., 1961, naturalized, 1971; d. Julio Lorenzo and Laudelina (Vazquez) Inchaustegui; m. John Robert Redruello, Dec. 14, 1972; 1 child, Michelle. A.A., Miami-Dade Community Coll., 1972; B.S., Fla. Internat. U., 1974. Cert. systems profl. With Fla. Power & Light Co., Miami, 1975—, records analyst, 1981-84, sr. records analyst, 1984—; cons. United Bus. Records, Miami, 1985—. Editor South Fla. Record newsletter, 1983-86; editor, producer Files Mgmt. video tape, 1984-85. Rotary Club scholar, 1970. Mem. Assn. Records Mgrs. and Adminstrs. (chpt. chmn. bd. 1985—, chpt. mem. of yr. 1985), Assn. for Info. and Image Mgmt., Exec. Female, Nuclear Info. and Records Mgmt. Assn. (Appreciation award 1985). Republican. Roman Catholic. Avocations: swimming; jazzercise; reading. Office: Fla Power & Light Co 9250 W Flager St Miami FL 33174

REEB, DEBBIE MARIE, art educator, artist; b. Stanley, Wis., July 29, 1955; d. Anton Sylvester and Beverly June (McManus) Penk; m. D. Joe Reeb, Aug. 23, 1980. Comml. Art Assoc. Degree, Western Wis. Tech. Inst., 1975; B.S., U. Wis.-Stout, 1978. Cert. tchr., Wyo. Dietitian Eau Claire Health Care Ctr., Wis., 1977; sec. Kelley Girl Temporary Service, Denver, 1978; tchr. elem. art Natrona County Sch. Dist. 1, Casper, Wyo., 1978-80; tchr. art Natrona County High Sch., Casper, 1980—, chmn. art dept., 1980—; mem. Art Curriculum Com., Casper, 1983—, Humanities Com., Casper, 1984—, Faculty Adv. Com., Casper, 1983—. One woman shows include Am. Nat. Bank, 1984; exhibited in group shows at S.D. Juried Art Show, 1985, Nebr. Juried Art Show, 1985, Mont. Juried Art Show, 1984, Casper West Wind Art show 1984. Active Casper Symphony Orch. Assn., 1984-85, Home Builders Assn., Casper, 1978—. Recipient 1st place holiday decoration award Casper City Council 1984. Mem Wyo. Arts Edn. Assn., Casper Artists Guild. Roman Catholic. Avocations: camping; photography; stain glass; travel. Home: 1564 Begonia Casper WY 82604

REECE, CHERI DODSON, nurse, educator; b. Altoona, Pa., Apr. 17, 1946; d. Paul Francis and Evelyn Pearl (Brown) Dodson; diploma in nursing Western Pa. Hosp. Sch. Nursing, Pitts., 1967; B.S. in Nursing, Cedar Crest Coll., Allentown, Pa., 1969; postgrad. in nursing Kent State U., 1979-83; postgrad. Case Western Res. U., 1984—; m. David Alan Reece, June 21, 1969; 1 dau., Michelle Lynn. Nurse coll. infirmary, 1967-69; staff nurse Western Pa. Hosp., 1968; pvt. duty nurse, 1969, 78, 84; staff nurse Nason Hosp., Roaring Spring, Pa., 1969; instr. inservice edn. N.D. State Hosp., Jamestown, 1969-71; staff nurse Santa Clara Valley Med. Center, San Jose, Calif., 1971-72; instr. nursing San Jose Hosps. and Health Center, 1972-74; instr. nursing Kent State U., 1974-75, 78-84, Ohio Valley Hosp., Steubenville, Ohio, 1975-77; staff nurse Ashtabula (Ohio) Medicare Center, 1977-78; instr. adult edn. Ashtabula Joint Vocat. Sch., 1978-79; phys. exam. nurse Phys. Measurements, Inc., Ashtabula, 1978; grad. asst. Case Western Res. U., 1985; continuing edn. instr.; cons. well-baby care. Active in campaign U.S. Rep., Am. Cancer Soc., Am. Heart Fund; patron Straw Hat Theatre; councilmatic aide Ashtabula City Council, 1981-83; head Center Shop at Ashtabula Arts Center, also patron. Mem. Nat. League Nursing, AAUW (sec. chpt. 1980-82, treas. 1983-85), Alumni Assn. Claysburg-Kimmel High Sch., Women's Service League.

REECE, REBECCA ROSE, educator; b. Knoxville, Tenn., July 25, 1947; d. Thomas Josuah and Imogene (Evans) Rose; m. Alvin Davis Reece, Jr., Apr. 29, 1967; children—Alvin Davis, III, Amy Rose. B.S., Lincoln Meml. U., 1970; M.S., East Tenn. State U., 1983. Social worker Head Start, 1967-68, head tchr., 1968-70; tchr. TNT Primary Sch., New Tazewell, Tenn., 1971—; assoc. funeral dir. Reece Funeral Home and Valley Chapel, Harrogate, Tenn. Democrat. Baptist. Lodges: DAR, Eastern Star. Home: Tazewell TN 37829 Office: Harrogate Sch New Tazewell TN 37825

REED, BARBARA ANN, reporter, editor; b. South Pittsburg, Tenn., Mar. 8, 1937; d. Jacob Harding and Estelle Leslie (Young) Burroughs; m.; children—Roberta Ann, Frank Edward. Student, Northwestern U., 1954, U. Ala., 1955-56. Freelance writer, 1964-66; bur. chief Norwich Bull. (Conn.), 1966-68; food editor, staff writer The Day, New London, Conn., 1968—; pub. relations cons. New London County Daycare, 1982-83. Author: A Time to Remember, 1976. Recipient Herbert Bayard Swope Meml. award 3d pl., 1978; Nat. Merit award Sudden Infant Death Syndrome Found., 1970. Mem. Noank Hist. Soc. (pres. 1972-73, 79-80, past program chmn., past sec., founder), Southwestern Conn. Women's Network, Mystic Seaport Marine Mus., Sigma Delta Chi. Independent. Methodist. Office: 47 Eugene O'Neill Dr New London CT 06320

REED, BETTY JO, microbiologist; b. Houston; d. James Henry and Annie M. (Waite) Reed; B.S., Tulane U., 1966, M.S., 1968, postgrad., 1968-71. Instr. infectious diseases Tulane U. Sch. Medicine, New Orleans, 1968-74; chmn. immunology dept. Universidad Del Valle, Cali, Colombia, 1968-74; microbiologist W. Jefferson Hosp., New Orleans, 1974-80, Montelepre Meml. Hosp., New Orleans, 1980—; cons. WHO; infection control instr.; lectr. alcohol and drug abuse program LWV, 1978—. USPHS fellow, 1966-71; HEW cert. in environ. control. Mem. Am. Soc. Med. Technologists, Am. Soc. Microbiologists, Am. Soc. Clin. Pathologists. Republican. Methodist. Author: Manual of Infection Control, 1975. Home: 206 E Mapleridge Metairie LA 70001 Office: 3125 Canal St New Orleans LA 70119

REED, CAROL MAY, public relations executive; b. Allentown, Pa., Apr. 20, 1948; d. Oliver Lamar and Maria (Schmoyer) Trumbauer; m. Gerald Wayne Reed, Aug. 25, 1968; children—Laura Ann, Angela Sue. Student Calif. Luth Coll., 1964-67. Vice chmn. Dallas County Republican Party, Tex. Fedn. Rep. Women, U.S. Congressman Jim Collins, Tex., U.S. Congressman Alan Steelman, Tex., U.S. Senator Harrison Schmitt, N.Mex., 1975-77; regional coordinator Texans for Tower, 1977-79; owner Carol Reed Assocs., Dallas, 1980—; exec. dir. Americans for Change, 1980, Republican Senatorial Com., 1981; mgr. campaign Kay Bailey Hutchison for Congress, 1981-82; head Dallas City Council campaigns, 1982-83; head fundraising Dallas Republican Host Com. for Republican Nat. Conv., 1983—; polit. dir. Phil Graham for Senate. Mem. Cerebral Palsy Bd., Dallas, 1981—; mem. Parkland Burn Ctr. Aux., Dallas, 1982—; mem. Dallas Cable TV Bd., 1983. Republican. Mem. Ch. of Christ. Home: 6538 Red Pine St Dallas TX 75248 Office: Carol Reed Assocs 3030 McKinney St #1001 Dallas TX 75204

REED, CAROLYN CAPRON, publisher; b. Newton, Mass., Feb. 20, 1941; s. Charles Hassler and Henrietta (Clogston) Capron; m. Kenneth Maurice Reed, Jan. 30, 1960; children—Kenneth Scott, Kimberly Lyn, Melissa Brace. A.S., Endicott Coll., 1960; student Cazenovia Coll., 1979. Adminstrv. asst. Reed Indsl. Sales, Cazenovia, N.Y., 1978-83; pres. Capron Pub. Co., Wellesley, Mass., 1981—. Clinic asst. Planned Parenthood, Syracuse, N.Y., 1968-70, bd. dirs., 1974-77, chmn. spl. giving, 1980-81. Mem. Wellesley C. of C. Republican. Avocations: reading; tennis; swimming; gardening. Home: 6 Huntington Dr Cazenovia NY 13035 Office: Capron Pub Corp 3 Seaward Rd Wellesley Hills MA 02181

REED, CATHY JANE, truck line executive, consultant; b. Bedford, Ind., Jan. 16, 1957; d. Carl M. and Vivian M. (Asciutto) Bridges; m. Frederick D. Reed, Aug. 14, 1976. Student pub. schs., Dayton. Rate clk. Helms Express, Dayton, 1974-75; transp. dispatcher Dayton Press, Inc., 1975-78; ops. mgr. U.S. Navigation, Cin., 1978-80; pres. Mad River Transp. Inc., Dayton, 1980—; v.p. Custom Freight Sales, Inc., Dayton, 1980—, Peerless Transp., Dayton, 1985—; cons. transp. Democrat. Roman Catholic. Avocations: travel; gardening; woodworking. Office: Mad River Transp Inc 1440 Miami Chapel Rd Dayton OH 45401

REED, CYNTHIA JEAN, educational administrator, consultant; b. Rochester, N.Y., Nov. 24, 1956; d. Russell Roger and Jean Carolyn (Strobridge) R. B.S. in Elem. Edn., SUNY-Oswego, 1978, M.S. in Edn., 1985; postgrad. SUNY-Cortland. Cert. elem. tchr., N.Y. Tchr., Fulton City Schs., N.Y., 1978-79; substitute tchr. Oswego and Fulton Schs., Oswego County, N.Y., 1979-80; tchr. for gifted Mexico Central Schs., N.Y., 1980-81; coordinator gifted edn. Jefferson-Lewis Bd. Coop. Ednl. Services, Glenfield, N.Y., 1981-82; tchr., coordinator gifted edn. Oswego County Bd. Coop. Ednl. Services, Mexico, N.Y., 1982-84; coordinator gifted edn. Cortland-Madison Bd. Coop. Ednl. Services, N.Y., 1984—. Mem. exec. com. Oswego County Environ. Mgmt. Council, 1980-81; mem. Cortland County Environ. Mgmt. Council, 1985-86. Mem. Assn. Supervision and Curriculum Devel., Advocacy for Gifted and Talented Edn., Central N.Y. Coordinators of Gifted Assn., Phi Delta Kappa. Avocations: reading; hiking; camping; cooking. Office: Cortland-Madison Bd Coop Ednl Services 1710 State Route 1 Cortland NY 13045

REED, DONNA LOUISE, public relations executive; b. Wichita, Kans., May 10, 1935; d. Joseph Melvin and Dorothy Yetta (Leben) Kogan; m. William Eugene Reed, Feb. 17, 1968; 1 dau., Allison Lynn. Student, So. Meth. U., 1952-53, Dallas Coll. of So. Meth. U., 1955-56. Profl. registered parliamentarian. Vice pres. pub. relations Preferred Printers, Inc., Dallas, 1960-68; dir. pub. relations Dallas Area Respiratory Health Assn., 1969-71; free lance pub. relations, 1972-78; v.p. pub. relations and mktg. Preferred Printers, Inc., 1979—; mem. nat. pub. relations adv. by-laws com. Nat. Tb and Respiratory Disease Assn., N.Y.C., 1970-71, mem. Dallas Communications Council, 1983-84. Contbr. articles to profl. jours. Mem. Dallas Republican Forum, 1983-84; mem. Lake Highlands Republican Women's Club, 1980—. Recipient Nat. Pub. Relations award Nat. Tb and Respiratory Disease Assn., 1970; Matrix award Women in Communications, 1976; Gridiron awards Dallas Press Club, 1969, 71, 72, 74, 77, 80. Mem. Women in Communications (chpt. pres. 1973-74), Am. Inst. Parliamentarians, Nat. Assn. Parliamentarians, North Tex. Registered Parliamentarians, Tex. Assn. Parliamentarians (editor Tex. Parliamentarian 1981, 2d v.p. 1983, 1st v.p. 1984), Dallas Communications Council, Dallas Fedn. Women's Clubs. Clubs: Dallas Women's Ballet, Dallas Opera Guild, Dallas Mus. Fine Art, Dallas Symphony Orch. League, Dallas Summer Musicals Guild, The 500. Republican. Episcopalian. Lodges: Order Eastern Star (worthy matron 1971-72, 82-83, state officer 1972—), Daus. of the Nile (queen 1979-80), Ladies Oriental Shrine of N. Am. (high priestess 1972-73), S.O.O.B., Order of the Rainbow for Girls (mother advisor 1972-73, 75-76, adult state officer 1981—), Past Matrons and Patrons Assn. Dallas (pres. 1980-81). Home: 9318 Faircrest St Dallas TX 75238 Office: Preferred Printers Inc 1207 Gano St Dallas TX 75215

REED, DORRIS HULL, television consultant; b. Phila., Sept. 7, 1924; d. Claude Lewis and Genevieve Marie (Turner) Hull; student Mich. State U., 1942-43, U. Mich., 1943-44; m. Willard James Musson, July 2, 1948 (dec. 1967); children—Willard James Musson, Julie Anne Musson Booth, Scott Hull Musson; m. John LeRoy Reed, Jr., May 12, 1972. Radio broadcaster Minute Parade, Detroit, 1947-50; TV traffic mgr. Sta. WWJ-TV, Detroit, 1950-54; v.p. adminstrn., corporate sec.-treas. McHugh & Hoffman, Inc., Fairfax, Va., 1969—. Mem. regional council Nat. Capital area United Way of Fairfax-Falls Church, 1983—; mem. Fairfax City Council, 1986—. Mem. Central Fairfax C. of C. (pres. 1982, co. rep. 1978—), Am. Women in Radio and TV (Washington chpt.), Fairfax Profl. Women's Network. Republican. Episcopalian. Office: 4009 Chain Bridge Rd Fairfax VA 22030

REED, EDITH THERESA, actuary, employee benefits consultant; b. N.Y.C., Aug. 16, 1927; d. John James and Carolyn (Siebert) R. B.A., St. Joseph's Coll., 1949; postgrad. U. Mich., 1949-50. Actuarial asst. George B. Buck Cons. Actuaries, Inc., N.Y.C., 1950-57, asst. actuary 1957-74, assoc. cons. actuary, 1974-79, cons. actuary, 1979—. Fellow Conf. Actuaries in Pub. Practice; mem. Am. Acad. Actuaries, Actuaries Club N.Y. (N.Y.C.), Internat. Actuarial Assn., Internat. Platform Assn., Kappa Gamma Pi. Roman Catholic. Club: Zonta of N.Y. (sec. 1985-86). Home: 300 E 40th St New York NY 10016 Office: George B Buck Cons Actuaries Inc 2 Pennsylvania Plaza New York NY 10121

REED, ELVIRA ARMAN, automobile agency executive; b. Italy, Jan. 11, 1921; came to U.S., 1927, naturalized, 1927; d. Louis Victor and Palmira (Machiovecchio) Cacio; grad. high sch.; m. Dallas R. Arman, Sept. 17, 1940 (dec.); children—Donna, Barbara; m. 2d, Clarence C. Reed, Dec. 21, 1973. With Lamerdin Pontiac (name changed to Arman Pontiac Inc. 1969), Compton, Calif., 1949-82, gen. mgr., 1950-67, owner, 1967-82; owner Compton Toyota (Calif.), 1970-82; gen. mgr. W. I. Simonson Inc., Mercedes Benz, 1982—; dir. Community Savs. & Loan, Long Beach. Mem. Pontiac Nat. Dealer Council, 1972-73, 76-77; chairwoman Los Angeles Internat. Automobile Show, 1972; mem. Calif. New Motor Vehicle Bd., 1976—, pres., 1978. Pres., YMCA, 1970-72; mem. UCLA Chancellor's Assocs., 1975—. Recipient Import Auto Dealer of Distinction award Sports Illustrated, 1979, AI ADA, 1980; Quality Dealer award Time mag., 1981. Mem. Compton C. of C. (pres. 1978—), So. Calif. Pontiac Dealers Assn. (pres. 1970, treas. 1975-80), Motor Car Dealers Assn. So. Calif. (treas., dir. 1973—), Long Beach Motor Car Dealers Assn., Compton Motor Car Dealers Assn. Club: Friday Morning (treas. 1984-85) (Los Angeles). Home: 1300 Oxford Rd San Marino CA 91108 Office: 1626 Wilshire Blvd Santa Monica CA 90403

REED, JANNENE GRIFFITH, newspaper editor, publisher; b. Wayne, Nebr., Feb. 8, 1929; d. Frank Marion and Pearl (Stone) Griffith; m. Donald R. Reed, Apr. 5, 1953; children—Cameron Leigh, Barbara Jayne. B.A., Wayne State Coll., 1951; student Kearney State Coll., 1956. Woman's feature editor Wayne (Nebr.) Herald, 1947-53; comml. artist Gen. Telephone, Chgo., 1953-55; instr. art Vermillion (S.D.) Schs., 1955-59; copywriter C.S. Wo Co., Honolulu, 1971-73; program dir. Gospel Light Publs., Glendale, Calif., 1975-78; stringer Pasadena (Calif.) Star-News, 1975-78; editor San Marino (Calif.) Tribune, 1978-80; editor, pub. Sierra Madre (Calif.) News, 1980—. Bd. dirs. Meth. Hosp. So. Calif., Arcadia, 1983—. Named Editor of Yr., SAR, 1982-83; SAR Community Spirit award; One Earth award Sierra Madre Environ. Action Council. Mem. Soc. Profl. Journalists, Sigma Delta Chi. Republican. Presbyterian. Office: Sierra Madre News 9 Kersting Ct Sierra Madre CA 91024

REED, JEAN SALAS, school principal; b. Torreon, N.Mex., Aug. 30, 1940; d. Ross Ray and Cora (Lopez) S.; m. Clifton Arlow Reed, July 19, 1974. B.A., Sienna Heights Coll., 1969; M.A., U. N. Mex., 1972, Ednl. Adminstrn. Edn. Specialist, 1974. Tchr., Co. of Mary, Los Angeles, 1960-70; counselor Jobs for Progress, Albuquerque, 1970-72; tchr. Los Lunas Pub. Schs., N. Mex., 1972; edn. specialist N. Mex. Dept. Edn., Santa Fe, 1972-74; prin. Santa Fe Pub. Schs., 1974—. Named Prin. of Year in Honor of Excellence, Burger King 1985. Delta Kappa Gamma scholar 1973. Mem. N. Mex. Adminstrs. Bd., Nat. Assn. Secondary Sch. Prins. (Excellence award 1985), N. Mex. Assn. Secondary Sch. Prin. (pres. 1981-82, Prin. of Year 1985), Phi Delta Kappa, Delta Kappa Gamma. Democrat. Roman Catholic. Avocations: swimming; piano playing; collecting bottles. Home: 1915 Camino Lumbre Santa Fe NM 87501

REED, JOANNE, telephone company executive; b. Olton, Tex., June 22, 1931; d. Willis Eugene and Sally S. (Thetford) Wright; student Tex. Tech. U., 1975; U. Kans., 1978, various mgmt. schs.; children—Dennis, Joni. Service rep., operator Gen. Telephone Co. of S.W., Ralls, Tex., 1950-63, chief operator, 1963-67; operator services mgr. Denton Gen. Telephone (Tex.), 1967-73, area bus. office supr., 1973-74, div. mgr., Sulphur Springs, Tex., 1974-76, div. mgr., Denton, 1976-78; div. mgr. Gen. Telephone Co. S.W., Garland, Tex., 1978-82, gen. mgr. North Central div., 1982—; dir. Republic Bank, Garland, Tex. Precinct chmn. Republican Party, 1980-81; mem. adv. com. Salvation Army, 1980—, chmn., 1983-84; bd. dirs. Met. YMCA, 1980-82, 83-85, Garland Symphony, 1980; chmn. United Way, 1976-80, Am. Cancer Soc., 1978; mem. Garland Indsl. Devel. Bd., 1982; 1st v.p. New Beginnings Ctr., 1983; mem. Dallas County Parks and Open Space Com., 1985-86. Mem. Tex. Assn. Bus. (sec.-treas. 1983-84), C. of C. (v.p. 1986—). Republican. Clubs: Soroptimists, Bus. and Profl. Women's, Eastern Hills Country. Home: 913 Fair Oaks St Garland TX 75040 Office: PO Box 461308 Garland TX 75046

REED, JUDY JONES, educational administrator; b. Biltmore, N.C., Oct. 27, 1947; d. Roy Lee and Ruth Madeline (Corpening) J.; m. Ronald Roy Reed, Feb. 3, 1978. B.S. in Bus. Adminstrn., We. Carolina U., 1971, M.A. in Edn.-Bus., 1975, Edn. Specialist-Adminstrn., 1977. From instr. to dean students to dean acad. affairs, Cecils Jr. Coll., Asheville, N.C., 1971-84; exec. dir. Blanton's Jr. Coll., Asheville, 1984-85, Miller-Motte Bus. Coll., Gastonia, N.C., 1985—; coll. insp. for Assn. Independent Colls. and Schs., Washington, 1975—. Mem. N.C. Assn. Independent Colls. and Schs. (past treas., pres. elect, pres., bd. dirs. 1981-85), Southeastern Bus. Coll., (dean of yr. 1977), Nat. Bus. Edn. Assn., N.C. Bus. Edn. Assn., Asheville C. of C. (small bus. council 1984—). Democrat. Baptist. Avocations: needlepoint, sewing. Home: 9-D Binwhe Estates Gastonia NC 28052 Office: Miller-Motte Business Coll 160 W Franklin Ave Gastonia NC 28052

REED, KATHLYN LOUISE, occupational therapist; b. Detroit, June 2, 1940; d. Herbert Curtis and Jessie Ruth (Krehbiel) R.; student U. Wis., 1958-61; B.S., U. Kans., 1964; M.A., Western Mich. U., 1966; Ph.D., U. Wash., 1973. Temporary supr., occupational therapist Vis. Nurse Assn., Beloit, Wis., 1964; staff occupational therapist Kans. U. Med. Center, Kansas City, 1964-65; instr. U. Wash., Seattle, 1967-70; research assoc. Child Devel. Center, Seattle, 1972-73; chmn., prof. dept. occupational therapy U. Okla., Oklahoma City, 1973-85; cons. HEW Pub. Health grant to Ohio State U., 1970-71, NIH grant to Am. Occupational Therapy Assn., 1972-73; cons. Okla. Dept. Health, 1976-77, Oklahoma City Pub. Schs., 1979-81; acting instr. U. Puget Sound, Tacoma, 1971. Telephone worker, counselor Open Door Clinic, 1968-72; mem., co-chmn. citizen's bd. Seattle Mental Health Center, 1970-72, mem. exec. bd., 1971-72. Recipient Elmer H. Wilds award Western Mich. U., 1966, Traineeship Dept. HEW-Rehab. Services Adminstrn., 1970-72. Fellow Am. Occupational Therapy Assn. (nominating com. chmn. 1972, bylaws chmn. 1979-81, chmn. standards and ethics commn. 1983—, award of merit 1983 Eleanor Clarke Slagle lectr. 1985); mem. Am. Assn. Mental Deficiency, Council Exceptional Children (chpt. treas. 1970-72, chpt. v.p. 1976-77), Am. Pub. Health Assn., Okla. Assn. for Severely Handicapped, Okla. (practice chmn. 1973-74, pres. 1974-76, del. 1976-79), Wash. (del. 1968-73) occupational therapy assns., Am. Assn. Higher Edn., Am. Soc. Allied Health Professions, World Fedn. Occupational Therapists, Sigma Kappa, Pi Lambda Theta, Alpha Eta. Co-author: Concepts of Occupational Therapy, 1980, rev. edit., 1983; author: Models of Practice in Occupational Therapy, 1984. Home: 8800 Rolling Green Oklahoma City OK 73132

REED, LUEDA CAROLE, psychologist, real estate broker; b. Dallas, Oct. 14, 1942; d. Truman Jesse and Rebecca Ida (Culver) Johnson; children—William Scott, Megan Carole. Assoc. Arts & Sci., Richland Coll., 1984; B.A. magna cum laude, U. Tex.-Dallas, 1985; doctoral candidate clin. psychology Calif. Sch. Profl. Psychology. Travel agt. Profl. Travel Co., Dallas, 1970-72; real estate broker, v.p. Phyllis Everett Realtors, Dallas, 1972-79; real estate broker Better Homes Realtors, Dallas, 1979-80; owner Lueda Reed, Realtor, Dallas, 1980—; teaching asst. Richland Coll., Dallas, 1983—, psychol. asst., 1984—, lectr., 1985; real estate instr. Homes for Living Metroplex Council, Dallas, 1977-78, head real estate sch., 1978-79. Contbr. to poetry collections. Recipient Top Producer award Phyllis Everett, Realtors, Dallas, 1977-79, Sales Assoc. of Year, 1978, 79, Salesman of Yr., 1978, Salesman with a Purpose, 1978. Mem. Dallas Bd. Realtors (edn. com. 1978-79), Nat. Honor Soc., Nat. Dean's List, Psi Chi, Phi Theta Kappa. Club: Dallas Ski. Office: Social Sci Div Richland Coll 12800 Abrams Dallas TX 75243

REED, MARGARET CAROL, nurse; b. Frankfort, Ky., Nov. 29, 1935; d. Regis Francis and Margaret Frances (Moore) Whitehead; m. Clyde E. Reed, May 9, 1964 (div.); children—Suzanne, Rebecca Lynn. Diploma, Nazareth Sch. Nursing, 1958. Registered nurse, Ky.; lic. ins. rep., Ky. Head nurse critical care unit, intensive care unit King's Daus. Hosp., Frankfort, Ky., 1970-77; sr. regional adminstr. Ky. Peer Rev. Orgn., Louisville, 1977-81, assoc. care service dir., 1982—; dir. Assoc. Care Service, 1983-85; health care cons., 1985—. Pres. Franklin County (Ky.) Republican Women, 1966, 78; 4th v.p. Ky. Fedn. Rep. Women, 1979; activities dir. Good Shepherd Parish Council, 1976, 77, 78. Mem. Ky. Nurses Assn. (bd. dirs. polit. action com., 1979). Roman Catholic.

REED, MARLENE MINTS, educator; b. San Antonio, Sept. 25, 1937; d. Woodie John and Heloise (Pittman) Mints; B.B.A., Baylor U., 1959; M.B.A., N.E. La. U., 1977; D.B.A., La. Tech. U., 1981; m. Bill J. Reed, Aug. 29, 1958; children—Lisa Rochelle, William Barclay. Various positions in industry, Houston, Ft. Worth, Monroe, La., and Birmingham, Ala., 1959-73; asst. prof. mgmt. N.E. La. U., 1979-81; assoc. prof. mgmt. and econs. Sch. Bus., Samford U., Birmingham, 1981—; cons. small bus. Named Most Disting. Prof. Bus., Alpha Kappa Psi, 1982, J. Buchanan disting. tchr. Samford U., 1984. Mem. Acad. Mgmt., S.W. Small Bus. Inst. Assn., Nat. Bus. Edn. Assn., Beta Gamma Sigma, Omicron Delta Epsilon, Delta Pi Epsilon, Pi Omega Pi, Kappa Kappa Gamma, Omicron Delta Kappa. Republican. Baptist (Sunday Sch. tchr.). Home: 1582 Panorama Dr Birmingham AL 35216 Office: Samford U Sch Bus 800 Lakeshore Dr Birmingham AL 35229

REED, MARSHA LEE, personnel agency executive, consultant; b. Pitts., Sept. 8, 1953; d. Milton and Ruth (Farber) Denmark; m. David P. Reed, Sept. 4, 1977; children—Diane, Robert. B.Gen. Studies, Ohio U., 1975. Cons. Devonshire Personnel, Garden Grove, Calif., 1977-79, Mgmt. Recruiters, Miami, Fla., 1979-80; unit mgr. Dunhill Personnel, Miami, 1980-82; owner, pres. Markett Personnel, Miami, 1982—. Mem. Nat. Assn. Personnel Cons., Nat. Assn. Female Execs., Nat. Assn. Female Bus. Owners, Fla. Assn. Personnel Cons., Bus. and Profl. Women, Greater Miami Jewish Fedn., Kappa Delta (social chmn. 1973-75). Democrat. Club: Hadassah (Miami). Avocations: reading; piano playing. Home: 11124 SW 132d Ct Miami FL 33186 Office: Markett Personnel PO Box 162-211 Miami FL 33116

REED, MARTHA ANN, educator; b. Tremont, Miss., May 9, 1942; d. Harold Abney and Vervie Clytee (Parker) Pitts; m. John Howell Reed, June 8, 1963; children—Kimberly, Melanie, Jennifer. Student Bob Jones U., 1960-61, Free Will Baptist Bible Coll., 1961-63. Cert. tchr. Southeast Accrediting Assn. Christian Schs. Bookkeeper, West Duplin Christian Acad., Warsaw, N.C., 1971-75, tchr., 1980-83; tchr. Palmetto Christian Acad., Florence, S.C., 1978-80; tchr. Emmanuel Christian Sch., Dunn, N.C., 1984—, dir., 1984—. Music coordinator Prospect Free Will Bapt. Ch., Dunn, 1983—, church organist, 1983—, dir. adult choir, 1983—, tchr. Sunday sch., 1984—. Home: Route 3 Box 676 Dunn NC 28334 Office: Emmanuel Christian Sch PO Box 340 Dunn NC 28334

REED, MARTHA ANN, public affairs specialist; b. Houston, Sept. 8, 1930; d. Emmett Conway and Evelyn Ysleta (Spurlock) Swain; student Tex. Christian U., 1948-50; A.A., U. Houston, 1956; m. Charles G. Reed, Apr. 20, 1974; children by previous marriage—Rebecca Hemphill Sanders, Ann Hemphill Byrns, Steven Earl. Tchr., Oakdale, La., 1956-60, Goose Creek, Tex., 1962-64; assoc. editor Oakdale Jour., 1959-62; women's editor Baytown (Tex.) Sun, 1963-70; lifestyle editor Beaumont (Tex.) Enterprise & Jour., 1970-77; dir. pub. info. Lamar u., 1977-79; spl. asst. to supt. Port Arthur (Tex.) Ind. Sch. Dist., 1979-82; pub. affairs dir. John E. Gray Inst., Beaumont, Tex., 1982-85; pub. relations coordinator McFaddin-Ward Hist. House Mus., 1985—. Mem. spl. grand jury, Jefferson County, Tex. Named, Sagamore of the Wabash, 1979, Ky. Col., 1981, Adm. Nebr. Navy, 1981; named to Southeast Tex. Women's Hall of Fame, 1984. Mem. Nat. Fedn. Press Women (past pres.), Tex. Press Women (past pres.), Southeast Tex. Press Club, Internat. Assn. Bus. Communicators, Beaumont Art Mus., Beaumont Symphony Assn., Beaumont Heritage Soc., Lamar U. Friends of Arts, Beta Sigma Phi (hon. internat. mem.). Contbr. articles in field. Office: 1906 McFaddin Ave Beaumont TX 77701

REED, MARY LOU, state legislator. Mem. Idaho State Senate, dist. 2, 1985—. Democrat. Office: State Capitol Boise ID 83720*

REED, NANCY RICHEY, educator, consultant; b. San Augustine, Tex., Dec. 29, 1940; d. Joseph Walter and Anna Blanche (Polk) Richey; m. James Earl Reed, May 20, 1972 (div. Dec. 1980). B.B.A., Sam Houston State U., 1962, M.B.A., 1969. Tchr., Galena Park (Tex.) Schs., 1962-69; adminstr., instr. McMahon Coll., Houston, 1969-75; instr. English for ct. reporters Alvin (Tex.) Community Coll., 1975—; cons. reporting firms, Houston, 1975—; sponsor Word Droppers Club, Alvin, Tex., 1983-84. Named Outstanding Woman of Tex., 1983. Mem. Tex. Jr. Coll. Tchrs. Assn., Nat. Shorthand Reporters Assn., Tex. State Tchrs. Assn., Alvin Community Coll. Tchrs. Assn., Alpha Delta Pi. Methodist.

REED, ROSEMARY, distribution company executive; b. Worcester, Mass., Dec. 11, 1952; d. George Albion and Rosa Mae (Duncan) R. B.S. in Speech, Emerson Coll., 1974; M.Ed., Worcester State Coll., 1976; postgrad. U. Mass., 1980; M.B.A., Anna Maria Coll., 1986. Cert. tchr., Mass. Communication instr. Suffolk U., Boston, 1976-78, 81-83, Fitchburg State Coll., Mass., 1978-80; edn. adminstr. Option Program, Haverhill, Mass., 1981-83; edn. dir. Stetson Sch., Barre, Mass., 1983-85; corp. recruiter Positions Inc., Westborough, Mass., 1985; tchr. Butler Ctr., Westborough, 1985—; tng. mgr. Future Products, Worcester, 1986—. Author, editor accreditation programs. Second v.p. Quabin Community Arts Council, Barre; mem. Barre Players. Mem. Am. Soc. Tng. and Devel. Avocations: acting; reading; vegetarian cooking; program development research. Home: Station Rd Barre MA 01005 Office: Future Products 110 Lovell St Worcester MA 01603

REED, SALLY, foundation executive; b. Lynwood, Calif., May 20, 1955; d. William H. and Sally Frances (Hayes) Gibson. A.A., Cooke County Coll., 1975; B.S.Ed., Southwestern U., 1978. Tchr. civics Killeen High Sch., Tex., 1978-81; dir. devel. Nat. Conservative Polit. Action Com., Alexandria, Va., 1981-83; founder, chmn. Nat. Council for Better Edn., Alexandria, Va., 1983—. Pres., Conservative Youth Found., Alexandria, 1984—, Profl. Educators Guild, 1984—. Author: NEA: Propaganda Front of the Radical Left, 1983; A Parent's Survival Guide to the Public Schools, 1985. Republican. Roman Catholic. Office: Nat Council Better Edn 1800 Diagonal Rd Alexandria VA 22314

REED, SELINA MAE, telephone company executive; b. Youngstown, Ohio, Dec. 16, 1946; d. Dorris Hightower; m. Charles Pickard, Oct. 16, 1965 (div. 1970); m. John Andrew Reed, Feb. 28, 1975; children—Latya Nicole, Jada Kawren. Operator, Ohio Bell Co., Youngstown, 1964-67, supr., 1967-69, service observer, 1969-71, asst. mgr., 1971-72, group chief operator, 1972-79, mktg. dir., 1972-82, asst. mgr., 1982—; dir., credit chmn. Saints Savs. & Trust. Fin. chmn. Republican Women, Youngstown, 1985—. Mem. Assn. Female Execs., Am. Film Inst., Nat. Trust for Hist. Preservation, Am. Entrepreneurs Assn. Mem. Apostolic Pentecostal Ch. Avocations: collecting brass figures, bells, crystal figurines, elephants, stamps, Goebel statues. Home and Office: 1149 Timbercrest Dr Youngstown OH 44505

REED, SUE ASSUNTA NUGENT, school principal; b. Bklyn., Aug. 15, 1933; d. Joseph and Anna (Merola) Montella; m. Scott Gordon Reed, Jan. 9, 1974; children—Jessica Lindsay, Scott Gordon. B.A., Hunter Coll., 1955; M.S.Ed., 1956; Ph.D., N.Y.U., 1973. Tchr., public schs., N.Y.C., 1956-65, asst. prin., 1965-73; prin. Congers Elem. Sch. (N.Y.), from 1973, Little Tor Sch., 1985—; adj. asst. prof. Hunter Coll., 1973, Coll. New Rochelle, 1980—. Mem. Clarkstown Bicentennial Commn., New City, N.Y., 1975-76; counselor Vol. Counseling Service, New City, 1975-76. NDEA grantee, U. PR., 1965; Danforth fellow, 1975; Nat. Humanities Faculty grantee, 1975; Ford Found./Am. Assn. Sch. Adminstrs. grantee, 1977; Inst. for Devel. Ednl. Activities fellow, 1982; Primary Mental Health Project scholar, 1981. Mem. Am. Assn. Sch. Administrs., Assn. Suprs. Curriculum Devel., Internat. Reading Assn., Nat. Council Accreditation Tchr. Edn., Bus. and Profl. Women's Assn. (chmn. young careerist com.) Phi Delta Kappa, Kappa Delta Pi. Club: Soroptimist (pres. 1982-84). Home: 9 Van Houten Fields West Nyack NY 10994 Office: 57 Lake Rd Congers NY 10920

REED-BEAUREGARD, PATRICIA ANN, systems analyst, consultant; b. Nashville, Aug. 23, 1941; d. Charles Francis and Martha Cordelia (Jones) Clark; m. James Kingston Reed, Oct. 1, 1960 (div. 1980); 1 child, Jeffrey Kingston; m. Thomas Donald Beauregard, Aug. 23, 1980 (dec. 1983). Student UCLA, 1960-62, Coll. DuPage, 1980-81. Prin., Pat's Hats, Glen Ellyn, Ill., 1978-80; data processing mgr. Universal Coach, Northlake, Ill., 1980-81; mgmt. info. systems adminstr. The Equity Group, Chgo., 1981-84; pres. P.C. Bus. Cons., Glen Ellyn, 1984—; instr. Coll. of DuPage, 1985-86. Contbr. articles to profl. jours. Patentee in designer hats. Founder Suddenly Single, Glen Ellyn, 1984. Mem. Glen Ellyn Women's Book Club, Illini Mothers Assn. (chmn. DuPage County 1986—). Presbyterian. Avocations: refinishing furniture; writing; mind games; golf; bowling. Home and Office: 670 Western Ave Glen Ellyn IL 60137

REEDER, DONNA JEAN BENEDICT, investment company executive; b. Dallas, Jan. 21, 1943; d. Bill C. Benedict and Vesta Frances (Long) Collins; children—Gary, David, Julie, Robert, Mikal. Student pub. schs., Dallas. Decorator, bookkeeper, Dallas, 1967-79; v.p. Benedict Industries, Inc., Dallas, 1981-83, exec. v.p., 1983, pres., 1984—; v.p., treas. Century Ready Mix, Inc., Wylie, Tex., 1983—, Century Fleet Maintenance & Parts, Inc., Dallas, 1981-84. Baptist. Office: Benedict Industries Inc 13515 N Stemmons Freeway Dallas TX 75234

REED-GROSS, PATRICIA ELAINE, educator; b. Charleston, S.C., Dec. 17, 1952; d. David and Theodocia (Kennedy) Reed; m. Neil Gross, Sept. 26, 1980. B.S., Winthrop Coll., 1974, M.Ed., 1976; postgrad. U. S.C., Columbia Coll., S.C., 1978—. Head spl. edn. Chester County Pub. Schs., Chester, S.C., 1976-77; spl. edn. cons. Winthrop Coll., Rock Hill, S.C., 1977-78; tchr. aphasic children S.C. Sch. for Deaf and Blind, Spartanburg, 1978-79; tchr. juvenile delinquents Spartanburg Boys' Home, S.C., 1979-80; tchr. learning disabled Springdale Sch., Camden, S.C., 1981-84; tchr. emotionally handicapped Hillcrest High Sch., Sumter, S.C., 1984-85; head tchr. autistic adults Pine Grove Sch., Elgin, S.C., 1985—; tchr. adult edn. Manning Correctional Instn., Columbia, 1981—; companion Columbia Area Mental Health, 1981-84. Mem. Nat. Assn. Female Execs. Baha'i. Avocations: swimming; camping. Home: 120 Windmill Orchard Rd Columbia SC 29223 Office: Pine Grove Sch Elgin SC 29045

REED-RANDOLPH, SHIRLEY FAY, state public health administrator; b. Peoria, Ill., Sept. 19, 1936; d. Charles Edward and Ruby Fay (Williams) Sanders; m. Willard Franklyn Reed, Dec. 31, 1960 (dec. July 1971); children—Franklin Edward, Charles Thomas; m. 2d, Verdun Randolph, Oct. 16, 1982. B.S., U. Ill.-Champaign-Urbana, 1958; M.S. in Pub. Health, U. Mo.-Columbia, 1968. Continuity writer, traffic mgr. Sta. WPEO, Peoria, Ill., 1958-60; continuity writer Sta. WMAY, Springfield, Ill., 1960-61; copywriter McKay Advt. Agy., Phoenix, 1961-62; mem. pub. relations staff Motorola Semi-Conductor Products div., Phoenix, 1962-63; staff writer Ill. State Jour. and Register, Springfield, 1963-65; with Dept. Pub. Health State Ill., Springfield, 1965, adminstrv. asst. Bur. of Personal and Community Health, 1973-74, exec. asst. Office Health Services, 1974-76, chief div. local health services, 1976-79, assoc. dir., 1979—; guest lectr. Sangamon State U., Springfield, 1979—, now adj. prof. health services adminstrn.; preceptor dept. community health St. Louis U. Contbr. articles to profl. jours. Bd. dirs. Family Planning of Sangamon County, Inc., Springfield, 1969-71; bd. dirs. Ounce of Prevention Fund, Chgo., 1982—. Mem. Am. Pub. Health Assn. (governing council 1978-81, chmn. health adminstrn. sect. 1986), Ill. Pub. Health Assn. (mem. exec. bd. 1969-71, sec. 1977-79, program chmn. 1980-81), Ill. Soc. Health Educators (pres. 1974-75). Methodist. Office: Ill Dept Pub Health 535 W Jefferson St Springfield IL 62761

REED-ROWE, HELEN PATRICIA, mgmt. assistance co. exec.; b. Balt., Oct. 22, 1949; d. John Walter and Gladys Rebecca Reed; B.A., U. Md., 1971; M.B.A. candidate Southeastern U., 1982; children—Nikkia Tenee, Kevin Anthony. Adult edn. instr., Balt., 1971-72; EEO specialist Dept. Agr., 1972-73; personnel mgmt. specialist Md.-Nat. Capital Park and Planning Commn., Silver Spring, Md., 1973-81; pres., chief exec. officer Libscor Assos., Inc., Balt., and Washington, 1981—. Pres. Balt. City Wide Republican Club, 1981; mem. Balt. City Rep. Central Com., 1981, Md. Rep. State Central Com., 1981; co-chmn. membership com. Md. Fedn. Rep. Women; mem. Cherry Hill Devel. Corp. Recipient Community Service award Balt. Police Dept., 1980; Md. Senatorial scholar, 1969-71. Mem. Nat. Assn. Female Execs., Md. Assn. Affirmative Action Officers, NAACP, Am. Soc. Tng. and Devel., Nat. Assn. Human Rights Workers, Internat. Personnel Mgmt. Assn., LWV, Cherry Hill Improvement Assn., Alpha Kappa Mu, Alpha Kappa Alpha. Presbyterian. Club: 4th Dist. Women's Polit. Office: Libscor Assocs 644 Hillview Rd Baltimore MD 21225

REEPMEYER, MARIE CHRISTINA, librarian; b. Cohoes, N.Y., Oct. 4, 1947; d. Herman John and Marion Lula (Debien) Reepmeyer; A.A., Stephens Coll., 1967; B.A. in Sociology, SUNY-Buffalo, 1969; M.L.S., SUNY-Albany, 1974. Caseworker, central intake, Erie County Dept. Social Services, Buffalo, 1969-70; head legal services librarian Upstate N.Y., Legal Aid Soc., Albany, 1977-79; asst. librarian N.Y. State Dept. Law, Albany, 1979—; wholesale dir. We Care Mink Oil Products, Albany, 1971—; Shaklee distbr., 1984—; cons. Legal Aid Soc., Albany, 1979. Chmn., Miss Mo. Young Republicans Queen Contest, 1966-67; bd. dirs. Albany br. YWCA, 1982-83, chmn. world mutual service com. 1982-83; tertiary, vol. librarian Secular Order Discalced Carmelites, Schenectady, 1982—; sponsor Mother Teresa and Concerned Women Am. Recipient Mem. AAUW (dir. Albany br. 1980-82, corr. sec., newsletter editor 1980-82, nominating com. 1983-84, del. Centennial Conv. 1981, vice chmn. Eastern Area Interbranch Council 1981-82), Nat. Assn. Female Execs. (network dir. 1980-81), Am. Assn. Law Libraries, Assn. Law Librarians of Upstate N.Y., Alumni Assn. SUNY, Albany, Kateri Tekakwitha League, Blue Army of Our Lady of Fatima, Sacred Heart Automobile League, Padre Pio Prayer Group. Roman Catholic. Club: C.O.M.E.T.S. (newsletter editor 1981-82) (Albany). Home: 18 Bertha St Albany NY 12209 Office: NY State Dept Law Library The Capitol State St Albany NY 12224

REES, MARCIA, lawyer; b. San Francisco, Jan. 30, 1941; d. Gordon Ingraham and Virginia Martha (Meier) Gould; m. Peter William Rees, Aug. 3, 1963; children—Megan, Michael Morgan. B.A., U. Calif.-Berkeley, 1962; M.Ed., U. Del., 1972; J.D., Temple U., 1980. Bar: Del. 1980, Pa. 1981. Layout artist Fibreboard Paper Products, San Francisco, 1962-63; social worker Alameda County Welfare Dept., Oakland, Calif., 1963-66; tchr. Newark Sch. Dist. (Del.), 1970-76; law clk. Franta & Funk, Newark, 1978; atty. Prickett, Jones, Elliott, Kristol & Schnee, Wilmington, 1979-84; dep. atty. gen., counsel for State Bd. Edn., Del. Dept. Justice, Wilmington, 1984—. Sec., 22d Rep. Dist. Democratic Com., Newark, 1984; leader 22d Dist. Biden Adv. Commn., 1983-84; sec. bd. dirs. Arthritis Found. Del., Wilmington, 1984, Mem. ABA, Del. Bar Assn., Wilmington Women in Bus., Del. Trial Lawyers Assn., Am. Trial Lawyers Assn. Office: Dept Justice 820 French St Wilmington DE 19801

REES, NORMA S., university administrator, speech pathology and audiology educator; b. N.Y.C., Dec. 27, 1929; d. Benjamin and Lottie (Schwartz) Delgado; m. Raymond R. Rees, Mar. 19, 1960; children—Evan, Raymond. B.A., Queens Coll., 1952, M.A., Bklyn. Coll., 1954; Ph.D., NYU, 1959. Assoc. prof. speech, dir. speech and hearing ctr. Queens Coll., CUNY, 1954-67; prof. speech and hearing scis., dir. ctr. communication disorders Hunter Coll., CUNY, 1967-72, exec. officer Ph.D. program in speech and hearing scis., 1972-74, assoc. dean grad. studies, 1974-76, dean grad. studies, 1976-82; vice chancellor acad. affairs and prof. speech pathology U. Wis.-Milw., 1982—, acting chancellor, 1985—. Contbr. chpts. to books, articles to profl. jours. Recipient award N.Y. State Speech and Hearing Assn., 1978. Fellow Am. Speech-Lang.-Hearing Assn. (v.p. 1957-77, pres. 1979); mem. N.Y. State Speech and Hearing Assn. (pres. 1971), Wis. Speech and Hearing Assn., AAAS. Clubs: University, Tempo (Wis.). Office: U Wis-Milw PO Box 413 Milwaukee WI 53201

REESE, ELLEN PULFORD, psychologist, writer; b. Hartford, Conn., Aug. 30, 1926; d. Alfred Ely and Katherine Cary (Cook) P.; m. Thomas Whelan Reese, Dec. 17, 1949. B.A., Mt. Holyoke Coll., South Hadley, Mass., 1948, M.A., 1954. Lic. psychologist, Mass. Research asst. Mt. Holyoke Coll., 1948-56, asst. dir. psychol. labs., 1956-64, dir. psychol. labs., 1964-69, lectr.

psychology, 1970-80, assoc. prof., 1980-85, prof., 1986—; v.p. Hampshire Communications, Amherst, Mass., 1969-76. Author books including: Human Behavior, 1978; (with Beth Sulzer-Azaroff) Applying Behavior Analysis, 1982; author, dir. ednl. films including: Behavior Theory in Practice, 1965, Imprinting, 1968; mem. editorial bd. Behavior Modification, 1977—. Trustee Cambridge Ctr. Behavioral Studies, Cambridge, Mass., 1981—, Loomis Chaffee Sch., Windsor, Conn., 1973—. Recipient award for disting. contbn. to edn. in psychology Am. Psychol. Found., 1986; Mt. Holyoke Coll. grantee, 1970, 71, 75, 77, 81, 83, 84. Fellow Am. Psychol. Assn. (mem. exec. com. Div. 25 1973-75 77-79), Assn. for Behavior Analysis (mem. council 1981-86, pres. 1984), Animal Behavior Soc., N.Y. Acad. Scis., Sigma Xi. Office: Mount Holyoke Coll South Hadley MA 01075

REESE, KATHLEEN E., utility executive; b. Chgo., Feb. 17, 1949; d. David Jenkins and Shirley Lois (Kaltneger) B.; m. Wilson A. Reese; children—Elizabeth Alexandra, Christopher John, Melanie Suong, Sheryl Louise. B.S., U. Wis., 1972; M.B.A., Nova U., 1984. Project specialist U. Wis., 1972-73, research asst., 1968-72; water quality control technician City of Ft. Lauderdale, Fla., 1974-75; treatment plant operator II Broward County (Fla.) Utilities Dept., Lauderdale Lakes, 1975-80, treatment plant mgr., 1980-84, spl. projects coordinator II, Pompano Beach, 1984-86, spl. project coordinator III, 1986—. Mem. Am. Water Works Assn., Am. Soc. Pub. Adminstrn., Fla. Water and Pollution Control Operators Assn., Nat. Water Well Assn., AAUW, Fla. Renaissance Guild, Nat. Assn. Female Execs. Clubs: Fla. Renaissance Guild, Eastern Star. Contbr. articles to profl. publs. Office: 2401 N Powerline Rd Pompano Beach FL 33069

REESE, KATHLEEN LEANN, marketing and promotion executive, consultant; b. Akron, Ohio, Nov. 7, 1954; d. Bruce Maynard and Margaret Ann (Gebert) R. B.A. in Communication, Bowling Green State U., 1977. Comml. copywriter WTOL TV Sta., Toledo, 1977-78; advt. specialist Andersons, Maumee, Ohio, 1978-79, pub. relations specialist, 1979-81; dir. on-air promotion KXAS TV Sta., Dallas, Ft. Worth, 1981-83; creative services dir. WAVY TV Sta., Portsmouth, Va., 1983—. Promotion coordinator Norfolk Com. for Prevention Child Abuse Celebrity Night Fundraiser, 1984, 85, 86; bd. dirs. Assn. Retarded Citizens, Norfolk, 1984; bd. dirs. AMC Cancer Research Ctr., Hampton Roads Chpt., 1986; bd. dirs. Campus East Community Assn., pres., 1986. Recipient Silver award Advt. Club Toledo, 1980. Mem. Broadcast Promotion Mktg. Execs. (Gold medallion, Merit award 1985), Advt. Fedn. Greater Hampton Roads, AD 2 Toledo (pres. 1980), Am. Women in Radio and TV (v.p. 1980), Kappa Delta. Avocations: writing; sailing; camping; softball. Office: WAVY TV Sta 801-Wavy St Portsmouth VA 23704

REESE, MARTHA GRACE, lawyer; b. Newark, Ohio, Feb. 27, 1953; d. John Gilbert and Louella Catherine (Hodges) R.; m. William Pulliam Harman; children—Benjamin Victor Harman, Elizabeth Lang Harman, B.A. with high distinction, DePauw U., 1975; J.D. magna cum laude, Ind. U., 1980. Bar: Ind. 1980, U.S. Dist. Ct. (so. dist.) Ind. 1980, U.S. Ct. Appeals (7th cir.) 1981. Law clk. U.S. Dist. Ct. (so. dist.) Ind., 1980-82; assoc. Baker & Daniels, Indpls., 1982-83; ptnr. Wilson, Hutchens & Reese, Greencastle, Ind., 1984—. Steering com. Ind. Leadership Celebration, 1983—, sec., 1985—. Mem. ABA, Ind. State Bar Assn., Indpls. Bar Assn., Putnam County Bar Assn., Phi Beta Kappa. Home: 1006 S College Ave Greencastle IN 46135 Office: Wilson Hutchens & Reese 16 S Jackson St Greencastle IN 46135

REESE, MARY LUCILLE, nurse; b. Mobile, Ala., June 30, 1933; d. Cleveland and Irma (Pearson) Wolfe. R.N. diploma Kansas City Gen. Hosp. 2, Mo., 1955. R.N., Mo. Staff nurse City Hosp., Mobile, 1960-65; staff nurse Mobile Infirmary Med. Ctr., 1965-73, asst. dir. nursing service, 1973-82, dir. nursing service, 1982—. Lodge: Order Eastern Star. Office: Mobile Infirmary PO Box 2144 Mobile AL 36652

REESE, ROBERTA ANN, legal assistant; b. Emporia, Kans., June 28, 1943; d. Ivan Lowell and Helen Marie (Fearl) Shawick; m. James R. Melvin, Sept. 10, 1965 (div. Aug. 1971); m. Charles Hamilton Reese, Nov. 5, 1971; 1 child, Curtis James. A.A., Fullerton Coll., 1983; student U. Calif.-Irvine, 1985—. Exec. sec. Inter-Polymer Ins., Los Angeles, 1970-71; legal sec. Welsh & Farris, Buena Park, Calif., 1971-72, Fonte & Warren, Buena Park, 1972-78, pension asst. Hunt-Wesson Foods, Fullerton, Calif., 1978-83; adminstrv. asst. Butterfield Securities Corp., Brea, Calif., 1983; legal asst. William Hinz, Atty., La Habra, Calif., 1983—. Mem. Orange County Legal Secs. Assn. (pres. 1979-80, 85-86, Mem. of Yr. 1983), Orange County Bar Assn. (paralegal sect. 1985-86). Republican. Lutheran. Avocations: reading; swimming; traveling; family.

REESOR, JOAN LOUISE, veterinarian; b. Grand Rapids, Mich., Dec. 4, 1954; d. Hillis Eugene and Betty Louise (Worpel) R. B.S., Mich. State U., 1979, D.V.M., 1979. Small animal intern U. Pa., Phila., 1979-80; assoc. veterinarian Roseland Animal Hosp., South Bend, 1981—. Mem. Am. Vet. Med. Assn., Am. Animal Hosp. Assn., Michiana Vet. Med. Assn. Lutheran. Home: 619 Travers Circle Apt B Mishawaka IN 46545 Office: Roseland Animal Hospital 424 Dixieway N South Bend IN 46637

REEVE, HEATHER HOUSTON, lawyer; b. Portland, June 11, 1955; d. Gerald Polk Houston and Marilyn Ada (Gleason) Lundborg; m. David Houston Reeve, Dec. 27, 1981. B.A., U. So. Calif., 1979; J.D., Loyola U. of Los Angeles, 1982. Bar: Calif. 1982, Wash. 1983, U.S. Ct. Appeals (9th cir.) 1982. Judicial externship U.S. Dist. Ct. (cen. dist.) Los Angeles, 1981; law clk. Calif. Ct. Appeals 4th Dist., San Bernardino, Calif., 1982-83; law clk. Wash. State Supreme Ct., Olympia, 1983-84; assoc. Reed, McClure, Moceri Thonn & Moriarty, P.S., Seattle, 1984—; intern UN Non-Govt. Liaison Service, N.Y.C., 1980. Mem. exec. com. Today's Costn. and You, 1984—. Mem. ABA, Calif. Bar Assn., Wash. Bar Assn., Seattle-King County Bar Assn., World Affairs Council Seattle, Cticlub, Phi Beta Kappa. Democrat. Episcopalian. Home: 1733 N 128th St Seattle WA 98133 Office: Reed McClure Moceri Thonn and Moriarty PS 1700 Bank of Calif Ctr Seattle WA 98104

REEVE, JACQUELINE ANNE, nurse; b. Warren, Ohio, Apr. 10, 1951; d. James Arnold and Thelma Joyce (Trask) R.; A.A. in Nursing, Kent State U., Ashtabula, 1971. Nursing supr. Char-Lotte Nursing Home, Inc., Rock Creek, Ohio, 1971-79; team leader Northeastern Ohio Gen. Hosp., North Madison, 1979-80; dir. nursing Con-Lea Nursing Home, Geneva, Ohio, 1980-81, Good Samaritan Nursing Home Corp., East Peoria, Ill., 1982; dir. nursing service Wickliffe (Ohio) Country Pl., 1982-86; pvt. practice cons. for nursing homes; profl. reviewer med. records: mem. Ohio Health Care Assn. peer rev. survey team, 1981-83. Active ACLU, Cleve.; mem. Jefferson Vol. Fire Dept. Rescue Squad, 1978—. Mem. Nat. League Nursing, Nursing in Long-Term Care (treas. 1985-86), N.Y. Acad. Scis., Cleve. Area Citizens League Nursing Dirs., Nat. Assn. Female Execs., Nat. Honor Soc., Quill and Scroll. Organizer, condr. inservice courses in field. Home: PO Box 93 Jefferson OH 44047 also 141 Steele Ave Apt 203 Painesville OH 44077

REEVES, CAROLINE BUCK, civic worker, author; b. St. Louis; d. Philo Melvin and Aletheia (Hall) Buck; A.B., Wellesley Coll., U. Wis., 1928; M.A., Columbia, 1934; m. William Harvey Reeves, Aug. 29, 1931; children—Aletheia Nevius, H. Van Kirk. Editorial, coll. depts. Henry Holt & Co., pubs., N.Y.C., 1928-31; indsl. economist U.S. Govt., Washington, 1942-45, Rockefeller U., 1970-83. Pres. bd. mgrs. Home for Old Men and Aged Couples (name changed to Isaac H. Tuttle Fund 1981), N.Y.C., 1955-58, bd. dirs., 1951—, sec. bd., 1960-62, trustee, 1969—, mem. com. on aging Fedn. of Protestant Welfare Agys., N.Y.C., 1951-58; mem. hobby show com. Community Council of Greater N.Y., 1955-63; mem. N.Y. Com. Frontier Nursing Service, Inc.; bd. dirs. The Bargain Box, Inc., 1962-69; bd. dirs. Amsterdam Nursing Home Corp., 1974—. Mem. Colonial Dames Am., Delta Delta Delta. Club: Colony. Author: Impact of War on Tri-City Area, 1917-19, 1943; Impact of World War I on Hampton Roads Area, 1944, Disposition of Surplus Machine Tools by the War Department following World War I, 1944, also articles. Home: Apt E505 200 E 66th St New York NY 10021

REEVES, KATHRYN RANDALL, nurse; b. Albion, Mich., Nov. 8, 1934; d. Tom R. and Eleanor (Householder) Randall; student Albion Coll., 1952-54; A.D.N., Fullerton Coll., 1964; B.S., Calif. State U., 1969; B.A., Calif. State U., Fullerton, 1982, M.A., 1985; m. George I. Reeves, June 25, 1954; children—Thomas Charles, Mary Kathryn, Susan Elisabeth. Charge nurse, asst. dir. nursing Childrens Hosp., Orange County, Calif., 1964-73, head nurse adolescent unit, med. surg. supr., 1973-76; adminstrv. dir. emergency dept. St. Joseph Hosp., Orange, 1976—. Vol. nurse ARC; bd. dirs. Muckenthaler Cultural Ctr., Fullerton Library Council. Cert. emergency nurse, nurse adminstr. Mem. Nat. Critical Care Inst., Emergency Nurses Assn. (pres. Orange County chpt. 1982-83), DAR, Orange County Geneal. Soc., Mensa, Alpha Lambda Delta, Alpha Gamma Sigma, Psi Chi, Delta Gamma. Democrat. Episcopalian. Home: 201 Friar Pl Fullerton CA 92635 Office: 1100 Stewart Ave Orange CA 92668

REEVES, MICHAELYN MARIE, communications technician; b. S.I., N.Y., Nov. 3, 1956; d. Clyde James and Dorothy Grace (Brown) Tuggle; m. Robert Owen Reeves, Sept. 24, 1976 (div. Apr. 1978). Cashier I. Magnin, Pasadena, Calif., 1979-80; communication technician AT&T Communications, Los Angeles, 1980—. Served with USAF, 1974-79. Roman Catholic. Home: 14634 Vose St Van Nuys CA 91405

REEVES, VIRGINIA ANN, laboratory executive; b. San Jose, Calif., Octr. 13, 1957; d. Carl and Helen Belle (Williams Reeves McKeany; m. Daniel R. Stone, Dec. 4, 1976 (div. Aug. 1979). Student Sacramento City Coll., 1981-86. Cosmetician, Sears Roebuck Co., Sacramento, 1977-78, Raleys, 1978-80; sales rep. Schmid Labs., Sacramento, 1980-85, dist. sales mgr., 1985—. Mem. Nat. Assn. Profl. Saleswomen, Nat. Assn. Female Execs. Democrat. Lutheran. Club: Toastmasters. Avocations: camping; sewing; woodworking. Home: PO Box 2272 Citrus Heights CA 95611 Office: Schmid Labs Route 46W Little Falls NJ 07424

REFUERZO, CHARITO MANZA, newspaper executive; b. Davao City, Davao, Mindanao, Philippines, Oct. 2, 1927; came to U.S., 1969; d. Ramon V. and Mercedes (Jayme) Manza; m. Serafin Refuerzo, Mar. 10, 1971 (dec.); 1 son, Joseph. A.A., Tchrs. Coll., Tacloban City, Leyte, Philippines, 1952; B.A. in English, U. So. Philippines, Cebu City, Cebu, 1960, cert. secretarial sci., 62, postgrad. in English, 1968-69. Sec. to dir. and chmn. bd. trustees Tchrs. Coll., Tacloban City, 1950-52; sec. to chmn. bd. trustees, pres. and exec. v.p. U. So. Philippines, Cebu City, 1955-69, part time instr. commerce/secretarial, 1955-69, acting head secretarial dept., 1967-69; sec. to mgr. and exec. v.p. Hild Floor Machine Co., Los Angeles, 1969-73; part-time instr. MTI Bus. Sch., Hollywood, Calif., 1969-71; with computer dept. Los Angeles Times, 1973—. Mem. Nat. Com. to Preserve Social Security and Medicare; mem. research council Scripps Clinic and Research Found., La Jolla, Calif. Recipient silver pin Los Angeles Times, 1984. Mem. Nat. Assn. Female Execs., Ladies Aux. of U.S. Navy, Smithsonian Instn. (assoc.), Am. Film Inst., Los Angeles County Mus. Art. Republican. Roman Catholic. Address: PO Box 1804 Los Angeles CA 90053

REGALADO, ELISA, university administrator; b. Remedios, Cuba, Dec. 2, 1940; d. Rene Mederos and Rafaela (Rodriguez) Mederos Sales; children—Elisa, Jose. B.A., U. Villanueva (Cuba), 1960; M.B.A., U. Miami (Fla.), 1983. Dir. med. budgeting and fin. reporting U. Miami Med. Sch. (Fla.), 1966—. Mem Nat. Assn. Accts., Am. Mgmt. Assn., Nat. Assn. Female Execs., Assn. Am. Med. Colls. (group bus. affairs). Republican. Roman Catholic. Club: U. Miami Bowling (sec. 1979, treas. 1980). Office: U Miami Sch Medicine PO Box 016960 D2-3 Miami FL 33101

REGAN, ELIZABETH ANN, insurance company executive; b. Paterson, N.J., May 6, 1942; d. Gerard and Elizabeth (VanLenten) Oorthuys; m. Charles E. Regan, Jan. 26, 1963; children—Keith Eugene, Meredith Margaret, Deanne Elizabeth. A.A. Green Mountain Coll., 1962; B.S., U. Conn., 1971, M.A., 1977, Ph.D., 1982. Export sec. United Technologists, East Hartford, Conn., 1962-67; instr. U. Conn., Storrs, 1973-80; systems analyst IBM, Boulder, Colo., 1981; sr. project mgr. Mass. Mut. Life Ins. Co., Springfield, Mass., 1982—. Contbr. articles to profl. jours. Bd. dirs. Alumni Bd. Green Mountain Coll., Poultney, Vt., 1968-79; chmn. nominating com. Hockanum Valley Community Services Council, Vernon, Conn., 1972-73. Recipient Nat. Research award Delta Pi Epsilon, 1984, Grad. Leadership Devel. award Dept. Vocational Edn., 1980-81, Bus. Edn. Merit award Nat. Bus. Edn. Assn., 1971. Mem. Assn. Info. System Profls. (edn. com.), Office Systems Research Assn. (research com.), Am. Vocational Assn., Pi Lambda Theta, Omicron Tau Theta. Democrat. Club: Suburban Women's (Vernon, Tolland, Ellington, Conn.) (pres. 1970-73). Avocations: skiing, tennis. Home: 49 Center Rd Tolland CT 06084 Office: Mass Mut Life Ins Co 1295 State St Springfield MA 01111

REGAN, ELLEN FRANCES (MRS. WALSTON SHEPARD BROWN), ophthalmologist; b. Boston, Feb. 1, 1919; d. Edward Francis and Margaret (Moynihan) R.; A.B., Wellesley Coll., 1940; M.D., Yale U., 1943; m. Walston Shepard Brown, Aug 13, 1955. Intern, Boston City Hosp., 1944; asst. resident, resident Inst. Ophthalmology, Presbyn. Hosp., N.Y.C., 1944-47, asst. ophthalmologist, 1947-56, asst. attending ophthalmologist, 1956-84; instr. ophthalmology Columbia Coll. Physicians and Surgeons, 1947-55, asso. ophthalmology, 1955-67, asst. clin. prof., 1967-84. Mem. Am. Ophthal. Soc., AMA, Am. Acad. Ophthalmology, Assn. Research Ophthalmology, N.Y. Acad. Medicine, N.Y. State, Mass. med. socs. Clubs: River, Wellesley. Home: Tuxedo Park NY 10987 Office: Box 632 Tuxedo NY 10987

REGAN, HELENE, career counseling agency executive; b. Bklyn., Nov. 12, 1938; d. Abraham Bernard and Yetta (Pepper) Straussman; ed. Baruch Coll.; children—Scott Lawrence, Keith Martin, Andrea Beth. Coordinator display advt. Blaine-Thompson, N.Y.C., 1957-59; pres. Regan Assocs. Ltd., N.Y.C., 1967—; owner, mgr. Fabulous Furs by Helene, N.Y.C., 1967-76; 2d v.p. Prescott & James, personnel agy., N.Y.C., 1976-83; cons. Regan Assocs. Inc., 1983—; fashion coordinator for fur industry. Active in fundraising Cancer Care, NAACP, United Jewish Appeal, and Orgn. Rehab. and Tng., N.Y.C. Recipient 12 medals for achievement Women's Am. Orgn. for Rehab. and Tng., 1969-74. Mem. Internat. Platform Assn. Republican. Office: 4 Lexington Ave Suite 4-N New York NY 10010

REGAN, MARY DESMOND, personnel executive; b. Wilmington, Del., Sept. 20, 1935; d. Daniel F. and Mary (Nee) Desmond; m. John F. Regan, Aug. 20, 1960; children—Sean F., Maureen A., Kevin D. B.S., U. Del., 1957; postgrad. U. Pa., 1958-60. Acct., Hercules, Inc., Wilmington, Del., 1971-76, office mgr., 1976-79; salary/benefits adminstr. Boots Hercules, Wilmington, 1979-81; personnel mgr. Nor-Am Chem. Co., Wilmington, 1981—. Mem. Am. Soc. Personnel Adminstrs., Adminstrv. Mgmt. Soc., AAUW. Roman Catholic. Home: 1613 N Franklin St Wilmington DE 19806 Office: Nor-Am Chem Co 3509 Silverside Rd PO Box 7495 Wilmington DE 19803

REGAN, MAUREEN JUNE, publisher; b. Kansas City, Kans., Sept. 25, 1959; d. Patrick Joseph and M. June (Bolinger) R. B.S. in Journalism, U. Kans., 1982. Corp. sales mgr. Brock Hotel Corp., Dallas, 1982-84; pub. Women's Yellow Pages Directory, Denver, 1984—, Colorado Springs Women's Yellow Pages, 1986. Mem. Mayor's Commn. on Women, 1984. Mem. Bus. Women Resources Network (bd. dirs. 1983-84), Women's Bus. Owners Assn. (bd. dirs., 1985-86). Democrat. Roman Catholic. Avocations: reading; travel; skiing. Home: 645 Bellaire St Denver CO 80220 Office: Women's Yellow Pages Inc 1758 Emerson Denver CO 80218

REGAN, MILDRED GEAR, radio station manager; b. Cleve., May 22, 1933; d. Carroll James and Helen (Hower) Gear; m. Harley Ray Regan, Mar. 13, 1954; children—Donna Rae, Leslie Lynne, Jeanette Jay. Grad. high sch., Rock Creek, Ohio, 1952. Owner, The Regan's Book Store, Houma, La., 1967-71; office mgr. KHOM Radio, Houma, 1971-76, asst. mgr., 1976-79, sta. mgr., 1979—. Served with USN, 1952-54. Club: Altrusa Internat. (pres. 1982-84) (Houma). Avocations: reading; sewing; gardening; little theatre. Office: KHOM Radio 2306 W Main St Houma LA 70360

REGAN, SUZANNE MARIE, marketing executive; b. Camden, N.J., May 11, 1950; d. Cornelius Joseph and Jeannette (Way) R.; B.S., U. Conn., 1972; M.B.A., Drexel U., 1978; m. Ronald L. Feldberg, Apr. 10, 1976. Acctg. procedures analyst Campbell Soup Co., Camden, N.J., 1972-74, mktg. research analyst, 1974-77, asst. mktg. mgr. Swanson div., 1977-78, mktg. mgr. Swanson div., 1978-81, mktg. mgr. pet foods, 1981-85, gen. mgr. pet foods, 1985—; pres. Champion Valley Farms, 1985; bd. dirs. Pet Food Inst., 1985—. Mem. Nat. Assn. Female Execs., Am. Mgmt. Assn. Home: 59 Woodhurst Dr West Berlin NJ 08091 Office: Campbell Pl Camden NJ 08101

REGES, MARIANNA ALICE, media and public relations executive; b. Budapest, Hungary, Mar. 23, 1947; came to U.S., 1956, naturalized, 1963; d. Otto H. and Alice M. R.; A.A.S. with honors, Fashion Inst. Tech., 1967; B.B.A. with high honors, Baruch Coll., N.Y.C., 1971, M.B.A. in Stats., 1978; m. Charles P. Green, Feb. 15, 1975; children—Rebecca Reges, Charles P. III. Media research analyst Doyle, Dane, Bernbach Advt., N.Y.C., 1967-70; research supr. WCBS-TV, N.Y.C., 1970-71; research mgr. Woman's Day Mag., N.Y.C., 1971-72; asst. media dir. Benton & Bowles Advt., N.Y.C., 1972-75; mgr. research and sales devel. NBC Radio, N.Y.C., 1975-77; sr. research mgr. Ziff Davis Pub. Co., N.Y.C., 1977-84; mgr. media research Bristol-Myers Co., 1984—. Mem. Vt. Natural Resources Council, 1977—; mem. Nature Conservatory, 1980—; advisor Baruch Coll. Advt. Soc., 1975—. Mem. Am. Mktg. Assn., Am. Advt. Fedn., Media Research Dir. Assn., Radio and TV Research Council, Women in Communications, Advt. Women N.Y., Beta Gamma Sigma, Sigma Alpha Delta. Home: 10 Stuyvesant Oval New York NY 10009 Office: 345 Park Ave New York NY 10154

REGET, IONE HOZENDORF, business services company executive, enrolled agent; b. Jackson, Miss., Sept. 19, 1937; d. Glenn Frederick and Ione Belle (Lowry) Hozendorf; m. Francis John Reget, Jan. 17, 1967; children—Diane Michele, Philip Francis, Michael Trahern. B.A. cum laude, U. Minn., 1959; postgrad. U. Calif.-Berkeley, 1978, Coll. Fin. Planning, 1984—; Pres., East Sierra Bus. Services, Inc., Bishop, Calif., 1980—; corp. sec. Frank J. Reget Accountancy Corp., 1972—; sec.-treas. Meyer Cookie Co., Inc. Soprano, Bishop Community Chorus, 1974-78; treas. Calvary Bapt. Ch., Bishop, 1975—, choir dir., 1980—; chmn. mem. Civic Arts Commn., City of Bishop, 1984—. Mem. Nat. Assn. Enrolled Agts., Calif. Soc. Enrolled Agts., Calif. Assn. Ind. Accts., Aircraft Owners and Pilots Assn., DAR, Mensa. Republican. Club: Playhouse 395. Home: Route 1 146 North St Bishop CA 93514 Office: 150 N Main St Bishop CA 93514 Mail Address: PO Box 448 Bishop CA 93514

REGNART, CLAUDIA SWANNACK, educator; b. Spokane, Wash., Aug. 11, 1937; d. John William and Leone Estelle (Roth) Swannack; B.A., U. Puget Sound, 1959; postgrad. East Wash. Coll. Edn., summers 1958, 60, U. Wash., summer 1966, Alaska Pacific U., 1968-69, U. Alaska, summers 1972, 74, fall 1982; m. Ronald I. Regnart, Nov. 21, 1962; children—Jeffrey, Patrick. Tchr., Anchorage Sch. Dist., 1959-63, 64-65, 67, Nome (Alaska) Sch. Dist., 1963-64; tchr., owner Rabbit Creek Pre-Sch., Anchorage, 1972—. Chmn. PTA, Anchorage, 1970—; den mother Boy Scouts Am., 1973-79; vol. worker Cancer Fund, Heart Fund, FISH, Little League. Mem. Alaska Edn. Assn., NEA, Am. Assn. for Edn. of Young Children. Methodist. Club: Order Eastern Star. Home: 4900 Rabbit Creek Rd SRA Box 5476A Anchorage AK 99516

REGNER, BETH ELLEN, stock trader; b. Burlington, Wis., Feb. 22, 1951; d. John Lewis and Beatrice Marie (Lehsten) Regner; m. Richard Thomas Vrchota, Jr., Nov. 2, 1985. B.S. in Nursing, U. Wis.-Milw., 1974; M.S. in Bus. Mgmt., Cardinal Stritch Coll., Milw., 1984. R.N. Pub. health nurse Pub. Health Dept., Milw., 1974-77; from staff nurse to head nurse emergency room and cardiac rehab. unit Columbia Hosp., Milw., 1977-84; project mgr. Datacare, Inc., Milw., 1984-86; stock trader, preferred stock dept. Milw. Co., 1986—; vol. cardiac rehab. nurse Mt. Sinai Rehab. Program, Milw., 1977-81. Roman Catholic. Avocations: tennis, aerobics, biking, walking, reading. Home: 3659 W College Ave Apt 54 Milwaukee WI 53221 Office: Preferred Stock Dept Milwaukee Co 250 E Wisconsin Ave Milwaukee WI 53202

REGNIER, CLAIRE NEOMIE, marketing and business consultant; b. Fort Riley, Kans., May 2, 1939; d. Eugene Arthur and Claire Janet (Macfarlane) Regnier; B.S. cum laude in Journalism, Trinity U., San Antonio, 1961. Advt. cons., San Antonio, 1961-68; editor Paseo del Rio Showboat newspaper, San Antonio, 1968-81; exec. dir. San Antonio River Assn., San Antonio, 1968-81; pres. Metro Cons., San Antonio, 1981—. Chmn. Centro 21 Downtown Revitalization Task Force, San Antonio; rep. San Antonio River Corridor Com.; mem. Fiesta San Antonio Commn., San Antonio Parks and Recreation Adv. Bd.; bd. dirs., chmn. public relations com. San Antonio Area council Girl Scouts U.S.A. Recipient awards of excellence for Showboat, Alamo Bus. Communicators, 1970, 71, 73, 74; Headliner award San Antonio chpt. Women in Communications, 1980. Mem. Internat. Assn. Bus. Communicators (Bronze Quill award 1986), Women in Communications (Southwest region banner award 1981, Proliner awards 1984-86), Tex. Public Relations Assn., Alamo Bus. Communicators (Communicator of Yr. 1977), San Antonio Mus. Assn., San Antonio Conservation Soc. Clubs: Altrusa, Univ. Roundtable. Home: 7772 Woodridge St San Antonio TX 78209 Office: 8122 Datapoint Suite 301 San Antonio TX 78229

REGNIER, JOYCE ANNE, nursing administrator; b. Ottawa County, Kans., July 22, 1940; d. Bernice Allen and Venita LoRee (Pitts) Bartley; B.S.N. cum laude, Marymount Coll., Salina, Kans., 1973; M.S., Kans. State U., 1983; N.H.A., Barton County Community Coll., 1985; m. J. Lucien Regnier, Aug. 6, 1958; children—Bernard, Douglas, Michelle. Staff nurse, charge nurse Ottawa County Hosp., Minneapolis, Kans., 1973-76; dir. nursing Kenwood View Nursing Home, Salina, Kans., 1977-79; nursing instr. Marymount Coll., Salina, 1979-81; ICU nurse, 1982-83; adminstr. Manor of Kansas City (Kans.), 1983—; adv. bd. vocat. tech. sch., Salina, 1977, Ottawa County Health Dept., Kans., 1976; mem. planning and coordination com. for continuing edn. for nurses, Kans. Mem. Sigma Theta Tau. Methodist. Home: 7458 Isabel Ct Kansas City KS 66112 Office: 3231 N 61st St Kansas City KS 66104

REHAGEN-HUFF, ANDREA LEE, career consulting, outplacement company executive, consultant; b. St. Louis, Nov. 20, 1949; d. Clemens John and Margaret Mary (Sheridan) Rehagen; m. S. Michael Huff, Jan. 11, 1969; 1 child, Jeffrey Michael. B.A. in Sociology, So. Ill. U., 1971; M.A. in Counseling, Washington U., St. Louis, 1975. Career counselor State of Ill., Granite City, 1971-73; counselor RHS, Inc., St. Louis, 1973-75, Womanhelp, San Francisco, 1975-77; dir. career devel., career cons. Career Planning Services/Woman's Way, San Rafael, Calif., 1977-80; pres., career cons. CareerWorks, San Francisco, 1980—. Mem. Am. Soc. Tng. and Devel. (chmn., founder career devel. div. 1979-81), No. Calif. Human Resources Council, Women Entrepreneurs, Career Planning and Adult Devel. Network. Democrat. Avocation: collector of early 20th century art and furnishings. Office: CareerWorks 100 Spear St Suite 810 San Francisco CA 94105

REHBERG, IRENE LEE, elastic materials exec.; b. Shanghai, China, Feb. 22, 1946; came to U.S., 1969, naturalized, 1982; d. Kam Yee and Chang Hing (Ho) Lee; B.S., Ohio U., 1973; m. John Thomas Rehberg, Aug. 24, 1980; 1 son, Eric Lee. Lab. specialist Fusion, Inc., Willoughby, Ohio, 1973-77; profl. chemist SCM-Gidden Metals, Cleve., 1977-78; sr. chemist Tremco, Cleve., 1978-80; v.p., dir. Elastic Materials, Inc., Medina, Ohio, 1980—; tchr. Chinese culture; soldering and brazing cons. Recipient award for outstanding contbn. to Lakeland Community Coll., 1974. Mem. Delta Phi Alpha. Roman Catholic. Patentee various fields. Home: 20735 White Bark St Strongsville OH 44136 Office: 2552 Lester Rd Medina OH 44256

REHER, ANNE MARIE SULLIVAN, civic worker; b. Denver, Dec. 25, 1915; d. Dennis Francis and Mary Ellen (Malone) Sullivan; m. Sven Helge Reher, Apr. 11, 1942 (div. 1984); children—Thomas, Kathleen, David, Vincent, Mary Regina. B.A. in History and Philosophy, Loretto Heights Coll., 1937; B.A. in Music, UCLA, 1942; M.A. in Music, Mt. St. Mary's Coll., 1952. Concert pianist, 1942—; accompanist for Sven Reher, concert violist, goodwill ambassador Gen. Petroleum Corp., Union Bank; tchr. Graland Country Day Sch., Denver, Marymount Grade and High Sch., Los Angeles; community coordinator Adult Edn. Programs UCLA; founder women's com. Braille Inst.; commr. Dept. Municipal Arts, City of Los Angeles, 1974-80. Bd. dirs. Community Relations Conf. So. Calif., NCCJ, Am. Jewish Com., Urban League, NAACP, Christian Friends of Palestine; pres. UN Assn. Beverly Hills; v.p. UN Assn. Los Angeles; founder Christines, The Commonweal Club, Catholic Peace Assn.; founding bd. dir. Catholic Human Relations Council, Loyola Human Relations Workshop, Friendship Day Camp; mem. Clergy and Laity Concerned, Blue Ribbon Com. of Music Ctr., Assistance League, Women's Com. of Los Angeles Philharm. Orch., Women's Internat. Com. of UCLA, Faculty Wives of UCLA, Los Angeles County Mus. Assn., Friends of CalTech, Westwood Community Plan Adv. com., Girl Scouts USA, PTA. Recipient Los Angeles City Council Commendation, 1980; named Calif. Child Study Found. Woman of Yr., 1984. Mem. Sigma Alpha Iota, Delta Omicron. Roman Catholic. Clubs: Immaculate Heart College Mothers'; Loyola Mothers'; Paulist Mothers'. Avocations: music, drama, art, writing, politics. Home: 911 Malcolm Ave Los Angeles CA 90024

REIBMAN, JEANETTE FICHMAN (MRS. NATHAN L. REIBMAN), state senator; b. Ft. Wayne, Ind., Aug. 18, 1915; d. Meir and Pearl (Schwartz) Fichman; B.A., Hunter Coll.; LL.B., Ind. U.; LL.D. (hon.), Lafayette Coll., Cedar Crest Coll., Wilson Coll., Lehigh U.; m. Nathan L. Reibman; 3 children. Atty. tax amortization br. U.S. War Dept., Washington; atty. U.S. War Prodn. Bd., 1941-44; mem. Pa. Ho. of Reps., 1954-56, 58-66, sec. com. of welfare, chmn. com. on edn., 1959-62, com. on twps., 1965; mem. Pa. Senate, 1966—, chmn. edn. com., 1967-80. Pa. commr., Edn. Commn. of States; mem. Pa. Adv. Com. on Probation. Del. White House Conf. on Problems of Aging, White House Conf. on Children; mem. Gov.'s Citizens Commn. on Basic Edn.; mem. Joint State Govt. Commn. on Decedents' Estates; mem. Pa. Council Arts; mem. Pa. coordinating com. Internat. Women's Yr., 1976, del. nat. conf., 1977; mem. Fed. Citizen's Com. for Dept. Edn., 1977. Trustee, Lafayette Coll., St. Luke's Hosp. of Bethlehem; mem. commonwealth bd. Med. Coll. Pa.; bd. dirs. Pa. Higher Edn. Assistance Agy. Named Disting. Dau. Pa.; elected to Hunter Coll. Alumni Hall of Fame; recipient State of Israel-City of Jerusalem Peace award, 1977. Mem. AAUW, LWV, Delta Kappa Gamma, Sigma Delta Tau, Phi Delta Kappa. Democrat. Home: 514 McCartney St Easton PA 18042

REIBMAN-MYERS, FRANCINE LEE, business executive; b. N.Y.C., Dec. 5, 1949; d. Abe and Katherine C. (Glass) Reibman; m. Jay H. Myers, May 31, 1980; 1 child, Benjamin Alexander Reibman-Myers. B.A. cum laude, CUNY. Assoc. dir. Nat. Student Lobby, Washington, 1972-74; dir. govt. ops. Continental Mktg., Washington, 1972-74; acting dir. vets. affairs CUNY, 1974-75; chmn. bd. Culpepper, Inc., Millburn, N.J., 1983-86; pres. Fran Reibman & Assocs., Millburn, 1976—; cons. House Select Com. on Aging, 1977-78, Triathalon Products, Inc., 1985—, Cons. Mennen Med. Inc., 1986—. Patentee rehab. gym, 1985. Candidate for N.Y. State Assembly, 1972; bd. dirs. John F. Kennedy Democratic Club, Jamaica, N.Y., 1978-84; adv. People to Rehabilitate and Integrate the Disabled, 1973-78; sec. Council on Internat. Relations for UN, 1972-73; Democratic county committee person, Queens, 1972-74; bd. govs. Queensborough Pres.'s Council for Tenants, 1972-73. Mem. Am. Assn. Advancement of Med. Instrumentation, Nat. Assn. Female Execs. Jewish. Avocations: horseback riding; golf; sailing; building; reading.

REICH, JOANNE LEE, business and marketing consultant; b. Oakland, Calif., Aug. 30, 1945; d. Herbert and Wanda Jane (Porter) R. B.A., UCLA, 1967; postgrad. Babson Coll., Wellesley, Mass., 1982—. Programmer analyst, cons. various orgns., Los Angeles, 1969-73; sr. programmer analyst Compata, Inc., Canoga Park, Calif., 1973-75; systems engr. Data Gen. Corp., El Segundo, Calif., 1975-78; project mgr., bus. planning Honeywell Info. Systems, Billerica, Mass., 1978-82; bus. planning cons. Wang Labs., Inc., Lowell, Mass., 1982-86; mktg. mgr. Direct Products div. Data Gen. Corp., Westboro, Mass., 1986—; market research cons. Micro Tech. Research, Chelmsford, Mass., 1984—. Mem. Am. Mgmt. Assn., Nat. Assn. Female Execs. Avocations: oil painting, drawing, community theater production activities. Office: Data Gen Corp 4400 Computer Dr Westboro MA 01580

REICH, KATHLEEN JOHANNA, Librarian, educator; b. Mannheim, Germany, May 1, 1927; came to U.S., 1955, naturalized, 1958; d. Robert and Luise Charlotte Helene (Kurowsky) Weichel; M.A.T. in English, Rollins Coll., 1976, Ed.S., 1981; 1 son, Robert Weichel. With Orlando (Fla.) Pub. Library, 1955-57; cataloguer, instr. U. Detroit, 1957-60, Trinity U., San Antonio, 1960-61; adminstr. Fla. Book Processing Center, Orlando, 1961-68; bur. chief, div. library services Fla. State Dept., Winter Park, 1968-71; assoc. prof. library sci. Rollins Coll., Winter Park, 1971-83, asst. dean faculty, 1981-83, dir. overseas studies, 1983-84; spl. collections librarian, acting archivist Rollins Coll., 1983—; acad. dean Prev Prep. Sch., Sarasota, Fla., 1983—. Mem. AAUP, African Literature Assn., Nat. Assn. Fgn. Student Affairs, Am. Water Ski Assn., Soc. Am. Archivists, Kappa Delta Pi. Home: 211 Fawsett Rd Winter Park FL 32789 Office: Rollins College Winter Park FL 32789

REICH, MYRA ANN REARDON, food services company executive; b. Ft. Sill, Okla., Nov. 24, 1929; d. Michael Reardon and Myra (Dunn) Hudson; m. Albert Lee Reich, Feb. 22, 1947 (div. May 1980); children—Sharon Reich Wiggins, Karen Reich Taylor, Catherine Reich Ragusa. Student pub. schs., Nowata, Okla. Cert. food service mgr. Food handler, asst. mgr. Macke-Progressive Co., Houston, 1957-67; asst. mgr. Ara Services, Texas City, Tex., 1967-69; operator, mgr. Denny's Inc., Houston, 1969-73; dir. food service Ara Services, Orange, Tex., 1973-77; food dir. Morrison Mgmt. Services, Inc., Mobile, Ala., 1980—. Contbr. articles to profl. jours. Active Mus. Fine Arts, Houston, Morrison Polit. Action Com., Mobile, Mothers' Against Drunk Drivers. Mem. Nat. Assn. Female Execs., Inc., Exec. Profl. Services Inc., Am. Bus. Women's Assn. Republican. Baptist. Clubs: Single-Adult-Christian Group (telephone chmn. Houston 1983—); Resort Condominiums Internat., Downtown Meth. Singles. Home: 10110 Forum Park Dr #158 Houston TX 77036 Office: Tex Research into Mental Scis Tex Inst of Rehab and Research 1333 Moursund Houston TX 77026

REICHEL, LEATRICE IDA, banker; b. Erie, Pa., Jan. 31, 1930; d. Jacob Charles and Ida Eva (Bovee) Seib; student pub. schs.; widow. With Security Bank, Erie, 1948—, asst. sec., 1970-75, personnel officer, 1972-84, asst. v.p., 1975-84; personnel officer Pennbank, Titusville, Pa., 1984; personnel officer, affirmative action officer Pennbancorp, Titusville, 1986—. Mem. personnel com. Erie chpt. ARC, 1980—, chmn., 1983-85; mem. Erie Merit Rev. Bd. Mem. Nat. Assn. Bank Women (past chmn. N.W. Pa. group), Am. Soc. Personnel Adminstrn., Personnel Assn. N.W. Pa. (pres. 1981-82). Clubs: Aviation Country, Erie Maennerchor Aux., East Erie Turners, Order Eastern Star. Office: 801 State St Erie PA 16501

REID, CHARLOTTE T., business consultant; b. Kankakee, Ill., Sept. 27, 1913; d. Edward Charles and Ethel (Stith) Thompson; m. Frank R. Reid, Jan. 1, 1938 (dec. 1962); children—Patricia, Frank, Edward, Susan. Student Ill. Coll., 1931-32; LL.D. (hon.), John Marshall Law Sch., Ill. Coll., Aurora Coll. Vocalist, NBC, Chgo., 1936-39; mem. Ho. of Reps., Washington, 1962-71; mem. Commn. on FCC, Washington, 1971-76; dir. Liggett Group, N.Y.C., 1977-80, Midlantic Banks, Inc., Edison, N.Y., 1977—, Motorola Inc., Schaumburg, Ill., 1978-84. Mem. Presdl. Task Force on Internat. Pvt. Enterprise, 1983-85; mem. com. Def. Adv. Com. on Women in the Services, 1982-85; bd. overseers Hoover Instn., 1984—. Republican. Club: Capitol Hill (dir. 1968-82).

REID, JEANNE MARIE, nutritionist; b. Tampa, Fla., Oct. 8, 1923; d. William Clarence and Christine Alicia (Mahoney) Reid; B.S., U. Ala., 1945; M.S., U. Md., 1962; postgrad. U. Minn., 1969. Dietetic intern N.Y. Hosp.-Cornell Med. Center, N.Y.C., 1946; asst. dietitian Charity Hosp., New Orleans, 1946-47, assoc. dir. therapeutic dietetic services, 1947-51; chief therapeutic dietitian Jackson Meml. Hosp., Miami, Fla., 1951-53; research dietitian Clin. Center, NIH, Bethesda, Md., 1953-57, metabolic research dietitian, out-patient clinic dietitian, 1957-67, research nutritionist Nat. Inst. Arthritis, Metabolism and Digestive Diseases, 1967—. Mem. Am. Dietetic Assn., Nat. Assn. Uniformed Services, Am. Inst. Nutrition, Commd. Officers Assn. USPHS, Nutrition Today Soc., D.C. Dietetic Assn., Assn. Mil. Surgeons, Sigma Xi. Contbr. articles in field to profl. jours. Office: National Institute of Arthritis Metabolism and Digestive Diseases National Institutes of Health 9000 Rockville Pike Bldg Room 4B-58 Bethesda MD 20205

REID, JUDY DOROUGH, electronics company executive; b. Pell City, Ala., Sept. 17, 1945; d. David Newton and Gaynell Whitfield (Braden) Dorough; m. Robert Gordon Reid, Feb. 24, 1979. Student, Samford U., 1963-64, Clayton Jr. Coll., 1976-78, Alverson-Draughrom Sch., 1964-65. Programmer, Ala. Farm Bur., Montgomery, 1967-69; system engr. Central Computer Service, Birmingham, Ala., 1969-73; asst. v.p. Bandata Inc., Atlanta, 1973-81; programmer analyst ETS, Atlanta, 1981-82; asst. v.p. NWGA Computer Service, Calhoun, Ga., 1982-86; programmer analyst Electronic Processors Ltd., Birmingham, 1986—. Designer data processing system of automated banking, 1973. Mem. Nat. Assn. Female Execs. Baptist. Home: 3210 9th Ave N Pell City AL 35125 Office: Electronic Processors Ltd 1225 5th Ave N Birmingham AL 35203

REID, KATHERINE LOUISE, art educational supervisor; b. Port Arthur, Tex., Mar. 25, 1941; d. Clifton Commodore and Helen Ross (Moore) Reid. B.A., Baylor U., 1963; postgrad. in design and illustration, Kans. City Art Inst., 1964; M.Ed., U. Houston, 1973; cert. supervision U. Houston-Clear Lake City, 1980; postgrad. San Jacinto Coll., 1982. Cert. art educator, profl. supr., Tex. Litho reproduction artist Hallmark Cards, Kansas City, Mo., 1963-64; tchr. art high sch. Pasadena Ind. Sch. Dist. (Tex.), 1964-77, supr. art, gifted and talented and photography, 1977-85; supr. art and photography InterAct, 1985—; head crafts, asst. dir. dir. winter discovery program-ski camp Cheley Colo. Camps, Denver, Estes Park, 1967-74; staff artist, media workshop, Tex. Edn. Agy., Austin, summer 1961; art enrichment tchr. Port Arthur Ind. Sch. Dist. (Tex.), summer 1961; head crafts Camp Waluta, Silsbee, Tex., summer, 1960. Mem. Friends of Fine Arts-Baylor U., Waco, Tex., 1981—; mem. Scholastic Art awards Regional Bd., Houston, 1978-84; bd. dirs. Houston Council Student Art Awards, Inc., 1984—. Named Tchr. of Yr. Pasadena Ind. Sch. Dist., 1975; Outstanding Secondary Educator of Am., 1975; Tex. Art Educator of Yr., 1985. Mem. Nat. Art Edn. Assn. (rep., editor newsletter 1982-85, chmn. supervision div. 1982-83, v.p. membership 1978-80, chmn. pub. info. com., regional chmn. youth art month 1980-82; regional chmn. membership com. 1976-78, pres. 1987—), Tex. Alliance for Arts Edn. (bd. vice chmn. 1984-86), Nat. Art Edn. Assn. (conv. com. 1977, 85), Houston Art Edn. Assn. (sec. 1969), Nat. Assn. for Supervision and Curriculum Devel., Delta Kappa Gamma (2d v.p. 1984-86). Baptist. Home: 106 Ravenhead Houston TX 77034

REID, LYNNE MCARTHUR, pathologist; b. Melbourne, Australia, Nov. 12, 1923; d. Robert Muir and Violet Annie (McArthur) Reid; M.D., U. Melbourne, 1969; M.D. (hon.), Harvard U., 1976. Pathologist-in-chief The Children's Med. Center, Boston; S. Burt Wolbach prof. pathology Harvard U. Fellow Royal Coll. Physicians, Royal Coll. Pathologists, Royal Australian Coll. Physicians, Can. Thoracic Soc.; mem. Am. Assn. Pathologists, Am. Pediatric Soc., Fleischner Soc., Brit. Thoracic Soc., Am. Thoracic Soc. Clubs: University Women's (London); Harvard (Boston). Office: 300 Longwood Ave Boston MA 02115

REID, NINA MAE BARNEY, county official; b. Escalante, Utah, July 7, 1933; d. Royal and Lilly (Mooseman) B.; m. Omer Arthur Reid, June 25, 1952; children—Terry, Kim, Wendy. Student Brigham Young U., 1963-64. Dep. county assessor Utah County, Utah, 1951-53, exec. sec. to bd. county commrs., 1967-69, county recorder, 1969—, also county boundary commr., 1979—; mem. Utah State Human Resource Steering Com., 1979-81; mem. Utah State Plat Standards Com.; mem. Utah State Cadastral Mapping Cert. Com. Past del., past corr. sec. Utah County Women's Legis. Council; active Springville Civic and Federated Faits Bien Club; past mem. Springville Coordinating Council; past pres. Springville City Council Club Pres.; past mem. Springville Art Bd.; past sec. Com. on Children and Youth; chmn. Mountainlans Area Agy. Coordinating Council on Aging, 1975-79; dist. Republican sec., 1956; Utah County Rep. sec., 1968; bd. dirs. Mental Health Assn. Utah County, 1980-83; Named to Outstanding Young Women Am., U.S. Jaycees, 1965; recipient Nat. Achievement award Nat. Assn. Counties, 1979, 80. Mem. Utah Assn. Counties (lady v.p. 1974-75, bd. dirs. 1975-76, 70-84, sec. human services legis. com. 1978-80, Outstanding County Ofcl. award 1981), Utah Assn. County Recorders (pres. 1980-81), Nat. Assn. Counties, Nat. Assn. Recorders and Clks. (chmn. nat. land-title records com. 1982—), Am. Soc. Pub. Adminstrs. (bd. dirs. 1978—, pres. Central Utah chpt. 1982-83), Nebo First Dist. Federated Women's Clubs (2d v.p.). Mormon. Avocations: oil painting; camping; golfing; writing poetry; hiking.

REID, PATRICIA MARY, marketing research company executive; b. Winnipeg, Man., Can., Nov. 7, 1929; d. Charles Lamont and Ethel Judith (Mason) R. B.Sc., U. Manitoba. 1953, B. Pedagogy, 1953. Research trainee Cockfield Brown, Montreal, Que., Can. and Toronto, Ont., Can., 1954-57; advt. research mgr. MacLaren Advt., Toronto, 1958-68; pres. Mktg. Insights, Winnipeg, 1970—. Contbr. articles to profl. jours. Bd. dirs. YWCA, Winnipeg, 1974-76. Mem. Winnipeg C. of C., Am. Mktg. Assn. (pres. chpt. 1973-74), Profl. Mktg. Research Soc., Can. Advt. Research Found., Mktg. Research Assn., Zeta Tau Alpha (pres. 1951-52). Anglican. Avocations: needle crafts; history. Office: Mktg Insights 1485 Portage Ave Winnipeg MB R3G 0W4 Canada

REIDY, MARY ANN, laboratory administrator, technologist; b. Tulsa, Okla., Dec. 29, 1939; d. Martin Joseph and Eileen Patricia (O'Flaherty) R. B.S. in Edn., U. Tulsa. Cert. technologist, Am. Med. Technologist, Am. Soc. Clin. Lab. Technologists, St. Louis. Lab. dir. Am. Assn. Bioanalysts, St. Louis, 1965—; owner, dir. Plaza Med. Lab., Bartlesville, Okla., 1973—. Democrat. Roman Catholic. Home: 4412 E Frank Phillips Bartlesville OK 74005 Office: Plaza Med Lab Inc 3850 E Frank Phillips Bartlesville OK 74005

REIER, REBECCA ANN, data processing executive; b. Miamisburg, Ohio, Aug. 29, 1948; d. Jacob E. and Ruth (Evanshine) Allen; m. Charles E. Reier, Oct. 20, 1973; 1 son, Benjamin. A. B.S., U. Charleston, 1979; R.N., Miami Valley Hosp., 1970; nurse anesthesia Ohio State U., 1973; postgrad. bus. adminstrn. W.Va. Coll. Grad. Studies, 1980-81. Cert. registered nurse anesthetist. Clin. instr. Charleston Area Med. Ctr., W.Va., 1976-80; v.p. Med-Stat Mgmt. Assn., Charleston, 1979-81; pres. Med. Econ Inc., Greenville, 1981—; data processing cons. Anesthesia Assocs. Dayton, 1983. Chmn., Jobs Tng. Partnership Program, Greenville, 1984. Bus. Profl. Womens Club scholar, 1966. Mem. Med. Group Mgmt. Assn., Ohio Med. Group mgmt. Assn., Data Processing Mgmt. Assn., Assn. Women in Comptuign, Am. Assn. Nurse Anesthetists, Bus. and Profl. Women Club, AAUW. Avocations: Fishing; boating; travel. Home: 955 Sunset Dr Greenville OH 45331 Office: Med Econ Inc PO Box 460 Greenville OH 45331

REILAND, KATHLEEN ELLEN, airline administrator; b. Corona, Calif., June 26, 1956; d. James Allen and Barbara Ellen (Brunson) Reiland; m. Robert Samuel Beck, June 22, 1980. Cert. psychiat. technician, West Valley Coll., Saratoga, Calif., 1976; B.S. in Human Relations and Organizational Behavior, U. San Francisco, 1983. Psychiat. technician Atascadero State Hosp., Calif., 1976-77; with Pacific Southwest Airlines, 1977—, flight attendant, 1977-79, tng. instr., San Diego, 1979-81, supr. in-flight, Los Angeles, 1981-83, mgr. in-flight adminstrn., San Diego, 1983, mgr. in-flight systems and procedures, San Diego, 1983—, mgr. contract negotiations, San Diego, 1982-83. Mem. Los Angeles City C. of C. Home: 221 24th Place Manhattan Beach CA 90266

REILLY, ANN LYNN, horticulture executive; b. Bklyn., Jan. 24, 1944; d. Rolf Theodore and Marguerita Bernadette (Griffin) Bjornson; m. Thomas Jerard, Dec. 14, 1968; children—Patrick, Lynn. B.A., Rosemont Coll., Pa., 1965; postgrad. St. John's U. Sch. Bus., Jamaica, N.Y., 1966-68; cert. horticulturist, SUNY. Research chemist Charles Pfizer and Co., Bklyn., 1965-69; advt. exec. Costich & McConnell, Hauppauge, N.Y., 1975; owner, operator Hort. Communications, Massapequa Park, N.Y., 1976—; hort. photographer; pub. relations counsel Bedding Plants Inc., Am. Assn. Nurserymen, Council Tree and Landscape Appraisers. Author: Success with Seeds, 1978 (best gardening book of yr. award Garden Writers Assn. Am., 1979); Roses You Can Grow, 1978; Step by Step Guide to Gardening, 1986; contbr. some 200 articles on hort. to mags. Mem. Am. Rose Soc. (dir. 1982-85, outstanding cons. rosarian award 1979), Am. Soc. Assn. Execs., Nursery Assn. Execs., Mailorder Assn. Nurserymen (past exec. dir.), N.Y. State Turfgrass Assn. (exec. dir.), Greenhouse Suppliers Assn. (exec. dir.), Garden Writers Assn. Am. (dir. 1985—), Am. Hort. Soc., Bklyn Botanic Garden (instr.), N.Y. Botanic Garden (dir.), Planting Fields Arboretum (instr.), L.I. Flower Growers Assn. (past dir.), L.I. Hort. Soc., Met. Retail Florists Assn. (past dir.), N.Y. State Flower Industries (former dir.) Am. Philatelic Soc., Met. Golf Course Supts. Assn. (hon.), Phi Theta Kappa, Beta Kappa Sigma. Home and Office: 210 Cartwright Blvd Massapequa Park NY 11762

REILLY, ANTOINETTE DIRAIMONDO, accounting manager, accountant; b. Bklyn., Jan. 21, 1956; d. Peter and Jennie (Palumbo) DiRaimondo; m. William Patrick Reilly, Nov. 11, 1978. B.S., St. John's U., 1977; M.B.A., Pace U., 1986. Staff acct. Deloitte Haskins & Sells, N.Y.C., 1977-79; sr. acct. Salomon Bros., N.Y.C., 1979-81, supr. acctg., 1981-83, acctg. mgr., 1983-85, group mgr., v.p., 1985—. Roman Catholic. Office: Salomon Bros Inc One New York Plaza New York NY 10004

REILLY, CATHERINE REGINA, information manager; b. Cooperstown, N.Y., July 22, 1949; d. John Patrick and Catherine Regina (Dempsey) Reilly; B.A., Coll. of Mt. St. Vincent, 1970; M.L.S. magna cum laude, Pratt Inst., 1972. With Chase Manhattan Bank, N.Y.C., 1972—, research supr., 1975, asst. treas., mgr. research library, 1977, 2d v.p., mgr. info. center, 1981-84, bus. systems officer legal dept., 1984, v.p., legal dept. adminstr., 1985—; chmn. Janus Seminar, 1983. Trustee Massapequa Pub. Library, 1985—, sec., 1985—. Mem. Nat. Info Conf. (mem. program com. 1980), Spl. Libraries Conf. (coordinator fin. insts. rountable 1979), Spl. Libraries Assn. (program chmn. N.Y. chpt. 1980-81), ALA, Am. Soc. Info. Sci., Assn. Info. Mgrs., Phi Beta Mu. Editor, Biz-dex, 1975-80; editor Bus. and Fin. Newsletter, 1980-82. Office: 1 Chase Manhattan Plaza New York City NY 10081

REILLY, JOAN, nursing educator; b. Johnson, Wash., May 2, 1931; d. Jacob and Vernice Althea (Marine) Steiner; m. Robert Joseph Reilly, June 20, 1960; children—Sean Michael, Patrick Joseph, Bridget Colleen. B.S.N., Wash. State U., 1953; M.S.N., St. Louis U., 1970. R.N. Staff nurse VA Hosp., Spokane, 1953-55, 1962-63; office nurse pediatrician's office, Spokane, 1955-56; nursing supr. Bakersfield Meml. Hosp. (Calif.), 1956-58; instr. St. Luke's Sch. Nursing, Spokane, 1958-60; staff nurse Ireland Army Hosp., Ft. Knox, Ky., 1961-62; instr. St. Joseph Sch. Nursing, Tacoma, 1964-65, 66-67, nursing service staff asst. St. Joseph Hosp., Tacoma, 1970; charge nurse St. Peter Hosp., Olympia, Wash., 1973-74; vis. nurse Tacoma Gen. Hosp., 1974-77; instr. Tacoma Community Coll., 1977—. Unit service chmn. ACS, Tacoma, 1977; mem. corp. Hospice of Tacoma, 1981—; vol. ARC, Karlsruhe, Germany, 1971; mem. Tacoma Zool. Soc., 1983; mem. Friends of Library, Steilacoom, Wash., 1983; mem. Steilacoom Hist. Mus. Soc., 1983; key person United Way, Tacoma, 1983-84. Mem. Wash. State Nurses' Assn. (chmn. Ways and Means Com. 1982-83, bd. dirs. 1981-84), N.W. Nurses Soc. on Chem. Dependency, Alcoholism Profl. Staff Soc. of Wash., Phi Kappa Phi. Clubs: Ft. Steilacoom Running, Irish Cultural (pub. com. Tacoma 1982-83). Home: 711 First St Steilacoom WA 98388 Office: Tacoma Community Coll 5900 S 12th St Tacoma WA 98465

REILLY, MAUREEN GRIFFITH, media specialist, educator; b. Jamaica, N.Y., Nov. 17, 1942; d. George Thomas and Joan Loretta (Curley) Griffith; m. Thomas Patrick Reilly, Nov. 18, 1967; children—Maryanne, Brian, Megan. B.A., Albertus Magnus Coll., 1964; M.S., Central Conn. State U., 1980, 6th yr. certification, 1985. Tchr., Levittown Pub. Schs. (N.Y.), 1964-68, Summit Pub. Schs. (N.J.), 1969, Wethersfield Pub. Schs. (Conn.), 1979; media specialist Hartford Pub. Schs. (Conn.), 1980, Lewis Mills High Sch., Burlington, Conn., 1980—, coordinator library handbook, 1981-85, coordinator video programs, 1980—; coordinator library skills curriculum Burlington Pub. Schs., 1982-83. Author: (with Betty Billman) Selected Resources for Teachers in Connecticut, 1980. Bd. dirs. Farmington Pub. Library (Conn.), 1976-80, Farmington Mus., 1976-80. Newspaper Fund scholar NYU, 1966; Pub. Sch. Coop. Libraries grantee Dept. Edn., State of Conn., 1982; Carlton W.H. Erickson award Conn. Ednl. Media Assn., 1983. Mem. ALA, Assembly on Lit. for Adolescents, Conn. Ednl. Media Assn. (sec. 1982-83, v.p. 1983-85) Albertus Magnus Coll. Alumnae Assn., LWV, Phi Delta Kappa. Democrat. Roman Catholic. Club: Red Oak Hill. Home: 48 W District Rd Farmington CT 06032 Office: Library Lewis Mills High Sch Route 4 Burlington CT 06013

REILLY, NINA-MARIE, illustrator, author; b. Bayonne, N.J., Nov. 6, 1954; d. Edward Joseph and Olga (Antuck) Reilly. B.A. in Theatre, Mary Washington Coll., Va., 1976; student in comml. art No. Va. Community Coll., 1976-78, fashion design Barbizon Sch., Chevy Chase, Md., 1980, Grad. in Lit., George Mason U., 1981-83, Profl. Acting Workshop, U. Conn., 1983. Supr., Wolf-Trap Filene Ctr., Vienna, Va., 1972-78; researcher Traffic Service Corp., Washington, 1976-77; free-lance artist, Vienna, Va., 1977—; illustrator System Devel. Corp., McLean, Va., 1980—; actor, designer numerous community groups. Author; (film script) Mary Who?, 1976; (play) The Light of Bethlehem, 1980; artist (designer dolls) Lovaboos, 1984; (film) narrator; YWCA-Please Get in the Water, 1984. Instr. CPR, ARC, Fairfax County, 1982-86; sponsor Greenpeace, Washington, 1984-86. Recipient numerous awards for art and illustration, most recent: Achievement in Art, System Devel. Corp., McLean, Va., 1986. Mem. Nat. Assn. Female Execs., Am. Theatre Assn., Nat. Trust Historic Preservation, Am. Film Inst., Vienna Theatre Co. (bd. dirs. 1982-86, sec. 1982-84). Avocations: theatre; art; sailing; swimming; tennis; reading; music. Home: 1842 Foxstone Dr Vienna VA 22180

REIMER, LINDA MARY, art dealer, jewelry importer; b. Elgin, Ill., Dec. 4, 1951; d. William C. and Marilyn S. Reimer; B.A., So. Ill. U., Carbondale, 1972; M.P.A., George Washngton U., 1975. Supr. med. programs Pfizer Med. Systems, Inc., Columbia, Md., 1976-78; mgr. med. ops. Pfizer, Inc., N.Y.C., 1978-81; pres. LMR Enterprises Inc., N.Y.C., 1981—. Vice pres. Sutton Area Community, Inc., N.Y.C., 1983—. Mem. Mcpl. Art Soc., Nat. Assn. Women Bus. Owners. Office: 60 Sutton Pl S New York NY 10022

REIMER, SUSAN MARTIN, lawyer; b. Long Beach, Calif., Aug. 7, 1953; d. Ival Eugene and Ernestine (Flinn) Martin; m. Robert A. Reimer, Aug. 21, 1982. Student Clemson U., 1971-73; J.D., John Marshall Law Sch., Savannah, Ga., 1979. Bar: Ga. 1979. Legal asst. Moss Creek Devel. Corp., Hilton Head, S.C., 1974-76, Sea Pines Plantation, Hilton Head Island, 1976-78, Bouhan, Williams & Levy, Savannah, 1979; assoc. Stephen E. Curry, Augusta, Ga., 1980-82; sole practice, Augusta, 1982-85; assoc. Paine, Dalis, Smith & McElreath, P.C., Augusta, 1985—. Pres., dir. Central Savannah River council Girl Scouts U.S.A., 1983-86; elder Covenant Presbyterian Ch. Mem. Augusta Bar Assn., Ga. Bar Assn., Ga. Trial Lawyers Assn., ABA, Nu Beta Epsilon (Frat. Achievement award 1979). Home: 2416 Cherokee Rd Augusta GA 30904 Office: 312 Wheeler Exec Ctr Augusta GA 30909

REIMERS, LINDA LEA, nurse; b. Loup City, Nebr., Oct. 6, 1959; d. Lee Harold and Phyllis Marie (Beran) R. Lic. practical nurse, CTCC Sch. Nursing, Kearney, 1978; student Kearney State Coll., 1980; R.N. Diploma, Mary Lanning Sch. Nursing, 1983. R.N., Nebr. Nurse's aid Lutheran Hosp., Grand Island, Nebr., 1977; lic. practical nurse St. Francis Med. Ctr., 1978-80; practical nurse Good Samaritan Hosp., Kearney, Nebr., 1980-81, staff nurse, 1983—. Mem. Am. Legion Aux., Mary Lanning Alumni. Republican. Roman Catholic. Avocations: bicycling; swimming; sewing; painting. Home: 310 W 27th St Kearney NE 68847 Office: Good Samaritan Hosp 31st and Central Kearney NE 68847

REIN, CATHERINE AMELIA, lawyer; b. Lebanon, Pa., Feb. 7, 1943; d. John and Esther (Scott) Shultz; B.A. summa cum laude, Pa. State U., 1965; J.D. magna cum laude, NYU, 1968; m. Barry B. Rein, May 1, 1965. Bar: N.Y. 1968, U.S. Supreme Ct. 1971. Assoc., Dewey, Ballantine, Bushby, Palmer & Wood, N.Y.C., 1968-74; with Continental Group, Stamford, Conn., 1974—, sec., sr. atty., 1976-77, sec., asst. gen. counsel, 1978-80, v.p., gen. counsel, 1980—, v.p. gen. counsel Continental diversified ops., Stamford, Conn., 1978—. Mem. ABA, Assn. Bar City N.Y., Conn. Bar Assn. Episcopalian. Office: 1 Harbor Plaza Stamford CT 06904*

REINA, DOROTHY LEE FORRESTER, ceramic company executive; b. Crockett, Tex., Feb. 10, 1932; d. Emmett Ray and Grace Lee (Hallmark) Forrester; children—Teri Nanette, James Dennis, Catherine Lee. Student Rice U., 1954-55, U. Houston, 1958. Sec. Engrs. & Fabricators, Inc., Houston, 1958-63; sec., office mgr. Interkiln Corp. Houston, 1963-70, ptnr., v.p. fin., 1970—; ptnr., pres. Reina & Co., 1983—; pres. Advanced Ceramics, Inc., Houston, 1986—; dir. various fgn. cos. Mem. Gulf Coast Council Fgn. Affairs, Asia Soc., Nat. Assn. Accts., UN Assn. U.S.A., Am. Ceramic Soc. Episcopalian. Clubs: University, Magic Circle Republican Women's, Warwick (Houston); Les Ambassadeurs (London).

REINBOLD, PATRICIA MARLENE, jewelry store executive; b. Goodland, Kans., July 1, 1953; d. Richard L. and Betty D. (Wright) Roth; 1 child, Kelli M. Reinbold. Student pub. schs., Dodge City. Salesperson (part-time) Roth Jewelers, Dodge City, Kans., 1966-72, Vernon Jewelers, Salina, Kans., 1972-73; salesperson, 1973-76, mgr., 1976—. Bd. dirs. Greater Downtown Salina Inc., 1981—, 2d v.p., 1985-87, promotion com., 1984—. Mem. Kans. Jewelers Assn., Salina C. of C. (retail activities com. 1984-85). Republican. Avocations: scuba diving; fishing; archaeology. Office: Vernon Jewelers of Salina 123 N Santa Fe Salina KS 67401

REINER, MARY ELISABETH, public relations specialist; b. N.Y.C., Apr. 19, 1931; d. Francis Drake and Ethel B. (Pleis) Wells; m. John Paul Reiner, July 27, 1961; children—Mary E., Clark B. B.A., Middlebury Coll., 1953; M.A. in Anthropology, NYU, 1955; diploma Russian Inst., Columbia U., 1960, M.A. in Pub. Law and Govt., 1960. Prof. govt. Notre Dame campus St. John's U., N.Y.C., 1960-62; editor UNICEF, N.Y.C., 1973-77; info. officer U.S. Com. for UNICEF, N.Y.C., 1977-79; dir. pub. info. Internat. Human Assistance Programs, N.Y.C., 1979-81; devel. dir. Nat. Child Labor Com., N.Y.C., 1981-83; dir. resource devel. Internat. Inst. Rural Reconstrn., N.Y.C., 1984—. Editor newsletter News of the World's Children, 1977-79, NGO-UNICEF Newsletter, 1973-77. Nat. bd. dirs. Girl Scouts U.S.A., 1975-81; chmn. devel. World Leisure and Recreation Assn., 1980-83; del. Care, Inc., 1979—; mem., head team of reps. at UN, World Assn. Girl Guides and Girl Scouts, 1969-78, hon. assoc. world com., London, 1978. Mem. Women Execs. in Pub. Relations, Pub. Relations Soc. Am. (chpt. pub. service council 1979—), Nat. Soc. Fund-Raising Execs., Women in Communications, N.Y. Jr. League (dir. 1969-70, chmn. sustaining mems. com. 1973-74). Republican. Roman Catholic. Home: 340 E 72d St New York NY 10021 Office: Internat Inst Rural Reconstrn 1775 Broadway New York NY 10019

REINER, VERNA LYNNE CAHILL, advertising executive; b. St. Louis, Mar. 21, 1954; d. Richard Joseph and Dorothy Jane (Deal) Cahill; m. Richard Edward Reiner, Mar. 31, 1972; children—Christopher, Angela, Michael, Douglas. Student, Washington U., St. Louis, 1974-76. Editor, Lee's Summit Jour., 1976-79, creative dir. group communications, 1979-81, v.p. advt. mktg. and media services, 1981-82; account exec. Minturn Advt., Kansas City, 1982—. Bd. dirs. Lee's Summit (Mo.) Safety Town. Presbyterian. Home: 4104 SW Pryor Rd Lee's Summit MO 64063 Office: Minturn Advt 1 W Armour St Suite 311 Kansas City MO 64111

REINERT, KATHLEEN HERRON, analytical chemist; b. Santa Monica, Calif., July 1, 1956; d. Thomas James and Virginia (Owen) Herron; Alumni scholar, Pomona Coll., 1974-78; m. Ted Reinert, Aug. 25, 1979. With Beckman Instruments, 1976, U.S. Borax Research, 1977-78; analytical chemist Burroughs Corp., Carlsbad, Calif., 1978-82, microelectronics complex, San Diego, 1982-86; sr. scientist Gen. Dynamics Convair div., San Diego, 1986—. Mem. Am. Chem. Soc., Inst. Environ. Scis., ASTM. Home: 4851 Regency Circle Oceanside CA 92056

REINHARD, LISA MARIE, market research analyst, consultant; b. Austin, Tex., Oct. 6, 1956; d. Erwin Arthur and Irene Cecilia (Salzman) R. B.S. in Mktg. magna cum laude, U. Ala.-Tuscaloosa, 1978; M.B.A., U. Ala.-Birmingham, 1982. Inside sales rep., estimator Watts Engring. Sales, Inc., Birmingham, Ala., 1978-79; market research analyst S. Central Bell Telephone Co., Birmingham, 1979-84; mgr. market research BellSouth Services, Birmingham, 1984-85, mgr. competitive analysis, 1985—; cons. Connections, Inc., Birmingham, 1983. Active Republican Party, Birmingham; com. chmn. Children's Hosp. Telethon Adv. Com., 1983—. Named Outstanding Mktg. Student (first woman), Birmingham Sales and Mktg. Execs., 1978. Mem. Am. Mktg. Assn. (sec. Birmingham 1982-83, v.p. membership and collegiate relations 1983-84, pres. 1984-85), Jefferson County U. Ala. Alumni Assn., Beta Gamma Sigma, Alpha Lambda Delta, Phi Eta Sigma, Zeta Tau Alpha. Roman Catholic. Clubs: Civitan (Outstanding Service award Met. Club Birmingham 1983). Home: 603 Forrest Dr Birmingham AL 35209 Office: BellSouth Services 2101 6th Ave N Birmingham AL 35203

REINHARDT, CINDY LOU, real estate development consultant; b. Ft. Worth, Apr. 2, 1950; d. Marvin and Marjeree (Downing) R.; B.A. in Polit. Sci., S.W. Tex. State U., 1971; M. Urban and Regional Planning, Tex. A&M U., 1975. Program dir. South/West Planning Assos., Bryan, Tex., 1973-75; community planner Houston-Galveston Area Council, 1975-76; dir. planning and policy devel. Houston Housing Authority, 1976-79, dep. exec. dir., 1979-80; pres. Creative Transitions Inc., Houston, 1980-81; v.p. Realm Devel. Corp., Houston, 1982-86; adj. prof. city planning Tex. So. U., 1979-81. Vice pres. Young Democrats Tex., 1972. Mem. Am. Inst. Cert. Planners (charter), Am. Planning Assn. (chmn. profl. devel. com. Tex. chpt. 1980-82). Home and office: 4235 Case Houston TX 77005

REINHARDT, REBECCA KATHLEEN, nurse; b. Oakland, Calif., Apr. 24, 1959; d. William Charles and Shirley Jean (Choate) R. B.S. in Nursing, Harding U., 1982. R.N., Ark. Med.-surg. and labor-delivery nurse Mercy San Juan Hosp., Carmicheal, Calif., 1982—, nursing preceptor, 1985—. Republican. Mem. Ch. of Christ. Avocations: team sports; needlework. Home: 8909 Twin Falls Dr Sacramento CA 95826 Office: Mercy San Juan Hosp Nursing 6501 Coyle Ave Carmicheal CA 95608

REINHART, KELLEE CONNELY, journalist; b. Kearney, Nebr., Dec. 15, 1951; d. Vaughn Eugene and Mary Jo (Mullen) Connely, B.A., U. Ala., 1972, M.S., 1974; m. Stephen Wayne Reinhart, June 15, 1974; children—Keegan Connely, Channing Mullen. Advt. copywriter Stas. WTBC-AM, WUOA-FM, 1970-72; asst. mgr. Ala. Press Assn., 1972-74; asst. to the editor Antique Monthly mag., 1974-75, mng. editor, 1975-77, editorial dir. Antique Monthly and Horizon mags., 1977—. Mem. Soc. Profl. Journalists, Am. Soc. Mag. Editors, Sigma Delta Chi, Art Table. Office: 1305 Greensboro Ave Tuscaloosa AL 35401

REINIG, ALICE BENITA, clinical psychologist; b. Panama, Iowa, May 23, 1932; d. John G. and Margaret (Schwery) R., B.A., Mt. St. Scholastica Coll., 1954; M.A., U. Denver, 1969, Psy.D., 1979; children—Deborah Ann Muenchrath, Jean Marie Muenchrath, Mary Carol Muenchrath. Lic. clin. psychologist, Calif. Tchr. Denver Public Schs., 1967-69, St. Mary's Acad., Denver, 1969-71; psychotherapist J.G. Benedict, Ph.D. and Assocs., Denver, 1974-79; instr. Chapman Coll., San Diego, part-time 1979-80, U. of LaVerne, San Diego, 1980; postdoctoral fellow Mercy Hosp. and Med. Center, San Diego, 1979-80; pvt. practice clin. psychology, San Diego, 1980—; mem. staff Grossmont, Alvarado, Mercy, Mesa Vista, Scripps Meml., Harbor View hosps.; cons. Interfaith Counseling Inst. Mem. Am. Psychol. Assn. (divs. 12, 29, 42), Calif. Psychol. Assn., Acad. San Diego Psychologists, Am. Assn. Pastoral Counselors and Pacific Region, Am. Assn. Sex Educators, Counselors, and Therapists, San Diego Soc. for Sex Therapy and Edn., Giving and Receiving Orgn. for Women. Club: Internat. Elite. Author: Self-Testing in Clinical Psychology Graduate Training Programs: Practices and Issues. Home: 434 8th St Del Mar CA 92014 Office: 4313 La Jolla Village Dr San Diego CA 92122

REINING, BETH (BETTY) LAVERNE, public relations counselor, executive, consultant; b. Fargo, N.D., Nov. 4, 1921; d. George Washington and Grace Emma (Twiford) Reimche; m. John R. Toohey, Dec. 12, 1942 (div. 1958); 1 child, Carolyn Ray Toohey Hiett; m. Jack Reining, Oct. 3, 1976 (div. 1984). Student U. Minn., 1940-41, Glendale Community Coll., 1967-68, Yavapai Coll., 1981-82, Ariz. State U. Account exec. Comco Pub. Relations, Phoenix, 1970-72; pres., owner, Janzik Pub. Relations, Scottsdale, Ariz., 1972-75, JB Communications, Phoenix, 1975-84, Media Communications, Phoenix, 1984—; cons. in field; hostess-reporter for KPAZ-TV, 1971-73; lectr. in field. Columnist Today's Newspapers, 1974-75, Ariz. Republic, 1968. Patentee tension twist footlet. Chmn., pres., founder Ariz. Youth Resources Inc., Phoenix, 1975; sec.-treas. Quadroma, Inc., Escondido and San Diego, Calif., 1979-82; coordinator clean air seminars State of Ariz., 1978. Recipient awards Ariz. Press Women, 1970-83; Good Citizen award State of Ariz., 1969; others. Mem. Am. Mgmt. Assn., Pub. Relations Soc. Am. (cert. cons.), Nat. Fedn. Press Women (pres.), Ariz. Press Women (pres. 1982), Phoenix Press Club, Nat. Acad. TV Arts and Scis., Phoenix C. of C., Cottonwood C. of C. (chmn. tourism, bd. dirs. 1985—), Gamma Phi Beta (thespian). Republican. Club: Ariz. Youth Resources (chmn., pres. 1975-76). Avocations: ice skating; hiking; collecting rocks and coins; sketching; dancing; travel. Home: PO Box 1822 Cottonwood AZ 86326 also PO Box 10509 Phoenix AZ 85064 Office: Media Communications 1000S Main St Cottonwood AZ 86352 also 5425 E Thomas Suite 173 Phoenix AZ 85018

REINISCH, JUNE MACHOVER, psychologist, educator; b. N.Y.C., Feb. 2, 1943; d. Mann Barrett and Lillian (Machover) B. B.S. cum laude, NYU, 1966; M.A., Columbia U., 1970, Ph.D. with distinction, 1976. Vice-pres. rock music promotion co.; assoc. prof. psychology Rutgers U. (N.J.); dir. Kinsey Inst. for Research in Sex, Gender and Reproduction, Ind. U., Bloomington, 1982—. Contbr. articles to profl. jours. NIMH trainee, 1971-74, grantee, 1978-80; Ford Found. grantee, 1973-75; Erikson Ednl. Found. grantee, 1973-74; Nat. Inst. Child Health and Human Devel. grantee, 1981-88. Mem. Am. Psychol. Assn., AAAS, Internat. Acad. Sex Research (charter), Internat. Soc. Psychoneuroendocrinology, Internat. Soc. Research Aggression, Sigma Xi. Address: Kinsey Inst for Research in Sex Gender and Reproduction Morrison Hall Ind U Bloomington IN 47405*

REISER, LYNN WHISNANT, psychiatrist; b. Charlotte, N.C., July 28, 1944; d. Ward William and Susan (Richardson) Whisnant; B.S., Duke U., 1966; M.D., Yale U., 1970; m. Morton F. Reiser, Dec. 19, 1976. Intern, Hosp. of St. Raphael, New Haven, Conn., 1970-71; resident in psychiatry, Yale U., 1971-74, asst. clin. prof., 1975-83, assoc. clin. prof., 1983—, assoc. dir. undergrad. edn., 1978-85, dir. undergrad. edn., 1985—. Diplomate Am. Bd. Psychiatry and Neurology. Fellow Am. Psychiat. Assn.; mem. Internat. Coll. Psychosomatic Medicine, Am. Psychosomatic Soc., Am. Psychoanalytic Assn., Western New Eng. Psychoanalytic Soc. Contbr. articles in field to profl. jours. Home: 99 Blake Rd Hamden CT 06517 Office: Yale Medical School Dept Psychiatry New Haven CT 06511

REISINGER, SANDRA SUE, journalist, lawyer; b. Washington Court House, Ohio, Feb. 27, 1946; d. Dale E. and Elinor Jean (McMurray) R. B.S., Ohio State U., 1968, M.A., 1969; J.D., U. Dayton (Ohio), 1980. Bar: Ohio 1980. Teaching asst. Ohio State U., 1968-69; with Dayton Daily News, 1969-81, asst. mng. editor, 1976-81; mng. editor The Miami News, 1981—. Mem. ABA. Office: The Miami News PO Box 615 Miami FL 33152

REISLER, HELEN BARBARA, publishing company executive, career counselor, television personality; b. N.Y.C., June 21; d. George and Elizabeth Lois (Schultz) Gottesman; B.S. in Edn., N.Y. U., 1954; M.S. in Edn., Reading and Critical Thinking, L.I. U., 1978; various certs., profl. seminars; m. Melvin Reisler, June 5, 1955; children—Susan-Jo, Karen-Jane, Keith James. Elem. tchr., N.Y.C., 1954-78; instr. Grad. Sch. Edn. and adj. lectr. L.I. U., Bklyn. Ctr., 1978; account exec. N.Y. Yellow Pages, Inc., N.Y.C., 1979, personnel mgr., 1979, adminstrv. dir., 1980-83, v.p. adminstrn./personnel, 1984-85, also dir.; staff specialist/market and sales support N.Y. Yellow Pages, Southwestern Bell Publs., 1985—; moderator weekly cable TV show N.Y. Bus. Forum, N.Y.C.; panel lectr. Career Conf. for Women, NOW. Recipient Ptnr. in Edn. award N.Y.C. Bd. Edn., 1984; subject of articles The Mktg. Letter, Sales and Mktg. Mgmt. mag., Nat. Bus. Employment Weekly, Wall Street Jour., Savvy. others. Mem. Sales Execs. Club N.Y. (bd. dirs.), Adminstrv. Mgmt. Soc., Execs. Assn. Greater N.Y., Nat. Assn. Female Execs., Women Bus. Owners N.Y. Club: NYU. Home: 47 Plaza St Park Slope Brooklyn NY 11217 Office: New York Yellow Pages-Southwestern Bell Publs New York NY 10003

REISMAN, JUDITH A., institute president; b. Hillside, N.J., Apr. 11, 1985; M.A. in Speech Communication, Case Western Res. U., 1976, Ph.D. in Speech Communication, 1980. Faculty dept. anthropology and sociology, 1981-83; research prof. sch. edn. Am. U., Washington, 1983-85; founder, exec. dir. research and edn. br. Inst. Media Edn., 1985—, lectr. Contbr. articles to profl. jours. Co-recipient Scholastic Mag. awards: Dukane award, 1982, Gold Camera award, 1982, Silver Screen award 1982, Filmstrip of Yr. award, 1981-82, Silver Plaque award, 1982; 1st pl. award local TV series, 1974; Best of 1965 award, 1965. Mem. AAAS, Am. Assn. Composers, Authors and Pubs., Internat. Communication Assn., N.Y. Acad. Scis., Soc. Sci. Study Sex, Nat. Black Child Devel. Inst., World Assn. Infant Psychiatry and Allied Disciplines. Office: Inst Media Edn PO Box 7404 Arlington VA 22207

REISS, DALE ANNE, real estate executive; b. Chgo., Sept. 3, 1947; d. Max and Nan (Hart) R.; B.S., Ill. Inst. Tech., 1967; M.B.A., U. Chgo., 1970; m. Jerome L. King, Mar. 5, 1978; 1 son, Matthew Reiss King. C.P.A., Ill.; cert. mgmt. cons. Cost acct. First Nat. Bank of Chgo., 1967; asst. controller City Colls. Chgo., 1967-70; dir. fin. Chgo. Dept. Public Works, 1970-72; prin. Arthur Young & Co., Chgo., 1972-80; sr. v.p., controller Urban Investment and Devel. Co., Chgo., 1980-85; mng. ptnr. Chgo. office Kenneth Leventhal & Co., 1985—. Fund raiser Grad. Sch. Bus., U. Chgo.; dir., sec./treas. Info. Tech. Research Center, Mus. Sci. and Industry. Mem. Fin. Execs. Inst., Urban Land Inst., Am. Inst. C.P.A.s, Ill. Soc. C.P.A.s (real estate com., savs. and loan com.), Nat. Assn. Real Estate Cos. (dir., com. chmn.), Chgo. Fin. Exchange, Am. Woman's Soc. C.P.A.s., Lincoln Park Zool. Soc. Clubs: Economic, Chicago, Chgo. Yacht, Exec. Chgo., Metropolitan. Office: 30 S Wacker Dr Chicago IL 60606

REISS, ELAINE SERLIN, lawyer, educator; b. N.Y.C., Oct. 27, 1940; d. Morris A. and Dorothy (Gever) Serlin; m. Joel A. Reiss, Sept. 1, 1963; children—Joshua A., Naomi L. B.A., NYU, 1961; LL.B., Columbia U., 1964; LL.M., NYU, 1973. Legal editor, mgr. dept. Doyle, Dane, Bernbach, N.Y.C., 1965-68; mgr. legal dept. Ogilvy & Mather, N.Y.C., 1968-72, v.p., mgr. legal dept., 1972-77, sr. v.p. legal dept., 1977-82, gen. counsel, 1982—, exec. v.p., 1984—; instr. NYU Tisch Sch. of Arts, 1981—. Named to Acad. of Woman Achievers, YWCA, N.Y.C., 1983. Mem. Bar Assn. City N.Y. (mem. corp. law com. 1981-85, chmn. advt. industry com.), Am. Assn. Advt. Agys. (chmn. legal com. 1979-81). Office: Ogilvy & Mather 2 E 48th St New York NY 10017

REITER, ELAINE MARY, state. ofcl.; b. Ellsworth, Minn., July 12, 1928; d. Jacob Nicholas and Esther Suzanne (Kappes) R; B.S. in Bus. Adminstrn., Marquette U., Milw., 1953; M.Ed. in Counseling, U. Mo., Columbia, 1967, M.P.A., 1976. Personnel asst. Square D Co., Milw., 1953-56; exec. asst. Psychol. Service Corp., St. Louis, 1957-63; services mgr. Psychol. Assos., St. Louis, 1963-64; counselor Mo. Employment Service, St. Louis, 1964-68; dep. dir. Mo. Office Aging, Jefferson City, 1968-72; cons. adult services to State of Mo., 1973-76; regional adminstr. Mo. Div. Family Services and Aging, 1977-81, service access mgr. Mo. Div. Aging, 1981—; bd. dirs. Mo. Green Thumb, 1978; mem. nat. protective services task force Adminstrn. Aging, 1982; del. White House Conf. Aging, 1971. Recipient various service awards. Mem. Am. Public Welfare Assn. (chmn. membership Mo. chpt. 1976-77), Mo. Assn. Social Welfare (dir. 1975-82, exec. com. 1976-79, chmn. aging task force 1975-80, chmn. Kansas City div. 1981-82), AAUW, Geront. Soc., Mo. Assn. Prevention Adult Abuse, Mid-Am. Congress Aging. Roman Catholic. Club: Lakewood. Office: Broadway State Office Bldg Jefferson City MO 65102

REIVITZ, LINDA, state official; B.S. in Polit. Sci., U. Wis., 1965, M.A. in Bus., 1982; postgrad. U. Mich. Survey Research Ctr., 1966. Caucus analyst Wis. Legis., 1967-68; asst. to pres. N.Y.C. Bd. Edn., 1969; legis. asst. to Congressman David Obey, Washington, 1969-74; exec. asst. to sec. Wis. Dept. Adminstrn., 1975; exec. asst. to sec. Wis. Dept. Natural Resources, 1976-77, adminstr. div. mgmt. services, 1979-80; sec. Wis. Dept. Employment Relations, 1978; student/adminstrv. asst. U. Wis. Hosp. and Clinics, Madison, 1981, asst. supt., 1982; sec. Wis. Dept. Health and Social Services, Madison, 1983—. Office: Wis Health and Social Services Dept PO Box 7850 Madison WI 53707

REMICK, LEE, (MRS. WILLIAM RORY GOWANS), actress; b. Quincy, Mass., Dec. 14; d. Frank E. and Margaret (Waldo) R.; student Barnard Coll., 1953; D.H.L., Emerson Coll., 1975; m. William A. Colleran, Aug. 3, 1957 (div. 1969); children—Kate, Matthew; m. 2d, William Rory Gowans, Dec. 18, 1970. Broadway debut in Be Your Age, 1953, other Broadway plays include Anyone Can Whistle, 1964, Wait Until Dark, 1966; films include A Face in the Crowd, 1956, The Long Hot Summer, 1957, Anatomy of a Murder, 1959, Wild River, 1959, Sanctuary, 1960, Experiment in Terror, 1961, Days of Wine and Roses, 1961, The Wheeler Dealers, 1962, Baby The Rain Must Fall, 1963, Hallelujah Trail, 1965, No Way to Treat a Lady, 1967, The Detective, 1968, Hard Contract, 1969, Loot, 1972, A Delicate Balance, 1973, Hennessy, 1974, The Omen, 1976, Telefon, 1977, The Europeans, 1979, The Competition, 1980, Tribute, 1980; appeared in TV prodn. Jennie, Lady Randolph Churchill, 1975; appeared TV series Wheels, 1978, TV mini-series Haywire, 1981, The Women's Room. Address: care Internat Creative Artists 8899 Beverly Blvd Los Angeles CA 90048

REMINGTON, ROBERTA ANNE, registered nurse, association executive, consultant; b. Springfield, Mo., Apr. 5, 1941; d. William Robert and Annabelle (Collier) O'Connell; 1 dau., Julie Anne. Student S.W. Mo. State U., 1959-61, Drury Coll., Springfield, 1965; diploma St. John's Hosp. Sch. Nursing, Springfield, 1963. Psychiat. nurse St. John's Hosp., Springfield, 1963-65; clinic nurse, asst. to gen. surgeon Ferrell-Duncan Clinic, 1963-67; Greene County maternal health nurse, Springfield, 1972-75; maternal-child health nurse Springfield Dept. Pub. Health and Welfare, 1975-77, community health programs coordinator, 1977-78; cons. maternal child health and child abuse City-County Health Dept., 1976-78; coordinator legis/econ. and gen. welfare programs Mo. Nurses Assn., 1978-79; indsl. hygienist Mo. Div. Labor Standards, 1980; adv. victim/witness assistance program, Springfield-Greene County, 1980; dir. med. affairs Am. Cancer Soc. Mo. Div., Inc., Jefferson City, 1980—; cons. CODAC, Springfield, 1974; nurse cons. Springfield Cerebral Palsy Ctr., 1976-77; owner The Crazy Quilt Boutique, Washington Crossing, Pa., 1971-72; conf. participant; guest lectr. child sexual abuse U. Mo., 1977—; cons. Founder, bd. dirs. The Family Ctr., 1975-79; vol. adviser for Mo., Nat. Found. March of Dimes, 1974-80, bd. dirs. Ozark Mountain chpt., 1972-76, service award, 1976; mem. state cabinet Mo. Found. March of Dimes, 1975-80; maternal-infant health task force Health Systems Agy., 1977; adv. bd. Springfield Park Central Hosp., 1977-78, Childbirth Without Pain, 1977-79; mem. Gov.'s Ad Hoc Com. on Sudden Infant Death Syndrome, 1977-79; bd. dirs. Ozark region Nat. Kidney Found., 1977-78; bd. dirs. Child Advocacy Council, 1977-78; dir. Park Central Found., 1978; adv. bd. Planned Parenthood, 1978, Battered and Abused Women, 1978; med. adv. bd. Cerebral Palsy of Mo., 1979; bd. dirs. Hospice, Jefferson City; bd. dirs. Central Mo., Mo. Assn. Social Welfare, 1982; bd. dirs. Springfield Civic Ballet, 1977. Recipient Curator's award U. Mo., 1959; Community Service award USNR, 1975; Disting. Service award Springfield Jaycees, 1976; named Outstanding Young Woman of Yr., Jaycee Wives, 1976. Mem. Oncology Nursing Soc., Mo. Pub. Health Assn. (dir., chmn. health care sect.), Mo. Soc. Assn. Execs. Office: Am Cancer Society Mo Div PO Box 1044 3322 American Ave Jefferson City MO 65102

REMLAND, MARJORIE ELLEN (MRS. KEITH P. REMLAND), communications company executive; b. Bklyn., Sept. 13, 1943; d. Murray and Ann Rae (Weisman) Block; B.S., CCNY, 1964; M.B.A., Fairleigh Dickinson U., 1978; postgrad. Pace U.; m. Keith Peter Remland, Mar. 5, 1967. Researcher, assoc. producer CBS News, N.Y.C., 1964-67; pub. relations assoc. Am. Lung Assn., N.Y.C., 1968-73, Warner-Lambert Co., Morris Plains, N.J., 1973-77; editor Morris Plains News and Warner Lambert World, until 1977; mgr. employee communications Schering-Plough Corp., Kenilworth, N.J., 1977-79; staff mgr. bus. market ops. AT&T, Basking Ridge, N.J., 1979-82; staff mgr. capital planning and analysis Am. Bell, Morristown, N.J., 1983; mgr. fin. matters orgn. AT&T Info. Systems, Morristown, 1984—. Pub. relations cons. Am. Occupational Therapy Assn., 1968-71, Assn. Children with Learning Disabilities, 1973; mem. Lincoln Park (N.J.) Environ. Control Com., 1970-73; chmn. Morris County (N.J.) Selective Service Bd. 37. Mem. Internat., N.J. assns. bus. communicators. Club: Ramapo Kennel (trustee). Home: 8 Brightwood Rd Lincoln Park NJ 07035 Office: 100 Southgate Pkwy NJ 07960

REMSEN, ANN TRAPANI (MRS. FRANK TALLARICO), educator; b. Bklyn.; d. S. James and Helen I. (Marx) Trapani; B.S., Bklyn. Coll., 1941; M.S., Hofstra U., 1959; postgrad. State U. Tchrs. Coll., Genesco, N.Y., 1959; Ph.D., N.Y. U., 1974; m. John Remsen, Nov. 1936; 1 dau., Charlene Remsen Haroche; m. 2d, Frank Tallarico, Aug. 9, 1967. Tchr., Hicksville Sch. System, 1955-56; tchr. West Hampstead Pub. Schs., 1956-58, remedial reading tchr. elementary grades, 1958-59; reading clinician Hofstra U., 1957-58; dist.-wide reading cons. elementary and jr. high sch. Syosset Sch. System, 1959-62, developmental reading tchr. South Woods High Sch., 1960; asst. prof., supr. student tchrs. St. John's U., Jamaica, N.Y., 1962—, sec. interdeptl. com. on linguistics; numerous lectures; cons. CAUSE, 1972-73; sec. Nassau Reading Council, 1964-65; tchr. Peace Corps Workers for Jamaica B.W.I., summer 1965; cons. project LAWYER, Westbury Sch. System, 1970—. Pres. Albany Ave. Sch. PTA, 1954-55; tchr. rep. PTA Bd., 1958-59. Mem. NEA, West Hempstead Tchrs. Assn. (past treas.), Internat. Reading Assn., St. John's U. Faculty Assn. (sec., dir. 1974-81), Kappa Delta Pi (adviser). Home: 63A Independence Ct Yorktown Heights NY 10598

REMSON, JANE FRANCES, charitable assn. exec.; b. New Orleans, Sept. 15, 1940; d. Marcel and Josephine Marie (Frey) R.; B.S., St. Mary's Dominican Coll., 1964. Intern, Mercy Hosp., New Orleans, 1964-65; chief Blood Bank, St. Joseph Hosp., Thibodaux, La., 1965-67; set up hosp. lab. Holy Child Hosp., Dumaguete City, Philippines, 1967-69, dir., co-founder Mt. Carmel Mobile Clinic, 1978-80; research technologist Tulane U. Med. Center, 1970-77; dir. Bread For the World, New Orleans, 1982—; mem. Mayor's Nutrition Task Force, 1983—; mem.steering com. New Orleans Pax Christi; tchr. hematology, hunger edn. Mem. Am. Soc. Clin. Pathologists, Am. Soc. Med. Technologists. Democrat. Roman Catholic. Home: 420 Robert E Lee St New Orleans LA 70124 Office: Inst of Human Relations PO Box 12 Loyola U New Orleans LA 70124

REMY, ELAINE VIRGINIA (GINGER), construction company executive; b. Pasadena, Calif., Apr. 27, 1951; d. Lawrence Edward and Virginia Lee (Davis) R.; m. Kenneth Anson Wood, Nov. 14, 1981 (div. 1983). Student U. So. Calif., 1969-71. Clk., Bechtel Power Corp., Norwalk, Calif., 1972-73; engring. aide, constrn. engr. C.F. Braun & Co., Alhambra, Calif., 1973-77; constrn. engr., estimator Fluor Engring. and Constrn. Co., Irvine, Calif., 1977-79; project engr. Koll Co., Newport Beach, Calif., 1979-83; constrn. project mgr. Equidon Contractors, Irvine, 1983-85; project mgr. Walsh Constrn. Co., Portland, Oreg., 1985—. Recipient Leadership award Elks, 1969. Mem. Bldg. Industry Assn. Republican. Presbyterian. Avocations: swimming; bicycling; landscaping; photography; travel. Home: 3023 SE Olsen St Milwaukie OR 97222 Office: Walsh Constrn Co 3015 SW 1st Ave Portland OR 97201

REMY, IRMA MARJORIE, educational administrator; b. Maywood, Calif., Oct. 16, 1925; d. Charles Henry and Irma (Page) Bowers; m. Edward Earl Remy, Oct. 3, 1946; children—Christine Ann, Shelly Katherine. Student U. Redlands, 1943, Long Beach City Coll., 1959-60, Pepperdine U., 1974; B.A., Calif. State U.-Long Beach, 1963; M.A., 1966. Cert. secondary tchr., adminstr. Calif. Tchr. home econs. Westminster High Sch., Huntington Beach (Calif.) Union High Sch. Dist., 1963-72, dept. chmn., 1967-72, dist. dept. chmn., 1970-72; coordinator home econs., women's occupations Orange County Dept. Edn., Santa Ana, Calif., 1972-73; regional supr. home econs. vocat. cons. Specialist Regional Occupational Ctrs./Programs, State of Calif. Dept. Edn., Los Angeles, 1973-82, regional coordinator (so. region) vocat. edn., 1982-84; asst. supt. So. Calif. Regional Occupational Ctr., Torrance, 1984—. Mem. Am. Vocat. Assn., Calif. Assn. Vocat. Adminstrs., Calif. Assn. Regional Occupational Programs/Ctrs., So. Calif. Council Vocat. Edn. Adminstrs., Calif. Assn. Vocat. Educators. Democrat. Mem. Ch. Jesus Christ of Latter-day Saints. Office: 2300 Crenshaw Blvd Torrance CA 90501

RENAKER, JANE ANN, golf course executive; b. Dayton, Ohio, Dec. 3, 1922; d. Herbert Elmer and Luella Carolyn (Burkhardt) Quiggle; m. Allan Frazier Renaker, Jan. 24, 1942 (dec. Mar. 1984); children—Carol Anne, Joyce Lynn, Stephen Allan. Grad. high sch., Dayton, Ohio. Bookkeeper, Delco Products, Dayton, 1941-43; bookkeeper, part owner Al's Super Service & Used Cars, Dayton, 1945-56, Renaker Chevrolet & Oldsmoble, Brookville, Ind., 1956-67; operator, part owner Brook Hill Golf Course, Brookville, 1973-83, sole owner, 1983—. Republican. Methodist. Club: Delta Theta Tau. Lodge: Eastern Star (page 1957). Home and Office: Rural Route 3 Box 120 Brookville IN 47012

RENDA, SHARON LEE, personnel placement service executive; b. Rochester, N.Y., Dec. 11, 1946; d. Richard Garrett and Elaine Frances (Robinson) Blake; m. Vincent G. Renda, Aug. 16, 1968 (div. 1984). Diploma Katharine Gibbs Sch., Boston, 1967; student Nazareth Coll., 1977-79. Legal sec. Salzman & Salzman, Rochester, 1967-68; adminstrv. asst. Friden div. Singer Co., Rochester, 1968-69; office mgr. Internat. Sales Mgmt., Miami, Fla., 1969-71; v.p., gen. mgr. Plaza Careers, Inc., Rochester, 1971-80; bus. affairs mgr. Gates Music, Inc., Rochester, 1980-81; pres., owner Renda Personnel Cons., Inc., Rochester, 1981—. Mem. adv. bd. Alfred State Coll., 1984—, Greece Central Schs., 1985—, Salvation Army, 1984—, Blue Cross, 1984—, Better Bus. Bur., 1981—. Mem. Nat. Personnel Cons., Inc., Internat. Assn. Personnel Women, Am. Soc. Personnel Adminstrn., Rochester Temporary Services Assn., Rochester Sales and Mktg. Execs. Club, Rochester C. of C., Adminstrv. Mgmt. Soc. (pres. 1984-86), Rochester Women's Network. Republican. Presbyterian. Club: Jewish Community Ctr. Avocations: tennis; jogging; gourmet cooking. Home: 639 French Rd Rochester NY 14618 Office: 401 Triangle Bldg 335 Main St E Rochester NY 14604

RENDL-MARCUS, MILDRED, artist, economist; b. N.Y.C., May 30, 1928; d. Julius and Agnes (Hokr) Rendl; B.S., N.Y. U., 1948, M.B.A., 1950; Ph.D. (Dean Bernice Brown Cronkhite fellow 1950-51), Radcliffe Coll., 1954; m. Edward Marcus, Aug. 10, 1956. Economist, Gen. Electric Co., 1953-56, Bigelow-Sanford Carpet Co., Inc., 1956-58; lectr. econs. evening sessions CCNY, 1953-58; research investment problems in tropical Africa, 1958-59; instr. econs. Hunter Coll., 1959-60; lectr. econs. Columbia U., 1960-61; research econ. devel. Nigeria, W. Africa, 1961-63; sr. economist Internat. div. Nat. Indsl. Conf. Bd., 1963-66; asst. prof. Grad. Sch. Bus. Adminstrn., Pace Coll., 1964-66; assoc. prof. Borough of Manhattan Community Coll., City U. N.Y., 1966-71, prof., 1972-85; vis. prof. internat. econs. Fla. Internat. U., Miami, 1986 prin. MRM Assos., Rendl Fine Art; corp. art econ. cons.; participant Internat. Economical Meeting, Amsterdam, 1968, Econs. of Fine Arts in Age of Tech., 1984. One man oil animal abstracts shows: Carriage Barn, New Canaan, Faber Birren Oil Show, 1985; exhibited New Canaan Art Show, 1982, 83, 84, New Canaan Soc. for Arts Ann., 1983, Miami Beach, 1986, Dade County, 1986. Bd. dirs. N.Y.C. Council on Econ. Edn., 1970—. Recipient Disting. Service award CUNY, 1985. Fellow Gerontol. Assn.; mem. Am. (vice chmn. ann. meeting 1973), Met. (sec. 1954-56) econ. assns., Indsl. Relations Research Assn., Allied Social Sci. Assn. (vice chmn. conv. 1973), Womens Econ. Round Table (N.Y.C. Women in the Arts award 1986), AAUW, N.Y. U. Grad. Sch. Bus. Adminstrn. Alumni (sec. 1956-58). , Clubs: Radcliffe; Women's City (art and landmarks com.). Author: (with husband) Investment and Development of Tropical Africa, 1959, International Trade and Finance, 1965, Monetary and Banking Theory, 1965; Economics, 1969; (with husband) Principles of Economics, 1969; Economic Progress and the Developing World, 1970; Economics, 1978; also monographs and articles in field. Econ. and internat. research on industrialization less developed areas, internat. debtor nations and workability of buffer stock schemes. Home: 928 West Rd New Canaan CT 06840 Office: PO Box 814 New Canaan CT 06840 also 7441 Wayne Ave Miami Beach FL 33141

RENDON, JOSEFINA MUNIZ, municipal court judge; b. San Juan P.R., June 17, 1949; d. Francisco V. Muniz-Souffront and Gloria (Vazquez de) Muniz; m. Ruben Rendon, June 29, 1974; children—Daniel Ruben, Raquel Ischel. Student U. Tex., 1967-68, Universidad Interamericana, San Juan, P.R., 1968-69; B.A., U. Houston, 1972, J.D., 1976. Bar: Tex. 1977, U.S. Dist. Ct. (so. dist.) Tex. 1979, U.S. Ct. Appeals (5th cir.) 1979. Legal process clk. Pub. Defenders Office, San Francisco, 1977-78; ptnr. firm Rendon & Rendon, Houston, 1978-83; mcpl. ct. judge City of Houston, 1983—; commr., vice-chmn. Civil Service Commn., Houston, 1980-83. Newspaper legal columnist, La Voz de Houston, 1980-83. Bd. dirs. Pub. Interest Advocacy Council, Houston, 1979-81; pres. SER-Jobs for Progress Bd., Houston, 1983—; dist. legal adviser League United Latin Am. Citizens, Houston, 1980-83. Recipient awards League United Latin Am. Citizens; Outstanding Service to Community award City of Houston, 1983; named One of Houston's Most Interesting People, Houston City Mag., 1984. Mem. Am. Judges Assn., Tex. Mcpl. Cts. Assn., ABA, Tex. Bar Assn., Houston Bar Assn., Mex.-Am. Bar Assn., Am. Immigration Lawyers Assn., Puerto Rican Assn. Office: Mcpl Ct 1400 Lubbock St Houston TX 77002

RENEGAR, EDITH MAURINE, insurance company executive; b. Knoxville, Feb. 8, 1936; d. John Leonard and Mary Mildred (Dillon) DeLozier; m. Douglas Renegar, Dec. 27, 1957 (dec. Oct. 1978); children—Douglas Christian, David Leigh, James Andrew, Marnie Paige. Student U. Tenn.-Chatanooga, 1955; bus. cert. McKenzie Bus. Coll., 1957. Sec., Burlington Industries, Greensboro, N.C., 1957-58; sec. Duke U., Durham, N.C., 1958-59; sales rep. Life of Va., Greenville, 1983-84; spl. agt. Northwestern Mut. Life Ins. Co., Greenville, 1984—. Mem. Nat. Assn. Life Underwriters. City of Chattanooga scholar, 1954-56. Republican. Presbyterian. Club: Foxcroft Garden. Avocations: gardening; yoga; sewing. Home: 18 Red Fox Dr Greenville SC 29615 Office: Northwestern Mut Life Ins Co 7N Laurens St Greenville SC 29602

RENEHAN, KAREN MARIE, nurse; b. Providence, Jan. 11, 1956; d. Dante and Dorothy Ellen (Bonn) DiCaprio; m. Richard Joseph Renehan, Aug. 6, 1977 (div.); 1 son, Matthew David. Assoc. in Sci. and Nursing, Community Coll. R.I., 1981; B.S.N., R.I. Coll., 1987. Nurses aide Kent County Hosp., Warwick. R.I., 1973-76, nursing asst., 1976-81; staff nurse Roger William's Hosp., Providence, 1981, Kent County Hosp., Warwick, R.I., 1981—. Republican. Roman Catholic. Avocations: reading; baseball; basketball; swimming; bike riding; football; skiing. Home: 15 Janet Dr West Warwick RI 02893 Office: Kent County Meml Hosp 455 Tall Gate Rd Warwick RI 02886

RENNER, BRENDA LORETTA, auto dealer; b. Greeneville, Tenn., July 22, 1950; d. U.L. and Ida Belle (Blazer) R. B.S., East Tenn. State U., 1972, postgrad., 1984-85. Bus. mgr. Cocke County Meml. Hosp., Newport, Tenn., 1973-76; bus. mgr. and corp. sec.-treas. Bewley Oldsmobile-Subaru, Inc., Greeneville, Tenn., 1976—. Dir. Tenn.-Caroline Fair Assn., Newport, Tenn., 1983-86. Named Bus. Mgr. of Quar., Subaru Top Achievement Recognition Club, 1982. Mem. Nat. Assn. Female Execs., Oldsmobile Bus. Mgmt. Club, Jaycees (v.p. Cocke County 1985-86), Epsilon Sigma Alpha (Tenn. state pres. 1986-87, named Outstanding Mem. 1981, 84). Republican. Baptist. Avocations: travel; reading. Home: Route 2 Box 195 Parrottsville TN 37843 Office: Bewley Oldsmobile-Subaru Inc 535 Tusculum Blvd Greeneville TN 37743

RENNER, MELINDA LEE SWETT, association executive; b. Atlanta, May 12, 1946; d. James Alexander and Dorothy Ellen (Sigman) Lee; m. Roy Albert Swett, Jr., July 5, 1965 (div. 1970); m. Stephen Alan Renner, Aug. 4, 1979 (div. 1984). Student Ga. So. Coll., 1965-66; B.A., Emory U., 1968, M. Librarianship, 1969; specialist in library service Atlanta U., 1976; postgrad. in legal research and info. sci. Catholic U., 1980-82. Group chief supr. So. Bell Tel.&Tel., Atlanta, 1967-69; serials and microforms librarian DeKalb Community Coll., 1969-75, pub. services librarian, 1975-77; asst. to program coordinator U.S. Nat. Commn. on Library and Info. Sci., White House Conf. on Libraries and Info. Services, Washington, 1977; library program officer tng. and profl. devel. USIA, Washington, 1977-81; tech. info. cons. Nat. Council on Radiation Protection and Measurements, Bethesda, Md., 1981; library and tech. info. mgr. Atomic Indsl. Forum, Washington, 1981-82, assoc. tech. mgr. Nat. Environ. Studies Project, 1982-85, mgr. spl. projects, 1985—; editor NESP Newsletter, 1982—; contbg. editor Pub. Utilities Reports/Analysis of Investor-Owned Electric and Gas Utilities, 1985. Contbr. articles to library jours. Mem. adv. bd. Friends of Libraries, Washington, 1981-83; advisor House of Ruth, home for battered women, Washington 1982-85; mem. adv. bd. Sta. WETA-TV, Atlanta, 1975-77; active Arthritis Found., Columbia Hist. Soc. Ga. State Regents scholar, 1964; Emory U. scholar, 1966-68; HEW fellow, 1968-69, 75. Mem. D.C. Library Assn. (exec. bd. 1982-84, treas. 1982-84), ALA (standing com. on library edn. 1980-81, chmn. Nat. Library Week 1981-82), Soc. for Risk Analysis, Ga. Library Assn. (govtl. affairs chmn. 1975-77), Am. Soc. for Info. Sci., Elec. Women's Round Table, Greater Washington Soc. Assn. Execs., Women in Energy, Nuclear Energy Women, Spl. Libraries Assn., NOW, Nat. Abortion Rights Action League, Planned Parenthood, Mensa, Phi Beta Kappa, Eta Sigma Phi, Beta Phi Mu. Home: 3711 Windom Pl NW Washington DC 20016 Office: Nat Environ Studies Project Atomic Industrial Forum 7101 Wisconsin Ave Bethesda MD 20814

RENNICK, ANNE C., lawyer; b. Galesburg, Ill., Jan. 12, 1951; d. John Donald and Mary Jeanne (Verdun) Rennick; m. Charles A. Schoenheider, Apr. 25, 1981. B.S., U. Ill., 1973; J.D., John Marshall Law Sch., Chgo., 1976. Bar: Ill. Ptnr., Rennick & Rennick, Wyoming, Ill., 1976—. Pres., Willow Lake Village Homeowners Assn., Peoria, Ill., 1980; sec. Willow Tree Condominium Assn., Peoria, 1977-80. Mem. ABA, Ill. Bar Assn. (chairperson real estate broker-lawyer accord com.), Stark County Bar Assn. (Law Day chairperson 1977-81), DAR, St. Thomas Bowling League (pres. 1979), Jr. League of Peoria. Office: Rennick & Rennick Box 90 Wyoming IL 61491

RENNINGER, MARY KAREN, librarian; b. Pitts., Apr. 30, 1945; d. Jack Burnell and Jane (Hammerly) Gunderman; m. Norman Christian Renninger, Sept. 3, 1965 (div. 1980); 1 son, David Christian. B.A., U. Md., 1969, M.L.S., 1975, M.A., 1972. Tchr. English West Carteret High Sch., Morehead City, N.C., 1969-70; grad. asst. instr. English U. Md., College Park, 1970-72; head network services NLS, Library of Congress, Washington, 1974-78, asst. for network support, 1978-80; mem. fed. women's program com., chief library div. VA, Washington, 1980—; mem. Fed. Library Com., 1980—, USBE Personnel Subcom., 1982-84. Recipient Meritorious Service award Library of Congress. 1974; Spl. Achievement award Library of Congress, 1976; Performance award VA, 1982, 83, 84, 85, Adminstr.'s Commendation award, 1985. Mem. Med. Library Assn., (govt. relations com. ex-officio rep. to FLICC 1984—), D.C. Library Assn., NOW, Phi Beta Kappa, Alpha Lambda Delta, Beta Phi Mu. Home: 840 College Pkwy Rockville MD 20850 Office: Library Div (142D) VA 810 Vermont Ave NW Washington DC 20420

RENOUD, DOROTHY IDA, publishing company executive; b. Far Rockaway, N.Y., Aug. 11, 1933; d. Herbert William and Elizabeth (Fischer) Owen; m. David Francis Renoud, Jan. 18, 1958; children—David, Douglas. Sales service mgr. Reinhold Pub., N.Y.C., 1951-61; circulation dir. United Tech. Pub., Garden City, N.Y., 1961-80; v.p. Coastal Communications, N.Y.C., 1980—. Recipient Fraundorf award Long Beach Fire Dept., N.Y., 1979. Mem. Nat. Bus. Circulation Assn. (bd. dirs. 1981—). Avocation: camping. Home: 527 W Chester St Long Beach NY 11561 Office: Coastal Communications Corp 488 Madison Ave New York NY 10022

RENTER, LOIS IRENE HUTSON, librarian; b. Lowden, Iowa, Oct. 23, 1929; d. Thomas E. and Lulu Mae (Barlean) Hutson; B.A. cum laude, Cornell Coll., Iowa, 1965; M.A., U. Iowa, 1968; m. Karl A. Renter, Jan. 3, 1948; children—Susan Elizabeth, Rebecca Jean, Karl Geoffrey. Tchr. Spanish, Mt. Vernon (Iowa) High Sch., 1965-67; head librarian Am. Coll. Testing Program, Iowa City, Iowa, 1968—; vis. instr. U. Iowa Sch. Library Sci., 1972—. Mem. Am. Soc. Info. Sci., ALA, Spl. Libraries Assn., Phi Beta Kappa. Methodist. Home: 1125 29th St Marion IA 52302 Office: Box 168 Iowa City IA 52243

RENTERIA, ESTHER G., public relations company executive; b. East Los Angeles, Calif., May 1, 1939; reared by Daryl and Jane Locey; A.A., East Los Angeles Coll., 1958; B.A., Calif. State U., Los Angeles, 1974; m. Martin Renteria, Feb. 13, 1971; children—Christopher, David. Reporter, Alhambra (Calif.) Post Advocate, 1959-61; reporter, soc. editor East Los Angeles Tribune & Gazette, 1962-68; desk editor, newswriter Sta. KNX, Los Angeles, 1968; asso. producer, hostess-moderator Ahora! TV Series, Public Broadcasting Sta. KCET, 1969-70; public info dir. East Los Angeles Coll., 1970-83; pres. Esther Renteria Pub. Relations, Inc., Los Angeles, 1983—; producer Sta. KNXT TV Series: Bienvenidos and The Siesta is Over, 1970-74, ednl. cons. bilingual edn. series Juntos, 1979-82; sec., dir. Future Broadcasting Corp., 1980—; sec.-treas. Trojan Security Services, Inc.; instr. UCLA Extension. Bd. dirs. Plaza de la Raza Cultural Center; mem. East Los Angeles Service Center Adv. Council; bd. dirs. Bilingual Found. of the Arts, Cleland Ho. of Neighborly Service; bd. dirs. East Los Angeles Regional Occupational Center Adv. Bd.; public relations dir. Los Angeles Street Scene Festival, 1978—. Sec. Hollywood chpt. Hispanic Acad. of Media Arts and Scis. Mem. Hispanic Pub. Relations Assn. (sec.). Democrat. Roman Catholic. Club: Job's Daus. Home: 301 Dochan Circle Montebello CA 90640-2649 Office: 5400 E Olympic Blvd Suite 250 Los Angeles CA 90022

RENWANZ, GRACE DANIELLE, nurse; b. Bklyn., Aug. 30, 1923; d. Daniel F. and Mary Elizabeth (Madden) Luna; R.N., Somerset Hosp., Somerville, N.J., 1944; m. Roger A. Renwanz, May 10, 1947; children—Andrea G., Marsha E., Ingrid J., Mark R. Staff nurse Somerset Hosp., 1944-45; mem. staff Muhlenberg Hosp., Plainfield, N.J., 1965—, ICU, 1969-79, intravenous therapy specialist, 1980-81, sr. staff nurse emergency room, 1981-83, radiology nurse, 1983—; trustee Somerset Valley Vis. Nurses Assn., 1961—, sec., 1968—. Sec., Bound Brook (N.J.) Recreation Commn., 1954-56; v.p. Bound Brook Republican Club, 1962-64. Served to 1st lt., Nurse Corps, AUS, 1945-47; PTO. Recipient various service awards. Mem. Assn. Critical Care Nurses. Presbyterian. Home: 155 Farm Ln Bound Brook NJ 08805 Office: Muhlenberg Hosp Randolph Rd Plainfield NJ 07061

RENZ, FAYE WYRICK, canvas goods company executive; b. Peoli, Ohio, Sept. 1, 1931; d. Emmet Miller and Mary Isabel (Foster) Wyrick; m. Harry Oliver Neilly, Jan. 30, 1955 (dec. May 1976); children—Alvin L., Andrew W., Adam G., Alec H.; m. Charles Frank Renz, June 25, 1977. B.S. in Biology, Mt. Union Coll., 1953; postgrad. in med. tech. Los Angeles County Gen. Hosp., 1953-54. Cert. med. technologist Am. Soc. Clin. Pathology. Med. technologist Shadyside Hosp., Pitts., 1955-56; owner Neilly Canvas Goods Co., Pitts., 1976—. Republican. Presbyterian. Avocation: violinist in Wilkinsburg Civic Symphony. Home: 1527 Old Beulah Rd Pittsburgh PA 15235 Office: Neilly Canvas Goods Co 2709 Penn Ave Pittsburgh PA 15222

REPASKY, B. NADINE, temporary service firm executive; b. New Castle, Pa., Jan. 22, 1931; d. John Donald and Beulah Mae (Balmer) Bartlett; m. Robert Stephen Repasky, 1952 (div. 1961); children—Timothy Gene, Mark Douglas, Suzan Rene. A.A., New Castle Bus. Sch., 1952. With Martin Marietta Aerospace Co., Orlando, Fla., 1961-81, cost control analyst, 1975-81; owner, operator Temp World, Inc., Orlando, 1981—; del. White House Conf. Small Bus., 1986. Coordinator Salvation Army drive Martin Marietta Aerospace Co., Orlando, 1973, adviser Jr. Achievement, 1975; coordinator Foster Children's Christmas gift giving, Orlando, 1983; sponsor-coordinator Foster Children's ann. picnic, Orlando, 1984; speaker on success Women's Network, Orlando, 1985. Mem. Horizon Club div. Citrus Club Orlando (founding), Am. Bus. Women's Assn. (treas. 1983-84, chpt. Woman of Yr. award 1984), Nat. Assn. Female Execs., Better Bus. Bur., Orlando Area C. of C., U.S. C. of C. Republican. Methodist. Avocations: golf; fishing; biking; tennis; swimming. Office: Temp World Inc 7000 Lake Ellenor Dr Suite 123 Orlando FL 32809

REPETTI, SUSAN LEONARD, lawyer; b. Boston, Jan. 4, 1956; d. Jerome M. and Virginia R. (Curley) Leonard; m. James R. Repetti, Aug. 16, 1980; 1 child, Jane Elizabeth. B.A. in Econs., Wellesley Coll., 1977; student London Sch. Econs., 1975-76; J.D., Boston Coll., 1980; LL.M., Boston U., 1984. Bar: Mass. 1980, U.S. Dist. Ct. Mass. 1981, U.S. Tax Ct. 1982. Assoc. law firm Sullivan & Worcester, Boston, 1980—. Editor Boston Coll. Law Rev., 1979-80. Alumnae liaison Wellesley Coll. AC-CESS Assocs., 1981-85; mem. Wellesley Coll. Career Assocs., 1980—. Durant scholar, 1977. Mem. ABA, Mass. Bar Assn., Boston Bar Assn., Order of Coif, Phi Beta Kappa. Roman Catholic. Club: Hyannisport. Office: Sullivan & Worcester 1 Post Office Sq Boston MA 02109

REPKE, DONNA LEE, medical equipment company executive; b. Elizabeth, N.J., Jan. 28, 1954; d. William Otto and Dorothy Joan (Wilcox) R. B.S. in Nursing, Duke U., 1976. Staff nurse III, Emory U. Hosp., Atlanta, 1976-80; clin. specialist Datamedix, Sharon, Mass., 1980-81, sales rep., 1981, sales coordinator, 1982; regional sales mgr. Diagnostic Med. Instruments Co., East Syracuse, N.Y., 1982—. Mem. Am. Assn. Critical Care Nurses, Nat. Assn. Female Execs., Duke Alumni Assn., Delta Delta Delta. Avocations: tennis; reading; travel. Home: 6124 Wintergreen Rd Norcross GA 30093 Office: Diagnostic Med Instruments 6602 Joy Rd East Syracuse NY 13057

REPLIN, RICKI MARILYN, lawyer; b. Denver, Dec. 8, 1953; d. Phillip and Shirlee (Simon) Goldman; m. Norman Stanley Replin, Aug. 8, 1976 (div. Mar. 1978); m. Gordon Lee Miller, Apr. 19, 1986. B.S., U. Colo., Boulder, 1975; postgrad. U. Okla., Norman, 1975-76; J.D., U. Tulsa, 1978. Bar: Okla. 1978. Sole practice, Tulsa, 1978-79, 82—; assoc. James C. Pinkerton, Tulsa, 1980-82; mentor Tulsa Pub. Schs. Div. Instructional Support, 1981-82; alt. mcpl. judge City of Tulsa, 1985—. Bd. dirs., v.p. Domestic Violence Intervention Services, Tulsa, 1978-81; docent Tulsa Mcpl. Zoo, 1983—; vol. Tulsa Alliance for Classical Theater, 1982—, v.p., 1986—; mem. Tulsa Ballet Theater Guild, 1985-86; bd. dirs. Tulsa Area Women Owned Bus., 1986—. Recipient Am. Jurisprudence award in property U. Okla., 1976. Mem. ABA, Tulsa County Bar Assn., Assn. Trial Lawyers Am., Okla. Bar Assn., Okla. Trial Lawyers Assn. Republican. Jewish. Clubs: Leads (asst. coordinator 1983), Profl. Resources Orgn. (v.p. 1983—) (Tulsa). Office: Ricki M Replin PC 1310 S Denver St Tulsa OK 74119

REPLOGLE, LAURE LEE, funeral home executive; b. Altoona, Pa., Nov. 17, 1947; d. Warren Henry and Janet Ann (Cassidy) R.; m. Russell Howard Baker, Sept. 25, 1976; 1 child, Warren Russell Baker. A.Liberal Arts, Robert Morris Jr. Coll., 1969; B.B.A. in Mgmt., Robert Morris Coll., 1972; B.Mortuary Sci., Pitts. Inst. Mortuary Sci., 1974. Funeral dir. Warren H. Replogle Funeral Home, Altoona, Pa., 1974-82, owner, 1982—, prefinancing rep., 1982—. Compiler cookbooks, 1976, 77. Mem. Keystone Funeral Dirs. Assn. (chmn. Floral com. 1984—), Pa. Funeral Dirs. Assn., Nat. Funeral Dirs. Assn., Allegheny Luth. Home Women's Aux., Altooona Hosp. Women's Aux. Republican. Baptist. Club: Altoona Bus. and Profl. Women's (chmn. ways and means, historian). Lodges: Order of Eastern Star, Shriners, K.T. Women's Aux. Avocations: music; camping; physical fitness; walking; weightlifting. Home: 2700 W Chestnut Ave Altoona PA 16601 Office: Warren H Replogle Funeral Home 2636 W Chestnut Ave Altoona PA 16601

REPLOGLE, ROSE ELEANOR, oriental rug restoration expert; b. Omaha, Jan. 14, 1909; d. John Isaiah Taminosian and Ellen G. Taminosian Cook; grad. Omaha Tech., 1927; m. Fahy Norris Replogle, Jan. 10, 1931; children—Ronald, Richard Harold, Charles Martin. Sec. to pres. Nebr.-Iowa Grain Co., Omaha, 1927-31; apprentice to Ellen G. Cook, oriental carpet restorer, 1955-65; owner Replogle Oriental Rug Restoration, Kansas City, Mo., 1968—; cons./appraiser oriental carpets, tapestries; commd. to restore four tapestries U. Kan. Art Mus., Lawrence, 1977; restorer oriental carpets and tapestries Kan. City Club, 1958—. Mem. Outreach Council, Country Club Christian Ch. Mem. Women's C. of C. of Kansas City Mo. (sec., chmn. constitution/by-laws 1982, dir.), Smithsonian Instn., Art Study Club (1st v.p.), Friends of Zoo. Republican. Clubs: Soroptimists, P.E.O. (historian 1986), P.E.O., Kings Daus. and Sons Internat. (1st v.p.), Woman's City, Red Mitten Writers (pres.), Adult Friendship (corr. sec.). Address: 6821 Brookside Rd Kansas City MO 64113

REPPERT, NANCY LUE, county official; b. Kansas City, Mo., June 17, 1933; d. James Everett and Iris R. (Moomey) Moore; student Central Mo. State U., 1951-52, U. Mo., Kansas City, 1971-75; cert. legal asst., Rockhurst Coll., Kansas City, Mo., 1980; cert. risk mgr., 1979; m. James E. Cassidy, 1952 (div.); children—James E., II, Tracy C. With Kansas City (Mo.) chpt. ARC, 1952-54, N. Central region Boy Scouts Am., 1963-66, Clay County Health Dept., Liberty, Mo., 1966-71, City of Liberty, 1971-80; risk mgr. City of Ames (Iowa), 1980-82; risk mgr. City of Dallas, 1982-83; dir. Dept. Risk Mgmt., Pinellas County, Fla., 1984—; mem. faculty William Jewell Coll., Liberty, 1975-80; vis. prof. U. Kans., 1981; seminar leader, cons in field. Lay minister United Meth. Ch., 1965—; dir. youth devel. Hillside United Meth. Ch., Liberty; co-chmn. youth dir. Collegiate United Meth. Ch., mem. Council of Ministries; advancement chmn. Mid-Iowa Council Boy Scouts Am., membership chmn. White Rock Dist. council, health and safety chmn. West Central Fla. council, 1985—, skipper Sea Explorer ship, 1986—. Recipient Order of Merit, Boy Scouts Am., 1979, Living Sculpture award, 1978,79; Service award Rotary Internat., 1979. Mem. Am. Mgmt. Assns., Internat Platform Assn., Risk and Ins. Mgrs. Soc., Public Risk and Ins. Mgmt. Assn., Am. Soc. Profl. and Exec. Women, Am. Film Inst., U.S. Naval Inst., Nat. Assn. Female Execs., Nat. Inst. Mcpl. Law Officers. Author: Kids Are People, Too, 1975. Pearls of Potentiality, 1980; also articles. Home: Blind Pass Marina 9555 Blind Pass Rd St Petersburg Beach FL 33706 Office: 315 Court St Clearwater FL 33516

RESNICK, ALICE ROBIE, state judge; b. Erie, Pa., Aug. 21, 1939; d. Adam Joseph and Alice Suzanne (Spizarny) Robie; m. Melvin L. Resnick, Mar. 20, 1970. J.D., U. Detroit, 1964; Ph.B., Siena Heights Coll., 1961. Bar: Ohio 1964, Mich. 1965, U.S. Supreme Ct. 1970. Asst. county prosecutor Lucas County Prosecutor's Office, Toledo, 1964-75; judge Toledo Mcpl. Ct., City of Toledo, 1976-83; judge 6th Dist. Ct. Appeals, State of Ohio, Toledo, 1983—; instr. U. Toledo, 1968-69. Trustee, Siena Heights Coll., Adrian, Mich., 1982—; organizer Citizen's Adv. Com. on Crime Stopper Program, Crime Control, Toledo, 1981—; bd. dirs. Toledo-Lucas County Safety Council; bd. dirs. Vol. Am.; mem. Zonta of Toledo I; mem. Toledo Mus. Art; Internat. Inst. Toledo. Mem. Toledo Bar Assn., Lucas County Bar Assn., ABA, Nat. Assn. Women Judges, Am. Judicature Soc., Toledo Women's Law Forum, Ct. of Appeals Judges Assn., Dem. Bus. Profl. Women's Club, Mcpl. Judges Assn. Roman Catholic. Office: 6th Dist Ct of Appeals 800 Jackson St Toledo OH 43624*

RESNICK, CYNTHIA BILT, speech and lang. pathologist; b. Bklyn., Mar. 8, 1946; d. Murray and Helen Francis (Rubin) Bilt; B.A. cum laude, Marymount Manhattan Coll., 1976; M.S. in Speech Pathology, Tchrs. Coll., Columbia U., 1978; m. Jerry Resnick, June 17, 1967 (dec. 1972). Trainee in speech and language clin. pathology Marymount Manhattan Coll., N.Y.C., 1975, Columbia U., N.Y.C., 1976-77, Kennedy Child Study Center, N.Y.C., 1977, Beth Abraham Hosp., Bronx, N.Y., 1977; speech and language clinician L.I. Jewish-Hillside Med. Center, New Hyde Park, N.Y., 1977; tchr. speech and hearing handicapped Good Shepherd Sch., Inwood, N.Y., 1977-78; mem. staff Bur. Speech Improvement, N.Y.C. Bd. Edn., 1978; speech/lang. pathologist Lorge Sch., N.Y.C., 1978-80 Summit Sch., N.Y.C., 1980; speech/lang. cons. Forest Hills Nursing Home, 1980-85; speech/lang. cons. Coll. Nursing Home, Flushing, N.Y., 1983-85; pvt. practice, Rego Park, N.Y., 1981—. Recipient hon. mention for acad. excellence in speech sci., Marymount Manhattan Coll., N.Y.C., 1976; citizenship award Roosevelt Prep. Sch., Stamford, Conn., 1963. Mem. Am. (cert.), N.Y. State speech and hearing assns., Mass. Speech Lang. Hearing Assn., Speech Communication Assn., Internat. Assn. Logopedics and Phoniatrics. Address: 94-11 59 Ave Suite A7 Rego Park NY 11373

RESNICK, RHODA BRODOWSKY, psychotherapist; b. Mar. 22, 1930; d. Isador and Rose (Wasserman) Brodowsky; B.S., CCNY, 1951; M.S., Queens Coll., 1973; postgrad. Hunter Coll.; m. Jack H. Resnick, May 21, 1950; children—Steven E., Caryn B. Tchr., N.Y.C. Bd. Edn., 1960-80, guidance counselor, 1980—; psychotherapist L.I. Cons. Center, 1973-77; pvt. practice psychotherapy, 1975—. L.I. Inst. Mental Health fellow, 1975. Mem. Am. Personnel and Guidance Assn., United Fedn. Tchrs. Home: 340 E 64th St New York NY 10021 Office: Bd Edn 347 Baltic St Brooklyn NY 11201

RETZER, MARY ELIZABETH HELM, retired librarian; b. Balt.; d. Francis Leslie C. and Edna (Smith) Helm; B.A., Western Md. Coll., 1940; M.A., Columbia U., 1946; postgrad. George Washington U., Ind. U., U. Ill., Ill. State U., Bradley U.; Ph.D., Western Colo. U., 1972; m. William Raymond Retzer, June 28, 1945; children—Lesley Elizabeth, Apryl Christine. Mem. faculty Rockville (Md.) Bd. Edn., 1940-47, elementary supr., 1945-47; mem. staff Peoria Public Library, 1957-63, homebound librarian, 1961-63; cons. librarian Bergan High Sch., 1964-67; condr. library sci. course in reference Bradley U., 1966—; librarian Hines Elementary Sch., 1963-66, Roosevelt Jr. High Sch., 1966-69; head media center Manual High Sch., Peoria, Ill., 1969-82. Instr. water safety courses ARC, summers 1940—; pres. women's bd. Salvation Army, 1952-54; pres. Peoria Nursery Sch. Assn., 1953-54; mem. legis. action com. Ill. Congress PTA, 1955-56; mem. Crippled Children's Adv. Com., Peoria, 1957-60; active various community drives; mem. women's adv. bd. Peoria Jr. Star, 1970-73. Mem. Ill. Valley Librarians Assn. (pres. 1971-72), ALA, Ill. Library Assn., Ill. Assn. Media in Edn. (certification com. 1973—), NEA, Ill., Peoria edn. assns., Ill. Audiovisual Assn., AAUW, Internat. Platform Assn. Republican. Presbyterian. Clubs: Order Eastern Star, Ill. State U. Adminstrs., Willowknolls Country. Home: 1317 W Moss Ave Peoria IL 61606 also winter residence 2221 Beneve Terr Sarasota FL 33582

REUBEN-LOCKERMAN, GENEVA LORENE, professional services specialist; b. Silverstreet, S.C., Nov. 4, 1928; d. James and Matilda (Stewart) Reuben; B.A., Benedict Coll., 1949; M.A., Columbia U., 1950, postgrad. Tchrs. Coll., 1982; postgrad. N.Y. U., 1951, 59; m. Joseph Howard Lockerman, June 10, 1953; 1 son, Joseph Howard. Freshman counselor Fla. A & M U., Tallahassee, 1951-53; service rep. N.Y. Tel. Co., 1954-55; tchr. Jersey City Bd. Edn., 1958-64; edn. specialist Jersey City Can Do, 1965-68; asso. dir. students Jersey City State Coll., 1968-71, psychologist-counselor, 1971-75, counselor I, 1975-85, profl. services specialist I, 1986—; lectr. Dartmouth Coll., Hanover, N.H., 1971-74, supr. counselors Dartmouth Edn. Center, 1975-76. Active, NAACP; chmn. bd. dirs. Jersey City Ednl. Center; chmn. affirmative action com. Jersey City State Coll.; mem. Jersey City Bd. Personnel Practices; bd. dirs. Action for Sickle Cell Anemia of Hudson County, Inc.; chmn. nominating com. of Sr. Companion Program of North Jersey. Recipient Mary McCleod Bethune award, Sojourner Truth award, 1983; Profl. Merit award Jersey City State Coll., 1985. Mem. Am. Assn. Counseling and Devel., Assn. Multicultural Counseling and Devel., NEA, Nat. Vocat. Guidance Assn., Jersey City State Coll. Faculty Assn. (sec. 1977-78), Assn. Counselor Edn. and Supervision, Assn. Multicultural Counseling and Devel., Assn. Non White Concerns in Personnel and Guidance, Black Women in Higher Edn. Democrat. Baptist. Home: 144 Bayview Ave Jersey City NJ 07305 Office: 2039 Kennedy Blvd Jersey City NJ 07305

REUTHER, ROSANN WHITE, advertising agency executive; b. Nashville, Nov. 24, 1943; d. Wiley Butler and Mildred Elizabeth (Little) White; student George Peabody Coll., 1961-64; m. Peter Martin Reuther, Oct. 3, 1964. Advt. copywriter WHMA Radio, Anniston, Ala., 1964-65, Bapt. Sunday Sch. Bd., Nashville, 1965-72, Thomas Nelson Pubs., Nashville, 1972-73; account exec. Holder-Kennedy Pub. Relations, Nashville, 1973-74; pub. relations dir. T. Nelson, Nashville, 1974-75; pension adminstr. Wood, Bateman, Nord, Assos., Nashville, 1975-76; owner, pres. In-Vision Advt. and Pub. Relations, Nashville, 1976—; lectr. Tenn. State U., 1978-79; part-time instr. Nashville State Tech. Inst.; faculty Tenn. Entrepreneur Forum, 1984. Worker, Carter for Pres. campaign, Tenn., 1976. Recipient Paul M. Hinkhous award of excellence in advt., 1974. Mem. Nashville Advt. Fedn., Am. Women in Radio and TV (pres. Nashville chpt. 1981-82, dir. dist. B, 1982-83). Baptist. Home: 1315 Haber Dr Brentwood TN 37027 Office: 20 Academy Pl Nashville TN 37210

REUTHER, RUTH ELIZABETH, author, ret. educator b. Gainesville, Tex., Feb. 27, 1917; d. Edwin Jerry and Grace (Patrick) Huffaker; A.A., Gainesville Jr. Coll., 1936; B.S., N. Tex. State Coll., 1938; m. J. R. Reuther, Jan. 26, 1941; 1 dau., Alma Grace. Tchr. English, Valley View (Tex.) Ind. Sch., 1944-46; tchr. Sam Houston Elem. Sch., 1957-58, tchr. reading and lit., Wichita Falls, Tex., 1958-74; ret. Author: Wife of Four Hobbies, 1956; (juvenile) Gray C. Circus Horse, 1970; (poetry) Texas is My Home, 1982; (history) A Century of Faithful Witness, 1983; also short stories, articles on visual tng. profl. jours. Mem. Visual Tng. Assts. Congress, Ft. Worth. Named to North Tex. Woman's Hall of Fame, 1985. Mem. Tex. State Tchrs. Assn., Circus Fans Assn. Am., NEA, Assn. Childhood Edn., Woman's Forum, Wichita Falls (pres.), Tex. poetry socs., Internat. Reading Assn., Wichita County Hist. Commn., Delta Kappa Gamma. Baptist. Clubs: Order Eastern Star, Poetry (Wichita Falls). Home: 4450 Phillips Dr Wichita Falls TX 76308

REVEAL, ARLENE HADFIELD, librarian, consultant; b. Riverside, Utah, May 21, 1916; d. Job Oliver and Mabel Olive (Smith) Hadfield; children—James L., Jon A. B.S., Utah State U., 1938; grad. in librarianship San Diego State U., 1968; M.L.S., Brigham Young U., 1976. librarian, Calif. Social case worker Boxelder County Welfare, Brigham City, Utah, 1938-40; office mgr. Strawberry Inn, Strawberry, Calif., 1950-65, Dodge Ridge Ski Corp., Long Barn, Calif., 1948-65; adminstrv. asst. Mono County Office of Edn., Bridgeport, Calif., 1961-67; catalog librarian La Mesa-Spring Valley Sch. Dist., La Mesa, Calif., 1968-71; librarian Mono County Library, Bridgeport, Calif., 1971—. Author: Mono County Courthouse, 1980. Recipient John Cotton Dana award H.W. Wilson Co., 1974. Mem. Delta Kappa Gamma (pres. Epsilon Alpha chpt. 1984—), Beta Sigma Phi (treas. Xi Omicron Epsilon chpt. 1981, 83-85, pres. 1982, 85—). Lodge: Rebekah (treas. 1973—). Home: PO Box

532 Bridgeport CA 93517 Office: Mono County Free Library PO Box 398 Bridgeport CA 93517

REVER, BARBARA L., medical educator, consultant, researcher; b. Bklyn., Dec. 18, 1947. B.A., Barnard Coll., 1969; M.P.H., U. Calif.-Berkeley, 1970; M.D., N.Y. Med. Coll., 1974. Diplomate Am. Bd. Internal Medicine, Splty. Nephrology. Intern, Los Angeles Community Hosp., U. So. Calif., 1974-75; resident in internal medicine, Los Angeles County Hosp., 1975-76, Kaiser Found. Hosps., Los Angeles, 1976-77; fellow in nephrology U. Calif., Los Angeles Sch. Medicine, 1978-80; spl. cons. Calif. State Dept. Pub. Health, summer 1970; research assoc. Dept. Community and Preventive Medicine, N.Y. Hosp. Coll., summer 1971; instr. biology and physiology Community Health Medic Tng. Program, Indian Health Service Hosp., N. Mex., summer 1972; asst. prof. medicine, asst. dir. renal transplantation div. nephrology UCLA, 1980—. Office: 230 San Jose St Suite 30 Salinas CA 93901

REVIS, FRANCES W., retired educator; b. Colbert, Okla., Dec. 10, 1910; d. Harvey R. and Ophelia (Dane) Williamson; B.S., Southeastern State Tchrs. Coll., 1931; M.A., Tex. State Coll. Women, 1950; Ed.D., Tex. Woman's U., 1958; m. Sidney M. Revis, Jan. 19, 1963. (dec. Aug. 1983). Tchr. home econs. Checotah (Okla.) High Sch., 1931-33; county dir. pub. welfare, Cotton, Logan, LeFlore counties, Okla., 1933-40; tchr. vocat. homemaking Colbert (Okla.) High Sch., 1940-57; faculty mem. Southeastern Okla. State U., Durant, 1958-76, asst. prof. home econs., 1958-65, assoc. prof., 1965-69, prof., head home econs., dept., 1969-76, prof. emeritus, 1976—. Sec.-treas. western sect., So. Regional Conf. Coll. Food and Nutrition Tchrs., 1957-76; bd. dirs. Colbert Hist. Soc. Named Outstanding Tchr., Southeastern State U., 1973-74. Mem. Am., Okla. home econs. assns., Okla. Edn. Assn., AAUP, Higher Edn. Alumni Council Okla., N.E.A., AAUW, Am., Okla. voca. assns., Am., Okla. Sch. food service assns., Ret. Tchrs. Assn., Durant Hist. Soc., Nat. Council Adminstrs. Home Econs. Soc. Nutrition Edn., Delta Kappa Gamma. Home: PO Box 70 Colbert OK 74733

REXIN, RUTH ANNETTE, social service agency executive; b. Fremont, Nebr., Mar. 15, 1951; d. Wilber Hoye and Marcella Mae (Stuchmer) Paasch; m. Samuel Arthur Rexin, Aug. 31, 1973; children—Joseph, David. Student Drake U., 1969-70, Kearney State Coll., 1970-71; B.S. in Social Welfare, U. Nebr.-Omaha, 1972, M.S.W., 1976. Social worker Archbishop Bergan Mercy Hosp., Omaha, 1972-74; social worker Luth. Family Services, Omaha, 1976-83, area adminstr., 1983-84, interim exec. dir., 1984-85, exec. dir., 1985—; exec. dir. Indian/Chicano Health Clinic, Omaha, 1984—; practicum instr. Grad. Sch. Social Work, U. Nebr.-Omaha, 1983. Mem. Incest Network, Child Abuse Council. Mem. Nat. Assn. Social Workers, Luth. Social Service Program Dirs. (treas. 1985), Coalition of Execs., Wildewood Edn. Assn., U. Nebr.-Omaha Alumni Assn., Chi Omega Alumni Assn. Lutheran. Avocations: golf; reading; bridge. Home: 6223 S 79th Circle Omaha NE 68127 Office: Luth Family Services 120 S 24th St Omaha NE 68102

REXRODE, SUSAN ORR, city official; b. Henderson, N.C., Aug. 16, 1950; d. Elmer Roscoe and Pearl Lee (Woodlief) Orr; m. Edward Douglas Rexrode, Jan. 1, 1979; 1 child from previous marriage, Tonya Carol Sharron. Student Western Carolina U., 1968-69; A.A., Louisburg Coll., 1970; B.S., East Carolina U., 1972, postgrad., 1972-73; postgrad. N.C. State U., 1979. Tchr. biology, chemistry Scotland Neck High Sch., N.C., 1973-74, Norlina High Sch., N.C., 1974-75; lab. technician City of Henderson, N.C., 1976-79, wastewater supt., 1979-80; wastewater supt. City of Havelock, N.C., 1980—; instr. Annual Wastewater Sch., N.C. Water Pollution Control Assn., U. N.C.-Chapel Hill, 1982—; instr. lab. ops. N.C. Div. Environ. Mgmt. and Coastal Carolina Community Coll., Jacksonville, N.C., 1982; co-developer various wastewater plant improvements, 1982-85. Active Girl Scouts Am. Teaching fellow East Carolina U., 1972-73. Mem. Water Pollution Control Fedn. (William D. Hatfield award 1984), Am. Water Works Assn., N.C. Profl. Wastewater Operations Assn. (chairperson 1984-85), N.C. Water Pollution Control Assn., N.C. Water Works Operators Assn. Democrat. Baptist. Avocations: personal Computing; hiking; reading. Office: City of Havelock Hatteras Ave Havelock NC 28532

REYES, CECILIA MAGSINO, auditor; b. Bauan, Batangas, Philippines, Feb. 28, 1937; came to U.S., 1972, naturalized, 1977; d. Dominador A. and Filomena (Caringal) Magsino; m. Nazario Diaz Reyes, Oct. 18, 1964; children—Reymel, Ruel, Rachel. B.S. B.A., U. Philippines, 1957. C.P.A., Philippines, Tex., Calif. Asst. mgr. Bauan Rural Bank, Inc., Philippines, 1958-67; instr. various colls., Philippines, 1958-72; acct. Nat. Health Enterprises, San Francisco, 1972-73; gen. ledger in charge Wells Fargo Bank, San Francisco, 1973-74; acctg. analyst Mt. Zion Hosp., San Francisco, 1974-76; cost analyst Schlage Lock Co., San Francisco, 1976-82; auditor Office Insp. Gen., HUD, San Francisco, 1982—. Treas., Philippine Am. Council San Francisco, 1981, Philippine Independence Com., 1981-82; bd. dirs. Filipino Adult and Youth Cath. Orgn. San Francisco, 1982-83; fin. com. Filipino Ams. of No. Calif., 1983-84. Recipient award of Distinction, Filipino Adult and Youth Cath. Orgn., 1982; award of Service, Filipino Ams. of No. Calif., 1983. Mem. Filipino Accts. Assn., (exec. v.p. 1976-81). Roman Catholic. Home: 112 Leland Ave San Francisco CA 94134 Office: Office Inspector Gen Audit Dept HUD 1375 Sutter St San Francisco CA 94104

REYES, MARCIA STYGLES, medical technologist; b. Winchester, Mass., July 15, 1950; d. Bernard Francis and Eleanore Cecilia (Nicgorska) Stygles; B.S. in Med. Tech., Merrimack Coll., North Andover, Mass., 1972; M.S. in Health Scis. (Kellogg Found. grantee), SUNY, Buffalo, 1977; m. Carlos Reyes, Aug. 5, 1978. Sr. med. technologist Symmes Hosp., Arlington, Mass., 1970-73; sr. microbiologist and serologist Mt. Auburn Hosp., Cambridge, Mass., 1973-75; asst. prof., clin. coordinator Quinnipiac Coll., Hamden, Conn., 1976-81; lab. supr. Canberra Clin. Labs., Meriden, Conn., 1981—; cons. in med. tech. Mem. Am. Soc. Clin. Pathologists, Am. Soc. Med. Tech., Conn. Soc. Med. Tech. (Speaker awards), Am. Soc. Microbiology, Am. Soc. Allied Health Profls. Home: 199 Dover St New Haven CT 06513

REYHER, REBECCA HOURWICH, writer, lectr., educator; b. N.Y.C., Jan. 21, 1897; d. Isaac A. and Lisa (Joffe) Hourwich; student Columbia U., N.Y. Sch. Social Work; B.A., U. Chgo.; m. Ferdinand Reyher, July 13, 1917 (div. 1934); 1 dau., Faith Reyher Jackson. Woman's suffrage worker for Women's Polit. Union, Nat. Woman's Party, N.Y., Boston, Chgo., and 30 states, 1915-23; feature writer Hearst's Internat. mag., Africa, 1923-24; advt. writer, editor J. Walter Thompson & Co., 1927-29; pub. relations asst. Joseph McKee (pres. bd. aldermen, later mayor), N.Y., 1930-31; cons., adviser Sears, Roebuck & Co., 1931-33; regional dir., profl., service, arts projects Fed. Works Progress Adminstrn., N.Y., N.E., 1935-37; asst. to dir., dir. motion pictures Info. Service, W.P.A., 1937-39; exec. sec., mem. bd. dirs. Dominican Rep. Settlement Assn. Inc., 1939-43; weekly broadcast City Fun with Children, Sta. WYNC, N.Y.C., 1945-49, also radio series Behind the Scenes with UN, 1946; mem. faculty New Sch. Social Research, N.Y.C., 1963-70; cons. Internat. Inst. Women's Studies, Washington, 1971—. Mem. flying caravan del. People's Mandate Com. Inter-Am. Peace and Cooperation throughout 17 countries, S. and C.Am., 1937. Author: The Stork Run, 1944; Babies and Puppies are Fun, 1944; My Mother is the Most Beautiful Woman in the World, 1945; Zulu Woman, 1948 (paperback edit. 1972); The Fon and His Hundred Wives, 1953; Search and Struggle for Equality and Independence; editor anthology: Babies Keep Coming, 1947; contbr. articles leading mags. and newspapers. Traveled South and Portuguese East Africa to gather material for books and articles, 1924-25, North Africa, Europe, Russia, Egypt, Greece, Turkey, Near East, 1929. Nigeria, Brit. Cameroons, 1949-50, South Africa, 1950-51, Belgian Congo, Nigeria, Uganda, Kenya, Pakistan, India, Ceylon, Europe, 1957, 13 African countries, 1965, France, 1966; contbr. biography to oral history project on personal experience in suffrage movement and Equal Rights Amendment from its beginning U. Calif. Address: care Jackson Fenwick Free Saint Inigoes MD 20684

REYMOND, SUSAN GEORGETTE, public relations executive; b. Milw., Mar. 28, 1941; d. Louis Anthony and Anne Victoria (Zayac) Reymond; m. Michael E. Fillichio, 1962 (div. 1967); 1 dau., Susan Georgette. B.A., Rosary Coll., 1963; M.B.A., Northwestern U., 1966; postgrad. Loyola U., Chgo., 1983—. Dir. fashion and publicity Hart Schaffner & Marx, Chgo., 1968-75; pres. Suzanne, Ltd., Chgo., 1975-77; dir. publicity and fashion Bonwit Teller, Chgo. and N.Y.C., 1977-79; pres. S. Reymond Enterprises, Inc., Chgo., 1979-82; dir. pub. relations Ritz-Carlton, Chgo., 1982—; instr. Internat. Acad. Merchandise and Design, Chgo. and Toronto, 1979—. Mem. hospitality com. United Cerebral Palsy Telethon; mem. telethon com. Muscular Dystrophy; publicity chmn. Nat. Com. for Prevention Child Abuse. Fellow Pub. Relations Soc. Am., Publicity Club Chgo., Chgo. Network; mem. Fashion Group Chgo. (dir. publicity 1980-81). Republican. Roman Catholic. Club: University. Office: Ritz Carlton Hotel 160 E Pearson St Chicago IL 60611

REYNES, WENDY WARNER, pub. co. exec.; b. Boston, Sept. 29, 1944; d. Philip Russell and Elizabeth (Patton) Warner; A.A., Conn. Coll., 1966; m. Jose (Tony) Antonio Reynes, III, Apr. 26, 1969; children—Jose (Tad) Antonio, Gabrielle Elizabeth. With Foote, Cone, Belding, N.Y.C., 1966-68; advt. sales rep. Cosmopolitan Mag., N.Y.C., 1968-69, Co-Ed Mag., N.Y.C., 1969-70; asst. product mgr. Avon Products, N.Y.C., 1970; advt. sales rep. Mag. Networks, N.Y.C. and Chgo., 1970-72; midwest mgr. advt. sales Girl Talk Mag., Chgo., 1972-75; div. mgr. advt. sales Pattis Group, Chgo., 1975-79; pres. Reynes & Assos., Inc., 1979—, Sales Unltd., Inc., 1985—. Bd. dirs. Multiple Sclerosis, 1974-79, St. Joseph's Sch. PTA, 1979-80, Marriage Encounter, 1976—; active Jr. League Greenwich, Conn., 1965-67, Jr. League N.Y.C., 1967-75. Mem. Agate Club (dir.), Advt. Assn., Women's Advt. Club Chgo. (co-chmn.). Clubs: Chgo. Advt., Wilmette Tennis, East Bank, Women's Advt. Chgo. Home: 460 Ash St Winnetka IL 60093

REYNOLDS, BETTY JEAN, government official; b. Portland, Oreg., Jan. 14, 1948; d. James Bossuet and Lois Pearl (Leatherwood) R.; m. Mark J. Waletich, 1966 (div. 1970); 1 child, Kari Lynn. B.S. magna cum laude, Oreg. State U., 1972; M.S., U. Oreg., 1973; cert. J.F.K. Sch., Harvard U., 1982. State affairs dir. Oreg. State U., Corvallis, 1966-72; grad. teaching fellow U. Oreg., Eugene, 1972-73; budget, mgmt. analyst exec. dept. Oreg., Salem, 1973-79; exec. dir. Govt. Ethics Commn. of Oreg., Salem, 1977—. Bd. dirs. Salem Tourism and Conv. Assn., 1984-85, Salem Non Profit Housing Corp., 1977-78; vol. Retarded Teens, Elderly Nutrition, Salem, 1974-75. Mem. State Mgmt. Assn. (bd. dirs. 1983-84), Council of Govt. Ethics Laws (bd. dirs. 1981-82), Am. Soc. Pub. Adminstrn. (cert. of award 1983), Salem Area C. of C. (bd. dirs. 1985), Phi Kappa Phi. Lodge: Zonta. Avocations: sports; arts; outdoor hobbies. Office: Oreg Govt Ethics Commn 155 Cottage NE Salem OR 97310

REYNOLDS, BONNIE LEE, publishing company official; b. Erie, Pa., Aug. 5, 1943; d. Aubrey Edward and Clara Sybil (Burns) R.; student Coll. of Sch. Ozarks, Point Lookout, Mo., 1963, 64, U. Ark., 1964, 65, 67, Ark. Tech. U., Russellville, 1967, 68. Bookkeeper, Cenla Community Action Com., Alexandria, La., 1966; bookkeeper Wheatley Brothers Auto Supply, Hot Springs, Ark., 1964; prodn. mgr. The Hot Springs News, 1969-79; office mgr. LaVilla Publs., Hot Springs, 1979-84, layout mgr., 1979—; ad compositor Sentine Record Publs., 1984—. Recipient Ark. Writers Conf. Alice Leight Night 1st prize, 1976; 1st prize Ark. Poetry Day, 1980. Mem. Nat. Fedn. State Poetry Socs., Poets' Roundtable Ark. (pres. 1982-83, Ark. award of merit 1985), Ark. Authors, Composers and Artists Soc. (1st prize for oil painting 1981, 83), Am. Acad. Poets, Poets Study Club Terre Haute. Baptist. Author: A Touch of Wonder, 1977; Hurry Dawn, 1984; editor: Where Did They Go? (poetry), 1984; editor Sun Rise Herald, 1985—. Contbr. poetry to numerous publs. Home: 107 Euclid St Hot Springs AR 71901 Office: Star Route 10 Box 490A Hot Springs AR 71901

REYNOLDS, CAROLE ANN, insurance agent; b. Torrington, Conn., June 16, 1943; d. Edwin Michael and Alice Elizabeth (Becker) Fadoir; m. David Roger Reynolds, Nov. 29, 1963; children—Deborah Rena, Scott Joseph. Lic. ins. agt., Conn. Clk., sec. Burns, Brooks & McNeil, Torrington, 1961-75, office mgr., 1975-81, asst. sec. to corp., 1977-79, sec. to corp., 1979-80; sec. part-time to corp. Harold J. Burns Realtor, 1981—; customer service rep., lic. ins. agt. DeVoe Ins. Agy., Danbury, Conn., 1981-84; comml. account exec. Peter M. Bakker Ins. Agy., Inc., West Hartford, Conn., 1984—; pres. Ins. Women of Litchfield County, Torrington, 1982—; pres. Ins. Women Club, Torrington, 1963-75. Active March of Dimes Telethon, St. Jude's Telethon, others. Mem. Nat. Assn. Ins. Women, Ind. Ins. Agts. Conn. (sec. 1979—). Club: Altrusa. Roman Catholic.

REYNOLDS, CAROLE LEE, lawyer; b. Washington; d. Vernon and Elizabeth (James) R. B.A., Am. U., 1971; M.A., New Sch. Social Research, 1973; J.D., Northeastern U., 1977. Bar: Va. 1977, D.C. 1978. Atty., FTC Bur. Consumer Protection, Washington, 1977—. Author: The Mortgage Money Guide; How to Advertise Consumer Credit. Recipient Meritorious Service award. Mem. ABA. Office: FTC Div Credit Practices Washington DC 20580

REYNOLDS, CHERYL LOUISE, lawyer; b. Burbank, Calif., Dec. 27, 1944; d. Frank Hale and Sadie Louise (Risien) Reynolds; m. Lawrence E. Myhre, Dec. 19, 1963 (div. 1973); children—Jeffrey Reynolds Myhre, Laura Louise Myhre. Student Calif. State Poly., 1962-64; B.A., Rutgers U., 1976; J.D., 1979. Bar: N.J. 1980. Assoc. law firm Wharton, Stewart & Davis, Somerville, N.J., 1979-80; ptnr. law firm Thiele & Reynolds, Somerville, N.J., 1980-82; group counsel Data Systems Group, The Perkin-Elmer Corp., Holmdel, N.J., 1982-85; counsel Concurrent Computer Corp., Holmdel, N.J., 1985-86; legal cons. C.L. Reynolds and Assocs., Monmouth Beach, N.J., 1986—. Author: Introduction to Computer Graphics, 1976; The Self-Executing License, 1984; editor: Rutgers Jour. Computers and the Law, 1978-79, tech. cons., 1981-82; mem. adv. bd. Computer Law Reporter; contbr. articles to profl. jours. Mem. ABA, N.J. State Bar Assn., N.J. Assn. Women Bus. Owners, Somerset County Womens Bar Group, Computer Law Assn. Republican. Unitarian.

REYNOLDS, ELIZABETH (BETTY) JEAN, state official; b. Portland, Oreg., Jan. 14, 1948; d. James Bossuet and Lois Pearl (Leatherwood) R.; m. Mark Waletich (div.); 1 child, Kari Lynn Waletich. B.S. magna cum laude, Oreg. State U., 1972; M.S., U. Oreg., 1973; postgrad. Harvard U., 1982. State affairs dir., work-study grader Oreg. State U., Corvallis, 1966-72; grad. teaching fellow U. Oreg., Eugene, 1972-73; budget, mgmt. analyst Oreg. Exec. Dept., Salem, 1973-79; exec. dir. Oreg. Govt. Ethics Commn., Salem, 1979—; Bd. dirs. Salem Non-Profit Housing Corp., 1977-78, Nat. Council Govt. Ethics Law, 1981-83, Salem Conv. and Visitors Assn., 1984—; vol. Fairview Hosp., Salem, 1974-75. Named One of 100 Most Powerful Women in Oreg., Oreg. Mag., 1981; Oreg. State U. scholar, 1972. Mem. Salem C. of C. (bd. dirs. 1985—), Oreg. State Mgmt. Assn. (bd. dir. 1984—), Salem Conv. and Visitors Assn. (bd. dirs. 1984—), Phi Kappa Phi. Lodge: Zonta Internat. Office: Oreg Govt Ethics Commn 155 Cottage St NE Salem OR 97310

REYNOLDS, ESTELLA MARY HENRY, nursing educator; b. Acree, Ga., Dec. 27, 1936; d. John Marion and Wessie Mae (Hawkins) Henry; m. Charles McKinley Reynolds, Jr., Aug. 19, 1956; children—Eric Charles, Gregory Preston. B.S., Tuskegee Inst., 1960; M.S., Wayne State U., 1962; doctoral student Old Dominion U., 1982—. R.N., Va. Charge nurse Grady Meml. Hosp., Atlanta, 1960, staff nurse/clin. instr. Sch. Nursing, 1960-61; instr. practical nursing Monroe Area Vocat.-Tech. Sch., Albany, Ga., 1962-65; clin. instr. St. Joseph Infirmary Sch. Nursing, Atlanta, 1965-68, med.-surg. nursing coordinator, 1968-70; asst. prof. Ga. State U., Atlanta, 1970-75; assoc. prof. Hampton Inst. (Va.), 1975—; mem. com. Area Health Edn. Ctr., Norfolk, Va., 1981—. Bd. dirs. Tidewater chpt. Am. Heart Assn., 1976—; mem. Urban League, NAACP. Named Tchr. of Yr., Monroe Area Vo-Tech Sch., 1963; recipient Service award ARC, 1974. Mem. Am. Nurses Assn., Va. Nurses Assn., Va. League Nursing (resolution com. 1981-83), Nat. League Nursing, AAUW, Sigma Theta Tau, Chi Eta Phi. Baptist. Clubs: Norfolk Moles (pres. 1981-83, nat. fin. sec. 1984—), Girlfriends (fin. sec. 1981-83), Links, Jack and Jill of Am. (Norfolk). Home: 4504 Kelley Ct Virginia Beach VA 23462 Office: Hampton Inst Hampton VA 23668

REYNOLDS, EVELYN CAROL, dental educator; b. Littlefield, Tex., Feb. 3, 1941; d. Aubrey Franklin and Helen Mae (Carrico) Willis; m. Tom Reynolds, Jan. 5, 1962; children—Darla Deann, Merriel Denise. B.S., No. Ariz. U., 1974; A.A., Glendale Community Coll., 1969; Dental Asst., Blair Coll., Phoenix, 1968. Pvt. dental cons., Phoenix, 1978—; head instr. Apollo Coll., Phoenix/Tempe, 1980-82; adminstrv. asst., dir. dental edn. Crestwood Acad., Tempe, 1983-84; dir. dental edn. Biosystems Inst., Tempe and Denver, 1984—. Author: Expanded Functions Assisting, 1984; columnist Tempe mag. Contbr. articles to profl. jours. Chmn. dental edn. com. PTA, 1985—. Mem. Am. Dental Assisting Assn. (former editor 1980-81), Nat. Assn. Female Execs (bd. dirs. 1983—), Nat. Dental Assisting Assn. Avocations; sailing; oil painting; prospecting. Home: 5050 W Beverly Ln Glendale AZ 85306 Office: BIosystems Inst 1701 S 52d St Tempe AZ 85282

REYNOLDS, JANE ELLEN, nursing administrator; b. Washington, Dec. 17, 1938; d. Lisle L. and Edith F. (Barker) Riner; m. Roger F. Reynolds, Mar. 28, 1953; children—Rick Lee, Terry Lynn. A.S., Santa Rosa Jr. Coll., 1974; B.S.N., Calif. State U.-Sonoma, 1976; M.S.N., U. Calif.-San Francisco, 1978; M.H.S./F.N.P., U. Calif.-Davis, 1979; Ph.D., Walden U., 1982. Cert. tchr. Asst. adminstr., nursing dir. Warrack Hosp., Santa Rosa, Calif., 1965-69; supr., inservice head nurse Los Guilucos Youth Authority, 1965-69; ednl. dir. nursing adminstrn. Sonoma County Mental Health, 1969-78; research and clin. coordinator VA Hosp., Menlo Park, Calif., 1978-80; asst. adminstr., dir. Nursing Agy. Calif., Santa Barbara, 1980—. Active Alcohol and Drug Awareness/Mental Health Action, 1980—; mem. Redwood Empire Hosp. Planning Commn., 1980—. NIMH grantee. Mem. Mental Health Nursing Support Group (bd. dirs.), Calif. Nursing Assn., Am. Acad. Med. Adminstrs. (life). Democrat. Club: Toastmasters. Lodge: Optimists (women's club). Author: Self-Directed Learning Groups, 1978; Nurses Attitudes with Alcoholics; Quality Care: A Community Health Study. Office: 4129 State St Suite F Santa Barbara CA 93110

REYNOLDS, JANET DUNBAR, medical center administrator; b. Medford, Mass., Dec. 15, 1944; d. Dale Ogden and Mildred Louise (Dunbar) R.; m. Frank Burton Lloyd, Nov. 19, 1972 (div. Dec. 1981); children—Jennifer Dunbar, Jamie Gibson. Student West Valley Coll., Saratoga, Calif., 1984—. Sr. flight attendant World Airways, 1967-70; med. sec. specialist Stanford U. Med. Ctr., Palo Alto, Calif., 1970-72; sales adminstr. Telesensory Systems Inc., Palo Alto, Calif., 1972-76; tax acct. Los Altos, Calif., 1976-80; adminstr. New Mgmt. Ctr., Palo Alto, 1980-81; adminstr. Hand Therapy & Rehab. Assocs., Inc., Campbell, Calif., 1983-86; adminstrv. mgr. Berryesea Med. Ctr., San Jose, Calif., 1986—. Troop record keeper Girl Scouts Santa Clara County, 1984-85, asst. service unit mgr., 1986. Mem. Nat. Assn. Female Execs., Occupational Therapy Assn. Calif. (asst. to treas. 1983-86, assoc.), Indsl. Claims Assn. Democrat. Avocations: calligraphy; reading; aerobics; crafts.

REYNOLDS, JO ANN, advertising and marketing specialist; b. Chgo., June 16, 1941; d. Harry and Elaine Kinzelberg; married. B.A., U. Ill., 1965. Interior designer, Chgo., 1970-73; mem. woman's bd. Chgo. Mus. Contemporary Art, 1971-73; sr. sales/mktg. cons. Dun & Bradstreet, Oak Brook, Ill., 1974-79; indsl. real estate salesman Arthur Rubloff & Co., Chgo., 1979-80; Midwest advt. salesperson Crain Communications, Inc., Chgo., 1980-83; gen. mgr. Hdqrs. Cos., 1983—; regional mktg. mgr. Sure-Mail and Coupon Co., Inc. Recipient Nat. award AIA, 1970. Home: 2053 Broadway San Francisco CA 94115

REYNOLDS, JO S(CHOLZE), educational administrator; b. Sarasota, Fla., Aug. 15, 1941; d. Joseph Wendling and Frances (Amsden) Scholze; m. James Hooks Reynolds, Dec. 27, 1959 (div. May 1985); children—Jamie Jo, James Burton. A.A., Palm Beach Jr. Coll., 1967; B.S., Fla. Atlantic U., 1968, M.Ed., 1973; postgrad. Nova U., 1983—. Tchr. J.I. Leonard High Sch., Lake Worth, Fla., 1968-73; dean Conniston Jr. High Sch., West Palm Beach, Fla., 1973-76, Congress Middle Sch., Boynton Beach, Fla., 1976-79; asst. prin. Forest Hill High Sch., West Palm Beach, 1979-83; prin. Palm Beach pub. sch., Fla., 1983—; chmn. county secondary curriculum com., 1985-86. Contbr. poetry to various publs. Former Tchrs. Sarasota scholar, 1959; Selby Found. scholar and grantee, 1967. Mem. Nat. Assn. Secondary Sch. Prins., fla. Assn. Secondary Sch. Prins., Am. Assn. Sch. Adminstrs., Palm Beach C. of C. Democrat. Baptist. Office: Palm Beach Pub Sch Cocoanut Row and Seaview Palm Beach FL 33480

REYNOLDS, KARYN CHERYL, banker, consultant; b. N.Y.C., Mar. 10, 1945; d. Leonard John and Harriette (Cohen) R.; m. Elliott Wolk, Dec. 27, 1970 (div.); 1 dau., Harmony. B.S., Hofstra U., Hempstead, N.Y., 1965, M.B.A., 1977. Programmer, Control Data, Bloomington, Minn., 1967; project mgr. Phoenix Computer Tech., N.Y.C., 1968-69; pvt. practice computer applications cons., 1969-72; pres. Kth Dimension, Beechurst, N.Y., 1973-82; v.p., Chase Manhattan Bank, N.Y.C., 1982—; assoc. prof. computer applications, mgmt. sci. LIU, Greenvale, N.Y., 1976-82; assoc. prof. Hofstra U., 1978-81, 84; chmn. Kacie Trading, N.Y.C., 1972. Author poems. IBM fellow, 1978. Fellow Beta Gamma Sigma, Pi Alpha Alpha; mem. Assn. Computer Machinery. Club: Mensa (dir. 1976-77). Office: Chase Manhattan Bank 1 Chase Plaza New York NY 10081

REYNOLDS, KATHRYN ANNE, accountant; b. Kalamazoo, July 31, 1957; d. Ronald Louis and Patricia Anne (Mathers) Blaul; m. Lee Michael Reynolds, Aug. 4, 1979; children—Daniel, Stephani, Joseph. Student McHenry Community Coll., 1975-76, Knox Coll., 1976-77; B.B.A. in Acctg., U. Wis.-Whitewater, 1979. C.P.A., Wis. Mem. staff Baillies, Denson, Erickson & Smith, C.P.A.s, Lake Geneva, Wis., 1980-82, sr. acct., 1983-84; dir. acctg. Rubidell Recreation Inc., Elkhorn, Wis., 1984—. Rotary exchange student, France, 1973-74. Mem. Am. Inst. C.P.A.s, wis. Inst. C.P.A.s, Nat. Assn. Accts., Nat. Assn. Female Execs. Home: 39335 93d St Route 1 Box 130 Genoa City WI 53128 Office: Rubidell Recreation Inc 39 N Washington St Elkhorn WI 53121

REYNOLDS, KATHY LOU, pediatrician; b. Mpls., July 16, 1952; d. Maynard Clinton and Donna Lou (Gleason) Reynolds. B.A., U. Minn., 1973, B.S., 1976, M.D., 1978. Diplomate Am. Bd. Pediatrics. Resident, Hosp. Sick Children, Toronto, Ont., Can., 1978-80, Stanford U., Palo Alto, Calif., 1980-81; practice medicine specializing in pediatrics, Los Gatos, Calif., 1981—; vice chmn. dept. pediatrics Los Gatos Hosp., 1983-84. Mem. Am. Med. Women Assn., Santa Clara County Med. Soc., Bay Area Physicians for Human Rights. Office: 777 Knowles Dr #11 Los Gatos CA 95030

REYNOLDS, LINDA CAROLINE, writer, educator; b. Ft. Worth, Jan. 20; d. James Daniel and Martha Caroline (Valigura) Little; B.B.A., Tex. Christian U., 1965, M.B.A., 1970. Tchr., Ft. Worth Pub. Schs., 1965-73; instr. Tarrant County Jr. Coll., 1974-75, Tex. Christian U., Ft. Worth, 1976-85; self-employed writer, lectr. and cons., Ft. Worth, 1976—. Bd. dirs. Mus. Western Transp.; active Van Cliburn Council, Opera Guild. Mem. Am. Vocat. Assn., Am. Bus. Communication Assn., Tex. Bus. Edn. Assn., Nat. Bus. Edn. Assn. Author: Snow Country Typewriting Practice Set, 1974; Air Country Typewriting Practice Set, 1980; Dimensions in Personal Development, 1976; Dimensions in Professional Development, 1982. Office: 3817 Overton Park E Fort Worth TX 76109

REYNOLDS, NANCY BRADFORD DUPONT (MRS. WILLIAM GLASGOW REYNOLDS), sculptor; b. Greenville, Del., Dec. 28, 1919; d. Eugene Eleuthere and Catherine Dulcinea (Moxham) duPont; student Goldey-Beacom Coll., Wilmington, Del., 1938; m. William Glasgow Reynolds, May 18, 1940; children—Kathrine Glasgow Reynolds Sturges, William Bradford, Mary Parminter Reynolds Savage, Cynthia duPont Reynolds Farris. Exhibited one-woman shows: Rehoboth (Del.) Art League, 1963, Del. Art Mus., Wilmington, Caldwell, Inc., 1975, Wilmington Art Mus., 1976; exhibited group shows: Corcoran Gallery, Washington, 1943, Soc. Fine Arts, Wilmington, 1937, 38, 40, 41, 48, 50, 62, 65, NAD, N.Y.C., 1964, Pa. Mil. Coll., Chester, 1966, Del. Art Center, 1967, Met. Mus. Art, N.Y.C., 1977, Lever House, N.Y.C., 1979; represented in permanent collections: Wilmington Trust Co., E.I. duPont de Nemours & Co., Children's Home, Inc., Claymont, Del., Goldsborough Bldg., Wilmington, Children's Bur., Wilmington, Stephenson Sci. Center, Nashville, Lutheran Towers Bldg., Travelers Aid and Family Soc. Bldg., Wilmington, Bronze Fountain Head, Longwood Gardens, Kennett Square, Pa. Guide, mem. research staff Henry Francis DuPont Winterthur Mus., 1955-63. Organizer vol. service Del. chpt. ARC, 1938-39; chmn. Com. for Revision Del. Child Adoption Law, 1950-52; pres. bd. dirs. Children Bur. Del.; pres., trustee Children's Home, Inc. Recipient Confrerie des Chevaliers du Tastevin Clos de Vougeot-Bourgogne France, 1960; Hort. award Garden Club Am., 1964, medal of Merit, 1976; Dorothy Platt award Garden Club of Phila., 1980; Alumni medal of merit Westover Sch., Middlebury, Conn. Mem. Pa. Hort. Soc., Wilmington Soc. Fine Arts, Mayflower Descs., Del. Hist. Soc., Colonial Dames, League Am. Pen Women, Nat. Trust Hist. Preservation. Episcopalian. Clubs: Garden of Wilmington (past pres.), Garden of Am. (past asst. zone 4 chmn.), Vicmead Hunt, Greenville Country, Chevy Chase (Washington); Colony (N.Y.C.); Catherine Lorillard Wolfe Art (N.Y.C.). Author: Needlepoint Kneelers. Contbr. articles to profl. jours. Address: PO Box 3919 Greenville DE 19807

REYNOLDS, NANCY IRENE, county registrar; b. Kansas City, Mo., Feb. 26, 1942; d. Chester Earl and Martha Louise (Laverentz) Jacobs; m. Frank J. Reynolds, Jr., Apr. 29, 1962; 1 child, Penelope Ann. Sec. to probate judge Hiawatha, Kans., 1965-66; abstractor Finley & Miller, Attys., 1967-68; clk. County Treas., Hiawatha, Kans., 1976-77; registrar deeds Brown County (Kans.), Hiawatha, 1977—; treas. Northeast Kans. Emergency Med. Tech., 1985—. Disaster chmn. Brown County chpt. ARC, 1984—. Mem. Hiawatha

Bus. and Profl. Women's Orgn. (pres. 1985—, Woman of Yr. award 1983), Hiawatha High Sch. Alumni Assn. (treas. 1983—), Kans. Register of Deeds Assn. (treas. 1985-86). Avocations: needlecrafts; reading. Home: 608 N 3d St Hiawatha KS 66434 Office: Brown County Register of Deeds Office Courthouse Hiawatha KS 66434

REYNOLDS, PATRICIA ANN, construction company executive; b. Detroit, Sept. 23, 1936; d. John Franklyn Bush and Mary Edna (Dever) Bush Ward; m. Kevin B. Reynolds, July 1955 (div. 1984); children—Kevin Jr., Shawn, Todd, Robin. Grad. high sch., Grand Rapids, Mich. Billing and payroll clk. Schoonbeck Inc., 1955-57; credit dept. Fox Jewelry, 1958-60. receptionist, switchboard operator Super Foods, Grand Rapids, 1962-66, Purchase Electric, Grand Rapids, 1966-71; purchase estimator Diversified Industries, Grand Rapids, 1972-77; owner, ptnr. Reynolds Bldg. Maintenance, Grand Rapids, 1976-84; gen. mgr. Superior Installation, Madisonville, Tenn., 1977—. Mem. Am. Bus. Womans' Assn. Avocations: boating; fishing. Home: Route 1 Vonore TN Office: Superior Installation Co Inc Kefauver Dr Madinsonville TN 37354

REYNOLDS, PATRICIA FOLEY, real estate broker; b. Boston; d. William J. and Theresa (Liston) Foley; m. George I. Reynolds, May 28, 1965 (div. 1975); 1 dau., Janet Liston. B.A., Manhattanville Coll., 1949; LL.D., Boston U., 1952; M.B.A., Northeastern U., 1962. Lic. real estate broker, Conn.; bar: Mass., U.S. Supreme Ct. Trial lawyer Mahony-Brier Coffin, Boston, 1952-54; securities lawyer, lectr. John Hancock Life, Boston, 1954-65; dir. Mid Hudson Valley Cablevision, N.Y.C., 1966-69; real estate salesman Katz Realty, Westport, 1976-81; real estate broker, developer Country Agy., Westport, 1982—. Pres., Nature Ctr. Women's League, Westport, Conn., 1969-70; trustee Nature Ctr. for Environ., Westport, 1969-70; Mem. ABA, Inter-Am. Bar Assn., Westport-Weston Bd. Realtors (atty.-broker com.). Republican. Roman Catholic. Clubs: Fairfield County Hunt (Westport); Harvard (N.Y.C.). Home: 84 Wilton Rd Westport CT 06880 Office: The Country Agy 238 Post Rd E Westport CT 06880

REYNOLDS, RUTHIE GRACE, educator; b. Covington, Ga., Dec. 3, 1945; d. Horace Joe and Lucille (Freeman) R,; A.S., Mary Holmes Jr. Coll., 1965; B.S., U. Dubuque, 1967; M. Acctg., U. Ariz., 1970; Ph.D., Ga. State U., 1981; children—Reiko Renee Tate, Thomas Anthony Tate, Jr. Tax tecnician IRS, Atlanta, 1967-68; auditor Touche Ross & Co., San Francisco, 1970-71; auditor U. Calif., Berkeley, 1971-72; instr. Tenn. State U., Nashville, 1972-75; acct. R.G. Reynolds, C.P.A., Nashville, 1973-75; asst. prof. U. Tenn., Nashville 1976-77, Ga. Inst. Tech., Atlanta, 1981—. C.P.A., Tenn.; John Hay Whitney fellow, 1968-69; Arthur Andersen & Co., fellow, 1980. Mem. Am. Inst. C.P.A.s, Am. Acctg. Assn., Tenn. Soc. C.P.A.s. Office: Coll Mgmt Ga Inst Tech 225 North Ave Northwest Atlanta GA 30332

REYNOLDS, SANDRA LYNN, banker; b. Norwalk., Conn., Oct. 20, 1949; d. Kendall Wright and Norma Louise (Caswell) Reynolds; B.A. with high honors in Sociology, U Conn., 1973; grad. New Eng. Sch. Banking, 1982. With First Bank of New Haven, 1973-84, asst. to mgr., Waterford br., 1977, officer, asst. mgr., 1977, asst. trust officer trust dept., 1978, trust officer, 1981-84; trust officer Conn. Nat. Bank, 1984—; mem. trust curriculum com. New Eng. Sch. Banking, Williams Coll., 1982. Vol. Library of Congress, Library for Blind and Physically Handicapped, 1979—; treas. Central Conn. Bus. and Estate Planning Council. Vice chmn. legacy and planned giving com. Am. Cancer Soc.; corporator Middlesex Meml. Hosp. Recipient YWCA Women in Leadership award, 1979. Mem. Am. Inst. Banking, Nat. Assn. Bank Women (chmn. Conn. group 1980-81, state edn. and tng. chmn. 1981-82, state membership chmn. 1982-83, New Eng. regional membership chair 1983-84, pres. Conn. council 1984-85, nat. dir. 1985-86, treas. Ednl. Found. 1986-87), Phi Beta Kappa. Office: Conn. Nat. Bank 363 Main St Middletown CT 06457

REYNOLDS, SARAH (SALLY) SUZANNE, art dealer; b. Spartanburg, S.C., Apr. 3, 1946; d. George Dewey and Janet Louise (Bone) Cooksey; m. Thomas Clifford Knudson, June 27, 1967 (div. May 1978); children—Christopher Michael, Suzanne Rainey; m. Norman Towner Reynolds, July 4, 1982. Student U. Calif.-Santa Barbara, 1964-67; B.A., Calif. State U.-Fresno, 1972. Cons. to chief chaplain U.S. Naval Acad., Annapolis, Md., 1974-75; community relations Tex. Eastern Corp., Houston, 1975-76; corp. relations coordinator Zapata Corp., Houston, 1976-77; owner Sally K. Reynolds, Dealer in Fine Art, Houston, 1977—; exec. dir. Art League of Houston. Trustee, Carnegie Mus., Hanford, Calif., 1971-73, Mus. of Art of Am. West; bd. dirs. Hanford Community Theater, 1971-73; mem. council for visual and performing arts U. Tex. Health Sci Ctr.; mem. visual arts adv. panel Tex. commn. for Arts. Recipient Resolution of Recognition, Gov. Tex., 1980. Episcopalian. Clubs: River Oaks Country (Houston); Cosmopolitan (N.Y.C.). Home: 2704 West Ln Houston TX 77027 Office: PO Box 22146 Houston TX 77227

REYNOLDS, W(YNETKA) ANN, university administrator; b. Coffeyville, Kans., Nov. 3, 1937; d. John Ethelbert and Glennie (Beanland) King, Jr.; children—Rachel Rebecca, Rex King; m. Thomas H. Kirschbaum. B.S. in Biology and Chemistry, Kans. State Tchrs. Coll., 1958; M.S. in Zoology, U. Iowa, 1960, Ph.D. in Zoology, 1962; Sc.D. (hon.), Ind. State U., 1980, Ball State U.; D.H.L. (hon.), McKendree Coll., Ill. Asst. prof. biology Ball State U., Muncie, Ind., 1962-65; asst. prof. anatomy Coll. Medicine, U. Ill., 1965-68, assoc. prof., 1968-73, prof., 1973—, research prof. ob-gyn, 1973—, acting assoc. dean for acad. affairs, 1977, assoc. vice chancellor for research, dean Grad. Coll., 1977-79; prof. ob-gyn Ohio State U., 1979-82, prof. anatomy, 1979-82, provost, 1979-82, pres. Research Found., 1979-82; chancellor Calif. State U. System, Long Beach, 1982—, prof. biology, Dominguez Hills, 1982—; hon. prof. biol. scis. San Francisco State U., 1982—; clin. prof. ob-gyn. UCLA Sch. Medicine, 1985—; dir. Gen. Telephone Calif., Am. Electric Power Co., Abbott Labs.; mem. Assn. Gov. Bds. Adv. Council of Presidents, 1983—; mem. Am. Council Edn., Commn. on Higher Edn. and Adult Learner, 1981—; trustee Nat. Joint Council Econ. Edn., 1983—; chmn. Econ. Lit. Council Calif., 1983-84. Contbr. articles to profl. jours. Mem. citizens adv. council Congl. Causes for Sci. and Tech., 1983—; mem. exec. council So. Calif. Council, Invest-in-Am., 1983; mem. Bill of Rights Commemoration Com., 1983—; mem. Calif. Alliance for Arts Edn., 1984—; bd. dirs. Regional Research Inst. So. Calif., 1984—, Californians Preventing Violence, 1983—, Calif. Econ. Devel. Corp., 1984—; nat. chmn. Higher Edn.-Industry Savings Bond Campaign, 1985, 86; mem. Nat. Commn. on Role and Future of State Colls. and Univs., 1985—; nat. adv. bd. Okla. Network Continuing Higher Edn., 1985—; mem. Nat. Commn. on Excellence in Ednl. Adminstrn., 1985—. Recipient Honoree award Women's Employment Options Conf., 1983; Honoree award Women's Opportunity Week, 1983, Disting. Alumna award Kans. State Tchrs. Coll., 1972; Central Assn. Obstetricians and Gynecologists grantee, 1968; NSF fellow, 1958-62, Woodrow Wilson fellow (hon.), 1958. Fellow Calif. Acad. Scis., Am. Coll. Obstetricians and Gynecologists; mem. AAAS, Am. Assn. Anatomists, Am. Diabetes Assn., Am. Soc. Zoologists, Endocrine Soc., Perinatal Research Soc., Soc. Exptl. Biology and Medicine, Soc. Gynecologic Investigation, Am. Assn. State Colls. and Univs. (com. policies and purposes, 1983—, nat. commn. continuing higher edn. leadership 1985—), Soc. Gynecologic Investigation, Am. Assn. Higher Edn. (bd. dirs. 1984—), Sigma Xi, Phi Kappa Phi. Office: Calif State U 400 Golden Shore Long Beach CA 90802

RHEINHEIMER, JOYCE SCHULTZ, psychologist; b. Chgo., June 11, 1944; d. Albert Matthew and Bridget (Brown) Schultz; B.A., U. Ill., Chgo., 1970; M.S., Ill. Inst. Tech., 1974, Ph.D., 1976; m. John Peterson, Jan. 11, 1986; children—Robert, Kimberly, Scott, Kelly. Ednl. cons. Behavioral Research Labs., Chgo., 1973-75; instr. Chgo. State U., 1975; sch. psychology intern Sch. Dist. 62, Des Plaines, Ill., 1975-76; instr. Little Co. of Mary Hosp., Evergreen Park, Ill., 1976; clin. psychologist Roth Group, Northbrook, Ill., 1975-78; instr. Lewis U., Lockport, Ill., 1978, DePaul U., Chgo., 1979; psychotherapist in pvt. practice, Tinley Park, Ill.; cons. psychologist Libra Sch., Riverside, Ill. Mem. South Subarea Adv. Council, Health Services Agy., 1979—, vice chmn., 1980—; co-chmn. Mental Health Coalition South Cook County, 1979-83; prin. Joyce Rheinheimer, Ph.D. & Assoc., Inc., 1984—. Panel mem. South Suburban YMCA Encore Program. Cert. sch. psychologist. Mem. Am. Psychol. Assn., Ill. Psychol. Assn., Chgo. Psychol. Assn. (pres. 1979), Women in Mgmt. South Suburban Network, Am. Soc. Clin. Hynosis. Home: 16464 Laura Ln Oak Forest IL 60452 Office: 16820 Oak Park Ave Tinley Park IL 60477

RHEINLANDER, MARY LINDA, assn. exec.; b. Evansville, Ind., Nov. 7, 1941; d. Clarence Joseph and Margaret Lucille (Herron) Behme; student parochial schs., also continuing edn. classes; m. Robert Edward Rheinlander, Jan. 14, 1961; children—Karen Lynn, Kristine Louise, Keith Edward, Kami Jo. Sec., Whirlpool Corp., 1960; asst. Evansville's Future, Inc., 1965-67; interviewer students Evansville Vanderburgh Sch. Corp., 1974; coordinator job placement service Ind. State U., Evansville, 1970-73; exec. sec. Ind. U. Med. Sch., Indpls., 1975-78; exec. dir. Sheet Metal Contractors Assn., Evansville, 1978—; mem. council Evansville Area Labor-Mgmt. Com.; speaker in field. Pres. Parish Council, mem. Cath. Sch. Bd. Mem. Nat. Assn. Women in Constrn., Ind. Sheet Metal Council, Nat. Assn. Sheet Metal and Air Conditioning Contractors, Nat. Assn. Female Execs., U.S. C. of C., Evansville C. of C., Ind. Lawyers Wives Assn., Evansville Lawyers Wives Assn., Am. Soc. Assn. Execs. Roman Catholic. Home: 5318 West Haven Dr Evansville IN 47712 Office: PO Box 6201 Evansville IN 47712

RHO, SHIN-SOON CHANG, physician; b. Korea, July 13, 1931; d. Eui-Se and Hyun-Sook (Oh) Chang; m. Yong-Myun Rho, Dec. 13, 1958; 4 sons, John I., Robert B., David S., Walter A. M.D., Korea U. Coll. Medicine, 1955. Attending physician St. Joseph's Hosp., Flushing, N.Y., 1980—, Terrace Heights Hosp., Hollis, N.Y., 1980-84, La Guardia Hosp., Forest Hills, N.Y., 1985—; practice internal medicine, Ozone Park, N.Y., 1980—. Diplomate Am. Bd. Internal Medicine. Mem. AMA, Med. Soc. County of Queens, Am. Soc. Internal Medicine. Home: 5 Randall Pl Pelham Manor NY 10803 Office: 79-20 Pitkin Ave Ozone Park NY 11417

RHOADES, CAROL LYNN, controller; b. Logansport, Ind., June 16, 1941; d. Paul William and Olive May (Miller) Settlemyre; m. Norman Ray Rhodes, Sept. 18, 1960; children—William A., Karen S. Student Ind. Bus. Coll., 1959. Controller Wolf Service Ctr., Logansport, 1959—. Pres. Logansport Community Sch. Bd., 1985—; sec. Logansport Park Bd., 1984—; active Girls Softball Assn., Logansport, 1982-84, Girls Pixie League, Logansport, 1982-84; pres., sec., treas. Columbia PTA, Logansport, 1970-82. Mem. LWV, Profl. Secs. (pres., Sec. of Yr. 1979), Delta Theta Chi (sec. 1982-84). Republican. Methodist. Lodge: Eagles Aux. Avocations: camping; latch hooking; gardening. Home: 1413 Liberty St Logansport IN 46947 Office: Wolf Service Ctr 101 Wolf Rd Logansport IN 46947

RHOADES, ELLEN A., nonprofit agency administrator; b. N.Y.C., Dec. 29, 1945; d. Leonard and Thyra (Silverstein) Levine; m. Darrell T. Rhoades, Mar. 17, 1968 (div. 1978); 1 child, Benjamin. B.A., Oglethorpe U., 1967; M.Ed., Emory U., 1971; Ed.S., Ga. State U., 1974, postgrad., 1976-80. Cert. edn. for deaf. Cons., City Bd. Edn., Atlanta, 1971; tchr. DeKalb County Schs., Atlanta, 1971-74; coordinator infant program Atlanta Speech Sch., 1974-76; instr. Emory U., Atlanta, 1978; grantwriter, dir. Unisensory Project, Atlanta, 1980-83; founder, exec. dir. Auditory Ednl. Clinic, Atlanta, 1977—. Mem. adv. bd. Beebe Speech Hearing Ctr., Easton, Pa., 1979—; cons. Cath. Archdiocesan Schs., Atlanta, 1975, Tex. Tech U., 1976. Mem. citizens adv. bd. So. Bell, 1983—; mem. disabilities task force Human Services Planning Adv. Council, 1982, disabled childrens task force Council Children Ga., 1982; state coordinator Children's Rights Com., 1980—. Recipient Outstanding Disabled Georgian award Ga. Council Devel. Disabilities, 1982; Outstanding Non-Profit Mgmt. award Metro Atlanta Community Found., 1985; named Profl. Handicapped Woman of Yr., Pilots, 1981, Deaf Woman of Yr., Quota Club, Atlanta, 1979; Emory U./Ga. State U. fellow, 1970-71, 78-79. Mem. A.G. Bell Assn. for Deaf (bd. dirs. 1980—), Auditory Verbal Internat. (exec. com. 1978—), Council Exceptional Children, Ga. Soc. Assn. Execs. Avocations: tennis; reading; fine arts; chess; theatre. Home: 8565 St Charles Ave Atlanta GA 30306 Office: Auditory Ednl Clinic 3016 Lanier Dr Atlanta GA 30319

RHOADES, KAROLYN SUE, broadcasting sales director, civic worker; b. Mattoon, Ill., Dec. 30, 1938; d. Robert Alma and Juanita Maxine (Fort) Gass; m. William Rhoades, Aug. 4, 1984; children—Kimberly, Matthew. Respiratory techician Okeechobee Gen. Hosp., Fla., 1974-78; emergency med. technician Emergency Med. Service, Okeechobee, 1974-78; sales dir. Okeechobee Broadcasters, 1979—; owner Rhoades Flooring. Bd. dirs. St. Lucie Women's Bowling Assn., 1983-84, local chpt. ARC, 1979-80; publicity dir. Am. Cancer Soc. and Hospice, 1983-84; pageant coordinator Miss Speckled Perch Beauty Contest, 1985—; chmn. Toys for Tots. Mem. Okeechobee C. of C. (dir. 1985, exec. dir. 1986), Am. Bus. Women's Assn. (chmn. ways and means com. 1985). Avocations: Bowling; byclying. Office: Sta WOKC 2700 S US 441 Okeechobee FL 33472

RHOADES, NANCY ANN, air force officer; b. Fort Campbell, Ky., June 16, 1959; d. Glen Lee and Mary Josephine (Lasell) R.; m. Leo Kenneth Anderson, Jr., Jan. 7, 1984. B.S. in Astro Engring., U.S. Air Force Acad., 1981; M.S. in Aero. and Astronaut. Engring., Stanford U., 1985. Commd. 2d lt. U.S. Air Force, 1981, advanced through grades to capt., 1985; satellite test engr. space div. Los Angeles, 1981-84; instr. dept. astronautics U.S. Air Force Acad., Colorado Springs, Colo., 1985—. Recipient Medal of Merit, Nat. Air Force Assn., 1985. Mem. Air Force Assn., AIAA, Soc. Women Engrs. Avocations: aerobics; long distance running; sewing. Home: 17485 Paver Way Monument CO 80132 Office: US Air Force Acad Dean Faculty Astronautics Colorado Springs CO 80840

RHOADS, GERALDINE EMELINE, editor; b. Phila., Jan. 29, 1914; d. Lawrence Dry and Alice Fegley (Rice) R.; A.B., Bryn Mawr Coll., 1935. Publicity asst. Bryn Mawr (Pa.) Coll., 1935-37; asst. Internat. Students House, Phila., 1937-39; mng. editor The Woman mag., N.Y.C., 1939-42; editor Life Story mag., 1942-45; editor Today's Woman mag., N.Y.C., 1945-52, Today's Family mag., 1952-53; lectr. Columbia U., 1954-56; asso. editor Readers Digest, 1954-55; producer NBC, 1955-56; assoc. editor Ladies Home Jour., 1956-62; mng. editor, 1962-63; exec. editor McCall's mag., 1963-66; editor-in-chief Woman's Day Mag., 1966-82, editorial dir., 1982-84, v.p., 1972-77, editorial dir. Woman's Day Resource Ctr.; v.p. consumer publs. CBS, N.Y.C., 1977-84. Home: 865 1st Ave New York NY 10017

RHODES, ANN L(OUISE), construction company executive; b. Ft. Worth, Oct. 17, 1941; d. Jon Knox and Carol Jane (Greene) R.; student Tex. Christian U., 1960-63, 75—. Vice pres. Rhodes Enterprises, Inc., Ft. Worth, 1963-77; owner-mgr. Lucky R Ranch, Ft. Worth, 1969—; pres., chmn. bd. ALR Enterprises, Inc., Ft. Worth, 1977—, pres. Sunergos Prodns. div., 1983—; owner Ann L. Rhodes Investments, Ft. Worth, 1976—. Bd. dirs. Tarrant County Council on Alcoholism, 1973-78, hon. bd. dirs., 1978—, named Outstanding Vol., 1972, recipient Vol. Service awards, 1970-78; bd. dirs. N.W. Tex. chpt. Arthritis Found., 1977—; mem. exec. com. Tarrant County Republican Com., 1964-69; mem. adv. bd. Circle Theatre, 1984—. Mem. Am. Mgmt. Assn., Nat. Fedn. Ind. Bus., Am. Horse Council, Jr. League Fort Worth, Kappa Kappa Gamma. Episcopalian. Office: ALR Enterprises Inc Suite 908 Republic Bank Ridglea Fort Worth TX 76116

RHODES, ARBIE COOK, educational administrator; b. Sylva, N.C., Feb. 1, 1931; d. John Lewis and Ellen (Watson) Cook; m. Woodfin Chester Rhodes, June 19, 1954; 1 child, Judy Rhodes. B.S., Western Carolina U., 1960, M.A. in Ednl. Adminstrn., 1973. Tchr. Buncombe County, Asheville, N.C., 1960-73, in-service coordinator, 1972-74; prin. Biltmore Elem. Sch., Asheville, 1973-80, Valley Springs Sch., Arden, N.C., 1980—; presenter So. Assn. Colls. and Schs., 1984. Named Prin. of Yr., Buncombe County Classroom Tchrs., 1979. Mem. N.C. Assn. Sch. Adminstrs. N.C. Assn. Educators, Buncombe County Prins. Assn. (Prin. of Yr. award 1980), Phi Beta Kappa, Kelta Kappa Gamma (officer 1976—). Democrat. Presbyterian. Club: Money Makers Investment (vice pres. 1984—) (Asheville). Avocations: music, reading, investment clubs. Home: Ball Gap Rd Arden NC 28704 Office: Valley Springs Middle Sch Route 1 Box 16 Arden NC 28704

RHODES, CYNTHIA STRAHLER, telephone company official; b. Allentown, Pa., May 28, 1947; d. George Robert and Janet Gordon Strahler; student Ursinus Coll., 1965-66, U. Md., 1970, Lafayette Coll., 1982-84; m. Robert Wesley Rhodes, Oct. 22, 1966; children—Danielle Renee, Robert Carver. Supr. network engring. AT&T Long Lines, 1972-75, market adminstr., 1975-78, supr. spl. communications project, 1978-79, supr. service costs, Bedminster, N.J., 1979-81, staff supr. tariff planning and adminstrn., 1981-82, staff mgr. interstate tariff implementation, 1982-86, mgr. interstate access cost intervention, 1986—. Mem. Nat. Assn. Female Execs. Republican. Moravian. Club: Chrysalis Dancers. Office: 2C210 Bedminster NJ 07921

RHODES, JACQUELINE YVONNE, marketing executive; b. Fairfield, Ala., Mar. 3, 1949; d. Lee Oliver and Jimmye Lucille (Warren) Rhodes. Student pub. schs., Cleve. Bus. services rep. Ohio Bell Telephone Co., Cleve., 1969-82, bus. officer instr., 1973-74, spl. communications cons., 1974-76, account exec. II, 1976-80, personnel mgr., 1980-82; account exec. American Bell, Cleve., 1983; dir. sales and mktg. Psychassess, Inc., Cleve., 1983—; telecommunications analyst Clev. Clinic Found., 1985—; sec. Turner & Knight, Inc., Cleve., 1981-83. Vice pres. Harambee: Services to Black Families, Cleve., 1983. Mem. Nat. Assn. Female Execs., Citizens' League, Women's City Club. Baptist. Home: 17722 Tarkington Ave Cleveland OH 44128

RHODES, JERI ELIZABETH, college official; b. Lewiston, Maine, June 10, 1951 d. William Gerard and Audrey Mae (Atherton) Norris; m. Roy Louis Rhodes, May 20, 1973; children—Matthew, Keith. B.A. in History, Am. U., 1973; B.A. in Fin., U. Calif.-Riverside, 1980. Acctg. supr. City of Corona, Calif., 1978-80, Marriott Corp., Bethesda, Md., 1981-83; asst. controller Colorfax, Silver Spring, Md., 1980-81; treas. St. John's Coll., Annapolis, Md., 1983—. Mem. Inst. Mgmt. Acctg. (cert. mgmt. acct.), Am. Soc. Women Accts. (officer local chpt. 1981—). Home: 10108 Frederick Ave Kensington MD 20895 Office: St John's College 60 College Ave Annapolis MD 21404

RHODES, MARTA KORWIN, publisher, educator, pianist; b. Wilno, Poland, July 22; came to U.S., 1950, naturalized, 1964; d. Henryk Lipkowski and Helen Korwin-Milewski. M.M., Music Conservatory, Kraokow, Poland, 1938; diploma London Sch. Econs., 1944; B.S.C., Group SW, Toronto, 1945; M.S.W., U. Pa., 1956; postgrad. Cath. U., Washington. Prin. coll. UNRRA, Hagen, Fed. Republic Germany, 1945-50; instr. Psychiat. Inst., Balt., 1956-59; asst. prof. Fla. State U., Tallahassee, 1959-62; assoc. prof. William and Mary Coll., Richmond, Va., 1963-75; researcher Govt. of Regina, Can. Sub Arctic Circle, 1975; assoc. prof. George Washington U., 1976-78; pub., founder Perspectives, Inc., Polish-Am. Ednl. and Cultural Bi-Monthly, Washington, 1970—. Author: In Spite of Everything; The Mask of Warriors, 1977. Contbr. articles to profl. jours. Decorated Silver Cross of Merit Polish Govt., Golden Cross of Merit Polish Army, Mil. Cross Polish Army, Cross of Merit of Sovereign Order of Knights of Malta 1st class. Mem. Polish Am. Arts Club (founder, 1st pres., life mem.). Avocations: gardening; walking; skiing; reading. Address: Perspectives Inc 700 7th St SW Washington DC 20024

RHODES, MARY BERRYMAN, computer systems executive; b. LaGrande, Oreg., Feb. 2, 1947; d. Joseph Leslie and Bonnie Bertha (Osborn) Berryman; 1 child, Barney Justin. B.S. in Secondary Edn./Math. Eastern Oreg. State Coll., 1969; postgrad. Oreg. State U., 1969-71, Eastern Oreg. State Coll., 1983-85. Programer, Oreg. State U., Corvallis, 1969-71; sec. Morrow County Extension, Heppner, Oreg., 1972-75; ins. agt. Grange Ins., Union County, Oreg., 1978-81; mgr. regional software E.O.S. Coll., LaGrande, Oreg., 1979-80; systems analyst Computer Ctr., Eastern Oreg. State Coll., 1980-85; system mgr., 1985—, coordinator accad. computing systems, 1985—. Author: OS-3: A User's Manual, 1968, ALGOL: A User's Manual, 1969, OSCAR: A User's Manual, 1969. Den Mother Cub Scouts Den 3, LaGrande, 1984—. Oreg. State U. grad. research assistantship in math., 1969-71. Mem. N.W. Council for Computers in Edn. (treas. 1980-81), Internat. Council for Computers in Edn., Sigma Alpha Chi (treas. 1967-68). Democrat. Methodist. Avocations: oil painting; wildflowers; refinishing old furniture. Office: Computer Center Eastern Oreg State Coll 8th and K LaGrande OR 97850

RHODES, MARY ELIZABETH FRECHTLING (MRS. IRWIN S. RHODES), former editor; b. Madison, Ind., May 3, 1911; d. George William and Laura (Lory) Frechtling; student Butler U., 1928-30, Herron Art Sch., 1925-30; m. Irwin S. Rhodes, Dec. 12, 1941; children—Elana Susan, Irwin Lawrence. With Marx-Flarsheim Advt. Co., Cin., 1930-32; exec. sec. Perfect Mfg. Co., Cin., 1932-36; sales promotion, real estate mgmt. Am. Service Assos., Cin., 1936-40; asst. editor The Papers of John Marshall, U. Okla. Press, 1969, The Papers of Roger B. Taney, 1970-81. Chmn. Cin. Fine Arts Dr., 1947-59, Cin. Summer Opera Women's Com., 1966-67; mem. adv. bd. Air Pollution Control League, 1958-62; adv. com. Cin. Juvenile Ct., 1960—; mem. exec. com. Am. Cancer Soc. Balls, 1966-78; chmn., v.p. Women's Com. Cin. Symphony Orch., 1959-64; sponsor Irwin S. and Elizabeth F. Rhodes Legal History Collection, U. Okla. Mem. Soc. Ind. Pioneers, Cin., Ky., Md., Lancaster County (Pa.) hist. socs., DAR, Nat. Press Club, Cin. Art Mus., Am. Soc. Profl. and Exec. Women, Ky. Soc. Washington. Editor C.A.R. Nat. Mag., 1966-67. Home: 3815 Erie Ave Cincinnati OH 45208

RHODES, MARY JANE, nurse; b. Frenchburg, Ky., Aug. 20, 1960; d. Joseph Sherman and Wilma Jean (Bryant) R. Assoc. Nursing, Cumberland Coll., 1980. Registered nurse Central Baptist Hosp., Lexington, Ky., 1980-85, staff devel. and quality assurance coms., 1984-86; nursing supr. Mary Chiles Hosp., Mt. Sterling, Ky., 1985—. Democrat. Baptist. Avocations: singing; writing; bowling; volleyball; swimming. Home: 2220 Devonport Dr I-43 Lexington KY 40504 Office: PO Box 7 110 Sterling Ave Mount Sterling KY 40353

RHODES, PAULA RENETTE, legal educator, consultant; b. New Orleans, July 18, 1949; d. Leroy Louis and Marie M. (Richard) R. B.A. cum laude, Am. U., 1971; J.D., Harvard U., 1974. Bar: La. 1975, D.C. 1978, U.S. Supreme Ct. 1980. Law clk. New Orleans Legal Assistance Corp., summer 1972; legal cons. Am. Friends Service Com., St. Louis, 1973; staff atty. La. Dept. Justice, New Orleans, 1974-77; assoc. Dorsey & Marks, New Orleans, 1975-77; atty./demonstration project mgr. Legal Service Corp., Washington, 1977-79, prof. Mid Atlantic Legal Edn. Opportunity Program, Washington, summer 1980; assoc. prof. Howard U. Sch. Law, Washington, 1979—; adj. prof. U. Bridgeport Sch. Law, Conn.; vis. prof. San Diego Sch. Law, 1983-84; legal cons. Inst. Food and Policy Devel., 1982, U.S. Dept. Energy, 1980-81, D.C. Pub. Service Commn., 1979-80, U.S. Adminstrn. on Aging, 1978, Friends World Com. on Consultation, 1981. Assoc. editor The Forum, 1982-83; contbr. articles to legal jours. Bd. dirs. Am. Friends Service Com., 1982—, mem. exec. com. internat. div., 1981—, mem. nat. women's program com., 1980—, affirmative action rev. com., 1982-84, vice clk. peace edn. div., 1984—; co-chmn. Third World coalition, 1983—; mem. Pesticides Action Network Internat., Black Women's Agenda, So Others May Eat (SOME), Transafrica; trustee Friends Meeting of Washington; mem. D.C. Solar Task Force, D.C. Commn. on Women, Friends Com. on Nat. Legislation, Debt Crisis Network. Mem. D.C. Bar Assn., La. Bar Assn., Internat. Bar Assn., Fed. Bar Assn. (chpt. dir., continuing legal edn. com.; nat. council 1980-81; participant Bill of Rights program 1980), ABA. Quaker. Office: Howard U Law Sch 2900 Van Ness St NW Washington DC 20008

RHODUS, IDA KATHERINE, steel company executive; b. Richmond, Ky., July 21, 1956; d. Robert Buford and Imogene (Adams) Rhodus; m. Gary Paul Howard, Dec. 9, 1983. Student Eastern Ky. U., 1973, U. Ky., 1978. Teller, Bank Commerce, Lexington, Ky., 1974-75; sales/estimator Mid State Steel Co., Lexington, 1975-78, Harry Gordon Steel Co., Lexington, 1978-81; estimator Mosher Steel Co., Houston, 1981-82, Galaxy Steel Co., Houston, 1982-84; mgr. estimating Republic Iron Works, Houston, 1984—; mgr. sales/estimating Superior Iron Works Inc., Houston, 1984—. Named Ky. Col. Mem. Women in Constrn. (dir. 1978-82). Democrat. Home: 6401 Bayou Glen Houston TX 77057 Office: Superior Iron Works Inc 9523 Fairbanks N Houston Rd Houston TX 77064

RHOTEN, JULIANA THERESA, school principal; b. N.Y.C., June 28; d. Julius Joseph and Gladys Maude (Grant) Bastian; B.A., Hunter Coll., 1954; M.S., 1956; Ed.S., U. Wis., Milw., 1977; m. Marion Rhoten, Aug. 7, 1956; 1 son, Don Carlos. Tchr. elem. schs., Milw., 1957-65, reading specialist, 1965-71, adminstr., 1971-80; prin. Ninth St. Sch., Milw., 1980-83, Parkview Sch., Milw., 1983—. Mem. Assn. Supervision and Curriculum Devel., Internat. Reading Assn., Nat. Council Tchrs. English, Adminstrs. and Suprs. Council, Phi Delta Kappa, Alpha Kappa Alpha. Home: 7222 N 99th St Milwaukee WI 53224 Office: 10825 W Villard Ave Milwaukee WI 53225

RHYNE, OPAL MAE, cleaning company executive; b. Hope, N.Mex., May 15, 1928; d. James Lewis and Eva Ann (Jones) Stephens; m. Harvey Lynn Rhyne, Apr. 8, 1947 (div. Jan. 1963); children—Cynthia Ann, Sandra Lynn. Student U. Tex.-Brownwood, 1948-49, Artesia Christian Coll., 1981-82, Eastern N.Mex. U., 1983-86. File clk. U.S. Air Force, Roswell, N.Mex., 1944-46; snack bar mgr. Renfro Drug Co., Brownwood, Tex., 1947-49; owner, mgr. Fashion Cleaners, Artesia, N.Mex., 1959—; free-lance writer on care of wearing apparel. Newspaper columnist, 1982-83. Mem. Community Choir, adv. bd. dirs. Good Samaritan; bd. dirs. United Way; mem. Arts Council; adv. bd. dirs. Am. Security Council, 1981—, U.S. Congl., 1981—; mem. Republican Nat. Com. Recipient Artesia Businessmen's Assn. (awards 1963, 64, 65, 66, 67, other awards. Baptist. Club: Gun (Artesia). Lodge: Altrusa (pres. 1963-64). Avocations: writing; painting; creative sewing; coin collecting; guns. Office: Fashion Cleaners 105 S 5th St Artesia NM 88211

RHYNE-REESE, DEBORAH ANN, school counselor; b. Gaslonia, N.C., Nov. 13, 1949; d. Dane Samuel and Anne Laurie (Lewis) Rhyne. B.A. in Psychology, Sacred Heart Coll., 1971; M.Edn., U. N.C., 1972; postgrad. U. Oslo, Johns Hopkins U. Cert., Nat. Bd. Cert. Counselors. Sch. counselor Gaston County Schs., Gastonia, 1972-76, elem. counseling cons., 1979—; social dir. Maisons-Sur-Mer Resort Commn., Myrtle Beach, S.C., 1976-78; employment counselor State of Md. Dept. Human Resources, Balt., 1978-79. Active, Little Theatre of Gastonia, bd. dirs., 1979-83; pres. Sacred Heart Alumni Assn., 1972-73; mem. Pres.'s Counsil Sacred Heart Coll., 1967-71; mem. community research com. Jr. League of Gaston County, Gastonia, 1982-83, mem. arts com., 1983, 84; mem. Gaston County Art and History Mus., Art Guild, Gaston County Arts and Sci. Council; bd. dirs. Gaston Community Action, Gastonia, 1980-83; pres. Gaston County chpt. Sacred Heart Coll. Alumni Assn. Mem. Am. Personnel Guidance Assn., Am. Sch. Counselor's Assn., N.C. Personnel and Guidance Assn., Invitational Edn. Assn. Democrat. Presbyterian. Home: 208 W 4th Ave Gastonia NC 28052 Office: Gaston County Schs Box 1397 Gastonia NC 28052

RIBBLE, ANNE HOERNER, information representative; b. Balt., Oct. 30, 1932; d. Jerold Kiser and Helen Blythe (Miller) Hoerner; B.A., Smith Coll., 1954; M.A., Harvard U., 1955; m. John C. Ribble, July 26, 1974; 1 dau. by previous marriage—Helen Blythe Strate. Tchr. English, Weston (Mass.) High Sch., 1955-57, tech. asst. IBM, N.Y.C., 1958-63, editor, Armonk and White Plains, N.Y., 1969-75, mgr. editorial services data processing div., White Plains, 1976-77, program adminstr. systems communications div., N.Y.C., 1977-78, staff tech. edn., fed. systems div., Houston, 1978-80, info. rep., 1980—. Mem. Manhattan County Com., Democratic party, 1961-62; co-chmn. English Teaching Program, N.Y. Jr. League, 1965-67, honored vol., 1968, bd. dirs. 1968-69; bd. dirs. Stanley Isaacs Community Center, 1968-72; vestry Ch. of Holy Trinity, N.Y.C., 1976-78. Mem. Internat. Assn. Bus. Communicators (pres. Houston chpt. 1982), Women's Profl. Assn. (bd. dirs. 1980-81, 84). Home: 6200 Willers Way Houston TX 77057 Office: IBM 1322 Space Park Dr Houston TX 77058

RIBBS-DAVIS, ALMA, marketing manager; b. San Jose, Calif., Jan. 24, 1960; d. William T. and Geraldine A. (Henderson) Ribbs; m. Darby Allen Davis, Sept. 25, 1982. B.A., Stanford U., 1982. Assoc., B.L. McTeague & Co., Hartford, Conn., 1981; mktg. communications coordinator Grid Systems Corp., Mountain View, Calif., 1982-83; account supr. Ketchum Pub. Relations, Palo Alto, Calif., 1984-86; product mktg. mgr. Sun Microsystems, Mountain View, 1986—; guest lectr. San Jose State U., 1986; cons. Capital Solutions, Palo Alto, 1984-85; dir. Gilcrest & Green, Marin, Calif., 1986. Vol. local mayoral campaign; vice-chair Stanford Students for Kennedy, 1979-80. Mem. Pub. Relations Soc. Am. (assoc.), Internat. Assn. Bus. Communicators, Nat. Assn. Female Execs. Democrat. Episcopalian. Lodge: Lioness (San Jose) Avocations: reading; sports. Home: 1256 G Vicente Dr Sunnyvale CA 94086 Office: 2550 Garcia Ave Mountain View CA 94043

RIBELIN, ROSEMARY BINGHAM, college bookstore and campus center administrator; b. Indpls., Ind., Aug. 8, 1933; d. Remester Alexander and Joy Dorothy (Reed) Bingham; m. Richard Grant Ribelin, Aug. 16, 1957; children—Pamela Joy, Karen Sue. Student Indpls. schs. Sec. to mgr. Phoenix Mut. Life Ins., Indpls., 1952-61, office supr., 1971-76; sec. to pres. Franklin Coll., Ind., 1976-79, bookstore/campus ctr. dir., 1979—. Leader Hoosier Capital council Girl Scouts U.S.A., 1965-75; canvasser Multiple Sclerosis Soc., Am. Cancer Soc., Am. Heart Assn., 1965-77; canvasser Channel 20 Pub. Broadcasting Service, Indpls., 1968; active com. mem. J. K. Lilly School PTA, Indpls., 1965-75, pres., 1972; canvasser United Fund, Indpls., 1968-75, pres., 1971. Moneyraiser, poll worker Republican Party, Indpls. Deacon, Sunday Sch. tchr. and supt. First Presbyn. Ch. of Franklin. Mem. Philanthropic Nat. Soc. (pres. 1983-85), Delta Theta Tau (treas. Lambda Eta chpt. 1981-82, v.p. 1982-83, pres. 1983-85). Lodges: Daus. of Nile, Order Eastern Star, Oriental Shrine. Avocations: Hooking rugs, reading, crocheting, playing cards, embroidery. Office: Franklin Coll Bookstore Campus Ctr Franklin IN 46131

RIBNER, MURIEL S., business executive, lawyer; b. N.Y.C., Mar. 8, 1924; d. Nathan Lewis and Lillian (Titan-Rubin) Solomon; B.A., N.Y. U., 1945, LL.B., 1951; m. H. J. Coman, Aug. 13, 1943 (div. 1950), m. 2d Lloyd D. Ribner, Jan. 24, 1952 (div. 1978); children—Andrew B., Lloyd D. Sec. editor Bronxville Rev.-Press, 1941-42; AP researcher Rockefeller Pl., N.Y.C., 1942-43; admitted to N.Y. State bar, 1951; partner Ribner Bus. Systems, N.Y.C., 1954-58; pres. Estey Corp., Englewood, N.J., 1976-80; v.p. Merry Traders, N.Y.C., 1981—; active trustee family trusts and investments. Bd. dirs. Starr-Anne Found. Democrat. Address: 444 E 57 St New York NY 10022

RICCELLI, CARLENE VICTORIA, college program administrator, health educator; b. St. Johnsbury, Vt., May 10, 1948; d. Carmen Joseph and Arline Muriel (Young) R. B.A., U. Mass., 1970, M.Ed., 1975, Ed.D., 1978. Cert. guidance counselor, high sch. prin., English tchr. gen. supr., Mass. Guidance counselor Amherst Regional High Sch., Mass., 1976-79, prin., 1979-80; supr. guidance Brookline Schs., Mass., 1980-81; dir. prevention ctr. Dept. Pub. Health, Boston, 1981-82; coordinator alcohol edn. Univ. Health Services, U. Mass., Amherst, 1982—, asst. prof. edn., 1985—. Contbr. articles to profl. jour. Bd. dirs., chmn. publicity Com. for a Better Chance, Amherst, 1978—; mem. Youth Council, Northampton, Mass., 1980-81; bd. dirs. Valley Light Opera, 1984—; mem. town meeting Amherst, 1978-80. Recipient Excellence in Alcohol Programming award Nat. Assn. Sch. Personnel Adminstrs., 1985; Gov.'s citation for programming to reduce accidents and alcohol-related fatalities. Mem. New Eng. Coll. Alcohol Network (founding, treas. 1984—), Am. Coll. Health Assn. (1990s objectives com.). Avocations: community theatre and opera; softball; contra-dance music; dancing; piano; gardening. Home: 270 Northeast St Amherst MA 01002 Office: Univ Health Services U Mass Amherst MA 01003

RICCI, JERRI, artist; b. Perth Amboy, N.J.; d. Ulysses Anthony and Caroline (Ricci) Ricci; student Mt. St. Mary's Acad., Plainfield, N.J., 1931-34, N.Y. Sch. Applied Design, 1935; Art Students League N.Y., 1935-38; m. Arnold W. Knauth, II, May 29, 1948. Four one man shows Milch Galleries, N.Y.C., one Fairleigh Dickenson Coll.; exhbns. Addison Gallery, Andover, Mass., Artists for Victory, N.Y.C., Toledo Mus. Art, Milch Galleries; represented in permanent collections Parrish Mus., Southampton, L.I., Am. Acad. Arts and Letters, N.Y.C., Clark U., Worcester, Mass., Butler Art. Inst., Youngstown, Ohio, Ranger Fund. Recipient Gold Medal of Honor, Allied Artists, 1942, Arthur E. Friedrichs award, 1948; E.J. Tonsberg prize Rockport (Mass.) Art Assn., 1942, Hayward Neidringhaus award, 1945, Clara Stroud award Am. Water Color Soc., 1947, Herbert Pratt purchase prize, 1950, Charles H. Stuart Meml. purchase prize, 1953; William Publicover award North Shore Art Assn., 1949; purchase Butler Art, Inst., 1950; Bronze Medal of Honor, Corcord (Mass.) Art Assn., 1953; Silver Medal, Catherine Lorrilard Wolfe Club, N.Y.C. 1954; Clara Obrig award N.A.D., 1954. Mem. N.A.D., North Am. Water Color Soc., Audubon Artists, Allied Artists Am., Phila. Water Color Club, Rockport, North Shore, St. Augustine art assns. Home: 1 Atlantic Ave Rockport MA 01966

RICCIARDI, JULIE CLEVELAND ARNOLD, lawyer; b. Kansas City, Mo., Dec. 5, 1949; d. Eugene Keasling Jr. and Dawn (Cleveland) Arnold; m. Mark Joseph Ricciardi, June 6, 1981; 1 child. A.B., Smith Coll., 1972; M.S. in Pub. Adminstrn., U. Mo., 1977; J.D., Washington U., 1981. Bar: Mo. 1981. Computer programmer State of Mo. State Auditor, Jefferson City, 1975-76, systems analyst and programmer, Office of Adminstrn., 1976-78; staff lawyer St. Louis County Probate Ct., St. Louis, 1981—. Second v.p. Young Democrats, Jefferson City, 1976; bd. dirs. Support Dogs for the Handicapped, St. Louis, 1984—. Mem. ABA, Met. Bar Assn. St. Louis, Greater St. Louis Tng. Club, Phi Delta Phi. Episcopalian. Home: 815 Berick Dr Saint Louis MO 63132 Office: Saint Louis County Probate Div 7900 Carondelet St Saint Louis MO 63105

RICCIO, KATHRYN BLOOMER LUCAS, manager; b. North Salem, N.Y., July 25, 1956; d. Warren Bloomer and Elizabeth (Hassett) Lucas; m. David Mark Riccio, Nov. 1981. B.A., Pace U., 1978. Mgr. med. edn. Boehringer Ingelheim Pharms., Ridgefield, Conn., 1978. Photographer, North Salem Hist. Soc., N.Y., 1978; mem. organizing com. Spl. Olympics, Somers, N.Y., 1973; bd. dirs. Conn. chpt. Am. Lung Assn., 1986—, chair planning com., 1986-87. Mem. Nat. Assn. Female Execs. (area dir. 1985—), Health Care Exhibitors Assn., Am. Mgmt. Assn., Pharm. Mfrs. Assn., Meeting Planners Internat., Profl. Conv. Mgmt. Assn., Am. Coll. Chest Physicians (adv. panel). Republican. Roman Catholic. Avocations: painting; golf; karate; water skiing.

RICE, BARBARA POLLAK, advertising and marketing executive; b. Ft. Scott, Kans., Nov. 11, 1937; d. Olin N. and Jeanette E. (Essen) Brigman; student N. Central Coll., 1955, Elmhurst Coll., 1956; B.A. in Communications, Calif. State U., Fullerton, 1982; m. Stanley Rice, Apr. 28, 1978; 1 dau., Beverly Johnson. Art dir. Gonterman & Assos., St. Louis, 1968-71; advt. mgr. Passpoint Corp., St. Louis, 1971-73; advt., pub. relations mgr. Permaneer Corp., St. Louis, 1973-74; advt. cons., advt. mgr. Hydro-Air Engring., Inc., St. Louis, 1974-76; mgr. mktg. services Hollytex Carpet Mills subs. U.S. Gypsum Co., City of Industry, Calif., 1976-79; pres. B.P. Rice & Co., Inc., Cerritos, Calif., 1979—. Recipient Designer Best Exhibit award Nat. Farm Builders Trade Show. Mem. Am. Advt. Fedn., Los Angeles Advt. Women (pres., dir.), Bus. Profl. Advt. Assn., Calif. State U.-Fullerton Sch. Communications Alumni Assn. (bd. dirs.), Beta Sigma Phi (past pres., outstanding mem.). Author: Truss Construction Manual, 1975. Home: 8178 Havasu Circle Buena Park CA 90621 Office: 13079 Artesia Blvd Suite 228 Cerritos CA 90701

RICE, BEVERLY ANN (MRS. LARRY T. RICE), department store executive; b. Evansville, Ind., Feb. 2, 1934; d. Howard H. and Grace M. (Sawin) Boegaholtz; B.S., Ind. U., 1956; m. Larry T. Rice, Aug. 6, 1961. Asst. to fashion dir. L.S. Ayres & Co., Indpls., 1956-59, buyer, designer, 1959-65, fashion dir., 1965-66, div. mdse. mgr. better apparel, 1966-69, div. v.p., 1969-73, v.p., 1973-76, v.p., gen. mdse. mgr. apparel and small wares, from 1976; now v.p., gen. mgr. Gidding Jenny, Indpls.; mem. N.Y. Fashion Group, 1965—. Bd. fellows Northwood Inst., recipient Disting. Woman award, 1976. Mem. Women's com. Ind. Symphony Soc. Mem. Women's C. of C., Ind. U. Alumni Assn., Indpls. Mus. Art Alliance, Alpha Omicron Pi, Beta Gamma Sigma. Presbyterian. Home: 4532 N Pennsylvania St Indianapolis IN 46205 Office: 8702 Keystone Crossing Indianapolis IN 46240

RICE, BOBBYLYNE, school social worker; b. Selma, Ala., Oct. 5, 1936; d. Robert Henry and Pauline (Heade) R.; student Ala. State U., 1953-54, 70; B.A., Calif. State U., San Francisco, 1973; M.S.W., San Francisco State U., 1975; 1 dau., Deirdra. Various positions in industry, 1963-71; tchr. San Francisco Unified Sch. Dist., 1972-76, sch. social worker, 1976-85, dean of students, 1985-; chmn. alumni community support group, dept. social work edn. San Francisco State U., 1978—; mem. com. child care relative issues, joint legis. task force Nat. Assn. Social Workers-Calif. Assn. Sch. Social Workers, 1978—. Mem. Nat. Assn. Social Workers, Calif. Assn. Sch. Social Workers (treas., dir. 1978-79), San Francisco Alliance Black Educators, San Francisco Classroom Tchrs. Assn. Democrat. Roman Catholic. Home: 1305 Laguna St San Francisco CA 94115 Office: 135 Van Ness Ave Educators San Francisco CA 94102

RICE, CANDACE KOHLES, shopping center executive; b. Twin Falls, Idaho, Apr. 29, 1948; d. Fabian Sebastian and Bessie Inez (Chesnut) Kohles; m. William Warren Rice, Jan. 30, 1948; children—Dannell, Kathryn. B.A., Calif. State U.-Fullerton, 1970. Lic. real estate broker; cert. mktg. dir. Ptnr., v.p. Cube, Inc., Los Angeles, 1974-77; asst. mgr. World Trade Ctr., Los Angeles, 1974-78, Buena Park Mall, Calif., 1979-81; centre mgr. Richard Ellis, London, 1982-83; leasing and devel. mgr. Donahue Schriber, Costa Mesa, Calif., 1984—. Patentee plexiglass cubes. Bd. dirs. Boys Club Buena Park, 1979-81; bd. dirs. Visitors and Conv. Bur. Buena Park, 1979-81. Recipient President's award Boys Club Buena Park, 1980. Mem. Internat. Council Shoppings Ctrs. (Maxi award 1980), Assessment Treatment Services Ctr. (com. chmn. Santa Ana 1984-86), So. Calif. Mktg. Dirs. Assn. (bd. dirs. Los Angeles 1979-81), Alpha Chi Omega (Outstanding Woman of Orange County award 1970). Republican. Avocations: tennis, skiing, cycling, riding. Home: 1524 Serenade Terr Corona del Mar CA 92625 Office: Donahue Schriber 3200 Bristol St Suite 660 Costa Mesa CA 92626

RICE, CATHLEEN BLANCHARD, health care administrator, consultant; b. Hartford, Vt., Sept. 5, 1921; d. Seth Elwell and Alice Mary (Wylie) Blanchard; m. Stanley Edward Rice, Feb. 11, 1942; children—Thomas Edward, Susan Alice Rice Ranney, Stephen Charles. Grad. Hanover Sch. Practical Nursing, N.H., 1962; student Northeastern U., Vt. Coll., U. Vt., also continuing edn. courses. Lic. health care adminstr., practical nurse, N.H., Fla., Vt. Aircraft communicator CAA, Lebanon, N.H., 1943-50; office mgr. Rice Trucking Co., White River Junction, Vt., 1946-53; operator New Eng. Telephone Co., White River Junction, 1955-57; pvt. duty nurse, White River Junction, 1961-62; founder health care adminstr. Brookside Nursing Home, White River Junction, 1963-84, pres., cons., 1979—, v.p., treas., 1967-79; cons. Hartford Vocat. Sch., White River Junction, committeewoman Vt. Agy. Human Services, 1978. Leader Brownies Swiftwater council Girl Scouts U.S.A., White River Junction, 1955-59; Sunday sch. tchr. Methodist Ch., White River Junction, 1966-67. Recipient Bus. Woman of Yr. award Bus. and Profl. Womens Club, 1979; Community Service award Vt. Grange, 1985. Fellow Am. Coll. Health Care Adminstrs.; mem. Lic. Practical Nurses Assn., Nat. Assn. Practical Nurses, Am. Health Care Assn., Vt. Health Care Assn., DAR. Republican. Avocations: horses; interior decorating; reading; travel; camping. Home: 4063 NE Skyline Dr Jensen Beach FL 33457 Office: Brookside Nursing Home Inc 120 Christian St RFD White River Junction VT 05001

RICE, DOROTHY PECHMAN, medical economist; b. Bklyn., June 11, 1922; d. Gershon and Lena (Schiff) Pechman; student Bklyn. Coll., 1938-39; B.A., U. Wis., 1941; D.Sc. (hon.), Coll. Medicine and Dentistry N.J., 1979; m. John Donald Rice, Apr. 3, 1943; children—Kenneth D., Donald B., Thomas H. With hosp. and med. facilities USPHS, Washington, 1960-61; med. econs. studies Social Security Adminstrn., 1962-63, health econs. br. Community Health Service, USPHS, 1964-65; chief health ins. research br. Social Security Adminstrn., 1966-72, dep. asst. commr. research and stats., 1972-75; dir. Nat. Center Health Stats., Rockville, Md., 1976-82; prof. dept. social and behavioral scis. Sch. Nursing, U. Calif., San Francisco, 1982—. Recipient Social Security Adminstrn. citation, 1968, Disting. Service medal HEW, 1974; award Jack C. Massey Found., 1978. Fellow Am. Public Health Assn. (Domestic award for excellence 1978), Am. Statis. Assn.; mem. Inst. Medicine, Am. Econ. Assn., Population Assn. Am., LWV. Developer health ins. research program Social Security Adminstrn. Contbr. articles to profl. jours. Home: 1055 Amito Ave Berkeley CA 94705 Office: Sch Nursing N631 San Francisco CA 94143

RICE, EDGENIE HIGGINS, educational and arts consultant; b. Worcester, Mass., Feb. 8, 1942; d. Milton Prince and Alice Lord (Coonley) Higgins; A.A., Bradford Coll., 1962; cert. Ecole du Louvre, France, 1963; B.A., Boston U., 1965; m. Donald Sands Rice, Aug. 27, 1966; children—Alice Higgins, Edgenie Reynolds. Exhibits coordinator Smithsonian Inst. Traveling Exhibition Service, 1966 67; visual arts coordinator N.Y. State Council on the Arts, N.Y.C., 1967-70; asst. dir. Community Environments, N.Y.C., 1970-71; cons. Mus. Collaborative, N.Y.C., 1972; originator, dir. UN-US Mother-Child Workshop, N.Y.C., 1972-81. Bd. dirs. YWCA, N.Y.C., 1972-85, chmn. vol. com., 1979-81, exec. com., 1976-77, 78-82; mem. program com. World Mut. Service Com., 1972-76, vice chmn. program com., 1982-83, chmn. visitors service for nat. bd., 1971-72; mem. jr. council Mus. Modern Art, 1973-76; mem. grants com. Ch. of the Heavenly Rest, 1979-81; mem. benefit com. Cooper-Hewitt Nat. Mus. Design, Legal Aid Soc., YWCA-YMCA Camping Council; parents league rep. Chapin Sch., 1980-81; trustee, mem. arts and student affairs coms., acad. affairs, chmn. hon. degrees com. Clark U., Worcester, Mass., 1981—; pres. Civitas, 1982—. Clubs: Cosmopolitan, The River. Home: 1120 Fifth Ave New York NY 10128

RICE, ELIZABETH FISCHER, financial executive; b. Highland Park, Ill., Mar. 25, 1953; d. Thomas Clark and Nancy (Knight) Fischer; m. Larry Alan Rice, Feb. 25, 1984. B.A., Coe Coll., 1975; M.B.A., Northwestern U., 1977. Fin. analyst Xerox Corp., Rochester, N.Y., 1977-81, plant controller, Oak Brook, Ill., 1981-85, program fin. mgr., Rochester, 1985—. Mem. Nat. Assn. Female Execs., Xerox Mgmt. Assn., Omicron Delta Epsilon, Delta Delta Delta. Republican. Episcopalian. Avocations: racquetball; running; reading. Home: 134 Beckwith Terr Rochester NY 14610 Office: Xerox Corp 1350 Jefferson Rd Henrietta NY 14623

RICE, ELLEN FRANCES, career development and vocational counselor; b. Gettysburg, Pa., May 14, 1941; d. John Stanley and Grace Luene (Rogers) R. B.A. in English, Gettysburg Coll., 1964; M.A. in Christian Edn., Wheaton Grad. Sch., Ill., 1966; M.S. in Guidance and Counseling, Nova U., 1973. Cert. tchr., Fla. Dir. Christian edn. Greenville Community Reformed Ch., Scarsdale, N.Y., 1966-69; tchr. St. Mark's Episcopal Sch., Ft. Lauderdale, 1969-70; youth dir. First United Methodist Ch., Ft. Lauderdale, 1972-74; vocat. counselor Christian Counseling Ministries, Pompano Beach, Fla., 1986—. Sec., bd. dirs. Ctr. of Pastoral Counseling and Human Devel., Ft. Lauderdale, 1973-78; vol. North Ridge Gen. Hosp. Aux., Ft. Lauderdale, 1977-81; mem. nat. bd. Med. Coll. Pa., Phila., 1976-82. Mem. AAUW, Delta Gamma. Clubs: Ft. Lauderdale Yacht, Lago Mar Beach. Home: 1750 S Ocean Ln Fort Lauderdale FL 33316 Office: Ctr of Christian Counseling Ministries 1625 NE 28th St Pompano Beach FL 33064

RICE, GERI E., law office managment consultant; b. Chgo., Apr. 13, 1947; d. Benjamin Louis and Perle Bertha Friedman; Legal Asst. Cert. with honors, Mallinckrodt Coll., 1975; B.S., B.A. with distinction, U. Phoenix, 1983. Legal asst. law dept. Urban Investment and Devel. Co., Chgo., 1972-79; law office mgr. Coffield Ungaretti Harris & Slavin, Chgo., 1979-80; law office adminstr. Dinkelspiel & Dinkelspiel, San Francisco, 1980-82; mgmt. cons., San Francisco, 1982—; mem. faculty Practising Law Inst., N.Y.C., 1978-79; mem. adv. com., lectr. Mallinckrodt Coll., Harper Coll., 1977-79; mem. faculty Paralegal Tng. and Resource Center, San Francisco, 1981-82, San Francisco State U., 1982—; speaker, trainer in field. Author articles. Mem. Ill. Paralegal Assn. (dir. 1976-79; pres. 1977-79), Nat. Fedn. Paralegal Assns. (chmn. com.), Assn. Legal Adminstrs. (co-chmn. edn. com., dir. 1981—, treas. 1982-83), Internat. Platform Assn. Author articles in field. Office: GER Cons 1908 1/2 Green St San Francisco CA 94123

RICE, JENNIFER SUSAN, development, public relations executive; b. Houston, Jan. 18, 1951; d. Myer and Rose (Forrest) R.; B.A. with honors, U. Tex., Austin, 1972, M.A. in Communications, 1974. Dist. exec. dir. Am. Cancer Soc., Austin, Tex., 1974-75, br. dirs., Miami, Fla., 1975-76; dir. public info./research Urban League Greater Miami, 1976-77; mental health planning cons., communications coordinator Miami Jewish Home and Hosp. for Aged, 1977-79; dir. public relations and devel. James Archer Smith Hosp., Homestead, Fla., 1979-81; assoc. dir. N.J. region Deborah Hosp. Found., Browns Mills, N.J., 1981-83; mktg. mgr. West Coast Reply-o/Kennedy Sinclair, Wayne, N.J., 1983-84; exec. dir. Ocean County Coll. Found., Toms River, N.J., 1984—. Mem. public edn. com. Am. Cancer Soc.; mem. Child Abuse Task Force, Mental Health Assn. NIMH fellow, 1972. Mem. Public Relations Soc. Am., Nat. Assn. Hosp. Devel., Nat. Soc. Fund Raising Execs., Fla. Hosp. Assn., S. Fla. Hosp. Public Relations Assn., Internat. Assn. Bus. Communicators (pres. S. Fla. chpt.), Phi Kappa Phi. Home: 1205 Haynes Run Medford NJ 08055 Office: Ocean County Coll Found College Dr CN2001 Toms River NJ 08763

RICE, JOY KATHARINE, clinical psychologist, educator; b. Oak Park, Ill., Mar. 26, 1939; d. Joseph Theodore and Margaret Sophia (Bednarik) Straka; student Rosary Coll., 1956-57; B.F.A. with high honors, U. Ill., 1960; M.S., U. Wis., Madison, 1962, M.S. (teaching fellow, Knapp fellow), 1964, Ph.D. (USPHS predoctoral fellow), 1967; m. David Gordon Rice, Sept. 1, 1962; children—Scott Alan, Andrew David. Asst. dir. U. Wis. Counseling Center, Madison, 1966-74, dir. Office of Continuing Edn. Services, 1972-78, prof. ednl. policy studies and women's studies, 1974—; pvt. practice psychology, 1967—; mem. State of Wis. Ednl. Approval Bd., 1972-73, Office of Career Edn. Adult Edn. Commn., Washington, 1978. Office of Edn. instnl. grantee, 1974-77. Mem. Am. Psychol. Assn., Wis. Psychol. Assn., Nat. Register Health Service Providers Psychology, Am. Ednl. Research Assn., Adult Edn. Assn. (merit service award 1978, 79, 80, 82), Am. Assn. Higher Edn., Internat. Council Psychologists, Nat. Assn. for Women Deans, Adminstrs. and Counselors (editorial bd. 1984—), Phi Delta Kappa. Author: Living Through Divorce: A Developmental Approach to Divorce Therapy, 1985; mem. editorial bd. Lifelong Learning, 1979—; contbr. articles to profl. jours. Home: 4230 Waban Hill Madison WI 53711 Office: 243 Education Bldg University of Wisconsin Madison WI 53706

RICE, JUDY ERWIN, insurance company executive; b. Houston, Sept. 9, 1947; d. Hal and Uva Marie (Loftis) Burton Erwin; m. Michael Allen Teague, Mar. 17, 1967 (div. Feb. 1973); children—Michael, Kathy, Jennifer; m. John Franklin Rice, Sept. 28, 1973. Student Stephen F. Austin U., 1966-67. Cert. ins. counselor. Personal lines clk. Liberty Mut., Houston, 1967-68, CEM Agys., Houston, 1968-72; multi-lines clk. Atkinson Bros., Houston, 1972-73, Reliable Ins. Agy., Temple, Tex., 1975-77; owner Rice Enterprises, Temple, Tex., 1977-80; account exec. Reliable Ins., Temple, 1980—. Vice-pres. Temple Civic Ballet, Tex., 1979; bd. dirs. Cen-Tex. Zool. Soc., Waco, 1978. Mem. Fedn. Ins. Women, Nat. Assn. Female Execs., Temple Ins. Women (treas., sec. 1982), Temple Agts. Assn. (sec.-treas. 1984). Republican. Methodist. Club: Lake Belton Yacht (sec.-treas. 1984) (Temple). Avocations: needlework; reading; gardening. Home: 141 Woodland Trail Belton TX 76513

RICE, LILLIAN HART, furniture manfacturing company executive, mathematics educator; b. Canaan, W.Va., Mar. 26, 1942; d. Hartzel Meredith and Nellie Blanche (Watson) R. A.B., Glenville State Coll., 1965; M.S., W.Va., U., 1968. Grad. teaching asst. W.Va. U., Morgantown, 1965-66; instr. math. Radford Coll., Va., 1966-67; asst. prof. math. Bluefield State Coll., W.Va., 1968-72; sr. research analyst Lane Co. Inc., Altavista, Va., 1972-84, dir. mktg. research and prodn. ordering, 1984—. Bd. dirs. Altavista Sheltered Workshop, 1975—. Mem. Am. Mktg. Assn., Assn. Women Mathematicians, Beta Sigma Phi. Home: 207 B E Hurt Rd Hurt VA 24563 Office: Lane Co Inc Frankin St Altavista VA 24517

RICE, LINDA TILLMAN, administrative assistant; b. Orlando, Fla., June 3, 1943; d. Thomas John and Stella Frances (Block) Tillman; student Valencia Community Coll., Orlando, 1973-74, Fla. Jr. Coll., Jacksonville, 1976-78, U. North Fla., 1983-84. Exec. sec. to mgr. advance systems engring. Martin Marietta Aerospace Corp., Orlando, 1963-69; exec. sec. to pres., also office mgr., fashion coordinator and writer Act II Jewelry Inc., Orlando, 1969-76; legal asst., sec. Howell, Howell, Liles, Braddock & Milton, Jacksonville, Fla., 1976-78; exec. asst. to owners and developers Regency Sq. Shopping Center, Jacksonville, 1978-79; free-lance legal sec. and asst., Jacksonville, 1979-80; adminstrv. asst. to sr. v.p. human resources and labor relations Seaboard System R.R., Jacksonville, 1980-83. Hospitality chmn., v.p. Women of Jacksonville Art Mus., 1977-80, publicity chmn., 1981-82; mem. Republican Nat. Com. Nat. Secs. Assn. (asst. treas. 1973-74, sec. 1974-75), Women's Guild of Cummer Gallery, Women's Guild Jacksonville Mus. Arts and Scis., Nat. Assn. Ry. Bus. Women (pres. 1984-85). Recipient Dist. VI Railway Bus. Woman of Yr., 1986. Episcopalian. Home: 10754-8 Scott Mill Rd Jacksonville FL 32217

RICE, MARY ALICE, aviation maintenance training company executive; b. Sabetha, Kans., Nov. 23, 1932; d. Edward Martin and Mary Margaret (Mohan) Boeding; m. James William Rice, June 9, 1956; children—Michael, Catherine, Mark, Patrick, Timothy, Eileen. Student dietetics Benedictine Coll., Atchison, Kans., 1950-52; student aviation San Jacinto Coll., 1974, bus. U. Houston, 1976. Reservations and flight control positions Braniff Airways, Kansas City, Mo., 1952-56; chairperson bd. A & J Enterprises, Houston, 1971—. Editor Aviation Technician Edn. Council Newsletter, 1978-83. State treas. Ch. Women United, Tex., 1980-84, fin. chairperson, 1984-86. Mem. Nat. Assn. Women Bus. Owners. Democrat. Roman Catholic. Avocations: reading, travel, golf. Home: 18727 Point Lookout Dr Houston TX 77058 Office: A & J Enterprises Inc 8880 Telephone Rd Houston TX 77061

RICE, PATRICIA BYRNE, tannery executive, taxidermy executive; b. Yuba City, Calif., July 31, 1939; d. Onslow Anthony and Margaret Pearl (Baeta) Byrne; children—Christine Marie, Deborah Lee, Michelle Lyn. Student Vallejo Jr. Coll., 1957. Apt. mgr. Metzger Bros., Columbus, Ohio, 1971-72; sec., treas. Midwest Custom Tannery, Columbus, 1972-81, pres., owner, 1981—. Co-chmn. Ohioans for Wildlife Conservation, Columbus, 1976-77. Mem. Ohio Taxidermist Trade Register (bd. dirs. 1980-82), Taxidermist Suppliers Assn. (sec.-treas. 1983—), Profl. Tanners Guild (v.p. 1984—), Nat. Rifle Assn., Ducks Unltd. (booklet chmn. 1984). Republican. Roman Catholic. Lodge: Women of Moose (jr. regent 1964-65). Avocations: fishing; leather work; hunting. Office: Midwest Custom Tannery Inc 464 W Gay St Columbus OH 43215

RICE, RAMONA GAIL, aquatic physiologist, ecological phycologist, educator, consultant; b. Texarkana, Tex., Feb. 15, 1950; d. Raymond Lester and Jessie Gail (Hubbard) R. B.S., Ouachita U., 1972; M.S., U. Ark., 1975, Ph.D., 1978; postgrad. Utah State U., 1978-80. Undergrad. asst. Ouachita U., Arkadelphia, Ark., 1970-72; grad. teaching asst. U. Ark., Fayetteville, 1972, 77-78, grad. research asst., 1973-77; asst. research scholar, scientist Fla. Internat. U., Miami, 1980-85; research coordinator, faculty Pratt Community Coll., Kans., 1985—; adj. instr. Miami Dade Community Coll., 1984-85. Contbr. articles to profl. jours. Judge Dade County Sci. Fair, Fla., 1981-85;

tchr. Sunday Sch. First Baptist Ch., South Miami, Fla., 1982-85, leader girls in action, 1982-83, youth chaperone, 1982-85. Grantee, NSF, 1981-83, Fla. Dept. Environ., 1981-83, EPA, 1983-85. Mem. Fla. Acad. Scis., AAAS, Phycological Soc. Am., Soc. Limnology and Oceanography, Sigma Xi. Democrat. Avocations: pianist; crochet; needlework; photography; reading. Office: Dept Biol Scis Pratt Community Coll Pratt KS 67124

RICE, ROMA JEAN, magazine editor; b. Lincoln, Nebr., Sept. 14, 1936; d. Conrad and Elizabeth (Brumm) Leichner; B.S. in Bus. Adminstrn., U. Nebr., 1958. Buyer, Macy's Mo.-Kans., 1958-65; adminstrv. asst. City Mgrs. Office Kansas City (Mo.), 1965-69; editor The Workbasket, Modern Handcraft, Inc., Kansas City, 1977—. Mem. Fashion Group, Independence Young Matrons, Eastern Jackson County Bar Aux., AAUW, Phi Chi Theta. Office: 4251 Pennsylvania Ave Kansas City MO 64111

RICE, ROSE-ANNE, safety equipment manufacturing executive, designer; b. Flandreau, S.D., Feb. 22, 1921; d. Vincent Archibald Doyle and Olga (Andersen) Doyle-Hartigan; m. Ashley Weston Rice, Feb. 24, 1949 (dec. Feb. 1966); stepchildren—Michael, Steven, Timothy, Patricia, Barbara. Student Augustana Coll., Sioux Falls, S.D., 1939-40; B.F.A., U. Wash., 1943; M.A., Art Ctr. Sch., Los Angeles, 1945; postgrad. U. Calif.-Northridge, 1957-59. Asst. buyer shoes Frederick & Nelson, Seattle, 1938-43; advt. designer Doyle Design, Los Angeles, 1945-49; art dir. Broadway Dept. Store, Los Angeles, 1949-55, TAT Advt., Burbank, Calif., 1955-57; designer Rice Mfg. Co. Inc., Van Nuys, Calif., 1949-66, pres., owner, designer, 1966—. Designer silk banner (AIA award 1958, exhibited in Nat. Gallery Art, 1958). Vice pres., program chmn. Delphian Soc., Los Angeles, 1955-68; active Van Nuys Women's Club, Calif., 1955-63, United Way Fund, Van Nuys, 1955-63; program chmn. 22d Dist. Republican Assembly, Los Angeles, 1958-59. Recipient Woman of Yr. in Bus. award Delphian Soc., 1967; Newman Endowment grantee U. Wash., Seattle, 1943. Mem. Soc. Plastics Engrs. (program chairperson Los Angeles chpt. 1967-68, Pioneer in Plastics award 1969), Van Nuys C. of C., AAUW. Democrat. Lutheran. Developed vinyl glove, 1948-49, vinyl traffic cone, 1960. Avocations: gardening; photography; painting; reading. Office: Rice Mfg Co Inc 14941 Oxnard St Van Nuys CA 91409

RICE, SUSAN JOETTE, nurse; b. Topeka, Nov. 15, 1946; d. Claude Harvey and Martha May (McClellan) R.; student Pasadena Nazarene Coll., 1964-66; B.S. in Nursing, Calif. State U., Los Angeles, 1969, M.S.N., 1982; postgrad Cambridge Grad. Sch. Psychology, Los Angeles, 1985—. Staff nurse Children's Hosp. Los Angeles, 1969-75, asst. head nurse, 1972-74, nurse mgr., 1974-75; nursing unit coordinator newborn and neonatal intensive care nurseries, perinatal clinician Glendale (Calif.) Adventist Med. Center, 1976-78; neonatal clin. specialist Huntington Meml. Hosp., Pasadena, 1981-85; staff nurse mental health unit Glendale Adventist Med. Ctr., 1985—. Vol. counselor Pasadena Mental Health Ctr., 1985—. Mem. Am. Assn. Critical Care Nurses, Calif. Perinatal Assn., Nat. Assn. Neonatal Nurses. Republican. Mem. Nazarene Ch. Home: 133 E Pamela Rd Monrovia CA 91016

RICE, VIRGINIA DOCKING, civic worker; b. Columbus, Miss., Nov. 22; d. Thomas Grant and Annie Strong (Duncan) Blackwell; m. George Docking, Jan. 25, 1925 (dec. Jan. 1964); children—Robert, George Richard; m. Carl V. Rice, Aug. 4, 1978. B.S., Kans. U. Columnist Kans. newspapers, 1958-61. Exec. bd. Mid-Am. Art Alliance, Kansas City, 1979—; pres. Friends of Kans. Library, Lawrence, 1968-70, Friends of Kansas City Library, 1980-82; bd. dirs. City Beautiful Commn. of Kansas City, Kans.; adv. bd. Kans. Arts Commn., 1965—, Gold Medal Club, Kans.; trustee William Allen White Found., Sch. Journalism, U. Kans. Mem. Women in Communication (hon.), Nat. Assn. Am. Pen Women, Kans. Authors Club, Daus. of Cincinnati, DAR, P.E.O., Beta Sigma Phi (hon.), Gamma Phi Beta. Democrat. Home: 2108 Washington Blvd Kansas City KS 66102

RICE-AVILA, PATRICIA ANN, general accounting manager; b. Aldrich, Mo., Aug. 24, 1946; d. William Wayne and Wilda Mae (Lowery) Rice; A.A., Southwest Baptist U., Bolivar, Mo., 1966; B.A., Southwest Mo. State U.; postgrad. Calif. State U.-Fullerton; m. Anthony Avila III; children—Jessica Jean, Clifford Wayne, Jacqueline Marie, Alicia JoAnne. Office mgr. Patscheck-Veiga Constrn. Co., Tustin, Calif., 1972-75; asst. to controller Richards West Co., Newport Beach, Calif., 1976-78; acctg. supr. Warner Lambert Co., Anaheim, Calif., 1978-80, supr. fin. analysis and planning, 1980; mgr. fin. control Pepsi Cola, Torrance, Calif., 1980-82; sr. fin. adminstr. Microdata Corp., (name changed to McDonnel Douglas Computer Systems Co.), Newport Beach, Calif., 1982-86, gen. acct. mgr. Printronix, Irving, Calif., 1986—. Bd. dirs. Real Reasons Homes for Abused Children. Mem. Nat. Assn. Female Execs., Am. Prodn. and Inventory Control Soc., Am. Mgmt. Assn., AAUW, NOW (chpt. program chmn. 1977), LaLeche League (chpt. publicity chmn. 1972-73). Democrat. Roman Catholic. Home: 29805 Rustic Oak Laguna Niguel CA 92677 Office: 30100 Town Center Dr Suite 102 Laguna Niguel CA 92677

RICE-MOORE, CHERYL LEIGH, accountant, business administrator; b. Phila., Oct. 26, 1949; d. Junius Marcus Emerson and Sylvia Lorraine (Rice) Ferguson; m. Acel Moore, Oct. 19, 1974; B.S. in Mktg. and Acctg., LaSalle Coll., 1980. Nat. pub. relations officer Nat. Assn. Black Accts., Inc., Washington, 1980; fiscal field specialist/pre-audit monitor Opportunities Industrialization Ctrs. Am., Inc., Phila., 1980-81; fiscal corp. adminstr. Gaudenzia, Inc., Phila., 1982-85; controller Hamlyn Assocs., Inc., Phila., 1985—; vis. lectr. U. Pa. Community Wharton Edn. Program, Phila., 1981, 82, 83-84. Mem. Nat. Assn. Black Accts., Inc. (2d v.p. local chpt. 1982, 83, Eastern regional treas. 1983, 84, scholarship awards dinner chmn. local chpt. 1979, 80, 81; outstanding mem. award 1981). Baptist. Home: 6618 Greene St Philadelphia PA 19119 Office: Hamlyn Assocs 210 Church St G Philadelphia PA 19106

RICH, HELEN WALL (MRS. ARTHUR L. RICH), educator; b. Chester, S.C., May 4, 1912; d. George Addison and Georgia (Hardin) Wall; student Queen's Coll., 1930-32; B.S. summa cum laude, Catawba Coll., 1934; diploma in piano playing Juilliard Sch. Music, 1938; diplomas Christiansen Choral Sch., 1950, 51; m. Arthur Lowndes Rich, July 26, 1934; children—Arthur Lowndes, Ruth Anne. Instr. music Catawba Coll., Salisbury, N.C., 1934-43; univ. organist Mercer U., Macon, Ga., 1944-50, asst. prof. music, 1950-73, prof. emeritus, 1973—; organ recitalist throughout S.E.; v.p. Tudor Apts., Inc., Atlanta, 1960-73; pres. Biscayne Apts., Atlanta, 1976—. Mem. Federated Music Clubs (hon.; chmn. scholarship contest), Ga. Piano Tchrs. Guild, Nat. Assn. Schs. Music (asso.), Am. Coll. and Univ. Concert Mgrs. Assn. (asso.), Cardinal Key Soc. Mercer U. (hon.), Delta Omicron. Club: Morning Music (Macon, dir.). Home: 369 Candler Dr Macon GA 31204

RICH, INA, travel agency executive, consultant; b. N.Y.C., Oct. 22, 1932; d. Alfred and Lillian (Blumenson) Heller; m. Allen Norman Rich, Aug. 30, 1952; children—Donna Devore, Michele Esman. B.A., Queens Coll., 1953. Cert. travel cons. Tchr. N.Y.C. Schs., 1953-56; tour leader Metric Tours, Scarsdale, N.Y., 1961-65, dir., 1961-80, pres. Metric Travel, 1980; pres. Rich Worldwide Travel, Scarsdale, 1980—; mem. adv. bd. dirs. Pan Am, White Plains, N.Y., 1983—, Eastern Airlines, N.Y.C., 1982—; coordinator Inst. Cert. Travel Agts., Scarsdale, 1980-82. Leader Girls Scouts U.S.A., New Rochelle, N.Y., 1963; bd. dirs. PTA, New Rochelle, 1964-70. Mem. Am. Soc. Travel Agts. (program com. 1973—), Assn. of Westchester Travel Agts. (advisor 1980—), 41-74 Women in Travel, Pacific Area Travel Agts. Jewish. Lodge: Women's Am. Ort Temple Israel (pres. 1966-68, editor 1970-75). Avocations: golf; reading. Home: 38 Amherst Dr New Rochelle NY 10804 Office: Rich Worldwide Travel 1495 Weaver St Scarsdale NY 10583

RICH, JEANNE GADOUA, excavation and construction company executive; b. Clinton, Mass., Mar. 18, 1958; d. Maurice and Mary Frances (Vienneau) Gadoua; m. Paul Francis Rich, Sept. 6, 1981; children—Tania Jeanne, Joseph Paul. A.S. in Law Enforcement with honors, Mount Wachusett Community Coll., 1978; B.S. in Criminal Justice, U. Lowell, 1980; postgrad. Clark U., 1982. Lic. locksmith; lic. real estate salesperson. Adminstrv. asst. to dir. Clinton Parks and Recreation, Mass., 1974-80; security officer Norton Co., Worcester, Mass., 1979-82; owner P.F. Rich Co., Lancaster, Mass., 1981-83, ptnr., 1983—; spl. police officer Lancaster Police Dept., 1984-85, Worcester Police Dept., 1980-82. Author report writing tng. manual, 1981. Pres., Clinton Woman's Softball Assn., 1983. Mem. U.S. C. of C. Avocations: skiing, gardening, horseback riding, reading, softball. Home and Office: 307 Centerbridge Rd Lancaster MA 01523

RICH, JUDITH G. HEMPHILL, insurance sales representative, rental property owner; b. Murphy, N.C., June 23, 1947; d. Ray Mauney and Mary Grace (Colwell) Hemphill; m. Sidney F. Rich, July 3, 1965 (div. 1970); 1 child, Cary R. Student Kennesaw Coll., 1977-78. Lic. ins. agt., real estate agt. Sales rep. Combined Ins. Co., Chgo., 1972-76; policy service rep. Prudential Property and Casualty Ins., Atlanta, 1976-77; sales rep. Fran Hale Ad Agy., Marietta, Ga., 1977-79, Atlantic and Pacific Life Ins., Atlanta, 1979-80; dist. sales mgr. Mut. of Omaha, College Park, Ga., 1980-84; sales rep. Hagan & Assocs., Marietta, 1984—. Recipient awards Combined Ins., 1973, 74-75 Mut. of Omaha, 1982-83. Mem. Ins. Women of Cobb County (pub. relations chmn. 1986—). Mem. Ch. of God. Avocation: collecting old family photographs. Home: 146 Riverchase Dr Woodstock GA 30188 Office: Hagan & Assocs 16 Norcross St Bldg 1 Roswell GA 30075

RICH, MARCIA R., lawyer; b. N.Y.C., Dec. 29, 1948; d. Jack and Beatrice (Fishman) R. B.A., Bard Coll., 1970; J.D., Bklyn. Law Sch., 1973. Bar: N.Y. 1974, U.S. Dist. Ct. (ea. dist.) N.Y., 1976. Staff atty. juvenile rights div. Legal Aid Soc. N.Y.C., 1973-77; assoc. law asst. to justices Supreme Ct. 1st Jud. Dist., N.Y.C., 1977—. Vol. Am. Heart Assn., N.Y.C., 1979—. Mem. New York County Lawyers Assn. (com. law reform 1983—), ABA, N.Y. State Bar Assn., Assn. Law Assts. City N.Y. (exec. bd. 1980-81), N.Y. Women's Bar Assn. Office: Law Dept Supreme Ct 1st Jud Dist 60 Centre St New York NY 10007

RICH, SUSAN ABBY, efficiency consultant; b. Bklyn., Apr. 11, 1946; d. Milton and Jeanette (Merns) Rich. B.A., Bklyn. Coll., 1967, M.A., 1976, advanced cert. in administrn. and supervision, 1977; cert. indsl. relations UCLA, 1981. Tchr. speech, theater N.Y.C. Bd. Edn., 1967-77; employee relations supr. Crocker Nat. Bank, 1977-81; plant personnel mgr. Boise Cascade Corp., 1981-82; cons. office efficiency and productivity Get Organized, Get Rich, Playa del Rey, Calif., 1982—. Mem. Women's Referral Service (Mem. of Year award 1985), The Network Group, Venice Area C. of C. (bd. dirs.). Office: Get Organized Get Rich 7777 W 91 St Suite 1154B Playa del Rey CA 90293

RICHARD, ANITA LOUISE, management consultant; b. Willard, N.Y., June 22, 1951; d. Mervin Gerald and Illene (Rosenberg) Isaacson; m. J. Ernest Richard, May 16, 1981; stepchildren—Christine, Chad. Student, U. Fla., 1969-70, Bklyn. Coll., 1972-74, Bernard Baruch Coll., 1974-76; B.A. magna cum laude, Golden Gate U., 1982. Mktg. mgr. Exxon Office Systems, N.Y.C., 1976-77, program mgr., Dallas, 1977-78, br. mgr., Pasadena, Calif., 1978-79, br. sales mgr., Century City, Calif., 1979, regional sales program mgr., Marina Del Rey, Calif., 1979-81, mktg. mgr., San Francisco, 1981-82; product mgr. Wells Fargo, San Francisco, 1984; mgmt. cons. J. Richard & Co., Hillsborough, Calif., 1984—. Mem. Am. Mgmt. Assn., Am. Compensation Assn., Am. Mktg. Assn., Group Health Assn. Am., No. Calif. Human Resource Council, No. Calif. Health Care Mktg. Assn. Republican. Jewish. Clubs: Los Angeles Athletic; Decathlon (Santa Clara, Calif.). Avocations: photography; piano; hiking. Home: 25 W Avondale Rd Hillsborough CA 94010 Office: J Richard & Co 25 W Avondale Rd Hillsborough CA 94010

RICHARD, BETTY BYRD, geriatric fitness educator, consultant, writer; b. Charleston, W.Va., Aug. 30, 1922; d. Ernest O'Farrell and Blanche Elizabeth (Davenport) Byrd; m. Samuel Jackson Richard, Jr., June 12, 1943; children—Caroline Byrd Richard Rossman, Samuel Jackson III. B.A. in Sociology, U. Charleston (W.Va.), 1977. Research assoc. exercise planning and design Frankel Found., Charleston, 1966-70; assoc. adminstr., 1970-79; cons. geriatric fitness W.Va. Commn. on Aging, 1979-83; dir. Gerokinetics, Charleston, 1984—; W.Va. co-originator co-dir. Preventicare program, 1970-79; coordinator 1st Appalachian Conf. on Phys. Activity and Aging, 1973; coordinator Gerokinesiatrics Conf. on Aging, 1977; author books including: Be Alive as Long As You Live, rev. edit. 1977; Age and Mobility, 1979; contbr. to Guide to Fitness After Fifty, 1977; producer gerokinetics program on audio cassette, 1980, gerokinetics slide/tape program, 1985; featured on weekly pub. TV series on exercise programs for sr. citizens, 1974-75. Recipient Gov.'s Sr. Service award, 1982. Mem. So. Gerontol. Soc., Nat. Council on Aging. Republican. Presbyterian. Club: Edgewood Country (Charleston). Lodge; Eastern Star. Home: 321 Mountain View Dr Charleston WV 25314 Office: Gerokinetics 401 4th Ave South Charleston WV 25303

RICHARD, DARLENE DOLORAS, marketing firm executive, banker; b. Mansfield, Ohio, Jan. 4, 1946; d. Charles Alvertis and Marjorie Elaine (Foster) Swander; m. David Allen Richard, Aug. 14, 1965 (div.). A.A., Famous Artist Sch., 1964; B.A. in Edn., Ohio State U., 1969. Asst. to controller Johnstown Properties, Atlanta, 1978-79, adminstrv. mgr. TCG Communications, Atlanta, 1979; promotional dir. Am. Health Cons., Atlanta, 1979-82; pres. Direct Mktg./R&D, Ltd., Atlanta and Buffalo, 1982—, Marine Midland Bank N.A., Buffalo, 1985—. Mem. Newsletter Assn. Am., Atlanta Ad Club, Nat. Assn. Female Execs., AAUW, Am. Mgmt. Assn., Internat. Oceanographic Found. Republican.

RICHARD, DIANA MARIE, army officer; b. Dallas, Mar. 24, 1958; d. Dee Will and Dorothy Mae (Scott) R. B.S. with honors, Tex. Coll., 1980; student Dallas Bapt. Coll., 1975-76; M.S., Boston U., 1985. Commd. 2d lt., U.S. Army, 1980, advanced through grades to capt., 1983, bn. chem. officer, Stuttgart, Germany, 1983, corps officer, Nellingen, Ger., 1984-86. Mem. Soc. Chem. Officers, NAACP, Delta Sigma Theta. Democrat. Baptist. Lodge: Mem. Order Eastern Star. Home: 6032 Golden Gate Circle Dallas TX 75241

RICHARD, GINGERLYN CARLENE, oil company accountant, consultant; b. Austin, Tex., Mar. 26, 1949; d. Carl Edward and Helen LaVerne (Smith) R. B.S., Tex. Woman's U., 1972. Registered occupational therapist. Asst. chief occupational therapy-psychiatry Meth. Hosp., Houston, 1973-78; acct. Exxon Pipeline Co., Houston, 1981—; staff instr. teaching intern program Meth. Hosp/Tex. Woman's U., 1977-78. Staff mem. adv. bd. outreach Houston YWCA, 1972-79. Mem. Am. Occupational Therapy Assn. Republican. Home: Houston TX 77043 Office: Exxon Pipeline Co 800 Bell St Houston TX 77002

RICHARDS, ALYS PRICE, educational administrator; b. Fort Worth, Nov. 12, 1937; d. Duel Robert and Wilene (Wilson) Price; m. George Arthur Richards, Aug. 13, 1960; children—Lyn Ann, George Arthur II. B.A., So. Meth. U., 1960. Cert. tchr., Tex. Elem. tchr. Dallas Ind. Sch. Dist., 1960-62, 65-66; mgr., owner Green & Price Co., Italy, Tex., 1972-80; bus. mgr. Dr. George Richards, Richardson, Tex., 1980—; owner, mgr. farm, Italy, Tex., 1975—; personnel asst. So. Meth. U., Dallas, 1982-84, worker's compensation coordinator, 1983-84, coordinator spl. events, 1984—. Bd. dirs. Dallas County Dental Aux.; pres. bd. dirs. Richardson Symphony Orch. (Tex.), 1979-80, Richardson Symphony Orch. Guild, 1971-73, Tex. Women's Assn. for Symphony Orch., 1976-77; mem. adminstrv. bd., chmn. council on ministries 1st United Methodist Ch., Richardson. Recipient Five-Yr. award, 1976, Ten-Yr. award, 1981, both Richardson Symphony Orch.; Cert. of Appreciation, Exchange Club, 1982. Mem. Alpha Delta Pi (pres. 1968-69), Zeta Phi Eta. Clubs: Richardson's Woman's, Prairie Greek Garden (pres. 1976-77), Criterion Book (pres. 1977-78), Mustang, So. Meth. U. Staff. Home: 4 Forest Park Dr Richardson TX 75080 Office: So Meth U Dallas TX 75275

RICHARDS, ANN WILLIS, state official; b. Waco, Tex., Sept. 1, 1933; d. Cecil and Ona Willis; m. David R. Richards; children—Cecile, Dan, Clark, Ellen. B.A., Baylor U., 1954; cert. U. Tex.-Austin, 1955. Adminstrv. asst. to Tex. State Rep. Sarah Weddington, 1973-75; co-commr. Travis County Tex., 1977-82; mem. Pres.'s Adv. Com. on Women, 1978-80, Spl. Commn. on Delivery of Human Services in Tex., 1979-80, Tex. Criminal Justice Adv. Bd., 1981-82; state treas. State of Tex., 1983—; chair Tex. State Depository Bd., 1983—; mem. Tex. State Banking Bd., 1983—, Travis County Democratic Party; govt. and history tchr. Austin Ind. Sch. Dist., 1955-57; mem. Austin Transp. Study, 1977-82. Recipient Woman of Yr. award Women in Communications, 1978; One of Austin's 10 Most Influential Citizens award Austin Am-Statesman, 1978; Outstanding Woman of Central Tex. award AAUW, 1979; Woman of Yr. award Tex. Women's Polit. Caucus, 1981. Mem. Nat. Assn. State Treas., Nat. Assn. Unclaimed Property Adminstrs., Nat. Women's Polit. Caucus, Sierra Club. Address: Treasury Dept PO Box 12608 Capitol Station Austin TX 78711*

RICHARDS, BETTY JANE, employee relations executive; b. Twinsburg, Ohio, July 9, 1930; d. Albert William and Kathryn Irene (Harding) Reese; m. Paul S. Richards, Sept. 4, 1948; children—Leslie, Dolores, Jane, Carol. Student Kent State U., 1974-76. With Ins. Co. N.Am., Cleve., 1948-49; dental asst. Dr. Hammel, Hudson, Ohio, 1949-50; sec. Tom Moore Tractor Co., Mantua, Ohio, 1960-62; inventory control sec. Carlon Products Co., Aurora, Ohio, 1962-65; exec. sec. to pres. Mantaline Corp., Mantua, 1965-73; employee relations mgr. Eaton Corp., Mantua, 1973—. Mem. Pvt. Industry Council, Portage County, Ohio, 1980-83, trustee, 1983; mem. adv. com. Maplewood Area Vocat. Sch., Ravenna, Ohio, 1980-83. Mem. Am. Soc. Personnel Adminstrn. (pres. 1979). Democrat. Home: 3851 Mennonite Rd Mantua OH 44255 Office: Eaton Corp IPP Div Main and Orchard St Mantua OH 44255

RICHARDS, BEVERLY JONES, psychotherapist; b. Phila., May 8, 1946; d. Harry H. and Apolonia (Lima) Darden Williams; m. Lester Van Jones, Sept. 6, 1969 (div. 1980); m. Lawrence Mark Richards, June 23, 1984; stepchildren—Hope, Malaika, Heather. B.S., Cheyney U., 1968; M.S. in Edn., Antioch U., 1974. Cert. Am. Assn. Marriage and Family Therapy, Eastern Pa. Psychiat. Inst., Sch. Family Psychiatry. Caseworker Dept. Pub. Assistance, Phila., 1968-70; tchr. English high sch. Phila. Bd. Edn., 1970-75, counselor, 1975-85, cons., 1985; psychotherapist Women in Transition, Phila., 1980—, cons., trainer, 1981-84; pvt. practice psychotherapy J.S. Assocs., Phila., 1983—; cons. Harambee Inst., Phila., 1980-83, Elaine Carter Assocs., N.Y.C., 1980-81; Bd. dirs. Spruce Family Planning, Phila., 1982-85, Spruce Adolescent Counseling, Phila., 1982-85; vol. lectr. Holmesburg Prison, Pa., 1980. Mem. Am. Assn. Marriage and Family Therapy, Pupil Personnel and Guidance Assn. Phila. Democrat. Episcopalian. Avocations: gardening; art; travel; reading. Office: JS Assocs 1427 Spruce St Philadelphia PA 19102

RICHARDS, CHRISTINE-LOUISE, author, artist, composer, pianist; b. Radnor, Pa., Jan. 11, 1910; d. Joseph Ernest and Catherine (Fletcher) R.; student pvt. schs., art schs., N.Y.C., Munich, Ger. One-woman shows: Stockbridge, Mass., 1947, 48, 52, 53, Oneonta, N.Y., 1960, 61; group shows include: Stockbridge Art Assn., 1931-32; represented in collections, Calif., Mass., N.Y.; owner, founder, pres. Blue Star Music Pub. Co., Pittsfield, Mass., 1946—, now Morris, N.Y. Recipient Silver medal Internat. Inst. Community Service, Cambridge, Eng.; prize of Golden Centaur, others. Fellow Internat. Biog. Assn.; mem. Phila. Art Alliance, Am. Fedn. Musicians, Nightingale-Bamford Alumni Assn., Academia Italia delle arte e del Lavoro (2 gold medals, hon. diploma Master of Painting), Met. Mus. Art, Audubon Soc., Nat. Assn. Composers USA, Emergency Aid of Pa., Pa. Acad. Fine Arts, Nat. Mus. Women in Arts, Acad. Natural Scis., Phila. Mus., Friends N.Y. Pub. Library, Pa. Hort. Soc., Am. Hort. Soc., Bklyn. Bot. Gardens, Met. Opewra Guild, Glimmerglass Opera Theatre, Nat. Trust, Nat. Arbor Day Found., Save the Redwoods, others. Club: Peale (Phila.). Author and Illustrator: The Blue Star Fairy Book of Stories for Children; The Blue Star Fairy Book of More Stories for Children; The Blue Star Fairy Book of New Stories for Children, 1980; Branches, 1983. Composer: (song) What Makes Me Dream of You, 1950, numerous others. Contbr. portrait to Artists U.S.A., 1970-71, 76. Address: Springslea PO Box 188 Morris NY 13808

RICHARDS, CORY DANA, mktg. exec.; b. Los Angeles, July 30, 1955; d. Alfred and Meryl Jean (Weinman) R.; B.A. with honors in Advt./Communications (Calif. State scholar 1973-77, Ballet Assn. scholar 1973-77), U. Calif., Santa Cruz, 1977; postgrad. Loyola Marymount U. Account exec. Public Media Center, San Francisco, 1974-77; public affairs adv. Calbe Channel 6, San Francisco, 1976-77; cons. on public affairs to radio stas., Los Angeles, 1977-78; dir. mktg., product mgr. MCA Records, Los Angeles, 1978-80; dir. mktg. Hang Ten Internat., San Diego, after 1980; now asst. to chmn., dir. advt. Carole Little for Saint Tropez West; asso. producer Live from Gilley's radio show; speaker on women in music UCLA Extension. Vol. nutritionist, tchr. slim living program, fund-raising team capt. YMCA, Los Angeles. Recipient spl. recognition award Cowell Health Center, 1976. Mem. Interfaith Council San Fernando Valley, Women in Bus., Nat. Country Music Assn., Sales and Mktg. Execs., Now. Club: N.Y. Publicity. Office: Los Angeles CA 90048 Home: 536 N Sweetzer Ave Los Angeles CA 90048

RICHARDS, DEBORAH DAVIS, technical writer and editor; b. St. Augustine, Fla., Dec. 9, 1943; d. Philip A. and Ann (Winship) Davis; m. James Lincoln Richards, June 12, 1965 (div. Aug. 1984); 1 dau., Christine. B.A., Wellesley Coll. (Mass.), 1965. Vol., Peace Corps, India, 1966-67, tng. assoc., 1967; clinic dir. Planned Parenthood, Washington, 1968-69; co-founder, dir. Action for Child Transp. Safety, N.Y.C., 1972-82; videotex analyst Buckner News Alliance, Seattle, 1981—; newsletter writer, editor Am. Acad. Pediatrics, Evanston, Ill., 1981—, Nat. Child Passenger Safety Assn., Washington, 1983—; mem. nat. hwy. safety adv. com. U.S. Dept. Transp., 1979-83; cons. Nat. Hwy. Traffic Safety Adminstrn., Washington, 1981-83. Author and narrator (ednl. film) Don't Risk Your Child's Life, 1978, revised, 1980, 83; author, editor (program manual) Protecting Our Own, 1983. Mem. Nat. Child Passenger Safety Assn. (sec. bd. dirs., regional rep. 1981-83). Democrat. Unitarian. Clubs: The Mountaineers, Wellesley (Seattle).

RICHARDS, DONNA FRANCES, advertising agency executive; b. Nacogdoches, Tex., Dec. 3, 1958; d. Don Bruce and Juanita Joy (Booker) R. B.A., Abilene Christian U., 1981. Account exec. BTD Directory Mgmt., Dallas, 1981-82; mktg. mgr., personnel mgr., office mgr. Autofleet Underwriters Agy., Inc., Dallas, 1982-85; nursing aide Skelton Haven Ranch, Princeton, Tex., 1985; owner, operator Ads To Riches, Dallas, 1985—. Ptnr., St. Jude Children's Research Hosp., Memphis, 1984—. Abilene Christian U. communication scholar, 1980. Mem. Nat. Assn. Female Execs. Baptist. Avocations: reading, writing, swimming, snow skiing.

RICHARDS, JANE AILEEN, rehabilitation nursing consultant; b. Oakland, Calif., Oct. 19, 1948; d. John Donald and Mary Dolores (Peters) R. B.S. in Nursing, U. San Francisco, 1970; M.S. in Nursing, San Jose State U., 1976. R.N.; cert. ins. rehab. specialist. Staff nurse ICU Mills Meml. Hosp., San Mateo, Calif., 1970-73; asst. head nurse ICU, 1973-76, edn. specialist, 1976-80, mgr. acute rehab. ctr., 1980-83; rehab. nursing cons. J.R. Assocs., San Mateo, 1983—; cons. Hannah & Brophy Law Firm, San Francisco, 1984—. Pres. United Cerebral Palsy Assn., Palo Alto, Calif., 1983-85, 79-81, bd. dirs., vice chmn. vol. devel. com., N.Y.C., 1983—. Mem. Assn. of Rehab. Nurses, Calif. Assn. Rehab. Profl., Nat. Rehab. Assn., Rehab. Ins. Nurse Group, Sigma Theta Tau (Alpha Gamma chpt.). Republican. Avocations: golf, camping. Home and Office: JR Assocs 456 Mariner's Island Blvd Suite 210 San Mateo CA 94404

RICHARDS, JEANNE ELIZABETH, lawyer; b. Pine Bluff, Ark., Apr. 17, 1956; d. Walter Rankin and Alyine (Proctor) R. B.A., Henderson State U., 1977; J.D., U. Ark., 1980. Bar: Ark. Assoc. firm Gill & Johnson, Dumas, Ark., 1980-83; city atty. City of Gould (Ark.), 1982-83, City of Grady (Ark.), 1982-83; dep. pros. atty. 11th jud. dist., Pine Bluff, Ark., 1982-83, 6th jud. dist., Little Rock, 1983-86; assoc. Wood Law Firm, North Little Rock, Ark., 1986—; assoc. dir. Christian Civic Found.; dir. Freeway of Ark, Inc. Group Leader Park Hill Bapt. Ch., North Little Rock, 1983-84, Lauback tutor, 1984; Sunday sch. tchr., com. mem. Pike Avenue Bapt. Ch., North Little Rock. Mem. ABA, Ark. Bar Assn., Assn. Trial Lawyers Am., Ark. Mcpl. League, Delta Theta Pi. Office: Wood Law Firm PO Box 5606 North Little Rock AR

RICHARDS, JUDITH G., business service owner; b. Kalamazoo, Oct. 20, 1939; d. Robert H. and Mary R. (Slumkoski) Richards. A.A.S., Ferris State Coll., 1960. Legal sec. Bush & Bush., Attys., Sturgis, Mich., 1965-77; owner Executives Bus. Service, Sturgis, 1978—. Bd. dirs. ARCH Rehab. Facility, 1979—; city commr. Sturgis City Commn., 1983—. Methodist. Avocations: traveling; sailing; gourmet cooking. Office: Executives Business Service 207 W Chicago Rd Sturgis MI 49091

RICHARDS, KATHERINE MARY, librarian; b. Longview, Wash., Oct. 31, 1941; d. William Robert and Tessie Margaret (Winn) Enright; m. Joe McCall Richards, June 30, 1961 (div. 1966). B.A., Marylhurst Coll., 1964; M.L.S., Ind. U., 1968; cert., Johns Hopkins U., 1969. 73, Cath. U. Am., 1968-69, Columbia U., 1981. Asst. librarian Dental Sch. U. Oreg., Portland, 1965-67; asst. hist. librarian Med. Sch. Yale U., New Haven, 1969-70; hist. librarian Health Sci. U. Med., Balt., 1970-77; mgr. library Emergency Care Research Inst., Plymouth Meeting, Pa., 1978-79; dir. library Cooper Med. Ctr., Camden, N.J., 1979-80; assoc. librarian N.Y. Hist. Soc., N.Y.C., 1981—; mem. preservation com. Research Library Group, Stanford, Calif., 1983—, mem. pub. services com., 1983—. Author article. Sec., Trentcentun Corp., Bronx, N.Y., 1983, pres., 1983—; bd. dirs. NOW Md. State, 1975-76, Balt. chpt., 1974-76. Fellow Johns Hopkins U., 1968. Mem. ALA, Spl. Library Assn. (adv. bd. N.Y.C. 1983—, sec.-treas. Museum of Art and Humanities of N.Y.C. 1983—), Am. Printing History Assn., Am. Assn. History of Medicine. Republican. Unitarian. Home: 3001 Henry Hudson Pkwy Riverdale Bronx NY 10463 Office: NY Historical Soc 170 Central Park W New York NY 10024

RICHARDS, LACLAIRE LISSETTA JONES (MRS. GEORGE A. RICHARDS), social worker; b. Pine Bluff, Ark.; d. Artie William and Geraldine (Adams) Jones; B.A., Nat. Coll. Christian Workers, 1953; M.S.W., U. Kans., 1956; postgrad. Columbia U., 1960; m. George Alvarez Richards, July 26, 1958; children—Leslie Rosario, Lia Mercedes, Jorge Ferguson. Psychiat. supervisory, teaching, community orgn., adminstrv. and consultative duties Hastings Regional Center, Ingleside, Nebr., 1956-60; supervisory, consultative and adminstrv. responsibilities for psychiat. and geriatric patients VA Hosp., Knoxville, Iowa, 1960-74, field instr. for grad. students from U. Mo., EEO counselor, 1969-74, 78—, com. chmn., 1969-70, Fed. women's program coordinator, 1972-74; sr. social worker Mental Health Inst., Cherokee, Iowa, 1974-77; adj. asst. prof. dept. social behavior U. S.D.; instr. Augustana Coll.; outpatient social worker VA Med. and Regional Office Center, Sioux Falls, S.D., 1978—; EEO counselor. Mem. Knoxville Juvenile Adv. Com., 1963-65, 68-70, sec., 1965-66, chmn., 1966-68; sec. Urban Renewal Citizens' Adv. Com., Knoxville, 1966-68; mem. United Methodist Ch. Task Force Exptl. Styles Ministry and Leadership, 1973-74, mem. adult choir, mem. ch. and society com.; counselor Knoxville Youth Line program; sec. exec. com. Vis. Nurse Assn., 1979-80; canvasser community fund drs., Knoxville; mem. Cherokee Civil Rights Commn.; bd. dirs., pub. relations, membership devel. and program devel. cons. YWCA, 1984-85. Named S.D. Social Worker of Yr., 1983. Mem. Nat. Assn. Social Workers (co-chmn. Nebr. chpt. profl. standards com. 1958-59), Acad. Cert. Social Workers, S.D. Assn. Social Workers (chmn. minority affairs com., v.p. S.E. region 1980, pres. 1980-82 exec. com. 1982-84, mem. social policy and action com.), Nebr. Assn. Social Workers (chmn. 1958-59), AAUW (sec. Hastings chpt. 1958-60), AMA Aux., Seventh Dist. S.D. Med. Soc. Aux., Coalition on Aging, NAACP (chmn. edn. com. 1983—). Methodist (Sunday sch. tchr. adult div.; mem. commn. on edn.; mem. Core com. for adult edn.; mem. Adult Choir; mem. Social Concerns Work Area). Home: 1701 Ponderosa Dr Sioux Falls SD 57103

RICHARDS, MARTA ALISON, lawyer; b. Memphis, Mar. 15, 1952; d. Howard Jay and Mary Dean (Nix) Richards; m. Jon Michael Hobson, May 5, 1973 (div. Jan. 1976); m. 2d, Richard Peter Massony, June 16, 1979; 1 child, Richard Peter Massony, Jr. Student Vassar Coll., 1969-70; A.B. cum laude, Princeton U., 1973; J.D., George Washington U., 1976. Bar: Assoc., Phelps, Dunbar, Marks, Claverie & Sims, New Orleans, 1976-77; assoc. counsel Hibernia Nat. Bank, New Orleans, 1978; assoc. Singer, Hutner, Levine, Seeman & Stuart, New Orleans, 1978-80, Jones, Walker, Waechter, Poitevent, Carrere & Denegre, New Orleans, 1980-84; ptnr. Mmahat Duffy & Richards, 1984, Montgomery, Barnett, Brown, Read, Hammond & Mintz, 1984—; lectr. paralegal inst. U. New Orleans, 1984 . Contbr. articles to legal jours. Treas. alumni council Princeton U., 1979-81. Mem. ABA, La. Bar Assn., Fed. Bar Assn., New Orleans Bar Assn., Princeton Alumni Assn. New Orleans (pres. 1982—). Episcopalian. Home: 1133 8th St New Orleans LA 70115 Office: Montgomery Barnett Brown Read Hammond & Mintz 1800 First Nat Bank Commerce Bldg New Orleans LA 70112

RICHARDS, MILDRED VERONNEAU, real estate broker; b. Meriden, Conn., Dec. 5, 1918; d. Henry August and Mary Theresa (Wollschlager) Veronneau; student Pequod Bus. Sch., 1936-37; grad. Realtors Inst., 1969; m. Joseph Maurice Richards, Oct. 26, 1940; children—Joseph M., Mark O., Christine M., Deborah R. Owner, mgr. Richards Agency, Meriden, 1961—; v.p. Invesco, Inc., Meriden, 1974-81, pres., 1981-82; sec. People's Mortgage of Meriden, Inc., 1972-73. Treas. Meriden Council Catholic Women, 1950-51; pres. St. Mary's Ch. Aux., 1952-53; bd. dirs. Meriden chpt. ARC, 1979-81, Wallingford-Meriden chpt., 1982—; bd. dirs. Meriden Public Health and Vis. Nurse Assn., 1950-55, 62-64, sec., 1954-55; mem. Meriden Bd. Edn., 1982—; mem. Conn. Task Force Housing for the Elderly. Cert. real estate brokerage mgr. Mem. Meriden Hosp. Women's Aux., Conn. Assn. Bds. Edn. (dir. 1983), Greater Meriden C. of C. (dir. 1977-80), Central Conn. Bd. Realtors (past pres., sec. and treas., Realtor of Year award 1973, 76, 83), Conn. Assn. Realtors (dir. 1968—, sec. 1974-78, sr. v.p. 1978, pres.-elect 1978, pres. 1979, Realtor of Yr. 1983), Nat. Assn. Realtors (regional v.p. 1984), Realtors Nat. Mktg. Inst., Nat. Inst. Farm and Land Brokers, Women's Council Realtors (pres. local chpt. 1976—, nat. gov. 1977-78, chmn. by-laws com. 1978). Clubs: Meriden Women's, Charity. Home: 14 William Ave Meriden CT 06450 Office: 247 S Broad St Meriden CT 06450

RICHARDS, PAMELA MOTTER, lawyer; b. Columbus, Ohio, Feb. 24, 1950; d. L. Clair and Mildred Jo (Williams) Motter; m. John W. Richards, II, Mar. 1, 1975 (div. 1984); children—Christine Elizabeth, Teresa Jo. B.A., DePauw U., 1972; J.D., Ohio No. U., 1975. Bar: Ga. 1975. Assoc., Cowart, Varner & Harrington, Warner Robins, Ga., 1977-82; ptnr. Cowart, Varner, Harrington & Richards, Warner Robins, 1982-83, Cowart, Varner & Richards, 1983—. Bd. dirs., sec. Kids Stuff Learning Ctrs. of Am., Warner Robins, 1983—, Warner Robins Day Care Ctr., 1976-80, Am. Cancer Soc., 1981—; v.p. Warner Robins C. of C., 1981-82, dir., 1980-82. Mem. State Bar of Ga., Houston County Bar Assn., ABA. Club: Civitan. Office: PO Box 818 Warner Robins GA 31099

RICHARDS, PENELOPE JAY, nurse; b. Princeton, N.J., Apr. 12, 1959; d. Henry and Judith (Odell) R. A.A.S., Mercer County Community Coll., Trenton, N.J., 1980. Staff nurse Middlesex Gen. Univ. Hosp., New Brunswick, N.J., 1980-82, asst. head nurse, 1982—. Mem. Jamesburg First Aid Squad, N.J., 1977-80. Presbyterian. Avocations: sewing, crafts. Office: Middlesex Gen Univ Hosp Somerset St New Brunswick NJ 08901

RICHARDS, PHYLLIS ANDERSON, nurse, health service executive; b. Stuart, Iowa, Sept. 9. 1929; d. John Edward and Verna Mae (Hully) Anderson; m. Herbert Montaque, Mar. 16, 1956; children—Pamela, Herbert, III, Patricia, John. B.S. in Nursing, U. Wash., 1948-53. Surgery nurse Swedish Hosp., Seattle, 1953-54, 1954-56; delivery nurse Kapiolani, Honolulu, 1954; nurse Hawaii Prep. Acad., Kamuela, 1969—; bd. dirs. Hawaii Island Hosp. Council, 1960-70, Lucy Henriques Med. Center, Kamuela, 1981—. Bd. dirs., instr. ARC, 1970-83; instr. Am. Heart Assn. Hawaii, 1983; bd. dirs. Girl Scouts council Pacific Hawaii, 1939—. Recipient Alumni award Hawaii Prep. Acad. Alumni, 1983. Mem. Am. Nurses Assn. Club: Hawaiian Republican. Home: Kahua Ranch Box 837 Kamuela HI 96743 Office: Hawaii Preparatory Acad Kamuela Hawaii 96743

RICHARDS, RHODA ROOT WAGNER, civic worker; b. Phila., Oct. 2, 1917; d. Edward Stephen and Rhoda Earley (Root) Wagner; student U. Pa., 1937-39; A.A., Wildcliff Jr. Coll., 1938; m. J. Permar Richards, Jr., May 18, 1940; children—Patricia A.V. Richards Cosgrave, J. Permar III. Profl. artist; founder, chmn. Hosp. Corps, Navy League Service, 1941-43; chmn. ARC Nurses Aide Corps, Jacksonville, Fla., 1944-45, Long Beach, Calif., 1945-46; founder, chmn. Fiesta Benefits, Hahnemann Hosp., 1950-57; former chmn. jr. com. Met. Opera; bd. dirs. Phila. Lyric Opera Co.; chmn. Ring for Freedom Republican Campaign of S.E. Pa., 1960; pres. Emergency Aid of Pa., 1961-64; v.p. bd. dirs. Inglis House, Phila., 1977-82; pres. women's bd. Phila. div. Am. Cancer Soc., 1978-81, hon. life mem.; founder, chmn. Community Activities Calendar, 1970-80; gen. chmn. 1st Ann. Washington Crossing Assembly, 1978; trustee Baldwin Sch.; co-chmn. fundraising com. Ambulatory Service Pavilion, Presbyn.-U. Pa. Med. Center; vice chmn. Women's Commn. for Bicentennial, 1976; bd. dirs., mem. Appleford Commn. Parsons-Banks Arboretum; bd. dirs. St. Johns Settlement House, 1954-86, Vol. Services for Blind, Phila. div. Am. Cancer Soc., 1978-86, Phila. chpt. Lupus Found., 1980-81; mem. Delaware Valley women's bd. Freedoms Found. at Valley Forge; past v.p. women's assn., past chmn. fin. com., chmn. centennial spl. event and gen. com. for the celebration Bryn Mawr Presbyn. Ch.; hon. col. corps of cadets Valley Forge Mil. Acad. and Jr. Coll.; founder, chmn. Rittenhouse Preservation Coalition, 1982—; v.p., asst. treas. Preservation Coalition of Greater Phila.; mem. Hospitality, Phila. Style; chmn. bd. dirs. Emergency Aid of Pa. Found. Recipient Crusade award Am. Cancer Soc., 1976; spl. award for community service St. John's Settlement House, 1977; Florence A. Sanson award for patriotism, 1986; named Disting. Dau. of Pa., 1985. Mem. Phila. Mus. Art, Pa. Acad. Fine Arts, Woodmere Art Gallery, Hahnemann Hosp. Women's Assn., DAR, Daus. of the Cincinnati, Dames of Loyal Legion, Nat. Soc. Colonial Dames of XVII Century, Dames Sovereign Mil. Order Temple of Jerusalem, Honolulu Mus. Art, Geneal. Soc. Pa., Am. Hist. Soc., Nat. Trust for Historic Preservation, Smithsonian Instn. Clubs: Sedgeley, Cosmopolitan, Peale, Safari, Bald Peak Colony. Home: 1250 Lafayette Rd PO Box 608 Bryn Mawr PA 19010

RICHARDS, TERESA GAIL, lawyer; b. Birmingham, Ala., Mar. 8, 1955; d. Harold Linn and Mona (Martin) R. A.A., Jefferson State Jr. Coll., 1975; B.A., Troy State U., 1977; J.D., U. Ala., 1980. Bar: Ala. Law clk. Juvenile Ct., Tuscaloosa, Ala., 1978-80; law clk. to judge U.S. Bankruptcy Ct., Montgomery, Ala., 1980-82; counsel Ala. Commn. Higher Edn., Montgomery, 1982—; congl. intern to U.S. Senator Howell Heflin, Washington, summer 1979. Advisor Tri-Hy-Y, Montgomery, 1983-84. Recipient George C. Wallace Leadership scholarship Gov. Ala., 1975. Mem. ABA, Ala. Bar Assn., Montgomery County Bar Assn., Phi Delta Phi. Home: 2333 College St Montgomery AL 36106 Office: Ala Commn on Higher Edn One Court Sq Montgomery AL 36197

RICHARDSON, BARBARA KATHRYN, social worker; b. Magnet Cove, Ark., Nov. 28, 1936; d. Fred Lee and Lillian Catherine (Adkins) R.; B.A., Mary Hardin-Baylor U., 1961; M.S.W., Washington U., St. Louis, 1965. Sec., Dyke Bros., Little Rock, 1953-55; legal sec. Donalson, Bullard & Kucera, Dallas, 1955-57; public welfare worker Henderson County Public Welfare, Hendersonville, N.C., 1961-62; child welfare worker Tex. Dept. Public Welfare, Belton, 1962-63, adoption worker, Tyler, 1965-66, asst. dir. child welfare, Houston, 1966-69; dir. adoptions Hope Cottage Children's Bur., Dallas, 1970-74; dir. emergency-crisis unit Dallas County Mental Health-Mental Retardation, 1974-76; ednl. contract specialist, continuing edn. bur. Tex. Dept. Human Services, 1977-81, project developer Office Research, Demonstration and Eval., 1981—; Democratic precinct del., Dallas, 1972. Mem. Nat. Assn. Social Workers (state dir. 1974-75), Acad. Cert. Social Workers, Council on Social Work Edn. (ho. of dels. 1980-82), Tex. Public Employees Assn. Home: 719 A Harris Ave Austin TX 78705 Office: Tex Dept Human Services PO Box 2960 Austin TX 78769

RICHARDSON, BERNICE TANNER, teacher educator; b. Talladega, Ala., Dec. 17; d. Groce Warwick and Mattie (Green) Turner; m. F. C. Richardson, Aug. 5, 1975; 1 child, Darrell DeCarlton. Student Ala. A&M Coll., 1953-55, St. Joseph's Coll., East Chicago, Ind., 1960-61; B.S. in Elem. Edn., Ind. U. N.W., Gary, 1968, M.S. in Elem. Edn., 1973, adminstrn. cert. in elem. edn., 1978; postgrad. U. Notre Dame, summer 1974. Tchr. St. Hedwig Catholic Sch., Gary, 1965-73, prin., tchr., 1973-78; asst. prin. Gary Community Schs., 1979-84, also interim prin. schs., 1980, 81, 82; prin. Chase Elem. Sch., Gary, 1984-85; asst. prof. edn., minority student adviser Moorhead State U., 1986—; summer adminstr. Gary Manpower Program at St. Hedwig Cath. Sch., 1976-78. Mem. Gary Inter-Greek Council, 1975-80; mem. Ind. U. N.W. Alumni Bd., 1977-82; bd. dirs. YWCA, 1975-80, Lake County Assn. for Mentally Retarded, 1982-84. Recipient Nat. Award of Merit, Grade Teacher Mag., 1969, Devoted Service award St. Hedwig PTA, 1978, Profl. Achievement award Ind. Assn. Elem. Sch. Prins., 1983, award for meritorious service rendered at Williams Sch., PTO, 1984. Mem. Gary Elem. Princ.'s Assn., Urban League N.W. Ind. Guild, Nat. Council Negro Women, Zeta Phi Beta (officer). Home: 401 Horn Ave Moorhead MN 56560

RICHARDSON, BOBBI, professional support services executive; b. Evansville, Ind., July 1, 1945; d. Julius John and Anna Louise (Griggs) Steinkamp; children—Amy Griggs Richardson, Michael Lawrence Richardson. Student Lockyear Bus. Coll., 1963, U. So. Ind. Cert. med. staff coordinator. Exec. sec. Citizens Nat. Bank, Evansville, Ind., 1964-69; legal sec. Newkirk, Keane, Kowalczyk & Leal, Ft. Wayne, Ind., 1971-72; sec. Mead Johnson & Co., Evansville, 1977-78; med. staff coordinator Deaconess Hosp., Evansville, 1978-85, cons., 1985—; exec. dir. Share-In Care, Inc., Evansville, 1985; owner, pres. Profl. Support Service, Evansville, 1985—; cons. Builders' Spltys., Evansville, 1984—. Mem. Am. Entrepreneur Assn., Nat. Assn. Female Execs., Network of Evansville Women, Women in Networking (recorder, historian 1985-86). Republican. Roman Catholic. Avocations: skiing, reading, traveling. Home: 10110 Lindar Ln Evansville IN 47712 Office: Profl Support Services 10110 Lindar Ln Evansville IN 47712

RICHARDSON, BRENDA, museum administrator; b. Howell, Mich., July 15, 1942; d. Robert Burr and Helen Isabel (Wright) R. B.A., U. Mich., 1964; M.A., U. Calif.-Berkeley, 1966. Curator, asst. dir. University Art Mus., Berkeley, 1964-75, Balt. Mus. Art, 1975—. Author exhbn. catalogues: Mel Bochner, 1976, Frank Stella, 1976, Barnett Newman, 1979, Bruce Nauman: Neons, 1982, Gilbert & George, 1984, Oskar Schlemmer, 1986, Scott Burton, 1986. Recipient Disting. Alumni Lectureship, U. Calif.-Berkeley, 1973. Office: Balt Mus Art Art Museum Dr Baltimore MD 21218

RICHARDSON, CHERYL BEATRICE, personnel administrator; b. Phila., Feb. 18, 1945; d. Clinton Walter and Ruth Pearl (Simons) Lott; children—Joseph R., Kailei A. B.A., Glassboro State U., 1967; M.S., SUNY-Binghamton, 1981. Tchr., Cherry Hill pub. schs. (N.J.), 1967-76; indsl. relations asst. Revere Copper & Brass, Rome, N.Y., 1979-81; sr. personnel adminstr. Pitman-Moore, Inc., Washington Crossing, N.J., 1981-84; sr. adminstr., corp. exec. officer Johnson & Johnson Corp., New Brunswick, N.J., 1984—. Co-chmn. Delaware Valley United Way, Trenton, N.J., 1982-84, Bus. Adv. Council, Princeton, N.J., 1983-84. Named Woman of Yr., Women's Club of Palmyra, 1968. Mem. Tri-State Personnel Assn. (pres. 1984—), Delaware Valley Personnel Assn., Am. Soc. Personnel Adminstrn., Lambda Kappa Mu, Delta Sigma Theta. Roman Catholic. Home: 217 B Willow Turn Mount Laurel NJ 08054 Office: Johnson & Johnson Corp One Johnson & Johnson Plaza New Brunswick NJ 08933

RICHARDSON, DEBORAH GAIL, administrator; b. Biloxi, Miss., Dec. 18, 1950; d. Woten Tenneson and Willie Marie (Wesley) R. B.A. in French, Tex. So. U., 1974. Recreation leader Rome State Sch. for Retarded (N.Y.), 1970; computer programmer, analyst trainee Johnson & Johnson Co., Sherman, Tex., 1971-72; recreation leader City of Houston Parks Dept., 1973-74; application specialist computing Allied Bank Tex., Houston, 1974-77; asst. mgr. prodn. U. Houston Computing Ctr., 1977—. Vol., Miss Deaf Tex. Pagent, Houston, 1980, City of Houston Parks Dept., 1980-81. Mem. Zeta Phi Beta. Office: U Houston Computing Ctr 4213 Elgin Houston TX 77004

RICHARDSON, DOROTHY VIRGINIA, accountant; b. Bennington, Okla., Sept. 26, 1937; d. William Lycurgus and Mittie Mae (Richardson) Ray; student Eastern Okla. A&M, 1955-56; B.B.A., U. Alaska, 1974; m. Charles Howard Richardson, Dec. 28, 1958; children—Charles Timothy, Michael Todd. Asst. acct. Peat, Marwick, Mitchell & Co., Omaha, 1975-76; gen. acct. U. Alaska Statewide System, Fairbanks, 1976; asst. bus. mgr. Geophys. Inst., Fairbanks, 1976-77; dir. grant and contract services U. Alaska, Fairbanks, 1977-80; controller Alaska Legal Services Corp., Anchorage, 1980-81; bus. mgr. div. community colls., rural edn. and extension U. Alaska, Anchorage, 1981-83; assoc. controller U. Fla., Gainesville, 1983—. Active Cub Scouts, Mothers March of Dimes, PTA; pres. Alachua County Geneal. Soc., Am. Cancer Soc. Served with USAF, 1957-59. Mem. Am. Inst. C.P.A.s, Soc. Research Adminstrs., Council on Govtl. Relations (costing policies com.), Nat. Council Univ. Research Adminstrs. Office: 128 Grinter Hall U Fla Gainesville FL 32611

RICHARDSON, EMILIE WHITE, manufacturing company executive, investment company executive; b. Chattanooga, July 8; d. Emmett and Mildred Evelyn (Harbin) White; B.A., Wheaton Coll., 1951; 1 dau., Julie Richardson Morphis. With Christy Mfg. Co., Inc., Fayetteville, N.C., 1952—, sec. 1956-66, v.p., 1967-74, exec. v.p., 1975-79, pres., chief exec. officer, 1980—; pres. E. White Investment Co., 1968—; cons. Aerostatic Industries, 1979—; v.p. Gannon Corp., 1981—; cons. govt. contacts and offshore mfg., 1981—; lectr., speaker in field, 1983—. Vice pres. pub. relations Ft. Lauderdale Symphony Soc., 1974-76, v.p. membership, 1976-77, adv. bd., 1978—; active Atlantic Found., Ft. Lauderdale Mus. Art, Beaux Arts, Freedoms Found.; mem. E. Broward Women's Republican Club, 1968—, Americanism chmn., 1971-72. Mem. Internat. Platform Assn., Nat. Speakers Assn., Fla. Speakers Assn. Presbyterian. Green Valley Country. Home: 1531 NE 51st St Fort Lauderdale FL 33334 Office: PO Box 35375 Fayetteville NC 28303

RICHARDSON, GRACE ELIZABETH, consumer products company executive; b. Salem, Mass., Nov. 22, 1938; d. George and Julia (Sheridan) R.; m. Ralph B. Henderson, Mar. 3, 1979. B.S., Simmons Coll., 1960; M.S., Cornell U., 1962; M.B.A., NYU, 1981. Textile technologist Harris Research Lab., Washington, 1962-65; instr. Simmons Coll., Boston, 1965-66; dir. consumer edn. materials J.C. Penney, N.Y.C., 1966-73; dir. residential conservation Con Edison, N.Y.C., 1974-81; dir. consumer affairs Chesebrough-Ponds, Greenwich, Conn., 1981-85; dir. consumer affairs Colgate Palmolive, N.Y.C., 1985—. Named Nat. Bus. Home Economist of Yr., Home Economists in Bus., 1979; recipient Consumer Edn. award Major Appliance Consumer Action Panel, 1977. Mem. Am. Home Econs. Assn. (v.p. external affairs 1983-85), Cornell U. Council, Nat. Coalition Consumer Edn. (bd. dirs. 1983—). Home: 531 Main St New York NY 10044 Office: Colgate Palmolive Co 300 Park Ave New York NY 10022

RICHARDSON, JEAN MCGLENN, civil engr.; b. Everett, Wash., Nov. 15, 1927; d. Clayton Charles and Marie Elizabeth (Mellish) McGlenn; B.S.C.E., Oreg. State U., 1949; registered profl. engr., Ala., Oreg.; m. William York Richardson, II, June 11, 1949; children—William York III, Paul Kress II, Clayton McGlenn. Engr., Walter Schoel Engring. Co., Birmingham, Ala., 1950-54; office engr. G.C. McKinney Engring. Co., San Jose, Calif., 1972-74; civil design leader Harland Bartholomew & Assocs., Birmingham, 1974-78, Rust Engring. Co., Birmingham, 1978-82; owner, prin. Jean Richardson and Assocs. Inc., cons. engrs., 1983—; women's engring. del. to China and USSR, Sept. 1984; counselor to female students on engring. as a career; regional chmn. Mathcounts, 1986; math. vol. pub. schs. Mem. Soc. Women Engrs. (sr. sect. rep. to nat. bd.), Am. Cons. Engrs. Council (Ala.), Nat. Soc. Profl. Engrs., Alpha Phi. Republican. Episcopalian. Clubs: Inverness Country, Women's Golf Assn. Office: PO Box 59533 2830 19th St S Birmingham AL 35209

RICHARDSON, KAREN LEROHL, lawyer; b. Albuquerque, Sept. 15, 1950; d. John Kenneth and Ann (Castleman) Lawrence Lerohl; B.A., Coll. William and Mary, 1972; J.D., Am. U., 1978; postgrad. George Washington U., 1980-82. Admitted to Va. bar, 1979, U.S. Ct. Claims bar, 1980, U.S. Supreme Ct., 1982, U.S. Ct. Appeals (4th cir.) 1982, Calif., 1984; supr. law dept. Prudential Ins. Co., Washington, 1972-74; law clk. Arnold and Porter, Washington, 1975-78; atty. Def. Logistics Agy., Alexandria, Va., 1978-80; atty. Office Sec. Def., Washington, 1980-84; counsel TRW Inc., 1984—. Recipient Presidential Sports award, 1980; Disting. Youth award Dept. Army, 1976. Mem. Am. Bar Assn. (dep. chmn., mem. subcom. 1980—), Fed. Bar Assn., Va. Bar Assn., ACLU, Assn. Old Crows, Am. Corp. Counsel Assn., Nat. Contract Mgmt. Assn., Calif. Bar Assn., Los Angeles County Bar Assn., Nat. Women's Polit. Caucus DaCamera Soc., others. Club: Cameron Station Tennis (pres. 1980). Office: One Space Park Redondo Beach CA 90278

RICHARDSON, LYNN KAREN, lawyer; b. Trenton, N.J., Oct. 31, 1953; d. John and Joan Mae (Duenger) Richardson. B.A., Franklin and Marshall Coll., Lancaster, Pa., 1971-74; M.A., U. Tex. Med. Br.-Galveston, 1974-78; J.D., So. Tex. Coll. Law., Houston, 1976-80. Bar: Mich. 1980, U.S. Dist. Ct. (ea. dist.) Mich., 1981, U.S. Dist. Ct. (no. dist.) Calif. 1984, U.S. Ct. Appeals (6th cir.) 1981, U.S. Ct. Appeals (9th cir.) 1984. Research asst. Rice U., Houston, 1976-78; research assoc. U. Mich. Sch. Pub. Health, Ann Arbor, Mich., 1980, cons. 1982; jud. law clk. U.S. Dist. Ct., Detroit, 1981-82; asst. U.S. Atty. U.S. Atty.'s Office, Detroit, 1982-84, San Francisco, 1984—; instr. Atty. Gen.'s Adv. Inst., Washington, 1984—. Author govt. documents, 1975, 80; contbr. articles to profl. jours. Mem. State Bar Assn. Mich., ABA, Fed. Bar Assn. Democrat. Presbyterian. Office: U S Atty's Office 450 Golden Gate Ave San Francisco CA 94102

RICHARDSON, MARILYN JO, mortgage company executive; b. Muncie, Ind., Apr. 20, 1947; d. Roy Berryman and Vera Lavonne (Smedley) Weyland; m. Willie Caldwell Frazier, Feb. 18, 1974 (div. 1979); children—Kristi Irene, Jason Caldwell; m. George Emerson Richardson, Jr., Sept. 17, 1983; stepchildren—Stuart, Joyce, Judy. With First Mortgage, Anaheim, Calif., 1967-71; processing supr. Mason-McDuffie So. Calif., Santa Ana, 1971-74; adminstrn. mgr. Mason-McDuffie, Berkeley, Calif., 1974-78, ptnr., 1978-82; chief adminstrn. officer Mason-McDuffie Mortgage Corp., Walnut Creek, Calif., 1982-83, chief operating officer, 1983—. Named Boss of Yr., Assn. Profl. Women No. Calif., 1984. Mem. Mortgage Assn. Am. Avocations: reading; horseback riding. Home: PO Box 601 Diablo CA 94528 Office: Mason McDuffie Mortgage Corp 1550 Parkside Dr Walnut Creek CA 94596

RICHARDSON, MARTHA, nutrition analyst; b. Noble, La., Apr. 22, 1917; d. Alexander M. and Olive (Barlow) R.; A.B., U. Mo., 1938, Ph.D., 1953; M.S., Kans. State U., 1939. Dietitian, William Newton Meml. Hosp., Winfield, Kans., 1940-42, Molly Stark Sanatorium, Canton, Ohio, 1942-47; asst. dir. residence halls, instr. home econs. U. Mo., 1947-50, instr. home econs., 1951-53; head of foods and nutrition U. Utah, 1953-55; nutrition analyst Agrl. Research Service, Washington, 1955-80. Named Disting. Alumna, U. Mo., 1968. Fellow AAAS; mem. Am. Dietetic Assn., Am. Home Econs. Assn., Am. Med. Writers Assn., Am. Inst. Food Techologists, Am. Chem. Soc. Am. Assn. Cereal Chemists, Am. Forestry Assn., AAUW, N.Y. Acad. Scis., Sigma Xi, Gamma Sigma Delta, Phi Upsilon Omicron, Sigma Delta Epsilon. Contbr. articles to profl. jours. Home: 403 Russell Ave #309 Gaithersburg MD 20877

RICHARDSON, MARY ELEANORE BRZEZICKI, manufacturing company executive; b. Pittsfield, Pa., Mar. 13, 1932; d. Joseph E. and Eleanore Victoria (Battko) Bosko; student Kans. State U., Manhattan, 1952-53, Rosary Hill Coll., Buffalo, 1972, U. Pitts., 1978-79; m. Robert Edward Brzezicki, June 2, 1956 (div. Feb. 1974); children—Michael Joseph, Suzanne Marie; m. 2d, Carl Lindsey Richardson, July 9, 1983. Various secretarial positions, 1956-59, 75; engaged in real estate sales, 1972-74; freelance community corr. Buffalo Evening News, 1972-74; exec. sec. to pres. and chief exec. officer, editor corp. newsletter Struthers Wells Corp., Warren, Pa., 1975-83; owner M.E. Brzezicki Enterprises, Volant, Pa., 1983—; Warren County corr. Erie Times News, 1981-83. Exec. bd. West Falls (N.Y.) Sch. Assn., 1969-72, 2d v.p., public relations chmn. East Aurora (N.Y.) Middle Sch. Assn., 1972-73; pres. New Horizons, Warren, 1977, 80-82; bd. dirs. Warren YWCA, 1982-83, pres., 1982-83. Mem. Warren Bus. and Profl. Women's Club (pres. 1982—; Woman of Year award 1982-83), Pa. Assn. Notaries, Kappa Delta. Republican. Roman Catholic. Home and Office: RD 2 Box 122A McNulty Rd Volant PA 16156

RICHARDSON, MYRTLE, abstractor, former judge; b. Jefferson County, Ohio, July 2, 1907; d. Thomas and Blanche (Whitecotton) Heinselman; student Kans. State Tchrs. Coll., 1926; A.A., Dodge City Community Coll., 1978; m. Harold E. Richardson, Mar. 4, 1929 (div.); 1 dau., Nancy Lee Richardson Ridgway. Tchr. public schs., Edwards County, Kans., 1924-28; reporter, advertiser Kinsley (Kans.) Graphic, 1928-35, mgr., 1937-41; editor, advt. mgr. So. Standard, McMinnville, Tenn., 1935-36; abstractor H. F. Thompson, Kinsley, 1943-54; editor Kinsley Mercury, 1954-57; abstractor, Kinsley, 1957-84; probate judge, Kinsley, 1958-69; judge Mcpl. Ct. Kinsley, 1958-69. Bd. dirs. United Drive, 1947-57, Edwards County chpt. ARC, 1940-50; community and project leader 4-H Club, 1943-52; community and project leader Edwards County 4-H Who's Who Club, 1943-52; pres. PTA, 1940-44. Vice chmn. Edwards County Democratic Com. 1956-84; pres. Edwards County Fedn. Dem. Women's Club, 1970-74, 76—; chmn. Dem. Central Com., Edwards County, 1981; dist. dir. South 1st Dist. Fedn. Dem. Women's Clubs, 1981. Mem. C. of C. (sec.-mgr. 1947-54), Edwards County Hist. Soc. (historian), S. Central Kans. Probate Judges Assn. (pres. 1966). Author: Oft Told Tales-A History of Edwards County, Kansas from 1873 to 1900, 1976; The Great Next Year Country, 1983. . Home: 120 N 2d St Kinsley KS 67547

RICHARDSON, ROBERTA NUTTALL, nurse; b. Newport, N.J., Oct. 15, 1941; d. Robert and Ann Elizabeth Haviland Nuttall Slimmer; R.N. Cooper Hosp. Sch. Nursing, Camden, N.J., 1965; student Diablo Valley Coll.; law student J.F. Kennedy U., Orinda, Calif., 1984—; children—Joyce Ann, Stuart, Judy. Pub. health nurse on-call, Clinton County (Ind.) Hosp., 1967-69, Rochelle (Ill.) Community Hosp., 1973-76, Americana Healthcare Center, Rochelle, 1974-76; dir. nursing Hacienda Convalescent Hosp., Concord, Calif., 1977-79; dir. nursing Casa San Miguel Rehab. Center, Concord, 1979-84; acting nursing supr. acute psychiat. hosp. 1st Hosp. of Vallejo (Calif.), 1984—; legal/med. cons. for Terence G. Cady, Atty. at Law, Pleasant Hill, Calif. Pres., United Meth. Women, 1974-75, sec., 1975-76; pres. Campfire Girls, Rochelle, 1971-76, Crippled Children, Ind., 1968; leader Cub Scouts, 1970-76; mem. Contra Costa County Continuing Care Forum. Mem. Beta Sigma Phi. Republican. Clubs: Moose, Order Eastern Star. Home: 4005 Santa Fe Ct Concord CA 94521 Office: Psychiatric SNF 1st Hosp of Vallejo 525 Oregon St Vallejo CA 94590

RICHARDSON, RUTH DELENE, business educator; b. New Orleans, May 27, 1942; s. Daniel Edgar and Allie Myrtle (Skinner) R.; B.S., Mars Hill Coll., 1965; M.S., U. Tenn., Knoxville, 1968, Ed.D. (EPDA fellow), 1974. Tchr., LaFollette (Tenn) High Sch., 1965-66; instr. Clinch Valley Coll., Wise, Va., 1967-68, U. S.C., Union, 1968-69, Tenn. Wesleyan Coll., Athens, 1969-71, Roane State Community Coll., Harriman, Tenn., 1971-73; assoc. prof., chmn. dept. bus. edn. and office adminstrn. Ala. State U., Montgomery, 1974-75;

assoc. prof. U. South Ala., Mobile, 1975-80; assoc. prof. adminstrv. office services U. North Ala., Florence, 1980—; cons. career edn.; employment tester. Mem. Assn. for Bus. Communication, Nat. Bus. Edn. Assn., Profl. Secs. Internat., Delta Pi Epsilon, Omicron Tau Theta, Phi Delta Kappa, Pi Lambda Theta, Pi Omega Pi. Lutheran. Contbr. articles to profl. jours. Home: 2026 Greenbrier Rd Florence AL 35630 Office: U N Ala Box 5180 Florence AL 35632

RICHARDSON, SALLY KEADLE, state health care administrator; b. Huntington, W.Va., Mar. 2, 1933; d. Okey P. and Viola Miriam (Graybeal) Keadle; m. Don Rule Richardson, Dec. 15, 1961; children—Miriam Paige, Ruth Evan. A.B., Vassar Coll., Poughkeepsie, N.Y., 1954. Regional pub. info. rep. Columbia Gas System, Charleston, 1958-62; dir. Children's Mus., Charleston, 1963; coordinator space-related sci. project Kanawha County Schs., Charleston, 1967-68; vol. dir. Rockefeller for Gov. Campaign, Charleston, 1972, program dir., 1976, 1980; dir. admissions W.Va. Wesleyan Coll., Buckhannon, 1974-75; spl. asst. Office of Gov. State of W.Va., 1977, dep. commr. Dept. Welfare, 1978-79, dep. dir. Dept. Health, 1979-83; chmn. W.Va. Health Care Cost Rev. Authority, Charleston, 1983—; W.Va. rep. Task Force on So. Children, So. Growth Policies Bd., 1978-79; co-chmn. exec. com. W.Va. Internat. Yr. of Child, 1979; staff mem. Com. on Human Resources Nat. Gov. Assn., 1983—. Mem. Am. Health Planning Assn., W.Va. Pub. Health Assn. Democrat. Episcopalian. Office: W Va Health Care Cost Rev Authority State Capitol Complex Charleston WV 25305

RICHARDSON, SHIRLEY MAXINE, newspaper editor; b. Rising Sun, Ind., May 3, 1931; d. William Fenton and Mary (Phillips) Keith; m. Arthur Lee Richardson, Feb. 11, 1950; children—Mary Jane Hamm, JoDee Mayfield, Steven Lee Richardson. Personnel mgr. Mayhill Pubs., Knightstown, Ind., 1967—, prodn. mgr., 1975—, editor, 1967—. Mem. Newspaper Farm Editors of Am., Am. Agrl. Editors' Assn., Profl. Journalists of Am. Republican. Avocations: traveling; reading; boating; quilting. Home: 366 E Carey St Knightstown IN 46148 Office: Mayhill Pubs 27 N Jefferson St Knightstown IN 46148

RICHARDSON, STEPHANIE JEAN, nurse; b. St. Paul, Apr. 20, 1954; s. Downie Stevens and Harriet Louise (Schilling) R. B.S. in Pub. Health Edn., U. Calif.-Davis, 1976; B.S. in Nursing, Calif. State U.-Sacramento, 1978; postgrad. U. Utah, 1983—. R.N., Utah. Staff nurse, dept. inservice dir., triage nurse specialist emergency dept. Cottonwood Hosp., Murray, Utah, 1978-80; staff nurse, mem intra-aortic balloon pump team, mem. flight team, quality care rep. ICUs, Holy Cross Hosp. Salt Lake City, 1980—; teaching asst., clin. instr. advanced medicine-surgery, lectr., tutor U. Utah Coll. Nursing, 1984-85; advanced cardiac life support provider Am. Heart Assn., Salt Lake City, 1978—, instr. advanced cardiac life support, 1984—; presenter Nursing Research Conf., Salt Lake City, 1984. Contbr. to Pathophysiology 1986. NIH grantee, 1983-85; advanced research fellow U. Utah, 1985, 86. Mem. Utah Nurses Assn., Am. Assn. Critical Care Nurses (participant Nat. Teaching Inst. 1982), Nat. Assn. Female Execs., Utah Bus. and Profl. Women, Sigma Theta Tau (research in progress award). Democrat. Roman Catholic. Home: 627 3d Ave Apt 3 Salt Lake City UT 84103

RICHARDSON, SUZANNE ROST, financial consultant; b. El Campo, Tex., Oct. 30, 1955; d. Robert Rudolph and Roberta (Streger) Rost; m. Richard Blakely Richardson, Jr., July 14, 1979. B.B.A., U. Houston, 1978. Asst. mktg. dept. RepublicBank Houston, 1979-81, regional market devel. officer, 1981-82, asst. v.p. comml. market devel., 1982-84, v.p., regional mktg. mgr., 1984-85; cons. Prime Mktg., Houston, 1985—; organizing dir. RepublicBank Eldridge, Houston, 1984-85. Sec. Camp Logan Civic Club, Houston, 1984—. Mem. Am. Mktg. Assn., Bank Mktg. Assn. (1st v.p. Gulf Coast chpt. 1985—, 2d v.p. 1984-85, treas. 1983-84, sec. 1982-83). Republican. Avocations: deep sea fishing; ethnic cooking. Home: 6513 Westcott St Houston TX 77007 Office: Prime Mktg 1669 S Voss Suite 351 Houston TX 77057

RICHARDSON, VIRGINIA LEE, business executive; b. Salina, Kans., Nov. 5, 1933; d. Burton W. and Mae E. (Dent) Valentine; m. George A. Richardson, Dec. 22, 1950. Student Columbia U., Ind., 1961-63, Kans. State Tech. Inst., 1975-76. Bookkeeper, Asbury Hosp., Salina, 1956-60, acctg. supr., 1960-66; office mgr. Vernon Jewelers, Salina, 1966-72; store mgr. Vernon's Supply Co., Inc., Salina, 1972-75, pres., 1975—; v.p. Vernon's Print Shoppe, Salina, 1982—; pres. Vernon's Photo ID Systems, Salina, 1975—, also dir. mktg. govt. sales; cons. Author: Christian Learning Guide, 1970. Active March of Dimes; attendance sec. Grace Bapt. Temple, Salina, 1985—. Recipient letter of commendation Whiteman AFB, Mo., 1973. Mem. Salina C. of C., Midstates Printers Assn., Salina Police Wives Assn. (pres. activities 1969-70). Republican. Club: Civitan (Salina). Avocations: poetry; drawing; fishing; boating; skeet shooting. Office: PO Box 2777 Salina KS 67402

RICHARDS-STOWER, NANCY ANN, lawyer; b. Springfield, Mass., Mar. 29, 1951; d. Carl Joseph and Sarah Ann (Morazzini) Richards; m. Richard M. Stower, Sept. 15, 1973 (div.); 1 child, Jonathan Douglas. B.A., George Washington U., 1973; J.D., Franklin Pierce Law Center, 1976. Bar: Va. 1976, N.H. 1978. Legal intern com. on banking, housing and urban affairs U.S. Senate, Washington, 1976; assoc. Law Offices Robert Fitzpatrick, Washington, 1976-77; ptnr. Rines and Rines, Concord, N.H., 1978—; v.p. New Eng. Fish Farming Enterprises, Inc., Concord, 1983-84; pres. Allor Project Co., Inc., 1985—. Founding editor Obiter Dictum, 1974-75. Mem. N.H. Commn. on Human Rights, Concord, 1979-85, chmn., 1980-85; founder N.H. Com. to End Handgun Violence, 1982; chmn. N.H., McGovern for Pres. campaign, 1983-84; mem. N.H. Democratic State Com., 1984—. Mem. ABA, N.H. Bar Assn. Home: 7 Cross St Merrimack NH 03054 Office: Rines and Rines 81 N State St Concord NH 03054

RICHEY, DOROTHY LOUISE, physical education educator; b. Mobile, Ala., Oct. 1, 1943; d. Oscar and Adeline (Morris) Richey. B.S., Tuskegee Inst., 1966; M.S., Ind. State U.-Terre Haute, 1967; Ed.D., Nova U., 1979. Instr., coach Ind. State U., 1968-72; coordination recreation, instr. Chgo. State U., 1972-74, asst. dir. athletics, 1973-74, dir. athletics, 1974-77; prof. phys. edn. Community Coll. of Allegheny County, W. Mifflin, Pa., 1978—; ofcl. Caffifesta Games, Barbados, W.I., 1982; asst. Women's Olympic Tng. Camp, U. Ill.-Champaign, 1972; ofcl. USA Can. Women's Track and Field Meet, U. Ill.-Champaign, 1972, numerous other meets, competitions; mem. U.S. Olympic Com. on Coaches Edn., 1984—. Mem. Women's Track and Field Coaches Assn., Eastern Dist. Assn. Health, Phys. Edn., Recreation and Dance, Am. Assn. Health, Phys. Edn., Recreation and Dance, Nat. Assn. Female Execs., Nat. Assn. Girls and Women in Sport (pres.-elect), Zeta Phi Beta, Delta Psi Kappa. Address: PO Box 99973 Pittsburgh PA 15233

RICHIE, SHARON, army nursing officer; b. Phila., Dec. 14, 1949; d. William Joseph and Helen Lucille (Oglesby) R.; m. Paul Henri, Jan. 1, 1986. B.S., Wagner Coll., 1971; M.S., U. Tex. Grad. Sch. Nursing, San Antonio, 1976. Commd. 2d lt. U.S. Army, advanced through grades to lt. col., 1984; clin. staff nurse Walter Reed Army Med. Ctr., Washington 1971-74; hosp. pschiat. nurse cons., head nurse 5th Gen. Hosp., Landstuhl, Germany, 1976-77; psychiat. clin. nurse specialist Alcholism Treatment Facility, Stuttgart, Germany, 1977-79; cons. alcohol and drug abuse nursing U.S. Army Surg. Gen., The Pentagon, Washington, 1980, also clin. liaison officer; asst. dir. edn. and rehab. Office Drug and Alcohol Abuse Prevention, Dept. Def., Pentagon, 1980-82; White House fellow, 1982-83; asst. chief nurse evenings/nights Letterman Army Med. ctr., San Francisco, 1983-84, chief ambulatory nursing service, 1984-85, dir. quality assurance, dept. nursing, 1985-86; PROFIS chief nurse, 8th Evacuation Hosp., Fort Ord, Calif., 1984-86; asst. chief nurse Kimbrough Army Hosp., Ft. Meade, Md., 1986—; cons. Regional Commrs. Pres's Commn. on White House Fellow, 1985, 86. Named Alumni of Yr., Wagner Coll., S.I., 1983; White House fellow, 1982; Meritorious medal sec. Def., 1982. Mem. Nat. Black Nurses Assn., Am. Nurses Assn., Am. Nurses Found., Drug/Alcohol Nurses Assn., Assn. U.S. Army, Assn. U.S. Mil. Surgeons, Sigma Theta Tau. Clubs: Presidio Officers (co chmn. council 1985-86), Rocks (Washington) (v.p.). Avocations: weight lifting; collecting miniature camels; indoor gardening. Home: 6302 49th Ave Riverdale MD 20737 Office: Kimbrough Army Hosp Dept Nursing Ft Meade MD 20755

RICHMAN, GERTRUDE GROSS (MRS. BERNARD RICHMAN), civic worker; b. N.Y.C., May 16, 1908; d. Samuel and Sarah Yetta (Seltzer) Gross; B.S., Tchrs. Coll. Columbia U., 1948, M.A., 1949; m. Bernard Richman, Apr. 5, 1930; children—David, Susan. Vol. worker Hackensack Hosp., 1948-70; mem. bd. dirs. YM-YWHA, Bergen County, N.J., 1950-75, bd. mem. emeritus, 1975—; chmn. Leonia Friends of Bergen County Mental Health Consultation Center, 1959; founder, hon. pres. Bergen County Serv-A-Com., affiliated with women orgns. Div. Nat. Jewish Welfare Bd.; v.p. N.J. sect. Nat. Jewish Welfare Bd., 1964-71; hon. trustee women's div. Bergen County United Jewish Community; mem. adv. council Bergen County Office on Aging, 1968-83, reappointed, 1984—; mem. Hackensack Bd. Edn., 1946-51; mem. pub. relations com. Leonia Pub. Schs., 1957-58; N.J. del. White House Conf. on Aging, 1971; trustee Mary McLeod Bethune Scholarship Fund; v.p. Bergen County nat. women's com. Brandeis U., 1966-67. Recipient citation Nat. Council Jewish Women and YWCA in Bergen County, 1962; citation Nat. Jewish Welfare Bd., 1964, Harry S. Feller award N.J. Region, 1965; 14th Ann. Good Scout award Bergen council Boy Scouts Am., 1977; Woman Vol. of Distinction, Bergen County council Girl Scouts, 1979; Human Relations award Bergen County sect. Nat. Council Negro Women, 1982. Mem. Kappa Delta Pi.

RICHMAN, JOAN, television producer; b. St. Louis, Apr. 10, 1939; d. Stanley M. and Barbara (Friedman) R.; B.A., Wellesley (Mass.) Coll., 1961. Asst. producer WNDT, N.Y.C., 1964-65; researcher, CBS News, N.Y.C., 1961-64, researcher spl. events units, 1965-67, mgr. research Republican and Democratic nat. convs., 1968, assoc. producer spl. events, 1968; producer spl. events CBS News, 1969-72; sr. producer The Reasoner Report, ABC News, 1972-75; exec. producer CBS Sports Spectacular, 1975-76, CBS News weekend broadcasts, 1976-82, v.p., dir., exec. producer spl. events, 1982—. Recipient Nat. TV Acad. Arts and Scis. Emmy award for CBS News space coverage, 1970-71, 71-72; Alumnae Achievement award Wellesley Coll., 1973. Mem. Nat. Acad. TV Arts and Scis., Wellesley Coll. Alumnae Assn. (pres. class of 1961, 1966-70). Home: 228 W 22d St New York NY 10011 Office: CBS News 524 W 57th St New York NY 10019

RICHMAN, PHYLLIS CHASANOW, newspaper editor and critic; b. Washington, Mar. 21, 1939; d. Abraham and Helen (Lieberman) Chasanow; children—Joseph, Matthew, Libby. B.A., Brandeis U., 1961; postgrad. U. Pa., 1961-62, Purdue U., 1967-71. Research asst. U. Pa., Phila., 1961-62; social analyst Phila. Redevel. Commn., 1962-63; researcher Diagnostic and Relocation Ctr., Phila., 1963-65; freelance writer, Washington, 1971-76; restaurant critic Washington Post, 1976—, exec. food editor, 1980—. Author: Barter, 1976; Best Restaurants and Others: D.C., 1980, 82, 84. Syndicated columnist Richman's Table. Mem. Washington Ind. Writers (dir., adv. bd.), Las Dames d'Escoffier (officer). Home: 5311 38th St NW Washington DC 20015 Office: Washington Post 1150 15th St NW Washington DC 20071

RICHMAN, SELMA, microbiologist; b. Bklyn.; d. Joseph and Leah (Kennis) R. B.S., Bklyn. Coll.; M.A., Central Mich. U., 1979. Successively lab. technician Queens Gen. Hosp., Jamaica, N.Y.; jr. microbiologist Cumberland Hosp., Bklyn.; asst microbiologist Queens Hosp. Ctr., Jamaica; prin. microbiologist Coney Island Hosp., Bklyn., 1965—; cons. in field. Author: Case Study on Aeromonas Hydrophila, 1982. Mem. Am. Soc. Clin. Pathologists, Am. Soc. Microbiology, Med. Mycology Soc. Am., Nat. Assn. Female Execs. Avocations: knitting; tennis; racquetball; swimming; music. Office: Coney Island Hosp 2601 Ocean Pkwy Brooklyn NY 11235

RICHMOND, ELIZABETH LEAH, interior design and planning firm executive; b. Val D'Or, Que., Can. Aug. 16, 1951; came to U.S., 1979; d. James and Christina J. (Toscani) Dent; m. Richard E. Richmond, Dec. 18, 1971 (div. Aug. 1978); m. Terry Lee Coffin, Mar. 3, 1984. Cert. in Interior Design, Humber Coll., Toronto, Ont., Can., 1974. Space planner IMCO, Toronto, 1974-76; cons. Can. Govt., Toronto, 1976-77; designer PAJ, Toronto, 1977-79; project mgr. EPR, San Francisco, 1979-80, Dodson & Henry, San Diego, 1980-81; owner, operator Facilities Planning Assn., San Diego, 1981—; mem. exec. com. Interior Designers Can. Toronto, 1977-79. Bldg. design and interiors pub. in profl. jours. Asst. Renaissance Fair, San Diego, 1982. Mem. San Diego C. of C., Inst. Bus. Designers. Republican. Baptist. Avocations: swimming; sailing; riding; biking; reading. Office: Facilities Planning Assn 2202 4th Ave San Diego CA 92101

RICHMOND, JOYCE CORTRIGHT, medical librarian; b. Hackensack, N.J., Dec. 14, 1947; d. Charles Vernon and Sara (Sigel) Cortright; m. Karl Sharp Richmond, Nov. 27, 1971; children—Scott Sharp, Benjamin Charles. B.A. cum laude, Fairleigh Dickinson U., 1969; student Wroxton Coll., Eng., 1968; M.L.S., U. Md., 1974; cert. in English lit. Exeter Coll., Oxford, Eng., 1970. Advanced profl. cert., Md. Dept. Edn. Grad. asst. librarian U. Md., College Park, 1973-74; head librarian Severna Park Sr. High Sch., Md., 1974-77; substitute librarian Anne Arundel County Pub. Schs., 1977-82; med. librarian Anne Arundel Gen. Hosp., 1982—; chmn. state media exhibit Md. Ednl. Media Orgn., 1976; mem. Middle States Evaluation Team, 1977. Sec., Hillsmere Shores Improvement Assn., Annapolis, Md., 1983-84; mem. exec. bd. Key Parent League, Annapolis, 1983-84, sec., 1984-85. Mem. Ednl. Media Assn. Anne Arundel County (treas., newsletter editor 1977-84), Md. Ednl. Media Orgn., ALA, Md. Tchrs. Assn., Med. Library Assn., Balt. Consortium for Resource Sharing, Md. Assn. Health Sci. Librarians, Phi Zeta Kappa, Beta Phi Mu, Phi Omega Epsilon. Home: 513 Harbor Dr Annapolis MD 21403 Office: Anne Arundel General Hosp Franklin and Cathedral Sts Annapolis MD 21401

RICHMOND, PHYLLIS ALLEN, library science educator; b. Boston, Jan. 5, 1921; d. Charles Francis Hitchcock and Elberta (Currie) Allen; m. James Hugh Richmond, Sept. 24, 1949 (dec.). A.B., Western Reserve U., 1942, M.S.L.S., 1956; A.M., U. Pa., 1946, Ph.D., 1949. Curator history Rochester Mus., N.Y., 1943-45, 47; asst. to dir. Inst. History of Medicine, Johns Hopkins U., Balt., 1952; librarian U. Rochester, N.Y., 1955-68; prof. library sci. Syracuse U., N.Y., 1969-70, Case Western Res. U., Cleve., 1970-85; vis. prof. UCLA, spring 1985, Columbia U., N.Y.C., spring 1986; speaker in field. Author: PRECIS for North American Usage, 1981. Mem. editorial bd. several library jours. Contbr. numerous articles to profl. jours. Recipient award of Merit Am. Soc. Info. Sci., 1972; Margaret Mann citation ALA, 1977; predoctoral fellow Am. Council Learned Socs., Cornell U., 1948. Mem. ALA (held several offices), Am. Soc. Info. Sci. (several offices), History of Sci. Soc., Spl. Libraries Assn., Phi Beta Kappa. Republican. Presbyterian. Avocations: travel, ham radio, computer. Home: 6628 Aintree Park Dr Apt 202 Cleveland OH 44143

RICHMOND, SUZIE MARIE, nurse; b. Rochester, N.Y., Aug. 3, 1953; d. Eugene Francis and Mary Aileen (Coleman) Atwood; m. Daniel Paul Richmond, Mar. 17, 1978. Assoc. Degree in Nursing, Monroe Community Coll., 1974. Lic. nephrology nurse; cert. hemodialysis nurse. Med. surg. staff nurse St. Mary's Hosp., Rochester, 1974-77, CCU staff nurse, 1977-78; hemodialysis staff nurse Rochester Gen. Hosp., 1979-82, nurse mgr., instr., 1982—. Recipient Medal of Life award Am. Heart Assn., 1984. Mem. Am. Nephrology Nurses Assn. Roman Catholic. Avocations: aerobics; Nautilus; swimming. Home: 245 Black Walnut Dr Rochester NY 14615 Office: Rochester Gen Hosp 1425 Portland Ave Rochester NY 14621

RICHMOND-SELL, ADRIANNE, film production executive, writer; b. Bklyn., Feb. 29, 1944; d. Milton George and Florence (Rosen) Henry; m. Paul Bradley Richmond, Oct. 18, 1963 (div. July 1974); children—Wendy Joan, Bruce Richmond; m. Jack M. Sell. B.A., NYU, 1965. Creative dir., v.p. Introspect, Inc., Chgo., 1974-78; v.p., creative dir. Haddon Advt., Chgo., 1978—; v.p. Metrofilms, Chgo., 1981—, asst. dir. feature films, 1980—. Mem. adv. bd. Thayne Lyman Endowment Fund, 1984—. Recipient Gold award Houston Film Festival, 1985; Silver, Gold and Bronze medals N.Y. Internat. Film Festival, various yrs. Mem. TV Acad. Chgo. Jewish. Club: Inner Circle (Washington).

RICHTER, JACKIE WILSON, business executive; b. Hornbeck, La., Oct. 30, 1933; d. Jack Caraway and Marie (Self) Wilson; grad. Nacogdoches Bus. Coll., 1951; student Victoria Coll., 1951, 72, Del Mar Coll., 1978-80; m. Clyde Joseph Richter, Dec. 12, 1952; children—Lisa Anne, Clyde Joseph, Sarah Elizabeth. With R.W. Hill Co., Victoria, Tex., 1952, So. Pacific R.R., 1953-57; co-owner, Richter's Precision Air Co., Victoria, 1962—, Intra-Coastal Enterprises, Corpus Christi, Tex., 1975—. Alt. del. Republican State Conv., 80, del., 1982, 84; regional walk coordinator Collins for U.S. Senate, 1982; del. Tex. Fedn. Rep. Women Conv., 1983; v.p. Corpus Christi Rep. Women's Club, 1983-84, pres., 1984; mem. Corpus Christi Symphony Guild, Art Mus. South Tex., Art Community Center; patron Harbor Playhouse. Mem. Refrigeration Engr.'s Soc. (aux. pres. 1967) C. of C., Tex. Restaurant Assn., Better Bus. Bur., Tex. Retail Grocers Assn., DAR (2d vice regent 1984-85, regent) Colonial Dames XVII Century (sec. 1983-85), Daus. Am. Colonists, Daus. Republic Tex., Photog. Soc. Ams. (Internat. Salon Silver medal, San Antonio, 1981, Silver medal, Richmond, Va., 1983, Endres Silver medal 1981). Lutheran. Club: Corpus Christi Camera (past dir.). Office: PO Box 226 909 N Staples Corpus Christi TX 78403*

RICHTER, MARGARET, health products and services consultant, author; b. Paterson, N.J., Aug. 5, 1948; d. Joseph and Florence (Zafeman) R.; student Princeton (N.J.) Hosp., 1968, Fordham U., 1975-78. Staff nurse Princeton Hosp., 1968-70; leadership and staff nurse Mt. Sinai Med. Center, N.Y.C., 1970-76; health care analyst L.I. Coll. Hosp., Bklyn., 1976-77; exec. asst. N.Am. Railco, Inc., N.Y.C., 1977-78; health records analyst Beth Israel Med. Center, N.Y.C., 1978-79; project coordinator, health facilities cons. Duffy, Inc., Planners and Designers, N.Y.C., 1979-81; project dir., health facilities cons. Henry Meltzer Group, Inc., N.Y.C., 1981-82; founder, pres. Margaret Richter Assocs. Inc., 1982—, freelance writer. Mem. AIA, Women Bus. Owners N.Y. (dir.), AT&T: Orgn. Effectiveness Group, Nat. Ctr. for Barrier Free Environment. Office: 1700 York Ave New York NY 10128

RICHTER, MARY JANE, school administrator, consultant; b. Red Bank, N.J., Oct. 17, 1937; d. Ross Eckman and Esther Jackson (Herr) Wiley; m. John Edward Richter, Aug. 11, 1956; children—Jacqueline Richter-Menge, Andrea Ross. B.S., U. Del., 1980, postgrad., 1982—. Cert. tchr., Del. Dir. Little Sch., Dover, Del., 1975—. Bd. dirs. Kent Gen. Hosp., Dover, Dover Acad., 1982—; trustee Del. Fedn. Retarded Children, Wilmington, 1978—. Mem. Nat. Assn. Edn. Young Children, Del. Assn. Edn. Young Children, Internat. Reading Assn., AAUW, Omicron Nu. Republican. Lutheran. Club: Dover Century. Avocations: tennis; fitness; reading. Home: 733 Oak Dr Dover DE 19901 Office: Little Sch Inc 308 N Queen St Dover DE 19901

RICHTER, ROBERTA BRANDENBURG (MRS. J. PAUL RICHTER), educator; b. Osborn, Ohio, Dec. 29; d. Warren F. and Mary M. (Davis) Brandenburg; student Miami-Jacobs Coll., 1930, Wittenberg U., 1930-31, Coll. Music, U. Cin., 1931-32, U. Dayton, 1954, 64; B.S., Miami U., Oxford, Ohio, 1958, M.Ed., 1959; postgrad. Wright State U., 1966-70; doctoral candidate Ohio State U., 1969; m. Jean Paul Richter, Oct. 6, 1934; 1 son, James Paul. Bus. mgr. T.D. Peffley, Inc., 1929-32; sec., prodn. mgr. Delco Products div. Gen. Motors, 1932-34; exec. sec. Meth. Union, 1932-38, LWV, 1935-38, Elder & Johnston Dept. Store, 1938-40; ct. reporter Common Pleas Ct. Montgomery County, 1940-46; adminstrv. asst. Ch. Fedn. Greater Dayton, Ohio, 1946-50; audio-visual cons. schs., chs. Twyman Films, 1950-53; legal asst. Nadlin Law Offices, 1953-58; instr. stenotype, office practice Miami-Jacobs Coll., Dayton, 1941-48; tchr. stenotype, guidance counselor Stebbins High Sch., Dayton, 1958-82; vocat. guidance coordinator Mad River Planning Dist., Montgomery County, Ohio, 1968-73. Instr. workshops in stenotype for ct. reporting Wright State U., Dayton, 1970—; 1st cellist youth div. Symphony Orch.; dir. Lang. Unlimited, Inc., Lake Forest, Ill. Supt., tchr., adviser youth div. Grace United Meth. Ch., Dayton, 1942-72, sec. adminstrv. bd., 1940—, council on ministries, 1972-74, past pres. Excel Club, circle leader, hospitality chmn., pres. homebuilders class, program chmn., laywoman chmn. Christian higher edn.; instr., counselor Camp Miniwanca, Am. Youth Found., 1949-68. Mem. Am., Ohio, Miami Valley personnel and guidance assns., Nat., Ohio bus. tchrs. assns., Am., Ohio sch. counselor assns., Nat., Ohio edn. assns., Nat. Vocat. Guidance Assn., Dayton Area Bus. Soc. (v.p. 1969-82), Nat. Shorthand Reporters Assn., Delphian Soc. (past pres.), Pub. Speaker Bur., Council World Affairs, AAUW, LWV (past pres. and treas.), Internat. Platform Assn., World Trade Club (1st woman), Greater Dayton C. of C., Bus. and Profl. Women (past pres.), Pi Omega Pi. Clubs: Order Eastern Star, Progressive Mothers (chmn. program Dayton 1969-70). Author ednl. handbooks, pamphlets. Contbr. articles to profl. jours.; lectr. in field. Home: 3865 Seiber Ave Dayton OH 45405

RICHTER, SUSAN ELIZABETH, nurse; b. Salt Lake City, Jan. 12, 1944; d. Joseph Leo and Sara Jane (Bero) Shalvoy; R.N., St. Vincent's Sch. Nursing, 1964; B.S. U. New Haven, 1984; m. Edward Frederick Richter, Jr., Nov. 6, 1965; children—Meghan, Heidi, Edward, Kathleen, Colin. Staff nurse St. Vincent's Med. Center, Bridgeport, Conn., 1964-71, evening supr., 1972-78, evening adminstrv. dir., 1978-82, dir. community health relations, 1982—. Chmn., Community Projects Com., 1979-84; sch. vol. Assn. of Bridgeport, 1977—, bd. dirs. 1977—, chmn., 1979-80; co-leader Jr. Girl Scout Troop, 1974-77; bd. dirs. Fairfield County chpt. Am. Heart Assn., 1980-82; mem. Bridgeport Coalition on Hypertension Control, 1980-83. Mem. St. Vincent's Sch. Nursing Alumni Assn. (corr. sec. 1983—), Alpha Sigma Lambda. Republican. Roman Catholic. Clubs: St. Vincent's Med. Center Aux., Home Sch. Assn. of Assumption Sch., Am. Diabetic Assn. (rec. sec. Bridgeport chpt. 1983—), Am. Cancer Soc. (bd. dirs., exec. com. Conn. div.), Conn. Hosp. Assn., Conn. Pub. Health Assn., Am. Soc. Perspective Medicine, Nat. Ctr. Health Edn., Bus. and Industry Council, New Eng. Health Promotion Mgrs. Council, Barnum Festival Soc.

RICHTMEYER, KAREN SUE, telecommunications account executive; b. Bad Axe, Mich., Apr. 9, 1953; d. Lorin C. and Grace M. (Ruegsegger) R. B.Music Edn., B.Elem. Edn., No. Mich. U., Marquette, 1974; M.B.A., Mercer U., Atlanta, 1984. Cert. industry cons. communications. Regional music assessor Mich. Edn. Assn., Lansing and Marquette, Mich., 1975; dining room mgr. Holiday Inn, Marquette, 1975-78; mktg. adminstr. Nev. Bell Telephone Co., Reno, 1979-80, account exec., 1980; account exec. So. Bell Telephone Co., Atlanta, 1981-82; account exec., industry cons. AT&T Info. Systems, Atlanta, 1982—. Co-organizer fund drive Am. Cancer Soc., Reno, 1979. Named Outstanding Account Exec. for July and Dec., So. Bell Telephone Co., 1982, recipient Account Exec. Challenge of the Yr. award, 1981; recipient Bus. Mktg. Sales award Nev. Bell Telephone Co., 1980; named Outstanding High Sch. Musician, USMC Found., 1971. Mem. Nat. Assn. Female Execs., AT&T Achievers Club, Wire Assn. Internat., Nat. Assn. Women in Constrn., Musicians Union Am. Methodist. Club: Atlanta Track. Office: AT&T Info Systems 2300 Northlake Center Tucker GA 30084

RICKARD-RIEGLE, BARBARA KATHERINE, journalist, news broadcaster; b. Los Angeles, May 1, 1931; d. Thomas and Katherine Elizabeth (Blackburn) Rickard; student pvt. schs., Santa Rosa, Calif.; children—Katherine, Karen, Christopher, Melissa, Richard. Editor, Phenix City (Ala.) Herald, 1957-58; news broadcaster, editor WRBL-Radio-TV, Columbus, Ga., 1958-62; polit. reporter Esquire Broadcasting Co., Sta. WQXI, Atlanta, 1962-63; news commentator Sta. WAII-TV, Atlanta, 1962-63; polit. writer, columnist Los Angeles Herald Examiner, 1963-66; Congressional news sec., Washington, 1966-67; news writer, guest broadcaster Stas. KNXT, KABC-TV, Hollywood, Calif., 1964-67; broadcaster, women's news editor Sta. KNX-CBS, 1967-71; news broadcaster, producer, reporter, bur. chief Westinghouse Broadcasting Corp., Sta. KFWB, Hollywood, 1971—; guest broadcaster Pub. Broadcasting System, Sta. KCET, 1975—; propr., pres. Calico Feature Prodns., Anaheim, Calif., 1969—; instr. journalism Calif. State U., Fullerton, 1972-73. Republican candidate for Calif. State Assembly, 1976. Named Journalist of Year, Cypress Coll., 1980; recipient Angel of Distinction award City of Los Angeles, 1973, John Swett Journalist of Yr. award Calif. Tchrs. Assn., 1974, 79. Mem. Am. Women in Radio and TV (chpt. pres. 1982-83; chairperson bus. and industry forum Ednl. Found. 1979), Nat. Women's Polit. Caucus, Investigative Reporters and Editors, Orange County Press Club (dir. 1979—, pres. 1984-85), Women in Communications (award 1979), Pioneer Broadcasters W., Sigma Delta Chi. Author: The Long Hot Summer of 1962; Something is Missing: The Majority Sex, 1971; Dinner for One: Soupçon for Singles, 1977. Home and office: 2512 W Chain Ave Anaheim CA 92804

RICKARDS, NANCY WOOD, educator; b. Cortland, N.Y., Oct. 20, 1953; d. Gordon Fowler and Ruth (Lewis) Wood; m. Harold Albert Rickards, Jr., Mar. 24, 1984. B.S., U. Vt., 1975; M.Edn., Fla. Atlantic U., 1979. 5th grade tchr. Okeechobee County, Fla., 1975-78, Title I reading tchr., 1978-79, 4th grade tchr., grade chmn., 1979—. Sec., treas. Oak Lake Villas Homeowners Assn., Okeechobee, 1984. Named Okeechobee County Tchr. of Yr., 1981-82, Outstanding Social Studies Tchr. Okeechobee County, 1984-85. Mem. Delta Kappa Gamma. Republican. Methodist. Avocations: scuba diving; snow and water skiing; needlework. Home: 2201 SW 28th St Villa 81 Okeechobee FL 33474 Office: North Elem Sch 3000 NW 10th Terr Okeechobee FL 33472

RICKBEIL, CLARA EVELYN SHELLMAN (MRS. RAYMOND E. RICKBEIL), club woman; b. Gibson City, Ill.; d. Kilian and Anna Marie (Johnson) Shellman; grad. Brown's Bus. Coll., Champaign, Ill., 1922; student U. Ill., 1927-28; m. Raymond Earl Rickbeil, May 8, 1930. Office sec. Ford County Farm Bur., Gibson City, 1922-26; secretarial position Raymond E.

Rickbeil, C.P.A., Springfield, Ill., 1928-61, Ernst & Ernst, Springfield, 1961-65. Mem. bd. King's Daus.; adv. bd. Am. Security Council; mem. Community Concert Assn., Nat. Fedn. Republican Women, Rep. Women's Club Sangamon County, Sangamon County Farm Bur. Recipient award for work pub. acctg. legis. Ill. Soc. C.P.A.s, 1956. Mem. U. Ill. Alumni Assn., U. Ill. Pres.'s Club, Am. Legion Aux., Meml. Hosp. Aux., Sangamon County Hist. Soc. Republican. Presbyterian. Clubs: Woman's (reception com. 1962-63, social com. 1963-64, corr. sec. 1972-75, dist. program chmn. dist. 21 1968-69, dist. corr. sec. 1969-72), Mariama (vice chmn. chpt. 5 1966-67, chmn. 1967-72), Amateur Musical, Order Eastern Star, Zonta (treas. 1954-57, fin. com. 1965—, fin. chmn. 1957-63, 64, service chmn., mem. service com. 1953-62), Sangamo (asso.); Three Hills Extension Homemakers (reporter) (Kerrville, Tex.). Home: 937 Feldkamp Ave Springfield IL 62704

RICKENBAUGH, MARY KATHERINE, insurance company executive; b. Bellevue, Ohio, June 12, 1944; d. Kent Fleet and Charlotte Mitchel (Seltzer) Dillon; student Smith Coll., 1962-63; B.A., Western Res. U., 1966; M.B.A., Case Western Res. U., 1983; m. Richard Carl James, Sept. 10, 1966 (div. 1984); children—Carl, Daniel; m. Donald Rickenbaugh, 1985. Personnel asst. Fisher Foods, Inc., Cleve., 1966-69, payroll asst., 1973-75, asst. tax mgr., 1975-76, accounts payable supr., 1977; acct., C.P.A., Cohen & Co., Cleve., 1977-80; bus. mgr. Hathaway Brown, Shaker Heights, Ohio, 1980-82; fin. ops. mgr. Progressive Casualty Ins. Co., Cleve., 1982—. C.P.A., Ohio. Mem. Am. Inst. C.P.A.s, Ohio Soc. C.P.A.s, Nat. Assn. Female Execs., Republican. Episcopalian. Home: 36002 Derby Downs Solon OH 44139 Office: 6300 Wilson Mills Rd Mayfield Village OH 44143

RICKETTS, BARBARA HARRINGTON, nursery school administrator; b. Worcester, Mass., July 17, 1922; d. Roy Peck and Henrietta Katrina (Meyers) Harrington; m. Edward William Ricketts, June 19, 1943; children—David Kenneth, Jonathan Edward, Pamela Dianne Ricketts Menard. Student Framingham State Coll., 1963-64, Worcester State Coll., 1966-67, Quinsigamond Community Coll., 1981-82. Sec., McCoy Lumber Co., Worcester, Mass., 1942-45; sec., substitute tchr. Oxford Pub. Schs., Mass., 1953-58; owner, operator Merry Morning Nursery Sch., Oxford, 1958-81; owner, dir. Merry Morning Presch. Ctr., North Oxford, Mass., 1981—. Chmn. service team Girl Scouts U.S.A., Oxford, 1958-84; supt. ch. sch., Oxford, 1958-80; pres. Women's Soc. Christian Service, Oxford, 1952-54, 60-61; sec. Sch. Bldg. Com., Oxford, 1974-76. Recipient Thanks Badge, Mass. council Girl Scouts U.S.A., 1984. Republican. Methodist. Club: Oxford Women's (pres. 1951-53). Avocations: skiing; biking. Home: 5 West St Oxford MA 01540 Office: Merry Morning Presch Ctr Norwood Ct North Oxford MA 01537

RICKIN, SHEILA ANNE, personnel executive; b. N.Y.C., Oct. 13, 1945; d. Louis and Ethel (Schmuckler) Bernstein; B.A., CCNY, 1966; postgrad. N.Y.U.; M.B.A. candidate Pace U. Research asst. pre-baccalaureate program CCNY, 1966-68; placement counselor Elaine Revell, Inc., N.Y.C., 1968; adminstr. asso. to chief exec. officer Planned Parenthood Fedn. of Am., N.Y.C., 1969-74; personnel mgr. Family Circle Mag./N.Y. Times Mag. Group, 1974—. Mem. Am. Soc. Personnel Adminstrs., Am. Mgmt. Assn., Met. N.Y. Assn. for Applied Psychology, N.Y. Human Resources Planners, N.Y. Personnel Mgrs. Assn., Mag. Pubs. Assn. (personnel com.). Club: N.Y. Health and Racquet. Office: Family Circle Inc 488 Madison Ave New York NY 10022

RICKS-JEFFERSON, CAMILLE ANTOINETTE, broadcast production executive; b. Washington, Dec. 29, 1954; d. William James and Juanita Elizabeth (Turner) Ricks; m. Orin Randell Jefferson, Oct. 6, 1984; 1 child, Omari Jahi. B.A., U. Md., 1977; grad. Barbizon Modeling Sch., 1971; postgrad. Southeastern U., Washington, 1983-84. Broadcast engr., Westinghouse Sta. KYW, Phila., 1979-80; relief broadcast engr. Sta. WRC-TV, Washington, 1980; legal asst. U.S. Atty. Office, Washington, 1981-82; broadcast engr. Taft Broadcasting Sta. WDCA, Washington, 1982-84; prodn. mgr., pub. affairs dir. Sta. WNJR, Hillside, N.J., 1985—. Active Big Bros. and Big Sisters of Am., Washington, 1978—. Mem. Nat. Assn. Female Execs. Club: Options Unltd. (Washington). Avocations: gourmet cooking; sewing; walking.

RIDDER, MARY ANN, insurance company executive; b. East Chicago, Ind., Dec. 21, 1942; d. Edward Joseph and Ann Theresa (Dwyer) Dolatowski, m. Richard L. Ridder, Feb. 11, 1984. B.A., Ind. U. C.L.U. Underwriter, Guarantee Res. Life, Hammond, Ind., 1963-66; field payroll coordinator Morrison Constrn. Co., Hammond, 1966-68; adminstrv. asst. to v.p. Underwriters Nat., Indpls., 1968-70; office mgr. Gregory & Appel Life Agy., Indpls., 1970-81; v.p. employee benefits div. Brougher Life Ins. Co., Greenwood, Ind., 1981—; v.p. Sterling Investors Life Ins. Co., 1985—; v.p. Brougher Ins. Group Inc. Vol., Indpls. Mus. Art. Recipient award Polit. Sci. Dept., Ind. U., 1981, Cavanaugh award Sch. Liberal Arts, 1981. Mem. Am. Soc. C.L.U.s, Ind. U. Sch. Liberal Arts Alumni Assn. (pres. 1982-83), Gold Key Soc., Pi Sigma Alpha. Editorial adv. bd. The Self-Insurer. Contbr. articles to trade publs. Home: 1025 Collingwood Dr Indianapolis IN 46208 Office: Brougher Agy Inc 2528 US 31 S Greenwood IN 46142

RIDDER, STEPHANIE, lawyer, educator; b. Paris, Nov. 28, 1951; came to U.S., 1952; d. Walter Thompson and Marie (Wasserman) R. B.A. cum laude, Harvard U., 1974; J.D., U. Va., 1977. Admitted to Va. bar, 1977. Staff atty. Legal Services Corp., Fredericksburg, Va., 1977-79, Harrisonburg, Va., 1979-80, Culpeper, Va., 1980-83; adj. prof. Law Sch. Cath. U. Am., Washington, 1984, Law Sch. George Washington U., Washington, 1984—. Bds. dirs. Virginians Against Domestic Violence, Richmond, 1980—, Child Care and Learning Ctr., Washington, Va., 1981—; mem. Democratic Com. Rappahannock County, Va., 1983-84. Mem. Va. Women Attys. Assn. Home: Route 1 Box 555 Amissville VA 22002

RIDDICK, MILDRED MAVIS, consultant; b. Roanoke Rapids, N.C., Jan. 2, 1954; d. Willie B. and Christine (Mason) High; B.S., Coppin State Coll., 1977; M. Social Service (scholar 1977, 78), Bryn Mawr Coll., 1979; 1 child, Stacie Christine. Community organizer Phila. Council Neighborhood Orgns., 1977-78; asst. to exec. dir. Big Sisters Phila., 1978-79; staff asst. Congressman Parren J. Mitchell, 7th Congressional Dist. Balt., 1979; research assoc. Mayor's Office Manpower Resources, Balt., 1979-82; clin. dir. Urban Cardiology Research Center, Balt.; adminstrv. research assoc. Joline, Inc., health and edn. systems analysts. Contbr. articles to Bapt. Leader mag. Evangelist New Shiloh Bapt. Ch., youth superintendent Sat. ch. sch.; adv. Harlem Park youth council NAACP. Recipient Pres. Emeritus Human Relations award Coppin State Coll., 1977. Mem. Student Council Exceptional Children (v.p. in charge publs. 1976-77), Nat. Assn. Social Workers (Bryn Mawr Coll. liaison Pa. chpt. 1978-79), Alpha Kappa Mu. Baptist. Dept. editor Edn. and Tng. of Mentally Retarded, 1976-77. Home: 4501-C Wakefield Rd Baltimore MD 21216 Office: Urban Cardiology Research Center 924 W North Ave Baltimore MD 21216

RIDDLE, CONSTANCE CHRISTINE, educational administrator, consultant; b. Wichita, Kans., Oct. 7, 1923; d. Chester Victor and Evalyn Eugenia (Billinger) Stippich; m. George Archibald Riddle, Jr., June 25, 1944; children—George Archibald III, Michael Christopher, Penelope Diane, David Payne. B.A. in Journalism, U. Okla., 1944; postgrad. in edn. U. Houston, 1968, M.Ed. in Curriculum and Instrn., 1970. Tchr. 3d grade Houston Ind. Sch. Dist., 1963-67, tchr. minimally brain injured, 1967-71, diagnostic tchr., 1972-74, chmn. adv. com., 1973-74, adminstrv. supr., 1974-79, tng. coordinator spl. edn., 1975-79, program adminstr., 1980-82, asst. dir. proposal devel., 1982-85, mem. adv. bd. Vols. in Pub. Schs., 1984-86; exec. dir. Literacy Advance, Houston, 1985—; cons. Am. Women in Radio/TV, Houston, 1983—, Shearer Pub. Co., 1986. Author, editor. Developing Motor Skills, 1979; Reading Management System, 1979; co-author, editor Parent Education Workshop Modules, 1983. Bd. dirs. Houston chpt. Am. Heart Assn., 1961-72; pres., bd. dirs. Literacy Advance Houston, 1979-81; Tex. rep. South Central Literacy Action, 1985—; chmn. nat. long range planning com. Laubach Literacy Action, 1985—; flotilla comdr. U.S. Coast Guard Aux., Seabrook, Tex., 1984-85. Recipient Bell Ringer award Literacy Advance Houston, 1982-84. Mem. Women in Communications (exec. com. 1983-84), Houston Profl. Adminstrs. (exec. com. 1982-83), Delta Kappa Gamma (pres. 1976-78; scholar 1974), Phi Delta Kappa, Kappa Delta Pi. Home: 5238 Ariel Houston TX 77096 Office: Literacy Advance of Houston Inc 4433 Bissonnet Bellaire TX 77401

RIDDLE, DEBORAH FAY, personnel representative; b. Durham, N.C., Oct. 24, 1956; d. Grady L. Riddle and Daisy (Reynolds) Riddle Robinson. B.S. in Edn., N.C. Central U., 1978; M.B.A., Brenau Coll., 1982. Sec. Durham Manpower Co., 1975; clk. typist Dept. H.E.W., 1976-78; substitute tchr. Durham City Pub. Schs., 1978, Atlanta pub. schs., 1979; personnel rep., Mgmt. Tng. Corp., Atlanta, 1979—. Mem. Nat. Assn. Female Execs., Delta Sigma Theta (historian 1976). Baptist. Home: 872 Oglethorpe Ave SW Atlanta GA 30310

RIDDLE, DOROTHY IRENE, international management educator; b. Chgo., Jan. 12, 1944; d. Charles Wainwright and Katharine Elsie (Parker) R. B.A. summa cum laude, U. Colo., 1964; M.B.A., U. Ariz., 1981; Ph.D., Duke U., 1968. Asst. prof. psychology Coll. William and Mary, Williamsburg, Va., 1968-70; asst. prof. Richmond Coll.-CUNY, S.I., N.Y., 1970-72; ptnr., psychologist Alternatives for Women, Tucson, 1973-75; assoc. in clin. tng. U. Ariz., Tucson, 1976-80; assoc. prof. internat. services and cross-cultural communication Am. Grad. Sch. Internat. Mgmt., Glendale, Ariz., 1981—; chief psychologist Marana Community Clinic, Ariz., 1976-80; intercultural cons. Thunderbird Mgmt. Ctr., Glendale, 1981—; cons. UN Conf. on Trade and Devel., Geneva, 1985—, Sistema Economico Latinoamericano, Caracas, 1986—. Author: Service-led Growth: The Role of the Service Sector in World Development, 1986. Contbr. articles to profl. jours. Pres. Group Health of Ariz. (PimaCare) Tucson, 1977-79. Named Tempe All-Am. Woman, 1985. Mem. Acad. Mgmt., Am. Psychol. Assn., Acad. Internat. Bus., Services World Forum, European Found. Mgmt. Devel., Soc. Intercultural Edn., Tng. and Research. Democrat. Avocations: music; hiking. Office: Am Grad Sch Internat Mgmt Glendale AZ 85282

RIDDLES, LIBBY N., sled-dog racer, trainer and breeder; b. Madison, Wis., Apr. 1, 1956; d. Willard Parker and Mary (Reynolds) R. Grad. high sch., St. Cloud, Minn. Finished 18th place in Iditarod Sled-Dog Race, 1980, 20th place, 1981, completed and finished 1st place, 1985; finished 7th place in Kusko 300 Sled-Dog Race, 1982, 5th place, 1984. Recipient Leonard Seppala Humanitarian award Alaska Airlines, 1985, Victor awards for excellence in sports, 1985; honored by Gov. Alaska with proclamation of Libby Riddles Day, Mar. 21, 1985. Democrat. Home: Box 545 Teller AK 99778

RIDDLES, MARGO ANN, real estate broker; b. Waco, Tex., Nov. 24, 1941; d. Karl Carter Southern and Gladys (Bell) Southern Tuttle; m. Timothy Leon Riddles, Sept. 19, 1980 (div. Mar. 1983); children—Robert, Randy, Kristi, Jennifer Cole. Student Cameron U., 1975, Okla. Sch. Real Estate, 1978. Teller, First Nat. Bank, Liberal, Kans., 1972-73, Seneca State Bank, Wichita, Kans., 1973-74; sec. So. Kirby Co., Lawton, Okla., 1974-75; sales assoc. Lawton (Okla.) Real Estate, 1975-78; broker assoc. Crossroads Realty, Lawton, 1978-80, Century 21 Lawton Real Estate, 1980—. Chmn. Community Housing and Equal Opportunity Com., 1984. Named to Million Dollar Club, Century 21 Real Estate, 1976-77; Million Dollar Producer, Crossroads Realty, 1978-79; recipient Top Listings award Century 21 Lawton Real Estate, 1982. Mem. Nat. Assn. Realtors, Okla. Assn. Realtors, Lawton Bd. Realtors (grievance com. 1977-82). Democrat. Office: Century 21 Lawton Real Estate 1902 Cache Rd Lawton OK 73501

RIDE, SALLY KRISTEN, astronaut; b. Los Angeles, May 26, 1951; d. Dale Burdell and Carol Joyce (Anderson) Ride; m. Steven Alan Hawley, July 24, 1982. B.S., Stanford U., 1973, B.A. in English, 1973, M.S., 1975, Ph.D., 1978. Astronaut, NASA, Johnson Space Ctr., Houston, 1978—; teaching asst., research asst. physics dept. Stanford U.; on-orbit capsule communicator STS-2 and STS-3 missions, NASA; astronaut STS-7, Kennedy Space Ctr., Fla., 1983, ST3-41G, 1984. Office: NASA/Johnson Space Ctr Houston TX 77058

RIDENOUR, SUZANNE SWENSON, executive search firm executive; b. Tallahassee, Feb. 15, 1943; d. Allen Edward and Margaret (Salley) Swenson; m. James Lee Ridenour, Dec. 28, 1968 (div. 1980). Student Bradley U., 1960-62. Terr. sales mgr. Am. Express Co., Chgo., 1968-69; sales rep. grocery products The Quaker Oats Co., Chgo., 1969-70; office mgr. Staff Builders Temporary Help Service, Chgo., 1970-71; placement dir. Robert Morris Coll., Chgo., 1971-76; pres. Gillick-Ridenour & Assocs., Chgo., 1976-82; pres., chief exec. officer Ridenour & Assocs., Chgo., 1982—; del. trade mission to promote export service industries Dept. Commerce, SBA, Nat. Assn. Women Bus. Owners, London, Frankfurt, Fed. Republic Germany, Madrid, 1985. Ill. del. White House Conf. on Small Bus., 1986; bd. govs. Anti-Cruelty Soc., Chgo., 1983—; bd. dirs. Chase House, Chgo., 1983-85; mem. nat. council advisers Coll. Bus. Adminstrn., Bradley U., Peoria, Ill., 1984—; mem. exec. com., aux bd. Lincoln Park Zool. Soc., Chgo., 1984—. Mem. Direct Mktg. Assn. (world direct trade council, conf. program adv. com., judge ECHO creative awards), Brit. Direct Mktg. Assn., European Direct Mktg. Assn., Internat. Bus. Council Mid-Am., Mid-Am. Swedish Trade Assn. (dir.), Chgo. Assn. Direct Mktg (officer and bd. dirs. 1979—, pres. 1984-85, founding trustee ednl. found. 1985—), Direct Mktg. Ednl. Found. (trustee 1985—), Nat. Assn. Women Bus. Owners (dep. chairperson internat. com. 1985—, chpt. dir.). Republican. Office: Ridenour & Assocs 230 N Michigan Ave Chicago IL 60601

RIDER, MARILYN ANN, stockbroker; b. Conrad, Mont., Dec. 15, 1941; d. Louis E. and Emmi V. (Markuson) Schroer; diploma acctg., Gt. Falls (Mont.) Comml. Coll., 1960; m. Joe Raunig, Jan. 2, 1960 (div. 1971); children—Christina M., Rodney B., Brett R.; m. 2d, Lloyd D. Keith, Apr. 19, 1972 (dec. July 1973); m. 3d, Bruce A. Rider, Dec. 10, 1977 (div. 1979); 1 son, Marc D. Engaged in acctg., 1960-74, 75-77; owner Keith Enterprises, Chester, Mont., 1974-75; account exec. Merill Lynch, Pierce Fenner and Smith, Spokane, from 1977, asst. v.p., fin. cons., tchr. courses in field. Mem. core team New Life. C.P.A., Wash. Mem. Wash. Soc. C.P.A.s, Am. Women's Soc. C.P.A.s. Roman Catholic. Clubs: Spokane Duplicate Bridge (dir. 1976), Pres.' of Merrill Lynch. Home: N 7927 Pine Meadow Nine Mile Falls WA 99026 Office: 1st Ave and Wall St Spokane WA 99201

RIDGE, CLAIRE LILLIAN, general contractor; b. Bklyn., Jan. 2, 1936; d. William Carl and Elizabeth Claire (Braun) Edwards; student Palm Beach Jr. Coll., 1981—; m. William J. Ridge, Nov. 6, 1968; children by previous marriage—Glenn A. Simonin, Diane C. Graziano. Lic. real estate broker; notary pub. Real estate saleswoman Provident Properties, Inc., 1965-67; owner, real estate broker Piper Realty, Inc., 1967-73; owner, builder St. Mark's Estates, Inc., Fieldcrest Homes, Inc., 1971—; owner, builder Sunshine Custom Builders, Inc. and Sunshine Builders of Palm Beach, Inc., 1977—; owner C. Ridge Realty, Inc. Mem. Singer Island Civic Assn.; mem. minority bus. enterprise staff com. Palm Beach County Commrs. Mem. North Palm Beach County Bd. Realtors, Home Builders Assn. Palm Beach County, Nat. Assn. Notaries, Nat. Assn. Women in Constrn., Palm Beach Gardens C. of C. Republican. Lutheran. Club: Frenchmen's Creek Country. Home: 1037 Morse Blvd Singer Island Riviera Beach FL 33404 Office: 1960 W 9th St Riviera Beach FL 33404

RIDGEWAY, HAZEL LEE, librarian; b. Gilbertown, Ala., Dec. 24, 1934; d. Brewister Kable and Helen (Phylon) Scruggs; m. Johnnie Tyrone Ridgeway, Aug. 11, 1959; children—Ivar Konrad, Irvin John. B.A., Tenn. State U.-Nashville; M.S. in L.S., U. So. Calif. Cert. community jr. coll. instr., Calif. Tchr. pre-sch. City of Los Angeles Dept. Parks and Recreation, 1966-68; librarian intern Los Angeles Pub. Library, 1972-73; librarian Inglewood Pub. Library (Calif.), 1973—; cons. Internat. Yr. of the Child, Inglewood, 1979. Coordinator, Neighborhood Watch Program, Cerritos, Calif., 1983. Recipient cert. of appreciation City of Los Angeles, 1971, March of Dimes Found., 1981; cert. of recognition City of Inglewood, 1981. Mem. ALA, Calif. Library Assn., Librarians Black Caucus (treas. 1981-83). Democrat. Baptist. 20130 S Mapes Ave Cerritos CA 90701 Office: Inglewood Pub Library 101 W Manchester Blvd Inglewood CA 90301

RIDGEWAY, JANICE MCCULLOUGH, librarian; b. Pelham, Ga., Apr. 17, 1949; d. John Arthur McCullough and Gladys (Ward) McCullough Sapp; m. Garry C. Horton, Mar. 21, 1970 (div.); m. Lonnie D. Ridgeway II, Feb. 17, 1979; 1 child, Leah Kathleen. Student Harvard U., summer 1968, Yale U., summer 1969; B.A., Albany State Coll., 1970; M.L.S., Emory U., 1972; postgrad. SUNY-Albany, 1975. Tchr. English, Dooly County Bd. of Edn., Vienna, Ga., 1970-71; head reference dept. Anchorage Mcpl. Library, 1972-77; co-founder, ptnr. BiblioSearch, Anchorage, 1976-79; asst. mcpl. librarian pub. services Anchorage Mcpl. Libraries, 1977-85, project mgr. for hdqrs. library, 1985—; owner, researcher Ridgeway Research Services, Anchorage, 1979—; dir. Anchorage Opportunity and Indsl. Ctr., 1976. Organizer Jesse Owens Games, Anchorage, Anchorage Debutant Ball; activist Anchorage Community Schs., Anchorage Community Council. Recipient Miss Albany State Coll. award, 1969-70. Mem. ALA, Alaska Library Assn. (exec. bd. 1974-75), Nat. Assn. Female Execs., Alpha Kappa Mu, Beta Phi Mu. Democrat. Club: Quota. Office: Anchorage Municipal Libraries 3600 Denali Anchorage AK 99503

RIDGWAY, ROZANNE LEJEANNE, foreign service officer, former ambassador; b. St. Paul, Aug. 22, 1935; d. H. Clay and Ethel Rozanne (Cote) R.; m. Theodore E. Deming. B.A., Hamline U., 1957, LL.D. (hon.), 1978. Commd. fgn. service officer Dept. State, 1957; various assignments in Washington, 1957-59, 64-67, 70-73, dep. asst. sec., ambassador for oceans and fisheries, 1975-77; various fgn. assignments in Manila, 1959-61, Palermo, Italy, 1962-64, Oslo, 1967-70; dep. chief of mission, Nassau, 1973-75; ambassador to Finland, Helsinki, 1977-80; counselor Dept. State, Washington, 1980-81, spl. asst. to sec. state, 1981-82; ambassador to German Democratic Republic, 1982-85; asst. sec. U.S. Dept. State, 1985—. Recipient citations Dept. State, 1967, 70, 75, 81; Person of Yr. award Nat. Fisheries Inst., 1977; Joseph C. Wilson award for achievement in internat. relations, 1982. Office: US Dept State 2201 C St NW Washington DC 20520*

RIDINGS, DOROTHY SATTES, national organization executive; b. Charleston, W.Va., Sept. 26, 1939; d. Frederick Lyle and Katharine Elizabeth (Backus) Sattes; m. Donald Jerome Ridings, Sept. 8, 1962; children—Donald Jerome Jr., Matthew Lyle. Student Randolph-Macon Woman's Coll., 1957-59; B.S. in Journalism, Northwestern U., 1961; M.A., U. N.C., 1968; D. Pub. Service, U. Louisville, (hon.), 1985. Editor Ky. Bus. Ledger, Louisville, 1977-83; communications cons., Louisville, Washington, 1983—; pres. U.S. LWV, Washington, 1982—; v.p. Nat. Mcpl. League, 1985—. Bd. dirs. Independent Sector, Nat. Com. Against Discrimination in Housing, Commn. Nat. Elections, Leadership Conf. on Civil Rights, Com. on Constl. System, Com. for Study of Am. Electorate, Leadership Ky., Leadership Louisville, Bretton Woods Com., others. Democrat. Presbyterian. Office: US LWV 1730 M St NW Washington DC 20036

RIDLEY, BETTY ANN, Christian Science practitioner, educator, lecturer; b. St. Louis, Oct. 19, 1926; d. Rupert Alexis and Virginia Regina (Weikel) Steber; m. Fred A. Ridley, Jr., Sept. 8, 1948; children—Linda Drue Ridley Archer, Clay Kent. B.A., Scripps Coll., Claremont, Calif., 1948. Christian Sci. practitioner, 1973—; mem. Christian Sci. Bd. Lectureship, worldwide, 1980-85, C.S. tchr., 1982—; mem. Found Bibl. Research and Preservation Primitive Christianity. Mem. Jr. League Am. rm. Home: 7908 Lakehurst Dr Oklahoma City OK 73120 Office: 3000 United Founders Blvd Suite 100-G Oklahoma City OK 73112

RIDLEY, LANI SUE, sales executive; b. Altadena, Calif., Mar. 21, 1948; d. Mahuel Joseph and Vera Jean (Van Steenwyk) Pedrini; B.A., UCLA, 1971; M.Bus., U. So. Calif., 1973; 1 son, Jason Michael. Free lance graphic designer/comml. artist, 1966-77; prodn. mgr., comml. artist Lloyd's Fashion Advt., Los Angeles, 1972-73; advt. prodn. mgr. McMahan's Furniture Co., Santa Monica, Calif., 1973-75; media dir./prodn. mgr. Walgers & Assos. Advt., Inc., Hollywood, Calif., 1975-77; account exec./media dir./prodn. mgr. Darryl Lloyd Advt., Inc., Encino, Calif., 1977-78; mktg. rep. Memorex Corp., W. Los Angeles, 1978-79; sales mgr. Prime Computer Inc., Culver City, Calif., 1980-83; western regional sales mgr. Symbolics, Inc., Westwood, Calif., 1983—; pres. LRS, Inc.; condr. seminars in field. Recipient Quota Club-Prime Computer Million Club Award, 1980, 81. Rookie of the Yr. award, Prime Computer Inc., 1980, Top Producer in Western Region award, 1981, Book to Ship award, also 1st system award Symbolics, Inc., 1984, others. Mem. Nat. Assn. Female Execs., Am. Soc. Profl. and Exec. Women, Working Women Soc., Research Inst. Am., Assn. Women in Computing, Assn. Computing Machinery, Am. Def. Preparedness Assn., Data Processing Mgmt. Assn., Career Guild, Alpha Phi. Clubs: Data Processing, Personal Profit. Office: 1401 Westwood Blvd 2d Floor Los Angeles CA 90024

RIEDL, LINDA ELIZABETH, insurance agency executive; b. Marlboro, Mass., Apr. 16, 1947; d. Harold Andrew and Ethel Virginia (Libby) Kelly; m. Robert J. Riedl, June 20, 1971; children—Robert James, Joanna Lee. A.A., Green Mountain Coll., 1967. Investment broker Moseley, Hallgarten & Estabrook, Boston, N.Y.C., 1969-76; ins. broker Robert J. Riedl Ins. Agy., Dennisport, Mass., 1976-80, treas., 1980—. Mem. exec. bd. Cape Cod and Islands Council Boy Scouts Am., Hyannis, Mass., 1982-83; v.p. Am. Field Service, Harwich, Mass., 1977-78. Mem. Mass. Assn. Ins. Women, Ind. Ins. Agents Mass., Profl. Ins. Agents. Republican. Roman Catholic. Club: Harwich Jr. Womans (pres. 1978-79). Office: Robert J Riedl Ins Agy Inc PO Box 128 24 Route 134 Dennisport MA 02639

RIEGEL, MARILYN RUTH, management consultant; b. Chgo., Oct. 13, 1944; d. Sam and Reva Levine; B.A., Northeastern Ill. U., 1969; Ed.M., U. Ill., 1977; postgrad Northwestern U., 1977-79, Loyola U., 1983-84. Tchr., Chgo. Bd. Edn., 1970-77; dir. staffing and employee relations Urban Investment & Devel. Co., 1977-84; exec. v.p. James H. Lowry & Assocs., 1984-86; v.p. Pearl M. Tabbert Assocs., 1986—. Past pres. Affirmative Action Assn. Mem. Am. Soc. Tng. and Devel., Internat. Assn. Personnel Women, OD Network. Home: 6145 N Sheridan Rd Apt 17C Chicago IL 60660 Office: 3 First National Plaza Suite 1616 Chicago IL 60602

RIEGER, ELLEN LUNDE, commodity exchange executive; b. N.Y.C., June 30, 1952; d. Steen and Barbara A. (Baylis) Lunde; m. Peter C. Brathauer, Aug. 17, 1974 (div. Sept. 1977); m. Thomas Muller Rieger, June 22, 1983. B.A. cum laude, St. John's U., N.Y.C., 1974. Asst. to ptnr. East View Co., N.Y.C., 1980-84; v.p. Windsor-Birch, Ltd., N.Y.C., 1983-86; exec. asst. to pres. Commodity Exchange, Inc., N.Y.C., 1986—. Mem. DAR (regent Peter Minuit chpt. 1984-86, chmn. Greater N.Y. Regent's Round Table 1986-87). Home: 1192 Park Ave New York NY 10128 Office: Commodity Exchange Inc 4 World Trade Ctr New York NY 10048

RIEGER, ROSALYS MCCREREY, county official, piano teacher; b. Falls City, Nebr., Apr. 12, 1920; d. Alexander and Maude Lillian (Bateman) McCrerey; m. Leslie Ivan Rieger, Apr. 12, 1940; 1 child, Christopher Philip. B. of Music in Piano, U. Kans., 1946; M.A. in Polit. Sci., Kans. State U., 1977; postgrad Washburn Law Sch., Topeka, Kans., 1977-78. Head records dept. Remington Arms, Kansas City, Mo., 1941-43; social worker Brown County Social Welfare Dept., Hiawatha, Kans., 1944-46; sec. engring. dept. Harvard U., Cambridge, 1944; music tchr. Powhattan Grade and High Sch., Kans., 1946-48, Res. Grade and High Sch., Kans., 1958-59; pvt. piano tchr., Manhattan, Kans., 1960—; county commr. Riley County, Manhattan, 1979—. Co-author: Music Handbook, 1978. Mem. Riley County-Manhattan Health Bd., 1978—, Downtown Redevel. Adv. Bd., Manhattan, 1980—; Democratic precinct committeewoman, Riley County, Manhattan, 1974-78; pres. Kans. Council on Crime and Delinquency, 1984—; mem. Manhattan Arts Council, 1974—, Kans. for ERA, 1973—, Riley County Mental Health Assn., 1972—. Mem. Kans. Music Tchrs. Assn., Manhattan Area Music Tchrs. League (co-founder, charter pres. 1972), World Federalist Assn., LWV, Mu Phi Epsilon, Pi Kappa Lambda. Presbyterian. Avocations: ceramics, knitting, reading, attending concerts, playing piano. Home: 1908 Blue Hills Rd Manhattan KS 66502 Office: Riley County 110 Courthouse Plaza Manhattan KS 66502

RIEKER, ANNE ELLORA, judge, humanitarian; b. Elmira, N.Y., Sept. 27, 1923; d. Eric Wendell and Viola Della (Hinckly) Phillips; m. Thomas Henry Rieker, Nov. 6, 1943; children—Constance Anne, Carla Anne, Thomas Eric. A.S., Hershey Jr. Coll., 1943; postgrad. Washburn U., 1958-59, Nat. Jud. Coll. U. Nev., 1982, 85. Dir. recreation therapy Extended Care Facility, Andover, N.J., 1967-70; exec. dir. Office on Aging, Sussex County, N.J., 1970-74; surrogate judge County of Sussex, Newton, N.J., 1975—. Trustee Knoll Heights Sr. Citizens Housing, Sparta, N.J., 1975—; chmn. March of Dimes, Morristown, N.J., 1978-79; bd. dirs. Sussex County Family Services, Frankford Twp., N.J., 1983—. Named Outstanding Citizen of Yr., VFW, 1975; Vol. award March of Dimes, 1981, 82, 83, 84, 85. Mem. N.J. Assn. County Officers (pres. 1979-81), Nat. Coll. Probate Judges, Nat. Judges Assn., Internat. Assn. Clks. Recorders Election Ofcls. and Treas., N.J. Assn. Counties (4th v.p. 1985), N.J. Bar Assn. (assoc.), N.J. Assn. Elected Women Ofcls. (bd. dirs. 1981-83). Democrat. Episcopalian. Clubs: Soroptimist Internat. (v.p. 1985), Newton Country. Avocations: music; golf; handcrafts; travel. Office: Hall Records 4 Park Pl Newton NJ 07860

RIELY, PHYLLIS ELEANOR, microbiologist, consultant; b. Welshfield, Ohio, Jan. 25, 1918; d. Clifford James and Ethel (Corliss) Brunton; student Capital U., 1936-39; grad. Sch. Med. Tech. Huron Rd. Hosp., 1941; m. Charles T. Riely, Nov. 28, 1942 (div.); children—Terrence, Patricia, Maura, Shawn. Systems microbiologist Fairchild Hiller Co., Farmingdale, N.Y., 1960-66; life support coordinator Pall Corp., Glen Cove, N.Y., 1966-69; mgr. med. product devel. Internat. Paper Co., Tuxedo, N.Y., 1969-71; dir. med. products

East-West Med. Products Co., Hauppage, N.Y., 1971-73; mgr. biomed. regulatory affairs Pall Corp., Glen Cove, 1973-74; mgr. microbiol. devel. Marion Labs., Kansas City, Mo., 1974-81; mgr. tech. edn. Marion Sci. div. Marion Labs., Kansas City, Mo., 1981-82. Mem. Am. Soc. Microbiology, Royal Soc. Health. Republican. Methodist. Patentee in field; author book; contbr. articles to profl. jours. Home: 12818 Maplewood St Sun City West AZ 85375

RIEPE, CHARLEINE WILLIAMS, educator; b. Lackawanna, N.Y., Oct. 28, 1924; d. Edward and Dorothy Hayd (Van Allen) Williams; m. Dale Maurice Riepe, May 24, 1948; children—Katharine Leigh Herschlag, Dorothy Lorraine. B.A. cum laude, D'Youville Coll., 1945; M.A., U. Mich., 1948; A.B.D., SUNY-Buffalo, 1969. Tchr. Holy Angels Acad. Buffalo, N.Y., 1945-47; instr. classics Carleton Coll., Northfield, Minn., 1950-52, U. S.D., Vermillion, 1952-54, SUNY-Buffalo, 1963-69; instr. English Tsuda Coll., Tokyo., 1958; instr. classics, research librarian in sci. U. N.D., 1959-60; tchr. Latin and English, Tappan Middle Sch., Ann Arbor, Mich., 1960-61; tchr. English and classics Oyster Bay High Sch., 1962-63; tchr., chmn. fgn. langs. Amherst Central High Sch., Buffalo, 1971-85; cons. N.Y. state regents exams., 1978-80. Editor reading selections for Latin level III, 1973; mng. editor, sec., treas. Arethusa, 1968-71. Recipient Teaching Excellence award Amherst PTA, 1978; regents scholar, 1942-46. Mem. Classical Assn. Empire State (exec. council), Classical Assn. New Eng. States, Nat. Jr. Classical League, N.Y. Assn. Fgn. Lang. Tchrs., N.Y. State Classical League, Pompiiana, Univ. Women of SUNY, Classical Assn. Western N.Y. (v.p. 1972-74, 84—, exec. council 1974-76), West N.Y. Fgn. Lang. Educators (life), LWV, Delta Kappa Gamma. Avocations: travel and living abroad; still photography; swimming; flower arrangement; cooking. Home: 48 Capen Blvd Buffalo NY 14214 Office: Amherst Central High Sch Main St Amherst NY 14226

RIFAS, GAYLEN GOLDSTEIN, lawyer; b. Cin., Dec. 28, 1943; d. Leonard Jack and Gratian Dorothy (Block) Goldstein; B.A. (Dean's Merit scholar) U. Miami (Fla.), 1966, J.D., 1969; m. Earle V. Rifas, Sept. 28, 1968 (div.); children—Kobi, Eagan, Evan. Admitted to Fla. bar, 1969; individual practice law, Miami, 1969—; Mem. bd. local PTA, 1975—. Mem. ACLU, Audubon Soc., Izaak Walton League. Democrat. Jewish. Home: 13975 SW 73d Ct Miami FL 33158 Office: 13975 SW 73d Ct Miami FL 33158

RIFFLE, LYNDA FREHNER, accountant; b. Cedar City, Utah, Oct. 9, 1947; d. Orlin Frehner and Lucille (Demille) Johannesen; m. Austin Neal Riffle, Mar. 29, 1968; children—Steven Neil, David Scott, Leah Ann. Student Boise State U., 1974-75; B.S., So. Utah State U., 1982; postgrad. Carroll Coll., 1982-83, U. Utah, 1983. C.P.A., Mont., Utah. Staff acct. Anderson-Zirmuehlen Co., Helena, Mont., 1980-82, tax sr., 1982-84; tax supr. Schmitt, Griffiths, Anderson, Smith & Co., Ogden, Utah, 1984—. Bd. dirs. YWCA, 1984—. Mem. Am. Soc. Women Accts. (v.p.-pres. elect 1983-84; outstanding service award), AAUW, Women in Mgmt., Am. Soc. C.P.A.s, Mont. Soc. C.P.A.s. Utah Assn. C.P.A.s, Ogden C. of C. Avocations: swimming; gardening; oil painting; NBA basketball. Office: Schmitt Griffiths Anderson Smith & Co 4155 Harrison Blvd Suite 300 Ogden UT 84403

RIFKIND, ARLEEN B., physician, medical researcher; b. N.Y.C., June 29, 1938; d. Michael C. and Regina (Gottlieb) Brenner; m. Robert S. Rifkind, Dec. 24, 1961; children—Amy, Nina. B.A., Bryn Mawr Coll., 1960; M.D., NYU, 1964. Diplomate Nat. Bd. Med. Examiners. Intern Bellevue Hosp., N.Y.C., 1964-65, resident, 1965; clin. assoc. Nat. Inst. Child Health and Human Devel. Endocrine br. Nat. Cancer Inst., 1965-68; research assoc., asst. resident physician Rockefeller U. Hosp., 1968-71; asst. prof. medicine Cornell U. Med. Coll., N.Y.C., 1971-82, assoc. prof. medicine, 1983—, asst. prof. pediatrics, 1971-75, asst. prof. pharmacology, 1973-78, assoc. prof., 1978-82, prof., 1983—; chmn. Gen. Faculty Council Cornell U. Med. Coll., 1984-86, Nat. Inst. Environ. Health Scis. Rev. Com., 1985-86. Contbr. articles to profl. jours. Chmn. Friends of the Library, Jewish Theol. Sem. Am., 1985—; trustee Dalton Sch., 1986—. Recipient Andrew W. Mellon Tchr.-Scientist award, 1976-78; USPHS spl. fellow, 1968-70, 71-72. Mem. Endocrine Soc., Am. Soc. Clin. Investigation, Am. Soc. Pharmacology and Exptl. Therapeutics, AAAS, Soc. Toxicology. Office: Cornell U Med Coll Dept Pharmacology 1300 York Ave New York NY 10021

RIGAS, HARRIETT BADAKER, electrical and computer engineering educator; b. Winnipeg, Man., Can., Apr. 30, 1934; came to U.S., 1956; d. Max and Helen (Pasternak) Badaker; m. Anthony L. Rigas, Feb. 14, 1959; 1 son, Marc. B.Sc. in Elec. Engring., Queen's U., Can., 1956; M.S. in Elec. Engring., U. Kans., 1959, Ph.D. in Elec. Engring., 1963. Elec. engr. biophysics Mayo Clinic, Rochester, Minn., 1956-57; sr. research engr. aerodynamics Lockheed Missiles, Sunnyvale, Calif., 1963-66; program dir. systems theory NSF, Washington, 1975-76; from asst. prof. to prof. Wash. State U., Pullman, 1966-84, dept. chair elec.-computer engring., 1979-84; dept. chair elec.-computer engring. Naval Postgrad. Sch., Monterey, Calif., 1984—; mem. com. Nat. Acad. Sci., 1979—. Co-editor Jour. Computers and Elec. Engring., 1982—; contbr. articles to profl. jours. Recipient Disting. Engring. Service award U. Kans., 1983. Fellow IEEE (governing bd. 1984-86; Engr. of Yr. 1980, 83) Soc. Women Engrs. (Achievement award 1982), Sigma Xi (chpt. pres. 1981-82), Tau Beta Pi (Disting. Engr. award). Office: Naval Postgrad Sch Supt Code 62 Monterey CA 93943*

RIGAUD, MARIE-CLAUDE, psychiatrist; b. Port-Au-Prince, Haiti, Jan. 24, 1939; came to U.S. 1964; d. Antoine Dolbrise and Charlotte (Aarons) Saint-Jean; m. Andre Rigaud, Sept. 30, 1961; children—Carl, Ralph, J-Philippe, Cassandre, Joseph, Claudine. Bachelor, Pensionnat Sterose de Lima, Haiti, 1956; M.D., U. Haiti, 1962. Diplomate Am. Bd. Psychiatry and Neurology. Resident in pub. health, Plaisance, Haiti, 1962-63, Pont-Sonde, Haiti, 1963-64; resident in psychiatry Seton Psychiat. Inst., Balt., 1966-69, sr. staff supr., 1970-73; house physician in medicine and obstetrics Provident Hosp., Balt., 1965-66; staff psychiatrist Spring Grove State Hosp., Balt., 1969-70; med. dir. Psychiat. Day Hosp., Seton Inst., 1971-73; practice medicine, specializing in psychiatry, 1973—; psychiat. cons. to med. dept. and EAP program, Western Electric Co., Aurora, Ill., 1979-84; clin. dir. Suburban Psychiat. Assocs, Naperville, occupational cons., Lombard, Ill.; sr. psychiat. cons. Kane-Kendall Mental Health Ctr., Aurora, Ill., Cardiac Rehab. Program, Copley Meml. Hosp., Aurora; cons. staff, adviser cancer support program Copley Meml. Hosp.; med. staff Mercy Ctr. for Health Care Services, Aurora; lectr. in field. Bd. dirs. Fox Valley Pastoral Counseling Ctr. of Aurora; trustee Rosary High Sch., others. Mem. Balt. County Med. Assn., Med. and Chirurg. Faculty State of Md., Ill. Psychiat. Soc., Am. Psychiat. Soc., Md. Soc. Liaison Psychiatrists, Kane County Med. Soc., AMA, Assn. Haitian Physicians Abroad (pres.), Women in Mgmt., Internat. Med. Council of Ill., others. Roman Catholic. Address: 103 S Highland Ave Aurora IL 60506 Office: PO Box 2816 Aurora IL 60507

RIGER, ELEANOR SANGER, TV producer, writer; b. Hong Kong, Sept. 15, 1929; d. Richard and Lonni (Wernicke) Sanger; B.A. magna cum laude, Smith Coll., 1950; postgrad. Russian Inst., Columbia U., 1951-52; m. Robert Riger, June 10, 1950 (div. July 1981); children—Christopher, Victoria Riger Phillips, Robert, Charlotte Riger Hull; m. Peter L. Keys, Feb. 11, 1985. Mgr. public affairs Sta. WNBC-TV, N.Y.C., 1957-60; writer ABC news, 1967; mgr. client relations, asso. producer ABC Sports, 1966-69; free lance TV documentary producer, writer, 1969-70; producer, writer Tomorrow Entertainment, N.Y.C., 1971-73; staff producer, writer, dir. ABC Sports, N.Y.C., 1973—. Bd. dirs. Women's Sports Found., Wonder Woman Found. Recipient Emmy award for sports, 1976, for summer olympics, 1977, for Wide World of Sports, 1980, for winter olympics NCAA Football, 1981; Smith Coll. medal, 1982; named ABC-YWCA Woman Achiever of Yr., 1983. Mem. Acad. TV Arts and Scis., Writers Guild Am., Am. Women in Radio and TV, Women in Communications, Dirs. Guild Am., Phi Beta Kappa. Democrat. Episcopalian. Office: ABC 1330 Avenue of Americas New York NY 10019

RIGER, FRANCINE WOLF, personnel administrator; b. Yonkers, N.Y., May 12, 1945; d. Samuel and Dorothy (Fondillier) Wolf; m. Peter S. Riger, May 31, 1965; children—James B., Gerald David. B.S. summa cum laude, Mercy Coll., 1980; A.B.S., Vernon Coll., Jr. Coll., 1965. Mgr. Daisy Ltd., Yonkers, 1973-77; benefits officer Lehman Coll., CUNY, Bronx, 1981-85; mgr. staff benefits N.Y. Pub. Library, N.Y.C., 1985—. Active Boy Scouts Am. Mem. Internat. Found. Employee Benefits, Am. Personnel Assn., Sigma Iota Pi, Alpha Chi. Republican. Jewish. Avocations: music; dance; painting; sculpture. Home: 5414 Arlington Ave Riverdale NY 10471

RIGG-GORDON, P. MICHELE, computer company executive; b. San Juan, P.R., June 23, 1951; d. Alvin Lewis and Ruth (Epstein) Gross; m. James E. Gordon, Mar. 13, 1984. Diploma, Bishops-Arno, Bolsta, Sweden, 1970; B.A., Tufts U., 1972, M.P.A., 1973. Mgr. field personnel ITEK Corp., Rochester, N.Y., 1973-78; mgr. personnel Kaiser Electronics Co., San Jose, Calif., 1978-82; dir. Molecular Computer, San Jose, 1982-84; v.p. Altos Computer Systems, San Jose, 1984—; pres. R & H Assocs., Los Gatos, Calif., 1980—; cons., trainer in field, San Jose, 1978—; mem. adv. bd. dirs. Tech. Tng. Ctr., San Jose, 1983. Travelli scholar, 1970; Zonta Club scholar, 1970; U. Uppsala research fellow, 1971. Mem. No. Calif. Tech. Personnel Com. (chmn. 1981-83), Am. Soc. Personnel Adminstrn., Am. Electronics Assn. (dir. Palo Alto, Calif. 1983—). Club: Decathlon (Santa Clara, Calif.). Office: 251 River Oaks Pkwy San Jose CA 95134

RIGGINS, LOIS, museum administrator; b. Nashville, Nov. 18, 1939; d. Percy Leon and Lula Belle Prather (Traughber) Von Schmitton; 1 son, Nicholas. B.S., Belmont Coll., 1968; postgrad., U. Western Ky., 1969-72, George Washington U., 1978. Cert. tchr., Ky., Tenn. Tchr. Ky. Pub. Schs., Adairville, 1962-71; tour supr. Tenn. State Capitol, Nashville, 1972-74; curator of extension services Tenn. State Mus., Nashville, 1975-77, curator edn., 1977-81, dir., 1981—; chmn. Mus. Educator's Forum, 1979-81. Editor: newsletter Open Eye, 1978-81; author: adminstrn. tng. manual Handicapped Acessibility, 1979-80. Chmn. Nashville Flight of Tenn. Friendship Force, Caracas, Venezuela, 1977, Tenn. Am. Revolution Bicentennial Arts Competition, 1976. Mem. Southeastern Mus. Conf. (edn. com., rep. to Am. Assn. Mus. council, publs. advt. com. 1983), Inter Mus. Council of Nashville (chmn. edn. 1980-81), Am. Assn. Mus. Baptist. Home: 403 McAdoo St Nashville TN 37205 Office: Tenn State Mus 505 Deaderick St Nashville TN 37219

RIGGS, ANNA CLAIRE, metals service center executive; b. Danville, Ind., Jan. 22, 1944; d. Leland Wesley and Mary Alice (Miller) Cox; m. Michael Ross Riggs, Dec. 10, 1983; 1 child, Matthew. B.S. in Edn., Ind. U., 1966. Credit tng. and promotion mgr. L.S. Ayres, Indpls., 1966-74, cons., credit dept., 1984; credit ops. mgr. Burdine's, Miami, Fla., 1974-77; br. mgr. Centaur Metals, Indpls., 1977-85; resident mgr. Copper & Brass Sales, Indpls., 1985—. Children's choir dir. and Sun sch. tchr. United Meth. Ch., Danville, Ind. Mem. Nat. Assn. Female Execs., Beta Sigma Phi (pres., advisor). Avocations: travel; sewing; reading. Home: 107 Martin Dr Danville IN 46122 Office: Copper & Brass Sales 8002 Woodland Dr Indianapolis IN 46278

RIGGS, CONSTANCE KAKAVECOS, college administrator; b. Indpls., Apr. 6, 1928; d. James Eustace and Dorothy Amelia (Boren) Kakavecos; B.A., St. Mary-of-the-Woods Coll., Terre Haute, Ind., 1975; m. Kenneth Wesley Riggs, Dec. 4, 1947 (dec.); children—Ken Roger, Yvonne Denise Riggs Rench, James Cary, Vicki Catherine, Constance Amelia, Jeffrey Allan. Med. edn. coordinator St. Vincent Hosp., Indpls., 1967-72; asst. to pres. Wabash Coll., Crawfordsville, Ind., 1972-78; asst. v.p. for devel. St. Mary-of-the-Woods Coll., 1978-79; asst. to pres. Rollins Coll., Winter Park, Fla., 1979—; lectr. in field. Bd. dirs. Montgomery County (Ind.) United Fund, 1973-75, Terre Haute YWCA, 1978; trustee Ind. Council for Advancement and Support of Edn., 1978. Hon. fellow Ind. Collegiate Press Assn. Mem. Fla. Freelance Writers Assn., Nat. Fedn. Press Women. Greek Orthodox. Club: Altrusa (pres. 1983-84). Author: Sam Shue and the Seven Satchels, 1976. Editor: Montgomery County Remembers, 1976; editorial bd. Vigo County Hist. Soc., 1978; columnist Orlando Sentinel, 1981—, Winter Park Outlook, 1984—, Senior Voice, 1985—. Home: 200 St Andrews Blvd Apt 3503 Winter Park FL 32792 Office: Rollins Coll Winter Park FL 32789

RIGGS, JEANETTE TEMPLETON, civic worker; b. Little Rock, Mar. 13, 1933; d. Donald M. and Fay (Templeton) Brewer; student Little Rock U., 1950-51, Tex. Coll. for Women, 1951-52; B.S., U. Ark., 1955; m. Byron Lawrence Riggs, June 1955; children—Byron Kent, Ann Templeton. Founder, Rochester (Minn.) Ballet Guild, 1970, pres., 1974; mem. establishing bd., exec. bd. Rochester Arts Council, 1972, producer, dir. T.S. Elliot's The Rock, 1970; founder, performer So. Minn. Ballet Co., 1974; sponsor Nat. Ballet Cos., Rochester, 1970-75; exec. bd. for restoration 1875 Pattern Book House, Rochester Heritage Assn., 1975-77; exec. bd. Savino Ballet Nat., 1975-78; founder, exec. bd. Citizens Action Com., 1977-79; asso., commentator Women, Cable TV Program for Women, Rochester, 1979; mem. Mayor's Com. on Drug Abuse, 1979-80; mem. Olmsted County Steering Com. for George Bush, 1979-80, a founder, mem. exec. bd. Olmsted County Republican Women's Orgn., 1979—, mem. Olmsted County Rep. Central Com., 1979—, exec. bd. issues com., 1979-80. Home: 432 SW 10th Ave Rochester MN 55901

RIGNEY, JANE, journalist; b. Flushing, N.Y., Dec. 4, 1948; d. William J. and Janet C. (Teesink) R. B.A., U. Ill., 1971; student Juilliard Sch., 1979-81. Reporter, mag. editor Daily News-Gazette, Champaign, Ill., 1968-71; women's world editor Anchorage Daily Times, 1971-72; part-time reporter N.Y. Voice, Flushing, 1977-78; asst. dir. pub. relations Juilliard Sch., N.Y.C., 1977-81; copy editor Hudson Dispatch, Paterson, N.J., 1982-83; night copy chief N.Y. Tribune, 1983-84, dance critic, 1983-86; freelance dance critic, 1986—; editor Dance Horizons, Bklyn., 1978—; freelance copy editor Village Voice, N.Y. Daily News, Jersey Jour., Am. Banker, Fairchild Publs.; also freelance writer. Mem. Catholics for Free Choice, N.Y.C., 1977—, NOW, 1980—, Nat. Abortion Rights Action League, 1980—. Recipient Outstanding Vol. award Alaska March of Dimes, 1972; Ann. Press award Alaska Scholarship, Inc., 1972. Mem. Nat. Writers Union, Nat. Press Club, Editorial Freelancers Assn., Women in Communications, N.Y. Press Club, Dance Critics Assn., Soc. Profl. Journalists. Democrat. Roman Catholic.

RIKLEEN, LAUREN STILLER, lawyer; b. Winthrop, Mass., Apr. 29, 1953; d. Joseph Stiller and Elaine Lillian (Brodie) Stiller; m. Sander A. Rikleen, May 25, 1975. Student Clark U., 1971-73; B.A., magna cum laude, Brandeis U., 1975; J.D., Boston Coll., 1979. Bar: Mass. 1979, U.S. Dist. Ct. Mass. 1980, U.S. Ct. Appeals (1st cir.) 1980, U.S. Supreme Ct. 1984. Asst. dir. Flaschner Jud. Inst., Boston, 1979-81; atty. enforcement div. EPA, Boston, 1981-82, Office Regional Counsel, 1982-84; asst. v.p. for negotiations Clean Sites, Inc., Alexandria, Va., 1984—. Contbr. articles to legal publs. Mem. Wayland Planning Bd., Mass., 1980-83; mem. Met. Area Planning Council, Boston, 1980-84. Recipient Merit award EPA, 1982. Mem. ABA (natural resources com.). Democrat. Jewish. Office: Clean Sites Inc 1199 N Fairfax St Alexandria VA 22314

RILEY, BARBARA POLK, librarian; b. Roselle, N.J., Nov. 21, 1928; d. Charles Carrington and Olive Bond P.; A.B., Howard U., 1950; B.S., N.J. Coll. Women, 1951; M.S., Columbia U., 1955; m. George Emerson Riley, Feb. 23, 1957 (dec.); children—George E., Glenn C., Karen O. Asst. librarian, Fla. A&M U., 1951-53; with Morgan State Coll., 1955; with Dept. Def., 1955-57, S.C. State Coll., 1957-59, U.Wis., 1958-59; asst. librarian Atlanta U., 1960-68; asst. dir. Union County Anti Poverty Council, 1968; librarian Union County Tech. Inst., Scotch Plains, N.J., 1968-82, Scotch Plains campus, Union County Coll., 1982—. Mem. Roselle Bd. Edn., 1976-78; bd. dirs. Union County Anti Poverty Council, 1969-72, Black Women's History Conf. Steering Com., 1985—; mem. Roselle Human Relations Commn., 1971-73; bd. dirs. Plainfield Sci. Center, 1974-76, Union County Psychiat. Clinic, 1980-83, Pinewood Sr. Citizens Council, 1981-85. Mem. N.J. Library Assn., Council Library Tech., ALA (Black caucus), N.J. Black Librarians, Coalition of 100 Black Women (bd. dirs. N.J. chpt. 1986), Black Librarian Network N.J. (bd. dirs. 1985—), Alpha Kappa Alpha. Mem. A.M.E. Ch. Clubs: Just-A-Mere Lit.; Whatever. Home: 114 E 7th Ave Roselle NJ 07203 Office: 1033 Springfield Ave Cranford NJ 07016

RILEY, CATHERINE IRENE, state senator; b. Balt., Mar. 21, 1947; d. Francis Worth and Catherine (Cain) R. B.A., Towson State U., 1969. Bacteriologist Balt. City Hosp., 1969-72; legis. aide Md. Ho. of Dels., Annapolis, 1973-74, del., 1975-82; mem. Md. Senate, 1982—; cons. Md. State Div. Alcoholism Control, 1973; mem. House Environ. Matters Com., 1975-82; mem. Spl. Joint Com. Energy, 1977-83, chmn. 1978-79, 1980-83; mem. Adminstrv. Exec. and Legis. Review Com. 1978—, senate chmn., 1983—, mem. So. Legis. Conf. Energy Com. 1978, Environ. Com., 1983—, vice chmn., 1985—; mem. So. Environ. Resource Council, 1978, Power Plant Siting Adv. Com., 1977—, State of Md. Energy Conservation Bd., 1978-83, Fire Safety Subcom., 1981-83; mem. BiState Cheasapeake Bay Commn., 1981-83, chmn. 1982; chmn. Forest Land Task Force, 1981-84, Budget and Taxation Senate Com., 1983—, Subcom. Edn., Health, and Human Resources, 1983—, Nat. Conf. State Legis. Energy Commn., 1983—; senate chmn. adminstrv. exec. and legis. review com., 1983—, Ho. of Dels. mem. 1978-83. Contbr. articles to profl. jours. Mem. adv. com. State Edn. Policy Seminars Adv. Com., 1983—, Protective Services to Children and Families, 1983—; exec. bd. Balt. Area Council Boy Scouts Am., 1983—; hon. chmn. Am. Cancer Soc., 1982-83; mem. Harford County Child Protection Council, 1978-80, vice chmn. 1980; mem. Harford County Council Community Services, 1976—, Harford County legis. del., 1975—, chmn. 1976, 1980-82; mem. Md. Order Women Legislators, 1975—, sec. 1976-79; mem. adv. bd. Susquehanna State Park, 1975—; mem. Joppatowne Womens Club, 1975—, No. Md. Assn. for Retarded Citizens, Inc., 1975—, Upper Cheasepeake Watershed Assn., Inc., 1975—. Recipient Disting. Service award Md. State Troopers, 1980; Community Service award, United Way, 1978; Disting. Service award Jaycees, 1976; Liberty award Harford Christian High Sch., 1975; Cert. of Appreciation Md. Mcpl. League, 1984; William P. Coliton Outstanding Community Service award Johns Hopkins U., 1985; named Young Democrat of Yr. State of Md., 1975; Women of Yr. Soroptimist Club, 1980. Mem. AAUW, Towson State U. Alumni Assn. (admissions council 1975—, chmn. fund drive 1980), Md. Jaycee Women, Izaak Walton League. Roman Catholic. Avocations: golf; sailing; stamp collecting. Office: State Senate 20 Office Bel Air MD 21014

RILEY, CHARLOTTE KAY ANDRUS, utilities company administrator; b. Tulia, Tex., June 9, 1950; d. Charles Royce and Bobbie J. (Starnes) A.; m. Larry Edward Riley, July 4, 1970; 1 child, Andrea Cathleen. B.B.A. in Acctg., U. Tex.-Arlington, 1982. Assoc. acct. Tex. Electric Service Co., Ft. Worth, 1982-84, acct., 1984; programmer Tex. Utilities Services Inc., Dallas, 1984—. Mem. Acct. Alumni Assn. of U. Tex.-Arlington. (bd. dirs. 1983-85, pres. 1984-85, appreciation award 1984). Avocation: photography. Home: Route 13 Box 416 Fort Worth TX 76119 Office: Tex Utilities Services Inc 2001 Bryan Tower Dallas TX 75101

RILEY, DOROTHY COMSTOCK, state Supreme Court justice; b. Detroit, Dec. 6, 1924; d. Charles Austin and Josephine (Grima) Comstock; m. Wallace Don Riley, Sept. 13, 1963; 1 child, Peter Comstock. B.A. in Polit. Sci., Wayne State U., 1946, LL.B., 1949. Bar: Mich. 1950, U.S. Dist. Ct. (ea. dist.) Mich. 1950, U.S. Supreme Ct. 1957. Atty. Wayne County Friend of Ct., Detroit, 1956-68; ptnr. Riley and Roumell, Detroit, 1968-72; judge Wayne County Cir. Ct., Detroit, 1972, Mich. Ct. Appeals, Detroit, 1976-82; justice Mich. Supreme Ct., Detroit, 1982-83, 1985—; mem. U.S. Jud. Conf. Commn. on State-Fed. Ct. Relations. Contbr. articles to profl. jours., chpt. to books. Appointed to local adv. com. Citizenship Edn. Study, 1946-50. Fellow Am. Bar Found.; mem. ABA (family law sect., com. juvenile justice gen. practice sect. 1975-80, judicial adminstrn. sect., mem. standing com. fed. ct. improvements), Am. Judicature Soc., Mich. State Bar Assn. (state bar found., civil liberties com., 1954-58, family law sect. 1966—), Detroit Bar Assn. (pub. relations com. 1955-56, program com. 1954-58, friend of ct. and family law com. 1965-75, chmn. 1974-75, author Detroit Lawyers Com. in Action column, 1955), Nat. Women Judges Assn., Nat. Women Lawyers Assn., Women Lawyers Assn. Mich. (pres. 1957-58). Club: Women's Economic. Recipient Disting. Alumni award Wayne State U. Law Sch., 1977, Headliner award Women of Wayne, 1977. Republican. Roman Catholic. Avocations: reading; gardening. Office: Mich Supreme Ct 1425 Lafayette Bldg Detroit MI 48226

RILEY, GAILYA NAN, educator; b. Slidell, Tex., Aug. 30, 1934; d. Homer Bedford and Lucetta Constance Winstead; B.S., N. Tex. State U., Denton, 1955, M.Ed., 1979; m. John Howard Riley, June 4, 1955; children—John Steven, Brenda Gail, Richard Scott, Mark Allan. Tchr. schs. in Tex., 1955—; tchr. social studies, English and reading Hurst-Euless-Bedford Ind. Sch. Dist., 1968-80, secondary curriculum cons., 1980—; reviewer reader fed. grants proposals. Chmn. heritage com. Euless Bicentennial Commn., 1978-80; historian First Baptist Ch., Euless, 1975-78. Recipient Educator medal Freedom Found., 1980; named Hurst-Euless-Bedford Tchr. of Yr., 1977; Tex. Tchr. of Yr., 1978. Mem. Nat. Council Social Studies, Tex. Council Social Studies (pres.), Assn. Suprs. and Adminstrs., Tex. Assn. Supervision and Curriculum Devel. (pres. chpt.), Nat. Assn. Gifted, Studies, Tex. Hist. Assn. (adv. bd.), So. Hist. Soc., Tex. Assn. Gifted and Talented, Northeast Hist. Soc., Phi Delta Kappa. Club: Soroptimist Internat. (pres.). Author articles in field, sch. musicals. Home: 707 Royce Dr Euless TX 76039 Office: 1849 Central Dr Bedford TX 76021

RILEY, GLENDA, history educator; b. Cleve., Sept. 9, 1938; d. George F. and Lillian B. (Knafels) Gates; 1 child, Sean Gates. B.A., Western Res. U., 1960; M.A., Miami U., Oxford, Oxio, 1963; Ph.D., Ohio State U., 1967. Instr. Denison U., Granville, Ohio, 1967-68; vis. asst. prof. Ohio State U., Columbus, 1968-69; successively asst. prof. history, assoc. prof., prof., dir. women's studies program U. No. Iowa, Cedar Falls, 1969—. Author: Frontierswomen: The Iowa Experience, 1981; Women and Indians on the Frontier, 1984; Inventing the American Woman, 1985. Contbr. articles on women's history to profl. jours. NEH pilot grantee, 1980-81, NEH summer fellow, 1984; recipient Palladin Writing award Mont. Hist. Soc., 1984. Mem. Orgn. Am. Historians, Nat. Council Pub. History, Nat. Women's Studies Assn., Am. Assn. State and Local History, Western History Assn. (nominating bd. 1984-86). Avocations: horseback riding; traveling. Home: 718 Orchard Dr Cedar Falls IA 50613 Office: Dept History U No Iowa Cedar Falls IA 51614

RILEY, JOCELYN CAROL, writer; b. Mpls., Mar. 6, 1949; d. G.D. Riley and D.J. (Berg) Riley Jacobson; m. Jeffrey Allen Steele, Sept. 4, 1971; children—Doran Riley, Brendan Riley. B.A. in English, Carleton Coll., 1971. Mng. editor Carleton Miscellany, Northfield, Minn., 1971; mktg. asst. Beacon Press, Boston, 1971-73; scriptwriter Am. Family Insurance Co., Madison, Wis., 1983-85; freelance writer, editor, speaker, 1973—. Author: Only My Mouth Is Smiling (ALA Best Books of 82 award, A. Tofte award 1982), 1982; Crazy Quilt, 1984; Page Proof, 1987; also articles in Christian Sci. Monitor, Pubs. Weekly, Writer, other publs. Mem. Women in Communications (pres. Madison chpt. 1984-85, nat. del. 1983, Writers Cup 1985), Council for Wis. Writers, Authors Guild, Madison Assn. for Multi-Image (pres. 1986-87). Address: PO Box 5264 Hilldale Madison WI 53705

RILEY, LINDA MARIE, government program analyst; b. Alameda, Calif., Dec. 26, 1940; d. William Barton and Marie Elizabeth (Hales) Johnson; m. Donald Boyd Hunt, July 12, 1958 (div. July 1977); children—Terisa Lynn Hunt Rademacher, Jon Larr Hunt; m. David LeRoy Riley, Jan. 13, 1978; stepchildren—Roxanne Riley Saylor, Michael Donovan, Russell Lloyd, Daryl David. With U.S. Army, Yuma Proving Ground, Ariz., 1959—, statis. asst., 1981-82, mgmt. analyst, 1982-85, program analyst, 1985—; speaker, mgr. Fed. Women's Program, Yuma, 1982-84. Author/trainer tng. man., 1985. Leader, trainer, cons. Ariz. Cactus-Pine council Girl Scouts U.S. Recipient Thanks badge Ariz. Cactus-Pine council Girl Scouts U.S., 1976, TECOM Professionalism award Yuma Proving Ground Test and Evaluation Command, 1983. Mem. Federally Employed Women (pres. Eleanor McCoy chpt. 1986-87, co-chmn. tng. seminar 1983, Am. Soc. Mil. Comptrollers (chpt. organizer 1985), Nat. Assn. Female Execs. Mem. Christian Ch. Lodge: Toastmasters. Avocations: camping; public speaking. Home: 661 S 6th Ave Yuma AZ 85364 Office: US Army Yuma Proving Ground Attention: STEYP-RM-B Yuma AZ 85365

RILEY, MATILDA WHITE, sociologist; b. Boston, Apr. 19, 1911; d. Percival and Mary (Cliff) White; m. John Winchell Riley, Jr., June 19, 1931; children—John W., III, Lucy Ellen Riley Sallick. A.B., Radcliffe Coll., 1931, M.A., 1937; D.Sc., Bowdoin Coll., 1972; L.H.D. (hon.), Rutgers U., 1983. Research asst. Harvard U., Cambridge, Mass., 1932; v.p. Mktg. Research Co. Am., N.Y.C., 1938-49; chief cons. economist War Prodn. Bd., 1941-43; research specialist Rutgers U., N.Y.C., 1950, prof., 1951-73, prof. emeritus, 1973—, dir. sociology lab., 1959-73; prof., chmn. dept. sociology and anthropology Bowdoin Coll., Brunswick, Maine, 1973—, D.B. Fayerweather prof. polit. economy and sociology, 1974-81, prof. emeritus, 1981—; assoc. dir. Nat. Inst. on Aging, Bethesda, Md., 1978—; sr. mem. Inst. Medicine, Nat. Acad. Scis., 1978—; faculty Harvard U., summer 1955; asso. and dir. on aging and society Russell Sage Found., N.Y.C., 1964-73, staff sociologist, 1974-77; vis. prof. NYU, 1956-61; cons. Nat. Council on Aging, Acad. Ednl. Devel.; mem. study group NIH, 1971-78, chmn. working group on health and behavior; mem. study group Social Sci. Research Council Com. on Life-course Perspectives, 1973—; mem. adv. bd. Carnegie Corp. Aging Soc. Project, 1983—; trustee Big Sisters Assn. Author: (with P. White) New Product Research, Gliding and Soaring, 1931; (with Riley and Toby) Sociological Studies in Scale Analysis, 1954; Sociological Research, vol. I, II, 1964; (with others) Aging and Society, vol. I, 1968, vol. II, 1969, vol. III, 1972; (with Nelson) Sociological Observation, 1974; Aging from Birth to Death: Interdisciplinary Perspectives, 1978; (with R. Merton) Sociological Traditions from Generation to Generation, 1980; Aging from Birth to Death: Sociotemporal

Perspectives, 1982; (with Hess and Bond) Aging in Society, 1983. Contbr. articles to profl. jours. Fellow Center Advanced Study in Behavioral Scis., 1978-79; recipient Lindback research award Rutgers U., 1970; Social Sci. award Andrus Gerontology Center, U. So. Calif., 1972. Mem. Am. Sociol. Assn. (exec. officer 1949-60, pres. 1985-86, 1st Ann. award for Sociol. Practice 1983, commonwealth award, 1984), AAAS (chmn. sect. social and econ. scis. 1975-77), Am. Assn. Public Opinion Research (sec.-treas. 1949-51, disting. research award, 1983), Eastern Sociol. Soc. (v.p. 1968-69, pres. 1977-78), Sociol. Research Assn., D.C. Sociol. Soc. (co-pres. 1983-84), Phi Beta Kappa, Phi Beta Kappa assns. Office: Assoc Dir NIH Inst on Aging 9000 Rockville Pike Bethesda MD 20205

RILEY-DAVIS, SHIRLEY MERLE, advertising agency executive, writer; b. Pitts., Feb. 4, 1935; d. William Riley and Beatrice Estelle (Whittaker) Byrd; m. Louis Davis; 1 child, Terri Judith. Student U. Pitts., 1952. Copywriter, Pitts. Mercantile Co., 1954-60; exec. sec. U. Mich., Ann Arbor, 1962-67; copy supr. N.W. Ayer, N.Y.C., 1968-76, assoc. creative dir., Chgo., 1977-81; copy supr. Leo Burnett, Chgo., 1981—; Writer of print, radio, and TV commercials. Former bd. dirs. Epilepsy Services Chgo. Recipient Grand and First prize N.Y. Film Festival, 1974, Gold and Silver medal Atlanta Film Festival, 1973, Gold medal V.I. Film Festival, 1974, 50 Best Creatives award Am. Inst. Graphic Arts, 1972, Clio award, 1973, 74, 75, Andy Award of Merit, 1981, Silver medal Internat. Film Festival, 1982; Senatorial scholar. Mem. Women in Film, Facets Multimedia Film Theatre Orgn. (bd. dirs.), Nat. Assn. Female Execs., Greater Chgo. Council for Prevention of Child Abuse (bd. dirs.). Democrat. Roman Catholic. Avocations: dance; poetry; design. Office: Leo Burnett USA Prudential Plaza Chicago IL 60601

RIMES, SUZIE WILMA BELLE, educator, consultant; b. Houston, Dec. 20, 1941; d. Cecil Anton and Mae Belle (Chambers) Means; m. Robert Jack Rimes, June 16, 1962; children—Cynthia J., Robert J. B.S., Sam Houston State Tchrs. Coll., 1964; M.Ed., Sam Houston State U., 1968. Tchr., Houston Ind. Sch. Dist., 1964-66, reading specialist, 1966-68, tchr. 5th grade, 1968-69, curriculum coordinator, 1970-73, prin. Clear View Acad., Houston, 1974-76; cons. Wesley Elem. Sch., 1977—, yr.-round sch. coordinator, 1984-85. Named Outstanding Tchr., Readers Digest Children's Book Club, 1965, Outstanding Instr., Sci. Research Assocs., Chgo., 1980. Mem. Houston Assn. for Children with Learning Disabilities, Delta Kappa Gamma (pres. 1986—). Democrat. Lutheran. Club: Lutheran Women. Home: 2403 Brookmere St Houston TX 77008

RINALDI, RENEE ZAIRA, physician; b. N.Y.C., Dec. 10, 1949; d. John James and Concetta (Vecchio) Rinaldi; m. Kenneth Robert Ballard, June 16, 1977; children—Claudia Michele, Celeste Noelle. B.A., Barnard Coll., Columbia U., 1971; Ed.M., Harvard, 1973; M.D., N.Y. Med. Coll., 1976. Diplomate Am. Bd. Internal Medicine and Rheumatology. Intern, Met. Hosp., N.Y.C., 1976-77; resident medicine San Fernando program UCLA, Sepulveda Campus, 1977-79, adj. asst. prof. medicine, 1982-83; staff internist Olive View Hosp., Van Nuys, Calif., 1979-80, fellow rheumatology UCLA, 1980-82; practice medicine specializing in rheumatology, Los Angeles, 1983—; asst. clin. prof. medicine UCLA, 1983—. Jane Wyman Clin. fellow, 1981. Mem. So. Calif. Rheumatology Soc., Los Angeles County Women's Med. Assn., Am. Rheumatology Assn. Office: 8631 W 3d St Suite 420 E Los Angeles CA 91403

RINALDI, SANDRA BRUCE, travel consultant; b. Inglewood, Calif., Apr. 27, 1948; d. Robert Glen and Florence Taylor (Fuller) Bruce; student Foothill Coll., 1966-68, Golden Gate U., 1976; m. William Rinaldi, Aug. 17, 1968. Teller, Crocker Nat. Bank, San Rafael, Calif., 1969-71, loan clk., 1971-72, sr. loan clk., 1972-73, installment loan specialist, 1973-75, sr. installment credit specialist, 1975-77, asst. br. mgr., corp. officer, 1977-79, retail banking officer, 1979-83; travel consultant Cruise & Leisure Travel, San Rafael, 1983-85, mgr., 1985—. Mem. Nat. Assn. Female Execs., Individual Travel Agts. Republican. Episcopalian.

RINALDO, HELEN, interior designer; b. Manville, N.J., July 5, 1922; d. Zigmond and Kate (Szymanski) Ossowski; student summer and evening classes N.Y. Sch. Interior Design, 1964; student N.Y. U., 1964, Somerset County (N.J.) Coll., 1973-76, m. Nicholas Rinaldo, Feb. 7, 1948; children—Linda Ann, Lorraine Ann. Interior designer W. & J. Sloane, Red Bank and Short Hills, N.J., 1981, Lord & Taylor, Paramus, N.J., 1974; owner Rinaldo Interiors, Scotch Plains, N.J., 1959-65; designer local firms; speaker career day local sch. Mem. Hist. Commn. Twp. of Branchburg (N.J.), until 1982. Mem. Allied Bd. Trade (N.Y.C.), Internat. Platform Assn. Home and Office: 69 Partridge Lane Cherry Hill NJ 08003

RINALDO, ROBERTA, educational administrator; b. Syracuse, N.Y., Dec. 6, 1936; d. Robert L. Sardino and Florence May (Owen) Krupa; m. Carmen Leonard Rinaldo, Sept. 15, 1956; children—Elizabeth Ann, Diane. B.A., Mary Washington Coll., 1961; M.A., U. Iowa, 1965; Cert. Advanced Study, SUNY-New Paltz, 1975; doctoral student Fordham U., 1984—. Cert. tchr., N.Y. Supr. spl. projects, tchr. Wiltwyck Residential Treatment Ctr., Yorktown, N.Y., 1969-81; dir. reading and gifted edn. Wappingers Central Sch. Dist., Wappingers Falls, N.Y., 1981-84, jr. high sch. prin., 1984—; cons. No. Westchester BOCES, Yorktown Heights, N.Y., 1975-81. NDEA grantee 1974; Mary Washington Coll. grantee, 1960-61; NDEA fellow 1964-65, grantee, 1968; Mary Washington Coll. scholar 1961. Mem. Wappingers Adminstrs. Assn. (v.p. 1984—), Assn. Westchester Adminstrv. Women, Internat. Reading Assn., Phi Delta Kappa. Avocation: movie memorabilia. Home: 25 Sherwood Ave Ossining NY 10562 Office: Van Wyck Jr High Sch Hillside Lake Rd Wappingers Falls NY 12590

RIND, SHERRY, writer; b. Seattle, Mar. 29, 1952; d. Martin B. and Bernice (Mossafer) Rind; m. John F. Welliver. B.A., U. Wash., 1973, M.A., 1977. Instr. writing Bellevue Community Coll., Wash., 1978—, also other community colls. Author: The Hawk in the Backyard 1985 (Anhinga prize for poetry 1984); The Whooping Crane Dance, 1981. Bd. dirs. Seattle Zool. Soc., 1984—, Books Mercaz, Seattle, 1983-85. Recipient Louisa Kern award, 1982. Avocation: aviculture.

RINEHART, JOAN MARIE, nursing educator; b. Montgomery, W.Va., June 6, 1934; d. Bernard F. and Clara I. (Congleton) Rinehart; m. Warren L. Green, Nov. 21, 1981. B.S., U. Va., 1958; M.S., Cath. U., 1968; Ph.D., U. Md., 1972. R.N. Asst. prof. nursing Cath. U., Washington, 1972-75; assoc. prof. W.Va. U., Morgantown, 1975-77; assoc. prof., acting head Pa. State U., State College, 1977-83; assoc. prof. Widener U., Chester, Pa., 1983-86. Mem. editorial bd. Advances in Nursing Sci., 1980—. Contbr. articles to profl. jours., chpt. in book. Mem. Nat. League Nursing, Sigma Theta Tau. Methodist. Home: 235 New Castle Dr Shillington PA 19607

RINEHART, NITA, state senator; b. Tex. Mem. Wash. State Ho. of Reps., 1979-82; mem. Wash. State Senate, 1983—, vice chmn. edn. com., mem. rules, ways and means, govtl. ops. coms. Democrat. Office: Wash State Capitol Bldg Olympia WA 98504*

RING, BARBARA ANN, marketing and health care services consultant; b. St. Louis, Mar. 7, 1945; d. Oliver C. and Ann (McCarron) Garleb; A.A. in Nursing, El Camino Coll., 1964; B.A., UCLA, 1967, J.D., 1971; B.S. in Mgmt., Pacific Christian Coll., 1978; m. Douglas Ralph Ring; 1 son, Michael Francis. With Harbor Gen. Hosp., Torrance, Calif., 1964-66, Gardena Meml. Hosp., 1967-68, UCLA Med. Center, 1969-70, Brotman Meml. Hosp., Culver City, 1971-73; cardiac specialist Calif. Hosp. Med. Center, Los Angeles, 1974-77; asst. dir. nurses Fountain Valley Community Hosp. (Calif.), 1978-79; cons. Upjohn Health Care Services, 1980-84; pvt. nursing cons., 1984—. Youth camp dir. YMCA, also caravan dir. Bank Am. scholar, 1962; Westment Coll. scholar, 1962. Mem. Am. Mgmt. Assn., Nat. Assn. Female Execs., Critical Care Nurses Assn.

RING, ELEANOR LOUISE, county clerk; b. Capron, Okla., Jan. 7, 1934; d. Henry F. and Phoebe Eleanor (Dickey) Schwerdtfeger; m. William J. Ring, Aug. 17, 1951; children—Renetta Kay Ring Benson, Bryan Lee. Grad. high sch., Capron, 1951. Sec., Alva C. of C., Okla., 1953-60, sec., mgr., 1960-62; dep. county clk. Woods County, Okla., 1968-77, county clk., 1977—; cons. handbook state auditor and insp., Okla., 1984—. Chmn. precinct Woods County, 1978-80; county sec. Republican Party, Woods County, 1980-81. Mem. N.W. Dist. County Clk.'s. Assn. (pres. 1979-80), Okla. County Clk.'s Assn. (legis. com. 1980-81, edn. com. 1981-82, 84-85), N.W. Dist. County Officers Assn. (v.p. 1985). Methodist. Avocations: plants; gardening. Office: Woods County Clk PO Box 386 Alva OK 73717

RING, KAREN JENTOFT, travel school executive; b. Mpls., Oct. 9, 1939; d. Albert B. and Else Jentoft (Lindholm); B.A., Colby Coll., 1961; children by previous marriage—Timothy R., Marcie L. Sales agt. Northwest Airlines, Inc., Mpls., 1962; office mgr. Travel Center, Inc., Mankato, Minn., 1963-72, Champions Travel, Inc., Louisville, 1972-73; gen. mgr. Dittmann Tours, Northfield, Minn., 1973; Hennessey Travel Service, Excelsior, Minn., 1973-74; div. mgr. Diamonds Co., Phoenix, 1974-80; instr. SST Travel Schs., Phoenix, 1981-82; mgr. Davidson Travel, Phoenix, 1982; dir., v.p. AIT Travel Sch., Scottsdale, Ariz., 1983—. Bd. dirs. YWCA camps, 1955-57; instr. water safety ARC; mem. Mankato First Bapt. Ch. Bd. Edn., 1968-69; chmn. Republican 5th Precinct Com., 1968-71, Neighbor to Neighbor Fund Drive, 1969-71; alt. del. Rep. State Conv., 1970. Mem. AAUW (state conv. housing chmn. 1966), Am. Soc. Travel Agts. (treas. 1976-80), Inst. Cert. Travel Counselors (cert travel counselor), Ariz. Women in Travel, Pacific Area Travel Assn. Home: 6625 E Granada Rd Scottsdale AZ 85257 Office: 6900 E Camelback Rd Suite 330 Scottsdale AZ 85251

RINGQUIST, JUDY PATRICE, lawyer; b. Budapest, June 14, 1945, came to U.S., 1950; LL.B., Western State U., 1977. Bar: Calif. 1977, Md. 1979, R.I. 1981, U.S. Dist. Ct. R.I., 1981, U.S. Ct. Appeals (1st cir.) 1985, U.S. Supreme Ct. 1982. Sole practice, Newport, R.I., 1981-86; tchr. R.I. Coll., Providence, 1982; adv. bd. Legal Aid Soc., San Gabriel Valley, Calif., 1973. Dir. Pomona (Calif.) chpt. LWV, 1973, pres., 1974, steering com., Newport County, R.I., 1983. Recipient Am. Jurisprudence award, 1976. Mem. Assn. Trial Lawyers Am., ABA, Fed. Bar Assn. (asst. sec. R.I. chpt. 1981-82), Calif. Bar Assn., Md. Bar Assn., R.I. Bar Assn. Office: 120 W Main Rd Middletown RI 02840

RINI, MARY ANN, lawyer; b. Lorain, Ohio, Oct. 9, 1947; d. Stanley Paul and Kathleen M. (Feeley) Olewinski; m. Gusty A. Rini, July 9, 1947; children—Aaron Christopher, Blaire Elizabeth, Drew Adam. B.A. in English, Notre Dame Coll., Cleve., 1969; M.A. in English, John Carroll U., 1973; J.D., Cleve. State U., 1978. Bar: Ohio 1979, U.S. Dist. Ct. (no. dist.) Ohio. Tchr. Cleve. Bd. Edn., 1969-72, Lakewood High Sch., Cleve., 1972-77; asst. pub. defender, Cleve., 1978—; sole practice, Cleve., 1978—. Mem. Cleveland Heights Democratic Club, 1982—, Garfield Heights Dem. Club, 1982—. Nat. Inst. Trial Advocacy scholar, 1981. Mem. Young Lawyers Cuyahoga County Bar Assn. (chmn. 1982-83), Cuyahoga County Bar Assn., Nat. Legal Aid and Defenders Assn., Criminal Def. Lawyers Assn., ABA (com. alternative sentencing). Roman Catholic. Home: 3866 Tyndall St University Heights OH 44118 Office: 3570 Warrensville Center Rd Suite 103 Shaker Heights OH 44122

RINK, KATHLEEN CLARE, insurance company official; b. Hinsdale, Ill., Feb. 8, 1954; d. Virgil William and Patricia Jane (Donahue) R. B.A., St. Mary's Coll., Notre Dame, Ind., 1976; J.D., DePaul U., 1979; LL.M. in Estate Planning, U. Miami, 1980. Bar: Ill. 1979; C.L.U. Trust adminstr. State Nat. Bank, Evanston, Ill., 1981-82; assoc. dir. advanced underwriting The Equitable, Oak Brook, Ill., 1982-85; advanced underwriting cons. N.Y. Life, Bannockburn, Ill., 1985—; speaker estate planning various profl. orgns. Co-author play: Naperville Live, 1981. Mem. ABA, Ill. Bar Assn. Roman Catholic.

RINN, MARILYN HALL, employment agency executive, educator; b. Dexter, Maine, Jan. 30, 1933; d. Charlie Everett and Leona Ruth (Peavy) Hall; m. Samuel William Rinn III, June 28, 1953 (div. 1977); children—Kathryn Ann, Nancy Hall, Marilyn Louise, M. Jane. B.A. in Polit. Sci., U. Pitts., 1976, M.Ed., 1976. Counselor Churchill High Sch., Pa., 1975-76; trainer, counselor Contact Teleministries, Inc., Pitts., 1972-75; quality control mgr. Nike, Inc., Exeter, N.H., 1980-81, internat. quality control mgr., 1982-83; owner Ameribiz Employment, Portsmouth, N.H., 1985—. Coordinator, bd. dirs. Wilkinsburg Community Ministry, 1972-73. Mem. Portsmouth C. of C. (bus. and edn. com.), Am. Assn. Counseling and Devel., Nat. Assn. Employment Counselors, Nat. Assn. Female Execs. Republican. Avocations: treasure hunting; study and practice of metaphysics. Home: Sawyers Mill Apts Box 82 One Mill St Dover NH 03820 Office: Ameribiz Employment Samuel Beck House The Hill Portsmouth NH 03801

RINSLEY, JACQUELINE ANN, nurse; b. Chgo., Apr. 5, 1933; d. John Lancelot and Margaret Elizabeth (Zeilinger) Louk; student Washington U., St. Louis, 1951-52; diploma in nursing St. Luke's Hosp. Sch. Nursing, 1955. Psychiat. nurse Topeka State Hosp., 1955-56, sect. head nurse, 1955-56; gen. and pediatric nurse St. John's Hosp., Springfield, Mo., 1956-57, Burge Hosp., 1957-58; head pediatric nurse Stormont-Vail Hosp., Topeka, 1958-60; psychiat. nurse Kans. Neurol. Inst., Topeka, 1960-70, adminstr., 1970-80, dir. nursing edn., 1980-82; legal sec. Dist. Atty.'s Office, 1984—. Mem. Am., Kans. nurses assns., Am. Assn. Mental Deficiency, Nat. Rehab. Assn., Nat. Audubon Soc., Am. Mus. Nat. History, Smithsonian Assos., Nat. Fedn. Bus. and Profl. Women's Clubs, Zeta Tau Alpha. Republican. Lutheran. Home: 923 SE Bay Blvd #28 Newport OR 97365 Office: 225 W Olive Newport OR 97365

RINZLER, CAROL GENE EISEN, lawyer, writer; b. Newark, Sept. 12, 1941; d. Irving Y. and Ruth (Katz) Eisen; m. Carl Rinzler, July 21, 1962 (div. 1976); children—Michael Franklin, Jane Ruth Amelia. A.B., Goucher Coll., 1962; J.D., Yale U., 1980. Bar: N.Y. 1981. Editor, Charterhouse Books, Inc., N.Y.C., 1971-73, pub., 1973-74; articles editor Glamour Mag., N.Y.C., 1974-77; assoc. Cahill Gordon & Reindel, N.Y.C., 1980-86; of counsel Rembar & Curtis, 1986—; instr. pub. law N.Y.U., 1983—. Author: Frankly McCarthy, 1969; Nobody Said You Had to Eat Off the Floor, 1971; The Girl Who Got All the Breaks, 1980; Your Adolescent: An Owner's Manual, 1981; book critic Washington Post, 1974—; columnist Ladies' Home Jour., 1977-80, Mademoiselle, 1981—, Cosmopolitan, 1983—; contbr. articles, revs. to various periodicals; contbg. editor Pubs. Weekly, 1983—; bd. dirs. Feminist Press, 1981—. Mem. Assn. Bar City of N.Y., Friends of Scarlett O'Hara, Women's Media Group (pres. 1984-85), Nat. Book Critics Circle, PEN (exec. com. 1986—). Jewish. Club: Cosmopolitan (N.Y.C.). Office: 19 W 44th St New York NY 10036

RIORDAN, FRANCIS ELLEN, linguist, educator, nun; b. Solomon, Kans., Oct. 24, 1915; d. Patrick Francis and Ella (Barret) R.; A.B., Marymount Coll., 1936; M.A., Cath. U. Am., 1945, Ph.D., 1952. Joined Sisters St. Joseph, 1937; directress St. Mary Acad., Silver City, N.Mex., 1950-51; prin. Luckey High Sch., Manhattan, Kans., 1951-53, Cathedral High Sch., Salina, Kans., 1953-57; prof. French, chmn. fgn. langs. dept. Marymount Coll., Salina, 1962-83, chmn. humanities div., 1980-83, dir. interdisciplinary program, 1973-76; mem. faculty Northwestern Coll., Orange City, Iowa, 1983-84, Ctr. for Peace Concerns, 1984—. Mem. coordinating com. State of Kans. Women's Meeting, 1977. Lang. dept. fellow Cath. U., 1948-49. Mem. Am. Assn. Tchrs. of French, Kappa Gamma Pi. Author: Concept of Love in the French Catholic Literary Revival, 1952; The Brave Walk Single File, pageant, 1959. Home: 108 N Estates Dr Salina KS 67401

RIPIN, MAUREEN CATHERINE, data processor; b. N.Y.C., Oct. 14, 1929; d. Joseph Benedict and Mary (Clarke) Matthews; B.S., C. W. Post Coll., 1970; m. Frederick Ripin, Mar. 15, 1975; children—Colleen, Maureen, Patricia. Sci. programmer Data Master, L.I., N.Y., 1966-69; dir. data processing Harry Winston, Inc., N.Y.C., 1970—; founder Christie Clarke—Beautiful Things for Your Home, Washington Depot, Conn. Mem. Data Processing Mgmt. Assn., Am. Mgmt. Assn., Women in Info. Processing, NOW, Alpha Sigma Lambda. Office: Harry Winston Inc 718 Fifth Ave New York NY 10019

RIPLEY, JAYNE POORE, educator, consultant, lecturer; b. Evanston, Ill., Oct. 9, 1931; d. Earl Yates and Mabel Claire (Ransom) P.; m. William Lee Ripley, Aug. 25, 1952 (div. 1969); children—Mark, Trent, Kirk, Paul. B.A. in Psychology, U. Ark., 1952, M.S.E. in Childhood Edn., 1957; Reading Specialist Cert., Ind. U., 1979. Gen. elem. tchr. North Little Rock Pub. Schs., Ark., 1952-55; lectr. Ark. Bapt. Sch. Nursing, Little Rock, 1956-57, Vincennes U. Bedford extension, Ind., 1980; substitute tchr. Lawrence County Schs., Ind., 1961-68; reading tchr. and cons. Mitchell Community Schs., Ind., 1969—; discussion leader Jr. Great Books, Mitchell, 1984—. Pres., bd. dirs. Bedford Little Theater, 1966-67; founder, 1st pres. Citizens for a Better Environment, Bedford, 1970-71. Mem. Internat. Reading Assn. (founding mem. R.E.A.D. council, rec. sec. 1979-81). Unitarian. Avocations: gourmet cooking; fitness. Home: 121 Edgewood Dr Bedford IN 47421 Office: Mitchell Jr High Sch 1010 Bishop Blvd Mitchell IN 47446

RIPPER, RITA JO (JODY), financial executive; b. Clarion, Iowa, May 8, 1950; d. Carl Phillip and Lucille Mae (Stewart) Ripper; B.A., U. Iowa, 1972; M.B.A., N.Y.U., 1978. Contracts and fin. staff Control Data Corp., Mpls., 1974-78; regional mgr. Raytheon Corp., Irvine, Calif., 1978-83; v.p. Caljo Corp., Des Moines, Iowa, 1983-84; asst. v.p. Bank of America, San Francisco, 1984—. Vol. and alt. del. Republican Party, Edina, Minn., N.Y.C., 1975—; vol. Cancer, Heart, Lung Assns., Edina, N.Y.C., Calif., 1974-78, 84—. Mem. Internat. Mktg. Assn., World Trade Ctr. Assn., Acctg. Soc. (pres. 1975-76), Mensa, Beta Alpha Psi (chmn. 1977-78), Phi Gamma Nu (v.p. 1971-72) Presbyterian. Home: 22 Marinero Circle #46 Tiburon CA 94920 Office: Bank of America 2 Embarcadero Ctr San Francisco CA 94111

RIPPY, FRANCES MARGUERITE MAYHEW (MRS. N. MERRILL RIPPY), educator; b. Ft. Worth, Sept. 16, 1929; d. Henry Grady and Marguerite Christine (O'Neill) Mayhew; B.A., Tex. Christian U., 1949; M.A., Vanderbilt U., 1951, Ph.D., 1957; postgrad. (Fulbright scholar), U. London, 1952-53; m. Noble Merrill Rippy, Aug. 29, 1955 (dec. 1980); children—Felix O'Neill, Conrad Mayhew, Marguerite Hailey. Instr., Tex. Christian U., 1953-55; instr. to asst. prof. Lamar State U., 1955-59; asst. prof. English, Ball State U., Muncie, Ind., 1959-64, assoc. prof., 1964-68, prof., 1968—, dir. Ph.D. studies in English, 1966—, editor Ball State U. Forum, 1960—; vis. asst. prof. Sam Houston State U., 1957; vis. lectr., prof. U. P.R., summers 1959, 60, 61; cons.-evaluator North Central Assn. Colls. and Schs., 1973—, New Eng. Assn. Colls. and Schs., 1983—. Recipient McClintock award, 1966; Danforth grantee, summer 1964, asso., 1965—; Ball State U. research grantee, 1960, 62, 70, 73; Lilly Library summer research grantee, 1978. Mem. MLA, Coll. English Assn., Johnson Soc. Midwest (sec. 1961-62), AAUP, Nat. Council Tchrs. English, Am. Soc. 18th Century Studies, Ind. Coll. English Assn. (sec.-treas. 1982-83, v.p. 1983-84, pres. 1984-85). Author: Matthew Prior, 1986. Contbr. articles to profl. jours., chpt. to anthology. Home: 4709 W Jackson Muncie IN 47304

RISHEIM, WANDA JOAN, educator, artist, pilot, real estate broker; b. July 11, 1935; d. Arthur J. and Meta C. Wands; A.B., Lincoln Christian Coll., 1961; M.S., Ft. Hays State Coll., 1963. Tchr. high schs. in Mo., Ill. and Calif., 1963-74; tchr. San Dieguito High Sch. Dist., Encinitas, Calif., 1976—; area dir. mktg. Jim Rohn Prodns., 1981; one-woman exhbn. Clayton Gallery, St. Louis, 1970; group exhbn. Art Inst. San Diego, 1974-75. Mem. Nat. Assn. Female Execs., NEA, Nat. Art Edn. Assn., Women in Sales, Women in Mgmt., Calif. Tchrs. Assn., AAUW. Club: Toastmasters. Address: 1123 Santa Helena Park Ct Solana Beach CA 92075

RISINGER, DOROTHY EXAAH, social worker, educator; b. Mansfield, La., Sept. 10, 1919; d. Marlin and Mary Iva (McBride) R.; A.B.A., Stephens Coll., 1938; B.A., La. State U., 1940; M.S.W., Tulane U., 1954. Exec. sec. and home service dir. ARC, Mansfield, La., 1940-46; welfare caseworker, Mansfield, 1950-52, New Orleans, 1954-55; clin. social worker, instr. in rehab. and comprehensive care Tulane U. Sch. Medicine, New Orleans, 1955-60, coordinator disability evaluation study, 1960-65, asst. coordinator rehab. teaching program, 1965-66; asst. prof., asst. coordinator Office of Dean, La. State U. Sch. Medicine, Shreveport, 1966-75, asst. prof., med. social cons., clin. social worker, 1975-80; joint faculty Tulane U. Sch. Public Health, 1957-60, Sch. Social Work, 1955-66; faculty dept. medicine La. State U. Sch. Medicine, 1968-75; cons. N.W. La. Comprehensive Health Planning Council, 1969, N.W. La. Rehab. Center, 1967-75, Mollie E. Webb Regional Speech and Hearing Center, 1972-76; pvt. practice clin. social work, med.-social cons. Bd. dirs. Community Council, Inc., Shreveport, 1968-74, 76—, chairperson agy. conf. com., 1980—. Recipient Service award ARC, 1945, Am. Cancer Soc., 1962, 65, Arthritis Found., 1973. Mem. Nat. Rehab. Assn., Nat. Assn. Social Workers (pres. La. chpt. 1980—), Family Relations Council La. (pres. 1972-74), Mental Health Assn., Soc. Hosp. Social Work Dirs., Am., La. hosp. assns., AMA (spl. affiliate), Nat. Council Family Relations, Nat. Assn. Retarded Citizens, AAUP, Phi Beta Phi. Democrat. Episcopalian. Contbr. articles on rehab. to profl. jours. Home: 957 Monrovia St Shreveport LA 71106 Office: Suite 1118 Fountain Towers Shreveport LA 71101

RISKIND, SUSAN ELIZABETH, executive recruiter; b. San Antonio, Dec. 17, 1951; d. Morris Samuel and Ruth (Sholtz) Riskind; B.A. in English, U. Tex.-Austin, 1975. Tchr., Am. Sch. Lugano, Switzerland, 1976-77; propr. Mama Says No Antiques, Dallas, 1977-79; personnel placement exec. Snelling & Snelling, Dallas, 1979-80; exec. recruiter Lamber Personnel, San Francisco, 1980-82; free lance exec. recruiter, San Francisco, 1982—; copywriter K.E.P.S. Radio, Eagle Pass, Tex., 1968-69; instr. in field. Producer, dir. Poetry Playhouse, 1970. Cuban/Hispanic liaison Congl. campaigns 1975-76, Montgomery County, Md.; mem. Raol Wallenberg Democratic Club, San Francisco, 1983; organizer, mgr. bilingual project Model Cities, Eagle Pass, Tex., 1968-69. Model Cities grantee, 1972; recipient Soroptomist award, 1970. Mem. Nat. Assn. Female Execs., Exec. Search Network (founder). Democrat. Club: Jewish Fedn. Office: 233 24th Ave San Francisco CA 94131

RISLEY, EDYTH C., petroleum geologist; b. Little Rock, Oct. 12, 1928; d. Elmer J. and Lillie L. (McNeill) R.; student Randolph-Macon Woman's Coll., 1945-47; B.S., So. Meth. U., 1949; postgrad. U. Colo., 1949; M.S., Stanford U., 1951. Jr. geologist McAlester Fuel Co., Magnolia, Ark., 1949; geologist Continental Oil, Midland, Tex., 1951-56; sr. geologist, cons. McCord & Assocs., Dallas, 1957-63; sr. sci. reference librarian Dallas Public Library, 1963-75; hdqrs. staff geologist Holly Corp., Dallas, 1975-77; sr. geologist Ray Holifield & Assos., Dallas, 1977-85, cons. geologist, 1977—. Mem. Am. Assn. Petroleum Geologists (ho. of dels. 1981-84, rec. sec. 1983-84), Dallas Geol. Soc. (sec. 1979-80), West Tex. Geol. Soc., Nat. Audubon Soc., Energy Club of Dallas, Pi Beta Phi. Contbr. publs. in field. Home: 2905 University Blvd Dallas TX 75205 Office: 2905 University Dallas TX 75205

RISO, EUNICE ESTELLE, city official; b. Milford, Conn., Feb. 16, 1932; d. Thomas G. and Mildred E. (Almquist) Riso; student U. Conn., 1950-52. Recreation supr. Milford, 1953-55, Visalia (Calif.), 1955-60, Bridgeport (Conn.), 1960-62; supt. recreation Visalia, 1963-70, dir. leisure services, 1970-84, dir. adminstrn., 1984—. Vice chmn. Tulare County Commn. Status Women, 1976-80, chmn., 1980—; fund drive chmn. Golden Valley council Girl Scouts U.S.A., 1972. Mem. Calif. Parks and Recreation Soc. (dist. pres. 1967, Outstanding Recreator award 1970), AAU, Amateur Softball Assn. (commr.), Visalia C. of C. (Woman of Yr. 1984), Calif. Assn. Retarded Children (state and dist. bowling dir. 1968-74), Chi Kappa Rho (dist. pres. 1979-80), Tulare County Women's Trade Club (charter). Club: Visalia Soroptimist (past pres., Regional Women Helping Women award 1983). Home: 2020 E Vassar St Visalia CA 93277 Office: 707 W Acequla Visalia CA 93291

RISS, TONI PALLETT, communications systems executive; b. Kans. City, Mo., Dec. 4, 1952; d. Richard Roland and Freda Gale (Hunt) Riss. B. Humanities with highest honors, New Coll. Calif., 1978; postgrad. Loretto Heights Coll., 1971-73, U. Colo., 1973-74, Columbia Sch. Broadcasting, 1980; cert. telecommunications mgmt. Golden Gate U., 1984. Network communications specialist Network, San Francisco, 1979-81; telecommunications operator Bechtel, San Francisco, 1981-83, network customer service coordinator 1983—; cons. Home Office Corp., San Francisco, 1983-84. Mem. Bay Area Com. Against Briggs Initiative, San Francisco, 1978; mem. Abalone Alliance, San Francisco, 1981—; mem. ARC, San Francisco, 1981-83. Mem. Women in Telecommunications. Democrat. Jewish. Club: Rosicrucian Order (San Francisco). Author (poetry) Seasons of Myself, 1978. Composer, singer, musician (record album) Fire and Wind, 1984. Home: 1402 Guerrero St San Francisco CA 94110

RISSO, ELLA, real estate and insurance executive; b. Atlantic City, Aug. 22, 1938; d. Edward and Mary (Bowen) Peterson; m. John D. Risso, Mar. 21, 1959 (div. 1984); children—Linda Sue, Carolyn Louise, Patricia Marie, Arlene Gay. Student in Ins. and Real Estate, Rutgers U., Camden, N.J., Stockton State Coll., Pomona, N.J. Salesperson, agt. Risso Real Estate & Inc., Brigantine, N.J., 1963—, Ned Carrier & Sons, Inc., Brigantine; pres. Ella Risso Ins. Mem. Ins. Women Atlantic County (pres. 1983-84). Republican. Roman Catholic. Lodges: Sons of Italy (3d v.p. 1983-85), Ladies Lions (treas. 1984-85) (Brigantine). Home: 219 S Roosevelt Blvd PO Box 672 Brigantine NJ 08203 Office: 3300 Brigantine Blvd Brigantine NJ 08203

RISTOW, LINDA SUE, city official; b. Osceola, Iowa, May 17, 1947; d. Robert David and Mary Ellen (Sawyer) Musson; student Calif. State U., Fullerton, 1965-66, Fullerton Jr. Coll., 1966-67; m. Paul Gary Ristow, Sept. 2, 1966 (div. Oct. 1985). Programmer, Transam. Ins. Co., Los Angeles, 1967-68;

programmer/analyst Thom McAn Shoe Co., Worcester, Mass., 1969-70, Hunt Wesson Foods, Inc., Fullerton, 1971-77; project leader Santa Fe Internat., Orange, Calif., 1977-79; mgr. bus. systems Braegen Corp., Anaheim, Calif., 1979-81; mgr. info. services City of Irvine, Calif., 1981—. Chmn., Coalition of Neighborhood Assns., Laguna Beach, Calif., 1978-84; pres. Arch Beach Heights Assn., Laguna Beach, 1978—; mem. adv. com. for Laguna Canyon Rd., Orange County Bd. Suprs., 1978-79; exec. v.p. Laguna Greenbelt, 1979-85; mem. adv. com. Laguna Beach Gen. Plan, 1979-81; chmn. Orange County Coastal Coalition, 1981. Cert. in prodn. and inventory control mgmt. Mem. Calif. Data Base Mgmt. Assn. (sec.), Assn. Mcpl. Data Processing Dirs. (pres.), Am. Prodn. and Inventory Control Soc., Data Processing Mgmts. Assn. Democrat. Methodist. Home: 917 Quivera Laguna Beach CA 92651 Office: City of Irvine Data Processing Office 17200 Jamboree Rd Irvine CA 92713

RITCH, KATHLEEN, diversified company executive; Harbor Beach, Mich., Jan. 23, 1943; d. Eunice (Spry) R.; B.A., Mich. State U., 1965: student Katharine Gibbs Sch., 1965-66. Exec. sec., adminstrv. asst. to pres. Katy Industries, Inc., N.Y.C., 1969-70; exec. sec., adminstrv. asst. to chmn. Kobrand Corp., N.Y.C., 1970-72; adminstrv. asst. to chmn. and pres. Ogden Corp., N.Y.C., 1972-74; asst. sec., adminstr. office services, asst. to chmn. Ogden Corp., N.Y.C., 1974-81, corporate sec., adminstr. office services, 1981-84, v.p., corporate sec., adminstr. office services, 1984—; part-owner Unell Mfg. Co., Port Hope, Mich., 1966—. Mem. Am. Soc. Corporate Secs. Home: 500 E 77th St New York NY 10162 Office: 277 Park Ave New York NY 10172

RITCHIE, INGRID MARIA, environmental health scientist, educator; b. Munich, W.Ger., May 26, 1949; came to U.S., 1952; d. Curtis Huey and Johanna Leokadia (Kroll) Ritchie; A.S., Murray State Coll., 1969; B.S. summa cum laude, Southwestern State U., 1971; M.S., U. Minn., 1973, Ph.D. (USPHS fellow), 1980. Research scientist Air Quality Minn. Pollution Control Agy., Mpls., 1974-76, Regional Copper-Nickel Study, Mpls., 1976-79, health risk assessment Minn. Dept. Health, Mpls., 1979-82; asst. prof. Sch. Pub. and Environ. Affairs, Ind. U., Indpls., 1982—; vice chmn. Sci. and Tech. Resource Adv. Council to Minn. Joint Legis. Com. on Sci. and Tech.; mem. Indpl. Air Pollution Control Bd.; mem. task force on Kerosene heaters Underwriters Labs., Inc. Mem. Am. Pub. Health Assn., Nat. Air Pollution Control Assn. Office: Ind U BS-SPEA Room 4083 801 W Michigan St Indianapolis IN 46223

RITCHIE, JUDITH ANN, consultant in health care education and systems design; b. Cumberland, Wis., Mar. 23, 1943; d. David and Ruth Genvieve (Elmberg) Wallace Hobscheid; m. Philip R. Ayres, Jan. 1, 1983; m. Lary Wayne Ritchie, Aug. 10, 1963 (div. 1981); 1 child, David Wayne. R.N., Hennepin County Gen. Hosp., Mpls., 1964; student U. Minn., 1961-63, Nat. U., 1983—. Paramedic coordinator Bay Hosp., Chula Vista, Calif., 1970-77, Mercy Hosp., San Diego, 1977-79; dir. field ops. Hartson Ambulance Service, San Diego, 1979-83; trauma coordinator County San Diego, 1984-85; exec. dir. Judith Ritchie & Assocs., San Diego, 1983—; instr. Southwestern Coll., Chula Vista, 1973-76, U. Calif.-San Diego, 1978-83. Bd. dirs. Twin Forum YWCA, San Diego, 1985—; chmn. exec. com. Mexican Am. Found., San Diego, 1985—. Leadership scholar YWCA, 1982, Emergency Nurses Assn., 1984. Mem. Emergency Nurses Assn. (bd. dirs. 1980-84, membership chmn. 1985—), Profl. Network, Council for Long Term Care Nurses, Calif. Assn. Hosp. Facilities (assoc.), County Paramedic Agys. Com. (vice chmn. 1981-83). Republican. Clubs: Ena Pronet. Avocations: jazz; photography. Home: 4641 Calle de Vida San Diego CA 92124

RITCHIE, MARY MOORE MEACHAM, court reporter, business executive; b. Mecklenburg County, N.C., Oct. 4, 1939; d. James Bess and Christine Neilson (Rosebro) M.; A.A.S., Sullins Coll., 1959; m. Barron L. Ritchie, Jr., Mar. 19, 1960; children—Barron III, James Mark, Virginia Brooke. Sec., tax dept., Belk Stores Services, Charlotte, N.C., 1959-61, legal sec., 1962-63; com. clk. Ho. of Reps., N.C. Gen. Assembly, 1967; owner, mgr., pres. Ct. Reporting Services, Inc., Raleigh, N.C., 1969—, Sir Walter Center Exec. Suites, Raleigh, 1980—; instr. Meredith Coll., 1979-80. Mem. Nat. Stenomask Verbatim Reporters Assn. (past chmn. bus. mgmt. com.), Nat. Assn. Women Bus. Owners (past pres. Triangle chpt.), Raleigh C. of C., Nat. Assn. Sec. Services, Profl. Assn. Sec. Services, Assn. Info. System Profls. Republican. Presbyterian. Clubs: MacGregor Downs Country, Capital City. Home: 1809 Falls Church Rd Raleigh NC 27609 Office: PO Box 1729 Raleigh NC 27602

RITENOUR, SHIRLEY JEANNE, construction company executive; b. Seward, Pa., Jan. 28, 1938; d. Peter Harold and Mabel Claire (Stephens) Bouch; m. Ray Ritenour, June 30, 1956; children—Suzanne Jane, Ray Alden, Dorothy Claire, Ernest Clinton. Pvt. sec., estimator, asst. Royal Plate Glass, Johnstown, Pa., 1955-57; constrn. estimator Five R Excavating, New Florence, Pa., 1971—, stockholder, 1969—, sec., treas., 1971—, chief exec. officer, 1979—. Committeewoman Democratic Party, St. Clair Twp., Pa. Decorated grand cross of color Order of Rainbow Girls. Mem. Assn. Bus. and Profl. Women in Constrn. (dir. publicity 1985—), Constructors Assn. Western Pa., Assoc. Pa. Constructors, NOW. Democrat. Presbyterian. Lodges: Order Eastern Star, White Shrine of Jerusalem, Knights Templar Aux. Avocations: reading; travel; photography. Home: PO Box 387 New Florence PA 15944 Office: Five R Excavating Inc PO Box 387 New Florence PA 15944

RITSON, DONNA DIANE, communications administrator; b. Chgo., Feb. 22, 1955; d. Raymond Bernard and Elaine Marion (Englund) Nietschmann; m. Scott Campbell Ritson, Feb. 25, 1978; 1 stepchild, Carrie Stewart Ritson. B.S. with honors, Roosevelt U., Chgo., 1983; postgrad., 1983—; cert. bus. communicator. Sec. Baxter-Travenol Labs., Deerfield, Ill., 1973-76, advt. asst., 1976-80, conv. coordinator, 1980-83; communications coordinator Angus Chem. Co., Northbrook, Ill., 1983-84, communications mgr., 1984—. Mem. Bus. Profl. Advt. Assn., Nat. Assn. Female Execs., Am. Mktg. Assn. Club: Chgo. Yacht. Avocations: skiing, sailing, scuba diving, boating. Home: 131 Windsor Dr Vernon Hills IL 60061 Office: Angus Chem Co 2211 Sanders Rd Northbrook IL 60062

RITTENBERRY, GAY NELL, realtor, construction company executive; b. Franklin, Ky., Apr. 12, 1947; d. Charles Roland and Bessie Lee (Mayes) Deweese; m. Jack Gordon Rittenberry, May 31, 1969; children—Elizabeth Gayle, Charles Gordon, Emily Lee. B.S. in English, Austin Peay State U., 1969, postgrad. 1971-73. Tchr. English, Hopkinsville High Sch., Ky., 1969-73; owner, operator Better-Built Constrn., Hopkinsville, 1977—; realtor, auctioneer Century 21 Town & Country, Hopkinsville, 1978—. Mem. Christian County Bd. Edn., Hopkinsville, 1977-81; rep. Hopkinsville Human Relations Commn., 1978-81; mem. Christian County Recreation Dept., Hopkinsville, 1980-81; mem. resolution com. Ky. State Bd. Edn., Frankfort, 1980; chmn. Pritchard Com. on Edn. for Christian County, Hopkinsville, 1984. Mem. Christian County Bd. Realtors (sec., bd. dirs. 1979-81), Ky. Bd. Realtors, Nat. Assn. Realtors. Democrat. Baptist. Avocations: reading, water skiing, sailing. Home: 1723 S Main St Hopkinsville KY 42240 Office: Century 21 Town and Country PO Box 1001 Hopkinsville KY 42240

RITTENHOUSE, SHIRLEY BASH, university administrator; b. Champaign, Ill., Nov. 23, 1928; d. Elmer Clarence and Alice Josephine (Lee) Bash; B.S. in Chemistry with honors, U. Ill., Champaign-Urbana, 1950; m. Warren L. Rittenhouse, Nov. 29, 1975; children—Janice L. Woodward, Barbara A. Pfaller. Research asst. phys. chemistry Parke-Davis Co., Detroit, 1950-52; teaching asst. chemistry U. Ill., 1959-60, research asst. biochemistry, 1960-65, staff asst. president's office, 1965-79, staff assoc., 1979-85. Mem. Phi Beta Kappa, Iota Sigma Pi, Sigma Delta Epsilon, Kappa Alpha Theta. Home: 5 Imperial Ct Champaign IL 61820

RITTER, ANN L., lawyer; b. N.Y.C., May 20, 1933; d. Joseph and Grace (Goodman) R. B.A., Hunter Coll., 1954; J.D., N.Y. Law Sch., 1970; postgrad. Law Sch., NYU, 1971-72. Bar: N.Y. 1971, U.S. Ct. Appeals (2d cir.) 1975, U.S. Supreme Ct. 1975. Writer, 1954-70; editor, 1955-66; tchr., 1966-70; atty. Am. Soc. Composers, Authors and Pubs., N.Y.C., 1971-72, Greater N.Y. Ins. Co., N.Y.C., 1973-74; sr. ptnr. Brenhouse & Ritter, N.Y.C., 1974-78; sole practice, N.Y.C., 1978—. Editor N.Y. Immigration News, 1975-76. Mem. ABA, Am. Immigration Lawyers Assn. (treas. 1983-84, sec. 1984-85, vice chair 1985-86, chair 1986-87), N.Y. State Bar Assn., N.Y. County Lawyers Assn., Assn. Trial Lawyers Am., N.Y. State Trial Lawyers Assn., N.Y.C. Bar Assn. Democrat. Jewish. Home: 47 E 87th St New York NY 10128 Office: 420 Madison Ave New York NY 10017

RITTER, DEBORAH BRADFORD, lawyer; b. Boston, Nov. 4, 1953; d. Edmund Underwood and Priscilla (Rich) R. B.A., Yale U., 1974; J.D., Boston Coll. Law, 1980. Bar: N.H. 1980, Mass. 1981. Assoc. firm McLane, Graf, Raulerson & Middleton, Manchester, N.H., 1980-82, Singer, Stoneman, Kunian & Kurland, P.C., Boston, 1983—; dir. N.H. Legal Assistance Corp., Concord, N.H., 1982-84. Sec., bd. dirs. N.H. Performing Arts Ctr., Manchester, 1980-85, Yale Alumni Schs. Com., Boston, 1982—. Mem. ABA, Mass. Bar Assn., N.H. Bar Assn. Home: 413 Hammond St Chestnut Hill MA 02167

RITTER, LUCY ELIZABETH, retired business executive; b. Shanghai, China, Sept. 10, 1910 (parents Am. citizens); d. Ovid Herbert and Lucy (Corker) R.; A.B., Stanford U., 1930, M.A., 1931. Research sec. Calif. Taxpayers Assn., 1931-34; security analyst Calif. Western States Life Ins. Co., Sacramento, 1935-43, asst. treas., 1943-54, 2d v.p., asst. treas., mgr. securities dept., 1954-68, v.p. securities, 1968-75, now ret. Bd. dirs. Sacramento Community Chest, 1953-56, Sacramento Children's Home, 1949-55; dir. nat. exec. bd. Stanford Alumni Assn., 1955-58; life mem., bd. govs. Mercy Hosps. Found., 1971—; bd. dirs. Crocker Art Mus., Sacramento, 1974-83; trustee Sacramento Symphony Trust Fund Found.; mem. bd. regents U. Pacific, 1974—; mem. vis. libraries com. Stanford U., 1976-82; mem. Calif. Pub. Employee's Retirement Bd., 1961-69; alt. del. Democratic Nat. Conv., 1956, 64; chmn. woman's Citizens for Kennedy, 3d congl. dist., 1960. Mem. Inst. Chartered Fin. Analysts, Security Analysts of San Francisco, Crocker Art Mus. Assn. Clubs: Del Paso Country, Sacramento, Metropolitan, San Francisco. Author: Lucy's Twentieth Century, 1974; An Ode to Common Sense, 1977; Lucy Goes to South America, 1979; contbr. articles to profl. jours. Home: Capitol Towers 1500 7th St Sacramento CA 95814

RITTERMAN, SHAREN BRUNEAU, audiologist; b. Boston, May 1, 1949; d. Roger Joseph and Arlene Frances (Weisend) Bruneau; A.A., Manatee Jr. Coll., 1969; M.S., U. South Fla., 1972; m. Stuart I. Ritterman, Sept. 2, 1977; 1 son, Joshua Nathaniel. Audiologist, Hillsboro County Public Schs., Tampa, Fla., 1972-75; vis. instr., clin. supr. U. South Fla., Tampa, 1975; clin. audiologist/program dir. audiology Central Fla. Speech and Hearing Clinic, Lakeland, 1976-77; speech/lang. pathologist Pasco County Schs., Dade City, Fla., 1977-83; pres. Cypher Research Consortium, 1985—. Recipient cert. clin. competence Am. Speech and Hearing Assn.; cert. of registration in audiology, Fla. Mem. Fla. Speech, Lang. and Hearing Assn., Am. Speech, Lang. and Hearing Assn. Roman Catholic. Address: 181 Ellerbee Rd Wesley Chapel FL 34249

RIVARD, PHYLLIS KELTGEN, graphic arts and printing broker, publisher; b. Mankato, Minn., Aug. 23, 1943; d. Leo M. and Catherine M. (Peters) Keltgen; student Mankato State U., 1961-64, Metro State U., 1978-79; children by previous marriage—Alan, (dec.), Daniel. With DM Printing, Inc., Mankato, Minn., 1960—, newsletter editor, 1962-80, mgr. art dept., 1962-77, instr. inservice tng., 1977-80, v.p. sales, 1977—, co-propr., 1961—; v.p. mktg. The Press, Inc., Chanhassen, Minn., 1981-82; graphic arts broker, pub. Par Cons., Inc., Mpls. 1977—. Mem. All-America City Com., 1978; bd. dirs. Jr. Achievement, Mankato chpt., 1980—. Mem. Sales and Mktg. Execs. of Mpls., Entrepreneur's Network, Minn. Women's Network, Mankato C. of C. (dir. 1977-80), Mankato State Alumni Assn. (pres. 1978-79, dir. 1976—). Home and Office: 1920 S First St Minneapolis MN 55454

RIVELLI, GIOCONDA MARIA CATHERINE, artist, jewelry designer; b. Florence, Italy, d. Lorenzo and Catherine Anderson (Lester) R.; student Istituto Santa Reparata, Istituto della Santissima Annunziata al Poggio Imperiale Florence; m. Eric Richards Rippel, Nov. 6, 1974; 1 child, Schoenly Shearer Alexandra. Mem. pub. relations staff S. Ferragamo, Florence, 1959-63; pub. relations fashion coordinator Irene Galitzine couture, Rome, 1963-67, Titti Brugnoli, 1967-69; owner, mgr. Gioconda, N.Y.C., 1969—; editor Harpers Bazaar, Italy, 1969-71. Mem. organizing com. Scuola d'Italia, N.Y.C., 1977; one-woman shows: Aaron Faber Gallery, N.Y.C., 1978, Martha, Park Ave, N.Y.C., 1985; painting exhbn. Essex Art Gallery, 1979; collage exhbn. Rizzoli Art Gallery, N.Y.C., 1980; collage and jewelry show Gallery Il Borro, Florence, Italy, 1981; jewelry exhbn. Am. Mus. Natural History, N.Y.C., 1980, coordinator Pompeii A.D. '79 Show, 1982, Art Students League, N.Y.C. Mem. Pres.'s Council Vis. Nurses, N.Y.C.; mem. coms. N.Y. Infirmary-Beekman Downtown Hosp., N.Y.C.; mem. com. Internat. Inst. Rural Reconstrn., N.Y.C.; bd. control Art Students League, 1985-86. Club: Circolo Nautico E Della Vela, Porto Ercole, Italy.

RIVERA, ANNA MERCEDES, psychiatric social worker; b. Santruce, P.R., July 9, 1945; d. Jose A. and Ana D. (Real) Rivera. B.A., Adelphi U., 1969; M.S.W., Fordham U., 1979. Lic. clin. social worker, Fla. Joined Sisers Holy Family of Nazareth, 1972, left order, 1979. Social worker Little Flower Children's Services, Wading River, N.Y., 1969-71; psychiat. social worker Catholic Family and Community Services, Bridgeport, Conn., 1972-82; asst. dir. Hispanic unit psychiat. social worker Greater Bridgeport Community Mental Health Ctr., 1982-83; clin. social worker Hernando County Mental Health Ctr., Inc., Brooksville, Fla., 1983—; cons. in field. Advisor, chairperson, bd. dirs. Southwest Neighborhood Health Council, Inc., Bridgeport, 1975-80; bd. dirs. Mental Health Services Coordinating Com., 1980-82, exec. com., 1981-82; mem. adv. bd. Ret. Sr. Vol. Program, Brooksville, Fla., 1985—, Multi-Service Ctr., Brooksville, 1986—. William Conley scholar Council of Catholic Women, Bridgeport, 1976-79; recipient Outstanding Service award for Leadership South-West Neighborhood Health Council, Inc., 1979. Mem. Nat. Assn. Social Workers, Fla. Soc. Clin. Social Workers, Nat. Assn. Female Execs., Democrat. Roman Catholic. Avocations: photography; singing; music; reading; nature; sports. Office: Hernando County Mental Health Ctr Inc 5333 Commercial Way (US 19) Spring Hill FL also Citrus Counseling Services PO Box 157 Beverly Hills FL 32665

RIVERA, CHITA, actress, singer, dancer; b. Washington, Jan. 23, 1933; d. Pedro Julio Figuerva del Rivero; m. Anthony Mordente. Student, Am. Sch. Ballet, N.Y.C. Broadway debut: Call Me Madam, 1952; appeared on stage in: Guys and Dolls, Can-Can, Seventh Heaven, Mister Wonderful, West Side Story, Father's Day, Bye Bye Birdie, Three Penny Opera, Flower Drum Song, Zorba, Sweet Charity, Born Yesterday, Jacques Brel is Alive and Well and Living in Paris, Sondheim-A Musical Tribute, Kiss Me Kate, Ivanhoe, Chicago, Bring Back Birdie, 1981, Merlin, 1983, The Rink, 1984 (Tony award 1984), Jerry's Girls, 1985; performed in cabarets and nightclubs around world; starred in: film Sweet Charity, 1969; numerous TV appearances include The New Dick Van Dyke Show, 1973-74. Office: William Morris Agy 1350 Ave of Americas New York NY 10019

RIVERA, CHRISTINE RACHAEL, banker; b. Pocatello, Idaho, Aug. 30, 1953; d. Mike F. and Aurelia (Garcia) R.; student Idaho State U., Boise State U., Mundelein Coll., Chgo. With 1st Security Bank of Idaho, N.A., Boise, 1971—, beginning as clk., successively mgmt. trainee, teller, teller supr., ops. officer, affirmative action officer, 1971-81, installment loan officer, comml. loan officer, asst. br. mgr., 1981—. Bilingual edn. com. Students Econ. Edn. Assn.; student advisor Idaho Bus. Assn.; former pres. Idaho Assn. Affirmative Action; mem. Minority Bus. Devel. Assn., YWCA. Mem. Am. Inst. Banking, Nat. Assn. Bank Women (N.W. regional scholar). Democrat. Roman Catholic. Club: 300 Main St. Home: 162 Valleywood Dr Sun Valley ID Office: PO Box 2117 Ketchum ID 83340

RIVERA, NINA JEANNE, lawyer; b. Milw., Oct. 26, 1946; d. Walter Gustav and Norma Jane (Goode) Nauman; m. Roger Eli Parsons, June 19, 1967 (div. Jan. 1975); children—Lisa Shawn, Johanna Janta. m. Jose de Jesus Rivera, June 19, 1978; children—Martin Arturo, Mira Adelia. B.A. magna cum laude, Ariz. State U., 1976; J.D. with honors, Ariz. State U., 1979; student Occidental Coll., 1965-67. Bar: Ariz. 1979. Atty., SBA, Phoenix, 1979-82; spl. asst. U.S. Atty. U.S. Dept. Justice, Phoenix, 1982—; dist. counsel SBA, Phoenix, 1982—; mem. Insp. Gen.'s Adv. Council, 1981-82; mem. bankruptcy rules com. Ariz. State Bar, 1982-83. Contbg. author: ABA Bankruptcy Forms Manual, 1982; also articles. Recipient letter of commendation Pres. Reagan, 1982; Merit award SBA, 1981; Am. Jurisprudence award, 1979. Mem. ABA, Ariz. Bar Assn., Maricopa County Bar Assn., Ariz. Assn. Women Lawyers, ACLU. Democrat. Roman Catholic. Home: 5502 N 6th St Phoenix AZ 85012

RIVERS, BRENDA JOYCE, retail executive; b. Plant City, Fla., Oct. 27, 1949; d. Eddie Lee and Joan (White) R.; B.A. (Univ. scholar 1967-70), Fisk U., 1971; M. Urban and Regional Planning (R.F. Mellon fellow), U. Pitts., 1972. Program asst. Urban League Pitts., 1972-73; urban planner U. Miami Center Urban Studies, Coral Gables, Fla., 1974-75; planner, City of Miami, 1975-78; asst. project mgr. Polizzi Heery Constrn. Mgrs., Coral Gables, 1979-80; planner, coordinator Ferendino, Grafton, Spillis, Candela, Coral Gables, 1980-81; owner, mgr. Airport Ice Cream Shoppe, 1982—. Bd. dirs. Greater Miami Urban League, 1977-83, Community Action Agy. Dade County, 1978-83, Leadership Miami Alumni Assn., 1981-82, Dade Econ. and Employment Devel. Corp., 1982—, YWCA Greater Miami and Dade County, 1984—. Urban League fellow, 1973. Mem. Greater Miami C. of C. (leadership class 1980), Women's C. of C. (bd. dirs. 1984—), Am. Planning Assn., Delta Sigma Theta. Democrat. Clubs: Toastmistress, Ebony (pres. 1980-81). Home: 3420 Franklin Ave Miami FL 33133 Office: Miami Internat Airport PO Box 592873 Miami FL 33159

RIVERS, DENISE ZASOWSKI, state management specialist; b. Buffalo, N.Y., Feb. 6, 1953; d. Walter Bernard and Jean Rita (Sadaj) Zasowski; m. Charles Guy Rivers, Jr., Sept. 27, 1980. B.A., Daemen Coll., Amherst, N.Y., 1971-75; M.A. in Polit. Sci., SUNY-Buffalo, 1977, postgrad., 1976-78. Instr. environ. studies, SUNY, Buffalo, 1978; budget examiner State of N.Y., Albany, 1978-80, sr. budget analyst, 1980-83, mgmt. specialist, Buffalo, 1983—; ind. distbr. Shaklee Corp., Albany, 1980—; telemktg. rep. Monarch Fin. Services, Buffalo, 1984—. Auction vol. Sta. WNED-TV, Buffalo, 1973—; mem. Orchard Park Democratic Com., N.Y., 1984—. Kosciuszko Found. grantee, 1974-75. Mem. Polish Am. Hist. Assn., U.S. Jaycees, N.Y. State Jaycess (mgr. time dynamics individual devel. program 1985-86), Orchard Park Jaycees (bd. dirs. 1985, sec., 1985-86, recipient numerous awards), Pi Gamma Mu, Delta Epsilon Sigma. Democrat. Roman Catholic. Club: Fansfor 17 (Buffalo). Lodge: Polish Union of Am. (treas. white Eagles Youth div. 1976-77, sec. 1977-78, v.p. 1978, editor in chief newsletter 1976-78). Avocations: photography; latchooking. Home: 60 Shadow Ln Apt 7 Orchard Park NY 14127 Office: 500 Ellicott Sq Bldg Buffalo NY 14203

RIVERS, JOYCE MANSFIELD, lawyer; b. Fairbanks, Alaska, Aug. 30, 1935; d. Ralph Julian and Carol (Caldwell) Rivers; m. John Tracy Mansfield, Sept. 15, 1956 (div. Oct. 1974); children—Eugenie Mansfield Zgraggen, Ralph Douglas Mansfield. B.A., Brandeis U., 1958; J.D., U. of Pacific, 1977. Bar: Calif. 1977, Alaska, 1978. Sec., tech. writer asst. for various businesses and law firms, Fairbanks, 1950-58, Los Angeles, 1959-70, Sacramento, 1971-73; legal asst. to county counsel, Sacramento, 1973-77; asst. atty. gen. civil div. Office Atty. Gen. Alaska, Anchorage, 1978-79; corp. staff atty. Alascom, Inc., Anchorage, 1979-83, legal affairs specialist, 1984—, corp. sec., 1985—; assoc. atty. firm Hughes, Thorsness, Gantz, Powell & Brundin, Anchorage, 1983-84. State coordinator NOW, Alaska, 1980-82, sec., 1985—; chmn. ERA task force for Alaska, 1980-84; 1st v.p. Anchorage Area Democratic Council, 1982-84; mem. Spl. Citizens Com. Alaska Mini-Title IX, 1981-82; nat. del. for Alaska, White House Conf. on Families, 1980; mem. Anchorage Women's Commn., 1985—, Anchorage Sch. Dist. Sex Equity Adv. Com., 1985—. Mem. Anchorage Assn. Women Lawyers, Nat. Assn. Women Lawyers, NOW, Nat. Womens Polit. Caucus. Democrat. Home: 2741 W 42d Pl Anchorage AK 99517 Office: Alascom Inc PO Box 196607 Anchorage AK 99519-6607

RIVES, SUSAN RAE, insurance company executive; b. Amarillo, Tex., Nov. 30, 1944; d. Forrest A. and Rubie Tom (Jordan) Gibbs; m. Ray Gilbert Besing, Aug. 1975 (div. Dec. 1980); m. Jon Matthew Rives, Mar. 4, 1983; 1 child, Tiffany. B.A., San Angelo State Coll., 1967. Sec. Cooper Airmotive, Dallas, 1972-75; simulation services adminstr. Simuflite Tng. Co., Dallas, 1981-84; mgr. office services Legion Cos., Dallas, 1985—. Asst. White House Advance Staff, Dallas, 1979; mem. advance publicity staff John Hill Gubernatorial Campaign, Dallas, 1979; pres. Walker Middle Sch. PTA, Dallas, 1979-80. Mem. Nat. Assn. Female Execs. Democrat. Episcopalian. Office: Legion Companies 12700 Park Central Suite 1770 Dallas TX 75251

RIVETTE, MICHELE LYN, sales executive; b. Paw Paw, Mich., Sept. 18, 1961; d. Lynn Vincent and Anita Marie (St Pierre) R. B.A. in Advt., Mich. State U., 1983. Sales rep. Procter & Gamble Co., Cleve., 1983-85, dist. field rep., Detroit, 1985, unit sales mgr., Detroit, 1985—. Big Sister Detroit Big Brother-Big Sister Orgn., 1986. Mem. Nat. Assn. Female Execs., Mich. State U. Alumni Assn. Avocations: refinishing antiques, reading, travel. Office: Procter & Gamble Co 26935 Northwestern Hwy Suite 500 Southfield MI 48086

RIVLIN, ALICE MITCHELL, economist; b. Phila., Mar. 4, 1931; d. Allan C. G. and Georgianna (Fales) Mitchell; B.A., Bryn Mawr Coll., 1952; M.A., Radcliffe Coll., 1955, Ph.D., 1958; m. Lewis Allen Rivlin, 1955 (div. 1977); children—Catherine Amy, Allan Mitchell, Douglas Gray. Research fellow Brookings Instn., Washington, 1957-58, staff econ. studies div., 1958-66, sr. fellow, 1969-75; dir. Congl. Budget Office, 1975-83; dir. econ. studies Brookings Instn., Washington, 1983—; dep. asst. sec. program coordination HEW, Washington, 1966-68, asst. sec. planning and evaluation, 1968-69. Staff, Adv. Commn. on Inter-govtl. Relations, 1961-62. Mem. Am. Econ. Assn. (pres. 1985). Author: The Role of the Federal Government in Financing Higher Education, 1961; (with others) Microanalysis of Socioeconomic Systems, 1961; The U.S. Balance of Payments in 1968, 1963; Systematic Thinking and Social Action, 1971; (with others) Setting National Priorities: The 1974 Budget, 1973; Economic Choice 1987, pub. 1986. Editor: Economic Choices, 1984. Office: Brookings Instn 1775 Massachusetts Ave NW Washington DC 20036

RIZZO, MARY ANN FRANCES, international trade executive, former educator; b. Bryn Mawr, Pa., Jan. 11, 1942; d. Joseph Franklyn and Armella Louise (Grubenhoff) R.; B.A. magna cum laude (N.Y. State scholar), Marymount-Manhattan Coll., 1963; M.A. (fellow), Yale U., 1965, Ph.D. (Lounsbury-Cross fellow), 1969; grad. smaller co. mgmt. program Harvard U. Bus. Sch., 1979. Instr., Romance langs. and lit. Yale U., New Haven, 1966-70; asst. prof. Finch Coll., N.Y.C., 1971-73; v.p. Joseph F. Rizzo Co., Fla., 1969—; mem. bd. adv. Assn. Internat. des Etudiants en Sciences Economiques et Commerciales, Ariz. State U. Charter mem. bd. regents Catholic U. Am. Mem. Am. Assn. Tchrs. of Italian, MLA, Am. Assn. Univ. Profs. Italian, Am.-Italy Soc., Il Circolo Italian Cultural Club (Palm Beach, Fla.), Fgn. Trade Council Palm Beach County (charter mem.), Ariz. World Trade Council, Scottsdale C. of C., Alpha Chi. Republican. Roman Catholic (community council 1972-74). Clubs: Harvard Bus. Sch. Greater N.Y., Yale (N.Y.C. and Phoenix); Yale of Palm Beaches; Cercle Français de Palm Beach (Fla.): Ariz. Harvard Bus. Sch. Translator: From Time to Eternity, 1967; bibliographer: Italian Literature-Roots and Branches, 1976. Home: Villa Serein 2170 Ibis Isle Rd Palm Beach FL 33480 also 5665 N 74th Pl Scottsdale AZ 85253 Office: PO Box 1376 Lake Worth FL 33460 also 5111 N Scottsdale Rd Scottsdale AZ 85253

RIZZO, MARY CATHERINE, pension plan administrator; b. Milw., Apr. 17, 1943; d. John Henry and Catherine (Beyer) Conrad; m. Ronald Stephen Rizzo, Sept. 10, 1963; children—Ronald Stephen, Michael Robert. A.A., Pasadena City Coll., 1979; B.S., U. So. Calif., 1982. Treas., FMR Corp. (McDonalds), Orange, Calif., 1967-70; v.p., treas. RSR Inc., Los Angeles, 1980—; v.p. Atty.'s Pension Systems, La Canada, Calif., 1982—, chief fin. officer, 1985—. Mem. legal aid com. Lawyers Wives of Pasadena, Courthouse tour docent. Mem. Am. Mgmt. Assn., U. So. Calif. Acctg. Circle, Internat. Found. Employee Benefits, Beta Gamma Sigma. Home: 1101 Singingwood Dr Arcadia CA 91006 Office: Atty's Pension System Inc 4529 Angeles Crest Hwy La Canada CA 91011

RIZZO, TERRIE LORRAINE HEINRICH, aerobic fitness executive; b. Oneonta, N.Y., Dec. 15, 1946; d. Steven Joseph Heinrich and Grace Beatrice (Davis) Chamberlin; m. Michael Louis Rizzo, Dec. 28, 1968; 1 child, Matthew Michael. B.A., Pa. State U., 1968; M.A., Johns Hopkins U., 1971. Tchr. Balt. County Sch. System, 1968-79; asst. dir. univ. relations U. Md., Catonsville, 1980-81; exec. dir. Aerobic Danse de Belgique, Brussels, 1981—; pres. Eurobics Inc., Sunnyvale, Calif., 1984—; aerobics dir. Green Valley Health Clubs, San Jose, Calif., 1985; pres. Personally Fit, 1986; cons. Belgian Ministry Sport, Sabena Airlines, others. Author: Sittercise, 1985. Contbr. articles to profl. jours. Pres. Internat. Study Group, Brussels, 1983-84. Mem. Internat. Dance Exercise Assn., Assn. for Fitness in Bus., Aerobics and Fitness Assn. Am., Pa. State Alumni Assn. (bd. dirs. 1979-85), Brussels and Sunnyvale C. of C., Mensa, Pi Gamma Mu, Phi Alpha Theta. Democrat. Roman Catholic. Clubs: Am. Women's (Brussels) (dir. 1983-84); San Jose Quota. Avocations: travel; oenology; gourmet cooking. Home: 1503 Harrison Ct Sunnyvale CA 94087 Office: 108 E Fremont Ave Sunnyvale CA 94087

ROACH, KATHLEEN LOUISE, management analyst, auditor, consultant; b. Washington, Sept. 9, 1956; d. Carl Vincent and Violet Louise (Chandler) Flowers; m. Anthony Joseph Anastasi, Jan. 25, 1975 (div. Aug. 1979); 1 child, Anthony Lee Roach. Grad. Behavioral Mgmt., Frostburg State Coll., Md., 1974; postgrad. Montgomery Coll., Rockville, Md., 1975—. Budget analyst, bookkeeper Hydrographic/Topograchic Ctr. Def. Mapping Agy., Washington,

1977-79, personnel clk., 1977-80, personnel asst., 1980-82, personnel asst. Office of Distribution Services, 1982, computer programmer/analyst, 1982-84, mgmt. analyst Hydrographic/Topographic Ctr., 1984—, mem. affirmative action com., 1985—. Mem. Bd. Suprs. of Elections Montgomery County, Md., 1980—. Recipient numerous awards. Mem. Federally Employed Women (pres. 1985—), Am. Mgmt. Assn., Am. Soc. Mil. Comptrollers, Nat. Assn. Female Execs. Republican. Club VFW Ladies Aux. Avocation: hockey. Home: 3711 May St Wheaton MD 20906 Office: Def Mapping Agy Code: CMM Washington DC 20315

ROAKE, JILL, personnel executive; b. Portland, Oreg., Apr. 16, 1950; d. Robert F. and Jeannette (Pook) Roake. B.S. in Home Econs., Oreg. State U., 1972; postgrad. Portland State U., 1979—. Dept. mgr. Liberty House, San Francisco, 1973-74; field rep., asst. dist. mgr. Southland Corp., Dallas, 1974-77; sr. personnel adminstr. Evans Products, Portland, 1977-80; sr. compensation analyst Nerco Inc., Portland, 1980-82, corp. compensation adminstr., 1982-84, dir. benefits, 1984-85; mgr. compensation and benefits Wacker Sutronic Corp., 1985—; ski instr. Powder Hounds, Portland, 1976—; cons. in field Treas., bd. dirs. Tri County Affirmative Action Assn., Portland, 1978-86, mem. research bd., 1986—; study group com. City Club of Portland, 1982; bd. dirs. Portland Youth Philharmonic, 1983—. Am. Soc. Personnel Adminstrs., Am. Compensation Assn., Pacific N.W. Ski Instrs. Assn., Delta Delta Delta. Club: Jr. League Portland. Home: 12085 SW Settler Way Beaverton OR 97005

ROBB, LYNDA JOHNSON, writer; b. Washington, Mar. 19, 1944; d. Lyndon Baines and Claudia Alta (Taylor) Johnson; B.A. with honors, U. Tex., 1966; m. Charles Spittal Robb, Dec. 9, 1967; children—Lucinda Desha, Catherine Lewis, Jennifer Wickliffe. Writer, McCall's mag., 1966-68; contbg. editor Ladies Home Jour., 1968-80; lectr. Bd. dirs. Reading Is Fundamental, 1968—, Lyndon B. Johnson Family Found., 1969—; mem. Woodlawn Bd. Historic Trust; chmn. Pres.'s Adv. Com. for Women, 1979-81; chmn. Va. Women's Cultural History Project, 1982—; bd. dirs. Nat. Home Library Found.; chmn. Va. Women's Cultural History Project, 1982—; mem. So. Govs. Task Force on Infant Mortality; chair Va. Task Force on Infant Mortality. Mem. Zeta Tau Alpha. Democrat. Episcopalian. Office: 612 Chain Branch Rd McLean VA 22107

ROBBINS, ANN CAROTHERS, nursing consultant; b. Detroit, May 21, 1936; d. George Gregory and Pauline Elise (Tucker) Carothers; m. Theodore C. Robbins, Nov. 14, 1959; children—Susan Catherine, Karen Elizabeth, Thomas Charles. R.N., Norfolk Gen. Hosp., 1959; B.S.N., Tex. Woman's U., 1973, M.S.N., 1976. Supr. Woodlawn Hosp., Dallas, 1973-75; instr. Tex. Woman's U., Denton, 1975-79; cons. U. Tex. Health Scis. Ctr., Dallas, 1980-81; cons. Buckner Baptist Nursing Home, Dallas, 1982-83; asst. prof. Dallas Baptist Coll., 1981-83; dir. nurses Parkland Hosp., Dallas, 1983-85; cons., Dallas, 1980—; mem. disaster nursing team ARC, Dallas, 1981-82; mem. Tex. Nurses' Coalition for Action in Politics, Dallas, 1975—. Mem. Am. Nurses Assn., Tex. Nurses Assn. (treas. dist. 4, 1981-82, pres. 1983-84), Sigma Theta Tau. Republican. Methodist. Contbr. articles to profl. jours., chpts. to books. Office: 9809 Vistadale Dr Dallas TX 75238

ROBBINS, ANN TURNER, educational administrator; b. Athens, Ala., Aug. 23, 1940; d. Frank Patterson and Ora Lee (Rose) Turner; m. James Woodrow Robbins, Oct. 28, 1956; children—James Woodrow, Joseph Howell II. B.S. in Elem. Edn. cum laude, Samford U., 1969, M.S. in Elem. Edn., 1972; advanced degree in edn. leadership U. Ala.-Birmingham, 1978. Cert. tchr. grades 1-8, cert. ednl. adminstr. kindergarten-12, Ala. Tchr. Vestavia Elem. Sch., Ala., 1969-71; tchr. Pizitz Middle Sch., Vestavia, 1972-77, tchr., adminstrv. asst., 1977-78; prin. Edgewood Elem. Sch., Homewood, Ala., 1978—. Mem. Homewood Prins. Assn. (v.p. 1984-86), Ala. Assn. Elem. Sch. Prins. (dist. v.p. and pres.-elect 1986-88), Nat. Assn. Sch. Prins., Ala. Assn. Sch. Adminstrs., Assn. Supervision and Curriculum Devel., Women Educators Network, Montevallo In-Service Ctr. (adminstr. governing bd.), Ala. Council Computer Edn., Kappa Delta Pi. Republican. Baptist. Avocations: cooking; reading; physical fitness. Office: Edgewood Elem Sch 901 College Ave Homewood AL 35209

ROBBINS, BARBARA SCHWARTZ, insurance executive; b. N.Y.C., June 3, 1952; d. Sigmund and Miriam Schwartz; B.A., Herbert H. Lehman Coll., 1973. Group sales rep. Conn. Gen., N.Y.C., 1974-78; asst. v.p. The Kaye Group, 1978-82; asst. v.p. Robbins Orgn., N.Y.C., 1982—. C.L.U. Mem. Group Ins. Assn. (sec.-treas.). Office: 708 3d Ave New York NY 10017

ROBBINS, BETTY-JANE, publishing company executive; N.Y.C., Nov. 11, 1955; d. Jack Elliot and Marilyn Robbins; m. Robert Fields, June 26, 1983; 1 child, Jenna Kafe. B.A. magna cum laude U. Rochester, 1977; student U. Sussex, Eng., 1975-76. Publicity asst., media specialist Simon and Schuster, N.Y.C., 1977-79; publicist M. Evans and Co., N.Y.C., 1979-81; publicity mgr. Harcourt, Brace, Jovanovich, N.Y.C./San Diego, 1981-82, mktg. dir., San Diego, 1982-85, publicity dir., editor HBJ New York, 1985—; tchr. publicity and advt. U. Calif-San Diego. Recipient Susan W. Williams Meml. award U. Rochester, 1977. Mem. Pubs. Publicity Assn., Pubs. Ad Club, Phi Beta Kappa. Office: Harcourt Brace Jovanovich 111 Fifth Ave New York NY 10003

ROBBINS, CAREY ANGELYN MAY, nurse; b. Fayette, Ala., Feb. 24, 1952; d. Carey Milton and Billie Angelyn (Wilson) May; m. Berlin Jackson Robbins, Jr., June 5, 1980; 2 sons, Berlin Jackson, John Michael; 1 son by previous marriage, William Alan Potter. Student Athens Coll., 1970-72, B.S.N., U. Ala.-Birmingham, 1974. B.S. supr. Bryce Hosp., Tuscaloosa, Ala., 1974-75, 76-78, nurse recruiter, 1975-76; psychiat. charge nurse Huntsville Hosp. (Ala.), 1978-80, staff nurse emergency dept., flight nurse, 1980—. Mem. Huntsville Civic Ballet Assn., Huntsville Historic Soc. Served with Army Res. Mem. Am. Nurse Recruiters Assn. Republican. Baptist. Home: 6100 University Dr Huntsville AL 35806 Office: 2124 S Memorial Pkwy Huntsville AL 35801

ROBBINS, CARRIE F(ISHBEIN), theatrical, interior designer, costume design, educator; b. Balt., Feb. 7, 1943; d. Sidney W. and Bettye A. (Berman) Fishbein; m. Richard D. Robbins, Feb. 15, 1969. B.S. and B.A., Pa. State U., 1964; M.F.A., Yale Drama Sch., 1967. Costume designer Saturday Night Live, 1985-86, (2 Tony nominations), also 19 Broadway shows, N.Y.C., 1968—, San Francisco Opera, 1980, Opera Co. of Boston, 1975, 76, 86, Hamburg State Opera (W.Ger.), 1979, Washington Opera Soc., 1975, 4 shows N.Y. Shakespeare Festival, 10 shows Lincoln Ctr. Repertory V. Beamont Theatre, 3 shows Tyrone Guthrie Theatre, Mpls., 3 shows Mark Taper Forum, Los Angeles, 9 shows various regional theatres U.S., 7 shows Chelsea Theatre Ctr., Bklyn., 3 shows John Houseman's City Ctr. Acting Co., Juilliard Sch., N.Y.C., 5 shows sta. WNET and cable TV, 5 Off-Broadway Theatres, N.Y.C.; vis. guest lectr. on costume design U. Ill., UCLA, Oberlin Coll., others; master tchr. costume design NYU, 14 yrs. Solo exhibit art work, Central Falls Gallery, N.Y.C., 1980; participant group exhbns. Cooper Hewitt Mus., Pa. State U., Wright-Hepburn Gallery, N.Y.C., Scottsdale, Ariz., Central Falls Gallery, 1983; illustrations and calligraphy pub. annual calendar Soc. of Scribes competition, also Ms. mag.; work chosen to hang in juried show Salmagundi Club (Fine Arts Soc.), 1983, 84; original costume work photographed in books: Costume Design, 1983, Fabric Painting and Dyeing for the Theatre, 1982; original drawing reproduced Time-Life Series: The Ency. of Collectibles; designer loft conversions, comml. lobby space, studios, numerous others. Named Disting. Alumna, Pa. State U., 1979; recipient Drama Desk award, Am. Theatre Wing, N.Y.C., 1971, 72, Maharam award for design, Joseph Maharam Found., N.Y.C., 1975, Juror's Choice award for surface design, Fashion Inst. of Tech., 1980, Dramalogue Critics' award for Outstanding Achievement in Theatre, Los Angeles, 1982, Silver Medal, 6th Triennial of Theatre Design, Novisad, Yugoslavia, 1981. League N.Y. Theatres, N.Y.C., 1971-72, 73-74. Steering com. League Profl. Theatre Tng. Programs, 1977-84. Mem. Profl. Women in Theatre, Graphic Artists Guild, Soc. Scribes, Am. Soc. Interior Designers, United Scenic Artists Local 829. Home and Office: 11 W 30th St 15th Floor New York NY 10001

ROBBINS, JANE LEWIS, educator; b. New Iberia, La., Dec. 14, 1942; d. William Lewis and Maurine (James) R. B.S., U. Okla., 1965; M.E., So. Methodist U., 1971; postgrad. Tex. Women's U., 1981, 83, 85. Tchr., Lone Grove Ind. Sch. Dist. (Okla.), 1964-65, Concord-Carlisle (Mass.) Regional Sch. Dist., 1966-67, Newton (Mass.) Pub. Schs., 1967-68, Highland Park Ind. Sch. Dist., Dallas, 1968—; instr. reading clinic So. Meth. U., 1972-75, Sch. Edn., summer 1978, adj. prof. Div. Ednl. Studies; chmn. English dept. McCulloch Middle Sch.; coach coordinator Tex. Acad. Pentathlon, 1985, 86. Mem. Tex. Assn. Improvement Reading, Tex. Assn. Gifted and Talented, Assn. Children with Learning Disabilities, Internat. Reading Assn. (North Tex. Council), Tex. Middle Sch. Assn., Pi Beta Phi, Delta Kappa Gamma. Republican. Episcopalian.

ROBBINS, JANE TURNEY, banker; b. Santa Barbara, Calif., Apr. 27, 1943; d. Chauncey and Doris (Turney) R.; B.A., Duke U., 1965; M.A. (Univ. fellow), Yale U., 1970; postgrad. Taiwan Normal U., Taipei, 1972. China analyst Dept. State, Washington, 1970-71; mgr. Citibank, N.A., Internat. Banking Group, N.Y.C., Taiwan and Philippines, 1973-76; polit. risk ins. officer Overseas Pvt. Investment Corp., Washington, 1977-80; country officer Asian Devel. Bank, Manila, 1980-84; with Shannon and Luchs Co., Washington, 1986—. U.S. Govt. Title IV fellow, 1967-68. Mem. Mass. Soc. Mayflower Descs., NOW, Foster Parents Plan, Washington Assn. Realtors, Cum Laude Soc., Phi Beta Kappa, Kappa Alpha Theta. Republican. Episcopalian. Home: 2231 39th Pl NW Washington DC 20007

ROBBINS, JOAN RAFF, real estate executive; b. Newark; d. Morry and Florence (Lubin) Raff; m. Jay Howard Robbins, Apr. 15, 1961; children—Jonathan David, Jeffrey Michael, Joshua Benjamin. A.A. in Nursing, Fairleigh Dickinson U., 1960; grad. Realtors Inst. Md., 1980. R.N. Dir. nursing Bethesda-Silver Spring Nursing Ctr., Chevy Chase, Md., 1967-69; real estate sales Snider Bros., Inc., Potomac, Md., 1976-79; sales mgr. Lewis & Silverman, Potomac, 1980-81, Peck Properties, Potomac, 1981-83; broker of record, salesperson Joan Robbins Realty, Bethesda, Md., 1983—; lectr. sales incentive, mktg. techniques, 1977-84. Mem. Nat. Assn. Realtors, Md. Assn. Realtors, Realtors Nat. Mktg. Inst. (cert. real estate broker), Montgomery County Bd. Realtors (Top 1st Yr. licensee 1977, Million Dollar Sales Club 1979, profl. standards com. 1984—), Nat. Assn. Female Execs. Republican. Jewish. Avocations: swimming; reading; antique collecting; creative artwork/graphics. Home: 8209 Gainsborough Ct W Potomac MD 20854 Office: Joan Robbins Realty Inc 4835 Del Ray Ave Bethesda MD 20854

ROBBINS, KATHERINE KINGSLAND, television producer; b. Washington, Oct. 30, 1951; d. Edward Southward and Dorothy K. (Davis) Robbins. B.A., Washington U., St. Louis, 1973. Travel dir. Maritz Travel Co., St. Louis, 1974-77; writer/photographer Washington U. Sch. Medicine, St. Louis, 1977-79; exec. producer Sta. KTVI, St. Louis, 1979-82; TV producer Nat. Geog. Soc., Washington, 1983-84; pres. Kingsland Prodns., Inc., Washington, 1984—; prodn. coordinator films: The Sky's the Limit, 1983, Irving Johnson: High Seas Adventurer, 1983.; producer The Extra Mile, 1984. Mem. Jr. League Washington, Am. Women in Radio and TV, Women in Communications, Women in Film and Video. Bd. dirs. Recs. for the Blind, Inc., 1984—. Episcopalian. Office: Nat Geographic Soc 17th and M Sts NW Washington DC 20036

ROBBINS, PAULA ANN IVASKA, university dean; b. Teaneck, N.J., Dec. 13, 1935; d. Paavo Waldemar Topias and Anna Maria Margareta (Snellman) Ivaska; m. Michael D. Robbins, 1956 (div. 1968), children—Jeffery Paul, Matthew Llewellyn. Ph.D., U. Conn., 1977. Dir. student employment Radcliffe Coll., Cambridge, Mass., 1962-64; dir. career counseling Trinity Coll., Hartford, Conn., 1970-75; instructional design assoc. Hartford Grad. Ctr., 1975-77; edn. policy fellow Inst. Ednl. Leadership, George Washington U., Washington, 1977-78; assoc. dir. grad. studies Fitchburg State Coll. (Mass.), 1977-80; mgr. software tech. writing and documentation Computervision Corp., Bedford, Mass., 1981-82; postdoctoral fellow Finnish Ministry Edn., Helsinki, 1981; vis. lectr. U. Helsinki, 1982; asst. dean Grad. Sch., U. Lowell (Mass.), 1983—. Author: Successful Mid-Life Career Change, 1978. Chmn. Concord Democratic Town Com. (Mass.), 1970; del. Mass. Dem. Conv., 1970, 81, 82; mem. adv. bd. Concord-Carlisle Adult and Community Edn., 1980—. Mem. Phi Kappa Phi, Phi Delta Kappa. Office: Grad Sch U Lowell Lowell MA 01854

ROBBINS, RIMA, journalist, public relations consultant; b. N.Y.C., Apr. 3, 1934; d. Maurice and Ruth (Ackerman) Robbins; m. Michael John Greenberg, June 10, 1954; children—Peter A., John K., Karl P. B.A. in Lit., Fla. State U., M.A. in East Asian Studies; M.S. in Journalism, Boston U. Writer, editor Career Edn. Ctr., Fla. State U., Tallahassee, 1973-77, info. specialist Fla. Dept. State, Tallahassee, 1977-80; dep. dir. pub. info. Fla. Hosp. Cost Containment Bd., Tallahassee, 1980-81; tech. editor Planning Research Corp., Jacksonville, Fla., 1982-83; pub. relations coordinator St. Augustine Gen. Hosp. (Fla.), 1983; pres. The Shadow, St. Augustine, 1983—; adj. prof. English, Flagler Coll., St. Augustine, 1985-86. Contbr. articles to various newspapers, newsletter, book reviews. Legislative adminstr. LWV of Fla., Tallahassee, 1974-75; mem. Leon County Democratic Women's Club, Tallahassee, 1977-80. Mem. Soc. Tech. Communication, Inc., Fla. Pub. Relations Assn., Women in Communications, Inc. (coordinator, radio documentary sect. Clarion competition 1986), Am. Med. Writers Assn., Pub. Relations Soc. Am. Democrat. Home: Route 1 Box 112B Saint Augustine FL 32086

ROBBINS-CARTER, JANE BORSCH, library educator; b. Chgo., Sept. 13, 1939; d. Reuben August and Pearl Irene (Houk) Borsch; m. John M. Carter, Dec. 23, 1975; 1 dau., Molly Warren Robbins. B.A., Wells Coll., 1961; M.L.S., Western Mich. U., 1966; Ph.D., U. Md., 1972. Asst. prof. library and info. sci. U. Pitts., 1972-73; asso. prof. Emory U., Atlanta, 1973-74; cons. to the bd. Wyo. State Library, 1974-77; asso. prof. La. State U., Baton Rouge, 1977-79, dean, 1979-81; prof., dir. Sch. Library and Info. Studies, U. Wis., Madison, 1981—. Author: Public Library Policy and Citizen Participation, 1975, Public Librarianship: A Reader, 1982; contbr. numerous articles to profl. jours.; Editor: Library and Information Science Research, 1982—. Mem. ALA (councilor 1976-80), Am. Soc. Info. Sci., Assn. for Library and Info. Sci. Edn. (dir. 1979-81, pres. 1984), Wis. Library Assn. (pres. 1986). Democrat. Episcopalian. Address: Sch Library and Info Studies U Wis Madison WI 53706

ROBERGE, M. SHEILA, state senator. Mem. N.H. Senate, 1985—. Del., Republican Nat. Conv., 1980, Rep. nat. committeewoman from N.H. Office: NH State Capitol Bldg Concord NH 03301*

ROBERSON, EDITH PEGRAM, nurse; b. Forsyth County, N.C., Sept. 19, 1933; d. Arnold Wade and Annie Sue (Gravette) Pegram; R.N., City Meml. Hosp. Sch. Nursing, 1954; m. Charles E. Roberson, Sept. 6, 1957; children—Charles David, Robert Joseph. Staff nurse City Meml. Hosp., Winston-Salem, 1960-64; adminstrv. supr. Forsyth Meml. Hosp., 1964-66, clin. specialist, 1964-66, asst. dir. nursing, 1966-81, asso. dir. nursing, 1981—. Registered nurse, N.C. Mem. City Meml. Hosp. Alumni Assn., Forsyth County Heart Assn., Quill and Scroll. Democrat. Baptist. Club: NC. Farm Bur. Contbr. articles to profl. jours. Home: PO Box 1 Walkertown NC 27051 Office: 3333 Silas Creek Pkwy Winston Salem NC 27103

ROBERSON, ELIZABETH WILLOUGHBY, marketing research executive; b. Phila., Dec. 15, 1927; d. Jason Theodore and Elizabeth Bell (Sullivan) R.; student Columbia U., 1947-50. Research trainee Young & Rubicam Inc.; mgmt. cons. The Diebold Group; field dir. Market Facts, Inc., The NPD Group, Stockton & Ott, Inc., N.Y.C., 1979—. Elder, Fifth Avenue Presbyn. Ch. Mem. Market Research Assn. (President's award). Home: 52-40 39th Dr Woodside NY 11377 Office: The NPD Group 900 W Shore Rd Port Washington NY 11050

ROBERSON, FRANCES VIRGINIA, educational administrator; b. Townsend, Ga., Apr. 11, 1947; d. Harold Hampton and Virginia Dare (Ryals) Rozier; m. James William Howard, June 9. 1968 (div. 1974); 1 child, Virginia Frances; m. James Everett Roberson, Jan. 6, 1983; 1 child, Jordan; stepchildren—Mark, Miranda. B.S. in Home Econs., U. Ga., 1969, M.Ed., 1976, Ed.S., 1980, Ed.D., 1986. Tchr.-student asst. U. Ga., 1965-68; tchr. sci. Wayne County Jr. High Sch., Jesup, Ga., 1969-70; instr. St. Leo's Coll., Ft. Stewart, Ga., 1977; instr. home econs., dept. head Bradwell Inst., Hinesville, Ga., 1970-81; vocat. dir. Liberty County, Hinesville, 1981—; pres. bd. dirs. Family Housing Corp., Hinesville, 1983-85; dir., sec.-treas. Liberty Loan Co. Inc. Mem. South Eastern Vocat. Adminstrs. (bd. dirs. 1984-85, dir. innovative programs 1985-86), Ga. Assn. Secondary Vocat. Adminstrs. (charter; sec. 1985-86), Pvt. Industry Council, Hinesville C. of C., Ga. Vocat. Assn., Am. Vocat. Assn., Ga. Assn. Supervision and Curriculum Devel., Kappa Delta Pi, Phi Kappa Phi. Republican. Methodist. Clubs: Ga. Bulldog, Bradwell Boosters, Cherokee Rose Country. Home: 256 Topi Trail Hinesville GA 31313 Office: Bradwell Inst 100 Pafford St Hinesville GA 31313

ROBERSON, KIM ELIZABETH, nurse; b. Seattle, Sept. 20, 1955; d. Frank Tracey and Zetta Elizabeth (Jacobson) R. B.S. in Nursing, Seattle U., 1977. Commd. 2d lt., U.S. Army, 1977, advanced through grades to capt., 1980; asst. head nurse, Frankfurt-W.Ger., 1980-81, chief nurse Health Clinic, 1981-83, clin. staff nurse, San Francisco, 1983-85; ret., 1985; house supr. Seattle VA Med. Ctr., 1985—; mem. affiliate faculty Am. Heart Assn., San Francisco, 1984-85. Decorated Commendation medal. Mem. Nurses Orgn. of VA. Avocations: kayaking; study of wines, study of music; reading. Home: 8730 Wabash Ave S Seattle WA 98118 Office: Seattle VA Med Ctr 1660 S Columbian Way Seattle WA 98108

ROBERSON, SHIRLEY LOIS, nonprofit management executive; b. Worcester, Mass., Apr. 26, 1935; d. Paul T. Salmonsen and Ruth Mildred (Hofstra) Shimkus; m. William Virgil Roberson, June 20, 1961 (div. Nov. 1979); children—Kimberly, Marika. B.A. magna cum laude, Wheaton Coll., 1957; M. Edn., Worcester State U., 1960; postgrad. U. San Francisco. Tchr. Oxford Schs., Oxford, Mass., 1957-60, Army Dependent Schs., France, 1960-62, Laney Jr. Coll., Oakland, Calif., 1968-72; ptnr., cons. Roberson/Smit Assoc., Oakland, 1975-79; exec. dir. A Central Place, Oakland, 1977—. Pres., LWV, Oakland, 1973-75, conv. chmn., 1977; v.p. Community Devel. Commn., Oakland, 1976-78; program mem. Nonprofit Mgmt., San Francisco, 1980—; bd. dirs. YMCA, Oakland, 1981-84; pres. bd. The Support Ctr., San Francisco, 1985; elder Montclair Presbyn. Ch., Oakland, 1985—. U. San Francisco scholar, 1984. Mem. Devel. Execs. Roundtable, Nonprofit Mgmt. Group, Wheaton Alumnae (council 1980—). Club: Last Monday (council 1976—) (Oakland). Avocations: skiing; backpacking; traveling; house construction; drama; painting. Home: 44 Cortez Ct Oakland CA 94611 Office: A Central Place 477 15th St Oakland CA 94612

ROBERSTON-SMITH, MARY PATRICIA (PEIRCE) (MRS. JOHN A. SMITH), community college dean; b. Key West, Fla., Jan. 10, 1942; d. Robert P. and Jemeile (Seamon) Peirce; B.S. magna cum laude (Centennial Honor scholar), La. State U., 1963, M.S., 1964; M.Ed., Southeastern La. U., 1973; Ed.D., Rutgers U., 1982; m. John A. Smith; children—Stephanie Dawn, Debbie, Diane, John. Young adult librarian Enoch Pratt Free Library, Balt., 1964-65, adminstrv. asst., 1965-66; instr. Balt. Jr. Coll., 1966-67; library specialist and tchr. Ednl. Media Center, Covington, La., 1967-70; instr. NASA Miss. Test Facility, 1967-68; field librarian St. Tammany Parish Sch. Bd., Covington, 1967-70; chief librarian S.E. La. Hosp., Mandeville, 1970-73, coordinator adult edn., 1972-73; asst. prof. library and learning resources Bergen Community Coll., Paramus, N.J., 1973-79, assoc. prof., 1979-81, asst. dean instructional services, 1979-81, assoc. dean instructional services, 1981-82, dean instructional services, 1982—; tchr., cons. in reading, library work and spl. edn.; prodn. asso. CBS summer semester, 1974-75; mem. Gov.'s Com. Libraries; mem. acad. council Thomas A. Edison State Coll. Staff instr. 1st Army Instr. Tng. Sch., USAR, 1975, 76, 77. Trustee Bergen County Health and Welfare Council, treas. bd., 1986—; chmn. fin., bd. dirs. Sherbruke Co-op; state sec.-treas., v.p., pres. Acad. Offiers Assn. Mem. AAUW (v.p.), Mensa, Delta Kappa Gamma, Kappa Delta Pi, Mu Sigma Rho, Beta Phi Mu, Alpha Lambda Delta, Kappa Delta Pi, Tau Kappa Alpha. Contbg. editor: The Special Child, 1976. Home: 125 Prospect Ave Hackensack NJ 07601 Office: Bergen Community Coll 400 Paramus Rd Paramus NJ 07652

ROBERTS, BARBARA, state government official; b. Corvallis, Oreg., Dec. 21, 1936; d. Robert M. and Carmen L. (Murray) Hughey; m. Frank N. Sanders, Dec. 26, 1954 (div. 1972); children—Mike, Mark; m. Frank L. Roberts, June 29, 1974. Acctg. office mgr. various constrn. firms, Portland, Oreg., 1965-75; campaign dir. for candidate for atty. gen., Portland, 1975-76; commr. Multnomah County, 1978; mem. Oreg. Ho. of Reps., 1981-85, majority leader, 1983-84, mem. legis. adminstrn. com., 1983-84, legis. rules and ops. com., 1983, revenue and sch. fin. com., 1981-83, speaker's policy com., 1981-84; sec. of state State of Oreg., Salem, 1985—. Contbr. articles to jours. Mem., past chmn. Parkrose Sch. Bd., 1973-83; mem. Democratic Precinct Com., 1966-85, del. Nat. Dem. Convs., 1980, 84; bd. dirs. Edgefield Lodge, 1977-80, pres., 1979; bd. dirs. Mt. Hood Community Coll., 1978-82, chmn., 1979; chmn. East Multnomah County Youth Ctr. Com., 1979-80, Juvenile Services Commn. Multnomah County, 1979-82; trustee Woodland Park Hosp., Eastmoreland Hosp.; bd. dirs. Morrison Ctr., Nat. Com. for Prevention Child Abuse; mem. Mt. Hood Community Health Ctr. Recipient Civil Civil Liberties award ACLU, 1980, 81, Eagle award Mt. Hood Community Coll., 1981, Outstanding Service award Community Colls. Oreg. Students Assn., 1981, Pres.'s award Oreg. Speech and Hearing Assn., 1982, Founder's award Oreg. Grad. Sch. Psychology, 1982, Disting. Service award Oreg. Commn. for Handicapped, 1984. Mem. LWV, Oreg. Fair Share, Citizens for Children, 1000 Friends of Oreg., Oreg. Women's Polit. Caucus, Oreg. Environ. Council, Parry Ctr., Nat. Soc. Autistic Children, Oreg. Women in Ednl. Adminstrn., Oreg. Downtown Devel. Assn., Friends of Columbia Gorge. Office: 136 State Capitol Bldg Salem OR 97310

ROBERTS, BARBARA ANN, telephone company official; b. Milw., Feb. 21, 1929; d. Andrew Max and Ersilia (Celia) Gertrude (Comparoni) Maglio; student Milw. public schs.; m. Albert Lloyd Roberts, Sept. 3, 1949; children—Marybeth, Bradley J, David L. With Wis. Telephone Co., Milw., 1961—, now group mgr. operator services; v.p., sec. Sports Dome, Inc. Mem. Bus. and Profl. Women Milw. (pres. 1979-81), Wis. Bus. and Profl. Women (dist. dir. Eastern Dist. 8 1981-82). Home: 8411 W Cheyenne St Milwaukee WI 53224 Office: 2140 Davidson Rd Waukesha WI 53186

ROBERTS, BETTY, state supreme court justice; b. Arkansas City, Kans., Feb. 5, 1923; d. David Murray and Mary Pearl (Higgins) Cantrell; m. John W. Rice, Sept. 25, 1942 (div. Feb. 1960); children—Dian Odell, John Rice, Jo, Randall; m. Keith D. Skelton, June 15, 1968. B.S., Portland State U., 1958; M.S. in Polit. Sci., U. Oreg.-Eugene, 1962; J.D., Northwestern Sch. Law, Portland, 1966. Bar: Oreg. 1967. Tchr., Reynolds High Sch., Portland, 1958-60, Centennial High Sch., 1960-62, David Douglas High Sch., 1962-67, mem. Oreg. Ho. of reps., 1964-69; tchr. Mt. Hood Community Coll., Portland, 1967-76; ptnr. Skelton & Roberts, Portland, 1967-77; mem. Oreg. Senate, 1969-77; judge Oreg. Ct. Appeals, Salem, 1977-82; justice Supreme Ct. Oreg., Salem, 1982—. Author: (with Keith D. Skelton) Abortion and the Courts, 1971. Named Citizen of Yr., Oreg. Edn. Assn., 1975; Woman of Yr., Oreg. Women's Polit. Caucus, 1975; recipient Liberty award Oreg. Conf. Seventh-Day Adventists, 1976; Outstanding Citizen, U. Oreg., 1984. Mem. ABA, Oreg. Bar Assn., Multnomah Bar Assn., Nat. Assn. Women Judges, Oreg. Women's Polit. Caucus. Democrat. Office: Oreg Supreme Ct Supreme Court Bldg Salem OR 97310

ROBERTS, CAROL ANTONIA, mayor; b. June 22, 1936; m. Hyman J. Roberts, Aug. 9, 1953; children—David, Jonathan, Mark, Stephen, Scott, Pamela. Student Palm Beach Jr. Coll., Palm Beach Atlantic Coll., Tufts U., U. Fla. Commr., City of West Palm Beach, Fla., 1975—, vice mayor, 1976-77, 84-85, mayor, 1985—; co-founder pub./relations firm Denman, Roberts & Ross, 1978—; pres. Sunshine Acad. Press., Inc.; pres., broker VIP Mgmt. and Realty, Inc. Mem. Intergovtl. Relations Com., Task Force for Growth in Fla., Dist. 9 Mental Health Bd.; mem. exec. bd. Palm Beach County Mcpl. League; bd. dirs. Dist. 20 Mental Health Bd. Task Force; mem. Adv. Bd. Health and Rehab. Services; vice chmn. Met. Planning Orgn. of Palm Beach County, 1985; mem. pres.'s council U. Fla.; founder Jewish Community Day Sch. of Palm Beaches, 1974; bd. dirs. Palm Beach County Comprehensive Community Mental Health Ctr. Bd., Goodwill Industries, Jewish Fedn. of Palm Beach County; mem. Fla. Crime Prevention Commn., 1985. Named Woman of Yr. Bus. and Profl. Women of Palm Beaches, 1985, Sisterhood of Temple Beth El, 1986, Leading Lady in Mcpl. Govt., Network Connection, 1985; recipient appreciation award Tri-County Nat. Bus. League, 1985. Mem. Palm Beach County Med. Soc. Aux., Jewish Fedn. of Palm Beach County. Club: Zonta. Office: Office of Mayor Palm Beach FL 33407

ROBERTS, CELIA ANN, librarian; b. Bangor, Maine, Feb. 6, 1935; d. William Lewis and Ruey Pearl (Logan) R.; A.A., U. Hartford, 1957, B.A., 1961; postgrad. So. Conn. State Coll., 1963—. With catalog, acquistion and circulation depts. U. Hartford Library, 1956-65; librarian Simsbury (Conn.) Free Library, 1965; reference librarian Simsbury Public Library, 1969—. Tchr. ballet classes, 1965-66; ballet mistress Ballet Soc. Conn., Inc., 1968-70; with corps de ballet Conn. Opera Assn., 1963-64; active in prodns. Simsbury Light Opera Assn., 1964, 69. Mem. ALA, Conn. Library Assn., Simsbury Hist. Soc., Ont. Geneal. Soc., New Eng. Historic and Geneal. Soc., AAUW (past pres. Greater Hartford br.), Pro Dance, DAR (Abigail Phelps chpt.), Conn. Soc.

Genealogists, Soc. Mayflower Descs. Conn., Dance Masters Am. Universalist. Office: 725 Hopmeadow St Simsbury CT 06070

ROBERTS, CHRISTINE WYSMIERSKI, health care executive, health care design consultant; b. Chgo., Sept. 11, 1951; d. Chester Frank and Sophie (Nejman) Wysmierski; m. John Nathan Roberts, July 10, 1971 (div.). B.A. in English, U. Iowa, 1972. Group sales rep. Conn. Gen. Life Ins. Co., Boston, 1975-76; employee benefits cons. Alex and Alex, Boston, 1976-78; mgr. employee benefits Nixdorf Computer Co., Burlington, Mass., 1978-79; v.p. Nat. Med. Enterprises, Los Angeles, 1979-85; nat. dir. provider relations and adminstrn. Am. Med. Internat., Beverly Hills, Calif., 1985—; cons. employee benefits, Los Angeles, 1982—; guest speaker. Recipient cert. of achievement YWCA, Los Angeles, 1983. Mem. Hosp. Council So. Calif. (employee benefits com. 1982-83), Nat. Assn. Female Execs. Democrat. Office: Am Med Internat Inc 9665 Wilshire Blvd Beverly Hills CA 90010

ROBERTS, DORIS EMMA, epidemiologist, consultant; b. Toledo, Dec. 28, 1915; d. Frederic Constable and Emma Selina (Reader) R.; nursing diploma Peter Bent Brigham Sch. Nursing, Boston, 1938; B.S., Geneva Coll., Beaver Falls, Pa., 1944; M.P.H., U. Minn., 1958; Ph.D., U. N.C., 1967. Staff nurse Vis. Nurse Assn., New Haven, 1938-40; sr. nurse Neighborhood House, Millburn, N.J., 1942-45; supr. Tb Baltimore County Dept. Health, Towson, Md., 1945-46; Tb cons. Md. State Dept. Health, 1946-50; cons., chief nurse Tb program USPHS, Washington, 1950-57; cons. div. nursing USPHS, 1958-63; chief nursing practice br. Health Resources Adminstrn., HEW, Bethesda, Md., 1966-75; adj. prof. Sch. Pub. Health, U. N.C., 1975-84; cons. WHO, 1961-84, VA Health Professions Scholarship Program, 1982-85. Mem. Pub. Citizen, Inc. Served with USPHS, 1945-75. Recipient Disting. Alumna award Geneva Coll., 1971; Disting. Service award USPHS, 1971; Outstanding Achievement award U. Minn., 1983. Fellow Am. Pub. Health Assn. (v.p. 1978-79, Disting. Service award PHN sect., 1975, Sedgwick Meml. medal 1979); mem. Inst. Medicine of Nat. Acad. Scis., Common Cause, Delta Omega. Home: 6111 Kennedy Dr Chevy Chase MD 20815

ROBERTS, DOROTHY HYMAN, apparel company executive; b. N.Y.C., Dec. 6, 1928; d. Edgar C. and Theresa M. (Marks) Hyman; B.A., Conn. Coll., 1950; m. Paul M. Roberts, June 18, 1950 (dec.); children—Lynn, Steven; m. Paul M. Cohen. With Echo Design Group, Inc. (formerly Echo Scarfs, Inc.), N.Y.C., 1950—, pres., 1978—. Mem. The Fashion Group, Am. Mgmt. Assn. (trustee). Office: 10 E 40th St New York NY 10016

ROBERTS, EILEEN DORIS FRAHM, graphic designer, illustrator; b. N.Y.C., June 3, 1933; d. Walter Frederick and Gertrude May (Meyer) Frahm; m. Stanton Harvey Roberts, Jr., Sept. 13, 1953; children—Jodi Lynn, Stanton Harvey, Brent Walter. Student Pratt Inst., 1951-52, SUNY-Buffalo Coll. for Tchrs., 1952-54, Albright Art Sch., 1952-54, N.Y. Sch. Interior Design, 1965, Mira Costa Coll., 1971-73, Palomar Jr. Coll., 1979, U. Calif.-San Diego, 1984. Comml. artist Art Design Assocs., Mountainview, Calif., 1959-60; illustrator Ford Found., N.Y.C., 1964-65; craft coordinator Recreation Dept. City of Carlsbad, Calif., 1972; math. aide Oceanside Unified Sch. Dist., Calif., 1976-78; owner, artist Roberts Design Studio, Carlsbad, 1977—; art cons. gifted children Oceanside Pub. Schs., 1973-74. Designer, illustrator: Self-Hypnosis, A Guide To, 1983, May Centers Safety Book, 1983; painter: Misty (best of show award 1969); 1st woman contbr. to Combat Art Program USMC, Quantico, Va., 1967—. Arts and crafts assn. Prince William County Fair, Va., 1967-68; artist-in-residence Oceanside Bicentennial Com., 1975-76; chmn. Meet the Americans, Oceanside, 1975-76; mem. Invisable Univ., U. San Diego, 1984—, San Diego Art Inst. Mem. Nat. League Am. Pen Women, Nat. Assn. Female Execs., Artist Equity Assn., Book Publicists of San Diego. Avocations: hiking; bicycling; painting; jogging; cooking; reading. Home: 344 Leeward Ct Oceanside CA 92054 Office: Roberts Design PO Box 1261 Carlsbad CA 92008

ROBERTS, ELIZABETH H., podiatrist, author; b. Bklyn. m. Nathan Wasserheit (dec.); 1 dau., Judith N. Wasserheit. D. Podiatric Medicine, L.I. U., 1943. Pvt. practice podiatry, N.Y.C., 1943—; prof. emeritus, N.Y. Coll. Podiatric Medicine; established diabetic foot clinic N.Y. Infirmary, 1949; chairperson dept. regional anatomy, M.J. Lewi Coll. Podiatric Medicine, 1954-66, chairperson dept. practice adminstrn., 1945-51. Trustee N.Y. Coll. Podiatric Medicine. Author: Manual of Practice Administration, 1949; On Your Feet, 1975, put on cassettes for blind, 1977; contbr. articles to profl. publs. Fellow Am. Soc. Podiatric Medicine, Am. Acad. Podiatry, Am. Assn. Podiatry Adminstrn.; mem. N.Y. State Bd. Podiatry (chairperson 1979-81). Home: 210 W 90th St New York NY 10024 Office: 133 E 58th St New York NY 10022

ROBERTS, ERICA SUE, electronic data processing auditor; b. N.Y.C., Nov. 30, 1960; d. Joel S. and Rene (Farkas) Balsam; m. James J. F. Roberts, Nov. 28, 1982. B.A., NYU, 1981. Cert. info. system auditor. EDP auditing specialist Blue Cross-Blue Shield, N.Y.C., 1981; EDP auditor Dean Witter Reynolds, N.Y.C., 1982, Hazeltine Corp., Greenlawn, N.Y., 1983-84, L.I. Savs. Bank, Centereach, N.Y., 1984-85, NortonCo., Worcester, Mass., 1985—; EDP cons., Huntington, N.Y., 1982—. Mem., Harbor Heights Civic Assn., 1982—. N.Y. State Regents scholar, 1977. Mem. Securities Industry Assn. (rec. sec. 1982), EDP Auditors Assn., Nat. Assn. Female Execs., NYU Alumni Assn. Office: 1 New Bond St Worcester MA 01606

ROBERTS, EVELYN FREEMAN, composer, conductor, musician; b. Cleve., Feb. 13, 1919; d. Ernest A. and Gertrude (Richardson) Freeman; B.Mus., Cleve. Inst. Music, 1941; grad. student Calif. State U., Los Angeles, 1964-66, UCLA, U. So. Calif., 1967-70; m. Thomas S. Roberts; children—Anita, Ernest, Claire, Lisa. Tchr. music Karamu Ho., Cleve., 1937-40; performed Cafe Soc., N.Y.C., Town and Country, Club Elegante, Bklyn., Dunes Hotel, Las Vegas, Desert Inn Hotel Hilton, Las Vegas, Harrah's, Reno, Sahara-Tahoe; appeared in movies, including Toys in The Attic, A Clash of Cymbals, Choose Me; TV appearances include Jonathan Winters, Ed Sullivan shows, Andy Griffith Spl., Profiles in Courage, numerous local shows, spls.; staff arranger Leslie Uggams Show; spl. performance at White House, 1970; recorded albums; arranger for numerous rec. stars; co-founder, dir., program coordinator Young Saints Acad. Performing Arts and Skills, Los Angeles, 1971—. Bd. dirs. Calif. Confedn. of Arts. Recipient numerous commendations, citations, awards from civic orgns. Mem. Am. Soc. Composers and Pubs., Songwriters Guild, Am. Musicians Union (life). Methodist. Home and Office: 2000 Wellington Rd Los Angeles CA 90016

ROBERTS, GEORGIA LEE, real estate broker, developer; b. Houston, Dec. 27, 1925; d. George W. and Myrtle Lee (Gilliland) Faulkner; m. Grady Leon Roberts, Sept. 22, 1972 (div. 1981); 1 child, Pamela Lyn. Student Am. Coll. Real Estate, Bryan, Tex., 1981. Assoc., Roberts and Assocs., Madisonville, Tex., 1979-81, broker, 1981—; developer Madison Sq. Shopping Ctr., Madisonville. Avocations: horticulture; boating; fishing; interior decorating. Office: Roberts and Assocs Real Estate 1619 E Main St Madisonville TX 77864

ROBERTS, GERALDINE DUKES, mathematics educator; b. Smith County, Miss., Dec. 27, 1932; d. John B. and Ora B. (Arender) Dukes; m. M. Sam Roberts, Jan. 18, 1953; children—Steven S., Patricia Roberts Hudson, Teresa A. B.S., Miss. Coll., 1970, M.Ed., 1975; Ph.D., U. Miss., 1984. Cert. math. tchr. Music tchr. Sch. for Retarded, Jackson, Miss., 1965-70; math tchr. Council Schs., Jackson, 1970-73, Jackson Pub. Schs., 1973-79; pres., founder Roberts Rental, Inc., Jackson, 1983—; math. prof., acting chair dept. Belhaven Coll., Jackson, 1979—. Mem. Nat. Council Tchrs. of Math., Miss. Council Tchrs. of Math., Phi Delta Kappa, Delta Kappa Gamma (chpt. pres. 1981-83, chair music com. 1983-85). Lodge: Order Eastern Star (worthy matron 1970-71, grand organist 1984-85). Office: 1500 Peachtree St Jackson MS 39202

ROBERTS, HELEN LAURA, trade association executive; b. Pontiac, Mich., Jan. 11, 1916; d. D.J. and Laura I. (Skidmore) Hood; m. Lloyd Dale Roberts, May 27, 1937 (dec. 1960); children—Judith L. Roberts Seaman, Jacqueline G., Garrett L. B.S., Wayne U., 1936. Sec., Detroit, 1935-40; adminstrv. asst. AMI, Grand Rapids, Mich., 1945-53; exec. sec. Nat. Container Corp., Jacksonville, Fla., 1953-60; dir. sales Thunderbird Motel, Jacksonville, 1960-66, Am. Hotel, Atlanta, 1966-67; spl. catering rep. Atlanta Marriott, 1967-82; pres. Atlanta Women's C. of C., 1981-82; sec.-treas. Nat. Assn. Catering Execs., 1969-83, adminstr., 1983—. Mem. Atlanta Women's C. of C. (pres. 1981-82), Zeta Beta Chi (pres. 1972-73). Avocations: reading; bridge; knitting; cooking. Home and Office: 3008 Horseshoe Ct Orlando FL 32822

ROBERTS, HELEN PATRICIA, lawyer; b. Summit, N.J., Jan. 20, 1955; d. Thomas and Margaret R. (Martin) Walthier; m. William Louis Roberts, Aug. 7, 1980. B.S. in Nursing, U. Ariz., 1977, J.D., 1982. Bar: Ariz., 1982. Nurse intensive care unit Univ. Hosp., Tucson, 1977-78; nurse intensive care unit Tucson Gen. Hosp., 1978-79; law clk. Rabinovitz Dix & Rehling, Tucson, 1981, assoc., 1983—. Sec. Health and Environ. Law League, Tucson, 1981. Mem. Ariz. Bar Assn., ABA, Ariz. Women Lawyers Assn., Pima County Med. Soc. Aux., Sigma Theta Tau.

ROBERTS, HELEN WYVONE, city official; b. Kirksville, Mo., Jan. 9, 1934; d. William Lawrence and Lectie Beryl (Boley) Chitwood; m. Philip C. Roberts, Jan. 9, 1952 (div. 1976); children—Christy, Cheryl, Gayla. Secretarial degree Chillicothe Bus. Sch., 1951; B.S., Lindenwood Coll., 1983. Exec. sec. McDonnel-Douglas Aircraft, St. Louis, 1962-65, Transit Homes, Inc., Greenville, S.C., 1970-76; exec. sec. City of St. Peters, Mo., 1976-79, asst. planning and devel. coordinator, 1979-81, adminstrv. asst. to city adminstr., 1981-84, asst. to city adminstr., 85—, purchasing agt., 1984—. Mem. Nat. Assn. Female Execs., Internat. Cities Mgmt. Assn., Am. Pub. Works Assn., Am. Mgmt. Assn., Am. Bus. Women's Assn., Mo. Indsl. Devel. Council, Alpha Sigma Tau. Baptist. Avocations: horseback riding; sports; reading. Home: 329 Karen St Saint Charles MO 63301 Office: City of St Peters PO Box 9 Saint Peters MO 63376

ROBERTS, JAYNE KELLY, lawyer; b. N.Y.C., Sept. 30, 1948; d. William Frederick and Kathleen (Kelly) Mueller; m. Malcolm Jersome Roberts, Oct. 10, 1972; children—Chris, Karyn, Paul, Mark, Michael, Seth. B.A., U. Calif.-Berkeley, 1977; J.D., U. San Francisco, 1980. Bar: Calif. 1981, U.S. Dist. Ct. 1981. Assoc., Sandwick & Martin, Oakland, 1981; sole practice, San Francisco, 1981—. Bd. govs. Bard Coll., Annandale on Hudson, N.Y., 1982; bd. dirs. Presidio Hill Sch., San Francisco, 1983—. Mem. Am. Assn. Trial Lawyers, Calif. Assn. Trial Lawyers, San Francisco Assn. Trial Lawyers, Queen's Bench. Democrat. Office: 4 Embarcadero Center San Francisco CA 94111

ROBERTS, JEAN REED, lawyer, business executive; b. Washington, Dec. 19, 1939; d. Paul Allen and Esther (Kishter) Reed; m. Thomas Gene Roberts, Nov. 26, 1958; children—Amy, Rebecca, Nathanial. A.B. in Journalism, U. N.C., 1966; J.D., Ariz. State U., 1973. Bar: Ariz. 1974. Assoc. Bates and O'Steen, Phoenix, 1974-75; sole practice, Scottsdale, Ariz., 1975-84; founding ptnr. Simon, Reeves & Roberts, 1985—; legal dir., advisor to gov. Ariz.-Mex. Commn., 1980—; judge pro tem Superior Ct., Maricopa County, Ariz., 1979—. Editor: Scottsdale Bar Practice Manual, 1981. Sec. Charter 100 Phoenix, 1983-84; dir. Soroptimist Internat. Scottsdale, 1982—; judicial chair Ariz. Women's Polit. Caucus, 1981-83; adv. bd. Ariz. Displaced Homemakers, Phoenix, 1981-82; mem. Bd. of Adjustment, Town of Paradise Valley, 1984—. Mem. State Bar Ariz. (founder art law sect. 1979-81), Scottsdale Bar Assn. (dir. 1980-82), ABA (sec. com. mem.), Ariz. Women Lawyers (judicial chair 1982-83). Democrat. Jewish. Home: 6655 E Hummingbird Ln Paradise Valley AZ 85253 Office: Law Office Jean Reed Roberts Suite A-1 7110 E McDonald Dr Scottsdale AZ 85253

ROBERTS, JEANNE ADDISON, literature educator; b. Washington; d. John West and Sue Fisher (Nichols) Addison; m. Markley Roberts, Feb. 19, 1966; children—Addison Cary Steed Masengill, Ellen Carraway Masengill Coster. A.B., Agnes Scott Coll., 1946; M.A., U. Pa., 1947; Ph.D., U. Va., 1964. Instr. Mary Washington Coll., 1947-48; instr. chmn. English Fairfax Hall Jr. Coll., 1950-51; tchr. Am. U. Assn. Lang. Center, Bangkok, Thailand, 1952-56; instr. Beirut Coll. for Women, Lebanon, 1956-57, asst. prof., 1957-60, chmn. English dept., 1957-60; instr. lit. Am. U., Washington, 1960-62, asst. prof., 1962-65, assoc. prof., 1965-68, prof., 1968—, dean faculties, 1974; lectr. Howard U., 1971-72; seminar prof. Folger Shakespeare Library Inst. for Renaissance and 185h Century Studies, 1974; dir. Nat. Endowment Humanities Summer Inst. for High Sch. Tchrs. on Teaching Shakespeare, Folger Shakespeare Library, 1984, 85, 86. Author: Shakespeare's English Comedy: The Merry Wives of Windsor in Context, 1979; Editor: (with James G. McManaway) A Selective Bibliography of Shakespeare: Editions, Textual Studies, Commentary, 1975; contbr. articles to scholarly jours. Danforth Tchr. grantee, 1962-63; Folger Sr. fellow, 1969-70. Mem. MLA (chmn. Shakespeare div. 1981-82), Renaissance Soc. Am., Milton Soc., Shakespeare Assn. Am. (trustee 1978-81, pres. 1986-87), AAUP (pres. Am. U. chpt. 1966-67), Southeastern Renaissance Conf. (pres. 1981-82), Mortar Board, Phi Beta Kappa, Phi Kappa Phi. Episcopalian. Home: 4931 Albemarle St NW Washington DC 20016 Office: Dept Lit Am U Washington DC 20016

ROBERTS, JO CONWAY, marketing executive; b. San Francisco, Apr. 8, 1951; d. Russell John and Anna Josephine (Goodson) Conway; m. Dale Roberts, Feb. 25, 1978. B.A. in Bus. Adminstrn., Calif. State U., 1973. Cert. profl. ins. woman. Tour clk. Calif. State Auto Assn., Berkeley, 1970; fin. aid asst. Calif. State U., Chico, 1970-73; prodn. rep. Continental Ins., San Francisco, 1973-76; mktg. rep. Royal Ins., San Francisco, 1976-80, mktg. supt., 1980-83, mktg. coordinator, 1983—; instr. Xerox PSS, Royal Ins., 1974—; exec. dir. Royal PAC, N.Y.C., 1983—; lectr. in field. Compiler, editor: NAIW Legislative Program, 1982; contbr. articles to profl. jours. Mem. mem. Coalition to Stop the Canal, Concord, 1982; mem. ad hoc com. for campaign reform, Contra Costa County, 1983; bd. dirs. Alcoholism Council Contra Costa County, 1983. Named Young Career Woman, Mt. Diablo Bus. and Profl. Women, 1977, 80. Mem. Ins. Women of Contra Costa County (pres. 1982-83; Ins. Woman of Yr. 1982), East Bay Field Assn. (pres. 1979-80), Nat. Assn. Ins. Women, Oakland Ins. Forum (pres. 1980-81). Republican. Roman Catholic. Club: CAVE. Home: 1942 Maybelle Dr Pleasant Hill CA 94523 Office: Royal Ins 595 Market St San Francisco CA 94105

ROBERTS, JOSIE CALHOUN, med. technologist; b. Bryceland, La., Jan. 29, 1946; d. June Crawford and Zelda (Pecor) Calhoun; student La. Inst. Tech., 1964-66; B.S., So. State Coll., 1968; cert. Confederate Meml. Med. Center, 1968; m. George Hamilton Roberts, Aug. 13, 1966; children—Amy Michelle, Kelley Ruchelle, John Brandon. Phlebotomist, Confederate Meml. Med. Center, Shreveport, La., 1967-68; med. technologist Willis Knighton Hosp., Shreveport, 1968, Assoc. Pathologist Lab., El Dorado, Ark., 1969, U. Miss. Med. Center, 1970, Union Meml. Med. Center, El Dorado, 1971-75, Drs. Beauregard, Irwin, Daniels, Monroe, La., 1980-81; relief med. technologist Dr. Ed Brown, Monroe, 1980-82, St. Francis Med. Center, 1982—. Mem. Am. Soc. Med. Tech., La. Soc. Med. Tech., Lambda Tau. Democrat. Baptist. Home: Route 2 Box 257B West Monroe LA 71291

ROBERTS, JOY, controller; b. Kansas City, Mo., Dec. 12, 1928; d. William and Francis (Swanson) Woods; student St. Teresea's Coll., 1958, UCLA, 1975, 76, 78, 79; 1 dau., Paula. Media supr. Selders, Jones, Covington, Kansas City, Mo., 1958-60; acct. Barickman, Selders Advt., Kansas City, 1960-64; controller Sheldom Marks Assos., Los Angeles, 1965-70; gen. mgr., controller Foster, Gilbert, Rumar, Inc., Santa Monica, Calif., 1970-75; owner, mgr. Joy Assos., Advt., Los Angeles, 1975—; corp. controller Jenkins Covington Newman, Los Angeles, N.Y.C., 1977-82; fin. mgr. and bus. cons., 1982—. Mem. Women in Bus., Women in Communications, Women in Mgmt.

ROBERTS, JUDITH MARIE, librarian, educator; b. Bluefield, W.Va., Aug. 5, 1939; d. Charles Bowen and Frances Marie (Bourne) Lowder Alberts; m. Craig Currence Jackson, July 1, 1957 (div. 1962); 1 son, Craig, Jr.; m. 2d, Milton Rinehart Roberts, Aug. 13, 1966. B.S., Concord State Tchrs. Coll., 1965. Librarian, Cape Henlopen Sch. Dist., Lewes, Del., 1965—. Pres. Sussex Help Orgn. for Resources Exchange, Georgetown, Del., 1984-85, Friends of Lewes Pub. Library, 1986—; chmn. exhibits Gov. Conf. Libraries and Info. Services, Dover, Del., 1978. Mem. ALA, NEA, Del. State Edn. Assn., Cape Henlopen Edn. Assn., Del. Library Assn. (pres. 1982-83), Del. Learning Resources Assn. (pres. 1976-77). Methodist. Home: 42 DeVries Circle Lewes DE 19958 Office: Cape Henlopen High Sch Kings Hwy Lewes DE 19958

ROBERTS, KAREN KAY, real estate executive; b. Sunbury, Pa., Nov. 24, 1944; d. Thomas LaVerne and Anne Elizabeth (Hoover) R. B.S. in Journalism and Pub. Relations, Utica Coll., 1967; M.A. in Liberal Studies, SUNY-Stony Brook, 1972; M.A. in TV Communication, Christian Broadcasting Network U., 1983. Lic. Nat. Assn. Security Dealers, Pa.; lic. real estate agt., N.Y., Pa.; lic. ins. agt., Pa. Dir. continuity and traffic Sta. WRUN, 1967; elem. tchr., 1968-80; grad. coll. tutor, 1981-82; host TV talk show L.I. Insights, 1979; actress Sta. CBN-TV Another Life, 1981-83; anchorwoman, producer, 1982, asst. casting dir. commls., 1983; fin. cons. Equitable Fin. Services, Northumberland, Pa., 1984-85, trainer new cons.; mgr. Joseph Lincoln Ray Real Estate Agy., 1985—; real estate agt. and cons.; cons. pub. relations; researcher Christian drama; publicity chmn. Tri-County chpt. Am. Cancer Soc., 1985-86; lay speaker United Meth. Ch., 1981—. Author: (TV screen play) Quest For Love, 1983. Co-founder Tri-City Singles, co-chmn., 1984; mem. Sun-Contact phone ministry, charter, rep. speaker bur., 1984; vol. Sunbury Hosp. Sta. CBN grantee, 1983; CBN U. scholar, 1981-83. Mem. Christian Drama Assn. of Writers, NEA, N.Y. State Ret. Tchrs. Assn. Republican. Clubs: Sunbury Social, Shamokin Valley Country. Home: PO Box 301 204 Ninth Ave Shamokin Dam PA 17876

ROBERTS, KAREN RUTH, industrial engineer; b. Austin, Tex., Jan. 24, 1951; d. Roy Edward and Nellie Margaret (Asher) Butz; m. Michael Lee Roberts, Mar. 13, 1981; children—Chris Lee, Christi Renae, Craig Alan, Casey Michael. B.A., Ottawa U., 1973; M.S., U. Tex., 1978. Tchr. math. Meadowbrook Jr. High Sch., Shawnee Mission, Kans., 1973-76; research asst. Applied Research Labs., Austin, Tex., 1976-78; engr. Southwestern Pub. Service Co., Amarillo, Tex., 1978-81, supervisory engr., 1981-82, sr. engr., 1982—. Bd. dirs. YMCA Running Club, 1981-84, v.p., 1985-86. Recipient Presdl. scholarship Ottawa U., 1969-73. Mem. Ops. Research Soc. Am. Baptist. Home: 4220 Roxton St Amarillo TX 79109 Office: PO Box 1261 Amarillo TX 79170

ROBERTS, KATHERINE ANN, nursing educator; b. Beaumont, Tex., Nov. 6, 1952; d. William A. and Dorothy Lee (Hall) Wood; m. Gregory Lee Roberts, Jan. 4, 1974; children—Amanda Leigh, Matthew Joseph. B.S.N., U. Tex.-Houston, 1976; M.S.N., Tex. Women's U., 1981; student Lamar U., 1971-73. Registered nurse, Tex. Staff nurse M.D. Anderson Hosp., Houston, 1976, Women-Children's Hosp., Beaumont, Tex., 1976; nursing instr. Lamar U., Beaumont, 1976—. Tchr. Sun. Sch., First Ch. Nazarene, Beaumont, 1983-84. Mem. U. Tex. Alumni Assn., Nat. League Nursing, Am. Nurses Assn., Tex. Assn. Coll. Tchrs., Am. Cancer Soc., Am. Heart Assn., Sigma Theta Tau, Alpha Delta Pi. Office: Lamar Univ PO Box 10081 Beaumont TX 77710

ROBERTS, KATHLEEN JOY DOTY, educator; b. Jamaica, N.Y., Apr. 19, 1951; d. Alfred Arthur and Helen Caroline (Sohl) Doty; B.A. in Edn., Queens Coll., 1972, M.S. in Spl. Edn., 1974; cert. of advanced study in ednl. adminstrn. Hofstra U., 1982; m. Robert Louis Roberts, Nov. 24, 1974; children—Robert Louis, Michael Sean. Cert. in math., N.Y. State. Tchr. health conservation Woodside Jr. High Sch., 1973-77; coordinator spl edn. dept. Ridgewood Jr. High Sch., N.Y., 1977-81; resource room tchr. Grover Cleveland High Sch., Ridgewood, 1981—. Cert. N.Y. State Dept. Mental Hygiene; cert. N.Y. State sch. dist. adminstr., ednl. adminstr., ednl. supr., spl. edn. supr. Mem. NEA, N.Y. State Tchrs. Assn., Council for Exceptional Children, Soc. Mayflower Descs., Nat. Soc. Colonial Daus. of 17th Century (pres. 1985—), DAR, AAUW, Phi Delta Kappa. Republican. Baptist. Author: Closed Circuit Television and Other Devices for the Partially Sighted, 1971. Home: 52 Hicksville Rd Massapequa NY 11758 Office: 2127 Himrod St Ridgewood NY 11385

ROBERTS, LORI GAYE, soft drink marketing executive; b. Manitowoc, Wis., Nov. 9, 1955; d. Albert William and Betty Lou (Brunner) Benishek; m. Ronald W. Roberts, Dec. 1985. Student U. Wis., Madison, 1973-75; B.B.A., U. Wis.-Milw., 1977. Ter. sales mgr. Coca-Cola USA, Chgo., 1977-79, sales devel. mgr., Madison, 1979-80, asst. mgr. market planning, Atlanta, 1980-84, mgr. telemarketing and direct mail, 1981—; lectr. in field. Profl. women's fund raiser Atlanta Symphony Orch., 1984; youth edn. advisor Jr. Achievement, 1981-84; counselor Rape Crisis Ctr., Madison, 1974. Mem. Sales and Mktg. Execs. (exec. mem., dir.), Pi Sigma Epsilon (nat. dir.). Clubs: Coca Cola Running, Atlanta Travel. Home: 331 Wood Ridge Dr Atlanta GA 30339 Office: Coca-Cola USA PO Drawer 1734 Nat 19 Atlanta GA 30301

ROBERTS, LOUISE NISBET, philosopher; b. Lexington, Ky., Apr. 21, 1919; d. Benjamin and Helen L. Nisbet; A.B., U. Ky., 1942, M.A., 1944; Ph.D. (univ. scholar 1945-46, Delta Delta Delta fellow 1946-47, AAUW fellow 1947-48), Columbia U., 1952; m. Warren Roberts, June 14, 1952; children—Helen Ward, Valeria Lamar Roberts Emmett. Instr. philosophy Fairfax Hall, Waynesboro, Va., 1943-44, Fairmount Casements, Ormond Beach, Fla., 1944-45; mem. faculty Newcomb Coll., Tulane U., 1948—, prof. philosophy, 1969-85, prof. emeritus, 1985—, head dept., 1969. Mem. Am. Philos. Assn., Southwestern Philos. Soc., So. Soc. Philosophy and Psychology, Am. Soc. Aesthetics, AAUP (chpt. sec.-treas. 1966-68), Phi Beta Kappa (chpt. pres. 1956-57), Delta Delta Delta. Democrat. Episcopalian. Author articles in field. Office: Newcomb Coll 1229 Broadway New Orleans LA 70118

ROBERTS, MARGARET KOPLINSKI, building contractor, accountant; b. Plant City, Fla., Mar. 13, 1932; d. Larry J. and Pearl C. (Gouley) Koplinski; m. J. Frank Roberts, Jr., July 3, 1953; children—Lorrie Roberts Wheeler, Steven J. Cert. bldg. contractor, Fla. Acct. Logan Lumber Co., Tampa, Fla., 1962-65; controller PKS Constrn., Tampa, 1965-74; controller Creative Products, Tampa, 1974-83, asst. sec.-treas., 1975-83; sec.-treas. Bay Area Constrn., Inc., Tampa, 1979-84, pres., 1984—, also dir. Avocations: reading; crossword puzzles; travel; exercise; championship bowling. Office: Bay Area Constrn Inc PO Box 14176 Tampa FL 33690

ROBERTS, MARGOT MARKELS, business executive; b. Springfield, Mass., Jan. 20, 1945; d. Reuben and Marion (Markels) R.; children—Lauren B. Phillips, Debrah C. Herman. B.A., Boston U. Interior designer Louis Legum Furniture Co., Norfolk, Va., 1965-70; buyer, mgr. Danker Furniture, Rockville, Md., 1970-72; buyer W & J Sloane, Washington, 1972-74; pres. Bus. & Fin. Cons., Palm Beach, Fla., 1976-80, Margot M. Roberts & Assocs., Inc., Palm Beach, 1976—; v.p., dir. So. Textile Services Inc., Palm Beach. Pres. Brittany Condominium Assn., Palm Beach, 1983—; v.p. South Palm Beach Civic Assn., 1983—, South Palm Beach Pres.'s Assn., 1984—; vice chmn. South Palm Beach Planning Bd., 1983—. Mem. Nat. Assn. Women in Bus., Palm Beach C. of C. Republican. Jewish. Home: 3575 S Ocean Blvd Palm Beach FL 33480 Office: Margot M Roberts & Assocs Inc 230 Royal Palm Way Suite 211 Palm Beach FL 33480

ROBERTS, MARY BELLE, consulting social worker; b. Akron, Ohio, Sept. 27, 1923; d. Joseph Gill and Inez Wilson (Garvey) Roberts; B.S., U. Mich., 1948, M.S.W., 1950. Instr. dept. psychiatry U. Ala. Med. Coll., 1950-53; psychiat. social worker div. mental hygiene Ala. Dept. Pub. Health, 1950-52, acting dir., dir., 1952-53; sr. psychiat. social worker bur. mental health div. community service Pa. Dept. Welfare, 1954-55; cons. psychiat. social work community service br. NIMH, USPHS, HEW, 1955-64; pvt. practice psychiat. social work, 1964-68; caseworker Family Service, Miami, Fla., 1968-70, Family and Childrens Service, Miami, 1971-75; casework cons. United Family and Childrens Services, Miami, 1975-85, Family Counseling Services, Miami, 1985—. Cert. social worker, Md.; lic. clin. social worker, Fla. Home: 501 Valencia Ave #2 Coral Gables FL 33134 Office: 2190 NW 7th St Miami FL 33125

ROBERTS, MARY WENDY, state official; b. Champaign, Ill., Dec. 19, 1944; d. Frank and Mary C. R.; student (Nat. Def. Fgn. Lang. fellow) Chinese Japanese Inst., U. Colo., 1964; B.A. in Polit. Sci., U. Oreg., 1965; M.A., U. Wis., 1971; div.; 1 dau., Alexandra Louise McKay Prentice Bullock. Social worker Children's Services Div., 1967-71; counselor Juvenile Ct., 1971; mem. Oreg. Ho. of Reps., 1973-75; mem. Oreg. Senate, 1975-79; Oreg. Commr. Labor and Industries, 1979—. Mem. Democratic Nat. Com., del. nat. conv., 1980, 84, vice chmn. Oreg. del.; mem. Gov's Jobs Partnership Tng. Act Council, 1985—. Recipient Mary Rieke award, 1978; award for affirmative action and equal opportunity Nat. Am. Soc. Pub. Adminstrn., 1985. Mem. Portland Art Assn., Oreg. Hist. Soc., Nat. Assn. Govt. Labor Ofcls., Am. Council Young Polit. Leaders, Women Execs. in State Govt. Office: Bur Labor and Industries 1400 SW 5th Ave Portland OR 97201

ROBERTS, MYRNA PATRICIA, systems analyst, programmer, documentation specialist; b. Christiansted, St. Croix, V.I., Oct. 9, 1949; d. Paul Azariah and Cynthia Adaphnie Jane (Martin) James; m. Thomas Wilson Roberts, Sr., Dec. 29, 1973; children—Myrna Letecia, Cynthia Akita, Thomas Wilson, Jr. B.S. in Math., Morgan State Coll., Balt., 1972; M.A. in Math, Morgan State U., Balt., 1979. Cert. computer programming. Math. instr. N.Y. Pub. Schs., Bklyn., 1972, Balt. Pub. Schs., 1972-73. Prince Georges Pub. Schs., Prince Georges County, Md., 1973-74, D.C. Pub. Schs., Washington, 1974-80; analyst Computer Sci. Technicolor Assn., Seabrook, Md., 1980; systems analyst Vitro Corp., Silver Spring, Md., 1980—; proprietor, operator wedding cons. Myrna's House of Petals, Glenn Dale, Md., 1983, fashion designer Essence Unlimited, Glenn Dale, 1984; co-dir. Math Lab., Washington; income tax preparer,

1985—; real estate agt., 1985—. Campaign worker Democratic Party, New Carrollton, Md., 1976, Washington, 1984. Mem. Bus. and Profl. Woman So. Prince George's County, NAACP (Columbia, Md.), ACLU. Club: V.I. Advocate (membership com. 1984-85). Avocations: floral design, fashion design, sewing, party planning, travel. Home: 6900 Glenn Dale Rd PO Box 400 Glenn Dale MD 10769 Office: Vitro Corp 14000 Georgia Ave Silver Spring MD 20910

ROBERTS, NINA MARGHERITA, engineer's analyst; b. N.Y.C., Jan. 18, 1958; d. Michael Charles and Margaret Ethel (Barrett) Vuocolo; m. Terry Lee Roberts, May 26, 1984. A.A., Valencia Community Coll., 1977; B.B.A., U. Cen. Fla.-Orlando, 1979. Group sales mgr. Foley's Dept. Stores, Houston, 1979-81; engineer's analyst Ryder Scott Co., Houston, 1981—. Mem. Am. Mktg. Assn., Omicron Delta Kappa, Phi Theta Kappa. Republican. Methodist. Home: 2425 Holly Hall #E63 Houston TX 77054 Office: Ryder Scott Co 1100 Milam St Suite 3232 Houston TX 77001

ROBERTS, PATRICIA HENNECART, travel agent; b. Atlantic City, Apr. 13, 1922; d. Baron Charles Eduard and Ellen Dorothy (Bach) Hennecart; m. John Alexander Roberts, Sept. 5, 1942; 1 child, Antoinette Roberts Brewster. Student Cambridge U., 1938, Sorbonne, 1939. Travel agt. Travel Bur., Inc., N.Y.C., 1968-76; v.p. Fredrics Helton Travel, N.Y.C., 1976-83; pres. Frederics Helton Service Inc., N.Y.C., 1983—. Bd. dirs. Vis. Nurse Service N.Y.C., 1961-76, Internat. Social Service, N.Y.C., 1960-74; chmn. sponsors N.Y. Jr. League Ball, 1961. Named Fgn. Woman of Yr., Republic South Korea, 1959, Outstanding Vol. award Jr. League N.Y., 1962. Mem. Am. Soc. Travel Agts. Republican. Episcopalian. Club: Rockaway Hunting (Cedarhurst, N.Y.). Avocations: Travel; golf; theatre; books. Home: 75 East End Ave New York NY 10028 Office: Frederics Helton Travel 509 Madison Ave New York NY 10022

ROBERTS, PRISCILLA WARREN, painter; b. Glen Ridge, N.J., June 13, 1916; d. Charles Asaph and Florence Mary R.; student Art Students League, 1936-43, NAD, 1939-43. One-woman shows: Grand Central Art Galleries, N.Y.C., 1961, 81, Westmoreland County Mus., Pa., 1984, Canton Art Inst., Ohio, 1985; group shows include: NAD, N.Y.C., ann. 1945—, Carnegie Instn., Pitts., 1946, 47, 48, 49, Rutgers U., New Brunswick, N.J., 1982; represented in permanent collections: Met. Mus. Art, N.Y.C., Butler Inst., Youngstown, Ohio, Dallas Mus., Canton (Ohio) Art Inst., others. Mem. NAD, Catherine Lorillard Wolfe Assn. (hon.).

ROBERTS, RENEE, computer company executive, consultant; b. N.Y.C., Dec. 26, 1948; d. Jack and Celia (Kipnis) Cooper; m. Mark Usher Roberts, Sept. 20, 1974; 1 child, Gretchen. B.A., NYU, 1967; M.A. cum laude, Columbia U., 1970; postgrad. Boston U. Curriculum coordinator Kent Denver Sch., 1981-82; dir. jr. sch. Walnut Hill Sch., Natick, Mass., 1982-83; pres. Access To Computers, Inc., South Dennis, Mass., 1983—; cons. U.S. Coast Guard, Mashpee, Mass., 1985. Author: Backgammon for Beginners, 1981. Editor, contbg. author: Backgammon, 1979. Ford scholar NYU, 1965; univ. scholar Boston U., 1982. Office: Access To Computers Inc 44 Old County Rd Harwich Port MA 02646

ROBERTS, SALLY JOANN, relocation company executive; b. Terre Haute, Ind., Jan. 31, 1938; d. Frances Wayne and Berniece Ernestine (Scanlon) Hatfield; m. Ronald Leroy Roberts, June 8, 1957; children—Terri Lynn, Timothy Lee, Cynthia Ann, Christopher Allen. Student Ind. State U., 1955-57. Relocation mgr. Employee Transfer Corp., Chgo., 1977-79; mgmt. cons. C21 No. Ill. Region, Rosemont, 1979-80; v.p. Baird & Warner, Chgo., 1980-83; v.p., co-owner Profl. Relocation, Oak Brook, Ill., 1983-85; pres. Profl. Relocation, Bloomingdale, Ill., 1985—; bd. mem. I.C.R. Referral Network, Kansas City, Kans., 1981-83; mem. adv. bd. Am. Bound Pubs., Los Angeles, 1986—. Author: Homebuyers Guide, 1980, Relocation, 1981-85. Mem. Nat. Assn. Realtors (life mem. million dollar sales 1977, cons. Chgo. 1983-86), Employee Relocation Council (com. mem. 1981-85), Relocation Dirs. Council (com. mem. 1981-85), Chgo. Assn. Commerce and Industry. Republican. Lutheran. Avocations: sailing; golfing; bridge. Office: Profl Relocation Group 261 E Lake St Bloomingdale IL 60108

ROBERTS, SANDRA BROWN, realty company executive; b. Boston, May 26, 1939; d. Frederick Thomas and Christine (Peyton) Brown; m. Joseph Peter Roberts, Aug. 26, 1962 (div. May 1984); children—Christine, Joseph, Paul. B.A., Boston Coll., 1981. Lic. real estate broker, Mass. Owner, mgr. real estate, Wellesley, Mass., 1963—; pres. Riverview Realty, Wellesley, 1970—; comml. realtor, Boston, 1974—; cons. Berkshire Hathaway, New Bedford, Mass., 1983—. Founder, pres., bd. dirs. Friends of Ft. Washington; active Friends of Boston Ballet, 1983—; mem. Boston U. Woman's Council. Mem. New Eng. Women in Real Estate, DAR (Boston Tea Party chpt. regent 1983-84, 84—), Mass. DAR Ex-Regents Club, Navy League of U.S., New Eng. Hist. Geneal. Soc. Republican. Roman Catholic. Lodge: Order of Crown of Charlemagne (life mem.). Home: 52 Kenilworth Rd Wellesley MA 02181 Office: Riverview Realty 51 River Street Wellesley MA 02181

ROBERTS, SUSAN BROWNING, editor; b. Summit, N.J., May 27, 1941; d. Roland Browning and Geraldine Harper (Davidson) R.; A.B., Grinnell Coll., 1963; M.A., U. Idaho, 1982; m. Louis A. Hieb, June 8, 1963 (div. June 1975); children—Matthew Alan, John Andrew. Soc. news writer New Haven Register, 1963-64; asst. young adult and teen program dir. New Haven YM-YWCA, 1964-65; reporter, sch. editor The Princeton (N.J.) Packet, 1965-70; corr. Spokane (Wash.) Daily Chronicle, Pullman, 1974-75; editor Forest Wildlife and Range Expt. Sta. U. Idaho, Moscow, 1975-84; ext. publs. editor Wash. State U., 1984—; editorial adv. Jour. Interpretation, 1982-84. Bd. deacons First Presbyn. Ch., Moscow, 1980-82; den mother Lewis Clark council Boy Scouts Am., 1976-77, 81-83, awards chmn., 1977-79, sec.-treas., 1983-84. Mem. Agrl. Communicators in Edn. (awards for excellence 1979, 80), Am. Sociol. Assn. Democrat. Presbyterian. Office: 401 Hulbert Hall Agrl Info Wash State U Pullman WA 99164

ROBERTS, VIRGINIA CLAIRE, network and communications systems representative; b. Eden, Tex., Sept. 9, 1957; d. William Benjamin and Mary Virginia (Rodgers) Roberts. B.B.A. in Indsl. Mgmt., U. Tex., 1979; M.B.A., U. Houston at Clear Lake, 1981. Personnel intern Exxon Co. U.S.A., Houston, 1978; grad. asst. U. Houston at Clear Lake, 1980-81; controls engr. Brown & Root, Inc., Houston, 1981-84; systems rep. Comnet, Inc., Houston, 1984—. Vol. United Way Big Sisters Program, Houston, 1984; bd. dirs. Terra Condominiums Assn., Houston, 1984—. Grad. fellow U. Houston, 1981. Mem. Am. Bus. Women's Assn. (Hand award 1982, treas. 1983-84), Tex. Orgn. Profl. Sales Women, Soc. for Women Mgrs. (pres. 1980-81), Omicron Delta Kappa, Sigma Iota Epsilon, Phi Chi Theta, Beta Sigma Phi. Democrat. Home: 3100 Walnut Bend Ln # 202 Houston TX 77042

ROBERTSHAW, JANE, lawyer; b. Houston, Nov. 20, 1952; d. John Charles and Lois Caroline R. B.A. magna cum laude with distinction in Anthropology, Colo. Coll., 1974; J.D., U. Colo., 1980. Bar: N.Mex. 1980. Mem. Sutin, Thayer & Browne, Albuquerque, 1980—. Mem. ABA, Albuquerque Bar Assn., Phi Beta Kappa, Pi Gamma Mu, Alpha Lambda Delta. Office: Sutin Thayer & Browne PO Box 1945 Albuquerque NM 87103

ROBERTSON, CELESTE BERNARDINE, foreign service officer; b. Portsmouth, Va., Feb. 27, 1947; d. Eddie and Mildred Virginia (Harris) R.; m. John Kofi Abu, June 12, 1983; 1 child, Nichole Rochelle Robertson. B.A., Norfolk State U., 1971; M.Ed., Tex. So. U., 1973. Personnel mgmt. specialist Dept. Navy, Harrisburg, Pa., 1969-70; vol. Peace Corps, Ivory Coast, W. Africa, 1971-74; coordinator English Lang. Inst., Ivory Coast, 1974-77; internat. devel. specialist AID/Dept. State, Washington, 1979-82, asst. program officer, Niger, W. Africa, 1982-85, dep. program officer, Mali, W. Africa, 1985—. Publicity officer Internat. Women's Assn. Mali, 1986—. Recipient 10 Yr. Service award AID/Dept. State, 1985. Mem. Nat. Assn. Female Execs., Smithsonian Inst., Nat. Trust for Historic Preservation, Nat. Wildlife Preservation and Trust, Profl. Women of Mali Assn., NAACP. Democrat. Baptist. Avocations: gourmet cooking; reading. Office: USAID/BAMAKO (ID) Dept State Washington DC 20520

ROBERTSON, KAREN LEE, county administrator, acoustical consultant; b. Whittier, Calif., Mar. 21, 1955; d. Lethal Greenhaw Robertson and Lloydine Ann (Pierce) Robertson-Reese; 1 dau., Kimberlee Ann Kubski. Student Calif. State U. Acoustical technician Hilliard & Bricken, Santa Ana, Calif., 1977-79, John J. Van Houten, Anaheim, Calif., 1979; prin. Robertson & Assocs., Boulder, Colo., 1980; acoustical technician David Adams & Assocs., Denver, 1980; v.p. engring. John Hilliard & Assocs., Tustin, Calif., 1985—; acoustical specialist County of Orange, Santa Ana, 1980—. Co-author Land Use/Noise Compatibility Manual, 1984; editor Noise Element of General Plan, 1984. Speaker in field. Mem. Acoustical Soc. Am. (bd. dirs. 1985—), Transp. Research Bd. (tech. mem. 1985—), Nat. Assn. Noise Control Ofcls., Community/Indsl. Noise Control Assn., Inst. Noise Control Engring. (affiliate), Calif. Assn. Window Mfrs. (STC Task Group 1985). Republican. Home: 220 N Kodiak #B Anaheim CA 92807 Office: County of Orange-EMA/Regulation 12 Civic Center Plaza Santa Ana CA 92702-4048

ROBERTSON, MARY ELLA, ednl. adminstr., social worker; b. Lake Charles, La., Sept. 5, 1924; d. John and Mildred (Gardner) Robertson; B.A. summa cum laude, Xavier U., 1947; M.S.W., Atlanta U., 1949; advanced cert. in social work, Smith Coll., 1955; research fellow Adminstrv. Sci. Center, U. Pitts., 1959-60; D.Social Work, U. Pitts., 1962. Psychiat. social worker VA, Montrose, N.Y., 1949-53; supr. social services Family Service Assn., Ann Arbor, Mich., 1953-54; asst. prof. Case Western Res. U. Sch. Social Work, Cleve., 1955-57; exec. dir. Cleve. Guidance Center, 1957-59; asst. dean, asso. prof. U. Pitts. Grad. Sch. Social Work, 1962-66; vis. prof., asst. dean curriculum devel. U. Wis., Milw., 1966-67; dean, prof. Howard U. Sch. Social Work, Washington, 1967-69; prof. Boston Coll. Grad. Sch. Social Work, Chestnut Hill, Mass., 1969-72; prof. social service Ind. U.-Purdue U. at Indpls., 1972-74; v.p. for community services at Gov.'s State U., Park Forest South, Ill., 1974-77; prof. social policy Kent Sch. Social Work, U. Louisville, 1977—, dir. continuing edn. and community programs, 1977—; cons. social services various state and govt. agys.; dir. John Hancock Mut. Life Ins. Co. Mem. adminstrv. rev. panel child welfare policies Office of Children and Youth, Harrisburg, Pa., 1964-65; mem. com. on profl. edn. Comprehensive Mental Health Study Com. for Pa., 1964-66; mem. adv. com. to pres. Mt. Mercy Coll., Pitts., 1965-68; mem. adv. com. to sec. labor and industry Commonwealth of Pa., 1965-66; mem. adv. com. on population HEW, 1972-76; mem. adv. com. on youth employment U.S. Dept. Labor, 1978-80; mem. exchange groups in social welfare policy to Kenya, Somalia, Trinidad, People's Republic of China, 1978-81. Bd. dirs. Human Life Found., Washington, Parents and Childrens Services Children's Mission, Boston. Named Pitts. Woman of Year Mayor's Com. on Public Service, 1965; Outstanding Alumna, Atlanta U. Sch. Social Work, 1969; Dau. Commonwealth of Pa. Mem. Nat. Assn. Social Workers, Council on Social Work Edn. (past chmn. nat. com. on admissions, mem. dean's adv. com., mem. Ho. of Dels. 1967-70), Pitts. Commn. Cath. Charities (del. assembly), Kappa Gamma Pi, Alpha Kappa Mu. Contbr. articles to profl. jours. Home: 800 S 4th St Louisville KY 40203 Office: Kent Sch Social Work U Louisville Louisville KY 40208

ROBERTSON, SARAH GREENSHIELDS, banker; b. Easterhouse, Scotland, Oct. 30, 1930; came to U.S., 1954, naturalized, 1969; d. George and Mary Walker (Kirkwood) Greenshields; student U. Glasgow, 1947-49, Am. Inst. Banking, 1971-77, U. Wis., Madison, 1978-80; m. William Robertson, Dec. 26, 1952 (div.); children—William Duncan, Deborah May. Bookkeeper-teller Bank of Hinsdale (Ill.), 1969-71, note teller, 1971-73, bookkeeping supr., 1973-74, ops. supr., 1974, asst. cashier, 1974-77, asst. v.p., 1977, cashier, 1977-79, v.p., cashier, 1979—; pres. OPN. Bd. mem. PTA, 1968-69; vol. art appreciation instr. Hinsdale Grade Sch., 1963-66, library helper, 1965-67. Mem. Bank Adminstrn. Inst. (dir. pres. 1985-86), Chgo. Bank Women's Assn., Hinsdale C. of C. (bd. adv. 1982-84). Presbyterian. Club: Junior Women's (Hinsdale), Pachyderm West, Exec. Breakfast (Oakbrook, Ill.). Lodges: Katherine Legge Aux.; Daus. Brit. Empire in Ill. (3d v.p. 1986). Office: 400 E Ogden Ave Hinsdale IL 60521

ROBERTSON, THELMA OLIVE, county official; b. Hinsdale, Mont., Feb. 17, 1933; d. Henry Earl and Mary Christina (Meharry) Mix; m. Clare John Robertson, July 7, 1955; children—Roy Clare, Randy Earl, Rodney Ray. B.A., No Mont. Coll., 1971; M.E., U. Mont., 1981. Elem. tchr. Sch. Dist. 22, Ledger, Mont., 1953-54, Kremlin, Mont., 1954-55, Sch. Dist. 8, Kevin, Mont., 1960-62, Sch. Dist. 22, Ledger, 1962-63, Sch. Dist. 14, Shelby, Mont., 1964-77; supt. of schs. Toole County, Mont., 1978—; mem. Ednl. Excellence Forum, Mont. State U. Adv. Council on Tchr. Edn. Treas. Shelby Internat. Tng. in Communication, 1984; v.p. Toole County Democratic Women, 1984. Mem. Sch. Adminstrs. of Mont., Mont. Assn. County Supts. (sec. 1981-82, v.p. 1982-83, pres. 1984—), Delta Kappa Gamma (2d v.p.), Kappa Kappa Iota. Lutheran. Avocation: reading. Home: 1010 2d St N Shelby MT Office: Toole County Seat County Courthouse Shelby MT 59474

ROBEY, CARLA LEANN, horse breeder and shower; b. Chickasha, Okla., Aug. 6, 1952; d. James and JoAnn (Irwin) Watson; m. Bart Robey; 1 child, Bart Jay. B.S. summa cum laude, Okla. Coll. Liberal Arts, 1972; M.S., Kans. State U. Chemist Kerr-McGee Oil Co., Edmond, Okla., 1974-76; tchr. Oklahoma City, 1976-78; co-owner Bart Robey Quarter Horses, Purcell, Okla., 1974—. Named Outstanding Tchr. in Oklahoma City, 1978. Recipient many circuit awards for horses. Mem. Am. Quarter Horse Assn., Okla. Quarter Horse Assn. Home and Office: Bart Robey Quarter Horses PO Box 924 Purcell OK 73080

ROBEY, KATHLEEN MORAN (MRS. RALPH WEST ROBEY), club woman; b. Boston, Aug. 9, 1909; d. John Joseph and Katherine (Berrigan) Moran; B.A., Trinity Coll., Washington, 1933; m. Ralph West Robey, Jan. 28, 1941. Actress appearing in Pride and Prejudice, Broadway, 1935, Tomorrow is a Holiday, road co., 1935, Death Takes a Holiday, road co., 1936, Left Turn, Broadway, 1936, Come Home to Roost, Boston, 1936; pub. relations N.Y. Fashion Industry, N.Y.C., 1938-43. Mem. Florence Crittenton Home and Hosp., Women's Aux. Salvation Army, Gray Lady, ARC; mem. Seton Guild St. Ann's Infant Home. Mem. Christ Child Soc., Fedn. Republican Women of D.C. English-Speaking Union. Republican. Roman Catholic. Clubs: City Tavern, Cosmos (Washington), Nat. Woman's Republican. Home: 4000 Cathedral Ave NW Washington DC 20016

ROBICHAUD, PHYLLIS IVY ISABEL, artist, educator; b. Jamaica, West Indies, May 16, 1915; came to U.S., 1969, naturalized, 1977; d. Peter C. and Rose Matilda (Rickman) Burnett; grad. Tutorial Coll., 1933, Kingston, Jamaica, Munro Coll., St. Elizabeth, Jamaica, 1946; student Central Tech. Sch., Toronto, Ont., Can., 1960-63, Anderson Coll., Can., 1968-69; m. Roger Robichaud, July 22, 1961; children by previous marriage—George Wilmot Graham, William Henry Heron Graham, Mary Elizabeth Graham Watson, Peter Robert Burnett Graham. Sec. to supr. of Agr., St. Elizabeth, 1940-50; loans officer and cashier Confederation Life Assn., Kingston, 1950-53; tchr. art Jamaica Welfare Ltd., 1963; tchr. art recreation dept. New Port Richey, Fla., 1969-77; tchr. art Pasco Hernando Community Coll., New Port Richey, 1977—; propr., mgr. Band Box Dress Shop, Kingston, Jamaica, 1954-57; numerous one-woman shows of paintings including various banks, libraries, Kingston, 1963-64, 67, Toronto, 1968, New Port Richey, 1969, 70, 73, 76, Tampa, Fla., 1974, 75, 76, Omaha Cattle Company restaurant, Clearwater Fla., 1982; numerous group shows, latest being: Sweden House, Tampa, 1977-78, Chasco Fiesta, New Port Richey, 1977, Magnolia Valley Golf and Country Club, New Port Richey, 1978, W. Pasco Art Guild, New Port Richey, 1978, 79, other cities in Fla.; executed murals, New Port Richey and Kingston; represented in permanent collections: New Port Richey C. of C., Magnolia Valley Golf and Country Club, also pvt. collections. Patron, St. Alban's 4H Club, 1942; sec. Sunday sch. Ch. of Eng., Kingston, 1937-39. Recipient award T. Eaton Co. of Can., 1961, cert. of merit, Mayor of New Port Richey, 1976, appreciation award New Port Richey Recreation Dept., 1977; award Fla. Heart Fund. Mem. Nat. League Am. Pen Women (v.p. Tampa br. 1978-80, dir. 1969—), West Pasco Art Guild (Blue ribbons 1978, 79), Fla. Fine Arts Guild. Republican. Roman Catholic. Address: 1053 Lenox Circle New Port Richey FL 33552

ROBILLARD, FLORENCE, state senator. Former mem. Vt. Higher Edn. Planning Commn., Adv. Council on Comprehensive Health Edn.; mem. Vt. Senate, 1985—. Office: Vt State Captiol Bldg Montpelier VT 05602*

ROBINETTE, SHEREE, subcontractor; b. Tampa, Fla., Mar. 12, 1957; d. William J. and Patricia Ann (Gearhart) R. A.A., Hillsborough Community Coll., 1977; B.A.B.A., U. South Fla., 1980. Mgr., Fontaine Supply, Tampa, 1977-80; owner/mgr. Tampa Accessory Corp., 1980—. Mem. Nat. Assn. Women in Constrn., Nat. Assn. Profl. Estimators. Republican. Baptist. Avocations: ballet; swimming; cycling; collectibles. Office: 5700 Memorial Hwy Tampa FL 33615

ROBINS, CAROL LANGFORD, pediatrician; b. Chgo., July 20, 1940; d. Robert Erwin and Beatrice (Hall) Langford; B.A., Stanford U., 1962; M.D., U. Chgo., 1969; m. Arthur G. Robins, June 14, 1969; children—Sebastian, Jeremy. Pediatrician Roxbury Dental and Med. Group Boston, 1977-82; pediatrician Roxbury Comprehensive Community Health Ctr., 1984—; instr. psychiat. day hosp., Tufts U, Boston, 1979-81; instr. pediatrics New Eng. Sch. Acupuncture, Boston, 1981-82; herbal and acupuncture cons. Whole Health Assocs., Watertown, Mass., 1981-83; health book reviewer New Age mag. Den mother Boy Scouts Am.; tour leader, vol. Arnold Arboretum. May C. Willett fellow in child neurology, 1975-77. Diplomate Am. Bd. Pediatrics, Mem. Mass. Med. Soc., Mass. Acupuncture Soc., Fla. Native Plant Soc., Boston Mycological Club, Sierra Club, Audubon Soc., Friends of the Farlow. Mem. Assembly of God Ch. Author booklet: Aloe Vera Queen of Medicinal Plants, 1980. Office: ABM Acupuncture 385 Harvard St Brookline MA 02146

ROBINS, JUDY ROSELYN, interior designer, fine art consultant; b. Cleve., Sept. 2, 1948; d. Stanley and Esther (Resnick) Waxman; A.A.S., Fashion Inst. Tech., 1969; B.S., N.Y. U., 1970, M.A., 1972; m. Kenneth M. Robins, Sept. 26, 1971. Fabric coordinator Celanese Corp., N.Y.C. 1970-71; merchandiser Bayly Corp., Denver, 1973-74; free-lance interior designer, 1975—; instr. interior design Met. State Coll., Denver, 1977-81, Judy Robins Interiors, Inc., Denver, 1977—; dir. Waxman Industries. Mem. Young Womens Leadership Cabinet United Jewish Appeal, 1977-82; bd. dirs. Jewish Family and Childrens Service Colo., 1978-83, sec., 1981-82; v.p. Allied Jewish Fedn., 1981-84, chmn. Leadership Roundtable, exec. com., bd. dirs.; gen. campaign chmn. women's div. Allied Jewish Fedn., 1987; bd. dirs. Congregation B.M.H., 1981-83; bd. dirs. Am. Jewish Com., 1980-81; mem. women's bd. Nat. Jewish Hosp., 1978-80; steering com. Alliance for Contemporary Art; mem. collections com. Denver Art Mus., trustee, 1986—; mem. bd. Nat. Jewish Ctr. for Immunology and Respiratory Medicine, 1984—. Recipient Young Leadership award Allied Jewish Fedn., 1977. Democrat. Home and Office: 755 Lafayette St Denver CO 80218

ROBINS, MARJORIE MCCARTHY (MRS. GEORGE KENNETH ROBINS), civic worker; b. St. Louis, Oct. 4, 1914; d. Eugene Ross and Louise (Roblee) McCarthy; A.B., Vassar Coll., 1936; diploma St. Louis Sch. Occupational Therapy, 1940; m. George Kenneth Robins, Nov. 9, 1940; children—Carol Robins Von Arx, G. Stephen, Barbara A. Robins Foorman. Mem. Mo. Library Commn., 1937-38; mem. bd. St. Louis Jr. League, 1945, 46; mem. bd. Occupational Therapy Workshop of St. Louis, 1941-46, pres., 1945, 46; mem. bd. Ladue Chapel Nursery Sch., 1957-60, 61-64, pres. bd., 1963, 64; past regional chmn. United Fund; past mem. St. Louis Met. Youth Commn., St. Louis Health and Welfare Council; bd. dirs. Internat. Inst. of St. Louis, 1966-72, 76—82, 83—, sec., 1968, v.p., 1981; bd. dirs. Mental Health Assn. St. Louis, 1963-70, Washington U. Child Guidance and Evaluation Clinic, 1968-78; bd. dirs. Central Inst. for Deaf, 1970—, v.p., 1975-76, pres., 1976-78; bd. dirs. Met. St. Louis YWCA, 1954-63, 64-74, pres. bd., 1960-63, trustee, 1977—; mem. nat. bd. YWCA, 1967-79, nat. v.p., 1973-76; vol. tchr. remedial reading clinic St. Louis City Schs., 1968-71, trustee John Burroughs Sch., 1960-63, John Burroughs Found., 1965-80, Roblee Found., 1972—, Nat. YWCA Retirement Fund, 1979—; bd. dirs. Gambrill Gardens United Meth. Retirement Home, 1979-85, Thompson Retreat and Conf. Center, 1981—; bd. dirs. Springboard to Learning Inc., 1980—, v.p., 1980—. Mem. Archeol. Inst. Am. (bd. dirs., treas. St. Louis chpt. 1985—). Clubs: Vassar (sec. and pres. 1939-40), Wednesday (dir. 1968-70, 77-79, 80-81) (St. Louis). Home: 45 Loren Woods Saint Louis MO 63124

ROBINS, MIRIAM CLAIR, interior design consultant; b. Denver, Sept. 19, 1935; d. H. Rupard and Mildred L. (Opie) Robins; B.A., Colo. Coll., 1957; M.A., U. Denver, 1959. Instr. piano, organ, Denver, 1957-62; v.p., dir. Olinger Life Ins. Co., Denver, 1961-63, exec. v.p., dir., 1963-73, pres., dir., 1973-78, vice chmn. bd., 1978-85; v.p., dir. Robins Agy., Inc., Denver, 1963-85; cons. Cherry Creek Interiors, Denver, 1984—. Tchr., music arranger for talent competition Miss America, 1958. Vice pres. Colo. Life Conv., Denver, 1966-67. Mem. AAUW, Denver Art Mus., Kappa Delta Pi, Mu Phi Epsilon, Kappa Alpha Theta. Republican. Clubs: Denver, Denver Athletic, Garden of the Gods, Cherry Hills Country, Met. (U. Denver); Palmer Assocs., (Colo. Coll.) Home: Polo Club N 2552 E Alameda Ave 61 Denver CO 80209

ROBINS, NATALIE, writer, poet; b. Bound Brook, N.J., June 20, 1938; d. Louis and Mildred (Levy) R.; m. Christopher Charles Herbert Lehmann-Haupt, Oct. 3, 1963; children—Rachel, Noah. B.A., Mary Washington Coll., 1960. Mem. adj. faculty Grad. Sch., Bank Street Coll. Edn., N.Y.C., 1978—. Author: (poetry) Wild Lace, 1960; My Father Spoke of His Riches, 1966; The Peas Belong on the Eye Level, 1972; Eclipse, 1981; (with Steven M.L. Aronson) Savage Grace, 1985. Address: care ICM 40 W 57th St New York NY 10019

ROBINSON, AGNES CLAFLIN, civic worker; b. N.Y.C., Oct. 2, 1918; d. Crittenden Hull and Agnes Sanger (Claflin) Adams; student Radcliffe Coll., 1936-39; A.B., Barnard Coll., 1941; M.S., N.Y. U., 1949; m. Albert Lewis Robinson, (div.); children—Nicholas Adams, John Claflin, Hugh Wesley, James Allen, Lewis Stewart. Tech. asst. Bell Telephone Labs., Whippany, N.J., 1943-44; v.p. Family Service Assn., Morristown, N.J., 1946-48; bd. dirs. Adult and child Guidance Clinic, San Jose, Calif., 1955-58; v.p. Palo Alto Mental Health Soc., 1959-63; pres. PTA, Palo Alto, Calif., 1961-63; trustee Palo Alto Unified Sch. Dist., 1963-73, pres., 1965-67; chmn. Drug Abuse Bd., Palo Alto, 1971-74; mem. adv. bd. Nairobi Day Schs., East Palo Alto, 1969-72; mem. adv. bd. Child Care Now, 1972-73; mem. Calif. Post-Secondary Edn. Commn., 1974-80, chmn., 1978-80; advisor to pub. affairs com. YWCA, 1974—; mem. Mid-Peninsula Com. for Integrated Edn., 1974-80; bd. dirs. Addiction Research Found., 1974-78, pres., 1974-77; bd. dirs. Mid-Peninsula Learning Ctr. 1980-83; pres. New Ways to Work, 1976-79; mem. spl. legis. com. Calif. Student Fin. Aid Study Group, 1979; mem. Palo Alto Human Relations Commn., 1981-82; bd. govs. Calif. Community Colls., 1982—, pres., 1986-87. Mem. Sierra Club (life), NAACP (life), PTA (life). Democrat. Clubs: Radcliffe of Mid-Peninsula, Palo Alto. Author: (with Ruth McAneny Loud) New York, New York! A Knickerbocker Holiday for You and Your Children, 1946. Home: 1765 Fulton St Palo Alto CA 94303

ROBINSON, ANNE DURRUM, human resources development consultant; b. Hugo, Okla., May 14, 1913; d. William Landon and Effie Anne (Lear) Durrum; B.J., Tex. Women's U., 1935; M.A., U. Tex., 1960; m. Harold G. Robinson, June 6, 1945; 1 dau., Marye Lear. Staff writer NBC, Hollywood, Cal., 1945; continuity editor KTBC, Austin, 1942-44, KNOW Radio, Austin, 1946-49; KASE, hostess TV program Sta. KTBC-TV, Austin, 1955-56; editor Sta. KASE, Austin, 1959-61; hostess KLRN-TV, Austin, 1961-63, KHFI-TV, Austin, 1966-67; mng. editor jour., writer Travis County Med. Soc., Travis County Med. Soc. Blood Bank and Med. Exchange, Austin, 1961-63; free-lance writer, lectr., performer, tchr., 1968; copywriter, office mgr. David G. Benjamin, Inc., 1963-68; asst. dir. curriculum devel. Tex. Dept. Human Services, Austin, 1973-77, edn. dir. mgmt. tng. div., 1977-78; ind. cons. human resource devel., 1978—. Grantee research Women in Communications, Inc., 1959, 71, nat. one-act play prize Hermit Club, Cleve., 1947, 1948, three-act play prize Houston Little Theatre, 1947, song lyrics award Nat. Five Arts award, 1947, numerous poetry prizes. Mem. Women in Communications (chpt. pres. 1952, named Outstanding Woman in Continuing Edn., Austin chpt. 1977), Am. Soc. Tng. and Devel., Intergovtl. Tng. Council, Inst. Noetic Scis., World Future Soc., ESP Research Assocs. Found., Nat. Assn. Gifted Children, AAAS, Menninger Found., Tex. Public Employees Assn., Women's Symphony League, Center Positive Prayer. Author: Symphony for Simple Simon; Never the Twain Shall Eat. Home and Office: 2309 Shoal Creek Blvd Austin TX 78705

ROBINSON, BARBARA METZGER, management consultant; b. Summit, N.J., Feb. 11, 1945; d. Fred and Millicent (Stamler) Metzger; m. Sherman Robinson, Dec. 20, 1969; 1 child, Matthew Noble. B.A., Mt. Holyoke Coll., 1966; M.L.S., Simmons Coll., 1969; postgrad. Cath. U. Am., 1973, Rutgers U. Grad. Sch. Library Service, 1976. Prodn. asst. Sta. WGBH-TV, Boston, 1966-67; cons. children's Mus., Boston, summer 1969; librarian Runkle Sch., Brookline, 1969; editorial assoc. juvenile div. Puffin, Penguin Books, London, 1970-71; cons. Woodrow Wilson Sch., also Firestone Library, Princeton U., summer 1971; reference and young adult librarian Princeton Pub. Library (N.J.), 1971-73; cons. Devel. Adv. Service, Harvard U., summer 1972; dir. info. ctr. Pub. Tech., Inc., 1973-75; acting asst. librarian spl. projects Princeton U. Library, 1975-76; research assoc. Nat. Enquiry into Scholarly Communication, Princeton, 1976; cons. Machlup Info. Research, N.Y.C., 1976-77, NSF, Directorate Applied Sci. and Research Applications, 1977, Peat, Marwick,

Mitchell & Co., 1984-85; ind. cons. to small bus. and libraries, 1985—; exec. sec. Council Computerized Library Networks, Washington, 1979-80; chief of library programs Met. Washington Council of Govts., Washington, 1977-83; alt. from D.C., White House Conf. on Library and Info. Services, 1979; del. Mayor's Pre-White House Conf. on Libraries and Info. Services, 1978; advisor HEW Office of Libraries and Learning Resources, 1977-78, Research Library Adv. Group, Nat. Ctr. Edn. Stats., 1980, AID/NSF-Funded Egyptian Tng. Project, 1980-81, Ctr. Telecommunications Studies for George Washington U., 1983; participant in workshops. Contbr. articles to profl. jours. Recipient H.W. Wilson award, 1982; Carnegie Found. grantee, 1965. Mem. Calif. Library Assn., Spl. Libraries Assn. (rep. network adv. com. to Library of Congress 1982-84, mem. Task Force on Role of Spl. Libraries in Nationwide Network 1981-82), ALA (sect. chmn. 1981-82, program com. chmn. 1979-80, nominating com. 1979-80), Continuing Library Edn. Network and Exchange, Am. Soc. Info. Sci. (networking com. 1982-83), Women's Nat. Book Assn., Beta Phi Mu. Democrat. Home and office: 3009 Hillegass Ave Berkeley CA 94705

ROBINSON, BRENDA COOMBS, city official; b. Goldsboro, N.C., Dec. 16, 1947; d. Rhem Horace and Mary Kathleen (Davis) Coombs; student Meredith Coll. 1965-67; B.S. in Bus. Adminstrn. U. Central Fla. 1977, M.A. in Econs., 1979; children—Lisa Reed Donnan, Christopher Scott Donnan, Allison Ann Robinson. Grad. asst. U. Central Fla. 1978-79; sr. planner manpower div. County of Seminole, Fla. 1979, sr. budget and mgmt. analyst 1979-81; dir. fin. City of Altamonte Springs, Fla. 1981-83; mgmt. and budget ofcl. City of Orlando, Fla., 1983—. Recipient Orlando C. of C. Gold Telephone award 1976. Mem. Govtl. Fin. Officers Assn., Beta Gamma Sigma, Omicron Delta Kappa. Republican. Presbyterian. Home: 186 Monterey Isle South Longwood FL 32779 Office: 400 S Orange Ave Orlando FL 32801

ROBINSON, BRENDA PERRY, metals company executive; b. Richlands, Va., June 21, 1946; d. Joseph Franklin and Irene (Jessee) Perry; student public schs., Va. and Md., also various seminars; m. Walter Warren Robinson, Aug. 24, 1977; 1 dau. by previous marriage, Lori Kay White. File clk. Tabb Brockenborough & Ragland, Richmond, Va., 1963-64; acctg. clk. So. states R.H. Donnelley Co., Richmond, 1965; with Reynolds Metals Co., Richmond, 1966—, mgr. employee med. benefits, 1978-81, mgr. adminstrv. services, mgr. office systems implementation, 1981-84, mgr. office automation cons. and edn., 1981-86; pres. Innovative Resources, 1985—; v.p. sales Riddick Communications/MGI, 1986—; condr. seminars in field. Editor INNOVATA. Chmn. adv. council State of Va. Dept. Bus. Edn.; sec. Miss Softball Am., Richmond; co. rep. United Way, Richmond; substitute rep. Va. Nutrition Com.; project bus. cons. Jr. Achievement, 1985; mem. adv. com. Incubator Task Force, 1986, to Congressman Bliley, 1986. Named Boss of Yr., Am. Businesswomen's Assn., 1976. Mem. Adminstrv. Mgmt. Soc. (speakers' bur., chmn. edn. com.), Office Automation Roundtable, Va. Advanced Tech. Assn. (bd. dirs.), Richmond Office Automation Roundtable (sec.), Women's Network, Nat. Assn. Female Execs. Baptist. Home: 702 Sleepy Hollow Rd Richmond VA 23229 Office: 6601 W Broad St Richmond VA 23261

ROBINSON, CAROL LEE, librarian, teacher; b. New Rochelle, N.Y.; d. Richard and Dorothy (Clark) Word; m. Curtis Robinson, June 19, 1977 (dec.); children—Ujima, Zakiyyah. B.A., Northeastern U., 1976; postgrad. Prat Inst., 1981-82; M.L.S., Queens Coll., 1983. Library intern Library of Congress, Washington, 1973; mus. intern MIT Hist. Coll., Cambridge, 1974-76; library asst. Coopers & Lybrand, Washington, 1976-78; tchr. pub. schs., Washington, 1978-80; librarian trainee Mt. Vernon Library, N.Y., 1981-83, reference librarian, 1983—. Queens Coll. fellow, 1982-83. Mem. New York Black Librarians Caucus, Westchester Library Assn., ALA, Phi Alpha Theta. Club: Mt. Vernon Day Care. Office: Mount Vernon Pub Library 28 S 1st Ave Mount Vernon NY 10050

ROBINSON, CAROL SUSAN, advertising agency executive; b. Detroit, Oct. 28, 1938; d. Allen Lawrence and Sally (Cutler) R.; student Mich. State U., 1956-57; B.S., Boston U., 1960; student Soc. Arts and Crafts, Detroit, Calif. Coll. Arts and Crafts, Oakland, Otis Art Inst., Los Angeles; m. Richard Allen Clarke, Mar. 23, 1974; stepchildren—Richard, Janis Clarke Meldahl, William, Robert; 1 child, Kendall Elizabeth Robinson Clarke. Tchr. public schs., Sharon, Mass., 1960, Woodland Hills and Granda Hills, Calif., 1960-61; art buyer, exec. sec. Foote, Cone & Belding, Los Angeles, 1961-65; copy chief, continuity dir. KFOX, Long Beach, Calif., 1966-68; mgr. visual design Mattel, Inc., Los Angeles, 1968-75; pres. Seven Fleet St., Ltd., San Francisco, 1975-77; ptnr., v.p. King, Robinson & Clarke, San Francisco, 1978; pres., treas. bd. Robinson-Clarke, Inc., San Francisco, 1978—. Mem. Nat. Assn. Female Execs., NOW, San Francisco Art Comm., Los Angeles County Mus. Art, Oakland Art Mus., San Francisco Advt. Club. Office: Pier 9 San Francisco CA 94111

ROBINSON, CATHERINE L., government official; b. Titusville, Pa., Nov. 5, 1948; d. William A. and Frances (Zdarko) Lauer; m. James W. Robinson, May 25, 1968 (div. 1981); 1 child, Melissa C. Robinson. Student Jamestown Bus. Coll., N.Y., 1966-68, George Mason U., No. Va. Community Coll., 1972-73. Payroll clk. Cyclops Spl. Steel Co., Titusville, 1969-70; payroll specialist U.S. Dept. Navy, Washington, 1971-74; payroll liaison U.S. Dept. State, Washington, 1974-78; health liaison specialist HEW, Washington, 1978-79; grants specialist Dept. Edn., Washington, 1979-83; procurement analyst U.S. Marshals Service, McLean, Va., 1983—. Recipient Outstanding Performance award U.S. Dept. Edn., 1982; Outstanding Performance award U.S. Marshals Service, 1983; Outstanding Young Woman of Yr., 1983. Mem. Nat. Assn. Female Execs., Bus. and Profl. Women's Assn. Roman Catholic. Avocations: swimming; walking; sight seeing; travel. Home: 7700 Tremayne Pl Apt 301 McLean VA 22102 Office: US Marshals Service One Tysons Corner Ctr McLean VA 22102

ROBINSON, CHERYL ARLENE, accountant; b. Franklin, Tenn., Jan. 18, 1958; d. George Howard and Mary Frances (Matthews) Robinson. B.S. in Bus. Adminstrn. summa cum laude, Ala. A&M U., 1980; M.B.A. magna cum laude, Tex. So. U., 1984. Karate instr. Ala. A&M U., Normal, 1978-81, grad. asst., 1980; tax acct. Shell Oil Co., Houston, 1981-83; sr. acct. Sohio Petroleum Co. div. Standard Oil Ohio, Houston, 1983—. Acad. scholar Ala. A&M U., 1976-80. Mem. Assn. M.B.A. Execs., No. Shaolin Kung-Fu Assn. (asst. instr. Houston 1981—), Tang Soo Do Susik Assn. (Black Belt 1980, instr. Houston 1981—), Martial Arts Soc. (Acad. Black Belt 1977, instr. 1978—), Alpha Kappa Mu (scholar 1979-81), Delta Mu Delta (scholar 1980). Democrat. Baptist. Office: Sohio Petroleum Co PO Box 4587 5151 San Felipe St Houston TX 77210

ROBINSON, DEBRA ANN, marketing executive; b. Chgo., Sept. 27, 1957; d. Louis Harold and Irma Mildred (Weiner) Robinson. B.F.A., U. Ill., 1979; M.B.A., DePaul U., 1984. Promotion coordinator Success Mag., Chgo., 1979-82; assoc. account exec. Marcoa Direct Advt./BBDO Internat., Chgo., 1982-83; asst. mktg. mgr. Las Vegas MTI Vacations, Oak Brook, Ill., 1983—. Illustrator: Recreational Therapy Journal, 1978. Simon Litman scholar, 1978. Mem. Soc. Typog. Arts, Women in Design, Chgo. Assn. Direct Mktg. (3d prize award 1983), Direct Mail/Mktg. Assn. Jewish. Home: 671 W Wrightwood Chicago IL 60614 Office: MTI Vacations 1220 Kensington Oak Brook IL 60521

ROBINSON, EDITH BIRT, nursing administrator; b. Langley, S.C., June 30, 1940; d. Augustus and Julia (Brown) Birt; m. Levi Robinson, July 16, 1958 (div. 1967); children—Levi Robinson, Erwin Maurice. A.S., U. S.C.-Aiken, 1977. R.N. Sec. to prin. Jefferson High Sch., Bath, S.C., 1965-75; staff nurse Med. Coll. Ga.-Augusta, 1977-80; realtor Aiken (S.C.) Bd. Realtors, 1981—; staff nurse Univ. Hosp., Augusta, Ga., 1982—; R.N. supr. United Mchts., Clearwater, S.C., 1979—. Editor: Nursing Procedure Manual, 1983. Mem. U. S.C. Ednl. Found., 1983; com. leader Jacksonville Community Ctr./Park, Aiken, 1970-83; program coordinator Young Storm br. Baptist Ch., Langley, S.C., 1969-83. Mem. Am. Assn. Occupational Nurses, S.C. State Assn. Occupational Nurses, Nat. Bd. Realtors, Aiken Bd. Realtors. Democrat. Baptist. Club: Choir Club (past pres.). Home: PO Box 510 Huber Clay Rd Langley SC 29834 Office: United Mchts Inc Clearwater Plant Belvedere Rd Clearwater SC 29822

ROBINSON, ELAINE, lawyer; b. Schuykyll, Pa., Jan. 14, 1955; d. Neal Benjamin and Florence Elaine (Thomas) Robinson. B.A. in Journalism and Econs., Wichita State U., 1977; J.D., NYU, 1980. Bar: D.C. 1981. Assoc., Wald Harkrade & Ross, Washington, 1980-82; trial atty. Commodity Futures Trading Commn., Chgo., 1982—. Mem. ABA, Delta Sigma Theta. Office: Suite 4600 233 S Wacker Dr Chicago IL 60606

ROBINSON, ELEANOR GRACE, trucking company executive; b. Onalaska, Wis., Apr. 9, 1916; d. Howard T. and Mina C. (Christofferson) Kinney; m. Ellsworth M. Robinson, Nov. 30, 1939 (dec. Aug. 1974); children—Penny E. Robinson Silha, Paul M. B.S. in Elem. Edn., U. Wis.-LaCrosse, 1936. Tchr. Walker Sch., West Salem, Wis., 1936-37; prin. Elm Grove Sch., La Crosse, Wis., 1938-48; critic tchr. U. Wis.-La Crosse, 1937-50; mem. faculty rural-elem. dept. U. La Crosse, 1940-50; v.p. sec. Robinson Transfer, La Crosse, 1935-58; v.p., sec. Robinson Transfer Co. Inc., La Crosse, Wis., 1958-74, pres., 1974—. Bd. dirs. YWCA, La Crosse; moderator John Knox Presbytery, 1978-79, Synod of Lakes and Prairie, Presbyn. Ch., 1979-80, vice moderator gen. assembly, 1985, mem. nominating com., 1980-85, elder local ch., 1967—. Recipient Century Farm award State of Wis., 1978; Vol. in Mission award Presbyn. Ch., N.Y.C., 1978, 79, Wild Irish Rose award Shamrock Club of La Crosse, 1983. Mem. Am. Trucking Assn., Nat. Fedn. Ind. Bus., Contract and Common Carrier Conf., La Crosse Area Flyers (historian, La Crosse County Hist. Soc., Onalaska Hist. Soc. (life), La Crosse Archaeol. Soc., LWV (bd. dirs.), La Crosse Area Jazz Soc. Republican. Clubs: Fauver Hill Study (Onalaska, Wis.); Shamrock (treas. 1981-82, 85—, sec. 1983-84) (La Crosse). Home: 1923 N Kinney Coulee Onalaska WI 54650 Office: Robinson Transfer Co Inc 1809 St James St Box 25 La Crosse WI 54602

ROBINSON, ETHEL LUVENIA, air force officer; b. Chgo., Aug. 20, 1948; d. David Herman Sands and Dorothy (Boyd) Bailey; m. Clarence Jerome Robinson, Nov. 6, 1982. B.A., U. Md., 1970, M.L.S., 1971, M.A., 1975. Commd. 2d lt. U.S. Air Force, 1981, advanced through grades to capt., 1986; chief personnel utilization McGuire AFB, N.J., 1982-83; instructional analyst, Tinker AFB, Okla., 1983-85; career field mgr. Air Tng. Command, Randolph AFB, Tex., 1985—; arts specialist NEA, Washington, 1979-81. Editor reference books. Vol. mediator consumer div. Okla. Atty. Gen.'s Office, Oklahoma City, 1985. Mem. Nat. Soc. Performance and Instrn., Air Force Assn., Nat. Assn. Female Execs., Toastmasters, Tuskegee Airman Assn., Kappa Delta Pi. Avocations: antiques and collectibles. Home: PO Box 471 Randolph AFB TX 78148 Office: Hdqrs Air Tng Command Randolph AFB TX 78148

ROBINSON, GAY ELIZABETH CLARA, clergywoman; b. Stamford, Conn., Aug. 13, 1933; d. Theodore Alfred, Sr. and Elizabeth (Majher) Guilmette; student L.I.F.E. Coll., 1951-52; A.A., Orange Coast Coll., 1966; B.A., Calif. State U., 1968, M.A., 1970; postgrad., Golden State U., 1980—; m. Gary Garth Robinson, Feb. 3, 1952; children—Joy Leah Robinson Thornton, Clayton David. Asst. credit mgr. Phelps-Terkel, 1951-52; exec. adminstrv. asst. Pozzo Constrn. Co., 1952-53; ordained to ministry Internat. Ch. Foursquare Gospel, 1962; assoc. pastor Perris, Calif., 1955-58, SW Dist. Conf. rep., 1958-60, Worldwide Mission rep. 48 countries, 1965—; pastoral staff Ch. by the Sea, Huntington Beach, Calif., 1960—; founder Breath of Life, 1975; founder, dir. Dynamic Life Seminars; instr. Irvine Coll., 1976-78; SW dist. sec., 1960-78; broadcaster sta. KYMS, 1979—; tour dir., 1977—; participant exec. mgmt. seminars, 1976—. Mem. Republican Women's Nat. Com. Scholarship Chapman Floating Coll. of the Seas, 1966; scholar Pepperdine U., 1951-55. Mem. Nat. Assn. Evangelicals, Western Psychol. Assn., World Pentecostal Conf., United Foursquare Women (program chmn.), L.I.F.E. Alumni Assn. (past alumni sec.). Club: Temple City Jr. Women's (devotion leader, sec., 1957-60). Author: The Inner Woman, 1978; What is Your God Concept?, 1982; contbr. book revs., articles to publs. in field. Office: 715 Lake St Huntington Beach CA 92648

ROBINSON, GLADYS MABEL CHAMBERS (MRS. CARL TAPLEY ROBINSON), educator; b. New Orleans, Dec. 5, 1909; d. Oscar Louis and Susie Elizabeth (Lang) Chambers; A.B., Northwestern State Coll., 1929; M.S., U. Chgo., 1931, postgrad., 1947, 68; postgrad. Tulane U., 1932, Marine Biol. Lab., Woods Hole, Mass., 1938, U. Ill., 1955-57, Ill. Inst. Tech., 1964-65; D.Sc. (hon.), George Williams Coll., 1984. Asst. prof. biology Tougaloo (Miss.) Coll., 1931-41, U. Akron (Ohio), 1942-48; instr. George Williams Coll., Downers Grove, Ill., 1949-50, prof. biology, 1959-75, prof. emeritus, 1975—, dir. div. natural scis., 1965-73; instr. Cook County Sch. Nursing, Chgo., 1950-59. Recipient Golden Apple award for excellence in teaching, student body George Williams Coll., 1972. Ford Found. scholar, 1953, NSF scholar, 1964-65, 65, 68. Mem. Bot. Soc. Am., Am. Inst. Biol. Sci., Assn. Midwest Coll. Biology Tchrs., Ill. Acad. Sci., Nature Conservancy, Phi Sigma, Sigma Delta Epsilon. Democrat. Baptist. Gladys C. Robinson Marsh, George Williams Coll., named in her honor. Home: 7920 S Lafayette St Chicago IL 60620

ROBINSON, IDA CAMMON, nursing educator; b. Chgo., Feb. 11, 1920; d. Judge and Lee Ruth (Moses) Cammon; m. Lewis A. Robinson, Nov. 18, 1948; children—Lewis A. Jr., Beverley, Daoud Rasheed. Diploma Freedmen's Hosp. Sch. Nursing, Washington, 1945; B.S. in Nursing, Catholic U. of Am., 1948, M.S. in Nursing, 1958. R.N.; cert. phlebotomy technologist. Supr. surg. nursing Freedmen's Hosp., Washington, 1956-57, dir. in-service edn., 1959-60, dir. edn., 1963-73; dir. edn. and tng. Children's Hosp., Nat. Med. Ctr., Washington, 1973-81; edn. cons. The Pendleton Group, Washington, 1981—; dep. dir. edn. Nat. Phlebotomy Assn., Washington, 1982—; instr. ARC, Washington, 1963-73, Am. Heart Assn., Washington, 1963—; cons. Nat. League for Nursing, N.Y.C., 1967-70; adv. cons. D.C. Long Term Care Facility, Washington, 1982—; pres. D.C. Bd. Nurse Examiners, 1963-73; edn. cons. Am. Nurses Assn., Kansas City, Mo., 1974-79; nurse cons. AID, Washington, 1965, Fed. City Coll., Washington, 1967-70. Vol. D.C. Pub. Schs. Career Devel., 1970— (Apple award 1984). Recipient Alumni Leadership award Freemen's Hosp. Sch. Nursing Alumni, 1970, Community Service award Howard U., 1973, Outstanding Community Service award Black Nurses Assn., 1983, Gold Pin award for acad. excellence U. of D.C., 1981. Mem. D.C. Nurses Assn. (v.p. 1971-72, Outstanding Service award 1971), Nat. Phlebotomy Assn. (dep. dir. 1982—, Disting. Service award 1984), Chi Eta Phi (nurse recruitment chmn. 1963—, Community Service award 1975), The Medettes. Democrat. Presbyterian. Avocations: dramatics; writing; sewing; travel. Home: 325 Anacostia Ave NE Washington DC 20019 Office: Nat Phlebotomy Assn 1833 Monroe St NE Washington DC 20018

ROBINSON, JANET ANDREWS, development administrator; b. Salt Lake City, Aug. 17, 1935; d. James William and Katherine (Nichol) A.; m. George Thomas Heisel, Jan. 31, 1971 (div. Aug. 1979); children—Andrea Eileen, John Thomas; m. John Glass Robinson, Dec. 4, 1980. B.S., U. Utah, 1957. Adminstrv. asst. St. Luke's Hosp., Phoenix, 1963-66; manpower planner Health Council of Monroe County, Rochester, N.Y., 1966-67; dir. rev. Genesee Regional Health Planning Council, Rochester, 1969-73; dir. devel. Highland Hosp., Rochester, 1980—; treas. bd. Blue Shield Rochester, 1979—; chmn. Rochester Hosp. Services Bd., Rochester, 1983-85; v.p. Highland Hosp., Rochester, 1981-84. Author manuals. Mem. Nat. Soc. for Fund Raising Execs. (bd. dirs. 1983—). Republican. Roman Catholic. Club: Genesee Valley (Rochester). Avocations: squash; golf; tennis; music; art. Home: 69 Green Valley Rd Pittsford NY 14534 Office: Highland Hosp Found South at Bellevue Dr Rochester NY 14620

ROBINSON, JEAN RUTH, educator; b. Rockford, Ill., Dec. 9, 1925; d. Albert Eric and Eleanor Cora (Peterson) Anderson; B.A., Beloit Coll., 1947; M.A., Radcliffe Coll., 1952, Ph.D., 1953; m. Kenneth Leon Robinson, July 10, 1954; children—James Carl, Alan Eric. Lectr., Wells Coll., 1954-56; faculty Cornell U., Ithaca, N.Y., 1965—, lectr., sr. lectr., 1965-81, prof. consumer econs. and housing, 1981—, dept. chmn., 1981—; trustee Citizens Savs. Bank, 1983—. Trustee Village of Cayuga Heights, 1976-79, 80-84; bd. dirs. N.Y. State Council Econ. Edn. Lutheran. Office: 121 MVR Cornell Univ Coll Human Ecology Ithaca NY 14853

ROBINSON, JUDITH LYN, insurance brokerage executive; b. Charlottesville, Va., June 26, 1943; d. Jesse Montgomery and Averil (Kelley) R.; m. Stephen David Brodsky, May 19, 1971. C.P.C.U. Vice pres. Robinson & Robinson, Inc., N.Y.C., 1965-73, pres., 1973-78; treas. Silver Eureka Corp., N.Y.C., 1973-78; v.p. H & R Phillips, Inc., N.Y.C., 1978-83, pres., 1983—; chmn. N.Y. chpt. Jonathan Trumbull Council of Hartford Ins. Co., 1980—; mem. adv. council Atlantic Mut. Ins. Co., N.Y.C., 1984—; bd. dirs. Preventive Medicine Inst./Strong Clinic. Mem. Am. Soc. C.P.C.U.s, Ins. Soc. N.Y. Republican. Baptist. Home: 157 E 57th St New York NY 10022 Office: H & R Phillips Inc 622 3d Ave New York NY 10017

ROBINSON, JUDY LYNN, nurse; b. Houston, July 10, 1958; d. James Perry and Vera Inez (Blanton) R. B.S., Dillard U., 1980; M.S., Tex. So. U., 1984. Assoc. clin. nurse Park Plaza Hosp., Houston, 1979, clin. nurse, 1980-81; sch. nurse Codwell Elem. Sch., Houston, 1981—. Sponsor, instr. ARC, Houston, 1982-83. Mem. Chi Eta Phi (corr. sec. 1979), Alpha Kappa Alpha (antibasileus 1978). Baptist. Lodge: Courts of Calanthe. Home: 4619 Galesburg St Houston TX 77051 Office: Codwell Elem Sch 5225 Tavenor Houston TX 77048

ROBINSON, JULIE ANN, lawyer; b. Omaha, Jan. 14, 1957; d. Marvin Harold and Charlene Helen (Womack) Robinson. B.S. in Journalism, U. Kans., 1978; J.D., 1981 Bar: Kans. 1981, Mo. 1983. Law clk. Schnider, Shamberg & May, Fairway, Kans., 1981; law clk. to chief judge U.S. Bankruptcy Ct., Kansas City, Kans., 1981-83; asst. atty. U.S. Dept. Justice, Kansas City, 1983—. Reporter, writer U. Kans. Daily Kansas newspaper, 1977-78. Recipient Black Woman of Distinction award Yates br. YWCA, Kansas City, 1982. Mem. ABA, Kans. Bar. Assn., Am. Judicature Soc. (student leader award 1980), Phi Delta Phi, Delta Sigma Theta. Methodist. Office: 812 N 7th St Kansas City KS 66101

ROBINSON, KATHERINE PRENTIS WOODROOFE, editorial director; b. Detroit, Oct. 20, 1939; d. Robert William and Lindsay Prentis Woodroofe. B.A. magna cum laude, Smith Coll., Northampton, Mass., 1961. With Scholastic Mags., Inc., N.Y.C., 1961—; asst. editor Lit. Cavalcade Mag., 1963-64; assoc. editor, mng. editor Scholastic Scope Mag., 1965-67, editor, 1967-85, editorial dir. lang. arts mags., 1985—, also editor Scope Play Series, 1971, 75, 86, Scope Activity Kits, 1975, 76, 77, 78, 79. Home: 156 W 88th St New York NY 10024 Office: Scholastic Scope 730 Broadway New York NY 10003

ROBINSON, KATHLEEN MARIE, personnel executive; b. Milw., July 22, 1946; d. John Henry and Dorothy Ellen (Dunlavy) Robinson. B.S., U. Cin., 1968, M.A., 1970. Head resident U. Wis., Oshkosh, 1970-72, U. Tenn., Knoxville, 1972-73; asst. to dir. Opportunities Indsl. Ctr., Springfield, Ohio, 1975-78; EEO supr. Internat. Harvester, 1978-81; sr. personnel mgr., mgr. compensation and staff relations Citicorp., Denver and Phoenix, 1982-85, compensation and benefits analyst, St. Louis, 1985—. Bd. dirs. Springfield Urban League, Project Woman, Springfield. Mem. Am. Compensation Assn. (cert.), U. Cin. Alumni Assn., Alpha Chi Omega. Office: Citicorp 670 Mason Ridge Center Dr Saint Louis MO 63141

ROBINSON, LAURA A., realtor; b. Portland, Oreg., Dec. 13, 1919; d. James and Edith (Prensk) Ashrow; m. Edgar S. Robinson, June 25, 1920; children—Tamar, David. Student Reed Coll., 1938-40; B.A., U. Oreg., 1942; M.A., Columbia U., 1945. Personnel rep. U.S. Civil Service, Portland, then N.Y.C., 1940-44; asst. dir. speakers bur. United Jewish Appeal, N.Y.C., 1946-48; exec. dir. Hadassah med. sch. campaign Hebrew U., N.Y.C., 1948-52; realtor, owner Laura Robinson Real Estate, Washington, 1960—; cons. fair housing, Washington, 1964-70. Mem. Nat. Bd. Realtors, Washington Bd. Realtors. Democrat. Avocations: tennis; swimming. Home and office: 3512 Northampton St NW Washington DC 20015

ROBINSON, LEATRICE CRAIG, educational administrator; b. Cleve., Apr. 16, 1933; d. Lafayette Manual and Lula (Reed) Craig; B.S. in Edn., Bowling Green State U., 1955; m. Emerson Robinson, Sept. 1, 1956; 1 son, Jon. Service rep. Ohio Bell Telephone Co., Cleve., Dayton, 1951-61; tchr. Glenville High Sch., Cleve., 1961-67, Mumford High Sch., Detroit, 1967-79, head fgn. lang. dept., 1978-79; pres., exec. dir. dir. Robinson's Advantage Inst. for Children, Inc., Detroit, 1977—; co-founder Mach-Kit Shoppe. Pres., Pinehurst Block Club, 1969-81; active United Negro Coll. Fund dr., 1982; bd. dirs. Foster Grandparent Program. Recipient cert. of award for outstanding Bus. Achievement and Community Service Mich. Dept. Commerce. Mem. Black Econ. Trade Assn., Nat. Assn. Female Execs. NAACP, Nat. Black Child Devel. Inst., Nat. Assn. for Edn. Young Children, Mich. Assn. Child Care Adminstrs., Detroit-Wayne County Child Care Coordinating Council, Nat. Assn. Women Bus. Owners, Booker T. Washington Bus. Assn. (bd. dirs.), Alpha Kappa Alpha. Roman Catholic. Club: Thursday Luncheon Group. Office: 20503 Washburn St Detroit MI 48221

ROBINSON, LILIEN FILIPOVITCH, educator; b. Ljubljana, Yugoslavia, Feb. 7, 1940; d. Milenko and Branka Filipovitch; B.A. with distinction, George Washington U., 1962, M.A., 1965; Ph.D., Johns Hopkins U., 1978; m. David Robinson, June 8, 1974. Grad. teaching fellow George Washington U., 1962-64, lectr. in art history, 1964-65, asst. prof. art history, 1965-71, asso. prof., 1971-76, prof., 1979—, chmn. dept. art, 1976—. Mem. Coll. Art Assn. Am., Phi Beta Kappa, Omicron Delta Kappa, Delta Gamma. Serbian Orthodox. Office: Art Dept George Washington U Washington DC 20052

ROBINSON, LILLIAN ARBELL, insurance agency executive; b. Rome, Ga., Aug. 2, 1922; d. Malvin Roeser and Birdie Lee (Draper) Brown; m. Glen G. Robinson, Mar. 3, 1942; children—Glenda Lee Robinson Stanley, Robert Gary. Student Gregg Bus. Coll., Phoenix, 1940-41, Ins. Inst. Am., Phoenix, 1978-83, Soc. Cert. Ins. Counselor, Tempe, Ariz. 1981. Acct. Thunderbird Flight Sch. Glendale, Ariz., 1941-42; co-owner Glenzona Ins., Glendale, 1960-80, office mgr., 1975-80, owner, mgr., 1980—; co-dir., owner H & R Assocs. Investments, Glendale, 1947—; co-owner, bd. dirs. Lake Mary Park Investments, 1960—. Pres. Women's Soc. Bethany Bible, Phoenix, 1960-65; bd. dirs. Camelback Girls Residence Aux., Phoenix, 1970-71. Mem. Kachina West Ins. Women, Nat. Assn. Ins. Women (cert. profl. ins. woman). Republican. Office: Glenzona Ins 5751 W Glendale Ave Glendale AZ 85301

ROBINSON, LINDA ROGERS, hospital executive; b. New Hebron, Miss., Jan. 5, 1941; d. Hardye Monroe and Juanita Theresa (Lee) Rogers; m. George Edward Robinson, June 2, 1961 (div. Sept. 1979); children—Tenley, Sydney Anne, Joy Theresa. Student, Jackson Comml. Coll., 1959, Houston Community Coll., 1983. Vice pres. Robinson Oil Equipment Co., Jackson, Miss., 1967-78, pres., 1979-81; mktg. asst. Sam Houston Meml. Hosp., Houston, 1982-83, mktg. dir., 1983-85; mktg. dir. Pasadena Gen. Hosp., Tex., 1985—. Mem. Am. Mktg. Assn., Nat. Assn. Female Execs., Tex. Soc. Hosp.d Pub. Realtions and Mktg. Baptist. Home: 6000 Reims Apt 3606 Houston TX 77036 Office: Pasadena Gen Hosp 1004 Seymour Pasadena TX 77506

ROBINSON, LOIS HART, public relations executive; b. Freeport, Ill., Aug. 9, 1927; d. Seril N. and Cora (Stabenow) Hart; m. Noel M. Henze, Nov. 15, 1947 (div. 1964); m. Jack Fay Robinson, July 16, 1968; children—Susan Henze Bentley, Cynthia Henze Berkeley, Charles Henze. Student Oakton Community Coll., 1976-77, Northwestern U., 1977-81. Med. sec. Freeport Meml. Hosp., 1945-47; sec. No. Ill. Corp., 1947-49; adminstrv. asst. to supt. schs. Community Sch. Dist. 303, St. Charles, Ill., 1962-68; exec. sec. Bell & Howell Co., Chgo., 1969-73, supr. corp. relations, 1973-79, mgr. corp. communications, 1979-85, mgr. corp. communication services, 1985—; pres., dir. Bell & Howell Found., 1983—. Recipient Effie award Am. Mktg. Assn., 1983. Mem. Internat. Assn. Bus. Communications. Congregationalist. Home: 2614 Lincolnwood Dr Evanston IL 60201 Office: 5215 Old Orchard Rd Skokie IL 60077

ROBINSON, MABEL CRENSHAW, health education educator; b. Birmingham, Ala., Jan. 11, 1930; d. Oliver Gordon and Mabel Carlile (Crenshaw) R.; A.B., Birmingham-So. Coll., 1953; M.A., U. Ala., 1962, A.A., 1965, Ed.D., 1970, postgrad., 1975-76. Public sch. tchr., Ala., 1953-65; grad. asst. U. Ala., University, 1965-66; cons. health, phys. edn. and recreation, Ala. Dept. Edn., Montgomery, 1966-73, profl. devel. specialist, 1973-75, health edn. specialist, 1976-78, tchr. edn. advisor, regulatory services, 1978-80; asst. dean, prof. health edn. Sch. Edn., U. Ala., Birmingham, 1980—; after sch. girls sports leader YMCA, Mountain Brook, Ala., 1954-63; dir. Mountain Brook Summer Recreation Program, Birmingham, 1958-59; girls program dir. Shades Valley br. YMCA, Birmingham, 1963-65; owner-dir. Mabel Robinson Day Camp at Mary Munger, Inc., 1964-66; adj. prof. U. Montevallo, 1971, Troy State U., Montgomery, 1979; cons. schs., Ala., Mich. Dept. Edn.; chmn. health edn. sect. Ala. state tchrs. exit exam., Ala. Dept. Edn.; chmn. profl. preparation com. Ala. Health Adv. Com.; mem. adv. com. Nat. Task Force for Preparation and Practice of Health Educators. Resource material preparation adv. com. Ala. affiliate Am. Heart Assn., 1975—, vol. fundraiser, 1976-77; bd. dirs. Imagination Celebration, Birmingham, 1980—. Recipient award Ala. Assn. Intercollegiate Athletics for Women, 1976, Mobile Coaches Assn., 1980. Mem. Am. Sch. Health Assn., Am. Assn. for Supervision and Curriculum Devel., Ala. Assn. for Supervision and Curriculum Devel. (task force for profl. devel., liaison with Am. Assn. 1973-74), Assn. Tchr. Educators, AAHPER and Dance and So. Dist. (honor award 1978), Soc. State Dirs. Health, Phys. Edn. and Recreation (honor award 1979), Nat. Center Health Edn. (role delineation adv. com. sch. health edn. project Bur. Health Manpower), Capstone Coll. Edn.

Soc., Phi Delta Kappa, Kappa Delta Pi, Kappa Delta Epsilon, Kappa Delta. Methodist. Club: Birmingham Country. Coordinator nat. profl. conf., 1981; contbr. writings to profl. publs. and newsletters; mem. writing teams publs.; co-author: A Physical Education Guide for Secondary Schools, 1967. Home: 2519 Park Lane Ct S Birmingham AL 35223 Office: Univ Alabama Birmingham AL 35294

ROBINSON, MARION SWETT, banker; b. Boston, Aug. 3, 1947; d. Albert Hersey and Mary (Stewart) Swett; B.A., Wellesley Coll., 1969; M.B.A., Stanford U., 1979; M.A., Stanford Food Research Inst., 1979; m. Lawrence R. Robinson III, June 30, 1979; 1 son, Albert Hersey. Sr. asst. dir. Morgan Grenfell & Co. Ltd., London, 1970-77; asst. v.p. Mfrs. Hanover Trust, N.Y.C., 1979-80; v.p. Bankers Trust Co., N.Y.C., 1980—. Republican. Congregationalist. Club: Fairfield Villages Wellesley. Office: 1 Bankers Trust Plaza New York NY 10015

ROBINSON, MARY LOU, federal judge; b. Dodge City, Kans., Aug. 25, 1926; d. Gerald J. and Frances Aynn (Pierce) Strueber; student Amarillo Coll., 1946; B.A., U. Tex., 1948, LL.B., 1950; m. A.J. Robinson, Aug. 28, 1949; children—Rebecca Aynn Robinson Gruhlkey, Diana Ceil, Matthew Douglas. Admitted to Tex. bar, 1949; individual practice law, 1950-55; judge County Ct., Potter County, Tex., 1955-59; judge 108th Dist. Ct., 1961-73; asso. justice Ct. Civil Appeals, 7th Supreme Jud. Dist. Tex., 1973-77, chief justice, 1977-79; judge U.S. Dist. Ct. for No. Dist. Tex., 1979—. Elder Westminster Presbyn. Ch. Named Tex. Women of Yr. Tex. Fedn. Bus. and Profl. Women, 1973, one of 10 Outstanding Panhandle Women, W. Tex. State U., 1976. Mem. Nat. Assn. Women Lawyers, Amarillo Bar Assn., Tex. Bar Assn., Am. Bar Assn., Delta Kappa Gamma. Office: PO Box 13248 Amarillo TX 79189*

ROBINSON, MARY LOUISE, management company executive; d. Francis J. and Frances (Sikerzycki) Wazeter; B.A., Wellesley Coll., 1963; M.B.A., Harvard U., 1970. Product devel. mgr. Dansk Designs, Ltd., Mt. Kisco, N.Y., 1970-73; product group mgr. Clairol, Inc., N.Y.C., 1974-76; sr. product mgr. Matchabelli, Cheseborough Ponds, Greenwich, Conn., 1977; exec. v.p. 800 Spirits, Inc., N.Y.C., 1980—; pres. M. Robinson Assos., N.Y.C., 1979—, dir. 1980—; v.p. Chase Investors Mgmt. Corp. Mem. Women Bus. Owners of N.Y. (bd. dirs. 1979-81), Women in Bus. Clubs: Harvard, Vanderbilt Toastmasters (pres. 1980). Contbr. articles to profl. jours. Address: 160 E 48 St New York NY 10017

ROBINSON, NAOMI JEAN, training systems analyst; b. Storm Lake, Iowa, Oct. 10, 1951; d. Wendell and Norma (Wright) R.; B.A., Buena Vista Coll., 1973; M.A.Ed., George Washington U., 1978. Cert. tchr., Iowa. Tchr., elem. schs., Storm Lake, Iowa, 1973-75; edn. specialist intern U.S. Army, Fort Monroe, Va., 1976-78, edn. specialist, Fort Eustis, Va., 1978-79, tng. systems analyst, White Sands Missile Range, N.Mex., 1979-83, tng. effectiveness analysis study coordinator, 1983-85, sr. analyst, 1985—, edn. and tng career program mgr., 1983—. Vice pres., Young Republicans, 1972-73. Mem. Nat. Assn. Exec. Females, Federally Employed Women (v.p. Three Crosses chpt. 1982-83, v.p. and chmn. membership 1984-85), Human Factors Soc., Iowa Edn. Assn. Republican. Presbyterian. Club: Bus. and Profl. Women. Author: Guidelines for Development of Skill Qualification Tests, 1977. Home: 2850 Fairway Dr Apt 4 Las Cruces NM 88001 Office: US Army TRASANA attn ATOR-THE White Sands Missile Range White Sands NM 88002

ROBINSON, NELL BRYANT, nutrition educator; b. Kopperl, Tex., Oct. 15, 1925; d. Basil Howell and Lelia Abiah (Duke) Bryant; m. Frank Edward Robinson, July 14, 1945 (dec.); 1 child, John Howell Robinson. B.S., N. Tex. State U., 1945; M.S., Tex. Woman's U., 1958, Ph.D., 1967. Registered dietitian, Tex. Tchr. Comanche High Sch., Tex., 1945-46, Kopperl High Sch., Tex., 1946-48; county extension agt. Agrl. Extension Service, Tex., 1948-56; prof. nutrition Tex. Christian U., Fort Worth, 1957—, chmn. dept. nutrition and dietetics, 1985—. Contbr. chpt. to book. Named Top Prof., Tex. Christian U. Mortar Bd., 1978. Mem. Am. Dietetic Assn. (del., council on edn., ethics com. 1985—), Am. Home Econs. Assn., Tex. Dietetic Assn. (pres., 1972-73, Disting. Dietetican 1981), Tex. Home Econs. Assn. (pres. 1978-80, Home Economist of Yr. 1975). Club: Fort Worth Women. Lodge. Order Eastern Star. Home: 5729 Wimbleton Way Fort Worth TX 76133 Office: Tex Christian U PO Box 32869 Fort Worth TX 76129

ROBINSON, PAMELA SUE, sales representative; b. Fresno, Calif., Nov. 2, 1959; d. Doyle Franklin and Nancy Jo (Price) R.; m. Gerald Allen Anderson, Feb. 15, 1986. Student San Jose Bible Coll., 1980-84, Fresno City Coll., 1978-79. Receptionist, sec., office mgr. Airport Plaza Exec. Suites, San Jose, Calif., 1980-83; computer salesperson Datalease Systems, Sunnyvale, Calif., 1983-84; office mgr., sales rep. Semiconductor Tools, San Jose, 1984-85; Western regional sales rep. Semiconductor Services, San Jose, 1985; corp. sales rep. Holiday Inn, San Jose, 1986—; securities asst. sales rep. Bateman, Eichler, Hill & Richards, 1986—. Mem. Nat. Assn. Female Execs., Soc. Female Execs. Avocations: playing instruments; singing; sign language. Home: 3510 Moorpark Ave #129A San Jose CA 95117 Office: 99 Almaden Blvd San Jose CA 95113

ROBINSON, PEGGY MADSEN, administrative librarian, archivist; d. Carl Westergard and Margaret (Kennedy) Madsen. A.A., Stephens Coll.; B.A., Loretto Heights Coll., 1973; M.L.S., U. Denver, 1973, archival cert., 1975. Asst. librarian Loretto Heights Coll., Denver, 1973-77, art curator, 1974-77; adminstrv. librarian U.S. Dept. Army, Germany, 1977-79; tech. process intern Jefferson County Sch. Dist., Denver, 1980; archivist, 1981-82; dir. N.E. Colo. Regional Library, Wray, 1983-84; adminstrv. librarian Friends of Children-Viet Nam Internat. Adoption Orgn., Denver, 1984—; instr. English U. Without Walls, Denver, 1973-77. Mem. ALA, Colo. Library Assn. Mountain Plains Library Assn., Soc. Scholarly Pub., SLA, AAUW (rep. commn. women, publicity chair), Wyoming Hist. Soc. (v.p. Washakie chpt.), U. Denver Alumni Assn. (sec.), Stephens Coll. Alumni Assn. (pres.).

ROBINSON, SALLY HALE, marketing company executive; b. Longview, Tex., Oct. 3, 1944; d. Mahlon Frances and Evelyn Baxter (Snook) Dempewolf; m. William Thomas Robinson, June 2, 1984; m. William J. Hale, Aug. 11, 1965 (div. Sept. 1979); 1 child, Elizabeth Dempewolf Hale. A.S., U. Palm Beach, 1963; student U. S.C., 1965-67. Congl. asst., Atlanta, 1967-69; sales assoc. Estee Lauder Corp., Augusta, Ga., 1978-79; sales mgmt. staff Hilton Internat., Augusta, 1983-84; sales assoc. Ellis Branch Realtor, Ocean Springs Miss., 1984—; mktg. dir. Bob Edwards Prodns., Ocean Springs, 1985—; dir. sales Audubon Mktg. Co., New Orleans, 1985—; model Belks Inc., Augusta, Ga., 1979-84. Pres., Med. Aux., Ocean Springs, Miss., 1985-86. Mem. Bd. Realtors Ocean Springs, Nat. Assn. Female Execs. Republican. Episcopalian. Avocations: writing; art; travel; training thoroughbreds; sailing. Mailing Address: 1121 Van Cleave Rd Ocean Springs MS 39564 Home: 6705 Belle Fountaine Beach Ocean Springs MS 39564 Office: Ellis Branch Realtor 734 Hwy 90 W Ocean Springs MS 39564

ROBINSON, SALLY WINSTON, artist; b. Detroit, Nov. 2, 1924; d. Harry Lewis and Lydia (Kahn) Winston; B.A., Bennington Coll., 1947; student Cranbrook Acad. Art, 1949; grad. Sch. Social Work, Wayne U., 1948, M.A., 1972; M.F.A., Wayne State U., 1973; m. Eliot F. Robinson, June 28, 1949; children—Peter Eliot, Lydia Winston, Suzanne Finley, Sarah Mitchell. Psychol. tester Detroit Bd. Edn., 1944; pyschol. counselor and tester YMCA, N.Y.C., 1946; social caseworker Family Service, Pontiac, Mich., 1947; instr. printmaking Wayne State U., Detroit, 1973—. One person shows U. Mich., 1973, Wayne State U., 1974, Klein-Vogol Gallery, 1974, Rina Gallery, 1976, Park McCullough House, Vt., 1976, Williams Coll., 1976, Arnold Klein Gallery, 1977; exhibited group shows Bennington Coll., Cranbrook Mus., Detroit Inst. Art, Detroit Artists Market, Soc. Women Painters, Soc. Arts and Crafts, Bloomfield Art Assn., Flint Left Bank Gallery, Balough Gallery, Detroit Soc. Women Painters, U. Mich., U. Ind., U. Wis., U. Pittsburg, Toledo Mus., Krannert Mus.; represented in permanent collections, Detroit, N.Y.C., Birmingham, Bloomfield Hills; tchr. children's art Detroit Inst. Art, 1949-50, now artistic advisor, bd. dirs. drawing and print orgn. Bd. dirs. Planned Parenthood, 1951—, mem. exec. bd., 1963—; bd. dirs. PTA, 1956-60, Roeper City and Country Sch., U. Mich. Mus. Art, 1978; trustee Putnam Hosp. Med. Research Inst., 1978; mem. Gov.'s Commn. Art in State Bldgs., 1978-79; mem. art and devel. coms. So. Vt. Art Ctr.; mem. vol. com. Marie Selby Gardens. Mem. Detroit Artists Market (dir. 1956—), Bennington Coll. Alumnae Assn. (regional co-chmn. 1954), Detroit Soc. Women Painters, Birmingham Soc. Women Painters (pres. 1974-76), Bloomfield Art Assn. (program co-chmn. 1956), Founders Soc. Detroit Inst. Art. Unitarian (mem. Council 1963—). Clubs: Village Women's (Birmingham, Mich.); Women's City (co-ordinator art shows 1950) (Detroit); Garden (Bennington, Vt.). Home: 7 Monument Circle Old Bennington VT 05201 also 708 Pine Run Dr Osprey FL 33559

ROBINSON, SANDRA LAWSON, physician, state department administrator; b. New Orleans, Mar. 22, 1944; d. Alvin James Lawson and Elvera (Stewart) Lawson Martin; m. Carl Robinson; children—Michael, Carla. B.A., Howard U., 1965, M.D., 1969; M.P.H., Tulane U., 1977. Intern in pediatrics Children's Hosp. Nat. Med. Ctr., Washington, 1969-70, resident in pediatrics, 1970-71; resident in pediatrics, fellow in ambulatory care U. Calif.-San Francisco, San Francisco Gen. Hosp., 1971-72; coordinator minority affairs La. State U. Med. Ctr., 1979; med. dir. Neighborhood Health Clinics, New Orleans, 1973-77; dir. ambulatory care and outpatient services Charity Hosp., New Orleans, 1977-81; dir. ambulatory care service Children's Hosp. New Orleans, 1981-84; sec. and state health officer La. Dept. Health and Human Resources, Baton Rouge, 1984—; clin. asst. prof. pediatrics La. State U. and Tulane U. Schs. Medicine, 1974—; adj. asst. prof. Tulane U. Sch. Pub. Health and Tropical Medicine, 1977—. Recipient Region V award Howard U. Alumni; Outstanding Community Service award Black Orgn. Leadership Devel.; Outstanding Service award Tangipahoa Voters League; Woman's Day Honor award Mt. Zion United Meth. Ch. Mem. New Orleans Med. Soc., Pediatric Soc. of New Orleans, Tulane Women's Assn., Orleans Parish Women's Med. Assn., New Orleans Grad. Med. Assembly, Ambulatory Pediatric Soc., Nat. Med. Assn., La. Women's Network, Inc., Assn. State and Terr. Health Ofcls., Nat. Women's Forum, Delta Sigma Theta (Community Service award, Pub. Service award). Democrat. Roman Catholic. Avocations: skiing; reading. Office: Dept Health and Human Resources PO Box 3776 Baton Rouge LA 70802

ROBINSON, SARAH BONHAM, artist, art educator, therapist; b. Somerville, N.J., Mar. 16, 1939; d. Robert Daniel and Eleanor Cammann (McMurtry) Bonham; m. Bruce Mitton Robinson, Aug. 28, 1961 (div. 1975); children—Christopher Day, David Brooke, Megan Louise, Andrew Cornell. B.A., Wilson Coll., 1961; M.F.A., U. Pa., 1962; art edn. cert. Kean Coll., 1973. Asst. art instr. Wilson Coll., Chambersburg, Pa., 1960-61; art educator Newark Acad., Livingston, N.J., 1966-68; adj. instr. Rutgers U., New Brunswick, N.J., 1967; art therapist J.E. Runnells, Berkeley Heights, N.J., 1974; creative arts therapist dept. psychiatry Elizabeth Gen. Med. Ctr. (N.J.), 1974—, dir. activity therapy, 1976—, clin. chief partial hosp., 1978—, chmn. quality assurance psychiatry 1980-83, asst. dir. rehab. services, 1983—; art therapy cons. Children's Specialized Hosp., Mountainside, N.J., 1976—. Producer, editor film strip: Changes, 1974. Illustrator: Miller-Cory Colonial Cooking, 1975. Paintings exhibited in U.S. and abroad, 1960—, including World's Fair 1965, Moscow, 1985. Artist, Miller-Cory Hist. Orgn., Westfield, N.J., 1969-79; artist, mem. Sane, Union County, N.J., 1969—. Woodrow Wilson fellow, 1961. Mem. Am. Assn. Partial Hosps., N.J. Assn. Partial Hosps. (regional chmn. 1983—, co-founder), N.J. Psychiat. Rehab. Assn. Democrat. Home: 235 Sinclair Pl Westfield NJ 07090

ROBINSON, SHERLENE FRANCES, industrial manufacturing company official; b. San Angelo, Tex., Apr. 16, 1959; d. Donald George and Frances Cleo (Reynolds) R.; m. Lance T. McKenzie, July 16, 1977 (div. May 1985). A. Applied Arts in Bus., Cisco Jr. Coll., 1984. B.B.A. in Mgmt., Hardin-Simmons U. Student clk. City of Fort Stockton, Tex., 1976-77; clk./sec. Zales Jewelers, Abilene, Tex., 1977-78; purchasing clk. U.S. Brass Corp., Abilene, 1978-82, asst. buyer, 1982-83, buyer, 1983—. Mem. Abilene All-Am. Bus. and Profl. Women (1st v.p. 1986—), Alpha Chi. Republican. Mem. Ch. of Christ. Avocations: running; reading; water skiing. Office: US Brass Corp 2117 Interstate 20 Abilene TX 79601

ROBINSON, VIVIAN MARIE, electrical distributor executive; b. Los Angeles, Oct. 15, 1944; d. Bertrand Olander White and Myrtle Louise Lucas; m. Ray Robinson, June 26, 1979 (div. 1980). B.A. in Urban Tchr. Edn., Governor State U., 1976, M.A. in Human Relation Services, 1979, postgrad. in media communications, 1980—. Tchr. City Colls. of Chgo., 1978-82; mktg. and sales rep. Satellite Communications, Chgo., 1982-83; mktg. cons. Sonicraft, Chgo., 1983-84, pres., chmn. bd. dirs. Midwest Communications Supply Co., Chgo., 1984—. Mem. adv. bd. Olive Harvey Coll., Chgo., 1984—; Ill. del. White House Conf. on Small Bus., 1986. Mem. Soc. Cable TV Engrs., Chgo. Minority Assn. Cable Contractors, Betty Winfield Baldwin Fedn. Women's Clubs, Chatham Bus. Assn., Ill. Assn. Black Women Bus. Owners (pres.), Phi Theta Kappa. Home: 5471 Hyde Park Blvd Chicago IL 60615 Office: Midwest Communications Supply Co 140 W 62d St Chicago IL 60621

ROBINSON, WILDA JUANITA, educational administrator; b. Allendale, S.C., Sept. 27, 1947; d. Wilbur and Eloise Virginia (Mitchell) R.; 1 child, Tshaka Ali. B.S. in History, Voorhees Coll., Denmark, S.C., 1970; M.Ed., U. S.C., 1975, also postgrad. Cert. tchr., S.C. Tchr., Estill Elem. Sch., S.C., 1970-71, Allendale County Schs., S.C., 1973-84; research cons. Sta. WAFR-FM, Durham, N.C., 1971-73; prin. Allendale Elem. Sch., 1984—. Vice chmn. Rural Health Inc., Allendale, 1977—; ex-officio mem. Allendale County Devel. Bd., 1981—; mem. exec. com. S.C. State Devel. Bd., Columbia, 1981-86; mem. edn. com. Voorhees Coll. Bd. Trustees, 1983—; sec. Allendale County Democratic Com., 1980—. Mem. S.C. Assn. Sch. Adminstrs., S.C. Assn. Elem. Sch. Prins., Nat. Assn. Female Execs., S.C. Edn. Assn. (Outstanding County Educator of Yr. award 1978), NEA, AAUW, NAACP, Voorhees Coll. Alumni Assn., U. S.C. Alumni Assn. Mem. Ch. of Christ. Home: PO Box 786 Allendale SC 29810 Office: Allendale Elementary Sch Hwy 278 E Allendale SC 29810

ROBIRDS, GAY WARREN, advertising agency executive; b. Houston, Apr. 1, 1956; d. Eugene Wesley and Dorothy Jean (Gay) Warren; m. Stephen Dale Robirds, June 17, 1978; 1 dau., Rebecca Gay. B.F.A., U. Tex., 1977; postgrad. Ga. State U., 1982. Art dir., copywriter The Richards Group, Dallas, 1977-78; dir. pub. relations Baylor U. Med. Center, Dallas, 1978-80; mktg. dir. Leadership Dynamics, Inc., Atlanta, 1980-82; v.p. Fellers, Lacy & Gaddis, Austin, Tex., 1982—; mktg. cons. Christian Fin. Mgmt., Atlanta, 1981-82; art dir. Christian Career Counseling, Atlanta, 1981-82; creative cons. Austin Women's Ctr., 1983—. Cons. advt. George Strake for Tex. Lt. Gov., 1983. Art Study fellow Richmond Coll., 1974. Recipient Award of Merit, Print Mag., 1977; named Outstanding Student, U. Tex., 1977. Mem. Women in Communications, Austin Assn. Advt. Agy. Prins., Laguna Gloria Arts Guild, Phi Beta Phi. Republican. Methodist. Clubs: Jr. Austin Women's Dental Aux., Texas-Ex-Students Assn., Austin Country (Austin). Office: Fellers Lacy & Gaddis 2211 IH 35 South Suite 400 Austin TX 78741

ROBISON, ANN GREEN (MRS. ADOLF ROBISON), textile co. exec.; b. N.Y.C., Nov. 19, 1904; d. Boris and Mary (Sugarmen) Green; B.A., U. Maine, 1924, L.H.D., 1975; M.A., Columbia, 1936; grad. woman's inst. Jewish Theol. Sem. Am., 1959; m. Adolf Robison, Aug. 28, 1927; children—Peter Jordan, Michael Douglas. Tchr. French, Mattanawcook Acad., Lincoln, Maine, 1924-25. New Rochelle, N.Y., 1925-38; v.p. Robison Industries, 1966—; Mem. adv. com. dept. Herbraic studies Rutgers State U. of N.J., chmn. spl. com. scholarships and grants. Accredited observer at UN in U.S. and France, 1947-52; lectr. U.S. Del., Milan, Italy, 1951. Mem. women's div. Am.-Israel Cultural Found., mem. program, interfaith and univ. coms; v.p. Robison Found., 1956-83; mem. state com. Radio Free Europe; exec. com. Am. Israel Pub. Affairs Com., sec., 1973—; mem. bd., exec. com., sec. Bergen-Passaic Lung Assn., 1974-76, chmn. by-laws and fund-raising coms., mem. exec. com.; v.p., bd. dirs., exec. com., chmn. public relations com. Am. Lung Assn. of N.J.; mem. bd., co-chmn. Adult Center Jewish and Related Studies, YM-YWHA of Bergen County; mem. bd. Community Mus. of Bergen County; nat. v.p. Nat. Jewish Community Relations Adv. Council, 1973-77, chmn. membership com., mem. exec. com., 1979—; mem. community adv. bd. Easter Seal Soc., 1977-81. Vice pres. Jewish Fedn. for Community Services Bergen County; mem. alumni council and exec. com. Tchrs. Coll., Columbia, 1980; bd. dirs. Republican Women's Clubs of Bergen County; chmn. Bergen County Rep. Campaign Com.; bd. dirs. woman's div. United Jewish Community, 1978—. Recipient medal merit Fairleigh Dickinson U., 1966, Ann Robison House named in her honor 1964; Nat. citation Jewish Nat. Fund, 1968; 1st Woman of Year, YM-YWHA, 1970; Brandeis award Zionist Orgn. Am., 1972; award Jewish War Vets., 1972; honored with husband Israel Bonds, 1978. Mem. UN Assn. (dir. N.J. div. 1980—), AAUW (nat. com. on internat. relations, area program chmn. 1977—, mem. bd. No. Valley br., 1st v.p. in charge program 1969-70, fellowship chmn. 1974-77, chmn. internat. relations 1977—, Ann Robison fellowship named in her honor 1968), Synagogue Council Am. (mem. UN com.), Nat. Council Jewish Woman (nat. dir., chmn. nat. internat. affairs 1968-76, chmn. 85th anniversary com. 1977, chmn. Israel priority task force 1979-82, mem. bd. Mid-Atlantic dist., mem. numerous coms.), Internat. Council Jewish Women (U.S. rep. resolutions com., hospitality and pub. relations chmn. conv. 1969, chmn. resolutions com. 1969-75, v.p. 1972-79, editor Newsletter 1974—), Internat. Relations for Federated Woman's Clubs N.J. (div. chmn.), Hadassah (life), Brandeis U. Womens Assn. (life), Internat. Program Assn., Phi Beta Kappa, Phi Kappa Phi. Club: Teaneck Coll. (program chmn., mem. bd.). Author weekly column On the Go in the Jewish Standard, 1966—. Home: 554 S Forest Dr Teaneck NJ 07666 Office: Robison Industries 33 New Bridge Rd Bergenfield NJ 07621

ROBISON, JUDY KAY, nursing home administrator; b. Rosebud, Tex., Mar. 26, 1947; d. Edwin Jerry and Mildred Nadine (Tawater) Slovacek; m. James Harold Cunningham, Mar. 19, 1971 (div. Aug. 1976); 1 child, Jena Cassidie; m. Donnie Ray Robison, Dec. 20, 1976 (div. July 1982). Student LaSalle Extension U., 1966, U. Tex., 1976; A.A.S., McLennan Community Coll., 1980. Designer Green Flower Shop, Rosebud, 1961-65; exec. sec. Gary Job Corps Ctr., San Marcos, Tex., 1965-74; asst. adminstr. Rosebud Med. Services, 1975-77, adminstr., 1977-82; Community adminstr. Hosp. Assn. of Tex., Inc., Rosebud, 1982—. Adv. bd. Foodservice Research Ctr., 1984, Temple Jr. Coll., Tex., 1982, 85; TV telethon coordinator Easter Seal Soc., 1985. Mem. Am. Coll. Nursing Home Adminstrs. Club: Rosebud Ex-Students (sec., treas. 1982—). Avocations: music; horticulture; tennis; skiing; dancing. Home: 503 E Ave G Rosebud TX 76570 Office: Community Hosp Assn Tex Inc Heritage House Corner of College and Ave F Rosebud TX 76570

ROBISON, MARSHA GAIL, counseling company executive; b. Charleroi, Pa., Nov. 24, 1953; d. Lou H. and Marian Alice (Robinson) Skokut; children—Justin, Maya. Student in Mech. Engring., Mt. San Antonio U., 1977-80. CAD packaging designer Gen. Dynamics, Pomona, Calif., 1972-80, Singer Librascope, Glendale, Calif., 1980-81; ind. cons. Hughes, ITT, Rockwell, Los Angeles, 1981-83; pres. CAD Counsel, North Hollywood, Calif., 1982—. Mem. Nat. Computer Graphics Assn. Avocation: back-packing. Office: CAD Counsel 5032 Lankershim Blvd North Hollywood CA 91601

ROBISON, PAULA JUDITH, flutist; b. Nashville, June 8, 1941; d. David Victor and Naomi Florence R.; student U. So. Calif., 1958-60; B.S., Juilliard Sch. Music, 1963; m. Scott Nickrenz, Dec. 29, 1971; 1 dau., Elizabeth Hadley Nickrenz. Soloist with various maj. orchs., including N.Y. Philharmonic; mem. Orpheus Trio, 1970-80; prin. ann. recital series: Paula and . . ., 1976-82; co-dir. chamber music Spoleto Festivals, Charleston, S.C., Melbourne, Australia and Spoleto, Italy; mem. faculty Juilliard Sch. Music. Commd. concertos for flute and orch. by L. Kirchner, T. Takemitsu, O. Knussen, R. Beaser; performances at White House, Live from Lincoln Ctr., others; recs. for CBS Masterworks, Vanguard, Musicmasters. Recipient First prize Geneva Internat. Competition, 1966, Pegasus award Spoleto Festival, 1985; profiled on CBS Sunday Morning; named Musician of Month, Musical Am., 1979; Martha Baird Rockefeller grantee, 1966. Mem. Chamber Music Soc. Lincoln Center (founding). Address: care Shaw Concerts Inc 1995 Broadway New York NY 10023

ROBLEDO, MARIA SOFIA, educational administrator; b. Mercedes, Tex., June 28, 1948; d. Bernardo and Guadalupe (Casas) R. B.A., Calif. State U.-Sacramento, 1971; M.A. in Edn., Stanford U., 1972. Tchr., Sacramento City Unified Sch. Dist., Sacramento, 1972-74, human relations advisor, 1974-77, dean students high sch., 1977, vice prin. high sch., 1977-80, prin. middle sch., 1980-83, prin. high sch., 1983—. Bd. dirs. Stanford Home for Children, Sacramento, 1970-82, Sacramento Concilio, 1976-78, Jane Lathrop Sch., Sacramento, 1985—; mem. Mexican Am. Polit. Assn., Sacramento, 1983—. Recipient Scholarship, Stanford U., Palo Alto, Calif., 1971; named Secondary Adminstr. of Yr., Sacramento City Adminstrs. Assn., 1981. Mem. Assn. Mexican Am. Educators (sec., pres.). Democrat. Roman Catholic. Club: Stanford of Sacramento. Avocation: golf. Office: Hiram W Johnson High Sch 6879 14th Ave Sacramento CA 95820

ROBLES, XENIA CASILDA, physical therapist; b. Barceloneta, P.R., Mar. 27, 1950; d. Enrique and Esther (Rodriguez) Vargas; m. Juan Antonio Robles, July 25, 1975; children—Grisel Marie, Maricelle. Student U. P.R., 1972. Mem. physiotherapy staff Physician Phys. Therapy Services, Gary, Ind., 1972-74; clin. instr. VA West Side Med. Ctr., Chgo., 1974-76, 1978-84; dir. phys. therapy Norwegian Am. Hosp., Chgo., 1984—; mem. faculty U. Ill.-Chgo., 1979—. Mem. Am. Phys. Therapy Assn., Chicagoland Dirs. Forum. Democrat. Roman Catholic. Avocation: embroidery; volley ball. Home: 2418 W Marquette Rd Apt 3 Chicago IL 60629 Office: Norwegian Am Hosp 1044 N Francisco Ave Chicago IL 60622

ROCCO, STEPHANIE ANNE, human resources administrator; b. Allen Park, Mich., Sept. 4, 1950; d. Gordon S. and Eleanor Jane (Tierney) R. B.A. in Social Sci., Fla. Atlantic U., 1972; M.A. in Human Resources Mgmt., Pepperdine U., 1977. Counselor, South County Drug Abuse Found., Delray Beach, Fla., 1974-78; human research mgr. BMI Textron, Lake Park, Fla., 1978-84; employee relations mgr. Uninet Inc., Lenexa, Kans., 1984—. Mem. Am. Soc. Personnel Adminstrn., Info. Exchange, Phi Theta Kappa. Republican. Mem. Unity Ch. Avocations: photography; equitation; travel.

ROCHA, MARILYN EVA, clinical psychologist; b. San Bernardino, Calif., Oct. 23, 1928; d. Howard Ray Gonding and Laura Anne (Johanson) Walker; m. Hilario Ursala Rocha, Mar. 25, 1948 (dec. Feb. 1971); children—Michael, Sherry, Teri, Denise. A.A., Solano Jr. Coll., 1970; B.A., Sacramento State U., 1973, M.A., 1974; Ph.D., U.S. Internat. U., 1981. Psychologist, Naval Drug Rehab. Ctr., U.S. Navy, San Diego, 1975-85, chief psychologist, 1983-84; staff clin. psychologist Calif. Youth Authority, Sacramento, 1986—; dir. Self-Help Agys., San Diego, Author short story. Vol. counselor Hamonium, San Diego, 1976-77; leader Vacaville council Cub Scouts Am., Calif., 1957-62, 4-H, also Brownie's. Mem. Calif. Scholastic Fedn., PTA (hon. life), Am. Psychol. Assn., Am. Assn. Suicidology, Delta Zeta. Democrat. Unitarian. Home: 3703 H St Sacramento CA 95816 Office: Calif Youth Authority No Reception Ctr Clinic 3001 Ramona Ave Sacramento CA 95826

ROCHE, SISTER DENISE ANN, college president; b. Buffalo, Sept. 17, 1942; d. Vincent Joseph and Mary Elizabeth (Crehan) R. B.A., D'Youville Coll., 1967; M.A., Boston U., 1968; Ph.D., U. Mass., 1977. Tchr., Our Lady of Fatima Grade Sch., L.I., N.Y., 1964-66; instr. D'Youville Coll., Buffalo, 1968-71, asst. prof., 1975-78, assoc. dean for continuing studies, 1978-79, pres., 1979—; teaching assoc. U. Mass.-Boston, 1972-75; mem. adv. bd. Business First, Buffalo, 1985—. Trustee Marygrove Coll., Detroit, 1981—; bd. dirs. Lafayette Gen. Hosp., Buffalo, 1980—, ARC, Buffalo, 1979—; chmn. coll. and univ. div. United Way Appeal, Buffalo, 1983—; mem. Task Force on Acute Care in Erie County, Buffalo, 1981-82, Erie County Legis. Task Force on Unemployment, Buffalo, 1984—. Named Citizen of Yr. N.Y. Soc. Profl. Engrs., 1984; recipient Pub. Service award SUNY-Buffalo Alumni Assn., 1985. Mem. Ind. Coll. Fund N.Y., Western N.Y. Consortium Higher Edn. (v.p.), Western N.Y. Regional Edn. Ctr. for Econ. Devel. Roman Catholic. Club: Zonta. Home: 320 Porter Ave Buffalo NY 14201

ROCHEROLLE, EUGENIE KATHERINE, composer, lyricist, pianist, educator; b. New Orleans, Aug. 24, 1936; d. Gustave Joseph and Katherine Lucille (Schlegel) Ricau; m. Didier Andre Rocherolle, May 14, 1960; children—Valerie, Laurent, Damien, Justin. B.A. in Music, Sophie Newcomb Coll. Tulane U., 1958. Composer, lyricist 40 anthems for chorus, 3 band works, 1 work for band and chorus; composer 17 books for piano; composer musicals, chamber works, string orch. work, radio commls.; commd. piano solo Clavier Mag., 1983; commd. anthem Wilton Congregational Ch. (Conn.), 1976; featured Am. composer, judge Audrey Thayer Meml. Piano Competition Avon, Conn., 1986. Mem. Women's Republican Club, Wilton, 1980—, exec. bd., 1982—; mem. exec. bd., sec. Wilton Orch., 1983—. Recipient prize for Fanfare, South Coast Choral Soc., 1985. Mem. Nat. League Am. Penwoman (co-state chmn. music, 1983-85, 1st prize 1986), Nat. Fedn. Music Clubs (judge jr. festivals 1982-85), ASCAP, Conn. Composers Inc. Roman Catholic. Club: DAR (chaplain Drum Hill chpt. 1982—).

ROCHETTO, EVELYN MARIE, state ofcl.; b. Chgo.; d. Lucius J. and Clara M. (Jung) Young; Ph.B., Northwestern U., 1952; m. Paul A. Rochetto, June 9, 1937. Profl. musician, 1930-50; membership sec. Internat. Soc. Gen. Semantics, 1950-55, exec. sec., from 1955, dir., from 1952; now counseling specialist State of Ill. Mem. AAUW (pres. Chgo. br. 1956, 58, 64—, mem. bd. 1953—), Chgo. Story League (pres. 1970—), Am. Legion (dir.), Friends Mentally Ill (pres. 1958—), Alpha Sigma Lambda (dir.). Club: Woman's Univ. (pres. 1966—). Home: 5240 N Sheridan Rd Chicago IL 60640

ROCHIRA, NANCY MARY, public housing administrator; b. Lawrence, Mass., May 1, 1944; d. Walter Richard and Anna (Kuchuruk) Kibildis; m. Joseph Rochira, Nov. 25, 1962 (dec. Jan. 1984); 1 dau., Teresa Anne. Cert. McIntosh Bus. Sch., 1962; student N.H. Coll., 1975, 77, U. N.H., 79, Castle Jr. Coll., 1984, Inst. for Practicing Real Estate, 1985. Receptionist, exec. sec. Supervisory Union, Atkinson, N.H., 1961-68; sales assoc. Salem-Derry Cable Co., Salem, N.H., 1971; asst. to mgr. Lancelot Assos., Salem, 1974; exec. dir. Salem Housing Authority, 1974—, sec. bd. commrs., 1974—. Area leader Heart Fund, 1980-81; mem. Salem Assn. Retarded Citizens, Salem, 1975—; mem. adv. com. Town and Country Theatre, 1985. Recipient Certificate of Recognition, Green Thumb Nat. Farmers Union, 1980, Cert. of Recognition, N.H. Housing Commn., 1978. Mem. N.H. Assn. Exec. Dirs., N.H. Assn. Housing Authorities, Nat. Assn. Female Execs., Nat. Assn. Housing and Redevel. Ofcls. Avocations: swimming; gardening; cooking. Home: 117 Haverhill Rd Salem NH 03079 Office: 44 Millville St Salem NH 03079

ROCHON, SANDRA PALMA, banker; b. Laredo, Tex., Sept. 16, 1947; d. Edward Anthony and Ofelia (Dickinson) Palma; A.A., San Antonio Jr. Coll., 1967. Credit dept. mgr. Del Rio Bank & Trust Co. (Tex.), 1964-71; mgmt. trainee Household Fin. Corp., Silver Spring, Md., 1975; asst. v.p., comml. loan officer Dominion Nat. Bank, Vienna, Va., 1975-79; v.p., compliance officer, br. adminstr., collections supr. Town & Country Bank & Trust Co., (name now Enterprise Bank) Falls Church, Va., 1979-84; sr. v.p., asst. sec. to bd., mortgage loan officer, br. ops. supr. compliance and security officer Fairfax Saving Bank, 1984—. Sec. Reflection Homeowners Assn., 1980-81, pres. 1981—.Mem. Nat. Assn. Bank Women chmn. No. Va. chpt.). Office: 6206 Rolling Rd Springfield VA 22152

ROCK, CARMELLA MARIE, computer/data processing supplies company executive; b. Auburn, N.Y., Mar. 31, 1936; d. Peter A. and Agnes (O'Hora) Maneri; 1 child, Michelle. B.S., Syracuse U., 1957; postgrad. CCNY, 1959-62, NYU, 1981-83. Sales rep. NCR, N.Y.C., 1960-66; br. sales mgr. Victor Bus. Products Syracuse, N.Y., 1974-78; nat. sales mgr. Tebniha Corp., N.Y.C., 1978-80; gen. mgr. PCR Mfg. Corp., N.Y.C., 1980—; owner, pres. Profl. Computer Resources, Bklyn., 1986—. Mem. Nat. Assn. Female Execs., Am. Mgmt. Assn., Nat. Owners and Pilots Assn. Roman Catholic. Avocations: flying; music; sailing; reading; gardening; cooking; swimming. Office: PCR Mfg Corp 2255 Broadway New York NY 10024

ROCK, JUDITH ANN, property management company marketing director, interior decorator; b. Marion, Ohio, Oct. 14, 1940; d. Paul Emerson and Nellie Ada (McAdams) Miller; m. Matthew William Rock, June 23, 1962 (div. Dec. 1973); children—Matthew Paul, Christopher Andrew. Grad. United Air Lines Stewardess Sch., 1959; B.S., Heidelberg Coll., Tiffin, Ohio, 1967. Reservationist, ticket agt. United Air Lines, N.Y.C., 1959-60, stewardess, Chgo., 1960-62, career speaker, 1967-73; TV personality Tele Communications, Marion, Ohio, 1968-80; account sales rep. Thomson Newspapers, Marion, Ohio, 1980-84; regional mktg. dir. First Property Mgmt., Columbus, Ohio, 1984—. Columbus Library fellow. Mem. Am. Assn. Mktg., Market Dirs. Ohio, Nat. Assn. Female Execs. (bd. dirs. 1985—). Republican. Lutheran. Club: Clipped Wings. Avocations: reading; dollhouse minatures; football; basketball; swimming. Office: First Property Mgmt 4650 Wakeford St Columbus OH 43214

ROCKAFELLOW, SUSAN SIMON, speech and language pathologist; b. Alma, Mich.; d. Benjamin William and Marjorie (Graff) Simon; m. Larry Lynn Rockafellow, Aug. 6, 1972; 1 child, Any Lynn. B.A., U. Mich., 1970; M.S., U. Okla., 1972. Speech therapist Fremont Pub. Schs., Calif., 1970-71; speech-lang. pathologist VA Hosp., Ann Arbor, Mich., 1972-73; counselor Ypsilanti Pub. Sch., Mich., 1973-75; dir. speech pathology Gratiot Community Hosp., Alma, Mich., 1975-77; speech pathologist in pvt. practice, Indpls., 1977-80; adminstr. Northside Rehab. Assn., Indpls., 1981—; cons. Rehab. Agy., Hilton Head, S.C., 1984. Mem. com. Jewish Community Ctr. Israelfest, Indpls., 1985. Mem. Am. Speech/Lang. and Hearing Assn. (ins. network), Ind. Speech/Lang. and Hearing Assn., Greater Indpls. Speech/Lang. and Hearing Assn., Nat. Assn. Bus. Women Owners, Nat. Assn. Rehab. Agencies. Democrat. Jewish. Avocations: running; sailing; biking; swimming. Home: 2028 Bechtel Indianapolis IN 46260 Office: Northside Rehab Assn 1717 W 86th St Suite 120 Indianapolis IN 46260

ROCKEFELLER, REGINA STRAZZULLA, lawyer; b. Boston, Mar. 31, 1951; d. Philip and Anne Leonore (Silvestro) Strazzulla; m. Godfrey Anderson Rockefeller, Jr., Aug. 3, 1974; children—Victoria Hamilton, Lisa Anderson. B.A. in Polit. Sci. magna cum laude, Tufts U., 1973; J.D. cum laude, Boston Coll., 1976. Bar: Fla. 1977, Mass. 1977. Mem. Hutchins & Wheeler, Boston, 1976—; mem. faculty Health Law Update, 1984; dir. Strazzulla Bros. Co. Inc., Ft. Pierce, Fla., 1979—. Contbr. articles to profl. jours. Trustee Waltham Weston Hosp. and Med. Ctr., 1980—; bd. dirs. Hospice West, Inc., 1985—. Mem. ABA, Mass. Bar Assn. (chmn. health care delivery systems 1983—), Fla. Bar Assn., Nat. Health Lawyers Assn. Office: Hutchins & Wheeler One Boston Pl Boston MA 02108

ROCKFORD-MAURER, WENDY, dental insurance services executive; b. Syracuse, N.Y., June 14, 1947; d. Julius and Beatrice (Lichtenstein) Marx; m. Richard Ira Rockford, Aug. 10, 1969 (div. June 1975); 1 child, Lee David; m. Lawrence Maurer, Feb. 10, 1981. B.S., Syracuse U., 1969; postgrad. Harvard U., 1966; M.S., Queens Coll., 1971. Cert. secondary tchr. English, N.Y. Tchr. English N.Y.C. Bd. Edn., 1969-72; officer mgr. Island Dental Group, Plainview, N.Y., 1975-83; cons. Ac-Claim Dental Services, Great Neck, N.Y., 1983—; adminstr. Dedicated Dental Services, Great Neck, 1984-85, 86—; mgr. Northeast Health Assocs., Jamaica, N.Y., 1985—; lectr. in field; cons. in field. Mem. Nat. Assn. Female Execs., Nat. Geog. Soc., Democrat. Jewish. Avocations: reading; camping. Home: 23 Schenck Ave Great Neck NY 11023

ROCKHILL, SANDRA MARIE, real estate company executive, consultant; b. Prince Frederick, Md., June 9, 1950; d. Malcolm Erwin and Eunice (Lewis) R. B.A., Trinity Coll., 1972; postgrad. in mktg. UCLA, 1976, in art, 1983. Mgr. advt. Benos Dept. Stores, Los Angeles, 1972-75; budget coordinator Benton & Bowles Advt., Los Angeles, 1975-77; corp. sec-treas. Temp Tronix, La Jolla, Calif., 1977-78; asst. gen. mgr. Univ. Stereo, Los Angeles, 1978-81; v.p. Rovi Cos., Los Angeles, 1981—; dir. Rovi Pacific Corp., Los Angeles, Rovi Leasing Corp., Los Angeles, M.E. Rockhill, Inc., Long Beach, Md., Rovi Land Corp., Los Angeles, Rovi Film Corp., Los Angeles; cons. office mgmt. Recipient Star Crest, Bob Buquor Meml. Found., 1977. Mem. Nat. Notary Assn., Nat. Antivivisection Soc., Los Angeles County Mus. Art, Calif. Vols. for Literacy, Friends of Animals. Democrat. Home: 9752 W Olympic Blvd Beverly Hills CA 90210 Office: Rovi Pacific Corp Suite 1111 1801 Century Park E Los Angeles CA 90067

ROCKMAN, ILENE FRANCES, librarian, researcher, reviewer, author, lecturer; b. Yonkers, N.Y., Nov. 9, 1950; d. Leon and Margaret (Klein) R. B.A., UCLA, 1972; M.S. in L.S. U. So. Calif., 1974; M.A., Calif. Poly. State U., 1978; Ph.D., U. Calif.-Santa Barbara, 1985. Librarian, Wash. State U., Pullman, 1974-75, Calif. Poly. State U., San Luis Obispo, 1975—; adj. prof. Cuesta Coll., San Luis Obispo, 1982—; abstracter Women Studies Abstracts, Rush, N.Y., 1976—. Contbr. articles to profl. jours. Active Mozart Festival, San Luis Obispo, 1981—, Symphony Assn., San Luis Obispo, 1976—. Recipient scholarship Calif. PTA, Los Angeles, 1973. Mem. ALA, Calif. Library Assn., Assn. Coll. and Research Libraries, Am. Ednl. Research Assn., Total Library Exchange (pres. 1979-80), Library Assocs. Calif. Poly. State U. (exec. sec. 1981-83). Democrat. Home: 654 Rancho Dr San Luis Obispo CA 93401 Office: Calif Poly State U San Luis Obispo CA 93407

ROCKSTEAD, SUZANNE ELAINE, volunteer services administrator; b. Indio, Calif., June 26, 1946; d. Frederick Wilson Smee and Dorothy Lorene (Coleman) Butler; m. Clifford Alan Rockstead, Sept. 7, 1967; children—Courtney Coleman. B.S. in Social Work cum laude, Utah State U., 1967; M.S. in Guidance and Counseling cum laude, U. Tenn., 1975. Tchr. Copperas Cove Schs., Tex., 1969-70; health researcher Evaluation, Survey and Health Research Corp., Nashville, 1972-74; dir. food program Downtown Assn. Chs., Nashville, 1976; Social worker Salvation Army, Nashville, 1974-76; psychiat. social worker Tenn. Dept. Metal Health/Mental Retardation, Nashville, 1976-82, dir. of vols., 1982—; bd. dirs. Progress, Inc., Nashville, 1984-85, ARC, Nashville, 1983—, Home 2, Inc., Nashville, 1976-82, Dhaman House, Nashville, 1980-82. Editor Internat. Symposium of First Lang. Acquisition, 1974. Mem. Clover Bottom Parent-Guardian Assn., 1976—. Mem. Met. Council Dir. of Vols., Tenn. State Employees Assn., Internat. Assn. Bus. Communicators. Club: Donelson Bus. and Profl. Women. Avocations: interior design; snorkeling; skiing; swimming; furniture refinishing. Office: Tenn Dept Mental Health-Mental Retardation 275 Stewarts Ferry Pike Donelson TN 37214

ROCKWELL, ELIZABETH DENNIS, financial executive; b. Houston; d. Robert Richard and Nezzell Alderton (Christie) Dennis; divorced. Student Rice U., 1939-40, U. Houston, 1938-39, 40-42. Asst. purchasing agt. Standard Oil Co. Tex., 1942-66; with Heights Savs. Assn., Houston, 1966-82, asst. sec., 1967-70, asst. v.p., 1970-75, v.p. mktg. 1975-82; v.p., fin. planner Oppenheimer & Co., Inc., Houston, 1982—; 2d v.p. Desk and Derrick Club Am., 1960-61; instr. Coll. of Mainland, Texas City, Tex.; instr. Downtown Coll. and Continuing Edn. Center, U. Houston, also mem. savs. and loan adv. com. Downtown Coll., mem. adv. com. Coll. Bus. Adminstrn., pres. Women's Interest Network, also mem. dean's adv. bd. Bd. dirs. ARC. Named Outstanding Woman of Yr., Mem. Am. Savs. and Loan League (state dir. 1973-76, chpt. pres. 1971-72, pres. S.W. regional conf. 1972-73, Leaders award 1972), Savs. Inst. Mktg. Soc. Am. (Key Person award 1974), Inst. Fin. Edn., Fin. Mgrs., Soc. Savs. Instns., U.S. Savs. League, Houston Heights Assn. (charter, dir. 1973-77), Houston North Assn., Rice U. Bus. and Profl. Women, Heritage Soc., Internat. Platform Assn. Clubs: River Oaks Bus. Women's Exchange. Author articles. Home: 3617 Yoakum Blvd Houston TX 77006 Office: M Corp Plaza 333 Clay St Suite 4700 Houston TX 77002

ROCKWELL, RAMONA THORSON, lawyer; b. Dubuque, Iowa, Apr. 22, 1933; d. John Anderson and Eva Elizabeth (Castaneda) Thorson; m. Dwight Rockwell, Jan. 2, 1960 (div. 1973); children—Thorson, Castaneda, Cornelius. B.A., Vassar Coll., Poughkeepsie, N.Y., 1955; J.D., U. Denver, 1977. Bar: Colo. 1977. Treas., Rockwell & Newell Inc., N.Y.C., 1970-71; dir. found. solicitation Outward Bound Inc., Greenwich, Conn., 1973-74; legal asst. Summers & Fourer, P.C., Denver, 1976; assoc. DeMuth, Eiberger, Kemp & Backus, Denver, 1977-78; trust officer First Nat. Bank Denver, 1979-82; sole practice, Denver, 1983—; cons. to gen. counsel Empire Savs. Building & Loan Assn., Denver, 1979; cons. Alpha Group Inc., Laguna Beach, Calif., 1983—. Assoc. editor Denver Law Jour. 1976-77. Pres. class 1955, Vassar Coll., 1968-80; vol. Sloan Kettering Meml. Hosp., N.Y.C., 1969-74; mem. Denver Art Museum. Recipient Am. Jurisprudence award Lawyers Coop. Pub. Co., Rochester, N.Y., Bancroft-Whitney Co., 1976. Mem. Denver Bar Assn., Colo. Bar Assn., ABA, ACLU. Republican. Episcopalian. Clubs: Vassar of Colo. (bd. dirs., program chmn. 1975-77). Home: 935 Steele St Denver CO 80206 Office: 935 Steele St Denver CO 80206

ROCQUE, BERNICE L., administrator; b. Norwich, Conn., Aug. 28, 1950; d. Michael William and Gabrielle Jean D'Arc (Picard) Janovicz; m. Christopher Grey Rocque, Jan. 12, 1973. B.A., U. Conn., 1972; M.L.S., Syracuse U., 1975. Circulation asst. Conn. Coll. Library, New London, 1972-74; young adult/reference librarian Simsbury Pub. Library (Conn.), 1976-79; supr. corp. library and info. services Texaco Inc., Harrison, N.Y., 1979-80, coordinator corp. library and info. services, 1980-81, coordinator corp. library network, 1981-83, area coordinator info. analysis and devel., 1983-86, area coordinator tng. and devel., 1986—; mem. Westchester adv. council Grad. Sch. Library and Info. Sci., Pratt Inst., Bklyn., 1980-86. Pres. Pine Hill Manor Condominium Assn., Stamford, 1983—, treas., 1981-83, v.p., 1979-80; Texaco team mem. Westchester Women's Indsl. Tennis Assn., 1982—; gov. Texaco Forum, 1981-83. Gaylord Bros. Co. scholar, 1974-75. Mem. Am. Soc. Info. Sci., Spl. Libraries Assn., ALA, Conn. Young Adult Materials Discussion Group, (chairperson 1978), Beta Phi Mu. Home: 57 Pinewood Trail Trumbell CT 06611 Office: Texaco Inc Corp Services Dept 2000 Westchester Ave White Plains NY 10650

RODA, ADELE, medical market researcher; b. Phila., July 27, 1929; d. George A. and Nancy (Elefont) Stein; m. David F. Roda, Dec. 27, 1949; children—Paul, Marc, Robert. Student Temple U. Dir. field ops. Intersearch, Cheltenham, Pa., 1971-78; pres. Roda Mktg. Research, Inc., Wyncote, Pa., 1978—. Elected majority insp. Cheltenham Bd. Elections, 1977; vol. tchr. for the blind Logan's Sch. Mem. Mktg. Research Assn., Am. Mktg. Assn., Pharm. Advt. council, Pharm. Mktg. Research Group, Elkins Park Sisterhood (treas. 1978-80). Republican. Jewish.

RODABAUGH, MARY JANE, emeritus teacher educator; b. Napoleon, Ohio, Aug. 2, 1917; d. Daniel and Sophia Wilhemina (Ruetz) Gorman; B.A., B.S. in Edn., Capital U., Columbus, Ohio, 1939; M.A., Ohio State U., 1945; m. James H. Rodabaugh, Nov. 9, 1946. Tchr. social studies and English, Mt. Zion (Ohio) High Sch., 1939-43; tchr., chmn. history dept. Columbus Sch. for Girls, 1955-63; instr. Kent (Ohio) State U., 1963-65, asst. prof., 1965-67; instr. Miami U., Oxford, Ohio, 1967-69, asst. prof. dept. tchr. edn., from 1969, now prof. emeritus. John Hay fellow Williams Coll., 1965. Mem. Am. Assn. Ret. Persons (state legrs. com.), Ohio Council Social Studies, LWV, AAUW, Phi Delta Kappa. Author: (with James H. Rodabaugh) Nursing in Ohio: A History, 1951; (with Parker LaBach) Common Learnings: Core and Interdisciplinary Team Approaches, 1969. Home: 7 Chestnut Hill Oxford OH 45056

RODDA, LYNN EDITH, pharmacist; b. Spokane, Wash., May 30, 1942; d. Robert Arthur and Lois Helen (Sylvester) Fisher. m. Thomas Cook Rodda, July 6, 1974; children—Paula Ruth, Kabrena Eileen. Student Whitmore Coll., 1960-62; B.S., Portland State U., 1964; B.Pharm., Wash. State U., 1977. Tchr. jr. high sci. and math., Beaverton, Oreg., 1964-65, St. Louis Park, Minn., 1965-66, Rochester, Minn., 1966-67; pharmacist Drug Fair, Moscow, Idaho, 1976-78, Pay 'n Save Corp., Fairbanks, Alaska, 1978-80, head pharmacist, 1979-80; staff pharmacist Teamster Health Care Corp., Anchorage, 1980, Pay 'n Save Corp., Anchorage, 1980-81; acting interim asst. dir. pharmacy Providence Hosp., Anchorage, 1981-83, acting dir. pharmacy, 1984-85, asst. dir. pharmacy, 1985—. Active Anchorage Poison Control Center. Recipient Bristol award, 1985. Mem. Am. Pharm. Assn., Am. Soc. Hosp. Pharmacists, Alaska Pharm. Assn. (chmn. profl. affairs com.). Republican. Episcopalian. Office: Providence Hosp Pharm 3200 Providence Dr Anchorage AK 99502

RODEHEAVER, OLAH ANITA, county official; b. Houston, Sept. 27, 1923; d. Charles Lee and Olah Hunter (West) Robertson; m. James Harvey Rodeheaver, Nov. 1, 1943; children—Margaret Dianne Rodeheaver Dupont, Nancy Ruth Rodeheaver Luksa. Grad. John H. Reagan High Sch., Houston, 1941. Exec. asst. to clk. Harris County, Houston, 1961-78, clk., 1979—; mem. faculty Internat. Ctr. Election Law and Adminstrn., 1985. Bd. dirs. New Directions, Inc., Houston, 1982—; mem. adminstrv. bd. Collins United Methodist Ch., Houston, 1984—. Recipient Outstanding Achievement to Community and Manking award Ethel Ransom Literary Club, 1985. Mem. Internat. Assn. Clks. Recorders, Election Ofcls. and Treas. (2d v.p. 1985), County and Dist. Clks. Assn. Tex. (co-chmn. legis. com. 1979—), Nat. Assn. Counties. Democrat. Club: Bayou City Democratic Women. Lodge: Order Eastern Star. Avocations: fishing; crocheting; enjoying children and grandchildren. Home: 4514 Mountwood St Houston TX 77018 Office: County Clk PO Box 1525 1001 Preston St Houston TX 77251

RODEKOHR, KATHY LEE, vocal music educator; b. Star City, Ark., Jan. 5, 1953; d. Robert Lee and Clarrean (Robertson) McFalls; m. Larry Stephen Rodekohr, July 14, 1979. B.S.Edn. in Speech Pathology and Music Edn., U. Central Ark., 1975; postgrad. U. Wyo., 1984, U. No. Colo., 1984. Entertainer, USO, N.Y.C., 1975; field rep. Delta Zeta Sorority, Columbus, Ohio, 1975-76; speech pathologist North Little Rock Schs., Ark., 1978-79; instructional aide, substitute tchr. Laramie County Sch. Dist. 1, Cheyenne, Wyo., 1980-83, vocal music instr., 1983—. Exec. dir., bd. dirs. Miss Wyo. Scholarship Pageant, 1984—; active Cheyenne Little Theatre Players, Cheyenne Christian Players; pianist, choir mem. First Baptist Ch., Cheyenne, 1980—. Mem. Music Educators Nat. Conf., Am. Choral Dirs. Assn., Wyo. Music Educators, Cheyenne Tchrs. Assn., Wyo. Educators Assn., NEA, Delta Zeta (nat. standards chmn. 1981-85). Democrat. Avocations: piano, performing, needlepoint, collecting wooden ornaments and music boxes. Home: 829 Pike St Cheyenne WY 82009 Office: Carey Jr High Sch 1780 E Pershing Blvd Cheyenne WY 82001

RODENBAUGH, MARCIA LOUISE, educator; b. Pitts., Nov. 11, 1942; d. F. Thomas and Lucy Indiana (Fry) Wimer; m. John Anthony Lee, Mar. 21, 1964 (div. Nov. 1971); m. Richard Allan Rodenbaugh, Aug. 3, 1975; stepchildren—Ken, Tiffany, Tricia. B.A. in Edn., Westminster Coll., New Wilmington, Pa., 1964, M.Ed. in Remedial Reading, 1966. Tchr., North Hills Sch. Dist., Pitts., 1964-70, Central Bucks Schs., Doylestown, Pa., 1970—. Author children's books: Marci Books (set of 5), 1983. Pres. Maple Leaf Day Care Ctr. Bd., Warminster, Pa., 1971; pres. Wesley Coll. Parents Assn., Dover, Del., 1985-86. Mem. Pa. Edn. Assn., NEA, Central Bucks Edn. Assn., Nat. Assn. Female Execs., AAUW. Republican. Presbyterian. Avocations: skiing; sailing; writing; piano; church choir. Home: 7-16 Aspen Way Doylestown PA 18901 Office: Central Bucks Sch Dist 315 W State St Doylestown PA 18901

RODGERS, AUDREY PENN, local government official; b. Berkeley, Calif., Aug. 8, 1923; d. Lewis and Edith Penn; A.B., U. Calif., Berkeley, 1944; m. David Leigh Rodgers, June 13, 1943 (div. Mar. 1982); children—Timothy Leigh, Janice Leigh Rodgers Bracken. Research asst. U. Rochester (N.Y.) Sch. Medicine, 1943-46, 49-51, NIH, Bethesda, Md., 1948-49; design/cons. landscaping pvt. homes and gardens, 1960-69; pres. Campaign Data Service, Inc., San Francisco, 1970-80; public info. dir. East Bay Infiltration/Inflow Study, San Francisco, 1980-85; pub. info. officer East Bay Infiltration/Inflow Correction Program, Wet Weather sect. East Bay Mcpl. Utility Dist., 1986—. Mem. San Francisco Charter Revision Com., 1968-70; chmn. design group Seward St. Park Task Force, Eureka Valley Promotion Assn., 1970-73; chmn. Dolores Hts. Spl. Use Dist. Com., 1978-80; bd. dirs. The Urban Sch., 1968-69, Dolores Hts. Improvement Club, 1962-64, San Francisco Planning and Urban Research Assn., 1968-78. Mem. LWV (dir. San Francisco 1966-67), Acad. Polit. Sci., Public Relations Soc. Am. (accredited), Women in Communication, Inc., Calif. Press Women, Orgn. Women in Landscape, Calif. Native Plant Soc. (v.p. Bay chpt. 1985), Sierra Club, People for Open Space, Nature Conservancy, Alpha Xi Delta. Democrat. Club: Met. Office: PO Box 24055 care EBMUD Oakland CA 94623

RODGERS, ELIZABETH STUART, photography studio executive; b. Indpls., June 6, 1922; d. William Russell and Gertrude (Ellinwood) Stuart; m. John Boyd Rodgers, July 11, 1946 (div. Apr. 1983); children—Betsy, Holly Anne, John Boyd III, William Stuart. B.S. in Journalism, Northwestern U., 1944. Founder, Betty Stuart Studio, Evanston, Ill., 1945 (now Stuart-Rodgers Studio), br. in Chgo., 1965—; asst. prof. photography Medill Sch. Journalism, Northwestern U., 1962-78. Author: Altar Bound, 1960; contbr. articles to profl. jours. Mem. woman's bd. North Shore Country Day Sch., Winnetka, Ill., 1969-85; pres. World Adoption Info. Fund, 1960-62. Mem. Profl. Photographers Am., Kappa Alpha Theta. Republican. Clubs: Garden of Illinois (program chmn. 1965, 66), 40 Acres Garden (pres. 1957-59); Little Garden (Barrington, Ill.) (progam chmn. 1965-69). Avocations: gardening; writing; photography. Home: 330 Diversey Pkwy Chicago IL 60657 Office: 2504 Greenbay Rd Evanston IL 60201

RODGERS, KATHERINE JEAN, insurance company analyst, consultant; b. Jacobs Creek, Pa., Mar. 6, 1934; d. Francis E. and Charlotte (Kelly) Semko; m. Robert James Rodgers, Jan. 4, 1953; children—Cecilia, Robert James, Elizabeth, Eileen, Jeanine, Kathleen. Student in med. tech. Franklin Sch. Sci. and Arts, 1953. Floating corr. Beneficial Ins. Co., Phila., 1974-75, asst. to mgr. 1975; corr. Penn Mut. Life Ins. Co., Phila., 1975-76, annuity technician, 1976-78, research analyst, 1978-82, sr. mktg. info. analyst, 1982—; owner Target Assocs., Marlton, N.J., 1983—. Contbr. poetry to various publs. Dir. membership Women's Resource Group, Penn Mut. Life Ins. Co., 1981-83. Fellow Life Mgmt. Inst.; mem. Am. Mktg. Assn. (treas. chpt. 1982-85, dir. 1985-87), Nat. Assn. Female Execs., Network of Women in Computer Tech., N.J. Assn. Women Bus. Owners, Am. Bus. Communications Assn. Office: Penn Mut Life Ins Co Independence Sq Philadelphia PA 19172

RODGERS, KATHERINE VIRGINIA, scientific supervisor; b. Moorehead, Miss., June 16, 1937; d. Robert Denver and Annie Laurie (Griffing) Rodgers. B.S., Quachita Bapt. Coll., 1959; postgrad. U. Houston. Cert. tchr., Tex. Clin. chemist Meml. Bapt. Hosp., Houston, 1959; nuclear med. technologist U. Tex. Med. Sch., Galveston, 1960-61; research chemist U. Tex. Dental Sch., Houston, 1961; research asst. Rice U., Houston, 1961-62, 64-65; med. technologist Tex. Children's Hosp., Houston, 1963; tchr. secondary sch. sci. Houston Inc. Sch. Dist., 1962-65, edn. cons., 1968-69; sr. engr. Lockheed Electronics Co., Houston, 1966-72, sr. scientist, 1972-79, sci. supr. engring. and mgmt. services, 1979—. Contbr. articles to profl. jours. Recipient Apollo Achievement award NASA, 1969. Mem. Am. Chem. Soc., Tex. Tchrs. Assn., Nat. Mgmt. Assn., Alpha Chi, Gamma Sigma Epsilon. Home: 18034 Bal Harbour Dr Houston TX 77058 Office: Lockheed Engring & Mgmt Services Co 1830 Nasa Rd Houston TX 77058

RODGERS, KIM MICHELLE, lawyer; b. Inglewood, Calif., Mar. 27, 1957; d. Gilbert Raymond and Beverly (Whitaker) Rodgers; m. Christopher M. Westhoff, Sept. 1, 1984. B.A., U. So. Calif., 1978; J.D., Southwestern U., 1981. Bar: Calif. 1982. Law clk. Coulter, Vernoff & Pearson, Pasadena, Calif., 1979-82; assoc. Weissman & Weissman, Los Angeles, 1982—. Mem. Barristers (Los Angeles), Los Angeles County Bar Assn., Calif. State Bar Assn., ABA, Jr. League of Pasadena, Alpha Omicron Pi (chpt. adv., Los Angeles, 1981-83, v.p., 1983-84), Democrat. Roman Catholic. Office: Weissman & Weissman 6922 Hollywood Blvd Los Angeles CA 90028

RODGERS, MARY COLUMBRO, English educator, chancellor; b. Aurora, Ohio, Apr. 17, 1925; d. Nicola and Nancy (DeNicola) Columbro; m. Daniel Richard Rodgers, July 20, 1965; children—Daniel Robert, Mary Patricia, Mary Kristine. B.A., Notre Dame Coll., Cleve., 1957; M.A., Western Res. U., 1962; Ph.D., Ohio State U., 1964; Ed.D., Calif. Nat Open U., 1975, D.Litt., 1978. Tchr. English, Cleve. schs., 1945-61; instr.-supr. English, Ohio State U., Columbus, 1962-64; research fellow, lectr. Facolta di Mgistero, U. Rome, Italy, 1964-65; asst. prof. English, U. Md., College Par, 1965-67; assoc. prof. English, Trinity Coll., Washington, 1967-68; prof. English, U. D.C., Washington, 1968—; founder, chancellor Open U. Am. System, Hyattsville, Md., 1965—. Author 94 monographs and books including: State Supervision of English and Reading Instruction, 1967; New Design in the Teaching of English, 1972; English Pedagogy in the American Open University, 1983; Design for Personalized English Graduate Degrees in an Urban University, 1984; Open University English Teaching, 1945 to 1985: Conceptual History and Rationale, 1985; History of the American Open University, 1965-85, 1985. Contbr. articles to profl. jours. Dean Am. Open Univ. Acad., Hyattsville, Md., 1965—. Ohio State U. fellow, 1962-64; Fulbright fellow, 1964-65. Fellow Fellowship of Cath. Scholars; mem. Am. Ednl. Research Assn., Nat. Council Tchrs. English, Poetry Soc. Am. Roman Catholic. Avocations: piano; clarinet; swimming. Home and Office: 3916 Commander Dr College Heights Estates Hyattsville MD 20782

RODGERS, NANCY LUCILLE, businesswoman; b. Denver, Aug. 22, 1934; d. Francis Randolph and Irma Lucille (Budy) Baker; student public schs.; m. George J. Rodgers, Feb. 18, 1968; children by previous marriage—Kellie Rae, Joy Lynn, Timothy Francis, Thomas Francis. Mgr., Western Telearm, Inc., San Diego, 1973—; pres. Rodgers Police Patrol, Inc., San Diego, 1973-83; br. mgr. Honeywell Inc., Protection Services div., San Diego, 1977-79; pres. Image, Inc., Image Travel Agy., Cairo, Egypt, 1981-83, Western Solar Specialties, 1979-80; founder, pres. Internat. Metaphysicians Associated for Growth through Edn., San Diego, 1979; founder, dir. Point Loma Sanctuary, 1983-86; co-founder, producer Zerciee Unltd., 1986—; co-founder, producer, dir. mktg. Zerciee Prodns., 1986—; cons., mem. speakers' bur. MOVE, Profl. Women's Center. Bd. dirs. Central City Assn. Mem. Am. Soc. Indsl. Security Assn., Western Burglar and Fire Alarm Assn., Nat. Burglar and Fire Alarm Assn., Calif. Assn. Lic. Investigators, Sales and Mktg. Execs. Internat., Am. Soc. Women Execs., Nat. Assn. for Holistic Health, Profl. Women's Assn., Apt. Rental and Owners Assn., Am. Bus. Women's Assn., Am. Union Metaphysicians, Nat. Assn. Women Contractors. Republican. Clubs: San Diego Yacht, Soroptimist Internat. Home: San Diego CA Office: 744 G St Suite 206B San Diego CA 92101

RODGERS, PATRICIA ANN, lawyer; b. Pitts., Nov. 17, 1952; d. Thomas Edwin and Patricia Marlene (Wagner) Rodgers; m. David Hampton Cullis, Aug. 31, 1979. B.A., Indiana U. of Pa., 1974; J.D., U. Toledo, 1977. Bar: Ohio 1978, Pa. 1978, U.S. Dist. Ct. (no. dist.) Ohio 1979, (we. dist.) Pa. 1980, U.S. Ct. Appeals (3d cir.) 1983. Assoc. Nina Sherman law firm, Toledo, 1978; ptnr. Rodgers & Zurawsky, Greensburg, Pa., 1978-79; pres., dir. Rodgers, Rodgers, Morava & Cullis, P.C. and predecessor firm, Greensburg, 1979—; instr. law Westmoreland County Community Coll., Youngwood, Pa., 1978-79. Contbg. author: Executive Report, 1985. Mem. continuing edn. adv. bd. Seton Hill Coll., Greensburg, 1982-84; chmn. Women's Adv. Commn., Westmoreland County, Pa., 1983-85; bd. dirs. Life Mgmt. Assocs., Greensburg, 1984—, Westmoreland County Community Coll., 1986—. Named Bus. Person of Week, WHJB/WOKU Radio and Pitts. Nat. Bank, 1983. Mem. ABA (family law com.), Pa. Bar Assn. (family law com.), Ohio Bar Assn., Westmoreland County Bar Assn. (family law com., civil rules com., constn. and by-laws com.), Greensburg Bus. and Profl. Women (program chair 1982-83, 1st v.p. 1982-83, pres., dir. 1983—, asst. dir. dist. 3), Phi Alpha Theta, Pi Gamma Mu. Office: Rodgers Rodgers Morava & Cullis PC 600 Rugh Ave Suite A Greensburg PA 15601

RODIGER, GEORGIANA GLENN, psychotherapist; b. Cambridge, Mass., Feb. 11, 1931; d. C. Leslie and Georgiana (Sibley) Glenn; B.A., Pomona Coll., 1952; postgrad. George Washington U., 1951, U. So. Calif., 1953; M.A., Fuller Theol. Sem., 1975; Ph.D., Fuller Grad. Sch. Psychology, 1980; m. William B. Rodiger, Jan. 31, 1953, (div. 1976); children—Georgiana, William B., James, Margaret, John. Field dir. Pasadena Area Girl Scouts U.S.A., 1952-53; developmental disabilities cons., trainer, research asst. Bur. Training and Manpower Devel. Sect., Calif. Dept. Health, Sacramento, 1973-76, psychol. asst., 1977-79; intern psychiat. div. Children's Hosp., 1978-80, trainer hospice vols., 1978-79; psychotherapist in pvt. practice, exec. dir. Georgiana Rodiger Center, Pasadena, 1980—; cons. Pasadena Unified Sch. Dist., 1979-81; faculty Pacific Oaks Coll., 1980-82, Rosemead Sch. Psychology, 1982-84. Co-founder, Hospice of Pasadena, 1979, Candlelighters, 1981; adviser Women in the Middle, 1981, Anorexic Bulemic Group, 1981-84; active United Way, PTA, Vis. Nurse Assn., others. Recipient Nat. award, United Community Funds and Councils of Am., 1968; Newton D. Baker Cert. of Recognition. Mem. Am. Psychol. Assn. Episcopalian. Club: Pasadena Jr. League. Home: 1102 Arden Rd Pasadena CA 91106 Office: 69 N Catalina St Pasadena CA 91106

RODINO, ELAINE ANN, psychologist; b. N.Y.C., Apr. 16, 1940; d. Americo Joseph and Rachel (Cafiero) Lamberti; B.S. cum laude, C.W. Post Coll., L.I. U., 1961; M.A., Hofstra U., 1963; Ph.D., Calif. Sch. Profl. Psychology, 1978; m. Robert J. Rodino, July 3, 1965; 1 dau., Michelle Lynn. Sch. psychologist Long Beach (N.Y.) City Sch. Dist., 1964-67, 70-71, Roslyn (N.Y.) Sch. Dist., 1971-76, Gt. Neck (N.Y.) Sch. Dist., 1973-75; mem. supervisory staff Center for Legal Psychiatry, Santa Monica, Calif., 1978-83; pvt. practice clin. psychology, Santa Monica, 1978—; psychologist Los Angeles Suicide Prevention Center, 1978-84; psychologist, clin. dir., 1982-84; mem. Calif. Task Force on Positive Parenting, 1978-79. Mem. Los Angeles County Psychol. Assn. (pres. 1983), Am. Psychol. Assn., Calif. State Psychol. Assn. (media psychology div.), Western Psychol. Assn., Am. Assn. Suicidology, Pi Gamma Mu, Psi Chi. Office: 233 Wilshire Blvd Suite 910 Santa Monica CA 90401

RODMAN, ELLEN RENA, broadcasting executive; b. Boston, July 5, 1940; d. Samuel and Edith (Aronson) Blumsack; m. William Bryant Rodman, Sept. 2, 1962; children—Pamela Beth, Keith Andrew. B.S., Simmons Coll., 1962; M.A., Columbia U., 1964; Ph.D., NYU, 1980. Dir. theatre arts various pvt. schs., N.Y.C., 1970-74; features writer N.Y. Daily News, N.Y. Times and McCalls mag., N.Y.C., 1974-79; children's entertainment reviewer N.Y. Times, 1974-79; dir. children's info. services NBC, N.Y.C., 1980-82, dir. corp. info. services, 1982-84; dir. corp. communications Westinghouse Broadcasting and Cable, Inc., 1984-85; v.p. corp. communications Children's TV Workshop, 1985—; dir. Nat. Assn. for Industry-Edn. Coop., Washington, 1983—. Author: (with Richard Flaste) The N.Y. Times Guide to Children's Entertainment, 1976; contbr. chpts. to books, articles to profl. jours., mags. Mem. Women in Communications, Am. Women in Radio and TV, Internat. Radio and TV Soc., Nat. Assn. Broadcasters (children's TV com. 1983-84). Office: Children's TV Workshop 1 Lincoln Plaza New York NY 10023

RODMAN, IRENE BETTY, association executive; b. Bklyn., Nov. 5, 1924; d. Frederick Sheldon Clark and Frances (Rice) Emmont; m. Warren Edward Rodman, June 27, 1943; children—Warren Lee, Donald Edward, Justin Leslie, Barbara Lynn. Profl. trainer N.Y.S. Quarterhorse Assn., Ghent, Buskirk, N.Y., 1952-76; teacher, coordinator Cottage Crafts Handspuns, Greenwich, N.Y., 1976-79; mgr. admissions Bennington Mus., Inc., Old Bennington, Vt., 1980-83; dir. caretaker Historic Preservation Old Bennington, 1983-85; exec. dir. Am. Cancer Soc., Hudson Falls, N.Y., 1986—; dir. Goodrich Quarter Horse Farms, Buskirk, 1965-70; cons. Peter Mattison Tavern, Shaftsbury, Vt., 1977-85, Mus. Old Bennington, 1978—. One-woman shows at Loveland Mus., Colo., 1984, Autumn Retreat Festival, Colo., 1984; represented in permanent collections at Bennington Mus., Inc., Peter Matteson Tavern. Contbr. articles to profl. publs. Co-author: Herbs to Infinity, 1979. Mem. Co. Mil. Historians, Chapman Mus., Hyde Collection, Inc., Bennington Mus., Inc. Republican. Methodist. Avocations: collecting military miniatures; writing; snowshoeing; gardening. Home: Box 126 RD#3 Kenyon Rd Greenwich NY 12834

RODMAN, JANE E., editor; b. Washington County, Ind., June 7, 1921; d. Glenn O. and Pearl E. (Bartlett) R. A.B., Evansville Coll., 1942; M.A., Ind. U., 1946. History tchr. Huntingburg High Sch. (Ind.), 1942-44, Evansville Coll. (Ind.), 1946-47; editorial asst., researcher to prof. Ind. U., Bloomington, 1947-53; sec., editorial asst. Ind. U. Press, Bloomington, 1953-55, asst. editor, 1955-69, assoc. editor, 1969-77, editor, 1977—. Editor: The Pictorial History of Indiana, 1980; author hist. articles. Mem. Bloomington Restorations, Hoosier Heritage Mus. Soc., Hist. Landmarks Found. Ind. Mem. Ind. Hist. Soc., Women in Communications. Republican. Mem. Ch. of Christ. Clubs: Women's Faculty, University (Bloomington). Home: 722 E University St Bloomington IN 47401 Office: Ind Univ Press 10th and Morton Sts Bloomington IN 47405

RODMAN, LINDA FRANK, employee relations executive; b. N.Y.C., Feb. 6, 1952; d. Eugene David and Doris (Lane) Frank; m. Lawrence Bernard Rodman, June 25, 1978; 1 child, Tara Alexa. B.A. cum laude, Yale U., 1973, M.A., 1975. Orgn. devel. cons. Mfrs. Hanover Trust, N.Y.C., 1975-77; mgmt. devel. assoc. Exxon Internat. Co., N.Y.C., 1977-79; sr. compensation analyst Exxon Corp., N.Y.C., 1979-81, personnel advisor corp. planning, 1981-83, employee resources coordinator, 1983-86, exec. compensation coordinator, 1986—. Contbr. articles to profl. jours. Bd. dirs., sec., chmn. mgmt. com. Children's Mus. of Manhattan, 1985—; mem. friends com. Lenox Hill Hosp., N.Y.C., 1983—; class chmn. Campaign for Yale, N.Y.C., 1980; rep. Yale U. Alumni Schs. Com., N.Y.C., 1975—; class agt. Yale U. Alumni Fund, N.Y.C., 1973—. Mem. Human Resources Planning Soc. (dir. 1980-84, chmn. com. on regional affiliates 1980-83, mem. nominating, profl. devel., constn. coms., orgn. sponsor, conf. coms. 1979-84), N.Y. Human Resource Planners (charter pres. 1978-80, exec. com. 1981—). Home: 50 Riverside Dr New York NY 10024 Office: Exxon Corp 1251 Ave of Americas New York NY 10020

RODMAN, SANDRA HUDLOW, editor; b. Arlington, Tex., Oct. 1, 1942; d. Paul Bennett and Sadie (Reedy) Hudlow; student U. Tex., 1961-67; Baylor U., 1963; m. Thomas J. Rodman, Oct. 7, 1967 (div.). Founding mem. Phoenix House Found., N.Y.C., 1967, coordinator program devel., 1971-72, exec. asst. to sr. v.p., 1973-78, bus. officer Calif. div., 1979-81, dir. adminstrn., 1981-83; exec. editor Strategic Learning Systems Pub., N.Y.C., 1981—; program devel. cons. Samaritan Village, N.Y.C., 1983-84; asst. instr. Phoenix Inst. Fin. Mgmt., 1978. Mem. N.Y. State Drug Abuse Fin. Task Force, Albany, 1977; chmn. Nat. Therapeutic Communities Task Force on Program Planning, 1981-83; trustee Potter's Field Theatre Co., N.Y.C., 1981-82. Recipient Nat. Radio-TV Best Actress award U. Tex., 1967. Mem. Nat. Assn. Female Execs., World Fedn. Therapeutic Communities, Phi Kappa Phi, Alpha Lambda Delta. Playwright/composer: The Mullions, 1966; Cosmic Cowboys, 1979. Office: 130 Hardenburgh Ave Demarest NJ 07627

RODMAN, SUE (ARLENE), wholesale Indian crafts company executive, artist; b. Fort Collins, Colo., Oct. 1, 1951; d. Marvin F. and Barbara I. (Miller) Lawson; m. Alpine C. Rodman, Dec. 13, 1970; 1 child, Connie Lynn. Student Colo. State U., 1970-73. Silversmith Pinel Silver Shop, Loveland, Colo., 1970-71; asst. mgr. Traveling Traders, Phoenix, 1974-75; co-owner, co-mgr. Deer Track Traders, Ltd., Loveland, 1975-85, exec. v.p., 1985—. Author: The Book of Contemporary Indian Arts and Crafts, 1985. Mem. Republican Presdl. Task Force, 1982—; mem. U.S. Senatorial Club, 1982—. Beta Loveland Women's Club scholar, 1969; Valley Airpark, Inc. Gordon M. Walker aviation meml. scholar, 1970. Mem. Nat. Assn. Female Execs., Indian Arts and Crafts Assn. Baptist. Club: Crazy Horse Grass Roots (S.D.). Avocations: museums; recreation research; fashion design; reading. Office: Deer Track Traders Ltd PO Box 448 Loveland CO 80539

RODMANN, DOROTHY ELLEN, association adminstr.; b. Washington, Feb. 1, 1930; d. Michael Albert and Georgie Rebecca (Stant) Peters; B.A., George Washington U., 1954, postgrad., 1954-55; m. Horst Rodmann, June 7, 1958; children—Leslie Ann, Karen Lynn. Adminstr. asst. Am. Polit. Sci. Assn., Washington, 1954-58; personnel asst. NEA, Washington, 1959-69, personnel assoc., 1969-71, employment mgr., 1971-72; personnel mgr. Nat. League Cities-U.S. Conf. of Mayors, Washington, 1972-76; personnel dir. Am. Chem. Soc., 1977—. Mem. Washington Personnel Assn., Conf. Instl. Adminstrs., Greater Washington Soc. Assn. Execs., Alpha Delta Pi. Club: Arminius Social (Washington). Home: 8428 Georgian Way Annandale VA 22003 Office: 1155 16th St NW Washington DC 20036

RODRIGUEZ, GILDA ENA, lawyer; b. Santurce, P.R.; Feb. 20, 1952; d. Ismael and Ena (Perez) R. B.A. in History, Fordham U., 1973; J.D., NYU, 1979. Bar: N.Y. 1981, D.C. 1980, U.S. Dist. Ct. (so. dist.) N.Y. 1983, U.S. Dist. Ct. (ea. dist.) N.Y. 1983, U.S. Dist. Ct. D.C. 1981, U.S. Ct. Appeals (D.C. cir.) 1981. Atty., Bur. Competition, FTC, Washington, 1979-82; asst. atty. gen. N.Y. State Dept. Law, N.Y.C., 1982-83; atty. AT&T, N.Y.C., 1983—; mem. staff N.Y. U. Rev. Law and Social Change, 1977-78. Helena Rubenstein Found. scholar, 1977-79. Mem. ABA, N.Y. State Bar Assn., D.C. Bar Assn.

RODRIGUEZ, JULIE LAYNE, computer-aided design specialist, mechanical engineer; b. Schenectady, Sept. 25, 1959; d. Phil Arroya and Mary Lou (Talbot) R. B.S.M.E., Ohio State U., 1982. Heating, ventilating and air-conditioning design engr. N.Y. State Office Gen. Services Div. Design and Constrn., Albany, 1982-84, sr. computer-aided design/drafting devel. specialist, 1984—. Mem. Am. Soc. Women Engrs., ASME Ohio State U. Alumni Club of Upstate N.Y. (pres. 1985—). Avocations: travel; racquetball; skiing; dance; photography. Home: 33 Lakeshore Dr Apt 2A Watervliet NY 12189 Office: New York State Office Gen Services Div Design and Constrn Empire State Plaza Corning Tower 34th Floor Albany NY 12242

RODRIGUEZ ORENSTEIN, ROSA MARIA, lawyer; b. Juarez, Chihuahua, Mexico, Jan. 5, 1956; came to U.S., 1961, naturalized, 1975; d. Alejo and Carmen (Montalvo) Rodriguez; m. James David Orenstein, May 20, 1979; children—Louis Thomas, Sara Lucia. B.A. in Econs., Stanford U., 1978; J.D., U. Calif.-Berkeley, 1981. Bar: Tex. 1982. Assoc., Gardere & Wynne, Dallas, 1982—. Mem. Dallas Hispanic C. of C., ABA, Tex. Bar Assn., Mexican Am. Bar Assn. Democrat. Roman Catholic. Clubs: Chicana Law Caucus, La Raza Law Students. Office: Gardere & Wynne 1700 Republic Bank Bldg Pacific and Ervay Sts Dallas TX 75201

ROE, CHERI LEE, physical education and health educator; b. Paterson, N.J., June 30, 1953; d. James William and Dorothy Helen (Johnson) R. B.S., Ashland Coll., 1975; M.A., U. Denver, 1976. Tchr., coach Felician Coll., Lodi, N.J., 1977, Lakeland Regional High Sch., Ringwood, N.J., 1980-81, Passaic County Tech. and Vocat. High Sch., Wayne, N.J., 1977—; volleyball coach Passaic County Tech. and Vocat. High Sch., 1983—; field hockey coach Lakeland High Sch., Wanaque, N.J., 1977-80, track and field coach, 1981. Mem. Democratic County Com. Women, Wayne, N.J., 1982-83; vol. Girl Scouts, North Jersey, 1975-84. Served to 2d lt. USNG, 1975—. Recipient Leadership award N.J. Mil. Acad. 1983. Mem. Discom Officers Assn. (treas. 1984—), Signal Officers Assn., N.J. N.G. Orgn., N.J. Edn. Assn., Passaic County Vocat. and Tech. Edn. Assn. (v.p. 1984—). Avocations: sports; travel. Home: 167 Lake Dr W Wayne NJ 07470

ROE, DONNA JENSEN, sales executive; b. Akron, Ohio, Nov. 22, 1930; d. John Davidson and Helen Graves (Shipley) Miller; student Kent State U., 1949-51; C.P.S., Ariz. State U., 1962; A.A., Phoenix Coll., 1974; postgrad. Grad. Sch. Bus., U. Wis.-Madison, 1980; m. Robert B. Roe, July 5, 1975 (dec.); children—Pamela, Christopher. Community, communication specialist Sperry Flight Systems, Phoenix, 1957-76; appointments sec. Gov. Wesley Bolin, State of Ariz., Phoenix, 1977-78; corr. sec. Gov. Bruce Babbitt, State of Ariz., Phoenix, 1978; asst. to dir. Ariz. Dept. Econ. Security, Phoenix, 1978-79; asst. exec. dir. Samaritan Med. Found., Phoenix, 1979-82; dir. catering sales Camelback Inn, Scottsdale, Ariz., 1983—. Mem. exec. bd. Theodore Roosevelt Council, Inc. Boy Scouts Am., 1977—; Mem. Ariz. Soc. Assn. Execs., Internat. Assn. Bus. Communicators, Women in Communications, Inc., Phoenix Art Mus. League, Phoenix Symphony Guild, Phoenix Opera Dames, Heard Mus. Republican. Presbyterian. Home: 77 E Missouri Ave Phoenix AZ 85012

ROE, RAMONA JERALDEAN, lawyer; b. Gassville, Ark., May 27, 1942; d. Roy Arlington and Wanda Jeraldean (Finley) Roe. B.A., U. Ark.-Fayetteville, 1964; J.D., U. Ark.-Little Rock, 1976. Bar: Ark. 1976. Mng. ptnr. Roe & Hunt, Rogers, Ark., 1977-81; assoc. firm Richardson & Richardson, Little Rock, 1981-82; sole practice, Little Rock, 1982-84; dep. exec. dir. Ark. Workers Compensation Commn., 1984—; city atty. City of Lowell (Ark.), 1978; instr. English composition North Ark. Community Coll., Rogers, 1980. Assoc. editor Ark. Law Rev., 1974-76; contbr. articles to profl. jours. Sec.-treas. Women's Circle, United Meth. Ch., Pea Ridge, Ark., 1980-81. Mem. AAUW (treas. 1980), ABA, Ark. Bar Assn., Ark. Assn. Women Lawyers, Mensa, Beaver Lake Bus. and Profl. Women (v.p. and treas. 1977-80), Napoleonic Soc. Am., Pulaski County Hist. Soc., Mensa, Delta Theta Phi, Lambda Tau. Methodist.

ROEHM, MARYANNE EVANS, nurse, university dean; b. Vigo County, Ind., Nov. 29, 1925; d. Herbert Elmer and Reba Fern Evans; m. Joseph L Roehm, Aug. 10, 1947. Diploma Union Hosp. Sch. Nursing, 1946; B.S., Ind. State U., 1953, M.S., 1957; M.S.N., Ind. U., 1965, Ed.D., 1966. Instr. and asst. dir. Union Hosp. Sch. Nursing, Terre Haute, Ind., 1946-55; asso. dir. edn. St. Anthony Hosp. Sch. Nursing, Terre Haute, 1957-64; asst. prof., then asso. prof. Ind. State U. Sch. Nursing, Terre Haute, 1966-70, dir. continuing edn., 1970-77, interim dean and dir. continuing edn., 1977-78, dean, 1978—; mem. Ind. State Bd. Nurses Registration and Nursing Edn., 1978-81, pres., 1980-81; mem. adv. com. Master's Degree program Ind. U. Sch. Nursing, 1981; mem. adv. com. hypertension project Vigo County Health Dept., 1981; mem. health occupations adv. com. Ind. Vocat. Tech. Coll., 1970—; mem. tech. adv. panel Ind. Commn. Higher Edn., 1979-80; mem. Ind. Council Baccalaureate and Higher Degree Deans and Dirs., Ind. Council Asso. Degree Deans and Dirs.; mem. adv. com. pediatric nurses asso. program Ind. U. Sch. Nursing, 1972-78; numerous workshops and confs. Asso. editor Nursing Digest, 1973-75. Contbr. articles to profl. jours. Mem. Vigo County Blood Donor Council, 1980; mem. community adv. council Terre Haute Center for Med. Edn. at Ind. State U., 1977—; mem. Vigo County Home Citizens Com., 1970—; vice-precinct committeeman; active ARC, Baptist Ch., CD; chmn. cancer prevention study Vigo County chpt. Am. Heart Assn., 1982. Named Nurse of Yr., Ind. Citizens League Nursing, 1978; cert. of recognition Ind. State Nurses Assn., 1977. Mem. Am. Nurses Assn. (council continuing edn.), Ind. Nurses Assn., Nat. League Nursing, Ind. League Nursing, AAUP, Am. Assn. Higher Edn., Am. Assn. Collegiate Deans, Midwest Alliance Nursing, Ind. U. Alumni Assn., Ind. State U. Alumni Assn., Union Hosp. Sch. Nursing Alumni Assn., Pi Lambda Theta, Sigma Theta Tau, Kappa Delta Pi, Phi Kappa Phi. Club: Altrusa. Republican. Home: Rural Route 22 Box 561 Terre Haute IN 47802 Office: 8th and Chestnut Sts Terre Haute IN 47809

ROELKER, NANCY LYMAN, history educator; b. Warwick, R.I., June 15, 1915; d. William Greene and Anna R. (Koues) Roelker; A.B., Radcliffe Coll., 1936; Ph.D., Harvard U., 1953. Tchr. history Winsor Sch., Boston, 1941-63; asst. prof. history Tufts U., 1963-65, asso. prof., 1965-69, prof., 1969-71; prof. European history Boston U., 1971-80; adj. prof. Brown U., 1979—. John Simon Guggenheim fellow, 1965-66; recipient medal for disting. achievement Radcliffe Coll., 1970, Metcalf prize Boston U., 1974, Gold medal City of Paris, 1985. Mem. Am. Hist. Assn., (v.p. research div. 1975-78, chmn. internat. activities com., U.S. del. to Internat. Congress Hist. Scis. 1982—), Soc. French Hist. Studies (pres. 1977-78), Am. Soc. Reformation Research, Am. Acad. Arts and Sci. Author: The Paris of Henry of Navarre, 1958; Editor, translator In Search of France, 1963, From Wilson to Roosevelt: American Foreign Policy 1913-1945, 1963; Queen of Navarre, Jeanne d'Albret, 1528-1572, 1968. Contbr. articles to profl. jours. Home: 777 Love Ln East Greenwich RI 02818 Office: Box N Brown U Providence RI 02912

ROELOFS, ALICE RUTH, human services non-profit company executive; b. LeMars, Iowa, Sept. 21, 1946; d. Edgar John and BettyJo (Clark) R.; m. Kenneth H. Kreps (div.); children—Alexis John, Erik Kevin; m. Joseph Dragun. B.A., Calif. State Coll., San Bernardino, 1968; elem. edn. cert. Met. State Coll., Denver, 1974; M.A., Eastern Mich. U., 1985. Tchr., Aurora Pub. Schs., Colo., 1970-74; program coordinator Coll. for Living, Met. State Coll., Denver, 1974-80; dir. Alternative Services, Royal Oak, Mich., 1980; chief exec. officer Adult Learning Systems, Inc., Ypsilanti, Mich., 1981—; mem. adv. bd. Ind. Living Commn., Mich. Dept. Social Services, 1985-86. Author: College for Living, 1978; Whole Life Program: Adult Learning, 1984; Adult Learning: Whole Life Living Skills Curriculum, 1984; World of Work: Job Club for ESL, 1985. Contbr. articles to profl. jours. Mem. Central Am. Edn. Action Com., Ann Arbor, Mich., 1984—; coordinator Washtenaw County, Mich. Coalition Against the Death Penalty, 1985-86. Grantee Mich. Dept. Edn., 1985, Mich. Dept. Mental Health, 1985-86. Mem. Am. Assn. Mental Deficiencies, Nat. Assn. Female Execs., Amnesty Internat. (regional membership coordinator Mich. 1984—), NOW. Avocations: movies; cooking; exercising; writing; dancing. Home: 1324 Marlborough St Ann Arbor MI 48104 Office: Adult Learning Systems Inc 813 E Michigan Ave Suite 207 Ypsilanti MI 48198

ROELOFS, BONNIE DOUGAL, manufacturing company executive, consultant; b. London, Nov. 21, 1954; came to U.S., 1956; d. Robert Elliot and Catherine (Fearnow) Dougal; m. James Leroy Roelofs, Aug. 20, 1976. B.B.A., Pan Am. U., 1976. Recruting coordinator Missile-Ordinance div. Tex. Instruments, Richardson, Tex., 1976-79; human resource specialist Office Systems div. Mead Corp., Richardson, 1979-81; western region sr. staffing rep. Tektronix, Inc., Irving, Tex., 1981-84, human resource specialist III, 1984-86, eastern region human resource mgr., 1986—; guest lectr. Pan Am. U., Edinburg, Tex., 1976-79, 81—, Skyline High Sch., Dallas, 1983; corp. rep. interview skills workshops and career days at various univs., 1976—. Fedn. Women's Club scholar, 1972; Kappa Delta scholar, 1974-76. Mem. Am. Soc. Personnel Adminstrs., Dallas Personnel Assn., Am. Compensation Assn., Panhellenic Council, Greek Council, Pi Omega Pi (charter mem., pres. 1974-76), Kappa Delta (v.p. 1973-75, Most Ideal Kappa Delta award 1975). Home: 2923 Silverton St Dallas TX 75229 Office: Tektronix Inc 1551 Corporate Dr Irving TX 75038

ROEPKEN, KAREN ELIZABETH, marketing executive; b. Chgo., Feb. 2, 1956; d. Henry Theodore and Sigrid (Pfaue) Roepken. B.S., U. Ill., 1978, M.S., 1979. Project dir. Burke Mktg. Research, Cin., 1979-81; research analyst S.C. Johnson, Racine, Wis., 1981-82; research analyst, assoc. mgr. market research, Helene Curtis Industries, Inc., Chgo., 1982-84; asst. dir. mktg. and econ. research United Dairy Industry Assn., Rosemont, Ill., 1984-86, sr. v.p. mktg. and econ. research, 1986—. Mem. Am. Mktg. Assn., U. Ill. Alumni Assn., Kappa Tau Alpha. Home: 428 North Ave Barrington IL 60010 Office: UDIA 6300 N River Rd Rosemont IL 60018

ROESCH, BETTY LOU, county offical, appraiser; b. Ipswich, S.D., Feb. 20, 1930; d. Quintin John and Anna Elizabeth (McGuckin) Founder; m. Donald Lloyd Stevens, Aug. 22, 1949 (div. Dec. 1969); children—Terry Lynn, Donna Marie, Scott David, Charles Lee; m. Donald Frederick Roesch, Aug. 14, 1979. Student No. State U., Aberdeen, S.D., 1947-48. Cert. assessor, S.D.; lic. real estate appraiser, 1986. Elem. tchr. rural area, Ipswich, 1948-50; dep. dir. equalization Edmunds County, Ipswich, 1965-75, dir. of equalization, 1975—. Bd. dirs. Ipswich Community Hosp., 1986. Contbr. articles to taxation mags. Mem. S.D. Assessor's Assn. (pres. dist. #7 level 1978-83; treas. state level 1983-84, 2nd v.p. 1984-85), Cert. S.D. Assessor (state pres. 1986). Democrat. Roman Catholic. Clubs: Arts and Crafts, Extension (Edmunds County pres. 1964-67, dist. #6 pres. 1968-70; rep. nat. conv. 1969). Lodge: Moose. Avocations: reading, travel. Office: Dir of Equalization 210 2d Ave Box 62 Ipswich SD 57451

ROESCHLAUB, JEAN (MARIAN) CLINTON, restaurant chain exec.; b. Berkeley, Calif., June 1, 1927; d. Clifford E. and Nelda M. (Patterson) Clinton; A.A., Stephens Coll., 1944; m. David J. Davis III, June 26, 1946 (dec. 1963); children—David J. Davis IV, Diane J., Bruce Clinton Davis; m. 2d, Ronald Curtis Roeschlaub, Jan. 9, 1965; 1 son, Ronald W. Civilian cons. on loan to Q.M. Gen., 1944-45; co-owner, dir. foods, v.p. Clinton's Restaurants, Inc., operators Clinton's Cafeterias, Los Angeles, 1944—; dir. Glendale Fed. Savs. and Loan Assn. Chmn. bd. curators Stephens Coll.; bd. dirs., mem. exec. com. Assistance League of So. Calif.; mem. aux. Braille Inst. Am., Los Angeles. Mem. Nat. Restaurant Assn., Calif. State Restaurant Assn. Republican. Presbyterian. Clubs: Orphanage Guild, Los Angeles Country, Los Angeles Athletic. Home: 5005 Los Feliz Blvd Los Angeles CA 90027 Office: 515 W 7th St Los Angeles CA 90014

ROESS, ALICE GUION, investment executive; b. St. Petersburg, Fla., May 20, 1943; d. William Rhinelander and Martha Alice (Kithcart) Wood; m. Martin John Roess, Jr., Nov. 21, 1981; 1 child, Florence Alice Roess. B.A. in Real Estate, Eckerd Coll., St. Petersburg, Fla., 1985. Cert. property mgr., real estate broker Fla. Property mgr. Kuhlman & Gentry, St. Petersburg, Fla., 1977-78; condominium mgr. Isla Del Sol, St. Petersburg, 1978-80; pres. Guaranty Mgmt., Assocs., Inc., St. Petersburg, 1982-83, Tour Hosts Mgmt., Inc., St. Petersburg, 1983—, v.p. Ocean Club of Palm Beach Shores, Inc., St. Petersburg, 1983—; supervisory mgmt. cons. A. Clinton Brooks & Co. Inc., St. Petersburg, 1980—; founding sec.-treas. Lenders Nationwide Mortgage Corp., St. Petersburg, 1984-86; pres. Gabriella Corp., St. Petersburg, 1984—. Mem. DAR, Tampa Mus. Fine Arts, St. Petersburg Mus. Fine Arts, Nat. Assn. Realtors, Inst. Real Estate Mgmt., Community Assns. Inst., Valuers, St. Petersburg Bd. Realtors, Fla. Assn. Realtors, Mensa. Republican. Episcopalian. Clubs: St. Petersburg Yacht, Intertel, Treasure Island Tennis and Yacht, Ocean (Palm Beach Shores). Home: The Lido 4450 Gulf Blvd Saint Petersburg FL 33706 Office: 1301 66th St N Saint Petersburg FL 33710

ROESSLER, P. DEE, lawyer; b. McKinney, Tex., Nov. 4, 1941; d. W.D. and Eunice Marie (Medcalf) Powell; m. George L. Roessler, Jr., Nov. 16, 1963; (div. Dec. 1977); children—Laura Diane, Trey. Student Austin Coll., 1960-61, 62-64, Wauland Bapt. Coll., 1961-62; B.A., U. West Fla., 1968; postgrad. East Tex. State U., 1975, U. Tex.-Dallas, 1977; J.D., So. Meth. U., 1982. Bar: Tex. 1982, U.S. Dist. Ct. (ea. dist.) Tex. 1983, U.S. Dist. Ct. (no. dist.) Tex. 1983. Tchr., Van Alstyne Ind. Sch. Dist., Tex., 1968-69; social worker Dept. Social Services, Fayetteville, N.C., 1971-73, Dept. Human Services, Sherman and McKinney, Tex., 1973-79, 81; mem. firm Abernathy & Roeder, McKinney, Tex., 1982-85, Ronald W. Uselton, Sherman, 1985—; instr. Collin County Community Coll., McKinney, 1986—; mem. Collin County Shelter for Battered Women, 1984—, chmn., 1984-85; v.p. Collin County Child Welfare Bd., 1985—; Republican judicial candidate Collin County, 1986; chmn. bd. Tri County Consortium Mental Health Mental Retardation, 1984-85; mem. Tex. Area 5 Health System Agy., 1979; mem. Collin County Mental Health Adv. Bd., 1978-79. Mem. Collin County Bar Assn., Collin County Women's Bar (chmn. 1984-85), Grayson County Bar Assn., Grayson County Social Services Assn. Baptist. Avocations: dancing; tennis; golf; reading; writing. Home: 2218 Chippendale St McKinney TX 75069 Office: Collin County Community Coll 2200 W University St McKinney TX 75069

ROFFEY, LEANE ELIZABETH, insurance company systems analyst programmer; b. Chgo., Mar. 17, 1949; d. Joseph Andrew and Ethel Antoinette (DeSalvo) Accomando; m. Arthur Roffey, 1972 (div. 1973). B.A., Wayne State U., 1972. Indsl. cons. Computype Corp., Ann Arbor, Mich., 1976-77; project leader Manufacturing Data Systems, Ann Arbor, 1978-80; info. mgmt. supr. First Variable Life Ins. Co., Little Rock, 1980-82; programmer/analyst First Pyramid Life, Little Rock, 1982-83, Ark. Blue Cross and Blue Shield, Inc., Little Rock, 1983-85, Am. Security Life Ins. Co., San Antonio, 1985—. Fellow Life Mgmt. Inst.; mem. Mensa. Republican. Episcopalian. Avocations: vocal coach.

ROGALSKI, ADRIENNE ALICE, cell biologist, educator; b. Chgo., Aug. 2, 1953; d. Edward Joseph and Viola Veronica (Komen) R.; B.A., U. Chgo., 1975; Ph.D., U. Ill., 1981. Sr. research technician U. Chgo., 1975-76; research asst., Univ. fellow U. Ill., 1976-81; NIH fellow U. Calif., San Diego, 1981-85; asst. prof. dept. anatomy U. Ill.-Chgo., 1985—. Mem. Am. Soc. Cell Biology, AAAS, Sigma Xi. Office: U Ill Chgo Dept Anatomy Box 6998 808 S Wood St Chicago IL 60680

ROGALSKI, LOIS ANN, speech and language pathologist; b. Bklyn., Dec. 17, 1947; d. Louis J. and Filomena Evelyn (Maro) Giordano; B.A., Bklyn. Coll., 1968; M.A., U. Mass., 1969; Ph.D., N.Y. U., 1975; m. Stephen James Rogalski, June 27, 1970; children—Keri Anne, Stefan Louis, Christopher James, Rebecca Blair. Speech and lang. pathologist Rehab. Center of So. Fairfield County, Stamford, Conn., 1969, Sch. Health Program-P.A. 481, Stamford, 1969-72; pvt. practice speech and lang. pathology, Scarsdale, N.Y., 1972—; cons. Bd. Coop. Ednl. Services, 1976-79, Handicapped Program for Preschoolers for Alcott Montessori Sch., Ardsley, N.Y., 1978—; research methodologist Burke Rehab. Center, 1977. Mem. profl. adv. bd. Found. for Children with Learning Disabilities, 1978—. Lic. speech and lang. pathologist, N.Y. State; Rehab. Services Adminstrn. fellow, 1968-69; N.Y. Med. Coll. fellow, 1972-75. Mem. N.Y. Speech and Hearing Assn., Westchester Speech and Hearing Assn., Am. Speech, Hearing and Lang. Assn. (cert. clin. competence), Council for Exceptional Children, Assn. on Mental Deficiency, Am. Acad. Pvt. Practice in Speech Pathology and Audiology (bd. dirs., treas.), Internat. Assn. Logopedics and Phoniatrics, Sigma Alpha Eta. Contbr. articles to profl. jours. Office: PO Box 1242 Scarsdale NY 10583

ROGELL, IRMA ROSE, harpsichordist; b. Malden, Mass.; d. M. Edward and Sara (Freedman) Rose; A.B., Radcliffe Coll.; student Wanda Landowska; m. Bernard C. Rogell (dec. 1964); children—Gerald, Gillian, Michael. Profl. debut Boston Jordan Hall, 1960; N.Y. debut, 1961; soloist with symphony orchs. including: Boston Symphony Orch., Brazil Symphony; European concert tours; radio-TV appearances; rec. artist Titanic Records, Protone; mem. faculty CUNY, 1973-78, Ethical Culture Sch. of N.Y.; guest lectr.-recitalist at various colls. and univs. Mem. Coll. Music Soc., Piano Tchrs. Congress N.Y. (sec.). Jewish. Club: Harvard (N.Y.C.). Home and Studio: 165 West End Ave New York NY 10023

ROGERS, AILENE KANE, educator; b. Jamaica, N.Y., Jan. 17, 1938; d. Daniel H. and Helen (Shirkey) Kane; B.A., Middlebury Coll., 1959; M.S., Am. U., 1963; m. Edward Lee Rogers, Nov. 18, 1961; children—Ruth, John, Helen, Daniel. Asst. dir. program Student Conservation Assn., Charlestown, N.H., 1959-60; dir., 1960; teaching asst. Am. U., Washington, 1961-62, naturalist Nat. Park Service 1966-68; tchr. sci. Hauppauge (N.Y.) Middle Sch., 1972-73; tchr. sci. Oak Grove Coburn Sch., Vassalboro, Maine, 1974-75, head sci. dept., 1976-79; tchr. sci. lower sch. Nat. Cathedral Sch., Washington, 1979-82, tchr. sci. upper sch., 1982—; counselor Sci. Camp, The Potomac Sch., McLean, Va., summers 1982—, head, 1986—. Founder Setauket Environ. Center, 1970, bd. govs., 1970-72; bd. dirs. Student Conservation Program, 1970-79; cons. Sch. Wide Environ. Edn. Program, N.Y.C., 1978; cons. edn. programs Nat. Geog. Soc., 1980—; founder, chmn. Pittston (Maine) Conservation Commn., 1975-78; co-pres. McLean High Sch. Student-Parent-Tchr. Assn., 1982-84. NSF grantee, 1962. Mem. Nat. Parks and Conservation Assn., Student Conservation Assn., Nature Conservancy (dir. Maine chpt. 1976-78). Club: The Grange (Pittston, Maine). Home: 6601 Jerry Pl McLean VA 22101 Office: National Cathedral School for Girls Mt St Albans Washington DC 20016

ROGERS, ALICE BRADSHAW, public relations and advertising executive; b. Dayton, Tex., Sept. 18, 1911; d. William Benjamin and Mannie Willis (Davis) Bradshaw; m. Evert A. Rogers, Aug. 17, 1934 (div. May 1950); children—Jane Rogers Matthews, Elizabeth Rogers Bannister, Nancy Lynn Rogers Stephanow. Student U. Tex., 1927-29, U. Houston, 1953, 59. Sec., Henry L. Doherty, stocks and bonds, 1930-33, L.E. Norton Real Estate, 1933-34, Fisk Electric Co., 1934-37; sec.-treas. Art Engraving Co., 1937-49, pres., 1949-50; pres. Advt. Arts Bldg. Corp., 1952-54, Houston Tradetypers, 1955-57, Goodwin-Dannenbaum Advt. Agy., 1957; dir., sec.-treas., pres. Art Engraving Co., Inc.; dir., pres. Advt. Arts Bldg. Corp.; pub. relations dir. Houston Youth Symphony, 1962-64; bus. relations dir. Better Bus. Bur., Houston; community club awards dir. Houston Chronicle, 1963-64; activities coordinator Houston Club, editor, bus. mgr. The Houston Clubber, 1964-83. Mem. adv. bd. Achievement Rewards Coll. Scientists Found.; dist. chmn. publicity bd. Girl Scouts U.S.A., 1946-50; mem. publicity com. United Fund, 1952-54; mem. advt. program com. Pin Oak Horse Show, Houston Fat Stock Show. Mem. Advt. Fedn. Am. (dir. 10th dist. 1955-81, Sterling Silver award 1978), Houston Advt. Fedn. (Outstanding Woman of Yr. award 1981, Alice B. Rogers Ednl. Fund established 1982), Houston Soc. Assn. Execs., Houston Advt. Club (v.p., dir., sec.-treas., Disting. Service mem., Silver medal award 1979), Harris County Heritage Soc., Houston C. of C., Gamma Alpha Chi. Clubs: Press (life) (Houston); Mothers (Zeta Tau Alpha). Home: 2501 Lazy Hollow Apt 110B Houston TX 77063

ROGERS, BEATRICE ANNE, real estate consultant; b. Trenton, N.J., May 7, 1917; d. Marshall H. and Laura (Thompson) Johnson; m. (dec. June 1980); children—Beatty Ann, Elizabeth Laura. B.S.Ed., Trenton State Coll., 1939. Tchr. pub. schs., Woodstown, N.J., 1938-45; realtor Rogers Realty Co., Woodstown, 1942—; tchr. real estate Salem Community Coll., Penns Grove, N.J., 1983. Mem. Salem Bd. Realtors, (sec. 1985). Republican. Clubs: Salem Country, Woodstown Womens. Avocations: travel; bridge; needlecraft. Home: 12 West Ave Woodstown NJ 08098 Office: Rogers Realty Co 14 West Ave Woodstown NJ 08098

ROGERS, CAROL JEAN, computer system consultant; b. St. Paul, Oct. 3, 1940; d. John Edward and Luella Grace (Holland) Christensen; grad. Estelle Compton Inst., Mpls., 1964, also specialized courses; m. Donald DeeRogers, Jan. 28, 1971; 1 son, Wade William; children by previous marriage—Sue Ann, Roxanne Leigh. Data entry specialist Hennepin County Dept. Ct. Services, Mpls., 1959-63; scheduling coordinator Sta. WTCN-TV, Mpls., 1963-65; coordinator for Minn., Miss Am. Teenager, St. Paul, 1967-69; upper Midwest coordinator Miss Universe, St. Paul, 1967-69; dir., instr. Mary Lowe Modeling Sch., Mpls., 1969-70; mktg. services coordinator Naidas Girl's Modeling Agy., Mpls., 1970-72; system flow tech. analyst Super Valu Stores, Inc., Hopkins, Minn., 1974-78, systems cons., 1980—; ind. systems cons., Wayzata, Minn., 1979—; adv. council Sawyer Sch. Bus., Mpls.; instr. Minn. public schs. Sunday sch. tchr. Grace Lutheran Ch., Deephaven, 1980-84. Mem. Nat. Assn. Female Execs., Am. Bus. Women's Assn. (chpt. pres.). Home: 3305 Shores Blvd Wayzata MN 55391 Office: 101 Jefferson Ave Hopkins MN 55343

ROGERS, CHRISTINE DUFFY, lawyer; b. Elizabeth, N.J., Jan. 23, 1955; d. John Francis and Olga Matlaga Duffy; m. David Michael Rogers, Aug. 9, 1980; 1 child, Joshua Patrick. B.A. cum laude, Harvard U., 1977; J.D., N.Y. U., 1980. Bar: N.Y. 1981, U.S. Dist. Ct. (so. dist.) N.Y. 1982, U.S. Dist. Ct. (ea. dist.) N.Y. 1982. Assoc. Donovan Leisure Newton & Irvine, N.Y.C., 1980—. Alumni interviewer admissions N.Y.C. Harvard/Radcliffe Schs. Com., 1978—. Mem. ABA. Democrat. Roman Catholic. Home: 250 E 87th St Apt 8A New York NY 10128 Office: Donovan Leisure Newton & Irvine 30 Rockefeller Plaza New York NY 10112

ROGERS, DEBRA DALE, hospital official; b. Inglewood, Calif., Nov. 8, 1941; d. Alfred F. and Janet (Agard) McKim; m. Michael Hall, Feb. 14, 1972; m. Danny L. Rogers, Dec. 26, 1959 (div. 1970); children—Darren, Laura, Gary, Cheryl, Gail. B.S., U. Phoenix, 1984. Registered respiratory therapist. With Queen of Valley Hosp., West Covina, Calif., 1971—, coordinator respiratory therapy, 1982-83, asst. mgr., 1984-85, asst. mgr. div. pulmonary and cardiovascular service, 1986—. Mem. Am. Assn. Respiratory Therapists, Calif. Soc. Respiratory Therapists, Mensa. (del.). Republican. Mailing Address: Box 3053 San Dimas CA 91773 Home: 1550 Cataract Ave San Dimas CA 91773 Office: Queen of Valley Hosp 1115 S Sunset Ave West Covina CA 91773

ROGERS, DOLORES MCMANUS, training company executive; b. Bellflower, Calif., Mar. 31, 1936; d. Joseph John and Thelma Joanne (Hinds) McManus Miller; m. Micahel Creighton Rogers, Nov. 26, 1971; children—Michael Creighton II, Eric Grinnell, Blake Lawrence. m. Clinton Lewis Byers, Jr., Aug. 2, 1958 (div. Mar. 1971). B.S., UCLA, 1957. Sales promotion staff Georgia Bullock, Inc., Los Angeles, 1957-62, v.p. sales promotion, 1962-66; dir. sales promotion Travilla, Los Angeles, 1966-71; owner, mgr. Exec. Assocs., Sherman Oaks, Calif., 1975—. Bd. dirs. Coldwater Counseling Ctr., Studio City, Calif., 1974-76; rec. sec. Las Donas, Los Angeles, 1979—. Mem. Am. Soc. Tng. and Devel., Fashion Group, AAUW. Republican. Episcopalian. Clubs: Sherman Oaks C. of C., UCLA Alumni Assn., Kappa Kappa Gamma. Avocations: cooking; reading; travel; golf; needlework. Home: 3906 Stone Canyon Rd Sherman Oaks CA 91403 Office: Executive Assocs 15015 Ventura Blvd Sherman Oaks CA 91403

ROGERS, DOROTHY SARA, college official; b. Melrose, Mass., Feb. 1, 1929; d. Robert J. and Sadie (Gardner) Nathan; m. Alan David Rogers, Jan. 21, 1951; children—Joan Rogers Leopold, Leslie S. B.S., Simmons Coll., 1950; student NYU, 1965, N.H. Coll., 1962. Trainee, service exec. Jordan Marsh Co., Boston, 1950-51; buyer sportswear and dresses Rogers Co., Inc., Manchester, N.H., 1952-55; fashion cons. Internat. Shoe Corp., St. Louis and Manchester, 1955-56; promotion cons. Pandora Industries, N.Y.C. also Manchester, 1956-57; fashion dir. Manchester Union Leader Corp., 1959-60; cons. sales tng. and fashion promotion The Lynch Co., Manchester, 1957-58; instr. distributive edn. City of Manchester, 1955-56; instr. principles of mktg. and retailing N.H. Coll., 1958-66, dir. coop. edn., 1976-83, dir. Office of Coop. Edn.-Internships-Placement, 1983—; cons. New Eng. Mut. Life Ins. Co., Boston, 1981-83; reviewer Addison, Wesley, Reading, Mass., 1966—, Houghton, Mifflin, Boston, 1966—, Holt, Rinehart, Winston, N.Y.C., 1966—, McGraw Hill, N.Y.C., 1966—, Random House, N.Y.C., 1966—, Richard D. Irwin, Inc., Homewood, Ill., 1966—, Prentice Hall, Inc., Englewood Cliffs, N.J., 1966—; prin., ptnr. RG Consultants, Manchester, N.H., 1976—; assoc. Phoenix Enterprises, Armonk, N.Y., 1983—; speaker various assns.; cons. Northeastern U., Boston, 1980, 1984; mem. Com. for Internat. Student Exchange, U.S. Dept. State, 1980. Author: Fashion: A Marketing Approach, 1983. Mem. Cooperative Edn. Assn., New Eng. Assn. Cooperative Edn. and Field Experience, Nat. Soc. Internships and Exptl. Edn., Am. Mktg. Assn., Nat. Retail Merchants Assn., Am. Collegiate Retailing Assn., N.H. Com. for Vocat. Edn. (dir.), AAUP, N.H. Women in Higher Edn., Eastern Coll. Personnel Officers. Republican. Jewish. Office: New Hampshire Coll 2500 N River Rd Manchester NH 03104

ROGERS, HELEN EVELYNWAHRGREN, newspaperwoman; b. Tacoma, Wash., Jan. 24, 1924; d. John Sigurd and Emma Elina (Carlson) Wahrgren; B.A., U. Wash., Seattle, 1946; m. Charles Dana Rogers, July 24, 1948. Volume I: Mem. editorial staff Holiday mag., Phila., 1946; civilian public relations writer, Ft. Lewis, Wash., 1946-47; asst. society editor Tacoma News Tribune-Sunday Ledger, 1947-51, radio-TV editor-columnist, 1951—. Mem. Newspaper Guild, Tacoma-Pierce County Geneal. Soc., Wis. State General Soc. Democrat. Lutheran. Author: What's Your Line?, Volume I: Delila Sprague Sherburne Harrington: Her Ancestors and Descendants. Home: 2906 N 24th St Tacoma WA 98406 Office: 1950 S State St Tacoma WA 98411

ROGERS, IRENE, librarian; b. Yonkers, N.Y., Oct. 12, 1932; d. Franklyn Harold and Mary Margaret (Nealy) R.; B.S. in Edn., New Paltz State Tchrs. Coll., 1954; M.L.S. (N.Y. State Tng. grantee), Columbia U., 1959. Tchr., West Babylon (N.Y.) Sch. System, 1954-57, Yonkers Sch. System, 1957-58; reference librarian Yonkers Pub. Library, 1959-67, adult services coordinator, 1967-73, asst. library dir., 1973—. Mem. Mayor's Adv. Com. Consumer Edn., Yonkers, 1970—; active United Way of Yonkers; mem. curriculum adv. com., report card revision com. Office Supt. Schs., 1982; mem. Yonkers unit Am. Cancer Soc. West Library System grantee, 1966. Mem. ALA, Westchester, N.Y. library assns. Club: Soroptimist (pres. 1978-79, 80-81, sec. dist. I North Atlantic region), Bus. and Profl. Women's (Yonkers). Home: 41 Amackassin Terr Yonkers NY 10703 Office: 7 Main St Yonkers NY 10701

ROGERS, JANET CARLENE SARGENT, county extension agent; b. Lubbock County, Tex., Jan. 20, 1948; d. Carl Walter and Alice Marie (Killingsworth) Sargent; B.S. in Home Econs. Edn. (Ethel Foster scholar, Elizabeth and Wylie Brisco Found. scholar), Tex. Tech. U., 1969, M.S. in Home Econs. Edn., 1970; postgrad. W. Tex. State U., 1973-74; Specialist cert. in aging, N. Tex. State U., 1982; m. Donald Ray Rogers, Sept. 3, 1977. Nursery sch. aide Cissie's Nursery Sch., Lubbock, 1966, 67-69; waitress Youngblood's Restaurant, Lubbock, 1969; grad. research asst. Home Econs. Instrnl. Materials Center, Tex. Tech. U., 1970; homemaking tchr. Canyon (Tex.) Ind. Sch. Dist., 1970-71, 71-76; county extension agt. home econs. Tex. Agrl. Extension Service, Big Spring, 1976-82; tchr. cons. Tex. Edn. Agy., Home Econs. Instrnl. Materials Center, Tex. Tech. U., 1975. Assoc. dir. Howard County Fair, Big Spring, 1976-82; advisor Howard County Council on Aging, 1976-82, bd. dirs., 1982-85. Named Boss of Yr., Big Spring chpt. Am. Bus. Women's Assn., 1981. Provisionally cert. in vocat. homemaking, cert. in profl. vocat. homemaking, Tex. Mem. Tex. Assn. Extension Home Economists, Am. Home Econs. Assn., Phi Upsilon Omicron. Presbyterian. Author articles and instructional materials. Home: Route 1 Box 144 D-5 Midland TX 79701

ROGERS, JANSIE, art and decorating company executive; b. Lenoir, N.C., Feb. 22, 1939; d. Raymond L. and Ruth (Henley) Setzer; m. G.R. Walter Rogers, June 23, 1963; (div. July 1984); children—Rob, Sharon. B.A., James Madison U., 1961. Cert. interior accessory designer. Pub. sch. tchr., Baltimore County, Md., 1960-63, Perryville, Md., 1975-77; accessory designer Transart Industries, Woodstock, Ga., 1977-78, design dir., 1978-82, nat. dir. Trans Designs, Woodstock, 1982—. Bd. dirs. YMCA, Nat. Multiple Sclerosis Soc., Arthritis Found. Recipient awards including trips abroad, mink coats, diamonds TransDesigns, 1977-86. Mem. The Female Exec., LWV. Democrat. Avocations: tennis, racquetball. Home and Office: 7554 Weatherworn Way Columbia MD 21046

ROGERS, JENNIFER ENGLES, producer, director; b. Batesville, Ark., July 28, 1943; d. Jake Raymond and Bess Ermine (Goodin) Engles; B.A., Ark. Coll., 1965; M.A., Memphis State U., 1973; m. Francis Xavier Rogers, Jr., Jan. 26, 1974; 1 son, Joshua Francis. Debate, drama tchr. Malden (Mo.) High Sch., 1965-66; sec. Dan River Mills, N.Y.C., 1966; drama tchr. Bald Knob (Ark.) High Sch., 1966-68; entertainer Silver Dollar City, Branson, Mo., 1967-69; actress Bloody Mama, Mt. Home, Ark., 1969; asst. mgr. Melba Theatre, Batesville, Ark., 1969-70; actress H & H Productions, So. states, 1970; remedial reading tchr. Newark (Ark.) Elem. Sch., 1970-71; producer, dir. Sta. WREG-TV, Memphis, Tenn., 1973-81; asst. prof. broadcasting Okla. State U., Stillwater, 1981-83; producer, dir. Cox Cable OKC, Oklahoma City, 1983-84. Named Miss Ark. Coll., 1965. Mem. Batesville Community Theatre (pres.), Alpha Psi Omega. Republican. Mem. Ch. of Christ. Author: The Autobiography of Miss Punkin Jones, 1977. Office: 2CSU/PSTV 100 N University Edmond OK 73034

ROGERS, JUANITA, media specialist; b. Oxford, N.C., July 16, 1947; d. Andrew Lewis and Clara (Hopkins) R. B.S., Fayetteville State U., 1967. Tchr. high sch., Hoke County Schs., Raeford, N.C., 1967-69; tchr. Mecklenburg County Schs., Clarksville, Va., 1969-77, librarian, La Crosse, Va., 1977-78; media specialist Vance County Schs., Henderson, N.C., 1978—. Vol., Richard H. Thorton Library, Oxford, 1980—. Recipient Community Sch. Vol. award Vance County Schs., 1981, Library Service award, 1982-85. Mem. N.C. Assn. Educators, NEA, Vance County Library Assn., Delta Sigma Theta. Democrat. Baptist. Clubs: Mary Potter. Avocations: photography; antiques; tennis; reading. Home: 117 Orange St Oxford NC 27565

ROGERS, JUDY, social worker; b. Newark, Jan. 29, 1943; d. John Oliver and Grace (Daniels) R.; A.B. with honors in Sociology, Dickinson Coll., 1965; M.S.W., N.Y.U., 1970; 1 child. Kimani. Coordinator social rehab., anti-recidivism project, Jersey City. 1967-68; therapist Bklyn. Psychiat. Centers, 1970-72; counselor VIP Med. Assocs., N.Y.C., 1972-73; clin. coordinator Harlem Center for Child Study, Harlem Hosp., N.Y.C., 1973—, co-chmn. staff devel. com., 1983-85; therapist family support demonstration project Psychiat. Inst. N.Y.; field instr. Sch. Social Work, Columbia U.; mem. profl. adv. com. James Weldon Johnson Mental Health Center, 1980—. First v.p. Parents Assn., Hunter Coll. Elem. Sch. 1981-82, pres. Black Parents Group, 1982-84; treas. Black Task Force on Child Abuse; active Operation Crossroads Africa, 1963, U.S. Youth Council, 1966-68. Recipient Gaylord H. Patterson Meml. prize for sociology, 1965. Mem. Nat. Assn. Social Workers (bd. dirs. N.Y.C. chpt., chmn. child and family advocacy com.), Nat. Assn. Black Social Workers. Office: 121 W 128th St New York NY 10027

ROGERS, JUDY ANN, company executive; b. Pontiac, Mich., May 25, 1948; d. Charles Michael and Virginia (Perna) Crickon; m. Ronald Richard Rogers, Aug. 30, 1967; 1 dau., Anne Michelle. Drug Sci. scholar, U. Mich., 1965; B.A. summa cum laude, Oakland U., Rochester, Mich., 1978; postgrad. Wayne State U. Law Sch., 1978-79. Office mgr. Holforty Assocs., Inc., Rochester, 1970-76; adminstr. asst. to controller Perry Drug Stores, Inc., Pontiac, 1976-78; officer mgr. Artcraft Blueprint Co., Pontiac, 1978-81; plant acct. Gates Rubber Co., Pontiac, 1981-83, v.p. Bus. Brokers, 1983-85; mgr., owner Fantastic Sam Lake, Orion, 1984—. Columnist. Mem. Orion Twp. Environ. Task Force, Fantastic Sams Owners Council of Mich.; active Republican party. Recipient silver Poet award, 1986; Walter Reuther Meml. Fund scholar, 1978. Mem. Nat. Assn. Exec. Females (v.p. programs univs. women 1981), Women in Commercial Real Estate, Am. Bus. Women, Mich. Profl. Women's Network. Club: Deer Lake Racquet. Contbr. to The Poet, Our Twentieth Century's Greatest Poems, Today's Greatest Poems. Home: 4383 Morgan Rd Pontiac MI 48055

ROGERS, KATE ELLEN, educator; b. Nashville, Dec. 13, 1920; d. Raymond Lewis and Louise (Gruver) R.; M.A. in Fine Arts, George Peabody Coll., 1947; Ed.D. in Fine Arts and Fine Arts Edn., Columbia U., 1956. Instr., Tex. Tech. Coll., Lubbock, 1947-53; co-owner, v.p. Design Today, Inc., Lubbock, 1951-54; student asst. Am. House, N.Y.C., 1953-54; asst. prof. housing and interior design U. Mo., Columbia, 1954-56, assoc. prof., 1956-66, prof., 1966-85, emeritus, 1985—, chmn. dept. housing and interior design, 1973-85; mem. accreditation com. Found. for Interior Design Edn. Research, 1975-76, chmn. standards com., 1976-82, chmn. research, 1982—. Nat. Endowment for Arts research grantee, 1981-82. Mem. Interior Design Educators Council (pres. 1971-73, chmn. bd. 1974-76, chmn. research com. 1977-78), Am. Soc. Interior Designers, (hon.), Am. Home Econs. Assn., Soc. Archtl. Historians. Democrat. Author: The Modern House, USA, 1962; editor Jour. Interior Design Edn. and Research, 1975-78.

ROGERS, KATHARINE MUNZER, educator; b. N.Y.C., June 6, 1932; d. Martin and Jean (Thompson) Munzer; B.A. summa cum laude, Barnard Coll., 1952; Fulbright scholar, Newnham Coll., Cambridge U., 1952-53; Ph.D., Columbia U., 1957; m. Kenneth C. Rogers, Aug. 4, 1956; children—Margaret, Christopher, Thomas. Instr. English, Skidmore Coll., Saratoga Springs, N.Y., 1954-55, Cornell U., 1955-57; lectr. to prof. English, Bklyn. Coll., 1958—; mem. doctoral faculty City U. N.Y. Mem. MLA. Author: The Troublesome Helpmate: A History of Misogyny in Literature, 1966; William Wycherley, 1972; Feminism in Eighteenth Century England, 1982. Editor anthologies: Before Their Time: Six Women Writers of the Eighteenth Century, 1979; The Signet Classic Book of 18th and 19th Century British Drama; Selected Writings of Samuel Johnson, 1981. Contbr. articles to profl. jours. Home: Hoxie House Stevens Inst Hoboken NJ 07030 Office: Dept English Bklyn Coll Brooklyn NY 11210

ROGERS, KATHERINE SQUIRES, public relations specialist; b. Bellefonte, Pa., Feb. 11, 1960; d. Burton Elliott and Mary Elizabeth (Reinoehl) Squires; m. Christopher David Rogers, June 26, 1982. B.A., Allegheny Coll., 1981. Copy editor Am. Physiol. Soc., Bethesda, Md., 1981-82; dir. pub. relations and publs. U. New Eng., Biddeford, Maine, 1983-85; coordinator guest relations Osteo. Hosp. of Maine, Portland, 1985—; Editor: Coastlines, alumni mag., 1983-85. Mem. Maine Media Women (pres. 1985-86), Maine Health Pub. Relations Assn., Bus. and Profl. Women, Soc. Tech. Communication, Am. Osteo. State Exec. Dirs., Nat. Soc. Patient Reps. Avocations: sailing; scuba diving. Home: 34 Hollis Rd Portland ME 04103 Office: Osteo Hosp Maine 335 Brighton Ave Portland ME 04102

ROGERS, LORETTA GAIL, mfg. co. exec.; b. Proctorville, Ohio, Mar. 10, 1936; d. Sanford Dale and Beatrice Emily Brumfield; student Huntington (W. Va.) Bus. Coll., 1962-63, Ohio U., Athens, 1975; m. Charles L. Rogers, Dec. 7, 1963; children—Michael, Kimberly, Steven. Various clerical and secretarial positions, 1966-77; with Anchor Hocking Corp., 1977—, indsl. relations mgr., Lancaster, Ohio, 1977—; mem. exec. council hosp. intervention program Nat. Safety Council, 1978. Adv. bd. Lancaster Vis. Nurses Assn., 1981. Recipient Cameron award safety, 1979. Mem. Lancaster-Fairfield County Personnel Assn., Fairfield County Safety Assn. Republican. Club: Lady Lions. Office: Anchor Hocking Corp Industrial Relations Dept 109 N Broad St Lancaster OH 43130

ROGERS, LYNNE GREER, construction company executive; b. Harlan, Ky., July 30, 1951; d. Perry Lee and Velma Kay (Ritchie) Greer; m. Carl Hagins Rogers, Jr., June 20, 1970; children—Carl Hagins III, Greer Blake. Student Fugazzi Bus. Sch., 1969-70. Acctg. clk. PH. Owens Co., Lexington, Ky., 1971-73; acctg. auditor Kaneb Coal Div., 1974-76, Lexington Ctr. Corp., 1976-78; bus. mgr. Ridgeview Constrn. Co., Lexington, 1978—; sec., cons. Tripper Lee Enterprises, Lexington, 1980—. Bd. dirs. Lexington Hearing & Speech Ctr., 1976-79; mem. Steeplechase com. Children's Cancer Research Fund; mem. com. Lexington Charitable Fund. Mem. Nat. Assn. Realtors, Ky. Assn. Realtors. Republican. Presbyterian. Avocations: tennis; sewing; reading; gardening; snow skiing. Home: 1600 Ferguson Rd Lexington KY 40511

ROGERS, MARGARET GAY, insurance executive; b. Ketona, Ala., Mar. 25, 1937; d. James Elbert and Margaret Louis (Nolde) Haigler, Jr.; student Massey Bus. Coll., 1957; m. Douglas Earl Rogers, June 30, 1975. Tng., inventory clk. Goodwill Industries, Ft. Wayne, Ind., 1959; with Ala. Title Co., Inc., Birmingham, 1963, file clk., asst. bookkeeper, 1965, policy clk., asst. bookkeeper, 1966, asst. bookkeeper, exec. asst. to pres., 1975—. Supporter numerous civic orgns. Mem. Nat. Assn. Female Execs., Nat. Fraternal Soc. of the Deaf. Republican. Lutheran. Home: 111 2d St Robinwood Birmingham AL 35217 Office: 615 N 21st St Birmingham AL 35203

ROGERS, MARIANNE EDITH, insurance broker, insurance agency executive; b. Clinton, Mass., Mar.4, 1948; d. George Milton and Marion (Hayes) R. B.A., Clark U., 1970. CPCU Broker, corp. officer George M. Rogers Ins. Agy., Inc., Boylston, Mass., 1972—, corp. clk., 1984—, pres., 1986—. Bd. dirs., mem. human rights com. Worcester Area Assn. Retarded Children (Mass.), 1981-86; area coordinator for South Worcester County, Mass. Spl. Olympics; bd. dirs. Worcester Foothills Theatre Co., 1981-82, Little Theatre Stage Co. Inc., Worcester, 1983-84; mem. exec. com. March of Dimes, Worcester, 1983-84; mem. adv. bd. Occupational Tng. Ctr., Worcester, 1984-86; mem. diocesean communications com. Episcopal Diocese of Western Mass., 1979; mem. vestry, lay reader Episcopal Ch. of the Good Shepherd, Clinton, Mass. Named Outstanding Young Leader, Worcester Jaycees, 1982. Mem. Soc. C.P.C.U.s (edn. coordinator Central Mass. chpt. 1980-84, chpt. tchr. 1981-84, chpt. pres. 1983-84), Profl. Ins. Agts. New Eng. (Mass. steering com. 1983, 84, bd. dirs., chmn. community relations com.; Presdl. citation 1985), Ind. Ins. Agts. Worcester County (bd. dirs. 1982-84). Republican. Club: Worcester Exec. Home: 1053 Pleasant St Worcester MA 01602 Office: George M Rogers Ins Agy Inc 545 Main St Boylston MA 01505

ROGERS, MARY VIRGINIA, nurse; b. Clarendon, Ark., Jan. 11, 1938; d. Leonard Velva and Mary Ailene (Booker) Rogers. R.N., St. Joseph Sch. Nursing, Memphis, 1959; B.S. in Nursing, U. Tenn., 1977, M.S., 1979. Staff nurse St. Joseph Hosp., Memphis, 1959-61, head nurse, 1961-65; head nurse Bland, Bland & Van Fossen, M.D.s, Memphis, 1965-72; head nurse, bus. mgr. Helen Key Van Fossen, M.D., P.C., Memphis, 1972-79, clin. specialist, 1979—; panel mem. Nursing 83, Spring House, Pa., 1982-83. Guarantor, Met. Opera, Memphis, 1982; patron Mid-South Opera Guild, Memphis, 1982—. Mem. Am. Nurses Assn., Tenn. Nurses Assn., Soc. Gastrointestinal Assts. (mem. faculty N.Y.C. 1980), Tenn. Soc. Gastrointestinal Assts. (treas. 1982-86, mem. faculty 1980-82, 85, sec. 1984-85, chmn. West div.), English Speaking Union, Nat. Beta Club. Republican. Episcopalian. Home: 4317 Burgundy Rd Memphis TN 38111 Office: Helen Key Van Fossen MD PC 920 Madison St Suite 501 Memphis TN 38103

ROGERS, REBECCA LAINE, nursing home adminstr.; b. Anniston, Ala., Sept. 2, 1952; d. Wilmer L. and Myrthel A. (Hill) R.; B.S. in Accounting, Jacksonville State U., 1973; postgrad. in Health Care Adminstrn., George Washington U., 1976. Sec., C. of C., Anniston, Ala., 1970-74; accountant Marvin Burke C.P.A., Anniston, 1974-75; adminstr. Golden Springs Nursing Facility, Anniston, 1975—. Ala. state chmn. Rock N Roll Jamboree, Am. Heart Fund. Mem. Ala. Nursing Home Assn. (sec., conv. com., chmn. pub. relations com. 1980), Am. Coll. Nursing Home Adminstrs. (treas. Ala. chpt.), Altrusa. Republican. Baptist. Office: PO Box 1790 Anniston AL 36201

ROGERS, ROWENA EMERY, state land administrator; b. Denver, Dec. 8, 1921; d. Roe and Jeanette (Carpenter) Emery; B.A., Vassar Coll., 1943; m. Ranger Rogers, Nov. 1, 1944; children—Susan, Jeannette, Roxana, Lorna, Robert, Sarah. Pres., mem. Colo. State Bd. Parks and Outdoor Recreation, Denver, 1971-75; pres. Colo. Bd. Land Commrs., 1986; mem. adv. com. Nat. Strategic Materials and Minerals Program, 1984-86; bd. dirs. Student Conservation Assn., 1986—; mem. Natural Areas Council, Denver, 1978-83; mem. State Recreational Trails Com., Denver, 1979-82; chairperson public lands com. Interstate Oil Compact Commn., Denver, 1982-86. Dist. commr. Platte Valley Pony Club, 1956—; vice chmn. Arapahoe County Republicans, 1966-68, Rep. 2d Dist. Com., 1962-64; bd. dirs. Met. Denver YWCA, 1968-72, Kent Sch., 1960-62; bd. dirs. Greenwood Village Open Space Commn., 1974-76. Mem. Western States Land Commrs. Assn. (pres. 1980-82), Colo. Womens Forum, Phi Beta Kappa. Episcopalian. Clubs: Arapahoe Hunt (hon. sec.); Vassar of Colorado. Home: 3011 Willamette Ln Littleton CO 80121 Office: 1313 Sherman St Room 620 Denver CO 80203

ROGERS, RUTH LOTTE, fashion consultant; b. Vienna, Austria, Dec. 31; came to U.S., 1938; d. Arnold and Elsie (Zemanek) Karplus; m. Martin C. Rogers, 1938 (div. 1950); m. Hans C. Altmann, Oct. 8, 1965; children—Susan Friedman, Victoria Thorson. Diploma Kunst Gewerbe Akadamie, Vienna. Design cons. Herzmansky, Vienna, White Stag, N.Y.C., Koret of Calif., N.Y.C.; exec. v.p. R.R.J. Industry, N.Y.C.; now pres. Ruth Rogers Enterprises Internat., N.Y.C.; cons. Met. Mus. Costume Inst., N.Y.C.; panelist Am. Woman's Econ. Devel. Corp., N.Y.C.; lectr. Shenkar Coll., Tel-Aviv, Israel, Fashion Inst. Tech., N.Y.C. Author fashion and color forecast Burlington Industry; columnist: Knit Notes. Mem. Fashion Group Inc. (chairperson knits com. forecasting trendbook), Fashion News Workshop, Designers Group Nat. Knitwear and Sportswear Assn. (exec. com.), Woman's Fashion Network (charter mem.). Avocations: painting; skiing; art. Home: 71 Park Ave New York NY 10016 Office: Ruth Rogers Enterprises Internat 71 Park Ave New York NY 10016

ROGERS, SHARON J., university librarian; b. Grantsburg, Wis., Sept. 24, 1941; d. Clifford M. and Dorothy L. (Beckman) Dickau; m. Evan D. Rogers, June 15, 1962 (div. 1980). B.A. summa cum laude in Social Sci., Bethel Coll., 1963; M.L.S., U. Minn., 1967; Ph.D. in Sociology, Wash. State U., 1976. Lectr. and instr. Alfred U., N.Y., 1972-76; coordinator library programs U. Toledo Libraries, Ohio, 1977-80; assoc. dean Bowling Green State U. Libraries, Ohio, 1980-84; univ. librarian George Washington U., Washington, 1984—. Contbr. articles to profl. jours. Bd. dirs. Toledo chpt. ACLU, 1978-84, state ACLU, Ohio, Columbus, 1982-84. NSF trainee, 1969-72; Jackson fellow U. Minn., 1964-65. Mem. Assn. Coll. and Research Librarians (pres. 1984—), Am. Assn. Higher Edn., Am. Sociol. Assn. Office: Gelman Library George Washington U 2130 H St NW Washington DC 20052

ROGERS, SHARON MARIE, manufacturing company executive, safety executive; b. Phila., July 22, 1960; d. Glenn Howard Borden and Jean Marie (Kaczorowski) Borden Costello; m. Alfred Pepper Rogers, Jan. 9, 1982. B.S. in Bus. Adminstrn., Phila. Coll. Textiles and Sci., 1981. Spl. projects engr. Caron Internat., Rochelle, Ill., 1981, dyehouse lab. supr., 1982-83, quality control mgr., 1983-84, quality assurance mgr., 1984-85; plant safety coordinator Aigner, An Avery Internat. Co., Rochelle, 1986—, mfg. supr., 1985—; advisor Rock Valley Jr. Achievement, Rochelle, 1984-85; dir. Rochelle Community Child Care Ctr., Rochelle, 1985; student recruiter Phila. Coll. Textiles and Sci., 1983—; speaker profl. confs., civic orgns. Contbr. articles to profl. jours. Com. mem. Hillcrest Zoning Bd., Ill., 1984; mem. adv. bd. community child care com. Rochelle Area C. of C., 1985. Recipient Presidential award Pres. Richard Nixon, Washington, 1974, Frank Leslie Honor award Textile Vets. Assn., Phila., 1981, Rochelle Young Career Woman award Rochelle Bus. and Profl. Women, 1983; W. W. Smith Found. acad. scholar, Phila., 1980-81, Manpower Found. scholar, Milw., 1980-81. Mem. Nat. Fedn. Bus. and Profl. Women (pres. Rochelle chpt. 1985-86), Ill. Fedn. Bus. and Profl. Women (program chmn. 1985, assoc. dir. 1985-86, dist. VI program award 1985), Am. Assn. Textile Chemists and Colorists (reception chair 1984 Internat. Tech. Conf. and Exhbn. 1982-84), Internat. Assn. Quality Circles (v.p. Kishwaukee Valley chpt. 1983), U.S. Jaycees (sec. Rochelle chpt. 1985). Democrat. Lutheran. Clubs: Young Adults (mem. steering com. 1985), Faith Lutheran Ch. Women (Rochelle). Avocations: counted cross-stitch; gardening; camping; swimming. Home: 219 River Rd Rural Route 1 Rochelle IL 61068 Office: Aigner An Avery Internat Co 1 Aigner Pkwy Rochelle IL 61068

ROGERS, SHARYN GAIL, lawyer; b. DuBois, Pa., Aug. 5, 1948; d. John (Heberling) Rogers; 1 dau., Kristyn Leigh. B.A., SUNY-Buffalo, 1970, M.A., 1972, J.D., 1977. Bar: N.Y. 1978. Law clk. to county atty. Erie County, Buffalo, N.Y., 1977, asst. dist. atty., 1978-79; assoc. firm Damon & Morey, Buffalo, 1979—. Mem. ABA, N.Y. State Bar Assn., Erie County Bar Assn. Methodist. Office: Damon & Morey 1600 Main Place Tower Buffalo NY 14202

ROGERS, VIRGINIA MARIEBUXTON, industrial psychologist; b. Phila., May 18, 1952; d. Robert Stevens and Dorothy Louise (Miller) B.; B.S., Pa. State U., 1974; M.A., U. Md., 1977, Ph.D., 1979. Research cons. Personnel Decisions Research Inst., Mpls., 1978-79; personnel research specialist Standard Oil Co. (Ohio), Cleve., 1979-81, staff tng. assoc., 1981-83, mgr. assessment services, 1983—. Lic. psychologist, Ohio. Mem. Am. Psychol. Assn. (indsl. organizational psychology). Home: 11687 River Ridge Strongsville OH Office: 10F3655 Sohio Bldg 200 Public Sq Cleveland OH 44114-2375

ROGGE, RENA WOLCOTT, librarian; b. Bklyn., Nov. 3, 1920; d. Ralph Stratton and Mona Florence (Shannon) Wolcott; m. Carl Frederick Rogge Jr., Aug. 4, 1942; 1 son, Carl Frederick Rogge. B.A., Elmira Coll., 1941; M.L.S., Rutgers U., New Brunswick, N.J., 1966; M.A.L.S., New Sch. Social Research, N.Y.C., 1972. Sec. Sch. Dist. South Orange, Maplewood, N.J., 1958-65; head reference librarian Cranford (N.J.) Pub. Library, 1966-68; readers' advisor Jersey City, 1968-69; reference librarian Newark State Coll., Union, N.J., 1969—; reference coordinator Kean Coll. Library, sec. faculty senate, 1978-79, archivist faculty senate, 1979—, chmn. constn. revision, 1982—, grad. research com. 1983—. Recipient Outstanding Pub. Employee award, State of N.J., 1972, merit Award, 1983; online research grantee, Kean Coll. N.J., 1979. Mem. N.J. Library Assn., Am. Soc. Indexers, N.J. State Coll. Librarians' Assn., Kean Coll. Fedn. Tchrs. (exec. com.). Club: Elmira Coll. Office: Home: 27 Bodwell Terr Millburn NJ 07031 Office: Nancy Thompson Library Morris Ave Kean Coll NJ Union NJ 07083

ROGOFF, BARBARA, design executive; b. N.Y.C., Nov. 21, 1949; d. Philip and Fay (Zucker) Rosenhause; m. Manus Warren Rogoff, Nov. 8, 1974; children—Stephanie, Adam. Assoc. Applied Sci., Fashion Inst. Tech., 1968. Designer, stylist Maxwell Industries, N.Y.C., 1968-72; stylist Cohama Fabrics, N.Y.C., 1972-75; owner, pres. Print Directions, N.Y.C., 1975-77; stylist J. P. Stevens, N.Y.C., 1977-80; design dir., v.p. Fieldcrest Mills, N.Y.C., 1980—. Mem. Fashion Group, Nat. Home Fashions League, Color Mktg. Group, Am. Women's Econ. Devel. Club: Southampton Bath and Tennis (N.Y.). Avocations: antique collections. Home: 445 E 86th St New York NY 10028

ROGOZINSKI, TINA MARIE, pharmaceutical company marketing executive; b. Oklahoma City, Dec. 10, 1962; d. Leonard Peter and Mildred Helen (Little) R. B.S. in Internat. Mktg., Quinnipiac Coll., 1984, cert. in export mktg., 1983. Advt. coordinator Healthkraft, Inc., Danbury, Conn., 1983-85; mktg. mgr. Tishcon Corp., Westbury, N.Y., 1985—. Contbr. poems to mags. Conn. State scholar, 1980. Mem. Nat. Assn. Female Execs., Am. Women Entrepreneurs. Avocations: writing; tennis; skiing. Home: 24 St Paul St Bethpage NY 11714 Office: Tishcon Corp 29 New York Ave Westbury NY 11590

ROHDE, JEAN CATHERINE, social worker; b. N.Y.C., June 27, 1948; d. John Francis and Nancy Anastasia (Robuck) R.; B.A. cum laude, Fairleigh Dickinson U., 1970; M.S.W., N.Y. U., 1975; Postgrad. Columbia U., 1979—, Psychoanalytic Inst. for Clin. Social Workers, 1978-79. Group leader Manhattan Psychiat. Center, N.Y.C., 1972-73, supr., 1975-77, outpatient program coordinator, 1977-79; program asst. Council on Social Work Edn., N.Y.C., 1980-81; research asso. Columbia U. Sch. Social Work, Indsl. Social Welfare Center, N.Y.C., 1981-82; lectr. dept. sociology Barnard Coll., 1982-84; research assoc., runaway and homeless youth project Council on Accreditation of Services for Families and Children, 1983-84; social worker, field placement supr. Spl. Ednl. Services Program, L.I. U., 1985—; guest speaker on treatment of mentally ill. N.Y. State Dept.; conducted stress workshops for disabled coll. students L.I.U., 19896. Mental Hygiene scholarship awardee, 1973-75; NIMH trainee, 1979-80. Mem. Council on Social Work Edn., Nat. Assn. Social Workers, Acad. Cert. Social Workers, Am. Orthopsychiat. Assn. Home: 52 W 56th St Apt 4R New York NY 10019 Office: Long Island Univ Brooklyn Campus Brooklyn NY 11201

ROHLA, TRUDI PHILLIPS, public relations agency executive; b. Los Angeles, Dec. 7, 1949; d. Paul Lunsford and Helen (Koziol) Phillips; B.A., Calif. State Poly. U., Pomona, 1976, postgrad., 1976-78; M.B.A., Pepperdine U., 1978; m. Gary D. Rohla, Dec. 27, 1969; (div.); 1 dau., Caroline Michelle. Script analyst motion pictures Paul Kohner, Inc., Los Angeles, 1970-75; news reporter Pasadena Star News/Foothil Intercity Newspapers, 1974-76; with Lenac, Warford, Stone, Inc., Irvine, Calif., 1975-77, dir. pub. relations, 1977-78; v.p. RW/Allen, Inc., Costa Mesa., Calif. and Los Angeles, 1978-79; with Burson-Marstellar, Los Angeles, after 1979, v.p., creative dir., Santa Clara, Calif.; now founder Rohla and Ptnrs. Mem. Pub. Relations Soc. Am. Home: 273 Portola Rd Portolo Valley CA Office: 1040 Noel Dr Menlo Park CA

ROHM, JESSICA DEE, public relations and marketing firm executive; b. N.Y.C., Feb. 26, 1956; d. Edward J. and Tereza Ann (DiPiazza) Zive; m. Eberhard Heinrich Rohm, Sept. 22, 1984. B.A., Barnard Coll., 1976. Reporter trainee N.Y. Times, 1976-77; pres., owner Jessica Dee Communications, N.Y.C., 1977—. Office: Jessica Dee Communications 160 E 56th St New York NY 10022

ROHRBAUGH, EILEEN FAYE, retail clothing executive; b. York, Pa., Nov. 26, 1944; d. Russell Wilford Eppley and Genevieve Rose (Quickel) Eppley Holtzapple; m. Richard Eugene Rohrbaugh, Feb. 22, 1962; children—James Edward, Mark Russell, Brian Patrick, Melissa Marie. Grad. high sch., York. Expeditor Tioga Textiles, York, 1964-72; dept. mgr. K-mart, York, 1976-79; asst. mgr. Jewel-T Discount Grocery, Camp Hill, Pa., 1979-82; mgr. Formfit Rogers, Inc., York, 1983—. Den mother, leader local Boy Scouts Am., 1974-82; leader, organizer local council Girl Scouts U.S.A., 1979-82. Mem. Am. Bus. Women's Assn. (chpt. rec. sec. 1985-86, treas. 1986—), Nat. Assn. Female Execs. Democrat. Avocations: travel; arts; reading; crafts. Home: 2577 Broad St York PA 17404 Office: Formfit Rogers Inc 2142 S Queen St York PA 17403

ROHRER, MARY ANNE SCHOBER, human resource consulting company executive; b. Milw., Apr. 10, 1946; d. Herman Frederick and Bernice Louise Schober; m. Arthur Thomas Harrison, June 15, 1974 (div. July 1981); children—Zachary Watkins, Jesse Josef; m. 2d, Dallas L. Rohrer, May 31, 1984; step-children—Sonya M. Rohrer, Dion P. Rohrer. B.S.W., U. Calif.-Berkeley, 1970. Customer service rep./mgr. tng. program Blue Cross-Blue Shield, Oakland, Calif., 1967-68; pub. relations dir. Phipps Land Co., Atlanta, 1972-74; sec.-treas. Village Planter, Inc., Atlanta, 1974-76; exec. v.p. I.D., Inc., Atlanta, 1979-81; pres., cons. Fin. Service Corp. Cons. Services, Inc., Atlanta, 1982—; pres. S.C.R., Inc. Counselor underprivileged teens, YWCA, emotionally disturbed-mentally retarded Goodwill Industries, Milw., 1966-67; counselor Berkeley Suicide Prevention Ctr., 1970-71; counselor, facilitator Pacific Psychotherapy, San Francisco, 1970-71; vol. tchr. Fulton County Schs., Atlanta 1974-75. Mem. Am.Soc. Personnel Adminstrs., Sales and Mktg. Execs., Alpha Chi Omega. Home: 1145 Edgewater Dr NW Atlanta GA 30328 Office: SCR Inc PO Box 550263 Atlanta GA 30355

ROHRER, SUSAN JANE, educational administrator; b. Springfield, Ill., Apr. 30, 1945; d. Russell Shriver and Margaret (Shumaker) Rohrer. A.B., MacMurray Coll., 1967; M.S., U. Ill., 1971, Ph.D., 1973. Cert. tchr. spl. K-14, High Sch., Gen. Adminstvr. K-12, Ill. Instr., Virden Jr. High Sch., Ill., 1967-69; asst. to dean U. Ill. Coll. Medicine-Urbana, 1974-75, adminstrv. assoc., 1975-80; asst. prin. Virden Jr. and Sr. High Schs., 1983-84, prin., 1984—; sports writer News Gazette Newspaper, Champaign, Ill., 1973-74. Methodist. Home: 121 West Hill St Virden IL 62690 Office: Virden Jr Sr High Sch 231 W Fortune St Virden IL 62690

ROHRMAN, SUSAN ELEANORA VITULLO, lawyer; b. Cin., May 2, 1948; d. Rudolph William and Clelia Frances (Rapisardi) Vitullo; m. Douglass Frederick Rohrman, Aug. 7, 1982; children—Kathryn Anne, Elizabeth Clelia. B.A., U. Chgo., 1970; J.D. cum laude, Loyola U., 1975. Bar: Ill. 1975; law clk. to justice Ill. Appellate Ct., Chgo., 1975-76; assoc. Keck, Mahin & Cate, 1976-81; staff counsel Household Internat., Inc., Prospect Heights, Ill., 1981-86. Contbr. articles to profl. jours. Mem. ABA, Ill. Bar Assn., Chgo. Bar Assn., Democrat. Roman Catholic. Office: Household Internat Inc 2700 Sanders Rd Prospect Heights IL 60070

ROJAS, NANCY MARTHA, bank executive; b. San Diego, May 21, 1961; d. John and Guillermina (Patino) R. B.B.A., U. San Diego, 1983. Staff acct. Armando Martinez & Co., Chula Vista, Calif., 1982-83, sr. acct., 1984-85; staff acct. Price Waterhouse, San Diego, 1983-84; auditor Bank of Am., San Diego, 1985—. Mem. Am. Inst. C.P.A.s, Calif. Soc. C.P.A.s, Nat. Assn. Female Execs, Kappa Gamma Pi. Republican. Roman Catholic. Club: Summit Orgn. (San Diego). Avocation: Taekwon-do. Home: 222 H St #3 Chula Vista CA 92010 Office: Bank of Am 3633 Camino del Rio S San Diego CA 92108

ROLAND, SHARON LOUISE, librarian; b. Riverton, Wyo., Apr. 9, 1939; d. Arthur C. and Genevieve L. (Ward) White; m. Leon H. Roland, Dec. 22, 1967; 1 son, Scott. A.A., N.W. Community Coll., Powell, Wyo., 1959; B.A., U. No. Colo., 1961; M. Librarianship, U. Wash., 1972; postgrad. Eastern Mont. Coll., 1965—. Cert. sch. librarian, elem. tchr., Mont. Tchr. first grade Franklin-McKinley Dist., San Jose, Calif., 1961-63, Springfield Pub. Schs. (Oreg.), 1963-64; tchr. first grade Billings Pub. Schs. (Mont.), 1964-67, 68-77, high sch. librarian, 1978—; tchr. first grade Powell Pub. Schs., (Wyo.), 1967-68; instr. in librarianship Eastern Mont. Coll., Billings, fall 1981; mem. library media task force Office Pub. Instruction Mont., 1982—, Mem. ALA, Mountain Plains Library Assn., Mont. Library Assn. (chmn. membership 1983-84, chmn. membership/publicity com. 1984—), Mont. Edn. Assn., NEA. Methodist. Home: 1846 Bitterroot Billings MT 59105 Office: Billings Sr High Sch 425 Grand Ave Billings MT 59101

ROLFE, ELAINE ANDERSON, accountant; b. Kansas City, Mo., July 10, 1936; d. Harold Joseph and Marguerite (Snyder) Anderson; m. Robert Edward Rolfe, Dec. 22, 1956 (div. Aug. 1982); children—Harold Edward, Frank Edwin. B.S., U. Tex.-Dallas, 1981. Assoc. analyst ARCO Oil and Gas Co., Dallas, 1981—. Home: 3439 Northaven Rd Dallas TX 75229

ROLL, VIRGINIA LEE, heating company owner; b. Tell City, Ind., Jan. 3, 1927; d. Percy Sylvester Sprinkle and Mary Louise (Sweat) Sprinkle Walters; m. Colvert Lee Roll, Sr., July 6, 1946; children—Colvert Lee, Gary Lee, Jennifer Lee Roll Hines. Long distance operator, sec. employment office AT&T Co., Louisville, 1945-46; owner Grocery Mart, New Albany, Ind., 1946-49; office mgr. Lee's Heating Service, Cape Girardeau, Mo., 1962-78, owner, 1978—. Watch capt. Neighborhood Watch, Cape Girardeau, 1983. Commd. Hon. Order Ky. Cols. Mem. C. of C., Metro Assn., VFW Aux. Republican. Baptist. Home: 1435 Luce St Cape Girardeau MO 63701 Office: Lee's Heating Service 28 S Spanish St Cape Girardeau MO 63701

ROLLER, CATHERINE ANN, residential maintenance company executive; b. San Francisco, Nov. 4, 1954; d. Billy Dean and Mae Rita (Lambert) Bottger, m. Richard Albert Roller, Feb. 9, 1975; children—Patricia Ann, Victoria Ann, Stephanie Ann. A.S. in Bus., Victor Valley Coll., 1984; B.S. in Bus. Adminstrn. U. Redlands, 1985. Driver's lic. asst. Dept. Motor Vehicles, Sacramento, 1972-77; adminstrv. asst. Commissary U.S. Air Force, Karamursel, Turkey, 1977-78, communications officer, Berlin, Fed. Republic Germany, 1978-79, social actions, 1979-80, contracting dept., George AFB, Calif., 1981-84; sr. buyer King Hi-Tech, Victorville, Calif., 1985-86; owner, operator Mr. Mom's Service; residential maintenance company, 1986—. Service unit chmn. Girl Scouts U.S.A., George AFB, 1981-82. Recipient Outstanding Contracting Support award Tactical Air Command, U.S. Air Force, 1981. Mem. Nat. Assn. Female Execs., Air Force Assn., Beta Sigma Phi. Democrat. Roman Catholic. Home: 15991 N Culver Victorville CA 92392 Office: Mr Mom's Service Victorville CA 92392

ROLLIN, MARGUERITE CLARA, costume jewelry designer, manufacturing company executive; b. Vienna, Oct. 18, 1905; came to U.S., 1941, naturalized, 1946; d. Mosco and Elsa (Russo) Galimir; m. Paul Rollin, 1943 (dec. 1963). Grad. Conservatory of Music, Vienna, 1935; diploma Sorbonne U., Paris, 1939. Owner, designer, mgr. Mille Fleurs, Inc., N.Y.C., 1943—. Fin. sec. Gracie Sq. chpt. B'nai B'rith, 1973—; active mem. Park Ave. Synagogue. Recipient Cert. of Honor, B'nai B'rith, 1984.

ROLLINGS, JOANN, nurse, army officer; b. St. Louis, Feb. 13, 1947; d. Edward Charles and Dorothy Jane (Horak) R. B.S. in Nursing, Baylor U., 1969; M.S. in Nursing, U. Tex.-El Paso, 1982; postgrad. U. Calif.-San Francisco, 1984—. Registered nurse, Tex. Commd. Nurse Corps, U.S. Army, 1969, advanced through grades to lt. col., 1986; clin. staff nurse Irwin Army Hosp., 1969-70, 95th Evacuation Hosp., DaNang, Vietnam, 1970-71; chief nursing inservice edn. and tng. Letterman Gen. Hosp., 1971-72; asst. prof. Walter Reed Army Inst. of Nursing, U. Md. Sch. Nursing, Washington, 1974-78; critical care clin. nurse specialist William Beaumont Army Med. Ctr., 1979-82; chief clin. nursing service U.S. Army Community Hosp., Seoul, Korea, 1982-83; quality assurance cons. Letterman Army Med. Ctr., 1985—; adj. clin. faculty Sch. Nursing, U. Tex.-El Paso, 1980-82, Sch. Nursing, San Francisco State U., 1983-84. Contbr. articles to profl. jours. Health cons. Girl Scouts U.S.A., Rockville, Md., 1975-77. Decorated Bronze Star medal, Army Commendation medal with oak leaf cluster, Meritorious Service medal with 2 oak leaf clusters; Commendation medal (Vietnam); U.S. Army Nurse Corps scholar, 1985. Mem. Am. Nurses Assn., Am. Assn. Critical Care Nurses, Calif. Nurses Assn., Officers Christian Fellowship, Sigma Theta Tau.

ROLLINS, BARBARA ANN, real estate broker; b. Bklyn., Feb. 8, 1935; d. Thomas Bartley and Frances Josephine (McVeigh) Ure; m. James Thomas Campbell, Sept. 10, 1955 (div. 1969); children—Thomas, Susan, James, Elaine, Patricia; m. Charles McCausland Rollins, June 2, 1979. Cert. Grad. Realtors Inst., 1984. Sec., sales assoc. Percy Oliver Real Estate, Plaistow, N.H., 1971-75; ptnr., broker Clement & Assocs., Raymond, N.H., 1975—. Mem. Rockingham Bd. Realtors (v.p. 1981, pres. 1982, Realtor of Yr. 1981). Democrat. Roman Catholic. Home: 10 Smith Corner Rd Newton NH 03865 Office: Clement & Assocs Realty Raymond Shopping Ctr Raymond NH 03077

ROLLINS, OTTILIE HIRT, librarian; b. Vienna, Austria, Nov. 18, 1915; d. Alfred and Christine (Cepelak) Hirt; came to U.S., 1935, naturalized, 1944; B.S. cum laude (Achelis scholar), Russell Sage Coll., 1945; M.S. in Library Sci., Western Res. U., 1960; m. John Pletcher Rollins, Sept. 5, 1945; children—Alfred Hirt, Christopher John. Acad. sec., tchr. German, Putney (Vt.) Sch., 1935-42; instr. phys. edn. Russell Sage Coll., Troy, N.Y., 1945-48; sec. Clarkson Coll. Tech. (now Clarkson U.), Potsdam, N.Y., 1948-50, cataloger, asst. librarian, acting librarian, 1961-67, asso. prof., head librarian, 1967-80, asso. dir. Ednl. Resources Center/library info. resources, 1980-81, lectr. German, 1958-60, 61-65, dir. Clarkson Eldenhostel, 1982-86; cons. Mem. AAUW (past pres., treas. 1983-85). ALA, N.Y. Library Assn. (legis. com.), Spl. Libraries Assn., Am. Soc. Engring. Edn., North Country Reference and Research Resources Council (past chmn. bd. trustees), No. Folk Dancers (leader), Beta Phi Mu. Home: 44 Bay Potsdam NY 13676 Office: Clarkson Univ Potsdam NY 13676

ROLPH, SHARON MURIEL, data processing administrator; b. Anacortes, Wash., Nov. 7, 1947; d. Harry Donald and Ruth Marie (Cohrs) R.; student N.W. Coll., 1966-67; cert. Northwestern Sch. Bus., 1967; A.Tech. Arts, Edmonds Community Coll., 1979; B.A., City U., 1982. Acctg. clk. Peoples Bank, Royal City, Wash., 1965; asst. bookkeeper N.W. Coll., Kirkland, Wash., 1966; proof operator People's Bank, Seattle, 1967; computer operator, lead data control clk. Nat. Bank Commerce, Seattle, 1968-72; computer operator GTE Data Services, Everett, Wash., 1972-73, scheduler, 1973-76, data control technician, 1976-78, programmer, 1978-79, programmer analyst, 1979-80; methods analyst Gen. Telephone N.W., Everett, Wash., 1980-82, methods adminstr., 1982-84, systems analyst, 1984—. Emcee, mem. exec. com., co-chmn., chmn. Pacific N.W. Christian Singles Conv., 1980—, drama producer, 1979. Club: Fellowship Christian Adult Singles II. Office: 1800 41st St Everett WA 98201

ROMAIN, MARGARET ANN, accountant; b. Mercer, Pa., Jan. 1, 1940; d. Peter Paul and Susie Anne (Murcko) Kutcher; student Youngstown (Ohio) State U., 1957-58, 68-69; cert. LaSalle Extension U., Chgo., 1963, 64, 66, 67; postgrad. Pa. State U., 1974; m. Joseph Romain, Jr., Nov. 23, 1968; children—Lucretia Ann, Kimberly Rose, Annette Marie. Sec., bookkeeper Voytik Constrn. Co., Sharpsville, Pa., 1957-58; bookkeeper Ernst, Inc., Sharon, Pa., 1958-60, Mort-Bohn & Assos., C.P.A.s, Sharon, 1960-62, D.G. Reed & H. Hudson, public accts., Sharon, 1962-64; asst. office mgr. J.V. McNicholas Transfer Co., Youngstown, 1965-66; partner Reed-Romain & Assos., 1966-70; pvt. practice acctg., Sharpsville, 1970-76, 78—; partner Romain-Pendel & Assos., Public Accts., 1976-78; owner, partner RP Computer Services and Romain-Pendel Office Rental, 1976-80; mem. Pa. Pub. Accts. Adv. Com., 1977—. Asst. treas. St. John's Episcopal Ch., Sharon, 1974, 75; exec. bd. Episc. Churchwomen, 1977-79; 4H Club leader, 1977—. First runner-up Queens Contest, chairwoman Children's Pet Parade, Sharpsville Centennial, 1974. Mem. Internat. Graphoanalysis Soc. (cert., Pa. chpt.), Ohio Soc. Enrolled Agts., Nat. (assoc. state dir. 1977—), Pa. (state bd. dirs. 1973—, state sec. 1978—, editor Pa. Acct. 1980-84, numerous coms., sec.) socs. public accts., Nat. (sec. 1972-73), Pa. (pres. 1972-74, exec. dir. 1975—) assns. enrolled fed. tax accts., Nat., Pa. (exec. dir.) assns. enrolled agts., Shenango Valley C. of C. Democrat. Clubs: Baldwin Organ (pres. 1969) (Sharon, Pa.); Quota (Sharon) (treas. 1985—Saddlemates Saddle (treas. 1979) (Transfer, Pa.). Home: 125 Koehler Dr Sharpsville PA 16150 Office: 2048 Buckeye Dr Sharpsville PA 16150

ROMAKER, JANET JUNE, newspaper editor; b. Toledo, Nov. 4, 1952; d. Charles Edward and Barbara Ann (Russell) Romaker; B.S., Bowling Green State U., 1974. Reporter, The Blade Newspaper, Toledo, 1974-75, 76-79, asst. regional editor, 1979, regional editor, 1979—; editor Swanton Enterprise Newspaper, Swanton, Ohio, 1976; faculty Sch. Journalism, Bowling Green State U., 1982-83. Chmn. fund drive Am. Heart Assn., 1980. Mem. Soc. Profl. Journalists (treas. 1981-82), Ohio Newspapers Women's Assn. (1st place newswriting category 1982), Sigma Delta Chi. United Methodist. Club: Toledo Press. Office: 541 N Superior St Toledo OH 43660

ROMAN, CAMILLE, writer, English educator; b. LaPlatta, Md., Feb. 18, 1948; d. Arthur Robert and LaNelle (Bugg) R.; m. Chris D. Frigon, Aug. 9, 1975. B.A., U. Mich., 1970; M.A., Boston Coll., 1985; postgrad. Brown U., 1985—. Writer, copy editor Quincy (Mass.) Patriot Ledger, 1969-72; community relations dir. Cambridge (Mass.) Pub. Library, 1972-73; editorial cons., Cambridge, 1973-76; publicity coordinator G.K. Hall & Co., Boston, 1976-78; editorial cons., Boston, 1978—; instr. English, Aquinas Jr. Coll., Newton, Mass., 1978-85. Author: Women Alive! (poetry), 1983; editor: (with Chris Frigon) Twayne Music Series, 1983—; contbr. articles revs., essays and poetry to newspapers, mags., jours., newsletters, TV and radio programs. Bd. dirs. Cambridge YWCA, 1970-72. Recipient John Cotton Dana award ALA, 1973. Mem. MLA, Women in Communications (v.p. Boston 1973-74, Edward Bernays award 1975), D.H. Lawrence Soc., Phi Theta Kappa (adv. 1982-85). Office: Brown U Dept English Box 1852 Providence RI 02912

ROMAN, SUSAN KOLBE, nursing educator; b. Elizabeth, N.J., Aug. 8, 1946; d. Charles Clayton and Ruth Martell (Leonard) Kolbe; m. Philip Randall Shannon, Aug. 3, 1968 (div. 1972); m. 2d, Stephen Edward Roman, June 19, 1976. B.S.N., U. Va., 1968. R.N., N.J., Va. Flight attendant Overseas Nat. Airways, Jamaica, N.Y., 1971-73; pediatric clinic nurse Beth Israel Hosp., Newark, 1973-74; instr. lic practical nurses Perth Amboy (N.J.) Adult Skills Tng. Ctr., 1974-76; pub. health nurse MCOSS Nursing Service, Red Bank, N.J., 1976-77; instr. lic. practical nurses Middlesex County Bd. Edn., East Brunswick, N.J., 1977-82; pvt. practice health cons., Cream Ridge, N.J., 1982—; coordinator Health Occupations Students Assn., East Brunswick, 1981. Co-chmn. Cream Ridge Bd. Health, 1977—; sec. Garwood (N.J.) Bd. Health, 1974-75; co-chmn. consumer health adv. com. Perth Amboy Hosp., 1976; mem. Manalapan Twp. (N.J.) Consumer Protection Bd., 1978. Teagle scholar, 1964-68. Mem. NOW, N.J. Health Occupations Educators Assn. Home: RD 1 PO Box 136G Cream Ridge NJ 08514

ROMANANSKY, MARCIA CANZONERI, book company executive; b. Bklyn., Apr. 22, 1941; d. Nicholas C. and Ellen (Zukas) Canzoneri; m. Robert Edward Romanansky, June 1, 1963. B.A. in History, Coll. Misericordia, Dallas, Pa., 1962; M.L.S., Pratt Inst., 1969; M.A. in Edn., Seton Hall U., 1973; postgrad. Fairleigh Dickinson U., 1980—. Acquisitions librarian St. Peter's Coll., Jersey City, 1963-68; sch. librarian Roselle High Sch. (N.J.), 1968-72; selection librarian Baker & Taylor, Somerville, N.J., 1972-74, chief librarian, 1974-80, asst. mgr. program services, 1980-81, mgr. program services, 1981—. Mem. publicity com., Showhouse, Aux. Muhlenberg Hosp., Plainfield, N.J., 1982, 84; mem. steering com. Plainfield Hist. Dist. Tours, N.J. Mem. ALA (tech. services com. 1982-84), Beta Phi Mu. Contbr. articles to profl. jours. Home: 994 Oakland Ave Plainfield NJ 07060 Office: 6 Kirby Ave Somerville NJ 08876

ROMANO, CHRISTINE DOROTHY PROVENZALE (MRS. CHARLES F. ROMANO), businesswoman, civic worker; b. Bklyn.; d. Leonardo and Concetta (Marino) Provenzale; student Bklyn. Coll., 1956, Mitchell Coll., 1962; B.A. in Bus. Adminstrn., William Paterson Coll.; m. Charles F. Romano, Oct. 16, 1938; children—Charles, Katherine. Treas., Red Stack Towing Co., Bklyn., 1956-58, v.p., 1958, pres., 1958-61, dir., 1956-61; sec.-treas. New London Towing Co., Bklyn., 1956-58, v.p., 1958-61, dir., 1956-61; sec. A&R Towing Co. Ltd., Bklyn., 1969—; v.p., sec. Smoke Rise (N.J.) Shipping, S.A. Sec., Bergen Beach Civic Assn., 1950-56, pres. 1956-62, dir., 1950-62; mem. Bklyn. Civic Council, 1956-62, dir., 1958-62; mem. 40th Sch. Dist. Sch. Bd., 1958-62, sec., 1959-62; chmn. ARC, 1956-63, vol. worker, Smoke Rise, 1964-66; vol. Heart Fund, Smoke Rise, 1964-66; chmn. Mothers March of Dimes, N.J. state rep., 1967-68; vice-chmn. No. N.J. chpt. Paterson Gen. Hosp. Aux., 1973—; chmn. Greater Paterson Gen. Hosp. Charity Ball, 1977. Clubs: Women of Smoke Rise, Smoke Rise Garden. Home: 734 Ridge Rd Smoke Rise NJ 07405

ROMANOFF, MARJORIE REINWALD, educator; b. Chgo., Sept. 29, 1923; d. David E. and Gertrude (Rosenfield) Reinwald; student Northwestern U., 1941-42, 43-45, Chgo. Coll. Jewish Studies, 1942-43; Ed.B., U. Toledo, 1947, Ed.M., 1968, Ed.D., 1976; m. Milford M. Romanoff, Nov. 6, 1945; children—Bennett S., Lawrence M., Janet Beth (dec.). Tchr., Old Orchard Elem. Sch., Toledo, 1947-48; substitute tchr. Toledo public schs., 1965-68; tchr. McKinley Sch., Toledo, 1964-65; cons. curriculum revision in lang. arts Toledo public schs., 1966, ethnic studies program, 1976-77; supr. student tchrs. U. Toledo, 1968-73, 85—; instr. Am. Lang. Inst., 1978—; adj. asst. prof. Bowling Green State U., 1978—, U. Toledo Coll. Edn., 1985—; cons. Toledo Hebrew Acad. Elem. Sch., 1968—; instr. reading Mary Manse Coll., Toledo, 1974; tchr. temple religious sch., Congregation Shomer Emunin, Toledo, 1947-73, bd. dirs.

temple sisterhood, 1958-62; bd. dirs. Hadassah, 1952—, pres. Toledo chpt., 1961-64; trustee Lucas County Children's Services Bd., 1974-76; trustee Cummings Treatment Center for Adolescents, 1976-81, pres. 1978-81; trustee Toledo Bd. Jewish Edn., 1975—, v.p., 1975-79, pres., 1982-84; trustee Big Sisters, 1978-79; trustee Jewish Family Service, 1978-85, v.p., 1982-85; bd. dirs. Jewish Welfare Fedn. Budget and Planning Commn., 1977-81, Toledo Community Planning Council, 1980-85; v.p. women's bd. Jewish Welfare Fedn., 1984-86; trustee Toledo Family Life Edn. Council, 1984-87; mem. allocations com. Mental Health and Retardation Bd., 1980-82. Named 1 of 10 Outstanding Women in Toledo, Guild of St. Vincent Med. Ctr., 1984. Mem. Nat. Soc. for Study Edn., Assn. for Supervision and Curriculum Devel., Internat. Reading Assn., Am. Ednl. Research Assn., Tchrs. English to Speakers of Other Langs., Toledo Assn. Children's Lit., Orgn. for Rehab. Through Tng. (1 of 6 Outstanding Women in Toledo 1984), Toledo Zool. Soc., Toledo Orch. Aux., ACLU (dir. 1968-78), Women's Internat. League for Peace and Freedom, Common Cause, Northwestern U. Alumni Assn. Phi Kappa Phi, Kappa Delta Pi (past pres.), Phi Delta Kappa, Pi Lambda Theta (pres. 1976-78, nat. membership chmn. 1978-84). Contbr. to Children's Lit. Assn. Quar., 1982. Home: 2514 Bexford Pl Toledo OH 43606 Office: Am Lang Inst U Toledo CEC 1006 Toledo OH 43606

ROMBERG, LESLIE HOLMES, international marketing management company executive; b. Bklyn., Aug. 11, 1941; d. Alton Butler and Margaret Nichol (Arnett) H.; m. Jon Word Blaschke, Aug. 20, 1966 (div. June 1968); m. Conrad Louis Romberg, Jan. 6, 1985. Student, Baylor Coll. Dentistry, 1959-60, U. Tulsa, 1962-64; B.S. in Chemistry and Biology, Central State U., Edmond, Okla., 1966; Ph.D. in Chemistry, U. Okla., 1968. Head internat. ops. New Eng. Nuclear Corp., Boston, 1969-77; sales engr. Tracor Analytic, Des Plaines, Ill., 1977-79; internat. mktg. and product mgr. Zoecon Industries, Dallas, 1979-80; owner, operator Tex-Am. Internat., Dallas, 1980—. Vice pres. Richardson Unitarian Ch., 1985-86, pres., 1986-87; bd. dirs. DeSoto Equestrian Ctr. Named Most Outstanding Former Student Central State U., 1975. Mem. Dallas C. of C., North Dallas Network Career Women. Republican.

ROME, FLORENCE MILES, author; b. Chgo., Sept. 24, 1910; d. Maurice David and Rose Miles; student, U. Ill., 1927-29; m. Harold Rome, Feb. 3, 1939; children—Joshua David, Rachel Miles. Author: The Scarlett Letters, 1971; The Tattooed Men, 1975, Arlene Francis, 1978; contbr. articles and short stories to profl. jours. Home: 1035 Fifth Ave New York NY 10028

ROMENSKI, KATHRYN B., physical therapist administrator; b. Pawtucket, R.I., Aug. 13, 1948. B.S., Boston U., 1970. Staff phys. therapist Allied Services for the Handicapped, Scranton, Pa., 1970-71, asst. chief phys. therapist, 1971-74, chief phys. therapist, 1974-77, dir. patient services, 1977-79, dir. phys. therapy, 1979—; pres. Allied Services Fed. Credit Union, 1984—, bd. dirs. 1970—. Mem. Am. Phys. Therapy Assn. (ho. of dels. 1973), Pa. Phys. Therapy Assn., Am. Mgmt. Assn., Nat. Rehab. Assn., Am. Acad. Orthotics and Prosthetics, Nat Rehab. Adminstrs. Assn., Internat. Rehab. Inst., Nat. Assn. Female Execs., Nat. Assn. Mgmt.

ROMEO, JOANNE JOSEFA MARINO, educator; b. Youngstown, Ohio, Nov. 21, 1943; d. Joseph James and Ann Marie (Bonamase) Marino; B.S., Ohio State U., 1965; postgrad. Youngstown State U., 1969-70; M.S., Purdue U., 1974; postgrad. in computer sci. U. Tenn., Knoxville; m. John Homer Romeo, Aug. 14, 1965; children—Christopher, Chrisanne, Jonathan. Substitute tchr. Grove City Schs., Columbus, Ohio, 1964-65; tchr. geometry, math. and French, Hamilton Sch. Dist., Columbus, 1965-66; tchr. gifted children Bluegrass Elem. Sch., Knoxville, Tenn., 1976-77; tchr. math. and sci. Webb Sch., Knoxville, 1977-85, also developer computer sci. program; headmistress Greenbrier Acad., Sevierville, Tenn., 1985—. Religious edn. dir. Sacred Heart Parish, Knoxville, 1979—. Mem. Nat. Council Tchrs. Math., Nat. Cath. Edn. Assn., Nat. Council Parish and Religious Coordinators and Dirs., Nat. Sci. Tchrs. Assn., Ohio State U. Alumni Assn., Purdue U. Alumni Assn., Alpha Gamma Delta. Republican. Home: 1708 Capistrano Dr Knoxville TN 37922 Office: Greenbrier Acad 217 Bruce St Sevierville TN 37862

ROMERO, ELIZABETH RIVERA, public health nurse; b. Manila, Jan. 10, 1958; came to U.S., 1973; d. Vivencio Delapaz and Erlinda (Magalona) Rivera; m. Oscar Dedios Romero, Feb. 14, 1978. B.S. in Nursing cum laude, San Francisco State U., 1980. R.N., Calif. Staff nurse St. Lukes Hosp., San Francisco, 1980-85; pub. health nurse St. Mary's Hosp., San Francisco, 1984-85, Doctor's Hosp. of Pinole, Calif., 1984—. Mem. Am. Nurses Assn., Calif. Nurses Assn., Golden Gate Nurses Assn., Am. Heart Assn. (Contra Costa chpt.), Filipino Nurses Assn. of Calif., Calif. Scholarship Fedn. Roman Catholic. Avocations: dancing; travel; camping; photography.

ROMERO, JULIA MARIE, international conference administrator; b. Washington, July 18, 1951; d. Albert R. and Clara Elsie (Goltz) R. Student Stanford U., 1985. Adminstrv. asst. Am. Forest Inst., Washington, 1975-77, House Select Com. on Intelligence, Washington, 1977-78; exec. dir. Nat. Jour., Washington, 1978-86; dir. spl. programs The Govt. Research Corp., Washington, 1986—. Tutor Washington Literacy Council, 1986. Mem. Nat. Assn. Female Execs., Nat. Fedn. Bus. and Profl. Women (chmn. legis. com. 1983-84, editor D.C. chpt. Capital Women newsletter 1985—). Republican. Roman Catholic. Avocations: travel; movies. Home: 3221 Connecticut Ave NW Apt 402 Washington DC 20008 Office: Govt Research Corp 1250 Connecticut Ave NW Suite 600 Washington DC 20036

ROMERO, LUISA JOSEFINA, banker; b. San Diego, Oct. 30, 1951; d. Pietro Guido and Anna Hermina (Foradori) Serena; m. Ricardo Javier Romero, Apr. 27, 1974; 1 son, Erik. With Security Pacific Nat. Bank, San Diego, 1972—, internat. ops. officer, 1976-81, asst. v.p. charge overall ops., 1981-82, asst. v.p., account officer, 1982-84, v.p., mgr., 1984—, bank rep. Western Council Internat. Banking, 1979—. Mem. World Trade Assn. San Diego, Nat. Assn. Bank Women, Hispanic Bankers Assn. San Diego. Home: 10360 Moorpark St Spring Valley CA 92078 Office: 1200 3d Ave Suite 220 San Diego CA 92101

ROMICK, INA SUE HIRSCH, lawyer; b. Chgo., May 1, 1944; d. Jerome Herman and Lillian (Schwartz) Hirsch; m. Jerome Michael Romick, Aug. 8, 1971; children—Stephanie Alisha, Kate Hilary. B.S., U. Houston, 1966; M.S., Tex. A & I U., 1968; J.D., Capital U., Ohio, 1976. Bar: Ohio 1976, U.S. Dist. Ct. (so. dist.) Ohio 1977. Tchr., Nat. Tchrs. Corps, Corpus Christi, Tex., 1966-68; counselor Job Opportunities for Youth, Houston, 1968-69; counselor Group Guidance Program, Houston, 1969-71; adminstrv. asst. Artromick Unit Dose Systems Internat., Columbus, 1976-79; sole practice, Columbus, 1979—. Bd. dirs. East Area Mental Health, Columbus, 1978-79; mem. women's issues com. S.W. Community Mental Health, 1978-79; chairperson pub. affairs, community services Nat. Council Jewish Women, Columbus, 1981-83; mem. Israel-Judaic and membership coms. Leo Yassenoff Jewish Ctr., Columbus, 1983-84. Recipient Am. Jurisprudence award, 1976. Mem. ABA (immigration law com.), Ohio Bar Assn., Women Lawyers Franklin County, Nat. Council Jewish Women (nat. continuing edn. subcom. 1982-83). Office: 20008 Zettler Rd Columbus OH 43232

ROMMER, BARBARA RUTH, physician; b. Newark, Jan. 20, 1944; d. Jack Jay and Isabella (Stern) R.; m. S.W. Pepitone, Oct. 23, 1971; 1 son, William S. B.A., Upsala Coll., 1965; student Adelphi U., 1962-63; M.D., Chgo. Med. Sch., 1970. Intern Mt. Siani Hosp. Med. Center, Chgo., 1970-71; resident in internal medicine Manhattan VA Hosp., N.Y.C., 1971-72; resident in gastroenterology U. Pa. Grad. Hosp., Phila., 1972-73; practice medicine, specializing in internal medicine and gastroenterology, Ft. Lauderdale, Fla., 1973—; mem. attending staff Holy Cross Hosp., Ft. Lauderdale, 1973—, vice chief med. dept., 1975-76; attending staff Imperial Point Hosp., Ft. Lauderdale, 1973—. Adv. bd. Mt. Scott Inst., 1971-80. NIMH grantee 1969-70. Mem. Broward County Med. Assn., Fla. Med. Assn., Broward County Soc. Internal Medicine, Am. Women's Med. Assn., ACP (assoc.), Internat. Med. Assn. for Reciprocal Assistance. Columnist, Fla. Made mag. Office: 2633 E Commercial Blvd Fort Lauderdale FL 33308

RONALDER, NINA WALKER, geologist; b. Fort Worth, July 1, 1955; d. John and Virginia (Stiles) Walker; m. Ronnie Lee Ronalder, Dec. 30, 1978; children—Katrina Michelle. B.S., Baylor U., 1977; M.S., U. Tex.-Arlington, 1982. Geologist Mobil Exploration Producing Services Inc., Dallas, 1971-81, prodn. geologist, Midland, Tex., 1985, staff ops. engr., Midland, 1986—. Mem. Am. Assn. Petroleum Geologists, Soc. Petroleum Engrs., West Tex. Geol. Soc., AAUW, Baylor Alumni Assn., Chi Omega. Baptist. Office: Mobil Producing Tex and New Mexico Inc PO Box 633 Midland TX 79702

RONAN, ELENA VINADÉ (MRS. WILLIAM JOHN RONAN), real estate broker; b. Havana, Cuba; d. Ricardo Poblet and Virtudes (Alpérez-Inclán) Vinadé; B.A., N.Y. U., 1943; m. William John Ronan, May 29, 1939; children—Monica Ronan Nourie, Diana Ronan Quasha. Asst. v.p. Douglas, Elliman, Gibbons & Ives, N.Y.C., 1976—; pres. Comillas Corp., N.Y.C., 1982—. Clubs: Cosmopolitan; Maidstone (East Hampton, L.I.); Knickerbocker; Winged Foot Golf; Creek. Home: 655 Park Ave New York NY 10021 Office: 575 Madison Ave New York NY 10021

RONDEAU, DORIS JEAN, entrepreneur, consultant; b. Winston-Salem, N.C., Nov. 25, 1941; d. John Delbert and Eldora Virginia (Klutz) Robinson; m. Robert Breen Corrente, Sept. 4, 1965 (div. 1970); m. Wilfrid Dolor Rondeau, June 3, 1972. Student Syracuse U., 1959-62, Fullerton Jr. Coll., 1974-75; B.A. in Philosophy, Calif. State U.-Fullerton, 1976, postgrad., 1976-80. Ordained to ministry The Spirit of Divine Love, 1974. Trust real estate clk. Security First Nat. Bank, Riverside, Calif., 1965-68; entertainer Talent, Inc., Hollywood, Calif., 1969-72; co-founder, dir. Spirit of Divine Love, Capistrano Beach, Calif., 1974—; pub., co-founder Passing Through, Inc., Capistrano Beach, 1983—; instr. Learning Activity, Anaheim, Calif., 1984—; chmn. bd., prin. D.J. Rondeau, Entrepreneur, Inc., Capistrano Beach, 1984—; co-founder, dir. Spiritual Positive Attitude, Inc., Moon In Pisces, Inc., Vibrations By Rondeau, Inc., Divine Consciousness, Expressed, Inc., Capistrano Beach. Author, editor: A Short Introduction To The Spirit of Divine Love, 1984; writer, producer, dir. performer spiritual vignettes for NBS Radio Network, KWVE-FM, 1982-84. Served with USAF, 1963-65. Recipient Pop Vocalist First Place award USAF Talent Show, 1964, Sigma chpt. Epsilon Delta Chi, 1985, others. Mem. Hamel Bus. Grads., Smithsonian Assocs., Am. Mgmt. Assn., nat. Assn. Female Execs. Avocations: long-distance running; body fitness; arts and crafts; snorkeling, musical composition.

RONDO, PHILLISTINE WARD, educational administrator; b. Edmondson, Ark., Mar. 26, 1926; d. Granville William and Bertha Cleveland (Hicks) Ward. B.E., Chgo. Tchrs. Coll., 1965; postgrad., U. Calif.-Riverside, 1965-71; NDEA Inst., Calif. State Coll., Northridge, 1968; M.S. in Edn./Sch. Adminstrn., U. Calif.-Fullerton, 1975, UCLA, 1985. Elem. tchr. Corona-Norco Sch. Dist., Calif., 1965-72, prin. summer sch., 1972, tchr., 1972-76, Title I coordinator, 1976-77, coordinator elem. edn., 1977-78, dir. headstart prof., 1978-80, elem. prin. Lincoln Elem. Sch., 1978-80, adminstrv. asst. instr. services, 1980-84, adminstrv. dir. instructional services, 1984-85, adminstrv. dir. personnel and eval. services, 1986—. Author handbooks and catalogues in field. Mem. NEA, Calif. Assn. Compensatory Edn., Internat. Reading Assn., Calif. Reading Assn., Calif. Assn. Tchrs. Other Langs., AAUW, Corona-Norco Mgmt. Assn., Assn. Calif. Sch. Adminstrs., Assn. Supervision and Curriculum Devel., Western Assn. Adminstrs. State and Fed. Edn. Progs., Am. Assn. Sch. Adminstrs., Am. Assn. Sch. Personnel Adminstrs. Methodist. Office: 300 Buena Vista Ave Corona CA 91720

RONEY, SHIRLEY FLETCHER, retail co. exec.; b. Atlanta, Dec. 3, 1935; d. Grady Franklin and Grace Ilene (Camp) Fletcher; student public schs., Atlanta; m. Sept. 19, 1953 (div.); 1 son, Joseph Clay. Collection corr. GMAC, Atlanta, 1953-64; sales rep. Washburn Realty, Atlanta, 1964-67; sec.-treas. Frank Jackson Lincoln Mercury, Inc., Sandy Springs, Ga., 1967-79, sec. treas., 1971—, comptroller, 1979—, pres., gen. mgr., 1983—; v.p., dir. J&J Investment Corp., 1975—; v.p., dir. Rivergate Corp., 1979—; sec. treas., dir. Ajax Rent a Car, Sandy Springs Toyota. Div. vice chmn. United Way, 1979; bd. dirs. Ga. Spl. Olympics. Mem. Am. Bus. Womens Assn., Am. Contract Bridge League. Home: 1520 Northcliff Trace Roswell GA 30076 Office: 7555 Roswell Rd Atlanta GA 30338

RONGO, LUCILLE LYNN, medical center executive; b. N.Y.C., Sept. 15, 1958; d. Vincent Frank and Lucy Ann (Guilano) R. B.S., Mercy Coll., Dobbs Ferry, N.Y., 1984. Asst. supr. accounts receivable Montefiore Med. Ctr., Bronx, 1978-81, asst. mgr. accounts payable, 1981-83, payroll mgr., 1983—. Mem. Nat. Assn. Female Execs. Avocations: drying, preserving and framing flowers; collecting miniatures; art; dance. Office: Montefiore Med Ctr 111 E 210th St Bronx NY 10466

RONHOVDE, VIRGINIA SEDMAN, political and civic worker; b. Missoula, Mont., Dec. 17, 1909; d. Oscar Alfred and Harriet Laura (Rankin) Sedman; student U. Mont., 1925-27; B.A., Wellesley Coll., 1929; M.A., Columbia U., 1930; postgrad., 1930-33; postgrad. (Columbia U. fellow) U. Berlin, 1933-35; m. Andreas G. Ronhovde, Apr. 7, 1936; children—Erik Sedman, Andrea Rankin, Nora Montana Ronhovde Hohenlohe, Kent McGregor. Instr. sociology and labor problems Rutgers U., 1935-36; salesman Boss and Phelps, Inc., Simmons Properties, Washington, 1954-76. Sec., League Republican Women, Washington, 1969-71, bd. dirs., 1971-73, 75-77, 1st v.p., 1973-75; del. Nat. Fedn. Rep. Women Conv., Dallas, 1975; del., mem. permanent orgn. com. Rep. Nat. Conv., 1976; mem. central com. D.C. Rep. Com., 1976-80, 80-84, alt. nat. committeewoman, 1980-84; mem. Missoula Design Rev. Bd. Mem. Kappa Kappa Gamma. Episcopalian. Club: Missoula County Rep. Women (bd. dirs. 1986). Home: 600 Beverly Ave Missoula MT 59801

RONSTADT, LINDA MARIA, singer; b. Tucson, July 15, 1946; d. Gilbert and Ruthmary (Copman) Ronstadt. Recorded numerous albums, including Evergreen, 1967, Evergreen Vol. 2, 1967, Linda Ronstadt, The Stone Poneys and Friends, Vol. 3, 1968, Hand Sown, Home Grown, 1969, Silk Purse, 1970, Linda Ronstadt, 1972, Don't Cry Now (Gold album), 1973, Heart Like a Wheel (Gold album, Platinum album), 1974, Prisoner In Disguise (Gold album, Platinum album), 1975, Hasten Down the Wind (Gold album, Platinum album), 1976, Greatest Hits (Gold album, Platinum album), 1976, Vol. 2 (Gold album), 1981, Simple Dreams (Gold album, Platinum album), Blue Bayou (Gold single), 1977, Living in the U.S.A. (Gold and Platinum albums), 1978; Mad Love (Gold album, Platinum album), 1980; Greatist Hits, Vol. II (Gold album), 1980, Pirates of Penzance Cast Album, 1981, Get Closer (Gold album), 1982, What's New (Gold album, Platinum album), 1983; Lush LIfe (Gold album, Platinum album), 1984; appeared on Broadway as Mabel in Pirates of Penzance, 1981, and in movie, 1982. Recipient Grammy awards for best country vocal female, 1975, best pop vocal female, 1976, Am. Music award, 1978. Address: care Peter Asher Mgmt Inc 644 N Doheny Dr Los Angeles CA 90069

ROOD, KATHRYN ANN (MINETT), businesswoman; b. Clinton, Ind., Apr. 21, 1927; d. Thomas Everett and Francis Ann (Dyrval) Minett; student Terre Haute Comml. Coll., 1944-45; m. Robert Enoch Rood, Jan. 29, 1946; children—Robert Thomas, Larry Warren, Ronald Irvin, Richard Alan (dec.). Sec., Lammers Paint and Glass Co., Terre Haute, Ind., 1945-46; office mgr., corp. sec. Eurich Home Improvement Inc., Saginaw, Mich., 1969-78, also dir.; sec.-treas., mem. exec. com. Saginaw County Republican Com. from 1979—; now owner K.A.R. Enterprises. Mem. Saginaw Human Planning Commn., 1975—, sec., 1975-76, chmn., 1977-78, 85-86; jury commr. Mich. State, 1979—; bd. dirs. Civic Center, Saginaw, 1980—, Neighborhood Housing Services, 1978—. Recipient award Saginaw Neighborhoods Inc., 1980. Mem. LWV (v.p. chpt. 1969-71, chpt. bull. editor 1969-74, county fin. chmn., 1969-74). Clubs: Bus. and Profl. Women's, (pres. 1986-87), Saginaw Rep. Women's, Order Eastern Star. Home and Office: 2712 Morgan Saginaw MI 48602

ROODKOWSKY, TATIANA, governmental affairs consultant; b. N.Y.C., Sept. 21, 1951; d. Nikita Dimitri and Alice May (Juenger) R.; B.A., Newton Coll. Sacred Heart, 1973; M.A. in Internat. Affairs Cath. U. Am., 1984; m. Donald D. Evans, Jr., Nov. 25, 1977. Research analyst NRA, Washington, 1975-77; Washington rep. Synthetic Organic Chem. Mfrs. Assn., 1977-78; assoc. dir. U.S. C. of C., Washington, 1978-83; pres. Thornton Assocs., 1983—. Chmn., Mass. Coll. Young Republicans, 1970-72; elected mem. Natick (Mass.) Town Meeting, 1973. Mem. Women in Govt. Relations (sec. 1981-82), Nat. Assn. Environ. Profls., Pi Sigma Alpha, Pi Gamma Mu. Byzantine Rite Catholic. Home: 4006 Thornton St Annandale VA 22003

ROOKARD, GLORIA M., home health care agency executive; b. Akron, Ohio, Jan. 3; d. Claude H. and Maurine (Witherspoon) Shuler; m. Howard J. Rookard, July 3, 1952; children—Howard J., Douglas S., David W., Derrick A., Deanna M. Diploma Akron Gen. Hosp., 1952; cert. Pediatric Nurse Practitioner, Good Samaritan Hosp., Cin., 1971; postgrad. in Bus. Adminstrn., U. Akron, 1978-84. Chmn. Teenage Pregnancy Ctr., Akron, 1969-72; founder, pres. Universal Nursing Services, Inc., Akron, 1982—; mem. Gov.'s Task Force on Minority Health Issues, 1986—. Author, co-author biographies, biog. sketches, 1980, 83, 84. Active Wesley Temple African Methodist Episcopal Ch., Akron, NAACP. Mem. Nat. Black Nurses Assn. (invited founder, treas. 1978-84, Nurse of Yr. 1985), Ohio Pediatric Nurses Assn. (pres. 1972-74), Akron Black Nurses Assn. (founder, chmn. cancer com. 1986), Contemporary Nurses Edn. Found. Avocations: Bridge; sewing; writing. Home: 645 Roslyn Ave Akron OH 44320 Office: Universal Nursing Services Inc 201 W Cedar St Akron OH 44307

ROONEY, MARY FRANCES, parliamentarian, lawyer; b. Chgo., Nov. 1, 1952; d. Francis A. and Cele M. (Looney) R. B.A., Marquette U., 1974; J.D., John Marshall Sch. Law-Chgo., 1981. Bar: Ill. 1981. Project analyst City of Milw., 1975; adminstrv. asst. to lt. gov. Ill., Chgo., 1976; staff asst. Ill. Senate, Chgo. and Springfield, 1977-82, legis. asst., 1982-83, parliamentarian, legal counsel, 1983-84; mem. firm Richard S. Jalovec & Assocs., Chgo., 1985—; parliamentarian, legal counsel Ill. Democratic Party, Chgo. and Springfield, 1983-84; legal counsel Waste Mgmt. of Ill., 1986—. Pres. Dem. Party of Rogers Park and Edgewater, Chgo., 1983-84; mem. Chgo. Area Pub. Affairs Council, 1983-84; fundraiser Dem. Nat. Com., 1984—. Mem. ABA, Ill. State Bar Assn., Chgo. Bar Assn. Roman Catholic. Home: 1041 W North Shore Ave Chicago IL 60626 Office: Waste Mgmt Ill 7300 W College Dr Palos Heights IL 60463

ROONEY, PATRICIA KAY, human resources executive; b. Pittsburg, Calif., June 18, 1954; d. Henry Joseph and Blanche Unice (Graham) Rooney; m. Kevin J. McGrath, Aug. 13, 1976. Student Holy Name Coll., 1972-74; B.A., Calif. Poly. State U., 1976; postgrad. Golden Gate U., 1980—. Research asst. dept. polit. sci. Calif. Poly. State U., San Luis Obispo, 1974-76; personnel asst. Intel Corp., Sunnyvale, Calif., 1976-77; v.p. human resources Ramtek Corp., Santa Clara, Calif., 1977—. Adv. com. mem. Electronics Assn. Calif., Sunnyvale, 1983-84. Mem. No. Calif. Human Resource Council, Am. Soc. Personnel Adminstrs., Phi Kappa Phi. Democrat. Roman Catholic. Clubs: Corinthians Sailing, Island Yacht. Office: Ramtek Corp 2211 Lawson Ln Santa Clara CA 95050

ROONEY-CARTER, JUDY ANN, educator; b. New Orleans, Jan. 9, 1954; d. Joseph and Frances Louise (Hertzock) Rooney; m. Anthony Eric Carter, Feb. 24, 1973; children—Anthony Eric, Donielle Frances. B.A. Phys. Edn., Calif. State U.-Los Angeles, 1979, B.A. English, 1979, M.A., 1984. Tchr., Compton Unified Sch. Dist., Calif., 1979, Los Angeles County Edn. Ctr., Downey, 1980-82, Inglewood Unified Sch. Dist., Calif., 1982-83; tchr. Los Angeles Unified Sch. Dist., 1982-83, chmn. dept. English Angel's Gate Sr. High Sch., 1983—. Author short stories and plays: Anthony and Judy: Afro-American Teenagers, 1971; poetry: Stuck here in my Afroninity: Black Girl in America, 1984; I Am Proud of Both Lands, 1984. Asst. exec. dir. Brown's Group Home, Los Angeles, 1983—; counseling asst. John Muir Jr. High LAUSD, 1978-79; mem. United Tchr. Los Angeles/Calif. Assn. Tchrs. English, 1983—; mem. Olympic Games vols., others. Mem. Am. Soc. Profl. and Exec. Women, Calif. Assn. Tchrs. English, Dance Educators Calif., Computer Using Educators, ALA, Pi Lambda Theta, Delta Sigma Theta. Democrat. Roman Catholic. Clubs: Pyramid 1000, Writer's Workshop (pres.). Home: 815 N La Brea Apt 159 Inglewood CA 90302 Office: LAUSD Continuation Sr High Div 450 N Grand Ave Los Angeles CA

ROOS, LINDA PILLSBURY, psychotherapist; b. St. Louis, July 4, 1946; d. Fred Hobart and Anne (Larsen) Pillsbury; B.A. in Edn., William Jewell Coll., 1968; M.A. in Guidance and Counseling, U. Mo., St. Louis, 1974; m. Howard Norman Roos, Sept. 23, 1972; 1 son, Nelson Thomas. Tchr. phys. edn. public schs., St. Louis, 1968-73; tchr. phys. edn. Parkway East Jr. High Sch., St. Louis, 1974-75; counselor Parkway Central Sr. High Sch., St. Louis, 1975-76, Parkway South Sr. High Sch., Ballwin, Mo., 1976-82; pvt. practice counseling, Kirkwood, Mo., 1981—. Mem. adv. bd. Met. Sch.; trustee 3d Baptist Ch., 1975-77; sec. bd. Northside Team Ministry, 1985, v.p., 1986; mem. Commn. for Future, William Jewell Coll. Mem. Am. Assn. for Counseling and Devel., Mo. Psychol. Assn., Am. Mental Health Counselors Assn., Am. Fedn. Musicians, NEA, Mo. Nat. Edn. Assn., Mo. Assn. Counseling and Devel., AAUW, P.E.O., Sigma Alpha Iota. Home: 1199 Clayton Pl Town and Country MO 63131 Office: 10502 Manchester Rd Kirkwood MO 63122

ROOT, JOAN SCHIMPF, civic worker, museum trustee; b. Phila., Jan. 25, 1926; d. Henry Leonard and Josephine Abbott (Sibson) Schimpf; B.A., Skidmore Coll., 1947; m. Stanley W. Root, Jr., Sept. 3, 1949; children—Henry W., Louise A., Walter W. (dec.). Chmn. mus. guide program Phila. Mus. Art, 1971-74, exec. com. Friends of Mus., 1975-77, pres. women's com., 1977-80, ex-officio mem. bd. trustees, 1977-80, trustee, mem. exec. com., 1980—; port warden, mem. exec. com. Phila. Maritime Mus., 1979—; bd. dirs. Friends Ind. Nat. Hist. Park, 1975-78, mem. capital projects com., 1980, mem. intern selection com., 1981—; mem. trustee com. Mus. Council Phila., 1981; exec. com. U.S. Assn. Mus. Vols., 1980-82; bd. dirs. Goldie Paley Design Ctr., Phila. Coll. Textiles and Sci., 1982—. Mem. Internat. Council Mus., Am. Assn. Mus., Vol. Com. Art Mus., Eastern Nat. Parks and Monuments Assn., Am. Craft Council, Nat. Trust Historic Preservation. Republican. Episcopalian. Clubs: Acorn, Sedgeley. Address: 16 Hounds Run Ln Blue Bell PA 19422

ROOT, LINDA ALICE, lawyer; b. Cleve., Apr. 24, 1939; d. Robert Emmett and Elizabeth Lenore (Patterson) Fetterly; m. Christopher Gerald Root, children—Jolie Kristin Garcia, Michael Curt-Root, Russell Allen Root. Student Pomona Coll., 1957-59; B.S. in Law magna cum laude, Western State U., 1981, J.D. magna cum laude, 1981. Bar: Calif. 1982. Law firm adminstr. Turney & Turney, National City, Calif., 1969-73; legal asst. Ralph Gano Miller, Jr., San Diego, 1973-75; freelance portrait artist, Chula Vista, Calif., 1977-79; teaching asst. Western State U., San Diego, 1979, tutor, reader, 1980-81; dep. dist. atty. San Bernardino County, Barstow-Victorville, Calif., 1982-84, Morongo Basin, 1984; lectr. on women and law. Contbr. poetry to various publs.; artist watercolors in pvt. collections. Co-mem. Republican Presdl. Task Force, Washington, 1982-83; mem. Nat. Congl. Com., 1982-83. Mem. ABA, Calif. Bar Assn., San Diego County Bar Assn., High Desert Bar Assn., Calif. Dist. Attys. Assn., San Bernardino County Prosecutors Assn., Western State Alumni Assn. Home: PO Box 787 Joshua Tree CA 92252 Office: Offices of District Atty 6527 White Feather Rd State Route 1 Box 60 Joshua Tree CA 92252

ROOT, NINA J., librarian; b. N.Y.C., Dec. 22; d. Jacob J. and Fannie (Slivinsky) Root; B.A., Hunter Coll.; M.S. in L.S., Pratt Inst.; postgrad. U.S. Dept. Agr. Grad. Sch., 1964-65, City U. N.Y., 1970-75. Reference and serials librarian Albert Einstein Coll. Medicine Library, Bronx, N.Y., 1958-59; asst. chief librarian Am. Cancer Soc., N.Y.C., 1959-62; chief librarian Am. Inst. Aeros. and Astronautics, N.Y.C., 1962-64; head reference and library services sci. and tech. div. Library of Congress, Washington, 1964-66; mgmt. cons. Nelson Assocs., Inc., N.Y.C., 1966-70; chmn. dept. library services Am. Mus. Natural History, N.Y.C., 1970—; free-lance mgmt. cons. and library planning, 1970—. Trustee Barnard Found., 1984—; mem. library adv. council N.Y. State Bd. Regents, 1984—. Recipient Meritorious Service award Library of Congress, 1965. Mem. ALA (preservation com. 1977-79, chmn. library/binders com. 1978-80, chmn. preservation sect. 1980-81, mem. council 1983—), Spl. Libraries Assn. (sec. documentation group N.Y. chpt. 1972-73, 2d v.p. N.Y. 1975-76, treas. sci. and tech. group N.Y. 1975-76, mus. arts and humanities div. program planning chairperson-conf. 1977), AAAS, Am. Sci. Info. Sci., Archons of Colophon (convener 1978-79), Soc. History of Natural History (N. Am. rep. 1977-85), N.Y. Acad. Scis. (mem. publs. com. 1975-80, archives com. 1976-78, search com. 1976). Club: Grolier (mem. exhbn. com. 1977-79, admissions com. 1979-81). Home: 400 E 59th St New York NY 10022 Office: Library of American Museum of Natural History Central Park W at 79th St New York NY 10024

ROPER, PAMELA KAY, nurse; b. Gary, Ind., July 2, 1956; d. Philip Edward and Emily Ruth (Wittig) R. A.A. in Applied Sci., Purdue U., 1977. R.N.; cert. critical care nurse. Teaching asst. Purdue U., West Lafayette, Ind., 1976-77; charge nurse Gary and Broadway Methodist Hosp., 1978, Porter Starke Services, Valparaiso, Ind., 1978; on call nurse Staff Builders Nursing Registry, Los Angeles, 1980—; nursing supr. Kaiser Mental Health Ctr., Los Angeles, 1981, relief supr. Edgemont Hosp., Los Angeles, 1982-83; critical care nurse Pacific Hosp., Long Beach, Calif., Hollywood Presbyterian Hosp., Los Angeles, 1984—. Participant Multiple Sclerosis Ski Marathon, Glendale, Calif., 1984, Easter Seals Dance Marathon, Santa Monica, Calif., 1980, Am. Diabetes Assn. Bike Marathon, Valparaiso, 1979. Named Nurse of Month, Staff Builders Nursing Registry, 1980. Mem. Purdue Alumni Assn. Club: Purdue Los Angeles. Avocations: playing classical and contemporary piano.

ROPKEY, ANN SAMONIAL, educator, lecturer; b. Vincennes, Ind., Jan. 31, 1917; d. Charles Edward and Martha Ann (Love) Samonial; A.A., Vincennes

U., 1936; B.S., Peabody Coll., 1938, M.A., 1941; postgrad. Vanderbilt U.; Litt.D. (hon.), Steed Coll., 1957; m. Stewart Winning McClelland, Aug. 2, 1947 (dec. Feb. 1977); m. 2d, F. Noble Ropkey, Aug. 16, 1980. Tchr., Bogalusa (La.) High Sch., 1938, Holmes High Sch., Covington, Ky., 1939-45; instr. Okla. Coll. Women, 1938-39; dean women Lincoln Meml. U., 1945-47; sponsor Dale Carnegie courses, Fla., Ind., 1947—; assoc. with Mrs. Dale Carnegie in Dorothy Carnegie Courses Women, 1956—. Pres. Decorative Arts Soc. (program chmn.), Indpls. Mus. Art; state chmn. DAR Mus., Washington; mem. adv. bd. Pompeiiana, Inc. Recipient faculty citation Vincennes U., 1983. Fellow Royal Soc. Arts (London); mem. Indpls. Propylaeum (past pres.), Internat. Platform Assn., AAUW, Wedgwood Internat. Seminar, Wedgwood Soc. (London), English Speaking Union, DAR (past chmn. Wheel and Distaff, chmn. nat. def. com. 1984-85, past hon. regent Caroline Scott Harrison chpt. 1975-77, lifemem. and past pres. Ind. Officers Club), Children's Mus. of Ind., Hon. Order Ky. Cols., Blair Mus. Lithophanes, Indpls. Mus. Art, Am Ceramic Circle, Kappa Kappa Kappa, Pi Gamma Chi. Republican. Roman Catholic. Clubs: Fortnightly, Contemporary, Alpha Beta Latreian (Indpls.). Authority on Coin glass, Lithophanes and Wedgwood. Home: 6360 W 79th St Indianapolis IN 46278

RORISON, MARGARET LIPPITT, reading consultant; b. Wilmington, N.C., Feb. 6, 1925; d. Harmon Chadbourn and Margaret Devereux (Lippitt) R.; A.B., Hollins Coll., 1946; M.A., Columbia U., 1956; Diplôme de langue, L'Alliance Française, Paris, 1966; postgrad. U. S.C., 1967-70, 81—. Market and editorial researcher Time, Inc., N.Y.C., 1949-55; classroom and corrective reading tchr. N.Y.C. public schs., 1956-65; TV instr. ETV-WNDT, Channel 13, N.Y.C., 1962-63; grad. asst., TV instr. U. S.C., Columbia, 1967-70; instrnl. specialist in reading S.C. Office Instrnl. TV and Radio, S.C. Dept. Edn., Columbia, 1971-81; reading cons. S.C. Office Instructional Tech., 1982—. Active Common Cause. Mem. Internat. Reading Assn., Am. Ednl. Research Assn., Assn. Supervision and Curriculum Devel., Nat. Soc. Study of Edn., AAUW. Phi Delta Kappa, Delta Kappa Gamma. Episcopalian. Author instrnl. TV series: Getting the Word (So. Ednl. Communications Assn. award 1972, Ohio State award 1973, S.C. Scholastic Broadcasters award 1973), Getting the Message, 1981. Home: 1724 Enoree Ave Columbia SC 29205

RORKE, MARCIA LYNNE, research firm executive; b. Albany, N.Y., Nov. 17, 1942; d. Gerald Dean and Bernice Elizabeth (Ferguson) Bouton; m. Jerome Alan Grad, Sept. 1966 (div. Jan. 1971); m. John Joseph Rorke, III, May 3, 1980; children—Blys Lien Grad, John Joseph. B.A., U. Denver, 1969, M.A., 1975. Pres., Mohawk Research Corp., Lake Forest, Ill., 1979—; research asst. dept. mass communications U. Denver, 1967-69; instr. dept. history Trinity Coll., Burlington, Vt., 1971-72; research asst. spl. edn. program U. Vt., Burlington, 1971-73; writer/editor Behavior Assocs., Tucson, Ariz., 1973-74; research social scientist Social Systems Research and Evaluation Div. and Ctr. for Social Research and Devel., Denver, 1975-79; treas., dir. Inventors Council Chgo., 1983-86; dir. Ind. Bus. Assn. Ill., 1983-86; cons. The World Bank, Washington, 1977-79, U.S. AID, Dept. State, Washington, 1978, Entrepreneurship Inst., Columbus, Ohio, 1978-79, Owens-Corning Fiberglas, Granville, Ohio, 1977-78, Coler Engring. Co., N.Y.C., 1977-81. Contbr. articles to profl. jours. Mem. alumni exec. bd. Am. Field Service Internat. Scholarships, N.Y.C., 1971-73, exchange student scholar, 1960. Mem. Lic. Execs. Soc., AAAS, Tech. Transfer Soc., Inventors Council. Office: Mohawk Research Corp 679 Green Briar Ln Lake Forest IL 60045

RORKE, MARIE MOORE, financial executive; b. N.Y.C., Oct. 6, 1933; d. William J. and Cleo (Kascpre) Moore; student Hunter Coll., 1951-52; A.S. in Bus. Mgmt., Adelphi U.; m. Charles Rorke, May 15, 1953 (dec.); 1 son, C. William. Exec. sec. Avis Car Leasing Co., Plainview, N.Y., 1964-66; bus. office rep. N.Y. Telephone Co., Huntington, 1966-67; corp. sec., asst. treas., corp. controller Geotel, Inc., Amityville, N.Y., 1967—; dir. AFP Industries. Sec., Heatherwood Civic Assn., Huntington, 1965—. Mem. Am. Inst. Corp. Controllers, Am. Soc. Profl. and Bus. Women. Home: 79 Knolls Dr Stony Brook NY 11790 Office: 185 Dixon Ave Amityville NY 11701

ROSADO, PEGGY MORAN, actress, singer, dancer, educator; b. Canton, Ohio, Apr. 16, 1946; d. Clarence Ellsworth and Mabel Cecilia (Kearns) Moran; student Northwestern U.; B.S., Kent State U., M.A., Hunter Coll., 1969; student Arthur Mitchell, Dance Theatre of Harlem, 1971, 76— Am. Ballet Theatre, 1972-74; m. Richard Robert Garcia di Magpiong, Apr. 7, 1979. Dir., lead dancer New World Dancers Inc., N.Y.C., 1971—; dancer Dance Theatre of Harlem, 1976 ; dance tchr. performing arts program Franklin K. Lane High Sch., Bklyn., 1970-71; dance tchr., choreographer Lincoln Sq. Community Center, N.Y.C., 1971—; tchr. vocal music and musical theatre La Guardia High Sch. Music and Performing Arts, Lincoln Ctr., N.Y.C., 1985—; student head NBC Theatre Workshop, N.Y.C., 1960-61; film appearances Serpico, Dog Day Afternoon, Nunzio, Prince of the City, So Fine, Ragtime, Cotton Club, Fame. Mem. Actors Equity Assn., Screen Actors Guild, AFTRA, AGVA, Assn. Am. Dance Cos., Am. Indian Community House. Roman Catholic. Choreographer New World Journey, 1971, The Creation, 1982. Home and Office: 345 W 58th St New York NY 10019

ROSAR, VIRGINIA WILEY, librarian, educator; b. Cleve., Nov. 22, 1926; d. John Egbert and Kathryn Coe (Snyder) Wiley; m. Michael Thorpe Rosar, Apr. 8, 1950 (div.); children—Bruce Wiley, Keith Michael, James Wilfred. B.A., U. Puget Sound, 1948; M.S., Long Island U., 1971. Music programmer Sta. WFAS, White Plains, N.Y., 1948; prodn. asst. Sta. NBC-TV, N.Y., 1948-50; tchr. Portledge Sch., Locust Valley, N.Y., 1967-70; librarian Syosset Schs. (N.Y.), 1970-71, Smithtown Schs., (N.Y.), 1971—; pres. World of Realia, Woodbury, N.Y., 1969-85; founder Cygnus Pub., Woodbury, 1985; guest lectr. C.W. Post Coll., L.I. U., 1975, Southampton Coll., L.I. U., 1976. Author: Perthes and Parents, 1963. Fund raiser ARC, Huntington, N.Y., 1960-63; membership com. Community Concert Assn., Huntington, 1960-66; fund raiser Leukemia Soc. Am., Hicksville, N.Y., 1978—. Mem. AAAS, ALA, N.Y. Acad. Scis., Suffolk Sch. Library Media Assn. Republican. Presbyterian. Club: Long Island Alumnae of Pi Beta Phi (pres. 1964-67). Home: 10 Warrenton Ct Huntington NY 11743 Office: Cygnus Pub PO Box 25 Woodbury NY 11797

ROSBERGER, ANNE WALDMAN, psychotherapist; b. N.Y.C., Nov. 23, 1932; d. Joseph and Susan (Wagner) Waldman; B.A., Bklyn. Coll., 1953; M.S., Columbia U., 1955; postgrad Yeshiva U., 1977—; m. Henry Rosberger, Oct. 12, 1958; children—Daniel, Richard. Sr. caseworker, supr. Salvation Army Family Service Bur., N.Y.C., 1955-59; field instr., 1968-69; chief cons., supr. Widows Consultation Center, N.Y.C., 1971-76; pvt. practice psychotherapy, N.Y.C., 1958—; exec. dir. Bereavement and Loss Center of N.Y., N.Y.C., 1976—; cons. St. Vincent's Hosp. Hospice, N.Y.C., 1979—; lectr. in field. Contbr. articles to profl. jours. Mem. Nat. Assn. Social Workers, Acad. Cert. Social Workers, Columbia U. Sch. Social Work Alumni Assn. (dir.), Alpha Kappa Delta. Office: 170 E 83d St New York NY 10028

ROSCOE, BETH HORVATH, computer company executive; b. N.Y.C., Aug. 22, 1952; d. Alvin Lenore (Gold) Elias; m. Harris Horvath, June 3, 1977 (dec. July 1977); m. Douglas A. Roscoe, Mar. 13, 1981. A.A., Miami Dade Jr. Coll., 1971, Assoc. of Sci.-Ct. Reporting, 1973. Registered profl. reporter, cert. shorthand reporter Nat. Shorthand Assn. Exec. v.p. Computer Classifieds, Inc., North Miami Beach, Fla.; pres., chief adminstr. Horvath & Horvath, Inc., Miami, Fla.; vice chmn. secretarial sci. dept. Miami-Dade Jr. Coll., Miami, 1982-83; chmn. spinal cord injury research U. Miami, 1983—, exec. dir. The Miami Project-A Fund to Cure Paralysis. Bd. dirs. U. Miami, 1983—; co-chmn. Elizabeth Arden Golf Classic for Cancer, Miami, 1984—; mem. com. Sunshine chpt. Nat. Asthma Ctr., Miami, 1983—. Mem. Dade County Freelance Reporters Assn. (pres. 1977-82), Builders Assn. South Fla. Democrat. Jewish. Office: Computer Classifieds Inc 17830 State Rd 9 North Miami Beach FL 33162

ROSDOLSKY, CHRISTINE DORA, fashion designer; b. Phila., Dec. 6, 1953; d. John and Mary (Grosseibl) R.; student Drexel U., 1971-73, Parsons Sch. Design, 1973-74. Design asst. Vera Maxwell, N.Y.C., 1974-76; asst. designer Hooper-Bleyle, N.Y.C., 1976-78; designer Talbott-Givenchy, N.Y.C. and Paris, 1978-79; designer Anne Fogarty, 1979-80; designer Dary Sue Fashions/David Strauss Fashions, N.Y.C., 1981-83; head designer Soko Separates, N.Y.C., 1983-84; designer, merchandiser Emotion Sportswear, N.Y.C., 1984—. Mem. Costume Soc. Am., Nat. Assn. Female Execs.

ROSE, ANITA CARROLL, educator; b. New Bedford, Mass., Oct. 14, 1922; d. Louis Arthur and Aline (Chicoine) Carroll; m. Anthony E. Rose, Sept. 24, 1955; children—Anthony David, Stephen Arthur. B.A., Southea. Mass. U., 1971; M.A.T., R.I. Coll., 1975. Exec. Sec. Berkshire-Hathaway, Inc., New Bedford, 1941-55, New Bedford Cancer Soc., 1956-59; tchr. French and English, New Bedford Pub. Schs., 1971—. Pres., New Bedford Jr. Women's Club, 1950-51; v.p. Catholic Women's Club, 1957-59; pres. Fairhaven Mothers' Club, 1967-69; mem. Fairhaven Town Meeting, Mass., 1965—; rec. sec. Fairhaven Improvement Assn., 1982—; sec. Fairhaven Republican Town Com., 1980—; trustee Millicent Library, Fairhaven, 1980—; treas. St. Joseph's Couples' Clubs, 1985-86. Mem. New Bedford Educators' Assn., Mass. Tchrs.' Assn., NEA, AAUW (pres. Coll. Club New Bedford Inc. 1983-85, del. nat. conv. 1981, 83, 85). Avocations: travel; music; theater. Home: 49 Laurel St Fairhaven MA 02719 Office: New Bedford High Sch 230 Hathaway Blvd New Bedford MA 02740

ROSE, DENISE BEYE, ins. co. official; b. Portsmouth, Va., Oct. 22, 1953; d. Fred Lewis and Donna Kathleen (Luing) Beye; B.A., U. Ark., 1974; m. Andy Murray Rose, Nov. 23, 1979. With Nationwide Ins., Denver, 1974-75; with Ins. Co. of N.Am., 1975-77, bond underwriter, Dallas, 1976-77; resident mgr. states of Tenn., Ky., Lawyers Surety Corp., Nashville, 1977-85, Allstate Ins. Co., 1985—. Cert. profl. ins. woman, profl. agt. Mem. Nat. Assn. Ins. Women, Tenn. Ins. Assn., Surety Assn. Nashville, Profl. Ins. Agts. Tenn., Nat. Assn. Female Execs., Ark. Alumni Assn. Republican. Baptist. Club: 1752 (v.p. 1980, pres. 1981, sec.-treas. 1982-84, treas. 1985-86). Home: 4019 Moss Rose Dr Nashville TN 37216 Office: PO Box 164527 Nashville TN 37216

ROSE, EDITH SPRUNG, lawyer; b. N.Y.C., Jan. 7, 1924; d. David L. and Anna (Storch) Sprung; m. David J. Rose, Feb. 15, 1948; children—Elizabeth Rose Stanton, Lawrence, Michael. B.A., Barnard Coll., 1944; LL.B., Columbia U., 1946. Bar: N.Y. 1947; N.J. 1973; U.S. Tax Ct. 1975. Adminstr., Practising Law Inst., N.Y.C., 1947-48; ptnr. Smith Lambert, Hicks & Miller, Princeton, N.J., 1974—. Mem. ABA, N.J. Bar Assn., Princeton Bar Assn., Women's Law Caucus of Nercer County. Club: Princeton. Home: 201 Lambert Dr Princeton NJ 08540 Office: Smith Lambert Hicks & Miller 1 Palmer Sq Box 627 Princeton NJ 08540

ROSE, EMILY HUNTINGTON, county court official; b. Chilmark, Mass., Jan. 28, 1936; d. Elon Gale and Mildred Aurelia (Tilton) Huntington; m. Peter Folsom McFarlin, May 29, 1959 (div. 1966); m. Ronald Joseph Rose, Oct. 2, 1967; children—Stephanie Gale, Jonathan Joseph. B.A. in Music, U. Rochester, N.Y., 1956; postgrad. Boston U., 1957-59. Research asst. Harvard U., Cambridge, Mass., 1957-65; legal sec., title abstractor Hill & Barlow Law Firm, Edgartown, Mass., 1966-70; ind. title abstractor, 1970-73; register of probate Dukes County Probate and Family Ct., Edgartown, 1973—. Social columnist Vineyard Gazette, Edgartown, 1966-73; writer, performer radio program Our Musical Heritage, Sta. WBUR, Boston, 1958-59. Mem. fin. com. Town of West Tisbury, Mass., 1968-70; mem. Tisbury Republican Town Com., 1975-76; mem. Mass. Pub. Info. Research Group, Boston, 1983—. Mem. Mass. Registers Assn., Alpha Epsilon Rho (hon.). Avocations: music, writing, bridge. Home: 45 Hines Point RD 2 Box 20 Vineyard Haven MA 02568 Office: Probate and Family Ct Main St Edgartown MA 02639

ROSE, ETHEL LOUISE, alcohol liaison coordinator; b. Los Angeles; d. Alvero Walter and Beatrice (Conklin) Maxfield; m. Donald A. Haas (div. May 1973); 1 child, Luanne Haas Pitcher. A.S., Westchester Community Coll., White Plains, N.Y., 1958; B.S., N.H. Coll., 1981; M. Human Service Adminstrn., Antioch/New Eng. Grad. Sch., Keene, N.H., 1984. Med. asst., George Greiner, M.D., Kent, Conn., 1974-76; human service counselor Scovill Mfg. Co., Waterbury, Conn., 1976-77; alcohol counselor St. Mary's Hosp., Waterbury, 1977-83, alcohol liaison coordinator, 1983—. Sec. Morris Found., Waterbury, 1982-84, officer, 1984—. Mem. Assn. Labor Mgmt. Adminstrs. and Consultants on Alcoholism, Conn. Fedn. Alcohol Counselors. Avocation: dogs. Home: 901 Watertown Ave Waterbury CT 06708 Office: Saint Mary's Hosp Joseph Ctr 56 Franklin St Waterbury CT 06702

ROSE, GAIL ELAINE, wholesale trade company manager; b. Chgo., Sept. 14, 1949; d. Edward Vincent and Ollove Lorraine (Ruska) Ruzicka. A.A.S., Morton Coll., 1969; B.A., Nat. Coll. Edn., Evanston, Ill., 1984. Dental asst. Merrill Shepro, D.D.S., LaGrange Park, Ill., 1968-71; dental asst. instr. Morton Coll., Cicero, Ill., 1969-71; dental asst. Bernard C. Marker D.D.S., Niles, Ill., 1971-73, adminstrv. asst. KYD Corp. Am., Oak Brook, Ill., 1973-78, adminstrv. mgr., Lombard, Ill., 1978—. Mem., assoc. Ill. Sheriffs' Assn., 1982-86; mem. Republican Nat. Com., Washington, 1980—. Mem. Am. Mgmt. Assn., Nat. Assn. Female Execs., Japan Am. Soc. Chgo. Roman Catholic. Lodge: Women of Moose. Avocations: physical fitness, bicycling, reading. Office: KYB Corp Am 901 Oak Creek Dr Lombard IL 60148

ROSE, GLADYS DORTCH, cytotechnologist; b. Memphis, Sept. 6, 1939; d. William Tell and Lillie (Thompson) Dortch; B.S., LeMoyne Coll., 1959; cert. in cytotech. U. Tenn., 1961; M.S. in Organizational Psychology, So. Ill. U., Edwardsville, 1978; m. Lucius Victor Rose, June 17, 1967; 1 dau., Gladys Ann. Substitute tchr. Memphis Public Schs., 1959, 61; supr. cytology Western Bapt. Hosp., Paducah, Ky., 1961-67; part-time cytotechnologist Cardinal Glennon Hosp., St. Louis, 1979-82; ednl. coordinator profl. edn. in cytology St. Louis U. Sch. Medcine, 1980-81; supr. cytology lab. St. Luke's Hosp., St. Louis, 1967—; assoc. adminstrv. dir. Labs. St. Louis Regional Med. Ctr., 1984—; cons. in field. Vol., YWCA. Recipient various service awards. Mem. Am. Soc. Clin. Pathology, Am. Cytology Soc., St. Louis Cytology Soc., St. Louis Med. Tech. Soc., Am. Public Health Assn., LWV, Nat. Assn. Univ. Women, Sigma Gamma Rho. Mem. A.M.E. Ch. Club: Order Calanthe. Author articles in field. Home: 7006 Stanford St St Louis MO 63130 Office: 5535 Delmar St St Louis MO 63112

ROSE, JACQUELINE DIANE, public relations company executive; b. Ft Dix, N.J., Dec. 11, 1945; d. Anthony Theodore and Carolyn (King) R. B.S., Syracuse U., 1967; M.S., U. Wis.-Madison, 1970. Analyst editor Nat. Better Bus. Bur., N.Y.C., 1967-68; med. writer Roche Labs., Nutley, N.J., 1970-72; asst. dir. consumer affairs Pharm. Mfrs. Assn., Washington, 1972-73; med. writer Winthrop Labs., N.Y.C., 1974-77; account exec. Hill and Knowlton, Inc., N.Y.C., 1977-80, account mgr., Chgo., 1983-85; dir. pub. relations Barnum Communications, Inc., 1981-82; founder Jacquie Rose Assocs., West New York, N.J., 1985; dir. pub. relations Barnum Communications, Inc., N.Y.C., 1981-82. Bd. dirs. Am. Cancer Soc., N.Y.C., 1982—, mem. pub. edn. com., Chgo.; mem. communications com. Muscular Dystrophy Assn. Fellow Am. Med. Writers Assn. (bd. dirs. 1979—, pres. N.Y.C. 1982-83), N.Y. Bus. Group on Health, Women in Communications, Healthcare Businesswomen's Assn., Pharm. Advt. Council, Nat. Speakers Assn. . Office: Jacquie Rose Assocs 6040 Boulevard E Suite 9A West New York NJ 07093

ROSE, JANET SHIRLEY, nurse, educator; b. Holdenville, Okla., May 22, 1938; d. Jack Philson and Audrey (Moses) Rose. B.S., Barry U., 1981. R.N.; cert. emergency and trauma nurse. Staff nurse psychiatry Norton Meml. Infirmary, Louisville, 1959-60; asst. head nurse psychiatry Cleve. Clinic Hosp., 1960-63; head nurse intensive care Winter Haven Hosp. (Fla.), 1963-70; office mgr. for physician, Winter Haven, 1970-72; supr. nursing Lake Wales Hosp. (Fla.), 1972-73; staff nurse emergency dept. Parkway Regional Med. Center, North Miami Beach, Fla., 1973-83, nursing educator, 1983-86, utilization rev. nurse, 1986—. Mem. Nat. Assn. Female Execs., Nat. Assn. Educators, Emergency Dept. Nurses Assn. (sec., dir. edn. 1981-83), Nat. Emergency Dept. Nurses Assn., Am. Nurses Assn., Fla. Nurses Assn., Am. Assn. Critical Care Nurses. Republican. Episcopalian. Office: 979 NW 1st St Miami Beach FL 33128

ROSE, JOANNA SEMEL, cultural board member; b. Orange, N.J., Nov. 22, 1930; d. Philip Ephraim and Lillian (Mindlin) Semel; m. Daniel Rose, Sept. 16, 1956; children—David S., Joseph B., Emily, Gideon G. Cert. Shakespeare Inst., U.K., 1951; B.A. summa cum laude, Bryn Mawr Coll., 1952; postgrad. St. Hilda's Coll., Oxford U., 1953. Chmn. adv. bd. Partisan Rev., N.Y.C.; former pres. bd. dirs. current bd. dirs. Paper Bag Players, N.Y.C.; current bd. dirs. Poets and Writers, Inc., N.Y.C., Project for Pub. Spaces, N.Y.C., Nat. Dance Inst., N.Y.C., British Inst., N.Y.C., Musical Theatre Works, N.Y.C., Guild Hall, East Hampton, N.Y., Ctr. for Visual History, N.Y.C. Assoc. fellow Berkeley Coll., Yale U. Bryn Mawr European fellow Oxford U., 1952-53. Clubs: Cosmopolitan, Bryn Mawr (N.Y.C.). Home: 895 Park Ave New York NY 10021

ROSE, KATHERINE CAST, civic worker; b. Akron, Ohio; d. John Frederick and Amy (Motz) Cast; A.B., Wellesley Coll., 1929; m. Horace Chapman Rose, Oct. 1, 1938; 1 son, Jonathan Chapman. Actress, Cleve. Play House, Chautauqua Repertory Co., 1929-36; trustee Goodrich Social Settlement, 1936-43, Jr. League Cleve., Nat. Cathedral Assn., Washington, 1948-56, 59-65, Children's Theatre of Washington, 1947-49, Cleve. Internat. Youth Leaders, Cleve. Playhouse; chmn. stage com. Washington Stage Door Canteen, 1943-46; chmn. box com. Nat. Symphony Orch., 1947-48; mem. adv. council Nat. Inst. Mental Health, 1956-59; co-chmn. Ohio Citizens for Eisenhower, 1952, 56; vice chmn. women's div. Nat. Citizens for Eisenhower's Congl. Com., 1954; mem. adv. council Nat. Accident Prevention Bur., 1959-63; chmn. Blueprint for Life, Cleve., 1963. Republican. Episcopalian. Clubs: Intown (Cleve.); Sulgrave (Washington). Home: 2701 31st St NW Washington DC 20008

ROSE, LINDA JANSEN, human resources management administrator; b. Atlantic City, July 21, 1950; d. Herman and Dorothy (Kreider) Jansen; m. Allan Rose; 3 children. Student Stockton State Coll., 1979, Northeastern U., Boston, 1983-85. Human resources adminstrv. asst. Spencer Gifts, Inc., Atlantic City, 1977-81; employee legal licensing adminstr. Playboy Elsinore Assocs., Inc., Atlantic City, 1981; personnel specialist Boston Fin. Data Services, N. Quincy, Mass., 1982, mgmt. exec. recruiter, 1982-83, human resources mgmt. adminstr., 1983-85; cons., dir. personnel human resources Rose Prodns., Coral Springs, Fla., 1985—; Vol., Coral Springs Schs., Broward County, 1985-86, Broward County Bd. Elections, 1986. Mem. Internat. Assn. Personnel Women, Nat. Assn. Female Execs., Am. Soc. Tng. and Devel., Am. Mgmt. Assn. Avocations: calligraphy; outdoor activities; video prodn.

ROSE, LISA, interior designer; b. N.Y.C., Jan. 22, 1950; d. Marte and Elisabeth (Carradonna) Previti; B.S., Cornell U., 1971; student N.Y. Sch. Interior Design, 1975. Asst. designer Braswell-Willoughby, N.Y.C., 1976-78; designer Jay Spectre Inc., N.Y.C., 1978-80; pres. Aubergine Interiors Ltd., N.Y.C., 1980—. Interior design projects pub. by various publs., including N.Y. Times, Interior Design, Home Beautiful, Cosmopolitan, Maison Francaise, Home mag., Design mag., Diversion mag., Ladies Home Jour., Designer mag. Mem. Internat. Soc. Interior Designers, Women Bus. Owners, Women in Design. Office: Aubergine Interiors Ltd 201 E 83d St New York NY 10028

ROSE, ROSEMARY CATHERINE, company executive; b. Antigo, Wis., Jan. 2, 1931; d. Ernest J. and Rose F. Slizewski; secretarial cert. Bryant-Stratton Sch., Milw., 1953; real estate course Spencerian Sch., Milw., 1964-65; cert. Am. Inst. Paralegal Studies, 1986; 1 son, Ted R. Adminstrv. asst. H. R. Salen, Waukesha, Wis., 1951-55; owner, operator motel, Brookfield, Wis., 1955-65, restaurant and dry cleaning plant, Lannon, Wis., 1960-65; exec. sec. E.P. Hoyer, New Berlin, Wis., 1967-70; owner, operator Sanitation Service Inc., Menomonee Falls, Wis., 1970-75, North Twin Supper Club, Phelps, Wis., 1975-79; v.p. systems O.L. Schilffarth Co. div. Crown Industries, Milw., 1979-82; owner, operator R-Service Co., Germantown, Wis., 1980—; broker, prin Alrose Realty Co.; gen. mgr. Hotel Rogers, Beaver Dam, Wis., 1982-83; exec. housekeeper Park East Hotel, 1984-85; office mgr. Cedar Disposal, Inc., 1985—. Lic. real estate broker, Wis. Mem. Internat. Platform Assn., Paralegal Assn. Wis., Nat. Assn. Female Execs., Nat. Rifle Assn., Nat. Mus. for Women in Arts, Am. Biog. Inst. Home: N105 W15750 Hamilton Ct Germantown WI 53022 Office: N60 W 16280 Kohler Ln Menonomee Falls WI 53051

ROSE, SADIE MARIE, real estate broker; b. Cairo, Ill., Sept. 6, 1940; d. Cloyd Thomas and Alma Gertrude (Lewis) Ross; m. Robert Lee Rose, June 6, 1959; children—Balaver Donell, Reginald Lloyd, Wayne Thomas, Maurissa DeLynn. Student Am. Real Estate Acad., Detroit, 1974, Bus. Mgmt. and Mktg. Inst., Detroit, 1976, Russels Sch. of Real Estate, Southfield, Mich., 1979. Sales assoc. Sears Real Estate Co., Detroit, 1974-75, Grand Oaks Realty, Detroit, 1976-78, sales mgr. Bowers Realty, Detroit, 1978-80; assoc. broker Welton and Assocs., Detroit, 1980-81; real estate broker S & R Rose Investment Co., Detroit, 1981—. Den mother Boy Scouts Am., 1970; counselor Teenage Youth Orgn., Detroit, 1980; vol. March of Dimes, Detroit, 1979; contbr. Black United Fund, Detroit, 1984—; Sunday sch. tchr. New Hope Missionary Baptist Ch., Southfield, 1984—. Named Top Producer Grand Oaks Realty, 1975, Top Salesman of Month Grand Oaks Realty, 1977. Mem. Nat. Assn. Realtors, NAACP, PTA, Detroit Council Realtors, United Nat. Realtors Assn., Million Dollar Sales Club. Avocations: cooking; reading; bowling; traveling; aerobics. Office: S & R Rose Investment Co 19763 James Couzens St Detroit MI 48235

ROSE, SHIELA ANNE, graphic artist; b. Missoula, Mont., Feb. 27, 1954; d. Robert Sayre and Coralie Mae (Segraves) R. B.A., Graceland Coll., Iowa, 1976. Records specialist Gallatin County, Mont., 1977-79; prodn. supr. High Country News, Bozeman, Mont., 1979-81; prodn. specialist Insty-Prints, Bozeman, 1981-82; press supr. Star Printing, Gillette, Wyo., 1982-83; owner Rose Enterprises, Wright, Wyo., 1983—. Mem. Am. Inst. Design and Drafting (state sec. 1984-85, assoc. editor D&D News 1983-84), NOW, AAUW, Women in Bus., Nat. Assn. Female Execs. Avocation: graphic arts/photography. Office: PO Box 119 Wright WY 82732

ROSE, SHIRLEY, publisher; b. Kansas City, Mo., Mar. 12, 1921; d. Harry G. and Esther (Mendelson) Mallin; B.A., U. Mo., 1941; m. Stanley Jay Rose, Oct. 7, 1942; children—Roberta Susan, Stephen Frederick. Co-founder, co-pub. Sun Newspapers, Overland Park, Kans., 1950—; sec., dir. Sun Publs. Inc., 1973—. Treas. Kans. div. Am. Cancer Soc.; pres. Johnson County Cancer unit; mem. adv. bd. U. Kans. Med. Ctr., CASA. Recipient Bea Johnson Meml. cancer award, 1975, 76, honoree for outstanding achievement in journalism Women in Communication, 1979. Mem. Overland Park C. of C. (dir.), Theta Sigma Phi. Republican. Club: Soroptimist. Home: 8600 Mission Rd Shawnee Mission KS 66207 Office: Sun Publs Bldg 7373 W 107th St Overland Park KS 66212

ROSELIN, NANCY WOODS, film producer, realty executive; Boston, Nov. 24, 1932; s. John James and Belle (Singer) Worswick; student public schs.; m. Alvin M. Roselin, Nov. 3, 1957; children—Phillip, Jonathan, Joel, Stephan. Fashion cons. Catalina, Inc., Boston, 1955-57; prodn. mgr. sunnybrook Sportswear, N.Y.C., 1957-59; asst. editor Printing News, N.Y.C., 1966-76; v.p. Planned Communication Services, N.Y.C., 1976—; pres. Nanal Realty, Spring Valley, N.Y., 1977—; seminar leader in field. Recipient Bronze award Internat. Film Festival, 1981. Office: care Planned Communication Services 12 E 46th St New York NY 10017

ROSELLE, SUE E., health care adminstr.; b. Tarentum, Pa., June 30, 1947; d. William John and Suzanne Esther (Clever) R.; B.S., Pa. State U., 1968; M.S.W., U. Ill., Urbana-Champaign, 1977; M.S., Robert Morris Coll., 1985; m. Kenneth E. Worstell, Sept. 6, 1969; 1 dau., Beth. Adminstrv. asst. Upward Bound, Pa. State U., 1970; social worker Norfolk (Va.) Family Planning Project, 1972-74, Burnham City Hosp., Champaign, Ill., 1976-77; sr. social worker S. Hills Health System Home Health Agy., Homestead, Pa., 1977-78, dir. allied health services, 1978-81; exec. dir. Emergency Med. Service Inst., Pitts., 1981-86; exec. dir. Women's Health Services, Pitts., 1986—. Mem. Nat. Assn. Social Workers (state dir.), Acad. Cert. Social Workers, Phi Kappa Phi. Home: 160 Lloyd Ave Pittsburgh PA 15218 Office: 5937 Broad Street Mall Suite 224 Pittsburgh PA 15206

ROSEN, CATHERINE PICARD, lawyer; b. N.Y.C., Jan. 8, 1940; d. Jean Jacques and Maria (Roth) Picard; m. Sanford Jay Rosen, June 22, 1958; children—Caren Emma, R. Durelle, Ian Douglas, Melissa Simone. Student Vassar Coll., 1957-58, Cornell U., 1958-59; B.A., Conn. Coll., 1961; J.D., Yale U., 1964. Bar: Tex. 1971, Calif. 1974. Assoc. firm Heller, Ehrman, White & McAuliffe, San Francisco, 1975—. Mem. Order of the Coif, Phi Beta Kappa. Home: 3504 Clay St San Francisco CA 94118 Office: Heller Ehrman White & McAuliffe 44 Montgomery St San Francisco CA 94104

ROSEN, JAYNE HALPERN, corporate executive; b. N.Y.C., Nov. 10, 1944; d. Max J. and Rosalind Halpern; m. Paul I. Rosen, June 21, 1970. Student U. Wis., 1962-63; B.S., Boston U., 1966. Assoc. editor Pyramid Pubs., 1966-67; assoc. dir. beauty clinic Good Housekeeping, 1967-68; asst. beauty editor Seventeen Mag., N.Y.C., asst. fashion editor Town & Country, N.Y.C., 1968-72; assoc. fashion editor Bride's Mag., N.Y.C., 1972-76; owner Jayne Rosen Pub. Relations, N.Y.C., 1976-81; dir. pub. relations Charles of the Ritz Group, Ltd., N.Y.C., 1981-83; now with creative promotions and mktg. J.R. Prodns. Mem. Fashion Group, Cosmetic Exec. Women. *

ROSEN, KAREN, interior designer; b. N.Y.C., Jan. 14, 1946; d. Leon D. and Beatrice (Willett) Miller; 1 child, Meredith Lauren. Student Boston U., 1964-66; B.S. in Elem. Edn., NYU, 1968; cert. N.Y. Sch. Interior Design, 1971.

Pres., KMR Design Group, Inc., full service design firm, N.Y.C., 1973—; color cons. to various mfrs. and showrooms in design field; interior design work ranges from residential to pub. and comml.; designer custom furnishings; guest lectr. various coll. and real estate courses; numerous radio and TV appearances; work featured in several major design mags. and newspapers. Recipient S.M. Hexter award for best residential interior, 1981. Mem. Am. Soc. Interior Designers (assoc.), Internat. Soc. Interior Designers. Office: KMR Design Group Inc 27 E 63d St Suite 1B New York NY 10021

ROSEN, PHYLLIS, art dealer, appraiser; b. Boston, May 31, 1937; s. Samuel and Lillian (Smith) Bornstein; student U. Heidelberg, Germany, 1956-58; m. Theodore Rosen. Dir., Obelisk Gallery, Inc., Boston, 1961—, Parker 470 Gallery, Boston, 1971-74, Harcus Krakow Rosen Sonnabend Gallery, Boston, 1972-74, Sculpture to Wear, Inc., N.Y.C., 1973-76; appraiser, cons. 20th Century art, Appraisal Services, 1976—. Office: 90 Commonwealth Ave Boston MA 02116

ROSEN, SHERRILL LYNN, lawyer; b. Denver, Jan. 26, 1955; d. Maynard Charles and Sandra Marilyn (Collinger) R. B.S. in Journalism, U. Colo., 1975; J.D., U. Mo., 1978. Bar: Mo. 1979, U.S. Dist. Ct. (we. dist.) Mo. 1979. Pub. relations asst. Bicentennial Horizons of Am. Music, St. Louis, 1975-76; legal researcher Ctr. Research and Social Behavior, U. Mo.-Columbia, 1976-77; staff Ind. Legal Services Assn., Columbia, 1976-77, dir., 1977-78; atty. Legal Aid Western Mo., Kansas City, 1978-82; sole practice, Kansas City, 1982—; lectr. Rockhurst Coll., 1982—; cons. Adult Abuse Remedies Coalition, Columbia, 1978-80. Bd. dirs. Housing Assistance, Inc., Kansas City, 1984—, sec., 1985; vice chmn. Jackson County Bd. Domestic Violence Shelters, 1984-85, sec., 1986. Recipient Vol. award Central Mo. Counties Human Devel. Corp., 1978; Criminal Justice award Rose Brooks Ctr., Inc., 1981; Margit Lasker award, 1982. Mem. ABA (exec. mem. family law sect., domestic violence com. 1984-85, co-chmn. 1985-86, 86-87), Mo. Bar Assn. (family law com.), Kansas City Bar Assn. (adv. com. family law com. 1983—), Sigma Delta Chi, Kappa Tau Alpha. Office: 818 Grand Suite 210 Kansas City MO 64106

ROSENBAUER, DONNA LOUISE, writer; b. Boston, Oct. 26, 1936; d. Oscar E. and Mary C. R.; B.A., Emmanuel Coll., 1958; M.Ed., State Tchrs. Coll., Boston, 1969; J.D., New Eng. Sch. Law, 1979. Children's librarian Bookmobile Service, Boston Public Library, 1958-60; tchr. 4th grade, public schs., Boston, 1960-63; instr. Hickox Secretarial Sch., Boston, 1965-68, Boston U. Sch. Journalism, 1971-72; editor Allyn & Bacon, Inc., Boston, 1963-66; sr. editor Ginn Pub./Xerox, Lexington, Mass., 1966-75; free-lance writer ednl. and legal materials, Boston, 1975—; guest lectr. journalism Northeastern U.; vol. high sch. tchr. for writing, basic English. Cert. tchr., Mass. Mem. Internat. Reading Assn., Nat. Ret. Tchrs. Assn., Nat. Writers Club. Author books, including: Introduction to Fire Protection Law, 1978; Exploring Language with the Dictionary, 4 book workbook series, 1979; Fire Science Series, 5 books on arson, 1982. Home: 16 Hunting Hill Lane Ashland MA 01721

ROSENBAUM, ARLENE, direct marketing services executive; b. Bklyn., Feb. 17, 1944; d. Milton and Clara (Spector) Pollack; m. Steven Alan Rosenbaum, Apr. 5, 1964; children—Laura Ellen, Michelle Lynn. B.S., CCNY, 1964. Software programmer Gen. Foods, White Plains, N.Y., 1966-71; pres., cons. Starline Systems, Inc., New City, N.Y., 1972—; v.p. Magi, Elmsford, N.Y., 1983-85, pres., 1985—. Mem. Direct Mktg. Assn. Office: Magi 3 Westchester Plaza Elmsford NY 10523

ROSENBAUM, BELLE SARA, personal property appraiser, interior designer, educator; b. N.Y.C., Apr. 1, 1922; d. Harry and Hinda (Sits) Heimowitz; m. Jacob H. Rosenbaum, Mar. 12, 1939; children—Linda Zelinger, Simmi Brodie, Martin, Arlene Levene. Cert. N.Y. Sch. Interior Design, 1945. Sr. mem. Am. Soc. Appraisers, Washington, 1979—; tchr./Judaica, Yeshiva U., 1984—; pres. Jarvis Designs, Inc., Union City, N.J., 1955-75, Design Assocs., BLS., Monsey, N.Y., 1970-78; v.p. Lord & Lady Inc., Union City, 1955-70, Cardio-Bionic Scanning, Inc., Spring Valley, N.Y., 1975-78; v.p., treas. Rapitech Systems, Inc., 1985. Author of short stories, 1947-48; contbr. articles on interior design to profl. jours. Bd. dirs. Migdal Ohr Schs., 1971—. Named Woman of Valor State of Israel, 1960. mem. Internat. Soc. Artists (founding mem.), Yeshiva of North Jersey Women (hon. pres. 1955). Clubs: Amit Women (pres. 1955-57) (N.J.), AMI Women (treas. 1948-78), Community Synogogue-Monsey (v.p. 1982—). Avocations: collector of art, antiques, Judaica, artist, gardening, communal and charity work. Home: Monsey NY

ROSENBAUM, JOAN HANNAH, museum director; b. Hartford, Conn., Nov. 24, 1942; d. Charles Leon and Lillian (Sharasheff) Grossman; m. Peter S. Rosenbaum, July 1962 (div. 1970). A.A., Hartford Coll. for Women, 1962; B.A., Boston U., 1964; student, Hunter Coll. Grad. Sch., 1970-73; cert., Columbia U. Bus. Sch. Inst. Non Profit Mgmt., 1978. Curatorial asst. Mus. Modern Art, N.Y.C., 1966-72; dir. mus. program N.Y. Council on Arts, N.Y.C., 1972-79; cons. Michal Washburn & Assocs., N.Y.C., 1979-80; dir. Jewish Mus., N.Y.C., 1980—. Bd. dirs. Artists Space, 1980—; mem. policy panel Nat. Endowment for Arts, 1982-83. European travel grantee Internat. Council Mus., 1972. Mem. Am. Assn. Mus. (cons. 1979—), N.Y. State Assn. Museums (v.p., council 1983), Art Table N.Y. Office: Jewish Mus 1109 Fifth Ave New York NY 10028

ROSENBAUM, LOIS OMENN, lawyer; b. Newark, Apr. 10, 1950; d. Edward and Ruth (Peretz) Omenn; m. Richard B. Rosenbaum, Apr. 4, 1971; children—Steven, Laura. A.B., Wellesley Coll., 1971; J.D., Stanford U., 1974. Bar: Calif. 1974, Oreg. 1977, D.C. 1974. Assoc., Fried, Frank, Harris, Shriver & Kampelman, Washington, 1974-75, Orrick, Herrington, Rowley & Sutcliffe, San Francisco, 1975-77; assoc. Stoel, Rives, Boley, Fraser & Wyse, Portland, Oreg., 1977-81, ptnr., 1981—. Mem. nat. legal com. Am. Jewish Com., 1982—, also bd. dirs. Wellesley Coll. scholar, 1971. Mem. ABA, Multnomah County Bar Assn., Am. Arbitration Assn. Clubs: Multnomah Athletic, Jewish Community Ctr. Office: Stoel Rives Boley Fraser & Wyse 900 S W 5th Ave Portland OR 97204

ROSENBERG, ELIZABETH HARTWELL, direct mail pub. and mktg. co. exec.; b. Rome, N.Y., July 19, 1949; d. Walter H. and Carolyn (Searle) Hartwell; B.A. in Sociology, Elmira Coll., SUNY, Buffalo, 1971; m. Jack A. Rosenberg, May 19, 1979; children—Kathryn Elizabeth, Ryan Andrew. Account rep. customer service Xerox, Buffalo, 1972-74, sales rep. mktg., 1974-76, sr. sales exec., product specialist mktg., Los Angeles, 1976-78; sales specialist mktg. Compugraphic, Los Angeles, 1979-81; account exec. mktg. Anaconda Ericsson, Santa Ana, Calif., 1981-82; mktg. exec., advt. coordinator, owner, ptnr. Kiwee Kidswear, 1982-83; pres. Horizons Internat., Long Beach, Calif., 1984—. Home and Office: 123 Syracuse Walk Long Beach CA 90803

ROSENBERG, JO, psychiatric social worker, psychoanalyst; b. Albany, N.Y., June 12, 1948; d. Irving H. and Madeline P. Rosenberg; B.A., Goucher Coll., Towson, Md., 1970; M.S., Columbia U., 1973; psychoanalysis cert. (fellow 1975-79), Postgrad. Center Mental Health, N.Y.C., 1979; postgrad. N.Y.U., 1981—. With maternal and child health dept. Bronx (N.Y.) Mcpl. Hosp. Center, 1973-76, coordinator emergency services children dept. child psychiatry, 1976-79; field work instr. N.Y.U. Sch. Social Work, 1977-79; sr. psychiat. social worker div. child and adolescent psychiatry N.Y. Hosp.-Cornell Med. Center, Westchester div., White Plains, N.Y., 1979-82, social work coordinator, 1982—; faculty Cornell U. Med. Sch., 1982—pvt. practice psychoanalysis and psychotherapy, N.Y.C. Fellow N.Y. State Soc. Clin. Social Work Psychotherapists; mem. Nat. Assn. Social Workers, Acad. Cert. Social Workers, Am. Orthopsychiat. Assn., Am. Group Psychotherapy Assn. Contbr. articles on group therapy to profl. jours. Home: 22 E 10th St New York NY 10003 Office: NY Hosp White Plains NY 10605

ROSENBERG, RITA FRANCES, accountant; b. Perth Amboy, N.J., Mar. 19, 1928; d. Meyer William Jaffe and Sylvia (Tenenbaum) Lewiss; m. Leonard Rosenberg, Dec. 21, 1947; children—Michael Leonard, Stephen Douglas, Mark Fletcher. B.S. in Acctg., Rutgers U., 1962. C.P.A., N.J. Ptnr. Eisner and Tenenbaum, C.P.A.s, Woodbridge, N.J., 1983—. Contbr. articles to profl. jours. Mem. Am. Inst. C.P.A.s, N.J. Soc. C.P.A.s (mem. acctg. rev. services com., tech. services subcom., quality control com., report rev. com., intercom. liaison), Am. Acctg. Assn., Am. Soc. Women Accts., N.Y. State Soc. C.P.A.s, Nat. Assn. Female Execs., N.J. Assn. Women Bus. Owners, N.J. Women's Network. Home: 216 Lincoln Ave Highland Park NJ 08904 Office: Eisner and Tenenbaum 900 Route 9 Suite 301 Woodbridge NJ 07095

ROSENBERG, SHELI, lawyer; b. N.Y.C., Feb. 2, 1942; d. Stephen Bernard and Charlotte (Laufer) Zysman; B.A., Tufts U., 1963; LL.B., Northwestern U., 1966; m. Burton X. Rosenberg, Aug. 30, 1964; children—Leonard, Marcy Joy. Admitted to Ill. bar, 1966, U.S. Tax Ct., 1973; asso. Cotton, Watt, Jones, King & Bowlus, Chgo., 1966-70; mem. firm Schiff, Hardin & Waite, Chgo., 1970-73, partner, 1973-81; v.p., gen. counsel Equity Fin. & Mgmt. Co., Chgo., 1981—. Mem. Fed. Judiciary Selection Com., 1970—; mem. hearing bd. Atty. Registration Commn., 1978—. Mem. Am. Bar Assn., Ill. Bar Assn., Chgo. Council Lawyers, Legal Club.

ROSENBERG, SUSAN, lawyer; b. Bklyn., July 24, 1945; d. Harold and Kitty (Paris) Schildkraut; m. Neil David Rosenberg, June 10, 1967; children—Lonnie Stuart, Seth Ian. A.B., Washington U., 1967; J.D. cum laude, Marquette U., 1983. Bar: Wis. 1983. Tchr. history Balt. City Pub. Schs., 1967-70; assoc. Samster, Aiken, & Mawicke, S.C., Milw., 1983—. Bd. dirs. Women to Women, Inc., Milw., 1984—. Thomas More scholar, 1981-83; Adolph I. Mandelker scholar, 1982-83. Mem. Wis. Acad. Trial Lawyers, Am. Trial Lawyers Assn., Wis. Bar Assn., ABA, Assn. Women Lawyers, Kappa Delta Pi, Alpha Sigma Nu. Jewish. Mem. Marquette U. Law Rev., 1981-83. Office: Samster Aiken & Mawicke 1509 N Prospect Ave Milwaukee WI 53202

ROSENBERGER, JUDITH BRAILEY, psychotherapist, psychoanalyst; b. Columbus, Ohio, Mar. 24, 1943; d. Lester George and Helen Cornelia (Castle) Brailey; B.S., Purdue U., 1965; M.A., U. Mich., 1967, Ph.D., 1973; M.S.W., Hunter Coll., 1976; cert. psychoanalysis, Center for Mental Health, 1982; m. Ernst H. Rosenberger, June 10, 1978; children—John Brailey, anne Elizabeth. Intern in counseling, student services counseling center, U. Mich., Ann Arbor, 1967-70; counselor Wayne State U., Detroit, 1970-71; lectr. Herbert H. Lehman Coll., City U. N.Y., 1971—; pvt. practice psychotherapy and psychoanalysis, N.Y.C., 1978—; staff Postgrad. Center for Mental Health, N.Y.C., 1978-82, supr., 1982-84, faculty, 1985—; adj. asst. prof. Hunter Coll., 1985-86, asst. prof. 1986—; summer faculty Smith Coll. Sch. Social Work, 1985—; Profl. project dir. Profl. Staff Congress, Bd. Higher Edn. research project, 1977-79. Cert. psychologist, Mass.; cert. social worker, N.Y. Mem. Am. Psychol. Assn. (div. psychoanalysis), AAUP, Acad. Cert. Social Workers, N.Y. Soc. Clin. Social Work Psychotherapists, Nat. Assn. Social Workers, Postgrad. Psychoanalytic Soc., Nat. Assn. for Advancement of Psychoanalysis. Author: The Identity Experience of College Women: Some Contributing Factors, 1973; Women Who Aspire to be Police Officers, 1979. Home: 315 E 68th St New York NY 10021 Office: 150 E 84th st New York NY 10028

ROSENBLATT, LOUISE MICHELLE, emeritus educator; b. Atlantic City, Aug. 23, 1904; d. Samuel and Jennie (Berman) R.; B.A. with honors, Barnard Coll., 1925; certificat d'etdes francaises, U. Grenoble, France, 1926; D.Comparative Literature, U. Paris, 1931; postgrad. in Anthropology, Columbia U., 1932-34; m. Sidney Ratner, June 1932; 1 son, Jonathan. Instr., English, Barnard Coll., 1927-38; asst. prof. English Bklyn. Coll., 1938-48; asso. chief Western European sect., chief central reports sect. Bur. Overseas Intelligence, Office War Info., 1943-45; prof. English edn. N.Y. U., 1948-72, prof. emeritus, 1972—; vis. prof. Rutgers U., 1972-75; mem. faculty insts. in English, Mich. State U., U. Pa., U. Ala., U. Alta. (Can.), Auburn U., U. Mass., 1978—; cons. in field. Franco-Am. Exchange fellow, 1925-26; Guggenheim fellow, 1942-43; recipient N.Y. U. Great Tchr. award, 1972; Nat. Council Tchr. English Disting. Service award, 1973; Russell award for disting. research, 1980; Leland Jacobs award for Lit., 1981. Mem. MLA, Am. Soc. Aesthetics, AAUP, Nat. Council Tchrs. English, Nat. Conf. Research in English, Am. Comparative Literature, Internat. Comparative Lit. Assn., Phi Beta Kappa. Author: L'Idee de l'Art pour l'Art, 1931, reprinted, 1976; Literature as Exploration, 1938, 3d rev. edit., 1976, 4th edit., 1983; (with William S. Gray) Reading in an Age of Mass Communication, 1949; Research Development in the Teaching of English, 1963; The Reader. The Text. The Poem: The Transactional Theory of the Literary Work, 1978; (with Robert Parker) Developing Literacy, 1983; (with Charles Cooper) Researching Response to Literature, 1984; (with Patricia Demers) The Creating Word, 1985; also articles in reading theory, theory & composition, criticism, teaching of lit. Home: 11 Cleveland Ln Princeton NJ 08540

ROSENBLITH, JUDY FRANCIS, psychology educator; b. Salt Lake City, Mar. 20, 1921; d. John Edward and Mary Louise (Slack) Francis; m. Walter A. Rosenblith, Sept. 27, 1941; children—Sandra Y., Ronald F. Student Occidental Coll., 1938-40; A.B., UCLA, 1942; M.A., Radcliffe Coll., 1950, Ph.D., 1958. Asst. prof. psychology Simmons Coll., 1951-52; New Eng. supr. Nat. Opinion Research Center, 1953-57; teaching fellow social relations Harvard U., 1948-50, Grad. Sch. Edn., 1953-56, instr., 1956-57, lectr., 1962-63; asst. prof. psychology Brown U., 1957-61, asst. mem. to mem. Inst. Life Scis., 1961-75, sr. research investigator div. biol. and med. scis., 1975-77; assoc. psychology dept. psychiatry Harvard Med. Sch., 1961-64, clin. assoc., 1965-67; assoc. prof. Wheaton Coll., Norton, Mass., 1965-68, prof. psychology, 1968-84, prof. emerita, 1984—; mem. maternal and child health research adv. com. Nat. Inst. Child Health and Human Devel., 1974-78. Author: (with Judith Sims Knight) In the Beginning: Development in the First Two Years, 1985. Adv. editor Contemporary Psychology, 1979-80; sr. editor: The Causes of Behavior: Readings in Child Development and Educational Psychology, 3 edits., 1962, 66, 72. Named Meneely Prof., Wheaton Coll., 1972-74; N.Y. Acad. Scis. fellow, 1976; grantee NIMH, 1958-60, Neurol. Diseases and Blindness, 1961-64, Child Health and Human Devel., 1966-70, Grant Found., 1971-77. Fellow Am. Psychol. Assn. (mem. bd. social and ethical responsibility for psychology 1977-81, mem. pub. info. com. 1981-84) mem. Soc. for Research in Child Devel. (sec. 1965-69, chmn. conv. arrangements 1979-81), Internat. Assn. Cross-Cultural Psychology, Internat. Assn. Applied Psychology, Internat. Soc. Study of Behavioral Devel., Psychonomic Soc., New Eng. Psychol. Assn., Eastern Psychol. Assn., Sigma Xi. Home: 164 Mason Terr Brookline MA 02146 Office: Wheaton Coll Norton MA 02766

ROSENBLOOM, NORMA FRISCH, lawyer; b. N.Y.C., Dec. 2, 1925; d. Jacob Frisch and Anna (Fox) Frisch Schwartz; B.A., New Sch. Social Research, 1951; J.D., Rutgers U., Newark, 1979; m. Philip Rosenbloom, Oct. 31, 1946; children—David, James, Eric. Mem. faculty, head dept. music Ranney Sch., Tinton Falls, N.J., 1962-74; admitted to N.J. bar, 1979, N.Y. State bar, 1980; chief law clk. Monmouth County (N.J.) Prosecutor's Office, 1979-80; assoc. firm Karasic & Karasic, P.C., Oakhurst, N.J., 1980-82, Abrams & Gatta, Ocean Twp., N.J., 1982—. Sec., mem. exec. bd. Temple Beth Miriam, Elberon, N.J., 1969-74; mcpl. leader Monmouth Beach (N.J.) Democratic Com., 1973—; del. Dem. Nat. Conv., 1976; freeholder rep. to Monmouth County Community Action Program, poverty program, 1975-76; bd. dirs. Central Jersey Regional Health Planning Bd., 1973-75, Planned Parenthood Monmouth County, 1981—. Recipient award for community involvement Asbury Park-Neptune Youth Council, 1970. Mem. ABA, Monmouth County Bar Assn., N.J. State Bar Assn., N.Y. State Bar Assn., Women Lawyers Monmouth County. Home: Channel Club Tower Monmouth Beach NJ 07750 Office: 1127 Hwy 35 Ocean NJ 07712

ROSENDAHL, PATRICIA MCGARVEY, journal editor; b. Galveston, Tex., Sept. 1, 1952; d. James Ligon and Elvera (McCoy) McGarvey; m. Torben Erik Rosendahl, July 3, 1976; children—James, Erik, Alicia. A.A., Palomar Coll., 1974; B.A., U. Tex., 1975; postgrad. U. Houston Law Sch., 1984—. Cert. social worker. Med. social worker Tex. Dept. Health, Galveston, 1977-84; head articles editor Houston Jour. Internat. Law, 1986—. Mem. ABA, State Bar Tex., Order of Barons, Admiralty Law Soc. (sec. 1985—), Health Law Orgn., Phi Delta Phi, Phi Kappa Phi. Episcopalian. Avocations: travel; writing; reading. Home: 1807 Austin Dr LaMarque TX 77568

ROSENFELD, IRENE CAROLE, photographic equipment manufacturing company executive; b. Bklyn., May 26, 1939; s. Murray and Alice (Stern) R.; m. Harold Irwin Rosenfeld, Apr. 3, 1960; children—Philip, Laura. A.A.S., Fashion Inst. Tech., 1960; B.F.A., SUNY, 1975. Fashion designer, Henry St. Artwear, Merrick, N.Y., 1975-80; sec. Bestwell Optical, Merrick, 1975-78, v.p., 1978-80, pres., 1980—. Democrat. Jewish. Avocations: painting, sculpting, pottery, photography, crafts. Home: 46 Henry St Merrick NY 11566 Office: PO Box 396 Merrick NY 11566

ROSENFELD, JOANN, physician; b. Savannah, Ga., Jan. 25, 1954; d. Paul G. and Judith (Bram) R. B.A., Johns Hopkins U., 1975, M.D., 1978. Diplomate Am. Bd. Family Practice. Intern Case Western Res. U. Hosp., Cleve., 1978-79, resident in family practice, 1979-81; physician Cecil-Kent Health Ctr., Cecilton, Md., 1981-85; asst. dir. family practice residency program St. Francis Hosp., Wilmington, Del., 1985—. Fellow Am. Acad. Family Physicians. Home: 1059 Frenchtown Rd Elkton MD 21921 Office: St Francis Hosp Family Practice 7th St and Clayton St Wilmington DE 19805

ROSENFELD, REBA, retired educator; b. Balt.; d. Max and R. Clara (Shorr) Rosenfeld; student Goucher Coll., Johns Hopkins U., 1954-56, 61; B.F.A., Md. Inst. Coll. Art, 1956; M.Ed. in Guidance and Personnel, U. Md., 1962; postgrad. Johns Hopkins, summer 1965, 66-67. Social worker Dept. Pub. Welfare, Balt., 1944-45, ARC, 1945-46; tchr. pub. schs., Balt., 1946-54, 56-59, counselor, 1959-79. Former med. field agt. SSS. Am. Assn. Ret. Persons, Nat. Ret. Tchrs. Assn. Home: 3422 Barry Paul Rd Randallstown MD 21133

ROSENHEIM, MARGARET KEENEY, social welfare educator, lawyer; b. Grand Rapids, Mich., Sept. 5, 1926; d. Morton and Nancy (Billings) Keeney; student Wellesley Coll., 1943-45; J.D., U. Chgo., 1949; m. Edward W. Rosenheim, June 20, 1947; children—Daniel, James, Andrew. Admitted to Ill. bar, 1949; mem. faculty Sch. Social Service Adminstrn., U. Chgo., 1950—, asso. prof., 1961-66, prof., 1966—, Helen Ross prof. social welfare policy, 1975—, dean, 1978-83; lectr. law U. Chgo. Law Sch.; vis. prof. U. Wash., 1965, Duke U., 1984; acad. visitor London Sch. Econs., 1973; cons. Pres.'s Commn. Law Enforcement and Adminstrn. of Justice, 1966-67, Nat. Adv. Commn. Criminal Justice Standards and Goals, 1972; mem. Juvenile Justice Standards Commn., 1973-76. Bd. trustees Children's Home and Aid Soc. Ill., 1981—, Nat. Inst. Dispute Resolution, 1981—, Carnegie Corp., N.Y.C., 1979—. Ford Found. grantee, 1967-68, 84. Mem. Chgo. Bar Assn. Editor, contbr.: Justice for the Child, 1962; Pursuing Justice for the Child, 1976; contbr. articles and book revs. to profl. jours. Address: 969 E 60th St Chicago IL 60637

ROSENKRANTZ, BARBARA GUTMANN, science historian; b. N.Y.C., Jan. 11, 1923; s. James and Jeanette (Mack) G.; A.B., Radcliffe Coll., 1944; Ph.D., Clark U., 1970; m. Paul Solomon Rosenkrantz, Apr. 19, 1950; children—Louise, Judith, Deborah. Microbiologist, Springfield (Mass.) Hosp., 1955-57, Wesson Meml. Hosp., Springfield, 1958-63; lectr. Harvard U., 1972-73, asso. prof. history of sci., 1973-75, prof., 1975—; mem. Inst. of Medicine, Nat. Acad. Sci., 1981—; former master Currier House, Harvard U.; trustee Clark U. Radcliffe Inst. fellow, 1967-69; NIH/Nat. Library Medicine grantee, 1971-72; Rockefeller humanities fellow, 1979-80. Mem. History of Sci. Soc., Am. Hist. Assn., Soc. Am. Historians, Am. Public Health Assn., Sigma Xi. Jewish. Author: Public Health and the State: Changing Views in Massachusetts 1842-1936, 1972; editor: (with William A. Koelsch) American Habitat: A Historical Perspective, 1973; numerous titles in Public Health in America series. Office: Dept Public Health Harvard U 677 Huntington Ave Boston MA 02115*

ROSENSTIEL, JOYCE BERGMAN, school principal; b. Chgo., Nov. 7, 1926; d. Harry and Estelle (Adelman) Bergman; m. Edward Bernard Rosenstiel, Sept. 7, 1947; children—Karina, Beth, Tom. Student Carleton Coll., 1944-45, U. Chgo., 1946-47; B.A., UCLA, 1949; M.A., Coll. Notre Dame-Belmont, Calif., 1980. Tchr., Ravenswood High Sch., East Palo Alto, Calif., 1966-69, Woodside High Sch., Calif., 1969-79, instructional v.p., 1979-82; instructional v.p. Menlo Atherton High Sch., Atherton, Calif., 1982-84, prin., 1984—. Mem. Sequoa Dist. Mgmt. Assn., Assn. Calif. Sch. Adminstrs., Phi Delta Kappa. Avocations: needlework; tennis; travelling; swimming; theatre-going. Office: Menlo Atherton High Sch 555 Middlefield Atherton CA 94025

ROSENSTOCK, JUDITH DEAN, special educator adminstrator, consultant; b. Syracuse, N.Y., Sept. 17, 1947; d. Jacob A. and Pearl (Rugg) Naistadt; m. Harvey Allan Rosenstock, May 9, 1982; children—Benjamin Leipzig, Deborah Elise Leipzig, Amara, Aaron and Marc Rosenstock. Student Boston U., 1965-67; B.S., NYU, 1969; M.S., Va. Commonwealth U., 1975; Ph.D., Syracuse U., 1980. Counselor, Overbrook State Hosp., Cedar Grove, N.J., 1968-69; asst. dir. St. Joseph's Adolescent Unit Program, Syracuse, 1970-71; tchr. learning disabled B.O.C.E.S., Syracuse, 1969-73; Child Find coordinator Syracuse Sch. Dist., 1975-76; N.Y. state adminstrv. intern N.Y. State Edn. Agy., Syracuse, 1975-76; asst. prof. U. Houston Clear Lake, 1979-84; dir. Teaching and Learning Ctr. Tex., Houston, 1983—; trainer, cons. N.Y. State Dept. Edn., Albany, 1976-77; cons. Bur. Indian Affairs, Washington, 1978; accreditation mem. Nat. Council for Accreditation of Tchr. Educators, Washington, 1982—; field reader Office Spl. Edn. and Rehab., Washington, 1983. Author: (with Harvey Rosenstock) Helping Parents Cope with Quarreling Siblings, 1983, Play: Important at Any Age, 1984, Your Stay in the Hospital, 1984; Childhood Friendships, 1985. Mem. community relations com. Jewish Fedn.; bd. dirs. Beth Yeshurun Schs., Houston, 1983, I. Weiner Sch., Houston, 1983, Beth Jacob, Galveston, Tex., 1978, D. Miller Found. Dr. Ivan Vasey fellow, 1967; Center on Human Policy fellow, Syracuse, 1971; Va. Commonwealth U. fellow, Richmond, 1974; Bur. Edn. of Handicapped fellow, Washington, 1975. Mem. Council for Exceptional Children, Council for Assoc. of Sch. Exec. Adminstrs., Profs. Sch. Adminstrn., Phi Delta Kappa. Jewish. Office: Teaching and Learning Ctr Tex PO Box 35553 Houston TX 77035

ROSENTHAL, CAROL A., financial planner; b. Ephrata, Pa., Mar. 22, 1942; d. James Whiteside and Marian Isabel (Shiffer) Magruder; m. Albert L. Rosenthal, July 31, 1969; children—Robert, Jill, Bruce. B.A., Rider Coll., 1973, A.A., 1962. Exec. sec. RCA Labs., Princeton N.J., 1962-69; fin. planner Albert L. Rosenthal, M.D., P.A., Lawrenceville, N.J., 1969—. Pres., Friends of N.J. State Mus., Trenton, 1983—, v.p. fine arts, 1980-83; bd. dirs. McCarter Assocs., Princeton, 1985—, Shakespeare 70, 1985—. Mem. Mus. Modern Art, Friends of Phila. Mus., Newark Mus., Trenton City Mus. Office: Albert L Rosenthal MD PA 74 Franklin Corner Rd Lawrenceville NJ 08648

ROSENTHAL, MARILYN SILVER, publishing exec.; b. N.Y.C., Aug. 15, 1940; d. Jack and Isabel (Rosenfeld) Silver; A.B., Boston U., 1961; M.A., Am. U., 1962; Ph.D., Georgetown U., 1973; m. Jacob Rosenthal, Apr. 6, 1963; children—John Nicholas, Anne Wallace. Asst. prof. linguistics York Coll. and Grad. Center, City U. N.Y., 1973-76; mgr. English lang. teaching dept. Oxford U. Press, N.Y.C., 1976—. Mem. TESOL, Nat. Assn. Female Execs. Author: The Magic Boxes: Children and Black English, 1977. Office: Oxford U Press 200 Madison Ave New York NY 10016

ROSENTHAL, MARTHA NEWMAN, special projects and events consultant; b. N.Y.C., Oct. 8, 1956; d. Norman and Janice (Newman) R.; m. Adorno Sclano, Mar. 2, 1978 (div.). B.A., Sarah Lawrence Coll., 1978. Jr. copywriter McCann-Erickson, Inc., N.Y.C., 1978-80; office mgr. Ed Libonati Prodns. Inc., N.Y.C., 1980-82; dir. spl. events and pub. relations Sch. Am. Ballet, N.Y.C., 1982-85; spl. cons. Am. Ballet Theatre, N.Y.C., 1986—. Writer, editor, designer newsletters, 1982; writer, designer mailing pieces, 1982; editor, designer advt. jour., 1985. Club: Doubles. Avocations: travel; languages; cultural institutions. Home: 47 E 87th St New York NY 10128 Office: American Ballet Theatre 890 Broadway New York NY 10003

ROSENTHAL, MARYLYN JOAN, chemical company official; b. N.Y.C., Aug. 31, 1937; d. Dan and Lena (Green) Vogel; B.S. in Edn. magna cum laude, Bklyn. Coll., 1957, M.A. in Edn., 1960; m. Howard Rosenthal, Mar. 29, 1959; children—David, Caryn. Tchr. elem. sch., N.Y.C., Edison, N.J., 1957-72; sales asst. Ball Bros. Research Corp., N.J., 1974-75; chem. trader, sales mgr. Parlin Chem., Parlin, N.J., 1975-82, gen. mgr., 1982-85; materials mgr. CPS Chem. Co., 1985—. Den mother Cub Scouts, 1969-72; chmn. fund raising Temple Emanu-El Sisterhood, 1973-74, 1st v.p., 1974-75, trustee, 1975-78. Certified elem. tchr., K-8, N.Y. State, N.Y. Mem. Northeastern Chem. Assn. (pres. 1985, past v.p., treas., rec. sec., exec. bd., membership chmn.), Phi Beta Kappa, Kappa Delta Pi. Office: Old Waterworks Rd Old Bridge NJ 08857

ROSENTHAL, NAOMI BRAUN, sociology educator; b. Chgo., Aug. 27, 1940; d. Morris and Rose (Erenberg) Braun; m. Joel Thomas Rosenthal, Apr. 29, 1962; children—Jessica, Joshua, Matthew. B.A., U. Chgo., 1963; M.S. in Econ. History, London Sch. Econs., 1966; Ph.D. in Sociology, SUNY-Stony Brook, 1976. Vis. asst. prof. SUNY, Stony Brook, 1972-73; instr. Am. studies SUNY, Old Westbury, 1975-77, asst. prof., 1977-80, assoc. prof., 1980—. Contbr. articles to profl. jours. Mem. exec. bd. Brookhaven Women's Ctr., Port Jefferson, N.Y., 1983-85. CETA grantee, 1978-79; NSF grantee, 1981, 83; NEH summer fellow, 1976; NSF summer grad. fellow, 1978. Mem. Am. Sociol. Assn., Berkshire Conf. Home: 116 Jones Ave Port Jefferson NY 11777 Office: SUNY Old Westbury NY 11568

ROSENTHAL, ROBIN FELICE, newspaper executive; b. Bklyn., Oct. 2, 1951; d. Herman Louis and Carolyn (Moskowitz) R.; B.A., Barnard Coll.,

1973; M.B.A., Harvard U., 1981. Prodn. supr. Ballantine Books, N.Y.C., 1973-76; mng. editor Berkley Publ. Corp., N.Y.C., 1976-77, publ. adminstr., 1977-78; dir. subs. rights Berkley/Jove Pub. Group, N.Y.C., 1978-79; asst. to v.p. advt. and circulation N.Y. Times Regional Newspaper Group, Atlanta, 1981-83; gen. mgr. Gainesville Sun (Fla.), 1983—. Bd. dirs. WUFT-FM, Gainesville, 1984. Mem. Gainesville Area C. of C. (dir. 1984—), Am. Bus. Womens Assn. Democrat. Jewish. Home: Box 58 Turkey Creek Alachua FL 32615 Office: Gainesville Sun 2700 SW 13th St Gainesville FL 32610

ROSENTHAL, RONNIE ANN, surgeon, educator; b. N.Y.C., Aug. 20, 1947; d. David and Doris (Larack) R.; m. Dana Kimball Andersen, Oct. 22, 1983; B.S. in Elec. Engring., CCNY, 1969; M.S., Columbia U., 1970; M.D., Downstate Med. Ctr., SUNY-Bklyn., 1977. Design engr. Cons. & Designers, N.Y.C., 1970-71; prodn. mgr. Julie Research Labs., N.Y.C., 1971-72; research asst. NYU Med. Ctr., 1972-73; asst. instr. surgery Downstate Med. Ctr., SUNY, Bklyn., 1977-81, asst. prof., 1982—, attending surgeon, 1982—; attending surgeon Kings County Med. Ctr., N.Y., 1982—. Contbr. chpt. to book. Diplomate Am. Bd. Surgery; NDEA fellow, 1969-70. Fellow ACS; mem. Assn. Acad. Surgery, Eta Kappa Nu, Tau Beta Pi. Office: Downstate Med Ctr Box 40 450 Clarson Ave Brooklyn NY 11203

ROSENTHAL, YONINA KOLLER, education and training consultant; b. Los Angeles, May 24, 1934; d. Irving M. and Doris S. Koller; m. David Walter Rosenthal, July 6, 1952; children—Gabriella, Albert, Aliza, Oren. B.A., Boston U., 1955; M.Ed., Rutgers U., 1963; Ph.D., U. N.C., 1974. Instr., U. N.C., 1965-71, Louisberg (N.C.) Coll., 1974, N.C. State U., 1975; ptnr. E. F. R. Assocs., 1975-81; program coordinator dept. human resources Duke U. Med. Ctr., 1979-81; tng. dir. Boston Counseling Assocs., 1981; mem. staff dept. staff devel. and edn. Melrose-Wakefield Hosp., Melrose, Mass., 1982—; tchr. Boston Ctr. Adult Edn., 1981-83; instr. New Eng. Hosp. Assembly, 1982, adj. prof. Mass. Bay Community Coll., 1981—. Mem. Gov.'s Adv. Bd. N.C.-Israel Vis. Scholars program, 1979-81; mem. N.C. Council on Social Legislation, 1979-81; mem. N.C. Council Woman's Orgn., 1978-81; mem. Glenwood Task Force, City of Raleigh, 1976-81. Mem. Am. Soc. Tng. and Devel., AAUW, Am. Soc. Health Care Edn. and Tng., U.N.C. N.C. Alumni Assn., Am. Mgmt. Assn., Boston U. Alumni Assn., LWV. Clubs: Hadassah. Home: 233 Clark St Brookline MA 02146 Office: Melrose-Wakefield Hosp 585 Lebanon St Melrose MA 02176

ROSENWALD, DOROTHY SHUBART, civic worker; b. Denver, May 15, 1916; d. Benedict and Daisy (Newhouse) Shubart; B.A., Mills Coll., 1936; m. Robert E. Rosenwald, Aug. 9, 1937; children—Richard S., Robert L. (dec.). Pres., LWV, Kansas City, 1943-44, state v.p. Mo., 1944-46; state conf. chmn. Mo. Assn. Social Welfare, 1957; pres. Nat. Council Jewish Women, Kansas City, 1953-55, dist. pres., 1963-65, nat. dir., 1963-75, v.p. nat. bd., 1971-75, hon. life dir.; mem. Jackson County Child Welfare Adv. Com., 1966-72, 74-76; bd. dirs. Internat. Council Jewish Women; 1975-81; mem. Mo. State Day Care Adv. Com., 1971-75, Gov.'s Com. for Children and Youth, 1978-81; chmn. Mo. Adv. Com., White House Conf. Families, 1980; mem. Jackson County Commn. on Children's Services 1964-67. Recipient Outstanding Service award Mo. Assn. Social Welfare, 1981. Mem. AAUW, Phi Beta Kappa. Democrat. Reform Jewish. Home: 111 W 68th St Kansas City MO 64113

ROSETT, JACQUELINE BERLIN, financial executive; b. N.Y.C., Aug. 28, 1945; s. Marshall Hamilton and Lenore (Berlin) Rosett. B.S. in Physics, Columbia U., 1967. With George B. Buck Inc., N.Y.C., 1967-68; pres. Jacqueline Rosett Assocs., N.Y.C., 1968—; cons. in internat. investments. Photographer: The African Ark, 1974. Vol. counselor N.Y.C. Opera Guild, 1982—; sponsor San Diego Zool. Soc., 1975—. Mem. Am. Soc. Profl. and Exec. Women, Nat. Assn. Female Execs. Democrat. Jewish. Club: Camerata (events chmn.). Office: Jacqueline Rosett Estate and Trust 165 E 72d St New York NY 10021

ROSEVEAR, PAMELA ADELE, director airline passenger services, restaurant consultant; b. Corvallis, Oreg., Nov. 26, 1953; d. Reginald, III, and Tomoko (Nonoue) R.; m. Robert Keith Suder, May 27, 1984. Student in Advanced Japanese, U. Hawaii, 1973, 77-78, B.S., U. Oreg., 1977, postgrad. in Advanced Japanese, El Camino Community Coll., 1985, 86. Flight attendant Braniff Internat. Airline, Dallas, 1978-81; mgr. Wendy's Inc., Houston, 1982; mgr., trainer Hungry Tiger, Houston, 1982-84; flight attendant Hawaii Express, Los Angeles, 1983; trainer, interpreter Chyuitsuya Co., Tokyo, 1983, cons., 1983—; dir. passenger services and inflight, Total Air, Los Angeles, 1984—. Mem. Mortar Board, Kappa Alpha Theta. Republican. Mem. United Ch. of Christ. Avocations: marathon running; cooking; education. Home: 218 28th St Hermosa Beach CA 90254 Office: Total Air 5534 Westlawn Los Angeles CA 90066

ROSHER, JERELENE, cytotechnologist; b. Safety Harbor, Fla., Jan. 29, 1945; d. John Louis and Alberta (Crockam) R.; A.A., Indian River Community Coll., 1966; grad. Bethune-Cookman Coll., 1984. Cytotechnologist, Halifax Hosp. Med. Center, Daytona Beach, Fla., 1967-78; supr. cytology dept. Asso. Med. Labs., Ormond Beach, Fla., 1978-83; practical nurse North Miami Gen. Hosp., 1985-86. Cert. cytotechnologist. Mem. Fla. State Soc. Cytology, Am. Soc. Clin. Pathologists. Baptist.

ROSHNOW, KATHERYN ANN CAMENISCH, computer company executive; b. Madison, Ind., May 15, 1950; d. Herman John and Louise Valeska (Aust) Camenisch; student Purdue U., 1968-69; B.S. in Bus. Adminstrn., Ind. U., 1972; M.B.A., U. Mich., 1977; m. George Nickolas Roshnow, Oct. 23, 1973. Sales mgr. Sheraton Motor Inn, Woodhaven, Mich., 1973-75; market research analyst Kerr Mfg. Co., Romulus, Mich., 1976; mktg. rep. IBM, Detroit, 1977-80, account rep., 1980-81, mktg. mgr., Seattle, 1981-82, sr. product planner, Boulder, Colo., 1982-85, group product adminstr. ISG Bus. Systems, Norwalk, Conn., 1986—. Adviser Jr. Achievement Southeastern Mich., 1980; mem. founders soc. Detroit Inst. Arts. Mem. Assn. M.B.A. Execs., Ind. U. (life), U. Mich. alumni assns. Presbyterian. Home: 27 Lindstrom 6C Stamford CT 06904 Office: IBM Corp Dept BBF 301 Merritt 7 Corp Park/5N12 Norwalk CT 06856

ROSHONG, DEE ANN DANIELS, psychologist, educator; b. Kansas City, Mo., Nov. 22, 1936; d. Vernon Edmund and Doradell (Kellogg) Daniels; B.Mus.Ed., U. Kans., 1958; M.A. in Counseling and Guidance, Stanford U., 1960; postgrad. Fresno State U., U. Calif.; Ed.D., U. San Francisco, 1980; m. Richard Lee Roshong, Aug. 27, 1960 (div.). Counselor, psychometrist Fresno City Coll., 1961-65; counselor, instr. psychology Chabot Coll., Hayward, Calif., 1965-75; coordinator counseling services Chabot Coll., Valley Campus, Livermore, Calif., 1975-81, asst. dir. student personnel services, 1981—; writer, coordinator symposia including: I, a Woman, 1974, Feeling Free to be You and Me, 1975, All for the Family, 1976, I Celebrate Myself, 1977, Person to Person in Love and Work, 1978; Healthy Person in Body, Mind and Spirit, 1979; Feelin' Good, 1980, Change 1981; Sources of Strength, 1982; Love and Friendship, 1983, Self Esteem, 1984; Trust Your Neighbor and Tie Up Your Camelat Night, 1985; Prime-Time: Making The Most of the Present Time in Your Life, 1986; mem. cast TV prodns. Eve and Co., Best of Our Times, Cowboy; chmn. Calif. Community Coll. Chancellor's Task Force on Counseling; chmn. commn. on student services Calif. Assn. Community Colls.; presenter state-wide confs. Calif. Assn. Community Colls-Calif. Community Colls. Counseling Assn., 1980—. Mem. Assn. Humanistic Psychologists, Western Psychol. Assn., Nat. Assn. Women Deans and Counselors, Calif. Assn. Counseling and Devel., Alpha Phi. Author: Counseling Needs of Community College Students, 1980. Home: 808 Comet Dr Foster City CA 94404 Office: 3033 Collier Canyon Rd Livermore CA 94550

ROSIER, JACQUELINE GILLIARD, utilities manager; b. Bklyn., Mar. 21, 1948; d. Lee and Beatrice (Reid) Gilliard; m. Alcindor R. Rosier, 1968; children—Alcindor, II, Jaquis Nicole, Christopher Joseph. B.S., Fla. A&M U., 1968; student So. Meth. U., 1979-82. Cert. industry cons. Trainee, Southwestern Bell Telephone Co., Dallas, 1972-73, mktg. mgr., 1973-75, sr. account exec., 1975-77, staff specialist, 1977-79, account exec., industry cons., 1981-83; account exec., industry cons. AT&T, Dallas, 1979-83; staff mgr. Nynex Corp., White Plains, N.Y., 1983—. Named Outstanding Young Woman of Am., 1975, mem. Pres. Club Southwestern Bell Telephone Co., 1980; recipient Award of Appreciation, Women in Mgmt., 1981. Mem. Alpha Kappa Alpha pres. 1985-86). Roman Catholic. Club: Jack & Jill, Inc. (Dallas). Home: 111 Shelter Rock Rd Stamford CT 06903 Office: 65 W Red Oak Ln White Plains NY 10604

ROSLANSKY, PRISCILLA FENN, microbiologist; b. Rochester, N.Y., Nov. 24, 1925; d. Wallace Osgood and Clara Bryce (Comstock) Fenn; B.A., Smith Coll., 1947; M.A., Radcliffe Coll.-Harvard U., 1948; Ph.D., U. Rochester, 1952; m. John Dale Roslansky, June 20, 1953; children—Louise, John Wallace, William Fenn., Clara Ruth. Clin. lab. technician, Calif., N.J., part-time, 1952-59; research asso. U. Calif., Berkeley, 1953-55; NIH fellow, Copenhagen, 1959-60; research asso. U. Ill., Urbana, 1960-63; research asso. Marine Biol. Lab., Woods Hole, Mass., 1964-68, 75-79, research on ultrastructure of nerves; research asso. U. Saarlandes, Homburg-Saar, W.Ger., 1968-69; clin. lab. technician Falmouth Med. Assos., 1969-75, fellow Bunting Inst. of Radcliffe Coll., 1981-83; dir. research Assocs. of Cape Cod, 1983—. Vice pres. Woods Hole Community Assn., 1976; mem. Woods Hole Civic Assn., 1967-68. Mem. Am. Soc. Microbiology, LWV (observer corps 1979—), Sigma Xi. Club: Woods Hole Women's. Contbr. articles to profl. jours. Home: 57 Buzzards Bay Ave Woods Hole MA 02543

ROSNESS, BETTY JUNE, advertising and public relations agency executive; b. Oklahoma City, Mar. 4, 1924; d. Thomas Harrison and Clara Marguerite (Stubblefield) Pyeatt; student Oklahoma City U., 1940-41; m. Joseph H. Rosness, Aug. 5, 1960; children—Melody L. Johnson (dec.), Michael C., Randall L., Melinda Rosness Mason, John C. Continuity dir. Sta. KFBI, Wichita, Kans., 1957-58; sales exec. Sta. KFH, Wichita, 1958-60; U.S. senatorial press sec., 1961-66; dir. advt. and public relations Alaska State Bank, Anchorage, 1966-68; prin. Rosness Advt. Assocs., Goleta, Calif., 1968—; dir. Fin. Corp. Santa Barbara (Calif.), Santa Barbara Savs. & Loan. Pres., Goleta Valley Girls Club, 1972-75, Ret. Officers Womens Assn., 1970; v.p. Santa Barbara Symphony Assn., 1977-80; bd. dirs. Channel City Womens Forum, 1976—, Goleta Valley Community Hosp.; Chmn. U. Calif. at Santa Barbara Affiliates; bd. dirs. Cancer Found., Santa Barbara, 1978-82, chmn. community edn. com., founding mem. Goleta Beautiful, Club West Track and Field; mem. allocations com., bd. dirs. United Way, Santa Barbara; founding mem., bd. dirs. Children's World of Hospice; mem. evangelism com. Good Shepherd Lutheran Ch. Recipient Disting. Sales award Kans. Sales Exec. Assn., 1959, 60; named Woman of Year, Santa Barbara County, 1978, Affiliate of Yr., U. Calif.-Santa Barbara, 1983-84. Mem. Greater Santa Barbara Advt. Club. (past v.p.), Goleta Valley C. of C. (past dir.), Santa Barbara C. of C. (bd. dirs. 1982—), Goleta Valley C. of C. Address: 669 Larchmont Pl Goleta CA 93117

ROSS, ADALENE BOWMAN, travel columnist, fashion show producer, public relations consultant; b. Oak Park, Ill., Dec. 14, 1919; d. Harry Bertram and Ida (Rundle) Bowman; m. George Ross, Aug. 2, 1942 (dec.); children—Nancy Lee, Lee Thornton, Lynn Louise. Student, San Mateo Jr. Coll., 1937-39. Internat. fashion show commentator, producer for maj. stores, designers, bus. and industry, movies and TV, 1948—; pub. relations cons., event creator various internat. firms, 1950—; travel columnist Addie's World, for San Mateo Times, 1969—; dir. pub. relations Bullock's No. Calif., 1970-80; v.p. pub. relations Joseph Magnin Stores Calif., Nevada, Colo., 1980-82; lectr. in field. Founding mem. San Mateo County Soc. Crippled Children and Adults, Inc. Recipient City of San Francisco Pub. Service awards, 1959-70; San Francisco Conv. Bur. Silver Cable Car award, 1969. Mem. AFTRA (founding mem. San Francisco br.), Jr. League. Reublican.

ROSS, BARBARA HUSER, real estate company executive; b. Lamar, Colo., Nov. 13, 1943; d. Archie and Mona Belle (Robinson) Huser; m. John T. Ross, Nov. 29, 1971. Student, Drury Coll., Mo., 1982-83. Lic. real estate broker Mo., Ark. Personnel sec. Ford Aeroneutronics, Newport Beach, Calif., 1963-64; mgr. gen. Family Farm, Mt. Vernon, Mo., 1964-65; field sec. Strout Realty Inc., Springfield, Mo., 1965-67, exec. sec., 1967-79, adminstrv. asst., 1979-82, asst. v.p., 1982-85, v.p., 1985—; seminar speaker/lectr., 1982—. Author-developer: Nat. Listing System, 1983; (manual) Branch Office Computer System Manual, 1984; contbr. articles to profl. jours. Mem. Nat. Assn. Realtors, Nat. Assn. Female Execs., Mo. Assn. Realtors (bd. dirs. 1986), Springfield Bd. Realtors (chair com. 1985-86), C. of C. (bd. dirs. Springfield, Mo. 1970-74). Lodge: DAR. Avocations: reading; travel; antique collector. Home: 4151 Tanglewood Rd Rogersville MO 65742 Office: Strout Realty Inc 1736 E Sunshine Springfield MO 65804

ROSS, BETTY GRACE, medical distribution company executive; b. N.Y.C., July 14, 1931; d. Philip and Nancy Anna (Meredith) Boccella; R.N., Presbyn. Hosp., 1952; student Ariz. State U., 1960-62; m. Robert W. Ross, Mar. 1, 1968 (div. July 1976). Sr. operating room nurse Roosevelt Hosp., N.Y.C., 1953-58; pvt. surg. nurse Neurosurgery Group, Orthopedic Group, Phoenix, 1960-64; sales assoc. Zimmer, Inc., Phoenix, 1964-71, distbr., owner Zimmer Ross Assocs., Phoenix, 1971—, Zimmer-Ross-Ltd., 1978—. Past pres. bd. dirs. Gloria Dei Luth. Ch.; charter mem., past pres. Center for Living of Paradise Valley. Mem. Assn. Operating Room Nurses of Phoenix (charter), Bloomfield Coll. Alumni Assn. Republican. Home: 5713 N Cattletrack St Scottsdale AZ 85253 Office: 1232 E Missouri St Phoenix AZ 85014

ROSS, BETTY JEAN, jewelry manufacturing company executive; b. Kansas City, Mo., Aug. 6, 1928; d. George W. and Ida Mae (Wolf) Terry; student Phillips U., 1946-47, LaSalle Extension U., 1954-55, U. N.Mex., 1970-71; m. Bob L. Ross, Feb. 19, 1950; children—Lee, Elizabeth, Eric, Eden. Mem. prodn. and control staff Black, Sivalls & Bryson, Kansas City, Mo., 1946-50; purchasing and credit mgr. Maisel Co., Albuquerque, 1956-72; credit mgr. Sunbell Corp., Albuquerque, 1972—. Block chmn. Am. Heart Assn., Am. Cancer Soc.; funding chmn. Bric Ross Meml. Library. Mem. Am. Mgmt. Assn., Nat. Assn. Credit Mgmt., Nat. Assn. Female Execs., Comml. Law League, Am. Collectors Assn., Dun & Bradstreet Credit Roundtable. Republican. Methodist. Home: 1501 Betts St NE Albuquerque NM 87112 Office: Sunbell Corp 7500 Bluewater Rd NW Albuquerque NM 87104

ROSS, CAROLYN MARIE, medical services supervisor; b. Bay St. Louis, Miss., Feb. 13, 1954; d. Elvin Andrew and Helena Carolyn (Lind) Asher. Assoc., Miss. Gulf Coast Jr. Coll., 1974. Cert. in occupational health nursing. Staff nurse Ocean Springs Hosp. (Miss.), 1974-75, South Miss. Home Health and Rehab. Agy., Pascagoula, 1975-76; med. services supr. Degussa Corp., Theodore, Ala., 1977—. Mem. Am. Assn. Occupational Health Nurses, South Ala. Assn. Occupational Health Nurses. Roman Catholic. Home: 4017 #36 Cottage Hill Rd Mobile AL 36609 Office: Degussa Corp PO Box 606 Theodore AL 36590

ROSS, CAROLYN THAYER, lawyer; b. Cin., June 5, 1948; d. Edward Miller and Carolyn (Warner) Thayer. B.A., U. Pa., 1970; J.D., Boston Coll., 1975. Bar: Mass. 1975, Ga. 1980, U.S. Dist. Ct. Mass. 1976, U.S. Supreme Ct. 1983. Tchr., Springside Sch., Phila., 1970-72; assoc. Abraham & Pappas, Boston, 1975-76, Bowker, Elmes, Perkins, Mecsas & Gerrard, Boston, 1976-81; sole practice, Boston, 1981-82; v.p., gen. counsel Yankee Oil & Gas Inc., Boston, 1982-84; sr. v.p., gen. counsel Yankee Cos., Inc., 1984—. Home: 60 Temple St Boston MA 02114 Office: Yankee Cos Inc 49 Margin St Cohasset MA 02025

ROSS, CATHERINE JANE, history educator, social policy analyst; b. N.Y.C., Dec. 27, 1949; d. Alexander I. and Wilma (Saltzman) R.; m. Jonathan Rieder, Mar. 14, 1981. B.A., Yale Coll., 1971; Ph.D., Yale U., 1977, J.D., 1986. Post doctoral fellow/research assoc. Yale Bush Ctr. in Child Devel. and Social Policy, New Haven, 1977-79; asst. prof. Yale Child Study Ctr., New Haven, 1979—; cons. Adminstrn. for Children Youth and Families, HEW, 1979, Conn. Dept. Children and Youth Services, 1978—, ednl. films and radio programs. Joint editor: Child Abuse: An Agenda for Action, 1980. Del., Conn. Task Force on Juvenile Justice, 1979-80; com. mem. Conn. Task Force on Foster Care, 1979-81. Mellon fellow Aspen Inst. for Humanistic Studies, 1983-84; grantee Edna McConnell Clark Found., 1981-82, Herman and Amelia Ehrmann Found., 1979-82, Ford Found., 1980-82, John and Catherine MacArthur Found., 1981. Jewish. Office: Yale Child Study Ctr PO Box 3333 New Haven CT 06510

ROSS, CHARLOTTE PACK, suicidologist; b. Oklahoma City, Oct. 21, 1932; d. Joseph and Rose P. (Traibich) Pack; m. Roland S. Ross, May 6, 1951 (div. July 1964); children—Beverly Jo, Sandra Gail. Ed. U. Okla., 1949-52, New Sch. Social Research, 1952-53. Cert. tchr. Exec. dir. Suicide Prevention and Crisis Ctr. San Mateo County, Burlingame, Calif., 1966-85; pres., exec. dir. Youth Suicide Nat. Ctr., Washington, 1985—; co-chmn. Nat. Com. for Youth Suicide Prevention, 1984, Calif. Senate Adv. Com. Youth Suicide Prevention, 1982—; speaker Menninger Found., 1983, 84; instr. San Francisco State U., 1981-83; conf. coordinator U. Calif.-San Francisco, 1971—; cons. univs. and health services throughout world. Contbg. author: Group Counseling for Suicidal Adolescents, 1984; Teaching Children the Facts of Life and Death, 1985. Mem. editorial bd. Suicide and Life Threatening Behavior, 1976—. Mem. regional selection panel Pres.'s Commn. on White House Fellows, 1975-78; mem. CIRCLON Service Club, 1979—, Com. on Child Abuse, 1981—; founding mem. Women for Responsible Govt., co-chmn., 1974-79. Recipient Outstanding Exec. award San Mateo County Coordinating Com., 1971; Koshland award San Francisco Found., 1984; named to San Mateo County Women's Hall of Fame, 1985. Mem. Internat. Assn. Suicide Prevention (sec. gen. 1977—, v.p. 1985—), Am. Assn. Suicidology (sec. 1972-74), bd. govs. 1976-78, accreditation com. 1975—, chair region IX, 1975-82), Assn. United Way Agy. Execs. (pres. 1974), Assn. County Contract Agys. (pres. 1982). Democrat. Jewish. Club: Peninsula Press Club. Office: 1811 Trousdale Dr Burlingame CA 94010 also 1825 I St NW Suite 400 Washington DC 20006

ROSS, CORINNE MADDEN, writer; b. Newton, Mass., May 17, 1931; d. A.L. and Corinne (Bodwell) Madden; m. Charles Kenneth Ross, 1957 (div. 1960); m. 2d, Ralph Crosby Woodward, Dec. 31, 1982. Grad. Mt. Ida Jr. Coll., Newton, Mass., 1951. Editor, Charles D. Spencer & Assoc., Chgo., 1953-63; advt. and promotion mgr. Childrens Press, Chgo., 1963-66, New Horizons Pubs., Chgo., 1966-68; freelance writer, Chgo. and Boston, 1968—; books include: Christmas in Britain, 1978; Christmas in Mexico, 1976; Christmas in Italy, 1979; Christmas in Scandinavia, 1977; The New England Bed and Breakfast Book, 1986; Christmas in France, 1980; To Market, To Market: Six Walking Tours of the Old and New Boston, 1980; New England: Off the Beaten Path, 1981; The Southern Bed and Breakfast Book, 1986; The Mid-Atlantic Bed and Breakfast Book, 1986; contbr. numerous articles to periodicals; author children's stories. Episcopalian. Home: 45 Wayside Inn Rd Framingham MA 01701

ROSS, DEBRA, interior design executive; b. Bessemer, Ala., Jan. 22, 1952; d. Printis and Fredericka (Swan) B.; div. 1984; children—Ksenia D., Darron L., Erik, Viveca M. Computer cert. U. So. Calif., 1970; B.A., Los Angeles Bus. Coll., 1976. Teller Sumitomo Bank, Los Angeles, 1970-71; fgn. and domestic advisor Bank of Calif., Los Angeles, 1971-73; loan asst., utility exec. Tokai Bank, Inglewood, Calif., 1976-78; asst. mgr. Brunschwig & Fils, Los Angeles, 1979—. Mem. PTA, Nat. Assn. Female Execs., Single Working Mother Group (pres., founder Hawthorne, Calif. 1986). Democrat. Avocations: reading, cooking, Bible study. Office: Brunschwig & Fils 8687 Melrose Ave Los Angeles CA 90069

ROSS, DENISE GUINN, pathologist; b. San Antonio, Feb. 21, 1946; d. John Alonzo and Bessie Alice (Mitchell) Guinn; m. William Bruce Ross, Aug. 2, 1969; children—Rebecca, Christina, Michael Guinn. B.A., B.S., Tex. Woman's U., 1967; M.D., U. Tex.-Dallas, 1971. Diplomate Am. Bd. Pathology in Anatomic and Clin. Pathology, Blood Banking. Rotating intern, resident in pathology Naval Regional Med. Ctr., Portsmouth, Va., 1971-76, staff pathologist, 1976-79; instr. pathology Eastern Va. Med. Sch., Norfolk, 1972-78, asst. prof. pathology, 1978-85, assoc. clin. prof. pathology, 1985—; staff pathologist DePaul Hosp., Norfolk, 1978-81; asst. med. dir. ARC, Norfolk, 1981, med. dir., 1982—. Contbr. sci. articles to med. jours. Served from ensign to comdr., M.C., USNR, 1970-79. Recipient scholastic achievement award Kiwanis Internat., Denton, Tex., 1967, Physician's Recognition award AMA, 1977, 80, 83. Fellow Am. Soc. Clin. Pathologists (pathology continuing med. edn. award 1977, 80, 83); mem. Am. Assn. Blood Banks, Am. Soc. Cytology, Am. Soc. Apheresis, Mid-Atlantic Assn. Blood Banks (bd. dirs. 1985—), Va. Soc. Pathology, Va. Soc. Cytology, Va. Soc. Hematology, Tidewater Pathology Soc. Presbyterian. Office: Am Red Cross Blood Services PO Box 1836 Norfolk VA 23501

ROSS, DIANA, singer, actress, entertainer; b. Detroit; d. Fred Earl and Ernestine Ross; grad. high sch. Lead singer Diana Ross and the Supremes; now soloist; star motion picture Lady Sings the Blues, 1972, Mahogany, 1975, The Wiz, 1978; appeared Broadway An Evening with Diana Ross, 1976; TV spl. Diana, 1981. Recipient citation Vice Pres. Humphrey for efforts on behalf Pres. Johnson's Youth Opportunity Program; citation Mrs. Martin Luther King and Rev. Abernathy for contbn. to So. Christian Leadership Conf. cause; awards Billboard, Cash Box and Record World as worlds outstanding singer; named Female Entertainer Yr., NAACP, 1970; Grammy award as Top Female Singer Yr.; London Musical Express Poll winner as Top Female Singer in World; nominee Acad. award for best actress, 1972; Golden Globe award Hollywood Fgn. Press Assn., 1972; Image award for Best Actress, NAACP, 1972; Entertainer of Yr., Cue mag., 1972; Cesar award French Acad. Cinema Arts and Technique, 1976; Female Entertainer of Century, Billboard mag., 1976; Antoinette Perry award, 1977; star placed in Hollywood's Walk of Fame, 1982. Office: care RCA Records 1133 Ave of the Americas New York NY 10036

ROSS, DONA RUTH, speech pathologist; b. Hot Springs, S.D., June 17, 1930; d. Gordon Richard and Margaret Elizabeth (Emery) Bartell; student Aims Jr. Coll., 1968-69; B.A. (state scholar), U. No. Colo., 1972, M.A., 1973; postgrad. U. S.D., 1975—, Black Hills State Coll., 1974-75, No. State Coll., 1981, U. Eastern N.Mex., 1973; children—Judy, Barbara, Dale, Peggy, Randall. Speech pathologist Shannon County Schs., Pine Ridge Indian Reservation, Batesland, S.D., 1973-76, Yankton (S.D.) Schs., 1976-77; prin. New Underwood (S.D.) Schs., 1977-80; prin. Pierre (S.D.) Indian Learning Center, 1980-81, speech, lang. and hearing specialist Coop. Service Unit, 1983-85; speech pathologist Office Indian Edn. Programs, Bur. Indian Affairs Schs., Pine Ridge (S.D.) Indian Reservation, 1981-83; cons. Oglala Sioux Tribe Early Childhood Programs, 1973-80. Sec. Shannon County Democratic Party, 1975-76. Mem. Am. Speech, Lang. and Hearing Assn., Council for Exceptional Children. Democrat. Congregationalist. Home: Box 625 Metlakatla AK 99926 Office: Annette Island Schools Metlakatla AK 99926

ROSS, DORIS G., civic worker; b. Thompsonville, Conn.; d. Philip A. and Eva (Saffir) Sisitzky; student Barnard Coll., Max Reinhardt Drama Workshop, N.Y. U. Radio Workshop, Lee Strasberg Theatre Inst., Royal Acad. Dramatic Arts; m. Lewis H. Ross, Jan. 4, 1942; children—Phyllis, Allyne. Dir. New Eng. Zionist Youth Com., 1943-45; dir. theatre arts Manchester Inst. Arts and Scis., 1947-48; pres. Manchester Girls Clubs, 1950-51, dir., 1949-53, 54-58, 59-69, chmn. nat. adv. bd. Girls Clubs Am., 1955-57, v.p., 1956-57, pres., 1957-59, chmn. 15th Ann. Conf., 1960, first acting chmn. past pres. com., 1974, 1st pres. past pres. club, 1975-77, chmn. 15th ann. conf., 1960, chmn. silver jubilee com., 1969-70, chmn. directions and social concerns com., 1978-79, founder Children's Creative Theatre, 1978, chmn., 1979-81; hon. mem., 1981—; exec. com. Girls Clubs N.Y., 1970-73, bd. dirs., 1970-73, sustaining dir., 1973—, co-chmn. long range planning com., 1970-71; 1st pres. Theatre Art Players, Temple Emanuel, N.Y.C., 1970-71; trustee Actors Studio, 1978-82, originated Actors Studio Achievement awards celebration, 1981; dir. Manchester Settlement Assn., 1951-54, Manchester Vis. Nurses Assn., 1955-61; del. Nat. Soc. Welfare Assembly, 1957-59, White House Conf. on Children and Youth, 1960, voting del. nat. council state coms., 1960, mem. N.H. state exec. com., 1960, N.H. state sub-com. on Leisure Times Activities chmn., 1960; charter colleague Nat. Assembly Nat. Voluntary Health and Welfare Orgns., Inc., 1976—, mem. Nat. Juvenile Justice Program Collaboration, Mem. Pres.'s Citizens Adv. Com. on Fitness of Am. Youth, 1958-60; mem. exec. com. Gov.'s Com. on Children and Youth, 1961-63; Gov.'s rep. to Pres.'s Conf. on Youth Fitness, 1962; pres. Manchester Garden Club, 1963-64; dir. Opera League New Hampshire, Inc., 1964-69; trustee Actors Studio, 1978-82. Mem. Hadassah (pres. Manchester chpt. 1943-44, dir. Manchester chpt. 1942-49, New Eng. regional v.p. 1944-46). Address: 985 Fifth Ave New York NY 10021

ROSS, DOROTHY MARIE, assn. exec.; b. Whiteford, Md.; grad. high sch. Floor supr. heel dept. Bata Shoe Factory, Belcamp, Md., 1939-40; with Civil Service Commn., 1940; office clk. George F. Muth Co., Washington, 1941-47; with Am. Automobile Assn., Washington, 1947-62, supr. hotel-motel reservations, 1947-62; pres. Automotive Hall of Fame, Inc. (formerly Automotive Orgn. Team, Inc. and Automotive Old Timers, Inc.), Midland, Mich., 1963-80, pres., 1980—, editor AOT News, 1966—. Hon. bd. dirs. Boys Home of South, Greenville, S.C. Recipient Disting. Women's award Northwood Inst., 1971, Automotive Replacement Edn. award, 1978; Disting. Service citation Automotive Orgn. Team, 1972, Nazarene (Sunday sch. supt. 1956-60, sec. ch. bd. 1955-60, treas. 1954-56). Mem. Soc. Automotive Historians. Home: 5300 Perrine Rd Midland MI 48640 Office: PO Box 1742 Midland MI 48640

ROSS, ELEANORA (BETSY), consultant, speaker, writer, counselor; b. Washington, Iowa, Jan. 3, 1932; d. Roy Lloyd and Erna Machan (Spera) Miller; m. Robert E. Anderson (div. Jan. 1971); children—R. Daryl, Rebecca, David; m. William Wayne Ross, June 26, 1972 (dec. Aug. 1975). B.Gen. Studies with honors, U. Iowa, 1979; M.A., U. Iowa, 1983; M.Div., M.A. in

Organizational Design and Adminstrn., Synthesis Sch. for Social Research, 1986. Advt. design and graphic arts, 1960-72; founder, dir. Ray of Hope, Inc., Iowa City, Iowa, 1976—, workshop presentor, cons., counselor, group facilitator, pub. relations, 1976—. Author: After Suicide: A Ray of Hope, 1986; writer, producer videotapes: After Suicide: A Unique Grief Process, 1980; Survivorship After Suicide, 1984. Grantee Ella Lyman Cabot Trust, 1983, Kaltenborn Found., 1984, others; recipient Edn. awards P.E.O., 1974, 82, Bus. and Profl. Women, 1984. Mem. Forum for Death Edn. and Counseling, Am. Assn. Suicidology, Am. Assn. Retired Persons, Inst. Human Potential (bd. dirs. 1983—), Omicron Delta Kappa. Avocations: dancing; drama; poetry and fiction writing; music; travel; horseback. Office: Ray of Hope Inc PO Box 2323 Iowa City IA 52244

ROSS, ELISE JANE, newspaper executive; b. Manchester, Conn., Aug. 29, 1943; d. Harry and Sophia J. (Osher) R. B.A., NYU, 1965. Programmer, Met. Life Ins. Co., N.Y.C., 1965-69; systems analyst Bache, N.Y.C., 1969-70; mgr. systems and programming Omniswitch, Inc., Lake Success, N.Y., 1970-73; v.p. info. systems The N.Y. Times, N.Y.C., 1973—. Office: The NY Times 229 W 43d St New York NY 10036

ROSS, EUNICE LATSHAW, judge; b. Bellevue, Pa., Oct. 13, 1923; d. Richard Kelly and Eunice (Weidner) Latshaw; m. John Anthony Ross, May 29, 1943 (dec. Jan. 1978); 1 child, Geraldine Ross Coleman. B.S., U. Pitts., 1945, LL.B., 1951. Bar: Pa. 1952. Atty., Pub. Health Law Research Project, Pitts., 1951-52; atty. jud. asst., law clk. Ct. Common Pleas, Pitts., 1952-70; adjunct law prof. U. Pitts., 1967-73; dir. family div. Ct. Common Pleas, Pitts., 1970-72; judge Ct. Common Pleas of Allegheny County, Pitts., 1972—; mem. Bd. Jud. Inquiry and Rev., Commonwealth of Pa.; mem. Gov.'s Justice Commn., 1972-78. Author: (with others) Survey of Pa. Public Health Laws, 1952. Contbr. articles to legal publs. Com. person, vice chmn. for 14th ward Democratic Com., Pitts., 1972; exec. com. bd. trustees U. Pitts., 1980—; adv. bd. Animal Friends, Pitts., 1973—; bd. mem. The Program, Pitts., 1983—. Recipient Disting. Amumna award U. Pitts., 1973; named Girl Scout Woman of Yr., Pitts. council Girl Scouts U.S., 1975; cert. of Achievement Pa. Fedn. Women's Clubs, 1975, 77. Mem. Allegheny County Bar Assn. (vice chmn., exec. com. young lawyers sect. 1956-59), Pitts. Bus. and Profl. Women's Club, Pa. State Trial Judges Conf., Western Pa. Hist. Soc. Club: Monday Luncheon. Home: 1204 Denniston Ave Pittsburgh PA 15217 Office: 802 City-County Bldg Pittsburgh PA 15219

ROSS, EUNICE(SALLY), city official; b. Minneapolis, Kans., Dec. 29, 1923; d. Grover Frederick and Frana Delora (Jones) Best; m. Wayne A. Ross, Sept. 27, 1944; children—Jerry Wayne, Rodger David, Melody Hope Parker, Robin Eunice Mooney. Grad. Bus. Coll., Tulsa, 1942; grad. in bus. and edn. Bethany Peniel Coll., Okla., 1945. City clk., Tahlequah, Okla., 1979—. Treas. Cherokee County Fedn. Democrat Women, 1977-79, pres., 1983-85; del. Nat. Conv. Dem. Women, 1984; precinct chmn. Democratic party, 1983-86; mem. County Improvement Com., 1984-86. Recipient Dist. award Okla. Fedn. Dem. Women, 1983, Big T award, 1984. Mem. Internat. Inst. Mcpl. Clks. (dir. region IV), Okla. Mcpl. League (resolutions com. 1983-85, mcpl. action com. 1982-85, legis. com. 1983-86, resolutions com. 1983-85), Okla. Women in Mcpl. Govt. (exec. bd. 1982-86), Cherokee County Hist. Preservation Soc. (treas. 1982-86), Indian Territory Geneal. and Hist. Soc. (pres. 1980-84), DAR (pres. officers' club 1984-86, Cherokee Capital regent 1986—, congl. com. 1983-85). Baptist. Club: Soroptimist (Tahlequah) (pres. 1985-86; Athena award 1985-86). Home: 402 W Shawnee St Tahlequah OK 74464 Office: City of Tahlequah 111 S Cherokee Ave Tahlequah OK 74464

ROSS, GAIL SHARON, pediatric psychologist, educator; b. Paterson, N.J., Nov. 19, 1946; d. Samuel Michael and Matilda (Gershon) R.; B.A. magna cum laude with honors in Psychology, Barnard Coll., 1968; M.A., U. Chgo., 1969; Ph.D., Harvard U., 1978; m. Robert Jay Schwartz, Jr.; children—Matthew Alexander, Michael Benjamin, Alexandra Ross. Assoc. in research in psychology Yale U., New Haven, 1976-78; research assoc. in psychiatry and pediatrics Cornell U. Med. Coll., N.Y.C., 1978-80, instr. psychiatry and pediatrics, 1980, asst. prof. pediatrics, 1982—, staff psychologist Perinatology Center, N.Y. Hosp., N.Y.C., 1978—; dir. Early Childhood Direction Center of Manhattan and Bronx, 1980-82. NDEA Title IV fellow, 1968-69; NIMH grantee, 1972-76; N.Y. State Developmental Disabilities grantee, 1979-82. Mem. Am. Psychol. Assn., Am. Acad. Scis., N.Y. Acad. Scis., Soc. Research in Child Devel., Am. Assn. Women in Psychology, Phi Beta Kappa, Phi Delta Kappa. Contbr. articles to profl. jours.; research in devel. of normal and highrisk infants. Office: Perinatology Center 525 E 68th St New York NY 10021

ROSS, GWEN JANETTE, owner temporary help agency; b. Sweetwater, Tex., Nov. 12, 1929; d. Willard Bruce and Jenell (Whitworth) Gibson; m. M. Mark Hagood, Sept. 3, 1951 (div. Sept. 1962); children—Michael S., Gail Lynn; m. Robert F. Ross, Oct. 17, 1969. B.F.A., U. Tex., 1951. Sec. Austin Sch. System, Tex., 1948-52; ins. agt. Gwen Hagood Ins. Agy., Austin, 1956-62; real estate agt. G. Hagood Real Estate, Austin, 1958-62; owner, pres. Manpower, Inc. of Austin, 1962—. Mem. Temporary Help Services Assn. of Tex., Assn. Manpower Franchise Owners. Republican. Methodist. Avocations: travel; reading; stained glass. Office: Manpower Inc of Austin 609 W 6th St Austin TX 78701

ROSS, HELAINE SWERDLOFF, television producer and director; b. N.Y.C., Apr. 1, 1949; d. Carl Swerdloff and Miriam (Feldman) Swerdloff Levin; m. Robert I. Ross, Apr. 18, 1984. B.S. cum laude, Temple U., 1971. Prodn. asst. Ralph Lopatin Prodns., Phila., 1970-72, film editor, 1972-75; prodn. asst. Mike Douglas Show, Phila., 1975-77, sr. talent coordinator, Los Angeles, 1978-80; sr. producer Entertainment Tonight, Los Angeles, 1980-83; writer, producer Rona Barrett Show, Los Angeles, 1983; producer, dir. Lifestyles of the Rich and Famous, Los Angeles, 1983-85; producer network Movie of Week, Calif., 1985—; lectr. UCLA. Editor films: American Asset, 1975 (N.Y. Film and TV Soc. Silver medal); Athens Achievement (N.Y. Film and TV Soc. Bronze medal). Fundraiser Danny Thomas Leukemia Found., Phila., 1975-77, Am. Cancer Soc., Los Angeles, 1983. Mem. Dirs. Guild Am., Nat. Assn. Female Execs. Jewish. Avocations: writing; reading; cooking; tennis; movies. Home and Office: 14006 Palawan Way Apt 6-204 Marina del Rey CA 90292

ROSS, HOPE SNIDER, physician; b. Vonore, Tenn., May 23, 1910; d. Henry Tipton and Iris (Ellis) Snider; B.S., Maryville (Tenn.) Coll., 1931; M.D., U. Okla., 1935; m. George T. Ross, June 4, 1931; children—Julia, Jerry, Mary. Intern, U. Okla. Hosps., 1935-36; resident anesthesiology North Hudson Hosp., Weehauken, N.J., 1936-37; practice medicine specializing in family practice, Enid, Okla., 1937-78, in gynecology, Enid, 1980-86; physician Okla. del. Nat. Democratic Conv., 1964-80, 84. Named Woman of Yr. Enid YWCA, 1981. Fellow Am. Acad. Family Practice; life mem. Okla. Med. Assn. Democrat. Methodist. Address: 28 Woodlands St Enid OK 73701

ROSS, JUDITH PARIS, life insurance company executive; b. Boston, Dec. 23, 1939; d. Max and Ruth P.; ed. Boston U., 1961, UCLA, 1978; grad. Life Underwriting Tng. Council, 1978; 1 son, Adam Stuart. Producer, co-host Checkpoint TV show, Washington, 1967-71; hostess Judi Says TV show, Washington, 1969; brokerage supr., specialist impaired risk underwriting Beneficial Nat. Life Ins. Co., Beverly Hills, Calif., 1973-82; ins. specialist salary savs. plans, v.p., sec. West Los Angeles Life Underwriters, 1981-82, sec., v.p., 1982-84; dir. mktg. Brougher Life Ins. Co., Beverly Hills, 1982—; speaker ins. industry meetings and convs. Active local PTA, local politics, Boy Scouts Am.; mem. early childhood edn. adv. com. Beverly Hills Unified Sch. Dist., 1977. Mem. Nat. Assn. Life Underwriters, Calif. Assn. Life Underwriters (dir. W. Los Angeles 1980—, chmn. public relations). Office: 9465 Wilshire Blvd Suite 603 Beverly Hills CA 90212

ROSS, KAREN LEE, educator, health care consultant; b. Detroit, Jan. 25, 1953; d. Stewart L. and Joann (Megyesi) McCallum. B.S., Western Mich. U.; M.A., U. Mich. Sr. adult program coordinator City of Farmington Hills (Mich.), 1975-78; asst. project dir. Madonna Coll., Livonia, Mich., 1978-82, asst. prof., field supr., 1978—; coordinator, state activity dir. tng. Health Care Assn. Mich., Lansing, 1982—. Mem. Nat. Council Aging, Alzheimers Disease and Related Disorders Assn. (adv. bd. 1982—). Home: 32165 W 12 Mile Farmington Hills MI 48018 Office: Madonna Coll 36600 Schoolcraft Livonia MI 48150

ROSS, KATHERINE BALL, editor; b. Washington, Feb. 25, 1944; d. Frederic Joseph and Juelda (Watson) Ball; m. John Munder Ross, Aug. 17, 1974; 1 son, Matthew Munder Ball Ross. B.A., Wellesley Coll., 1965. Assoc. editor, articles Redbook Mag., N.Y.C., 1970-76, sr. editor, 1976-78, contbg. editor, 1978-80; articles editor Mademoiselle Mag., N.Y.C., 1980-83, assoc. editor, 1983—. Mem. Am. Soc. Mag. Editors, Women's Media Group, Women in Communications, Soc. Profl. Journalists. Home: 277 West End Ave New York NY 10023 Office: Mademoiselle Mag 350 Madison Ave New York NY 10017

ROSS, KATHLEEN ANNE, nun, college administrator; b. Palo Alto, Calif., July 1, 1941; d. William Andrew and Mary Alberta (Wilburn) R. B.A., Fort Wright Coll. 1964; M.A., Georgetown U., 1972; Ph.D., Claremont Grad. Sch., 1979. Joined Sisters of the Holy Names of Jesus and Mary, Washington Province, 1960. High sch. tchr. Holy Names Acad., Spokane, Wash., 1964-70, 1972-73; secondary edn. personnel specialist Sisters of the Holy Names, Wash. State, 1971-73; acad. v.p., Ft. Wright Coll., Spokane, 1973-76, 1978-81; research assoc. Claremont Grad. Sch., Calif., 1977-78; founding pres. Heritage Coll., Toppenish, Wash., 1981—; cons. U. San Francisco, 1976-78; cons., trainer Yakima Indian Nation, Wash. State, 1974—; dir. Holy Names Coll., Oakland, Calif.; internat. chmn. Gen. Chpt. Sisters of Holy Names of Jesus and Mary, Montreal, Can., 1980-81. Author: (with others) Multicultural Pre-School Curriculum for Yakima Indian Nation, 1978; Success and Failure of American Indian Students in Higher Education, 1979 (P.L. Spencer/Phi Delta Kappa award 1980). Invited lectr. Serving Hispanics and Indians in Higher Edn. in the 1990's. Recipient Hausam-Fiske award Claremont Grad. Sch., 1977; Claremont Grad. Sch. assistantship, 1977-78; Georgetown Grad. Sch. fellow, 1970-71; S. I. Anthon award Altrusa Club, 1985. Mem. Soc. Intercultural Edn. Research and Tng., Am. Assn. for Higher Edn., AAUW. Roman Catholic. Avocations: violinist; needlework. Office: Heritage Coll Route 3 Box 3540 Toppenish WA 98948

ROSS, KENDRA ANN, nursing educator; b. Coldwater, Mich., Oct. 6, 1940; d. Clyde Kenneth and Betty Ann (Barnes) Dryer; m. William Alexander Reid Wilson, Apr. 21, 1962; children—Kendra Ann, Laura, Bill; m. 2d, Stuart Charles Ross, June 18, 1982. B.S. in Nursing, U. Mich., 1962; M.S. in Nursing, No. Ill. U., 1979. Head nurse, med.-surg. ICU, Annapolis Hosp., Wayne, Mich., 1962-65, evening supr., instr. medication course for practical nurses, 1965-68; practical nurse coordinator Ann Arbor Practical Nurse Center, 1963-64; instr. staff devel. Borgess Hosp., Kalamazoo, 1970-71; instr. assoc. degree nursing program Kalamazoo Valley Community Hosp., 1970-71; instr. diploma nursing program Copley Sch. Nursing, Aurora, Ill., 1975-78; clin. specialist, nurse practitioner-neurology, cons. neurol. nursing, tchr. practitioner Rush-Presbyn.-St. Luke's Med. Center, Chgo., 1980-82; instr. assoc. degree nursing program Coll. Dupage, Glen Ellyn, Ill., 1982-84; instr. diploma nursing program St. Joseph Med. Ctr., Joliet, Ill., 1984—; instr., course developer Pharmacotherapeutics Coll. Dupage, Glen Ellyn, Ill., 1984, physical assessment adult client correlating normal and abnormal findings and nursing diagnosis. Co-author: Physical Assessment: A Nursing Diagnosis Approach, Fundamentals of Nursing: A Learning Guide. Mem. bd. Dupage County Health Dept., Wheaton, Ill., 1975; active local councils Girl Scouts U.S., 1948-51, 71-73; co-founder Naperville chpt. Nat. Assn. Learning Disabilities, 1971-75. Mem. Soc. Nursing Profls., Nat. League Nursing, DAR. Republican. Congregationalist. Home: 104 Foxcroft St Naperville IL 60565

ROSS, KHADIJA ELIZABETH RUSSELLA, major asset manager, liquidation specialist; b. Bremerton, Wash., June 27, 1949; d. Donald Alonzo Ross, Jr. and Geraldine Russella (Kent) Ross Osorio; m. Francis A. Dahmer, Jr., Mar. 1968 (div. 1976); 1 child, Cory. B.A., Ga. So. Coll., 1976; M.Ed., U. Wash., 1982. Dir. ESL program Army Community Services, Ft. Stewart, Ga., 1975-76; asst. store mgr. K-Mart, San Jose, Calif., 1982-83; income property loan adminstr. Westside Fed. Savs. & Loan, Seattle, 1984-85; loan servicing specialist Fed. Savs. and Loan Ins. corp., Seattle, 1985—; admitted Wash. State Supreme Ct., ltd. practice officer, 1984. Mem. Seattle Art Mus., Seattle Sci. Ctr., Greenpeace. Served with U.S. Army, 1967-68. Mem. Nat. Assn. Female Execs., Alumni Assn. U. Wash., NOW, Mensa. Shi'ite Moslem. Avocations: writing; traveling; studying. Office: Fed Savs and Loan Ins Corp-Receiver for Westside 400 SW 152nd St Seattle WA 98148

ROSS, LEABELLE I. (MRS. CHARLES R. ROSS), ret. psychiatrist; b. Lorain, Ohio, Feb. 11, 1905; d. Charles E. and Harriet (Dobbie) Isaac; A.B., Western Res. U., 1927, M.D., 1930; m. Charles R. Ross, Sept. 23, 1941; children—Charles R., John Edwin. Surg. intern Lakeside Hosp., Cleve., 1931-32; resident obstetrics and gynecology Iowa State U. Hosp., 1932-33; resident obstetrics and surgery N.Y. Infirmary, N.Y.C., 1933-34; pvt. practice, Cleve., 1935-40; staff physician Cleve. State Hosp., 1938-42; dir. student health Bowling Green (Ohio) State U., 1942-45; psychiatrist Bur. Juvenile Research, Columbus, Ohio, 1946-47; psychiat. cons., 1948-51; psychiatrist Mental Hygiene Clinic, Columbus VA, 1951-55; dir. med. services Juvenile Diagnostic Center, 1955-59, acting supt., 1958, 61-62, dir. psychiat. services, 1959-62, clin. dir., 1962-70. Mem. Am. Psychiat. Assn., Ohio Psychiat. Assn., Am. Group Psychotherapy Assn., Tri-State Group Psychotherapy Soc., Neuropsychiat. Assn. Central Ohio, Assn. Physicians Div. Mental Hygiene and Correction (pres. 1963-64), Alpha Sigma Rho, Nu Sigma Phi. Club: Soroptimist. Home: 1289 Gold Ridge Rd Sebastopol CA 95472

ROSS, LINDA DIANNE, retail business owner, childbirth educator; b. Torrance, Calif., Feb. 18, 1956; d. Leland Douglas and Barbara Jean (Henderson) Roberts; m. Michael Kent Ross, Aug. 7, 1976; children—Michael Jason, Stacey Lynn, Gregory Brian, Jacob Lee. Cert. Alternative childbirth educator. Personnel asst. Deutsch Co., Gardena, Calif., 1974-75; purchasing sec., mktg. sec. Skyclimber, Inc., Lynwood, Calif., 1975-76; homemaker, Norwalk, Calif., 1976-83; owner, mgr. Whole Birth Store, Monrovia, Calif., 1985—; v.p. Archtl. Lamination and Fabrication Co., Paramount, Calif., 1983—. Contbr. column on childbirth and pregnancy to local newspaper. Mem. Nat. Assn. Parents and Profls. for Safe Alternatives in Childbirth, Internat. Childbirth Educators Assn., Alternative Childbirth Educators (promotional com. 1985—). Republican. Avocations: travel; reading; writing; camping.

ROSS, LOIS INA, manufacturing and distributing company executive, new products marketing consultant; b. Boston, Nov. 5, 1947; d. Harry and Esther (Kashuck) Sadow; m. Paul M. Ross, Aug. 25, 1968; children—Gregory, Nicole. Student, Boston U. Asst. office mgr. Waldoroth Label Mfg., Mattapan, Mass., 1965-67; mem. union labor relations com., Stop & Shop, Hyde Park, Mass., 1967-68; office and personnel mgr. Friends Baked Beans, Malden, Mass., 1968-69; community relations rep. McDonalds Restaurant, Syracuse, N.Y., 1978-80; pres., owner Your Hats Desire, Inc., Manlius, N.Y., 1981—; speaker Syracuse U., 1984. Recipient Super Achiever award Admanco Mfg., 1984. Mem. Am. Camping Assn., Advt. Specialty Inst., Women Bus. Owners, Syracuse C. of C. Democrat. Jewish. Clubs: Women's Am. (Syracuse). Avocations: bridge; aerobics; tennis; theater. Office: Your Hats Desire Inc PO Box 434 102 Washington St Manlius NY 13104

ROSS, MADELYN ANN, newspaper executive; b. Pitts., June 26, 1949; d. Mario Charles and Rose Marie (Mangieri) R. B.A., Indiana U. of Pa., 1971; M.A., SUNY-Albany, 1972. Reporter, Pitts. Press., 1972-78, asst. city editor, 1978-82, spl. assignments editor, 1982, mng. editor, 1983—; instr. Community Coll. of Allegheny County, Pitts., 1973-79. Mem. program com. Leaderhship Pitts., 1985; mem. Columbus Day Parade Com., Pitts., 1985; mem. World Affairs Council, Pitts., 1983—. Democrat. Roman Catholic. Avocations: music; art. Office: Pitts Press 34 Blvd of Allies Pittsburgh PA 15230

ROSS, MARY COWELL (MRS. JOHN O. ROSS), lawyer; b. Oklahoma City, Okla., Oct. 1, 1910; d. Sears F. and Elizabeth (Van Zwaluwenburg) Riepma; A.B., Vassar Coll., 1932; LL.B., Memphis State U., 1938; LL.D., U. Nebr., 1973; m. Richard N. Cowell, Mar. 1, 1946 (dec. Jan. 1953); m. 2d, John O. Ross, Mar. 31, 1962 (dec. June 1966). Bar: Tenn. 1938, D.C. 1944, N.Y. 1947. Atty. U.S. Govt., Washington, 1940-44; pvt. practice Cromelin & Townsend, Washington, 1944-46. Royall, Koegel & Rogers and predecessors, N.Y.C., 1946-61; individual practice law, 1961—; treas., dir. 39 E. 79th St. Corp., 1966-73; treas., dir. 795 Fifth Ave. Corp., 1977—; mem. adv. com. N.Y. Commn. on Estates, 1965-67. Bd. dirs. Silver Cross Day Nursery, N.Y.C., 1963-70, Cunningham Dance Found., 1969-72, Central Park Community Fund, 1977-81; trustee U. Nebr. Found., 1966—, bd. dirs., 1974-79; hon. trustee Nebr. Art Assn. Mem. Am. Bar Assn., N.Y. Women's Bar Assn. (pres. 1955-57, dir. 1957-63, 74-80, adv. council 1963—), Bar Assn. City N.Y. (surrogate cts. com. 1961-65, library com. 1965-78, com. on profl. responsibility 1972-75), Nat. Assn. Women Lawyers (assembly del. 1962-64, 73-74, UN observer 1965-67, v.p. 1967, chmn. 1971 ann. conv., distinguished service award 1973), Vassar Coll. Alumnae Assn., Phi Alpha Delta, Delta Gamma. Address: 2 E 61st St New York NY 10021

ROSS, NANCY ANN, educator; b. Des Moines, Sept. 13, 1942; d. Harold Ahlstedt and Margaret (Peniston) Swihart; m. Randy Hale Ross, June 7, 1963; children—Leslie Diane, Andrew James. A.A., Grand View Coll., 1962; B.S. with honors in Edn., Drake U., 1973. Mktg. sec., editor News, Capital City Bank, Des Moines, 1962-69; tchr. assoc. Des Moines Pub. Schs., 1969-71, tchr., 1977—; new account rep. Advance Mortgage, Des Moines, 1974-76. Gifted and talented bldg. coordinator Des Moines Schs., 1984—. Mem. Council for Exceptional Children, NEA, Iowa State Edn. Assn. Home: 3011 SW 39th Des Moines IA 50321

ROSS, NELL TRIPLETT, financial consultant; b. Winterville, Miss., Feb. 14, 1922; d. Ethel Earl and Myrtie (Harrison) Triplett; B.A., Millsaps Coll., 1942; m. William Dee Ross, Jr., July 25, 1944; 1 son, William Dee III. Tchr., Consol. Sch. of Chatham (Miss.), 1942-43, Glen Allan (Miss.) Consol. Sch., 1943-46; sec. econs. dept. Duke U., Durham, N.C., 1946; tchr. Durham High Sch., 1947, E.K. Powe Sch., Durham, 1947-48, Lakewood Elem. Sch., Durham, 1948-49; with purchasing dept. La. State U., Baton Rouge, 1949-50; enrollment officer La. Hosp. Service, Inc., Baton Rouge, 1950-51; co-owner Mentone Plantation, Erwin and Chatham, Miss., 1961—; owner, dir., sec. Fin. Cons. Services, Inc., 1970—. Methodist. Clubs: Baton Rouge Country, Camelot, Bocage, Piedmont. Home: 2738 McConnell Dr Baton Rouge LA 70809

ROSS, PATTI JAYNE, physician; b. Sharon, Pa., Nov. 17, 1946; d. James J. and Mary N. Ross; B.S., DePauw U., 1968; M.D., Tulane, U., 1972; m. Allan Robert Katz, May 23, 1976. Asst. prof. U. Tex. Med. Sch., Houston, 1976-82, asso. prof., 1982—, dir. adolescent obstetrics and gynecology, 1976—, also dir. phys. diagnosis; speaker in field. Bd. dirs. Pituitary Found., 1982—; mem. Rape Council. Diplomate Am. Bd. Ob-Gyn. Mem. Tex. Med. Assn., Harris County Med. Soc. So. Perinatal Assn., Houston Obstetric and Gynecologic Soc., Assn. Profs. Obstetrics and Gynecology, Soc. Adolescent Medicine, AAAS, Am. Women's Med. Assn., Orgn. Women in Sci., Sigma Xi. Roman Catholic. Clubs: River Oak Breakfast, Profl. Women Execs. Contbr. articles to profl. jours. Office: 6431 Fannin St Houston TX 77030*

ROSS, PEGGY, marketing executive; b. Dayton, Ohio, Mar. 18, 1936; d. Guy Bryan Pickett and Clyda (Prather) Pickett Whitehead; m. Paul Henry Ross, Apr. 2, 1955 (div. Aug. 1977); children—Paul Bryan, Paula Page, Preston Blake, Errol Brady; m. 2d, Thomas Robert Fortney, Oct. 10, 1981. Student U. Cin., 1971-74, Chatfield Coll., St. Martin, Ohio, 1971-74. Freelance writer, Bethel, Ohio, 1971-76; staff reporter Cin. Post, 1976-78; dir. mktg. McGill & Smith, Inc., Amelia, Ohio, 1978-82; pres. PR:PR, Milford, Ohio, 1982-83; v.p. TechneGrowth, Inc., Milford, 1983—. Editor: Caught in Time, 1976. Mem. adv. bd. Cancer Family Care, Batavia, Ohio, 1982-83; dir. publicity United Appeal, Clemont-Brown Counties, Ohio, 1983. Mem. Soc. for Mktg. Profl. Services (trustee 1982-83), No. Ky. C. of C., Greater Cin. C. of C., Clermont County C. of C. (dir. 1983—). Republican. Clubs: Women's Investment Group, Cin. Women's Network (Cin.).

ROSS, REBECCA ANN, sales executive; b. Jackson, Miss., Apr. 10, 1952; d. Robert Bryan and Betty Lou (Mize) R. B.S. in Bus. Adminstrn., U. So. Miss., 1974. Buyer, McRaes Dept. Stores, Jackson, 1974-76, Sanger Harris Dept. Store, Dallas, 1976-78; sales mgr. Internat. Playtex Co., Dallas, 1978-83; regional sales mgr. Rush Hampton Industries, Inc., Dallas, 1983-84; sales mgr. So. region Liz Claiborne Hosiery div. Kayser-Roth Hosiery Inc., Dallas, 1984-85; sales mgr. LDS Metromedia, Dallas, 1985—. Home: 18040 Midway Rd #201 Dallas TX 75252

ROSS, ROBERTA MAYE, diversified company executive; b. Santa Paula, Calif., Jan. 9, 1928; d. Theodore Arthur and Minnie Thelma Stangland; student Ventura Jr. Coll., 1946; Calif. State U., Los Angeles, 1952-56; B.A., LaVerne U., 1972; m. John Paul Ross, June 20, 1959; children—Theodore David, Victoria Lou. Office mgr. Southport Engring. Co., Los Angeles, 1949-57; controller Framing Contractors Ltd. also Trent Meredith Inc., Oxnard, Calif., 1957-60; owner Adminstrv. Assts., Oxnard, Calif., 1960-78, sr. partner, 1978-81, sec.-treas., 1981—; sec.-treas. Victoria Land Co. Inc. Gard Trucking, Inc., C-D Woodworks Inc., Santa Paula, Calif.; v.p. OSW & F Inc. Cert. profl. sec. Mem. Profl. Secs. Internat., Am. Soc. Women Accts. Clubs: Mediodia Bus. and Profl. Women's Altrusa (gov. Dist. 11, 1985-87). Address: Administrative Assistants Inc PO Box 2128 Oxnard CA 93030

ROSS, SHEILA MAUREEN HOLMES, sales manager; b. San Jose, Calif., Nov. 1, 1951; d. Douglas F. and Mary A. (Zager) Murphy; B.A., San Jose State U., 1973; m. Lawrence Richard Ross, Dec. 20, 1981; 1 child, Vanessa Katherine Ross. Exec. sec. J.M. Mfg., Santa Clara, Calif., 1972-74; mktg. coordinator Chick, Orthopedic/Hosmer-Dorrance, Campbell, Calif., 1974-75; mgr. mktg. adminstrn. Consol. Video Systems, Sunnyvale, Calif., 1975-83; regional mgr., Pacific dist. sales mgr. ADDA Corp., Los Gatos, Calif., 1977-83, N.W. regional mgr., 1983-84; broadcast sales mgr. Aurora Systems, San Francisco, 1984—. Mem. Internat. Platform Assn., Soc. Motion Pictures and TV Engrs. Home: 28 Dartmouth Pl Danville CA 94526

ROSS, SUSAN JULIA, lawyer; b. Phila., July 24, 1943; d. Herbert Joseph and Susan Eshleman (Reese) R.; B.A., magna cum laude, U. Pa., 1965, J.D. magna cum laude, 1969; postgrad. N.Y. U. Law Sch., 1972-75. Admitted to N.Y. bar, 1971, N.Mex. bar, 1976; asso. firm Dewey, Ballantine, Bushby, Palmer & Wood, N.Y.C., 1969, 71-76; partner firm Natelson & Ross, Taos, N.Mex., 1976—; vis. asso. prof. law U. Oreg., 1978; dir. Beneficial Corp., Wilmington, Del., 1979—. Trustee Millicent Rogers Mus., Taos. Thouron-U. Pa. fellow, Oxford U., 1969-70; Am. Scandinavian Assn. fellow, Stockholm U., 1970. Mem. Phi Beta Kappa, Order Coif. Contbr. in field articles to jours.

ROSS, SUZANNE IRIS, fund raising executive; b. Chgo., Feb. 2, 1948; d. Irving and Rose (Stein) R. B.A. in Secondary Edn., Western Mich. U., 1971. Dir. youth employment Ill. Youth Services Bur., Maywood, Ill., 1978-79; exec. dir. Edn. Resource Ctr., Chgo., 1979-82; asst. dir. devel. Art Inst. Chgo., 1982-83, mgr. govt. affairs, 1983-84, dir. govt. affairs, 1984-85; v.p. devel. Spertus Coll. Judaica, Chgo., 1985—; lectr. Sch. Art Inst., Chgo., 1982-85, Ill. Fire Inspectors Assn., Mt. Prospect, Ill., 1982-84, Episcopalian Archdiocese, Chgo., 1984; instr. Columbia Coll., Chgo., 1980—. Mem. adv. council Citizens Com. on Media, Chgo., 1978-80; adv. panelist Chgo. Office Fine Arts, 1981-82; mem. adv. council Greater Chgo. Food Depository, 1984-85; exec. com. Chgo. Coalition Arts in Edn., 1981-82; mem. info. services com. Donor's Forum of Chgo. Mem. Nat. Soc. Fund Raising Execs., Am. Assn. Mus., Am. Council Arts, Ill. Arts Alliance. Democrat. Jewish. Avocation: Attending cultural events. Home: 3709 N Janssen #2RB Chicago IL 60613 Office: Spertus Coll Judaica 618 S Michigan Ave Chicago IL 60605

ROSS, TIA SHEREE, writer, editor; b. Washington, June 29, 1963; d. William James Ross and Shirley Ann (Chiles) Bush. Student Trinity Coll., Washington, summer 1981, Montgomery Coll., 1986; B.A. in Print Journalism, Howard U., 1985. Reporter, editorial asst. Walter Reed, Washington, 1981-85; intern U.S. Congress, Washington, 1984; equal opportunity asst. Dept. Transportation, Washington, 1985, writer-editor, 1985—. Editor: Construction Manual, 1986, Saudi Arabian manual on Uniform Traffic Control Devices, 1986; reporter, writer numerous newspaper articles. Jr. fellow Office of Personnel Mgmt., 1981; Fleishman scholar, 1984, Trustees' scholar Howard U., 1985. Mem. Women in Communications (treas. Howard U. chpt. 1984-85), Nat. Assn. Female Execs. Democrat. Baptist. Avocations: writing poetry; skiing. Home: 13825 Castle Blvd #41 Silver Spring MD 20904 Office: Dept Transportation 400 7th St SW Washington DC 20950

ROSS, VIRGINIA R., business executive; b. Los Angeles; d. Roy Renwick and Olivia Marie (Macbride) Wilson; B.S., U. Redlands; M.A., Calif. State U.; children—Will, Brian, Darrell, Leslie. Writer-editor, fiber artist, 1965-70; product mgr. A Stitch 'n' Time, San Marino, Calif., 1970-75; product mgr. research and devel. Hazel Pearson Handicrafts, Industry, Calif., 1976-81. Editor, REC, Inc., Arcadia, Calif., 1983-86. Mem. Am. Crafts Council, Surface Design Assn. Republican. Presbyterian. Home: 1350 Winston San Marino CA 91108

ROSS, ZOLA HELEN, writer; b. Dayton, Iowa, May 9, 1912; d. Sherman Andrew and Bertha Ellen (Iles) Girdey; m. Frank William Ross, May 28, 1934. B.A., MacMurray Coll., 1930. Writing tchr. Lake Washington Vocat.-Tech.

Inst., Kirkland, Wash., 1957—. Author: 26 adult novels (hists. and mysteries, some under pseudonym Helen Arre Bert Iles), 11 juvenile novels (with Lucile McDonald). A founder Pacific Northwest Writers Conf., 1956, trustee and program chmn. 16 years, pres., 1962, advisor, 1964—. Recipient Book of Yr. award State of Wash., 1948; Theta Sigma Phi award, 1948; Woman of Achievement and Spl. award Women in Communications, 1982; Lit. and Teaching award Wash. State U., 1983. Mem. Western Writers Am., Mystery Writers Am., Soc. Children's Book Writers, Nat. League Am. Penwomen, Free Lancers, Women in Communications. Methodist. Home: 16907 72d Ave NE Bothell WA 98011

ROSSER, PATRICIA ANNE, association executive; b. Savannah, Ga., June 29, 1948; d. Hoyt Paul and Annie Alberta (Cobb) Canady; B.A., Ga. So. Coll., 1970; M.Ed., Ga. State U., 1973; m. David Jere Rosser, Jan. 4, 1975; step children—Barbara Lynn, Michael Judson, Jennifer Claire; foster children—Janice Claire Jendrynski, Kevin S. Barbour. Personnel and devel. asst. Crawford Long Hosp., Atlanta, 1970-72; tchr. Holy Innocents Episcopal Sch., Atlanta, 1972-76, Harding Acad., Nashville, 1976-77; saleswoman NLT Computer Services Co., Nashville and Clearwater, Fla., 1978-81, Western Res. Fin. Services Co., also Western Res. Life Ins. Co., Clearwater, 1980-81; exec. dir. Channel Markers for Blind, Clearwater, 1981-86, Pinellas Ctr. for Visually Impaired; cons., 1986—; seminar leader in field. Bd. dirs., former treas. Found. Mental Health; former pres. Mental Health N. Pinellas; bd. dirs. Sr. Citizens Services; mem. Hosp. Women's Adv. Bd. Mem. Concerned Women Am., Leadership Pinellas, Clearwater C. of C., Delta Zeta (nat. treas.). Democrat. Baptist. Office: 1609 Indian Rocks Rd Clearwater FL 33516

ROSSER, RACHELLE KAREN, cable TV executive; b. Cleve., Jan. 21, 1955; d. Alvin Ramond and Barbara E. (Roth) R. Student (Rotary exchange student) S. Wiltshire Sch. for Girls, Salisbury, Eng., 1972-73, Mt. Holyoke Coll., 1973-75; B.B.A. in Mktg. cum laude, U. Pa. Wharton 1983. Sales rep. Anixter Pruzan, Wharton, N.J., 1976-77, Cable TV Supply Co., Los Angeles, 1977-79, account exec. Jerrold div. Gen. Instrument Corp., Hatboro, Pa., 1979-81; regional sales mgr. Pioneer Communications Am., Columbus, Ohio, 1981-84, dir. corp. accounts, 1984—. Author publs. in field. Recipient Salesman of Yr. award Jerrold Electronics Co., 1981; Salesperson of Yr. award Pioneer Com., 1982, 85. Mem. Soc. Cable TV Engrs., Phila. Cable Club (exec. com.), Women in Cable (dir.), N.J. Cable TV Assn. (assoc. dir. 1983-84), Sigma Kappa Phi. Home: PO Box 268 Haddonfield NJ 08033 Office: 2200 Dividend Dr Columbus OH 43228

ROSSI, ELISABETH-ANN ROONEY, travel agency executive; b. Worcester, Mass., Aug. 29, 1946; d. Francis Joseph and Evelyn Esther (Rosenlund) Rooney; m. Paul Joseph Rossi, July 25, 1969; children—Nicole, Victoria. Student U. Aix-Marseilles, Aix-en-Provence, France, 1966-67; B.A., Hartwick Coll., 1968; M.A., Clark U., 1975. Tchr. English, Shrewsbury High Sch., Mass., 1968-70; travel agt. Rosenlund Travel Service Inc., Worcester, Mass., 1970-80, pres., treas., 1980—. Vol. worker United Way Central Mass., Worcester, 1983-84. Mem. Am. Soc. Travel Agts. Lutheran. Lodge: Quota. Avocation: travel. Office: Rosenlund Travel Service Inc 332 Main St Worcester MA 01608

ROSSI, MARIE THERESA, marketing company executive; b. N.Y.C., Apr. 19, 1939; d. Dominick and Theresa (Marino) Porco; B.A., Coll. New Rochelle (N.Y.), 1960; m. Louis F. Rossi, June 11, 1960 (dec.); children—Donna, Laura. Dir. alumnae relations Coll. New Rochelle, 1973-75, dir. ann. giving/estate planning, 1975-77; dir. sales and mktg. Aero-Vend, Inc., Portchester, N.Y., 1977-80; pres. Organized Bus. Techniques, Inc., OBT, Inc., Valhalla, N.Y., 1979—. Bd. dirs. Coll. New Rochelle. Mem. Valhalla C. of C. (pres. 1980-81), Meeting Planners Internat., Women in Sales Assn. (founder 1979), Sales and Mktg. Execs. Westchester (exec. dir. 1980-83, bd. dirs.), Am. Soc. Assn. Execs., Sales Exec. Club N.Y. Roman Catholic. Author articles in field. Office: 8 Madison Ave Valhalla NY 10595

ROSSINI, CARLOTTA, advertising agency executive; b. N.Y.C., Apr. 21, 1944; d. Luigi and Hulda (Lefridge) R. Student Columbia U. Sch. Gen. Studies, 1963-64. Mgmt. trainee InterPub. Group of Cos., N.Y.C., 1966; media planner Wunderman, Ricotta & Kline Inc., N.Y.C., 1967; pres. Rossini/Steven Assocs., N.Y.C., 1967-70; v.p., mgmt. supr. Ogilvy & Mather Advt., N.Y.C., 1970—. Recipient Addy award Am. Advt. Fedn., 1968, Effie award Am. Mkgt. Assn., 1981; named to Outstanding Young Women Am., U.S. Jaycees, 1977. Mem. NOW, ACLU. Office: Ogilvy & Mather Advt 2 E 48 St New York NY 10017

ROSS-JACOBS, RUTH ANN, golf and country club executive; b. Milw., Mar. 10, 1934; d. Arthur Theodore and Mary Marilyn (Digert) Kamman; m. Warren Ross, Aug. 9, 1957 (div. Sept. 1972); 1 child, Michael Edward; m. Albert Jacobs, June 28, 1973 (dec. Apr. 1978). B.S., U. Miami, Coral Gables, Fla., 1958; M.S., Wayne State U., 1961; postgrad. U. Wis., 1967-69. R.N., Fla., Wis., Mich. Staff nurse Lafayette Clinic, Detroit, 1958-59; instr. Milw. Inst. Tech., 1962-67; dir. inservice edn. St. Mary's Hosp., Milw., 1963-69; cons. Hearthside Rehab., Milw., 1968-69; owner Peddler Stores, Milw., 1969-72; pres. Jacobs & Densmore Ltd., Toronto, Ont., Can., 1978-83; v.p. Vaughn Ltd., Toronto, 1978—. Author: Inservice Education, 1967; Nursing Procedures, 1969. Pres. PTO, Boca Raton, Fla., 1973-76; mem. Republican Nat. Com., Washington, 1984-85; mem. Inner Circle, Washington, 1984-85. Recipient stipend NIH, Bethesda, Md., 1959. Mem. Sigma Theta Tau. Republican. Lutheran. Club: Boca Raton. Avocations: real estate investments; travel; charity. Home: 2000 S Ocean Blvd Penthouse K Boca Raton FL 33432

ROSSMAN, JOANNE WALKER, artist; b. Los Angeles, Aug. 27, 1937; d. Harold Norman and Ruth Mary (McDowell) Walker; student Woodberry Coll., Los Angeles, 1955-57, Cerritos (Calif.) Coll., 1971-72; children—Brenda, Dean, Dan, Daryl. Asst. advt. mgr. Buzza Greeting Card Co., Anaheim, Calif., 1972-75; asst. advt. prodn. mgr. Star Crest Co., Costa Mesa, Calif., 1976; portrait artist Knotts Berry Farm, Buena Park, Calif., 1976—; owner, mgr. Comml. Center, Fullerton, Calif., 1974-78, Med. Center Rossman Med. Plaza, Santa Ana, Calif., 1978—, Tom and Jerri's Dance Studio, Long Beach, Calif., 1977-80; owner Dancin DeLights, mobile sound system, 1978—. Recipient various dance awards. Mem. Nat. Assn. Female Execs. Address: 2932 Cottonwood St Apt 19 Orange CA 92665

ROSSMAN, MARLENE LAURA, marketing executive, educator; b. N.Y.C., July 4, 1948; d. David and Anne (Stoltz) R.; m. Elliot Silverman, June 29, 1980. B.A., Pace U., 1972, M.B.A., 1982; M.A., NYU, 1974. Counselor George Wingate High Sch., Bklyn., 1972-76; mng. dir. Wingate English Acad., Bklyn., 1976-80; mgmt. cons. Rossman, Graham Assocs., N.Y.C., 1980—; mktg. mgr. Port Authority Trading Co., N.Y.C., 1983—; adj. prof. mktg. NYU, N.Y.C., 1984—; adj. prof. internat. mktg. Iona Coll., 1986—; adj. prof. CUNY, 1973-74; seminar leader Am. Mgmt. Assn., N.Y.C., 1984; speaker in field. Author: The International Businesswoman: A Guide to Success in the World Marketplace, 1986. Com. mem. Women's Funding Coalition, N.Y.C., 1984—, Overseas Edn. Fund, Washington. Mem. Fin. Women's Assn., AAUP, Am. Mktg. Assn., Women Bus. Owners N.Y., Omicron Delta Epsilon. Club: NYU (N.Y.C.). Home: 201 E 17th St New York NY 10003

ROSSNER, JUDITH, novelist; b. N.Y.C., Mar. 31, 1935; d. Joseph George and Dorothy (Shapiro) Perelman; student CCNY, 1952-55; m. Robert Rossner (div.); children—Jean, Daniel; m. 2d, Mordecai Persky (div.). Author: (novels) To the Precipice, 1966; Nine Months in the Life of an Old Maid, 1969; Any Minute I Can Split, 1972; Looking for Mr. Goodbar, 1975; Attachments, 1977; Emmeline, 1980; August, 1983; also short stories. Address: care Julian Bach Agy 747 3d Ave New York NY 10017

ROSTOW, ELSPETH DAVIES, political science educator; b. N.Y.C.; d. Milton Judson and Harriet Elspeth (Vaughan) Davies; m. Walt Whitman Rostow, June 26, 1947; children—Peter Vaughan, Ann Larner. A.B., Barnard Coll., 1938; A.M., Radcliffe Coll., 1939; M.A., Cambridge (Eng.) U., 1949; L.H.D. (hon.), Lebanon Valley Coll.; LL.D. (hon.), Austin Coll. Lectr. Am. studies Barnard Coll., 1939-41, instr. govt., dir., 1941-43; instr. govt., 1945-47; mem. social sci. faculty Sarah Lawrence Coll., 1945-47; tchr. Salzburg (Austria) Seminar, 1947; supr. in history, Univ. lectr. Cambridge U., 1949-50, 58-59; research asso. dept. econs. and social sci. M.I.T., 1950-52, asst. prof. history, 1952-65, on leave, 1961-65; asso. prof. history Am. U., 1961-69; lectr. grad. history faculty Georgetown U., 1961-62; faculty asso. Fgn. Service Inst., 1967-69; assoc. prof. govt. U. Tex., Austin, 1969-76, prof., 1976—, Stiles prof. Am. civilization and govt., 1984—, acting dir. Am. studies, 1970-71, chmn. comparative studies, 1972-74, acting dean div. gen. and comparative studies, 1974-75, dean div., 1975-77; dean Lyndon B. Johnson Sch. Public Affairs, 1977-83; mem. Pres.'s Adv. Com. for Trade Negotiations, 1978-82, Pres.'s Commn. for a Nat. Agenda for the Eighties, 1979-81; research asso. OSS, Washington, 1943-45; Geneva corr. London Economist, 1947-49; lectr. Air War Coll., 1963-81, Army War Coll., 1965, 68, 69, 78, 79, 81, Nat. War Coll., 1962, 68, 74, 75, Indsl. Coll. Armed Forces, 1961-65, Naval War Coll., 1971, Fgn. Service Inst., 1974-77, Dept. State, Europe, 1973. Author: Europe's Economy After the War, 1948, (with others) America Now, 1968, The Coattailless Landslide, 1974; contbr. articles, revs., poems to scholarly jours., newspapers, mags. Trustee Sarah Lawrence Coll., 1952-59; bd. dirs., trustee Overseas Edn. Fund, 1961-74; bd. dirs. Barnard Coll., 1962-66, London Baines Johnson Found., 1977-83; trustee nat. com. The Coll. Bd., 1978-82; mem. adv. council Am. Ditchley Found., 1980; bd. dirs. Salzburg Seminar, 1981—. Recipient award Air U.; Woman of Accomplishment award Harper's Bazaar, 1967; Outstanding Woman award Women in Communications, Austin, 1973. Mem. Nat. Acad. Public Adminstrn., Tex. Philos. Soc., Nat. Assn. Schs. Public Affairs and Adminstrn. (dir. exec. council 1978-80), Assn. Public Policy Analysis Mgmt. (policy council 1980—), Phi Beta Kappa, Phi Nu Epsilon (hon.), Mortar Bd. (hon.), Omicron Delta Kappa. Club: Headliners (Austin). Home: One Wild Wind Point Austin TX 78746 Office: Drawer Y University Station Austin TX 78712

ROSZAK, SARAH, sculptor; b. N.Y.C., Aug. 26, 1947. Cert., Pa. Acad. Fine Art, 1969; B.F.A., U. Pa., 1969; M.F.A., Columbia U., 1972. Exhibited in group shows Pa. Acad. Fine Art, Phila., 1970, Nat. Inst. Arts and Letters, N.Y.C., 1973; Harold Ernst Gallery, Boston, 1973, Kalliope Gallery, West Hampton, L.I., N.Y., 1974; Marion Locks Gallery, Phila., 1974, Art in Pub. Spaces, N.Y.C., 1977; represented in permanent collections St. Luke's Hosp., N.Y.C., N.Y.C. Hosp. Project, John C. Davis Collection, Lexington, Ky., Drs. Sandra and Arnold Gold Collection, Englewood, N.J.; Dante Cuccinello Collection, N.Y.C., Lewis Beck Collection, Tel Aviv. Louis Comfort Tiffany Found. grantee, 1972; MacDowell Colony fellow, 1974; Am. Acad. and Inst. Arts and Letters grantee, 1978. Address: One St Luke's Pl New York NY 10013

ROSZEL, JANE GATEWOOD, personnel executive; b. Atlanta, Jan. 16, 1931; d. Richard Loren and Eliza (Ramey) Gatewood; m. Norman Fitzwilliam Roszel, Oct. 3, 1953; 1 child, Richard Fitzwilliam. B.A., Hollins Coll., 1952. Advt. salesperson Times Herald Newspapers, Washington, 1952-53; caseworker State of La., Franklin, 1954-55; research analyst Rich's Dept. Store, Atlanta, 1955-60, retirement specialist, 1962-74, employee benefits mgr., 1974—. Com. chmn. Atlanta Health Care Coalition, 1983—; bd. dirs. Downtown Atlanta Sr. Services, 1982-83; del. Fulton County Rep., Atlanta, 1962; mem. Collier Hills Civic Assn., Atlanta, 1980—. Mem. Internat. Soc. Pre-Retirement Planners (dir. 1978-84). Episcopalian. Clubs: Boxwood Garden, Little Theatre Franklin (dir. 1954-55). Avocations: camping; gardening; ch. activities. Office: Rich's 45 Broad St Atlanta GA 30302

ROTCHSTEIN-KORN, NANCY, travel agent; b. Cin., July 15, 1945; d. Edwin Charles and Vera Amanda (Hesterberg) Schadewald; m. Errol Richard Korn, May 27, 1983; m. Stephen L. Rotchstein, Oct. 22, 1966 (div. Oct. 1973); 1 child, April A. Grad. Nursing Coll. Mercy, San Diego, 1968; B.A., Bus., Nat. U., 1979, M.A., 1984. R.N.; lic. real estate, ins. sales. Nurse, U. Calif.-San Diego Med. Ctr., 1968-72, project mgr., 1972-77; sales rep. Ayerst Labs., N.Y.C., 1977-79; sales assoc. Practices Sales and Locations, Irvine, Calif., 1978-82; owner, Nanko Internat. Advt., San Diego, 1983—; pres. Seaport Village Travel, Inc., 1983—; ptnr., Getaway Tours San Diego, 1984—; instr. Nat. U., San Diego, 1984-85. Asst. editor The Getaway newsletter, 1983—. Mem. Entrepreneurs Club, Am. Soc. Travel Agts., Nat. Mgmt. Assn. (treas. local chpt. 1978-79), Central City Assn. Club: Women in the Know (sec. 1984—). Avocations: Skiing; scuba diving; running; travel. Home: 4650 W Point Loma Blvd #304 San Diego CA 92107 Office: Seaport Village Travel Inc 853 W Harbor Dr San Diego CA 92101

ROTEPEL, PATRICIA VICTORIA, accountant; b. Jersey City, Aug. 1, 1957; d. Henry Victor and A. Dolores (Motyleski) R.; m. Daniel Gordon Weaver, Sept. 14, 1986. B.S. in Acctg. with high honors, Rutgers U., 1985. Adminstrv. asst. U.S. Army, Munich, Federal Republic of Germany, 1975-78; prodn. mgr.'s asst. Cosmair Inc., Piscataway, N.J., 1978; acctg. asst. Chevron Chem. Co., Perth Amboy, N.J., 1978-85; personnel and adminstrv. supr. USAR, Edison, N.J., 1978—; acct. Chicopee div. Johnson & Johnson Inc., Dayton, N.J., 1985—. Participant Hands Across Am., New Brunswick, N.J., 1986, Hand in Hand/One on One, Edison, 1980-83. Served with U.S. Army, 1975-78, ETO. Mem. Alpha Sigma Lambda. Democrat. Roman Catholic. Avocations: reading; theater; swimming; bicycling; exercising. Home: 376 Carlton Ave Piscataway NJ 08854 Office: Chicopee Div Johnson & Johnson Inc 2351 US Route 130 Dayton NJ 08810

ROTERT, DENISE ANNE, occupational therapist, army officer; b. Sioux Falls, S.D., Nov. 18, 1949; d. Leonard Joseph and Irene Winnifred (Jennings) R.; B.S., U. Puget Sound, 1971; M.A., U. No. Colo., 1975. Commd. 2d lt. Med. Specialist Corps, U.S. Army, 1970, advanced through grades to maj., 1983; staff occupational therapist Tripler Army Med. Center, Honolulu, 1973-76, officer in charge occupational therapy sect. Ireland Army Hosp., Fort Knox, Ky., 1976-77; clin. supr. occupational therapy sect. Letterman Army Med. Center, Presidio of San Francisco, 1977-79; chief instr. occupational therapy asst. course Acad. Health Scis., Ft. Sam Houston, Tex., 1979-84; chief occupational therapy Tri-Service Alcohol Recovery Dept., Naval Hosp., Bethesda, Md., 1984—. Mem. Am. Occupational Therapy Assn., D.C. Occupational Therapy Assn., World Fedn. Occupational Therapists. Roman Catholic. Office: Occupational Therapy Tri-SARD NHBETH Bethesda MD 20814

ROTH, EDITH ELIZABETH, sales office manager, political campaign consultant; b. Budapest, Hungary, June 2, 1935; came to U.S., 1949; d. Edmond and Mary (Bertalan) Rockenstein; m. Mickey Moshe Roth, Apr. 9, 1964; children—Leonora Rose, Adrienne Haddassah. B.A., Cleve. State U., 1981; M.A., Kent State U., 1982. Coordinator re-entry women's program Cleve. State U., 1981; pvt. practice campaign cons., Ohio, 1982—; div. mgr. First Investors Corp., 1985—; co-owner Imagination in Plastic, Cleve., 1982—. Trustee Heights Community Congress, Cleveland Heights, Ohio, 1977-80; chairperson Severance Devel. Commn., Cleveland Heights, 1978; pres. Millikin Neighbors, Inc., Cleveland Heights, 1978-82; mem. fin. com. City Council, Cleveland Heights, 1979-81. Mem. Pi Sigma Alpha. Clubs: Cleveland Heights Democratic. Home: 3691 Blanche Rd Cleveland Heights OH 44118 Office: First Investors Corp 153 E Erie St Painesville OH 44077

ROTH, GLORIA WEISER, educator; b. N.Y.C., Aug. 7, 1949; d. Max and Eva (Cuttler) Weiser; m. Henry James Roth, July 20, 1975; children—Nanci Heather, Michelle Diana. B.S. in Edn. and Psychology, Herbert Lehman Coll., 1971, M.Ed., 1973. Elem. tchr. Bd. Edn., N.Y.C., 1971-78, asst. trainer, tchr. mgmt., 1976-77, tchr., 1977-78, tchr. inservice course in math. games, 1971; tchr. toddler YM & YWHA, N.Y.C., 1984—; pres. Mitchell Lama Co-op, N.Y.C., 1980—; bd. dirs. Inwood Terr., Inc., coop. apts., N.Y.C., 1979—, v.p., 1979, pres., 1980—. Jewish. Lodge: Hadassah (chpt. bd. dirs. 1979—, chpt. v.p. 1982-83). Office: Inwood Terr Inc 99 Hillside Ave New York NY 10040

ROTH, JOAN ELISE, beauty/fashion market consultant; b. Allentown, Pa., Jan. 17, 1935; d. Charles Edward and Christina (Wallace) Decker; m. Garrison Daniel Roth, Sept. 8, 1956 (div. 1982); children—Tucker, Kimberly, Jillian. Student, Miss Porter's Sch., Farmington, Conn., 1953; B.A., Moravian Coll. for Women, 1955; student, Grace Down's Sch., 1955-57. Designer, owner Gigi Ltd., Washington, 1969-73; designer, fashion coordinator, ptnr. Studio J., Inc., Washington, 1973-76; owner, mgr. Ego Trip, Inc., Washington, 1976-78; asst. buyer designer salon Saks-Jandel, Chevy Chase, Md., 1979; cons. Congl. Fitness Ctr. of Capitol Hill, France Internat., Saga Club, Washington, Sports Vision, Ltd., Watergate Hair Salon, Suissa Hair Salon, Georgetown, Salon at Mayflower Hotel, Washington. Mem. Am. Assn. Fitness Dirs. Bus. and Industry, Nat. Assn. Women Bus. Owners, Nat. Assn. Female Execs. Fashion Group Internat., Republican. Episcopalian. Avocations: swimming; bicycling; cross country skiing.

ROTH, JUNE LEVIN, lawyer, business executive; b. Cleve., Nov. 30, 1922; d. Harry B. and Rose (Cohn) Levin; m. Henry E. Roth Nov. 4, 1946 (dec. Nov. 1966); children—Dennis, William, Deborah. B.A., Western Res. U., 1943, LL.B., 1945. Bar: Ohio 1945. Atty., OPA, Cleve., 1945-46; v.p. Sidney Tanning Co., Ohio, 1959-66, pres., 1966—; Bd. dirs. Planned Parenthood Fedn. Am., N.Y.C., 1980—, Alan Guttmacher Inst., N.Y.C., 1984—. Mem. Tanners Council Am. (bd. dirs. 1976-79, 84—), Order of Coif. Home: Rural Route 5 Sidney OH 45365 also 44 Gramercy Park New York NY 10010 Office: Sidney Tanning Co 218 N Ohio Ave Sidney OH 45365

ROTH, MARLEN DEANNE VILAS, state official, simultaneous translator; b. Havana, Cuba, Nov. 19, 1949; came to U.S., 1961, naturalized, 1971; d. Manuel Vilas and Gladys R. Diaz; m. Karl Paul Roth, Apr. 19, 1980. Grad. Cosmopolitan Prep. Sch., 1969. Free-lance translator, writer, 1966—; assoc. editor, art critic Chgo. Hispaño Newspaper, 1973-77; asst. producer, air personality La Cuba de Ayer radio show, 1975; dir. pub. relations, dancer Ballet Azteca, 1977-78; art critic, interviewer, air personality, news announcer, dir. spl. reports Sta. WOPA, 1978-83; office mgr., adminstrv. asst. to dir. Ill. Gov.'s Office Interagy. Coop., 1977-78, adminstrv. aide on women, 1977-84; asst. to dep. dir. for mktg. Ill. Dept. Commerce and Community Affairs, Chgo., 1984—; frequent guest on local TV and radio shows; frequent speaker for numerous civic, polit., bus. groups. Mem. Ill. Commn. on Status Women, 1981-83; active Minority Women's Employment Confs., 1981, 82; numerous Republican activities, current ones being chmn. Hispanic Council, Ill. Rep. State Com., 1981—, dep. committeeman for Hispanic Affairs, Proviso Twp., Ill., 1984—. Mem. Pan Am. Council (bd. dirs. 1977-78, exec. v.p. 1978-84, pres. 1984—), Am. Soc. Notaries (govt. relations com.), Spanish-Am. Pro Art and Culture Soc. (dir. pub. relations, bd. dirs.), Nat. Assn. Cuban Journalists (Chgo. chpt.). Avocation: travel.

ROTH, REGINA SARAH, psychologist; b. Lake Forest, Ill., Mar. 6, 1950; d. Richard James and Shirley (White) R.; A.B. with honors, Conn. Coll., 1972; M.A., NYU, 1974, Ph.D. (NIMH trainee), 1976; postdoctoral student Northwestern U. Med. Hosp. Inst. Psychiatry, 1978-79. Staff cons. clin. div. Worthington Hurst & Assocs., Chgo., 1977-78; psychology postdoctoral trainee Hines (Ill.) VA Hosp., 1979; psychology postdoctoral trainee West Side VA Hosp., Chgo., 1979-80; pvt. practice clin. psychology, 1980—. Mem. Am. Psychol. Assn., Ill. Psychol. Assn., Nat. Register Mental Health Service Providers, Chgo. Assn. Psychoanalytic Psychology, Am. Group Psychotherapy Assn. Home: 3001 S King Dr Apt 508 Chicago IL 60616 Office: 333 N Michigan Ave Suite 1928 Chicago IL 60616 also 1701 E Lake Ave Suite 445 Glenview IL 60025

ROTH, STEPHANIE CAMILLE (STEPHANIE STEPHENS), on-air personality; b. Asheville, N.C., Oct. 18, 1952; d. John Frances and Mary Louise (Phillips) Roth. B.A. cum laude, Wake Forest U., 1974; M.A., NYU, 1980; exchange student U. London, 1974. Adminstrv. asst. Jefferson Prodns., Charlotte, N.C., 1975-76; prodn. asst. CBS-TV, N.Y.C., 1977; project/news bur. coordinator United Airlines, N.Y.C., Chgo., 1977-80; mgr. media relations Tex. Internat. Airlines, Houston, 1980-81; mgr. media relations/mktg. promotions Continental Airlines, Houston, 1980-85; on-air personality, media relations and promotions mgr. KTFM, Waterman Broadcasting Corp., San Antonio, Tex., 1985—; free-lanceon-camera talent; spl. events master of ceremonies. Recipient Corp. award of Merit, United Airlines, Chgo., 1980. Mem. Pub. Relations Soc. Am. (Silver Anvil award 1984), Aviation Space Writers Assn., Internat. Assn. Bus. Communicators, Soc. Am. Travel Writers, Am. Women in Radio and TV. Office: KTFM PO Box 18128 San Antonio TX 78218

ROTHBAUM, VIRGINIA EDEL, therapist, adminstr., artist; b. Savannah, Ga., Jan. 30, 1924; d. Herman Myers and Riette (Levy) Edel; A.A., Armstrong Jr. Coll., 1943; A.B in Journalism, U. N.C., Chapel Hill, 1945; A.S. in Mental Health, Armstrong State Coll., U. Ga., 1978, pediatric devel. studies, 1979-81; children—Stephen Ira, Peggy Ann, John Edel. Public relations Bell Telephone-System, 1945-48, Savannah, Phila. and Woodbury, N.J., 1952-53; substitute tchr., Phila., 1948-49; owner, br. adminstr. Diners/Fugazy Travel, Savannah, 1970-72; advt. sales Savannah Mag., 1972; reading therapist Royce Reading Center, Savannah, 1971-76, 79-83, assoc. dir., 1976-78; edn. therapist asst. Ga. PsychoEd Network, 1978-79; participant learning disability seminars Armstrong State Coll., 1972, 74-82; tutor Savannah Area Literacy Tng. Program, 1983—; life counselor Am. Cancer Soc., Savannah, 1977—, coordinator Reach to Recovery, 1979-82; counselor Hospice of Savannah, 1978-81; mem. ad hoc com. Savannah Alliance for Mentally Ill, 1980-82; docent Hist. Savannah, 1983—. Active Parent Tchr. Orgn./PTA, Girls Scouts U.S.; mem. community adv. com. World Coll. West, Marin County, Calif., 1977—. Founding sponsor, 1980. Mem. AAUW, Savannah Artists Guild, Savannah Art Assn., Ga. Assn. Children with Learning Disabilities, Orton Soc. Jewish. Watercolor artist; one woman show Newsweek Gallery, N.Y.C., 1967, Heritage Gallery, Savannah, 1982, also illustrator, designer.

ROTHBELL, JOAN SPITZER, employment company executive; b. Newark, June 17, 1937; d. Harold Saller and Mildred (Weinreich) Spitzer; m. Samuel Furman, Aug. 20, 1960 (div. July 1970); children—Laurie, Jill; m. Earle Norris Rothbell, Nov. 10, 1970. A.S., Endicott Coll., 1957; student Lab. Inst. Mdse., 1958. Buyer, cons. Barbizon Lingerie, N.Y.C., 1958; asst. mgr. Saks Fifth Ave, Springfield, N.J., 1959-60; owner, pres. R & K Employment Assocs., Inc., Rahway, N.J., 1980—. Vice pres. Woodbridge Gifted Parent Assn., N.J., 1978-79. Mem. Nat. Council Jewish Women (v.p.), Handra, N.J. State Dental Aux. (pres.). Office: R & K Employment Assocs Inc 75 E Cherry St Rahway NJ 07065

ROTHBERG, RYNA HELAINE, librarian; b. Hartford, Conn., Apr. 22, 1936; d. George S. and Ceil Mann; m. Jack A. Rothberg, Apr. 2, 1960. B.A. cum laude, U. Conn., 1958, postgrad., 1958-60; M.L.S. with distinction, U. Wash., 1971. Standard teaching credential in secondary English, Calif. Children's librarian Ventura County Library Services Agy., Simi, Calif., 1964-68, br. head, Moorpark, Calif., 1968-69; br. supr. Newport Beach Pub. Library (Calif.), 1972-73, coordinator children's services, 1973-83, coordinator adult services, 1983-85; asst. dir. Ontario City Library, Calif., 1985—; lectr. Coastline Community Coll., Orange County, Calif., 1975-83, Chapman Coll., judge U. Calif.-Irvine Friends of the Library Orange County Author Awards, 1978; speaker in field. Compiler-author bibliography: Selected Bibliography of Juvenile Fiction Portraying the Handicapped, 1979; Books and the Teen-age Reader, 2d rev. edit., 1980; contbr. articles to profl. jours.; columnist book revs. West Coast Jewish News, 1977-79. Adv., Orange County March of Dimes Reading Olympics, 1979, 81, Orange County chpt. UNICEF Internat. Yr. of Child Com., 1978. Mem. ALA (Newbery Medal com. 1981), Calif. Library Assn. (children's services chpt. pres. 1974, 80, chair continuing edn. com. 1984), So. Calif. Council Lit. for Children and Young People (dir. 1980-82, 3d v.p. 1983-84, chairperson 1984 Awards Com., treas. 1985—), Young Adult Reviewers So. Calif. (chairperson booklist com. 1972, treas. 1977-78, pres. 1981), Pub. Library Execs. Assn. So. Calif., Friends of the Library, Profl. Women's Network of Orange County, AAUW (Newport-Cost Mesa br. program v.p. 1983-85), Gem Theatre Guild (dir. 1985, treas. 1984, newsletter editor 1986), Kappa Delta Pi, Phi Beta Mu. Home: 12271 Oakwood St Garden Grove CA 92640 Office: Ontario City Library 215 East C St Ontario CA 91764

ROTHCHILD, NINA, state official; b. N.Y.C., Mar. 5, 1930; d. Robert Lee and Mary Todd (McCall) Peek; m. Kennon Rothchild, Sept. 22, 1951; children—Kennon, Mary Todd, Sally. A.B. magna cum laude, Smith Coll., 1951. Mem. community faculty Met. State U., St. Paul, 1973-76; exec. dir. Council Econ. Status of Women, St. Paul, 1976-82; commr. employee relations State of Minn., St. Paul, 1983—. Author: Sexism in Schools: A Handbook for Action, 1973. Mem. Mahtomedi Bd. Edn. (Minn.), 1970-76; bd. dirs. St. Paul YWCA, 1977-82; v.p., bd. dirs. Planned Parenthood of Minn., St. Paul, 1972-78; del. Internat. Women's Yr. Conv., Houston, 1977; founder, bd. dirs. Minn. Women's Consortium, St. Paul, 1981—. Recipient Outstanding Achievement award Adminstrv. Women in Edn., St. Paul, 1978; Outstanding Leadership in Govt. award St. Paul YWCA, 1981; Disting. Service to State Govt. award Nat. Govs. Assn., 1984. Mem. NOW, Minn. Women's Polit. Caucus, Minn. Women's Econ. Roundtable, Minn. Working Women 9 to 5, LWV, Phi Beta Kappa, Sigma Xi. Office: Employee Relations 444 Lafayette Saint Paul MN 55101

ROTHENBERG, SAUNDRA, day care center administrator, business executive; b. N.Y.C., May 30, 1943; d. Harold and Etta (Isaacs) Hamm; m. Max P. Rothenberg, Feb. 21, 1965; children—Dana, Jordan. B.A., Bklyn. Coll., 1965; B.R.E., Tchrs. Inst. for Women, N.Y.C., 1964. Tchr., Ramaz Sch., N.Y.C., 1963-65, N.Y.C. Pub. Schs., 1965-67, Hebrew Acad., Miami Beach, Fla., 1967-68, Dade County Pub. Schs., North Miami Beach, Fla., 1968-70; prin., adminstr. Red and White Sch. House, Hollywood, Fla., 1972—, Golden Glades Day Sch., Opa Locka, Fla., 1980—; lectr. in field. Bd. dirs. Hillel Day Sch., North Miami Beach, 1970-84, Hebrew Acad., Miami Beach, 1984-86, Central

Agy. Jewish Edn., Dade County, 1985—; chmn. scholarship dinners Hillel Day Sch. and Hebrew Acad.; mem. adv. bd. Broward County 4-H, Fla., 1975-77, Broward Assn. Children Under Six, 1980—, Broward County Kindergarten and Nursery Assn., 1980—; pres. Galil chpt. Am. Mizrachi Women, North Miami Beach, 1969-72, v.p. Vered chpt., North Miami Beach, 1972-83, pres. S.E. Fla. council, 1983—; del. So. Fla. Community Relations Bd., 1984-85; alt. del. Internat. Conf. on Women, Nairobi, Kenya, 1985. Recipient numerous awards including Am. Mizrachi Women; Builders award Hillel Community Day Sch., 1981; Community Service award Shaaray Tefliah, 1983; Key to City Miami Beach Service award, 1985, Mayor's Service award, 1985. Mem. Dade Fedn., South Broward Fedn., Women's Study Group North Miami Beach (chmn. 1980-84). Jewish. Avocations: travel, tennis; bowling; swimming; gourmet cooking. Office: Red and White Sch House 4200 NW 65th Ave Hollywood CA 33024

ROTHENBERG, SUSAN, painter; b. Buffalo, Jan. 20, 1945. B.F.A., Cornell U., 1966. One-person shows Three Large Paintings, N.Y.C., 1975, Willard Gallery, 1976, 77, 79, Matrix, Univ. Art Mus., Berkeley, Calif., 1978, Walker Art Ctr., Mpls., 1978; Mayor Gallery, London, 1980, Galerie Rudolf Zwirner, Cologne, 1980, Five Heads, Willard Gallery, 1981, Akron Art Mus., 1981-82; Stedelijk Mus., Amsterdam, 1982; group exhbns. include Art Inst. Chgo., 1982, Zeitgeist, Martin-Groupius-Bau, Berlin, 1982, Milw. Art Mus., 1982-83; represented in permanent collections Mus. Modern Art, N.Y.C., Albright-Knox Art Gallery, Buffalo, Whitney Mus. Am. Art, N.Y.C., Walker Art Ctr., Des Moines, Art Mus. South Tex., Corpus Christi, Mus. Fine Arts, Houston, Akron Art Mus., Munson-Williams Proctor Inst., Utica, N.Y.; featured in numerous popular and profl. mags. Am. Acad. and Inst. Arts and Letters grantee in art, 1983. Address: 138 Watts St New York NY 10013

ROTHERMEL, JOAN EBERT, lawyer; b. N.Y.C., Feb. 22, 1948; d. Edmund Francis and Lathelia Marie (Keesey) Ebert; m. Timothy Simes Rothermel, Aug. 11, 1974; children—Sara Ebert, David Edmund. B.A. cum laude, Goucher Coll., 1970; postgrad. Law Ctr. George Washington U., 1971-72; J.D. cum laude, Fordham U., 1976. Bar: N.Y. 1977, U.S. Dist. Ct. (so, ea. dists.) N.Y. 1977, D.C. 1980, U.S. Ct. Appeals D.C. 1981. Legis. asst. Congressman Bradford Morse, Washington, 1970-72; spl. asst. to Undersec. Gen. Polit. and Gen. Assembly Affairs, UN, N.Y.C., 1972-76; law clk. Surrey, Karasik, Morse & Seham, N.Y.C., 1976-77; assoc. Surrey, Karasik, Morse & Seham, N.Y.C., 1977-79; assoc. Seham, Klein & Zelman, N.Y.C., 1979-83, ptnr., 1983—. Recipient Thaddeus Stevens award Fordham U., 1976, West Pub. Co. award in constl. law, 1976. Mem. ABA, Assn. Bar City of N.Y., D.C. Bar Assn., Phi Beta Kappa. Episcopalian. Home: 245 E 40th St New York NY 10016 Office: Seham Klein & Zelman 485 Madison Ave New York NY 10022

ROTHMAN, DEANNA, electroplating company executive; b. Bklyn., Sept. 20, 1938; d. Frank Philip and Elsie (Goldstein) Dukofsky; m. Edward Rothman, Dec. 8, 1956 (div. July 1984); children—Jeffrey Scott, Michele Dawn, Robert Jay. B.A., Bklyn. Coll., 1968. Exec. Bronzemaster Co., Bklyn., 1969-80, Perma Plating Co. Inc., Bklyn., 1980-84; pres. Duratron Finishing Corp., Bklyn., 1984—. Sec. Tenants Assn., S.I., 1973-77; v.p. Orgn. Rehab. and Tng., Woodmere, N.Y., 1978-80. Mem. Masters Electroplating Assn., Am. Metal Finishers, Nat. Assn. Female Execs., NOW. Republican. Jewish. Avocations: painting; collecing art deco; dance; theatre.

ROTHMAN, ESTHER POMERANZ, social agency executive, psychologist; b. N.Y.C., Nov. 25, 1919; d. Max and Anne (Reiner) Pomeranz; m. Arthur M. Rothman, Apr. 13, 1946; 1 dau., Amy. B.A., Hunter Coll., 1942; M.A., Columbia U., 1944; M.A., CCNY, 1946; Ph.D., NYU, 1958. Cert. psychologist, N.Y. Tchr., N.Y.C. Bd. Edn., 1944-57, prin., 1957-80; exec. dir. Glie Youth Program, N.Y.C., 1980-85; exec. dir. Correctional Edn. Consortium, 1985—; research psychologist Tchrs. Hot Line, N.Y.C., 1972-74. Author: Angel Inside Went Sour, 1972; Troubled Teachers, 1974; co-author: Disturbed Child, 1967. Mem. Citizens Com. for Children, N.Y.C., 1972—. Recipient Valley Forge Freedom award, 1976. Fellow Am. Assn. Orthopsychiatry (sec. 1976-79); mem. Am. Psychol. Assn. Home: 200 E 16 St New York NY 10003 Office: Correctional Edn Consortium 29-10 Thomson Ave Long Island NY 11101

ROTHMAN, JUDITH DIANE, children's television writer, b. Bklyn., Sept. 27, 1952; d. Irwin and Dorothy (Kleinman) R.; m. Howard Lee Zellman, Mar. 16, 1980 (div. 1984). B.A., U. N.Mex., 1973, M.A., 1977. Ednl. media producer Walt Disney Telecommunications, Burbank, Calif., 1981-82; dir. program devel. Disney Channel, Burbank, 1982-84; producer Hyperion Films, Los Angeles, 1984—; cons. Siriol Animation, Cardiff, Wales, 1985. Author: The $90 Overalls, 1985. Co-author TV program: Superted: The Bear Cares, 1985; author: Dumbo's Circus, 1985. Co-producer TV film Mr. Nobody, 1985. Mem. Women in Cable, Women in Film. Democrat. Jewish. Avocation: travel.

ROTHMAN, SHEILA, banker, accountant, educator; b. N.Y.C., Oct. 12, 1931; d. Joseph Charles and Henrietta (Horowitz) Handshoe; m. Frank Rothman, Sept. 2, 1956; children—Andrew Steven, Richard Robert. B.B.A., C. Coll. N.Y., 1952, M.B.A., 1959; postgrad., 1959-64. Tchr. L.D. Brandeis High Sch., N.Y.C., 1966-68; controller Goodwill Inds. and Sheltered Workshop Inc., Bridgeport, Conn., 1974-77, Cable Mgmt. Services, Bridgeport, 1978-79, Conn. Community Bank (formerly Conn. Women's Bank), Greenwich, 1983—; sr. acct. Moore Mccormack Bulk Transport, Inc., Stamford, Conn., 1980-83; mem. Selectman's com. to Research Tax Relief for the Elderly, Westport, Conn., 1975; dir., sec. Conn. Research Group, Inc., Westport, 1984—. Exec. com., lobbyist Caucus of Conn. Democrats, Hartford, New Haven, 1968-73; statewide treas. Joseph D. Duffey U.S. Senatorial campaign, Hartford, 1969-71; state coordinator McGovern for Pres., Conn., 1971; mem. Women's Polit. Caucus, Westport, Conn., 1971-74, Westport Democratic Town com., 1971-74; Sunday Sch. tchr., prin. Congregation for Humanistic Judaism, Westport, 1971-75. Mem. Nat. Assn. Accts. Avocations: physical fitness activities, new age holistic health activities. Home: 38 Oak St Westport CT 06880 Office: Conn Community Bank 100 Mason St Greenwich CT 06830

ROTHROCK, JANE CLAIRE, nursing educator; b. Abington, Pa., Mar. 20, 1948; d. John Richard and Dorothea Ethel (Leser) Lynch; m. Joseph Rothrock, III, Apr. 17, 1977. B.S.N., U. Pa., 1974, M.S.N., 1978. Staff nurse Hosp. U. Pa., Phila., 1969-71, staff developer, 1971-74; dir. operating room Grad. Hosp., Phila., 1974-76; clin. instr. U. Pa., Phila., 1976-77; dir. operating room, Bryn Mawr Hosp., Pa., 1978-79; assoc. prof. Delaware County Community Coll., Media, Pa., 1979—; pres. Quest RN Inc., Wallingford, Pa., 1985—; mem. adv. bd. Edn. div. Am. Sterilizer Co., Erie, Pa., 1984—. Bd. dirs. Community Mental Health Ctr., Chester, Pa., 1980—. Author: Chesapeake Odysseys, 1984; editor: The RN First Assistant, 1986; contbr. articles to profl. jours. Assn. Operating Rm. Nurses scholar, 1974, 85-86. Mem. Am. Nurses Assn., Pa. Council Operating Rm. Nurses (pres. 1984-86), Assn. Operating Rm. Nurses (edit. bd. 1983-86), Soc. Research in Nursing Edn. Republican. Methodist. Clubs: Pine Ridge Garden, Jr. Womens. Avocations: Sailing; skiing; needlework. Office: Delaware County Community Coll Rt 252 Media PA 19063

ROTHSCHILD, AMALIE RANDOLPH, filmmaker, producer, director; b. Balt., June 3, 1945; d. Randolph Schamberg and Amalie Getta (Rosenfeld) R.; B.F.A., R.I. Sch. Design, 1967; M.F.A. in Motion Picture Production, N.Y. U., 1969. Spl. effects staff in film and photography Joshua Light Show, Fillmore E. Theatre, NYC, 1969-71; still photographer TWA Airlines Pub. Relations Dept., Village Voice newspaper Rolling Stone magazine, Newsweek magazine, After Dark, N.Y. Daily News, numerous others, 1968-72; co-founder, partner New Day Films, distbn. coop., 1971—; owner, operator Anomaly Films Co., NYC, 1971—; mem., co-founder Assn. of Independent Video and Filmmakers, Inc., NYC, 1974, bd. dirs., 1974-78; instr. in film and TV, N.Y. U. Inst. of Film and TV, 1976-78; cons. in field to various organizations including Youthgrant Program of Nat. Endowment for Humanities, Washington, 1973-76; motion pictures include: Woo Who? May Wilson, 1969; It Happens to Us, 1972; Nana, Mom and Me, 1974; Radioimmunoassay of Renin, Radioimmunoassay of Aldosterone, 1973; Conversations with Willard Van Dyke, 1981; Richard Haas: Work in Progress, 1984; editor: Doing It Yourself, Handbook on Independent Film Distribution, 1977. Active mem. Community Planning Bd. 1, Borough of Manhattan, N.Y.C., 1974-86. Recipient spl. achievement award Mademoiselle mag., 1972; independent filmmaker grant, Am. Film Inst., 1973; film grantee N.Y. State Council on the Arts, 1977, 85, Nat. Endowment Arts, 1978, 85, Md. Arts Council, 1977, Ohio Arts and Humanities Councils, 1985. Mem. Internat. Film Seminars (trustee 1975-80), Independent Cinema Artists and Producers (bd. dirs. 1976-84), Univ. Film and Video Assn., N.Y. Women in Film. Democrat. Address: 135 Hudson St New York NY 10013 also Via delle Mantellate 19 Rome 00165 Italy

ROTHSCHILD, DIANE, advertising agency executive; b. Apr. 11, 1943; d. Morton Royce and Marjorie Jay (Simon) R.; m. John R. Spencer, Aug. 12, 1976; 1 child, Alexandra Rothschild. B.A., Aldephi U., 1965. Copywriter Doyle Dane Bernbach Advt., Inc., N.Y.C., 1967-73, v.p., 1973-79, sr. v.p., assoc. creative dir., 1979-85, exec. v.p., creative dir., 1985—. Recipient maj. advt. awards. Mem. YWCA Acad. Women Achievers. Office: Doyle Dane Bernbach Inc 437 Madison Ave New York NY 10022

ROTHSCHILD, LINDA MAY, hospital nursing administrator; b. Palmerton, Pa., Apr. 21, 1947; d. Willard Bryfogle and Margaret Catherine (Thomas) Blocker; m. Joseph Steven Rothschild, Sept. 17, 1982; 1 child, Michael. B.A., Gordon Coll., 1971; Assoc. Sci. in Nursing, Gwynedd-Mercy Coll., 1975, B.S., 1977; M.S., Pa. State U., 1982. Asst. dir. nursing Park West Manor Nursing Home, State College, Pa., 1977-78; dir. nursing Mount Holly Ctr., N.J., 1979-81; asst. dir. nursing service Germantown Hosp. and Med. Ctr., Phila., 1981-82; dir. med.-surg. nursing Chestnut Hill Hosp., Phila., 1982—; faculty continuing edn. Pa. State U., 1979, Villanova U., Pa., 1981; faculty seminar series Resource Applications, Inc., Balt., 1982; clin. assoc. grad. program Villanova U. Coll. Nursing, 1984—. Contbr., clin. cons. Helping Geriatric Patients, 1982. Mem. Am. Orgn. Nurse Execs., Nat. League for Nursing, Pa. League for Nursing, Sigma Theta Tau, Phi Kappa Phi. Avocations: gardening; cooking; playing piano. Home: 7902 Ronaele Dr Elkins Park PA 19117

ROTHSCHILD, MARY CASPE, sales and marketing executive; b. Des Moines, July 11; d. Sam and Sarah Caspe; m. Joseph Maximillian Rothschild Sept. 2, 1939 (div. 1952). Grad. high sch., Des Moines. Mem. radio staff Cowles Stas., Des Moines, 1932-36, Hearst Sta., Los Angeles, 1936-39, Sta. KFWB, Warner Bros., Los Angeles, 1939-52; with Sta. KTLA-TV, Golden West, Los Angeles, 1952-57; pres. Cross & Rothschild, Inc., Los Angeles, 1955-85; ptnr. Rothschild/Robertson Ptnrs., Los Angeles, 1985—. Author: (poetry) Call Me Mary, Sin, Gin & Lohengrin. Democrat. Club: Mission Hills Country (Rancho Mirage, Calif.). Avocations: cooking; poetry. Office: Rothschild/Robertson Ptnrs 7013 Willoughby Ave Los Angeles CA 90038

ROTHSTEIN, BARBARA JACOBS, fed. judge; b. Bklyn., Feb. 2, 1939; d. Solomon and Pauline Jacobs; B.A., Cornell U., 1960; LL.B. (winning oralist Ames Moot Ct. competition), Harvard U., 1966; m. Ted L. Rothstein, Dec. 28, 1968; 1 son, Daniel Glen. Admitted to Mass. bar, 1966, Wash. bar, 1968; pvt. practice, Boston, 1966-68; asst. atty. gen. Wash. Gen. Consumer Protection Div., 1968-77; mem. faculty U. Wash. Law. Sch., 1975-77; judge Wash. Superior Ct., 1977-80; judge U.S. Dist. Ct. Western Dist. Wash., 1980—. Officer, bd. dirs. Seattle Mental Health Inst., Seattle Treatment Center; trustee Am. Jewish Com. Named Cornell Woman of Year, 1978. Mem. Am. Judicature Soc., Am. Bar Assn., Am. Trial Lawyers Assn., Nat. Assn. Women Judges, Wash. Bar Assn., Seattle-King County Bar Assn. (trustee young lawyers sect. 1971-72), Urban League, Mcpl. League. Club: Cornell (officer, dir.) (Seattle). Address: US Courthouse Seattle WA 98104

ROTHSTEIN, EVELYN BIERMAN, educational consultant; b. N.Y.C., Dec. 12, 1928; d. David and Clara Kane Bierman; B.S., CCNY, 1953, M.A., 1961; D.Ed., Columbia U., 1974; m. Eugene L. Rothstein, June 16, 1951; children—Andrew, Mitchell, Richard, Miriam. Classroom tchr. N.Y.C. Schs., 1953-54; reading specialist Nyack (N.Y.) Pub. Schs., 1958-67; prof. reading and linguistics CCNY, SUNY, Briarcliff Coll., 1967-76; ednl. cons., Nyack, N.Y., 1976—; owner Evelyn Rothstein Assocs., pubs. ednl. materials, Nyack, 1977—. Mem. Internat. Reading Assn., Assn. Supervision and Curriculum Devel., Assn. Children with Learning Disabilities, Nat. Council Tchrs. English, NOW (del. state orgn.), Kappa Delta Pi. Author: Teaching Writing: A Developmental Systematic Approach, 1982; Easy Writer Student Worksheets, 1982. Home: Terrace Dr South Nyack NY 10960 Office: PO Box 650 Nyack NY 10960

ROTHSTEIN, MARILYN SIMON, advertising and writing agency executive; b. Bklyn., May 11, 1953; d. Leo and Freida (Hammer) Simon; m. Alan Miles Rothstein, Jan. 24, 1976; children—Sharyn Pamela, Marisa Shana. B.A., NYU, 1974. Staff writer Seventeen Mag., N.Y.C., 1974-77; copy supr. Gabriel Industries, N.Y.C., 1977-78; copywriter Mintz & Hoke, Avon, Conn., 1978-81; owner Rothstein Advt. Writers, Avon., 1981-84; pres. Simon Advt. & Writing, Inc., Avon, 1984—. Recipient awards for advt. and copywriting Advt. Club Greater Hartford, Advt. Club Western Mass., Conn. Art Dirs. Club; Retail Advt. Conf. TV award of Merit, Nat. Com. on Films for Safety. Mem. Women in Communications (program chmn. Central Conn. chpt. 1981-83, v.p. 1983-84, pres. 1984-85), Conn. Art Dirs., Greater Hartford Jewish Fedn. Bus. Profl. Women, NOW. Club, Advt. Club of Greater Hartford, Probus of Greater Hartford. Home: 592 Lovely St Avon CT 06001 Office: Simon Advt & Writing Inc 41 Old Avon Village Avon CT 06001

ROTHWEILER, THERESA MARIE, nursing educator; b. Neola, Iowa, Feb. 18, 1929; d. Robert Francis and Margaret (Burns) Cavanaugh; m. George Anton Rothweiler, Jr., Sept. 12, 1953; children—Beatrice, Gregory, Steven, Paul, Joan. B.S.N., Lorretto Heights Coll., 1951; M.S., U. Minn., 1972; Ph.D., U. Minn., 1980. Nurse, St. Anthony Hosp., Denver, 1952-53; asst. head nurse Miller Hosp., St. Paul, 1953-54; nurse educator Anoka Ramsey Community Coll., Coon Rapids, Minn., 1972-74; nurse educator Gustavus Adolphus Coll. St. Peter, Minn., 1975-80; asst. prof. nursing U. Minn., Mpls., 1980—; founder Profl. Stress Mgmt. Inc., 1985; lectr. in field. Adviser, Washington County Community Health, 1977-82. Mem. Minn. Nurses Assn. (edn. commn. 1979-81, 83—, dist. bd. dirs. 1977-83), Sigma Xi, Sigma Theta Tau. Office: Sch Nursing U Minn 308 Harvard St Minneapolis MN 55455

ROTONDO, JANE, beauty salons executive; b. Momence, Ill., Apr. 9, 1922; d. Lee and Ruth Hazel (Hazlette) Snapp; children—Maria Jane Santos, Charles J. II (dec.). Student Champaign Beauty Sch., 1943. Lic. beautician. Sec., supt. Def. Plant, Elwood, Ill., 1940-43; hairdresser, Champaign, Ill., 1943-45; hairdresser for funeral homes, Champaign, from 1955; owner beauty salons in nursing homes, Essex County, N.J., 1964—; fin. sec. Columbus Hosp., Newark, 1965-67; owner, pres. Caravan of Beauty and Caravan by Jane, Essex County, 1966—. Vice pres. Parents without Partners, Essex, N.J., 1968-73 (Woman of Yr. 1970). Home: 417 Abington Ave Bloomfield NJ 07003

ROTWEIN, SUZANNE, med. record adminstr.; b. Jackson, Miss., Apr. 9, 1952; d. Abe Arthur and Helene Rose (Ascher) R.; B.S., U. Ala., Birmingham, 1975; M.S., Southwest Tex. State U., 1985; postgrad. U. Tex.-Dallas. Dir. med. record dept. New Vaughan Meml. Hosp., Selma, Ala., 1975-78; dir. med. record dept. Druid City Hosp. Regional Med. Center, Tuscaloosa, Ala., 1978-82; dir. med. record dept. Bexar County Hosp. Dist., San Antonio, 1982-84, San Antonio Children's Ctr., 1984-85; mem. adj. faculty dept. health services adminstrn. U. Ala., Birmingham; cons. to hosps.; leadership lectr. U. Ala. Capstone Sch. Nursing. Chmn. apt. complex Am. Cancer Soc. Fund Dr., Tuscaloosa. Mem. Am. Med. Records Assn., Ala. Med. Record Assn. (editor newsletter 1977-78), Tex. Med. Records Assn., Tex. Hosp. Assn., AAUW, Am. Hosp. Assn., Assn. Records Mgrs. and Adminstrs., Hadassah (life), Delta Phi Epsilon. Home: 700 Custer Rd #188 Richardson TX 75080

ROUDYBUSH, ALEXANDRA BROWN (MRS. FRANKLIN ROUDYBUSH), author; b. Hyères, Côte d'Azur, France, Mar. 14, 1911 (parents Am. citizens); d. Constantine and Ethel (Wheeler) Brown; B.A., London Sch. Econs., 1930; m. Franklin Roudybush, May 22, 1941. Corr., London Evening Standard, Washington, 1931; sec. to Drew Pearson, 1932; asst. Agence Havas, 1935; research news analyst Time mag., N.Y.C., 1936; sec. to chief news dept. CBS, 1936; White House corr. MBS, 1940; asst. to sect. head Nat. Acad. Scis., Washington, 1957-60; adminstr., sec. firm Dewey, Ballantine, Bushby, Palmer & Wood, attys., Paris, 1965-80. Mem. Mystery Writers Am. Author: Before the Ball was Over, 1965; Death of a Moral Person, 1967; A Capital Crime, 1969; The House of the Cat, 1970; A Sybaritic Death, 1972; Gastronomic Murder, 1973; Suddenly in Paris, 1975; The Female of the Species, 1978; Blood Ties, 1981. Home: 15 Ave du President Wilson Paris 16e France Office: 45 Ave George V Paris 8e France also Sauveterre de Rouerque 12 Aveyron France

ROUKEMA, MARGARET SCAFATI, congresswoman; b. Newark, Sept. 19, 1929; d. Claude Thomas and Margaret (D'Alessio) Scafati; B.A. with honors in History and Polit. Sci., Montclair State Coll., 1951, postgrad. in history and guidance, 1951-53; postgrad. program in city and regional planning Rutgers U., 1975; m. Richard W. Roukema, Aug. 23, 1951; children—Margaret, Todd (dec.), Gregory. Tchr. history, govt., public schs., Livingston and Ridgewood, N.J., 1951-55; mem. 97th-99th Congresses from 7th N.J. Dist. Vice pres. Ridgewood Bd. Edn., 1970-73; bd. dirs., co-founder Ridgewood Sr. Citizens Housing Corp.; trustee Spring House, Paramus, N.J., Leukemia Soc. No. N.J., Family Counseling Service for Ridgewood and Vicinity; mem. Bergen County (N.J.) Republican Com.; NW Bergen County campaign mgr. for gubernatorial candidate Tom Kean, 1977. Mem. Bus. and Profl. Women's Orgn. Clubs: Coll. of Ridgewood, Ridgewood Rep. Office: 226 Cannon House Office Bldg Washington DC 20515*

ROULEAU, CAROLYN FERNAN, field systems coordinator; b. Miami, Fla., Jan. 1, 1950; d. Philip A. and Joanne Fernan; m. Kenneth E. Rouleau, Mar. 3, 1973 (div. Feb. 1980); children—Tiffany Ann, Joseph Philippe. Student Fla. Atlantic U., 1969-71, Fla. Internat. U., 1972-73, U. Miami, 1985—. Coordinator, Conservation Found. Air Quality Workshop, Miami, Fla., 1970-71; city field systems coordinator Hertz Corp., Miami, 1971—; dir. Colleen Mine, Balt., 1983—. Patron, Greater Miami Opera; active Girl Scouts USA. Mem. Nat. Assn. Female Execs., LWV, Beta Gamma Sigma. Club: Miami Woman's. Avocations: sailing; golf; gardening.

ROULEAU, MONA MARY, medical management executive; b. Barre, Vt., Oct. 18, 1953; d. Albert Joseph and Yvette R. (Dubuc) R. Assoc. Applied Sci. in Medicine, Springfield Tech. Community Coll., Mass., 1973, Assoc. Applied Sci. in Bus., 1978; B.B.A., Baruch Coll., CUNY, 1985. Mgr. surg. dept. Surgeons Ltd., Springfield, 1974-80; practice mgr. for J. Prutting, C. Caggiono, N.Y.C., 1980-84; dir. Cardiac Extension, Inc., N.Y.C., 1984-85; v.p., chief operating officer Elite Surg. Suites, Inc., N.Y.C., 1985—. Mem. Nat. Assn. Female Execs. (dir. workshop), Am. Mgmt. Assn. Office: Elite Surg Suites Inc 611 Henry St Brooklyn NY 11231

ROULETTE, HEDL DRESDNER, advertising executive, communications consultant; b. Trenton, N.J., Oct. 23, 1930; d. Karl George and Miriam Virginia Dresdner; B.A., Elmira Coll., 1950; postgrad. Wharton Sch., U. Pa.; m. William Roulette, Dec. 28, 1953 (div.); children—Karla Roulette Rauch, William Brooke. With public relations dept. Princeton (N.J.) U., 1950-53; owner Hedl Yuletree Farm, sculpture and design in brass, Coopersburg, Pa., 1965-79; dir. advt. Quakertown (Pa.) Free Press, 1973-79; dir. advt. The Trentonian, Trenton, N.J., 1979-83; print media advt. cons., 1983—. Active, Jr. League, Delaware Valley United Way; vol. St. Luke's Hosp.; bd. govs. Trenton Symphony; vol. Citizens for Eisenhower; bd. dirs. George Washington council Boy Scouts Am.; active YWCA, Princeton. Mem. N.J. Press Assn., Pa. Newspaper Pub. Assn., Internat. Newspaper Advt. Assn., Interstate Newspaper Advt., Suburban Phila. Newspaper Advt. Assn.. S. Jersey Newspaper Advt., DAR (dir. George Washington chpt.), Nat. Assn. Republican Women, Trenton C. of C. Presbyterian. Club: Soroptimist (dir. Trenton 1980-81). Home: 105 Penn Valley Terr Yardley PA 19067

ROUND, BETTYE HAMMONS (MRS. THORNTON EDGERLY ROUND), retired realtor; b. Barberville, Fla.; d. Benjamin Abner and Alice Adella (Ward) Hammons; grad. high sch.; student various courses in real estate, decorating, bus. mgmt.; degree U. Fla., 1951; m. Thornton Edgerly Round, July 27, 1961 (dec.); 1 dau., Alice Adair Gilbert (Mrs. Darrell D. Brown). Free-lance interior designer, Coral Gables, Miami, Fla., 1935-39; agt., Independence Life Ins. Co., Orlando, Fla., 1950-51; broker Homestead Devel. Co., 1952-56; owner real estate broker firm Bettye H. Gilbert, 1956-61, Bettye H. Round Realtor, after 1961; owner, Windsor Manor, Inc., Orlando, after 1961; co-owner Lee's Inn, Highlands, N.C., 1961-69. Mem. Vis. Nurses Assn., 1962—; mem. Orlando Day Nursery, 1964-72; mem. women's com. Fla. Symphony Orch., 1964-78; mem. Central Fla. Civic Theatre Guild. Fellow Internat. Assn.; mem. Orlando Winter Park Bd. Realtors (sec. 1958, pres. women's council 1959-60), Fla. Bd. Realtors (corr. sec. 1958), Nat. Soc. Lit. and Arts, Internat. Platform Assn, AAUW. Democrat. Episcopalian. Clubs: Sorosis, Dubsdread Country, Orlando Country (Orlando). Home: 722 Alameda Ave Orlando FL 32804

ROUNDS, MARTHA GILTNER, fitness and nutrition counseling company executive; b. Joplin, Mo., Apr. 12, 1919; d. Frank Phillips and Berry Frances (Barnes) Giltner; m. Francis Joseph Rounds; children—Berry R. Lane, Kevin T., Tracy A. B.S. in Bus., Miami U., Oxford, Ohio, 1941. Buyer John Shillato Co., Cin., 1941-44, Stix, Baer & Fuller, St. Louis, 1945-49; owner, pres. Martha Rounds Slimnastics, St. Louis, 1962—, Martha Belle, Ltd., St. Louis, 1975—, Martha Rounds Acad. for Children, St. Louis, 1983—; dir. Mark Twain State Bank, Bridgeton, Mo. Bd. dirs. Delta Gamma Found., 1953-57; mem. aux. bd. St. Louis U. Hosps., 1967-75; co-chmn. Salvation Army Tree of Lights project, 1976-77; mem. pres.' adv. cabinet Girl Scouts U.S., 1980. Recipient Shield award Delta Gamma Found., 1983; named Woman of Yr., Nat. Fedn. Bus. and Profl. Women's Club, 1979. Home: 12 Southcote St Brentwood MO 63144 Office: Martha Belle Ltd 1801 Parkridge Brentwood MO 63144

ROUNDTREE, JACQUELINE WASHINGTON, public relations executive, government official, consultant; b. Rock Hill, S.C., Dec. 19, 1949; d. Jack H. Washington and Mary (Washington) McGhee; m. Joe L. Bolder, Oct. 17, 1969 (div. 1983); m. Eugene V.N. Roundtree, Nov. 12, 1983; 1 child, Mary Margaret. B.A., Howard U., 1971, Ph.D., 1975. Reporter, editor Washington Star, 1969-78; part-time coll. instr. Howard U., Washington, 1975-81; spl. asst. sec. Dept. Commerce, Washington, 1978-80; dep. chief pub. affairs Minority Bus. Devel. Agy., Washington, 1980-82; regional; pub. affairs officer HUD, Boston, 1983—; pub. relations cons. United Community Planning Corp. Boston, 1982-83, All-Stainless Corp., Hingham, Mass., 1982—. Bd. dirs. Urban League Guild Eastern Mass., 1982—; Md. state commr. Internat. Women's Yr., 1977-78; vol. United Way Mass. Bay, 1984—; bd. dirs. Mass. Assn. for Mental Health, 1985—, chmn. communications com., 1984—. Recipient Balt./Washington Newspaper Guild Front Page award for news series, 1972; named Outstanding Employee, HUD, 1985. Mem. Women in Communications (bd. dirs., newsletter editor 1985), Howard U. Alumni Club, Alpha Kappa Alpha, Gamma Sigma Sigma (Alumnus of Yr. 1981). Republican. Baptist. Avocations: reading, writing; golf. Home: 108 Heritage Ln East Weymouth MA 02189 Office: HUD John F Kennedy Fed Bldg Room 800 Boston MA 02114

ROUNTREE, ELIZABETH COFFEE, librarian; b. Alto, Ga., July 13, 1937; A.B. in English, Piedmont Coll., 1958; M.A., U. Ill., 1959; Diploma Advanced Studies Librarianship, Emory U., 1971; M.P.A. U. New Orleans, 1984. Dir., Piedmont Coll. Library, 1959-65, N.E. Ga. Regional Library, 1965-72, Brunswick-Glynn County Regional Library, 1972-77; asst. librarian New Orleans Pub. Library, 1977-83; dir. St. Tammany Parish Library, 1984—. Contbr. articles to profl. jours. Mem. ALA, S.W. Library Assn., La. Library Assn., Greater New Orleans Library Club, Beta Phi Mu. Address: St Tammany Parish Library 402 N Jefferson Ave Covington LA 70433*

ROUNTREE, MARY MARTIN, educator; b. Atlanta, Sept. 26, 1931; d. Robert Emory and Mary (Thompson) Martin; A.B., U. Ga., 1952, M.A. in French, 1954; M.A. in English, U. Pitts., 1963, Ph.D. in English, 1965; m. Dec. 18, 1953; children—Ashley Everett, Meredith Martin. Asst. prof. English and Am. studies Mt. Holyoke Coll., South Hadley, Mass., from 1966, then assoc. prof., now prof.; Fulbright prof. U. Toulouse (France), 1970-71, U. Tunis (Tunisia), 1981-82; lectr., Africa. Mem. MLA, South Atlantic MLA, Phi Beta Kappa. Democrat. Research, publs. on fiction Conrad Aiken, poetry of Jean de Boschere. Home: 19 Hadley St South Hadley MA 01075 Office: Dept English Mount Holyoke Coll South Hadley MA 01075

ROUP, BRENDA JACOBS, nurse, army officer; b. Petersburg, Va., July 8, 1948; d. Eugene Thurman and Sarah Ann (Williams) Jacobs; m. Clarence James Roup, May 8, 1976. B.S.N., Med. Coll. Va., Richmond, 1970; M.S.N., Cath. U. Am., 1977. Commd. 2d lt. U.S. Army, 1970, advanced through grades to maj., 1980; chief infection control Brooke Army MEDCEN, San Antonio, 1983-86; chief infection control Walter Reed MEDCEN, Washington, 1986—; nurse con. in infection control to U.S. Army Surgeon Gen., 1986—. Mem. Assn. Practitioners in Infection Control, Assn. Mil. Surgeons, Sigma Theta Tau. Jewish. Avocations: reading; swimming; cooking. Office: Walter Reed Army Med Ctr 16th St Washington DC 20307

ROUPE, BARBARA DOYLE, lawyer; b. Oakland, Calif., May 27, 1937; d. Morris MacKnight and Juliet (Clapp) Doyle; m. George Allen Roupe, Sept. 12, 1959; children—Julie, Thomas Allen. B.A., Stanford U., 1959, J.D., 1976. Bar:

Calif. 1976. Ptnr., Kelley & Roupe, San Jose, Calif., 1976-78; assoc. Adams & Etienne, Saratoga, Calif., 1978—; mem. adv. council Community Found., Santa Clara County, Calif., 1978—, Peninsula Open Space Trust, Menlo Park, Calif., 1978-80, 83—. Bd. dirs. Villa Montessori Sch., San Jose, 1968-70, San Jose Mus. Art, 1976-78, Peninsula Open Space Trust, Menlo Park, 1980-83; mem. Jr. League San Jose. Mem. ABA, Calif. State Bar, Santa Clara County Bar Assn. Republican. Episcopalian. Club: Saratoga Tennis (dir.).

ROURKE, ROSEMARIE FRITSCHI, plastics co. exec.; b. Karlsruhe, W.Ger., Nov. 17, 1942; d. Ernst and Annemarie Fritschi; abitur Lessinggymnasium, Karlsruhe, 1962; m. Lowndes Edward Rourke, Mar. 19, 1964; 1 dau., Loren Lynn. Mgr., Berlitz Sch. Langs., Karlsruhe, 1962-67; chief adminstr. Freedman Bros., Bridgeport, Conn., 1967-72; controller Norfield Corp., Danbury, Conn., 1972-74, v.p., 1974-78, v.p., gen. mgr. Norfield div. Fallek Chem. Co., 1978-82, pres., 1982—; dir., sec. Corp. Devel. Systems, Inc. Mem. Am. Mgmt. Assn. Republican. Roman Catholic. Patentee plastics. Office: 36 Kenosia Ave Danbury CT 06810

ROUSE, BEATRICE A., epidemiologist; b. Easton, Pa.; d. Paul and Teresa Arcadi. B.A. summa cum laude, U. Fla., 1957, M.Ed., 1964; Ph.D., U. N.C., 1980. Research assoc. U. N.C. Sch. Medicine, Chapel Hill, 1964-69, Ctr. for Alcohol Studies, 1969-80; research asst. prof. Boston U. Sch. Medicine, 1980-82; epidemiologist VA Med. Ctr., Durham, N.C., 1983, Nat. Inst. Drug Abuse, Rockville, Md., 1983—, vis. scholar, 1980-82; cons. Dept. Def., Washington, 1984—; mem. med. reimbursement ADAMHA, Rockville, 1983-84. Editor: Drinking-Alcohol Use in American Society, 1978. Contbr. articles to profl. publs., chpt. to book. Mem. Disabled Vets. Comdrs. Club, Washington, 1984—; charter mem. Nat. Mus. Women in Arts, Washington, 1985—. Fellow USPHS, 1974-75, 76-77. Mem. Acad. Behavioral Medicine Research, N.Y. Acad. Scis., AAAS, Soc. Epidemiologic Research, Am. Pub. Health Assn., Nat. Assn. Female Execs. Club: Parklawn Sailing Assn. Md. Avocations: volunteer teaching. Office: 11-A-55 Parklawn Bldg 5600 Fishers Ln Rockville MD 20857

ROUSE, CORA ELIZABETH, retail store executive; b. Kinston, N.C., Aug. 10, 1960; d. Raymond Edward and Bethenia Leora (Maye) R. Student York Coll., 1978-79, Wagner Coll., 1981-84. Asst. tchr. Merrick Y Day Care, Jamaica, N.Y., 1978-79; supr. Floreal, N.Y. Inc., Jamaica, 1983-85; owner, operator Lu Ray's, Albany, N.Y., 1985—. Youth coordinator Godian Fellowship Ch., Jamaica, 1983—; cons. Godian Food Ctr.; bd. dirs. Christian Ch. Movement, N.Y.C., 1983—. Mem. Nat. Assn. Female Execs., Actor's Workshop. Democrat. Avocations: theatre; bowling; opera; ice skating. Home: 135-27 129 St S Ozone Park New York NY 11420

ROUSE, DORIS JANE, research institute executive; b. Greensboro, N.C., Oct. 3, 1948; d. Welby Corbett and Nadia Elizabeth (Grainger) R.; B.A. in Chemistry, Duke U., 1970, Ph.D. in Physiology and Pharmacology, 1980; m. Blake Shaw Wilson, Jan. 6, 1974; 1 dau., Nadia Jacqueline Wilson. Sci. instr. Peace Corps, Liberia, 1970-71; research scientist Burroughs Wellcome Co., Research Triangle Park, N.C., 1971-76; dir. biomed. applications team NASA, Research Triangle Inst., Research Triangle Park, 1976-83, dir. Ctr. for Tech. Applications, 1983—; adj. asst. prof. U. N.C. Sch. Medicine, 1983—; adminstr. wheelchair standards com. Am. Nat. Standards Inst., 1984—; cons. VA. Mem. adv. bd. Assn. Retarded Citizens. Recipient group achievement award NASA, 1979. Mem. Assn. Advancement Med. Instrumentation, Rehab. Engring. Soc. N.Am., Am. Soc. Aging (tech. adv. bd. 1983—), Am. Congress Rehab. Medicine. Club: Triangle Dive. Contbr. articles profl. jours. Home: 2410 Wrightwood Ave Durham NC 27705 Office: PO Box 12194 Research Triangle Park NC 27709

ROUSE, ELOISE MEADOWS, foundation executive; b. Shreveport, La., July 22, 1931; d. Curtis Washington and Lucille Eloise (Loyd) Meadows; m. Dudley Lee Rouse, Aug. 26, 1952; children—Deborah L., Lee, Elizabeth M. B.Mus. Ed., Baylor U., 1952. 1st grade tchr. Brentwood Elementary Sch., Austin, Tex., 1953-55; v.p., dir., mem. grants rev. com. The Meadows Found., Dallas, 1979—. Mem. honor bd. New Horizons Ranch & Center Home for Troubled Youth, Goldthwaite, Tex.; mem. exec. bd. Meadows Sch. of the Arts, So. Meth. U.; mem. exec. com., bd. dirs. Dallas Summer Musicals, mem. adv. com. Baylor U. Sch. Music; mem. Baylor U. Devel. Council, Dallas Mus. Art; active First Bapt. Ch. Dallas. Mem. Village Gardeners Garden Club (1st v.p.), Wadley Guild, Marianne Scruggs Garden Club (Crystal Charity Ball com.), Park Cities Hist. Soc., Dallas Summer Musicals Guild, DAR, Internat. Platform Assn., Nat. Trust Historic Preservation. Clubs: Dallas Country (Women's Tennis Assn.), Dallas Women's; Tournament Players, Ponte Vedra (Fla.). Home: 4540 Lorraine Ave Dallas TX 75205 Office: The Meadows Found 2922 Swiss Ave Dallas TX 75204

ROUSE, JACQUELINE ANNE, history educator, editor; b. Roseland, Va., Feb. 1, 1950; d. John Henry and Fannie (Thompson) R. B.A., Howard U., 1972; M.A., Atlanta U., 1973; Ph.D., Emory U., 1983. Sr. instr. Palm Beach Jr. Coll., Lake Worth, Fla., 1973-78; guest lectr. Ga. Inst. Tech., Atlanta, 1983; asst. prof. history Morehouse Coll., Atlanta, 1983—; guest lectr. Jackson State U., 1984; panelist NEH, Washington, 1985. Editorial intern Jour. of Negro History, 1979-83, asst. editor, 1983—. Smithsonian Instn. fellow 1982, 83; NEH fellow, 1984; grantee United Negro Coll. Fund, 1985, Mellon Found., 1985. Mem. Assn. Black Women Historians (regional dir. 1984—), Assn. Social and Behavioral Scientists (mem. exec. council 1984—), Assn. Study Afro-Am. Life and History, So. Hist. Assn., Nat. Women's Studies Assn., Howard U. Alumni Assn. Democrat. Baptist. Avocations: reading, spa-aerobics, writing, music. Home: 887 F Gatehouse Dr Decatur GA 30032

ROUSE, JOHNNIE ANITA, automated data processing adminstr.; b. Liberty, S.C., June 5, 1943; d. John Henry and Bernice (McDowell) R.; B.S., Howard U., 1965; M.A., Am. U., 1967. Computer specialist Dept. Army, Washington, 1966-72, Bur. Labor Stats., Dept. Labor, Washington, 1972-74; chief br. employment service data systems D.C. Dept. Manpower, Washington, 1974-79; chief div. mgmt. data systems D.C. Dept. Employment Services, 1979—; dir. Black Ski, Inc.; pres. Diversified Interiors. Vol. tutor for jr. high and high sch. students; vol. hospitality coms., local hosps. Recipient plaque for outstanding performance D.C. Dept. Manpower, 1976, Performance award, 1978; also numerous commendations for systems designed, 1968-81. Mem. Internat. Assn. Personnel in Employment Security, Automated Data Processing Mgrs. Assn., Nat. Assn. Female Execs., Delta Sigma Theta. Democrat. Baptist. Office: Dept Employment Services/OMIDS Room 411 500 C St NW Washington DC 20785

ROUSE, SARAH DASHIELL, motion picture and broadcasting librarian; b. Richmond, Va., Nov. 5, 1949; d. Parke Shepherd and Elizabeth Marshall (Gayle) R.; m. Patrick Joseph Sheehan, Apr. 16, 1984. B.A., Randolph-Macon Woman's Coll., 1971; M.L.S., Cath. U. Am., 1974. Film catalog editorial asst. Am. Film Inst., Washington, 1974-75; film archivist London Film Sch., Eng., 1975-76; film/TV cataloger Library of Congress, Washington, 1976-82, motion picture and broadcasting archivist and librarian, 1982—. Editor: Thirty Years of Television: TV Holdings in the Library of Congress, 1985. Contbr. articles and film revs. to library jours. Blood donation keyworker ARC, Washington, 1981—. Mem. On-Line Visual Catalogers, Library of Congress Profl. Assn. Democrat. Episcopalian. Office: Motion Picture Film & Recorded Sound Div Library of Congress 10 1st St SE Washington DC 20540

ROUSE, SUE THOMPSON, emeritus educator; b. Ulman, Mo., Aug. 28, 1920; d. Clyde Waldo and Retta (Darr) Thompson; A.B., Harris Tchrs. Coll., St. Louis, 1942; M.A., U. N.C., Chapel Hill, 1950; Ed.D. (fellow 1960), George Peabody Coll., Nashville, 1963; postgrad. U. Minn.; m. Linwood I. Rouse, Aug. 29, 1945 (div.). Elem. sch. tchr., Mo. and N.C., 1947-59; mem. faculty U. S.C., Columbia, 1961—, prof. edn., 1974-86, disting. prof. emerita, 1986—; cons. infield. Chmn., S.C. Commn. Ministry for Christian Ch. (Disciples of Christ), 1973-80; mem. regional bd. Christian Chs. in S.C., 1979-83, moderator, 1980-82; pres. Regional Assembly Christian Chs. in S.C., 1977-78; mem. nat. adv. com. ministry Christian Ch., 1978-82, nat. bd. dirs. Div. Homeland Ministries, 1981-87. Served with USCGR, 1943-46. Fellow Am. Assn. Mental Deficency; mem. NEA (life), S.C. Edn. Assn., Council Exceptional Children, S.C. Psychol. Assn., S.C. Mental Health Assn., Nat. Audubon Soc., Delta Kappa Gamma, Phi Delta Kappa. Democrat. Author articles in field, chpts. in books.

ROUSE, SUSAN KINGSNORTH, radio station executive, computer consultant; b. Memphis, Aug. 27, 1943; d. Neil George and Louise (Harlow) Kingsnorth; m. Ray Richard Rouse, July 30, 1966. A.A., Stephens Coll., 1963; B.S. in Elem. Edn., Syracuse U., 1965; M.S. in Reading, U. Bridgeport, 1971. Cert. tchr., N.Y., Conn., Mo. Tchr. West Hartford Pub. Schs., Conn., 1965-66, Knob Noster Pub. Schs., Mo., 1966-68, Springfield Pub. Schs., Mo., 1968-69, Greenwich Pub. Schs., Conn., 1969-83; tchr., cons. computers Tipton Pub. Schs., Mo., 1983—; co-owner, program dir. Sta. KZMO AM & FM, California, Mo., 1983—, notary public, 1984—. Bd. dirs. Moniteau County Cancer Soc., California, Mo., 1985—. Mem. Nat. Assn. Broadcasters, Mo. Broadcasters Assn., California C. of C. Clubs: Colony Walking Horse Assn. New England (bd. dirs., pres. 1974-83), New England Walking Horse Assn. (bd. dirs., 1974-83). Avocations: riding; swimming; woodworking; golf. Home: Country Club Rd California MO 65018 Office: KZMO AM & FM PO Box 307 California MO 65018

ROUSH, ANNE FRANCES, social worker; b. Carroll, Iowa, Nov. 20, 1930; d. Lawrence James and Frances Xavier (Whalen) Lane; R.N., Mercy Hosp. Sch. Nursing, Des Moines, 1951; B.S., St. Louis U., 1953; M.S.W., U. Hawaii, 1968; m. Howard Patrick Roush, Aug. 6, 1955; children—Mary Frances, Louise Catherine, Jenny Elizabeth, Frederick Lawrence, Martin Louis. Head nurse Barnes Hosp., asst. in nursing Washington U., St. Louis, 1953-54; instr. St. Marys Hosp. Sch. Nursing, Tucson, 1955-56; psychiat. social worker So. Ariz. Mental Health Center, Tucson, 1968—, mental health treatment team leader, 1982—; field instr. Sch. Social Work Ariz. State U., Tempe; cons., co-founder, mem. bd. COPE, 1975-81. Recipient Field Instr. award, 1982. Mem. Nat. Assn. Social Workers (chmn. nominations com. Ariz. chpt. 1982-84), Acad. Cert. Social Workers. Mem. Holy Resurrection Orthodox Ch. Research in manpower in social work, 1968. Home: 6260 N Oasis St Tucson AZ 85704 Office: 1930 E 6th St Tucson AZ 85719

ROUSS, RUTH, lawyer; b. Des Moines, May 21, 1914; d. Simon Jacob and Dora (Goldin) R.; m. Dennis O'Rourke, Jan. 21, 1940; children—Susan Jerene, Kathleen Frances, Brian Jay, Dennis Robert, Ruth Elizabeth, Dolores Ann. B.A., Drake U., 1934, J.D., 1937. Bar: Iowa 1937, U.S. Supreme Ct. 1945, Colo. 1946, D.C. 1971. Counsel Jay N. Darling, Des Moines, 1937-38; atty. Office of Solicitor, USDA, Washington, 1938-45, asst. to solicitor, 1940-45; sole practice, Colorado Springs, Colo., 1946, 50-69; ptnr. Williams and Rouss, Colorado Springs, 1946-50; assoc. Sutton, Shull and O'Rourke, Colorado Springs and Washington, 1969-72; ptnr. Rouss and O'Rourke, Colorado Springs and Washington, 1972—. Active in Colorado Opera Festival, 1976-78, Colorado Springs Chorale, 1976—; bd. dirs., chmn. Human Relations Com., Colorado Springs, 1968-73, Colorado Springs Community Planning and Research Council, 1972-78. Mem. World Affairs Council, Urban League, Am. Lung Assn., Com. Protection Human Rights, El Paso County Bar Assn., Colo. Bar Assn., D.C. Bar Assn., Am. Law Inst., Internat. Fedn. Women Lawyers, Phi Beta Kappa. Home: 8 Heather Dr Colorado Springs CO 80906 Office: Rouss & O'Rourke 231 E Vermijo Ave Colorado Springs CO 80903

ROVELSTAD, MATHILDE VERNER, educator; b. Kempten, Ger., Aug. 12, 1920; d. George and Therese (Hohl) Hotter; came to U.S., 1951, naturalized, 1953; Ph.D., U. Tübingen, 1953; M.S. in L.S., Catholic U. Am., 1960; m. Howard Rovelstad, Nov. 23, 1970. Cataloger, Mt. St. Mary's Coll., Los Angeles, 1953; sch. librarian Yoyogi Elementary Sch., Tokyo, 1954-56; mem. faculty Cath. U. Am., 1960—, prof. library sci., 1975—; vis. prof. U. Montreal, 1969. Research grantee German Acad. Exchange Service, 1969. Mem. ALA (internat. relations com. 1977-79), Internat. Fedn. Library Assns. and Instns. (standing adv. com. library schs. 1975-81), Assn. for Library and Info. Sci. Edn. Author: Bibliotheken in den Vereingten Staaten, 1974; Bibliography: An Inquiry Into Its Definition and Designations, 1980. Contbr. profl. jours. Home: 11 Banbury Rd Gibson Island MD 21056 Office: Sch Library and Info Sci Catholic Univ Am Washington DC 20064

ROVET, JOANNE FRANCES, psychologist; b. Montreal, Que., Can., Feb. 24, 1946; d. David George and Jane (Adelman) Rigler; B.Sc. magna cum laude, York U., 1968; Ph.D., U. Toronto, 1974; m. Ernest Rovet, Dec. 26, 1967; children—Benjamin, Heather, Jennifer. Asst. prof. Ont. Inst. Studies in Edn., Toronto, 1974-75; postdoctoral fellow Hosp. Sick Children, Toronto, 1975-78, research asso., 1978-83, asst. prof., 1983-86; asst. prof. spl. edn. Ont. Inst. Studies in Edn., 1983-86, assoc. prof., 1986—. Recipient Lionel Charlesworth prize York U., 1965; York U. scholar, 1964, Can. Council doctoral fellow, 1971-73, Med. Research Council postdoctoral fellow, 1975-78, Ont. Mental Health Found. fellow, 1981-82; Health and Welfare Can. research scholar, 1983—. Mem. Soc. Research Child Devel., Behavior Genetics Soc., Internat. Neuropsychol. Soc., Am. Psychol. Assn., Can. Psychol. Assn., Ont. Bd. Examiners Psychology, Turner Syndrome Soc. Contbr. articles to profl. jours. Home: 399 Glengrove Ave Toronto ON M5N 1W8 Canada Office: 555 University Ave Toronto ON M5G 1X8 Canada

ROWE, DOLORES WINIFRED, educational consultant; b. Turkeyford, Okla., Sept. 1, 1918; d. James Ora and Maude Mae (Phenix) Rowe. Student NE Okla. Jr. Coll., 1936-38; B.S., Northeast State Coll., Tahlequah, Okla., 1942; M.S., U. Okla., 1949. Elem. and jr. high tchr., pub. schs., Wyandotte, Okla., 1938-43, Seneca, Mo., 1943; asst. supr. social scis. NE State Coll., Tahlequah, 1943-48, supr. social sci. dept., 1948-54, asst. dir. reading lab., 1954-56, dir., 1956-57; ednl. cons. Houghton Mifflin Co., Boston and Dallas, 1957—. Contbr. stories and adaptations to reading textbooks, 1960-64. Vol. worker local draft bd., World War II. Mem. Cherokee Hist. Soc., AAUW, Delta Kappa Gamma. Republican. Methodist. Mailing address: 9042 Villa Park Circle Dallas TX 75225

ROWE, DOROTHY LEE, educator; b. Huntington, W.Va., Oct. 30, 1920; d. McKinley Leander and Mabel Mae (Ferris) Rowe; B.S. in Edn., Ohio U., 1941; postgrad. Harvard Grad. Sch. Edn., 1953, Purdue U., summer, 1956; M.A., U. Chgo., 1958; postgrad. Bowdoin Coll., summer, 1962. Tchr. math. Chesapeake, Ohio, 1941-43, Ironton (Ohio) High Sch., 1943-46, Gallia Acad. High Sch., Gallipolis, Ohio, 1946-58; instr. math. Miami U., Oxford, Ohio, 1958-73, sr. instr., 1973-78, prof. emeritus math. and stats., 1978—. Nat. adv. bd. Am. Security Council, 1978-86; sustaining mem. Republican Nat. Com., 1971-86; active McCullough-Hyde Hosp. Aux., Friends of Lane Public Library. Ford Found. fellow, 1952-53; Gen. Electric fellow, summer, 1956; NSF fellow, 1957, 58, summer 1962. Mem. AAUW, AAUP, Math. Assn. Am., NEA, Nat. Ret. Tchrs. Assn., Ohio Ret. Tchrs. Assn., Pi Lambda Theta, Pi Mu Epsilon, Delta Kappa Gamma, Kappa Delta Pi. Republican. Presbyterian. Address: 4741 Nottingham Court Ashland KY 41101

ROWE, GENEVA LASSITER, psychotherapist, counseling center administrator; b. Atlanta, Aug. 11, 1927; d. Hoyt Cleveland and Tinie (Gresham) Lassiter; m. Fred Earnest Rowe, May 3, 1958; children—Carol, Vickie, Randall. B.A., Oglethorpe U., 1968; M.S.W., U. Ga., 1970; Ph.D., Fla. State U., 1978; C.P.C., Parkwood Hosp. Accredited Acad. Cert. Social Workers; lic. marriage and family therapist, Ga. Alcohol and drug counselor Georgian Clinic, Atlanta, 1968; outpatient counselor DeKalb Guidance Clinic, Atlanta, 1969; protective services supr. DeKalb Family and Children Services, Decatur, Ga., 1970-72; marriage and family therapist Fla. State U., 1977; lectr. sociology Oglethorpe U., 1978-81; psychotherapist, dir. Northeast Counseling Ctr., P.C., Atlanta, Marietta and Lawrenceville, Ga., 1978—; clin. supr. master's students in practicum Ga. State U., 1980—; allied health profl. CPC Parkwood Hosp. Fellow Am. Orthopsychiat. Assn., Internat. Council Sex Edn. and Parenthood; mem. Am. Assn. Marriage and Family Therapy (clin. mem.), AAUW, Ga. Assn. Marriage and Family Therapy (pub. relations chmn. 1984-86), Gwinnett County C. of C., Cobb County C. of C., Young Women of Arts. Methodist. Home: 2005 Woodsdale Rd NE Atlanta GA 30324 Office: Northeast Counseling Ctr PC 2995 Lawrenceville Hwy Lawrenceville GA 30245 also 3823 Roswell Rd NE Marietta GA 30062

ROWE, MAE IRENE, investment company executive; b. Gardner, Mass., Dec. 6, 1927; d. Clifford Wesley and Mertie (Moore) Mann; m. Willard Chase Rowe, June 18, 1951 (div. 1979); children—Gail B. Rowe Simons, Bruce C. B.A. with high honor, Am. Internat. Coll., 1949. Cert. real property adminstr. Social worker City of Montague, Turners Falls, Mass., 1949-51; mgr. Park Investment Co., Cleve., 1979—. Pres., v.p., bd. dirs. Park Ridge Counseling Service, Ill., 1972-76; clerk Village of Kildeer, Ill., 1977; bd. dirs. Maine Township Mental Health Service, Park Ridge, 1975-76. Mem. Cleve. Bldg. Owners Mgrs. Assn. (mem. edn. com. 1983—), Bldg. Owners Mgrs. Assn. Internat., Soc. Real Property Adminstrs. (cert.), LWV (v.p., mem. city adv. com. 1973-76), Republican. Unitarian. Club: Cleve. Racquet. Avocations: tennis; computer study and operation. Home: 34108 Chagrin Blvd Apt 5103 Moreland Hills OH 44022 Office: Park Investment Co 907 Park Bldg Cleveland OH 44114

ROWE, MARGARET STEED, hospital supply manager; b. Los Angeles, July 5, 1947; d. Robert Franklin and Margaret Anne (Martin) Steed; m. Charles R. Rowe, III, July 9, 1977; 1 dau., Courtney Renee. B.S., Calif. State U.-San Diego, 1970; M.S., U. Mo.-Columbia, 1975. Dietetic intern Colo. State U., 1970-71; adminstrv. dietitian U. Mo., Columbia, 1971-74, teaching asst., 1974-75; food systems mgr. Am. Dietary Products div. Am. Hosp. Supply Corp., Santa Ana, Calif., 1975-82, dietary systems mgr., 1982-83; nat. dietary systems mgr., McGaw Park, Ill., 1983-84, nat. systems mgr., 1984—; speaker profl. confs. Mem. Am. Dietetic Assn., Dietitians in Bus. and Industry, Women in Bus. Home: 1448 Lawrence Ave Lake Forest IL 60045 Office: 1425 Waukegan Rd McGaw Park IL 60085

ROWE, PATRICIA J., medical technologist; b. Carbondale, Pa., July 17, 1941; d. John Lucas and Glennice Edith (Schaeffer) Gershey; m. David Charles Rowe, Aug. 17, 1963; children—Dawn, David. B.S., Denver U., 1963; postgrad. Georgetown U., 1962, Ft. Lewis Coll., 1965. Cert. tchr., N.Mex. Radioisotopes lab. asst. Denver U., 1963; med. technologist Mercy Hosp., Durango, Colo., 1964-66; med. technologist U. Colo., 1966—, assoc. instr., 1971-76, rep. staff council, 1984—, chmn. staff council award com., 1985; mem. student mgmt. trainee program Front Range Community Coll., Broomfield, Colo., 1985—. Author: (course manual) Introduction to Medical Technology, 1971. Mem. vice chancellor search com. U. Colo., 1980; vol. prop. mgr. puppet program Bethany Baptist Ch., Boulder, 1984. Denver U. scholar, 1959; Ford Found fellow, 1963. Mem. Am. Chem. Soc., Colo. Assn. Continuing Med. Lab. Edn., Phi Alpha Theta. Republican. Avocations: writing; art. Home: 3775 Silver Plume Ln Boulder CO 80303

ROWE-MAAS, BETTY LOU, real estate investor; b. San Jose, Calif., Apr. 2, 1925; d. Horace DeWitt and Lucy Belle (Spiker) Rowe; children—Terry Lee, Clifford Lindsay, Craig Harrison, Joan Louise. Real estate investor, Saratoga, Calif., 1968—. Mem. Nat. Trust Hist. Preservation, Smithsonian Instn., San Jose Mus., Saratoga Mus., San Francisco Mus., Los Gatos Mus., San Jose Symphony, Moltalvo; bd. dirs. Valley Inst. Theater Arts, San Jose City Ctr. Ballet, 1984-86; treas. Route 85 Task Force, 1978—; treas. Traffic Relief for Saratoga; mem. Saratoga Good Govt., 1970—. Mem. LWV. Clubs: Commonwealth of California, Los Gatos Republican, Saratoga Country. Home: 20360 Saratoga Los Gatos Rd Saratoga CA 95070

ROWEN, RUTH HALLE, musicologist, educator; b. N.Y.C., Apr. 5, 1918; d. Louis and Ethel (Fried) Halle; B.A., Barnard Coll., 1939; M.A., Columbia U., 1941, Ph.D., 1948; m. Seymour M. Rowen, Oct. 13, 1940; children—Mary Helen Rowen Obelkevich, Louis Halle Rowen. Mgr. ednl. dept. Carl Fischer, Inc., N.Y.C., 1954-63; assoc. prof. musicology CCNY, 1967-72, prof., 1972—; mem. doctoral faculty in musicology City U. N.Y., 1967—. Mem. ASCAP, Am. Musicol. Soc., Music Library Assn., Coll. Music Soc., Nat. Fedn. Music Clubs (nat. musicianship chmn. 1962-74, nat. young artist auditions com. 1964-74, N.Y. state chmn. Young Artist Auditions 1981, Liberty Dist. coordinator 1984, N.Y. state pres. 1985—), Phi Beta Kappa. Author: Early Chamber Music, 1948, reprinted, 1974; (with Adele T. Katz) Hearing—Gateway to Music, 1959; (with William Simon) Jolly Come Sing and Play, 1956; Music Through Sources and Documents, 1979; (with Mary Rowen Obelkevich) Instant Piano, 1979, 80, 83, Beethoven's Parody of Nature, 1984; Glinka's Tour of Folk Modes, 1984. Home: 115 Central Park W New York NY 10023

ROWER, MARGARETTA FRANCISCA, audiologist, speech pathologist, educator; b. N.Y.C; d. Alfred H. and Katherine (Messmer) R.; B.S., SUNY, New Paltz, 1964; M.S., Ithaca Coll., 1972; postgrad. (Noyes Found. fellow), Cornell U., 1972-74; 1 dau., Nancy. Tchr. pub. schs., N.Y. State, 1964-72; audiologist, mobile audiology clinic Ithaca (N.Y.) Coll., 1972-73, instr., clin. supr., dept. speech pathology and audiology, 1973-75, grad. instr., part-time, 1975—; chief of speech pathology and audiology Broome Devel. Services, N.Y. State Dept. Mental Hygiene, Binghamton, N.Y., 1975—; tchr. Dept. Def., Okinawa (Japan) and Würzburg (Germany), 1981-82. adj. prof. Broome Community Coll., Dept. Def., Bitburg Air Base, W.Ger., 1984—; Fruehauff Found. grantee, summer 1971; lic. audiologist, N.Y. State; lic. tchr., N.Y. State. Mem. Am. Assn. Mental Deficiency, Am. Speech and Hearing Assn. (cert. of clin. competency), Assn. Speech Pathologists and Audiologists of Mental Hygiene. Contbr. articles to profl. jours. Home: 1005 Baylor Dr Binghamton NY 13903 Office: Bitburg American Schools DODDS Federal Republic of Germany APO 09132

ROWLAND, CAROLE ANN, air force officer; b. Oskaloosa, Iowa, Mar. 30, 1952; d. Willis Marion and Majorie Ann (Lamb) R. B.S. in Edn., Northeast Mo. State U., 1975, M.A. in Phys. Scis., 1976; grad. Squadron Officer Sch., Montgomery, Ala., 1985. Prof. sci. Northeast Mo. State U., Kirksville, 1975-76; asst. maintenance supr. Davis-Monthan AFB, Ariz., 1978-81; chief equipment allowance sect. Hdqrs. TAC, Langley AFB, Va., 1981-84; officer-in-charge maintenance br. 363 Tactical Fighter Wing, Shaw AFB, S.C., 1984-85, maintenance supr., 1985—, officer's club rep., 1985—; resident cons. for mil. women Davis-Monthan AFB, Ariz., 1980-81. Editor film Grand Canyon Adventure, 1975; also articles; mural artist. 4-H leader, Sumter, S.C., 1985—; base donation organizer ARC, Tucson, 1978-81. Served to capt. USAF, 1976—. Mem. Nat. Assn. Female Execs., Fed. Women's Program (program and publicity com.), Nat. Wildlife Fedn. (life), Nat. Parks and Conservation Assn. (life), Alpha Sigma Tau, Sigma Zeta. Avocations: photography; basketball; racquetball; art; softball.

ROWLAND, JEFFIE LANDERS, artist; b. Murray Cross, Ala., July 10, 1924; d. Eli Jefferson and Pearl Dorsey (Baskin) Landers; B.S., Jacksonville (Ala.) State Tchrs. Coll., 1945; postgrad. U. Ga., Athens; pupil of Lamar Dodd; m. Jack Lamb Rowland, Dec. 23, 1947; children—Mary Jane, Nancy Eugenia, Alice Alden. Elem. sch. tchr., Athens, 1947-48, 1st schs. art supr., 1948-52; 1st schs. art supr. Clarke County schs., Athens, 1952-62; art cons. North Ga. elem. schs., 1962-80; chmn. docents U. Ga. Mus. Art, Athens, 1978—, sch. coordinator for docents program, 1981—, also mem. bd. Friends of Mus.; illustrator Belle Meade Fox Hunt, 1985-86; one-woman show Jacksonville State Tchrs. Coll., 1948; group exhbns. include High Mus. Art, Atlanta, S.E. Art Assn. Mem. show com. Renfrew Hunter-Jumper Shows. Recipient Belle Meade Fox Hunt Hammerhead award, 1982, Staff award, 1983; other art awards. Mem. DAR, Arts Alliance, Greater Atlanta Dressage Assn. (coordinator Pony club). Republican. Presbyterian. Club: Belle Meade Fox Hunt (Thomson, Ga.). Author articles in field; book: Fox Hunt Cartoons, 1983. Address: Beech Haven Athens GA 30606

ROWLAND, PATRICIA BRITTINGHAM, real estate broker; b. Guyton, Ga., July 14, 1941; d. Kenneth L. and Faye (McClelland) Brittingham; student DeKalb Coll., U. Ga.; m. Jimmie Dave Rowland; children—Philip Charles, Debora Faye, Jeffrey Allan. Various corp. sec.-treas. and controller positions, positions, 1970-78; pres. Charles S. Roberts & Co., Atlanta, 1978-82; office mgr., Salesperson Adams Realty Inc., Royston, Ga., 1982-84; real estate broker Pinehurst Realty Co., Lavonia, Ga., 1984-86, WaterMark Realty Co., 1986—; corp. sec. Spalding & Co., Securities Brokers, Atlanta, 1980-81. Democrat. Episcopalian. Home: 155 Teepee Ln Lavonia GA 30553 Office: WaterMark Realty Co PO Box 613 Lavonia GA 30553

ROWLEY, ELLEN SUSANNE, broadcast executive, consultant; b. San Francisco, July 8, 1951; d. Robert Norman and Florence Susanne (Curtis) Rowley. B.A. in Sociology, U. Calif.-Berkeley, 1974; M.B.A., Golden Gate U., 1980. C.P.A., Calif. Controller, bus. mgr. Audience Research and Devel., San Francisco, 1978-80; sr. tax cons. Touche Ross & Co., San Jose, Calif., 1980-83; asst. bus. mgr. UTV San Francisco, Inc., Sta. KBHK-TV, San Francisco, 1984—; cons. Burchardt & Assocs., Campbell, Calif., 1983—, Ellen S. Rowley, C.P.A., Fremont, Calif., 1983—. Chmn. Youth for a New Am., Sacramento, 1969. Calif. State scholar, 1969-71; Mary Phleger Meml. scholar, 1972. Mem. Am. Inst. C.P.A.'s, Calif. Soc. C.P.A.'s, Am. Mgmt. Assn., AAUW. Republican. Mem. Christian and Missionary Alliance Ch. Home: 889 Mowry Ave No 188 Fremont CA 94536 Office: UTV of San Francisco Inc KBHK-TV 420 Taylor St San Francisco CA 94536

ROWLEY, MAXINE LEWIS, educator, writer; b. Provo, Utah, Sept. 23, 1938; d. Max Thomas Lewis and Illa Lewis Sanford; B.A. (Ford Found. scholar, merit scholar), Brigham Young U., 1960; B.S., U. Utah, 1974; M.A., Utah State U., 1979; m. Arthur William Rowley, Sept. 23, 1960; children—

Anne, Jenefer. Promotion writer sta. KCPX-TV, 1960; extension home economist USDA, 1961; grad. asst. Brigham Young U., Provo, 1965; mgmt. trainee Deseret Book Co., Salt Lake City, 1967; chmn. dept. Patricia Stevens Career Coll., Salt Lake City, 1969; chmn. consumer and homemaking dept. Weber Sch. Dist., Roy, Utah, 1974, learning experience designer, 1975-78; mem. consumer and homemaking faculty Utah State U., Logan, 1978-79, spl. appointee to Utah State U. by Utah State Bd. Edn., 1978-86, cons. Utah Vocat. Bd. Edn., instrumental writer Utah State U. Found., 1979; mem. Faculty Brigham Young U., 1980; author texts and teachers guide CHECS, 1979; author curriculum guide Operation: Free Enterprise, 1977; author filmstrips on consumer econs. and career exploration, 1977. Active ward, stake and region positions Ch. of Jesus Christ of Latter-day Saints; leader 4-H Club, mem. councils and adv. bds.; leader Girl Scouts U.S.A., Young Homemakers; mem. State Text Book Evaluation Com., 1978-84, U. Utah Evaluation Com., 1979. Named Outstanding Leader Am. Edn., 1976, Nat. Tchr. of Yr., 1977, Outstanding Tchr. in Dept., Brigham Young U., 1985, 86. Mem. Nat. Assn. Vocat. Home Econs. Tchrs., Am. Home Econs. Assn. (cons., author yearbook 1934), Am. Vocat. Assn., NEA, Utah Home Econs. Assn., Utah Vocat. Assn., Utah Council for Improvement of Edn., Utah Edn. Assn. (award for womens' awareness task force project 1976), County Welfare Com., Home Econs. Edn. Assn., Vocat. Home Econs. Tchrs. (nat. chmn. public relations and legis. coms. 1978), Mortarboard (pres. 1960), Omicron Nu, Phi Kappa Phi, Spurs, Gamma Phi Omicron. Mem. Republican Party. Home: 3308 Charing Cross Rd West Jordan UT 84084 Office: Smith Family Life Bldg Brigham Young U Provo UT 84321

ROWLEY, ROSEMARIE MARGARET, executive search consulting firm manager; b. Oceanside, N.Y., Dec. 30, 1949; d. Michael Joseph and Elizabeth Ann (Cassidy) R. B.S., Central Conn. State U., 1971. Various staff positions, Ernst & Whinney, N.Y.C., 1976-81, supr., 1981-83, mgr., 1983—; mem. Vol. Urban Cons. League, N.Y.C., 1982—. Contbr. article to newspaper. Mem. Nat. Assn. Profl. and Corp. Recruiters, Am. Soc. Personnel Adminstrs. (nat. and N.Y.). Roman Catholic. Club: Cornell. Office: Ernst & Whinney 153 E 53rd St New York NY 10022

ROY, BABETTE CHARLOTTE, artist; b. N.Y.C., Apr. 29, 1922; d. Frederick Christian and Emma Josephine (Sengele) Maasch; m. Francis Albert Roy, May 27, 1944; 1 child, Allan Gregory. Cert., Famous Artists Sch., Westport, Conn., 197-173; student Traphagen Sch. Design, 1938-40, John Pike Watercolor Sch., 1970-78. Legal sec. Cravath, Swain & Moore, N.Y.C., 1941-44; census taker U.S. Census Bur., Orange County, N.Y., 1950; sec. Supt. Schs., Warwick, N.Y., 1954-65; artist, 1955—. One woman shows in Middletown, N.Y., 1983, Warwick, N.Y., 1965, 72, 80, Florida, N.Y., 1978, Goshen, N.Y., 1983; exhibited in group shows at Goshen, 1963-85, Newburgh, N.Y., 1980-85, N.Y.C., 1968, 70, Old Forge, N.Y., 1982; represented in permanent collections at Orange County Community Coll., Middletown, Pine Island, N.Y., Scottsdale, Ariz. Mem. Warwick Hist. Soc., N.Y., 1985, Warwick Beautification Com., 1985, Hosp. Aux., Warwick, 1985, Humane Soc., 1985. Recipient Dedication and Leadership award Orange County Art Fedn., 1982. Mem. Salmagundi Club, Hudson Valley Art Assn., Knickerbocker Artists, Orange County Watercolor Soc. (co-founder, pres. 1975-83), Am. Artists Profl. League, Orange County Art Fedn. (pres. 1976-80). Republican. Episcopalian. Club: Officers (West Point Mil. Acad.). Lodge: Parrish Mus. Avocations: reading; gardening; sailing; travel. Home: 3 Robin Brae Warwick NY 10990 also Pine Hall Mathews VA 23109

ROY, BARBARA JEAN, marine corps officer; b. Webster County, W.Va., Sept. 16, 1938; d. Ross Edward and Kathleen Louise (Aggleson) R.; B.S. in Recreation, Fairmont State Coll., 1960; postgrad. U. Va., 1961, Am. U., 1972-73. Commd. 2d lt. U.S. Marine Corps, 1960, advanced through grades to col., 1980; public affairs officer Marine Corps Schs., Quantico, Va., 1960-63; head, asst. head public affairs br. Hdqrs. 8th Marine Corps Dist., New Orleans, 1963-67; projects coordinator Def. Adv. Com. on Women in the Services, Office of Asst. Sec. Def., 1967-69, exec. sec., 1978-79; asst. G-1, Office of Asst. Chief of Staff G-1, Camp S.D. Butler, Okinawa, 1970-71; community relations officer, spl. projects officer, spl. asst. for women marine affairs div. info., Hdqrs. U.S. Marine Corps, Washington, 1971-74; dep. dir. Woman Officer Sch. Edn. Center, Quantico, 1974-75, asst. test and evaluation officer acad. dept., 1975, protocol officer hdqrs. edn. ctr. Marine Corps Devel. and Edn. Commn., Quantico, 1975-77; mil. asst. to asst. sec. def. for manpower, res. affairs and logistics Dept. Def., 1977-79; asst. dir., dir. Marine Corps Extension Sch., Hdqrs. Edn. Center, Quantico, 1979-81, asst. chief of staff for leadership instrn., 1980-81, asst. chief staff personnel and services, hdqrs. edn. ctr., 1981-82; recorder, presiding officer Naval Discharge Rev. Bd., Naval Council Personnel Bds., Washington, 1982—; mem. Augmentation/Retention Bd., Navy Phys. Rev. Council, Commd. Officers Mess Adv. Bd., Council of Advs. on Profl. Edn., Family Assistance Adv. Council, Gen. Ct.-Martial Bd. and numerous other bds. Mem. Quantico Mil-Civilian Community Relations Council; mem. Sleepy Hollow Citizens Assn.; active Young Republicans; life mem. Girl Scouts U.S.A. Decorated Def. Meritorious Service medal, Joint Services Commendation medal, Nat. Def. Service medal, Navy Meritorious Unit commendation. Mem. Nat. Assn. Female Execs., Nat. C. of C. for Women, Wolf Trap Farm Park (assoc.), Smithsonian Instn. (resident assoc.), Nat. Zoo (assoc.), U.S. Naval Acad. Athletic Assn., Fairfax County Police Dept. Neighborhood Watch Assn., Marine Corps Combat Corrs. Assn., Ret. Officers Assn., Marine Corps Assn., Woman Marines Assn. (life), Nat. Thespians Soc., Nat. Trust Hist. Preservation, Humane Soc. U.S., Washington Humane Soc., Statue of Liberty Ellis Island Found., Franklin Mint Collectors Soc., Sigma Sigma Sigma. Editorial bd. Marine Corps Gazette. Home: 6426 Eppard St Falls Church VA 22044 Office: Naval Council Personnel Bds Washington DC 22203

ROY, ELSIJANE TRIMBLE, judge; b. Lonoke, Ark., Apr. 2, 1916; d. Thomas Clark and Elsie Jane (Walls) Trimble; J.D., U. Ark., 1939; 1 child, James Morrison. Admitted to Ark. bar, 1939; mem. firm Reid, Evrard & Roy, Blytheville, Ark., 1947-54, Roy & Roy, Blytheville, 1954-63; atty. Ark. Revenue Dept., Little Rock, 1939-64; law clk. Ark. Supreme Ct., Little Rock, 1963-65; judge Pulaski County Circuit Ct., Little Rock, 1966; asst. atty. gen. State of Ark. Little Rock, 1967; sr. law clk. U.S. Dist. Ct., Little Rock and Ft. Smith, 1968-74; asso. justice Ark. Supreme Ct., Little Rock, 1975-77; U.S. dist. judge East and West Dists. of Ark., Little Rock, 1977—. Mem. med. adv. com. U. Ark. Med. Center, 1952-54; mem. chmn. com. Ark. Constnl. Commn., 1967-68. Committeewoman Democratic party 16th Jud. Dist., 1940-42; vice-chmn. Ark. Dem. State Com., 1946-48. Named Woman of Yr. for Ark., 1976; recipient Disting. Alumna award U. Ark., 1977. Mem. Nat. Assn. Women Lawyers, Ark. Bar Assn., Am. Assn. U. Women, Little Rock Women Lawyers (pres. 1939, 42), U. Ark. Alumni Assn. (dir. 1946-48), Ark. Women Lawyers (pres. 1940-1941), Mortar Bd., P.E.O., Chi Omega. Office: US Post Office and Courthouse PO Box 3255 600 W Capital Little Rock AR 72203

ROY, KAREN JAMES, computer engineer; b. Summit, N.J., Aug. 19, 1955; d. Arthur Richard, Jr. and Joyce Doyle (Murphy) R. Student Houston Community Coll., 1977-79, 81-82. Service sec. Palmetto Ford Truck Sales, Miami, Fla., 1974-75; credit and accounts receivable mgr. Isabell Gerhart Co., Houston, 1975-77; info. systems mgr. C.J. Thibodeaux & Co., Houston, 1978-84; data base engr. InteCom Inc., Allen, Tex., 1984-85, fin. analyst, 1985—; sec. Hewlett Packard-Greater Houston Regional Users Group, Houston, 1982-84. Mem. Women in Data Processing, Nat. Assn. Female Execs. Democrat. Roman Catholic. Home: 2500 Park Blvd 3Q Plano TX 75074 Office: 601 InteCom Dr Allen TX 75002

ROY, LOIS D., government official; b. Graniteville, Vt., Aug. 17, 1932; d. John K. and Blanche Morrison Campbell; student U. Vt., 1973-74; m. Donald G. Roy, Feb. 1, 1968 (dec.); children—Debra Jane, Gregory Scott. Clk., U.S. Post Office, 1951-52; sec., clerical supr. Immigration and Naturalization Service, U.S. Dept. Justice, 1955-69, personnel staffing specialist, 1973-75, personnel mgmt. specialist, 1976-77, employee relations specialist, Burlington, Vt., 1977-82, EEO program mgr. Eastern region, 1985-86; sec. IRS, 1969-73; pres., dir. Personal Devel. Assn., Inc., Burlington, Vt.; dir. U.S. Govt. Employees Credit Union, 1973-79. Fund raiser Public Broadcasting System, Burlington. Mem. Nat. Assn. Female Exec., Vt.-N.H. Field Fed. Safety and Health Council (founding), Burlington Bus. & Profl. Womens Club (past pres., recipient Women award 1975). Republican. Clubs: Altrusa Internat. (v.p. 1979-80, pres. 1981-82), Christian Women's Council (chmn. 1984). Home: 101 Dale Rd Burlington VT 05401

ROY, MOLLIE DUNN, lawyer; b. Marion, Ohio, Apr. 16, 1953; d. Thomas Joseph and Mary Martha (Wade) Dunn; m. Charles John Roy, Aug. 21, 1976. Student Marquette U., 1971-72; B.S., Georgetown U., 1975, J.D., 1982. Bar: D.C. 1983. Adminstrv. asst. U.S. ERDA, Washington, 1975-78; paralegal U.S. Dept. Energy, Washington, 1978-82; assoc. Rogers, Hoge & Hills, Washington, 1982-83, Pillsbury, Madison & Sutro, Washington, 1983—. Mem. ABA, Women's Bar Assn. D.C., D.C. Bar Assn., Phi Beta Kappa, Alpha Sigma Nu. Democrat. Roman Catholic. Office: Pillsbury Madison & Sutro 1667 K St NW Washington DC 20006

ROY, SYLVIA RAY, real estate broker; b. Meridian, Miss., Mar. 19, 1936; d. Charles Adrian and Martha (Singley) Ray; B.A., Sophie Newcomb Coll., 1957; M.Ed., Tulane U., 1968; m. John Overton Roy, Jr., Dec. 26, 1959; children—Charles Overton, John Parker. Tchr. secondary schs., New Orleans, 1957-67; with Trade-Mark Realty, New Orleans, 1968-75; broker, pres. Sylvia Roy Properties, Ltd., New Orleans, 1975—; asst. prof. Loyola U. of the South, New Orleans, 1979—. Mem. Nat. Assn. Realtors, La. Realtors Assn. (dir.), Real Estate Bd. New Orleans (dir.), Women's Council Realtors (dir.), Grad. Realtors Inst., Republican. Clubs: Orleans, D.A.R. Home: 70 Audubon Blvd New Orleans LA 70118 Office: 737 State St New Orleans LA 70118

ROYE, BETHANN, health care system administrator; b. Cleve., Jan. 2, 1952; d. William K. and Sally Ann (Hammond) Daniel; M. Jesse Earnest Roye, Jr., Oct. 19, 1974. B.S.N., Tex. Christian U., 1974; M.B.A., Houston Bapt. U., 1983, M.S.M. candidate, 1983—. Head nurse Spring Branch Meml. Hosp., Houston, 1977-78; cardiac rehab. specialist Meth. Hosp., Houston, 1978-79; patient care coordinator Midland Meml. Hosp., Tex., 1979-81; health systems cons. Meml. Care Systems, Houston, 1981-83, dir. operating room services, 1983—. Mem. Tex. Hosp. Assn., Assn. Operating Room Nurses. Republican. Avocation: sports. Home: 22422 S Rebecca St Katy TX 77449 Office: Meml Hosp System 7600 Beechnut St Houston TX 77079

ROYER, MARLENE MILDRED, nurse; b. Sun Prairie, Wis., Mar. 21, 1941; d. Floyd Gerald and Sylvia Inga (Halverson) Gallagher; L.P.N., N.H. Vocat. Tech. Coll., 1975; m. Raymond Arthur Royer, June 4, 1960; children—Daniel R., William Raymond. Seamstress, Jack Winter Garment Co., Colubus, Wis., 1958-60; factoryworker Clarostat Mfg. Co. and United Tanners, Inc., Dover, N.H., 1960-68; nurses aide Riverside Rest Home, Dover, 1969-74; nurse Wentworth Douglass Hosp., Dover, 1975-76; nurse, charge nurse Mapleshade Nursing Home, East Lebanon, Maine, 1976; nurse, charge and med. nurse Riverside Rest Home, Dover, 1976—. Denmother Boy Scouts Am. N.H. nursing grantee, 1974-75. Lutheran. Home: Box 254 County Farm Cross Rd Dover NH 03820

ROZELL, JUDITH ALMA, accounting officer, financial system executive; b. Lansing, Mich., Dec. 1, 1940; d. Andrew Melancthon and Mary Gladys (Brown) Rozell; student Mich. State U., 1958-59, Lansing Community Coll., 1978-79; 1 son, Andrew Wayne. Mgr. F.W. Woolworths Restaurant, Lansing, Mich., 1961-65; raw steel schedular Diamond Reo Trucks, Lansing, 1965-68; accrual acct. Am. Bank & Trust, Lansing, 1968-73, acctg. supr., Lansing, 1973-78, acctg. officer, fin. system mgr., 1978-83; acctg. officer, data processing mgr. 1st of Am. Bank, Ludington, Mich., 1983-85, asst. v.p., controller, 1985—. Mem. Community div. Lansing Safety Council, 1981-82; safety chmn. Mt. Hope Sch., 1981-82; den mother Cub Scouts Am., 1978-81, cubmaster, 1981-82; treas. CIC Allen Sch., 1978-79. Mem. Am. Inst. Banking, Parents Without Partners, Mason County Hist. Soc., Zonta Internat. Republican. Methodist. Home: 602 Ressequie St Ludington MI 49431 Office: 130 E Ludington Ave Ludington MI 49431

ROZICH, ILEENE SHAFFER, clubwoman; b. Greenville, Pa., Jan. 5, 1932; d. Charles Tennyson and Elizabeth Irene (McClimans) Welk; student Youngstown State U., 1950-51; m. John Henry Shaffer, Dec. 1, 1951 (dec.); children—Kathy Charlene Spadin, Marybeth Dawn Lang, Jon Mark; m. 2d, William Steve Rozich, Feb. 14, 1975; stepchildren—Ken Shaffer, Karen Allen. With G.M. McKelvey, Youngstown, Ohio, 1948-51; with Livingston's, Youngstown, 1951-53; with Tippecanoe Country Club, Canfield, Ohio, 1965-73; pres. Girard Republican Club, 1979—; precinct committee person, Girard City, Ohio, 1965—; mem. exec. com. Trumbull County, Ohio, 1968—; mem. Dames of Malta, 1955—, Queen Esther, 1961; mem. Protectors Club, pres., 1971-75; mem. Mahoning chpt. DAR; Charter mem. Tjaatje De Witt Chpt. Colonial Dames XVII Century, 1982. Republican. Lutheran. Mem. Ohio Geneal. Soc. (First Families Ohio), Mercer County Geneal. Soc. (pres. 1980, VFW Aux. Author: Welk Family History. Home: 362 Iowa Ave Girard OH 44420

ROZIER, JACQUELINE BAZILE, federal government employee; b. Bklyn., Aug. 29, 1953; d. Jean Marie and Eunice Benita (Whitehead) Bazile; m. Johnnie Edward Rozier, Jr., Mar. 12, 1976; children—Jean Edward Marie, Jacques Etien. B.B.A., U. Md., 1978; M.S. in Adminstrn., Ga. Coll., 1983, M.P.A., 1986. Resources mgr. U.S. Air Force, 1974-78; vet. services U.S. Dept. Agr., Atlanta, 1980; purchasing agt. Commodities, Robins AFB, Ga., 1981-83, quality assurance specialist electronics Warfare Quality Sect., 1983—. Founder, cons. Fort Hawkins Neighborhood Assn., Macon, Ga., 1985—; asst. sec. Blacks in Govt., Warner Robins, Ga., 1985—; vol. Harriet Tubman Mus., Macon, 1985—. Served as sgt. USAF, 1974-78. Mem. NAACP, Nat. Assn. Female Execs., Better Mgmt. Assn., Quality Circles, Lambda Kappa Mu. Democrat. Episcopalian. Clubs: Bullish Investment Group (co-buyer 1985—), Warner Robins. Lodges: Eastern Star, Daus. of Isis. Home: 109 Barnesdale Dr Warner Robins GA 31093 Office: Electronics Warfare Quality Sect WR-All/MAQIA Robins AFB GA 31098

ROZRAN, ANDREA RICE, health care company executive; b. Chgo., Dec. 17, 1941; d. Robert W. and Vivian Hope (Elstein) Rice; m. Jack L. Rozran, Sept. 6, 1965 (div. 1980); m. Marshall Stewart Yablon, Feb. 12, 1981; 1 child, Alexis. B.A., U. Mich., 1962; M.A., UCLA, 1967; postgrad. U. Chgo., 1965-71. Statis. cons. dept. edn. U. Chgo., 1967-69, Scott, Foresman and Co., Glenview, Ill., 1970; staff assoc. Woodstock Inst., Chgo., 1977-79; pres. Andrea R. Rozran and Assocs., Chgo., 1979-80, Diversified Health Resources, Inc., Chgo., 1980—; cons. City of Chgo., 1979; corp. bd. mem. Blue Cross of Ill., Chgo., 1981—. Author: (monograph) The Planner's Role in Facilitating Private Sector Reinvestment, 1979. Mem. Ill. Health Facilities Planning Bd., Springfield, 1974-79; mem. Ill. adv. com. to U.S. Civil Rights Commn., Chgo., 1979-84; co-chmn. Profl. Health Services div. Jewish United Fund, Chgo., 1985; mem. priorities com. United Way of Met. Chgo., 1976-79; Mem. LWV (v.p., chmn. various coms., 1972-77), Am. Health Planning Assn., Soc. for Hosp. Planning, Women's Health Execs. Network (chmn. by-laws com. 1981-83). Home: 1209 N Astor St Chicago IL 60610 Office: Diversified Health Resources Inc 620 N Michigan Ave Suite 550 Chicago IL 60611

RUARK, ELEANOR ROSE, banker; b. Athens, Ga., June 25, 1924; d. Elwood and Zora Mae (Williams) Kirk; student U. Ga. Banking Sch., 1968; m. Rexford G. Ruark, Oct. 23, 1944; children—Elaine, Stanley, Karen. With Farmers Bank, Union Point, Ga., 1956—, asst. v.p. Greensboro br., 1980—; sec. to supt. Greene County Bd. Edn., 1976-77. Mem. Nat. Assn. Bank Women (charter, chmn. N.E. Ga. group 1970-71), Bank Adminstrn. Inst. (chpt. treas. 1962), Ga. Bankers Assn. (women's com.). Baptist (treas. ladies aux. 1975-78). Club: Greene County Country. Office: Farmers Bank 202-A S Main St Greensboro GA 30642

RUARK, THEODORA WILMA, hospital administrator; b. Flandreau, S.D., Jan. 22, 1935; d. Theodore and Louella Lenora (Paul) Lathrop; B.S., U. Houston, Clear Lake, 1986; m. Vernon R. Ruark, May 16, 1976; children—Julie, Dwain, Darrell, Kenneth, Patrick. From credit mgr. to dir. hosp. bus. services U. Nebr. Med. Center, Omaha, 1962-80; mgr. hosp. bus. systems Lifemark Corp., Houston, 1980-85; asst. dir. bus. services St. Mary's Hosp., Galveston, 1985—. Mem. Internat. Comsumer Credit Soc., Am. Guild Patient Account Mgrs. (treas. elect 1981; award individual achievement, 1979, 80), Hosp. Fin. Mgmt. Assn., Am. Hosp. Assn., Am. Mgmt. Assn., Mensa. Republican. Methodist. Contbr. column to jour., 1979-85. Home: 543 Pompano Dr Hitchock TX 77563 Office: St Mary's Hosp Galveston TX 77550

RUBACKY, MARJORIE MCLAUGHLIN, career mgmt. co. exec.; d. Francis Michael and Agnes (Whelan) McLaughlin; m. Gerald E. Rubacky. B.A., Catholic U. Am. Product mgr. United Jersey Bank, Hackensack, N.J., 1972-75; sr. assoc. Career Mgmt. Assocs., N.Y.C., 1975-76; pres. Rubacky Assocs., N.Y.C., 1976-80; prin. Gallagher Mgmt. Assocs., 1980-83; corp. dir. Mainstream Access, Inc., N.Y.C. 1983—. Mem. Women's Econ. Round Table, Am. Soc. Personnel Adminstrn., Am. Women's Econ. Devel. Corp. Club: Montclair Golf. Home: 125 Lorraine Ave Upper Montclair NJ 07043 Office: 535 Fifth Ave New York NY 10017

RUBB, PEGGY-GRACE PLOURD, dancer, artistic director; b. Hartford, Conn., Sept. 27, 1931; d. Launcelot J. and Margaret (Feeney) Plourd; m. Milton Robert Rubb, June 6, 1953; children—Bonnie Leigh, Eric John, Michael Robert. Student Hartt Conservatory of Music, Hartford, 1938-49, Shenandoah Conservatory, Winchester, Va., 1949-51, Froman Profl. Ballet Sch., New London, Conn., 1959-62, Hampton Acad. Ballet, Va., 1962-63, Nat. Ballet, Washington, 1963-66. Tchr., R.H. Lee Elem. Sch., Glen Burnie, Md., 1951-52; dancer Common Glory Jamestown Corp., Williamsburg, Va., 1963; accompanist Annapolis Modern Dance Assn., Md., 1973; ballet mistress dance studio, Crofton, Md., 1974-78; dance instr. gymnastics camp Washington Coll., Chestertown, Md., 1977; dance coach Glen Burnie Artistic Skate Club, 1980-81; artistic dir. Crofton-Bowie Sch. of Ballet and affiliated cos., 1978—; choreographer Tom Thumb Players, Annapolis, 1972; dancer Hampton Roads Civic Ballet, Va., 1962-63. Choreographer; composer; lyricist. Bd. dirs. Annapolis Children's Theatre, 1977-78. Mem. Md. Council for Dance, Nat. Assn. Female Execs., Phi Beta Sigma. Club: U.S. Naval Acad. Class '53 Wives (pres. San Diego 1957-58, pres. New London 1959-60). Avocations: sketching; painting. Office: 2411 Crofton Ln Chelsea House Suite 2 Crofton MD 21114

RUBENSON, LYNN BETH, public relations and marketing consultant; b. New Castle, Pa., Oct. 3, 1952; d. Sander Harold and Shirley Rose (Malkin) Rubenson; m. Benny Richard Benjamin, Sept. 8, 1984. B.S.J., Ohio U., 1974. Mgr. public relations WPXI-TV, Pitts., 1976-77; nat. pub. relations mgr. WQED-TV PBS, Pitts., 1978-80; account supr., dir. Creamer Dickson Bas Ford, Providence and Boston, 1980-84, Cone & Co., Boston, 1984-86; sr. cons. Rubenson Communications, Providence, 1986—. Mem. pub. relations com. Keep Providence Beautiful, 1984. Mem. Public Relations Soc. Am. (founding mem. bd. dirs. S.E. New Eng. 1982-84), Soc. Profl. Journalists, Boston Ad Club, Nat Assn. Exec. Women. Jewish. Avocations: photography; creative writing; swimming. Home: 228 Doyle Ave Providence RI 02906

RUBENSTEIN, ELIZABETH SUAREZ, cosmetic mfg. exec.; b. Lucena City, P.I., Dec. 28, 1942; d. Inocencio Bolos Suarez and Eufrocina Laceste Quinsaat; came to U.S., 1969, naturalized, 1975; B.S. in Chem. Engring., U. Santo Tomas, Manila, 1964; m. Leslie Ronald Rubenstein, July 2, 1976; 1 dau., Lisa Anne. Chemist, H. Kohnstamm, N.Y.C., 1969; analytical chemist Allied Testing & Research, Hillsdale, N.J., 1970; research dir. Chromex Chem. Corp., Bklyn., 1970-75; tech. dir. Chem. Spray (A.T.I.), Totowa, N.J., 1975, Krueger (Cosmetic) Corp., Bklyn., 1975-78, Paramount Cosmetics, Union City, N.J., 1978—. Mem. Am. Inst. Chem. Engrs., Am. Chem. Soc., Soc. Cosmetic Chemists, Cosmetic Toiletry and Fragrance Assn. Home: 153 Freeman St Brooklyn NY 11222 Office: 3710 Hudson Ave Union City NJ 07087

RUBIDO, ESPERANZA, university official, writer; b. Havana, Cuba, Jan. 27, 1950; came to U.S., 1967, naturalized, 1973; d. Pedro and Maria Nieves (Matias) R.; A.A. with honors, Miami Dade Community Coll., 1974; B.A. cum laude, U. Miami, 1979, postgrad., 1979—. With U. Miami (Fla.), 1973—, staff coordinator, 1978—; owner Bestours Travel Services, 1986—. Recipient Appreciation cert. City Miami, 1976, YMCA, 1976; Carilda Oliver Labra poetry award, Madrid, 1983; others. Mem. MLA, So. Hollywood Poetry Inst., Círculo Ednl. Profls. Art, Cruzada Educativa Cubana, Círculo Ignacio Agramonte, Nat. Hispanic Assn., Gala Poetry Assn. Roman Catholic. Author: Más Allá del Azul, 1976, Antología Poética Hispanoamericana, 1978; En un mundo de nombres, 1984; La mujer en La poesia Hispanica, 1984; 9 Poetas Cubanos, 1984; contbr. poetry to anthologies. Office: PO Box 450 264 Miami FL 33145

RUBIN, ALICE FISHER, state official; b. Bklyn., June 8, 1940; d. Harold L. and Betty Fisher; B.A., St. John's U., 1964, M.A. (Ford Found. scholar), 1968; m. Lowell M. Rubin, Dec. 7, 1972; children—David Fisher, Emily Claire. Research asst. N.Y. State Conf. Mayors, Albany, 1966; spl. asst. Nassau County (N.Y.), 1967; research and liaison coordinator N.Y.C. Comptroller's Office, 1970-74; asst. commr. Agy. for Child Devel., N.Y.C., 1974-78; asst. sec. to Gov. N.Y. State for intergovtl. relations Exec. Chamber N.Y. State, N.Y.C., 1978-83; adj. lectr. City U. N.Y., 1971-82; adj. asst. prof. Grad. Sch. Pub. Adminstrn., L.I. U., 1984. Bd. trustee Bklyn. Pub. Library, 1975—; bd. dirs. Bklyn. chpt. ARC, 1977—, N.Y.C. Tech. Coll. Found., 1982; founder Jewish Women's Leadership Caucus, Bklyn., 1981. Mem. AAUW. Home: 141 Argyle Rd Brooklyn NY 11218

RUBIN, CYNTHIA ELYCE, museum curator; b. Lowell, Mass., Nov. 7, 1944; d. M. Michael and Gladys (Cohen) Weinberg. A.B., Vassar Coll., 1966; Equivalence du Baccalaureat and Equivalence du Certificat d'Etudes Littéraires Générales, U. Paris, 1967; Ed.M., Boston U., 1968-71; postgrad. NYU, 1983—. Exec. v.p. Emporium Publs., Inc., Boston, 1970-81; curator spl. project Mus. Am. Folk Art, N.Y.C., 1984—; guest curator, 1979, 82—; U. N.C. fellow Mus. Early So. Decorated Arts Summer Inst., Winston-Salem, 1981. Author: Old Boston Fare, 1975; Shaker Miniature Furniture, 1979; Mission Furniture, 1980. Compiler, editor: Southern Folk Art, 1985. Mem. Culinary Historians Boston, Authors Guild. Club: Vassar.

RUBIN, IDA ELY, art cons., writer; b. N.Y.C., Nov. 27, 1923; d. Thurston Van Vechten and Elizabeth Boomer (Scheffer) Ely; B.A. with high honors, Wells Coll., Aurora, N.Y., 1944; postgrad. Inst. Fine Arts, NYU, 1944-49; m. Jerome Sanford Rubin, Mar. 1, 1957; children—Richard Ely, Alicia Mirella. Exec. dir. XX Internat. Congress Art History, N.Y.C., 1959-61; dir. devel. Inst. Fine Arts, 1962-63; dir. visual arts Inter-Am. Found. Arts, N.Y.C., 1963-64; spl. cons. Art Gallery Center Inter-Am. Relations, N.Y.C., 1965-68; dir. visual arts Inst. Contemporary Hispanic Art, N.Y.C., 1973-77; art cons., curator pvt. collections, 1970-80; fgn. corr. Arte en Colombia; mem. selection com., mem. Jury Contemporary Painting, Drawing, Sculpture and Photog. Exhbns., 1960—; mem. faculty Manhattanville Coll., Purchase, N.Y., 1970-71; lectr. in field. Fellow Belgium-Am. Edn. Found., Brussels, 1951; vice chmn. visual arts com. N.Y.C. Cultural Council, 1969-72; mem. exec. com. Drawing Soc. N.Y.C., 1961-82; chmn. mus. acquisitions com. Council on Arts, MIT, 1972-84; v.p. U. Andes Found., 1981-84; mem. exec. com. Americas Found., 1981-84; mem. internat. art selection com. UNICEF, 1983-84. Clubs: Nat. Arts (gov.), Cosmopolitan (N.Y.C.). Editor: Acts of XX Internat. Congress of Art History, 4 vols., 1963; Drawings of Morris Graves, 1974; Catalogue of the Guennol Collection, 1976. Author articles, books, catalogues. Address: 158 Indian Head Rd Riverside CT 06878

RUBIN, JANICE ANN, lawyer; b. Newark, Nov. 12, 1941; d. Carl and Helen Edith (Baletin) Edelstein; m. Burton Jay Rubin, Feb. 17, 1974; 1 dau., Jennifer Sidell. A.B. cum laude, Smith Coll., 1964; J.D., George Washington U., 1973. Bar: Va. 1974, U.S. Supreme Ct. 1979. Editor McKinsey & Co., Washington, 1971-72; editor Bur. Nat. Affairs, Inc. Patent, Trademark & Copyright Jour., Washington, 1972-74; legis. atty. Am. Law div. Congressional Research Service, Library of Congress, Washington, 1974—; antitrust cons. Contbr. in field. Mem. Fed. Bar Assn. (2d v.p. D.C. cir., v.p. 1983-84, pres. elect 1985-86), ABA. Club: Smith Coll. Washington. Office: 101 Independence Ave SE Washington DC 20540

RUBIN, KAREN ELIZABETH, real estate appraisal and consulting firm executive; b. Stamford, Conn., Oct. 12, 1957; d. James Elwood and Cecile (Frankel) Rubin. B.S. with distinction, Cornell U., 1981; student Brandeis U., 1975-76, New Sch. for Social Research, 1974-75, 76-77. Lic. salesperson in real estate, N.Y. Asst. mgr. Ashley's Inc., N.Y.C., 1976-78; mgr. Seventh Ave. South, Inc., N.Y.C., 1978-79, Hienkel's Inc., Darien, Conn., 1981-82; cons. and valuation analyst Hospitality Valuation Services, Inc., Mineola, N.Y., 1982-84, sr. v.p., 1984—; guest lectr. NYU, Real Estate Inst., 1985—; alumni interviewer Cornell U., 1985—; cons. fin. High Ridge Plaza, Stamford, Conn. Author/developer newsletter Rubin Report on Hospitality Econometrics, 1984—. Cornell U. Dean's scholar, 1979, 80, 81. Mem. Cornell Soc. Hotelmen, Inst. Propery Taxation. Avocations: jazz dancer; creative writer; guitarist. Office: Hospitality Valuation Services Inc 372 Willis Ave Mineola NY 11501

RUBIN, LOIS CAROL, lawyer; b. N.Y.C., July 27, 1950; d. Maxwell Aaron and Hyacinth Marsha (Rothenberg) R.; m. Henry Ferstenberg, Sept. 3, 1972 (div. 1977). B.A., NYU, 1972; M.S., U. So. Calif.-Brussels Extension, 1974; J.D., St. John's U., 1979. Bar: N.Y. 1980; cert. social studies tchr. Tchr. Brussels Am. Sch., 1974-76; assoc. firm Shearman & Sterling, N.Y.C., 1979-86, Weil, Gotshal & Manges, 1986—. Mem. St. John's Law Rev.; contbr. articles to legal publs. Dean's acad. scholar, 1977. Mem. ABA, N.Y. State Bar Assn., New York County Bar Assn. Democrat. Jewish. Office: Weil Gotshal & Manges 767 Fifth Ave New York NY 10153

RUBIN, MARCIA J. SOLOMON, financial consultant; b. N.Y.C., June 17, 1952; d. Raymond and Dorothy (Goldman) Solomon; m. Stuart N. Rubin, Sept. 1, 1973; children—Craig, Brian. B.A. in Psychology, Queens Coll. CUNY, 1973; M.A. in Personnel Adminstrn., Columbia U., 1974; M.A. in Pub. Adminstrn., NYU, 1976. Student activities mgr. Queens Coll., Flushing, N.Y., 1973-75; chief recreation services USAF, Madrid, Spain, 1975-79; city mgr., Kingwood, Tex., 1980-82; dir. fin. Met. YWCA Houston, 1982-83; fin. cons., tax preparer, Houston, 1983—; cons. to various businesses, 1983—. Mem. Kingwood Civic Assn., 1980-82; bd. dirs. Hearthstone Homeowners Assn., Houston, 1983-84. Mem. Nat. Assn. Female Execs., Women's Adv. Council. Jewish. Home: 7523 Cart Gate Dr Houston TX 77095

RUBIN, ROCHELLE ELISA, copywriter; b. Bklyn., Feb. 5, 1957; d. Arthur and Madeline (Grossman) Rubin; m. John N. Palumbo, Feb. 23, 1980 (div. 1982). Student Goucher Coll., 1975-76, R.I. Sch. Design, 1975; B.S. in Mktg. Mgmt., NYU, 1979; postgrad. Sch. Visual Arts. Pvt. med. cons., N.Y.C., 1980-82; freelance writer, Dallas, 1982; copywriter Cunningham & Walsh, Dallas, 1983-84, Bozell & Jacobs, Dallas, 1984-86, John Brown & Ptnrs., Seattle, 1986—; writer nat. advt. consumer campaign La Quinta Motor Inns. Recipient Cert. of Achievement, Art Dirs. Club Houston, 1983, 1 show cert. merit ADS Mag. Jewish. Home: 900 Queen Anne Ave N Apt 209 Seattle WA 98109 Office: John Brown & Ptnrs Inc 51 University St Suite 200 Seattle WA 98101

RUBIN, VERA COOPER, astronomer; b. Phila., July 23, 1928; d. Philip and Rose Anna (Applebaum) Cooper; m. Robert J. Rubin, June 25, 1948; children—David, Judith Rubin Young, Karl, Allan. B.A., Vassar Coll., 1948; M.A., Cornell U., Ithaca, N.Y., 1951; Ph.D., Georgetown U., 1954; D.Sc. (hon.), Creighton U., 1978. Research asst. Georgetown U., Washington, 1955-61, asst. prof., 1961-65; astronomer dept. terrestrial magnetism Carnegie Instn. of Washington, 1965—; physicist U. Calif.-La Jolla, 1963-64; disting. vis. astronomer Cerro Tololo Inter Am. Obs., Chile, 1978; chancellor's disting. prof. U. Calif.-Berkeley, 1981; mem. vis. com. Nat. Radio Astronomy Obs., 1975-79, dept. astronomy Harvard U., 1976-82, 84-85; bd. dirs. Assn. Univs. for Research in Astronomy, 1973-76; mem. Smithsonian Instn. Council, 1979-84. Author numerous papers on dynamics of galaxies; editor Astrophys. Jour. Letters, 1977-82; editorial bd. Sci. mag., 1979—. Phi Beta Kappa scholar, 1982-83. Mem. Am. Astron. Soc. (councilor 1977-80), Internat. Astron. Union (pres. galaxy commn. 1982-85), U.S. Nat. Acad. Scis., Am. Acad. Arts and Scis., Phi Beta Kappa. Office: Dept Terrestrial Magnetism Carnegie Instn Washington 5241 Broad Branch Rd NW Washington DC 20015

RUBINSTEIN, SHIRLEY JOY, nursing service executive; b. Toronto, Ont., Can., Nov. 19, 1927; came to U. S., 1928, naturalized, 1948; d. Harry Hyman and Ida Ruth (Albert) Adel; m. Philip F. Rubinstein, Aug. 17, 1947; children—David Brian, Wendy Sue, Hope Terri. With Jewish Agy. for Palestine, Washington, 1947-49; coordinator Nursing Staff, Inc., 1975-78; co-founder, pres. Nursing Services, Inc., Silver Spring, Md., 1978—; pres., founder Fantasy Factory, Inc., 1985—, Pegasus Limousine service Inc., 1985—. Democrat. Jewish. Club: B'nai Birth. Office: PO Box 4133 Silver Spring MD 20904

RUBIO, ELENITA IGNACIO, physician; b. Cavite, Philippines, May 22, 1943; d. Pedro Ignacio and Francisca San Miguel (Reyes) Ignacio; A.A., U. St. Tomas, 1962, M.D., 1967; m. Nunilo G. Rubio, June 20, 1970; children—Nunilo, Noel, Nathaniel. Intern, Swedish Hosp., Mpls., 1968-69; resident in internal medicine Hines (Ill.) VA Hosp., 1970-72; attending physician, 1972—; practice medicine, specializing in internal medicine, Chgo. and Franklin Park, Ill., 1973—; co-owner Chgo. Hamlin Med. Center, 1974—; co-owner, treas. RVR Med. Splty. Group Ltd., 1974—; clin. instr. Loyola Stritch Sch. Medicine, 1972—. Mem. AMA, Ill., Chgo. med. socs., Philippine Med. Soc. Chgo., (bd. dirs.), U. St. Tomas Med. Alumni (bd. dirs.). Club: Indianhead Park Village. Home: 6555 Cochise Dr Indianhead Park IL 60525 Office: 3758 W Chicago Ave Chicago IL 60631

RUBLE-TROTTER, ANN, clergywoman; b. Seattle, Oct. 26, 1953; d. Monte Rahe and Stella (Terefinko) Ruble; m. Francis Michael Trotter, Aug. 29, 1984. Cert. sec. Met. Bus. Coll., Seattle, 1972. Ordained to ministry Ch. of Scientology, 1980. Minister, Ch. of Scientology, Seattle, 1980—, dir. pub. affairs, 1983; pres. Ch. of Scientology of Wash. State, 1984—. Bur. chief Jour. Freedom News, 1984—. Bd. dirs. Citizen's Commn. Human Rights, Seattle, 1984—; mem. Com. on Religious Liberties, Seattle, 1985—. Office: Ch of Scientology of Wash State 2004 Westlake Ave Seattle WA 98121

RUBSCHLAGER, JOAN SNIDER, baking corporation executive; b. Pontiac, Ill., Jan. 16, 1938; d. George W. and Jewel (Underwood) Snider; m. Paul A. Rubschlager, June 29, 1963. B.S. in Elem. Edn., Ill. Wesleyan U., 1960; postgrad. Nat. Coll. Edn., 1971. Tchr. pub. schs., Park Ridge, Ill., 1960-71, tchr. lang. arts, 1971-75, dir. gifted program, 1975-77; sec., treas. Rubschlager Baking Corp., Chgo., 1977—. Mem. Nat. Restaurant Assn., (exhibitors adv. bd. 1980-83), Nat. Food Distributors Assn. (mfrs. council 1982—), Ill. and Chgo. Food Mfg. Council, City of Hope (v.p. 1981-84, chmn. bd. dirs. 1984-86), Alpha Lambda Delta, Phi Kappa Phi, Delta Omicron. Office: Rubschlager Baking Corp 3220 W Grand Ave Chicago IL 60651

RUBY, LOIS ANN HARRIET, gift shop owner; b. Minneapolis, Dec. 23, 1929; d. Clair Luvern and Mae Jeanette (Sather) R. Student Mpls. Art Inst. (now Coll. Art and Design), 1949-55, Atelier Lack, Studio Sch. Fine Arts, Mpls., 1982. Sec., office mgr. Brown Fire Equipment Co., Des Moines, 1948-49; art dir. Treasure Masters, Mpls., 1949-63; creative artist Peck, Inc., St. Paul, 1964-68; mgr. Held's Gift Shop, Mpls., 1968-70; gift shop mgr. Eitel Hosp., Mpls., 1970-82; freelance artist and owner Left Hand Center Gifts, St. Louis Park, Minn., 1982—. Recipient 1st Prize package design for Valentines, U.S. Packaging Awards, 1967. Mem. Health Care Gift Shop Assn. (sec. 1979-80). Republican. Lutheran. Club: Lefthander's of Greater N.W. (asst. chmn. 1982-83). Office: Left Hand Center Gifts 4400 Excelsior Blvd Saint Louis Park MN 55416

RUBY, SALLY ANNE, city official; b. Hershey, Pa., Sept. 25, 1944; d. Edward Mark and Sarah Ellen (Tobias) Keeney; B.S., Labanon Valley Coll., Annville, Pa., 1973; M.Ed., Millersville (Pa.) State Coll., 1974; m. Herbert L. Weed. Counselor, Fla. Div. Corrections, 1974-76; compliance coordinator City of Clearwater (Fla.), 1976—. Bd. dirs., v.p., chair personnel com. Pinellas County Counsumer Credit Counseling Service, 1981-84; mem. Tampa Bay Open Housing Coalition, 1980-81; mem. human rights com. Pinellas Opportunity Council, 1979-81; sec. Clearwater Urban League Guild, 1980-81; mem. loan com. Neighborhood Housing Service, Clearwater; mem. bi-racial com. and spl. attendance permit com. Pinellas County (Fla.) Sch. Bd.; mem. cons. Council FACE. Mem. Nat. Assn. Human Rights Workers, Fla. Assn. Community Relations Profls. (sec. 1981-85), NOW, Nat. Abortion Rights League, Nat. Assn. Female Execs., LWV, Millersville State Coll. Alumni Assn. Unitarian-Universalist. Home: 416 N Lincoln Ave Clearwater FL 33515 Office: PO Box 4748 Clearwater FL 33518

RUCKELSHAUS, ELIZABETH TIMMINS, knitwear manufacturing company executive; b. Anna, Ill., Apr. 28, 1947; d. Claire Henry and Marie Isabel (Ammon) Timmins; m. William Chalmers Ruckelshaus, Sept. 2, 1967; stepchildren—Sarah Littell Ruckelshaus Gordon, Peter Boone, A.B., Pa. State U., 1969; postgrad. Phila. Coll. Textiles and Scis., 1976. Tchr. French, Upper Dublin Sch. Dist., Fort Washington, Pa., 1969-76; dir. mktg. Wenco, Inc., N.Y.C., 1977-78; mfr., designer Patterncraft Corp., Norristown, Pa., 1978—. Author instrns. of knitting patterns Vogue Knitting Mag., Good Housekeeping Knitting Mag., Reynolds Yarns, Bucilla Yarns, Plymouth Yarns, Gemini Yarns, Perry Ellis Yarn Kits, Phildar Yarns, Bernat Yarns, 1978—. Avocations: sewing and knitting; reading. Home: PO Box 123 Eagleville PA 19408 Office: Patterncraft Corp 311 W Marshall St Norristown PA 19401

RUCKER, HELEN BORNSTEIN (MRS. B. WALLACE RUCKER), author; b. Seattle; d. Maurice Sello and Julia (Gyle) Bornstein; grad. Nat. Park Coll., 1923; student Cornish Sch. Allied Arts, 1934-35, 46-47, 55-56, U. Wash.; m. B. Wallace Rucker, Jan. 30, 1932; children—B. Wallace, Stephen Morley. Author: Cargo of Brides, 1956, 69; The Wolf Tree, 1960; also short stories. Unit chmn. ARC, 1940-45; trustee, membership chmn., sec., corrs. sec., chmn. programs spastic children Seattle Jr. Programs, 1941-56; trustee Cornish Sch. Allied Arts, 1935-38, Friends Seattle Public Library, 1957-60, Franklin Guild Children's Orthopedic Hosp.; chmn. N.W. Authors Bookshelf, Seattle Public Library, 1964-66; bd. dirs. Wash. State Jewish Hist. Soc., 1980. Mem. Nat. League Am. Pen Women (sponsoring com. Spirit of Seattle 1949 for Mus. History and Industry), Seattle Free-Lance Writers, N.W. Internat. Writers Conf., Pioneer Assn. State Wash., Friends of Crafts, Phi Delta Nu. Clubs: Soroptimist (Seattle; co-chmn. student loan fund 1968-69, Achievement award Past Pres. Assembly 1960), Seattle Tennis, Wash. Athletic. Editor: The Bull., Friends Seattle Public Library, 1958-60. Home: 1620 43d Ave E Apt 9B Seattle WA 98112

RUCKER, MARGARET MARIE, postal service executive; b. Cleve., July 15, 1939; d. Theodore and Doretha (Jones) Mason; m. Freddie Rucker, July 12, 1963 (div. 1969); children—Terrance F., Anthony C. Student Cuyahoga Community Coll., 1973-75; B.A. in Fin. Mgmt., Governors State U., Park Forest, Ill., 1983; cert. Exec. Devel. Program, U. Ill., 1983. Clk., U.S. Postal Service, Cleve., 1959-73, specialist, 1973-77, mgr. procurement services office, Chgo., 1977-82, mgr. contracts and supply mgmt. br., Central Region, Chgo., 1982—, facilitator, Chgo. Post Office Women's Program 1981-83, mem. coordinating com. Regional Employee Involvement, Chgo., 1983-84. Trustee Second Baptist Ch. of Wheaton, 1983; mem. NAACP, Urban League. Recipient cert. of appreciation Younger Girls Activity Club, Chgo., 1980; Am. Logistics Assn. scholar, 1982. Mem. Federally Employed Women, Nat. Assn. Female Execs., Black Fine Arts Performers Wheaton (steering com. 1981-84). Democrat. Office: Contracts and Supply Mgmt Branch USPS Central Regional Headquarters 433 W Van Buren Room 1104 Chicago IL 60699

RUCKER, SUZANNE JUNE, fund raiser; b. Coral Gables, Fla., June 27, 1945; d. Thomas John, Jr. and June Ethel Agusta (Stones) R.; B.B.A., Fla. Atlantic U., 1971, M.B.A., 1975. Assoc. dir. Am. Soc. Cons. Pharmacists, 1971-73; chpt. specialist Epilepsy Found. Am., 1973-74; assoc. dir. devel. Fairfax Hosp. Assn. Found., Springfield, Va., 1974-81; dir. devel. Arlington Hosp. Found. (Va.), 1982—; instr. George Washinton U.; seminar speaker in field. Bd. dirs. Crittenton Services, Salvation Army Aux. Washington, Republican Working Women's Forum. Lic. real estate agt. Fellow Nat. Assn. Hosp. Devel. Republican. Office: 1701 N George Mason Dr Arlington VA 22205

RUCKER-HUGHES, WAUDIEUR ELIZABETH, educator; b. Washington, July 30, 1947; d. Jeter and Jeannette Belle (Toomer) Rucker; B.S., D.C. Tchrs. Coll., 1969, M.A. in Edn., U. Redlands, 1974; 1 child, Telicee E.M. Tchr. history J.W. North High Sch., Riverside, Calif., 1969-76, dean students, 1976-79; lectr. Afro-Am. history Riverside City Coll., 1972-74; exec. dir. Inland Area Opportunities Industrialization Center, Riverside, 1979—; cons. in field. Commr. Community relations City of Riverside, 1972-76; sec. State Inter-Group Relations Educators, 1976-77; pres. Coalition of Urban Peoples, 1978-80; lay mem. Riverside County Jud. Selection Com., 1978—, Calif. State Bar ct. referee, 1979—. NSF fellow, 1970-71; Center for Leadership Edn. grantee, 1978. Mem. NAACP, Urban League, Riverside Women's Polit. Caucus, Nat. Women's Polit. Caucus, Exec. Dirs. Assn. (sec. 1983-84), Nat. Council Negro Women, Delta Kappa Gamma. Mem. C.M.E. Ch. Club: The Thurs. Group. Author: Canine Capers, 1976; A Book to Match our Diversity, 1980. Home: 8907 Delano Dr Riverside CA 92503 Office: 2222 Kansas Ave Riverside CA 92507

RUCKER-LOTT, BARBARA VICTORIA, insurance analyst; b. Newark, May 29, 1956; d. Walker Rucker and Manora Naomi (Brown) Rucker; m. Richard Earl Lott, June 27, 1981; 1 dau., Ashley Nicole. B.A. in Psychology, Fisk U., Nashville, 1977; M.B.A. in Acctg., Atlanta U., 1979. Programmer trainee Sun Ins. Service, Atlanta, 1980-81; prodn. analyst Richway Dept. Stores, Atlanta, 1981-83; tech. support analyst Mass. Indemnity Life Ins. Co., Norcross, Ga., 1983—; cons. intern Legal Services Corp., Atlanta, 1978. Vol. Democratic mayorial campaign, Atlanta, 1982. Mem. Am. Bus. Women, Women's C. of C., Soc. Advancement Mgmt., Acctg. Soc. (sec. 1977-78), Democrat. Methodist. Club: Toastmasters Internat. (v.p. 1977-78). Home: 395 Benjamin Circle Fayetteville GA 30214

RUCKER-REED, ELIZABETH ANNE, state official; b. Murfreesboro, Tenn., Nov. 18, 1949; d. John Richardson and Margaret Eleanor (Wolfe) Rucker; m. Dwight Todd Reed, Oct. 28, 1969 (div. May 1976); children—D. Todd, Jr., M. LeeAnne. Student Middle Tenn. State U., 1967-68, 76-86, U. Tenn., 1968-69. Paying and receiving teller/br. mgr. First Tenn. Bank, Murfreesboro, 1976-77; asst. dir. admitting Rutherford Hosp., Murfreesboro, 1977-79; clin. supr., bookkeeper Primary Care Mgmt. Corp., Murfreesboro, 1979-80; sec., bookkeeper Stoner River Equipment Co., Murfreesboro, 1980-81; adminstrv. asst. USC Data Systems, Murfreesboro, 1981-84; adminstrv. officer Tenn. Dept. Labor, Nashville, 1984—. Mem. Murfreesboro Little Theater, 1978-81; campaign asst. Councilman Robert Corlew, Murfreesboro, 1982; county coordinator Senator John Rucker Campaign, 16th Dist., State Tenn., 1976, 80; troop leader Girl Scouts Am., 1982-84, 83-85; com. mem. Boy Scouts Am., 1981-86, troop com. chmn., 1983-85; co-leader Girl Scouts Am., 1985-86, troop organizer, 1985-86. Mem. Nat. Assn. Female Execs. Democrat. Mem. Ch. of Christ. Avocations: boating; skiing; camping; reading; theater. Home: 1510 Bradyville Pike Murfreesboro TN 37130 Office: Tenn Dept Labor Manpower Div 1800 JK Polk Bldg 505 Deaderick St Nashville TN 37219

RUDACILLE, SHARON VICTORIA, med. technologist; b. Ranson, W. Va., Sept. 11, 1950; d. Albert William and Roberta Mae (Anderson) R.; B.S. cum laude, Shepherd Coll., 1972. Med. technologist VA Center, Martinsburg, W. Va., 1972—, instr. Sch. Med. Tech., 1972-76, asso. coordinator edn., 1976-77, edn. coordinator, 1977-78, quality assurance officer clin. chemistry, 1978-80, lab. service quality assurance and edn. officer, 1980-84, leader clin. chemistry sect., 1984—; mem. adj. faculty Shippensburg (Pa.) State Coll., 1977-78. Mem. Am. Soc. Med. Technologists, Am. Soc. Clin. Pathologists, W.Va. Soc. Med. Technologists, Shepherd Coll. Alumni Assn., Sigma Pi Epsilon. Baptist. Home: PO Box 14 Ranson WV 25438 Office: Route 9 Martinsburg WV 25401

RUDBERG LOWE, PAULA MARIE, marketing communications editor; b. Bellingham, Wash., Jan. 26, 1956; d. William Peter and Margaret Marie (Buerstatte) Rudberg; m. Daniel Roy Lowe, Apr. 24, 1981. A.A., Highline Community Coll., 1976; B.A., Wash. State U., 1978. Lic. Broadcaster FCC. Ski instr. Ski Masters Ski Sch., Bellevue, Wash., 1974-76; swim instr., lifeguard King County Parks, Seattle, 1975-80; news dir., announcer sta. KENE, Toppenish, Wash., 1978-79; sec. Highline Community Coll., Midway, Wash., 1979-81; writer, photographer Olympia News (Wash.), 1981-82; asst. editor North Thurston Sch. Dist., Lacey, Wash., 1982-84; editor St. Joseph Hosp., Tacoma, 1984—. Recipient awards for publs. Mem. Women in Communications (pres. Tacoma-Olympia profl. chpt. 1982-84, coordinator regional meeting 1982-83, cert. commendation 1983). Club: Toastmistress (publicity coordinator 1982-84). Home: 5202 Rumac St SE Olympia WA 98503 Office: St Joseph Hosp Mktg Communications PO Box 2197 Tacoma WA 98401

RUDEN, VIOLET HOWARD (MRS. CHARLES VAN KIRK RUDEN), Christian Sci. tchr., practitioner; b. Dallas; d. Millard Fillmore and Henrietta Frederika (Kurth) Howard; B.J., U. Tex., 1931; C.S.B., Mass. Metaphys. Coll., 1946; m. Charles Van Kirk Ruden, Nov. 24, 1932. Radio continuity writer Home Mgmt. Club broadcast Sta. WHO, Des Moines, 1934; joined First Ch. of Christ Scientist, Boston, 1929; C.S. practitioner, Des Moines, 1934—; C.S. minister WAC, Ft. Des Moines, 1942-45; 1st reader 2d Ch. of Christ Scientist, Des Moines, 1952, Sunday sch. tchr., 1934—; instr. primary class in Christian Sci., 1947—. Trustee Asher Student Found. Drake U., Des Moines, 1973. Mem. Women in Communications, Mortar Bd., Orchesis, Cap and Gown. Republican. Club: Des Moines Women's. Home and Office: 5808 Walnut Hill Dr Des Moines IA 50312

RUDER, SANDRA LEE, advertising agency executive; b. Joliet, Ill., July 27, 1953; d. Irvin Alfred and Dorothy Lee (Moore) R. B.A., Fla. Atlanta U., 1982. Cert. travel agt. cons. Salesman, Allied Radio, Park Forest, Ill., 1970-71; salesman Marshall Field & Co., Park Forest, 1972-73; prodn. control analyst Universal Metal Service, South Holland, Ill., 1973-81; travel cons. Bank of Park Forest, 1981; pres. Dynamics USA Inc., Boca Raton, Fla., 1982—. Chmn., pub. info. specialist Am. Cancer Soc., Boca Raton, 1985—. Mem. Nat. Assn. Women Bus. Owners, Advt. Splty. Inst., Nat. Family Bus. Council (bd. dirs. 1979-80). Republican. Club: Royal Palm Polo (Boca Raton). Avocations: swimming; tennis; scuba diving; traveling. Home: 5517 Pacific Blvd Apt 4413 Boca Raton FL 33432

RUDERMAN, ANNE TULLY, hypnoanalyst; b. Wilmington, Del., June 26, 1927; d. James Joseph and Adeline (Van Buren) Tully; B.A., Antioch Coll., 1948; postgrad. Yale U., 1949-50; M.S.W., Smith Coll., 1952; m. S.G. Ruderman, July 23, 1947; children—James Michael, Dan Tully. Clin. social work psychotherapist Westchester County Div. Mental Hygiene, 1952-54; pvt. practice psychotherapy, 1954—; sr. staff therapist, practicum supr. Morton Prince Center, Inst. Research in Hypnosis, N.Y.C., 1970-77; co-founder, co-dir. Cancer Counseling and Tng. Center of Westchester, Scarsdale, N.Y., 1977—; disting. lectr., guest lectr. orgns., colls. and univs. Cert. in hypnotherapy and hypnoanalysis Inst. Research in Hypnosis; cert. social worker N.Y.; cert. masterpractitioner in Neuro-Linguistic Programming; cert. Acad. Cert. Social Workers. Fellow Soc. Clin. Social Work Psychotherapists; mem. Nat. Assn. Social Workers, Soc. Clin. and Exptl. Hypnosis, Internat. Soc. Hypnosis. Home and Office: 29 Quentin Rd Scarsdale NY 10583

RUDERMAN, JEANNE WENDY, pediatrician, neonatologist; b. Los Angeles, June 30, 1953; d. George Lawrence and Ruth (Bornstein) Ruderman. B.S. in Biol. Scis., U. So. Calif., 1974; M.D., UCLA, 1978. Diplomate Am. Bd. Pediatrics. Intern, resident in pediatrics Los Angeles County-U. So. Calif. Med. Ctr., Los Angeles, 1978-81; fellow in neonatology Cedars-Sinai Med. Ctr., Los Angeles, 1981-83, attending staff neonatologist, 1983—; asst. prof. pediatrics UCLA Sch. Medicine, 1984—. Contbr. articles to med. jours. Fellow Am. Acad. Pediatrics; mem. Calif. Perinatal Assn., Phi Beta Kappa. Office: Cedars-Sinai Med Ctr Dept Pediatrics Room 4310 8700 Beverly Blvd Los Angeles CA 90048

RUDIN, ANNA NOTO, mayor; b. Passaic, N.J., Jan. 27, 1924; m. Edward Rudin, June 6, 1948; 4 children. B.S. in Edn., Temple U., 1945, R.N., 1946; M. Pub. Adminstrn., U. So. Calif., 1983. Nursing educator Temple U. Sch. Nursing, Phila., 1946-48, Mt. Zion Hosp., San Francisco, 1948-49; mayor City of Sacramento, 1983—. Mem. Democratic State Central Com., Calif., 1984-85; bd. dirs. Sacramento Commerce Trade Orgn., Sacramento, 1984-85. Recipient Woman of Yr. award Soroptimist Club, 1976; Women in Govt. award U.S. Jaycee Women, 1984; Woman of Distinction award Sacramento Area Soroptimist Clubs, 1985. Mem. U.S. Conf. Mayors, LWV, Calif. Elected Women's Assn. (pres. 1976). Avocations: music; sewing. Office: City of Sacramento 915 I St Sacramento CA 95814

RUDINE, FRANCINE CAREN, filmmaker; b. Dallas, July 2, 1946; d. Francis Lumbard and Lois (Sustala) Rudine; m. Peter Edward Wittman, Aug. 25, 1973. B.F.A. in Film and TV, So. Methodist U., 1968; M.S. in Communications, Syracuse U., 1972. Copywriter, girl Friday Horn Advt., Dallas, 1969-70; freelance producer, writer, Syracuse, N.Y., 1971-72; owner, operator Tel-Assocs., Syracuse, 1972-73, Rudine-Wittman Prodns., Dallas, 1973—; pres. Rudine-Wittman Films, Inc., Dallas, 1983—; chmn. USA Film Festival, Dallas, 1984; bd. advisors KD Studio, Dallas, 1985—. Producer: (sponsored film) The Forgotten Freedom (Gold award), Out of Conflict ... Accord, (Silver award); (feature motion pictures) Play Dead, 1981, Ellie, 1983. Mem. acquisition com. USO 1985 (45th Anniversary Gala), Dallas, 1985; chmn. Communicator of Yr. Gala, Dallas, 1984. Mem. Soc. Theatrical Artists Guidance and Enhancement (bd. dirs.), Dallas Communications Council, USA Film Festival, Women in Communications (speaker), Women in Film (speaker), North Dallas C. of C. (speaker), Alliance Francaise, Women For Change (v.p. Dallas 1974). Democrat. Methodist. Avocations: skiing; travel. Office: Rudine-Wittman Films Inc 6309 N O'Connor Rd #104 Irving TX 75039

RUDKO, FRANCES HOWELL, lawyer; b. Elgin, Okla., Nov. 25, 1935; d. Paul Basil and Bertie Eleanor (Maggart) Howell; m. Michael Rudko, Aug. 21, 1956; children—Michael, Stephen Craig, Peter Gregory. B.A., So. Meth. U., 1959; J.D., U. Ark., 1973, M.A. in History, 1983. Bar: Ark. 1973, U.S. Dist. Ct. (we. dist.) Ark. 1973. Tchr. English, Grand Prairie Schs. (Tex.), 1959-60; sole practice law, Fayetteville, 1973—; judge Prairie Grove Mcpl. Ct. (Ark.), 1976. Bd. dirs. Arts Center Ozarks, Springdale, 1976-77, North Ark. Symphony Soc., 1981—, Butterfield Trail Retirement Center, 1981—. Mem. Washington County Bar Assn. (sec. treas. 1977), Ark. Bar Assn (chmn. family law sect. 1975-76), Fayetteville C. of C., ABA, Am. Assn. Women Lawyers, AAUW, Phi Beta Kappa. Methodist. Clubs: Altrusa (treas. 1979-81), Washington County Med. Aux. (pres. 1980-81). Home: 1410 Oakcliff St Fayetteville AR 72701 Office: 3000 Market St Suite B Fayetteville AR 72701

RUDNICK, CYNTHIA JANE VAN HOUSER, consumer products company manager; b. Nashville, Oct. 1, 1953; d. Roger William and Ange Merrill (King) Vanhooser; m. M. Jack Rudnick, Sept. 4, 1982; children—Matthew, Andrew. B.S., Middle Tenn. State U., 1977, M.B.E., 1980. Mktg. tchr. Marshall County Schs., Lewisburg, Tenn., 1977-78; mktg. instr. Columbia State Coll., Tenn., 1978-81; adj. faculty Syracuse U., Utica, N.Y., 1983-85; sales rep. Far East and Pacific, Oneida Silversmiths, N.Y., 1981-83, asst. mktg. mgr., 1983-84, product mgr., 1984—. Bd. dirs. Oneida County Civic Center, N.Y., 1985-86; pres. Marshall County Tchrs. for Democrats, Lewisburg, 1977-78. Runner-up, Miss. Tenn., 1973; named Miss Marshall County, C. of C., 1971. Mem. Nat. Assn. Female Execs., World Commerce Assn., Distbrv. Edn. Clubs of Am. (nat. advisor 1977-81), Pi Omega Pi, Delta Pi Epsilon. Democrat. Ch. of Christ. Avocations: tennis; snowskiing; calligraphy; gardening; cooking. Home: East Seneca St Sherrill NY 13461 Office: Oneida Silversmiths Kenwood Ave Oneida NY 13421

RUDNICK, IRENE KRUGMAN, lawyer, former state legislator; b. Columbia, S.C., Dec. 27, 1929; d. Jack and Jean (Getter) Krugman; A.B. cum laude, U. S.C., 1949, LL.B., 1952; m. Harold Rudnick, Nov. 7, 1954; children—Morris, Helen Gail. Admitted to S.C. bar, 1952; individual practice law, Aiken, S.C., 1952—; instr. bus. law U. S.C., Aiken, 1962—; tchr. Warrenville Elem. Sch., 1965-70; supt. edn. Aiken County, 1970-72; mem. S.C. Ho. of Reps., 1972-78, 80-84. Active, Aiken County Democratic Party, S.C. Dem. Party. Recipient Citizen of Yr. award, 1976-77, Bus. and Profl. Women's Career Woman of Yr., 1978, Aiken County Friend of Edn. award. Mem. NEA, S.C. Tchrs. Assn., Aiken County Tchrs. Assn., Am. Bar Assn., Aiken County Bar Assn., Nat. Order Women Legislators, AAUW, Alpha Delta Kappa. Jewish. Clubs: Order Eastern Star, Hadassah, Am. Legion Aux., Lioness. Office: Box 544 224 Park Ave Aiken SC 29801

RUDNICK, PAULETTE FENTON, educational administrator; b. N.Y.C., May 7, 1947; d. William Nelson and Beatrice June (Lee) Fenton; m. Philip Rudnick, Aug. 28, 1966; children—Danielle Hope, William Alan. B.S., L.I. U., 1974. Adminstrv. asst. Queens Day Prep. Sch., Sunnyside, N.Y., 1964-74; asst. prin. Boro Hall Acad., Bklyn., 1975-82, dir., 1982—. Office: Boro Hall Acad 17 Smith St Brooklyn NY 11201

RUDNIK, SISTER MARY CHRYSANTHA, college official; b. Winona, Minn., Dec. 2, 1929; d. Basil John and Sarah (Knopick) Rudnik; student Loyola U., 1951-52, Felician Coll., 1952-54, Cardinal Stritch Coll., 1954-57, Coll. St. Francis, 1957; Ph.B., DePaul U., 1958; postgrad. Mundelein Coll., 1959-60; M.A., Rosary Coll., 1962; postgrad. Northeastern Ill. U., 1964. Joined Congregation of the Sisters of St. Felix of Cantalice (Felician Sisters), 1948. Page, clk. Hill Reference Library, St. Paul, 1946-48; tchr. Holy Innocents Sch., Chgo., 1948-49, 50-54, St. Bruno Sch., Chgo., 1954-55, Holy Family Sch., Cudahy, Wis., 1955-57, Good Counsel High Sch., Chgo., 1958-67; instr. Felician Coll., Chgo., 1963—, librarian, 1957-82, dir. devel. and public relations, 1975—. Organizer, coordinator Felician Library Service, 1966-74, coordinator instl. self-study for accreditation North Central Assn.; mem. task force for study of instl. research for Ill. Assn. Community and Jr. Colls., 1968; library cons. St. Clement Sch., 1969; del. Ill. White House Conf. on Library and

Info. Services, 1978; Rev. Andrew Bowhuis, meml. scholar Cath. Library Assn., 1960. Mem. Nat. Soc. Fund Raising Execs. (cert. fundraising exec.), Cath. Library Assn. (life, chmn. No. Ill. unit 1968-69, exec. bd. 1981—), Art Inst. Chgo. (life), Council on Library Tech. (v.p. 1970, pres. 1971), Council for Advancement and Support of Edn. Address: 3800 Peterson Ave Chicago IL 60659

RUDNITZKY, SANDRA ROSENBLOOM, social worker; b. Pitts.; d. Howard and Thelma (Lewine) Rosenbloom; m. Elliot Rudnitzky, Aug. 12, 1973; children—Robyn Helene, Michelle Randi, Jillian Shira. B.Mus. cum laude, Boston U.; M.A., Columbia U.; M.S.W., Hunter Coll. Tchr. music, Queens schs., N.Y.C.; recreation therapist Montefiore Hosp. and Med. Ctr., Bronx, N.Y., social work asst., then student intern, 1971-74, med. social worker, 1974-75; pediatric social worker Perth Amboy Gen. Hosp., N.J., 1976-77; chmn. Middlesex County Child Placement Rev. Bd., N.J., 1979—; seminar leader employee assistance program Johnson & Johnson, spring 1986; bd. dirs., N.J. chpt. sponsor Middlesex County chpt. Parents Anonymous, 1977—; mem. social service adv. bd. Middlesex County Head Start, 1979—. Bd. dirs. Jewish Family Service of No. Middlesex County, v.p., 1981-83, pres. bd. dirs., 1985—; bd. dirs. Middlesex County Human Services Council; mem. Perth Amboy Family Preservation Council; mem. budget panel United Way of Central Jersey, 1984. Mem. Nat. Assn. Social Workers, Assn. Children N.J., Acad. Cert. Social Workers, Mental Health Assn. N.J., Nat. Council Jewish Women, Women's Am. ORT. Office: Middlesex County Child Placement Rev Bd 98 James St Edison NJ 08837

RUDOLPH, BEVERLY ANN, customer relations service and consulting company executive; b. Waukesha, Wis., Dec. 15, 1941; d. George William and Marjorie (Held) Seidl; m. Forest Rudolph, Jr., Nov. 28, 1959 (div. July 1966); children—Ronald George, Rebecca Lynne. Student public schs. Oconomowoc, Wis., 1959. Dancer, entertainer, nightclubs, Milw., 1968-70; exec. sec., agt. Mut. Trust Life Ins. Co., Brookfield, Wis., 1970-73; adminstrv. asst., paraprofl. counselor Counseling Ctr., Milw., 1973-77; dist. sales mgr. Automated Mktg. Systesm, Inc., Detroit, 1979-83; customer relations mgr. Bob Carter Ford Inc., Inver Grove Heights, Minn., 1983-84; pres. Custom Follow-up Inc., South St. Paul, 1984—. Coordinator personnel, sec. bd. dirs. Underground Switchboard crisis line, Milw., 1971-76. Mem. Wilderness Soc., Nat. Assn. Female Execs., Nat. Wildlife Fedn., Sierra Club, St. Paul C. of C. Avocations: Hiking; backpacking; horseback riding Office: Custom Follow-up Inc 450 Southview Blvd #250 South St Paul MN 55075

RUDOLPH, SONDRA, zoological society executive; b. Phila., Jan. 2, 1934; d. Irving S. and Nettie (Gruman) Bernstein; m. Howard Victor Rudolph, Oct. 3, 1954; children—Steven Paul, Andrew Lawrence. B.S., Temple U., 1955. Vice pres. mktg. U.S. Postal Service Fed. Credit Union, Washington, 1978-83; personnel dir. CMG Telemarketing (formerly Campaign Mktg. Group), Alexandria, Va., 1983-84; dir. dept. human resources Friends of Nat. Zoo, Nat. Zool. Park, Washington, 1985—; mem. Credit Union Promotional Com. Greater D.C., 1981-82. Recipient Golden Mirror award Credit Union Exec. Soc. for newsletter, 1981, for handbook, 1981, for membership brochure, 1982, for splty. advt., 1982. Mem. Am. Mktg. Assn., Am. Soc. for Personnel Adminstrn. Republican. Jewish. Home: Box 23621 Washington DC 20026 Office: Friends of Nat Zoo Washington Zoological Park Washington DC 20008

RUDULPH, MIMI, journalist, civic worker; b. Boston, Oct. 29, 1923; d. Frank Newell and Frederica (Lord) Terhune; B.A., U. N.H., 1944; postgrad. Juilliard Sch. Music, 1944-45, Columbia U., 1945, Boston U., 1948; H.H.O. (hon.), Northwood Inst., Dallas, 1983; m. Burwell Blount Rudulph, Dec. 30, 1948; 1 dau., Frederica Lord Rudulph. Founder Sunday Afternoon Concerts, Palm Springs (Calif.) Desert Mus., 1963, mem. performing arts and women's coms.; founder Palm Springs Friends of the Los Angeles Philharmonic, Met. Opera Showcase Concert, 1977; co-founder Palm Springs Opera Guild; producer-host weekly radio interview program: Window to the Arts, 1977-84; coordinator Festival of the Desert, 1980-82; music critic Desert Sun, 1962-83; arts columnist Sand to Sea mag., 1974—; mem. first community adv. bd. sta. KCET (PBS), 1979-82; arts advisor Coll. of the Desert, coordinator MGM lecture series, author People to People Day Proclamation, 1971; founder Walk for Devel., 1968, Freedom From Hunger, 1969, Internat. Friendship Fiesta, 1967-72; pres. Desert Chpt., People to People, 1972-77; chmn. Books and Authors Luncheon, 1973; mem. regional bd. Western Opera Theater, 1973-77; co-chmn. Welcome N.Z., 1972, Welcome Israel, for Conv. and Visitors Bur., 1973; mem. adv. panel Valley Solar Environ. Grant. Named Mother of Yr., recipient C. of C. award, 1961; honored testimonial luncheon, various civic groups, 1967; recipient vol. award Patton Hosp. various yrs., Betty Ford award Coll. of Desert, 1981, B'nai B'rith award, 1975, Am. Soc. Interior Designers award, 1977, 20th Year Outstanding Citizen award, Coll. of Desert, 1982; Vol. of Yr. award Palm Springs Women's Press Club, 1982; Woman of Yr. award Women United Internat., 1985. Proclamation Palm Springs Desert Mus., 1986; named Leading Women of Desert in arts category Palm Springs Life mag., 1986; day named in her honor by mayor of Palm Springs, Mar. 16, 1986. Mem. Music Critics Assn., World Affairs Council (bd.), Met. Opera Nat. Council. Clubs: Palm Springs Pathfinders. Writer on the arts; sonnet Two Silent Watchers used by composer Ernst Krenek for his Opus 222, 1975, author: Inside the Iron Lung, 1985. Home and Office: 729 High Rd Palm Springs CA 92262

RUDWICK, LYNNE MADELENE, stockbroker; b. N.Y.C., Aug. 14, 1950; d. Marvin Ira and Wilma Arlene (Halpern) Rudwick; m. Ralph Michael Pernick, June 6, 1971 (div. 1974). B.A. cum laude, SUNY-Binghamton, 1971; M.A., NYU, 1973. Various positions Lehman Bros. Kuhn Loeb, N.Y.C., 1975-81; account exec. Liss Tenner & Goldberg, Clifton, N.J., 1981-82, Purcell Graham & Co., N.Y.C., 1982-83, Butcher & Singer Inc., N.Y.C., 1983—. Jewish. Home: 101 W 12th St Apt 12Z New York NY 10011 Office: Butcher & Singer Inc 65 Broadway New York NY 10003

RUDY, RUTH CORMAN, state legislator; b. Millheim, Pa., Jan. 3, 1938; d. Orvis E. and Mabel Jan (Stover) Corman; m. C. Guy Rudy, Nov. 21, 1956; children—Douglas G., Donita Rudy Koval, Dianna F. Degree in x-ray tech. Carnegie Inst., 1956; student Pa. State U., 1968-71. Clk. of cts. County of Centre (Pa.), Bellefonte, 1976-82; rep. Pa. Gen. Assembly, Harrisburg, 1982—. Mem. Democratic Nat. Com., 1980—; pres. Pa. Fedn. Dem. Women, Harrisburg, 1985; 1st v.p. Nat. Fedn. Dem. Women, 1981—. Named Woman of Yr., Pa. Fedn. Dem. Women, 1982. Methodist. Office: Pa Ho of Reps PO Box 115 Harrisburg PA 17120

RUETENIK, SAMMY JEAN, educator; b. Monroe, Mich., June 23, 1929; d. Samuel Jether and Alta Ruth Rubley; B.A., U. Mich., 1950; M.A., Oakland U., 1971; m. David Gibbons Ruetenik, Aug. 25, 1950 (div. 1983); children—Katheryn, Christopher, Heidi, Daniel, Bennett. Tchr., Lansing (Mich.) Schs., 1950-51, Lakewood (Ohio) Schs., 1963-67; tchr. Bloomfield Hills (Mich.) Schs., 1967-78, 79-82, asst. prin., coordinator early entrance program Bloomfield Sch., 1978-79; owner MSSAM, 1979—. Vice-pres. Lakewood Safety Council, 1959; regional dir., bd. dirs. Mich. Reproductive Freedom Council, 1981-83; bd. dirs. Mich. Women's Hall of Fame. Cleve. Council Human Relations grantee, 1963. Mem. Mich. Edn. Assn. (women's task force, pres. women's caucus), NEA (regional coordinator, v.p. women's caucus, pres. women's caucus), Mich. Women's Studies Assn., Coalition for Non-Sexist Edn., NOW, Nat. Women's Polit. Caucus, Mich. Women's Polit. Caucus, Mich. Social Studies Council. Democrat. Presbyterian. Author: The Family, 1979. Address: 244 Neptune Walled Lake MI 48088

RUFF, JOAN R(OBERTA), lawyer; b. Clay Center, Kans., Sept. 17, 1947; d. Carl Henry and Evelyn Wava (Cate) R.; m. Dennis Paul Wilbert, Dec. 30, 1971; 1 dau., Kimberly A. Ruff-Wilbert. B.S. in Journalism, Kans. U., 1970, J.D., 1973; LL.M. in Taxation, NYU, 1975. Admitted to Kans. bar 1973, Mo. bar 1983. Assoc. firm Hackler Londerholm Corder Martin & Hackler, Olathe, Kans., 1973-78; atty. Panhandle Eastern Pipe Line Co., Kansas City, Mo., 1978-81, sr. atty., 1981—. Bd. dirs. Panhandle Employees Credit Union, 1982—. Trustee Kans. City Mus., 1984—. Mem. Am. Petroleum Inst. (income tax com. 1981—), Kans. U. Law Soc. (bd. govs. 1976-79), Kansas City C. of C. (centurion 1983—). Republican. Clubs: Central Exchange, Zonta. Home: 6601 Willow Ln Shawnee Mission KS 66208 Office: Panhandle Eastern Pipe Line Co 3444 Broadway Kansas City MO 64141

RUFFINO, BARBARA CASEY, bank executive; b. Washington, Jan. 13, 1943; d. Ralph Edward and Virginia Mae (Weddleton) Casey; m. Russell G. Ruffino, Aug. 1, 1970; children—Michael G., Jane R. B.A., Hood Coll., 1965; M.A., Columbia U., 1966. Sr. planner Appalachian Regional Commn., Washington, 1967-71; sr. assoc. Kirschner Assocs., Washington, 1971-77; mgmt. cons. Barbara Ruffino Assocs., Hingham, Mass., 1977-82; mgmt. devel. specialist Fidelity Investments, Boston, 1982-83; asst. v.p. State St. Bank, Boston, 1984—. Mem. Sch. Site Planning and Constrn. Com., Hingham, 1983—; bd. dirs. Continuum, Newton, Mass., 1985—; pres. Parent Tchr. Student Orgn., Hingham, 1984-85; mem. steering com. life endowment Hood Coll., Frederick, Md., 1985. NEA research fellow, 1968. Mem. Am. Soc. Tng. and Devel. (mem. program com.). Roman Catholic. Avocation: historical travel. Home: 31 Park Circle Hingham MA 02043 Office: State St Bank and Trust Co PO Box 351 Boston MA 02101

RUFFINO, CAROLYN LOUISE, district court judge; b. Bryan, Tex., Oct. 3, 1945; d. Preston and Callie (Fazzino) Ruffino. Student bus. adminstrn. Baylor U., 1972-74; J.D., 1976. Bar: Tex. 1977. Asst. trust office First Nat. Bank, Bryan, 1976-77; sole practice, College Station, Tex., 1978-80; asst. dist. atty. Dist. Atty.'s Office, Bryan, 1980-82; judge Brazos County Ct. at Law, Bryan, 1983—; judge 361st Dist. Ct., 1986—; mem. Brazos County Juvenile Bd., 1983—. Chmn. bd. Brazos County Rape Crisis Ctr., 1982-85; mem. steering com. Tex. Dem. Com. for Women, Austin, 1984; youth dir. St. Anthony's Ch., Bryan, 1980—, sec. Altar Soc., 1977-78; chmn. community affairs Austin Diocese Catholic Women, Austin, 1981-82. Named Outstanding 4-H Girl, Brazos County 4-H Clubs, Bryan, 1963, Outstanding Woman Brazos County, LWV, 1981. Mem. ABA, State Bar Assn. Tex., Brazos County Bar Assn., AAUW, Bryan-College Station C. of C. (adv. bd. leadership program 1983-85). Home: 305 Dunn St Bryan TX 77801 Office: 300 E 26th St Bryan TX 77802

RUGE, MARIAN CAST, public health nutritionist; b. Beaver Crossing, Nebr., Nov. 19, 1943; d. Marvin William Cast and Lois Margaret (Biltoft) Cast Hohnbaum; m. W. Alan Ruge, Dec. 10, 1977; children—Ian, Alex. B.S. in Home Econs., U. Nebr., 1965, M.S. in Nutrition, 1976. Registered dietitian. Community devel. vol. Peace Corps, Ain el Aouda, Morocco, 1965-67; extension agt. Coop. Extension Service, Albion, Nebr., 1968-69; tchr. home econs. Am. Girls Coll., Izmir, Turkey, 1969-72; regional nutritionist Internat. Voluntary Services, Lae, Papua New Guinea, 1976-79; women, infants and children nutritionist Pub. Health Dept., Grand Island, Nebr., 1981—; mem. vocat. edn. adv. council Grand Island Pub. Schs., 1983—. Bd. dirs. YWCA, Grand Island, 1981-83. Fulbright-Hays research grantee U.S. Dept. State, Morocco, 1974-75. Mem. Am. Dietetic Assn. Republican. Presbyterian. Home: 275 S Kimball St Grand Island NE 68801 Office: G I Hall County Health Dept 105 E 1st St Grand Island NE 68801

RUGG, ROSEANNE MILLER, market researcher; b. Phila., June 10, 1953; d. Francis Joseph and Rosemary Theresa (Griffin) Miller; m. James A. Rugg, Nov. 28, 1981. B.S., Cabrini Coll., Radnor, Pa., 1975; M.B.A., U. Miami, 1983. Assoc. research scientist Dade div. Am. Hosp. Supply Corp., Miami, Fla., 1976-80, mkt. research analyst, 1980-85; mkt. research coordinator Cedars Med. Ctr., Miami, 1985—. Mem. Am. Mktg. Assn., Am. Assn. Clin. Chemists, Beta Beta Beta. Home: 13925 SW 52d Lane Miami FL 33175 Office: Cedars Med Ctr 1400 NW 12th Ave Miami FL 33136

RUGGIERI, HELEN, poet, editor, publisher, educator; b. South Plainfield, N.J., Aug. 30, 1938; d. James Gordon and Lily (Middleton) Mitchell; m. Ford Francis Ruggieri, Mar. 9, 1963; children—Maria T., Ford M., Andrea G. B.A., Pa. State U., 1960; M.A., St. Bonaventure U., 1972. Editor, pub. Allegany Mountain Press, Olean, N.Y., 1974—; instr. in writing Jamestown Community Coll., Olean, 1981—. Author: The Poetess, 1982; Concrete Madonna, 1983; Rock City Hill Exercises, 1984. Mem. Niagara Erie Writers (county coordinator 1978-85). Avocations: gardening; herb lore. Home: 111 N 10th St Olean NY 14760

RUGGIERO, MARIA, marketing research analyst; b. Bronx, N.Y., July 14, 1956; d. Mark Anthony and Ann L. (Mangini) Dondero. B.S. in Mktg., St. John's U., 1978. Catalog inventory control specialist J.C. Penney Co., Inc., N.Y.C., 1978-81, market research analyst, 1981-83, communications research analyst, 1983-84, mktg. programs analyst, 1984, mktg. sr. research analyst, 1984—. Mem. Am. Mktg. Assn. Roman Catholic. Home: 12 Buckingham Meadow Rd East Setauket NY 11733 Office: JC Penney Co 1301 Ave of Americas New York NY 10019

RUGH, ALISA P(URDY), business executive; b. N.Y.C., June 21, 1907; d. Reginald Fairn and Mary Elizabeth (Davis) Purdy; m. Kenneth Augustine Rugh, July 16, 1938 (dec.); 1 child, Alberta Hope Rugh Kerin. Student U. Ill., 1923-25, U. Mo., 1926. Credit mgr. Schweig-Engel Corp., St. Louis, 1926-33; trader C. J. Devine Co., St. Louis, 1933-38; pres. Mace Springs Water Co., Bolivar, Pa., 1969-85, Garfield Refractories, Bolivar, 1969—, Rugh-Hillcrest Farms, New Cumberland, W.Va., 1969—, Patton Refractories, Pa., 1969—. Group leader Meml. Hosp. Aux., Johnstown, Pa., 1972-73; mem. Sch. Bd. Authority, Johnstown, 1982—; bd. dirs. Johnstown Symphony, 1969-80, ARC, Johnstown, 1970-71. Republican. Presbyterian. Clubs: Sunnehamma Country (Johnstown); Duquesne (hon. life mem.) (Pitts.). Avocations: golf; bridge. Home: 5420 N Ocean Dr Apt 2203 Singer Island FL 33404

RUHE, SHIRLEY LOUISE, government official; b. Des Moines, Mar. 20, 1943; d. Merritt Elton and Grace Alberta (Crabtree) Bailey; B.S., Iowa State U., 1965, M.S., 1969; m. Jonathan Mills Ruhe, Feb. 28, 1970; children—Alix-Nicole, Jonathan G. B. Wire editor, photographer Ames (Iowa) Daily Tribune, 1968-69; legis. asst. Congressman John Culver, 1969-72; staff asst. Congressman John Blatnik, 1973-75; dep. dir. budget com. U.S. Ho. of Reps., Washington, 1976—; spl. asst. Budget Process Task Force, 1976-77, chief budget process, 1978-79, dir. task force, 1979—; co-staff dir. Reconciliation Task Force, 1981—; adviser Spl. Rules Com. Task Force on Budget Process, 1982-83. Ford Found. grantee, 1969. Mem. Delta Sigma Phi, Phi Kappa Phi. Democrat. Home: 3915 N Woodstock St Arlington VA 22207 Office: 203 House Annex 1 Washington DC 20515

RUIZ, DEBRA ANN, educator; b. New Orleans, Mar. 19, 1952; d. Hugh Raymond and Audrey Mae (Ragas) Benvenutti; m. Gregory Paul Ruiz, Dec. 16, 1972; children—Gregory, Jr., Beau Raymond, Kristin Ann. B.A., Southeastern La. U. Legal sec. Levy, Smith, Pailet, New Orleans, 1973-74; tchr. St. Bernard Parish Sch., Chalmette, La., 1974-75, 76-77; tchr. Promised Land Acad., Braithwaite, La., 1977—. Bd. dirs. St. Bernard Catholic Ch. Parish Council, La., 1985—. Recipient dedication of yearbook Promised Land Acad., 1985. Democrat. Avocations: needlepoint; reading; swimming; softball; tennis. Home: 111 W Park Blvd Braithwaite LA 70040 Office: Promised Land Acad Route 1 Box 109 Braithwaite LA 70040

RUIZ, LISBETH JEAN, chamber of commerce official, editor, writer; b. Los Angeles, June 26, 1949; d. Louis and Laura Elvira (Peterson) Ruiz; 1 dau., Sofia Ruiz. Student Niagara U., 1969-71; B.J., U. Mo., 1973. Proofreader, Bee Publs., Williamsville, N.Y., 1969-70; editorial asst. Niagara Observer, Niagara Falls, N.Y., 1970-71; editor Parent Edn. Assn., Columbia, Mo., 1972-73; patient services coordinator N.C. Burn Ctr., U. N.C. Sch. Medicine, Chapel Hill, 1975-77, asst. to dir., mgr. skin bank, 1977-79; adminstrv. dir. econ. policy and nat. chamber found. C. of C. U.S., Washington, 1980—. Mem. Sigma Delta Chi. Republican. Home: PO Box 65280 Washington DC 20035 Office: Chamber of Commerce of USA 1615 H St NW Washington DC 20062

RUIZ-VALERA, PHOEBE LUCILE, librarian; b. Barranquilla, Colombia, Jan. 27, 1950; d. Ramon and Marion (Mehlman) Ruiz-Valera; m. Thomas Patrick Winkler, Mar. 27, 1981. B.A. cum laude, Westminster Coll., 1971; M.L.S., Rutgers-The State U., 1974; M.A., NYU, 1978. Library trainee Passaic (N.J.) Pub. Library, 1973-74, reference librarian, 1974; library assoc., cataloger NYU Law Library, N.Y.C., 1974-79, asst. curator, cataloger, 1979-81; librarian III, cataloger Rutgers U. Library, New Brunswick, N.J., 1981-82; chief cataloger Assn. Bar City N.Y., 1982-85, head tech. services, 1985—. Mem. ALA, Am. Assn. Law Libraries, Law Library Assn. Greater N.Y., Reforma, Salalm. Democrat. Presbyterian. Office: Assn Bar City NY 42 W 44th St New York NY 10036

RULE, ANN, author; 4 children. Grad. U. Washington with Deg. in English, 1954, postgrad. in police sci. Former policewoman, Seattle; free-lance writer newspapers, True Detective, Cosmopolitan, others; vol. Seattle Crisis Clinic; author non-fiction books: The Stranger Beside Me, 1980, The I-5 Killer, Want-Ad Killer, Lust Killer, Beautiful Seattle, 1984, novel Possession, 1983, Small Sacrifices, 1986; occasional pseudonym, Andy Stack; speaker on subject of serial killers. Address: care New Am Library 1633 Broadway New York NY 10019

RULE, BARBARA JEAN, marketing research executive; b. Wilmington, Del., Mar. 22, 1957; d. Joseph McBath and Jean Elizabeth (Tuckerman) R. B.S. in Biology, Emory U., 1979; M.B.A. in Mktg., Ga. State U., 1982. Research analyst Majers Corp., Atlanta, 1982-83; mgr. market research Stone Mfg. Co., Greenville, S.C., 1983-85; asst. mgr. sales research L'eggs Products, Inc., Winston-Salem, N.C., 1985—; cons. Edwards Baking Co., Atlanta, 1982. Mem. Am. Mktg. Assn., Alpha Mu Alpha, Chi Omega (pres. chpt. 1978-79, sec. 1977-78). Club: Symphony Chorale (Winston-Salem). Avocations: singing; ice skating; swimming; sports. Office: L'eggs Products Inc 5660 University Pkwy Winston-Salem NC 27105

RULE, VETA FRANKLIN TURNER (MRS. EDGAR WRIGHT RULE, JR.), writer, civic worker; b. Montgomery, Ala.; d. William Prescott and Lucy Houston (Reynolds) Turner; student U. Denver, 1927-31; m. Edgar Wright Rule, Jr., May 18, 1932; children—Lucie (Mrs. Gordon Lee Kidd, Jr.), James Randolph. Free lance writer, 1927—; pres. Denver Press Council, 1968—; writer, promoter original steering com. for Channel 6, Denver Ednl. TV, 1951-53; publicity dir. Colo. br. Am. Ch. Union, 1963-65; mem. Denver Civic Theater; mem. pub. relations staff, Presbyn. Hosp. Aux., 1951-55. Mem. Nat. League Am. Pen Women (pres. Denver br. 1956-58), Poetry Soc. Colo. (pres. 1969-70, asst. in compilation Golden Anniversary anthology), Nat. Assn. Parliamentarians, Nat. Fedn. State Poetry Socs. (conv. del. 1973-75), Denver Press Council (hon.), Alpha Gamma Delta. Anglican. Contbr. articles to profl. jours. Home: 2467 S Milwaukee St Denver CO 80210

RULTENBERG, ROSEANNE, librarian; b. Phila., May 27, 1950; d. Max and Mildred Gert (Rabinowitz) R. B.A. in Fine Arts cum laude, Hofstra U., 1971; M.S. in Info. Sci., Drexel U., 1975; studied painting with John Laub, 1980-83. Cataloger, Free Library of Phila., 1975-77, reference librarian for young adults, 1977-78, children's librarian, 1978—, head br. library, 1984—, storyteller, performer, 1978—, chmn. printed book lists, 1980, 84; cons. programs for gifted students Sch. Dist. of Phila., 1983-84. Exhibited paintings and photographs Bushrod Library, Phila., 1982, Frankford Women's Clubs, Phila., 1983, Cheltenham Art Ctr. (Pa.), 1983; illustrator: The Work, 1970, 71. Judge photography show Northeast Regional Library, Phila., 1979. Mem. ALA, Women's Caucus on the Arts. Office: Free Library of Phila 19th St and Benjamin Franklin Pkwy Philadelphia PA 19103

RUMLEY, FRANCINE CASANOVA, realtor; b. Charleston, S.C.; d. Ernest Casanova and Eugenia Rose (Passailaigue) Gibbs; m. Willard Lee Rumley; children—Jeffery Lane, Willard Lee III, Gary Beecher. Secretarial Sci., King's Bus. Sch., 1964; N.C. Real Estate for Brokers, Pitt Community Coll., 1976. Cert. real estate broker, N.C. Reference librarian George H. & Laura Brown Library, Washington, N.C., 1974-83; real estate broker The Rich Co., Washington, N.C., 1978—; cons. career Beaufort Community Coll., Washington, N.C., 1981—, area high schs., Washington, N.C., 1979—; cons. hist. George H. Brown Library, Washington, N.C., 1972-83. Co-chmn. county Heart Fund Dr., 1975; appointed mem. Hist. Dist. Commn., 1984—. Mem. Washington Bd. Realtors (pres. 1982-83), N.C. Bd. Realtors, Nat. Bd. Realtors, Washington Jr. Women's Club (Pres.'s award 1974, pres. 1975-76). Democrat. Presbyterian. Home: 212 W 12th St Washington NC 27889 Office: The Rich Co Route 1 Box 17 Washington NC 27889

RUMMEL, SUE ANN, medical technologist; b. Nampa, Idaho, Dec. 3, 1949; d. Talma Henry and B. Jeanne (Mitchell) Rummel; B.S. cum laude in biology, Bethany Nazarene Coll., 1971; M.S., U. Mo., 1981; postgrad. U. Kans. Sch. Medicine, 1984—. Med. technologist Bapt. Meml. Hosp. Clin. Lab., Kansas City, Mo., 1972-75, asst. supr. hematology lab., 1975-81; instr. Affiliated Sch. Med. Tech., Kansas City, Mo., 1981-84, dir. Research/Devel. Dept. Clin. Labs., 1982—; lectr. in field. Cert. med. technologist, specialist in hematology. Mem. Am. Soc. Clin. Pathologists. Office: 6601 Rockhill Rd Kansas City MO 64131

RUMPEL, BARBARA MARIE WEIMER, radio station executive; b. LaPort, Ind., Sept. 21, 1948; d. Warren George and Dorothy May (McDermott) Weimer; m. John H. Rumpel, Nov. 18, 1977. Student U. Ill., 1966-67, Kendall Coll., 1967-68. Media buyer/planner various advt. agencies, Chgo., 1968-73; account exec. Field Broadcasting, WFLD-TV, Chgo., 1973-76, Field Spot Sales, N.Y.C., 1976-79; nat. sales mgr. East Shore Broadcasting, WRCN FM/AM, Riverhead, N.Y., 1979-81, Island Broadcasting, WALK FM/AM, Patchogue, N.Y., 1981-84, gen. sales mgr., 1984—. Mem. Sr. Choir, 1st Presbyn. Ch., Southampton, N.Y., 1985. Mem. L.I. Radio Broadcasters Assn. (sec. 1983-85), N.Y. Market Radio Assn., others. Republican. Office: Island Broadcasting Co WALK FM/AM PO Box 230 Patchoque NY 11772

RUMPEL, HELEN BARBARA, artist; b. Lancaster, Pa., Mar. 31, 1937; d. Paul Hophni and Olive Deane (Morris) Johnson; m. Clarence Arthur Henry Rumpel, June 14, 1959; children—Warren Dean, Wesley Morris. A.A., Stephens Coll., 1957; B.S. in Art Edn., U. Wis., 1959. Art tchr. Santa Fe Pub. Schs., 1959-61; free-lance in contemporary embroidery, painting and clay, Santa Fe, 1960—; color cons. Register & Assocs. Architects, Inc., Santa Fe, 1977-84; tchr., lectr. mus. and guilds, U.S.A. and abroad, 1978—. Contbr. cover to Delta Kappa Gamma Internat. Bull., 1984. Participant 11th ann. Biennial Needlework Show, Indpls. Art Mus., 1984; one-woman shows include Sheldon Meml. Fine Arts Mus., U. Nebr., 1978, N.Mex. Govs. Gallery, Santa Fe, 1980, Wichita Art Assn., Kans., 1983, Baker Fine Art Gallery, Lubbock, Tex., 1984, 85, 86, Kokopelli II Galleries, Inc., Albuquerque, 1985, Sol del Rio, San Antonio, 1984-85, N.Mex. State U., 1986; group show: Pittsburg Art Ctr., 1985; represented in permanent collections Sheldon Meml. Gallery U. Nebr., Fine Arts Mus. of Mus. N.Mex., N.Mex. State Fair (purchase award), St. Luke's United Methodist Ch., Oklahoma City, Wichita Art Assn. Mem. Nat. Artist Equity Assn. (pres. 1972-74), Designer Craftsmen of N.Mex. (pres. 1974-76), Nat. Standards Council Am. Embroiderers (nat. tchr.), Embroidery Guild Am. (nat. tchr., exhibitor), DAR (officer Heritage chpt.), AAUW (past officer), Pilots Club Internat. (speaker), Dig and Hope Garden Club, Westerners (Santa Fe chpt.), Delta Kappa Gamma, Delta Zeta. Republican. Presbyterian. Home: 320 Cadiz Rd Santa Fe NM 87501 Office: Rumpel Art Studio PO Box 1552 Santa Fe NM 87501

RUMPFF, BARBARA BRYANT, marketing executive, consultant; b. Orlando, Fla., Sept. 25, 1951; d. Allen Leroy Bryant and Trudy (Whittington) McGarity; m. Cornelis J. Rumpff, May 15, 1976. B.S., Fla. State U., 1972, M.B.A., 1974; student U. Valencia, Spain, 1971, U. Belgrade, Yugoslavia, 1973. Research asst. Chevron Petroleum, The Hague, Holland, 1974; field mgr. Procter & Gamble, Cin., 1975-77; sales promotion mgr. Internat. Playtex, Stamford, Conn., 1978; pres. European Am. Mktg. Corp., Atlanta, 1979—. Pres. Assn. Internat. Students in Econs. and Commerce, Tallahassee, Fla., 1970-74. Mem. Am. Mktg. Assn. Office: European Am Mktg Corp 669 Gunby Rd Marietta GA 30067

RUMSEY, F. M. CLAIRE, painter, sculptor, poet; b. N.Y.C., May 11, 1916; d. David and Frances (Davidge) Rumsey; grad. N.Y. Sch. Applied Design for Women, 1937, Degree in Advanced Window Display, 1939; money mgmt. student SUNY, 1978-79. One-woman shows: Warner Pub. Library, 1974, 75, Greenburgh Pub. Library, 1975, County Ct. House, White Plains, N.Y., 1977; group shows include: Guild Hall, E. Hampton, N.Y., 1960, Expn. Intercontinentale, Monaco, 1965, 66, Katonah (N.Y.) Gallery, 1958-69; represented in pvt. collections; creator painted poems; contbr. poems to numerous mags. Mem. NOW. Home: 3 Byram Brook Pl Armonk NY 10504

RUNGE, CATHERINE PARKER, bottling company executive; b. Balt., Aug. 2, 1931; d. Thaddeus Cornelius and Catherine Marie (Ross) Parker; m. Patrick Eugene O'Gara, June 2, 1951 (div. Mar. 1981); children—Patrick Michael, Walter Casey, Cathleen Camille, Timothy Sean; m. William Howard Runge, Sept. 10, 1983. Student Fla. State U., 1948-49, U. Fla., 1949-50. Travel counselor AAA, Tampa, Fla., 1950; file clk. Hankins Realty, Tampa, 1950; sec. Pepsi-Cola Bottling Co., Tampa, 1951, exec. sec. to chief exec. officer, 1982-83, dir. pub. relations, 1983—; vol. worker Navy Relief Soc., Fla., Ga., Tex., Fla., 1966-80; real estate salesperson Ross Keith Realty, Falls Church, Va., 1973-74; office mgr. Dental Office, Sanford, Fla., 1981-82. Recipient Meritorious Service award NavyRelief Soc., 1970, 79. Mem. Sarasota C. of C. (ambassadress 1985, 86), Sarasota Tourism Assn., Venice Area C. of C. (Fla.), Better Bus. Bur.

Republican. Roman Catholic. Lodge: Zonta. Avocations: music; gourmet cooking; golf; public speaking.

RUNGE, MARY MUNSON, pharmacist; b. Donaldsonville, La., July 25, 1928; d. John Harvey and Mary Leona (Brown) Lowery; m. Wilbert Percy Munson, Dec. 13, 1947 (div. 1976); 1 dau., Katharine Marie; m. Alfred Joseph Runge, Sept. 4, 1976. B.S. in Pharmacy, Xavier U., New Orleans, 1948; D.Sc. (hon.), Mass. Coll. Pharmacy, 1980; D.Pharmacy (hon.), Ohio No. U., 1984. Pharmacist Roddicks Pharmacy, Richmond, Calif., 1949-51, Contra Costa County Hosp., Martinez, Calif., 1951-65, Brookside Hosp., San Pablo, Calif., 1965-71, Apothecary, Oakland, Calif., 1971—; mem. adv. council Smith Kline Corp., Phila., 1974-77; corp. mem. Calif. Blue Shield, San Francisco, 1980—; mem. Calif. Bd. of Pharmacy, Sacramento, 1983-87; Melendy lectr. U. Minn., Mpls., 1979. Adviser Pres. Reagan's Health Policy Commn., Washington, 1980. Named Hosp. Pharmacist of Yr., Calif. Hosp. Pharmacists Assn., 1968. Mem Am. Pharm. Assn. (pres. 1979-80 5 chmn. bd. 1980), Calif. Pharmacist Assn. (pres. 1974-75, Pharmacist of Yr. 1978), Calif. Pharmacist Ednl. Found. (pres. 1978—), Calif. Soc. Hosp. Pharmacists (pres. 1967-68), Inst. Medicine. Office: The Apothecary 10850 MacArthur Blvd Oakland CA 94601

RUNION, ROBERTA LYNN, editor, communications professional; b. Alexandria, Va., May 24, 1957; d. Wayne Godolphin and Gladys Roberta (Whetzel) R. B.A., George Mason U., Fairfax, Va., 1979. Editorial asst. Am. Hist. Assn., Washington, 1981-82; editorial asst. Washingtonian Mag., Washington, 1982-83, also contbr. articles; freelance editor/writer, 1983-85; assoc. editor Soc. Neurosci., 1985-86. Editorial asst. Writings on Am. History, 1980-81, Recently Pub. Articles, 1981-82; asst. editor: Guide to Departments of History, 1981-82; editor: Neuroscience Training Programs in North America, 1986; assoc. editor: Call for Abstracts. Mem. Washington Edn. Press Assn. Home: Route 1 Box 548 Chantilly VA 22021

RUNKEL, JANE ELIZABETH, educator; b. Port Washington, Wis., Aug. 27, 1952; d. Paul David and Jean (Goettmann) R.; A.B., Ripon Coll., 1974, also postgrad.; M.Ed., U. Wis., Oshkosh, 1979; postgrad. Northwestern U. Admissions counselor Ripon Coll., 1974-77, asst. dean admissions, 1977-78, asst. dean admissions, asst. career planning, 1978-79, asst. dean admissions, asst. dir. career planning and placement, 1979-80, asst. dean students, dir. career planning, 1980-82, dir. career planning and placement, affirmative action officer, 1982-84; practicum dir. Northwestern U., 1984-86, teaching assoc., 1986-87, also class rep. Sch. Edn. Alumni Bd. Mem. Nat. Assn. Women Deans, Adminstrs. and Counselors, Am. Ednl. Research Assn., New Eng. Historic and Geneal. Soc., DAR (Wis. Outstanding Jr. 1984), Soc. Colonial Dames, Phi Delta Kappa, Kappa Delta Pi, Alpha Delta Pi. Club: Bowne House Restoration. Office: Sch Edn Northwestern U Andersen Hall 2003 Sheridan Rd Evanston IL 60201

RUNOWICZ, CAROLYN DILWORTH, physician; b. Willimantic, Conn., May 1, 1951; d. S. Robert and Aline (Bergeron) Dilworth. B.A., U. Conn., 1973; M.D., Jefferson Med. Coll., 1977. Resident ob-gyn Mt. Sinai Hosp., N.Y.C., 1977-81, fellow gynecol. oncology, 1981-83, clin. instr., 1983-85; asst. prof., dir. gynecol. oncology dept. ob-gyn Albert Einstein Coll. Medicine, Montefiore Med. Ctr., N.Y.C., 1985—; lectr. in field. Contbr. articles and chpts. to med. publs. Galloway fellow Sloane-Kettering Meml. Hosp., N.Y.C., 1980. Fellow Am. Coll. Obstetricians and Gynecologists; mem. AMA, Am. Med. Woman's Assn., N.Y. County Med. Soc., Phi Beta Kappa, Alpha Omega Alpha, Phi Kappa Phi. Club: Metropolitan (N.Y.C.). Office: Albert Einstein Coll Medicine Dept Ob-Gyn Belfer Bldg Room 501 1300 Morris Park Ave Bronx NY 10461

RUNSTAD, JUDITH MANVILLE, lawyer; b. Ontario, Oreg., July 15, 1944; d. Gerry Wright and Jean (Thurston) Manville; m. 2d, H. Jon Runstad, Dec. 3, 1977. B.S., U. Idaho, 1966, M.S., 1967; J.D., U. Wash., 1974. Bar: Wash. 1974. Tchr., Shorecrest High Sch., Seattle, 1967-71; legal intern King County Pros. Atty., Seattle, 1972-73; assoc. Foster, Pepper & Riviera, Seattle, 1974-79, ptnr., 1979—; dir. Safeco Mut. Funds Bd., Seattle. Bd. govs. Griffin Coll., Seattle, 1982—; trustee Downtown Seattle Assn., 1982—, v.p., 1985-86, pres., 1986-87; bd. dirs. ACT Theater, Seattle, 1979—, treas., 1984—, trustee Seattle Art Mus., 1984—, Seattle Repertory Theatre, 1985—. Mem. ABA, Wash. Bar Assn. (dir. land use sect.), Urban Land Inst., Seattle C. of C. (treas. 1984—, gen. counsel 1985-86), Lambda Alpha, Phi Beta Kappa. Episcopalian. Exec. editor: Law Rev. Clubs: Seattle Tennis, Seattle Yacht, Wash. Athletic.

RUNTE, ROSEANN, university administrator; b. Kingston, N.Y., Jan. 31, 1948; came to Can., 1971; d. Robert B. and Anna L. (Schorkopf) O'Reilly; m. Hans Rainer Runte. B.A. summa cum laude, SUNY-New Paltz, 1968; M.A., U. Kans., 1969, Ph.D., 1974. Lectr. Bethany Coll., W.Va., 1970-71; lectr. adult studies St. Mary's U., Halifax, N.S., Can., 1971-72; prof. Dalhousie U., Halifax, 1972-83, asst. dean., chmn. French dept., 1980-83; pres. U. St. Anne, Pointe-de-l'Eglise, Nouvelle-Ecosse, 1983—; mem. pubs. com. Hannah Inst., Toronto, Ont., 1984—. Author: Brumes bleues, 1982; Faux-Soleils, 1984. Editor: Studies in 18th Century Culture, (vols. VII, VIII, IX), 1978, 79. Contbr. articles to profl. jours. Bd. dirs. N.S. Art Gallery, Halifax, 1985—. N.Y. State Regents scholar, 1965-68; NDEA grantee, 1968-72. Mem. Can. Fedn. for Humanities (past pres.), Internat. Soc. for 18th Century Studies (assoc. treas. 1983—), N.S. Soc. for Study of Ethnicity (v.p. 1985—), Atlantic Assn. Univs. (exec. bd. 1985—), Bus. and Profl. Women's Assn., Association des Professeurs de Français des Universités et Collèges, MLA, Can. Comparative Lit. Assn., Internat. Assn. for Comparative Lit. (treas. 1985—), Can. Soc. for 18th-Century Studies (past pres.), Atlantic Soc. for 18th-Century Studies (past pres.), others. Roman Catholic. Office: U Sainte Anne Pointe de l'Eglise NS B0W 1M0 Canada

RUNYON, ALICE LOUISE MINNERLY, restoration research, educator, musician; b. North Tarrytown, N.Y., June 12, 1902; d. Percy Charles and Phernetta Elizabeth (Miller) Minnerly; B.S., N.Y. U., 1943, M.A., 1947; grad. Guilmant Organ Sch., 1940; m. James Garfield Runyon, June 30, 1928 (dec. 1955). Tchr. pub. sch., 1921-46; asst. dir. Philipse Castle restoration, 1943-47; head research for restoration Sunnyside, Washington Irving's home, 1945-47; asso. dir. Philipse Castle and Sunnyside, 1947-51, Sleepy Hollow Restorations, Inc., 1951-55, corp. sec., trustee, 1951-55; dir. Specialized Research, 1956—. Curator Horace Greeley Mus., 1958-68; genealogist Dutch Colonial of Del., 1967-71. Organist and choir master Christ Evang. and Ref. Ch., N.Y.C., 1942-52; lectr. Sec., v.p. USO, The Tarrytowns, World War II. Mem. Am. Guild Organists, Hist. Soc. Tarrytowns (dir., sec.), Sons and Daus. Pilgrims (organizing pres. past nat. officers club, 1st dep. gov. gen., N.Y. State gov., dep. gov., treas., sec., nat. bd. mem.), Am. Hist. Soc., Patriotic Women Am., Daus. Am. Colonists, Colonial Daus. 17th Century, DAR (chmn. Jr. Am. Citizens, registrar, historian, dir.), Daus. Founders and Patriots Am. (life; N.Y. pres., v.p., nat. councillor, nat. chmn. hist. edn., nat. corr. sec.), Daus. Colonial Wars (pres. N.Y. State, nat. historian, mem. nat. exec. bd., rec. sec., 2d v.p. Nat. Officers Club), Ams. Armorial Ancestry (nat. councillor, nat. pres., nat. treas., nat. registrar, genealogist), Soc. Holland Dames, Ames. Royal Descent (past nat. councillor, 3d v.p. gen.), Colonial Dames Am., Huguenot Soc. Am. (nat. registrar, council), Descs. Knights of Garter, Women's Nat. Republican Club, Am. Friends Lafayette, Daus. Union 1861-1865, Order of Washington, Order Three Crusades, Descs. William the Conqueror, Women Descs. Ancient and Honorable Arty. Co., N.Y. State Hist. Assn. (organizer 1st jr. chpt.), Westchester County, Chappaqua (former trustee), Somers (hon.) hist. socs., Nat. Gravel Soc. (v.p.), Kappa Delta Pi. Author: Minne Johannes and Some of his Descendants; Frederick Miller of Colchester and Some of His Kin; others. Contbr. articles to various publs. Historian village of N. Tarrytown, N.Y., 1947-81; asst. registrar gen., past archivist Order of Crown of Charlemagne in Am. Home: 483 Munroe Ave North Tarrytown NY 10591 Office: Specialized Research PO Box 187 North Tarrytown NY 10591

RUPER, JERAY MARIAN, accountant; b. Painesville, Ohio, May 10, 1952; d. Richard Lewis and Nancy Jean (Few) Bunnell; m. Daniel Lynn Eiler, Dec. 7, 1973 (div. 1980); children—Heather Lynn, Heidi Marie; m. Ronald Thomas Ruper, June 6, 1981. B.A. in Acctg., Thiel Coll., 1974; postgrad. W.Va. U., 1985—. C.P.A., Pa., Ohio, W.Va. Acct., Rex Walker & Assocs., Grove City, Pa., 1976-78; mgr. fin. acctg. Harris Wholesale Co., Solon, Ohio, 1978-83; spl. asst. to chief fin. officer W.Va. U., Morgantown, 1983-84, mgr. mgmt. analysis, 1984—; cons. fin. systems Human Interface, Morgantown, 1983—. Mem. Am. Inst. C.P.A.s, W.Va. Soc. C.P.A.s, Ohio Soc. C.P.A.s. Republican. Roman Catholic. Avocation: travel. Office: WVa U Stewart Hall Morgantown WV 26505

RUPERT, CAROLA GAY, museum administrator; b. Washington, Jan. 2, 1954; d. Jack Burns and Shirley Ann (Orcutt) R. B.A. in History, Bryn Mawr Coll., 1976; M.A., in Am. History and Mus. Studies, U. Del., 1978. Personnel mgmt. trainee Naval Material Command, Arlington, Va., 1972-76; Hagley fellow Hagley Mus., Wilmington, Del., 1977; asst. curator exhibits Hist. Soc. of Del, Wilmington, dir. Macon County Mus., Decatur, Ill., 1978-81; dir. Kern County Mus., Bakersfield, Calif., 1981—; advisor Kern County Heritage Com., Bakersfield, 1981—; mem. Kern County Hist. Records Com., 1981—. Treas. Arts Council of Kern, 1984—, bd. dirs., 1983—, pres. elect, 1986; bd. dirs. Kern County Mgmt. Council, 1983—; chmn. and co-chmn. County Employees United Way Campaign, Bakersfield, 1981-83; bd. dirs. Calif. Com. Promotion of History, Sacramento, 1984—. Bryn Mawr Coll. Alumnae Regional scholar, 1972-76. Mem. Am. Assn. for State and Local History, Am. Assn. Museums (MAP surveyor 1985—), Nat. Trust for Hist. Preservation. Avocations: swimming; camping. Office: Kern County Mus 3801 Chester Ave Bakersfield CA 93301

RUPERT, ELIZABETH ANASTASIA, library science educator; b. Emlenton, Pa., July 12, 1918; d. John Hamilton and Eva Blanche (Elliott) R. B.S. in Edn., Clarion U., 1959; M.S. in L.S., Syracuse U., 1962; Ph.D., U. Pitts., 1970. Cert. library sci., Pa. Sec., Quaker State Oil Refining, Emlenton, 1939-56; tchr., librarian Oil City Area Schs., Pa., 1959-61; librarian Venango Campus Clarion State Coll., 1961-62, prof. library sci., 1962-70; prof., dean library sci. Clarion U., 1970—, interim pres., 1977; acct. William Rupert Mortuary, Inc., Knox, Pa., 1948—. Mem. ALA, Assn. for Library and Info. Sci. Edn., Pa. Sch. Library Assn., Pa. Library Assn. (trustee, regional chmn. 1975-78). Republican. Mem. Ch. of God. Home: Drawer H Knox PA 16232 Office: Coll Library Sci Clarion U Pa Wood St Clarion PA 16214

RUPRECHT, MARY MARGARET WYANT, office automation mgmt. cons.; b. O'Neill, Neb., Oct. 20, 1934; d. Charles Ellsworth and Mary Loretto (Cuddy) Wyant; student Coll. St. Benedict, 1952-54; cert. Am. Inst. Banking, 1970; m. Gregory Earl Ruprecht, Sept. 24, 1955; children—Mary Debra, Sharie Marie. Dist. clk. U.S. Soil Conservation, Aitkin, Minn., 1956-68; comml. loan sec. No. City Nat. Bank, Duluth, Minn., 1965-71; office mgr. Fryberger, Buchanan Law Firm, Duluth, 1971-72; pvt. practice word processing and mgmt. cons., Duluth, 1972-76; v.p., prin. Altman & Weil, Inc., mgmt. cons., 1976-79; pres. Mary M. Ruprecht & Assocs., 1979—; tchr. Am. Inst. Banking. Mem. adv. council Minn. State Bd. Edn., Duluth Office Edn. Assn., Coll. Applied Scis. at Miami U., Oxford, Ohio, Ball State U., Muncie, Ind. Fin. dir. 8th Congressional Dist. Dem.-Farm Labor Party, 1972-73. Cert. mgmt. cons. Mem. Internat. Word Processing Assn. (internat. pres. 1974-75), Am. Inst. Banking (nat. chmn. women's com. 1970-71), Adminstrv. Mgmt. Soc., Am. Mgmt. Assn., Office Systems Research Assn. (conf. chmn. 1985), Bus. and Profl. Women's Assn., Internat. Platform Assn. Co-Author: Managing Office Automation; Office Automation: Concepts and Principles; Office Automation: A Management Approach. contbr. articles to profl. jours. Home: 140 W Myrtle St Duluth MN 55811

RUSCITELLA, MARIA MARTHA, lawyer; b. Phila., May 9, 1954; d. Ulysses Thomas and Joan Marie (Hagner) Ruscitella. B.A., Elmira Coll., 1975; J.D., Delaware Law Sch., Wilmington, 1978. Bar: Pa. 1979. Sole practice, Wayne, Pa., 1979-80; corp. counsel C.D.M. Inc., Hatboro, Pa., 1980-82; sole practice, Paoli, Pa., 1982-83; gen. counsel Theriault's Inc., Annapolis, Md., 1983—. Contbr. monthly newsletter The Dollmasters, 1983; contbr. The Law Forum, 1976—. Mem., Annapolis Law Ctr., 1983—. Mem. ABA, Pa. Bar Assn., Women's Bar Assn. Md., Delta Theta Phi. Republican. Roman Catholic. Club Young Republicans. Home: 15 Nutwell Rd Lothian MD 20711 Office: Theriault's Inc 1981 Moreland Pkwy Annapolis MD 21401

RUSH, JULIA ANN HALLORAN (MRS. RICHARD HENRY RUSH), artist, writer; b. St. Louis, Oct. 25, 1927; d. Edward Roosevelt and Flavia Hadley (Griffin) Halloran; m. Richard Henry Rush, Aug. 15, 1956; 1 child, Sallie Haywood. Student Washington U., St. Louis, 1945-47; B.A., George Washington U., 1949. One man shows: Fort Amador Officers Club, Panama Canal Zone, El Panama Hotel, Panama, George Washington U., Statler Hotel, Roosevelt Hotel, Washington, Newspaper Women's Club, Washington, Waukegan Library, Ill., Epworth Heights Hotel, Ludington, Mich., exhibited in group shows: Panama Art League, Corcoran Gallery; represented in permanent collections: U. Panama; also pvt. collections; model John Robert Powers Agy., 1950; sec.-treas., dir. N.Am. Acceptance Corp., 1956-58; v.p. Rush and Halloran, Inc., 1957-58, ptnr., 1954-57; research asst. to husband's bi-weekly newsletter Art/Antiques Investment Report, 1973—. Illustrator: Antiques As An Investment (author Richard H. Rush), 1968; research asst.: Investments You Can Live With and Enjoy (author: Richard H. Rush), 1974, 2d, edit., 1975, 3d edit., 1976; Photographer: Automobiles as an Investment, 1982; Investing in Classic Cars, 1984. Recipient 1st prize (Panama) Newspaper Women's Club, 1953; First Prize Panama Art League, 1953. Mem. DAR, Nat. League Am. Penwomen, Florence Crittenton Circle (rec. sec. 1968-69), Kappa Kappa Gamma. Club: Washington. Office: Villa Cornaro at Piombino Dese PD Italy 35017

RUSH, SARAH MAY, federal government financial official; b. Kokomo, Ind., Nov. 23, 1953; d. Lawrence Wayne and Eva Lenor (Burns) R. Tech. degree Ind. Vocat. Tech. Coll., 1979; B.S., Ind. U.-Kokomo, 1982. Owner, operator farm, Windfall, Ind., 1974—; instr. logistics U.S. Army Res., Indpls., 1984—; personnel clk. Dept. of Army, Indpls., 1984-85, operating acct., 1985—. Chmn. mil. units Seed City Jamboree Com., Windfall, 1982—. Serve with U.S. Army Res., 1975—. Mem. DAV (life), Nat. Assn. Female Execs., Fraternal Order Police (assoc.), Am. Soc. Mil. Comptrollers, Am. Legion (1st vice comdr. 1983-85, comdr. 1985—). Republican. Lodge: Tecumseh (life). Avocation: metaphysics study. Home: Route 1 Box 47 Windfall IN 46076 Office: US Army Fin and Acctg Ctr Bldg 1 FINCO-CB Indianapolis IN 46249-1326

RUSHFORD, MARION DIANE, nurse; b. Milw., Dec. 22, 1943; d. Archie Rude and Francis Ilene (Thompson) Hanson; R.N., St. Luke's Hosp., Racine, Wis., 1975; student Parkside U., Kenosha, Wis., 1972-75, also specialized nursing courses; m. Oct. 31, 1984; children—David, Diana. R.N., So. Wis. Center, Union Grove, 1975; patient care coordinator Brookside Geriatrics Center, Kenosha, 1977; inservice coordinator charge tng. and edn. Westview Nursing Home, Racine, 1978; dir. staff devel. Lincoln Luth. Home, Racine, 1979; dir. nursing Shady Lawn West, Kenosha, Algoma Hosp. and Western Village, Green Bay, Wis., 1981-83; adminstr. Western Village, 1983—; real estate saleswoman, also owner, operator floral design shop Rose Palace. Mem. Gateway Bd. Fire Tng. State of Wis. grantee, 1972-75; lic. nursing home adminstr., Wis. Mem. Wis. Soc. Health, Manpower, Edn. and Tng., Long Term Care Dirs. Greater Milw., Kenosha Dirs. Long Term Care, Nat. Assn. Female Execs., Am. Nurses Assn., Internat. Platform Assn. Lutheran. Address: 4650 Stagecoach Rd Green Bay WI 54301

RUSK, MARGARET SENER, manager of houses; b. Balt., Mar. 25, 1928; d. Alexander Proudfit and Anna (Sener) Rusk; 1 child, Christian. B.A., Wellesley Coll., 1948; M.Ed., Harvard U., 1951; M.L.S., Syracuse U., 1962. English tchr. Universidad del Atlántico, Barranquilla, Colombia, 1956-57; lab. tech. Upstate Med. Ctr., Syracuse, N.Y., 1957-58; cataloguer Syracuse U. Library, N.Y., 1963-72; coordinator draft-mil. counseling Am. Friends Service Com., Syracuse, 1975-77, counselor, 1970—; mgr. houses, Syracuse, 1978—. Contbr. articles and field notes to The Kingbird, publ. of Fedn. of N.Y. State Bird Clubs, 1959—. Contbr. articles to Peace Newsletter, Syracuse Peace Council, 1970—. Bird censuser Onondaga Audubon Soc., Syracuse, 1953—; active Syracuse Peace Council, Syracuse, 1953—; mem. Fedn. N.Y. State Bird Clubs, 1955—, permanent rep. from Onondaga Audubon Soc., 1975—. Recipient Disting. Service award Onondaga Audubon Soc., 1983; Peace award Syracuse Peace Council, 1984. Mem. Beta Phi Mu. Avocations: birdwatching; herb collecting.

RUSK, PEGGIE JOY, personnel executive; b. Piney Flats, Tenn., Mar. 6, 1941; d. Kenneth George and Hazel Erma (Williams) Walker; m. David Earl Rusk, Aug. 2, 1964; 1 child, Ginger Faye. Student Mount Vernon Bus. Sch. Sales sec. Galion (Ohio) Iron Works, 1957-59; classified advt. mgr. Mount Vernon News (Ohio), 1959-67; exec. sec. Turner & Shepard, Columbus, Ohio, 1967-77; personnel rep. Alexander & Alexander, Columbus, 1977-79, personnel mgr., 1979—, asst. v.p., 1984—. Named Ms. Exec., Columbus Dispatch, 1983; awards Ohio Newspaper Assn., 1965, 67. Mem. Am. Soc. Personnel Assn., Central Ohio Personnel Assn., Columbus Compensation Group. Republican. Presbyterian. Lodge: Order Eastern Star. Home: 222 Apache Circle Westerville OH 43081 Office: Alexander & Alexander 17 S High St Columbus OH 43215

RUSKELL, VIRGINIA ANN, librarian, educator; b. Nashville, June 4, 1948; d. George Channing Ruskell and Douglass (McFerrin) Rudkoff; A.A., Reinhardt Coll., 1967; B.A. in history, Emory U., 1969; M.L.S., George Peabody Coll., 1970; M.A. in English, West Ga. U., 1975. Library asst. George Peabody Coll. Library Sch., 1969-70; interlibrary loan librarian West Ga. Coll., Carrollton, 1970-76, bibliog. instrn. librarian, 1977-80, reference coordinator, 1980—, assoc. prof., 1980—. Treas., LWV, Carrollton, 1975-77; chmn. social concerns St. Andrew United Meth. Ch., Carrollton, 1981-82, fin. sec., 1980-81, chmn. fin. com., 1982. Council Library Resources Library Services Enhancement grantee, 1976-77. Mem. Southeastern Library Assn., AAUP (sec. 1974-75, v.p. 1975-76), AAUW (v.p. programs 1982—), Beta Phi Mu, Phi Kappa Phi. Democrat. Home: PO Box 844 Carrollton GA 30117 Office: West Ga Coll Library Carrollton GA 30118

RUSNACK, SANDRA ELAINE, energy consulting company executive; b. Hammond, Ind., June 6, 1950; d. Roy Edward and Joan Elaine (Imes) Thon; m. Robert William Rusnack, Sept. 11, 1971. B.S. in Acctg. and Mgmt., Calumet Coll., 1981. Acctg. clk. Cert. Concrete Inc., East Chicago, Ind., 1971-72; staff acct. Ind. Forge and Machine Co., East Chicago, 1973-77; asst. treas. HYCRUDE Corp., Chgo., 1980-81; instr. Ind. Vocat. Tech. Coll., Gary, 1982-83; mgr. acctg. GDC, Inc., Chgo., 1977—, treas. GDC Internat., Inc., 1981—. Treas., Citizens for Community Improvement, Whiting, Ind., 1975. Mem. Nat. Assn. Female Execs. Office: GDC Inc 10 W 35th St Chicago IL 60616

RUSSELL, ANN NICHOLS, college administrator; b. Birmingham, Ala., May 10, 1940; d. Olas Clarence and Emma (Spurgeon) Nichols; m. Jim W. Russell, May 14, 1961 (div. 1979); children—Mark Acton, Craig Nichols. Student, Auburn U., 1958-61; B.A., Am. U., 1965; M.Ln., Emory U. 1981; postg. Ednl. asst. First United Meth. Ch., Cedartown, Ga., 1970-73; pub. relations rep. Ethel Harpst Home, Cedartown, 1973-78; TV producer Tri-County Regional Library, Rome, Ga., 1978, pub. relations/grants coordinator, 1978-81; grants coordinator Berry Coll., Mt. Berry, Ga., 1981-82, dir. corp. and found. programs, 1982—; mem. state planning com. Am. Council on Edn. Nat. Identification Program, 1983—; info. cons. Infosearch, Rome, 1981—; project cons. Ga. Com. for Humanities and NEH, 1980. Contbr. articles to profl. jours.; producer video series Folk Art: Bridge Between The Mountains and the Plains, 1978. Pres., Jr. Service League, Cedartown, Ga., 1975-76; mem. adv. com. Congressman Newt Gingrich, 1982; chmn. bd. dirs. Polk Tng. Ctr. Mentally Retarded, 1972-75, First United Meth. Presch., 1977-78. Recipient Cokesbury Grad. award Emory U., 1980; John Whouley fellow, 1980. Mem. Council for Advancement and Support of Edn., ALA, AAUW (editor/br. pres. 1976-77), Rome Area C. of C., Leadership. Club: Cherokee Golf and Country. Home: 318 W Girard Ave Cedartown GA 30125 Office: Berry Coll Mount Berry GA 30149

RUSSELL, ANNE DORA, ednl. adminstr.; b. Daleville, Ala., Jan. 7, 1931; d. Curtis G. and Annie B. (Engram) Robinson; B.S., Ala. State Coll., 1958; M.S., U. Mich., 1969, postgrad., 1972-79; children by previous marriage—John, Shirley Jenkins. Tchr. English and bus. edn. public schs., Enterprise, Ala., 1958-62; substitute tchr. Pontiac (Mich.) Bd. Edn., 1962-63, tchr. English and bus. edn., 1965-71; sec. U. Mich. Med. Sch., Ann Arbor, 1963-64; dir. health edn. and welfare Pontiac Area Urban League, 1964-65; part-time instr. secretarial sci. Wayne Community Coll., Mich., 1977; asst. prin. Pontiac Central High Sch., 1971-80, Pontiac No. High Sch., 1980-83, Pontiac Central High Sch., 1983—. Del. 48th Precinct, Pontiac, 1974-76; bd. dirs. Newman Non-Profit Housing Corp., 1965—. Recipient cert. of award Jefferson Jr. High Sch., 1968, You Can award Pontiac Adult Edn., 1975, cert. of appreciation Mich. State U., 1974. Served with USAF, 1952-53. Mem. Nat. Assn. Secondary Sch. Prins., Pontiac Assn. Sch. Adminstrs. (cert. of appreciation 1976), NAACP, Ala. State U. Alumni Assn., U. Mich. Alumni Assn., Delta Kappa Gamma. Democrat. Methodist. Author: Blacks in Pontiac, 1975; Builders of Detroit, 1978. Home: 1158 Dudley St Pontiac MI 48057 Office: 300 W Huron St Pontiac MI 48053

RUSSELL, BONNIE F., manger and research executive; b. Ft. Edward, N.Y., June 20, 1939; d. G. Wright and Edna J. (Marshall) R. Student Central Coll., Fayette, Mo., 1957-59; B.S., Ohio No. U., 1961. Lic. lab. technologist, Fla.; lic. lab. supr., radiation safety officer, Calif. Med. technician Glens Falls (N.Y.) Hosp., 1961-63; dental technician Williams Ceramic Lab., Glens Falls, 1963-73; med. technologist Orlando (Fla.) Plasma Ctr., 1976-77, mgr., 1977-78; asst. mgr. Houston Plasma Ctr., 1978-79; v.p. med. affairs Lopapa Inst., Inc., Los Angeles, 1979—. Inventor plasma expressor, 1977. Committeeman Glens Falls Democratic Party, 1968; mem. City-State Renter Adv. Com., Los Angeles, 1982—; mem. citizens' adv. council Am. Inst. Cancer Research; mem. Women's Marathon Olympic Com.; research council Scripps Clinic and Research Found. Mem. Calif. Bus. Women Network (v.p.), Nat. Assn. Female Execs., Am. Mgmt. Assn., N.Y. Acad. Scis., Found. Christian Living. Lodge: Rebekahs (v.p. 1972). Home: 722 S Ardmore St 36 Los Angeles CA 90005 Office: Researchers 3400 W 6th St Los Angeles CA 90020 also Fashion Dynamics 1155 Triton Dr Foster City CA 94404

RUSSELL, CAROLYN ANN, artist, former art gallery owner; b. Peoria, Ill., Oct. 7, 1937; d. Frank Louis and Frances Mary (Gula) Cinotto; m. William Merle Russell, Aug. 29, 1959, children—William Gregory, David Franklin, Susan Marie. B.A., Whitworth Coll., 1959. Art tchr. Spokane Pub. Schs. Washington, 1959-60; owner The Art Studio, Sumner, Wash., 1968-71; represented by Colorado Springs Fine Arts Ctr., Holiday Sales Gallery, 1984. One-woman show Penrose Library, Colorado Springs, 1983; exhibited in group shows at Colorado Springs Art Guild, 1977, Colorado City Art Show, 1978, Colorado Springs Mothers' Art Show, 1979. Young life leader Young Life, non-denominational Christian group, Spokane, Wash., 1956-58, Renton, Wash., 1964, Colorado Springs, 1982-84. Recipient 1st prize Colorado Springs Art Guild, 1st prize Colorado City Art Show, 1st prize Colorado Springs Mothers' Art Show. Republican. Presbyterian. Clubs: Kinnikiniks Antique, Bon Vivants. Home: 1132 Park St Sumner WA 80909

RUSSELL, CAROLYN JEAN, lawyer; b. Dallas, Mar. 27, 1949; d. John Thomas and Zeta Blondell (Turner) R. B.S., Howard U., 1969; M.A., George Washington U., 1972; J.D., Harvard U., 1977. Bar: Mass. 1977, D.C. 1980. Spl. asst. Office Sec. Def., Washington, 1969-72; dir. urban environ. programs EPA, Washington, 1972-74, dir. office civil rights and urban affairs, Atlanta, 1977-80; dir. office civil rights HHS, Atlanta, 1980-82, inter-govtl. affairs cons., 1982-83; atty., policy analyst Council State Govts., Atlanta, 1983-85; intergovtl. affairs cons. HHS, Atlanta, 1985—; lectr. Spelman Coll., Atlanta, 1984; rep. Pres.'s Council on Children and Youth, Washington, 1971. Bd. dirs. Coalition Internat. Programs, Atlanta, 1983—; mem. allocation panel United Way, 1982, 83-84. Recipient bronze medal EPA, 1980, Outstanding Service award Combined Fed. Campaign, 1981, Minority Bus. Opportunity Com./Atlanta Fed. Exec. Bd., 1979. Mem. ABA, Nat. Bar Assn., Ga. Assn. Black Women Attys., Harvard U. Alumni Assn., Delta Sigma Theta. Republican. African Methodist Episcopalian. Home: 1038 Oglethorpe Ave SW Atlanta GA 30310 Office: HHS 101 Marietta Tower Atlanta GA 30323

RUSSELL, CATHY ANN, furniture company manager; b. Chgo., Apr. 3, 1953; d. Paul Eugene and Gaycina Elizabeth (Trager) R. B.A. in Mktg., U. Fla., 1975. Asst. buyer, mgr. Burdines Dept. Stores, Miami, Fla., 1976-81; dir. pub. relations Intro Prodns., Inc., North Miami, Fla., 1981; funding chmn. Miami Design Preservation League, Miami Beach, Fla., 1981-82; adminstrv. asst. ops. Montgomery Ward Co., Hialeah, Fla., 1982-83; standard procedures mgr. Levitz Furniture Corp., Boca Raton, Fla., 1983—; mem. Employment Relocation Council, Washington, 1984-85. Mem. cultural arts bd. Miami Beach C. of C., 1981-82. Recipient Outstanding Service award Miami Design Preservation League, 1982. Mem. Nat. Assn. Female Execs., Miami Design Preservation League. Club: Bus. Unit Group-Boca Raton Mus. Art. Office: Levitz Furniture Corp 6111 Broken Sound Pkwy NW Boca Raton FL 33431

RUSSELL, DORA LEE, seafood industry executive; b. Sanford, Fla., Nov. 11, 1935. Lobbyist Organized Fishermen of Fla., Tallahassee, 1970-77, bd. dirs., 1969—; asst. to dir. research and policy Office of Gov., State of Fla., 1977-78; pres., owner Russell Seafood, Inc., Kissimmee, Fla., 1968—, Russell Seafood Shoppes, Inc., Kissimmee, 1985—. Mem. Gulf and South Atlantic Fisheries Devel. Found., 1984—; Central Fla. Commn. Status of Women, 1978-79; bd. dirs. Ballet Guild of Sanford-Seminole, 1965—, Kissimmee Bd. Adjustments, 1983—; chmn. dist. bd. trustees Seminole Community Coll., 1981—. Mem. Southeastern Fisheries Assn., Beta Sigma Phi. Democrat. Baptist. Avocations:

reading; flying; travel. Office: Russell Seafood Inc 810 Penfield St Kissimmee FL 32741

RUSSELL, ELAINE CLAUDIA, city official; b. Genesee, Idaho, Mar. 23, 1940; d. Estel M. and Claudia I. (Carbuhn) Collins; m. Sheldon W. Russell, Oct. 8, 1960; children—Brent D., Monte B. Student Kinman Bus. Coll., 1959. City clk., dep. treas. City of Moscow, Idaho, 1967—. Sec. bd. dirs. U. Idaho Fed. Credit Union, Moscow, 1983-84. Mem. Idaho City Clks. and Fin. Officers Assn. (dist. dir. 1981-82, 2d v.p. 1982-83, 1st v.p. 1983-84, pres. 1984—, chmn. awards com. 1978-82, cert.), Internat. Mcpl. Clks. Assn. Avocations: gardening; sewing; baking; motorcycling. Home: 1933 Vandal Dr Moscow ID 83843 Office: City of Moscow 122 E 4th St Moscow ID 83843

RUSSELL, GAIL HUTCHISON, banker; b. Wilmington, Del., Apr. 16, 1952; d. James Hervey, Jr. and Dorothy (Holton) Hutchison; m. Robert Ehmer Russell, Mar. 17, 1973; 1 child, Kyle James. B.A., U. Del., 1973, M.B.A., 1981. Various supervisory positions Farmers Bank, Wilmington, 1973-77; office mgr. Adria Labs., Wilmington, 1977; mgr. customer service and acctg. Blue Cross-Blue Shield Del., Wilmington, 1978-81; asst. v.p. deposit and payment services Morgan Bank Del., Wilmington, 1981-86; v.p. deposit acctg. Morgan Christiana Corp., 1986—. Active various neighborhood civic orgns. Mem. Wilmington Women in Bus., Daus. of Colonial Wars. Home: 108 Tall Pines Dr Newark DE 19713 Office: Morgan Bank 902 Market St Wilmington DE 19801

RUSSELL, HARRIET SHAW, social worker; b. Detroit, Apr. 12, 1952; d. Louis Thomas and Lureleen (Hughes) Shaw; m. Donald Edward Russell, June 25, 1980; children—Lachante Tyree, Krystal Lanae. Assoc.Bus., Detroit Bus. Inst., 1976; B.S., Mich. State U., 1974. Factory employee Gen. Motors Corp., Lansing, Mich., 1973; student supr. tour guides State of Mich., Lansing, 1974; mgr. Ky. Fried Chicken, Detroit, 1974-75; unemployment claims examiner State of Mich. Dept. Labor, Detroit, 1975-77, asst. payment worker, 1977-84, social services specialist, 1984—. Vol., Mich. Cancer Soc., East Lansing, 1970-72, Big Sisters/Big Bros., Lansing, 1972-73; speaker Triumphant Bapt. Ch., Detroit, 1976-80; chief union steward Mich. Employees Assn., Lincoln Park, 1982-83. Recipient Outstanding Work Performance Merit award Mich. Dept. Social Services, 1979. Mem. Nat. Assn. for Female Execs., Delta Sigma Theta. Democrat. Baptist. Office: State of Mich Dept Social Services 999 Fort St Lincoln Park MI 48146

RUSSELL, HAZEL M. HAWKINS, teacher educator; b. Cedar Lake, Tex., June 11; d. Nelse and Evelyn (Gee) Hawkins; m. James Russell, June 19, 1946; children—Beverly Ann, Vicki Rochelle. B.A., Prairie View State Coll., 1944; M.A., Redlands U., 1965; PhD., U.S. Internat. U., 1974. Elem. tchr., Lubbock, Tex., 1944-46, Riverside Schs., Calif., 1947-69; cons. pupil services Riverside Sch. Dist., 1970-74, adminstr., 1975-82; asst. prof. Calif. State U.-Fullerton, 1982—; lectr. Calif. State U.-San Bernardino, 1974-81; adj. faculty U. Calif.-Riverside, 1974-80, Redlands U., 1983-84; cons. Co-author: Black Women Speak Out, 1980. Bd. dirs. Riverside County Mental Health Assn., 1984—; mem. Atty. Gen.'s Com. on Race, Ethnicity and Minorities and Religious Violence, 1984—; edn. chair NAACP, 1980—. Recipient Edn. award NAACP, 1985; Community Service award Alpha Kappa Alpha, 1984, YWCA Riverside, 1980, Nat. Council Negro Women, 1985. Mem. NEA, AAUW, AAUP, Assn. Calif. Sch. Adminstrs., Calif. Faculty Assn., Assn. Calif. Intergroup Relation Educators (pres. 1979), Alpha Kappa Alpha (vp. 1985, Ida L. Jackson grad. achievement award 1985), Delta Kappa Gamma. Democrat. Avocations: travel; reading; camping; writing; public speaking. Home: 2094 Carlton Pl Riverside CA 92507

RUSSELL, JOAN DELIGHT, hospital administrator, realtor, investor; b. Youngstown, Ohio, July 20, 1933; d. Jack Leonard and Pauline Frances (Cox) Burris; m. Herbert A. Cook, Dec. 12, 1964 (div. May, 1981); children—Scott, Vicki, Todd, Herbert, Jr., Tami, Susan; m. Camp Wells Russell, May 16, 1981. Student St. Paul Bible Coll., Minn., 1951-56; diploma in nursing Grant Hosp., Columbus, Ohio, 1955. Registered nurse; cert. nursing home administrator. Post-operative specialist open heart surgery various hosps., 1956-61; in-service coordinator I.V. therapist various hosps., 1962-64; owner, dir. of nurses, hops. adminstr. Convalescent Hosp., Long Beach, Calif., 1964-72; v.p. Circle Convalescent Hosp., Calif., 1972-82, Leisure Convalescent Hosp., Calif., 1972-82, Hac-Con Corp., Long Beach, 1972-82; sec. Pacific Coast Convalescent Hosp. Corp., Long Beach, 1972-82; pvt. practice investments, real estate, office bldg. mgmt., Long Beach, 1972-84; pres. Delight Investment, Inc., Long Beach, 1981—; owner, operator Calif. Convalescent Hosp., Long Beach, 1984—; speaker schs. and seminars. Weekly radio broadcast, 1965-72. Del., Am. Nurses Assn., Calif. Nurses Assn.; organist West Lakewood Baptist Ch., Sunday sch. tchr.; mem. Campus Crusade, Campus Life; pres. Point Loma Coll. Women's Aux. Mem. Nursing Home Adminstrs., Registered Nurses Assn., Real Estate Assn. Republican. Club: Youth for Christ (exec. bd.). Avocations: music, boating, motor home camping. Home: 5421 El Cedral Long Beach CA 90815 Office: Calif Convalescent Hosp 3850 E Esther St Long Beach CA 90815

RUSSELL, JUDITH ANNE, manufacturing company official; b. Chgo., Jan. 29, 1961; d. Sheila Maryce (Enright) Russell. B.S. in Mgmt., Bradley U., 1981. Sales asst. IBM, Peoria, Ill., 1981; contract adminstr. Tex. Instruments, Dallas, 1982—. Mem. Order of Omega, Sigma Delta Tau. Democrat. Roman Catholic. Office: Tex Instruments Inc PO Box 226015 Dallas TX 75266

RUSSELL, KATHRYN ANN, baking company executive; b. Port Huron, Mich., June 16, 1950; d. Calvin Arthur Mausolf and Janet Ann (Lillis) Goodrich; m. John C. Russell, Aug. 8, 1970 (div. Feb. 1982). Student No. Ill. U., 1968-70, Elmhurst Coll., 1982—. Receptionist/switchboard operator Keebler Co., Elmhurst, Ill., 1971-74, purchasing analyst, asst. to v.p. purchasing, 1974-77, purchasing agt., 1977—. Roman Catholic. Office: Keebler Co 1 Hollow Tree Ln Elmhurst IL 60126

RUSSELL, LOUISE BENNETT, economist; b. Exeter, N.H., May 12, 1942; d. Frederick Dewey and Esther (Smith) Bennett. B.A., U. Mich., 1964; Ph.D., Harvard U., 1971. Economist Social Security Adminstrn., Washington, 1968-71, Nat. Commn. on State Workmen's Compensation Laws, Washington, 1971-72, Dept. Labor, Washington, 1972-73; sr. economist Nat. Planning Assn., Washington, 1973-75; sr. fellow Brookings Instn., Washington, 1975—; mem. various adv. groups. Author: Technology in Hospitals, 1979; The Baby Boom Generation and the Economy, 1982; Is Prevention Better Than Cure?, 1986; author numerous pub. papers. Mem. Nat. Acad. Scis. Inst. Medicine. Office: Brookings Instn 1775 Massachusetts Ave NW Washington DC 20036

RUSSELL, MARY ANN, nurse, educator; b. Hamden, Conn., Aug. 24, 1930; d. Felice Vincenzo and Josephine Angela (Festa) Sagnella; m. Warren Edward Russell, Feb. 5, 1955; children—Lynn Marie, Sharon Lee. Diploma in Nursing, Hartford Hosp. Sch. Nursing, Conn.; B.S. in Nursing Edn., Central Conn. State U., New Britain. R.N., Conn. Staff nurse Hartford Hosp., Conn., 1951-52, asst. head nurse, 1952-53, head nurse, 1953-54, staff devel. instr., 1967-77, nursing supr., 1977—, co-editor nursing newsletter, 1978—; office nurse to cardiovascular surgeon, Hartford, 1954-59; vol. nurse Farmington, Conn. ARC. Vol. East Hartford Meals on Wheels. Mem. Hartford Hosp Alumnae Assn. Roman Catholic. Club: East Hartford Women's. Avocations: reading; crafts; singing; cooking; tennis. Home: 31 Andover Rd East Hartford CT 06108 Office: Hartford Hosp 80 Seymour St Hartford CT 06115

RUSSELL, MARY HELEN, publishing company executive, youth counselor; b. St. Louis, Aug. 9, 1939; d. George Kelly and Sarah Mae (Belion) Fugh; m. Charles David Russell, June 6, 1968; children—Sararetha, Anthony, Cedric. Student Thornton Community Coll., Harvey, Ill., 1958-59; Southwestern Coll., Dowagiac, Mich., 1981. Technician, Consol. Lab., Chicago Heights, Ill., 1960-64, Sue Ann Food Labs., Chgo., 1964-65; med. sec. Huntington Meml. Hosp., Pasadena, Calif., 1965-68; pub. Society mag., Harvey, Ill., 1968-70; youth dir., counselor Cass Youth Service Bur., Cass County, Mich., 1970-81; pres. C & M Pub., Kalamazoo, 1983—. Author: Black Achievers Vol. I. 1983, Vol. II, 1985; (plays) Old Time Religion, 1967, Our People, 1968. Treas. Cass Mental Health Bd., Cassopolis, Mich., 1970-81; dir. efectiveness tng. Youth Service Bur., Cassopolis, 1970-81; mem. Cass Zoning Bd., Cassoplis, 1974-81; mem. Kalamazoo Human Relations Bd., 1981-82; chmn. action audit com., bd. dirs. YWCA, Kalamazoo, 1984—; sec., program and music dir. 2d Baptist Ch., Harvey, Ill., 1959-73; campaign dir. Harvey Democratic Com., 1975. Recipient plaque YMCA, Harvey, 1975; cert. YWCA, Kalamazoo, 1985, Human Relations Commn., Kalamazoo, 1981. Mem. Kalamazoo Women's Network. Presbyterian. Avocations: singing; fashion coordinator; tennis; sewing; ceramics. Office: C & M Publishing PO Box 191 Oshtemo MI 49077

RUSSELL, MARY PATRICIA, advertising agency executive; b. Columbus, Ohio, Mar. 16, 1942; d. James Francis and Mary Alice (Skenyon) Shea; m. Bobby G. Russell, July 22, 1965; children—Mary Alice, Bobby Gene II. Student Catherine Spalding Coll. (formerly Nazareth Coll.), 1962-63, Ohio State U., 1972-74, continuing edn. cert. in indsl. mktg. mgmt., 1980. With Ohio Bell Telephone, Columbus, 1960-62; radio engr., disco jockey Sta. WSIB, Beaufort, S.C., 1967-68; with Sta. WTVN, Columbus, 1968-69; owner, founder Dale City Telephone Answering Service, Woodbridge, Va., 1970-71; media dir. Kight, Cowman, Abram Advt., Columbus, 1974-79; promotion mgr. Dispatch and Citizen-Jour. daily newspapers, Columbus, 1980-81; communications cons., 1981-86; owner, pres. Patty Russell Mktg. Media Co., Inc., Columbus, 1982-86; pres. Russell, Luke, Mercier Advt. Agy., Columbus, 1986—; ptnr./pres. PR Media/Promotion, Inc., 1983; cons., speaker SBA; SCORE/ACE cons. Bd. dirs. Columbus Area Council on Alcoholism, 1981-82; pres. bd. dirs. One-To-One, 1982-83. Served with USMC, 1963-65. Mem. Columbus Advt. Fedn. (trustee 1977—), Central Ohio Indsl. Marketers (dir. 1981, 82), Mensa. Republican. Roman Catholic. Home: 3008-A Riverside Dr Columbus OH 43221 Office: 3021 Bethel Rd Columbus OH 43220

RUSSELL, MATTIE UNDERWOOD, librarian; b. Randolph, Miss., May 14, 1915; d. William Vance and Mattie Pearl (Underwood) R.; B.A., U. Miss., 1937, M.A., 1940; Ph.D., Duke U., 1956. Tchr. social studies high schs., Miss. 1937-43; asst. prof. history Mars Hill (N.C.) Coll., 1943-46; asst. curator manuscripts Duke U., Durham, N.C., 1948-52, curator 1952-85; vis. assoc. prof. library sci. U. N.C., Chapel Hill 1969-78. Fellow Soc. Am. Archivists (chmn. C.F.W. Coker prize subcom. 1984); mem. Historic Preservation Soc. Durham (archivist), So. Hist. Assn. (rep. to Nat. Archives Adv. Council 1978-83), Nat. Trust Historic Preservation, Hist. Soc. N.C., (pres. 1974), N.C. Lit. and Hist. Assn., Assocs. Nat. Archives. Democrat. Contbr. in field.

RUSSELL, NANCY GILLESPIE, home health agency executive, management consultant, nurse; b. Fremont, Ohio, Dec. 22, 1937; d. R. Philip and Margaret E. (Miller) Gillespie; m. Daryl E. Powell, July 16, 1958 (div. 1969); children—Deborah, Susan, Emily, Jennifer; m. James F. Russell, Nov. 15, 1980. R.N. diploma Toledo Hosp. Sch. Nursing, 1958; B.S., St. Francis Coll., Joliet, Ill., 1981. R.N., Ohio. In various nursing positions, Toledo, 1958-71; rehab. nurse Parkview Hosp., Pueblo, Colo., 1972-74; nurse adminstr., owner Russell Health Services, Pueblo, 1974—; cons., prin. Russell & Assocs., Pueblo, 1982—; Pres. bd. dirs. Coordinating Com., Pueblo, 1984, Pueblo Suicide Prevention, 1985, 86; instr. Pueblo Community Coll. Ctr. Small Bus., 1985. Pres. bd. dirs. Women's Sailing Clinic, So. Colo. Yacht Club, Pueblo, 1985-86; bd. dirs., active in program planning United Way, Pueblo. Mem. Pueblo C. of C. Republican. Avocations: sailing; skiing; jazz. Home: 1508 Berkley Pueblo CO 81004 Office: Russell Health Services 110 East D St Pueblo CO 81004

RUSSELL, PATRICIA EILEEN, accountant; b. Washington, Sept. 16, 1941; d. Eugene Victor and Charlotte Frances (Shipman) Hartman; div.; children—Cecile Colette, Simone Renee. A.A., Montgomery Jr. Coll., Takoma Park, Md., 1981; M.A., Central Mich. U., 1982; B.Individualized Study, George Mason U., 1981. Acctg. asst. Door Systems, Lorton, Va., 1974-79; controller Oldelft Corp., Fairfax, Va., 1979-83; program mgr. TRW, McLean, Va., 1983-84; dir. fin. and adminstrn. Micro Research, Falls Church, Va., 1984-85; owner Acctg. Services for Small Businesses, Warrenton, Va., 1985—; mem. adj. faculty No. Va. Community Coll., Manassas, 1982—. Writer textbook modules for Small Business Students Text, 1985. Actress The Loft, Warrenton, 1985; treas. Va. Involved Exec. Women, Fairfax, 1984-85. Mem. Am. Mgmt. Assn., Nat. Assn. Accts., Nat. Soc. Pub. Accts., Rappahannock Assn. for Arts in Community, Piedmont Environ. Council, Phi Theta Kappa, Sigma Iota Epsilon. Club: Ski (Washington). Avocations: camping, skiing. Office: Accounting Services for Small Businesses Route 5 Box 174-B Warrenton VA 22186

RUSSELL, PATRICIA HOLLY, anesthesiologist; b. Columbia, Mo., July 30, 1934; d. Bert Francis and Alma Elizabeth (Sample) Holly; m. William Alton Russell, Jr., Aug. 28, 1955; children—Holly Ann, William Alton III. M.D., Emory U., 1957. Diplomate Am. Bd. Anesthesiology. Resident in anesthesiology; from instr. to assoc. prof. George Washington U., Washington, 1960-73; chmn. dept. emergency medicine Greater S.E. Community Hosp., Washington, 1977-79; from med. officer to dir. div. surg.-dental drug products FDA, Rockville, Md., 1980, 83—. Contbr. articles to profl. jours. Bd. dirs. CARE, N.Y., 1980—, also sec. Robert Wood Johnson Clin. scholar George Washington U., 1975-77. Mem. Am. Soc. Anesthesiologists, Internat. Anesthesia Research Soc., Md.-D.C. Soc. Anesthesiologists, PEO. Republican. Presbyterian. Office: FDA Div Surg-Dental Drug Products HFN-160 5600 Fishers Ln Rockville MD 20895

RUSSELL, PAULINE MARIE, insurance administrator; b. York, Nebr., Oct. 20, 1932; d. Loyal Roosevelt and Iola Pauline (Hatfield) Rhoads; m. Richard Lee Russell, July 24, 1956; children—Richard Kent, Susan Marie Russell Payne, Dennis Dale, Brenda Lyn Russell Hathaway. Office-key person ins. dept. 1st Trust Co; York, Nebr., 1951-57; auto rater Travelers Ins. Co., Santa Ana, Calif., 1963-65; personal accounts rep. Russ & Lake Ins., Fullerton, Calif., 1966-69, Manassas Ins. Agy. (Va.), 1969-70; office mgr. Summerlin Ins. Agy., Jacksonville, N.C., 1970-72; personal accounts rep. Republic Ins. Brokers, Santa Ana, 1972-75; comml. accounts rep. Continental Gen. Ins. Brokers, Anaheim, Calif., 1975-80; comml. accounts service rep. Serdinsky Ins. Agy., Anaheim, 1980—. Mem. Nat. Assn. Ins. Women, Ins. Women Orange County (ins. women of yr. award 1982, rec. sec. 1978-79, v.p. 1979-80, pres. elect 1980-81, pres. 1981-82, bd. dirs. 1983-84). Clubs: Pop Warner Assn. (pres. women's aux. 1973-74, bd. dirs. 1974-76); Royal Neighbors Am. (sec. 1955-56). Office: Serdinsky Ins Agy 2576 W Woodland Dr Anaheim CA 92801

RUSSELL, ROSALIND CORINNE, naturopathic physician; b. Los Angeles, Jan. 12, 1945; d. George Bruce Angelo and Dorrie Anne (Newbern) Russell; m. James Hedgecock, May 13, 1972; stepchildren—Mary Ellen, Jeffrey. A.A., El Camino Coll., 1963; B.A. in Edn., Pepperdine U., 1967, M.A. in Psychology and English, 1972; postgrad. Pasadena Chiropractic Coll., 1973-76; diploma naturopathy U. London, 1978. Owner, operator specialty restaurants, Hawaii, 1967-68; stewardess Braniff Airline Co., 1968; nutritional advisor, officer mgr., exec. adminstr. Hedgecock Chiropractic Corp., Newport Beach and Pasadena, Calif., 1972—; sec.-treas. Cardinal Air Services, 1981—, chmn., 1984—, helicopter pilot, 1981-83; pres. R. Star Prodns.; mem. adv. bd. Polstar, Inc.; lectr. Parker Chiropractic Sch. for Profl. Success, 1982, 83, 84, 85, 86. Mem. Parker Chiropractic Research Found., Acupuncture Soc. Am. Republican. Clubs: Leads, Prime Time. Office: 4321 Birch St E Newport Beach CA 92660

RUSSELL, SUSAN REIDGREENE, university executive; b. Buffalo, Nov. 27, 1940; d. John F. and Madeleine (Breinig) Reid; student Ohio Wesleyan U., 1958-59; B.A. magna cum laude, Syracuse U., 1962; postgrad. SUNY, Buffalo, 1965-66; m. James Wilson Greene, II, June 15, 1962; children—Timothy Taylor, Elizabeth Claussen; m. Clifford Springer Russell, Sept. 7, 1985. Field adminstr. Survey Research Center, U. Mich., 1962-64; faculty recruiter SUNY, Buffalo, 1964-65, instnl. researcher, 1965-68; pres. Assn. Jr. Leagues, Inc., N.Y.C., 1976-78; exec. dir. Alliance for Volunteerism, Washington, 1978-79; v.p. programs Youth for Understanding, Internat. Student Exchange, Washington, 1979-82; dir. instl. relations Resources for The Future, 1982-86; dir. devel. and pub. affairs Vanderbilt Inst. Pub. Policy Studies, Nashville, 1986—; cons. organizational devel., 1975-79. Pres. Jr. League, Buffalo, 1972-73, mem. nat. bd. dirs., 1974-78; chmn. Erie County (N.Y.) Devel. Coordination Bd., 1973-76, 78-79; vice chmn. Erie and Niagara Counties Regional Planning Bd., 1974-75, chmn., 1975-76; chmn. Fedn. Regional Planning and Devel. Bds. for State N.Y., 1978-79; elder Westminster Presbyn. Ch., Buffalo, 1977-79; bd. dir., nat. adv. com. Nat. Sch. Vol. Program 1976—. Nat. Center for Vol. Action, President's Commn. on Employment of Handicapped, 1976-78; bd. dirs. Big Sisters Washington Met. Area, 1982-85, Nashville Symphony, 1986—. Recipient Community Service award SUNY, Buffalo, 1975, Arents Pioneer medal Syracuse U., 1977, Nat. Vol. Activist award Nat. Center for Vol. Action, 1977. Mem. U.S. Figure Skating Assn., Assn. Vol. Action Scholars, Assn. for Vol. Adminstrn. LWV, Jr. League, Phi Beta Kappa, Kappa Alpha Theta. Kappa. Office: Vanderbilt Inst Pub Policy Studies 1208 18th Ave S Nashville TN 37212

RUSSELL, VIRGINIA DEGANAHL, public relations exec., consultant; b. N.Y.C., Apr. 2, 1931; d. Joe and Josephine (Coombs) deGanahl; student Mt. Vernon Sem. and Coll., 1949-52, U. Calif. extension, George Washington U., 1951; m. Thomas Hale Russell, June 21, 1952; children—George, Sarah, Edward, Josephine, Charles, Michael, Kenneth. Mem. bd. Vt. Symphony Orch., Burlington, 1970-81; pres. Dvorak Internat. Fedn., Brandon, Vt., 1976-79, pres., 1981—; art historian on Jacob van Ruisdael and 17th century Holland. Mem. Otter Valley (Vt.) Sch. Bd., 1976-77; bd. dirs. Girl Scouts U.S.A., 1967-69, Brandon chpt. Am. Cancer Soc., 1967-70, Mem. Am. Nat. Standards Inst. (chmn. com.), World Future Soc. Democrat. Episcopalian. Clubs: Arts (Washington); Dutch-Am. Acad. Soc. (Boston). Home: 11 Pearl St Brandon VT 05733

RUSSO, IRMA HAYDEE ALVAREZ DE, pathologist; b. San Rafael, Mendoza, Argentina, Feb. 28, 1942; came to U. S., 1972, naturalized, 1982; d. Jose Maria and Maria Carmen (Martinez) de Alvarez; B.A., Escuela Normal M.T.S.M. de Balcarce, 1959; M.D., U. Nat. of Cuyo, Mendoza, 1970; m. Jose Russo, Feb. 8, 1969; 1 dau., Patricia Alexandra. Intern, Sch. of Medicine Hosps., Argentina, 1969-70; resident in pathology Wayne State U. Sch. Medicine, Detroit, 1976-80; research asst. and instr. Inst. of Histology and Embryology Sch. Medicine U. Nat. of Cuyo, 1963-71, asso. prof. histology Faculty of Phys., Chem. and Math. Scis., 1970-72; research asso. Inst. for Molecular and Cellular Evolution, U. Miami, Fla., 1972-73; research asso. exptl. pathology lab. div. biol. scis., Mich. Cancer Found., Detroit, 1973-75, research scientist, 1975-76, vis. research scientist, 1976-82, asst. mem., pathologist, 1982—, co-dir. pathology reference lab., 1982—; chief resident physician dept. pathology Wayne State U. Sch. Medicine, 1978-80, asst. prof., 1980-82; mem. staff Harper-Grace Hosps., Detroit, 1980-82; Rockefeller grantee, 1972-73; Nat. Cancer Inst. grantee, 1978-81, 84—; guest lectr. dept. obstetrics Sch. Medicine U. Nat. of Cuyo, 1965-71. Diplomate Am. Bd. Pathology. Mem. Coll. Am. Pathologists, Am. Soc. Clin. Pathologists, Am. Assn. for Cancer Research, Mich. Soc. Pathologists, AMA, Electron Microscopy Soc. Am., Mich. Electron Microscopy Forum, Sigma Xi. Roman Catholic. Contbr. numerous articles on pathology to profl. jours. Office: 110 E Warren Ave Detroit MI 48201

RUSSO, LESA LYNN, public relations executive, bookkeeper, music teacher; b. Corsicana, Tex., Oct. 19, 1955; d. James Aubrey and Wanelle (Warren) Starkes; m. Robert Joseph Russo, Nov. 21, 1980. B.A. in Piano Performance, Baptist Bible Coll., 1978; postgrad. in Secondary Edn., Pensacola Bible Coll., 1979. Comml. tchr. First City Bank, Garland, Tex., 1979; bookkeeper Dallas Life Found., 1979—, pub. relations exec., 1985—; bookkeeper Jupiter Rd. Baptist Ch., Garland, 1979—, dir. childrens choirs, 1980-85. Republican. Baptist. Home: 3305 S Glenbrook Dr Garland TX 75041 Office: Dallas Life Foundation PO Box 2203 Dallas TX 75221-2203

RUSSO, MARIE DOLORES, municipal official; b. Fairview, N.J., July 5, 1925; d. Joseph Anthony and Rose Bertha (Casamento) Trivisonno; m. Carl Paul Russo, Aug. 15, 1948; children—Peter, Paul (twins). Student pub. schs., Cliffside Park, N.J. Sec. personnel dept Aluminum Co. Am., Edgewater, N.J., 1943-61; registered mcpl. clk. Borough of Palisades Park, N.J., 1977—. Mem. Bergen County Mcpl. Clks. Assn., N.J. Assn. Mcpl., Clks. Internat. Inst. Mcpl. Clks., Palisades Park Republican Club, Women's Rep. Club (Palisades Park). Roman Catholic.

RUSSO, MERI LOUISE, graphics and printing consulting company executive, artist; b. Detroit; d. Silveo Angelo and Margaret (Klein) Basta; 1 child, Daniel Charles. Student Macomb County Community Coll., Warren, Mich., 1970-72; student mktg. Rutgers U., 1985. Graphic artist Creative Universal, Detroit, 1971-72; freelance graphic designer, N.J., Pa., 1972-73; graphic designer Sexton Studios, Cherry Hill, N.J., 1973-74; art dir. Mainline Graphic Arts Co., Mount Laurel, N.J., 1974-76; account mgr. Mainline Graphic Arts Co., Mount Laurel, 1976-78; owner, pres. Graphic Design Service, 1978-81; account exec./cons. Thomason Press Inc., 1981-85; account exec. L.P. Thebault Co., Parsippany, N.J., 1985-86; prin. Meri Russo Graphics Cons., Moorestown, N.J., 1985—; Eastern regional sales mgr. John Roberts Co., 1986—; freelance comml. artist, 1976—; graphics cons./broker, N.Y.C., N.J., Pa., Va., 1978—. Recipient Graphics gold award NEO, 1977. Mem. Women in Communications, Nat. Assn. Female Execs. Avocations: horseback riding; tennis; sailing; golf; skiing. Home: 26 W Central Ave Moorestown NJ 08057 Office: One Greentree Ctr Suite 201 Marlton NJ 08053 also: The John Roberts Co 9687 E River Rd Minneapolis MN 55433

RUSSO, NANCY MARGARET, lawyer; b. Cleve., Oct. 6, 1956; d. Humbert and Maureen Helen (McCaffery) R.; m. Joel F. Sacco. A.B. in Polit. Sci., W. Liberty State Coll., 1977; J.D., Cleveland-Marshall Law Sch., 1981. Bar: Ohio 1982, U.S. Dist. Ct. (northeastern dist.) Ohio 1982. Investigator Lake County Narcotics, Painesville, Ohio, 1977-78; with Marriott Inn, Cleve., 1978-79; legal sec. Bartunek, Garofoli, Cleve., 1979-81; paralegal/litigation asst. Calfee, Halter & Griswold, Cleve., 1981-84; atty., fin. and fraud investigator Blue Cross/Blue Shield of Northeast Ohio, 1984—. Contbg. author ref. book: Ohio Family Law, 1984. Vol. atty. Cleve. Attys. Seeking Equity, 1983—; participant legal clinic staff Law Day, Cleve., 1980-86. Mem. ABA, Am. Trial Lawyers Assn., Greater Cleve. Bar Assn., Ohio Bar Assn. Met. Crime Bur., Fraud Investigators Assn., W. Liberty State Coll. Alumni Assn. Roman Catholic. Home: 3151 W 160th St Cleveland OH 44111 Office: Blue Cross/Blue Shield of Northeast Ohio 2060 E 9th St Cleveland OH 44114

RUSSO, SUSAN J., nurse, chiropracter, author; b. N.Y.C., May 3, 1946; d. Louis and Dolly (DelGaudio) R. A.A.S., Bronx Community Coll., 1965, R.N., 1965; B.A. in Psychology, Mt. St. Vincent, 1971; D.Chiropractic X-Ray and Spinography, Columbia Inst., 1973. R.N., 1965; diplomate in chiropractic. Psychiat. nurse St. Vincent's Hosp., Harrison, N.Y., 1968-69, neurol. nurse, 1969-70; mem. rehab. staff VA Hosp., N.Y.C., 1970-71; mgr. owner Mr. Waffles, N.Y.C., 1971-74; chiropractic physician Renaissance Ctr., Hoboken, N.J., N.Y.C., 1974-80; internat. lectr., author on holistic economics, stress and arthritis, 1980—. Author: The Warbabies' Statement, 1976. Charter mem. Republican Presdl. Task Force, Washington, 1982-84. Recipient Woman of Achievement award NJ Jour., 1974; Samuel Rubin Found. scholar, 1963-65. Mem. Internat. Acad. Nutritional Cons. (charter), Am. Assn. Fin. Profls., Liberty Lobby, N.Y. Chiropractic Soc., N.J. Chiropractic Soc. Republican. Roman Catholic. •

RUSSO, VIVIAN ALFONSINA, cosmetic company executive, creative consultant; b. Bklyn., Apr. 21, 1949; d. Louis Anthony and Iole Primetta (Barbaglia) R.; m. Robert Ferro, May 26, 1968 (div. 1975). Student Bernard Baurch Coll., 1966, Brooklyn Coll., 1967, Fashion Inst. Tech., 1971-77. Assoc. advt. mgr. Kayser-Roth Corp., N.Y.C., 1968-77; advt. and sales promotion mgr. GAF Corp., N.Y.C., 1977-80; sales promotion and merchandising mgr. Revlon, N.Y.C., 1980-82; dir. creative services Del Labs., Farmingdale, N.Y., 1982—; lectr. Briarcliff Bus. Coll., Hicksville, N.Y., 1985. Creative dir. (coop. program) Co-op Advt. Credit Card Program (Sales and Mktg. Mgmt. Mag. award), 1976, (sampling program) Excello Shirts-Fabric Swatch (Sales and Mktg. Mgmt. Mag. award), 1977, (product catalogue) View-Master Catalogue (Nat. Endowment Arts award), 1978, GAF Star-Vinyl Floors Catalogue (Nat. Endowment Arts award), 1980. Friend of Bd. Nat. Found. Ileitis and Colitis, Inc., N.Y.C., 1981. Recipient Mgmt. award Am. Mgmt. Assn., 1979. Mem. Cosmetic Exec. Women, Advt. Women N.Y., Inc., The Fashion Group, Theatre Guild Assn. Republican. Roman Catholic. Avocations: Tennis; painting; photography; fishing. Office: Del Labs 565 Broadhollow Rd Farmingdale NY 11735

RUST, LIBBY KAREN, charitable organization administrator; b. York, Maine, Feb. 8, 1951; d. Myron Davis and Meta Mildred (Libby) R.; B.A., Wheaton Coll., 1973; M.S., Columbia U., 1977. Daycare field asst. Childhood Ednl. Enrichment Program, Waterville, Maine, 1974-75; cons. Center for Community Planning and Cons., N.Y.C., 1975-76; intern Morgan Guaranty Trust Co., N.Y.C., 1976; staff asst. subcom. on mental health Task Force on N.Y.C. Fiscal Crisis, 1976-77; auditor AT&T, N.Y.C., 1977; budget examiner Legis. Office of Budget Rev., N.Y.C., 1977-78; exec. dir. Strafford County Human Services, Dover, N.H., 1978-79; allocations dir. United Way, Inc., Portland, Maine, 1979-82, planning and allocations div. dir., 1982-84, exec. dir. Seacoast United Way, 1984—. Mem. budget com. Town of York, 1979-80. Republican. Clubs: Portland Wheaton, Portland, Portland Jr. League. Home: Linnea Ln York Harbor ME 03911

RUST, RACHEL LOUISE, family therapist; b. Wharton, Tex., Oct. 18, 1955; d. Lloyd Gates and Rose Marie (Dominy) R. B.Social Work, U. Tex.-Austin, 1978; M.S., U. Tex.-Dallas, 1981; M.S. in Social Work, U. Tex.-Arlington, 1983. Cert. social worker, Assn. Cert. Social Workers. Group counselor Salesmanship Club Youth Camps, Palestine, Tex., 1978-80; case mgr. Juliette Fowler Home, Inc., Dallas, 1981-82; family therapist Salesmanship Club Ctr., Dallas, 1983—. Mem. Nat. Assn. Social Workers, Mental Health Assn., Tex. Corrections Assn. Presbyterian. Club: 500 Inc (Dallas). Home: 6249 Belmont

St Dallas TX 75214 Office: Salesmanship Club Dallas Ctr 4730 Harvest Hill Dallas TX 75234

RUTENBERG-ROSENBERG, SHARON LESLIE, journalist; b. Chgo., May 23, 1951; d. Arthur and Bernice (Berman) Rutenberg; student Harvard U. Summer Sch., 1972; B.A., Northwestern U., 1973, M.S.J., Medill Grad. Sch. Journalism, 1975; m. Michael J. Rosenberg, Feb. 3, 1980; children—David Kaifel, Jonathan Reuben (twins). Bus. mgr. Northwestern U. Yearbook, 1971-72; reporter-photographer Lerner Home Newspapers, Chgo., 1973-74; corr. Medill News Service, Washington, 1975; reporter-newsperson UPI, Chgo., 1975—; mem. exec. bd. Northwestern U. Student Adv. Council, 1972-73. Vol. worker Chgo.-Read Mental Health Center. Recipient Peter Lisagor award exemplary journalism in print feature category, 1980, 81; Golden Key award Nat. Adv. Bd. to Children's Oncology Services, Inc., 1981; Chgo. Hosp. Pub. Relations Soc. awards for news story and feature story, 1983, 84; cert. student pilot, cert. scuba diver. Mem. Hadassah, Hon. Order Ky. Cols., Sigma Delta Chi, Sigma Delta Tau. Covered Pres. of U.S., the Pope, prime minister of Israel. Home: 745 Marion Ave Highland Park IL 60035 Office: 360 N Michigan Ave Chicago IL 60601

RUTGERS, KATHARINE PHILLIPS (MRS. FREDERIK LODEWIJK RUTGERS), dancer; b. Butler, Pa., Sept. 2, 1910; d. Thomas Wharton and Alma (Sherman) Phillips; diploma Briarcliff Coll., 1928; student L'Hermitage, Versailles, France, 1929-30; pupil ballet Vera Trefilova, Paris, Carl Raimund, Vienna, Varga Troyanoff, Budapest; pupil modern dance with Iris Barbura, Bucharest Ballet, Vincenzo Celli, N.Y.C., Igor Schwezoff, N.Y.C., Mme Huapola, Hawaii, Jean Yazvinsky, N.Y.C.; m. Frederik Lodewijk Rutgers, Feb. 2, 1942; children—Alma Rutgers Bulazel, Corinne Rutgers Tolles. Performed dance concerts Bucharest, 1937-40, U.S., 1941—; repertoire includes religious, patriotic, dramatic, poetical dances; dance therapist St. Barnabas Hosp., N.Y.C., 1965-70. Chmn. ethnol. dance dept. Bruce Museum Assos., Greenwich, Conn., 1970—. Bd. dirs. Bruce Museum. Recipient citation for promoting culture with dance programs Nat. Fedn. Music Clubs, 1973. Mem. N.Y. Fedn. Music Clubs (chmn. dance dept. 1979-80), Nat. League Am. Pen Women (local pres. 1980—), Alliance Francaise, Sacred Dance Guild, Colonial Dames Am., D.A.R., Internat. Biog. Soc. Clubs: Regency (N.Y.C.), Indian Harbor (Greenwich, Conn.). Author numerous pamphlets on the dance, also verses for choreographies; styled nat. dances for stage. Home: La Cova Pecks Land Rd Greenwich CT 06830 Studio: 211 W 58th St New York NY 10023

RUTHANN, ARON, lawyer, real estate developer; b. Bklyn., Oct. 24, 1942; d. David and Freida (Freedman) Greenzweig; m. Barry Aron, Dec. 19, 1965; children—Dana Stacey, Joshua Todd. B.S., Cornell U., 1964; M.A., NYU, 1967; J.D., Catholic U. Am., 1980. Bar: Md. 1980. Project dir. market research Oxtoby-Smith, N.Y.C., 1967-68; sr. marketing assoc. Continental Can Co., N.Y.C., 1969-70; prin., pres. Aron Research Co., Rockville, Md., 1973-75; assoc. Lerch, Early & Roseman, Bethesda, Md., 1980-81; pres. Development Research, Inc., Rockville, Md., 1981—; mortgage financing, brokerage and devel. cons. Washington Met. area, 1980—. Bd. dirs. Washington Hebrew Congregation, Washington, 1983-86; pres., bd. dirs. W. Montgomery County Citizens Assn., Potomac, Md., 1980-83; issues chmn. Repub. Central Com., Rockville, Md., 1982; vol. Reagan Campaign, Washington, 1980; vol. Ronald Reagan for Pres. Campaign, Washington, 1980, 84; mem. Women's com. Nat. Symphony Orchestra, Washington, 1981—, Potomac (Md.) Women's Rep. Club., 1979—. Mem. ABA, Md. Bar Assn., Montgomery County Bar Assn. Club: Cornell of Washington. Office: Development Research Inc 17 W Jefferson St Suite 5 Rockville MD 20850

RUTLEDGE, VIRGINIA ALICE, bus. services co. exec.; b. Grant Tower, Ill., Dec. 15, 1919; d. Emora F. and Dora A. (Davis) Howe; children by former marriage—Walter, Patricia. Corporate pres. Gateway Account Service Inc., St. Louis, 1968—; lectr. in field. Pres. bd. trustees Mo. Consumer Credit Ednl. Found., 1979. Recipient exec. achievement award Asso. Credit Burs. Inc., 1976. Mem. Mo. (pres. 1974-75, credit exec. of yr. award 1973), Internat. (distinguished service award 1975) consumer credit assns., Mo. Collector Assn. (pres. 1973-74), Soc. Consumer Credit Execs., Asso. Credit Burs. Inc. Nat. leader in consumer credit. Office: 8460 Watson Rd St Louis MO 63119

RUTMAN, SUSAN H., visual artist; b. Bklyn., Jan. 16, 1948; d. Hyman L. and Judy (Sontag) R.; m. Arthur H. Johnson, Sept. 18, 1970 (div. 1974). B.F.A., Boston U., 1969. Sculptor, art tchr. Pub. Schs., Watertown, Mass., 1969-72; owner, sculptor The Craft Arcade, St. Johnsbury, Vt., 1972-76; free-lance photographer, N.Y.C., 1976-81; pres. The Townhouse Collection, N.Y.C., 1981—. Mem. Nat. Assn. Female Execs., Small Bus. Service Bur., Am. Craft Council, NOW. Democrat. Jewish. Avocation: fine art photography. Home: 145 E 72d St Apt 3F New York NY 10021

RUTT, MELANIE GAY, educator; b. Gordonville, Pa., July 12, 1943; B.A., Millersville U., 1970, M.Ed. in Gifted Edn., 1984, M.Ed. in Elem. Edn., 1985; m. Jan C. Rutt, June 21, 1966; children—Bryan Edward, Marcus Ian. Resource room aide Manheim Twp. Schs., 1980-81; project coordinator, asst. to dir. program for devel. intellectual potential Franklin and Marshall Coll., Lancaster, Pa., 1980-82; tutor Center for Academic Devel., Millersville U., 1982; tchr. Jenkins Early Childhood Center, 1982-84; tchr. gifted Intermediate Unit 13, 1985—. Exhibited group shows Lancaster Open Award Art Shows, 1979—, Lancaster County Art Assn. Shows, 1979-81; represented in pvt. collections. Mem. Pa. Assn. Gifted Edn., Assos. Sisters of the Holy Cross, Nat. Assn. for Edn. Young Children, Lancaster County Art Assn., Holy Cross Alumnae of Sacred Heart Acad. (dir. 1980-81, corr. sec. 1978-80), Pi Lambda Theta. Address: 80 Knollwood Dr Lancaster PA 17601

RUTTY, BRIDGET, programmer analyst; b. Elmira, N.Y., Dec. 20, 1944; d. John Francis and Anna Mae (Sprague) R.; student pub. schs., Syracuse, N.Y.; cert. data processing. Computer operator Rae Oil Co., Rochester, N.Y., 1966-67; programmer Security Trust Co., Rochester, 1967-68; systems analyst SCM Corp., Syracuse, 1968-84; sr. programmer, analyst Syracuse U., 1984—. Recipient Service award Data Processing Mgmt. Assn., 1977. Mem. U.S. Dressage Fedn., Data Processing Mgmt. Assn. (pres. chpt. 1975-76; Service award 1984), Assn. Computing Machinery (vice chmn. chpt. 1985-87), Nat. Taxpayers Union. Assn. Inst. Cert. Computer Profls., Am. Assn. Individual Investors. Republican. Office: 214 Machinery Hall Syracuse NY 13244

RUYFFELAERT, BETTE J., telecommunication network executive; b. Southbridge, Mass., Aug. 4, 1944; d. Earl W. and Dorothy (Feige) Krueger; m. Michael E. Ruyffelaert, Nov. 21, 1975; children—Shawn M. B.A. in German, Clark U., 1966, M.B.A., 1985. Claims auditor Paul Revere Inc., Worcester, Mass., 1966-67, programmer, 1967-69; sr. programmer Tom McAn, Worcester, 1969-74; sr. programmer, analyst Am. Opt., Southbridge, Mass., 1974-78; sr. software engr. Digital Equipment, Maynard, Mass., 1978-79, mgr. info. systems, 1979-85. Mem. Nat. Assn. Female Execs., Coast Guard Aux., Women's Support Group. Methodist. Avocations: reading; cross country-downhill skiing; canoeing; hiking. Home: 228 Wellman Ave North Chemsford MA 01863 Office: Digital Equp Cpr 555 Virginia Rd Concord MA 01742

RUYLE, LYDIA MILLER, artist, educator; b. Denver, Aug. 4, 1935; d. David Jacob and Lydia (Alles) Miller; m. Robert A. Ruyle, Sept. 15, 1957; children—Stephen Robert, Margaret Lee, Robin Lee. B.A. magna cum laude, U. Colo., 1957; M.A., U. No. Colo., 1972. Research assoc. Bur. State and Community Service, U. Colo., Boulder, 1957-59; paralegal Miller and Ruyle Law Offices, Greeley, Colo., 1968-70; dir. Creative Arts Ctr., Greeley, 1970-75; artist-in-residence, instr. printmaking U. No. Colo., Greeley, 1980-82, art history instr., 1984—; artist, Greeley, 1965—; dir., v.p. Wild County Dist. Six Bd. Edn., Greeley, 1975-77; mem. Colo. Council Arts and Humanities, Denver, 1977-83; chmn. Art in Pub. Places, 1979-82; chmn. Community Arts Councils of Colo., 1980-81, chmn. grants-in-aid, 1981-82; commr. Colo. Commn. Higher Edn., Denver, 1983—; bd. dirs. No. Colo. Found., 1984—, Colo. Found. Arts, 1984—; organizing com. Colo. Group Nat. Mus. Women Arts, Washington, 1984—. Illustrator, Küche Kochen cookbook, 1973. Sculptor bronze armillary sundial Rutherford Hill Winery Napa Valley, Calif., 1972; exhibitor UN Conf. on Women, Nairobi, Kenya, 1985; contbr. The Birth Project, Judy Chicago, 1985. Chmn. Citizens Task Force Cultural Affairs, Greeley, 1977-80, Residential Ch., United Way, Weld County, 1972-73; vice chmn. Weld County Democratic Central Com., Greeley, 1968-72. Recipient Jurors award Manhattan Nat. Print Exhbn., 1984. Named Parent of Yr., U. Colo. Alumni Assn. 1983, Community Service award, 1985; Boettcher Found. scholar 1953-57. Mem. AAUW (chmn. Nat. Art Mart, Greeley br. 1970, 82-85), Artists Equity Assn., Nat. Assn. Women Artists, Los Angeles Printmaking Soc., World Print Council, Phi Beta Kappa, Gamma Phi Beta, Pi Gamma Mu, Delta Phi Delta. Avocations: cooking; knitting; skiing; travel. Home: 2101 24th St Greeley CO 80631 Studio: 2101 24th St Greeley CO 80631

RUZICKA, ANNE CULTON, accounting company executive; b. Lexington, Ky., Aug. 17, 1946; d. Eugene and Anne Elizabeth (Vaughan) Culton; m. Anthony J. Ruzicka, Jr., Nov. 30, 1974; children—Carrie Culton, Annette Lynne. B.S. in Acctg., U. Ky.-Lexington, 1968, M.S. in Acctg., 1969. C.P.A., Ill. Audit mgr. Arthur Young & Co., Chgo., 1969-76; ptnr. Ruzicka & Assocs., Chgo., 1976-82, v.p., 1982—; dir., v.p., treas. Chgo. Fin. Exchange, 1982—; dir., v.p. C.P.A.s Pub. Interest, Chgo., 1983—. Contbr. in field. Bd. dirs. Coalition on Non-Profit Acctg., Chgo., 1980-83; tchr. Glencoe Union Ch. (Ill.), 1981-83. Recipient award Ernst & Ernst, 1967; Charlotte Danstron Meml. award, 1984. Mem. Am. Inst. C.P.A.s, Exec. Club Chgo., Chgo. Soc. Women C.P.A.s (pres. 1977), Am. Women Soc. C.P.A.s, Nat. Assn. Women Bus. Owners, Women in Mgmt. (bd. dirs., pres., treas. 1983—), Beta Gamma Sigma, Beta Alpha Psi. Home: 580 Jackson Ave Glencoe IL 60022 Office: Ruzicka & Assocs Ltd 8 S Michigan Ave Chicago IL 60603

RUZICKA, VICKI P., marketing executive; b. Chgo., Apr. 30, 1945; d. Victor Hugo and Ellyn Marie (Doyle) Reid. B.S., Northeastern Ill. U., Chgo., 1976. Prodn. mgr. Signature Direct Response Mktg., Evanston, Ill., 1981-82, purchasing mgr., 1983-84; credit promotions media mgr. Montgomery Ward, Chgo., 1982-83; fulfillment purchasing mgr. The Signature Group, Schaumburg, Ill., 1984—. Author: Trips: Head, Bod and Side, 1968, Poetry Magazine, 1970; author standardized test measuring male attitudes toward women. Served with USAF, 1979-83. Mem. Nat. Assn. Purchasing Mgrs., Direct Mail Mktg. Assn., Printing Inst. Ill., Chgo. Assn. Direct Mktg., Women's Direct Response Group. Roman Catholic. Avocations: sailing; golf; classical piano; baseball. Office: The Signature Group 200 N Martingale Rd Schaumburg IL 60194

RYALL, JO-ELLYN M., psychiatrist; b. Newark, May 25, 1949; d. Joseph P. and Tekla (Paraszczuk) R.; B.A. in Chemistry with gen. honors, Douglass Coll., Rutgers U., 1971; M.D., Washington U., St. Louis, 1975. Resident in psychiatry Washington U., 1975-78, psychiatrist Student Health, 1980-84, clin. instr. psychiatry, 1978-83, clin. asst. prof., 1983—; inpatient supr. Malcolm Bliss Mental Health Center, St. Louis, 1978-80, psychiatrist outpatient clinic, 1980-82; pvt. practice medicine specializing in psychiatry, St. Louis, 1980—. Bd. dirs. Women's Self Help Center, St. Louis, 1980-83, Manic Depressive Assn., St. Louis, 1982—. Diplomate Am. Bd. Psychiatry and Neurology. Mem. Am. Psychiat. Soc. (pres. Eastern Mo. Dist. Br. 1983-84), Am. Med. Women's Assn. (pres. St. Louis Dist. br. 1981-82, regional gov. 1985—), AMA, St. Louis Met. Med. Soc. (del. to state conv. 1981—, councilor 1985—). Roman Catholic. Club: Washington U. Faculty. Office: 9216 Clayton Rd Suite 105 Saint Louis MO 63124

RYALS, MARY JOHNSTON, business executive; b. Pampa, Tex., Oct. 29, 1934; d. James Wayne and Olive Jo (Miller) Johnston; student Baylor U., 1953-54, Colo. Coll., 1956; m. Carthy R. Ryals, Sept. 5, 1953 (div.); children—R. Dawne, C. Ronway, Carthy R. Owner, mgr. Amarillo Travelodge, 1965-70; adminstrv. coordinator of continuing edn. U. Tex. Southwestern Med. Sch., Dallas, 1972-78; dir. postgrad. edn. San Diego Radiology Research & Edn. Found., 1978-82; pres. Ryals and Assocs., 1982—; v.p. J2R Computer Software, 1979-82; v.p. Savvy Spouse, 1980—. Recipient Merit award, Travelodge, 1965. Mem. Meeting Planners Internat. (dir. San Diego chpt. 1981-82), Nat. Assn. Female Execs., Inc., Profl. Conv. Mgmt. Assn., Am. Soc. Assn. Execs. Republican. Baptist. Club: Winners Circle. Office: PO Box 920113 Norcross GA 30092-0113

RYAN, DEBORAH JEANNE, lawyer; b. Miami, Fla., Sept. 20, 1949; d. Ewell Deltz and Lilah Fern (Sutton) R. A.A., Miami-Dade Jr. Coll., 1969; B.B.A., Fla. Internat. U., 1976; J.D., U. Miami, 1984. Bar: Fla. 1984. Staff purchasing dept. Fla. Power & Light Co., Miami, 1974-77, contract agt., 1977-80, fleet adminstrv. supr. automotive dept., 1980-82; law clk. to U.S. bankruptcy judge So. Dist. Fla., 1984—. Vol. local polit. activities. Recipient various Buyer of Month awards Fla. Power & Light Co., first female purchasing agt., contracts agt., automotive supr. Mem. Good Govt. in Mgmt. Assn., YWCA Women's Network, Am. Bus. Women's Assn., Fla. Assn. Women Lawyers NOW, Zeta Tau (pres 1968-69). Cert. scuba diver. Office: US Bankruptcy Ct So Dist Fla 51 SW First Ave Rm 1411 Federal Bldg Miami FL 33130

RYAN, DOROTHY BARGER, writer; b. Lancaster, Pa., Oct. 24, 1942; d. Clay Miller and Dorothy Esther (Barger) R.; B.A. magna cum laude, Pa. State U., 1964, postgrad., 1964-65; M.A. in English, U. Del., 1983; children by previous marriage—Lisa, Jon, Craig Miller. Freelance writer, 1970—; editor Subject Guide to Books in Print, R.R. Bowker & Co., Lancaster, Pa., 1961-65, Gotham Book Mart Monograph Series, 1977—; instr. English, Goldey Beacom Coll., Wilmington, Del., 1979-80; instr. English U. Del., 1980-81, intern Office of Devel., 1981-82; asst. to dirs. Med. Soc. Del., 1983-84; tech. editor Morton Thiokol/Elkton div., 1985—; editor Solid Facts, 1985—; exhibited rare Am. postcards Gotham Book Mart Gallery, 1976, Valentine postcards Rockwood Mus., Wilmington, Del., 1978. Named Woman of Yr., Postcard History Soc., 1979. Mem. Hist. Soc. Del., Chester County (Pa.) Hist. Soc., Lancaster County (Pa.) Hist. Soc., Del. Art Mus., Met. Postcard Collectors Club, S. Jersey Postcard Club, Deltiologists of Am., Phi Beta Kappa, Phi Kappa Phi, Sigma Tau Delta, Alpha Lambda Delta. Episcopalian. Author: Picture Postcards in the United States, 1893-1918, 1976, 2d edit., 1982; Philip Boileau Painter of Fair Women, 1980; contbr. numerous articles on postcards as hist. data to various mags.; contbr. revs. to publs. on antiques. Home: 91 Ritter Ln Newark DE 19711 Office: Morton Thiokol Elkton Div Box 291 Elkton MD 21921

RYAN, ELEANORE A., clinical psychologist; b. Chgo.; B.S. with honors in Chemistry, Mundelein Coll.; Ph.D. in Clin. Psychology, Northwestern U., 1978; children—Robert, James, Mark, John, Christopher, Marynel. Staff psychologist Porter-Starke Services, Valparaiso, Ind., 1978-80; psychol. cons. Gary (Ind.) Community Mental Health Center, 1980-81; pvt. practice clin. and cons. psychology, Clarendon Hills, Ill., 1981—; psychologist Hines VA Hosp. (Ill.), 1983—; mem. faculty Ill. Benedictine Coll., Elmhurst Coll. Cert. psychologist, Ill., Ind. Mem. Am. Psychol. Assn., Ill. Psychol. Assn., Midwest Psychol. Assn., Assn. DuPage Psychologists (pres.), Nat. Register Health Service Providers in Psychology, Soc. for Clin. and Exptl. Hypnosis, Chgo. Psychologists in Addictive Behavior, Consortium Vietnam Vet. Service Providers. Roman Catholic. Home and office: 215 Coe Rd Clarendon Hills IL 60514

RYAN, ELIZABETH ANN, nurse; b. Syracuse, N.Y., Sept. 22, 1950; d. John W. and Catherine Mary (James) R. Diploma Crouse Irving Meml. Hosp. Sch. Nursing, Syracuse, 1971; student Syracuse U. Nurse, Plaza Nursing Home, Syracuse, 1971-79; critical care staff nurse Crouse-Irving Meml. Hosp., Syracuse, 1979—. Republican. Roman Catholic.

RYAN, EVELYN MARIE, sales and marketing management consultant; b. Mayaguez, P.R., Sept. 21, 1936; d. Arturo R. Oppenheimer and Georgina Castro; m. Michael John Ryan, Jan. 7, 1956; children—Michael, Terence, Cathy, Darren, Jennifer, Arthur, Karl. Grad. with honors in Secretarial Sci. Havana Bus. U., Cuba, 1955; B.S. in Econs. St. Thomas Vilanova U., Cuba, 1955; cert. in Comml. Edn., U. P.R., 1966. Cert. personnel cons., 1985. Translator, adminstrn. asst. M.W. Kellog Co., N.Y.C., 1957-59; translator, interpreter, Tucson, Ariz., San Diego, Calif., 1959-66; comml. edn. tchr. Manpower Bus. Tng. Inst., San Juan, P.R., 1970-75, admissions officer, 1975-77; sales, mktg. mgmt. cons. Careers Inc., Hatorey, P.R., 1977—. Contbr. articles to local newspapers. Surveyor New Progressive Political Party, San Juan, 1974. Mem. Am. Mktg. Assn. (pres., founding mem. P.R. chpt. 1985—, bd. dirs. 1984-85, sec. 1983-84), Am. Business Women Assn., Sales and Mktg. Execs., Mfrs. Assn., P.R. Products Assn., San Juan C. of C. Democrat. Roman Catholic. Club: Cafe del Puerto (San Juan). Avocations: reading, music, camping, beach activities, painting, drawing, writing, training others. Office: Careers Inc 1919 Banco Popular Center Hato Rey PR 00918

RYAN, JOAN SUE, business educator; b. Klamath Falls, Oreg., Mar. 28, 1948; d. John and Susan Elvara (Fenton) Cacka; m. Tom Edward Ryan, Feb. 20, 1976; children—Michael Edward, Christie Susan. B.S., So. Oreg. Coll., 1970; M.S., Oreg. State U., 1976. Teaching, vocat. cert., Oreg. Legal sec. Luvaas, Cobb & Richards, Eugene, Oreg., 1970-73; escrow closer Lane County Escrow Dept., Eugene, 1974; tchr. jr. high sch. Bethel Sch. Dist., Eugene, 1974-78, high sch., 1978-81; instr. bus. Lane Community Coll., Eugene, 1982—; speaker ednl. confs., Calif., Idaho, Utah, Oreg., Mont., 1983—. Author: Managing Your Personal Finances, 1985, Personal Business Management, 1986; creator bus. math. video tapes for computer interactive telecourse Lane Community Coll., 1984. Mem. Oreg. Bus. Edn. Assn. (sec. 1986-87), Delta Pi Epsilon (v.p. Gamma Omicron chpt. 1985-86). Democrat. Baptist. Avocation: oil painting. Home: 1305 Flintridge PO Box 5354 Eugene OR 97405 Office: Bus Dept Lane Community Coll 4000 E 30 Ave Eugene OR 97405

RYAN, JOANNE WINONA, college official and dean, educator, artist; b. Jersey City, May 24, 1932; d. James Joseph and Josephine Veronica (Di Blasi) R. B.A., Caldwell Coll., 1963; M.A., U. Notre Dame, 1969; Ph.D., NYU, 1981. Elem. tchr. Archdiocese of Newark, Newark and West Orange, N.J., 1951-60; secondary tchr., chmn. art dept. Mount St. Dominic Acad., Caldwell, N.J., 1960-70; instr., dir. art edn. Caldwell Coll., N.J., 1972-75, acad. dean, 1975-78, assoc. prof., 1975-81; dean acad. affairs, prof. Phila. Colls. Arts, 1982—, acting pres., summer 1983, v.p., 1984—; exec. dir. Internat. Soc. for Advancement of Living Traditions in Arts, Middle Atlantic region, N.Y.C., 1981—. Mem. Pa. Humanities Council, Phila., 1984—; mem. bd. advisors New Sch., N.Y.C., 1975-83. Author: The Aesthetic Dimension in Process Philosophy, 1972. One-woman shows Caldwell Coll., 1972, Muhlenberg Coll., Pa., 1973, 80 Washington Square East Galleries, N.Y.C., 1980, 81; exhibited in group shows U. Notre Dame, 1969, Nutley Art Festival, N.J., 1972, Catholic Fine Arts Soc., 1972, Miniature Art Soc., 1972 (1st prize), Art Ctr. of Oranges, N.J., 1972; artist/writer in residence W.S. Davis Estate, Orient, N.Y., 1972-73. Research grantee NYU/John D. Rockefeller III Fund, N.Y.C., 1972. Visceglia Found., Raritan, N.J., 1982. Mem. Am. Council on Edn., Coll. Art Assn., Women's Caucus for Art, Nat. Art Edn. Assn., Catholic Fine Arts Soc. (sec.-treas. 1970-72), Nat. Assn. Schs. Art and Design (instl. rep.), Middle State Assn. Colls. and Schs. (instl. rep.), Pa. Art Edn. Assn. Office: Phila Colls Arts Broad and Pine Sts Philadelphia PA 19102

RYAN, JUDITH LYNDAL, educator; b. Sydney, Australia, Apr. 6, 1943; d. William Matthew and Kathleen (Ferris) O'Neil; m. Lawrence Ryan, Feb. 24, 1964 (div. 1985); children—Antony Lawrence, Vanessa Lyndal. B.A. with honors, U. Sydney, 1964; Dr.Phil., U. Muenster (W. Ger.), 1970. Mem. faculty Smith Coll., 1967-85, prof., 1980-85, Doris Silbert prof. humanities, 1982-85; prof. Harvard U., Cambridge, Mass., 1985—; vis. asso. prof. Brown U., 1979-80. Author: Umschlag and Verwandlung: Rilkes Lyrik der mittleren Periode, 1972; The Uncompleted Past, 1983; also articles. Mem. MLA, Am. Assn. Tchrs. German, New Eng. MLA, AAUP. Office: Harvard U Boylston Hall Cambridge MA 02138

RYAN, LAVONNE BLINDERMAN, speech pathologist; b. Southampton, N.Y., Aug. 2, 1932; d. Leo M. and Gwen (Smith) Blinderman; B.S., SUNY-Buffalo, 1954; M.A., Coll. St. Rose, 1963; postgrad. SUNY, Albany, 1963; m. F. Paul Ryan, July 4, 1955; children—Kathleen Ryan Goodwin, Laura Marie, Scott Paul. Speech therapist Buffalo Public Schs., 1954; speech lang. therapist Norfolk (Va.) Cerebral Palsy Center, 1955, 56, Bethlehem Central Sch. Dist., Delmar, N.Y., 1969 74; supr. clin. practicum, dept. speech pathology and audiology SUNY-Albany, 1975-76; chief ednl. therapist VA Hosp., Albany, N.Y., 1977; speech lang. pathologist South Colonie Sch. Dist., Albany, 1978—; pvt. practice speech pathology, 1958-69. Bd. dirs. YWCA, 1962-70. Mem. 3d Dist. Dental Soc. Aux. (dir. 1959-69), Am. Speech and Hearing Assn., N.Y. State Speech Lang. Hearing Assn., Kappa Delta Pi. Home: 49 Thorndale Rd Slingerlands NY 12159 Office: 100 Hackett Ave Albany NY 12205

RYAN, MARLEIGH GRAYER, educational administrator; b. N.Y.C., May 1, 1930; d. Harry and Betty (Hurwick) Grayer; B.A., N.Y. U., 1951; M.A., Columbia U., 1956, cert. E. Asian Inst., 1956, Ph.D. (Ford fellow), 1965; m. Edward Ryan, June 3, 1950; 1 son, David Patrick. Lectr., asst. prof., assoc. prof. Japanese, Columbia U., N.Y.C., 1960-72; chmn. dept. Asian langs. and lit. U. Iowa, Iowa City, 1972-81, assoc. prof., 1972-75, prof., 1975-81; chmn. Columbia U. Seminar on Modern Japan, 1985-86; dean Liberal Arts and Scis., prof. Japanese, SUNY-New Paltz, 1981—. Japan Found. fellow, 1973; Nelson A. Rockefeller Inst. Govt. fellow, 1985—. Mem. Assn. Asian Studies (dir. 1975-78), Assn. Tchrs. of Japanese (sec. 1962-71), MLA (del. assembly 1979—, exec. com. Asian lit. 1981—, chair 1984). Author: Japan's First Modern Novel, 1965; The Development of Realism in the Fiction of Tsubouchi Shoyo, 1975; editor Jour. Assn. Tchrs. of Japanese, 1971-75. Office: FT614 SUNY New Paltz NY 12561

RYAN, MARY JANE, nursing administrator, consultant; b. Mishawaka, Ind., Sept. 27, 1925; d. William A. and Johanna M. (Vanderbosch) Thallemer; m. George T. Ryan, Aug. 25, 1951; children—Theresa, Christine, Kathryn, Joanna, Timothy. Diploma St. Vincent's Sch. Nursing, Indpls., 1947; student St. Louis U., 1948; cert. in mgmt. Pacific Luth. U., Tacoma, 1976. Head psychiat. nurse St. Vincent's Sanitarium, St. Louis, 1947-49; supr. surg. chest and Tb Healthwin Hosp., South Bend, Ind., 1949-51; supr. psychiatric care Crestview Hosp., St. Paul, 1954-56; dir. nursing St. James Hosp., Chicago Heights, Ill., 1965-73; dir. nursing for Hosp. Corp. Am., Nashville, 1973—, cons. nursing adminstrn., 1978-79; dir. nursing North Shore Hosp., North Miami, Fla., 1973-74, Holy Family Hosp., Spokane, Wash., 1974-78, Castleview Hosp., Price, Utah, 1979—; mem. adv. com. Prairie State Coll., Chicago Heights, 1966-67, Spokane Community Coll., 1974-78; mem. faculty Coll. Eastern Utah, Price, 1979—, also mem. adv. com. Mem. Assn. Nurse Execs. (charter mem.; membership com.), Washington Assn. Nurse Adminstrs. (bd. dirs. 1977-78), Fla. Assn. Nurse Adminstrs. Republican. Roman Catholic. Avocations: cross-country skiing; swimming; reading. Office: Castleview Hosp 300 Hospital Dr Price UT 84501

RYAN, NANCY JEAN, hotel sales executive; b. Chgo., Nov. 25, 1952; d. Edward Charles Ryan and Mary (Simpson) Ryan Townsend; student John Carroll U., 1970-72, Rome Center of Loyola U. of Chgo., 1972-73; B.S. in Mktg./Bus. Adminstrn., Bradley U., 1974. Reservations mgr. Ambassador West Hotel, Chgo., 1975-78, asst. exec. mgr., 1978-79; front office mgr. Tremont Hotel, Chgo., 1979-80; front office mgr. Mayfair Regent Hotel, Chgo., 1980-81, sales rep./corp. accounts, 1981-82; sales mgr. Grand Met. and Forum hotels, 1982-84; nat. sales mgr. Howard Johnson Co., 1984—. Active Stritch Sch. Medicine Jr. Service League, 1969—, Presentation Ball Jr. Aux., Chgo., 1970, Northwestern Meml. Hosp. Service Bd., 1978-81, Presbyterian-St. Luke's Hosp. Vol. Services, Chgo., 1981-82; mem. Landmarks Preservation Council Ill., 1982-83; mem. Gov. James R. Thompson Re-election Com., 1979, 82. Named to Outstanding Young Women Am., 1982. Mem. Hotel Front Office Execs. Assn. (sec.-treas. 1979-80), Ill. Opera Guild, Chgo. Drama League, Meeting Planners Internat., Midwest Bus. Travel Assn. Clubs: Jr. League Chgo., Chgo. Travel Women's. Home: 1550 N Lake Shore Dr Chicago IL 60610

RYAN, PATRICIA, editor. B.S. in History, Columbia U. With Sports Illustrated mag., 1960-78, sr. editor, 1970-78; sr. editor People mag., 1978-80, asst. mng. editor, 1980-81, exec. editor, 1981-82, mng. editor, 1982—. Office: People Weekly Time and Life Bldg Rockefeller Center New York NY 10020*

RYAN, PATRICIA A., insurance company administrator, psychologist; b. Troy, N.Y., Aug. 2, 1958; d. Edward Joseph and Alice Mae (Van Slyke) R. B.A. in Psychology cum laude, Siena Coll., 1984. Dir. vol. speakers bur. St. Peter's Hosp. Alcoholism Treatment Ctr., Albany, N.Y., 1980-81; psychopharmacology research asst. Capitol Dist. Psychiat. Ctr., Albany, 1981-82; clin. research asst. dept. psychiatry Albany Med. Ctr., 1982-83; oncology data mgr. Albany Med. Coll., 1984; psychophysiology research asst. Albany VA Med. Ctr., 1984-85; claims rep. Farmers Ins. Group of Cos., Simi Valley, Calif., 1986—; cons. post-traumatic stress disorders in Vietnam veterans VA, Albany, 1984-85. Contbr. articles to profl. publs. Mem. Alpha Kappa Alpha, Psi Chi. Republican. Club: Siena Coll. Women's. Avocations: home improvement, arts, travel. Home: 22832 Hilton Head St Apt 100 Diamond Bar CA 91765 Office: Farmers Ins Group of Cos 3041 Cochran St Simi Valley CA 93099

RYAN, ROSEMARY BENFORD, nurse, educator; b. Lynch, Ky., Mar. 3, 1946; d. Patrick A. and Elizabeth (Benford) Ryan. Diploma in nursing Conemaugh Valley Meml. Hosp., Johnstown, Pa., 1967; B.S. in Nursing, Duquesne U., 1970; M.S. in Nursing, U. Colo., 1973; postgrad. U. Mo.-Kansas City, 1983. R.N. Staff nurse Conemaugh Valley Meml. Hosp., 1967-68; asst. instr., 1971-72; U.S. fed. trainee, 1972-73; asst. prof. U. Nebr., Omaha, 1973-76; clin. nurse specialist VA Med. Ctr., Topeka, 1976-78; med.-surg., then acute care nursing supr. VA Med. Ctr., Kansas City, Mo., 1978-84; asst. chief nursing service VA Med. Ctr., Omaha, 1984—; adj. asst. prof. U. Kans. Coll. Health

Scis., Kansas City, 1981—. Contbr. articles to profl. jours. Bd. dirs. Myasthenic Gravis Found., Kansas City, Mo., 1983—. Recipient letter of commendation VA Med. Ctr., 1979, spl. advancement for performance, 1979, spl. advancement for achievement, 1983; Nat. Student Nurses Assn. scholar, 1970. Mem. Student Nurses Assn. Pa. (grad. advisor 1967-68), Am. Soc. Health, Manpower, Edn. and Tng., Am. Women's and Bus. Club, Conemaugh Valley Meml. Hosp. Alumnae Assn., Nat., State and Dist. Nurses Assn. (dir., chmn. state by-laws, mem. recruitment com., dist. by-laws chmn.). Republican. Roman Catholic. Home: 4235 N 127th Ct Box 104 Omaha NE 68164 Office: Omaha VA Med Ctr 4401 Woolworth Ave Omaha NE 68105

RYAN, SHEENA ROSS, school executive; b. Perth, Scotland, Aug. 1, 1944; came to U.S., 1972; d. Douglas George Haig and Johanna Adams (Brown) Ross; m. Raymond John Ryan, Dec. 17, 1978 (div. Feb. 1985); 1 child, Ross McCarthy. Assoc., Inst. Bankers, Glasgow, Scotland, 1964; B. Profl. Studies, Pace U., 1985. Banker, Clydesdale Bank, Glasgow, 1962-65; acct. Newmont Pty. Ltd., Melbourne, Australia, 1965-72; acctg. mgr. Hertz Internat., N.Y.C., 1972-73; asst. controller M&M Internat., N.Y.C., 1974-76; v.p. human research planning Marsh & McLennan, N.Y.C., 1976-80; founder, dir. New Eng. Sch. of Needle Art, Wilton, Conn., 1985—; dir. Rotondo Real Estate, Katonah, N.Y. Editor: Human Resource Planning newsletter, 1979. Mem. Embroiderers Guild Am., Mensa. Avocation: reading.

RYBICKI, MARY ANN FELDHAUS, printing products co. exec.; b. St. Louis, Mar. 9, 1951; d. Darvin Lambert and Lucille Edna (Berghold) F.; B.S. summa cum laude in Mktg., St. Joseph's Coll., 1973; M.B.A., U. Pa., 1976; m. Roger A. Rybicki; 1 child, Michael E. Procurement systems support analyst Re-entry and Environ. Systems div. Gen. Elec. Co., Phila., 1973-75; mktg. ops. analyst 3M Corp. Mktg. Analysis & Systems, St. Paul, 1976-78, mktg. planning supr. Printing Products div., 1978-81, mktg. services supr., 1981, mktg. services mgr., 1981—; tchr. Bus. and Econ. Edn. Found. Mem. exec. com. Careers Workshop Greater Mpls. council Girl Scouts U.S.A., 1980; vol. Ind.-Republican City Alderman campaign, 1979, mem. steering com. Mpls. Ind. Rep. City Alderman campaign, 1981, precinct chairwoman, 1982-83. Mem. Am. Mgmt. Assn. Club: Wharton Alumni of Minn. (dir. 1983-84). Office: 3M Co 3M Center Bldg 223-2N Saint Paul MN 55144

RYBURN, BETTY CORNETT, sociology educator; b. Northfolk, W.Va., Jan. 12, 1935; d. Clyde Jefferson and Berthelda Alice (Northen) Cornett; 1 dau., Pam. A.S., Marshall U., 1955, B.A., 1957; M.A., Ohio U., 1958; Ph.D., Laurence U., 1975. Mem. faculty Towson State Coll. (Md.), 1959-61, 67-68, U. Md.-Balt., 1967, George Mason U., 1970-75, Am. Tech. U., 1979-82; pvt. practice Family Counseling Service, Harker Heights, Tex., 1979-82; assoc. prof. sociology Mobile Coll. (Ala.), 1982-86, assoc. dean extended programs, 1984-86, assoc. prof. sociology and psychology, 1986—; cons., lectr. on human relations, leadership skills and mil. families. Author: The Relationship Between Certain Sociological Factors and Grade Achievement, 1958; Alienation: Generative Social Structural Conditions, Role Conflict/Strain, and Resulting Social Consequences, 1975; contbr. articles to profl. jours., papers to profl. confs. Chmn. Am. Heart Assn. Drive, Am. Cancer Soc. Drive; bd. advisers U. West Fla. Ctr. on Aging. Mem. Am. Sociol. Assn., Mid-South Sociol. Assn., So. Sociol. Soc., Ala.-Miss. Sociol. Assn., AAUP, AAUW, Alpha Lambda Delta, Alpha Kappa Delta. Baptist. Home: 25 Cobblestone Way W Mobile AL 36608 Office: Mobile Coll Dept Sociology Coll Pkwy Mobile AL 36613

RYCHECK, JAYNE BOGUS (MRS. ROY RICHARD RYCHECK), former ednl. adminstr.; b. Schenectady; d. Peter and Sylvia (Cywinski) Bogus; M.A., N.Y. U., 1953; B.S., State U. N.Y., Albany, 1941; postgrad. Syracuse U., 1957-66; m. R. Richard Rycheck, July 26, 1942. Tchr. various schs., 1935-43; elementary sch. tchr. Schenectady (N.Y.) City Schs., 1943-51, leadership intern, 1951-52, elementary sch. prin., 1952-61, dir. spl. edn., 1961-72. Instr. Russell Sage Coll., 1955-58, State U. N.Y., Oneonta, 1956; cons. bur. handicapped children N.Y. Edn. Dept., 1966-76, mem. commrs. and hoc coms., 1964-72, State Planning Com. Insts. for In-Service Edn., 1964-67; rep. to Community Welfare Council Schenectady County, 1961-62; adv. council N.Y. State Joint Legislative Com. Mental and Phys. Handicapped, 1970-72; mem. adv. com. Schenectady County Office for Aging, 1976-81, vice chmn., 1977-78, chmn., 1978-81; advisory com. Older Ams. Act program N.Y. State Office of Aging, 1977-80. Trustee, chmn. edn. Schenectady Mus., 1974-77; mem. human services adv. com. Schenectady County Community Coll., 1977—. Recipient Humanitarian service awards United Cerebral Palsy Schenectady County, 1966, 67, Capital dist. Assn. for Brain-Injured Children, 1967; Meritorious Alumni award State U. N.Y. Coll. at Oneonta, 1972; Capitol Dist. Speech and Hearing award, 1972; Distinguished Service award N.Y. Fedn. chpts. Council for Exceptional Children, 1972; Joseph P. Kennedy, Jr. Found. award for outstanding activity for the mentally retarded, 1972, achievement award for contbns. to quality of life for sr. citizens N.Y. State Legislature, 1979; Disting. Service award Council Adminstrs. Spl. Edn., 1980. Mem. N.Y. State (sec. 1967-68), Nat. councils adminstrs. spl. edn., Assn. Childhood Edn. (state sec. 1952-55, state exec. bd. 1951-59), Council Exceptional Children (mem. chpt. regional and state bds. 1966-78, state regional dir. 1966-68, state adv. bd. 1966-72, v.p. 1968-69, state pres. 1970), Schenectady County Assn. Childhood Edn. (treas. and v.p. 1952), N.Y. State Assn. Childhood Edn. Internat. (sec., v.p. 1962-65), Am. Assn. Mental Deficiency, N.Y. State Assn. Brain-Injured Children (state adv. bd. 1963-67, dist. adv. bd. 1966-72), Nat. Soc. Autistic Children, Assn. Retarded Children (adv. bd.), Gifted Children Soc. (adv. com.), Schenectady C. of C. (edn. com.), Schenectady County Ret. Tchrs. Assn. (v.p. 1973, pres. 1974-76), Am. Assn. Ret. People (program com. chpt. 1973-76, legis. chmn., dir. 1981-84), AAUW (topic chmn. 1977-79, chpt. Name Grant honoree 1981), N.Y. Assn. Elementary Prins. (hon. life), N.Y. State Ret. Tchrs. Assn. (county dir. Eastern zone, del. state conv. 1974-76), Schenectady County Hist. Soc. (rec. sec., dir. 1982-84), Delta Kappa Gamma (chmn. chpt. profl. affairs com. 1972-76, del. state legis. forum 1974-79, mem. state com. profl. affairs 1974-75). Contbr. articles to publs. Home: 1537 Kingston Ave Schenectady NY 12308

RYDALCH, ANN, state senator. Mem. Idaho Senate, 1985—. Past mem. Idaho Bicentennial Commn.; former vice chmn. Idaho Republican Com. Office: Idaho Senate State Capitol Boise ID 83720*

RYDBERG, MARSHA GRIFFIN, lawyer; b. Tampa, Fla., Dec. 11, 1946; d. Jack and Nibia (Santana) Griffin; m. Thomas Henry Rydberg, Jan. 25, 1975; children—Kristen Elizabeth, Nancy Marshall. B.A., Emory U., 1968; J.D. cum laude, Stetson U., 1976. Bar: Fla. 1976, U.S. Dist. Ct. (mid. dists.) Fla. 1977, U.S. Dist. Ct. (so. dist.) Fla. 1983, U.S. Ct. Appeals (11th cir.) 1977, U.S. Supreme Ct. 1983. Youth worker Young Life Campaign, Tampa, 1968-70; youth dir. 1st Presbyn. Ch., Tampa, Fla., 1970-73; assoc. Gibbons, Tucker, McEwen, Smith, Cofer & Taub, Tampa, 1976-79; assoc., then ptnr. Taub & Williams, Tampa, 1979—. Contbr. articles to legal jours. Atty. to Jr. League of Tampa, Inc., 1983-85; bd. dirs. Drug Abuse Comprehensive Coordination Office, Tampa, 1981—; elder Temple Terrace Presbyn. Ch. (Fla.), 1982-85. Recipient Disting. Achievement award Internat. Acad. Trial Lawyers; Judge Joe Morris award Stetson U. Mem. Fla. Bar (vice-chmn. news editorial bd. Fla. Bar Jour. 1980-83, chmn. 1984—), ABA (com. on condemnation, zoning and property use, chmn. Law Student div.), Hillsborough County Bar Assn. (chmn. Fed. Ct. liaison com. 1982), Phi Alpha Delta (Outstanding Scholastic Achievement award). Democrat. Contbr. articles to profl. jours. Office: Taub & Williams PO Box 3430 201 E Kennedy Blvd Suite 1700 Tampa FL 33601

RYDER, GEORGIA ATKINS, educator, university dean; b. Newport News, Va., Jan. 30, 1924; d. Benjamin Franklin and Mary Lou (Carter) Atkins; B.S., Hampton (Va.) Inst., 1944; Mus.M., U. Mich., 1946; Ph.D., N.Y. U., 1970; m. Noah Francis Ryder, Sept. 16, 1947; children—Olive Diana, Malcolm Eliot, Aleta Renee. Resource music tchr., Alexandria, Va., 1945-48; faculty music dept. Norfolk State U., 1948—, prof., 1970—, head dept., 1969-79, dean Sch. Arts and Letters, 1979—. Bd. dirs. Va. Symphony, ctr. Black Music Research, Columbia Coll., Chgo., Nat. Consortium Arts and Letters for Hist. Black Colls. and Univs., Norfolk Commn. Arts and Humanities, Southeastern Va. Arts Assn.; mem. advisory com. Norfolk chpt. Young Audiences. Grantee So. Fellowship Fund, 1967-69, Consortium Research Tng., 1973; recipient award Norfolk Com. Improvement Edn., 1974. Mem. Music Educators Nat. Conf., Coll. Music Soc., Intercoll. Music Assn., Va. Music Educators Assn., Delta Sigma Theta. Contbr. articles to profl. jours. Office: Norfolk State U Norfolk VA 23504

RYDER, SANDRA SMITH, communications specialist; b. Great Lakes, Ill., July 6, 1949; d. Dennis Murrey and Olga (Grosheff) Smith; m. Nicholas Grafton Ryder, Feb. 26, 1977 (div. 1981). B.S., Northwestern U., 1971; postgrad. U. So. Calif., 1983—. Reporter, columnist Camarillo Daily News (Calif.), 1971-76; editor Fillmore Herald (Calif.), 1976-78; editorial asst. Ventura County Farm Bur., (Calif.), 1978-80; pub. info. officer Oxnard Union High Sch. Dist. (Calif.), 1980-82; pub. info. officer Ventura Coll., 1982-83; pub. relations dir. Murphy Orgn., Oxnard, Calif., 1983-84; pub. affairs rep. Gen. Telephone Calif., Santa Monica, 1984—. Mem. Ventura County Commn. for Women, 1981—. Mem. Nat. Sch. Pub. Relations Assn., Women in Communications, Soc. Profl. Journalists, Pub. Info. Communication Assn., Greater Los Angeles Press Club. Home: 177 W Green Vale Dr Camarillo CA 93010 Office: Gen Telephone 100 Wilshire Blvd Santa Monica CA 90406

RYE, VIRGINIA KATHERINE BRYAN, retired nursing educator, consultant; b. N.Y.C., Dec. 25, 1918; d. Arthur Melvyn and Alvina Mary (Glocker) Bryan; m. William Rye, Mar. 13, 1943 (div. 1977); children—Susan Goodwin, Bryan (dec.), Deidre, Kathleen Malin, John (dec.). R.N., Pa. Hosp., 1942; A.A., Old Dominion Coll., 1951; B.S., So. Conn. State Coll., 1968; M.S., U. Md., 1971; tchrs. cert. Glassboro State Coll., 1965. Dir., tchr., sch. nurse Pvt. Nursery Sch., Arco Felici, Italy, 1951-56; asst. dir. nursing Cherry Hill (N.J.) Hosp., 1958-60; classroom tchr. pub. sch., Ashland, N.J., 1960-66; supervisory psychiat. nurse St. Elisabeths Hosp., Washington, 1971-73; assoc. prof., asst. dir. U. D.C., Van Ness campus, Washington, 1974-77; asst. prof. Grad. Maternal-Child Imperial Health Sci. Ctr., Tehran, Iran, 1978-79; asst. prof. psychiat. nursing U. Tex. Health Sci. Ctr., San Antonio, 1979-83, ret., 1983; review tutor, dir. spl. classes for state bd. pool exam. Vol. VA Hosp.; active local Democratic politics. Served as 2d lt. U.S. Army Nurse Corps, 1943-44. Recipient Commendation, Luth. Gen. Hosp., 1983; award for excellence in teaching under very difficult circumstances Imperial Health Sci. Ctr., Tehran, Iran, 1979; Commendation for Excellence in Nursing, Doctor Hosp., Washington, 1973; award for excellence in design of nursing program St. Elisabeths Hosp., Washington, 1973; Recognition for Excellence in Teaching Upward Bound, U. D.C. Van Ness Campus, 1976; named Tchr. of Yr., Voorhees Twp., N.J., 1965. Mem. Nat. League Nursing. Democrat. Roman Catholic. Home: 7450 Stonefruit San Antonio TX 78240

RYERSON, MARGERY AUSTIN, painter; b. Morristown, N.J., Sept. 15, 1886; d. David Austen and Mary McIlvaine (Brown) R. A.B., Vassar Coll., 1909; studied, Art Students League, N.Y.C. Painter, etcher and lithographer. Represented prints in permanent collections, Smithsonian Instn., other mus., U.S. and abroad; exhibited paintings in collections, N.J. Hist. Soc., painting in collections, Norfolk Mus. Arts and Scis., Va., prints in collections. Abbot Labs., painting in collections, NAD, paintings in collections, Vassar Coll., Philbrook Art Ctr., Tulsa, Frye Mus., Seattle, Va. State Coll., Union Theol. Sem.; contbr.: Arts in Am., The Am. Scholar, Am. Artist, The Artist, N.Y. Herald Tribune, N.Y. Times Book Rev.; compiler: The Art Spirit, by Robert Henri; co-editor: Hawthorne on Painting; illustrator: Winkie Boo. Recipient 1st prize (oil) Hudson Valley Art Assn., 1956, 57, 58, Gold medal for oil portrait Nat. Arts Club, 1957, 62, 69, Silver medal, 1971, Maynard portrait prize NAD, 1959, 1st prize Balt. Water Color Club, 1960; portrait prize (oil) Silvermine Guild, 1960; recipient Hook Meml. Am. Watercolor Soc., Talens N.J. Watercolor Soc., 1963, Winsor and Newton, 1968, Stevenson prize (oil) Nat. Arts Club, 1967, Grumbacher, 1972, Clinedinst medal Artist Fellowship, 1971, Holton Meml. Watercolor prize Knickerbocker Artists, 1974, prize for graphics, 1978, Dole prize Am. Artists Profl. League, 1973, prize for graphics Am. Artists Profl. League, 1974, Albany Print Club prize, 1973, N.A., 1959; painter mem. Grand Central Art Galleries. Mem. Am. Watercolor Soc., Balt. Water Color Club, Knickerbocker Artists, Soc. Am. Graphic Artists, Allied Artists Am. (v.p. 1952-53), Audubon Artists (corr. sec. 1958-59), N.J. Watercolor Soc., Print Club Albany, Pen and Brush. Address: care Condon 3 Dingletown Rd Greenwich CT 06830

RYKER, JOHANNE LACEAL, business executive; b. Turlock, Calif., Dec. 7, 1946; d. John Wilson and Bette Louise (Slack) Dickinson; children—Dale Alan Ryker, Chad Allen Ryker. Cert. in retail merchandising Coll. of Marin, 1968; B.S. in Bus. Edn., Mktg. and Acctg., San Francisco State U., 1971. Mgr.-acct. San Jose Flight Sch. (Calif.), 1971-72; acct.-comptroller Youritan Constrn. Co., Palo Alto, Calif., 1972-77; owner Ryker Enterprises, Sunnyvale, Calif.; fin. cons. Youth adviser YMCA, 1967; active PTA, Baymonte, Valley Christian, Allen Schs., 1979-83, Foster Care. 1979. Recipient Community Devel. award in Indian affairs VISTA, 1967, marksmanship award Nat. Rifle Assn., 1961; named Foster Parent of Santa Clara County, 1979. Mem. Antique Dealers and Collectors Assn., DAR Republican. Clubs: Optomists, Order Jobs Daus. (hon. mem. Bethel 234).

RYLAND, CHACHI PAGANO, data processing manager; b. Camagüey, Cuba, Jan. 9, 1938; came to U.S., 1938; d. Nicholas and Pearl (Norman) Pagano; B.A. (Altrusca Club scholar), U. Fla., 1959; M.S., U. So. Calif., 1979; m. Walter Moncure Ryland, III, Aug. 27, 1961; children—William Norman, Robert Walter, Ada Virginia. Mathematician, RCA, Cape Canaveral, Fla., 1960-62; supervisory acct., Verdun, France, 1963-64; programmer/analyst Macro Services Corp., Boston, 1968-69; computer specialist U.S. Army Computer Systems Command, Ft. Eustis, Va., 1970-71; programmer/analyst Nev. Power Co., Las Vegas, 1974-75; cons. data processing, Yuba City, Calif., 1976-79; systems engr. Electronic Data Systems Corp., Dallas, 1979-81, system mgr., 1981-82, applications cons., 1982-85, info ctr. mgr., 1985—. Mem. Yuba City Ad Hoc Com. on Status of Women, 1977; mem. Sutter County (Calif.) Welfare Adv. Bd., 1977; bd. dirs. Women's Issues Network, Dallas, 1980—, sec., 1983-85. Recipient cert. of achievement U.S. Army Computer Systems Command, 1971. Mem. Data Processing Mgmt. Assn., Am. Mgmt. Assns. Democrat. Developed program to facilitate locating data on magnetic disks, 1975. Home: 4024 Fechin Circle Plano TX 75023 Office: 7171 Forest Ln Dallas TX 75230

RYLES, NANCY, b. Portland, Oreg., Dec. 18, 1937; d. William Dunn and Madlyn (Nutting) Wyly; m. Vernon B. Ryles, Jr., 1957; children—Scott, Ashley. Ed. Willamette U., 1955-56, Portland State U., 1969-72. Former mem. Oreg. Ho. of Reps.; now mem. Oreg. Senate. Mem. Beaverton Dist. 48 Sch. Bd., Oreg., 1972-78; mem. Gov.'s Commn. on Status Women, 1973-75; mem. state adv. council Career and Vocational Edn., 1975-78. Recipient Human Rights award Oreg. Edn. Assn., 1974; Excellence in Action award Delta Kappa Gamma, 1976; 1st Citizen award Beaverton, 1977; Disting. Service award Oreg. Vocat. Assn., 1978. Mem. Beaverton C. of C. (bd. dirs.), Washington County Pub. Affairs Forum, Oreg. Women's Polit. Caucus. Republican. Office: Oreg Senate State Capitol Salem OR 97310*

RYMAN, ELLA-MARY MARGARET, mathematics educator; b. Jersey City, Dec. 13, 1944; d. Earnest Fred and Genevieve Agnes (Byrnes) R. B.A. in Math. Edn., Jersey City State Coll., 1967, M.A., 1970, postgrad., 1978. Cert. prin., supr., N.J. Tchr. math. Union Hill High Sch., Union City, N.J., 1967—. Vol. Riverside Gen. Hosp. Mem. NEA, N.J. Edn. Assn., Union City Edn. Assn. (treas. 1979—), Am. Legion Aux. (pres. 1970-71, 75-76, treas. 1980-82, v.p. 1983—, Plaque for Outstanding Leadership 1980), Bus. and Profl. Women, Hudson County Air Force Assn. Republican. Roman Catholic. Lodges: North Hudson Lioness (v.p. 1982-83, Plaque for Dedicated Service 1982), K.C. Home: 716 10th St Union City NJ 07087 Office: Union Hill High Sch 3800 Hudson Ave Union City NJ 07087

RYMER, PAMELA A., judge; b. Knoxville, Tenn., Jan. 6, 1941; d. Bowen and Helen (Keller) R. A.B., Vassar Coll., 1961; LL.B., Stanford U., 1964. Dir. polit. research and analysis Citizens for Goldwater Com., Washington, 1964; assoc. Lillick, McHose & Charles, Los Angeles, 1966-72, ptnr., 1973-75; ptnr. Toy and Rymer, Los Angeles, 1975-83; judge U.S. Dist. Ct. for Central Dist. Calif., Los Angeles, 1983—. Chmn. postsecondary edn. com. State of Calif. Mem. ABA, Calif. Bar Assn., Los Angeles Bar Assn., Assn. Bus. Trial Lawyers. Office: US Courthouse 312 N Spring St Los Angeles CA 90012*

RZEWNICKI, JANET C., state official; b. Akron, Ohio, May 21, 1953; d. Robert Myers; m. Victor Rzewnicki, June 3, 1973. B.S., U. Del. Sr. acct. Peat, Marwick Mitchell, Wilmington, Del., 1978-80; corp. acct. Hercules Inc., Wilmington, 1980-81; acctg. instr. U. Del., Newark, 1980-82; dir. Whisman & Assocs., Wilmington, 1981-82; state treas. State of Del., Dover, 1983—. Columnist Del. Bus. Rev. Treas., bd. dirs. March of Dimes, Newark, 1979—; bd. dirs. United Way of Del., Wilmington, 1980-82; active Gov.'s Council on Devel. Fin., 1982-85. Mem. Nat. Assn. State Treas., Am. Inst. C.P.A.s, Del. Soc. C.P.A.s, Pa. Inst. C.P.A.s, Am. Soc. Women Accts. (dir. 1981), Beta Gamma Sigma. Republican. Office: Office of State Treas Thomas Collins Bldg PO Box 1401 Dover DE 19903*

SAAD, DOROTHY STURGES, nursing home administrator; b. Norfolk, Va., Apr. 23, 1919; d. Phillip Gordon and Anna (Taylor) Sturges; m. John Elias Saad, Nov. 14, 1942; children—E.J., Barbara, Alex, Dorothy Ann, Greg, Lee, Gordon (dec.). R.N., South Balt. Gen. Hosp., 1939; student U. Md., 1940-42. R.N., Ala.; lic. nursing home adminstr., Ala. Hosp. nurse Lee Meml. Hosp., Norfolk, 1939-42, Steinberger Hosp., Greensboro, N.C., 1939-42; active vis. nurses, hosp. nursing, pvt. duty nursing, supr., Mobile, Ala., 1946—; dir. nurses, owner Heritage Nursing and Convalescent Ctr., Inc., Mobile, 1968—; also owner Heritage Hospice, Southeastern Alimentation, Home Nursing Services, Saad's Med. Equipment, Gordon Oaks Retirement Ctr.; mem. bd. accreditations and standards com.; mem. Ala. Bd. Examiners for Nursing Home Adminstrs. Mem. area agy. on aging, Mobile; mem. Ridgefield Neighborhood Community Watch, Mobile; guarantor Mobile opera guild, 1979-82; mem. health com. Mobile United Way, 1978. Recipient Ala. Gerontol. Nurse of Yr. award, 1982, Excellence Profl. Nursing Practice award Mobile County Nurse's Soc., 1985; named Outstanding Career Woman of Mobile, Gayfers Career Club, 1985. Served to capt. Nurse Corps, U.S. Army, 1942-46, PTO. Mem. Physicians and Community Nurses Assn., Am. Nurses Assn., Ala. Nursing Home Assn., Ala. Nurses Assn., Am. Gerontol. Soc., Ala. Gerontol. Soc., Lebanese-Am. Club (Woman of Yr. award 1978), Ala. Medicaid Liaison Council, Nat. Assn. State Bd. Examiners for Nursing Home Adminstrs., Shriners Ladies Assn. Democrat. Episcopalian. Avocations: playing with grandchildren; traveling; rose gardening. Home: 5913 Shenandoah Rd N Mobile AL 36608 Office: Heritage Nursing Convalescent Ctr Inc 954 Navco Rd Mobile AL 36690

SAARMANN, LEMBI, nurse, educator; b. Geislingen, Germany, July 7, 1948; came to U.S., 1950; d. Lembit and Heli (Mald) Saarmann. B.S., Adelphi U., 1969, M.S., 1973; Ed.D., Columbia U., 1986. Staff nurse Albert Einstein Coll. Hosp., Bronx, N.Y., 1969-72; clin. nurse specialist LaGuardia Hosp., Forest Hills, N.Y., 1973-74; clin. nurse specialist Mercy Hosp., Rockville Centre, N.Y., 1974-77, acting asst. dir. nursing, 1977-78; asst. prof. Molloy Coll., Rockville Centre, N.Y., 1978-86; asst. prof. Sch. Nursing, San Diego State U., 1986—; bd. dirs. Nassau Assn. Nurses for Polit. Action, Nassau County, N.Y., 1971-73. Mem. Nurses Coalition for Action in Politics, Washington, 1983—. Mem. N.Y. State Nurses' Assn. (mem. Task Force on Outcomes of Edn. Programs, mem. council on legislation Albany), Am. Nurses Assn., Soc. Nursing History (sec. 1980-83), N.Y. Acad. Sci., Nat. League for Nursing, AAUP, Orgn. Am. Historians, Sigma Theta Tau (chpt. historian 1982-84, 3d v.p. 1985-86). Baptist. Contbg. author: Manual of Nursing Practice, 1983. Office: Sch Nursing San Diego State U San Diego CA 92182

SABAU, CARMEN SYBILE, chemist; b. Cluj, Romania, Apr. 24, 1933; naturalized U.S. citizen; d. George and Antoinette Marie (Chiriac) Grigorescu; m. Mircea Nicolae Sabau, July 11, 1956; 1 dau., Isabelle Carmen. M.S. in Inorganic and Analytical Chemistry, U. C.I. Parhon, Bucharest, Romania, 1955; Ph.D. in Radiochemistry, U. Fridericiana, Karlsruhe, W.Ger., 1972. Chemist, Argonne (Ill.) Nat. Lab., 1976—. Internat. Atomic Energy Agy. fellow, 1967-68; Humboldt fellow, 1970-72. Mem. Am. Chem. Soc., Am. Nuclear Soc., Am. Romanian Acad. Arts and Sci., Assn. for Women in Sci., N.Y. Acad. Sci., Sigma Xi. Author: Ion-exchange Theory and Applications in Analytical Chemistry, 1967; contbr. articles to profl. jours. Home: 6902 Martin Dr Woodridge IL 60517 Office: Argonne Nat Lab 9700 S Cass Ave Bldg 205 Argonne IL 60439

SABLE, BARBARA KINSEY, educator; b. Astoria, L.I., N.Y., Oct. 6, 1927; d. Albert and Verna Rowe Kinsey; B.A., Coll. Wooster, 1949; M.A., Tchrs. Coll. Columbia U., N.Y.C., 1950; D.Mus., U. Ind., 1966; m. Arthur J. Sable, Nov. 3, 1973. Office mgr., music dir. sta. WCAX, Burlington, Vt., 1954; instr. Cottey Coll., 1959-60; asst. prof. N.E. Mo. State U., Kirksville, 1962-64; asst. prof. U. Calif., Santa Barbara, 1964-69; now prof. music U. Colo., Boulder, Mem. Nat. Assn. Tchrs. Singing (past state gov., asso. editor bull.), AAUP, Colo. State Music Tchrs. Assn. Democrat. Author: The Vocal Sound, 1982. Home: 3430 Ash Ave Boulder CO 80303 Office: Coll Music Campus Box 301 U Colo Boulder CO 80309

SABOE, ELENA PROTA, hosp. info. systems mgr.; b. Phila., July 6, 1943; d. Joseph Thomas and Elena (Perri) Prota; B.A., Cabrini Coll., Radnor, Pa., 1965; m. Jon Saboe, Mar. 29, 1969; 1 dau., Kirsten Elyn. Tchr. English, Bishop McDevitt High Sch., Wyncote, Pa., 1966-72; mng. editor Franklin Inst. Research Labs., Phila., 1975-79; mgr. documentation SMS, Malvern, Pa., 1979-81, tng. cons., 1982-84, mgr. edn., 1984—. Mem. Soc. Tech. Communications, Network Women in Computer Tech., Nat. Assn. Tng. Devel. Office: 51 Valley Stream Pkwy Malvern PA 19355

SABOL, SUZANNE KAY, lawyer, educator; b. Union City, Pa., Oct. 7, 1953; d. Richard Lee and Shirley Ann (Clute) Donnell; m. Garry Albert Sabol, June 17, 1978. B.S. in Edn., Edinboro U., 1975; M.Ed., Gannon U., 1978; J.D., Capital U., 1982. Bar: Ohio 1983. Intake counselor Serenity Hall, Inc., Erie, Pa., 1975-76; tchr. socially, emotionally disturbed Northwest Tri-County Intermediate Unit, Edinboro, Pa., 1976-78; tchr. severe behaviorally handicapped Columbus City Schs. (Ohio), 1978—; sole practice law, Columbus, 1982—. Recipient award Spl. Edn. Dept. Columbus City Sch., 1983. Mem. ABA, Ohio Bar Assn., Columbus Bar Assn., Columbus Edn. Assn. Democrat. Mem. Assembly of God Ch. Office: 1681 River Bend Rd Columbus OH 43223

SABOTTKE, HELEN LOUISE AHLBERG, educator; b. Middletown, Conn., Dec. 7, 1926; B.S. in Bus. Edn., Central Conn., State Coll., New Britain, 1949; M.S. in Elementary Edn., So. Conn. State Coll., New Haven, 1967, diploma in reading, 1971; certificate in adminstrn., U. Bridgeport, Conn., 1974; children—Craig, Mark. Tchr., Trumbull (Conn.) Bd. Edn.; 1963-70, cons. reading, 1970-74, coordinator, reading and lang. arts, 1974—; owner Craigmark Creations. Cert. elem. edn., reading cons., emergency med. technician. Title IV grantee. Mem. Internat. Reading Assn., New Eng. Reading Assn., NEA, Conn. Edn. Assn., Conn. Assn. of Reading Research, Nat. Assn. Tchrs. English, Smithsonia Assos., Jenny Lind Doll Club, United Fedn. Doll Clubs, Doll Club N.Y., Doll Artisan Guild, Kappa Delta Pi, Delta Kappa Gamma (pres. Beta chpt. 1978-80). Home: 17 Old Orchard Ln Trumbull CT 06611 Office: Trumbull High Sch Strobel Rd Trumbull CT 06611

SABOYA, MARIA ELENA, banker; b. Palma Soriano-Oriente, Cuba, May 27, 1951; came to U.S., 1960, naturalized, 1970; d. Casimiro and Irma (Gross) S.; student in data processing mgmt. Automated Bus. Coll., Harvard U., 1971-72; A.A. in Acctg., Miami Dade Jr. Coll., 1981; M.B.A., Barry U. Computer clk. Sears Roebuck, Chgo., 1972-74; tax clk. Met. Dade County (Fla.), 1974; with Capital Bank, 1974-85, v.p. North Miami Beach office, 1980-81, v.p., br. mgr. North Bay Village office, 1981—; v.p. Miami office Bayshore Bank, 1985—; notary public; mem. faculty Am. Inst. Banking 1982. Mem. North Dade C. of C., North Miami Beach C. of C., Latin C of C. Democrat. Roman Catholic. Home: 1329 71 St Miami Beach FL 33141 Office: 10800 Biscayne Blvd Miami FL 33161

SACCA, HARRIET WANDS, music educator; b. Pittsfield, Mass, July 21, 1919; d. Harry J. and Anna F. (Mara) Wands; B.S., Coll. St. Rose, 1939, M.A., 1962; student SUNY, Albany, Oneonta. Tchr. pub. schs., Albany, N.Y., 1942-66; instr. Coll. St. Rose, 1962-63; dir. music edn. Albany (N.Y.) Bd. Edn., 1966—; bur. assoc. examiner personnel N.Y. State Dept. Edn. Past pres. Soroptimist Internat., 1969-70, City Club Albany, Inc., 1974-75; active Albany County Democratic Com., 1962—; jud. del. 3d Jud. area N.Y. State, 1975-86; mem. Albany Local Devel. Corp.; bd. dirs. St. Joseph's Housing Corp., Youth Emergency Shelter, Albany Tulip Festival; adv. bd. mem. capital Region Ctr. Arts in Edn., 1983—; mem. adv. bd. Albany County Alternatives to Incarceration, 1985-86; bd. dirs. Coop. Extension Community Resources Devel., bd. dirs. 7 County Youth Symphony Orch., 1970-84. Recipient Citizen of Yr. award Ford Motor Co., 1971; Women Helping Women award

Soroptimist, 1975; Disting. Service award N.Y. State PTA, 1985. Fellow Harry Truman Library; mem. Music Educators Nat. Conf., N.Y. State Sch. Music Assn., Capitol Hill Choral Soc. (dir.), Albany Adminstrs. Assn., Albany Civic Auditorium (dir.), Delta Kappa Gamma, Delta Epsilon. Democrat. Roman Catholic. Clubs: Bus. and Profl. Women's, Soroptimist, Club of Albany, Cath. Women's Service League, Coll. St. Rose Alumni, Pres.'s Soc. Home: 226 Morris St Albany NY 12208 Office: Albany Bd Edn Academy Park Albany NY 12207

SACCO, MARY ELIZABETH, employment agency executive; b. Allentown, Pa., May 19, 1960; d. Richard John and Agnes Jane (Nixon) Bazewick; m. Joseph Francis Sacco, Nov. 27, 1982; 1 child, Joseph Gimmie. Assoc. Applied Scis. in Bus., Broome Community Coll., 1980. Waitress, Mister Donuts, Binghamton, N.Y., 1976-78; sales Sears Roebuck & Co., Johnson City, N.Y., 1978-80, Acme Cash Register Co., Johnson City, 1980-82; advisor, mgr. Wildwood Personnel, Johnson City, 1982-83; owner, mgr. Crest Personnel Agy., Johnson City, 1983—. Mem. Broome County C. of C., Nat. Assn. Female Execs. Avocations: ceramics, camping. Office: Crest Personnel Agy 435 Main St PO Box 495 Johnson City NY 13790

SACCOMAN, PATRICIA LINDEN, Arabian horse breeder, writer; b. Chgo., Mar. 27, 1933; d. John Wendell and Ruth (Blanchard) Linden; m. William John Saccoman, June 11, 1964; children—Melinda, Joseph, John, Mark. Student San Diego State U., U. Ariz. Founder, pres. Pied Piper Tours for Children, San Diego, 1967-71; owner, mgr. Lazy Diamond Ranch, Jerome, Idaho, 1971-82; owner, mgr., pres. Stallion Oaks Arabians, El Cajon, Calif., 1975—, Stallion Oaks Enterprises, El Cajon, 1980—; chmn. bd. The Adventures of Studley, El Cajon, 1984—. Author: Studley Sets his Goal, 1984; The Runaways, 1985. Bd. dirs. Salvation Army, El Cajon, 1982—, YMCA HDD Dept., San Diego, 1970-73. Recipient cert. of appreciation Salvation Army, 1983, YMCA, 1976, Purple Rag award. Mem. Internat. Arabian Horse Assn. (youth com.), Arabian Horse Regis-ry, Arabian Horse Trust (regent 1975—), Arabian Riders and Breeders (del., bd. dirs. 1981—), Desert Arabian Horse Assn., Star World of Arabians, San Diego Med. Aux., Delta Gamma. Republican. Avocations: swimming; tennis; aerobics; music. Home: 5816 Stallion Oaks Rd El Cajon CA 92021 Office: Stallion Oaks Enterprises 505 N Mollison El Cajon CA 92021

SACHSE, BARBARA KAY, home economist; b. Milw., May 18, 1961; d. Thomas Edward and Joyce (Heck) S. B.S., U. Wis.-Stout, 1983. Unit mgr. Szabo Foodservice, Columbus, Ohio, 1983; food service mgr. Saga Corp., Racine, Wis., 1984; research and devel. home economist Croissant Etc. Corp., Milw., 1984-86; home economist Alto-Shaam, Inc., Menomonee Falls, Wis., 1986—. Leader Lutheran Rangerettes, Milw., 1985-86. Recipient chancellor's award U. Wis., Stout, 1983. Mem. Nat. Assn. Female Execs., Home Econs. Profl. Improvement Council, Home Econs. in Bus. (chmn. profl. devel. coll. and univ. relations). Avocations: aerobics; outdoor activities; reading; sports. Office: Alto-Shaam Inc PO Box 450 W164 N9221 Water Menomonee Falls WI 53051

SACHSE, ELINOR YUDIN, economist; b. N.Y.C., Sept. 10, 1940; d. Lazarus Simon and Genevive (Goldberg) Yudin; B.A. with honors in Econs., Barnard Coll., 1962; M.A., Columbia U., 1964, Ph.D., 1968; m. Harry R. Sachse, Nov. 30, 1975; children—Michael Judah, Marianna Victoria. Mem. faculty dept. econs. N.Y. U., N.Y.C., 1966-69; various positions World Bank, Washington, 1969-79, chief internat. economy div., 1974-78; sr. staff economist internat. trade Council Econ. Advs., White House, 1980-82; cons. EYS Assocs., Washington, 1982—. Ford Found. fellow, 1965-66; Internat. Econs. Workshop fellow, 1963-64, 64-65; Francis M. Dibblee scholar, 1962-63. Author: Human Capital Migration, Direct Investment and the Transfer of Technology, 1976; also articles. Mem. Am. Econs. Assn. Jewish. Home: 2934 Newark St NW Washington DC 20008

SACHTLEBEN, BETTY JUNE, social services administrator; b. Centralia, Ill., Oct. 29, 1929; d. William Charles and Nellie Josephine (Winstead) Sissom; B.S., Washington U., 1962, M.S.W., 1966; m. Roland Sachtleben, Feb. 9, 1951; children—Stewart Gary, Cynthia Barbara, Sherwood Roland, Sanford Stanley, Kristin Charles. Psychiat. social worker Malcolm Bliss Mental Health Center, St. Louis, 1966-67; with div. pupil personnel St. Louis Public Schs., 1967-68; supr. social service dept. Parkway Sch. Dist., Chesterfield, Mo., 1969-72; social worker Family and Children's Service, St. Louis, 1972-73, pvt. practice psychiat. social work, St. Louis, 1973-75; exec. dir. Mo. Counseling Service, Bridgeton, Mo., 1975-81, REACH Internat. Communications Horizons, Creve Coeur, Mo., 1981—; adj. asst. prof. St. Louis U.; instr. Washington U. Bd. dirs. New Hope Found. for Retarded Children, 1972-73; dir., sec. Sunshine Found., 1973-79; dir. Parents Without Partners, 1975-79. Mem. Nat. Assn. Social Workers, Am. Assn. Marriage and Family Therapists. Lutheran. Home: 12669 Northwinds Dr Creve Coeur MO 63146 Office: Creve Coeur MO 63141

SACINO, SHERRY WHEATLEY, public relations executive; b. Wilmington, Del., July 14, 1959; d. Lawrence McClusky and Carolyn Aria (Alexander) W. B.A., Ariz. State U., 1980. Pub. relations exec. Phoenix Pro Soccer, 1980-81; owner, pres. Wheatley Advt. and Pub. Relations, Phoenix, 1981-83; owner, pres. Sherry Wheatley Saciro, Inc., 1983—; acct. supr. Wood, Cohen, Leonard & Bush Advt. and Pub. Relations, Tampa, Fla., 1983—; founder, exec. dir. Tampa Bay Council for Internat. Visitors, Inc., 1984—; exec. dir. Internat. Culinary Festival, Tampa, 1984; owner Ariz. Coaching Acad., Phoenix, 1981-83; pub. relations dir. Richard Simmons Concert, Phoenix, 1982, Phoenix Clean Community System, 1982-83; nat. spokesperson McDonald's Restaurant, 1977. Creator Ruby Slippers Kit, 1983. Vol. pub. relations coordinator Muscular Dystrophy Assn., Ariz. and Fla., 1974-84, Arthritis Assn., Ariz. and Fla., 1980-84; pub. relations dir. Dan Fogelbert Concert for Ariz. Gov. Babbitt, Phoenix, 1982; mem. Ariz. Gov.'s Council on Health and Fitness, 1983; bd. dirs. Pinellas County March of Dimes; mem. Tampa Bay Internat. Trade Council. Recipient award Phoenix Clean Community System, 1982. Mem. Phoenix AD2 Club (v.p. 1983), Sigma Delta Chi (sec. 1978-80). Republican. Roman Catholic. Home: 2507 Pass-A-Grille Way Pass-A-Grille Beach FL 33706 Office: PO Box 46438 Pass-a-Grille FL 33741

SACKETT, DONNA GUARDISON, editor; b. Bklyn., Nov. 26, 1947; d. Benjamin R. and Florence M. (Bender) Gurdison; A.A. with high honors, Brookdale Community Coll., 1975; B.A. with high honors, Douglass Coll., 1977; M.S., Rutgers U., 1981. Staff sec. Bell Telephone Labs., Holmdel, N.J., 1965-75; student intern employee devel. dept. Johnson & Johnson, Skillman, N.J., 1977; personnel cons. Prudential Property & Casualty Ins. Co., Holmdel, 1977-84, editor The Prudential, 1985—; cons. U.S. Army Res., 1981; instr. Brookdale Community Coll., Lincroft, N.J., 1978—. Mem. adv. bd. Women's Ctr., Brookdale Community Coll. Mem. Indsl. Relations Alumni Assn. (treas.), Network Working Women. Eastern Communication Assn. (chmn. applied communication div. 1980). Home: Box 94 Little Sliver NJ 07739 Office: 213 Washington St Newark NJ 07101

SACKETT, MARILYN HEDRICKS, radiologic technician; b. Jacksonville, Tex., Oct. 15, 1943; d. Ben N. and Otha Fay (Simmons) Hedricks. Cert., Nan Travis Meml. Hosp., Jacksonville, Tex., 1964; B.S. with honors, Lamar U., 1974; M.Ed., U. Houston and Baylor Coll. Medicine, 1978. Registered radiologic technologist, registered emergency med. technician, Tex. Staff technologist Nan Travis Meml. Hosp., 1964-65; chief technologist Gen. Mexia Hosp., Mexia, Tex., 1964-71; program coordinator Lamar U., 1971-75; instr. Houston Community Coll., 1975-77; div. chmn. health scis. San Jacinto Coll., Pasadena, Tex., 1977-81; mgr. radiation health and safety Dresser Atlas Oilfield Services Group, Houston, 1981-82; v.p., cons., Houston EMS Acad., 1982-83; tech. dir. radiology Methodist Hosp., Houston, 1983—; accreditation surveyor Joint Rev. Com. on Edn. in Radiologic Technology, Chgo., 1974-80; mem. wireline services subcom. Tex. Radiation Control Adv. Bd., 1982-84; cons., lectr. in field. Contbr. in field. Recipient cert. of recognition North Mexican Congress of Radiologic Technologists, Monterrey, 1978. Mem. Am. Soc. Radiologic Technologists (curriculum task force com. 1977-78, chmn. 1979-80), Tex. Soc. Radiologic Technologists (chmn. nominating com. 1970-71, chmn. edn. com. 1971-73, 2d v.p. 1971-73, chmn. edn. alliance, 1972-74, sec. 1975-77, preos. 1979-80, chmn. exec. bd. 1980-82, legis. co-chmn. 1982-83, asst. ann. meeting program chmn. 1983-84), Houston Area Radiologic Technologist Soc. (chmn. exec. bd. 1977-78, chmn. long range planning com. 1984), Bay Area Imaging Modality Soc., Dallas Area Radiologic Technologist Soc. (chmn. exec. bd. 1968-69), Radiation Service and Suppliers Assn (sec. 1982-84), Health Physics Soc. Republican. Office: Methodist Hosp 6565 Fannin St Houston TX 77030

SACKETT, SUSAN DEANNA, motion picture production assistant, writer; b. N.Y.C., Dec. 18, 1943; d. Maxwell and Gertrude Selma (Kugel) S. B.A. in Edn., U. Fla., 1964, M.Ed., 1965. Tchr. Dade County Schs., Miami, Fla., 1966-68, Los Angeles City Schs., 1968-69; asst. publicist, comml. coordinator NBC-TV, Burbank, Calif., 1970-73; prodn. asst. STAR TREK coordinator Gene Roddenberry, Hollywood, Calif., 1974—; lectr. and guest speaker STAR TREK convs. in U.S., Eng., Australia, 1974—. Author and editor: Letters to Star Trek, 1977; co-author: Star Trek Speaks, 1979; The Making of Star Trek-The Motion Picture, 1979; You Can Be a Game Show Contestant and Win, 1982; Say Good/Night Gracie, 1986. Mem. Acad. Sci. Fiction, Fantasy and Horror Films, ACLU, Mensa, Sierra Club. Democrat. Office: Paramount Pictures 5555 Melrose Ave Hollywood CA 90038

SACKETT-BLACK, MARY LOU, chiropractor; b. Ann Arbor, Mich., May 12, 1949; d. Lester Walter and Helen Beeken (Miller) S.; m. Wayne Edward Black, Dec. 17, 1983; children—Samantha Lou, Terry Lee Knoll; stepchildren—Rose Nicole, Chad Edward Black. A.S., Monroe County Community Coll., 1975; D.Chiropractic, Palmer Coll. Chiropractic, Davenport, Iowa, 1979. Chiropractor, Hillsdale (Mich.) Family Chiropractic Life Center, 1980—. Diplomate Am. Bd. Chiropractic Examiners. Mem. Internat. Chiropractic Assn. Home and Office: 2806 Carleton Rd Hillsdale MI 49242

SACKLOW, HARRIETTE LYNN, advertising agency executive; b. Bklyn., Apr. 12, 1944; d. Sidney and Mildred (Myers) Cooperman; m. Stewart Irwin, July 2, 1967; 1 son, Ian Marc. B.A., SUNY-Albany, 1965, postgrad., 1967-69; postgrad. Union Coll., 1969-70, Telmar Media Sch., N.Y.C., 1981. Tchr. math. Guilderland Central Schs. (N.Y.), 1967-76; v.p., media dir. Wolkcas Advt., Inc., Latham, N.Y., 1975—; supr. internship programs Coll. St. Rose, Albany, N.Y., 1981; lectr. to area colls., Albany, 1981—. Vice pres. Sisterhood Congregation Ohav Sholom, Albany, 1981—; mem. bd. Congregation Ohav Sholom, Albany, 1983—. Mem. Am. Women in Radio and TV (pres. 1982-84, chmn. task force for new mem. acquisition, speaker). Club: Advt. of the Capital District, Albany Yacht (Albany). Office: Wolkcas Advt Inc 435 New Karner Rd Albany NY 12205

SACKS, PATRICIA ANN, librarian, consultant; b. Allentown, Pa., Nov. 6, 1939; d. Lloyd Alva and Dorothy Estelle (Stoneback) Stahl; m. Kenneth LeRoy Sacks, June 27, 1959. A.B., Cedar Crest Coll., 1959; M.S. in L.S., Drexel U., 1965. News reporter Call-Chronicle, Allentown, 1956-59, 1961-63; reference librarian Cedar Crest Coll., Allentown, 1964-66, head librarian, 1966-73; dir. libraries Muhlenberg and Cedar Crest Colls., Allentown, 1973—; del On Line Computer Library Ctr. Users Council, Columbus, Ohio, 1977—; cons. colls./health care orgns., 1981—. Mem. editorial bd. Jour. Acad. Librarianship, 1982-84. Trustee Cedar Crest Coll., 1985—. Named Outstanding Acad. Woman, Lehigh Valley Assn. for Acad. Women, 1984. Mem. ALA (chmn. copyright com. 1985—), Assn. Coll. and Research Libraries (chmn. standards and accreditation com. 1976-78, 81-84), Eastern Pa. Health Systems Council, Lehigh Valley Assn. Ind. Colls. (chmn. librarians sect. 1967-81), AAUP, AAUW, LWV Lehigh Valley Conservancy, Phi Alpha Theta, Phi Kappa Phi, Beta Phi Mu. Democrat. Home: 2997 Fairfield Dr Allentown PA 18103 Office: Cedar Crest and Muhlenberg Colls 30th and Walnut Sts Allentown PA 18104

SACRE, MARY ALICE, employee benefits executive; b. St. Louis, Apr. 8, 1933; d. Homer E. and Alice E. (Cameron) Klipstine; m. Byron Lee Sacre, Nov. 21, 1959. A.A., Harris Tech. Coll., 1953. Night supr. Mercantile Trust Co., St. Louis, 1952-53; asst. to sales mgr. Shampaine Co., St. Louis, 1953; policy writer Pearl Assurance Co., Los Angeles, 1953-54; personnel specialist, editor Honeywell, Inc., Gardena Calif., 1954-67; indsl. relations mgr. Interform Inc., 1967-73; pension adminstr. So. Calif. Rapid Transit, Los Angeles, 1973-78; corp. benefits mgr. Denny's Inc., La Mirada Calif., 1978-86; exec. dir. Wash. Counties Ins. Fund, Olympia, 1986—. Mem. Self Ins. Inst. Am. (dir. 1984-86), Am. Soc. Personnel Adminstrs. Office: Wash Counties Ins Fund 206 10th Ave SE Olympia WA 98501

SADDLEMYER, (ELEANOR) ANN, educator; b. Prince Albert, Sask., Can., Nov. 28, 1932; d. Orrin Angus and Elsie Sarah (Ellis) S.; B.A., U. Sask., 1953; M.A., Queen's U., 1956, LL.D., 1977; Ph.D., U. London, 1961. Lectr., Victoria (B.C.) Coll., 1956-57, instr., 1960-62, asst. prof., 1962-65; asso. prof. U. Victoria, 1965-68, prof. English, 1968-71; prof. English, Victoria Coll., U. Toronto, 1971—, dir. Grad. Centre for Study of Drama, 1972-77, 85-86, sr. fellow Massey Coll., 1975—; Berg prof. N.Y.U., 1975; dir. Theatre Plus, Colin Smythe Pubs. Can. Council scholar, 1958-59, fellow, 1968; Guggenheim fellow, 1968, 77. Fellow Royal Soc. Can.; mem. Internat. Assn. Study Anglo-Irish Lit. (chmn. 1973-76), Assn. Can. Theatre History (pres. 1976-77), Can. Assn. Irish Studies, Humanities Assn., Assn. Can. Univ. Tchrs. English, Can. Assn. Univ. Tchrs., Assn. Can. and Que. Lit. Author: The World of W.B. Yeats, 1965; In Defence of Lady Gregory, Playwright, 1966; Synge and Modern Comedy, 1968; J.M. Synge Plays Books One and Two, 1968; Lady Gregory Plays, 4 vols., 1970; Letters to Molly: Synge to Maire O'Neill, 1971; Letters from Synge to W.B. Yeats and Lady Gregory, 1971; Theatre Business, The Correspondence of the First Abbey Theatre Director, 1982; Collected Letters of J.M. Synge, Vol. I, 1983; Vol. II, 1984 co-editor: Theatre History in Canada; editorial bds. Modern Drama, 1972-83, English Studies in Can., 1973-84, Themes in Drama, 1974, Shaw Rev., 1977, Research in the Humanities, 1976, Irish Univ. Rev., 1970; contbr. articles to profl. jours. Home: 100 Lakeshore Rd E Oakville ON L6J 6M9 Canada Office: Dept English Victoria Coll U Toronto Toronto ON M5S 1K7 Canada

SADICK, BARBARA ANN, publishing production manager; b. Bklyn., July 31, 1952; d. Richard L. and Marion (Weiss) S. B.A. summa cum laude, NYU, 1974. Asst. editor Bus. Research Pubs., N.Y.C., 1977-80; prodn. mgr., editor MacRae's Blue Book, 1980-84; prodn. mgr. Bus. Research Publs., N.Y.C., 1982-84, Media Horizons, N.Y.C., 1985—. Mem. Women in Prodn., NOW. Office: Media Horizons 50 W 23d St New York NY 10010

SADLE, AMY ANN, watercolorist, printmaker; b. Council Bluffs, Iowa, Aug. 3, 1940; Student State U. Iowa, U. R.I.; studied with Fritz Eichenberg, Claude Croney, Virginia Cobb, Ed Whitney, Naoko Matsubra, and others. One woman shows U. N.D., 1986, San Diego Print Club, 1985, others; exhibited U. Kans., Dartmouth Coll., N.H., St. Johns, Nfld., Midwest Watercolor Club, U. N.D., and others; represented in permanent collections Statue of Liberty, Tulsa Library, Des Moines Art Ctr., Nebr. Hist. Commn., Nebr. Indian Commn., St. Mary's Torrington, Wyo., St. Theresa, Mitchell, Nebr. Recipient Best of Show award San Diego Print Club, 1984, mem. Artists Equity, San Diego Print Club, Phila. Print Club, World Print Council, N.J. Internat. Print Club, Midwest Watercolor. Author: Home of Wooden Men and Iron Men.

SADLER, B(ARBARA) SUSAN, criminal investigator; b. Dallas, Aug. 15, 1947; d. Weldon Glenn and Helen Lillian (Bukosy) Sadler. B.S., E. Tex. State U., 1972. Criminal investigator Tex. Dept. Human Services, Dallas, 1973—; res. officer Dallas Police Dept., 1975-77, res. sgt., 1977-82; chairperson Forest Hills Assn. Crime Prevention, 1980-83, v.p., 1983, pres., 1983—. Recipient Merit cert. Dallas Police Dept., 1980. Mem. Nat. Welfare Fraud Assn., Forgery Investigators Assn. Tex., United Council on Welfare Fraud, White Rock Bus. and Profl. Women's Club (pres. 1985—), Hist. Preservation League, VFW Aux. Democrat. Methodist. Office: Tex Dept of Human Resources 2727 Inwood Rd Suite 200 Dallas TX 75235

SADLER, KIM MARTIN, writer; b. N.Y.C., Sept. 4, 1956; d. Ned William and Janie (Goodwin) Martin; m. Paul Hobson Sadler, Oct. 10, 1981. B.A., Howard U., 1978. Promotions specialist Nat. Assn. Social Workers, Silver Spring, Md., 1979—. Editor-in-chief Plymouth Prompter newsletter, Plymouth Congl. United Ch. of Christ, Washington, 1982—, also mem. bd. social action. contbr. articles to various publs. Mem. Nat. Black Media Coalition, Women in Communications Transafrica, Delta Sigma Theta (editor/writer Washington alumnae chpt. newsletter), Theta. Club: Capital Press. Office: Nat Assn of Social Workers 7981 Eastern Ave Silver Spring MD 20910

SADLER, RENEE KELLEY, educational administrator; b. Macon, Ga., June 26, 1961; d. Joseph A. and Grace (Fountain) Kelley; 1 child, Brian David. A.S., Macon Jr. Coll., 1980; B.S., Ga. Coll., 1982, M.S., 1985. Dir., prin. Briarwood Acad., Macon, 1982—. Recipient Excellence award Bd. Dirs. Briarwood Acad., 1983. Mem. Nat. Council Social Studies. Home: 3979 San Juan Ave Macon GA 31206 Office: Briarwood Acad 800 Lackey Dr Macon GA 31206

SADOCK, POPSY (EILEEN), journalist; b. Greensburg, Pa., Sept. 26, 1927; d. Samuel and Rhoda (Abramson) Friedlander; m. Martin Theodore Sadock, May 2, 1949; children—Jamie, Seth, Jonathan. Student Sch. Journalism, Pa. State U., 1945-48. Soc. editor, women's editor Tribune Rev., Greensburg, Pa., 1948-50, freelance columnist, writer, 1956-73; talk show hostess Sta. WHJB, Greensburg, 1966; editor Focus mag. Tribune Rev., 1973-80, feature writer, consumer editor, 1980—. Co-chmn. Greensburg Open Tennis Tournament, 1969-79; pres. Nat. Council Jewish Women, Greensburg, 1959-61. Recipient journalistic award Am. Cancer Soc., 1983; 3d place award for feature writing Women's Press Assn., 1984. Mem. Pa. Women's Press Assn. (award 1982, 83, 84), Pa. Newspaper Pubs. Assn. (Keystone Press award 1976, 77, 82), Women's Press Club, Sigma Delta Chi (exec. com. 1984—), Pitts. Press Club. Republican. Home: 127 Underwood Ave Greensburg PA 15601 Office: Tribune Review Cabin Hill Dr Greensburg PA 15601

SADOCK, VIRGINIA ALCOTT, psychiatrist; b. Sofia, Bulgaria, Nov. 25, 1938; came to U.S., 1941, naturalized, 1947; d. Fred and Rica (Boni) Alcott; A.B., Bennington Coll., 1960; M.D., N.Y. Med. Coll., 1970; m. Benjamin J. Sadock, Oct. 20, 1963; children—James, Victoria. Intern, N.Y. Med. Coll.-Met. Hosp. Center, N.Y.C., 1970-71, resident, 1971-73; dir. human sexuality program, asst. prof. clin. psychiatry N.Y. Med. Coll., 1973-80; practice medicine specializing in psychiatry, N.Y.C., 1973—; mem. staff N.Y.U. Hosp., Bellevue Hosp.; assoc. prof. clin. psychiatry, dir. grad. edn. in human sexuality N.Y.U. Med. Center, 1980—. Diplomate Am. Bd. Psychiatry and Neurology. Fellow Am. Psychiat. Assn.; mem. AMA, Am. Med. Women's Assn., N.Y. State Med. Soc., N.Y. County Med. Soc. Contbr., asst. to editors: Comprehensive Textbook of Psychiatry, 2d edit., 1975, 4th edit., 1984. Office: 4 E 89th St New York NY 10028

SADOFSKY, STELLA, social worker; b. Vienna, Austria, June 9, 1927; came to U.S., 1940; d. Max and Nellie (Benedek) Streit; m. Harold Irving Sadofsky, Sept. 1, 1947; 1 dau., Melanie. B.A., Bklyn. Coll., 1949; M.S.W., Case Western Res. U., 1951. Case worker, supr. Travelers Aid Soc., N.Y.C., 1951-61; sr. caseworker Mass. Soc. for Prevention of Cruelty to Children, Salem, 1961-63; adoption counselor N.J. Home Soc., Camden, 1964-66; clin. social worker Mt. Laurel Schs. (N.J.), 1966—; adj. prof. Glassboro State Coll., Camden County Community Coll., 1974-76; adolescent and adult group therapist, Haddonfield, N.J., 1984—. Bd. dirs. Assn. Retarded Citizens, Burlington County, 1983—; mem. adv. com. Planned Parenthood of So. N.J., Camden, 1981—. Mem. Nat. Assn. Social Workers, Acad. Cert. Social Workers, Acad. Clin. Social Workers, N.J. Assn. Sch. Social Workers, Alpha Kappa Delta. Home: 421 Covered Bridge Rd Cherry Hill NJ 08034 Office: Mt Laurel Sch System 330 Mt Laurel Rd Mount Laurel NJ 08054

SADOVSKY, ANNE B., marketing executive; b. McKinney, Tex., Nov. 17, 1941; d. Herbert Archie Browne and Trannie Laura (Headrick) Lee; children—Jerry Wayne Morgan, Scott Alan Morgan. Student Eastfield Coll., Dallas, 1974, Richland Coll., Dallas, 1975. Vice-pres. mktg. Lincoln Property Co., Dallas, 1973-81, J. Stiles, Dallas, 1980-81; pres. Anne Sadovsky & Co., Dallas, 1981—. Pub. Metroplex Apartment Directory, 1983-84; contbr. articles to profl. jours. Mem. womens bd. Northwood Inst., Dallas, 1983-84. Named Boss of Yr., Am. Bus. Women, 1981. Mem. Nat. Apt. Assn. (past dir.), Tex. Apt. Assn. (past dir.), Apt. Assn. greater Dallas (dir. products and services 1983-84), Sales and Mktg. Execs. (dir. 1983-84), Nat. Assn. Home Builders, Nat. Speakers Assn. Home: 7155 Helsem Bend Dallas TX 75230 Office: Anne Sadovsky & Co 12720 Hillcrest Rd Suite 305 Dallas TX 75230

SAEMAN, BERNICE HENSEL, plumbing and heating company executive; b. Arcadia, Wis., Apr. 29, 1912; d. Hiram Edgar and Elizabeth B. (Meier) Hensel; m. Vincent Victor Saeman, June 25, 1938 (dec. Mar. 1984); children—Ellen Saeman Martino, William Henry. B.E., Whitewater U., Wis., 1933. Lic. tchr. Instr. comml., band condr. Middleton High Sch., Wis., 1933-38; ptnr. Saeman Plumbing & Heating Co., Cross Plains, Wis., 1938—. Bd. dir. Madison Catholic Women, Wis., 1980-82; treas. Council of Catholic Women, Cross Plains, 1952-53; mem. Friends of WHA-TV, Madison, Friends of Library, Cross Plains, 1972—, Hist. Soc., Cross Plains, 1978—. Mem. Wis. Master Plumbing Aux. (bd. dir. 1972—), Alumni Assn. Whitewater State U., Am. Legion (organizer, condr. band Cross Plains, 1939-49). Republican. Clubs: U. Wis.-Whitewater Century, State of Wis. Garden Fedn. (fin. bd. dir. 1977—), Nat. Council State Garden, Olbrich Bot. Soc., Madison Dist. Wis. Garden Fedn. (treas. 1972-76, vice dir., dir., 1981-83, adviser 1983-85), Middleton Garden (v.p. 1957-58, 70-73, pres. 1959-60, mem. nominating com. 1985—). Lodges: K.C. Friends; Elks Widows. Avocations: club meetings, bridge, travel. Home: 1804 Cross St Cross Plains WI 53528 Office: Saeman Plumbing and Heating Co 2112 Water & Park Cross Plains WI 53528

SAENZ, NANCY ELIZABETH KING, civic worker; b. Greenville, Tex., Jan. 28, 1930; d. Henry M. and Vallie (Wheatley) King; m. Michael Saenz, July 28, 1950; children—Michael King, Cynthia Elizabeth Saenz Ward. A.B. with honors, Tex. Christian U., 1950, B.S. magna cum laude, 1952; postgrad. Hartford Sem. Found., 1952-53, Escuela de Idiomas, 1953; Lexington Theol. Sem., 1953. Missionary, United Christian Missionary Soc., Indpls., Served in P.R., 1954-57; chmn. dept. Christian edn. Christian Chs., P.R., 1962-64, sec., 1959-61, state dir., 1963; with dept. Christian edn. P.R. Council Chs., 1959-64, sec., 1959-60; sec. and counselor State Christian Women Fellowship of Christian Chs., P.R., 1955-57, 59-63, dist. chmn., Indpls., 1968-71; dist. cons., mem. adminstrv. com. Christian Women's Fellowship in Tex., 1972-75; mem. nominating com. Internat. Christian Women's Fellowship, 1974-78; pres.-elect Christian Ch. in S.W., 1974-76, pres., 1976—; mem. gen. bd. Christian Ch. in U.S. and Can., 1974-81, dir. Vol. Ctr. Met. Tarrant County, 1982—. Author: Winds of Change, 1968; Step by Step to a Successful Volunteer Program, 1984. Sec., Disciples of Christ Acad. PTA, Bayamon, P.R., 1962-63; mem. state com. Home for Aged, United Ch. Women, P.R., 1963; bd. dirs. Ft. Worth Area Council Chs., exec. interim dir., 1979; women's com. Ind. State Symphony Soc., 1967—; mem. women's com. Internat. Christian U. Japan, 1962-64, 65—, pres. Indpls. chpt. 1967-68; mem. exec. bd. Indpls. council PTA, 1967-70; mem. vocat.-tech. adv. council Laredo Ind. Sch. Dist., 1971—; vol. coordinator Am. Bible Soc., 1974—; mem. Laredo Mercy Hosp. Aux., 1973-75, pres.-elect, 1974-75; mem. Tarrant County Vol. Ctr. Com., 1975—, vice chmn., 1978-79, chmn., 1980-81; bd. dirs. Hostesses to Overseas Guests, 1982—. Bd. dirs. Greater Indpls. Fedn. Chs., 1970-71; pres.-elect Tarrant Area Community of Chs., 1980, pres., 1981-82; bd. sponsors Laredo Civic Ballet Soc., 1971-75; bd. dirs. Laredo Planned Parenthood Assn., 1972-75, v.p., 1973-74, pres.-elect, 1974-75; bd. dirs. Ruth Be. Cowle Rehab. Ctr., 1974-75; mem. adv. council Vols. in Pub. Schs., Ft. Worth, 1977-78, chmn., 1981-82; bd. dirs., mem. ch. fin. council Christian Ch., Disciples of Christ, 1978—, mem. exec. com., 1981-82; chmn. emergency assistance com. United Way of Met. Tarrant County, also mem. allocations com. Mem. Irvington Union of Clubs (exec. bd. 1966—, 2d v.p. 1968-60), Young Mothers Club Irvington (v.p. 1965, pres. 1967), Marion County Guardian Home Guild (pres. 1968-70), Art Assn. Indpls., Thistle Hill Docent Guild, Art League, Irvington, AAUW, Laredo and Ft. Worth Table II, Ch. Women United (pres. Fort Worth 1980-81), Pan Am. Roundtable, Alpha Chi, Phi Sigma Iota. Clubs: Rotary Anns, Women's Coll. (P.R.); Tex. Christian U. Women Execs. (Ft. Worth); Irvington Women's Laredo Tuesday Music and Lit. (pres. 1973); Women's City. Home: 4201 Westmont Ct Fort Worth TX 76109 Office: 210 E 9th St Forth Worth TX 76102

SAFEWRIGHT, JUDY KAY, travel consultant; b. Rushville, Ind., Oct. 29, 1944; d. Orval Lee and Evalyn Dora (Dearinger) S. Diploma, Atlantic Airline Career Tng. Sch., 1964; Cert. Am. Airlines Sabre Sch., 1984. Travel cons. Muncie Travel Service, Ind., 1964-68; v.p., mgr. Adventure Travel of Pompano Beach, Fla., 1968-79; pres., mgr. Judy Safewright Travel Ctr., Pompano Beach, 1979—. Campaign dir. Republican Club, Pompano Beach, 1984; mem. parade com. Diamond Jubilee, 1983. Named Woman of the Year, Am. Bus. Women's Assn., 1971. Mem. Pompano Beach C. of C. (bd. dirs. 1983—, edn. com.

1983-84, Bus. Woman of Yr. 1983) Am. Soc. Travel Agts., Bon Vivants of Broward County. Republican. Lodges: Soroptimist (v.p. 1983-85), Jobs Daus. Avocations: travel; swimming; dancing.

SAFFELL, MARTHA LOUISE, company executive; b. Dallas, Mar. 19, 1920; d. Claude Hutchins and Lula Jane (Thompson) Butler; m. Robert Lee Rhodes, Feb. 19, 1936 (div. 1940); 1 son, Gary Lloyd; m. 2d. Donald Earl Saffell, Dec. 1, 1940; children—Glenn Leeland, Donna Darlene, Douglas Wayne, Donald Charles, Jonathan Donald. Student Dallas Bapt. Coll. Comptometer operator Agriculture Adjustment Adminstrn., College Station, Tex., 1939; sec., treas. Saffell Plumbing and Air Conditioning, Inc., Dallas, 1946—. Case aide Am. Cancer Soc., Dallas, 1970—; counselor Contact-Dallas Telephone Counseling, 1977—. Republican. Episcopalian. Lodge: Hillcrest Eastern Star (Adah 1952-55). Home: 2105 White Cliff Ln Richardson TX 75080 Office: Saffell Plumbing and Air Conditioning Inc 3901 San Jacinto Dallas TX 75204

SAFFER, SALLY JOAN, training company executive; b. Lowville, N.Y., Feb. 8, 1943; d. Bernard Theodore and Mary Ann (Strong) Martzloff; m. Lee F. Davis, May 20, 1978; children—Debra Ann, Kristen Margit. B.A. in Bus. Adminstrn., Empire Coll., SUNY-Rochester, 1972. In mktg. support IBM, Rochester, N.Y., 1972-75, mktg. rep., 1975-79; cons. office automation Word Processing/Office Systems, 1979-82; v.p. product devel. Integrated Tng. Systems, Inc., Rochester, 1982-85, pres., 1982. Author, producer, dir. curriculum materials/textbooks: Word Processing and The Changing Office Environment, 1984; Insight Into Office Automation, 1985. Contbr. articles to trade, ednl. mags. Mem. Profl. Mktg. and Sales Execs. Club, Am. Soc. Tng. and Devel. Avocations: reading; golf. Home: 18 Winding Wood Pittsford NY 14534 Office: Integrated Tng Systems Inc 530 Cross Keys Office Park Fairport NY 14450

SAFFY, EDNA LOUISE, educator; b. Jacksonville, Fla., Mar. 8, 1935; d. Habib Solomon and Sadie Daumit Saffy; m. Grady Earl Johnson, Aug. 9, 1969. B.A., U. Fla., 1966, M.A., 1968, Ph.D., 1976. Asst., then instr. English, U. Fla., 1967, speech, 1972-75; prof. rhetoric Fla. Jr. Coll., Jacksonville, 1968-72, 75—; speaker, guest lectr., cons., polit. activist. Mem. Democratic exec. com. Duval County; del. to Dem. Nat. Conv., 1979; exec. bd. dirs. Jacksonville Citizens for a Nuclear Freeze, 1982-83; mem. State of Fla. Dem. Com. Affirmative Action Com., 1983; mem. Jacksonville Planning Commn., 1979. Recipient various recognition awards. Mem. S. Atlantic Modern Lang. Assn., Speech Communication Assn., So. Speech Communication Assn., Fla. Speech Communication Assn., Fla. Coll. English Assn., U. Fla. Grad. Speech Assn. (pres. 1975), Fla. Women's Network (dir.), Jacksonville Women's Network (founder), U. Fla. Alumni Assn., NOW (dir., co-convenor Jacksonville chpt. 1970, dir. convenor Gainesville U. of Fla. chpt. 1973), Fla. Women's Polit. Caucus pres. 1978-79, ERA Jacksonville (pres., 1976-77), Alachua County Women's Polit. Caucus (charter mem.), Duval County Women's Polit. Caucus (v.p. 1983), Nat. Women's Polit. Caucus (chmn. So. Dem. Task Force 1983—), Gen. Fedn. Women's Clubs, Alpha Chi Omega. Club: Women's (Jacksonville). Home: 3451 Remington St Jacksonville FL 32205 Office: Fla Jr Coll South Campus Beach Blvd Jacksonville FL 32216

SAFI, DEBORAH CAVAZOS, lawyer; b. Dallas, Feb. 8, 1953; d. Arnaldo Nelson and Ila Mae (Rinn) Cavazos; m. Hazim Jawad Safi, July 28, 1979; 1 son, Jawad Joseph. B.A., Baylor U., 1975, J.D., 1977. Bar: Tex. 1977. Assoc., Andrews & Kurth, Houston, 1977-81; corporate atty. Transco Energy Co., Houston, 1981-83; sole practice, Houston, 1983—. Co-leader Blue Bird's Camp Fire Girls, Waco, Tex., 1972-73. Mem. ABA, State Bar Tex., Houston Bar Assn., Houston Young Lawyers Assn. (dir. 1982-84, treas. 1984-85, co-chmn. luncheon program for corp. counsel sect. 1980-81, chmn. entertainment sect. 1981-82), Delta Delta Delta. Home: 1200 Smith Houston TX 77002

SAFIAN, JOYCE LYNN, health care executive; b. Porterville, Calif., July 3, 1948; d. Lee Gum and Soo (Gong) Quock; R.N. diploma O'Connor Hosp. Sch. Nursing, San Jose, Calif., 1969; family nurse practioner cert. U. Calif.-Davis, 1977; B.A. in Health Services Adminstrn., St. Mary's Coll., Moraga, Calif.; M.A. in Health Services Adminstrn., Antioch U. West, 1979; 1 son, Christian. Asst. dir. nurses Arroyo Vista Hosp., Santa Rosa, Calif., 1971; clin. nurse cons. Sonoma State Hosp., Elderidge, Calif., 1973-77; cons. phys. assessment, Santa Rosa, 1977-82; dir. employee/employer health services Santa Rosa Meml. Hosp., 1977-82; pres., chmn. Corp. Health Services, Inc., indsl. and occupational medicine, Santa Rosa, also Larkspur, Petaluma, 1982—; owner Joyce Safian and Assocs., Occupational Health Cons. Sec., Sonoma County (Calif.) Bd. on Alcoholism, 1977-80. Mem. Assn. Hosp. Employee Health Profls. (founder, exec. pres. 1981—), Am. Public Health Assn., (governing council), Sonoma County Forum, Nat. Assn. Female Execs. Democrat. Roman Catholic. Author articles. Home: 123 Hidden Valley Ct Santa Rosa CA 95404 Office: 95 Montgomery Dr Suite 114 Santa Rosa CA 95404

SAFIAN, SHELLEY CAROLE, advertising agency executive; b. Bklyn., May 29, 1954; d. Jack Israel and Harriet Sara (Cohen) S. B.F.A., Parsons Sch. Design/New Sch. for Social Research, 1975. Asst. art dir. Axelrod and Assocs., N.Y.C., 1975-77; art dir. Sta. WDBO-TV-AM/FM, Orlando, Fla., 1978-80; owner, pres. Safian Communications Services, Inc., Orlando, 1981—; mem. adv. com. Career Edn., Orange County, Fla., 1981—, chmn., 1982-83; advt. cons. post-secondary vocat. and community edn. div. Orange County Pub. Schs., 1983-84. Active govs. council on phys. fitness/Sunshine State Games, 1983; exec. producer/dir. March of Dimes Telethon, Orlando, 1984; exec. dir. United Cerebral Palsy Telethon, Orlando, 1984; pub. relations Liaison-United Cerebral Palsy, Orlando, 1983-84; founder Career Dir. for the Deaf, Orlando, 1985. Recipient 2 First Place Addy awards Orlando Advt. Fedn., 1981; First Place Addy award, 2 pl. awards (2), merit awards (2), Orlando Advt. Fedn., 1982. Mem. Broadcast Promotion and Mktg. Execs. Assn. (Silver Medallion 1983), Broadcast Designer's Assn. (bd. dirs. 1980-82), Am. Women in Radio and TV (bd. dirs. 1980-81). Republican. Avocation: horseback riding. Office: Safian Communications Services Inc 7040 Lake Ellenor Dr Orlando FL 32809

SAFIRSTEIN, AMANDA, lawyer; researcher, dental nurse; b. Montreal, Que., Can., Apr. 6, 1909; came to U.S., 1914; d. Ephraim Leon and Sophie Miriam (Lewis) Ackerman; m. Samuel Safirstein, Dec. 19, 1929; children—G. Richard, Jared Jack, Arnold Alan. B.A., Seton Hall U., 1978, J.D., 1981. Bar: N.J. 1982. Asst. editor Fisher Maritime Cons., South Orange, N.J., 1977-79, Inst. Continuing Legal Edn., Newark, 1979-81; Contbr. articles to various publs. Republican County committeewoman, South Orange; v.p., pres. Faith of Israel Synagogue, East Orange. Mem. ABA, Assn. Trial Lawyers Am., Essex County Bar Assn., Nat. Assn. Investment Clubs (dir. No. N.J. region). Lodge: Hadassah. Jewish.

SAFKO, DEBORAH LEE, health care administrator; b. Alliance, Ohio, Sept. 19, 1951; d. Joseph Paul Safko and Doris Marie (Wolf) Sniegocki; m. Samuel John Costa, Jr., Sept. 2, 1972 (div. April 1984); children—Mario Benjamin, Jeremy Michael. B.S. magna cum laude in Human and Social Scis., Drexel U., 1974; M.B.A. in Health Adminstrn., Temple U., 1972. Bus. mgr., mktg. dir. Occupational Health Services, Pennsauken, N.J., 1983-86; unit mgr. Children's Hosp., Phila., 1986—. Active mem. Phila. Com. on City Policy, 1972—. Recipient Am. Coll. Hosp. Adminstrs. award, 1981; grantee Pub. Health Services Traineeship, 1980, 81. Mem. Nat. Assn. Female Execs., Phi Mu. Democrat. Roman Catholic. Home: 1206 Manning St Philadelphia PA 19107

SAFRAN, CLAIRE, writer, editor; b. N.Y.C., Mar. 18, 1930; d. Simon and Flora (Rand) S.; m. John Milton Williams, June 8, 1958; 1 child, Scott Edward. B.A. cum laude, Bklyn. Coll., 1951. Editor-in-chief In mag., N.Y.C., 1965-67; assoc. editor Family Weekly, N.Y.C., 1967-68; editor-in-chief Coronet mag., N.Y.C., 1968-71; contbg. editor Redbook mag., N.Y.C., 1974-76, 79-81, exec. editor, 1977-78; roving editor Reader's Digest, Pleasantville, N.Y., 1983—. Author: New Ways to Lower Your Blood Pressure, 1984. Contbr. to mags. Recipient Media award Am. Psychol. Found., 1977, Merit award in Journalism Religious Pub. Relations Council, 1978, Journalism award Am. Acad. Pediatrics, 1979, Media award Odyssey Inst., 1979, 80, Journalism award Am. Acad. Family Physicians, 1984, William Harvey award, 1984. Mem. Am. Soc. Journalists and Authors (Weissinger award 1984), Women in Communications (Matrix award 1982, 83, 84), NOW. Home: 53 Evergreen Ave Westport CT 06880

SAGE, DIANE F., designer, research and design director; b. Nelson, B.C., Can., Nov. 13, 1940; came to U.S., 1961; d. Cecil Albert and Myrtle Cora (Fisher) S. Student Vancouver Sch. Art, 1959-61, Chouinard Inst. Fine Art, 1961-63. Artist, Custom Craft Printing, Vancouver, B.C., Can., 1959-60; fashion designer James Chambers Mfg. Co., Vancouver, 1962-67; fashion designer, owner The Sage Way, Vancouver, 1967-69; dir. fashion and edn. Simplicity/Style Patterns, Toronto, Ont., Can., 1968-78; arts coordinator Vernon Community Arts Council, Vernon, B.C., Can., 1979-80; dir. research and design The Creative Circle, Gardena, Calif., 1981—; free lance artist, designer, Can. and U.S., 1969-86. Designer fashions, accessories, graphics D. Sage Originals, 1967-86, Serene fashion collection, 1977; contbg. designer Canadian Living mag., 1978, 79; editor catalogs Creative Circle Collection, 1982, 83, 84, 85. Named Designer of Tomorrow, Dominion Textiles/Can. Pacific Airlines, 1964, Designer of Yr., Creative Circle, 1983. Avocations: arts; gardening; reading; bicycling; cooking. Office: Creative Circle 15777 S Broadway Gardena CA 90248

SAGE, ROBIN DALE, lawyer; b. Longview, Tex., Aug. 25, 1958; d. Roger E. and Della Dale (Baxter) S. B.A., Baylor U., 1980, J.D., 1981. Bar: Tex. 1981, U.S. Dist. Ct. (ea.dist.) Tex. 1983. Assoc., Sharp, Ward, Ross, McDaniel & Price, Longview, Tex., 1981-83; sole practice, Longview, 1983—. Mem. ABA, State Bar Tex., Gregg County Bar Assn., Acad. Family Mediators, Nat. Assn. Women Lawyers, Orthopsychiat. Assn. Baptist. Club: Zonta (Longview). Home: 2708 Patio Dr Longview TX 75605 Office: Whaley at Center Longview TX 75606

SAGGESE, TERESA ANN, lawyer, business executive; b. Macon, Ga., July 9, 1949; d. Robert Francis and Woodie Mozelle (Branan) S. B.F.A., U. Ga.-Athens; J.D., Mercer U., Macon. Bar: Ga. Paralegal, Gambrell Russell & Forbes, Atlanta, 1973-76; asst. to v.p. Nat. Bank of Ga., Atlanta, 1976; asst. to pres. Cumberland Mortgage, Atlanta, 1977; assoc. Savell, Williams, Cox & Angel, Atlanta, 1980-84; ptnr. Glass, McCullough, Sherrill & Harrold, Atlanta, 1984—; owner, cons. Corp. Identity for Women, Atlanta, 1983—. Assoc. editor: Mercer Law Rev., 1979-80; contbr. articles to profl. jours. Vol., Humane Soc., Athens and Atlanta, 1971, Atlanta Retardation Ctr., 1976, Atlanta Area Services for Blind, 1976. Mem. ABA, State Bar Ga., Atlanta Bar Assn., Lawyers Club of Atlanta, Order Barristers, Phi Delta Phi. Methodist. Home: 38 Cantey Pl NW Atlanta GA 30327 Office: Glass McCullough Sherrill & Harrold 1409 Peachtree St NE Atlanta GA 30309

SAIA, DIANE PLEVOCK DIPIERO, paralegal, nutritionist; b. Boston, Oct. 2, 1941; d. Charles and Monica (Alexandravich) Plevock; B.S., Framingham (Mass.) State Coll., 1962; M.S., Simmons Coll., Boston, 1969; doctoral candidate U. Mass., 1974-75; married; 1 son, David. Field nutritionist Mass. Dept. Edn., Boston, 1962-64; nutrition cons., sch. program coordinator New Eng. Dairy and Food Council, Boston, 1964-67, sr. staff and nutrition edn. cons., program coordinator, Springfield, Mass., 1970-83; pres. Food/Nutrition Consignments, Springfield, Mass., 1981—; tchr. Weymouth (Mass.) Schs., 1967-70; mem. faculty Springfield Coll., 1970—, assoc. prof. nutrition, 1970—; pres. Food and Nutrition Consignments, 1979—; mem. faculty, cons. Baystate Med. Center, Springfield; mem. faculty Western N.E. Coll., 1982-84; producer TV shows, radio and consumer edn. programs. Mem. Home Econs. Assn., Soc. Nutrition Edn., Home Economists in Bus., New Eng. Public Health Assn., Mass. Home Econs. Assn. (exec. bd. 1972—, pres. 1978-79), Sales and Mktg. Execs. (bd. dirs.; membership chair), Mass. Bar Assn. Roman Catholic. Clubs: Valley Press (asso. dir. 1976-79, chmn. scholarship ball 1977-79), Pioneer Valley Racquet. Home: 7 Berkeley Dr Long Meadow MA 01006 Office: 55 State St Springfield MA 01103

SAIBARA, MARJORIE LYNN, accountant; b. Houston; d. Robert and Rola Saibara; B.B.A., U. Houston, 1972. C.P.A., Tex. Joint venture acct. Union Oil of Calif., Houston, 1973-74; joint interest, revenue accountant Coastal States Gas Corp., Houston, 1974-78; Dept. Energy liaison for controller's dept. revenue crude oil and gas processing supr., spl. projects acct., asst. mgr. revenue acctg., project leader for revenue acctg. software installation Cabot Corp., Houston, 1978—; counselor U. Houston Career Day. Chmn. worship ministry Presbyn. Ch. of Covenant, 1980—; Presbytery del., 1980; ruling elder Presbyn. Ch., mem. pulpit nominating com., 1982, mem. worship ministry 1985. Mem. Am. Soc. Women Accts. (dir., membership chmn.), Petroleum Accts. Soc. of Houston (membership com. 1981-82, membership chmn. 1982-83, 83-84, 84-85, 85-86, picnic com. and golf tournament 1984-85, 85, 86), Tex. Soc. C.P.A. (Houston chpt.), Phi Mu (treas., v.p.). Office: 550 West Lake Pk Blvd Suite 900 Houston TX 77079 and PO Box 4544 Houston TX 77210-4544

SAIKI, PATRICIA (MRS. STANLEY MITSUO SAIKI), state senator; b. Hilo, Hawaii, May 28, 1930; d. Kazuo and Shizue (Inoue) Fukuda; B.S., U. Hawaii; m. Stanley Mitsuo Saiki, June 19, 1954; children—Stanley Mitsuo, Sandra S., Margaret C., Stuart K., Laura H. Tchr., Dept. Edn. Hawaii, 1959-66; research asst. Hawaii State Senate, 1966-68; mem. Hawaii Ho. of Reps., 1968-74, Hawaii State Senate, 1974-82. Dir. Amfac, Inc., Hawaiian Airlines. Mem. Pres.'s Adv. Council on Status of Women, 1969-76; mem. Nat. Commn. Internat. Women's Year, 1969-70; commr. Western Interstate Commn. on Higher Edn.; fellow Eagleton Inst., Rutgers U., 1970. Mem. Kapiolani Hosp. Aux. Sec. Hawaii Republican Com., 1964-66, vice chmn., 1966-68, chmn., 1983-85; del. Hawaii Constl. Conv., 1968; alt. del. Rep. Nat. Conv., 1968, del., 1984; Rep. nominee for lt. gov. Hawaii, 1982; mem. Fedn. Republican Women. Trustee Hawaii Pacific Coll.; bd. dirs. Nat. Fund for Improvement of Post-Secondary Edn., 1982-85. Hawaii Visitors Bur., 1983-85; trustee U. Hawaii Found., 1984—. Episcopalian. Address: 784 Elepaio St Honolulu HI 96816

ST. AMAND, GLENDA WEAVER, social worker, counselor; b. Akron, Ohio, Apr. 17, 1923; d. Christian and Selma Fridfelt (Johnson) Weaver; m. Leonard M. St. Amand, Mar. 24, 1951; children—Janet G., David G. B.A., Houghton Coll., 1945; M.S.W., Columbia U., 1947; postgrad. Marywood Coll., 1974-81, Pa. State U., 1981. Cert. social worker, N.Y. Social worker Family Service Bur., Bklyn., 1945-49; med. social worker Roosevelt Hosp., N.Y.C., 1949-51; dir. social service People's Hosp., Akron, Ohio, 1951; med. social work cons. State of N.J., Trenton, 1964-67; sch. social worker Joint Bd. for Exceptional Children, Bucks County (Pa.), 1967-72; guidance counselor Neshaminy Sch. Dist., Langhorne, Pa., 1972-86; supr., treas. Presbyn. Counseling Service, Morrisville, Pa., 1976-78. Author: (handbook) Navy Relief Volunteer, 1951. Leader Freedom Valley council Girl Scouts U.S.A., Cub Scouts, Lower Makefield, Pa.; committeeman Lower Makefield Republican Com. Salvation Army fellow, 1946. Mem. Nat. Assn. Social Workers, NEA, Neshaminy Edn. Assn., Pa. Edn. Assn., Am. Personnel and Guidance Assn., Historic Morrisville Soc. Republican. Presbyterian. Clubs: Lower Makefield Women's (welfare dir.); Buck County Women's (welfare dir.). Home: 20 Oakdale Blvd Morrisville PA 19067 Office: Neshaminy Sch Dist 2001 Old Lincoln Hwy Langhorne PA 19047

ST. AUBIN, PHYLLIS ANN, agri bus. exec.; b. Camden, Mo., Dec. 24, 1938; d. Charles Dan and Alberta (Archer) Feeney; student (Lion Oil Co. scholar) Memphis State U., 1956-57; m. Forrest Edmund St. Aubin, Nov. 26, 1971; 1 dau., Pamela DeAnn Gooch Schultz; stepchildren—Mark Randall, Leslie Alexandra St. Aubin Brown. Advt. asst. Mobay Chem. Corp., Kansas City, Mo., 1968-80; mgr. coop. sales devel. Farmland Industries, Kansas City, Mo., 1980—. Recipient Voice of Democracy award Lion Oil Co., 1955. Mem. Nat. Agri Mktg. Assn. (dir. Mo.-Kans. chpt.), Nat. Assn. Female Execs., Kansas City Ad Club. Republican. Baptist. Home: 8715 Sycamore Kansas City MO 64138 Office: Farmland Industries 3315 N Oak Hwy Kansas City MO 64116

ST. CLAIR, HELEN ALLISON, association executive; b. Stevenson, Ala., July 23, 1932; d. George Milton and Frances Carolyn (Grider) Allison; student U. Ala., 1949-52, U. Va., 1961-62; m. Fred Weems St. Clair, Aug. 4, 1950 (div. July 1984); children—Loyce Anne, Fred Weems, Thomas Reid. Supr., Camp LeJeune (N.C.) Sitting Service, 1956-60; tchr. pub. schs., Prince William County, Va., 1960-64, substitute tchr., 1967-69; mem. spl. activities staff Miss. Optometric Assn., 1974-76, exec. dir., 1976—; cons. internat. assn./interprfl. com. Am. Optometric Assn. Mem. Miss. Council on Aging, 1976-80, mem. Inst. on Aging, 1976—; trustee So. Coll. Optometry, Memphis, 1979-82; bd. dirs. Central Miss. chpt. ARC, vice chmn. community vol. service com., 1981-82, chmn., 1982-83, mem. exec. com., chmn. vols. Central Miss. chpt., 1985—; chmn. Central Miss. Sub Area council Miss. Health Systems Agy., 1981-83, vice chmn., 1980-81. Mem. Am. Soc. Assn. Execs., Internat. Assn. Optometric Execs. (v.p., pres. 1980), So. Council Optometric Execs., Am. Public Health Assn., Miss. Gerontol. Assn., Miss. Soc. Assn. Execs. (dir. 1982-83, v.p. 1983-84), Am. Soc. Assn. Execs. (membership devel. com. 1981-83, bd. dirs. 1983—), LWV. Methodist. Club: Miss. Women's (ofcl.). Contbg. editor So. Jour. Optometry, 1976—. Home: 102 Meadow Ln Lake Cavalier Route 3 Jackson MS 39213 Office: 5420 I-55 N Suite D Jackson MS 39236

ST. GERMAIN, JEAN MARY, med. physicist; b. N.Y.C.; d. Herbert and Mary J. (Newman) S.; B.S., Marymount Manhattan Coll., 1966; M.S., Rutgers U., 1967. Fellow radiol. health USPHS, Rutgers U., New Brunswick, N.J., 1967; fellow dept. med. physics Meml. Hosp., N.Y.C., Cornell U. Med. Coll., 1967-68, asst. physicist, 1968-71, instr. radiology (physics), 1971-78, clin. asst. prof., 1979—; asst. attending physicist Meml. Sloan-Kettering Cancer Center; cons. in field. Diplomate Am. Bd. Health Physics. Mem. Health Physics Soc. Am. Assn. Physicists in Medicine (sec., dir.), Soc. Nuclear Medicine, Radiol. Soc. N.Am., N.Y. Acad. Scis., Radiol. and Med. Physics Soc. N.Y. (past pres.), Iota Sigma Pi (pres. V chpt.). Author: The Nurse and Radiotherapy, 1978; contbr. articles, chpts. to med. jours., texts. Office: 1275 York Ave New York NY 10021

ST JEAN, CATHERINE, advertising agency executive, consultant; b. Dubuque, Iowa, Oct. 10, 1950; d. Harvey Dale and Mary Theresa (Heinz) Avery; m. Kenneth Roland St Jean, June 24, 1978 (div. May 1983). B.A. in Communications, Loyola U., Chgo., 1977. Sec. Needham, Harper & Steers, Chgo., 1977, video editor, 1978, creative coordinator, 1979, presentations services mgr. Needham, Harper & Steers/U.S.A., Chgo., 1980, v.p., corp. dir. communications services Needham, Harper & Steers, Inc., N.Y.C., 1982-86, asst. dir. creative services, v.p., 1986—. Author, art dir. direct mail brochure: How to Keep the Heart in New York for Tri-State United Way (Merit award 1982, bronze medal N.Y. Internat. Film and TV Festival 1984), 1982. Mem. Advt. Women in N.Y. (editor 1984, chmn. 1984, bd. dirs. 1-yr. dir. 1985, 2-yr. dir. 1986—), Women In Communications (chmn. 1984). R Office: Needham Harper Worldwide 909 3d Ave New York NY 10022

ST JEAN, JUDITH SUZANNE, research institute administrator; b. Pitts., May 15, 1950; d. Albert Anton and Wanda Amelia (Mistarz) Heidish; m. Joseph Alfred St Jean, Jr., Nov. 30, 1974. B.A., Duquesne U., 1973; M.A., Slippery Rock U., 1982. Ednl. coordinator Midwestern Intermediate Unit, Grove City, Pa., 1978-81; asst. dir. admissions Point Park Coll., Pitts., 1982; legis. asst. Pa. Ho. of Reps., Harrisburg, 1983; telethon coordinator Youngstown Hosp. Assocs., Ohio, 1983-84, interim corp. dir. devel., 1984; v.p. Am. Inst. Cancer Research, Falls Church, Va., 1985—. Recipient Publ. Design awards Pa. Sch. Bds. Assn., 1980, Nat. Sch Pub. Relations Assn., 1978, 79, Pa. Sch Bds. Assn., 1979, Interiors award Better Homes & Gardens, 1982. Democrat. Mem. AAUW, Hoyt Inst. Fine Arts, Lawrence County Hist. Soc., Psi Chi. Roman Catholic. Avocations: house restoration; running. Home: 1504 Highland Ave New Castle PA 16105

ST. LAURENT, NANCY LOUISE, pharmaceutical company executive; b. West Chester, Pa., Mar. 15, 1944; d. William and Louise (Gray) Hetherington; m. Norman Nelson St. Laurent, June 5, 1971. B.S. in Chemistry, Ursinus Coll., 1966; postgrad. Villanova U., 1973, Widener U., 1977-79, Phila. Coll. Pharmacy and Sci., 1968-69. Chemist, Wyeth Labs. div. Am. Home Products Corp., West Chester, Pa., 1966-69, supr. packaging, 1969-73, mgr. finishing mfg., 1973-75, tng. specialist, Radnor, Pa., 1975-76, personnel mgr. Wyeth Labs., 1976-79, dir. pharm. prodn. Ft. Dodge Labs., (Iowa), 1979—; mem. process engring. subcom. Parenteral Drug Assn., Phila., 1980—. Commr. Ft. Dodge Mcpl. Housing Agy., 1981—; bd. dirs. Lakota Girl Scouts U.S.A., Ft. Dodge, 1982—, leader cadette troop, 1981—; mem. fin. com., 1981—. Mem. Animal Health Inst. Lutheran. Club: La Sertoma (pres. 1982-83). Home: 344 Country Club Dr Fort Dodge IA 50501 Office: Fort Doge Labs Div AHPC 800 5th St NW Fort Dodge IA 50501

ST. OURS, SANDRA LOU, banker; b. Escanaba, Mich., Nov. 30, 1957; d. Wayne Anthony and Roberta Lou (Hardy) Jacques; m. Thomas J. St. Ours, Apr. 30, 1977. Student No. Mich. U. Sch. Banking, 1981-82, Am. Inst. Banking, 1982. Bookkeeper, First Nat. Bank, Escanaba, 1975, teller, 1975-76, head teller, 1977-79, br. mgr., 1980-82, asst. cashier, 1983-85, asst. v.p., 1985—. Mem. Mich. Bank Pac, Bus. and Profl. Women's Orgn. (bd. dirs. 1984-85, found. chmn., 1985-86), Nat. Assn. Female Execs., Am. Inst. Banking (sec. Bay de Noc chpt. 1979-82), Altrusa. Democrat. Roman Catholic. Avocations: cake decorating; cross country skiing. Office: First Nat Bank and Trust Co 1205 Ludington St Escanaba MI 49829

ST. PAUL, TINA DIANE, manufacturing company manager; b. Bakersfield, Calif., Mar. 8, 1948; d. Harold B. and Beverly M. (Reichel) Leydenfrost; div.; 1 child, Tracy Andrea. Legal sec., Hollywood, Calif., 1972-75; paralegal, Century City, Calif., 1975-78; owner/cons. Corporation Update, Los Angeles, 1978-83, 85-86; contracts adminstr. McDonnell Douglas Helicopter Co., Culver City, Calif., 1983-85, mgr. export control, 1985—. Author manuals. Vol., Californians for Brown, 1978-79; bd. dirs. Women's Legal Def. and Edn. Fund, 1978-79, Women's Movement, Los Angeles, 1978-79. Mem. Women in Def. (bd. dirs. 1983-86). Avocations: nutrition; cake decorating; reading; hiking; swimming. Office: McDonnell Douglas Helicopter Co Centinela Ave and Teale St Culver City CA 90230

ST. PIERRE, CHARLOTTE EATON, social worker, consultant; b. Cooperstown, N.Y., Apr. 22, 1955; d. Charles William and Katherine Mildred (Pentz) Eaton; m. Ronald Donald St. Pierre, Sept. 5, 1981. B.A. cum laude, SUNY-Geneseo, 1977; M.S.W., SUNY-Albany, 1982. Cert./lic. social worker, cert. in secondary edn., N.Y. Med. claims approver Met. Group Health, Utica and Colonie, N.Y., 1978-83; social service dir. Silver Haven Nursing Home, Rotterdam, N.Y., 1983-85; med. social worker, social services dir. James Eddy Geriatric Ctr., Troy, N.Y., 1985—; group leader Alzheimers Disease and Related Disorders, Troy and Albany, 1985—; cons. fin. planning to families of elderly and/or Alzheimers victims. Vol. Utica Psychiat. Ctr., N.Y., 1977-78. Mem. Nat. Assn. Social Workers, Devon Cattle Assn. Democrat. Avocations: ceramics; quilting; collecting antiques. Home: 8 Drake Ct Waterford NY 12188 Office: Eddy Meml Geriatric Ctr 2256 Burdell Ave Troy NY 12180

ST. ROSE, EDWINA J. LOSEY, lawyer, employee relations and development specialist; b. Charlottesville, Va., Aug. 25, 1952; d. Edward Lee and Emma Jane (Brown) Losey; m. Dennis Anthony St. Rose, Oct. 6, 1979; 1 child, Dennis Anthony. B.A., Barnard Coll., N.Y.C., 1974; J.D., George Washington U., 1977. Bar: Pa. 1979, D.C. 1984. Legal editor Bur. Nat. Affairs, Washington, 1977-80; atty., advisor Social Security Adminstrn., Arlington, Va., 1980-83; employee relations and employee devel. specialist Naval Intelligence Command, Washington, 1983-85; pvt. practice EEO investigator, 1985—. Mem. ABA, D.C. Bar Assn., Pa. Bar Assn. Home: 209 E Tantallon Dr Fort Washington MD 20744

ST. TAMARA (TAMARA KOLBA), painter, printmaker; b. Navahradak, Byelorussia; came to U.S., 1950, naturalized, 1956; d. Alexander and Maria (Boris) Stahanovich; m. Alexander Kolba, Feb. 22, 1958. B.A., Western Coll., Oxford, Ohio, 1954; M.F.A., Columbia U., 1956. Free-lance printmaker, artist, 1956—. One-woman shows include: Western Coll., 1955, Aenle Gallery, N.Y.C., 1956, Avanti Galleries, N.Y.C., 1968, Asbury Park (N.J.) Art Mus., 1973, Free Pub. Library of Woodbridge (N.J.), 1975, Guild of Creative Art, Shrewsbury, N.J., 1975, 77, West Long Branch (N.J.) Library, 1979; exhibited in group shows Young Printmakers traveling exhbn., 1967-69, Herron Sch. Art, Indpls., Nat. Print and Drawing Exhbn., DeKalb, Ill., 1968, UNICEF, N.Y.C., 1969, 74, 76, 79, Audubon Artists, N.Y.C., 1971, 79, Davidson (N.C.) Nat. Print and Drawing Competition, 1972, 73, First Miami (Fla.) Graphics Biennial, 1973, G.W.V. Smith Mus., Springfield, Mass., 1973, 74, 76, 77, 3d Hawaii Nat. Print. Exhbn., Honolulu, 1975, 65th Ann. Exhbn., Wadsworth Atheneum, Hartford, Conn., 1975, Va. Highlands Festival, Abington, Va., Salmagundi Club, N.Y.C., 1979, 11th Ann. Biennial Nat. Art Exhbn., Valley City, N.D., 1979, 81, Printmaking Council of N.J., Somerville, 1981, Charlotte (N.C.) Printmakers Soc., 1981, 1st Ann. Juried Show, Southport, N.C., 1981, Nat. Miniature Show, Cuyahoga Falls, Ohio, 1982, 14th Nat. Art Show, La Junta, Colo., 1982, Lever House, N.Y.C., 1982. Illustrator: Biography of a

Polar Bear, 1972; Come Visit a Prairie Dog Town, 1976; Animal Games, 1976; Save that Raccoon, 1978; author, illustrator: Asian Crafts, 1970; Chickaree—A Red Squirrel, 1980. Mem. Guild Creative Art, Byelorussian Inst. Arts and Scis., Catherine Lorillard Wolfe Art Club, Print Club of Albany. Home: 235 Hockhockson Rd Tinton Falls NJ 07724

SAIZAN, PAULA THERESA, oil company executive; b. New Orleans, Sept. 12, 1947; d. Paul Morine and Hattie Mae (Hayes) Saizan; B.S. in acctg. summa cum laude, Xavier U., 1969; m. George H. Smith, May 26, 1973 (div. July 1976). Systems engr. IBM, New Orleans, 1969-71; acct., then sr. acct. Shell Oil Co., Houston, Tex., 1971-76, sr. fin. analyst, 1976-77, fin. rep., 1977-79, corp. auditor, 1979-81, treasury rep., 1981-82, sr. treasury rep., 1982—. C.P.A.; notary public. Mem. Am. Inst. C.P.A.s, Tex. Soc. C.P.A.s, Nat. Assn. Accts., Inwood Forest Improvement Assn., Houston Area Urban League, Nat. Assn. Black Accts., LWV of Houston, Xavier U. Alumni Assn. (membership dir.), Phi Gamma Nu. Roman Catholic. Home: 5426 Long Creek Ln Houston TX 77088 Office: 4095 One Shell Plaza PO Box 2463 Houston TX 77001

SAKAC, SISTER ANN, college administrator. Pres., Mount St. Mary Coll., Newburgh, N.Y. Office: Mount Saint Mary Coll Powell Ave Newburgh NY 12550*

SAKS, JUDITH-ANN, artist; b. Anniston, Ala., Dec. 20, 1943; d. Julien David and Lucy-Jane (Watson) S.; student Tex. Acad. Art, 1957-58, Mus. Fine Arts, Houston, 1962, Rice U., 1962; B.F.A., Tulane U., 1966; postgrad. U. Houston, 1967; m. Haskell Irvin Rosenthal, Dec. 22, 1974; 1 son, Brian Julien. One-man shows include: Alley Gallery, Houston, 1969, 2131 Gallery, Houston, 1969; group shows include: Birmingham (Ala.) Mus., 1967, Meinhard Galleries, Houston, 1977; Galerie Barbizon, Houston, 1980, Park Crest Gallery, Austin, 1981; represented in permanent collections including: L.B. Johnson Manned Space Mus., Clear Lake City, Tex., Harris County Heritage Mus., Windsor Castle, London, Smithsonian Instn., Washington: commns. include: Pin Oak Charity Horse Show Assn., Roberts S.S. Agy., New Orleans; curator student art collection U. Houston, 1968-72; artist Am. Revolution Bicentennial project Port of Houston Authority, 1975-76. Recipient art awards including: 1st prize for water color Art League Houston, 1969, 1st prize for graphics, 1969, 1st prize for sculpture, 1968. Mem. Art League Houston, Houston Mus. Fine Arts, DAR (curator 1983-85). Home: PO Box 1793 Bellaire TX 77401

SALAMAN, MAUREEN KENNEDY, nutritionist; b. Glendale, Calif., Apr. 4, 1936; d. Ted and Elena (Peters) Kennedy; m. Frank Salaman; children—Sean, Coleen. M.Sc. in Nutrition, Donsbach U., Huntington Beach, Calif., 1981. Hostess show Gift of Health Sta. KFAX AM, 1977—, Totally Yours with Maureen Salaman, Sta. KEST-AM, San Francisco, 1977—, West Coast Report, Sta. WMCA-AM, N.Y.C., 1980—; feature writer Let's Live mag., 1978 ; pres. Nat. Health Fedn., Monrovia, Calif., 1982—; cons., lectr., researcher on cancer research and metabolic medicine, nutrition; freedom of choice lobbyist; v.p. Project Freedom; vice presidential candidate Populist Party, 1984. Author: Nutrition: The Cancer Answer, 1983. Editor: Choice Mag., 1972-77, Public Scrutiny, 1978-80, Health Freedom News, 1982-86. Contbr. articles to profl. jours. Developer nutrition programs for radio and TV. Decorated Freedom Fighters medal Korean Govt.; recipient Patrick Henry Liberty award Nat. Health Fedn. Office: Nat Health Fedn 212 W Foothill Blvd Monrovia CA 91016

SALAMON, LINDA BRADLEY, educator; b. Elmira, N.Y., Nov. 20, 1941; m. 1964; 2 children. A.B., Radcliffe Coll., 1963; M.A., Bryn Mawr Coll., 1964, Ph.D., 1971. From lectr. to asst. prof. Dartmouth Coll., 1967-72; asst. prof. Smith Coll., 1972-73, Bennington Coll., 1974-75, U. Pa., 1977-79; assoc. prof. Washington U., St. Louis, 1979—; fellow Bunting Inst., 1973-74; dean Coll. Arts and Scis., Washington U., 1979. Recipient Penrose award Am. Philos. Soc., 1975. Author: Nicholas Hilliard's Arte of Limning, 1983; contbr. articles to profl. jours. Address: Washington Univ PO Box 1117 Saint Louis MO 63130*

SALAS, CLARA MARIA, state official, social work consultant; b. Santiago de Cuba, Cuba, May 31, 1947; came to U.S., 1961, naturalized, 1970; d. Justo Eduardo and Rosario (Saez) S. B.A., Queens Coll., CUNY, 1971; M.S.W., Fordham U.-Lincoln Ctr., 1977. Psychiat. social worker Office Mental Health State of N.Y., Manhattan Psychiat. Ct., Ward's Island, N.Y., 1977-77, family care coordinator, 1977-80, dir. vol. services, 1983—; social work cons. Young Adult Inst. and Workshop, N.Y.C., 1983—. Author: (bilingual children's book) Coqui and Juan, 1972. Second vice chairperson community adv. bd. City Hosp. at Elmhurst, N.Y., 1984—; mem. Community Bd. 4, Elmhurst-Corona, 1985—. Recipient Spl. Project award United Hosp. Fund, 1984. Mem. N.Y. Assn. Dirs. Vol. Services (sec. 1984-85), N.Y. State Assn. Dirs. Vol. Services, N.Y. Assn. Adminstrs. Vol. Services. Avocations: reading; opera; archeology; history; computers. Office: Office of Mental Health State of NY Manhattan Psychiat Ctr Ward's Island NY 10035

SALAVERRIA, HELENA CLARA, educator; b. San Francisco, May 19, 1923; d. Blas Saturnino and Eugenia Irene (Loyarte) S.; A.B., U. Calif.-Berkeley, 1945, secondary teaching cert., 1946, M.A., Stanford U., 1962. High sch. tchr., 1946-57; asst. prof. Luther Coll., Decorah, Iowa, 1959-60; prof. Spanish, Bakersfield (Calif.) Coll., 1961-84, chmn. dept., 1973-80. Vol., Hearst Castle; mem. srs. adv. group edn. Cuesta Coll. Community Services. Mem. Calif. (dir. 1976-77), Kern County (pres. 1975-77) fgn. lang. tchrs. assns., NEA, Union Concerned Scientists, Natural Resources Def. Council, Calif. Tchrs. Assn. (chpt. sec. 1951-52), AAUW (edn. com.), Yolo County Council Retarded, Amnesty Internat., Common Cause, Sierra Club, Prytanean Alumnae, U. Calif. Alumni Assn., Kern County Basque Club, Am. Farmland Trust. Democrat. Presbyn. Address: PO Box 63 Cambria CA 93428

SALAZAR, ADELA NORA, med. technologist; b. Pueblo, Colo., Nov. 14, 1953; d. Petronillo and Sarah (Madrid) S.; B.S. in Med. Tech., N.Mex. Highlands U., 1975. Intern, Meml. Gen. Hosp., Las Cruces, N.Mex., 1974-75; med. technologist St. Vincent Hosp., Santa Fe, 1975—. Mem. Am. Soc. Clin. Pathologists, N.Mex. Soc. Med. Tech. Democrat. Roman Catholic. Office: 455 St Michael's Dr Santa Fe NM 87501

SALAZAR, NINFA ALICIA REYES, janitorial services company executive; b. Dexter, Mo., May 27, 1959; d. Juan Q. and Eloisa (Rodriguez) Reyes; m. Julian Salazar Sr., Sept. 10, 1979; 1 child, Julian Jr. Ed. Prarie State Coll., Sawyer Coll. Bus. With Davis Temporaries, Chicago Heights, Ill., 1980-82; office mgr. E&B Painting, Harvey, Ill., 1981-82; owner, pres. J&N's Janitorial Services, Chicago Heights, 1982—. Court watcher Cook County Ct. Watcher's Project, Chicago Heights, 1985. Mem. Women in Mgmt., Women's Referral Services, Entrepreneur Assn. Am., Notaries Assn. Am., Chicago Heights C. of C. Avocations: bicycle riding; skating; dancing. Home: 175 Thelma Ln Chicago Heights IL 60411 Office: J&N's Janitorial Service PO Box 353 Park Forest IL 60466

SALAZAR, ROSE ANN, pay television executive, entrepreneur; b. Madison, Wis., Aug. 16, 1934; d. Joseph John Koltes and Ethel M. (Powers) Kelly; m. div.; children—Edward Jr., Kathleen Salazar Gould, Thomas, Gregory. Student Citrus Coll., 1962-66. Credit central mgr. Sears, Roebuck & Co., Canoga Park, Calif., 1966-82; dir. On TV-Nat. Sub TV, Glendale, Calif., 1982-85; dir. Selectv of Calif., Marina del Rey, 1985—; owner Still Looking, La Crescenta, Calif., 1983—; seminar leader Glendale Community Coll., 1984—. Author: Selectv Credit Collections, 1985, Selectv Customer Service, 1985. Chairperson United Way, Covina, Calif., 1976. Recipient Spl. Services award Handicap Rotary Olympics, 1979. Mem. Soc. Profl. Credit Mgrs., Montrose C. of C., Nat. Assn. Female Execs. Republican. Lutheran. Avocations: gourmet cooking; writing poetry and fiction; bowling. Home: 4636 Dyer St La Crescenta CA 91214 Office: Selectv of Calif 4755 Alla Rd Marina del Rey CA 90292

SALDAÑA, ELSA ANTONIA, advertising agency executive; b. Brownsville, Tex., Oct. 13, 1950; d. Juan Angel and Blasita (Garza) Saldaña. B.S. with spl. honors, U. Tex., 1973. Media planner Compton Advt., N.Y.C., 1977-78; sr. media planner Grey Advt., N.Y.C., 1978-79; supr. Young & Rubicam, N.Y.C., 1979-83; assoc. media dir. Young & Rubicam/Dentsu, Los Angeles, 1983-85; assoc. media dir., v.p. McCann-Erickson, 1985—. Mem. Women in Communications, Nat. Assn. Female Execs. Club: Advt. Office: McCann-Erickson 6420 Wilshire Blvd Los Angeles CA 90048

SALE, LILLIAN, marketing communications consultant; b. Los Angeles, Dec. 30, 1936; d. Leonard and Muriel (Stansfield) Weiss; student in bus. UCLA, 1954-58. Mgr. public relations non-profit found., Oakland, Calif., 1970-73; account exec. Ross Wurm & Assos., public relations agy., Modesto, Calif., 1974-76; prin., chief cons. Lillian Sale Communication Services, pub. relations, mktg., sales promotion, direct mail, advt., publs., audio-visual services, Los Angeles, 1976—. Mem. Public Relations Soc. Am. (accredited counselor, PRISM award 1984), Publicity Club Los Angeles (PRO awards 1980, 82), Nat. Direct Mktg. Assn., Direct Mktg. Club of So. Calif., Women in Bus. Author: How To Talk Banker-ese, 1979. Address: PO Box 48439 Los Angeles CA 90048

SALERNO, EVELYN, cons. pharmacist; b. Passaic, N.J., Dec. 14, 1936; d. John C. and Elvira (Infante) S.; B.S., Rutgers U., 1958; D.Pharmacy, Mercer U., 1975. From clk. to part-time registered pharmacist Martini's Pharmacy, Hackensack, N.J., 1956-60; chief pharmacist Pascack Valley Hosp., Westwood, N.J., 1960; pharmacist Prescription Pharmacy, Hialeah, Fla., 1961-63; registered pharmacist, asst. mgr., dir. pharmacy South Fla. State Hosp., Hollywood, 1963-74, dir. profl. services, asst. dir. hosp. pharmacies, 1975—; with RCW Cons., Inc., 1975-82; dir. clin. services Nursing Home Assos., Inc., 1981-82; vis. lectr. U. Miami Sch. Nursing, asso. prof., 1977—; cons. Hospice S. Fla., Sunrise, community for retarded. Mem. Am. Pharm. Assn., Am. Soc. Hosp. Pharmacists, Am. Inst. History Pharmacy, Southeastern Soc. Hosp. Pharmacists, S. Fla. Soc. Hosp. Pharmacists, Fla. Pharm. Assn., Fla. Soc. Hosp. Pharmacists, Rutgers U. Alumni Assn., Mercer U. Alumni Assn., Am. Pharm. Assn. Acad. Pharmacy Practice, Heart Assn. Greater Miami. Democrat. Roman Catholic. Author papers in field, profl. reviewer; contbr. chpt. to Pharmacology in Nursing, 17th edit.; columnist Fla. Jour. Hosp. Pharmacy. Office: 8768 SW 131st St Miami FL 33176

SALERNO, SUSAN CORINE, accountant; b. Burlington, Wis., Sept. 22, 1950; d. Richard L. and Ardine B. Haugen Hebron; m. F. Robert Salerno, Sept. 6, 1975. B.S., U. Wis., 1971; M.B.A., Roosevelt U., 1982. Office mgr., Hertz Corp., Milw., 1972-75; fleet adminstr. Digital Equipment Corp., Maynard, Mass., 1975-78; adminstrv. mgr. The Trane Co., Chgo., 1978-81; fin. analyst-metals ARCO Metals, Rolling Meadows, Ill., 1981—; div. controller metal and ore ACLI Internat, a Donaldson, Lufkin & Jenrette Co., White Plains, N.Y., 1982-85; acctg. supr. Malcolm Pirnie, Inc., environ. engrs., White Plains, 1985—; workshop panelist, cons. in field. Author brochure, booklet in field. Mem. Women in Communications, Nat. Assn. Fleet Adminstrs., Nat. Assn Van Pool Operators (co-editor newsletter; mem. internat. communications com., bd. dirs. 1978—), Nat. Safety Council (cert. instr. def. driving course). Home: 84 Locust Rd Pleasantville NY 10570 Office: 2 Corporate Park Dr White Plains NY 10602

SALESI, ROSEMARY ANN, university administrator, educator; b. Troy, N.Y., Aug. 6, 1942; d. Frank P. and Estelle Alma (Kushman) D'Agostino; m. Robert Joseph Salesi, June 25, 1964. B.S., SUNY-Oswego, 1963; M.L.S., U. Maine, 1970; Ed.D., U. Ga., 1977. Cert. tchr., library media specialist. Classroom tchr. Jordan-Elbridge Sch., N.Y., 1963-67, Sch. Dist. 22, Hampden, Maine, 1967-71; from instr. to asst. prof. edn. U. Maine, Orono, 1971-78, assoc. prof., 1979-86, prof., 1986—; asst. dean Grad. Sch., 1982-84, assoc. dean, 1984—; reviewer ERIC/RCS Clearinghouse, 1973—; cons. Author: Odyssey: An HSB Literature Program, 1982; also articles. Mem. Bangor Symphony Women, 1975—. Recipient Faculty Achievement award U. Maine, 1980. Mem. ALA, Maine Reading Assn., New Eng. Reading Assn. (exec. bd. 1978—, treas. 1982-85, v.p. 1985-86), Nat. Council Tchrs. of English (cons.), Children's Lit. Assembly (dir., treas. 1985—), Internat. Reading Assn. (chair internat. edn. com. 1983-85). Democrat. Home: PO Box 427 Hampden ME 04444 Office: U Maine 2 Winslow Hall Orono ME 04469

SALGUEIRO, CARMEN ESCUDÉ, educator, concert pianist, piano instructor, accompanist; b. Santiago-de-Cuba, May 11, 1950; came to U.S., 1962, naturalized, 1972; d. Juan and Maria del Carmen (Ramos) Escude; m. Robert Da Costa Salgueiro, Nov. 18, 1973. B.M., Catholic U., 1971; M.M., Manhattan Sch. Music, 1973; Degree in Theory & Solfege, Conservatory Music, Santiago, Cuba, 1961. Cert. Tchr. Vocal Music K-12, Bilingual-Bicultural Edn., Elem. Edn., Tchr. English as Second Language, N.J. Tchr. piano and theory Villa Walsh Acad., Morristown, N.J., 1971; elem. vocal music tchr. Lafayette St. Sch., Newark, 1972-75, Hawkins St. Sch., Newark, 1975-76; elem. bilingual tchr. South St. Sch., Newark, 1980-84; elem. summer sch. tchr. Oliver St. Sch., Newark, 1984, tchr. English as Second Language, Newark, 1984—; concert pianist (solo and orchestra), Cuba, U.S., Italy, 1933—, Organist Our Lady of Mercy Ch., Park Ridge, N.J., 1982; choir dir. Student Community Concerts, Newark, 1984—. Sec. Congress of Portuguese Speaking Peoples, Newark, 1974, Peter Francisco Meml. Commn., Newark, 1976; mem. Portuguese-Am. Scholarship Found., Newark, 1973—, scholarship com., 1984—. Scholar Villa Victoria Acad., 1962-67, Manhattan Sch. Music, 1971, Catholic U., 1967-71, Kean Coll., 1979-82, Seton Hall U., 1979-81; Master Tchr. Status Newark Bd. Edn., 1985. Mem. N.J. Tchrs. Assn., Newark Tchrs. Union, Sigma Alpha Iota. Republican. Roman Catholic. Club: España. Avocations: traveling, swimming, composing, astronomy, philology.

SALHANICK, BRENDA CRANE, pension consultant; b. Keene, N.H., Aug. 2, 1951; d. Clayton Howard and Anita (Barry) Crane; B.A. cum laude, St. Anselm Coll., 1974; paralegal and para-actuary studies Bentley Coll. 1977, C.L.U. Northeastern U. 1978; student Suffolk U. Law Sch.; m. Joel Alan Salhanick, Sept. 16, 1978. With Jules Meyers Assocs., Chestnut Hill, Mass. 1975-83, dir. pension dept. 1977-83, v.p. Employee Benefit Plan Services 1979-83. Instr. first aid ARC 1972-81. Mem. Nat. Assn. Security Dealers. Republican. Clubs: New England Aquarium Dive (past pres. and newsletter editor), St. Anselm Coll. Century.

SALING, STELLA MARIA, clin. psychologist; b. Wildflecken, Germany, Feb. 1, 1948; d. Louise Saling; B.A., U. Calif., Riverside, 1970; M.A., U.S. Internat. U., 1975, Ph.D., 1978. Psychologist, Grosse Pointe (Mich.) Psychol. Center, 1978-79; staff New Alternatives, San Diego, 1980-81; pvt. practice psychotherapy and psychodiagnosis, 1981—; cons. residential assessment and treatment child abuse victims. U. Calif. Pres.' scholar, 1967-68. Mem. Am. Psychol. Assn., San Diego Psychology and Law Soc., San Diego Mental Health Assn. Club: Sierra. Contbr. to Sr. Life Newspaper, 1980-81. Office: 7290 Navajo Rd Suite 209 San Diego CA 92119

SALINGER, JOAN MARIE, data processor; b. New Rochelle, N.Y., Mar. 14, 1949; d. John Gerard and Dorothea Eleanor (Lucy) Kelleher; B.A. in Math., Coll. New Rochelle, 1970; M.S. in Computer Sci., Poly. Inst. N.Y., 1978. With AT&T Co., White Plains, N.Y., 1971—, tng. mgr. long lines, 1978-80, data processing mgr. long lines, 1980—; lectr. Coll. New Rochelle. Mem. Ursuline Alumnae Assn. (class agt.). Democrat. Roman Catholic. Office: AT&T 99 Church St White Plains NY 10601

SALISBURY, ALICIA LAING, state senator; b. N.Y.C., Sept. 20, 1939; d. Herbert Farnsworth and Augusta Belle (Marshall) Laing; m. John Eagan Salisbury, June 23, 1962; children—John Eagan Jr., Margaret Laing. Student Sweet Briar Coll., 1957-60; B.A., Kans. U., 1961. Mem. Kans. Senate, 1985—, chmn. adminstrv. rules and regulations com., vice chmn. edn. com., mem. assessment and taxation com., legis. and congl. apportionment com., legis. econ. devel. commn. local govt. com., pub. health and welfare com. Elected mem. State Bd. Edn., Topeka, 1981-85; mem. edn. task force Midwestern Conf. of Council State Govts.; pres. Jr. League of Topeka, 1961—; trustee Leadership Kans., 1982—; bd. dirs. Topeka Community Found., 1983—, Kans. Council on Employment and Tng., 1985—; mem. adv. commn. Juvenile Offenders Program, Kans., 1985—; mem. adv. bd. Kans. Action for Children, 1982—, Kans. Ins. Edn. Found., 1984—; former bd. dirs. Topeka C. of C., United Way Greater Topeka, ARC, Family Service and Guidance, Topeka, Shawnee County Mental Health Assn., Florence Crittenton Services, Topeka, Kans. Action for Children, Topeka City Commn. Govtl. Adv. Com. Mem. Nat. Conf. State Legislators, Nat. Republican Legislators' Assn., Shawnee County Rep. Women, Kappa Kappa Gamma. Episcopalian. Avocations: tennis; downhill skiing; water sports; horseback riding; spectator sports. Office: Kans State Senate State Capital Bldg Topeka KS 66612

SALITERMAN, LAURA SHRAGER, pediatrician; b. N.Y.C., June 26, 1946; d. Arthur M. and Ida Shrager; A.B. magna cum laude, Brandeis U., 1967; M.D., N.Y. U., 1971; m. Richard Arlen Saliterman, June 15, 1975. Intern, resident in pediatrics Montefiore Hosp. and Med. Center, Bronx, N.Y., 1971-74; pediatrician Morrisania Family Care Center, Bronx, 1974-75, Share Health Plan, St. Paul, 1975—, dir. pediatrics, 1976-82; clin. instr. pediatrics U. Minn., 1975-81, clin. asst. prof. pediatrics U. Minn., 1981—. Mem. nat. women's com. Brandeis U., 1975—, Sherwood Forest Neighborhood Assn., 1977—. Recipient Greenberg Meml. Sci. award Brandeis U., 1967; diplomate Am. Bd. Pediatrics. Mem. Am. Acad. Pediatrics, N.Y. U. Sch. Medicine Alumni Assn., Phi Beta Kappa. Clubs: Oak Ridge Country (Hopkins, Minn.); Minneapolis. Home: 11911 Live Oak Dr Minnetonka MN 55343 Office: 1020 Bandana Blvd W Paul MN 55108

SALKIN, GERALDINE (JERI) FAUBION, dancer, dance therapist, educator; b. Denver, Mar. 18, 1916; d. George Everett and Hanna Viola (Harvey) Faubion; student Lester Horton Dance Theater, Carmelita Maracci, Trudi Schoop, Los Angeles, 1937-47, Doris Humphrey, N.Y.C., 1952-53, Rudolf Von Laban, London, 1956-57, Hanna Fenichel, Ph.D., 1965-70, UCLA, 1959-60; Ph.D., 1978; m. Leo Salkin, June 29, 1936; 1 dau., Lynn Salkin Sbiroli. Concert dancer Lester Horton Dance Group, Los Angeles, 1937-47, tchr. creative modern dance, 1939-47; tchr. creative modern dance Dance Assos., Hollywood, Calif., 1949-53, Am. Sch. of London (Eng.), 1956-57, Jeri Salkin Studio and Center for Child Study, Hollywood, 1968-73; developer body ego technique Camarillo (Calif.) State Hosp., 1957-64; movement specialist Nat. Endowment Arts grantee, 1973—; dir., body ego technique dept. Cedars-Sinai Thalians Community Mental Health Center, Los Angeles, 1965—; dance cons., tchr. Nat. Head Start Program, Calif., 1964; dir. workshops, mem. aux. faculty Goddard Coll., Antioch Coll., various hosps. and univs. Calif. Dept. Mental Hygiene grantee, 1960-63. Mem. Am. Dance Therapy Assn., AAHPER, Calif. Dance Educators Assn., Calif. Assn. Health, Phys. Edn. and Recreation, Nat. Assn. Edn. Young Children, Child Devel. Specialists, Com. Research in Dance. Democrat. Author: Body Ego Technique, an Educational and Therapeutic Approach to Body Image and Self-Identity, 1973; author, choreographer film (with Leo Salkin and Trudi Schoop) Body Ego Technique, 1962 (U.S. Golden Eagle Council on Internat. Nontheatrical Events award 1963). Home: 3584 Multiview Dr Hollywood CA 90068 Office: 8730 Alden Dr Los Angeles CA 90048

SALLEY, VIRGINIA SUTTON, business executive; b. Miami, Fla.; d. Durward Belmont and Sarabelle (Burns) Sutton; student Sullins Coll., Rollins Coll.; m. George H. Salley, Aug. 28, 1961. Asso., jr. partner D.B. Sutton Jewelry Co., Miami, 1948-50; singer (Gloria Manning, profl. name) with Vincent Lopez Orch., Ben Ribble Orch., 1951-60; owner, operator Wiscasset Antiques, 1960-62; owner, mgr., pres. Sutton Manning Corp., 1962—; guest artist WOR-TV, N.Y.C.; currently appearing on club singing engagements, Miami Beach. Co-author: Royal Bayreuth China. Mem Met. Dade County Zoning Apls. Bd., 1966-70, vice-chmn. 1970-71; mem. pres.'s adv. council Barry Coll., 1978-79; community advisor Beaux Arts, U. Miami, Lowe Art Mus., 1975-78; bd. dirs. Big Bros., 1971-72, Gilded Lilies Dade County Soc. Crippled Children, 1982-83; founder, pres. Theatre Arts League, 1959, Jr. Theatre Guild of Miami, 1961. Mem. Nat. League Am. Pen Women, Am. Guild Variety Artists, Screen Actors Guild, DAR, Soc. Arts and Letters N.Y.C., Women's Guild of U. Miami. Mem. Christian Ch. Clubs: Miami Yacht, Bath, Surf, Indian Creek, Boothbay Harbour Yacht. Contbr. articles to profl. jours. Office: Sutton Manning Corp 100 N Biscayne Blvd Suite 700 Miami FL 33132

SALLING, SANDRA KAY, travel agency executive; b. Whitesboro, Tex., Apr. 28, 1946; d. Ralph Louis and Velma Odessa (Guess) S.; m. Doyle G. Dobbins, July 29, 1966 (div. 1976); 1 child, Deidre Salling. Mgr. North Tex. Travel Co., Sherman, 1967-72, Assoc. Travel, Inc., Sherman, 1972-75, Gelco Travel Services, Dallas, 1980-82; vacation mgr. Great Southwest Travel, Arlington, Tex., 1975-79; v.p. Travel Funtastic, Inc., Dallas, 1979-80; owner, mgr. Internat. Tours Park Plaza, Ft. Worth, 1982—. Mem. Inst. Cert. Travel Agts., Am. Soc. Travel Agts., Am. Bus. Women's Assn. Mem. Ch. of Christ. Avocations: piano, guitar; flying; singing. Office: Internat Tours Park Plaza 2501 Parkview Dr Suite 111 Fort Worth TX 76102

SALLOT, LYNNE MARIE, marketing communications corporation executive, writer; b. Cleve., Jan. 26, 1948; d. Kenneth Charles Funk and Rose Marie (Shoup/Clark) Pyle; m. Jeffry George Sallot, Oct. 5, 1968 (div. Dec. 1974); 1 child, Kenneth Edward. B.A., Kent State U., 1970. Editorial asst. Cleve. Press, 1967-68; bur. reporter Beacon-Jour., Akron, Ohio, 1969-71; asst. editor Maclean-Hunter, Toronto, Ont., Can., 1973-73, editor Southam Publs., Toronto, 1975-76; N.Am. mgr. Internat. Mktg. Ptnrs./Cayman Islands News Bur., Miami, Fla., 1977-80; v.p., dir. Creative Resources, Inc., Miami, 1980—; freelance writer contbg. to Redbook, Chatelaine, Quest, Miami Herald, others, U.S., Can., 1972 . Author: Bearwalk, 1977. Promotion, publicity activities for various charity orgns. including Am. Cancer Soc., City of Hope, Cystic Fibrosis Found., 1973—. William Randolph Hearst Found. scholar, 1969, award for feature writing, 1970; Scripps-Howard Found. scholar, 1968; Can. Arts Council grantee, 1977; Nat. Gaspar award Am. Cancer Soc., 1984; spl. award Ronald McDonald House, 1985. Mem. Women in Communications. Democrat. Home: 7550 S W 60th St Miami FL 33143 Office: Creative Resources Inc 2000 S Dixie Hwy Miami FL 33133

SALMON, ALICE SULLIVAN, nurse; b. N.Y.C., July 22, 1949; d. James Stephen and Ellen Hanna (Smith) Sullivan; B.S. in Nursing, Molloy Coll., 1971; M.A. in Nurse Edn., N.Y. U., 1975; m. Francis W. Salmon, Oct. 12, 1975. Staff nurse Jack D. Weiler Hosp. Albert Einstein Coll. Medicine, 1971-72, asst. head nurse, 1972-74, asst. dir. II, 1975-80, asst. dir. nursing, 1980-84, assoc. dir. nursing, 1984—. Mem. Am. Nurses Assn., Nat. League Nursing, Sigma Theta Tau. Office: 1825 Eastchester Rd Bronx NY 10461

SALMON, PHYLLIS WARD, computer company executive; b. Dallas, Aug. 10, 1948; d. Clinton David and Reba (Gilbert) Ward; m. James Y. Barbo, Dec. 12, 1970 (div. Jan. 1975); m. William Wellington Salmon, Jan. 21, 1977. A. in Acctg., Richland Coll., 1977; B.S. in Edn., Stephen F. Austin U., 1971. Cert. tchr. secondary edn., Tex. Cost acct. Jackson-Shaw, Dallas, 1975-79, Dal-Mac Devel., Dallas, 1979-81; store mgr. Shepard & Vick, Dallas, 1983-84; mktg. coordinator Tex. Instruments, Dallas, 1984-85; pres. Computer Expertise, Richardson, Tex., 1985—. Mem. Nat. Assn. Female Execs., Tex. Computer Dealers Assn. (organizing mem.), Dallas Needlework and Textile Guild. Republican. Episcopalian. Club: St. Clare's Guild (bd. dirs. 1980-81)(Dallas). Avocations: needlepoint; photography; travel. Office: Computer Expertise Inc 301 S Sherman Suite 119 Richardson TX 75081

SALMON, WILMA HOPE, lawyer; b. Corbin, Ky., Nov. 8, 1922; d. David Monroe and Laura Edna (Warren) Salmon. B.A., U. Ky., 1943; M.S.W., Tulane U., 1951; J.D., Loyola of South, 1982. Case worker ARC, New Orleans, 1943-47; case worker, supr. Bd. Pub. Welfare, Washington, 1947-49, Child Welfare-Orleans Parish, Childrens Div., New Orleans, 1949-63; dir. Orleans P-D Pub. Welfare, New Orleans, 1963-73, social analyst, until 1973; foster care adoption analyst Day Care Human Resources, Baton Rouge, 1973-79; state program chief La. Dept. Human Resources, Baton Rouge; legal services developer La. Govs. Office Elderly Affairs, Baton Rouge, 1982—; field work instr. Tulane U., La. State U., New Orleans, 1950-58; mem. La. Health Planning Adv. Council, Baton Rouge, 1972; sec. exec. com. New Orleans Health Plan Council, 1973-76. Author: Task Centered Case-Work in a Public Social Service Agency, 1976. Vice pres. Tulane Sch. of Social Work Alumni, New Orleans, 1961; bd. dirs. St. Marks Community Ctr., New Orleans, 1970-72; group leader Goals to Grow, New Orleans, 1972; mem. LWV, New Orleans, 1978—. Mem. ABA, La. State Bar Assn., Nat. Assn. Social Workers (bd. dirs. 1968-70). Club: Vieux Carre Property Owners (New Orleans). Office: Governor's Office Elderly Affairs 4528 Bennington St Baton Rouge LA 70898

SALMONS, JOANNA, nursing administrator; b. Smiths Grove, Ky., Nov. 7, 1933; d. Walter Scott and Birdie Wilma (Jackson) Parker; m. William L. Salmons, June 6, 1970; children by previous marriage—Robert B. Morrow, Scott Alan Morrow. R.N., Fla. Hosp. Sch. Nursing, 1954; student So. Missionary Coll., 1979; cert. in health systems mgmt. Harvard U., 1980, Yale U., 1985; B.S.N. SUNY, 1982; postgrad. Trinity Coll. Dir. nursing Larkin Gen. Hosp., Miami, Fla.; adminstr., Fort Walton Beach (Fla.) Hosp., 1974-75; dir. surg. nursing Fla. Hosp., Orlando, 1976-78; v.p. profl. standards Adventist Health Systems/Sunbelt Corp., Orlando, 1978-79; sr. v.p. Fla Hosp. Med. Ctr., Orlando, 1979—; dir. Health Care Mgmt. Corp., Adventist Health System/Sunbelt; cons. in field. Mem. A Thousand Plus com. Am. Cancer Soc. Recipient Outstanding Achievement award, Larkin Gen. Hosp., Miami, 1969 Mem. Fla. Nurses Assn. (bd. dirs. 1980-81, 83-84), Am. Heart Assn., Retarded Children's Assn. Orange County, Fla. Hosp. Assn., Am. Nurses Assn. (cert. nurse adminstr.), Fla. Orgn. Nursing Execs., Am. Orgn. Nursing Execs., Assn. Seventh-Day Adventist Nursing Execs. (bd. dirs.). Club: Buena Ventura Lakes

Golf and Tennis. Home: Knollwood 1212 Waverly Way Longwood FL 32750 Office: 601 Rollins St Orlando FL 32803

SALSBURY, GLENNA RUTH, speaker, cons.; b. Peoria, Ill., Sept. 13, 1937; d. Glenn Albert and Helen Bethia (Lake) Arnold; B.S., Northwestern U., 1959; M.A., UCLA, 1961; M.A., Fuller Theol. Sem., Pasadena, Calif., 1977; m. James W. Salsbury, Feb. 10, 1979; children by previous marriage—Monica Osborn, Melissa Osborn, Michelle Osborn. Pres., Cameo Tapes and Books, Santa Ana, Calif., 1972-77; v.p. human resources Tarbell Realtors, Tustin, Calif., 1977-80; pres. Salsbury Enterprises, El Toro, Calif., 1980—; mgmt. and sales tng. cons. Mem. Nat. Speakers Assn., Sales and Mktg. Execs. Republican. Mem. Christian Ch. Author: Reflections, 1977; The Bible: Fact or Fiction?, 1968; Can Humans Be Christians?, 1972; Have You Considered Job?, 1972. Home and office: 22135 Debra El Toro CA 92630

SALSE, ELIZABETH LANDON, cross-cultural communication executive; b. Rio de Janeiro, Aug. 19, 1929; d. Archie Blake and Ambrosina (Salse) Landon; B.A., Andrews U., 1949; M.S., No. Ill. U., 1978; m. Eduardo A.B. Salse, Dec. 25, 1956 (div.); children—Elise Landon Johnson, Victoria Lynne Switzer, John Blake, Angela Marie. Instr., Harper Coll., Palatine, Ill., 1971-77; developed high sch. English as 2d lang. program Joliet (Ill.) Jr. Coll., 1977; coordinator English as 2d lang. program Mundelein Coll., Chgo., 1977-78; pres., owner Sales Cross-Cultural Communication, Arlington Heights, Ill., from 1978; now personnel mgr. MBL Chemi-Flex, Lombard, Ill. Mem. Soc. Human Resource Profls., Mem. Intercultural Edn., Tng. and Research. Home and Office: 306 N Carlyle Pl Arlington Heights IL 60004

SALSTROM, SARA-JANE, medical technologist; b. Youngstown, Ohio, May 19, 1946; d. Martin and Edna Hazel (Theis) Mueller; B.S., Kent State U., 1971; 1 dau., Valerie Jean. Intern in med. tech. Akron (Ohio) City Hosp., 1970-71, staff med. technologist, 1971-74, research med. technologist specializing in infectious disease research, 1974—. Mem. Am. Soc. Clin. Pathologists (cert. med. technologist), Am. Soc. Microbiology, Nat. Rifle Assn. Republican. Lutheran. Club: Zeppelin Rifle. Contbr. articles to profl. jours. Office: Akron City Hosp 75 Arch St Suite 204 Akron OH 44304

SALTIEL, NATALIE, accountant; b. Chicago, Mar. 19, 1927; d. Henry Carl and Dorothy (Maremont) S.; m. Sidney D. Levin, Oct. 13, 1963; 1 child, Erica Saltiel Levin. B.B.A. with highest distinction, Northwestern U., 1948. C.P.A., Ill. Staff acct. firm, Chgo., 1948-52; practice acctg., Chgo., 1952—. Bd. dirs., mem. exec. com., com. chmn. United Way Chgo., 1979-85, United Way/ Crusade of Mercy, 1980—; mem. adv. council, chmn. com. W.B.E.Z. Chicagoland Pub. Radio, 1981—. Mem. Am. Inst. C.P.A.s, Ill. C.P.A. Soc., Chgo. Women's Soc. C.P.A.s, Chgo. Fin. Exchange, Beta Gamma Sigma. Office: 105 W Madison St Chicago IL 60602

SALTZ, RITA SEPLOWITZ, computer services company executive; b. Willimantic, Conn., Aug. 20, 1939; d. Samuel and Anna Ida (Nadel) Seplowitz. B.A., Smith Coll., 1960; M.S., Eastern Conn. State Coll., 1968. Tchr. pub. schs., Conn., 1962-66; exec. dir. The New Hope Ctr., Inc., Keene, N.H., 1966-68; cons., N.H., Mass., W.Va., 1968-70; tech. writer, user relations specialist W.Va. U. Computer Ctr., Morgantown, 1971-79; mgr. info. services W.Va. Network for Ednl. Telecomputing, Morgantown, 1979-80, asst. dir., 1980—. Author: The WVUCPU WATRJE Primer, 1971. Editor The WVNET Newsletter, 1971-79. Contbr. articles to profl. jours. Mem. Assn. Computing Machinery (editor newsletter spl. interest group on univ. and coll. computing services 1979-80), Am. Soc. Tng. and Devel. Home: PO Box 1078 Morgantown WV 26507-1078

SALVERSON, CAROL ANN, church adminstrator, librarian; b. Buffalo, June 30, 1944; d. Howard F. and Estella G. (Zelie) Heavener. Student Syracuse U., 1962-64; B.A., SUNY-Buffalo, 1966; M.S., Syracuse U., 1968; grad. Sacred Coll. Jamilian Theology and Div. Sch., Internat. Community Christ, Reno, 1976. Ordained to ministry Internat. Community of Christ, 1974. Library trainee SUNY Med. Ctr., Syracuse, 1966-67; research asst. Inst. for Advancement Biomed. Communication, Syracuse, 1966-67; asst. editor SUNY Union List of Serials, Syracuse, 1967-68; readers services librarian, asst. prof. Jefferson Community Coll., Watertown, N.Y., 1968-75; adminstr. pub. services dept., dir. Theol. Research Library, Internat. Community of Christ, Reno, 1975—; trustee North Country Reference and Research Resources Council, Canton, N.Y., 1974-75; mem. faculty Sacred Coll. Jamilian U. of Ordained, Internat. Community of Christ, Reno, 1979—, Jamilian Parochial Sch., 1978—; chmn. Survey of User Edn. in N.Y. State Acad. Libraries, 1971. Asst. editor Union List of Serials SUNY, 2d edit., 1967; contbr. articles on library sci. to profl. jours. Chmn. survey transp. needs in Watertown, LWV, 1969-70; asst. dir. religious edn. All Souls Unitarian-Universalist Ch., Watertown, 1969-70, chmn. religious edn. com., 1970-71, trustee, treas., 1974-75; founder, coordinator Life Ctr., Watertown, 1973-75. Mem. ALA, Nat. League Concerned Clergywomen, Nev. Library Assn., Club: College Women's (Watertown). Home: 2025 La Fond Dr Reno NV 89509 Office: Chancellery Internat Community of Christ 643 Ralston St Reno NV 89503

SALVESON, CATHERINE JANE KENNEDY, writer; b. South Bend, Sept. 27; d. William Jackson and Cassandra (Wood) Kennedy; m. John Theodore Salveson, Jr., Oct. 14, 1949 (dec.); children—John Theodore III, Jill Theresa, William Jackson. Student Immaculate Heart Coll., Hollywood, Calif., Compton (Calif.) Jr. Coll. Actress, dancer, stage and screen, 1932-46; radio personality, Hollywood, Calif., 1946-51; advt. mktg. rep. TMG for DuPont, Miami, Fla., 1965-72; owner, operator Kenmae Apt. Hotel, Miami Beach, Fla., 1962-72; 1st asst. mgr. N.Y. Hilton Hotel, N.Y.C., 1974-83; writer, N.Y.C., 1983—; contbr. articles and short stories to periodicals. Committeewoman, Republican Com. Dade County, 1967-70; pres. Rep. Women of Miami Beach, 1967-70; co-chmn. library com. Women's Nat. Rep. Club, N.Y.C., 1972, pub. relations co-chmn., 1973; committeewoman Rep. Exec. Com. of N.Y. County, 1984—; mem. benefit com. Millay Colony for the Arts, 1974—. Roman Catholic. Club: LaGorce Country (Miami Beach). Home: 205 3d Ave New York NY 10003

SALVETTI, SUSAN, lawyer; b. N.Y.C., Feb. 22, 1955; d. Sergio and Emma (Fucini) S.; m. Peter James Palenzona, Apr. 5, 1981; 1 dau., Marisa Danielle. B.A. summa cum laude, Fordham U., 1976, J.D., 1979. Bar: N.Y. 1980. Student asst. U.S. Attys. Office, N.Y.C., 1978, Manhattan Dist. Attys. Office, N.Y.C., 1979; assoc. Newman, Tannenbaum, Helpern & Hirschtritt, N.Y.C., 1980-82, Martin, Clearwater & Bell, N.Y.C., 1982-85, Zwerling, Schachter & Zwerling, N.Y.C., 1985—. Generoso Pope scholar, 1975. Mem. N.Y. State Bar Assn., Parents League N.Y., Phi Beta Kappa.

SALYARDS, DENISE ANN, bank official; b. Providence, Feb. 10, 1954; d. William Bradford and Dorothy Mary (Thibodeau) Smith; student Providence Coll., 1975-79; m. Michael Jeffrey Salyards, Dec. 29, 1979; children—Michael Jeffrey, II, Kristina Alaine. Clk.-typist money market dept. Indsl. Nat. Bank, Providence, 1972, bookkeeper, 1972-75, asst. fin. analyst, 1975-76, market research asst., 1976-78, market research analyst, 1978-79; dir. market research Hamilton Bank, Lancaster, Pa., 1979-82; mgr. market research 1st Nat. Exchange Bank, Roanoke, Va., 1982; asst. v.p., dir. market research Dominion Bankshares Corp., 1982-83; asst. v.p., retail mktg. systems mgr. Barnett Banks Fla., Inc., Jacksonville, 1983-85; v.p., dir. mktg. Barnett Bank of South Fla. N.A., Miami, 1985—; cons. Strategic Planning Task Force, 1981, Hamilton Bank, 1982—. Mem. Am. Mktg. Assn. (chpt. pres. 1981-82, bd. dirs. South Fla. chpt. 1985—), Bank Mktg. Assn., Nat. Assn. Bank Women, Nat. Assn. Female Execs. Roman Catholic. Home: 2890 SW 139th Way Davie FL 33330 Office: 800 Brickell Ave Miami FL 33131

SALZMAN, MARIAN LYNN, business journalist, consultant, writer, lecturer; b. N.Y.C., Feb. 15, 1959; d. Norman Erwin and Ruby Valerie (Freeman) S. B.A., Brown U., 1980. Editor Mgmt. Review, Am. Mgmt. Assns., N.Y.C., 1984-85; editorial dir. and co-founder Career Insights Inc., Providence, 1980-83; lectr. coll. campuses and corps. Author: Inside Management Training, 1985; MBA Jobs, 1986. Contbr. articles on career and management topcs to profl. jours. and consumer mags. Trustee Brown Univ. Club N.Y., 1984—. Dorot Found. fellow 1980.

SAMANICH, NANCY COLETTE, advertising and yacht charter executive; b. Cleve., July 27, 1938; d. Robert George and Mary Margaret (Borie) Tischler; m. Nick E. Samanich, Oct. 5, 1957 (div. Oct. 1982); children—Nicholas, Michael, David, Barbara, Jennifer, Robert. Student Cleve. State U., 1973-78. With NASA, Cleve., 1956-58; news room asst. WKYC-NBC, Cleve., 1975-76; media buyer, planner Wyse Advt., Cleve., 1976-78; media dir., account exec. Image Advt., Westlake, Ohio, 1978-81; pres., mktg. dir. Forte Communications, Inc., Cleve., 1981—, also dir.; dir. Champagne & Roses, Cleve. Active local Boy Scouts Am., 1964-66, Girl Scouts U.S., 1968-72, Am. Field Services, 1982-83. Mem. Sales and Mktg. Execs. Cleve. (speaker 1983—, asst. dir. 1984—), Communicators Club Cleve. Avocations: sailing, flying, traveling, reading. Home: 229 Yacht Club Dr Rocky River OH 44116 Office: Forte Communications Inc 1330 Old River Rd Cleveland OH 44113

SAMBERG, SHIRLEY, sculptor; b. N.Y.C., May 18, 1920; d. Julius and Bessie (Greenhaus) Klein; widowed; children—Jesse, Wendy. Cert., N.Y. Sch. Interior Design, 1950. Tchr. sculpture North Shore Community Art Ctr., Gt. Neck, N.Y., 1969-79, Wunch Art Ctr., Glen Cove, N.Y., 1979-82; guest lectr. Peking U., China, 1982. Solo exhbns. include: Unicorn Gallery, N.Y.C., 1978, Gallery 33, N.Y.C., 1976, Bryant Library, Roslyn, N.Y., 1976; group exhbns. include: Mus. Eskiltuna, Sweden, 1976, Gallery Kristianstad, Stockholm, Sweden, 1976, Royal Acad., Stockholm, 1973, Avery Fisher Hall, N.Y.C., 1975, Heckscher Mus., Hunting, N.Y., 1973, Silvermine Guild, New Canaan, Conn., 1972, Cayman Gallery, N.Y.C., 1980, Hempstead Harbor Artists Assn., Glen Cove, N.Y., 1984; represented in permanent collections: Rockefeller U., Art Publ. Archives, Peking, China; also numerous pvt. collections. Mem. Nat. Assn. Women Artists (judge 1985-86), Profl. Artists Guild. Address: 22 Barnyard Ln Roslyn Heights NY 11577

SAMBOLD, MARGIE LOU, banker; b. McKees Rocks, Pa., Nov. 22, 1935; d. Fred and Anna Louise (Gernandt) Enghardt; student Am. Inst. Banking; m. Albert James Sambold, May 1, 1956; children—Albert James, Sylvia Ann, Angela Janine. Bookkeeper, proof operator Commonwealth Trust, McKees Rocks, Pa., 1952-56; teller First Nat. Bank Topeka, 1956-59, Bank of Bellevue (Nebr.), 1962-66; teller, credit analyst, loan officer, br. mgr., asst. cashier Bank Meridian (formerly Hampton Nat. Bank), 1971—, also fin. services officer, br. adminstr., now asst. v.p. Active Boy Scouts Am., Friends of Library; Hampton Housing Authority, 1977-78. Mem. Am. Inst. Banking (dir. eastern N.H. chpt., treas. eastern dist.), Nat. Assn. Bank Women, Bus. and Profl. Women's Club, (past pres., chmn. state fin. com.), N.H. Bus. and Profl. Women's Club (state treas.). Republican. Clubs: Catholic Women's, Officers Wives, Band Boosters. Home: 35 Milbern Ave Hampton NH 03842 Office: 100 Winnacunnet Rd Hampton NH 03842

SAMBOR, CYNTHIA JANIS, logistic analyst; b. Johnstown, Pa., Apr. 12, 1957; d. Frank John Sambor and Janis Louise (Barron) Sambor Melvin. B.S. in Bus., U. Md.; cert. in fashion merchandising Bradford Sch., 1976. Buyer Glosser Bros., Johnstown, Pa., 1976-77; store mgr. The Ltd., Columbus, Ohio, 1977-82; fin. analyst ASG, Silver Spring, Md., 1982-83; logistic analyst Ketron, Inc., Arlington, Va., 1983—. Co-editor: Small Store Strategy, 1981; author: Logistic Element Manager Plan, 1983. Bd. dirs. Pa. State Soc., Washington, 1983-85; majorette advisor Connemaugh Twp. Area High Sch., Davidsville, Pa., 1976, 77; teen bd. advisor The Ltd., Wheaton, Md., 1980, 81, 82. Recipient Outstanding Achievement award The Ltd., Greensburg, Pa., 1980. Mem. Soc. Logistic Engrs. Republican. Roman Catholic.

SAMBRANO, FLORA T., equal employment official; b. El Paso, Tex., Dec. 14, 1935; d. Narciso Saenz and Josefina (Granados) Trillo; m. Gus Sambrano, Sr., July 17, 1955; 1 child, Gus., Jr. B.S. in Edn., U. Tex. Equal opportunity specialist, Ft. Bliss, Tex., 1973-77, 85—; U.S. customs officer U.S. Dept. Treasury, El Paso, 1977-82; mgr. Fed. Woman's Program, Ft. Bliss, 1982-83; equal opportunity officer William Beaumont Army Med. Ctr., El Paso, 1983-85; cons. in field, 1981—; mem. Nat. Hispanic Speakers Bur., Washington, 1980—; presenter workshops. Author Travel Tips, 1983-85. Editor, Equal Opportunity Bull., 1985—. Chmn. Selective Service Bd., El Paso, 1982—; co-chmn. personnel com., bd. dirs. YWCA, El Paso, 1985—; bd. dirs. El Paso Women's Employment and Edn., 1984—; mem. Pres.'s Com. for the Handicapped, 1986; adv. bd. Hispanic Com. Recipient numerous local and nat. awards in field of equal opportunity and human relations; named Feminist of Yr., El Paso Polit. Women's Caucus, 1978. Mem. Profl. Women's Network, Exec. Forum, Exec. Women's Internat., Profl. Women-El Paso C. of C. Democrat. Roman Catholic. Home: 1389 Adabel Dr El Paso TX 79936 Office: Equal Opportunity Office Attn: ATZC-DCE-EO Bldg 114 Fort Bliss TX 79916

SAMIIAN, BARAZANDEH, corporate executive; b. Tehran, May 13, 1939; came to U.S., 1958. B.A., Woodbury U., Los Angeles, 1961; B.A., Immaculate Heart Coll., Los Angeles, 1979; M.A., Webster U., Geneva, 1981. Cons., Design & Architecture, Tehran, 1965-72; bus. cons. multinat. corps., Calif., 1970-77; co-owner Samiian and Solomon Assocs., Geneva, 1978—; adj. prof. Webster U., Geneva, 1981-82; cons. and lectr. human resources devel. Named Woman of Yr., 1983. Office: B Samiian Assocs PO Box 5918 Bethesda MD 20814

SAMIOS, CORINNE, fabric/wallpaper company design director; b. N.Y.C.; d. John Pythagoras and Ruth Charlotte S.; Student Traphagen Sch. Fashion, N.Y.C., 1955-57; student interior design Art Students League, 1955-60. Colorist Old Deerfield Fabrics, 1957-63, Everfast, 1963-66, Cohama, 1966-69; stylist Cyrust Clark, 1969-74; stylist Brunschwig & Fils, N.Y.C., 1974—, now design dir.; condr. seminars Phila. Coll. Sci. and Textiles; speaker Am. Assn. Textile Colorists and Chemists. Developed fabric/wallpaper collections based on hist. documents of Brighton Pavillion, Eng., 1980, Old Westbury Gardens, N.Y.C., 1981; Cooper-Hewitt Mus., 1982; Musée des Arts Decoratifs, Paris, 1983; work covered in various publs.; develops musical portraits of people. Active West Side Block Assn., N.Y.C.; tchr. art to handicapped Bird S. Coler Hosp., N.Y.C., 1960-63. Mem. Am. Soc. Interior Designers, Nat. Home Fashions League. Office: Brunschwig & Fils 979 3d Ave New York NY 10022

SAMMARTINO, SYLVIA (MRS. PETER SAMMARTINO), retired university official; b. Boston, Dec. 5, 1903; d. Louis J. and Anna E. (Bianchi) Scaramelli; A.B., Smith Coll., 1925; M.A., Columbia U., 1926; LL.D., Kyung Hee U., Seoul, Korea, 1964; D.H.L., Fairleigh Dickinson U., 1966; m. Peter Sammartino, Dec. 5, 1933. Tchr. pub. high sch., N.Y.C., 1927-28, 1933-35; treas. Scaramelli and Co., Inc., N.Y.C., 1928-33; ednl. editor Atlantica 1933-35; circulation mgr. La Voix de France, N.Y.C., 1935-37; registrar Fairleigh Dickinson U., 1942-50, dir. admissions, 1950-59, dean of admissions, after 1959. Chmn. N.J. Commn. on Women, 1971. Bd. govs. N.Y. Cultural Center; chmn. bd. trustees Integrity Inc.; pres. Garden State Ballet; mem. Restore Ellis Island Com.; trustee Newark Symphony Hall, William Carlos Williams Center for Performing Arts. Recipient Amita award, 1960; medal Smith Coll., 1967; Pres.'s medal Mercy Coll.; named Citizen of Yr., Rutherford C. of C., decorated officer Ordre National (Ivory Coast); Order of Star of Africa (Liberia); officer Order of Merit (Italy). Mem. Internat. Assn. Univ. Pres., Nat. Orgn. Italian-Am. Women (hon. trustee). Home: 140 Ridge Rd Rutherford NJ 07070

SAMMET, JEAN E., computer scientist; b. N.Y.C.; d. Harry and Ruth S.; B.A., Mount Holyoke Coll., Sc.D. (hon.), 1978; M.A., U. Ill. Group leader programming Sperry Gyroscope, Great Neck, N.Y., 1955-58; sect. head, staff cons. programming Sylvania Electric Products, Needham, Mass., 1958-61; with IBM, 1961—, Boston adv. program mgr., 1961-65, program lang. tech. mgr., 1965-68, programming tech. planning mgr. Fed. Systems div., 1968-74, programming lang. tech. mgr., 1974-79, software tech. mgr., 1979-82, programming lang. tech. mgr., 1983—; chmn. history of computing com. Am. Fedn. Info. Processing Socs., 1977-79. Author: Programming Languages: History and Fundamentals, 1969; editor-in-chief Assn. Computing Machinery Computing Revs., 1979—; contbr. articles to profl. jours. Mem. Assn. Computing Machinery (pres. 1974-76, Disting. Service award 1985), Math. Assn. Am., Nat. Acad. Engring., Upsilon Pi Epsilon. Office: IBM Fed Systems Div 6600 Rockledge Dr Bethesda MD 20817

SAMMS, EVA DOLORES, educator; b. Quitman, Ga., Mar. 25, 1937; d. Benjamin Franklin and Ruby Lee (Mitchell) Watts; children—Rory C. Thomas, Enrique S. Samms. B.A., Shaw U., Raleigh, N.C., 1976; M.S., Nova U., Ft. Lauderdale, 1978, Ed.S., 1982, postgrad., 1982—. Cert. vocat. and adult edn. tchr. Fla. Legal sec. Legal Services of Greater Miami, Fla., 1967-70, Storer Broadcasting Co., Balharbour, Fla., 1970-72; sec., bookkeeper Dade County Pub. Schs., Miami, 1973-76, bus. tchr., 1976-84, vocat. and adult edn. tchr., 1984—; curriculum writer Dade County Schs., 1982—, software evaluator, 1986; pres., cons. Triangle Mgmt., Miami, 1985—. Author: (curriculum) Professional Secretary, 1978. Precinct capt. Democratic Party, Miami, 1977-83, com. woman, 1984—; dep. registrar Voter Registration, Miami, 1980—; pres. Minority Women, Miami, 1982, 84. Recipient Outstanding Service Plaque, Miami Lakes Jr. High Sch., 1981, Service award United Tchrs. of Dade County, 1984, 85; Letter of Commendation, Area Supt., North Miami, 1984. Mem. Vocat. Bus. Edn. Assn., Assn. Supervision and Curriculum Devel., Booker T. Washington Alumni (Miami, pres. 1984-85), Phi Delta Kappa, Beta Tau Zeta. Democrat. Am. Baptist. Club: Scruples (Miami). Avocations: gardening; sports; dancing; people. Office: Lindsey Hopkins Vocat and Tech Ctr 750 NW 20 St Miami FL 33127

SAMPIETRO, GABRIELLE LOUISE MACKINNON, fashion designer, fashion manufacturing company executive; b. Chalfont St. Giles, Buckinghamshire, Eng., Feb. 20, 1954; U.S. citizen since birth; d. James Bowie and Gabrielle Augusta Patricia Young-Mackinnon; m. Miguel C. Sampietro, Oct. 4, 1974; children—Alanna Gabrielle, Alexis Tamara. Student St. George's-Clarens, Switzerland, 1971, Acad. of Fine Arts, Mallorca, Spain, 1972. Asst. to pres. Worldmart, World Trade Ctr., N.Y.C., 1975; mgr. retail div. Charles Jourdan, Inc., N.Y.C., 1976-79; pres., founder Gabani, Inc., N.Y.C., 1978—. Anglican. Avocations: snow skiing, horseback riding, all water sports, painting. Office: Gabani Inc 53 E 74th St New York NY 10021

SAMPLE, DOROTHY EATON, state representative; m. Richard L. Sample; 3 children. B.A. in Econs., Duke U., J.D. Bar: N.C.; cert. tchr., real estate salesperson, Fla. Sec. to law firms, law clk.; asst. atty. HOLC; sec., dept. mgr. automobile fin. co.; now mem. Fla. Ho. of Reps. Mem. Fla. State Children's Commn.; mem. adv. council on conservation and environ. Fla. Dept. Natural Resources; mem. state adv. com. on coastal zone mgmt. Dept. Environ. Regulations; Founder Alliance for Conservation of Natural Resources; pres. Save Our Bays; pres. PTA, Pasadena Property Owners Assn., Band Boosters (3 schs.); mem. adminstrv. bd. dirs. Pasadena Community Ch.; legis. chmn. LWV; leader Girl Scouts U.S.A.; sponsor Jr. Coll. Service Club; bd. dirs. Gulf Coast and Fla. State Tb Assn.; bd. dirs. CONA (Council of Neighborhood Assn.); v.p. West St. Petersburg Property Owners Assn.; bd. dirs. Community Welfare Council; bd. dirs. March of Dimes, Mothers' March of Dimes VIP chmn., publicity chmn.; legal asst. Soc. for Prevention Cruelty to Animals; bd. dirs. St. Petersburg Hist. Soc.; area chmn. Sci. Ctr., Easter Seal Guild, Toy Shop, Friends of Library, Multiple Sclerosis, United Fund drives; mem., officer Republican Clubs; bd. dirs. Suncoast Active Vols. for Ecology; mem. Citizens Council on Crime, St. Petersburg Bicentenial Com.; mem. adv. bd. dirs. Pinellas Parkway; mem. Blue Ribbon Charger Com.; chmn. Coast Coordinating Council; mem. Pinellas County Edn. Study Commn; trustee Gulf Coast chpt. Nat. Multiple Sclerosis Soc.; assoc. bd. dirs. Mental Health Assn. in Pinellas County; bd. dirs. Nat. Handicapped Freedom Found., Inc.; mem. Cons. Council of FACE Learning Ctr., Inc. Recipient Good Govt. award Conservative Union, 1981, Tampa Women for Responsible Legis. Freedom award, 1982, Outstanding Pub. Ofcl. award St. Petersburg Beach Homeowners Assn., 1982, service award March of Dimes, 1984, also others. Mem. Fla. Wildlife Fedn. (v.p., regional dir.; spl. service award 1977), AAUW (legis. chmn.), Pan Hellenic Assn., Duke U. Alumni Assn. (chmn.), Pinellas C. of C. (govt. action com.), Chi Phi, Delta Phi Rho Alpha. Clubs: St. Petersburg Yacht; Sinawik (pres.).

SAMPLE, DOROTHY ELLIOTT, psychol. counselor, educator; b. Winfield, Ala., Nov. 1, 1938; d. John Belton and Annie Earl (Franks) Elliott; B.A., F.W. Bapt. Coll., 1961; A.B., U. Mich., 1966, M.A., 1967, Ph.D., 1976; Th.D., Toledo Sem., 1973; m. Richard Howard Sample, Aug. 27, 1961; children—Richard Howard, Scott Elliott, Lisa Deanne. Tchr., Linden (Mich.) Community Schs., 1963-65, Flint (Mich.) Community Schs., 1967-82; faculty John Wesley Coll., Owasso, Mich., 1973-75, adj. prof. psychology, 1973-75; tchr. Center for Christian Studies, Flint, 1979-80; tchr. piloted jr. high gifted edn. program Flint Schs., 1977; profl. counselor Personality Dynamics, Flint and Southfield, 1977—; lectr. Pres., Women's Missionary Union, So. Bapt. Conv., 1981; mem. exec. bd. Bapt. State Conv. Mich., 1977-80, mem. exec. com., 1978-80, mem. com. bds., 1979-80; vol. counselor County Jail, Flint, 1978-80. Recipient Delta Epsilon Chi Outstanding Student Merit award, 1961; Lit. Soc. award, 1961. Mem. U. Mich. Alumni Assn., AAUW, Christian Assn. Psychol. Studies, Mich. Edn. Assn., Delta Kappa Gamma, Phi Kappa Phi, Delta Epsilon Chi. Baptist. Co-author: Life in the Fifth Dimension; contbr. articles to profl. jours. Home: 3119 Prospect St Flint MI 48504 Office: 600 N 20th St Birmingham AL 35203

SAMPSON, ELLANIE SUE, librarian, editor; b. Ft. Monmouth, N.J., July 30, 1953; d. Arnold Ingvold and Edith Louise (Johnston) Sampson; m. H. Gordon Solberg, June 1, 1982. B.A. in Fine Arts, U. N.Mex., 1974; M.L.S., U. Okla., 1975. Slide librarian Sch. Art, Okla. U., Norman, 1975-78; adminstr. Northeast Mo. Library Service, Kahoka, 1978-79; librarian, dir. Truth or Consequences Pub. Library (N.Mex.), 1979—; cons. depts. history, English, architecture, Norman, 1975-78, Herron Sch. Art, Purdue U., Indpls., 1977. Mng. editor Dry Country News, 1983-85; compiler/calligrapher/editor: Salad Out with Jazzworks, 1983. Bd. dirs., bookkeeper Black Range Food Coop., Truth or Consequences, 1982—; chairperson Ret. Sr. Vol. Program Adv. Council, Truth or Consequences, 1983—; founder Womanswork, 1983—; organizer Stephen King Day, Truth or Consequences, 1983. Mem. N. Mex. Library Assn., ALA, U. Okla. Sch. Library Sci. Alumni Assn., Am. Bus. Women's Assn. (rec. sec. chpt. 1977-78), Grand River Library Conf. (v.p. 1979), Wellness N.Mex. Assn. Club: Jazzworks. Home: 409 Grape St Truth or Consequence MN 87901 Office: Truth or Consequences Pub Library 501 McAdoo St PO Box 311 Truth or Consequences NM 87901

SAMPSON, JUNE ELISABETH, historical museum administrator; b. Phila., May 31, 1946; d. William Herbert and Helen Elizabeth (Whitall) Stafford; B.A. in History, Earlham Coll., Richmond, Ind., 1968; M.A. in History Mus. Tng., SUNY, Oneonta, 1972; m. Earl Sampson, Jan. 22, 1972; stepchildren—Earl Brett, Daniel C., Shawn, Indira. Mus. curator S.D. State Hist. Soc., Pierre, 1969-72; asst. dir. W.H. Over Mus., U. S.D., Vermillion, 1972-73, dir., 1973-79; dir. Western Heritage Center, Billings, Mont., 1980-83; grant writer Powell County Mus. and Arts Found., Deer Lodge, Mont., 1983-84; dir. The Danish Immigrant Mus., Elk Horn, Iowa, 1984—; instr. dept. anthropology U. S.D., 1973-79. Mem. Landmarks, Inc., Billings, 1980—. Mem. Am. Assn. Mus., Ioua Mus. Assn., Am. Assn. for State and Local History. Quaker. Office: The Danish Immigrant Mus Box 178 Elk Horn IA 51531

SAMPSON, PATSY HALLOCK, college president; b. Picher, Okla., July 9, 1932; d. Daniel Webster and Mary Gladys (Whitehead) Hallock; children—Catherine, Jacquelyn, Rebecca. B.A. with spl. distinction, U. Okla., 1961; Ph.D. in Psychology, Cornell U., 1966. Asst. prof. SUNY-Binghamton, 1965-66; NIMH postdoctoral fellow Cornell U., 1966-67; asst. prof. Wellesley Coll., (Mass.), 1967-70; prof., chmn. dept. psychology Calif. State Coll.-Bakersfield, 1970-73; adminstr. Nat. Inst. Child Health and Human Devel., Bethesda, Md., 1973-75; psychologist Nat. Inst. Alcohol Abuse and Alcoholism, Washington, 1975-77; dean faculty, prof. psychology Pitzer Coll., Claremont, Calif., 1977-80; dean Coll. Liberal Arts, Drake U., Des Moines, 1980-83; pres. Stephens Coll., Columbia, Mo., 1983—. Mem. Phi Beta Kappa, Sigma Xi. Office: Office of the Pres Stephens Coll Columbia MO 65215

SAMPSON, SHERLYN KAYE, county official; b. Clay Center, Kans., Dec. 19, 1950; d. Leonard Wayne and Genevieve Virginia Adeline (Frigon) McIntosh; m. Gary Wayne Sampson, Mar. 28, 1970; children—James Vincent, Jan Annette. Student Ft. Hays Kans. State Coll., 1969. Clk.-stenographer elem. edn. dept. Ft. Hays, 1970-71; sec., chmn. div. edn., 1971-72; legal sec. Oyler and Paddock, Lawrence, Kans., 1972; dep. clk. dist. ct. Douglas County,

Kans., 1972-74, clk. of dist. ct., 1975—; mem. jury standards com. Supreme Ct., Topeka, 1983. Recipient Liberty Bell award Douglas County Bar Assn., 1984. Mem. Kans. Assn. Dist. Clks. and Ct. Adminstrs. (legis. com. 1984—), Kans. Bus. and Profl. Women (treas. 1983), Fraternal Order of Police Ladies Aux. (pres. 1977-78, sec. 1979, treas. 1980). Democrat. Methodist. Office: Douglas County Dist Ct 111 E 11th Room 179 Lawrence KS 66044

SAMPSON, SUSAN RAE, lawyer; b. Myrtle Point, Oreg., June 11, 1947; d. Reynold Vake and Mildred Esther (Goers) Sampson; m. Robert Blaine Martin, Mar. 25, 1967 (div. 1975); children—Eric Blaine, Brook Ian. Student Oreg. State U., 1965-68; B.A. with honors in English, U. Wash., 1969; J.D., 1974. Bar: Wash. 1974, U.S. Dist. Ct. (we. dist.) Wash. 1974, U.S. Ct. Appeals (9th cir.). Clk. Western Auto Hardware Store, Florence, Oreg., part-time 1965, 66; legal editor Book Pub. Co., Seattle, 1972-74; asst. atty. gen. State of Wash., Seattle, 1974-77; asst. city atty. City of Seattle, 1977-84; assoc. Oles, Morrison, Rinker, Stanislaw & Ashbaugh, 1984—; bd. dirs. Seattle Mgmt. Assn., 1983, 84, v.p., 1983, newsletter editor, 1982, 83, 84; lectr. pub. personnel law, 1982-84. Contbr. articles to law jours. Mem. 32d Legis. Dist. Democrats, Seattle, 1982-84; asst. scoutmaster Troop 164 Chief Seattle council Boy Scouts Am., 1984. Mem. ABA, Wash. Women Lawyers Assn. (legis. com.), Wash. State Bar Assn. legis. com. 1981-83).

SAMS, DORIS LAVERNE, college counselor; b. Youngwood, Pa., Apr. 26; d. Benjamin F. and Lucinda (Myers) S.; B.A., Seton Hill Coll., 1950; M.Ed., U. Pitts., 1959. Lic. mental health counselor, Fla., nat. bd. cert. counselor Nat. Acad. Cert. Clin. Mental Health Counselors. Employment interviewer Conn. State Employment Service, Thompsonville, 1950-53; tchr. Hempfield Area Schs., Greensburg, Pa., 1953-58, sch. psychologist, 1958-66; prof., counselor Broward Community Coll., Ft. Lauderdale, Fla., 1966—; human potential seminar leader Rational Behavior Therapist Workshops. Mem. Gov.'s Com. on Handicapped. Frick scholar. Mem. Am. Mental Health Counselors Assn., Am. Psychol. Assn. (assoc.), Nat. Assn. Cert. Clin. Mental Health Counselors, Am. Assn. Counseling and Devel., Humane Soc., Pet Rescue. Republican. Home: 1400 SW 19th St Fort Lauderdale FL 33315 Office: Broward Community Coll Fort Lauderdale FL 33024

SAMS, MARY ANN PACELLA, educational adminstr., corp. exec.; b. Chgo., Sept. 14, 1933; d. Carmen Harold and Helen Frances (Strauk) Pacella; A.B. cum laude, Mundelein Coll., 1958; M.Ed., U. Puget Sound, 1970; postgrad. U. San Francisco, 1977—; certificate San Francisco State U., 1973, Central Wash. State Coll., 1969, Am. Montessori Tchr. Tng. Inst., 1966, U. Kans., 1964, Chgo. Tchrs. Coll., 1960; m. Wendell M. Sams, Aug. 12, 1973; 1 son, Derek John. Spl. services tchr. Chgo. Pub. Schs., 1958-61; social and personal adjustment tchr. Vocat. Rehab. Div., Topeka, Kans., 1962-64; tchr. kindergarten, primary grades Chgo. Pub. Schs., 1964-66; master tchr., tchr.-trainer Park Ridge (Ill.) Montessori Sch., 1966-67, Spring Valley Montessori Sch., Federal Way, Wash., 1967-68; tchr. Annie Wright Sem., Tacoma, 1968-69; instr. U. Puget Sound, Tacoma, 1968-70; early childhood specialist Franklin Pierce Pub. Sch. Dist., Tacoma, 1969-70; project mgr. Project Learn, Behavioral Research Labs., Menlo Park, Calif., 1970-71; dir. Sullivan Presch. and Sullivan Sch. Redwood City, Calif., 1971, exec. dir. curriculum and personnel Sullivan Presch. and Sullivan Elem. Sch., Irving, Calif., 1971-73; coordinator reading and English as second lang. Dept. Def., Mil. Dependents Schs., Japan, 1973-74; program dir. Western Region, Mini-Skools Ltd., Irving, Calif., 1974-75; supr. personnel San Francisco Unified Sch. Dist., 1975-78, program mgr. Children's Centers Dept., 1978-79; dir. Children's Centers Dept., Oakland (Calif.) Unified Sch. Dist., 1979-80, adminstr. child devel. Piedmont Children's Center, 1981—; grad. instr. early childhood edn. U. San Francisco; cons. in field; ofcl. U.S. del. Sino-Am. Child Devel. Educators del. to Peoples Republic China, 1985; lectr. in field. Recipient Cert. of Appreciation, San Francisco Unified Sch. Dist. Bd. Edn., 1978; Tribute, Oakland Unified Sch. Dist. Bd. Edn., 1980; Appreciation award Oakland Dept. Children's Centers, 1980. Mem. Calif. Child Devel. Adminstrs. Assn. (state exec. bd. 1979-81, Cert. of Excellence 1980, Keeper of Dream award 1981), United Adminstrs. of Oakland Schs., Nat. Assn. for Edn. of Young Children, Council for Exceptional Children, Am. Assn. Sch. Personnel Adminstrs., Am. Soc. for Personnel Adminstrs. Bay Area Sch. Personnel Assn., Am. Montessori Soc., Nat. Black Child Devel. Inst., Assn. Montessori Internationale, Assn. Calif. Sch. Adminstrs., Phi Delta Kappa. Roman Catholic. Contbr. articles in field to profl. jours. Office: 86 Echo Ave Oakland CA 94611

SAMUEL, BARBARA JOAN, business administration educator; b. Scranton, Pa., Dec. 31, 1955; d. David Edward and Joan Elizabeth (Evans) S. B.S., Susquehanna U., 1977; M.B.A., U. Scranton, 1982; postgrad. Syracuse U., 1983—. Traffic mgr. Scranton Broadcasters, 1977-78; account exec. AT&T Info. Systems, Kingston, Pa., 1978-83; doctoral teaching asst. Syracuse U., N.Y., 1983-85; lectr. in mktg. U. Scranton, 1986—. Mem. Am. Mktg. Assn. Republican. Home: 1010 Woodland Way Clarks Summit PA 18411

SAMUELS, JANET LEE, lawyer; b. Pitts., July 18, 1953; d. Emerson and Jeanne (Kalish) Samuels; m. David Arthur Kalow, June 18, 1978; 1 dau., Margaret Emily. B.A. with honors, Beloit Coll., 1974; J.D., NYU, 1977. Bar: N.Y. 1978, D.C. 1980. Staff atty. SCM Corp., N.Y.C., 1977-80, corp. atty., 1980-83, sr. corp. atty., 1983—, assoc. gen. counsel Allied Paper div., 1983—. Advisor NYU Law Sch. Student Advisor Program, N.Y.C., 1982—. Mem. ABA, Assn. Bar of City N.Y., Assn. Trial Lawyers Am., N.Y. State Bar Assn., Phi Beta Kappa.

SAMUELS, SHIRLEY CHASINS, psychotherapist; b. Bronx, N.Y., Dec. 6, 1930; d. Rubin and Clara (Traub) Chasins; B.S., Syracuse U., 1952, M.S., 1957; Ed.D., Columbia U., 1969; postgrad. Child Psychoanalysis, Center for Preventive Psychiatry, 1974; m. Stanley Samuels, Sept. 9, 1951; children—Jeffrey, Nita, Mark. Tchr., Syracuse (N.Y.) U. Nursery Sch., 1955-57, Maywood Nursery Sch., Hartsdale, N.Y., 1961-63; dir. Mt. Vernon (N.Y.) YM-YWHA Nursery Sch., 1963-65; dir. early childhood program Conservative Synagogue of Riverdale, Bronx, N.Y., 1966-68; adj. asst. prof. Hunter Coll., N.Y.C., 1968-74; asso. prof. edn. Manhattan Coll., Purchase, N.Y., 1969-80; child psychotherapist Center for Preventive Psychiatry, White Plains, N.Y., 1974-80, clin. supr. 1980—; adj. prof. Coll. New Rochelle (N.Y.), 1978—, Pace U., 1986—; pvt. practice psychotherapy, White Plains, 1977—; mem. adv. bd. Tuckahoe Counseling Ctr., N.Y., 1985—; cons., lectr. in field. Bd. dirs. Union Day Care, Greenburgh, N.Y., 1981—, Westchester Assn. Young Children, White Plains, 1974—, Early Childhood Resource and Info. Center, N.Y.C. Libraries, 1981—; pres. Youth Bd. Westchester County, 1981—; mem. adv. bd. therapeutic activity program Grasslands Hosp., Valhalla, N.Y., 1981—. Recipient award Youth Bd. Westchester County, 1981—, Proclamation Service award, 1981. Mem. Assn. Marriage and Family Therapy (corr. sec. 1983-85); mem. Assn. Child Psychoanalysis, Am. Psychol. Assn., Am. Orthopsychiat. Assn. Democrat. Jewish. Author: Enhancing Self-Concept in Early Childhood, 1977, Disturbed Exceptional Children: An Integrated Approach, 1981, 2d edit., 1986. Mem. editorial bd. Jour. Preventive Psychiatry, 1981—. Home: 10 Crest Dr White Plains NY 10607 Office: 19 Greenridge Ave White Plains NY 10601

SAMUELSON, ARLENE ANN, personnel consultant; b. South Bend, Ind., Sept. 16, 1947; d. Carl and Ruby Arlene (Jones) Haring; m. Jerry Benson Samuelson, July 21, 1967; children—Jay Bruce, Chris Allen. B.A., Ind. U.-Ft. Wayne, 1969. Tchr., Logansport Community Schs., Ind., 1969-70; mgr. Fabulous Figure, Inc., Anderson, Ind., 1972-74; area supr. Boddee Shoppe, Inc., Ft. Wayne, Ind., 1972-74, owner, Lebanon, Ind., 1974-81; personnel cons. Century Personnel, Indpls., 1980-82, Dimension Personnel, Indpls., 1982—. Asst. editor Flightline newsletter, 1981—; editor newsletter Fishnet, 1984-85. Active mem. Advanced United Ch. Christ, Ind., 1977—, deaconess, counselor conf. laity com. Named Counselor the Month, Century Personnel, 1980-82, Dimension Personnel, 1983-85. Lodge: Zonta (pres. 1980-81). Avocations: reading; counted cross stitch. Home: 904 N Jameson St Lebanon IN 46052 Office: Dimension Personnel Inc 120 E Market St #450 Indianapolis IN 46204

SAMZ, JANE DEDE, science writer, editor; b. Closter, N.J., Jan. 2; d. Benjamin and Ruth (Burstein) Samz. A.B. in Math., Smith Coll., 1969, postgrad., U. Ky., 1969-70; M.A. in History of Sci., U. Wis.-Madison, 1971. Teaching asst. physics dept. U Ky., Lexington, 1969-70; editorial asst. Sci. World Mag., Scholastic Mags., Inc., N.Y.C., 1972-73, asst. editor, 1973-76, assoc. editor, 1976-79, editor, 1979—; lectr. communications dept. Stanford U., Calif., 1979; freelance writer Grolier, 1977-79, Funk and Wagnalls, 1981-83, Prentice-Hall, Inc., 1983-84; cons. in field. Author: Matter-Science World Visuals, 1975; (co-author) Voyage to Jupiter, 1980. Contbr. articles to profl. jours. Camille and Henry Dreyfus Found. fellow, 1978-79; NSF grantee, 1965; grantee advanced placement program Cornell U., 1964. Mem. Smith-Princeton Chamber Singers European Concert Tour, 1968, Mexican Concert Tour, 1969, Masterwork Chorus, 1970's. Mem. N.Y. Acad. Scis., AAAS, N.Y. Newspaper Guild, Am. Mus. Natural History, Planetary Soc. Home: 749 Scotland Rd Apt 6E Orange NJ 07050 Office: Sci World Scholastic Inc 730 Broadway New York NY 10003

SAN ANGELO, MARY, artist; b. Port Arthur, Tex., Dec. 4, 1915; d. George Manos and Katherine (Whitcher) Manos; m. Joseph San Angelo, Apr. 19, 1934; children—Thomas, George (dec.) David. Student Chester Snowden Art Class, Houston, 1964-67, Lowell Collins Sch. Art, Houston, 1968-71, Art League, Houston, 1967—. Profl. artist, Houston, 1968—; group shows include: Mus. Fine Arts, Houston, 1970, Tex. Fine Arts Assn., Art League Gallery, 1974; represented in permanent collections: Art League Houston, Allen Ctr., Houston. Recipient First award Tex. Women in Art, Houston, 1976. Mem. Art League of Houston (awards 1969-73). Roman Catholic. Home: 6502 Mercer St Houston TX 77005

SANBORN, ANN, ship's captain, import/export company executive; b. Portsmouth, Va., May 28, 1954; d. Richard Wellington and Ruth Ann (Chenoweth) S. B.S., Tex. A&M U., 1979. Master, U.S. Steam or Motor Vessels. Third officer Exxon Co. USA, Houston, 1979-80; 2d officer U. Wash./Seattle, 1980-81; chief officer Mobil E & P, Dallas, 1982-85; lectr. Tex. A&M U., Galveston, 1985; pres. Sanborn Indusutries, Inc., Tampa, Fla., 1985—. Mem. Mensa. Democrat. Episcopalian. Avocations: sewing; cooking; history; skiing.

SANBORN, ANNA LUCILLE, pension and ins. cons.; b. Bklyn., Mar. 29, 1924; d. Peter Francis and Matilda M. (Stumpp) Galligen; B.A., Bklyn. Coll., 1945; 1 son, Dean Sanborn. Head dept. benefit and estate planning Union Central Life Ins. Co., N.Y.C., 1949-51; adminstr. employee benefits Seaboard Oil Co., N.Y.C., 1952-56; with Frank J. Walters Assocs., Inc., N.Y.C., 1957—, pres., 1970—. Bd. dirs. Archdiocesan Service Corp. Mem. Am. Acad. Actuaries, Republican. Roman Catholic. Home: 58-11 Seabury St Elmhurst NY 11373 Office: 509 Madison Ave New York NY 10022

SANBORN, BEVERLYJEAN, pain center administrator; b. Akron, Ohio; d. Jean Ross Pennington and Carmen Juanita (Parsons) Leivdal; m. Robert Edward Bator, May 23, 1964 (div. 1977); 1 child, Lisa Lynn; m. Richard Hugh Sanborn, Aug. 19, 1978. Office mgr. News Tribune, Ft. Pierce, Fla., 1981-85; fin. adminstr. Comprehensive Pain Ctr., Sebastian, Fla., 1985—. Avocation: raising and breeding Yorkshire and Airedale terriers. Home: 6606 Pensacola Rd Fort Pierce FL 33451

SANBORN, CHARLOTTE JEAN HOLBROOK, counselor, educator, consultant; b. Concord, N.H., Mar. 14, 1925; d. Charlie Rollin and Mary Alice (Wood) H.; m. Thomas F. Perry, Jr. (div. 1966); m. Donald E. Sanborn III, Apr. 2, 1969 (div. Dec. 1976); children—Joan Perry Miller, John Holbrook, Martha Jane. B.A., U. Oreg., 1946; A.A. in Bus. Adminstrn., Pierce Coll., 1957; B.Ph.D., Pacific Western U., 1981. Biostatistician, State of N.H., 1957-67; research assoc. dept. psychiatry Closed Cir. TV Consultation, 1967-70; dir. N.H.-Vt. Closed Cir. Med. Interactive TV Project, 1970-75; dir. community services Dartmouth-Hitchcock Mental Health Ctr., 1975-77; dir. consultation/edn. West Central Mental Health, Hanover, 1977-80; dir., counselor faculty-employee assistance program Dartmouth Coll., Hanover, 1979—, asst. prof. clin. psychiatry, 1977—; cons. health care tech. div. Nat. Ctr. Health Services, Research and Devel., NIMH, 1972-75, region 1, HEW, Mental Health Ctr. Site Visits, 1980-81; cons. employee assistance programs Johns Hopkins U., Middlebury Coll., Mt. Holyoke Coll., Duke U., DePauw U., Anaheim Meml. Hosp., Calif., Boise Cascade, Cold Regions Research Lab., Hanover, 1983-85. Editor, contbr. Assessment Community Mental Health Movement, 1977, Law and the Mental Health Professions, 1979, Case Management in Mental Health, 1983; editorial cons. Jour. Suicide and Life Threatening Behavior, 1982—; contbr. articles to profl. jours. Mem. Democratic Com., Hanover, 1981—. Mem. LWV, Am. Assn. Suicidlogy (bd. mem. 1981-84, sec. 1985—), Am. Med. Record Assn., N.H. Med. Record Assn. (pres. 1972-73, 77-78), N.H. Mental Health Assn. (bd. dirs.), Assn. N.H. Mental Health Agys. (pres. 1977—), Nat. Assn. Female Execs., Assn. Labor Mgmt. Adminstrs. and Cons. in Alcoholism, Internat. Assn. Suicide Prevention, Am. Soc. Health Care Edn. and Tng., Nat. Assn. Womem Deans, Adminstrs. and Counselors, N.H. Social Welfare Council. Roman Catholic. Avocations: reading; hiking; music; traveling; sports spectator. Home: 1 Curtiss Rd Hanover NH 03755 Office: Dept Psychiatry Dartmouth Med Sch 9 Maynard St Hanover NH 03756

SANBORN, DIANE LOWLINE, real estate broker; b. McPherson, Kans., Oct. 11, 1935; d. Lowell Kenneth and Irma Pauline (Johnson) Hawley; m. Malte Kent Sanborn, Oct. 8, 1955; children—Dirk, Blake, Dana. Student U. Kans., 1953-55; grad. Realtors Inst., Mo., 1979. Salesman, Carriage Realtors, Rolla, Mo., 1973-80; broker, salesman Town and County Realtors, Rolla, 1980-82; broker, co-owner Countryside Real Estate, Rolla, 1982—. Pres., Phelps County Panhellenic, Rolla., 1976, Club TEAC, Rolla, 1980-82; dir. Planned Parenthood of the Ozarks, Rolla, 1974-78. Named Mo. Realtor Assoc. of the Year, Mo. Assn. Realtors, 1980. Mem. Mo. Assn. Realtors (vice chmn. mktg. 1983—; mem. exec. com. 1980-82), Realtors Nat. Mktg. Inst. (cert. residential specialist), Rolla Bd. Realtors (chmn. various coms.). Republican. Episcopalian. Office: Countryside Real Estate 219 Hwy 72 W Rolla MO 65401

SANBORN, DOROTHY CHAPPELL, librarian; b. Nashville, Apr. 26, 1920; d. William S. and Sammie Maude (Drake) Chappell; m. Richard Donald Sanborn, Dec. 1, 1943; children—Richard Donald, William Chappell. B.A., U. Tex., 1941; M.A., George Peabody Coll., 1947; M.P.A., Golden Gate U., 1982. Asst. cataloger El Paso Pub. Library, Tex., 1947-52, Library of Hawaii, Honolulu, 1953; cataloger Redwood City Pub. Library, Calif., 1954-55, 57-59, Stanford Research Inst., Menlo Park, Calif., 1955-57; librarian Auburn Pub. Library, Calif., 1959-62; cataloger Sierra Coll., Rocklin, Calif., 1962-64; reference librarian Sacramento City Library, 1964-66; county librarian Placer County, Auburn, Calif., 1966—; chmn. Mountain Valley Library System, 1970-71, 75-76, 85-86; cons. county librarian Alpine County Library, Markleeville, Calif., 1973-80. Served with WAVES, 1944-46. Mem. ALA, Calif. Library Assn., AAUW (pres. chpt. 1982-84). Democrat. Mem. Ch. of Christ. Club: Soroptimists. Home: 135 Midway St Auburn CA 95603 Office: Auburn-Placer County Library 350 Nevada St Auburn CA 95603

SANBORN, KIMBERLEE RAE, nurse; b. Bangor, Maine, Mar. 29, 1955; d. Robert Newton and Roxanna (Starbuck) Yarrow; m. Gary Sanborn, Aug. 18, 1984. A.A. in Nursing, Quinnipiac Coll., Hamden, Conn., 1980. R.N., Conn. Dietary aide Luth. Home, Middletown, Conn., 1970-72, nurses aide, 1972-78; security dispatcher Quinnipiac Coll., Hamden, Conn., 1976; nurses aide New Britain Gen. Hosp., Conn., 1979, staff nurse, 1980-82, asst. head nurse, 1982—. Avocations: skiing; nature; art; macrame; camping. Home: 18 Lake St Middletown CT 06457

SANCHEZ, CORDELIA CHAVEZ, educator; b. Albuquerque, Mar. 22, 1926; d. Elfido and Gregorita M. Chavez; B.A., U. N.Mex., 1946; postgrad. U. Albuquerque, 1964-78; children—Kenneth John, Margaret Marie. Tchr., Albuquerque Public Schs., 1946-51, 65—, Prince George's County, Md., 1959-60, Washington Schs., 1958-59; Mem. juvenile parole bd. N.Mex., 1978, chmn. Com. Children and Youth, 1976-78; mem. adv. council N.Mex. Employment Security Commn., 1977-78; vice chmn. N.Mex. Dem. Party, 1978-82; del. Nat. Dem. Party Conf., Kansas City, Mo., 1974, Memphis, 1978; del. Nat. Dem. Conv., 1976, 80. Recipient Distng. Woman of N.Mex. award N.Mex. Women's Polit. Caucus, 1976. Mem. NEA. Roman Catholic. Home: 6500 Rio Grande NW Albuquerque NM 87107

SANCHEZ, JESUSA, lawyer; b. Alice, Tex., July 3, 1955; d. Juan Ortiz and Zenaida (Cantu) Sanchez. B.B.S., Tex. A&I U., 1976; J.D., Tex. So. U., 1980. Bar: Tex. 1981. Asst. county atty. Jim Wells County, Alice, Tex., 1980-84, county atty., 1984—. State committeewoman Tex. Dem. Party, Austin, 1982-84; mem. exec. bd. Mexican-Am. Dems., Austin, 1982-84; mem. Tex. Woman's Polit. Caucus, Austin, 1982—; mem. Jim Wells County Dems., Alice, 1982. Democrat. Roman Catholic. Home: 743 W 1st St PO Box 3070 Alice TX 78332 Office: Jim Wells County Atty PO Box 2080 Alice TX 78332

SANCHEZ, ROSIE LEE, business educator; b. St. Joseph, La., Apr. 7, 1944; d. Ike Bellows, Jr. and Ophelia (Hartley) Bellows McDonald; div., 1 child, Darryl. B.S. in Bus. Edn., Langston U., 1967; M.A. in Bus. Edn., Govs. State U., University Park, Ill., 1981. Cert. bus. edn. instr., Ill. Tchr. 4th and 5th grades McClellan Sch., Chgo., 1967-68; tchr. coordinator Headstart Sch., Hominy, Okla., 1972-74, PREP Progam, Joliet, Ill., 1978-79; instr. STAT-TAB Tng. Ctr., Chgo., 1982-83, curriculum specialist, 1983-86; employment assessor Govs. State U., 1985—, instr. summer youth program in career edn., 1979. Recipient Coop. Vocat. Edn. commendation Chgo. Bd. Edn., 1983. Baptist. Avocations: reading, sports, horticulture. Home: 709 Burnham Dr Apt 4B University Park IL 60466 Office: Regional Employment Network Govs State U Stuenkel Rd University Park IL 60466

SANCHEZ, SARA MARIA, librarian, bibliographer; b. Havana, Cuba; d. Ramiro Jesus and Sara Maria (Rodriguez-Baz) S.; B.A., U. Villanova, 1957; B.L.S., U. Havana, 1960; M.L.S., SUNY-Geneseo, 1974. Librarian, Merici Acad., Havana, 1959-61; librarian Cuban Nat. Library, 1960-67; asst. prof. library sci. U. Miami, 1970-83, assoc. prof., 1984—. Mem. ALA, Am. Council Coll. and Research Libraries, Latin Am. Studies Assn., Met. Mus. Miami, Coalition Hispanic Am. Women, Dade County Library Assn. (sec. 1979-81), Fla. Library Assn., Assn. Caribbean Univ. and Research Libraries, Cuban Mus. Arts. Democrat. Roman Catholic. Home: 1860 SW 22d St #10 Miami FL 33145 Office: Library Univ Miami Coral Gables FL 33124

SANDAGE, ELIZABETH ANTHEA, market research executive, educator; b. Larned, Kans., Oct. 13, 1930; d. Curtis Carl and Beulah Pauline (Knupp) Smith; student Okla. State U., 1963-65; B.S., U. Colo., 1967; M.A., 1970; Ph.D. in Communications, U. Ill., 1983; m. Charles Harold Sandage, July 18, 1971; children by previous marriage—Diana Louise Danner (Mrs. Vern White), David Alan Danner. Public relations rep., editor Martin News, Martin Marietta Corp., Denver, 1960-63, 65-67; retail advt. salesperson Denver Post, 1967-70; instr. advt. U. Ill., 1970-71, vis. lectr. advt., 1977-84; v.p., dir. pubs. Farm Research Inst., Inc., Urbana, 1984—. Mem. Pres.'s Council, U. Ill. Found.; active Carle Hosp. Aux.; mem. adv. council Crescendo Club, Champaign Nat. Bank, 1985-86. Mem. Assn. for Edn. in Journalism and Mass Communications, Am. Acad. Advt., Friends of U. Ill. Found., Sigma Delta Chi, Kappa Tau Alpha. Republican. Presbyterian. Editor: James Webb Young Fund Newsletter, 1970-71; Occasional Papers in Advertising, 1971; The Sandage Family Cookbook, 1976, 2d edit., 1986; The Inkling, Carle Hosp. Aux. Newsletter, 1975-76. Home: 106 The Meadows Urbana IL 61801

SANDAHL, BONNIE BEARDSLEY, pediatric nurse practitioner; b. Washington, Jan. 17, 1939; d. Erwin Leonard and Carol Myrtle (Collis) B.; m. Glen Emil Sandahl, Aug 17, 1963; children—Cara Lynne, Cory Glen. B.S.N., U. Wash., 1962, M.N., 1974, cert. pediatric nurse practitioner, 1972. Dir. Wash. State Joint Practice Commn., Seattle, 1974-76; instr. pediatric nurse practitioner program U. Wash., Seattle, 1976, course coordinator quality assurance, 1977-78; pediatic nurse practitioner/health coordinator Snohomish County Head Start, Everett, Wash., 1975-77; clin. nurse educator (specialist) Harborview Med. Ctr., Seattle, 1978—, dir. child abuse prevention project, 1986—. Mem. Task Force on Pharmacotherapeutic Courses, Wash. State Bd. Nursing, 1985—; Puget Sound Health Systems Agy., 1975—, pres., 1980-82; mem. child devel. project adv. bd. Mukilteo Sch. Dist., 1984-85; mem. parenting adv. com. Edmonds Sch. Dist. chmn. hospice-home health task force Snohomish County Hospice Program, Everett, 1984-85, bd. dirs. hospice, 1985—; mem. Wash. State Health Coordinating, Council, 1977-82; mem. Nat. Council Health Planning and Devel., HHS, 1980—; mem. adv. com. on uncompensated care Wash. State Legislature, 1983-84; mem. Joint Select Com., Tech. Adv. Com. on Managed Health Care Systems, 1984-85. Pres., Alderwood Manor Community Council, 1983—; treas. Wash. Women's Polit. Caucus, 1983-84. Named Nurse of Yr., King County Nurses Assn., 1985; recipient Golden Acorn award Seattle-King County PTA, 1973. Mem. Am. Nurses Assn. (pediatric nurse practitioner subcom. Com. Examiners Maternal-child Nursing Practice, 1986—, hon. award), Wash. State Nurses Assn., King County Nurses Assn., Wash. State Soc. Pediatrics, Sigma Theta Tau. Democrat. Methodist. Home: 1814 200th St SW Alderwood Manor WA 98036 Office: Harborview Med Ctr 325 9th Ave MS ZA-53 Seattle WA 98104

SANDAHL, VIRGINIA CLARE, congressional aide; b. Alexandria, Va., June 1, 1945; d. Clifford Fredrick and Clara Alvina (Amend) S. A.A., Marion Jr. Coll., 1965; postgrad. U. Ga., 1966-67. Congl. aide to Congressman J. Rarick, U.S. Ho. of Reps., Washington, 1967-72, to Congressman W. Powell, 1972-74, to T. Guyer, 1974-81, to Delbert L. Latta, 1981—. Bd. dirs. Republican Women of Capitol Hill, 1979-80, v.p., 1980-81, pres., 1981-83; 1st v.p. Arlington County Republican Women, Arlington, Va., 1983-84. Recipient Fashion Show award Republican Women of Capitol Hill, 1984. Lutheran. Club: Jr. Woman's (3d v.p. 1985-86, pres. 1986-87) (McLean, Va.). Avocations: writing; reading; needlepoint; traveling. Home: 6803 Nesbitt Pl McLean VA 22101 Office: 2309 Rayburn House Office Bldg Washington DC 20515

SANDER, SUSAN BERRY, environmental engineering corporation executive; b. Walla Walla, Wash., Aug. 26, 1953; d. Alan Robert and Elizabeth Ann (Davenport) Berry; m. Dean Edward Sander, June 3, 1978. B.S. in Biology with honors, Western Wash. U., 1975; M.B.A. with honors, U. Puget Sound, 1984. Biologist, graphic artist Shapiro & Assocs., Inc., Seattle, 1975-77, office mgr., 1977-79, v.p., 1979-84, pres., 1984—, dir., 1980—. Merit scholar Overlake Service League, Bellevue, Wash., 1971, Western Wash. U., Bellingham, 1974, 75, U. Puget Sound, 1984. Mem. Soc. Mktg. Profl. Services, Seattle C. of C. Club: Washington Athletic (Seattle). Avocations: skiing; swimming; hiking; traveling; painting. Office: Shapiro & Assocs Inc 1812 Smith Tower Seattle WA 98104

SANDERLIN, OWENITA HARRAH, author, educator; b. Los Angeles, June 2, 1916; d. Owen Melville and Marigold (Whitford) H.; B.A. summa cum laude, Am. U., 1937; postgrad. U. Maine, U. Calif., San Diego State U.; m. George William Sanderlin, May 30, 1936; children—Frea Elizabeth, Sheila Mary, David George, John Owen. Freelance writer, speaker, 1940—; tchr. English, U. Maine, 1942, 46; head dept. speech and drama Acad. of Our Lady of Peace, San Diego, 1961-68; cons. gifted programs San Diego city schs., 1971-73, 80—; author: Jeanie O'Brien, 1965; Johnny, 1968; Creative Teaching, 1971; Teaching Gifted Children, 1973; Tennis Rebel, 1978; Match Point, 1979; co-author: Gifted Children: How to Identify and Teach Them, 1979. Recipient Poetry award Alpha Chi Omega, 1936; Double Ruby award Nat. Forensic League, 1965. Mem. Nat. Assn. Gifted Children, Assn. San Diego Educators of Gifted, San Diego Natural History Museum, Scripps Clinic and Research Found., Mortar Bd. Clubs: San Diego State U. Women's; Singing Hills Tennis. Address: 997 Vista Grande Rd El Cajon CA 92021

SANDERS, DORIS SAGAR, nursing administrator; b. Yonkers, N.Y., Mar. 26, 1924; d. Yates and Elizabeth (Megaughin) Sagar; m. Warren Herbert Sanders, Mar. 7, 1945 (div. 1961); children—Warren John, Kathleen Sanders Willson. R.N., R.I. Hosp., 1945; B.S. in Nursing, U. S.C., 1980; M.Health Scis., Med. U. S.C., 1984. Staff nurse Spartanburg Gen. Hosp., S.C., 1946-66, area supr., 1966-80; nursing adminstr. St. Luke's Hosp., Tryon, N.C., 1980-83; charge nurse Doctors Meml. Hosp., Spartanburg, 1983-84; nurse exec. assoc. AMI, Palm Beach Gardens, Fla., 1984-85; nursing adminstr. Byrd Meml. Hosp., Leesville, La., 1985—. Mem. Council on Aging, Spartanburg, 1966. Mem. Dist. 5 State Nurses Assn. (treas. 1947). Republican. Club: Pilot (Spartanburg). Lodge: Order Eastern Star. Avocation: amateur artist.

SANDERS, DOROTHY ELAINE, home nursing service executive, consultant; b. N.Y.C., Mar. 2, 1928; d. Fitzgerald Antonio and Daisy Belle (Mamby) Wiltshire; m. Frank N. Sanders, Nov. 13, 1949 (dec. Apr. 1979); children—Carolyn, Dorothea, Vera. A.S. in Applied Sci., N.Y.C. Tech. Coll., 1973; B.S. in Nursing, Medgar Evers Coll., Bklyn., 1986. Registered profl. nurse, N.Y. Staff nurse City Hosp., N.Y.C., 1958-60, asst. head nurse, 1977-82; head nurse nursing home, Bronx, N.Y., 1960-77; staff nurse pvt. hosp., N.Y.C., 1964-73; supr. nurse Home Attendant Programs, N.Y.C., 1982-84, asst. dir., 1984—; cons. home care, 1985—. Recipient service honor, social work service dept. Presbyterian Hosp., N.Y.C., 1985. Avocations: dancing; reading. Home: 2175 Lacombe Ave Bronx NY 10473 Office: Central Harlem Meals on Wheels HAP 2090 7th Ave New York NY 10027

SANDERS, ESTHER JEANNETTE, retired aerospace company executive; b. Ogden, Utah, Feb. 19, 1926; d. Warren Lynn and Esther Marguerite (Harris) Garner; B.A., U. Colo., 1948; m. Thomas Wesley Sanders, Jan. 10, 1946. With Calif., Inst., Tech. Coop. Wind Tunnel, Pasadena, 1948; with Sperry Gyroscope Co., Point Mugu, Calif., 1949-55; with Propulsion Research Corp., Santa Monica, Calif., 1955-57; with TRW, Redondo Beach, Calif., 1957-84, head engrng. test data analysis sect., retired. Home: 15405 Callahan Ranch Rd Reno NV 89511

SANDERS, FRANCES BEYER, ct. reporter; b. Iowa City, Iowa, June 11, 1923; d. Henry Frederick and Wilma Carolina (Beckjorden) Beyer; student Mason City Jr. Coll., 1942-43, Mcht. Marine Ct. Reporting Sch., 1944, Tampa U., 1945-46; m. James Chesley Sanders, Apr. 27, 1946; children—James Chesley, Gary H., Kari Mayre. Ct. reporter USCG, Tampa, Fla., 1944-46; freelance ct. reporter, Tampa, 1947-48; high sch. and adult edn. tchr. typing, shorthand and bookkeeping, Southport, N.C., 1953-54; office mgr. Yaupon Beach, Southport, 1954-59; legal sec., Juneau, Alaska, 1959-62; asst. sec. Alaska Senate, Juneau, 1962; freelance ct. reporter, operatior Taku Reporters, Juneau, 1962-86; co-owner, operator S & S Ceramics, 1978—. Bd. dirs. Juneau Receiving Home, 1970-73, Greater Juneau Arts and Humanities Council, 1968-71, 75—. Served with USCG, 1943-45. Decorated citation for outstanding performance of duty. Mem. Nat. Shorthand Reporters Assn. Democrat. Presbyterian. Clubs: Eastern Star; Women of Moose, Sons of Norway. Home: 9358 Lee Smith Dr Juneau AK 99803 Office: PO Box 2340 Juneau AK 99803

SANDERS, GLORIA JEAN, court reporter; b. Gainesville, Fla., Oct. 7, 1948; d. Clarence Richard and Betty Ellen (Lamb) S.; student U. S.C., 1978-82. Stenographer, FBI, Columbia, S.C., 1966-67; legal sec. Atty. Harvey L. Golden, Columbia, 1967-73; freelance typist, Columbia, 1971-75; court reporter S.C. Public Service Commn., Columbia, 1973-82; freelance court reporter, Columbia, 1974-82; pres. Sanders Stenographics, Orange, Tex., 1982—. Mem. Nat. Stenomask Verbatim Reporters Assn. (past pres., instr., cert. examiner, Cert. of Merit 1978, 3d place Nat. Speed Contest 1980, 1st place 1981, 82), DAR, Interesting Women in S.C. (founder, dir.). Club: Altrusa Internat. Office: PO Drawer 7 Orange TX 77630

SANDERS, JACQUELYN SEEVAK, psychologist, educator; b. Boston, Apr. 26, 1931; d. Edward Ezral and Dora (Zoken) Seevak; 1 son, Seth. B.A., Radcliffe Coll., 1952; M.A., U. Chgo., 1964; Ph.D., UCLA, 1972. Counselor, asst. prin. Orthogenic Sch., Chgo., 1952-65; research assoc. UCLA, 1965-68; cons. Osawatomie State Hosp. (Kans.), 1965-68; asst. prof. Ctr. for Early Edn., Los Angeles, 1969-72; assoc. dir. Sonia Shankman Orthogenic Sch., U. Chgo., 1972-73, dir., 1973—; curriculum cons. day care ctrs. Los Angeles Dept. Social Welfare, 1970-72; instr. Calif. State Coll., Los Angeles, 1972; lectr. dept. edn. U. Chgo., 1972-80, sr. lectr., 1980—; instr. tchr. edn. program Inst. Psychoanalysis, Chgo., 1979-82. Contbr. articles to profl. jours. UCLA Univ. fellow, 1966-68; Radcliffe Coll. Scholar, 1948-52. Mem. Am. Assn. Children's Residential Ctrs. (program chair 1977-79, treas. 1979-81), Am. Ednl. Research Assn., Am. Orthopsychiat. Soc., Am. Psychol. Assn., Nat. Soc. Study Edn. Jewish. Clubs: Quadrangle, Raquet (Hyde Park, Ill.). Home: 5842 S Stony Island Ave Apt 2G Chicago IL 60637

SANDERS, JANET LYNN, public relations exec.; b. Louisville, June 25, 1948; d. Lloyd Thomas and Willie Mae (Guinee) S.; B.A. with honors, Trinity Coll., Washington, 1970; M.A., U. Colo., Boulder, 1972. Writer/reporter Edn. Commn. States, Denver, 1972-73; copywriter/pub. relations asst. Mefford Weir Advt., Denver, 1973-77; writer/asst. account exec. Francis X. Kohler Pub. Relations, Marina del Rey, Calif., 1978-79; account exec. Reeds & Farris, Los Angeles, 1979; corp. pub. relations mgr. Allstate Savs. & Loan Assn., Glendale, Calif., 1979-81; nat. mktg. services mgr. Ticor Title Insurers, Los Angeles, 1981—; teaching asso. U. Colo., Boulder, 1972; instr. English, Community Coll. Denver, 1973. Mem. Women in Communications, Publicity Club Los Angeles. Office: Ticor Title Insurers 6300 Wilshire Blvd Los Angeles CA 90048

SANDERS, MARLENE, television correspondent; b. Cleve., Jan. 10, 1931; d. Mac and Evelyn R. (Menitoff) S.; student Ohio State U., 1948-50; m. Jerome Toobin, May 27, 1958 (dec. Jan. 1984); children—Jeff, Mark. Writer, producer various programs on WNEW-TV, N.Y.C., 1955-60, P.M. program Westinghouse Broadcasting Corp., N.Y.C., 1961-62; asst. dir. news and pub. affairs Radio Sta. WNEW, N.Y.C., 1962-64; news corr. ABC, 1964-72, producer numerous documentaries; writer, producer documentaries Children in Peril, 1972, Population: Boom or Doom, 1973, hour-long spl. Woman's Place (Golden Eagle certificate CINE, Clarion award), 1973, Womens Health: A Question of Survival, 1975, The Right to Die (Ohio State award, Front Page award, Writers Guild Am. award), 1974; v.p., dir. TV documentaries ABC News, 1976-78; corr., producer CBS Reports, CBS News, N.Y.C., 1978—; anchor woman, gen. corr. Saturday Edition Newsbreak, 1981—. Recipient Headliner award Nat. Press Club award for Lawyers: Guilty as Charged?: documentary, 1976, Matrix award N.Y. Women in Communications for outstanding achievement in broadcast industry, 1976, N.Y. State Broadcasters Assn. award, 1976, Deadline award Deadline Club of N.Y. chpt. Soc. Profl. Journalists, Sigma Delta Chi, 1977, 2 Emmy awards, others. Mem. Women in Communications (past pres.), Am. Women in Radio and TV, Women's Forum, Sigma Delta Chi. Office: CBS News 524 W 57th St New York NY 10019

SANDERS, MARVIS CLAIRE, travel journalist; b. Fairland, Okla., Dec. 10, 1930; d. Jacob Monroe and Jessie Augusta (James) England; m. Delmer Marion Sanders, Apr. 10, 1950; children—George Gregory, Marcia Lynn. Student Contra Costa Jr. Coll., 1968; B.A., Calif. State U.-Fresno, 1981; A.A., Coll. Sequoias, 1976. Library clk. City of Richmond, Calif., 1966-71; with Contra Costa County, Richmond; 1971; reporter Mineral King Publs., Exeter, Calif., 1971-80, editor, 1980-85. Leader, Campfire Girls, Richmond, 1964-66; chmn. Alvarado Sch. PTA Library, Richmond, 1962-68. Mem. Calif. Congress of Parents and Tchrs. (hon. life). Democrat.

SANDERS, MICHELE GARSIDE HENSILL, school system superintendent; b. Richmond, Calif., Nov. 10, 1942; d. John R. and Inez Sophia (Lonquist) Garside; B.A., Chico State U., 1964; M.A., San Francisco State U., 1973; postgrad. U. Calif., Berkeley; m. Steven Neil Sanders, Apr. 3, 1979. Tchr., Belmont and Richmond, Calif., 1964-76; adminstrv. asst. to supt. Belmont Sch. Dist., 1976-78, prin. Ralston Intermediate Sch., 1978-82, also dist. adminstr. communications; asst. supt. Portola Valley (Calif.) Sch. Dist., 1982-83; supt. Portola Valley Sch. Dist., 1983—; instr. U. Calif., Berkeley Extension, U. San Francisco, Dominican Coll., 1974-79; instr. art therapy Coll. Notre Dame; instr. San Francisco State U., 1983—; cons. theatre arts, motivation, communications, curriculum, mgmt. Co. mem. Lamplighters, San Jose Civic Light Opera, 1975—; bd. mgrs. Carlmont YMCA, 1978-80; pres. bd. dirs. Homeowners Assn., 1977-78; auctioneer Sta. KQED, 1976—; chmn. fin. Belmont Faculty Assn., 1975-76; bd. dirs. U. Calif. Berkeley Inst. Sch. Adminstrs. Bank of Am. grantee, 1979, 84. Mem. Assn. Calif. Sch. Adminstrs. (achievement award 1978), Assn. for Humanistic Psychology, Assn. Supervision and Curriculum Devel., Calif. Assn. Gifted, PTA (Service award 1981), Sierra Club, Alpha Delta Kappa, Phi Delta Kappa. Pub. Belmont Reports, 1976-78. Office: 4575 Alpine Rd Portola Valley CA 94107

SANDERS, PATRICIA KUTZER, municipal aide; b. Jacksonville, Fla., Mar. 16, 1953; d. Melvin Daniel and Rebecca Dean (Rogers) Kutzer; m. Michael Evans Monroe, Mar. 17, 1973 (div. 1980); 1 child, Aron Michelle; m. Johnny Michael Sanders, July 25, 1984. B.S.S., Fla. Jr. Coll., 1975. Sec. Jacksonville Electric Authority, 1975-76, sec. Office of Mayor, City of Jacksonville, 1976-78, adminstrv. asst., cons. pub. employees union negotiations 1980-82, adminstrv. asst. to city acct., 1978-79, adminstrv. asst. to city treas., 1979-80, council aide to City Council, 1980—. Author DAR essay, 1978. Mem. LWV, Jacksonville, 1985—, Jacksonville Women's Network, 1985—, Duvul Democratic Assn., Jacksonville, 1985—; pres., v.p. Lioness Club, Jacksonville, 1975. Mem. Profl. Secs. Assn. (v.p. 1980-81). Methodist. Avocations: raising plants, exercise, gunsmithing, home improvements. Home: 2061 Camden Ave Jacksonville FL 32207 Office: City Council Office 220 E Bay St Jacksonville FL 32202

SANDERS, PHYLLIS ADEN, radio/TV broadcaster; b. Buenos Aires, Argentina, June 27, 1919; d. Fred and Anna Almeda (Pettit) Aden; B.A., Occidental Coll., 1941; M.A., Scarritt Coll., 1943; m. Olcutt Sanders, Apr. 8, 1947; children—Lynn Edwin, Marta Almeda, Jay Olcutt, Fred Aden, R. Elizabeth. Formerly tchr.; lectr., workshop leader on changing roles of women, 1973-75; producer/host weekly radio interview show Changing World of Women, Sta. WNYC, N.Y.C., 1972-79; TV reporter/host/commentator on women's issues Sta. WNYC-TV, N.Y.C., 1975-78; regular weekly commentator Prime of Your Life, NBC-TV, N.Y.C., 1979-83; reporter Age Whys, AM Phila., Sta. WPVI-TV, 1981-83; producer, host weekly series Growing Older with Style, WCAU-TV, Phila., 1983—, feature reporter Noonbreak, 1983—; producer, host series on aging WHYY-TV, 1984—; reporter, interviewer TV series on aging, nat. PBS-TV. Community relations dir. Town of New Castle (N.Y.), 1972-73, originator, coordinator Community Day, New Castle, 1971; coordinator N.Y.C. women's adv. com. on meeting with network mgmt., 1976-77. Recipient award N.Y. chpt. NOW, 1973, N.J. Women, 1976; named to Phila. Mayor's Sr. Citizen Honor Roll, 1984. AFTRA, Nat. Acad. TV Arts and Scis., Women's Inst. for Freedom of Press, ACLU, Friends Com. on Nat. Legis., NOW, Older Women's League. Mem. Soc. of Friends. Home: 135 S 20th St #305 Philadelphia PA 19103

SANDERS, ROBIN RENEE, diplomat; b. Hampton, Va., July 5; d. Robert M. and Geneva (Machoney) Sanders. B.A., Hampton Inst.; M.A., Ohio U., 1979, M.S., 1979. Broadcast lic. FCC 3d class. Editor Essence Mag., N.Y.C., 1974-76, Fgn. Broadcast Info. Service, Washington, 1976-77; intern account exec. Burson-Marsteller Co., N.Y.C., 1977-78; pub. relations assoc. Seventeen mag., N.Y.C., 1979-80; polit. and counselor officer Am. embassy, Dominican Republic, 1980-83, consular officer Am. consulate, Oporto, Portugal, 1983-85; cons. Profl. Women's Seminar, 1983, 84; speaker U. Oporto, 1983; Oporto, lectr. Am. Lang. Inst., Oporto, 1983; researcher dept. internat. relations Ohio U., 1978; TV producer dept. gerontology Hampton Inst., 1976-77. Mem. Nat. Council Negro Women, 1980-82, Black Caucus, 1980—, Mus. African Art, 1980—. Recipient 1st place award for painting Two Faces, Scholastic Art Bd., 1981; journalism scholar Syracuse U, 1970. Mem. Women in Communications, Pub. Relations Soc. Am., Am. Fgn. Service Assn., Alpha Kappa Alpha, Alpha Kappa Mu. Consular Corps (Oporto); Diplomatic (Santo Domingo), Thursday Luncheon Group, Capital Press (Washington). Home: 110 E Bloomfield St Rome NY 13440 Office: Am Consulate Oporto Portugal APO NY NY 09678

SANDERS, SHARON MICHELLE, business official; b. Sheffield, Ala., Aug. 2, 1955; d. Charles William Sanders and Gloria Belle (Peters) Sanders Blount. B.A. in Theatre Arts, Calif. State U.-Fullerton, 1977. Sales rep. Bonne Bell Cosmetics, Lakewood, Ohio, 1973-79; sr. asst. mgr. Household Fin. Corp., Pasadena, Calif., 1980-82; sales rep. Drackett sub. Bristol-Myers, Cin., 1982-84; sales rep. Kerr Dental, Romulus, Mich., 1984-86, dist. mgr., 1986—. Recipient Miss Duarte award City of Duarte, Calif., 1972-73. Mem. Nat. Assn. Female Execs. Avocations: bicycling; reading; skiing. Home: 148 N Stedman Pl Monrovia CA 91016 Office: Kerr Dental Products 28200 Wiak Rd Romulus MI 48174

SANDERS, SUZANNE NANNETTE, nurse, health company executive; b. Tacoma, Mar. 17, 1945; d. Thomas Benton and Eleanor Nannette (Vaughan) Wilson; B.S. in Nursing with high honors, U. Tex., 1975; M.S., Tex. Woman's U., Houston, 1982; m. James L. Sanders, Jan. 25, 1974; children—Jeanene Cooper, Charlotte Cooper, Marilyn Cooper, Lindsey Sanders. Research asst. zoology dept. U. Tex., 1969-71, M.D. Anderson Hosp., Tex. Med. Center, Houston, 1971; nurse St. Joseph's Hosp., Houston, 1975; dir. nursing Richmond (Tex.) State Sch., 1979; pres., owner Liftercise Inc., Sugar Land, Tex., 1980—; mem. bd. Office of Early Childhood Devel., 1977, chmn. bd., 1980-81. Vice pres. Mcpl. Utility Dist. No. 13, 1980, bd. mem., 1977-81; mem. Mus. Natural Scis. Mem. Sigma Theta Tau. Democrat. Club: Sugar Land Lioness (charter mem.). Various radio and TV appearances: author: Liftercise: A Program for Women Using Weights with Exercise, 1980. Office: 339 Southwestern Blvd Sugar Land TX 77478

SANDERS-CLARDY, THELMA ELIZABETH, lawyer; b. Okemah, Okla., Jan. 11, 1955; d. Hobart Curtis and Maurine Yvonne (Lee) Sanders; m. James Edward Clardy, June 28, 1980 (div. Feb. 1986). B.S. cum laude, Tenn. State U., 1975; J.D., Tex. So. U., 1979. Bar: Tex. 1979. Law clk. NASA, Houston, 1977; sec. to dean women Tenn. State U., Nashville, 1976; staff atty. Office for Civil Rights, U.S. Dept. Edn., Dallas, 1979—. Bd. dirs. N.Central Tex. Legal Services Found., Dallas, 1982-84; mem. policy council Dallas Area Women's Polit. Caucus, 1983-85. Recipient Pro Bono award Dallas Bar Assn. and N. Central Tex. Legal Services Found., 1983. Mem. United for Action (parliamentarian 1983, mem. of yr. 1982), ABA, Tex. State Bar, Dallas Bar Assn., Dallas Assn. Black Women Attys. (pres. 1981-83). Democrat. Baptist. Home: 6526 Maryibel Circle Dallas TX 75237 Office: Office for Civil Rights Dept Edn 1200 Main Tower Suite 1930 Dallas TX 75202

SANDERSON, GLENDA JOYCE, histotechnologist; b. Chickasha, Okla., Feb. 2, 1947; d. Parley Ohlow and Christine Tula (Cornelius) Sanderson; cert. histology Wesley Med. Center, 1971; student Labette County Community Jr. Coll., 1974-75. Staff histologic technician Associated Labs., Wichita, Kans., 1971-74; head histology dept. Labette County Med. Center, Parsons, Kans., 1974-76; chief histotechnologist Hertzler Clinic, Halstead, Kans., 1976—. Mem. Nat. Soc. for Histotech., Inc. (charter mem., region V sec., health, safety, membership coms., chmn. nomination and election com., Kans. del. to ho. of dels., past mem. awards com.), Kans. Soc. for Histotech., Inc. (pres. 1982—, past pres., sec., chairperson of membership com., charter mem.), Am. Soc. Clin. Pathologists (affiliate mem., cert. histologic technician and histotechnologist). Baptist. Home: 725 Spruce Apt #4 Halstead KS 67056 Office: 327 Chestnut St Halstead KS 67056

SANDERSON, SANDRA LEE, computer software executive; b. Los Angeles, Nov. 28, 1944; d. Carl Foree and Mildred Anna (Bailey) S.; m. Willis L. Pitkin, Jr., June 9, 1965 (div. 1981; children—Joseph Reeves, Sara Love, Mara Faith; m. Howard Grant Sanderson, July 19, 1983. B.A., Whittier Coll., 1965, M.A., 1966. Reading specialist Whittier Sch. Dist., 1966-69; real estate agt., Logan, Utah, 1979-80; owner Gold Key Realty, Logan, 1981-82; real estate broker, mgr. Caldwell Banker, Logan, 1982-83; founder Sanderson Data Systems, Soquel, Calif., 1983—; nat. trainer Women's Council Realters, Chgo., 1984—. Contbr. articles to profl. jours. Recipient Realtor of Yr. award Logan Bd. Realtors, 1981; Pres.'s award Utah State Women's Council Realtors, 1983; Woman of Yr. award Logan Bd. Women Council Realtors, 1983. Democrat. Quaker. Avocations: ice skating; skiing; hiking; learning; astrology. Home: 1730 Day Valley Rd Aptos CA 95003 Office: Sanderson Data Systems 2912 Daubenbiss Soquel CA 95073

SANDIN, CAROLINE TOWLEY, county commissioner; b. St. Peter, Minn., Nov. 18, 1915; d. Gabriel Heiberg and Victoria Louise (Almen) Towley; m. Howard Victor Sandin, July 20, 1941; children—Caroline, Howard II, Sarah, Victoria, Catherine, Martha, Elizabeth. Student pub. schs. Comml. instr. S.W. Bell Telephone Co., East St. Louis, Ill., 1941-44; comml. rep. N.W. Bell Telephone Co., Shakopee, Minn., 1939-41; part-time clk. Windmill Art Gallery, Ashland, Wis., 1983—; county commr. Ashland County Bd., 1978—. Pres., founder LWV, Ashland, 1956-60; mem., pres. Bd. Edn., Ashland, 1961-83; mem. bd. regents U. Wis. system, Madison, 1968-77; mem. Ashland Common Council, 1978—; mem. bd. visitors U. Wis.-Superior, 1978—, pres., 1983-85; mem. Bay Area Rural Transit Commn., 1978—, v.p., 1978, sec., 1984-85; mem. Family Forum Bd., 1984—; mem. Unified Services Bd., 1980—, pres., 1985—. Recipient Disting. Alumni award U. Wis.-Superior, 1977. Named Woman of Yr., C. of C., 1979; Outstanding Citizen of Yr., Chequamegon VFW, 1984. Republican. Lutheran. Club: Rod and Gun (Ashland). Home: 703 W 7th St Ashland WI 54806

SANDLAN, BRENDA CHAMBERLIN, nurse; b. Brattleboro, Vt., Sept. 1, 1948; d. Thomas and Bernice (Fairbanks) Chamberlin; A.L.A., Pensacola Jr. Coll., 1973, A.S. in Nursing, 1973; B.S., St. Joseph's Coll., Maine, 1980. Nursing asst. Brattleboro (Vt.) Meml. Hosp., 1965-66, practical nurse, 1967-69; nurse Extended Care Facility, Tallahassee, 1969-71, Univ. Hosp., Pensacola, Fla., 1971-73; nurse Reconstrn. Home, Ithaca, 1974-75; relief indsl. nurse Nat. Cash Register Co., Ithaca, 1975-76 Ithaca Gun Co., 1976; charge nurse, relief supr. Oak Hill Manor Nursing Home, Ithaca, 1976-77, asst. dir. nursing services, 1977-81, dir. nursing services, 1981—, nurse coordinator, 1981—. Health cons. Tompkins County Agrl. and Hort. Soc.; mem. adv. com. profl. nursing program Tompkins-Cortland Community Coll.; religious edn. instr. Roman Cath. Ch.; vol. ARC, 1967, nurse, 1974, chpt. chairperson, 1979-81; mem. Vt. State 4-H Hon. Soc. Mem. Nurses United for a Respectfully Supportive Environ., Cath. Daus. Am. Office: Oak Hill Manor Nursing Home 602 Hudson St Ithaca NY 14850

SANDMAN, KATHLEEN ELLEN, chiropractic physician, writer; b. Warren, Ohio, June 4, 1947; d. Cecil Ford and Ethel M. (Rayle) Parthemer; m. Peter Terrance Betras, May 13, 1967 (div. July 1977); children—Jennifer Jacqueline, Robin Nicole; m. 2d, Terry Dale Sandman, Sept. 1, 1979 (div. Mar. 1984); 1 son, Jason Terrence. Student Geneva Coll., Beaver Falls, Pa., 1966-67, Youngstown U. (Ohio), 1971-73; D.C., Nat. Coll. Chiropractic, Lombard, Ill., 1977, B.S. in Human Biology, 1977. Mem. faculty Nat. Coll. Chiropractic, 1979-81; writer biomed. communications, 1981-83; owner, clinic dir. Sandman Chiropractic Clinic, Wheaton, Ill., 1982—. Contbr. articles to profl. jours. Mem. Am. Med. Writers Assn., Am. Chiropractic Assn., Nat. Coll. Alumni Assn., Ill. Chiropractic Assn., AAUW, Women in Mgmt., Nat. Assn. Women Bus. Owners. Office: Sandman Chiropractic Clinic 233 E Ontario St Chicago IL 60611

SANDS, BARBARA LEE, golf company executive, outdoor writer; b. N.Y.C., June 28, 1932; d. Jack D. and Hylda A. (Aptheker) Levine; student Hunter Coll., 1949-52; m. Lawrence Sands, Apr. 6, 1968; children—David, Lori, Doria. Mng. editor True Experience Mag., 1968-70; outdoor editor Sporting Guide mag., 1970-71; N.Y. State editor, columnist Outdoor Jour., 1970—; outdoor video news reporter WFMJ-TV; pres. Par-Mate Golf Gloves, 1972—; corp. dir. Jack D. Levine Inc.; freelance writer various nat. outdoor mags. Mem. Outdoor Writers Assn. Am., N.Y. State Outdoor Writers Assn. (Excellence of Craft award for outstanding achievement 1982), Nassau County Outdoor Writers Assn., Mensa. Office: Par-Mate 4 Willow Park Ctr Farmingdale NY 11735

SANDS, KITI, financier, designer, realtor, beauty/health consultant; b. N.J.; d. Frank and Muriel (Kulla) Reiner; m. Ira Sands, 1975; children—Nelson Anthony, Tiffany Ivy, Summer Paige. Cosmetology and Estheticians Sch., 1962, Wilsey Sch. Design, 1974, NYU, 1974. Cert. cosmetologist and esthetician, 1962. Asst. to Monsieur Jacques as dir. of Antoines de Paris; pres. La Grande Femme Inc.; ptnr. Claredon Capital Group, N.Y., Fla.; pres. Tiffany Ivy Yacht Interiors Inc., Tiffany Ivy Interiors Inc., Tiffany Sands, Inc.; pres. Bio Cellular Systems, Inc., 1981; v.p. New Capital Properties, Inc., New Capital Mgmt. Inc., 1980—; sec., dir. L.K. Inc., Fla.; design and costume cons., N.Y.C., 1974—; propr. Park Ave. Salon for Hair Color Cons., N.Y.C., 1974-81; dir. Bio-Med Acne Ctr., Fla.; commr. of deeds N.Y.C., to 1981; researcher and developer of skin care and haircoloring processes and formulae, columnist and feature writer; lectr. on image creation for the working person, including Dressing For Your Career. Aquacade swimmer, 1960-62. Recipient Disting. Service citation Indsl. Home for Blind, 1976; Disting. Mem. award City of Hope, 1977; Cert. Achievement for Acad. and Inst. by Clairol; Clairol Certs. of award for Outstanding Hair Coloring Expertise; Certs. Achievement for Higher Edn. in the art of Profl. Coloring. Mem. Congress of Colorist (qualified), Ind. Cosmetic Mfrs. and Distbrs. Office: Miami FL

SANDS, LU ALICE, librarian; b. Montgomery County, Tenn., Dec. 30, 1926; d. Bailey Gay and Betty Marable (Minor) Lyle; m. John Earl Sands, Nov. 25, 1947; 1 child, Alan Minor. B.A., George Peabody Coll., 1947; M.A., Fla. State U., 1961; postgrad. Emory U., 1967, Oxford U., Eng., summer 1983. Head children's services South Ga. Regional Library, Valdosta, 1956-59; dir. library and learning resources North Fla. Jr. Coll., Madison, 1960—; cons. in field. Trustee Suwannee River Region Library, Live Oak, Fla., 1972-74. Mem. Fla. Library Assn., Southeastern Library Assn. Democrat. Methodist. Author: Basic Materials for Junior College Libraries: Books: Philosophy, Religion, Art, and Music, 1963. Editor: Fla. Libraries, 1971-72. Home: 115 Hancock St SE Madison FL 32340 Office: North Florida Jr Coll Madison FL 32340

SANDSTROM, ALICE WILHELMINA, accountant; b. Seattle, Jan. 6, 1914; d. Andrew William and Agatha Mathilda (Sundius) S.; B.A., U. Wash., 1934. Office mgr. Star Machinery Co., Seattle, 1935-43, Howe & Co., Seattle, 1943-46; practice as C.P.A., Seattle, 1945—; controller Children's Orthopedic Hosp. and Med. Center, Seattle, 1948-75, asso. adminstr. fin., 1975-81; lectr. U. Wash., Seattle, 1957-72. Mem. Wash. State Title XIX Adv. Com., 1975-82; mem. Wash. State Vendors Rate Adv. Com., 1980—; mem. Mayor's Task Force for Small Bus., 1981-83; pres. Seattle YWCA, 1986—; bd. dirs. YWCA, Seattle, 1981—, Children's Orthopedic Hosp. Found., 1982—; Sr. Services Seattle King County, 1985, treas., 1986. C.P.A., Wash. Fellow Hosp. Fin. Mgmt. Assn. (charter; state pres. 1956-57, nat. treas. 1963-65, Robert H. Reeves merit award 1970, Frederick T. Muncie award 1985), Wash. State Hosp. Assn. (treas. 1956-70), Am. Soc. Women Accts. (pres. Seattle 1946-48), Am. Soc. Women C.P.A.s. Club: Women's Univ. (Seattle). Home and Office: 5725 NE 77th St Seattle WA 98115

SANDSTROM, BODEN (BARBARA) C., sound engineer; b. Rochester, N.Y., Sept. 19, 1945; d. Louis Charles and Marion (Gridley) S.; B.A. (N.Y. State Regents scholar 1963-67), St. Lawrence U., 1967; A.M.L.S. (Work-Study scholar), U. Mich., 1968; grad. in Synergetic Audio Concepts, Washington, 1977, grad. in advanced rec. Omega Rec. Studio, Silver Spring, Md., 1977. M.S. in Audio Tech., Am. U., 1984. Librarian, San Jose State Coll., 1968-69; head circulation dept. Northeastern U. Library, 1969-72; librarian lit. div. Martin Luther King Library, Washington, 1972-75; owner, operator Woman Sound, Inc., Washington, 1975—; sound engr. Mich. Women's Music Festival, 1977-78, 81-84, Nat. Women's Writers Conf., 1977, 3d, 4th, 5th and 7th Nat. Women's Music Festivals, West Coast and So. Women's Music and Comedy Festivals, 1981-84, 82, Am. Folk Life Festivals, 1981, 83, Lilly Tomlin tour, 1983, Chris Williamson tour, 1982, Casse Culver tour, 1980; tchr. concert sound engrng. privately and at Am. U.; office mgr. Female Liberation, Boston, 1970-72. Mem. Audio Engring. Soc., Acoustical Soc. Am., Nat. Assn. Women Bus. Owners, Mortar Bd. Home: 19 Logan Circle A NW Washington DC 20005 Office: PO Box 1932 Washington DC 20013

SANDWEISS, MARTHA A., museum curator, author; b. St. Louis, Mar. 29, 1954; d. Jerome Wesley and Marilyn Joy (Glik) S.; B.A. magna cum laude, Radcliffe Coll., 1975; M.A. in History, Yale U., 1977, M. Phil. in History, 1981, Ph.D., 1985. Smithsonian-Nat. Endowment Humanities fellow, Nat. Portrait Gallery, Washington, 1975-76; curator photographs Amon Carter Mus., Ft. Worth, 1979—. Author: Carlotta Corpron: Designer with Light, 1980; Masterworks of American Photography, 1982; Laura Gilpin: An Enduring Grace, 1986; catalogue Pictures from an Expedition: Early Views of the American West, 1979; editor: Historic Texas: A Photographc Portrait, 1986; Contemporary Texas: A Photographc Portrait, 1986. Ctr. for Am. Art and Material Culture fellow Yale U., 1977-79. Office: Amon Carter Mus PO Box 2365 Fort Worth TX 76113

SANDY, CATHERINE ELLEN, librarian; b. Italy; d. Felice Antonio and Guglielma Elena Santaniello; student Rosary Coll., 1933-34, U. Florence, Italy, 1951; B.S., Columbia U., 1953. Librarian, Port Washington (N.Y.) Pub. Library, 1926-73. Bd. dirs. Art Adv. Council, Port Washington Pub. Library; trustee, charter mem. Cow Neck Peninsula Hist. Soc. Recipient Alumni medal Columbia, 1970. Mem. Am., N.Y., N.C. library assns., UN Assn., Gen. Studies Alumni Assn. Columbia. Roman Catholic. Editor: Cow Neck Peninsula Hist. Jour. Home: 35 Davis Rd Port Washington NY 11050

SANFORD, ISABEL GWENDOLYN, actress; b. N.Y.C., Aug. 29; d. James Edward and Josephine (Perry) S.; m. William Edward Richmond (dec.); children—Pamela (Mrs. Eddie Ruff), William Eric, Sanford Keith. Ed. pub. schs. Stage appearances in Off-Broadway prodns., also in, Los Angeles; Broadway appearance in Amen Corner; films appearances include Guess Who's Coming to Dinner, 1968, Pendulum, 1969, Stand Up and Be Counted, 1972, The New Centurions, 1972, Love at First Bite, 1979; TV appearances include Supertrain; co-star The Jeffersons, 1974 . Mem. Kwanza Found. Address. care Lemack & Co 7060 Hollywood Blvd 206 Los Angeles CA 90028

SANFORD, PEGGY POWELL, lawyer, educator; b. Ft. Myers, Fla., Feb. 25, 1945; d. W.E. and Florabelle (Loveless) Powell; m. Robert A. Sanford, Oct. 7, 1967; children—Jacob John, Daniel Douglas. B.A., Miss. State U., 1967; M.A., Pepperdine U., Los Angeles, 1973; J.D., Fla. State U., 1981. Bar: Fla., 1981. Intern Office State Atty., 2nd Jud. Cir., Quincy, Fla., 1981; assoc. Woods,

Johnston & Carlson, Tallahassee, 1981-82; forensic gen. counsel Fla. State Hosp., Chattahoochee, Fla., 1982-83, legal counsel, 1983—; city atty., Malone, Fla., 1982—; adj. prof. Fla. A&M U., Tallahassee, Fla., 1975-79, 82—; instr. Chipola Jr. Coll. Law Enforcement Tng. Ctr., Marianna, Fla., 1981-85; psychologist Jackson County Guidance Clinic, Marianna, Fla., 1973-75; staff Psychologist Arthur G. Dozier Sch., Marianna, 1975-78. Bd. dirs. Jackson County Guidance Clinic, 1983-85. Mem. ABA, Panhandle Bar Assn., Order of Coif. Democrat. Presbyterian. Club: Pilot (Marianna) Home: 227 Sylvia Dr Marianna FL 32446 Office: Florida State Hosp Chattahoochee FL 32324

SANFORD, RUTH COOPER, educator, counselor; b. North Warren, Pa., Dec. 26, 1906; d. Elden Oscar and Elma Miretta (Dorn) Cooper; B.A., Lebanon Valley Coll., 1930; M.A., Columbia U., 1938; postgrad. N.Y. U., Rutgers U., Columbia U.; m. Daniel Seymour Sanford, Aug. 7, 1940; 1 dau., Mei-Mei Elma Cooper. Tchr., head dept. English, Lakewood (N.Y.) High Sch., 1930-37; asst. to sec. Tchrs. Coll., Columbia U., 1938-40; guidance officer, assoc. prof. We. Md. Coll., Westminster, Md., 1944-49; dir. guidance and counseling services Lakewood (N.J.) High Sch., 1952-55; chmn. guidance and counseling services, West Hempstead, N.Y., 1955-72; co-dir. Center Interpersonal Growth, Port Jefferson, N.Y., 1979—; adj. prof. LIU, 1972—, Hofstra U., 1980—, Union for Experimenting Colls. and Univs., 1986—; facilitator person-centered workshops with Dr. Carl R. Rogers, U.S. and abroad, 1978—. Recipient Peter Zenger award in pub. service and journalism, 1976, award for outstanding contbn. to edn. Lebanon Valley Coll., 1975; named Counselor of Yr., N.Y. State Assn. Counseling and Devel., 1976. Mem. Am. Assn. Counseling and Human Devel., N.Y. State Assn. Counseling and Human Devel., Assn. Humanistic Edn., Assn. Humanistic Psychology, Assn. for Devel. Person-Centered Approach. Democrat. Author: Creativity and Intelligence: Implications for Counselors, 1965; Intimacy in a Person-Centered Way of Being: Paradigm for Change, 1982; Unconditional Positive Regard: A Misunderstood Way of Being, 1984; Evolution of Client-Person Centered Psychotherapy, 1985; co-author (with Dr. Carl Rogers) Journey to the Heart of Africa, 1982; contbg. author: Freedom to Learn (Carl R. Rogers), 1983; Comprehensive Textbook of Psychiatry IV, 1985; weekly columnist As I See It, 1975-81. Home and Office: 2023 Cecilia Pl Seaford NY 11783

SANGER, MARY ROSE, computer educator; b. Waukesha, Wis., Nov. 19, 1951; d. Joseph Louis and Mary (Recs) Inzeo; m. Richard Edgar Sanger, July 19, 1975; 1 child, Kristin Mary. B.S. magna cum laude, Carroll Coll., 1974. Lic. tchr., Wis. Tchr. St. Mary Sch., Waukesha, 1974-83; computer cons. All About Computers, Hales Corner, Wis., 1983—; pres. KMR Computer Classrooms, Hales Corners, 1983—; tchr. St. Mary Sch., Hales Corners, 1984—. Treas. Hales Corners Friends of Library, 1984-85, v.p., 1985—; friend Pub. Broadcasting System TV, Milw., 1982—; del. 2d level Wis. Democratic Caucus, Milw., 1984; campaign worker Adelman for Congress, Hales Corners, 1984. Mem. Nat. Fedn. Ind. Bus. Roman Catholic. Avocations: cross country skiing; bicycling; reading. Home: 10833 W Liberty St Hales Corners WI 53130 Office: KMR Computer Classrooms Inc 5665 S 108th St Hales Corners WI 53130

SANJABI, SHEILA RUTH, educational administrator; b. Worcester, Mass., Feb. 3, 1944; d. Walter John and Virginia Clare (Weller) Dulmaine; m. Fereidun Bakhtiar Sanjabi, Dec. 19, 1966 (div. Oct. 1976). Diplome, Universite D'Aix Marseilles, Aix-en-Provence, France, 1964; B.S., Georgetown U., 1965; J.D., Am. U., 1980. Bar: D.C. 1981. Documentation coordinator Communications Satellite Corp., Washington, 1965-69; dir. bus. affairs Nat. Assn. Coll. and Univ. Bus. Officers, Washington, 1969-83; comptroller Chaminade U., Honolulu, 1983—. Mem. ABA, Nat. Assn. Coll. and Univ. Bus. Officers, D.C. Bar Assn. Home: 430 Keoniana St Apt 709 Honolulu HI 96815 Office: St Louis-Chaminade Edn Ctr 3140 Waialae Ave Honolulu HI 96816

SANJENKO, GRACE LORETTA, health adminstrator; b. Saskatoon, Can., Jan. 9, 1943; d. Fred and Ruth SanJ.; came to U.S., 1963; B.S., Calif. State U., Northridge, 1971, M.S.P.H., 1973; M.P.A., U. So. Calif., 1978; m. Malcolm David Cobb, May 21, 1978. Tech. editor Children's Hosp. Los Angeles, 1972-73; adminstrv. asst. Central Los Angeles Health Project, 1973; dist. dir. community health edn. Los Angeles County Dept. Health Services, 1973-75; mem. faculty dept. health sci. Calif. State U., Northridge, 1974—, faculty supr. grad. resident and intern program, 1974—; risk mgr. Los Angeles County Dept. Health Services, 1975-78; assoc. prof. Chapman Coll., 1978—, dir. Office Quality Assurance, Children's Hosp. Los Angeles, 1980-81; adminstr. health programs Internat. Tech. Corp., 1984-85; pres. Med. Risk Mgmt. Assocs., 1985—. Mem. Am. Public Health Assn., Soc. Profl. Health Educators (nat. chpt. rep. 1976-78), Los Angeles County Health Assn. (v.p. 1974-76), Am. Mgmt. Assn., Am. Hosp. Assn. Risk Mgrs. Author: Implementation of Risk Management for Reduction of Malpractice Costs in Public Hospitals, 1977. Home: 13212 Schoenborn St Sun Valley CA 91352 Office: Chapman Coll Regional Edn Center WLA 8740 La Tijera Blvd Los Angeles CA 90045

SANNA, LUCY JEAN, writer; b. Menomonie, Wis., Apr. 20, 1948; d. Charles Albert and Margaret Sheila (McGee) S.; B.A., St. Norbert Coll., 1969; postgrad. U. Wis., Madison, 1970-74; m. Peter Lawrence Frisch, Jan. 2, 1971; 1 dau., Katherine Sanna. Asst. editor Scott Foresman & Co., Glenview, Ill., 1970-73; freelance editor, Palo Alto, Calif., 1973-75; editor FMC Corp., San Jose, Calif., 1975-78; supr. corp. advt. Memorex Corp., Santa Clara, Calif., 1978-79, exec. presentations adminstr., 1979; mgr. communications services Electric Power Research Inst., Palo Alto, 1980—. Mem. adv. council Energy Source Edn. Program; mem. Calif. Energy Edn. Forum. Office: EPRI PO Box 10412 Palo Alto CA 94303

SANNER, ALICE MATHILDA, machine tool co. exec.; b. Dubuque, Iowa, Oct. 31, 1913; d. Louis A. and Emma (Gross) Sanner; grad. high sch., Dubuque. With Rockford Machine Tool Co. (Ill.) subs. Greenlee Bros. & Co., 1942—, advt. mgr., 1946-75, ret., 1975, editor Hot Chips mag., 1951-80, also advt. mgr. Machine Tool Products-Greenlee Group, 1972-75; editor publ. Greenleaves, 1972-75. Mem. Rockford Art Assn., Chgo. Art Inst., Orch. Guild of Rockford Symphony Orch., Inc., Rockford Mus. Assn., Friends of Rockford Mus., Cath. Woman's League, St. James Altar and Rosary Soc., No. Ill. Communicators. Roman Catholic. Contbr. short stories coll. and popular publs. Home: 122 N Chicago Ave Rockford IL 61107

SANS, JUDITH, cosmetics manufacturing and salon francise executive; b. Hungary, Feb. 13, 1930; came to U.S., 1936; d. Michael Dubosh and Elaina Takache; children—David, Daniel. Ed. Monmouth Coll., 1953. Vice pres. Belmar Motors, from 1951; v.p. sales Magnolia Inn, from 1960; pres. Atlantis Isle of Beauty, Inc., from 1963, Fair Lady, Inc., from 1967; founder, pres. Judith Sans Internationale, Inc., Atlanta, 1968—; dir. skin care Glemby Internat., from 1973; cons. skin care; guest speaker, lectr., worldwide; TV, radio appearances; del. to confer on nutrition, health and diet U.S. Dept. Commerce to Poland and Romania, 1968, to China, 1979, also Egypt and Moscow; dir. tng. seminars Stellenbosch Acad. South Africa, 1980; founder Sans Inst. Internat., Inc., Atlanta, 1982; mem. adv. bd. cosmetologists and aestheticians State of Ga. 1982-83. Columnist Atlanta Women's News, 1984—; author book; featured in newspapers, mags., worldwide; developed products for use in U.S. Winter Olympics, 1980; Pres. Reagan's liaison to pvt. sector for initiative on women bus. owners, 1984; liaison for pvt. sector SBA, 1983; mem. U.S. Commn. on Aging, HHS, 1984—; mem. DeKalb County Communications Com. (Ga.), 1983—; mem. econ. task force com. Ga. Sec. of state 1983-84; mem. bus. adv. com. for mktg. and distributive edn. Ga. State U., Atlanta, 1983-84; chairperson Enterprise Atlanta, 1983—; mem. fundraising com. Atlanta Cancer Soc.; bd. dirs. Women's Bus. Owners Ednl. Council, State of Ga., 1984—. Named Woman Bus. Owner of Yr., 1980, 81; recipient awards various cosmetic cos. Mem. Com. of 200, Atlanta Women Bus. Owners (pres. 1981-82), Committee Internationale de Esthetique et de Cosmetology (founding), Committee Internationale de Esthetique et de Cosmetology pioneer mem. U.S. chpt.), Aestheticians Internat. Assn., South African Inst. Health and Beauty Therapists, KOSMETIK, Internationale de Esthetica Bologna (Italy), Societe les esthetique (Paris), Soc. Aroma Therapy—Herbal Ltd. of Eng., Brit. Confedn. Estheticians, Fashion Group (Atlanta chpt.), Internat. Visitors (Atlanta chpt.), Sigma Pi Epsilon. Clubs: Atlanta Women's Commerce (founder, dir.), One Hundred. Office: Judith Sans Internationale 3853 Oakcliffe Industrial Ct Atlanta GA 30340

SANSBURY, PAMELA ALTMAN, computer supply industry executive; b. Greensboro, N.C., May 1, 1953; d. James Albert and Lila Doris (Farmer) Altman; m. Robert Alan Sansbury, June 5, 1976. B.S. in Home Econs., Miss. State U.-Starkville, 1974. With buyers tng. program Sanger-Harris, Dallas, 1975-78; saleswoman Sandy Hancock Enterprises, Dallas, 1978-79; dist. mgr. Syncom div. Schwan Sales, Dallas, 1979-82; regional mgr. Wabash DataTech, Inc., Dallas, 1982-85; nat. sales mgr. Perfect Data Corp., 1985—. Republican. Methodist.

SANSING, MARIANNE HIGGINS, advertising agency executive; b. LaGrange, Ga., July 1, 1952; d. William Charles and Margaret Louise (Wall) H.; m. Robert Alex Sansing, Sept. 7, 1974; 1 dau., Christy Robin. B.F.A., Auburn U., 1974. Artist, Auburn U., 1974-75; mgr. The Framery, Pensacola, Fla., 1975-76; art dir. So. Pub. Co., Pensacola, Fla., 1976-78; asst. art dir. Dodson, Craddock & Born, Pensacola, Fla., 1978-80, account exec., 1980—. Vice pres., bd. dirs. Gulf Coast Children's Med. Found., Pensacola, 1981-84, Fla.'s Jr. Miss, Inc., Pensacola, 1982-84. Mem. Fla. Pub. Relations Assn., W. Fla. Advt. Council. Baptist. Home: 1105 Peperidge Dr Pensacola FL 32504 Office: Dodson Craddock & Born Advt Inc 4711 Scenic Hwy Pensacola FL 32504

SANTANDREA, MARY FRANCES, lawyer; b. Melrose Park, Ill., Apr. 14, 1952; d. Francis Paul and Agnes Rose (Franch) S. B.A. (James scholar), U. Ill.-Urbana, 1974, M.A., 1976; J.D. cum laude, Santa Barbara Coll. Law, 1982. Bar: Calif. 1982. Legal researcher Cavalletto, Webster, Mullen & McCaughey, Santa Barbara, Calif., 1979-80; legal researcher M.J. Treman, Santa Barbara, 1980-81; legal researcher Bargiel & Carlson, Santa Barbara, 1981-82; research atty. Halde, Thomas, Kallman & Hulse, Santa Barbara, 1982-83; litigation atty. Anderson & Geller, Santa Ana, Calif., 1983-85, Ambrosi & Lavoie 1985-86, Smith & Smith, Costa Mesa, Calif., 1986—. Mem. ABA, Orange County Bar Assn., Orange County Women Lawyer's Assn. Democrat. Roman Catholic. Office: Smith & Smith 695 Town Center Dr Costa Mesa CA 92626

SANTANGELO, ANNE CELESTE, public relations, career placement company executive; b. Norristown, Pa., Feb. 12, 1943; d. Alphonso and Anna Margaret (Kramer) Santangelo; m. Elhag M. Hamed, July 14, 1985. B.A. in History, Cabrini Coll., 1965; M.L.S., U. Wash., 1966; Cert. Bus. Data Processing, U. Calif.-Berkeley, San Francisco, 1982. Lic. profl. librarian, N.Y. Children's librarian N.Y. Pub. Library, N.Y.C., 1972-74; coordinator children's services Contra Costa County Library System, Pleasant Hill, Calif., 1974-80; personnel counselor Pacific Personnel Service, San Francisco, 1980; placement rep. Control Data Inst., San Francisco, 1980-82; data processing recruiter Allied Recruiters, San Francisco, 1982-83; owner, operator St. Angelo Resume and Small Bus. Service, San Francisco, 1982—; symposium storyteller N.Y. Pub. Library, 1974. Mem. Nat. Assn. Female Execs., ALA (counselor-at-Large 1972-74, chmn. children's services div. booksellers and book distbrs. liaison com. 1971-73), Calif. Library Assn. (bd. dirs., exec. bd. children's services div.), N.Y. Library Assn. (scholarship com. 1970-73), Westchester Library Assn. (publicity chmn. 1971). Address: 1635 Gough St Apt 104 San Francisco CA 94109

SANTANGELO, SUSAN HILLEBRANDT, educational administrator; b. Houston, Oct. 29, 1937; d. Leslie Robert and Anne Delilah (Corrigan) Hillebrandt; m. Donald Kenneth Roberts, July 2, 1960 (div. 1963); m. 2d, Giuseppe Salvatore Santangelo, July 11, 1968; 1 son, Giuseppe Salvatore. B.A., Wellesley Coll., 1959; postgrad. Boston U., 1960; M.A., U. Houston, 1966. Tchr., Westford Acad. (Mass.), 1959-60, Needham High Sch., 1960-62; spl. events dir. Tiffany & Co., Houston, 1963-67; fgn. student advisor U. Houston, 1967-72; dean of girls Kinkaid Sch., Houston, 1976—; cons., writer After Dinner Players, Houston, 1963—. Author: For Friends & Then Some, 1966; Kinkaid and Houston: 75 Years, 1981. Mem. Houston Model Cities Bd., 1972; judge Christian Scriptwriters Contest, Mpls., 1977; Mem. Am. Assn. for Counseling and Devel., Houston Ballet Assn. Episcopalian. Clubs: River Oaks Tennis, Downtown (v.p. 1979-80) (Houston). Office: The Kinkaid Sch 201 Kinkaid School Dr Houston TX 77024

SANTEE, CAROL ANN, nurse; b. South Bend, Ind., Jan. 11, 1950; d. Joseph F. and Shirley M. (Carter) Buzolitz; m. James Howard Santee, Oct. 7, 1972. R.N. diploma, Holy Cross Sch. Nursing, South Bend, 1971; postgrad. Harper Coll., 1977-78, McHenry County Coll., 1982-83. Cert. occupational health nurse. Supr. emergency room Meml. Hosp., South Bend, 1971-72; surg. nurse Sherman Hosp., Elgin, Ill., 1972-74; occupational health nurse Sun Electric Corp., Crystal Lake, Ill., 1974-77, Chgo. Magnet Wire Corp., Elk Grove, Ill., 1977-82; owner, mgr. Tri-County Occupational Health Cons., Cary, Ill., 1982—. Mem. article rev. panel Nursing Life Mag., Springhouse, Pa., 1983-85. Vol. nurse Crystal Lake Rescue Squad, 1972-75; vol. blood pressure nurse Cary-Grove Sr. Citizen Ctr., 1980—; vol. tchr. No. Ill. Spl. Recreation Assn., Crystal Lake, 1981—; tchr., care minister Sts. Peter and Paul Ch., Cary, 1981—; instr. first aid, CPR and nutrition ARC, 1975—; instr. CPR, Chgo. Heart Assn., 1982—; mem. OHN com. Nat. Safety Council, 1984—. Named Vol. of Yr., McHenry County, Crystal Lake, 1983. Mem. Suburban Chgo. Assn. Occupational Health Nurses (charter, membership chmn. 1977-79, dir., publicity chmn. 1978-80, 1st v.p., newsletter editor 1980-81, pres. 1981-85), Ill. Assn. Occupational Health Nurses (corr. sec. 1984-86), Women's Adv. Council (membership chair), Nat. Assn. Female Execs. Roman Catholic. Lodge: Cary Lioness (bd. dirs. 1977-78, rec. sec. 1978-79, v.p. 1979-80, community calendar chmn. 1983-84). Home: 24675 N Jensen Ave Cary IL 60013 Office: Tri-county Occupational Health Cons 24675 N Jensen Ave Cary IL 60013

SANTELL, MADELEINE CAROL, artist; b. Earl Park, Ind., Aug. 19, 1932; d. Leo Oliver and Ocie (Coffel) Worland; m. John Joseph Santell, Jr., Oct. 6, 1951; children—Rebecca, Kimberly. Student U. Miami, 1950-51, Dade Jr. Coll., 1960-62. One woman shows Galerie Laurens, Paris, 1983, Galerie Bernheim-Jeune, Paris, 1983, Marbella Gallery, N.Y.C., 1984, Galerie Montfleury, Cannes, France, 1984; exhibited in group shows Paris, N.Y.C., Calif.; represented in permanent collections. Mem. Societes des Artistes Independants Paris, Republican. Roman Catholic. Club: DAR. Address: 5900 Reseda Blvd Tarzana CA 91356

SANTELL, ROBERTA (RICKIE), political worker; b. Los Angeles, July 23, 1937; d. Hyman and Sue (Fields) Thompson; student Los Angeles City Coll., 1955-56; m. Richard Alfred Santell, June 17, 1956; children—Mitchell James, Lisa Gaye. Sec. criminal div. Office of Los Angeles County Clk., 1955, CBS-TV, Los Angeles, 1956. Exec. bd. Covina Valley Fair Housing Council, 1969-70; co-organizer Police Community Relations Bd., La Puente area, 1970; mem. Los Angeles County Democratic Central Com., 1976—; assembly dist. chmn., regional vice-chmn. Calif. State Central Com., 1978—, co-chmn. credentials com.; del. Dem. Nat. Conv., 1980, 82, also mem. credentials com.; mem. community relations com. Jewish Fedn. Council of Greater Los Angeles, Eastern Region, 1984—. Recipient Dem. Women of Year award, 1971-72, Los Angeles County Central Com. Dem. of Year award, 1980. Jewish. Home: 336 S Barranca St West Covina CA 91791

SANTEN, ANN HORTENSTINE, broadcasting executive, music producer; b. New Orleans, May 23, 1938; d. Jacob L. and Martha Taylor (Grace) Hortenstine; m. Harry H. Santen, Oct. 4, 1958; children—Edward, Sally, Matthew. Student Smith Coll., 1956-58; B.F.A., U. Cin., 1979. Assoc. producer Sta.-WGUC, Cin., 1974-77, chief music producer, 1977-79, music dir., 1977—, internat. coordinator, 1981—; cons. Radio Nederlan, The Netherlands, 1978—, Deutsche Welle, Fed. Republic Germany, 1980—; dir. Am. Pub. Radio. Producer radio programs, including A Conductor Looks at Aida (Corp. Pub. Broadcasting award 1977), Hanukah Program (Corp. Pub. Broadcasting award 1980); producer radio series Festival! (Oebie award 1982). Adviser Cin. Composers Guild League, 1979—; panelist Ohio Arts Council, Columbus, 1985; trustee Cin. Opera, 1980-84; panelist Ohio Arts Council, 1985—. Named Producer of Yr., Ohio Ednl. Broadcasters, 1983. Mem. Coll. Conservatory Music Alumni Assn. (trustee 1981-85). Avocations: skiing; climbing. Office: WGUC-FM 1223 Central Pkwy Cincinnati OH 45214

SANTIAGO, JOANNE ANDRE, chiropractor; b. Hornel, N.Y., Mar. 8, 1949; d. Joseph Anthony and Vivian Eleanore (Nicholson) Santiago; m. Jude Vincent Lombardi, Oct. 7, 1979. B.A., Rutgers U., 1971; Dr. Chiropractic, Columbia Inst. Chiropractics, N.Y.C., 1974; M.S. Nutrition Biology, U. Bridgeport, 1979. Gen. practice chiropractic medicine, Bloomfield, Conn., Iselin, N.J., after 1974; mem. vis. faculty N.Y. Chiropractic Coll., Old Westbury, 1976—. Vol. counselor Middlesex Probation Office, New Brunswick, N.J., 1975-78; team physician Pop Warner Football, Iselin, Colonia, 1978—. Recipient Outstanding Alumnus award N.Y. Chiropractic Coll., 1980. Mem. Am. Chiropractic Soc. (assoc.), N.J. Chiropractic Soc. (disting. service award 1979), N.Y. Chiropractic Acad., Chiropractic Sports Council, Union Middlesex Somerset Chiropractic Assn. (pres. 1974—, dir. 1974—, service award 1978, outstanding award 1980), N.Y. Chiropractic Alumni Assn. (pres. 1979-81, sec. 1982, dir. 1983—, Conn. Chiropractic Assn. (dist. dir. pub. relations). Office: 20 E Main St PO Box 1430 Avon CT 06001 and 1430 Oak Tree Rd Iselin NJ 08003

SANTIAGO, ROSA EMILIA, sales and marketing executive; b. Havana, Cuba, Nov. 17, 1935; came to U.S., 1960; d. Emilio and Rosa (Fernandez) S.; m. Pedro P. Llaguno, July 19, 1963 (div. 1976); children—Rosa E., Peter E., Paul E. B.A. with honors, Fla. Internat. U., 1977. With sales and mktg. dept. Holiday Inn, Coral Gables, Fla., 1975-78, mktg. dir., 1982—; sales mgr. Holiday Rent-a-Car, Miami, Fla., 1976-79, v.p., 1981; mktg. dir. Ramada Inn/Airport, Miami, 1981; S.E. dist. mktg. dir. Holiday Rent-a-Car System, Miami, 1981-82; pres. U.S. Aviation Showcase, 1983—; instr. div. tourism Biscayne Coll., (now St. Thomas U.), Miami, 1979—, also mem. Women's Concern Com. assoc. editor tourism mag., 1976—; free-lance rep., vice dist. chmn. Tequesta dist. Boy Scouts Am.; past membership chmn., chmn. pub. relations; mem. Coalition Hispanic Am. Women, Council for Internat. Visitors; past mem. Congl. Citizens Council on Hispanic and Minority Affairs. Recipient Wood badge Boy Scouts Am., 1978, Dist. award of merit, 1984, Silver Beaver award, 1985. Mem. Women's C. of C. South Fla. (charter mem.), Coral Gables C. of C., Alexander von Humboldt Soc. Ams. (v.p.), Internat. Platform Assn., Venezuelan C. of C., Brazilian C. of C., Miami Forum, Phi Lambda Pi. Democrat. Roman Catholic. Home: 9412 SW 4th Ln Miami FL 33174 Office: Holiday Inn 2051 LeJeune Rd Coral Gables FL 33134

SANTIAGO, VIVIANA PELICOT, financial consultant; b. N.Y.C., Aug. 17, 1949; d. Jose Antonio and Lidia Ester (Perez) Pelicot; m. Louis G. Santiago, Apr. 30, 1976. A.B. in Bus. Adminstrn., U. P.R., 1969; B.A. in Mgmt. and Mktg. St. Peter's Coll., Englewood Cliffs, N.J., 1983. Adminstrv. asst. to pres. S.Am.-Internat., Nabisco Brands Inc., N.Y.C., 1978-82; ptnr., v.p. Silent Type Inc., Englewood, N.J., 1982-83; fin. cons. Merrill Lynch Pierce Fenner & Smith, Wayne, N.J., 1983—; instr., seminar speaker at high schs., colls., 1985—. Mem. Hispanic C. of C. of Paterson (fin. adviser 1985—, Hispanic C. of C. of N.J. State (fin. adviser, 1985—), N.J. Network for Bus. and Profl. Women, Career Women's Network, Nat. Assn. Female Execs. Lodge: Soroptimists (local treas. 1986—). Avocations: languages; tennis; golf. Office; Merrill Lynch Pierce Fenner & Smith 201 Willow Brooke Wayne NJ 07470

SANTIRE, HELEN (ATHENA), mathematics educator; b. Providence, Sept. 28, 1946; d. Nestor and Lillian (Nicholopoulos) Garabedian; m. Stanley Paul Santire, June 25, 1967; 1 dau., Heather Michele. B.S., George Washington U., 1968; M.Ed., Prairie View A&M U., 1974. Cert. math. tchr., guidance counselor, Tex. Tchr. algebra Prince George's County Schs., Washington, 1968-69; tchr. geometry Austin Ind. Schs. (Tex.), 1969-72; tchr. math. Galveston Ind. Schs. (Tex.), 1972-77; tchr. algebra and geometry Spring Branch Ind. Schs., 1977-79; dir. spl. services Internat. Sch., Riyadh, Saudi Arabia, 1979-82; tchr. geometry Alief Ind. Schs., Houston, 1982—; mem. Tex. Textbook Com., Houston 1983-84. Bd. dirs. YWCA, Galveston, 1975-76. Mem. LWV, Galveston Hist. Found., NEA, Tex. Tchrs. Assn., Alief Edn. Assn. Democrat. Greek Orthodox. Lodge: Daus. of Penelope (sec. Galveston 1972-73). Home: 201 Wilcrest St Apt 2507 Houston TX 77042

SANTOPADRE, MARYELLEN, pharmaceutical distributing company executive; b. Red Bank, N.J., Aug. 27, 1961; d. Morris Joseph and Elinor Catherine (Ryan) Tetro; m. Gil G. Santopadre, July 21, 1984. B.S. in Mktg. and Advt., Monmouth Coll., 1983, postgrad. Computer mgr. Ketchum Distbg. Inc., Cranford, N.J., 1983-85, sales mgr., 1985—. Mem. Nat. Assn. Female Execs., Rutgers Pharmacy Conf., Wholesale Druggists Assn. of N.J. Avocations: skiing; racquetball. Home: 778 Hwy 36 Hazlet NJ 07730 Office: Ketchum Distbrs Inc 40 S Ave West Cranford NJ 07016

SAO, MARIA DA CONCEICAO, fashion designer; b. Evora, Portugal, Apr. 27, 1946; came to U.S., 1974, naturalized; d. Manuel Mendes and Diamantina Maria (Sequeira) Ginja; m. Georg Bo Andresen, June 11, 1964 (div. 1976); m. John Patrick Heininger, Aug. 24, 1976. Artist/designer, Aarhus, Denmark, 196472; designer Sophie Boutique, Aarhus, 1973-74; owner/designer Sao's Studio, Washington, 1975-84; pres. SAO Ltd., N.Y.C., 1983—; exhibitor/lectr. Corcoran Gallery, Washington, 1980, Smithsonian Inst., Washington, 1975-83, Textile Mus., Washington, 1979, R.I. Sch. Design, Providence, 1981, Am. Ctr. Arts, Paris, 1981. Author: Wearable Art, 1979, also articles and catalogues. Nat. Endowment Arts grantee, 1981; D.C. Commn. Arts fellow, 1981; recipient Design award Woman in Design Internat., 1981. Roman Catholic. Avocations: horseback riding, exercise. Office: SAO Ltd 202 W 40th St Suite 1201 New York NY 10018

SAPINSLEY, LILA MANFIELD, state official; b. Chgo., Sept. 9, 1922; d. Jacob and Doris (Silverman) Manfield; B.A., Wellesley Coll., 1944; D. Pub. Service, U. R.I., 1971; D.Pedagogy, R.I. Coll., 1973; m. John M. Sapinsley, Dec. 23, 1942; children—Jill Sapinsley Mooney, Carol Sapinsley Rubenstein, Joan Sapinsley Lewis, Patricia. Mem. R.I. Senate, 1972-84, minority leader, 1974-84; dir. R.I. Dept. Community Affairs, 1985; chmn. R.I. Housing and Mortgage Fin. Corp., 1985—. Mem. R.I. Gov.'s Commn. on Women; commr. Edn. Commn. of States; pres. bd. trustees Butler Hosp., 1978-84; trustee R.I. State Colls., 1965-70, chmn., 1967-70; trustee U. R.I., R.I. Coll. Found.; bd. dirs. Miriam Hosp., Hamilton House, Trinity Repertory Co., Lincoln Sch., Wellesley Center for Research on Women, 1980. Recipient Alumnae Achievement award Wellesley Coll., 1974; Outstanding Legislator of Yr. award Republican Nat. Legislators Assn., 1984. Republican. Jewish. Home: 25 Cooke St Providence RI 02906

SAPIR, SELMA GUSTIN, psychologist, educator; b. N.Y.C., Aug. 6, 1916; s. Max and Sally F. (Lookstein) Gustin; m. Robert I. (dec. July 1973); children—Marc, Judith Sapir Novick. B.S., NYU, 1935; M.A., Sarah Lawrence Coll., 1956; Ed.D., Columbia U., 1984. Cert. sch. psychologist, guidance counselor, tchr., adminstr., N.Y. Research asst. Columbia U., 1963-70; psychologist Bd. Coop. Ednl. Services, West County #2, Ardsley, N.Y., 1956-60; psychologist Mamaronak Pub. Sch., N.Y., 1965-70; prof. psychology Bank St. Coll., N.Y.C., 1968—; research lectr. Belgium Research Scientists, 1979; Fulbright prof. U. Anahuac, Mexico City, 1980; psychology cons. Alcott Sch., Ardsley, N.Y., 1982—; lectr. N.Y. Acad. Scis., 1984. Author: A Professionals Guide, 1978; Children with Special Needs, 1983; Clinical Teaching Model, 1985; Editor: Children With Learning Problems, 1973. Recipient Study award Ford Found., 1955. Mem. Internat. Council Psychologists (bd. dirs. 1985-87, UN del. 1982—), Am. Psychol. Assn., Multidisciplinary Acad. Educators (mem. council 1983). Avocations: theatre; art. Home: 60 Biltmore Ave Yonkers NY 10710 Office: Bank Street Coll Edn 610 W 112th St New York NY 10025

SAPP, BARBARA DIANE, utility company data resource administrator, realtor; b. Wenatchee, Wash., Nov. 27, 1940; d. John Franklin and Dorothy Doris (Kelsay) Cool; m. Leroy Sapp, Dec. 12, 1959 (div. 1975); children—Michael, Patrick, Stephen. B.S. in Bus. Adminstrn., U. Redlands, 1979. Tape clk. GTE Data Services, Marina del Rey, Calif., 1975-76, IM-programmer, 1976-77, IM-programmer analyst, 1977-79, IM-systems analyst, 1979-80, IM-sr. tech. analyst, 1980-81; IM-supr. data resource mgmt. Gen. Telephone, Marina Del Rey, 1981—. Mem., organizer Canejo Valley Community Ctrs., Newbury Park, Calif., 1976. Mem. Gen. Telephone Good Govt. Club, Beta Sigma Phi (pres. 1974-75). Republican. Methodist. Avocations: flying; backpacking. Home: 3441 Frankie Dr Newbury Park CA 91320 Office: General Telephone of Calif 4750 Lincoln Blvd Marina del Rey CA 90292

SAPPENFIELD, DIANE HASTINGS, development company executive civic worker; b. Marion, Ohio, Apr. 22, 1940; d. Edgar Dean and Marguerite Elizabeth (Alexander) Hastings; B.A. in Sociology and Econs., Mills Coll., 1962; tchr.'s cert. Calif. State U., Los Angeles, 1963; M.S. in Fin. and Real Estate, Am. U., 1986; m. Ronald Eugene Sappenfield, July 6, 1962; children—Derek Ronald, Ann Elizabeth. Tchr. elem. sch., El Segundo, Calif., 1963-66; asst. dir. admissions Mills Coll., 1972-74; v.p., dir. DDA Assos., Inc., McLean, Va., 1978—; asst. to chmn. bd. Watergate Complex, Washington, 1979-81; dir. corp. mktg. Watergate Devel. Inc., McLean, 1981-82. Vol. tchr. Saugatuck Elem. Sch., Westport, Conn., 1976-79; active benefits for Corcoran Sch. Art, Nat. Symphony Orch., Women's Bd. Am. Heart Assn., Hope Ball, Meridian House, Washington; bd. dirs. Westport-Weston Arts Council, 1973-79, Young Concert Artists, 1984—; mem. Levitt Pavilion Governing Com., 1974-79; pres. Friends of Levitt Pavilion, 1977; trustee Stauffer-Westport Fund, 1976-79; mem. Westport Young Woman's League, 1969-79, pres., 1975-76; bd. dirs. Stamford-Norwalk br. Jr. League, 1977-78. Mem. Mills Coll. Club N.Y., Washington Jr. League. Home: 7612 Georgetown Pike McLean VA 22102

SARAFIAN, SYLVIA ANNETTE, computer systems specialist; b. Newton, Mass., June 16, 1931; d. Antranig Arakel and Elizabeth (Zorian) S.; B.A., Mt. Holyoke Coll., 1953. Chemist, Mass. Meml. Hosps., Boston, 1953-56; programmer, Honeywell Inc., Newton, Mass., 1956-58, System Devel. Corp., Santa Monica, Calif., 1958-61, Bedford, Mass., 1961-64, computer systems specialist, Santa Monica, 1966-71; programmer Bolt, Benarek & Newman, Cambridge, Mass., 1964-66; owner COMPUFARM and The Aurora, Marina Del Rey, Calif., 1971—, Advanced Bus. Microsystems, Marina Del Rey, 1981—; speaker symposium on computers in agr.; participant programs in field. Asso. mem. Calif. Republican State Central Com., 1975-76, 78; bd. dirs. Marina Rep. Club, 1982; mem. Dornan for Congress campaign, 1976, 78, 80; active Calif. Women for Agr., 1977-79. Mem. Armenian Apostolic Church. Club: Appalachian Mountain. Author CompuFARM, computer system for agr., written for time-sharing, 1971, for microcomputers, 1981; author: The Aurora, written for time-sharing, 1977, for microcomputers, 1982; prodn. asst. for TV show Face to Face, 1976. Home: 13856 Bora Bora Way #105C Marina Del Rey CA 90292 Office: PO Box 9352 Marina Del Rey CA 90295

SARALEGUI, CRISTINA MARIA, magazine editor; b. Havana, Cuba, Jan. 29, 1948; came to U.S., 1960; d. Francisco and Cristina (Santamarina) S.; 1 dau., Cristina Amalia; m. 2d, Marcos Avila, June 9, 1984. Student mass communication U. Miami. Features editor Vanidades Continental, Miami, Fla., 1970-73; editor Cosmpolitan Spanish, Miami, 1973-76, editor-in-chief, 1979—; dir. entertainment Miami Herald, 1976-77; editor-in-chief Intimidades mag., Miami, 1977-79, 83—. Mem. jury Miss Venezuela Pageant, 1983. Featured in bestseller Latin Beauty, 1982; keynote speaker Union Am. Women, P.R., 1981. Mem. Legendary Women of Miami. Republican. Roman Catholic. Club: Jockey (Miami). Office: Editorial America SA 6355 NW 36th St Virginia Gardens FL 33166

SARANAC, WINNIE B., educator; b. N.Y.C., Jan. 30, 1929; d. Jack and Pauline (Weisman) Brokaw; m. George Eugene Saranac, Sept. 30, 1949; 1 dau., Paula Beth. B.S. in Journalism, Ohio U., 1949; M.S., C.W. Post Coll., 1978. Tchr. Farmingdale Schs., N.Y., 1969-78, tchr. spl. edn., 1978—. Mem. Spl. Edn. Parent-Tchr. Assn., Theta Sigma Phi. Avocations: skiing; tennis; biking; traveling.

SARANDON, SUSAN ABIGAIL, actress; b. N.Y.C., Oct. 4, 1946; d. Phillip Leslie and Lenora Marie (Criscione) Tomalin; m. Chris Sarandon, Sept. 16, 1967 (div.). B.A. in Drama and English, Cath. U. Am., 1968. TV appearances include series Calucci's Department, Search For Tomorrow, miniseries AD, 1985, Mussolini: The Decline and Fall of Il Duce, 1985; theatre appearances include: An Evening with Richard Nixon, A Coupla White Chicks Sittin' Around Talkin'; motion pictures include: The Great Waldo Pepper, Rocky Horror Picture Show, Pretty Baby, King of the Gypsies, Loving Couples, Agnes of God, 1985, Compromising Positions, 1985. Mem. AFTRA, Screen Actors Guild, Actors Equity, Acad. Motion Picture Arts and Scis., NOW, Amnesty Internat., ACLU. Office: care William Morris Agy Inc 1350 Ave of the Americas New York NY 10019

SARDINA, MARTA ISABEL, engineer; b. Havana, Cuba, June 28, 1952; came to U.S., 1972, naturalized, 1981; d. Alberto and Guadalupe (Zuniga) S.; B.S. in Math., UCLA, 1977; M.S. in Program Mgmt., West Coast U., 1981. Sr. tracking system analyst Bendix Field Engring. Corp., Pasadena, Calif., 1978-80, project leader, sr. engr., 1980-82; sr. engr. system definition and requirements group Convair div. Gen. Dynamics, San Diego, 1982-85; sr. engr. Cubic Corp., 1985—. Recipient Cert. of Achievement, Bendix-Jet Propulsion Lab., 1979; NASA-Group Achievement award, 1981. Mem. Nat. Assn. Female Execs., Soc. Women Engrs., AAUW. Home: 5517 Caminito Katerina San Diego CA 92111 Office: Cubic Corp 9333 Balboa Ave San Diego CA 92123

SARGENT, ALICE GOLDSTEIN, consultant, author; b. Cin., Feb. 5, 1939; d. Harold D. and Adele (Linch) Goldstein; B.A. in English Lit., Oberlin Coll., 1960; M.A., Brandeis U., 1963; M.Ed. in Group Dynamics, Temple U., 1966; Ed.D., U. Mass., Amherst, 1974; m. G. Dann Sargent, June 2, 1963 (dec. 1976); 1 dau., Elizabeth. Cons. to orgns., Washington, current clients include E.I. Dupont de Nemours, U.S. Dept. Treasury, Treasury Exec. Inst., Fed. Exec. Inst., U.S. Dept. Energy, Nat. Tng. Labs., EPA; mem. faculty Am. U. Sch. Govt. and Pub. Adminstrn., U. So. Calif. Sch. Pub. Adminstrn.; project coordinator Nat. Project on Women in Edn., Office of Asst. Sec. Edn., HEW, Washington, 1975-76; dir. M.B.A. program Trinity Coll., Washington 1976-77; seminar leader Australian Inst. Mgmt. Mem. Acad. Mgmt., Hong Kong Mgmt. Assn., Am. Psychol. Assn., Organizational Devel. Network (bd. dirs.). Author: Beyond Sex Roles, 1976, 2d edit., 1985; The Androgynous Manager, 1981, pub. in 5 langs., 1983. Home: 4819 Dexter Terr NW Washington DC 20007

SARGENT, BARBARA GATES, medical technologist; b. Rosebud, Tex., Jan. 8, 1937; d. John Wesley and Lucille (Johnson) Gates; m. Waldo Sargent, Aug. 6, 1965. Student Prairieview A&M Coll., 1955-58, Commonwealth Coll. Sci., Houston, 1958-59. Med. technologist Spring Branch Hosp., Houston, 1959-61, Bellaire Gen. Hosp., Houston, 1961-69, Bellaire Med. Plaza, Houston, 1969-76; chem. supr. Bellaire Gen. Hosp., 1976-82, asst. lab. mgr., 1982-83, lab. mgr., 1983—. Mem. Am. Soc. Med. Technologists, Nat. Cert. Agy. Clin. Lab. Scientists, Am. Med. Technologists (cert.), Eta Phi Beta. Episcopalian. Club: Select Set (Houston). Home: 502 Detering St Houston TX 77007 Office: Bellaire General Hosp 5314 Dashwood Houston TX 77081

SARGENT, CAROLINE LOUISE, edni. adminstr.; b. Richmond, Ind., Nov. 7; d. George Andrew and Margaret (Kromer) S.; Mus.B., Wittenberg U., 1972; postgrad. Cath. U. Am., 1972-74, N.Y.U., 1979. Asst. adminstr. Sch. Engring. and Arch., Cath. U. Am., Washington, 1973-76; nat. program clk. Foster Grandparent Program Hdqrs., Washington, 1977-78; coordinator public relations and vols. Montclair (N.J.) Community Hosp., 1979; public relations asst. Bloomfield (N.J.) Coll., 1979-80, asst. dir. devel., 1980-82; dir. devel. and pub. relations Far Brook Sch., Short Hills, N.J., 1982—. Alida Attwell scholar, 1968. Mem. Council Advancement and Support Edn., Nat. Assn. Female Execs., N.J. Press Women. Office: Far Brook Sch 52 Great Hills Rd Short Hills NJ 07078

SARGENT, DIANA RHEA, bookkeeper; b. Cheyenne, Wyo., Feb. 20, 1939; d. Clarence and Edith (de Castro) Hayes; grad. high sch.; m. Charles Sargent, Apr. 17, 1975; children—Rene A. Coburn, Rochelle A. Weldy Riddle, Clayton R. Weldy, Christopher J.; stepchildren—Laurie E. Sargent, Leslie E. Sargent. IBM proof operator Bank Am., Stockton, Calif., 1956-58, gen. ledger bookkeeper, Modesto, Calif., 1963-66; office mgr., head bookkeeper Central Drug Store, Modesto, 1966-76, Sargent & Sargent, Modesto, 1976—. Mem. Haven Stanislaus Women's Refuge Center. Mem. NOW, San Francisco Mus. Soc., Nat. Soc. Public Accts., Merced Accts. Soc. Democrat. Humanist. Address: PO Box 919 Modesto CA 95353

SARGENT, MARGARET HOLLAND, artist; b. Hollywood, Calif., Dec. 30, 1927; d. Cecil Claude and Norma Mary Holland; student U. Calif., Los Angeles, 1946-47, 54-55; studied with Herbert Abrams, N.Y.C., John Howard Sanden, N.Y.C.; m. Howard Leroy Sargent, June 22, 1947; children—Christopher Lee, Kenneth Dean. One women shows Frye Art Mus., Seattle, 1971, 84, Woodside Gallery, Seattle, 1972, Excelsior, N.Y., 1975, Turkish-Am. Assn., Ankara, 1963, Art League No. Va., 1968; group shows include: Salmagundi, N.Y.C., 1974, 75, 76, Overseas Press Club, N.Y.C., 1975; represented in permanent collections: West Point Mus., Pentagon, Washington; owner Sargent Portraits; commd. by Time, Inc. for covers of Gerald Ford, Margaret Thatcher, Karen Quinlan; staff lectr. Nat. Portrait seminar, N.Y.C. Recipient numerous awards; cert. Am. Portrait Soc. Producer videos on art instrn., 1983-84. Home: 2750 Glendower Ave Los Angeles CA 90027

SARGENT, SARAH DAVIS, writer, educator; b. Roanoke, Va., Mar. 15, 1937; d. Francis Atwell and Mary Taylor (Dupuy) Davis; m. Seymour Herbert Sargent, Aug. 26, 1962; children—Edgar Guy, Alice Marshall. B.A., Randolph-Macon Woman's Coll., 1959, M.A., Yale U., 1961. Instr. English, U. N.D., Grand Forks, 1961-62, U. Vt., Burlington, 1963-67; lectr. U. Wis.-Oshkosh, 1968-76; children's books include: Edward Troy and the Witch Cat, 1978; Weird Henry Berg (Friends of Am. Writers Juvenile Book Merit award 1980, listed among best books Sch. Library Jour. 1980), 1980; Secret Lies (ALA Notable book), 1981; Lure of the Dark, 1984; Watermusic, 1986. Woodrow Wilson fellow, 1959-60. Mem. Phi Beta Kappa. Democrat. Home: 627 Ceape Ave Oshkosh WI 54901

SARLAT, GLADYS, public relations executive; b. Elizabeth, N.J., July 22, 1923; d. Max and Dora (Levin) S. B.S., U. Wash., 1946. Asst. fashion coordinator Kay Sullivan Assocs., N.Y.C., 1949-50; fashion dir. Warsaw & Co., N.Y.C., 1950-54; asst. fashion dir. Emporium Dept. Store, San Francisco, 1955-56; asst. prodn. mgr. Cunningham & Walsh Advt., San Francisco, 1958-59; v.p., pub. relations dir. Harwood Advt., Tucson and Phoenix, 1959-68; pres. Godwin & Sarlat Pub. Relations, Tucson, 1970—. Mem. Tucson Tomorrow, 1980—, Adv. com., Downtown Devel. Corp., Tucson, 1979-84; v.p. Tucson Trade Bur., 1977-80. Named Woman of Yr. for Bus., Ariz. Daily Star, Tucson, 1963; Lulu award Los Angeles Women in Advt., 1962. Mem. Tucson Met. C. of C. (chmn.-elect 1985-86), Pub. Relations Soc. Am. (dir. 1980-81, mem. Counselors Acad.), Fashion Group Inc. Republican. Jewish. Clubs: Old Pueblo, La Paloma Country. Home: 5530 N Camino Aremosa Tucson AZ 85718 Office: Godwin & Sarlat Pub Relations 120 W Broadway Tucson AZ 85701

SARNO, PATRICIA ANN, educator; b. Ashland, Pa.; d. John Thomas and Anna (Harvest) S.; B.S., Pa. State U., 1966, M.Ed., 1971; postgrad. Bucknell U., 1967, Bloomsburg U., 1970. Programmer planetarium, tchr. sci. Pottsville (Pa.) High Sch., 1967; tchr. biology Schuylkill Haven (Pa.) Area High Sch., 1967—, sci. chmn., coordinator sci. dept. computer programming, 1973—; cons. Pa. Edn. Dept., career program Pottsville Hosp.; evaluator, sci. chmn. Middle Atlantic States Accreditation of Colls. and Secondary Schs. Assn., 1977-85. Dow Chem. Co. grantee, 1971. Mem. Pa. Edn. Assn. (exec. bd.), AAAS, Nat. Assn. Biology Tchrs., Am. Mus. Natural History, Nat. Tchrs. Assn., Pa. Tchrs. Assn., NEA, Am. Inst. Biol. Scis., Pa. Acad. Scis., Smithsonian Assocs., Pa. State U. Alumni Assn., Schuylkill Haven Edn. Assn., Phi Sigma, Delta Kappa Gamma. Contbr. to profl. jours. Discoverer spider species Atypus snetzingeri, 1973. Home: 49 S Balliet St Frackville PA 17931 Office: Schuylkill Haven High Sch Schuylkill Haven PA 17972

SARNOFF, LILI-CHARLOTTE DREYFUS (LOLO SARNOFF), artist, business exec.; b. Frankfurt, Germany (Swiss citizen), Jan. 9, 1916; d. Willy and Martha (Koch von Hirsch) Dreyfus; grad. Reimann Art Sch. (Germany), 1934, U. Berlin, 1935; student U. Florence (Italy), 1936-37; m. Stanley Jay Sarnoff, Sept. 11, 1948; children—Daniela Martha, Robert B.L. Came to U.S., 1941, naturalized, 1944. Research asst. Harvard Sch. Public Health, 1948-54; research asso. cardiac physiology Nat. Heart Inst., Bethesda, Md., 1954-59; pres. Rodana Research Corp., Bethesda, 1958-61; v.p. Catrix Corp., Bethesda, 1958-61; inventor FloLite light sculptures under name Lolo Sarnoff, 1968; one-woman shows: Agra Gallery, Washington, 1969, Corning Glass Center Mus., Corning, N.Y., 1970, Gallery Two, Woodstock, Vt., 1970, Gallery Marc, Washington, 1971, Hood Coll., Frederick, Md., 1972, Internat. Art Mart, Basel, Switzerland, 1972, Franz Bader Gallery, Washington, 1976, Art Barn, Washington, 1976, Art Fair, Washington, 1976, Gallery K, Washington, 1978, 81, Washington Project for Arts, 1980, Alwin Gallery, London, 1981, Galerie von Bartha, Basel, Switzerland, 1982, Gallery K, Washington, 1982, 83, 84, 85, La Galerie L'Hotel de Ville, Geneva, Switzerland, 1982, Palm Beach Galleries, New Orleans, 1984, Washington Women's Art Ctr., 1985, Ctr. Internat. d'Art Contemporain, Paris, 1985, Pfalzgalerie, Kaiserlautern, W. Ger., 1985; represented in collections: Fed. Nat. Mortgage Assn., Washington, Corning Glass Center Mus., Nat. Air and Space Museum, Washington, David Lloyd Kreeger Collection, Washington, Kennedy Center, Washington, Nat. Acad. Sci., Chase Manhattan Bank, N.Y.C., Israel Mus., Jerusalem, others. Past trustee Nat. Ballet, Mt. Vernon Coll., Washington; trustee Art Barn; bd. dirs. Fgn. Student Service Council, Washington Performing Arts Soc. Mem. women's com., trustee Corcoran Gallery of Art. Recipient Gold medal Accademia Italia delle Arti e del Lavoro, 1980. Club: City Tavern (Washington). Democrat. Co-inventor electrophrenic respirator; inventor flowmeter. Home: 7507 Hampden Ln Bethesda MD 20814 also Barnard VT 05031

SAROSDY, JANE GRAFFEO, lawyer; b. Dallas, June 22, 1953; d. Joseph Victor Graffeo and Margaret Jane (Dunn) Graffeo Uchman; m. Randall Louis Sarosdy, Oct. 29, 1983. B.A. summa cum laude with honors, Newcomb U. of Tulane U., 1975, postgrad., 1977-78; J.D., Stanford U., 1980. Bar: D.C. 1981. Law clerk to presiding justice U.S. Ct. Appeals, D.C., Washington, 1980-81; assoc. Covington & Burling, Washington, 1981-84; atty.-adviser Office Internat. Tax Counsel, U.S. Dept. Treasury, Washington, 1984—. Sr. articles editor Stanford Law Rev., 1979-80. Active NOW, Washington, 1980—, Women's Legal Def. Fund, Washington, 1980—. Recipient Pierce Butler prize Tulane U., 1975, alumni medal, 1978; Belcher Evidence award Stanford U., 1980. Mem. ABA, Women's Bar Assn. D.C., Women in Employee Benefits, Phi Beta Kappa. Democrat. Roman Catholic. Home: 2450 N Ohio St Arlington VA 22207 Office: Office Internat Tax Counsel Main Treasury Room 4013 Bldg 15th and Pennsylvania Ave NW Washington DC 20220

SARSON, PATRICIA ANNE, computer consulting firm executive, author; b. London, June 6, 1946; came to U.S., 1973, naturalized, 1975; d. Francis Charles and Anne Brown (Nisbet) Sarson; m. Christopher Peter Gane, Apr. 1, 1975. B.Sc. in Zoology, U. London, 1969. Systems engr. IBM, London, 1967-72; cons., lectr. Yourdon Inc., N.Y.C., 1973-75; asst. v.p. Mfrs. Hanover Trust Co., N.Y.C., 1976; exec. v.p. Improved System Tech., N.Y.C., 1977-81; ptnr. Gane-Sarson, N.Y.C., 1981—. Co-author: Learning to Program 1975; Structured Systems Analysis, 1977; (ednl. methodology) STRADIS, 1979; (ednl. video tapes) Analysis and Design, 1979. Avocations: sailing; walking; classical music; collecting antiques. Office: Gane-Sarson 245 E 50th St PH New York NY 10022

SARTON, MAY, author, poet; b. Wondelgem, Belgium, May 3, 1912; brought to U.S., 1916, naturalized, 1924; d. George Alfred Leon and Eleanor Mabel (Elwes) Sarton; student Shady Hill Sch., Cambridge, Mass., Inst. Belge de Culture Francaise, Brussels, 1924-25; grad. Cambridge High and Latin Sch., 1929; Litt.D. (hon.), Russell Sage Coll., 1959, Clark U., 1975, U. N.H., 1976, Bates Coll., 1976, Colby Coll., 1976, Thomas Starr King Sch. Ministry, 1976, U. Maine, 1981, Bowdoin Coll., 1983, Bucknell U., 1985. Lectr. poetry U. Chgo., Harvard U., U. Iowa, Colo. Coll., Wellesley Coll., Beloit Coll., U. Kans., Denison U., others; Briggs-Copeland instr. composition Harvard U., 1950-52. Awarded Golden Rose for poetry, 1945; Edward Bland Meml. prize Poetry Mag., 1945; Alexandrine medal Coll. St. Catherine, 1975; Avon/COCOA Pioneer Woman award, 1983; Fund for Human Dignity award, 1984; Am. Book award, 1985; Bryn Mawr fellow in poetry, 1953-54; Guggenheim Found. fellow, 1954-55; Nat. Found. Arts and Humanities grantee, 1967. Fellow Am. Acad. Arts and Scis.; mem. N.E. Poetry Soc., Poetry Soc. Am. (Reynolds lyric award 1953). Author: Encounter in April, 1937; The Single Hound, 1938; Inner Landscape (poems), 1939; The Bridge of Years, 1946, The Lion and The Rose (poems), 1948; Shadow of a Man, 1950; The Leaves of the Tree (poems), 1950; A Shower of Summer Days, 1952; The Land of Silence (poems), 1953; Faithful Are the Wounds, 1955; The Birth of a Grandfather, 1957; In Time Like Air, 1957; The Fur Person (fiction), 1956; I Knew a Phoenix, 1959; The Small Room, 1961; Cloud, Stone, Sun, Vine, 1961; Joanna and Ulysses, 1963; Mrs. Stevens Hears the Mermaids Singing, 1965; A Private Mythology (poems), 1966; Miss Pickthorn and Mr. Hare, 1966; As Does New Hampshire (poems), 1967; Plant Dreaming Deep (autobiography), 1968; The Poet and the Donkey, 1968, Kinds of Love, 1970; A Grain of Mustard Seed (poems), 1971; A Durable Fire (poems), 1972; Journal of a Solitude, 1973; As We Are Now, 1973; Collected Poems, 1974; Punch's Secret, 1974; Crucial Converstaions (novel), 1975; A World of Light (autobiography), 1976; A Walk Through the Woods, 1976; The House by the Sea (a journal), 1977; A Reckoning (novel), 1978; Halfway to Silence (poems), 1980; Recovering (a journal), 1980; Writings on Writing (essays), 1980; A Winter Garland (poems), 1982; Anger, 1982; At Seventy, A Journal, 1984; (poems) Letters from Maine, 1984; The Magnificent Spinster, 1985.

SARTOR, CYNTHIA MARIE, social worker; b. Battle Creek, Mich., Nov. 23, 1948; d. Ambrogio and Domenica Theresa (Conto) S.; B.A. Mercy Coll., Detroit, 1971; M.S.S.W., U. Louisville, 1979. Patient advocate St. Lawrence Community Mental Health Center, Lansing, Mich., 1971-74; devel. disabilities specialist, social work outpatient therapist Mountain Comprehensive Care Center, Prestonburg, Ky., 1974-78; dir. econ. devel. Ctr. for Housing Alternatives and Socio-Econ. Options, David, Ky., 1977-79; instr. social work, sociology Pikeville (Ky.) Coll., 1979-80; asst. prof. social work Ind. State U., Terre Haute, 1981—. Bd. dirs., chmn. policy com. David Community Devel. Corp. (Ky.), 1975-77; mem. Christian Service Ministry, Prestonsburg, 1975-78; bd. dirs., chmn. crisis team com. Sexual Abuse Victim Assistance, Inc. Mem. Vigo County Assn. Retarded Citizens, Nat. Assn. Social Workers, Ind. Assn. Social Work Educators, Council on Social Work Edn., Phi Kappa Phi, Alpha Delta Mu. Office: Dept Sociology and Social Work Ind State U Terre Haute IN 47802

SARVAS-PALM, ARLENE FRANCES, educational program administrator; b. Bethlehem, Pa., July 2, 1947; d. James Stephen and Elizabeth (Petanovics) Sarvas; m. Vincent John Palm, July 4, 1985. B.S., Pa. State U., 1970, D.Ed., 1976; M.Ed., Lehigh U., 1973. Cosmetology instr. Bethlehem Area Vocat. Tech. Sch., Pa., 1970-73; asst. dir. Franklin County Area Vocat. Tech. Sch., Chambersburg, Pa., 1975-76; supr. instrn. Bethlehem Area Vocat. Tech. Sch., 1976-81; dir. Carbon County Area Vocat. Tech. Sch., Jim Thorpe, Pa., 1981-85; dir. Baldy View Regional Occupation Program, Claremont, Calif., 1985—; instr. Lehigh U., Bethlehem, 1973-74, Pa. State U., University Park, 1974-75. Co-author: Evaluation of Vocational Technical Schools, 1977. Mem. Am. Assn. Sch. Adminstrs., Nat. Council Local Adminstrs., Calif. Assn. Health Career Educators, Pa. Vocat. Assn. (life, pres.-elect 1985), Calif. Assn. Regional Occupational Ctrs. Programs, Pi Lambda Theta, Iota Lambda Sigma, Phi Delta Kappa. Club: Soroptimist (v.p. 1975). Office: Baldy View ROP 135 S Spring St Claremont CA 91711

SASAKI, PATRICIA ANN, state official; b. Honolulu, Feb. 19, 1950; d. Chester H. and Barbara M. (Takata) Akamine; B.A., U. Hawaii, 1973; m. Randall M. Sasaki, Apr. 5, 1980. Exec. asst., U. Hawaii InterArts Festival and Hawaii Dance Theatre, 1976-77, U. Hawaii Multicultural Curriculum Project, 1977; info. specialist State Manpower Commn., Honolulu, 1978-80; payroll clk. Lola of Hawaii, Honolulu, 1978-82; program specialist Office Gov., Exec. Office Aging, Honolulu, 1980—; pres. partner, co-owner Peppovision, Inc., Honolulu, 1980—. Pres., 2M Community Council, 1978-80; vol. Moiliili Community Center, 1972-82. Mem. Women in Communications, Inc. (sec. Hawaii prof. chpt. 1980), Japanese Women's Soc., Honolulu Japanese Jaycees.

SASEK, GLORIA BURNS, educator; b. Springfield, Mass., Jan. 20, 1926; d. Frederick Charles and Minnie Delia (White) Burns; B.A., Mary Washington Coll. of U. Va., 1947; Ed.M., Springfield (Mass.) Coll., 1955; postgrad. Sorbonne, summer 1953; A.M., Radcliffe Coll., 1954; postgrad. Università per Stranieri, Perugia, Italy, summer 1955; m. Lawrence Anton Sasek, Sept. 5, 1960. Tchr. high sch. English in Conn. and Mass., 1947-60; mem. faculty La. State U., Baton Rouge, 1961—, asst. prof. English, 1971—, chmn. freshman English, 1969-70. Recipient George H. Deer Distinguished Tchr. award La. State U., 1977. Mem. Modern Lang. Assn., AAUP, South Central Modern Lang. Assn., South Central Renaissance Soc., NEA. Roman Catholic. Home: 1458 Kenilworth Pkwy Baton Rouge LA 70808 Office: Dept English 219 Allen Hall La State U Baton Rouge LA 70803

SASSER, SUE LYNN, bank executive; b. Lawton, Okla., Oct. 2, 1954; d. C.W. and Alfa B. (Dutton) S. B.A. in Journalism, Central State U., 1976, M.S. in Profl. Services in Home Econs., 1980; Ph.D. in Consumer Scis., Tex. Woman's U., 1983. Real estate salesperson The 89er Real Estate Co., Oklahoma City, 1976-78; grad. asst. Central State U., Edmond, Okla., 1979-80, Tex. Woman's U., Denton, 1981-82; program evaluator U.S. GAO, Dallas, 1983-85; econ. edn. specialist Fed. Res. Bank of Dallas, 1985—, Coordinator Adopt-A-School Activities, 1985—. Recipient Spl. Achievement commendation U.S. GAO, 1983; Claudia G. Williams scholar, 1981-82, McMahon scholar, 1972-74, Central State U. Grad. Home Econs. scholar, 1980. Mem. Am. Home Econs. Assn., Tex. Home Econs. Assn., Am. Council on Consumer Interests, Soc. of Consumer Affairs Profls., Southeastern Regional Assn. Family Econs.-Home Mgmt. Profls. Baptist. Avocations: sports; gourmet cooking; reading. Office: Fed Res Bank of Dallas Pub Affairs Dept 400 S Akard Sta K Dallas TX 75222

SASSIN, LYNN BONNIE, lawyer; b. N.Y.C., Feb. 29, 1956; d. Benjamin and Rose (Lipsky) Sassin. B.A., U. Md., 1978; J.D., U. Md.-Balt., 1981. Bar: Md. 1981. Jud. clk. presiding justice Cir. Ct. Balt. (formerly Supreme Bench Balt.), 1981-82; assoc. Frank, Bernstein, Conaway & Goldman, Balt., 1982—. Mem. Charles Village Civic Assn., Balt., 1983, Associated Jewish Charities of Balt.-Young Leadership Council, Balt., 1983-84, Women's Law Ctr. Mem. Balt. Bar Assn., Md. State Bar Assn., ABA. Democrat. Home: 3000 Guilford Ave Baltimore MD 21218 Office: Frank Bernstein Conaway & Goldman Baltimore Federal Bldg 300 E Lombard St Baltimore MD 21202

SASSO, CASSANDRA GAY, lawyer; b. Washington, Feb. 5, 1946; d. Philip Francis and Lois Aileen (Ayers) Sasso; m. David John Stephenson, Jr., Feb. 12, 1982; 1 son, Gabriel David. B.S. magna cum laude, U. Nebr., 1967; M.A., U. Calif.-Santa Barbara, 1970; J.D., Northwestern U., 1974. Bar: Ill., 1974, Colo., 1976. Law clk. Schiff Hardin & Waite, Chgo., 1973; assoc. Sidley & Austin, Chgo., 1974-75; instr. antitrust and securities U. Denver Sch. Law, 1978-79, 85-86; instr. trial practice U. Colo. Law Sch., Boulder, 1983-84; ptnr., trial lawyer Sherman & Howard, Denver, 1975—. Bd. dirs. Colo. Lawyers Com., Denver, 1980-82, Legal Aid Soc. Met. Denver, 1981-83; bd. dirs. Colo. Jud. Inst., 1982-85, v.p., 1984-85; mem. Denver Com. Fgn. Relations, 1981-84; chmn. bd. dirs. Colo. chpt. ACLU, Denver, 1982-83; mem. steering com. Colo. Lawyers for Nuclear Arms Edn., Denver, 1982-84. Mem. Colo. Women's Bar Assn., Chgo. Council Lawyers (sec. 1974-75), Colo. Bar Assn. (bd. govs. 1980-83), Denver Bar Assn. (trustee 1978-81), Colo. Trial Lawyers Assn. (bd. dirs. 1983-85), ABA, Mortar Bd., Alpha Omicron Pi. Democrat. Presbyterian. Home: 1781 Holly St Denver CO 80220 Office: Sherman and Howard 633 17th St Suite 2900 Denver CO 80202

SASSO, ELEANOR CATHERINE, state senator; b. Fall River, Mass., Dec. 9, 1934; d. Robert Charles and Ellen (O'Hare) Ashworth; m. Louis Anthony Sasso, 1957; children—Ellen Marie, Ann Marie, Robert. B.S., Immaculata Coll., Pa., 1957. Mem. R.I. State Senate, 1979—; researcher Bur. Nat. Affairs, from 1978. Chmn. Cranston Recycling Commn., 1972-73; mem. Cranston Transvan Com., from 1973; mem. Spl. Gov.'s Commn. To Study Entire Election Process, 1977-78. Mem. LWV, Met. Nursing and Health Assn. (bd.), Common Cause, Save the Bay. Democrat. Roman Catholic. Office: RI Senate State Capitol Providence RI 02903*

SASSO, MARIA DOLORES, export-import management and marketing company executive; b. Kingston, Jamaica, Apr. 21, 1949; came to U.S., 1954, naturalized, 1960; d. Donald Abraham and Maria Concepcion (Oliver) S.; m. Michael Eugene Richardson, June 12, 1971; children—Desiree M., Tatyana M. B.A. in History, French, Mt. St. Mary Coll., Newburgh, N.Y., 1970; M.A. in Internat. Relations, U. Ark., Ramstein AFB, W. Ger., 1974. Tchr., Army Edn. Ctr., Baumholder, W. Ger., 1972-75, adminstr., 1975-76; dir. ops. Bouton Brady Corp., Manassas, Va., 1979-80; internat. sales Knudson Mfg. Inc., Denver, 1981—; pres. M.S. Internat. Corp., McLean, Va., 1982—; ptnr. MMJV Enterprises, Arlington, Va., 1985—. Author: English as a Second Language, 1975. Tchr., Confraternity of Christian Doctrine, Vienna, Va., 1985—. Recipient Cert. of Appreciation/Meritorious Service, Baumholder Mil. Community, 1976. Mem. Washington Internat. Trade Assn., Suburban Md. Internat. Trade Assn., Nat. Assn. Female Execs., No. Va. Internat. Trade Assn. (bd. dirs. 1985—), Nat. Assn. Women Bus. Owners, Va. Assn. Female Execs. (exec. v.p.), Career Women's Network (founding bd. dirs., membership dir.). Roman Catholic. Club: Fort George G. Meade Officer Wives (2d v.p. 1978-79). Avocations: horseback riding; painting. Home: 8512 Jeffersonian Ct Vienna VA 22180 Office: M S Internat Corp PO Box 9143 McLean VA 22102

SASSOON, MAUREEN HANNAH, loss control specialist; b. Hollywood, Calif., Jan. 23, 1956; d. Moe George and Margaret Joyce (Eardley) S. B.S., Calif. State U.-Northridge, 1979, M.S., 1980, M.P.H. in Edn., 1985. Cert. community coll. thcr., Calif. Intern in health and safety CSUN, ARLI, Globe Battery, 1978-79; health and safety coordinator Globe Battery Co., Fullerton, Calif., 1979-81; indsl. hygiene and loss control specialist Cal-Surance Assoc., Torrance, Calif., 1981—. Instr., ARC, Los Angeles, 1979—, Am. Cancer Soc., West Los Angeles, 1985—. Recipient award for services above and beyond ARC, 1981. Mem. Am. Soc. Safety Engrs. (treas. 1981-82, 2d v.p. 1982-83, pres. 1984-85), Am. Indsl. Hygiene Assn. (mem. respirator com. 1983—), Nat. Environ. Health Assn., Calif. Environ. Health Assn. Republican. Mem. Covenant Ch. Office: Cal-Surance Assoc 3537 Torrance Blvd Torrance CA 90503

SATAKE, DALE MATSUI, realty company executive, consultant; b. Oakland, Calif., Jan. 30, 1947; d. Shichiro and Satsuki May (Hirano) Matsui; m. Robert Shigeo Satake, June 16, 1968. B.A. in Polit. Sci., U. Calif.-Berkeley, 1968, life teaching credential, 1969. Tchr. Lafayette (Calif.) Sch. Dist., 1969-72; co-owner Boardwalk Market, Inc., Tiburon, Calif., 1972-78; dir. mktg. Clark and Assocs., Columbia, Md., 1980, relocation dir., 1980-81; cons. on relocation, Columbia, 1982, Balt., 1983—; mgr. corp. relocation services

Merrill Lynch Realty, Severna Park, Md., 1982—. Mem. Howard County Econ. Devel. Adv. Council, 1983—, Howard County Human Services and Bus. Task Force, 1984; trustee Columbia found., 1985—; bd. dirs. United Way Partnership 1985—; mem. allocations com. United Way of Central Md., 1985—. Mem. Marin Found., Kappa Alpha Theta (v.p. chpt. 1967-68). Office: Merrill Lynch Realty 1407 York Rd Suite 105 Timonium MD 21093

SATARO, PATRICIA ANN, organization nursing administrator; b. Coaldale Pa., Sept. 19, 1941; d. Joseph John and Anna Agnes (Borovsky) Pavlick; m. Thomas Louis Sataro, May 4, 1968; children—Gina Marie, Christina Maria. Diploma Fordam Sch. Nursing, 1962; B.S., Adelphi U., 1970; M.S., Hartford Grad. Ctr., 1984. Head nurse Albert Einstein Hosp., Bronx, N.Y., 1966-68; asst. dir., adminstr. ARC, Farmington, Conn., 1979-81, dir. nursing, 1981—. Mem. Am. Assn. Blood Banking, Am. Nurses Assn. (cert.), Conn. Nurses Assn. Office: ARC 209 Farmington Ave Farmington CT 06119

SATCHELL, LISA BOLING, healthcare executive; b. Panama City, Fla., Sept. 18, 1960; d. William Wallace and Juanita Lee Ruth (Hannah) Boling; m. Richard John Satchell, Oct. 26, 1985. B.A., Belmont Coll., 1982. Dir. ops. Envoy Corp., Nashville, 1983-85; mgr. customer service Synercom Computers, Brentwood, Tenn., 1985-86; installation analyst Health America, Nashville, 1986—. Mem. Nat. Republican Com., 1985, 86, MADD (Mothers' Against Drunk Drivers), 1982—; participant Dance for Heart, Am. Heart Assn., Nashville, 1986. Mem. Nat. Assn. Female Execs., Sigma Tau Delta. Avocations: photography; aerobics; travel. Office: Health America 3310 West End Ave Nashville TN 37203

SATCHFIELD, LINDA KAYE, municipal purchasing agent, administrative manager; b. Coldwater, Mich., Feb. 3, 1951; d. Paul Edward and Winifred May (Carroll) Satchfield; m. Eugene Earl Eastlick, Dec. 26, 1977 (div. 1983). B.B.A., Western Mich. U., 1980, M.B.A., 1983. Asst. mgr. Mursch Sports, San Antonio, 1971-73; buyer U. Tex., San Antonio, 1973-74, central stores mgr., 1974-78; purchasing analyst City of Kalamazoo, 1980-83, purchasing agt., 1983—; mem. bd. Mich. Pub. Purchasing Assn., 1984—. Mem. Mich. Pub. Purchasing Officers (sec. 1983—), So. Mich. Purchasing Mgmt. (bd. dirs.). Lutheran. Avocations: computers; hiking; reading; writing. Home: 110 E Candlewyck Kalamazoo MI 49001 Office: City of Kalamazoo 241 W South St Kalamazoo MI 49007

SATELL, MARGARET COX, speech pathologist; b. Bklyn., Jan. 28, 1947; d. Jere Coleman Cox and Jane Dunseath (O'Neill) C.; m. Edward M. Satell, July 7, 1985. Student Chatham Coll., 1965-67; B.A. cum laude and with distinction, Mt. Holyoke Coll., 1969; M.A., Northwestern U., 1971. Speech pathologist Berkshire Rehab. Center, Pittsfield, Mass., 1972-78, clin. supr., 1978; speech pathologist Hosp. U. Pa., Phila., 1979—, chief speech pathology, 1985—; instr. dept. otorhinolaryngology Med. Sch. U. Pa., 1979—; cons. Ashmere Manor Nursing Home, Hinsdale, Mass., 1975-78, Bennington (Vt.) Convalescent Center, 1975-77. Rehab. Services Adminstrn. trainee, 1969-71; recipient award for continuing edn., 1983. Mem. Am. Speech Lang. and Hearing Assn. (cert. clin. competence 1973), Pa. Speech-Lang.-Hearing Assn., Southeastern Pa. Speech and Hearing Assn. Republican. Presbyterian. Clubs: Mendelssohn, Women's Faculty U. Pa., Mt. Holyoke Alumnae. Home: 1158 West Valley Rd Wayne PA 19087 Office: 3400 Spruce St Philadelphia PA 19104

SATHER, LINDA ANN, college administrator; b. Joliet, Ill., June 8, 1954; d. Robert H. and Dolores Ann (Conway) Johnson; m. John W. Sather, July 30, 1977. A.A.S., Joliet Jr. Coll., 1974; B.A. in Speech, Theatre and Edn., Lewis U., 1976. Secondary teaching cert., Ill. Tchr. speech Plainfield High Sch., Ill., 1976-77; clk. Joliet Pub. Library, 1977-80; sec. Rialto Square Theatre, Joliet, 1981-84; alumni coordinator Joliet Jr. Coll., 1984-85; coordinator clin. experience Lewis U., Romeoville, Ill., 1984—, adminstrv. asst., project smart, 1985. Avocations: sewing; reading; movies. Home: 1209 Oneida St Joliet IL 60435 Office: Lewis U Route 53 Romeoville IL 60441

SATINOVER, TERRY KLIEMAN, lawyer; b. Chgo., Apr. 25, 1936; d. Charles D. and Mary (Klieman) S.; student Shimer Coll., 1952-54; B.A. cum laude, U. Chgo., 1955, J.D. magna cum laude (Weymouth Kirkland scholar), 1958; m. Richard Ross Fagen, June 15, 1958 (div. June 1970); children—Sharon, Ruth, Elizabeth, Michael. Admitted to Ill. bar, 1970; practice in Chgo., 1971—; partner firm Pope, Ballard, Shepard & Fowle, Ltd., Chgo., 1971-78; mem. inquiry panel Ill. Disciplinary and Registration Com. Bd. dirs. Charles Satinover Fund, Akiba Schechter Day Sch., Chgo. chpt. Am. Friends of Hebrew U. Mem. Am., Ill., Chgo. (sec. exec. and real taxation subcoms. of real property com. 1972-73, mem. exec. subcom. 1973-74, co-chmn. newsletter) bar assns., Order of Coif, Phi Beta Kappa. Jewish (officer, trustee congregation). Home: 155 N. Harbor Dr Apt 4207 Chicago IL 60601 Office: 69 W Washington St Suite 3200 Chicago IL 60602

SATLOW, MARCIA FAITH E., neurologist, educator; b. Jamaica, May 1, 1949; d. Godfrey C. and Monica (Nicholson) Lawrence; m. Stephen J. Satlow, Apr. 2, 1974 (div.); 1 son, Aaron James. M.B., B.S. U. W.I., 1973. Diplomate Am. Bd. Psychiatry and Neurology. Intern Univ. Hosp. of the W.I., Jamaica, 1973-74; resident in Neurology Ottawa (Ont., Can.) Civic Hosp., 1975-77, Nassau (N.Y.) County Med. Ctr., 1977-79; asst. instr. dept. neurology SUNY-Stony Brook, N.Y., 1978-79, instr., fellow, 1979-81; vis. fellow Electromyography Neurol. Inst. of N.Y., N.Y.C., 1979-80, asst. prof., 1981—; mem. exec. bd. Muscular Dystrophy Assn., Long Island, N.Y., 1981—. Mem. AMA, N.Y. Acad. Scis, Am. Acad. Neurology, Am. Assn. Electromyography and Electrodiagnosis. Anglican. Office: Dept Neurology SUNY Health Sciences Ctr T12 020 Stony Brook NY 11794

SATO, EUNICE NODA, city official; b. Livingston, Calif., June 8, 1921; d. Bunsaku and Sawa (Maeda) Noda; A.A., Modesto Jr. Coll., 1941; B.A., Colo. State Coll. Edn., 1944; M.A., Columbia U., 1948; m. Thomas Takashi Sato, Dec. 9, 1950; children—Charlotte Patricia, Daniel Ryuichi, Douglas Ryuji. Tchr. public schs., Alpha, Mich., 1944-47; ednl. missionary, Yokohama, Japan, 1948-50; community vol., Long Beach, Calif., 1958-75; mem. Long Beach City Council, 1975-86, mayor, Long Beach, 1980-82; corp. sec. Health Systems Agy. Los Angeles County, 1978-79. Bd. dirs. ARC, 1974—, United Way Region III, 1975-80, Goodwill Industries, 1978-81, Sr. Care Action Network, 1978-80, Women's Council of Long Beach C. of C., 1977-86; trustee St. Mary's Hosp., 1977—; pres. Long Beach Council of Chs., 1973-75, Long Beach PTA Council, 1973-75; pres. Industry Edn. Council, Long Beach, treas. So. Calif. consortium, bd. dir. Calif. unit; mem. State Adv. Group on Juvenile Deliquency Prevention; mem. Gov.'s Council on Criminial Justice, Task Force on State Gang Violence Recipient Outstanding Lay Woman of Yr. award Long Beach Area Council of Chs., 1976; Outstanding Woman of Yr. award Women's Council of State C. of C., Calif., 1979; Community Service award Long Beach Coordinating Council, 1969; Medal of Honor, DAR, 1981; Woman of Yr. award Los Altos YMCA, 1982, Long Beach Internat. Bus. and Profl. Women's Club, 1982. Mem. Calif. State PTA (hon. life), Nat. PTA (hon. life), Calif. Assn. Elected Women in Edn. and Research, League Calif. Cities (pub. safety policy com.), AAUW. Republican. Methodist. Contbr. monthly articles for neighborhood papers. Home: 2895 Easy Ave Long Beach CA 90810 Office: 333 W Ocean Blvd Long Beach CA 90802

SATTERBERG, CAROL ANNE, nursing educator; b. Wenatchee, Wash., Mar. 10, 1932; d. Raymond H. and Virginia (Leedy) Lund; m. Richard A. Satterberg, Aug. 1, 1953; children—Karen, Daniel, Shelly. B.S. in Nursing, U. Wash., Seattle, 1954, M.Nursing, 1969. R.N. Staff nurse Swedish Med. Ctr., Seattle, 1954; office nurse Wenatchee Valley Clinic, Wenatchee, 1955-56; nursing faculty Nashville Gen. Hosp., 1956-57; mem. nursing faculty Highline Community Coll., Midway, Wash., 1969—. Author: Nursing Skills Manual, 1978; supplemental text Obstetrical Nursing, 1980; Nursing Clinical Aide-Drug Prototypes, 1981. Mem. Nurses Assn. of Am. Coll. Obstricians and Gynecologists (local program com., state workshops) Democrat. Presbyterian. Home: 12544 Shorewood Ln SW Seattle WA 98146 Office: Highline Coll 240th Pac Hwy S Midway WA 98031

SATTERFIELD, MARY (YARBROUGH) MCADEN, retired educator, civic worker; b. Semora, N.C., Mar. 15, 1911; d. John H. and Ella T. (Yarbrough) McAden; A.B., Meredith Coll., 1931; postgrad. N.C. State U., 1965, U. Va. Extension, 1965, U. N.C., summer, 1963; m. Lynn Banks Satterfield, Nov. 29, 1933; children—Lynn Banks, John De Berniere. Tchr. Caswell County (N.C.) elem. schs., 1931-34; tchr. sci. Caswell County high schs., 1934-36; postmaster U.S. Post Office, Milton, N.C., 1936-41; tchr. elem. grades Caswell County Pub. Schs., 1962-71. Clk., Town of Milton, 1959-61, sec. bd. of elections, 1976, registrar bd. of elections, 1979-81, registrar Town Bd. of Elections, 1983; mem. Caswell County Transp. Efficiency Council, 1981-83. Named Caswell County Mother of Yr., 1980. Mem. N.C., Caswell County (pres. 1962-64, sec. 1977-86) hist. assns., N.C. Assn. Educators, Nat. Ret. Tchrs. Assn., Semora Homemakers Extension, Mus. Assos. of N.C., UDC. Democrat. Baptist. Clubs: Milton Woman's (pres. 1961-62, v.p. 1962-64, sec. 1965—), Milton Community (sec. 1937-44, pres. 1965-67), Order Eastern Star.

SATTERFIELD, ROCHELLE KRILL, psychologist, clinical social worker; b. Cleve., Dec. 22, 1938; d. Harold J. and Hilda (Davis) Krill; B.A., U. Calif., San Diego, 1964; M.S.W., Calif. State U., San Diego, 1969; Ph.D., U. Tex.-Austin, 1984; m. Ben Satterfield, June 22, 1958 (div.); 1 son, Jeffrey Mark. Psychiat. social worker Brown Schs., Oaks Treatment Center, Austin, Tex., 1969-79; pvt. practice psychology, Austin, 1974—; cons. Transitional Treatment Center, Austin, 1978-81. Mem. Austin Group Therapy Assn. (pres., exec. com.), Am. Psychol. Assn., Southwestern Group Psychotherapy Assn. (exec. com., sec.), Am. Group Psychotherapy Assn., Nat. Assn. Social Workers. Home: 5500 Windward Dr Austin TX 78723 Office: 1500 W 6th St Austin TX 78703

SATTERLEE, JUANITA RUTH, consulting firm company executive; b. Wadena, Minn., Dec. 19, 1933; d. Charles Vivian and Hattie Alene (Austin) Phillips; m. Charles Gifford Satterlee, Oct. 14, 1954 (div. June 1973); children—Nan, Mark, Scott. Student, Macalester Coll., 1951-53. Research coordinator Countryside Council, South West State U., Marshall, Minn., 1974-77; commr. Minn. Public Utilities Commn., 1977-83; cons. Northwestern Bell, Diversified Energy, Mpls., 1984—; pres. Mid Am. Regulatory Commrs., 1982; vice chmn. Minn. Pub. Utilities Commn., 1978-81. Active in Minn. Women's Polit. Caucus, St. Paul, 1977—, St. Paul Urban League, 1977—, Minn. Women's Consortium and Campaign Fund, St. Paul, 1977—, Minn. Hist. Soc., St. Paul, 1977—, Jefferson Forum, St. Paul, Mpls., 1977—. Mem. Minn. Telephone Assn., Nat. Assn. Regulatory Commrs. Democrat. Congregational. Clubs: Minn., Bohemian (Des Moines). Avocations: fishing; reading; antiques. Home: 504 Selby Saint Paul MN 55102 Office: Direct Dialogue 100 S 5th St Suite 660 Minneapolis MN 55402

SATTERTHWAITE, HELEN FOSTER, state legislator; b. Blawnox, Pa., July 8, 1928; d. Samuel J. and Lillian (Schreiber) Foster; B.S. in Chemistry, Duquesne U., 1949; m. Cameron B. Satterthwaite, Dec. 23, 1950 (div. July 1979); children—Mark Cameron, Tod Foster, Tracy Lynn, Keith Alan, Craig Evan. Biol. technician U.S. Dept. Agr., 1967-68; research asst. Iowa State U. Coll. Agr., 1971; lab. technician U. Ill. Coll. Agr., 1968-70; research chemist E.I. duPont de Nemours & Co., Wilmington, Del., 1951-53; research asst. Gulf Research and Devel., Harmarville, Pa., 1950; natural sci. lab. technician U. Ill. Coll. Vet. Medicine, 1971-74; rep. Gen. Assembly Ill., 1974—, chairperson House com. on higher edn., 1983—, vice-chairperson elem. and secondary edn.; mem. Commn. on Mental Health and Devel. Disabilities, 1975-85, mem. exec. com., 1977-85, vice chairperson, 1979-85; mem. Commn. to Visit and Examine State Instns., 1977-85. Bd. dirs. East Central Ill. Health Systems Agy., 1977-79; bd. dirs. Champaign County (Ill.) United Way, 1970-74, mem. budget com., 1973-74, mem. joint rev. com. on funding Champaign County Mental Health Programs, 1973; co-chairperson Task Force on Mental Retardation for Champaign County Mental Health Bd., 1973; mem. Ill. Developmental Disability Advocacy Authority, 1977-85, vice chmn., 1979-80; chairperson Ill. House Democratic Study Group, 1979-81; mem. Edn. Commn. of the States, 1985—; mem. Nat. Conf. State Legis. Commn. on Labor and Edn., 1985—. Recipient Freshman Legislator of Yr. award Ill. Edn. Assn., 1975; commendation Ill. State's Attys. Assn., 1975; Best Legislator award Ind. Voters Ill., 1976, 78, 80, 82, 84; cert. honor Assn. Students Govts., 1977; Disting. Service cert. Am. Vets. World War II, Korea and Viet Nam, 1977; Environ. Legis. of Yr. award Ill. Environ. Council, 1977, 79, 81, 83; Meritorious Service award Champaign County Council on Alcoholism, 1978; Perfect Voting Record award Ill. Credit Union League, 1979, Ill. Wildlife Fedn., 1979; cert. spl. recognition Ill. Women's Polit. Caucus, 1979, 80, Public Service award Izaak Walton League, 1980; named Person of Yr., Champaign County Mental Health Assn., 1981, Pub. Citizen of Yr., Illini Dist. and Ill. chpt. Nat. Assn. Social Workers, 1981. Mem. Ill. Conf. Women Legislators (co-convenor 1981-83), Nat. Order Women Legislators (dir. Region IV 1982, treas. 1983-84), Delta Kappa Gamma. Quaker. Office: 2049 Stratton Office Bldg Springfield IL 62706 also 118 E University Ave Champaign IL 61820

SATTLER, JANIECE DONNA, sales executive; b. Avon, S.D., Jan. 28, 1932; d. Fred James and Fannie Grace (Durma) S.; student Colo. State U., 1965-66, City Coll., Seattle, 1979-80. Bookkeeper, King Lumber Co., Loveland, Colo., 1950-53; legal stenographer Seaman & Ball, Attys. at Law, Loveland, 1953-54; statis. clk. U.S. Bur. Reclamation, Loveland, 1955-64; sec. dept. radiology and radiation biology Colo. State U., Ft. Collins, 1964-67; asst. dir. Continuing Edn. Lab. Personnel, Wash./Alaska Regional Med. Program, Seattle, 1967-71; adminstrv. coordinator dept. pathology Providence Med. Center, Seattle, 1971-80, purchasing mgr., 1980-82; supr. sales Advanced Tech. Labs., Inc., Bellevue, Wash., 1983-84, sales dir. Hewlett Packard, 1984—. Mem. Nat. Writers Club. Republican. Author: A Practical Guide to Financial Management of the Clinical Laboratory, 1980, 2d edit., 1986; contbr. articles to various publs. Home: 1035 156th Ave NE #8 Bellevue WA 98007 Office: 15815 SE 37th Bellevue WA 98006

SAUER, DEBORAH PAULINE, nurse; b. Oklahoma City, Mar. 29, 1957; d. Louis Edward and Marjorie Ann (Hollman) Johnston; m. Ronald Dean Sauer, May 30, 1975; children—Rebecca Ann, Adam Edward. Diploma, St. Anthony's Sch. Nursing, Oklahoma City, 1979. R.N. Nurse's aide St. Anthony's Hosp., 1976-78; nurse intensive and cardiac care units South Community Hosp., Oklahoma City, 1979-82; nurse Newcastle Elem. Sch. (Okla.), 1982—; basic rescuer Am. Heart Assn., Oklahoma City, 1979-83, CPR instr., 1983—. Recipient achievement cert. South Community Hosp., 1979, 80. Mem. NEA, Okla. Edn. Assn., Sch. Nurse Orgn. Okla., Nat. Assn. Sch. Nurses. Democrat. Baptist. Home: PO Box 667 Newcastle OK 73065 Office: Newcastle Elementary Sch PO Box 709 Newcastle OK 73065

SAUER, ELISABETH RUTH, lawyer; b. Charleston, W.Va., July 27, 1948; d. Gordon Chenoweth and Mary Louise (Steinhilbur) S. B.A., Northwestern U., 1970; J.D., U. Mo., 1975. Bar: Mo. 1975. Assoc. firm Campbell, Erickson, Cottingham, Morgan & Gibson, Kansas City, Mo., 1975-80, ptnr., 1980—. Bd. dirs. Planned Parenthood Western Mo. and Kans., 1978—, v.p., 1983-84; bd. dirs. Kansas City Met. Regional Com. on Status of Women, 1976-78. Mem. ABA, Mo. Bar Assn., Kansas City Bar Assn., Assn. Women Lawyers of Greater Kansas City. Club: Rockhill Tennis-Kenwood. Office: Campbell Erickson Cottingham Morgan & Gibson 4901 Main Suite 414 Kansas City MO 64112

SAUER, POLLY ANNE, marketing executive; b. Monroe, Wis., Aug. 2, 1954; d. Remfrey Eugene and Leah Gertrude (Flannery) Sauer. B.S. in Theatre Arts, U. Wis.-Stevens Point, 1977, B.S. in Communications with honors, 1977. Div. mktg. mgr. Ency. Britannica, Milw., 1978-79, Los Angeles, 1979-81, regional mktg. mgr., Western Region U.S., 1981-83, nat. mktg. mgr., 1983-85, dir. nat. mktg., 1985-86, asst. to exec. v.p., 1986—. Named Player of the Yr., Players Orgn. U. Wis., 1975-76, 76-77. Student Technician of the Year, 1975-76, 76-77, Best Student Dir., 1975-76, 76-77. Mem. Am. Mgmt. Assn., Nat. Assn. Female Execs. Club: Players (pres. 1976-77). Home: 1540 N LaSalle St Suite 2004 Chicago IL 60610 Office: Ency Britannica USA 310 S Michigan Chicago IL 60604

SAUER, SUSAN MARIE, manufacturing company official; b. Geneva, Ill., Nov. 21, 1952; d. Walter Francis and Margaret Marie Sauer; B.S., Ill. State U., 1974; postgrad. in bus. adminstrn. No. Ill. U. With Container Corp. Am., Chgo., 1974—, casualty mgr., 1979-80, mgr. workers compensation and regional claims coordinator, internat. ins. coordinator, 1980-82, mgr. workers' compensation, 1983—; mem. bd. Ill. Insolvency Fund. Mem. Nat. Council Self-Insurers (bd. dirs.). Lutheran. Office: 1 First National Plaza Chicago IL 60603

SAUERBREY, ELLEN ELAINE RICHMOND, state legislator; b. Balt., Sept. 9, 1937; d. Edgar Arthur and Ethel Frederika (Landgraf) Richmond; A.B. summa cum laude in Biology and English, Western Md. Coll., 1959; m. Wilmer John Emil Sauerbrey, June 27, 1959. Biology instr., chmn. sci. dept. Baltimore County Sch. System, 1959-64; Baltimore County dist. mgr. U.S. Census, 1970; mem. Md. Ho. of Dels. from 10th Legis. Dist., 1978—. Del., Rep. nat. convs., 1968, 76, 84, mem. credentials com., 1984. vice chmn. Rep. State Central Com. of Balt. County, 1966-71; trustee Md. Council Econ. Edn. Mem. Md. Fedn. Rep. Women, Am. Legis. Exchange Council (Md. chmn., nat. bd. dirs.), Nat. Taxpayers Union, Md. Farm Bur., Women Legislators of Md., So. Legis. Conf. (consumer protection com., mem. agr. and rural affairs com.), Md. Conservative Union, Nat. Tax Limitation Com., Beta Beta Beta. Presbyterian. Office: House Office Bldg Annapolis MD 21401

SAUERBRUNN, KATHLEEN HANDLEY, lawyer, govt. ofcl.; b. Little Silver, N.J., Oct. 18, 1917; B.A., Douglass Coll., 1939; LL.B., So. Meth. U., 1962; m. Bertram J.L. Sauerbrunn; children—Randa Meredith, Sharon Doyle, Jennifer Harper. Admitted to Tex. bar, 1962, U.S. Supreme Ct. bar, 1965, D.C. bar, 1979; asst. dist. atty., 1962-63; asso. counsel firm Boyd, Veigel and Gay, McKinney, Tex., 1963-65; atty.-adv. higher edn. br., Office Gen. Counsel, HEW, Washington, 1965-67; atty.-adv., adminstrv. law br., Office Gen. Counsel, HUD, Washington, 1967-70, dir. adminstrn., mng. partner functions for gen. counsel, 1971-72, asst. gen. counsel for land sales, ins. and disaster assistance, 1972-77, asso. gen. counsel for regulatory programs, 1977-83. Recipient Disting. Alumna award Douglass Coll., 1978; charter mem. Sr. Exec. Service, 1979. Mem. Am. Bar Assn., Tex. Bar Assn., D.C. Bar Assn., Exec. Women in Govt., Fed. Bar Assn. Clubs: Tantallon Golf and Country, Laconia Country, Women's Golf Assn. Home: 1315 Swan Harbour Rd Fort Washington MD 20744

SAUERESSIG-RIEGEL, SUZANNE, veterinarian, newspaper columnist; b. Nuremberg, Germany, Feb. 4, 1925; came to U.S., 1955; d. Josef and Elizabeth (Walsch) Saueressig; m. Richard T. Riegel, Dec. 26, 1955. D.V.M., Munich U., 1953, Dr. Med. Vet., 1954. Nurse, U.S. 6th Army, W.Ger., 1946-49; staff veterinarian Humane Soc. of Mo., St. Louis, 1955-65, chief of staff, 1965—. Author weekly column Ask the Pet Doctor, St. Louis Globe Democrat, 1980—; author (booklet) Salmonella in Shellfish, 1954; co-author collaboration research papers St. Louis U. Med. Sch. 1959-61; contbr. article to mag. Served as nurse German Army, 1943-46. Recipient spl. leadership award profl. category YWCA, St. Louis, 1983, 25 yrs. service award Humane Soc. Mo., 1980. Mem. AVMA, Am. Animal Hosp. Assn., Assn. Woman Veterinarians (Woman Vet. of Yr. 1972), Assn. Feline Practitioners, Mo. Acad. Vet. Medicine, Am. Assn. Lab. Animal Sci., Vet. Oncology Soc., Am. Vet. Cardiology Soc., Mo. Control Officers Assn., Mo. Vet. Med. Assn. Roman Catholic. Office: Humane Soc of Mo 1210 Macklind Ave Saint Louis MO 63110

SAUL, SHURA, gerontologist; b. N.Y.C., July 8, 1920; d. Froim Camenir and Rose (Lisenco) Rudin; B.A., Hunter Coll., 1940; M.S.W., Columbia U., 1963, Ed.D., 1972; m. Sidney R. Saul, Dec. 14, 1941; children—Mark, Jonathan, Jennifer, Tchr. kindergarten N.Y.C. Bd. Edn., 1943-48; dir. Bronx River Child Care Center, 1948-49; group worker Jewish Guild for Blind, N.Y.C., 1954-61; cons. social worker United Hosp. Fund, N.Y.C., 1964-67; mem. faculty Sch. Social Work, N.Y.U., N.Y.C., 1967-69; mem. faculty Brookdale gerontology program Adelphi U., Garden City, N.Y., 1975—, Wurzweiler Sch., N.Y.C., 1981—; dir. student unit Self Help Community Services, N.Y.C., 1969-71; coordinator profl. services Kingsbridge Heights Nursing Home, Bronx, 1971-78, ednl. coordinator, 1978—; cons. psychogeriatrics and edn. Borders Health Bd., others, Scotland, 1974—, Chaim Sheba Med. Ctr., Israel, 1982—. Chmn. bd. dirs. Bronx-North Manhattan Coalition for Elderly and Long Term Care, 1981-82; observer, del. White House Conf. on Aging, 1981. Recipient Woman of Yr. award Jewish Welfare Bd., Bronx, 1954. Mem. Goldens Bridge Community Assn. (history com. 1978—), Nat. Assn. Social Workers, Nat. Council on Aging, Am. Group Psychotherapy Assn. Author: The Right To Be Different, 1962, Aging: An Album of People Growing Old, 1974, 2d edit., 1983 Sophia Moses Robison, Woman of the Twentieth Century, 1981; editor: Social Group Work for Frail Elderly, 1982; producer, editor: (videotape series) Enhancing the Quality of Life for Institutionalized Elderly, Scotland, 1980, other videotapes on aging, 1976, 82; contbr. articles to profl. publs. Home: Box 281 Goldens Bridge NY 10526

SAULTER-HEMMER, JANET LYNN, computer programmer; b. Glen Ridge, N.J., Nov. 25, 1954; d. Lajoie Alvin and Nancy Harriet (Leatherberry) Saulter; m. Benjamin Joseph Singerline, Dec. 11, 1976 (div. 1981); 1 son, Scott Benjamin; m. 2d Thomas Paul Hemmer, Oct. 7, 1984. A.A., Thomas A. Edison Coll., Trenton, N.J., 1977, B.A., 1983; grad. Chubb Inst. Computer Tech., Parsippany, N.J. Sec. to v.p. Rapidata Co., Fairfield, N.J., 1974-76, office mgr. Scottish Pedlar Co., South Orange, N.J., 1976-77; contract adminstr. McGraw-Edison Service, Fairfield, 1979-84; computer programmer Dun's Mktg. Services div. Dun & Bradstreet, 1984—, now sr. programmer, analyst. Recycling co-ordinator Presbyn. Ch., West Caldwell, N.J.; organizer, N.J. state pres. Orgn. Enforcement Child Support, West Caldwell; mem. Essex County Adv. Commn. on Status of Women chmn. Foster Grandparents Program, West Caldwell; former dir. Camp Fatima N.J., Livingston; youth adv. del. Presbytery of Newark; elder Presbyn. Ch. of West Caldwell. Mem. Jaycee-ettes (state dir. 1979-80, officer yr. 1980). Democrat. Club: Jr. Woman's (West Essex, N.J.) Lodge: Order Easter Star (Caldwell #61). Home: 8 Maple Ln Lake Hiawatha NJ 07034 Office: Dun's Mktg Service 3 Century Dr Parsippany NJ 07054

SAUNDERS, ALMA ANNETTE, educator; b. Brunswick, Ga., Sept. 24, 1930; d. William Van and Cora Mae (Young) Gunter; B.Bus.Edn., Ga. State U., 1971, M.Bus. Edn., 1978; m. William J. Saunders, Dec. 11, 1948 (dec. 1977); children—Amanda Lou Robertson, Michael William. Sec., United Electric Co., Jacksonville, Fla., 1957-58; bookkeeper Blue Marlin Co., Key West, Fla., 1959-60; billing clk. Hoffmann-La Roche, Inc., Decatur, Ga., 1965-66; statis. asst. Tb program Center for Disease Control, Atlanta, 1966-68; tchr. Blayton Bus. Coll., Atlanta, 1971-72; tchr. bus. edn. Fulton County Sch. System, Atlanta, 1972—; cons., lectr. in field. Mem. exec. bd. North Springs United Methodist Ch., Atlanta, 1979, adult Sunday sch. tchr., 1979. Recipient Educator of Yr. award 5th congl. dist. Ga. Vocat. Assn., 1977, 81; Outstanding Service award Ga. Dept. Edn., Bus. and Office Edn., 1979, 81. Mem. Internat. Soc. Bus. Edn., Nat. Bus. Ednl. Assn., Ga. Bus. Edn. Assn., Am. Vocat. Assn., Ga. Vocat. Assn., Am. Soc. for Tng. and Devel., North Fulton C. of C., Am. Council on Consumer Interests, Delta Pi Epsilon. Home: 6987 J Roswell Rd Atlanta GA 30328 Office: 1131 Alpharetta St Roswell GA 30075

SAUNDERS, BEATRICE NAIR (MRS. DERO AMES SAUNDERS), editor, association executive; b. New Britain, Conn., Dec. 26, 1915; d. Frank and Sophie (Adler) Nair; B.A., Smith Coll., 1936; m. Dero Ames Saunders, May 23, 1936; children—David Nair, Richard Ames. Tchr. pub. schs., New Britain, 1936; editorial asst. Cordon Co., N.Y.C., 1937-39, Family Welfare Assn. Am., N.Y.C., 1939-42; supr. editorial div. publs. div. ARC, Washington, 1943-46; free-lance editor various publs. N.Y.C., 1946-50; editor-in-chief, publs. dept. Girl Scouts U.S.A., N.Y.C., 1950-55; dir. publs. dept., editor Social Work, Nat. Assn. Social Workers, N.Y.C., 1955-82, publs. cons., 1982—; mem. adj. faculty Grad. Sch. Social Services, Fordham U., Lincoln Center, N.Y.C., 1982—. Founding editor Affilia, Jour. Women and Social Work, 1986—. Vol., ARC, Freeport, L.I., 1946-47, Child Care Center, Freeport, 1946-47; chmn. parents assn. Downtown Community Sch., 1948-50; chmn. 22d-21st St. Community Council, 1954-58, 62-63; chmn. com. on existing housing Chelsea Community Council, 1957-60; vice chmn. Chelsea Com. for Neighborhood Devel., 1960-63, chmn., 1963-65. Clubs: Smith Coll., Heights Casino. Home: 446 W 22d St New York NY 10011 Office: Grad Sch Social Service Fordham Univ Lincoln Ctr New York NY 10023

SAUNDERS, BETH PENN, advertising executive; b. Asher, Okla., Dec. 9, 1932; d. Floyd Glenn and Florence E. (Seckinger) Embry' B.F.A., Art Center, 1952; m. Robert D. Saunders, Dec. 13, 1975; children from previous marriage—Kathryn Elizabeth, Wesley Alan, David Embry. Art dir. Gottschalks, Fresno, Calif., 1952, Scope Advt., 1965-67; advt. dir. BuildMart Corp., 1967-75; head AD-Vantage Advt., Chino, Calif., 1975—; pres. Embryline Inc., Mut. Advt. Corp. Mem. Republican Women of Long Beach (Calif.). Mem. Bus. and Profl. Women. Home: 8441 Wilson Ct Alta Loma CA 91701 Office: 13364 Central Ave Chino CA 91710

SAUNDERS, CANDACE A., marketing representative, consultant; b. Fort McClellan, Ala., Oct. 16, 1956; d. John Richard and Jane Alice (Thurman) Arnold; m. Russell Scott Saunders, Aug. 23, 1980. B.S. magna cum laude, UCLA, 1978. Asst. v.p. Pritikin Longevity Center, Santa Monica, Calif., 1979-83; sec., treas. Saunder Electric Inc., West Los Angeles, 1982—; cons. Rental Industry Mgmt. Systems, Pasadena, Calif., 1983—; mktg. rep. Integrated Systems Mgmt., San Diego, 1983—; cons. 10:40 Tax Preparation Services, Santa Monica, 1981—. Mem. AAU, Alpha Lambda Delta. Republican. Episcopalian. Club: Santa Monica Track (Women's rep. 1980). Home: 7447

Vanalden Ave Reseda CA 91335 Office: Integrated Systems Mgmt 2515 Camino Del Rio S Suite 300 San Diego CA 92108

SAUNDERS, CLARA IRENE, publisher, writer; b. Entiat, Wash., Aug. 20, 1917; d. Leroy and Laura Marie (Murdock) Foote; ed. public schs., spl. courses; children—Dianne, Donna, Nancy, Eugene, David. Practical nurse, World War II; mgr. South Kitsap C. of C., 1964-69; pub. Who, 1974-75; freelance writer; poetry includes: This Is Me, 1975; Remembering You, 1980; Very Personal, 1982; children's books include: The David Stories, 1982; David and His Friends, The Once in Awhile, 1974. Coordinator Kitsap Mental Health Group; organizer crisis clinic and office Kitsap County Council on Aging, 1962-65. Named Citizen of Day, Sta. KIXI, Seattle, 1981. Mem. Grey Panthers. Republican. Episcopalian. 2440 Snyder Ave Bremerton WA 98312

SAUNDERS, JACQUELINE, nurse; b. Camden, N.J., Sept. 25, 1960; d. John Arthur and Betty Frances (Coleman) S. B.S. in Nursing, Rutgers U., 1983. R.N., Pa., N.J., Va. Staff nurse St. Agnes Med. Ctr., Phila., 1983; charge nurse Our Lady of Lourdes Med. Ctr., Camden, 1983-85; operating room intern Med. Coll. Va., Richmond, 1985—. Mem. Delta Phi Epsilon. Democrat. Home: 1501 Wildwood Ave Camden NJ 08103

SAUNDERS, JEANNE DOUGHERTY, development and fund raising executive; b. Kansas City, Mo., Nov. 14, 1924; d. Lewis Bissell and Nancy (Moore) Dougherty; m. Louis Alexander Saunders, Jan. 1, 1952; children—Susan, John Stephen, James. Student William Jewell Coll., 1942-43; B.A., U. Mo., 1946; M.A., Columbia U. and Union Theol. Seminary, 1952. Cert. fundraiser. Short term missionary to Philippines, Presbyn. Bd. Fgn. Missions, N.Y.C., 1946-50; instr. religion dept. Tex. Christian U., Ft. Worth, 1958-64, dir. religious activities, 1961-64; dir. pub. info. Vis. Nurse Assn., Dallas, 1973-82; dir. capital campaign Christian Ch., Ft. Worth, from 1982, now v.p. charitable devel. Vis. Nurse Assn. chmn. bd. dirs. Juliette Fowler Homes, Inc., Dallas, 1981-82. Mem. exec. com. Nat. Benevolent Assn., St. Louis, 1981-82; sec., bd. dirs. Fowler Christian Apts., Ind., Dallas, 1978-82; mem. sr. services com. Community Council Greater Dallas, 1979-82; mem. com. on aging Greater Dallas Community Chs., 1980-82. Mem. Mortar Bd., Kappa Kappa Gamma. Democrat. Mem. Christian Ch. Home: 10207 Best Dr Dallas TX 75229 Office: Vis Nurse Assn 8200 Brook River Dr Suite 200N Dallas TX 75247

SAUNDERS, NINA ALEXANDER, interior designer; b. Lemberg, Poland, Jan. 1, 1934; came to U.S., 1951, naturalized, 1955; d. Leopold and Ann (Erbsen) Alexander; m. Roger Alfred Saunders, Oct. 4, 1953; children—Gary L., Jeffrey G., Todd R., Tedd R. Student CCNY, 1951-52, NYU, 1952-53. Ptnr., J & N Interior Design, Brookline and Chestnut Hill, Mass., 1971-79; pres. Interior Design Assocs. Boston, 1979—; Jr. League showhouse invitee, Newton, Milton and Brookline, 1975, 76, 77; dir. Hotels of Tradition, Boston, 1980—; judge nat. lodging-hosp. design awards, 1983. Bd. dirs. women's div. Combined Jewish Philanthropies, Boston, 1985—, Friends of Pub. Garden, Boston, 1985—; trustee New Eng. Aquarium, Boston, 1981—, Met. Opera Boston, 1982—; mem. exec. bd. Mus. Fine Arts Ladies Com., Boston, 1982—. Honored by proclamation Nina A. Saunders Day, Mayor of Boston, 1981. Clubs: Longwood Cricket (Chestnut Hill); Belmont Country (Mass.); Algonquin, Badminton and Tennis (Boston). Avocations: tennis; skiing; painting; travel; entertaining. Office: Interior Design Assocs 64 Arlington St Boston MA 02117

SAUNDERS, PATRICIA SUSAN, psychologist, psychoanalyst; b. White Plains, N.Y., Sept. 20, 1944; d. Sanford and Isabell (Friedlander) S.; m. Arthur Grossman, Oct. 9, 1975 (div. Mar. 1978). B.A., Adelphi U., 1965; M.S., Rutgers U., 1967, Ph.D., 1969. Lic. psychologist, N.Y.; cert. psychoanalyst. Clin. psychologist in pvt. practice, N.Y.C., 1971—, Hillside Hosp., Glenoaks, N.Y., 1971-74, Jewish Bd. Family and Children's Services, N.Y.C., 1974-84, Postgrad. Ctr. for Mental Health, N.Y.C., 1978—; supervising psychologist New Hope Guild Assocs., N.Y.C., 1984—; research cons. Rosenfeld Heart Found., N.Y.C., 1975—. Postdoctoral fellow in clin. psychology NIMH, Albert Einstein Med. Coll., 1969-71. Mem. N.Y. State Psychol. Assn., Postgrad. Psychoanalytic Soc. Democrat. Avocations: photography, tennis, running, literature, piano and guitar. Home: 412 E 55th St Apt 3E New York NY 10022 Office: 135 E 50th St Room 103 New York NY 10022

SAUNDERS, PAULA RONNIE, computer consultant, educator; b. Bklyn., Mar. 16, 1944; d. Arthur Jay and Terry (Soipher) S. B.A., Hofstra U., 1967; cert. Apex Tech. Sch., N.Y.C., 1980, Control Data Inst., N.Y.C., 1981. High sch. English tchr., N.Y.C. Pub. Schs., 1967-80; technician Xerox Corp., N.Y.C., 1981-82, 3M Co., N.Y.C., 1982-83; computer instr. Royal Bus. Sch., N.Y.C., 1983—; computer cons., 1982—. Mem. Sr. Action Gay Environment, NOW, Nat. Assn. Female Execs., Women in Computing, Women in Data Processing, N.Y. Amateur Computer Club, IBM PC Club. Avocations: guitar; singing; poetry; writing short stories. Home: 220 W 24th St New York NY 10011

SAUNDERS, PHYLLIS S., consultant; b. N.Y.C., May 2, 1932; d. Jack and Bella (Bader) Bloom; widowed; children—Todd B., Dean B. Student, U. Miami. Broker, cons. to bus. in Caribbean and Central Am., 1955—. Mem. Am. Bus. Women's Assn., Nat. Assn. Women Bus. Owners, Am. Liver Found., Am. Jewish Com., Nat. Home Asmatic Children, PTA, Cub Scouts Am., Khoury League, Salvation Army, Hope Ctr. Mentally Retarded, Hebrew Home for the Aged, Arthur Ford Acad., U. Miami AIDS Research Ctr., Little Theatre Groups, Fla. Feminist Bank. Republican. Avocations: golf; tennis; aerobics; fishing; boating. Address: 1570 Madruga Ave Suite 216 Coral Gables FL 33146

SAUNDERS, PHYLLIS TIPKER, university official; b. Sewickley, Pa., July 20, 1918; d. George Edward and Margaret (Springer) Tipker; m. Henry A. Saunders, Apr. 17, 1943 (div.). B.S., Slippery Rock U., 1946; M.S., Barry U., 1964. Cert. elem. tchr., Pa. Tchr. Moon Area Schs., Coraopolis, Pa., 1937-46, prin., 1946-49; tchr. Dade County Pub. Sch., Miami, Fla., 1949-66, elem. asst. prin., 1966-75; ret., 1975; coordinator pub. affairs Barry U., Miami Shores, Fla., 1976-82, dir. pub. info., 1982—, editor The Flame, 1982—. Mem. NEA, Women in Communication, Hialeah-Miami Springs Area C. of C. Democrat. Presbyterian. Club: Spotlight (Hialeah, Fla.).

SAUNDERS, RUBIE AGNES, writer, educator; b. N.Y.C., Jan. 31, 1929; d. Walter St. Clair and Rubie Gwendolyn (Ford). B.A., Hunter Coll., 1950. Editor children's mag. Parent's Mag. Enterprises, N.Y.C., 1950-80; freelance writer, New Rochelle, N.Y., 1980—; instr. Inst. Children's Lit., Redding Ridge, Conn., 1980—. Nominating com. chmn., bd. dirs. The Feminist Press., N.Y.C., 1984—. Editor Mag. Young Miss, 1965-80; The Calling All Girls Party Book, 1966, The Concise Guide to Baby Sitting, 1972; Smart Shopping and Cosumerism for Teen-Agers, 1973; The Beauty Book, 1982; and many more. Contbr. articles to profl. jours. and chpts. to books. Sec., New Rochelle Council on Arts, 1976—; sec. Bldg. Permit Adv. Commn.; leader pack Bklyn. council Cub Scouts Am., 1960—. Recipient Outstanding Grad. award Hunter Coll., 1960; name to Hall of Fame, Hunter Coll., 1972. Avocations: gardening; cooking; reading. Home and Office: 26 Glenwood Ave New Rochelle NY 10801

SAUNDERS, RUTH ELLEN, nurse; b. Marlinton, W.Va., May 16, 1955; d. Ether James and Maggie Virginia (Myers) Tyson; m. Jerry O'Neil Saunders, Aug. 16, 1975; children—Tina Danielle, Kevin O'Neil. B.A. magna cum laude, W. Va. State Coll., 1976; student Va. Western Community Coll., 1980-82; A.Applied Sci., Dabney S. Lancaster Community Coll., Clifton Forge, Va., 1983. R.N., Va. Credit interviewer Sears Roebuck & Co., Roanoke, Va., 1976-77; credit loan clk. 1st Nat. Exchange Bank, 1977-78; ins. sales agt. Mut. of Omaha Ins. Co., 1978; nursing asst. Community Hosp. Roanoke Valley, 1978-80; R.N., Lewis Gale Hosp., Roanoke, 1983—. Recipient Superior Cadet Decoration award Army ROTC, 1973-74; Cert. of Commendation, Health Scis. Unltd., 1981; Nat. Coll. scholar, 1973. Mem. Am. Assn. Critical Care Nurses. Baptist. Avocations: biking; singing. Home: 3810 Green Springs Ave NW Roanoke VA 24017 Office: Lewis Gale Hosp 1900 Electric Rd Salem VA 24153

SAUNDERS, RUTH LYNCH, psychiatric social worker; b. Longview, Wash., Nov. 4, 1927; d. Harry Hudson and Marion Lucille (Gibson) Lynch; B.S., UCLA, 1949; M.S.W., Columbia U., 1976; cert. Psychoanalytic Tng., Inst. for Contemporary Psychotherapy, 1979; m. Frank A. Saunders, May 24, 1958; 1 son, Anthony David. Projects editor The Sat. Rev. of Lit., N.Y.C., 1960-65; asst. med. editor McCall's, N.Y.C., 1965-67; editor Warner Bros., N.Y.C., 1967-69, Roche Med. Image, 1969-73; psychotherapist Inst. for Contemporary Psychotherapy, N.Y.C., 1976—; mem. staff Center for the Study of Anorexia and Bulimia, N.Y.C., N.Y., 1979—; pvt. practice, N.Y.C. Mem. Manhattan adv. bd. N.Y. Urban League, 1962-74, pres. Lucy Stone League, 1972-74. Cert. social worker. Mem. Phi Beta Kappa, Alpha Mu Gammaa. Clubs: Sankaty Head Golf, Siasconset Casino (Nantucket, Mass.). Home: 680 West End Ave New York NY 10025 also Box 248 Siasconset MA 02564 Office: 940 Park Ave New York NY 10028

SAUNDERS, SALLY LOVE, poet, therapist; b. Bryn Mawr, Pa., Jan. 15, 1940; d. Lawrence and Dorothy (Love) S. Student Temple U., Phila., 1962-63, Sophia U., Tokyo, summer 1963, W. Ill. U., African tour, summer 1964; B.S., George Williams Coll., Downers Grove, Ill., 1965; postgrad. in poetry writing New Sch. of Social Research, N.Y.C., 1968-69. Group worker Margaret Fuller House, Cambridge, Mass., summers 1951-61; Univ. House, Phila., 1961-63; social worker asst. Dorchester Settlement House, Mass., 1959, Ten Acre Sch., Wellesley, Mass., 1960-61; freelance writer, lectr., N.Y.C., Phila., San Francisco. Author: Pauses, 1978; Fresh Bread, 1982. Contbr. poetry to mags. Mem. NOW, Phila., 1985—, Free Women's Sch., Phila., 1985—. Recipient Poetry award Wilory Farm Contest, 1981; recipient numerous grants for group poetry therapy. Mem. Assn. Poetry Therapy, The Nat. Writers Club, Press Club of San Francisco, Acad. Am. Poets, Ina Coolbrith Poetry Circle, Assn. for Poetry Therapy, Poets' and Writers' Guild, N.Y.C., Poetry Soc. Am., Pen and Pencil Club, Phila. Home: 1420 Locust St 36C Philadelphia PA 19102 Office: 209 Summit Rd Malvern PA 19355

SAUNDERS, SANDRA JEAN, lawyer; b. Cleve., Jan. 1, 1944; d. Alexander V. and Rosemary (Sunyog) Toth. B.A., Brown U., 1964; M.A., Fordham U., 1965; J.D., Lewis and Clark Law Sch., 1978. Bar: Oreg. 1979. Securities analyst various cos., N.Y.C., Boston, Chgo., 1964-73; econ. cons., Portland, 1973-76; pvt. practice law, Portland, 1979—. Sec. bd. dirs. Pittock Mansion Soc., Portland, 1981—; trustee Leukemia Assn. Oreg., 1984—; area rep. Nat. Alumni Schs. Program, Brown U., 1981—; mem. Portland Met. Citizens Cable TV Com., 1973-74; pres. Women's Assn., Oreg. Mus. Sci. and Industry, Portland, 1974, mem. council, 1984—; mem. women's council Portland Art Assn., 1973—; bd. dirs. Vol. Braille Services, Inc., Portland, 1985—. Law rev. staff Environ. Law, 1977. Recipient Am. Jurisprudence award, 1978. Mem. Oreg. State Bar, Multnomah County Bar Assn., Oreg. Trial Lawyers Assn., Oreg. Young Attys. Assn. (dir. 1981-83), ABA, Phi Alpha Delta. Clubs: Portland City, Multnomah Athletic. Office: 660 Morgan Bldg 720 SW Washington St Portland OR 97205

SAUNDERS, SUSAN GODWIN, consulting company executive; b. N.Y.C., Jan. 4, 1953; d. Louis Alexander and Jeanne (Dougherty) S. B.A. in Anthropology and Sociology, Mills Coll., 1975; M.P.A. in Econs. and Fin., Am. U., 1978. Mem. staff Internat. Vol. Services, Dacca, Bangladesh, 1975-76; mktg. specialist Nat. Econ. Devel. Assn., Washington, 1977; sr. assoc. TRITON Corp., Washington, 1978-80, dir. internat. devel., 1981-82, v.p. internat. accounts, corp. officer, 1983—, self-employed mgmt. cons., 1984—; worked in Nepal, Thailand, Philippines, Pakistan, Egypt, Ecuador, Peru, Panama, Mexico; 1st student of So. Meth. U. Ethnographic Field Sch. in N.Mex. to live on Indian reservation and conduct ethnographic study of the Pueblo, summer 1973; advisor to bd. dirs. Andromeda (Hispanic mental health orgn.), Washington, 1982. Mem. Am. Pub. Health Assn. Mem. Disciples of Christ Ch. Home: 2130 P St NW Apt 819 Washington DC 20037

SAUNTRY, SUSAN LYNN, lawyer; b. Bangor, Maine, May 7, 1943; d. William Joseph and Emily Joan (Guenter) Schaefer; m. John Philip Sauntry, Aug. 18, 1968; 1 dau., Mary Katherine. Student Hood Coll., 1961-62; B.S. in Fgn. Service, Georgetown U., 1965, LL.M., 1975. Bar: D.C. 1975. Mem. Congl. liaison staff OEO, Washington, 1966-68; program analyst EEOC, Washington, 1968-70; mgmt. analyst U.S. Dept. Army, Okinawa, 1970-72; assoc. firm Morgan, Lewis & Bockius, Washington, 1975-83, ptnr., 1983—. Editor Georgetown U. Law Jour., 1974-75; co-author: Employee Dismissal Laws Forms and Procedures, 1986; contbr. articles to profl. publs. Active Nat. Women's Party. Mem. ABA, D.C. Bar Assn., AAUW, Corcoran Gallery of Art., Nat. Fedn. Bus. and Profl. Women, Phi Beta Kappa, Pi Sigma Alpha. Democrat. Office: Morgan Lewis & Bockius 1800 M St NW Suite 800N Washington DC 20002

SAUSEDO, ANN ELIZABETH, newspaper librarian; b. Douglas, Ariz., Nov. 19, 1929; d. Eugene Ephraim and Bertha Evelyn (Kimpton) Bertram; m. Richard Edward Sausedo, July 22, 1952 (div. 1966); 1 dau., Robin Marie. Student Calif. schs. Asst. librarian Stockton Record (Calif.), 1948-51, head librarian, 1955-67; stewardess Calif. Central Airlines, 1951; library dir. Washington Star, 1967-76; free-lance organizer file systems, Palo Alto, Calif., 1976-78; library dir. Los Angeles Herald Examiner, 1978—. Contbr. chpt. to book in field. Mem. Spl. Libraries Assn., Nat. Assn. Female Execs., Calif. Bus. Women's Network. Office: Los Angeles Herald Examiner 1111 S Broadway Los Angeles CA 90015

SAUVÉ, JEANNE, government official; b. Prud'homme, Sask., Can., Apr. 26, 1922; d. Charles Albert and Anna (Vaillant) Benoit; m. Maurice Sauve, Sept. 24, 1948; 1 son, Jean-François. Grad., U. Ottawa; diploma, U. Paris, 1952; D.Sc. (hon.), N.B. U., 1974, LL.D., U. Calgary, 1982, McGill U., 1984, U. Toronto, 1984; L.H.D., Mt. St. Vincent U., 1983. Nat. pres. Jeuness Etudiante Catholique, Montreal, 1942-47; tchr. French London County Council, 1948-50; asst. to dir. youth sect. UNESCO, Paris, 1951; journalist, broadcaster, 1952-72; bd. dirs. Union des Artistes, Montreal, 1961, v.p., 1968-70, Canadian Inst. on Pub. Affairs, 1962-64, pres., 1964; mem. Canadian Centennial Commn., 1967; gen. sec. Fedn. des Auteurs et des Artistes du Can., 1966-72; founding mem. Inst. Polit. Research, 1969-72; mem. Parliament for Ahuntsic (Montreal), Parliament for Laval-des-Rapides, 1972-84; speaker House of Commons, 1980-84; gov.-gen. of Can., 1984—; minister of state for sci. and tech., 1972, minister of state in charge of sci. and tech., 1972-74, minister of environment, 1974-75, minister of communications, Ottawa, 1975-79; advisor for external affairs Sec. of State, 1978. Hon. fellow Royal Archtl. Inst. Can. Mem. Liberal Party of Can. Roman Catholic. Office: Ottawa ON K1A 0A6 Canada

SAVAGE, JOAN LEONHARDT, oil shale development company executive; b. Milw., Aug. 18, 1924; d. Lawrence Edwin and Lucille Eva (Brandeis) Leonhardt; R.N., Columbia Sch. Nursing, 1945; m. John William Savage, Aug. 6, 1950; children—John, Roy Edward, Marshall Thomas, Daniel. Pres. Savage Oil Shale Devel. Co., Rifle, Colo., 1950—, Savage Ranches, 1957—, Shale Inc., 1981—; gen. partner JOJO Oil Shale Devel., 1957—, Buffalo Basin Ltd., 1973—; sec.-treas. Rifle Ski Corp., 1973—; chmn. bd. Quality Time Audio Bookstores. Active Tb Assn., 1960-75; Colo. Mental Health Assn., 1972-75; mem. citizens adv. council Mesa Coll., 1974-75, also Rifle High Sch.; mem. Grand Valley Sch. Bd., 1959-62; adv. com. Colo. Office Emergency Conservation, 1986. Served with Cadet Nurse Corps, 1942-45. Mem. Nat. Woman's Forum, Alliance for Colo., Arabian Horse Assn., Colo. Assn. Housing and Bldg. (dir.), Rifle C. of C., Colo. Woman's Forum. Clubs: Colo. W. Arabian Horse, 20. Home: 5953 320 Rd Rifle CO 81650 Office: 1122 293 Rd Rifle CO 81650

SAVAGE, MARIE BONITA, nurse; b. Charleston, S.C., Feb. 7, 1953; d. Harold Tobias and Corinne Bare (Farrell) Hazel; m. John Alfred Savage, Dec. 29, 1978. B.S., Hampton Inst., 1975; M.P.H., Emory U., 1984. R.N., Ga., Va. Home health care aide instr. and program developer CETA, Hampton, Va., 1978; dir. edn. and tng. Southwest Community Hosp., Atlanta, 1979-82; staff relief nurse Grady Meml. Hosp., Atlanta, 1983—; nursing cons., Atlanta, 1983—. Bd. dirs. Mid-Atlanta unit Am. Cancer Soc., 1982-83. Mem. Am. Soc. for Health Manpower and Tng., Delta Sigma Theta. Democrat. Roman Catholic.

SAVAGE, VANDOLYN JOYCE, librarian; b. Truscott, Tex., Aug. 7, 1929; d. Van Wyck and Mabel Lee (Craig) Browning; m. Vernon Howard Savage, Sept. 8, 1951 (div. 1978); children—Van Howard, Lynn Monroe, Jan Lee. B.A., North Tex. State Coll., 1950; M.L.S., North Tex. State U., 1968. Asst. music librarian North Tex. State Coll. Library, Denton, 1950-52; catalog librarian U. Tex. Library, Austin, 1952-54, sr. cataloger, 1968-70, asst. chief, catalog dept., 1970-73, head librarian end process sect., 1973-74, head librarian, automated bibliographic processing unit, 1974-76, head librarian acquisitions and processing dept., 1976-78; jr. high sch. librarian Quanah (Tex.) Pub. Schs., 1954-55; reference librarian Tarleton State Coll. Library, Stephenville, Tex., 1959-61, cataloger, 1962-67; asst. documents librarian North Tex. State U. Library, Denton, 1968; asst. dir. tech. services U. Houston Univ. Park Libraries, Houston, 1978-85; assoc. dir. Bibliographic Resource Ctr., AMIGOS Bibliographic Council, Inc., Dallas, 1985—; chmn. tech. services com. Houston Area Research Libraries Consortium, 1979-80. Mem. ALA, Assn. Coll. and Research Libraries (sec. chpts. council 1982), Library Adminstrn. and Mgmt. Assn., Tex. Library Assn. (chmn. coll. and univ. libraries div. 1980-82), Tex. Assn. Coll. Tchrs. (vice chmn. U. Houston chpt. 1980-81), Beta Phi Mu, Phi Kappa Phi. Democrat. Mem. Disciples of Christ. Home: 12484 Abrams Rd 1702 Dallas TX 75243 Office: AMIGOS Bibliographic Council Inc 11300 N Central Expressway Suite 321 Dallas TX 75243

SAVAR, DEBORAH ESTHER, health care administrator; b. Phila., Mar. 31, 1951; d. Morton and Veronica (Napiorkowski) S. B.A., Douglass Coll., 1973; M.B.A., Temple U., 1978. Operational auditor N.J. Legislature, Trenton, 1973-76; supervising budget analyst N.J. Dept. Human Services, Trenton, 1976-77, asst. to dep. commr., 1978-81, dir. legal and regulatory affairs, 1981-82; dir. mgmt. info. service N.Y.C. Health & Hosps. Corp., 1982, exec. asst. to v.p. fin., 1983, dir. revenue mgmt., 1984; adminstr. Temple U. Health Scis. Ctr., Phila., 1985—. Chmn. social services task force Florio for Gov. N.J. campaign, 1981. Recipient Outstanding New Program award Phila. Jaycees, 1981; Mem. Health Care Fin. Mgmt. Assn., Med. Group Mgmt. Assn., Am. Pub. Health Assn. Democrat. Jewish. Avocations: reading, ice skating, horseback riding. Home: 204 Elkins Rd Cherry Hill NJ 08034

SAVARIEGO, BERTA KOZOLCHYK, foreign language educator; b. Havana, Cuba, Nov. 1, 1946; d. Mane and Flora (Kirstein) Kozolchyk; m. Alberto Savariego, Sept. 5, 1965; 1 dau., Donna. B.A. in Spanish with minor in English, Tex. Woman's U., Denton, 1967, M.A. in Spanish, 1968; Ph.D. in Spanish, Tex. Tech. U., 1974. Instr. Spanish, San Antonio Coll., Dallas, 1968-70; instr. Spanish and English, Richland Coll., Dallas, 1973-76, El Centro Coll., Dallas, 1973-76; translator Rimco, Inc., Dallas, 1976-77; instr. Spanish Miami Dade Community Coll., 1977-79; instr. Spanish, So. Meth. U., Dallas, 1979—. Recipient Matrix award Women in Communications, Inc., 1981; Golden Reel of Merit award Internat. TV Assn., 1981; Bronze award Internat. Film and Festival N.Y., 1981. Mem. Am. Assn. Tchrs. Spanish and Portuguese, MLA, South Central Modern Lang. Assn., AAUW, Am. Translators Assn., Am. Lit. Translators Assn., Phi Kappa Phi, Phi Sigma Iota, Pi Delta Phi. Author fiction and textbooks. Home: 6102 Calm Meadow Dallas TX 75248 Office: Bilingual Programs Adult and Community Edn Dade County Pub Schs 1450 NE 2d Ave Miami FL 33132

SAVIANO, BERNADETTE, clergywoman, computer company graphic arts manager; b. Fall River, Mass., May 10, 1948; d. Jesse Medeiros and Rosaline (Aguiar) Tavares. A.A., R.I. Jr. Coll., 1968; mech. drafting cert. Hall Inst., 1978; student psychology and mgmt. Salve Regina Coll., 1981—. Account exec. Co-Art Ad Agy., Providence, 1973-75; account exec., ptnr. Argentieri Assocs. Advt. Providence, 1975-77; mktg. cons. Christian's, Providence, 1977-78; mgr. graphics dept. Purvis Systems (Computer Systems Engring. Co.), Middletown, R.I., 1978-86; minister adult edn., outreach and evangelism Lawndale Bapt. Ch., Greensboro, N.C., 1986—. Author: (poems) Desert Songs, 1982; exhibited photographs Newport Art Mus., 1983. Mem. Nat. Contract Mgmt. Assn. Home: 19016 Ashwood Ct Suite 116 Greensboro NC 27408 Office: 3505 Lawndale Ave Greensboro NC 27408

SAVINO, ELLEN KAYE, cable television producer; b. N.Y.C., Aug. 6, 1948; d. Gilbert Mankowski and Bertha Kitover; m. Paul Savino, Sept. 1969 (div. 1975). B.A., Fordham U., 1981. Cert. systems profl. Supr. data entry Group Health Inc., N.Y., 1974-77; dir. budget control People & Properties, N.Y., 1977-79; adminstrv. asst. Hellmuth, Obata & Kassabaum, N.Y., 1979-81; supr. data entry Home Box Office, N.Y., 1981—; asst. dir. Cable Follies for Women in Cable, N.Y.C., 1983; asst. producer Follies Classic for Internat. Radio and TV Soc., N.Y.C., 1984. Mem. prodn. com. Olympics "Superskates", Madison Square Garden, N.Y.C., 1979-83. Mem. Assn. for Systems Mgmt. (cert., N.Y., chpt. publicity chmn 1981-82, sec. 1982-84, v.p., 1984-85, pres. 1986—, editor edn. brochure 1983, 84, 85, Outstanding Service award 1983-84, Cert. Appreciation award 1984), Nat. Assn. For Female Execs. Home: 340 West End Ave New York NY 10023 Office Home Box Office 1114 Ave of the Americas 1034 New York NY 10036

SAVIT, CHRISTINA ERIKA, diversified company exec.; b. Syracuse, N.Y., Nov. 13, 1953; d. Irving James and Erika Margaret (Engelhardt) June; B.S., Cornell U., 1975; m. Jeffrey Bruce Savit, May 8, 1978. Research technician Cornell U., Ithaca, N.Y., 1975-78; product mgr. Informatics, Inc., Fairfield, N.J., 1978-79, mktg. mgr., 1979-80; teleprocessing and planning group leader Exxon Corp., Florham Park, N.J., 1980—; v.p. Savvy Comp., Inc., Upper Montclair, N.J., 1981-82. Sponsor, Futures for Children, Albuquerque, 1974-84. Mem. Assn. Computing Machinery, AAAS, Nat. Wildlife Fedn. (life), Nat. Audubon Soc., Animal Protection Inst., Sierra Club (life), Nature Conservancy (life), N.J. Kung Fu Acad. Office: Exxon Corp PO Box 153 Florham Park NJ 07932

SAVITT, SUSAN SCHENKEL, lawyer; b. Bklyn., Aug. 21, 1943; d. Edward Charles and Sylvia (Dlugatch) Schenkel; children—Andrew Todd Savitt, Daniel Cory Savitt. B.A. magna cum laude, Pa. State U., 1964; J.D., Columbia U., 1968. Bar: N.Y. 1968. Atty., Nassau County Legal Services, Freeport, N.Y., 1973-74; assoc. Bernardo & Farrauto, Yonkers, N.Y., 1975-77; asst. corp. counsel City of Yonkers, 1977-78; adj. prof. Elizabeth Seton Coll., Yonkers, 1982-83; ptnr. Epstein Becker Borsody & Green, P.C., N.Y.C., 1978—. Bd. dirs. Hastings-on-Hudson Sch. Bd., N.Y., 1984—, Westchester County ACLU, White Plains, 1976-77; v.p. Pa. State Alumni Club/Westchester County, 1985—. Recipient Cert. of Appreciation, Office of County Exec., 1985. Mem. Westchester County C. of C., N.Y. State Bar Assn., ABA, N.Y. State Women's Bar Assn., N.Y. State Sch. Bd. Attys. Assn., N.Y. State Pub. Employer Labor Relations Assn., Phi Beta Kappa, Alpha Kappa Delta, Phi Gamma Mu., Pa. State U. Alumni Assn. (v.p.). Office: Epstein Becker Borsody & Green 250 Park Ave New York NY 10177-0077

SAVOIE, BRIETTA DOLORES, librarian; b. Milw., Aug. 28, 1933; d. Walter and Vera Margaret (Rueger) Giger; m. Edmond Albert Savoie, Oct. 11, 1959; children—Philip Edmond, Raymond Walter, Anne-Marie Margaret. B.A., Ohio State U., 1955; M.S.L.S., Columbia U., N.Y.C., 1957. Profl. librarian's cert., N.Y., N.J. Librarian, Bklyn. Pub. Library, 1957-59; cataloger, reference librarian New Sch. Social Research, N.Y.C., 1959-60; children's librarian Teaneck Pub. Library, N.J., 1981—. Voter registration chmn. Glen Rock LWV, N.J., 1978-81; v.p. United Way of Ridgewood, Glen Rock, Hohokus and Midland Park, N.J., 1980-81; pres. Ridgewood chpt. UN Assn., N.J., 1981-85. Mem. N.J. Library Assn., N.J. Audubon Soc., So. Poverty Law Ctr. Klanwatch Project, UN Assn., LWV, Sierra Club. Democrat. Unitarian Universalist. Avocations: international relations; environmental protection; bicycling; gardening; cooking. Home: 654 Doremus Ave Glen Rock NJ 07452 Office: Teaneck Pub Library 840 Teaneck Rd Teaneck NJ 07666

SAVOLT, LOUANN SUE, ladies shop owner; b. Ft. Wayne, Ind., Sept. 28, 1942; d. Harold Edwin and Norma Esther (Mertz) Hartman; m. Larry Gene Savolt, Sept. 6, 1980; children by previous marriage—Neil Reith, Sheila Reith. A.Nursing, Garden City Community Coll., 1977. R.N., Kans. Coll. health nurse Garden City Community Coll., Kans., 1977-80; staff nurse St. Catherine Hosp., Garden City, 1983; owner, mgr. Personally Yours Lingerie, Garden City, 1984—. Hot line vol. Family Crisis Services, Finney County, Kans., 1982-84; pub. edn. chmn. Am. Cancer Soc., Finney County, 1978-84; co-chmn. Coalition for Prevention of Child Abuse and Neglect, Finney County, 1978-79, chmn., 1979-80. Recipient Service award Finney County Am. Cancer Soc., 1981, Family Crisis Services, 1984. Mem. Women's C. of C., C. of C., Nat. Retail Mchts. Assn., Nat. Assn. Female Execs. Lutheran. Avocations: reading; snowmobiling; traveling. Home: Route 2 Box 50 Holcomb KS 67851 Office: Personally Yours Lingerie 1514 E Harding Garden City KS 67846

SAWADA, SUZANNE RONI, lawyer; b. Chgo., Apr. 17, 1951; d. Fred Hiroshi and Susanne Kazuko (Matsumura) Sawada; m. Leonard Stephen Joy, Dec. 29, 1973. B.A. in Math., U. Rochester (N.Y.), 1973; J.D., U. Chgo., 1977. Bar: Ill., 1977, U.S. Dist. Ct. (no. dist. Ill.), 1977. Research asst. U. Rochester, 1973-74; assoc. Schiff Hardin & Waite, Chgo., 1977-83, ptnr., 1984—. Assoc. editor U. Chgo. Law Rev., 1976-77. Trustee, First Presbyterian Soc. Evanston, 1983—, sec., 1983, pres., 1984. Recipient Joseph Henry Beale prize U. Chgo., 1975. Mem. ABA, Chgo. Bar Assn., Chgo. Council Lawyers. Office: Schiff Hardin & Waite 7200 Sears Tower Chicago IL 60606

SAWDEY, CARMEN RITA, educator, administrator; b. Anchorage, May 1, 1947; d. Thomas Charles and Esther Norma (Ona) Cianfrani; m. Stephen Dale Sawdey, May 31, 1968; children—Kam Genet, Courtney Maryn. Student, Carthage Coll., summer 1968; B.A., Cedarville Coll., 1968; postgrad. U. Idaho, fall 1975, Eastern Wash. U., winter 1979, Seattle Pacific U., 1980; cert., Central Wash. U., 1980. Tchr., Chgo., 1969, Anchorage, 1969-70, Jacksonville, Fla., 1970, Middletown, R.I., summer 1971, 71-72; with bookkeeping dept. Seattle First Nat. Bank, Pullman, 1973; instr. dog obedience classes, 1973—; mgr., bookkeeper, exercise dir. for ladies health spa, Moscow, Idaho, 1973; tchr., Idaho, 1973-76; adult tutor Right to Read, Moses Lake, Wash., 1976-77; organizer, operator day care ctr., 1977; tchr., adminstr. Warden Hutterite Sch., Warden, Wash., 1977—; Dir. tours Hutterite Colony, founder, first aid, CPR instructional program, 1977-78. Avocations: horseback riding; playing piano/accordian; singing; dog obedience instruction; breeding/raising Gt. Danes. Home: Route 1 Box 233 Warden WA 98857 Office: Warden Hutterite Sch Route 1 Box 93 Warden WA 98857

SAWYER, DIANE, television journalist; b. Glasgow, Ky., Dec. 22, 1945. B.A., Wellesley Coll., 1967. Reporter Sta. WLKY-TV, Louisville, Ky., 1967-70; with White House Press Office, 1970-74; mem. Nixon-Ford transition team, 1974-75; asst. to former Pres. Nixon in writing his memoirs, 1975-78; with CBS News, 1978—, corr., from 1980, co-anchor morning news, from 1981, early morning news, from 1982, now co-editor 60 Minutes program, 1984—. Office: care CBS News 51 W 52d St New York NY 10019*

SAWYER, GENE, journalist; b. Danvers, Mass., Sept. 9, 1910; d. Morse Leon and Harriet Elizabeth (Adams) Lewis; grad. Cushing Acad., Ashburnham, Mass., 1928; student Syracuse U., 1928-30; m. W.P. Sawyer, Sept. 9, 1930. Radio announcer, writer, producer, Honolulu, N.Y.C., China, 1937-49; officer U.S. Fgn. Service, Burma, Cambodia, Indonesia, Washington, 1950-65; corr. in Honolulu, Voice of Am., Washington, 1966-71; student interviewer manuscripts Hawaii Pacific Coll. and East West Center, Honolulu, 1972-79; editor original material on Burma and Cambodia, U. Hawaii, 1980-81. Vice-pres., Hawaii div. U.N. Assn., 1971-73, bd. dirs., 1975—. Recipient cert. of Merit, Sr. Achievement, 1980; named Vol. of Yr., East West Ctr., 1985. Mem. Women in Communications, Honolulu Acad. Arts, Fgn. Service Assocs., Friends of East-West Ctr. (life), Theta Sigma Phi. Author: Celebrations, Asia and the Pacific, 1978. Home: 1465 Aala St Apt 802 Honolulu HI 96817

SAWYER, HELEN ALTON, painter; b. Washington; d. Wells Moses and Kathleen Alton (Bailey) Sawyer; student at Master's School, Dobbs Ferry, 1914-18; studied art with Johansen and Hawthorne; m. Jerry Farnsworth, Aug. 26, 1925. Painter, artist in oil and water color, lithographer; exhibited at principal galleries and museums of U.S. Represented permanent collections numerous museums including Whitney Mus. Am. Art, Pa. Acad., Toledo Mus., Syracuse U. Mus., John Herron Mus., Indpls., Atlanta Mus., Amherst Coll. Mus., Williams Coll. Mus. Art, Chrysler Mus., others, IBM collection, Library of Congress, C. & O. R.R. collections; oil painting Clown Still Life owned Norfolk Mus. Recipient numerous awards, honors. Mem. N.A.D., Nat. Arts Club, Provincetown, Yonkers, Sarasota art assns., Audubon Artists, Nat. Assn. Women Artists. Contbr. articles and verse to jours. Has painted in U.S., Spain, France, Mexico. Home: 3482 Flamingo Sarasota FL 33581

SAWYER, KATHERINE H. (MRS. CHARLES BALDWIN SAWYER), librarian; b. Cleve., July 11, 1908; d. Willard and Martha (Beaumont) Hirsh; A.B., Smith Coll., 1930; M.S. in Library Sci., Western Res. U., 1956; m. Charles Baldwin Sawyer, Aug. 19, 1933; children—Samuel Prentiss, Charles Brush, William Beaumont. With Cleve. Pub. Library, profl. librarian hosps., instns. dept., 1956-61; med. librarian St. Luke's Hosp., Pittsfield, Mass., 1965-66; library cons. Ministry of Health, Guyana, S.Am., 1966-68; curator Sophia Smith Collection, Smith Coll., 1970-71; parish librarian St. Paul's Episcopal Ch., Cleveland Heights, Ohio, 1971-79, mem. vestry, 1974-77. Library chmn. exec. com. Garden Center of Greater Cleve., 1959-65; chmn. Friends of Western Res. Hist. Library, 1972-77. Bd. mgrs. Episcopal Ch. Home, 1954-64, pres., 1961-64, trustee, 1965—; bd. govs. Western Res. U., 1957-66, bd. visitors Sch. Library Sci., 1958-68, 69—; trustee Friends of Cleve. Pub. Library, 1962-67, Christian Residences Found., 1976-82. Mem. Western Res. Hist. Soc. (trustee 1979—), Archeol. Inst., Spl. Libraries Assn. Clubs. Union, Intown. Co-author (talking books for blind) Gardening for Blind Persons, 1962; Beauty, Glamour and Style, 1963. Home: 2 Paseo del Mundo Green Valley AZ 85614

SAWYER, KRISTIN LEE, executive search consultant; b. Salem, Mass., July 12, 1951; d. Jack Nichols and Carol Margary (Forsyth) Arnold; m. Alan Irwin Sawyer, Nov. 12, 1972 (div. Nov. 1985); children—Carrie Lee, Jeremy Scott. Student Harbor Jr. Coll., San Pedro, Calif., 1969, El Camino Coll., Redondo Beach, Calif., 1970, Monserrat Sch. Visual Art, Beverly, Mass., 1975. Vice pres., sales Custom Clean, Topsfield, Mass., 1975-77; mfrs. rep. Sawyer Assoc., Topsfield, 1977-79; account exec. Exxon Office Systems, Waltham, Mass., 1979-80; facility cons. M. Brown, Inc., Boston, 1980-83; pres. The Sawyer Co., Topsfield, 1984—; cons. in field. Speaker, Mass. Com. to Ratify E.R.A., 1975. Mem. Nat. Assn. Personnel Cons., North Shore Women in Bus., Nat. Assn. Female Execs., Ms. Found. for Women, NOW. Club: Ipswich Bay Yacht. Avocations: sailing; skiing; horseback riding.

SAWYER, SANDRA MCCOMMAS, lawyer, former judge; b. Tulsa, Sept. 1, 1937; d. Franklin Delmar and Irene (Adams) McCommas; student Tex. Tech. Coll., Draughon Bus. Sch., LL.B., Oklahoma City U., 1967; m. L.L. Sawyer, Mar. 6, 1981; children—Lise Dyann, Richard Owen, Whitney Michelle. Legal sec., 1956-64; admitted to Okla. bar, 1967, Oreg. bar, 1983; legal asst. to U.S. Ct. Appeals judge, 1964-67, law clk., 1967-68; bill drafter Okla. Legislature, 1969-70; chief traffic ct. project Okla. Supreme Ct., 1970-75; individual practice law, Oklahoma City, from 1967; partner firm Moran & Johnson, Oklahoma City; referee juvenile div. Okla. County Dist. Ct., 1977-78, spl. dist. judge, 1978-80; assoc. Grant, Ferguson & Carter, P.C.; adj. prof. So. Oreg. State Coll.; lectr. Okla. Center Continuing Legal Edn., 1969-75, Okla. Bar Found. Legal Secs. Ednl. Series, 1974; mem. Okla. Legislature Interim. Com. Municipal Cts. Revision, 1973-74. Sunday Sch. tchr., supt. Resurrection Episcopal Ch., Oklahoma City; pres. regional adv. com. So. Oreg. State Coll.; mem. So. Oreg. Drug Awareness Com. Recipient Outstanding Civic Contbn. award Modern Woodmen Am., 1977. Mem. Am. (nat. v.p. law student div. 1966; Gold Key award 1965, 66), Okla. (Outstanding Grad. Law Student award 1967, grievance com. 1977-78), Okla. County, Oreg. bar assns., Oklahoma City U. Law Sch. Alumni Assn. (sec. 1971), Iota Tau Tau, Zeta Tau Alpha. Author, editor in field; spl. cts. reporter Am. Judicature Soc., 1974-78. Home: 585 Thornton Way Ashland OR 97520 Home: 585 Thornton Way Ashland OR 97520

SAWYERS, ELIZABETH JOAN, library administrator; b. San Diego, Dec. 2, 1936; d. William Henry and Elizabeth Georgianna (Price) S.; A.A., Glendale Jr. Coll., 1957; B.A. in Bacteriology, UCLA, 1959, M.L.S., 1961. Intern, Nat. Library Medicine, 1961-62, asst. head acquisition sect., 1962-63, head, 1963-66, spl. asst. to chief tech. services div., 1966-69, spl. asst. to assoc. dir. for library ops., 1969-73; asst. dir. Univ. Libraries for Tech. Services SUNY, Stony Brook, 1973-75; dir. Health Scis. Library Ohio State U., 1975—. Mem. Med. Library Assn., Assn. Acad. Health Scis. Library Dirs. (sec. 1981-83, pres. 1983-84), Am. Soc. Info. Sci., Spl. Libraries Assn., Ohio Library Assn., Acad. Library Assn. Ohio. Home: 135 W Kenworth Rd Columbus OH 43214 Office: 376 W 10th Ave Columbus OH 43210

SAX, MARY RANDOLPH, speech pathologist; b. Pontiac, Mich., July 13, 1925; d. Bernard Angus and Ada Lucile (Thurman) TePoorten; B.A. magna cum laude, Mich. State U., 1947; M.A., U. Mich., 1949; m. William Martin Sax, Feb. 7, 1948. Supr. speech correction dept. Waterford Twp. Schs., Pontiac, 1949-69; lectr. Marygrove Coll., Detroit, 1971-72; pvt. practice speech and lang. rehab., Wayne, Oakland Counties, Mich., 1973—; mem. sci. council stroke Am. Heart Assn. Grantee Inst. Articulation and Learning, 1969, others. Mem. Am. Speech-Lang.-Hearing Assn., Mich. Speech Pathologists in Clin. Practice, Mich. Speech-Lang.-Hearing Assn. (com. community and hosp. services), Mich. Heart Assn., AAUW, Internat. Assn. Logopedics and Phoniatrics (Switzerland), Founders Soc. of Detroit Inst. Arts, Mich. Humane Soc., Theta Alpha Phi, Phi Kappa Phi, Kappa Delta Pi. Contbr. articles to profl. jours. Home and Office: 31320 Woodside Franklin MI 48025

SAXION, SANDRA LEE, communications executive; b. Cleve., Sept. 6, 1947; d. Robert and Louise A. (Schotsch) Dangel; B.A. in Social Sci. and Edn., Heidelberg Coll., Tiffin, Ohio, 1969; m. Barry Dean Saxion, May 10, 1980. Sales rep. N.J., Gillette Co., 1973-76; mktg. mgr. Warner-Amex Cable Co., N.Y.C., 1977-79; dir. mktg. Teleprompter Manhattan Cable TV, N.Y.C., 1979-80; dir. mktg. UTV Cable Network, Fair Lawn, N.J., 1981-83; pres. Saxion, Inc., 1983—; speaker in field. Mem. Women in Cable, LWV, Bus. and Profl. Women (1st v.p. 1984-85). Republican. Methodist. Home: 137 Rockaway Valley Rd Boonton NJ 07005

SAXON, LINDA LEE, purchasing official; b. Chgo., Oct. 28, 1948; d. George William and Shirlee Joan (Francioni) Simpson; children—Susan Lynn, Jeffrey Scott. Student Roosevelt U., Coll. Lake County, Harper Coll., U. Nev. Coordinator, Baxter Travenol Labs., Deerfield, Ill., 1976-81; buyer Evang. Hosp. Systems, Oakbrook, Ill., 1981—. Mem. Nat. Assn. Purchasing Mgmt., Female Execs. Am., Poets/Writers, Inc., Western Writers Am., Soc. Children's Writers, Washington Ind. Writers. Republican. Roman Catholic. Home: 6558 S Valley View Las Vegas NV 89118 Office: Evangelical Hosp Assn 2025 Windsor Dr Oakbrook IL 60615

SAXTON, CATHERINE PATRICIA, public relations executive; b. Sheffield, Eng., July 5, 1944; d. Clifford and Kate Ann (Ruane) S. B.A. cum laude, Fordham U., 1978. Account supr. The Rowland Co., N.Y.C., 1980; Mgr. corporate communications Westinghouse Broadcasting & Cable Co., N.Y.C., 1981-82; prin., pres. Saxton & Assocs., N.Y.C., 1983—; chief exec. officer Potter/Saxton Assocs., Inc., 1985—; prof. pub. speaking Katharine Gibbs Coll., N.Y.C., 1977—. Mem. exec. com. Mayor's Commn. for a Vietnam Vet's Meml., 1982—; chmn. N.Y. Women in Communications/NYU Cable Conf., 1983; bd. dirs. Vets. Ensemble Theatre Co. Mem. Internat. Radio and TV Soc., N.Y. Women in Communications, Nat. Acad. TV Arts and Scis. Roman Catholic. Home: 325 E 90th St New York NY 10128

SAYAD, PAMELA MIRIAM, lawyer; b. San Francisco, Apr. 13, 1949; d. Samuel D. and Charlotte (Yonan) Sayad. A.B. in Polit. Sci., U. Calif-Berkeley, 1970; J.D., U. Notre Dame, 1973. Bar: D.C. 1974, U.S. Ct. Appeals (D.C. cir.) 1974, Mass. 1980, U.S. Dist. Ct. Mass. 1980, Calif. 1982, U.S. Dist. Ct. (no. dist.) Calif. 1981, U.S. Ct. Appeals (9th cir.) 1981. Atty., Gen. Counsel's Office, HEW, Washington, 1973-74, Solicitor's Office div. Indian Affairs, Dept. of Interior, Washington, 1974-77; asst. U.S. atty. for D.C., Dept. of Justice, Washington, 1977-80; assoc. Swartz & Swartz, Boston, 1980, Archer, Rosenak & Hanson, San Francisco, 1981-82, Bourhis, Lawless & Harvey, San Francisco, 1982-83; ptnr. Sayad & Trigero, San Francisco, 1983—. Contbg. author: Criminal Practice Institute Manual, 1980. Bd. dirs. Found. Study of Electoral Reform, San Francisco, 1983—; trustee Calif. Indian Legal Services, 1984—; mem. Jr. League San Francisco. Recipient Recognition grant U. Notre Dame Law Sch., 1972-73. Mem. ABA, San Francisco Bar Assn., Calif. Trial Lawyers Assn., Assn. Trial Lawyers Am., Calif. Women Lawyers, Gamma Phi Beta. Democrat. Presbyterian. Club: San Francisco Tennis. Office: Sayad & Trigero 444 Market St Suite 930 San Francisco CA 94111

SAYLOR, BETTY ASHBY, educator; b. Houston, Aug. 9, 1930; d. James Curtis and Rachel Alma (McCown) Ashby; children—Mark Leroy King, Richard Burns Saylor. B.A., Ouachita Bapt. Coll., Arkadelphia, Ark., 1954; M.Ed., M.Ed., U. Houston, 1969. Cert. tchr., Tex. Tchr., Pasadena Ind. Sch. Dist., (Tex.), Aldine Ind. Sch. Dist., Houston; spl. edn. resource tchr. Bowie Elem. Sch. Lamar Consol. Ind. Sch. Dist., Rosenberg, Tex., Taylor Ray Intermediate Sch., 1979—. Recipient Valley Forge Tchrs. medal Freedoms Found. at Valley Forge, 1971. Mem. Tex. PTA (active), Tex. Classroom Tchrs. Assn. Baptist. Lodge: VFW Ladies Aux. (chmn. Voice of Democracy 1968-70; named Tex. Tchr. of Yr. 1970).

SAYLOR, DUELL KELLY, retired sewing industry executive; b. Arab, Ala., Mar. 20, 1914; d. Marshall Livingston and Ella (Waldrop) Kelly; m. John D. Saylor, Dec. 12, 1931 (dec. 1979); 1 child, Michael. Diploma, Internat. U., 1953; postgrad. Howard Coll., 1969-70; cert. communication Ala. Dept. Edn., 1960-85. Owner, mgr. cafe, Arab, 1933-40; clk., mgr. dry goods store, Arab, 1940-47; supr. sewing plant Blue Bell, Inc., Arab, 1949-60, supr., tng. coordinator, 1960-71, mgr., 1971-79; cons., 1979—; tchr. oil painting, Arab, 1981—. Designed outside Christmas lighting display, 1968, 69, 72, 75 (1st prize). Pres. Mothers Club 1, Arab, 1957-60; organizer, pres. Marshall County Indsl. Group, Ala., 1977; mem. adv. bd. North Ala. Mental Health Systems, 1978—; mem. vocat. adv. council Arab City Sch., 1979—. Recipient cost sav. award, quality award, improving methods award Blue Bell Inc.; Cert. of Appreciation Gov. of Ala., 1986. Mem. Homemakers of Ala. (chmn. publicity com.), Bus. and Profl. Women Arab (pres. 1968), Lodge: Order Eastern Star. Avocations: oil painting; sewing; travel; reading; gardening. Home: 803 7th St NE Arab AL 35016

SAYLOR, NANCY LEE, educator; b. Tucson, May 11, 1941; d. Ellmont Meredith and Margaret Ann (Simmons) Saylor. B.S. in Health, Phys. Edn. and Recreation, Tex. Woman's U., 1962. Cert. tchr. secondary edn., phys. edn. and recreation, driver edn., elem. edn., Tex. Tchr. elem. and phys. edn. Dallas Ind. Sch. Dist., 1963-76, tchr. phys. edn. and gymnastics, coach, 1976—; asst. dir. recreation Denton State Sch. (Tex.), 1962-63. Mem. project 1000, Tex. Educators Polit. Action Com., Austin, 1983—. Recipient Favorite Tchr. award Positive Parents of Dallas, 1983. Mem. Classroom Tchrs. of Dallas (dist. dir. 1983-85), Tex. Tchrs. Assn., NEA, Dallas Assn. for Health, Phys. Edn. and Recreation (pres. 1981-83), Tex. Assn. for Health, Phys. Edn., Recreation and Dance, AAHPERD. Mormon. Home: 1415 Matagorda Dallas TX 75232 Office: WE Greiner Middle Sch 625 S Edgefield Dallas TX 75208

SAYLOR, TERRI AMMERMAN, media consultant; b. Altoona, Pa., Nov. 18, 1953; d. Dan Sheridan and Mary Theresa (Graca) Ammerman; m. Alvin Norman Saylor, Jr., Aug. 27, 1983; 1 child, Sheridan Joy. Student U. Houston, 1972-74, Houston Bapt. U., 1981-84. Model, radio and TV talent, Dallas and Houston, 1976-79; personnel cons. Talent Tree Personnel, Houston, 1979-81; asst. gen. mgr., media trainer Ammerman Enterprises, Houston, 1981—; TV hostess Houston Monthly Mag., 1983. Mem. Am. Women in Radio and TV, Nat. Orgn. Female Execs. Republican. Presbyterian. Club: Toastmasters (ednl. v.p. 1983). Home: 11715 Dorrance St Stafford TX 77477 Office: Ammerman Enterprises Inc 4800 Sugar Grove Blvd Suite 400 Stafford TX 77477

SAYRE, JOAN MARIE, speech pathologist, educator; b. Columbus, Ohio, May 25, 1933; d. Robert Edison and Pauline Vivian (Southard) S. B.S., Bowling Green State U., 1955; M.Ed., Kent State U., 1960. Tchr. hearing impaired Pub. Schs. Cin., 1955-56; speech and hearing therapist Pub. Schs. West Carrollton (Ohio), 1956-57; orthopedic therapist Pub. Schs. Dayton (Ohio), 1957-60; instr. speech pathology audiology Miami U., Oxford, Ohio, 1960-66, asst. prof. speech, 1966-72, acting chmn., assoc. prof. speech and hearing scis. and pediatrics, 1973-74; prof. speech and hearing, chmn. dept. Coll. Arts and Scis., assoc. prof. pediatrics U. Miami Sch. Medicine, Coral Gables, Fla., 1973-78, assoc. prof. dept. pediatrics, 1973—, also mem. grad. faculty; speech pathology cons. Miami Jewish Home and Hosp. for Aged; co-chmn. Communications Problems of Aging Conf., 1977; mem. adv. bd. Fla. State Dept. Edn., 1974-76. Bd. dirs. Hearing and Speech Ctr. Miami, 1973—. Mem. Internat. Listening Assn., Speech Communication Assn., Am. Speech and Hearing Assn., Fla. Speech and Hearing Assn., Am. Gerontol. Soc., Quota Club, Fla. Communications Assn., Sigma Alpha Eta. Democrat. Roman Catholic. Contbr. articles to profl. jours.; author: Teaching Language Through Sight and Sound; Helping Older Adults with Acquired Hearing Loss; Handbook for Older Adults with Impaired Hearing; also filmstrips, videotapes. Office: Dept Communications Univ Miami Coral Gables FL 33124*

SAYRE, MICHELE ROBINSON, radio consultant; b. Glen Cove, N.Y., Feb. 12, 1954; d. Henry Lewis and Dorothy Benson (Smith) Robinson; m. Joseph Robert Sayre, July 8, 1981. A.A., Miami Dade Community Coll., 1975. Head cashier Pantry Pride Stores, Miami, Fla., 1973-76; music dir. Sta. WINZ-FM, Miami, 1976-79, Sta. WSHE, Ft. Lauderdale, Fla., 1979-80; asst. to editor Album Network, Los Angeles, 1980-81; asst. program dir. Sta. KLOL, Houston, 1981-83, program dir., 1983-84; music dir., radio cons. Shane Media Services, Houston, 1984—. Adminstrv. asst. Concerned Democrats, Miami, 1972. Am. Legion scholar, 1968. Mem. Nat. Assn. Female Execs., Phi Theta Kappa. Methodist. Office: Shane Media Services 7703 Windswept Houston TX 77063

SCAHILL, PATRICIA LOUISE, actuary, consultant; b. Indpls., Aug. 15, 1948; d. William Glenn and Minna Belle (Seidensticker) Batchelder; m. Edwin Carl Scahill, Mar. 5, 1971 (div. Jan. 1984); m. Gary Allen Larreategui, July 6, 1985. B.A. in Math., Ind. U., 1970. Statistician/programmer State of Ind., Indpls., 1970-72; actuary Jefferson Nat. Life, Indpls., 1972-76; actuary, v.p. The Nyhart Co., Indpls., 1976-84; actuary, assoc. William M. Mercer-Meidinger, Columbus, Ohio, 1984-85, Balt., 1985—. Sec., bd. mem. Common Cause, Ind., 1980-84, bd. mem., Ohio, 1984-85; crisis intervention worker Suicide Prevention Service, Columbus, 1984-85. Fellow Soc. Actuaries; mem. Am. Acad. Actuaries, Conf. Actuaries in Pub. Practice, Soc. Mayflower Descs. (recording sec., bd. dirs. 1980-85), DAR, Mensa, Sierra Club. Avocations: reading; writing; scuba diving; swimming. Home: 6432 Elffolk Terrace Columbia MD 21045 Office: William M Mercer-Meidinger 300 E Lombard St Suite 1200 Baltimore MD 21202

SCALABRINI, PAMELA ANN, association administrator; b. Santa Monica, Calif., Oct. 8, 1956; d. Benso Albert and Helen (Behare) S. A.A., El Camino Jr. Coll., 1977; B.A., Calif. State U.-Long Beach, 1980. Therapist devel. disabled Social Vocat. Services, Hermosa Beach, Calif., 1980-83, program evaluator coordinator, 1983-84; exec. dir. Soc. to Aid Retarded, Torrance, Calif., 1986—; cons. in field. Mem. Quo Vadis Family Counseling Ctr., Torrance, 1984—. Mem. Nat. Assn. Female Execs., Nat. Assn. for Autistic Children, Delta Delta Delta. Democrat. Roman Catholic. Avocations: skiing; tennis; water skiing; sewing; cooking.

SCALES, ERMA JEAN, educator; b. Houston, July 8, 1934; d. Andrew Eugene and Laura (Sylvester) Young; m. Nelson G. Scales, Apr. 21, 1962; children—Adrian Eugene, Christal Louise, Tanya Renee. B.A. in Elem. Edn., Tex. So. U., 1956; M.S., Prairie View A&M U., 1964. Spl. edn. tchr. A.B. Anderson Elem. Sch., Houston, 1964-67, trainable and educable edn. tchr., 1960-67; resource and mentally retarded tchr. MacArthur Elem. Sch., Galena Park, Tex., 1967—. Mem. Houston Housing Bd. Appeals, 1981—. Named Terrific Tchr. of the Year, Dist. XI PTA, 1984, Galena Park Classroom Tchr. Mem. NEA, Tex. Tchrs. Assn. Glanea Park Classroom Tchrs. Assn., Galena Park Edn. Assn., Tex. Classroom Tchrs. Assn., Iota Phi Lambda. Democrat. Baptist. Lodge: Order Eastern Star. Address: 6812 McWilliams St Houston TX 77088

SCALESE, ELLEN RENEE, maintenance company executive; b. Newton, Mass., Aug. 31, 1954; d. Anthony J. and Evelyn (Spicer) Cardarelli; m. Fred J. Scalese, Jr., June 2, 1973; children—Leah, Michael, Jenna. B.A., U. Mass., 1974; cert. U. Perugia, Italy, 1969. Comml. loan officer Shawmut Bank, Waltham, Mass., 1974-78; co-owner, pres. Coastal Cleaning Service, Plymouth, Mass., 1978—. Editor: Handicap Directory U. Mass., 1974. Counselor, U. Mass., Amherst, 1972-74, handicap counselor, 1972-74. Mem. Bldg. Service Contractors, Plymouth C. of C. (bd. dirs. 1984-85), Greater Boston C. of C., Small Bus. Assn. Home: 9 Alison Circle Plymouth MA 02360 Office: Coastal Cleaning Service 9 Alison Circle Plymouth MA 02360

SCALETTA, MARION WITTE, travel co. exec.; b. Fargo, N.D., Apr. 20, 1948; d. Alvin Glenn and Wilma Marion (Serum) Witte; B.S. summa cum laude in Bus. Adminstrn. U. N.D., 1969; m. Paul John Scaletta, Apr. 4, 1981. Mgr., Touche Ross & Co., C.P.A.s, Mpls., 1969-76; v.p. Internat. Travel Arrangers, St. Paul, 1977—. Bd. dirs. Minn. Acctg. Aid soc., 1979—; treas. Breconwood Homeowners Assn., 1980—. C.P.A., Minn., N.D. Mem. Nat. Assn. Accts. (past pres. Mpls. Viking chpt.), Am. Soc. Women Accts. (past pres. Mpls./St. Paul chpt.), Am. Inst. C.P.A.s, Am. Women's Soc. C.P.A.s, Minn. Soc. C.P.A.s, Beta Alpha Psi, Alpha Lambda Delta. Office: Internat Travel Arrangers 666 Transfer Rd Saint Paul MN 55114

SCAMACCA, ROSEMARIE, insurance agent; b. Buffalo, Sept. 13, 1941; d. Salvatore and Marie (Del Nuovo) Bellomo; m. Michael J. Scamacca, Sept. 30, 1960; children—Michael R., Frank, Marie. Ins. agt. Insuramerica, Tonawanda, N.Y., 1978—. Committeewoman Tonawanda Twp. Democratic Com., 1982—, state committeewoman 140th Assembly Dist., State N.Y., 1982—, chmn. ways and means com., 1983—; commr. Buffalo and Fort Erie Peace Bridge Authority, 1983—. Mem. Bus. and Profl. Women Assn., Profl. Ins. Agts. Assn. Club: Eleanor Roosevelt Democratic Women's. Home: 1390 Colvin Blvd Kenmore NY 14223 Office: Insuramerica 2343 Sheridan Dr Tonawanda NY 14150

SCANLAN, SHARON ANN, retail store manager; b. Madison, Wis., Feb. 1, 1948; d. William Emmett and Mary Jane (Murrish) Brewer; m. Stephen Robert Scanlan, Oct. 22, 1974; children—Karen Lynn, Christopher Robert. B.S., U. Wis., 1970; student Hamline U., St. Paul, 1966-67. Store mdse. mgr. Sears, Roebuck and Co., Glendale, Calif., 1977-78, group mdse. mgr., Alhambra, Calif., 1978-80, territorial mdse. mgr., 1980; store mgr., San Luis Obispo, Calif., 1981-84, group operating mgr., Phoenix, 1984—. Bd. dirs. Pvt. Industry Council, San Luis Obispo, 1981-84, San Luis Obispo County Symphony, 1981-84, Crossroads Methodist Ch., Phoenix, 1986—. Republican. Clubs: Toastmistress, Soroptomist. Avocations: golf; reading; sewing. Home: PO Box 26419 Phoenix AZ 85068 Office: Sears Roebuck & Co PO Box 2922 Phoenix AZ 85062

SCANLON, DOROTHY THERESE, history educator; b. Bridgeport, Conn., Oct. 7, 1928; d. George F. and Mazie (Reardon) S.; A.B., U. Pa., 1948, M.A., 1949; M.A., Boston Coll., 1953; Ph.D., Boston U., 1956; postdoctoral scholar Harvard U., 1962-64, 72. Tchr. history and Latin Marycliff Acad., Winchester, Mass., 1950-52; tchr. history Girls Latin Sch., Boston, 1952-57; prof. Boston State Coll., 1957-82, Mass. Coll. Art, 1982—. Recipient Disting. Service award Boston State Coll., 1979, Faculty Award of Excellence, Mass. Coll. Art, 1985. Mem. Pan-Am. Soc., Latin Am. Studies Assn., Am. Hist. Assn., Orgn. Am. Historians, Am. Studies Assn., Am. Assn. History of Medicine AAUP, AAUW, Phi Alpha Theta, Delta Kappa Gamma. Author: Instructor's Manual to Accompany Lewis Hanke, Latin America: A Historical Reader, 1974; contbr. Biographical Dictionary of Social Welfare, 1986. Home: 140 Thornton Rd Chestnut Hill MA 02167 Office: Mass Coll Art Dept History 621 Huntington Ave Boston MA 02115

SCANLON, ROSEMARY, economist; b. Inverness, N.S., Can., Dec. 25, 1939; d. Donald Angus and Mary Agnes (MacDonald) MacLellan; A.B., St. Francis Xavier U., N.S., 1959; M.A. (Ford Found. Scholar) U. New Brunswick, 1960; P.M.D., Harvard Bus. Sch., 1981; m. Michael Scanlon, 1965 (div. 1979); children—Sean Donald, Jennifer; m. Louis H. Masotti, 1985. Instrn. econs. Coll. of William and Mary, Williamsburg, Va., 1960-63; asst. prof. Old Dominion U., Norfolk, Va., 1963-65; econ. analyst Port Authority of N.Y. and N.J., 1969—; sr. economist for regional research, 1977-80, mgr. econ. devel. planning, N.Y.C., 1980—, chief economist, 1983, asst. dir., 1984; chairperson Women's Equity, 1979; adv. bd. Kellogg Sch. Mgmt., Northwestern U. Recipient Salute to Women in Business award YWCA of N.Y.C., 1980. Mem. Nat. Council for Urban Econ. Devel. (bd. dirs.), N.Y. Regional Economists Assn. Club: Harvard Bus. Sch. of Greater N.Y. Author: The Regional Economy, 1985; Regional and Economic Development Strategies, 1979; The Arts as an Industry in N.Y.-N.J., 1983. contbr. articles to profl. jours. Home: 10 Clinton St Apt 9T Brooklyn NY 11201 Office: 1 World Trade Center Floor 54 E New York NY 10048

SCAPPATICCI, DIANE, business school president; b. Porchester, N.Y., Nov. 9, 1946; d. Hugo and Carmella (Rigano) S. B.A., SUNY-Albany, 1968; M.B.A. with distinction, Pace U., 1978. Word processing mgr. Text Communications Corp., N.Y.C., 1968-69; asst. to div. mgr. Rob Roy Co., N.Y.C., 1969-72; v.p., adminstr. Drake Bus. Schs., N.Y.C., 1972-77, exec. v.p., 1977-80, pres., 1980—; cons. and speaker to various groups. Pres., dir. Eastside Young Republican Club, N.Y.C.; v.p. N.Y. Republican County Com., N.Y.C., 1983—; pres., dir. 25 W 13th Corp., N.Y.C., 1981-84; battered women com. vol. Jr. League City N.Y., 1982; mem. Jr. League City N.Y. Speakers' Bur. for Abused Women, 1983-85; mem. alumni bd. dirs. SUNY-Albany, 1983. Recipient 2d Place award Idea Exchange, Workforce Creative Service; named Bus. Educator of Yr., Equal Rights Council, N.Y.C., 1984. Mem. Registered Bus. Schs. Assn. (bd. dirs., pres. 1984—), Assn. Ind. Colls. and Schs. (com. mem., speaker 1981—, disting. service award 1985), Bus. Edn. Assn. N.Y. (bd. dirs. 1981—), Am. Mgmt. Assn., The Pres. Assn., Nat. Bus. Edn. Assn., Eastern Bus. Edn. Assn., Bus. Tchrs. Assn. N.Y. State. Clubs: Westside Tennis, La Rande Beach. Avocations: tennis; skiing; reading; exercising. Office: Drake Bus Schs 10 E 38th St New York NY 10016

SCARBOROUGH, JUNE MOZELLE DOZIER, lawyer; b. Fulton, Ala., Apr. 12, 1947; d. Slater Matthew and Annie Mozelle (Ryan) Dozier; m. William George Scarborough, Jan. 8, 1972; children—Elizabeth Mozelle, William Matthew. B.A., U. Ala., 1969; J.D., Duke U., 1972. Bar: N.Y. 1973, U.S. Dist. Ct. (so. dist., ea. dist.) N.Y. 1973. Assoc., Sherman & Sterling, N.Y.C., 1972-74; v.p., asst. sec. Mfrs. Hanover Leasing Corp., N.Y.C., 1974—. Mem. alumni council Duke U. Law Sch., 1979-82; lay reader Incarnation Episcopal Ch., Morrisville, Pa., 1983—. Mem. ABA, Phi Beta Kappa, Alpha Lambda

Delta, Kappa Delta Epsilon, Alpha Xi Delta (Honor ring 1969). Office: Manufacturers Hanover Leasing Corp 270 Park Ave New York NY 10017

SCARBOROUGH, LINDA MARIE, county court official; b. Dalton, Nebr., Apr. 26, 1943; d. Lawrence Andrew and Thelma Marie (Arnold) Houston; m. Paul Everet Scarborough, May 27, 1961; children—Kay Lynn, Donald Paul. Grad. high sch., St. Paul, Nebr. Sec. Haggart and Haggart law firm, St. Paul, 1966-73; assoc. county judge Howard County, Nebr., 1973—. Democrat. Avocation: genealogy. Office: Howard County Ct Box 94 Saint Paul NE 68873

SCARBOROUGH, RUTHANN, educator; b. Marion, Ill., July 30, 1936; d. Floyd and Aretha (Stilley) Jent; B.A., So. Ill. U., Carbondale, 1956; M.R.E., Southwestern Bapt. Theol. Sem., Ft. Worth, 1958; m. Curtiss C. Scarborough, Nov. 23, 1955; children—Karol Ruth, Keith Curtiss. Tchr., Odessa (Tex.) Public Schs., 1958-59, St. Mark's Mini Sch., Florissant, Mo., 1966-72; early childhood edn. dir. North Side Baptist Ch., 1972-82; organizer North Side Day Care Center, 1972, dir. programs, 1972-82; dir. Weekday Early Edn. Center, minister childhood edn. Third Bapt. Ch., St. Louis, 1982-85; minister presch. edn. 1st Bapt. Ch. of Ferguson, Mo., 1985—; leader tchr. tng. workshops Mo. Bapt. Conv. and So. Bapt. Conv., presch. skill workshops, Taiwan, 1982, parenting groups Christian Civic Found.; tchr. Drug, Alcohol, Tobacco and Edn. Inc. Mem. Nat. Assn. Edn. of Young Children, Metro St. Louis Weekday Early Edn. Dirs. (pres.). Baptist. Contbr. to Ounce of Prevention, 1979; contbr. articles to Bapt. Sunday Sch. Bd. Home: 2476 Buttonwood Ct Florissant MO 63031 Office: 1st Baptist Ch 333 N Florissant Rd Saint Louis MO 63135

SCARBROUGH, DAPHNE, designer; b. Long Beach, Calif., June 24, 1954; d. Delayne Myers and Marjory Alice (Nunnery) Scarbrough. B.A., U. Tex.-Austin, 1978. With Sakowitz, Houston, 1979-80; designer, gen. mgr., buyer George Allen's Brass Wks., Houston, Dallas, 1980-82; owner, designer The Brass Maiden, Houston, 1982—; instr. D. Nollner & Assocs., Dallas, 1982. Vol., Bill Clements for Gov., Tex., 1979, John Connally campaign, 1980; designer Muellar House for Retarded, Cypress, 1983. Mem., Tex. Hist. Soc., Houston Zool. Soc., Nat. Fedn. Ind. Bus., Houston C. of C., Mus. Fine Arts, Soc. Antonio Mus. Fine Arts, Children's Mus., Nat. Trust for Hist. Preservation, Art League Houston, Pi Sigma Alpha. Methodist. Club: Engle Rodeo Assn., Houston Livestock Show and Rodeo.

SCARBROUGH, DOROTHY LORELLE, nursing educator, consultant; b. Cottonwood, Ala., Sept. 17, 1932; d. Theo and Bonnylin Elizabeth (Adams) Ray; m. John William Scarbrough, June 1, 1952; children—Mary Jane, Lisa Ann, Tina Marie. B.S. in Nursing, U. Ala., 1954, M.S. in Nursing, 1960. R.N.; cert. gerontol. nurse. Instr. U. Ala., Tuscaloosa, 1954-59, asst. prof. nursing, 1962-69; staff nurse Druid City Hosp., Tuscaloosa, part-time 1960-62; dir. reality orientation tng. program Tuscaloosa VA Med. Ctr., 1969-81, nursing supr., 1981—; mem. adv. bd. reality orientation project Am. Hosp. Assn., Chgo., 1973-74; workshop coordinator, cons. Hillhavan Found., Tacoma, also VA med. ctrs., 1973-80; mem. adv. com. Region IV Nationwide Edn. Ctr., Raleigh, N.C., 1975-77; workshop planner, participant Southeastern Region Med. Edn. Ctr., Birmingham, Ala., 1976-83; lectr. N.B. (Can.) Dept. Health, Fredericton, 1982; cons., lectr. Internat. Ctr. for Disabled, N.Y.C., 1982-83; tech. advisor films on reality orientation; co-producer workbook and cassette. Co-author self-instruction materials; author chpt. in book; contbr. articles to profl. jours. Ala. del. White House Conf. on Aging, Washington, 1971; participant Southeastern Assembly, Am. Assembly Columbia U., Sea Island, Ga., 1972; mem. profl. adv. bd. Tuscaloosa County Mental Health Assn., 1980—; mem. adv. council Ret. Sr. Vol. Program, Tuscaloosa, 1981—; co-organizer Tuscaloosa Alzheimer's Support Group, 1983. Recipient Meritorious Service award Tex. Assn. Homes for Aging, 1974. Mem. Ala. League Nursing (state treas. 1956-58, dir. 1956-58), Am. Nurses Assn. (local nomination com.), U. Ala. Capstone Coll. Nursing Honor Soc., Gerontol. Soc., Sigma Theta Tau. Democrat. Methodist. Home: 8 Forest Hill Tuscaloosa AL 35401

SCARFONE, ELEANOR LEE, real estate investment broker, nurse, consultant; b. St. Petersburg, Fla., Sept. 30, 1953; d. Rosario Carmine and Eleanor Gray (Lewis) S. Assoc. Sci., St. Petersburg Jr. Coll., 1973. Intensive care nurse Clearwater Community Hosp., Fla., 1974-78; recovery room nurse Med. Ctr. Hosp., Largo, Fla., 1978-81; nurse coordinator Home Health Care of Pinellas County, St. Petersburg, 1981-84; pres. Scarfone Investment Realty, Inc., Clearwater, 1984—, Scarfone Investment Realty, Inc. Mortgage Fin. Services, Clearwater, 1985-86. Mem. Foster Parents Plan, Tampa chpt., 1981—. Mem. Nat. Assn. Female Execs., Am. Mgmt. Assn., Clearwater C. of C. Roman Catholic. Avocations: ballroom dancing; writing. Home: PO Box 3093 Clearwater Beach FL 33515 Office: Scarfone Investment Realty Inc 1321 US 19 S Suite 508 Clearwater FL 33546

SCARNE, STEFFI NORMA, English educator, games company executive; b. Englewood, N.J., Jan. 18, 1925; d. Leo Patrick and Marie Elizabeth (Duffy) Kearney; m. John Scarne, 1956 (dec. 1985); 1 child, John Teeko. B.S. magna cum laude, Seton Hall U., 1971, M.A., 1973; Ph.D., Pacific Western U., 1986. Vice pres., editor, cons. John Scarne Games Inc., North Bergen, N.J., 1950—; exec. sales rep. Hamilton Shoe Co., N.Y.C., 1954-68, Grove Co., N.Y.C., 1968-71; English tchr. North Bergen High Sch., 1971—. Recipient Dean's Gold Medal for Acad. Excellence, Seton Hall U., 1971. Mem. NEA, Am. Fedn. Tchrs., Nat. Assn. Female Execs. Office: John Scarne Games Inc 4319 Meadowview Ave North Bergen NJ 07047

SCARROW, PAMELA KAY, health care manager; b. Washington, Nov. 4, 1949; d. Edward Charles and Elsie Lorine (Kay) Scarrow; m. Antonio Joseph Franz, Sept. 3, 1979; 1 child, Vanessa Motil Franz. A.A., Navarro Coll., Tex., 1981; B.S., Golden Gate U., 1983. Adminstrv. asst. Trust Territory of the Pacific Islands, Saipan, Mariana Islands, 1976-79; adminstrv. asst. Navarro Coll., Corsicana, Tex., 1979-81; staff asst. San Francisco Symphony, 1981-82; med. staff liaison Calif. Med. Assn., San Francisco, 1982—. Editor: Contracting Resource and Assistance Dept., Inc., Economic Resource Guide, 1986. Mem. Nat. Assn. Med. Staff Services. Democrat. Roman Catholic. Office: Calif Med Assn 44 Gough St San Francisco CA 94103

SCARZAFAVA, NETTIE JEAN, lawyer; b. Bee Branch, Ark., Mar. 22, 1946; d. Robert Harry and Sylvia Yetive (Linn) Chambers; m. Robbie Ray Atkinson, Dec. 22, 1967 (div. 1978); children—Angela Linn, Amy Raye, Amber Jean; m. John Francis Scarzafava, Nov. 16, 1978. B.S., U. Central Ark., 1968; J.D., St. Mary's U., 1975. Bar: Tex. 1976, N.Y. 1981, U.S. Dist. Ct. (no. dist.) N.Y. 1981. Tchr. West Memphis Jr. High Sch., Ark., 1968-70, Alfred Beech Jr. High Sch., Savannah, Ga., 1970-71; sole practice, San Antonio, 1975-76, Oneonta, N.Y., 1981—; adminstrv. law judge Tex. Employment Commn., San Antonio, 1976-81; asst. gen. counsel Govt. Employees Credit Union, San Antonio, 1981; town justice Town of Oneonta, 1981—. Bd. dirs. Otsego County Family Services, 1982-84. Mem. AAUW, LWV, Assn. Trial Lawyers Am., N.Y. State Trial Lawyers Assn., Otsego County Magistrates Assn. (v.p. 1983-84), N.Y. State Magistrates Assn., Delta Theta Pi, Alpha Chi. Democrat. Methodist. Office: 48 Dietz St Oneonta NY 13820

SCATES, ALICE YEOMANS, former government official, consultant; b. Pitts., Jan. 21, 1915; d. William E. and Georgiana L. (Lloyd) Yeomans; B.S., State Tchrs. Coll., Glassboro, N.J., 1936; M.Ed., Duke U., 1949; Ed.D., George Washington U., 1963. Tchr. elem. sch., Haddon Heights, N.J., 1937-43; civilian personnel officer Sedalia Army Airfield, Mo., Greenville Army Air Field, S.C., 1944-46; tng. officer VA Center, Dayton, Ohio, 1947-48; research asso., dir. Am. Council on Edn. Staff for Office Naval Research Projects, 1949-53; asst. dir. Nat. Home Study Council, 1954; editor, research asst. Office of Edn., HEW, 1955, research analyst and coordinator coop. research program, 1956-64, program planning officer occupational research program, 1965-66, dir. basic research br. secondary edn., 1967-69, program planning and eval. officer Nat. Center Ednl. Research and Devel., 1969-71, eval. specialist Office Program Eval., 1971-80; eval. officer Office of Mgmt., U.S. Dept. Edn., 1980-82; cons., 1982—. Served to capt. U.S. Army, 1943-46. Fellow AAAS; mem. Am. Sociol. Assn., Am. Anthrop. Assn., Am. Acad. Polit. and Social Sci., Am. Ednl. Research Assn. Adult Edn. Assn., Kappa Delta Pi, Phi Delta Gamma. Author research reports, articles in field. Home: 560 N St SW Washington DC 20024 Office: Box N-501 560 N St SW Washington DC 20024

SCATTOREGGIO, ESTHER, flexographic printing company executive; b. Bronx, N.Y., Aug. 10, 1941; d. Richard and Tillie (Mullin) O'Donnell; m. Alan Goldman, July 4, 1959 (div. 1970); children—Richard, Felecia Hillary; m. John Joseph Scattoreggio, Mar. 12, 1978. Student various bus. courses. Sales clk. Waring Envelope, Bklyn., 1969-70, sales service mgr., 1970-71; exec. sec. to nat. sales mgr. Saxon Adhesive Products, Long Island City, N.Y., 1971-72, asst. nat. sales mgr., 1972-74; office mgr. flexographic co., Nassau, N.Y., 1974-75, asst. v.p. ops., 1976-77, v.p. ops., 1977-79; co-owner/operator JES Label & Tape, Inc., Hollis, N.Y., 1979—. Active girls softball league, Little League; ice hockey league. Mem. Navigators, Club of Printing Women. Avocations: bowling; swimming; tennis; racquetball. Home: North Hills NY 11040 Office: JES Label & Tape Inc 205-11 Jamaica Ave Hollis NY 11423

SCAVO, MARYBETH, maid service executive; b. Menomonie, Wis., Feb. 1, 1948; d. Bernard Owen and Jean Frances (Stoll) Hughes; m. Ronald Frank Scavo, Dec. 28, 1968; children—Marc Bryan, Angela Jo. B.S. with honors, Central Mich. U., 1970. Cert. secondary tchr., Mich. tchr. Grand Blanc High Sch., Mich., 1970-80; pres., gen. mgr. The Maids, Inc., Corpus Christi, Tex., 1980—. Author: Your Maids' Franchise: an Operations Manual, 1985. Pres., St. Pius X PTO, Corpus Christi, 1984-86; mem. St. Pius X Sch. Bd., 1984-86; sec.-treas. St. Pius X Roman Catholic Ch. Altar and Rosary Soc., 1983-85; mem. personnel com. YWCA, Corpus Christi, 1985. Mem. Exec. Women Internat. (membership com. 1984-85). Clubs: Altrusa, New Neighbors. Lodge: Elks Does. Avocations: reading; piano; Spanish. Home: 5009 Goldeneye St Corpus Christi TX 78413 Office: The Maids Inc 5009 Goldeneye St Corpus Christi TX 78413

SCERBO, FRANCES CAROLYN GARROTT, architectural technician; b. Bowling Green, Ky., Mar. 10, 1932; d. Irby Reid and Carrie Mae (Stahl) Cameron; m. Leslie Othello Garrott, Oct. 12, 1951 (dec. Feb. 1978); children—Dennis Leslie, Alan Reid; adopted children—Carolyn Maria, Karen Roxana; m. 2d, Raymond William Scerbo, May 31, 1978. Student Fla. State U., 1951, St. Petersburg Jr. Coll., 1962-74; grad. Pinellas Vocat. Tech. Inst., 1975. With Sears, Roebuck and Co., Rapid City, S.D., 1951-52, St. Petersburg, Fla., 1961-62; bookkeeper Ohio Nat. Bank, Columbus, 1953-54, Sunbeam Bakery, Lakeland, Fla., 1955-56; with Christies Toy Sales, Pennsauken, N.J., 1958-60; exec. sec. Gulf Coast Automotive Warehouse, Inc., Tampa, Fla., 1970-73, office mgr., 1975-78; sec.-treas., chief pilot, co-owner Tech. Devel. Corp., St. Petersburg, Fla., 1970-78; freelance archtl. draftsman and designer, archtl. cons., constrn. materials estimator, 1975—, Fla. state judge Vocat. Indsl. Clubs of Am. Skills Olympics, 1986. Nat. Assn. Women in Constrn. scholar, 1974. Mem. Nat. Assn. Women in Constrn., Alpha Chi Omega. Democrat. Home and Office: 11298 53d Ave N Saint Petersburg FL 33708

SCHAAF, BARBARA CAROL, writer, consultant; b. Chgo., Dec. 17, 1940; d. William and Mary Anne (Krutilla) S. B.G.S. cum laude, Roosevelt U., 1971; M.B.A., U. Chgo. Exec. Program, 1976. Free-lance writer, Harvey, Ill., 1977—; cons. health care delivery systems, transp., housing, taxation, labor and econs., including to Continental Air Transport, 1979-80, Cook County treas., 1980—, Chgo. Health Maintenance Orgn., 1983-85; lectr. urban and ethnic history, English medieval history; lectr. on urban and ethnic history USIA, 1978; mem. adv. com. Artists in Residence Program, Chgo. Council Fine Arts, 1979-83; bd. dirs. Chgo. Ctr. Hosp., 1982—; treas., bd. dirs. Chgo. Ctr. Health System, 1985—. Author: Mr. Dooley's chicago, 1977 (Carl Sandburg award 1978, also nominee Am. Hist. Assn. Gershoy award and Pulitzer prize); also articles to newspapers, mags. Press sec. Eleanor McGovern, 1971-72, Richard M. Daley campaign, Chgo., 1979-80; treas. Harvey Pub. Library Bd. Trustees, 1977—, R. F. Kennedy presdl. campaign and other polit. campaigns, Ill., 1978. Nat. Found. for Humanities fellow Writing in Chgo. Program, 1978. Mem. Nat. Book Critics Circle, Richard III Soc. Democrat. Roman Catholic. Ind. scholarship in urban history, English medieval history, and military history. Home and Office: 400 Streamside Dr Harvey IL 60426

SCHACH, CARRINGTON COEBURN, communications specialist; b. Balt., Feb. 16, 1956; d. William Oscar and Harriet Frances Sawtelle (Ratchford) S. Student Ellis Sch., Florence, Italy, 1974; B.A., Wheaton Coll., 1978. Lic., N.Y. State Ins. Dept. Brokerage cons. Conn. Gen., N.Y.C., 1979-80; mgr. sales promotion Monarch Resources Inc., N.Y.C., 1980-83, dir. corp. communications, 1983—; freelance mktg. communications and pub. relations counseling, N.Y.C., 1983—. Author article in profl jour. Sculptor bronze Female Nudes, 1978. Vol. tchr. Home for Crippled Children, Pitts., 1970-74; fund raiser Sta. WQED Pitts., 1970-74; fund raiser Reagan/Bush campaign, N.Y.C., 1980. Mem. Nat. Assn. Securities Dealers (cert.), Nat. Assn. Female Execs., Pub. Relations Soc. Am., Fin. Communications Soc., Life Communicators Assn. Clubs: Rolling Rock (Ligonier, Pa.); Rockaway Hunting (Lawrence N.Y.); Pitts Golf. Office: Monarch Resources Inc 780 Third Ave 20th Fl New York NY 10017

SCHACHTEL, ELLEN MERRILL, sales executive; b. N.Y.C., Nov. 25, 1945; d. Irving Ira Schachtel and Elinor Leeds (Weiler) Krach. B.A. in Psychology, Fordham U., 1976. Sales mgr. Wilbur-Ellis Co., N.Y.C., 1978-80, Sweetheart Cones Co., Bklyn., 1980—. Mem. AAUW (chmn. women 1982—, membership v.p. 1984). Royal Oak Found. N.Y.C., Archaeol. Inst. America, Nat. Assn. Profl. Saleswoman.

SCHACHTER, ESTHER RODITTI, lawyer; writer; b. Los Angeles, Feb. 7, 1933; d. David and Lucy Roditti; m. Oscar H. Schachter, Aug. 8, 1957; children—Charles David, Susan Dayana. B.A., UCLA, 1954; J.D., Harvard U., 1957. Bar: N.Y. 1959. Assoc. Stickles, Hayden and Kennedy, N.Y.C., 1957-62; asst. dir. Legis. Drafting Fund Columbia U., N.Y.C., 1962-65, cons., 1965-67; cons. N.Y.C. Air Pollution Control Dept., 1965-67; instr. and cons. New Sch. for Social Research, N.Y.C., 1968-70; cons. Internat. League for Rights of Man, N.Y.C., 1969, Rand Inst., N.Y.C., 1969, U.S.-Societ Environ. Studies Program, UN Assn., N.Y.C., 1969; sr. research assoc. Ctr. for Policy Research Columbia U., 1970-73; sr. program officer Ford Found., N.Y.C., 1972-78; pres. Esther Roditti Schachter, P.C., N.Y.C., 1978-83; ptnr. Schachter & Froling, N.Y.C., 1983—; speaker, lectr., panelist profl. assn. confs., forums, workshops, U.S., Can., Tokyo. Author: N.Y.C. Air Pollution Control Code Annotated, 1965; Enforcing Air Pollution Controls, 1979; Financial Support of Women's Programs in the 1970's, 1979; Computer Contracts Reference Directory, 1979-83; co-author: Charities and Charitable Foundations, 1974; author, co-author articles in field; legal editor: Computer Economics Report, 1983—; Computers for Design and Construction, 1983—. Nat. governing bd. Common Cause, 1979-82, mem. state governing bd., N.Y., 1982-84; mem. com. on urban environ. Citizens Union, N.Y.C., 1969-73; mem. West Side Democratic Club, 1958-63. Ford Found. grantee, 1970; NSF grantee, 1971; recipient Award for Outstanding Service Brandeis U., Nat. Women's Com., 1973. Mem. ABA (sect. sci. and tech. com. on law relating to computers), Assn. Bar City N.Y. (founder, chmn. com. on computer law 1980—), N.Y. State Bar Assn. (banking corp. and bus law sect., computer law subcom.), Computer Law Assn., Phi Beta Kappa. Club: Panther (Alamuchy, N.J.).

SCHAEFER, LEE ASTRID, counseling hypnotherapist; b. Chgo., Apr. 1, 1927; d. Paul N. Hagstrom and Hedvina R. (Anderson) Blom; m. Raymond L. Schaefer, Aug. 12, 1950; children—Karen, Anita, Sonja. Student U. Chgo., 1945; diploma Art Inst. Chgo., 1950; student Amundsen-Mayfair, Chgo., 1969-70; B.A. in Psychology with honors, Northeastern U., Chgo., 1974, M.A. in Social Sci., 1983. Dress designer, fashion model, Chgo., 1944-58; counselor Omni House, Youth Services Bur., Arlington Heights, Ill., 1976; pvt. practice counseling hypnotherapist, Arlington Heights, 1973—; tchr. self-hypnosis Northeastern Ill. U., 1975—, faculty asst., 1975-77; pres. Autohypnotic Behavioral Conditioning, Arlington Heights, 1980—; chmn. program Midwest Hypnosis Conv., Elmwood Park, Ill., 1975-80, chmn., 1977. Contbr. articles to profl. jours. Mem. Assn. to Advance Ethical Hypnosis (sec. 1976-77, pres. local chpt. 1978), Assn. Humanistic Psychology, Psi Chi (sec., treas. Northeastern U. chpt. 1973-76). Unity. Home: 404 N Windsor Dr Arlington Heights IL 60004 Office: ABC Inc 404 N Windsor Dr Arlington Heights IL 60004

SCHAEFER, MARGARET MARY, nurse; b. Breese, Ill., Oct. 17, 1949; d. John Anthony and Annie Catherine (Wolters) Niemann; m. Henry Arnold Schaefer, Apr. 12, 1969; children—James, John, Dan. A.A., Belleville Area Coll., 1969. Nurses' aide St. Joseph Hosp., Breese, 1967-69; staff nurse St. Joseph's Hosp., Clinton County Hosp., 1969-72; staff nurse Samaritan Meml. Hosp., Macon, Mo., 1973-83, night supr., 1983—. Leader 4-H Club, Atlanta, Mo., 1983—. Mem. Mo. Nurses Assn., Am. Nurses Assn. Roman Catholic. Avocations: hiking; canoeing; quilt-making. Home: Route 2 Box 103 Atlanta MO 63530

SCHAEFER, PATRICIA, librarian; b. Ft. Wayne, Ind., Apr. 23, 1930; d. Edward John and Hildegarde Hartman (Hormel) S.; B.Mus., Northwestern U., 1951; M.Mus., U. Ill., 1958; M.A. in Library Sci., U. Mich., 1963. Typist U.S. Rubber Co., Ft. Wayne, Ind., 1951-52; sec. to promotion mgr. sta. WOWO, Ft. Wayne, 1952, sec. to program mgr., 1953-55; coordinator publicity and promotion Home Telephone Co., Ft. Wayne, 1955-56; sec. Fine Arts Found., Ft. Wayne, 1956-57; library asst. Columbus (Ohio) Public Library, 1958-59; audio-visual librarian Muncie (Ind.) Public Library, 1959—, asst. library dir., 1981—; chmn. Ind. Library Film Circuit, 1962-63; sec. Ind. Library Film Service, 1969-70, exec. bd., 1981-82, treas., 1983-85; exec. bd. Ind. Film Council, 1981-82, v.p., 1982-83, pres., 1983-84; mem. Ind. State Library Audio-Visual Task Force, 1979-80; cons., adv. two-yr. technicians program library sci. dept. Ball State U.; dir. Franklin Electric Co., Inc. Bd. dirs. Muncie Symphony Assn., 1964-74, 85—, Del. County Council for Arts, 1985—; mem. community adv. com. Ball Brothers Found. Cultural Ctr.; mem. adv. com., bookshop dir. Midwest Writers' Workshop, 1976-77; pres. Del. County Council for Arts, 1979-81; bd. dirs. Muncie YWCA, 1977-82, 84—, treas., 1981-82; gen. chmn. Ind. Renaissance Fair, 1978, 79; vice chmn. Sta. WBST Community Adv. Com.; pres. Eastern Ind. Area Library Services Authority; mem. trustees adv. Council Milton S. Eisenhower Library, Johns Hopkins U. Mem. ALA, Ind. Library Assn. (dist. chmn. 1972-73, chmn. Ind. Library Assn.-Ind. Library Trustee Assn. library planning com. 1969-73, treas. 1973-75, chmn. awards and hons. com. 1977-80, sec. div. women in Ind. Libraries 1983—, v.p., pres.-elect), Dist. Library Assn. (chmn. 1972-73), Nat. League Am. Pen Women (pres. Muncie Br. 1974-78), Delta Zeta. Republican. Roman Catholic. Clubs: Am. Recorder Soc., Northeastern Ind. Recorder Soc., Muncie Matinee Musicale (pres. 1965-67), Ind. Fedn. Music Clubs (dist. sec.-treas. 1967-68), Riley-Jones (charter mem.), Altrusa (pres. Muncie). Program annotator E.Central Ind. Community Singers, 1980—, Muncie Symphony Orch., 1963—. Home: 405 S Tara Ln Muncie IN 47304 Office: 200 E Main St Muncie IN 47305

SCHAEFER, PATRICIA ANN, librarian; b. Lebanon, Ohio, Jan. 22, 1933; d. Riley Ray and Louise Collette (Fraher) Freeze; B.S., Miami U., Oxford, Ohio, 1954; m. William H. Schaefer, Aug. 11, 1956; children—Susan P., Nancy A., William H. III (dec.). Med. technologist Mercy Hosp., Hamilton, Ohio, 1954-58, Middletown (Ohio) Hosp., 1958-62; librarian Middletown City Schs., 1979—, intermediate librarian McKinley Sch., 1982—. Active, YMCA, pres., 1977-79; bd. dirs. Middletown Symphony, 1974-78, Arts in Middletown, 1983—; hon. bd. dirs. Am. Cancer Soc., 1961—; chmn. legis. City Charter Rev. Com., 1970; residential chmn. United Way, 1976; chmn. Sch. Tax Levy, 1978; mem. Middletown City Commn., 1983—; mem. exec. com. Ohio-Ky.-Ind. Regional Council, 1986. Recipient Stuart Ives Service to Youth award, 1980. Mem. Am. Soc. Clin. Pathologists, Registry Med. Technologists, Am. Bus. Women's Assn. (pres. 1961-62), Middletown C. of C., LWV (pres. 1962-63), PEO, Sigma Sigma Sigma. Methodist. Club: Browns Run Country. Home: 1909 Antrim Ct Middletown OH 45042

SCHAEFFER, BARBARA HAMILTON, transportation company executive; travel consultant; b. Newton, Mass., Apr. 26, 1926; d. Peter Davidson Gunn and Harriet Bennett (Thompson) Hamilton; m. John Schaeffer, Sept. 7, 1946; children—Laurie, John, Peter. Student, Skidmore Coll., 1943-46; A.B. in English, Bucknell U., 1948; postgrad. Montclair State U., 1950-51, Bank St. Coll. Edn., 1959-61, Yeshiva U., 1961-62. Cert. primary, secondary tchr., N.J. Dir. Pompton Plains Sch., N.J., 1959-62; adviser Episcopal Sch., Towaco, N.J., 1968-70; v.p. Deltona-DeLand Trolley, Orange City, Fla., 1980-81; pres. Monroe Heavy Equipment Rentals, Orange City, 1981—; cons. TLC Travel Club, Orange City, 1981—; lectr. on children's art, 1959-70. Contbr. articles to profl. publs. Mem. Small Bus. Devel. Regional Ctr. (Stetson U. chpt.), DeLand Area C. of C. (transp. com. 1981-85). Episcopalian. Avocations: restoring old home; oil painting; piano. Home: 400 Foothill Farms Rd Orange City FL 32763 Office: Monroe Heavy Equipment Rentals Inc 400 Foothill Farms Rd Orange City FL 32763 also 2425 Enterprise Rd Orange City FL

SCHAEFFER, SUSAN FROMBERG, author, educator; b. Bklyn., Mar. 25, 1941; d. Irving and Edith (Levine) Fromberg; B.A., U. Chgo., 1961, M.A. with honors, 1963, Ph.D. with honors, 1966; m. Neil J. Schaeffer, Oct. 11, 1970; children—Benjamin Adam, May Anna. Instr. English, Wright Jr. Coll., Chgo., 1964-65; asst. prof. Ill. Inst. Tech., Chgo., 1965-67; successively asst. prof., asso. prof., prof. Bklyn. Coll., 1967—; guest lectr. U. Chgo., Cornell U., U. Ariz., U. Maine, Yale U., U. Tex., U. Mass. Recipient E.L. Wallant award, Friends of Lit. award.; Prairie Schooner's Lawrence award; Poetry award Centennial Rev. Mem. PEN, Authors Guild, Poetry Soc. Am. Democrat. Jewish. Author novels: Falling, 1973; Anya, 1974; Time In Its Flight, 1978; Love, 1981; The Madness of a Seduced Woman, 1983; Mainland, 1984; poetry: The Witch and the Weather Report, 1972; Alphabet For the Lost Years, 1976; Granite Lady (nominee Nat. Book award), 1974; Rhymes and Runes of the Toad, 1975; The Bible of the Beasts of the Little Field, 1980; short stories: The Queen of Egypt and Other Stories, 1980. Address: 783 E 21st St Brooklyn NY 11210

SCHAFER, LINDA RENEE, lawyer; b. Riverside, Calif., Oct. 3, 1952; d. Thomas Coy and Lillian Lucille (Jordan) Ramsey; m. Robert Joseph Schafer, Mar. 19, 1977; children—Alicia Dawn, Shannon Renee. B.S., Western Bapt. Coll., 1973; J.D., Willamette U., 1977. Bar: Oreg. 1978. Title examiner Pioneer Nat. Title Ins., Albany, Oreg., 1978-79; sole practice, Salem, Oreg., 1979-84; assoc. Annala, Carey, Hull & Van Koten, Hood River, Oreg., 1985—; adv. counsel Trade Adv. Com., Salem, 1980-83. Mem. ABA, Trial Lawyers Assn. Am., Oreg. State Bar, Oreg. Pub. Defenders Assn. Democrat. Baptist. Office: 305 Cascade Hood River OR 97031

SCHAFFHAUSEN, FLORENCE PLATT, environmental writer, columnist; b. Woodbridge, N.J., Nov. 30, 1908; d. George Gilbert and Eva Antoninette (Smith) Platt; m. Joseph Frank Schaffhausen, Apr. 3, 1936 (dec.); children—Eric Platt, Caroline Chandler Schaffhausen Tyrrell. Student N.J. Coll. for Women, 1927-30; B.F.A., Am. Inst. Graphic Arts, NYU. Reporter, advt. mgr. Metuchen Recorder (N.J.), 1933-35; spl. writer Albuquerque Tribune, 1936; reporter Daily Intelligencer, Doylestown, Pa., 1963-70, environmental writer, 1970—, environmental columnist, 1971—; environmental advisor Conservation Alliance of Bucks County, Doylestown, 1970— (writing award 1982). Chmn. Citizens Adv. Com. on Gen. Govt., Dobbs Ferry, N.Y., 1957-59; founder, mem. Dobbs Ferry Com. for Selection of Sch. Bd. Candidates, 1955-58; charter mem. Bucks County Council on the Arts, Doylestown, 1973-81. Recipient Keystone Press award, 2d place, Pa. Soc. Newspaper Editors Pa. Newspapers Pubs. Assn., 1969; Disting. Service Citation Bucks County Soil and Water Conservation Dist., 1970; EPA award, 1980. Mem. Pa. Women's Press Assn. (1st place award for editorial, 1976, many others), Bucks County Council on Arts. Republican. Presbyterian. Office: Daily Intelligencer N Broad St Doylestown PA 18901

SCHAFFHAUSEN, JANE IMBS, apparel manufacturing company executive; b. Paris, France, Sept. 17, 1929; came to U.S., 1939; d. Bravig and Valeska (Balbarishky) Imbs; m. Henry W. Trimble, Oct. 4, 1984; children—Wellington D. Watters, Valeska A. Watters. M.B.A., Vassar Coll., 1951. Pres., Village Store, Birmingham, Mich., 1953-67, N.Y.C., 1961-77; pres. Belle France, Inc., N.Y.C., 1974-82, chmn., 1982—. Recipient Entrepreneur Woman's award Women in Bus., 1981. Mem. Phi Beta Kappa. Office: Belle France Inc 530 7th Ave New York NY 10018

SCHAFFNER, ARLENE RUTH, office administrator, dental hygienist; b. Chgo., Nov. 4, 1930; d. Morris and Esther (Nathan) Ginsburg; m. Gerald Schaffner, Apr. 6, 1952; children—James H., Sue A., Ellen B. Dental hygienist Drs. Kobernick & Chionis, San Diego, Calif., 1970—. Bd. dirs., past pres. Phoenix Jewish Community Ctr. Aux., past leader Cub Scouts, Girl Scouts U.S., Campfire Girls; mem. Brandeis, San Diego. Mem. Am. Contract Bridge League, San Diego Starlight Assn. Lodge: B'nai B'rith Women (life, past pres.) Avocations: tennis; hiking; bridge.

SCHAFLIN, BARBARA ANN, ins. co. exec.; b. Newark, Feb. 24, 1943; d. Edward Paul and Mary Ann (Vrabel) Filipowski; student Seton Hall U., 1964-65; cert. dance tchr. Dance Educators Am., 1966; student Mommouth Coll., 1978, Am. Coll., 1982—, Inst. Children's Lit., 1980-82; m. Ernest J. Schaflin, July 22, 1967; children—John Ernest, Christina Ann, Peter James. Dance tchr. June and Don Stirling Talent Center, Newark, 1964-67; adminstrv. asst. Interstate Adminstrs., Inc., Red Bank, N.J., 1978-81; spl. agt. Prudential Life Ins. Co. Am., Ocean, N.J., 1981-83; ind. agt. life, health and fin. services B.A. Schaflin & Co., 1983—; Sales assoc. Heritage House Realty & Cons., 1985—. Trustee Middletown Twp. Hist. Soc.; mem. leader and devel. com. Monmouth County 4-H Assn.; lector St. Mary's Ch.; pres. Lincroft Sch. PTA, 1976-78; mem. Middletown Twp. Community Devel. Com. Mem. Nat. Assn.

Life Underwriters, Monmouth Assn. Life Underwriters, Women's Network, N.J. Fedn. Bus. and Profl. Women (state treas. 1985-86, former state councilor on future of women in workplace, asst. dist. dir., long range plan com.), Beta Sigma Phi (chpt. pres. 1966-69, 71-72, 78-79, Order of Rose degree 1980, Outstanding Young Women of Am. award 1975, Who's Who in East award 1983-84, 85-86). Home: 10 Rose St Lincroft NJ 07738 Office: 1411 Hwy 35 Ocean NJ 07712

SCHALANSKY, JANET KAY, state official; b. Denver, Oct. 20, 1950; d. Melvin Curtis and Florence Marie (Jones) P.; m. James Lee Schalansky, July 20, 1974; children—Jay Patrick, Jill Marie, Julie Ann. B.A. in Pre-medicine, Emporia State U., 1972; M.S. in Rehab., 1973; postgrad. U. Kans., 1983—. Cert. rehab. counselor. Disability examiner Kans. Div. Vocat. Rehab., Topeka, 1973-76; adminstrv. officer Kans. Div. Mental Health/Mental Retardation, Topeka, 1976-79; exec. dir. Developmental Disabilities Council, Topeka, 1979-84; dir. adult services Kans. Dept. Social and Rehab. Services, 1984—. Mem. Kans. Conf. on Social Welfare, Am. Assn. Mental Deficiency. Democrat. Methodist. Home: 906 Glendale Dr Topeka KS 66606 Office: Adult Services State Complex West 2700 W 6th St Topeka KS 66606

SCHALK, BEVERLY VANDYKE, nurse educator; b. Hillsboro, Oreg., Aug. 13, 1959; d. Ervin Aloysius and Jane Margaret (Bernards) Van Dyke; m. David Charles Schalk, Aug. 20, 1983; 1 child, Laura Beverly. B.S., Oreg. State U., 1982; A.S. in Nursing, Chemeketa Community Coll., 1984. Coordinator vols. escape field studies program U. Oreg., Eugene, 1979-80; fetal alcohol syndrome directory coordinator Benton-Linn Council on Alcohol, Corvallis, Oreg., 1982; early pregnancy instr. March of Dimes, Salem, Oreg., 1982-84; staff nurse Salem Hosp., 1983-84, nurse perinatal educator, 1984—; stress mgmt. workshop designer/facilitator U. Oreg., 1982, Salem Sr. Ctr., 1983. Mem. pub. health edn. com. March of Dimes., 1982-84. Nurses Assn. of Am. Coll. Obstetricians and Gynecologists, Mem. Am. Soc. for Psychoprophylaxis in Obstetrics, Oreg. Assn. for Advancement of Health Edn., Salem Childbirth Edn. Assn., Eta Sigma Gamma (pres. chpt. 1980-82). Democrat. Roman Catholic. Home: 5080 Fir Dell Ct SE Salem OR 97306 Office: General Unit Salem Hosp 2561 Center St NE Salem OR 97301

SCHALLER-DRAKE, GLORIA JEAN, marketing executive; b. Chgo., Aug. 2, 1953; d. George Joseph and Dolores (Riley) Schaller; m. Thomas G. Drake, July 21, 1984. B.S., Western Ill. U., 1975; M.B.A., Keller Grad. Sch. Mgmt., 1982. Market research analyst Allied Van Lines, Broadview, Ill., 1975-77, sr. market research analyst, 1977-78; mktg. mgr. Allied Air Freight, Broadview, 1978-81; mktg. specialist Continental Bondware, Rolling Meadows, Ill., 1981-83, mgr. mktg. and internat. sales 1983—. Mem. Am. Mktg. Assn., Chgo. Council Fgn. Relations, Women in Foodservice. Club: Variety. Office: 1701 Golf Rd Tower Three Rolling Meadows IL 60008

SCHANDER, MARY LEA, municipal government official; b. Bakersfield, Calif., June 11, 1947; d. Gerald John Lea and Marian Lea Coffman; B.A. (Augustana fellow), Calif. Luth. Coll., 1969; M.A., UCLA, 1970; m. Edwin Schander, July 3, 1971. Staff aide City of Anaheim Police Dept. (Calif.), 1970-72, staff asst., 1972-79, sr. staff asst., 1979-80, mgmt. auditor, 1980-82; asst. to pub. safety dir. City of Pasadena Pub. Safety Agy. (Calif.), 1982-85; asst. to police chief City of Pasadena, 1985—; lectr. Calif. Luth. Coll.; freelance musician. Mem. LWV, Am. Mgmt. Assn. Club: Los Angeles Athletic. Author publs. in field. Home: 275 Waverly Dr Pasadena CA 91105 Office: PO Box 50151 Pasadena CA 91105

SCHARF, LORI BETH, business systems executive; b. Queens, N.Y., Apr. 19, 1955; d. Jerome Donald and Phyllis Joan (Elfenbein) Lovitts; m. Sanford Scharf, July 1, 1982. Student SUNY-Buffalo, 1973-74; A.A.S. in Applied Sci., Sullivan County Community Coll., 1976. Various positions with hotel chains in Catskills (N.Y.), 1974-76; corporate sec., fin. adviser, estimator, officer mgr. Landhill Press, N.Y.C. and Westbury, N.Y., 1976-81; officer mgr. Rotary Bus. Systems, Farmingdale, N.Y., 1981—. Office: 590 Smith St Farmingdale NY 11735

SCHAROLD, MARY LOUISE, psychoanalyst, educator; b. Wichita Falls, Tex., Mar. 3, 1943; d. Walter John and Louise Helen (Hartman) Baumgartner; m. William Ballew McCollum, Aug. 23, 1964 (div. 1981); m. Harry Karl Scharold, June 19, 1982; children—Margaret Louise, Walter Ballew. B.A. with highest distinction, U. Kans., 1964; M.D., Baylor Coll. Med., 1968; postgrad. Topeka Inst. for Psychoanalysis, 1981. Diplomate Am. Bd. Psychiatry and Neurology. Intern Meml. Baptist. Hosp., Houston, 1968-69; resident in psychiatry Baylor Coll. Med., Houston, 1969-72, chief resident, 1971-72; practice of medicine specializing in psychoanalysis, Houston, 1972—; asst. prof. Baylor Coll. Med., Houston, 1973-76, asst. clin. prof., 1981-84, assoc. clin. prof., 1984—; dir. Baylor Psychiat. Clinic, Houston, 1973-76; co-dir. Rice U. Psychiat. Service, Houston, 1981-82; asst. clin. prof. U. Kans. Sch. Medicine, Kansas City, 1977-81; teaching assoc. Topeka Inst. Psychoanalysis, 1980-81; instr. Houston-Galveston Psychoanalytic Inst., 1984—. Adv. bd. Leavenworth Mental Health Assn., Kans., 1977-81. Watkins scholar U. Kans., 1961-64. Fellow Am. Psychiatric Assn. (chmn. Tex. peer review 1984—); mem. Am. Psychoanalytic Assn. (cert. 1982, peer rev. com. 1985—), Am. Group Psychotherapy Assn., Houston Psychiatric Soc. (v.p. 1984-85, pres. elect 1985-86), Houston-Galveston Psychoanalytic Soc. (sec.-treas. 1984-86, pres.-elect 1986-88), Houston Group Psychotherapy Soc. (adv. bd. 1984-85), Mortar Bd., Phi Beta Kappa, Delta Phi Alpha, Alpha Omega Alpha, Hilltopper, Pi Beta Phi Alumni Assn. Republican. Lutheran. Office: 4101 Greenbriar Dr Suite 240 Houston TX 77098

SCHAROSCH, KAREN MAURENE, child care center director; b. Scottsbluff, Nebr., June 18, 1938; d. Gerald Francis and Thelma (Mae) Hanlon; m. David Patrick Scharosch, June 27, 1964; children—Jody Anne, Jill Marie, Janet Louise, John David, Jerry Patrick. A.A., Western Nebr. Jr. Coll., 1959; B.A., No. Colo. Coll., 1963. Tchr. Dix Pub. Schs., Nebr., 1959-61, Centralia Sch. Dist., Anaheim, Calif., 1961-64; vol., Hayward, Calif., 1965-66; dir. Kiddie Kollege Day Sch. and Kindergarden, Salem, Oreg., 1973—; mem. adv. bd. career devel. South Salem High Sch., 1975-78; mem. local sch. adv. com. Leslie Middle Sch., Salem, 1983-85. Leader Camp Fire, Salem, 1973-79, co-chmn. leaders assocs., 1978-79; mem. Child Care Action Project-Salem Keizer Sch. Dist. Mem. Oreg. Assn. Day Care Dirs., Salem Assn. Edn. Young Children (pres. 1977-78). Republican. Roman Catholic. Club: Am. Field Service (Salem). Avocations: music; marimba; young children. Office: Kiddie Kollege 669 Vista Ave SE Salem OR 97302

SCHATZ, HELEN D., county official; b. McClusky, N.D., Aug. 10, 1936; d. Edwin Walter and Esther Mae (Lee) Zinke; m. Darryl Dean Schatz, Dec. 26, 1953; children—Marian Lee, Darryl Dean, Jr. Clk., Burleigh County, Bismarck, N.D., 1962-75, dep. treas., 1975-79, treas., 1979—. Mem. N.D. Assn. Counties (pres. 1981-82), N.D. County Treas. Assn. (pres. 1980-82), Zonta Internat. Lutheran. Avocations: sewing, knitting, boating, camping. Office: Burleigh County Courthouse Bismarck ND 58501

SCHATZ, PAULINE, dietitian; b. Sioux City, Iowa, Sept. 25, 1923; d. Isaac and Haya (Kaplan) Epstein; B.S., UCLA, 1945, M.S., 1950, M.S. in Public Health, 1963; Ed.D., U. So. Calif., 1984; m. Hyman Schatz, Sept. 2, 1951; children—Barbara, Larry. Head dietitian VA, 1946-54; asso. prof. Los Angeles City Coll., 1958-68; prof. home econs. Calif. State U., Los Angeles, 1968-83, prof. emeritus, 1983—, dir. center dietetic edn., 1979—. Grantee VA, Kellogg Found., HEW. Mem. Am. Dietetic Assn., Am. Home Econs. Assn., Calif. Dietetic Assn. (Disting. Service award 1986), Los Angeles Dietetic Assn., Omicron Nu. Author: Manual for Clinical Dietetics, 1978, 3d edit., 1983. Office: Dept Home Econs Calif State Univ Los Angeles CA 90032

SCHAUB, MARILYN MCNAMARA, theology educator; b. Chgo., Mar. 24, 1928; d. Bernard Francis and Helen Katherine (Skchan) McNamara; m. R. Thomas Schaub, Oct. 25, 1969; 1 child, Helen Ann Schaub. B.A., Rosary Coll., 1953; Ph.D., U. Fribourg, Switzerland, 1957; diplome Ecole Biblique, Jerusalem, 1967. Asst. prof. classics Rosary Coll., River Forest, Ill., 1957-69; vis. prof. theology LaRoche Coll., Allison Park, Pa., 1970-73; prof. theology Duquesne U., Pitts., 1973—; adminstrv. dir. Expedition to S.E. Plain of Dead Sea, Jordan, 1981—. Author: Friends and Friendship for Augustine, 1964. Translator: (with H. Richter) C. Spicq, Agape in the New Testament, 3 vols., 1963-65. Contbr. articles to profl. jours. Trustee Am. Schs. Oriental Research, 1981-85. Hon. assoc. Am. Schs. Oriental Research, Jerusalem, 1966-67, Danforth assoc., St. Louis, 1975-81. Mem. Soc. Bibl. Lit. (mem. council 1981-85), Am. Acad. Religion, Cath. Bibl. Assn., Israel Exploration Soc. Democrat. Roman Catholic. Avocations: archaeol. excavations in the Middle East. Home: 25 McKelvey Ave Pittsburgh PA 15218 Office: Theology Dept Duquesne U Pittsburgh PA 15282

SCHAUBERT, LAUREL VIRGINIA, med. illustrator; b. Portland Oreg., Aug. 3, 1923; d. John and Mildred (Hall) Karg; student Reed Coll., 1940-43, U. Calif., 1947-49, Art League San Francisco, 1950-53, U. Calif. San Francisco Med. Center, 1953-55; m. Arvid D. Schaubert, Nov. 10, 1962; children—Gay Lee Schaubert Giannini, Leslie May (dec.). Med. illustrator Ft. Miley VA Hosp., 1955; sr. illustrator dept. surgery U. Calif., San Francisco, 1955-69; prin. illustrator Lange Med. Publs., Los Altos, Calif., 1961—; now also co-owner, pres. Biomed Arts Assocs., Inc., San Francisco; instr. U. Calif., 1959-61, 74-78. Recipient cert. of commendation Calif. Dist. Attys. Assn., 1977; Merit award Fedn. Biocommunication Socs., 1979. Mem. Assn. Med. Illustrators (Outstanding Service award 1972; chmn. bd. govs. 1971-72, v.p. 1975-76, pres. 1976-77), Graphic Artists Guild. Co-author: Scientific Illustration: Standards for Publication; contbr. med. illustrations and articles to textbooks, profl. jours. Office: 350 Parnassus Ave Suite 905 San Francisco CA 94117

SCHAUER, CATHARINE GUBERMAN, author, editor, columnist; b. Woodbury, N.J., Sept. 24, 1945; d. Jack and Anna Ruth (Felipe) Guberman; m. Irwin Jay Schauer, July 4, 1968; children—Cheryl Anne, Marc Cawin. A.B., Miami-Dade Jr. Coll., 1965; B.Ed., U. Miami, 1967; postgrad. Mercer U., 1968. Writer, Miami (Fla.) News, 1962-63; tchr. Dade County Schs., Miami, Fla., 1967-68; coordinator pub. info. Macon Jr. Coll. (Ga.), 1968-69; writer Atlanta Jour., 1969-72; editor Ridgerunner newspaper, Woodbridge, Va., 1973-75; pub. info. specialist Dept. Interior, Washington, 1980-82; writer Dept. Army, Ft. Belvoir, Va., 1982-84, chief prodn., design and editorial, publs. div., 1984-85; head writer-editor SE region U.S. Naval Audit Service, Virginia Beach, Va., 1986—; columnist, writer Potomac News, Woodbridge, 1972-85. Contbr. articles to profl. jours. Historian, publicity chmn. PTO, Woodbridge, 1974; publicity chmn. Boy Scouts Am., Woodbridge, 1974-83, Girl Scouts U.S.A., Woodbridge, 1974-79; bd. dirs. Congregation Ner Tamid, Woodbridge, 1984-85. Recipient Outstanding Tng. Devel. Support award U.S. Army, 1983; 1st place news writing award and 1st place for advt. design Fla. Jr. Coll. Press Assn., 1964, 1st place feature writing award, 1964. Mem. Va. Press Women, Women in Communications Nat. Fedn. Press Women, Sigma Delta Chi (1st place news writing award 1965). Democrat. Jewish. Home: 10 N Valasia Rd Poquoson VA 23662 Office: US Naval Audit Service Southeast Region 5701 Thurston Ave Virginia Beach VA 23455

SCHAUMBURG, JANET LEE, mining engineer; b. Rupert, Idaho, Mar. 17, 1953; d. Ronald K. and Florence Arlene (Roselius) Kofoed; m. Robert Clyde Miller, June 23, 1984; m. Gary Lee Schaumburg, Oct. 7, 1974 (div. Mar. 1980). Shift supr. Anaconda Copper Co., Butte, Mont., 1977-79; surface mining engr. Exxon Minerals Co., Douglas, Wyo., 1979-81, planning analyst, N.Y.C., 1981-83, sr. staff mining engr., Houston, 1983-84; sr. community rep. LaBarge Project, Exxon Co. U.S.A., Frontier, Wyo., 1984—. Adviser, U. Idaho, Moscow, 1981—. Bd. dirs. United Way, Sweetwater County, Wyo., 1986. Newmont Mining Co. scholar, 1973-76; Womens Aux. Soc. Mining Engrs. scholar, 1975. Mem. Soc. Mining Engrs. (nat. tech. papers com. 1982-85), Nat. Soc. Profl. Engrs. (v.p. Butte 1979), Soc. Women Engrs. (nat. long range planning com. 1981-82), Bus. and Profl. Womens Club (pres. chpt. 1979), C. of C. Kemmerer (membership chmn. 1986). Republican. Lodge: Eastern Star. Avocations: cross country skiing; playing piano; reading; racquetball; tapdancing. Office: Exxon Co USA PO Box 98 Frontier WY 83121

SCHEAF, KATHERINE LAUREL, association trainer; b. Columbus, Ohio, Mar. 23, 1946; d. Oral Judson and Mildred (Van Fossen) Scheaf. B.S., U. Wis., 1967. Various office and sales mgmt. positions, San Francisco, 1967-71; pres., chief exec. est, San Francisco, 1971-75, corp. officer, bd. dirs., trainer, 1975-81; trainer Werner Erhard & Assocs., San Francisco, 1981—; founding mem. Hunger project, 1972; founding mem. Holiday Project, San Francisco, 1971. Lutheran. Office: 765 California St San Francisco CA 94108

SCHECK, ROSANNE A., educator; b. N.Y.C., Sept. 19, 1949; d. Joseph Dominick and Theresa Marie Leone; m. Donald Gordon Scheck, July 30, 1972; children—Anne Catherine, Caitlin Ashley. B.A. magna cum laude, Fairleigh Dickinson U., 1971; M.A., Dartmouth Coll., 1981. Tchr. Robert Erskine Sch., Ringwood, N.J., 1972-75, Cornish (N.H.) Elem. Sch., 1975-77, J.M. Hill Sch., East Stroudsburg, Pa., 1977-82. Active parent involvement program Growing Concern Montessori Presch., Reeders, Pa. Grantee State N.J. Dept. Edn., 1974. Mem. Childbirth Edn. Assn. Poconos, La Leche League Internat., Pa. Assn. Lawyers Wives. Home: East Dogwood Ln Mountainhome PA 18342

SCHEELE, MARY ALICE HAHN, business executive; b. Milw., Mar. 25, 1947; d. Elmer Paul and Marguarite Cecilia (Hitchings) Hahn; student U. Wis., Whitewater, 1964, Wash. State U., 1970-71, Eastern Mich. U., 1977-78; A.B. with honors, U. Mich., 1979; m. Robert F. Scheele, Sept. 6, 1964; children—Michael, Jonathan, Jeffrey. Dir., producer news, public affairs WEMU-Radio, Ypsilanti, WCBN-Radio, Ann Arbor, 1974-77; asst. producer WXYZ-TV, Southfield, Mich., 1978; public relations women's athletics U. Mich., 1979; promotion specialist Univ. Microfilms Internat., 1980; account exec. Widerschein Strandberg Assos., Toledo, 1981-83; customer service rep. tech. info. communications Info. Mktg. Internat., Oak Park, Mich., 1983—; announcer women's basketball games Crisler Arena, 1978. Asst. dir. Sex Info. Clinic, Pullman, Wash., 1971; publicity vol. presdl. campaign, 1976; participant public auction KQED, San Francisco, 1980, KGO-TV Cystic Fibrosis Telethon, 1980; chmn. sch. fund-raising activities, 1978. Mem. Women in Communications, Nat. Assn. Profl. Saleswomen, Kappa Tau Alpha. Democrat. Lutheran. Club: Toledo Advt. Office: Info Mktg Internat 13271 Northend Oak Park MI 48237

SCHEER, JANICE CAPACCIO, psychologist; b. Newark, July 25, 1933; d. Frank and Fannie (DeMarco) Capaccio; m. Norman Scheer, Oct. 22, 1955; children—Mark, Lisa, Suzanne. B.A., Douglass Coll., 1955; M.A., Fairleigh Dickinson U., 1970; D.Psychology, Rutgers U., 1982. Social worker Div. Youth and Family Services, Newark, 1956-58; sch. psychologist Wharton Bd. Edn. (N.J.), 1972—; pvt. practice psychology, Livingston, N.J., 1982—; cons. N.J. chpt. ARC, 1972-75, N.J. Pre-Schs. Programs, 1975—. Recipient Outstanding Psychologist award Morris County Assn. Sch. Psychologists, 1981. Mem. N.J. Assn. Sch. Psychologists (del. exec. bd. 1975-83), Council Jewish Women (life), N.J. Assn. Retarded Citizens (life). Home and office: 6 Highview Dr Livingston NJ 07039

SCHEETZ, MARY JOELLEN, college president; b. Lafayette, Ind., May 20, 1926; d. Joseph Albert and Ellen Isabelle (Fitzgerald) S.; A.B., St. Francis Coll., Ft. Wayne, Ind., 1956; M.A., U. Notre Dame, 1964; Ph.D., U. Mich., 1970. Joined Sisters of St. Francis of Perpetual Adoration, Roman Cath. Ch., 1946; high sch. tchr., 1956-67; dean of girls Bishop Luers High Sch., Ft. Wayne, 1967; acad. dean St. Francis Coll., 1967-68, pres., 1970—; pres. Ind. Conf. Higher Edn. Mem. Assn. Cath. Colls. and Univs., Conf. Small Colls. Address: 2701 Spring St Fort Wayne IN 46808

SCHEFFER, BARBARA LOUISE, nurse; b. Cin., Apr. 8, 1943; d. George Granville and Mildred Dorothy (Chesney) Rose; m. Ronald Edward Scheffer, Sept. 13, 1969; children—Caroline, James, Thomas. B.S. in Nursing, U. Cin., 1965. R.N., Ind. Staff nurse ICU, Gen. Hosp., Cin., 1968-69; staff nurse Cameron Hosp., Angola, Ind., 1971-79, 81—, staff devel., 1980-81; nurse co-ordinator Community Sheltered Workshop, Angola, 1979-80; cons. Well Child Clinic, Angola. CPR instr. Am. Heart Assn., Angola, 1980—; diabetic instr. Cameron Hosp., Angola, 1980—; bd. mem. Am. Cancer Assn. Angola area., 1983—. Mem. Angola Bus. and Profl. Women (chmn. various coms.). Served to ensign USN, 1966-68. Avocations: reading; needlework; biking; aerobics. Home: 302 Stony Ridge Dr Angola IN 46703 Office: Cameron Meml Community Hosp 416 E Maumee St Angola IN 46703

SCHEFFER, CHERI ROSE, artist; b. Kansas City, Mo., Nov. 12, 1950; d. Jules Emile and Frances Wilhelmina (Doman) S.; 1 child, Tangi Katzer. Student Kans. State Tchrs. Coll., 1969-71. Lic. real estate agt., Fla. Treas. Island Art Shoppe, Dunedin, Fla., 1974—, v.p. Scheffer Studio, Inc., Dunedin, 1980—; assoc. Surfcoast Realty, Dunedin, 1984—; cons. Nat. Edn. Ctr., Tampa, Fla., 1983—. Sculptor The Protected Child, 1981. Bd. dirs. Pinellas County Arts Council, Fla., 1984—. Recipient cert. of achievement Minolta Corp., 1985. Mem. Contractors and Builders Assn., Nat. Assn. Female Execs., Ducks Unlimited. Republican. Avocations: photography; yachting; media research. Home: 1897 Stancel Dr Clearwater FL 33546 Office: Scheffer Studio Inc 240 Causeway Blvd Dunedin FL 33528

SCHEIMER, JANICE SCHAEFER, financial consultant, planner; b. Alva, Okla., Sept. 21, 1948; d. Andrew August and Ruth Ida (Boyce) Schaefer; m. Gary Lee Scheimer, Aug. 10, 1968; children—Scott Allen, Eric Lee. B.S., Ariz. State U., 1971, M.B.A., 1972. Cert. fin. planner. Rate analyst Northwest Pipeline, Salt Lake City, 1976-78; mktg. mgr. Western Fed. Savs., Colorado Springs, 1979-82; fin. cons. Shearson Am. Express, Gimsbach, Fed. Republic Germany, 1982-83, Colorado Springs, 1985—, Integrated Resources, Gimsbach, 1983-85; v.p., treas. Golden Horizons, Inc., Cheyenne Wells, Colo., 1979—; instr. U. Md., Fed. Republic Germany, 1984-85; cons. Pro-Trac, 1984; v.p., treas. S.S. & N. Inc., Cheyenne Wells, 1984—. Soccer team mother Am. Youth Assn., Ramstein, Fed. Republic Germany, 1982-85; mem. Homebuilders Assn., Colorado Springs, 1985—. Mem. Inst. Cert. Fin. Planners. Republican. Clubs: Officers Wives (U.S. Air Force Acad.); Officers Wives (Ramstein) (treas. 1984-85). Avocations: ice skating; skiing; water skiing; travel; needlework; interior decorating. Home: 365 Allegheny Pl Colorado Springs CO 80919 Office: Shearson Am Express 101 N Tejon #401 Colorado Springs CO 80903

SCHEIN, SALLY JOY, special services-learning consultant, marriage, family counselor; b. Chgo., July 6, 1930; d. Rudolph James and Lillian (Cohen) Good; m. Michael Schein, Apr. 9, 1955; children—Jack Edward, David Lee. B.A., U. Chgo., 1950; M.S., CCNY, 1953; Ed.S., Seton Hall U., 1982, also postgrad.; postgrad. Nova U., 1986—. Occupational therapist Monmouth Meml. Hosp., Longbranch, N.J., 1953-54; tchr. nursery kindergarten N.Y. Dept. Welfare, N.Y.C., 1954-55; tchr. kindergarten Yonkers Pub. Sch., N.Y., 1955, Dumont Pub. Sch., N.J., 1955-56; learning disabilities teaching cons. Haworth, N.J., 1968-72, Caldwell, N.J., 1972-79, Cranford Pub. Sch., N.J., 1979—; psychologist extern North Caldwell, Closter, N.J., 1976-77; counselor Community Mental Health Ctr., Dumont, 1981-82. Author: Welcome to Danish International Studies, 1979; (with E. Riley et al) Sparking Divergent Ability, 1985. Founding mem. bd. Community Mental Health Ctr., Dumont, 1958-60. Mem. Am. Assn. Marriage and Family Therapists, Bergen County Assn. Sch. Psychologists, Assn. Learning Cons., Council Exceptional Children, Orton Soc. Avocations: Sculpting; art; jogging; travel. Home: 4 Harding Ave Dumont NJ 07628

SCHEIN, VIRGINIA ELLEN, organizational psychologist, educator; b. Rahway, N.J., June 23, 1943; d. Jacob Charles and Anne Schein; B.A. cum laude, Cornell U., 1965; Ph.D., NYU, 1969; 1 son, Alexander Nikos. Sr. research asso. Am. Mgmt. Assn., N.Y.C., 1969-70; mgr. personnel research Life Office Mgmt. Assn., N.Y.C., 1970-72; dir. personnel research Met. Life Ins. Co., N.Y.C., 1972-75; asso. prof. Case Western Res. U., Cleve., 1975-76; vis. asso. prof. Yale U., New Haven, 1976-77; asso. prof. mgmt. U. Pa., Phila., 1977-80; cons., pvt. practice organizational psychology, 1975—; assoc. prof. psychology Baruch Coll., CUNY, 1982-85; assoc. prof. mgmt. Gettysburg Coll., 1986—. Mem. Internat. Assn. Applied Psychology, Am. Psychol. Assn., Met. N.Y. Assn. Applied Psychology (pres. 1973-74), Acad. of Mgmt. (dir.), Organizational Dynamics, Acad. Mgmt. Rev. Psi Chi. Contbr. articles to profl. jours. Office: Dept Mgmt Gettysburg Coll Gettysburg PA 17325

SCHEINMAN, LESLIE KASS, account executive; b. Flushing, N.Y., Oct. 27, 1953; d. Ralph R. and Geraldine N. (Rothberg) Kass; m. William T. Scott, III, May 25, 1975 (div. Oct. 1981); m. Gerald Lynn Scheinman, July 1, 1984; 1 child, Lee Jacob (dec.). Student Boston U.; B.F.A., U. R.I. Store mgr. McDonald's Corp., Raleigh, N.C., 1976-78; media dir. Martin J. Simmons Advt., Chgo., 1978-79; asst. dir. advt. Penta Investments, San Diego, 1979; account exec. Gemini II Advt., San Diego, 1980; media planner/buyer Cole & Weber, Los Angeles, 1980-83; account exec. McGavren Guild Radio, Los Angeles, 1983—; cons. to small advt. agys. Leader/organizer Young World Devel./Am. Freedom from Hunger Found., 1971; patron Los Angeles County Mus. Art, 1984—. Boston U. scholar, 1971, 72. Mem. Nat. Assn. Female Execs., Advt. Industry Emergency Fund, Mortar Bd. Republican. Jewish. Avocations: crafts; sculpture; sports. Office: McGavren Guild Radio 6420 Wilshire Blvd Los Angeles CA 90048

SCHELBY, ERIKA KATE, international business consultant; b. Berlin, Oct. 31, 1935; came to U.S., 1970; d. Kurt H. and Edith (Winkler) Mueller; m. Frederick Schelby, June 6, 1982; children by previous marriage—Ulrike, Susanne. B.A., Kans. State U., 1977; M.S., U. Ill., 1978. Asst. to dir. Georg Jensen Silver, Dusseldorf, W.Ger., 1959-60; v.p. Nordlys Ohg., Dusseldorf, 1960-64, pres., 1964-70; bus. research mgr. Goodyear Tire & Rubber Co., Akron, Ohio, 1978-80, mktg. mgr. Mo. Research Labs., Albuquerque, 1980-82; pres. Interteam Assocs., Albuquerque, 1982—. Mem. Am. Mktg. Assn., Greater Albuquerque C. of C., Phi Beta Kappa, Phi Kappa Phi, Gamma Theta Upsilon. Office: Interteam Assocs 1214 Jackson SE Albuquerque NM 87108

SCHEMMEL, EVELYN ANN, college administrator; b. Albany, N.Y., Dec. 18, 1940; d. Raymond and Helen Edith (Brockley) Nickel; m. Gerald Bernard Schemmel, Aug. 24, 1963. B.S. in Bus. Edn., SUNY-Albany, 1963. Instr., dept. head Mary Immaculate High Sch., Key West, Fla., 1965-67; dean of instrn. Kelsey-Jenney Coll., San Diego, 1970-72, dir., 1972-73; dir. acad. affairs Cannon's Bus. Coll., Honolulu, 1974, pres., dir. colls. Cannon's Bus. Coll. and Educators of the Pacific, 1974—. Recipient Cert. of Recognition, State of Hawaii, Commn. on Manpower and Full Employment, 1980. Mem. Western Bus. Edn. Assn. (pres. 1985—), Hawaii Bus. Edn. Assn. (pres. 1978-79, Dist. Service award 1980), Nat. Bus. Edn. Assn. (exec. bd. 1985-86). Club: Pilot of Downtown Honolulu (pres. 1984-85). Home: 1430 Laukahi St Honolulu HI 96821 Office: Cannon's Bus Coll 1500 Kapiolani Blvd Honolulu HI 96814

SCHENK-ZIEBELMAN, CYNTHIA MARIAN, import executive; b. Fort Worth, Jan. 18, 1954; d. Eugene F. and Florence (Klein) S.; m. Peter H. Ziebelman, Sept. 1, 1985. B.S., Tex. Christian U., 1976. Asst. mgr. Foxmoor Casuals, Livingston, N.J., 1972-75; owner Klein Signs, Fort Worth, 1975-76; asst. mdse. mgr. Pier 1 Imports, Fort Worth, 1976-77, mdse. mgr., 1977-81; v.p. Intercontinental Art, Inc., Gardena, Calif., 1981-85; pres. Designer Ideas Inc Redondo Beach, Calif., 1985—. Mem. Nat. Assn. Female Execs. Roman Catholic. Avocations: travel; swimming; windsurfing; needlepoint. Office: Designer Ideas 635 Paseo Playa Suite 306 Redondo Beach CA 90277

SCHEPPS, VICTORIA HAYWARD, lawyer; b. Brockton, Mass., June 11, 1956; d. William George and Lucy Victoria (Mitcheroney) Hayward; m. Frank Schepps, Sept. 18, 1982. B.A., Suffolk U., 1977; J.D., U. San Diego, 1981. Instr., Northeastern U., Boston, 1981-83; assoc. Hoffman & Hoffman, Boston, 1983-85, Mark J. Gladstone, P.C., 1985—; mem. adv. bd. Northeastern U. Paralegal Program, Boston, 1982—. Mem. Mass. Bar Assn., ABA, Mass. Conveyancing Assn., Forum Com. Entertainment and Sports Law. Democrat. Roman Catholic. Home: 11 Overlook Rd Randolph MA 02368 Office: Mark J Gladstone PC PO Box 788 402 N Main St Randolph MA 02368

SCHERER, ANITA MARTHA STOCK, advertising agency executive; b. Cleve., Sept. 20, 1938; d. William John Stock and Gertrud Clara (Kaufmann) Bacher; m. Richard Phillip Scherer, Nov. 25, 1961; children—William Richard, Christopher Howard. Student U. Cin., 1956-57; Assoc.Bus., Jones Bus. Coll., 1958. Account sec. Northlich, Stolley, Inc., Cin., 1978-79, account asst., 1979-80, asst. account mgr., 1980-81, account mgr., 1981-84, mktg. service assoc., 1984—; lectr. local schs., univs., Cin. 1980—. Co-editor: monthly newsletter Badge, 1967-72; designer, created assorted notepads, 1986. Lector, Out Lady of Victory Roman Cath. Ch., Cin., 1972—; pres. Delhi Hills Community Council, Cin., 1974-75; adv. bd. mem. Coll. Mount St. Joseph, Ohio, 1974-80; v.p. adminstrn. Stagecrafters, Cin., 1983-85, publicity chmn., 1984—; mktg. bd. mem. Contemp. Arts Ctr., 1985—. Winner nat. competition Am. Assn. Advt. Agys., 1980; recipient Outstanding Performance award Assn. Community Theatres, Cin., 1983, Excellence in Acting award Ohio Community Theatres Assn., 1984. Mem. Nat. Assn. Female Execs., Am. Mktg. Assn., Acad. Health Services Mktg., Cin. C. of C. (lectr. 1984—). Club: Ohio Valley Direct Marketing. Avocations: travel, reading medieval/renaissance history, community theater. Office: Northlich Stolley Inc 200 W 4th St Cincinnati OH 45202

SCHERER, JEANNE CATHERINE, nurse, author; b. Buffalo, Apr. 8, 1928; d. Albert and Florence Rose (Steinman) Scherer. R.N., Buffalo Gen. Hosp. Sch. Nursing, 1954; B.S. in Nursing, D'Youville Coll., 1966; M.S., Canisius Coll., 1972. Staff nurse various hosps., 1954-66; clin. instr. Sisters Hosp. Sch. Nursing, Buffalo, 1966-68, 78—, asst. dir., med. surg. nursing coordinator, 1968-78. Author: Introductory Clinical Pharmacology, 1975, 2d edit., 1982; Introductory Medical-Surgical Nursing, 1977, 4th edit., 1986 Lippincott's

Nurses' Drug Manual, 1985; also student work manuals. Mem. Nat. League Nursing. Republican. Roman Catholic.

SCHERER, MARITA ROSE, repertory theatre adminstr.; b. Indpls., July 30, 1947; d. John Edward and Patricia Marie (Spragg) S.; B.S., Ind. U., 1971; 1 dau., Heather Patricia Schneider. Editor Sportlite newspaper, Louisville, 1975; asst. mgr. Scherer Market, Morristown, Ind., 1976-78; supr., tchr. Thrift Shop, Shelby County Assn. Retarded Citizens, Shelbyville, Ind., 1978-79; community affairs dir. Fairbanks Hosp., 1979-80; exec. asst. Ind. Repertory Theatre, Indpls., 1980-81, dir. devel., 1981—. Pres., Morristown Dodds Hall Players, 1977; pres. Shelby Arts Council, Shelbyville, 1979. Mem. Public Relations Soc. Am., Ind. Bus. Communicators, Ind. Council Fund Raising Execs. Inc., Shelby Arts Council. Roman Catholic. Club: Dodds Hall Players (pres.). Office: 140 W Washington St Indianapolis IN 46204

SCHERGER, MOZELLE SPAINHOUR (MRS. GEORGE RICHARD SCHERGER), librarian; b. Forsyth County, N.C., Dec. 17, 1916; d. Earnest Sidney and Mertie Blanche (Hauser) Spainhour; B.S., Appalachian State Tchrs. Coll., Boone, N.C., 1937; B.S. in L.S., U. N.C., 1943; m. George Richard Scherger, Feb. 23, 1946; children—Teresa Ann (Mrs. Richard Martin), George Richard, Joseph John, Daniel M. Tchr. English and French, sch. librarian Cramerton (N.C.) High Sch., 1937-42; librarian Laurinburg-Maxton AFB, 1943, Piedmont Jr. High Sch., 1944, Pope Field AFB, 1945-46, Charlotte (N.C.) Coll., 1957-64; documents and serials librarian U. N.C. at Charlotte, 1965-69, asst. reference librarian, 1969-78, reference librarian, 1979-80. Mem. AAUP. Home: 701 St Julien St Charlotte NC 28205

SCHERL, ELLEN JANICE, physician; b. N.Y.C., Nov. 9, 1952; d. Siegfried and Lila (Lesnick) Scherl. B.A. cum laude, Barnard Coll., 1974; M.D., N.Y. Med. Coll., 1977. Intern, resident Beth Israel Hosp., Mt. Sinai Med. Ctr., N.Y.C., 1977-81, attending in gastroenterology, 1983—; fellow in gastroenterology Mt. Sinai Med. Ctr., N.Y.C., 1981-83; cons. panel United Store Workers, 1983—, Equitable Life Assurance Soc. U.S., Exec. Health Examiners. Contbr. articles to profl. jours. Mem. ACP, AMA, Am. Gastroent. Assn., Am. Soc. Gastroenterologic Endoscopy, AAAS, Am. Soc. Gastrointestinal Endoscopy. Club: Barnard Columbia.

SCHERMER, BONNIE L., marketing representative; b. Encino, Calif., May 27, 1959; d. Sam and Lucille (Lewis) S. B.S. in Bus. Adminstrn., U. So. Calif., 1981. Sales asst. IBM, Los Angeles, 1980-81, mktg. rep., 1981—; legis. asst. U.S. Ho. of Reps., Washington, 1980. Capt. March of Dimes Walk America '86, Los Angeles; dir. Magic Days Found. Christmas Charity Party for Skid Row, Los Angeles, 1985. Named to 100% Club, IBM, 1982, 83, 84, 85. Mem. Am. Mktg. Assn., Nat. Assn. Female Execs., U. So. Calif. Commerce Assocs., U. So. Calif. Bus. Sch. Alumni, U. So. Calif. Alumni Assn. Republican. Avocations: piano; tennis; jogging; aerobics; travel. Office: IBM South-West Marketing Div 355 S Grand Ave 17th Floor Los Angeles CA 90060

SCHERMER, KATHY WILSON, lawyer; b. Rome, Ga., Mar. 31, 1956; d. O. Maex and Julia N. (Johnson) Wilson; m. Robert Charles Schermer, June 16, 1979. B.A., Davidson Coll., 1974; J.D., U. Ala., 1981. Bar: Ga. 1981, Fla. 1983. Ptnr., Schermer & Schermer P.C., Atlanta, 1981-83; assoc. Law Offices Peter DeMamio, Sarasota, Fla., 1984; in-house legal counsel Palmetto Fed. Savs. and Loan Assn., a Goldorre Co., 1984—; corporate sec., 1984—; corporate sec. 600 Investment, Inc., 1984—. Mem. ABA, Ga. Bar Assn., Fla. Bar Assn. Democrat. Presbyterian. Office: Palmetto Fed Savs and Loan Assn 600 8th Ave Palmetto FL 3356

SCHETLIN, ELEANOR M., university administrator; b. N.Y.C., July 15, 1920; d. Henry Frank and Elsie (Chew) Schetlin; B.A., Hunter Coll., 1940; M.A., Tchrs. Coll., Columbia, 1942, D.Edn., 1967. Playground dir. Dept. of Parks, N.Y.C., 1940-42; librarian Met. Hosp. Sch. Nursing, N.Y.C., 1943-44, dir. recreation, 1944-48, dir. recreation and guidance, 1948-59; coordinator student activities State U. N.Y., Plattsburgh, 1959-63, asst. dean students, 1963-64; asst. prof., coordinator student personnel services City U. N.Y., Hunter Coll., 1967-68; asst. dir. student personnel Columbia U., Coll. Pharm. Scis., N.Y.C., 1968-69, dir. student personnel, 1969-71; asso. dean for students, health scis. center State U. N.Y. at Stony Brook, 1971-73, asst. v.p. student services, 1973-74, assoc. dean for students, dir. student services, 1974-85. Mem. So. N.Y. League Nursing (dir. 1954-56, 64-66), Student Nurse Assn. N.Y. State (adviser 1955-59), Nat. Assn. Women Deans, Adminstrs. and Counselors. Contbr. articles to profl. jours. Home: 20 Barberry Ln Sea Cliff NY 11579 Office: Health Scis Center State U Stony Brook NY 11794

SCHETTER, JANE A., county official; b. Sheboygan, Wis., May 14, 1951; d. Daniel C. and Elizabeth Marie (Kleefisch) Graff; m. Thomas J. Schetter, May 17, 1974. Clk./typist Sheboygan County, Wis., 1969-74, ct. sec., 1974-82, clk. of cts., 1983—. Bd. dirs. ARC, Sheboygan. Mem. Wis. Clks. of Circuit Ct. Assn. (sec.-treas. 1983-85, v.p. 1985—). Republican. Roman Catholic. Club: Athletic (Sheboygan). Avocations: swimming; biking; running; cross-country skiing. Home: 1516 S 21st St Sheboygan WI 53081 Office: 615 N 6th St Sheboygan WI 53081

SCHETTINO, ELAINE FRANCES, sales training company executive; b. White Plains, N.Y., Dec. 4, 1956; d. John Salvatore and Rita Marion (De Gennaro) Schettino. B.F.A., NYU, 1979, M.B.A., 1983. Sales rep. Equitable Life Ins. Co., Bklyn., 1979, The Runner mag., N.Y.C., 1979-80; N.Y.C. assoc. editor Singles Critique mag., Hollywood, Calif., 1979-80, T.G.I.F. mag., Hollywood, 1978-81; pres., cons. E.F. Schettino Co., White Plains, 1982—; cons. Northeast Div., Southland Corp., other various orgns. Chmn. communications and outreach subcom. Westchester Small Bus. Council, County C. of C., White Plains, 1982-84. Recipient Founders' Day award NYU, 1979. Mem. Westchester County Assn., Am. Soc. Tng. and Devel. (treas. chpt., coordinator sales and mktg. subgroup 1984—), Advt. Club of Westchester (seminar coordinator), Sales Execs. Club N.Y., Internat. Radio and TV Soc., Better Bus. Bur., Westchester County Bd. Realtors, Women in Sales Assn. Republican. Roman Catholic. Club: Toastmasters (sec., exec. bd.). Home: 320 E Columbus Ave White Plains NY 10604 Office: E F Schettino Co PO Box 28 East White Plains Br White Plains NY 10604

SCHEUERMANN, MONA, educator; b. N.Y.C., June 6, 1946; d. Philip and Irene Rifkin; B.A., Queens Coll., 1967; M.A., Hunter Coll., 1969; Ph.D., SUNY-Stony Brook, 1974; m. Peter Scheuermann, Dec. 28, 1973. Asst. prof. English, York Coll., 1974-75; asst. prof. J.S. Reynolds Community Coll. 1974-76; asst. prof. Oakton Community Coll., Des Plaines, Ill., 1976-79, assoc. prof. 1979-84, prof., 1984; guest prof. U. Hamburg, 1985; vis. prof. U. Utrecht. NDEA fellow. Mem. MLA, Am. Assn. Eighteenth-Century Studies, Keats-Shelley Assn., Wordsworth Soc., Phi Beta Kappa. Author: The Novels of William Godwin, 1980; Social Protest in the Eighteenth-Century English Novel, 1985; contbr. articles to profl. jours. Office: 1600 E Golf Rd Des Plaines IL 60016

SCHEWEL, ROSEL HOFFBERGER, educator; b. Balt., Mar. 1, 1928; d. Samuel Herman and Gertrude (Miller) Hoffberger; m. Elliot Sidney Schewel, June 12, 1949; children—Stephen, Michael, Susan. A.B., Hood Coll., 1949; M.Ed., Lynchburg Coll., 1974; Ed.S., 1982. Reading resource tchr. Lynchburg Pub. Schs., Va., 1967-75; adj. prof. edn. Lynchburg Coll., 1973-79; cons., seminar leader Woman's Resource Ctr., Lynchburg, 1980—; asst. prof. edn. Lynchburg Coll., 1980—. Trustees Hood Coll., Frederick, Md., 1985; trustee, exec. com. Lynchburg Coll., Va., 1985, Va. Found. for Humanities and Pub. Policy, 1985; trustee, exec. com. Va. Women's Cultural History Project; trustee Va. Mus. of Fine Arts, 1985, Nat. Fedn. Temple Sisterhoods, 1980-84. Recipient Disting. Service award NCCJ, 1973. Mem. Assn. of Children with Learning Disabilities (dir.), Internat. Reading Assn., Lynchburg Area Counselors Assn. Democrat. Jewish. Address: 4316 Gorman Dr Lynchburg VA 24503

SCHIAVI, ROSEMARY FILOMENA, educator; b. Syracuse, N.Y., Feb. 20, 1947; d. Stefano and Rose (Falso) Schiavi; A.A., Maria Regina Coll., 1967; B.A., Brescia Coll., 1969; M.S., Syracuse U., 1973; postgrad. in tchr. edn. and curriculum devel. Tchr., Syracuse City Sch. Dist., 1969—, tchr. Meachem Sch., 1980-83, acting prin., 1979; asst. office of profl. devel. and field programs Syracuse U., 1984-85; adminstrv. intern West Genesee/Syracuse U. Teaching Ctr., Bus. Ednl. Exchange Com. Mem. exec. bd. Maria Regina Coll., pres. exec. alumni assn. Mem. Assn. for Supervision and Curriculum Devel., Am. Fedn. Tchrs., N.Y. United Tchrs. Assn., Syracuse Tchrs. Assn., N.Y. State Assn. Tchr. Educators, Brescia Coll. Alumni Assn., Syracuse U. Alumni Assn., Am. Edn. Research Assn., Assn. Tchr. Educators, Assoc. Photographers Internat., Nat. Assn. Female Execs., Audubon Soc., Phi Delta Kappa. Home: 237 Stafford Ave Syracuse NY 13206 Office: Syracuse U Sch Edn 150 Marshall St Syracuse NY 13210

SCHIAVINA, LAURA MARGARET, artist; b. Springfield, Mass., Nov. 27, 1917; d. Joseph A. and Egidia (Bernini) Schiavina; student Traphagen Sch. of Fashion, 1944-46, U. R.I., 1967, Cornell U., 1968, Art Students League, 1973-74. With Eastern States Farmers Exchange, Springfield, 1935-44; with Marsh & McLennan, 1944-75, adminstrv. asst., 1971-75, librarian Wm. M. Mercer, Inc. subs., 1975-80; one-man shows at Little Gallery, Barbizon Hotel, N.Y.C., 1968, Galerie Internat., N.Y.C., 1969; exhibited in group shows at Westfield (Mass.) Coll., 1968, Nat. Acad., N.Y.C., 1969; Lever House, N.Y.C., 1973, 74, 83, 84, 85, 86, Queensboro Community Coll. Gallery, 1984, Cork Gallery, N.Y.C., 1984, Westbeth Gallery, N.Y.C., 1985, Nat. Arts Club, 1986, Isis Gallery, 1986, also various exhbns. with Wall St. Art Assn., Nat. Art League and Jackson Heights Art Club, Snug Harbor Cultural Ctr., S.I., N.Y., 1984, Audubon Artists; represented in pvt. collections. Recipient numerous prizes, awards. Mem. Wall St. Art Assn. (v.p. 1972-76), Am. Artist Profl. League, Nat. Art League, Burr Artists Inc., Nat. League Am. Pen Women, Cath. Artists of 80's, Eleanor Gay Lee Gallery Found. Inc. Club: Jackson Heights Art (pres. 1970-71), Salmagundi (N.Y.C.). Home: 35-25 78th St Jackson Heights NY 11372

SCHIEMEL, JOAN MARIE, aerospace engineer; b. N.Y.C., June 19, 1936; d. Frank and Florence Marie (MacDowell) S.; A.A., Concordia Collegiate Inst., 1955; B.A., Queens Coll., 1957; postgrad. Columbia U., 1957-58; M.S., L.I. U., 1971; postgrad. Adelphi U., 1973-79. Student social worker Luth. Social Services, N.Y.C., 1957-58; with Fairchild Republic Co. (and predecessor cos.), 1958—, flight test engr., 1958-63, sci. programmer, 1963-65, sr. sci. programmer/analyst, 1965-69, flight dynamics analyst, 1969-78, flight simulation engr., 1978-85, sr. sect. chief digital flight simulation, sr. mgr. Flight Systems Simulation Lab., Farmingdale, N.Y., 1985—. Mem. AIAA (council 1979-85, exec. sec. 1981-83), Math. Assn. Am., IEEE, Assn. Old Crows, Air Force Assn., Am. Def. Preparedness Assn. Contbr. articles to profl. jours. Office: Route 110 and Conklin St Farmingdale NY 11735

SCHIER, MARY JANE, science writer; b. Houston, Mar. 10, 1939; d. James F. and Jerry Mae (Crisp) McDonald; B.S. in Journalism, Tex. Woman's U., 1961; m. John Christian Schier, Aug. 26, 1961; children—John Christian, II, Mark Edward. Reporter, San Antonio Express and News, 1962-64; med. writer Daily Oklahoman, also Oklahoma City Times, 1965-66; reporter, med. writer Houston Post, 1966-84; sci. writer, univ. editor U. Tex. System Cancer Ctr., 1984—. Recipient award Tex. Headliners Club, 1969, Tex. Med. Assn., 1972-74, 76, 78, 79, 80, 82 Tex. Hosp. Assn., 1974, 82, Tex. Public Health Assn., 1976, 77, 78, others. Lutheran. Club: Houston Press (pres. 1974-75). Home: 9742 Tappenbeck St Houston TX 77055 Office: 6723 Bertner Ave Houston TX 77030

SCHIESS, BETTY BONE, priest; b. Cin., Apr. 2, 1923; d. Evan Paul and Leah (Mitchell) Bone; B.A., U. Cin., 1945; M.A., Syracuse U., 1947; M.Div., Rochester Ctr. for Theol. Studies, 1972; m. William A. Schiess, Aug. 28, 1947; children—William A. (dec.), Richard Corwine, Sarah. Ordained priest Episcopal Ch., 1974; priest assoc. Grace Episc. Ch., Syracuse, N.Y., 1975; mem. Gov.'s Task Force on Life and Law, 1985—. Recipient Gov.'s award Women of Merit in Religion, 1984; U. Cin. Disting. Alumna award, 1984; chaplain Syracuse U., 1976-78, Cornell U., Ithaca, N.Y., 1978-79; rector Grace Episc. Ch., Mexico, N.Y., 1984—; writer, lectr., cons. religion and feminism, 1979—. Bd. dirs. People for Public TV in N.Y., 1978, Religious Coalition for Abortion Rights; mem. infant care rev. com. Crouse-Meml. Hosp.; trustee Elizabeth Cady Stanton Found., 1979; mem. policy com. Council Adolescent Pregnancy; NOW (past pres. Syracuse), Internat. Assn. Women Ministers (dir. 1978, pres. 1985—), Clergy Assn. Diocese of Central N.Y. (v.p. 1985—), Mortar Bd., Theta Chi Beta. Democrat. Contbr. article to religious jour. Home: 107 Bradford Ln Syracuse NY 13224

SCHIESSWOHL, CYNTHIA RAE SCHLEGEL, lawyer; b. Colorado Springs, July 7, 1955; d. Leslie H. and Maime (Kascak) Schlegel; m. Scott Jay Schiesswohl, Aug. 6, 1977; 1 dau., Leslie Michelle. B.A. cum laude, So. Meth. U., 1976; J.D., U. Colo.-Boulder, 1978; postgrad. U. Denver, 1984. Bar: Colo. 1979, U.S. Dist. Ct. (Colo.) 1979, U.S. Ct. Appeals (10th cir.) 1984, Wyo. 1986. Research clk. City Atty.'s Office, Colorado Springs, 1976; investigator Pub. Defender's Office, Colorado Springs, 1976; dep. dist. atty., 4th Jud. Dist. Colo., 1979-81; sole practice law, Grand Junction, Colo., 1981-82, Denver, 1983-84; assoc. Law Offices of John G. Salmon P.C., 1984-85; sole practice, Laramie, Wyo., 1985—; guest lectr. Pikes Peak Community Coll., 1980. Staff U. Colo. Law Rev., 1977. Advisor, Explorer Law Post, Boy Scouts Am., 1980-81; mem. ch. devel. com. Central Rocky Mt. region Christian Ch. (Disciples of Christ), 1986—; vol. Project Motivation, Dallas, 1974. Mem. AAUW, ABA, Wyo. State Bar Assn., Colo. Bar Assn. (ethics com. 1984-85, long range planning com. 1985—), Pi Sigma Alpha, Alpha Lambda Delta, Alpha Delta Pi. Republican. Methodist (mem. fin. com. youth and music depts. 1979-81). Office: 1151 Banock Dr Laramie WY 82070

SCHIFF, HELEN D., clothes designer; b. Bklyn., May 17, 1947; d. Harry Bale and Esther Genin; m. Stuart B. Schiff, Oct. 22, 1972. student Fashion Inst. Tech., SUNY, 1964-67. Designer infantswear Playmore Knits, 1971-72, Little Topsy, 1972-73, Catton Bros., 1973-76; dir. design Mayfair Infantswear, N.Y.C., 1976-85; fashion merchandiser, China import dir. David Pik Internat., 1985—. Pres. Par-Troy chpt. Cancer Care, Inc., 1980-82, v.p. regional fundraising, N.J., 1979-80, fundraising co-chmn., vice chmn. chpts. coordinating com., 1985-86leadership tng. co-chmn., 1983-84. Recipient various awards Cancer Care, Inc. Office: David Pik Internat 1450 Broadway New York NY 10018

SCHIFFMAN, NANCY ELIZABETH, corporate executive; b. Everett, Mass., May 6, 1937; d. Joseph Coelho and Helen (Buchanan) Perry; B.A. cum laude, Boston U., 1973, M.S. in Urban Affairs, 1976; m. Yale M. Schiffman, June 23, 1974; children—David, Steven. Community relations specialist YWCA, Natick, Mass., 1975-76; regional transp. planner Central Mass. Regional Planning Commn., Worcester, 1977-79; Congressional research staff Rockwell Internat., Arlington, Va., 1980-82; v.p. SES, Inc., Springfield, Va., 1982-84, chief exec. officer, 1984—. Mem. women's and minority com. Area Manpower Planning Bd., Marlboro, Mass., 1976; mem. subcom. Sudbury Housing Authority, 1977; chairperson bd. dirs. Offender Aid and Restoration of Arlington, Va., 1980; mem. Republican County Com., Fairfax, Va., 1982, chmn. Springfield dist.; mem. exec. com. Fairfax Rep. Com.; candidate for Va. Senate, 1983. Mem. Am. Pub. Transit Assn. (council on preserving urban motility), Nat. Fedn. Rep. Women (patron). Contbr. articles to profl. jours. Home: 7406 Forest Hunt Ct Springfield VA 22153

SCHIFLETT, MARY FLETCHER CAVENDER, researcher/educator; b. El Paso, Tex., Sept. 23, 1925; d. John F. and Mary M. (Humphries) Cavender; 1 son, Joseph Raymond. B.A. in Econs. with honors, So. Meth. U., 1946, B.S. in Journalism with honors, 1947; M.A. in English, U. Houston, 1971. Writer, historian Office Price Adminstrn., Dallas, 1946-47; asst. editor C. of C. Publs., Dallas, 1947-48; bus. writer Houston Oil, 1948-49; market analyst Cravens-Dargan, Ins., Houston, 1949-52; bus. writer Bus. Week and McGraw-Hill Pub. Co., Houston, 1952-56; freelance writer in bus. econs., banking and ins., 1956-68; spl. projects coordinator Center for Human Resources, Houston, 1969-73; dir. publs. Energy Inst., U. Houston, 1974-78; sr. research assoc. Inst. Labor and Indsl. Relations, 1973-80, adj. faculty Coll. Architecture, 1976—, dir. Ctr. for Health Mgmt., Coll. Bus. Adminstrn., 1980-83; assoc. dir. research and planning Tex. Med. Ctr., Inc., Houston, 1984; dir. pub. affairs Tex. Med. Ctr., 1985—. Pres., Houston Ct. Humanities, 1978-80; project dir. Houston Meets Its Authors I-IV, 1980-84; pub. program dir. Houston: Internat. City, 1980-83. Mem. Internat. Council Indsl. Editors, World Future Soc., Tex. Folklore Soc., Friends of the Library, Houston C. of C. (future studies com. 1975-84, small bus. council 1981-83), Nat. Assn. Bus. Economists, AIA (profl. affiliate; profl. devel. com., health com.), Cultural Arts Council Houston, Mortar Bd., Theta Sigma Phi, Alpha Theta Phi, Delta Delta Delta. Methodist. Author: (with others) Dynamics of Growth, 1977, Applied Systems and Cybernetics, 1981. Office: Tex Med Ctr 406 Jesse H Jones Library Bldg Houston TX 77030

SCHIFTER, MARGARET EILEEN, lawyer; b. Darby, Pa., June 1, 1946; d. John Charles and Elizabeth (Cummings) Elliott; children—David Schifter. B.A. cum laude, Hunter Coll., 1974; J.D., Hofstra U., 1977. Bar: Pa. Owner mini-fleet of city cabs, N.Y.C., 1974-78; pvt. practice law, Phila. Chmn. fund raising St. Agnes High Sch., N.Y.C., 1983-84. Mem. ABA, Pa. Bar Assn., Am. Immigration Lawyers Assn., Assn. Trial Lawyers Am., Sigma Tau Delta. Republican. Roman Catholic.

SCHILKE, SHIRLEY PLATT, corporate executive; b. Berlin, Pa., July 23, 1925; d. Frank I. and Matilda H. (Baughman) Platt; student Strayers Bus. Coll., Washington, 1943, High Mus. Sch. Art, Atlanta, 1948; m. Carl Richard Schilke, Dec. 3, 1944; children—Kristie Lee, Wendy Lee, Richard Frank. Civilian sec., fin. officer Ft. Belvoir, Va., 1942-46; with Harcar Aluminum Products Co., Sanford, Fla., 1957—, now sec.-treas.; co-owner, v.p. Schilke Enterprises, Inc., Sanford, Fla., 1975-78, pres., 1978—. Past pres. Seminole Meml. Hosp. Aux., Women of First Presbyn. Ch., Sanford; mem. chmn.'s com. U.S. Senatorial Bus. Adv. Bd., 1981, 82; past sec. Seminole County PTA Council, Seminole-DeBary Heart Council; trustee Washington Legal Found.; South Seminole Med. Center; past bd. dirs. United Fund of Seminole County; mem. adv. bd. Salvation Army, Golden Arms, Inc. Mem. Fla. C. of C., Sanford C. of C. (chmn. bd. dirs.), Greater Seminole County C. of C., C. of C. U.S., Nat. Fedn. Ind. Bus., Internat. Platform Assn., Smithsonian Assocs., U.S. Senatorial Club, Nat. Soc. Lit. and Arts. Club: Women's of Sanford (life). Author: (poetry) The Many Facets of Love, 1976. Home: 107 Country Pl PO Box 2101 Sanford FL 32771 Office: 1201 Cornwall Rd PO Box 1148 Sanford FL 32771

SCHILLER, ARDITH MARLENE, secretarial/bookkeeping consultant; b. Jackson, Minn., Oct. 12, 1939; d. Thomas William and Maxine Dorothy Raine; A.A. in Bus. Adminstrn. and Office Occupations, U. Alaska, 1979, A.A.S. in Bus. Adminstrn., 1980; m. Jerome J. Schiller, Oct. 11, 1968; 1 dau., Gretchen Susan. Stenographer, Prudential Ins. Co., Winona, Minn., 1957, First Nat. Bank, Winona, 1959; sec., stenographer Monarch Marking System Co., Garden Grove, Calif., 1960-62; exec. sec. Acoustica Assos., Inc., Los Angeles, 1962-65; adminstrv. sec. Fgn. Services, Dept. State, Washington, 1965-67; sec., office mgr. U.S. Army Europe Hdqrs. Polit. Adv.'s Office, Dept. Army, Heidelberg, W.Ger., 1968-69, Hamilton Bros. Oil Co., Anchorage, 1971-83; owner, mgr. Bus. Cache, Anchorage, 1974-81; dir., sec. C.C. Hawley and Assos., Inc., 1974; freelance bus. and fin. mgr., 1983—. Cert. profl. sec. Mem. Nat. Assn. Female Exec., Am. Entrepreneurs Assn. Catholic. Research on mgmt. techniques for small bus. Home: 5320 Shaun Circle Anchorage AK 99516

SCHILLER, MARY ROSITA, dietitian; b. Mich., June 14, 1936; d. Edmund Martin and Julia Catherine (Greiner) S.; B.S., Mercy Coll., Detroit, 1959; M.S., Mich. State U., 1966; Ph.D. (Hattie Margaret Anthony fellow, Mich. Home Econs. Assn. scholar, Mary Swartz Rose fellow, Hazel Williams Lapp fellow, provisional univ. dissertation yr. fellow), Ohio State U., Columbus, 1972. Joined Sisters of Mercy, Roman Cath. Ch., 1952; dietetic intern Henry Ford Hosp., Detroit, 1959-60; hosp. dietitian Mercy Community Hosp., Manistee, Mich., 1960-62; adminstrv. dietitian St. Lawrence Hosp., Lansing, Mich., 1962-66; from instr. to assoc. prof. Mercy Coll., 1966-78, program dir. dietetics, 1972-78; prof. dietetics, dir. med. dietetics div. Ohio State U., Columbus, 1978—; pres. Detroit Dietetic Assn., 1969-70; chmn. nutrition com. Mich. Heart Assn., 1975-76; mem. task force dietetic edn. VA, 1975-77. Mem. Am. Dietetic Assn. (chmn. commn. accreditation 1978-79, program chmn. region IV council edn. 1975-76, editorial reviewer jour. 1975—; Mary Zahasky Meml. scholar 1977), Nutrition Today Soc., Am. Soc. Allied Health Professions, Soc. Nutrition Edn., Am. Soc. Health Manpower Edn. and Tng., Ohio Dietetic Assn. (chmn. 1980-81), Ohio Home Econs. Assn., Columbus Dietetics Assn. Author articles in field. Office: 1583 Perry St Columbus OH 43210

SCHILLING, KATHERINE LEE TRACY, educator; b. Mitchell, S.D., May 31, 1925; d. Ernest Benjamin and Mary Alice (Courier) Tracy; B.A., Dakota Wesleyan U., 1947; M.A., U. S.D., 1957; postgrad. U. Wyo., U. Nebr., Kearney State Coll.; m. Clarence R. Schilling, Oct. 14, 1951; 1 dau., Keigh Leigh. Tchr. elementary and secondary schs., also colls., S.D. and Nebr.; now with specially funded project for disadvantaged children Winnebago Indian reservation, Nebr. Mem. staff S.D. Girls' State, 1950-51; mem. S.D. Gov.'s Com. on Library, Nebr. Gov.'s Com. on Right to Read. Recipient Outstanding Tchr. award S.D. High Sch. Speech Tchrs., 1966. Mem. NEA, Nebr., Thurston County (pres.) edn. assns., Winnebago Tchrs. Assn., Delta Kappa Gamma. Mem. Order Eastern Star. Club: Internat. Toastmistress (internat. dir. 1963-65, Mitchell Toastmistress of Year 1959). Contbr. articles to profl. jours., also poetry. Home: 39 S Harmon Dr Box 578 Mitchell SD 57301 Office: Winnebago Public Sch or Nebraska Indian Community Coll Winnebago NE 68071

SCHILLINGER, ELISABETH HUPP, journalism educator, editor, author, graphic designer; b. Springfield, Ill., Mar. 28, 1943; d. Walter Wayne and Joyce Dayle (Hartwig) Hupp; B.S. in Journalism, U. Ill., 1965; m. John A. Schillinger, Aug. 28, 1965; children—Liesl Katharine, Justin Hupp, Nathaniel Hartwig. Tech. editor U. Ill. Coll. Engring., 1965-67; writer, editor U. Wis. Office Publs., 1967-70; asst. dir. info. Saginaw (Mich.) Valley State Coll., 1970-73; tech. writing, design cons., 1973-75; engring. editor Purdue U. Schs. Engring., 1975-82; editor Okla. State U. Publs. Office, 1982-84, asst. prof. Okla. State U. Sch. Journalism, 1984—. Co-author: Men and Ideas in Engineering, 1967. Contbr. articles to profl. publns. Home: 2015 N Husband St Stillwater OK 74075 Office: Okla State U 206 Paul Miller Bldg Stillwater OK 74078

SCHILZ, YVONNE ELIZABETH, air force officer; b. Waco, Tex., Nov. 23, 1958; d. John D. and Charleen K. (Leaverton) Wilhelm; m. Michael T. Schilz, May 29, 1981. B.S., U.S. Air Force Acad., 1981; M.Ed., S.D. State U., 1985. Commd. 2d lt. U.S. Air Force, 1981, advanced through grades to capt., 1985, air traffic control trainee 1872 Sch. Squadron, Keesler AFB, Miss., 1981, 2021 Communications Squadron, Tyndall AFB, Fla., 1981-82; chief air traffic control tng. 2148 Info. Systems Squadron, Ellsworth AFB, S.D., 1982-83, dep. chief air traffic control ops., 1983-84, chief, 1984; chief air traffic control ops. Offutt AFB, Neb., 1985—. Contbr. articles to profl. publs. Mem. Air Force Assn. (life). Republican. Roman Catholic. Avocations: piano; tennis; softball; skiing; latchhooking.

SCHIMBERG, MARTHA, market research executive; b. Boston, Dec. 10, 1933; d. Harold Sherman and Romayne (Marcus) Goldberg; m. Lee Schimberg, June 14, 1955; children—Deborah, William, Daniel, David. B.A., Wellesley Coll., 1955; M.A., Xavier U., 1977. Vice-pres. Action Data, Inc., Cin., 1977-82; pres. Answer Group, Cin., 1982—. Mem. Am. Mktg. Assn. Jewish. Home: 130 Linden Dr Cincinnati OH 45215 Office: Answer Group 11161 Kenwood Rd Cincinnati OH 45242

SCHIMMEL, ANN ELIZABETH, travel agency executive; b. York, Pa., Sept. 19, 1953; d. Robert Frederick and Elizabeth (Brooks) S. B.A., Bucknell U., 1975. Travel cons. Taos Travel, 1976-78, Neiman Marcus, Dallas, 1978-79; internat. travel cons. Gelco Travel, Denver, 1980-81; pres., mng. ptnr., founder Travel Connections Denver, 1981—; v.p., co-founder Denver Fin. Partnership, 1984-85. Grad. Leadership Denver, 1983; mem. exec. com Club 250, Denver, 1983-85. Mem. Am. Soc. Travel Agts., Denver C. of C. (chmn. bus. after hours 1983-85), Colo. Assn. Commerce and Industry (founding; chmn. Chmn.'s Club 1985), Denver Jr. League (chmn. 1984-85). Republican. Presbyterian. Avocations: skiing; golf; travel. Home: 9700 E Iliff J-117 Denver CO 80231 Office: 303 16th St Suite 280 Denver CO 80202

SCHINDEL, RONNIE SUSAN LEVINE, advertising executive, writer; b. N.Y.C., Oct. 14, 1939; d. Harold and Ada (Simon) Levine; m. Samuel M. Schindel, July 2, 1960; children—Robert Harold, Shari Jill. B.S. magna cum laude, NYU, 1960; M.A., Columbia U., 1962. Tchr. Pub. Sch. 125, Manhattan,

N.Y.C., 1960-62, Walker AFB Elem. Sch., Roswell, N.Mex., 1962-64; freelance writer, Huntington, N.Y., 1964—; movie reviewer Radio Sta. WGSM, Huntington, 1977—, Women's Record, Roslyn, N.Y., 1985—; creative dir. Ray Adell Media Enterprises, Inc., Greenlawn, N.Y., 1977—, v.p., 1982—. Author: (children's books) I Am Jungle Soup, 1967, Hermit Crab, 1967; also programmed reading instruction materials, radio commls., movie revs. Pres., Woodhull Sch. PTA, Huntington, 1975-76, Kehillath Shalom Synagogue, Cold Spring Harbor, N.Y., 1976-77; vol. Sta. WGSM Call for Action, Huntington, 1975-77. Recipient Founders Day award NYU, 1960; grantee Columbia U., 1960-62. Mem. Delegation L.I. Bus. and Profl. Women (bd. dirs. 1986—, co-chair publicity 1985), L.I. Ctr. for Bus. and Profl. Women, Nat. Assn. for Female Execs., L.I. Communicators Assn., Am. Bus. Assocs. Office: Ray Adell Media Enterprises Inc 103 Broadway Greenlawn NY 11740

SCHIVEK, ELAINE RONA, legal researcher; b. Boston, Mar. 9, 1930; d. Rueben and Sarah (Berch) Weinberg; m. James Schivek, Oct. 30, 1949 (dec. Feb. 1982); children—Helene Marcia Schivek Demeo, Alan Jay, Howard Richard. B.A. in Edn. cum laude, Suffolk U., 1953, M.Ed. in Adminstrn. and Supervision magna cum laude, 1980; postgrad. Boston U., 1953, 65, 68, Boston State Coll., 1967-69, Simmons Coll., 1968-69, Lesley Grad. Sch., 1976-78, Commonwealth Sch. Law, 1986—. Lic. tchr., cert. in adminstrn., spl. edn., Mass. Elem. tchr. Boston Sch. Dept., Boston and Roxbury, Mass., 1957-69, Westwood Elem. Sch., Mass., 1969-70, Revere Sch. Dept., Mass., 1970-71; office mgr. Storm/Check Aluminum Co., Hyde Park, Mass., 1971-79; elem. and secondary tchr. Cambridge (Mass.) Schs., 1979-84; legal researcher Registry of Motor Vehicles, Boston, 1984—; pvt. tutor Randolph Sch. Dept., Mass., 1983—; Mem. Randolph Clean Up Com., 1985-86; candidate for sch. com. Randolph Sch. Dept., 1986; active Mass. Polit. Caucus Women's Group, Boston, 1985-86, Women's Democratic Networking Group, Newton, Mass., 1985-86; fundraiser Senator John Kerry's Campaign, Boston, 1984-86, Gerald D'Amico for lt. gov., Mass., 1986—; fundraiser, campaign mgr. state rep. candidate, Mass., 1986—; past v.p. and pres. Jewish War Vets. of Milton, Mass.; bd. dirs. Combined Jewish Philanthropies Career Div., 1985—. Five undergrad. scholarships Suffolk U., Boston, 1948-53; teaching fellow Suffolk U. Grad. Sch., 1979-80; Ednl. coll. Greater Mass. intern, Brookline, Mass., 1984-85. Mem. Mass. Deans, Counselors and Adminstrs., Suffolk U. Alumnae (fundraiser), Mass. Caucus for Women, Knights of Pythias (bd. dirs., trustee, 1960-75). Club: Brandeis U. (bd. dirs. 1976-80). Avocations: travel; reading; writing. Office: Registry Motor Vehicles 18 Country Club Dr Boston MA 02368

SCHLACHTER, GAIL ANN, publishing company executive, author; b. Detroit, Apr. 7, 1943; d. Lewis E. and Helen (Blitz) Goldstein; children—Sandra, Eric. B.A., U. Calif., 1964; M.A. in History and Edn., U. Wis., 1966, M.L.S., 1967; Ph.D. in Library Sci., U. Minn., 1971; M.Pub. Adminstrn., U. So. Calif., 1979. Asst. prof. library sci. U. So. Calif., Los Angeles, 1971-74; head social sci. dept. Calif. State U. Library, Long Beach, 1974-76; asst. univ. librarian U. Calif.-Davis, 1976-81; dir. Am. Bibliog. Ctr., ABC-Clio Info. Services, Santa Barbara, Calif., 1981-82, v.p. publs., 1982-83, v.p., gen. mgr., 1983—, also cons., 1980-81; acting exec. dir. Info. Inst., Santa Barbara, 1981-82; pres. Reference Services Press, Santa Barbara, 1976—. Author: Minorities and Women (reference book), 1976; Reference Sources in Library and Information Services, 1984; Directory of Financial Aids for Women (reference series), 1978—; exec. editor reference serial: Hist. Abstracts, 1981—; Am.: History and Life, 1981—. Named Outstanding Prof., U. So. Calif. Library Sch., 1973. Mem. ALA, Calif. Library Assn. (councillor 1980—, pres. chpt. Acad. and Research Librarians 1977-78). Home: 1533 Manitou Rd Santa Barbara CA 93105 Office: ABC-Clio Info Services 2040 APS Santa Barbara CA 93103

SCHLAERTH, SALLY ANNE GALLAGHER, newspaper librarian; b. Erie, Pa., May 23, 1928; d. Raymond Aloyisius and Eleanor (Curriden) Gallagher; m. Joseph Donald Schlaerth, Nov. 27, 1954; children—Kathi, Sharon, Sally Jo, Joseph Donald. B.A. cum laude, D'Youville Coll., 1950; postgrad. Canisius Coll., 1950-51; M.L.S., SUNY-Buffalo, 1969. Tchr. English, McMahon High Sch., Buffalo, 1950-51; service rep. N.Y. Telephone Co., Buffalo, 1951-55; librarian Kaegebein Sch., Grand Island, N.Y., 1968-73; chief librarian Buffalo News, 1973—. Mem. Spl. Library Assn., Kappa Gamma Pi, Sigma Delta Chi. Roman Catholic. Home: 47 Milton St Williamsville NY 14221 Office: Buffalo News One News Plaza Buffalo NY 14240

SCHLAFLY, PHYLLIS STEWART, author, lawyer; b. St. Louis, Aug. 15, 1924; d. John Bruce and Odile (Dodge) Stewart; B.A., Washington U., St. Louis, 1944, J.D., 1978, M.A., Harvard U., 1945, LL.D., Niagara U., 1976; m. Fred Schlafly, Oct. 20, 1949; children—John F., Bruce S., Roger S., Liza S. Forshaw, Andrew L., Anne V. Bar: Ill. 1979, D.C. 1984, Mo. 1985. Author, pub. Phyllis Schlafly Report, 1967—; broadcaster Spectrum, CBS Radio Network, 1973-78; commentator Matters of Opinion Sta. WBBM, Chgo., 1973-76; syndicated columnist Copley News Service, 1976—; TV commentator Cable News Network, 1980-83. Del. Republican Nat. Conv., 1956, 64, 68, 84, alt., 1960, 80; pres. Ill. Fedn. Rep. Women, 1960-64; 1st v.p. Nat. Fedn. Rep. Women, 1964-67; mem. Ill. Commn. on Status of Women, 1975-85; mem. Adminstrv. Conf. U.S., 1982—; nat. chmn. Stop ERA, 1972—; pres. Eagle Forum, 1975—; mem. Pres. Reagan's Def. Policy Adv. Group, 1980; mem. Commn. on Bicentennial of U.S. Constn., 1985—. Recipient 10 Honor medals Freedoms Found.; Brotherhood award Nat. Conf. Christians and Jews, 1975; named Woman of Achievement in Public Affairs, St. Louis Globe-Democrat. 1963; named one of 25 most influential woman in U.S. in social action World Almanac, 1978—; named one of 10 most admired women in World Good Housekeeping Mag. Poll, 1977—. Mem. ABA, Ill. Bar Assn., DAR (nat. chmn. Am. history 1965-68, nat. chmn. bicentennial com. 1967-70, nat. chmn. nat. def. com. 1977-80, 83—), Phi Beta Kappa, Pi Sigma Alpha. Author: A Choice Not an Echo, 1964; The Gravediggers, 1964; Strike From Space, 1965; Safe Not Sorry, 1967; The Betrayers, 1968; Mindszenty The Man, 1972; Kissinger on the Couch, 1975, Ambush at Vladivostok, 1976; The Power of the Positive Woman, 1977; Equal Pay for UNequal Work, 1984; Child Abuse in the Classroom, 1984. Address: 68 Fairmount Alton IL 62002

SCHLEGEL, BETH ANN, retail executive; b. St. Louis, Aug. 23, 1952; d. Harold August and Dorothy May (Gehl) Schlegel. B.A., Fontbonne Coll., 1974. Exec. trainee Famous Barr, St. Louis, 1974, asst. buyer, 1974-76, multiple dept. mgr., 1976-77; merchandiser Gateway Apparel, St. Louis, 1977-79, mdse. mgr., 1979—. Editor, contbg. author Merchandise Manual, 1977—. Vice pres. 13th Ward Republican Orgn., St. Louis, 1984-85, mem. exec. bd. 11th Ward, 1984-85. Mem. Nat. Assn. Female Execs., LWV. Roman Catholic. Avocations: swimming; travel; reading; sewing; needlework. Office: Gateway Apparel 8500 Valcour Saint Louis MO 63123

SCHLEICHER, ESTELLE ANN, lawyer; b. Buffalo, Sept. 28, 1947; d. Martin Edward and Peggy (Lewin) S. B.A., SUNY-Brockport, 1969; J.D., U. Pacific, 1979. Research asst. SRI Internat., Menlo Park, Calif., 1969-72; clk. Wallace J. Smith Inc., Sacramento 1976-78; assoc., 1980-81; sole practice, Sacramento, 1981—; judge pro tem Sacramento County Claims Ct.; instr., Pacific Coll. Legal Careers, Sacramento, 1982-85. Bd. dirs. Sacramento County Law Library Found. Judge, coach high sch. Law-related Ednl. Conf., Sacramento, 1982-84. Soroptimist scholar, 1978; McGeorge scholar, 1977-79. Mem. Sacramento Young Lawyers Assn. (dir. 1982-85), Sacramento County Bar Assn., Calif. Trial Lawyers Assn. (assoc. editor CTLA Forum), Capitol City Trial Lawyers Assn. (dir. 1986—), ABA. Jewish. Office: 2201 21st St Sacramento CA 95816

SCHLEIFER, ALISON PEDICORD, educational consultant; b. Norristown, Pa., Nov. 6, 1942; d. Harry William and Adah (Alison) Pedicord; A.B., Mt. Holyoke Coll., 1964; certs. U. Paris, 1962, 63; M.S., So. Conn. State Coll., 1975; m. James Thomas Schleifer, Aug. 15, 1964; children—Katharine Alison, Margaret Elizabeth. Tchr., Amity Regional Sch. Dist., Woodbridge, Conn., 1964-71, dept. chmn. fgn. langs., 1968-71, tchr. French, part-time, 1976-77; ednl. cons., New Haven, 1976—. Bd. dirs. YWCA, 1971-76, v.p. bd. dirs., 1976; bd. dirs. Downtown Comparative Ministry, 1971—, pres., 1973-75, v.p., 1976-82; del. gen. synod United Ch. of Christ, 1975, 77; chair of allocations United Way Greater New Haven. Mem. Ind. Ednl. Counselors Assn. Mem. United Ch. of Christ. Club: Mt. Holyoke. Contbr. articles to profl. jours. Address: 220 Alston Ave New Haven CT 06515

SCHLEIMER, SHIRLEY BRASSAW, accountant; b. Saginaw, Mich., Sept. 2, 1926; d. Guy Edward and Helen (Siller) Brassaw; student Walton Sch. Commerce, 1947-51; m. Edward C. Schleimer, Dec. 22, 1951 (dec. 1975); 1 dau., Jane Elizabeth. Pvt. practice acctg. Shirley B. Schleimer, C.P.A., Saginaw, 1954-75; ptnr. Rehmann, Robson, Osburn & Co., Saginaw, 1976—. Treas., Saginaw YWCA, 1980-82; treas. Salvation Army, 1981-82, chmn., 1984—; mem. Saginaw Community Found. C.P.A., Mich. Mem. Am. Inst. C.P.A.s, Am. Women's Soc. C.P.A.s (Nat. Public Service award 1980), Am. Soc. Women Accts. (chpt. pres. 1952-54, 76-78), Mich. Soc. C.P.A.s, Networking (founder, treas. 1979-81). Lutheran. Club: Zonta (state treas. 1980-82, internat. treas. 1982-83, Saginaw Woman of Yr. 1982). Office: PO Box 2025 Saginaw MI 48605

SCHLEIN, MIRIAM, author; N.Y.C.; d. William and Sophie (Bigleisen) S.; children—Elizabeth Weiss, John Weiss. B.A. in Psychology, Bklyn. Coll., 1947. Author over 60 books for children, natural sci. books, concept books, story books, picture books, including: Shapes, 1952, It's About Time, 1955, The Way Mothers Are, 1963, I, Tut: The Boy Who Became Pharaoh, 1978, Antarctica, the Great White Continent, 1980, Project Panda Watch, 1984 (Children's Sci. Book award N.Y. Acad. Scis. 1985), Giraffe, The Silent Giant (Children's Book of Yr. Child Study Assn. 1976), What the Elephant Was, 1986, The Dangerous Life of the Sea Horse, 1986; author adult fiction and non-fiction in publs. including Redbook, McCall's, Ladies Home Jour., Good Housekeeping, Univ. Rev., Creative Living, Colorado Quar.; included in anthologies; transl. into Danish, Swedish, Italian, French, Dutch, Norwegian, German, Braille. Awards include: Outstanding Sci. Trade Book for Children, Nat. Sci. Tchrs. Assn./ Children's Book Council Joint Com. for: Snake Fights, Rabbit Fights, and More, 1979, Lucky Porcupine, 1980; Billions of Bats, 1982; Virginia Kirkus 100 Best Books and Westchester Library Best Children's Books 1974-75 for What's Wrong with Being a Skunk?, 1974; Children's Book Showcase Title/Children's Book Council for Giraffe, The Silent Giant, 1976; Jr. Lit. Guild selections include: The Four Little Foxes, 1952, Elephant Herd, 1954, City Boy, Country Boy, 1955, The Big Cheese, 1957, The Pile of Junk, 1962; Herald Tribune Honor Book award for Elephant Herd, 1954; Boys' Clubs Am. Jr. Book Award for Fast Is Not a Ladybug, 1953; Children's Books of Yr. award Child Study Assn. for Giraffe, The Silent Giant, 1976; honor book N.Y. Acad. Scis. for Project Panda Watch, 1985. Mem. Authors Guild, PEN Am. Center, Forum of Writers for Young People (pres. 1975-76). Author filmstrip materials Guidance Assocs.; textbook editor Harcourt Brace Jovanovich, 1980; editor Scribner Ednl. Pubs., 1985. Home and Office: 19 E 95th St New York NY 10128

SCHLENOFF, MARJORIE LITWIN, psychoanalyst; b. Atlantic City, Feb. 27, 1948; d. Theodore S. and Julia T. Litwin; B.A. in Psychology summa cum laude, U. Md., 1969; M.S.W., Columbia U., 1973; m. Larry B. Schlenoff, June 8, 1969; children—Lauren, Jessica. Psychiat. social worker No. Westchester Guidance Ctr., Mt. Kisco, N.Y., 1973-75; supervising social worker Rockland County Mental Health Clinic, Pomona, N.Y., 1973-77; co-founder Family Service Group of Putnam Community Ctr., Carmel, N.Y., 1977-78; clin. intern, sexual treatment and edn., dept. psychiatry Cornell U. Med. Ctr., N.Y.C., 1978-79; faculty mem., field work coordinator Inst. Counseling and Therapy, Found. Religion and Mental Health, Briarcliff Manor, N.Y., 1979-82; pvt. practice psychoanalytic psychotherapy and treatment of sexual dysfunctions, 1974—; cons. N.E. Counseling Center; adj. clin. instr. Wurzweiler Sch. Social Work, Sch. Social Work Hunter Coll.; developer, host weekly program Let's Talk about Sex, Sta. WVIP, 1982-83; mem. edn. com. Planned Parenthood. Fellow Soc. Clin. Social Work Psychotherapists; mem. Psychoanalytic Assn. of Westchester Ctr. for Psychoanalysis and Psychotherapy (cert. in psychoanalysis 1984), Sex Info. and Edn. Council U.S., Am. Assn. Sex Educators, Counselors and Therapists, Phi Beta Kappa, Alpha Epsilon Phi (outstanding nat. mem. 1969). Democrat. Jewish. Contbr. article to profl. jour. Home: Patterson Rd Pound Ridge NY 10576 Office: 16 Dakin Ave Mount Kisco NY 10549

SCHLESINGER, JANET ROSE, physical therapist; b. N.Y.C., Aug. 18, 1952; d. George and Erika (Kopalt) S.; m. Charles Lee Gerard, Mar. 11, 1973 (div. Dec. 1975); m. Edward N. McClure, Feb. 19, 1984; 1 child, Miriam Allison. B.S. in Phys. Therapy, Quinnipiac Coll., 1974; M.S. in Phys. Therapy, L.I.U., 1978. Phys. therapist Kalamazoo Valley Intermediate Sch. Dist., Mich., 1974-76, State of N.Y., Staten Island, 1976-77, Little Co. Mary Hosp., Torrance, Calif., 1978-80, Med. Ctr. Phys. Therapy, Torrance, 1980—; phys. therapist Expert Connection, Torrance, 1985. Mem. Am. Phys. Therapy Assn. Jewish. Avocations: skiing; swimming; exercise; reading. Home: 4627 Milne Dr Torrance CA 90505 Office: Med Ctr Phys Therapy 4201 Torrance Blvd #670 Torrance CA 90503

SCHLETTE, SHARON ELIZABETHKUNZ, utility company executive; b. Bklyn., May 25, 1945; d. Albert Valentine and Dorothy Lee (Jacobs) Kunz; student St. Johns U., 1978-82; m. Arthur F. Schlette, Oct. 12, 1985. With Consol. Edison Co., 1963 , dist. office teller, 1967-69, acctg. clk., customer service area, 1967-72, asst. supr. Manhattan customer service, 1972-78, unit mgr. Br. III-Westside, Manhattan customer service, 1978-81, unit mgr. Lincoln Center Br., 1981-82, unit mgr. Yorkville Br., 1982—. Mem. Consol. Edison Engring. Soc., Nat. Rifle Assn., Aircraft Owners and Pilots Assn. (lic. pilot). Republican. Home: 446 Madison Ave Brentwood NY 11717 Office: 1555 3d Ave New York NY 10028

SCHLICHTING, CATHERINE FLETCHER NICHOLSON, librarian, educator; b. Huntsville, Ala., Nov. 18, 1923; d. William Parsons and Ethel Louise (Breitling) Nicholson; B.S., U. Ala., 1944; M.L.S., U. Chgo., 1950; m. Harry Fredrick Schlichting, July 1, 1950 (dec. Aug. 1964); children—James Dean, Richard Dale, Barbara Lynn. Asst. librarian U. Ala. Edn. Library, Tuscaloosa, summers 1944-45; librarian Sylacauga (Ala.) High Sch., 1944-45, Hinsdale (Ill.) High Sch., 1945-49; asst. librarian Centre for Children's Books, U. Chgo., 1950-52; instr. reference dept. library Ohio Wesleyan U., Delaware, 1965-69, asst. prof., 1969-79, asso. prof., 1979-85, prof., 1985—, student personnel librarian, 1966-72, adviser Mortar Bd., 1969-72, mem. exec. com., 1973-79, 85—, sec. com., 1973-74, 76-77. Mem. adminstrv. bd. Methodist Ch., 1963-81, chmn. adminstrv. bd., 1985—, mem. Council on Ministries, 1975-81, chmn., 1975-77. Recipient Algernon Sidney Sullivan award U. Ala., 1944. Ohio Wesleyan U.-Mellon Found. grantee, 1972-73, 84-85; GLCA Teaching fellow, 1976-77. Mem. ALA, Ohio Library Assn., Midwest Acad. Librarian Conf., Acad. Librarians Assn. Ohio (dir. 1984—), AAUP (chpt. sec. 1967-68, chpt. exec. com. 1973-78), Kappa Delta Pi, Alpha Lambda Delta. Democrat. Clubs: Ohio Wesleyan U. Womans (exec. bd. 1969-72, 77-79, 81-84, pres. 1969-70, sec. 1977-78), History (pres. 1971-72, v.p. 1978-79), Fortnightly (pres. 1975-76), Am. Field Service (pres. Delaware chpt. 1975-76) (Delaware). Author: Introduction to Bibliographic Research: Basic Sources, 4th edit., 1983; Checklist of Biographical Reference Sources, 1977; Audio-Visual Aids in Bibliographic Instruction, 1976; Introduction to Bibliographic Research: Slide Catalog and Script, 1980; also articles. Home: 414 N Liberty St Delaware OH 43015 Office: LA Beeghly Library Ohio Wesleyan U Delaware OH 43015

SCHLICHTING, MARY JOAN, information systems account executive, consultant; b. Akron, Ohio, Feb. 9, 1952; d. Hans Louis and Adelaide Anne (Karr) Schlichting. B.A. in Fine and Applied Arts, U. Akron, 1974. Spl. events coordinator U. Akron (Ohio), 1968-71; with Fisher Fazio's, Akron, 1970-78; account exec. AT&T, Cleve., 1978—, nat. account exec. AT&T Info. Systems, 1983—; cons. Jeno Inc., Chgo., 1983. Pres., Ohio chpt. Sunshine Found, Cleve., 1982-83. Mem. Nat. Assn. Female Execs. Democrat. Roman Catholic. Office: AT&T Info Systems 333 S Beandry Suite 1101 Los Angeles CA 90017

SCHLITT, ANNELIES JEANNE, software engineer; b. New Rochelle, N.Y., May 27, 1943; d. Matthew Marcellus and Aukje Hillegonde (Hoogeveen) Dorenbosch; B.S., Columbia U., 1967; m. Gerd Herbert Schlitt, Feb. 27, 1974; children—Lawrence Matthew, Alexander Paul. Systems programmer Ciba-Geigy Corp., Ardsley, N.Y., 1968-70, Basel, Switzerland, 1970-71, Wehr, W.Ger., 1971-73; self-employed systems cons., Wehr, 1973-78; software engr. Intel Corp., Santa Clara, Calif., 1979-84, system engr., Munich, W.Ger., 1984-86; self-employed systems cons., 1986—. Home: 22996 Standing Oak Ct Cupertino CA 95014

SCHLOBOHM, JULIA ANN, nutrition educator, consultant; b. Kansas City, Mo., Jan. 9, 1952; d. Earnest Lee and Joy Ellen (Gerth) Groves; m. Richard W. Sizer, Jan. 29, 1971 (div. Mar. 1981); 1 child, Scott W.; m. H. Alan Schlobohm, Nov. 24, 1984. B.S., Washburn U., 1982; M.S. in Tech. Tchr. Edn., Pittsburg State U., Kans., L.P.N., Kans. Staff nurse St. Francis Med. Cgr., Topeka, Kans., 1979-81; cook's asst. Dorothy's Kitchen, Topeka, 1981; dietetic technician Kans. U. Med. Ctr., Kansas City, Kans., 1982; quality control technician Fleming Co., Topeka, 1982; asst. mgr. Grandmas Apron, Topeka, 1983; instr. nutrition Kaw Area Vo-Tech Sch., Topeka, 1984—; vol. nutrition cons. Head Start, Topeka, 1986. Mem. Am. Home Econs. Assn., Kans. Council on Nutrition, Nat. Assn. Female Execs., Topeka Restaurant and Purveyors Assn. Republican. Lutheran. Sec. First Lutheran Youth Com., Topeka 1985-86. Avocation: aerobic fitness. Office: Kaw Area Vo-Tech Sch 5724 Huntoon Topeka KS 66604

SCHLOFF, KAY DAVID, lawyer; b. Wyandotte, Mich., Mar. 18, 1937; d. Harold Charles and Agatha Florence (David) S.; Ph.B. cum laude, U. Detroit, 1959, J.D. magna cum laude, 1962. Admitted to Mich. bar, 1963; mem. firm Raymond, Chirco, Fletcher & Donaldson, Detroit, 1962-64; law clk. U.S. Dist. Judge Talbot Smith, 1965-71; dep. fed. defender Fed. Defender Office, Detroit, 1972-74, dir. legal tng., dir. Criminal Justice Inst., 1974-76, supr. asst. corp. counsel, 1977—; mem. Mich. Bd. Law Examiners, 1974-79. Mem. Mich. Bar Assn., Detroit Bar Assn., Women Lawyers Assn., Pub. Corp. Law Council, Mich. Assn. of Professions (dir. 1979-81). Democrat. Roman Catholic. Home: 9000 E Jefferson St Apt 21-14 Detroit MI 48214 Office: City of Detroit Law Dept 1010 City County Bldg Detroit MI 48226

SCHLOSNAGLE, CAROL ANN, communications executive; b. Carlisle, Pa., Dec. 23, 1950; d. Eugene Stanley and Ethel Mae (Smeltzer) S.; B.A. in English Lit., Hood Coll., 1972. Photojournalist, feature writer Carlisle Evening Sentinel, Carlisle, 1968-71, Frederick (Md.) News-Post, 1971-72; v.p. public relations Cole & Weber, Inc., Seattle, 1974-82; v.p. communications Group Health Coop., Seattle, 1982—. Publicity dir., fund raiser Am. Expdn. to K2, Pakistan, 1978; v.p. bd. dirs. Pike Market Community Clinic; mem. recruitment and pub. relations coms. Leadership Tomorrow; bd. dirs. Nat. Coop. Bus. Found. Mem. Seattle Advt. Fedn., Public Relations Soc. Am. (Wash. State chpt. award of Merit, 1978), Am. Hosp. Assn., Mktg. Exec. Communicators Internat. Republican. Presbyterian. Clubs: Washington Athletic, Seattle Press, Seattle Athletic, City. Publicity and travel writer and photographer for consumer and trade mags., newspapers. Home: 2728 Fairview Ave E Seattle WA 98102 Office: 300 Elliott Ave West Seattle WA 98119

SCHLOSS, JO ANN BOCK, entrepreneur; b. Denver, Aug. 9, 1932; d. Samuel and Rose Bock; B.A. in Communications, U. Colo., 1972, M.A. in Orgnl. Behavior and Communications (grad. fellow 1975), 1975; m. Charles M. Schloss, Jr., Dec. 19, 1948; children—Charles M., III, Sindi Jo, Kristy Anne. Community relations cons. Denver Commn. Community Relations, 1972-73, project dir. commn. youth, 1973-75; with Central Bank of Denver, 1976-82, v.p. staff relations and devel., 1979-81, v.p. human resources planning and devel., 1981-82; chief operating officer Schloss & Shubart, Inc., 1983-84; pres., chief exec. officer Profitable Decisions, Inc., Aurora, Colo., 1985—. Bd. dirs. U. Colo. Alumni and Friends, 1979-80, Center for Women and Work, 1980-81; mem. Arap. County Pvt. Industry Council. Mem. Nat. Assn. Bank Women, Am. Soc. Tng. and Devel., Internat. Assn. Bus. Communicators, Human Resources Planning Soc., Internat. Assn. Quality Circles, Am. Soc. Personnel Adminstrs., NOW, Leadership Denver, Women's Forum Colo., World Future Soc., Women Bus. Owners Assn., Phi Beta Kappa. Home: 801 E Radcliffe Ave Englewood CO 80110 Office: 3198 Nome St Aurora CO 80010

SCHLOSS, KARLA FAITH, educational administrator; b. Malden, Mass., Apr. 7, 1952; d. Marvin Lawrence and Ann Frances (Kendell) Schloss. B.S., Emerson Coll., 1974; M.A., Calif. State U.-Northridge, 1975. Program specialist Los Angeles County Div. of Spl. Edn., Downey, Calif., 1978-80; regional edn. coordinator spl. edn. Mass. Dept. Edn., Northeast Regional Edn. Ctr., North Reading, 1980-83; prin. Perley Elem. Sch., dir. spl. edn. Georgetown pub. schs. (Mass.), 1983—; tchr./specialist lang. disordered jr. high aphasic/autistic pre-sch. diagnostic Los Angeles County Div. Spl. Edn., Downey, 1975-78; trainer Nat. Assn. Autistic Children, Mass. Dept. Edn., 1981-83. Active Am. Cancer Soc., Lynn, Mass., 1982—; mem. Nat. Tay Sachs Found., Newton, Mass., 1980—. Recipient Disting. Service award Emerson Coll., 1973; 100 Hours Services award Boston Children's Hosp., 1973. Mem. Am. Speech and Hearing Assn., Mass. Elem. Prins. Assn., Mass. Speech and Hearing Assn., Adminstrs. of Spl. Edn. Assn. Jewish. Office: Perley Elem Sch 51 North St Georgetown MA 01833

SCHLOSSBERG, DIANE EGUIA, nursing educator; b. Houston, Jan. 10, 1952; d. Ernest L. and Maria O. (Martinez) Eguia, m. Jack Larry Schlossberg, Sept. 2, 1979; 1 son, Mark Andrew. B.S., U. Houston, 1982; R.N., San Jacinto Coll., 1973. Staff operating room nurse M. D. Anderson Hosp., Houston, 1973-77; head nurse surgery renal transplant urology Hermann Hosp., Houston, 1977-80, instr. Houston Community Coll., 1981-83, San Jacinto Coll., Pasadena, Tex., 1980-81, 83—. Mem. Assn. Operating Room Nursing, Tex. Jr. Coll. Tchrs. Assn., Am. Urology Assn. Allied (pres. 1982), Assn. Surg. Tech. Instrs. Roman Catholic. Club: Oak Forest Civic (Houston). Home: 3803 Thonig St Houston TX 77092

SCHLOSSER, ANNE GRIFFIN, librarian; b. N.Y.C., Dec. 28, 1939; d. C. Russell and Gertrude (Taylor) Griffin; m. Gary J. Schlosser, Dec. 28, 1965. B.A. in History, Wheaton Coll., Norton, Mass., 1962; M.L.S., Simmons Coll., 1964; cert. archives adminstrn. Nat. Archives and Records Service, Am. U., 1970. Head UCLA Theater Arts Library, 1964-69; dir. Louis B. Mayer Library, Am. Film Inst., Los Angeles, 1969—, dir. film/TV documentation workshop, 1977—. Project dir.: Motion Pictures, Television, Radio: A Union Catalogue of Manuscript and Special Collections in the Western United States, 1977. Active Hollywood Dog Obedience Club, Calif. Numerous grants for script indexing, manuscript cataloging, library automation. Mem. Soc. Am. Archivists, Soc. Calif. Archivists (pres. 1982-83), Theater Library Assn. (exec. bd. 1983—), Assn. Entertainment Industry Computer Profls. (bd. dirs. 1986—). Democrat. Episcopalian. Avocations: running; swimming; reading; dog obedience training. Office: Am Film Inst Louis B Mayer Library 2021 N Western Ave Los Angeles CA 90027

SCHLOTFELDT, ROZELLA MAY, nursing educator; b. DeWitt, Iowa, June 29, 1914; d. John W. and Clara C. (Doering) S.; B.S., State U. Iowa, 1935; M.S., U. Chgo., 1947, Ph.D., 1956; D.Sc. (hon.), Georgetown U., 1972, Adelphi U., 1979, U. Ill. at Med. Ctr., 1985; L.H.D. (hon.), Med. U.S.C., 1976; Sc.D. (hon.), Wayne State U., 1984. Staff nurse State U. Iowa, VA Hosp., 1935-39; instr., supr. maternity nursing State U. Iowa, 1939-44; asst. prof. U. Colo. Sch. Nursing, 1947-48; asst., then asso. prof. Wayne State U. Coll. Nursing, 1948-55, prof., assoc. dean Coll. Nursing, 1957-60; dean Frances Payne Bolton Sch. Nursing, Case Western Res. U., 1960-72, prof., 1960-82, ref., 1982, prof., dean emeritus, 1982—. Spl. cons. Surgeon Gen.'s Adv. Group on Nursing, 1961-63; mem. nursing research study sect. USPHS, 1962-66; mem. Nat. League for Nursing-USPHS Com. on Nursing Edn. Facilities, 1962-64; mem. com. on health goals Cleve. Health Council, 1961-66; mem. Cleve. Health Planning and Devel. Commn., 1969-72; adv. com. div. nursing W.K. Kellog Found., 1959-67; v.p. Ohio Bd. Nursing Edn. and Nurse Registration, 1970-71, pres., 1971-72; mem. Nat. Health Services Research Tng. Com., 1970-71; mem. supply and edn. panel Health Manpower Com., 1966-67, rev. com. Nurse Tng. Act, 1967-68; bd. visitors Duke U. Med. Center, 1968-70; mem. council, exec. com. Inst. Medicine of Nat. Acad. Scis., 1971-75; mem. nat. adv. health services council Health Services and Mental Health Adminstrn., 1971-75; mem. def. adv. com. on women in services Dept. Def., 1972-75; bd. dirs., treas. Nursing Home Adv. and Research Council, from 1975; mem. adv. panel Health Services Research Commn. on Human Resources, Nat. Acad. Sci., from 1977; cons. Walter Reed Army Inst.; adv. council on nursing U.S. VA, 1965-69, chmn., 1966-69; mem. Yale U. Council Com. on Med. Affairs, 1981-86. Served to 1st lt. Army Nurse Corps, 1944-46. Recipient Disting. Service award U. Iowa, 1973. Fellow Am. Acad. Nursing (v.p. 1975-77), Nat. League Nursing; mem. Am. Nurses Assn. (chmn. commn. on nurse edn. 1967-70, mem. com. for studying credentialling 1976-79, adv. com. W. K. Kellogg Nat. Fellowship program 1981-85), Sigma Theta Tau (nat. v.p. 1948-50, chmn. com. to select disting. lectrs. 1986—), Pi Lambda Theta. Mem. editorial bd. Nursing Leadership, Advances in Nursing Sci.; contbr. numerous articles to profl. jours. Home: 1111 Carver Rd Cleveland Heights OH 44112 Office: Sch Nursing Case Western Reserve U Cleveland OH 44106

SCHLUNDT, VIRGINIA MONA, lawyer; b. Washington, Nov. 26, 1949; d. Arthur and Virginia Mary (Stroia) Schlundt. B.A., Ohio Wesleyan U., 1971; J.D., Am. U., 1974. Bar: Mass. 1974. Inquiry recorder Congl. Research Service, Library of Congress, Washington, 1971; legis. asst. Congressman Donald W. Riegle, Washington, 1972, Congressman James Corman, Washington, 1973-74; atty. Inter-Am. Devel. Bank, Washington, 1974-75; sr. legis. asst. Congressman Yvonne Burke, Washington, 1975-76; counsel Com. Fgn. Affairs, Washington, 1977-80; subcom. staff dir. subcom. internat. ops., Washington, 1980-84; pres.

Strategic Vision: The Internat. Communications and Info. Group, 1984—. Contbr. articles to profl. jours. Mem. ABA, Mass. Bar Assn., Am. Soc. Internat. Law.

SCHMALTZ, KATHLEEN MARY, TV news anchor, writer; b. Detroit, Apr. 7, 1958; d. Donald Edward and Gwendolyn Rita (Strotz) S. B.A. in Communication Arts, Criminal Justice, Mich. State U., 1980. Promotion asst., coordinator tour guides WJBK-TV2, Detroit, 1974-76; news, sports, pub. affairs Mich. State Radio Network, East Lansing, Mich., 1976-79; news reporter, announcer WKAR-AM-FM, East Lansing, 1978-79, WITL-AM-FM, Lansing, Mich., 1979—; news anchor, writer WILX-TV, Lansing and Jackson, Mich., 1979—; ascertainment study researcher Mich. State Radio Network, East Lansing, 1978—; guest speaker various orgns. Mem. Mich. State U. Student Adv. Group, 1977-79. Mem. Women in Communications. Office: WILX-TV 10 PO Box 30380 Lansing MI 48909

SCHMEES, HAZEL KOEHNE, medical technologist; b. Hamilton County, Ohio, June 20, 1934; d. Arthur and Ethel (Poertner) Koehne; B.S., Ohio U., 1956; M.T., Mt. Carmel Hosp. Sch. Med. Tech., 1956; m. William B. Schmees, June 6, 1959; 1 son, Douglas Benard. Med. technologist Children's Hosp., 1959-60, Jack Kirschner, M.D., Cin., 1961; night supr. EPP Meml. Hosp., 1961-63; dept. head St. Francis Hosp., Cin., 1963-65; lab. supr. Drs. Clin. Lab., Cin., 1965-78; acting lab. dir. Biederman Allergy Clinic, Cin., 1978-83; clin. instr. Ohio Coll. Bus. and Tech., 1983—, dept. head, 1985—. Republican precinct exec., 1966-69; mem. ch. council St. Peter's United Ch. of Christ, 1983—, recorder, 1984-85, 86. Cert. med. technologist. Mem. Am. Soc. Clin. Pathologists, Ohio Soc. Med. Technologists (membership chmn. dist. 8 1957-61), Am. Assn. Bioanalysis, Internat. Soc. for Lab. Tech., Am. Bd. Bioanalysis, South Central Assn. Microbiologists. Republican. Clubs: Ohio U. Alumni (dir. 1982—), St. Peter's Women's Guild (pres. 1970-78, treas. 1979-84, pres. 1984—. Home: 886 Krupp Dr Fayetteville OH 45118 Office: 415 W Court St Cincinnati OH 45203

SCHMEICHEL, CAROL LYNN, college dean; b. Jamestown, N.D., Nov. 23, 1947; d. Milton Raymond and Dorothy Elaine (Otto) Lochow; m. Russel Lee Schmeichel, June 13, 1969; children—Donald, Jennifer, David. B.A., Jamestown Coll., 1969; M.E.D., S.D. State U., 1971. Caseworker Barnes County Welfare Dept., Valley City, N.D., 1969-70; coll. instr. Central Ariz. Coll., Coolige, Ariz., 1971-74; adult edn. Jamestown Pub. Schs., Jamestown, N.D., 1975-76; counselor, dir. student services Jamestown Coll., 1976-85, dean students, 1985—. Mem. Displaced Homemakers Adv. Com., Bismarck, N.D., 1985—, Adult Edn. Adv. Bd., Jamestown, 1985—. Mem. Am. Assn. Counseling and Devel., N.D. Coll. Personnel Assn. (pres. 1982-83), N.D. Personnel Deans Assn. (pres. 1985—), AAUW. Clubs: Quilters Guild N.D., Jamestown Quilters (treas. 1983—), Buffalo City Running (Jamestown). Avocations: quilting; running; biking. Home: 405 6th Ave NE Jamestown ND 58401 Office: Jamestown Coll Box 6096 Jamestown ND 58401

SCHMERTZ, PHYLLIS KANE, television, radio production executive; b. N.Y., Mar. 2, 1949; d. Martin and Rhoda Kane; m. Robert Jospeh Schmertz, June 7, 1975 (dec. July 1975). B.S., NYU, 1971. Dir. vol. ops. Dem. Nat. Conv., N.Y.C., 1976; fundraiser, dir., Speakers Bus., Israel Bonds Women's Div., N.Y.C., 1971-81; dep. campaign mgr. Mayor Abe Beame Re-Election Com., N.Y.C., 1977; mayor's rep., co-founder 1st Ann. Wold Banking Congress, N.Y.C., 1977; pres. Embassy News Publs., Washington, 1977-82; vice chmn., treas. Universal Video Enterprises, Ltd., N.Y.C., 1982—. Author mag. Embassy News, 1979. Mem. Democratic House and Senate Council, Washington, 1978—; co-chmn. Robert J. Schmertz Meml. Games, Toms River, N.J., 1976—; mem. Mondale for Pres., N.Y.C., 1983—; v.p., bd. govs. Broadcasting Found. Am., 1982—; mem. N.Y.C. Hall of Sci., Flushing Meadow Devel. Corp. Mem. Internat. Platform Assn. Jewish. Home: 1020 5th Ave New York NY 10028

SCHMERZLER, BARBARA HARLIB, real estate broker; b. Bklyn., Nov. 23, 1933; d. Abraham S. and Yetta (Goldstein) H.; m. Seymour Barash Schmerzler, Jan. 26, 1958; children—Alan Matthew, Robert Alexander, David Laurence, Daniel Harlib. Prodn. asst. NBC-TV, N.Y.C., 1951-58; writer TV quiz show Walt Framer Prodns., N.Y.C., 1958-59; realtor, assoc. U.S. Homefinders, Inc., Westport, Conn., 1972-77, pres., 1977—. Mem. Westport Bd. Realtors (pres. 1984-86, Realtor of Yr. 1982, 85), Conn. Assn. Realtors (state conv. chmn. 1984, 85), Nat. Assn. Realtors. Jewish. Avocations: creative writing; singing; tennis.

SCHMIDT, BENNA, medical transcriptionist, company executive; b. Toronto, Ont., May 6, 1947; came to U.S., 1976; d. Moses and Shirley Sarah (Malcoff) Kisin; m. Gary Charles Schmidt, Oct. 3, 1976 (div.). Student in English, Communications, Seneca Coll., 1967. Med. transcriptionist York-Finch Hosp., Toronto, 1970-76; character model, actress, Southfield, Mich., 1977—; freelance transcriptionist, Southfield, 1977-80; exec. adminstr. Cardioscan Corp., Southfield, 1980-82; owner Dial and Dictate, Oak Park, Mich., 1982—. Mem. Am. Assn. Med. Transcription (newsletter editor 1984—), Nat. Assn. Female Execs., Assn. Info. Systems Profls. Jewish.

SCHMIDT, BETTY JO, motel and trailer court executive; b. Kearney, Nebr., Sept. 3, 1938; d. LaVerne Ivan and Vivian Jane (Johnson) Banks; student U. Wyo., B.B.A. in Acctg. U. San Diego; m. Aug. 25, 1954; children—LaVerne, Dennis, Linda. Owner, mgr. Blue Ribbon Cafe & Lounge, Meeteetse, Wyo., 1976-78; mgr. Schmidt Ranch and Limousin Cattle Co., Meeteetse, 1965-78, Don Neet Limousin Cattle Co., Meeteetse, 1970-76; head bookkeeper First State Bank, Cody, Wyo., 1968-71; bookkeeper Barling Constrn. Co., Meeteetse, 1971-73; owner, mgr. Sagebrush Motel and Trailer Ct., Wamsutter, Wyo., 1978—; chief fiscal officer Legal Aid Soc. San Diego, 1985-86. Mem. Wyo. Limousin Assn., Nat. Assn. Limousin Breeders, Wyo. Stockgrowers Assn., Beta Alpha Psi. Republican. Lutheran. Home and office: 8110 Stadler La Mesa CA 92041

SCHMIDT, CAROL, writer, communications consultant; b. Dearborn, Mich., Sept. 10, 1942; d. Emmett R. and Lorraine G. Schmidt; B.A. magna cum laude, Marygrove Coll., 1964; postgrad. U. N.C., 1964-65, UCLA extension, U. So. Calif. City editor Mich. Chronicle Newspaper, Detroit, 1965-68; communications cons. Chrysler Corp., Detroit, 1968; edn. editor Macomb Daily Newspaper, Mt. Clemens, Mich., 1969-70; feature editor, sales promotion mgr. Brentwood Pub. Co., Los Angeles, 1971-78; communications dir. Research and Edn. Inst., Inc., Harbor-UCLA Med. Center, Torrance, Calif., 1978-84; founder, ptnr. Words & Numbers, 1984—; free-lance writer, polit. speech writer, cons.; part-time instr. Wayne County Community Coll., Detroit, 1969-70. Pub. relations dir., co-coordinator Sunset Junction Neighborhood Alliance and St. Fairs; state del. Democratic Party, Mich., 1968-69; mem. Los Angeles Women's Community Chorus. Recipient First prize Nat. Newspaper Pubs. Assn., 1967. Mem. Am. Soc. Assn. Execs., Am. Hosp. Assn. (communications sect.), Soc. for Hosp. Public Relations, Nat. Mgmt. Assn. (v.p. Harbor-UCLA chpt.), Women in Communications, Am. Med. Writers Assn., Feminist Women's Writers Guild, White Women Against Racism, CORE, NOW (pres. Beach Cities 1979-80, state bd. dir. 1977-81), Ginny Foat Def. Fund. Office: 3924 W Sunset Blvd Suite A Los Angeles CA 90029

SCHMIDT, CAROL SUZANNE, hospital administrator; b. River Rouge, Mich., Aug. 8, 1936; d. J. T. Grant Vaden and Virginia Jean (Senker) Vaden Webster; m. Ronald Lee Schmidt, Aug. 18, 1957; children—Karen Suzanne Schmidt Chymych, Linda Lee, Ronald Lee. R.N. diploma Hinsdale Hosp. Sch. Nursing, Ill., 1958; B.S.N. cum laude, Met. State Coll., Denver, 1981; M.A. cum laude, Webster U.-Denver, 1984. R.N., Colo. Operating room nurse Porter Meml. Hosp., Denver, 1961-69, charge relief nurse, 1975-76, adminstrv. supr., 1976-77, head nurse ortho/neuro unit, 1977-82; disease control nurse Vis. Nurse Assn., Denver, 1961-63; nurse Denver Gen. Hosp., 1966-67; office mgr., bookkeeper Timber Ridge Constrn., Evergreen, Colo., 1967-79; asst. dir. nursing Boulder Meml. Hosp., Colo., 1982-83, dir. nursing, 1983-84, v.p. patient care, 1984—. Tchr. Seventh Day Adventist Ch., Boulder and Denver, 1958-85; vol. Colo. Health Fair, Denver, 1979, 80; tchr. basic life support Am. Heart Assn., Denver, 1980-82. Recipient Dist. Nurse of Yr. award Colo. Nurse Assn., 1975. Mem. Am. Coll. Hosp. Execs. of Am. Hosp. Assn., Am. Orgn. Nurse Execs., Assn. Seventh Day Adventist Nurses (bd. dirs. 1984-86), Colo. Soc. Nurse Execs. (active image of nursing 1985), Bus. and Profl. Women (legis. com. 1985). Avocations: needlework; travel. Office: Boulder Meml Hosp 311 Mapleton Ave Boulder CO 80302

SCHMIDT, CHRISTINE RUNYON, social services director; b. Newark, June 2, 1941; d. Ernest Peter and Emma (Runyon) Schmidt. B.A., U. Colo., 1966; M.S.W., U. Mich., 1972. Caseworker, Huerfano County Dept. Social Services, Walsenburg, Colo., 1966-72, social service supr., 1972-73, dir., 1973—. Treas. Walsenburg Civic League, 1978—; mem. Huerfano County Sch. Bd., 1983—; pres. Huerfano County Hist. Soc., LaVeta, 1978—. Mem. Colo. Dirs. County Dept. Social Services Assn. (sec. 1974-76). Avocations: drawing; painting; reading; sports. Office: Huerfano County Dept Social Services 121 W 6th St Walsenburg CO 81089

SCHMIDT, ELISABETH BODROG, dietitian; b. Rankin, Pa., Mar. 27, 1932; d. John and Anna S. (Fuga) Bodrog; B.S., Carlow Coll., Pitts., 1954; M.Ed., U. Pitts., 1967; Ph.D., Pa. State U., 1982; m. Lawrence Lichti Schmidt, Nov. 11, 1959; 1 son, Lawrence Paul. Menu planning dir. Sky-Chefs, Inc., N.Y.C., 1958-60; dist. dietitian Inter-State United, Pitts., 1961-63; adminstrv. dietitian Johns Hopkins Hosp., Balt., 1965-67; asso. prof., chmn. dept. food sci. mgmt. Indiana (Pa.) U., 1967-71; asso. prof. food and nutrition East Carolina U., Greenville, N.C., 1971-74; dir. ops. services health care div. Macke Co., Cheverly, Md., 1975-76; asst. prof. Coll. Bus., Hotel and Restaurant Mgmt., Fla. State U., Tallahassee, 1976—; treas., dir. Pita Taxi, Inc.; past mem. adv. com. Pa. Nutrition Steering Com.; mem. Nat. Com. Serving Size Standards for Nutritional Labeling, Steering Com. Geriatric Feeding Programs; condr. workshops, cons. in field. Mem. Nat. Restaurant Assn. (exec. dir. 1968-69; found. fellow 1970), Am. Dietetics Assn., Am. Mgmt. Assn., Council Hotel, Restaurant and Indsl. Edn., Soc. Hosts (hon.). Mem. Russian Orthodox Ch. Club: Toastmistress. Author papers in field. Office: 204 DIN Fla State Univ Tallahassee FL 32306

SCHMIDT, JANE EMILY, nurse; b. El Paso, Tex., Nov. 17, 1948; d. Gilbert Wright and Martha Bell (Brown) Reschenthaler; m. Peter Schmidt, Sept. 6, 1966 (div. Apr. 1980); children—Peter, Eric; m. Marcus Erle Schmidt, Apr. 11, 1982. A.S. in Nursing, Triton Coll., 1975; B.S. in Nursing, Lewis U., 1979; postgrad. Wichita State U., 1985. R.N., Ill., Kans. Staff nurse Loyola U. Med. Ctr., Maywood, Ill., 1975-79; staff nurse VA Hosp., Hines, Ill., 1970-81, 82-83, clin. nurse adminstr., 1981-82; staff nurse VA Hosp., Wichita, Kans., 1985—. Bd. dirs. Make-A-Wish, Wichita, 1984. Mem. Sigma Theta Tau. Mem. Ch. of Nazarene. Office: VA Med Ctr 5500 E Kellogg St Wichita KS 67214

SCHMIDT, JANET LOUISE, credit union executive; b. Beresford, S.D., Dec. 6, 1933; d. George E. and Ethel Mae (Bonine) Roberts; m. Harry V. Schmidt, Dec. 21, 1952; children—Rick J., Lori Lynn Schmidt Benedict. Student Hillsborough Community Coll., part-time 1970-77. Cert. credit union exec., 1983. Asst. mgr. Transp. Industry Credit Union, Tampa, Fla., 1959-72, asst. treas., 1972-82, v.p., 1982-84, pres., 1984—. Mem. Fla. Credit Union League (edn1. devel. and mktg. com. 1985—), Inst. Cert. Credit Union Execs. (dir., treas. 1983—), Fla. Credit Union Mgmt. Inst. (v.p. 1978-80), Computer Services Users Adv. Council, Credit Union Exec. Soc., Credit Mgrs. Assn. Methodist. Avocations: water skiing; boating; sailing; gardening. Office: 410 Ware Blvd Suite 516 Tampa FL 33619

SCHMIDT, JOANNE HARPER, Realtor; b. Tullahoma, Tenn., June 20, 1938; d. J. W. and Dortha Mae (Poe) Harper; m. Muray Ray Schmidt, Apr. 12, 1958; children—Karen Denise, Lamar Richard. Student U. Fla., 1962-65, U. Central Fla., 1977-79. Sec. Shands Teaching Hosp., Gainesville, Fla., 1961-65; real estate salesperson Windover Farms, Titusville, Fla., 1978-83; city councilwoman, vice mayor City of Titusville, 1979-85; prin. Joanne H. Schmidt, Lic. Real Estate Broker, Titusville, 1983—. From bd. dirs. to pres. Brevard League of Cities, Brevard County, Fla., 1979-83; bd. dirs. Fla. League Cities, Tallahassee, 1981-85, 2d v.p., 1984-85, mem. exec. bd. Task Force on Future Fla., 1983-84, bd. dirs. Fla.'s Future, Quality Cities, 1984-85; pres. Keep Brevard Beautiful, Titusville, 1985-86; pres. Young Republicans, Titusville, 1970-73. Mem. Titusville Bd. Realtors (key contact 1981—), Nat. Assn. Realtors, North Brevard Devel. Council, Titusville Area C. of C. (Better Bus. Div. award 1978, Govt. Leadership Outstanding Community Service award 1982. Home: 449 N Dixie Ave Titusville FL 32796 Office: Joanne H Schmidt Lic Real Estate Broker 4401 S Hopkins Ave Suite 103 Titusville FL 32780

SCHMIDT, MARIA CERES, educator, lawyer; b. Newark, June 28, 1950; d. Joseph Michael and Edith (Primamore) Ceres; m. Robert Edward Schmidt, Aug. 23, 1970. B.A., Montclair State Coll., 1972, M.A., 1975; J.D., Seton Hall U., 1978. Bar: N.J. 1979. Tchr. Westfield (N.J.) Sr. High Sch., 1972—; sole practice, Livingston, N.J., 1979-80, 81—; ptnr. Gray, Schmidt & Van Pelt, Plainfield, N.J., 1980-81; Committeewoman Essex County Republican Party, 1981-84. Mem. Westfield Edn. Assn., NEA, N.J. Edn. Assn.

SCHMIDT, MARILYNN JO, speech pathologist; b. Fostoria, Ohio, July 11, 1931; d. George William and Dorothy (Fry) S.; B.S. in Secondary Edn., Bob Jones U., 1954; M.A. in Speech Pathology, Denver U., 1960, Ph.D. in Speech Pathology, 1972. Tchr., Russellville (Mo.) High Sch., 1954-56, Boonville (Mo.) High Sch., 1956-59; tchr. Denver U., 1960-62; asst. prof. speech pathology Central Mo. State U., Warrensburg, 1962-73, asso. prof., 1973-78, prof., 1978—; cons. in field. Office Vocat. Rehab. fellow, 1959-60; VA grantee, 1971-72. Mem.Am. Speech-Lang.-Hearing Assn., Mo. Speech-Lang.-Hearing Assn., P.E.O., Phi Delta Kappa. Methodist. Home: 409 10th St Warrensburg MO 64093 Office: Speech and Hearing Clinic Central Mo State U Warrensburg MO 64093

SCHMIDT, MARY LOU, community college administrator; b. Spokane, July 28, 1934; d. Rafael Guillermo and Lucia Olive (Button) Ferrer; m. Herbert William Schmidt, Aug. 18, 1956; children—Mark Rafael, Crystal Marie. B.A., Wash. State U., 1955, M.Ed., 1960. Tchr., Wash. Jr. High Sch., Yakima, 1955-59; instr. Davis Sr. High Sch., Yakima, 1959-61; instr. English Yakima Valley Community Coll., 1961-74, div. chmn. langs. and lit., 1974-81, assoc. dean instrn., 1981—. Trustee, Wash. Commn. Humanities, 1976-80. Mem. Democratic Com. Yakima County, 1973. Producer, dir. TV shows Women in American Life, 1974-75. Danforth fellow, 1969. Mem. Wash. Assn. Devel. Edn. (pres. 1985—), Coll. Leaders Assn., Adult Edn. Dirs., Phi Beta Kappa, Phi Kappa Phi, Phi Delta Kappa. Office: Yakima Valley Community Coll Box 1647 Yakima WA 98907

SCHMIDT, RETA MAE, educator; b. Sturgeon Bay, Wis., Oct. 15, 1933; d. Vernon Edward Olson and Gertrude Jennie Johnson; m. Frederick James Schmidt, June 28, 1968 (div. 1975); 1 dau., Mary Ann. Student U. Wis., 1952-53, Prospect Hall Secretarial Sch., Milw., 1953-54; B.S. in Elem. Edn., U. Wis.-Oshkosh, 1958. Tchr., Racine (Wis.) Pub. Schs., 1958-59, Neenah (Wis.) Pub. Schs., 1959-68, Broward Pub. Schs., Ft. Lauderdale, Fla., 1968-69; tchr. Sturgeon Bay (Wis.) Pub. Schs., 1978—, 1st grade tchr. Sunrise Elem. Sch., 1978—. Mem. Wis. Edn. Assn., NEA, Internat. Platform Assn. Republican. Mem. Moravian Ch. Club: Order Eastern Star. Home: 845 S 16th Ct Sturgeon Bay WI 54235 Office: Sunrise Sch Sturgeon Bay WI 54235

SCHMIDT, RUTH CAROLINE, civic worker; b. Appleton, Wis., Apr. 2, 1922; d. William Gustavus and Gladys (Emily) Richter Gust; m. Robert Walter Schmidt, Nov. 14, 1941; 1 child, David Robert. Student Appleton Bus. Coll., 1940-41. Contbr. articles to ednl. jours. and newspapers. Pres. Elkhart Lake Sch. Bd., Wis., 1964-82; pres. Wis. Assn. Sch. Bds., Madison, 1978; del., mem. steering com. White House Conf. on Libraries, 1978-83; pres. Wis. PTA, Madison, 1983-85; chmn. Council of Library and Network Devel., Madison, 1981—; bd. dirs. Nat. PTA, Chgo., 1983-85; organizer student assistance program Drug and Alcohol Abuse Program, Elkhart Lake, 1983—; founder Am. Field Service Program, Elkhart Lake. Recipient Recognition of Service award Wis. Sch. Library Assn., 1978, Reading for Excellence award Sch. Bd., Elkhart Lake, Wis., 1984, Citation, Wis. Legislature, 1982. Mem. Nat. PTA (hon. life), Wis. PTA (hon. life), Wis. Assn. Sch. Bds. (life). Republican. Mem. United Ch. of Christ. Clubs: Elkhart Lake Study (pres.), Quit Quie Golf (Elkhart Lake) (pres.). Lodge: Order Eastern Star. Avocations: golf; swimming; bridge; reading. Home: 220 Crystal Lake Dr Plymouth WI 53073

SCHMIDTMANN, NANCY K., librarian, educator; b. N.Y.C., Apr. 13, 1940; d. Charles Bernard and Anna Mary (Gorman) Koonmen; A.B. cum laude, Chestnut Hill Coll., 1961; M.A., St. John's U., 1962, M.L.S., 1982; m. Otto S. Schmidtmann, Dec. 26, 1962; children—Lucie Ann, Mary Catherine, Peter, Emily Jean, Charles. Research asst. St. John's U., Jamaica, N.Y., 1961-62, 80-81; tchr. English Francis Lewis High Sch., Flushing, N.Y., 1962-63; copywriter Barth-Spencer Corp., Valley Stream, N.Y., 1968-70; editor/copywriter Barron's Ednl. Series, Woodbury, N.Y., 1970-72; sch. media specialist Our Lady of Mercy Sch., Hicksville, N.Y., 1973—; part-time children's librarian Syosset Pub. Library; panelist Nassau Suffolk Library Inst., 1980; audio-visual reviewer Sch. Library Jours., 1980—; cons. in field. Mem. exec. bd. PTA, Plainview Old-Bethpage pub. schs., 1967-70; 4-H leader, Nassau County, N.Y., 1970—; vol. Roman Cath. Diocese of Rockville Centre, 1965—. Recipient Freedoms Found. award, 1957; Ancient Order of Hibernians award, 1956; N.Y. State Coll. Teaching fellow, 1961-62; St. John's U. grad. assistantship, 1961-62, 80-81. Mem. Cath. Library Assn. (chpt. pres., nat. adv. bd.), Nat. Cath. Edn. Assn., Nassau County Library Assn., ALA, Delta Epsilon Sigma, Beta Phi Mu. (v.p.). Contbr. articles to profl. jours. Home: 149 Orchard St Plainview NY 11803 Office: 520 S Oyster Bay Rd Hicksville NY 11801

SCHMITT, BETTY JO, airline company executive, consultant; b. Chattanooga, May 22, 1936; d. Kenneth Harold Chadwick and Ruby Ellen (Shadrick) O'Neil; m. Arno George Schmitt, Nov. 9, 1957; children—Alan, Michelle, Kenneth, Eric, Glenn. Student U. Havana, Cuba, Suffolk County Coll. Payroll clerk Hoffman Beverage, N.Y.C., 1956-58; clk. N.Y. Airways, LaGuardia Airport, 1966-70, mgr. customer relations, 1970-74, mgr. interline, 1974-79, N.Y. Helicopter, Garden City, N.Y., 1980-84; mgr. interline sales Virgin Atlantic Airways, N.Y.C., 1984-85; dir. interline N.Y. Helicopter, Garden City, 1985—. Mem. Nat. Assn. Female Execs., Airlines Interline Mgrs. (program chairwoman 1986), Airline Sales Mgrs. Sect. N.Y. (treasurer, v.p. 1983-85, hon. mem.), Nat. Assn. Airline Mgrs. Exec. Secs. (1st hon. mem. 1985, bd. dirs. 1983-85), L.I. Area Reps. of N.Y. Republican. Avocations: creative writing; bowling; sewing; homemaking. Home: 43-10 Kissena Blvd Apt 14A Flushing NY 11355 Office: New York Helicopter North Ave Garden City NY 11520

SCHMITT, JOY MARY, microbiologist, photographer; b. Evergreen, Ill., Sept. 16, 1952; d. Robert Joseph and Shirley Elizabeth (Burns) S. B.S. in Med. Tech., Ind. U., 1974; B.A. in Photography, Brooks Inst., 1982. Cert. med. technologist. Med. technologist South Bend Med. Found., Ind., 1974-76, Bloomington Hosp., Ind., 1976-79; comml. photographer Knepp Studio, Mishawaka, Ind., 1982-83; microbiologist, photographer No. Ind. Med. Lab. Services, Michigan City, 1983—; photographer, tech. cons., pres. The Tech. Image, Michigan City, 1985—. Recipient Merit of Excellence award, Brooks Inst. Photography Indsl. Dept., 1982. Mem. Am. Soc. Clin. Pathologists, Am. Soc. Mag. Photographers. Avocations: photography; fishing; sailing; racquetball. Home: 330 Southwood Dr Michigan City IN 46360 Office: No Indiana Medical Lab Services 422 Franklin St Michigan City IN 46360

SCHMITZ, EUGENIA EVANGELINE, librarian, educator; b. Grand Rapids, Mich.; d. Joseph A. and Eugenia (Newhouse) S.; A.B., Western Mich. U.; B.S., Coll. St. Catherine; A.M., U. Mich., Ph.D., 1966. Br. librarian Grand Rapids Public Library; librarian, Creston High Sch., Grand Rapids, Sr. High Sch., Benton Harbor, Mich.; lectr. dept. library sci. U. Mich., 1963-67, asst. prof., 1967-68; asst. prof. library sci. U. Wis. at Oshkosh, 1968-70, assoc. prof., 1970-75, prof., 1975—, chmn. dept. library sci., 1968-80. Mem. ALA, Wis. Library Assn., Phi Beta Kappa, Phi Kappa Phi, Beta Phi Mu, Pi Lambda Theta, Sigma Pi Epsilon. Contbr. book revs. to Best Sellers, Jour. Acad. Librarianship, others.

SCHMITZ, SHARON ANN, nurse; b. Caledonia, Minn., Oct. 20, 1943; d. Leo Peter and Antoinette Eva (Bouquet) Schlitz; m. Paul Francis Schmitz, June 4, 1966; children—Christine, Julie, Lisa. B.S.N., Avila Coll., 1979; diploma St. Francis Sch. Nursing, LaCrosse, Wis., 1965. Nurse, St. Francis Hosp., LaCross, Wis., 1968; nurse Mary Greeley Meml. Hosp., Ames, Iowa, 1969-71, Bapt. Meml. Hosp., Kansas City, Mo., 1971-78; cons. Schmitz Assocs., Kansas City, 1979; dir. inservice edn. United Nurses Inc., Kansas City, 1979-80; nurse Menorah Med. Ctr., Kansas City, Mo., 1980—. Chmn., Kansas City Young Matrons, 1983; usher, team leader Folly Theatre, 1983; mem. Mo. Repertory Theatre Guild, 1983. Mem. Am. Nurses Assn., Mo. Nurses Assn., Ophthalmic Nurses Assn., Jr. Womens Symphony Assn. Roman Catholic. Home: 6640 Cherry St Kansas City MO 64131 Office: Menorah Med Center 4949 Rockhill Rd Kansas City MO 64110

SCHMITZ, SHIRLEY GERTRUDE, marketing and sales executive; b. Brackenridge, Pa., Dec. 19, 1927; d. Wienand Gerard and Florence Marie (Grimm) S. B.A., Ariz. State U., 1949. Tchr., guidance counselor Mesa High Sch., Ariz., 1949-51; area mgr. Field Enterprises Ednl. Corp., Phoenix, 1951-53, dist. mgr., 1953-55, regional mgr., 1955-57, br. mgr., Montreal, Que., Can., 1957-61, nat. supr., Chgo., 1961-63, asst. sales mgr., 1963-65, nat. sales mgr., 1965-70; v.p., gen. sales mgr. F.E. Compton Co. div. Ency. Brit., Chgo., 1970-71, exec. v.p., dir. sales, 1971-73; pres. CHB Port-A-Book Store, Inc., 1973-76; gen. mgr. Bobbs-Merrill Co., Inc., Indpls., 1976-82; v.p. sales U.S. Telephone Communications of Midwest, Inc., Chgo., 1982-83; exec. v.p. sales Entertainment Publs., Inc., Birmingham, Mich., 1983—. Mem. Internat. Platform Assn., Am. Mgmt. Assn., Am. Soc. Tng. and Devel., Kappa Delta. Republican. Roman Catholic. Office: 1400 N Woodward Ave Birmingham MI 48011

SCHMUCKER, RUBY ELVA, educator; b. Sugarcreek, Ohio, Nov. 17, 1923; d. Walter F. and Carrie M. (Mizer) Ladrach; R.N., Aultman Hosp. Sch. Nursing, 1945; B.S.N. magna cum laude, U. Akron, 1970, M.S., 1973; m. Nelson Schmucker, Oct. 20, 1945; children—Gary, David, Barbara, Steven. Staff nurse, head nurse, instr. Aultman Hosp., Canton, Ohio, 1942-74; instr. Coll. Nursing, U. Akron (Ohio), 1974-76; instr. Div. Nursing Edn., Akron Children's Hosp., 1976-77; psychiat. nurse, ward mgr. and supr. Massillon (Ohio) State Hosp., 1977-80, cons. to nursing service 1980-81, dir. nursing edn. 1981—; cons. Student Nurse Assn., 1972-74. Active ARC. Mem. Ohio League Nursing (steering com.), Nat. League Nursing, Am. Nurses Assn., Am. Personnel and Guidance Assn., Am. Coll. Personnel Assn., Aultman Hosp. Alumni Assn., Alpha Sigma Lambda, U. Akron Alumni Assn. Mem. United Ch. of Christ. Home: 4214 Bellwood Dr NW Canton OH 44708 Office: 3000 Erie St Massillon OH 44646

SCHNABL, MARTHA BARNETT, civic worker, parliamentarian; b. Jacksonville, Fla., June 3, 1916; d. Leroy Stewart and Bera (Odum) Barnett; m. John Hampton Hickman, (div. Dec. 1952); children—John Hampton III, Bera Barnett; m. Rolf Richard Schnabl, Nov. 5, 1954. Parliamentarian Dist. IV Fla. Fedn. Women's Clubs, 1980—, Garden Club Jacksonville, 1981—, Dist. IV Fla. Fedn. Garden Clubs, 1985—; mem. Jacksonville Mayor's Commn. on Aging, 1982-84; pres. North Jacksonville Woman's Club, Forest-Dale Woman's Club; active Woman's Club Jacksonville, Friday Musicale, Jacksonville. Mem. Nat. Assn. Parliamentarians, Fla. Assn. Parliamentarians (bd. dirs.), Mace Unit Parliamentarians. Democrat. Episcopalian. Avocation: camping. Home: 317 W 69th St Jacksonville FL 32208

SCHNACK, GAYLE HEMINGWAY JEPSON (MRS. HAROLD CLIFFORD SCHNACK), corp. exec.; b. Mpls., Aug. 14, 1926; d. Jasper Jay and Ursula (Hemingway) Jepson; student U. Hawaii, 1946; m. Harold Clifford Schnack, Mar. 22, 1947; children—Jerrald Jay, Georgina, Roberta, Michael Clifford. Skater, Shipstead & Johnson Ice Follies, 1944-46; v.p. Harcliff Corp., Honolulu, 1964—, Schnack Indsl. Corp., Honolulu, 1969—, Nutmeg Corp., Cedar Corp.; ltd. partner Koa Corp. Mem. Beta Sigma Phi (chpt. pres. 1955-56, pres. city council 1956-57). Established Ursula Hemingway Jepson art award, Carlton Coll., Ernest Hemingway creative writing award, U. Hawaii. Office: PO Box 3077 Honolulu HI 96802 also 1200 Riverside Dr Reno NV 89503

SCHNALL, EDITH LEA, mycologist, educator; b. N.Y.C., Apr. 11, 1922; d. Irving and Sadie (Raab) Spitzer; A.B., Hunter Coll., 1942; A.M., Columbia U., 1947, Ph.D., 1967; m. Herbert Schnall, Aug. 21, 1949; children—Neil David, Carolyn Beth. Clin. pathologist Roosevelt Hosp., N.Y.C., 1942-44; instr. Adelphi Coll., Garden City, N.Y., 1944-46; asst. med. mycologist Columbia Coll. Physicians and Surgeons, N.Y.C., 1946-47, 49-50; instr. Bklyn. Coll., 1947; faculty Sarah Lawrence Coll., Bronxville, N.Y., 1947-48; lectr. Hunter Coll., N.Y.C., 1947-67; adj. asso. prof. Lehman Coll., City U. N.Y., 1968; asst. prof. Queensborough Community Coll., City U. N.Y., 1967, asso. prof. microbiology, 1968-75, prof., 1975—, adminstr. Med. Lab. Tech. Program, 1985—; vis. prof. Coll. Physicians and Surgeons, Columbia U., N.Y.C., 1974; advanced biology examiner U. London, 1970—. Mem. Alley Restoration Com., N.Y.C., 1971—; mem. legis. adv. com. Assembly of the State of N.Y., 1972. Mem. Community Bd. 11, Queens, N.Y., 1974—; public dir. of bd. dirs. Inst. Continuing Dental Edn. Queens County, Dental Soc. N.Y. State and ADA, 1973—. Research fellow NIH, 1948-49; faculty research fellow, grantee-in-aid Research Found. of SUNY, 1968-70; faculty research grant Research Found. City U. N.Y., 1971-74. Mem. Internat. Soc. Human and

Animal Mycology, AAAS, Am. Soc. Microbiology (v.p. 1984-86), Med. Mycology Soc. N.Y. (archivist 1974—, fin. advisor 1983—, pres. 1969-70, 79-80, 81-82), Bot. Soc. Am., Med. Mycology Soc. Americas, Mycology Soc. Am., N.Y. Acad. Scis., Sigma Xi, Phi Sigma. Clubs: Torrey Botanical (N.Y. State); Queensborough Community Coll. Women's (pres. 1971-73) (N.Y.C.). Editor: Newsletter of Med. Mycology Soc. N.Y., 1969-85; founder, editor Female Perspective newsletter of Queensborough Community Coll. Women's Club, 1971-73. Home: 214-06 29th Ave Bayside NY 11360

SCHNASE, ANNEMARIE CHARLOTTE RISCHKE, antiquarian bookseller, publisher, researcher; b. Neisee, W.Ger., May 1, 1905; came to U.S., 1956; d. Alfred Ernst and Margaretha Anna (Franke) Rischke; m. Paul J. Schnase, Oct. 5, 1929 (dec. Sept. 1951); children—Brigitte Schnase Loeing, Gisela Schnase Kretschmann. Grad. Muche Lyzeum, Berlin, 1922. Apprentice, Paul Gottschalk, Berlin, 1922-24, antiquarian bookseller, 1925-32; owner Annemarie Schnase, Berlin, 1950-56, Scarsdale, N.Y., 1956—; pub. reprint editions of music periodicals, 1960—. Author, editor: Music Catalogs #1-37, 1960-84, Index Sheetmusic collections Sammlung v. Musikstucken alter und neuer Zeit, 1967. Recipient Bronze medal N.Y. Pub. Library, 1961. Mem. Internat. League Antiquarian Booksellers, Antiquarian Books Assn. Am., Internat. Assn. Music Libraries, Internat. Musicol. Soc., Am. Musicol. Soc. Office: Annemarie Schnase PO Box 119 Scarsdale NY 10583

SCHNEBLY, DIXIE JEAN, management consulting firm executive; b. Denver, Nov. 10, 1941. Grad. Parks Sch. of Bus., 1960; B.S.B.A., U. Denver, 1959-63; interior designer, Chgo. Sch. Interior Design, 1974. Lic. real estate broker. Exec. sec. various oil cos., Denver, 1961-77; truck driver Mobile Pre Mix Co., Denver, 1977-80; cons. Unique Designs & Interiors, Denver, 1968-77; pres. DHS Trucking, Inc., Wheat Ridge, Colo., 1980-84; pres. Dixie Corp., Wheat Ridge, 1984—. Active Witness for Peace, Denver, 1985—. Mem. Nat. Assn. Female Execs. (exec. sec. 1984—). Republican. Avocations: poetry writing, photography. Office: Dixie Corp PO Box 433 Wheat Ridge CO 80033

SCHNECK, HERMINIA MALARET, college counselor; b. Preston, Cuba, July 6, 1925; d. Pedro Salvador and Herminia (Ponce de Leon) Malaret; B.A., Bryn Mawr Coll., 1946; M.A., 1948; m. George W. Schneck, Sept. 17, 1949 (div. June 1978); children—Karen Elizabeth, Laura Isabel; m. 2d Vladimir Trenka. Psychometrician, Johnson O'Connor's Human Engring. Lab., Phila., 1947-48; research worker U. Pa. Press, Phila., 1948-50; translator Sharp & Dohme, Inc., Phila., 1950-52; tchr. St. John Sch., San Juan, P.R., 1958-62; prof. English Catholic U., Bayamon, P.R., 1966-68; tchr. English and history Academia del Perpetuo Socorro, Miramar, P.R., 1968-69, guidance coordinator, 1969-80; prin. St. John's Sch., 1980-81, Baldwin Sch., 1981-83, guidance counselor, 1983-84; now ind. coll. counselor; mem. Middle States regional council Coll. Bd., 1980-81. Mem. adv. com. Title IV Dept. Edn., chmn. coordinating com. Cath. Schs. Guidance Services, 1976-77. Mem. Caribbean Counselors Assn. (pres. 1976-79, v.p. 1979—, program dir.). Mem. Partido Nuevo Progresista (Statehood Party). Home: Box 3957 Bayamon Gardens Sta PR 00620 Office: Baldwin Sch PR Box 1827 Bayamon PR 00619

SCHNEE, AMANDA MERYL MACNAB, physician; b. North Berwick, Scotland, Dec. 3, 1945; came to U.S., 1975; d. Hamish Stuart Duncan and Marjorie Daphne Croal (McDonald) M.; M.B., Ch.B., St. Andrews U., Scotland, 1968; m. Mark Schnee, Oct. 21, 1967; children—Samantha Joanne, Jicky Miranda, Pippa Meryl, Briony Amanda. Intern, Ballochmyle Hosp., Mauchline, Ayrshire, Scotland, 1968-69; resident in family practice Ayrshire Central Hosp., Irvine, Ayrshire, 1969-71; gen. practice medicine, Glasgow, Scotland, 1971-75; physician USAF, Omaha, 1975-77; mem. faculty U. Tex. Med. Sch., Houston, 1977-81. asst. prof. dept. family practice, 1979-81; dir. Student Health Center, Rice U., Houston, 1981—. Diplomate Am. Bd. Family Practice. Mem. Am. Acad. Family Practice, Am. Med. Women's Assn. Home: 2318 Underwood Blvd Houston TX 77030 Office: Rice U Student Health Center Houston TX 77251

SCHNEE, ELAINE SHARON, computer consulting company executive; b. Bklyn., Mar. 27, 1945; d. Sydney William and Rebecca (Kaiser) Landau; m. David Z. Schnee, June 29, 1969; children—Hal, Dennis, Matthew, Mark. B.S., Bklyn. Coll., 1967, M.S., 1969. Corp. mgr., pres. Dynax Resources, Inc., Port Washington, N.Y., 1973—; tchr. Hunter Coll. High Sch., N.Y.C., 1967-69. Mem. bd. edn. Old Westbury Hebrew Congregation, N.Y., 1979—; treas. Willets Rd. Sch. PTO, Roslyn Heights, N.Y., 1984, North Shore Hebrew High Sch., Roslyn Heights, 1984—. Recipient Service award Am. Legion of N.Y., 1959. Mem. Child Devel. Research (movement notator 1971-75). Avocations: archery; racquetball. Home: 40 Hemlock Ln Roslyn Heights NY 11577 Office: Dynax Resources Inc 44 Harbor Park Dr Port Washington NY 11050

SCHNEEBERG, HELEN BASSEN, retired educator; b. Phila., Apr. 5, 1920; d. Carl and Minnie (Aion) Bassen; m. Norman Grahn Schneeberg, Nov. 3, 1940; children—Susan, Karen. B.A., U. Pa., 1941, Cert. of Advanced Studies, 1984; M.L.S., Drexel U., Phila., 1966. Cert. librarian. Bacteriologist, Mount Sinai Hosp., Phila., 1941-43; librarian West Phila., High Sch., 1966-67, Temple U., Phila., 1967-68; research asst. Franklin Inst. Research Lab., Phila., 1968-69; teaching assoc. Temple U., Phila., 1970-71; dir., listen-read project Sch. Dist., Phila., 1971-76. Contbr. articles to research rports. Bd. dirs. Please Touch Mus., Phila., 1979-81; steering com. Physicians for Social Responsibility, Phila., 1982-84; area legis. coordinator Women's Agenda, Phila., 1984—. Mem. N.Y. Acad. Scis., Soc. Research in Child Devel., Infant Mental Health of De. Valley. Democrat. Avocations: travel, reading, music, theatre, sailing, swimming. Home: 2010 Rittenhouse Sq Philadelphia PA 19103

SCHNEIDER, ADELE GOLDBERG, librarian, educator; b. N.Y.C., May 13, 1924; d. Abraham and Anna (Levy) Goldberg; B.A., Bklyn. Coll., 1945; M.L.S., Pratt Inst., 1965; M.A., L.I.U., 1971; m. Noel Schneider, Jan. 1, 1950; children—Adam Matthew, Tracy Lynn. Field interviewer Gallup Poll, N.Y.C., 1941-48; social worker N.Y.C. Dept. Social Services, 1949-52; editor Bklyn. Coll. Alumni Quarterly, 1961-65; instr. Kingsborough Community Coll. CUNY, 1965-70, asst. prof. dept. library, 1970-72, assoc. prof., 1972—. Contbr. articles to profl. jours. Mem. ALA, Library Assn. City U. N.Y., N.Y. Tech. Services Librarians, Beta Phi Mu. Home: 124 Oxford St Brooklyn NY 11235 Office: 2001 Oriental Blvd Brooklyn NY 11235

SCHNEIDER, CLAUDINE, congresswoman; b. Clairton, Pa., Mar. 25, 1947; B.A., Windham Coll., 1969; m. Eric D. Schneider, 1973. Exec. adminstr. Concern, Inc., Washington, 1969; founder R.I. Com. on Energy, 1973; exec. dir. Conservation Law Found., 1974; fed. coordinator R.I. Coastal Zone Mgmt. Program, 1978; producer, hostess public affairs program Sta. WJAR-TV, Providence, 1978-79; mem. 97th-99th Congresses from 2d R.I. Dist., 1979—. State chmn. spl. events Am. Cancer Soc., 1979. Named Outstanding Young Person of Year, South County Jaycees, 1979; Woman of Year, R.I. Women's Polit. Caucus, 1978. Office: Room 1512 Longworth House Office Bldg Washington DC 20515

SCHNEIDER, DEBORAH JO, journalist, researcher; b. Beech Grove, Ind., Mar. 20, 1951; d. Robert Davis and Corrine Mae (Webb) S. Student U. Iowa, 1969-71, U. Ga., 1971-73, DeKalb Coll., Decatur, Ga., 1973-75; postgrad. in communications Barry U., 1986—. Corrections officer Atlanta Bur. Corrections, 1973-76, liaison officer, 1975-76; cameraperson, technician Sta.-WETV, Atlanta, 1975-76; journalist, technician Sta.-WAGA-TV, Atlanta, 1976-80, KABC-TV News, Hollywood, Calif., 1980-81; journalist covering Caribbean and Latin Am., NBC News, Miami, Fla., 1981—; cons. Rio Hondo Coll. (Calif.), 1980. Recipient Best Crew award Los Angeles Press Club, 1980, AP award, 1980, UPI award, 1980. Mem. Sigma Delta Chi. Home: 152 NE 92d St Miami Shores FL 33138 Office: NBC News 1666-79th St Causeway Miami FL 33141

SCHNEIDER, ILENE ANNE, public relations consultant; b. Cleve., Nov. 15, 1949; d. Jules E. and Sylvia G. (Schaffer) Spector; B.A. in Polit. Sci., U. Pa., 1971; m. Bruce J. Schneider, July 12, 1975; 1 child, Liora Yael. Editor, Cleve. edit. TV Guide mag., 1971-72; assoc. editor Sch. Product News mag., Penton/IPC, Cleve., 1972-78; contbg. editor, 1978—; sr. pub. relations rep. Beckman Instruments, Inc., Fullerton, Calif., 1978-85; propr. Schneider the Writer Communications Service, Irvine, Calif., 1980—. Media coordinator-Rothschild for Mayor Campaign, University Heights, Ohio, 1977; sec. 22d Congressional Dist. Caucus, Cleve., 1973-75; asst. coordinator seminar series Youth in Politics, Dyke Coll., Cleve., 1974. Recipient Clarion award Women in Communications, 1978. Mem. Women in Communications, Public Relations Soc. Am., Am. Soc. Bus. Press Editors, Council Exceptional Children, Assn. Children with Learning Disabilities. Jewish. Lodge: B'nai B'rith Women (pres. Coastline chpt.). Contbr. articles to various publs. Home and Office: 21 Almond Tree Ln Irvine CA 92715

SCHNEIDER, JILL, physician, research administrator; b. Cin., July 27, 1947; d. Harold J. and Mary R. Schneider; m. Arthur N. Petrou, Feb. 13, 1977; 1 dau., Marissa H. B.A., U. Rochester, 1969; M.D., Mt. Sinai Sch. Medicine, 1974. Diplomate Am. Bd. Pediatrics. Intern, Bellevue Hosp., N.Y.C., 1974-75, resident, 1975-76; fellow Johns Hopkins Hosp. and Med. Sch., Balt., 1976-78; assoc. physician, assoc. dir. Rockefeller U. Hosp., N.Y.C., 1978-82; assoc. dir. clin. research Am. Cyanamid, Pearl River, N.Y., 1982—. Recipient Am. Chem. Soc. award, 1969; Burroughs-Welcome scholar, 1978-82. Mem. Endocrine Soc., AAAS, N.Y. Acad. Scis. Contbr. articles to profl. jours. Office: American Cyanamid Med Research Div Pearl River NY 10965

SCHNEIDER, LOIS JANE, real estate broker; b. Phila., Jan. 7, 1932; d. Robert H. and Margaret Mary (Quinn) Keough; m. Alan W. Schneider, Sept. 20, 1952; children—Laureen Lauber, Karen Michele. Student Drexel U., 1949-51. Sec. criminal squad FBI, Phila., 1951-53; real estate sales person Walter A. McNamara, Summit, N.J., 1962-76; pres., broker Lois Schneider, Realtor, Inc., Summit, 1976—. Chmn. prof. div. Summit United Way, 1985; pres. Overlook Hosp. Aux., 1980—. Mem. Nat. Assn. Realtors, N.J. Assn. Realtors (bd. dirs. 1984—), Women's Council Realtors, Internat. Fedn. Realtors, Am. Soc. Exec. Women, Real Estate Leaders Am., Summit C. of C. (Mayor's Blue Ribbon Com. 1984), Summit Bd. Realtors (pres. 1983—; Realtor of Yr. 1980). Club: Canoe Brook Country. Home: 25 Glendale Rd Summit NJ 17901 Office: Lois Schneider Realtor Inc 441 Springfield Ave Summit NJ 17901

SCHNEIDER, PHYLLIS LEAH, magazine editor; b. Seattle, Apr. 19, 1947; d. Edward Lee Booth and Harriet Phyllis (Ebbinghaus) Booth Russell; m. Clifford D. Schneider, June 14, 1969; 1 child, Pearl Brooke. Student Highline Coll., 1965-67; B.A., Pacific Lutheran U., 1969; M.A., U. Wash., 1973. English lang. tchr. Zion Sch., Bellville, Ill., 1971-72; features, fiction editor Seventeen Mag., N.Y.C., 1975-80; mng. editor Weight Watchers Mag., N.Y.C., 1980-81; editor-in-chief YM Mag., Gruner and Jahr, U.S.A., N.Y.C., 1981—. Contbr. articles to mags. Mem. Am. Soc. Mag. Editors. Avocations: writing fiction; cross-country skiing. Office: Young Miss Mag Gruner and Jahr USA 685 3d Ave New York NY 10017

SCHNEIDER, SANDRA JEAN, shopping mall executive; b. Ft. Madison, Iowa, Oct. 4, 1956; d. Francis D. and Delores A. (Moone) Rippenkroeger; m. Donald J. Schneider, July 21, 1979; 1 child, Brandon A. (dec.). B.A. in Fashion Merchandising, Columbia Coll., 1979. Spl. events coordinator trainee Traveling Lawrence Hall of Sch. Mktg., 1979-80; ops. dir.-in-tng. Golden Ring Mall, Balt., 1980-81; ops. dir., tenant coordinator La Plaza Mall, McAllen, Tex., 1981-83; asst. mgr. Pekin Mall, Ill., 1983-84; mall mgr. Heritage Park Mall, Midwest City, Okla., 1984—. Bd. dirs. United Cerebral Palsy, Oklahoma City, 1984, 85, 86. Mem. Nat. Assn. Female Execs. Avocations: boating; horseback riding; biking; gardening; sewing. Home: 1128 Oakhill Dr Midwest City OK 73110 Office: Heritage Mall Co 6801 E Reno St Midwest City OK 73110

SCHNEIDER, VALERIE LOIS, speech educator; b. Chgo., Feb. 12, 1941; d. Ralph Joseph and Gertrude Blanche (Gaffron) S., B.A., Carroll Coll., 1963; M.A., U. Wis., 1966; Ph.D., U. Fla., 1969; cert. advanced study Appalachian State U., 1981. Tchr. English and history Montello High Sch. (Wis.), 1963-64; dir. forensics and drama Montello High Sch., 1963-64; instr. speech U. Fla., Gainesville, 1966-68, asst. prof. speech, 1969-70; asst. prof. speech Edinboro (Pa.) State Coll., 1970-71; assoc. prof. speech East Tenn. State U., Johnson City, 1971-76, prof. speech, 1976—; instr. newspaper course Johnson City Press Chronicle, 1979. Chmn. AAUW Mass Media Study Group Com., Johnson City, 1973-74. Recipient Creative Writing award Va. Highlands Arts Festival, 1973; award Kingsport (Tenn.) Times News, 1984, 85, Tri-Cities Met. Advt. Fedn., 1983, 84; Danforth assoc., 1977. Mem. Speech Communication Assn. (Tenn. rep. to states adv. council 1974-75), So., Tenn. (exec. bd. 1974-77, publs. bd. 1974-78, pres. 1977-78), Religious Speech Communication Assn. (Best article award 1976), Tenn. Basic Skills Council (exec. bd. 1979-80, v.p. 1980-81, pres. 1981-82), AAUW (v.p. chpt. 1974-75, pres. 1975-76, corp. rep. for East Tenn. State U. 1974-76), Am. Assn. Continuing Higher Edn., Bus. and Profl. Women's Club (chpt. exec. bd. 1972-73, v.p. 1976-77), Nat. Assn. Remedial Developmental Studies in Post Secondary Edn., Mensa, Delta Sigma Rho-Tau Kappa Alpha, Phi Delta Kappa, Delta Kappa Gamma, Pi Gamma Mu. Presbyterian. Assoc. editor: Homiletic, 1974-76; columnist Video Visions, Kingsport Times-News (Tenn.), 1984-86; contbr. articles on speech to profl. jours. Home: C-5 Greenwood Apts 1409 Colony Park Dr Johnson City TN 37601

SCHNEIDERHAN, ELIZABETH ROSALIN, community services administrator; b. Niagara Falls, Ont., Can., July 4, 1927; d. Joseph Alphonse and Mary Lucy (Pappaianni) Madia; m. Charles William Schneiderhan, Apr. 7, 1956; children—Charles Joseph, John William. B.A., Toronto U., 1948; M.A. candidate Western Conn. State Coll., 1970. Translator, adminstrv. asst. Carborundum Co., Niagara Falls, N.Y., 1949-56; instr. Bruce High Sch., Westernport, Md., 1957, St. Jude Apostle Sch., Atlanta, 1965-66; legal asst. M.E. Zacharias, Atty., Wilton, Conn., 1975; exec. dir. Ridgefield Community Ctr. (Conn.), 1976-80; specialist program devel. YWCA, Fairfax County, Va., 1981-83; founder, dir. Ridgefield Community Ctr. Adult Edn., 1976-80, editor newsletter, 1976-80; founder, coordinator YWCA Women's Network, Fairfax County, Va., 1982; YWCA Artisan's Studio, Fairfax County, 1982; founder, owner Victorian Inn at Harwich, Harwich Center, Mass. Founder, coordinator Ridgefield Community Ctr. Arts Festival, 1979-80, Ridgefield Arts Council Community Arts Calendar, 1979-80, Ridgefield Arts Council, 1979. Mem. Women in Communications, Am. Soc. Tng. and Devel., AAUW, Fairfax County Council Arts, Darien Community Assn. (treas. 1967-69). Roman Catholic. Home: 102 Parallel St PO Box 340 Harwich MA 02645

SCHNEIER, DONNA FRANCES, retail executive; b. St. Louis, Mar. 30, 1938; d. Irwin H. and Bertha (Gershbock) Makovsky; B.S. summa cum laude, Brandeis U., 1959; M.F.A., N.Y. U., 1964; m. Arthur Schneier, Jan. 12, 1958; children—Marc Steven, Karen Anne. Pres., Gallery 6M, N.Y.C., 1966-73, Donna Schneier, Inc., N.Y.C., 1973-80, B&D Jewelry Corp., N.Y.C., 1977-80, Una Donna Ltd., N.Y.C., 1977—, Donna Schneier Fine Arts, 1980—. Bd. dirs. Yeshiva U., 1973—, Park East Synangogue, 1962—. Mem. Photog. Dealers Am., Nat. Assn. Catalog Showroom Merchandisers, Jewelers Bd. Trade. Office: 910 Fifth Ave New York NY 10010

SCHNEYER, CHARLOTTE ALPER, physiologist, educator; b. St. Louis, Nov. 21, 1923; d. Nathan and Anna (Schoenfeld) Alper; m. Leon H. Schneyer, June 11, 1945 (dec. 1976). A.B., Washington U., 1945; M.S., NYU, 1947, Ph.D., 1952. Assoc. prof. physiology U. Ala., Birmingham, 1965-67, prof. dentistry, 1964—, prof. physiology, 1967—, dir. lab. exocrine physiology, sr. scientist Cystic Fibrosis Research Found., 1981—; grant reviewer NIH, Bethesda, Md., 1969—, site visitor. Co-editor: Secretory Mechanisms of Salivary Glands, 1967. Contbr. articles to profl. jours. Adj. curator art glass Birmingham Mus. Art, 1985—. Nat. Inst. Dental Research grantee, 1984—. Mem. Am. Physiol. Soc., Soc. for Exptl. Biology and Medicine, AAAS, N.Y., Acad. Sci. Avocations: painting; enameling; art glass; composing music. Office: Univ Ala Dept Physiology University Station Birmingham AL 35294

SCHNITTGER, INGELA, internist, cardiologist; b. Risinge, Sweden, May 5, 1951; came to U.S., 1978; d. Jan Rydh and Ulla (Forsberg) Schnittger; m. (Timothy) Warren Schweitzer, Sept. 6, 1978. B. Medicine, Karolinska Inst., Stockholm, 1971, M.D., 1975. Diplomate Am. Bd. Internal Medicine. Intern, Karolinska Inst., Stockholm, 1975-76; fellow in cardiology Stanford U. Hosp., Calif., 1976-77, 80-83, resident, 1980, staff physician cardiology div., 1983—; resident in medicine Karolinska Inst., 1978, U. Conn., Farmington, 1979. Contbr. papers on cardiac ultrasound, cardiac arrythmia models, to profl. jours. Recipient Nat. Research Service award NIH, 1981-83. Mem. Am. Heart Assn., Am. Coll. Cardiology, AMA. Lutheran. Club: Fremont Hills Country (Los Altos Hills). Office: Cardiology Div Stanford Univ Hospital Stanford CA 94305

SCHNITZER, ARLENE DIRECTOR, art dealer; b. Salem, Oreg., Jan. 10, 1929; d. Simon M. and Helen (Holtzman) Director; m. Harold J. Schnitzer, Sept. 11, 1949; 1 son, Jordan. Student U. Wash., 1947-48. Founder, Fountain Gallery of Art, Portland, Oreg., 1961-86; sr. v.p. Harsh Investment Corp., 1951—. Bd. dirs. Oreg. Symphony Assn.; v.p. Oreg. Symphony; exec. com. U.S. Dist. Ct. Hist. Soc.; mem. exec. com., bd. dirs. Artquake; mem. adv. bd. New Beginnings; trustee Reed Coll., Portland; nat. trustee Nat. Symphony Orch., 1985—. Recipient Aubrey Watzek award Lewis and Clark Coll., 1981; Met. Arts Commn. award, 1985; Pioneer award U. Oreg., 1985; Pioneer award U. Oreg., 1985; honored by Portland Art Assn., 1979. Clubs: Univ., Multnomah Athletic (Portland). Office: 117 NW 21st Portland OR 97209

SCHNITZER, BARBARA LEVIN, public relations executive, investor, consultant; b. N.Y.C.; d. Harold and Denia R. Levin; m. Ralph Schnitzer, Aug. 8, 1953 (div.); children—Lynn, Frank. A.A., Briarcliff Coll., 1951; student Sophie Newcomb Coll., 1952. Owner, operator Candy Tree, Houston, 1960-63; pvt. investor, N.Y.C., 1969—; dir. pub. relations Livia Sylva, Inc., 1981—; cons. Fugazy Travel Corp., 1980—. Home: 245 E 63d St New York NY 10021 Office: 133 E 54th St New York NY 10022

SCHNORR, MARCIA ANNETTE, nursing educator; b. Oregon, Ill., Sept. 3, 1944; d. Edward Lawrence and Emily LaVerne (Cann) Schnorr. Diploma, Swedish Am. Hosp. Sch. Nursing, 1965; B.S., No. Ill. U., 1976, M.S., 1977, postgrad. in adult edn. Charge nurse Rochelle (Ill.) Community Hosp., 1965-70, supr. intensive care unit, 1970-76; mem. faculty Kishwaukee Coll., Malta, Ill., 1976—, instr. nursing, 1978—; social ministry ombudsman St. Paul Luth. Ch., Rochelle, Ill., 1978—; lectr. continuing edn. workshops, 1977—. Chmn. community edn. and service Ill. Heart Assn., 1970-76. Recipient Appreciation award No. Ill. Dist., Luth. Ch.-Mo. Synod, 1983, Service award, Bethesda Luth. Home, 1983; named Outstanding Educator Kiswaukee Coll., 1980. Mem. Ill. Nurses Assn., Am. Nurses Assn., Transcultural Nurses Assn., Am. Assn. Critical Care Nurses, Wholistic Health Assn., Sigma Theta Tau, Kappa Delta Pi. Republican. Home: 212 Southview Dr Rochelle IL 61068 Office: Kishwaukee Coll Malta Rd Malta IL 60150

SCHNURPEL, HELEN MAMIE PERSELL (MRS. HANS KARL SCHNURPEL), ret. realtor; b. Omaha, Aug. 25, 1902; d. John Alva and Mamie Ethel (Davis) Persell; student U. Nebr., 1930; certificate in real estate UCLA, 1959; m. Hans Karl Schnurpel, May 10, 1937. Co-owner Lynwood Realty Co. (Calif.), 1945-81, Real Estate Sch. So. Calif., Lynwood, 1951-81. Mem. Compton-Lynwood Bd. Realtors (hon. life mem., sec.-treas. 1966-67, dir.; pres. 1970), Nat. Assn. Realtors (hon. life), Calif. Assn. Realtors (hon. life), Lynwood C. of C. (treas. 1978-80, hon. life), Internat. Platform Assn. Republican. Club: Lynwood Womens (pres. 1975-76). Home: 14143 Dunrobin Ave Bellflower CA 90706

SCHOBER, DOROTHY FLORENCE, former educator; b. Green Bay, Wis., Sept. 19, 1910; d. Max William and Addie (Stone) Schober; B.A., U. Wis., 1932; M.P.H., Yale U., 1948; m. Ralph E. Hoffmeyer, Sept. 3, 1982. Visitor, dist. supr., dist. dir. Fla. Welfare Bd., Jacksonville, 1932-37; dir. Public Welfare Dept., Green Bay, 1937-42; cons. Div. Public Assistance, Wis. Dept. Pub. Welfare, Madison, 1942-44; counselor USPHS, 1944-45; health edn. cons. Council Social Agys., New Haven, 1946-49; heart work cons. State Com. on Tb and Public Health, N.Y., 1949-52; program cons., exec. asst. Am. Heart Assn., 1952-64, asst. dir. affiliate relations and services, 1964-65, asst. dir. dept. councils and internat. program, 1965-70, asso. dir., 1970-73, asso. dir. div. sci. affairs, chief sci. councils, 1973-75. Recipient Gold Heart Bracelet in appreciation 10 yr. service Staff Conf. Heart Assn., 1962. Fellow Am. Public Health Assn.; mem. Phi Kappa Phi, Alpha Kappa Delta. Home: 58-B Calle Cadiz Laguna Hills CA 92653 also 1114 11th Ave Albany GA 31707

SCHOCH, JACQUELINE LOUISE, university official; b. DuBois, Pa., July 17, 1929; d. Horace Gordon and Cora (Wineberg) S.; B.Sc. in Health and Phys. Edn., Pa. State U., 1951, M.Ed. in Counseling and Psychology, 1960, D.Ed. in Counseling and Psychology, 1965; cert. Inst. Ednl. Mgmt., Harvard U., 1979. Tchr. girls' phys. edn. Jr.-Sr. High Sch., Ford City, Pa., 1951-52; tchr. girl's phys. edn., acad. U.S. history DuBois Area Sr. High Sch., 1952-56, girls' guidance counselor, 1956-65; dir. guidance DuBois Area Sch. Dist., 1965-67, dir. instrn., 1967-70; asst. dir. for resident instrn. DuBois campus Pa. State U., 1970-76, asso. dir. acad. affairs, 1976—, dir. DuBois campus, 1978-83, campus exec. officer, 1983—, also mem., chmn. univ. coms., faculty senate. Instr. polit. action courses local C. of C., 1963; instr. adult swimming classes local YMCA, 1953-55; instr. continuing edn. program Pa. State U., 1967-70, also asst. prof. edn., 1970—. Cons. Appalachia project, W.Va., 1967-68; mem. evaluating teams for evaluating secondary schs. Middle States Evaluation Com., 1960-62. Bd. dirs. DuBois area United Fund, co-chmn. fund raising campaign, 1967-68, 2d v.p., 1970—; bd. dirs. DuBois council Girl Scouts, 1954-56, Family Life Center-Luth. Services, 1972-76; treas. DuBois Ednl. Found., 1981—; bd. dirs. DuBois Area YMCA, Clearfield County Area Agy. on Aging; deacon United Ch. of Christ. Named Boss of Yr., Internat. Secs. Assn., 1977. Delta Mu Sigma, Delta Psi Omega, Iota Alpha Delta, Delta Kappa Gamma, Pi Lambda Theta, Phi Delta Kappa. Office: DuBois Campus Pa State U DuBois PA 15801

SCHOCKET, EVE, lawyer; b. Chgo., Apr. 18, 1938; d. Theodore and Sophie (Feldman) Kaplan; m. Lee I. Schocket, Oct. 30, 1960; children—Eric Neal, Luanne Elizabeth. B.S., U. Wis., 1958, M.S.W., 1960; J.D. with distinction, U. Ariz., 1977. Bar: Ariz., 1977. Psychiat. social worker, Wis., Colo., Ariz., 1958-65; lawyer State Ariz. Ct. of Appeals, Tucson, 1977-78, Rabinowitz & Dix, P.C., Tucson, 1978-79, ptnr. Kerry, Schocket & Dusenberry, Tucson, 1979—. Bd. dirs. Law Coll. Assos., U. Ariz., Tucson, 1983—; mem. bd. edn. Catalina Foothills Sch. Dist., Tucson, 1978-84, clk., 1981-82, pres., 1983. Mem. ABA, Ariz. State Bar, Pima County Bar, Ariz. Women Lawyers (pres. So. Ariz. chpt. 1985-86), Nat. Assn. Social Workers, LWV (bd. dirs. 1970-74), Exec. Women's Council. Home: 2815 E Cerrado Los Palitos Tucson AZ 85718 Office: Kerry Schocket & Dusenberry 2949 E Broadway Tucson AZ 85716

SCHOECK, PATRICIA HUGHES, publishing company executive; b. Norfolk, Va., Nov. 26, 1952; d. George Maurice and Sallie Epps (Moss) Hughes; m. Stephen Richard Schoeck, Aug. 17, 1974; children—William Meredith, Robert Hughes. B.A., Agnes Scott Coll., 1975. Grad. admission counselor Ga. Inst. Tech., Atlanta, 1974-75; sr. telemarketing rep. D.C. Heath & Co., Atlanta, 1975-84, coordinator sales services, Lexington, Mass., 1984—. Editor: Training and Procedures Manual, 1985. Lane Found. scholar, 1973. Republican. Episcopalian. Avocations: reading; cooking; needlework. Home: 13 Dennison St Waltham MA 02154 Office: DC Heath and Co 125 Spring St Lexington MA 02173

SCHOEN, JOAN ESTHER, municipal clerk, treasurer; b. Southampton, N.Y., Apr. 9, 1938; d. Reynold Nielson and Christine Joan (Remkus) Hulse; children—JoAnn, Deborah, Christine, Jon A. B.S. in Acctg. magna cum laude, Southampton Coll. L.I. U., 1981. Cert. mcpl. clk., Internat. Inst. Mcpl. Clks., 1983. Clk., treas. Village of Sag Harbor (N.Y.), 1971—. Treas., mem. Sag Harbor Community Band, 1956—; treas., v.p. Ladies Village Improvement Soc., 1980, 81, 83. Recipient scholarship Syracuse U., 1981-83. Mem. L.I. Clks. and Treas. Assn. (dir. 1983—), N.Y. State Fin. Officers Assn. (dir. 1983), N.Y. State Clks. Assn. (chmn. com. 1983). Mem. N.Y. State Assn. City and Village Clks., N.Y. State Soc. Mcpl. Fin. Officers, Internat. Inst. Mcpl. Clks., N.Y. State Assn. Mcpl. Purchasing Ofcls., Suffolk County Village Ofcls. Assn. Republican. Roman Catholic. Home: South Redwood Rd Sag Harbor NY 11963 Office: Village of Sag Harbor Main St PO Box 660 Sag Harbor NY 11963

SCHOENBERG, BARBARA, family therapist; b. N.Y.C., Aug. 3, 1931; d. Max and Mollie (Blazer) Zuckerman; m. Lawrence J. Schoenberg, June 24, 1956; children—Douglas, Eric, Julie. B.A., Bklyn. Coll., 1953; M.S.W., Boston U., 1955. Social worker Jewish Bd. Guardians, N.Y.C., 1956-59, Youth & Family Counseling, Westfield, N.J., 1963-70, Jewish Family Service, Elizabeth, N.J., 1970-77; pvt. practice family therapy, Berkeley Heights, N.J., 1977—. Mem. N.J. Assn. Women Therapists (newsletter editor 1984-85), Nat. Assn. Social Workers. Office: 310 Springfield Ave Berkeley Heights NJ 07922

SCHOENFELD, CLARE ANN, investment banker; b. Boston, Feb. 11, 1951; d. Richard John and Mary Julie (Carrigan) S. B.S.B.A. summa cum laude, Boston Coll., 1972; postgrad. Babson Coll., 1975. Systems analyst Exxon USA, Houston, 1972-74; fin. analyst Exxon Internat., N.Y.C., 1975-77; mgr. Arthur Andersen & Co., N.Y.C., 1977-79; mgr. info. systems planning and advanced tech. Am. Express Co., N.Y.C., 1979-82; chief exec. liaison Goldman Sachs & Co., N.Y.C., 1982—. Trustee, Boston Coll., 1980—. Mem. Manhattan Bus. Group (dir. 1976-84), Boston Coll. Club of N.Y. (advisor). Clubs: Toastmasters (treas. 1975-76). Home: 429 E 52nd St #24D New York NY 10022 Office: Goldman Sachs & Co 85 Broad St New York NY 10022

SCHOENWETTER, JANET LOREE, claims manager; b. Des Moines, Iowa, June 30, 1956; d. Wilbur Alfred and Margaret Loree (Audehelm) Musson; m. Randall Robert Schoenwetter, Aug. 14, 1976. Cert. in Fashion Mdsg., Patricia Stevens Career Coll., Milw. Claims processor Aetna Life and Casualty, Milw., 1977-79, sr. claims processor, 1979-80, claims specialist, 1980-81, auditor, trainer, 1981-82; claims supr. NBP Inc., Milw., 1982-85; claims mgr. Primecare Health Plan of Wis. Inc., Milw., 1985—; cons. NBP Inc., Milw., 1985—. Mem. Village of Elm Grove Artists, Wis., West Allis Art Alliance, Wis. Mem. Nat. Assn. Female Execs., Smithsonian Instn. Republican. Avocations: Painting; softball; swimming; fishing; sewing. Home: 204 S Hartwell Waukesha WI 53186 Office: 1233 N Mayfair Rd Milwaukee WI 53226

SCHOESSOW, DONNA KAY, tax and financial services company executive; b. Los Angeles, Mar. 25, 1943; d. Theodore Charles and Hildegarde Alice (Albrecht) Schoessow. Student Santa Monica City Coll., 1961-62, Fullerton Jr. Coll., 1963-65, Coll. of San Mateo, 1973-74, Cabrillo Coll., 1977-78. Lic. real estate salesman, Calif. Constrn. coordinator Walter Beeson & Assocs., Fullerton, Calif., 1965-70; coordinator partnership affairs Fox and Carskadon Fin., Menlo Park, Calif., 1972-74; dir. land acquisition and planning McKeon Constrn., San Mateo, Calif., 1975-78; systems coordinator Concordia Devel. Corp., San Bernardino, Calif., 1978-80; sec., gen. mgr. Vesper Corp., Downey, Calif., 1980—; corp. officer Elizabeth Gardens Homeowners Assn., Cudahy, Calif., 1982—. Author: To See or Not To See, 1982; editor: How To Become a Developer, 1983. Pres. Fish of Fullerton, 1983-86, v.p., 1986—; bd. dirs. Emergency Med. Info., Inc., Santa Ana, Calif. Mem. Nat. Assn. Women in Construction (corr. sec. 1979-80, pres. 1981-82, 85-86, dir. 1982-83, scholarship chmn. 1981-82, 85-86, chmn. profl. edn., 1979-81, chaplain 1982-83), Juvenile Diabetes Found. Republican. Lutheran. Home: 4237 E Alderdale Ave Anaheim CA 92807 Office: Vesper Corp 9625 Lakewood Blvd Downey CA 90240

SCHOFF, ANABEL RICHARDSON, dance company executive; b. Dubuque, Iowa, Oct. 31, 1935; d. Willard and Florence Lillian (White) Richardson; m. Leland Elton Schoff, Aug. 4, 1955; 1 child, Litzi Lyons. Student Rockford Coll., 1953-55; B.A., No. Ill. U., 1982. Mng. dir. Rockford Dance Co., Ill., 1983—. Pres. bd. dirs. Rockford YWCA, 1977-79, mem. fin. com., 1980—; mem. nominating com. Rock River Valley Council Girl Scouts U.S., 1984—, mem. long range camp devel. com., 1985, chmn. camp devel. implementation com., 1985—. Mem. Ken Rock Gem and Mineral Club, Rock River Valley Gem and Mineral Club, YWCA Met. Women's Network. Lodge: Eastern Star. Avocations: needlework; reading; traveling and camping; rock-hounding; theatre and concerts. Office: Rockford Dance Co 401 S Main St Rockford IL 61101

SCHOFIELD, BARBARA DAY, real estate investment company executive; b. Cleve., Jan. 21, 1949; d. Joseph James and Grace (Nemec) Day; m. John Bell Schofield, Aug. 16, 1969; children—Jennifer Tucker, Levi Franklin, Douglas Franklin IV. Corp. officer Mountain Air Inc., Ft. Collins, Colo., 1973—; mng. gen. ptnr. Schofield Family Partnership, Fort Collins, 1980—. Bd. dirs. Downtown Devel. Authority, Ft. Collins, 1981—, chmn., 1983-84, 85-86; bd. dirs. Ft. Collins Symphony, 1983-84. Mem. Ft. Collins Area C. of C. (bd. dirs. 1983—, v.p. 1986). Republican. Avocations: skiing; biking; hiking; art. Home: 1801 Lakeshore Circle Fort Collins CO 80525 Office: Schofield Family Partnership 323 S Coll Ave Suite 8 Fort Collins CO 80525

SCHOLL, CHERYL ANN, insurance company representative; b. Cleve., Feb. 20, 1950; d. Francis and Marjorie Florence (Fix) Stefanick; m. Edwin James Scholl, Mar. 1, 1975. Student Santa Fe Community Coll., Gainesville, Fla., 1969-70, St. Petersburg Jr. Coll., Fla., 1968-69. Casualty claim rep. Allstate Ins. Co., St. Petersburg, 1974-78; claims rep. State Farm Ins. Co., Gainesville, 1979-81, Allstate Ins. Co., Gainesville, 1981—. Mem. Nat. Assn. Female Execs. Avocations: reading, needlework, woodworking, travel. Home: Rural Route 2 Box 332 Fort White FL 32038 Office: Allstate Ins Co 1109 NW 13th St Gainesville FL 32601

SCHOLL, DEBRA LYNN, sales executive; b. Myrtle Point, Oreg., Sept. 29, 1956; d. Elsworth Leroy Nelson and Sandra Jean (Roberson) Nelson Elbert; m. Douglas Kent Scholl, Aug. 25, 1984. Student Chapman Coll., 1976-77, Saddleback Coll., 1980; teaching cert. J.R. Powers Trade Sch., 1978. Personnel asst. Chapman Coll., Orange, Calif., 1976-78; personnel asst. Kimstock, Inc., Santa Ana, Calif., 1978-79, sales rep., 1979-84, sales mgr. for So. Calif., 1984—. Active fund raising for City of Hope, Los Angeles, 1983—. Mem. The Exec. Female. Republican. Avocations: sewing, reading. Home: 24671 Sadaba Mission Viejo CA 92692 Office: Kimstock Inc 2200 S Yale St Santa Ana CA 92704

SCHOLL, JUDITH T. (LOIS), legal educator, high technology company executive, educator; b. N.Y.C., Nov. 2, 1949; d. Harry and Deena (Israel) Teitelbaum; m. Frederick William Scholl, May 23, 1978. B.A., SUNY-New Paltz, 1971; J.D., Bklyn. Law Sch., 1974; LL.M., NYU, 1979. Bar: N.Y. 1976, U.S. Dist. Ct. (so. dist.) N.Y. 1981. Assoc. prof. law Del. Law Sch., Wilmington, 1975-79; asst. div. mgr., contracts and services coordinator Optical Info. Systems, Exxon Enterprises, Inc., Elmsford, N.Y., 1977-79; v.p., gen. counsel, gen. mgr., dir. Codenoll Tech. Corp., Yonkers, N.Y., 1980-85; assoc. prof. Jacob D. Fuchsberg Law Ctr., Touro Coll. Sch. Law, N.Y.C., 1980—. Contbr. articles to profl. jours. Mem. ABA, Order of Barristers, Phi Alpha Delta. Home: 2575 Palisade Ave Riverdale NY 10463

SCHOLL, PRISCILLA IRENE, nursing administrator; b. Amherst, Wis., Mar. 17, 1925; d. Charles Gerald and Lydia Francis (Schrader) Shanklin; grad. Deaconess Hosp. Sch. Nursing, 1946; student Milw. Tech. Coll., 1957-58, U. Wis., Milw., 1958-71; B.S. in Health Arts, Coll. of St. Francis, 1981; m. Robert Philip Scholl, May 22, 1948; children—Judith Ann, Susan. Staff nurse Deaconess Hosp., Milw., 1946-49, staff nurse circulating evenings, 1956-57, asst. clin. instr. and nursing service supr., 1957-64, inservice supr., 1964-67, supr. and instr. of renal program, 1966—; guest lectr. on renal failure to various nursing orgns. and lay orgns., 1970-78. Bd. dirs. Kidney Found. of Wis., 1973—, mem. med. and sci. com., 1973—, patient services com., 1971-75, chmn., 1974-75. Mem. Am. Nurses Assn., Am. Assn. Nephrology Nurses and Technicians (organizer Wis. chpt. 1978, pres. 1985-86), Network 13 (sec.-treas. exec. com. 1984-86). Pioneer in nephrology nursing. Office: Good Samaritan Med Ctr 2000 W Kilbourn Ave Milwaukee WI 53233

SCHOLTZ, ELIZABETH, botanical garden administrator; b. Pretoria, South Africa, Apr. 29, 1921; came to U.S., 1960, naturalized, 1978; d. Tielman Johannes and Vera Vogel (Roux) Roos-Scholtz; B.Sc., Witwatersrand U., 1941; D.H.L., Pace U., 1974; D.Sc., L.I. U., 1981. Technician, South African Inst. Med. Research, Johannesburg, 1942-44; technician dept. medicine, Johannesburg and Pretoria gen. hosps., 1944-46; with Groote Schuur Hosp., Capetown, as technician charge student labs., 1948-52, technician charge hematology lab., 1952-60; mem. staff Bklyn. Bot. Garden, 1960—, asso. curator instrn., 1964-71, acting dir., 1972-73, dir., 1973-80, v.p., 1980—; trustee Independence Savs. Bank. Recipient Arthur Hoyt Scott Garden and Horticulture award, 1981. Mem. Am. Hort. Soc., Am. Assn. Bot. Gardens and Arboreta (dir. 1976-79). Clubs: Brooklyn Heights Casino, Cosmopolitan. Office: 1000 Washington Ave Brooklyn NY 11225

SCHOLTZ, EVELYN, medical technologist, educator; b. Paterson, N.J., Aug. 17, 1943; d. Frank and Stephanie (Malinkiewicz) S.; A.S. in Chem. Tech., Fairleigh Dickinson U., 1963, B.S. in Med. Tech., 1965; M.A. in Biology, St. Joseph Coll., 1970; M.S. in Health Care Mgmt., Hartford Grad. Center, 1983; M.B.A., Rensselaer Poly. Inst., 1984. Med. technologist bacteriology lab. Hartford (Conn.) Hosp., 1965-67, supr. serology-microscopy lab., 1967-68; edn. coordinator med. lab. asst. program, 1968-71, program dir. lab. edn. Sch. Allied Health, 1979—; mgr. microbiology lab. Hartford Hosp., 1986—; adj. faculty mem. U. Conn., Storrs, West Conn. State Coll., Danbury, U. Bridgeport (Conn.), St. Joseph Coll., West Hartford, Conn. Bd. dirs. Cromwell Hills Assn., 1974-77. T. Stewart Hamilton fellow, 1976. Mem. Conn. Soc. Med. Tech., Am. Soc. Med. Tech., AAUW. Contbr. articles to profl. publs. Home: 29 Margo Ct Cromwell CT 06416 Office: 80 Seymour St Hartford CT 06115

SCHOOLEY, DOLORES HARTER, artist manager; b. Nora Springs, Iowa, May 2, 1905; d. Amil A. and Elizabeth (Sefert) Zemke; m. Leslie J. Harter, June 5, 1934 (dec. 1963); m. Charles Earl Schooley, Apr. 1, 1966. B.E., B.A., U. Colo., 1927; M.A., Northwestern U., 1931. Tchr. high sch. Consol. Schs., Johnstown, Colo., 1927-28, Byers, Colo., 1928-29, Clayton, Mo., 1931-34; theatrical makeup, 1937—; instr. theatrical makeup, dramatic clubs, N.J. Theatre League; lectr., demonstrator theatrical makeup, dramatic and women's clubs, high schs., N.J. and N.Y. area, 1937-53; dir., entertainer mil. posts First Army, 1951-53; dir. mil. project Phi Beta, 1951-61, nat. officer, mem. nat. council, 1956-61, cons. radio broadcast series WNYC, 1962-65; dir. community relations Wingspread Summer Theatre, Colon, Mich., 1955; co-chmn. Valley Shore Community Concerts, Conn., 1958-61; artist mgr., 1959—; chmn. benefit ball Sharon Hosp., 1970; founder, pres. Berkshire Hills Music and Dance Assn., 1970-78; mem. Music Mountain Corp., Falls Village, Conn., 1975-81. Trustee Sharon Creative Arts Found., 1970-73; hon. trustee Bar Harbor Festival, 1968—; founder, pres. Wingspread Found., 1977—. Mem. Alpha Omicron Pi, Phi Beta. Congregationalist. Clubs: Montclair (N.J.) Dramatic (chmn. makeup, instr. makeup); Rehearsal (program chmn.); Women's (dir. plays, chmn. drama dept.) (Glen Ridge, N.J.); Sharon Women's, Sharon Republican Women's (pres. 1982-85), Sharon Country (Conn.); Metropolitan (N.Y.C.). Address: 204 West Lake Summit Dr Winter Haven FL 33880 also 10 Moland Dr Etowah NC 28729

SCHOOLS, ANNA LOUISE, town official; b. Littleton, Maine, May 17, 1915; d. Thomas Allen and Hannah Teresa (Rugan) Schools. Student public schs. Houlton, Maine. Town mgr. City of Littleton, Maine, 1945—, collector, treas., 1943—, town clk., 1944—. Mem. Maine Town and City Mgrs. Assn. Democrat. Roman Catholic. Clubs: So. Aroostook Campers (past pres.), Sno-Rovers Inc. (sec. treas.). Avocation: Camping. Home: 3 Watson Ave Houlton MA 04730 Office: Town Littleton RFD 1 Box 70 Monticello ME 04760

SCHOON, DORIS VIVIEN, ophthalmologist; b. Luverne, Minn., Dec. 31, 1928; d. Jacob and Esther Viola (Hansen) S. B.A., U. Minn., 1950, M.D., 1954. Intern, Kings County Hosp., Bklyn., 1954-55; physician Embudo Presbyterian Hosp. (N. Mex.), 1955-57; resident in clin. pathology U. Colo. Med. Ctr., Denver, 1957-58; gen. practice medicine, Anaheim, Calif., 1958-61; resident in ophthalmology Los Angeles Eye and Ear Hosp. at Hollywood Presbyn. Hosp., 1961-64; practice medicine specializing in ophthalmology, Anaheim, 1965-75; dir. Electrophysiology Lab. of Ophthalmology Dept. U. Calif., Irvine, 1978—. Research in field of using fast random stimuli to obtain electroretinograms and visually evoked potentials. Diplomat Am. Bd. Ophthalmology. Fellow Am. Acad. Ophthalmology and Otolaryngology; mem. Am. Women's Med. Assn., N.Y. Acad. Scis., Internat. Soc. Clin. Electroretinography in Vision. Republican. Presbyterian. Lodge: Order Eastern Star. Office: 19732 MacArthur Blvd Irvine CA 92715

SCHOR, MARY ANN MCCARTHY (MRS. WARREN SCHOR), public relations exec.; b. Washington; d. Jeremiah John and Ann (Horstkamp) McCarthy; grad. George Washington U., 1962, grad. publ. specialist program, 1977; EPS Program, Trinity Coll., 1982; m. Warren Schor, May 2, 1964; 1 dau., Elizabeth Ann. Public relations, various accounts, Washington, 1962-66; dir. public relations program Met. Police Dept., Washington, 1966-69; public relations D.C. Dept. Public Health, Washington, 1979-70, D.C. Police Dept., Washington, 1970-75; public relations cons., 1976—. Mem. public relations com. D.C. Tb and Respiratory Disease Assn., 1969—. Mem. Am. Newspaper Women's Club (treas. 1982-83), Advt. Club Washington, Zonta. Roman Catholic. Editor: Rambling thru Georgetown, 1978-80; Rambling thru Alexandria, 1978-80. Home: 6206 Wedgewood Rd Bethesda MD 20034

SCHOR, OLGA SEEMANN, mental health counselor, real estate broker; b. Havana, Cuba, Mar. 2, 1951; came to U.S., 1961; d. Olga del Carmen (Hernandez) S.; m. David Michael Schor, Apr. 22, 1979; 1 child, Andrew. A.A., Miami Dade Community Coll., 1971; B.A., U. Fla.-Gainesville, 1973; M.Edn., U. Miami, Fla., 1976; Psy.D., Nova U., 1981; cert. Bert Rodgers Sch. Real Estate, Miami, 1981. Lic. mental health counselor; lic. real estate salesperson. Teaching asst. U. Fla., Gainesville, 1972-73; counselor U. Miami, Fla., 1974-79; assoc. psychotherapist Linda H. Jamrozy & Assocs., Miami, 1976-78, Interactive Systems, Miami, 1978-79; psychometrist Jackson Meml. Hosp., Miami, 1978-79; assoc. psychotherapist Behavioral Medicine Inst., Miami, 1979-85, Tony Ciminero & Assocs., Miami, 1985—; lectr. U. Miami, 1976-78, Jackson Meml. Hosp. Sch. Nursing, Miami, 1976; real estate broker The Keyes Co. Realtor, Coral Gables, 1981—; sec./treas. bd. dirs. BODS Inc., Miami. Mem. Am. Psychol. and Guidance Assn., Keyes Comml. Roundtable, Coral Gables Bd. Realtors, Dade County Mental Health Assn. Club: South Fla. Sailing Assn. (Miami). Avocations: sailing; diving; reading; running; theater; acting; tennis. Office: 5975 Sunset Dr Suite 601 Miami FL 33143

SCHORNACK-SMITH, JUDITH ANN, lawyer; b. Detroit, Aug. 13, 1953; d. Harold Albert and Mary Julia (Garavaglia) Schornack; m. Christopher John Smith, June 9, 1979. B.A. with distinction, U. Mich.-Dearborn, 1976; J.D., Wayne State U., 1981. Bar: Mich. 1982. Claims analyst Washington Nat. Ins. Co., Southfield, Mich., 1973-75; intern office of state rep. Jeffrey Padden, 1976, 16th Dist. Ct. Probation Dept., State of Mich., 1976; sec., bookkeeper State Rehab. Services Livonia, Mich., 1976-77; adminstrv. asst. Pres.'s Office, U. Detroit, 1977-81; legal asst. Office of City Atty., Royal Oak, Mich., 1981-82; in-house counsel Plymouth Indsl. Ctr. (Mich.), 1982-84; atty. Jaques Admiralty Law Firm, P.C., Detroit, 1985—; advisor U. Mich. Dearborn Polit. Internship Alumni Adv. Council, 1977-84. Precinct del. Democratic Party, Redford Twp., Mich., 1976. Mem. ABA, Mich. Bar Assn., Detroit Bar Assn. Democrat. Roman Catholic. Clubs: Wolverine (news editor 1983), Polit. Awareness (sec. 1975-76). Home: 16693 Pomona Dr Redford Twp MI 48240 Office: 1370 Penobscot Bldg Detroit MI 48226

SCHORNSTEIN, FLORENCE WEILAND, city official, civic worker; b. New Orleans, Aug. 8, 1934; d. Aubrey August and Fannie (Kahn) Weiland; m. Richard Schornstein, Sept. 3, 1955; children—Susan Schornstein Piper, Wendy Schornstein Good, Ellen Schornstein Williams. B.A., Newcomb Coll., 1956. Adminstrv. asst. New Orleans City Council, 1974-80; cons. Sup. Ct. La., 1980; supt. Parkway and Park Commn. City of New Orleans, 1982—; speaker in field. Mem. exec. com. City of New Orleans Human Relations Com.; founder, mem. exec. com. Children's Arts Council; officer Dryades St. YMCA, New Orleans; bd. dirs. Jewish Fedn. Greater New Orleans; bd. dirs., nat. v.p. Nat. Council Jewish Women, pres. Greater New Orleans sect. and so. dist., chmn. Nat. Fund Raising and Fin. Devel.; bd. dirs. Jewish Family Service, Family Service Soc., Jewish Endowment Found., La. Nature and Sci. Ctr., Ind. Women's Orgn., United Way, Touro Infirmary. Recipient Bicentennial award YWCA, 1976; Hannah G. Solomon award Nat. Council Jewish Women, 1979; Women Achievers award Women's Career Council, 1983; Israel Bonds Jerusalem City of Peace award, 1985; Weiss award NCCJ, 1985. Mem. Nat. Recreation and Park Assn., Urban Parks and Recreation Alliance, Phi Beta Kappa. Democrat. Avocations: swimming, walking, reading, music. Home: 1679 Soniat St New Orleans LA 70115 Office: Parkway and Park Commn 2829 Gentilly Blvd New Orleans LA 70122

SCHORR, BEVERLY HELEN, counselor; b. Phila., Aug. 23, 1934; d. Isadore and Anne (Greber) Rubin; m. David Jay Schorr, Aug. 31, 1952; children—Alan, Michael, Steven, Devra. B.A., Villanova U., 1975, M.A., 1977. Dir. adult programs Villanova U., Pa., 1976-83; treas. D.J.S. Assocs., Inc., Abington, Pa., 1982—; salesperson Milton Levy Real Estate. Chmn. Lower Southampton Commn., Trevose, Pa., 1978-83; bd. dirs. Beth Sholom Synagogue Sisterhood. Mem. Am. Conf. Higher Edn., Am. Edn. Assn., AAUW, Am. Personnel and Guidance Assn., Nat. Assn. Women Deans, Adminstrs., Counselors (Nat. directorate for continuing edn. 1981-83), Phila. Women's Network, Bus. and Profl. Women's Assn. Office: 1603 Old York Dr Abington PA 19001

SCHOTTENSTEIN, DIANE STEINBERG, lawyer; b. N.Y.C., June 13, 1957; d. Max and Shirley (Minaker) Steinberg; m. Edwin Michael Schottenstein, Oct. 16, 1983. B.S., Cornell U., 1978; J.D., NYU, 1981, LL.M. in Taxation, 1986. Bar: N.Y. 1982, U.S. Dist. Ct. (so. and ea. dists.) N.Y. 1982, N.J. 1983, Fla. 1983, U.S. Tax Ct. 1985. Clk., N.Y. Pub. Library, N.Y.C., 1975; banking clk. Lincoln First Internat. Bank, N.Y.C., 1976; advt. asst. Fairchild Publs., N.Y.C., 1978; law clk. N.Y.C. Dept. Health Adminstrv. Tribunal, N.Y.C., 1979; law clk. Citicorp, N.Y.C., 1979-81; assoc. atty. Matays Hughes & Brown, N.Y.C., 1981-86; assoc. atty. Law Offices of Arthur I. Frankel, P.C., N.Y.C., 1986—; intern N.Y. State Office Lt. Gov., Albany, 1977. Trustee Brooklyn Heights Synagogue. Mem. ABA, Assn. Bar City of N.Y., Bklyn. Women's Bar Assn., Bus. Women's Golf Assn. Phi Kappa Phi. Jewish. Home: 27 Grace Ct Apt 11 Brooklyn Heights NY 11201 Office: Law Offices of Arthur I Frankel PC 110 E 59th St New York NY 10022

SCHOTZKO, JUDITH GILBERT, nurse, lawyer; b. Rosiclare, Ill., Nov. 19, 1938; d. Maurice Clement and Naomi (Kibler) Gilbert; R.N., St. Luke's Sch. Nursing, 1959; B.A., Met. State U., 1977; J.D., U. Minn., 1980; m. John Rudolph Schotzko, July 16, 1963; children—Clay John, Jonna Marie, Molly Ann, Lee Gilbert. Surg. and psychiat. nurse, U. Minn. Hosp., Mpls., 1959-65; research asst. U. Minn. Law Sch., Mpls., 1979-80; admitted to Minn. bar, 1981; asso. firm Frundt, Frundt & Johnson, Blue Earth, Minn., 1980-82; pvt. practice law, Blue Earth, 1982—; mem. Minn. Ethical Practice Bd., 1980—, chmn., 1982-83; sec.-treas. Nat. Council on Govtl. Ethics Laws, 1982-83, chmn., 1983-84. Pres., Minn., Mental Health Assn., 1975-76, nat. bd. dirs. 1976-82, nat. regional v.p., 1981-82; chmn. Faribault County Rep. Party, 1972-77, alt. del. nat. conv., 1976. Recipient Blue Earth Women of Achievement award, 1973; Vol. of Yr. award Minn. Mental Health Assn., 1976. Mem. Minn. Student Nurses Assn. (v.p. 1958), Minn. Student Bar Assn., Minn. Bar Assn., Faribault County Bar Assn. (pres. 1985-86), 17th Jud. Dist. Bar Assn. (sec. 1985-86). Clubs: Med. Aux. Minn. Med. Student Wives (pres. 1966-67), Blue Earth Valley Med. Aux., Nat. Med. Student Wives (sec. 1967-68), Am. Legion Aux., Mitchell Chautaqua Circle. Home: Route 1 PO Box 42 Blue Earth MN 56013 Office: 223 S Main St Blue Earth MN 56013

SCHOWENGERDT, PEGGY DIANE, business systems consultant; b. Altus, Okla., Oct. 20, 1955; d. James Marshall and June (Heacock) Gosa. Diploma in Acctg., Oklahoma State Tech., 1976, A.A. in Acctg., 1980; student U. Tex., 1984—. Budget analyst Control & SW Corp., 1976-84; programmer analyst Mary Kay Cosmetics, Dallas, 1984-85; tech. cons. CIGNA Systems, Dallas, 1985—. Mem. Republican Nat. Com. Mem. Data Processing Mgmt. Assn. (chmn. attendance com. 1982-83), Nat. Assn. Female Execs. Office: CIGNA Systems 4115 Keller Springs Rd Suite 200 Dallas TX 75234

SCHRADE, ROLANDE MAXWELL YOUNG, composer, pianist, educator; b. Washington, Sept. 13; d. Harry Robert and Isabelle Martha (Maxwell) Young; pupil Harold Bauer, N.Y.C., Vittorio Giannini; student Manhattan Sch. Music, Juilliard Sch. Music; m. Robert Warren Schrade, Dec. 21, 1949; children—Robelyn, Rhonda Lee, Rolisa, Randolph, Rorianne. Debut as concert pianist Town Hall, N.Y.C., 1953, Nat. Gallery, Washington, 1954; founder, dir. ann. performances Sevenars Concerts, Inc., Worthington, Mass., 1968—, music dir., 1975—, also broadcasts, 1984, 85; recitalist radio sta. WGMS-FM, Washington; mem. music faculty Allen-Stevenson Sch., N.Y.C., 1968—; v.p., treas. Sevenars Music House, Inc., N.Y.C., 1968—. Concerts include Lincoln Ctr., 1980, Serenar's Concerts, Inc., annual music festival, Worthington, Mass., tour, N.Z., 1982, 84; appearances PM Mag., TV, 1980, 81. Mem. ASCAP, DAR (Bicentennial award 1972), Mut. Artists Mgmt. Alliance (founder, bd. dirs.). Episcopalian. Composer, pub. and recorded over 100 songs, most recent being album America 76; editor: songs of Carrie Jacobs Bond, Boston Music Co., 1958. Home and office: 30 E End Ave New York NY 10028 also Sevenars Worthington MA 01098

SCHRAG, JUDITH LANELLE, county official; b. Richland, Wash., Sept. 12, 1949; d. Thomas Francis and Esther Lola (Leavell) Walsh; student Columbia Basin Coll., Pasco, Wash., 1967-68, 74-75; M. Vernon Duane Schrag; Feb. 25, 1984. children—Gary William, Tamara Lynn, Rebecca Anne. Police, fire and emergency med. dispatcher City of Richland, 1972-75, 76-77; dep. sheriff, Franklin County Sheriff's Office, 1975-76; dir. Benton County Emergency Dispatch Center, Kennewick, Wash., 1977—; instr. Wash. Tng. Commn., Wash. Assn. Fire Chiefs; trustee, chmn. communications Mid-Columbia Emergency Med. Services Council. Mem. Assn. Public Safety Communication Officers (chpt. pres. 1979-81, nat. exec. com. 1981-82), Tri-Cities Mycol. Soc., Am. Mus. Natural History (assoc.), Nat. Assn. Female Execs., Wash. State Snowmobile Assn., Blue Mountain Snowmobile Assn., Order Eagles. Clubs: Altrusa, Finley Saddle. Office: PO Box 6108 Kennewick WA 99336

SCHRAGER, MINDY RAE, business executive; b. Paterson, N.J., Jan. 18, 1958; d. Julius Maxwell and Miriam (Max) S. Student Middlebury Coll., 1977, Inst. European Studies, Nantes, France, 1977-78; B.A., Dickinson Coll., 1979; M.B.A., Babson Coll., 1981. Cons., Nolan Norton & Co., Lexington, Mass., 1981-86; mgr. sales support Logos Corp., Wellesley, Mass., 1986—. Mem. Nat. Assn. Female Execs., Am. Mgmt. Assn. Avocations: reading; travel; sewing; needlepoint; music. Home: 135 Bedford St Burlington MA 01803

SCHRALL, LINDA ANNE, medical technologist, air force officer; b. Pitts., Apr. 11, 1960; d. Kenneth Joseph and Mary Ann (Urschler) S. B.S., Gannon U., 1982; M.S., U. Ark., 1986. Med. technologist Montefiore Hosp., Pitts., 1982-84; comm. 2d lt. U.S. Air Force, 1983; missile launch officer, Little Rock, 1984-86, med. technologist, 1986—. Vol. ARC, Little Rock, 1985—, Vol. Income Tax Assistance Program, Little Rock, 1986. Mem. Air Force Assn., Nat. Assn. Female Execs., Am. Soc. Clin. Pathologists (cert.). Republican. Roman Catholic. Avocations: gourmet cooking; aerobics; motorcycles; Miniature Schnauzer breeding. Home: 126 Lonsdale Circle Jacksonville AR 72076

SCHRAM, ELIZABETH JEAN, transportation executive; b. Chgo., Jan. 23, 1925; d. George Love and Lucile (Harris) Love Moeller; m. Robert Joseph Schram, Nov. 17, 1948; children—Margaret Jean, Ellen Louise, Paul Thaddeus. Student Ind. U.-Ft. Wayne, 1973-76. Vice pres., chief exec. officer Ft. Wayne All States, 1962-76; pres., chief exec. officer Gulf So. Services, Ft. Wayne and Tampa, Fla., 1976-84; v.p. Truck Maintenance, Inc., Ft. Wayne, 1979-85; regional mgr. Transport Drivers, Inc., Bensenville, Ill., 1984-85. Active Limberlost council Girl Scouts U.S.A., 1935-85; bd. dirs. St. Francis Coll., Ft. Wayne, 1980-84. Mem. Driver Leasing Council Am. (pres. 1974-76), Pvt. Carrier Conf., Pvt. Truck Council, Ont. Geneal. Soc. Roman Catholic. Clubs: Summit, Olympia (Ft. Wayne). Avocations: genealogy; gourmet cooking. Home: 515 E Washington Center Rd Fort Wayne IN 46825 Office: Transport Drivers Inc 4640 Speedway Dr Fort Wayne IN 46825

SCHRAMM, VERA MINELLI, member mental health center staff; b. East Chicago, Ind., June 7, 1934; d. Leonard Anthony and Jennie Marie (Crispi) M.; m. Kenneth Eugene Schramm, Oct. 23, 1954; children—Linda, Douglas, Diane, Anita. Sec. to registrar Purdue U., Hammond, Ind., 1952-55; vol. coordinator Riverbend Ctr. for Mental Health, Florence, Ala., 1972-78, coordinator community relations, 1978—, adminstrv. coordinator cardiac rehabs., 1982—, fin. counselor, 1984—; chairperson Ala. Council of Consultation and Edn. Dirs., 1982; mem. adv. com. Midsouth Home Health, Florence, 1983-84. Bd. dirs. council Roman Catholic Parish, Tuscumbia, Ala., 1982-85; agy. mem. United Way of Shoals, Florence, 1983-84; chairperson council Florence Community Services, 1984. Mem. Muscle Shoals Advt. Fedn. (Addy for excellence in advt. 1982, 83, bd. dirs. 1983-84). Republican. Clubs: Arlithom Study (pres. 1970-71), Inclusive Study (pres. 1974) (Sheffield, Ala.). Home: 108 Rivermont Dr Sheffield AL 35660 Office: Riverbend Ctr for Mental Health 635 W College St Florence AL 35631

SCHREIBER, EILEEN SHER, artist; b. Denver; d. Michael Herschel and Sarah Deborah (Tannenbaum) Sher; student U. Utah, 1942-45, N.Y.U. extension, 1966-68, Montclair (N.J.) State Coll., 1975-79; also pvt. art study; m. Jonas Schreiber, Mar. 27, 1945; children—Jeffrey, Barbara, Michael. Exhibited Morris Mus. Arts and Scis., Morristown, N.J., 1965-73, N.J. State Mus., 1969, Lever House, N.Y.C., 1971, Paramus (N.J.) Mus., 1973, Newark Mus., 1978, Am. Water Color Soc., Audubon Artists, N.A.D. Gallery, N.Y.C., Pallazzo Vecchio Florence (Italy); represented in permanent collections Morris Mus., Seton Hall U., Bloomfield (N.J.) Coll., Barclay Bank of Eng., N.J., Somerset Coll., NYU, Morris County State Coll., Broad Nat. Bank, Newark, IBM, Am. Telephone Co., RCA, Johnson & Johnson, Champion Internat. Paper Co., SONY, Mitzubichi, Data Control, Sperry Univac, Ga. Pacific Co., Public Service Co. N.J., others; also pvt. collections. Recipient awards N.J. Watercolor Soc., 1969, 72, Nat. Assn. Women Artists, 1970; 1st award in watercolor Hunterdon Art Center, 1972, Best in Show award Short Hills State Show, 1976, Tri-State Purchase award Somerset Coll., 1977, numerous others. Mem. Nat. Assn. Women Artists (chmn. watercolor jury; Collage award 1983), Nat., N.J. artists equity, Nat. Painter and Sculptors Assn., Hunterdon Art Center. Home: 22 Powell Dr West Orange NJ 07052 Office: Reece Galleries 24 W 57th St New York NY 10019 also Pason-Weisberg Gallery 822 Madison Ave New York NY 10021 also Dumont Landis Gallery New Brunswick NJ

SCHREIBER, FLORA RHETA, theatre arts and speech specialist, author, educator; b. N.Y.C., Apr. 24, 1918; d. William and Esther (Aaronson) Schreiber; B.S., Columbia, 1938, M.A., 1939; certificate Central Sch. Speech Tng. and Dramatic Art, U. London, 1937, N.Y. U. Radio Workshop, 1942. Instr., speech and dramatic art dept. Bklyn. Coll., 1944-46; creator-producer Bklyn. Coll. Radio Forum on WNYC, N.Y.C., 1944-46; drama critic Players mag., 1941-46; instr. Exeter Coll., U. Southwest, Eng., 1937; asst. prof. speech and dramatic arts dept. Adelphi Coll., Garden City, L.I., 1947-53, dir.

radio-TV div. Center Creative Arts, 1948-51; lectr. New Sch. Social Research, 1952—, now prof. English and speech, John Jay Coll. Criminal justice; mem. lecture circuit Brown U., Boston U., St. John's U., Oxford U., Yale U., others. Cornelia Otis Skinner scholar, 1937. Mem. AAUP, AAUW, Speech Assn. Am., ANTA, Speech Assn. Eastern States, Am. Soc. Journalists and Authors (sec. 1963, v.p. 1972-73, 75-76), Authors League Am. Author: Wm. Schuman (biography), 1954; Your Child's Speech, 1956; Jobs With a Future in Law Enforcement, 1970; Sybil, 1973 (pub. in 17 countries); The Shoemaker, 1983 (pub. in 7 countries); also short stories, plays, opera libreti and art songs. Contbr. nat. mags. including Cosmopolitan, Reader's Digest, Good Housekeeping, The Freeman, Redbook, Mademoiselle, Am. Mercury, N.Y. Times, Quar. of Film, Radio, and Television, Family Weekly, Today's Health, Woman's Day, others; formerly psychiatry editor Sci. Digest; columnist Bell-McClure, United Features, N.Y. Times Spl. Features. Producer radio forum on Community Theater for NBC, 1949; numerous radio and TV appearances in U.S., Can., London, Edinburgh. Office: John Jay Coll of Criminal Justice City U NY 444 W 56th St New York NY 10019

SCHREIBER, H. STEPHANIE, insurance representative; b. Akron, Ohio, Oct. 4, 1954; d. Steve Stanley and Wilma Eve (Mahalko) S. B.S. in Bus. Adminstrn. magna cum laude, U. Akron, 1976. Sales rep. Gen. Electric Co., Mpls., 1976-78; home office rep. Northwestern Nat. Life Ins. Co., Mpls., 1978, group field rep., Houston, 1978-82, sr. group field rep., 1982-84; account exec. Conn. Gen. Life Ins. Co., Cleve., 1984—. Mem. membership com. Encorps—Symphony Support Group, Houston, 1982—; active Mus. Fine Arts, Houston. Recipient Key award, Sales and Mktg. Execs. award. Mem. Mortar Board, Beta Gamma Sigma, Omicron Delta Epsilon. Phi Chi Theta.

SCHREIBER, VIRGINIA ANN, health care furnishings company executive, consultant; b. St. Louis, Feb. 23, 1946; d. Robert Hume and Josie May (Pence) Thompson; m. Don Merrill Schreiber, Dec. 26, 1967 (div. 1976). Student Western Mich. U., 1964-66, Mich. State U., 1966-67; B.A., U. Iowa, 1969. Buyer, Chittenden & Eastman Co., Burlington, Iowa, 1970-76; dist. mgr. Amedco Contract, Inc., St. Louis, 1977-82, regional mgr., 1982-84, v.p. nat. accounts, 1984-85; v.p. sales H. Robert Shampaine, Inc., St. Louis, 1986—. Big Sister, Marygrove Sch., St. Louis, 1979-80; mem. Women's Polit. Caucus, Metro St. Louis Women's Polit. Caucus. Recipient Million Dollar Sales award, Amedco Contract, Inc., 1980, 81, 82, Amedco Exec. Officer ring, 1984. Mem. AAUW, Nat. Assn. Female Execs., Am. Health Care Assn. (affiliate). Presbyterian. Avocations: Entertaining; concerts; films; plays; skiing; swimming; walking; racquetball; travel. Office: H Robert Shampaine Inc 3100 Gravois Saint Louis MO 63118

SCHREIBER-GARZA, ADRIA ANITA, power company executive; b. Tucson, Oct. 9, 1958; d. Paul Robert and Elizabeth Antoinette (Leich) Schreiber; m. Ricardo Aristeo Garza, July 12, 1980. B.S. in Edn., U. Tex., 1980. Load research analyst Central Power & Light Co., Corpus Christi, Tex., 1981-86, mgr. load research, 1986—. Mem. Nat. Assn. Female Execs. Avocations: Costume design; writing. Office: Central Power & Light Co 120 N Chapparal PO Box 2121 Corpus Christi TX 78403

SCHREINER, BEVERLY ETHEL, medical transcriptionist; b. Spokane, Wash., Dec. 7, 1931; d. Charlie P. and M. Jerrine (Cannon) Nolasco; m. George J. Schreiner, Feb. 4, 1951 (div. Feb. 1961); children—Michael, David, Judy. Student Franklin Hosp. Sch. Nursing, 1951, San Francisco City Coll., 1953, Am. Inst. Banking, San Francisco. Certified med. transcriptionist. Sec. Darrell Kammer, M.D., Nampa, Idaho, 1967-73; supr. med. records Idaho State Sch. and Hosp., Nampa, 1966-75; self-employed med. transcriptionist, Nampa, 1984—; med. sec. Caldwell Internal Medicine, Idaho, 1976—; supr. evening shift med. records office Mercy Med. Ctr., Nampa, 1967—. Mem. Nat. Assn. Med. Transcriptionists, Idaho Assn. Med. Transcriptionists. Mem. Coll. Ch. of the Nazarene. Avocations: reading; sewing; ceramics; grandma. Home: 320 Nectarine St Nampa ID 83651 Office: Mercy Med Ctr 1512 12th Ave Rd Nampa ID 83651 also Caldwell Internal Medicine 222 E Elm St Caldwell ID 83605

SCHREINER, KATHY JANE, retail clothing executive; b. N.Y.C., Sept. 16, 1953; d. Ernest and Ruth (Schnurmann) Schreiner. Student Stern Coll.-Yeshiva U., 1971-72; cert. NYU Inst. Retailing, 1978; postgrad. Fashion Inst. Tech., 1978—. Asst. buyer-ladies S. Klein's, N.Y.C., 1972; asst. buyer-menswear Steinbach's, Asbury Park, N.J., 1972-75; asst. mgr. Hit or Miss, Toms River, N.J., 1975; assoc. buyer menswear Feldman/Wechsler, Toms River, 1975-76; buyer menswear Clothiers Corp., N.Y.C., 1976-79, David Atkind Assocs., N.Y.C., 1979-80; buyer, owner KJS Enterprises, N.Y.C., 1980-85; exhibit coordinator Nat. Assn. Men's Sportswear Buyers, N.Y.C., 1982—. Contbr. articles on retailing to profl. jours. Active Jewish Nat. Fund, United Jewish Assn.-Young Leadership. Mem. Nat. Assn. Female Execs. Home: 305 West End Ave New York NY 10023 Office: NAMSB 535 Fifth Ave New York NY 10017

SCHREYER-THOMSON, CAMELLA JOY, artist, editor, corporate executive; b. Lawrence, Kans., July 17, 1949; d. George Maurice and Camella Inez (Burnette) Schreyer; B.A. cum laude, Pfeiffer Coll., 1971; M.A., East Carolina U., 1974; research studies Europe and Gt. Britain; m. Douglas Arthur Thomson, May 6, 1973. One-woman shows: Allas Art Galleries, Charlotte, N.C., 1971, Pfeiffer Coll. Gallery, 1975, 79; group shows include: Durham (N.C.) Art Guild, Fayetteville (N.C.) Mus. Art, Shooren's, Rockport, Mass., East Carolina U.; represented in permanent collection Pfeiffer Coll., also pvt. collections; editor-in-chief Am. Biog. Inst., Raleigh, N.C., 1973—; class agt. Pfeiffer Coll. Alumni Assn., 1976—. Mem. citizens adv. council Am. Inst. Cancer Research. Cert. tchr. kindergarten through 9th grades, N.C. Mem. Am. Fedn. Arts, Nat. League Am. Pen Women, Stanly County Art Guild, Durham Arts Council, Nat. Wildlife Assn., Raleigh C. of C., Raleigh Bus. and Profl. Women, Societe Suisse de Phaleristique (hon.), Order Sundiae, Phi Delta Sigma. Methodist. Contbr. poems to lit. jours.; art editor The Phoenix of Pfeiffer Coll., also various annuals. Address: 5436 Pine Top Circle Raleigh NC 27612

SCHROCK, JANET MARIE MOREHOUSE, interior designer; b. Carlisle, Pa., June 30, 1942; d. Harley Francis and Helen Elizabeth (Kitzmiller) Morehouse; B.S., Indiana U. of Pa., 1964; M.Ed., Pa. State U., 1971; M.S., Okla. State U., 1973; Ph.D., U. Mo., 1978; m. Jay Rupert Schrock, Aug. 3, 1968. Elem. art tchr., Leighton, Pa., 1964-66; art tchr., Chitose, Japan, 1969-70; instr. interior design. Kans. State U., 1974-76; instr. housing and interior design U. Mo., 1976-78; asst. prof. housing and interior design Tex. Tech. U., Lubbock, 1978-86, assoc. prof., 1986—. Teaching Devel. grantee Tex. Tech. U., 1982. Mem. Am. Assn. Housing Educators (exec. com., rec. sec.), Interior Design Educators Council, Am. Assn. Home Econs., Am. Soc. Interior Designers. Contbr. articles profl. jours. Office: 265 Home Economics Dept Family Man and Consumer Science Texas Tech University Lubbock TX 79509

SCHRODER, REGINA JABLONSKI, lawyer; b. Riverhead, N.Y., June 15, 1955; d. Zygmont and Jean (Jalbrzykowski) Jablonski; m. Henry Carl Schroder, July 19, 1975. B.A., U. Calif.-Davis, 1979, J.D., 1982; LL.M. in Taxation, McGeorge Sch. Law, Sacramento, 1984. Bar: Calif. 1982. Legal sec. Horan, Lloyd, Dennis Farr, Monterey, Calif., 1974; teller, clk. Security Pacific Bank, Carmel, Calif. and Davis, Calif., 1974-76; clk. Fin. Aids Office, U. Calif.-Davis, 1976-77; researcher, bibliographer Office of Adminstrn. of Criminal Justice, U. Calif.-Davis, 1978-80; law clk. Weintraub, Genshlea, Esqs., Sacramento, Calif., 1981; atty. tax and securities Van Camp & Johnson, Sacramento, Calif., 1983-86, Wilke, Fleury, Hoffelt, Gould & Birney, Sacramento, 1986—. U. Calif. grantee, 1976-78, Calif. Scholarship awardee, 1976-79; Bing Crosby Meml. Fund Scholarship, 1979; recipient Internat. Relations Outstanding Grad. award, 1979. Mem. ABA, Calif. State Bar Assn. (tax sect., adv. com. taxation 1985-86), Women Lawyers of Sacramento, Phi Beta Kappa, Phi Kappa Phi. Office: Wilke Fleury Hoffelt Gould & Birney 300 Capitol Mall 13th Floor Sacramento CA 95814

SCHROEDER, BETTY LOUISE, bookkeeper; b. Aldrich, Mo., Apr. 20, 1937; d. Raymond Fenton and Josie Margaret (Redman) Slagle; m. Earl Freddie Schroeder, Mar. 8, 1958 (div. 1981); children—Kathryn, David, Robert. Student pub. schs., Pleasant Hope, Mo. Head sec. Jackson Extension Ctr., Independence, Mo., 1964; typist MWM Colorpress, Aurora, Mo., 1965; income tax preparer, H&R Block, Aurora, 1969-77, preparer, owner, 1977-83, preparer, owner, West Plains, Mo., 1984—. Fund raiser Houn Dawg Band, Aurora, 1975-85. Baptist. Avocation: handcrafts. Office: H&R Block-Schroeder Bookkeeping 1406 Kentucky St West Plains MO 65775

SCHROEDER, CAROLYN RUTH, nurse; b. Mitchell, S.D., Mar. 11, 1948; d. Virgil Wayne and Louise Elizabeth (Harrison) Clemetson; m. Edward Meryl Schroeder, Nov. 29, 1975. B.S. in Nursing, S.D. State U., 1971; student Grace Coll. of Bible, Omaha, 1972-73. R.N., Nebr., Iowa. Staff nurse McKennan Hosp., Sioux Falls, S.D., 1971-72; float nurse Nebr. Meth. Hosp., Omaha, 1972-73; sch. nurse Grace Coll. of Bible, 1972-73; missionary nurse Africa Evang. Fellowship, Zambia, 1974; staff nurse Univ. Med. Ctr. Hosp., Omaha, 1975; staff nurse, acting supr. St. Catherine's Nursing Home, Omaha, 1976-77; charge nurse Skyline Villa/Manor, Omaha, 1977-79; pvt. duty nurse Kelly HealthCare, Omaha, 1979—, chairperson adv. bd., 1983; pvt. duty nurse Upjohn Health Care Service, Omaha, 1983—; mem. Nebr. Consortium of Hosps. Schs. of Nursing, Omaha, 1983-84. Sec. Child Evangelism Fellowship, Omaha, 1979-82, interim dir., 1980-82; vol. nurse ARC, Omaha, 1982. Republican. Baptist. Office: Upjohn HealthCare Service 8031 W Center Rd Omaha NE 68124

SCHROEDER, ELIZABETH CARSON, corporate training director; b. Havre de Grace, Md., Sept. 21, 1943; d. Omar L. and Catharine (Smith) Carson; m. John W. Schroeder, Jr., Sept. 15, 1984. B.A., Gettysburg Coll., 1965; M.Ed., Loyola Coll., 1971. Cert. rehab. counselor. Counselor to supr. Md. Div. Vocat. Rehab., 1968-79; cons. tng., Balt., 1979-84; corporate trainer MCI, Washington, 1984-85; dir. tng. Nat. Corp. Housing Partnerships-Property Mgmt., Inc., Washington, 1985—. Mem. Nat. Assn. for Rehab. Counseling-Mid Atlantic (pres. 1971-72), Am. Assn. Tng. and Devel. Democrat. Lutheran. Avocations: raising husky dogs, sports-volleyball, softball.

SCHROEDER, LAURA MAY, consultant; b. Greenville, Maine, July 2, 1932; d. Ralph Herbert and Bertha Rowe (Wintle) Given; grad. high sch.; m. Roscoe Schroeder, Nov. 26, 1971 (dec.); children—Linda, Ellen, Malcolm, Ann, Rodney, Helen, James, Roscoe. Co-owner, Folsomi's Air Service, Greenville, 1950-65; auditor Dept. Army Finance, Ft. Knox, Ky., 1969-71; adminstrv. asst. USPHS Hosp., Kanakanak, Alaska, 1971-74; fin. dir. City of Dillingham (Alaska), 1975-78; city mgr., 1978-83; acct. Dillingham Schs., 1983-84; prin. Nushagak Cons., 1984—. Payroll worker Native Villages, 1973-82; tech. adv. com. Bristol Bay Area Hosp., 1980-81; ex-officio mem. Dillingham Planning Commn., 1978-82; mem. Dillingham Sch. Bd., 1977, Bristol Bay Area Econ. Devel. Bd., 1978-81; apptd. mem. Alaska State Land Use Adv. Com., 1985—. Recipient various award including letter of appreciation City of Dillingham, 1978, USPHS, 1972. Mem. Alaska Mgmt. Assn., Am. Mgmt. Assn. Methodist. Home: Main St Dilingham AK 99576

SCHROEDER, MARY MURPHY, judge; b. Boulder, Colo., Dec. 4, 1940; d. Richard and Theresa (Kahn) Murphy; B.A., Swarthmore Coll., 1962; J.D., U. Chgo., 1965; m. Milton R. Schroeder, Oct. 15, 1965; children—Caroline Theresa, Katherine Emily. Admitted to Ill. bar, 1966, D.C. bar, 1966, Ariz. bar, 1970; trial atty. Dept. Justice, Washington, 1965-69; law clk. Hon. Jesse Udall, Ariz. Supreme Ct., 1970; mem. firm Lewis and Roca, Phoenix, 1971-75; judge Ariz. Ct. Appeals, Phoenix, 1975-79; judge U.S. Ct. Appeals, 9th Circuit, Phoenix, 1979—; vis. instr. Ariz. State U. Coll. Law, 1976, 77, 78. Mem. Am. Bar Assn., Ariz. Bar Assn., Fed. Bar Assn., Am. Law Inst., Am. Judicature Soc. Democrat. Club: Soroptimists. Contbr. articles to profl. jours. Office: 6421 Federal Bldg 230 N 1st Ave Phoenix AZ 85025

SCHROEDER, NANCY JANE, financial executive; b. Camp Kilmer, N.J., May 7, 1952; d. Donald Quentin and Barbara Ann (Colwell) Carmichael; m. Mark Schroeder, Apr. 20, 1985. B.S., Fla. State U., 1974. C.P.A., Fla. Supr. audit Coopers & Lybrand, Miami, Fla., 1974-78; mgr. audit Deloitte Haskins & Sells, Miami, 1978-83; mgr. corp. control and analysis Ryder System, Inc., Miami, 1983-85; mgr. tech. acctg. services PepsiCo., Inc., Purchase, N.Y., 1985—. Mem. Am. Inst. C.P.A.s. Republican. Roman Catholic. Home: 603 Steamboat Rd #2 Greenwich CT 06830 Office: PepsiCo Anderson Hill Rd Purchase NY 10577

SCHROEDER, RITA MOLTHEN, chiropractor; b. Savanna, Ill., Oct. 25, 1922; d. Frank Joseph and Ruth Jessie (McKenzie) Molthen; student in chem. engrng. Immaculate Heart Coll., 1940-41, UCLA, 1941; D.C., Palmer Sch. Chiropractic, 1949, Cleve. Coll. Chiropractic, 1961; m. Richard Henry Schroeder, Apr. 23, 1948; children—Richard, Andrew, Barbara, Thomas, Paul, Madeline. Engrng.-tooling design data coordinator Douglas Aircraft Co., El Segundo, Santa Monica and Long Beach, Calif., 1941-47; practice chiropractic, Bklyn., N.Y., 1949-59, Fresno, Calif., 1961—; pres. Schroeder Chiropractic, Inc., Fresno, 1982—. Bd. dirs. Pacific States Chiropractic Coll., 1978-80, pres., 1980-81. Recipient awards Pacific States Chiropractic Coll., others. Mem. Internat. Chiropractic Assn., Calif. Chiropractic Assn., Assn. Am. Chiropractic Coll. Pres. Republican. Roman Catholic. Office: 2535 N Fresno St Fresno CA 93703

SCHROEDER, TERRI LEA, city manager, educator; b. Elgin, Ill. Mar. 11, 1955; d. Earl and Caroline Louise Christensen. Student William Rainey Harper Coll., 1973-77; B.S. in Edn., No. Ill. U., 1977, M.A. in Pub. Adminstrn., 1979. Lic. pub. water supply operator Ill. EPA Class C; cert. water treatment plant operator Iowa Dept. Environ. Quality Grade I. Tchr., English, Sch. Dist. 202, Plainfield, Ill., 1977-78; adminstrv. asst. to village mgr. Village of Deerfield (Ill.), 1978-79; asst. village mgr. Village of Lincolnshire (Ill.), 1979-81, village mgr., 1981-82; city mgr. City of Iowa Falls (Iowa), 1982—; cons. exec. dir. Lake County Youth Service Bur., Lake Villa, Ill., 1979-80; communications and pub. relations coordinator Univ. Health Ctr., DeKalb, Ill., 1977-78; legal asst. Winnebago County Legal Aid, Rockford, Ill., spring 1979; feature speaker KIFG Radio Sta., fall 1982. Trustee, mem. budget com. 1st Congl. Ch., Iowa Falls, 1982—; bd. dirs., mem. leadership com. Com. of 80's Iowa Falls, 1982—; mem. DeKalb Human Relations Commn., 1977-79; lobbyist for Student Assn. on Higher Edn. Appropriations, 79th Gen. Assembly, Washington; chairperson for polit. awareness week, DeKalb, 1977; mem. Gov.'s Com. on Future of Econ. Growth of Iowa. Named Iowa's Young Career Woman of 1982-83, Iowa Fedn. Bus. Profl. Women, 1983; named Outstanding Young Working Woman, Glamour Mag., 1984; Esper A. Peterson Found. scholar, 1976-79; Gen. Assembly scholar. Mem. Bus. Profl. Women (Young Career Woman, chmn. dist. IV northwest Iowa 1983—), Internat. City Mgmt. Assn. (assoc.), Iowa City Mgmt. Assn. (newsletter editor 1983—), North Central Iowa City Mgmt. Assn. (founder, exec. bd. dirs.), Mcpl. Fin. Officers Assn., Am. Pub. Works Assn., Internat. Mcpl. Clks. Home: 315 Estes St Iowa Falls IA 50126 Office: City of Iowa Falls IA 315 Stevens St PO Box 698 Iowa Falls IA 50126

SCHROEN, FRAN BRANT, police department administrator; b. Salt Lake City, July 21, 1945; d. Albert Lynn and Julia (Rees) Brant; 1 child, Joseph Thomas; m. John Richard Schroen, May 19, 1970. Student, U. Utah. Research technician Geneol. Soc., Salt Lake City, 1963-65; exec. sec. Lang Wang Equipment Co., Salt Lake City, 1969-70; sec. E-Systems, 1971-72; legal sec., 1981-82; supr., examiner Salt Lake City Police Dept., 1972—; cons. in document examination for other Utah police depts. Contbr. articles to profl. publs. Treas. Salt Lake City Ctr./World Messianity, 1984—. Internat. Graphoanalysis Soc. scholar, 1984. Mem. Independent Assn. Document Examiners, World Assn. of Document Examiners, Nat. Assn. Female Execs., Utah Bus. Women, Sigma Alpha Gamma. Avocations: racquetball; horseback riding; weight lifting. Office: Salt Lake City Police Dept 450 S 300 E Salt Lake City UT 84111

SCHROPP, MARY LOU, public relations company executive; b. Havre-de-Grace, Md., Aug. 13, 1947; d. Howard James and Maude Elizabeth (Parker) S. Student, George Washington U., 1965-66. Vice pres. Snyder Assoc., Inc., Washington, 1969-76; pres. Health Communications, Inc., Washington, 1976-80; creative services project mgr. U.S. Catholic Conf., Washington, 1980-81; pres., owner MLS Creative Services, Falls Church, Va., 1981—. Editor: Electronic Media, Popular Culture and Family Values, 1985; Rehabilitation Facilities Sourcebook, 1984, 85; periodicals, textbooks. Exec. producer videotapes, 1982. Coordinator World Communications Day, Washington, 1982—; cons. Catholic Communication Campaign, Washington, 1982-84; fund raising cons. Nat. 4-H Council, Chevy Chase, Md., 1985—, Aviation Research and Edn. Found., Herndon, Va., 1985—. Mem. Pub. Relations Soc. Am., Washington Independent Writers, Religious Pub. Relations Council (v.p. local chpt. 1981-82, DeRose-Hinkhouse Communications award 1981, 82, 80), Nat. Soc. Fund Raising Execs. Democrat. Roman Catholic. Office: MLS Creative Services 7711 Trevino Ln Falls Church VA 22043

SCHROTH, EVELYN MARY, educator; b. Ellington, Wis., Aug. 5, 1919; d. Henry A. and Clara M. (Komp) Schroth; B.S., U. Wis., 1940; M.S., U. Ill., 1948, A.M., 1955; Ph.D., Pacific Western U., 1979. Tchr., Rhinelander (Wis.) High Sch., 1940-42; chmn. English dept. Waupun (Wis.) High Sch., 1942-44; tchr. Chgo. pub. schs., 1953-63, chmn. dept. English, Lindblom High Sch., 1956-62; instr. dept. English, U. Ill., Urbana, 1948-50; lectr. Northeastern U., Chgo., 1962-63; asso. prof. English, Western Ill. U., Macomb, 1963—. Program dir. U.S.O., 1946-48. John Hay fellow, 1961. Mem. Linguistic Soc. Am., Nat. Council Tchrs. English, Ill. Tchrs. English, AAUP, Phi Beta, Phi Kappa Phi. Home: 139 Kurlene Dr Macomb IL 61455 Office: 226 I Simpkins Hall Western Ill U Macomb IL 61455

SCHUBARTH, LINDA DALE, property management and homebuilding company executive; b. Price, Utah, July 28, 1950; d. Vernon Gerald and Merlin Mae (Davis) Lyons; m. Clyde Stanley Schubarth, Jan. 17, 1970; children—Spring May, Tyrone Raymond. Cert. of stenography Coll. of Eastern, 1969. Clk., stenographer Def. Dept., Ogden, Utah, 1969-72; sec. Colo. Western Devel., Monument, 1972; adminstrv. asst. Woodmoor Corp., Monument, 1972-74; reporting stenographer Lowry AFB, Denver, 1974-75; office mgr. Roark Assocs., Denver, 1975-76; v.p. Medema Homes, Inc., Denver, 1977-83; pres. Mgmt. Link Assocs., Denver, 1983—; 2d v.p. Presdl. Homes, Inc., 1983-84. Author: FHA/VA Processing, 1982. Leader 4-H Clubs, Ogden, 1972, Girl Scouts U.S.A., Denver, 1980. Mem. Community Assns. Inst. (pres. 1982-83). Mem. Church of Jesus Christ of Latter-day Saints. Home: 4405 S Biscay Way Aurora CO Office: Management Link Assocs PO Box 4997 Englewood CO 80155

SCHUBERT, ELIZABETH M(AY), paralegal adminstrv. asst.; b. Hamilton, Ohio, Sept. 10, 1913; d. A(ndreas) Gordon and Grace Symmes (Laxford) S.; B.S. in Edn. cum laude, Miami U., 1933. Sec., Beta Kappa Nat. Frat., Oxford, Ohio, 1931-38; adminstrv. asst. to dir. Ohio State Employment Service, Columbus, 1938-45, supr. procedures, 1945-47; adminstrv. asst. to pres. Schaible Co., Cin., 1948-50; paralegal adminstrv. asst. to Gordon H. Scherer, Atty.-at-Law, mem. U.S. Congress, U.S. del. to UN, U.S. rep. to exec. bd. UNESCO, Paris, 1950—. Mem. Phi Beta Kappa. Republican. Presbyn. Home: 1071 Celestial St Apt 1701 Cincinnati OH 45202 Office: 1071 Celestial St Suite 2103 Cincinnati OH 45202

SCHUBERT, NANCY ELLEN, beauty industry executive, management consultant, franchise director; b. Chgo., June 25, 1945; d. Raymond James and Kathleen Mary (Gibbons) Nugent; m. Emil Joseph Schubert, Jan. 14, 1967; children—James Bryant, Erin Heather, Shannon Kathleen. B.F.A., Mundelein Coll., 1968. Freelance artist, Chgo., 1968; tchr. St. Pius X Sch., Lombard, Ill., 1975-76; pres., treas., dir. Super Style, Inc., Hoffman Estates, Ill., 1981—, Super Six, Inc., Glendale Heights, Ill., 1983—, N.E.S. Mgmt. Inc., Schaumburg, Ill., 1985—, Super Style III, Inc., Berwyn, Ill., 1985—; created and developed Super Style concept and system of operation; created SuperStyle logo and design trademarked in 1983. Republican. Roman Catholic. Avocations: painting, sculpting, downhill skiing, horseback riding, flying. Office: Super Style Inc 707 W Golf Rd Hoffman Estates IL 60194

SCHUBERT, RUTH CAROL HICKOK, artist; b. Janesville, Wis., Dec. 24, 1927; d. Fay Andrew and Mildred Willamette (Street) Hickok; m. Robert Francis Schubert, Oct. 20, 1946; children—Stephen Robert, Michelle Carol Schubert Kump. A.A., Monterey Peninsula Coll., 1974; B.A. with honors, Calif. State U. San Jose, 1979. Council research dir. Monterey Peninsula Mus. Art, Monterey, Calif., 1975-76; owner, mgr. Casa de Artes Studio Gallery, Monterey, Calif., 1977—; cons. artist Monterey county Cultural Council, 1984; slide lectures, painting demonstrations through U.S.; rep. by Village Art Gallery, LaHaina, Maui, Hawaii, Rose Rock Gallery, Carmel, Calif., Valley Art Gallery, Portola Valley, Calif. One-woman shows include: Wells Fargo Bank, Monterey, Calif., 1975, 78, 79, Degl. Agostiniani, Rome, 1977, San Francisco Bay Nat. Wildlife Refuge Show, 1979, Periwinkle Gallery, Monterey, 1980, Art Intrigues Gallery, Pacific Grove, Calif., 1980, Village Gallery, LaHaina, Maui, Hawaii, 1983, Valley Gallery, Portola Valley, Calif., 1985; also group shows; represented in permanent collections: Monterey Peninsula Mus. Art, Monterey, Muscular Dystrophy Assn., San Francisco, Nabisco Brands, Inc., San Jose Calif. and N.Y.C. Recipient award Am. Artists, 1978, Monterey County, 1979, Mus. Natural History, 1980, Central Calif. Biennial, 1983, Nat. Art Appreciation Soc., 1984. Mem. Artists Equity Assn., Am. Watercolor Soc. (assoc.), Audubon Artists, Inc. (assoc.), Soc. Western Artists, Nat. League Am. Pen Women (pres. 1984-85), Central Coast Art Assn. (pres. 1977-78, 1st award 1977, 2d award 1979, 3d award 1980), Art Alumni San Jose State U., Monterey Civic Club. Republican. Episcopalian. Lodge: Order Eastern Star. Avocations: swimming; aerobics; travel. Home and Studio: 134 Dunecrest Ave Monterey CA 93940

SCHUCK, MARJORIE MASSEY, publisher, editor, authors' consultant; b. Winchester, Va., Oct. 9, 1921; d. Carl Frederick and Margaret Harriet (Parmelee) Massey; student U. Minn., 1941-43, New Sch., N.Y.C., 1948, N.Y. U., 1952, 54-55; m. Ernest George Metcalfe, Dec. 2, 1943 (div. Oct. 1949); m. 2d, Franz Schuck, Nov. 11, 1953 (dec. Jan. 1958). Mem. editorial bd. St. Petersburg Poetry Assn., 1967-68; co-editor, pub. poetry Venture Mag., St. Petersburg, Fla., 1968-69, editor, pub., 1969-79; co-editor, pub. Poetry Venture Quar. Essays, Vol. I, 1968-69, Vol. 2, 1970-71; pub., editor poetry anthologies, 1972—; founder, owner, pres. Valkyrie Press, Inc. (name changed to Valkyrie Pub. House 1980), 1972—; cons. designs and formats, trade publs. and ann. reports, lit. books and pamphlets, 1973—; founder Valkyrie Press Roundtable Workshop and Forum for Writers, 1975-79; established Valkyrie Press Reference Library, 1976-80; pub., editor The Valkyrie Internat. Newsletter, 1986—; lectr. in field. Judge poetry and speech contests Gulf Beach Women's Club, 1970, Fine Arts Festival dist. 14. Am. Fedn. Women's Clubs, 1970, South and West, Inc., 1972, The Sunstone Rev., 1973, Internat. Toastmistress Clubs, 1974, 78, Beaux Arts Poetry Festival, 1983; judge Fla. Gov.'s Screenwriters Competition, 1984—. Corr.-rec. sec. Women's Aux. Hosp. for Spl. Surgery, N.Y.C., 1947-59; active St. Petersburg Mus. Fine Arts (charter), St. Petersburg Sister City Com., St. Petersburg Arts Center Assn.; mem. Orange Belt express com. 1988 Centennial Celebration for St. Petersburg, mem. Com. of 100 of Pinellas County, Inc., exec. bd., 1975-77, membership chmn., 1975-77; pub. relations chmn. Soc. for prevention Cruelty to Animals, 1968-71, bd. dirs., 1968-71, 75-77; mem. Pinellas County Arts Council, 1977-79, chmn., 1977-78; mem. grant rev. panel for lit. Fine Arts Council of Fla., 1979. Named One of 76 Fla. Patriots, Fla. Bicentennial Commn., 1976; a recipient 1st ann. People of Dedication award Salvation Army, Tampa, 1984. Mem. Acad. Am. Poets, Fla. Suncoast Writers' Confs. (founder, co-dir., lectr. 1973-83, adv. bd. 1984—), Fla. Poets Assn., Com. Small Mag. Editors and Pubs., Coordinating Council Lit. Mags., Friends of Library of St. Petersburg, Suncoast Mgmt. Inst. (exec. bd.; chmn. Women in Mgmt. 1977-78), Pi Beta Phi. Democrat. Episcopalian. Author: Speeches and Writings for Cause of Freedom, 1973. Contbr. poetry to profl. jours. Home: 8245 26th Ave N Saint Petersburg FL 33710 Office: 2135-2149 1st Ave S Saint Petersburg FL 33712

SCHUCK, VICTORIA, former college president; b. Oklahoma City, Mar. 16, 1909; d. Anthony B. and Anna (Priebe) S.; A.B. with great distinction, Stanford U., 1930, M.A., 1931, Ph.D., 1937; L.H.D. (hon.) Mt. Vernon Coll., 1980. Univ. fellow, Stanford U., 1931-33, teaching asst., 1934-35, acting instr., 1935-36, instr., 1936-37; asst. prof. Fla. State Coll. for Women, 1937-40; asst. prof. Mt. Holyoke Coll., South Hadley, Mass., 1940-44, assoc. prof., 1944-50, prof. polit. sci., 1950-75; pres. Mt. Vernon Coll., Washington, 1977-80; prin. program analyst OPA, Washington, 1942-44; cons. Office Temporary Controls, 1945-47; vis. lectr. Smith Coll., 1948-49; vis. prof. Stanford U., summer 1952; guest scholar The Brookings Instn., Washington, 1967, 68, summers 1968, 70; Woodrow Wilson Internat. Ctr. for scholars, 1980; resident scholar polit. sci. Stanford U., 1982, 83, 84—; regional editor Ency. Brit., 1958-61; mem. Mass. Bd. Higher Edn., 1976-77. Mem. internat. secretariat, UN Conf., San

Francisco, 1945; mem. Mass. Commn. on Interstate Cooperation, 1957-60, Mass. adv. com. to U.S. Commn. on Civil Rights, 1962-78, Berkshire Community Coll. Planning Com., 1964-68, Greenfield Community Coll. Planning Com., 1965-67, D.C. Commn. Postsecondary Edn., 1979-80; mem. council Nat. Mcpl. League, N.Y.C., 1977—; mem. Planning Bd. South Hadley, 1959-67, chmn., 1961-67; mem. Pres.'s Commn. on Registration and Voting Participation, 1963; trustee U. Mass., 1958-65, mem. bldg. authority, 1960-68; mem. Commn. on Adminstrv. Rev. of U.S. Ho. of Reps., 1977, educator cons. panel U.S. Gen. Acctg. Office, 1980-82. Haynes Found. grantee, 1951-52; Asia Soc. grantee, 1971-72. Mem. Am. Soc. Pub. Adminstrn., AAUP (pres. Mt. Holyoke 1962-64), AAUW (pres. Mass. 1946-50, nat. chmn. legis. program com., nat. dir. 1965-69), New Eng. (pres. 1950-51), Am. (sec. 1959-60, v.p. 1970-71 rep. U.N. World Conf., 1985), Northeastern (v.p. 1971-72, pres. 1972-73) polit. sci. assns., Assn. Asian Studies, Washington Independent Writers, Mortar Bd., Chi Omega, Phi Beta Kappa. Club: Cosmopolitan (N.Y.C.); Women's Nat. Democratic. Contbr. articles to profl. jours.; co-editor: Women Organizing: An Anthology, 1979, New England Politics, 1981; regional editor Ency. Brit., 1958-61. Address: 4000 Cathedral Ave NW Washington DC 20016

SCHUCKETT, SANDY, librarian; b. Los Angeles, Aug. 20, 1937; d. Max M. and Bluma (Kreisberg) S. B.A., U. Calif.-Berkeley, 1960; M.A., Calif. State U.-Los Angeles, 1978. Cert. tchr., Calif., 1969. Tchr., Los Angeles pub. schs., 1962-66, librarian, 1966-74, media coordinator, 1974—; sec. White House Conf. Library and Info. Services Task Force, Washington, 1982—. Pres. Friends of Children and Lit., 1979—; active PTA, Los Angeles Sch. Library Assn. Mem., ALA, NEA, Am. Assn. Sch. Librarians, Calif. Library Assn., Educare; Kappa Delta Pi. Democrat. Jewish. Office: Los Angeles Unified School Dist 4112 E Olympic Blvd Los Angeles CA 90023

SCHUENAMAN, JACQUELINE PRYOR, Realtor, international financier; b. Lorain, Ohio, June 12, 1938; d. Harold Ellsworth and Ruth Magdeline (Newcomer) Pryor; m. Howard Roland Schuenaman, Apr. 9, 1960 (div. Oct. 1982); children—Scott, Sherri, Susan. Tchr., Lorain Public Schs., 1959-60; office adminstr., law firms, Lorain, 1979-81; office mgr., property cons. Nat. Sand & Gravel, Lorain, 1981-84; realtor Ray Haff, Inc., 1979—; pres. Pryor Properties, Lorain, 1959—; v.p. Behrens & Assocs., Lorain, 1985—; dir. Nat. Sand & Gravel, Lorain. Bd dirs. Lorain County United Fund Planning Bd., 1976-79. Mem. Internat. Soc. Financiers, Nat. Assn. Realtors, AAUW (pres. 1973-75, editor Ohio div. newspaper 1975-77), Bus. and Profl. Women. Avocations: Swimming; skiing; music. Office: Behrens & Assocs 333 W 25th St Lorain OH 44052

SCHUERMAN, CYNTHIA SUSAN, hardware company executive; b. Berwyn, Ill., May 8, 1957; d. Richard Charles and Patricia Ann (Kolf) Dunning; m. Joseph K. Schuerman, Apr. 22, 1979; 1 child, Nicole Renee. B.A., Millikin U., 1979. Pres. Schuerman Key Shop, Inc., Decatur, 1981—; sec.-treas. SKS Sales, Inc., Decatur, 1983—. Presbyterian. Home: 1895 Commonwealth Ave Decatur IL 62521 Office: Schuerman Key Shop Inc 141 N Jasper St Decatur IL 62521

SCHUH, JANICE SUE, manufacturing company executive; b. Marysville, Kans., Dec. 14, 1942; d. Frederick John William and Violet Clara (Yaussi) Millenbruch; B.S. in Home Econs. and Journalism, Kans. State U., 1966; m. Dec. 31, 1970; 1 son Jeffrey Scott. Successively women's reporter Racine (Wis.) Jour.-Times, asst. women's editor Pioneer Press, Wilmette, Ill., food and feature reporter Chgo. Daily News, public relations asso., editorial home economist Kitchens of Sara Lee, Deerfield, Ill.; with Ekco Products, Inc., Wheeling, Ill., 1972—, mgr. advt. promotion and design, 1974-81, mgr. mktg. communications, 1981-84; pres. Creative Practical Services, 1984—. Hearst scholar. Mem. Greater O'Hare Assn., Advt. Splty. Assn. Women in Mgmt. Address: 1013 Duxbury St Schaumburg IL 60193

SCHUHART, ANNE DASHLEY (SUSAN), actress; b. Rochester, N.Y., June 10, 1947; d. Richard Quinabert and Aynn (Miller) Schuhart; m. Frank John Zito, June 23, 1984. B.A. in English and Drama, Nazareth Coll., 1969. Asst. to Robert and Barbara Taylor Bradford, Bradford Enterprises, N.Y.C., 1981. Appeared in Hold Me!, Phila., 1978, Vanities, Chgo., 1979. Recipient Comdrs. award Nat. Catholic Theatre Conf., 1965. Mem. Actors Equity, AFTRA, Screen Actors Guild. Democrat. Roman Catholic. Office: Bradford Enterprises 450 Park Ave New York NY 10022

SCHUHLE, MARIANNE, machining company executive, real estate broker; b. Brownsville, Pa., Oct. 18, 1931; d. Ewing Elton and Vergie Marie (Brown) Stuart; m. Walter John Schuhle, June 23, 1951; children—Pamela Susan, Scott Allan, John Todd. Real estate tng. Marist Coll., Hyde Park, N.Y. Real estate broker, N.Y., Ariz. Personnel clk. Fed. Res. Bd. Govs., Washington, 1950-51; office sec. FAA, Washington, 1951-52; real estate salesman, Poughkeepsie, N.Y., 1968-74, broker, 1974-80; real estate broker, Tucson, 1980—; owner, mgr. Ariz. Custom Machining, Tucson, 1984—. Chmn. LaGrange Democratic Com., N.Y., 1976. Mem. Tucson C. of C., Nat. Fedn. Ind. Bus. Republican. Avocations: miniature making; traveling; decorating; ballooning. Home: 8341 E Big Horn Trail Tucson AZ 85715 Office: Ariz Custom Machining 2100 N Wilmot Rd #217 Tucson AZ 85712

SCHULER, ALISON KAY, lawyer; b. West Point, N.Y., Oct. 1, 1948; d. Richard Hamilton and Irma Sophia (Sancken) Schuler; m. Lyman G. Sandy, Mar. 30, 1974. B.A. cum laude, Radcliffe Coll., 1969; J.D., Harvard U., 1972. Bar: Va. 1973, D.C. 1974, N.Mex. 1975. Assoc. firm Hunton & Williams, Richmond, Va. and Washington, 1972-75; asst. U.S. atty., Albuquerque, 1975-78; assoc. firm Sutin, Thayer & Browne, Albuquerque, 1978-85, shareholder, 1981-85; shareholder Montgomery & Andrews, P.A., 1985—; adj. prof. law U. N.Mex., Albuquerque, 1983—. Bd. dirs. Am. Diabetes Assn., Albuquerque, 1980-86, v.p., 1981-82, chmn.-elect, 1982-84, chmn., 1984—; bd. dirs., pres. June Music Festival, Inc., 1980-85; mem. Albuquerque Com. Fgn. Relations, 1975—, chmn.-elect, 1983-84, chmn., 1984-85; mem. council St. Luke's Luth. Ch., 1976-80, 82-84, v.p., 1978-80, 82-84; mem. com. for profl. leadership Rocky Mountain Synod, Luth. Ch. in Am., 1981-86. Mem. ABA, State Bar N.Mex. (dir. corp., banking and bus. law sect. 1981-84, chmn. 1982-83), Albuquerque Bar Assn., Va. State Bar Assn., Fed. Bar Assn., D.C. Bar, Am. Soc. Internat. Law, Am. Judicature Soc., Nat. Assn. Women Lawyers, Harvard U. Alumni Assn. (regional dir. 1984, v.p. 1986—), Radcliffe Coll. Alumni Assn. (regional dir. 1983—). Club: Harvard-Radcliffe of N.Mex. (pres., dir. 1981—). Home: 632 Cougar Loop NE Albuquerque NM 87122 Office: Montgomery & Andrews PA PO Box 26927 707 Broadway Place Albuquerque NM 87125-6927

SCHULHAFER, JOAN ELLEN, publishing company executive; b. Elizabeth, N.J., Oct. 21, 1955; d. Herbert J. and Jean C. (Getchius) S. B.A. in English, Montclair State Coll., 1977. Publicity, advt. asst. Mason/Charter Pub., N.Y.C., 1977; publicity assoc. Dodd Mead & Co., N.Y.C., 1978-79, asst. dir. publicity John Wiley & Sons, N.Y.C., 1979-80; sr. publicist Simon & Schuster Inc., Pocket Books div., N.Y.C., 1980-81, publicity mgr., 1981-83, dir. publicity Silhouette Books div., N.Y.C., 1983—. Author: How to Write a Romance and Get it Published, 1983. Active Montclair Tenants Orgn., local Democratic politics. Mem. Publishers Publicity Assn., Women's Nat. Book Assn., Romance Writers Am., NOW, Nat. Assn. Female Execs. Roman Catholic. Office: Silhouette Books Simon and Schuster 1230 Ave of the Americas New York NY 10020

SCHULTE, DIANE JENNINGS, certified public accountant; b. Cedar Rapids, Iowa, July 14, 1953; d. William C. and Patricia Rose (Proskovec) Jennings. B.S., Mt. Mercy Coll., 1975; student Coe Coll., 1971-73; postgrad. U. Iowa, 1981—. C.P.A., Iowa. Bookkeeper (part-time) Eagles Grocery Store, Cedar Rapids, 1969-75; sr. acct. Bell & Van Zee, P.C., Cedar Rapids, 1975-81; treas. (part-time) Kenwood Park Ch., Cedar Rapids, 1977-78; controller LeaseAm. Corp., Cedar Rapids, 1981-82, asst. treas., 1982-84, v.p., chief fin. officer, 1984—. Mem. selection com. for Ramsey Scholarship Coe Coll., 1973, vol. Growth Fund Drive, 1981; vol. sr. citizen Thanksgiving dinner, Life Investors Inc., Cedar Rapids, 1983-85; mem. exec. com. Alumni Phonathon, Mt. Mercy Coll., Cedar Rapids, 1985; alumni career cons., 1984—. Mem. Nat. Assn. Accts. (Storm award 1985), Iowa Soc. C.P.A.s, Am. Women's Soc. C.P.A.s, Am. Inst. C.P.A.s, Nat. Assn. Female Execs. Roman Catholic. Avocations: running; bicycling; reading. Office: LeaseAm Corp 4333 Edgewood Rd NE Cedar Rapids IA 52499

SCHULTE, MYRNA MADGE, health coodinator; b. Ellinwood, Kans., Oct. 25, 1935; d. Carl William and Margaret Helena (Berscheidt) Schneider; m. Bernard Joseph Schulte, June 7, 1958; children—Mark Joseph, Catherine Ann. Student U. Kans., 1953-56. Sec., Southern/Anderson Law, Ellinwood, Kans., 1951-53, Republic Natural Gas, Summers 1953-56; sec. to dean U. Kans. Law Sch., Lawrence, winters 1953-56; sec., bookkeeper Manning Drilling Co., Ellinwood, 1952-53; airline hostess TWA, Kansas City, Kans., 1956-58, exec. sec., Newark, 1958-59; health coordinator Am. Heart Assn., Norwich, N.Y., 1979—, mem. legis. com. N.Y. State, 1983—. Contbr. articles to profl. jours. Mem. instnl. rev. bd. Chenango Meml. Hosp., 1979—, mem. aux. bd. dirs., 1962-72, 75—, decorator, 1979—; mem. council St. Paul's Parish, 1975-77; mem. supt.'s council Norwich High Sch., 1977-78. Recipient Outstanding Service award Am. Heart Assn., 1983; Panhellenic scholar, 1953. Mem. Am. Heart Assn. Nat. Staff Soc., Nat. Hon. Soc., Norwich Aux., Chenango Meml. Hosp. Aux. (v.p. 1964-66), Heart & Stroke Club (cons. 1984—). Republican. Roman Catholic. Club: Garden (pres. 1964-65). Avocations: piano; singing; gardening; dancer; organ. Home: Box 42 Edgewood Dr Norwich NY 13815 Office: Am Heart Assn Box 128 Norwich NY 13815

SCHULTER-ELLIS, FRANCES PIERCE, anatomist, educator; b. Chilton County, Ala., Sept. 22, 1923; d. William Mack and Lena Roberta (Varden) Pierce; B.S., Birmingham So. Coll., 1952; M.S., Emory U., 1954; Ph.D., George Washington U., 1972; m. Spencer P. Ellis, Apr. 1, 1977; children by previous marriage—Jenny Schulter Varden, Peter Alan Schulter. Instr. biology Chamblee (Ga.) High Sch., 1960-61; instr. biology Marjorie Webster Jr. Coll., Washington, 1961-65; teaching fellow in anatomy George Washington U. Med. Sch., 1966-71; asst. prof. anatomy U. Md. Sch. Medicine, Balt., 1972-80, assoc. prof., 1984—; research collaborator div. phys. anthropology Smithsonian Instn.; vis. prof. anatomy St. George U., Grenada, W.I.; cons. forensic sci. Md. Med. Examiners Office; book reviewer sci. books and films AAAS. Vol. worker Balt. Symphony Orch., 1973-76, Center Stage Theatre, Balt., 1973-75, George Washington U. Alumni Assn., 1975—, Anne Arundel County (Md.) Mental Health Assn., 1977—, Am. Cancer Soc., 1977—. Recipient Faculty of Yr. award U. Md. Sch. of Medicine, 1974, 78, 86; award for outstanding service and contbn. Student Nat. Med. Assn. of U. Md., 1978, Grad. Sch. Research award U. Md., 1974, 76, 78. Fellow Human Biology Council; mem. Am. Assn. Anatomists, Am. Assn. Phys. Anthropologists, Am. Acad. Forensic Scis., Am. Anthrop. Assn., Md. Soc. Med. Research, So. Soc. Anatomists, N.Y. Acad. Scis., AAUP, Phi Sigma, Beta Beta Beta, Theta Chi Delta. Clubs: Bay Hills (Md.) Golf, Annapolis Yacht, U.S. Naval Acad. Officers and Faculty. Contbr. articles to profl. jours. Home: 570 Foxpaw Trail Annapolis MD 21401 Office: 655 W Baltimore St Baltimore MD 21201

SCHULTZ, DIANE MARIE, food company executive; b. Buffalo, Dec. 23, 1948; d. Richard Frank and Genevieve Mary (Nowak) Buczkowski; m. Clifford Frank Schultz, Jr., July 4, 1975; 1 child, Jennifer Lynn. Student Sumter Area Tech. Coll. Accounts payable clk. Union Carbide Corp., Tarrytown, N.Y., 1969-71; bookkeeper East Aurora Tire Corp., N.Y., 1972-74; sr. account payable clk. Moog, Inc., Hydra-Point Inc., Cheektowaga, N.Y., 1974-75; sr. accounts payable clk. lead purchasing clk., programmer trainee Campbell Soup Co., Sumter, S.C., 1975-85, buyer expediter, 1985—. Mem. welcoming com. St. Ann Catholic Ch., Sumter, 1985. Mem. Purchasing Assn., Nat. Assn. Female Execs. Avocations: Organist; cross stitch; sewing. Office: Campbell Soup Co 2050 Hwy 15 S Sumter SC 29150

SCHULTZ, EILEEN HEDY, graphic designer; b. N.Y.C.; d. Harry A. and Hedy E. (Morchel) S.; B.F.A., Sch. Visual Arts, N.Y.C., 1957; postgrad. Columbia U., Art Students League, New Sch., Acad. des Beaux Arts. Comml. artist C.A. Parshall Studios, N.Y.C., 1957-58; editorial art dir. Paradise of the Pacific mag., Honolulu, 1958-59; art dir. Good Housekeeping mag., N.Y.C., 1959-82, creative dir. advt. and sales promotion, 1982—; creative dir. Hearst mags., 1981-85, promotion, 1985—; instr. graphic design Sch. Visual Arts; vis. prof. Syracuse (N.Y.) U. Recipient Outstanding Achievement award Sch. Visual Arts Alumni Soc., 1976, Youth award Art Students League, 1976. Mem. Soc. Illustrators (chmn. ann. exhbn. 1978), Art Dirs. Club N.Y.C. (pres. 1975-77), Joint Ethics Com. N.Y.C. (chmn. 1980-82), Am. Inst. Graphic Arts, Soc. Publ. Designers. Author monthly column Art Direction mag., 1970—; art dir., designer, editor 50th Ann. Advt., Editorial and TV Art and Design, 1971. Home: 450 E 63d St Apt 4M W New York NY 10021 Office: 959 8th Ave Suite 457 New York NY 10019

SCHULTZ, ELIZABETH ANNE CRIMMINS, nurse; b. Guelph, Ont., Can., Apr. 28, 1922; came to U.S., 1957, naturalized, 1969; d. Daniel and Elizabeth (Roth) Crimmins; diploma St. Joseph's Sch. Nursing, 1943; cert. teaching and supr. psychiat. nursing U. Toronto, 1954; B.S. in Nursing, U. Pitts., 1963, M. Nursing Edn., 1966; Ph.D., Walden U., Fla., 1981; m. Joseph Anthony Schultz, Nov. 25, 1972. Staff nurse St. Joseph's Hosp., Guelph, Ont., Can., 1943-44; pvt. duty nurse, Guelph, 1944-46; staff nurse King Edward Meml. Hosp., Bermuda, 1946-47, asst. head nurse, 1947-48, head nurse, 1948-49; staff nurse Vancouver Gen. Hosp., 1949-51; staff nurse, supr. Homewood Sanitarium, Guelph, 1951-53; head nurse, clin. tchr. Toronto Psychiat. Hosp., 1954-57; staff nurse, head nurse Western Psychiat. Inst., Pitts., 1957-62, asst. dir. nursing, affiliate edn., 1962-64; dir. nursing Western Restoration Center, 1966-69; asst. prof. psychiat. nursing Allegheny Community Coll., Pitts., 1969-71; asst. prof. dept. nursing Duquesne U., Pitts., 1971-75, assoc. prof., 1975-78; assoc. prof. dept. nursing Slippery Rock (Pa.) U., 1978-84; dir. health services Sistenco, Inc., 1984—; cons. psychiat., mental health nursing McKeesport Hosp., 1970-71; cons., lectr. psychiat., mental health nursing Slippery Rock U., 1975. Mem. AAUP, Advanced Practitioners Psychiat. Nursing, Am. Assn. Sex Edn. and Counselors, Am., Pa. nurses Assn., Nat., Pa. leagues nursing, U. Toronto Alumni Assn., U. Pitts. Alumni Assn. Home: 3 Shannopin Dr Pittsburgh PA 15202 Office: PO Box 4196 Pittsburgh PA 15202

SCHULTZ, HELEN MARY, instrument company executive; b. Duncan, Okla., Sept. 22, 1922; d. Paul Joseph and Martha Jane (Melton) Kelly; student U. Iowa, 1939-41; m. Charles J. Schultz, Sept. 29, 1944 (div. Feb. 1973); children—Cathryn Jane, Christy Jean, Charles David. Sales sec. G.T. Collatz Co., Inc., Wellesley, Mass., 1964-68; sales office mgr. Amicon Corp., Lexington, Mass., 1968-73; sales mgr. Tensitron, Inc., Harvard, Mass., 1973-75, mktg. dir., 1975-77, v.p., 1977-81, pres., gen. mgr., dir., 1981—. Home: 34 Country Club Ln Milford MA 01757 Office: Depot Rd Harvard MA 01451

SCHULTZ, KAREN LEE, fire and water restoration company executive; b. Hempstead, N.Y., June 24, 1953; d. Odd Andre and Irene Mae (Cortez) Solbakken; 1 child, Miakoda Li. Sr. recreation therapist Posada del Sol, Tucson, 1977-81; pres., owner Intimate Luxury, Tucson, 1981-85; gen. mgr. Global Restoration, Tucson, 1985—. Pres. Activities Dirs. Assn. Tucson, 1979-80; mem. candidate evaluation com. C. of C., Tucson, 1984-86; asst. leader Girl Scouts U.S.A., 1984-85. Mem. Tucson Bus. and Profl. Women, (pres., chmn. Trade Fair 1985-86), Tucson Women's Symposium, So. Ariz. Claims Adjusters, Nat. Assn. Female Execs. Democrat. Office: Global Restoration 4211 Santa Rita Tucson AZ 85714

SCHULTZ, LORRAINE HELENE, association executive; b. North Tonawanda, N.Y., Oct. 23, 1930; d. Francis and Michalina Sofia (Jok) Szemraj; student Alma Coll., 1948-50; m. Arthur Henry Schultz, June 18, 1955; children—Brian, Tracey. Stewardess, Eastern Airlines, 1953-55; v.p. Slenderella Internat., 1955-64; pres., owner Detroit Model Bur., 1964-69; dir. Am. Express Travel Club, Mich., 1969-73; pres., owner LHS Assocs., Birmingham, Mich., 1975—; dir. AutoLeather Guild, Birmingham, 1975—. Bd. dirs. Juvenile Diabetes Assn. Com.; pres. People Reaching Out, March of Dimes; mem. Republican Leadership Com. of Oakland County. Mem. Nat. Assn. Female Execs., Am. Soc. Profl. and Exec. Women, Nat. Council Career Women, Women's Assn. for Detroit Symphony Orch. (bd. dirs.), Oakland Citizen's League, Birmingham/Bloomington Bd. Realtors, Fashion Group Detroit (regional dir. 1985-86), Publicity Club N.Y. Roman Catholic. Clubs: Village Players, Rolls Royce Owners (newsletter editor region), Ferrari Owners. Home: 776 Waddington St Birmingham MI 48009 Office: 2501 M St NW Washington DC 20037

SCHULTZ, PAMELA KAY, supermarket bookkeeper; b. Madison, Wis., Oct. 21, 1947; d. Charles Floyd and Delores Marie (Rector) Duane; student Madison Area Tech. Coll., 1975; m. James Mallory Schultz, Jan. 22, 1966; children—Julie Katherine, Jennifer Kay, Karen Elizabeth. Sec. to v.p. Nat. Mut. Benefit Life Ins. Co., Madison, 1965-66; sec., bookkeeper Family Market Enterprises, Inc., DeForest, Wis., 1966—, v.p., 1986—; real estate broker, DeForest; founder Win-Fore Women's Investment Club. Leader, Blackhawk council Girl Scouts U.S.A., 1974, 75, 77, 79-80; a founder DeForest Area Hist. Soc., 1975, active membership dr., 1975-79, sec.-treas., 1975-79, bd. dirs., 1975-81; treas. DeForest Moravian Ch., 1977-83. Recipient Small Bus. award U. Wis., 1986. Mem. DeForest C. of C. (dir. 1984-85, pres. 1986). Home: 305 Meadow Ln DeForest WI 53532 Office: 302 N Main St DeForest WI 53532

SCHULZ, ELSA RUTH, educational administrator; b. Diamante, Argentina, Dec. 25, 1942; came to U.S., 1973; d. Miguel and Emma (Hardy) Esparcia; m. Victor A. Schulz, Jan. 25, 1967; children—Ronald A., Leroy Ed. B.A. in Music Edn., River Plate Coll., Argentina, 1963, B.A. in Edn., 1965; postgrad. Ind. U., 1982, Valparaiso U., 1981; M.A., Andrews U., Mich., 1979. Lic. tchr., Ind. Sch. prin. and tchr., Argentina, 1963-73; acting dir. and bilingual resource tchr. Hobart Sch. Corp., Ind., 1979-82; ESL coordinator Ivy Tech. Coll., Gary, Ind., 1982-85, dept. chair, 1985—. Author: Practical Classroom Suggestions, 1982; Curriculum Guide for Reading Instruction, 4 vols., 1983; numerous film appearances as singer. Mem. Nat. Assn. Female Execs., Nat. Assn. Bilingual Edn., Internat. Conf. Bilingual Edn., Nat. Conf. Bilingual Edn. Avocations: singing; organ and piano. Home: 3296 W 75th Pl Merrillville IN 46410 Office: Ivy Tech Coll 5727 Sohl Ave Hammond IN 46410

SCHULZ, KAREN GAYLE, financial planner; b. Wessington Springs, S.D., Nov. 16, 1959; d. Walter William and Lois Augusta (Thomas) S. B.S., S.D. State U., 1982. Asst. mgr., Lerner Shops, Rapid City, S.D., 1982-84, mgr., Denver, 1984-85; fin. planner IDS/Am. Express, Northglenn, Colo., 1985—. Mem. Bus. & Profl. Women's Orgn. (treas.), Metro North C. of C. Lutheran. Avocations: skiing; swimming. Home: 13467 N Osage St Northglenn CO 80234 Office: IDS/Am Express 11990 Grant St Suite 110 Northglenn CO 80233

SCHULZE, SUZANNE SIMS, archivist, librarian; b. Detroit, Jan. 14, 1922; d. Alfred Gapps and Christina Ruth (Stringer) Sims; m. Robert O. Schulze, Oct. 23, 1948; children—Peter, Elizabeth. B.A. in Polit. Sci., U. Mich., 1944, postgrad. Law Sch., 1947-48; M.P.A. in Pub. Adminstrn., Wayne U., Detroit, 1947; M.L.S., U. R.I., Kingston, 1971. Personnel examiner Wayne County Civil Service, Detroit, 1944-47; fgn. student adviser Columbia U., N.Y.C., 1950-51; fgn. student adviser U. Mich., 1952-55; librarian Bryant Coll., Smithfield, R.I., 1971-72; documents librarian U. No. Colo., Greeley, 1972-85, archives librarian, 1985—. Author: Century of the Colorado Census, 1976, revised, 1977; Population Information in 19th Century Census Volumes, 1983; Population Information in 20th Century Census Volumes, 1985, also others. Bd. dirs. LWV, Albuquerque, 1948-50, Mich. 1951-55, Providence, 1956-58, R.I., 1959-61; mem. R.I. Govs. Commn. on Reapportionment of Ho. of Reps., 1962; pres. Joint Legis. Council of R.I., Providence, 1967-71; bd. dirs., asst. v.p. OPPOSE (to oppose mandatory social security), Denver, 1981—. Grantee HEW, 1977, NEH, 1982. Mem. ALA (edn. chmn. govt. documents roundtable 1985—), Midwest Archives Conf., Colo. Pub. Employees Retirement Assn. (dir. 1980—), Mortar Board, Kappa Kappa Gamma. Democrat. Home: 1814 Reservoir Rd Greeley CO 80631 Office: Michener Library Archives U No Colo Greeley CO 80639

SCHULZE, THEODORA ECONOMOU, music director, educator, investment firm executive; b. Hammond, Ind., Sept. 19, 1930; d. Xenophon and Emilie (Mueller) Economou; oboist protege of Alfred Barthel and Kenneth Gekeler, 1943-53; m. Richard Schulze, Apr. 16, 1950; 1 son, Otto. Music dir., soloist The Telemann Soc., N.Y.C. and Ft. Lauderdale, Fla., 1955—; appearances at Carnegie Hall, Town Hall, N.Y. and other world centers, 1955—; dir. and soloist over 45 recs. on Vox, Nonesuch, Everest, Amphion, other U.S. and overseas labels, 1959—; taught at Carnegie Hall, 1954-63; pedagogical work published by Associated Music Pub., N.Y.C., 1970; sec. Philharm. Standard Corp., Acton, Mass., 1969-74; producer nat. syndicated radio show —The Age of Telemann—, 1961—; featured soloist Fla. Pops Orch.; appeared with Robert Goulet, Leonard Pennario, other major soloists, 1977—; treas. Amphion Recording Soc. Inc., 1982—, Wynwood Merc. Corp., 1982—. Office: 1 Financial Plaza Suite 1612 Fort Lauderdale FL 33301

SCHUMACHER, LEE K., educator, educational administrator; b. Chgo.; d. Bernard and Jean Kameron; m. William G. Schumacher, July 29, 1950; children—Karen, Brad, Guy, Craig. B.E. Chgo. Tchrs. Coll., 1952; M.S., No. Ill. U., 1967. Cert. adminstr. Tchr., Chgo. Pub. Schs., 1957; psychol., edn. diagnostic coordinator Dist. 54 Schs., Schaumburg, Ill., 1958-74; supr. spl. edn. Dist. 300 Schs., Dundee, Ill., 1974-77, Dist. U-46 Schs., Elgin, Ill., 1978—; examiner Orchard Sch., Niles, Ill.; clinician Luth. Gen. Hosp., Des Plaines, Ill., 1969-70; instr. De Paul U., Chgo., 1972-75, No. Ill. U., DeKalb, Ill., 1975. Contbr. articles to profl. publs. Bd. dirs. Hanover Youth Commn., Hanover Twp., Ill., 1981—. Named Outstanding Woman Educator Copley Newspaper, 1974, Mother of Yr. Univ. Ill., 1975. Mem. Assn. Children Learning Disabilities (state rep. 1974), Council Exceptional Children (chpt. pres. 1969), Delta Kappa Gamma (scholarship winner 1974, 83). Lodge: Elks. Avocations: bridge, travel, cooking. Home: 40 Glen Echo Rd Elgin IL 60120 Office: Dist U-46 355 E Chicago St Elgin IL 60120

SCHUMAN, MARY ELLEN, extension official; b. Columbia City, Ind., Jan. 18, 1935; d. Homer Earl and Dorothy Charlotte (Kanable) Schuman; B.S., Purdue U., 1957; M.S., Colo. State U., 1968. Merchandising trainee Morehouse Fashion Dept. Store, Columbus, Ohio, 1957-58; home demonstration agt. Purdue U., Portland, Ind., 1958-62, New Castle, Ind., 1962-69, area extension agt. youth, 1969-73; extension agt. youth, Marion County (Ind.), Indpls., 1973-81; area adminstr. Coop. Extension Service, 1981-84; dist. dir. Coop. Extension Service for Purdue U., 1984—. Mem. Ind. Youth Council, 1971. Mem. Nat. Assn. Extension Home Economists (Distinguished Service award 1972), Am., Ind. home econs. assns., Ind. Extension Agts. Assn. (sec. 1976-77, pres. 1978-79, Career award 1980), Ind. Extension Home Economists (pres. 1967), Nat. Assn. 4-H Agts. (Distinguished Service award 1972), Ind. Extension Youth Agts. (sec. 1976, pres. 1977), Purdue Alumni Assn., Epsilon Sigma Phi (v.p. 1983-84, pres. 1984-85), Gamma Sigma Delta. Club: Altrusa (Indpls.). Home: 3834 Wilderness Trail Indianapolis IN 46237 Office: 3510 E 96th St Suite 34 Indianapolis IN 46240

SCHUMANN, CLARA (MRS. FREDERICK JOHN SCHUMANN), civic worker; b. Detroit, Dec. 21, 1905; d. Otto Henry and Clara (Schultz) Helm; cert. Detroit Tchrs. Coll., 1926; B.S., Wayne State U., 1932; m. Frederick John Schumann, June 29, 1931; 1 dau., Linda Diane. Bd. dirs. LWV, Grosse Pointe, Mich., 1952-54; v.p. Keep Detroit Beautiful, 1958; Mayor's Com. Keep Grosse Pointe Park Beautiful; bd. dirs. Women's City Club of Detroit, 1941-43; pres. Coll. Women's Club of Detroit, 1936-37; Detroit pres. Women's Nat. Farm and Garden Assn., 1938-40; pres. Federated Garden Clubs of Mich., Inc., 1955-57, bd. dirs., 1970—; bd. dirs. Nat. Council State Garden Clubs, 1955-57; pres. Detroit Garden Center, 1943-44, bd. dirs., 1970—, pres., 1975, 78; sec. Grosse Pointe (Mich.) War Meml. Assn., 1956-58; pres. YWCA of Met. Detroit, 1959, now trustee; mem. world service council of nat. bd. YWCA, 1964; mem. council Internat. Inst. Met. Detroit, v.p., 1970—; pres. Mich. Questers; mem. adv. panel Sta. WTVS, Detroit, 1981—, Sta. WTVS-TV; bd. dirs. Adult Service Centers, 1982—. Mem. Alpha Sigma Tau. Unitarian. Home: 836 Harcourt Rd Grosse Pointe MI 48230

SCHUMANN, ROXY MAY, lawyer; b. Galesburg, Ill., Sept. 24, 1943; d. Gilbert Morris and Marguerite Ellen (Berry) Schumann; m. Lincoln James Nixon, June 10, 1961 (div. Nov. 1964); children—Anthony, Lincoln. Student Knox Coll., Galesburg, 1970-73; J.D., SUNY-Buffalo, 1977. Bar: Ill. 1978. Exec. dir. Carver Community Ctr., Galesburg, 1967-73; assoc. Braud, Warner, Neppl & Westensee, Ltd., Rock Island, Ill., 1978—, dir., 1979—. Bd. dirs. Mental Health 708 Bd., Rock Island, 1983. Mem. ABA, Ill. Bar Assn., Chgo. Bar Assn., Rock Island County Bar Assn., Assn. Trial Lawyers Am. Democrat. Mem. Unity Ch. Home: 3401 Black Hawk Rd Apt 1B Rock Island IL 61201 Office: Braud Warner Neppl & Westensee Ltd 1703 2d Ave Rock Island IL 61201

SCHUMER, MIRIAM HERNANDEZ, scientific journal editor; b. Aguas Buenas, P.R., Sept. 11, 1925, came to U.S., 1944; d. Ramon and Mary (Melendez) Hernandez; children—Gerard M. Soto, Leonard, Daniel Anthony, Naomi Nilza; m. William Schumer. Student U. P.R., Rio Piedras, 1942-43, CCNY, 1944-45, Brown's Bus. Coll. and Edison Ediphone Sch., N.Y.C., 1947-48, Sacramento Coll., 1965-67. Exec. sec. physics Meml. Cancer Ctr. and Sloan-Kettering Inst., N.Y.C., 1952-53, U.S. Vitamin Corp., N.Y.C., 1953-55; consumer columnist El Diario de Nueva York, N.Y.C., 1955-57; adminstrv. asst. dept. surgery Chgo. Med. Sch., 1960-65, U. Calif.-Davis, 1965-67, U. Ill. and VA West Side Hosp., Chgo., 1967-75; adminstrv. and editorial asst. dept.

surgery U. of Health Scis./Chgo. Med. Sch. and VA North Chicago (Ill.) Med. Ctr., 1975-80; asst. exec. editor dept. surgery U. of Health Scis./Chgo. Med. Sch., North Chicago, Ill., 1980—; asst. exec. editor Circulatory Shock jour., N.Y.C., 1979—; counselor equal opportunity employment 1976-79. Founder Beneficent Hispanic Soc. N.Y., 1947; founding mem. Hispanic Theater of N.Y., 1948; mem. Lake County Health Systems Agy., 1980-81. Recipient commendations VA, 1971, 79. Club: Espanol of North Shore. Home: 1995 Shore Acres Rd Lake Bluff IL 60044 Office: Dept of Surgery U of Health Sciences/The Chicago Med Sch 3333 Green Bay Rd North Chicago IL 60064

SCHUR, SUSAN DORFMAN, state legislator; b. Newark, Feb. 27, 1940; d. Norman and Jeanette (Handelman) Dorfman; B.A., Goucher Coll., 1961; children—Diana Elisabeth, Erica Marlene. Adminstr. fed. housing, fgn. aid, anti-poverty programs, 1961-67; mem. Mass. Housing Appeals Com., 1977-81; mem., v.p. Bd. of Alderman, Newton, Mass., 1974-81; mem. Mass. Ho. of Reps., 1981—; mem. Spl. Commn. on Divorce. Bd. dirs. Mass. chpt. Ams. for Democratic Action. Mem. Newton Democratic City Com., 1970—. Mem. LWV, Boston Network Women in Politics and Govt., Nat. Women's Polit. Caucus, Mass. Caucus Women Legislators. Office: State House Boston MA 02133

SCHURZ, RUTH DEAN, clinical social worker, sculptor; b. Elizabeth, N.J., Apr. 14, 1912; d. James Riddle and Marjorie Nott (Thatcher) S.; student Parson's N.Y. Sch. Fine and Applied Arts, 1930-32; sculpture student of Renzo Fenci, 1945-48; B.A. in Psychology, U. Calif., Santa Barbara, 1960; postgrad. U. Vienna, summer 1960; M.S.W., UCLA, 1962. Social worker Children's Home Soc. of Calif., Santa Barbara, 1962-67, Internat. Social Service, Athens, Greece, 1968-69, Family Service Agy. Santa Barbara, 1969-77; pvt. practice psychotherapy, Santa Barbara, 1977—; sculptor specializing in portrait busts, bronze, terra cotta, cast stone, Santa Barbara, 1948—, commns. include Maurice Abravanel, in Abravanel Hall, Music Acad., Santa Barbara, Symphony Hall, Salt Lake City, and Herbert P. Broida, in Broida Hall, U. Calif., Santa Barbara. Served with USN, 1943-44. Cert. social worker. Mem. Acad. Cert. Social Workers, Sculptors' Guild Santa Barbara. Episcopalian. Home and Office. 519 Peregrina Rd Santa Barbara CA 93105

SCHUSTER, EULA ELAINE, lawyer; b. Oklahoma City, June 8, 1936; d. John Otto and Eula Delone (Campbell) Schuster; A.B., Sweet Briar Coll., 1958; M.A., U. Okla., 1961, J.D., 1968. Prof. econs. Southeastern State U., Durant, Okla., 1961-65; admitted to Okla. bar, 1968; pvt. practice law Whitten & Whitten, Attys., Oklahoma City, 1968-71; asst. dist. atty. Oklahoma County, 7th Dist., 1972-78; partner firm Jones, Schuster & Flaugher, Oklahoma City, 1978—; lectr. in field. Mem. Oklahoma County Bd. Adjustment, 1978—, chmn., 1984-86, citizen mem. profl. liaison com. City of Oklahoma City, 1980—; mem. Bd. Edn., Oklahoma City Area Vocat. Tech. Sch., Dist. 22, 1982—, pres., 1984-85; mem. ch. bd. University Pl. Christian Ch., 1982—; bd. overseers Sweet Briar Coll., 1986-1990. Gen. Electric grantee, 1963. Mem. ABA, Okla. Trial Lawyers Assn., Fed. Bar Assn., AAUW (br. pres. 1978-80, Okla. div. bd. 1969-75, 81-83, 85-87), Oklahoma County Bar Assn., Okla. Bar Assn., Kappa Beta Pi, Delta Kappa Gamma. Office: 515 NW 13th St Oklahoma City OK 73103

SCHUTT, DAFNE LEE, real estate broker, photographer; b. Stockholm, Sweden, June 1, 1929; came to U.S., 1955; d. Gustaf H.E. and Adele Marie (Ytteborg) Von Hofsten; m. Donald Lee Schutt, Feb. 18, 1956; children—Lena, Lita, Nancy, Donald Jr., Ana, Otto. Student Orange Coast Coll., Costa Mesa, Calif., 1962-65. Lic. real estate broker, Calif. Photographer Ann Graf Studio, Long Beach, Calif., 1969-70, Jewell Studio, Gardena, Calif., 1970-72, Story Time Studio, Hollywood Calif., 1973-77; salesperson Century 21, San Pedro, Calif., 1977-81; broker, owner Available Real Estate, Torrance, Calif., 1981—; writer, photographer Wester Photographer, San Diego, 1985—. Author: Complete Modeling Guide, 1985. Avocation: breeding show dogs. Home: 1151 Sepulveda St San Pedro CA 90731 Office: Available Real Estate 25202 Crenshaw St Torrance CA 90505

SCHUYLER, JANE, educator; b. Flushing, N.Y., Nov. 2, 1943; d. Frank James and Helen (Oberhofer) S.; B.A., Queens Coll., 1965; M.A., Hunter Coll., 1967, Ph.D., Columbia U., 1972. Asst. prof. art history Montclair State Coll., Upper Montclair, N.J., 1970; coordinator fine arts, asst. prof. York Coll., City U. N.Y., Jamaica, 1973-77, 78—, C.W. Post Coll., L.I. U., Greenvale, N.Y., 1971-73, adj. asso. prof., 1977-78. Mem. Fine Arts Com. Internat. Women's Arts Festival, 1974-76. Columbia U. Summer Travel and Research grantee, 1969. Mem. Coll. Art Assn. Am., Women's Caucus for Art, AAUP, Nat. Trust Hist. Preservation, Renaissance Soc. Am. Democrat. Roman Catholic. Contbr. articles on occult and art to Cakes and Ale, 1978, Italian Quar., 1982, Secac Jour., 1983, 85. Author: Florentine Busts: Sculpted Portraiture in the Fifteenth Century, 1976. Home: 35 37 78th St Jackson Heights NY 11372

SCHWAB, CAROL ANN, lawyer; b. Washington, Mo., Mar. 2, 1953; d. Calvin George and Edith Emma (Starke) Schermann; m. Steven Joseph Schwab, May 31, 1975. B.A., Southeast Mo. State U., 1975; J.D., U. Mo., 1978; LL.M., Washington U., 1985. Bar: Mo. 1979, N.C. 1986. Law clk. Shook, Hardy & Bacon, Kansas City, Mo., 1979; law clk. U.S. Dist. Ct. Western Dist. Mo., Kansas City, 1979-82; assoc. Bryan, Cave, McPheeters & McRoberts, St. Louis, 1982-84; instr. legal writing St. Louis U. Sch. Law, 1984; assoc. Smith, Anderson, Blount, Dorsett, Mitchell & Jernigan, Raleigh, N.C., 1985—. Recipient John S. Divilbiss award U. Mo., 1977. Mem. ABA, N.C. Bar Assn., Mo. Bar Assn. Republican. Roman Catholic. Contbr. articles to profl. jours. Office: PO Box 12807 Raleigh NC 27605

SCHWAB, LYNNE SUSAN, teacher educator; b. Los Angeles, Aug. 15, 1944; d. Harold Norman, Marjorie (dec.), and Hilda (Gross) S.; B.A., UCLA, 1967, M.A., 1968; Ph.D., U. Wash., 1972. Researcher S.W. Regional Lab. Ednl. Research and Evaluation, Santa Monica and Inglewood, Calif., 1968; tchr. Santa Monica public schs., 1968-69; tchr., researcher U. Wash., 1969-72; tchr. human geography Western Wash. State Coll., spring 1972; mem. faculty U. N.Fla., Jacksonville, 1972—, asso. prof. elem. and secondary edn., 1976—; mem. vis. faculty Transp. Center, U. Tenn., 1970; cons. in field. Bd. dirs. Jacksonville YWCA, Jacksonville Job Readiness Program, Jacksonville Girls Club, active Children's Internat. Summer Villages. Grantee Edn. Professions Devel. Act, 1969, NSF, 1975, Mott Found., 1976, 77, 78. Mem. Am. Ednl. Research Assn., Nat. Council Social Studies, Assn. Curriculum and Supervision, Western Psychol. Assn., Nat. Council In-Service Edn., Phi Delta Kappa. Author textbooks, articles in field, chpts. in books. Office: Div Curriculum and Instrn U NFla Jacksonville FL 32216

SCHWABE, CLARA GONZALEZ, lawyer; b. Queens, N.Y., Apr. 15, 1947; d. Gustavo Jaime and Lila (Gonzalez) Schwabe; B.A., Syracuse U., 1968; J.D., Bklyn. Law Sch., 1973; Admitted to N.Y. bar, 1974; asso. firm Stanley E. Kooper, Bklyn., 1973-80; partner firm Kooper and Schwabe, Bklyn., 1980—. Mem. Community Bd. 2, Bklyn., 1973-80, chmn. by-laws com., 1977—. Mem. N.Y. State Trial Lawyers Assn. (editor Notes and Decisions 1980—), Bklyn. Bar. Assn. (co-editor-in-chief Bklyn. Barrister, 1981—), Bklyn. Council of Women Lawyers (founder, 1981, pres. 1981-82), N.Y. State Bar Assn., Puerto Rican Bar Assn., Bklyn. Law Sch. Alumni Assn. (exec. sec. 1980—, editor Veritas 1977—). Office: Kooper & Schwabe 16 Court St Suite 1704 Brooklyn NY 11241

SCHWABEL, MARY JANE, microbiologist; b. Buffalo, Oct. 9, 1946; d. Albert Thomas and Doris Katherine (Schottin) S.; B.S. in Biology, Daemen Coll., 1968; M.S. in Biology Edn., Canisius Coll., 1975; A.A.S. in Nursing, Trocaire Coll., 1983. Research asst. Erie County Virology Lab., SUNY, Buffalo, 1968-74; sr. serology techinican, supr. Erie County Lab., Buffalo, 1974-79; chief virologist dept. clin. microbiology and immunology Erie County Med. Center, Buffalo, 1979—. Mem. ASPCA, Nat. Wildlife Fedn., Internat. Wildlife Fedn., Am. Forestry Assn., Nat. Antivivisection Soc., North Shore Animal League, Western N.Y. Infection Control Soc., Nat. Am. Soc. Microbiology, Am. Public Health Assn., N.Y. State Assn. Public Health Labs., N.y. State Public Health Assn., AAAS, N.Y. State Nurses Assn., Beta Beta Beta, Republican. Roman Catholic. Office: 462 Grider St Buffalo NY 14215

SCHWAGER, ELAINE SUSAN, psychologist; b. Pitts., Aug. 3, 1949; d. Carl and Inge Susi (Weihl) S.; m. Marvin Hurvich, Nov. 1, 1981; children—Carl Harry, Julia Beth. B.A. cum laude in English Lit., CCNY, 1969; M.A. in English Lit., SUNY, Stony Brook, 1971; Ph.D. in Clin. Psychology, L.I.U., 1977; Ph.D., NYU, 1986, postdoctoral grad. in analytic tng., 1986. Intern, then postdoctoral fellow N.Y. Hosp. Cornell U. Med. Center, White Plains, 1975-79; asst. prof. psychology Downstate Med. Center, Bklyn., 1979—; staff psychologist Blueberry Treatment Center, Bklyn, 1980-81, ind. practice psychoanalytic psychotherapy, 1978—. Mem. Am. Psychol. Assn., Soc. Personality Assessment, N.Y. Psychol. Assn. Home: 79 W 12th St New York NY 10011 Office: 49 W 12th St New York NY 10011

SCHWALB, ANN WEISS, information specialist, photographer, editor, consultant; b. Modena, Italy, July 17, 1949; came to U.S., 1951, naturalized, 1959; d. Leo and Athalie (Schaefer) Weiss; m. Allen J. Schwalb, June 27, 1971; children—Julia Emily, Rebecca Lauren. B.A. magna cum laude, U. Rochester, 1971; M.A., Drexel U., 1973. Cert. med. librarian, pub. librarian, sch. librarian. Tchr. English, Bay Trail High Sch., Pittsford, N.Y.; cataloguer Drexel U., Phila., 1971-73; librarian Akiba Lower Sch., Merion, Pa., 1973; head children's dept. Tredyffrin Pub. Library, Strafford, Pa., 1973-79, head reference dept., 1979—; editor, chief cons. monographs, articles, freelance photographer, 1974—. Chief editor, cons. Puppetry and the Art of Story Creation, 1981, Puppetry in Early Childhood Education, 1982, Puppetry, Language and the Special Child: Discovering Alternative Language, 1984, Humanizing the Enemy... and Ourselves, 1986, Imagination, 1986. Photographer Bob Edgar's Campain U.S. Senate, 1985-86, David Landau's Congl. Campaign, 1986. Mem. ALA, Pa. Library Assn., ACLU, Free Wallenberg Alliance, Union Concerned Scientistists, SANE, Physicians for Social Responsibility. Home: 438 Barclay Rd Rosemont PA 19010 Office: Tredyffrin Pub Library 582 Upper Gulph Rd Strafford PA 19087

SCHWAM, LORI GAIL, physician; b. N.Y.C., June 1, 1955; d. Louis and Beverly (Katzman) Schwam. B.A., New Coll., 1978; M.D., Am. U. of Caribbean, 1982. House officer Beth Israel Med. Ctr., N.Y.C., 1983—. Mem. AMA. Jewish. Office: Dept Pathology Beth Israel Med Ctr 10 Nathan D Perlman Pl New York NY 10003

SCHWANER, ANNIE MAE GINN, state legislator; b. Carnesville, Ga., Apr. 24, 1912; d. Charles Holman and Mary Elizabeth (Terrell) Ginn; m. Nelson Marshall Schwaner (dec. 1967); children—Gordon Wesley, Audrey Mae, Susan Anne, Marsha Mae, Nelson Marshall II. Sec., Tubize Corp., Hopewell, Va., 1934-35; former reporter Hopewell News; former columnist Progress Index, Petersburg, Va.; mem. N.H. Ho. of Reps., 1963—, mem. mcpl. and county govt. com., 1963, mem. state constl. conv., 1964, 74-84, resources, recreation, and devel. com.; mem. exec. bd. Rockingham County Legis. Del., 1973—. Mem. State Security Task Force, also Price Stblzn. Bd., 1964—; founder, 1st pres. Plaistow (N.H.) Civic Orgn., 1959-60; chmn. vols. Greater Haverhill (Mass.) chpt. ARC, 1954-57, nat. del., 1955, exec. bd., 1954-57; com. chmn. PTA council, Worcester, 1947-48; exec. bd. Sea Coast Regional Plan, 1965-67; v.p. Seacoast Regional Devel. Assn.; mem. Diocesan Sch. Bd., 1965-71; chmn. various fund-raising drs.; mem. nat. fund raising and adv. bd. Am. Heart Assn.; mem. Rockingham County Selective System Draft Bd.; pres. Plaistow Women's Republican Club, 1964-66; bd. dirs. N.H. Heart Assn., state heart fund chmn., 1973; bd. dirs. Greater Salem Mental Health Clinic, 1976, So. Rockingham Mental Health Assn., 1975—; mem. N.H. Commn. on Status of Women. Recipient Bronze medal N.H. Heart Assn, 1959, cert. of merit Am. Mothers Com., 1960, cert. of honor N.H. DAV, 1965; citation White House, ARC. Mem. Cath. Daus. Am., Cath. Women's Guild (past pres.), Nat. Order Women Legislators (state pres. 1973). Roman Catholic (ch. adv. bd.).

SCHWARTZ, BARBARA SARA, interior designer; b. Bklyn., Apr. 10, 1935; d. Louis and Gladys (Sklarew) Gibson; m. Eugene Mark Schwartz, May 6, 1955; 1 son, Michael Holden. Student SUNY Sch. Applied Arts and Scis., N.Y.C., 1952-54, New Sch. Social Research, 1955-56. Pres. Dexter Design, Inc., N.Y.C., 1960—; charter mem. formica design adv. bd. Formica Corp., N.Y.C., 1978-83. Mem. assoc. council and com. on photography Mus. Modern Art, N.Y.C.; mem. 20th century com. Met. Mus. Art, N.Y.C.; mem. spl. events com., former chmn. events Whitney Mus. Am. Art, N.Y.C., mem. producer's council Bklyn. Acad. Music; bd. dirs., past v.p. Cunningham Dance Found., 1968—. Recipient Outstanding Interior of Yr. award, 1976; Best in Competition award I.B.D., 1980; named one of top 100 collectors in Am., Art and Antiques Mag., 1985-86. Mem. Am. Soc. Interior Designers (cert.). Avocation: art. Subject of numerous profl. articles. Office: Dexter Design Inc 133 E 58th St Suite 804 New York NY 10022

SCHWARTZ, CHERYL ANN, women's health lecturer, film and television producer, writer, actress; b. Cin., Sept. 4, 1949; d. Denny Lee and Alice Jane (Taylor) S. A.S., U. Cin., 1970, student 1967-72, student West Los Angeles Coll., 1977-79, Calif. State U.-Northridge, 1979-80, Pierce Coll., Woodland Hills, Calif., 1981-83. Publisher, editor The Well Woman, Beverly Hills, Calif., 1980—; lectr. Internat. Toxic Shock Syndrome Network, Beverly Hills, 1980—, also founder, dir.; dir. Hawaii Express, Los Angeles, 1982; owner, mgr. C.A. Schwartz & Assocs., Beverly Hill, 1982—; producer, host. The Well Woman, Encino, 1983-84, Cheryl & Co., Santa Monica, Calif., 1984—; pres. Cheryl A. Schwartz Prodns., Beverly Hills, 1983—; cons. Nat. Women's Health Network, Washington, 1981—. Author: In the Gutter Looking at Stars, 1980; exec. producer, writer Easy Does It: The Excercise Video for the Rest of Us. Mem. commn. on Status of Women, Los Angeles, 1980—; bd. dirs. Womens Equal Rights Legal Def. and Edn. Fund, 1983—; vol. UCLA Med. Center 1976-80; mem. Inter-Agy. Council on Child Abuse and Neglect, Los Angeles, 1983; mem. Wildlife Waystation. Mem. Am. Fedn. TV and Radio Artists, ASTM, Am. Film Inst., Screen Actors Guild, Aircraft Owners and Pilots Assn., Calif. Women's Health Network, Writers Guild Am., Empire State Consumer Assn., Nat. Consumers League. Republican. Clubs: Farkus (Beverly Hills); Los Angeles Polo. Office: PO Box 1248 Beverly Hills CA 90213

SCHWARTZ, CONSTANCE ANN, lawyer; b. N.Y.C., Jan. 22, 1947; d. Arnold Schwartz and Libby (Hirsch) Anninger. B.A., magna cum laude, Tufts U., 1969; M.A., NYU, 1971; M.L.S., Columbia U., 1971; J.D., Cardozo Sch. Law, 1979. Bar: N.Y., 1981. Librarian Princeton (N.J.) U., 1971-73, N.Y.U., 1973-75; lawyer Siemens Capital Corp., N.Y.C., 1979—. Mem. ABA, N.Y. Bar Assn., Women's Bar Assn. N.Y., N.Y.C. Bar Assn. Office: Siemens Capital Corp 767 Fifth Ave New York NY 10153

SCHWARTZ, DEBBIE GALIA, retired social worker; b. Bklyn., June 16, 1925; d. Israel Noah and Celia (Hendlin) Neiman; B.A., Bklyn. Coll., 1945; M.S.W., Columbia U., 1956; m. Sam Schwartz, Jan. 20, 1957; 1 son, Noah. Asst. dir. Bklyn. Jewish Youth Council, 1946-48; adminstr. public relations Youth Alyah, Jerusalem, 1951-52; group worker-health educator Hadassah Med. Orgn., 1952-54; hostess, moderator Fourth R, Sta. WCRA-TV, 1954-56; day camp dir., Hirschman YMHA of Coney Island, 1961-65, asst. exec. dir., 1965-68; exec. dir. Assn. Jewish Center Workers, N.Y.C., 1976-81; field work instr. Hunter Coll., 1961-68. Mem. Assn. Jewish Center Workers, Internat. Conf. of Jewish Communal Services, Columbia U. Sch. Social Work Alumni Assn., Jewish Public Soc.

SCHWARTZ, DORIS RUHBEL, public health nurse, geriatric nurse practitioner; b. Bklyn., May 30, 1915; d. Henry and Florence Marie (Shuttleworth) S. B.S., NYU, 1953, M.A., 1956; R.N., Methodist Hosp. Sch. Nursing, Bklyn. Staff nurse Vis. Nurse Assn., Bklyn., 1942-43, 48-51; editorial asst. Am. Jour. Nursing, N.Y.C., 1947-48; pub. health nurse Cornell U. Med. Coll., N.Y.C., 1951-62, tchr.-nurse practitioner, 1972-80, faculty pub. health nursing Cornell U.-N.Y. Hosp. Sch. Nursing, N.Y.C., from 1962; sr. scholar in nursing U. Pa., Phila., 1981—. Co-author: Family Handbook of Home Nursing; Cardiology for Nurses; The Elderly Ambulatory Patient, 1963; Gerontology and Geriatric Nursing (Am. Jour. Nursing Books of Yr. citation 1983), 1982. Chairperson welfare services com. Upper East Side Democratic Club, N.Y.C., 1960s; mem. N.Y.C. Health Research Council, late 1960s. Served to capt. Nurses Corps, U.S. Army, 1943-47; PTO. Rockefeller Found. fellow U. Toronto (Ont., Can.), 1949-50; NIH Fogarty fellow, Scotland, 1976. Mem. Am. Nurses Assn. (treas. Am. Jour. Nursing 1979, Pearl McIver medal 1980), Am. Pub. Health Assn. (Disting. Career award 1979), Nat. League for Nursing, Am. Acad. Nursing, (charter fellow), Inst. Medicine (sr.). Democrat. Unitarian.

SCHWARTZ, ELEANOR BRANTLEY, university dean; b. Kite, Ga., Jan. 1, 1937; d. Jesse Melvin and Hazel (Hill) Brantley; children—John, Cynthia. Student Mercer U., Ga. So. Coll., 1956-57; B.B.A., Ga. State U., 1961, M.B.A., 1963, D.B.A., 1969. Adminstrv. asst. Fin. Agy., 1954, Fed. Govt., Va., Pa., Ga., 1959-61; asst. dean admissions Ga. State U., Atlanta, 1961-65, asst. prof., 1965-70; assoc. prof. Cleve. State U., 1970-80, assoc. dean, 1975-80; dean, Harzfeld prof. U. Mo., Kansas City, 1980—; disting. vis. prof. Berry Coll., Rome, Ga., N.Y. State U. Coll., Fredonia, Mons U., Belgium; cons. pvt. industry, U.S., Europe, Can.; dir. Sentinel Consumer Products, Inc., Commerce Bank Blue Hills, Am. Carriers, Inc. Author: Sex Barriers in Business, 1971, Contemporary Readings in Marketing, 1974; (with Muczykand Smith) Principles of Supervision, 1984. Chmn., Mayor's Task Force in Govt. Efficiency, Kansas City, Mo., 1984; mem. community planning and research council United Way Kansas City, 1975-78; bd. dirs. Jr. Achievement, 1982—, Greater Kansas City ARC. Recipient Disting. Faculty award Cleve. State U., 1974, Cleve. Community Career Achievement award YMCA, 1980, 60 Women of Achievement Girls Scouts council Mid Continent, 1983. Mem. Am. Mktg. Assn., Acad. Internat. Bus., Am. Mgmt. Assn., Am. Case Research Assn., Internat. Soc. Study Behavioral Devel., Beta Gamma Sigma (bd. govts.). Office: Univ Mo Sch Bus and Public Adminstrn Kansas City MO 64110

SCHWARTZ, (ELLEN) SHIRLEY ECKWALL, chemist; b. Detroit, Aug. 26, 1935; d. Emil Victor and Jessie Grace (Galbraith) Eckwall; B.S., U. Mich., 1957; M.S., Wayne State U., 1962, Ph.D., 1970; B.S., Detroit Inst. Tech., 1978; m. Ronald Elmer Schwartz, Aug. 25, 1957; children—Steven Dennis, Bradley Allen, George Byron. Asst. prof. Detroit Inst. Tech., 1973-78, head div. math. sci., 1976-78; research staff mem. BASF Wyandotte Corp., Wyandotte, Mich., 1978-81, head sect. functional fluids, 1981; staff research scientist Gen. Motors Corp., Warren, Mich., 1981—. Corr. sec. Childbirth Without Pain Edn. Assn., 1962, Warren-Centerline Human Relations Council, 1968. Mem. Am. Soc. Lubrication Engrs. (treas. Detroit sect. 1981, chmn. sect. 1982-83, dir. 1985—), Am. Chem. Soc., Tissue Culture Assn., Soc. Automotive Engrs., Mensa, Sigma Xi. Lutheran. Contbr. articles to profl. jours.; patentee in field. Office: Gen Motors Research Labs Warren MI 48090

SCHWARTZ, ILENE, psychologist, educator; b. Phila., June 19, 1942; d. Israel Gerson and Jean (Soloway) Schiffman; m. Victor Louis Schwartz, Jan. 6, 1970 (div. 1980); 1 child, Amy Jill. B.S., Temple U., 1970; postgrad. U. Pa., 1981-82. Instr. psychology Pratt Inst., Bklyn., 1969-70; psychotherapist Phila. Mental Health Clinic, 1972-74, Phila. Consultation Ctr., 1974-80, Help, Inc., Phila., 1974-80; pvt. practice, Phila., 1980—; instr. Community Coll. Phila., 1974-80; cons. in field. Fellow Am. Psychol. Assn. Office: 201 S 18th St Philadelphia PA 19103

SCHWARTZ, JOAN WEINMAN, educational administrator; b. Phila., Oct. 2, 1942; d. Aaron L. and Amy (Lobel) Weinman; m. Jeffrey Byron Schwartz, Aug. 4, 1963; children—Kevin Jay, Jill Elaine. B.A. in English, U. Pa., 1963; M.A. in English, Am. U., 1971. Tchr., Tilden Jr. High Sch., Phila., 1964-65; tchr. English Walter Johnson High Sch., Bethesda, Md., 1965-68; instr. Dillard U., New Orleans, 1968-69; instr. Am U., 1971-72; coordinator fed. programs Pa. Dept. Edn., Harrisburg, 1975-79; exec. asst. to pres. Pa. Coll. Optometry, Phila., 1981—; legis. and fed. funding cons., 1979-81. Contbr. articles to profl. jours. Charter mem., organizer Harrisburg Area Rape Crisis Ctr., 1974-76; bd. dirs. LWV, Lower Merion, Pa., 1980—; dir. vols. McGovern for Pres. Campaign, 1972. Named Boss of the Yr., Keystone State Chtp. Am. Bus. Women's Assn., 1977. Mem. Am. Council on Edn., Nat. Identification Project for Women in Higher Edn. Adminstrn., Pa. Assn. Coll. and Univs. Democrat. Jewish. Avocations: tennis; sailing; reading; traveling. Home: 10 Radcliffe Rd Bala Cynwyd PA 19004

SCHWARTZ, JOYCE GENSBERG, pathologist; b. San Antonio, July 24, 1950; d. Frank and Sara Gensberg; B.A., U. Tex.-Austin, 1971, M.A., 1972; M.D., U. Tex.-San Antonio, 1980; m. Alan R. Schwartz, July 17, 1977. Speech pathologist Northeast Ind. Sch. Dist., San Antonio, 1971-73; vet. asst., 1973-74; resident in pathology Audie Murphy VA Hosp., San Antonio; pathology Faculty U. Tex. Health Sci. Ctr. at San Antonio, 1984. Mem. AMA, Coll. Am. Pathologists, Bexar County Med. Assn., Phi Kappa Phi. Jewish.

SCHWARTZ, JUDY ELLEN, navy cardiothoracic surgeon; b. Mason City, Iowa, Oct. 5, 1946; d. Walter Carl and Alice Nevada (Moore) Schwartz. B.S., U. Iowa, 1968, M.D., 1971. Diplomate Am. Bd. Surgery, Am. Bd. Thoracic Surgery. Intern, Nat. Naval Med. Center, Bethesda, Md., 1971-72, gen. surgery resident, 1972-76, thoracic surgery resident, 1976-78, staff cardiothoracic surgeon, 1979-82, chief cardiothoracic surgeon, 1982-83; chmn. cardiothoracic surg. dept. Naval Hosp., San Diego, 1983-85, quality assurance program dir., 1985—, exec. officer Rapidly Deployable Med. Facility Four, 1986; asst. prof. surgery Uniformed Services Univ. Health Scis., Bethesda, 1983—; cardiothoracic speciality cons. to naval med. command U.S. Navy, Washington, 1983-84. Contbr. articles to various publs. Fellow Am. Coll. Cardiology, Am. Coll. Surgeons; mem. Am. Thoracic Soc., Am. Med. Women's Assn., AMA, Uniformed Services Univ. Surg. Assocs. Lutheran. Office: Quality Assurance Unit Naval Hosp San Diego CA 92134

SCHWARTZ, KAREN MARCIA, clinical psychologist, counseling educator; b. Bklyn.; d. Bernard Leonard and Irene (Zanderer) S.; m. John Paddock, Sept. 5, 1982. B.S. summa cum laude in Psychology and Fine Arts, Tufts U., 1975; M.A. in Clin. Psychology, Emory U., 1978, Ph.D. in Clin. Psychology, 1980. Intern in psychology Emory U. Med. Sch.-Grady Meml. Hosp., Atlanta, 1979-80, Clayton Mental Health Ctr., Riverdale, Ga., 1980-81; asst. prof. counseling, counselor Counseling Ctr., Ga. State U., Atlanta, 1981—; pvt. practice family therapy, individual psychotherapy; cons. in field. Ga. State U. Urban-Life grantee, 1982-83, 83-84. Mem. Am. Psychol. Assn., Ga. Psychol. Assn. (chmn. div. women psychologists), Southeast Psychol. Assn., Phi Beta Kappa. Office: 2905 Piedmont Rd Suite B Atlanta GA 30303

SCHWARTZ, LAURIE KOLLER, association executive, development consultant; b. Munich, Germany, Oct. 19, 1947; came to U.S., 1949, naturalized, 1954; d. Felix and Sally (Wiernik) Koller; m. Michael Louis Schwartz, Aug. 20, 1967; children—Jonas David, Adam Avi, Samara Beth. Diploma in radiol. tech. Mercy Hosp., Balt., 1967; student U. Balt. Radiol. technologist Central Med. Ctr., Balt., 1967-68, Greenstein, Baitch & Friedman, Balt., 1968-70; ptnr. Creme de la Creme, Balt., 1976-78; bd. dirs., coordinator Mid-Atlantic region Internat. Assn. Near Death Studies, U. Conn., Storrs, 1982—; cons. Mgmt. Tng. Systems, Inc., Springfield, Va., 1985—. Active various polit. campaigns, Balt.; chmn. study group Hadassah Med. Orgn., Balt., 1975-76. Mem. Am. Register Radiol. Technologists, Exec. Women's Network, Nat. Alliance Female Execs., Second Generation-Children of Survivors of the Holocaust. Democrat. Jewish. Club: Mercantile (Balt.) Avocations: jazz and aerobic dancing; theatre reading; French cooking. Home: 7041 Concord Rd Baltimore MD 21208 Office: 800 N Charles St Suite 400 Baltimore MD 21201

SCHWARTZ, LINDA DORIEN, lawyer; b. Washington, Nov. 5, 1948; d. William and Yvette (Sperling) S.; m. Alan Hirsch Rosenthal, Oct. 23, 1977; children—Jeffrey Michael Ian, Kevin Hirsch. B.A. cum laude, U. Md., 1970; J.D., Am. U., 1973. Bar: Md. 1973, D.C. 1974. Assoc., Sheeskin & Hillman, P.C., Washington, 1973-76; asst. atty. gen. State of Md., Balt., 1976-77; assoc., then prin. Paley, Rothman & Cooper, Chartered, Chevy Chase, Md., 1977-82; sole practice, Chevy Chase, 1982—; lectr. Continuing Legal Edn., Rockville, Md., 1976-83; guest lectr. Am. U., 1973—. Editor Md. U. Handbook, 1970; contbr. articles profl. jours. Mem. Task Force Moderate Income Housing, Montgomery County, Md., 1978; lectr. Commn. for Women, 1980; panelist Sta. WETA-TV, Washington, 1973; mem. taskforce on young voters Democratic Central Com.; bd. dirs. Harbor Sch., Bethesda, Md. Mem. Montgomery County Bar Assn., (chmn. ethics com. 1983—), Md. Bar Assn. (ethics com. 1977-82), ABA, Am. Judicature Soc., Women's Bar Assn. Md., Phi Alpha Theta, Kappa Delta Pi. Office: 5530 Wisconsin Ave Suite 520 Chevy Chase MD 20815

SCHWARTZ, LINDA EDITH, educational materials company executive, writer; b. Charlotte, N.C., Apr. 26, 1943; d. William and Ina (Weinberg) Schwartz; m. Stanley E. Schwartz, Aug. 8, 1971; children—Stephen, Michael. B.A., U. Fla., 1964; M.A., Calif. State U.-Northridge, 1973. Cert. tchr., adminstr., supr., Calif. Tchr., Gulfstream Elem. Sch., Miami, 1964-65; tchr. Hickory Elem. Sch., Torrance, Calif., 1965-73; gifted cons. tchr. Mountain View Elem. Sch., Santa Barbara, Calif., 1973-75; founder, pres. The Learning Works, Santa Barbara, 1976—. Author: When I Grow Up; Mind Expanders; The Language Scoop, My Bar Mitzvah Keepsake, My Bat Mitzvah Journal, The Alphabet Circus, Creative Writing Rocket, Primary Teachers Pet, The Center Solution, Dictionary Dig, The Teacher's Pet, The Usage Sleuth, Short Vowel Voyage, Long Vowel Voyage, The Addition Magician, Hot Fudge Fractions, Math Marathon, Trivia Trackdown, Creative Capers, I Am Special, Mighty Math, others. Rec. sec. Temple B'nai B'rith, Santa Barbara, 1982-84, co-chmn. fundraising, 1984-85. Club: Zonta. Avocation: reading. Office: The Learning Works PO Box 6187 Santa Barbara CA 93160

SCHWARTZ, LITA LINZER, psychologist, educator; b. N.Y.C., Jan. 14, 1930; d. Aaron Jerome and Dorothy Claire (Linzer) Linzer; A.B., Vassar Coll., 1950; Ed.M., Temple U., 1956; Ph.D., Bryn Mawr Coll., 1964; diplomate Am. Bd. Forensic Psychology; m. Melvin Jay Schwartz, June 18, 1950 (div. 1983); children—Arthur Lee, Joshua David, Frederic Seth. Part-time instr., counselor Pa. State U., Ogontz Campus, Abington, 1961-66, asst. prof. ednl. psychology, 1966-71, assoc. prof., 1971-76, prof., 1976—; cons. in field. Recipient Humanitarian Award N.Y. Philanthropic League, 1973, Christian R. and Mary F. Lindback award for disting. teaching, 1982, Outstanding Tchr. award for 1981-82 Pa. State U. Coll. Edn. Alumni, 1982. Mem. Am. Psychol. Assn., Internat. Council of Psychologists, Am. Ednl. Research Assn., Council for Exceptional Children, Creative Edn. Found., Nat. Assn. for Gifted Children. Author: American Education, 1969, 74, 78; Educational Psychology, 1972, 77; The Exceptional Child: A Primer, 1975, 79; Exceptional Students in the Mainstream, 1984; (with Natalie Isser) The American School and The Melting Pot, 1985; contbr. articles to profl. jours. Office: Pa State U Ogontz Campus Abington PA 19001

SCHWARTZ, LORAINE HELEN, association executive; b. Chgo., Ill., June 15, 1918; d. William Albert Julius and Lydia Lena (Heinrich) Oldenburg; m. Paul Frederick Schwartz, Oct. 12, 1940; children—Lynn Williams, Gail Muffitt, Lauren Browning, Paul, Jr. Student Luther Inst., 1932-36. Pres. Park Lawn Sch. and Activity Ctr., Oak Lawn, Ill., 1980-84; now pres. Park Lawn Assn. for Retarded Children. Vol., Palos Community Hosp., Palos Hts., Ill.; bd. deacons Good Shepherd Luth. Ch., Palos Hts., 1973-79, chmn. bd. deacons, 1979-80. Republican. Lutheran. Home: 15405 Begonia Ct Orland Park IL 60462

SCHWARTZ, M. JANE, financial executive; b. Phila., Sept. 19, 1958; d. Donald and Mary Jane E. (Madden) S. A.A. in Bus. Adminstrn., Bucks County Community Coll., 1979; B.S. in Fin., LaSalle U., 1982; M.B.A. in Fin., St. Joseph's U., 1985. Loan servicing asst. SBA, Bala Cynwyd, Pa., 1976-82; dir. fin. Sparks Tune-Up (div. Maaco Enterprise), King of Prussia, Pa., 1982-86; sr. asset based lender Capital Impact Subs. City Trust Bancorp., Inc., 1986—; pvt. practice small bus. fin. cons., Feasterville, Pa., 1985—. Author, pub, newsletter: For Women Only, 1981-82. Mem. Pathways Condominium Fin. Com., Phila., 1985—. Recipient Fin. Sr. Acad. award, LaSalle U., 1982; named Nat. Empolyee of Yr. U.S. SBA, 1977, Regional Empolyee of Yr., 1977, Spl. Achievement award, Outstanding award, 1977-82. Mem. Nat. Assn. Female Execs., Phi Theta Kappa. Democrat. Roman Catholic. Avocations: Reading; softball; travel. Home: 136 A Turtle Run Stratford CT 06497 Office: Capital Impact 961 Main St Bridgeport CT 06601

SCHWARTZ, MONA, toy company sales executive; b. N.Y.C., Jan. 30, 1953; d. Harry and Annette (Ressler) S. B.A., Bklyn. Coll., 1974. High sch. tchr. biology N.Y.C. Sch. System, 1974-76; sales inventory person Eden Toys Inc., N.Y.C., 1976-77, salesperson, 1977-80, sales mgr., 1980—. Mem. Nat. Assn. Female Execs., Childrenswear Mfrs. Assn. Democrat. Jewish. Avocations: racquetball; boating; reading. Home: 1123 Sussex Rd Teaneck NJ 07666

SCHWARTZ, NATALIE LEVY, graphic designer, printing consultant; b. Newark, Feb. 10, 1938; d. Louis and Hilda Lillian (Waldstein) Levy; m. Harold Schwartz, Nov. 20, 1960 (div. July 1980); children—Mindy Claire, Gary Keith. B.S., Trenton State Coll., 1959. Cert. kindergarten and primary tchr., N.J. Elem. tchr., Watchung, N.J., 1959-61, Reno, 1963-64, Yokota AFB, Japan, 1964-65; paste-up and design staff Brooks-Johnson Printing, Bethesda, Md., 1974-75; owner-operator Prelude to Print, Kensington and Rockville, Md., 1975—. Co-author, editor, designer; (music book and calendar) Saluting the American Bicentennial, 1975. Mem. Women in Advt. and Mktg., Nat. Assn. Quick Printers, Big Band Soc. Republican. Jewish. Club: Reflections (area editor 1982-84) (Washington). Avocations: music, ballroom dancing, community theater. Office: Prelude to Print 6125 Executive Blvd Rockville MD 20852

SCHWARTZ, RHEA S., lawyer; b. Miami Beach, Fla., Sept. 27, 1950; d. Walter and Linda (Rosenthal) S.; B.A., Pa. State U., 1971; student U. Strasbourg, France, 1970; J.D., Georgetown U., 1974; m. Paul Martin Wolff, Oct. 9, 1976. Admitted to Ill. bar, 1974, D.C. bar, 1976; asso. firm Schiff, Hardin & Waite, Chgo., 1974-75; atty. Office of Solicitor, Dept. Labor, Washington, 1975-77; labor counsel U.S. Air, Inc., Washington, 1977-79; spl. asst. to Sec. Edn., Washington, 1979-80, asst. gen. counsel Dept. Edn., Washington, 1980—; atty. FDIC; lectr. continuing legal edn. program Georgetown U. Law Ctr.; adj. prof. law U. So. Calif. Grad. Sch. Pub. Adminstrn. Bd. dirs. HALT, Inc., Am. Jewish Com. Recipient Spl. Achievement award U.S. Govt., 1980-854. Mem. ABA, Ill. Bar Assn., D.C. Bar Assn., U.S. Figure Skating Assn. (del., governing council). Author: Women and Credit, 1974. Office: 550 17th St NW Washington DC 20429

SCHWARTZ, SANDY EICHELBAUM, legislative and political action specialist; b. Bronx, N.Y., May 14, 1945; d. Milton and Pauline Yetta (Rosen) Eichelbaum; A.A., San Antonio Jr. Coll., 1965; B.A., U. Tex., Austin, 1967; m. Leonard Jay Schwartz, July 4, 1965; 1 dau., Michele Fay. Tchr. pub. schs., Del Valle Ind. Sch. Dist., Austin, 1967-68, San Antonio, 1969-71; curriculum coordinator Edgewood Ind. Sch. Dist., San Antonio, 1971-72; govtl. services assoc. Ohio Edn. Assn., Columbus, 1972-80; govtl. relations Tex. State Tchrs. Assn., Austin, 1980—. Mem. exec. com. Franklin County Democratic party, 1978-80; mem. Internat. Women's Yr. Continuing Com., 1978-79, del.-at-large Nat. Women's Polit. Caucus, 1979-81; del. Dem. Nat. Conv., 1980. Mem. Nat. Assn. Legis. and Polit. Specialists in Edn. (pres. 1982-84), Nat. Council Jewish Women. Jewish. Club: U. Tex. Century. Home: 5800 Back Ct Austin TX 78731 Office: 316 W 12th St Austin TX 78701

SCHWARTZ, SUSAN HIRSCH, book publisher; b. N.Y.C., Mar. 30, 1946; d. Edwin Waixel and Patricia (Lamm) Hirsch; m. Charles P. Schwartz, Jr., Dec. 18, 1976; stepchildren—Alex, Ned, Debra, Emily. B.A., Skidmore Coll., 1968. Sr. publicist ABC-TV, Chgo., 1968-72; advt. and promotion dir. Follett Pub. Co., Chgo., 1972-75; pres. Susan Hirsch Pub. Relations, Chgo., 1975-81, Surrey Books, Inc., Chgo., 1981—. Author: How To Get a Job in Chicago, 1983. Bd. dirs. Michael Reese Hosp. Med. Research Inst., 1975—. Mem. Chgo. Advt. Club, Publicity Club Chgo., Publicity Club N.Y., Pub. Relations Soc. Am., Women in Communications, Pubs. Publicity Assn. Jewish. Clubs: Chgo. Press, Arts, Quadrangle (Chgo.). Home: 5546 S Dorchester Ave Chicago IL 60637 Office: Surrey Books 500 N Michigan Ave Chicago IL 60611

SCHWARTZ, SUSAN LYNN, television station executive; b. Columbus, Ohio, July 13, 1954; d. Martin and Ruth (Weisman) Wohlstein; m. Sanford Harold Schwartz, Sept. 12, 1976; children—Stephanie, Jonathan. B.A., Kent State U., 1976. Traffic clk. Sta. WTVN-TV, Columbus, 1976-77, film dir., 1977-78, pub. affairs dir., 1978-82, exec. producer, 1980-82, program mgr., 1982-85; program dir. Sta. KTUK-TV, Phoenix, 1985—. Trustee, corp. sec. Crime Solvers Anonymous, Columbus, 1979—; mem. exec. com. March of Dimes, Columbus, 1979; mem. pub. relations com. Heart Assn., Columbus, 1980-82; mem. edn. com. Multiple Sclerosis Soc., Columbus, 1979-80. Mem. Am. Women in Radio and TV, Nat. Assn. TV Program Execs. Democrat. Jewish. Avocations: tennis; skiing; running. Home: 6722 S Martin Ln Tempe AZ 85283 Office: Sta KTUK-TV 3435 N 16th St Phoenix AZ 85010

SCHWARTZ, SUSAN RENEE, lawyer; b. N.Y.C., June 5, 1954; d. Alexander and Martha (Gottesman) Schwartz. B.A. cum laude, Hunter Coll., 1977; J.D., U. Calif. Law Sch., Los Angeles, 1981. Bar: Calif. 1981, U.S. Ct. Appeals (9th cir.) 1982, U.S. Dist. Ct. 1982. Atty. Lawler Felix & Hall, Los Angeles, 1981-82, Hayes & Hume, Beverly Hills, Calif., 1983-84, Richards, Watson, Dreyfuss & Geshon, Los Angeles, 1985—; law clk. to judge U.S. Dist. Ct. (ce. dist.) Calif., Los Angeles, 1984-85. Mem. UCLA Law Rev.; editor: Fed Communication Law Jour., Fed. Communications Bar Assn., Washington, 1979-81. Chmn. Univ. Calif. Communications Bd., Los Angeles, 1979-80; bd. dirs. Hollywood-Wilshire Fair Housing Council, Los Angeles, 1982-83. Mem. Women Lawyers Los Angeles, ABA (vice chmn. com. on intellectual property). Office: Richards Watson Dreyfuss & Gershon 333 S Hope St 38th Floor Los Angeles CA 90071

SCHWARTZ, TILLIE, pediatrician; b. Winnipeg, Man., Can.; d. Leon and Sophie (Idell) Schwartz. B.A., U. Man., 1936, M.D., 1950. Rotating intern St. Boniface Hosp., Winnipeg, 1949-50; resident in medicine Gouverneur Hosp., N.Y.C., 1950-51; resident in pediatrics Met. Hosp., N.Y.C., 1951-52; Univ. Hosp., N.Y.C., 1952-53; practice medicine specializing in pediatrics, Kew Garden, N.Y., 1953—; asst. in clin. pediatrics N.Y. U., 1953-74, asst. prof. clin. pediatrics, 1974—; head pediatric allergy clinic Booth Meml. Hosp. Med. Center, Flushing, N.Y., 1958—. Fellow Am. Acad. Pediatrics, Am. Acad. Allergy; mem. AMA, N.Y. State Med. Assn., Queens County Med. Assn., Am. Med. Women Assn., N.Y. State Med. Women, N.Y.C. Med. Women, N.Y.C. Allergy Soc., Queens Pediatrics Soc. Home: 1620 Boathouse Circle Sarasota FL 33581

SCHWARTZ, VALERIE BREUER, interior designer; b. Senica, Czechoslovakia, May 13, 1912; came to U.S., 1928, naturalized, 1928; d. Jacob and Ethel (Weiss) Breuer; m. Leo Schwartz, Feb. 5, 1939; children—Catherine, Robert, William. Student States Real Gymnazium, Prague, 1925-28; Parsons N.Y. Sch. of Fine and Applied Arts, 1930-32. Cert. Am. Soc. Interior Designers. Self-employed interior designer, N.J., 1932—; guest on radio programs: Carol Reed Show, Barry Gray Show. Contbr. to various mags. including N.Y. Times, House & Garden, Cue Mag., Confort, Argentina. Mem. Hadassah (life). Talk show guest Carol Reed and Barry Gray shows.

SCHWARTZBERG, JOANNE GILBERT, medical director, physician; b. Boston, Nov. 30, 1933; d. Richard Vincent and Emma (Cohen) Gilbert; m. Hugh Joel Schwartzberg, July 7, 1956; children—Steven Jonathan, Susan Jennifer. B.A. magna cum laude, Radcliffe Coll., 1955; M.D., Northwestern U., 1960. Founder, bd. dirs., sec., med. dir. Home Health Service Chgo., No., 1972—; founder, bd. dirs., v.p., med. dir. Suburban Home Health Service, Chgo. area, 1975—; clin. asst. prof. preventive medicine and community health U. Ill. Coll. Medicine, 1985—. Mem. Health Planning Commn. Chgo., 1961-63; mem. Community Adv. Bd. Joint Youth Devel. Commn. Chgo., 1963-67; pres. Near North Montessori Sch., Chgo., 1972-75, bd. dirs., 1970—. Recipient Mayor's citation City of Chgo., 1963. Fellow Inst. Medicine; mem. AMA, Ill. Med. Soc., Chgo. Med. Soc., Am. Acad. Med. Dirs., Am. Geriatrics Soc., Chgo. Geriatrics Soc. (founding dir. 1984, sec.-treas. 1985), Am. Med. Women's Assn., Am. Pub. Health Assn., Ill. Pub. Health Assn., Alexander Graham Bell Assn. for Deaf (dir. 1984—; 2d vice-chmn. internat. parents orgn. 1984—, gen. chmn. internat. conv. 1986). Jewish. Contbr. articles to profl. jours. Home: 853 W Fullerton Pkwy Chicago IL 60614 Office: 33 W Grand Ave Chicago IL 60610

SCHWARTZ-SANDERSON, HARRIETTE JEANNE, television operations company executive; b. N.Y.C., Aug. 26, 1950; d. Max Alan and Gussie (Chasan) S.; m. Jay Gary Sanderson, Nov. 22, 1978. Student Announcer Tng. Studios, 1972. 3rd Class license FCC. Reporter special events dept. Radio Free Europe, N.Y.C., 1972-74; traffic, production mgr. Broadcasting Div., Inc., N.Y.C., 1974-76; post production, traffic supr. Video Prodns., Inc., N.Y.C., 1976-77; dir. TV ops. Fremantle Internat., Inc./Fremantle Corp., N.Y.C., 1977-85, v.p. global ops., 1985—. Mem. Nat. Assn. TV Program Execs. (assoc.). Avocations: poetry writing, lyric writing, personal greeting card writing, jogging, reading. Office: Fremantle Internat Inc/Fremantle Corp 660 Madison Ave New York NY 10021

SCHWARTZ-STEVENS, RONA LEE, transportation service executive; b. Phila., Apr. 14, 1957; d. Albert and Evelyn (Strauss) Schwartz; m. William P. Stevens Jr., Dec. 7, 1985. B.A., Am. U., 1979, M.A., 1981. Cert. tchr., Pa. Student aide U.S. Ho. of Reps., Washington, 1976-79, receptionist, 1979-81; data clk. fin. office, 1981-83; substitute tchr. Phila. Sch. System, 1983; mem. pub. relations staff Alert Transp. Service, Phila., 1983—, v.p. pub. relations, 1986—; v.p. Brocal Corp. Mem. Phila. Com. on City Policy, 1985—. Recipient cert. of appreciation Older Adults of Haddington, Phila., 1983, Sr. Wheels E., Phila., 1983, Puerto Rican Festival Week, 1985. Mem. Nat. Assn. Female Execs., Bus. Women's Nat. Com., Action Alliance, Carrie, B'Nai Brith Women Phila. Democrat. Jewish. Office: Alert Transp Service 218 N 13th St Philadelphia PA 19107

SCHWARTZTOL, HOLLY WECHSLER, psychologist; b. Washington, Dec. 20, 1946; d. James Arthur and Nancy (Fraenkel) Wechsler; B.A., Finch Coll., 1968; M.A., C. W. Post Coll., 1971; Ph.D., U. Miami, 1981; m. Robert Ira Schwartztol, Nov. 16, 1975; children—Laurence, Andrew. Instr. psychology C. W. Post Coll., Greenvale, N.Y., 1971; tchr. Yorktown High Sch., Yorktown Heights, N.Y., 1971-73; sch. psychologist Dade County Schs., Miami, Fla., 1973-84; pvt. practice psychology, Miami, 1982—; adj. asst. prof. counseling psychology U. Miami, 1984-85. Mem. Dade County Psychol. Assn., Fla. Psychol. Assn., Southeastern Psychol. Assn., Am. Psychol. Assn., Am. Mental Health Assn. Dade County, Citizens for Advancement of Mentally Ill. Democrat. Author: (with James A. and Nancy F. Wechsler) In a Darkness, 1972. Office: 9485 Sunset Dr Miami FL 33173

SCHWARZ, ESTHER DORIS, city official; b. Newark, Mar. 29, 1933; d. Benjamin and Ida (Margolis) Epstein; cert. in bus. adminstrn. Rutgers U., 1955; m. John Schwarz, Sept. 20, 1959; children—Bonnie, Michael, Perry. Office mgr., controller Manson Printers, Hillside, N.J., 1969-73, Classic Distbg. Co., Union, N.J., 1974-76; agt. N.J. Motor Vehicle Dept., 1978-82; councilman Town of Irvington, N.J., 1976—; adminstrv. analyst, investigator Essex County Div. Consumer Services. Instl. rep. Robert Treat council Boy Scouts Am., 1972-78; pres. Union Ave. Sch., Irvington, 1968-70, Frank H. Morrell High Sch., Irvington, 1975-76; crusade chmn. Irvington chpt. Am. Cancer Soc., 1980; bd. mgrs. Irvington Gen. Hosp., 1972-74; chmn. United Way, 1981; mem. Irvington Alcoholic Commn., 1976—, chmn., 1977-78; trustee mem. Irvington Adult Sch., 1976—; tchr. Congregation Oheb Shalom, South Orange, N.J., 1969—; mem. Citizens Commn. of Mental Health, 1973—. Recipient Disting. Service award Town of Irvington, 1974, Outstanding Citizenship award Jewish Civic League, 1977, Disting. CD Service award City of Newark, 1951, cert. of honor Congregation Oheb Shalom, 1979; cert. mcpl. tax collector, N.J. Mem. N.J. Motor Vehicle Agts. Assn. (1st. v.p. 1979—), Essex County Council PTA (pres. 1978-80), Nat. PTA (life), Police Athletic League, Nat. Council Jewish Women (legis. liaison chmn., v.p. adminstrn., pres. charter 1984-86, Hannah B. Solomon award for outstanding achievements in humanitarian efforts for children 1983), N.J. Elected Women Orgn. (charter), NAACP (charter). Democrat. Home: 117 Webster St Irvington NJ 07111 Office: Municipal Bldg Civic Sq Irvington NJ 07111

SCHWARZROCK, SHIRLEY LORRAINE PRATT, author, lecturer, educator; b. Mpls., Feb. 27, 1914; d. Theodore Ray and Myrtle Pearl (Westphal) Pratt; B.S., U. Minn., 1935, M.A., 1942, Ph.D., 1974; m. Loren H. Schwarzrock, Oct. 19, 1945 (dec. 1966); children—Kay Linda, Ted Kenneth, Lorraine V. Sec. to chmn. speech dept., U. Minn., Mpls., 1935, instr. in speech, 1946, team tchr. in creative arts workshops for tchrs., 1955-56, guest lectr. Dental Sch., 1967-72, asst. prof. (part-time) practice adminstrn. Sch. Dentistry, 1972 80; tchr. speech, drama and English, Preston (Minn.) High Sch., 1935-37, tchr. speech, drama and English, Owatonna (Minn.) High Sch., 1937-39, also dir. dramatics, 1937-39; tchr. creative dramatics and English, tchr.-counselor Webster Groves (Mo.) Jr. High Sch., 1939-40; dir. dramatics and tchr.-counselor Webster Groves Sr. High Sch., 1940-43; exec. sec. bus. and profl. dept. YWCA, Mpls., 1943-45; tchr. speech and drama Convent of the Visitation, St. Paul, 1958; editor pro-tem Am. Acad. Dental Practice Adminstrn., 1966-68; guest tchr. Coll. St. Catherine, St. Paul, 1969; cons. for dental med. programs Normandale Community Coll., Bloomington, Minn., 1968; cons. on public relations to dentists, 1954—; guest lectr. to various dental groups, 1966—; advisor profl. office mgmt.; tutor for speaking engagements. Author Effective Dental Assisting, 1954, 59, 67, (with J.R. Jensen), 1973, 78, 82; (with Lorraine Schwarzrock) Workbook for Effective Dental Assisting, 1979, 82, Manual for Effective Dental Assisting, 1978; (with Donovan F. Ward) Effective Medical Assisting, 1969, 76; Workbook for Effective Medical Assisting, 1969, 76; Manual for Effective Med. Assisting, 1969, 76; Contemporary Concerns of Youth, 1979; Facts and Fantasies about Drugs, 1984; Facts and Fantasies about Alcohol, 1984; Facts and Fantasies about Smoking, 1984; Some Common Crutches, 1984; Food as a Crutch, 1984; Can You Talk with Someone Else?1984; To Like and Be Liked, 1984; Changing Roles of Men and Women, 1984; Coping with Cliques, 1984; Living with Loneliness, 1984; Parents Can Be a Problem, 1984; Grades, What's So Important about Them, Anyway?, 1984, You Always Communicate Something, 1984; My Life, What Shall I Do with It?, 1984; Do I Know the Me Others See?, Crises Youth Face Today, 1984, Coping With Emotional Pain, 1984; Facts and Fantasies about Changing Roles of Men and Women, 1984; Appreciating People, 1984; Fitting In, 1984; Learning To Make Better Decisions, 1984; Coping with Personal Identity, 1984; Coping with Facts and Fantasies, 1984; Coping with Human Relationships, 1984; Coping with Teenage Problems, 1984. Pres., University Elem. Sch. PTA, 1955-56; vol. mgr. Eitel Hosp. Gift Shop, 1981-83. Mem. Minn. (hon. mem.) Acad. Dental Practice Adminstrn., Zeta Phi Eta (pres. 1948-49), Eta Sigma Upsilon. Home: 7448 W Shore Dr Minneapolis MN 55435

SCHWAUSCH, DORIS JEAN, educator; b. Georgetown, Tex., Nov. 12, 1947; d. Max Henry and Ida Elizabeth (Jansen) Schneider; m. Landon Kenneth Schwausch, June 17, 1967; 1 child, Jennifer Suzanne. B.S., U. Tex., Austin, 1970; M.Ed., U. Tex., 1981. Tchr. home econs., Jarrell Ind. Sch. Dist., Tex., 1970-78; tchr. home econs. Pflugerville Ind. Sch. Dist., Tex., 1978—; cons. Tex. Edn. Agy., Austin, 1981-85, also Tec. Tech. U., Lubbock. Tchr. Sunday Sch., Redeemer Lutheran Ch., 1975—. Mem. Vocat. Home Econs. Tchrs. Tex. (bd. dirs.), Am. Vocat. Assn., Kappa Delta Pi. Democrat. Home: 8035 Stillwood Ln Austin TX 78758 Office: Pflugerville High Sch 1301 W Pecan St Pflugerville TX 78660

SCHWEBEL, BERNICE LOIS, educator, executive; b. Hartford, Conn., Sept. 27, 1916; d. Joseph and Sara (Brewer) Davison; B.A., Russell Sage Coll., 1938; teaching cert. SUNY, 1949; M.A., N.Y.U., 1963; m. Milton Schwebel, Sept. 3, 1939; children—Andrew, Robert. Co-founder, dir. Counseling and Placement Services for Refugees, Jewish Community Center, Troy, N.Y., 1936; social case worker Troy Orphan Asylum, 1938-39; cottage mother Pleasantville (N.Y.) Cottage Sch., 1939-40; head tchr. Birnby Nursery Sch., N.Y.C., 1945-46; tchr. kindergarten, primary grades, Valley Stream, N.Y., 1950-67; supr. student tchrs. edn. dept. Douglass Coll., Rutgers U., New Brunswick, N.J., 1973-76; v.p. ednl. programs and materials Univ. Assocs., Columbus, Ohio, 1976—; treas. Continental Land Holding, 1984—. Trustee, Rutgers-Livingston Day Care Center, 1977-80; chmn. Rutgers-Old Queens Visitation Com., New Brunswick Tercentenary, 1979-80. Mem. Authors Guild, LWV, NOW, Women's League of Rutgers U., Russell Sage Alumnae Assn., N.Y.U. Alumni Assn. Co-author film script Resistance to Learning, 1962; author: Student Teachers Handbook, 1979; contbr. articles to various publs. Home: 1050 George St New Brunswick NJ 08901 Office: Univ Assocs 4123 Kendra Ct Columbus OH 43220

SCHWEBEL, JUDITH BEATRICE, petroleum company executive; b. Bakersfield, Calif., June 27, 1939; d. Ole Adsen and Mary Sohie (Leiva) Nelson; m. Jack Dean Schwebel, June 21, 1958 (dec. Jan. 1974); children—Scott, Jill, Elizabeth, Amy. Student Bakersfield Community Coll., 1957. Pres. Schwebel Petroleum, Inc., Bakersfield, 1974—; mem. Pvt. Industry Council, Bakersfield, 1981-83; mem. Employers Tng. Resources, Bakersfield, 1984; mem. Pub./Pvt. Task Force, Bakersfield, 1985. Founding mem. Calif. Living Mus., Bakersfield, 1983; exec. mem. Am. Cancer Soc., Bakersfield, 1983, bd. dirs., 1983-85. Mem. Dorian Soc. Republican. Roman Catholic. Clubs: Desk & Derrick, Petroleum (Bakersfield). Avocations: showing horses; reading; bridge. Office: Schwebel Petroleum Co Inc 3200 21st St Suite 201 Bakersfield CA 93301

SCHWECKE-SHERIDAN, ARDELL LORRAIN, business manager, actress, writer; b. Jersey City, Aug. 5, 1943; d. Frederick and Frances Ardell (Reicks) Schwecke. A.A.S., Fashion Inst. Tech., N.Y.C., 1963; B.A., Columbia Pacific U., 1982, M.A., Ph.D., 1983. Actress, writer, prodn. rep. Golden Beetle, Yugoslavia, 1968; actress Out to Lunch, PBS-TV, N.Y.C., 1970; actress, publicity cons. film The Godfather I, N.Y.C., 1971; co-star, actress, script editor The Super TV series, ABC, 1972; bus. mgr. Henrick-Hungwell Ltd., North Bergen, N.J., 1972—; dir. Sheridan Theatre Workshop, North Bergen, 1976—. Fellow Internat. Biog. Assn.; mem. Internat. Platform Assn., Audubon Soc. Office: Henrick-Hungwell Ltd 8200 Blvd E Suite 3G North Bergen NJ 07047

SCHWEDER, JEANNE ANN, editor; b. Elyria, Ohio, Jan. 2, 1947; d. Lawrence Allen and Dorothy Mae (Linden) Kuhl; student Calif. State U., Northridge, 1965-66, SUNY, Brockport, 1973-74; children—John Doyle, Jennifer Louise. With Empire State Weeklies, Webster, N.Y., 1967-82, reporter, editor, 1968-79, mng. editor, 1979-82; mgr. editorial services Nat. Alliance Bus., Washington, 1982—. Office: Nat Alliance Bus 1015 15th St NW Washington DC 20005

SCHWEINHAUT, MARGARET C., state senator; b. Washington; ed. George Washington U., Nat. U. Law Sch.; LL.D., St. Joseph Coll. Mem. Md. Ho. of Dels., 1955-61; mem. Md. Senate, 1961-63, 67—. Chmn. Md. Commn. on Aging, 1959-82. Bd. dirs. Nat. Council of Aging. Recipient Certificate of Merit, Nat. Council of Sr. Citizens; Margaret Schweinhaut Sr. Ctr. named in her honor, 1982. Mem. Internat. Gerontological Soc., Montgomery Retarded Children's Assn. Office: Maryland Senate State Capitol Annapolis MD 21401

SCHWEITZER, MARY-ELIOT SMITH (MRS. ROBERT SCHWEITZER, JR.), civic worker, electronics company executive; b. San Jose, Calif., July 7, 1927; d. Julius Avery and Elise (Peyton) Smith; A.A., Marymount Coll., 1948; Engring. Tech. degree Normandale Community Coll., 1981 m. Robert Schweitzer, Jr., Sept. 18, 1952; children—Mary-Eliot, James-Peyton, Mary-Neale. Sec., Teen-age Jr's, Stanford Convalescent Home, Palo Alto, Calif., 1944-45; receptionist, driver A.R.C., Palo Alto, 1947-51; mem. Jr. League, San Francisco, 1950-54; mem. Jr. League, N.Y.C., 1956-58; mem. Jr. League, Mpls., 1963—, bd. dirs., 1966-67. Leader, Girl Scouts U.S.A., Mpls., 1966-69; mem. Citizens Com. for Pub. Edn., Mpls., 1968-76, Citizens League, Mpls., 1968-80; docent Mpls. Inst. Arts, 1965-66, Hennepin County Hist. Soc., 1965-66; pres. Douglas Elementary Sch. P.T.A., 1968-70; v.p. West High Sch. P.T.A., 1970-71, pres., 1971-73; bd. dirs. Womens UN Rally, 1966-72; bd. dirs. Assos. James Ford Bell Library, 1968—, pres., 1972-75; bd. dirs. Friends Mpls. Inst. Arts, 1968-73; bd. dirs. Mpls. Council P.T.A.'s, 1969-76, treas., 1974-76; bd. dirs. Minn. World Affairs Center, 1969-76, UN Assn. of Minn., 1970-76; adv. bd. Childrens Theatre Co., Mpls., 1969-72, house mgr., 1971-72; vice chmn. Hennepin Lowry Council, 1972-74; chmn. bd. Jr. League Thrift Shop, 1966-67; mem. citywide adv. com. for ednl. facilities and plant planning Mpls. Pub. Schs., 1975-76; unit test mgr. Control Data Corp., Magnetic Peripherals, Inc., 1981—. Named Beautiful Activist, 1973. Mem. D.A.R., Mpls. Soc. Fine Arts, Womens Assn. Minn. Symphony Orch., Mpls. League Catholic Women (dir. 1974-80), League Women Voters, English Speaking Union, Univ. Hosps. Vol. Assn., West Dist. Schs. Assn. (vice-chmn. 1972-73, chmn. 1974-75), Peyton Soc. Va., Minn. Zool. Soc. Republican. Home: 5140 W 102d St Bloomington MN 55437

SCHWEITZER, N. TINA, writer, consultor in public relations, media relations, government relations; b. Hartford, Conn., Apr. 7, 1941; d. Abraham Aaron Morris and Ruth Blanche (Shifreen) S.; B.S., Emerson Coll., 1964. Free-lance writer, Boston and Washington, 1965-67; editor, chief prodn. maj. feature publ., mem. press-info. staff Embassy of Republic of Indonesia, Washington, 1967-68; researcher, writer Congl. Quar., Inc., Washington, 1969-70; owner Schweitzer Assocs., Hartford, Conn. and Washington, 1970-78, 79—; dir. community and govtl. relations Advocacy Services for the Deaf, West Hartford, Conn., 1978-79; del. White House Conf. Small Bus., 1986, profl. model, Mem. State-wide Health Coordinating Council, a U.S. Govt./Conn. Health Dept. project, 1978-80; adviser Conn. Office Advocacy to Handicapped; mem. legis. task force State of Conn.; del. first Conn. Gov.'s Conf. on Library and Info. Services, 1978; candidate Conn. Ho. of Reps., 1982; aux. police officer Hartford Police Dept., 1976-77; acting chmn. communications com. Unitarian Meeting House, West Hartford; dir. pub. relations Greater Hartford Com. UNICEF, 1984; affiliated Republican Town Com., Hartford. Contbr. articles to numerous govtl. and comml. publs.; author nat. Media Kit, 1978; writer, designer, producer series of TV videotape pub. service announcements on employment deaf or hard-of-hearing. Mem. Women in Communications, Nat. Press Photographers Assn., Community Council of the Capital Region, Mensa (Achievement award 1982), Sigma Delta Chi. Office: Schweitzer Associates 30 Woodland St Suite 9P Hartford CT 06105

SCHWENNSEN, TRISHA JOYCE, financial executive; b. Dallas, Aug. 17, 1954; d. Bill O. Tanner and Betty Joan (Sauls) Thompson; m. Arvel Gray McCulloch, May 24, 1975 (div. 1980); m. William Price Schwennsen, July 31, 1982. B.B.A., East Tex. State U., 1975, M.B.A., 1977; postgrad U. Tex.-Dallas, 1978. Acct. Tex. Oil and Gas Corp., Dallas, 1977-79; fin. analyst Gen. Dynamics, Ft. Worth, 1979-84; fin. mgr. Mostek/United Techs., Carrollton, Tex., 1984-85; controller Ideal Learning, Irving, Tex., 1986—. Mem. PEO Sisterhood, Alpha Phi, Alpha Phi Alumni. Roman Catholic. Avocations: physical fitness; needlework; entertaining; remodeling. Office: Ideal Learning Royal Port 5005 Royal Ln Irving TX 75063

SCHWIER, PRISCILLA LAMB GUYTON, television broadcasting company executive; b. Toledo, Ohio, May 8, 1939; d. Edward Oliver and Prudence (Hutchinson) L.; m. Robert T. Guyton, June 21, 1963 (dec. Sept. 1976); children—Melissa, Margaret, Robert; m. Frederick W. Schwier, May 11, 1984. B.A., Smith Coll., 1961; M.A., U. Toledo, 1972. Pres. Gt. Lakes Communications, Inc., 1982—; vice chmn. Seilon, Inc., Toledo, 1981-83, also dir.; pres.

Lamb Enterprises, Inc., Toledo, 1983—; dir. Lamb Enterprises, Inc., Toledo, 1976—. Contbr. articles to profl. jours. Trustee Wilberforce U., Ohio, 1983—, Planned Parenthood, Toledo, 1979-83, Maumee Valley Country Day Sch., Toledo, 1986—; mem. vestry St. Paul's Episcopal Ch., Maumee, Ohio, 1983—. Democrat. Episcopalian. Home: 345 E Front St Perrysburg OH 43551 Office: 1630 Ohio Citizens Bank Toledo OH 43604

SCHWIMMER, IRIS ANN, lawyer; b. N.Y.C., Sept. 25, 1950; d. David and May S.; m. Wilmer C. Butler, May 28, 1984. B.A., UCLA, 1975; J.D., Southwestern U., 1979; cert. Inst. Internat. and Comparative Law, U. San Diego and Oxford (Eng.) U., 1978. Bar: Calif. 1981. Law clk., assoc. Ellsworth & Bryan, Pasadena, Calif., 1981; sole practice, Los Angeles, 1981—; corp. counsel TV News Calif., Inc., Los Angeles, 1982—, Hyperion Films, Ltd., Los Angeles, 1982—; clk. to judge Superior Ct. Calif., 1978. Ignatius S. Parker scholar, 1978; Farmers Ins. scholar, 1979. Mem. ABA, State Bar Calif., Los Angeles County Bar Assn., Phi Alpha Delta. Republican. Office: 11752 San Vicente Blvd Los Angeles CA 90049

SCHWOPE, MARY KATHRYN, state legislator; b. Rock Springs, Wyo., July 21, 1917; d. Charles Alfred and Mary Frances (Moriarty) Vlox; student public schs., Green River, Wyo., 1923-35; m. Eldridge Lawson Schwope, July 15, 1940; children—Michael Lawson, Fachon J. Schwope Wilson, Patricia K. Schwope Murphy, Madalaine M. Schwope Connolly. With Union Pacific R.R., 1936-46; mem. Wyo. Ho. of Reps., 1975-76, 79—. Mem. Democratic Precinct Com., Cheyenne, 1957-67; vice chmn., dist. capt. County Dem. Com.; sec. City-County CD Council, 1962-63, Laramie County Fair Bd., 1966-76; mem. State Adv. Council Vocat. Edn., 1976-81; mem. Silver-Haired Legis. Adv. Com., 1982-83, Wyo. Gov.'s Task Force for Employment Older Ams., 1981—. Recipient nat. merit cert. Am. Revolutionary Bicentennial Adminstrn., 1976; Four Chaplains Legion of Honor, 1979. Mem. Am. Legion Aux. (state pres. 1968-69, nat. exec. com. 1969-70), Am. Assn. Ret. Persons, Wyo. Hist. Soc., Wyo. Wildlife Fedn., Cheyenne Sr. Citizens. Roman Catholic. Clubs: Zonta, Cheyenne Women's.

SCHYCKER-BAILEY, NANCY, educational consultant; b. Chgo., Jan. 4, 1941; d. Fredrick Peter Kinn and Bette Lee (Riha) Zamer; m. Richard Schycker, Fed. 10, 1963 (div. 1964); 1 child, Michael Vaughn; m. Jim D. Bailey, Jan. 14, 1984. Student U. Ill., 1959; A.A., Pasadena City Coll., 1960; B.A., Calif. State U., Los Angeles, 1962, M.A., 1972; Ph.D., Iowa State U., 1983. Cert. tchr., Calif. Tchr., Los Angeles Unified Sch. Dist., 1962-63, Covina Valley Unified Sch. Dist., Calif., 1964-67; master tchr. Garvey Sch. Dist., Calif., 1967-73, head start, state presch. dir., 1973-80, prin., 1980-81; research assoc. in sch. adminstrn. Iowa State U., Ames, 1981-83; adj. prof. Calif. State U.-Los Angeles, 1983—; cons. in staff devel., El Monte, Calif., 1984—. Author: Diagnostic and Prescriptive Inservices for Elementary Teachers, 1983. Contbr. articles to profl. publs. Mem. adv. com. Pasadena Area Community Coll. Dist., 1974-75; Head Start State Presch. Coordinators Council, 1979-80. Mem. Women in Ednl. Leadership, NEA, Am. Soc. Tng. and Devel., Phi Delta Kappa. Religious Scientist. Home and Office: 2504 Granada El Monte CA 91733

SCIANDRA, KATHLEEN DANIELS, lawyer; b. Bklyn., Dec. 19, 1950; d. Robert Joseph and Florence Marie (Crane) Daniels; m. Luigi Claudio Sciandra, Nov. 13, 1982; 1 dau., Claudia Simone. B.A., Cabrini Coll., 1972; J.D., Bklyn. Law Sch., 1975. Bar: N.Y. 1976. Assoc. firm Kirlin, Campbell & Keating, N.Y.C., 1975-80, ptnr., 1981—. Trustee Cabrini Coll., 1982-85. Mem. ABA, New York County Lawyers Assn., N.Y. Bar Assn., Nassau County Bar Assn., Maritime Lawyers Assn. Home: 160 Front St New York NY 10038 Office: Kirlin Campbell & Keating 14 Wall St New York NY 10005

SCIBEK, SUE TAYLOR, nurse, childbirth educator; b. San Saba, Tex., Oct. 21, 1944; d. Richard Sloan and Elizabeth Jane (Jester) Taylor; m. B.J. Eldridge, 1964 (div. 1968); m. Stanley William Scibek, Nov. 25, 1972; children—Richard, Ronald, Matthew; B.S. in Nursing, Mary-Hardin Baylor Coll., 1973. R.N., Tex. Staff nurse Scott & White Hosp., Temple Tex., 1973-75; head nurse obstetrics Wichita Gen. Hosp., Wichita Falls, Tex., 1975—; childbirth educator Prenatal Instrn. Assn., Wichita Falls, Tex., 1976—. Baptist. Home: 4604 Sierra Madre St Wichita Falls TX 76310 Office: Wichita Gen Hosp 1600 8th St Wichita Falls TX 76301

SCIMONE, PATRICIA LYNN, marketing executive; b. Amityville, N.Y., May 28, 1955; d. Thomas Mathew and Josephine (Galante) S. Student Fashion Inst., N.Y.C., 1974, Hunter Coll., 1975-76. Mdse. mgr. Diamond Co. Am., N.Y.C., 1976-79; buyer Service Mdse. Co., Nashville, 1979-81; new product mgr. Harlyn Products, Los Angeles, 1981-83; pres. Marriage Mktg., Encino, Calif., 1983—; mfg. cons. Harlyn Products, 1983; media and mktg. cons. Santa Monica C. of C. 1983. Mem. Am. Mgmt. Assn., Calif. Bus. Womens Assn., Nat. Assn. Female Execs., Sales and Mktg. Execs. Internat. Home: 5460 White Oak Ave Apt G301 Encino CA 91316

SCITOVSKY, ANNE AICKELIN, economist; b. Ludwigshafen, Germany, Apr. 17, 1915; came to U.S., 1931, naturalized, 1938; d. Hans W. and Gertrude Margarete Aickelin; student Smith Coll., 1933-35; B.A., Barnard Coll., 1937; postgrad. London Sch. Econs., 1937-39; M.A. in Econs., Columbia U., 1941; 1 dau., Catherine Margaret. Mem. staff legis. reference service Library of Congress, 1941-44; mem. staff Social Security Bd., 1944-46; with Research Inst., Palo Alto Med. Found. (Calif.), 1963—, chief health econs. div., 1973—; lectr. Inst. Health Policy Studies, U. Calif., San Francisco, 1975—; mem. Inst. Medicine, Nat. Acad. Scis.; mem. Pres.' Commn. for Study of Ethical Problems in Medicine and Biomed. and Behavioral Research; mem. U.S. Nat. Com. on Vital and Health Statistics, 1975-78; cons. HHS. Mem. Am. Econ. Assn., Am. Pub. Health Assn. Home: 161 Erica Way Menlo Park CA 94025 Office: Research Inst Palo Alto Med Found 860 Bryant St Palo Alto CA 94301

SCLAFANI, FRANCES ANN, lawyer, commissioner; b. N.Y.C., Aug. 25, 1949; d. Joseph John and Clementina Theresa (Polite) S. B.A. with honors, St. John's U., Jamaica, N.Y., 1971, J.D., 1974. Bar: N.Y. 1975, U.S. Dist. Ct. (ea. and so. dists.) N.Y. 1975, U.S. Ct. Appeals (2d cir.) 1975, U.S. Supreme Ct. 1978. Spl. congl. asst. U.S. Congress, Washington, 1971; asst. dist. atty. Suffolk Dist. Atty.'s Office, Riverhead, N.Y., 1974—, dep. chief felony trial bur., 1981-82, dep. chief major offense bur., 1982-83, chief adminstrv. asst. dist. atty. for Inter-Agy. Liaison, 1983—; commr. Pres.'s Commn. on Organized Crime, Washington, 1983—; mem. faculty U.S. Dept. Justice Ann. Drug Traffickers Prosecution Conf., Washington, 1983. Mem. adv. bd. Child Abuse Prevention Services Jr. League of LI. and Nat. Council Jewish Women; mem. Rape Victims Services Network Adv. Com., Hauppauge, N.Y.; candidate N.Y. state atty. gen., 1982. Mem. ABA (asst. sec. criminal justice sect. 1980-82, vice chmn. prosecution function com. 1981-82), N.Y. Bar Assn., N.Y. State Dist. Attys. Assn., Suffolk County Bar Assn., Suffolk County Criminal Bar Assn., Nat. Dist. Attys. Assn. (assoc. dir. 1981—). Republican. Roman Catholic. Office: Suffolk Dist Attys Office 222 Middle Country Rd Suite 222 Smithtown NY 11787

SCOFIELD, MARY ALICE GIGLIO, printing company executive; b. New Orleans, Oct. 28, 1925; d. James Peter and Mildred Agustus (Touzet) Giglio; m. Burt Ernest Scofield, Oct. 7, 1944 (dec. 1976); children—Scot Peter, Bryan Paul. B.S., Loyola U., New Orleans. Tchr., Cath. Diocese of New Orleans, 1945-61; founder, pres., owner Scofield Printing, Metairie, La., 1971—. Republican. Roman Catholic. Avocations: sailing, golfing, reading, dancing, theater. Home: 1495 Athis St New Orleans LA 70122 Office: Scofield Printing Co 3220 N Turnbull Dr Metairie LA 70002

SCOFIELD, SANDRA KAY, state senator; b. Chadron, Nebr., June 16, 1947; d. Maurice William and Mildred Elizabeth (Connell) S. B.S., U. Nebr., 1969, M.A., 1974. Tchr. Westside High Sch., Omaha, 1969-71; tech. writer Kentron Hawaii, Ltd., Honolulu, 1971-73; free-lance TV writer Lincoln, Nebr., 1974-81; career cons. Chadron State Coll., Nebr., 1978-79, 82, program adminstr., 1979-81, 83; mem. Nebr. Senate, 1983—. Writer (TV series) Survival Economics, 1974 (individual programs won nat. awards, 1974-76). Mem. Nebr. Environ. Control Council, Lincoln, 1983. Mem. AAUW, Delta Kappa Gamma. Democrat. Lodge: Eagles. Avocations: tennis; travel; hot air ballooning. Office: Nebr Legislature 2000 Capitol Bldg Lincoln NE 68509

SCOTT, ALICE FAYE, state housing development administrator; b. Arkansas, Feb. 26, 1943; d. Joseph and Lou Pearl (Kirby) Green; m. Nelson Eddie Scott, Aug. 31, 1963; children—Neysa Michelle, Kenyatta. Student Loop Jr. Coll., Chgo. Cert. real estate salesperson, Ill. Computer operator, asst. desk supr. Fed. Res. Bank, Chgo., 1976-77; asst. investment coordinator Ill. Devel. Authority, Chgo., 1976-78; sr. eligibility processing officer Ill. Housing Devel. Authority, Chgo., 1978—. Vice pres. Sammy Dyee Aux. Sch. of the Theater, Chgo., 1979—; bd. dirs., pub. relations com. St. Ignatius Coll. Prep. Mothers' Club, Chgo., 1982-84; chairperson fund raising com. Hales Franciscan High Sch., Chgo., 1985. Mem. Nat. Assn. Female Execs. Baptist. Avocations: primitive black art; antiques; jogging; bicycling; reading. Home: 5516 S Everett 2S Chicago IL 60637

SCOTT, ALICE HOLLY, library administrator; b. Jefferson, Ga.; d. Frank David and Annie (Colbert) Holly; m. Alphonso Scott, Mar. 1, 1959; children—Christopher, Alison. A.B., Spelman Coll., 1957; M.L.S., Atlanta U., 1958; Ph.D., U. Chgo., 1983. Librarian, Bklyn. Pub. Library, 1958-59; librarian Woodlawn br. Chgo. Pub. Library, 1955-60, br. head, 1961-72, dir. Woodson regional library, 1974-77, dir. community relations, 1978-81, dep. commr., 1982—. Com. Instl. Cooperation fellow, 1973. Mem. ALA (councillor 1982—), Ill. Library Assn., Chgo. Library Club, Beta Phi Mu. Democrat. Baptist. Office: Chgo Pub Library 425 N Michigan Ave Chicago IL 60611

SCOTT, ALICE JANE, nurse administrator, nurse; b. Cochecton, N.Y., Aug. 5, 1939; d. Milton Joseph and Minnie Alice (Campbell) Labar; m. Niles Charless Scott, Apr. 27, 1957 (div. Feb. 1972); 1 child, Harold Niles; m. Russell Berton Scott, Apr. 20, 1980. A.S. in Nursing, SUNY-Albany, 1981; B.S. in Human Services, U. Scranton, 1981, M.S. in Human Resource Adminstrn., 1984. R.N. Staff nurse CCU, Community Gen. Hosp., Harris, N.Y., 1981-82; nurse coordinator Beaumont Sch., Liberty, N.Y., 1981-82; dir. health service New Hope Rehab., Lock Sheldrake, N.Y., 1983-85; patient care coordinator Community Gen. Hosp., Harris, N.Y., 1985—. Mem. Delaware Valley Arts Alliance, Narrowsburg, N.Y., 1981—; leader Methodist Youth Fellowship-Damascus, 1984—. Recipient Outstanding Adult Higher Edn. award Pa. Assn. Adult Continued Edn., 1981; nursing scholar Community Gen. Hosp. Sullivan County, 1980. Mem. Mensa, Equinunk Hist Soc., Alpha Sigma Lambda. Republican. Methodist. Avocations: designing, needlecraft, reading, gardening. Home: PO Box 113 Callicoon NY 12723 Office: Community Gen Hosp Pediatric Dept Harris NY 12742

SCOTT, ANN BESSER, musicologist, educator; b. Newark, June 8, 1933; d. Hyman and Fannie (Bear) Besser; A.B., Radcliffe Coll., 1955; M.F.A., Brandeis U., 1957; Ph.D., U. Chgo., 1969; m. Gordon H.S. Scott, May 3, 1958; children—Ellen, Melinda. Instr., then asst. prof. music U. Chgo., 1968-73; mem. faculty Bates Coll., Auburn, Maine, 1973—, prof. music, 1979—, chmn. dept., 1974—, chmn. div. humanities, 1976-80; mem. music panel Maine Commn. Arts and Humanities, 1975-81; mem. Maine Humanities Council, 1981—, vice chmn., 1981—. Fellow Nat. Endowment Humanities, 1981. Mem. Am. Musicol. Soc. (sec. council 1974-79, editorial bd. jour. 1975-80, bd. dirs. 1985—), Coll. Music Soc., Phi Beta Kappa. Jewish. Author articles in field. Office: Box 1218 RFD 3 Winthrop ME 04634

SCOTT, ANNE BYRD FIROR, historian, educator; b. Montezuma, Ga., Apr. 24, 1921; d. John William and Mary Valentine (Moss) Firor; A.B., U. Ga., 1941; M.A., Northwestern U., 1944; Ph.D., Radcliffe Coll., 1958; L.H.D., Lindenwood Coll., 1968; m. Andrew Mackay Scott, June 2, 1947; children—Rebecca, David MacKay, Donald MacKay. Congl. rep., editor LWV of U.S., 1944-53; lectr. history Haverford Coll., 1957-58, U. N.C., Chapel Hill, 1959-60; asst. prof. history Duke U., Durham, N.C., 1961-67, assoc. prof., 1968-70, prof., 1971-80, W.K. Boyd prof., 1980—; vis. prof. Johns Hopkins U., 1972-73, Stanford U., 1974; Disting. vis. prof. Radcliffe Coll. and Harvard U., 1984; mem. adv. com. Schlesinger Library, Radcliffe Coll. Chmn. Gov.'s Commn. on Status of Women, 1963-64; mem. Citizens Adv. Council on Status of Women U.S., 1964-68. AAUW fellow, 1956-57; grantee Nat. Endowment for Humanities, 1967-68, 76-77, Nat. Humanities Center, 1980-81; Fulbright scholar, Australia, 1984; Ctr. for Advanced Studies in Behavioral Scis. fellow, 1986—. Mem. Am. Antiquarian Soc., Orgn. Am. Historians (mem. exec. bd. 1973-76, pres. 1983-84), So. Hist. Assn. (mem. exec. bd. 1976-79), Phi Beta Kappa. Democrat. Author: The Southern Lady, 1970; (with Andrew MacKay Scott) One Half the People, 1974, Making the Invisible Woman Visible, 1984; editor: Jane Addams, Democracy and Social Ethics, 1964; The American Woman, 1970; Women in American Life, 1970; Women and Men in American Life, 1976; mem. editorial bd. Am. Quar., 1974-78, Jour. So. History, 1978-84; contbr. articles to profl. jours. Office: Dept History Duke U Durham NC 27706

SCOTT, AUDREY M. WALL, lawyer; b. Geren, Miss., Nov. 18, 1947; d. Eugene Wilson and Mary Eliza (Flowers) Wall; m. O.C. Scott, Sept. 15, 1970; children—Daphne L., Lauren J. B.A., Howard U., 1973; J.D., Cath. U., 1977. Bar: Tenn. 1977, U.S. Supreme Ct. 1980. Staff atty. Memphis Area Legal Services, 1977, mng. atty., 1977-79; atty.-examiner EEOC, Memphis, 1979—. Arent and Fox fellow, 1974. Mem. ABA, Fed. Bar Assn., Nat. Bar Assn., Memphis-Shelby County Bar Assn., Black Women Forum. Methodist. Home: 1049 Colgate Rd Memphis TN 38106 Office: EEOC 1407 Union Ave Suite 502 Memphis TN 38104

SCOTT, BARBARA ANN, sociology educator, feminist, peace activist; b. N.Y.C., Jan. 3, 1937; d. Richard W. and Lia (Varell) Scott; m. Josiah Bartlett Page, June 8, 1958 (div. 1975); children—Evan Bartlett, Eric Scott. B.A. magna cum laude, Pembroke Coll., Brown U., 1958; M.A. in Sociology, Grad. Faculty New Sch. for Social Research, 1972, Ph.D. in Sociology, 1979. Elem. tchr. The Harley Sch., Rochester, N.Y., 1958-61, Poughkeepsie Day Sch., N.Y., 1968; instr. sociology SUNY-New Paltz, 1973-79, asst. prof., 1979-84, assoc. prof., 1984—, co-organizer, co-chmn. intercollegiate conf. Liberal Arts in a Time of Crisis; mem. bd. panelists NEH, 1980—; panelist 1st Internat. Conf. on Comparative, Hist. and Critical Analysis of Bureaucracy, Gottlieb Duttweiler Inst., Zurich, Switzerland, 1982; vis. scholar Ctr. Def. Info., Washington, 1986—. Author: Crisis Management in American Higher Edn., 1983 (Albert Salomon Meml. award 1980). Editor: The Liberal Arts in a Time of Crisis (forthcoming), 1986. Contbr. articles in profl. jours. Founder, coordinator Mid-Hudson chpt. Educators for Social Responsibility, 1983; cons., researcher for Democratic Congl. candidate Ed Bloch, 1985—; mem. adv. bd. Unison Learning Ctr., New Paltz, 1985—; trustee Shoreline Found. for Folk Lit. and Art, Branford, Conn., 1983—; alumni speaker Grad. Faculty New Sch. for Social Research, 1977. Mem. Am. Sociol. Assn., Assn. for Humanist Sociology (mem. nominating com. 1985—), N.Y. State Sociol. Assn. (bd. dirs. 1974-75), Mid-Atlantic Radical Historians Orgn. (regional assoc. 1979—), Eastern Sociol. Soc. (com. undergrad. teaching 1974-76), NOW, Women's Internat. League for Peace and Freedom, Union Concerned Scientists, Women's Action for Nuclear Disarmament, SANE. Home: Box 313 Rural Route 1 Hurley Rd Salt Point NY 12578 Office: Sociology Dept SUNY New Paltz NY 12561

SCOTT, BARBARA JEAN, personnel executive; b. Miami, Fla., Sept. 28, 1947; d. John Peter and Bertha Ann (Rutkowski) Nace; A.A., Broward Community Coll., 1970; B.A., U. Fla., 1972; M.Ed., U. S.C., 1980; m. Thomas William Scott, Dec. 18, 1971; 1 dau., Amanda Kristin. Adminstrv. asst. Am. Acad., Hollywood, Fla., 1972-73; instr. English, coordinator Am. Heritage Sch., Hollywood, 1973-77; statistician Greenville (S.C.) Tech., 1978-80, coordinator developmental edn., 1980; personnel asst. Builder Marts Am., Greenville, 1981—; pub. relations dir. Greenville Zoo, 1985; tchr. So. Plantation High Sch., 1986; cons. Publicity com. mem. Warehouse Theatre, Greenville, 1981, Greenville Library, Friends of the Zoo, 1981; vol. Assn. for Retarded Citizens. Mem. AAUW, Nat. Assn. Female Execs., Women's Network, Delta Kappa Gamma (pres.). Roman Catholic. Club: Greenville Bus./Profl. Women's. Home: 7672 NW 5th St Plantation FL 33324

SCOTT, BEVERLY ANN, distribution company official; b. Scottsbluff, Nebr., Dec. 27, 1941; d. Henry Clay and Illma Elizabeth (Moody) S.; m. Alan S. Davenport, Aug. 29, 1964 (div., 1980); 1 dau., Darby Layne. B.A. with honors in Sociology, U. Puget Sound, 1963; M.A. in Sociology, U. Iowa, 1966; postgrad. U. Mich., 1976-79. Instr., Cornell Coll., Mt. Vernon, Iowa, 1965-66, Coe Coll., Cedar Rapids, Iowa, 1966-67; program developer Linn Econ. Action Project, Cedar Rapids, 1967-68; exec. dir. Hawkeye Area Community Action Program, Cedar Rapids, 1968-70; program developer YWCA, Detroit, 1972; social planning and devel. analyst City of Detroit, 1972-75; cons. and edn. specialist Wayne County Community Coll., Detroit, 1975-76; sr. ptnr. Change HRD, Detroit, 1976-79; sr. assoc. Cons. Assocs., Detroit, 1979-81; corp. cons. Bendix Corp., Detroit, 1981; mgr. orgn. and mgmt. devel. McKesson Corp., San Francisco, 1982—. Mem. adv. bd. North End Concerned Citizens Community Council, 1973, dist. adv. com., 1975-76; chair YWCA, 1972-73, mem., 1971-81; fin. chair Montessorri Sch., 1972-73; chair social awareness group Faculty Women's Group U. Mich., 1972-73; pres. Women's Justice Ctr., 1979-80; co-chair Women's Equality Day Planning Com., 1980; steering com. UCS Met. Cam Council, 1977-81; chair program com. Detroit Women's Forum, 1977-80; mem. tng. team People Acting for Change Together, 1972-75; mem. Camping Unlimited com. Am. Camping Assn., 1976-77. Named Mgr. of Yr., McKesson Foods Group, 1983. Mem. NOW, Am. Soc. Tng. and Devel., Am. Sociol. Assn., Nat. Council Family Relations, Midwest Sociol. Assn., Youth Employment Service, Iowa Community Action Dirs., United Community Service Execs., Mich. Episcopal Tng. Network, Univ. Assocs., Women Decision Makers of Detroit, Women in Orgn. Devel., Orgn. Devel. Network (co-chmn. program com. 1985 conf.). Author: (with Ronald Kregoski) Quality Circles: How to Create them, How to Manage Them, How to Profit From them, 1982. Home: 166 Castro St San Francisco CA 94114 Office: 1 Post St San Francisco CA 94104

SCOTT, BEVERLY JANE, veterinarian; b. Columbia, Mo., July 4, 1951; d. D. and Norma Lou (Kilpatrick) Allen. B.S., Abilene Christian U., 1973; D.V.M., U. Mo., 1978. Owner, veterinarian Gilbert Vet. Clinic (Ariz.), 1978—. Treas., bd. dirs. Gilbert Econ. Devel. Assn., 1980-82; bd. dirs. YMCA, 1985-86, Chandler Area Council, 1985-86; chmn. United Way Gilbert area (prof. div.) 1985. Mem. AVMA, Am. Animal Hosp. Assn., Ariz. Vet. Med. Assn. (state dir. Nat. Pet Week 1983-84, com. chmn.), Central Ariz. Vet. Med. Assn. (bd. dirs. 1981-85, pres. 1986), Ariz. Acad. Vet. Medicine (v.p. 1982-83, bd. dirs. 1981-85), Soroptomist (charter mem., bd. dirs. 1983-86). Mem. Ch. of Christ. Office: Gilbert Vet Clinic 1717 S Gilbert Rd Gilbert AZ 85234

SCOTT, BONNIE KIME, English literature educator; b. Phila., Dec. 28, 1944; d. Roy Milford and Sheila (Burton) Kime; m. Thomas Russell Scott, June 17, 1967; children—Heather Sheila, Ethan Kime, Heidi Cathryn Molly. B.A., Wellesley Coll., Mass., 1967; M.A., U. N.C., 1969, Ph.D., 1973. Asst. prof. U. Del., Newark, 1975-80, assoc. prof., 1980—. Author: Joyce and Feminism, 1984; James Joyce, 1986. Contbr. articles to profl. publs. mem. Del. Humanities Council, 1983—. Recipient Excellence in Teaching award Mortar Bd., 1984. Mem. MLA, Am. Com. for Irish Studies (exec. com. 1981-83), James Joyce Found. (founder women's caucus 1983—), Phi Beta Kappa. Home: 216 Orchard Rd Newark DE 19711 Office: Univ of Del Dept of English Meml Hall Newark DE 19716

SCOTT, CATHERINE DOROTHY, librarian, consultant; b. Washington, June 21, 1927; d. Leroy Stearns Scott and Agnes Frances (Meade) Scott Schellenberg. A.B. in English, Catholic U. Am., 1950, M.S. in Library Sci., 1955. Asst. Librarian Export-Import Bank U.S.A., Washington, 1951-55; asst. librarian Nat. Assn. Home Builders, 1955-62, reference librarian, 1956-62; chief tech. librarian, Bellcomm, Inc., subs. AT&T, Washington, 1962-72; chief librarian Nat. Air and Space Mus., Smithsonian Instn., Washington, 1972-82, chief librarian Mus. Reference Ctr., 1982—; bd. visitors Catholic U. Am. Library Sci. Sch. and Libraries, 1984—; Editor: International Handbook of Aerospace Awards and Trophies, 1980, 81; Directory of Aerospace Resources, 1984; guest editor Spl. Collections in Aeronautics and Space Flight Collections, 1985. Vice-chmn. D.C. Republican Com., 1960-68; mem. platform com. Rep. Nat. Com., 1964, sec., 1968; del. Rep. Nat. Conv., San Francisco, 1964, Miami, Fla., 1968; Recipient Sec.'s Disting. Service award Smithsonian Instn., 1976, Alumni Achievement award Catholic U. Am., 1977. Mem. Spl. Libraries Assn. (pres. Washington chpt. 1973-74, cons. 1976—, chmn. aerospace div. 1980-81, Disting. Service award 1982, nat. dir. 1986—), Am. Soc. Info. Scis. (com. chmn.), Internat. Fedn. Library Assns. (del. 1976, 83, 85), Friends of Cath. U. Libraries (pres. 1984—), Nat. Fedn. Rep. Women, Rep. Women's Fed. Forum. Roman Catholic. Club: Capital Yacht (assoc. mem.) (Washington). Office: Smithsonian Instn A and I Bldg Room 2235 900 Jefferson Dr SW Washington DC 20560

SCOTT, DIANA, educator; b. Muncie, Ind., Aug. 6, 1943; d. Levan Ralph and Ogretta Mae (Clemens) Scott; B.S., Ball State U., 1965, M.A., 1968, Ed.D. (fellow), 1973. Tchr. elementary schs. Ft. Wayne (Ind.) Community Sch. System, 1965-67; instr. spl. edn. Ball State U., Muncie, 1968-70, asst. prof. elementary edn., 1973; asst. prof. lang. edn. and childhood edn. programs Fla. State U., Tallahassee, 1973-77, asso. prof., 1977—, head dept. childhood, reading and spl. edn., 1983-85; cons. to pub. schs. and tchr. edn. centers in various counties of Fla., 1974-77; tech. asst. for State of Fla. Right to Read Program, 1974-77. Mem. Nat. Council of Tchrs. English, Nat. Council for Exceptional Children, Fla. Reading Council, Internat. Reading Assn. Asso. editor Florida Reading Quar., 1973-77. Home: 348 Lexington Rd Tallahassee FL 32312 Office: Childhood Edn Dept Stone Bldg 115 Fla State U Tallahassee FL 32306

SCOTT, ELIZABETH LEONARD, statistics educator; b. Fort Sill, Okla., Nov. 23, 1917; d. Richard C. and Elizabeth (Waterman) S. B.A., U. Calif.-Berkeley, 1939, Ph.D., 1949. Research fellow U. Calif.-Berkeley, 1939-49, mem. faculty, 1949—, assoc. prof. stats., 1957-62, prof., 1962—, chmn. dept., 1968-73, asst. dean Coll. Letters and Sci., 1965-67, co-chmn. group in biostats., 1972—; mem. Commn. on Nat. Stats., Nat. Acad. Scis., 1971-77, Commn. on Women in Sci., 1977-82, Commn. on Applied and Theoretical Stats., 1981-84, Oversight Commn. on Radioepidemiologic Tables, 1983-85. Contbr. articles to profl. jours. Fellow Royal Statis. Soc. (hon.), Inst. Math. Stats. (council 1971-74, 76-79, pres. 1977-78); mem. Biometric Soc. (council 1978-81), Am. Astron. Soc., Internat. Astron. Union, Internat. Stats. Inst. (v.p. 1981-83), Internat. Assn. Stats. in Phys. Sci. (sci. sec. 1960-72), Bernoulli Soc. (council 1978-81, pres.-elect 1981-83, pres. 1983—), Astron. Soc. Pacific, AAAS (chmn. sect. U 1970-71, mem. council 1971-76). Office: Dept Stats U Calif Berkeley CA 94720

SCOTT, GERTRUDE ROSE, metals co. exec.; b. Pitts., Oct. 12, 1932; d. Leroy Lewis and Dorothea Margaret King; B.A. magna cum laude, U. Pitts., 1969, M.A., 1971. Public relations supr. Allegheny Gen. Hosp., Pitts., 1971-73; mgr. communications Jones & Laughlin Steel Corp., Pitts., 1973-76; v.p. corp. communication Meldrum & Fewsmith, Cleve., 1976-81; v.p. Steel Service Center Inst., Cleve., 1981—. Mem. Public Relations Soc. Am. (chpt. pres. 1982—). Office: Steel Service Center Inst 1600 Terminal Tower Cleveland OH 44113

SCOTT, IRENE FEAGIN, U.S. judge; b. Union Springs, Ala., Oct. 6, 1912; d. Arthur H. and Irene (Peach) Feagin; m. Thomas Jefferson Scott, Dec. 27, 1939; children—Thomas Jefferson, Irene (Mrs. Franklin L. Carroll III). A.B., U. Ala., 1932, LL.B., 1936, LL.D., 1978; LL.M., Catholic U. Am., 1939. Bar: Ala. 1936. Law Librarian U. Ala. Law Sch., 1932-34; atty. Office Chief Counsel, Internal Revenue Service, 1937-50, mem. excess profits tax council, 1950-52, spl. asst. to 1952-59, spl. asst. to head chief counsel, 1959-60; judge U.S. Tax Ct., Washington, 1960-82, sr. judge on recall, 1982—. Mem. ABA, Nat. Assn. Women Lawyers, Nat. Assn. Women Judges, Nat. Lawyers Club, Fed. Bar Assn., Ala. Bar Assn., D.C. Bar Assn. (hon.), Kappa Delta, Kappa Beta Pi. Office: US Tax Ct 400 2d St NW Washington DC 20217

SCOTT, JOAN WALLACH, historian; b. Bklyn., Dec. 18, 1941; d. Samuel and Lottie (Tanenbaum) Wallach; B.A., Brandeis U., 1962; M.A., U. Wis., Madison, 1964, Ph.D., 1969; m. Donald M. Scott, Jan. 30, 1965; children—Anthony Oliver, Elizabeth Rose. Asst. prof. history U. Ill., Chgo. Circle campus, 1970-72; asst. prof. Northwestern U., 1972-74; asso. prof. U. N.C., Chapel Hill, 1974-77, prof., 1977-80; Nancy Duke Lewis prof., prof. history Brown U., Providence, from 1980, now adj. prof.; dir. Pembroke Ctr. for Teaching and Research on Women, from 1981; now with Sch. Social Sci., Inst. for Advanced Study, Princeton, N.J.; dir. Summer Seminar for Coll. Tchrs., NEH, 1977, dir. Seminar for Coll. Tchrs., 1980-81; mem. Inst. for Advanced Study, Princeton, N.J., 1978-79. Social Sci. Research Council research tng. fellow, 1966-68; Nat. Endowment for Humanities fellow, 1975-76; Am. Council Learned Socs. grantee, 1978. Mem. Am. Hist. Assn. (chmn. com. on women historians 1978-80), Social Sci. History Assn., Soc. French Hist. Studies. Author: The Glassworkers of Carmaux, 1974 (Am. Hist. Assn. Herbert Baxter Adams prize 1974), (with Louise Tilly) Women Work and Family, 1978. Office: Inst for Advanced Study Olden Ln Princeton NJ 08540*

SCOTT, JOANN SULLIVAN, educator; b. Tyler, Tex., Aug. 20, 1932; d. Vernon Reid and Gladys Mabell (Turner) Sullivan; B.S. in Edn., U. Houston, 1963; postgrad. Houston Community Coll., 1980; bus. practices cert. Lockheed Tech. Inst., 1967, 70; 1 dau., Debra Ann Bloch. Assoc. scientist Lockheed Electronics, Johnson Space Center, NASA, Houston, 1966-70; career edn. cons., Houston Ind. Sch. Dist., 1970-74; pvt. practice, owner contract drafting service, Houston, 1974-75; coordinator tng. and graphics Internat. Field Data, Houston, 1975-76; geol./geophys. tech. asst. Mich. Wis. Pipe Line, Houston, 1976-81; instr., tng. coordinator, Women in Bus., Tex. Engring. Extension Service, Tex. A&M U. System, Houston, 1981-83; cons., tchr., life-career coordination and planning, 1983—; bus. developer, adult leisure learning, Free U., 1977-82. Officer Civic Club, 1974-77; coordinator literacy vol. tutor program Houston Community Coll.; adv. bd. R.E.A.D. (Reading Edn. and Devel.) Council; Vol. reading trainer. Recipient Man-on-Moon award, 1969. Mem. Am. Soc. Tng. and Devel., Nat. Soc. for Performance and Instrn., Houston Geol. Soc., Project Mgmt. Inst. Am. Mensa (service award, 1978), Gulf Coast Mensa (v.p. 1975-78, proctor, newsletter editor). Mem. Unity Ch. of Christianity. Author various curriculum bulletins, career devel. programs; researcher, author adult leisure courses. Home: 2501 Yupon St Houston TX 77006

SCOTT, JOSEPHINE BARNES, nursing administrator; b. Rocky Mount, N.C., June 28, 1954; d. William Henry and Cora (Smith) Barnes. B.S.N., Hampton Inst., 1976. Charge nurse Vanderbilt U. Med. Ctr., Nashville, 1976-79; supr. R.N. II, Nashville Regional Correctional Facility, 1979-81; supr. R.N. III Tenn. Reception and Guidance Ctr., Nashville, 1981-83; dir. nursing, mem. adv. bd. Family Care Home Health Services, Inc., Nashville, 1983—. Editor: Management of Effective Patient Care, 1978. Treas. Élan Civic Club, Nashville, 1981—; active YWCA, Nashville, 1984-85. Handy and Harman scholar, 1972-76; recipient Employee of Month award Quality Care Nursing Services, 1979, Award of Recognition, Elder Care, 1979. Mem. Tenn. Nurses Assn., Tenn. Assn. Home Health, Am. Nurses Found. Century Club, DAR (Mary Silliman chpt.). Democrat. Baptist. Avocations: reading; plays; music; fashion. Home: 1313 Kenmore Circle Nashville TN 37216 Office: 2001 Charlotte Ave Suite 202 Nashville TN 37203

SCOTT, JOYCE ELIZABETH, electronics technician; b. Mobile, Ala., Sept. 26, 1950; d. Johnnie and Levia Odell (Watts) Williams; A.A., Am. River Coll., 1974; B.A., San Francisco State U., 1979; M.A., U. Calif., Davis, 1981; m. Russell Alan Scott, July 5, 1980; children—Veronica, Jason. Exec. sec. constrn. br. U.S. Army C.E., San Francisco, 1970-73; adminstrv. asst. Calif. Office Mgmt. and Budget, Sacramento, 1974-75; sales mgr. Jocelyne Starr Accessories, Oakland, Calif., 1977-78; electronics technician Dept. Navy, Naval Air Rework Facility, Naval Air Sta., Alameda, Calif., 1978—, participant electronics apprentice program, 1978-82; tchr., vocat. counselor in field. Recipient Superior Performance award State of Calif., 1975. Mem. Federally Employed Women, Adminstrv. Assn., Assn. Mgrs. Democrat. Club: Order Eastern Star.

SCOTT, KAREN MICHELE, television producer; b. Saratoga Springs, N.Y., July 3, 1949; d. Alfred and Rosalie (Martin) Silberman; m. Guy B. Scott III, Aug. 20, 1973 (div. Nov. 1982). B.A. in Journalism, Ohio State U., 1971. Reporter, Sta. WRFD-WNCI Radio, Columbus, Ohio, 1971-73; assoc. producer Sta. WKBD-TV, Detroit, 1975-76; producer, news writer Sta. WXYZ-TV, Detroit, 1976-78; producer, exec. producer spl. projects Sta. WFSB-TV, Hartford, Conn., 1979-83; producer Sta. WNBC-TV, N.Y.C., 1983—. Mem. Radio-Television News Directors Assn., Women in Communications, Nat. Acad. TV Arts and Scis. Jewish. Office: WNBC-TV 30 Rockefeller Plaza New York NY 10020

SCOTT, LUCY, psychologist, consultant; b. Chgo., June 11, 1928; d. Amos H. and Fern (Irvin) Hoff; B.A., Ariz. State U., 1960, M.A., 1969; Ph.D., Fielding Inst., Santa Barbara, Calif., 1979; divorced; children—Cynthia, Susan. Tchr. jr. high sch., Phoenix, 1961-66; dir., tchr., counselor Cyesis Center, Phoenix Union High Sch. Dist., 1967-71; tchr., counselor, cons., trainer Family Life Edn. Project, Calif. Youth Authority, San Francisco, 1977-80; mem. faculty dept. health scis. San Jose State U., 1974-80; adj. faculty U. San Francisco, 1980—; dir. Parenthood After Thirty, Berkeley, Calif., 1980—; pvt. practice psychotherapy, Berkeley, 1974—; dir. Parents Place, San Francisco, 1985—; cons. in field; bd. dirs., adv. Calif. Youth Authority Task Force, Calif. Dept. Health Task Force, Calif. Family Life Edn. Program Devel. Project; lectr. in field. Mem. Assn. Women in Psychology, Internat. Assn. Applied Psychology, Am. Assn. Sex Educators, Counselors and Therapists, Am. Psychol. Assn., Am. Orthopsychiat. Assn. Author: Parenthood After Thirty; Resource Manual, 1981; Time Out for Motherhood, 1986.

SCOTT, LYNDA LEIGH, plastics company executive, communications consultant; b. Berlin, N.J., Oct. 22, 1961; d. Robert Edward and Elizabeth (Robertson) Honeywell S. B.A., Westminster Coll., 1983. Staff asst. Ams. for the Competitive Enterprise System, Erie, Pa., 1983-84, cons., 1983—; employee relations mgr. Westminster Mfg. Corp., Girard, Pa., 1984—. Editor Changing Tools, 1984-86. Inventor stencil art overlays, 1986. Mem. Internat. Assn. Bus. Communicators (sec. 1984-85, publicity 1985-86), Personnel Assn. N.W. Pa. Republican. Presbyterian. Avocations: racquetball; skiing; reading. Office: Westminister Mfg Corp 227 Hathaway St Girard PA 16417

SCOTT, MALORA COURTNEY, materials handling systems executive; b. Cin., Mar. 1, 1949; d. Court and Mildred Catherine (Neeley) C. Student So. Ohio Coll. Computer operator, invoice supr. Parke Davis div. Warner Lambert, Blue Ash, Ohio, 1967-83; mgr. data processing Micro Med, Inc., Fairfield, Ohio, 1983-85; credit mgr. Bobcat of Atlanta, Conley, Ga., 1985-86, Ogden Materials, Handling Systems, Inc., Atlanta, 1986—. Leader Campfire Girls Southwestern Ohio, Cin., 1974; mem. staff Muscular Dystrophy Assn., Cin., 1972-74; vol. ARC, Cin., 1968-70; sponsor GOP Victory Fund, 1984-86. Mem. Nat. Rifle Assn., Nat. Assn. Female Execs. Republican. Avocations: camping; music; needlework; swimming. Home: 704 Tree Mountain Pkwy Stone Mountain GA 30083

SCOTT, MARGARET JEAN, oil and gas company executive; b. Rapid City, Mich., Mar. 3, 1939; d. Robert Purcell and Nellie (Jerome) Morrison; m. Charles D. Scott, July 22, 1956; children—William D., Holly Jean, Christine Sue. Student Northwestern Mich. Coll., 1975-78. Mailwoman U.S. Postal Dept., Rapid City, Mich., 1960-68; sec. sales dept. Chef Pierre, Inc., Traverse City, Mich., 1968-69; legal sec., asst. Murchie Calcutt & Sondee, Traverse City, 1969-81; instr. Northwestern Mich. Coll., Traverse City, 1981-83; v.p. ops. Indsl. Natural Gas Corp., Traverse City, 1981—. Author, editor The Career Legal Secretary, 1980-81. The Career Legal Secretary-Advanced, 1980-82; editor, coordinator The NALS Docket, 1983. Named Legal Sec. of Yr., Mich. Assn. Legal Secs., 1977. Mem. Nat. Assn. Legal Secs. (state pres. 1981-83), Nat. Assn. Legal Assts.

SCOTT, MARGARET LOUISE, aerospace company graphics artist; b. Santa Monica, Calif., June 21, 1925; d. Earl Joseph and Stella May (Miller) Scott; student Los Angeles City Coll., 1947-51, El Camino Coll., 1973. Flight test analyst N.Am. Aviation, Los Angeles, 1943-51; graphics artist N.Am. Rockwell, Los Angeles, 1951-74; illustrations project coordinator Rockwell Internat., Los Angeles, 1974-75, dept. head graphics art dept., Los Angeles div., El Segundo, Calif., 1975—. Mem. trade adv. com. El Camino Coll., Glendale Community Coll., West Los Angeles Coll., 1975—. Home: 1601 Sunset Plaza Dr Los Angeles CA 90069 Office: 100 N Sepulveda El Segundo CA 90245

SCOTT, MARIANNE FLORENCE, national librarian of Canada; b. Toronto, Ont., Can., Dec. 4, 1928; d. Merle Redvers and Florence Ethel (Hutton) S. B.A., McGill U., Montreal, Que., Can., 1949, B.L.S., 1952, LL.D. (hon.), 1985. Asst. librarian Bank of Montreal, 1952-55; law librarian McGill U., 1955-73, lectr.-legal bibliography, 1964-74, law area librarian, 1973-74, dir. libraries, 1975-84; nat. librarian of Can., Nat. Library of Can., Ottawa, Ont., 1984—. Editor, co-founder Index to Can. Legal Periodical Lit., 1963—. Decorated Queen's Silver Jubilee medal. Mem. Que. Library Assn. (pres. 1961-62), Can. Assn. Law Libraries (pres. 1963-69, first hon. mem. 1980—), Can. Assn. Research Libraries (pres. 1978-79), Can. Library Assn. (pres. 1981-82). Office: Nat Library of Can 395 Wellington St Ottawa ON K1A ON4 Canada

SCOTT, MARY JANE GOMEZ, human resources specialist; b. Hartford, Conn., Aug. 12, 1944; d. Juan and Marion Priscilla (Jewett) Gomez; m. Jeffery Anderson Scott, Jan. 27, 1967. B.S.Ed., U. Conn., 1966. Tchr. elem. sch. Stamford Bd. Edn., 1966-69; coll. relations asst. Olin Corp., Stamford, 1969-73, compensation analyst, 1973-77, mgr. salary programs 1977-78, mgr. internal placement, 1978-80, mgr. salaried personnel, 1980-82; mgr. staffing GTE Communication Systems Corp., Stamford, 1982—. Mem. Employment Mgmt. Assn., Am. Compensation Assn., Am. Soc. Personnel Adminstrn. Home: 285 N Salem Rd Ridgefield CT 06877 Office: GTE Communication Systems Corp One Stamford Forum Stamford CT 06904

SCOTT, MELLOUISE JACQUELINE, media specialist; b. Sanford, Fla., Mar. 1, 1943; d. Herbert and Mattye (Williams) Cherry; m. Robert Edward Scott, Jr., July 1, 1972. B.A., Talladega Coll., 1965; M.L.S., Rutgers U., 1974, Ed.M., 1976, Ed.S., 1982. Media specialist Seminole County Bd. Edn., Sanford, 1965-72, Edison Bd. Edn. (N.J.), 1972—. Mem. ALA, N.J. Edn. Assn., NEA, Ednl. Media Assn. N.J. Baptist. Home: PO Box 8 Fords NJ 08863 Office: Edison Bd Edn Municipal Complex Edison NJ 08817

SCOTT, PATRICIA ANNE, nurse, educator; b. Miami, Fla., July 3, 1938; d. Francis Royal and Catherine Delores (Dunham) Scott; B.S., Columbia Union Coll., 1961; M.S. in Nursing, U. Pa., 1970; D.N.S., U. Calif., San Francisco, 1984; children—David Marc Freedman, Lesli Anne Freedman. Staff and charge nurse, various hosps., Washington, 1961-64; instr. Capital City Sch. Nursing, Washington, 1964-66; nurse Internat. Red Cross, London, 1966-68; asst. prof. Wesley Coll., Dover, Del., 1970-72; Loma Linda (Calif.) U., 1972-73; dir. nursing service SDA Hosp., Karachi, Pakistan, 1973-75; asst. prof., coordinator, So. Missionary Coll., Madison, Tenn., 1975-78, dir. sch. nursing Am. Hosp., Istanbul, Turkey, 1978-80; dean faculty of nursing Yarmouk U., Irbid, Jordan, 1985—. Mem. Am. Nurses Assn., Calif. Nurses Assn. (region 12), ARC, AAUP, Sigma Theta Tau. Episcopalian. Address: Yarmouk U Faculty of Nursing Irbid Jordan

SCOTT, PATRICIA LOUISE, sign manufacturing company executive; b. Chgo., Feb. 13, 1946; d. Gerald E. and Grace B. (Hauser) Doyle; m. Gregory L. Marshall, (dec. Oct. 1967); 1 child, Gregory L., II.; m. Don Scott, May 13, 1978. Adminstrv. asst. Sweda Internat., Chgo., Des Plaines, Ill., 1969-73; asst. credit mgr. Oce Industries, Chgo., 1974-77; gen. office staff Nutheme Co., Elk Grove, Ill., 1977-78, gen. mgr., 1978-83, pres., 1983—. Office: Nutheme Co 1461 D Lunt Ave Elk Grove Village IL 60007

SCOTT, ROSE ANNE, computer company executive; b. Pasadena, Tex., Dec. 19, 1948; d. William Hadley and Mary W. S. Mus.B., U. Tex., 1972. Tchr. music Austin Ind. Sch. Dist., Tex., 1972-74; employment cons. Hallmark Personnel, Houston, 1976-77; employment recruiter Aramco Services, Houston, 1977-83, employment supr., The Hague, Netherlands, 1982; employee relations rep. Compag Computer Corp., Houston, 1983—. Mem. Nat. Assn. Female Execs., Nat. C. of C. for Women, Am. Soc. Profl. Exec. Women, Houston Grand Opera Guild, Sigma Alpha Iota. Republican. Episcopalian. Home: 8331 La Roche Ln Houston TX 77036

SCOTT, WILLODENE ALEXANDER (MRS. RAY DONALD SCOTT), library administrator; b. Ethridge, Tenn., Sept. 4, 1922; d. Jesse Cary and Maud (Goff) Alexander; B.A., George Peabody Coll. for Tchrs., 1946, B.S. in L.S., 1947, M.A., 1949, Ed.S., 1972, now Ph.D. candidate; m. Ray Donald Scott, Nov. 27, 1959; 1 dau., Pamela Dean. Librarian, Sylvan Park Elem. Sch., Nashville, 1947-51, Waverly Belmont Jr. High Sch., Nashville, 1951-54, Howard High Sch., Nashville, 1954-62, Peabody Demonstration Sch., Nashville, 1962-63; librarian McCann Elem. Sch., Nashville, 1963-66; supr. instructional materials, library div. Metro Nashville-Davidson County Schs., Nashville, 1966-73, dir. instructional materials and library services, 1973—; lectr. Peabody Coll. Library Sch., Nashville, summers, 1950-66, 71-72, 76, U. Tenn., Nashville Center, 1970; Tenn. rep. White House Conf., 1970. Chmn. nat. alumni fund-raising George Peabody Coll. for Tchrs., 1975-76, nat. alumni pres., 1977-78, trustee, 1976-78; bd. dirs. Friends of Music, 1977-79; mem. vis. com. bd. trustees Vanderbilt U., 1979-85. Mem. ALA, Southeastern Library Assn. (scholarship com. 1968-70), Tenn. Library Assn. (membership chmn. 1955, 64, treas. 1977-78), Tenn. Edn. Assn. (library sect. pres. 1954), Met. Nashville Edn. Assn., NEA (life), Children's Internat. Edn. Center of Nashville (charter mem.-at-large), AAUW, Woman's Nat. Book Assn. (charter mem.), DAR (organizing treas. Buffalo River chpt. 1967-69), Delta Kappa Gamma (2d v.p. 1984-86). Baptist. Clubs: Order Eastern Star; Nashville Library (pres. 1952-53). Home: 525 Clematis Dr Nashville TN 37205 Office: 2601 Bransford Ave Nashville TN 37204

SCOTT-BATTLE, GLADYS NATALIE, psychiatric social worker; b. Cambridge, Mass., Sept. 16, 1933; d. Dudley Fairfax and Bessie Mae (Mitchell) Scott; m. James Henry Battle, Jr., Oct. 18, 1953 (div. 1975); children—Gregory, James, Jameel. B.A., Fordham U., 1975; M.S.W., Columbia U., 1978. Cert. social worker, tchr. N.Y. Program dir. Community Service Soc., N.Y.C., 1978-79; corp. liaison cities and schs., N.Y.C., 1979-80; psychotherapist Harlem Interfaith Counseling, N.Y.C., 1980-81; psychiat. social worker Met. Hosp., N.Y.C., 1981-83, N.Y.C. Bd. Edn., 1983—; cons. N.Y. State Disability Determinations, 1982—. Vice pres. Women Who Help Other People, N.Y.C., 1985; bd. dirs. Morningside Gardens Coop., N.Y.C., 1986; vol. Met. Mus. Art. Mem. Nat. Assn. Social Workers, Nat. Assn. Black Social Workers, United Fedn. Tchrs. Democrat. Avocations: visiting museums and art galleries, painting; theatre. Home: 524 W 123d St Suite 1W New York NY 10027

SCOTT-COHOON, JANICE LEE, health care executive; b. Oakland, Calif., Jan. 30, 1950; d. Royal M. and Betty Jean (Flynn) Scott; m. Stephen Michael Cohoon; 1 child, Caroline Scott. B.B.A., U. Tex., 1972. Auditor, Werner & Arendale, CPAs, Houston, 1972-73, Allstate Ins. Co., Menlo Park, Calif., 1973-74; acct. Santa Cruz County (Calif.), 1975-77; dir. acctg. San Jose Hosp. (Calif.), 1977-78; budget office mgr. North Colo. Med. Center, Greeley, Colo., 1978-79; asst. fin. mgr. Humana Hosp.-Garland (Tex.), 1979-80; asst. controller Methodist Hosps. of Dallas, 1980-81, dir. data processing, 1981-82, fin. analyst, 1982-83, v.p. data processing, 1983-84; mktg. dir. Infostat, Inc., Dallas, 1984-85; mktg. rep. Keane, Dallas, 1985—. Mem. Data Processing Mgmt. Assn., Tex. Hosp. Info. Systems Soc., Healthcare Fin. Mgmt. Assn. Office: Keane Inc PO Box 795063 Dallas TX 75279

SCOTT-MARTIN, LAURIE BETH, symphony development administrator; b. Syracuse, N.Y., Apr. 29, 1958; d. John Lawrence and Phyllis Marguerite (Sanderson) Scott; m. Stephen Andrew Martin, July 16, 1983. B.Mus. in Music Edn., U. Hartford, 1980. Mgr. Conn. Valley Youth Wind Ensemble, Hartford, Conn., 1980-81; mktg. dir. Nashville Symphony Assn., 1982-84; devel. dir. Buffalo Philharm. Orch., 1984—. Mem. steering com. Met. Arts Commn. Summer Lights Arts Festival, Nashville, 1983-84; resource com. mem. YWCA Try Angle House, Nashville, 1983-84; mem. Nashville Roundtable Investments, Inc., 1983. Agy. recipient Diamond award Nashville Advt. Fedn., 1982. Mem. Am. Symphony Orch. League (mgmt. fellow N.Y. Philharmonic, Nashville Symphony, Cleve. Orch. 1981-82), Nashville Area Jr. C. of C. (com. mem.). Presbyterian. Office: Buffalo Philharm Orch 71 Symphony Circle Buffalo NY 14222

SCOVILL, RUTH ALATHEA, TV facility executive; b. Hudson, N.Y., Nov. 26, 1950; d. Robert Barnard and Janet Patricia (Goodman) S.; B.F.A., San Francisco Art Inst., 1972; M.A., Calif. State U., 1976. Scheduler, One Pass Video, San Francisco, 1977-78, ops. supr., 1978-79; prodn. supr. Reeves Teletape, N.Y.C., 1979-80, mgr. studio facilities, 1980-82, gen. mgr. studio facilities, 1982-83; gen. mgr. remote facilities, 1983-85; dir. ops. One Pass Film and Video, 1985—. Mem. Profl. Women's Network, Bay Area Career Women, Am. Women in Radio and TV. Home: 1936 McAllister St San Francisco CA 94115 Office: One China Basin Bldg San Francisco CA 94107

SCREEN-BERRY, AUDREY BERNITA, nurse; b. Bklyn., May 1, 1955; d. Herbert and Helen Caroline (Moore) Screen; B.S. in Nursing, Russell Sage Coll., 1977; cert. in public adminstrn., Dyke Coll., 1982; m. Tommie Berry, Jr., May 12, 1978; children—Lenore Marie, Patrice. Staff nurse Univ. Hosps. Cleve., 1977-78; public health nurse Vis. Nurses Assn., Cleve., 1978-79, Maternity and Infant Care Project, Cleve., 1979-80; nurse, med. team mgr. Kenneth W. Clement Center Family Health Care, Cleve., 1980-84; nurse mgr. Huron Road Hosp., Cleve., 1984-86; pharm. sales rep. Smith Kline & French, 1986—. Registered nurse, Ohio. Mem. Cleve. Council Black Nurses, Am. Nurses Assn., Greater Cleve. Nurses Assn., Nat. Assn. Female Execs., AAUW. Lutheran.

SCRIBNER, BEVERLY KINNEAR, lawyer; b. Chandler, Okla., Mar. 8, 1941; d. Howard James and Helen Vista (Smith) Kinnear; m. Edward Leon Scribner, Aug. 26, 1961 (div. Aug. 1970); 1 son, John Edward; m. 2d, Don Martin Claunch, July 9, 1983; 1 stepdau., Diane Melissa. B.S. with distinction, U. Okla., 1963, J.D., 1977. Bar: Okla. 1977. Office mgr. McAfee & Taft, attys. at law, Oklahoma City, 1970-72; adminstr. asst. GHK Cos., Oklahoma City, 1972; legal asst. Hines & Smith, Oklahoma City, 1972-74; dir. legal asst. program U. Okla. Sch. Law, Norman, 1974-77; atty. Kerr Davis et al, Oklahoma City, 1977-79; ptnr. Bryant & Scribner, Oklahoma City, 1979-83, Claunch, Bryant & Scribner, Oklahoma City, 1983—; mem. adv. bd. legal asst. program Okla. U. Coll. Law, Norman, 1977—. Mem. ABA, Okla. Bar Assn., Oklahoma County Bar Assn., Oklahoma City Title Attys. Assn. (mem. exec. bd. 1983-84, treas. 1984, v.p. 1986), Oklahoma City Mineral Lawyers Soc. (pres. 1986-87), Oklahoma City Mgmt. and Profl. Women (pres. 1982). Republican. Presbyterian. Home: 10904 Maple Grove Oklahoma City OK 73120 Office: 710 Union Plaza 3030 Northwest Expressway Oklahoma City OK 73112

SCRIMA, VICTORIA MARIE, nurse educator; b. Bethlehem, Pa., Feb. 24, 1919; d. Donato and Michelina (Selvaggi) Scrima. Diploma in Nursing, Easton Hosp. Sch. Nursing, 1946; B.S., NYU, 1952, M.A., 1958, postgrad. 1964. Staff nurse Easton Hosp. (Pa.), 1946-47, head nurse, 1947-48, instr. Sch. Nursing, 1948-57; asst. prof. U. Utah Coll. Nursing, Salt Lake City, 1958-60; instr. NYU, N.Y.C., 1960-62; dir. confs. Am. Nurses Assn., N.Y.C., 1964-65, coordinator clin. conf., 1964-68; assoc. prof. nursing Niagara U. Coll. Nursing (N.Y.), 1968—; research assoc., cons., Roswell Park Meml. Inst., Buffalo, 1974-78. Contbr. articles to profl. jours. Recipient award for outstanding contbn. in cancer edn. Am. Cancer Soc., 1975; citation of merit as outstanding tchr. Niagara U., 1981; Victoria M. Scrima Research Day named in her honor Niagara U. and Sigma Theta Tau, 1984. Mem. Am. Nurses Assn., Am. Cancer Soc., Sigma Theta Tau, Alpha Sigma Lambda. Office: Niagara Univ Coll Nursing Niagara Univ NY 14109

SCRIVNER, BARBARA E., piano teacher; b. Oreg., May 25, 1931; student (piano student of Lawrence Morton), Bob Jones U., 1962-66; corr. student Inst. Children's Lit., Redding Ridge, Conn., 1974-76; children—R. Dick. Lawrence C., Barbara Ann, Betty Jo. Part time sec., Oreg., 1948-50, 60-62, 74-76, 80-82, 86—, Census Bur., S.C., 1974-76, 80-82; piano tchr., Greenville, S.C., 1963—. Active Republican Nat. Com., Nat. Rep. Senatorial Com., Nat. Rep. Congressional Com., S.C. Rep. Party. Mem. S.C. Music Assn., Music Tchrs. Nat. Assn., Liberty Found. Contbr. articles, letters to newspapers and columns; editor, pub. Golden Nuggets of Truth, 1982—.

SCRIVNER, DOROTHYE LUCILLE, nurse; b. Amoret, Mo., Jan. 20, 1915; d. Frederick William and Nora Agnes (Dale) Allman; R.N., Jane C. Stormont Hosp., 1939; m. Marvin J. Scrivner, Aug. 31, 1941; children—Lee Ann, William Nelson. Staff nurse U.S. Vets. Facility, Chilicothe, Ohio, 1940-41; operating room staff nurse Permanente Found. Hosp., Oakland, Calif., 1942-44; office nurse, operating room nurse Colorado Springs (Colo.) Med. Center, 1956-58, 61-65; asst. supr. med. floor Guadelupe Valley Hosp., Seguin, Tex., 1966; dir. nursing services Guadelupe Valley Nursing Home, Seguin, 1967-68; dir. nursing services Medalion Retirement Residence, Colorado Springs, 1970-75; dir. nursing Medalion W. Retirement Residence, Colorado Springs, 1976—; nurse cons. Sunny Acres Villa, 1976-77. Mem. Colo. Nurses Assn. Home: 2211 N Bonfoy Ave Colorado Springs CO 80909 Office: 417 E Kiowa St Colorado Springs CO 80903

SCRIVNER, JOYCE KAY, automated design engineer; b. Denver, June 12, 1950; d. Mansil Wayne and Harriet Lorraine (Webster) S.; S.S.T.P., Colo. Sch. Mines, 1967; student U. Colo., 1968-72; student Mich. State U., Clarion, 1974; B.S.C.S., Purdue U., 1976. Clk., U.S. Book Exchange, Washington, 1972-73, Govt. Printing Office, Washington, 1973-74; programmer SCADA group Leeds & Northrup Corp., North Wales, Pa., 1976-78; programmer/analyst Energy Mgmt. Systems div. Control Data Corp., Mpls., 1979-84; sr. design automated engr. Sperry, Mpls., 1984—; adminstr. Down Under Fan Fund, 1981-83; chmn. Plerglocon, Mpls., 1982; mem. corr. bd. Purdue U. Sch. Sci., 1984—. Mem. World Sci. Fiction Conv. Staff, 1977, 78, 80, 81, 82, 84, 85; chairperson art show Minicon, Mpls., 1980-81, 83. Down Under Fan Fund grantee, 1981. Mem. Assn. Women in Computing (program v.p. 1982-83, staff conf. 1982, 86), Minn. Sci. Fiction Assn., IEEE Computer Soc., Assn. Computing Machinery (staff conf. 1984). Editor mags.: Gypsy, 1979—, Of Such Are Legends Made, 1978—. Office: PO Box 64942 Mail Sta EBT4 Saint Paul MN 55164-0942

SCROGGIE, LOIS JEAN, writer, educator; b. Denver, Nov. 28, 1940; d. John and Ann Allison (Forsyth) Scroggie; B.A., U. Colo., 1964, M.A., 1966, postgrad., 1968, 73; m. Jan Whitinger, Dec. 25, 1975 (div.). Instr. English, Trinidad (Colo.) State Jr. Coll., 1966-82. Mem. AAUP, Modern Lang. Assn., Rocky Mountain Modern Lang. Assn., Women's Caucus for Modern Langs., Nat. Council Tchrs. English, English-Speaking Union, Am. Film Inst., Nat. Writer's Club, Soc. Children's Book Writers, City News Service. Author articles, poems. Home and Office: 777 Monaco Pwky Denver CO 80220

SCROGGINS, LEANN MARIE, nurse; b. Eads, Colo., July 15, 1947; d. Olly Sweeney and Rosena Clarice Scroggins. Diploma Bethel Sch Nursing, Meml. Hosp., 1969; B.S.N. magna cum laude, U. No. Colo., 1971; M.S., Tex. Woman's U., 1975. Registered nurse, Colo., Minn. Staff nurse Weisbrod Hosp., Eads, 1969, Weld County Gen. Hosp., Greeley, Colo., 1969-71, Meml. Hosp., Colorado Springs, 1971-72; instr. nursing Beth-el Sch. Nursing, Colorado Springs, 1972-74, 75-79; clin., nurse specialist St. Mary's Hosp., Rochester, Minn., 1979—; clin. preceptor U. Minn.-Rochester, 1982-83, 85, U. Wis.-Eau Claire, 1984-85. Mem. Am. Nurses Assn. Council Clin. Nurse Specialists, Am. Nurses Assn. (cert. clin. nurse specialist), Minn. Nurses Assn. (bd. dirs. dist. 6 1982-85), Midwest Nursing Research Soc. Mem. Ch. of Christ. Office: St Mary's Hosp 1216 SW 2nd St Rochester MN 55902

SCRUGGS, KAREN LAFRANCE, pediatrician; b. May 14, 1947; d. Samuel Hiley and Fannetta (McLean) S.; B.A. with honors, Macalester Coll., St. Paul, 1968; M.D., Washington U., St. Louis, 1973. Pediatric resident Mass. Gen. Hosp., Boston, 1973-75; pediatric endocrinology and metabolism fellow St. Louis Children's Hosp. (Washington U.), 1976-77; dir. community pediatrics St. Louis City Health Div., 1976-77; dep. asst. dir. child health services St. Louis County Dept. Community Health and Med. Care, 1977-81, program mgr. disease prevention services, 1981—; clin. instr. pediatrics Washington U. Med. Sch. Mem. leadership group St. Louis Metro Forum; elder, trustee Berea Presbyn. Ch., St. Louis. Fellow Nat. Endowment Humanities, 1977, Danforth Found., 1979-80; recipient Disting. Alumni citation Macalester Coll., 1982. Mem. Am. Public Health Assn., Mo. Med. Assn., Mo. Public Health Assn., St. Louis Pediatric Soc., St. Louis Public Health Assn., St. Louis Met. Med. Soc. Office: St Louis County Dept Community Health 801 S Brentwood Blvd Saint Louis MO 63105

SCRUGGS, MELVA CATHERINE HERNANDEZ, state social services administrator; b. Victoria, Tex., May 7, 1949; d. Marion and Catherine (Moraida) Hernandez; m. William Franklin Scruggs, Jr., Jan. 26, 1973; 1 son, William Franklin, III. A.A., Victoria Coll., 1969; B.A., U. Houston, 1976. Tchr., Children's Univ. Center, U. Houston, 1972; sales clk., cashier Foley's Dept. Store, Houston, 1972-73; welfare service technician II, Tex. Dept. Public Welfare, Houston, 1973-74, day care lic. rep., 1974—, instl. licensing rep., 1983—. Exec. com., vice chmn. fin. com. Harris County Democrats, 1981-82, vice chmn., 1982-84. Recipient Public Service award Tex. Dept. Human Resources, 1978. Mem. Nat. Assn. Edn. Young Children, Assn. Regulatory Adminstrn., Houston Area Assn. Young Children, Mental Health Mental Retardation Assn. of Harris County (bd. dirs. children's adv. council), Tex. Coalition for Juvenile Justice, Harris County Women's Polit. Caucus, Houston Dem. Forum, Harris County Heritage Soc., N. Woodland Hills Civic Assn. (bd. dirs.). Roman Catholic. Clubs: Bayou City Dem. Women, Kingwood Civic.

SCUDIERI, LORRAINE ALBERTO, educator; b. Montclair, N.J., Apr. 25, 1940; d. Harry and Evelyn C. (Palmerie) Alberto; B.A., Montclair State Coll., 1962; M.A., Rutgers U., 1966, now doctoral student; m. Bart Scudieri, Aug. 14, 1965; children—Laura, Matt, Chris, Tim, Patrick. Tchr., Pascack Valley High Sch., Hillsdale, N.J., 1962-65, Pascack Hills High Sch., Montvale, N.J., 1976-77, Montclair State Coll., Upper Montclair, N.J., 1966-68, 69-70, 71, 74, 79-83, 85—; instr. Fairleigh Dickinson U., 1969-72, 79-81, William Paterson Coll., Wayne, N.J., 1974-76, 82-83, Wyckoff (N.J.) Community Learning Center, 1979, Upsala Coll., East Orange, N.J., 1979-81; instr. decision scis. Rider Coll., Lawrenceville, N.J., 1983-85. Den mother Boy Scouts Am. NSF grantee, 1962-66. Mem. Ops. Research Soc. Am., Soc. Indsl. and Applied Math.

SCULL, MARIE LOUISE WALTER, commercial artist, designer; b. Stockholm, Sweden, Apr. 24, 1943; came to U.S., 1952, naturalized, 1973; d. Joseph Hilding and Martha (Noren) Walter; m. George Glenn Rodgers, Apr. 13, 1968 (div. 1972); 1 child: Kristina; m. Lynn Corson Scull, Sept. 18, 1980. Student Middlesex Community Coll., Conn. Sec., bookkeeper R.B. Spring Co., Essex, Conn., 1961-64; exec. asst. Hendel Mfg. Co., New London, Conn., 1964-65, Union Trust Co., Madison, Conn., 1965-72; artist, designer Mim-G Studios, Inc., Westerly, R.I., 1972—; pres. Employee Assn. Union Trust Co., Madison, 1967-68. Design art (book) Origins of Sea Terms, 1984, (poster) America's Cup 1987, 1985, (greeting card line) Captain Misty and Irving, 1985. Mem. New Eng. South Shore Artists Assn. Lutheran. Avocations: antiquing; gardening; canoeing; tennis. Home: 381 Noank Rd West Mystic CT 06388 Office: PO Box 147 West Mystic CT 06388

SCULL, ROBERTA AKIN, educational administrator, consultant; b. Columbus, Ga., Oct. 2, 1940; d. Robert Louis and Olive (Creekmore) A.; m. Herbert Meyer Scull, Aug. 17, 1963; children—Jason Alan, Dorothy Ann. B.A., U. Tenn., 1962; M.S., La. State U., 1969. Tchr. Alexandria Sch. System, Va., 1962-63, New Castle Schs., Del., 1963-67; librarian La. State U., Baton Rouge, La., 1969-82, dir. info. services Ctr. for Energy Studies, 1982—; vis. prof. U. Tenn., Knoxville, 1982; cons. Econ. Mgmt. and Planning Cons. Inc., Baton Rouge, 1979, Coastal Environment Inc., Baton Rouge, 1978—, Houston Pub. Library, 1977. Author: Bibliography of United State Government Bibliographies 1968-73, 1975; Bibliography of United States Government Bibliographies 1974-76, 1979, also articles. Mem. Depository Library Council to the Public Printer of the U.S., 1979-82, chmn. bibliographic control, 1981-82, sec. to council, 1980-81; room mother Parkview Sch., Baton Rouge, 1984—; dir. Girls in Action, Broadmoor Bapt. Ch., 1985-86; speaker to various groups and organs. throughout U.S. La. Dept. Natural Resources grantee, 1984. Mem. Special Library Assn., La Library Assn. (Mid-Career award 1981), Beta Phi Mu. Republican. Baptist. Club: Desk'N Derrick (Baton Rouge). Avocations: camping, boating, gardening. Home: 1089 Sinclair Dr Baton Rouge LA 70815 Office: Ctr for Energy Studies La State Univ Baton Rouge LA 70803-0301

SCULLY, CELIA G., writer; m. Thomas J. Scully, B.A., Trinity Coll., Washington, 1954; M.A., U. Nev., Reno, 1980, postgrad., 1981—. Writer, co-author: (with Thomas J. Scully) How to Make Money Writing about Fitness and Health, 1986; contbr. articles to mags.; contbg. editor Travel Agt. mag., N.Y.C., 1976-79; instr. non-fiction mag. writing Western Nev. Community Coll., Reno, 1977-78. Mem. Internat. Assn. Bus. Communicators, Authors Guild, Soc. Profl. Journalists, Am. Med. Writers Assn., Kappa Tau Alpha. Home: 1400 Ferris Ln Reno NV 89509

SCULLY, JULIA, editor, writer; b. Seattle, Feb. 9, 1929; d. Julius and Rose (Hohenstein) Silverman; B.A., Stanford U., 1951; M.A., N.Y. U., 1970; m. Edward Charles Scully, Aug. 3, 1963 (div. Jan. 1980). Assoc. editor U.S. Camera, 1956-61; editor Camera 35, 1961-66; editor Modern Photography, N.Y.C., 1966—. Tchr., New Sch. for Social Research, N.Y.C., Ramapo Coll. of N.J., Mahway. Author: Disfarmer: The Heber Springs Portraits, 1939-1946, 1976; Sutter Street Reverie, 1983; editor: The Family of Women, 1979. Office: 825 7th Ave New York NY 10019

SCULLYWEST, ELIZABETH MARY, geologist; b. Bklyn., Dec. 10, 1953; d. Michael R. and Mary L. (McQueeney) Scully; m. Edward Stember Scullywest, May 19, 1979. B.A. with honors, Skidmore Coll., 1976; M.S., U. Kans., 1978. Geologist, ArCo Exploration Co., Denver, 1978-80, sr. geologist, Lafayette, La., 1980-84, Midland, Tex., 1984-85; geologist U.S. Army C.E., Seattle, 1985—. Vol., Weicker for Senator, Conn., 1970. Mem. Geol. Soc. Am., Am. Assn. Petroleum Geologists, Sierra Club, Nat. Assn. Female Execs., Sigma Gamma Epsilon. Home: 19529 2d Dr SE Bothell WA 98012 Office: US Army CE 4735 E Marginal Way S Seattle WA 98134

SEABAUGH, CYNTHIA GAIL, editor, journalist, photographer; b. Jackson, Mo., Mar. 15, 1958; d. Willard Autlee and Virginia Marie (Proctor) S. Student S.E. Mo. State U., 1976-78. Bank Teller Security Bank, Sikeston, Mo., 1978-81; sec., receptionist Alcorn Real Estate, Sikeston, 1981; gen. reporter The Daily Standard, Sikeston, 1982, society editor, 1982—, freelance photographer, S.E. Mo., 1983—. Photographer for mags., other publs. Editor First Edit. mag., Sikeston area, 1984. Contbr. articles to local newspaper. Mem. Delta Area Blind, 1982—; active United Way, March of Dimes, United Cerebral Palsy; bd. mem. Am. Cancer Soc., Sikeston, 1984—; mem. Sikeston Community Choir, 1984, Sikeston Little Theatre, 1984—. Mem. Mo. Press Assn. (3d place spl. sect. 1985), Am. Bus. Womens Assn., Sikeston C. of C. (dir. 1986, Careerist of Yr. 1986), Mo. State Hwy. Patrol Press. Republican. Methodist. Lodge: Rotary Ann. Office: The Daily Standard 205 S New Madrid Sikeston MO 63801

SEABROOK, BONNIE MERCIER, risk and insurance executive; b. Atlanta, Oct. 13, 1947; d. D.B. and Louise (McCurry) Mercier; divorced; 1 son, Robert Hunter Seabrook. B.A., Clemson U., 1969; M.Ed., Clemson U., 1971. Tchr., Pickens County (S.C.) Sch. System, 1969-73; adult instr. Tri-County Tech, 1973-74; adminstrv. officer, personnel dir. W.B. Johnson Properties, Atlanta, 1976-77; mgr. of ins. McBurney Corp., Atlanta, 1978-85; owner, risk mgr. Indsl. Risk Mgmt. Services, Atlanta, 1985—, AIG Ins. Co., 1985—; ins. cons. Panhellenic House Corp. Assn., Emory U. Bd. dirs. Scholarship Atlanta Found., 1984—. Named Miss Summerville (S.C.), 1967, 68; participant Miss S.C. Pageant, 1967, 68. Mem. Risk and Ins. Mgmt. Soc., Jaycees (hon.), Assoc. Builders and Contractors of Ga. (chmn. safety com., 1984, 85; bd. dirs. 1985; Nat. award of excellence 1985), Angel Flight, Jr. League, Chi Omega (personnel advisor Emory U. chpt., nat. chmn. ins. 1982, 84 86, del. nat. conv. 1982, 84, 86, leader Firesides House Corp. 1983 del. 1985), Kappa Delta Pi (v.p. pub. relations 1986). Republican. Presbyterian. Home: 6830 Sunny Brook Ln Atlanta GA 30328

SEABROOK, MELISSE GILPIN, telephone co. ofcl.; b. Newark, July 7, 1948; d. Richard Bond and Claire Brownell (Treat) Gilpin; student public schs. With So. Bell Telephone Co., 1966—, 1st level electronic switching foreman, 1972-78, mgr. network adminstrn., Riviera Beach, Fla., 1980-82, mgr. toll and spl. services, 1982—. Mem. Women's Exec. Workshop. Republican. Presbyterian. Club: Zonta (Lake Worth, Fla.). Office: So Bell Telephone Co 3640 Ave E Riviera Beach FL 33404

SEABROOKS, CAROL TYRANCE, marketing consultant; b. Attleboro, Mass., May 2, 1946; d. Herman James and Marian Elizabeth (Taylor) Tyrance; B.A. in Econs., Howard U., 1967; postgrad. N.Y. U., 1969-73. Manpower analyst Dept. Labor, Washington, 1967-68; economist FPC, Washington, 1969; market research analyst Philip Morris, Inc., N.Y.C., 1971-74; campaign planner Avon Products, Inc., N.Y.C., 1974-77, new markets planning adminstr., 1977-78, sales estimator, 1978-80, sr. sales estimator, 1980-81, mgr. gift and decorative, 1981-84; freelance mktg. cons., 1985—. Bldg. capt. Fort Lee (N.J.) Tenants Assn., 1974-78, rec. sec., 1974-76. Martin Luther King fellow, 1968-70. Mem. Am. Mgmt. Assn., Alpha Kappa Alpha (chpt. v.p. 1977, 79, 80). Office: 9 W 57th St New York NY 10019

SEABROOKS, MARILYN SEBASTIAN, government program analyst; b. Allendale, S.C., Mar. 3, 1955; d. Ivory and Lily Bell (Daniels) S. B.A. in History, Ga. So. Coll., 1977; M.P.A., Bernard M. Baruch Coll., 1984. Tchr. Jenkin County Jr. High Sch., Millen, Ga., 1977-78; fin. counselor City of Savannah, Ga., 1978-80, spl. project coordinator, 1980-83, program coordinator, 1984-85; spl. asst. to dir. Dept. Human Services, Washington, 1983-84, program analyst, 1985—. Fellow Nat. Urban Fellows; mem. Am. Assn. Planners, Internat. City Mgr. Assn., Nat. Forum Black Pub. Adminstrs., Am. Soc. Pub. Adminstrs., Urban League, United Way Savannah, Psi Alpha Theta. Avocations: travel, sewing, antiquing. Home: 2352 Glenmont Circle Apt 201 Silver Spring MD 20902 Office: Dept Human Services 801 N Capitol St NE Washington DC 20002

SEABURG, JEAN, lawyer; b. Mpls., May 3, 1935; d. Gunnar Fredrick and Lorraine Elise (Otto) Dahlstrom; m. Paul A. Seaburg, July 27, 1957 (div. Jan. 1973); children—Mark David, Gunnar Paul; m. Richard J. Lee, Feb. 24, 1984. Student U. Minn., 1953-57; B.S.C.E., Marquette U., 1967, J.D., 1974. Bar: Wis. 1974, U.S. Dist. Ct. (ea. and we. dists.) Wis. 1974; registered profl. engr., Wis. Engr., Howard, Needles, Tammen & Bergendoff, Milw., 1967-71; law clk. Habush, Habush & Davis, Milw., 1973-74, assoc., 1974-77, ptnr., 1977—. Mem. ABA, Assn. Trial Lawyers Am., ASCE, Nat. Soc. Profl. Engrs. Lutheran. Office: Habush Habush & Davis 777 E Wisconsin Ave Milwaukee WI 53202

SEACORD, ELIZABETH DANIELLE, technical writer; b. Milford, Mass., Mar. 14, 1958; d. Daniel Freeman and Marietta Louise (Larney) S. B.S., Plymouth State Coll., 1980; student Newbury Jr. Coll., 1983-84, Northeastern U. 1984—, Stonehill Coll., 1986—. Mktg. asst. Riverbend Timesharing Co., Ashland, N.H., 1978-80; tech. communications asst. Cullinet Software Co., Westwood, Mass., 1980-81, editorial asst., 1981-83, copy editor, 1983, coordinating editor, 1983-84; tech. writer, mktg. design MIB Inc., Westwood, Mass., 1984—; sales cons. Webb Auto Sales, Mansfield, Mass., 1985—, design cons., 1985—. Plymouth State Coll. scholar, 1978. Mem. Nat. Assn. Female Execs., Boston Club Printing House Craftsmen (bd. dirs.), Pi Gamma Mu. Avocations: travel; writing. Home: 14 Alder Rd Norton MA 02766 Office: MIB Inc 160 University Ave Westwood MA 02090

SEAGER, HELEN PAYSON, political activist, consultant; b. Portland, Maine, Apr. 28, 1937; d. Thomas and Caroline Wood (Little) Payson; m. George Bradley Seager, Jr., June 22, 1963; children—Mary Davenport, Thomas Payson, Myra Ellen. B.A., Colby Coll., 1958; M.Ed., Harvard U., 1962. Dir. Pa. Commn. for Women, Harrisburg, 1979-83; treas. Season Sch. Cons., Inc., Pitts., 1975—; field dir. Western Pa., Women's Agenda. Author: Bishop's Bread, 1977; translator: Sibylan Prophets, 1965; contbr. articles to profl. jours. Coordinator of vols. Com. to Elect Barbara Hafer, Allegheny County, 1983; campaign mgr. Com. to Elect Ginny Connolly-Manhardt state bd. mem., pres. Pa. Women's Campaign Fund, 1984—; active city and state bds. ACLU, Pitts., 1983-86; state adv. com. U.S. Commn. on Civil Rights, Pa., 1982-85; founding mem. Mayor's Task Force on Women in Renaissance II, 1983—; active NOW, NAACP, Young Women's Christian Assn. Recipient Tribute to Honor Women in Govt. YWCA of Pitts., 1983; Legion of Honor award Chapel of the Four Chaplains, Valley Forge, Pa., 1979; Appreciation award Southwestern Pa. Council NOW chpts., 1985; Matrix award Pitts. Women in Communications, Inc., 1986. Mem. Phi Beta Kappa, Pi Lambda Theta. Republican. Episcopalian.

SEAHOLM, FRANCES CHARTERS, librarian; b. Chgo., June 30, 1933; d. John N. and Elizabeth (Stewart) Charters; m. John Edward Seaholm, Aug. 6, 1955 (widowed, 1979); children—Suzanne, Kathryn. Student Iowa State U., 1951-53; B.A., U. Minn., 1955, M.A.L.S., 1963. Reference librarian Aurora Pub. Library (Ill.), 1960-63, U. Oreg., Eugene, 1964-65, Bellwood Pub. Library (Ill.), 1965-66, Newburgh Pub. Library (N.Y.), 1966-68; reference librarian SUNY-New Paltz, 1968-80, 82—, cataloger, 1980-83, head circulation dept., 1983-85. Mem. ALA, SUNY Librarians Assn., Assn. Coll. Research Libraries. Republican. Mem. Reformed Ch. Am. Contbr. articles to profl. jours. Home: 1 N Manheim Blvd New Paltz NY 12561 Office: Circulation Dept Sojourner Truth Library SUNY College-New Paltz New Paltz NY 12561

SEAL, ANNA IRENE, nurse; b. Albany County, N.Y., Feb. 10, 1934; d. Wallace Jay and Dorothy Emma (Wood) Makely; A.S. in Nursing, U. State N.Y., 1977; A.A. in Liberal Arts with highest honors, Dutchess Community Coll., 1980; B.S. summa cum laude SUNY-New Paltz, 1983, postgrad., 1983—; m. Sylvester A. Seal, July 9, 1954; children—David, Richard, Christy Anne. Practical nurse to R.N. Dutchess County Dept. Health, Rhinebeck, N.Y., 1972-84, pub. health adviser, 1984—. Active lic. practical nurse program Dutchess County Bd. Coop. Ednl. Services; adv. com. Dutchess County Youth Bd. Cert. in community health nursing Am. Nurses Assn. Mem. Dutchess Community Coll. Alumni, U. State of N.Y. External Degree Alumni. Democrat. Home: Mills Cross Rd Staatsburg NY 12580 Office: 52 Market St Poughkeepsie NY 12601

SEALE, MARGARET RUTH, music educator, business executive; b. Knoxville, Ala., Apr. 20, 1915; d. James Andrew and Edna Lee (Phillips) Lamb; m. Clifton Carter Seale, Nov. 9, 1941; children—Clifton Carter, Joy Ruth, Robert Hamilton. Student Tulane U., 1958-59; B. Ch. Music, New Orleans Bapt. Theol. Sem., 1960, M. Ch. Music, 1962. Soloist, chorister New Orleans Opera Co., 1943-53; ch. soloist, concerts in New Orleans, Mobile, Ala., Meridian, Miss., others, 1944-70; contract tchr., voice and piano New Orleans Bapt. Theol. Sem., 1945-62; music therapist Willowood Home for Ret., 1972-74; owner, operator Marsile Music Co., New Orleans, 1974—; owner, dir. Marsile Mus. Pub. Co., New Orleans; pres. Big Parade Corp., 1975—. Mem. adv. bd. Delta Festival Ballet Co. Music Therapy Fund, 1950—; active LWV, 1972—. Recipient New Orleans Mayor's awards, 1971, 75. Mem. La. Council for Music and Performing Arts, Nat. Music Tchrs. Assn., La. Music Tchrs. Assn., New Orleans Music Tchrs. Assn. (exec. dir.), Nat. Music Council (bicentennial coordinator), Nat. Fedn. Music Clubs (bicentennial coordinator), La. Fedn. Music Clubs (New Orleans dist. coordinator 1964-74, v.p. 1972-74), Gottschalk Soc., Greater New Orleans Music Club, Jr. Philharmonic Soc., New Orleans C. of C. Aux., Gamma Xi, Mu Phi Epsilon. Composer songs: Welcome to New Orleans, Get-A-Going, Oh That Men Would Praise the Lord, Unworthy As I Am, All Things Work Together; author mus. prodn. Li'l Ol' Looziana; recs. include: In The Now, 1975; Love Song, It's Wonderful, Welcome to Louisiana; also sheet music. Home and Office: 4674 Franklin Ave New Orleans LA 70122

SEALS, LINDA, graphic designer; b. Dallas, May 26, 1951; d. Fred Clifford and Dorothy (Hardy) S. B.A., Colo. State U.-Ft. Collins, 1973. Co-founder B. Vader Phototypesetting, Fort Collins, Colo., ptnr., 1975-77, pres., gen. mgr., 1977-84, designer, owner, 1985—; mng. ptnr. The CLS Co., Ft. Collins, 1980—; co-founder Salt Cedar mag., art. dir., 1977-80. Designer poster in permanent collection Auschwitz Mus., Poland, 1985. Group shows include: Auschwitz Mus., 1985. Sponsor Ft. Collins Parks and Recreation teams, 1979-80; mem. Task Force on Alt. Trolley Routes, 1984-85, Pkwy. Preservation Soc., 1983—; judge bus. graphics competition Colo. Future Bus. Leaders Am., 1984. Mem. Typographers Internat. Assn. (recipient typographic execllence awards), Nat. Composition Assn. (recipient awards), Ft. Collins Hist. Soc., U.S. Tennis Assn., Ft. Collins Tennis Assn. Democrat. Avocations: tennis, gardening, reading. Office: B Vader Design Prodn 1331 W Mountain Ave Fort Collins CO 80521

SEAMAN, PEGGY JEAN, lawyer; b. New Orleans, Nov. 21, 1949; d. William David and Leah Catherine (Bourdet) Smith; m. Terry Noako Seaman, Dec. 22, 1970; children—Vanya Lianne, Ember Catherine. B.A., Rutgers U.-Camden, 1974; J.D., N.Y. Law Sch., 1978. Bar: N.Y. 1978, Va. 1980, U.S. Dist. Ct. Va., 1980, U.S. Dist. Ct. (so. and ea. dists.) N.Y. 1978. Assoc., Carol Lilienfeld, Esq., N.Y.C., 1978-79; gen. atty. Merit Systems Protection Bd., Office of Appeals, Washington, 1980-82, presiding ofcl., Washington Regional Office, Falls Church, Va., 1982-85, adminstrv. judge St. Louis Regional Office, 1985—. Recipient Sustained Superior Performance awards Merit Systems Protection Bd., 1982, 84. Mem. ABA, Athenaeum Honor Soc. Democrat. Home: 35 Aberdeen Place Clayton MO 63105 Office: Merit Systems Protection Board 1520 Market St Saint Louis MO 63103

SEARCY, JENNIFER J., newspaper publisher, editor; b. Covington, Ky., Dec. 7, 1956; d. Daniel L. and Mary Thomas (Glenn) S. B.A., Western Ky. U., 1978. Typesetter Grayson County News, Leitchfield, Ky., 1973-77; assoc. editor Grayson County News-Gazette, Leitchfield, 1977-80; pub., editor The Record, Leitchfield, 1980—. Pres., Grayson County Young Democrats, 1985-86. Mem. exec. bd. Ky. Young Dems., 1985-86. Named hon. Ky. Col., 1978; Outstanding Young Woman, Ky. Jaycee Women, 1985; Vol. of Yr., Grayson County Community Action Council, 1985. Mem. Ky. Press Assn. (recipient numerous awards for outstanding newspaper work), Grayson County Dem. Woman's Club, Grayson County Hist. Soc., Grayson County Community Arts Assn., Leitchfield C. of C. (bd. dirs. 1984-86), Jaycees (sec. 1985-86). Baptist. Avocations: reading, skiing, softball, tennis, target shooting. Office: The Record 68 Public Sq Leitchfield KY 42754

SEARIGHT, PATRICIA ADELAIDE, retired radio, TV cons.; b. Rochester, N.Y.; d. William Hammond and Irma (Winters) S. B.A., Ohio State U. Program dir. Radio Sta. WTOP, Washington, 1952-63, gen. mgr. info., 1964; radio and TV cons., 1964-84; ret., 1984; producer, dir. many radio and TV programs; spl. fgn. news corr. French Govt., 1956; v.p. Micro Beads, Inc., 1955-59; sec., dir. Dennis-Inches, Corp., 1955-59; exec. dir. Am. Women in Radio and TV, 1969-74. Mem. pres.'s council Toledo Mus. Art. Recipient Kappa Kappa Gamma Alumna achievement award. Mem. Am. Women in Radio and TV (program chmn.; corrs. sec.; dir. Washington chpt.; pres. 1958-60, nat. membership chmn. 1962-63, nat. chmn. Industry Info. Digest 1963-64, Mid-Eastern v.p. 1964-66), Soc. Am. Travel Writers (treas. 1957-58, v.p. 1958-59), Nat. Acad. TV Arts and Scis., Kappa Kappa Gamma. Episcopalian. Clubs: Soroptimist, Women's Advt. (2d v.p. Washington 1958-59, pres. 1959-60), Nat. Press. Home: 10549 E Desert Cove Ave Scottsdale AZ 85259

SEARLES, ANNA MAE HOWARD, educator, civic worker; b. Osage Nation Indian Terr., Okla., Nov. 22, 1906; d. Frank David and Clara (Bowman) Howard; A.A., Odessa (Tex.) Coll., 1961; B.A., U. Ark., 1964; M.Ed., 1970; postgrad. (Herman L. Donovan fellow), U. Ky., 1972—; m. Isaac Adams Searles, May 26, 1933; 1 dau., Mary Ann Rogers (Mrs. Herman Lloyd Hoppe). Compiler news, broadcaster sta. KJBC, 1950-60; corr. Tulsa Daily World, 1961-64; tchr. Rogers (Ark.) High Sch., 1964-72; tchr. adult class rapid reading, 1965, 80; tchr. adult edn. Learning Center Benton County (Ark.), Bentonville, 1973-77, supr. adult edn., 1977-79; tchr. North Ark. Community Coll., Rogers, 1979—, CETA, Bentonville, 1979-82; tchr. Joint Tng. Partnership Act, 1984—; coordinator adult edn. Rogers C. of C. and Rogers Sch. System, 1984—. Sec. Tulsa Safety Council, 1935-37; leader, bd. dirs. Girl Scouts U.S.A., Kilgore, Tex., 1941-44, leader, Midland, Tex., 1944-52, counselor, 1950-61; exec. sec. Midland Community Chest, 1955-60; gray lady Midland A.R.C., 1958-59; organizer Midland YMCA, Salvation Army; dir. women's div. Savings Bond Program, Midland; mem. citizens com. Rogers Hough Meml. Library, women's aux. Rogers Meml. Hosp.; vol. tutor Laubach literacy orgn., 1973—; sec. Beaver Lake Literacy Council, Rogers, 1973-83, Little Flock Planning Commn., 1975—, Benton County Hist. Soc., 1981—; pub. relations chmn. South Central region Nat. Affiliation for Literacy Advance, 1977-79; bd. dirs. Globe Theatre, Odessa, Tex., Midland Community Theatre, Tri-County Foster Home, Guadalupe, Midland youth centers, DeZavala Day Nursery, PTA, Adult Devel. Center, Rogers CETA, 1979-81; vol. recorder Ark. Hist. Preservation Program, 1984—. Recipient Thanks badge Midland Girl Scout Assn., 1948; Cert. of recognition, Rogers Pub. Schs., 1986; Instr. of Yr. award North Ark. Community Coll. West Campus Mem. NEA (del. conv. 1965), Ark. Assn. Public Continuing and Adult Edn. (pres. 1979-80), South Central Assn. for Lifelong Learning (sec. 1980—), PTA (life), Future Homemakers Am. (life; sec. 1980—), Delta Kappa Gamma. Episcopalian. Clubs: Altrusa (pres. 1979—), Apple Spur Community (Rogers). Home: Route 2 Rogers AR 72756

SEARLS, EILEEN HAUGHEY, lawyer, librarian, educator; b. Madison, Wis., Apr. 27, 1925; d. Edward M. and Anna Mary (Haughey) S.; B.A., U. Wis., 1948, J.D., 1950, M.S. in L.S., 1951. Admitted to Wis. bar, 1950; cataloger Yale U., 1951-52; instr. law St. Louis U., 1952-52, asst. prof., 1953-56, asso. prof., 1956-64, prof., 1964—, law librarian, 1952—. Mem. Wis. Bar Assn., Bar Assn. Met. St. Louis, Am. Assn. Law Librarians, Mid-Am. Assn. Law Libraries (pres.), Southwestern Assn. Law Libraries. Club: Altrusa. Office: 3700 Lindell Blvd Saint Louis MO 63108

SEARS, ALICE HART, company executive, consultant; b. Baden, Austria, Apr. 13, 1923 (parents Am. citizens); d. Benjamin and Augusta (Naswich) Hart; m. William R. Sears, Apr. 24, 1942; children—Richard C., Beth S., Catherine. Student NYU, 1941-43. Communications specialist UN Info. Ctr., N.Y.C., 1943-45; v.p. W.R. Sears, Inc., San Mateo, Calif., 1969—. Mem. IEEE. Republican.

SEARS, MARY HELEN, lawyer; b. Syracuse, N.Y., Nov. 30, 1929; d. James Louis and Helen Mary (Fitzgerald) Sears. A.B., Cornell U., 1950; J.D. with honors, George Washington U., 1960. Bar: Va., 1960, D.C., 1961, U.S. Supreme Ct., 1963. Chemist Allied Chem. and Dye Corp., Syracuse, N.Y., 1950-52, Hercules Powder Co., Wilmington, Del., 1952-55; patent examiner U.S. Patent Office, Washington, 1955-60; pvt. practice law, Washington, 1960-61; assoc. Irons, Birch, Swindler & McKie, Washington, 1961-69; mem. firm Irons and Sears, Washington, 1969-84; mem. Memel, Jacobs, Pierno, Gersh & Ellsworth, 1984—, chmn. trade regulation practice dept., 1984—; mem. adv. bd. Boardroom Reports, Inc., N.Y.C., 1980-85; mem. council Cornell U., 1981—; mem. council adminstrv. bd., 1984—; dir. Ventrex Labs., Inc., Portland, Maine, 1982-84. Contbr. articles to various publs. Recipient Outstanding Performance award U.S. Dept. Commerce, 1957. Mem. ABA, Am. Patent Law Assn., Am. Chem. Soc., Va. State Bar Assn., D.C. Bar Assn., Phi Alpha Delta. Republican. Office: 1800 M St NW Washington DC 20036

SEARS, SARAH, food company executive; b. Montclair, N.J., Jan. 23, 1950; d. William F. and Sarah L. (Booker) S.; B.A. in English with gen. honors, Douglass Coll., New Brunswick, N.J., 1972; M.B.A., Columbia U., 1976. Asst. brand mgr. Quaker Oats Co., Chgo., 1976-78, asst. product dir. Johnson & Johnson, New Brunswick, N.J., 1979-81, product dir., 1981-83; category mgr. Ciba Geigy Airwick Industries, Teterboro, N.J., 1983-84; product mgr. Gaines Foods Inc., Tarrytown, N.Y., 1984—. Home: 70 Ellington St East Orange NJ 07017 Office: 660 White Plains Rd Tarrytown NY 10591

SEARS, SUSAN ELNA, bedding manufacturing executive; b. Columbus, Ind., Dec. 29, 1946; d. Burton C. and Eloise (Albert) S.; m. John A. Herfort, 1976 (div. 1978); m. Gregory P. Sundberg, Mar. 31, 1984. B.A., Wellesley Coll., 1968; M.P.A., Harvard U., 1976. Asst., Boston City Council, 1970-72; dir. girls programs Mass. Dept. Youth Services, Boston, 1972-75; dir. juvenile program Tech. Devel. Corp., Boston, 1975; asst. v.p. N.Y. State Urban Devel. Corp., N.Y.C., 1976-80; cons. N.Y. Community Trust, 1980; pres. Domodidovo Ltd., N.Y.C., 1980—; Active Am. Field Service, N.Y.C., 1963—. Mem. Am. Women's Econ. Devel. Corp. Democrat. Avocations: reading, swimming. Home: 365 West End Ave New York NY 10024 Office: Domodidovo Ltd 365 West End Ave Suite 1403 New York NY 10024

SEAVER, MARY ANNE, cleaning company executive, meeting planner; b. Chgo., May 27, 1952; d. Albert C. and Betty Rose (Lewand) Schmidt; m. Thomas J. Hoppe, Aug. 18, 1973 (div. 1978); m. Richard Seaver, Oct. 11, 1985; children—Traci, Nicole. Student U. Calif.-San Diego, 1981-83, Nat. U., San Diego, 1984-85. Exec. sec. Gould, Inc., Rolling Meadows, Ill., 1979-80; asst. to pres. Solar Turbines, Inc., San Diego, 1980-84; pres. Profl. Meetings Unlimited, San Diego, 1984—; ptnr. Pro-Kleen, San Diego, 1986—; cons. Gt. Am. Savs. Bank, San Diego, 1985-86. Contrbr. articles to profl. publs. Loaned exec. United Way San Diego, 1983, account exec., 1984, 85; event coordinator San Diego Multiple Sclerosis Soc., 1984. Mem. Meeting Planners Internat (dir. 1985-86), Meeting Consultants Club, Nat. Assn. Female Execs., San Diego Zool. Soc. Republican. Roman Catholic. Avocations: swimming; dance. Office: Pro Kleen PO Box 12088 La Jolla CA 92037

SEBASTIANI, SUSAN MARIE, title insurance company executive; b. Trenton, N.J., Jan. 16, 1954; d. Louis Peter and Emma (Rendemonti) Carlucci; m. Anthony E. Sebastiani, Sept. 17, 1977. Student, Mercer County Community Coll., 1972. Sec. Eastern Abstract Co., Trenton, 1973-75; sec., title examiner Commonwealth Land Co., Trenton, 1975-77; asst. v.p. Continental Title Ins. Co., Trenton, 1977-84; pres. Mercer Title Services Agy., Inc., Trenton, 1984—. Mem. Mercer County Bd. Realtors, Mercer County Bar Assn. (affiliate), U.S. C. of C., N.J. Land Title Assn., Am. Land Title Assn. Home: 820 Fairmount Ave Trenton NJ 08629 Office: Mercer Title Services Agy Inc 5 Stults Ave PO Box 3710 Trenton NJ 08629

SEBEK, MARY LYNN, lawyer; b. Berwyn, Ill., Jan. 22, 1948; d. James Joseph and Henrietta Ann (Ruzicka) Sebek; m. Aurelio Luis Lucero, Jr., Jan. 7, 1984. Student U. Ibero Americana, Mexico City, summer 1967; B.A., Purdue U., 1969; J.D., DePaul U., 1976. Bar: Ill. 1976, D.C. 1979, U.S. Ct. Appeals (9th cir.) 1984. High sch. tchr. and sec., 1969-73; staff atty. SEC, Washington, 1976-78; trial atty. Dept. Justice, Washington, 1978-79; assoc. Coffield, Ungaretti, Harris & Slavin, Chgo., 1979-82; presiding ofcl. U.S. Merit Systems Protection Bd., Chgo., 1982-83; staff atty. U.S. Ct. Appeals (9th cir.), San Francisco, 1984-85; hearing examiner U.S. EEOC, Seattle, 1985—; pres., bd. dirs. Disability Law Clinic, Inc., Chgo., 1982-83. Author law rev. article. Actor, Second City Children's Theatre, Chgo., 1981-82, Victory Gardens Theatre Benefit, 1982; participant Ptnrs.-in-English, San Francisco, 1984. DePaul U. Law Sch. scholar, 1974-76; Women's Bar Found. of Ill. scholar, 1975-76. Mem. Kappa Delta Pi, Phi Beta Kappa.

SEBEST, EDWINA, nursing home administrator, real estate executive; b. McKeesport, Pa., May 19, 1941; d. Edward and Irene (Havanchak) S. B.A., Carlow Coll., 1963; M.A., DePaul U., 1966; Ph.D., U. Pitts., 1973. Lic. psychologist, Pa.; lic. nursing home adminstr., R.I. lic. real estate agt., R.I. Instr. Carlow Coll., Pitts., 1965-66; asst. chief testing services Pitts. Psychol. Counseling Ctr., 1966-67; chief psychologist S. Hills Child Guidance Ctr., Pitts., 1970-77; pvt. practice clin. psychology, Pitts., 1977-81; adminstr., pres. Catherine Manor Inc., Newport, R.I., 1981—; co-owner Brinley Victorian Inn, Newport, 1982—; instr. gerontology Salve Regina Coll., Newport, 1985; gen. ptnr. Real Estate Project, Newport, 1985. Mem. Guest House Assn. (pres. 1983-85), Am. Psychol. Assn., Pa. Psychol. Assn. Avocations: gardening; reading; boating. Home: 44 Catherine St Newport RI 02840

SEBEYRAN, JANE JOUVE, cosmetic company executive, educator; b. Clermontferrand, France, Feb. 23, 1926; came to U.S., 1969; d. Camille and Victoria Aline (Ducreux) Jouve; m. Gilbert Caussin, 1944 (div.); 1 child, Bernard L.; m. Pierre Jean Sebeyran, July 10, 1948; children—Martine, Eric. Student Sch. Immeuble des Societes Savantes, Paris, Profl. Edn. Francaise, Nice, U. de Beaute Cedib, Paris, U. de Soins Esthetiques du Corps, Paris, Ecole Internat. des Techniciennes de Beaute, Paris. Owner Jane J. Sebeyran Inst. de Beaute, Toulon, France, 1965-60; spl. contractor Waldorf Astoria Beauty Shop, N.Y.C., 1969-70; pres. Jane J. Sebeyran Ltd., N.Y.C., 1973-79; Jane J. Sebeyran Internat. Inc., Houston, 1980—; lectr. in field; columnist. Author: For You Madame. Active French Resistance, Chaumont, 1941-44. Avocations: swimming; reading, philosophy. Office: Jane J Sebeyran Internat Inc 14525 Memorial Dr Houston TX 77079

SEBRING, MARJORIE MARIE ALLISON, home furnishings executive; Burnsville, N.C., Oct. 8, 1924; d. James William and Mary Will (Ramsey) Allison Shockey; 1 child, Patricia Louise Banner Krohn. Student Mars Hill Coll., 1943, Home Decorators Sch. Design, N.Y.C., 1948, Wayne State U., 1953; grad. program U. Va., 1982. Dir. decorating div. Robinson Furniture, Detroit, 1949-57; head buyer Tyner Hi-Way House, Ypsilanti, Mich., 1957-63; head buyer Town and Country, Dearborn, Mich., 1963-66; instr. Nat. Carpet Inst., 1963-65; owner Adams House, Inc., Plymouth, Mich., 1966-72; exec. v.p. mktg. and sales, regional sales and mktg. mgr. Triangle Industries, Los Angeles, 1972-86; co-owner Markham-Sebring, Inc., St. Petersburg, Fla.; exec. dir. contract merchandising Kane Furniture, St. Petersburg. Trustee, Republican Presdl. Task Force. Recipient nat. sales awards, recognition for work with youth and aged. Mem. Internat. Home Furnishings Assn., Fla. Home Furnishings Rep. Assn. (officer), USCG Aux., Nat. Audubon Soc., Internat. Platform Assn. Contbr. creative display to Better Homes and Gardens, 1957-64. Address: 2601-3 Grist Mill Circle New Port Richey FL 33553

SECHRIST, LORI ANN, food company executive; b. York, Pa., July 24, 1955; d. George Stanley and Mary Alice (O'Donnell) Sechrist. B.S. in Food Sci., Pa. State U., 1977; M.B.A. in Mktg., Pace U., 1981. Sr. food technologist Gen. Foods Corp., Tarrytown, N.Y., 1977-81; new products mgr. Hershey Foods Corp. (Pa.), 1981—. Recipient Mktg. award Pace U., 1982. Mem. Am. Mktg. Assn., Am. Assn. Female Execs., Kennedy Ctr. Republican. Lutheran. Home: 4 Caledonia St Hershey PA 17033 Office: Hershey Foods Corp 19 E Chocolate Ave Hershey PA 17033

SECREST, VICKIE LYNN, nurse; b. Wheeling, W.Va., Aug. 6, 1954; d. Clyde Allen and Loretta Marlene (Hopkins) S. B.S.N., U. Ky., 1976; M.S., Ohio State U., 1979. R.N. Staff/charge nurse Mercy Hosp., Portsmouth, Ohio, 1976-78; head nurse, 1978; nurse coordinator Lexington VA Med. Ctr., Ky., 1979-81, asst. chief nurse trainee, 1981-83; asst. chief nursing service Shreveport VA Med. Ctr., La., 1983-84; assoc. chief nursing service Little Rock VA Med. Ctr., Ark., 1984—. Mem. parish council Roman Catholic Ch., Shreveport, 1983-84; active Lupus Found., Big Bros.-Big Sisters Program. Mem. Am. Soc. Nursing Service Adminstrs., Ohio State U. Alumni Assn., Nat. League Nursing, Sigma Theta Tau. Avocations: Creative writing; reading; needlepoint; walking; swimming.

SECRIST, DOLLY ALVAREZ, translator; b. Bucaramanga, Colombia, June 24; d. Justo Jose and Elvira Maria (Rodriguez) Alvarez; grad. John Robert Powers, 1966; A.A., El Camino Coll., 1971; student UCLA, 1971-73; B.S., U. Beverly Hills, 1982; postgrad. SUNY, 1983; m. Harold B. Secrist, Aug. 30, 1975. Varitypist, Biddle Publ. Co., Los Angeles, 1963-67; exec. sec. Alfred M. Lewis Co., Riverside, Calif., 1967-69; multilingual exec. sec. Gen. Electric TEMPO, Santa Barbara, Calif., 1969-71; multilingual exec. sec. UCLA, Westwood, Calif, 1971-73; adminstrv. asst., translator, expediter Bechtel Power Corp., Los Angeles, 1973-84; adminstrv. asst. Northrop Corp., 1984—. Mem. Soc. Logistics Engrs., Nat. Assn. Female Execs. Roman Catholic. Club: Toastmasters (officer). Home: 7579 Windsong Pl Rancho Cucamonga CA 91730 Office: 8900 E Washington Blvd Pico Rivera CA 90060

SECUNDA, LENORE, jewelry store owner; b. Bklyn., Aug. 27, 1938; d. Borah and Sylvia (Farowitz) Wydra; student Am. Inst. Antiques, 1967, Adelphi Bus. Sch., 1972, Kingsboro Community Coll., 1973-74; m. Allan Secunda, Mar. 4, 1961; children—Roy, Margo, Darcie. Owner, mgr. Lenore's Antique Jewelry, N.Y.C., 1966-72; store mgr. Brancusi Furniture, Los Angeles, 1976-78; pvt. practice interior designing, Los Angeles, 1976—; dir. showrooms Corsican Furniture Co., Los Angeles, 1978-85; owner Vintage Jewels, Los Angeles, 1986—. Democrat. Jewish. Home: 4536 Wilshire Blvd #1 Los Angeles CA 90010 Office: 8021 Melrose Ave Los Angeles CA 90046

SEDAR, BARI BIERN, actress, singer; b. Cin., Aug. 26, 1949; d. Harvey A. and Natalie A. (Smith) Biern; m. Scott Randall Sedar, Apr. 9, 1983. B.A., Stephens Coll., Columbia, Mo., 1970; M.F.A., Emerson Coll., 1973. Dir. sales Prodn. Media, Inc., Cin., 1974-75; account rep. J. Walter Thompson Co., Washington, 1975-78, copywriter, 1978-80, v.p., sr. copywriter, 1982-85; v.p., sr. copywriter Brouillard Communications, Washington, 1980-81; ptnr. Two Writers ... No Waiting; actress, singer, 1983—; actress in revue, 1983-84. Author, lyricist TV-print campaign for Am. Cancer Soc.: Draggin' Lady (Creative Excellence in Black Advt. award 1983), 1983. Mem. pub. relations com. Nat. Hospice Orgn., Washington, 1982-83; mem. internat. adv. council Children's Hospice Internat., Washington, 1983-84; vol. Washington Home Hospice, 1983-84.

SEDENQUIST, MARGARET ANNE HAGEMAN, real estate company executive; b. Douglas, Wyo., Jan. 17, 1927; d. Fred August and Ruth Elizabeth (Shaw) Hageman; m. Charles H. Sedenquist, Aug. 8, 1953; children—Mark C., Daniel F., Diana J. B.A., U. Wyo., 1948. Psychologist, Gen. Electric Co., Schenectady, 1948-51; tchr. Cody Pub. Schs., Wyo., 1952-54; owner, mgr. Margaret H. Sedenquist Realtor and Mohawk Mgmt. Co., Pasadena, Calif., 1972—; chmn. bd. dirs. Comml. Pacific Savs. & Loan Assn., 1984—, Sedenquist Froser, Inc. Jr. warden All Saints Episcopal Ch., Pasadena, 1980-81, sr. warden, 1981-82, mem. vestry, 1972-82; pres. Pasadena Chamber Orch., 1981-82; vice chmn. Inst. for Religion and Wholeness, Claremont Sch. Theology, 1985—; pres. bd. dirs. Pasadena Playhouse State Theater of Calif., 1981—. Mem. Calif. Assn. Realtors (bd. dirs. 1976-82), Soc. Exchange Counselors, Pasadena Bd. Realtors (pres. 1980), Los Angeles County Bd. Realtors (pres. 1982-83), Pasadena C. of C. Club: Zonta (bd. dirs. 1980—). Home: 1575 Riviera Dr Pasadena CA 91107 Office: 1386 E Walnut St Suite 202 Pasadena CA 91106

SEDERLOF, LEENA MARIA, orthodontist, b. Helsinki, Finland, Oct. 27, 1946; d. Unto Valter and Maria (Wolkoff) Pontynen; m. Hjalte S. Sederlof, Mar. 21, 1970; children—Lynn Marie, Mirah Lee. D.D.S., Helsinki U., 1971; M.S. in Orthodontics, Georgetown U., 1977. Practice dentistry, Helsinki, 1971-72; dentist Helsinki U. Student Health Ctr., 1972; vis. fellow NIDR, Bethesda, Md., 1974-75; practice orthodontics, Rockville, Md., 1977—, Washington, 1984—, Hyattsville, Md., 1984—. Mem. ADA, Am. Assn. Orthodontists, Am. Assn. Women Dentists, Finnish Dental Assn., Soc. Finnish Dentists, Montgomery County Dental Study Club, Greater Washington Acd. Women Dentists. Club: Kipina Kerho (Washington). Avocations: Ballet; gardening; music. Home: 3501 Davis St NW Washington DC 20007 Office: 4105 Wisconsin Ave NW Washington DC 20007

SEDGWICK, RAE, psychologist, nurse; b. Kansas City, Kans., Apr. 7, 1944; d. Chalres Rezin and Helen Hanway (Timmons) Sedgwick; student Bethany Sch. Nursing, 1965; B.S. in Nursing, U. Iowa, 1967; M.A., U. Kans., 1970, Ph.D. in Psychology, 1972, J.D., 1986. Nurse, Mercy Hosp., Iowa City, 1965-67, Community Mental Health, Kansas City, Kans., 1967-68; specialist Lab. Edn., Washington, 1971-72; coordinator Health C.A.R.E. Clinic, Pa. State U., University Park, 1974-76; clin. asso. Community Psychiatry, Altoona (Pa.) Mental Health Center, 1973-76; asst. prof. human devel. Pa. State U., University Park, 1972-76; resident psychologist Family Consulation Program, United Meth. Ch., Bonner Springs, Kans., 1976-80; pvt. practice psychology Sedgwick-Hildebrand Health Asso., Bonner Springs, 1976—; cons. in field; staff Bethany Med. Center, Kansas City, Kans., 1976—, Mid-Continent Psychiat. Hosp., Olathe, Kans., 1976-81, Cushing's Meml. Hosp., Leavenworth, Kans., 1976—, St. John Hosp., Leavenworth, 1976—. Mem. adminstr. bd. United Meth. Ch., Bonner Springs, Kans., 1976—; mem. Bonner Springs City Council, 1980—. Recipient Outstanding Young Woman award U. Kans., 1971; Bus. and Profl. Women's Clubs award, 1962; Nurse Scientist fellow and grantee, 1968-72; Bus. and Profl. Women's Club scholar, 1962; lic. psychologist, Kans.; registered nurse, Kans.; cert. clin. specialist in adult psychiat. and mental health nursing, in child and adolescent psychiat. and mental health nursing. Mem. Am. Nurses Assn., Am. Psychol. Assn., Council of Advanced Practitioners in Psychiatric-Mental Health Nursing, Council of Nurse Researchers, Ocean, Inc., Assn. Humanistic Psychologists, Kans. Psychol. Assn., Am. Heart Assn., Am. Orthopsychiat. Assn., AAAS, U. Kans. Alumni Assn., Intercollegiate Assn. Women Students (nat. resource bd. mem. 1972-73), Am. Assn. Psychiat. Services for Children, Am. Group Psychotherapy Assn. (del. to China 1982), Kans. Internat. Womens Yr. Commn., Bonner Springs C. of C. (dir.), Sigma Theta Tau. Club: Bus. and Profl. Women's. Author: Family Mental Health: Theory and Practice, 1980; White Frame House, 1980; asso. editor Jour. Corrective and Social Psychiatry, 1979-82; writer weekly column, An Ounce of Prevention, Bonner Springs Chieftain, 1977—; contbr. articles to profl. jours. Home: Box 377 Bonner Springs KS 66012 Office: PO Box 377 216 E 2d St Bonner Springs KS 66012

SEDLAK, ROBERTA KINCAID, controller; b. Bethlehem, Pa., Sept. 1, 1954; d. Robert Elwood and Caroline Vernice (Senovich) Kincaid; B.A. with high honors, Lehigh U., 1976; m. Richard John Sedlak, May 4, 1980. Sr. acct. Coopers & Lybrand, Phila., 1976-79; sr. internal auditor Siemens Corp., Iselin, N.J., 1979-81; mgr. gen. acctg. Siemens Hearing Instruments, Inc., Union, N.J., 1981-85, controller, 1985—. C.P.A., Pa., N.J. Mem. Am. Inst. C.P.A.s, Pa. Inst. C.P.A.s, N.J. Soc. C.P.A.s, Nat. Assn. Accts. Mem. Christian Ch. Club: Lehigh U. Town Alumni. Home: 1309 Murray Ave Plainfield NJ 07060 Office: 685 Liberty Ave Union NJ 07083

SEDLIS, MARGARET JOAN, architect; b. Boston, Dec. 6, 1950; d. Edward Gabriel and Cynthia Joy (Miller) S. B.F.A. in Environ. Design, Parsons Sch. Design, New Sch. for Social Research, 1972; M.Arch., Washington U., St. Louis, 1975. Jr. project mgr. Hoffman Partnership, St. Louis, 1976-77, John Cohen & Assocs., St. Louis, 1977-78; dir. space planning Planned Expansion Group/Architects, White Plains, N.Y., 1978-83; assoc./project dir. interiors Hellmuth, Obata & Kassabaum/Architects, N.Y.C., 1983—. Mem. Alliance of Women in Architecture. Home: 85 East End Ave New York NY 10028 Office: Hellmuth Obata & Kassabaum/Architects 1270 Ave of Americas New York NY 10020

SEDO, KATHRYN JENNETTE, legal educator, consultant, lawyer; b. Dearborn, Mich., May 13, 1950; d. Edward John and Helen (Ujinski) Sedo. A.B., U. Mich., 1974, J.D., 1976. Bar: Mich. 1976, Minn. 1982. Ptnr. firm Sedo and Darnton, Ann Arbor, Mich., 1976-79; clin. prof. U. Minn., Mpls., 1979—; dir. Internat. Alliance Sustaining Agr., Mpls., 1983-84; cons. Consumer and Workers Coops. in Midwest, 1979—, Distbg. Alliance Northcountry Coops., Common Health Warehouse Coop., Roots and Fruits Mem. ABA (legal edn. and admissions com.), Minn. Bar Assn. (legal edn. com., admissions and community relations com.), Hennepin County Bar Assn., Ramsey County Bar Assn., Nat. Lawyers Guild, Nat. Soc. Accts. Coops. Mem. Self Realization Fellowship Ch. Home: 701 Parkview Terr Minneapolis MN 55416 Office: U Minn Law Sch 229 19th Ave S Minneapolis MN 55455

SEEBER, ANN TERWILLIGER, movie theatre owner, real estate salesperson; b. Hoboken, N.J., Feb. 18, 1941; d. Harold DeNike and Mildred Emilia (Higgins) Terwilliger; m. John Robert Beck, May 23, 1960 (div. Sept. 1977); children—Debra Ann, Laura Jean; m. Frank Charles Seeber, Dec. 18, 1977. Student Pace Coll., 1959-60, Orange County Community Coll., 1985. Lic. in real estate. Proofreader, typesetter N.J. Herald, Newton, 1966-74, advt. sales, 1974-85; v.p. FAS Theater Corp., Warwick, N.Y., 1977—; pres. Chester Multi Theater, N.Y., 1985—. Scholar, Pace Coll., N.Y.C., 1959. Mem. NOW (nat. child care coordinator 1967-69, pres. Sussex County chpt. 1966-67), Nat. Assn. Theater Owners, N.Y. State Bd. Realtors, Orange County Bd. Realtors (realtor-assoc.), Women's Council Realtors. Lutheran. Office: Wifred L Raynor Inc 26 Main St Warwick NY 10990

SEEBERT, KATHLEEN ANNE, international trade consultant; b. Chgo.; d. Harold Earl and Marie Anne (Lowery) S.; M.A., U. Notre Dame, 1976; M.M., Northwestern U., 1983. Publs. editor ContiCommodity Services, Inc., Chgo., 1977-79, supr. mktg., 1979-82; dir. mktg. MidAm. Commodity Exchange, 1982-85; internat. trade cons. to Govt. of Ont., Can., 1985—; guest lectr. U. Notre Dame. Registered commodity rep. Mem. Futures Industry Assn. Am. (treas.). Republican. Roman Catholic. Clubs: Young Executives, Notre Dame of Chgo., Northwestern Mgmt. of Chgo. Office: 208 S LaSalle St Suite 1806 Chicago IL 60604

SEEGAR, CHARLON IONE, psychiatric social worker, educator; b. Denver, May 13, 1936; d. Wilner Hopson and Cordelia Ione (Lipham) S.; A.B., LaGrange Coll., 1959; M.S.W., U. N.C., Chapel Hill, 1964. Social worker Am. Nat. Red Cross Service to Mil. Hosps., Ft. Jackson, S.C., 1959-61, Maxwell AFB Hosp., Ala., 1962-63, Ft. Bragg Army Hosp., N.C., 1964-65, U.S. Army Hosp., Frankfurt Am Main, Germany, 1965-67, Charleston (S.C.) Naval Hosp., 1967; family planning cons. Dept. Family and Children Services, State of Ga., 1967-69; chief social worker maternal and infant care project, family planning project dept. ob-gyn Med. Coll. Ga., 1969-80, asst. prof., 1980—, social scientist, 1980—, coordinator outpatient div., 1980—; adj. instr. social work U. Ga., 1983—. Treas., SCLC, Augusta, Ga., 1969-73. Recipient Outstanding Young Woman of America, 1984; Lifefellow, Am. Biog. Inst. Research Assn.; mem. Nat. Assn. Social Workers (dir. 1969-75), Planned Parenthood E. Central Ga. (dir. 1975-80), Mental Health Assn. Ga., Mental Health Assn. Augusta, Ga. Conf. Social Welfare, Nat. Assn. Female Execs., Epilepsy Assn. Ga., Ga. Health Care Assn., AAUW. Home: 5 Lakeshore Loop August GA 30904 Office: 1515 Pope Ave Dept Psychiatry Med Coll Ga Augusta GA 30912

SEEGER, MELINDA WAYNE, occupational therapist; b. Albert Lea, Minn., Dec. 31, 1940; d. Oscar Earnest and Evelyn Josephine (Pihl) Wayne; B.S., U. Minn., 1963; m. Robert Charles Seeger, Mar. 16, 1964; 1 son, Jeffrey Wayne. Chief occupational therapy Rehab. Inst. Oreg., Portland, 1964-66; supr. phys. disabilities and gen. medicine and surgery occupational therapy Mpls. VA Hosp., 1966-68; supr. phys. disabilities occupational therapy Nat. Naval Med. Center, Bethesda, Md., 1968-71; assoc. chief rehab. services, dir. occupational therapy UCLA Med. Center, 1974-85, cons., prin. investigator rheumatology div. dept. medicine, 1985—. Mem. utilization rev. com. Vis. Nurse Assn. Los Angeles, 1975-85, mem. profl. adv. com., 1979-80; mem. exec. com. Allied Health Professions sect. Arthritis Found., 1980-85, chmn. edn. com., 1982-85, mem. profl. edn. com.; bd. dirs. Calif. Occupational Therapy Found., 1984-85. Recipient Spl. Achievement award Nat. Naval Med. Center, 1971, Outstanding Performance award, 1971; Spl. Performance award UCLA, 1980, 84; Addie Thomas Service award for outstanding service to rheumatology community Arthritis Found., 1986. Mem. Am. Occupational Therapy Assn., Occupational Therapy Assn. Calif., Allied Health Professions Assn. (chmn. edn. com. 1982—). Author, editor articles in field. Office: 10520 Strathmore Dr Los Angeles CA 90024

SEEKINGS, SARA M., industrial chemist; b. Mt. Vernon, N.Y., Jan. 22, 1953; d. John Kenneth and Irene Claire (Conner) Seekings. B.S., Framingham State Coll., 1974; M.B.A., Simmons Coll., 1984—. Research asst. Worcester Found. of Exptl. Biology, Shrewsbury, Mass., 1974-76; research technician GTE Labs., Waltham, Mass., 1976-77; research chemist Barnstead Co., W. Roxbury, Mass., 1977-78; assoc. scientist Polaroid Corp., Waltham, Mass., 1978-85, scientist, 1985—, vice chmn. affirmative action com. Chem. Ops. div., 1978-80, 85—. Patentee in field. Mem. Am. Chem. Soc., Nat. Assn. Female Execs., Support Women in Mgmt. Roman Catholic. Avocations: reading; music; guitar; tennis. Home: 39 Walcott Valley Dr Hopkinton MA 01748 Office: Polaroid Corp 1625 Main St W6 Waltham MA 02154

SEEKINS, ANNA MARIE, manufacturing executive; b. Lexington, Nebr., Oct. 22, 1948; d. Frederick Reo and Doris Louise (Hollibaugh) Green; m. James Lee Seekins, Jan. 3, 1969; children—Heidi Anne, Amy Marie. Grad. Westminster High Sch., Colo., 1966. With Forsythe & Dowis Carnival, 1950-64, Green's Amusements, 1964-68; collator, Joppesen Time-Mirror, Denver, 1967-73; typesetter AAA Marking, Colorado Springs, Colo., 1975-78; seamstress Camp 7, Longmont, Colo., 1978-80; co-owner AMS Products, Longmont, 1980—; order clk. Staydynamics, Longmont, 1982-84. Vol., Army Community Service Ctr., Colorado Springs. Republican. Baptist. Home: 2242 Sherman St Longmont CO 80501 Office: AMS Products 135 Gay St PO Box 1842 Longmont CO 80501

SEELBINDER, MARY LOUISE, nutrition products company salesperson; b. Waterford, Mich., July 28, 1929; d. Maynard Isreal and Velma Harriet (Smith) Beattie; m. Elmer Raymond Seelbinder, June 28, 1947; children—Thomas, Jane, Raymond, John, Nancy, Caroline, David. Student, Duberry Sch., 1946, Flint Jr. Coll., 1960-63. Pharmacy apprentice Des Jardins Drugs, Lapeer, Mich., 1945-47; with sales promotion staff Curtis Circulation, Lapeer County, Mich., 1953; fund raiser local chs. and charity, Ortonville, Mich., 1954; sales rep. Avon Products, Ortonville, 1955-63, dist. sales mgr., 1964-85; color cons. Shaklee Corp., Cin., 1985—. Recipient Circle of Excellence award Avon Products, 1971, 72, 73, 74, 77, 84. Mem. Beta Sigma Phi (sec. 1985—). Lutheran. Club: Luth. Women's (asst. dir. 1982-83) (Goodrich, Mich.). Avocations: square dancing; gardening; aerobics; hiking; snowmobiling. Home and Office: 114 Granger Box 187 Ortonville MI 48462

SEELEY, BARBARA GAIL, human services executive; b. Grand Forks, N.D., June 7, 1936; d. Alfred Thomas and Florence Micken S.; B.S., UCLA, 1957; M.S.W., U. So. Calif., 1970; now postgrad. in pub. adminstrn. Calif. State U.-Long Beach children—John Mark Doss, Timothy Stephen Doss, Elizabeth Gail Doss. Psychiat. social worker State of Calif., Pomona and Santa Ana, 1970-73; sr. clin. social worker Orange County Mental Health Dept., 1973-79, dep. dir. mental health, 1979-80, dep. regional mgr. human services agy., 1980-82, program mgr. mental health dept. Health Care Agy., 1982—; field educator San Diego State U. Sch. Social work; presenter internat. symposium, Jerusalem, 1983. Mem. Orange County (Calif.) Violence Prevention Task Force; mem. legis. and planning com. Regional Ctr. for Developmentally Disabled; mem. steering com. Community Support Systems Conf. Lic marriage, family and child counselor; lic. clin. social worker. Mem. Acad. Cert. Social Workers, Nat. Assn. Social Workers, Am. Soc. Pub. Adminstrn. (investigational rev. bd.), DAR. Methodist. Home: 3310 Seashore Dr Newport Beach CA 92663 Office: 1617 Westcliff Dr Newport Beach CA 92660

SEELEY, KIMBERLEY ANN, police officer; b. Urbana, Ill., Oct. 21, 1960; d. William Edward and Patricia Ann (Philbeck) Tarte; m. Ronald Eugene Seeley, Jan. 21, 1985. Assoc. Sci., Parkland Coll., 1981; B.S., U. Ill., 1982. Sec., bookkeeper Tarte's TV and Marine, Rantoul, Ill., 1972-78; police dispatcher City of Champaign, Ill., 1978-82, police officer, 1982—, mem. tactical unit, 1985-86. Recipient Merit award Champaign Police Dept., 1984. Mem. Police Protective and Benevolent Assn., Nat. Assn. Female Execs., Ill. Police Assn. Republican. Lutheran. Avocations: downhill snow skiing; target shooting. Office: Champaign Police Dept 82 E University St Champaign IL 61820

SEELEY, MARYANN DEL VISCO, communications and marketing executive; b. Newark, Oct. 14, 1948; d. James and Vincenzina (Cimirro) Del Visco; m. Timothy Allen Seeley, May 30, 1981; children—Vanessa Christina, Timothy Allen Jr. B.A. in English, Rutgers U., 1970; M.A. in Communications Arts, William Patterson Coll., 1974. Mgr. communications, asst. cashier Midlantic Nat. Bank div. Midlantic Banks, Inc., Newark, 1970-74; supr. info. N.J. Bell Telephone Co., Newark, 1974-75; exec. printing sales Newark Printing Co., 1975-76; sales rep. Xerox Corp., 1976-78, mgr. shareholder relations, 1978-81; co-owner, ptnr. T.A. Seeley Office Systems Co., Glens Falls, N.Y., 1981—. Assoc. editor N.J. Bell and Communication Mags., 1974-75; innovator in design of magapaper publs. Active communications group N.J. Bicentennial Celebrations Com. Recipient awards Publ. Design Writing, Soc. Publ. Designers, 1974, Financial World, 1974, N.Y. Bus. Communicators, 1974. Mem. Communicators Assn. N.J. (pres. 1973-75, dir. 1976-78, Publ. Design Writing award 1974), Internat. Assn. Bus. Communicators (Pub. Design Writing award 1974, speaker creative supervision ann. conf.), Art Dirs. Club N.J., Lake George Bus. and Profl. Women's Club (co-chair pub. relations 1985—). Office: 95 Broad St Glens Falls NY 12801

SEELHAMMER, CYNTHIA MAE, public relations specialist, writer; b. Fargo, N.D., Oct. 29, 1957; d. John Robert and Betty Jane (Brausen) S.; m. Barry Minett Robinson, May 31, 1980 (div. 1983); m. Douglas Lynn Myrland, Oct. 19, 1984. Student Kerevan Yhteskoulu, Kerava, Finland, 1975-76; B.A. in English, St. Cloud State U., 1976-80; postgrad. Golden Gate U., 1985—. Editor Sherburne City Hist. Soc., Becker, Minn., 1978-80; assoc. editor SCS Chronicle, St. Cloud, Minn., 1979-80; reporter Chandler Arizonan, Ariz, 1980-81; coordinator of pub. relations Bashas' Markets, Inc., Chandler, 1981-84; owner, mgr. Seelhammer Pub. Relations, Queen Creek, Ariz., 1984—; pub. info. specialist City Mesa, Ariz., 1984—. Author feature stories for papers, mags., 1980—. Editor: The Growth of Sherburn County, 1980. Officer Soroptimist Internat. Mesa, 1985; mem. Soroptimist Internat. Chandler, 1984; dept. registrar Pinal County Democrats, Florence, Ariz., 1983—; chmn. Chandler Neighborhood Council, 1981-82; bd. dirs. Chandler Boys Girls Club, 1985. Recipient Best Editorial award Minn. Newspaper Assn., 1980; MECCA fellow U. Denver, 1980. Mem. Internat. Assn. Bus. Communicators, Soc. Profl. Journalists (Best Editorial award Region 6 1980), Ariz. Press Women (v.p. pub. relations 1981-82, Best Feature award 1980). Democrat. Avocations: gourmet cooking; gardening; hiking; horseback riding. Home: Route 2 Box 576 Queen Creek AZ 85242 Office: City Mesa 55 N Center PO Box 1466 Mesa AZ 85201

SEELY, BETTY DARDEN, nurse anesthetist; b. Ephraim, Utah, Oct. 15, 1925; d. George Spafford and Maud Elizabeth (Hansen) Sumsion; m. John Speight Darden, Sept. 29, 1946 (dec. Oct. 1967); children—James E., Jon S., William D., Andrew S.; m. 2d, Joseph Boyd Seely, Feb. 6, 1979. R.N., U. Utah, 1946, nurse anesthetist, 1951, audiometer technician, 1972. Pub. health sch. nurse USPHS, Provo, Utah, 1950-51; obstet. nurse Latter-day Saints Hosp., Salt Lake City, 1951-52, nurse anesthetist, 1952-56; office nurse, Whittier, Calif., 1956-58; head indsl. nurse Sperry Univac, Salt Lake City, 1969-79; sch. nurse Provo (Utah) Canyon Sch., 1980—; author procedure book, instr. Deaconess Hosp. Youth Vol. Program, Great Falls, Mont., 1965-67, Cascade County Nursing Home Med. Aux. Vols., Great Falls, 1965-67. Pres. PTA, Woodstock Sch., Salt Lake City, 1961-62; program chmn. Great Falls (Mont.) Symphony Guild, 1965-67; pres. Cascade County Med. Aux., Great Falls, 1966-67; dir. vols. Deaconess Hosp., Great Falls, 1965-67; bd. dirs. John S. Darden Meml. Scholarship Fund. Recipient 30 Year Pin, ARC, Utah, Mont., 1946-79. Mem. Am. Nurses Assn. Am. Soc. Nurse Anesthetists, Utah State Nurse's Assn., Utah State Nurse Anesthetist Assn. Republican. Mormon. Clubs: Little League Booster (pres.) (Salt Lake City); Lady Lions, Riverside Country (pres. 1964-65) (Great Falls, Mont.). Lodge: Elks. Office: Provo Canyon Sch 4501 N University Ave Provo UT 84603

SEEMAN, CAROL MISCH, furniture sales and manufacturing company executive; b. Chgo., June 2, 1927; d. Charles E. and Selma (Herschman) Misch; m. Manfred Seeman, May 6, 1951; Children—Clarles Alan, William Henry. B.A., Goucher Coll., 1948. Sec., treas. Helikon Furniture Co., Inc., Taftville, Conn., 1959—; corporator Norwich Savs. Soc., Conn., 1978—. Bd. dirs. Sr. Citizens Job Bank, Norwich, 1983-85; hon. consul Republic of Haiti, Conn., 1979—. Democrat. Jewish. Home: 211 Harland Rd Norwich CT 06360 Office: Helikon Furniture Co Inc. 607 Norwich Ave Taftville CT 06360

SEEMANN-BEAUMONT, ROSALIE MARY, logistics consultant; b. St. Louis, July 30, 1942; d. Ulysses Sylvester and Helen Marie (Hootselle) Simon; ed. Lindenwood Colls., St. Charles, Mo., 1973-76, Harris Tchrs. Coll., St. Louis, 1961, U. Fla., Gainesville, 1964; m. Richard Vaughn, Jan 20, 1968 (dec.); 1 dau., Heather Elizabeth; m. Dennis Jon Beaumont, May 28, 1982. Records clk. McDonnell Aircraft Corp., St. Louis, 1962-64; vol. U.S. Peace Corps, Brazil, 1964-66; tech. analyst, group leader Conductron-Mo., St. Charles, 1966-71; self-employed, 1971-77; tech. analyst, maintenance engr. McDonnell Douglas Astronautics, St. Louis, 1977-78; mgr. supply support Northrop Def. Systems Div., Rolling Meadows, Ill., 1978-80; logistics mgmt. cons., Spring Grove, Ill., 1980-85; mgr. logistic support Recon/Optical, Inc., Barrington, Ill., 1985—. Adv. council Conductron-Mo. Affirmative Action Program; mem. ch. council, commr. ways and means St. John the Baptist Cath. Ch.; troop leader Sybaquay council Girl Scouts U.S.A. Recipient commendation Conductron-Mo., 1967. Mem. Soc. Logistics Engrs. (Mem. of Yr. award, sr. mem.), Assn. Old Crows, Lindenwood Colls. Assocs. Fine Arts, Nat. Assn. Female Execs., Northside Art Assn. (bus. mgr. News 1968-70). Republican. Home: 2910 Bay View Ln McHenry IL 60050 Office: 550 W Northwest Hwy Barrington IL 60010

SEFFER, YVONNE KATHRYN, financial consultant, import/export company executive; b. Chgo.; d. Urosh Lazar and Helen (Musulin) S.; B.A., Ohio U., 1972. Pres., Ivanka Internat. Imports, Chgo., 1973—; realtor asso. Coldwell Banker Co., Oak Brook, Ill., 1979—; internat. fin. cons., 1980—. Mem. Nat. Assn. Exec. Women, Nat. Assn. Realtors, Ill. Assn. Realtors, DuPage Bd. Realtors, La Grange Bd. Realtors, Internat. Sports Core, Internat. Order St. John of Jerusalem Hospitallers-Knights of Malta, Augustan Soc. Office: 1225 W 22d St Suite 110 Oak Brook IL 60521

SEGAL, ALETHEA BIGHAM, med. technologist; b. Rock Hill, S.C., Oct. 2, 1921; d. Boyce Hyatt and Sarah Dorcas (Whiteside) Bigham; B.S. in Chemistry and Zoology, Winthrop Coll., Rock Hill, 1942; M.T., Duke U., 1944; m. William Segal, July 28, 1950; children—Janet Cheryl Segal Fixel, Alethea Gail. Med. technician, office mgr. Dr. Louie Limbaugh and Dr. Karl Hanson, Jacksonville, Fla., 1944-60; med. technician The Clinic for Digestive Diseases, Jacksonville, Fla., 1960-62, clinic mgr., 1963-75, dir. patients accts., 1976—. Mem. Am. Soc. Clin. Pathologists, Fla. Soc. Med. Technologists, Credit Women Internat., Winthrop Coll. Alumni Assn., AAUW. Democrat. Baptist. Club: Ponte Vedra. Home: 5138 Rosebay Terr Jacksonville FL 32207 Office: 1610 Barrs St Jacksonville FL 32204

SEGAL, GERALDINE ROSENBAUM, sociologist; b. Phila., Aug. 26, 1908; d. Harry and Mena (Hamburg) Rosenbaum; m. Bernard Gerard Segal, Oct. 22, 1933; children—Loretta Joan, Richard Murry. B.S. in Edn., U. Pa., 1930, M.A. in Human Relations, 1963, Ph.D. in Sociology, 1978; M.S.L.S., Drexel U., 1968. Social worker County Relief Bd., Phila., 1931-35; sociologist, Phila., 1935—; cons. and lectr. in field. Author: In Any Fight Some Fall, 1975; Blacks in the Law, 1983. Bd. dirs. NCCJ, 1937-47, 82—, sec., 1983—; bd. overseers U. Pa. Sch. Social Work, 1983—, Juvenile Law Ctr.; chair Phila. Tutorial Project, 1966-68. Democrat. Jewish. Home: 2401 Pennsylvania Ave Apt 19-C-44 Philadelphia PA 19130

SEGAL, KATHLEEN RITA, advertising executive; b. Chgo., May 26, 1952; d. Harry L. and Margaret (Casey) Segal; m. Craig S. Baron, Oct. 16, 1982. B.A. in English, No. Ill. U., 1974. Broadcast buyer Lee King & Ptnrs., Inc., Chgo., 1974-77; media/research supr. Campbell Mithun, Inc., Chgo., 1977-79; assoc. media dir., v.p. BBDO Chgo., 1979—. Mem. NOW. Office: BBDO Chicago 410 N Michigan Ave Chicago IL 60611

SEGAL, LORE, writer, educator; b. Vienna, Austria, Mar. 8, 1928; came to U.S., 1951, naturalized, 1956; d. Ignatz and Franziska (Stern) Groszmann; m. David I. Segal, Nov. 3, 1960 (dec. 1970); children—Beatrice Ann, Jacob Paul. B.A., Bedford Coll., U. London, 1948. Adj. assoc. prof. creative writing Columbia U., N.Y.C., 1968-75, adj. prof., 1975-77; Hadley fellow Bennington Coll., Vt., 1972; lectr. Princeton U., N.J., 1973-77; prof. Sarah Lawrence Coll., Bronxville, N.Y., 1975-76; prof. creative writing U. Ill., Chgo., 1978—; vis. prof. Washington U., St. Louis, 1981; prof. Breadloaf Sch., Middlebury, Vt., 1975-79. Author: (novel) Other People's Houses, 1962-64; Lucinella, 1978; Her First American, 1985. Translator (tales) The Juniper Tree and other tales from Grimm, 1974; (juvenile) Tell Me a Mitzi, 1970; Tell me a Trudy, 1977; The Story of Mrs. Lovewright and Purrless Her Cat. Fellow Guggenheim Found., 1965-66, Nat. Council on Arts and Humanities, 1967-68, NEA, 1981, NEH, 1982. Mem. P.E.N. Internat., Associated Writing Programs, Poets and Writers. Home: 280 Riverside Dr New York NY 10025 Office: U Ill Box 4348 Chicago IL 60680

SEGER, GERALDINE, television hostess, nurse, realtor; b. Merrill, Mich., Dec. 18, 1938; d. Joseph Rudolph and Rose Marie (Prikosky) Lednicky; m. Dean W. Seger, Nov. 29, 1958 (dec. Jan. 1983); children—Mary, Brad, Craig, Clark Wayne; m. Glen Olmstead, Sept. 28, 1983. Diploma Mercy Sch. Practical Nursing, 1958; student Mid-Mich. Coll., 1980, Kirkland Community Coll., 1981. Cert. realtor, Mich. L.P.N., Mich. Sec. Blair Transit, Saginaw, Mich., 1956-57; nurse Mercy Hosp., Cadillac, Mich., 1975-78, Pub. Health Home Care, Lake City Mich., 1978-80; pvt. nurse, Cadillac, 1981-83; hostess Cable TV-3-GRK Prodns., Cadillac, 1985—. Active Scenic Trails council Boy Scouts Am., Lake City, 1967-80; past pres Med. Aux., Cadillac, 1958-83; fund raiser Mercy Hosp., Missaukee County Mich., 1965, various congressional candidates, 1962, 74, 83. Recipient Silver Beaver award Scenic Trails council Boy Scouts Am., 1977, Den Mother of Yr. award, 1976; Letter of Appreciation, USN, 1985, ARC, 1985; named Queen of Centennial, City of Lake City, 1968. Roman Catholic. Avocations: sailing; canoeing; water and snow skiing; cross country skiing; ceramics; wood refinishing; biking; walking. Home: 107 West Lake St PO Box N Lake City MI 49651

SEGER, MARTHA ROMAYNE, government official, economist; b. Adrian, Mich., 1932. B.B.A., U. Mich., 1954, M.B.A., 1955, Ph.D., 1971. Began career in econs. dept. Gen. Motors Corp.; later with Fed. Res. Bank Chgo., 3 yrs.; economist Detroit Bank & Trust Co., from 1967; v.p. Bank of Commonwealth, Detroit, from 1974; adj. assoc. prof. bus. econs. U. Mich., 1978-79; commr. fin. instns. State of Mich., from 1980; mem. bd. govs. FRS, Washington. Office: Federal Reserve System Office of Chairman 20th and C Sts NW Washington DC 20551*

SEGERSTROM, CELESTA MELODY THRONDSON, advertising executive; b. Oakland, Calif., Sept. 18, 1945; d. Albert Harold and Doris Irene (Galvin) Throndson; m. Karl Eric Segerstrom, Apr. 3, 1971 (div. July 1981). A.A., City Coll. San Francisco, 1965; B.F.A., Art Ctr. Coll. Design, 1969. Art dir., new product designer Cunningham and Walsh Inc., N.Y.C., 1969-70; ptnr., creative dir. Embryonics New Product Workshop, N.Y.C., 1970-72; instr. painting U. Nev. Community Coll. System, Winnemucca and Lovelock, 1974-76; art dir. Harrah's Hotels and Casinos, Reno, 1976-81; art dir., TV producer Gustin Curtis Advt. Co., Reno, 1981-82; v.p., creative group head Keller Crescent Co., Dallas, 1982—; free-lance illustrator, 1969—; free-lance painter Henry Conversano and Assocs., Oakland, Calif., 1976-78; owner Profiles Modeling and Talent Agy., Reno, 1977-80. Illustrator: Jay and the Americans (Saca award), 1970. Recipient Sweepstakes award for Overall Best Design, Communications Competition, 1982; 3 Bicentennial grants, 1976; Creativity 84 award. Mem. Art Ctr. Alumni Assn. (pres. N.Y. chpt. 1970-72), Reno Advt. Club, Nev. Artist Assn.

SEGERSTROM, JANE ARCHER, image consultant; b. Los Angeles, Feb. 1, 1930; d. Francis Gaden and Lyda Mary (Comer) Archer; m. Clifford Charles Segerstrom, Feb. 1, 1951; children—John Archer, Carol Anne. B.S., George Pepperdine U., 1951. Pres., Triad Interests, Houston, 1974—; founder-pres. Tri-D Consultants, Houston, 1983—; pub. Tri-D Signature Style, Houston, 1983—. Author: Look Like Yourself and Love It, 1980; Signature Style Books, 1986; also Tri-D cassettes. Mem. Nat. Speakers Assn., Assn. Fashion and Image Consultants, Profl. Image Consultants Internat., Color Image Consultants Internat., Home Economics in Bus. Republican. Presbyterian. Home: 10811 Riverview Dr Houston TX 77042 Office: Tri-D Consultants PO Box 42006 Houston TX 77242

SEGGERMAN, YVONNE ROSSON, producer, choreographer; b. Los Angeles, July 9, 1955; d. Harry Gurney Atha and Anne (Crellin) S.; m. Normand L. Beauregard, Sept. 8, 1984. B.A., Sarah Lawrence Coll., 1977. Dancer in film Zelig, N.Y.C., 1981; choreographer Nat. Assn. for Regional Ballet, Ark., Conn., N.Y.C., 1978-82; choreographer Ballet Today Co., N.Y.C., 1981-82; dir. sales and mktg. Mary Chess Perfumes, N.Y.C., 1980-83; assoc. producer Cumberland Co. for Performing Arts, Cumberland, R.I., 1983—, choreographic cons. N.Y. Renaissance Festival, Tuxedo, N.Y., 1980; mem. R.I. touring roster New Eng. Found. for Arts. Choreographer Hot Grog, 1981, The Canterbury Tales, 1981, The Would-Be Gentleman, 1983; research and reconstrn. of hist. Baroque and Renaissance dance. Monticello scholar Nat. Assn. Regional Ballet, Geneva, N.Y., 1982; R.I. State Council on Arts grantee, 1985, 86. Home: 161 W 95th St Apt 2F New York NY 10025 Office: Cumberland Co for the Performing Arts The Monastery Cumberland RI 02864

SEGIL, LARRAINE DIANE, materials company executive; b. Johannesburg, South Africa, July 15, 1948; came to U.S., 1974; d. Jack and Norma Estelle (Cohen) Wolfowitz; m. Clive Melwyn Segil, Mar. 9, 1969; 1 child, James Harris. B.A., U. Witwatersrand, South Africa, 1967, B.A. with honours, 1969; J.D., Southwestern U., Los Angeles, 1979; M.B.A., Pepperdine U., 1985. Bar: Calif. 1979, U.S. Supreme Ct. 1982. Cons. in internat. transactions, Los Angeles, 1976-79; atty. Long & Levit, Los Angeles, 1979-81; chmn., pres. Marina Credit Corp., Los Angeles, 1981-85; pres., chief exec. officer Electronic Space Products Internat., Los Angeles, 1985—; dir. Marina Bancorp, Marina Credit Corp., Colonial Thrift & Loan, Los Angeles, Maximed, Los Angeles. Bd. govs. Cedars Sinai Med. Centre, Los Angeles, 1984—; bd. dirs. So. Calif. Tech. Execs. Network. Mem. ABA (chmn. internat. law com. young lawyers div. 1980-84), Internat. Assn. Young Lawyers (exec. council 1979—, council internat. law and practice 1983-84). Club: Regency (house com.) (Los Angeles). Avocations: piano; horseriding. Office: ESPI 31194 La Baya Dr Suite 100 Westlake Village CA 91362

SEGNER, VENICE CHANDLER, psychologist; b. Sand Springs, Okla., Nov. 7, 1914; d. John Beverly and Beulah Virginia (Sewell) Chandler; B.A., U. Tulsa, 1962; Ph.D., U. Ga., 1968; m. O.E. Segner, Jan. 15, 1934 (dec. 1962); m. 2d Gilbert L. Stewart, Aug. 25, 1972; children—Jane (dec.), Leslie, Eugene (dec.), James. Staff psychologist Long Beach (Calif.) VA Med. Center, 1968-76, supervisory psychologist, 1976-80, ret., 1980; founder, pres. bd. dirs. The Middle Way, Inc., non-profit service orgn. for develop. disabled adults, including tng. in agrl. and related skills, Sebastopol, Calif., 1979—; clin. asso. U. So. Calif., 1973-80, Fuller Theol. Sem., 1977-80. Mem. Am. Psychol. Assn., Western Psychol. Assn. Democrat. Episcopalian. Home: 2759 Dyer Ave Sebastopol CA 95472 Office: 486 S Main Sebastopol CA 95472

SEGO, ARLENE F., educator; b. Cleve., Mar. 13, 1938; d. Henry John and Hazel Elizabeth (Kunkle) Frontroth; B.S., Indiana U. of Pa., 1959; M.Natural Scis., Ariz. State U., 1962. Tchr., West High Sch., Cleve., 1959-61, head dept. math., 1962-66; asst. prof. math. Cuyahoga Community Coll., Parma, Ohio, 1966-69, assoc. prof., 1969-72, prof., 1972—, also head dept., faculty marshall, 1972; pres. Typographics Group Inc. Program coordinator, dir. adult programs West High, Cleve., 1966-67, coordinator Head Start Program, 1966. Leader, Girl Scouts U.S.A., Cleve., 1962-64. Named Cleve. Businesswoman of Month, Bus. and Profl. Women Medina County Working Woman of Year, 1983; recipient AAUW award, 1983; Shell Merit fellow, 1965; Martha Holden Jennings scholar, 1963-64. Mem. Nat., Ohio, Greater Cleve. (pres. 1966-67) councils tchrs. math., Math. Assn. Am., AAUP, Brunswick C. of C. (dir., pres.), Ohio Assn. Community Jr. Colls. (sec. 1969-70), Assn. Women in Math., AAUW, Alpha Sigma Alpha, Delta Kappa Gamma (treas.). Club: Zonta. (dir., treas.). Author: Good Buddy. Home: 938 Penny's Dr Brunswick OH 44212 Office: 590 Pearl Rd Brunswick OH 44212

SEGOVIA, REGINA G., reporter; b. Birmingham, Ala., July 1, 1956; d. Johnny F. Davis and Betty S. (Mehaffey) Bloom; m. Robert John Segovia, Aug. 17, 1979 (div.); 1 son: Robert Frank. Student, Ind. U., 1976-77; B.A. English, Mundelein Coll.-Chgo., 1979. News writer, intern Sta. WGN, Chgo., 1978-79; newscaster, writer, producer Sta. WAAC, Terre Haute, Ind., 1979-80; women's resource ctr. coordinator, editor newsletter Ind. State U., Terre Haute, 1981; gen. assignment reporter Terre Haute Star, 1981-82; labor environment reporter Port Arthur News (Tex.), 1982—. Recipient 3d place award Hoosier Press Assn., 1982; UPI award, 1983; AP 3d place award, 1984; Tex. Press Assn. award, 1984. Democrat.

SEGOVIS, ELIZABETH WILSON, lawyer; b. Pasadena, Calif., Aug. 10, 1948; d. Frank Stedman and Jeannette Frances (MacKenzie) Wilson; m. James Courtney Segovis, Dec. 22, 1971; children—Colin Michael, Ian Patrick, Courtney Michelle. B.A., Cornell U., 1970; M.A., SUNY-Albany, 1973; J.D., So. Meth. U., 1978. Bar: Tex. 1978, U.S. Dist. Ct. (no. dist.) Tex. 1979. Social worker George Jr. Republic, Freeville, N.Y., 1970-72; felony probation officer Supreme Ct. N.Y., Bklyn., 1973-74; family ct. counselor Dallas County Juvenile Dept., Dallas, 1974-75; assoc. Johannes Robertson & Wilkinson, Dallas, 1976-79; asst. county atty. County Atty.'s Office, Sherman, Tex., 1979-84; assoc. Thompson, Green, Shaffer, Redwine, Denison, Tex., 1984-85; staff atty. North Tex. Central Legal Services Found., McKinney, Tex., 1985—; bd. dirs. Legal Services Found., Dallas, 1978-79, Women's Crisis Line of Grayson County, 1984—. Adv. bd. Grayson County Guidance Clinic, Sherman, Tex., 1984; trustee Grace United Meth. Sch., 1982-84. Mem. Grayson County Bar Assn. (v.p. 1980-81, 84-85), State Bar Tex., Collins County Bar Assn., ABA, Dallas County Bar Assn. Methodist. Home: 707 Concord Ln Allen TX 75002 Office: N Central Tex Legal Services Found 110 N Tennessee St McKinney TX 75069

SEGRAVES, IRENE ALBERTA, professional parliamentarian, educator, consultant; b. East St. Louis, Ill. Student U. Mex., 1935-41; B.E., Ill. State U., 1937; M.S., U. Ill., 1940; postgrad. U. Yucatan, 1950-53, 55. Profl. registered parliamentarian. Tchr. East St. Louis pub. schs., Ill., 1930-45; parliamentarian Ill. Heart Assn., 1950-82, Ill. Edn. Assn., 1973-80, Ill. Pharmacists, 1975—; founder Radio Info. Service, Belleville, Ill., 1972, pres., bd. for blind and print handicapped, 1982—; parliamentarian to bd. dirs. NOW, 1984; cons. Caseville Twp. Bd. Suprs., Ill., 1970—, Fairview Heights Bd. Aldermen, Ill. Author: (with Jeannette Collins) Through This Door to Democracy, 1968. By-law cons. Ill. Heart Assn., 1950—, v.p., 1970-80, by-law cons. Am. Heart Assn., 1950—. Recipient Leadership award Am. Heart Assn., 1960, Meritorious Service award, 1962; Disting. Service award Ill. Heart Assn., 1970. Mem. Nat. Assn. Parliamentarians (dist. dir. 1974), Am. Inst. Parliamentarians, Internat. Assn. Platform Speakers, Am. Arbitration Assn. (nat. panel), Gen. Fedn. Women's Clubs (bd. dirs. 1966-76), Ill. Fedn. Women's Clubs (pres. 1964-66), P.E.O. (v.p. GM chpt.). Republican. Clubs: Woman's (O'Fallon, Ill.) (pres. 1950-52), Wednesday (Belleville, Ill.) (pres. 1978-80). Home: 518 Lincoln Hwy Fairview Heights IL 62208 Office: Radio Information Service Shrine of Our Lady of the Snows 9500 W Route 15 Belleville IL 62223

SEGRAVES, JANE DIRENZO, lawyer; b. Alexandria, Va., Mar. 17, 1957; d. Vincent Neil and E. Linda (Schnellman) DiRenzo; m. Scott Jackson Segraves, Aug. 15, 1981. B.A., U. Va., 1978; postgrad. Northwestern U. Sch. Law, 1980-81; J.D., U. N.C., 1981. Bar: Ill. 1981. Assoc. firm Jenner & Block, Chgo., 1981-85; counsel MidCon Corp., 1985—. Mem. ABA, Ill. Bar Assn., DuPage County Bar Assn. Democrat. Roman Catholic. Office: MidCon Corp 701 E 22d St PO Box 1207 Lombard IL 60148

SEIBERT, MYRTLE CROSBY, travel consultant; b. Cadosia, N.Y., Feb. 11, 1921; d. Frank and Hattie Carolyn (Schaefer) Crosby; m. Robert D. Seibert, Sept. 15, 1940 (dec.); children—Robert C., Jane Ellen Seibert Andrus. Grad. Am. Soc. Travel Agents Sch., Am. Airlines Computer Sch.; student Berkshire Christian Coll. Pres. Catskill Travel Agy., Walton, N.Y., 1960—. Lay del. ann. Conf. United Methodist Ch., Walton, N.Y., 1984-85, 86-87. Mem. Am. Soc. Travel Agents, Nat. Assn. Female Execs. Democrat. Home: 22 Fancher Ave Walton NY 13856 Office: Catskill Travel Agy Inc 160 Delaware St Walton NY 13856 also 55 Main St Sidney NY 13838

SEID, JUDITH ANN, production manager publishing company; b. Balt., July 8, 1941; d. Eugene Baker and Helen Virginia (Wolford) Grossnickle; children—Karen Yvette, Jennifer Lynn, Laura Kathryn. A.A.S., Bergen Community Coll., 1978, A.A., 1976. Prodn. coordinator Med. Econs. Co., Oradell, N.J., 1978-80, prodn. and copy mgr., 1981-84, prodn. dir., 1984—. Mem. Am. Assn. Individual Investors, Phi Omega Epsilon. Democrat. Lutheran. Office: Medical Economics Co 680 Kinderkamack Rd Oradell NJ 07649

SEIDELMAN, SUSAN, film director. Attended Drexel Inst., NYU. Dir. films Smithereens, 1982, Desperately Seeking Susan, 1985; dir. debut with short film and You Act Like One, Too (Student film award Acad. Motion Picture Arts and Scis.). Address: care Sanford/Beckett 1015 N Gayley Suite 301 Los Angeles CA 90024*

SEIDEN, JEAN TRAGER, interior designer; b. Cin., July 21, 1941; d. Newton Junior and Louise (Goldsmith) Trager; student U. Miami (Ohio), 1959-60, U. Cin., 1960-63, Internat. Inst. Interior Design, 1974-76; m. Louis W. Seiden, Mar. 10, 1962; children—Ellen Louise, Richard Neal, Steven Alva. Owner, mgr. Jean T. Seiden Interior Design, Rockville, Md., 1975—; owner, v.p. Spectra Design Group, Ltd., 1985—; assoc. Potomac Designs, Rockville, 1973-77; v.p. Capitol Homes, Inc.; renovator hist. property, Washington, 1974-78. Bd. dirs. Civic Assn., 1965-66, Elem. Sch. PTA, 1966-69, Citizens Com. for Reading, 1972-74. Mem. Nat. Urban League, Nat. Home Fashion League, Nat. Hist. Soc., Nat. Women's Polit. Caucus, Bethesda-Chevy Chase Bus. and Profl. Women's Club, Mothers Against Drunk Driving, Nat. Trust Historic Preservation, Nat. LWV, NOW. Office: 1160 Rockville Pike Suite 211 Rockville MD 20852

SEIDERMAN, SUSAN LEVIN, publisher; b. Phila., Nov. 6, 1938; d. Leon and Ann (Vitz) Levin; m. Arthur Stanley Seiderman, Aug. 19, 1965; children—David, Leeann, E. Scott. Chief exec. officer Comp-Art, Phila., Welcomat, Phila., Review/Chronicle, Phila., 1979—. Bd. dirs. NCCJ, Phila., 1981-83; mem. com. on aging United Way, Phila., 1981-83; bd. dirs. YM-YWHA, Phila., 1982, Greentree Sch. Mem. Fedn. Bus. and Profl. Women (steering com. 1980-83). Democrat. Jewish. Office: Welcomat 1816 Ludlow St Philadelphia PA 19103

SEIDL, JEAN ELAINE, internist; b. N.Y.C., Sept. 26, 1927; d. Frank Norbert and Jennie (Vavra) Seidl; m. Richard H. Hamilton, Oct. 31, 1957; children—Elizabeth, Minard, Gordon. B.A., Barnard Coll., 1946; M.D., NYU, 1950; postgrad. U. Pa., 1972-73. Diplomate Am. Bd. Internal Medicine. Intern Bellevue Hosp., N.Y.C., 1952-54, resident in internal medicine, 1954-57; fellow in endocrinology NYU Med. Sch., 1957-58; practice medicine specializing in internal medicine, N.Y.C., 1958—; asst. prof. NYU Med. Coll., N.Y.C., 1958—; mem. staff NYU Hosp., Bellevue Hosp. Mem. AMA, N.Y. State Med. Soc., Am. Soc. Internal Medicine. Home: 63 E 66th St New York NY 10021 Office: 120 E 34th St New York NY 10021

SEIDL, PHYLLIS MIRIAM, advertising executive; b. Detroit, Oct. 12, 1955; d. Frank August and Emily Mary (Jacob) S. B.F.A., Calif. Coll. Arts and Crafts, 1975; pvt. tutor program Banff Sch. Fine Arts, Alta., Can., 1972. Pres., Visual Communications, Inc., Atlanta, 1975—; dir. Atlanta Zoo Carousel, Inc. Publs. chmn. The Atlanta Better Film Council, 1983-84; mem. Better Bus. Bur.; The English-Speaking Union of U.S., 1978; mem. Freedoms Found. at Valley Forge, 1979—, publs. com., 1982—, jr. com., 1984—; mem. Friends of Free China, 1979—, publs. chmn. 1982-84, v.p. 1985-86; mem. Am. Met. Opera Assn., Shoe String Opera Co., Pro-Mozart Soc. of Atlanta, 1980—, publs. chmn. 1981-84, publicity chmn., 1985-86; mem. Internat. Friends of Freedom Found.; Young Matrons' Circle, 1980—, publs. chmn. 1983-84; mem. Alliance Theatre Guild, 1980—, publicity chmn. 1982-83, publs. chmn. 1983-84; mem. Atlanta Alliance Children's Guild, 1980—, publicity chmn., 1981-83; mem. Atlanta Repertory Opera Co., 1981—, trustee, bd. dirs., 1982; jr. com. High Mus. of Art, Atlanta Symphony Assocs.; mem. Atlanta Ballet Guild, Atlanta Zool. Soc., Steinway Soc. Mem. Am. Bus. Assn., Nat. Acad. TV Arts and Scis., Young Women of Arts, Apt. Owners and Mgmt. Assn., Ga. Hospitality and Travel Assn., Buckhead Bus. Assn., Am. Film Inst., Atlanta C. of C. (internat. com.). Republican. Roman Catholic. Avocations: scuba diving; skiing; travelling; gourmet cooking; swimming. Office: Visual Communications Inc 550 Pharr Rd Suite 645 Atlanta GA 30305

SEIFERT, MARGARET FRANCIS, educational administrator; b. Brownwood, Tex., Nov. 17, 1944; d. Cabell Denny and Helen (Carroll) Francis; B.A., Transylvania Coll., 1966; M.A., Mankato State Coll., 1968; postgrad. Ind. U.; m. Ralph Louis Seifert, July 14, 1979; Adv., Mankato (Minn.) State Coll., 1966-68, head resident, 1967-68, ednl. coordinator, 1968-69, asst. dir. housing, 1969-70, dir. orientation, 1969-70; residence hall dir. Ball State U., Muncie, Ind., 1970-76, instr. directed admissions program, 1971-72, higher edn., 1972-74; assoc. dean students, dir. housing Hanover (Ind.) Coll., 1976-82; coordinator Learning Resource Center, Ind. Vocat./Tech. Coll., Madison, 1982-85, dir. instrn., 1985—; cons., adv. numerous univ. orgns., coms., bds. Mem. Hanover City Plan Commn., 1983-86, v.p., 198-86; participant Ind. Congress on Edn., 1983-84; bd. dirs. Jefferson County Girls Club, 1983-85, 86—, v.p., 1984, pres., 1985; mem. Gov.'s Literary Council, 1984-86. Mem. Am. Vocat. Assn., Ind. Vocat. Assn., Nat. Assn. Student Personnel Adminstrs. (rep. to Allerton conf. 1979), Nat. Assn. Women Deans, Adminstrs. and Counselors (sec. local arrangements com. for nat. com. 1980-82), Madison Hist. Soc., Assn. of Coll. and Univ. Housing Officers (program com. 1975—), Am. Coll. Personnel Assn. (mem. nat. conv. local arrangements com. 1974-76), Ind. Coll. Personnel Assn. (program presenter 1972—), Ind. Assn. Women Deans, Adminstrs. and Counselors (spring workshop com. 1974-75, membership chmn. 1977-78, v.p. 1978-79, pres. 1980-81, exec. bd., nominations chmn. 1981-82, hon. members chmn. 1982-83, by-laws chmn. 1983-84), Am. Personnel and Guidance Assn., AAUW (exec. council 1978-79, v.p. for program 1980-82, chmn. book fair 1982-83, pres. 1983-85), LWV, Muncie City Panhellenic (del. 1973-75), Pi Sigma Alpha, Alpha Lambda Delta (adminstrv. liaison Hanover Coll. 1981-82), Phi Eta Sigma, Delta Delta Delta (pres. alumni assn. 1974-75), Kappa Kappa Kappa (pres. 1986). Democrat. Club: Hanover Women's (pres. 1983) Home: PO Box 365 Hanover IN 47243 Office: Indiana Vocational-Technical Coll Madison IN 47250

SEIGER, MARILYN SANDRA, public relations and promotions executive; b. Washington, Jan. 20, 1945; d. Harry R. and Claire D. Seiger; B.S., Ohio State U., 1966; M.A., U. Pitts, 1967; M.B.A., Baruch Coll., 1986; m. Stan Amatucci, June 15, 1979. Editor, Holt, Rinehart & Winston, Inc., N.Y.C., 1969-73; editor/writer Redbook mag., N.Y.C., 1973-77; mng. editor 1,001 Decorating Ideas, N.Y.C., 1978-79; dir. public relations, promotion, advt. Brit. Consulate, N.Y.C., 1979-80; account supr. Peter Martin Assocs., N.Y.C., 1980-82; public relations mgr. Marriott Hotels, N.Y.C., 1982-85; dir. pub. relations and promotion CARE, N.Y.C., 1985—; cons., writer Singer Co., Reader's Digest, Formica, Martex. Lic. tchr., N.Y., Pa. Mem. Public Relations Soc. Am. (chmn. public relations workshops 1983, dir. N.Y. chpt. 1984—), Women Execs. in Pub. Relations. Office: 660 1st Ave New York NY 10006

SEITNER, RITA A., researcher, consultant; b. Milw., July 11, 1940; d. Robert and Esther (Steren) Seitner; m. Alfred F. Huete, Nov. 3, 1973 (div.). B.A., Beaver Coll., 1962; M.S., U. Wis.-Milw., 1977. Mktg. asst. Advanced Learning, Milw., 1972-75; adminstv. asst. J. Walter Thompson, N.Y.C., 1962-67; assoc. planner David M. Walker, Phila., 1967-68; urban analyst HUD, Phila., 1968-70; market analyst Gen. Electric, Milw., 1977-82; mgr. research Hoffman, York & Compton, Milw., 1982-84, pres. RS Research Cons., Inc., Milw., 1984—. Fellow Am. Mktg. Assn., Am. Mgmt. Assn., Direct Mktg. Club. Jewish. Office: 1219 N Jackson St Milwaukee WI 53202

SEITZ, KATHLEEN LYNNE, accountant; b. Cleve., Mar. 29, 1951; d. Gilbert Raymond Evans and Lois (Nuhn) Evans Kalman; m. Gerald R. Seitz, Oct. 6, 1973 (div. Feb. 1983); m. Frederick S. Watson, July 2, 1983. B.Adminstrv. Sci., Ohio State U., 1973. C.P.A., Ohio. Staff acct. Coopers & Lybrand, Columbus, Ohio, 1973, Wolf & Co., Atlanta, 1973-74; staff acct. Mannheimer, Seitz, Kate & Freiberg, Inc., Cleve., 1974-84, pres., owner, 1984—; trustee Mannheimer, Seitz, Kate & Freiberg, Inc. Profit Sharing Plan, 1980—, PEK Industries Profit Sharing Plan, Orlando, Fla., 1982—; dir. Applied Mgmt. Corp., Helena, Mont.; controller Commodore's Club Ltd. Partnership, Cleve., 1984—. Mem. Am. Inst. C.P.A.s, Ohio Soc. C.P.A.s, Nat. C.P.A. Network, Assn. Female Execs., Women's City Club. Methodist. Lodge: Altrusa. Avocations: boating; reading; computer programming. Office: Mannheimer Seitz Kate & Freiberg Inc 24100 Chagrin Blvd Suite 480 Cleveland OH 44131

SEITZ, LAURA RUTH, design studio executive, consultant; b. Detroit, Nov. 29, 1951; d. John Calvin and Charlotte Mary (Collins) S. Student Western Mich. U., 1969-72, Los Angeles Mcpl. Art Galleries, 1975-78, UCLA, 1978. Sales coordinator Edwards Bros., Ann Arbor, Mich., 1973-74; owner, designer Moonshadow Designs, Ann Arbor and Los Angeles, 1973-77; sec. Maher Elen Advt., Los Angeles, 1976-79, account exec., 1979-80, account supr., 1980-81; sales mgr. Sojourn Design Group, Pico Rivera, Calif., 1981-82; gen. mgr., owner Anselmo Design Assocs., Santa Monica, Calif., from 1982; now owner O'Mara/Seitz Design Group. Mem. Olympics Steering com. Muscular Dystrophy Assn., Los Angeles, 1979; mem. superwalk steering com. March of Dimes, 1981. Mem. NOW, Los Angeles Ad Club, Nat. Assn. Female Execs., Internat. Assn. Bus. Communicators. Office: O'Mara/Seitz Design Group 1321 7th St Santa Monica CA 90401

SELAME, ELINOR, packaging design company executive; b. Bklyn., Feb. 25, 1936; d. David and Nettie (Husney) Leventer; m. Joseph Selame, June 27, 1953; children—Theodore, Robert, Nadine. Student Bklyn. Coll., 1952-54, Boston U., 1965, Harvard U., 1966, Boston Coll., 1967. With Selame Design, Newton Lower Falls, Mass., 1967—, v.p. mktg., 1974-80, pres., 1981—. Author: So We Spin, 1970; Developing a Corporate Identity: How to Stand Out in the Crowd, 1975; Packaging Power, 1982. Contbg. author: Handbook of Modern Marketing, 1985; Marketing Managers Handbook, 1985. Contbr. articles to profl. jours. Bd. dirs. Artists Found.; mem. mktg. adv. council Babson Coll. Recipient Learning Materials award Am. Inst. Graphic Arts, Smaller Bus. Assn., 1972. Mem. Newton Art Ctr. (pres. 1981-82), Smaller Bus. Assn. (chmn. speakers bur. 1977), Internat. Platform Assn., Am. Mktg. Assn., Nat. Speakers Assn., Package Designer's Council. LWV. Office: Selame Design 2330 Washington St Newton Lower Falls MA 02162

SELBY, CECILY CANNAN, educator, scientist, exec.; b. London, Feb. 4, 1927; d. Keith and Catherine Anne Cannan; A.B. cum laude, Radcliff Coll., 1946; Ph.D. in Phys. Biology, M.I.T., 1950; m. Henry M. Selby, Aug. 11, 1951 (div. 1978); children—Norman, William, Russell; m. James Stacy Coles, Feb. 21, 1981. Teaching asst. in biology M.I.T., 1948-49; adminstrv. head virus study sect. Sloan-Kettering Inst., N.Y.C., 1949-50, asst. mem., 1950-55; research asso. Sloan-Kettering div. Cornell U. Med. Coll., N.Y.C., 1953-55, also instr. microscopic anatomy, 1955-57; tchr. sci. Lenox Sch., N.Y.C., 1957-58, headmistress, 1959-72; nat. exec. dir. Girl Scouts U.S.A., N.Y.C., 1972-75; acad. dean N.C. Sch. Sci. and Math., Durham, 1980-81; chmn. bd. advs., 1981-84; adv. com. Simmons Coll. Grad. Mgmt. Program, 1977-80;

mem. Com. for Corp. Support of Pvt. Univs., 1977-83; cons. U.S. Dept. Commerce, 1976-77; dir. Avon Products Inc., RCA, NBC, Loehmanns Inc., 1978-83; dir. Nat. Edn. Corp., 1984—; pres. Am. Energy Ind. Founder, chmn. N.Y. Ind. Schs. Opportunity Project, 1968-72; adj. prof. sci. edn. NYU, 1984—; trustee M.I.T., Bklyn. Law Sch., Radcliffe Coll.; mem. corp. Woods Hole Oceanographic Inst., 1981—, N.Y. Hall of Sci.; mem. council Rockefeller U., 1982—; mem. adv. council Yale U. Peabody Mus., 1983—; co-chmn. commn. Nat. Sci. Bd. on Pre-Coll. Edn. in Math., Sci. and Tech. Mem. Headmistresses of East (hon. mem.; pres. 1970-72), Cum Laude Soc. (past chpt. pres., dist. regent), Sigma Xi. Contbr. articles to profl. jours., chpt. to book. Clubs: Cosmopolitan (N.Y.C.); Women's Forum N.Y. Home: 45 Sutton Pl S New York NY 10022 Office: NYU Sch Edn Health Nursing and Arts Professions 933 Shimkin 50 W 4th St New York NY 10003

SELBY, NANCY CHIZEK, educator; b. South Bend, Ind., Sept. 15, 1935; d. Cletus and Mildred (Mauck) Chizek; m. David K. Selby, June 22, 1957; children—Pamela, Katherine, Susan, Elizabeth. B.S., Miami U., Oxford, Ohio, 1957. Instr., v.p. Verbal Communications, Dallas, 1972-79; founder, dir. Spine Edn. Ctr., Dallas, 1979—; mem. adv. bd. Dallas Safety Council, 1985—. Author: Care for Your Back, 1983; Back Injury Prevention Resource Handbook, 1984. Author videotape; Backache Blues, 1983. Telephone recruiter Republican Party, Dallas, 1976—, Friends of the Library. Mem. Am. Soc. Tng. and Devel., Tex. Safety Assn. (dir.), Am. Soc. Safety Engrs., Dallas County Med. Aux., Pi Beta Phi. Avocations: sailing; running; reading. Office: Spine Education Center 6161 Harry Hines Blvd Dallas TX 75225

SELESNICK, DENYSE CAROLE, publisher, trade exposition manager; b. Bath, Somerset, Eng., Oct. 1, 1938; came to U.S., 1947; d. William and Cecilly (Jacobs) Zeltzer; m. Marvin M. Selesnick, July 3, 1960; children—Stephanie Sue, Hillary Beth, Andrew Howard, Melanie Rachel. Student Los Angeles City Coll., 1956-57, UCLA, 1957-58, U. So. Calif. 1960-61. Assoc. editor Western Apparel Industry Mag., Los Angeles, 1958-60, mng. editor, 1960-72; publisher Apparel Industry Mag., Los Angeles, 1972-82; pres. Denyse and Co., Inc., Tarzana, Calif., 1971—; dir. gen. Notivest SA, Mexico City, 1980—. Mem. Women in Bus., Am. C. of C. Mexico City, Fashion Group, Nat. Assn. Expo Mgrs., Western Publs. Assn., Editorial Camara Mexico City, Am. Apparel Mfrs. Assn. (chmn. Calif.), Democrat. Jewish. Recipient Maggie award 1980. Avocations: Public speaking; international politics. Office: Denyse & Co Inc 5170 Garden Grove Ave Tarzana CA 91356

SELIG, MARTHA KEISER, social work consultant; b. N.Y.C., Dec. 25, 1912; d. Jacob H. and Sadie (Hammer) Keiser; B.A., Hunter Coll., N.Y.C., 1932; M.S., CCNY, 1933; postgrad. Columbia U., 1933-38; diploma N.Y. Sch. Social Work, 1939; m. Kalman Selig, Mar. 23, 1935; children—Judith Selig Rubenstein, Elaine Selig Gould. Clin. psychologist Edn. Clinic, CCNY, 1932-44; exec. dir. Jewish Community Services L.I., 1944-46; exec. dir. community services Fedn. Jewish Philanthropies N.Y., 1946-74; vis. prof. Adelphia U., Garden City, N.Y., also Jewish Theol. Sem., N.Y.C., 1974—; cons. health and welfare agys. and founds., 1974—, Health & Welfare Service, 1980—; exec. dir. S.H. and Helen R. Scheuer Family Found., 1980—; guest lectr. Columbia U., Wurzweiler Sch. Social Work, Hunter Coll. Sch. Social Work; exec. bd. Am. Jewish Com.; bd. dirs. Council Vol. Child Care Agys. N.Y.C., Henry Kaufman Campgrounds, Hebrew Arts Sch., Nat. Found. for Jewish Culture; mem. Mayor's Commn. on Child Care, N.Y. State Adv. Commn. on Welfare, N.Y. State Gov.'s Commn. on Alcohol and Drug Abuse. Recipient Naomi Lehman Meml. award, 1960, Samuel W. and Rose Hurowitz award Fedn. Jewish Philanthropies N.Y., 1975; named to Hunter Coll. Hall of Fame, 1976; hon. mem. psychol. assn., also edn. assn. CCNY. Mem. Nat. Assn. Social Workers, Acad. Cert. Social Workers, Nat. Conf. Jewish Communal Service (past pres.). Author papers in field. Home: 22 E 88th St New York NY 10028 Office: 120 W 57th St New York NY 10019

SELISTE, MARIE HELEN, financial executive; b. Bklyn., Oct. 27, 1946; d. Bruno Voldemar and Frances Ann (Castagna) S.; m. Frank Codispoti, Oct. 26, 1968 (div. 1982). Student DataPoint, N.Y.C., 1983. Auditing clk. Edward Thompson Co., St. Paul, 1964-68; full charge bookkeeper Arnessen Marine System, Bklyn., 1968-74; gen. mgr. Composite Films, N.Y.C., 1974-83; fin. comptroller Zaro Bake Shop, Bronx, N.Y., 1983-84; gen. mgr. A Cut Above Editorial, N.Y.C., 1984—. Bd. dirs. Marriage Encounter, Bklyn., 1974-77. Mem. Nat. Assn. Female Execs. Republican. Roman Catholic. Office: A Cut Above Editorial 17 E 45th St New York NY 10017

SELK, ELEANOR HUTTON, artist; b. Duboise, Nebr., Oct. 21, 1918; d. Anderson Henry and Florence (Young) Hutton; R.N., St. Elizabeth Hosp., Lincoln, Nebr., 1938; m. Harold Frederick Selk, Aug. 3, 1940; children—Honey Lou, Katherine Florence. Nurse, Lincoln, 1938-40, Denver, 1940-50; with Colo. Bd. Realtors, 1956-66; owner, mgr. The Pen Point, graphic art studio, Colorado Springs, 1974—; one-woman shows: Colo. Coll., 1970, 72, Nazarene Bible Coll., 1973, 1st Meth. Ch., 1971 (all Colorado Springs); exhibited in group shows: U. So. Colo., 1969, 70, 71, 72, Colorado Springs Art Guild, 1969-72, Pike's Peak Artists Assn., 1969-73, Mozart Art Festival, Pueblo, Colo., 1969-74, numerous others; represented in permanent collection U.S. Postal Service, Pen-Arts Bldg., Washington, Medic Alert Found. Internat. Hdqrs., Turlock, Calif. Rec. sec. Colo. chpt. Medic Alert Found. Internat., 1980-81, chairperson El Paso County and Colorado Springs chpt., 1980—, Colo. bd. dirs., 1980—, rec. sec., 1980—. Recipient 3d pl. award Nat. Tb and Respiratory Disease and Christmas Seal Art Competition, 1969, finalist award Benedictine Art competition Hanover Trust Bank, N.Y.C., 1970; numerous awards and certs. for pub. service and art. Mem. Nat. League Am. Pen Women (rec. sec. 1972-74; travelling art slide collection 1974—, awards for book cover art). Contbr. med. articles, short stories, poetry to newspapers. Home: 518 Warren Ave Colorado Springs CO 80906 Office: 333 N Tejon St Agora Mall Colorado Springs CO 80903

SELK, GAIL BARBARA, publisher; b. Rice Lake, Wis., Jan. 16, 1937; d. Robert John and Eleanor Irene (Massoni) Volck; m. Bruce Reynolds, Apr. 11, 1957 (div. 1959); 1 child, Michelle Elizabeth; m. James D. Selk, June 21, 1969. B.A., Macalester Coll., 1958; student U. Wis., 1980, 85. Account rep. Madison Newspapers, Inc., Wis., 1961-76; dir. advt. Consumer Publs., Madison, 1976-77; pub. Madison Mag., Wis., 1977—. Dir. Take I Civic Center, 1982; chmn. Advt. Fedn., Madison, 1982, Downtown Madison Advt., 1985; dir. Connection, Madison, 1982-85; sec. TEMPO, Madison, 1983-84. Active various fund raising orgns. Mem. Madison Bd. Realtors (chmn. advt. 1970-72). Clubs: Madison; Wisconsin (dir. 1985) (Madison). Avocations: windsurfing; swimming; boating; skiing. Home: 414 N Livingston St Madison WI 53703 Office: Madison Mag 123 E Doty St Madison WI 53703

SELK, VICKE FINCHER, college official; b. Pauls Valley, Okla., Jan. 6, 1946; d. Buford Lee and Naomi Alice (Gibbs) F.; m. John Erwin Selk, July 27, 1968; 1 child, Elizabeth Alliston Carrington. M.A., Claremont Grad. Sch., 1977. Dir. adminstrv. services, treas. Pitzer Coll., Claremont, Calif., 1971-83, v.p., treas., 1983—; cons. Am. Council on Edn., Washington, 1979-80. Bd. dirs. Claremont Presbyterian Day Care Ctr., 1984. Mem. Nat. Assn. Coll. and Univ. Bus. Officers, Western Assn. Coll. and Univ. Bus. Officers. Avocation: music. Office: Pitzer Coll 1150 Mills Ave Claremont CA 91711

SELKE, ELOISE WILDENTHAL, retired educator; b. Cotulla, Tex., Feb. 18, 1924; d. John and Lois (Pearce) Wildenthal; m. Harold E. Selke, Sept. 1, 1946 (Div. July 1966); children—Harold Edward, Kenneth Wayne. B.S. in Edn., U. Tex., Austin, 1945; M.Elem. Edn., Tex. A&M U., 1974. Trust dept. clk.-typist Frost Bank, San Antonio, 1945-46; clk.-typist R.R. Commn., Austin, 1946-47, Exxon Co., Corpus Christi, 1947-49; elem. tchr. Spanish and English, Houston Ind. Sch. Dist., 1966-84. Mem. Congress Houston Tchrs. (life), Tex. State Tchrs. Assn. (life), Sigma Delta Pi, Pi Lambda Theta. Democrat. Methodist. Home: 5010 Carew St Houston TX 77096

SELKREGG, LIDIA LIPPI, geologist; b. Florence, Italy, July 24, 1920; came to U.S., 1947, naturalized, 1951; d. Otello and Ida (Chiasserini) Lippi; B.S., Sci. Licee, Tunis, Tunisia, 1938; Dr. Natural Sci., U. Florence, 1942; m. Frederick Mills Selkregg, Sept. 15, 1945; children—Alicia L. (Mrs. R.E. Iden), Sheila (Mrs. J.E. O'Malley), Leif L. Geologist, Ill. State Geol. Survey, Urbana, 1952-58; geologist, engr. U.S. Army C.E., Anchorage, 1959-61; capital improvement coordinator City of Anchorage, 1968-70; planning officer Fed. Field Com. Devel. and Planning, Alaska, 1970-71; sr. scientist Arctic Environ. Info. and Data Center, U. Alaska, 1970-77, prof. resource econs. and planning, 1977-85, prof. emeritus, 1985—, founder, dir. Alaska Home Fed. Loan Assn. Mem. Greater Anchorage Area Borough Planning and Zoning Commn., 1965-75; mem. Alaska Growth Policy Council, Office of Gov., 1975-80; sci. com. Outer Continental Shelf adv. bd. Dept. Interior, 1979-81; mem. Alaska Coastal Zone Mgmt. Council, 1977-83; mem. Anchorage Mcpl. Assembly, 1975-83; adv. com. White House Conf. Balanced Nat. Growth and Econ. Devel., 1977-78; mem. Anchorage Geotech. Commn., 1984—; adv. Com. Alaska Land Use Council, 1984—. Recipient Spl. Achievement award for superior performance Dept. Commerce, 1970; lic. geologist, Alaska; cert. profl. geologist Am. Inst. Profl. Geologists. Mem. Alaska Planning Assn. (pres. 1974), Geol. Soc. Am., Alaska Press Club, AAAS, NEA-Alaska United Teaching Profession, Sigma Xi, Nat. Fedn. Bus. and Profl. Women's Clubs, NAACP. Democrat. Unitarian. Club: Anchorage Dem. Author: (with others) Urban Planning and the Reconstruction-Human Ecology vol. The Great Alaska Earthquake of 1964, 1972; Alaska Regional Profiles, 6 vols., 1974-77; editor: Environmental Atlas of Greater Anchorage Area Borough, 1972. Home: 5811 Radcliffe Dr Anchorage AK 99504 Office: University of Alaska 3210 Providence Dr Anchorage AK 99508

SELL, BETTY MARIE, library director, educator; b. Coplay, Pa., Oct. 31, 1928; d. William Frederick and Margaret Louisa (Wormick) Haas; m. Kenneth D. Sell, Sept. 17, 1949; children—Peter Daniel, Rebecca Anne. B.S., Ursinus Coll., Pa., 1950; M.R.E., Lancaster (Pa.) Theol. Sem., 1953; M.S., Fla. State U., 1967, A.M.L.S., 1976, Ph.D., 1981. Ednl. missionary United Ch. of Christ, Honduras, 1956-65; instr., asst. librarian Fla. State U., Tallahassee, 1966-68; instr., acquisitions librarian Livingston Coll., Salisbury, N.C., 1968-70; asst. prof. library sci. Catawba Coll., Salisbury, 1970-76, assoc. prof., 1976-83, prof., 1983—, library dir., 1970—. Co-author: Divorce in the U.S., Canada and Great Britian (Outstanding Reference Book of 1978 ALA; Choice Book of Yr., Family Relations jour.), 1978; Suicide: A Guide to Reference Sources, 1980; co-editor: (series) Social Problems and Social Issues, 1977-81; contbg. author: Library Effectiveness: State of the Art, 1980. Sec. LWV, Salisbury, 1968-70; nat. treas. Assn. Couples for Marriage Enrichment, 1977-81; v.p. So. chpt. Hist. Soc. Evang. and Ref. Ch., 1971—; pres. Salisbury-Rowan Family Life Council, 1977-79. U.S. Higher Edn. Act fellow, 1975-76. Mem. ALA, Southeastern Library Assn., N.C. Library Assn., Assn. Coll. and Research Libraries, Library Adminstrn. and Mgmt. Assn., Library Research Roundtable, AAUP (state pres. 1983-84), Delta Kappa Gamma, Beta Phi Mu. Democrat. Mem. United Ch. of Christ. Home: Route 9 Box 112 Salisbury NC 28144 Office: 2300 W Innes St Salisbury NC 28144

SELLERS, DEBORAH ANN CALLAWAY, nurse, educator; b. Oceanside, Calif., Mar. 12, 1956; d. Harold Cecil and Donna June (Mears) Callaway; m. Jeffery Douglas Sellers, Aug. 7, 1976. B.S. in Nursing, U. Kans., Lawrence, 1978; M.N. in Nursing, 1984. Charge nurse U. Kans. Med. Ctr., Kansas City, 1978; occupational health nurse Bendix Corp., Kansas City, Mo., 1979, Hallmark Cards Co., 1979, Bus. Industry Group, 1980; pvt. duty nurse, 1980-82; asst. dir. health services SLH Mgmt. Systems, Kansas City, Mo., 1983-84; instr. Research Coll. Nursing, Kansas City, Mo., 1984—; disaster nurse ARC, Kansas City, Mo., 1982—; site coordinator Greater Kansas City Health Fair, 1981. Co-author health care handbook. Co-chmn., Mental Health Assn. Johnson County, Overland Park, Kans., 1983; block capt. Neighborhood Watch Group, Mission, Kans., 1983. Mem. U. Kans. Nurses Alumni Assn., Greater Kansas City Assn. Occupational Health Nurses (sec. 1980-82, v.p. 1982-83), Kans. State Nurses Assn. (dist. 2 nominating com. 1983-84), Assn. Grad. Students Nursing (sec.-treas. 1981-82), LWV, U. Kans. Alumni Assn. Club: Med. Mates of U. Kans. (2d v.p. 1983-84, class rep. 1984-85) (Kansas City). Home: 9158 Somerset Overland Park KS 66207

SELLERS, JO ANN, human resources executive; b. Covington, Ky., Nov. 11, 1939; d. Walter Louis and Elsie May (Watkins) Schneider; m. Harry L. Sellers, May 29, 1986; 1 son, Terence Allen. Student Xavier U., 1969-70; student U. Cin., 1972-78, U. Mich., 1980, Am. Inst. Banking, 1969-75. Exec. sec. F.W. Dodge Corp., Cin., 1957-59, C.C. Bankemper & Assocs., Architects, Covington, Ky., 1960-67, No. Ky. Area Planning, Newport, 1967-69; with Fed. Res. Bank, Cin., 1969—, personnel asst., 1974-76, personnel coordinator, 1976-78, human resources mgr., 1978—. Cons. Community Chest, Cin., 1982-84; mem. policy com. Cin. Community Chest, 1983-84. Mem. Cin. Assn. Fin. Employers, Cin. Personnel Assn. (dir. 1983-85), Am. Inst. Banking, Am. Soc. Personnel Adminstrn., Employment Mgrs. Assn. Home: 5300 Hamilton Ave Apt 1106 Cincinnati OH 45224 Office: Fed Reserve Bank 150 E 4th St Cincinnati OH 45201

SELLERS, MARIE LYNN, management development company executive; b. Lake Charles, La., Dec. 19, 1948; d. Lawrence G. and Louise A. (Hanks) McLaren; m. M. Gerard Sellers, Dec. 27, 1967 (div. May 1972). B.A., McNeese State U., 1970, M.Ed., 1972; postgrad. Baylor Coll. Medicine, 1974-75. Assoc. sch. psychologist Harris County Dept. Edn., Houston, 1972-77; coordinator psychol. services LaPorte Schs. (Tex.), 1977-78; corp. dir. tng. Temporaries, Inc., Washington, 1978-82; cons. Successful Woman, Inc., Washington, 1979-82; pres. Transitions Unlimited, Houston, 1982—; lectr. in field. Contbr. articles on personnel tng. to profl. jours. Mem. com. Republican Gubernatorial campaign, Houston, 1982, Rep. Congl. campaign, Houston, 1983-84. Mem. Am. Soc. for Tng. and Devel. (nat. exec. com. 1984, v.p. Houston chpt. 1983), Nat. Assn. Temp. Services. Club: Hamilton Bus. (Houston). Home: 7555 Katy Freeway Apt 139 Houston TX 77024 Office: Transitions Unlimited Inc 2211 Norfolk Suite 700 Houston TX 77098

SELLERS, REGINA TERESA, educator; b. Pitts., Oct. 15, 1934; d. Herman Anthony and Gertrude Anne (Engel) Schwartz; A.A., San Antonio Jr. Coll., 1970; B.A., Incarnate Word Coll., 1973; postgrad. Our Lady of the Lake U., 1976, U. Sci. and Philosophy, 1976; children—John, Larry, Jerry, Joni, Jesse. Staff, Alcoholic Rehab. Center, San Antonio, 1972-73, San Antonio Children's Center, 1978; tchr. adutl edn. San Antonio Jr. Coll., 1976—; cons. to nursing homes, San Antonio, 1976—; pvt. practice clin. social work and hypnosis, San Antonio, 1976—. Served with USN, 1953-54. Recipient Better Life award in Edn., Tex. Nursing Home Assn., 1976; Public Welfare Dept. grantee, 1974-76. Mem. Acad. Cert. Social Workers, Nat. Assn. Social Workers, Tex. Psychotherapy Assn. Contbr. articles to profl. jours. Address: 427 Byrnes Dr San Antonio TX 78209

SELLMAN, DONNA DUVALL, educational administrator; b. Balt., Jan. 13, 1925; d. George Wilmer and Marion Mercedes (Brown) DuVall; m. Russell Armstrong Sellman, June 15, 1948; children—Maura Mercedes Sellman Sheridan, R. Thomas. B.A., Western Md. Coll., 1945; M.A., Columbia U., 1950. Cert. tchr., prin., Md. Tchr. Carroll County Bd. Edn., Westminster, Md., 1945-69, asst. prin., 1969-80; dir. alumni affairs Western Md. Coll., Westminster, 1980—; dir. Union Nat. Bank, Westminster. Mem. Council Advancement and Support Edn., Nat. Retired Tchrs. Am., Carroll County Retired Tchrs. Assn. (pres. 1985-87), AAUW (pres. Carroll County br. 1954-55), Phi Delta Kappa (pres. Towson State U. chpt. 1979-80), Phi Delta Gamma (pres. Psi chpt. 1978-80). Republican. Avocations: social dancing, travel, theater. Home: 59 Ridge Rd Westminster MD 21157 Office: Western Md Coll College Hill Westminster MD 21157

SELLS, JOSEPHINE COMPTON, moving and storage company executive; b. Iredell County, N.C., Nov. 13, 1926; d. Thomas Blaine and Neva Mozelle (Lippard) Compton; m. Haskell Lee Sells, July 27, 1944; children—Haskell Lee, William Conrad, Edith Andrewetta. Student, Dale Carnegie Inst., 1969, 73, Catawba Valley Tech. Inst., 1964, Mitchell Community Coll., 1973, 79, Midwestern Bapt. Coll., 1971, Bekins U. Sales and Mgmt., 1984. Telephone operator So. Bell, Statesville and Fayetteville, N.C., 1943-44; office supr. J.C. Penney Warehouse, Statesville, 1946-64; treas. Sells Service, Inc., Statesville, 1965-83, AAA Mini Warehouses, Statesville, 1979-83; pres. Sells Service, 1983—, AAA Mini Warehouse, 1983—. Mem. Am. Bus. Women's Assn. (pres. Lliederi chpt. 1984—), N.C. Movers Assn., Am. Movers Assn., Toastmasters Internat. Democrat. Baptist. Club: Catawba Valley Rock and Gem (Hickory, N.C.). Avocation: rock and gem collecting. Office: Sells Service Inc 2313 W Front St Statesville NC 28677

SELLS, JOYCE GREEN, nurse; b. Pensacola, Fla., Jan. 7, 1946; d. Elbert Paul Green, Jr. and Ellen (Chandler) Green Shryock; m. James Jerry Smothers, Aug. 12, 1961 (div. 1972); children—Sherry, Leigh, Kimberly, James; m. 2d Haskell Lee Sells II, Feb. 7, 1976. Intermittent student Jefferson State Jr. Coll., 1965-73, N.C. State U., 1978—; A.S. in Nursing, Wake Tech. Jr. Coll., 1979-81; cert. respiratory therapy U. Ala., 1974. R.N., N.C. Respiratory therapy technician South Highlands Hosp., Birmingham, Ala., 1974-76, Rex Hosp., Raleigh, N.C., 1976-79; nurse, respiratory therapy technician Wake Med. Ctr., Raleigh, 1980-82, Duke U. Med. Ctr. Hosp., Durham, N.C., 1982—. Active Raleigh chpt. NOW, 1976—, chairperson membership, 1978-79. Served with U.S. Army N.G., 1974-76. Mem. Am. Assn. Respiratory Therapy, N.C. Assn. Respiratory Therapy. Democrat. Contbr. to Am. Poetry Assn. Anthology, N.Y. Poetry Soc. Anthology.

SELTZER, META ELIZABETH, nursing educator; b. Allendale, N.J., Apr. 23, 1935; d. Harold Disturnell and Meta Elizabeth (Flagge) Brown; m. Morton Seltzer, Sept. 18, 1967 (div. Aug. 1980); 1 son, Randall Morton. R.N., Mountainside Hosp. Sch. Nursing, Upper Montclair, N.J., 1956; B.A. in Nursing, Jersey City State Coll., 1965; M.A. in Edn., Ariz. State U., 1972. Surg. nurse Good Samaritan Hosp., Suffern, N.Y., 1956-65; health edn. instr. No. Highlands Regional High Sch., Allendale, 1965-67; psychiat. nursing instr. Good Samaritan Sch. Nursing, Phoenix, 1968-69; med. surg. nursing instr. Maricopa Tech. Community Coll., Phoenix, 1974-79, dir. div. nursing, 1979—. Mem. State Wide Adv. Council Health Occupations, 1983—; chmn. Nursing Instructional Council Mariciopa County, 1982-83. Author: Basic Drug Calculations, 1979. Mem. Central Ariz. Health Systems Agy., Phoenix, 1980; maj. 403d Combat Support Hosp., Phoenix, 1978. Recipient Black and Gold award Maricopa Tech. Community Coll., 1983. Mem. Am. Assn. Women in Community and Jr. Colls., Council Nursing Edn. and Nursing Service, Ariz. Authors Assn., Res. Officer Assn., AAUW (chmn. global affairs 1973-74). Republican. Methodist. Home: 3506 N 25th Pl Phoenix AZ 85016 Office: Maricopa Tech Community Coll 108 N 40th St Phoenix AZ 85034

SELTZER, PHYLLIS ESTELLE, artist, designer; b. Detroit, May 17, 1928; d. Max and Lillian (Weiss) Finkelstein; m. Gerard Seltzer, May 30, 1953; children—Kim, Hiram. B.F.A., U. Iowa, 1952; postgrad. U. Mich., 1954-55, Case Western Res. U., 1966-70. Program coordinator Cleve. Coll. Case Western Res. U., 1969-71, Lake Erie Coll., Painesville, Ohio, 1970-72; art interior designer Dalton, Van Dijk and Johnson, Cleve., 1973-74; free lance designer, Cleve., 1975—. One woman shows: Vixseboxse Art Galleries, Cleve., 1983, Old Detroit Gallery, Cleve., 1985; group shows include: Hunterton Art Ctr., Clinton, N.J., 1978, Georgetown Coll., 1979, Mitchell Mus., Mount Vernon, Ill., 1979, Trumbull Art Guild, Warren, Ohio, 1980, Tri-C Coll., Cleve., 1981, Nationwide Gallery, Columbus, Ohio, 1983, Mansfield Art Ctr., 1984, Art Acad. Cin., 1984, Sandusky Figuarative Exhbn., Ohio, 1985, AAA, N.Y.C., 1986; represented in permanent collections: Ctr. for Contemporary Art, Cleve., Denis Conley Gallery, Akron, Rapp Gallery, Louisville, others. Vice pres. New Orgn. Visual Arts, Cleve. Recipient award Phila. Print Show; award Dayton Art Mus., 1952; Purchase award Cleve. Mus. Art, 1954, award Canton Art Inst., 1979, award Printworld, 1983, 84, 85-86, 87. Mem. Cleve. Print Club (pres. 1982-84). Home: 11225 Harborview Dr Cleveland OH 44102 Office: 1400 W 10th St Cleveland OH 44113

SELTZER, RONNI LEE, physician; b. N.Y.C., Apr. 24, 1952; d. Herbert M. and Marian Elaine (Willinger) S.; B.A., Syracuse U., 1973; M.D., Chgo. Med. Sch., 1977; m. Gary Broder, Jan. 20, 1980. Resident in psychiatry NYU Med. Center, Bellevue Hosp., 1977-81; pvt. practice medicine specializing in psychiatry, Englewood, N.J., 1981—; mem. med. staff Englewood Hosp., 1981—, Holy Name Hosp., 1984—; teaching asst. in psychiatry N.Y.U. Med. Center, 1980—. Mem. Am. Psychiat. Assn., N.J. Psychiat. Assn., Eastern Psychiat. Research Assn., AMA, Bergen County Med. Soc., Am. Med. Women's Assn., North Jersey Psychiat. Assn. (rec. sec. 1986-86, corr. sec. 1986-87), Chgo. Med. Sch. Alumni Assn. Contbg. editor: Ophthalmology Mgmt.; contbr. articles to profl. jours. Home: 200 Old Palisade Rd Fort Lee NJ 07024 Office: 200 Engle St Englewood NJ 07631

SELTZER, VICKI LYNN, physician; b. N.Y.C., June 2, 1949; d. Herbert Melvin and Marian Elaine (Willinger) S.; m. Richard Stephen Brach, Sept. 2, 1973; children—Jessica Lillian, Eric Robert. B.S., Rensselaer Poly. Inst., 1969; M.D., N.Y. U., 1973. Diplomate Am. Bd. Ob-Gyn, Intern, Bellevue Hosp., N.Y.C., 1973-74, resident in Ob-Gyn, 1974-77; fellow gynecol. cancer Am. Cancer Soc., N.Y.C., 1977-78, Meml. Sloan Kettering Cancer Center, N.Y.C., 1978-79; assoc. dir. gynecol. cancer Albert Einstein Coll. Medicine, N.Y.C., 1979-83; assoc. prof. Ob-Gyn, SUNY-Stony Brook, N.Y.C., 1983—; dir. Ob-Gyn, Queens Hosp. Center, Jamaica, N.Y., 1983—, pres. med. bd., 1986—. Editorial bd. Women's Life Mag., 1980-82; contbr. articles to profl. jours. Chmn. health com. Nat. Council Women, N.Y.C., 1979—; mem. Mayor Beame's Task Force on Rape, N.Y.C., 1974-76; mem. obstetric adv. com. Commr. of Health. Galloway Fund fellow 1975; recipient citation Am. Med. Women's Assn., 1973, Nat. Safety Council, 1978. Fellow N.Y. Obstet. Soc., Am. Coll. Ob-Gyn (gynecol. practice com. 1981); mem. Women's Med. Assn. (v.p. N.Y. 1974-79), Am. Med. Women's Assn. (com. chmn. 1975-77, 78-79, editorial bd. jour. 1985—), N.Y. Cancer Soc., N.Y. U. Med. Alumni Assn. (bd. govs. 1979—), Alpha Omega Alpha. Office: OB Gyn Queens Hosp Center 82-68 164th St Jamaica NY 11432

SELVAGGI, SUZANNE MARIE, pathologist; b. L.I.; d. Gerald Anthony and Gilda Mary (Ferraro) Selvaggi; m. Robert Bruce Washabaugh, June 10, 1978; 1 child, Sarah Jane. B.A. in Biology, Case Western Res. U., 1974; M.D., Albert Einstein Med. Coll., 1978. Diplomate Am. Bd. Pathology. Resident in pathology, teaching asst. NYU Med. Ctr., N.Y.C., 1978-83; asst. prof. pathology N.Y. Hosp.-Cornell U., N.Y.C., 1983—, mem. bd. medicine's record and accreditation com., 1983—. Editor Surg. Path. Quar. Index, 1981-83; contbr. articles to profl. jours. NYU fellow, 1980-82. Fellow Am. Soc. Clin. Pathologists; mem. AMA, Phi Beta Kappa. Office: Dept Pathology NY Hosp-Cornell Med Center 525 E 68th St New York NY 10021

SELVEY, WENDY KAY, researcher, crafts business executive; b. Willard, Ohio; d. David Eugene and Betty Jean Spaid; m. Guy Orlin Selvey, June 16, 1979; 1 child, William David. Student Firelands Coll., Huron, Ohio, 1976-78, Casper Coll., Wyo., 1979-80. Gen. office staff Landmark, Inc., Norwalk, Ohio, 1974; clk. Bellevue Music Ctr., Ohio, 1974-75; editor Med. Datamation, Bellevue, 1975, sec., shipping mgr., 1975-79, sec., 1980-81; researcher Health Cons. Assoc., Bellevue, 1981—. Mem. Soc. Prospective Medicine. Republican. Mem. Assembly of God Ch. Avocations: reading; square dancing; crafts. Home: 4910 C R 177 PO Box 53 Clyde OH 43410 Office: Health Cons Assocs 5433 Strong's Ridge Rd Bellevue OH 44811

SELZ, HARRIET MARION, plastics co. exec.; b. N.Y.C., Jan. 23, 1939; d. Phillip Charles and Muriel (Greenbaum) Gold; student Oneonta State Coll., 1956-58, Bloomfield Coll., 1975-78; m. Jay Selz, Oct. 20, 1957; children—Philip Charles, Bart Michael, Mark Lawrence, Pamela Carol. With Titan Plastics, Inc., East Rutherford, N.J., 1968—, prodn. mgr., 1974-75, purchasing mgr., 1975-79, asst. gen. mgr., 1979—, v.p., 1981—. Mem. legis. com. Montville (N.J.) Bd. Edn. Mem. Soc. Plastics Engrs. (voting rep. to blow molding div. of Soc. of Plastics Industry), Hadassah, Women's Am. Orgn. for Rehab. and Tng. Home: 142 Change Bridge Rd Montville NJ 07045 Office: 433 Murray Hill Pkwy East Rutherford NJ 07073

SEM, KAREN ELIZABETH, structural engineer; b. Bklyn., May 12, 1958; d. Jon Spoerk and Catherine (McGroarty) S. B.A., Fordham U., 1980; M.S., Fairleigh Dickinson U., 1983. Engring. aid Foster Wheeler Energy Co., Livingston, N.J., 1980-82; asst. structural engr. Nuclear Power Services, Secaucus, N.J., 1982-83; structural engr. LTV Aerospace & Def., Grand Prairie, Tex., 1983—. Democrat. Roman Catholic. Avocations: figure skating; horseback riding; sailing; volleyball. Home: 6601 Blackberry Dr Arlington TX 76016 Office: LTV Aerospace and Def 1701 W Marshall Dr Grand Prairie TX 75051

SEMON, DOROTHY GRACE PATTERSON, oil company executive; b. Shreveport, La., June 4, 1942; d. Harold Allen and Grace Winifred (Malven) Patterson; m. Phillip Ray Semon, July 18, 1964; 1 son, Ronald Scott. B.S., La. Tech. U., 1964. Sec. personnel Tex. Eastern Transp., Shreveport, La., 1964-66, sec. chief engr., 1970-71; sec. to dean Sch. Bus., La. Tech. U., Ruston, La., 1966-70; adminstrv. exec. R. Clyde Hargrove & J. Pat Beaird, Shreveport, La., 1973—; sec./treas., dir. Beaird Oil Corp., South Ridge Devel. Co., Inc., LMA Land Co., Inc., 1973—. Sec. ofcl. bd. Kings Hwy. Christian Ch., Shreveport, La., 1981—; mem. Am. Mother's Com., Shreveport, 1977—, Shreveport Symphony Women's Guild, 1975—; worker Shreveport Symphony ann. fund drive, 1979—. Mem. Red River Desk and Derrick (reservations chmn. 1983-84, treas. 1985). Democrat. Mem. Disciples of Christ Ch. Home: 6047 Fox Chase Trail Shreveport LA 71129 Office: R Clyde Hargrove & J Pat Beaird 1123 Commercial Nat Bank Bldg Shreveport LA 71101

SEMPLE, JANE FRANCES, paint manufacturing official; b. Lakewood, Ohio, Feb. 14, 1951; d. Frank Joseph and Margaret Eleanor (Carpenter) S.; m.

Nick N. Morana, June 24, 1977 (div. Sept. 1981). A.A.B., Cuyahoga Community Coll., Cleve., 1977; B.A., Baldwin-Wallace Coll., Berea, Ohio, 1980; M.B.A., Case Western Res. U., 1984. Adminstrv. asst. DeVilbiss Co., Cleve., 1969-77; br. ops. mgr. Ornyte Fiberglass, Cleve., 1977-79; project dir. Nat. Survey Research Ctr., Cleve., 1979-80; market research mgr. Sherwin-Williams Co., Cleve., 1980—; cons. Resource, Careers, Cleve., 1983. Mem. S.B. Anthony Soc. Womenspace, Cleve., 1980-83. Mem. Am. Mktg. Assn., Nat. Assn. Female Execs., NOW. Democrat. Club: Sherwin-Williams Women's. Home: 6207 Gilbert Rd Parma OH 44129 Office: Sherwin-Williams Co 101 Prospect Ave Cleveland OH 44114

SEMPLE, MARLENE COCKER, journalist; b. Sarasota, Fla., Feb. 10, 1932; d. Oswald McKellar and May (Branch) Cocker; student U. Miami, Fla., 1950-53; B.A., George Washington U., 1958; M.Ed., Loyola U., Chgo., 1983; m. William R. Cotton, Sept. 4, 1954; children—William R., David M., Lynn C.; m. 2d, Dale D. Semple, May 19, 1973. Reporter, Washington Post, 1964-67; editor Croft Ednl. Services, New London, Conn., 1967-69; sr. editor Follett Ednl. Corp., Chgo., 1969-70; ptnr. Other Words Writing and Editing Service, Chgo., 1971-75; editor Sci. Research Assocs., Chgo., 1975-78, test mktg. coordinator, 1979-81, project editor test devel., 1981-82, project adminstr., 1982-83; planner info. devel. IBM, 1983—. Mem. Soc. Tech. Communication, Chgo. Women in Pub. (pres. 1976). Author: Introductory Guide to Midwest Antiques, 1976. Office: IBM PO Box 1328 Boca Raton FL 33432

SEMPLE, MARY ANGELA, personnel executive; b. N.Y.C.; d. Henry Gordon and Mary Agnes (Flanagan) S.; A.B. in French, Coll. New Rochelle, 1961; cert. lang. study Laval U., Que., 1960. Asst. personnel mgr. Sci. Am., N.Y.C., 1965-70; personnel mgr. Psychol. Corp. subs. Harcourt, Brace, Jovanovich, N.Y.C., 1970-74; v.p., dir. of personnel Scribner Book Cos., N.Y.C., 1974-84; v.p. human resources Warren, Gorham & Lamont, Inc., N.Y.C., 1984—; lectr., cons. U. Denver Publ. Inst., 1978—. Republican County com. person for N.Y. County, 1983—. Mem. N.Y. Personnel Mgmt. Assn. (dir. 1982-84), Assn. Am. Publs. (trustee ins. com. 1978—). Club: N.Y. Jr. League. Home: 1365 York Ave New York NY 10021 Office: Warren Gorham & Lamont Inc 1633 Broadway New York NY 10019

SEMPLE, MURIEL V., retired educator, civic worker; b. Bklyn., Aug. 22, 1915; d. Michael James and Jennie Anne (Maguire) Campion; m. Robert L. Semple, Apr. 19, 1944 (dec. 1977); children—Edmund Campion, Susan Jane, Robert Louis, Michael James Semple. B.A., St. Joseph's Coll., Bklyn., 1937; M.D.H., Columbia U., 1939; M.S. in Edn., New Paltz State Coll., N.Y., 1961. Cert. tchr. N.Y., dental hygienist N.Y., cert. tchr. Fla. Dental hygienist Raymond M. Bristol, DDS, N.Y.C., 1939-42; tchr. dental hygiene Elwood Schs., N.Y., 1957; elem. tchr. Huntington, Port Jefferson, Copiague Schs., N.Y., 1957-80; vol. crime watch Citizens Crime Watch, Boca Raton, Fla., 1983-85, Covenant House, Fort Lauderdale, Fla., 1985; vol., resource person in field. Sec., Maidstone Park Springs Civic Assn., East Hampton, N.Y., 1970-72, Boca Towne Centre Owners Assn., 1982-83; mem. St. Joan of Arc Ch., 1984-85. Mem. Columbia U. Sch. Dentistry Alumni Assn., NEA, N.Y. State Tchrs. Assn.; mem. AAUW, S. Huntington PTA (Tchr. of Yr. 1980). Republican. Roman Catholic. Clubs: Royale Woman's (editor newsletter 1985, rec. sec. 1986—) (Boca Raton), Boca Raton Garden.

SEMRAU, JEANNINE ARAGON, librarian; b. Pueblo, Calif., Apr. 7, 1941; d. James and Carmen Caroline (Sibias) Aragon; m. Terry Semrau, Mar. 16, 1962 (div.); children—Milton, Becka, Stanley; m. 2d, Robert Clyde Parmeter, Mar. 1972; stepchildren—Diana, Susan, Tom, David. Student Fresno State U., 1974; B.S. in Sociology, Calif. State U., 1975, M.S. in L.S., 1977. Social worker aide Fresno Social Services (Calif.), 1967-68; library asst. Fresno County Free Library, 1968-74, librarian I, 1977-78, young adult coordinator, 1979-82, prin. librarian community libraries, 1982—, head central children's, 1979-82. Parent adv. bd. bilingual program Jefferson Sch., Fresno, 1977; pres. Fresno Area Library Council, 1986—. Recipient Innovative Teaching award Chancellors Office, Calif., 1976; Mex.-Am. Librarians scholarship Calif. State, 1976; Minority Intern Librarian award Pomona Pub. Library, 1976; Minority Mgmt. Seminar scholarship Calif. State Library, 1982; LSCA grantee, 1985. Mem. Calif. Library Assn., ALA. Democrat. Unitarian. Home: 242 N Yosemite Fresno CA 93701 Office: Fresno County Free Library 2420 Mariposa Ave Fresno CA 93721

SENDER, FLORENCE HARRIET, food marketing company executive; b. N.Y.C., Jan. 25, 1943; d. Egon and Sofie (Reich) Storch; m. Noam Sender, Nov. 16, 1983; children by previous marriage—Elyse Scherz, Josh Scherz, Ben Scherz. B.A., Hunter Coll., 1967. Owner, pres. Nibbles Internat., Inc. (formerly Nibbles, Inc.), Boston, 1974—. Mem. Eastern Dairy Deli Assn., New Eng. Dairy Deli Assn., Calif. Deli Council, Midwest Dairy Deli Assn., Internat. Cheese and Deli Seminar. Office: Nibbles Internat Inc 331 Watertown St Newton MA 02158

SENG, MINNIE ANNA, librarian, editor; b. Muskegon, Mich., Nov. 30, 1909; d. Edward and Ella Barbara (Pattie) Seng; student Muskegon Community Coll., 1927-29; A.B., U. Mich., 1932, A.B. in Library Sci., 1935, M.A. in Library Sci., 1943. Asst. med. librarian U. Iowa, 1935-39; cataloger Bay City Pub. Library (Mich.), 1939-40; order librarian Mich. Technol. U., Houghton, 1940-42; continuations cataloger U. Ark., 1943-44; head cataloger Calif. State U., Fresno, 1944-59; editor Edn. Index, H.W. Wilson Co., Pubs., Bronx, N.Y., 1959-66; head cataloger St. Ambrose Coll., Davenport, Iowa, 1967-72; periodicals librarian Frostburg (Md.) State Coll., 1972-74; ret., 1974. Mem. AAUW, Smithsonian Assos., Am. Hort. Soc. Democrat. Mem. Christian Ch. Home: 110 S Broadway Apt Q Frostburg MD 21532

SENGHOR, SHARON ALVENA WHITE, lawyer; b. N.Y.C., Sept. 28, 1952; d. Erman and Bernice Adela (Garth) W.; m. Keith Calhoun Senghor, June 23, 1984. B.A., Yale U., 1974; M.A., Columbia U., 1975; J.D., 1980. Bar: N.Y. 1981. Program dir. Internat. House, N.Y.C., 1975-77; research coordinator Nat. Inst. Advanced Studies, Washington, 1977; intern N.Y.C. Corp. Counsel, summer 1978; assoc. Steptoe & Johnson, Washington, summer 1979; asst. gen. counsel Smithsonian Instn., Washington, 1980—. Charles Evans Hughes fellow, 1979. Mem. D.C. Bar Assn. (chairperson art law com. 1984-85), N.Y. Bar Assn., ABA (mem. faculty). Democrat. Lutheran. Office: Office of Gen Counsel Smithsonian Instn 100 Jefferson Dr SW Washington DC 20008

SENIOR, SHEILA MATHILDA, nurse; b. Phila., May 28, 1947; d. Robert F. and Georgiana Marie (Stewart) Riskie; children by previous marriage—Harry Brooks, Georgianna Brooks; m. Matthew J. Senior (div. 1979); 1 child, Melissa. A.A.S., Delaware County Community Coll., Media, Pa., 1979. Staff med.-surg. nurse Hahnemann U. Hosp., Phila., 1979, cardiology staff nurse, 1979-82, nurse educator, cardiology, 1982-83, research nurse clinician, clin. cardiac electrophysiology, 1983—, head research nurse sudden death prevention program and clin. cardiac electrophysiology, 1985—; numerous presentations in field; coordinator First Nursing Presentation of the Yugoslav-U.S. Med. Assn., 1982; acting chmn. Third European Symposium on Cardiac Pacing, Torremolinos, Malaga, Spain, 1985; reviewer for jours. Author: (with P. Wilson) Understanding your Heart: Facts, Testing, Treatment, 1985; also articles. Vol. instr. for prison inmate reform Thresholds, 1977; mem. St. Francis Players; mem. choir St. Francis Roman Catholic Ch. Recipient Mayor's Service award, Phila., 1980, Humanitarian award Optimists Internat., 1980, Citizen of Yr. award Am. Legion, 1980. Mem. Am. Assn. Critical Care Nurses. Avocations: skiing; target shooting; dancing. Home: 257 N State Rd Apt 8C Springfield PA 19064 Office: Hahnemann U Broad and Vine Sts Philadelphia PA 19102

SENISI, ANN MCNULTY, nursing educator, community health educator; b. Bklyn., May 10, 1938; d. Michael and Teresa (Carron) McNulty; m. Daniel A. Senisi, July 2, 1960; children—Vincent, Margaret, Carolyn, Daniel, Michael, Kenneth. B.S., St. Josephs Coll., 1978; R.N., Prospect Heights Hosp., 1959; teaching cert. CUNY, 1976; M.A., Adelphi U., 1982. Head nurse Prospect Heights Hosp., Bklyn., 1959-63, Daleview Nursing Home, Farmingdale, N.Y., 1972-73, Lydia Hall Hosp., Freeport, N.Y., 1973-75; tchr. Nassau Tech-BOCES, Westbury, N.Y., 1975—; community health educator Am. Diabetic Assn., Melville, N.Y., 1982—, Multiple Sclerosis Found., Great Neck, N.Y., 1983—; advisor nat. analocal com. Health Occupation Students Am., N.Y., 1982—; curriculum writer Futuring Project Health Occupations, N.Y. State Dept. Edn. Mem. sch. bd. Our Lady of Lourdes Sch., Massapequa Park, N.Y., 1983, mem. adult folk choir. Mem. Am. Vocational Assn., Eta Sigma Gamma. Club: Lady Elks (pres. 1969-70) (Massapequa Park, N.Y.). Home: 226 Cypress St Massapequa Park NY 11762 Office: Nassau Tech-BOCES 1196 Prospect Ave Westbury NY 11596

SENN, DOROTHY JACQUELINE, newspaper editor, writer; b. Ardmore, Okla., Oct. 6, 1931; d. Lonzo L. and Esther J. (Truitt) Sartin; m. Ronald Lee Senn, May 8, 1953; children—Mark Ronald, David Lawrence, Stephen Lyle. B.A. in Journalism, U. Okla., 1953. Editor, Maryville Enterprise (Tenn.), 1954-56; freelance writer Oak Ridge, Tenn., 1956-68, 76—; reporter The Oak Ridger, 1968-71, Intermission editor, 1971-76, columnist, feature writer, fashion editor, 1976—; pub. relations cons; photographer. Contbg. author: An Encyclopedia of East Tennessee, 1981. Active Boy Scouts Am., 1965-74. Recipient Outstanding Service award Oak Ridge Children's Mus., 1983. Mem. Soc. Profl. Journalists, Dixie Council Authors and Journalists; Sigma Delta Chi. Democrat. Baptist (deacon). Lodge: Order Eastern Star. Office: The Oak Ridger 785 Oak Ridge Turnpike Oak Ridge TN 37830

SENN, JULIE JEAN, aerospace company executive; b. Faulkton, S.D., Aug. 15, 1958; d. George Arnold and Marilyn Helene (Boysen) S. B.S. in Engring., Harvey Mudd Coll., 1980; M.B.A., Ariz. State U., 1984. Assoc. engr. Garrett Turbine Engine Co., Phoenix, 1980-83, engr., 1983-84; sr. engr. Teledyne CAE, Toledo, Ohio, 1984-86, mgr. bus. devel., 1986—. Active Big Bros./Sisters Northwestern Ohio, Toledo, 1985-86; advisor Jr. Achievement, Toledo, 1985. Mem. Nat. Assn. Female Execs. Republican. Avocations: reading; weightlifting. Home: 648C W Sterns Rd Temperance MI 48182 Office: Teledyne CAE 1330 Laskey Rd Toledo OH 43612-0971

SENNET, DIANE CAROL, travel agency executive; b. N.Y.C., Mar. 28, 1948; d. Bernard and Marjorie Jean Sennet; B.A., U. Tenn., 1965-69; student Grace Downs Sch., 1969-70. Supr., Trans World Airlines, N.Y.C., 1970-75; owner, pres. Sennet Service Travel, N.Y.C., 1975—. Mem. adv. bd. Pan Am. Airways, 1983—, also TWA. Recipient awards TWA, Am. Airlines, Eastern Airlines. Mem. Internat. Air Traffic Assn., Air Traffic Conf. Am., Internat. Passenger S.S. Assn., N.Y. Assn. Women Bus. Owners, Travelsavers, Inc. Office: 34 W 32d St 5th Floor New York NY 10001

SENSENICH, ILA JEANNE, lawyer, magistrate; b. Pitts., Mar. 6, 1939; d. Louis E. and Evelyn Margaret (Harbourt) S.; B.A., Westminster Coll., 1961; J.D., Dickinson Sch. Law, 1964. Asso. firm Stewart, Belden, Sensenich and Herrington, Greensburg, Pa., 1964-70; asst. public defender Westmoreland (Pa.) County, 1970-71; U.S. magistrate for Western Dist. Pa., Pitts., 1971—; adj. prof. law Duquesne U., 1982—. Mem. Nat. Council U.S. Magistrates (sec. 1979-81, rec. sec. 1981-82), Fed. Bar Assn., Am. Bar Assn., Pa. Bar Assn., Allegheny County Bar Assn., Westmoreland Bar Assn., Nat. Assn. Women Judges. Author: Compendium of the Law of Prisoner's Rights, 1979. Contbr. in field. Office: 1026 US Post Office and Courthouse Pittsburgh PA 15219

SENSOR, MARY DELORES, hospital official, consultant; b. Erie, Pa., July 20, 1930; d. Sergie Pavl Malinowski and Leocadia Mary Francis (Machalinski) Harner; m. Robert Louis Charles Sensor, Apr. 21, 1945; children—Robert Louis Paul, Stephen Maxmillian Augustus, Therese Blaze, Katryn Anne. Student in Pre-Medicine, Gannon U., 1968-72, M.S. in Health Care Adminstrn., 1986; B.S. in Hosp. Adminstrn., Daemon Coll., 1972. Intern in hosp. adminstrn. Harvard U., Boston, 1972; dir. med. records St. Mary Hosp., Langhorne, Pa., 1972-74, Moses Taylor Hosp., Scranton, Pa., 1975-77, Erie County Geriatric Ctr., Fairview, Pa., 1977-82; dir. utilization rev. Millcreek Community Hosp., Erie, Pa., 1983—; bd. dirs. Christian Health Care Ctr., Erie, 1983-84; cons. prof. in-hosp. adminstrn. and med. records U. Pitts. and Temple U., 1972-74. Bd. dirs. St. John Kanty Prep. Sch., Erie, 1970-71, pres. Ladies Aux., 1970-71. Mem. Am. Med. Record Assn., Pa. Med. Record Assn., NW Pa. Med. Record Assn. (sec. treas. 1982-84), Nat. Assn. Quality Assurance Profls., Pa. Assn. Quality Assurance Profls. Roman Catholic. Club: Siebenburger Singing Soc. Avocations: Profl. classical dancing; researcher early man's migration patterns; gourmet cooking; collecting jazz. Home: 3203 Regis Dr Erie PA 16510

SENTER, SYLVIA, psychologist; b. N.J., Mar. 3, 1921; d. Samuel and Gertrude (Raphael) Kapralik; B.A., 1975; M.A., 1976; Ph.D. in Psychology, Goddard Coll., 1978; m. Jonas Senter, Sept. 30, 1941; children—Leigh Senter Saul, Jill. Intern, Temple U., now staff psychologist, lectr. behavior therapy unit, dept. psychiatry Temple U.-Eastern Pa. Psychiat. Inst., Phila.; dir. Behavioral Assocs., Greenwich, Conn.; former staff Bellevue Hosp., Univ. Hosp., NYU Med. Ctr. Author: Women at Work, 1982. Office: 27 Alden Rd Greenwich CT also 910 Fifth Ave New York NY 10021

SENTNER, FRANCES JEAN, utilities company executive; b. Cambridge, Mass., July 4, 1923; d. John Joseph and Mildred Veronica (Corbin) McCarthy; m. George Paul Sentner, July 23, 1949; children—Frank, George Jr., Judy, Kathy, Michael. B.A. in Econs., Rutgers U., 1973, M.A., 1976. Clerical staff Fed. Res. Bank, Boston, 1943-44; sec. to cost acct. ITT, Newark, also Clifton, N.J., 1944-49; customer service dept. Horn/Sales Inc., West Orange, N.J., part time 1960-73; assoc. acct. Public Service Electric and Gas Co., Newark, 1973-78, econ. staff asst., 1978—. Student adviser Jr. Achievement, Montclair, N.J., 1974-84, project bus. rep., 1985—; group leader United Fund Drive 1950-60; den mother Tamarack council Cub Scouts Am., Nutley, N.J., 1957-60. Mem. Tri-Town Bus. and Profl. Women (pres. 1985—), AAUW (life), Women's Polit. Caucus, V.F.W. Aux. (pres. 1981-82). Roman Catholic Club: Cath. Daus. Ams. (regent 1983-85, dist. dept. 1985—). Avocation: choir singing (church and company). Address: 72 San Antonio Ave Nutley NJ 07110 Office: Pub Service Elec and Gas Co 80 Park Plaza (T5A) Newark NJ 07101

SEPA, DEBBIE ANDINO, corporate secretary; b. Vega Baja, P.R., Aug. 8, 1945; d. Enrique and Antonia (Rosario) Andino; m. Luis Alberto Sepa Jr., Aug. 9, 1980; children—Louis Anthony, David James. A.A., John Jay Coll., Criminal Justice, 1979; B.A., Hunter Coll., 1982. Med. sec. Workmens Compensation Bd., N.Y.C., 1964-68; legal sec. Abraham E. Freedman Esq., N.Y.C., 1968-73; Richman and Rivera, Esq., Bronx, N.Y., 1973-75; exec. sec. Steven Jon Levine Esq., White Plains, N.Y., 1975-82; div. sec. NYNEX Corp., White Plains, N.Y., 1983—. Pres. Bilingual Vols. Am. City Coll., N.Y.C., 1980-82; mem. parish council St. Lucy's Ch., Bronx, 1983—, pres. spanish com., 1984—. Home: 635 Arnow Ave Bronx NY 10467

SEPAHPUR, HAYEDEH CHRISTINA, investment banker; b. Lincoln, Nebr., Dec. 8, 1958; d. Bahman and Marylin Lou (Duffy) S. B.S., Lehigh U., 1983. Analyst, Drexel Burnham Lambert Co., N.Y.C., 1982—. Sponsor, Jr. Statesmen of Am. Found., Washington, 1976—; charter mem. Nat. Mus. Women in the Arts, Washington, 1985—. Mem. Am. Film Inst., Am. Mensa Soc., Nat. Trust Hist. Preservation, Gamma Phi Beta. Club: Downtown Athletic (N.Y.C.). Home: Box E-3 444 E 86th St New York NY 10028 Office: Drexel Burnham Lambert Inc 60 Broad St 6th Floor New York NY 10004

SEPPALA, KATHERINE SEAMAN (MRS. LESLIE W. SEPPALA), business executive, clubwoman, b. Detroit, Aug. 22, 1919; d. Willard D. and Elizabeth (Miller) Seaman; B.A., Wayne State U., 1941; m. Leslie W. Seppala, Aug. 15, 1941; children—Sandra Kay, William Leslie. Mgr. women's bldg. and student activities adviser Wayne State U., 1941-43; pres. Harper Sports Shops, Inc., 1947-85, chmn. bd., treas., sec., 1985—; ptnr. Seppala Bldg. Co., 1971—. Mich. service chmn. women grads. Wayne State U., 1962—, 1st v.p., fund bd., active Mich. Assn. Community Health Services, Inc., Girl and Cub Scouts; mem. Citizen's adv. com. on sch. needs Detroit Bd. Edn., 1957—, mem. high sch. study com., 1966—; chmn., mem. loan fund bd. Denby High Sch. Parents Scholarship; bd. dirs., sec. Wayne State U. Fund; precinct del. Rep. Party, 14th dist., 1956—, del. convs.; mem. com. Myasthenia Gravis Support Assn. Recipient Ann. Women's Service award Wayne State U., 1963. Recipient Alumni award Wayne State U., 1971. Mem. Intercollegiate Assn. Women Students (regional rep. 1941-45), Women Wayne State U. Alumni (past pres.), Wayne State U. Alumni Assn. (dir., past v.p.), AAUW (dir. past officer), Council Women as Public Policy Makers (editor High lights) Denby Community Ednl. Orgn. (sec.), Met. Detroit Program Planning Inst. (pres.), Internat. Platform Assn., Detroit Met. Book and Author Soc. (treas.), Mortar Bd. (past pres.), Karyatides (past pres.), Anthony Wayne Soc., Alpha Chi Alpha, Alpha Kappa Delta, Delta Gamma Chi, Kappa Delta (chmn. cpht. alumnae adv. bd.). Baptist. Clubs: Zonta (v.p., dir.); Detroit Boat; Les Cheneaux. Home: 22771 Worthington Saint Clair Shores MI 48081 Office: 17157 Harper Detroit MI 48224

SERGE-QUIGLEY, GLORIA LOUISE, psychology educator; b. Bklyn., July 19, 1924; d. Anthony and Concetta (Sibilla) Serge; m. Walter P. Quigley, Nov. 20, 1954; children—Jean Margaret Quigley-Tully and Elizabeth Ann (twins). R.N., Kings County Hosp., 1946; B.S., St. John's U., N.Y.C., 1952, M.S., 1961, Ph.D., 1972. Biol. and phys. sci. instr. Bklyn. Hosp., 1951-52, Bklyn. State Hosp., 1952-54; assoc. prof. psychology Suffolk County Community Coll., Selden, N.Y., 1972-86, prof., 1986—. Mem. AAUP, Am. Psychol. Assn., Internat. Soc. Psychoneuroendocrinology, St. John's U. Alumni Assn., Disstaff Am. Med. Assn. Home: 136 Monroe Ave Patchogue NY 11772 Office: Suffolk County Community Coll Selden NY 11784

SERMOS, SYBIL FALK, artist; b. Boston, June 8, 1938; d. Edward I. and Etta (Goldman) Falk; m. Kemon A. Sermos, Apr. 4, 1968; children—Evan, Holly. B.F.A., Mass. Coll. Art, 1960. Tchr. Art Inst. Boston, 1962-69; pres. Holly Dolls by Sybil, Somerville, Mass., 1972-82; free-lance artist Harvard U. Med. Sch. News Office, Boston, 1981—, Larkin Publs., Chestnut Hill, Mass., 1981—. Group shows include Art Inst. Boston, 1967, Boston City Hall, 1977, Marlborough House Boston, 1978; works include Family of Dolls quilt (pub. in The National Bicentennial Quilt Exposition, 1976, and The Big Book of Applique, 1978). Mem., past chairperson Somerville Arts Lottery Council, 1980—; mem. Mass. Council on Arts and Humanities, 1984—; mem. Mass. Arts Lottery Council, 1985—. Recipient Richard R. Mitton award Jordan Marsh, 1960; 2d Place Crafts award Am. Mothers Com. Mass., 1976, 78; Best of Show Craft award Marblehead Art Festival, 1977, 1st prize Mixed Media award Winthrop Art Festival, 1978, 80, 82, 84, Spl. award for excellence in watercolor, 1984, 85. Mem. Winthrop Art Assn. (pres. 1981-83). Democrat. Jewish.

SERRALLES, MARJORIE ELAINE, financial analyst; b. Mexico City, Dec. 7, 1958; came to U.S., 1962; d. Juan Eugenio and Marjorie (Fletcher) S. B.S. in Bus. Adminstrn., Georgetown U., 1980. Lic. real estate, Fla.; C.P.A. Staff acct. Price Waterhouse, Miami, 1980-83; exec. asst. Thames Investment & Securities, London, 1983-84; sr. fin. analyst Ryder System, Miami, 1984—. Active Sta. WLRN, Pub. Radio, Miami, 1983, Georgetown U. Scholarship Com., Am. Cancer Soc. Republican. Mem. Georgetown U. Alumni Assn. (interview com.). Roman Catholic. Office: Ryder System Ins Div 8600 NW 36th St Miami FL 33166

SERRES, KATHLEEN ANN, savings and loan executive; b. Waukegan, Ill., Mar. 18, 1949; d. Robert Edwin and June Sylvia (Larson) Gaston; m. David Lee Serres, Oct. 5, 1968 (div. 1982); 1 son, Steven Lee. A.S., Seminole Jr. Coll., 1979. With 1st Fed. Savs. & Loan, Seminole, Okla., 1979—, asst. v.p., treas., 1983-85, asst. v.p., treas.-sec., 1985—. Mem. adv. bd. Seminole Salvation Army. Mem. Okla. Bus. and Profl. Women (pres. Seminole chpt. 1985-86), Nat. Assn. Female Execs., Seminole C. of C. Republican. Methodist. Lodge: Eastern Star. Avocations: sewing, needlepoint, reading. Home: 1824 Concord St Seminole OK 74868 Office: 1st Fed Savs & Loan PO Box 1391 Seminole OK 74868

SERSTOCK, DORIS SHAY, microbiologist, educator; civic worker; b. Mitchell, S.D., June 13, 1926; d. Elmer Howard and Hattie (Christopher) Shay; B.A., Augustana Coll., 1947; postgrad. U. Minn., 1966-67, Duke U., summer 1969, Communicable Disease Center, Atlanta, 1972; m. Ellsworth I. Serstock, Aug. 30, 1952; children—Barbara Anne, Robert Ellsworth, Mark Douglas. Bacteriologist, Civil Service, S.D., Colo., Mo., 1947-52; research bacteriologist U. Minn., 1952-53; clin. bacteriologist Dr. Lufkin's Lab., 1954-55; chief technologist St. Paul Blood Bank of ARC, 1959-65; microbiologist in charge mycology lab. VA Hosp., Mpls., 1968—; instr. Coll. Med. Scis., U. Minn., 1970-79, asst. prof. Coll. Lab. Medicine and Pathology, 1979—. Mem. Richfield Planning Commn., 1965-71, sec., 1968-71. Fellow Augusta Coll.; named to Exec. and Profl. Hall of Fame; recipient Alumni Achievement award Augustana Coll., 1977; Superior Performance award VA Hosp., 1978, 82; Golden Spore award Mycology Observer, 1985. Mem. Am. Soc. Microbiology, N.Y. Acad. Scis., Minn. Planning Assn. Republican. Lutheran. Clubs: Richfield Women's Garden (pres. 1959), Wild Flower Garden (chmn. 1961). Author articles in field. Home: 7201 Portland Ave Richfield MN 55423 Office: VA Hosp Minneapolis MN 55417

SESSLER, JERI DECARLO, technical researcher, corporate researcher, consultant; b. Oak Park, Ill., Oct. 6, 1953; d. Michael A. and Esther (Galucci) DeCarlo; m. Nicholas Eugene Sessler, Dec. 3, 1977; children—Michael Joseph, Nicole Christina. Student Loyola U., 1972-75; B.A. in Anthropology, No. Ill. U., 1976; cert. emergency med. technician, Kishwaukee Coll., 1976. Instr., fellow in anthropology No. Ill. U., 1973-76; emergency med. technician, paramedic Berz Ambulance Service, Chgo., 1976-77; trade fair coordinator Schenkers Internat., Schiller Park, Ill., 1977-79; research assoc. Staub Warmbold Co, Chgo., 1979-81; dir. research A.T. Kearney Inc Chgo., 1981—; adult edn. instr. Moraine Valley Community Coll., Orland Park, Ill., 1982. Mem. Am. Network of Exec. Women (pres. 1980-83), Nat. Assn. Female Execs., Am. Chem. Soc., Orgn. Devel. Network, Am. Soc. Tng. and Devel. Democrat. Roman Catholic. Home: 5167 Winona Ln Gurnee IL 60031 Office: A T Kearney Inc 222 S Riverside Plaza Chicago IL 60606

SESSOMS, JEAN BUTTS, insurance broker, real estate broker; b. Angier, N.C., July 22, 1935; d. John Tillman and Ruby (West) Butts; m. Bobby D. Sessoms, Sr., July 20, 1953; children—Bobby D., John Timothy. Student Campbell U., Buies Creek, N.C., 1953-1954. Cert. ins. counselor. Sec. C. of C., Fayetteville, N.C., 1956-57; mortgage processor Curtis E. Martin, Inc., Fayetteville, 1957-59, Provident Mortgaging Co., Florence, S.C., 1960-62; head spl. multi-peril dept. Woodbury & Co., Wilminton, N.C., 1969-75; v.p., sales mgr. J.S. Braddock Agy., Medford, N.J., 1977—; rep. Nat. Assn. Securities Dealers. Mem. Ramblewood Community Assn., Mt. Laurel, N.J. Mem. Soc. Cert. Ins. Counselors (trustee 1985-86), Profl. Ins. Agts., Ind. Agts. Assn., N.J. Woman Bus. Owners Assn., Medford Bus. Assn. (bd. dirs. 1985, 86), Cherry Hill C. of C. Republican. Methodist. Avocation: bridge. Home: 340 St Clair Ct Mount Laurel NJ 08054 Office: J S Braddock Agy 22 N Main St Medford NJ 08055

SETRELLA, DONNA MARIE, social worker, counselor; b. Waterloo, N.Y., Oct. 7, 1950; d. Louis Robert and Harriett Rose (LeVesque) Setrella; m. Michael Joseph John Burdick, Sept. 5, 1970 (div. Mar. 1973). Student Syracuse U., 1981; A.A., Onondaga Community Coll., Syracuse, N.Y., 1975; B.S. in Social Work, Slippery Rock U. (Pa.), 1979, cert. women's studies, 1979. Recreation specialist Dept. Parks and Recreation, City of Syracuse, summers 1973-79; peer counselor Slippery Rock U., 1977-79; spl. projects coordinator Syracuse Girls Club Inc., 1979-81; social worker Dept. Human Resources, State of Tex., Houston, 1981—. Asst. coach Sagemont Youth Soccer Orgn., Houston, 1983. Episcopalian. Home: 11710 Algonquin St 292 Houston TX 77089 Office: Tex Dept Human Resources 5530 Van Fleet St Houston TX 77033

SETTERINGTON, JERI LYNN, credit life insurance company executive; b. Lansing, Mich., Oct. 9, 1942; d. Melvin Andrew and Frances Marie (Rockette) Underwood; student Ferris State Coll., 1960-61, Mich. State U., 1963-64; children—Stefanie Lynn, Mark Thomas, Peter Charles. With Redmond Motor Div., Owosso, Mich., 1962-63; personnel asst., 1964-65; trainee Mid-Am. Life Assurance Co., Saginaw, Mich., 1974-77, supr., 1977-78, mgr., asst. sec., 1978-79, adminstrv. v.p. 1979-84, v.p., sec., 1984—. Home: 1458 Saxony SE Grand Rapids MI 49508 Office: 2901 Lucerne Dr Grand Rapids MI 49506

SETTLE, MARY LEE, author; b. Charleston, W.Va., July 29, 1918; d. Joseph Edward and Rachel (Tompkins) S.; student Sweet Briar Coll., 1936-38; m. William Littleton Tazewell, Sept. 2, 1978; 1 son, Christopher Weathersbee. Asso. prof. Bard Coll., Annandale-on-Hudson, N.Y., 1965-76; vis. lectr. U. Va., 1978, U. Iowa, 1976. Served with Womens Aux., RAF, 1942-43. Recipient Merrill Found. award, 1974, Nat. Book award, 1978. John Simon Guggenheim fellow, 1958, 60. Democrat. Author: The Love Eaters, 1954; The Kiss of Kin, 1955; O Beulah Land, 1956; Know Nothing, 1960; Fight Night on a Sweet Saturday, 1964; All The Brave Promises, 1966; The Clam Shell, 1971; Prisons, 1973; Blood Tie, 1977; The Scapegoat, 1981; The Killing Ground, 1982; Celebration, 1986. Office: care Farrar Straus and Giroux 19 Union Sq Wtive Mgmt New York NY 10003*

SETTLEMIRE, BEVERLY MAY, nursing home administrator; b. Allen County, Ohio, Jan. 3, 1933; d. Harry Franklin and Margurite (Brothers) Holden; R.N., Lima (Ohio) Meml. Hosp., 1954; B.S. in Nursing Arts, Findlay (Ohio) Coll., 1969; m. Robert Eugene Settlemire, June 11, 1955; children—

Edward Eugene, Larry Franklin. Part-time staff nurse Defiance (Ohio) City Hosp., 1958-64, Blanchard Valley Hosp., Findlay, 1964-69; dir. nurses Manley Manor, Findlay, 1972-75; adminstr. Fox Run Nursing Home, Findlay, 1976; dir. nursing Heritage Manor, Findlay, 1978-79; adminstr. Blakely Care Center, North Baltimore, Ohio, 1979-83; dir. nurses Hilton Nursing Home, Phoenix, 1985; dir. nurses Desert-Valley Rehab. Med. Ctr., 1986—. Pres. Definace and Hancock Counties Soc. Crippled Children and Adults, 1960-82; bd. dirs. Ohio Soc. Crippled Children and Adults, 1978-84. Mem. Phi Beta Lambda, Beta Sigma Phi. Episcopalian. Club: Findlay Country. Home: 5912 E Aire Libre Scottsdale AZ 85254

SETZMAN, EILEEN JUDITH, psychoanalyst; b. Phila., Nov. 26, 1942; d. Bernard and Eleanor (Cohen) S.; B.A., U. Pa., 1964; M.A., Temple U., 1967; Ph.D., NYU, 1973, cert. in psychoanalysis, 1979; m. Gary Wankoff. Lic. psychologist, N.J. NIMH grantee Phila. State Hosp., 1965-66; staff psychologist, therapist, ward adminstr. Bronx (N.Y.) Psychiat. Center, 1967-73; counselor, therapist Bklyn. Coll., 1973-74; pvt. practice individual and group psychotherapy, psychoanalysis and supervision, 1974—; asst. prof. Bklyn. Coll., 1973-74, Bloomfield Coll., 1975-77; adj. prof. Marymount-Manhattan Coll., 1973-75; mem. faculty L.I. Inst. for Mental Health, 1977-79, Met. Inst. for Tng. in Psychoanalytic Psychotherapy, 1979—; mem. faculty postdoctoral program for study and research in psychology (continuing edn.) N.Y.U., 1981—; cons. women's counseling project Barnard Coll., 1980-81; presenter workshops on sex role stereotypes, peer supervision, use of group modalities with coll. students and love to psychol. convs., 1972—. Mem. Am. Psychol. Assn., Psychoanalytic Soc. N.Y.U. Office: 320 W 86th St Apt 6A New York NY 10024

SEUBERT, CHRISTINE OLSON, physicist, consultant, costume designer; b. Seattle, Mar. 25, 1947; d. Clair Fred Olson and Joyce Evonne (Walter) Olson Bailey; m. Timothy Thomas Seubert, Nov. 2, 1968; 1 son, Harold Franklin. B.Sc., U. Houston, 1977; M.S., 1981. Lab. instr., research asst. U. Houston, 1977-78; physicist Exxon Prodn. Research Co., Houston, 1980-84; asst. costume designer, dancer S.W. Jazz Ballet Co., Houston, 1983—; costume designer Osborne Originals, 1984-85; computer cons. C.O.S. Assocs., Houston, 1984—; costume designer Accountrement, 1985—. Supernumerary Houston Grand Opera, 1983-85. NSF research grantee 1976; grantee U. Houston, 1976.Mem. Am. Geophys. Union, IEEE. Home: 2317 Ashland St Houston TX 77008 Office: 408 W 24th St Houston TX 77008

SEVER, SYBIL ELSA-MARIA, public relations executive; b. N.Y.C., Feb. 11, 1951; d. Joseph Paul and Elfriede Elsa-Anna (von Feuerstack) S.; B.A., UCLA, 1974; student Am. Film Inst., 1972. Asst. casting dir. 20th Century Fox Film Corp., Beverly Hills, Calif., 1970-71; asso. dir. public relations Operation Sail 1976, Inc., N.Y.C., 1976; dir. public relations Finnair, N.Y.C., 1977-79; sr. program publicist Showtime Entertainment, N.Y.C., 1980; dir. pub. relations and advt. St. James Enterprises, Inc., N.Y.C., 1981-83; sr. account exec. Ruder, Finn & Rotman, Inc., 1983-84; pub. relations mgr. Elizabeth Arden Co. Inc., 1985—. Chmn. pub. relations com. N.Y. Young Republican Club, 1979-80, editor newsletter, 1979-80; vol. Internat. Primate Protection League. Recipient Disting. Public Service award U.S. Coast Guard; cert. of appreciation Bd. Dirs. Operation Sail, Am. Revolution Bicentennial Adminstrn. Mem. Nat. Acad. TV Arts and Scis. (2 citations). Home: 223 E 50th St 4B New York NY 10022

SEVERY, JANAKI GAYLE (JANICE), special education secondary educator; b. Portland, Oreg., Aug. 17, 1948; d. Malcolm Moore and Ada Clare (McCall) S.; m. Anastassios Ioannis Bountalis, Aug. 16, 1980; children—Eleni Ashling, Alexandra Clare. B.A. in Drama and Edn., U. Wash., 1970, postgrad. in spl. edn., 1973-74; postgrad. in spl. edn. U. Ariz., 1977-79, Ed.M. in Counseling and Guidance, 1985. Cert. tchr., counselor. Supr. detention King County Juvenile Ct., Seattle, 1968-70; educator, program designer Juvenile Parole Services Sch., Seattle, 1970-73; dir., trainer Youth Services Bur. Sch., Seattle, 1974-75; spl. end. tchr. Seattle Pub. Schs., 1975-76, Tucson Pub. Schs., 1975-81, 84—; mgr., coordinator The Tng., Tucson, weekends 1979-80; instr. continuing edn. program U. Ariz., Tucson, 1979-81; wellness cons. various local businesses, Tucson, 1984—; speaker, facilitator Corondelet Health Services, Tucson, 1985—; condr. seminars, workshops Open U., Tucson, 1985—. Author: Women, The Inner Journey, workshop manual, 1985. Cons. Performax Systems Internat., Inc.; assoc. Prepaid Legal Services. Mem. Nat. Speakers Assn. (com. mem. Ariz.), Ariz. Counselors Assn., Nat. Assn. Female Execs., Action Linkage. Avocations: scuba diving; traveling; writing; reading; aerobics. Home: 2701 N Desert Ave Tucson AZ 85712

SEWALL, CHARLOTTE Z., state senator; b. Damariscotta, Maine, Nov. 28, 1947; d. Bernard Tucker and Anna (Bartlett) Zahn; m. Loyall F. Sewall, 1977. Ed. New Eng. Coll., U. Maine. With William L. Buyers, Inc., 1968-75, security ptnr., 1973-75; v.p. Electronic Countermeasures Maine, 1971-75; mem. Maine Ho. of Reps., 1974-80, Maine Senate, 1980—; pres. Keene Narrows Lobster, Inc. Trustee New Eng. Coll., Miles Health Care Found. Republican. Office: Maine Senate State Capitol Augusta ME 04333*

SEWARD, DEBRA VARNESE, college administrator; b. Leesburg, Fla., July 14, 1957; d. Lawrence and Earlene (Bethel) Seward. B.A., N.C. State U., 1979. Sales coordinator Southeastern Sight & Sound, Raleigh, 1979-81; office specialist St. Augustine's Coll., Raleigh, 1981-83; grants tech. asst. N.C. Central U., Durham, N.C., 1983-84; asst. dir. Wake Tech. Coll., Raleigh, 1985—. Mentor, YWCA, Raleigh, 1986—. Recipient award for best overall performance in original works N.C. State U., 1978. Mem. Nat. Assn. Female Execs., N.C. Assn. for Community Educators. Democrat. Baptist. Home: 108H Hunt Club Ln Raleigh NC 27606

SEWARD, KATHRYN ELLEN, county official; b. Flint, Mich., May 2, 1926; d. Benjamin Franklin Sharp and Edna Vigor (Davis) Sharp Smith; m. Orville Herbert Seward, June 28, 1947; children—Duane Orville, Keith Brian, Gayle Rene Seward Gibbs. Student Owosso Bus. Coll., 1943-44, Lansing Community Coll., 1973-77, Mich. State U., 1980, U. Mich. 1981. Clk. planning dept. Redmond Co., Mich., 1943-44, sec. methods dept., 1944-48, with operation and routing dept., 1948-52; assignment clk., clk. of ct. Shiawassee County, Mich., 1966-76, register of deeds, 1976—. Bd dirs. United Way, Owosso (Mich.), 1985—; v.p. Shiawassee County Republicans, 1979-80. Mem. Internat. Assn. Clks., Recorders, Election Ofcls. and Treasurers, Mich. Assn. Registers of Deeds (liaison chmn. chmn. legal forms and fees), United County Officers Assn., Shiawassee County Geneology Assn., Shiawassee County Hist. Soc. Methodist. Lodge: Zonta (sec. 1982-83) Avocation: genealogy and history of the county. Home: 4601 Simpson Rd Owosso MI 48867 Office: Shiawassee County Register of Deeds 208 N Shiawassee St Corunna MI 48817

SEWELL, BARBARA MOORE, delivery service company executive; b. Memphis, Oct. 9, 1932; d. Floyd Chester and Annie Laura (Curtis) Moore; m. George Norbin Johnson, Feb. 17, 1951 (div. May 1972); children—George Randall, Anthony Floyd, Jerald Curtis; m. John Edward Sewell, May 23, 1980; children—Kelly Dee, Edward Lee. Student Shelby State Community Coll., 1975. Acctg. asst. Ford Motor Co., Memphis, 1950-62; office asst., bookkeeper to Drs. Bringle and Young, Memphis, 1966-72; sec. acctg./personnel depts. Plough, Inc., Memphis, 1972-75; sec. personnel dept. Fed. Express Corp., Memphis, 1976-78, personnel asst., 1978-79, supr. personnel, 1979-82, personnel coordinator, recruiter, 1982—. Contbr. articles to profl. jours. Active Memphis Vol. Placement Program. Recipient numerous certs. of achievement Fed. Express Corp., 1978—. Mem. Am. Soc. Personnel Adminstrn. Home: 6583 Poplar Ave Germantown TN 38138 Office: Federal Express Corp 4009 Airways Module N Memphis TN 38194

SEWELL, ELIZABETH PERRY, investor, real estate broker; b. Odessa, Tex., Jan. 4, 1957; d. Charles Robert and Nancy Joanna (White) Perry; m. Richard William Sewell, Aug. 6, 1977; 1 child, Lauren Diane. B.B.A., Tex. A&M U., 1979, M.B.A., 1980. Teaching asst. fin. dept. Tex. A&M U., College Station, 1979-80; gas contract analyst United Tex. Transmission, subs. United Energy Resources, Houston, 1980-82; sr. fin. analyst United Energy Resources, Houston, 1982-84; chmn. bd. Ventura Realty, Inc., Houston, 1984—. Mem. Nat. Assn. Female Execs. Presbyterian. Avocations: snow skiing; car racing. Office: Ventura Realty Inc 10375 Richmond Ave Suite 1385 Houston TX 77042

SEWELL, MARSHA JUDITH, interior designer, product designer; b. Cleve., June 16, 1945. Student Kent State U., 1963-65; B.F.A., Royale Academiedes Beaux Arts, Brussels, 1966; postgrad. Cleve. State U., 1966-67. Cert. Nat. Council for Interior Design Qualification. Residential designer Teetzel Co., Grosse Pointe, Mich., 1971-74, various design firms, San Diego, 1974-77; owner Marsha Sewell and Assocs., San Diego, 1977—; pres. AEMESCO, Inc., San Diego, 1977—. Comml. renovations include: San Diego Civic Theatre (AIA/Am. Soc. Interior Designers Orchid award of Excellence 1980), Temple Emanu-El, San Diego, La Jolla Village Inn and Terrarium Restaurant, Sea Coast Inn, San Diego, Signatures de Paris retail store, La Jolla, Glorietta Bay Inn, Coronado, Calif., McBride Agy., La Jolla; new constrn. projects include condominiums, real estate and med. offices, furniture showroom. Contbr. numerous articles to design, interior decorating and gen. interest mags. Recipient Merit award for Forecast 80's, AIA, 1982; Design for Better Living award for Forecast 80's, Am. Wood Council, 1982; Appreciation award Youth Employment Program San Diego City Schs., 1980; named one of 85 San Diegans to Watch in '85, San Diego Mag. Mem. Am. Soc. Interior Designers (Presdl. citation for disting. service 1980, 81, bd. dirs. San Diego 1979-81, active various coms.), San Diego Hist. Soc. (designer for Showcase Ho. 1979-84). Address: 4250 A Morena Blvd San Diego CA 92117

SEWELL, PHYLLIS SHAPIRO (MRS. MARTIN A. SEWELL), corp. exec.; b., 1930; B.A. with honors, Wellesley Coll., 1952; 1 son, Charles Steven. With Federated Dept. Stores, Inc., Cin., 1952—, asst. research dir., 1958-61, research dir. store ops., 1961-65, sr. research dir., 1965-70, operating v.p. research, 1970-75, corp. v.p., 1975-79, sr. v.p. research and planning, 1979—; dir., mem. audit, exec. compensation coms. Lee Enterprises, Inc., Davenport, Iowa, 1977—; dir., mem. nominating and audit coms. Huffy Corp., Dayton, Ohio, 1981—. Bd. dirs., past pres. and treas. Cin. chpt. Nat. Cystic Fibrosis Found., 1963—; mem. cabinet, chmn. maj. firms div. Cin. United Appeal, 1982; mem. bus. adv. council Sch. Bus. Adminstrn., Miami U. of Ohio, 1982—; bd. dirs. Community Chest, 1984—, Jewish Vocat. Service, 1984. Recipient Outstanding Alumnae award Wellesley Coll., 1979; Disting. Cin. Bus. and Profl. Woman award, 1981; YWCA Career Woman of Achievement award, 1983; inducted into Ohio Women's Hall of Fame, 1982. Office: Federated Dept Stores Inc 7 W 7th St Cincinnati OH 45202

SEWELL, POLLY MCGINNIS, marketing executive; b. El Dorado, Kans., Mar. 5, 1935; d. Walter Fletcher and Wannah Alice (Mosier) McGinnis; m. Philip M. Sewell, Aug. 4, 1956 (div. 1986); children—Jeffrey Philip, Jennifer Sewell Fountain. Student U. Kans., 1953-56; B.A., Washburn U., 1957. Office mgr. James D. Watters, Dallas, 1975-79; mktg. rep. Ticor Title Ins., Dallas, 1979-82, mktg. mgr., 1983—, now v.p., sr. mktg. mgr. Bd. dirs. Jr. League, Topeka and Dallas, 1962—; bd. dirs. Salvation Army, 1967-70; sec., treas. Topeka Arts Council, 1966-70; precinct committeewoman Republican Party, Topeka, 1967-70; com. chmn. Guild, Wadley Inst., Dallas, 1976—. Mem. Women's Council Realtors (mem. coms. 1979—), Nat. Assn. Corp. Real Estate Execs. (mem. steering com. regional meeting 1983, sec.-treas. 1984-86), Nat. Assn. Indsl. and Office Parks, The Exec. Women's Forum (bd. dirs. 1983—), Chi Omega Alumni. Republican, Episcopalian. Home: 7810 Glen Albens Dallas TX 75225 Office: Ticor Title Ins 350 N St Paul Suite 2500 Dallas TX 75201

SEWTER, DOROTHEA LORETTA, recreation leader; b. Phila., Oct. 16, 1937; d. Thomas John and Dorothea Loretta (Houck) S.; m. William Swain Collier, Jr., June 30, 1956 (div. Mar. 1985); children—Mary, Dolores, William III, Thomas, John, Dorothea C. (dec.). A.A., Camden County Coll., 1976. Family therapist Family Counseling, Camden, N.J., 1977-78; recreation leader Sr. Citizens Day Ctr., Blackwood, N.J., 1980—. Editor Companion, 1981-85. Club: Elizabeth Haddon NOW, (Haddonfield, N.J.) (sec. 1984-85).

SEXAUER, ARWIN F.B. GARELLICK, librarian, poet, editor; b. Richford, Vt., Aug. 18, 1921; hon. diploma in arts and letters, Athens, Greece, 1979; D.Litt. (hon.), World U., World Acad. Arts and Letters, 1982; hon. diploma arts and letters Accademia Internazionale, Italy, 1982; m. Charles D. Bashaw, 1942 (dec.); children—Dawn Bashaw Mennucci, Alson C. Bashaw; m. 2d, Jack L. Garellick, 1963 (dec.); m. 3d, Howard T. Sexauer, 1979 (dec.). Asst. librarian Kellogg-Hubbard Library, Montpelier, Vt., 1966-73, head librarian, 1974-76; editor Vt. Odd Fellow mag., 1959-70; author: (book of poetry) Remembered Winds, 1963; poems in numerous anthologies; lyricist, monologist. Co-founder Music Mission Inc., 1963; past pres. United Meth. Ch. Women, Franklin County Pomona Grange, PTA; past v.p. Vt. 4-H Council; youth leader 4-H. Recipient numerous awards, including George Washington Honor medals, 1957, 59, 73, ASCAP Popular Panel awards (13), 1967-78, 82, citation, 1982; Richard Rodgers Music Found. award, Grand Ole Opry Trust Fund award, Dr. Arthur Hewitt Meml. award religious poetry, Virgilio-Mantegna medal, 1982; 2 spl. merit citations for poetry, 1982; spl. citation for poetry Internat. Congress Poets, 1982, numerous others. Fellow Internat. Acad. Poets (life), Anglo-Am. Acad. (hon.); mem. Accademia Leonardo da Vinci (diploma di benemerenza, diploma of honor The Glory, poet award, hon. rep.), World Poetry Soc. Intercontinental (disting. service citation, Vt. state rep.), Hellenic Writer's Club (life), Dr. Stella Woodall Poetry Soc. Internat., Calif. Fedn. Chaparral Poets, Poetry Soc. Vt., Gospel Music Assn., ASCAP, Vt. Library Assn., Internat. Press Assn., numerous others. Club: Rebekah (past noble grand). Poems, songs, other artifacts at Gleeson Library, U. San Francisco. Address: Idle Tide Cottage Box 303 Sanibel FL 33957

SEXTON, PATRICIA JOANNE, sporting goods mfg. co. exec.; b. Turlock, Calif., Aug. 24, 1943; d. Kennith Paul and Velma Faye (Rash) Herring; student Modesto Jr. Coll., 1962-68; children—Scott, Jill. Office mgr. various cos., 1971-75; mgr. retail fishing tackle store and saltwater fishing lure mfg., San Diego, 1982—. Mem. Dental Assts. Orgn., Women in Constrn. Republican. Office: PO Box 4875 San Diego CA 92104-0875

SEYBOLD, ADELE NEELY, former Democratic nat. committeewoman, civic worker; b. Comanche, Tex., Nov. 11, 1919; d. Eugene Gentry and Nell (Orand) Neely; B.A., U. Tex., 1940; tchrs. certificate U. Tex., 1940; m. Eugene Murphy Locke, Oct. 27, 1941; children—Aimee Locke Jacoble, John, Tom; m. 2d, William Dempsey Seybold, 1977. State chmn. women's activities Tex. gov.'s primary campaign, 1964; mem. Democratic Nat. Com., 1964-66, exec. com., 1964-66. Mem. hospitality bd. Met. Opera, Dallas, 1962-66, 69-70; mem. exec. com. Greater Dallas Council Chs., 1964-66; area chmn. Dallas Mental Health Assn., 1964; bd. dirs. women's group Dallas Council of World Affairs, 1970—, Bishop Mason Retreat and Conf. Center; hon. chmn. pub. edn. Tex. div. Am. Cancer Soc., also bd. dirs.; bd. dirs., sec. to bd. visitors U. Tex. System Cancer Center, M.D. Anderson Hosp. and Tumor Inst.; mem. found. adv. council Coll. Liberal Arts, U. Tex., Austin; mem. exec. com. chancellor's council U. Tex. Timberlawn Found.; mem. Fine Arts Commn., U.S. Dept. State. Mem. Daus. Republic Tex. (asso.), Ashbel Lit. Soc., Jr. League, Mus. Fine Arts, Young Women of the Arts, Dallas County Heritage Soc. (dir.), Dallas Jr. Assembly (dir. 1961-64). Soc. for Abandoned and Neglected Children, Mortar Bd., Phi Beta Kappa, Alpha Lambda Delta, Sigma Delta Pi, Phi Eta Sigma, Pi Lambda Theta, Pi Beta Phi. Episcopalian (edn. guild leader). Clubs: Dallas Country, Dallas Woman's; River Oaks Country; Houston, Houston City. Home: 3805 McFarlin Blvd Dallas TX 75205

SEYDELL, MILDRED, writer, lectr., traveler; b. Atlanta; d. Vasser and Elizabeth Cobb (Rutherford) Woolley; ed. Washington Sem., Atlanta, The Lucy Cobb Inst., Athens, Ga., and Sorbonne, Paris; m. Paul Bernard Seydel (dec.); children—Paul Vasser, John Rutherford; m. 2d, Max Seydel (dec.). Columnist Charleston (W.Va.) Gazette, 1921; rep. Hearst Crime Commn., in Europe, 1926, collecting data for series of articles and interviews; traveled in Belgium and Ireland, 1927, in Balkan States, Hungary, Turkey and Greece, 1929, Sweden, Germany and France, 1931; contributed Talks with Celebrities; made spl. study of liquor regulation in Sweden; traveled through Africa from Capetown to Cairo and into Palestine, 1934; made spl. study of history of diamonds and gold in S. Africa and native customs of Belgian Congo, investigation of activity of Jews in Palestine; adventure in friendship to South Sea Islands, New Zealand and Australia, 1937; Internat. News Service rep. in Germany and Czechoslovakia, 1938, Finland, 1939; corr. U.S. papers; adventures in Europe, 1955, Eng., Wales, 1956; pres. Mildred Seydell Pub. Co. Belgian dir. World Poetry Day. Mem. Ga. Mothers Com.; v.p. Meml. Day Com. Decorated knight Order Leopold (Belgium); recipient 1st Book of Golden Deeds award Roswell Exchange Club, 1978. Mem. Nat. League Am. Pen Women, Internat. Periodic Press (dir. poetry Belgian sect.), Friends of Emory U. Library (hon.), A.G. Rhodes Home (hon.), Beta Sigma Phi (hon.). Clubs: Peony Garden (hon.); American Women's (Brussels). Author: Secret Fathers, 1930; Then I Saw North Carolina, 1936; Chins Up, 1939; Come Along to Belgium, 1969; Keep the Courage, 1981. Editor: Poetry Profile of Belgium, 1960. Publisher: Silent Singing (poems); Essays Wise and Otherwise. Mem. adv. bd. Sunshine Mag., Fellowship in Prayer mag. Home: 9530 Scott Rd Route 2 Roswell GA 30076

SEYMOUR, ELLEN KATHLEEN, nursing educator; b. East St. Louis, Ill., Sept. 20, 1951; d. Edward Herman and Vivian Geraldine (Eisele) Schmitt; m. Harlan Francis Seymour, Aug. 17, 1973; children—Melissa Ann, Harlan Francis. R.N., DePaul Hosp., 1971; B.S. in Nursing, St. Louis U., 1977; M.S. in Nursing, U. Ill., 1981. Staff nurse Cardinal Glennon Children's Hosp., St. Louis, 1971-72; dist. nurse Vis. Nurse Assn., St. Louis, 1972-73, liaison nurse, 1973-77; liaison nurse Community Nursing Service, Lombard, Ill., 1977-78, spl. projects coordinator, 1980-81; instr. clin. nursing Ga. Baptist Hosp., Atlanta, 1982—. Mem. AAUW, Sigma Theta Tau. Roman Catholic. Home: 1662 Barn Swallow Pl Marietta GA 30062

SEYMOUR, PATTI FOX, trade association executive; b. N.Y.C., Mar. 14, 1953; d. Arthur T. Fox and Helen Fried; student Pratt Inst., 1970-72; B.F.A., Tufts U. and Sch. Mus. Fine Arts, 1974; m. Terry L. Seymour, Dec. 16, 1979; children—Terence Patrick, Ryan Samuel. Personnel dir. Internat. Weekends, Boston, 1974-76, Career Devel. Team, N.Y.C., 1976-78; asst. to pres., corp. adminstrv. mgr. Interglobal, N.Y.C., 1979-83; membership services dir. Direct Mktg. Assn., N.Y.C., 1983—. Contbg. author: Guerilla Tactics, 1978. Office: 6 E 43d St New York NY 10017

SEYMOUR, STEPHANIE KULP, U.S. judge; b. Battle Creek, Mich., Oct. 16, 1940; d. Francis Bruce and Frances Cecelia (Bria) Kulp; B.A. magna cum laude (Ford Found. grantee), Smith Coll., 1962; J.D., Harvard U., 1965; m. R. Thomas Seymour, June 10, 1972; children—Bart, Bria, Sara, Anna. Admitted to Okla. bar, 1965; asso. firms in Boston, Tulsa and Houston, 1965-71; assoc. firm Doerner, Stuart, Saunders, Daniel & Anderson, Tulsa, 1971-79, partner, 1975-79; circuit judge U.S. Ct. Appeals for 10th Circuit, Tulsa, 1979—. Mem. legal adv. panel Tulsa Task Force Battered Women, 1971-77; mem. various task forces Tulsa Human Rights Commn., 1972-76; mem. speakers bur. Oklahomans for ERA. Mem. Am. Bar Assn., Okla. Bar Assn. (assoc. bar examiner 1973-79), Phi Beta Kappa. Office: US Courthouse 333 W 4th St Tulsa OK 74103*

SHABACK, JEAN ANN, management consultant, technical documentation analyst; b. N.Y.C., July 14, 1952; d. Nicholas Shaback. B.S., Coll. Environ. Sci. and Forestry, SUNY-Syracuse, 1974; M.S., Rensselaer Poly. Inst., 1979. Research assoc. Eastman Dental Ctr., Rochester, N.Y., 1974-79; documentation analyst Xerox Corp., Webster, N.Y., 1979-81, sr. documentation analyst, 1981-82, tech. publ. planner, 1982-83; mem. tech. staff AT&T Info. Systems, Middletown, N.J., 1983-85; mgmt. cons. Bell Communications, Piscataway, N.J., 1985—; founder, dir. Princeton Grand Prix Cir. tennis, 1985. League dir. advanced Women's Winter Tennis League, Princeton, N.J., 1985—. Mem. Am. Soc. Tng. and Devel. (newsletter editor Rochester chpt. 1979-83). Avocations: tennis; horseback riding; sailing; travel. Home: 6 Academy Ct Pennington NJ 08534 Office: Bell Communications 6 Corporate Pl Piscataway NJ 08854

SHABAREKH, THERESA EVERS, retail management executive; b. St. Joseph, Tenn., Nov. 18, 1951; d. William Thomas and Cecilia Wilhemina (Halter) Evers; m. Robert Allen Shabarekh, July 3, 1976. Staff acct. Service Mdse. Co. Inc., Nashville, 1973-75, sr. acct., 1975-79, mgr. coop. advt., 1979-81, mgr. mdse. control, 1981-84, dir. mdse. control, 1984—. Mem. Am. Soc. Women Accts. (nat. bd. dirs. 1984-86, chpt. pres. 1980), Nat. Assn. Accts., Nat. Assn. Female Execs. Office: Service Merchandise Co Inc PO Box 24600 Nashville TN 37202

SHABEL, KAREN LIND, printing company executive; b. East Chicago, Ind., Oct. 3, 1948; d. Earl R. Lind; m. Dennis Shabel. A.B., Ind. U., 1970. Tchr. Gen. Edn. Devel. program OEO, 1970-72; dir. consumer div. Better Bus. Bur., Chgo., 1972-77; pres. Communicate, Inc., Westchester, Ill., 1977—; mem. faculty adult continuing edn. dept. Moraine Valley Community Coll., 1974-76; speaker various colls. and univs., civic and community orgns.; arbitrator constrn. panel Am. Arbitration Assn. Past bd. dirs., past sec. to bd. N.Am. Family and Ednl. Resources Found.; past trustee Ill. Council on Econ. Edn.; past bd. dirs. Family Fin. Counseling Service Greater Chgo.; past mem. nursing and health programs com. Mid-West chpt. ARC. Mem. Soc. Consumer Affairs Profls. (founding and charter mem.). Office: Communicate Inc 10407 W Cermak Rd Westchester IL 60153

SHACK, JUDY, data processing trainer; b. N.Y.C., May 6, 1949; d. Arthur and Estelle (Reich) S.; B.A. in Bus. Mgmt. and Econs., Hunter Coll., 1971; cert. in tng. and devel. N.Y.U. Sch. Continuing Edn., 1978. With Standard Security Life Ins. Co. N.Y., N.Y.C., 1971-79, dir. pension adminstrn., 1976-78, dir. pension ops., pension dept., 1978-79; cons. Modular Pension Systems, Metuchen, N.J., 1979-80; edn. coordinator computer/communications dept. Paine, Webber, Jackson, & Curtis, Inc., N.Y.C., 1980-81; edn. cons. computer ops. group Irving Trust Co., N.Y.C., 1981—. Vol., United Cerebral Palsy Telethon, N.Y.C. Mem. Am. Soc. Tng. and Devel. (past N.Y. Met. chpt. treas.), Tri-State Info. Mgmt. Educators. Author articles. Office: Irving Trust 61 Broadway New York NY 10015

SHACKELFORD, CYNTHIA KATE, university news bureau administrator; b. Columbus, Miss., Mar. 21, 1952; d. Manley King Shackelford and Willie Louise (Pearson) Shackelford Franks. B.S. magna cum laude, Miss. U. for Woman, Columbus, 1974. Staff writer Comml. Dispatch, Columbus, 1973-78; staff writer Miss. U. for Women, 1978-80, news editor pub. info., 1980-81, asst. dir. pub. info., 1981-83, dir. news bur., 1983—, tchr. journalism, 1980-81, 82-83, cons. Alumnae News, 1980—. Com. mem. Lowndes United Way, Columbus, 1985. Operation Tomorrow grad. Columbus/Lowndes C. of C., 1983. Recipient commendation cert. Miss. U. for Women, 1985. Mem. Coll. Pub. Relations Assn. Miss. (1st pl. photography award 1984, contest chmn. 1985— named Pub. Relations Practitioner of Yr. 1985), Pub. Relations Assn. Miss. (chpt. v.p. 1983-84, state v.p. 1985—), Mortar Board, Phi Kappa Phi. Democrat. Baptist. Avocations: fishing, gardening, reading. Home: 2702 Puckett Pkwy Columbus MS 39701 Office: Public Relations Miss Univ for Women 5th Floor Simmons Hall Columbus MS 39701

SHACKELFORD, LAUREL, editor; b. New Brunswick, N.J., Nov. 19, 1946; d. James Murdoch and Laura (Stevens) S.; m. Donald R. Anderson, June 18, 1971. Student Rutgers U., 1964, Upsala Coll., 1964-66; A.B., U. N.C., 1968. Writer Civil Rights Digest, Washington, 1968-69; reporter Louisville Times, 1969-73, 76-79, city editor, 1982-86; assoc. editor Courier Jour. and Times, 1986—; editor Appalachian Oral History, Pippa Passes, Ky., 1973-75; asst. city editor Courier Jour., Louisville, 1979-82. Contbr. articles to various publs.; editor: Our Appalachia: An Oral History (Weatherford award 1972), 1971. Nieman fellow Harvard U., 1981. Office: Louisville Times 525 W Broadway Louisville KY 40202

SHACOCHIS, BARBARA ANN, retail store executive; b. Pittston, Pa., Sept. 3, 1953; d. John Paul and Helen Mary (Levenoskie) S.; B.A. with honors, Mich. State U., 1971; M.A., U. San Francisco, 1980. Cert. fin. planner. Legal asst. coordinator McCutchen, Doyle, Brown & Enersen, San Francisco, 1976-79; mgmt. cons. Black, Borgman & Assos., Walnut Creek, Calif., 1979-80; dir. human resources Livingston Bros., Inc., San Francisco, 1980-83; regional personnel mgr. Mervyn's, Hayward, Calif., 1983-84, mgr. employee relations, 1984—; seminar leader Council on Edn. in Mgmt., Walnut Creek, 1979-80; mem. faculty U. Calif.-Berkeley and Santa Cruz, St. Mary's Coll., Moraga, Calif.; cons. to law firms, bus., 1977—. Corporate chmn. United Way. Mem. San Francisco Assn. Legal Assts. (dir. 1976-78), Calif. Alliance Paralegal Assns. (exec. dir. 1978-79), Am. Soc. Personnel Adminstrn. (accredited personnel specialist), Am. Compensation Assn., No. Calif. Indsl. Relations Council, Am. Soc. Tng. and Devel. Republican. Roman Catholic. Clubs: Commonwealth Calif., Golden Gate U. Assos. Home: 465 Centre Ct Alameda CA 94501 Office: 25001 Industrial Blvd Hayward CA 94545

SHADI, DOROTHY CLARKE, literary researcher, retired Spanish educator; b. Los Angeles, July 16, 1908; d. Thomas Tedford and Zilpha Jane (Dever) Clarke; m. Sundar Singh Shadi, Sept. 22, 1934; children—Zilpha Tedforda Shadi Paganelli, Ramona Rhea Shadi Miller, Verna. A.B., UCLA, 1929; M.A., U. Calif.-Berkeley, 1930, Ph.D., 1934. Prof. Spanish, Dominican Coll., San Rafael, Calif., 1935-37; lectr. in Spanish and Portuguese, U. Calif., Berkeley, 1945-48, asst. prof., 1948-55, assoc. prof., 1955-61, prof. Spanish, 1961-76, asst. dean Coll. Letters and Sci., 1963-66, summers 1964-70, prof. emerita, 1976—. Author: (under name of Dorothy Clotelle Clarke) A Chronological Sketch of

Castilian Versification, 1952; Morphology of Fifteenth Century Castilian Verse, 1964. Contbr. articles to profl. jours. Recipient Berkeley Citation U. Calif., 1976. Mem. MLA, Medieval Acad. Am., Modern Humanities Research Assn., Hispanic Inst. U.S., Dante Soc. Am., Hispanic Soc. Am. Home: PO Box 267 Berkeley CA 94701-0267

SHADINGER, JULIANNA MARIE, mental health services company executive; b. Kokomo, Ind., Aug. 2, 1952; d. Bern Milo and Jeanne Rosemary (Thomas) Lundin; m. David Allen Shadinger, July 10, 1977; 1 dau., Mae Marie. B.M.E., Ind. U., 1975, B.A., 1975. Adminstrv. asst., mayor's office City of Bloomington (Ind.), 1975-77; regional relations coordinator Ind. Vocat. Tech. Coll., South Bend, 1977-83; dir. community relations Madison Ctr., South Bend, 1983—; cons., lectr. St. Mary's Coll., also Ind. U.-South Bend. Contbr. articles to local mag. Bd. dirs. Scholarship Found., South Bend, 1979—, Century Ctr., South Bend, 1980—; dist. coordinator, no. region Mental Health Legis. Com. Ind., 1983-84; chmn. edn. policy com. Ind. Legislature, 1982-83; coordinator dist. 3 atty. gen. campaign, State of Ind., 1980; bd. exec. sec. YMCA, South Bend, 1979—; bd. mem. for communications United Way of St. Joseph County, 1981—; chmn. Family and Children's Concert, South Bend Symphony, 1983-84; bd. dirs. St. Joseph Med. Center Aux., Southold Dance Theater; bd. dirs., chmn. long range planning com. Michiana Opera Guild. Named Ind. Young Career Women, Ind. Bus. and Profl. Women, 1980; recipient 1st place communications award Ind. Press Fedn., 1981, 82, 83; ADI award Sales and Advt. Execs. St. Joseph Valley, 1982, 84. Mem. Women in Communications, Sales and Advt. Execs. (pres. 1984-85), South Bend C. of C., Mu Phi Epsilon. Democrat. Mem. Soc. of Friends. Clubs: Jr. League, Altrusa (South Bend). Lodge: Eastern Star. Home: 1703 Hoover Ave South Bend IN 46615

SHADLE, SUSAN BETH, security company executive; b. Pottsville, Pa., July 6, 1957; d. Irvin Elias and Louise Hilman (Reise) S. B.S., Pa. State U.-Middletown, 1979. Security supr. Marriott Hotel, Harrisburg, Pa., 1980-81; officer Paxtang Police Dept., Harrisburg, 1980-81; press attendant AMP Inc., Tower City, Pa., 1981; officer U.S. Secret Service, Washington, 1981-82; ops. supr. MVM Inc, Washington, 1982—, resident mgr. mass dept. pub. safety, 1984—. Mem. Nat. Assn. Female Execs. Republican. Home: 26 Chestnut W Randolph MA 02368 Office: MVM Inc 1731 Connecticut Ave NW Washington DC 20009

SHAFER, HELEN LOUISE, educational administrator; b. Athens, Tex., July 14, 1930; d. Horace Scott and Willouise (Low) Barron; m. Harvey Lee Shafer, Apr. 30, 1949; children—Julie Louise Shafer Kollhoff, Janet Lynn Shafer Boyanton, Edwin Scott. B.A., U. Tex., 1950; M.A., So. Meth. U., 1972; postgrad., N. Tex. State U., 1977-79. Cert. tchr., Tex. Tchr. biology and physics Adamson High Sch., Dallas, 1967-76; sci. instructional specialist, Dallas, 1976-78; adminstrv. planner Sci. Tech. High, Dallas, 1978-80; dean instrn. Bus. Mgmt. Ctr., Dallas, 1980-82; prin. Sci./Engring. Magnet High Sch., Dallas, 1982—; cons. edn. task force C. of C., Dallas, 1978-80; mem. Metroplex Alliance Engring. Edn., Dallas, 1982—, Dallas Alliance Minorities Engring., 1982—; panelist Minorities Engring. Symposium, Austin, Tex., 1984. Author: (with others) Career Oriented Pre-Technical Physics, 1975; Life Science, 1980. Ruling elder Wynnewood Presbyn. Ch., Dallas, 1979-81, 1984—, chmn. Christian edn., 1979-81, chmn. commitment com., 1984—; participant Goals Dallas, 1983-84. Grantee NSF, 1979, 1969-72. Mem. Nat. Sci. Tchrs. Assn., AAAS, Tex. Assn. Secondary Sch. Prins., Nat. Sci. Suprs. Assn., Mensa, Am. Assn. Physics Tchrs., N.Y. Acad. Scis., Am. Assn. Curriculum and Supervision, Dallas Sch. Adminstrs. Assn., Tex. Sci. Suprs. Assn., Phi Delta Kappa. Avocations: gardening; travel. Home: 1536 Bilco St Dallas TX 75232 Office: Sci Engring Magnet Sch 3700 Ross Ave Dallas TX 75204

SHAFER, PAQUITA MIGNON MORTON, journalist; b. Hopewell, Va., Aug. 23, 1918; d. Clarence Littleton Morton and Mignon Reed Osborne Bissell; student U. N.C.; m. Robert G. Shafer, June 27, 1981; children—Paquita Robin, Robert Edward, Deborah Mignon. Free-lance writer, 1950-57; asst. to state editor News and Observer, Raleigh, N.C., 1957-60; living trends editor Chapel Hill Newspaper, Chapel Hill, N.C., 1962-81; columnist, free-lance writer, 1981—lectr.; judge journalism contests; cons. Recipient numerous awards from various orgns., including Asso. Press, N.C. Press Women, Girl Scouts U.S.A., Lawyers of N.C., Jr. Service League, Nat. Newspapers Assn. Mem. N.C. Press Women's Assn. (pres. 1969-70), N.C. Press Assn., Sigma Delta Chi. Club: U. N.C. Woman's.

SHAFER, SHERRY R(AE), marketing and communication research company executive; b. Nebraska City, Nebr., June 27, 1941; d. Ken E. and Harriet V. (Johnson) Norris; children—Brent, Brad, Romy. B.A., Drake U., 1980, M.A. candidate, 1986. Paralegal staff mem. Leff, Leff, Leff, Iowa City, 1961-65; office mgr., physician's office, Los Angeles, 1971-75; account exec., pub. relations PEC, Des Moines, 1978; researcher IPBN, Des Moines, 1979; communication asst. City of Des Moines, 1979-80; asst. dir. pub. relations Iowa Methodist Med. Ctr., Des Moines, 1981-84; pres. K&S Assocs., West Des Moines, 1985—. Mem. Pub. Relations Soc. Am., (Iowa bd. dirs.), Women in Communication, Inc. (Iowa bd. dirs.), C. of C. (small bus. com.), Friday Forum, Round table, Theta Alumni Assn.

SHAFFER, ANITA MOHRLAND, educator, counselor; b. Racine, Wis., Apr. 5, 1939; d. Milton Arthur and Gudrun Amanda (Sundvoll) Stoffel; m. William Joseph Shaffer, June 22, 1963 (div. 1975); m. 2d, Ralph Otis Shankle, June 18, 1983 (dec. 1985); stepchildren—Gary, Kim. B.S. magna cum laude, U. Wis.-Madison, 1961; M.Ed., U. Wash., 1966; postgrad. Ariz. State U., 1971-76. Cert. in elem. edn., social sci. secondary edn., spl edn., Tex., Ariz.; lic. profl. counselor, Tex.; diplomate Internat. Acad. Profl. Counseling and Psychotherapy. Tchr. Racine Unified Dist. 1, 1961-63, Edmonds Sch. Dist. 15, Alderwood Manor, Wash., 1963-70; tchr. Ariz. Dept. Corrections, Phoenix, 1971-77; tchr. spl. edn. Pasadena Ind. Sch. Dist. (Tex.); 1977-78, spl. edn. counselor, 1978—. Patron Houston Mus. Fine Arts. Mem. Am. Assn. Counseling and Devel., Am. Mental Health Counselors Assn., Am. Sch. Counselor Assn., Tex. Assn. Counseling and Devel., AAUW, Nat. Assn. Female Execs., Smithsonian Instn. Beta Sigma Phi, Pi Lambda Theta. Home: 260 El Dorado Blvd Apt 801 Webster TX 77598 Office: Pasadena Ind Sch Dist Spl Services 3010 Bayshore Dr Pasadena TX 77502

SHAFFER, AUDREY JEANNE, medical records administrator, educator; b. Hutchinson, Minn., Nov. 24, 1929; d. Floyd R. and Edna C. (Seppman) Kleiman; m. Frank L. Shaffer, July 15, 1948; 1 child, Cynthia Louise Shaffer Wilkinson. B.S., Loma Linda U., 1973; M.A., Central Mich. U., 1982. Registered records adminstr. Med. records clk. San Bernardino County Hosp., Calif., 1948-50; radiology receptionist White Meml. Med. Ctr., Los Angeles, 1950-52; med. records clk. Portland Adventist Hosp., Oreg., 1952-53; med. record mgr. Tempe Community Hosp., Ariz., 1953-54; clin. faculty Loma Linda U., Calif., 1975—; dir. med. info. services Corona Community Hosp., Calif., 1973—; med. records cons. Calif., Utah and Philippines Pilot, med. asst. Liga Internat., Mex., 1964-68; chmn. Corona Blood Bank, 1957-68; chmn. vols. Corona Community Hosp. Aux., 1965-68; archaeology supr. Caesarea Expdn., Am. Schs. Oriental Research, Israel, summers 1974—. Recipient Vol. Service award Corona Community Hosp., 1968; Congeniality award Caesarea Archeol. Expdn., 1975. Mem. Loma Linda U. Med. Record Alumni (pres. 1979-81), Am. Med. Record Assn., Calif. Med. Record Assn. (quality assurance com. 1980-81), Nat. Assn. Quality Assurance Profls., Archeol. Inst. Am. Clubs: Women's Improvement (program chmn. 1960-61), Corona Flying (sec. 1960-68) (Corona). Home: 880 Encanto Dr Corona CA 91719 Office: Corona Community Hosp 800 S Main St Corona CA 91720

SHAFFER, DOROTHY BROWNE, educator, mathematician; b. Vienna, Austria, Feb. 12, 1923; d. Hermann and Steffy (Hermann) Browne; arrived U.S., 1940; naturalized, 1944; m. Lloyd Hamilton Shaffer, July 25, 1943 (dec. 1978); children—Deborah Lee, Diana Louise, Dorothy Leslie. A.B., Bryn Mawr Coll., 1943; M.A., Harvard U., 1945, Ph.D., 1962. Mathematician, MIT, Cambridge, 1945-47; tchg. fellow, research asso., Harvard U., Cambridge, 1947-48; asso. mathematician Cornell Aeronautical Lab, Buffalo, N.Y., 1948-58; mathematician Dunlap & Assoc., Stamford, Conn., 1958-60; lectr. grad. engring. U. of Conn. at Stamford, 1962; prof. math Fairfield (Conn.) U., 1963—; vis. prof. Imperial Coll. Sci. and Tech., London, fall 1978, U. Md., College Park, spring 1981; vis. prof. U. Calif.-San Diego, summer 1981; vis. scholar, 1986; NSF faculty fellow IBM-T.J. Watson Research Center, Yorktown Heights, N.Y., 1979. Contbr. numerous papers in math. analysis. Mem. Am. Math. Soc., Math. Assn. of Am., Assn. for Women in Math., London Math. Soc. Home: 156 Intervale Rd Stamford CT 06905 Office: Dept of Math and Computer Sci Fairfield U Fairfield CT 06430

SHAFFER, GAIL SUSAN, state official; b. Kingston, N.Y., Aug. 1, 1948; d. Robert Edwin and Marion Gertrude (Gallagher) S.; B.A. summa cum laude in Polit. Sci., Elmira U., 1970; student U. Paris, 1968-69. Editor, Sam Har Press, 1972-76; supr. Town of Blenheim, N.Y., 1975-77; spl. asst. to N.Y. State Commr. Environ. Conservation, 1977-79; exec. dir. N.Y. State Rural Affairs Council, 1979-80; mem. N.Y. State Assembly, 1980-82; sec. of state State of N.Y., 1983—. Mem. N.Y. State Democratic Com., 1976—. Mem. Ctr. for Women in Govt. (pres.), Phi Beta Kappa. Presbyterian. Office: NY State Dept State 162 Washington Ave Albany NY 12231

SHAFFER, JANE REGINA, assn. exec.; b. Peoria, Ill., June 4, 1933; d. Archie Henry and Ethel Ruth (Pedreyra) Hall; student Bradley U., Peoria, 1951-53; m. Roy Alvin Shaffer, Jan. 31, 1955; children—Jamie, Roy, Shawn. Sec.-treas., Diverco Corp., Winter Haven, Fla., 1957-70, Mansysco Corp., Peoria, 1970-72; divs. adminstr. Profl. Photographers Am., Inc., Des Plaines, Ill., 1972—. Chmn., Beautification Com. Winter Haven, 1968-69. Mem. Am. Photog. Artistans Guild, Nat. Assn. Female Execs., Nat. Soc. Assn. Execs., Nat. Mgmt. Assn. Democrat. Roman Catholic. Club: St. Mary's Women's. Home: 530 Springside Ln Buffalo Grove IL 60090 Office: 1090 Executive Way Des Plaines IL 60018

SHAFFER, JUDY ANN, data processing professional, educator; b. Boone, Iowa, Dec. 24, 1942; d. Vernon Sherwood and Josephine (Bean) Peterson; m. James Nelson Shaffer, Jr., Feb. 28, 1970. B.S., Morningside Coll., 1965; M.S., Iowa State U., 1969. Cert. tchr., Va. Tchr. math. Plaza Jr. High Sch., Virginia Beach, 1971; instr. Ivy Ind. Vocat. Tech. Coll., Ft. Wayne, Ind., 1973-74, Ind. Purdue U., Fort Wayne, 1974-76; programmer Bowmar, Fort Wayne, 1976-77; programmer analyst GTE Data Service, Fort Wayne, 1977-79, sr. programmer analyst Med. Mgmt. Systems Inc., Fort Wayne, 1979—; mem. assoc. faculty IPFW, Fort Wayne, 1984-85. Charter mem. Ft. Wayne Area Community Band, 1979—, personnel mgr., 1979-84; mem. Ft. Wayne Women's Bur., 1977—, Career Planners, Ft. Wayne, 1985—. Mem. PEO (treas. 1973-75), Kappa Mu Epsilon. Avocations: music; model railroading; gardening.

SHAFFER, SUSAN E., insurance company administrator; b. Nashville, Apr. 14, 1947; d. James G. and Esther W. Shaffer; m. Robert Gallinari, June 30, 1982. B.A. in English, Elmhurst (Ill.) Coll., 1969. Mem. claim dept. Allstate Ins. Co., 1971-76, unit mgr., Springfield, Pa., 1976-77, regional life claim mgr., Basking Ridge, N.J., 1977-79, dist. claim mgr., Latham, N.Y., 1979—. Mem. Albany Claim Mgrs. Council, Colonie C. of C., Life Office Mgmt. Assn., Ins. Inst. Am. (asso. in mgmt.). Office: 700 Troy Schenectady Rd Latham NY 12110

SHAFFER, SUSAN ELIZABETH, real estate executive, retailer; b. Detroit, Oct. 30, 1949; d. Robert William and Eleanor (Schwartz) Shaffer; m. Peter Nogueras, June 26, 1982. B.A., U. Mich., 1971; M.B.A. in Fin., Wayne State U., 1979. Asst. sec. Citizens Mortgage Corp., Southfield, Mich., 1972-75; mortgage officer Lambrecht Realty Co., Detroit, 1975-79; dir. fin. Maisel and Assocs., Southfield, 1979-81; ptnr. Nogueras and Assocs., Madison, Wis., 1981—; pres., dir. Shopping Ctr. Mgmt., Madison, 1984—; pres. Flair, Wisconsin Rapids, 1985—; ptnr. WR Joint Venture, Madison, 1984—. Mem. Internat. Council Shopping Ctrs., Mortgage Bankers Assn. (mem. young mortgage bankers com. 1978). Republican. Methodist. Home: 835 Richmond Way Nekoosa WI 54457 Office: Nogueras and Assocs 1000 E Riverview Expressway Wisconsin Rapids WI 54494

SHAFFER, SYBIL SNYDER, teen-ager pageant exec.; b. Greenville, S.C., Sept. 21, 1922; d. William Oscar and Nancy Louise (Walker) Snyder; student Jacksonville U., 1961; m. Edwin Gray Shaffer, May 28, 1966; 1 son, Richard Clyde. Chief clk. So. Rwy. Co., Greenville, S.C., 1943-53; mgr., fire, casualty agt. Spiers Ins. Agy., Columbia, S.C., 1960-66; traveling ins. auditor Agts. Acceptance Corp., Dallas, 1960-66, ins. auditor, Ponte Vedra Beach, Fla., 1966-71; founder, pres., nat. dir. Miss Nat. Teen-ager Pageant, 1971—; tchr. charm and improvement courses, 1959—. Bd. dirs. Cancer Assn., Crippled Children's Soc., Vets. Hosp., Cystic Fibrosis. Mem. Nat. Acad. TV Arts and Scis., Women in Film, Atlanta C. of C., Better Bus. Bur., Beta Sigma Phi (chpt. pres.). Methodist. Club: Ponte Vedra (Ponte Vedra Beach); Atlanta Press, Women's Commerce (founder). Writer Miss Nat. Teen-ager Mini-Modeling charm course Six Parts, 1972.

SHAFIA, GEORGIA, janitorial firm executive; b. Phila., Sept. 29, 1936; d. George L. and Isabel Cohen; m. Arnold Kushner, June 15, 1960 (div. 1964); m. Hass Shafia, July 9, 1968; children—Anabel, Louisa. B.A., Boston U., 1958; Ford Found. cert. U. Pa., 1960; M.L.S., Drexel U., 1963. Med. librarian Episcopal Hosp., Phila., 1963-64, chief med. librarian, 1964-66; chief med. librarian Queens Hosp., Jamaica, N.Y., 1964-66; med. librarian Samuel Bellet Library, Phila., 1974; pres./owner City Cleaning Co., Inc., Phila., 1977—; dir. Bldg. Service Contractors, Fairfax, Va. Chmn. annual giving Germantown Friends Sch., 1981-85. Mem. Forum for Exec. Women (membership com. 1984-85), Phila. Mus. Art, Acad. Fine Art. Clubs: Peale (Phila.); Germantown Cricket. Home: 3401 School House Ln Philadelphia PA 19144 Office: City Cleaning Co Inc 439 N 13th St Philadelphia PA 19123

SHAFTAN, BERNICE MILLER, shoe/handbag designer, consultant; b. N.Y.C.; d. Samuel David and Hannah (Averick) Miller; m. Gerald Wittes Shaftan, May 28, 1956; children—Richard Keith, Susan Debra. Student Art Students League, 1950-53. Designer, Carlisle Shoe Co., N.Y.C., 1950-52; dir. design, fashion dir. Hamilton Shoe Co., N.Y.C., 1952-57; pres. Bernice Shaftan Designs Ltd., N.Y.C., 1957—. Cons., dir. mktg., dir. Carr Leather Co., Lynn, Mass., 1978—; cons. interior design Hotel Montalembert, Paris, 1976—. Contbr. articles to profl. jours. Mem. county com. Conservative party, N.Y. County, 1982, 83; mem. Gramercy Park Assn., N.Y.C., Jr. League Brookdale Hosp. Med. Ctr., N.Y.C., 1983—. Recipient shoe design award Tanners Council Am., 1964. Mem. Shoe Women Execs. (chmn. bd. 1970-71, pres. 1969-70), Fashion Group, Footwear and Accessories Council (pres. 1980-81, chmn. bd. 1982-84), Internat. Platform Assn., Color Assn. U.S. Club: Nat. Arts. Home: 60 Gramercy Park N Apt 11A New York NY 10010 Office: Bernice Shaftan Designs Ltd Penthouse A-60 Gramercy Park N New York NY 10010

SHAH, BHARATI RASHMIKANT, physician; b. Junagadh, Gujrat, India, May 6, 1950; came to U.S., 1976; d. Nanalal Gulabchand Shah and Savita Liladhar Mehta; m. Rashmikant K Shah, Jan. 21, 1975; children—Tarak, Reema and Raagini (twins). M.B.B.S., Grant Med. Sch., Bombay, India, 1971, M.D. Pediatrics, 1975; diploma in child health Coll. Physicians and Surgeons, Bombay, 1973. Diplomate Am. Bd. Pediatrics. Fellow child psychiatry Gaebler unit Harvard Med. Sch., Boston, 1976-78; intern in pediatrics North Shore Children's Hosp., Salem, Mass., 1978-79; resident in pediatrics U. Mass., Worcester, 1979-81; pediatrician Bakersfield Family Med. Center (Calif.), 1982-83; practice medicine specializing in pediatrics, Bakersfield, 1982—. Mem. AMA. Home: 7800 Nairn Ct Bakersfield CA 93309 Office: 4580 California Ave Bakersfield CA 93309

SHALALA, DONNA EDNA, educator; b. Cleve., Feb. 14, 1941; d. James Abraham and Edna (Smith) S.; A.B., Western Coll., 1962; M.S.Sc., Syracuse U., 1968, Ph.D., 1970. Peace Corps. vol., Iran, 1962-64; asst. to dir. met. studies program Syracuse U. (N.Y.), 1965-69, instr. asst. to dean Maxwell Grad. Sch., 1969-70; asst. prof. dept. polit. sci. Bernard M. Baruch Coll., CUNY, 1970-72; assoc. prof. politics and edn. Tchrs. Coll., Columbia U., 1972-77; asst. sec. for policy devel. and research HUD, Washington, 1977-80; prof. polit. sci., pres. Hunter Coll. CUNY, 1980—; gov. Am. stock Exchange, 1981—. Trustee, Phipps Houses. Recipient Ohio Newspaper Women's scholarship, 1958, trustee scholarship Western Coll., 1958-62, Carnegie fellowship, 1966-68; Spencer fellow Nat. Acad. Edn., 1972—; Guggenheim fellow, 1975-76. Mem. Am. Polit. Sci. Assn., N.Y. Polit. Sci. Assn., Nat. Acad. Pub. Adminstrn., Am. Council Edn. (dir. 1980-84), social Sci. Research Council, Nat. Urban Coalition, Am. Arbitration Assn., Inst. Internat. Econs., Am. Ditchley Found., Children's Def. Fund, Fund City N.Y., N.Y.C. Partnership, Women's Forum (pres.). Author: Neighborhood Governance, 1971; The City and the Constitution, 1972; The Property Tax and the Voters, 1973; The Decentralization Approach, 1974. Office: 695 Park Ave New York NY 10021

SHALLOW, CHERYL ELAINE, electronics distributor and power supply manufacturing company executive; b. Meadville, Pa., Sept. 7, 1944; d. Richard and Jean Stroup; m. Richard Shallow, Feb. 23, 1968; children—Maria, Joe. Pres. J.S. Electronics, Inc., Garland, Tex., 1979—; dir. Andy's Plano Pest Control, Inc., 1983—, Central Exterminating, 1983—. Office: J & S Electronics Inc 1905 Copper St Garland TX 75042

SHANAHAN, ANN EDWARDS, educational administrator; b. Boston, Mar. 20, 1937; d. Herbert Edward and Elizabeth (Kennedy) Edwards; m. Edward Knobel Shanahan, Sept. 12, 1959; children—Edward K. Jr., Christopher E., Mark A. A.B., Smith Coll., 1959. Corr. Berkshire Eagle, Stockbridge, Mass., 1962-65; columnist Daily Hampshire Gazette, Northampton, Mass., 1971-75; staff writer Univ. Bulletin, U. Mass., Amherst, 1973-75; news dir. Smith Coll., Northampton, 1975-80, dir. pub. relations, 1980—. Bd. dirs. Northampton Ctr. Arts, 1984—, ARC Northampton, 1978-84, Volunteers Northampton Schs., 1982-84, Northampton Hist. Soc., 1981-84. Mem. Council Advancement and Support Edn. Democrat. Episcopalian. Avocations: reading; cooking. Home: 22 Paradise Rd Northampton MA 01060 Office: Smith Coll Elm St Northampton MA 01063

SHANAS, ETHEL, educator; b. Chgo., Sept. 6, 1914; d. Alex and Rebecca (Rich) S.; A.B., U. Chgo., 1935, M.A., 1937, Ph.D., 1949; L.H.D. (hon.), Hunter Coll., 1985; m. Lester J. Perlman, May 17, 1940; 1 son, Michael S. Sr. research analyst City of Chgo., 1952-53; instr. human devel., research asso. U. Chgo., 1947-52, sr. study dir. Nat. Opinion Research Center, 1956-61, research asso. prof. sociology, 1961-65; lectr. sociology U. Ill., Chgo. campus, 1954-56, prof., 1965-82, prof. emeritus, 1982—; prof. Med. Center, 1973-82; Kesten Meml. lectr. U. So. Calif., 1975. Vice chmn. UN Expert Com. on Aging, 1974; mem. U.S. Nat. Com. on Vital and Health Statistics, 1976-79; bd. govs. Chgo. Heart Assn., 1972-80; mem. City of Chgo. Adv. Council on Aging, 1972-78; bd. dirs. Schwab Rehab. Hosp., 1972-81, chmn. sect. on aging, 1985-86. Fellow Am. Sociol. Assn., Gerontol. Soc. Am. (pres. 1974, Kleemeier award 1977, Brookdale award 1981); mem. Ill. Sociol. Assn. (pres. 1971), Inst. Medicine of Nat. Acad. Sci., Midwest Sociol. Soc. (pres. 1980-81), Nat. Council on Family Relations (Burgess award 1978), Internat. Center of Social Gerontology (France). Author: The Health of Older People, 1962; (with others) Old People in Three Industrial Societies, 1968. Editor: (with G.F. Streib) Social Structure and the Family, 1965; (with R.H. Binstock) Handbook of Aging and the Social Sciences, 1976, 2d edit., 1985; (with M.B. Sussman) Family, Bureaucracy and the Elderly, 1977. Home: 222 Main St Evanston IL 60202 Office: U Ill at Chgo Box 4348 Chicago IL 60680

SHAND, RUSTLE GUNNING, municipal government official; b. Farmington, Mich., Oct. 29, 1927; d. Sidney David and Agnes Rustle (Bisset) Gunning; m. Robert E. Shand, July 3, 1954; children—Donovan Gunning, Robert Logg. B.A., Wayne U., Detroit, 1949. Fashion coordinator Winkelman's, Detroit, 1946-54, Patricia Stevens Schs., Detroit, 1965-75; fashion writer Observer-Eccentric Newspaper, Birmingham, Mich., 1975—; village clk. Village of Franklin, Mich., 1983—. Contbr. articles to fashion publs. Treas. Franklin Cemetery Assn., Franklin, 1980—; mem. Fashion Group, Detroit, 1975—. Mem. Oakland County Clks. Assn. Republican. Club: Village. Avocations: gardening, needlework. Home: 27080 Scenic Rd Franklin MI 48025 Office: Village of Franklin 32325 Franklin Rd Franklin MI 48025

SHANDERA, DOROTHY FRANCES, educator; b. Sardis, Miss., Nov. 8, 1929; d. George Monroe and Mary Browning (Chamblin) Hammitt; B.S., Miss. Women's U., 1951; postgrad. in Criminal Justice, U. Houston, 1971; M.Correctional Edn., Sam Houston State U., 1980; m. Charles Garland Shandera, Apr. 22, 1964; children—Deborah, Cindi. Tchr. high sch. and coll. All Saints Episcopal Coll., Vicksburg, Miss., 1951-52; high sch. tchr. Tyler (Tex.) Ind. Sch. Dist., 1955-59; Harris County probation officer, Houston, 1963-65; tchr. speech and drama Alvin (Tex.) Sch. Dist., 1965-68, Friendswood (Tex.) Sch. Dist., 1968-71; tchr. Spanish and English Round Rock (Tex.) Sch. Dist., 1973-76; bi-lingual instr. Windham Sch. Dist., Tex. Dept. Corrections, Huntsville, 1976-77, life skills instr., 1977-79, bi-lingual specialist, life skills coordinator, 1979—, participant Adkins Life Skills workshop, 1977; guest lectr. Sam Houston State U., 1979-80. Del., Tex. Women's Meeting, 1977, state del. Nat. Women's Conf., Internat. Women's Yr., Houston, 1977; del. Tex. Democratic Conv., 1980; state steering com. Texans for ERA; bd. dirs. Walker County Bd. Human Resources; mem. Tex. Women's Polit. Caucus; legis. aide for Sarah Weddington, 1973; vol. Green Acres Nursing Home; active PTA. Named one of outstanding career women Huntsville, 1978; recipient service cert. Windham Sch. Dist., 1979. Mem. AAUW (nat. del. 1975, travel grantee to conf. 1972, chpt. pres. 1974-76, coordinator state legis. conf.), Tex. Corrections Assn. (pres.-elect state orgn. 1981-82), NEA, Tex. State Tchrs. Assn. (state exec. com., pres.-elect), Windham North Assn. (pres., dist. VI legis. chmn.), Correctional Edn. Assn., Tex. State Ofcl. Ladies, Phi Delta Kappa. Democrat. Presbyterian (elder). Club: Bus. and Profl. Women. Contbr. articles to profl. publs. Office: Windham School District Texas Dept Corrections PO Box 99 Huntsville TX 77340

SHANE, DEBORAH LYNNE, broadcasting executive; b. Chgo., Mar. 24, 1950; d. Raymond and Francine Shane; student Bradley U., 1967-68; B.A., U. Miami, 1971, Ph.D., 1977. Performer, Theatre on the Lake, Chgo., summer 1967; asst. programming dir., disk jockey, audio engr. WRBU-AM, Peoria, Ill., 1967-68; asst. sta. mgr., audio engr. WTVP-TV, Peoria, 1967-68; performer, tech. adviser Ring Theatre Childrens Theatre Touring Co., Miami, Fla., 1968; asst. producer, dir. pub. affairs and childrens programming Learning Ladder, WPLG-TV, Miami, 1969-70; asst. programming dir. WINZ-AM, Miami, 1970-71; Midwest office mgr., dir. pub. relations and communications Gulf Leasing Corp., Chgo., 1971-72; comedy scriptwriter, guest performer Bozo's Circus, WGN-TV, Chgo., 1973-75; freelance writer, producer, dir. and performer for radio, television, films and theatre, Chgo., 1975-77; co-hostess, writer-producer television show Self Discovery from A to Z, WLRN-TV, Miami, 1977; v.p. broadcast and communications div. Asso. Leasing Internat. Corp., Ft. Lauderdale, Fla., 1977—; cons. Miami and S.E. Fla. area U.S. Inst. Theatre Tech.; guest author Lighting Dimensions mag.; guest author Backstage Mag.; asst. instr. U. Wis. Summer Speech Inst. Press coordinator Gov. Askew's Sunshine Amendment Day, Miami, 1976. Recipient B'nai B'rith Woman of Year award for pub. service to Greater Chgo. Met. Community, 1974; judge 17th Ann. Chgo. Emmy awards, 1975, 11th ann. Fla. Hosp. Pub. Relations awards, 1978; awarded Key to City of Miami Beach, 1979. Mem. Am. Women in Radio and TV (membership chmn., dir., 1976, pres. chpt. 1977-80, mem Speakers Bur. 1971—), AFTRA, Soc. Motion Picture and TV Engrs., Fla. Motion Picture and TV Assn. (rec. sec., dir., com. chmn. state bd.), Nat. Acad. TV Arts and Sci. (bd. govs.), Women in Communications, Playwrights Center (charter), Chgo. Women in Broadcasting (Spl. award for promoting better children's programming 1973, Radio and TV appreciation award 1978, 79), Panhellenic Assn. Ft. Lauderdale, Women's Fla. Assn. Broadcasters (pres. 1978-83), U. Miami Young Alumni Assn., Nat. Thespians Troupe 113 (life), Am. Soc. Notaries, Ft. Lauderdale/Broward County C. of C., Delta Zeta (Outstanding Alumni Recognition award 1977), Sigma Phi Epsilon (pres. Little Sisters Orgn.). Jewish. Clubs: B'nai B'rith Women (Chaverim chpt.); Cricket of Miami, Woodlands Country. Writer, hostess 24 episodes Self Discovery television talk show, 1976-77; writer, star 20 shows Debbie and Friends, 1973-74; screenplay collaborator The Eddie Faye Story. Office: Asso Leasing Internat Corp Presdl Plaza 4699 N State Rd 7 Fort Lauderdale FL 33319

SHANE, DORIS JEAN, respiratory therapist, administrator; b. Granite City, Ill., June 30, 1949; d. Elbert Paul and Arline Marie (Zitt) S. A.S. with clin. honors in respiratory therapy, Presbyn.-St. Luke's Hosp., Chgo., 1973. Registered respiratory therapist. Chief respiratory therapist Michael Reese Med. Ctr., Chgo., 1973-78; dir. respiratory therapy Edgewater Hosp., Chgo., 1978-81; dir. respiratory care services Mt. Sinai Med. Ctr., Miami Beach, Fla., 1981—; chmn. adv. council Respiratory Therapy Miami-Dade Community, 1984—; bd. dirs. Dade-Monroe Am. Lung Assn., 1982—, Sunny Shores Sea Camp, Miami, 1983—. Bd. dirs. Frank M. Rodde Community Ctr., Chgo., 1980; chmn. credit com. Mt. Sinai Fed. Credit Union, 1986. Mem. Fla. Soc. Respiratory Therapy (v.p. 1984-85), Am. Assn. Respiratory Therapy, Internat. Assn. Quality Circles, Am. Soc. Respiratory Care Adminstrs., Am. Bus. Women Assn., Nat. Assn. Female Execs. Democrat. Avocation: racquetball. Home: 312 NE 115th St Miami FL 33161

SHANE, LAURIE, public relations and advertising company executive; b. Los Angeles, Apr. 16, 1955; d. Robert Bernard and Joyce Ruth (Sasner) Sherman. B.A., Stanford U., 1977; postgrad. Canberra Coll., 1981; M.A., Pepperdine U., 1984. Mem. staff, minority specialist Paul N. McCloskey, U.S. Ho. of Reps.,

Palo Alto, Calif., 1975-77; dir. Australian Environment Ctr., Canberra, 1977-81; exec. dir., pres. The Communication Works, Inc., Los Angeles, 1982—; cons. Laguna Outreach, Laguna Beach, Calif., 1982—. Editor Bogong Mag., 1978-81, (award 1980). Contbr. to poetry mags. Mem. editorial bd. Lesbian News, Los Angeles, 1982—. Sec. Gay Press Assn., Los Angeles, 1982-84. Recipient Golden Advocate award Healthcare Pub. Relations and Mktg. Assn., 1985. Mem. Advt. Club of Am., Pub. Relations Soc. Am. (accredited; Prisms award 1984, award 1985), Nat. Assn. Bus. Councils (del.), Bus. and Profl. Assn. (pres.). Democrat. Jewish. Avocations: creative writing; yoga; hiking; camping; travel. Office: Communication Works 6421/2 N Robertson Blvd West Hollywood CA 90069

SHANE, SARAH POLIAKOFF, educator, administrator; b. Balt., Dec. 24, 1919; s. Raphael H. and Gussie H. (Schwartz) Poliakoff; m. Sylvan M. Shane, Mar. 14, 1943 (div. 1977); children—Betty Shane Ginsburg, Frank R., Ruth Shane Brandriss, Nancy Shane Fleischman. B.S., Towson State U., 1941; postgrad. U. Md., 1963-67. Tchr. Balt. Pub. Schs., 1940-45, pvt. schs., Balt., 1945-47, 62-67; coordinator program Jewish Big Bros./Big Sisters, Balt., 1980-81; counselor Assoc. Placement & Guidance Service, Balt., 1984-86; dir. vol. services Jewish Community Ctr. of Balt., 1986—. Past nat. bd. dirs. Am. Zionist Fedn., Conf. Pres. Major Am. Jewish Orgns., Jewish Nat. Fund, United Israel Appeal, Am. Israel Pub. Affairs Com., Israel Bonds, Am. Concil Vol. Agys. for Fgn. Services, Consortium for Community Self Help; past mem. Zionist gen. council World Zionist Orgn., also past mem. presidium; past bd. dirs. Balt. Zionist Fedn., pres., 1984—; past bd. dirs. Ladies' Aux. of Bais Yaakov Sch. for Girls, pres., 1963-65; past bd. dirs. Morris Rombro Free Loan Assn., pres., 1959-61; pres. Balt. chpt. Am. Mizrachi Women's Orgn., 1961-63; nat. pres. Amit Women, 1975-79; past rec. sec., treas. Luth. Hosp. Aux.; past assoc. sec. bd. Jewish Community Ctr; past chmn. big gifts Assoc. Jewish Charities and Welfare Fund Balt.; past v.p. Fedn. Jewish Women's Orgns. Md.; past pres. Jewish Community Ctr. Assocs.; past mem. Md. Gov.'s Commn. on Status of Women; past bd. dirs. Beth Jacob Congregation Sisterhood, Bais Yaakov Sch. PTA, Talmudical Acad. PTA, Women's Div. Israel Bonds. Avocations: knitting; embroidery, needlepoint; reading. Home: 29 Stonehenge Circle Apt 12 Baltimore MD 21208

SHANHOUSE, LINDA FILLINGHAM, savings and loan executive; b. Niagara Falls, N.Y., June 25, 1941; d. Kenneth Edward and Marian Georgina (Cooper) F.; m. Bill Shanhouse, Dec. 29, 1980. Asst. to v.p. Riggs Nat. Bank, Washington, 1965-73; exec. v.p., chief operating officer, dir. Friendship Savs. & Loan Assn., Chevy Chase, Md., 1973-84; sr. v.p. Ind. Am. Savs. Assn., Grand Prairie, Tex., 1984—. Trustee Studio Theatre (Washington). Mem. Mortgage Bankers Assn., U.S. League Savs. Assns., Md. Savs. and Loan League, Fin. Instns. Mktg. Assn., Bank Mktg. Assn., Women's Econ. Roundtable, Washington Women's Network, Women in Housing and Fin., Fin. Mktg. Council of Greater Washington. Republican. Home: 502 San Juan Dr Southlake TX 76092 Office: 530 S Carrier Pkwy Grand Prairie TX 75051

SHANK, CLARE BROWN WILLIAMS, former assistant chairman Republican National Committee; b. Syracuse, N.Y., Sept. 19, 1909; d. Curtiss Crofoot and Clara Irene (Shoudy) Brown; B.Oral English, Syracuse U., 1931; m. Frank E. Williams, Feb. 18, 1940 (dec. Feb. 1957); m. Seth Carl Shank, Dec. 28, 1963 (dec. Jan. 1977). Tchr., 1931-33; merchandising exec., 1933-42; Pinellas County mem. Rep. State Com., 1954-58; life mem. Pinellas County Rep. Exec. Com.; exec. com. Fla. Rep. Com., 1954-64; mem. exec. com. Rep. Nat. Com., 1956-64, asst. chmn. and dir. women's activities, 1958-64; alt., mem. exec. arrangements com. Rep. Nat. Conv., 1960; alt., program and arrangement coms. Rep. Nat. Conv., 1964; pres. St. Petersburg Women's Rep. Club, 1955-57. Mem. Def. Adv. Com. on Women in Services, 1959-65; trustee St. Petersburg Housing Authority, 1976-82. Recipient George Arents medal Syracuse U., 1959; citation for patriotic civilian service 5th U.S. Army and Dept. Def. Mem. AAUW, Gen. Fedn. Women's Clubs, DAR, Colonial Dames 17th Century, Fla. Fedn. Women's Clubs (dist. pres. 1976-78), Zeta Phi Eta, Pi Beta Phi (nat. officer 1945-48). Methodist. Clubs: Woman's (pres. 1974-76), Yacht (St. Petersburg). Home: 1120 North Shore Dr NE Apt 901 Saint Petersburg FL 33701

SHANK, MARY ANN, business analyst company executive; b. Santa Cruz, Calif., June 29, 1943. B.A., Calif. State U.-San Jose, 1967, M.A. in Librarianship, 1974. Vol., Peace Corps, Somalia, East Africa, 1967-69; sr. research librarian Santa Cruz, Calif., 1969-76; exec. v.p. Romac Western Corp., San Jose, 1976-81; pres. Trans-M Corp., Los Angeles, 1981—; speaker Small Bus. Clinic, San Jose, 1976—. Author: Financial Plans for Small Business, 1980, Financial Ratios in Small Business Planning, 1981. Columnist Small Bus. Jour., 1980—. Contbr. articles to profl. jours. Recipient Woman of Distinction award YWCA, 1985. Trustee The Roop Found. Fund, Montecito, Calif., 1981—. Mem. Internat. Assn. Fin. Planners, Amnesty Internat. Sierra Club. Mem. Self Realization Fellowship. Avocations: photography; bicycling. Office: Small Bus Clinic 1126 Coast Village Circle Montecito CA 93108

SHANK, SUZANNE, lawyer; b. Kansas City, Mo., Nov. 13, 1946; d. Howard Howe and Bettie Ann (Winkler) Hettick; m. Neil Alan Shank, Nov. 3, 1973; children—Andrew David, Michael Darrin, Pamela Suzanne. B.J., U. Mo., 1972; M.Pub.Adminstrn. in Health Adminstrn., U. Mo.-Kansas City, 1982, J.D., 1982. Bar: Mo. 1982. Journalist, U. Kans. Med. Ctr., Kansas City, 1972-73; asst. editor Am. Family Physician, Kansas City, Mo., 1973-75; exec. dir. Shank Med. Clinic, Kansas City, Mo., 1975-80; assoc. firm Shughart, Thomson & Kilroy, Kansas City, 1982—. Mem. Am. Soc. Hosp. Attys., Mo. Soc. Hosp. Attys., ABA, Mo. Bar Assn., Kansas City Bar Assn., Menorah Med. Center Aux., Kappa Tau Alpha. Home: 701 S Prairie Ln PO Box 686 Raymore MO 64083 Office: Shughart Thomson & Kilroy PO Box 13007 Kansas City MO 64199

SHANKS, KATHRYN MARY, health care administrator; b. Glens Falls, N.Y., Aug. 4, 1950; d. John Anthony and Lenita (Combs) S. B.S. summa cum laude, Spring Hill Coll., 1972; M.P.A., Auburn U., 1976. Program evaluator Mobile Mental Health, Ala., 1972-73; dir. spl. projects Ala. Dept. Mental Health, Montgomery, 1973-76; dir. adminstrn. S.W. Ala. Mental Health/Mental Retardation, Andulusia, Ala., 1976-78; adminstr. Mobile County Health Dept., 1978-82; exec. dir. Coastal Family Health Ctr., Biloxi, Miss., 1982—; ptnr. Shanks & Allen, Mobile, 1979—; cons. S.W. Health Agy., Tylertown, Miss., 1984—; preceptor Sch. Nursing, U. So. Miss., Hattiesburg, 1983, 84; advisor Headstart Program, Gulfport, Miss., 1984—, LPN Program, Gulf Coast Community Coll., 1984—; lectr. Auburn U., Montgomery, 1977-78. Bd. dirs. Mobile Community Action Agy., 1979-81; mem. S.W. Ala. Regional Goals Forum, Mobile, 1971-72, Cardiac Rehab. Study Com., Biloxi, Miss., 1983-84, Mothers and Babies Coalition, Jackson, Miss., 1983—, Gulf Coast Coalition Human Services, Biloxi, Miss., 1983—. Spring Hill Coll. Pres.'s scholar, 1972. Mem. Miss. Primary Health Care Assn. (pres.), Med. Group Mgmt. Assn., Biloxi C. of C., ACLU, Soc. for Advancement of Ambulatory Care, Spring Hills Alumni Assn. Avocations: tennis; home restoration. Office: Coastal Family Health Center PO Box 475 300 E Division St Biloxi MS 39530

SHANNON, BETTY ZIEGLER, dean technical institute; b. Memphis, Tenn., Aug. 1, 1927; d. Fred Bernard and Bessie Mae (Hambright) Ziegler; m. Robert Patrick Shannon, Aug. 27, 1950 (div.). B.A., U. S.C., 1948; postgrad. Emory U., 1950-52, Ga. State Coll., 1952-53, Oglethorpe U., 1956. Mgr. vets. affairs U. S.C., Columbia, 1948-50; owner Shannon Secretarial Service, Atlanta, 1950-56; field dir. W.H. Long Mktg., Inc., Greensboro, N.C., 1963-66; pres. Shannon Mktg., Greensboro, 1966-74; nat. research dir. Burger King Corp., Miami, Fla., 1970-74; research dir. Plantation Chamber (Fla.), 1974-76; research dir. Broward County Health Dept., Ft. Lauderdale, Fla., 1976-78; dean of students, adminstr. Keiser Inst. Tech., Ft. Lauderdale, 1978—. Cons., editor jour. Mem. Am. Mktg. Assn. (treas. 1964-65), Am. Assn. Pub. Opinion Research, Mktg. Research Assn., Am. Bus. Women's Assn. (pres. Woman of Yr. award 1985), Bus. and Profl. Women's Assn., Panhellenic Alumnae (corr. sec.), Delta Zeta. Democrat. Episcopalian. Clubs: Greensboro Women's Plantation Women's. Office: Keiser Inst Tech 4861 N Dixie Hwy Fort Lauderdale FL 33308

SHANNON, CAROLYN JEAN, interior designer, career enhancement consultant; b. Vincennes, Ind., Nov. 22, 1943; d. Melvin Eugene and Melita Harriet (Bair) Powell; children—Timothy Carl, Heather Caroline. B.A. in Telecommunications and Interior Design, Ind. U., 1985. Interior designer Buchanan & Sons Furniture, also Kitchen and Bath Ctr., also free-lance, Bloomington, Ind., 1975-81; sales mgr. Kittle's Ethan Allen, Bloomington and Indpls., 1981-82; owner, cons. The Profl. Woman, career enhancement seminars, Bloomington, 1982—; interior designer Interiors, Bloomington, 1984—. Rep. Local Council of Women, owners Bloomington Hosp., 1985-86. Phi Delta Kappa scholar, 1984. Mem. Nat. Assn. Female Execs., Golden Key, Psi Iota Xi, Phi Beta Kappa. Methodist. Avocations: bridge, travel, tennis. Home: 3871 Laurel Ct Bloomington IN 47401 Office: Interiors 300 E Kirkwood Ave Bloomington IN 47401

SHANNON, IRIS REED, nursing educator; b. Chgo.; d. Ira Paul and Iola Sophia (Williams) S.; B.S. in Nursing, Fisk U.-Meharry Med. Coll., 1948; M.A., U. Chgo., 1954; m. Robert Alwood Shannon, Aug. 21, 1953; Staff nurse Chgo. Bd. Health, 1948-50; instr. pub. health nursing Meharry Med. Coll., Nashville, 1951-56; tchr.-nurse, health coordinator child devel. Head Start, Chgo. Bd. Edn., 1957-66; dir. community nursing Mile Sq. Neighborhood Health Center, Presbyn.-St. Luke's Hosp., Chgo., 1966-69; co-dir. nurse asso. programs Rush Presbyn.-St. Luke's Hosp., 1971-76; chairperson community nursing Rush U., Chgo., 1972-77; asst. prof. pub. health nursing U. Ill., 1971-74; assoc. prof. community nursing Rush U., 1974—; mem. profl. adv. bd. Vis. Nurse Assn. Chgo., 1973-75; cons. Video Nursing, Inc.; mem. profl. adv. com. Mile Sq. Home Health Unit, Chgo., 1975-77; mem. Nat. Adv. Council on Nurse Tng., HEW, 1978-81. Mem. Nat. Task Force on Credentialing in Nursing, 1979-82; mem. Chgo. regional com. Ill. White House Conf. on Children, 1979-80. Recipient award of merit Ill. Public Health Assn., 1979; Hon. Recognition award Ill. Nurses Assn., 1979; Rockefeller fellow, 1953-54. Fellow Am. Pub. Health Assn. (chmn. pub. health nursing sect. 1977-79, governing council 1980—, H.A. Poindexter Disting. Service award Black Caucus Health Workers 1981), Am. Acad. Nursing; mem. Am. Nurses Assn., Am. Sch. Health Assn., Inst. Medicine of Nat. Acad. Scis., Delta Sigma Theta, Sigma Theta Tau. Office: Rush Univ Dept of Nursing 1753 W Congress Chicago IL 60612

SHANNON, JEANNE ANNETTE, county official; b. Independence, Iowa, Dec. 13, 1927; d. Milton Lorenzo and Marjorie Beth (Knowles) Cochran; m. Marshal L. Shannon, May 1, 1947 (dec. 1984); children—Judy Shannon Lentzkow, Dennis, Brent. Grad. high sch., Quasqueton, Iowa. With clk.-recorder's office Buchanan County, Iowa, 1957-65, county recorder, 1981—; sec. nursing edn. Mental Health Inst., Independence, 1965-69; sec. Craig Law Firm, Independence, 1969-75, Roberts Law Firm, Independence, 1975-81. Sunday sch. tchr. Immanuel Luth. Ch., Independence, 1983—; active Theos Widow's Support Group, Independence, 1984—, Hospice of Buchanan County, 1984—, Independence Women's Bowling Assn., 1971—; head Women for Harkin for Senator, Buchanan County, 1984—, mem. steering com., 1984; publicity chmn. Buchanan County Democratic Central Com., 1981—; publicity chmn. Buchanan County Easter Seal Soc. Iowa, 1986—; sec. Immanuel Luth. Ch. Women, 1986—; sec. for Dem. County Convs., Buchanan County, 1981—. Mem. Independence Bus. and Profl.Women (treas. 1979-80, 84—), Iowa Recorders Assn., Shalom Ch. Circle. Avocations: flowers; gardening; bowling; spectator sports. Home: 120 Terrace Dr Independence IA 50644 Office: Buchanan County Courthouse 210 5th Ave NE Independence IA 50644

SHANNON, LORIS KAY, association executive; b. Butte, Mont., Sept. 27, 1941; d. George Robert and Loris Marguerite (Brown) Powe; m. James Norman Bertelson, Aug. 8, 1964 (div. 1973); children—Christopher James, Bonnie Kay; m. Donald Sutherlin Shannon, Dec. 30, 1977; stepchildren—Stacey Eileen, Gail Alison, Michael Corbett. B.A. in English, Carleton Coll., 1963; M.A. in Teaching., Coll. St. Thomas, St. Paul, 1964; M.B.A., U. Ky., 1982. Tchr., Central Jr. High Sch., St. Louis Park, Minn., 1964-67; lab. technician U. Ky., Lexington, 1973-80, grad. research asst., 1980-81; assoc. editor Am. Assn. Individual Investors, Chgo., 1982-84, dir. communications, 1984—. Mem. Pub. Relations Soc. Am. Home: 1624 Elmwood Ave Wilmette IL 60091 Office: Am Assn Individual Investors 612 N Michigan Ave Chicago IL 60611

SHANNON, MARGARET RITA, educator; b. Cambridge, Mass.; d. James J. and Catherine M. (McDonough) Shannon; B.S., Mass. State Coll., 1936; M.Ed., Harvard U., 1947, Ed.D., 1959. Tchr. pub. schs., Cambridge, 1936-51; asst. prof. Mass. State Coll., Lowell, 1951-59, asso. prof. 1959-65, prof., 1965-74, chmn. dept. edn., 1969-74; dean Coll. Edn. U. Lowell, 1974-79, dean, prof. emerita, 1979—; sometime lectr. Recipient Alumni award, 1986. Mem. Internat. Reading Assn. (cons. nat. conf.), Am. Ednl. Research Assn., Nat. Council Tchrs. English (com. on linguistics and reading), Delta Kappa Gamma, Pi Lambda Theta (chpt. pres. 1958-61). Author textbooks; contbr. articles to profl. jours. Office: Coll Edn U Lowell W Campus Lowell MA 01854

SHANNON, REANER GIRTHENE, medical technologist, educator; b. Morrilton, Ark., Oct. 6, 1936; d. Hosea D. and Blanchie (Hardy) Gunnels; m. Henry Shannon, Jr., Mar. 20, 1960; 1 dau., Pamela Renee. Diploma Kansas City Gen. Hosp.'s Sch. Med. Tech., 1960; B.A., Park Coll., 1976; M.A., U. Mo.-Kansas City, 1978, Ph.D., 1983. Sr. med. technologist Kansas City Gen. Hosp., 1960-62, supr. hematology lab., 1962-69, dir. spl. hematology lab., 1969-74; instr. clin. hematology Kansas City Gen. Hosp.'s Sch. Med. Tech., 1962-68; instr. and research technologist U. Mo.-Kansas City City Sch. Medicine, 1974-79; asst. prof. med. tech., 1979—; lectr. profl. meetings; leader workshops. Co-author: Laboratory Evaluation of Hemostasis and Thrombosis, 1983; contbr. articles on hematology to profl. jours. Lay speaker Baptist Ch., tchr. Sunday Sch., dir. Outreach. Faculty fellow U. Kansas City Trustees, 1984-85. Mem. Am. Soc. Clin. Pathologists (registered med. technologist, faculty mem. regional workshop 1973, co-dir. regional workshop 1975, 80), Am. Soc. Coagulationists, Am. Soc. for Med. Tech. (speaker region VII meeting 1977), Urban League, NAACP, Coalition of 100 Black Women, Inc., Nat. Council Negro Women, Inc., Alpha Kappa Alpha. Home: 7601 E 73d Terr Kansas City MO 64133 Office: 2411 Holmes St M4-110 Univ Mo-Kansas City Sch Medicine Kansas City MO 64108

SHAPIRO, ANITA RAE, commissioner superior court; b. Omaha, May 16, 1941; d. Harry and Jesse (Shiloff) Lavine; m. Mark Howard Shapiro, June 8, 1961; children—David Gregory, Diane Elaine, Lisa Michelle. B.A., Mills Coll., Oakland, Calif., 1961; LL.B., U. Pa., 1965; student UCLA, summer 1959, U. Calif.-Berkeley, summer 1960, NYU Grad. Sch. Law Div., 1965-66. Bar: Calif. 1966, U.S. Dist. Ct. (cen. dist.) Calif. 1967, N.Y. 1969. Sole practice law, Pasadena, Calif., 1967; dep. city prosecutor City Prosecutor's Office, Pasadena, Calif., 1968; assoc. legal editor Lawyers Co-op Pub. Co., Rochester, N.Y., 1969-70; sr. jud. atty. Calif. Cts. Appeal, Los Angeles, 1971-76, San Bernardino, Calif., 1977-82; commr. Superior Ct., Los Angeles County, Calif., 1982—, asst. liaison commr., 1985-86; adj. prof. Western State U. Coll. Law, Fullerton, Calif., 1979-83. Editor: Calif. State Bar Jour., 1977-81. Vice-pres. Friends Outside, 1979-80, pres., 1980-81, nat. bd. dirs., 1978-81, 83-86; referee Calif. State Bar Ct., 1980-84; Judge Incamp lectr. Constl. Rights Found., 1983—; lectr. workshops and symposia. NYU Law Sch. scholar, 1965-66. Mem. Calif. State Bar Commn. on Corrs. (chmn. 1983-84, vice-chmn. 1982-83), Calif. State Bar Assn. (legis. com. familylaw sect. 1985—), Orange County Bar Assn., Los Angeles County Bar Assn., Los Angeles Women Lawyers Assn., Calif. Women Lawyers (past treas., bd. govs.) Women Lawyers Orange County, Inland Counties Women at Law (founder, pres. 1979-80), Calif. Ct. Commrs. Assn., Am. Judicature Soc. Office: Los Angeles Superior Ct 12720 Norwalk Blvd Norwalk CA 90650

SHAPIRO, DENISE LAURA, licensing/marketing firm executive, consultant; b. Oceanside, N.Y., Apr. 24, 1954; d. Arthur G. and Sylvia (Wieder) Cohen; m. Larence Lang Shapiro, Sept. 4, 1977. B.A., Syracuse U., 1975; M.A. in Mgmt., N.Y. U., 1977. Asst. Halston Enterprises, N.Y.C., 1976-77; asst. designer Malcolm Starr, N.Y.C., 1977; designer Salerno Handbag, N.Y.C., 1977; mdse. mgr. Honeybunch Handbag, N.Y.C., 1978-79; dir. ABC Inc., N.Y.C., 1979-82; pres. Preferred Lics. Ltd., N.Y.C., 1982—; v.p., gen. mgr. for licensing ops. ITT, 1984; developed retailing techniques for licensed product, nationwide, consumer advt. program for Statue of Liberty fund; instr. UN, N.Y.C., 1977-78; cons. in field. History guide Met. Museum Art, N.Y.C., 1978-79; bd. dirs. San Remo Tenants Corp., N.Y.C., 1980-83; active Pat Murphy for Judge Campaign, N.Y.C., 1983. Mem. Licensing Industry Assn., Women in Licensing. Clubs: Sandanona Hare Hounds (Millbrook, N.Y.); Greenwich Polo Players. Home: 146 Central Park W New York NY 10023 Office: Preferred Lics Ltd 146 Central Park W New York NY 10023

SHAPIRO, JOAN ISABELLE, laboratory administrator, nurse; b. Fulton, Ill., Aug. 26, 1943; d. Macy James and Frieda Lockhart; m. Ivan Lee Shapiro, Dec. 28, 1968; children—Audrey, Michael. R.N., Peoria Methodist Sch. Nursing, Ill., 1964. Nurse, Grant Hosp., Columbus, Ohio, 1975-76; nurse Cardiac Thoracic and Vascular Surgeons Ltd., Geneva, Ill., 1977—, mgr. non-invasive lab., 1979—; owner, operator Shapiro's Mastiff's 1976-82; sec.-treas. Sounds Services, 1976—, Mainstream Sounds Inc., 1980-84; co-founder, sec.-treas. Cardio-Phone Inc., 1982—; v.p., dir. Computer Specialists Inc., 1986—. Mem. Soc. Non-invasive Technologists, Soc. Peripheral Vascular Nursing (community awareness com. 1984—), Kane County Med. Soc. Aux. (pres. 1983-84, adviser, 1984-85). Lutheran. Office: Cardiac Thoracic and Vascular Surgeons Ltd 123 South St PO Box 564 Suite 100 Geneva IL 60134

SHAPIRO, JOANNE SILVERS, school psychologist, teacher; b. Middletown, N.Y., Mar. 14, 1937; d. Harry and Rose (Gorelikoff) Silvers; m. Joel Kenneth Shapiro, Sept. 3, 1956; children—Adam Mark, Jason Craig. B.A., Barnard Coll., 1958; M.S., Bklyn. Coll., 1961. Lic. sch. psychologist, N.J. Tchr. PS 155, Bklyn., 1958-63, Cumberland Sch., Great Neck, N.Y., 1963-64; part time play sch. tchr. Play Schs. Assn., N.Y.C., 1958-62; school psychologist Somerset Hills Sch., Warren, N.J., 1974-75, N.J. Assn. Retarded Children, Essex County, N.J., 1975-76, Oxford Central Sch., N.J., 1976-78, Alpine Pub. Sch., N.J., 1976—, Clifton Pub. Schs., N.J., 1983—. Mem. N.J. Assn. Sch. Psychologists. Avocations: tennis; golf. Home: 8 Canoe Brook Dr Livingston NJ 07039

SHAPIRO, JUDITH, anthropology educator; b. N.Y.C., Jan. 24, 1942. B.A., Brandeis U., 1963; postgrad. Ecole des Haute Etudes Institut d'Etudes Politiques, Paris, 1961-62; Ph.D., Columbia U., 1972. Asst. prof. U. Chgo., 1970-75; postdoctoral fellow U. Calif.-Berkeley, 1974-75; Rosalyn R. Schwartz lectr., asst. prof. anthropology Bryn Mawr Coll., Pa., 1975-78, assoc. prof., 1978—, chmn. dept., 1982—; mem. com. on social sci. personnel Social Sci. Research Council, 1977—. Contbr. articles to profl. jours., chpts. to books. Fellow Woodrow Wilson Found., 1963-64, Columbia U., 1964-65, NIMH, 1965-70, NEH Younger Humanist, 1974-75, Am. Council Learned Socs., 1981-82; grantee NSF summer field tng., 1965, NIMH, 1974-75, Social Sci. Research Council, 1974-75; Mem. Phila. Anthrop. Soc. (pres. 1983), Am. Ethnol. Soc. (nominations com. 1983—), Am. Anthrop. Assn. (com. on ethics 1976-79), Royal Anthrop. Inst., Phi Beta Kappa, Sigma Xi. Office: Dept Anthropology Bryn Mawr Coll Bryn Mawr PA 19010

SHAPIRO, LENORE, businesswoman; b. Balt., Nov. 30, 1933; d. Samuel and Beatrice (Polikof) Fried; m. Morton Shapiro, Aug. 21, 1955; children—Andrew, Tammy. B.A., Goucher Coll., 1955, M.Ed., 1956. Tchr. English and drama Roland Park Country Sch. for Girls, Balt., 1967-74; dist. mgr. World Book, Balt., 1976-80; founder, pres. Diversions, Inc., Balt., 1978—. Mem. bd. continuing edn. Goucher Coll., Balt., 1985—. Jewish. Address: 5 Springbriar Ln Baltimore MD 21208

SHAPIRO, LYNNE DIANNE, marketing research company executive; b. New Haven, Feb. 3, 1947; d. Bernard Louis and Marjorie (Clough) S. B.A. in Psychology, Russell Sage Coll., 1968; mgmt. cert. NYU, 1984. Sr. research exec. Grey Advt., N.Y.C., 1976-78; v.p. Stockton and Ott, Inc., N.Y.C., 1978-80; assoc. research dir. Dancer Fitzgerald Sample, N.Y.C., 1980-81; pres., owner L.D. Shapiro Mktg. Research., N.Y.C., 1981—; mktg. cons. Women's Sch. Learning, N.Y.C., 1985; research cons. N.Y. State NOW, 1985. Editor, pub. Write on Woman, 1977-79. Contbr. articles to profl. jours. and women's publs. Co-dir. Women's Equality Day Events, N.Y., 1980; event coordinator various feminist groups, N.Y., 1970-82. Mem. Am. Mktg. Assn., Nat. Assn. Female Execs., Women Against Pornography (founding mem, organizer, advt. cons., N.Y.C.). Democrat. Jewish. Home and Office: 345 W 87th St New York NY 10024

SHAPIRO, MARGE DIANA, lawyer; b. Sapporo, Japan, Jan. 12, 1949; d. Daniel William and Ruth (Hines) Rachal; m. Richard Stephen Shapiro, May 27, 1972. Student Agnes Scott Coll., 1966-68; B.A., Duke U., 1970; postgrad. U. S.C., 1970-72; J.D., Emory U., 1976. Bar: Ga. 1976. Teaching asst. U. S.C., Columbia, 1970-72; sole practice law, Decatur, Ga., 1977-80, Dunwoody, Ga., 1980-81; mng. atty. Hyatt Legal Services, Stone Mountain, Ga., 1981-85, UAW Legal Services Plan, 1985; sole practice law, Norcross, Ga., 1986—. Mem. adv. com. Ga. Vietnam Vets. Leadership Program, Atlanta, 1983, 84; legal adviser Atlanta Day Vets. Day's Parade, Atlanta, 1983. Mem. ABA, Ga. Bar Assn., Atlanta Bar Assn., Nat. Council Jewish Women (life), Jewish War Vets Aux., Delta Theta Phi (historian). Jewish.

SHAPIRO, NORMA SONDRA LEVY, federal judge; b. Phila., July 27, 1928; d. Bert and Jane (Kotkin) Levy; B.A. in Polit. Theory with honors, U. Mich., 1948; J.D. magna cum laude, U. Pa., 1951; m. Bernard Shapiro, Aug. 21, 1949; children—Finley, Neil, Aaron. Admitted to Pa. bar, 1952, U.S. Supreme Ct. bar, 1978; law clk. to judge Pa. Supreme Ct., 1951-52; instr. U. Pa. Law Sch., 1951-52, 55-56; asso. firm Dechert Price & Rhoads, Phila., 1956-58, 67-73, partner, 1973-78; judge U.S. Dist. Ct. for Eastern Pa., 1978—; assoc. trustee U. Pa. Law Sch., from 1978; trustee Women's Law Project, from 1978; mem. lawyer's adv. panel Pa. Gov.'s Commn. on Status of Women, 1974; legal adv. Regional Council Child Psychiatry. Pres., Lower Merion County (Pa.) Bd. Sch. Dirs., 1968-77, 77, v.p., 1976; v.p. Jewish Community Relations Council of Greater Phila., 1975-77; chmn. legal affairs com., 1978; past pres. Belmont Hills Home and Sch. Assn., Lower Merion Twp.; past legis. chmn. Lower Merion Sch. Dist. Intersch. Council; past mem. Task Force on Mental Health of Children and Youth of Pa.; past treas., chmn. edn. com. Human Relations Council Lower Merion; past v.p., parliamentarian, Nes Ami Penn Valley Congregation, Lower Merion Twp. Named Woman of Yr., Oxford Circle Jewish Community Center, 1979, Woman of Distinction, Golden Slipper Club, 1979; Gowen fellow, 1954-55. Mem. Am. Law Inst., Am. Bar Found., ABA (vice chmn. com. on law and mental health sect. family law), Pa. Bar Assn. (ho. of dels. from 1979), Phila. Bar Assn. (chmn. com. women's rights 1972, 74-75, chmn. bd. govs. from 1977, chmn. pub. relations com. 1978), Fed. Bar Assn., Nat. Assn. Women Lawyers, Phila. Trial Lawyers Assn., Am. Judicature Soc., Phila. Fellowship Commn., Order of Coif (chpt. pres. 1973-75), Tau Epsilon Rho. Guest editor Shingle, 1972. Office: US Courthouse Room 10614 601 Market St Philadelphia PA 19106*

SHAPIRO, PHYLLIS (MRS. ABRAHAM SHAPIRO), hotel adminstr.; b. Montreal, Que., Can., Mar. 12, 1922; d. Isadore and Sadie (Novack) Hochmitz; student Sullivan Bus. Coll., Montreal, 1939-41; m. Abraham Shapiro, Aug. 22, 1961; children—Gerri and Jewel (twins). Asst. mgr. Nat. Food Store Ltd., Montreal, 1942-45; office comptroller Dixon Watch Importing Co., 1945-48, adminstr. Bernard Schaeffer & Sons, importing agy., 1948-51; exec. sec. William Rosenberg, architect, 1951-57; exec. sec. Eugene Meth Assos., financier, 1957-61; adminstr. Twin City Motel, Brewer, Maine, 1968—; pres. The Carriage Inn, Pittsfield, Maine, 1978—. Jewish. Mem. B'nai Brith, Hadassah. Home: 58 Broadway Bangor ME 04401 Office: 453 Wilson St Brewer ME 04412

SHAPIRO, RICKI D., communications specialist; b. Schenectady, Apr. 4, 1952; d. A. Albert and Sandra Lee (Fichtner) S. A.B. in Journalism and Psychology, Syracuse U., 1974; postgrad. SUNY-Albany, 1981—. Reporter Schenectady Gazette, 1974-81; assoc. pub. relations Schenectady County Community Coll., 1981-85; communications coordinator Garden Way, Inc., Troy, N.Y., 1985—. Bd. dirs. Haven, Schenectady, 1983-85; mem. pub. relations com. ARC, Schenectady, 1983—. Mem. Internat. Assn. Bus. Communicators (vice chmn. programs 1985—), Schenectady C. of C. (mem. tourism council 1984—). Democrat. Jewish. Clubs: Ski (Schenectady); Women's Press of N.Y. (sec. 1982-84, bd. dirs. 1984-85). Avocations: photography; traveling; sailing; music; writing. Home: 2016 Eastern Pkwy Schenectady NY 12309 Office: Garden Way Inc 102d St and 9th Ave Troy NY 12180

SHAPIRO, SHARON, supply company executive; b. Chgo., Jan. 15, 1950; d. Harry H. and Miriam G. Shapiro. B.S. in Bus. Adminstrn. and Mktg., So. Ill. U., 1972; M.B.A. in Mktg., Roosevelt U., 1982. With Warren-Teed Pharms., Columbus, Ohio, 1972-74, Eli Lilly & Co., Indpls., 1974-76; therapeutic systems rep. Alza Corp., Palo Alto, Calif., 1976-78; hyperalimentation specialist Am. McGaw div. Am. Hosp. Supply Corp., Evanston, Ill., 1978-81, nutrition ter. mgr., 1981-82; mktg. cons. Video Intro, 1980-82; account Vicom Assocs., San Francisco, 1982—; guest lectr. Rancho La Puerta, Tecate, Mex. Mem. Med. Mktg. Assn. Office: Vicom Assocs 901 Battery San Francisco CA 94111*

SHARBEL, JEAN MARIE, editor; b. Lansford, Pa.; d. Joseph and Star (Nemir) Sharbel. B.A. in Journalism, Hunter Coll., N.Y.C. Editorial dir., v.p. Dauntless Books, N.Y.C., 1962-75; editor Modern Romances mag., Macfadden Women's Group, N.Y.C., 1976—. Address: Modern Romances Macfadden Women's Group 215 Lexington Ave New York NY 10016

SHARFMAN, CAROLINE SHARP, commercial paper credit analyst; b. Ann Arbor, Mich., Aug. 27, 1942; d. Mahlon Samuel and Mary Patricia (Potter) Sharp; m. William Lee Sharfman, Sept. 5, 1964 (div. 1985). B.A. with distinction, U. Mich., 1964; M.B.A., Columbia U., 1975. Assoc. Goldman, Sachs & Co., N.Y.C., 1975-80, v.p., 1980-83; v.p. Goldman Sachs Money Markets Inc., N.Y.C., 1983—. Mem. Phi Beta Kappa, Beta Sigma Iota, Beta Gamma Sigma. Episcopalian. Office: Goldman Sachs Money Markets Inc 85 Broad St New York NY 10004

SHARIAT-PANAHI, JALEH, physician; b. Mashad, Iran, May 24, 1945; came to U.S., 1972; d. Askavi and Narjes Movahed S.-P.; m. Ali Madani, Nov. 21, 1975; children—Leila, Mina, Susanne, Cyrus. M.D., Pahlavi U. Sch. Medicine (Iran), 1971. Resident in internal medicine U. Ala., Birmingham, 1973-75, fellow in infectious diseases, 1975-76; practice medicine, specializing in internal medicine and infectious diseases, Kingston, N.Y., 1978—; attending physician Kingston Hosp., 1978—, Benedictine Hosp., Kingston, 1978—. Office: 51 Hurley Ave Kingston NY 12401

SHARKE, INGRID, librarian; b. Troy, N.Y., July 21, 1951; d. Karl G.E. and Ann (Swensson) Sharke. B.A., The Western Coll.-Oxford, Ohio, 1973; M.L.S., SUNY-Geneseo, 1974. Librarian, Samaritan Hosp. Sch. Nursing, Troy, N.Y., 1976; asst. librarian The Times Record/The Sun. Record, Troy, N.Y., 1977-80; librarian The Times Record/Sunday Record, 1980—. Mem. ALA, Spl. Library Assn. Republican. United Ch. of Christ. Office: The Times Record 501 Broadway Troy NY 12181

SHARKO, JUDITH MCAULEY, rehabilitation services administrator; b. Boston, Jan. 25, 1942; d. Thomas Frances and Helen Clare (McKenna) McAuley; m. John Ralph Sharko, Jan. 9, 1971; 1 child, Tanya Dionis. B.S., Suffolk U., 1966; Med. Peripatology, Boston Coll., 1967, postgrad., 1976. Cert. in peripatology. Peripatologist, Pennhurst State Ctr., Spring City, Pa., 1967-70; self-employed cons., Paoli, Pa., 1970-76; cons. Bionic Instruements, Bala Cynwyd, Pa., 1976-78; v.p. Nurion, Inc., King of Prussia, Pa., 1978-82; pres. JMS Mobility Assocs., Inc., Wayne, Pa., 1982—; pres. Nat. Exhibits by Blind Artists, Paoli, 1983. Dir. com. to aid the blind Jr. League, Phila., 1978; v.p. Travel Aids for the Blind, Wayne, Pa., 1983—. Mem. Women's Sports Found., Assn. Edn. and Rehab. for Blind. Club: La Maison. Avocations: jogging; travel; biking; cross country skiing. Office: JMS Mobility Assocs Inc 175 Strafford Ave Suite 100 Wayne PA 19087

SHARLOW, THELMA FACEMIRE JACOBS, insurance agent; b. Centralia, W.Va., June 20, 1929; d. Guy Willard Facemire and Florence (Brady) Facemire Chasonis; m. Arthur F. Jacobs, Jr., Mar. 16, 1948 (dec. 1975); children—Betty Lou, Colleen, Randy, Arthur F. III. Student ins. courses Keene State Coll. (N.H.) Herd classification dept. Holstein-Friesian, Brattleboro, Vt., 1948-67, indexer, 1963-67; supr. comml. lines Richards, Inc., Brattleboro, 1967—. Mem. Nat. Assn. Ins. Women (past del. regional conv., bd. dirs., 2d v.p. regional assn.), Cert. Profl. Ins. Women. Baptist. Club: Evening Star Grange (officer) (Dummerston, Vt.). Home: 464 Western Ave Brattleboro VT 05301 Office: Richards Gates Hoffman & Clay 25 Harris Pl Brattleboro VT 05301

SHARP, ALICE ELIZABETH, management consultant; b. Miami, Mar. 7; d. Raymond B. and Willie Mae S.; B.S., U. Corpus Christi, 1959; M.A., U. Tex., Austin, 1961; Ph.D., Walden U., 1979. Tchr., marine sci. coordinator Corpus Christi Ind. Sch. Dist., 1961-66; mem. faculty Tarrant County Jr. Coll., Ft. Worth, 1967-69, also Del Mar Coll., Corpus Christi; dir. edn. Spohn Hosp., Corpus Christi, 1969-71; dir. edn. Maine Med. Center, Portland, 1971-76; regional edn. dir. AMI, Houston, 1976-81; owner, prin. MERS, cons. and tng. service, Houston, 1980—. Robert Welch Found. fellow, 1959-60. Mem. Houston C. of C., Am. Soc. Tng. Devel., Assn. Ednl. Communications Technology, Adult Edn. Assn., Am. Mgmt. Assn., Phi Sigma. Presbyterian. Contbr. articles to profl. jours. Office: PO Box 218356 Houston TX 77218

SHARP, ANNE CATHERINE, artist; b. Red Bank, N.J., Nov. 1, 1943; d. Elmer Eugene and Ethel Violet (Hunter) S.; B.F.A., Pratt Inst., 1965; M.F.A., Bklyn. Coll., 1973. One woman shows: Pace Editions, N.Y.C., 1974, Contemporary Gallery, Dallas, 1975, Eatontown (N.J.) Hist. Mus., 1980; group shows include: Mus. Modern Art, N.Y.C., 1975, 76, Arnot Art Mus., Elmira, N.Y., 1975, Bronx (N.Y.) Mus., 1975, Calif. Mus. Photography, U. Calif., Riverside, Cabo Frio Print Biennale, Brazil, 1985-86, Mus. Modern Art, Weddel, W. Ger., 1985, Mus. Contemporary Art of Campinas, Sao Paulo, Brazil, 1985-86, Kenkeleba Gallery, N.Y.C., 1985; represented in permanent collections: Smithsonian Instn., Nat. Air and Space Mus., Albright-Knox Gallery, Buffalo, Philip Morris, Inc., St. Vincent's Hosp., N.Y.C.; owner, mgr. Anne Sharp Studio, N.Y.C., 1970—; art tchr. Sch. Visual Arts, 1978—, Parson's Sch. Design, N.Y.C., 1984—, SUNY, Purchase, 1983. Mem. Artists Equity, Coll. Art Assn. Am., Nat. Mus. of Women in Arts, Nat. Space Inst., Women in the Arts. Home: 20 Waterside Plaza New York NY 10010

SHARP, DIANA LYNNE, civil administrator; b. Peru, Ind., Jan. 5, 1946; d. Vern Yates and Eva May (Layman) Gilbert; m. Larry Gene Sharp, Apr. 23, 1966; children—Brian Joseph, James Robert. With Peru Trust Co., Ind., 1964-73; dep. treas. Miami County, Peru, 1979-80, treas., 1981—. Sec., Miami County unit Am. Heart Assn., Peru, 1980—; treas. Parkview United Methodist Ch. Cub Scouts Am., Peru, 1982—; sec. Peru Little League, Inc., 1984—; past pres. Miami County Republican Women, Peru, 1981, 82. Mem. Ind. County Treas. Assn. (treas. 1982, 83). Lutheran. Avocations: sewing; counted cross stitch; camping. Home: 18 Graham Ave Peru IN 46970 Office: Miami County Treas 25 N Broadway Peru IN 46970

SHARP, GUN ANITA, public relations executive; b. Gothenburg, Sweden, Aug. 16, 1943; came to U.S., 1970; d. Andre Olof and Elsa Viola (Henrikson) B.A. in Advt. and Pub. Relations, Annonsbyra Foren Skola for Advt. and Public Relations, 1962; m. Roger Sharp, June 5, 1976; 1 son, Adam Mikael. Model, Europe, 1957-69; model Wilhelmina Model Agy., N.Y.C., 1970-72; free-lance broadcaster, newspaper journalist, Europe, 1966-69, U.S., 1970-74; with Bonnier Mag. Group Swedish Broadcasting, N.Y.C., 1970-74; head TV dept. R. Marston & Assocs., N.Y.C., 1974-78; pres. GRS Communications, Inc., N.Y.C., 1978—. Mem. Am. Women Radio and TV, Women in Communications. Clubs: Marstrand Yacht; Stamford Yacht; Royal Yacht of Gothenburg. Office: 211 E 43d St New York NY 10017

SHARP, MARY LUCILLE PEDEN, educational administrator; b. Kansas City, Mo., May 29, 1929; d. Clarence Allen and Laura Winifred (Henley) Peden; m. Richard Calvin Sharp, June 23, 1951; children—Richard Calvin, Robert Parker, Allen Russell Howland. B.S., Missouri Valley Coll., 1950; M.Ed., Central Mo. State U., 1970. Classroom tchr., Kans., Mo., Wash., 1950-69; reading specialist Kansas City (Mo.) Pub. Schs., 1969-74, adminstr. remedial reading program, 1974-76, cons. K-6 grades, 1976-77, instr. facilitator, 1977-80; prin. elem. schs., Kansas City, 1980—. Active local Boy Scouts Am., 1960-68, PTA, 1950—; sec. Elem. Schs. Meml. Fund Com., 1985—. Mem. Internat. Reading Assn. (treas. Kansas City chpt. 1975), Nat. Assn. Elem. Sch. Prins., Mo. Assn. Elem. Sch. Prins., Kansas City Assn. Elem. Sch. Prins. (pres. 1984-85), Assn. Supervision and Curriculum Devel., Kansas City Sch. Adminstrs. Assn., Delta Kappa Gamma (editor 1978-80, chmn. chpt. profl. affairs com. 1980-82, chmn. selective recruitment com. 1982-84, program com. 1984—). Episcopalian. Office: 11424 Gill St Sugar Creek MO 64054

SHARP, MONICA JENNIE, travel company executive; b. Dundee, Scotland, Apr. 30, 1941; came to U.S., 1962; d. Louis and Jeanie (Comerford) Proevost; m. Apr. 11, 1964. Sec., Brit. Airways, 1962-68; interline mgr. East African Airways, N.Y.C., 1969-74; pres., owner Cheetah Safaris, N.Y.C., 1975-80; v.p. Voyages Jules Verne, N.Y.C., 1980-83; pres., owner Gt. Journeys, N.Y.C., 1983—. Contbr. articles in field to profl. jours. Mem. Am. Soc. Travel Agents, Am. Soc. Peking. Club: St. Rule (St. Andrews, Scotland). Home: 6600 Boulevard E Wyn NJ 07093 Office: 2 W 45th St New York NY 10036

SHARP, SHARON BARTS, state official; b. Mishawaka, Ind., Oct. 7, 1939; d. Edwin J. and Gertrude E. (Maculski) Barts; student Holy Cross Central Sch. Nursing, South Bend, Ind., 1957-59; A.A.S., William Rainy Harper Coll., 1975; m. Donald L. Sharp, Sept. 12, 1959; children—Laura Sue, Christopher Barts. Free-lance writer, 1973-77; editor Elk Grove Twp. (Ill.) News, 1975-76; clk. Elk Grove Twp., 1975-79; spl. asst. on women to gov. State of Ill., Chgo., 1979-84; dep. dir. mktg. Ill. Dept. Commerce and Community Affairs, 1984—. Hon. co-chairwoman ERA Ill.; mem. Ill. Displaced Homemaker Adv. Bd.; mem. Cook County Republican Exec. Com., 1975—; co-chmn. Cook County Rep. Central Com., 1975—; Rep. nominee Ill. sec. of state, 1978; pres. Woman's Nat. Rep. Club, 1980—; bd. dirs. Ill. Fedn. Rep. Women; mem. Rep. Women's Task Force of Ill.; mem. Ill. Community Coll. Bd., 1976-79; mem. women's community adv. com. Northwestern U., 1982—; mem. women's bd. William Rainy Harper Coll. Mem. Chgo. Area Public Affairs Group, Women in Mgmt. (recipient Charlotte Danstron Women of Achievement award N.W. Suburban chpt.), Am. Econ. Devel. Council, Mid-Am. Econ. Devel. Council, LWV, Internat. Platform Assn., Ill. Devel. Council. Methodist. Clubs: City, Executive (Chgo.). Home: 1306 W Cedar Ln Arlington Heights IL 60005 Office: 100 W Randolph Rm 3-400 Chicago IL 60601

SHARPE, PAULINE, organization executive; b. Bklyn., Sept. 1, 1925; d. Harry and Esther (Gould) S. Student Bklyn. Coll., 1941-43, New Sch. for Social Research, N.Y.C., 1943-46. Editor N.Y. Petroleum Assn., N.Y.C., 1943-45, Ready-To-Wear, N.Y.C., 1945-47, Labor Relations Mgmt., N.Y.C., 1947-49; TV writer-dir. Sackett TV Prodns., N.Y.C., 1950-51; owner, mgr. Temporary Office Service, Miami, Fla., 1953-60; co-founder, exec. dir. Mark-Age, Inc., Ft. Lauderdale, Fla., 1960—. Author: Mark Age Period and Program, 1970, 2d edit., 1985; Evolution Of Man, 1971; Visitors From Other Planets, 1974; Angels and Man, 1974; Plan A Nation, 1975. Avocations: swimming; reading; sewing. Office: Mark-Age Inc PO Box 290368 Fort Lauderdale FL 33329

SHARPLES, VIRGINIA MITCHELL, engineering writing consultant; b. Indpls., July 3, 1942; d. James S. and Ruth K. Mitchell; B.A. (Operation Outstanding award 1974), Butler U., Indpls., 1964, M.S., 1970; m. Richard J. Sharples, Dec. 24, 1973; children—Allison Virginia, Scott Brydson, Gregory Mitchell, Glen Ryan. High sch. tchr., Phoenix, 1971-74, Tucson, 1974-75, Houston, 1977-78; customer services rep. Advanced Computer Techniques, Tucson, 1976-77; tech. services engr. SWACO div. Dresser Industries, 1978-81, engrng. writer Atlas div., Houston, 1981-82; copywriter Ogilvy & Mather, 1982-83; editor U.S. Woman Engr. Mag. seminar leader, engrng. writing cons. Mem. Soc. Women Engrs. Dallas (exec. bd. 1982-84), Soc. Petroleum Engrs. Episcopalian. Club: Dresser Toastmasters (pres. 1981, area gov. 1983-84). Author papers in field. Home and Office: 321 Yacht Club Dr Rockwall TX 75087

SHARROW, MARILYN JANE, library administrator; b. Oakland, Calif.; d. Charles L. and H. Evelyn S.; m. Lawrence J. Davis. B.S. in Design, U. Mich., 1967, M.A.L.S., 1969. Librarian Detroit Public Library, 1968-70; head fine arts dept. Syracuse U. Libraries, 1970-73; dir. library Roseville (Mich.) Public Library, 1973-75; asst. dir. libraries U. Wash., 1975-77, asso. dir. libraries, 1978-79; dir. libraries U. Man., Winnipeg, 1979-82; chief librarian U. Toronto, Can., 1982-85; univ. librarian U. Calif.-Davis, 1985—. Recipient Josenhans Pre-profl. award Detroit Public Library, 1968, Woman of Yr. in Mgmt. award Winnipeg YWCA, 1982. Mem. ALA, Calif. Library Assn. Office: U Calif-Davis 108 Shields Library Davis CA 95616

SHATAN, NORMA ALTSTEDTER, painter; b. N.Y.C., July 18, 1932; d. Irving Charles and Renee Rose (Green) Altstedter; student Academie de la Grande Chaumiere, Ecole du Louvre and Sorbonne, 1950-51; B.A., Goucher Coll., 1952; M.A., Columbia U., 1983; m. Chaim F. Shatan, May 29, 1955; children—Gregory, Gabrielle, Jessica, Jeremy. One-person exhbns. include: Prince St. Gallery, 1970, 72, 73, 76, 77, 82, 84, Paddlewicker Gallery, Lenox, Mass., 1977, 79; group shows include: Prince St. Gallery, Bklyn. Mus., Berkshire Mus, Salon des Comparaisons, Paris, Loch Haven Art Ctr., Orlando, Fla.; treas. Prince St. Gallery, 1970-80. Millay Colony for Arts fellow. Mem. Women in the Arts, Women's Caucus for Art. Translator: (with Alice Muehsam) The Sense of Form in Art (Heinrich Wolfflin), 1958. Home and Office: 415 Central Park W New York NY 10025

SHATTIL, ARLENE MARIE, public relations executive; b. Omaha, Nebr., July 12, 1920; d. John A. and Matilda (Bienstock) Solomon; m. Siegfried Shattil, Feb. 19, 1944; children—Ronald, Wendy, Daniel, Steven. Student U. Colo., 1938-41. Owner, pres. Scope Unltd., Chgo., 1969—; pub. relations cons. Circle Fine Art Corp., Chgo., 1979—. Ill. corr. Art Bus. News, 1984—. Vice pres. Jewish Council on Urban Affairs, Chgo., 1979—; mem. adv. bd. Ill. Youth Network Council Tng. Program, 1983—, bd. dirs. adv. council DePaul Goodman Sch. Drama, Chgo., 1983—; hon. bd. dirs. Women's Bd. Am. Cancer Soc., 1978—. Mem. Publicity Club Chgo. (bd. dirs. 1981—), Assn. Theatrical Press Agts. and Mgrs. Office: Scope Unlimited 2 E Oak St Suite 910 Chicago IL 60611

SHATTO, GLORIA MCDERMITH, college president, economist; b. Houston, Oct. 11, 1931; d. Ken E. and Gertrude (Osborne) McDermith; m. Robert J. Shatto, Mar. 19, 1953; children—David Paul, Donald Patrick. B.A. with honors in Econs., Rice U., 1954, Ph.D. (fellow), 1966. Market research Humble Oil & Refining Co., Houston, 1954-55; tchr. pub. sch., C.Z., 1955-56; tchr. Houston Independent Sch. Dist., 1956-60; asst. prof. econs. U. Houston, 1965-69, asso. prof., 1969-72; prof. econs., asso. dean Coll. Indsl. Mgmt., Ga. Inst. Tech., Atlanta, 1973-77; George R. Brown prof. bus. Trinity U., San Antonio, 1977-79; pres. Berry Coll., Mount Berry, Ga., 1980—; small bus. adv. com. U.S. Treasury, 1977-81; trustee Joint Council on Econ. Edn., 1985—; dir. Ga. Power Co., K-Mart Corp., Nat. Service Industries, So. Co. Contbr. articles to profl. jours.; Editor: Employment of the Middle-Aged, 1972; mem. editorial bd.: Ednl. Record, 1980-82. Mem. Tex. Gov.'s Commn. on Status of Women, 1970-72; trustee Ga. Tech. Research Inst., 1975-77, Berry Coll., Ga., 1975-79; mem. Ga. Gov.'s Commn. on Status of Women, 1975; mem. commn. on women in higher edn. Am. Council on Edn., 1980-82, chmn., 1982; mem. Ga. Study Com. on Public Higher Edn. Fin., 1981-82; v.p. Ga. Fund Ind. Colls., 1981, pres., 1982; mem. adv. bd. to Sch. Bus. Adminstrn., Temple U., Phila., 1981-83; mem. Study Com. on Ednl. Processes, So. Assn. Colls. and Schs., 1981-82, Ga. United Meth. Commn. on Higher Edn. and Campus Ministry, 1981—; trustee Redmond Park Hosp., Rome, Ga., 1981—. OAS fellow, summer 1968. Mem. Royal Econ. Assn., Am. Econ. Assn., So. Econ. Assn., Southwestern Econ. Assn. (pres. 1976-77), Am. Fin. Assn. (nominating com. 1976), Southwestern Social Scis. Assn., Fin. Execs. Inst. (chmn. Atlanta edn. com. 1976-77, mem. com. on profl. devel. 1981), AAUW (area rep. 1967-68, Tex. chmn. legis. program 1970-71, mem. internat. fellowships and awards com. 1970-76, chmn. 1974-76), Phi Beta Kappa, Phi Kappa Phi, Omicron Delta Epsilon. Address: Berry Coll Mount Berry GA 30149

SHATTUCK, BARBARA ZACCHEO, investment banking firm executive; b. New Rochelle, N.Y., Dec. 25, 1950; d. John Nicholas and Mary-Jane (Haller) Zaccheo; m. John Garrett Shattuck (div.). A.B., Conn. Coll., 1972; postgrad. NYU Sch. Bus., 1974-75. Bond analyst Standard & Poor's, N.Y.C., 1972-76; assoc. Blyth, Eastman Dillon & Co., N.Y.C., 1976; v.p. Goldman, Sachs, N.Y.C., 1976-82; ptnr. Cain Bros, Shattuck & Co., N.Y.C., 1982—; speaker Practicing Law Inst., Am. Hosp. Assn. Fundraiser Dem. Nat. Com., 1985-86; bd. dirs. Seltzer Found.; mem. friends of the collection com. Parrish Art Mus., Southampton, N.Y. Mem. Women's Econ. Round Table. Democrat. Episcopalian. Club: India House (N.Y.C.). Office: Cain Bros Shattuck & Co 101 Park Ave New York NY 10178

SHATTUCK, CATHIE ANN, lawyer; b. Salt Lake City, July 18, 1945; d. Robert Ashley and Lillian Francis (Culp) S.; B.A., U. Nebr., 1967, J.D., 1970. Bar: Nebr. 1970, Colo. 1971, U.S. Supreme Ct. 1975, D.C. 1984. Vice pres. Shattuck Farms, Inc., Hastings, Nebr., 1966-69, pres., 1969-70; atty., asst. project dir. Colo. Civil Rights Commn., Denver, 1971-73; trial atty. EEO Commn., Denver, 1973-77; partner firm Roybal & Shattuck, Denver, 1977-82; vice chmn. EEO Commn., Washington, 1982-84; ptnr. Epstein Becker Borsody & Green, Washington, 1984—; trainer, speaker in field. Mem. bd. fgn. service U.S. Dept. State, 1982-84; mem. sec.'s com. on vet.'s employment U.S. Dept. Labor, 1983-84; patron Denver Art Mus. Mem. Fed. Bar Assn., Am. Bar Assn., Nebr. Bar Assn., Colo. Bar Assn., Denver Bar Assn., Am. Judicature Soc., Nat. Assn. Women Lawyers, Alpha Xi Delta, Delta Sigma Rho, Tau Kappa Alpha (pres. 1966-67), Pi Sigma Alpha (v.p. 1966-67). Club: Denver. Office: Epstein Becker Borsody & Green 1140 19th St NW Suite 900 Washington DC 20036

SHATTUCK, RUTH ANN, property management executive; b. Carbondale, Ill., Apr. 14, 1950; d. Orville Drane Jackson and Ruth Irene (Tellor) Jackson Rafferty; m. Frederick Walter Shattuck, Mar. 29, 1982; children by previous marriage—Sallie Irena Woodard, Rebecca Ann Woodard, Lisa Michelle Woodard. Grad. high sch., Ft. Worth, 1968. Cert. in apt. mgmt. and profl. leasing. Clerical positions State of Tex., Ft. Worth, 1973-81; from leasing agt. to mgr. Carillon Mgmt. Co., Hurst and Ft. Worth, Tex., 1981-83; resident mgr. Stonehenge Apts., Ft. Worth, 1983-84, Country Oaks Apts./Herman Mgmt. Co., Ft. Worth, 1984, Spanish Meadows Apts./JG Mgmt., Ft. Worth, 1984-85; property supr. Tex. div. JG Mgmt., Ft. Worth, 1984—. Mem. Cert. Apt. Mgmt. Council (mem. speaker com. 1985-86), Tarrant County Apt. Assn. (mem. edn. com. 1982-86), Nat. Assn. for Female Execs. Republican. Baptist. Avocation: design and execution of individually numbered porcelain dolls. Home: 2210 E Loop 820 Apt 142 Fort Worth TX 76112 Office: Thorstar Inc PO Box 8623 Fort Worth TX 76124

SHAUGHNESSY, SISTER MARY ANGELA, principal, educator, consultant; b. Louisville, Dec. 16, 1949; d. Edward Michael and Corine Marie (Bratten) S. B.A., Spalding U., 1971, M.A., 1978; M.A., U. Louisville, 1976; Ph.D., Boston Coll., 1985. Joined Sisters of Charity of Nazareth, 1968; tchr., dept. head St. Mary's Acad., Leonardtown, Md., 1971-76; prin. Our Lady of Nazareth Acad., Wakefield, Mass., 1978—; adj. prof. Cath. Sch. Leadership program Boston Coll., Chestnut Hill, Mass., 1982—. Mem. Assn. Supervision and Curriculum Devel., Nat. Assn. Secondary Sch. Prins., Nat. Orgn. on Legal Problems of Edn. Home: 25 Winship Dr Wakefield MA 01880 Office: Our Lady of Nazareth Acad 14 Winship Dr Wakefield MA 01880

SHAVER, KATHRYN, advertising executive; b. LaFayette, Ala., July 5, 1945; d. Edwin Wood and Kathryn (Simmons) S.; m. Edwin Hampton Perry, May 25, 1976. B.A. in Visual Design, Auburn U., 1967. Creative dir. Fred Worrill Advt., Atlanta, 1968-71; creative dir. Pruitt Printing, Atlanta, 1971-73; art dir. David Advt., Louisville, 1973-75; chmn. K. Shaver Pub. Relations, Inc., Louisville, 1984—; pres. K. Shaver Advt., Inc., Louisville, 1975—; dir., exec. com. Heritage Corp., 1981—; cons. in field. Bd. dirs. Kidney Found., Louisville, 1979-82, Project Bus., Louisville, 1982-84; bd. dirs., treas. Better Bus. Bur., 1981—; bd. dirs. Leadership Louisville Found., 1985—, Louisville Orch., 1982—. Recipient numerous advt. industry awards. Mem. Advt. Club of Louisville (dir. 1977—, pres. 1984-85, chmn. 1985-86), C. of C. (vice chmn. 1984-86). Address: K Shaver Advt Inc 304 W Liberty Suite 300 Louisville KY 40202

SHAW, ARACELIS GOBERNA, educator; b. Pinar del Rio, Cuba, June 22, 1922; came to U.S., 1948, naturalized, 1955; d. Jose B. and Eloisa (Santiuste) Goberna; B.S., B.L., Inst. Pinar del Rio, 1941; Ph.D. and Letters, U. Havana, 1948; M.A., U. Fla., 1957; m. Steven J. Shaw, June 8, 1952. Instr., Berlitz Sch. Langs., Miami, Fla., 1949-52, N.Y.C., 1952-54; research asst. U. Fla., 1955-57; mem. faculty Columbia (S.C.) Coll., 1957—, prof. Spanish, 1963—, chmn. dept. fgn. langs., 1962—, head Intercultural and Lang. Center, 1977—; dir. lang. workshops, cons. in field. Pres. S.C. chpt. Partners of Americas, 1975-78, 81—. Recipient Cervantes award, 1976, S.C. Bicentennial award, 1976. Mem. Am. Assn. Tchrs. Spanish and Portuguese (pres. S.C. chpt. 1973-74), MLA, Southeastern Conf. Fgn. Lang. Tchrs. (adv. bd.), Nat. Council Fgn. Lang. Teaching, Southeastern Conf. Latin Am. Studies, Sigma Delta Pi. Roman Catholic. Club: Columbia Coll. Internat. Author: (for TV) El Espanol Paso a Pso, 1969; also workbooks, lab. manuals. Home: 4832 Forest Ridge Ln Columbia SC 29206 Office: Intercultural and Lang Center Columbia Coll Columbia SC 29203

SHAW, BETTY JOSEPHINE, housing development executive, housing consultant; b. Jonesboro, Ark., Sept. 5, 1945; d. Doyne J. and P. Ruth (Allison) Steinsiek; m. Jan. M. Shaw, Dec. 22, 1967 (div. Nov. 1980); 1 child, Misty Lynn. B. Music Edn., Ark. State U., 1967; postgrad. U. So. Miss., 1970, Ark. State U., 1969, U. So. Ark., 1975-77; cert. in mgmt. tng. U. Ala.-Birmingham, 1978; drug edn. tng. U.S. Dept. Edn. Sch. Medicine, Miami, Fla., 1973. Tchr., Judsonia Pub. Schs., Ark., 1967-69, Hattiesburg Pub. Schs., Miss., 1969-70; real estate sales Groves Realty, Magnolia, Ark., 1972-74; regional rep., mental retardation-developmental disabilities div. Ark. Dept. Human Services, Magnolia, 1974-77, adminstrv. asst. to dep. commr., 1977; mortgage loan underwriter Tenn. Housing Devel., Nashville, 1977-80; pres. Betty Shaw & Assocs., Jonesboro, 1980—; cons. on housing for disabled, 1980—; cons. to states of Ark., Idaho and Alaska, 1981, Utah and Pa., 1982, Tex., 1982-83, La., 1982—; cons. to numerous pvt. mental health orgns. and facilities, 1980—; project coordinator Harold Russell Assocs., Waltham, Mass., 1980-83; housing cons. Urban Systems Research & Engring., Inc., Cambridge, Mass., also Washington, 1985. Author, editor Accessing Housing manual, 1980; author: HUD Guidelines for Section 202 Housing for Developmentally Disabled Persons, 1985. County chmn. Ark. Heart Assn., 1972-73, mem. state bd. dirs., 1974-77; v.p. Nettleton Athletic Booster Club, Jonesboro, 1985—; Girls' State chmn. Nettleton unit Am. Legion Aux., 1985 ; vol. planner and worker 1st drug offenders program in Ark., 1973-74. Baptist. Avocations: judging gymnastics, raising horses, gardening. Home: PO Box 874 Jonesboro AR 72403

SHAW, DAISY K., educational administrator; b. N.Y.C., Sept. 26, 1913; d. Littman and Lena Katz; m. Frederick Shaw, Nov. 21, 1941; children—Richard, Ellen. B.A., Hunter Coll., 1933; postgrad. Columbia U., 1933-35, Cornell U., 1940, 61; M.A., NYU, Tchr. fgn. lang. Washington Irving High Sch., Benjamin Franklin High Sch., Long Island City High Sch. (all N.Y.), 1935-50; tchr. in charge Long Island City Evening High Sch., N.Y.C. Bd. Edn., 1944-47; coordinator Evening Guidance ctr., 1951-62, asst. prin. Simon Baruch Jr. High Sch., 1955-58, Washington Irving High Sch., 1958-62, dir. guidance Bur. Ednl. and Vocat. Guidance, N.Y.C. Pub. Schs., 1962-82, spl. asst. to exec. dir. div. pupil personnel services, 1982—; adj. assoc. prof. Hunter Coll., 1968-74. Recipient George Hutcherson award N.Y. State Personnel and Guidance Assn., 1975; ann. award Council Adminstrs. and Suprs., 1976; named to Hunter Coll. Hall of Fame, 1972; Bour e Bargy fellow to France, 1936; Ford Found. fellow, 1954-55. Mem. N.Y.C. Personnel and Guidance Assn. (pres. 1974-75), Large City Dirs. of Guidance (pres. 1973-74), Am. Personnel and Guidance Assn., Assn. Counselor Edn. and Supervision, Vocat. Guidance Assn., N.Y. Acad. Pub. Edn., Adminstrv. Women, Am. Assn. Sch. Adminstrs. Contbr. to Manual of Child Psychopathology, 1972; contbr. articles and revs. to profl. jours. Home: 41 Henry St Brooklyn NY 11201 Office: 362 Schermerhorn St Brooklyn NY 11217

SHAW, ELEANOR JANE, newspaper editor; b. Columbus, Ohio, Mar. 23, 1949; d. Joseph Cannon and Wanda Jane (Campbell) S.; B.A., U. Del., 1971; m. John M. Flanagan, Sept. 1, 1974. With News-Jour. newspapers, Wilmington, Del., 1970-82, acting bus. editor, 1976-77, editor HEW desk, asst. met. editor, 1977-80, bus. editor, 1980-82; topics editor USA Today, 1982-83; asst. city editor The Miami Herald, 1983-85; projects editor The Sacramento Bee, 1985—. Bd. dirs. Del. 4-H Found., 1978-83. Mem. Sigma Delta Chi. Office: The Sacramento Bee PO Box 15779 Sacramento CA 95852

SHAW, GEORGIA KAREN, family and youth worker; b. Houston, Aug. 20, 1953; d. Kara Vernon McQueen and Myrtle Lee (Shaw) Butler. B.A., U. Houston. Family and youth worker Hope Ctr. for Youth, Houston, 1977—. Mem. Nat. Assn. of Blacks in Criminal Justice, Tex. Council on Crime and Delinquency, Sigma Gamma Rho, Alpha Psi (fellow). Clubs: Lazy T Ranch (coordinator 1983—), YWCA, Urban Theater (Houston). Office: Hope Ctr for Youth 4115 Yoakum Houston TX 77006

SHAW, GRACE GOODFRIEND (MRS. HERBERT FRANKLIN SHAW), publisher; b. N.Y.C.; d. Henry Bernheim and Jane Elizabeth (Stone) Goodfriend; student Bennington Coll.; B.A. magna cum laude, Fordham U., 1976; m. Herbert Franklin Shaw; 1 child, Brandon Hibbs. Reporter, Port Chester (N.Y.) Daily Item; editorial coordinator World Scope Ency., N.Y.C.; asso. editor Clarence L. Barnhart, Inc., Bronxville, N.Y., 1950; free-lance writer for reference books, 1951-61; sr. editor, coll. dept. Bobbs-Merrill, N.Y.C., 1961-62, mng., editor, 1963-65; editing supr. World Pub Co., N.Y.C., 1965-68, mng. editor, 1968-69, sr. editor, 1969; mng. editor Peter H. Wyden Co., N.Y.C., 1969-70; asso. editor Dial Press, N.Y.C., 1971-72, sr. editor, 1972; sr. editor David McKay Co., N.Y.C., 1972-75; sr. editor Grosset & Dunlap, 1975-79, chief editor Today Press, 1977-79; exec. editor trade dept. Bobbs-Merrill Co., N.Y.C., 1979, pub., 1980-85; mng. editor Rawson Assocs., N.Y.C., 1985—. Mem. Overseas Press Club Am. Office: Rawson Assocs 115 Fifth Ave New York NY 10003

SHAW, JO AN, assn. exec.; b. Coshocton, Ohio, Feb. 3, 1929; d. Cleon K. and Daisy L. Shaw; student Bowling Green State U., 1947, 48, Kent State U., 1949-51. Recreational therapist Massillon (Ohio) State Hosp., 1952-60; recreational therapist Sunny Acres Hosp., Cleve., 1960-63; teen program specialist YWCA of Met. Detroit, 1964-69, creative and performing arts dir., 1969-71, public relations dir., 1971—. Coordinator, initiator Believe in Detroit Coalition, 1976-80; mem. community adv. bd. Channel 56, 1978-82. Mem. Detroit Women's Advt. Club (dir.), Detroit Press Club. Methodist. Home:

38768 Chartier St Mount Clemens MI 48045 Office: 2230 Witherell St Detroit MI 48201

SHAW, KATHLEEN ANN, journalist; b. Athol, Mass., Aug. 1, 1945; d. Alexander and Evelyn (Burwood) S. A.S., Becker Jr. Coll., 1965; student Assumption coll., 1985—, also intermittently Clark U., Anna Maria Coll. Reporter, Worcester Telegram & Gazette, Mass., 1964-81; writer lifestyle dept. Evening Gazette, Worcester, 1981-84, Time Out mag. staff, 1984—; reporter WCAT-AM, Orange, Mass., 1963. Solicitor, United Way, 1981—. Mem. Nat. Assn. Female Execs., Becker Jr. Coll. Alumni Assn. (chmn. nominating com. 1986, sec. 1986—). Roman Catholic. Avocations: reading; travel; swimming; Japanese language; Russian history studies. Home: 399 Unity Ave Athol MA 01331 Office: 20 Franklin St Worcester MA 01613

SHAW, MADELINE READ, machine tool company executive; b. Saginaw, Ala., July 16, 1910; d. Thomas H. and Eleanor (Satterwhite) Read; student U. Ala., 1919-22; m. Ralph M. Shaw Jr., June 15, 1927; 1 dau., Mary Eleanor Shaw Carretta (dec.). Tchr., Stafford Sch., Tuscaloosa, Ala., 1922-24; pvt. tchr. music, Gorgas, Ala., 1924-25; organist Paramount Publix Co., Miami, Fla. and N.Y.C., 1925-27; with Pedrick Tool & Machine Co., Riverton, N.J., 1939—, v.p. fin., 1940-79, pres., 1979—. Republican. Episcopalian. Club: Cosmopolitan of Phila. Home: Shawnee Hall Beverly NJ 08010 Office: 1518 Bannard St Riverton NJ 08077

SHAW, MARY ANN, psychologist; b. Dallas, July 5, 1937; d. Leon V. and Mabel (Bartlett) S.; B.S., U. Tex., 1959; M.Ed., U. Houston, 1966, Ed.D., 1973. Tchr. educable mentally retarded Spring Branch, Tex., 1959-64; vocat. counselor, Houston, 1964-66; psychometrist pvt. psychol. clinic, Houston, 1966-70; coordinator research Tex. Edn. Agency grant project, 1970-72; dir. psychol. services Tex. Scottish Rite Hosp. for Crippled Children, Dallas, 1972-82; dir. Dean Evaluation Ctr., Dallas, 1982-84; mem. clin. staff U. Tex. Health Sci. Center; cons. pvt. and public schs. Mem. Am. Psychol. Assn., Dallas Psychol. Assn., Assn. Pediatric Psychologists. Author: What Do I Do When; contbr. article to profl. jour.; research in field.

SHAW, MARY LEE, health care educator, consultant; b. Kokomo, Ind., Oct. 11, 1933; d. John Frederick and Mary Elizabeth (Bola) Maher; m. Thomas Arthur Shaw, Feb. 18, 1956 (div. 1975); children—Tracy Elizabeth, Susan Margaret, Kathryn Lee. A.A., William Woods Coll., 1952; A.B. in French, Ind. U., Bloomington, 1954, M.S., 1961. Instr. modern lang. dept. Purdue U.-Calumet, Hammond, Ind., 1961-70; tchr., cons. Burnham Pub. Schs., Hammond Pub. Schs., 1970-74; tng. specialist nursing edn. U. Tex., M.D. Anderson Hosp. and Tumor Inst., Houston, 1975-78; nurse recruiter, 1978-80, group supr., dept. tng. and devel., 1980—, supr. personnel tng. programs, 1986—; speaker in field. Mem. Alliance Française, Literacy Vols. Am., Phi Theta Kappa (pres. Fulton, Mo. chpt. 1951-52), Alpha Chi Omega (pres. Hammond chpt. alumni 1966-67). Home: 5227 Wood Creek Way Houston TX 77017 Office: MD Anderson Hosp and Tumor Inst 6723 Bertner Houston TX 77030

SHAW, NANCY ANN, lawyer; b. Pitts., May 15, 1955; d. Harry Edward and Patricia Ann (Hussey) S.; m. James A. Goldsmith, Sept. 10, 1983. B.A., U. Iowa, 1977; J.D., 1980. Bar: Ohio 1980. Assoc. firm Squire, Sanders & Dempsey, Cleve., 1980—. Articles editor Jour. Corp. Law, 1979-80. Mem. jr. womens com. Cleve. Playhouse. Mem. ABA, Ohio Bar Assn., Cuyahoga County Bar Assn., Def. Research Inst., Mortar Bd. Home: 19220 Lomond Blvd Shaker Heights OH 44122 Office: Squire Sanders & Dempsey 1800 Huntington Blvd Cleveland OH 44115

SHAW, NANCY LEE, myotherapist; b. Lincoln, Nebr., May 8, 1943; d. Donald Leland and Marie Helen (Jackson) Shaw. B.S., U. Nebr., 1966; M.A. cum laude, Trinity Evang. Div. Sch., 1976; Cert. myotherapist, Bonnie Prudden Sch. Phys. Fitness and Myotherapy, 1981. Instr., coach Horlick High Sch., Racine, Wis., 1966-71; coach Trinity Coll., Deerfield, Ill., 1971-73; instr., dept. chmn., coach Warren High Sch., Gurnee, Ill., 1973-77; instr., tutor, coach George Mason U., Fairfax, Va., 1977-79; program devel. specialist YWCA, Dunn Lorring, Va., 1979-80; instr. anatomy Bonnie Prudden Sch. Phys. Fitness & Myotherapy, Stockbridge, Mass., 1980; chief trigger point myotherapist Myofascial Pain Control Clinic, Springfield, Va., 1981—; faculty Shaw Myotherapy Inst., Springfield, Va., 1984—, dir., 1984—; lectr. in field; cons. Nat. Assn. Myotherapists, 1983—. Contbg. editor book, 1972. PTA of Nebr. scholar, 1962; named Coach of the Year, Warren High Sch., 1976. Mem. Nat. Assn. Myotherapists (past pres.), AAUW, Nat. Assn. Female Execs. Democrat. Methodist. Avocations: golf; cooking; swimming; camping; cycling. Home: 6810 Lois Dr Springfield VA 22150 Office: Myofascial Pain Control Clinic 6417 Loisdale Rd #309 Springfield VA 22150

SHAW, RENATA VITZTHUM, library administrator; b. Mantta, Hame, Finland, July 21, 1926; came to U.S., 1947, naturalized, 1957; d. Burghard and Helle (Sirén) Vitzthum von Eckstadt; m. Russell Ramon Shaw, Aug. 14, 1954; children—Rembert B.V., Lori R.H. M.A. in Art History, U. Chgo., 1949; Magister Philosophiae, U. Helsinki (Finland), 1951; Diploma in Museology, Ecole de Louvre, Paris, 1952; M.S. in L.S., Catholic U., 1962. With Library of Congress, Washington, 1962—, supervisory librarian, 1967-71, bibliog. specialist, 1971-82, asst. chief prints and photographs div., 1982-83, acting chief, 1983-84, asst. chief, 1984—, mem. Pennell purchasing com., 1983-84, mem. acquisitions com. 1985-86. Compiler: (bibliography) Picture Searching, 1973; (essays) Graphic Sampler, 1978, Century of Photographs, 1980; chmn. editorial com. Art Serials (D.C.), 1981, Washingtoniana, a guide to photog. resources in Prints and Photos Div., 1984-86. Recipient Meritorious Service award Library of Congress, 1975. Mem. ALA, Art Libraries Soc. N.Am., Washington Art Library Resources Com. (founder 1974), Spl. Libraries Assn. (dir. 1976-78), Huguenot Soc. S.C., Beta Phi Mu. Republican. Episcopalian. Home: 4850 Langdrum Ln Chevy Chase MD 20815 Office: Prints and Photographs Div Library of Congress 10 1st St SE Washington DC 20540

SHAW, SHARRILYN WHITING, perfume co. exec.; b. Mobile, Ala., Oct. 6, 1946; d. James Allen and Virginia G. (Hearn) Whiting; student U. Ala., 1965-67, U. South Ala., 1968-70, Sterling Inst., 1979, Tex. Tech. Profl. Devel. Center, 1981; m. Edwin Parker Shaw, Jr., Oct. 20, 1976; 1 son, Ivey. Writer, Nashville Tennessean, 1970, Mobile (Ala.) Press Register, 1968-69; account exec. The Pitluk Group, San Antonio, 1976-77; advt./promotion mgr. Sta. KSAT-TV, San Antonio, 1977-79; advt. mgr. Lone Star Brewing Co., San Antonio, 1979-80, mgr. mktg., 1980-82; v.p. mktg. Swiss Watch Distbn. Center, Inc., San Antonio, 1982; pres., chief exec. officer Dans Un Jardin Tex., Inc., Dallas, 1982—. Chmn., ABC-TV Network Promotion Adv. Bd., 1978-79, San Antonio Women's Edn. and Employment, Inc., 1981-82; commr. San Antonio Conv. and Visitors Bur., 1981-82; mem. steering com. Leadership San Antonio, 1981—; v.p. bd. dirs. Children's Hosp. Found., 1979—; bd. dirs. Monte Vista Hist. Assn., Tex. Women's Employment and Edn., Inc., others; mem. jr. com. San Antonio Symphony. Recipient Pro-Liner awards Women in Communications, 1980; award AP Ala., 1969; Addy awards, 1977, 78, 79; Internat. Assn. Bus. Communicators - Dallas award, 1981; Mem. Am. Mktg. Assn., Tex. Public Relations Assn., Women in Communications, (v.p. 1979-80), Alpha Chi Omega. Clubs: Bright Shawl, St. Anthony, Mills County Hunting & Fishing, First Wednesday Breakfast. Home: 303 W Gramercy Pl San Antonio TX 78212

SHAW, SUSAN JEAN, college administrator; b. N.Y.C., Sept. 30, 1943; d. Noah and Sylvia Charlotte (Troy) S.; B.Mus.Edn., Syracuse (N.Y.) U., 1965; postgrad. Hunter Coll., Columbia U. Tchrs. Coll.; M.Div., Alliance Theol. Sem., 1984; postgrad. Drew U., 1986—; divorced; children—Scott Lewis, Tamra Eileen. Tchr. music edn. public and pvt. schs., Westchester County, N.Y., 1966-73; placement counselor Fanning Personnel, N.Y.C., 1974-75; pres. Communiscope, Inc., Miami, Fla., 1976-77; exec. dir. Dental Health Services, Miami, 1977-79; propr. Shaw Enterprises, Inc., Miami and N.Y.C., 1979-81; communications specialist World Relief Corp., Nyack, N.Y., 1981-84; dir. coll. relations Berkshire Christian Coll., Lenox, Mass., 1984-86; exec. dir. Multiple Ministries, White Plains, N.Y., 1986—; cable TV producer The Psychotheology Hour; seminar leader, 1978—. Ridgeway Alliance Ch. scholar, 1980; William H. Nelson scholar, 1981. Mem. Profl. Bus. Women's Assn., Profl. Christian Women's Assn., Women in Ministry, Christian Singles Fellowship, AAUW, Pi Lambda Theta, Sigma Alpha Iota. Author articles, revs. in field. Home and Office: 5 Bryant Crescent 2K White Plains NY 10605

SHAW, UNEVA REAGAN, respiratory therapist; b. Chattanooga, Tenn., Sept. 21, 1956; d. Radford Burket and Susie Bernice (Flowers) Reagan; m. Charles Lee Shaw, Aug. 19, 1978. A.S. in Respiratory Care, Cleveland Community Coll., Tenn., 1976; B.S. in Mgmt., U. Tenn.-Chattanooga, 1987. Registered respiratory therapist. Staff therapist East Ridge Hosp., Chattanooga, 1976, Diagnostic Hosp., Chattanooga, 1976-79; mgr. respiratory therapy Hutcheson Med. Ctr., Ft. Oglethorpe, Ga., 1978-85; mgr. respiratory therapy and hosp. quality assurance NME-Metro Hosp., Chattanooga, 1985—; instr. Am. Heart Assn., 1981—, Chattanooga Tech. Coll., 1980-85. Mem. Am. Assn. Respiratory Therapy. Republican. Mem. Ch. of Christ. Avocations: skiing, photography, hiking. Home: PO Box 22576 Chattanooga TN 37422 Office: NME Met Hosp 511 McCallie Ave Chattanooga TN 37403

SHAWGO, PAULA MARIE, graphic designer; b. Celina, Ohio, Jan. 28, 1953; d. Thomas Leroy and Mary Grace (Turicchi) Bidwell; m. Barry Lee Ackom, June 15, 1970 (div.); 1 dau., Creon Nicole. Student Wright State U., 1971-72, San Antonio Coll., 1973-74. Advt. mgr. Gulf Pool Equipment Co., San Antonio, 1979, Refrigeration Engrng. Corp., San Antonio, 1980-82; v.p. advt. and pub. relations Genie Services Inc., San Antonio, 1982-83; graphic designer Inst. Texan Cultures, San Antonio, 1984—. Christian Scientist. Office: Inst Texan Cultures PO Box 1226 San Antonio TX 78294

SHAW-MCADAMS, AARONIA, marketing and business development consulting company executive; b. Burlington, N.C., Dec. 7, 1952; d. Aaron Vernard and Jennie Lee (Thompson) Shaw; 1 child, Thaddaeus D. Ed. Bennett Coll., 1971, Augusta Coll., 1978-80, Va. State U., 1978-80. Dir. bus. devel. Va. State Office of Minority Bus. Enterprise, Petersburg, 1977-80; various positions in internat. mktg. and European trade, Fed. Republic Germany, 1980-83; dir. Automated Scis. Group, Inc., Silver Spring, Md., 1985—; pres. The Exec. Link, Alexandria, Va., 1983—. Editor: ASG Technologies, 1985, 86; author report and manual. Mem. Nat. Assn. Female Execs., Armed Forces Communications and Electronics Assn., NAACP, Friends of Kennedy Center, Am. Soc. Profl. and Exec. Women, Assn. Female Bus. Owners. Democrat. Baptist. Avocations: tennis; swimming; travel. Home: Executive Link PO Box 15093 Alexandria VA 22309

SHEA, CHARLENE RIOPELLE, personal motivation speaker, consultant; b. Lawrence, Mass., Sept. 3, 1934; d. George Andrew and Ruth Knowlton (Pickard) Riopelle; B.S., U. Maine, 1957; m. Thomas Everett, Mar. 30, 1956; children—Valerie Ruth, Thomas Leon, Gwendolyn Beryl. Tchr. 1st grade, Okinawa, Japan, 1958-60, El Paso, Tex., 1961-65, Highland, N.J., 1965-68, Frankfurt, Germany, 1969-72; dir. sales tng. Mary Kay Cosmetics, Inc., Manchester, N.H., 1972-80; pres. Charlene Shea., Inc., motivational speaking and cons. firm, Manchester, 1980—; instr. U. N.H., Manchester, 1979—. Mem. fin. com. YWCA, 1981, bd. dirs., 1982-84; bd. dirs. WON, 1981. Recipient N.H. Woman in Bus. adv. award SBA, 1982; Cert. Speaking Profl. award, 1986. Mem. Internat. Platform Assn., Manchester C. of C., Nat. Speakers Assn., N.H. Women's Forum. Home and Office: 121 Allied St Manchester NH 03103

SHEA, DEBORAH HEATHER GUBNER, marketing executive; b. N.Y.C., Jan. 30, 1955; d. Richard Sigmund and Yvonne Lucille (Luke) Gubner; m. Bill Shea, Apr. 21, 1984 (div. 1986). B.A., U. South Fla., 1977; postgrad. in mktg. Northwestern U., 1979-81. First scholar First Nat. Bank Chgo., 1977-78, mgr. comml. mktg. communications, 1978-80, dir. internat. mktg., 1980-81; dir. mktg. planning and communications Arthur Andersen & Co., Chgo., 1981-83, dir. mktg. Rocky Mountain region, 1983-84; dir. Shea Cons. Group, 1984-86; dir. mktg. Cigna Healthplan, 1986—; profl. theatre actress, dir. Actors Studio, Circle in Square, N.Y.C., 1969-77. Bd. dirs. Goodman Theatre's Inner Circle, Chgo., 1979-81; mem. jr. governing bd. Chgo Symphony Recipient Eagle award for top fin. advt., Chgo Advt. Club, 1980, 81. Mem. Am. Mktg. Assn. (dir. Colo.) Direct Mktg. Assn., N.Am. Assn. Corp. Planners. Contbr. articles to profl. jours. Home: 2905 Mill Stream Ct Clearwater FL 33519 Office: Cigna Healthplan 2502 Rocky Point Rd Tampa FL 33623

SHEA, ELAINE EVANS, civic assn. exec.; b. Ithaca, N.Y., Aug. 1, 1935; d. William Arthur and Genevieve (Covert) Evans; A.A., Stephens Coll., 1955; m. Michael Henry Shea, June 28, 1956; children—Elizabeth Ann, Linda Evans, William Michael. Writer, film previewer Sta. KWTV, Oklahoma City, 1955-56; exec. dir. Save the Tallgrass Prairie, Inc., Shawnee Mission, Kans., 1974-84. Bd. dirs. Kans. Natural Resource Council, 1982-83; registered lobbyist, 1980-82; pres. Porter Sch. PTA, 1969; leader Girl Scouts; tchr. Sunday Sch., Shepherd deacon Village United Presbyn. Ch.; tract chmn. Am. Cancer Soc., 1982; exec. dir. Grassland Heritage Found., 1982-85, bd. dirs., 1985—; mem. Kans. Gov.'s Adv. Commn. on Environ., 1983—. Recipient Environ. Quality award EPA, 1978. Clubs: Stephens Coll. Dinner (pres. 1966), Prairie Planters Garden (pres. 1972), Kansas City Country. Editor: Tallgrass Prairie News, 1974-84. Home: 6025 Cherokee Dr Shawnee Mission KS 66205 Office: 5450 Buena Vista Shawnee Mission KS 66205

SHEA, PAMELA JANE, lawyer; b. Concord, N.H., Aug. 14, 1948; d. Ernest Francis and Cynthia Pamela (Horwood) Gaudreau; m. Dennis James Shea, Aug. 21, 1971; children—Kelly, Tracey. B.A. cum laude, Smith Coll., 1970; J.D., U. Mich., 1973. Bar: Mich. 1974. Law clk. organized crime, racketeering sect. U.S. Dept. Justice, Detroit, 1971; mem. firm Beier, Howlett, Hayward, McConnell, McCann, Jones, Kingsepp & Shea, Bloomfield Hills, Mich., 1973-79, ptnr., 1979—; mem. State Bar-Tort Law Rev. Com., 1983—, Circuit Ct. Com., Bloomfield Hills, 1983—; instr. I.C.L.E. Trial Advocacy Workshops, 1983—. Mem. Oakland County Bar Assn., State Bar Assn. Mich., ABA, Women's Bar Assn., Assn. Def. Trial Counsel, Sigma Xi. Republican. Episcopalian. Club: Smith (Birmingham-Bloomfield Hills). Home: 420 Dunston Rd Bloomfield Hills MI 48013 Office: Beier Howlett Hayward 74 W Long Lake Rd Suite 1 Bloomfield Hills MI 48013

SHEAHAN, CLAIRE MATHER, insurance company executive; b. Bridgeport, Conn., May 9, 1942; d. Robert Elston and Ruth Evelyn (Allen) S.; B.A., Vassar Coll., 1964. Copy editor Yale U. Press, New Haven, 1964-65; advt. press relations Tchrs. Ins. & Annuity Assn.-Coll. Retirement Equities Fund, N.Y.C., 1965-70, editor employee communications, 1970-72, communications specialist, 1972-78, corp. communications adminstr., 1978-80, asst. publs. officer, 1980-84, pub. info. officer, 1984-86, asst. v.p., pub. info. officer, 1986—. Mem. Fin. Communications Soc., N.Y. Women in Communications, Pub. Relations Soc. Am., N.Y. Fin. Writers Assn., Internat. Assn. Bus. Communicators, N.Y. Assn. Bus. Communicators, Nat. Investor Relations Inst., Am. Mgmt. Assn. Episcopalian. Clubs: Vassar (pres. emeritus), Women's City (N.Y.C.). Office: TIAA-CREF 730 3d Ave New York NY 10017

SHEARER, CATHERINE ELIZABETH, nursing educator, clinical specialist; b. Brookville, Pa., Nov. 28, 1943; d. James Edward and Esther Thelma (Minnich) Dwyer; m. Curtis Jennings Shearer, Jr., Nov. 28, 1963; children—Dawn Cherie, Curtis Jennings, III. A.S., Gloucester County Coll., 1975; B.S. in Nursing, Stockton State Coll., 1977; M.S. in Nursing, U. Del., 1983. R.N., N.J. Charge nurse Elmer (N.J.) Community Hosp., 1975-77; instr. Salem County Vo-Tech, Woodstown, N.J., 1976-78; dir. inservice, supr. Elmer Community Hosp. (N.J.), 1977-78; clin. specialist Ancora Psychiat. Hosp., Hammonton, N.J., 1982; instr. Cumberland County Coll., Vineland, N.J., 1982-83, Gloucester County Coll., Sewell, N.J., 1976—; pvt. practitioner, psychotherapist, Clayton, N.J., 1983—; guest lectr. to various orgns., 1976—. Author: Body Image and Self Concept of the Women with a Mastectomy, 1983. Chairperson pub. edn. Am. Cancer Soc., 1980-83, v.p., 1983, chmn. profl. edn., 1983—, chmn. bd., 1984—; mem. risk force Am. Heart Assn., Gloucester County, N.J., 1983-85. Recipient Sword of Hope, Am. Cancer Soc., 1982; Ruth Beaumont award in pub. edn. Am. Cancer Soc., 1983. Mem. Am. Nurses Assn., N.J. State Nurses Assn. (dir. 1980-81; mem. legis. com. 1977-80), Alumni Assn. Gloucester County (dir. 1983—). Home: 750 W Clayton Ave Clayton NJ 08312 Gloucester County Coll Salina and Tanyard Rds Sewell NJ 08080

SHEARER, DARLENE B., business executive, researcher; b. Albany, N.Y., Nov. 7, 1956; d. Carlo Michael Baggetta and Joyce Evelyn (Ward) Forscy. B.A. in Mgmt. and Bus. cum laude, Barat Coll., 1985. Customer service specialist Pyle Nat. Co., Chgo., 1977-78, product specialist, 1978-79, systms analyst, 1979-80, systems support supr., 1980, supr. customer service, 1981-83, mgr. customer service, 1983-84; v.p. ops. Tektac, Inc., 1984—; pres. Gina and Assocs., Riverside, Ill., 1980—. Mem. Republican Nat. Com., Washington, 1981-86; vol. '84 Presdl. campaign, Riverside, 1984. Mem. Delta Epsilon Sigma. Home: 116 Northgate Rd Riverside IL 60546

SHEARER, JOY BRAMPTON, lawyer; b. Bryn Mawr, Pa., Nov. 27, 1953; d. Andrew Willard Shearer and Joy Lorraine (Riley) McLeieer; m. John Robert Angstadt, Aug. 28, 1977; 1 son, John Robert. B.A., Fla. Atlantic U., 1973; J.D., U. Fla., Gainesville, 1975. Bar: Fla. 1976, U.S. Dist. Ct. (so. dist.) Fla. 1976, U.S. Ct. Appeals (11th cir.) 1981, U.S. Supreme Ct. 1981. Atty. Legal Aid Soc. Palm Beach County Inc., 1976-77; asst. atty. gen. Fla. Dept. Legal Affairs, West Palm Beach, 1977-83; bur. chief, 1983—. Contbr. chpt. to book. Mem. Fla. Assn. Women Lawyers (pres. Palm Beach County chpt. 1983-84), Fla. Bar Assn. (appellate rules com. 1982—), ABA, Palm Beach County Bar Assn. (vice chmn. law week com. 1983), Phi Alpha Delta. Office: Dept Legal Affairs 111 Georgia Ave Suite 204 West Palm Beach FL 33401

SHEBAR, ELINOR, wallcovering distbn. co. exec.; b. N.Y.C., June 24, 1936; d. David T. and Dorothy (Levine) Jacobson; A.A., Bklyn. Coll., 1956; m. Arthur Shebar, June 17, 1955; children—Eric, Mathew. Sales rep. Columbus Coated Fabrics, Rockville Centre, N.Y., 1971-74, W.R. Grace, Clifton, N.J., 1974-76; sales rep. Bayview Wall Coverings, Inc., Lindenhurst, N.Y., 1976-78, sales mgr., 1978—. Bd. dirs. Sterns Park, Freeport, N.Y., Union Reform Temple, Freeport, Republican Club, Freeport and Merrick, N.Y. Mem. Bus. and Profl. Woman's Assn., Wall Paper Distbrs. Assn., Paint and Wall Paper Dealers Assn., Color Mktg. Group, L.I. Computer Club, S100 Users Group. Clubs: B'nai B'rith, Hadassah. Office: Bayview Wall Coverings 41 E Sunrise Hwy Lindenhurst NY 11757

SHEDD, REBECCA LYNN, wholesale distribution company manager, literacy trainer; b. Toledo, Nov. 24, 1954; d. Richard George and Marjorie Ann (Lunn) S. B.A. in Edn., Depauw U., 1976; postgrad. U. Minn. Purchasing agt. Water Products Co., Eden Prairie, Minn., 1977—, mgr. data processing, 1984—; tutor, trainer Laubach Literacy, Mpls., 1979—. Tutor, trainer, bd. dirs. Minn. Literacy Council, Roseville, 1979—; lead trainer Mpls. Literacy Project, 1979—. Recipient Gold award Minn. Literacy Council, 1984. Mem. Laubach Literacy Action, Minn. Literacy Action, Am. Soc. Tng. and Devel. Methodist. Avocations: skiing. biking; swimming; reading; traveling. Home: 2427 E Lake of Isles Minneapolis MN 55405 Office: Water Products Co 15801 W 78th St Eden Prairie MN 55344

SHEEDY, KATHLEEN CROWLEY, med. technologist; b. Bridgeport, Conn., Mar. 23, 1950; d. Edward V. and Jeanne (Duhamel) Crowley; B.S., Western Conn. State Coll., 1972; student Danbury (Conn.) Hosp. Sch. Med. Technology, 1971-72, SUNY Upstate Med Center, Syracuse, 1973-74; m. Mark E. Sheedy; children—Paul C., John E. Lab. technologist, Danbury Hosp., 1972-73; instr. med. technology SUNY Upstate Med. Center, 1975-81, supr. blood bank, 1974-81; blood bank supr. Vassar Brothers Hosp., Poughkeepsie, N.Y., 1982—. Barlow House Council scholar, 1968. Mem. Am. Soc. Clin. Pathologists, Am. Assn. Blood Banks. Roman Catholic. Contbr. articles to profl. jours. Home: 24 Horseshoe Dr Hyde Park NY 12538 Office: Hosp Shared Services 191 Delafield St Poughkeepsie NY 12601

SHEEHAN, CATHE, marketing executive; b. Natick, Mass., Mar. 23, 1958; d. John Francis Sheehan and Marjorie Elizabeth (Werner) Picchi. B.S. in Econs. and Mgmt., B.A. in Psychology, Franklin Pierce Coll., 1980. Field dir. Media Stats., Inc., Silver Spring, Md., 1980-81; supr. domestic stats. Am. Textile Mfrs. Inst., Washington, 1981-82; dir. stats. Envelope Mfrs. Assn., Arlington, Va., 1982-83; office automation cons. Coopers and Lybrand, Washington, 1983-84; industry mktg. analyst Wang Labs., Lowell, Mass., 1984-86; dir. sales DBU, Inc., N.Y.C., 1986—. Contbg. author poetry anthology. Home: 825 N 29th St Apt 5D Philadelphia PA 19130 Office: 38 E 29th St New York NY 10016

SHEEHAN, DEBORAH ANN, radio station executive, theater executive; b. Paterson, N.J., Mar. 29, 1953; d. John J. and Ruth (Badertschier) S.; m. Emidio S. Quattrocchi, Mar. 15, 1985. B.A., William Patterson Coll., 1975. With radio Sta. WWDJ, Hackensack, N.J., 1980-83, Shadow Traffic, N.Y.C., 1981-83; dir. news, community affairs WPAT-AM/FM, N.Y.C., 1979—. Actress-tchr. Paterson Arts Ctr., 1975-79; host radio show Bus. Jour. N.J., 1984; host, producer radio show Debbie Sheehan mag., 1983; host FDU Focus, Cable Network N.J.; writer plays. Exec. dir., actress Learning Theater Co., Paterson, 1975—; sec. bd. dirs. YMCA Passaic Valley, Paterson, 1983—; mem. N.J. Legal Bd., Montclair, N.J., 1984—; mem. Paterson Edn. Found., 1984—; bd. dirs. United Way Passaic Valley, Conn., 1985. Recipient Edward R. Murrow Gold medal B'nai B'rith, 1983; Gold medal Internat. Radio Festival award, 1983; finalist Edward R. Murrow Gold medal B'nai B'rith, 1984-85; Best Reporter award Sigma Delta Chi, 1985; Best Feature award, 1985; Angel Excellence award, Los Angeles, 1985; Internat. Press Assn. fellow, Japan, 1985. Club: Zonta. Avocations: weaving; travel; acting. Office: WPAT-AM/FM 1396 Broad St Clifton NJ 07013

SHEEHAN, LINDA SUZANNE, educational administrator; b. Dayton, Ohio, Aug. 1, 1950; d. Paul J. and Betty L. (Fowler) King; m. J. Scott Sheehan, Dec. 18, 1971. 1 child Amy Elizabeth. B.S. in Edn. with honors, Ohio State U., 1971; M.Ed., U. Tex., 1974; adminstrn. cert. Houston Baptist U., 1983. Cert. tchr., Tex. Tchr. Upper Arlington Schs., Columbus, Ohio, 1971-72, Brown Sch., San Marcos, Tex., 1972-73, Comal Ind. Sch. Dist., New Braunfels, Tex., 1973-75, Alief Ind. Sch. Dist., Houston, 1975-79; asst. prin. Killough Middle Sch., Houston, 1979-84; prin. Olle Middle Sch., Houston, 1984—. Named Tchr. of Yr., Olle Middle Sch., Houston, 1978. Mem. Tex. Middle Sch. Assn. (dir. 1982—), Tex. Tchrs. Assn., Alief Edn. Assn., NEA, Houston Council Social Studies, Kappa Delta Pi (pres. 1984-85)., Phi Delta Kappa. Roman Catholic. Home: 11842 Cedar Pass Dr Houston TX 77077 Office: Olle Middle Sch 9200 Boone Rd Houston TX 77099

SHEEHAN, LORRAINE M., state official; b. Manchester, N.H., May 2, 1937. Mem. Md. Ho. of Dels., 1974-83, vice chmn. Prince George's County del., mem. ways and means com., subcom. on edn. of task force to study state/local fiscal relationships, humane practices commn., chmn. health care subcom., mem. Med. Assistance Program; sec. state State of Md., Annapolis, 1983—. Trustee Greater S.E. Community Hosp. Found.; bd. dirs. Suitland Local Devel. Corp. Recipient Margaret Sanger award Planned Parenthood Md., 1983; Disting. Service award Md. Mental Health Assn., 1985; Outstanding State Ofcl. award Young Democrats of Md., 1984. Mem. LWV, PTA, Marlboro Democratic Club, Kettering Civic Fedn., Greater Southeast Center for Aging. Club: Bus. and Profl. Women's (Woman of Yr. award 1984). Office: Office of Sec of State State House Annapolis MD 21404*

SHEEHAN, MARY AGNES, lawyer; b. St. Paul, Oct. 21, 1950; d. Donald Joseph and Patricia (Goodman) Sheehan; m. Anthony Francis Marra, Jr., June 5, 1982. Student U. Vienna, 1970-71; B.A., Creighton U., 1972, J.D. cum laude, 1975. Bar: Minn. 1975, D.C. 1980, U.S. Ct. Appeals (2d cir.) 1977, U.S. Ct. Appeals (3d cir.) 1977, U.S. Ct. Appeals (4th cir.) 1977, U.S. Ct. Appeals (5th cir.) 1977, U.S. Ct. Appeals (8th cir.) 1978, U.S. Ct. Appeals (9th cir.) 1978, U.S. Ct. Appeals (D.C. cir.) 1978, U.S. Ct. Appeals (1st cir.) 1978, U.S. Supreme Ct. 1979. Atty., Dept. Labor, Washington, 1975-80; ptnr. Garvey, Schubert, Adams & Barer, Washington, 1980—; gen. counsel Nat. Conf. State Societies, Washington, 1980-84, Minn. Soc., Washington, 1980-84. Recipient Disting. Achievement award Dept. Labor, 1978; Appreciation award Nat. Conf. State Societies, 1983. Mem. ABA, Fed. Bar Assn., Am. Trial Lawyers Assn., Women's Bar Assn., Washington Women's Network. Office: Garvey Schubert Adams & Barer 1000 Potomac St NW Washington DC 20007

SHEEHAN, PAMELA LUCY, landscaping executive; b. London, Aug. 26, 1930; d. William and Elsie (Marsh) Singleton; m. John Darlington Beecroft, Jan. 31, 1948 (div. Dec. 1969); children—Melanie Anne Beecroft McArthur, Peter J. Beecroft, Stephen Beecroft; m. John Gordon Myles (div. Jan. 1981); m. Robert Francis Sheehan, Dec. 29, 1984. Grad. high sch. Exec. asst. Doris Currie Personnel, Toronto, Ont., Can., 1969-70; office mgr. Summit Personnel, Toronto, 1970-71; pres. Superior Personnel, Toronto, 1972-83; pres. Rodeo-landscaping, Deerfield Beach, Fla., 1983—. Dir. pub. relations Victorian Order of Nurses, Ont., 1957. Mem. Fla. Builders Assn. (assoc.). Mem. Ch. of Eng. Club: Deer Creek Country (Deerfield Beach). Avocations: golf; tennis. Home and office: 2440 Lob-Lolly Ln Deerfield Beach FL 33442

SHEEHAN, SUSAN, writer; b. Vienna, Austria, Aug. 24, 1937; came to U.S., 1941, naturalized, 1946; d. Charles and Kitty C. (Hermann) Sachsel; m. Neil Sheehan, Mar. 30, 1965; children—Maria Gregory, Catherine Fair. B.A., Wellesley Coll., 1958. Editorial researcher Esquire-Coronet, N.Y.C., 1959-60; free-lance writer, N.Y.C., 1960-62; staff writer New Yorker mag., N.Y.C., 1962—. Author: Ten Vietnamese, 1967; A Welfare Mother, 1976; A Prison and a Prisoner, 1978; Is There No Place on Earth for Me?, 1982; Kate Quinton's Days, 1984. Contbr. articles to publs. including N.Y. Times Sunday Mag., Harper's, Atlantic, New Republic, McCall's, Holiday. Judge Robert F. Kennedy Journalism awards, 1980, 84; mem. adv. com. on employment and crime Vera Inst. Justice, 1978—; mem. lit. panel D.C. Commn. on Arts and Humanities, 1979—; mem. pub. info. and edn. com. Nat. Mental Health Assn., 1982—. Durant scholar Wellesley Coll.; Guggenheim fellow, 1975-76; fellow Woodrow Wilson Ctr. for Internat. Scholars, 1981; recipient Sidney Hillman Found. award, 1976, Gavel award ABA, 1978, Individual Reporting award Nat. Mental Health 1981, Pulitzer prize for gen. non-fiction, 1983, Feature Writing award N.Y. Press Club, 1984, Disting. Alumna award Wellesley Coll., 1984. Mem. Phi Beta Kappa. Office: New Yorker Mag 25 W 43d St New York NY 10036

SHEEHAN, VICTORIA SPANN, lawyer; b. St. Louis, July 25, 1953; d. Charles Wayne and Sue Pledge (Middleton) Spann; m. John Kevin Sheehan, Jan. 3, 1981; 1 dau., Meghan Catherine. Student U. Denver, 1971-72, Universidad de las Americas, Cholula, Puebla, Mexico, 1972-73; B.A. cum laude, U. N.H., 1975; J.D., Washington U., St. Louis, 1979. Bar: Mo. 1979, U.S. Dist. Ct. (ea. dist.) Mo. 1979. Bilingual paralegal Vista, East Chicago, Ind., 1975; law clk. Mo. Atty. Gen., St. Louis, 1978-79; assoc. atty. Kortenhof & Ely, St. Louis, 1979-84; v.p., gen. counsel Spann-Sheehan Co., St. Louis, 1984—; co-developer La Salle Bldg., St. Louis. Mem. ABA, Lawyers Assn., Assn. Def. Lawyers, Women Lawyers Assn., Mo. Bar Assn., Bar Assn. Met. St. Louis. Republican. Methodist. Office: Spann-Sheehan Co 2031 Olive St Saint Louis MO 63101

SHEEHEY, SHEILA CELESTE, mfg. co. exec.; b. Boston, May 13, 1924; d. Thommas Joseph and Charlotte Mary (Cronin) S.; B.A., N.Y.U., 1975. Asst. to social editor Newark News, 1947-56; asst. to advt. mgr. Handy & Harman, precious metal fabricator and refiner, N.Y.C., 1957-76, adv. mgr., 1976—. Mem. Bus. and Profl. Advt. Assn. Office: 850 3d Ave New York NY 10022

SHEEHY, MARYANN C., English educator; b. Greenwich, Conn., June 7, 1954; d. Joseph William and Mary Carol (Modugno) Gagon; m. Joseph John Sheehy, July 25, 1981. B.S. in English Edn., Western Conn. State U., 1976, M.S., 1983. Cert tchr., Conn. Tchr. English, New Milford High Sch., Conn., 1978—. Mem. Conn. Edn. Assn., NEA. Democrat. Roman Catholic. Avocations: writing; music; guitar; historic restoration.

SHEEHY, PATRICIA JANE, public relations consultant; b. Trenton, N.J., Oct. 23, 1946; d. William V. and Helen Mary (Dowd) S.; m. Martin P. Lombardo, Jan. 23, 1971 (div. May 1978); m. 2d, Michael J. Gallagher, Nov. 22, 1981; 1 dau., Patricia Sheehy Lombardo. B.A., Rider Coll., 1968. Sr. disability ins. examiner N.J. Dept. Labor and Industry, Trenton, 1968-74; media cons. Pub. News Service, N.Y.C., 1975-77; sr. editor Ednl. Testing Service, Princeton, N.J., 1977-80; pub. relations cons., Haddon Heights, N.J., 1981—; staff writer New Hope (Pa.) mag., 1982—. Contbr. articles to profl. jours. Chmn. Democratic borough council polit. campaigns, Princeton, N.J., 1972-77; v.p. Friends of Haddon Heights Library, 1983—. Mem. Phila. Women in Communications. Democrat. Roman Catholic. Clubs: Camden County Toastmasters Internat. (Haddonfield, N.J.); Village Playbox, Jr. Women's (program chmn. 1981-83) (Haddon Heights, N.J.). Home: 206 8th Ave Haddon Heights NJ 08035

SHEERAN, GAIL, travel agency owner; b. Winchester, Mass., May 10, 1936; d. Ralph Enoch and Helen Grace (Tetley) Wells; m. Kenneth Sheeran, Feb. 16, 1957 (div. Sept. 1983); children—Beverly Kaye, Debra Jean. Student Framingham State Coll., 1980-1981. Operator Northeast Telephone, Worcester, Mass., 1957-58; clk. Met. Life Ins., Worcester, 1958-59, Kanef Drug, Worcester, 1962-67; owner, pres. Gail's Childrens Apparel, Inc., Hudson, Mass., 1967-83, Uniglobe Best Way Travel, Inc., Marlboro, Mass., 1984—; corporator Hudson Savs. Bank, 1976-86; dancer, tchr. oriental dance, 1970-86; instr. exercise/aerobics, 1983-86. Co-chmn. Nostalgia Days-Hudson Merchants, 1980; worker mayoral campaign, Marlboro, 1985; bd. dirs. Quinsigamond Community Coll. Travel Sch., Worcester, Mass., 1986. Mem. Nat. Assn. Female Execs., Marlborough Bus. and Profl. Women's Club, Marlborough C. of C. (bd. dirs. 1985-86), Hudson Merchants Assn. (sec. 1977-79). Republican. Methodist. Clubs: 4-H, Grange (Oakham, Mass.). Avocations: dancing; jogging. Home: 1 Felton St Hudson MA 01749 Office: Uniglobe Best Way Travel Inc 530 Boston Post Rd Marlborough MA 01752

SHEETS, SUE LAURA, newspaper ofcl.; b. Dayton, Ohio, Nov. 15, 1929; d. Charles LeRoy and Dorothy Ethel (Leis) Schaaf; student Ohio State U., 1947-48, hon. degree Nat. Cash Register Posting Sch., Denver, 1952, student YMCA Coll. of Commerce, Newark, Ohio, 1968; grad. Inst. Children's Lit., Redding Ridge, Conn., 1982; m. R.E. Walters; children—Steven Mitchell, Douglas Charles, Gregg Joseph; m. 2d, Ralph D. Sheets, June 21, 1969. Sec. with Ohio Fin. Co., Dayton, 1948-50, Goulds Pumps, Seneca Falls, N.Y., 1950-52, 53-54; poster, Colo. Nat. Bank, Denver, 1952-53; reporter Ace News, Heath, Ohio, 1966-68; founding dir. LEADS, Buckeye Lake, Ohio, 1968-72; sec. with Garwood Industries, Heath, 1973-74; columnist, editor, editor bus. and farm page, The Advocate, Newark, Ohio, 1978-82, entertainment and TV editor, 1982—; tchr. painting oils and acrylics, owner, operator arts and crafts shop, Hebron, Ohio, 1968-77. Organizer sr. citizens group, Buckeye Lake, 1968. Mem. Licking County Art Assn., Friends of Daweswood, NRA. Democrat. Methodist. Clubs: Order Eastern Star (Hebron)., Land of Legend Rifle and Pistol. Home: 180 S 5th St Newark OH 43055 Office: 25 W Main St Newark OH 43055

SHEFFER, KAREN ELAINE, lawyer, investment broker; b. Winchester, Ind., May 4, 1953; d. Maurice Henry and Pauline Alberta (Baker) S. B.A., Ohio No. U., 1975; J.D., U. Cin., 1979. Bar: Ohio 1979, U.S. Dist. Ct. (no. dist.) Ohio 1983, U.S. Supreme Ct. 1984. Asst. prosecutor Crawford County, Bucyrus, Ohio, 1979-83; sole practice, Bucyrus, 1983-85; investment broker Edward D. Jones & Co., Bellevue, Ohio, 1985—; mem. law enforcement adv. bd. North Central Ohio Tech. Coll., Mansfield, 1983—. Mem. Youth Adv. Bd., Bucyrus, 1983—; v.p. unit Am. Cancer Soc.; site com. chmn. Crawford County Jail Betterment Com. Mem. ABA, Ohio State Bar Assn., Crawford County Bar Assn., Ohio Acad. Trial Lawyers, Fedn. Bus and Profl. Women. Republican. Methodist. Clubs: Altrusa, Bucyrus. Office: PO Box 147 Bellevue OH 44811

SHEFFIELD, ANN CORNELL, government official; b. N.Y.C., Oct. 17, 1941; d. Frederick and Carolyn (Blair) S.; m. Richard Lee Roth, Apr. 30, 1983. B.A., Smith Coll., 1963; M.A., Stanford U., 1966, Ph.D., 1973. Instr. class I, San Jose State Coll., 1964-65; teaching asst. Stanford U., 1966; instr. Smith Coll., 1966-69; instr. Barnard Coll., N.Y.C., 1969-73, asst. prof., 1973-77; humanist adminstr. NEH, Washington, 1977-79; program officer Woodrow Wilson Internat. Ctr. for Scholars, Smithsonian Instn., Washington, 1979-80, asst. dir. fellowships, program sec. history, culture and soc., 1980—; Trustee Paul Smith's Coll., 1979-85, Milton Acad., 1981—. Mellon Found. fellow Aspen Inst. Humanistic Studies, 1976. Mem. Am. Philol. Assn., Phi Beta Kappa. Office: The Wilson Ctr Smithsonian Instn 1000 Jefferson Dr SW Washington DC 20560

SHEFFIELD, JANET MCCABE, swim instructor; b. Primghar, Iowa, Mar. 24, 1944; d. Irving and Bess (Saxe) Lefkow; m. Richard Lee McCabe, Sept. 4, 1965 (div. June 1970); children—Bradley Samuel McCabe, Kevin Ira McCabe; m. Robert Langdon Sheffield, Aug. 31, 1975. B.A., U. Colo., 1966. Swim instr. Janet McCabe's Swim Sch., Boulder, 1964—; owner Mesa Swim Club, Boulder, 1974—; cons., com. mem. ARC, Boulder, 1980—; cons. pvt. swim pools, Denver, 1983—. Author: (with Cinda Kochen) Swimming, The First Three Years, 1986. Recipient Water Safety award ARC, Boulder, 1982. Mem. U.S. Swimming Found. Home: 4505 Apache Rd Boulder CO 80303 Office: Janet McCabe's Swim Sch 3080 Valmont St #210 Boulder CO 80301

SHEH, VIOLET MAE, journalist; b. Prince Rupert, B.C., Can., June 3, 1919; d. Mah Bon and Edith (Gee) Quen; student Mun Yew Sch. Chinese Studies, Toishan, Kwangtung, China, 1935-39; m. Kenneth Sheh, Feb. 19, 1948; children—Cheryl Irene Sheh DeHaan, Douglas Wayne, Kenneth Warren. Fgn. corr. Chinatown News, Vancouver, B.C., 1957-58; social and consumer columnist, gen. reporter, Richmond (B.C.) Rev., 1967-72, vol. writer, 1981—; writer travel articles from Fiji, Peru and Argentina, 1967-72; roving reporter Street Scene, 1981—. Home: 10251 Aintree Crescent Richmond BC V7A 3T9 Canada Office: 5811-A Cedarbridge Way Richmond BC V6X 2A8 Canada

SHEINBAUM, MATHILDE DATTELBAUM, association executive; b. Bklyn., Apr. 5, 1923; d. Maurice J. and Belle May (Klein) Dattelbaum; m. Herbert H. Sheinbaum, Feb. 22, 1953; children—Robert B., Susan C. Student Packer Collegiate Inst., Bklyn., 1936-42; B.A., Adelphi U., 1944; cert. Katherine Gibbs Sch., N.Y.C., 1945. Regional adminstr. Tablet & Ticket Co., N.Y.C., 1968-75; exec. dir. Assn. Ind. Camps, N.Y.C., 1975—. Bd. govs. Older Women's League, N.Y.C., 1983-84, exec. bd., 1984—. Mem. Met. Mus. Art., Friends of N.Y. Pub. Library, People for Am. Way. Jewish. Home: 541 E 20th St New York NY 10010 Office: Assn Ind Camps Inc 60 Madison Ave New York NY 10010

SHEININ, ROSE, biochemist, educator; b. Toronto, Ont., Can., May 18, 1930; d. Harry and Anne (Szyber) Shuber; B.A., U. Toronto, 1951, M.A. (scholar), 1953, Ph.D. in Biochemistry, 1956, L.H.D., 1985; D.H.L. (hon.), Mt. St. Vincent U., 1985; m. Joseph Sheinin, July 15, 1951; children—David Matthew Khazanov, Lisa Basya Judith, Rachel Sarah Rebecca. Demonstrator in biochemistry U. Toronto (Ont., Can.), 1951-53, asst. prof. microbiology, 1964-75, asst. prof. med. biophysics, 1967-75, prof. microbiology, 1975—, prof. med. biophysics, 1978—, assoc. prof. med. biophysics, 1975-78, chmn. microbiology and parasitology, 1975-82, vice dean Sch. Grad. Studies, 1984—; mem. Health Scis. Com.; vis. research assoc. chem. microbiology, Cambridge U., 1956-57, Nat. Inst. Med. Research, London, 1957-58; research assoc. fellow div. biol. research Ont. Cancer Inst., 1958-67; sci. officer cancer grants panel Med. Research Council Can.; mem. Can. Sci. Del. to People's Republic of China, 1973; mem. adv. com. Provincial Lottery Health Research Awards; mem. adv. com. on biotech. NRC Can., 1984—; mem. Sci. Council Can., 1984—; adv. com. on sci. and tech. CBC, 1980-85; vis. prof. biochemistry U. Alta., 1971. Nat. Cancer Inst. Can. fellow, 1953-56, 58-61; Brit. Empire Cancer Campaign fellow, 1956-58; recipient Queen's Silver Jubilee medal, 1978; Josiah Macy Jr. Faculty scholar, 1981-82; fellow Ligue Contre le Cancer, France, 1981-82. Fellow Am. Acad. Microbiology, Royal Soc. Can.; mem. Can. Biochem. Soc. (pres. 1974-75), Can. Soc. Cell Biology (pres. 1975-76), Am. Soc. Virology, Am. Soc. Microbiologists, Assn. Women in Sci., Scitech, Soc. Complex Carbohydrates, Toronto Biochem. and Biophys. Soc. (pres. 1960-70, council 1970-74). Assoc. editor Can. Jour. Biochemistry, 1968-71, Virology, 1969-72, Intervirology, 1974-85; editorial bd. Microbiol. Revs., 1977-80; author, co-author various publs. Office: Dept Microbiology Univ Toronto 150 College St Toronto ON M5S 1A8 Canada

SHEIRR, OLGA, artist; b. N.Y.C., June 7, 1931; d. Edward E. and Lillian (Tobias) S.; B.A., Bklyn. Coll., 1953; postgrad. Art Students League, Pratt Graphic Center, NYU, Itaglio Workshop, N.Y. Inst. Fine Arts; m. Maurice Krolik, Jan. 28, 1973. One-woman exhbns. include: Internat. Art Exchange, N.Y.C., 1962-63, Noho Gallery, N.Y.C., 1975-76, 78-80, 82, 83, Cicchinelli Gallery, N.Y.C., 1982, New Sch. Social Research, N.Y.C., 1984, Barbizon Gallery, Greenwich, Conn., 1984, Fairleigh Dickinson U., 1985; group shows Ken Keleba Gallery, 1985, Kipp Gallery, others; bd. dirs. Noho Gallery, 1975—, treas., 1982-83; exhbn. organizer Noho for the Arts, 1975-78; v.p., sec. Assn. Artists Run Galleries, N.Y.C., 1976-80, reviewer Artists View Art, 1976-80; group exhbns. include: A.A.A. Gallery, N.Y.C., 1965, 71, Silvermine Guild Artists, New Canaan, Conn., 1966, 76, Landmark Gallery, N.Y.C., 1976, The Arsenal, N.Y.C., 1978, Community Gallery, N.Y.C., 1980-81, 83, Springville (Utah) Mus. Art, 1981, 83, Riyadh, Saudi Arabia, 1982, Fairleigh Dickinson U., N.J., 1983, N.Y. Soc. Women Artists, 1984; represented in permanent collections: Mus. City of N.Y., St. Vincent's Hosp., N.Y.C., Greenville County (S.C.) Mus., NYU Hosp., others. Mem. Women's Caucus for Art, N.Y. Artists Equity (bd. dirs. 1985—), Women in the Arts, N.Y. Soc. Women Artists (rec. sec. 1984—). Subject of articles in mags. and newspapers. Home: 360 1st Ave 11 G New York NY 10010

SHELDON, BEATRICE EVERETT, political worker; b. Gunn, Miss., May 16, 1915; d. John Broadus and Pency Ann (Wooley) Everett; R.N., Dr. Willis Walley Sch. Nursing, Jackson, Miss., 1937; m. Anson H. Sheldon, Feb. 5, 1939; children—Patricia Ann Sheldon Strauss Ekstrom, Anson H., Lawson. Nurse, Kings Daus. Hosp., Canton, Miss., 1937, Greenville, Miss., 1937, Helena (Ark.) Hosp., 1938-39; sec.-treas. Machinery Inc., 1966—; County com. Miss. Republican Party, 1944-60; alternate del. to Rep. State Conv., 1948, 52, 56, 60. Trustee South Washington County Hosp., Hollandle, Miss., chmn. bd., 1985. Mem. Miss. Registered Nurse Assn. Episcopalian. Clubs: Longwood Community Culture (pres. 1975-78), Federated Women's. Home: Keystone Plantation Avon MS 38723

SHELDON, BROOKE EARLE, librarian, educator; b. Lawrence, Mass., Aug. 29, 1931; d. Leonard Hadley and Elsie Ann (Southerl) Earle; m. George Duffield Sheldon, Mar. 28, 1955 (dec.), children—L. Scott, G. Stephen. B.A., Acadia U., 1952, D.C.L. (hon.), 1985; M.L.S., Simmons Coll., 1954; Ph.D., U. Pitts., 1977. Youth librarian Detroit Public Library, 1954-55; base librarian, Ent AFB, Colorado Springs, Colo., 1955-57, U.S. Army, Germany, 1956-57; br. librarian Albuquerque Public Library, 1959-61; coordinator adult services Santa Fe Public Library, 1965-67; head library devel. N.Mex. State Library, Santa Fe, 1967-72; asst. dir. leadership tng. inst. U.S. Office Edn., Washington, 1971-73; head tech. services and tng. Alaska State Library, Juneau, 1973-75; dean Sch. Library Sci., Tex. Woman's U., Denton, 1977—, acting provost, 1979-80. Contbr. articles to profl. jours. Mem. ALA (pres. 1983-84), Tex. Library Assn., Beta Phi Mu. Democrat. Episcopalian. Office: School Library and Info Studies Texas Woman's University Denton TX 76204

SHELDON, ELEANOR HARRIET BERNERT, sociologist; b. Hartford, Conn., Mar. 19, 1920; d. M.G. and Fannie (Myers) Bernert; A.A., Colby Jr. Coll., 1940; A.B., U. N.C., 1942; Ph.D., U. Chgo., 1949; m. James Sheldon, Mar. 19, 1950 (div. 1960); children—James, John Anthony. Asst. demographer Office Population Research, Washington, 1942-43; social scientist U.S. Dept Agr., Washington, 1943-45; assoc. dir. Chgo. Community Inventory, U. Chgo., 1947-50; social scientist Social Sci. Research Council, N.Y.C., 1950-51, research grantee, 1953-55, pres., 1972-79; research assoc. Bur. Applied Social Research, Columbia, 1950-51; social scientist UN, N.Y.C., 1951-52; lectr. sociology Columbia U., 1951-52, vis. prof., 1969-71; research assoc., lectr. sociology UCLA, 1955-61, assoc. research sociologist, lectr. Sch. Nursing, 1957-61; sociologist, exec. assoc. Russell Sage Found., N.Y.C., 1961-72; vis. prof. U. Calif.-Santa Barbara, 1971; dir. Rand Corp., 1973-83, NL Industries, Equitable Life Assurance Soc., Citicorp, 1973-85, Citibank, 1973-85, Mobil Corp. Bd. dirs. Colby-Sawyer Coll., UN Research Inst. for Social Devel., 1973-79; trustee Rockefeller Found, 1978-86, Nat. Opinion Research Center; bd. dirs. Inst. East-West Security Studies. William Rainey Harper fellow U. Chgo., 1945-47. Fellow Am. Acad. Arts and Scis., Am. Sociol. Assn., Am. Statis. Assn. mem. U. Chgo. Alumni Assn. (Profl. Achievement award), Sociol. Research Assn. (pres. 1971-72), Council on Fgn. Relations, AAAS, Am. Assn. Pub. Opinion Research, Eastern Sociol. Soc., Internat. Sociol. Assn., Internat. Union. Sci. Study of Population, Population Assn. Am. (2d v.p. 1970-71), Inst. of Medicine (chmn. program com. 1976-77), Nat. Acad. Scis.-NRC Commn. on Behavior and Social Scis. Club: Cosmopolitan. Author: (with L. Wirth) Chicago Community Fact Book, 1949; America's Children, 1958; (with R.A. Glazier) Pupils and Schools in N.Y.C., 1965. Editor: (with W.E. Moore) Indicators of Social Change; Concepts and Measurements, 1968. Editor Family Economic Behavior, 1973. Contbr. articles to profl. jours. Home: 630 Park Ave New York NY 10021

SHELDON, GEORGIANA HORTENSE, government official; b. Lawrenceville, Pa., Dec. 2, 1923; d. William Franklin and Georgiana (Root) Sheldon; B.A., Keuka Coll., 1945; M.S., Cornell U., 1949; m. James R. Sharp, May 18, 1979. Dir. admissions Stetson U. Coll. Law, 1954-56; exec. asst. Republican Nat. Com., 1956-61; exec. sec. Hon. Rogers Morton (rep., Md.), 1962-69; dep. dir. Def. Civil Preparedness Agy., Washington, 1969-75; dir. Office Fgn. Disaster Assistance, dep. dir. internat. disaster assistance AID, 1975-76; vice chmn. CSC, 1976-77; mem. Fed. Power Commn., 1977—; mem. Fed. Energy Regulatory Commn., 1977-85. Presbyterian.

SHELDON, NANCY WAY, management consultant; b. Bryn Mawr, Pa., Nov. 10, 1944; d. John Harold and Elizabeth (Hoff) Way; B.A., Wellesley Coll., 1966; M.A., Columbia U., 1968, M. Phil., 1972; m. Robert Charles Sheldon, June 15, 1968. Mgmt. cons. ABT Assocs., Cambridge, Mass., 1968-70; mgmt. cons. Horbridge House, Inc., Boston, 1970-73, sr. asso., prin., N.Y.C., 1973-77, v.p., Los Angeles, 1977-79; mgmt. cons., pres. Resource Assessment, Inc., Los Angeles, 1979—; ptnr., real estate developer Resource Devel. Assocs., Los Angeles, 1980—; ptnr. Anubis Group Ltd., Los Angeles, 1980—. Registered, lic. pvt. investigator, Calif. Recipient achievement award Nat. Assn. Women Geographers. Mem. Am. Mining Congress, Am. Inst. Mining, Metall. and Petroleum Engrs., DAR, Nat. Audubon soc., World Wildlife Fund (charter). Clubs: Mt. Kenya Safari, Wellesley of So. Calif. Contbr. articles to profl. jours. Address: 1192 Kittiwake Circle Sanibel Island FL 33957

SHELINSKY, DEBRA ANN, lawyer; b. N.Y.C., Sept. 30, 1955; d. Philip and Sylvia (Silverstein) Shelinsky. B.A., Queens Coll., 1977; J.D., St. John's U., 1980. Bar: N.Y. 1981. Trademark atty. Morton-Norwich Products, Inc., Norwich, N.Y., 1981-82; trademark atty. Norwich Eaton Pharms., Inc. (subs. Procter & Gamble Co., Cin.), Norwich, 1982-83, trademark counsel, 1983—. Mem. N.Y. State Bar Assn., ABA (patent trademark copyright sect.), Pharm. Mfrs. Assn. (trademark copyright com.). Home: Hillside House Apts Norwich NY 13815 Office: Norwich Eaton Pharms Inc 17 Eaton Ave Norwich NY 13815

SHELL, BARBARA PAMPLIN, civic worker; b. Colonial Heights, Va., Sept. 3, 1928; d. Jennings Cornile and Blanche B. (Temple) Pamplin; B.S., Madison Coll., 1949; m. Louis Calvin Shell, Aug. 5, 1950; children—Pamela, Patricia. Tchr. chemistry, physics Chesterfield County Schs., 1949-51; chemist Brown and Williamson Tobacco Co., Petersburg, Va., 1951-52. Vice-mayor, Petersburg, 1976-78, mem. City Council, 1974-78; mem. Gov. Godwin's Local Govt. Adv. Council, 1977-78; legis. asst. to del. Va. Gen. Assembly, 1983—; pres. PTA Council, Petersburg, 1967-68; sec. State Va., Student Council Assns. Adv. Bd., 1968-70; chmn. dist. adv. com. Petersburg Public Schs., Emergency Sch. Assistance Act, 1974-75; pres. Women's Soc. Christian Service, St. Mark's United Meth. Ch., 1969-71, mem. adminstrv. bd., 1969-71, 84—, treas. United Meth. Women, 1980-81, pres., 1984—; mem. adv. bd. Salvation Army, 1972-75; mem. Va. Mcpl. League's Community Devel. Policy Com., 1975-78; mem. Nation's League of Cities Community Devel. Policy Com., 1976-78; mem. Interstate 95 Adv. Coms., 1974-82; mem. Crater Planning Dist. Commns. Legis. Com., 1976-78; mem. exec. bd. Va. Citizens Planning Assn., Inc., 1978-83, chmn. com. on regional work-shops for planning commrs., 1981-83; mem. state ethnic minority task force Va. ann. conf. United Meth. Ch., 1980—; v.p. govt. affairs Petersburg C. of C., 1980-81, bd. dirs., 1980-82; co-chmn. public employees div. United Way of Southside Va., 1981-82. Recipient Hon. Life Membership award Va. Congress Parents and Tchrs., 1966; Life Membership Award Women's Soc. Christian Service, 1967; named Petersburg Woman of Yr., Beta Sigma Phi, 1975.

SHELL, MARY KATHERINE JAYNES HOSKING (MRS. JOSEPH C. SHELL), county official b. Bakersfield, Calif., Feb. 9, 1927; d. Walter Charles and Mary Ellen (Young) Jaynes; student Bakersfield Coll., 1946-48; m. Richard Hosking, Aug. 21, 1948 (div. 1968); children—Geoffrey Richard, Timothy William (dec.), Meredith Katherine (dec.); m. 2d, Joseph C. Shell, Jan. 8, 1970. Mem. editorial staff Bakersfield Californian, 1944-45; mem. editorial staff Bakersfield News Bull., 1965-68, mng. editor, 1969; polit. columnist Bakersfield Californian, 1971-80; mayor City of Bakersfield, 1980-84; supr. Kern County, 1984—. Founding pres. Bakersfield Jr. Woman's Club, 1954-55. Mem. Kern County Republican Central Com., 1956-60; founder, state sec. United Reps. Calif., 1963; mem. Calif. del. Rep. Nat. Conv., 1964. Club: Kern Press (founder 1967). Home: 2930 21st St Bakersfield CA 93301 Office: County Adminstrv Bldg Truxtun Ave Bakersfield CA 93301

SHELL, (PETERSON) JUANITA, psychologist; b. Winston-Salem, N.C., Apr. 21, 1940; d. Douglas James and Sallie (Saunders) Shell; m. Alonza Peterson, Dec. 24, 1961; children—Lisa Peterson, Jason Peterson. B.A., CCNY, 1971; Ph.D., CUNY, 1977; postgrad. NYU, 1980—. Library asst. Bklyn. Pub. Library, 1959-64; sec. Haryou-Act, N.Y.C., 1965-67; psychotherapist Psychol. Ctr., N.Y.C., 1971-74; cons.-therapist Hale House, N.Y.C., 1974-77; psychology intern NYU-Bellevue Med. Ctr., N.Y.C., 1974-75; staff psychologist Bellevue Psychiat. Hosp., 1978—; clin. instr. dept. psychiatry NYU Sch. Medicine, 1978—; mem. faculty Bklyn. Coll., 1976-78; cons. Bklyn. Community Counselling Ctr., 1976—; mem. N.Y.C. Mayor's Adv. Subcom. on Mental Retardation and Devel. Disabilities, 1978—. Contbr. articles to profl. jours. Chairperson health com. N.Y.C. Community Bd. 4, 1979-81. Black Analysis Inc. fellow, 1975-76; NIMH grantee, 1971-74. Mem. N.Y. Acad. Sci., Am. Psychol. Assn., Jack and Jill Found. Am. (v.p. Met. chpt. 1984), Woman's Aux of North Gen. Hosp. Democrat. Episcopalian. Office: Dept Psychiatry NYU-Bellevue Med Ctr 30th St and 1st Ave New York NY 10016

SHELL, ROSALIE VIRGINIA, nurse; b. Terra Alta, W.Va., Feb. 13, 1925; d. Guy Allen and Della Emily (Hobb) Bell; m. Raymon Darrell Shell, Mar. 8, 1951; children—Vickie, Connie. Diploma, Union Protestant Sch., Clarksburg, W.Va., 1948. Staff nurse Iowa Meth. Hosp., Des Moines, 1949-51, Mercy Hosp., Marshalltown, Iowa, 1956-59; pvt. duty nurse Marshalltown Area Community Hosp. (Iowa), 1960-69; plant nurse Lennox Industries, Inc., Marshalltown, 1969—. Democrat. Lodges: Moose Aux., Eagles Aux. Office: Lennox Industries Inc 200 S 12th Ave Marshalltown IA 50158

SHELLER, REBEKAH MARIE, librarian; b. Rawlins, Wyo., Nov. 29, 1954; d. Robert A. and Bess (Robertson) S. B.S., U. Wyo., 1977; M.L.S., Clarion U. of Pa., 1982. Editor Basin Republican-Rustler (Wyo.), 1977-79; tech. asst. Big Horn County Library, Basin, 1979-81; grad. asst. dept. library sci. Clarion U. of Pa., 1981-82; youth services librarian Lewis and Clark Library, Helena, Mont., 1982—. Editor Rural Libraries, 1982—. Mem. ALA, Mont. Library Assn., Alpha Chi Omega, Beta Sigma Phi. Democrat. Episcopalian. Home: 1117 Pine Helena MT 59601 Office: Lewis and Clark Library 120 S Last Chance Mall Helena MT 59601

SHELLEY, CAROLE AUGUSTA, actress; b. London, Aug. 16, 1939; U.S., 1964; d. Curtis and Deborah (Bloomstein) S.; m. Albert G. Woods, July 26, 1967 (dec.). Studied ballet at, Arts Ednl. Sch., 1943-56; Prep. acad., R.A.D.A., 1956-57; studied voice with, Iris Warren. Trustee Am. Shakespeare Theatre., 1974-82. Appeared in: revues, films, West End comedies, including Mary Mary at the Globe Theatre; appeared as Gwendolyn Pigeon in: stage, film and TV versions of The Odd Couple; The Norman Conquests (Los Angeles Drama Critics Circle award 1975); appeared as Rosalind in: As You Like It; appeared as Regan in: King Lear; appeared as Neville in: She Stoops to Conquer, Stratford, Ont., Can., 1972; appeared as Mrs. Margery Pinchwife in: The Country Wife, Am. Shakespeare Festival, Stratford, Conn., 1973; as Nora in: A Doll's House, Goodman Theatre, Chgo.; appeared at, Shaw Festival, 1977, 80; appeared in The Play's the Thing, Bklyn. Acad. Music, 1978; other stage appearances include: nat. co. of The Royal Family (Los Angeles Drama Critics Circle award 1977); appeared in The Elephant Man (Outer Critics Circle award 1978-79 season, Tony award for best actress 1978-79 season); appeared in Bl the Spirit, Stratford (Ont.) Festival, 1982-83; appeared inaugural season, Robin Phillips Grand Theatre Co., London, Ont., Can., 1983-84; appeared on Broadway in the Misanthrope, 1983, Noises Off, 1984; films The Boston Strangler, The Odd Couple; created voice characters in Walt Disney films Robin Hood, The Aristocats. Recipient Obie Award for Twelve Dreams N.Y. Shakespeare Festival, 1982. Jewish. Child actress, beginning at age 3. Office: care Lionel Larner 850 7th Ave New York NY 10019

SHELLEY, HEATHER O., lawyer; b. Norfolk, Va., Oct. 19, 1957; d. Joseph Clifford and Doris Iren (Reedy) S. B.A. in History and Spanish, Washburn U., 1979, J.D., 1982. Bar: Kans. 1982. Law clk. State of Kans., Wichita, 1980; legal intern Sedgwick County, Wichita, 1981; legal intern Washburn Legal Clinic Topeka, 1981-82; asst. county atty. Barton County, Great Bend, Kans., 1982-83; staff atty. Kans. Dept. Social Rehab. Services, 1983—. Mem. Young Democrats Topeka, 1979. Mem. ABA, Kans. Bar Assn., Wichita Bar Assn., Assn. Trial Lawyers Am., Kans. Trial Lawyer's Assn., Wichita Area Women Lawyers, Washburn U. Topeka Alumni Assn., Washburn U. Sch. Law Alumni Assn., Alpha Phi (tng. adv. 1980-82), Phi Alpha Delta. Office: State of Kans Box 1620 Wichita KS 67201

SHELLY, DONNA MARIE LINTHICUM, nurse; b. Houston, Sept. 21, 1952; d. Bernard H. Linthicum and Gladys H. (Schneider) Albright. B.S.N., U. Tex., Austin, 1975; M.S. Tex. Woman's U., 1981. Staff nurse Children's Med. Ctr., Dallas, 1975-81; faculty assoc., pediatric clin. nurse specialist U. Tex. Health Sci. Ctr., Dallas, 1981—; pediatric nurse cons. Spl. Care Sch. for Devel. Disabled, Dallas, 1981—, Dallas East Ctr Devel. Disabled, 1983-84. Mem. Am. Nurses Assn., Tex. Nurses Assn., Am. Assn. Mental Deficiency, Maternal Child Health Interest Group, Assn. Care of Children's Health, Clin. Nurse Specialist Council Dallas (treas. 1982-84). Democrat. Lutheran. Club: Luth. Young Adults Tex. (sec. Dallas 1982-84). Co-author audio-visual ednl. materials. Home: 3270 Darvany Dr Dallas TX 75220 Office: U Tex Health Science Ctr Southwestern Med Sch Univ Affiliated Ctr 6011 Harry Hines Blvd Suite 102 Dallas TX 75235

SHELTON, BESSIE ELIZABETH, educator; b. Lynchburg, Va.; d. Robert and Bessie Ann (Plenty) Shelton; B.A. (scholar), W.Va. State Coll., 1958; student Northwestern U., 1953-55, Ind. U., 1956; M.S., SUNY, 1960. Young adult librarian Bklyn. Pub. Library, 1960-62; asst. head central reference div. Queens Borough Pub. Library, Jamaica, N.Y., 1962-65; instructional media specialist Lynchburg (Va.) Bd. Edn., 1966-74; ednl. research specialist, 1974-77; ednl. media assoc. Allegany County Bd. Edn., Cumberland, Md., 1977—. Guest singer Sta. WLVA, 1966—, WLVA-TV Christmas concerts, 1966—; cons. music and market research. Mem. YWCA, Lynchburg, 1966—, Fine Arts Center, Lynchburg, 1966—; ednl. adv. bd., nat. research bd. Am. Biog. Inst. Named to Nat. Women's Hall of Fame. Mem. NEA, Md. Tchrs. Assn., Allegany County Tchrs. Assn., Va. Edn. Assn., State Dept. Sch. Librarians, Internat. Entertainers Guild, Music City Songwriters Assn., Vocal Artists Am., Internat. Clover Poetry Assn., Internat. Platform Assn., Nat. Assn. Female Execs., Nat. Assn. Women Deans, Adminstrs. and Counselors, Intercontinental Biog. Assn., World Mail Dealers Assn., North Am. Mailers Exchange, AAUW, Am. Assn. Creative Artists, Am. Biog. Inst. Research Assn., Tri-State Community Concert Assn. Pi Delta Phi, Sigma Delta Pi. Contbr. poems to various publs. Democrat. Baptist. Clubs: National Travel, Gulf Travel. Home: PO Box 187 Cumberland MD 21502

SHELTON, BETSY CAMPBELL, financial executive; b. Redlands, Calif., May 1, 1949; d. Richard Bailey and Priscilla Alden (Simonds) Cook; student U. Calif., Santa Barbara, 1967-69; B.A. in Econs., U. Redlands, 1971; m. Robert Maurice Shelton, Feb. 8, 1975; 1 stepson, Scott Maurice. Adminstrv. asst. trust dept. Bank of Am., Los Angeles, 1971-72; sales asst./money market desk Goldman Sachs & Co., Los Angeles, 1972-74; sales liaison Bateman Eichler, Los Angeles, 1974-77; investment officer trust investment dept. Security Pacific Nat. Bank, Los Angeles, 1977-80; v.p., mcpl. bond trader Bateman Eichler, Los Angeles, 1980-82, v.p. instnl. sales, 1982-84; v.p. instnl. sales First Boston, Los Angeles, 1984—; outside instr. for securities test passing firm, 1981—. Bd. dirs. Sierra Madre Council Girl Scouts U.S.A. Mem. Los Angeles Mcpl. Bond Club, Los Angeles Assn. Investment Women. Office: 333 S Grand Los Angeles CA 90071

SHELTON, CYNTHIA WILSON, oil company executive; b. San Antonio, Tex., July 21, 1951; d. Victor Dugan Jr. and Peggy Sue (Phillips) Wilson; m. Michael Travis Shelton, July 10, 1982; 1 son, Matthew Travis. B.B.A. in Fin., U. Houston, 1980. With Getty Oil Co., Houston, 1973—, geol., geophys. sec., 1973-77, lease analyst, 1977, exploration mgr. sec., 1977-78, sec. to prodn. mgr., 1978, engring. tech., 1978-80, gas contract systems analyst, 1980-81, sr. gas contract systems analyst, 1981-82, contract adminstrn. supr., 1982—. Campaign worker Republicans to re-elect Gov. Bill Clements, Houston, 1982; recruitor vol. blood dr. Gulf Coast Regional Blood Ctr., Houston, 1978-80, 83. Mem. Desk & Derrick of Houston (chmn. 1977-80, dir. 1980-81, appreciation award 1980, 81), Nat. Assn. Female Execs., Nat. Gas Men of Houston. Home: 2845 Panagard St Houston TX 77082 Office: Getty Oil Co 500 Dallas St Ste 1510 Houston TX 77251

SHELTON, LUCY, soprano; B.A., Pomona Coll.; Mus. M. in Voice, New Eng. Conservatory Music, 1968. Asst. prof. voice Eastman Sch. Music, U. Rochester, 1979; vis. prof. Cleve. Inst. Music, 1986; appeared at Chamber Music N.W., Bethlehem Bach and Aspen music festivals, Casals Festival with Baroque ensemble; appeared as soloist with orchs., including Chgo., Boston, Denver, Houston, Balt., St. Louis symphonies, Los Angeles Chamber Orch., St. Paul Chamber Orch., Minn. Orch., BBC Proms in London, performance world premiere of Schwantner work with St. Louis Symphony, and nationwide tour as soloist with Helmuth Rilling and Los Angeles Chamber Orch.; also recitals, guest appearances with various groups, including Calliope and Twentieth Century Consort; recs. with Nonesuch Records, Vox, Vanguard, Grenadilla, Sonory, and Smithsonian Instn.; winner Walter W. Naumburg prize, 1977 (with Jubal trio) and 1980 (solo). Office: care Sheldon Softer Mgmt Inc 130 W 56th St New York NY 10019

SHELTON-COLBY, SALLY, banker, foreign policy analyst, former ambassador; b. San Antonio, Aug. 29, 1944; d. Harlan Bryan and Edith Angela (Pratka) S.; m. William E. Colby. B.A., U. Mo., 1966; M.A. (Univ. fellow), Johns Hopkins U., 1968; postgrad. (Fulbright scholar) Institut de Sciences Politiques, Paris, 1968, Georgetown U., 1969. Research asst. Brookings Instn., 1969; prof. internat. relations Iberomerican U. and Nat. Autonomous U. Mex., Mexico City, 1969-71; legis. asst. for fgn. policy to Sen. Lloyd Bentsen, 1971-77; dep. asst. sec. state for Latin Am., Washington, 1977-78; ambassador to Barbados, Grenada, Dominica, St. Lucia, and St. Vincent, 1979-81; spl. rep. to Antigua, St. Kitts-Nevis, Montserrat and Brit. V.I., 1979-81; v.p. Internat. Bus.-Govt. Counsellors, Inc., Washington, 1982-84; v.p. Bankers Trust Co., N.Y.C., 1984—; fellow Center Internat. Affairs, Harvard U., 1981-82. Bd. dirs. Nat. Endowment for Democracy, U.S. Com. of UN Fund for Women, Council Am. Ambassadors; trustee Mt. St. Mary's Coll. Italian Fgn. Ministry fellow; treas. Nat. Endowment for Democracy. NDEA fellow. Mem. Assn. Polit. Risk Analysts (bd. dirs.), NOW, Nat. Women's Polit. Caucus, Council Fgn. Relations, Fulbright Alumni Assn., Phi Beta Kappa. Democrat. Address: Bankers Trust Co 280 Park Ave 22 W New York NY 10017

SHEMER, MARTHA EVVARD, investment company executive; b. Ames, Iowa, Apr. 19, 1919; d. John Marcus and Martha (Cooper) Evvard; m. Jack Corvin Shemer, June 24, 1937 (dec. 1967); children—Jack Evvard, William Barry. Pioneer of properties, Phoenix, Scottsdale, Ariz., LaJolla, Calif. and Del Mar, Calif., 1941-75; pres. Shemer Enterprises, Phoenix, 1975-83, Shemer Investment Co., Phoenix, 1975—. Benefactor Shemer Art Ctr. and Mus. to City of Phoenix, 1984. Recipient Quill and Scroll nat. contest award, 1936. Republican. Avocations: helping humanity, bridge; poker; spite malice card games; reading; writing; travel; horses; inventing; needlepoint. Phoenix AZ

SHEMORRY, CORINNE JOYNES, marketng executive; b. Rolla, N.D., Jan. 24, 1920; d. William H. and Edna Ruth (Conn) Joynes; children—Gay, Jan. Publisher, Williston (N.D.) Plains Reporter, 1953-78; mktg. dir. Williston Credit Union, 1979—; journalist, lectr., cons., author, reporter. Recipient numerous awards in journalism on state and nat. level, including being named Outstanding Woman in Journalism in N.D., 1975. Mem. N.D. Press Assn., N.D. Press Women (past pres.), Nat. Press Women, Williston C. of C., Nat. Assn. Female Execs., Fin. Mktg. Assn. (charter), Sigma Delta Chi. Mem. United Ch. Club: Bus. and Profl. Women's (past pres.). Home: 210 E 14th St PO Box 1030 Williston ND 58801

SHENASSA, EDNA W., business executive; b. Bethesda, Md., Jan. 5, 1950; d. Sylvester M. and Mary Louise (Hollins) S. B.A., George Washington U., 1972, M.A., 1975. Acct. Redwing Acctg. Co., Arlington, Va., 1975-78, auditor, 1978-80; fin. cons. Edgewater Assocs., Washington, 1980-83, prin. Shenassa Bus. Services, Washington, 1983—. Active local conservation orgns. Mem. Am. Acctg. Assn., Nat. Assn. Women Execs., Nat. Trust for Historic Preservation. Address: Werik Bldg 733 15th St NW Suite 438 Washington DC 20005

SHENK, PATRICIA WOOTEN, adult care facility administrator; b. Chapmansville, W.Va., Apr. 17, 1935; d. Jasper W. and Hatha (Bays) Wooten; m. Raymond R. Shenk, May 23, 1959; children—Roanne Shenk Mazzucco, Ellen Shenk Perrotto, Mark Greenlee, Raymond Shenk, Timothy Shenk, Zachary Shenk. Rev. clk., mailroom supr. FBI, Washington, 1953-55; registration clk. Santa Clara Jr. Coll., part-time 1966; inventory control clk. Preiser Sci., Charleston, W.Va., 1967-69; owner, adminstr. Summit House, Alton, N.Y., 1973—; pres. Shenk Properties, Inc. Mem. Nat. Assn. Female Execs., Nat. Fedn. Ind. Bus., U.S. C. of C., Sodus C. of C., Empire State Assn. Adult Care Homes, Internat. Platform Assn. Republican. Methodist. Office: PO Box 194 Alton NY 14413

SHEPANEK, HELENE ANNA, educator; b. Regensburg, Germany, July 26, 1929; came to U.S., 1948, naturalized, 1950; d. Alfons and Alicia (Heidecker) Heiss; diploma Prinzessin von Arnheim Sch., Munich, 1947; B.A. summa cum laude, Am. U., 1972, M.A. with distinction, 1973; children—Marc Allen, Bruce Albert. Instr. German and French, C.I.A., Washington, 1965-66; teaching asst. Am. U., Washington, 1971-72, instr. German, 1972-78, professorial lectr., lang. specialist German studies, 1978—. Mem. AAUP, Am. Assn. Tchrs. of German, Am. Goethe Soc., Delta Phi Alpha, Phi Kappa Phi. Roman Catholic. Home: 850 Whann Ave McLean VA 22101 Office: Dept of Languages and Foreign Studies American University Washington DC 20016

SHEPARD, CYNTHIA JEAN, nurse; b. Cobleskill, N.Y., June 2, 1960; d. Clark James and Joanne Dorothy (Williams) S. Student Coll. of St. Rose, 1978-79; diploma; nursing Ellis Hosp. Sch. Nursing, 1983. R.N., N.Y. Nurse, Ellis Hosp., Schenectady, 1984—. Lutheran. Avocations: charcoal drawings; sewing; embroidery; crocheting; reading. Home: 943 Maple Ave Schenectady NY 12307 Office: Ellis Hosp 1101 Nott St Schenectady NY 12308

SHEPARD, GLORIA HARVEY, communications company executive; b. Ridgeland, S.C., June 20, 1932; d. Leroy Everett and Addie Gertrude (Gray) Harvey; m. Ray Lesler Shepard (dec.); children—Michael Ray, Glenn Eric. Student Armstrong Coll., 1950-52. Head bookkeeper Liberty Nat. Bank, Savannah, Ga., 1952-55; v.p. Hargray Telephone Co., Inc., Hilton Head Island, S.C., 1953-82, pres., 1982—; dir. Citizen & So. Nat. Bank of S.C. Bd. dirs. Better Bus. Bur., Hilton Head Heart Assn., Cultural Council Hilton Head Island. Mem. U.S. Telephone Assn., S.C. C. of C., S.C. Indsl. Developers Assn., Nat. Assn. Female Execs., Am. Mgmt. Assn., Independent Telephone Pioneers, Profl. Women's Club, Beta Kappa. Baptist. Club: Christian Women's. Avocations: biking; cards. Home: Hilton Head Island SC Office: Hargray Telephone Co Inc PO Box 5519 Hilton Head Island SC 29938

SHEPARD, LINDA MARY, real estate management company executive; b. Rochester, N.Y., Feb. 23, 1949; d. Angelo Anthony and Mary M. (Steiner) Costanza; m. Theodore L. Shepard, Jr., July 8, 1972; 1 son, Theodore James. A.A., Green Mountain Coll., 1969; B.A., U. Rochester, 1971. Vice pres. Glenbrook Manor Assocs., Rochester, 1972-83; pres. Shepard Signal, Inc., Canandaigua, N.Y., 1980-83, Costanza Enterprises, Rochester, 1983—; dir. Costanza Constrn. Co., Rochester, Shepard Bros., Inc., Canandaigua. Vol. Channel 21 Auction, Rochester, 1978; membership drive worker Rochester Philharm. Orch., 1980; counselor Planned Parenthood of Canandaigua, 1980; mem. Thompson Hosp. Vol. Program, 1980. Mem. Inst. Real Estate Mgmt., Bldg. Owners and Mgrs. Assn., Phi Theta Kappa. Avocations: sailing; tennis; writing. Office: Costanza Enterprises 14 Franklin St Rochester NY 14604

SHEPHERD, BARBARA JEAN, financial aid consultant; b. Macon, Ga., Aug. 15, 1954; d. Golston Cornelius and Mary Emma (Knight) Walker; m. Carl Newton Shepherd, III, Sept. 6, 1975; children—Jean Marie, Lauren Kay. Student pub. schs. Dir. fin. aid, organizational records Bauder Fashion Coll., Atlanta, 1975—; sec., treas. Precise Impressions, Atlanta, 1980—. Author pamplet Bauder's Guide to Financial Aid, 1983. Mem. Ga. Private Sch. Assn. (mem. adv. bd. 1982—, treas. 1984—), Ga. Assn. Fin. Aid Adminstrs., So. Assn. Fin. Aid Adminstrs. Republican. Baptist. Office: Precise Impressions Inc 1167 Zonolite Pl Atlanta GA 30306

SHEPHERD, ELSBETH WEICHSEL, operations engineer; b. Youngstown, Ohio, Dec. 5, 1952; d. Richard Henry and Lesley Frances (Lynn) Weichsel; B.S. in Math., Carnegie-Mellon U., 1974; M.B.A., U. Cin., 1978; m. Gordon Ray Shepherd, Aug. 28, 1976. Asst. indsl. engr. Armco, Inc., Middletown, Ohio, 1974-76, asso. indsl. engr., 1976-78, indsl. engr., 1978-82, sr. ops. engr., 1982-86, supr. process planning, 1986—. Mem. news mag. staff Jr. League Cin., 1980-81; vol. Miami Purchase Assn. Am. Iron and Steel Inst. fellow, 1978-81. Mem. Soc. Women Engrs. (pres. sect. 1981-82, provisional regional dir. 1983-84), Assn. Computing Machinery, Am. Inst. Indsl. Engrs. (v.p. services, pres. 1985-86), Tech. Socs. Council of Cin. (pres. 1986-87, 1st v.p. 1985-86, 2d v.p. 1984-85, treas. 1983-84). Home: 6255 Howe Rd Middletown OH 45042 Office: 1801 Crawford St Middletown OH 45043

SHEPHERD, GILLIAN MARY, physician; b. Belfast, U.K., Mar. 12, 1948; came to U.S., 1957; d. John Thompson and Helen (Johnston) S.; m. Eduardo Goar Mestre, Aug. 4, 1973; children—Laura Elena, Cristina Alicia., Eduardo Goar. B.A., Wheaton Coll., Norton, Mass., 1970, postgrad. Tufts U., 1970-73; M.D., N.Y. Med. Coll., 1976. Diplomate Am. Bd. Internal Medicine, Am. Bd. Allergy and Immunology. Intern, resident Lenox Hill Hosp., N.Y.C., 1976-79; fellow in allergy N.Y. Hosp./Cornell Med. Sch., N.Y.C., 1979-81; asst. prof. medicine Cornell U. Med. Coll., N.Y.C., 1981—; asst. attending physician N.Y. Hosp., N.Y.C., 1981—, head allergy assocs., 1982—; cons. allergy and immunology dept. medicine Meml. Hosp., N.Y.C., 1982—. Contbr. articles in field to profl. jours. Fellow Am. Acad. Allergy and Immunology (travel grantee 1981): mem. ACP, AMA, Am. Med. Women's Assn., Joint Council Allergy and Immunology, N.Y. Allergy Soc. (exec. com., chmn. com. on continuing med. edn. 1982—), N.Y. County Med. Soc. Office: NY Hosp-Cornell Med Ctr 525 E 68th St New York NY 10021

SHEPHERD, GRETA D(ANDRIDGE), educational administrator; b. Washington, Aug. 15, 1930; d. Philip J. and Bertha (Johnson) Dandridge; m. Clifton Murchison (div.); 1 dau., Michele M.; m. 2 Gilbert Shepherd (dec. Dec. 1983). B.S., Miner Tchr. Coll., Washington, 1951; M.A., D.C. Tchrs. Coll., 1961. Tchr. D.C. Pub. Schs., 1951-65, guidance counselor, 1965-66, asst. prin., 1966-69, prin., 1969-72; dir. East Orange Pub. Schs. (N.J.), 1972-80, acting supt., 1980-82; supt. Plainfield Pub. Schs. (N.J.), 1982-84; Mercer County supt. N.J. Dept. Edn., Trenton, 1984—; mem. Tchr. Corps, NEA, Jamaica, W.I. 1967; profl. field reader Office Civil Rights Title IV, Washington, 1978-79. Bd. dirs. YWCA of Essex and West Hudson, Orange, N.J., 1973-76, East Orange Pub. Library, 1980-82. Named Woman of Yr., Gamma Omicron chpt. Zeta Phi Beta, 1983. Mem. Am. Assn. Sch. Adminstrs., Nat. Assn. Fed. Program Adminstrs. (sec. 1981-83), Assn. Supervision and Curriculum Devel., N.J. Assn. Sch. Adminstrs., N.J. Coalition Ednl. Leaders. Baptist. Office: Mercer County Office Edn 2300 Hamilton Ave Trenton NJ 08619

SHEPHERD, JUDY CARLILE, retired government and communication official; b. Kansas City, Mo.; d. John Mercer and Mary Almeda (Chapin) Ellis; student Okla. State U., Tulsa U.; B.A., Am. U., Washington, 1960; m. Joseph Elbert Shepherd; 1 son from previous marriage, John Philip Carlile. Chief probation officer Tulsa County Ct., 1947-50; real estate broker United Farm Agy., 1952-58; bldg. fund campaign mgr. AAUW, Washington, 1958-59; govt. and public relations ofcl. Nat. Counsel Assos., Washington, 1959-61; congressional liaison Dept. Agr., Washington, 1961-65; public info. officer OEO, 1965-70, spl. asst. to dep. dir. ops. Head Start, elderly, Indian and migrant programs, 1970-73; dir. public relations Nat. Assn. Social Workers, Washington, 1973-74; social sci. analyst Congressional Research Service, Library Congress, Washington, 1976-85. Author: The Statutory History of the United States Capitol Police Force, 6 vols., 1985. Pres. bd. govs. Agr. Symphony Orch., 1961-64; bd. dirs. ARC, Boy Scouts Am., 1948-50; bd. dirs. Little Theatre, 1956-57. Recipient 1st place Fed. Editors Blue Pencil award, 1967; cert. humanist counselor. Mem. Nat. Press Club, Public Relations Soc. Am., Nat. Assn. Govt. Communicators, Am. Humanist Assn., Assn. Humanistic Psychology, Am. U. Alumni Assn., Okla. State Soc., Mo. State Soc., Ark. State Soc., Library Congress Profl. Assn., Humanist Assn. Nat. Capital Area (pres. 1977-78), Nat. Congress Am. Indians, DAR, Am. Soc. Access Profls. (charter). Club: Woman's Nat Democratic. Coordinator, Am. Discovers Indian Art exhbit, Smithsonian Instn., 1967. Home: 2365 N Oakland St Arlington VA 22207

SHEPHERD, MARY JANE, nursing educator, consultant; b. Indpls., Sept. 16, 1935; d. Donald Raymond, Sr., and Rose Ellen (Doll) Fargo; m. Vernon Lee Shepherd, May 30, 1953; children—Matthew Lee, Mark William, Lois Rose Shepherd Farley. A.A. in Nursing, Ind. U.-Indpls., 1970, B.S. in Nursing, 1976, M.S. in Nursing, 1981; postgrad. Ind. U., Bloomington, 1983—. R.N., Ind. Nursing attendant Muscatatuck State Hosp., Butlerville, Ind., 1962-68; camp nurse Camp James Whitcomb Riley, Martinsville, Ind., 1970-78; staff nurse Riley Hosp. for Children, Indpls., 1970-75; home service nurse United Cerebral Palsy Central Ind., Indpls., 1979-81, now cons.; lectr. nursing Ind. U., Indpls., 1976-81, asst. prof., 1981—. Author articles video rec., computer programs. Bd. dirs. United Cerebral Palsy Central Ind. Recipient Exceptional Achievement award United Cerebral Palsy Ind., 1978, Spl. Individual award, 1982; Outstanding Tchr. award Ind. U. nursing students, 1981. Mem. Am. Nursing Assn., Nat. League Nursing, Century Club Am. Nurses Found., Assn. Ind. Media Educators, Assn. Ednl. Communications Tech., Sigma Theta Tau. Republican. Episcpalian. Home: 5380 N 901 E Brownsburg IN 46112 Office: Ind U Sch of Nursing 610 Barnhill Dr NU 333 Indianapolis IN 46223

SHEPHERD, MICKI JO, commercial lending officer; b. Wheeling, W.Va., June 28, 1957; d. Paul Clayton and Bonnie (Dorsch) S. B.A., Ohio State U., 1977. Loan adminstr. Union Bank, San Diego, 1980-82, credit trainee, Los Angeles, 1982, credit mgr., 1982-83, loan analyst, 1984, sr. analyst, 1984, loan officer, Bakersfield, Calif., 1985—. Active United Republican Women of Calif., 1985, United Reps. of Calif., 1985. Mem. Nat. Assn. Accts., Nat. Assn. Female Execs. Methodist. Home: 6600 White Ln #39 Bakersfield CA 93309

SHEPHERD, NANCY KAY, financial planner; b. Belleville, Ill., Aug. 11, 1948; d. Richard George and Martha Lou (Cheek) Hamann; m. Michael David Shepherd, Oct. 20, 1973; children—Monika Michelle, Niklas David. B.A., Ill. State U., 1970; M.Ed. in Counseling, Boston U., 1977. Instr. North Greene High Sch., White Hall, Ill., 1970-73; bookkeeper Army and Air Force Exchange Service, Ft. Lewis, Wash., 1973-75; instr. Dept. Defense, Overseas Schs., Mannheim, W.Ger., 1975-80; instr. Trinidad High Sch., Colo., 1980-82; fin. planner IDS/Am. Express, Durango, Colo., 1982—; instr. San Juan Coll., Farmington, N.Mex., 1985-86, Women at Work Conf., Farmington, 1986. Fund raiser Civitan, Durango, Colo., 1984-85; organizer The Network, profl. women's org., Farmington; dir. Better Bus. Bur., Farmington, 1985-86; instr. Gov.'s Conf. for Women, Farmington, 1985. Named Div. Fin. Planner of Yr., IDS/Am. Express, Colorado Springs, 1983, 84. Mem. Inst. Fin. Planners, AAUW, P.E.O. (chaplain 1985-86). Club: Civitan (Durango, Colo.). (sec. 1985-86). Avocations: racquetball; crocheting; weight lifting; reading. Home: 2012 Smith Ln Farmington NM 87401 Office: IDS/Am Express 2120 N Sullivan St Farmington NM 87401

SHEPHERD, SAUNDRA DIANNE, physician; b. N.Y.C., July 16, 1945; d. Archibald Ethelbert and Sylvia Marguerite (Allman) Shepherd; m. Peter John Payne Finch, Nov. 24, 1973; 1 dau., Abi Jean Shepherd-Finch. B.S., CCNY, 1968; M.A., Hunter Coll., 1971; M.D., Yale U., 1975. Intern, 1975-76, resident, NYU/Bellevue Med. Ctr., 1976-78, fellow, 1978-79; fellow Columbia-Presbyterian Med. Ctr., N.Y.C., 1979-81, attending physician, 1980-81; attending physician St. Luke's Roosevelt Hosp. Ctr., 1982—, Harlem Hosp. Ctr., N.Y.C., 1982; asst. clin. prof. pediatrics and community medicine residency program in social medicine Montefiore Hosp., 1982—; mem. adj. faculty Sophie Davis Sch. Biomed. Edn., CCNY; social medicine residency program preceptor Martin Luther King Health Ctr., N.Y.C.; cons. physician Family Ct., N.Y.C., 1972—; cons. pediatrician Legal Aid Soc., 1972—; mem. Emergency Com. to Aid Lebanon; vol. physician, El Salvador; mem. First U.S.-Nicaragua Colloquium on Health, 1983. Bd. dirs. United Meth. City Soc. Mem. Physicians for Social Responsibility, AAUW, Am. Acad. Pediatrics, N.Y. Acad. Scis., Am. Med. Women's Assn. Home: 59 W 94th St New York NY 10025

SHEPPARD, POSY (MRS. JOHN WADE SHEPPARD), vol. social worker; b. New Haven, Aug. 23, 1916; d. John Day and Rose Marie (Herrick) Jackson; student Vassar Coll., 1938; m. John W. Sheppard, May 16, 1936; children—Sandra (Mrs. Allan Gray Rodgers), Gail (Mrs. S. Stinor Gimbel), Lynn (Mrs. William M. Manger), John W. Vol. field cons. for Conn. ARC, 1955-61, nat. bd. govs., 1960-66, vice chmn. bd. govs., 1962-66; rep. League Red Cross Socs. to UN, 1957-81; rep. Am. Nat. Red Cross to com. internat. social welfare Nat. Social Welfare Assembly, 1957-62; chmn. NGO Com. UNICEF, 1962-64, 71-73; social welfare com. White House Conf. Internat. Coop. Year.; chmn. exec. com. NGO/OPI Conf., UN, 1963-65; pres. conf. ECOSOC, 1966-69. Mem. Nat. Soc. Colonial Dames, Jr. League Greenwich (vice chmn.), Nat. Inst. Social Scis. Clubs: Round Hill, Field (Greenwich, Conn.); Cosmopolitan (N.Y.C.). Home: 535 Lake Ave Greenwich CT 06830

SHER, ILONA, systems manager; b. Montreal, Canada, May 20, 1955; d. Benjamin and Olga (Korec) Sher. B.A., McGill U., 1977; M.B.A., Wharton Sch., 1981. Systems programmer, analyst Can. Pacific Ltd., Montreal, 1977-79; cons. Grant Thornton, N.Y.C., 1981-85; systems mgr., Macmillan, Inc., N.Y.C., 1985—. Fund-raising chmn. Westside Action for Nuclear Disarmament, N.Y.C., 1985—. Office: Macmillan Inc 866 3rd Ave New York NY 10022

SHER, JOANN GIFFUNI, lawyer, insurance executive; b. N.Y.C., May 30, 1942; d. Joseph and Flora (Baldini) Giffuni; B.A., Jackson Coll., Tufts U., 1963; LL.B., Fordham U., 1966; postgrad. U. Va., 1977; m. Michael L. Sher, Feb. 2, 1970 (div. 1977). Bar: N.Y. 1968. With Mfrs. Hanover Trust Co., N.Y.C., 1966-71; atty. Tchrs. Ins. and Annuity Assn., Coll. Retirement Edn. Fund., N.Y.C., 1972-73, asst. counsel, 1973-74, assoc. counsel, 1974-76, counsel, 1976-78, v.p., 1978—; lectr. in field. Mem. Family Edn. Com., Community Service Soc., 1970-72, mem. com. on edn., 1972-77, bd. dirs., 1985—; bd. dirs. Women's Prison Assn., 1972-74, Turtle Bay Music Sch., 1982—, Pastel Soc. Am., 1977—. Mem. ABA, Assn. Bar City N.Y., Nat. Assn. Coll. and Univ. Attys. Club: Cosmopolitan. Office: 730 3d Ave New York NY 10017

SHER, JOANNA RUTH, physician; b. Winnipeg, Man., Can., May 23, 1933; came to U.S., 1949, naturalized, 1958; d. Joseph and Dorothy Hollenberg; A.B., U. Chgo., 1952, B.S., 1956, M.D., 1956; m. Norman Sher, Dec. 28, 1955; children—Jonathan Aaron, Katherine Amy. Rotating intern Kings County Hosp., Bklyn., 1956-57, resident pathology, 1957-58; fellow pathology Kings County Hosp., SUNY Downstate Med. Center, Bklyn., 1960-62; Nat. Inst. Neurol. Diseases spl. fellow in neuropath. SUNY Downstate Med. Center, 1962-64; asst. neuropathologist Kings County Hosp., Bklyn., 1964-70, dir. neuropath. lab., 1970—; prof. clin. pathology, Downstate Med. Center, Bklyn., 1977—, asst. dean, 1977-83; cons. depts. pathology Brookdale Hosp. and Med. Center, Bklyn., Maimonides Hosp. and Med. Center, Bklyn. Hosp., L.I. Coll. Hosp. Diplomate Am. Bd. Pathology. Fellow Am. Soc. Clin. Pathologists; mem. Internat. Acad. Pathology, Am. Acad. Neurology, Am. Assn. Neuropathologists, Phi Beta Kappa, Sigma Xi, Alpha Omega Alpha. Editor: (with D. Ford) Primary Intracranial Neoplasms, 1979; contbr. articles in field to profl. jours. Home: 2347 E 63d St Brooklyn NY 11234 Office: Box 25 Downstate Med Center 450 Clarkson Ave Brooklyn NY 11203

SHER, LINDA ROSENBERG, lawyer; b. Chgo., May 16, 1938; d. Sidney and Rebecca Rosenberg; B.A., U. Chgo., 1959; LL.B., Yale U., 1962; m. Stanley O. Sher, Aug. 11, 1963; children—Jeremy Jay, Hellyn Sue. Admitted to D.C. bar, 1962; counsel constl. rights subcom. Senate Judiciary Com., 1962-64; atty. NLRB, 1964-77, asst. gen. counsel supreme ct. br., 1977—. Office: 1717 Pennsylvania Ave NW Washington DC 20570

SHERBECK, CARMEN ANDERSON, artist; b. Seattle, May 25, 1920; d. Lars Oscar and Olga Theresa (Lovegren) Larson; m. Leander Adair Sherbeck, Feb. 14, 1943; children—Carmen Roxanne, Celia Martine, Jonathan Adair. Student Bethel Coll., St. Paul, 1938-39, Mary Baldwin Coll., Banft Sch. Art, 1945, I Hsiung Ju, 1970, Ed Whitney, 1982; studied with Hartwell Priest, 1965, Maxwell Starr, 1960. Pres. Va. Mus. Fine Arts, Waynesboro chpt., 1979-81. One-man shows Mus. Art, Edmonton, Can., 1946, Fairfax Hall, Waynesboro, Va., 1951, Harrigan's Restaurant, Washington, 1960, Collector's Gallery, Washington, 1961, Raymond Duncan Galeries, Paris, 1963, Fine Arts Ctr., Staunton, Va., 1964, Ligoa Duncan Galeries des Arts, N.Y.C., 1964, Va. Nat. Bank, Charlottesville; exhibited in group shows at Annual Royal Can. Acad. Exhibit, Montreal, 1947, Can. Women Artists, Riverside Mus., 1947, Nat. Exhibit, Tyler, Tex., 1962, Prix-de-Paris Exhibit, Raymond Duncan Galleries, Paris, 1963, Echeverrig-Duncan Gallery, Beach Haven, N.J., 1963, Ligoa Duncan Gallery, N.Y.C., 1963, Allied Artists Am., N.Y.C., 1963, Gallery of Modern Art, Fredericksburg, Va., 1964, Albemarle Art Assn.-Sears So. Arts Festival, Charlottesville, Va., 1964, Atlanta Mus. Art, 1964, Am. Group Show, Bruxelles, Belgium, 1964, Bohman-Konstgalleri, Stockholm, 1968, Lynchburg Fine Art Ctr., 1968, Salon d'Artistes Independence and Salon d'Automme, Grand Palais, Paris, 1968. Bd. dirs. Waynesboro chpt. Va. Mus., 1984—. Recipient 61 awards for art work including Judges Choice award Staunton Fine Arts Outdoor Show, 1985. Mem. Arts Club (pres. 1984-85), Art League Alexandria-Torpedo Factory, Va. Watercolor Soc., Albemarle Art Assn., Paletteers of Waynesboro (chmn. 1982). Baptist. Home and studio: 1826 Cherokee Rd Waynesboro VA 22980

SHERBELL, RHODA, sculptor; b. Bklyn.; d. Alexander and Syd (Steinberg) S.; student Art Students League, 1950-53, Bklyn. Mus. Art Sch., 1959-61; also pvt. study art, Italy, France, Eng., 1956; m. Mervin Honig, Apr. 28, 1956; 1 dau., Susan. Exhibited one-woman shows: Country Art Gallery, Locust Valley, N.Y., Bklyn. Mus.,Adelphia Coll., A.C.A. Galleries, N.Y.C., 1967, Capricorn Galleries, Rehn Gallery, Washington, 1968, Morris (N.J.) Mus. Arts and Scis., 1980, Palace Theatre of Arts, 1986, Bronx Mus. Art, N.Y.C., 1986; one-woman retrospective at N.Y. Cultural Center, 1970, Nat. Arts Collection, Washionton, 1970, Nat. Art Mus. of Sport, 1977, Jewish Mus., N.Y., 1980, Black History Mus., 1981, Queen Mus., 1981, Nat. Portrait Gallery, Washington, 1981, Bergen Mus. Art and Sci. (N.J.), 1984; two-woman shows at William Benton Mus. Art, Country Art Gallery, Rehn Gallery, Port Washington Library; exhibited group shows: Downtown Gallery, N.Y.C., Maynard Walker Gallery, N.Y.C., F.A.R. Gallery, N.Y.C., Provincetown Art Assn., Detroit Inst. Art, Pa. Acad. Fine Arts, Bklyn. and L.I. Artists Show, Old Westbury Gardens Small Sculpture Show, Audubon Artists, NAD, Albany State Mus. Art; Allied Artists, Heckscher Mus., Nat. Art Mus. Sports, Mus. Arts and Scis., Los Angeles, Am. Mus. Natural History, Chgo. Hist. Soc., NAD, others; represented permanent collections: Stony Brook (N.Y.) Mus., Colby Coll. Mus., Oklahoma City Mus., Montclair (N.J.) Mus., Colby Coll. Mus., Nat.

Arts Collection, Nat. Portrait Gallery, Mus. Am. Art, Smithsonian Instn., Baseball Hall of Fame, Nassau Community Coll., Hofstra U. Emily Lowe Gallery, Art Students League, Jewish Mus., Queens Mus., Black History Mus., Nassau County Mus., N.Y. Pub. Library, also pvt. collections; TV shows ABC, 1968, 81; ednl. TV spl. Rhoda Sherbell-Woman in Bronze, 1977; important works include Walking Ballerina, Adolescent Girl, The Sunday Hat, Standing Woman, Seated Ballerina; portraits Casey Stengel, Yogi Berra, Marguerite and William Zorach, The Gypsie Troupe, Aaron Copland. Cons., council mem. Emily Lowe Gallery, Hofstra U., Hempstead, N.Y., 1978, pres. bd., 1980-83; council mem. Nassau County Mus., 1978, trustee, 1st v.p. council; asso. trustee Nat. Art Mus. of Sports, Inc.; cons., community liaison WNET Channel 13, producer Fine Art Update, 1975—; producer, co-host radio show Not for Artists Only, N.Y.C., 1978-79; trustee Women's Boxing Fedn., 1978. Recipient Am. Acad. Arts, Letters and Nat. Inst. Arts and Letters grant, 1960; Louis Comfort Tiffany Found. grant, 1962; Alfred G. B. Steel Meml. award Pa. Acad. Fine Arts, 1963-64; Helen F. Barnett prize NAD, 1965; Jersey City Mus. prize for sculpture, 1961; 1st prize sculpture Locust Valley Art Show, 1966, 67; Ann. Sculpture prize Jersey City Mus.; Bank for Savs. 1st prize in sculpture, 1950; Ford Found. purchase award, 1964; MacDowell Colony fellow, 1976; 2 top sculpture awards Mainstreams 77; Cert. of Merit, Salmagundi Club, 1978, prize for sculpture, 1980, 81; award for sculpture Knickerbocker Artists, 1980, 81; top prize for sculpture Hudson Valley Art Assn., 1981. Fellow Nat. Sculpture Soc.; mem. Sculpture Guild (dir.), Nat. Assn. Women Artists (Jeffery Childs Willis Meml. prize 1978, Gold medal of honor 1980), Allied Artists Am. (dir.; M.M. Hexter award 1984, cert. merit 1984), Audubon Artists (Greta Kempton Walker prize 1965, Chaim Gross award, award for disting. contbr. to orgn. 1979, 80, Gold medal of honor 1985, Louis Weikum award; dir.), Woman's Caucus for Art, Coll. Art Assn., Am. Inst. Conservation Historic and Artistic Works, N.Y. Soc. Women Artists, Artists Equity Assn. N.Y., Nat. Sculpture Soc., Internat. Platform Assn., Profl. Artists Guild L.I., Painters and Sculptors Soc. N.J. (Bertrum R. Hulmes Meml. award), Am. Watercolor Soc. (award for disting. contbn. to orgn.), Catharine Lorillard Wolfe Club (hon. mention 1968), Nat. Arts Club. Appeared several TV shows; guest various radio programs. Contbr. articles to newspapers, popular mags. and art jours. Home: 64 Jane Ct Westbury NY 11590

SHERBIN, JAN, television and radio news broadcaster; b. Hartford, Conn. B.S. in Journalism, Boston U., M.S. in Journalism. Mgr., TV and radio dept. Henry Ford Mus., Greenfield Village, Detroit, 1980-82; reporter Sta. WPTA-TV, Fort Wayne, Ind., 1983-84; news dir. Sta. WFWQ, Fort Wayne, 1984—, host and producer TV Bus. News Program, 1984—; corr. AP, UPI, RKO networks and Network Ind. Freelance writer. Tchr. Jr. Achievement, Fort Wayne, 1985; speaker, contest judge numerous civic and charity groups. Recipient Best Radio News Series award AP, Ind., 1985; Best TV Investigative Report AP, Ind., 1984; Best TV Investigative Report UPI, Ind., 1984; Health Journalism award Am. Chiropractic Assn., 1985; Golden Mike award Am. Legion Aux., 1985. Mem. Am. Women in Radio and TV (pres. Detroit chpt. 1982), New England Women's Press Assn. (pres. 1977-79). Office: Sta WFWQ 2260 Lake Ave Suite 230 Fort Wayne IN 46805

SHERBURNE, ROSANNE ANGELILLO, welding company executive; b. Southington, Conn., Nov. 10, 1954; d. John Battista and Anna Theresa (Palmieri) Angelillo; m. Dennis Edward Sherburne, June 14, 1980; children—Dennis Edward Jr., Richard Allen. Student Tunxis Community Coll., 1972-73. Cost acct.'s asst. Gould Allied Control, Plantsville, Conn., 1974-76; prodn. planner Accurate Forging div. Delta, Bristol, Conn., 1976-81; quality control asst. Napco Inc., Terryville, Conn., 1981-83; v.p., co-owner Conn. Specialty Welding, Plantsville, 1983—. Author poems. Musician, technician Southington Community Orch., 1970-74; coach Terryville Little League, 1980-81; den leader Terryville Cub Scouts Am., 1980-83; coordinator St. Casmir's Renew Team, 1984-85. Mem. Southington C. of C. Roman Catholic. Clubs: Parents (Bristol); Mothers, Women's Guild (Terryville). Avocations: bowling; softball; writing; painting; traveling. Home: 200 Wonx Spring Rd Plantsville CT 06479 Office: Conn Specialty Welding PO Box 387 Plantsville CT 06479

SHERF, SANDEE CROFT, real estate developer; b. Okmulgee, Okla., Feb. 24, 1950; d. C. Don and Joyce Marie (Harris) Croft; m. Paul P. DeGeronimo, Nov. 4, 1970 (div. 1980); children—Shawn Dale, Aimee Vanessa; m. E.W. Sherf, May 15, 1983; 1 child, Summer Ashley. Student Maryville Coll., 1969. Flight attendant Piedmont Airlines, Salem, N.C., 1969-70; credit card mgr. Blount Nat. Bank, Maryville, Tenn., 1970-72; travel agt. AAA of Va., Lynchburg, 1972-76; real estate agr. Century 21, Houston, 1979-81; real estate developer E.W. Sherf Interests, Humble, Tex., 1981—; v.p. Reid Rd. Mcpl. Utility Dist., Houston, 1983—. Leader, San Jacinto council Girl Scouts U.S.A., 1983; mem. Champion Forest Civic Club, Houston, 1983, Mus. Fine Arts, Houston, Smithsonian Instn., Washington. Recipient Managerial Acctg. and Fin. Concepts award Bldg. Owners and Mgrs. Inst., 1983. Mem. Tex. Assn. Realtors, Nat. Assn. Realtors, Houston Bd. Realtors, Real Estate Securities and Syndications, Realtors Nat. Mktg. Inst. Writer's Guild. Republican. Baptist. Avocations: skiing; swimming; race car driving; dancing; writing. Office: EW Sherf Interests Inc 21330 Aldine Westfield Suite 102 Humble TX 77338

SHERIDAN, EMILY JEAN O'NEIL, banker; b. Jamaica, N.Y., Jan. 8, 1948; d. James Coyle and Emily (Olff) O'Neil; m. Paul Sheridan, Nov. 20, 1982; 1 child, Sarah Elizabeth. A.A., Suffolk County Community Coll., 1968; B.S., SUNY, Stony Brook, 1970; M.A., Adelphi U., 1975, cert. mgmt., 1977, M.B.A., 1980. Sales-person/cashier Rainbow Shops, Port Jefferson Station, N.Y., 1966-70; tchr. Sachem Sch. Dist., Holbrook, N.Y., 1970-72; tax examiner IRS, Holtsville, N.Y., 1973-77; adminstrv. systems analyst Nat. West USA, N.Y.C., 1977-80, unit mgr. planning and control, systems officer, 1980-84, group controller, asst. v.p., 1984—. Committee person Suffolk County Democratic Party, 1972-73; treas. Com. of People for Lutz, Brookhaven Twp., N.Y., 1978—; mem. com. Citizens Adv. Com., Brookhaven Twp., 1975-76; mem. Brookhaven Town Adv. Com. on Youth, 1976-77; mem. Brookhaven Town Youth Bur. Bd., 1977-82. Mem. Nat. Assn. Bank Women, Nat. Assn. Female Execs., AAUW. Roman Catholic. Home: 2 Essex Ln Hicksville NY 11801 Office: 3 Huntington Quadrangle Melville NY 11747

SHERIDAN, PATRICIA ELVIRA O'DOWDA MARTIN, lawyer, educator; b. Oak Park, Ill., Sept. 18, 1939; d. Harold Arpin and Elvira Eba Ada (Anderson) Martin; m. Robert Bliss Sheridan, Mar. 28, 1964; children—Jeffrey Bliss, Susanne Elvira O'Dowda, Barbara Jean Arpin. Student U. Ill.-Chgo., 1957-59; B.A. cum laude, Elmhurst (Ill.) Coll., 1961; postgrad. Lewis U. Coll. Law, 1978-79; J.D. magna cum laude, No. Ill. U., 1982. Tchr. cert.; bar: Ill. 1982, U.S. Dist. Ct. 1982. Tchr. elem. sch., Elmhurst, Ill., 1961-64, Glen Ellyn, Ill., 1964-66; coordinator arts and crafts Elmhurst Park Dist., 1963; assoc. Stephen D. Helm, Naperville, Ill., 1982-84; sole practice, Glen Ellyn, Ill., 1984—. Casenotes and comments editor No. Ill. U. Law Rev., 1981-82; contbr. articles to profl. jours. Co-dir. Valley View Arboretum Civic Assn., Glen Ellyn, 1975-76; rec. sec. Glen Ellyn Republican Women's Club, 1976-77; chmn. Com. for Round Meadow Park, Glen Ellyn, 1976-77; co-chmn. land and water com. Valley View Arboretum Civic Assn., Glen Ellyn, 1976-78. Recipient Alumni Assn. Achievement award, Outstanding Woman Student Leader award, 1981, Corpus Juris Secundum award No. Ill. U., 1982; Leslie A. Holmes scholar, 1981-82. Mem. ABA, Ill. Bar Assn., Ill. Trial Lawyers Assn., DuPage County Bar Assn., Naperville Heritage Soc., Chgo. Council Fgn. Relations, AAUW, LWV, Tau Epsilon Rho. Home: 3 S 201 Arboretum Rd Glen Ellyn IL 60137 Office: 201 Arboretum Rd 3S Glen Ellyn IL 60137

SHERIDAN, SUE DELIANE, lawyer; b. Bellefontain, Pa., Jan. 17, 1954; d. James Francis Sheridan and Peggy (Bishir) Black. B.A., Duke U., 1976; J.D., Vanderbilt U., 1979. Bar: Mass. 1980, D.C. 1985. Atty., U.S. Dept. Energy, Washington, 1979-83; staff Domestic Policy Council, White House, Washington, 1980; counsel subcom. fossil and synthetic fuels U.S. Ho. of Reps., Washington, 1983—. Contbr. articles to profl. jours. Recipient Am. Jurisprudence award, 1979. Mem. ABA, D.C. Bar Assn., Alpha Delta Pi. Democrat. Home: 2711 O St NW Washington DC 20007 Office: Subcom on Fossil and Synthetic Fuels Room 331 House Annex #2 2d and D Sts SW Washington DC 20515

SHERIFF, HILLA, physician; b. Easley, S.C., May 29, 1903; d. John Washington and Mary Lenora (Smith) Sheriff; student Coll. of Charleston (S.C.); 1920-22, H.H.D. (hon.), 1985; M.D., Med. U. of S.C., Charleston, 1926; M.P.H., Harvard U., 1937; m. George Henry Zerbst, July 10, 1940. Intern, Hosp. of Woman's Med. Coll., Phila., 1926-27, Children's Hosp., Washington, 1928-29, Willard Parker Contagious Disease Hosp., N.Y.C., 1929; practice pediatrics, Spartanburg, S.C., 1929-33; dir. Spartanburg County Health Dept., 1933-40; med. staff Spartanburg Gen. Hosp., med. dir. Am. Women's Hosp. Units in Spartanburg and Greenville Counties, S.C., 1931-36; med. dir. research study in Spartanburg County for Milbank Meml. Fund, N.Y.C., 1935-39; asst. dir. div. maternal and child health Dept. Health and Environ. Control, State of S.C., Columbia, 1940-41, dir., 1941—, chief bur. community health services, asst. state health officer, 1968-74, dep. commr. personal health services, past dir. crippled children's services; clin. prof. pediatrics Med. U. S.C., 1972—; clin. prof. medicine and preventive medicine and community health U. S.C., 1985—. Mem. S.C. State Youth Conservation Com., chmn. health and med. care sub com.; rep. from S.C. to White House Conf., 1940, 50, 60; mem. State Adv. Com. on Adult Edn., 1947. Mem. S.C. Council for Handicapped Children, Gov.'s Interagy. Council on Mental Retardation Planning; chmn. S.C. State Nutrition Com.; bd. dirs. Winthrop Coll. Found., Rock Hill, S.C. Recipient meritorious award S.C. Mental Health Assn., 1972, spl. pioneer award; Outstanding State Employee award S.C. State Employees Assn., 1974; award S.C. Hosp. Assn., 1975; William Weston award for disting. service in pediatrics Dept. Pediatrics, Sch. Medicine, U. S.C., 1983. Named to Order of Palmetto, Gov. of S.C. Diplomate Am. Bd. Preventive Medicine. Fellow Am. Public Health Assn. (council mem. maternal and child health sect., Ross award 1969), Am. Acad. Pediatrics (chpt. pres. 1972), Assn. State Maternal and Child Health and Crippled Children's Dirs. (pres. 1960-62), Am. Assn. Public Health Physicians, Columbia Med. Soc. (v.p. 1962), Am. Med. Women's Assn. (2d. v.p. 1946), Am. So., S.C. med. assns., S.C. Public Health Assn., (pres. 1947), Pan Am. Med. Women's Alliance, S.C. Obstet., and Gynecol. Soc. (hon. mem.), S.C. Pediatric Soc. (sec.-treas. 1941-46, pres. 1972-73), S.C. Mental and Social Hygiene Soc. (pres. 1948-49), S.C. Thoracic Soc., S.C. Conf. Social Work, Delta Kappa Gamma, Alpha Epsilon Iota. Episcopalian. Clubs: S.C. Fedn. of Women's, Business and Professional Women's (charter mem. Spartanburg club), Survey (Columbia, S.C.); Harvard of S.C. (sec.-treas. 1977-79). Home: 807 Hampton Hill Dr Columbia SC 29209

SHERK, LORRAINE MARTHA, nurse, educator; b. Washington, Mo., Nov. 1, 1922; d. William Frederick and Martha Wilhelmina (Dierking) Meyer; student Central Mo. State U., 1940-42; R.N., St. Luke's Hosp. Sch. Nursing, 1945; B.S. in Nursing, Washington U., 1947, M.Ed., 1963; m. George W. Sherk, Sept. 13, 1947; 1 son, George W. Office and pvt. duty nurse, Washington, Mo., 1946-57; instr. Deaconess Sch. Nursing, 1950; instr. St. Luke's Sch. Nursing, 1957-62, assoc. dir., 1962-71, dir. nursing edn., 1971—; past accreditation visitor Ind. State Bd. Nursing; past pres. Fedn. for Accessible Nursing Edn. and Licensure. Mem. Kirkwood Hist. Soc., Mo. Hosp. Assn. (com.), Hosp. Assn. Met. St. Louis (past com.), Mo. Citizens for Life, Humane Soc. Mo., Am. Heart Assn., Nat. League Nursing (past accreditation visitor, chmn. bd. rev. diploma programs), Mo. League Nursing (nominating com.), Assembly Hosp. Schs. Nursing (past mem. governing council, program com., chmn. resolutions com.), Show-Me State Diploma Nurse Educators (past chmn.), Deans and Dirs. St. Louis Sch. Nursing (past chmn.), St. Luke's Alumni Assn., Kappa Delta Pi. Presbyterian (deacon). Home: 643 E Jefferson Ave Kirkwood MO 63122 Office: 5535 Delmar Blvd Saint Louis MO 63112

SHERMAN, BEATRICE ETTINGER, business executive; b. N.Y.C., May 29, 1919; d. Max and Stella (Schrager) Ettinger; m. Herbert Jacob Howard, Feb. 15, 1942 (dec. 1971); children—Robert David Howard, Carolyn Howard Smith; m. Ernest John Sherman, Dec. 31, 1974. Student, Shimer Jr. Coll., Mt. Carroll, Ill., 1936-38; B.A., U. Miami, Fla., 1940; postgrad. Harvard U., 1940, Paris-Am. Acad., Paris, 1972, Alliance Française, Paris, 1973. Corp. sec., dir. Save Electric Corp., Toledo, 1940-67, Verd-A-Ray Corp., Toledo, 1944-67, Penetray Corp., Toledo, 1962-67; ptnr. Stella Assocs., Newark, 1960-80; pres. Besman Inc., Coral Gables, Fla., 1975—. Vol. worker Jewish Welfare Fedn., Toledo, 1942-69; nat. speaker United Jewish Appeal. Mem. Assoc. Telephone Answering Exchange, Telocator Network Am., Nat. Council Jewish Women (edn. v.p. 1962-63, bull. editor 1961-62), League City Mothers (v.p. 1953), Hadassah (chpt. v.p. 1963-64). Jewish. Home: 5108 SW 72d Ave Miami FL 33155 Office: Besman Inc 141 Aragon Ave Coral Gables FL 33134

SHERMAN, BERNICE MAE, educator; b. Brockton, Mass., Oct. 7, 1930; d. John Alfred and Gladys Josephine (Boyd) Swan; B.S. in Edn., Bridgewater State Coll., 1970, M.Ed. in Reading, 1975, postgrad. 1984; m. James Owen Pritchard, Feb. 12, 1955 (dec. 1963); 1 dau., Rhonda Mae; m. 2d Robert A. Sherman, Dec. 27, 1980. Tchr. Carver (Mass.) Pub. Schs., 1968-70; reading, learning disabilities specialist, 1970-76, dir. visual motor tng. program, 1973-76, coordinator in-service programs, 1973-76; reading, learning disabilities coordinator Plymouth (Mass.) Sch. System, 1976-82; coordinator programs for children with learning disabilities Fed. Furnace Sch., Plymouth, 1976-79; reading and learning disabilities coordinator Hedge Sch., Plymouth, 1979-83; cons. tchr. reading Hedge Sch. and Mt. Pleasant Sch., Plymouth, 1983—. Mem. Plymouth-Carver Edn. Assn., Plymouth-County Edn. Assn., Mass. Reading Assn., Mass. Tchrs. Assn., NEA, Internat. Reading Assn. Methodist. Club: Mem. Order Eastern Star. Home: 220 Bedford St Apt D8 Bridgewater MA 02324

SHERMAN, DEBORAH, lawyer; b. Glen Cove, N.Y., Nov. 23, 1955; d. Howard and Mary Edith (Coleman) S.; m. Edward William Ostan, Jr., Aug. 19, 1979 (div. 1984); m. Joel B. Harris, Apr. 1, 1986. B.A., SUNY-Stony Brook, 1978; J.D., Hofstra U., 1981. Bar: N.Y. 1982, U.S. Dist. Ct. (so. dist.) N.Y. 1982, U.S. Dist. Ct. (ea. dist.) N.Y. 1982; notary public. Assoc., Weil, Gotshal & Manges, N.Y.C., 1981-83, Gold, Farrell & Marks, N.Y.C., 1983-84. Editor Hofstra Law Rev., 1979-81. Sponsoring mem. Simon Wiesenthal Ctr., Los Angeles, 1984. Mem. ABA, N.Y. State Defenders Assn., Phi Beta Kappa, Alpha Kappa Delta. Office: 152 Remsen St Brooklyn NY

SHERMAN, ELAINE, marketing educator and consultant; b. N.Y.C.; d. Joseph and Beatrice (Silverstein) Goldman; m. Leon Schiffman; children—Bradley, Alan, Melissa. B.A., Bklyn. Coll.; M.B.A., Hofstra U., 1978; M.A., Baruch Coll., N.Y.C., 1982; Ph.D., CUNY, 1983. Owner small bus., N.Y.C., 1970-74; real estate broker, N.Y.C., 1974-83; prof. mktg. Hofstra U., Hempstead, N.Y., 1978—; cons. Market Discovery Group, 1982—; ednl. adviser Jour. Direct Mktg. Author: (with others) Retail Management: A Strategic Approach, 1983; Segmenting the Elderly Consumer, 1983; contbr. articles to profl. jours., chpt. to book. Am. Advt. Assn. fellow, 1981. Mem. Acad. Mktg. Sci., So. Mktg. Assn., Am. Mktg. Assn., Direct Mktg. Ednl. Council, Assn. for Consumer Research, Acad. Mktg. Sci., Am. Collegiate Retailing Assn., Ph.D. Alumni Assn. CUNY, Beta Gamma Sigma. Office: Hofstra U 107 Phillips Hall Hempstead NY 11550

SHERMAN, FRANCES BUCK, artist, photographer; b. Barahona, Santo Domingo; d. Harry Catlett and Elizabeth F. Buck (parents Am. citizens); student Sophie Newcomb Coll., New Orleans, 1936-37, St. Mary's Jr. Coll., Raleigh N.C., 1937, New Orleans Acad. Art, 1947-48, Atlanta Sch. Art., 1967-68, Jacksonville Mus. Art, 1976, N.Y. Inst. Photography, 1981; m. Walter Scott Sherman, Jr., Nov. 9, 1950; children—G. Scott, F. Carolyn; children by previous marriage—Thomas M. Frasier, Harry B. Frasier. Pvt. art tchr., New Orleans, 1947; pvt. practice modeling, New Orleans, 1947-48; staff fashion model Burdines Dept. Store, Miami, 1949-50, asst. fashion coordinator, 1951-52; fashion cons. Coronet Sch. Modeling, Miami, 1953-54; instr. art Tampa Realistic Artists Gallery (Fla.), 1969-70; one-woman shows: Tampa Realistic Art Gallery, 1970, St. Marys Episcopal Ch., Tampa, 1971, Britton Theatre Corp., Tampa, 1970, Royal Trust Bank, Jacksonville, Fla., 1980, 81; group shows include: Va. Mus. Fine Arts, Richmond, Mint Mus. Art, Charlotte, N.C., Isaac Delgado Mus. Art, New Orleans, Swan Coach House Gallery, Atlanta, Jacksonville Art Mus. (Fla.), 1979, St. Augustine Art Assn. (Fla.), 1979, St. Augustine Art Assn., 1980, 81; represented in permanent collections: Jacksonville Shipyards Corp., Robinson-Humphrey Investors, Atlanta, Jacksonville (Fla.) U.; hostess Jacksonville Art Assembly Art Festival, 1977. Active fund raising Pub. Broadcasting TV Sta., Tampa, 1970-71, Jacksonville, 1972-78; active Republican Campaign Hdgrs., Jacksonville, 1976; mem. Nat. Rep. Congl. Com., Duval County Rep. Women's Club. Recipient Certificate of Recognition, The Bicentennial Commn. Jacksonville, 1976; named Outstanding Patriot, Patriots of Am. Bicentennial, 1976. Mem. Am. Artists Profl. League, Inc., Nat. League Am. Pen Women, Inc. (pres. Jacksonville br. 1974-76; Fla. v.p. 1974-76), St. Augustine Art Assn., Fla. Poetry Soc., Arts Assembly Jacksonville, Jacksonville Art Mus., Jacksonville Coalition Visual Artists, Nat. Writers Club. Episcopalian. Contbr. poetry to books and mags. Home: 4331 San Jose Ln Jacksonville FL 32207

SHERMAN, JUDITH DOROTHY, owner-producer classical recording company, recording engineer; b. Cleve., Nov. 12, 1942; d. William Paul and Laverne (Spoerke) Luekens; m. Kenneth Sherman, Aug. 1, 1964 (div. Aug. 1972); m. 2d, Max Wilcox, Jan. 1, 1981. B.A., Valparaiso U., 1964; M.F.A., SUNY-Buffalo, 1971. Rec. engr. Edward at the Moog, N.Y.C., 1971-72; producer-music dir. WBAI-FM, N.Y.C., 1972-76; owner-producer Judith Sherman Prodns., N.Y.C., 1976—; rec. engr. Marlboro (Vt.) Music Festival, 1976—; vocalist Steve Reich and Musicians, 1971-72. Recipient Corp. Pub. Broadcasting award, 1976. Mem. Audio Engring. Soc. (dir. 1975-77), Assn. Classical Music. Democrat. Home and Office: 225 W 70th St New York NY 10023

SHERMAN, MARY ELLEN KENNEDY, personnel executive; b. Chgo., June 17, 1919; d. Robert Thomas and Mary Cecelia (Hammond) Kennedy; A.A., Los Angeles Valley Coll., 1966; B.S., Pepperdine U., 1973; M.B.A., 1974; AEP, Personnel Accreditation Inst., 1977; m. Lloyd McBean Sherman, Dec. 1, 1967; children—Tom D. Akins, Mary Patricia Kraakevik. Indsl. relations supr. Douglas Aircraft Co., Inc., Santa Monica, Calif., 1942-61; dir. personnel Helene Curtis Industries, Studio Girl, Glendale, Calif., 1961-65; dir. personnel Semtech Corp., Newbury Park, Calif., 1965-73, v.p., 1973—; lectr., cons. in field. Mem. Am. Mgmt. Assn., Internat. Assn. for Personnel Women (mem. of Yr. 1982), Am. Soc. Personnel Adminstrn., Personnel and Indsl. Relations Assn., Am. Bus. Women's Assn., Personnel Women of Los Angeles. Republican. Roman Catholic. Club: Zonta (dist. gov.). Office: Semtech Corp 652 Mitchell Rd Newbury Park CA 61320 Home: 6976 Platt Ave Canoga Park CA 91307

SHERMAN, MELINDA ANNE, advertising executive; b. Chgo., Sept. 17, 1946; d. Gerald Wilfred and Dorothy Anne S.; m. Nathan Butler Swift, Nov. 17, 1984. B.A., U. Colo., 1968; M.S.J., Northwestern U., 1973. High Sch. tchr. English, journalism and drama, Albion and Reading, Mich., 1968-70; account rep. Equitable Life Assurance Soc., Chgo., 1970-72, Young & Rubicam N.Y. Advt., 1973-76; v.p., account supr. Leo Burnett USA Advt., Chgo., 1976—; mem. faculty Keller Grad. Sch. Mgmt., Chgo., 1984, 85. Bd. dirs. Chgo. Opera Theater. Recipient Spl. Performance award Young & Rubicam Advt., 1975, 76. Mem. AAUW, Chgo. Drama League, Chgo. Advt. Club. English Speaking Union, Gamma Phi Beta. Clubs: Women's Athletic, Plaza (Chgo.). Home: 1560 N Sandburg Terr Chicago IL 60610 Office: Prudential Plaza Chicago IL 60601

SHERMAN, SARA LOUISE DELACY, computer applications analyst, consultant; b. Sioux Falls, S.D., Mar. 16, 1948; d. Edwin and Margaret Elayne (Ryger) Turowski; m. Madars I. Ozolins, Apr. 10, 1966 (div. Sept. 1974); children—John Erik Ozolins, Danielle Delacy Ozolins Bearman; m. Robert Vincent Sherman. Sec. to pres. Brewer and Assocs., Santa Barbara, 1981-83; fin. planner Estate Fin. and Money Mgmt., Santa Barbara, 1982-83; free-lance computer applications analyst, Santa Barbara, 1983-85; founder, pres. NETA, Inc.-The Legal Network, Santa Barbara, 1985—; cons. to govt., industry, panelist Am. Arbitration Assn., N.Y.C., 1982-86. Reporter Santa Barbara News Press, 1981-85. Inventor teledome, laser data system, Legal Network computer software. Mem. Santa Barbara Transp. Commn., 1983-84; mem. Sci. and Engring. Council, Santa Barbara, 1985; program chmn., bd. dirs. Santa Barbara Women's Club, 1985-86. Mem. Am. Mgmt. Assn., Channel City Women's Forum, Assn. Former Intelligence Officers, Air Force Assn., AAAS, N.Y. Acad. Scis., Armed Forces Communications and Electronics Assn., Nat. Trust Hist. Preservation. Roman Catholic. Office: NETA Inc-The Legal Network 19 E Mission Santa Barbara CA 93101

SHERN, STEPHANIE MARIE, accountant; b. Taylor, Pa., Jan. 7, 1948; d. Joseph and Stephanie (Malodovitch) Andrews; m. George Emil Shern, Sept. 25, 1971. A.A., Keystone Jr. Coll., 1967; B.S., Pa. State U., 1969. C.P.A., N.Y. Staff accountant to ptnr. Arthur Young & Co., N.Y.C., 1969—; dir. Met. Retail Fin. Execs., N.Y.C. Contbr. articles to profl. jours. Named Keystonian of Yr., Keystone Jr. Coll., 1984. Mem. N.Y. State Soc. C.P.A.s (bd. dirs. 1985—), Am. Inst. C.P.A.s, Women's Econ. Round Table, Beta Alpha Psi (mem. adv. forum 1984—). Republican. Ukrainian Orthodox. Club: Panther Valley Golf (Allamuchy, N.J.). Home: 113 Prospect St Little Falls NJ 07424 Office: Arthur Young & Co 277 Park Ave New York NY 10172

SHERREN, ANNE TERRY, chemistry educator; b. Atlanta, July 1, 1936; d. Edward Allison and Annie Ayres (Lewis) Terry; m. William Samuel Sherren, Aug. 13, 1966. B.A., Agnes Scott Coll., 1957; Ph.D., U. Fla.-Gainesville, 1961. Grad. teaching asst. U. Fla., Gainesville, 1957-61; instr. Tex. Woman's U., Denton, 1961-63, asst. prof., 1963-66; research participant Argonne Nat. Lab., 1973-80; assoc. prof. chemistry N. Central Coll., Naperville, Ill., 1966-76, prof., 1976—. Clk. of session Knox Presbyn. Ch., 1976—, ruling elder, 1971—. Mem. Am. Chem. Soc., Am. Inst. Chemists, AAAS, AAUP, Ill. Acad. Sci., Sigma Xi, Delta Kappa Gamma, Iota Sigma Pi (nat. pres. 1978-81, nat. dir. 1972-78). Presbyterian. Contbr. articles to field to profl. jours. Office: N Central Coll Naperville IL 60566

SHERRILL-EDWARDS, IVA, communications company executive, professional development consultant, financial planner; b. Little Rock, Aug. 18, 1937; d. Leroy and Beulah (Wardlow) Sherrill; m. John Moses Edwards, May 19, 1956 (div. Jan. 1979); children—Delmonte, Dennis, Tina Marie. B.A., The Union, Cin., 1985. Service rep. Cin. Bell, 1968-79, customer advisor, 1979-81, facilities coordinator, 1981—; instr. Discovery Learning Ctr., Cin., 1985—; image cons. Iva S. Edwards Cons., Cin., 1984—; fin. planner LBA Fin. Services, Cin., 1986—. Com. mem. Charter Party Cin., 1984; com. mem. allocations Community Chest, Cin., 1986. Mem. Nat. Assn. Female Execs. (network dir. 1985), Am. Bus. Women Assn. (com. mem. 1985). Republican. Mem. African Methodist Episcopal Ch. Avocations: tennis; swimming; reading; traveling. Office: LBA Fin Services & Cons 7374 Reading Rd Suite A-6 Cincinnati OH 45237

SHERRY, DIANE HEATHER, information technology executive; b. Washington, Oct. 5, 1953; d. Daniel I. and Ruth (Mordes) Sherry. B.S. in Zoology, U. Md., 1974, M.L.S. in Library and Info. Services, 1978; M.Mgmt., Kellogg Sch. Mgmt., Northwestern U., 1986. Phys. sci. technician U.S. Dept. Agr., Beltsville, Md., 1972-75; info. analyst Tracor-Jitco, Rockville, Md., 1975-76; info. specialist Franklin Inst., Phila. and Rockville, Md., 1976-79; info. mgr. Procter & Gamble, Cin., 1979-82, products research mgr., 1982-83; mgr. info. resource ctrs. Travenol Labs., Chgo., 1983—. Author: Coffee Bibliography, 1980; editor govt. documents 1976-79. HEW grantee, 1978. Mem. Am. Soc. Info. Sci., Associated Info. Mgrs., Soc. Tech. Communication, Nat. Assn. Female Execs. Home: 758 Judson Ave Highland Park IL 60035 Office: Travenol Labs Route 120 & Wilson Rds Round Lake IL

SHERRY, MARILYN MORIN, psychiatric social worker; b. Worcester, Mass., Mar. 25, 1935; d. Jacob and Gertrude (Greenberg) Morin; A.B., Clark U., 1956; M.S., Simmons Coll., 1958; m. Gerald B. Sherry, Jan. 3, 1960; children—Samuel, Trudy. Social worker Child and Family Services of Conn., Manchester, 1958-61, Hartford, Conn., 1966-71, Dept. Human Services, New Britain, Conn., 1977-79, social worker palliative care and geriatrics Mt. Sinai Hosp., Hartford, 1979-81; psychiat. social worker U. Conn. Health Center, Farmington, 1981—; pvt. practice social work, 1981—. Adv. bd. Encore, YWCA Post-mastectomy Program, 1980-81. Mem. Registry of Clin. Social Workers, Acad. Cert. Social Workers, Nat. Soc. Clin. Social Workers, Coalition Social Work Orgns. Conn. (founding mem., sec.-treas. 1981—), Nat. Assn. Advancement Group Psychotherapy, Nat. Registry Health Care Providers in Clin. Social Work, Am. Assn. for Marriage and Family Therapy. Home: West Hartford CT Office: Univ Conn Health Center H 1015 Farmington CT 06032

SHERWIN, JUDITH SCHWARTZ, lawyer; b. Chgo., Aug. 20, 1945; d. Louis and Lillian Diane (Scholl) Schwartz; m. Byron L. Sherwin, Dec. 24, 1972; 1 son, Jason Samuel. B.A., Roosevelt U., 1972, M.A., 1975; J.D., John Marshall Law Sch., 1978. Bar: Ill. 1978, U.S. Dist. Ct. (no. dist.) Ill. 1978, U.S. Ct. Appeals (7th cir.) 1978, U.S. Tax Ct. 1978, U.S. Supreme Ct. 1982, Fed. Trial Bar 1983. Assoc. Law Offices Solomon Gutstein, Chgo., 1978-80; ptnr. firm Gutstein & Schwartz, Ltd., Chgo., 1980-83, Gutstein & Sherwin, Chgo., 1983—. Bd. dirs. Project Leap, Chgo., 1978—. Mem. ABA, Chgo. Bar Assn., Ill. Bar Assn., Am. Trial Lawyers Assn. Democrat. Jewish. Office: Gutstein & Sherwin 180 N LaSalle St Chicago IL 60601

SHERWIN, ROBERTA MAE, physician; b. Phila., May 10, 1930; d. Robert S. and Matilda C. (Schweers) Sherwin; m. Raymond Sidney Jones, Jan. 27, 1962. B.S., Wheaton Coll. (Ill.), 1951; R.D., Med. Coll. Pa., 1955; M.S. in Medicine, Temple U., 1958. Intern, Episcopal Hosp., Phila., 1955-56; resident Temple U. Hosp., Phila., 1956-58; instr. medicine Temple U. Med. Ctr., Phila., 1960-66; practice medicine specializing in internal medicine and cardiology,

Cheltenham, Pa., 1960-76; physician Exxon Co. U.S.A., Houston, 1977-78, asst. med. dir., 1978-80, med. dir. refinery, Baytown, Tex., 1980-83; asst. med. dir. Exxon Chems. Am., Houston, 1983—; cons. Friends Hosp., Phila., 1970-77; staff physician Frankford Hosp., Phila., 1962-77, Jeanes Hosp., Phila., 1970-77; bd. dirs. Christian Med. Soc., Chgo., 1976-77. Mem. AMA, ACP, Am. Coll. Cardiology, Tex. State Med. Assn., Pa. State Med. Soc., Harris County Med. Soc., Philadelphia County Med. Soc., Bus. and Profl. Women. Club: Doctor's (Houston). Office: Exxon chem Americas PO Box 3272 Houston TX 77001

SHERWOOD, MADISEN, minister, writer, lecturer, counselor; b. Elgin, Oreg., Aug. 29, 1917; d. Calloway Cecil and Nellie Ann (Hug) Howard; m. William Gene Bellm, Oct. 21, 1961; children by previous marriage—Loren, Carolee, Melodie, Kaydence; stepchildren—Stephen, Melanie, Colleen. Ph.D., Inst. Creative Thinking, 1951; Mh.D. (hon.), U. Metaphysics, 1982. Ordained to ministry Ch. Universal of Master in Oakland, 1952. Founder, pres., bishop Esoterian Soc. (inc. 1968), Seattle, 1951—; pres. Nu-Manh Corp., Seattle, 1976—; treas. Priority One Co., Coeur d'Alene, Idaho, 1978—; Author: Carolee in Candyland, 1945; Tempered in Flame, 1970; Basic Disciplines, 1975; Karma Through the Eyes of a Seer, 1977; editor The Esoterian, 1971—. Home: PO Box 1336 Coeur d'Alene ID 83814 Office: Esoterian Soc Inc PO Box 1338 Coeur d'Alene ID 83814

SHERWOOD, MIDGE, author; b. Ironton, Ohio; d. Roy and Addie (Brace) Winters; m. Jack E. Sherwood, Jan. 19, 1946; children—Margaret Sherwood Simms, Melanie Winters. B.J., U. Mo., 1938. Women's editor Ironton Daily Tribune, 1933-38; city editor Ironton Daily News, 1938-40; asst. mgr. West coast news bur. TWA, Los Angeles, 1940-42; pub. relations dir. Western Air Lines, 1942-45; aviation columnist, corr. Skyways, So. Flight, 1945-48; owner, operator Midge Winters Agy., 1945-48; assoc. editor Matrix Mag., Women in Communications, 1950-55; book reviewer Los Angeles Times, 1963; free lance writer, 1958—. Author: And How it Grew, 1965; San Marino Ranch to City, 1977; Days of Vintage, Years of Vision, Vol. 1, 1982. Chmn. Hertrich Meml., Soc. Fellows of Huntington Library, 1967; founder, archivist San Marino Hist. Soc. Mem. Western Writers of Am., Women in Communication, PEO, Huntington Westerners (founder), Westerners Internat. (bd. dirs.), Phi Mu. Home: 1867 Windsor Rd San Marino CA 91108

SHEVELEV, IRENE, physician; b. Odessa, USSR, July 28, 1954; came to U.S., 1982; d. Leonid and Maria (Makh) Zeldovich; m. Simon Shevelev, Mar. 4, 1983. M.D., Pirogov Med. U., Odessa, 1977. Physician, First City Hosp., Odessa, 1977-78, Marsden Hosp., Sydney, Australia, 1980-81; physician Methodist Hosp., Bklyn., 1983—. Office: Methodist Hosp 506 6th St Brooklyn NY 11215

SHEVLAND, JEAN ELLEN, underwriter; b. St. Paul, July 15, 1922; d. William and Matilda Helen (Herning) Suiter; m. Charles William Shevland, June 23, 1945; children—Susan Jean, William Charles. Student, Globe Bus. Coll., 1941. Sec., F.M. Raver, Tacoma, Wash., 1942-45; sec., underwriter Rathbone King & Seeley, Portland, Oreg., 1951-54; accounts sec. Alfred J. Davis Co., Portland, 1954-57; underwriter United Pacific Ins. Co., Portland, 1957-61; underwriter, asst. comml. sec. Fire JBL&K Corp., Portland, 1962-70; sec. Saling Dodd Ins., Portland, 1971-85. Named Women of Yr., Portland Rose chpt. Am. Bus. Women's Assn., 1981. Mem. Ins. Women Mt. Hood (corr. sec. 1980-81, v.p. 1981-82), Am. Bus. Women's Assn. (chpt. pres. 1977-78, rec. sec. 1983-84). Democrat. Methodist. Address: 6114 NE Alameda Portland OR 97213

SHICK, LAURA JANE, product development and marketing consultant; b. Balt., May 27, 1950; d. George Roland and Harriet Regina (Wilson) De Hoff; m. Robert Francis Stuber, Dec. 28, 1971 (div. Apr. 1977); m. Richard Lee Shick, Aug. 8, 1980; children—Suzanne Lillian, Jonathan David. B.S. in Home Econs. and Textiles, U. Del., 1972, M.S. in Stats., 1981. Consumer research scientist Scott Paper Co., Phila., 1974-76, quality brand mgr., 1976-77; market research analyst Campbell Soup Co., Camden, N.J., 1978-79; mgr. market research Cigna Corp., Phila., 1979-84; pres. Laura Shick & Co., 1984—; cons. Ins. Inst. Am., Malvern, Pa., 1983—; vol. mktg. cons. Brandywine River Mus., Chadds Ford, Pa., 1981—, Historic Yellow Springs (Pa.), 1983—, Hedgerow Theatre, Moylan, Pa., 1984—. Sales vol. Greater Phila. C. of C., 1983; vol. cons. Bus. Vols. for Arts, Phila., 1983—. Named to Order of Link 4-H, 1970. Mem. Product Devel. Mgmt. Assn. (pres. Phila. 1983-84), Am. Mktg. Assn., Soc. Ins. Research, Am. Statis. Assn., Omicron Nu, Alpha Chi Omega. Republican. Presbyterian. Home and Office: 216 S Ridley Creek Rd Moylan PA 19065

SHIDELER, SHIRLEY ANN WILLIAMS, lawyer; b. Mishawaka, Ind., July 9, 1930; d. William Harmon and Lois Wilma (Koch) Williams; LL.B., Ind. U., 1964; 1 dau., Gail Shideler Frye. Legal sec. Barnes, Hickam, Pantzer & Boyd, Indpls., 1953-63; admitted to Ind. bar, 1964; practiced in Indpls., 1964—; assoc. firm Barnes & Thornburg, 1963-70, ptnr., 1971—. Active fund drives Indpls. Symphony, 1968—, Indpls. Mus. Art, 1969-79; bd. dirs. bus. unit gals Indpls. Mus. Art, 1973-80; bd. dirs. Indpls. Legal Aid Soc., 1982—, Community Hosp. Services Found., Central Newspapers Found. Fellow Am. Coll. Probate Council; mem. ABA, Ind. Bar Assn. (sec. 1975-76, chmn. probate, trust and real property sect.), Indpls. Bar Assn. (bd. mgrs. 1968-72, v.p. charge affairs 1972), Ind. Bar Found. (bd. mgrs. 1980—, sec. 1981-82, treas. 1981—), Indpls. Bar Found. (bd. mgrs. 1970-82, sec. 1972-77), Estate Planning Council. Club: Woman's Rotary (pres. 1969-71, dir. 1968-79) (Indpls.). Home: 5150 Hawthorne Dr Indianapolis IN 46226 Office: 1313 Merchants Bank Bldg Indianapolis IN 46204

SHIELDS, ADDIE LAWRENCE, county historian; b. Beekmantown, N.Y., June 24, 1916; d. Howard Clifton and Agnes Elizabeth (Dupee) Lawrence; m. Francis Matthew Shields, Nov. 21, 1940 Ddec. 1964); children—Charlotte Frances, Charles Howard. Lic. Plattsburgh State Normal Sch., 1937; B.S. in Early Childhood, SUNY-Plattsburgh, 1973. Tchr. Dist. 3 Beekmantown, 1937-41; farm operator, 1964-71; asst. dir. Migrant Mexican Day Care Ctr., 1973; historian Clinton County, Plattsburgh, 1978—; chmn. women's com. Farm Bur., mem. State Women's Com.; pres. Clinton County Farm Bur.; sec., treas. NE Local Dairymen's League. Editor: Landmark in a Passageway-Beekmantown, 1976. Compiler and editor: The Diary of John Jersey McFadden in year 1972, 1982; The John Townsend Addoms Homestead-Underground RR Station, 1981. Compiler: Account Book for the Farmer-1876-Amos Barber (1828-89), 1984. Author preface for M. Benoit Pontbriands Comte Clinton-Marriages a Repertory 1830-80. Dedication by author Morris Glenn-Glenn's History of Adirondacks (Essex County), 1980. Addie Shields Day named in her honor No. N.Y. Am.-Can. Geneal. Soc., 1985. Mem. Clinton County Hist. Assn., N.Y. State Assn. County Historians (sec.), North County Local Historians Assn. (assoc. mem.). Republican. Presbyterian. Home: Point au Roche Plattsburgh NY 12901 Office: County Government Ctr 137 Margaret St Plattsburgh NY 12901

SHIELDS, DOROTHY MCDONALD, library science educator; b. Rochester, Pa., Aug. 7, 1930; d. Charles Dwight and Florence Janetta (Jameson) McD.; m. Thomas Albert Shields, Dec. 16, 1950 (dec. 1956); 1 dau., Alison Shields Butterfield. B.A., Muskingum Coll., 1952; postgrad. U. Hawaii, 1959-61; M.S.L.S., Western Res. U., 1964; Ed.D., Brigham Young U., 1977. Library cons. Oberlin Coll. (Ohio), summer 1964; elem. librarian, pub. schs., Lexington, Mass., 1964-65; head librarian Liahona High Sch., Nuku'alofa, Tonga, 1965-67, Ch. Coll. N.Z., Temple View, 1968-72; asst. prof. library sci. Brigham Young U., Provo, Utah, 1974-82, assoc. prof., 1982—; presenter/dir. workshop on creative uses of books with children, 1980-83. Contbr. articles to profl. publs. Mem. ALA, Assn. Library Services to Children, Utah Library Assn., Mountain Plains Library Assn., Assn. for Library and Info. Sci. Edn., Beta Phi Mu (exec. council 1981-84), Delta Kappa Gamma. Mormon. Home: 211 Cherry Dr Orem UT 94058 Office: Sch Library and Info Scis 5042 HBLL Brigham Young U Provo UT 84602

SHIELDS, LAURA AULL, public relations counselor; b. Taylorville, Ill., Oct. 24, 1917 d. Leo Franklin (dec.) and Gladys Aull (Montgomery) (dec.) Aull; student Ill. Normal U., 1935; children—Deborah, Beth, Roger, Clark, Constance. Feature writer San Gabriel Valley Tribune, Covina, Calif., 1969—; owner Shields Communications, Santa Monica, Calif., 1976—. Mem. Counselors Acad., Public Relations Soc. Am., Women in Bus., Nat. Assn. Women Bus. Owners. Democrat. Home and Office: 159 Wadsworth Ave Santa Monica CA 90405

SHIELDS, TAMARA WEST-O'KELLEY, accounting firm executive; b. Lewiston, Idaho, Oct. 23, 1948; d. Brooks E. and Dona J. (Rogers) O'Kelley; m. William Henry Shields, Nov. 8, 1974; 1 child, Stewart Alan. B.B.A. cum laude, North Tex. State U., 1976. Staff acct. James C. Beach C.P.A., Carrollton, Tex., 1972-76, Deloitte, Haskings & Sells, C.P.A., 1976-77; chief fin. officer Comminications Systems, Inc., Irving, Tex., 1977-84; pvt. practice acctg., Dallas, 1984—; lectr. in field. Mem. Am. Inst. C.P.A.s (ethics com.), Tex. Soc. C.P.A.s, Beta Alpha Psi. Office: 4444 Spring Valley Suit 109 Dallas TX 75244

SHIELDS, WANDA LOU, university official; b. Ft. Worth, Sept. 13, 1940; d. B. Rex and Chrystle O. (Riddle) Shields; m. Melvin D. Holtzclaw, Dec. 27, 1966 (div.). Student U. Tex., 1958-60; B.S., Tex. Woman's U., 1962; M.A., 1968; Ed.D., U. Houston, 1978. Cert. tchr., adminstr., Tex. Tchr. Houston Ind. Sch. Dist., 1962-73, program cons., 1973-75, asst. dir., 1975-78, personnel coordinator, 1978-81, prin. intern, 1980-81; assoc. dean Coll. Edn. and Behavioral Studies, Houston, Baptist U., 1981—; also dir. M.Ed. and M.A. in Psychology Programs. Contbr. to Human Sexuality, 1968. Mem. Maplewood Civic Club, Houston, 1974—; bd. dirs. Se-Arama Marineworld, Galveston, 1980—; trustee N.W. Acad., Houston, 1983—; vol. Houston Leukemia Soc., 1980—, Houston Cancer Soc., 1981—; pres. adult choir 1st Bapt. Ch., Houston. Named Faculty Woman of Yr., Houston Bapt. U., 1982. Mem. Tex. Soc. Coll. Tchrs. Edn. (v.p. 1982), Houston Prins. Assn. (exec. bd. 1980-81), Religious Heritage Am., Phi Delta Kappa, Kappa Delta Pi. Office: Houston Baptist U 7502 Fondren Rd Houston TX 77074

SHIERY, JULIE ANN, auto-diesel machine shop owner, trainer and owner of thorobreds; b. Scottdale, Pa., July 31, 1963; d. George Edward and Toni Lee (Helmick) S.; 1 child, Clarissa Renee. Bus. grad. (hon.), Bus. Career Inst., Greensburg, Pa., 1982. Mgr., HY SY Stable, Connellsville, Pa., 1976-78, mgr./trainer Black Creek Stable, Connellsville, 1978-80; sec./machinist Bill's Performance Shop, New Alexandria, Pa., 1982-83, owner, 1983—; owner J.A.S. Stables, New Alexandria, 1984—; cons. to several auto racing orgns., 1983—. Teen leader Ripple Ridge 4-H Club, Scottdale, 1978-81. Named Grand Nat. Champion, Madison Sq. Gardens, N.Y.C., 1978; Grand Nat. Champion, All Am. Quarter Horse Congress, Ohio, 1979; Grand Champion Ky. Horse Trails, 1979; Grand Champion, Pa. State 4-H Show, 1977. Democrat. Avocations: stock car racing; drag racing; tractor/truck pulling; equestrian events. Home: RD 1 New Alexandria PA 15670 Office: Bill's Performance Shop RD 1 Box 61HX New Alexandria PA 15670

SHIGLEY, LOIS MARIE, banker; b. Seattle, May 17, 1943; d. Floyd Dwayne and Gloria Lois Stone; student Whittier (Calif.) Bus. Coll.; grad. Nat. Installment Credit Sch., U. Okla., 1979, Nat. Compliance Sch., 1980; m. Gerald F. Shigley, Sept. 5, 1971; children—John M., Robert A. Legal sec. Whittier City Attys., 1961-63; exec. sec., asst. office mgr. Fotomat Corp., LaJolla, Calif., 1969-71; adminstrv. asst. to pres. Beach —n— Towne Realtors, San Diego, Calif., 1971-72; mktg. research dept. Samsonite Corp., 1974-75; v.p., 1st Nat. Bank of Strasburg (Colo.), 1976-85, mktg. mgr., 1984-85. Home: 1301 Inverness Huntsville TX 77340

SHIH, JOAN FAI, artist, educator; b. Kwang Tong, China, Sept. 4, 1932; came to U.S., 1953; d. Henry Ken-Wai and Laura Suk-Wee (Chen) S. Student Art Students' League, N.Y.C., 1953; B.F.A., Kansas City Art Inst., 1956, M.F.A., 1961; post-grad. Pa. Acad. Fine Arts, 1957-59, 61-63. One man shows include: Brit. Council, Gloucer Bldg., Hong Kong, 1956; Cedar Crest Coll., Allentown, Pa., 1969; Danville Mus. Fine Arts, Va., 1986, exhibited in group shows including: Nelson and Atkins Mus. Art, Kansas City, Mo., 1954, Pa. Acad. Fine Arts, 1963, 69, 70, 72, 74, 76, 81, 83, Phila. Civic Center Mus., 1970, 74, 79, 80, 82, traveling exhbn. Nat. Assn. Women Artists, 1978-80, 80-82, 83-85, 85-87, Huntington Mus., N.Y.C., 1981, Bergen Mus., Paramus, N.J., 1983; represented in permanent collections including D.W. Newcomer's Sons Gallery, Kansas City, Mo., Meth. Hosp., Phila.; instr. Kansas City Art Inst. (Mo.), 1959-61, Converse Coll., Spartanburg, S.C., 1966-67; lectr. painting Rosemont Coll. (Pa.), 1969—. Kansas City Art Inst. grantee, 1959-61, Kansas City Art Inst. scholar, 1953-56; recipient 1st prize D.W. Newcomer's Sons Ann. Show, Kansas City, 1960, honorable mention Plastic Club Ann. Art Exbfn., Phila., 1985. Mem. Nat. Assn. Women Artists (Elizabeth Erlanger Meml. prize 1980), Fellowship of Pa. Acad. Fine Arts, Coalition of Women's Art Orgns., Phila. Watercolor Club, Hong Kong Art Club. Episcopalian. Home: 2013 Locust St Philadelphia PA 19103 Office: Rosemont College Rosemont PA 19010

SHILDNECK, BARBARA JEAN, accounting magazine editor; b. Waynesboro, Pa., Apr. 1, 1937; d. Barry Price and Helen Matilda (Armstrong) S. B.A. in English Lit., Wilson Coll., Chambersburg, Pa., 1959. Jr. prodn. asst. Am. Inst. C.P.A.s, N.Y.C., 1959-62, sr. prodn. asst., 1962-66, asst. editor Jour. of Accountancy, 1966-73, editor The C.P.A., 1969-73, manuscript editor Jour. of Accountancy, 1974-79, mng. editor Jour. of Accountancy, 1979-83, editor, 1984—; panelist video tape edn. program Dunwoody and Co. Chartered Accountants, Toronto, Ont., Can., 1977. Am. Inst. C.P.A.s, 1980, lectr. in field. Contbr. articles to profl jours. Mem. Am. Soc. Bus. Press Editors, Nat. Assn. Female Execs. Democrat. Avocations: painting; drama; art; reading; writing. Office: Am Inst CPAs 1211 Ave of Americas New York NY 10036

SHILLER, DORIS BARKER, lawyer; b. N.Y.C., May 9, 1933; d. Chester and Fay (Chasnoff) Barker; m. Jack Shiller, July 18, 1954 (div. 1981). A.B., Barnard Coll., 1954; J.D., Yale U., 1979. Bar: Conn. 1979, U.S. Dist. Ct. 1979, U.S. Ct. Appeals (2d cir.) 1982. Assoc., ptnr. Marsh, Day & Calhoun, Bridgeport, Conn., 1979-85; ptnr. Berkowitz, Balbirer, Weisman & Lubell, Westport, Conn., 1985—. Contbr. article to jour. Mem. Westport Bd. Edn. (Conn.), 1971-78; bd. dirs., pres. Coop. Ednl. Services Fairfield County, Darien Conn., 1972-76; bd. dirs. Child Care Council Westport, 1981-85, Westport Ctr. for Arts 1984-86. Recipient Provost Econs. prize Barnard Coll., 1954. Mem. Conn. Bar Assn., ABA. Democrat. Home: 10 Cypress Pond Rd Westport CT 06880 Office: Berkowitz Balbirer et al 253 Post Rd W Westport CT 06881

SHILLING, ESTHER, nurse, pacemaker clinician; b. Summit, N.J., Feb. 11, 1931; d. Charles and Mildred (Wright) Engel; m. Allan B. Shilling, Sept. 11, 1955; children—Jeffrey, Larry, Michael. R.N., Newark Beth Israel Hosp. Sch. Nursing, 1951; student Rutgers U., 1953-55. R.N., N.J. Operating room staff nurse Newark Beth Israel Hosp., Newark, N.J., 1951-53, asst. operating room supr., 1953-57; operating room scrub nurse Irvington Gen. Hosp., Irvington, N.J., 1958-59; sch. nurse New Providence High Sch., 1963-65; adminstr. pacemaker team Newark Beth Israel Med. Ctr., Newark, N.J., 1968-74, pacemaker clinician, 1974—; nurse adminstr. N.J. Regional Medico Program for Eval. Pacemakers, 1969-72; trustee Pacemaker Found. Inc., 1969-80; cons. ESB/Medcor Corp., Yardly, Pa., 1974-77; courtesy instr. Mountainside Hosp. Sch. Nursing, Montclair, N.J., 1973—. Editor: Heartbeat newsletter, 1972, 73, 74; editor Pacemaker Clinic Brochure, 1974—; contbr. articles to profl. jours; chpt. to book. Pres. sisterhood Jewish Community Ctr., Summit, N.J., 1965, 66, 67. Mem. N.Am. Soc. Pacing and Electrophysiology, Am. Assn. Critical Care Nurses, Am. Heart Assn., Newark Beth Israel Hosp. Alumni Assn. Democrat. Jewish. Home: 4 Lavina Ct Summit NJ 07901 Office: Newark Beth Israel Med Ctr Pacemaker Ctr 201 Lyons Ave Newark NJ 07112

SHILLING, KAY MARLENE, psychiatrist; b. Scottsbluff, Nebr., July 1, 1952; d. Harrison Gene and Rose Marie (Allen) Herber; m. Mark Randall Shilling, July 2, 1977. B.S., U. Nebr.-Lincoln, 1976; M.D., U. Nebr.-Omaha, 1980. Diplomate Nat. Bd. Med. Examiners. Resident in psychiatry Nebr. Psychiat. Inst., Omaha, 1981-84; practice medicine specializing in psychiatry, Ohama, 1984—; cons. Methodist Childrens Hosp Family Life Ctr., Ohama, 1985—; bd. dirs. Indian-Chicano Health Ctr., Omaha. Mem. Am. Med. Women's Assn. (pres. Omaha br. 1986-87), Am. Psychiat. Assn., AMA, Met. Omaha Med. Soc., Nebr. Med. Assn., Alpha Xi Delta. Avocations: gourmet cooking; interior decorating; house renovation. Home: 1103 S 80th St Omaha NE 68124 Office: 8300 W Dodge St Suite 423 Omaha NE 68114

SHILLING, SHIRLEY ROMAINE, insurance agent; b. Butler, Pa., Jan. 19, 1936; d. Arthur W. and Georgia Alberta (Hutzley) Percy; 1 dau., Pamela Kay Shilling Ebert. C.P.C.U. Underwriter, Nationwide Ins., Butler, 1953-59, Borgal Ins. Agy., Inglewood, Calif., 1961-69; office mgr. Fred E Cimino Ins. Agy., Inglewood, 1969-74; sec.-treas., partner Fred E. Cimino & Assocs., Inc., Los Angeles, 1974-83; owner C&S Ins. Services, Los Angeles, 1984—; mem. producer council Mercury Ins. Group, 1979—. Named Ins. Woman of Yr., Calif. Ins. Assn., 1972, Woman of Yr., Torrance YWCA, 1979. Mem. Nat. Assn. Ins. Women (pres. (past nat. pres., nat. bldg. chmn., Region VIII Ins. Woman of Yr. 1973), South Bay Assn. Ins. Women, Ins. Inst. Am. (exam. com.), Soc. CPCU (nat. candidate devel. commn., dir. chpt.), Profl. Ins. Agts., Ind. Ins. Agts. Am., Profl. Ins. Agts. Calif./New., Ind. Ins. Agts. Calif., Ind. Ins. Agts and Brokers Assn. Inglewood/Centinela Valley (dir., Ins. Woman of Yr. 1971, edn. chmn.), Ins. Women of Ingelwood-South Bay (past pres., dir.). Republican. Presbyterian. Contbr. articles to ins. trade jours. Office: C&S Ins Services PO Box 45056 Los Angeles CA 90045

SHILLINGSBURG, MIRIAM JONES, educator; b. Balt., Oct. 5, 1943; d. W. Elvin and Miriam (Reeves) Jones; B.A., Mars Hill Coll., 1964; M.A., U. S.C., 1966, Ph.D., 1969; m. Peter L. Shillingsburg, Nov. 21, 1967; children—Robert, George, John, Alice, Anne Carol. Asst. prof. Limestone Coll., Gaffney, S.C., 1967; asst. prof. Mississippi State (Miss.) U., 1970-75, asso. prof., 1975-80, prof., 1980—; Fulbright lectr. U. New South Wales, Duntroon, Australia, 1984-85. Nat. Endowment Humanities fellow in residence, Columbia U., 1976-77. Mem. MLA, Soc. Study So. Lit., Am. Studies Assn., Southeastern Soc. Eighteenth Century Studies. Mem. Editorial bd. Works of W.M. Thackeray; contbr. articles to profl. jours. and mags.

SHILLINGTON, ANN GRIFFIN, electronic manufacturing company executive; b. Macon, Ga., Feb. 21, 1937; d. Perry Lumpkin and Laura Mabel (Wilson) Griffin; m. Thomas Raymond Shillington, May 13, 1957; children—Lisa Ann, David Gary. Student U. Ala., Tuscaloosa, 1955-57; B.A. in Edn., Fla. Atlantic U., 1970; postgrad. in acctg. Ga. State U., 1975. Cert. prodn. and inventory mgmt. Tchr., Miami, Fla. and Atlanta, 1970-72; sec., treas. Shillington & Assocs., Atlanta, 1972-75; asst. to pres. Southeast Communications systems, Atlanta, 1975-76; adminstr., fin. asst. Greater Florence C. of C., S.C., 1976-80; materials, cost control mgr. Shaw, Walker Co., Florence, 1980-85; purchasing supr. OKI Telecom, Atlanta, 1985—. Vice chmn. campaign United Way, Florence, 1982-83, vice chmn. allocations, Florence, 1979. Mem. Am. Prodn. and Inventory Control Soc. (bd. dirs. 1982-85, Recognition award 1985), Purchasing Mgmt. Assn. Ga., Nat. Assn. Female Execs. Avocations: travelling; sports; theater. Home: 3777 Willow Wood Way Lawrenceville GA 30245

SHIM, KATHYLEEN SHERROD, public relations executive; b. Uniontown, Ala., Feb. 14, 1948; d. Benjamin Herndon and Kathyleen S.; B.S. cum laude, U. Fla., 1975; M.A., George Washington U., 1980; m. Kye Taik Shim, Dec. 12, 1980. Film prodn. asst. Barton Film Co., Jacksonville, Fla., 1969-70; writer Sta. WTLV-TV, NBC affiliate, Jacksonville, 1970-71; studio prodn. crew Sta. WUFT-TV, PBS affiliate, Gainesville, Fla., 1973-75; reporter, photographer Vero Beach (Fla.) Press Jour., 1975-78; writer press dept. U.S. Senator Bill Roth, 1978-80; press sec. U.S. Rep. Larry J. Hopkins, Washington, 1981-84; freelance newspaper columnist, 1983; communications and mktg. cons., 1984—; pub. affairs specialist Peace Corps, Washington, 1984—; dir. communications Indsl. Biotech. Assn., 1986—; v.p. C&C Food Service, Inc., Washington, Key Jobs, Inc., Lakeland, Fla. Recipient 2d place awards Nat. Better Newspaper Contest, 1977, 78; 1st place award Fla. Press Assn., 1979, 2d place award, 1977, 78, 79, Claudia Ross Meml. award, 1977, outstanding performance award Peace Corps, 1985. Mem. Republican Communications Assn., Senate Press Secs. Assn., Womens Polit. Caucus Capitol Hill. Home: 6591 Cypress Point Rd Alexandria VA 22312

SHIMADA, LINDA MICHI, insurance agency executive; b. Honolulu, Oct. 22, 1963; d. Glenn Atsuo Shimada and Amy Ayako (Takeda) Shimada Wong. B.B.A., U. Hawaii, 1985. Lic. life ins. solicitor, registered issuer of securities, Hawaii. Salesperson McInerny, Honolulu, 1982-83; clk. U. Hawaii Bd. Regents, Honolulu, 1982-84; sales rep. A.L. Williams, Honolulu, 1984, sales mgr., 1984-85, dist. mgr., 1985, div. mgr., 1986—. Mem. Am. Entrepreneurs Assn., Nat. Assn. Female Execs., Alpha Beta Chi (chpt. sec. 1983-84, chpt. pres. 1984-85). Democrat. Baptist. Office: A L Williams 401 Waiakamilo Suite 202 Honolulu HI 96817

SHIMANSKI, JANETTE MARIE, marketing educator, consultant; b. Mpls., June 14, 1956; d. Raymond Francis and Berma Kathleen (Gallery) S. B.B.A., U. Wis., 1978, M.S., 1980; postgrad. U. Minn., 1983—. Mktg. analyst 3M, St. Paul, 1980-81, sr. mktg. analyst, 1981-82, mktg. supr., 1982-83; instr. mktg. U. Minn., Mpls., 1983—; research cons. 3M, St. Paul, 1983—; mktg. cons. Vicki Reid & Assocs., St. Paul. Recipient award First Bank of Mpls., 1974. Mem. Am. Mktg. Assn., Beta Gamma Sigma. Roman Catholic. Club: Calhoun Beach. Home: 2915 Dean Pkwy #105 Minneapolis MN 55416 Office: Univ Minn 1220 Management and Econs 271 19th Ave S Minneapolis MN 55455

SHIMBERG, ELAINE FANTLE, writer; b. Yankton, S.D., Feb. 26, 1937; d. Karl S. and Alfreda (Edelson) Fantle; B.S., Northwestern U., 1958; m. Mandell Shimberg, Oct. 1, 1961; children—Karen, Scott, Betsy, Andrew, Michael. Continuity dir. WALT Radio, Tampa, Fla., 1959-60, WFLA Radio, 1960-61; freelance writer, 1961—; co-hostess WFLA-TV talk show Women's Point of View, Tampa, Fla., 1976-81; tchr. Writing for Publication and Profit, Hillsborough Community Coll., Tampa 1980-82. Mem. public info. com. Fla. div. Am. Cancer Soc., 1974—, mem. childhood cancer com. 1975-79; bd. devel. council St. Joseph Hosp., 1982—; bd. dirs. United Way, 1986—. Mem. Am. Soc. Journalists and Authors, Authors Guild, Women in Communication, Am. Med. Writers Assn., Athena Soc. Author: How to be A Successful Housewife/Writer, 1979; Two for the Money: A Woman's Guide to a Double Career Marriage, 1981; contbg. author: The Complete Guide to Writing Non-Fiction, 1983; Teenage Drinking and Driving: A Deadly Duo, 1984; Coping with Kids and Vacation, 1986. Contbr. articles to various mags.

SHIMOMURA, TERRI NOBUKO, banker; b. Honolulu, Apr. 3, 1957; d. Allen Yasunobu Shimomura and Alice Miyuki Nishimura; m. Francisco Javier de la Hoz Ulloa, June 18, 1982. B.A. magna cum laude, Princeton U., 1979. Credit trainee Chase Manhattan Bank, N.Y.C., 1979-80, credit auditor, 1980-81, relationship mgr. Chase Manhattan's Instnl. Portfolio in Mexico, Mexico City, 1982-83, 2d credit officer Chase Manhattan Bank in Mexico, Mexico City, 1983-84, relationship mgr. Chase Manhattan's Corp. Portfolio in Mex., 1984—. Recipient Lt. John A. Larkin Jr. Meml. prize for Polit. Economy Woodrow Wilson for Pub. and Internat. Affairs of Princeton U., 1979. Mem. Phi Beta Kappa. Club: Princeton of N.Y. Home: PO Box 521 care Chase-Mexico Bowling Green Station New York NY 10004

SHINE, BARBARA, advertising executive; b. Mpls., July 22, 1938; d. Monroe J. and Charlotte K. Shine. Ph.B. in Communications, Northwestern U., 1982; A.A., U. Minn., 1960. With Dow Jones & Co., Inc., Wall St. Jour., Denver, Los Angeles, Silver Spring, Md. and Chgo., 1962—, Midwest advt. coordinator Travel for Bus. and Pleasure, office mgr. classified advt. sales, 1980—. Com. mem. Mental Health Assn. Montgomery County, Kensington, Md., 1973-77; mem. mental health edn. adv. com. State of Md., Balt., 1975-77; com. mem. Mental Health Assn. Greater Chgo., 1977-78; mem. leadership com. U. Minn. Alumni Assn., Chgo., 1980—. Recipient Crystal Prism award Advt. Club, 1974. Mem. Am. Advt. Fedn. (recipient Citations for Meritorious Service 1972, 74, dir. 2d dist. 1971-76), Advt. Club Met. Washington (com. mem., dir. 1974-77, pres. 1973-74). Office: 1 S Wacker Chicago IL 60606

SHINEHOUSE, ELFREDA JANE, biologist, educator; b. Chestnut Hill, Pa., Apr. 13, 1931; d. Arthur Dewey and Elfreda Frances (Ross) Perreten; B.S., Ursinus Coll., 1952; postgrad. U. Pa., 1953; m. Robert R. Shinehouse, Apr. 5, 1952; children—Linda Anne, Patricia G., James P., Lisa Susan. Phys. therapist Montgomery County Hosp., Norristown, Pa., part time 1953, Phoenixville (Pa.) Hosp., part time 1958-60; instr. biology Ursinus Coll., Collegeville, Pa., part time 1960-77, asst. prof., 1977-83, assoc. prof., 1984—, asst. premed. adviser, 1981—. Sec., Home and Sch. Assn., 1961-62; tchr. aide Oaks Elem. Sch., 1977-78; Sunday Sch. tchr. St. James Episcopal Ch., 1978-79, chmn. Christian Women in Soc., 1979-80. Recipient Lindback award for disting. teaching Ursinus Coll., 1981; March of Dimes Found. grantee, 1952. Mem. Registry Am. Phys. Therapists, Sigma Xi (assoc.), Beta Beta Beta, Pi Nu Epsilon. Republican. Home: 1747 S Collegeville Rd Collegeville PA 19426 Office: 209 LSB Ursinus Coll Collegeville PA 19426

SHINER, JOSETTE ANN SHEERAN, editor; b. Orange, N.J., June 12, 1954; d. James J. and Sarah Ann (Gallagher) S. B.A., U. Colo., 1976. Nat. desk editor N.Y. News World, 1976-77; Washington bur. chief N.Y. News World, 1977-80, White House corr., 1980-82; Capital Life and mag. editor Washington Times, 1982-84, asst. mng. editor, 1984-85, dep. mng. editor, 1985—. Recipient Atrium award U. Ga., 1984. Mem. Nat. Press Club (newsmaker chmn. 1980-82; Meritorious Service award 1981, Vivian award 1981), Sigma Delta Chi. Office: Washington Times 3600 New York Ave NE Washington DC 20002

SHINGLER-DAVIS, LOU, accountant; b. Ashburn, Ga., Mar. 13, 1957; d. Clark Henderson and Martha (Gordy) Shingler; m. E.J. Davis, Jr., Jan. 11, 1986. A.S., Abraham Baldwin Coll., 1978; B.B.A., Ga. Southwestern Coll., 1980. Bookkeeper, Ashburn Bank, Ga., 1976-77, Pete-Mar Inc., Ashburn, 1979-80; employment interviewer Ga. Dept. Labor, 1980-83; cost acct. Merck & Co., Inc., Albany, Ga., 1983—; cons. and lectr. in bus., acctg., leadership effectiveness and GED Vocat. Edn., Albany, Ga., 1983—. Sect. chmn. Commerce & Industry div. United Way, Albany, 1983. Featured in newspaper article. Methodist. Clubs: Nat. Skeet Shooting Assn.; Ga. Skeet Shooting Assn. Avocations: working; fishing; skeet shooting; golfing; animal welfare. Address: Rt 4 Box 153 Dawson GA 31742

SHINK, SHARI FRANCINE, lawyer; b. Greensburg, Pa., Dec. 3, 1948; d. John Anton and Frances Marie (Ursic) S. B.S., U. Pitts., 1970; student Duquesne U., 1973; J.D., Rutgers U., 1975. Staff atty. Neighborhood Legal Services, Pitts., 1973-77, Child Advocacy Legal Aid, Pitts., 1977-79, mng. atty., 1979-81; exec. dir. Colo. Guardian Ad Litem Project, Denver, 1981—; mem. Gov.'s Commn. to Study Children's Code, Denver, 1983-84; mem. Colo. Social Services Com. to Establish Policy, 1983; field instr. Denver U. Sch. Social Work, 1982—; speaker Internat. Congress on Child Abuse, Paris, 1982. Bd. dirs. Met. Child Protection Council, 1982—, Chrysalis teen group home, 1982—. Scholar in residence, fellow Nat. Ctr. for Prevention Child Abuse, Denver, 1978. Mem. Nat. Assn. Counsel for Children (v.p., dir. 1979-81), Nat. Assn. Female Execs., Nat. Assn. Ct. Appointed Spl. Child Advocates, ABA, Pa. Bar Assn., Colo. Bar Assn. Democrat. Roman Catholic. Club: Colo. Mountain. Lodge: Nat. Slovene Benefit Soc. Office: Colo Guardian Ad Litem Project Denver Juvenile Ct City County Bldg 1460 Cherokee St Denver CO 80202

SHINN, MICHELE DIANE, retail company executive, consultant; b. Frackville, Pa., Oct. 15, 1949; d. Michael and Sophia Nellie (Studlick) Stetts; m. David William Shinn, July 7, 1973 (div. Nov. 1980). B.S. in Edn., Bloomsburg State U., Pa., 1971. Cert. elem. tchr., Pa., N.J. Tchr. spl. edn. Doylestown Elem. Sch., Pa., 1971-73, Tuckerton Sch. Dist., N.J., 1973-80; v.p., co-owner Marchele's, Ltd., Summerville, S.C., 1980—; instr. Trident Tech. Coll., Charleston, S.C., part-time 1981—, Rutledge Coll., Charleston, part-time 1985—; seminar leader Low Contry Seminar Network, Charleston, 1984—; pvt. practice communications cons., Charleston, 1985—. Mem. Am. Soc. Tng. and Devel., Summerville C. of C. (bd. dirs. 1983—). Republican. National Catholic. Club: Pilot of Greater Summerville (treas. 1982-85). Avocations: reading; playing the piano; water skiing; snow skiing; volleyball. Home: 2190 H Bees Ferry Rd Charleston SC 29407 Office: Marchele's Ltd 1185 Dorchester Rd Summerville SC 29483

SHIPLEY, SHELIA DAVIS, record company executive; b. Scottsville, Ky., Oct. 2, 1952; d. Robert Shelby Davis and Pauline (Powell) Willoughby; m. Bennie Ray Shipley, June 1, 1969; 1 child, Bennie Michael. Student U. Tenn., 1975-77, Nashville State Tech. Inst., 1978-79. Sales clk. Gibson's Discount Store, Scottsville, Ky., 1970-73; receptionist Monument Records, Nashville, 1976-79; promotion, sales coordinator RCA Records, Nashville, 1979-83; dir. career coordination Hallmark Direction Co., Nashville, 1983-84; nat. dir. promotion MCA Records, Nashville, 1984—. Author poetry. Mem. Country Music Assn., Acad. Country Music, Nashville Music Assn., Country Promotion Assn. Republican. Baptist. Office: MCA Records 1701 W End Ave Suite 400 Nashville TN 37203

SHIPLEY, SHIRLEY DAHL, oil co. exec.; b. Orange, N.J., Oct. 17, 1932; d. Conrad George and Sylvia Marion (Gronquist) D.; B.S., Cedar Crest Coll. Allentown, Pa., 1954; m. William Stewart Shipley II, July 2, 1955; children—William Stewart III, Linda Ann, Elizabeth Marion. Tchr., Radnor Twp. (Pa.) Schs., 1954-55, Sarasota County (Fla.) Schs., 1955-56; adminstrv. v.p. Shipley-Humble, Inc., York, Pa., 1977—. Pres., York Suburban Sch. Dist. Bd., 1973-79; bd. dirs. York Country Day Sch., York County Library System, York County Mental Health Center, Greater York, Inc., United Community Services, York County Literacy Council, ARC, Women's Assn. York Symphony Orch.; v.p. Childrens Home; trustee, mem. exec. com. York Coll. of Pa., 1972—; mem. York, Franklin and Adams County Intermediate Unit Sch. Bd. pres. Jr. League York, 1967-69; nat. bd. dirs. Assn. Jr. Leagues, 1970-72; mem. Pa. adv. council U.S. Commn. Civil Rights; trustee York Coll. Pa. Mem. Pa. Petroleum Assn., Petroleum Marketers Assn. Am. Republican. Presbyterian. Home: 1000 Clubhouse Rd York PA 17403 Office: 550 E King St PO Box 946 York PA 17405

SHIPLEY, V. FERN, personnel recruiting company executive; b. Manchester, Okla., Sept. 29, 1921; d. Charles C. and Oma (Ready) Wilson; m. David McNalley Shipley, Jan. 21, 1943 (div. Nov. 1968); children—Davon David, Sondra Fern Busch. Student U. Colo., 1961-62. Cons., Cartwright Employment Agy., Boulder, 1969-71, head cons., 1973-77; mgr. Western Permanent Services, Boulder, 1972; owner, mgr. Shipley Personnel Recruiting, Boulder, 1978—. Fund raiser Mountain View Methodist Ch., 1960; tchr. Sunday Sch., Meth. Ch., 1954-56, chmn. Bible Sch., 1954; leader, Colo. Muscular Dystrophy Research Fund Drive, 1955; mgr. telethon drive, Boulder, 1955. Republican. Avocations: Travel; sewing; oil painting; interior design; swimming. Home: 2820 Dover Dr Boulder CO 80303 Office: 1300 Canyon Blvd Suite 1 Boulder CO 80302

SHIPMAN, DIANNA LOUISE, lawyer; b. Houston, Dec. 18, 1949; d. Loyd Wayne and Dovie Louise (Screws) Shipman. B.A. magna cum laude, U. Houston, 1971; J.D., 1980. Bar: Tex. Legal asst., ins. positions, 1972-77; assoc. Parks, Tradd, Mulder & Miller, Houston, 1980-84, Shipman & Cox, P.C., Houston, 1984—. Vol., Kathy Whitmire Mayoral Campaign, Houston, 1980-81. Mem. Nat. Assn. Women Comml. Real Estate (parliamentarian 1983-84, pres. 1985-86), Houston Fin. Council for Women (rec. sec. 1984, treas. 1986), Alley Theater Guild). Clubs: Exec. Forum (pres. 1983-84) (Houston), Galleria Bus., Profl. Woman's (sec. 1982-83). Office: Shipman & Cox PC 3915 Essex Ln Suite 103 Houston TX 77027

SHIPP, MAURINE SARAH HARSTON (MRS. LEVI ARNOLD SHIPP), realtor; b. Holiday, Mo., Mar. 6, 1913; d. Paul Edward and Sarah Isabel (Mitchell) Harston; grad. Ill. Bus. Coll., 1945; student real estate Springfield Jr. Coll., 1962; student law LaSalle Extension U., 1959-62; m. Levi Arnold Shipp, Jan. 30, 1941; children—Jerome Reynolds, Patricia (Mrs. Rodney W. England). With Ill. Dept. Agr., Springfield, 1941-65, supr. livestock industry Brucellosis sect.; saleswoman Morgan-Hamilton Real Estate Co., Springfield, 1962-64; owner, mgr. Shipp Real Estate Agy., Springfield, 1965—. Prin. appraiser urban renewal HUD, 1971-72; mem. Public Bldg. Commn. Springfield. Bd. dirs. Springfield Travelers Aid, 1971—. Mem. Springfield Bd. Realtors, Nat., Ill. assns. real estate bds., NAACP, Urban League, Iota Phi Lambda. Episcopalian. Mem. Order Eastern Star. Club: Bridge. Home: 31 Bellerive Rd Springfield IL 62704

SHIPP, ROSE LEVADA, lawyer; b. Jersey City, N.J., Sept. 24, 1934; d. Anthony and Joyce Waldean (Gilbert) DeGregorio; m. David Crenshaw Shipp, Sept. 11, 1954; children—David Anthony (dec.) Sallie Dean, Daniel Linwood. B.A. magna cum laude, U. Louisville, Ky., 1970, J.D., 1972. Bar: Ky. 1973. Student intern U.S. Atty.'s Office, Louisville, 1971-72; solo practice, Louisville, 1973-76, Taylorsville, Ky., 1979—; asst. Commonwealth's atty., Louisville, 1976-78; chmn. bd. All Am. Assocs. Drinks, Inc., Ky., 1983—; chief exec. officer, chmn. bd. G.T. Mott, Inc., 1984—. Mem. Young Reps. Am., Louisville, 1968-72; treas., v.p. Republican Attys. of Louisville, 1973-75; precinct capt., 1974-75; audio tester Head Start, Louisville, 1964-65; Pres., Woodcock Honor Soc., U. Louisville, 1973. Mem. Ky. Bar Assn., Fed. Bar Soc., Assn. Trial Lawyers Am., Ky. Acad. Trial Lawyers, ABA. Clubs: Bus., Profl. Women's (Taylorsville, Ky.), Crescent Hill Women's (Louisville). Home: 2781 Maple Rd Louisville KY 40205 Office: Rose Levada Shipp Atty at Law PO Box 483 Main St Taylorsville KY 40071

SHIPPE, MARY LOU, instructional designer, developer; b. Kansas City, Mo., Nov. 25, 1942; d. Hiram Arthur and Clio (Robinson) Cooley; m. Donald Louis Shippe, Aug. 13, 1966; children—Kenneth Louis, Angela Lou. B.A., Kans. U., 1964; M.P.A., Okla. U., 1979; D.P.A. candidate Nova U., 1983—. Research technician Dept. Def., Md., 1964-66, analyst, 1970-71; substitute tchr. Howard County Schs., Md., 1972-76; instr. Los Angeles Community Coll. Overseas, Japan, 1976-79; asst. Pub. Today News Service, Washington, 1979; village mgr. Town Ctr. Community Assn., Md., 1980-83; instructional designer, developer computer based tng. Ford Aerospace and Communications Corp., Hanover, Md., 1983—. Mem. Columbia Forum, Md., 1980—, Housing and Human Services Task Force, Columbia, 1980-82. Mem. Am. Soc. Pub. Adminstrn., Am. Bus. Womens Assn. (v.p. 1985-86), Assn. Ednl. Communications and Tech., LWV. Club: Zonta (dir. 1982-86). Avocations: travel; theatre; boating. Home: 9573 Long Look Ln Columbia MD 21045 Office: Ford Aerospace and Communications Corp 2100 Standard Dr Hanover MD 21076

SHIRK, AUDREY HOPE, artist, painter; b. Rochester, N.Y., Sept. 18, 1921; d. David Daniel and Ethel Edith (Trinz) Salisch; m. Mortimer I Metzger, June 22, 1941 (div. Oct. 1964); children—Jane Metzger Laffend, Warren Stanley; m. Stanley Edgar Shirk, Nov. 23, 1965. Assoc., Parsons Sch. Fine and Applied Art, 1941. Instr., Parsons Sch. Fine and Applied Art, N.Y.C., 1943-44; centennial chmn. Nat. Assn. Women Artists, Inc., N.Y.C., 1983-85, exec. producer cable TV documentaries and videotapes, 1984, 85. Recipient Samuel Gelband award 1976, Woman Art award 1977, Medal Honor Nat. Assn. award 1983. Mem. Nat. Assn. Women Artists Inc. (chmn. traveling painting exhibitions 1978-82, bd. dirs. 1978—, pub. relations, 1982-85; honor award 1983), Sharon Creative Arts Found. (gallery dir. 1980-83, exec. com., bd. dirs. 1980-83, mem. exec. com. 1981-83). Avocations: skiing; swimming; travel; reading; theatre. Office: Box 151 Cornwall CT 06796

SHIRK, EVELYN URBAN, philosophy educator; b. Flushing, N.Y., Sept. 12, 1918; d. Amos Urban and Mary Jane (Welchans) S.; m. Justus Buchler, Feb. 20, 1943; 1 child, Katherine Urban. B.A., Wilson Coll., 1940; M.A., Columbia U., 1942, Ph.D., 1949. Instr. Bklyn Coll., 1942-48; asst. prof. Hofstra Coll., Hempstead, N.Y., 1949-53, assoc. prof., 1953-63; prof. Hofstra U. (formerly Hofstra Coll.), 1963—, dept. chmn., 1980—. Editor: (with others) Readings in Philosophy, 1946; Adventurous Idealism: The Philosophy of Alfred Lloyd, 1952; The Ethical Dimension, 1965; In Pursuit of Awareness, 1967. Mem. Am. Philos. Assn., Soc. Advancement Am. Philosophy (program chmn. 1976, exec. com 1977-79), L.I. Philos. Soc. (exec. com.), AAUP, Phi Beta Kappa. Home: 3 Homestead Ave Garden City NY 11530 Office: Hofstra U Dept Philosophy Soc Sci and Religion 1000 Fulton Ave Hempstead NY 11550

SHIRK, MARIANNE EILEEN, veterinarian; b. Detroit, Aug. 11, 1944; d. Wesley Emerson and Eleanor Jane (Grossman) Lickfeldt. Student U. Mich., 1962-64; D.V.M., Mich. State U., 1968, M.S. in Vet. Pathology, 1969. Diplomate Am. Bd. Vet. Practitioners. Grad. asst. Mich. State U., East Lansing, 1968-69; veterinarian Dandy Acres Vet. Clinic, Hartland, Mich., 1969-71, Quartz Mountain Animal Hosp., Scottsdale, Ariz., 1972—; speaker at various profl. meetings; host of twice monthly call-in talk show Pet-Vet, Sta. KTAR, Phoenix, 1982—. Author article in profl. jour. Recipient Disting. Alumnus award Mich. State U., 1985. Mem. Am. Acad. Vet. Dermatology, AVMA, Am. Animal Hosp. Assn., Ariz. Vet. Med. Assn. (pres.-elect 1982-83, pres. 1983-84, chmn. ann. state meeting 1979—, dir. 1980-81), Central Ariz. Vet. Med. Assn. (pres.-elect 1980-81, pres. 1981-82, dir. 1978-80), Ariz. Acad. Vet. Practice (Outstanding Continuing Edn. record 1983), Am. Assn. Equine Practitioners. Republican. Home: 6900 E Gold Dust Ave Scottsdale AZ 85254 Office: Sundown Animal Clinic 10606 N 71st Pl Scottsdale AZ

SHIRLEY, ELEANOR, social service agency executive; b. Adams, Mass., May 9, 1937; d. Joseph Lucian and Elsie (Barschdorf) Freeman; m. Edward Salmond Shirley, Aug. 10, 1963; 1 child, Rebecca Salmond. B.A., Wheaton Coll., Mass., 1959; M.A., Hartford Sem. Found., Conn., 1961; M.B.A., Tulane U., 1985. Dir. edn. St. Peter's Ch., Beverly, Mass., 1961-63; coll. work dir. Mt. Holyoke Coll., South Hadley, Mass., 1965-68; staff La. State U. Episcopal Chapel, Baton Rouge, 1969; dir. Women & Employment Program for Women, Baton Rouge, 1977-80, program devel. dir. Office of Women's Services, Baton Rouge, 1980—. Pres. LWV, Baton Rouge, 1972-75. Named Outstanding Woman, Links Inc. of Baton Rouge, 1975. Mem. Nat. Assn. Female Execs. Democrat. Episcopalian. Club: Episcopalian Ch. Women (pres. 1985-86, Baton Rouge). Home: 10203 Winterhue Dr Baton Rouge LA 70810 Office: Women's Services 200 Riverside Mall Baton Rouge LA 70802

SHIRLEY, NORMA, librarian, bibliographer; b. Chatham, N.Y., Mar. 22, 1935; d. George and Bertha (Shattuck) Shirley. B.A., Russell Sage Coll., 1962; M.L.S., SUNY-Albany, 1963, M.S. in Ednl. Adminstrn., 1980. Asst. reference librarian Jr. Coll. Albany, 1963-65; librarian Hudson Area Library (N.Y.), 1966-67; reference librarian Russell Sage Coll., Troy, N.Y., 1967-69; librarian Poughkeepsie High Sch. (N.Y.), 1970-71; library media specialist Spl. Edn. Ctr., Dutchess County BOCES, Poughkeepsie, 1971—. Co-author: Checklist of Serials in Psychology and Allied Fields, 1969; Serials in Psychology and Allied Fields, 1976. Mem. Dutchess County Library Assn. (past pres.), Sch. Library Media Specialists Southeastern N.Y. (pres), ALA, N.Y. Library Assn., NEA, Dutchess County Mental Health Assn., N.Y. State Tchrs. Handicapped. Home: PO Box 2401 Poughkeepsie NY 12603

SHISHIDO, KAREN LYNN, accounting company executive; b. Chgo., Aug. 11, 1951; d. Frank A. and Lorraine S. (Williams) Katzbeck; m. Carl A. Petersen, June 17, 1972 (div. June 1975); m. 2d, Jack L. Shishido, Dec. 10, 1982. B.S., U. Ill.-Chgo., 1976. C.P.A. Mem. tax staff Price Waterhouse, Chgo., 1977-78, tax sr./mgr., Tokyo, 1978-82, tax mgr., Los Angeles, 1982-83, sr. mgr., 1984—. Active Asia Pacific Council Am. Chambers, Tokyo, 1979-82. Recipient Pres.'s Leadership award Am. C. of C. in Japan, 1980. Mem. Am. Inst. C.P.A.s, Ill. C.P.A. Soc., Calif. C.P.A. Soc., Am. Soc. Women C.P.A.s, Japan-Am. Soc. Office: Price Waterhouse 400 S Hope St Los Angeles CA 90071

SHISHKOFF, MURIEL MENDELSOHN, educational administrator; b. Chgo., Mar. 5, 1917; d. Henry Robert and Anita (Arnow) Mendelsohn; B.A., U. Chgo., 1936; M.A., Northwestern U., 1940; m. Nicholas Shishkoff, Aug. 26, 1946; children—Andrew, Debra. Elem. tchr., Fond du Lac, Wis., 1936-41; personnel mgr. Twentieth Century Glove Co., 1946; tchr. Newport-Mesa (Calif.) Unified Sch. Dist., 1963-69; founding dir. Women's Opportunities Center, U. Extension, U. Calif., Irvine, 1970-72, asst. dir. Office Relations with Schs. and Colls., 1974-82. Vice pres. LWV, Palos Verdes Peninsula, Calif., 1963. Served to lt. USNR (W-VS), 1942-45. Recipient grant award Reachout, Dept. Mental Hygiene, Sacramento, 1972. Mem. Nat. Assn. Women Deans, Adminstrs. and Counselors, NOW, Women For. Home: 19542 Sandcastle Ln Huntington Beach CA 92648

SHISLER, ALICE HAFLING, dancer; b. Richmond, Va., Nov. 23, 1923; d. Jacob Mathew and Elise (Atkinson) Hafling; B.A. in French with distinction, U. Va., 1972, postgrad., 1972-75; m. James Douglas Shisler, Apr. 17, 1965; children by previous marriage—Elise Amory Crosswy, Otis Taylor Amory, III, Marcie Tuck Amory. Student, asst. Elinor Frye Dance Sch., Richmond, 1940-44; editorial sec. Commonwealth mag., 1944-46; owner dance sch. Acad. Dance Arts, Charlottesville, Va., 1947—; dir., choreographer Charlottesville Dance Co., 1973—; cons. in field. Docent Bayly Mus. of U. Va., 1984—. Recipient Appreciation award Charlottesville Lions Club Minstrel Shows, 1981. Mem. Dance Masters Am. Republican. Episcopalian. Club: Farmington Country. Author syllabi on dance. Address: 901 Rugby Rd Charlottesville VA 22903

SHISLER, KATHLEEN MARIE, oil company executive; b. Peoria, Ill., Dec. 20, 1960; d. Kent Rodney and Kari Ann (Karlsen) S. B.S. in Computer Sci., No. Ill. U., 1983. Resident asst. No. Ill. U., DeKalb, 1981-82, teaching asst., 1982-83; programmer Chevron Corp., Concord, Calif., 1983-85, service mgmt. analyst, San Ramon, Calif., 1985-86, programmer, analyst, 1986—, United Way rep., 1984, Gulf-Chevron merger user liason, Houston, San Ramon, Calif., 1985-86; host, interviewer Chevron Recruiting, Concord, 1983—. Mem. Nat. Assn. Female Execs. Republican. Lutheran. Club: Family Fitness Ctr. (Dublin, Calif.). Avocations: painting; running; traveling; photography; dancing. Home: 70 Fawn Pl Danville CA 94526 Office: Chevron Info Tech Co 2410 Camino Ramon San Ramon CA 95583-0953

SHIVELY, DOROTHY JEAN, educator; b. Sebring, Ohio, Mar. 19, 1930; d. Emmett Roosevelt and Evelyn Grace (Merrick) Garlock; m. Milton Lee Shively, July 7, 1951; children—Lisa, Merrick, Martin. B.A., Mt. Union Coll., 1952; postgrad. Kent State U., 1953, Akron U., 1955-56, Tufts U., 1974. Cert. tchr. Tchr. Sebring Schs., Ohio, 1953-55, Akron Schs., Ohio, 1955-57, Westminster Schs., Calif., 1968-69; tchr., dir. Stow Schs., Mass., 1970-74; tchr., team leader Maynard Schs., Mass., 1974—, cons., 1972-74; cons. Perley-Gilbert Architects, Lowell, Mass., 1972-74; adv. mem. Northeast Regional/Tufts U. Council on Early Edn., Maynard, 1974-76. Vol., ARC, Malmstrom AFB, Great Falls, Mont., 1960-63; mem. exec. council PTA, Garden Grove, Calif., 1963-68; troop leader Costa Mesa council Girl Scouts U.S.A., Westminster, 1965-68; edn. com. Stow Evangel. Ch., Stow, Mass., 1974-80. Mem. NEA, Mass. Edn. Assn., Maynard Edn. Assn., Mt. Union Alumni Assn. (fund-raiser). Presbyterian. Avocations: alpine skiing, travel, quilting, interior decorating, oil painting. Home: 20 Sudbury Rd Stow MA 01775

SHOAFF, BARBARA JANE, insurance company executive; b. Bronxville, N.Y., Mar. 25, 1950; d. Peter Carras and Jane (Cockburn) Malesardi. B.A., U. Fla., 1972. Owner, mgr. Fanning Personnel, Clearwater, Fla., 1972-74; sr. sales cons. Blue Cross Blue Shield, Jacksonville, Fla., 1975-78; chief exec. officer S&S Insurors Inc., Sarasota, Fla., 1979—, Third Party Adminstrs. of Sarasota, Inc., 1979—; cons. Keep Well Trust, Sarasota, 1983—, U.S. Security Benefits, Memphis, 1984. Author: Medical Self Insurance, 1985. Sec. Sarasota Meml. Pub. Hosp., 1980—, trustee, 1980—, chmn. by-laws com., 1980—. Mem. West Coast Health Coalition, Nat. Claims Assn., Fla. Claims Assn., Soc. Profl. Benefits Adminstrs., Nat. Assn. Life Underwriters, Fla. Assn. Life Underwriters, LWV. Republican. Episcopalian. Club: Altrusa. Avocations: tennis, jogging; biking; skiing; boating. Home: 1385 Harbor Dr Sarasota FL 33579 Office: PO Box 4105 .Sarasota FL 33578

SHOEMAKER, DOROTHY KAY, civic worker; b. Lanerch, Pa., May 5, 1897; d. Robert Gillespie and Mary (Scott) Kay; grad. Goucher Coll., 1920; m. Benjamin H. Shoemaker III, June 30, 1938; children—Robert Kay. Sec. Class 1915 Westtown Sch.; mem. Nat. Soc. Colonial Dames; bd. dirs. Germantown Settlement; mem. women's bd. Germantown Dispensary Hosp., 1930-60; bd. dirs. Ralston House, 1935—. Mem. Pi Beta Phi. Republican. Episcopalian. Home: 515 Locust Ave Germantown Philadelphia PA 19144

SHOEMAKER, MARY CAROLYN, nursing educator; b. Pekin, Ill., July 9, 1945; d. Honor K. and Millie L. (Gosnell) Little; m. Edward A. Shoemaker, June 14, 1964; 1 son, Mark E. R.N., Graham Hosp. Sch. Nursing, 1967; B.S., Bradley U., 1971; M.S., Tex. Woman's U., 1976; Ph.D. in Ednl. Adminstrn. and Founds., Ill. State U., 1985. Staff charge nurse Peoria State Hosp. (Ill.), 1967-71; instr. Graham Hosp. Sch. Nursing, Canton, Ill., 1971-73; instr. St. Francis Hosp. Sch. Nursing, Peoria, 1973-77, instr., dept. chmn., 1977-85; level 1 coordinator Saint Francis Med. Ctr. Coll. Nursing, Peoria, 1986—. Mem. Nat. League Nursing, Nat. Nurses Assn., Ill. League Nursing, Ill. Nurses Assn., Tex. Woman's U. Alumni Assn., Kappa Delta Pi. Methodist. Office: Saint Francis Med Ctr Coll Nursing 211 Greenleaf Peoria IL 61603

SHOEN, JUDITH ANNE, marketing company executive; b. Rockford, Ill., Dec. 25, 1940; d. Abe J. and Bertha Deborah (Polinsky) S. B.S., U. Wis., 1962. Editorial asst. Mademoiselle Mag., N.Y.C., 1962-63; food editor Restaurants & Instns. mag., Chgo., 1963-64, merchandising editor, 1964-66, sr. editor, 1971-74; Eastern editor, internat. editor Service World Internat. mag., N.Y.C., 1966-71, editor-in-chief, N.Y.C., 1967-71, Chgo., 1971-74; dir. pub. relations Dispenser Juice Distbrs./Consol. Foods, San Francisco, 1974-75; pres. Judith Shoen Assocs., San Francisco, 1975-78; v.p. Foote, Cone & Belding, San Francisco, 1978-81, also dir. FCB Foodservice; dir. mktg. Telstar Corp., San Francisco, 1981-82; pres. Foodservice Promotions, Inc., Mill Valley, Calif., 1982-85, Washington, 1985—. Mem. Internat. Foodservice Mfrs. Assn., Internat. Foodservice Editors Council, Les Dames d'Escoffier, Alpha Epsilon Phi, Theta Sigma Phi. Office: 5020 Lowell St NW Washington DC 20016

SHOENFELT, CATHERINE RUTH, marketing executive; b. Dallas, Dec. 9, 1954; d. Marion Justus and Nell (Harden) S. B.Music Edn., U. Tex.-San Antonio, 1980. Tchr. music Viva Musica, San Antonio, 1980-81, Northside Ind. Sch. Dist., San Antonio, 1981-84; mktg. mgr. Austin Pathology Assocs., Tex., 1984—; singer Chamber Choralet Symphony, San Antonio, 1982; vol. Symphony Designer Showplace, Austin, 1986, Healthfest-Pathology Booth, Austin, 1986. Mem. Nat. Assn. Female Execs. Republican. Lutheran. Club: Blair County Genealogy Soc. (Altoona, Pa.). Avocations: music; tennis; jazzercise; crewel; needlepoint; swimming; reading; cooking. Home: 7600 Wood Hollow Apt 1111 Austin TX 78731 Office: Austin Pathology Assocs 711 W 35th St Suite C-11 Austin TX 78705

SHOENIGHT, PAULINE ALOISE SOUERS, author; b. Bridgeport, Ill., Nov. 20, 1914; d. William Fitch and Carrie (Milhouse) Souers; B.Ed., Eastern Ill. U., 1937; m. James Richard Tracy, Sept. 18, 1946 (dec. Aug. 1972); m. 2d, Hurley F. Shoenight, June 25, 1976. Mem. hon. bd. advs. Am. Biog. Inst., Mem. Nat. Ret. Tchrs. Assn., Eastern Ill. Alumni Assn. (life), Friends of Foley Library, Friends of U. Mo. Libraries, PEO Sisterhood, Performing Arts Assn., Am. Poets Fellowship Soc. (hon. life mem.), The Pensters, Pleasure Island Sr. Citizens Club (charter), Am. Poetry League, Foley Extension Club, Baldwin Heritage Mus. Assn. (charter life), Ill. Poetry Soc. (charter), Book Club for Poetry, Ala. State Poetry Soc., Acad. Am. Poets. Republican. Baptist. Clubs: Baldwin Sr. Travelers, Foley Sr. Travelers. Author: His Handiwork, 1954; Memory is a Poet, 1964; The Silken Web, 1965; A Merry Heart, 1966; In Two or Three Tomorrows, 1968; All Flesh Is Grass, 1971; Beyond The Edge, 1973. Address: Route 3 Box 1107 W Riverwood Dr Foley AL 36535

SHOLLENBERGER, SYDNI (SYDNEY) ANN CRAWFORD, author, publicist; b. Cleve., June 23, 1940; d. Charles Burger and Carolyn Louise (Hull) Crawford; B.A., Allegheny Coll., 1962; m. Lewis W. Shollenberger, Jr., Aug. 18, 1962. Pub. info. officer and editor Space News Roundup, NASA, Houston, 1970-72. mng., editor Travel Publs., Am. Automobile Assn., Washington, 1972-74, freelance journalist, publicist, 1974—; adminstrv. asst. community relations Walnut-Creek Sch. Dist. Publicity dir. Falls Church Bicentennial Commn., 1976-81; bd. dirs. Falls Church Village Preservation and Improvement Soc.; publicity co-chmn. Falls Church Citizens for a Better City, 1978, fin. chmn., 1982 docent Cherry Hill Farm; pres. Broadmont Citizens Assn., 1978-79; press cons. Fisher for Congress campaign, 1978, 80; chmn. Falls Church Adv. Bd. on Parks and Recreation; community relations coordinator Fairfax County Reentry Women's Employment Center, 1979-83; sec. Welcome to Washington Internat. Club, 1978-80; mem. Va. Commn. on Status of Women, 1983. Mem. Capital Press Women (v.p. 1976-78), Pub. Relations Soc. Am., Calif. Sch. Pub. Relations Assn. Clubs: Zonta, Woman's Nat. Democratic, Capital Speakers (class pres. 1977, chpt. 3 pres. 1980-81).

SHOLTZ, KATHERINE LOUISE, librarian, chemist; b. Waukegan, Ill., July 14, 1931; d. E. Albin and Helmi Rachel (Salmi) Junnila; m. Paul N. Sholtz, Aug. 30, 1952; children—Karen, Peter. B.S., U. Ill., 1952, M.S., 1953; M.L.S., SUNY-Albany, 1967. Research assoc. Harvard U., Boston, 1953-55, Iowa State U., Ames, 1955-57; librarian IBM, Rochester, Minn., 1966-67; computer applications librarian Mayo Clinic, Rochester, 1967-72, assoc. dir. library, 1972-80; dir. library services Western Conn. State U., Danbury, 1980—. Contbr. articles to profl. jours. Chmn., Rochester Housing and Redevel. Agy., 1974-77; chmn. adv. bd. Council of Govt. Housing, Rochester, 1977-80; pres. LWV, Rochester, 1969-71. Recipient award for promotion of sci. research Sigma Xi, New Haven, 1983. Mem. ALA, Med. Library Assn., Conn. Library Assn. Lutheran. Home: Milltown Rd RD 5 Brewster NY 10509 Office: Ruth A Haas Library Western Conn State U 181 White St Danbury CT 06810

SHONK, DIERDRE LYNN, company executive, accountant; b. Columbus, Ohio, Dec. 17, 1959; d. Donald Archie and Joan Sandra (Speedie) Smith; m. Kevin David Shonk, Apr. 15, 1978. B.S. in Bus. Adminstrn. cum laude, Franklin U., 1979. Sr. asst. Deloitte Haskins & Sells, Columbus, 1979-81; corp. acct. Ranco, Inc., Dublin, Ohio, 1981-83; corp. controller Heinzerling Found., Columbus, 1983—. Trustee Colony Hill Recreation Assn., Columbus, 1980-85; treas. Colony Hill Condo Assn., Columbus, 1981-85. Leadership-Achievement scholar Franklin U., 1978-79; fellow Animal Protection Inst., Washington, 1978—. Mem. Am. Inst. C.P.A.s, Ohio Soc. C.P.A.s, Nat. Assn. Accts., Nat. Assn. Female Execs. Republican. Lutheran. Avocations: needlepoint; embroidery; swimming; scuba diving; sailing. Office: Heinzerling Found 1800 Heinzerling Dr Columbus OH 43223

SHONTZ, MARILYN LOUISE, library science educator; b. Cleve., Nov. 5, 1943; d. William Painter and Marie Rita (Kessler) S. B.A., Heidelberg Coll., 1965; M.L.S., Case Western Res. U., 1967; A.M.L.S., Fla. State U., 1982. Children's librarian Cleve. Pub. Library, 1965-67; sch. librarian Cleve. Pub. Schs., 1967-70; sch. library media specialist Marion County Schs., Ocala, Fla., 1970-80; asst. prof. library sci. Shippensburg (Pa.) U., 1982—, chmn. dept. library sci., 1983—, acting asst. dean Coll. Edn. and Human Services, 1986—. Teaching fellow Fla. State U., Tallahassee, 1981. Mem. ALA, Am. Assn. Sch. Librarians, Pa. Sch. Librarians Assn., Beta Phi Mu. Home: RD 1 Box 441 Newburg PA 17240

SHONTZ, PATRICIA JANE, restauranteur; b. Mercer, Pa., Mar. 29, 1933; d. Thomas Cloyd and Glaydes Evelyn (Pease) Buckley; student pub. schools,

Grove City, Pa.; m. George Edward Shontz, July 22, 1962; 1 dau. by previous marriage, Sandra Lee McCandless. Clerical asst. Am. News Co., Washington, 1950-51; acct., office mgr. Mundt Motors Chevrolet & Buick, Grove City, 1953-62; sec.-treas. Cajun Corp., Madeira Beach, Fla., 1972—; pres. John's Pass Seafood Festival Corp., 1981—. Madeira Beach City commr., 1973-79, vice mayor, 1977-79, co-chmn. planning bd., 1979-82; chmn. Bicentennial Com., Madeira Beach, 1975-76; mem. John's Pass Village Assn., 1970—, Pinellas County Tourist Devel. Council, 1978-79, Madeira Beach Taxpayers Assn., 1964—; mem. Republican Nat. Com. Named Madeira Beach Citizen of Yr., 1974, 79. Mem. Nat. Restaurant Assn., Fla. Restaurant Assn., Madeira Beach C. of C. (dir. 1965, 81-82, pres. 1967-69, 83). Presbyterian. Clubs: Bus. and Profl. Women, Soroptimist, Order Eastern Star, Order White Shrine. Office: 100 Madeira Way Madeira Beach FL 33708

SHORES, JANIE LEDLOW, justice Alabama Supreme Court; b. nr. Georgiana, Ala., Apr. 30, 1932; d. John Wesley and Willie (Scott) Ledlow; LL.B., U. Ala., 1959; A.B., Samford U., 1968; m. James L. Shores, Jr., May 12, 1962; 1 dau., Laura Scott. Sole practice, Selma, Ala., 1959-61; legal dept. Liberty Nat. Life Ins. Co. Birmingham, Ala., 1962-66; prof. law Cumberland Sch. Law, Samford U., 1966-74; assoc. justice Ala. Supreme Ct., Montgomery, 1975—. Former legal adviser Ala. Constn. Revision Commn., mem. Nat. Adv. Council on State Ct. Planning. Mem. Am. Judicature Soc., Am. Bar Assn. Democrat. Episcopalian. Contbr. legal articles to profl. jours. Office: PO Box 218 Montgomery AL 36101*

SHORR, MIRIAM KRONFELDT, artist; b. N.Y.C.; student Hunter Coll.; m. Eli Yale Shorr, 1931. Exhibited in ann. shows Audubon Artists, City Center Gallery, Bklyn. Mus., Nat. Soc. Painters in Casein, Norfolk Mus., Riverside Mus.; one man shows Brandeis U., Bklyn. Coll., U. Maine, Rutgers U., So. Ill. U., LaSalle Coll., Hillsdale U., Gettysburg Coll., others; group shows U. Houston, N.D. State U., Colo. Mountain Coll., Ottawa (Kans.) U., Washington and Jefferson Coll., others; traveling one-man shows throughout U.S. Recipient 1st prize for drawing Nat. Assn. Women Artists, 1962; Lena Newcastle award, 1961, 65; Aileen O. Webb prize, 1974; 1st prize Fibers and Fabrics Exhbn., Longboat Key Art Assn., 1979; 1st prize enamels Venice (Fla.) Art League, 1982; 2d prize Sarasota Art Assn., 1983; Longboat Key Art Center West Coast Parade of Prize Winners, 1982-86; 1st prize Venice Art League, 1985. Mem. Artists Equity Assn. (dir. 1958-64), Nat. Assn. Women Artists (dir. 1970-72), Sarasota Art Assn. (chmn. exhbns. 1976-78, editor The Bull. 1979-81), Art League Manatee County, Fla. Artists Group. Home: 7308 Broughton St Sarasota FL 33580

SHORS, SUSAN DEBRA, lawyer; b. Detroit, Nov. 23, 1954; d. Clayton Marion and Arlene Lois (Towle) S. B.A., Pitzer Coll., 1976; J.D., Golden Gate U., 1984. Bar: Calif. Extern, Calif. Supreme Ct., San Francisco, 1983; research atty. Calif. Ct. Appeal, San Francisco, 1984-85; appellate atty., San Francisco, 1985—; cons. Nob Hill Neighbors, San Francisco, 1982-86. Sr. editor Golden Gate Law Rev. Notes and Comments, 1985; mem. editorial bd. Barrister's Club Mag., 1986. Atty. Lawyers Com. for Urban Affairs/Asylum Project, San Francisco, 1986. Mem. ABA, Calif. Bar Assn., Calif. Women Lawyers, Bar Assn. San Francisco (mem. appellate com. 1986). Democrat. Office: Law Offices 2500 Clay St San Francisco CA 94115

SHORT, PAULA MYRICK, educational administration educator; b. Pinehurst, N.C., Feb. 25, 1945; d. John Howard and Ruby Pauline (Fields) Myrick; m. Rick Jay Short, Feb. 2, 1980; children—Jeffrey Brent, John Ryan, Rick Jay Jr. B.A., U. N.C.-Greensboro, 1967, M.Ed., 1970; Ph.D., U. N.C., Chapel Hill, 1983. Tchr., Greensboro City Schs., N.C., 1967-68, Orange County Schs., Hillsborough, N.C., 1968-69; media coordinator Alamance County Schs., Mebane, N.C., 1970-71; tchr. Neal Jr. High Sch., Durham, N.C., 1971-74, Chewing Jr. High Sch., Durham, 1977-79; system level media supr. Chapel Hill-Carboro City Schs., 1979-80; ednl. cons. div. ednl. media N.C. Dept. Pub. Instrn., Raleigh, 1980-82; asst. prof. ednl. adminstrn. Coll.Edn., Tex. Woman's U., Denton, 1984-85, Centenary Coll., Shreveport, La., 1985-86, U. Nebr. at Omaha, 1986—. Chmn. day care com. Chapel Hill Service League, 1977-78. Delta Kappa Gamma state scholar 1982. Mem. SW Ednl. Research Assn., La. Assn. Sch. Execs., Tex. Assn. Supervision and Curriculum Devel., Soc. Sch. Librarians Internat. (bd. dirs. 1985-86), Assn. Supervision and Curriculum Devel., N.C. Media Council (pres. 1982), Delta Kappa Gamma, Phi Delta Kappa, Pi Lambda Theta. Methodist. Home: 1701 Gentilly Dr Shreveport LA 71105 Office: Dept Ednl Adminstrn and Supervision Coll Edn 310 Kayser Hall U Nebr Omaha NE 68182

SHORT, SUSAN ALICE, legal educator, lawyer; b. Washington, Sept. 20, 1947; d. Lester Edward and Jacqueline Yvonne (Gangestad) S. B.A., U. Minn., 1969, J.D. cum laude, 1974. Bar: Minn. 1974, U.S. Dist. Ct. Minn. 1975. Clin. law tchr. U. Minn., Mpls., 1974-76, 78—; sole practice, Mpls., 1976-78; founder, v.p. Minn. Lesbian and Gay Legal Assistance, Mpls., 1979-82. Sec. adv. com. to Mayor and City Council Mpls. on Disabilities, 1980-83; dir. Minn. Com. Lesbian/Gay Rights, Mpls., 1974-83; del. State Democratic Conv., 1976, 82. Mem. Minn. Women Lawyers, ABA, Minn. State Bar Assn. (human rights com. 1980-83, legal assistance com. 1980-83). Democrat. Office: U Minn Law Sch 190 Law Center Minneapolis MN 55455

SHOTKIN, JANE DORIEN, nurse; b. Warren, Pa., Oct. 9, 1935; m. Louis M. Shotkin, Apr. 2, 1960; children—David, Adina, Sharona, Micah. R.N. diploma U. Rochester, 1956; B.S., Simmons Coll., Boston, 1958; postgrad. U. Md., 1984. Registered nurse. Asst. instr. Mass. Gen. Hosp., Boston, 1958-60; clin. nurse Upjohn Homemaker Health Care Service, Rockville, Md., 1976-79; clin. nurse Max Cohen, M.D., Surg. Oncologist, Washington, 1979-84; clin. nurse Walter Reed Army Med. Ctr., Washington, 1981-84, sr. clin. nurse, 1984—. Contbr. articles to profl. jours. Mem. Young Israel Shomrai Emunach, Silver Spring, Md., 1974—; mem. nursing edn. com. Montgomery County Heart Assn., 1980-81, chmn., 1982-83. Named Parent of Yr. Hebrew Acad. of Suffolk County, 1975; recipient spl. award Montgomery County Heart Assn., 1982. Mem. Sigma Theta Tau. Clubs: Hadassah (edn. v.p. chpt. 1969-72), Yeshiva High Sch. (dir. 1979-81). Home: 11517 Lovejoy St Silver Spring MD 20902

SHOUN (DYE), VICKI JANE, publishing company executive; b. Maryville, Tenn., Mar. 10, 1956; d. Thomas Jefferson and Fannie Jean (Greene) Shoun; m. Robert Ray Dye, Sept. 3, 1978 (div. June 1984). B.B.A., Memphis State U., 1977. Salesperson Brach's Candies, Tulsa, 1978-79, Hershey Chocolate Co., Oklahoma City, 1980-82; div. mktg. mgr. Ency. Brit., Oklahoma City, 1984—. Active Martin Nature Ctr., Oklahoma City, 1985-86, Young Republicans, Oklahoma City, 1986—. Mem. Soc. Advancement Mgmt. (v.p.), Am. Mktg. Assn., Phi Sigma Epsilon, Phi Gamma Nu (chpt. pres.). Home: 2201 NW 122d Apt 3113 Oklahoma City OK 73120 Office: Ency Britannica 5601 NW 72d St Oklahoma City OK 73132

SHOURDS, MARY ELIZABETH, exec. search firm exec.; b. Braddock, Pa., Nov. 7, 1942; d. Hugh Vincent and Mary Caroline (Denne) Gallagher; B.S. magna cum laude in Bus., Pepperdine U., 1973; postgrad. UCLA, 1982. Dir. personnel Rockwell Internat., El Segundo, Calif., 1964-75; co-founder, partner, v.p. Houze, Shourds & Montgomery, Inc., Los Angeles, 1977—; advisor UCLA Grad. Sch. Mgmt., 1979—. Bd. dirs. UCLA Exec. Program Assn., 1975—. Mem. Assn. Exec. Recruiting Cons., Orgn. Women Execs. Club: Univ.

SHOWALTER, CAROL DIANE, fiber optics manufacturing company executive; b. Pitts., Mar. 12, 1952; d. Louis John and Elinor Edwina (Clark) Kacinko; m. Ronald Lee Showalter, Mar. 12, 1981; 1 child, Tiffani Dawn; m. Merle Wray Powell, Jr., June 7, 1969 (div. Jan. 1981); 1 child, Erick Jon. A.S. with high honors Boyce campus Community Coll. Allegheny County, 1974; B.S. with honors, U. Pitts., 1979. Data base supr. Tex. Instruments, Dallas, 1980-83, E-Systems, Melpar, 1983; asst. dir. data processing, mgr. data base adminstrn., applications devel. and systems Vanguard Technologies, Fairfax, Va., 1983-85; data base adminstr. Siecor Corp., Hickory, N.C., 1985—. Mem. Data Processing Mgmt. Assn. (treas.), Am. Mgmt. Assn., IDMS Users Group, Phi Theta Kappa. Home: Route 11 Box 1488 Hickory NC 28601

SHOWALTER, IDA, accountant; b. Niota, Ill., Dec. 26, 1919; d. Roy C. and Ivy May (Hubbard) Sparrow; M.Accts., Gem City Coll., 1937; student Butler U., 1957; m. Russell W. Showalter, Feb. 23, 1945; children—Karen, Linda. Acct., Blessing Hosp., Quincy, Ill., 1937-46, The Gilfillan Clinic, Bloomfield, Iowa, 1946-48; med. sec. Eli Lilly & Co., Indpls., 1949; corp. sec./treas. Woollen Assocs., Inc., Indpls., 1960-80, corp. sec., 1980-83; pvt. practice acctg., Indpls., 1950-60, 84—; partner Majestic Partnership, Indpls., 1980—. Treas., missions chmn. Ch. of the Nazarene; v.p. P.T.O. Lic. profl. acct., Ind. Mem. Cert. Profl. Sec. Soc., Ind. Tax Practitioners Assn. Republican. Home and Office: 6062 East St Joseph St Indianapolis IN 46219

SHOWALTER, RONDA KERR, health educator; b. Lima, Ohio, Oct. 2, 1942; d. John Russell and Arnita Ruth (Baier) Kerr; m. Graham C. Showalter, Aug. 23, 1969; 1 child, Abigail. B.S., Capital U., 1964; M.S., Ind. U., 1968. Phys. edn. tchr. Spencerville High Sch., Ohio, 1964-65; phys. edn., health instr. Ohio No. U., Ada, 1965-68; asst. prof. health edn. Pa. State U., State College, 1968-72; fitness instr. West Br. YMCA, Milton, Pa., 1981-85. Author: It's Your Life, 1969; Health, Science and College Life, 1972. Pres., Linntown Parent-Sch. Assn., Lewisburg, 1981-82. Fellow; AAUW mem. NEA. Republican. Lutheran. Avocations: walking; swimming; aerobics, dancing. Home: 36 S 3d St Lewisburg PA 17837

SHREVE, ANNE HOOVER, painter; b. Charleston, W.Va., Feb. 1, 1926; d. Clarence Leet and Ethel May (Dodrill) Hoover; m. Harvey McKinley Shreve, Nov. 22, 1947; 1 adopted child, Anne McKinley. Student Mason Coll. Fine Art, 1943-45, Art Students' League, N.Y.C., 1983-84; student in art Morris Harvey Coll., 1943-47; studied with Nell Blaine, 1984. Advt. layout and design artist Charleston Daily Mail, 1943-50; asst. advt. mgr. Diamond Dept. Store, 1950-51; advt. mgr. Woodrum's, 1951-53; profl. painter, 1955—; mem. W.Va. Arts and Humanities comm., 1971-80; rep. by Mickelson Gallery, Washington, Miller Gallery, Cin. Exhibited in one-woman shows Gallery 1897, Lewisburg, W.Va., 1981, Mickelson Gallery, 1984, Miller Gallery 1985; group shows include Marietta Nat., 1981, Huntington Galleries, 1981, Three Painters and a Printmaker, Washington, 1982, Butler Midyear Nat., 1982, Mickelson Gallery, summers 1982-85, W.Va. Juried Exhbn., 1983, 85, Miller Gallery (two-artist show), 1983, Meadows Mus., Shreveport, La., 1984; rep. in permanent collections The Rockefeller Collection, Union Carbide, Beechwood Home, Cin. Home and Studio: Middle Ridge Route 2 Box 486-K Charleston WV 25314

SHREVE, SANDRA DIANE, educational administrator; b. Detroit, May 25, 1941; d. William Orlo and Gladys Lucille (Struthers) S.; B.S., Wayne State U., 1963, M.Ed., 1971; Ph.D. candidate U. Colo., 1978—. Tchr., Detroit Public Schs., 1963-70, career counselor, 1970-74; counselor Aurora (Colo.) Public Schs., 1975-81, adminstrv. intern., 1980-81, asst. prin., 1981-82, prin. Montview Elem. Sch., 1982-83, dir. certificated employment, 1983—. Mem. Colo. Assn. Sch. Execs., Nat. Assn. Elem. Sch. Prins., Sch. Execs. Aurora, NAACP, Nat. Council Negro Women, LWV, Am. Personnel and Guidance Assn., Assn. Curriculum Devel., Colo. Assn. Curriculum Devel., AAUW, Soroptimist Internat., Pi Lambda Theta, Phi Delta Kappa, Delta Sigma Theta. Democrat.

SHREVE, SUSAN RICHARDS, author, English literature educator; b. Toledo, May 2, 1939; d. Robert Kenneth and Helen (Greene) Richards; m. Porter Gaylord Shreve, May 26, 1962; children—Porter, Elizabeth, Caleb, Kate. B.A., U. Pa., 1961; M.A., U. Va., 1969. Prof. English lit. George Mason U., Fairfax, Va., 1976—; vis. prof. Columbia U., N.Y.C., 1982—; pres. PEN South-PEN Am. Ctr., 1983—. Author: (novels) A Fortunate Madness, 1974, A Woman Like That, 1977, Children of Power, 1979, Miracle Play, 1981, Dreaming of Heroes, 1984, Scouts of the Heart, 1986; (children's books) The Nightmares of Geranium Street, 1977, Family Secrets, 1979, Loveletters, 1979, The Masquerade, 1980, The Bad Dreams of a Good Girl, 1981, The Revolution of Mary Leary, 1982, The Flunking of Joshua T. Bates, 1984, How I Saved the World on Purpose, 1985, Lucy Forever and Miss Rosetree, Shrinks, Inc., 1985. Recipient Jenny Moore award George Washington U., 1978; John Simon Guggenheim award in fiction, 1980; Nat. Endowment Arts fiction award, 1982. Mem. Phi Beta Kappa. Democrat. Episcopalian. Home: 3518 35th St NW Washington DC 20016

SHRIVER, ROSALIA OLIVER, librarian; b. Balt., Oct. 14, 1927; d. Mark Owings and Rosalia (Oliver) S. B.A., Notre Dame Coll. of Md., 1967; M.L.S., Drexel U., 1971. Library profl. Enoch Pratt Free Library, Balt., 1967-69, 1970—. Author: Rosa Bonheur: with a checklist of her works in American collections, 1982. Mem. Nat. League Am. Penwomen. Home: 1101 Saint Paul St Baltimore MD 21202

SHROADS-SCHULTZ, CRYSTAL VIRGINIA, science educator; b. Joliet, Ill., Mar. 21, 1949; d. William Myron and Ada (Baldus) Shroads; m. Edward Anson Schultz, Aug. 13, 1977. B.S. in Biology, U. Miami, 1971, M.S. in Biology, 1974. Teaching asst. biology U. Miami, Coral Gables, Fla., 1971-72, 1972-73; tchr. marine biology Gulliver Acad., Coral Gables, 1973—, head sci. dept., 1980—; sec., treas. Tri-Beta Biol. Hon. Soc., 1970-71. Mem. Internat. Oceanographic Found., Tropical Audubon, Soc., Internat. Wildlife Fedn., Animal Protection Inst., Defenders of Wildlife, Zool. Soc., Am. Soc. Prevention Cruelty to Animals, World Wildlife Fund Cousteau Soc., Ctr. Environ. End. Defenders of Wildlife, Am. Soc. for Prevention Cruelty to Animals, Oceanic Soc., Nat. Audubon Soc., Zool. Soc., World Wildlife Fund, Animal Protection Inst. Republican. Lutheran. Home: 241 Buttonwood Dr Key Biscayne FL 33149 Office: Gulliver Acad Inc 12595 Red Rd Coral Gables FL 33156

SHUFFIELD, FRANCES MILLS, county official; b. Pflugerville, Tex., Nov. 12, 1926; d. August and Helen Wanda (Wieruscheske) Mills; m. Bunn M. Pelham, Apr. 10, 1943 (div. Jan. 1964); children—Diana Marie Pelham Carmean, Marcus Lee Pelham; m. Joseph Nelson Shuffield, May 20, 1964; 1 child, Joseph Nelson. Clk., typist SSS, Austin, Tex., 1943-50; asst. chief dep. Travis County Tax Office, Austin, 1956-66; chief dep. Midland County Tax Office, Midland, Tex., 1966-80, tax assessor, collector, 1981—; sec. Bd. Tax Profl. Examiners, Austin, 1981—. Bd. dirs West Tex. Youth Orch., Midland, 1983—. Mem. Tex. Assn. Assessing Officers, Inst. Cert. Tex. Assessors, Tax Assessors and Collectors Assn. Tex. Republican. Methodist. Club: Midland County Arts. Avocations: camping; travel; skiing; snow sports. Office: Midland County Tax Office PO Box 712 707 W Washington Midland TX 79701

SHUKLA, MOHINI, child psychiatrist; b. Nairobi, Kenya, Africa, Dec. 12, 1949; came to U.S., 1976, naturalized, 1982; d. Bhanuprasad and Pushpa (Gor) S.; m. Baldur Limburg, May 31, 1978; 1 son, Lars-Arun. M.D., Med. Coll. Baroda (India), 1975. Diplomate Am. Bd. Psychiatry and Neurology. Intern Shree Sayaji Gen. Hosp., Baroda, 1973-74, Maidenhead Gen. Hosp. (Eng.), 1975-76; clin. instr. Alcohol Clinic, Bklyn., 1976-77; resident in psychiatry Brookdale Hosp., SUNY, 1977-81; fellow child psychiatry North Shore U. Hosp., Cornell Med. Coll., N.Y., 1981-83, clin. instr. psychiatry, 1982—. Mem. Am. Acad. Child Psychiatry, Am. Psychiat. Assn. Home: 308 E Main St Centerport NY 11721 Office: 33 E Carver St Huntington NY 11743

SHULKO, PATSY LEE, nutrition consultant; b. Indpls., Sept. 24, 1934; B.S., Mich. State U., 1956, M.A., 1970; m. Richard M. Shulko, Aug. 4, 1973; 1 son, Gregory. Asst. prof. Med. Coll. Ga., Augusta, 1972-82; cons., 1982—. Mem. Am. Dietetic Assn., Ga. Dietetic Assn., Augusta Dietetic Assn., Am. Home Econ. Assn., Ga. Heart Assn., Ga. Nutrition Council, Soc. Nutrition Edn., Nutrition Today Soc. (charter), Nutritionists in Nursing Edn. (nat. chmn. 1983-84), AAUP, AAUW, Omicron Nu, Pi Beta Phi. Clubs: Houndslake Country, Racquet. Home: 425 Waverly Dr Augusta GA 30909

SHULMAN, CLAIRE LUCILLE, financial services executive; b. N.Y.C., Mar. 27, 1941; d. Jacob Morris and Beatrice Irene (Krieger) Epstein; B.A. in English, Hofstra U., 1961, M.S. in Secondary Edn., 1964; children—Scott, Brian, Russell. Tchr. English, social studies, pvt. and public schs., Westbury and Lawrence, N.Y., 1969-77; owner, operator Metro Hobby Shop, needlework design shop, Woodmere, N.Y. and Miami, Fla., 1969-77; dir. mktg. Ethnic Crafts, Miami, 1977-78; exec. dir. Fla. Regional Minority Purchasing Council, Miami, 1978-79; dir. exchange and travel Interval Internat., South Miami, Fla., 1979-80; adminstr. Island Developers, Ltd., South Miami, 1979-82; pres. Claire Shulman and Assocs., fin. services, 1981—; pres. Personal Introduction Services, Inc., 1985—; del. White House Conf. on Small Bus., 1979-80. Mem. Dade County (Fla.) Commn. for Status of Women; mem. steering com. Common Cause; mem. planning com. YWCA Women in Mgmt. Program, Miami; mem. women's concern com. Mental Health Bd., Miami, 1979. Recipient recognition for outstanding community service from Pres. Carter. Mem. Mensa (treas. Miami chpt.), Zonta (treas. Downtown Miami chpt.), Phi Delta Epsilon, Epsilon Tau Lambda. Democrat. Jewish. Author: How to Build a Successful Needlepoint Business, 1977; editor: Briarlake Newsletter. Home: 9184 SW 132d Ln Miami FL 33176

SHULMAN, TAMARA, psychologist; b. N.Y.C., Apr. 8, 1953; d. Bernard and Miriam S.; m. Barry J. Bendes, 1984. B.A. magna cum laude, Bklyn. Coll., 1973; M.A., Hofstra U., 1974, Ph.D., 1977; postgrad. NYU, 1981—. Diplomate in clin. psychology Am. Bd. Profl. Psychology; lic. psychologist, N.J., N.Y. Staff psychologist Mental Health Clinic of Passaic (N.J.), 1977-78; staff psychologist Elizabeth Gen. Hosp. Community Mental Health Clinic (N.J.), 1978-79, chief childrens services, 1979-81; pvt. practice psychology, Clifton, N.J., 1979—; consulting psychologist N.J. Div. Narcotics, 1978-84, Clifton Pub. Sch. System, 1981—; mem. allied clin. staff St. Mary's Hosp., Passaic, 1982—; adj. prof. C.W. Post Coll., Geeenvale, N.Y., 1977, Nassau Community Coll., Garden City, N.Y., 1975; assoc. clin. prof. Pace U., N.Y.C., 1986; field supr. N.J. Coll. Medicine and Dentistry, Newark, 1986. Contbr. articles to profl. jours. Mem. Am. Psychol. Assn., N.J. Psychol. Assn., Assn. for Advancement of Psychology, Phi Beta Kappa. Home: 340 E 64th St Apt 25A New York NY 10021Office: 66 Mt Prospect Ave PO Box 754 Clifton NJ 07015 also 340 E 64th St New York NY 10021 -1

SHULTZ, SUSAN FRIED, executive search consultant; b. N.Y.C., Mar. 25, 1943; d. L. Richard and Jane (Kent) Fried; B.A. in Govt. and Econs., U. Ariz., 1964; postgrad. in internat. affairs George Washington U., 1967. Congl. legis. asst., 1964-68; campaign and press dir. various polit. campaigns, 1968-78; pub. relations cons., 1974-81; contbr. editor Phoenix mag., 1973—; pres. Susan Shultz and Assocs., exec. search cons., Paradise Valley, Ariz., 1981—; cons. SS & A, Phoenix; writer Beverly Hills Diet and sequel, 1981-82. Mem. staff Republican Nat. Conv., 1964, 68, 80; charter mem. Charter 100, 1980; charter class mem. Valley Leadership, 1980; membership chmn. Village 5 Phoenix Planning Com., 1980; bd. dirs. Behavioral Health Found. Mem. Phoenix Com. Fgn. Relations (exec. com.), Ariz. Dist. Export Council, Jr. League of Phoenix. Episcopalian. Club: Phoenix City (bd. dirs.). Address: 6001 E Cactus Wren Rd Paradise Valley AZ 85253

SHUMATE, DOROTHY LEE, pharmacist; b. Oak Hill, W.Va., Feb. 4, 1956; d. Garland Lee and Betty Alice (Perry) Pugh; m. David Keith Shumate, Mar. 14, 1981. Student Concord Coll., 1974-76; B.S. in Pharmacy, W.Va. U., 1979. Registered pharmacist. Pharmacist, Rural Acres Pharmacy, Beckley, W.Va., 1979-81, Beckley Hosp., 1979, Fairway Drug, Addison, Ill., 1981-82, Martin Ave. Pharmacy, Naperville, Ill., 1982-85, Pulaski Drugs, Va., 1985—. Mem. Am. Pharm. Assn., Va. Pharm. Assn., AAUW, Rho Chi, Gamma Beta Phi, Alpha Chi, Lambda Kappa Sigma. Republican. Mem. Ch. of the Brethren. Avocations: ping pong; piano; organ; racquetball. Home: Rt 2 Box 8 Pulaski VA 24301

SHURE, MYRNA BETH, psychologist, educator; b. Chgo., Sept. 11, 1937; d. Sidney Natkin and Frances (Laufman) S.; student U. Colo., 1955; B.S., U. Ill., 1959; M.S., Cornell U., 1961, Ph.D., 1966. Asst. prof. U. R.I., head tchr. Nursery Sch., Kingston, 1961-62; asst. prof. Temple U., Phila., 1966-67, assoc. prof., 1967-68; instr. Hahneman Med. Coll., Phila., 1968-69, sr. instr. psychology, 1969-70, asst. prof., 1970-73, assoc. prof., 1973-80, prof., 1980—. NIMH research grantee, 1971-75, 77-79, 82—. Recipient Lela Rowland Prevention award Nat. Mental Health Assn., 1982; . lic. psychologist, Pa. Fellow Am. Psychol. Assn. (Disting. Contbn. award div. community psychology 1984); mem. Eastern Psychol. Assn., Soc. Research in Child Devel., Phila. Soc. Clin. Psychologists. Author: (with George Spivack) Social Adjustment of Young Children, 1974; (with George Spivack and Jerome Platt) The Problem Solving Approach to Adjustment, 1976; (with George Spivack) Problem Solving Techniques in Childrearing, 1978. Editorial bd. Jour. Applied Developmental Psychology. Office: 1505 Race St Philadelphia PA 19102

SHUTT, ELIZABETH ANNE, speech and language pathologist; b. Richmond, Va., Nov. 9, 1951; d. William Henry and Mary Virginia (Seal) Gill; B.S., Radford Coll., 1973; M.Ed., U. Va., 1978; m. Bernard Ray Shutt, Aug. 11, 1973; children—Christopher Ray, Kelley Virginia, Courteney Elizabeth. Tchr. hearing impaired Chesterfield County (Va.) Public Schs., 1973-74; speech pathologist Hanover County (Va.) Public Schs., 1974-76; speech/lang. pathologist Richmond (Va.) Cerebral Palsy Center, 1978-80; pvt. speech and lang. pathologist, Richmond, 1980—; speech and lang. pathologist/cons. Stuart Circle Hosp., Richmond, 1980—, Retreat Hosp., Richmond, 1982—; speech and lang. cons. Our Lady of Lourdes Parochial Sch., Richmond, 1984—; mem. staff Tutoring Cons., Inc., 1976—. Mem. Speech and Hearing Assn. Va., Am. Speech-Lang.-Hearing Assn., Council Exceptional Children (div. learning disabilities), Children With Communication Disorders. Roman Catholic. Home: 9327 Becton Rd Glen Allen VA 23060 Office: 9327 Becton Rd Glen Allen VA 23060

SHUTTE, MARILYN KAY, nurse practitioner, nursing educator; b. Eveleth, Minn., July 31, 1951; d. William Peter and Josephine Ann (Longar) S. B.A. in Nursing, Coll. St. Scholastica, 1973; M.S. in Primary Care Nursing, U. Wis.-Oshkosh, 1980. Cert. adult nurse practitioner. Staff nurse Theda Clark Regional Med. Ctr., Neenah, Wis., 1973-76, med.-surgical unit head nurse, 1976-77, coordinator A Breath of New Life pulmonary rehab. program, 1980—; nurse practitioner Assoc. F.L. Hildebrand, M.D., Nicolet Clinic, Neenah, 1977—; grad. instr. U. Wis., Oshkosh, 1985—. Mem. Fox Valley Health Profls. (sec.-treas. 1983—), Sigma Theta Tau. Roman Catholic.

SHUTTEE, ANNE KATHERINE, lawyer; b. Austin, Tex., Sept. 3, 1955; d. Walter Richard and Lois Elaine (Hayes) S. B.A., Trinity U., San Antonio, 1976; J.D., Harvard U., 1979. Bar: Mo. Law clk. to judge U.S. Dist Ct., Kansas City, Mo., 1979-80; assoc. Shook, Hardy & Bacon, Kansas City, 1980-85; assoc. Hughes & Luce, Dallas, 1985—. Mem. Mo. Bar Assn., Phi Beta Kappa. Democrat. Home: 6055 Martel Dallas TX 75206 Office: Hughes & Luce 1000 Mercantile Dallas Bldg Dallas TX 75201

SHUTTLESWORTH, JUNE, printing/graphics company executive; b. Beeville, Tex., June 23, 1936; d. Thomas Edward Hickman and Alma Ellen (Ikonen) Hickman Kostelnik; m. William Brooks Parker, Sept. 18, 1971 (div.); children—Eric, Suzanne; m. 2d, Kenneth Shuttlesworth, Sept. 24, 1983. Student Washington U.-St. Louis, 1956, Tampa U., 1958; cert. Inst. Advanced Advt. Studies, 1983. Comml. artist Saud Advt. Co., St. Louis, 1956-58; account exec. Clearwater Advt. Co. (Fla.), 1958-60, Dallas Art and Advt. Agy., 1965-67, Robinson Advt. Agy., Dallas, 1967-69; v.p. Case & Assocs., Dallas, 1969-83; pres. Intermediate Group, Tyler, Tex., 1983—. Active Tyler C. of C. Recipient advt. and design awards. Mem. Bus. and Profl. Advt. Assn., Printers Industries Assn., Tyler Network Exec. Women. Episcopalian. Home: Route 24 PO Box 2064 Tyler TX 75703 Office: Intermedia Group 3710 W Way Tyler TX 75703

SHWARTZ, SHEILA ALPERT, designer; b. New Bedford, Mass., Mar. 22, 1931; d. Simon and Della (Davidson) Alpert; A.B.A., Curry Coll., Boston, 1950; children—Peter D., Patti Diane. Founder, 1965, since pres. Faces of Time, Ltd., Inc., jewelry, personal and home accessories, N.Y.C.; pres. Faces of Time II, retail store, Dallas, 1986—. Pres. New Bedford chpt. Hadassah, 1958-60; bd. dirs. 40th St. Tenants Corp., 1983—. Mem. Exec. Female, LWV. Republican. Office: 32 W 40th St New York NY 10018

SHY, MARILYN MUSZALSKI, conservationist; b. Detroit, Jan. 9, 1954; d. Edmund Paul and Estelle Ann (Bielicki) M.; m. Gregory Bernard Shy, Mar. 14, 1980. B.A., Western Mich. U., 1975, M.S., 1981. Soil conservationist Soil Conservation Service, Fremont, Mich., 1981-83, dist. conservationist, Cadillac, Mich., 1983—. Western Mich. U. fellow, 1976. Mem. Soil Conservation Soc. Am., Audubon Soc., Nature Conservancy. Avocations: ornithology. Home: 356 Coster Rd Fife Lake MI 49633 Office: US Dept Agr Soil Conservation Service 3060 W 13th St Cadillac MI 49601

SHYMANSKI, CATHERINE MARY, psychiatric clinical nurse specialist; b. Omaha, Jan. 23, 1954; d. Leo Michael and Mildred Mary (Swank) Wshanski. A.A.S. in Nursing, Iowa Western Community Coll., 1977; B.S.N., Buena Vista Coll., 1978; B.F.A., Drake U., 1980; M.S.N., Columbia Pacific U., 1984. Staff nurse Menninger Found., Topeka, 1978-79; staff devel. instr., clin. coordinator Stormont Vail Regional Med. Ctr., Topeka, 1979-80; charge nurse Allen County Hosp., Iola, Kans., 1980-81; asst. dir. nursing Arkhaven at Erie, Kans., 1980; dir. shift ops. Truman Med. Ctr., Kans. City, Mo., 1983; nursing supr. Osawatomie State Hosp., Kans., 1981—. Mem. River City Players, Osawatomie, Kans., 1984—. Mem. Osawatomie Bus. & Profl. Women (pres. 1985-86, dist. dir.-elect 1986-87, Young Career Woman award 1982, 84, Woman of Year, 1982-83), AAUW. Democrat. Lutheran. Avocations: fishing and show cats; gardening; reading. Office: Osawatomie State Hosp Osawatomie KS 66064

SIBLEY, CAROL MORSE, medical communications consultant; b. San Antonio, Jan. 11, 1944; d. Edison Spencer and Cecile (Bernard) Morse; student U. Del., 1962-64; B.S., Hahnemann Med. Coll., 1966; m. Frederick Drake Sibley, Mar. 15, 1975; 1 dau., Janet Bernard. Med. writer internat. div. Bristol-Myers, N.Y.C., 1968-72; asso. biomed. communications Turner Assocs., Greenwich, Conn., 1972-73; clin. research assoc. Pfizer Pharms., N.Y.C., 1974-76, mgr. sci. communications, 1976; cons. pharm. industry, Montclair, N.J., 1976—; assoc. biomed. communications J.L. Shapiro Assocs., Metuchen, N.J., 1979-82; dir. sci. affairs Audio Visual Med. Mktg., N.Y.C., 1982-83. Committeeman, Republican party, Phila., 1965-66. Mem. Am. Soc. Microbiology, N.Y. Acad. Scis., Am. Soc. Clin. Pathologists. Republican. Episcopalian. Home and Office: 196 Christopher St Montclair NJ 07042

SIBLEY, CHARLOTTE ELAINE, pharmaceutical company executive; b. Holliston, Mass., June 11, 1946; s. C. Edward and Jane Forbes (Kelly) S. A.B., Middlebury Coll., 1968 M.B.A., U. Chgo., 1970. Market research mgr. Pfizer Inc., N.Y.C., 1970-73; security analyst Donaldson, Lufkin & Jenrette, N.Y.C., 1973-76; cons., N.Y.C., 1976-78; mktg. research mgr. Lipton Co., Englewood Cliffs, N.J., 1978-80; market research mgr. Johnson & Johnson Products Inc., New Brunswick, N.J., 1980-84; research dir. Med. Econs. Co. Inc., Oradell, N.Y., 1984—. Cons., Vol. Urban Cons. Group, N.Y.C., 1974-78. Vice pres., treas. St. Cecilia Chorus, N.Y.C., 1974—. Mem. Med. Surg. Market Research Group, N.Y. Soc. Security Analysts. Republican. Home: 225 E 36th St Apt 16J New York NY 10016 Office: Med Econs Co Inc 680 Kinderkamack Rd Oradell NJ 07649

SIBLEY, PATRICIA CATHERINE, advertising agency executive; b. San Bernardino, Calif., Nov. 9, 1952; d. Charles Leonidas and Catherine Louise (Coleman) S.; m. Peter R. Condo, May 18, 1974 (div. Apr. 1981). B.A., Fla. State U., 1974. Media buyer, planner Weltin Advt., Atlanta, 1974-77; sr. media buyer, planner Young & Rubicam Advt., Atlanta, 1977; media dir. Pringle Dixon Pringle Advt., Atlanta, 1977-78; media supr. Liller Neal Weltin Advt., Atlanta, 1978-82; dir. media and client services Wemmers Communications, Atlanta, 1982-83; pres. Sibley & McCulloch, Atlanta, 1983—; cons. Emory U. Exec. MBA Class, Atlanta, 1985, Giftabout Ga. Inc., Atlanta, 1985; founder, tchr. Media Buying Sch., 1984. Patron mem. High Mus. Art, Atlanta, 1983—, mem. jr. com., 1984—. Mem. Atlanta C. of C. (internat. com. 1983—), Atlanta Media Planners Assn., Am. Women in Radio and TV, Atlanta Broadcasting/Advt. Club (bd. dirs. 1984—), Zeta Tau Alpha Alumni Assn. Baptist. Clubs: Ansley Golf, Lake Lanier Sailing (Atlanta). Avocations: sailboat racing, golf, needlepoint. Home: 971 Dean Dr Atlanta GA 30318 Office: Sibley & McCulloch Inc 11 Piedmont Ctr Suite 810 Atlanta GA 30305

SIBSON-WARREN, EILEEN MARY, computer company executive; b. Framingham, Mass., Nov. 17, 1958; d. David Sidney and Virginia Francis (Kinnarney) Sibson; m. Rory Arthur Warren, June 25, 1983; 1 child, Christine Anne Warren. Student Univ. Coll. Cork, Ireland, 1978; B.A., U. Mass., 1980; postgrad. Clark U., 1981-82. Assoc. editor EDL services Digital Equipment Corp., Maynard, Mass., 1981-84, computer systems sales cons., Detroit, 1984—. Campaign worker United Way, Detroit, 1984, 85; participant March of Dimes Walk Am., Detroit, 1986. Mem. Nat. Assn. Women in Sales, Am. Mgmt. Inst., Alpha Lambda Delta (Mass. chpt.). Avocations: reading; history American industry; dance; equestrian sports; European folk culture. Office: Digital Equipment Corp 2133 Haggerty Rd Novi MI 48050

SICHLER, GAIL ANN, bookbinding company executive; b. Denver, July 9, 1954; d. Richard Robert and Rita Mathilda (Erslund) Lundquist; m. William Douglas Sichler, Apr. 8, 1973 (div. 1984); 1 child, Erica Ann. Student U. No. Colo., 1972-73. Corporate sec. Denver Bookbinding Co., 1972—; owner GASCO, a racing car co. Del., Small Bus. Conf., Colo., 1983. Mem. Library Binding Inst. (dir. 1978—). Republican. Club: Sports Car Am. (treas. 1984). Office: Denver Bookbinding Co 2715 17th St Denver CO 80211

SICILIANO, ANN P., cytologist; b. Neptune, N.J., Dec. 20, 1930; d. Gavino and Theresa Siciliano; asso. degree in med. tech. Wilson Jr. Coll., 1948; cert. in cytology Parkway Hosp., 1949; B.S., Northwestern U., 1962. With Parkway Hosp., Brookline, Mass., 1949-53; supr. cytology and isotopes labs. Highland Park (Ill.) Hosp., 1954-60; cytologist U. Ill. Med. Sch., Chgo., 1960-61; cytologist supr. Edgewater Hosp., Chgo., 1961-68, North Suburban Clinic, Skokie, Ill., 1964—. Mem. Internat. Acad. Cytology, Am. Soc. Cytotechnologists, Am. Soc. Clin. Pathology (assoc.), Am. Soc. Cytology (assoc.), Ill. Soc. Cytology (treas.). Roman Catholic. Office: PO Box 206 Kenilworth IL 60043

SICKEL, HARRIET FRANCES, nursing administrator; b. Harrisburg, Pa., Dec. 13, 1930; d. Charles Edward and Frances L. (Webster) Kunkle; m. Donald Oliver Sickel, Feb. 26, 1955 (Div. Sept. 1979); children—Jeffrey, Edward. R.N., Harrisburg Hosp., Sch. Nursing 1951; pub. health cert. U. Pa., 1956; student Elizabethtown Coll., Pa., 1976-80, Antioch U., Phila., 1984—. Cert. nurse adminstr. lic. nursing home adminstr. Staff nurse Harrisburg Hosp., 1951-52, Eastern Montgomery County Vis. Nurses Assn., Abington, Pa., 1955-60; dir. nurses Lakeside Nursing Home, Phila., 1964-65; adminstr., dir. nursing Livengrin Found., Bensalem, Pa., 1965—. Mem. addictive behavior com. J.F.K. Mental Health Ctr., Phila., 1985; bd. dirs. home health care sect. Homemakers-Upjohn, Langhorne, Pa., 1985. Served to lt. (j.g.) USN, 1952-55; Korea. Recipient Four Chaplains Legion of Honor, 1984. Mem. Am. Nurses Assn., Pa. Nurses Assn., Bucks County Nurses Assn., Nat. Fire Protection Assn., Drug and Alcohol Nurses Assn., ARC. Republican. Methodist. Club: Soroptimists (2d v.p. 1984-86) (Bucks County). Avocations: skiing; gardening; button and bottle collecting; swimming; theatre. Home: 4833 Hulmeville Rd Bensalem PA 19020 Office: Livengrin Found 4833 Hulmeville Rd Bensalem PA 19020

SICKMAN, MARY RIE, architectural engineer; b. Tokyo, Nov. 6, 1955; came to U.S., 1958, naturalized, 1962; d. Bernard Vincent and Masako (Hagiwara) Palmer; m. Thomas Dale Sickman, June 23, 1979; 1 child, Emily Jean. B.Arch., U. Cin., 1980. Draftsperson Alexander & Assocs., Mansfield, Ohio, 1975-77; architect student trainee VA Med. Ctr., Cin., 1978-80, engr. officer trainee, 1980-81; project engr. VA Med. Ctr., Atlanta, 1981-83; asst. chief engr. VA Med. Ctr., Lexington, Ky., 1983—. Advisor Med. Explorer Group Post 117 Boy Scouts Am., 1980-81. Named to Outstanding Young Women Am., U.S. Jaycees, 1981. Mem. Nat. Assn. Female Execs. Democrat. Methodist. Avocations: reading; baking; softball. Home: 1976 Twin Ridge Dr Lexington KY 40514 Office: Va Med Ctr Engring Service Cooper Dr Div Lexington KY 40511

SIDEY, MIRIAM KAY, town official; b. Indpls., Nov. 30, 1946; d. Paul Thomas and Mary Ellen (Mohler) Wildey; m. Billy Thomas Sidey, Apr. 20, 1968; 1 child, Aimee Jo. Student Ind. Bus. Coll., 1964-65, Ball State U., 1981. Cert. mcpl. clk. Acctg. clk. Nat. Cash Register, Indpls., 1965-71; clk.-treas. Town of Yorktown, Ind., 1973—. Vice-pres. Yorktown-Mount Pleasant Twp. Democratic Club, 1984-86; dist. organizer Delaware County Heart Assn., Muncie, Ind., 1976-77; mem. adv. com. Ball State U. Sch. Continuing Edn. and Pub. Service, 1985. Mem. Internat. Inst. Mcpl. Clks. (fin. com. 1984-85), Ind. Assn. Cities and Towns (legis. and nominating coms. 1984-85, exec. com. 1979-80), Ind. League Mcpl. Clks. and Treas. (v.p. 1984-85, pres. 1985-86), Ind. Govt. Fin. Officers Assn. (bd. dirs. 1985-86). Democrat. Roman Catholic. Avocations: reading; travel. Home: 210 Hunter Rd Yorktown IN 47396 Office: Town of Yorktown Inc 720 W Smith St Yorktown IN 47396

SIDLEY, LINDA CAROL, word processing company executive; b. Corpus Christi, Tex., Oct. 2, 1944; d. Hugh Alton and Alice Marie (Vaughn) Smith; m. Kenneth Roger Deats, June 3, 1967 (div. Aug. 1977); 1 child, Jonathan Beck; m. Thomas Hill Sidley, III, June 13, 1981. Student Chadek Conservatory Music, 1964-65, U. Ala.-Huntsville, summer 1965; B.A., Covenant Coll., 1966; postgrad. Am. U., summer 1968. Tchr. Phila.-Montgomery Christian Acad., 1966-67; counselor Med. Placement Co., Atlanta, 1974-75; supr. Kelly Girl Services, Huntsville, 1977; exec. sec. McDonnell Douglas, Huntsville, 1977-78, Teledyne Wah Chang, Huntsville, 1979-83; tchr. Westminster Acad., Huntsville, 1983-84; owner, prin. Word Broker, Huntsville, 1984—. Singer, Huntsville Community Chorus, 1960—; prin. singer Prince Georges County Community Opera, Md., 1973-75; soloist Bowie Madrigal Singers, Md., 1973-75; bd. dirs., cons. Inst. Bibl. Therapy, Huntsville, 1984—, Christian Services, 1985—. Mem. Nat. Assn. Female Execs. Republican. Presbyterian. Club: Crofton Christian Women's (music chmn. 1973-75). Avocations: reading, needlework, music. Home: 3411 Venona Ave Huntsville AL 35810 Office: Word Broker 3411 Venona Ave Huntsville AL 35810

SIEBERT, MURIEL, former state banking ofcl.; b. Cleve.; d. Irwin J. and Margaret Eunice (Roseman) S.; student Western Res. U., 1949-52; D.C.S. (hon.), St. John's U., St. Bonaventure U. Security analyst Bache & Co., 1954-57; analyst Utilities & Industries Mgmt. Corp., 1958, Shields & Co., 1959-60; partner Stearns & Co., 1961, Finkle & Co., 1962-65, Brimberg & Co., N.Y.C., 1965-67; pres. Muriel Siebert & Co., Inc., mems. N.Y. Stock Exchange, 1968-77, chmn., 1977-82; individual mem. (1st woman mem.) N.Y. Stock Exchange, 1967; trustee Manhattan Savs. Bank, 1975-77; supt. banks State of N.Y., N.Y.C., 1977-82; asso. in mgmt. Simmons Coll. Trustee, Manhattan Coll.; v.p., mem. exec. com. Greater N.Y. Area council Boy Scouts Am.; Rep. candidate for U.S. Senate from N.Y., 1982 primary; mem. N.Y. State Econ. Devel. Bd.; dir. Urban Devel. Corp., State N.Y. Mortgage Agy., Job Devel. Authority. Mem. N.Y. Soc. Security Analysts, Money Marketeers N.Y.U. (gov.), Sales Execs. Club (past v.p. dir.). Clubs: Wings (past dir., v.p.), Westchester County, El Morrocco. Office: Muriel Siebert & Co Inc 444 Madison Ave New York NY 10022*

SIEDLECKI, NANCY THERESE, lawyer, funeral director, embalmer; b. Chgo., May 30, 1954; d. LeRoy John and Dorothy Josephine (Wilczynski) Schielka; m. Jonathan Francis Siedlecki, June 18, 1977; children—Samantha Ann, Abigail Marie. Student Triton Jr. Coll., 1971-73; grad. funeral dir., Worsham Coll., 1974; student Loyola U., Chgo., 1974-76., U. Ill.-Chgo., 1976-77; J.D. with honors, Chgo.-Kent Coll. Law, 1980. Bar: Ill. Paralegal in real estate Rosenberg, Savner, & Unikel, Chgo., 1974-77; sole practice law, Burr Ridge, Ill., 1980—; cons. various small bus. corps., Chgo., 1980—. Mem. ABA, Ill. State Bar Assn., Chgo. Bar Assn. Roman Catholic. Home: 8219 Park Ave Burr Ridge IL 60521

SIEGAL, RITA DENA, interior plantscaper, florist; b. Jersey City, Feb. 24, 1947; d. Arthur and Shirley Estelle (Klemons) S.; m. James Lee D'Angelo, Aug. 1, 1971 (div. May 1983). Student U. S.C., 1967; A.A. in Retailing, Vernon Ct. Jr. Coll., 1968. Fashion coordinator Simplicity Pattern Co., N.Y.C., 1968-70; asst. to pub. Crane Communications, N.Y.C., 1970-71; pres., owner Dandelion, Ltd., Myrtle Beach, S.C., 1975—. Chmn. house and grounds com. Arcadian II Homeowners Assn., Myrtle Beach, 1984—; pres. Grand Strand Tips Club, Myrtle Beach, Myrtle Beach chpt. Hadassah; active Myrtle Beach Women's Club. Mem. Landscape Contractors Am. Jewish. Avocations: running; cooking; reading. Home: Arcadian II 7-D Myrtle Beach SC 29577 Office: Dandelion Ltd 515 W Broadway Myrtle Beach SC 29577

SIEGEL, BETTY LENTZ, college president; b. Cumberland, Ky., Jan. 24, 1931; d. Carl N. and Vera (Hogg) Lentz; B.A., Wake Forest Coll., 1952; M.Ed., U. N.C., 1953; Ph.D., Fla. State U., 1961; postgrad. Ind. U., 1964-66; Doctorate (hon.), Cumberland Coll., 1985, Miami U., 1985; m. Joel H. Siegel, June 6; children—David Jonathan, Michael Jeremy. Asst. prof. Lenoir Rhyne Coll., Hickory, N.C., 1956-59, asso. prof., 1961-64; asst. prof. U. Fla., Gainesville, 1967-70, asso. prof., 1970-72, prof., 1973-76, dean acad. affairs for continuing edn., 1972-76; dean Sch. of Edn. and Psychology, Western Carolina U., Cullowhee, N.C., 1976-81; pres. Kennesaw Coll., Marietta, Ga., 1981—; cons. to numerous sch. systems. Recipient Outstanding Tchr. award U. Fla., 1969; Mortar Bd. Woman of Yr. award U. Fla., 1973. Mem. Am. Psychol. Assn., Am. Ednl. Research Assn., Assn. for Supervision and Curriculum Devel., Am. Assn. Colls. of Tchr. Edn., Nat. Univ. Extension Assn., Adult Edn. Assn., Nat. Assn. State Univs. and Land Grant Colls., Phi Alpha Theta, Pi Kappa Delta, Alpha Psi Omega, Kappa Delta Pi, Pi Lambda Theta, Phi Delta Kappa, Delta Kappa Gamma. Republican. Baptist. Author: Problem Situations in Teaching, 1971; contbr. articles to profl. jours. Office: Kennesaw College Marietta GA 30061

SIEGEL, CAROL, lawyer; b. Bklyn., June 25, 1957; d. Leon and Sara (Berkofsky) Siegel; m. Mitchell L. Rosenblatt, Oct. 23, 1982. B.A., Bklyn. Coll., 1978; J.D., Western New Eng. Coll., 1981. Bar: N.Y. 1982, U.S. Dist. Ct. (ea. dist) N.Y. 1982, U.S. Dist. Ct. (so. dist.) N.Y. 1982. Assoc. firm Leonard H. Kaplan Esq., Bklyn., 1981-83; sole practice, Bklyn., 1983—. Mem. ABA, Bklyn. Bar Assn., Bklyn. Women's Bar Assn., Kings County Criminal Bar Assn., N.Y. County Lawyers Assn., Phi Delta Phi. Office: 44 Court St Brooklyn NY 11201

SIEGEL, DEBORAH ELIZABETH, public relations executive; b. Hempstead, N.Y., Sept. 1, 1954; d. Harry and Lillian Marie (Anderson) Siegel. Student N.Y. U., 1976-77; B.B.A. in Mktg., Bernard Baruch Coll. Product planning asst. Chase Manhattan Bank, N.Y.C., 1975-76; pub. affairs asst. McGraw-Hill, Inc., N.Y.C., 1976-79; communications asst. McGraw-Hill Publs. Co., N.Y.C., 1979-81, pub. relations assoc., 1981—. Mem. Women in Communications. Bus./Profl. Advt. Assn., Internat. Radio and TV Soc. Office: McGraw-Hill Publs Co 1221 Ave of the Americas New York NY 10020

SIEGEL, LEE, soft goods merchandise purchasing company executive; b. Bklyn., May 13, 1931; d. George and Rosella (Cohen) Siegel; children—Ira Stephen Blaufarb, Jonathan David Blaufarb. Asst. buyer Corn Buying Office, N.Y.C., 1953-56; buyer Sophie Feltz, N.Y.C., 1956-59, Steinberg-Kass N.Y.C., 1959-61, Bolton Stores, N.Y.C., 1961-65; pres. Lee Siegel Assocs. Inc., N.Y.C., 1965—. Home: 580 West End Ave New York NY 10024 Office: Lee Siegel Assocs 1 Times Sq New York NY 10036

SIEGEL, LORRAINE JUDY, librarian; b. N.Y.C.; A.A., Queensborough Community Coll., CUNY, 1971; B.A., Hunter Coll., CUNY, 1973; cert. online services tng Nat. Library Medicine, 1983; M.L.S., Pratt Inst., 1976. Reference librarian, cataloguer Frick Art Reference Library, N.Y.C., 1974-77; research librarian Joseph E. Seagram & Sons, N.Y.C., 1977; reference and research librarian Am. Arbitration Assn., N.Y.C., 1978-81; asst. librarian, computer operator Patterson, Belknap, Webb & Tyler, N.Y.C., 1981—; archivist N.Y. Soc. Ethical Culture, N.Y.C., 1977-78. Compiler appendixes Arbitration and the Licensing Process, 1981; researcher, compiler bibliography The Termination Handbook, 1981. Vol., Am. Ballet Theatre, 1983-84, Prison Reform Task Force of the N.Y. Soc. Ethical Culture, 1972-73. Mem. ALA, Am. Assn. Law Libraries, Law Library Assn. Greater N.Y., Spl. Library Assn., Japan Soc. Office: Patterson Belknap Webb & Tyler 30 Rockefeller Plaza New York NY 10112

SIEGEL, LYNNE FRANCINE, lawyer; b. Chgo., June 2, 1945. B.A. cum laude, U. Ill.-Chgo., 1965; M.A., U. Ill.-Urbana, 1966; J.D., Northwestern U., 1981. Bar: Ill. 1981. Tchr., Centennial High Sch., Champaign, Ill., 1966-68; asst. prof. Parkland Coll., Champaign, Ill., 1968-69; assoc. prof. English, St. Louis Community Coll., 1969-78; assoc. Seyfarth, Shaw, Fairweather & Geraldson, Chgo., 1981-83, Ross & Hardies, Chgo., 1983-85; gen. counsel Ill. Edn. Assn., 1985—. Notes and comments editor Northwestern U. Law Rev. Named Outstanding Educator, St. Louis Community Coll., 1974. Mem. ABA, Chgo. Bar Assn. Office: Ill Edn Assn 100 E Edwards St Springfield IL 62704

SIEGEL, MARLENA, lawyer; b. Phila., Apr. 7, 1953; d. Isadore Siegel and Libby (Oppenheim) Siegel Forman. B.A., Rutgers U., 1974; J.D., Temple U., 1979. Bar: Pa. 1979, U.S. Dist. Ct. (ea. dist.) Pa. 1979, U.S. Ct. Appeals (3d cir.) 1985. Law clk. firm Barsky, Golden & Remick, Phila., 1978-79, assoc., 1979-80; arbitrator Phila. Mcpl. Ct., 1982—; ptnr. Starr & Siegel, P.C., Phila., 1980-82, Zion & Siegel Assocs., 1986—; sole practice, Phila., 1982-85; instr. seminar, 1983. Bd. dirs. Phila. Ctr. Human Devel., Inc., 1982—, counsel to bd., 1982—. Mem. ABA, Pa. Bar Assn. (jud. adminstrn. com. 1985—), Phila. Bar Assn. (chmn. mcpl. ct. com. 1982—), Comml. Law League Am. (laws and legis. com. 1985—, pamphlet com. 1985—), Phila. Trial Lawyers Assn., Tau Epsilon Rho (exec. com. 1980—, asst. corr. sec. 1982-85, corr. sec. 1985—). Democrat. Club: Phila. Lawyers'. Home: 7314 Germantown Ave Philadelphia PA 19119 Office: Zion & Siegel 1422 Chestnut St Philadelphia PA 19102 also Rosemont Bus Campus 919 Conestoga Rd Bryn Mawr PA 19010

SIEGEL, MARSHA ELLEN, medical administrator; b. Phila., Feb. 6, 1949; d. Albert Samuel and Annette Elizabeth (Cohen) Miller; m. June 18, 1972 (div. July 1978); 1 child, Evan Andrew. A.S., Cherry Hill Sch. Med. Technology, 1968. Technologist, Thomas Jefferson U., Phila., 1968-69; supr. lab. Miami Heart Inst., Miami Beach, 1969-72; owner, v.p. Personnel Service, North Miami Beach, Fla., 1976-78; v.p., dir. ops. Med. Group Mgmt., Hollywood, Fla., 1981—. Treas., v.p. Affiliated Med. Providers Assocs. Inc., North Miami Beach, Fla., 1986. Mem. Hollywood C. of C., Am. Med. Care and Rev. Assn., Group Health Assn. Am. Avocations: Dancing; golf; fishing. Office: Med Group Mgmt 2500 Hollywood Blvd Hollywood FL 33020

SIEGLER, LORA CELIA, lawyer; b. Paterson, N.J., May 13, 1957; d. Harry and Helen (Fox) Siegler. B.A. in English, U. Pa., 1977; J.D., Rutgers U., 1980. Bar: N.Y. 1981, Utah 1983. Research asst. Rutgers U., Camden, N.J., 1978-80; securities analyst Utah Securities Div., Salt Lake City, 1980-83; sole practice law, Salt Lake City, 1983-85; ptnr. Siegler & Mason, 1985—; legal cons. Dept. Fin. Inst., Salt Lake City, 1983—. U. Pa. scholar, 1974. Mem. Utah State Bar, N.Y. State Bar Assn. (corp. sec. 1983—), Salt Lake County Bar Assn., ABA, ACLU. Office: 1399 S 700 E #12 Salt Lake City UT 84111

SIEH, MAURINE KAY, nurse; b. Leon, Iowa, Sept. 28, 1950; d. Vernon Charles and Dorothy Maxine (Akes) Dobson; B.S. in Nursing, N.E. Mo. State U., 1972; M.S. in Nursing, U. Miss.; m. Robert Hans Sieh, Nov. 18, 1972; children—Robert Carter, Jennifer Clarissa. Charge nurse psychiat. unit St. John's Hosp., Springfield, Mo., 1972-74; public health nurse Will County Health Dept., Joliet, Ill., 1974-75; unit nurse Mental Health Inst. Mentally Retarded Children, Park Forest, Ill., 1977-79; instr. Lamaze method childbirth, Park Forest, 1977-81; psychiat. nurse, chmn. nurse practice and standards com. Menninger Found., Topeka, 1981; nurse neuro-neurosurg. unit Univ. Med. Center, Jackson, Miss., 1981-82; prenatal nurse ob/gyn clinic U. Miss. Med. Ctr., 1982—; instr. Lamaze method. Mem. Nat. League Nursing, Am. Soc. Psychoprophylaxis in Obstetrics, Internat. Childbirth Edn. Assn., Audubon Soc., Nature Conservancy. Mem. Brethren Ch. Home: 4953 Oak Leaf Dr Jackson MS 39212

SIEKIERSKI, KAMILLA MALGORZATA, dental lab. technician; b. Warsaw, Poland, Aug. 4, 1938; came to U.S., 1963, naturalized, 1970; d. Tomasz and Janina W. (Sendzimir) Piotrowski; cert. dental technician Sch. Dental Technicians, Krakow, Poland, 1957; m. Kazimierz Siekierski, Nov. 25, 1959; children—Marzanna, Eva. Owner, operator Kama's Dental Lab., Krakow, 1963; dental technician Dan's Dental Lab., Waterbury, Conn., 1963-65, Wilcox Dental Lab., Wethersfield, Conn., 1965-68; pres. Dentek, Inc., Milford, Conn., 1980—. Mem. Conn. Dental Lab. Assn. (pres. 1977-79), Nat. Assn. Dental Labs., Conf. Dental Labs. Home: 350 Gulf St Milford CT 06460 Office: 158 Cherry St Milford CT 06460

SIEMON, CAROL RUTH, psychologist; b. St. Louis, Nov. 26, 1935; d. Ralph M. and Ruth A. (Burhop) S.; m. David L. G. Crockett, June 29, 1980; children—Christine R. Granger Campbell, Mark S. Granger. B.S., Concordia Coll., River Forest, Ill., 1957; M.S., So. Ill. U., 1973, Ph.D., 1979. Lic. clin. psychologist; cert. rehab. counselor; diplomate Internat. Acad. Profl. Counseling and Psychotherapy. Tchr., St. John Lutheran Sch., Hamlin, N.Y., 1957-58; editor social studies textbooks Fideler Pub. Co., Grand Rapids, Mich., 1964-67; tchr. Pinery Park Elem. Sch., Wyoming, Mich., 1967-71; mental health counselor Human Services, Inc., Chester, Ill., 1972-77; intern counseling center So. Ill. U., Carbondale, 1977-79; counselor, acting dir. counseling ctr. Christopher Newport Coll., Newport News, Va., 1979-80; pvt. practice clin. psychology, So. Ill. and Paducah, Ky., 1980—; stress counselor for adults and elderly, NIMH grantee Marion Tornado Disaster Relief Project, 1982-83; mem. faculty adult re-entry programs John A. Logan Community Coll., Carterville, Ill., 1980-83; part-time faculty Paducah Community Coll., 1986. Charter mem. U.S. Com. Against Nuclear War; mem. Am. Psychol. Assn. Office: 1401 Broadway Suite 2 Paducah KY 42001

SIEMON, JOYCE MARILYN, lawyer, writer; b. Bridgeport, Conn., Dec. 4, 1944; d. George Lewis and Rita (Siegel) Nissenson; 1 dau., Alyssa Karen. B.A. in English, Carnegie Inst. Tech., 1966; J.D. with high honors, Fla. State U., 1980. Bar: Fla. Instr. legal writing and research Coll. Law Fla. State U., Tallahassee, 1979-80; intern. Fla. Supreme Ct., 1980; law clk. Office Gen. Counsel, Fla. Dept. Gen. Services, Tallahassee, 1980; assoc. Young, Stern & Tannenbaum, P.A., North Miami Beach, Fla., 1981, Greenberg, Traurig, Askew, Hoffman, Lipoff, Quentel & Wolff, P.A., Miami, Fla., 1981-82, Hornsby & Whisenand, Miami, 1982-85; sole practice, North Miami Beach, Fla., 1985—; tech. writer, Computer Sci. Research Center Carnegie Inst. Tech., Pitts., 1966-67; tchr., Leesville Jr. High Sch. (La.), 1967-68, Leesville State Sch., 1968; mag. editor VanTrump, Zeigler and Shane, Pitts., 1969; news editor Pitts. Press, 1970; staff writer Dade County Pub. Safety Dept., Miami, 1971-75; reporter North Dade Jour., Miami, 1977; freelance writer, 1977—; mem. Dade County Task Force for Handgun Control Ordnance Rev. Editor: Lawrenceville: A Short History, 1969; author weekly humor column Siemon Says, North Date Jour., 1977; author employee manual, advt. brochures, newspaper articles and ads, book revs.; author, editor, contbr. articles to legal and non-legal publs. Dade County coordinator Network, 1983; corr. sec. Democratic Club of North Dade; del. Fla. Dem. Conv. Mem. ABA, Fla. Bar (various coms.), Am. Judicature Soc., Dade County Bar Assn., North Dade C. of C., Miami Bd. Realtors (communications and legis. coms.), Forum of North Dade, Order of Coif, Phi Alpha Delta. Office: Senator Bldg 13899 Biscayne Blvd North Miami Beach FL 33181

SIEMSGLUSZ, SUSAN JANE, sales representative; b. El Paso, Tex., Apr. 19, 1950; d. Walter Diedrick and Evelyn Young S. A.A., Southeastern Ill. Jr. Coll., 1978; B.S. in Bus. Edn., So. Ill. U., 1983. Cert. tchr., Ill. Exec. sec. David A. Kosh & Assocs., Washington, 1972-77; floor mgr. Woodward & Lothrop, Washington, 1972-76; sales clk. Design Store, Washington, 1976-77; bank teller 1st Nat. Bank, Harrisburg, Ill., 1978-81; instr. Hickey Sch., St. Louis, 1983-85; sales rep. Datamax, St. Louis, 1985—, Profl. Bus. Sch., St. Louis, 1985—. Pres. Regional Arts Council, Ill., 1978; pres. Harrisburg Arts League, 1978. Mem. Nat. Bus. Edn. Assn., St. Louis Bus. Edn. Assn., Phi Beta Lambda. Republican. Lutheran. Avocations: bowling; golf; needlepoint. Home: 6605 Clayton Ave Apt 112 Saint Louis MO 63139

SIETMAN, ANNETTE MARIE, enrolled tax agent; b. Akron, Ohio, Mar. 13, 1944; d. Orville George and Ann Marie (Kloskowski) Seaver; B.S.Ed., Ohio State U., 1966; m. William Howard Ashcraft, Nov. 4, 1966 (dec. Dec. 1972); children—Julie, Joel; m. 2d, J. David Sietman, Mar. 22, 1974. Music tchr. Atherton Community Schs., Flint, Mich., 1966-67; music and math. tchr. Field Schs., Brimfield, Ohio, 1967-68; adminstrv. asst. H & R Block, Akron, 1970-72; bookkeeper Town & Country Interiors, Tallmadge, Ohio, 1972-75; owner Ashcraft-Sietman Tax & Acctg. Service, Kent, Ohio, 1976—; income tax instr., 1971-72. Treas., St. Patrick Home and Sch. Assn., 80; mem. Kent City Income Tax Rev. Bd., 1982-86. Mem. Ohio Soc. Enrolled Agts. (pres. 1977-78, 78-79, dir. 1979-85), Nat. Assn. Enrolled Agts. (sec. 1979-80, dir. 1980-82, v.p. 1982-83). Democrat. Roman Catholic. Home: 724 Grove Ave Kent OH 44240

SIGERSON, MARJORIE LORRAINE, librarian; b. Pitts., June 11, 1923; d. Roy Allen and Myrtle Mae (Bering) Parke; student Carnegie Inst. Tech., 1941-42, U. Pitts., 1942-43; m. David Kinley Sigerson, Apr. 9, 1943 (div. Dec. 1985); children—Diane Parke, David Kinley. Librarian, Mus. Arts and Scis., Daytona Beach, Fla., 1963—, trustee, 1978—, pres. Guild, 1978-79. Mem. com. Halifax Art Festival, 1963—; mem. council Garden Clubs of Halifax Dist., 1965-67; charter mem. Ormond Beach (Fla.) Meml. Hosp. Aux., 1967-76; pres. Street Sch. P.T.A., New City, N.Y., 1958-59; leader Girl Scouts U.S.A., 1956-58. Recipient award for disting. service, Mus. Arts and Scis., 1977, 79, 80, 81, 82. Presbyterian. Clubs: Harvard Dames (sec. 1946-47), Cherry Laurel Garden (pres. 1966-67), Oceanside Country (v.p. 9-Hole Golf Group). Home: 410 John Anderson Dr Ormond Beach FL 32074 Office: Museum of Arts and Sciences 1040 Museum Blvd Daytona Beach FL 32014

SIGMAN, DEBORAH ELAINE, cosmetics and skin-care products company research executive. B.S.B.A., Loyola Coll., Balt., 1983. Market research analyst dept. market research Noxell Corp., Hunt Valley, Md., 1984, research guidance supr., 1984—, also mem. corp. packaging com., 1984—. Mem. ASTM. Office: Noxell Corp 11050 York Rd Hunt Valley MD 21030

SIGNER, GLORIA JOYCE, automobile and truck dealer; b. Portland, Oreg., Apr. 23, 1925; d. Wilfred and Hazel Lucille (Pretty) Watson; m. Richard Ernest Signer, Sept. 6, 1947 (dec. 1970); children—Donald Richard, Janet Signer Muller, Jeanine Signer Garrett. B.S., Oreg. State U., Corvallis, 1947. Tchr. pub. schs., Portland, Oreg., 1948-50; automobile and truck dealer Signer Motors, Inc., Corvallis, 1970—; corp. treas. Wheels Life Ins. Co. Ltd., Grand Cayman, W.I., 1985—. Mem. Corvallis City Budget Rev. Commn., 1978—; mem. adv. council Coll. Bus. Oreg. State U., Corvallis, 1985—. Named Retailer of Yr., Corvallis C. of C., 1979; Time Quality Dealer (Oreg.), Time mag., 1983. Mem. Nat. Automobile Dealers Assn., Oreg. Automobile Dealers Assn. (dir. 1974-77), Corvallis Automobile Dealers Assn. (pres. 1975-78), Women Entrepreneurs of Oreg. (sec. 1984-85). Office: Signer Motors Inc 705 NW Buchanan St Corvallis OR 97330

SIKES, CYNTHIA, actress. Film appearances: Ladies and Gentlemen the Fabulous Stains, 1982, The Man Who Loved Women, 1983, Goodbye Cruel World, 1983; TV series: Big Shamus, Little Shamus, 1979, Captains and the Kings, 1976-77. Address: care Triad Artists Inc 10100 Santa Monica Blvd 16 Fl Los Angeles CA 90067

SILA, JOAN LEE, social worker; b. Benton Harbor, Mich., Sept. 4, 1949; d. Frank T. and Viola D. Sila. A.A., Lake Mich. Coll., 1970; B.A., John Carroll U., 1974; M.S.S.A., Case Western Res. U., 1977; postgrad. John Marshall Law Sch., Cleve. State U., 1979—. Asst. dir. social services Salvation Army, Cleve., 1977-79, coordinator home group for boys, 1979-81, dir. child conservation council, 1981-82; social service supr. Youth Devel. Center, Hudson, Ohio, 1982, residential services dir., 1982—. Mem. Nat. Assn. Social Workers, Acad. Cert. Social Workers, Nat. Council Crime and Delinquency, Am. Psychiat. Assn. Children. Roman Catholic. Office: Youth Devel Center 966 Hines Hill Rd Hudson OH

SILBER, ELLEN S., French language and literature educator, women's studies educator; b. Hartford, Conn., Feb. 25, 1939; s. Samuel and Norma A. (Sandberg) Schnitzer; m. Alvin Daniel Silber, Nov. 29, 1960; 1 child, Kenneth David. A.B., Wellesley Coll., 1960; M.A. in Teaching, Columbia U., 1962, 80, Ph.D., 1968. Lectr. in French, Queens Coll., N.Y.C., 1964-66; assoc. prof. French, Marymount Coll., Tarrytown, N.Y., 1969—; adj. asst. prof. U. Hartford Extension, Westchester, N.Y., 1975; adj. assoc. prof. career devel., women's studies Cornell U., Purchase, N.Y., 1980-81; adj. assoc. prof. Coll. New Rochelle, N.Y., 1980-82. Contbr. articles to profl. jours. Recipient grant to improve fgn. lang. component of internat. studies program at Marymount Coll., U.S. Div. Edn., 1984-86; Exxon Edn. Found. grantee, 1985—. Mem. MLA, Am. Council on Teaching of Fgn. Lang., Am. Assn. Tchrs. French, AAUP, Nat. Women's Studies Assn. Democrat. Jewish. Home: 2757 Edgehill Ave Bronx NY 10463 Office: Marymount Coll Tarrytown NY 10591

SILBERBERG, SOPHIE COUSINS, publishing executive; b. Rochester, N.Y., May 15, 1913; d. Samuel and Sarah (Miller) Cousins; m. Samuel David Silberberg, Feb. 3, 1935; children—Michael C., Robert H. B.A., Hunter Coll., 1935. Asst. to buyer book dept. R.H. Macy & Co., N.Y.C., 1935-40; sales promotion asst. Rand McNally & Co., N.Y.C., 1940-43; dir. pub. relations Nassau Library System, Hempstead, N.Y., 1959-64; dir. library relations Rand McNally & Co., N.Y.C., 1964-68; dir. advt. and promotion children's books Thomas Y. Crowell, N.Y.C., 1968-77; dir. advt. and promotion children's books Random House, N.Y.C., 1977-78; exec. dir. Fund for Free Expression, N.Y.C., 1978—; coordinator Am. Through Am. Eyes Book exhibit Assn. Am. Pubs., Moscow Book Fair, 1979, 85, China, 1981; books include: Children's New York, 1939; contbr. articles to profl. jours. Mem. ALA, Freedom to Read Found. (dir. 1965-68, 76-79). Home: 70 E 10th St New York NY 10003 Office: Fund for Free Expression 36 W 44th St New York NY 10036

SILBERT, JACQUELINE, service company executive, accountant; b. Bklyn., Dec. 15, 1921; d. Leon and Mary Gittell; children—Laurence, Amy Silbert Block. B.A. in Edn. with honors, Hunter Coll., 1942. Co-founder MacClean Service Co. Inc., Bellerose, N.Y., 1953, pres., chief exec. officer, 1982—; dir. Liberty Nat. Bank, Conn. Editor: Hunter Coll. Alumni Newspaper, 1970-72. Contbr. articles to real estate publications. Mem. R.I. State Bd. Edn., 1950-52; bd. dirs., v.p. The Lighthouse, Queens, N.Y., 1970-74, chmn. fund raising, 1971-72; pres., bd. dirs. St. John's U. Aux., 1970—, co-chmn. fund raising, 1976—; bd. dirs. Walter Kaner's Childrens Fund, 1982—, Forest Hills Jewish Ctr. Aux., 1972-74. Named Woman of Yr., Nat. Conf. Christians & Jews, 1975; Pres. medal St. John's U., 1978. Mem. Bldg. Service Contractor's Assn., Internat. Sanitary Supply Assn., Service Employer's Assn. Club: Old Westbury Hebrew Congregation Bridge. Avocation: growing trees. Office: MacClean Service Co Inc 249-12 Jericho Turnpike Bellerose NY 11426

SILBURN, ELAINE GWENDOLYN, banker; b. Denver, June 3, 1937; d. Russell Edwin and Genevieve (Johnson) Seay; m. David L. Silburn, June 16, 1957; children—Carla Anne, James Russell. A.B.A., U. Denver, 1957; student Northwestern U., 1960, U. Okla., 1981. Trust officer United Bank of Denver, 1957-65; personal banker, personal banking officer, asst. v.p., v.p. United Bank of Skyline, Denver, 1978-83, sr. v.p., 1983—, dir., 1984—. Bd. dirs. Holistic Approaches to Independent Living, 1984-86; vol. Denver Pub. Schs., alumni fund campaign U. Denver, Channel 6 Pub. TV Auction, 1983, Am. Cancer Soc., mem. major gifts fund com. Denver Symphony Orch., 1984; mem. steering com. Denver Bus. Challenge, 1984; mem. fin. devel. com. Mental Health Assn. Colo.; adv. bd. Mile High United Way; del. Republican county and state assemblies. Mem. Nat. Assn. Bank Women, Leadership Denver Assn., Denver C. of C., Cultural Affairs Task Force, Gamma Phi Beta. Episcopalian. Club: Sweet Adelines, (High Country chpt.) (pres. 1977). Home: 3119 S Akron Ct Denver CO 80231 Office: United Bank of Skyline NA 1055 16th St Denver CO 80202

SILCOCK, MARY MARGARET, writer, secretary, accountant; b. Hayward, Calif., Mar. 11, 1944; d. Francis Ellsworth and Ruth (Wightman) Case; m. James Mitchell, Aug. 26, 1947 (div.); m. Russell D. Silcock, 1948; children—Russell D., Jeffrey D., Mandy R. B.A. in Theatre, Stella Rae Acad., 1959; postgrad. Brigham Young U., 1962-63, U. Ariz., 1975-76, U. Md., 1980-82. Travel/freight agent Greyhound Internat., Santa Clara, Calif., 1970-74; mgr. Kentucky Fried Chicken, Sierea Vista, Ariz., 1975-77; acct. FAO, Stuttgart, Germany, 1977-80, Washington, 1980-82; gen. mgr. DeAnza Properties, Inc., Los Gatos. Calif., 1983-84; payroll acct. Central Santa Clara Regional Occupational Agy., San Jose, Calif., 1984-85; adminstrv. sec. City of Mountain View, Calif., 1985—. Author Hullaballoo, 1980; The Lennon Connection, 1979. Editor community newsletter, Pattonville, Germany, 1978-80. Vol. Dem. Party for Ferraro, San Jose, 1984; pub. commr. dir. Latter Day Saints Ch., San Jose, 1980-85. Mem. Nat. Thespian Soc. (life), Nat. Forensic League (life), Nat. Assn. Female Execs., Nat. Notary Assn., Writers Connection. Clubs: Non-commd. Officers Wives (pres. Stuttgart, W. Ger. 1977-79, social sec. Ft. Bellvoir 1980-81). Avocations; writing; dance; theatre. Office: Mcpl Ops Center 231 N Whisman Rd Mountain View CA 94043

SILER, INA CATHY, trainer, educator; b. Washington, July 10, 1951; d. Floyd Howard and Helen (Gill) Siler. Student Fisk U., 1969-71; B.A. magna cum laude, Howard U., 1973, M.A., 1975; postgrad., Purdue U., 1976-77; Ph.D., U. Okla., 1980. Instr. Bowie (Md.) State Coll., 1975-76, U. D.C., 1975-76; communications specialist Nat. Park Service, Washington, 1975-77; asst. prof. No. Ill. U., DeKalb, 1980-83; account exec. trainer Home Box Office, Inc., Atlanta, 1983—; cons. Nat. Capitol Parks, Washington, 1976-77, Ill. Bd. Edn., Springfield, 1980-83; recruiter grad. sch. U. Okla., Norman, 1979-80. Vol. Stateville Correctional Ctr., Joliet, Ill., 1982, Dwight (Ill.) Correctional Ctr., 1983; com. mem. NAACP, Atlanta, 1983—. Named outstanding tchr. dept. communications, U. Okla., 1979; Nat. Fellowships Fund fellow, 1983—. Mem. Am. Soc. Tng. and Devel., Internat. Listening Assn., Ill. Speech and Theatre Assn. Mem. United Ch. of Christ. Office: Home Box Office Inc 3475 Lenox Rd NE Suite 1000 Atlanta GA 30319

SILER, PAULA VICTORIA, nurse, medical center administrator; b. San Pedro, Calif., July 18, 1957; d. Harold Harvey Siler and Pauline Margaret (Hashe) Siler Vander Burgh. B.S. in Nursing, Loma Linda U., 1980, B.S. in Biology, 1982; M.S. in Mktg. and Nursing Adminstrn., 1984. R.N., Calif. Critical care nurse St. Joseph Hosp., Orange, Calif., 1976—; instr. U. Phoenix, Phoenix, Ariz., 1983—; asst. dir. nursing Harbor-UCLA Med. Ctr., Torrance, Calif., 1985—. Editorial bd. Emphasis: Nursing, 1985—. Calif. Scholarship Fedn. scholar Loma Linda U., Calif., 1977, 78, 79. Mem. So. Calif. Nursing Diagnosis Assn., Am. Assn. Critical Care Nurses, Loma Linda Alumni Assn. (scholar Loma Linda U. 1983), Nat. Mgmt. Assn., Sigma Theta Tau (scholar Loma Linda U. 1983). Democrat. Presbyterian. Lodge: Job's Daus. (hon. mem.). Avocations: jewelry design; hand-made specialty crafts; travel. Home: 330 Univ Costa Mesa CA 92627

SILHAN, GAILYA S(UE), radio station executive; b. Salzburg, Austria, July 31, 1955; came to U.S., 1956; d. Ronald Thomas and Linda Gaye (Richards) Williams; m. Jerry Daniel Silhan, Dec. 3, 1982. Student pub. schs., Ft. Worth. Sec. Stewart Title Co., Ft. Worth, 1971-74, Tex. Title Co., Ft. Worth, 1974-75; sec./closer 1st Land Title, Ft. Worth, 1975-78; sales and account exec. Sta.-KPLX, Ft. Worth/Dallas, 1978-83, sales promotion dir. Stas.-KPLX/KLIF, Ft. Worth/Dallas, 1983-85, account exec., 1985-86; local sales mgr. Sta. WTXQ, CBS Radio, Dallas, 1986—. Named Top Salesperson, Susquehanna Broadcasting Co., 1981-83; named to Million Dollar Sales Club, 1983. Mem. Am. Women in Radio and TV (bd. dirs. Ft. Worth chpt. 1980-81), Assn. Broadcasting Execs. Tex. Home: 7017 Meadow Lake Dallas TX 75214 Office: 4131 N Central Expressway Suite 700 Dallas TX 75204

SILINSH, JOAN, publishing company executive; b. Mexico City, Nov. 13, 1937; came to U.S., 1948, naturalized; d. Alson Byron and Carmen Elena (Ramos) Keeler; m. John Silinsh, May 15, 1958 (div. 1979). Student U. Houston, 1955-58; B.A., Pace U., 1969. Asst. promotion mgr. Chem. Engring. Mag., N.Y.C., 1967-69, sales services mgr., 1969-76; assoc. mgr. communications McGraw-Hill, Inc., N.Y.C., 1976-79, mgr. communications, 1979-80, dir. mktg. communications, 1984—; dist. mgr. Internat. Mgmt. Mag., N.Y.C., 1980-84; guest lectr. internat. advt. and promotion Pace U., N.Y.C., 1981—. Contbr. articles to profl. jours. Mem. N.Y. Bus. Press Editors (2d v.p. 1978-79, 1st v.p. 1980-81), Bus./Profl. Advt. Assn., Am. Mktg. Assn., N.Y. Women Communications, Assn. Bus. Publs. (vice chmn. promotion).

SILKOTCH, CHERYL MAE, financial executive, consultant; b. Sioux City, Iowa, Oct. 15, 1948; d. Leland Leroy and Frances Elaine (Beaubien) Masters White; m. Stephen Paul Silkotch, June 1, 1973; children—Stephen Paul IV, Sheri Lynn. Student U. Alaska, 1969-70, Los Angeles Harbor Coll., 1983-84. Lobby desk clk. Polaris Hotel, Fairbanks, Alaska, 1968-69; sec. security Loomis Armored Car, Fairbanks, 1969; sec., asst. mgr. R & M Engring., Fairbanks, 1969-71; sec. acctg. E.W. Hahn, Inc., El Segundo, Calif., 1971-73; sales rep. Tri-Chem Inc., Newark, 1977-81; clk., acctg. cons. Silkotch Enterprises, Lomita, Calif., 1979—; bookkeeper, payroll clk. Snyder Constrn., Anza, Calif., 1981; sec., bookkeeper I. Alexander Wells, Anza, 1980-81; asst. dir. Children's Country Sch., Lomita, Calif., 1979-80. Vice-pres. PTA, Harbor City, Calif., 1981-82, 83-84; modeling coordinator Miss Anza Queen Com., 1980-82. Recipient Outstanding Service awards Lions Club Am., Anza, Calif., 1980, Anza C. of C., 1981; Outstanding Achievement award Los Angeles 10th Dist. PTA, Harbor City, 1983. Mem. Second Amendment Found., North Shore Animal League (Gold Club 1980-84), Anza C. of C. (bookkeeper new memberships 1981-83). Clubs: DeAnza Heritage (Anza); Postal Commemorative Soc. (Norwalk, Conn.). Home and office: 60710 Coyote Canyon Rd Star Route 1 Box 239 Anza CA 92306

SILL, GERTRUDE GRACE, art historian, writer, lecturer; b. Bklyn., Jan. 3, 1927; d. Edwin Joseph and Gertrude (Keating) Grace; m. Davis Andrews Sill, Sept. 9, 1950; children—Andrews, Lucinda. B.A., Smith Coll., 1948; M.A., Wesleyan U., Conn., 1978. Lectr., Met. Mus. Art, N.Y.C., 1975-76, cons., 1978-80; lectr. art history Conn. State Coll., New Haven, 1980-81; adj. prof. art history Fairfield U., Conn., 1978—; curator: George Cope, West Chester's Home Artist, 1978, John Haberle, Master of Illusion, 1985-86. Author: Handbook of symbols in Christian Art, 1975; Master Paintings of the Bible, 1977; contbr. articles to Connoisseur, Antiques, Art in America, Brooks newspapers. Pres., chmn. bd. Peqot Library, Southport, 1977-81; pres. bd. dirs. Westport Community Art Assn., 1954-58; mem. Bridgeport Archtl. Conservancy, 1980-83. Grantee Nat. Endowment Arts, 1978, 85; fellow Morgan Library, N.Y.C., 1976—. Mem. Coll. Art Assn., Assn. Am. Art Historians. Roman Catholic. Avocations: Collecting American 19th century paintings and drawings; travel. Office: Dept Art Fairfield Univ N Benson Rd Fairfield CT 06430

SILLAVAN, NANNIE SUE, nurse; b. Nashville, Ark., Sept. 20, 1934; d. Roy Lee and Martha Pearl (Gathright) King; m. William Donnie Sillavan, June 15, 1962; 1 son, Michael Dewayne. R.N., St. Joseph's Sch. Nursing, 1958. Head nurse St. Joseph Hosp., Hot Springs, Ark., 1958-59, Howard County Meml. Hosp., Nashville, Ark., 1960-63; surgery supr. Hempstead County Hosp., Hope, Ark., 1963-66; sch. nurse Hope Pub. Schs., 1966—; mem. adv. com. Red River Vocat.-Tech. Sch. Nursing, Hope, 1966—, Hempstead County Pub. Health Dept., Hope, 1970—. Sunday sch. tchr. Garrett Meml. Bapt. Ch., Hope, Democrat. Clubs: 3rd Dist. Arts and Crafts (treas. 1977—), Genealogical. Home: Route 1 PO Box 252 Springhill Rd Hope AR 71801

SILLEMAN, PAMELA TOBY, construction company executive; b. Napa, Calif., Mar. 8, 1957; d. Darrell Denver and Dorothy Helen (Rodgers) Toby; m. Glen Mogens Silleman, July 12, 1980. Student Napa Valley Coll., 1975-77; real estate courses King Coll., 1977-78. Fashion coordinator Clothes Hound, Inc., Napa, Calif., 1975-76; mem. pub. relations staff Western Title Co., Napa, 1976-77; realtor Classical Properties, Napa, 1977—; owner, design coordinator Silleman Constrn. Co., Napa, 1980—; design cons. Silleman Designs, Napa, 1982—. Co-founder Napa Valley Republican Bus. Council, 1984. Mem. Nat. Assn. Realtors, Calif. Assn. Realtors, Napa County Bd. Realtors (Outstanding Realtor of Yr. 1983), San Francisco Showplace Square. Republican. Avocations: painting; skiing; tennis. Office: Silleman Constrn 1750 1st St Napa CA 94559

SILLIMAN, ELAINE JOYCE RUBENSTEIN, speech language pathologist, educator; b. Buffalo, June 16, 1938; d. Joseph and Dorothy Fineberg Rubenstein; B.S., Syracuse U., 1960; Ph.D. (NDEA fellow), CUNY, 1976; m. Paul Harris Silliman, Jan. 28, 1961; children—Scott L., Dawn R. Speech-lang. clinician Bronx Mcpl. Hosp. Center, 1960-62; supr. speech-lang. services USPHS community health project Albert Einstein Coll. Medicine, Bronx, 1966-68; clin. supr. Center for Communication Disorders, Hunter Coll., CUNY, 1973-76, prof. Sch. Health Scis., 1976—, dir. communication scis. program, 1981-84, 85—, acting dean Sch. Health Scis., 1984-85, doctoral faculty CUNY program speech and hearing scis., 1984—. Fellow Am. Speech-Lang.-Hearing Assn. (cert. clin. competence); mem. N.Y. Acad. Scis., N.Y. State Speech-Lang.-Hearing Assn. (pres. 1982-84), Westchester Speech-Lang.-Hearing Assn., N.E. Ednl. Research Assn., Sigma Xi. Contbr. articles to profl. jours.; editorial bd. Lang., Speech & Hearing Services in Schools, 1983—. Office: Sch Health Scis Hunter Coll CUNY 425 E 25th St New York NY 10010

SILLS, BEVERLY (MRS. PETER B. GREENOUGH), opera company director, coloratura soprano; b. Bklyn., 1929; d. Morris and Sonia (Bahn) Silverman; grad. public schs.; student voice Estelle Leibling, piano Paolo Gallico, stagecraft Desire Defrere; hon. doctorates Harvard U., N.Y.U., New Eng. Conservatory, Temple U.; m. Peter B. Greenough, 1956; stepchildren—Lindley, Nancy, Diana; children—Meredith, Peter B. Radio debut as Bubbles Silverman on Uncle Bob's Rainbow House, 1933; appeared on Maj. Bowes Capitol Family Hour, 1938-41, Our Gal Sunday; operatic debut Phila. Civic Opera, 1947; toured with Shubert Tours, Charles Wagner Opera Co., 1950, 51; debut with N.Y.C. Opera Co., 1955, as Rosalinda in Die Fledermaus; debut San Francisco Opera, 1953, La Scala, Milan, 1969, Royal Opera, Covent Garden, London, 1971, Met. Opera, N.Y.C., 1975; debut, Paris, 1971; appeared throughout U.S., Europe, S.Am., including Vienna State Opera, Teatro Fenice, Venice, Teatro Colon, Buenos Aires, Deutsche Oper, West Berlin, Teatro San Carlo, Naples, 1966; guest appearances with Boston Symphony, Tanglewood Festival, 1968, 69, Robin Hood Dell, Phila., 1969, N.Y. Philharm., San Francisco Symphony, Cleve. Orch., Phila. Orch.; star roles in Handel's Julius Caesar, Manon, La Traviata, Tales of Hoffman, Lucia di Lammermoor, Roberto Deveraux, Anna Bolena, Maria Stuarda, Siege of Corinth, Thäis, Don Pasquale; gen. dir. N.Y.C. Opera, 1979—; ret. from opera and concert stage, 1980. Named One of America's 25 Most Influential Women in 1977, World Almanac, 1978; recipient Handel medallion, 1973; Pearl S. Buck Women's award, 1979; Medal of Freedom, 1980. Author: Bubbles-A Self-Portrait, 1976. Office: care Edgar Vincent Assos 124 E 40th St New York NY 10016

SILLS, NANCY MINTZ, lawyer; b. N.Y.C., Nov. 3, 1941; d. Samuel and Selma Annette (Kahn) Mintz; m. Stephen J. Sills, Apr. 17, 1966; children—Eric Howard, Ronnie Lynne. B.A., U. Wis., 1962; J.D. cum laude, Albany Law Sch., 1976. Bar: N.Y. 1977, U.S. Dist. Ct. (no. dist.) N.Y. 1977. Asst. editor fin. news Newsweek mag., N.Y.C., 1962-65; staff writer, reporter Forbes mag., N.Y.C., 1965; research assoc. for pub. relations Eastern Airlines, N.Y.C., 1965-67; asst. editor Harper & Row, N.Y.C., 1968-69; free lance writer, editor, N.Y.C. and Albany, 1967-70; confidential law sec. N.Y. State Supreme Ct., Albany, 1976-79; assoc. firm Whiteman, Osterman, & Hanna, Albany, 1979-81, Martin, Noonan, Hislop, Troue, & Shudt, Albany, 1981-83; ptnr. firm Martin, Shudt, Wallace & Sills, Albany, 1984; counsel firm Krolick and DeGraff, Albany, 1984—; asst. counsel N.Y. State Senate, 1983—; dir. Albany Law Sch. Estate Planning Inst., 1979—; cons. The Ayco Corp., 1975. Editor: Reforming American Education, 1969; Up From Poverty, 1968; researcher The Negro Revolution in America, 1963; contbr. articles to mags. Bd. govs. Fedn. Jewish Philanthropies Endowment, 1983—; bd. dirs. Albany Jewish Community Ctr., 1984—. Mem. ABA, N.Y. State Bar Assn., Bar Assn. Albany County, N.Y. Women's Bar Assn., Estate Planning Council Eastern N.Y., Women's Aux. Albany County Med. Soc., Albany Med. Coll. Faculty Wives, Women's Am. O.R.T., B'nai B'rith Women, Phi Beta Kappa, Sigma Epsilon Sigma. Clubs: Colonie Country, Hudson River (Albany). Home: 16 Hiawatha Dr Guilderland NY 12084 Office: Krolick and DeGraff One City Sq Albany NY 12207

SILLS, TONI MARIA, educator, adviser; b. Gravette, Ark., Mar. 27, 1948; d. Nesbert Levert and Bonnie Louise (Brown) Miller; m. Jerry Neal Sills, June 7, 1969; 1 child, Christy Allison. Student Radford Women's Coll., Va., 1966-68, Ark. Tech. U., 1968-69, 73, 84-85; B.A., So. Ill. U., 1973; M.S.E., U. Central Ark., 1977. Cert. tchr., Ark. English tchr. Gardner Jr. High, Russellville, Ark., 1974—; dir. Ark. Jr. High Sch. Journalism workshop, Russellville; workshop leader Ark. High Sch. Journalism Conv., Little Rock, 1985; cons. Ark. State Dept. Edn. Contbr. articles to profl. jours. Named State Semi-finalist NASA Tchr. in Space, 1985; Ark. Writing Project fellow, 1985. Mem. NEA, Ark. Edn. Assn., Russellville Classroom Teaching Assn., Ark. High Sch. Press Advisers Assn., Nat. High Sch. Press Advisers Assn., Columbia Scholastic Press Advisers Assn., Alpha Chi. Avocations: reading; writing; traveling; doll collecting. Home: 33 Dawn Heights Russellville AR 72801 Office: Forrest E Gardner Jr High Sch 1000 S Arkansas Ave Russellville AR 72801

SILLS-LEVY, ELLEN, marketing research executive; b. N.Y.C., Mar. 14, 1942; d. Lewis M. and Diana B. Sills; B.A. cum laude with honors in Econs., Bklyn. Coll., 1963; M.B.A., Columbia U., 1965. Market research analyst Gen. Foods Corp., White Plains, N.Y., 1965-67; v.p., sr. asso. research dir. BBDO, Inc., N.Y.C., 1967-77, etat dir. TEAM/BBDO, Dusseldorf, W. Ger., 1977-78; v.p., mgr. research and bus. devel. Needham, Harper & Steers, Inc., N.Y.C., 1979; v.p., dir. research TBWA, N.Y.C., 1979-80; v.p., dir. communications Citibank, N.Y.C., 1980-83; exec. v.p., ptnr. Bernard Engelhard & Assocs., N.Y.C., 1982-84; pres. Simmons Custom/Fin. Services, N.Y.C., 1985—; guest speaker Am. Mktg. Assn., Bank Mktg. Assn., Bank Adminstrn. Inst.; guest speaker Advt. Research Found., also mem. bd. dirs. Mem. alumni bd. Columbia U. Grad. Sch. Bus. Mem. Fin. Women's Assn. (past pres.) Advt. Women N.Y. (chmn. awards com.), Nat. Women's Econ. Alliance, Internat. Alliance Profl. Execs. Home: 64 E 86th St New York NY 10028 Office: 219 E 42d St New York NY 10017

SILTON, BARBARA J., ednl. center adminstr.; b. Fresno, Calif.; d. Joe and Leota S.; B.A., Calif. State U., 1972; M.A., U. San Francisco, 1980, doctoral candidate in psychology, 1983. Counselor, tchr. Yakima Indian Center, Santa Rosa, Calif., 1974-75; hosp.-home instrn. multi-handicapped Los Angeles Unified Sch. Dist., Berenece Carlson Sch., 1974-80; dir. Noble Ednl. Center, Inc., Woodland Hills, Calif., 1975—, dir. Ednl. Therapy Center and Clinic, 1975—, pres. Noble Ednl. Therapy Found.; cons. pvt. schs., including Montessori Sch. Santa Monica. Mem. Council Exceptional Children, Calif. Assn. Ednl. Therapists. Co-founder Noble Method, remediation system for learning disabilities. Office: 22008 Del Valle St Woodland Hills CA 91364

SILVA, BARBARA VIOLA, account executive, management consultant; b. Trieste, Italy, Sept. 28, 1949; d. Benjamin Stansbury and Luciana (Delise) Davis; m. Lee Roy Cox, Apr. 6, 1970 (div.); 1 son, Anthony Lee; m. 2d, Frank Jesus Silva, Mar. 24, 1981. B.A. in Mktg., San Jose State U., 1972; B.S. in Behavioral Sci., Santa Clara U., 1974. Customer support rep., tech. instr. Rolm Corp., Santa Clara, Calif., 1976-79; exec. v.p. Nor-Cal Pipeline Inc., Fremont, Calif., 1979-82; sr. account exec. Heuristics Search Inc., doing bus. as Patrick & Co., Santa Clara, 1982—. Notary pub. State of Calif., Santa Clara, 1980-84. Mem. Entrepreneurs Alliance, Nat. Assn. Female Execs. (area bd. dirs. 1983—), Fremont C. of C. (pub. affairs com. 1981-83). Democrat. Roman Catholic. Office: Patrick & Co 4633 Old Ironsides Dr Suite 300 Santa Clara CA 95050

SILVA, PHYLLIS C., state official; b. Woonsocket, R.I., May 6, 1928; d. Reuben Ballou and Alice (Carr) Cook; m. J. Camille Peloquin, Sept. 5, 1949 (div. 1973); children—J. Camille, Linda Peloquin Clayton, Ronald, Theodore; m. 2d John L. Silva, June 26, 1977. Student U. R.I., Catholic Tchrs. Coll. Reg. genealogist. Spinner Black Cotton Mill, Blackstone, Mass., 1944-49; lacquer sprayer Brier Mfg. Co., Providence, 1949-56; tchr. Woonsocket Sch. System (R.I.), 1956-67; asst. sec. of state in charge of archives Office of R.I. Sec. of State, Providence, 1967—; coordinator Hist. Records Adv. Bd. R.I., 1976—; lectr. on state archives, 1980—; coordinator Nat. Hist. Publs. and Records, 1976—. Bd. dirs. New Eng. Conservation Ctr., 1978-82. Named Brevet col. Newport Arty. (R.I.), 1976. Mem. R.I. Geneal. Soc. (1st v.p.), Soc. Am. Archivists, Bristol Hist. Soc. Roman Catholic. Office: Sec of State's Office State House Room 43 Providence RI 02903

SILVER, BELLA WOLFSON, day care center exec.; b. N.Y.C., Mar. 10, 1937; d. David Michael and Edith (Bienenstock) Wolfson; B.S., Adelphi U., 1958; postgrad. Bank St. Coll., 1958-59; m. Kenneth A. Silver, Oct. 19, 1958; children—James, Daniel. Kindergarten tchr., N.Y.C., 1958, Madison (Wis.) Public Schs., 1959-61, White Fish Bay (Wis.) Public Schs., 1961-65; nursery sch. tchr., Deerfield, Ill., 1975-77; substitute tchr. Deerfield Public Schs., 1975-77; founder., dir., pres. Deerfield Day Care Center, 1978—; corp. cons. Day Care/Child Care Services, 1983—; pub. speaker on child care to North Shore high schs., 1984. Mem. Deerfield Caucus; active Cub Scouts, Deerfield, Outstanding Service award 1973-77; mem. exec. bd. Jewish United Fund; sec. Parents-Tchrs. Orgn. Recipient award Bahais of Deerfield, 1981; teaching cert., Wis., Ill.; lic. tchr., N.Y.C. Mem. AAUW, Assn. Childhood Edn. Internat., Nat. Assn. Edn. Young Children, Chgo. Assn. Edn. Young Children, Nat. Assn. Female Execs., Deerfield C. of C., Phi Sigma Sigma (Pyramid award 1965). Jewish. Home: 309 Willow Ave Deerfield IL 60015 Office: 445 Pine St Deerfield IL 60015

SILVER, JOYCE ALAINE, business executive, banker, former pharmecutical manufacturing company executive; b. N.Y.C., Dec. 2, 1942; d. Leo and Ida Vera Silver; B.A., Simmons Coll., Adelphi U., 1962; M.S., L.I. U., 1973; Ph.D. candidate Cornell U. Med. Center, N.Y. U. Med. Center, 1973-76; div.; children—Edward Erik, Lisa Sheryl. Research fellow Cornell U.-N.Y. U. Med. Center, 1973-76; supervising engr., plant trouble shooter Ford Motor Co., Dearborn, Mich., 1976-79; with Pfizer, Inc., Bklyn., 1979-82, sr. mfg. supr. diagnostics and sterile products, 1981-82, mgr. materials resource planning, mgr. pharm. warehousing, distbn. ops., 1981-82; v.p. customer service Bankers Trust Co., N.Y.C., 1982-84, pres. contracting corp., L.I., N.Y., 1984—. Lobbyist, Continuation of NSF Funds, 1974; mem. Com. to Re-Elect Carol Berman, Senator, 1979. NIH Fellowship, 1973-76; L.I. U. Teaching Fellowship and Scholarship award, 1971-73. Mem. AAAS, Fedn. Am. Scientists, Engring. Soc. Detroit, N.Y. Acad. Sci., Women's Economic Club Detroit, N.Y. Women's Bus. and Profl. Group, N.Y. Networking.

SILVER, SUSAN BACON, management consultant; b. Los Angeles, Dec. 3, 1950; d. Ralph Frankel and Marilyn Marks; m. Donald Philip Silver. B.S. magna cum laude, U. So. Calif., 1972; M.A., Calif. State Poly. U., 1975. Cert., Calif. Tchr., Walnut Valley Unified Sch. Dist., Walnut, Calif., 1972-77; instr. Calif. State Poly. U., Pomona, 1976-77; adult edn. instr. Los Angeles Unified Sch. Dist., 1977-79; writer, editor for Disney, Glencoe Pub., Goodyear Pub., others, Los Angeles, 1977-79; pub. affairs-communications mgr. aircraft div. Northrop Corp., Hawthorne, Calif., 1979-84, lectr. in field; editor, writer, photographer trade publs. Community Report (12 awards) and Small Bus. Report (7 awards), 1981-83; founder, pres. Positively Organized!, Santa Monica, Calif., 1983—; profl. speaker corps., trade assns., colls., univs. Contbr. to Flowers & Mag., 1985—. Active Richstone Center for Prevention Child Abuse, Hawthorne, Calif., 1980—; vol. Internat. Med. Corps. Mem. Internat. Assn. Bus. Communicators (awards program co-chmn. 1982, hospitality chmn. 1982, Silver 6 Trophy 1982, speaker internat. confs. Montreal and Hawaii 1984), Internat. Platform Assn., So. Calif. Soc. Assn. Execs., Insiders Network (bd. dirs.), Santa Monica Area C. of C. (bd. dirs., chmn. com.), Calif. Press Women (3 awards 1982-83), Western Publs. Assn. (Maggie trophy 1982), Nat. Speakers Assn., Sierra Club, Leads Club. . Office: Positively Organized! 2850 Ocean Park Blvd Suite 300 Santa Monica CA 90405

SILVERBERG, HARRIET ANNE, publicist; b. Washington, Mar. 2, 1937; d. David Eleck and Sophie (Taetle) Snyder; student George Washington U., 1954-55; m. Stanley M. Silverberg, Aug. 28, 1955; children—Denise, Marc. Free-lance public relations work, Washington, 1955-80; advance public relations person Ladybird Johnson Train, 1964; with Smithfield Ham Products (Va.), 1962-75; part-time public relations asst. George Reedy, Lyndon Johnson Adminstrn., 1964-65; with L.N. Hill Co., Rockville, Md., 1968-70; dir. promotion WAVA FM radio, Arlington, Va., 1977-80; pres. Harriet Silverberg

Assos. Potomac, Md., 1980—. Bd. dirs. Washington chpt. Am. Diabetes Assn., 1959—, pres.-elect, nat. bd. dirs., 1975-81, vice chmn. communications com., 1976-77; chmn. publicity Montgomery County Youth Orch., 1975; treas. Congregation Beth El Sisterhood, 1965-70; bd. dirs. United Jewish Appeal Women's Div., 1980-82, Am.-Israeli Cultural Found., 1982—, Nat. Health Council, Washington, 1978-82. Recipient Maurice Protas award Am. Diabetes Assn., 1976. Mem. Public Relations Soc. Am. Democrat. Jewish. Club: Advt. of Washington. Address: 8401 Pittsfield Ct Potomac MD 20854

SILVER-MALYSKA, TARA ELIZABETH, retail store art director, fashion illustrator; b. Washington, Dec. 13, 1959; d. Robert Frances Silver and Cordelia Elizabeth (Foster) Titus; m. Robert Paul Malyska, Aug. 14, 1982. B.F.A., Va. Commonwealth U., 1982; postgrad. U. Houston. Asst. mgr. Country Legend, Alexandria, Va., 1981-82; freelance illustrator, Houston, 1982—; asst. art dir. Weiner's Stores Inc., Houston, 1982—. Mem. Nat. Assn. Female Execs., Art Dirs. Club Houston, Am. Mgmt. Assn. Republican. Episcopalian. Avocations: reading; collecting original art works; racquetball; tennis; swimming; decorating. Office: Weiner's Stores Inc 6005 Westview Houston TX 77252

SILVERMAN, BERNICE GRACE ABEL, steel products executive; b. Chgo., Apr. 19, 1932; d. Jacob Israel and Celia (Surkin) Abel; student U. Ill., U. Chgo., De Paul U., m. William J. Silverman, Mar. 14, 1959; children—Robin Lee Silverman Sturman, Jaci Lynn Friedlander. Owner, operator Best Locker Service, Washington, 1968—; pres., chief operating officer, dir. Best Steel Products, Inc., Washington, 1975—. Active Multiple Sclerosis Soc., Am. Cancer Soc. Mem. Nat. Automatic Merchandising Assn., Internat. Assn. Amusement Parks and Attractions, Internat. Council Shopping Centers, NOW, Nat. Fedn. Bus. and Profl. Women, Nat. Ski Area Assn., Am. Waterpark Assn. Clubs: Hadassah (life), B'nai B'rith (life). Home: 4606 Kenmore Dr NW Washington DC 20007 Office: 5540 Connecticut Ave NW Washington DC

SILVERMAN, BERYL A., professional hypnotist, writer; b. Newark, Aug. 4, 1938; d. Edward Edmund and Ruth (Schlesinger) Sacharow; m. Herbert L. Silverman, Oct. 1, 1967; children—Jennifer Leah, Laurence David. Student County Coll. Morris, 1978. Various secretarial positions, N.Y. N.J., Ohio, 1954-68; asst. dir. Ethical Hypnosis Tng. Ctr., Irvington, N.J., 1968-70; dir. Boonton Area Hypnosis Ctr., N.J., 1975—; bus. mgr. Internat. Soc. Profl. Hypnosis, N.Y.C., 1970-72, exec. dir., 1972-85. Author: Professional Hypnosis Training, vol. I, 1980 (Internat. Soc. Profl. Hypnosis award of Merit 1981), vol. II, 1985. Pres. John Hill Home and Sch. Assn., Boonton, 1979-81; sec. Boonton Band Boosters, 1985-86. Mem. Internat. Soc. Profl. Hypnosis (co-founder 1970, cert., chmn. bd. admissions 1970-85, conf. registration chmn. 1970-84, trustee and bd. dirs. 1970-85, Golden Pendulum award 1974), Assn. to Advance Ethical Hypnosis (membership chmn. 1967-70). Republican. Jewish. Avocations: gardening; handicrafts; reading. Home and office: 218 Monroe St Boonton NJ 07005

SILVERMAN, ELISE BLOOM, lawyer; b. N.Y.C., June 19, 1957; d. Leonard and Annette (Meilman) Bloom; m. Mitchell Sheldon Silverman, Nov. 21, 1982. B.A., U. Chgo., 1979; J.D., Emory U., Atlanta, 1982. Bar: Ga. 1982. Intern fed. defender Fed. Defender Program, Atlanta, 1981-82; assoc. Mitchell, Loggins, Campbell & Elsberry, Atlanta, 1982-84; assoc. Jackson, Lewis, Schnitzler & Krupman, N.Y.C., 1984—; atty. Vol. Lawyers for the Arts, Atlanta, 1982—. Chairperson Alumnae Schs. Com. U. Chgo., 1982-84. Mem. ABA, Ga. Bar Assn. Republican. Home: 20 Deepdale Dr Great Neck NY Office: Jackson Lewis Schnitzler & Krupman 261 Madison Ave New York NY

SILVERMAN, GAIL ANN, nurse, consultant; b. Los Angeles, Mar. 19, 1955; d. Stanley Irwin and Rita B. (Alexander) Silverman. A.A. in Liberal Arts, Los Angeles Valley Coll., 1974; A.A. in Nursing, 1976. Sales, asst. mgr. Bullock's, Sherman Oaks, Calif., 1972-75; nurse aide Los Angeles New Hosp., 1975-76; critical care nurse Motion Picture and TV Fund Hosp., Calabassas, Calif., 1982-84; critical care nurse Cedars-Sinai Med. Center, Los Angeles, 1976—; critical care cons. Motion Picture and TV Fund Hosp., Calabasses, 1982-84, critical care cons., 1982-84; ednl. cons. ARC, 1985—; legis. spl. cons. Am. Fedn. Nurses, Los Angeles, 1983 ; critical care cons. Am. Fedn. Nurses, Los Angeles, 1983—; ednl. cons. critical care Save a Heart Found., Los Angeles, 1984-86. Instr., Am. Heart Assn., Los Angeles, 1976—; vol. ARC, Los Angeles, 1976—, relief diaster supr., 1986—; mem. Jewish Labor Com., Los Angeles, 1983-85; Calif. state bd. mem. Nurses Alliance Calif., 1983-86; relief disater coordinator Multi-AID, 1986—; nursing supr. Calif. Spl. Olympics Summer Games, 1986—. Mem. Am. Assn. Critical Care Nurses, San Fernando Valley Assn. Critical Care Nurses, Am. Heart Assn. Democrat. Jewish. Home: 4424 Woodman Ave #103 Sherman Oaks CA 91423 Office: Cedars Sinai Med Center 8700 Beverly Blvd Los Angeles CA 90048

SILVERMAN, JUDITH, human resources administrator, author, consultant; b. Bklyn., Aug. 26, 1933; d. David and Shirley Beatrice (Maltz) Marks; m. Myron Bernard Silverman, July 3, 1955; 1 son, Brian Scott. B.A. cum laude, Bklyn. Coll., 1960; M.L.S., Pratt Inst., 1963; P.D., L.I.U. 1985. Sec. Fairchild Publs., N.Y.C., 1954-56; tchr., librarian N.Y.C. Bd. Edn., Bklyn., 1956-62; sr. librarian Bklyn. Pub. Library, 1964-68, Queens Borough Pub. Library, Queens, N.Y., 1973-76; asst. dir. personnel Baldwin (N.Y.) Pub. Library, 1976-80; exec. mgr. for personnel Bd. Cooperative Ednl. Services Nassau County, Westbury, N.Y., 1980—; cons. books R. R. Bowker Co., N.Y.C., 1971—. Author: Index to Collective Biographies for Young Readers, 1970, 3rd edit., 1979. Mem. N.Y. State/Sch. Personnel Adminstrs., L.I. Assn. Sch. Personnel Adminstrs., N.Y. Library Assn. (mem. com.), Nassau County Library Assn. (mem. com.), Beta Phi Mu. Office: Bd Cooperative Educational Services of Nassau County Valentines and The Plain Rds Westbury NY 11590

SILVERMAN, MARYLIN A., advertising agency executive; b. N.Y.C., Mar. 15, 1941; d. Morris George and Sophie (Betesh) Adler; m. Joseph Elias Silverman, May 30, 1965; children—Lisa, Jennifer. B.A., Ind. U.-Bloomington, 1962; student Baruch Grad. Sch. Bus., CUNY, 1963-65. Research analyst Compton Advt., N.Y.C., 1962-63; account research supr. Foote, Cone & Belding, N.Y.C., 1963-68; self-employed market research cons., N.Y.C., 1968-78; research group head Ogilvy & Mather, Inc., N.Y.C., 1978-82; sr. v.p., sr. assoc. research dir. Backer & Spielvogel, Inc., N.Y.C., 1982—; cons. Am. Assn. Advt. Agys., 1980-81, Boys Clubs Am., N.Y.C., 1984-85. Co-author: Marketing Review, 1980. Mem. exec. council Washington Sq. Park Council, 1969-74; mem. exec. bd. Friends Sem. PTA, N.Y.C., 1980-82. Mem. Am. Mktg. Assn., Women in Communications, Am. Assn. Advt. Agys. (research com.). Grenwich Ho. Potters and Sculptors Assn. Office: Backer & Spielvogel Inc 11 W 42d St New York NY 10036

SILVERMAN, WENDY B., technical writer; b. Phila., Oct. 17, 1956; d. Herman and Paulin (Wexler) S. Student Douglas Coll., 1974-76; B.A., William Paterson Coll., 1979. Methods and procedures analyst, personal methods and procedures analyst to v.p. real estate Prentice Hall, Englewood Cliffs, N.J., 1979-81; cost analyst Gen. Bearing, West Nyack, N.Y., 1981-82; cons. ins. systems, 1982-83; cons. GEISCO, Piscataway, N.J., 1983-85; tech. writer On-Line Software Internat., Fort Lee, N.J., 1985—. Mem. Nat. Assn. Female Execs. Democrat. Jewish. Avocations: piano; recorder; nutrition and homeopathy; weight training; swimming. Home: 333 Canterbury Ln Wyckoff NJ 07481 Office: On-Line Software Internat 2 Executive Dr Fort Lee NJ 07024

SILVERSTEIN, ELIZABETH BLUME, lawyer; b. Newark, Nov. 2, 1892; d. Selig and Goldie (Arahowitz) Blume; m. Max Silverstein, Aug. 23, 1934 (dec. 1955); 1 son, Nathan Royce. LL.B., N.J. Law Sch. (now Rutgers U. Sch. Law), 1911. Bar: N.J. 1913, U.S. Supreme Ct. 1921, U.S. Tax Ct. 1960. First woman lawyer in N.J. in practice law, 1913, 1st woman in N.J. to represent defendant, unassisted in homicide case, 1916, 1st woman on legal adv. bd. of Draft Bd. during World War I, Essex County, N.J. Del. First Am. Jewish Congress, 1916, 23, exec. bd. dirs., mem. immigration com., 1923, del. 1st World Jewish Congress, 1936; leader Balfour parade, Newark. Mem. Women's Lawyers Assn. (v.p. 1920s), ABA, Essex County Bar Assn., Am. Judicature Soc., N.J. State Bar Assn., Nat. Assn. Women Lawyers (N.J. state del.). Republican. (del. Republican conv. 1932). Club: Heinberg Rep. (pres. 1920's). Lodges: Ind. Order Brith Abraham (1st woman to serve nat. order exec. positions, asst. to Grand Master, chmn. Jewish rights, chmn. com. on disability), Louis D. Brandies Lodge (pres. 1920s). Home: 62 Osborne Terr Newark NJ 07108

SILVERSTEIN, SUSAN SOLOMON, human service consultant; b. Bklyn. Dec. 15, 1951; d. Herbert and Gerry (Bloom) Solomon; B.A. in Psychology, Hofstra U., 1973; M.S.W., Adelphi U., 1977; m. Clifford Silverstein, Mar. 15, 1980. Intake coordinator Woodward Sch. for Emotionally Disturbed, Freeport, N.Y., 1972-73; clin. coordinator Nassau House, Inc., Mineola, N.Y., 1976-78; dir. Women's Center of Central Nassau, Franklin Square, 1974-76; human service cons. Eli Silverstein Inc./Feetstreet Ltd., Huntington, N.Y., 1978—; founder, dir. Littlefolks Learning Center, 1982—; owner, dir. Kids Club Inc., 1985—. Recipient award for spl. achievement in personel motivation and communication Women's Center of Central Nassau, 1980. Mem. Nat. Assn. Female Execs. Home: Wooley Ln E Great Neck NY 11021 Office: 10 New St Huntington NY 11743

SILVERSTONE, DOROTHY LITTMAN, public relations executive, philanthropist; b. N.Y.C., Sept. 19, 1903; d. Samuel and Sarah Gertrude (Neustadt) Littman; m. Murray Silverstone, May 23, 1928 (dec. 1969); children—Marilyn R., Barbara E., Susan H. B.A., Fordham U., 1984. Community leader, founder Garden Party for Brit. War Relief, N.Y., 1941; founder Sarah Delano Roosevelt Children's Nursing Home, London; organizer Children to Palestine, Christian Jewish Com.; producer The Magnetic Tide, 1949, Vision of Peace in Painting; pres. Internat. Cultural Ctrs. Youth, Jerusalem, and U.S. Mem. Am. Mothers Inc. Jewish. Clubs: Scarsdale Womans, Brach Point. Avocations: landscape architecture; photography; writing; creating mediums for better human relations. Home: 128 Central Park S New York NY 10019 Office: Internat Cultural Ctrs Youth Inc Exec Office 128 Central Park S New York NY 10019

SILVERTHORN, PATRICIA MARIE, accounting manager; b. San Jose, Calif., Nov. 26, 1951; d. Leo Henry and Marguerite Marie (Arioto) S.; m. David John Botto, May 8, 1982. B.A. in Advt., San Jose State U., 1975; student U. So. Calif., 1979-80; Calif. State U.-Dominguez Hills, 1982-85. Acct., Arete Assocs., Sherman Oaks, Calif., 1979-80; supr. acctg. contracts Dynamics Technology, Inc., Torrance, Calif., 1980-85; cons. T.A. Carlson & Co., C.P.A.s, Springfield, Va., 1986; pvt. practice cons. ORI, Inc., Rockville, Md., 1985-86, Sci. Tech., Inc., Gaithersberg, Md., 1985-86. Mem. Nat. Contract Mgmt. Assn. Democrat. Office: ORI Inc 1375 Piccard Dr Rockville MD 20850

SILVEY, DORRY ANN, teacher, writer; b. Port Jervis, N.Y., Oct. 11, 1951; d. Kirkwood Allan and Eleanor Elizabeth (McCormack) Loske; m. Joseph Alexander Silvey, Sept. 17, 1976. A.A.S., Fulton-Montgomery Community Coll., 1971; B.S., SUNY-Brockport, 1973; M.Ed., Coll. St. Rose, Albany, N.Y., 1976. Cert. tchr., N.Y. Tutor Assn. Retarded Children, Johnstown, N.Y., 1975-76; tchr. spl. edn. Gloversville Sch. Dist., N.Y., 1976—; tchr. rep. Gloversville Com. of Handicapped, 1978-80. Mem. Internat. Women's Writing Guild, Edna St. Vincent Millay Soc. Avocations: sailing; gardening; weaving; flower arranging; transcendental meditation. Home: Box 174 Star Route Hagaman NY 12086

SIM, ELIZABETH ANN, commercial artist, administrative assistant; b. Bristol, Conn. A.A., Katharine Gibbs Sch., Boston, 1963; student Art Sch. U. Hartford, 1963-66, 74; student Am. Airlines Coll., 1963; student Graphic Arts and Advt., Tunxis Coll., 1974-75. Adminstrv. asst., head librarian to math., scis., edn. faculty Trinity Coll., Hartford, Conn., 1963-66; copywriter and illustrator Bowling Green State U. (Ohio), 1971, 72; research asst., common stock librarian Aetna Life and Casualty, Hartford, 1972, 73, comml. artist for pub. relations and advt., 1973, 74, sr. prodn. mgr., buyer pub. relations and advt., 1974, 75; adminstrv. asst. to v.p. Analytic Scis. Corp., Reading, Mass., 1982-83; profl. free lance illustrator, 1971-81. Writer feature articles Toledo Blade, 1971, 72; researcher nutritional relationship to blood sugar conditions; editor newsletter on diet and recipes, 1976; paintings shown group exhbns. New Eng., 1977-82. Founder nutrition council and help center for hypoglycemia, 1975-76; pres. Hopewell Sch. PTO, Glastonbury, Conn., 1977; bd. mem. Town Adv. Com., Glastonbury, 1977; ambassador to Israel, Germany and Eng., The Friendship Force, 1976, 79, 84 pres. Baton chpt., 1984; pub. relations coordinator, sex edn. tchr. elem. grades Glastonbury Pub. Schs., 1976-77; asst. coach and publicity dir. Lynnfield Girls' Softball, 1978-81; arts and crafts instr. sr. citizens and civic groups, Boston area, 1981-83; exec. bd. Women's Fellowship, treas., publicity dir. South Glastonbury Congl. Ch., 1974-78; leader Conn. Valley Council Girl Scouts U.S.A., 1974-78; speaker ch., bus. groups, clubs. Grantee, Environ. Studies Ctr., Bowling Green, 1971-72; cited for ind. research Huxley Inst., 1974-76; Best Speaking award, Dale Carnegie Inst., 1974. Clubs: Lynnfield Newcomers, Northeast Tennis Ctr. (tournament team mem. 1978-79), Thompson Country, Lynnfield Art Guild, Glastonbury Hills Country, Pike Brook Swim and Tennis.

SIMKIN, DIANA SUE, parent education company executive; b. Suffern, N.Y., Feb. 13, 1949; d. Edward R. and Sherli (Cohen) S.; m. David Kritchman, May 23, 1976. B.A., Cornell U., 1972; M.A., NYU, 1978. Cert. Am. Soc. for Psycho-prophylaxis in Obstetrics/Lamaze, 1980. Dancer, Rudy Perez Co., Phyllis Rose Co. and Lenore Lattimer, 1972-80; dir. The Elisabeth Bing Ctr. for Parents, N.Y.C., 1976-82; co-founder Family Focus, Inc., N.Y.C., 1982, dir., 1983—. Author: The Complete Pregnancy Exercise Program, 1980; The Complete Baby Exercise Program, 1985. Mem. Am. Women's Econ. Devel. Council, ASPO/Lamaze. Avocations: literature; travel. Office: Family Focus Inc 1370 Lexington Ave New York NY 10128

SIMKUS, BARBARA ANN, limousine service executive; b. Oak Park, Ill., Oct. 9, 1938; d. Oldrich and Libuse Sylvia (Kocian) Skaryd; m. Robert Peter Simkus, May 24, 1958; children—Karen, Sharyl, Laura, Robert Peter, Scott. Grad. high sch., Cicero, Ill. Sec., Martin Fan & Blower Co., Cicero, 1955-59; home-typist Monarch Printing Co., Chgo., 1967-79; reservationist West Suburban Limousine Service, Carol Stream, Ill., 1975-80, bus. mgr., 1980—. Editor Carol Stream News, 1967-79 (Village award 1979). Co-chmn., sec. Carol Stream 25th Anniversary Commn., 1983-84. Named Citizen of Yr., Community Improvement, Carol Stream, 1972, Spl. Citizen of Yr., Community Improvement, 1981. Mem. Carol Stream Hist. Soc. (sec. 1974—), Carol Stream Bus. and Industry (v.p. 1983—). Republican. Roman Catholic. Club: Carol Stream Woman's (pres. 1980-84). Avocations: bowling; reading; stichery. Home: 841 Papoose Ct Carol Stream IL 60188

SIMMONDS, MARY ANNE, oncologist; b. Danville, Pa., Nov. 16, 1949; d. Henry T. and Harriet Anne Lynn S.; A.B., Smith Coll., 1971; M.D., Med. Coll. Pa., 1975; m. Richard W. Stewart, June 7, 1975; 1 child, Anne Whitaker. Resident in internal medicine Geisinger Med. Center, Danville, Pa. 1975-78; fellow in hematology Thomas Jefferson U., Phila., 1978-80; fellow in oncology Hershey Med. Center (Pa.), 1980-81; asst. prof. oncology Pa. State U. Med. Coll., Hershey, 1981—. Bd. dirs. Pa. div. Am. Cancer Soc., 1981—. Am. Cancer Soc. jr. faculty fellow, 1981-84; Kate Hurd Mead fellow, 1982-83; diplomate Am. Bd. Internal Medicine. Fellow ACP; mem. AMA, Am. Fedn. Clin. Research, Central Pa. Oncology Group, Sigma Xi, Alpha Omega Alpha. Republican. Presbyterian. Club: Jr. League Harrisburg. Home: 1811 Warren St New Cumberland PA 17070 Office: Hershey Med Center Hershey PA 17033

SIMMONS, ADELE SMITH, college president; b. Lake Forest, Ill., June 21, 1941; d. Hermon Dunlap and Ellen I. (Thorne) Smith; m. John L. Simmons; children—Ian, Erica, Kevin. B.A., Radcliffe Coll., 1963; Ph.D., Oxford U., 1969; L.H.D. (hon.), Lake Forest Coll., 1976, Amherst Coll., 1977, Franklin Pierce Coll., 1978, U. Mass., 1982. Dean, Jackson Coll., Tufts U., Medford, Mass., 1970-72; dean of student affairs Princeton U., N.J., 1972-77, asst. prof. history, 1972-77; pres. Hampshire Coll., Amherst, Mass., 1977—; mem. council Internat. Exchange of Scholars, 1982-85; dir. Affiliated Pubs., Boston, Marsh and McLennan Co., N.Y.C., New Eng. Telephone Co., Boston. Author: Modern Mauritius, 1980. Contbr. articles to profl. jours. Chmn. bd. trustees Carnegie Found. for Advancement of Teaching, Princeton, 1978—; trustee Union of Concerned Scientists, Washington, 1983—, World Policy Inst., N.Y.C., 1983—; commr. Pres.'s Commn. on World Hunger, Washington, 1978-80. Mem. Council Fgn. Relations, Phi Beta Kappa. Clubs: Cosmopolitan, Princeton (N.Y.C.). Office: Hampshire Coll Amherst MA 01002

SIMMONS, ANNA MORGAN, retail furniture merchant, interior designer; b. Birmingham, Ala., Nov. 23, 1953; d. Albert Rufus and Irene Elizabeth (Mitchell) Morgan; m. William Cris Simmons, Sept. 28, 1975; children—Jessica Brie, William Courtney. B.S., U. Tenn., 1975. Interior designer Flack's Carriage House, Memphis, 1975-78; mgr. office Bristol Family Dental Practice, Tenn., 1980-83; owner, operator Simmons' Carriage House, Inc., 1984—. Treas., v.p. Bristol Ballet Co., Va., 1984-85, pres. 1985-86. Republican. Episcopalian. Avocations: swimming; aerobics; sewing; reading. Home: 619 Euclid Ave Bristol VA 24201 Office: Simmons' Carriage House Inc 1135 Volunteer Pkwy Bristol TN 37620

SIMMONS, CAROLINE THOMPSON, civic worker; b. Denver, Aug. 22, 1910; d. Huston and Caroline Margaret (Cordes) Thompson; A.B., Bryn Mawr Coll., 1931; M.A. (hon.), Amherst Coll., 1981; m. John Farr Simmons, Nov. 11, 1936; children—John Farr (dec.), Huston T., Malcolm M. Chmn. women's com. Corcoran Gallery Art, 1965-66; vice chmn. women's com. Smithsonian Assos., 1969-71; pres. Decatur House Council, 1963-71, Alianza Ibero-Americana, 1972-74; mem. bd. Nat. Theatre, 1979-80; trustee Washington Opera, 1955-65; bd. dirs. Fgn. Student Service Council, 1956-79; mem. Washington Home Bd., 1955-60; bd. dirs. Smithsonian Friends of Music, 1977-79; commr. Nat. Mus. Am. Art, 1979—; trustee Folger Shakespeare Library, 1979—, Dacor-Bacon House Found., 1977—; mem. Washington bd. Am. Mus. in Britain, 1970—; bd. dirs. Found. Preservation of Historic Georgetown, 1975—; trustee Amherst Coll., 1979—81; v.p. internat. council Mus. Modern Art, N.Y.C., 1978—; mem. council Phillips Collection, 1982—; bd. dirs. Alliance Francaise. Mem. Soc. Women Geographers. Presbyterian. Clubs: Sulgrave, Chevy Chase. Address: 1508 Dumbarton Rock Ct Washington DC 20007

SIMMONS, DIANE EILEEN, corporate executive; b. New Smyrna Beach, Fla., Jan. 28, 1950; d. George Andrew and Carolyn Margaret (Cross) Naser; A.A., Daytona Beach Community Coll., 1971; student U. N.C., 1978, U. South Fla., 1980; m. Paul L. Simmons, June 2, 1973; children—Thomas David (dec.), Paula Kay. Pres., Fla. Trade Publ., Daytona Beach, Fla., 1971-74; project engr. Pollak & Skan Inc., Rosemont, Ill., 1977-78; mgr. S.E. region, 1978-79; exec. dir. Internat. Soc. Pharm. Engrs., Tampa, Fla., 1979-81; exec. dir. Seminars, Inc., Tampa, Fla., 1978-84; exec. sec., treas. ROST Inc., 1977—; pres. Regulatory Info. Systems, Inc., 1983-84; sec.-treas. Tam-Rock Devel., Inc. Mem. Parenteral Drug Assn., ASME, Nat. Assn. Female Execs. Republican. So. Baptist. Pub., FACT mag., 1971-74; editor Pharm. Engring. Jour., 1979-81, Bio Process Engring., 1984-85. Office: 3802 W Ehrlich Rd Tampa FL 33624

SIMMONS, DONNA MARIE, histotechnologist, neurobiology researcher; b. Hartford, Conn., Oct. 13, 1943; d. John Henry and Ellen Louise (Meehl) Strayer; m. Corvin Gale Simmons, Sept. 17, 1964. Student U. Wash., Western Wash. State U., Tacoma Gen. Hosp. Sch. Med. Tech. Lab. technician U. Wash. Med. Sch., 1964; histologic technician Northgate Med. Lab., Seattle, 1964-67; research technologist Regional Primate Research Ctr., U. Wash., 1967-82; research asst. Devel. Neurobiology Lab. Salk Inst., La Jolla, Calif., 1982-85; sr. technician Neural Systems Lab. Salk Inst., 1985—; cons., lectr. in field. Author tech. articles, revs. in field; mem. editorial bd. Jour. Histotech.; lead sci. del. to People's Rep. of China, 1986. Recipient various service awards; best non-clin. pub. in field, 1985. Mem. Am. Soc. Clin. Pathologists (affiliate), Wash. State Histology Soc. (past pres., histology liaison Am. Soc. Med. Tech.), Nat. Soc. Histotech. (charter mem., regional dir. 1980-82, jucicial chair 1983-86), Calif. Soc. Histotech., Assn. Women in Sci. (San Diego charter mem., dir. 1985-86), Soc. for Neuroscience, Swiss Soc. for Histotechnology, N.Y. Acad. Sci., NOW. Office: 10010 N Torrey Pines Rd La Jolla CA 92037

SIMMONS, DORIS JEANETTE, chiropractic clinic executive; b. Tuscaloosa, Ala., May 22, 1949; d. Earnest Joseph and Elma Ree (Simpson) Watkins; m. William Van Simmons, May 8, 1971; children—Susan, Tricia, Doris, Ashley. Grad. phys. therapy asst. Tex. Chiropractic Coll., Padadena, Tex., 1975; grad. chiropractic asst. Parker Chiropractic Research, Ft. Worth, 1977; student U. Ala.-Tuscaloosa, 1976-77, Internat. Acad. of Neuro-Vascular Disease, Atlanta, 1980, Nat. Coll. Chiropractic, Lombard, Ill., 1982. Fashion model, 1968—; telephone operator S. Central Bell, Tuscaloosa, 1966-69, service analyst, 1969-71; exec. dir. Simmons' Chiropractic Clinic, Tuscaloosa, 1980—. Appeared in TV commls. Leader Tombigbee council Girl Scouts U.S.A., Tuscaloosa, 1976—. Named Chiropractic Wife of Yr., Ala. State Chiropractic Assn., 1983. Mem. Am. Chiropractic Aux., Ala. State Chiropractic Aux. (1st v.p. 1978-80, pres., 1980-82, parliamentarian 1982-84, raffle chmn. 1985—), Internat. Chiropractic Research Exchange, Nat. Assn. Female Execs. Episcopalian. Club: Soc. Fine Arts (Tuscaloosa). Avocations: modeling; tennis; dancing. Home: 17-709 Northwood Lake Northport AL 35476 Office: Simmons Chiropractic Clinic 2602 7th St Tuscaloosa AL 35401

SIMMONS, ELLAMAE, allergist; b. Mt. Vernon, Ohio, Mar. 26, 1919; d. Augustus Lawrence and Ella Sophia (Cooper) Simmons; R.N., Hampton Inst., 1940; B.S., Ohio State U., 1948, M.A., 1950; postgrad. Meharry Med. Coll., 1954-55; M.D., Howard U., 1959. Intern. Wayne County (Mich.) Gen. Hosp., Eloise, 1959-60, resident, 1960-62; resident U. Colo. Med. Center, 1962-63, resident in chest medicine Nat. Jewish Hosp., 1964, resident in allergy, 1965; psychiat. nurse Central State Hosp., Petersburg, Va., 1940-41; allergist Permanente Med. Group Kaiser Found. Hosp., San Francisco, 1966—; mem. admissions com. U. Calif. at San Francisco Sch. Medicine, 1974-78. Chmn. No. Calif. Mut. Real Estate Investment Trust, 1967-68. Served with nurses corps U.S. Army, 1942-46. Mem. Am. Acad. Allergy, Am. Coll. Allergy, Am. Assn. Clin. Allergy and Immunology, John Hale Med. Assn., AMA, Nat., Calif., San Francisco med. assns., Am. Med. Womens Assn., Am. Lung Assn., Am. Thoracic Soc. Unitarian. Home: 3711 Clay St San Francisco CA 94118 Office: 2200 O'Farrell St San Francisco CA 94115

SIMMONS, GAIL LINDSAY, lawyer; b. N.Y.C., June 15, 1949; d. James Lambert Simmons and Jacqueline (Chambers) Cook; m. Allen Howard Feldman, Jan. 5, 1980; children—Andrew Simmons, Thomas Simmons. Student U. London, 1968, Harvard U., 1970; B.A., Carnegie-Tech., Pitts., 1971; J.D., Case Western Res. U., Cleve., 1974. Bar: D.C. 1975, Ohio 1974, others. Law clk. Thurlow Smoot, Cleve., 1972-74; atty. U.S. Customs, Washington, 1974-75, U.S. Dept. Labor, Washington, 1975-79; asst. corp. counsel D.C. Govt., Washington, 1979-81; ptnr. Cotten, Day & Doyle, Washington, 1981—; fiduciary appointments D.C. Superior Ct., Washington, 1983—. Mem. Jr. League Washington, Don't Tear It Down, Washington, Preservation of Assateague Nat. Seashore (Va.). Mem. ABA, Fed. Bar Assn., D.C. Bar Assn., Trial Lawyers Assn. Am. Republican. Presbyterian. Home: 3708 Morrison St NW Washington DC 20015 Office: Cotten Day & Doyle 1899 L St NW Washington DC 20036

SIMMONS, HELEN MARIE, govt. ofcl.; b. Beaver City, Nebr., Aug. 22, 1920; diploma Lincoln (Nebr.) Sch. Commerce, 1938; m. Robert Owen Simmons, Oct. 5, 1947 (dec. Jan. 1979). Various secretarial positions, 1941-42; with Dept. Agr., 1942—, adminstrv. asst. Office Gen. Counsel, Shawnee Mission, Kans. and Kansas City, Mo., 1966-85; ret.; adminstr. Overland Park Christian Ch., Kans., 1985— (part time). Recipient Superior Service award Dept. Agr., 1964. Mem. Assn. Legal Adminstrs., Mem. Christian Ch. (Disciples of Christ). Home: 12021 W 66th St Shawnee KS 66216 Office: Overland Park Christian Ch 7600 W 75th St Overland Park KS 66204

SIMMONS, JANICE K., communications consultant; b. Johnstown, Pa., Jan. 16, 1951; d. Elnor J. Simmons. B.A. in English and Music, U. Pitts., 1972, postgrad. 1974-77, cert. personnel adminstrn. Grad. Sch. Bus., 1983. Staff writer and editor Pa. Electric Co./GPU, Johnstown, 1972-74, 74-76, dir. internal communication, 1976-78; mgr. employee communication Koppers Co., Inc., Pitts., 1978-81; sr. communications cons. Johnson & Higgins, Pitts., 1981-84; asst. v.p., communications mgr., 1984—. Mem. pub. relations com. Greater Pitts. Campfire Girls, 1983; advisor Internat. Order of Rainbow Girls, Pitts., 1980, 81; bd. dirs. Greater Johnstown YWCA, 1976, 77. Recipient Southwest Pa. Communications awards United Way, 1981. Mem. Internat. Assn. Bus. Communicators (v.p. membership 1981, dir. 1979-82, 84, Golden Triangle award of Excellence 1980, 82), Am. Assn. Personnel Adminstrs., Pitts. Personnel Assn., Am. Soc. Profl. and Exec. Women. Office: Johnson & Higgins of PA Inc 2600 One PPG Pl Pittsburgh PA 15222

SIMMONS, JEAN, actress; b. London, Eng., Jan. 31, 1929; d. Charles and Winifred Ada (Loveland) Simmons; ed. Orange Hill Sch., Burnt Oak, London; m. Stewart Granger, Dec. 20, 1950 (div. June 1960); 1 dau. Tracy; m. 2d, Richard Brooks, Nov. 1, 1960; 1 dau., Kate. Motion picture actress, appearing in English and Am. films, including Great Expectations, Black Narcissus, Hamlet, The Actress, Guys and Dolls, Young Bess, Adam and Evelyn, Big Country, 1958; Home Before Dark, 1958; Spartacus, Elmer Gantry, 1959; The Grass Is Greener, 1960; All the Way Home, 1963; Rough Night in Jericho; Divorce American Style; The Happy Ending; also theatre appearance A Little Night Music, Phila. and on tour, 1974; appeared in TV mini-series The Dain Curse, 1978, A Small Killing, 1981, Valley of the Dolls, 1981, The Thornbirds (Emmy award 1983). Office: care Morgan Maree 6363 Wilshire Blvd Los Angeles CA 90048

SIMMONS, LORETTA BLAIR, utility contractor; b. Hilton, N.Y., Jan. 16, 1926; d. F. Alvin Blair and I. Laura (Batty) Quinn; m. Eldon M. Simmons, Nov. 28, 1943. Ptnr. Alvin Blair & Co., Rochester, N.Y., 1953-58; v.p.-treas. Blair Supply Corp., Rochester, 1958-70, pres., treas., 1970—. Mem. Nat. Utility Contractors Assn. (nat. pres. 1985-86, Ditchdigger of Yr. 1984). Home and Office: Blair Supply Corp 785 Beahan Rd Rochester NY 14624

SIMMONS, MARY RUTH, computer specialist; b. Waldorf, Md., Apr. 7, 1925; d. Henry Dyer and Bertha Evelyn (Cooke) Middleton; student Am. U., 1967, Auburn U., 1977—; m. David Martin Simmons, June 26, 1943; children—David Martin, Robert Michael, Thomas Wayne, Carol Ann, Frank Paul, John Edward. Sec., Dept. Treasury, CSC, Washington, 1942-51; with Middleton & Middleton, Waldorf, Md., 1951-59; with Tri County Fed. Savs. & Loan Assn., Waldorf, 1959-65, asst. mng. officer, 1964-65; programmer, systems analyst USAF, Bolling AFB, Washington, 1966-70; computer specialist, Air Force Data Systems Design Center, Gunter AFS, Montgomery, Ala., 1970-84, chief software office, Washington, 1984—, team leader, 1979—. Mem. Assn. Computing Machinery, Data Processing Mgmt. Assn., Federally Employed Women (charter pres.). Republican. Roman Catholic. Clubs: Ballroom Dance (charter pres.), Toastmistress. Home: 4940 Rodman St NW Washington DC 20016 Office: Washington Area Computer Center (MAC) Andrews AFB MD 20331

SIMMONS, MONICA LESLIE, television executive; b. Washington, Aug. 19, 1958; d. Charles William and Sheilah Antoinette (Forsythe) S. B.A., Howard U., 1982. Advt. mgr. Heldref Publs., Washington, 1983; program asst. WDVM-TV, Washington, 1984-85, program adminstr., 1985—. Mem. Nat. Acad. TV Arts and Scis. Democrat. Episcopalian. Avocations: reading; ice skating; sewing. Office: WDVM-TV 4001 Brandywine St NW Washington DC 20016

SIMMONS, ROBERTA MILLBERRY, public school educator, educational consultant; b. Peabody, Mass., Oct. 15, 1926; d. Harold Kirk Edward and Alice Malcome (Parker) Millberry; div.; children—Steven Parker, Susan Carol, Sharon Alice. B.S., U. N.H., 1947; Ed.M., Salem State Coll., 1972; Ed.D., Boston U., 1984. Reading edn. specialist. Intermediate grade tchr. Wakefield Pub. Schs., Mass., 1966-85, high sch. reading specialist, 1985—; state gifted children coordinator Am. Mensa Ltd., Boston, 1978—; exec. dir. Millberry Assocs., Wakefield, 1985—. Editor EDUDATA newsletter, 1985; monthly columnist on gifted children Boston Mensa Beacon, 1978—. Bd. dirs. Eastern Middlesex Council for Children, Wakefield, 1978-85, sec. bd., 1984, recipient cert. of appreciation, 1985. Mem. Assn. for Supervision and Curriculum Devel., Mass. Assn. for Devel. Individual Potential, Mass. Tchrs. Assn., NEA, Nat. Assn. for Gifted Children, Ednl. Press Assn. Am., Nat./State Leadership Tng. Inst. on Gifted and Talented, Mensa, Phi Delta Kappa, Pi Lambda Theta. Avocations: reading, writing. Office: Millberry Assocs PO Box 1753 Wakefield MA 01880

SIMMONS, SHARON FALLER, journalist, advertising executive; b. Toledo, Ohio, Sept. 5, 1940; d. John A. and Shirley F. (Banks) Faller; m. Alan D. Simmons, Nov. 10, 1962 (div. 1980). B.B.A., U. Toledo, 1962. Media buyer Beeson-Reichert, Inc., Toledo, 1965-68; continuity dir. Sta.-WDHO-TV, Toledo, 1968; free lance writer, Toledo, 1968-75; publs. dir. Wendt Rotsinger Kuehnle, Inc., Toledo, 1979—; editor, pub. Village Voice of Ottawa Hills, 1975—. Com. chmn. Women's Opera Guild, Toledo, 1971-77; exec. bd. Sunset House Aux. Recipient Exemplar award Ohio State Bd. Edn., Columbus, 1980. Mem. Am. Advt. Fedn. (past 5th dist. gov., Medal of Merit, 1982); Sigma Delta Chi. Republican. Lutheran. Clubs: Advt. of Toledo (pub. editor 1972—, Sharon award 1980), Press of Toledo (hon. bd. govs.). Office: Wendt Rotsinger Kuehnle Inc 3450 W Central Ave Toledo OH 43606

SIMMONS, SUZANNE ISABELLE, educator; b. Akron, Ohio, Nov. 3, 1941; d. Willie Fate and Virgin Hazel (Varner) S.; B.A., Ohio U., Athens, 1963; M.A. in Teaching, Antioch Coll., Yellow Springs, Ohio, 1968. Tchr., Morgan Community Sch., Washington, 1967-69; counselor Project Crossroads, Washington, 1969-70; edn. dir. Council Econ. Opportunities, Cleve., 1972-74; tng. dir. Martin L. King Hosp., Los Angeles, 1974; exam. asst. Los Angeles Sch. Dist., 1974-75, summer 1976-77; tchr. Inglewood (Calif.) Sch. Dist., 1975—; mem. home econs. adv. council Cleve. Bd. Edn., 1973; bd. dirs Johnnie Tillmon Child Devel. Center, Los Angeles, 1974; cons. in field, rep. numerous ednl. coms. Chmn., Friends of the Avalon-Carver Community Center, Los Angeles, 1982; bd. dirs. Los Angeles Commn. Assaults Against Women, 1985. Recipient Service award Nat. Com. Children and Youth, 1970; grantee Nat. Tchr. Corps, 1976-78. Mem. Am. Fedn. Tchrs., Nat. Assn. Female Execs., Media Forum, Black Women's Forum, Women's Network, Alpha Kappa Alpha. Republican. Mem. A.M.E. Zion Ch. Home: 4335 Don Tomaso Dr Apt 3 Los Angeles CA 90008 Office: 3316 W 78th Pl Los Angeles CA 90043

SIMMONS, SYLVIA, advertising agency executive, author; b. N.Y.C.; B.A., Bklyn. Coll.; M.A. in English Lit., Columbia U.; m. Hans H. Neumann, 1962. Dir. sales promotion and direct mail div. McCann Erickson, Inc., N.Y.C., 1958-62; v.p., asst. to pres. Young & Rubicam, Inc., N.Y.C., 1962-73; sr. v.p., dir. spl. projects Kenyon & Eckhardt, Inc., N.Y.C., 1975—. Recipient Medal of Freedom, 1946, award for best radio comml. N.Y. Radio Broadcasters Assn., 1976-77, award for contbns. in direct mail promotions Sales Promotion Execs. Assn. Mem. Direct Mail Advt. Assn., Authors Guild, Propylaea, Sigma Tau Delta. Clubs: Sales Promotion Execs., Advt. Women of N.Y., Copy (N.Y.C.). Author: New Speakers Handbook, 1972; The Great Garage Sale Book, 1982; How To Be The Life of the Podium, 1982; (with Hans H. Neumann) The Straight Story on VD, 1974; Dr. Neumann's Guide to the New Sexually Transmitted Diseases, 1983; also articles. Office: Kenyon & Eckhardt 40 W 23d St New York NY 10010

SIMMONS, SYLVIA JEANNE QUARLES (MRS. HERBERT G. SIMMONS, JR.), college administrator; b. Boston, May 8, 1935; d. Lorenzo Christopher and Margaret Mary (Thomas) Quarles; B.A., Manhattanville Coll., 1957; M.Ed., Boston Coll., 1962; m. Herbert G. Simmons, Jr., Oct. 26, 1957; children—Stephen, Alison, Lisa. Montessori tchr. Charles River Park Nursery Sch., Boston, 1965-66; registrar Boston Coll. Sch. Mgmt., Chestnut Hill, Mass., 1966-70; dir. fin. aid Radcliffe Coll., Cambridge, Mass., 1970-75, asso. dean admissions and fin. aid, 1972-75, asso. dean admissions, fin. aid and women's edn., 1975; asso. dean admissions and fin. aid Harvard and Radcliffe, from 1975; assoc. v.p. for acad. affairs, central adminstrn. U. Mass., Boston, 1976—, spl. asst. to chancellor, 1979—; v.p. field services Mass. Higher Edn. Assistance Corp., 1982-84, sr. v.p., 1984—; mem. faculty Harvard U.; cons. Mass. Bd. Higher Edn., 1973—. Bd. dirs. Rivers Country Day Sch., Weston, Mass., Simon's Rock Coll., Great Barrington, Mass., Wayland (Mass.) Fair Housing, Cambridge Mental Health Assn., Family Service Greater Boston, Concerts in Black and White, Mass. Higher Edn. Assistance Corp.; trustee and alumnae bd. dirs. Manhattanville Coll. Mem. adv. com. Upward Bound, Chestnut Hill Boston Coll., 1972-74; Camp Chimvey Corners, Becket, Mass., 1971-77. Named One of Ten Outstanding Young Leaders, Boston Jr. C. of C., 1971; recipient Bicentennial medal Boston Coll., 1976; Achievement award Greater Boston YMCA, 1977. Mem. Women in Politics, Nat. (exec. council 1973-75), Eastern (1st v.p. 1973) assns. financial aid officers, Coll. Scholarship Service Council, Links, (pres. local chpt. 1967-69), Nat. Inst. Fin. Aid Adminstrs. (dir. 1975—), Jack and Jill Am. (pres. Newton chpt. 1972-74, Delta Sigma Theta, Delta Kappa Gamma. Club: Manhattanville (pres. Boston 1966-68). Home: 3 Dean Rd Wayland MA 01778 Office: 330 Stuart St Boston MA 02116

SIMMONS, VIRGINIA LEE COWAN, educational administrator; b. Ft. Wayne, Ind., May 17, 1921; d. James Clarence and Julia (Webster) Cowan; A.B., Ind. U., 1942, Ed.S., 1970; M.S., Butler U., 1957; postgrad. U. Wis., 1964-67; m. Eric L. Simmons, Apr. 25, 1943 (div. 1948); children—Nancy Lee (Mrs. Roy Green), Eric Leslie. Market research analyst McCann-Erickson, Chgo., 1944-48; retail mcht. Aquatic Galleries, Cin., 1949-52; sales, alvt. Empire Tropical Fish Import Co., N.Y.C., 1952-53; Direct Mail Advt., Halvin Products, Bklyn., 1953-55; tchr. Indpls. Sch. 76, 1955-60; asst. prin. Sch. 61, 1960-61, asst. prin. Sch. 101, 1962-63; prin. Lew Wallace Sch. 107, Indpls., 1964-72, Frances Bellamy Sch. 102, Indpls., 1972-74, William H. Evans Sch. 95, Indpls., 1974-80, G.B. Loomis Sch. 85, Indpls., 1980-82; cons. prin., Indpls., 1982—; program supr. audio-visual center Ind. U., Bloomington, 1961-62; lectr. Butler U., summer 1965; cons. Ind. U., summer 1969. Contbg. mem. Childrens Mus.; mem. Indpls. Mus. Art, Indpls. chpt. Project HOPE; sponsoring mem. Met. Indpls. TV Assn., Inc., 1969-73; coordinator Christmas gift and hobby show Indpls. Public Schs., 1969-75. Bd. dirs. Young Audiences of Ind., 1969-80, co-chmn., 1976-78, chmn., 1977-78; bd. dirs. Indpls. chpt. Freedoms Found. at Valley Forge, 1st v.p., 1971-73, 75-77, 83—, pres., 1973-75, v.p., 1977-83, also awards, 1977-83. Recipient Am. Educators medal Freedoms Found., 1972. Mem. NEA (life), Ind. U. Alumni Assn. (life), Indpls. Zool. Soc. (charter), Ind. Tchrs. Assn., Bus. and Profl. Women's Clubs, Inc., Indpls. Council Adminstrv. Women Edn., (dir.), Nat. Soc. Study Edn., Nat. Congress Parents and Tchrs., Butler U. Alumni Assn., Nat. Elem. Prin. Assn., Ind. Edn. Art Assn., Hoosier Salon, Assn. Supervision and Curriculum Devel., Internat. Reading Assn., Indpls. Art League, Brown County Art Gallery Assn., Watercolor Soc. Ind., AAUW, Izaak Walton League Am., DAR, Alpha Chi Omega, Delta Kappa Gamma, Phi Delta Kappa (hon.), Pi Lambda Theta. Methodist. Clubs: Ind. Schoolwomens; Century, Indpls. Propylaeum, Indpls. Athletic, Women's Dept. Author monographs. Compiler, editor: Elementary School Principals Handbook, 1985. Home: 5715 N Meridian St Box 688804 Indianapolis IN 46268

SIMMONS-WILLIS, BEVERLEY, social worker; b. Chgo., Sept. 30, 1941; d. Ward and Louise (Baskin) Simmons; A.A., Wilson Jr. Coll., 1962; B.A., Roosevelt U., Chgo., 1964; A.M., U. Chgo., 1970; m. Johnnie E. Willis, Oct. 8, 1966. Caseworker, supervising caseworker Cook County (Ill.) Dept. Public Aid, Chgo., 1964-72; caseworker, program coordinator Family Service Bur., United Charities Chgo., 1972-78; coordinator children and adolescent services Chgo. Health Dept., Mental Health Div., 1978—; family therapist, cons. parent effectiveness tng. Cert. social worker, Ill. Mem. Acad. Cert. Social Workers, Nat. Assn. Social Workers, Nat. Assn. Black Social Workers. Office: 1971 W 111 St Chicago IL 60643

SIMMS, SUSAN FAYE, nursing administrator; b. Bklyn., Nov. 25, 1939; d. Sol and Freda (Leventhal) Simms. Diploma in Nursing, Jewish Hosp. Bklyn. Sch. Nursing, 1956-59; B.S. in Nursing, Tchrs. Coll., Columbia U., N.Y.C., 1964; M. Profl. Services in Health Care Adminstrn., C. W. Post Coll., Long Island U., Greenvale, N.Y., 1975-77. Cons. Norman Jaspay Assn., N.Y.C., 1968-69; asst./dir. nursing Peninsula Hosp. Ctr., Queens, N.Y., 1969-72; asst. dir. nursing Kingsbrook Jewish Med. Ctr., Bklyn., 1973-76, assoc. dir. nursing, 1976-77; asst. prof. St. Francis Coll., Bklyn., 1976-77; v.p. nursing Arlington Hosp., Va., 1977—; cons. nursing edn. State Bd. Higher Edn. Ga., 1979; mem. govs. adv. com. Medicare and Medicaid, Va., 1982; adj. prof. George Mason U., Annandale, Va., 1980-81. Mem. Com. of 100, Arlington, Va., 1977-79; chmn. curriculum adv. com. nursing program Northern Va. Community Coll., 1980—. Served to capt. USAF, 1964-66. Regents scholar N.Y. State U., 1956, 60. Named Honoree Va. div. AAUW, 1985. Mem. Va. Nurses Assn. (lobbyist 1984; pres. 1984—), Am. Nurses Assn., Nat. League Nursing, Nat. Forum Adminstrs. Nursing Service, Va. Assn. Nursing Execs. (bd. dirs.), Am. Assn. Nurse Execs. Republican. Jewish. Club: Great Dane Rescue League (v.p. 1981-84) (Vienna, Va.). Avocations: cooking; traveling; gardening; writing. Home: 2904 Woodfern Ct Woodbridge VA 22192 Office: The Arlington Hosp 1701 N George Mason Dr Arlington VA 22205

SIMON, ALYCE, artist; b. N.Y.C.; d. Irving and Sophie Rothlein; student Pratt Inst., 1939-40, Bklyn. Mus. Art Sch., 1941-46, Art Students League, 1942-43, Syracuse U., 1943-44; children—Michael Scott, Russell Roy. Pres., Alyce Simon Art and Design, N.Y.C., 1974—; partner, art cons. Fred Kolber & Co., N.Y.C., 1981—; numerous one-man shows of paintings and/or sculpture including: Hunter Coll., N.Y.C., 1966-67, Smithsonian Instn., Washington, 1969-70, Ont. (Can.) Mus. Centennial Centre, 1970, Washburn Gallery, Hayden Planetarium, Boston, 1970-71, Palais de Exhibition, Geneva, 1971, Petit Palais Musee, Geneva, 1971, Marcus Jewelry, N.Y.C., 1972, Benson Gallery, Bridgehampton, N.Y., 1972, Weiner Gallery, N.Y.C., 1977, Crickett Club Gallery, Miami, Fla., 1976-79, UN Plaza, N.Y.C., 1980-81; numerous group shows Fine Arts Galleries, Carnegie Inst. Pa., 1942-45, Bklyn. Mus., 1946-50, 68-69, Jersey City Mus., 1964, Nat. Acad. Fine Arts, N.Y.C., 1967-68, 72, Audubon Artists, N.Y.C., 1967, Galerie Internationale, N.Y.C., 1972; represented in permanent collections: Chitose Corp., Tokyo, Albert Knox Mus., Buffalo, numerous pvt. collections. Dir. fin. Internat. Women's Arts Festival, Internat. Women's Yr., 1975-76. Recipient numerous art awards including Carnegie Inst., 1941-44, Bklyn. Mus., 1945, 46, 47, 49, 50, Citta di Reggio award Centro Internazionale di Arte e Cultura, 1982. Mem. Carmel Hist. Soc., Pacific Asian Soc., Nat. Com. on Am. Fgn. Policy, Womens Econ. Round Table, U.S. Trotting Assn., Women Bus. Owners of N.Y., Experiments in Art and Tech. Republican. Developer technique of using nuclear energy as an art form. Address: 860 United Nations Plaza New York NY 10017

SIMON, CARLY, singer, composer; b. June 25; d. Richard Simon; studied with Pete Seeger; m. James Taylor, 1972 (div. 1983); children—Sarah Maria, Benjamin Simon. Singer, composer, rec. artist, 1971—; albums include Carly Simon, 1971, Anticipation, 1972, No Secrets, 1973, Hotcakes 1974, Playing Possum, 1975, The Best of Carly Simon, 1975, Another Passenger, 1976 Boys in the Trees, 1978, Spy, 1979, Come Upstairs, 1980, Torch, 1981, Hello Big Man, 1983, Spoiled Girls, 1985; single records include Nobody Does it Better, 1977, Torch, 1981; appeared in film No Nukes, 1980. Recipient Grammy award as best new artist, 1971. Address: care Epic Records care CBS Records 51 W 52d St New York NY 10019*

SIMON, CAROLINE K(LEIN), lawyer; b. N.Y.C.; d. Julia (Feist) and David Klein; m. Leopold King Simon (dec. 1952); children—Lee, Cathy Simon Silver; m. Irving W. Halpern, 1953 (dec.). Grad. Columbia U.; LL.B., NYU; L.H.D. (hon.), Jewish Inst. Religion, Hebrew Union Coll., 1966. Bar: N.Y., U.S. Dist. Ct. (so. dist.) N.Y., U.S. Supreme Ct. Gen. practice, N.Y.C.; of counsel Decker Hubbard and Welden; sec. of state State of N.Y., 1959-63; judge N.Y. State Ct. Claims, 1963-70. Mem. spl. legis. com. on ct. reorgn. N.Y. State Senate; chmn. subcom. on the jury N.Y. Appellate Divs. 1st and 2d Depts.; mem. com. on discrimination in employment N.Y. State War Council, 1943-45; commr. State Workmen's Compensation Bd., 1944-45, State Commn. Against Discrimination, 1945-55, State Youth Commn., 1956-59; legal adviser U.S. del. UN Human Rights Commn., 1958; mem. White House Confs. on Children, 1950, 60; bd. dirs., exec. com. Com. on Modern Cts., Fund for Modern Cts.; mem. med. malpractice mediation panel 1st Jud. Dept.; adv. council Nat. Ctr. for State Cts.; past chmn. bd. trustees, mem. exec. com. Nat. Council on Crime and Delinquency, also mem. nat. adv. council; hon. bd. trustees, past chmn. com. on social affairs and pub. responsibility Jewish Bd. Family and Children's Services; life mem. exec. bd., mem. adminstrv. com. and bd. govs. Am. Jewish Com.; mem. Nat. Jewish Welfare Bd.; pres., chmn., trustee Fedn. Employment and Guidance Service; bd. dirs., former v.p. Willkie House; bd. dirs. USO of N.Y.; former bd. dirs., asst. treas. Freadom House, also exec. com. and counsel to bd.; trustee N.Y. County Lawyers Found.; hon. bd. dirs. Manhattan chpt. Brandeis U. Nat. Women's Com.; hon. v.p. Nat. Assn. Women Artists, Inc., 19—; trustee, exec. com. Fedn. Jewish Philanthropies; former chmn. Legacy com. Temple Emanu-El; candidate of Republican Party for pres. City Council of N.Y., 1957; Contbr. to books; contbr. articles on govt., law, social problems to publs. including N.Y. Times Mag., Jour. of Living, legal jours. Recipient Presdl. citation NYU, 1962. Outstanding Citizenship award Am. Heritage Found., 1961, citation and testimonial, Mass. Com. on Caths. Protestants and Jews, 1960. Bond Between Us Award for outstanding service to Israel, 1960, citation and testimonial dinner Assn. for Help of Retarded Children, 1960, Ann. Brotherhood award Temple Emanu-El, N.Y.C. 1961, Woman of Achievement award Fedn. Jewish Women's Orgns., Salute to Women award, 1962; named Woman of Achievement, Women's Internat. Exposition, 1957, Woman of Yr., Beth Israel Hosp. Sch. Nursing, 1960, Woman of History N.Y. State, 1980; named to Hall of Fame Mt. Vernon High Sch. (N.Y.), 1981. Mem. ABA (sect. jud. adminstrn., alt. del. to Internat. Bar Assn. 1966), N.Y. State Bar Assn. (sec. jud. administrn., former chmn. adminstrv. law com., currently mem. cts. and community com., com. on profl. issues and standards, editorial bd. jour.), N.Y. County Lawyers Assn. (coms. judiciary, forum, spl. com. profl. ethics, former mem. bd. dirs.), Assn. Bar City N.Y. (com. on profl. responsibility, joint com. on fee concilliation, sr. vol. lawyers com.), World Habeus Corpus (exec. com.), Nat. Assn. Spl. Ct. Judges, Nat. Ctr. for State Cts. (adv. council), Am. Arbitration Assn. (law com. comml. sect.), Delta Kappa Gamma (internat. hon.). Home: 200 E 66th St New York NY 10021 Office: 30 Rockefeller Plaza New York NY 10020

SIMON, CHERYL ANN, information systems executive; b. Pottsville, Pa., Dec. 23, 1950; d. Andrew George and Eleanor Helen (Pomian) Hauslyak; student Union County Coll., 1975-77; programming diploma Chubb Inst., 1982; m. Leo Simon, Dec. 11, 1971; children—Eleanor Louise, Christopher Andrew. Stenographer, Bell Telephone Labs., Piscataway, N.J., 1969-70; with Merck Sharp & Dohme Research Labs., Rahway, N.J., 1970—, group leader Vydec Machines, Med. Affairs Internat., 1975-79, supr. word processing/communications center, 1979-82, assoc. regulatory info. systems, 1982—; lectr. Named Sec. of Yr., Union County chpt. Profl. Secs. Internat., 1979-80, N.J. Div., 1980-81; Young Career Woman, Bus. and Profl. Women's Club, 1979; Mem. Assn. Info. Systems Profls., Internat. Soc. Wang Users, Internat. Info./Word Processing, Nat. Assn. Female Execs. Contbr. articles to profl. jours. Office: 485 Route 1 S Parkway Towers Bldg D Iselin NJ 08830

SIMON, CHRISTINE COPLEY, state ofcl.; b. Trenton, N.J., Dec. 18, 1948; d. George Dewey and Veronica Helene (Mislan) Simon; student Bucks County Community Coll.; B.A., Lehigh U., 1976, M.A., 1978; children—Stacey, Jack. With Proctor & Gamble, Trenton, N.J., 1969-72; summer cities youth counselor, Bethelehem, Pa., 1975; hist. interpretor U.S. Park Service, Ind. Nat. Park, Phila., 1976; research asst. Sch. Edn., Lehigh U., and Law Enforcement Assistance Agy., Bethelehem, Pa., 1976-77; teaching asst. Lehigh U., 1977-78; field housing service coordinator N.J. Dept. Community Affairs, Toms River, 1978-81, sr. project specialist, 1981—; cons. if field. Vol. researcher N.J. Network TV, Trenton, 1981. Univ. Trustee scholar, 1974-76. Mem. Internat. Reading Council, Ocean County Women's Network, Assn. for Female Execs., NEA, Ocean County Council Social Services. Club: Toms River High Booster's. Contbr. articles to profl. jours. Office: 240 Main St Toms River NJ 08753

SIMON, DEBRA WAGNER, accountant; b. Phila., July 24, 1959; d. Joseph and Annette (Schmerling) Wagner; m. Paul Stephen Simon, Sept. 5, 1982. B.S.B.A., Drexel U., 1982. C.P.A., Pa. Jr. acct. Mann Judd Landau, Phila., 1983-84, staff acct., 1984, sr. acct., 1985—. Mem. Surrey Pl. Civic Assn., Cherry Hill, N.J., 1985-86. Mem. Am. Inst. C.P.A.s, Pa. Soc. C.P.A.s, Am. Women's Soc. C.P.A.s. Jewish. Avocations: tennis; computers. Office: Mann Judd Landau 1401 Walnut St Philadelphia PA 19102

SIMON, DOROTHY ELAINE, educator; b. Madison, Wis., Nov. 17, 1931; d. William Rees and Beatrice Helena (Reque) Beckett; m. William Henry Simon, Oct. 1, 1955; children—Stephen Eric, William Edward. B.S., So. Conn. State U., 1954. Cert. elem. tchr., Conn. Tchr. grade 1 Center St. Sch., North Haven, Conn., 1954-57; tchr. grades 3-4 Clover St. Sch., Windsor, Conn., 1968—; cooperating tchr. Internship Program, U. Hartford and Central Conn. State U., 1973-85; unit leader Multi Unit Sch., Windsor, 1972—. Sec. Republican Women's Club, Windsor, 1965-68; corr. sec. Women's Aux. of Hartford Symphony, 1966-70; v.p. PTO, Windsor, 1965-68; co-chmn. Windsor Red Cross Drive, 1969. Recipient honorarium So. New Eng. Telephone. Mem. NEA, Conn. Edn. Assn., Windsor Edn. Assn., Nat. Assn. Individually Guided Edn. Episcopalian. Clubs: Green Mountain (Vt.); Millbrook Golf (Windsor). Avocations: sketching; writing; hiking; camping; bicycling. Home: 17 Priscilla Rd Windsor CT 06095 Office: Clover St Sch 57 Clover St Windsor CT 06095

SIMON, DOROTHY MARTIN, chemist, business executive; b. Harwood, Mo., Sept. 18, 1919; d. Robert William and Laudell (Flynn) Martin; A.B., S.W. Mo. State U., 1940; Ph.D., U. Ill., 1945; postdoctoral work Cambridge (Eng.) U., 1953-54; Sc.D. (hon.), Worcester Poly. Inst., 1971; D.Eng. (hon.), Lehigh U., 1978; m. Sidney L. Simon, Dec. 6, 1946 (dec. Nov. 1975). Grad. teaching asst. U. Ill., 1941-45; research chemist rayon div. E.I. Du Pont de Nemours & Co., Inc., Buffalo, 1945-47; chemist Oak Ridge Nat. Lab., 1947; asso. chemist Argonne (Ill.) Nat. Lab., 1948-49; aero. research scientist, group leader NACA, Cleve., 1949-53, asst. br. chief chemistry, 1954-55; group leader combustion fundamentals Magnolia Petroleum Co., Dallas, 1955-56; prin. scientist, tech. asst. to pres. research and advanced devel. div. Avco Corp., Greenwich, Conn., 1956-62, dir. corp. research def. and indsl. products group, 1962-64, group v.p. Avco Corp., 1964-68, corp. v.p. research, 1968-84; pres. Simon Assocs., 1984—. Marie Curie lectr. State U. Pa., 1962; dir. Conn. Nat. Bank, Crown Zellerbach Corp., Warner Lambert Co. Mem. NSF panel sci. and tech., 1973—; trustee Worcester Poly. Inst., Northeastern U.; bd. dirs. Draper Lab.; mem. vis. com. sponsored research, vis. com. for aeros. and astronautics M.I.T.; mem. overseers' com. for applied research Harvard U.; mem. nat. materials adv. bd. Nat. Acad. Scis./NRC; mem. Pres.'s Com. for Nat. Medal of Sci.; chmn. Daniel Guggenheim award bd., 1982; mem. def. policy adv. com. on trade Dept. Def., 1978-83, chmn., 1982; mem. vis. com. Nat. Bur. Standards, 1981. Recipient Rockefeller Public Service award, 1953; Outstanding Alumnus award S.W. Mo. State U., 1957; Outstanding Profl. Woman award Bus., Profl. Women's Club N.Y., 1966; Disting. Service in Engring. medal U. Mo., Columbia, 1980; Illini Achievement award U. Ill., 1983. Fellow AIAA (nat. dir.), Am. Inst. Chemists; mem. Am. Chem. Soc., Internat. Combustion Inst., Soc. Woman Engrs. (Achievement award 1966), N.Y. Acad. Scis., Conn. Acad. Scis. and Engring., Sigma Xi. Contbr. articles to profl. jours. and collected symposia books. Home and Office: 222 Stagecoach Rd Chapel Hill NC 27514

SIMON, ELIZABETH ANN, social worker; b. Kaplan, La., Mar. 21, 1949; d. Luke and Lucy (Marceaux) S.; B.A., St. Mary's Dominican Coll., 1971; M.S.W., Tulane U., 1972. Coordinator Satellite Clinics, Charters Mental Health Center, New Orleans, 1973-74, clin. social worker, 1974-77; field instr. Tulane U. Sch. Social Work, New Orleans, 1975-76; clin. cons., community edn. facilitator Family & Child Services, New Orleans, 1977-79; pvt. practice psychotherapy, New Orleans, 1977—; mem. La. State Bd. Cert. Social Workers; cons. YWCA Battered Women's Program, New Orleans, 1978-79, bd. dirs., 1979-80. Clin. fellow Tulane U., 1973. Mem. New Orleans Feminist Counseling Collective (founding mem. 1976), Women Against Violence Against Women (chmn. interium com. 1978-79, dir. 1981), La. Soc. Clin. Social Work, Assn. Women in Social Work, Acad. Cert. Social Workers, Nat. Assn. Social Workers (La. state bd. dirs. 1983-86, nat. com. mem., nat. com. on lesbian and gay rights 1985-86), ACLU, NOW. La. Gay Polit. Action Caucus (bd. dirs. 1981-82), Nat. Gay Task Force, Gay Rights Nat. Lobby, Council for Devel. of French in La. Feminist Writers Guild. Home: 220 S Gayoso New Orleans LA 70119 Office: 3500 St Charles Ave New Orleans LA 70115

SIMON, KATHRYN ALLYN, fashion designer, textile designer; b. Nov. 11, 1953; d. Kenneth Paul Simon and Elaine Doris (Rosenberg) Simon Post; m. Robin Poppelsdorff, Oct. 31, 1972 (div. July 1979). Student Rudolf Steiner Inst., Emerson Coll., Sussex, Eng., 1973-74. Clothing and sweater designer Elaine Post Ltd., N.Y.C., 1969-71; textile designer Ascher Fabrics, London, 1972-73, Galleon Fabrics, N.Y.C., 1974-75; freelance textile designer New Wave, N.Y.C., Los Angeles, N.Y.C., 1975-79, Paris, 1979-80; owner Kathryn Simon Inc., designer and mfr. women's high fashion clothing, N.Y.C., 1981—. Work featured in Woman's Wear Daily, Harpers Bazaar, Vogue, Elle, N.Y. Times. High sch. coordinator Vietnam Moratorium Com., N.Y.C., 1969. Mem. Fashion Council. Avocations: African/Brazilian dance, painting. Office: Kathryn Simon Inc 260 W 35th St New York NY 10001

SIMON, LORENA COTTS, music teacher, composer, poet; b. Sherman, Tex., Jan. 16, 1897; d. George Godfrey and Willie (Jones) Cotts; student Am. Conservatory, summer 1938, Juilliard Music Sch., summer 1939; diploma Sherwood Music Sch., 1941; Litt.D. (hon.), Internat. Acad. Leadership, Quezon City, Philippines; L.H.D. (hon.), No. Pontificial Acad., Malmo, Sweden, 1969; Mus.D. (hon.), St. Olav's Acad., Sweden, 1969; m. Samuel C. Simon, Nov. 6, 1918 (dec.). Tchr. violin, piano, theory and harmony, Port Arthur, Tex., 1919—. Organizer, dir. Schubert's Violin Choir, Port Arthur, 1919-55. Named Poet Laureate of Tex. 1961; Poet Laureate of Magnolia Dist., 1962-64; Poet Laureate of Port Arthur, 1962—; recipient gold plaque Tex. Fedn. Women's Club, 1962, spl. award 1st place in poetry and music Tex. heritage dept., 1963; medal of merit and diploma of merit Centro Studi Scambi Internat., Rome, Italy, 1965; Gold medal award, and hon. poet laureate-musician United Poets Laureate Internat., 1966, named Cath. Lady of Humanity, 1977; decorated Equestrian Order of Holy Sepulchre, 1981; inducted into Knights and Ladies of the Holy Sepulchre, Pope John II, 1982; recipient Greatness and Leadership award U. Manila, 1967; Silver medal, Gold medal, Diploma Centro Studi E Scambi—Internazionali, 1967; Gold Laurel Wreath, Gold medal, Karte of Award, 1966; named to International Poets' Hall of Fame, 1969, named most outstanding woman internationally Congress of Doctors, Quezon City, Philippines, 1969; named Cath. Poet Laureate of World, 1967. Mem. Nat., Tex. press women's assns., Nat. Council Cath. Women, Nat. Guild Piano Tchrs. (charter mem.; adjudicator), Am. Coll. Musicians (adjudicator), Internat. Guild Library, Am. Poetry League, Poets Soc. Tex. (critic judge), Am. Poets Fellowship Soc. Corp., UN Assn. U.S.A., Alpha Delta Kappa. Clubs: Writers' (pres. 1963-64), Symphony. Author: The Golden Keys, 1958; From My Heart (1st place award Ann. Poetry Writers Contest of Tex. Press Women's Assn. 1961), 1959; Children's Story Hour (1st place award Nat. Fedn. Press Women's Ann. Writers' Contest 1962), 1960. Songs pub. include: Live Expectantly, 1962, In Search for Growth, 1963, Freedom's Light, 1963, What Can I Do for Jesus, 1963, I Was a Star, I Was a Lamb, I Was a Donkey;

organ piece Mediation, 1967. Chmn. spl. editorial com. World Poets Laureate Anthology, 1969-70. Donor funds for constrn. of 9 churches in Africa. Home: 411 5th Ave Port Arthur TX 77642

SIMON, STEFANIE TASMANIA, computer analyst, consultant; b. Columbus, Ohio, Jan. 6, 1962; d. Salem Thaddeus and Tiney (Ray) S. B.S. in Econs., So. Meth. U., 1984. Assoc. analyst Pacific Bell Co., San Francisco, 1984-85, analyst, 1986—; cons. Jemmott Enterprises, Sacramento, 1984-85. Chair San Francisco Cost Savs. Info. Panel, 1986—. Mem. Nat. Assn. Female Execs., C.I.T.I.E.S. (Community Involvement Teams in Every Sector). Democrat. Baptist. Avocations: aerobics, tennis, water skiing, skiing, saxophone playing. Home: 4519 Lehigh Ct Sacramento CA 95841 Office: Pacific Bell Co San Ramon CA 94583

SIMON, THELMA BROOK, lawyer; b. Chgo., Oct. 16, 1916; d. John and Ida R. (Goodman) Brook; m. Harold M. Simon, Apr. 21, 1940; children—Elliott Martin, Justin Daniel. B.A., U. Ill., 1937; J.D. (scholar), U. Chgo., 1940. Bar: Ill. 1940, U.S. Supreme Ct. 1959, U.S. Ct. Appeals (7th cir.) 1980. Assoc. atty. firm Angerstein & Angerstein, Chgo., 1940-42; atty. U.S. Treasury Dept., Chgo., 1942; legal research asst. Supreme Ct. Ill., Springfield, 1946-62, 68-69; law clk. U.S. Dist. Ct. No. Dist. Ill., Chgo., 1962-65; asst. solicitor U.S. Dept. Labor, Chgo., 1971-72; prof. law John Marshall Law Sch., Chgo., 1972-74; chmn. Law Sch. alumni seminar U. Chgo. Law Sch., 1982. Contbr. articles to profl. jours.; asst. author: Uniform Jury Instruction Manual Federal Criminal Cases, 1963. Trustee Village of Wilmette (Ill.), 1961-69. Mem. ABA, Chgo. Bar Assn. (adminstrv. law com. 1979—, chmn. 1980-81, legis. com. 1982—), Ill. Bar Assn., Am. Judicature Soc., Women's Bar Assn. Ill. (pres. 1955-56), LWV, Phi Beta Kappa. Democrat. Address: 3119 Wilmette Ave Wilmette IL 60091

SIMON-GOODFRIEND, LYNN, nonprofit housing management executive; b. Chgo., Mar. 3, 1952; d. Jordan Oscar Simon and Rita Sargen-Simon; m. Jeffrey Jay Goodfriend, Nov. 2, 1980. B.S., Oberlin Coll., 1975. Mgr. Vincentian Villa, San Francisco, 1979-82; exec. dir. St. Vincent De Paul Housing, San Francisco, 1982—; dir. Indochinese Housing Devel. Corp., San Francisco, 1981—. No. Calif. alumni admissions coordinator Oberlin Coll., 1983. Mem. No. Calif. Assn. Nonprofit Housing (dir. 1980—, sec. 1980-81, pres. 1981-83, treas. 1983—), Nat. Assn. Nonprofit Retirement Housing (dir. 1981-83), Democrat. Jewish. Address: St Vincent De Paul Society 1825 Mission St San Francisco CA 94103

SIMON-MILLER, FRANÇOISE LOUISE, marketing educator, consultant; b. Cordemais, France, Dec. 27, 1946; d. Louis Joseph and Yvonne Emilie (David) Simon. Licence de Lettres magna cum laude, Univ. de Nantes, 1968, Maitrise summa cum laude, 1969; M. Phil. with distinction, Yale U., 1972, Ph.D. with distinction, 1980; M.B.A. with honors, Northwestern U., 1983; instr. Wellesley Coll., 1975-78; Mellon asst. prof. Northwestern U., Evanston, Ill., 1978-81; new product mgr. Abbott Labs., 1983-85, now mng. cons. Cresap, McCormick & Paget, N.Y.C.; adj. faculty U. Chgo. Grad. Sch. Bus., 1983-85, N.Y.U. Grad. Sch. Bus., 1985—. Contbr. book revs., articles to profl. jours.; finalist for award in mktg. excellence Biomed. Mktg. Assn., 1984. Mem. Am. Mktg. Assn. (internat. div. council), Assn. Consumer Research, Council Fgn. Relations. Recipient award Yale U. Concilium on Internat. Studies, 1974; Wellesley Coll. award, 1977; Faculty Research award Northwestern U., 1983, chpts. to books. Club: Yale of N.Y..

SIMONS, ELIZABETH R., biochemist, educator; b. Vienna, Austria, Sept. 1, 1929; came to U.S., 1941, naturalized, 1948; d. William and Erna Engle (Weisselberg) Reiman; B.Ch.E., Cooper Union, N.Y.C., 1950; M.S., Yale U., 1951, Ph.D., 1954; m. Harold Lee Simons, Aug. 12, 1951; children—Leslie Ann Mulert, Robert David. Research chemist Tech. Operations, Arlington, Mass., 1953-54; instr. chemistry Wellesley (Mass.) Coll., 1954-57; research asst. Children's Hosp. Med. Center and Cancer Research Found., Boston, 1957-59, research asso. pathology, 1959-62; research asso. Harvard Med. Sch., 1962-66, lectr. biol. chemistry, 1966-72; tutor biochemical scis. Harvard Coll., 1971—; asso. prof. biochemistry Boston U., 1972-78, prof., 1978—. Grantee in field. Mem. AAAS, Am. Chem. Soc., Am. Heart Assn., Am. Soc. Biol. Chemists, Am. Soc. Cell Biology, Am. Soc. Hematology, Am. Fedn. Clin. Research, Assn. Women in Sci., Biophys. Soc., Internat. Soc. Thrombosis and Hemostasis, N.Y. Acad. Sci., Sigma Xi. Contbr. in field. Office: Boston University Sch Medicine 80 E Concord St Boston MA 02118

SIMONS, GAIL M., publishing company executive; b. N.Y.C., Jan. 18, 1950; d. Edward Irving and Sylvia (Estrin) Madonick; B.A. in Econs., N.Y.U., 1971; M.B.A., City U. N.Y., 1977; m. A. James Simons, June 10, 1972; 1 dau. Jessica Lauren. Market and advt. research asso. Conde Nast Publs., N.Y.C., 1971-73; credit and fin. analyst European Am. Bank & Trust Co., N.Y.C., 1973-74; dist. lending rep. Nat. Bank of N.Am., N.Y.C., 1974-75; corp. budget analysis mgr. Readers Digest Assn., Inc., Pleasantville, N.Y., 1975-78, fin. mgr., 1979-83; pres. Health & Med. Guides, Inc., Irvington, N.Y., 1984—. Mem. Nat. Assn. Female Execs. Home: 290 Birch Ln Irvington NY 10533 Office: Health & Med Guides Inc PO Box 165 Irvington NY 10533

SIMONS, LYNN OSBORN, state official; b. Havre, Mont., June 1, 1934; d. Robert Blair and Dorothy W. (Briggs) Osborn; m. John Powell Simons, Jan. 19, 1957; children—Clay, Bill. B.A., U. Colo., 1956. Cert. tchr. Tchr., Jordan Sch. Dist., Midvale, Utah, 1956-57, Sweet Water Sch. Dist., Rock Springs, Wyo., 1957-58, Univ. of Wyo., Laramie, Wyo., 1959-61, Natrona Sch. Dist., Casper, Wyo., 1963-64; credit mgr. Gallery 323, Casper, 1972-77; state supt. pub. instrn. State of Wyo., Cheyenne, 1979—; dir. State of Wyo. Land Commn., Charities & Reform, Farm Loan Bd., Capital Bldg. Commn. Mem. Council Chief State Sch. Officers, Am. Assn. Sch. Adminstrs., Edn. Commn. of the States, LWV (pres. chpt. 1970-71). Democrat. Episcopalian. Home: Box 185 Cheyenne WY 82003 Office: Dept of Edn Hathaway Bldg Cheyenne WY 82003

SIMONS, SUSAN WILLINGHAM, state official; b. Nashville, Mar. 12, 1942; d. Ben Hill and Dorothy (Wells) Willingham; m. W. Lucas Simons, Sept. 5, 1964; children—Susan, Adele, Dede. B.A., Wellesley Coll., 1964. Chmn., Alcoholic Beverage Commn., Nashville, 1979-81; fin. dir. Alexander for Gov., (Tenn.), 1981-82; chmn. inauguration, Nashville, 1982-83; asst. to commr. Employment Security, Nashville, 1983; commr. Gen. Services Dept., Nashville, 1983—. Episcopalian. Home: 227 Deer Park Dr Nashville TN 37205

SIMONS, VIRGINIA MARIE, personnel director; b. Toledo, July 21, 1930; d. George Lee and W. Almeda (Braly) Patterson; m. Harold Henry Simons, Dec. 31, 1948 (dec. 1978); children—Harold Lee, Mark Anthony, Lynn Marie. Student Cleve. State Coll., 1974, Chattanooga State Coll., 1979-80, U. Tenn., 1973. Lic. investigator, Tenn., Ga. Pvt. investigator Pinkerton's Inc., Chattanooga, 1965-71, personnel supr., 1972—. Dale Carnegie grad. asst. awardee, 1973. Mem. Chattanooga Area Personnel Assn., Am. Soc. Personnel Assn., Am. Bus. Women's Assn. Club: Tenn. Valley Patroits (v.p. 1984). Address: Pinkerton's PO Box 21208 Chattanooga TN 37421

SIMONSON, DONNA MARIE, state official; b. Decatur, Ill., Jan. 25, 1948; d. Howard Joseph and Geneva Darlene Gleespen; student Alverno Coll., 1966-68; B.A., U. Ill., 1971, M.S.W., 1975. Mental health specialist Ill. Dept. Mental Health, Danville, 1971-74; student assoc. Com. on Women in Social Welfare, Nat. Assn. Social Workers, Washington, 1974; children's cons. Ill. Commn. Children, Springfield, 1975, exec. dir., 1977-85; planner Ill. Dept. Children and Family Services, Springfield, 1985—. Mem. Juvenile Justice Del., Citizen ambassador, People to People, USSR and Western Europe, 1982. Mem. Nat. Assn. Social Workers (various offices). Club: Altrusa of Springfield. Editor: Report of Com. on Youth and the Law, 1978; Report of Task Force on Drugs and Alcohol, 1979; Ill. Report White House Conf. on Children, 1980; Ill. Report Conf. on Children's Priorities for 80s, 1982. Office: Dept Children and Family Services IN Old State Capitol Plaza Springfield IL 62706

SIMONTON, GAIL MAUREEN, lawyer; b. Ripley, Tenn., July 5, 1951; d. William Christopher and Elizabeth Jane (Butler) Simonton. Student Centre Coll., Danville, Ky., 1969-71, Alliance Francaise, 1971, Institut Americain U., Avignon, France, 1971-72; B.A., U. Tenn.-Martin, 1975; J.D., U. Tenn.-Knoxville, 1977. Bar: Tenn. 1978. Intern, Bur. Ednl. and Cultural Affairs, U.S. Dept. State, Washington, 1973; law clk. to judge Tenn. Ct. Criminal Appeals, Covington, 1977-79; assoc. firm Thomason, Crawford & Hendrix, Memphis, 1979-82; asst. sec., staff atty. Guardsmark, Inc., Memphis, 1982-85; exec. dir. Com. Nat. Security Cos., Inc., 1985—. Research editor Tenn. Law Rev., 1976-77. Treas., bd. dirs. Covington Little Theater, 1977-78; youth league referee Covington Area Soccer Assn., 1978. Mem. ABA, Memphis and Shelby County Bar Assn. (dir. young lawyers sect. 1983), Tenn. Bar Assn., Am. Soc. Indsl. Security, Am. Soc. Assn. Execs., Tenn. Fedn. Bus. and Profl. Women (nominations chmn. 1981-82, legis. chmn. 1983-84), Raleigh Bus. and Profl. Women (pres. 1983-84, chmn. polit. action com. 1985-86, dist. dir. 1986-87). Club: Provida (Memphis). Home: 16 S Edgewood St Memphis TN 38104 Office: 2670 Union Ave Ext Suite 514 Memphis TN 38112

SIMPKINS, CAROL, social work administrator; b. N.Y.C., Sept. 2, 1947; d. Walter and Cleo (Coleman) S. B.S., N.C. Agrl. and Tech. State U., Greensboro, 1969; M.S., Columbia U., 1973. Cert. social worker. Counselor Victim Services Agency-Hot Line, N.Y.C., 1983—; program dir. Graham Windham Neighborhood Service Ctr., N.Y.C., 1984—. Treas., sec. Nat. Black Child Devel. Inst., N.Y.C., 1985. Democrat. Home: 25 Boerum St Brooklyn NY 11206 Office: Graham Windham Neighborhood Family Service Ctr 131 Kingston Ave Brooklyn NY 11213

SIMPKINS, MARY ELIZA, nurse; b. Edgefield, S.C., Nov. 13, 1933; d. Cornelous and Minnie Bell (Johnson) Chinn; diploma Phila. Gen. Hosp. Sch. Nursing, 1973; student Parkview Community Coll.; m. Albert Simpkins, July 8, 1953; children—Albert, David, Anthony, Mary. Nurse, Phila. Gen. Hosp., 1973-74; charge nurse in orthopedics Temple U., 1974-76; primary nurse, psychiat. group patients Hahneman Med. Coll. and Hosp., 1976-79; shift supr. Kelloggs Psychiat. Hosp., Corona, Calif., 1979-80; shift charge nurse, orthopedics, med.-surg. nurse Parkview Community Hosp., Riverside, Calif., 1980-83, shift charge nurse Intercept, 1983—. Republican. Adventist. Home: 4655 Minier Ave Apt 36B Riverside CA 92505

SIMPSON, ANDREA LYNN, energy company executive; b. Pasadena, Calif., Feb. 10, 1948; d. Kenneth James and Barbara Lois Simpson; B.A., U. So. Calif., 1969; grad. U. Colo. Sch. Bank Mktg., 1977; M.S., U. So. Calif., 1983. Asst. cashier mktg. First Interstate Bank of Calif., Los Angeles, 1969-73; asst. v.p. mktg. First Hawaiian Bank, Honolulu, 1973-78; v.p. corp. communications Pacific Resources, Inc., Honolulu, 1978—; guest lectr. U. Hawaii, 1974-82, Chaminade U., 1975-84. Dir. Hawaii Heart Assn., 1977-83; dir. Girl Scouts Pacific, 1982—; publicity chmn. Hawaii YWCA, 1982; mem. Hawaii State Commn. Status of Women, 1985—. Recipient Ursa Major Nat. Award Alpha Phi Internat., 1978; named Panhellenic Hawaii Woman of Yr., 1979; Outstanding Young Person of Hawaii Hawaii Jaycees, 1978; Outstanding Woman in Bus., YWCA, 1980; Outstanding Woman of Hawaii Girl Scout council of Pacific, 1985. Mem. Am. Mktg. Assn. (dir., v.p.), Public Relations Soc. Am. (dir., sec.), Honolulu Advt. Fedn. (Woman of Yr. 1984), Honolulu Press Club, Public Utilities Communicators Assn. Club: Outrigger Canoe. Office: 733 Bishop St #3100 Honolulu HI 96842

SIMPSON, CATHY ANN, land title company executive, real estate broker; b. Ripley, Miss., Aug. 6, 1953; d. Booth Obed and Annette Grace (Tapp) Simpson. m. Thomas Earl Jones, July 21, 1973 (div. Dec. 1981). B.A. with honors, Harding U., 1975. Real estate broker Houston Bd. Realtors, 1976—; mktg. broker cons. Capital Title Co., Houston, 1979-81; founder, owner The Settlers, 1979—, asst. v.p. Commerce Title Co., Houston, 1981-85; mktg. broker Capital Title Co., 1985—; faculty The Real Estate Sch. Mem. Tex. Real Estate Polit. Action Com. Mem. Nat. Assn. Realtors, Houston Bd. Realtors. Democrat. Mem. Ch. of Christ. Home: 11710 Bowlan Ln Houston TX 77035 Office: Capital Title Co 2929 Allen Pkwy Suite 200 Houston TX 77019

SIMPSON, CLAIRE RITTMEYER, speech-lang. pathologist; b. Cin., May 31, 1923; d. Harry Michael and Clara Elizabeth (Koenig-Wenning) Rittmeyer; student Seton Hill Coll., 1940-42; B.A., U. Cin., 1945; M.S., U. Vt., 1973; m. Lawrence A. Simpson, June 27, 1945; children—Michael Weir, Elizabeth Hay, Deborah Witt, John Gerard, Paula Wenning, Hilary Anne. Remedial reading specialist St. Albans-Fairfield Supervisory Union, St. Albans City Elem. Sch. System, Vt., 1966-68, adult basic edn. tchr., 1967-68, speech-lang. pathologist, 1968—, coordinator communication services, 1976—; adj. prof. dept. communication sci. and disorders U. Vt., 1979—; cons. Franklin County Home Health Agy., 1974—, St. Mary's Parish Lectors Assn., 1974—, Franklin County Vocat. Rehab. Div., State Agy. for Human Services, 1974—. ARC Gray Lady, 1951-61; den mother Cub Scouts, Boy Scouts Am., 1955-56, 61-62; county ways and means chmn. Kerbs Meml. Hosp. Aux., 1957-58; counselor Jr. Cath. Daus. of Am., 1960-65; active various charitable orgns.; music chmn. St. Mary's Parish, 1975-79. Vt. Dept. Spl. Edn. fellow, 1969, 70, 71. Mem. Am. Speech-Lang.-Hearing Assn., Vt. Speech-Lang.-Hearing Assn., Nat. Council for Exceptional Children, Vt. Council for Exceptional Children, NEA, Vt. Edn. Assn., St. Albans City Edn. Assn., Vt. Assn. Mental Health, Nat. Assn. Retarded Citizens, Vt. Children's Aid Soc., Nat. Fedn. Bus. and Profl. Women, AAUW, Seton Hill Coll. Alumni Assn., U. Cin. Alumni Assn., U. Vt. Alumni Assn., Delta Kappa Gamma, Zeta Tau Alpha. Republican. Roman Catholic. Clubs: Cath. Daus. Am., Autonöe. Author: Let's Talk Speech! A Handbook for Parents, 1969; Desensitization With and Without Biofeedback, 1973. Office: St Albans City Elem Sch Bldg Bellows St Saint Albans VT 05478

SIMPSON, DOROTHY JACOBSON, university administrator; b. Parkers Prairie, Minn., Feb. 11, 1938; d. Herman Gerhard and Clara (Sannes) Jacobson; m. Wayne Frederick Simpson, Aug. 23, 1958; children—Margaret, Stacy, Scott. B.A., St. Olaf Coll., 1960; M.S., St. Cloud State U., 1977; postgrad. Summer Inst. for Women in Higher Edn. Adminstrn., 1983. Piano instr. St. Cloud State U., Minn., 1974-76, Outreach coordinator, 1977-78, dir. ednl. confs., 1978-83, asst. to pres., 1983-85, v.p. univ. realtions, 1985—. Author: Guide for Piano Instruction for the Educationally Blind, 1979. Chmn., Minn. State Elderhostel, 1982-83; bd. dirs. Performing Arts Bd., Alexandria, Minn., 1983—, Minn. Orch. Bd., Coll. St. Benedict, 1984; vice chmn. campaign St. Cloud Area United Way, 1984—. Fellow Bush Found., summer 1983. Mem. Phi Kappa Phi (pres. 1983-85), Sigma Alpha Iota. Office: Saint Cloud State U Saint Cloud MN 56301

SIMPSON, DOROTHY MAE, educational administrator; b. Longview, Tex., Aug. 25, 1932; d. Duff and Eliza (Griffin) Hanson; m. Claude Simpson. B.S., Bishop Coll., 1953; M.Ed., Prairie View A & M U., 1978. Cert. tchr. mid-mgmt., Tex. Tchr., Dallas Ind. Sch. Dist., 1954-73, specialist in community relations, 1974-81, specialist in community affairs, 1982—; dir. NW dist. Bapt. Assn. North Tex., 1961—; dir. community relations Lincoln High Sch., Dallas, 1974-78; cons. Goodstreet Service Ctr., Dallas, 1981—. Author: BM&E Guide for Young People (Plaque 1970), 1969. Named Communicator of Yr., Dallas Ind. Sch. Dist., 1974; recipient Merit award Goodstreet Bapt. Ch., 1975, Merit award Bethel Bapt. Ch., 1981, Merit award R. L. Thornton Sch., 1982. Mem. Delta Sigma Theta. Democrat. Home: 5739 Old Ox Rd Dallas TX 75241

SIMPSON, HARRIETT STONER, personnel executive; b. Abbeville, S.C., Nov. 18, 1945; d. Guy Lafayette and Ethel (Brownlee) Stoner; m. C. Dennis Simpson, Jan. 28, 1971 (div. 1978); 1 son, Christopher. Student, Ga. Coll., 1964-65, Lander Coll., 1976-80. With Flexible Tubing, Abbeville, S.C., 1965—, personnel asst., 1971-79, employment mgr., 1979-84, personnel mgr., 1984—. Co-chmn. Abbeville County Spring Festival, 1984. Mem. Am. Soc. Personnel Adminstrn., Piedmont Area Personnel Assn., Riverbanks Zool. Soc. Republican. Baptist. Home: Route 5 PO Box 345 Abbeville SC 29620 Office: Flexible Techs Box 888 Abbeville SC 29620

SIMPSON, JUDITH KAY, construction company executive; b. Shelbyville, Tenn., Mar. 5, 1944; d. Albert Donald and Jessie Ruth (Castell) Snell. B.S. in Office Mgmt., Middle Tenn. State U., 1966. Prin. stenographer Tenn. Dept. Edn., Nashville, 1967-73; asst. office mgr. Lee Co., Nashville, 1977-81; controller Sharondale Constrn. Co., Brentwood, Tenn., 1981—; dir. William Vick & Assocs., Nashville. Vice pres. United Methodist Women, South End United Methodist Ch., Nashville, 1974, chmn. Council on Ministries, 1976-77; dir. prison ministry Ch. Women United, Nashville, 1975-76. Mem. Am. Mgmt. Assn., Constrn. Fin. Mgmt. Assn., Nat. Assn. Female Execs. Republican. Methodist. Avocations: music; reading; interior decorating. Office: Sharondale Constrn Co PO Box 576 Brentwood TN 37027

SIMPSON, KATHRYN JACQUIN, publishing company executive; b. Peoria, Ill., June 22, 1924; d. Wentworth Cory and Kathryn Mathilda (Niehaus) Jacquin; m. Howard M. Simpson, Nov. 25, 1948; children—John N., Cory Simpson Christian, Michael H., David M., Dana Simpson Lyddon. A.B., Bradley U., 1946. With Charles A. Bennett Co. (name changed to Bennett Publ. Co. 1975-76), 1946-83, also dir.; sec. Cabco, Inc., 1970-76. Bd. dirs. Heart of Ill. United Fund, 1961-66, sec. 1962-66; bd. dirs. YWCA, Peoria, 1966—, treas. 1970-71, vice pres. 1974-79, 83-85, chmn. planned giving 1984—, chmn. fin. development 1980-83; mem. ch. council St. Philomena Catholic Ch., 1981-85, sec. parish council, 1983. Mem. Nat. Council Boy Scouts Am., East Central Region Com. Boy Scouts Am., East Central Region Fin. Com. Boy Scouts Am., mem. W.D. Boyce council Boy Scouts Am., 1970—, v.p., 1974-79. Co-author: The United Way and the Local Council, 1979, rev. 1981. Recipient Silver Beaver award W.D. Boyce Council Boy Scouts Am., 1971, St. George Emblem award Nat. Council Boy Scouts Am., 1974. Mem. Jr. League Peoria, Women's Civic Fedn., Lakeview Ctr. for Arts and Scis., Theta Alpha Phi, Pi Beta Phi. Republican. Club: Willow Knolls Country. Home: Peoria IL

SIMPSON, LAURA EVELYN, accountant; b. Herrin, Ill., July 19, 1917; d. Roy and Mary (Trout) Wilson; student public schs., Ill.; diploma acctg., income tax and C.P.A. coaching LaSalle Extension U., 1952; m. Levi C. Simpson, Oct. 16, 1936; children—Doris I. Simpson Hill, Suzanne Simpson Barnett, Troy E., Joy. Bookkeeper, Atlas Powder Co., 1932-48; self-employed, 1934-41; with acctg. div. Sherwin Williams Def. Corp., 1942-45, Roy Barger Acctg. Service, Marion, Ill., 1945-52; propr. acctg. service, Marion and Harrisburg, Ill., 1953-79; part-time practice acctg., New Port Richey, Fla., 1980—. Treas., Sunday sch. tchr. Cedar Grove United Methodist Ch., Marion, 1946-79; pres. women's div. Holiday United Meth. Ch., New Port Richey, Fla., until 1984, chmn. missions commn., 1984—, also ch. treas.; leader 4-H Club, 1951, 52. Card holder IRS. Mem. Nat. Fedn. Ind. Bus. (chmn. Saline and Williamson County 1966, nat. adv. council 1971), Nat. Soc. Public Accts., Internat. Platform Assn. Republican. Home: 3634 Claremont New Port Richey FL 33552

SIMPSON, MARILYN JEAN, artist; b. Birmingham, Ala., Aug. 24, 1929; d. Homer Kyle and Ellen (Allan) Parker; student U. Ala., Art Students League N.Y., San Miguel, Mex., Robert Brackman Sch., Conn., Am. U., Avignon, France, Rome and Florence, Italy; children—Carol Leann, Charles Boyd. Dir., Acad. Fine Arts, Ft. Walton Beach, Fla., 1974-77; Marilyn Simpson Sch. Fine Art, Ft. Walton Beach, 1962-73, Artists Workshop, Ft. Walton Beach, 1982—; exhbns. include: Kotter Gallery, Nat. Arts Club, Lever House, Paula Insel Gallery (all N.Y.C.). Recipient award Am. Artist Profl. League, 1975; Gold medal, hon. degree Academia Italia, Rome, 1979, Golden Centaur award, 1982. Mem. Am. Artists Profl. League, Profl. Artists Guild. Address: Route 1 Box 43C Mary Esther FL 32569

SIMPSON, MARY ALICE, foundation executive; b. Kenefic, Okla., Dec. 5, 1937; d. William Ernest and Eunice Bessie (Lawson) Whitmire; m. Kenneth Ray Simpson, Apr. 28, 1956; children—Sandra Gail, Randal Dale. Student Draughon Coll., 1956-57, U. Okla., 1977, 78, 80, U. Tulsa, 1979, 82, Okla. State U., 1981, 84. Cert. fund raising exec. Sec., Nabisco, Oklahoma City, 1956-57, Bd. Edn., Oklahoma City, 1957-59; personnel cons., interviewer Snelling & Snelling, Oklahoma City, 1959-60; interviewer Regency Personnel, Oklahoma City, 1960-61; assoc. dir. devel. Okla. Med. Research Found., Oklahoma City, 1962—. Mem. Nat. Soc. Fund-Raising Execs. (v.p. Okla. chpt. 1985, bd. dirs., mem. exec. com. Okla. chpt. 1981—), Council for Advancement and Support of Edn., Nat. Assn. Female Execs. Democrat. Baptist. Avocations: reading; camping; gardening; crossword puzzles. Home: 1049 NW 105th St Oklahoma City OK 73114 Office: Okla Med Research Found 825 NE 13th St Oklahoma City OK 73104

SIMPSON, MARY MICHAEL, clergywoman, psychotherapist; b. Evansville, Ind.; d. Link Wilson and Mary Garrett (Price) Simpson; B.A.B.S., Tex. Women's U., 1946; grad. N.Y. Tng. Sch. Deaconesses, 1949; grad. Westchester Int. Tng. Psychoanalysis and Psychotherapy, 1976; S.T.M., Gen. Theol. Sem., 1982. Missionary, Liberia, 1950-52; mem. Order St. Helena, 1952-84 acad. head Margaret Hall Sch., Versailles, Ky., 1958-61; sister-in-charge convent, Liberia, 1962-67; dir. novices, 1968-74; pastoral counselor Cathedral St. John Divine, N.Y.C., 1974—, canon residentiary, canon counselor, 1977—; ordained priest Episcopal Ch., 1977; pvt. practice psychotherapy. Mem. Nat. Assn. for Advancement Psychoanalysis, N.Y. State Assn. Practicing Psychotherapists, N.Y. Assn. Clin. Psychologists. Contbg. author: Yes to Women Priests, 1978; author: The Ordination of Women in the American Episcopal Church, 1981. Address: 1047 Amsterdam Ave New York NY 10025

SIMPSON, VI, state senator; b. Los Angeles, Mar. 18, 1946; d. Lloyd M. and Helen (Chacon) Sentman; m. Kenneth N. Simpson; children—Jason, Kristina. B.A. in Bus., Calif. State U.-Hayward, 1968. Asst. to chmn. Com. on Status of Women, Calif., 1974-75; dir. pub. affairs Calif. Parks and Recreation Soc., Sacramento, 1975-77; county auditor Monroe County, Ind., 1980-84; mem. Ind. Senate, 1984—; pres. Vi Simpson and Co., Inc., Bloomington, Ind., 1983—. Editor: Equal Rights Monitor mag., 1974-76. Syndicated newspaper columnist Know Your Rights, 1975-76. Named Freshman Democrat Senator of Yr., Ind. broadcasters Assn., 1985, Legis. of Yr., Ind. State Employees Assn., 1985. Mem. Ind. Constructo Inc., NAACP, AAUW. Methodist. Avocations: jogging; skiing; camping; hiking. Office: Vi Simpson and Co Inc 5185 W State Rd 46 Bloomington IN 47401

SIMPSON, YVONNE MUMFORD, quality assurance specialist; b. Davenport, Iowa, Dec. 15; d. Decatur DeRoy Jr. and Evelyn Starr (Gleason) Mumford; m. Albert Austin Simpson, Dec. 24, 1947 (dec.); children—Albert Jr., Deborah, Doreene, Rebecca, Alec, Keith, Christopher, Elizabeth. B.A. cum laude in Criminal Justice, St. Ambrose Coll., 1980; student London U., 1979; M.A. in Law Enforcement Adminstrn., Western Ill. U., 1985. Ct. dep. Mcpl. Ct., Davenport, 1967-73, Scott County Dist. Ct., Davenport, 1973-77; asst. to v.p. research, St. Ambrose Coll., Davenport, 1978-81; quality assurance specialist hdqrs. U.S. Army Armament, Munitions and Chem. Command, Rock Island, Ill., 1981—; assigned to Rock Ready project Pine Bluff (Ark.) Arsenal, 1983—. Contbr. poetry to Poetry of Love Past and Present; Other Voices in American Poetry, 1980. Active Bicentennial Com., Davenport, 1976; campaign vol. Jim Leach for U.S. Congress, 1978-80; mem. criminal justice curriculum com. Muscatine Community Coll. Recipient letters of commendation. Mem. Acad. Caribbean Studies, Acad. Criminal Justice Studies, Federally Employed Women. Republican. Lutheran. Clubs: Toastmistress, Camera, Postcard. Lodges: Eastern Star, White Shrine, Amaranth, Cauldren. Home: 1404 Nancy St Pine Bluff AR 71602 Office: Pine Bluff Arsenal SMCPB-QAO Pine Bluff AR 71611

SIMS, BARBARA JEAN, management and information resource management consultant; b. St. Louis, Nov. 17, 1941; d. Vernon Elbert and Iva (Leslie) S. B.S., Northwestern U., 1963; M.Internat. Affairs, Columbia U., 1968, Ed.D., 1974; postgrad. George Washington U., 1981-82. Vol., Peace Corps, Morocco, 1963-65; escort-interpreter lang. services div. U.S. Dept. State, Washington, summer 1966, 68-69, 73-76; ednl. program specialist Bur. Ednl. Personnel Devel., Office Edn., Washington, 1970-71; ednl. program specialist to v.p. Warner & Warner Internat. Assocs., Inc., 1972-73; pvt. practice cons., 1973-75; Peace Corps dir., Mali, 1975-76; pvt. practice cons., Washington, 1977—. Translator, editor: Economic Development: Does Aid Help?, 1983; Changing Vistas in United States-Africa Economic Relations, 1981, AF:LOG African Interests of American Organizations, 1975. Ford Found. internat. fellow, 1967-68; fellow Internat. Inst. for Edn., 1967. Mem. Assn. for Fed. Info. Resources Mgmt., Pi Lambda Theta. Office: Creation 2130 P St NW 619 Washington DC 20037

SIMS, ELIZABETH BALLARD SIMS, court reporter; b. Bastonia, N.C., Aug. 17, 1944; d. Fred Wilson and Mabel Elizabeth (Allen) Ballard; m. Robert Vincent Sims, Sept. 4, 1964; 1 dau., Candace Elizabeth Sims Barkley. Student Gaston Meml. Hosp. Sch. Nursing, 1962-63, Gaston Coll. Dep. registrar deeds Gaston County, 1964-69; ofcl. ct. reporter, N.C., 1969-74; free-lance reporter, Dallas, N.C., 1974-86; ofcl. ct. reporter 26th Jud. Dist., State of N.C., 1986—; ofcl. ct. reporter U.S. Bankruptcy Ct. Western dist. N.C., Charlotte div., 1983-84; jud. div. 26th Jud. Dist. Superior Ct., State N.C., 1986—. Mem. com. Adminstrv. Office of Cts., 1977-78, N.C. Gov.'s Council on Status of Women, 1978—. Active Gaston County Democratic Women; Dem. precinct judge, 1973, youth rep. to area precinct meeting; chmn. Gaston County Mother's March of Dimes campaign, 1980-81. Mem. Nat. Shorthand Reporters Assn., N.C. Shorthand Reporters Assn. (legis. com.). Methodist. Home: 402 Sunset Circle Dallas NC 28034

SIMS, LORETTA JAMES, employment counselor; b. Holly Springs, Miss., Feb. 7, 1948; d. Sylvester and Elmer (Greer) James; 1 dau., Chyreese Tawana. B.S. in Bus. Edn. cum laude, Miss. Indsl. Coll., Holly Springs, 1971. Personnel mgmt. specialist, then personnel staffing specialist U.S. CSC, Jackson, Miss., 1971-78; equal opportunity specialist Office Fed. Contract Compliance Programs, Kansas City, Mo., 1978—. Mem. ACLU, Common Cause, Urban

Leaque, NAACP. Baptist. Home: 6102 E 126th St Apt 305 Grandview MO 64030 Office: DOL/OFCCP 1103 Grand St Room 1400 Kansas City MO 64106

SIMS, LYDIA THERESA, city affirmative action executive; b. Pennsgrove, N.J., Nov. 18, 1920; d. Clifton and Helen Elvira (Hoskins) Williams; student Wash. State U., 1971, Eastern Wash. State U., 1974-77; m. James M. Sims, Aug. 2, 1941; children—James M., Ronald C., Donald C. Stenographer, sec. YWCA, Spokane, Wash., 1951-63, Spokesman Rev., Spokane, 1964-66, Spokane Neighborhood Centers, 1966-68; dep. dir. Eastside Neighborhood Center, Spokane, 1968-70; manpower tng. specialist, personnel and affirmative action officer Community Action Council, Spokane, 1970-73; affirmative action dir. City of Spokane, 1975—. Precinct com. person Spokane County Central Democratic Com.; v.p. bd. dirs. Spokane YWCA; bd. dirs., chmn. world mut. services com. Spokane YWCA; v.p. Interstate Human Rights Task Force; mem. adv. com., dept. office tech. Spokane Community Coll.; N.W. Women's Law Center; chmn. affirmative action com. Spokane County Central Democratic Com.; mem. chmn. Eastern Wash. Agy. on Aging Minority Task Force. Recipient Human Relations award Fairchild AFB, 1977; award of appreciation Kiwanis, 1979; Leadership award YWCA, 1986. Mem. Am. Assn. Affirmative Action (treas. Region X), NAACP (pres. N.W. area 1980-82, pres. Spokane br. 1976-80, merit award, award of appreciation 1982), Nat. Mgmt. Assn., LWV, Personnel Mgmt. Assn. Baptist. Club: Links (treas.). Dir. research and devel. Black history slide show, 1979. Home: E 1218 5th Ave Spokane WA 99202 Office: W 808 Spokane Falls Blvd Spokane WA 99201-3333

SIMS, TERESSA CAMILLE, vocational counselor, consultant; b. Lynwood, Calif., Nov. 5, 1949; d. Robert Russell and Demettress (Butler) S. B.A. in Psychology, Tex. A&I U., 1971; M.A. in Criminology and Corrections, Sam Houston State U., 1973, postgrad., 1976-78. Adminstrv. asst. counsel for health resources devel. Mid-Trinity Valley, Huntsville, Tex., 1971-72; lectr. speech Sam Houston State U., Huntsville, 1972; correctional officer Tex. Dept. Corrections, Huntsville, 1972; tchr. consultant/coordinator Windham Sch. System, Tex. Dept. Corrections, Huntsville, 1972-79; life skills educator Windham Sch. System, Huntsville, 1979-82; vocat. counselor Windham Sch. Dist., Navasota, Tex., 1982—; cons. E. Tex. State U., 1978-79; news disseminator Women's Task Force on Corrections in Tex., 1981-82; seminar leader to civic orgns., pvt. businesses, Region Edn. Service Ctrs., 1982—. Author: Reality Adjustment Program Manual, 1973, Occupational Orientation Curriculum Guide, 1976, 79, Occupational Investigation in Texas Curriculum Manual, 1979, Employability Skills: Indirectly Learned Through Industrial Vocational Education or Not?, 1983. Law Enforcement Edn. Program grantee, Washington, 1971-73. Mem. Am. Correctional Assn., Correctional Edn. Assn. (constitution com. 1977, election com. 1978), Am. Vocat. Assn., Am. Tech. Vocat. Assn., NEA/Tex. State Tchrs. Assn. (dist. six pub. relations com. 1981-82, sec.-treas. Windham local 1981-82), Tex. Corrections Assn. (recording sec. state orgn. 1981-82), Tex. Vocat. Guidance Assn. (occupational orientation div. 1978-81, pres. area V 1978-80, vocat. counselor div. 1982—, mem. state conf. planning coms. 1983, 84, 85), Grimes County Corrections Assn., Tex. A&I U. Alumni Assn., Inst. Contemporary Corrections and Behavioral Scis. Alumni Assn., Sam Houston State U. Alumni Assn., Nat. Assn. Female Execs., Am. Judicature Soc., Smithsonian Assocs. Republican. Roman Catholic. Avocations: clothing; gardening; cooking; dancing; teaching gymnastics. Home: 707A Ruth Ct Navasota TX 77868 Office: Tex Dept Corrections Pack 2 Windham Sch System Route 1 Box 1000 Navasota TX 77868

SIMSON, VERONICA BYRNES CINELLI, civic worker, health services administrator, coloratura soprano; b. Birmingham, Ala.; d. Andrew Louis and Gladys (Foushee) Byrnes; student parochial schs., Atlanta; advanced studies in music and langs., N.Y.C.; m. Albert A. Cinelli (dec. 1972); m. 2d A.A.R. Simson, June 24, 1978. Bd. dirs. Gen. Health Info. Service, Inc., N.Y.C.; adminstrv. coordinator Med. and Surg. Specialists Plan, N.Y.C.; health adminstr. Health Counseling Service, N.Y.C.; founder Med. and Health Services, N.Y.C.; gen. chmn. scholarship fund benefits Italian Charities Am., Inc.; mem. Met. Opera Guild, Inc., ARC, Operatic Group. Office: 1021 Park Ave New York NY 10028

SIMUNICH, MARY ELIZABETH HEDRICK (MRS. WILLIAM A. SIMUNICH), public relations executive; b. Chgo.; d. Tubman Keene and Mary (McCamish) Hedrick; student Phoenix Coll., 1967-69, Met. Bus. Coll., 1938-40; m. William A. Simunich, Dec. 6, 1941. Exec. sec. sales mgr. KPHO radio, 1950-53; exec. sec. mgr. KPHO-TV, 1953-54; account exec. Tom Rippey & Assos., 1955-56; pub. relations dir. Phoenix Symphony, 1956-62; co-founder, v.p. Paul J. Hughes Pub. Relations, Inc., 1960-65; owner Mary Simunich Pub. Relations, Phoenix, 1966-77. Pub. relations dir. Walter O. Boswell Meml. Hosp., Sun City, Ariz., 1969-85; instr. pub. relations Phoenix Coll. Evening Sch., 1973-78. Bd. dirs. Anytown, Ariz., 1969-72; founder, sec. Friends Am. Geriatrics, 1977—. Named Phoenix Advt. Woman of Year, Phoenix Jr. Advt. Club, 1962; recipient award Blue Cross, 1963; 1st Pl. award Ariz. Press Women, 1966. Mem. Internat. Assn. Bus. Communicators (pres. Ariz. chpt. 1970-71, dir.), Pub. Relations Soc. Am. (sec., dir. 1976-78), Am. Soc. Hosp. Pub. Relations (dir. Ariz. chpt. 1976-78), Nat., Ariz. press women. Club: Phoenix Press. Home: 4133 N 34th Pl Phoenix AZ 85018

SINAY, RUTH DORIS, psychologist; b. Bklyn., Feb. 5, 1920; d. Maurice Howard and Marion Gertrude (Heller) Milman; A.A., Santa Monica City Coll., 1953; B.A. cum laude in Psychology, U. So. Calif., 1956, Ph.D. (NIMH fellow), 1967; m. Joseph Sinay, Mar. 7, 1961; 1 son, Frederick Allen Schiff. Tchr. pub. schs., Hawthorne, Calif., 1957-58; instr. psychology U. So. Calif. Sch. Medicine, Los Angeles, 1967-71, dir. child and adolescent psychol. tng. program, 1969—, acting dir. child and adolescent psychol. services, 1969-70, dir., 1971—, asst. clin. prof., 1971-79, asso. clin. prof., 1979—; asso. clin. prof. psychology Fuller Theol. Sem., Pasadena, Calif., 1969—; cons. in field. Mem. Los Angeles Mayor's Com. on Youth and Aging, 1974-75; chmn. Take A Giant Step, Los Angeles, 1977; active United Jewish Fund drives; alt. del. Muskie for Pres., 1972. Recipient Judas Magnos award Hebrew U., Jerusalem, Israel, 1977. Mem. Am., Western, Calif. State (sec. 1975-78), Los Angeles County psychol. assns., Psychologists in Pub. Service (sec. 1969-70), Pi Lambda Theta. Club: Los Angeles Variety. Author: (with H. Slucki and N. Tiber) The Really Easy Reader Game, 1974; contbr. articles to profl. jours. Home: 1025 Carolyn Beverly Hills CA 90210 Office: 1937 Hospital Pl Los Angeles CA 90033

SINCLAIR, BEVERLEY ANN, broadcast journalist; b. Saskatoon, Sask., Can., Jan. 22, 1955; d. Don Smith and Betty Elena S.; student B.C. Inst. Tech., 1973-75. Reporter, editor CBC Radio, Vancouver, 1973-75; reporter, editor Sta. CKIQ, Kelowna, B.C., 1975-77, public affairs, news dir. Sta. CJOV-FM, Kelowna, 1977-78; public affairs dir. Sta. C-FAX, Victoria, B.C., Can., 1978-86, talk show host, 1986—; host Mixed Co., CHEK-TV, Victoria, 1986—; guest lectr. B.C. Inst. Tech. Recipient Edward R. Murrow award for radio documentary of social significance, 1979. Office: CHEK-TV 780 Kings Rd Victoria BC V8T SA2 Canada

SINCLAIR, SHARON LEE, training manager; b. Battle Creek, Mich., June 21, 1947; d. William Dennis and Opal (Bowmer) S.; m. Rufe Sinclair Bynum, III, Oct. 21, 1974 (div.). A.B.S., Kellogg Community Coll., 1968; B.S., Western Mich. U., 1970. Research technician Gen. Foods, Battle Creek, 1968-72; fashion coordinator Neiman-Marcus, Dallas, 1972-74; servicing mgr. Am. Home Savs., Dallas, 1974-76; v.p. Tex. Mortgage Corp., Dallas, 1976-82; gen. mgr. Supercuts, Dallas, 1982-83; ctr. mgr., seminar dir. Werner Erhard & Assocs., Chgo., 1983—. Bd. dirs. Medallion Mchts. Assn., Dallas, 1982-83, B.H. Condominium Assn., Dallas, 1980-82; sec. Calhoun County Young Republicans, Battle Creek, 1968; participant Big Sisters Am., Dallas, 1974-82; mem. World Hunger Project, San Francisco, 1981—; contbr. Breakthrough Found., San Francisco, 1981—. Mem. Nat. Assn. Female Execs., Nat. Mortgage Bankers Assn. Republican. Roman Catholic. Clubs: Dallas 500, Cottilion. Office: Dallas Fort Worth Area Ctr 2035 Royal Ln Suite 250 Dallas TX 75229

SINDEROFF, RITA JOYCE, property management company executive, real estate salesperson; b. Bklyn., June 22, 1932; d. Joseph George and Mary (Cohen) Rothkopf; m. Arthur B. Schneider, Oct. 18, 1953 (div. Sept. 1973); children—Linda Ellen, Debra Carol. Degree in comml. art Pratt Inst., 1953; B.A. in Acctg. Bklyn. Coll., 1954. Controller Central Funding Co., Bklyn., 1973-80; owner, controller Riteway Mgmt. Inc., Coral Springs, Fla., 1980—, real estate salesperson, 1985—; cons. in field. Active Cancer Soc., Bklyn., 1954-73, March of Dimes, Bklyn., 1960-70. Recipient 1st art award City of N.Y., 1950. Democrat. Jewish. Avocations: reading; dancing; swimming. Office: Riteway Mgmt Inc 7920 Wiles Rd Coral Springs FL 33067

SINGER, ARLENE KOWEEK, computer company executive; b. New Rochelle, N.Y., Mar. 7, 1950; d. Maxwell and Hannah (Grabelsky) Koweek; m. Dana Jay Singer, Dec. 27, 1975 (div. Aug. 1983). B.A., U. Mass., 1972; M.I.L.R., Cornell U., 1974. Mgmt. trainee Citibank, N.Y.C., 1975, personnel cons., Brussels, 1976-79, personnel mgr., N.Y.C., 1979-80, asst. v.p., N.Y.C., 1980-81; compensation advisor ITT, N.Y.C., 1982-83, mgr. compensation, 1983—. Mem. Am. Soc. Personnel Adminstrs., Internat. Assn. Personnel Women (lectr. 1981), Cornell Indsl. and Labor Relations Sch. Alumni Assn., Phi Beta Kappa. Democrat. Jewish. Club: Hadassah (N.Y.C.). Home: 624 E 20th St #3A New York NY 10009 Office: ITT 320 Park Ave New York NY 10022

SINGER, CAROL LEE, advertising agency executive, photographer; b. Hammond, Ind., Nov. 20, 1947; d. Leo and Wanda (Barnas) S. B.S. with distinction, Ind. U., 1969. With media dept. Leo Burnett Co., Chgo., 1970-72, asst. account exec., 1972-73, account exec., 1973-78, account supr., 1978; v.p., account supr. Benton & Bowles, Chgo., 1978-83, v.p., mgmt. supr., 1983-85; v.p., mgmt. supr. D'Arcy Masius Benton & Bowles, Chgo., 1985—; also free-lance photographer. Contbr. photographs to sailing mag. covers., mags., books. Roman Catholic. Office: D'Arcy Masius Benton & Bowles 200 E Randolph Chicago IL 60601

SINGER, GLADYS MONTGOMERY, writer; b. Natick, Mass.; d. Charles Norton and Myrtle (Cates) Taylor; B.A., Wellesley Coll.; m. Alexander John Montgomery (dec. 1955); m. 2d, Russell E. Singer, 1975 (dec. 1975). Sci. and semi-tech. writer McGraw-Hill mags. in Washington office, 1942-61, Washington reporter editor Textile World, 1943-46, Washington reporter Electronics, 1943-44, Washington editor, 1944-57, Washington rep., Nucleonics, 1947-48, co-editor, 1949-52; Washington reporter Bus. Week, 1952-61; feature writer Sci. Illustrated, 1957-61; then freelance, now ret. Mem. Pres.'s Adv. Com. on Arts, Kennedy Center, 1970-76; bd. dirs. D.C. League Republican Women 1983-85; adv. com. Former Senator Margaret Chase Smith Library, 1984—. Recipient citation Armed Forces Communications and Electronics Assn., 1970. Mem. AAAS, Nat. Assn. Sci. Writers, Women's Nat. Press Club (pres. 1957-58), Am. News Women's Club, English-Speaking Union. Clubs: Sulgrave, Chevy Chase, Wellesley College (Washington). Home: 2725 29th St NW Apt 605 Washington DC 20008

SINGER, JANET COHN, lawyer; b. N.Y.C., Apr. 8, 1948; d. Nathan and Helen (Scherer) Cohn; m. Michael N. Singer, June 9, 1968; children—Deborah, Sarah. B.A., U. Rochester, 1969; J.D., Cornell U., 1976. Bar: N.Y. 1977, U.S. Supreme Ct. 1981. Assoc. firm Otterbourg, Steindler, Houston & Rosen, N.Y.C., 1976-77, Sarisohn, Sarisohn, Carner, Steindler & LeBow, Commack, N.Y., 1977-80; sole practice law, Huntington, N.Y., 1980—; guest lectr. Am. Sch. Real Estate, 1983—. Bd. dirs., legal chmn. Planned Parenthood Suffolk County, 1979—, Temple Beth El, Huntington, 1983—. Mem. N.Y. State Bar Assn., Suffolk County Bar Assn., Suffolk County Matrimonial Bar Assn., Suffolk County Women's Bar Assn. (dir.), NOW. Democrat. Home: 85 Holst Dr West Huntington NY 11743 Office: 205 E Main St Huntington NY 11743

SINGER, JEANNE (WALSH), composer, concert pianist; b. N.Y.C., Aug. 4, 1924; d. Harold Vandervoort and Helen (Loucks) Walsh; B.A. magna cum laude, Barnard Coll., 1944; artist diploma Nat. Guild Piano Tchrs., 1954; student in piano Nadia Reisenberg, 1945-60, composition, Douglas Moore, 1942-44, Ph.D. (hon.) in Music World U., 1984; m. Richard G. Singer, Feb. 24, 1945, dec.; 1 son, Richard V. Composer, concert pianist solo chamber ensembles N.Y., 1947—; tchr. piano Manhasset, N.Y., 1960—; lectr. in field. Recipient spl. award merit Nat. Fedn. Music Clubs, 1st prize in nat. competition Composers Guild, 1979, Grand prize Composers Guild, 1982, 1st prize Composers and Songwriters Internat., 1985, also various nat. awards; honored at all-Singer concert, Bogotá, Colombia, 1980; N.Y. Council Arts grantee. Fellow Internat. Biog. Assn.; mem. ASCAP (awards 1978-86), Am. Music Center, Internat. League Women Composers, Nat. League Am. Pen Women (nat. music chmn.), Composers, Authors and Artists Am. (v.p. N.Y.C., music mag. editor 1972-80, nat. award 1981), Am. Women Composers, Internat. Platform Assn., Phi Beta Kappa. Clubs: Barnard Coll. of L.I., Tuesday Morning Music Douglaston; Bohemians (N.Y.C.). Composed numerous instrumental, vocal works including: Summons (baritone), 1975, A Cycle of Love (4 songs with piano), 1976, Suite in Harpsichord Style, 1976, From The Green Mountains (trio), 1977, (choral work) Composers' Prayer, Nocturne for Clarinet, 1980, Suite for Horn and Harp, 1980, From Petrarch (voice, horn, piano), 1981, Quartet for Flute, Oboe, Violin, Cello, 1982, Trio for Viola, Oboe, Piano, 1984, Come Greet the Spring (choral), 1981; performed Lincoln Center, radio, TV. Home and office: 64 Stuart Place Manhasset NY 11030

SINGER, JULIE LYNN, public relations/broadcasting company executive; b. Reading, Pa., Nov. 9, 1956; d. Henry David and Anita M. (Klein) S. B.S. in Broadcast Journalism cum laude, Syracuse U., 1978; postgrad. Franklin and Marshall U., 1979, New Sch. Social Research, 1981-83. Radio news feature announcer Sta. WAER-FM, Syracuse, N.Y., 1976-78; TV documentary and news writer Sta. WPIX-TV, Syracuse, 1977; TV news anchor, producer, reporter Sta. WGAL-TV, Lancaster, Pa., 1978-80; v.p. Hill & Knowlton, N.Y.C., 1980-85; pres. Dorf & Stanton Broadcast Communications, 1985—. Mem. Internat. Radio and TV Soc., Women in Communication, Syracuse U. Profl. Publicity Group, Syracuse U. Alumni Assn. Jewish. Office: Dorf & Stanton Communications Inc 111 Fifth Ave New York NY 10003

SINGER, LYNN BUCHHOLZ, cons. co. exec.; b. Chgo., June 18, 1948; d. Alexander and Jean (Ross) Buchholz; B.A. cum laude, U. Mich., 1970, M.P.H., 1972; m. Steven M. Singer, Nov. 26, 1976; children—David Benjamin, Michael Lawrence. Program analyst USPHS, Chgo., 1972-73, regional program cons. migrant health, 1973-77, chief profl. consultation services, 1977-79; intergovtl. affairs specialist Dept. Health and Human Services, Chgo., 1980-81; v.p. Community Health Found., Skokie, Ill., 1981—; chairperson adv. com. HEW Fed. Women's Program, 1978, 79. USPHS trainee, 1970, recipient cert. outstanding performance, 1973, 76; citation Dept. Health and Human Services, 1980. Office: 9933 Lawler Skokie IL 60077

SINGER, MARTHA HOUX, marketing professional; b. Warrensburg, Mo., Feb. 7, 1942; d. James Robert and Doris Lorraine (Smith) Houx; m. Lawrence Alan Singer, July 22, 1967; children—Robert Alan, Michael Stuart. B.J., U. Mo., 1963; M.B.A., U. So. Calif., 1980. Advt. copywriter Sears, Roebuck & Co., Chgo., 1963-66; asst. to exec. dir. Chgo. Maternity Ctr., 1966-67; staff writer, spl. edit. editor Santa Monica (Calif.) Evening Outlook, 1969-75; pub. relations dir. West Los Angeles-Beverly Hills YWCA, 1975-77; cons. to various Los Angeles businesses, 1978-80; promotion mgr. Shepherd Machinery/POWER SYSTEMS, Los Angeles, 1980-83; dir. research Kessler & Assocs., Los Angeles, 1983—. Mem. Women in Communications (dir. 1976-6, chpt. recognition 1976), Am. Mktg. Assn. Lodge: P.E.O. Office: Kessler & Assocs 11661 San Vincente Blvd Los Angeles CA 90049

SINGER, MAXINE FRANK, biochemist; b. N.Y.C., Feb. 15, 1931; d. Hyman S. and Henrietta (Perlowitz) Frank; A.B., Swarthmore Coll., 1952, D.Sc. (hon.), 1978; Ph.D., Yale U., 1957; D.Sc., Wesleyan U., 1977; D.Sc., U. Md. Balt. County, 1985, D.Sc., Cedar Crest Coll., 1986; m. Daniel Morris Singer, June 15, 1952; children—Amy Elizabeth, Ellen Ruth, David Byrd, Stephanie Frank. USPHS postdoctoral fellow NIH, Bethesda, Md., 1956-58, research chemist (biochemistry), 1958-74, head sect. on nucleic acid enzymology Nat. Cancer Inst., 1974-79; chief Lab. of Biochemistry, Nat. Cancer Inst., 1979—; Regents vis. lectr. U. Calif., Berkeley, 1981; mem. sci. adv. bd. Internat. Inst. Genetics and Biophysics, Naples, Italy, 1982—. Bd. dirs. Found. for Advanced Edn. in Scis., 1972-78, 85-86; trustee Wesleyan U., Middletown, Conn., 1972-75, Yale Corp., New Haven, 1975—; bd. govs. Weizman Inst. Sci., Israel, 1979—; bd. dirs. Whitehead Inst., Cambridge, Mass., 1985—. Recipient award for achievement in biol. scis. Washington Acad. Scis., 1969, award for research in biol. scis. Yale Sci. and Engring. Assn., 1974, Superior Service Honor award HEW, 1975, Dirs. award NIH, 1977, Disting. Service award HHS, 1983; Dreyfus disting. scholar Swarthmore Coll., 1982. Fellow Am. Acad. Arts and Scis.; mem. AAAS, Am. Soc. Biol. Chemists, Am. Soc. Microbiologists, Am. Chem. Soc., Inst. Medicine of Nat. Acad. Scis., Nat. Acad. Scis. (council 1982-85). Editor: Jour. Biol. Chemistry, 1968-74; editorial bd. Sci. mag., 1972-81; chmn. editorial bd. Procs. of Nat. Acad. Scis. Contbr. articles to scholarly jours. Home: 5410 39th St NW Washington DC 20015 Office: Bldg 37 4E-28 Bethesda MD 20205

SINGER, PHYLLIS, editor; b. Newark, May 22, 1947; d. Carl N. and Marion (Heller) S.; m. Edward J. Lowe, Jr., Aug. 11, 1979; children—James, Daniel. B.S., Boston U., 1969. Mgr. print and broadcast traffic F. William Free & Co., advt., N.Y.C., 1969-70; researcher, reporter, editor L.I. Comml. Rev., Syosset, N.Y., 1970-72; with Newsday, L.I., 1972—, asst. editor, then sr. editor viewpoints, now asst. mng. editor features; mem. bd. Newspaper Features Council. Mem. Am. Assn. Sunday and Feature Editors (v.p.). Office: 235 Pinelawn Rd Melville NY 11747

SINGH, JOYCE HIDEKO, educator; b. Stockton, Calif., July 21, 1942; d. Ichiro and Mitsue (Nakai) Nakahara; m. Gurnam Singh, Aug. 22, 1970. B.A., San Jose State Coll., 1965, M.A., 1968; M.A., San Jose State U., 1976. Cert. kindergarten-primary tchr., adminstr., Calif. Substitute tchr. Alumn Rock Sch. Dist., San Jose, Calif., 1965; tchr. Northwood Elem. Sch., Berryessa Union Sch. Dist., San Jose, 1965—; summer sch. tchr.; congl. contact person Santa Clara County Service Ctr. Council Polit. Action Com.; coordinator Dist. Kindergarten Com., chmn., 1982-84; mem. Dist. Curriculum Council; chmn. Berryessa Dist. Election Com. Mem. Soc. Baptist Conv., 1960-67. Milpitas Metalcraft scholar, 1960. Mem. Calif. Tchrs. Assn. (women's caucus), NEA (women's caucus), Assn. Supervision and Curriculum Devel., Am. Edn. Assn., Calif. Tchrs. Assn. (sec. 1983-84), Asian Am. Educators Assn., Asian Am. Caucus of Calif. Tchrs. Assn.

SINGH, KALPANA, obstetrician, gynecologist; b. Patna, India, Aug. 22, 1949; came to U.S., 1973; d. Ras Bihari and Manna Rani S.; m. Rama S. Singh, Feb. 12, 1969; children—Tulika, Anjali. M.B. B.S., Prince of Wales Med. Coll., Patna, 1971. Intern, Prince of Wales Med. Coll., 1973; house physician Biscayne Med. Coll., Miami, Fla., 1975-76; resident in ob-gyn Mt. Sinai Hosp. Med. Coll., Chgo., 1977-79; practice medicine specializing in ob-gyn, Chgo., 1980—; instr. Rush Med. Coll., Chgo., 1980—. Fellow Am. Coll. Ob-Gyn; mem. AMA (Physicians Recognition award 1980), Chgo. Med. Soc., Ill. State Med. Soc. Home: 9912 S Kilpatrick St Oak Lawn IL 60453 Office: 2808 W 87th St Chicago IL 60652

SINGH, SUSHILA, artist; b. Fatehgarh, India, Aug. 29, 1940; came to U.S., 1969; d. Ramlal and Ramkumari Katiyar; m. Ramchandra Sitaram Singh, Dec. 12, 1964; children—Rajiv, Sanjay. B.A., Agra U., 1964, M.A., 1968; diploma advt. and illustrating art Art Instrn. Schs., Mpls., 1977, diploma in painting, 1978. One-woman shows include Dharam Samaj Coll., Aligarh, India, 1968, Indian Inst. Tech., Kanpur, India, 1968, U. Ill. Art Gallery, Urbana, 1969, 70, Zigler Mus., Jennings, La., 1977; represented in permanent collection: Spindletop Mus., Beaumont, Tex., Art Instrn. Schs., Mpls.; portrait of Prince Charles, accepted by same as gift; commd. to paint Dr. Denton Cooley, Houston. Lectr. art classes in community ctrs., 1977—; tchr. painting leisure learning program McNeese State U., 1979—. Recipient 3 Gold medals Agra U., 1st prize for painting Rhythm, Art Instrn. Schs., 1972. Mem. Art Assocs. Lake Charles. Address: 4801 Orleans St Lake Charles LA 70605

SINGHAUS, BARBARA L., accountant; b. Dover, Ohio, Sept. 16, 1956; d. Enos L. and Janet (Stonebrook) Loader; m. William David Singhaus, May 12, 1979. B.S. in Acctg., U. Akron, 1978. C.P.A., Ohio. Staff acct. Rea & Assocs., New Philadelphia, Ohio, 1976-79; ptnr. Harter, Singhaus & Co., North Canton, Ohio, 1979—. Mem. community planning com. United Way, Canton, 1980—; pres., bd. dirs. Planned Parenthood of Stark County, Canton, 1984—. Mem. Am. Inst. C.P.A.s, Ohio Soc. C.P.A.s. Presbyterian. Avocations: skiing, golf. Home: 2074 Beechtree Dr Uniontown OH 44685 Office: Harter Singhaus & Co 5902 Mayfair Rd North Canton OH 44720

SINGLETARY, PATRICIA ANN, minister, trust company executive; b. N.Y.C., Mar. 3, 1948; d. George and Minnie Juanita (Williams) Nickens; m. Edward Franklin Singletary, Feb. 5, 1966; children—Erik Franklin, Don Andrew. B.Th., New World Bible Inst. and Sem., 1984, M.R.E., 1986; postgrad. SUNY-Empire State Coll., 1985—. Sr. reorgn. underwriter Depository Trust Co., N.Y.C., 1968—; nat. corr. sec. Nat. Baptist Conv. U.S.A. Inc., Spiritual Life Commn. of Women Clergy; assoc. minister Morning Star Missionary Bapt. Ch. of Jamaica, N.Y. Editor: The Ekklesiastes, 1986. Recipient Vol. Services award City of N.Y., 1980. Mem. Nat. Assn. Negro Bus. and Profl. Women, Nat. Assn. Female Execs., Interdenominational Bd. Clergywomen (gen. sec. 1985—), Nat. Bapt. Women Ministers Conv. (bd. mgrs. 1983—), Eastern Bapt. Assn. (instr. 1981-83, v.p. evangelistic unit 1982-83). Office: Morning Star Missionary Bapt Ch 114-44 Merrick Blvd Jamaica NY 11434

SINGLETON, JANE GURLINE PACE, real estate company executive; b. Homestead, Fla., Jan. 6, 1928; d. Leander James and Julia (Laughter) Pace; B.A., Flora McDonald Coll., 1948; student U. Fla., 1952-53, Stetson U., Deland, Fla., 1955-56; children—Robert Maginnis, Nancy Maginnis, Joseph. Tchr. public schs., Orange County, Fla., 1954-59; mem. Bd. Edn., Sequatchie County, Tenn., 1970; county judge, Sequatchie County, 1970-72; ofcl. OEO, Washington, 1972; personal sec. Jeanne Dixon, Washington, 1973-74, Congressman John Duncan, Washington, 1973-74; legis. asst. White House, Washington, 1975-76; pres., mgr. Singleton Properties, Inc., Manalapan, Fla., 1977—; pres. Gold Coast Electric, Inc., Lantana, Fla. Precinct chmn. home precinct, 1976; v.p. bd. dirs. Council on Child Abuse and Neglect Palm Beach County, 1984; vice chmn. adv. bd. John F. Kennedy Hosp., Atlantis, Fla., 1984. Recipient Beautification and Renovation award Town of Lantana, 1981. Mem. Nat. Juvenile Judges Assn., C. of C., Internat. platform Assn. Republican. Presbyterian. Club: Zonta. Columnist: Signal Mountain (Tenn.) News, 1970. Home and Office: 1000 S Ocean Blvd Manalapan FL 33462

SINGLETON, SARAH MICHAEL, lawyer; b. Ann Arbor, Mich., Apr. 2, 1949; d. Palmer Christie and Susan (Ballard) Singleton. B.A., Sarah Lawrence Coll., 1971; J.D. with high honors, Ind. U., 1974. Bar: N.Mex. 1974, U.S. Circuit Ct (10th circuit) 1976, U.S. Supreme Ct. 1978. Atty., N.Mex. Pub. Defender, Santa Fe, 1974-76; adj. prof. U. N.Mex. Sch. Law, Albuquerque, 1978; atty. Singleton Law Offices, Santa Fe, 1976-85, Montgomery & Andrews P.A., Santa Fe, 1985—; chmn. Bd. Bar Examiners, Santa Fe, 1982—. Contbr. articles to profl. jours. Chmn. bd. trustees No. N.Mex. Legal Services, Taos, 1980. Recipient award for outstanding contbn. State Bar of N.Mex., 1983. Mem. State Bar of N.Mex., ABA, Trial Lawyers of Am., Bar Assn. First Judicial Dist. (pres. 1978). Democrat. Office: Montgomery & Andrews PA 325 Paseode Peratta PO Box 2307 Santa Fe NM 87501

SINIARD, SHEILA COSTNER, interior designer; b. Columbia, S.C., Sept. 8, 1954; d. Dennis Dale and Anita Louise (Whitener) Costner; 1 child, Robert Adam. B.S., Western Carolina U., Cullowhee, N.C., 1976. Asst. resident mgr. pub. relations/mktg. Club Regency/Governors Club, Myrtle Beach, S.C., 1976-78; designer, sales rep. S.S. Interiors, Myrtle Beach, 1978-83; comml. designer John Gore & Assocs., Myrtle Beach, 1983-84; designer, owner Design Dimension, Myrtle Beach, 1984-85; owner, designer Elizabeth Design Dimensions, Charlotte, N.C., 1985—. Mem. Am. Soc. Interior Designers, Inst. Bus. Designers, Nat. Assn. Female Execs. Avocations: art; golf; flying. Office: Elizabeth Design Dimensions 231 E Worthington Ave Charlotte NC 28203

SINK, ALVA GORDON (MRS. CHARLES A. SINK), clubwoman; b. Rose Twp., Mich.; d. Nathaniel J. and Ella M. (Highfield) Gordon; student Eastern Mich. U., summers 1914, 18; A.B., U. Mich., 1923; m. Charles A. Sink, June 18, 1923 (dec.). Tchr. pub. schs., Rose Center, Mich., 1914-17, Hickory Ridge, Mich., 1917-18, Holly, Mich., 1918-19, Canfield Pvt. Sch., Ann Arbor, Mich., 1919-22. Mem. Women's Republican Club, Ann Arbor. Dir. Washtenaw County chpt. ARC, 1943-48, 53-59, in charge First Aid and Accident Prevention, 1941-61; pres. Mich. House and Senate Club, 1929-30, U. Mich. Alumnae Club, 1931-33, Sara Browne Smith Group Alumnae Club, 1957-59, Women's Soc. Congl. Ch., 1946-48; regent Sarah Caswell Angell chpt. DAR, 1955-57. Recipient Red Cross citation, 1959, Alumnae Council award U. Mich., 1971, Disting. Alumni Service award U. Mich., 1978; Alva Gordon Sink Group of U. Mich. Alumnae named in her honor. Mem. Hist. Soc. Mich., Alumni Assn. U. Mich., French Huguenots, AAUW, Ann Arbor Art Assn., Henry P. Tappan Soc., P.E.O. Clubs: Art Study, Garden, Faculty Women, Presidents of U. Mich. (pres. emeritus 1975-76), Ann Arbor Women's City. Home: 1325 Olivia Ave Ann Arbor MI 48104

SINNARD, ELAINE JANICE, painter, sculptor; b. Fort Collins, Colo., Feb. 14, 1926; d. Elven Orestes and Catherine (Bennet) S.; student Art Students League, 1948, N.Y. U., 1953, Sculpture Center, N.Y.C., 1954, Academie de la Grande Chaumiere, Paris, 1956. Painter, sculptor; works exhibited Riverside Mus., N.Y.C., 1955, City Center, N.Y.C., 1954-56, Nat. Arts Club, N.Y.C.,

1959-82, Lord & Taylor, N.Y.C., 1963-78, Bergdorf Goodman, N.Y.C., 1980-85, Zantman Art Galleries, Carmel-by-the-Sea, Calif., 1970-73, Chevy Chase Gallery, Washington, 1981-86; one woman shows and group exhbns. include: Bergdorf Goodman Nena's Choice Gallery, Chevy Chase Gallery, Bjorn Lindgren Gallery, Sinnard Art Studios; tchr. open workshop for artists. Mem. Nat. Arts Club N.Y.C. Home and Studio: Box 304 New Hampton NY 10958

SINNEMAKI, ULLA ULPUKKA, nurse, educator; b. Antrea, Finland, Sept. 11, 1928; d. Otto William and Kaisa Viola (Jappinen) Spjut; m. Maunu Matti J. Sinnemaki, June 12, 1949 (div. Feb. 1968); children—Markku Taneli, Sirkka Astrid. B.A., NYU, 1972; B.S., SUNY-Stony Brook, 1976; M.Ed., McNeese State U., 1978, Ed.S., 1979, M.Ed., 1981. R.N., N.Y., La., Tex. Field interviewer Bur. Census, N.Y.C., 1973-75; Operating room asst. St. Charles Meml. Hosp., N.Y.C., 1965-72; staff nurse Lake Charles Meml. Hosp., La., 1976-77; head nurse South Cameron Hosp., Cameron, La., 1977-80, dir. nursing, 1983-84; staff nurse Humana Hosp., Oakdale, La., 1984. Translator books, articles from English to Finnish, 1961—; designer rya rugs. Mem. Com. 1000 Baton Rouge, 1983. Mem. Nat. League Nursing, Am. Nurses Assn., Assn. Ednl. Communictions and Tech., Assn. Supervision and Curriculum Devel., Nat. Assn. Female Execs. Democrat. Lutheran. Avocations: gardening; music; photography. Address: 332 W State St Lake Charles LA 70605

SINNREICH, NAOMI WENDY BRAININ, lawyer; b. Bronx, N.Y., Jan. 18, 1953; d. William David and Beatrice Roslyn (Horowitz) Brainin; m. Abraham Isaac Sinnreich, Aug. 10, 1975. B.A., SUNY-Stony Brook, 1974; J.D. cum laude, Benjamin N. Cardozo Sch. Law, 1981. Bar: N.Y. 1982. Legal adminstrv. asst. Garbarini, Scher & DeCicco, N.Y.C., 1974-75; law clk., legal asst. Mandel & Resnik, N.Y.C., 1975-80; assoc. firm Graubard Moskovitz McGoldrick Dannett & Horowitz, N.Y.C., 1981-83; corp. atty.-assoc. Lowenthal, Landau, Fischer & Ziegler, N.Y.C., 1983—. Editor moot ct. bd., 1980-81. Mem. ABA, N.Y. State Bar Assn., Assn. Bar City N.Y. Democrat. Jewish. Office: Lowenthal Landau Fischer & Ziegler 250 Park Ave New York NY 10177

SINUSAS, ROSEMARIE THERESE SPECIAN, pharmaceutical company executive; b. Somerville, N.J., Nov. 4, 1944; d. William Michael and Maryann (Dudek) Specian; m. Edward J. Sinusas, Jr. Dec. 28, 1985; B.S. in Home Econs. (Ella Mae Shellshy Holmes award), Albright Coll., Reading, Pa., 1966; M.S. in Human Behavior and Devel., Drexel U., Phila., 1971; M.B.A., Loyola-Marymount U., Los Angeles, 1980. Sales rep. Atlas Crown Brokerage, Los Angeles, 1973-75; regional rep. Reynolds Metals Co., Los Angeles, 1975-77; mktg. mgr. nat. accounts Glass Containers Corp., Anaheim, Calif., 1977-79; sr. package developer Lederle Labs., Pearl River, N.Y., 1980—. Recipient various sales awards. Mem. Am. Mktg. Assn., Packaging Inst., N.J. Mktg. Assn., N.J. Packaging Assn., AAUW. Home: 85 New Holland Village Nanuet NY 10954 Office: Lederle Labs N Middletown Rd Pearl River NY 10965

SIPE, ILENE GOLDBAUM, lawyer; b. Tucson, Mar. 8, 1954; d. Arthur and Miriam (Saltzman) Goldbaum; m. Dean Allen Sipe, Mar. 26, 1978. B.S. in Speech and Hearing Scis. with high distinctions and honors, U. Ariz., 1975, J.D., 1978. Bar: Ariz. 1978, U.S. Dist. Ct. Ariz. 1978. Assoc., Kenneth Allen, Tucson, 1979-81, Waterfall, Economidis, Tucson, 1981-83; sole practice, Tucson, 1983—; founder, dir. Pima County PrivaCourt, Inc., Tucson, 1983-85; speaker before profl. groups. Mem. ABA, Ariz. Bar Assn., Pima County Bar Assn., Ariz. Trial Lawyers Assn., Ariz. Women Lawyers Assn., Phi Kappa Phi. Democrat. Office: 1403 Home Fed Tower 32 N Stone Ave Tucson AZ 85701

SIPORIN, RAE LEE, university official; b. Detroit, Apr. 12, 1940; d. Morris and Zelda (Brown) Siporin; B.A., Wayne State U., 1962; M.A., U. Calif. at Los Angeles, 1964; Ph.D., 1968; certificate Inst. Ednl. Mgmt., Harvard U., 1977. Asst. prof. English, U. Pitts., 1968-72, asst. dean Coll. Arts and Scis., 1970-72, exec. asst. to vice chancellor planning and budget, 1973-75, dir. program planning, 1975-76; dean acad. affairs, prof. English, Franklin Pierce Coll., Rindge, N.H., 1976-78; dean gen. studies Stockton State Coll., Pomona, N.J., 1978-79; dir. undergrad. admissions and relations with schs. UCLA, 1979—; Am. Council Edn. adminstrv. acad. intern, asst. to pres. Ohio State U., 1972-73; chmn. adv. com. on research and devel. Coll. Bd., 1983—; cons. in field. Emma Wilson Richards fellow, 1967-68; Disting. scholar U. Calif. at Los Angeles, 1968. Mem. Am. Assn. Higher Edn., Am. Assn. Collegiate Registrars and Admissions Officers (chmn. EEO com. 1984-86), Phi Beta Kappa. Democrat. Author: Women and Education: The Conference as Catalyst, 1972. Editor: Female Studies V, 1972. Dir., initiator nat. conf. Women and Edn.: A Feminist Perspective, 1971. Office: UARS 1147 Murphy Hall UCLA Los Angeles CA 90024

SIRI, JEAN BRANDENBURG, citizen advocate; b. Lakota, N.D., Mar. 11, 1920; d. Tunis Orville and Edith Marion (Malloy) Brandenburg; m. William Yettergren (div.); m. William E. Siri, Dec. 6, 1949; children—Lynn Kimsey, Ann Kathryn. B.S., Jamestown Coll., 1942; postgrad. U. Calif.-Berkeley, 1946. Biologist, Lawrence Berkeley Lab., U. Calif., 1954-52; mem city council City of El Cerrito, Calif., 1980-85, mayor, 1982-83. Chmn. civil service Contra Costa Grand Jury, 1967; mem. state solid waste mgmt. and resource recovery adv. council, Sacramento, 1973-74; bd. dirs. stege San. Dist. Bd., El Cerrito, 1972-76, chmn., 1975. Served to lt. USNR, 1942-45. Recipient Sol Feinstone Nat. Environ. award Syracuse U., 1976-77; Clean Air Citizen award Am. Lung Assn., Santa Clara-San Benito Counties, 1976. Mem. West Contra Costa Conservation League (pres. 1968-85), Contra Costa Gray Panthers (environ. chmn. 1980-86). Home: 1015 Leneve Pl El Cerrito CA 94530

SIROF, HARRIET TOBY, writer, educator; b. N.Y.C., Oct. 18, 1930; d. Herman and Lillian (Miller) Hockman; m. Sidney M. Sirof, June 18, 1949; children—Laurie, David, Amy. B.A., New Sch. Social Research, 1962. Pvt. tutor Bklyn., 1962-76; instr. L.I. U., Bklyn., 1978-79, South Shore Adult Center, Bklyn., 1977-83, Bklyn. Coll., 1980-81, 1984—; instr. writing St. John's U., Jamaica, N.Y., 1978—. Author: The If Machine, 1978; A New Fashioned Love Story, 1977; Junior Encyclopedia of Israel, 1980; Save the Dam, 1981; That Certain Smile, 1982; The Real World, 1985; Anything You Can Do, 1986. Recipient Louis Weiss award New Sch. Social Research, 1962. Mem. Authors Guild, Internat. Womens Writing Guild, Soc. Children's Book Writers. Democrat. Jewish. Home: 792 E 21st St Brooklyn NY 11210

SIROTNAK, VIRGINIA LEO, lawyer; b. Scranton, Pa., Sept. 29, 1935; d. Joseph A. and Theresa (Sebilia) Leo; B.A., Marywood Coll., Scranton, 1957, M.S. in Edn., 1959; J.D., U. Detroit, 1970; m. Joseph M. Sirotnak, Dec. 24, 1974. Tchr. Latin, Scranton public schs., 1957-67; legal clk. orphans ct. Lackawanna County (Pa.), 1970-71; admitted to Pa. bar, 1971; spl. asst. atty. gen. Office Chief Counsel, Pa. Dept. Transp., 1973-79; pvt. practice, Scranton, 1971—; asst. city solicitor City of Scranton, 1982—; mem. pre-law adv. bd. Marywood Coll., also mem. faculty Grad. Sch. Public Adminstrn.; mem. panel Am. Arbitration Assn. Bd. dirs. Scranton YWCA; sec. Jefferson Found. Fulbright scholar, 1960. Mem. Pa. Bar Assn., Lackawanna County Bar Assn. (exec. com. of bd. dirs.), Lackawanna County Hist. Soc., AAUW (past chpt. pres.), Marywood Coll. Alumnae Assn. (past chpt. pres.), Scranton Bus. and Profl. Women's Club, Lackawanna County Fedn. Sportsmen (life), Slovak League Am. Democrat. Roman Catholic. Club: Century (Scranton). Office: 612 Connell Bldg Scranton PA 18503

SIROWER, BONNIE FOX, fundraiser; b. Bklyn., Jan. 9, 1949; d. Stanley S. and Harriet (Fischer) Fox; m. Martin Alan Sirower, Sept. 20, 1970; children—Kenneth, Daniel. A.B., Barnard Coll., 1970; M.A., Tchrs. Coll., Columbia U., 1971. Tchr., United Cerebral Palsy, N.Y.C., 1970-73, Bergen County Bd. Spl. Services, Paramus, N.J., 1973-76; spl. events coordinator Am. Heart Assn., Glen Ridge, 1979-81; dir. devel. Goodwill Industries, Astoria, N.Y., 1981-83; pres. Access Unltd., 1984-85; dir. devel. Cheshire Home, Inc., 1986—; cons. New Concepts for Living, Hillsdale, N.J., 1983. Pres. Sisterhood Temple Beth Haverim, Mahwah, 1976-77; co-chmn. Glen Rock Independence Day Assn., 1983. Mem. N.J. Soc. Fund Raising Execs., Women in Fin. Devel., Assn. Fund Raisers for Disabled (pres. 1981-83), N.J. Puzzlers' League (pres.), Phi Beta Kappa. Jewish. Home: 69 Godfrey Terr Glen Rock NJ 07452

SISCO, MARY ELIZABETH, lawyer, consultant; b. Fort Worth, Nov. 16, 1937; d. Daniel Louis and Mary Elizabeth (Blanton) Creson; m. William Theodore Sisco, Aug. 7, 1959; children—Christopher Theodore, Gregory Samuel, Lois Danine. B.A., Tex. Christian U., 1959; J.D., Tex. Tech U., 1979. Bar: Tex. 1979. Provisional secondary teaching cert., Tex. Tchr., Fort Worth Ind. Sch. Dist., 1959-61, Memphis Ind. Sch. Dist., 1961-65; ind. market researcher, Rochester, Minn., 1968-72; solo practice, Lubbock, Tex., 1979—; treas., bd. dirs. Y-Not Better Papers, Dallas, 1975—. Trustee, Lubbock Ind. Sch. Dist., 1980-86; bd. dirs. Caprock council Girl Scouts U.S.A., Lubbock, 1980—; rep. Tex. Legis. Cabinet, Girl Scouts U.S.A., Dallas, 1981-84; bd. dirs. Lubbock Civic Ballet, 1983-85; mem. West Tex. Mus. Assn., Tex. Tech. U., 1974—; co-chmn. Lubbock Assn. Concerned with Teenage Sexuality, 1984, pres., 1985; bd. dirs. Lubbock div. March of Dimes; mem. Vol. Lawyers and Accts. for the Arts; life mem. Lubbock PTA, Tex. PTA. Mem. ABA, Order of Coif, Alpha Chi, Delta Delta Delta. Methodist. Clubs: Lubbock Women's, Classic Toastmasters (v.p.). Office: 3607 22d St Lubbock TX 79410

SISCO, VERONICA ROBINSON, banker; b. Camden, N.J., Aug. 8, 1952; d. Stephen Henry and Mildred Levetta (Littleton) Robinson. B.A. in History, Washington Coll., 1974; postgrad. U. Del., 1984. Cert. tchr. social studies, Md. adult edn. instr., Del.; cert. paralegal asst. Tchr. history Kent County Bd. Edn., Chestertown, Md., 1974-79; coordinator tng. Del. Opportunities Industrialization Ctr., Wilmington and Dover, 1980-81; adult edn. instr. Christina Sch. Dist., Newark, Del., 1981-82; collector Md. Nat. Bank, Balt., 1982, Md. Bank, N.A., Newark, 1982, collection supr., 1982-84, credit supr., 1984-85, tng. mgr., 1985—, personal banking officer, 1985—. Mem. adv. bd. dirs. Occupational Services, Inc., Wilmington, 1983; host-parent Fresh Air Fund, Newark, N.Y.C., 1979-81; bd. dirs. West End Neighborhood House, Wilmington, Kingswood Community Ctr., Wilmington; vol. in polit. campaigns; election dist. capt. Dem. party, New Castle, Del., 1984. Mem. Del. Paralegal Assn., Am. Inst. Banking (adv. bd. dirs. Del. chpt. 1985-86), Del. Human Resources Group, Am. Soc. Notaries, Am. Soc. Tng. and Devel., Brandwine Profl. Assn. Avocations: travel; gardening; writing. Office: Md Bank NA 400 Christiana Rd Newark DE 19713

SISK, ELIZABETH A., insurance company executive; b. Mercedes, Tex., Oct. 12, 1951; d. Noa B. and Velva E. (Schnurbusch) S. B.A., U. Tex., 1974. Mem. entry level staff Farmers Ins. Group, Austin, Tex., 1976-77, policy service supr., 1977-78, auto underwriter, 1978-81, prematic supr., 1981-85, auto underwriting supr., 1985, policy service mgr., 1985—. Asst. dir., stage mgr. (local amateur theatre) The Ritz, 1982 (Best Comedy Prodn. Austin Cir. of Theatres 1982); editor-founder: (newsletter) The F.I.G. Leaflet, 1983-85. Officer Toastmaster Internat., Austin, 1983—; mem. Citizens' Traffic Safety Commn., Austin, 1985—. Named Competent Toastmaster, Toastmasters Internat., Austin, 1984; cert. in Gen. Ins., Ins. Inst. Am., 1984. Mem. Am. Soc. Tng. and Devel., Nat. Assn. Female Execs., Am. Mgmt. Assn., Austin Jr. C. of C. (bd. dirs. 1986-87). Republican. Presbyterian. Club: U. Tex. Ex-Students (Austin). Lodge: Order of Eastern Star. Avocations: sewing; handicrafts; collecting-reading books; travel; sports. Office: Farmers Ins Group 17105 FM 1325 Austin TX 78728

SISK, MELINDA ANN, geophysicist; b. Corpus Christi, June 30, 1953; d. Lyman and Violet Ann (Kennemer) S. Student U. Tex.-Arlington, 1971-72, Dallas Community Coll., 1973-79; B.S. in Geosci., U. Tex.-Richardson, 1981. Geophys. asst. Mobil Oil Co., Dallas, 1972-75; sales rep. Smitty's Sporting Goods, Dallas, 1975-76, Elgin B. Robertson Electronics, Dallas, 1976; geophys. asst. Mobil Oil Co., Dallas, 1977-80; exploration geophysicist Sun Exploration and Prodn. Co., Dallas, 1981—. Desk and Derrick grantee, 1980; Soc. Exploration Geophysicists grantee, 1980; Mobil Oil Corp. Srs. grantee, 1980-81. Mem. Soc. Exploration Geophysicist, Dallas Geophys. Soc., Assn. Women Geoscientists. Republican. Clubs: Alpine Ski Sports, Shelby Sports Car. Office: Sun Exploration and Prodn Co PO Box 2880 Dallas TX 75221

SISKO, MARIE FERRARIS, fund raising executive; b. N.Y.C., Feb. 3, 1928; d. Joseph and Jean (Boaro) F.; B.A., Queens Coll., 1975; postgrad. Adelphi U., 1976; m. Taisto Edward Sisko, Dec. 26, 1948; children—Warren Joseph, Robert Edward. Asst. acct. N.Y.C. Bd. Edn., 1968-69; dir. personnel Daypac Inc., 1969-70; exec. asst. Ponder & Best, 1971-73; sales adminstr. Ampacet Corp., 1973-75; mktg. rep. Better Bus. Bur., 1975-77; asst. exec. dir. Leukemia Soc. Am., 1978-82; pub. relations assoc., campaign dir. Ketchum, Inc., 1982-85; dir. maj. gifts Seton Hall U., South Orange, N.J., 1985—; v.p. Sisko Enterprises, N.Y. World's Fair, 1964-65; editor, salesperson Malba (N.Y.) News & Views Newspaper, 1969-80. Del. White House Conf. on Small Bus., N.Y.C., 1978. Mem. N.Y. Assn. Women Bus. Owners (founding 1976, edn. com.), Queens Coll. Alumni Assn. (trustee 1976—, pres. Ace chpt. 1977-79), Nat. Soc. Fund Raising Execs., AAUW. Lutheran. Home: 32 Center Dr Malba NY 11357 Office: Seton Hall U South Orange NJ

SISLER, NANCY JEAN, restaurant owner; b. Aurora, Ill., Nov. 30, 1932; d. Thomas Fraser and Helen (Petruchius) Fraser; m. Paul S. Braun, Nov. 27, 1954 (div. 1964); 1 dau., Lisa; m. 2d, James A. Sisler, July 1, 1967. Student No. Ill U., 1951. Owner Hillside Restaurant, Dekalb, 1955—. Home: 131 Ilehamwood Dekalb IL 60115 Office: 121 N 2d St Dekalb IL 60115

SISSON, BETTY LOU, diversified company executive; b. Burbank, Calif., Apr. 21, 1934; d. Harvey Orville and Isabel Miriam (Melville) Angermeir; m. James DeGrado, June 7, 1952 (div. 1975); children—James H., William F.; m. Everett A. Sisson, Apr. 7, 1984. Sales rep. Rich Port Realtor, Clarendon Hills, Ill., 1971-76, v.p., mgr. Oak Brook, Ill., 1976-78; exec. v.p., mktg. mgr. The Midwest Club Co., Oak Brook, 1979-83; exec. v.p. Am. Growth Devel. Corp., Oak Brook, 1979—; exec. v.p., dir. Selected Properties, Inc., Oak Brook, 1983—, Guildcrest Furniture Industries, Inc., Peru, Ind., 1984—; v.p., dir. Pringle & Booth Fashion Photography Studio, Chgo., 1986—; dir. Peru Properties, Inc., Am. Growth Industries, Inc., Oak Brook. Co-chmn. Am. Cancer Soc., Clarendon Hills, 1974. Affiliate mem. DuPage Bd. Realtors. Republican. Clubs: Michigan City Yacht (Ind.); Ocean Reef (Key Largo). Avocation: boating. Home: 1405 Burr Ridge Club Dr Burr Ridge IL 60521 Office: Pringle & Booth Inc 547 S Clark St Chicago IL 60605

SISSON, LORI MAE, industrial accountant; b. Warren, Pa., Sept. 2, 1958; d. Harry and Agatha M. (Johnson) Neizmik; m. Scott R. Sisson, Dec. 5, 1955. B.S. in Acctg., Robert Morris Coll., 1978; M.B.A., St. Bonaventure U., 1985. Staff acct., Seidman & Seidman C.P.A.s, Jamestown, N.Y., 1978-80; account sr. GTE, Warren, Pa., 1980-81, plant controller, 1981-84, div. mgr. fin. analysis I, 1984-85, div. mgr. fin. analysis II, Williamsport, Pa., 1985—. Mem. Nat. Assn. Female Execs. Republican. Avocations: sewing; bycycling; crafts. Home: RD 2 Box 307H Montoursville PA 17754 Office: 2401 Reach Rd Williamsport PA 17701

SISTERSON, JANET MARGOT, physicist; b. Edinburgh, Scotland, July 7, 1940; came to U.S. 1968, naturalized, 1985; d. Thomas James and Lucy Margaret (Smith) Brownlee; B.Sc., U. Durham, 1961; Ph.D., Imperial Coll. Sci. and Tech., U. London, 1965; m. L. Keith Sisterson, Oct. 23, 1965; children—James, Mark. Basic grade physicist London Hosp., 1964-66; sr. physicist Chelsea Hosp. for Women, London, 1966-68; research fellow Cambridge (Mass.) Electron Acceleator, 1968-73; research assoc. Harvard Cyclotron Lab., 1973—. Mem. exec. bd. Harrington Sch. PTA 1977-83. Mem. Am. Phys. Soc., Am. Assn. Physicists in Medicine, Am. Women in Sci. Contbr. articles to profl. jours. Office: 44 Oxford St Cambridge MA 02138

SITOSKI, JULIANN JOCELYN, lawyer; b. Hazleton, Pa., Nov. 30, 1953; d. Stanley John and Elsie Antoinette (Matusick) S. B.S. in Community Devel., Pa. State U.-University Park, 1975; postgrad. Boston U., 1978-79; J.D., U. Denver, 1981. Bar: Colo. Supreme Ct. 1983, U.S. Dist. Ct. (Colo.) 1983. Assoc., Kutak Rock & Campbell, Denver, 1981-85, Gorsuch, Kirgis, Campbell, Walker and Grover, 1985—. Articles editor: Denver Law Jour., 1980-81; contbr. articles to profl. jours. Recipient scholarships, 1972-74. Mem. ABA, Colo. Bar Assn., Denver Bar Assn. Office: Gorsuch Kirgis Campbell Walker and Grover 1401 17th St Suite 1100 Denver CO 80202

SITTENFELD, LINDA ROSE, television producer, lawyer; b. N.Y.C., Nov. 30, 1955; d. Curtis Joseph and Anita Paula S. B.A. in European Studies, Conn. Coll., 1977; J.D., Fordham U., 1981. Bar: N.Y. 1981. Project coordinator LINK Power & Machinery Corp., White Plains, N.Y., 1979-80; researcher/writer I.R.A.S. Devel. Corp., White Plains, N.Y., 1981-82; researcher/writer/producer Cable News Network, N.Y.C., 1982-83, writer, 1985—. Assoc. editor Fordham Internat. Law Jour., 1981; Contbr. articles to profl. jours. Mem. ABA, N.Y. State Bar Assn., New York County Bar Assn., AIAA, Smithsonian Assocs., Am. Mus. Nat. History. Jewish. Home: 263 West End Ave Apt 2G New York NY 10023

SITTER, CLARA MARIE LOEWEN, librarian, media specialist; b. Watonga, Okla., June 28, 1941; d. Arthur Harold and Virginia Mae (Wood) Loewen; m. Lester Dewey Sitter, Aug. 19, 1962; children—Susan Elizabeth, Scott Douglas. B.A., U. Okla., 1962; M.L.S., U. Tex., 1966; cert. advanced study Denver U., 1981; Ph.D., U. Colo.-Boulder, 1982. Cert. tchr., Colo. With U. Tex. Libraries, Austin, 1962-66; cataloger West Tex. State U., Canyon, 1967; librarian, assoc. dir. Amarillo (Tex.) Coll., 1968-71; library media specialist St. Mary's High Sch., Colorado Springs, Colo., 1971-73, Harrison High Sch., Colorado Springs, 1973-84, Sierra High Sch., Colorado Springs, 1984—. Contbr. articles profl. jours. Mem. ALA, Assn. Ednl. Communications and Tech., Colo. Library Assn., Colo. Ednl. Media Assn., Am. Assn. Sch. Librarians, AAUW, NEA, Colo. Edn. Assn., Harrison Edn. Assn., Chi Omega, Phi Delta Kappa. Methodist. Home: 5030 W Rowland Ave Littleton CO 80123 Office: Sierra High Sch 2250 Jetwing Dr Colorado Springs CO 80916

SITZES, MADELINE D'REE PENTON, lawyer; b. Corpus Christi, Tex., Aug. 13, 1942; d. Hewitt Hillard and Jo Thelma (Thomas) Penton; m. Charlie C. Sitzes, Mar. 31, 1967 (div. Dec. 1975). Student Fla. State U., 1960-62; B.S. magna cum laude, North Tex. State U., 1972; J.D., U. Houston, 1980. Bar: Tex. 1980, U.S. Ct. Appeals (5th cir.), U.S. Dist. Ct. (so. dist.) Tex. Flight attendant Delta Air Lines, Dallas, 1962-67, 73-76; supr., 1975-76; cattle rancher Paradise, Tex., 1967-75; substitute tchr. Bridgeport Ind. Sch. Dist. (Tex.), 1972-74; optometrist asst. Dr. Jack Vaughan, Dallas, 1976; prin. Madeline Sitzes & Assocs., Houston, 1980—; pvt. pilot, glider pilot, 1963—; pvt. instrn. tennis, Bridgeport, Dallas, 1967-76. Campaign mgr. Hogan Stripling for Judge, Houston, 1982; vol. Denton State Sch. Mentally Retarded, 1970-72. Mem. State Bar Tex., Harris County Criminal Def. Assn., Tex. Criminal Def. Lawyers Assn., Houston Bar Assn., Am. Trial Lawyers Assn., Tex. Trial Lawyers Assn. Phi Delta Phi. Republican. Episcopalian. Home: 9929 Warwana St Houston TX 77080 Office: Madeline Sitzes & Assocs 710 N Post Oak Rd Suite 312 Houston TX 77024

SIVERSON, JUDITH BUNT, clinical psychologist; b. Phila., June 27, 1935; d. Michael and Katherine (Lemon) Bunt; A.B. magna cum laude, Temple U., Phila., 1968; M.A., 1969, Ph.D. in Clin. Psychology, 1974; 1 dau., Michele Lyn. Staff psychologist rehab. medicine dept. Temple U. Hosp., 1971-72; staff psychologist alcoholism unit Diagnostic and Rehab. Center, Phila., 1972-73; staff psychologist Community Mental Health Center Gloucester County, Woodbury, N.J., 1973-75; chief psychologist rehab. medicine dept. Rolling Hill Hosp., Elkins Park, Pa., 1975-77; chief psychol. services rehab. medicine dept. Temple U. Hosp., 1977-80; pvt. practice psychology, cons., Glassboro, N.J., and Phila., 1980—; coordinator head injury rehab. program St. Lawrence Rehab. Center, Lawrenceville, N.J., 1983; adj. assoc. prof. Temple U. Served with WAC, U.S. Army, 1955-57. Lic. psychologist Pa., N.J. Mem. Nat. Acad. Neuropsychologists, Am. Psychol. Assn., Pa. Psychol. Assn., N.J. Psychol. Assn., Phila. Soc. Clin. Psychologists. Address: 22 Dickinson Rd Glassboro NJ 08028

SIVERTSEN, SHARON POWERS, lawyer; b. Washington, Apr. 30, 1957; d. Thomas Vincent and Ann (Milligan Crawford) Powers; m. B. Eric Sivertsen, Nov. 25, 1983. B.A. in Polit. Sci. and Fine Arts, Boston Coll., 1979; J.D., Duke U., 1982. Bar: Va. 1982. Assoc. firm Sedam & Herge, P.C., McLean, Va., 1982-83, Finkelstein, Thompson and Levenson, Washington, 1983—. Mem. Va. State Bar Assn. Roman Catholic. Home: 4237 S 32d Rd Arlington VA 22206 Office: Finkelstein Thompson Levenson 2828 Pennsylvania Ave NW Washington DC 20007

SIZEMORE, DEBORAH LIGHTFOOT, writer, editor; b. Lamesa, Tex., Mar. 18, 1956; d. Glenn Billy and Francis Earlene (Cable) Lightfoot; m. O.E. Gene Sizemore, June 19, 1981. B.S. in Agrl. Journalism summa cum laude, Tex. A&M U., 1977. Writer, Tex. Agrl. Extension, College Station, 1976-77; copy editor Abilene Reporter-News (Tex.), 1978; customer service rep. Motheral Printing Co., Ft. Worth, 1978-79; prodn. coordinator Graphic Arts, Inc., Ft. Worth, 1980-81; writer, editor, Crowley, Tex., 1981—; agrl. writer, editor Boy Scouts Am., Irving, Tex., 1981—; contbg. editor Dairymen's Digest, Arlington, Tex., 1981—. Longhorn Scene, Ft. Worth, 1982-84; writer, photographer Harvest Times, Dallas, 1983-84, Simbrah World, Ft. Worth, 1985—; contbg. editor Lone Star Horse Report, 1985—; contbr. photographs to mags.; contbr. articles mags. Women's issues chmn., v.p. membership, pub. info. officer, newsletter editor AAUW of Tarrant County, 1981-86; organizer nat. security pub. debate, Ft. Worth, 1983. Recipient Sr. Merit award in Agrl. Journalism, Tex. A&M U., 1978, Thomas S. Gathright Acad. Excellence award, 1976, certs. of merit Livestock Publs. Council, 1984. Mem. Tex. Women for Agr., Am. Agri-Women, Western Writers Am., Nat. Writers Club, Phi Kappa Phi, Gamma Sigma Delta. Club: Ft. Worth A&M. Office: 19 Frazier Ln Crowley TX 76036

SJOBERG ANDERSON, CYNTHIA FINKBEINER, speech and language pathologist; b. Hastings, Mich., Dec. 7, 1949; d. Charles Lavern and Lois Mae (Kenyon) Finkbeiner; m. Peter Carl Sjoberg, Sept. 6, 1974 (div. Dec. 1981); 1 child, Hilary Kenyon; m. Donald Anderson, Sept. 16, 1985. B.S., Western Mich. U., 1972, M.A., 1974. Dir. speech Hackley Hosp., Muskegon, Mich., 1974-75; speech pathologist Grand Haven Pub. Schs., Mich., 1975—; dir. Ambucs Summer Lang. Clinic, Grand Haven, 1984—. Creator summer lang. program. Pres. Kiddie Carousel, Grand Haven, 1983—; Stephen minister Christ Community Ch., Spring Lake, Mich., 1984—; big sister Grand Haven, 1975-80. Named Ambucs, Nat. Therapist of Yr., 1985. Mem. Am. Speech/Hearing/Lang. Assn. (cert.). Democrat. Home: 17554 G Parkwood Spring Lake MI 49456 Office: Grand Haven Pub Schs 1415 Beechtree Grand Haven MI 49417

SJOGREN, DEBORAH MARY, accountant; b. Ely, Minn., Aug. 1, 1953; d. Stanley Joseph and Justine Pauline (Korent) Boldine; m. Mark Robert Sjogren, Aug. 21, 1976. A.A., Vermillion Community Coll., 1973; B.S., St. Cloud State U., Minn., 1975. Br. acct. Montgomery Ward, St. Paul, 1975-77; fin. processing cons. region III Mgmt. Info. Service/Elem., Secondary, Vocat., St. Cloud, Minn., 1977-78; acctg. supr. Vision Ease Corp., St. Cloud, 1978-83; controller Franciscan Sisters of Little Falls, Little Falls, Minn., 1983—. Yugoslav Nat. Home scholar, 1971. Mem. Profl. Women's Orgn. (founder), Nat. Assn. Female Execs., Central Minn. Nat. Assn. Accts., Phi Chi Theta (charter). Avocations: horseback riding; needlecrafts; racquetball. Office: Franciscan Sisters of Little Falls 116 8th Ave SE Little Falls MN 56345

SJOLANDER, LINDA ARLENE, communications specialist, consultant; b. Portland, Oreg., Aug. 7, 1943; d. Nathaniel David and Ardis Margaret (Gisselberg) S.; m. James Earl Pennington, Aug. 7, 1965 (div. Sept. 1974); m. John Derek Lyons, Feb. 14, 1986. B.A. in English, U. Oreg., 1965; M.Ed. in English, Boston U., 1970. Tchr., David Douglas Schs., Beaverton, Oreg., 1965-69, Winchester Schs., Mass., 1970-73; co-dir., counselor John F. Kennedy Sch., Queretaro, Mex., 1973-74; asst. v.p. pub. relations Newspaper Advt. Bur., N.Y.C., 1975-76; self-employed, Boston, 1977; editor, writer Intermetrics, Inc., Cambridge, Mass., 1978-85; cons., propr., by Sjolander, Belmont, Mass., 1983-85, Sjolander Lyons Communications, Concord, Mass., 1986—; guest lectr. U. Lowell, Mass., 1985. Contbr. articles to profl. jours. Mem. Belmont Citizens Com., Mass., 1983-85. Recipient Outstanding Performance award Intermetrics, Inc. and NASA, 1983. Mem. Soc. Tech. Communications, Concord C. of C., Alpha Omicron Pi. Republican. Episcopalian. Avocations: people; art; music; dance; literature. Home and Office: 12 Hawthorne Village Concord MA 01742

SKABAR, RHONDA LEANN, nurse; b. Orrville, Ohio, Oct. 24, 1959; d. Daris Lee and Shirley Ann (Marks) Carr; m. Michael Joseph Skabar, Mar. 12, 1977 (div. Aug. 1978); 1 child, Jennifer LeAnn. Assoc. in Nursing, U. Charleston, 1984. Lic. R.N., Ohio. Recipient Basic Ednl. Opportunity grant, 1983; Pell grantee, 1982-84; grantee W.Va. Higher Edn., 1983-84, Supplementary Ednl. Opportunity grantee, 1983. Mem. Am. Nurses Assn. Republican. Roman Catholic. Avocations: tennis; running; cooking; exercising; dancing. Home: 1033 N Elm St Apt B Orrville OH 44667

SKALL, TERRY ROBERTSON, newspaper editor; b. Chgo., May 3, 1943; d. Robert Irving and Beatrice Hannah (Winter) Robertson; m. Richard A. Skall, May 23, 1963; children—Barbara, Jeffrey, David. Student Northwestern U., 1961-63; B.S., Western Res. U., 1966. News editor Chagrin Valley Pub. Co., Chagrin Falls, Ohio, 1974-80; editor-in-chief Chagrin Valley-Solon Times, Chagrin Falls, 1980—; freelance travel writer, 1983—. Mem. Sigma Delta Chi (award for editorial writing 1980, award for news reporting 1981). Office: Chagrin Valley/Solon Times Box 150 34 S Main St Chagrin Falls OH 44022

SKALSKY, SUSAN ELEANOR, pediatrician, hospital administrator; b. London, July 1, 1946; came to U.S., 1948, naturalized, 1953; d. Lewis L. and

Livia (Gluck) S. B.A. in Chemistry, C.W. Post Coll., Old Brookville, N.Y., 1968; M.D., N.Y. Med. Coll., 1972; M.P.H., Columbia U., 1985. Intern, then resident Roosevelt Hosp., N.Y.C., 1972-75; pediatrician Manhattan Children's Psychiat. Ctr., N.Y.C., 1975-79; chief med. services Manhattan Psychiat. Ctr., N.Y.C., 1979-81; clin. dir. med. services Essex County Hosp. Ctr., Cedar Grove, N.J., 1981—; asst. clin. pediatrics Columbia U. Coll. of Physicians & Surgeons, N.Y.C., 1976—; substitute med. dir. Turning Point, Cedar Grove, 1983—. Recipient Chemistry award C.W. Post Coll., 1968, Physician's Recognition award AMA, 1976, 79, 82, 85. Fellow Am. Acad. Pediatrics; mem. AMA, Am. Pub. Health Assn., N.Y. Lung Assn., Alumni Assn. N.Y. Med. Coll., Phi Eta. Avocations: tennis, swimming, traveling, reading, decorating, gardening, stock market, theater, movies, art dance. Home: 31 Gladding Rd Caldwell NJ 07006 Office: Essex County Hosp Ctr 125 Fairview Ave Cedar Grove NJ 17009

SKATTUM, DONNA WEIR, television executive; b. Arlington, Va., Feb. 19, 1960; d. Carl Lester and Margaret Mary (Morris) Weir; m. Jon Andrew Skattum, Sept. 25, 1983. B.A., Dickinson Coll., 1981. Asst., intern WHP-TV, Harrisburg, Pa., 1980-81; layout designer S.P. Dunham's, Trenton, N.J., 1981-83; news dir., anchor WCEE-TV, Mt. Vernon, Ill., 1983—. Roman Catholic. Home: 508 S Lincoln Blvd Centralia IL 62801 Office: WCEE-TV PO Box 1600 Mount Vernon IL 62864

SKEET CHARLES, NATALIE JEANETTE, information specialist; b. N.Y.C., Aug. 1, 1954; d. Lionel Theodore and Ruby (Birkett) Skeet; m. Enoch Llewellyn Charles, Nov. 26, 1982. A.A., Finch Coll., 1975; B.A., cert. in criminal justice, L.I.U., 1976; M.A., Columbia U., 1980, M.Ed., 1984. Fin. aid counselor Columbia U., N.Y.C., 1979, asst. dir. student aid, 1979-82; program analyst N.Y. State Higher Edn. Services Corp., Albany, 1982, coordinator, 1982-83, info. specialist, 1983—, adv. bd. dirs., 1982—; adv. bd. Fin. Aid for Colls. and Tech. Schs., N.Y.C., 1982—. Asst. adminstr. Bronx div. Council of Chs., 1981—; voter registrar J. Raymond Jones Democratic Club, N.Y.C., 1983. Clark Found. grantee, 1972-76. Mem. Alpha Kappa Alpha (v.p. 1975-76, merit and service award, fin. aid cons. 1982—). Home: 524 W 122d St Apt 3C New York NY 10027 Office: NY State Higher Edn Services Corp 99 Washington Ave Albany NY 12255

SKEETER, SHARYN JEANNE, writer, writing/literature educator; b. Yonkers, N.Y., July 12, 1945; d. Clarence Doyle and Jeanne Althea (Ryerson) S.; m. Clarence Major, July 11, 1975 (div. 1978); m. 2d, Michael Thomas Tucker, Oct. 16, 1982. B.A., CCNY, 1966, postgrad. Sch. Edn., 1966-68, Sch. Liberal Arts, 1973-75; M.B.A., Anna Maria Coll., Paxton, Mass., 1981. Tchr., N.Y.C. Bd. Edn., 1966-68; editorial asst. Mademoiselle mag., N.Y.C., 1969-70; fiction, poetry and books editor Essence mag., N.Y.C., 1970-76; asst. prof. writing, lit. and pub. Emerson Coll., Boston, 1980—; poetry/fiction reader, lectr. at various univs., colls., libraries. Co-editor arts jour. Departures, 1979; contbr. poetry, articles, bookrevs., fiction to various lit. jours.; Judge poetry competition United Negro Coll. Fund, N.Y.C., 1972; press rep. Phillis Wheatley Poetry Festival, Jackson, Miss., 1972. Mem. Nat. Council Tchrs. English, Women in Communications. Democrat. Unitarian-Universalist. Home: 30 Charles St Lexington MA 02173 Office: Emerson Coll 100 Beacon St Boston MA 02116

SKEFOS, CATHERINE HETOS, lawyer; b. San Antonio, Tex., Mar. 12, 1952; d. Nicholas Stephen and Maria (Galanos) Hetos; m. Harry J. Skefos, June 21, 1975; 1 dau., Chrystan Maria. B.A. cum laude, U. Pa., 1973, M.S. cum laude, 1973; J.D. Memphis State U., 1979. Bar: Tenn. 1980. Curator, U.S. Supreme Ct., Washington, 1973-77, cons., 1976-77; law clk. Chancery Ct. of State Tenn., 1979-80; assoc. Apperson Crump Duzane and Maxwell, Memphis, 1981-85; sole practice law, 1985—. Co-author, narrator, actor (film) Supreme Court, 1976. Mem. recruitment com. U. Pa., Phila., 1981—; bd. dirs. Memphis/Shelby County Mental Health Assn., 1981-82. Recipient Cert. of Appreciation, Young Lawyers of Va. Bar Assn., 1976, Am. Jurisprudence award in Domestic Relations, 1979. Mem. ABA, Tenn. Bar Assn. (membership chmn. 1984-85), Memphis and Shelby County Bar Assn., Republican. Greek Orthodox. Office: PO Box 111301 Memphis TN 38111

SKELLY, ELLEN BROWNE, nurse, educator; b. Longford, Ireland, Aug. 8, 1940; came to U.S., 1957; s. Robert Joseph and Ellen Rose (Keenan) B.; m. John James Skelly, Feb. 1, 1964; children—James Patrick, Peter Joseph. A.A.S. in Nursing, Hudson Valley Community Coll., Troy, N.Y., 1975; B.S. in Nursing, Russell Sage Coll., Troy, 1979, M.S. in Health Edn., 1983. Pvt. duty nurse, East Greenbush, N.Y., 1975-76; staff nurse Meml. Hosp., Albany, N.Y., 1976-80; nursing supr. Samaritan Hosp., Troy, 1980-83; nursing supr. Albany Med. Ctr., 1983—. Mem. Am. Nurses Assn., N.Y. State Nurses Assn., Sigma Theta Tau. Republican. Roman Catholic. Club: Schodack Country (N.Y.). Home: 299 Lape Rd Nassau NY 12123 Office: Albany Med Ctr 500 New Scotland Ave Albany NY 12208

SKELTON, DOROTHY GENEVA SIMMONS (MRS. JOHN WILLIAM SKELTON), educator; b. Woodland, Calif.; d. Jack Elijah and Helen Anna (Siebe) Simmons; B.A., U. Calif., 1940, M.A., 1943; m. John William Skelton, July 16, 1941. Sr. research analyst War Dept., Gen. Staff, M.I. Div. G-2, Pentagon, Washington, 1944-45; vol. researcher, monuments, fine arts and archives sect. Restitution Br., Office Mil. Govt. for Hesse, Wiesbaden, German, 1947-48; vol. art tchr. German children in Bad Nauheim, Germany, 1947-48; art educator, lectr. Dayton (Ohio) Art Inst., 1955; art educator Lincoln Sch., Dayton, 1956-60; instr. art and art edn. U. Va. Sch. Continuing Edn., Charlottesville, 1962-75; researcher genealogy, exhibited in group shows, Calif., Colo., Ohio, Washington and Va.; represented in permanent collections Madison Hall, Charlottesville, Madison (Va.) Center. Author: The Squire Simmons Family, 1746-1986, 1986. Mem. Nat. League Am. Pen Women, AAUW, Am. Assn. Museums, Coll. Art Assn. Am., Inst. for Study of Art in Edn., Dayton Soc. Painters and Sculptors, Nat. Soc. Arts and Letters (life), Va. Mus. Fine Arts, Cal. Alumni Assn., Air Force Officers Wives Club. Republican. Methodist. Clubs: Army Navy Country; Lake of the Woods (Va.) Golf and Country. Chief collaborator: John Skelton of Georgia, 1969. Address: Lotos Lakes Brightwood VA 22715

SKELTON, RHETA SHORTNACY, nursing home administrator; b. Oxford, Ala., Aug. 19, 1933; d. Robert Walter and Grayce Emelle (Sanders) Shortnacy; m. Frederick Tildon Skelton, Jr., Sept. 20, 1952; children—Frederick T. III, Cynthia Marie, Brian Lee, Loretta Joyce. Lic. health care adminstr., Ala. Sales rep. Freddy's Watch Shop, Birmingham, 1951-53; sec.-typist Agar Constrn. Co., Birmingham, 1957-62; bookkeeper South Haven Nursing Home, Birmingham, 1965-70, asst. adminstr., 1970-79, adminstr.-owner-pres., 1979—. Campaign worker Wallace for Gov., 1964-82, Reagan for Pres., 1980; spl. dep. Jefferson County Sheriffs Dept., Birmingham, 1980—. Fellow Am. Coll. Nursing Home Adminstrs.; mem. Ala. Nursing Home Assn., Am. Health Care Assn., Bus. and Profl. Women's Club, Birmingham C. of C., Bus. Women's Prayer Group, Am. Geriatric Soc. Republican. Baptist (teacher, mem. choir). Office: The South Haven Nursing Home 3141 Old Columbiana Rd Birmingham AL 35226

SKENDER, LAVERNE JANET, electric motor services co. exec.; b. Oak Park, Ill., Aug. 28, 1935; d. Edward Louis and Philamina Tillie (Baumruk) Stedron; A.A., Morton Jr. Coll., 1955; m. George Joseph Skender, June 9, 1956 (dec.); children—Jeffrey Scott, Patricia Diane, Edward George, Jacalyn Louise, Amy Lynn. Sec., Sears Roebuck, 1952-58; asst. purchasing agt. Prater Industries, 1967-69; sec. Dykema & Dykema, 1970-71; outside salesman DeBar Electric Motors, Chgo., 1971-83; pres. City Suburban Electric Motors, Inc., 1983—; dir. Stedcor Corp. Pres. U.S. Navy League, Forest Park, 1976, 77, 79, 81, 82; active NOW; bd. dirs. Fillmore Family Services. Named to scroll of honor U.S. Navy League. Mem. Elec. Apparatus Service Assn. (mem. mgmt.), Elec. Motor Distbrs., Assn. Elec. Machinery Trades, World Chpt. Elec. Assn., Am. Soc. Profl. and Exec. Women, Nat. Assn. Female Execs. Clubs: West Suburban Exec., West Suburban Breakfast (dir. 1980-82), Bus. and Profl. Women (legis. chmn. Cicero, 1976-77, 80-81, pres. 1974-75, 79-71, Nike award, dist. dir. 1976, state expansion chmn., 1980-81). First woman in outside motor sales, first woman shop foreman, first woman pres. of motor shop, first woman pres. U.S. Navy League Council. Home: 2211 W Clifton Pl Hoffman Estates IL 60195 Office: 2740 N Pulaski Rd Chicago IL 60639

SKENE, MARY LOUISE, lawyer; b. Jackson, Miss., Sept. 18, 1952; d. George Neil and Louise (Pate) Skene; m. William Josiah Neville, Jr., June 10, 1978; children—Mary Elizabeth, William Josiah III. B.A., Huntingdon Coll., 1974; J.D., Mercer U., 1977. Law clk. James Webb, Montgomery, Ala., 1976, George N. Skene, Macon, Ga., 1976-78; ptnr. firm Neville, Neville & Skene, Metter, Ga., 1978-79, Neville & Skene, Metter, 1979-85; recorder City of Metter, 1980—; solicitor State Ct. of Candler County, 1986—. Bd. dirs. Candler County Cancer Soc., Metter, 1979—, Metter-Candler County Welcome Ctr., Metter, 1979-85; mem. Foster Care Jud. Rev. Panel, Metter, 1984—. Huntingdon scholar Huntingdon Coll., 1970. Mem. State Bar Ga., Ga. Trial Lawyers Assn., Am. Trial Lawyers Assn., Bus. and Profl. Women (pres. 1980-81). Republican. Methodist. Home: Route 2 Metter GA 30439 Office: PO Box 791 Metter GA 30439

SKILLIN, VERONICA, college president. Pres. Coll. Notre Dame, Belmont, Calif. Office: Office of Pres Coll Notre Dame 1500 Ralston Ave Belmont CA 94002

SKINNER, MARY JUST, state legislator; b. South Bend, Ind., July 7, 1946; m. Scott Skinner, 2 children. A.B. cum laude, Barnard Coll., 1968; J.D., Columbia U., 1971. Bar: Vt., N.Y., Pa. Mem. Vt. State Senate, 1979—. Democrat. Office: Vt Senate State Capitol Montpelier VT 05602*

SKINNER, MARY THOMPSON, lawyer, accountant; b. Durham, N.C., Jan. 2, 1954; d. Elmer Cook and Amelia Archer (Farrior) Thompson; m. Charles Robertson Skinner III, May 16, 1981. B.S., U. N.C., 1976; J.D., 1981. Bar: N.C. 1981; C.P.A., N.C. Staff acct. Thomas, Knight, Trent King & Co., Durham, N.C., 1976-78; assoc. Newson, Graham, Hedrick, Bryson, Kennon & Faison, Durham, 1981-83; sole practice, Durham, 1983—; ptnr. Dougherty & Skinner C.P.A.s, Durham, 1983—. Bd. dirs. Nat. Pre Menstrual Syndrome Soc., Inc., 1983-84; bd. dirs., treas. YWCA, Durham, 1978-81. Mem. ABA, N.C. Bar Assn., Durham County Bar Assn., N.C. Assn. C.P.A.s, Estate Planning Council Durham. Democrat. Presbyterian. Club: Jr. League. Home: 3408 Hope Valley Rd Durham NC 27707 Office: Dougherty & Skinner CPAs 2634 Chapel Hill Blvd Suite 322 Durham NC 27707

SKINNER, PATRICIA MORAG, state legislator; b. Glasgow, Soctland, Dec. 3, 1932; d. John Stuart and Frances Charlotte (Swann) Robertson; m. Robert A. Skinner, Dec. 28, 1957; children—Robin Ann, Pamela. B.A., NYU, 1953; Mdse. trainee Lord & Taylor, N.Y.C., 1955-59; adminstrv. asst. Atlantic Products, N.Y.C., 1954-59; newspaper corr. Salem Observer, N.H., 1964-84; mem. N.H. Ho. of Reps., 1973—, chmn. labor, human resources and rehab. com., 1975—; chmn. N.H. Adv. Council Unemployment Compensation. Bd. dirs. Castle Jr. Coll., 1975, Swift Water council Girl Scouts U.S.; mem. adv. council N.H. Voc-Tech. Coll., Nashua, 1978-83; trustee Nesmith Library, Windham, N.H., 1982—. Mem. N.H. Fedn. Women's Clubs (parliamentarian, legis chmn. 1984—), N.H. Fedn. Republican Women's Clubs (pres. 1979-82). Christian Scientist. Club: Windham Woman's (pres. 1981-83). Lodge: Order Eastern Star. Office: 306 Legislative Office Bldg Concord NH 03301

SKINNER, SARAH HANBY, pianist; b. Port Arthur, Tex., July 28, 1941; d. Willard Skinner and Helen Gould (Langdon) Skinner Jenkins; m. Daniel Edgar Hanby, Feb. 5, 1977 (div. Oct. 1983); 1 son, Duncan Frederick Hanby-Skinner. B.Music, U. Tex., 1962, M.Music, 1966. Pianist, accompanist, 1959—; music educator, 1960—; mus. dir. Camelot Playhouse, Midland, Mich., 1974-75, 9th Ch. of Christ Scientist, Houston, 1975-76, 1st Ch. Religious Sci., Bellaire, Tex., 1981—. Composer songs. Mem. Houston Assn. Profl. Musicians, Mu Phi Epsilon. Democrat. Mem. Ch. of Religious Sci. Home: 12964 Trail Hollow Houston TX 77079

SKLAMBA, SHARON ANN, lawyer; b. New Orleans, Aug. 15, 1956; d. Carl John and Marjorie C. (Wimberly) Sklamba; m. Curtis R. Hearn. B.A. magna cum laude, Loyola U., New Orleans, 1977; J.D. cum laude, 1980. Bar: La. 1980, Tex. 1982. Law clk. to presiding judge U.S. Ct. Appeals Fed. Cir., Washington, 1980-81; assoc. Johnson & Swanson, Dallas, 1981-84, Kullman Inman Bee & Downing, New Orleans, 1984—. Recipient Am. Legion award, 1970; Tulane Law Sch. Merit award, 1978, 79. Mem. ABA, La. State Bar Assn., Tex. State Bar Assn., Dallas Women Lawyers Assn. Democrat. Roman Catholic. Home: 44 Swallow Ln New Orleans LA 70124 Office: Kullman Inman et al PO Box 615 New Orleans LA

SKLAR, KATHRYN KISH, historian; b. Columbus, Ohio, Dec. 26, 1939; d. William Edward and Elizabeth Sue (Rhodes) Kish; children—Leonard Scott, Susan Rebecca. B.A. magna cum laude, Radcliffe Coll., Harvard U., 1965; Ph.D., U. Mich., 1969. Lectr., asst. prof. U. Mich., Ann Arbor, 1969-74; assoc. prof. UCLA, 1974-81, prof. history, 1981—, chmn. com. to adminster program in women's studies Coll. Letters and Sci., 1974-81; adv. bd. So. Calif. Inst. Hist. Research and Services, 1981—; mem. Calif. Council for Humanities, 1981-85; Pulitzer Prize juror in history, 1976; fellow Newberry Library Family and Community History Seminar, 1973; NEH cons. in women's studies U. Utah, 1977-79, Santa Clara U., 1978-80, Roosevelt U., 1980-82; hist. cons. AAUW. Author: Catharine Beecher, A Study in American Domesticity (Berkshire Prize 1974), 1973; editor: Catharine Beecher, A Treatise on Domestic Economy, 1977; Harriet Beecher Stowe: Uncle Tom's Cabin, or Life among the Lowly: The Minister's Wooing: Oldtown Folks, 1981; Notes of Sixty Years: The Autobiography of Florence Kelley, 1859-1926, 1986; mem. editorial bd. Am. Quar., 1976-79, Jour. Am. History, 1978-81; guest editor Feminist Studies, 1976; scholarly adv. bd. Ms., 1980-84; contbr. articles to profl. jours. Woodrow Wilson fellow, 1965-67; Danforth grad. fellow, 1967-69; Ford Found. faculty research grantee, 1973-74; Radcliffe Inst. fellow, 1973-74; Nat. Humanities Inst. fellow, 1975-76; Daniels fellow Am. Antiquarian Soc., 1976; demonstration grantee NEH, 1976-78; Schlesinger Library grantee Radcliffe Coll., 1982; Rockefeller Found. humanities fellow, 1981-82; Woodrow Wilson Internat. Ctr. fellow, 1982; NEH fellow Newberry Library, 1982-83; UCLA Council for Internat. and Comparative Studies grantee, 1983; Guggenheim fellow, 1984. Mem. Am. Hist. Assn. (chmn. com. on women historians 1980-83, v.p. Pacific Coast br. 1986-87), Orgn. Am. Historians (exec. bd. 1983-86, Merle Curti award com. 1978-79, lectr. 1982—), Am. Studies Assn. (council mem.-at-large 1978-80), Berkshire Conf. Women Historians, Am. Antiquarian Soc., Phi Beta Kappa. Office: Dept History UCLA Los Angeles CA 90024

SKLAREK, NORMA MERRICK, architect; b. N.Y.C., Apr. 15, 1928; d. Walter and Amy (Willoughby) Merrick; m. Rolf Sklarek, Feb. 14, 1967; children—Gregory Ransom, David Fairweather, B.Arch., Columbia U., 1950. Architect Skidmore, Owings, Merrill, N.Y.C., 1955-60; dir. architecture Gruen Assocs., Los Angeles, 1960-80; project dir. Welton Becket Assocs., Santa Monica, from 1980; now ptnr. Siegel Sklarek Diamond, Los Angeles, mem. faculty N.Y.C. Community Coll., 1957-60, UCLA, 1972-78. Prin. works include Am. embassy, Tokyo, Pacific Design Center, Los Angeles, Courthouse Center, Columbus, Ind., Fox Plaza, San Francisco, City Hall, San Bernardino, Calif., Los Angeles Airport Terminal. Fellow AIA (v.p. Calif. chpt.). Office: Siegel Sklarek Diamond 10780 Santa Monica Blvd Suite 260 Los Angeles CA 90025

SKLOOT, BETSY A(NN), social services administrator; b. Batesville, Ind., Mar. 29, 1942; d. James Robert and Cynthia Hahn (Stocker) Lee; m. Floyd Steven Skloot, Aug. 10, 1970; children—Matthew Lee, Rebecca Lee. B.A. with high honors, So. Ill. U., 1966, M.A., 1970. Instr. in English, Carbondale High Sch. and So. Ill. U., 1966-72; budget analyst and mgr. State of Ill., Springfield, 1973-76, assoc. Medicaid adminstr., 1978-81, Medicaid adminstr., 1981-84; budget analyst and mgr. State of Wash., Olympia, 1976-78; dir. Multnomah County Dept. Human Services, Portland, Oreg., 1984—. Mem. State Medicaid Dirs.' Assn. (sec. 1982-84), Am. Pub. Health Assn., Am. Pub. Welfare Assn., Ill. Pub. Welfare Assn. Office: 3425 Thurman Ave NW Portland OR 97210

SKLUZACEK, GAYLE MARIE, fine art and wine appraiser/consultant; b. Loansdale, Minn., Mar. 29, 1953; d. Edward P. and Lucille E. (Hartmann) S. B.A. in art History, Barat Coll., 1975; postgrad. in architecture history U. Minn., 1973-77, in art history U. Chgo., 1977-80; cooking and wine apprentice, France, Ger., Italy, 1979. Cert. tchr., N.Y.C. Assoc. curatorial asst. Carnegie Instn., Pitts., 1980-81; staff tng. dir.-wine cons. Sardi's, N.Y.C., 1981—; dining room service and wine tasting tchr. N.Y.C. Bd. Edn., 1982—; dir. fine arts dept. Jason Rahm & Assocs., N.Y.C., 1983-85; research dir. Lawrence Gallery, N.Y.C., 1985—; pres., dir. fine arts div. Abigail Hartmann Assocs., N.Y.C., 1985—. Author newsletter Art Investment Strategies, 1984-85; author tng. manuals. Bd. dirs. Adv. Council Occupational Edn., 1982—; leader Girl Scouts, 1980; active Mondale Presdl. Campaign, 1984. Docent Oriental Inst., U. Chgo., 1980-81. Mem. Internat. Soc. Appraisers, Am. Assn. Appraisers, Les Amis du Vin, Mus. Modern Art, Met. Mus. Art, Am. Mus. Women in the Arts (charter). Democrat. Roman Catholic. Avocations: art; computers; gourmet cooking; wine; tennis. Home: 200 W 93d St Suite 6L New York NY 10025

SKONEY, SOPHIE ESSA, educational administrator; b. Detroit, Jan. 29, 1929; d. George Essa and Helena (Dihmes) Cokalay; Ph.B., U. Detroit, 1951; M.Ed., Wayne State U., 1960, Ed.D., 1975; m. Daniel J. Skoney, Dec. 28, 1957; children—Joseph Anthony, James Francis, Carol Anne. Tchr. elem. sch. Detroit Bd. Edn., 1952-69, remedial reading specialist, 1969-70, curriculum coordinator, 1970-71, region 6 article 3 title I coordinator, 1971-83, area E curriculum devel. specialist, 1984—; cons. in field. Mem. Wayne State U. Coll. Edn. Alumni Assn. (pres. bd. govs. 1979-80), Macomb Dental Aux. (pres. 1969-70), Mich. Dental Aux. (pres. 1980-81), Am.-Assn. Sch. Adminstrs., Wayne State U. Alumni Assn. (v.p. bd. dirs. 1985-86), Internat. Reading Assn., Mich. Reading Assn., Mich. Assn. State and Fed. Program Specialists, Profl. Women's Network (newsletter editor 1981-83, treas. 1983-85, pres. 1985-87), Delta Kappa Gamma, Beta Sigma Phi, Phi Delta Kappa. Roman Catholic. Newsletter editor Wayne State Coll. Edn. Alumni Assn., 1975-77, 81-87. Home: 20813 Lakeland St St Clair Shores MI 48081 Office: 1121 E McNichols St Detroit MI 48203

SKOPINICH, RENATA MARY, gemologist, financial executive; b. Mali Losinj, Yugoslavia, Aug. 8, 1955; came to U.S., 1963, naturalized, 1968; d. Joseph and Mary (Hroncich) S. Student La Guardia Coll., 1974-76. Asst. mgr. Albithel Jewelry Mfg. Co., N.Y.C., 1975-77; mgr. Steve Papps/LPG Gems, N.Y.C., 1978-81; sec.-treas., gemologist Hans-Dieter Haag Co., Inc., Los Angeles, Calif., 1982—. Mem. Am. Gem Trade Assn., Am. Jewelers, Gemological Inst. Am. Republican. Roman Catholic. Avocations: gourmet cooking; skiing; travel; languages. Home: 914 Arizona Ave #5 Santa Monica CA 90401 Office: Hans-Dieter Haag Co Inc 629 S Hill St 1206 Los Angeles CA 90014

SKORD, JENNIFER LYNNE, patent attorney; b. Chgo., Oct. 3, 1948; d. Joseph and Jean (Bobeyka) Skord; m. Karl Moulton, July 5, 1969 (div. 1975). B.A., Bradley U., 1970; Summer Cert. U. Exeter (Eng.) Law Sch., 1978; J.D., DePaul U., Chgo., 1980. Bar: Ill. 1980, Ind. 1985, U.S. Dist. Ct. (no. dist.) Ill. 1980, U.S. Dist. Ct. (no. dist.) Ind. 1985, U.S. Patent and Trademark Office 1982, U.S. Ct. Appeals, Fed. Cir., 1983, U.S. Supreme Ct. 1984. Lab. technician Pabst Brewing Co., Peoria, Ill., 1970-77; law clk. James Conlon & Assocs., Chgo., 1978-79, Kolar & Conte, Chgo., 1979-80; patent atty. Ladas & Parry, Chgo., 1980-83, Eltech Systems Corp., Chardon, Ohio, 1983-84, Miles Labs., Inc., Elkhart, Ind., 1984-86, Cryovac div. W.R. Grace & Co., Duncan, S.C., 1986—. Mem. Am. Chem. Soc., Mensa, ABA, Chgo. Patent Law Assn., Am. Intellectual Property Law Assn., AAUW, Phi Alpha Delta. Home: 201 Powell Mill Rd L-208 Spartanburg SC 29301 Office: Cryovac Div WR Grace & Co PO Box 464 Duncan SC 29334

SKOV-GORDON, ANDRÉA RIIS, computer exec.; b. Zurich, Switzerland, Sept. 10, 1952; d. Niels Aage and Camille Emery (Burleigh) Skov; B.S. in Physics, Northeastern U., 1973, M.S. in Physics, 1974; m. Michael Franklin Gordon, Aug. 30, 1980. Project engr. aerospace div. Gen. Electric Co., Hanscom AFB, Bedford, Mass., 1975-77; N.E. dist. salesman Ramtek Corp., Lexington, Mass., 1977-78, product mktg. mgr. color graphic terminals, Santa Clara, Calif., 1978-81; dir. product mgmt. Logical Bus. Machines, Sunnyvale, Calif., 1981-82, v.p. mktg. and ops. 1982-83; v.p. Structured Systems Group Inc., Oakland, Calif., 1983—. Mem. Soc. Women Engrs., Tech. Mktg. Soc. Am., NOW, Nat. Dance Tchrs. Assn. Republican. Unitarian. Home: 14970 Sobey Rd Saratoga CA 95070 Office: 1294 Hammerwood Ave Sunnyvale CA 94086

SKROBELA, KATHERINE CREELMAN, data processor; b. N.Y.C., Jan. 18, 1941; d. George Douglas and Marjorie Ethel (Broer) Creelman; A.B., Vassar Coll., 1962; M.L.S., Columbia U., 1964; m. Paul John Skrobela, May 23, 1970. Music cataloger Bklyn. Coll., 1964-71; music librarian Middlebury (Vt.) Coll., 1971-80; programmer ADT Co., N.Y.C., 1981-83; sr. cons. Marathon Software & Services, Inc., 1983—. Treas., bd. dirs. Middlebury Farmers Market, 1979; dir. St. Stephen's Motet Choir, Middlebury, 1975-78. Mem. Am. Soc. Info. Sci., ALA, Music Library Assn. (chmn. com. on cataloging, rep. to ALA catalog code revision com.), UFO Users Group (bd. dirs. Northeast region). Country Dance and Song Soc. Am. Editor Music Cataloging Bull., 1970-75. Home: 234 Lincoln Rd Brooklyn NY 11225 Office: 145 Porter Ave Bergenfield NJ 07621

SLAATEN, DORIS ADELE, educator; b. Charleston, N.D., Oct. 5, 1920; d. Alfred O. and Maude L. (Dukette) S.; B.S., Minot State Coll., 1949; M.A., Northwestern U., 1957; Ph.D., Colo. State U., 1975. Tchr. public schs., N.D., Mont., 1942-57; faculty Minot (N.D.) State Coll. Div. Bus., 1957-84, prof. bus., 1976-84, now prof. emeritus N.D. rep. to bd. dirs. Mountain Plains Bus. Edn. Assn., 1977-84; mem. Minot State Coll. Devel. Bd., 1977—, bd. regents, 1977—; bd. dirs. Minot Chamber Chorale, 1979-85, Minot Commn. on Aging, 1984—. Recipient Sigma Sigma Sigma Outstanding Alumni Recognition award, 1970; Alumni Golden award Minot State Coll., 1979; Nat. Bus. Edn. Meritorious Service award, 1979; 25-Yr. Profl. award Minot C. of C., 1979. Mem. N.D. Office Edn. Assn. (pres. 1969-70), Nat. Bus. Edn. Assn., N.D. Bus. Edn. Assn., NEA, Am. Vocat. Assn., Bus. and Profl. Women (Woman of Yr. 1979), Phi Beta Lambda, Pi Omega Pi, Pi Lambda Theta, Phi Delta Kappa, Delta Pi Epsilon, Delta Kappa Gamma. Lutheran. Club: M1000. Author: Office Education for Tomorrow's World, 1972; manual for N.D. office edn. coordinators, 1980. Address: 1000 20th Ave NW Apt B4 Minot ND 58701

SLACER, SUZANNE, banker; b. Buffalo, May 28, 1957; d. Phillip John and Josephine (LaBruna) Slacer. B.A. in Econs., SUNY-Buffalo, 1980; M.B.A., Canisius Coll. Supr. POS/ATM dept. Goldome, FSB, Buffalo, 1979-84, supr. demand deposit acctg., 1984-85, asst. mgr. item processing, 1986—; loaned exec. United Way of Buffalo and Erie County, 1985. Mem. panel health services div. United Way allocations, 1986, Sect. Chmn. civic and cultural agys. pub. and service div., 1986. Mem. Nat. Assn. Female Execs. Republican. Lutheran. Avocations: racquetball; skiing; needlework. Office: Goldome FSB One Fountain Plaza Buffalo NY 14203

SLACK, BEVERLY JEAN, cable television company executive; b. North Manchester, Ind., Sept. 18, 1936; d. Raymond B. and Imogene B. (Vickery) Schroll; m. Max E. Slack, Sept. 19, 1954; children—Jennifer L., Andrew E. Cert. GTE Secretarial Sch., 1965; Ameri-Comm CATV Tng., 1983. With Gen. Telephone-Ind., North Manchester and Wabash, 1956-79, central office supervisory asst., 1975-79; with Omega Communications, North Manchester, 1979-84, Three Rivers, Mich., 1984—, regional mgr., 1984-85, ops. mgr., 1985—. Mem. Women In Cable (bd. dirs. Ind.-Ill. unit 1982, v.p. Ind.-Ill. 1986—), North Manchester C. of C., Epsilon Sigma Alpha. Republican. Lutheran. Lodge: Order Eastern Star. Avocations: reading; snowmobiling; camping. Home: 1404 Villa Ct North Manchester IN 46962 Office: Omega of Mich Cable Co 1 N Main St Three Rivers MI 49093

SLACK, KAREN KERSHNER, advertising agency executive; b. Port Arthur, Tex., Aug. 28, 1951; d. High Cleveland and Eleanor Lucille (Beaty) Kershner; B.J., U. Tex., Austin, 1973; m. Jim Slack, Jr., May 12, 1979; children—Megan, James Ryan. Pub. relations dir. Lakeway Co., Austin, 1973-74; account coordinator, copywriter Point Communications, Inc., Houston, 1974-76; account exec., then v.p. Rochelle Mktg. Co., Inc., Houston, 1976-80; pres., owner Communications Plus, Houston, 1980—; mem. communications adv. com. Houston United Way, 1980—; chmn. steering com. Houston Festival, 1979—. Mem. Houston Advt. Fedn., Houston Prodn. Mgrs. Assn., Soc. Mktg. Profls., Internat. Assn. Bus. Communicators. Home: 204 Old Bridge Lake Houston TX 77069 Office: 2990 Richmond St Suite 525 Houston TX 77098

SLACKE, SALLY ANN, contracting company executive; b. S.I., N.Y., Apr. 16, 1933; d. Patrick and Mary G. (Granito) Magdalen; student Drake Bus. Sch., 1951, Adelphi U., 1968, Suffolk County (N.Y.) Community Coll., 1969; m. Felix P. Slacke, Oct. 8, 1955 (dec. 1975); children—Barbara, Diane, Carole Lynn. Sec., Netherland Trading Soc., N.Y.C., 1951-58; v.p. Slacke Drilling Co., Kings Park, N.Y., 1963-73; pres. Slacke Test Boring, Inc., Smithtown, N.Y., 1973—; dir. Allstate Life Ins. Co.; del. White House Conf. Small Bus., Washington. Coordinator sr. citizen activities Town of Smithtown, 1968-69; trustee L.I. Loves Bus., Inc.; chmn. L.I. Project Pride, 1981. Recipient L.I. Bus. Leadership award, 1980; Clara Barton Humanitarian award Suffolk County chpt. ARC, 1981; B'nai B'rith Youth Services award, 1982; AAUW Woman of Year award, 1982; Woman in Bus. Adv. of Year SBA, 1982; L.I. Achievers award, 1982. Mem. Nat. Assn. Female Execs. Inc., 110 Center for Bus. and Profl. Women, L.I. Assn. Commerce and Industry. Republican. Roman Catholic. Club: Zonta Internat. Office: 4 Main St Kings Park NY 11754

SLATCHER, DOLORES JONES, city manager; b. Milford, Del., Oct. 15, 1949; d. William E. and Pauline C. (Passwaters) Jones; m. William A. Slatcher, Aug. 4, 1984. Assoc. in Bus. Adminstrn. and Acctg., Del. Tech. and Community Coll. Acct. Moore Chevrolet-Olds Dealer, Lewes, Del., 1970-77; fin. dir. City of Seaford, Del., 1977-79, asst. city mgr., 1979-81, city mgr., 1982—. Republican. Methodist. Avocations: reading; softball; skiing; golf. Home: 414 Sussex Ave Seaford DE 19973 Office: City of Seaford 302 E King St Seaford DE 19973

SLATER, ALICE EVELYN, equal employment opportunity specialist; b. Hartford, Conn., July 23, 1949; d. Kenneth Lincoln and Adelaide Augustine (Rogers) Slater. B.S. in Human Relations and Organizational Behavior, U. San Francisco, 1985. Assigned risk automobile ins. rater Aetna Ins. Co., Hartford, 1967-68; personnel cons. Cosmopolitan Girl Employment Agy., Boston, 1970-71; community relations asst. Cambridge Econ. Opportunity Com., Mass., 1971; emergency room sec. City of Cambridge Hosp. and clk.-typist Bd. of Health, 1971-78; personnel clk., sec. Hdqrs., U.S. Dept. Army, San Francisco, 1979-85; EEO counselor U.S., Army Hdqrs., San Francisco, 1982-85; sec. HUD, San Francisco, 1985-86; EEO specialist/Hispanic employment program mgr. and fed. equal opportunity recruitment program mgr. Naval Weapons Sta., Concord, Calif., 1986—; owner, operator Slater's Secretarial Services, San Francisco, 1981—. Author: (research project) The Study of the Made Whole Concept of the Federal Equal Employment Opportunity Program on the Presidio of San Francisco, 1985. Artist (portrait) Contemplation, 1967 (Scholastic Art award 1967). Founder, dir. Slater Com. for Multiple Sclerosis, San Francisco, 1985—; mgr. Hispanic Employment Program Advocacy Task Force, 1986—; mem. Hispanic Employment Underrepresentation Task Force, 1986—; sec. United Negro Coll. Fund, San Francisco, Bay Area Inter-Alumni Council; 1984—; observer/reprter LWV, San Francisco Commn. on Status of Women, 1985—. Served with U.S. Army Res., 1976-84. Recipient Cert. of Appreciation, City of Cambridge, 1975; Best Speaker award Toastmasters Internat., 1981, 82, Best Evaluator award, 1982; numerous awards and commendations U.S. Army; Cert. of Appreciation, United Negro Coll. Fund, 1985. Mem. Federally Employed Women, Noncommnd. Officers Assn., Nat. Assn. Female Execs., Fed. Mgrs. Assn., Fed. Equal Employment Opportunity Adv. Council. Democrat. Clubs: Mensa, Commonwealth of Calif. Address: 901 Broderick St San Francisco CA 94115

SLATER, BARBARA RUTH, psychologist, educator; b. Potsdam, N.Y., Feb. 18, 1934; d. Gilson M. and Eleanor (Robinson) S.; B.A., St. Lawrence U., Canton, N.Y., 1955, M.Ed., 1959; Ph.D. in Sch. Psychology, Tchrs. Coll., Columbia U., 1966. Secondary sch. tchr. Port Dickinson (N.Y.) Schs., 1956-62; sch. psychologist, Pelham, N.Y., 1966-68; asst. prof. psychology Hofstra U., Hempstead, N.Y. 1968-71; prof. psychology, coordinator sch. psychology Towson (Md.) State U., 1971—; ind. practice psychology, 1967—. Diplomate in sch. psychology Am. Bd. Profl. Psychology. Mem. Am. Psychol. Assn., Nat. Assn. Sch. Psychologists, Md. Sch. Psychologists Assn., Eastern Psychol. Assn., Md. Psychol. Assn. Co-author: Cognitive Skills Assessment Battery; Psychodiagnostic Evaluation of Children. Home: 322 Jodyway Timonium MD 21093 Office: Dept Psychology Towson State U Towson MD 21204

SLATER, CONSTANCE, educator; b. Plymouth, Mass., Sept. 13, 1931; d. George Lewiston and Dorothy Mae (Darby) Finch; student Broward Community Coll., 1968-73; B.A., Shaw U., 1975; postgrad. Fla. Atlantic U., 1975-77; m. Fred Carl Slater, Nov. 22, 1952; children—Steven, Scott, Stacey Slater Owens, Sherrill Slater Barb. Office mgr. Comml. Union Assurance Co., Indpls., 1950, Family and Child Service Agy., San Bernardino, Calif., 1951, Gate City Sash and Door Co., Fort Lauderdale, Fla., 1952-54; tchr. aide Sundial Sch. for Retarded, Ft. Lauderdale, 1963-68; tchr. asst. Broward County Schs., Ft. Lauderdale, 1968-77, tchr. Wingate Oaks Center for Retarded, Ft. Lauderdale, 1977—; owner-dir. Tall Pine Camp for Exceptional Citizens, Coker Creek, Tenn., 1971—. Sec., Parents and Friends of Sunland Tng. Center, 1961-68; vice-chmn. Dist. 10, Fla. Human Rights Advocacy Com. on Mental Retardation, 1978—; tchr. rep. to N. Central Adv. Com., 1978-79, Supt. Schs. Dist. Adv. Com., 1979; bd. dirs. Broward County Assn. for Retarded Citizens. Vocat. Edn. for Handicapped fellow Fla. Internat. U., 1979-80. Mem. Council for Exceptional Citizens, Nat. Assn. for Retarded Citizens, Am. Assn. on Mental Deficiency. Democrat. Home: 6221 NW 17th St Fort Lauderdale FL 33313 Office: Wingate Oaks Center for Retarded Broward County Schs 1211 NW 33d Terr Fort Lauderdale FL 33311

SLATER, FRANCES MARIE, hospital manager; b. Galveston, Tex., Oct. 22, 1947; children—Julie, Denise, John. B.S., Domnican Coll., Houston, 1969; postgrad. Houston Bapt. U., 1985—. Head nurse St. Joseph Hosp., Houston, 1969-74, shift dir., 1974-75, infection control coordinator, 1975-81; asst. mgr. Methodist Hosp., Houston, 1981—. Mem. Kingwood Republican Women's Orgn., 1980—. Mem. Assn. Practitioners Infection Control (chpt. pres. 1978-80, chpt. treas. 1976-78). Republican. Roman Catholic.

SLAUGHTER, DIANA TERESA, educator; b. Chgo., Oct. 28, 1941; d. John Ison and Gwendolyn Malva (Armstead) Slaughter; B.A., U. Chgo., 1962, M.A., 1964, Ph.D., 1968. Instr. dept. psychiatry Howard U., Washington, 1967-68; research asso., asst. prof. Yale U. Child Study Center, New Haven, 1968-70; asst. prof. dept. behavioral scis. and edn. U. Chgo., 1970-77; asso. prof. edn. and African Am. studies Northwestern U., Evanston, Ill., 1977—; mem. nat. adv. bd. Fed. Center for Child Abuse and Neglect, 1979-82, Ednl. Research and Devel. Center, U. Tex., Austin; chmn. public policy program com. Chgo. Black Child Devel. Inst., 1982—, dir., 1982-84; dir. Ill. Infant Mental Health Com., 1982-83; mem. res. adv. bd. Chgo. Urban League, 1986—. Mem. Am. Psychol. Assn. (bd. ethnic and minority affairs), Soc. for Research in Child Devel. (governing council 1981-87), Am. Ednl. Research Assn., Assn. Black Psychologists, Groves Conf. Family, Delta Sigma Theta. Contbr. articles to profl. jours. Home: 835 Ridge Ave Evanston IL 60202 Office: 2003 Sheridan Rd Evanston IL 60201

SLAUGHTER, JANE MUNDY, author; b. Buchanan, Va., Oct. 2, 1905; d. Luther Thomas and Pearl Carnce (Karnes) Mundy; R.N., Jefferson Hosp., Roanoke, Va., 1926; m. Frank G. Slaughter, June 10, 1933; children—Frank G., Ramdolph M. Operating Room supr. Jefferson Hosp., 1923-24; pvt. duty nurse, 1924-33; freelance author, 1970—; author: Espy and the Catnappers, 1975; also 1st history of Fla. Med. Assn. Aux. Bd. dirs. Jacksonville (Fla.) YWCA, 1960-65. Mem. Fla. Hist. Soc., Jacksonville Hist. Soc., Fla. Fedn. Garden Clubs (life mem. Jacksonville), Fla. Med. Assn. Aux. (historian 1950). Democrat. Presbyterian. Club: Timuquana Country. Address: 5051 Yacht Club Rd Jacksonville FL 32210

SLAUGHTER, KATHERINE TRUDEAU, distribution company executive; b. Detroit, Sept. 30, 1955; d. Raymond Thomas and Sylvia Catherine (Rusinowski) Trudeau; m. James Bradley Slaughter, Sept. 1, 1984. B.A., U. Mich., 1977, M.B.A., 1980. Account exec. AT&T Communications, Troy, Mich., 1980-83, telemarketing cons., 1983-85; telemarketing supr. MMI Distbg. Inc., Dearborn, Mich., 1983-85, mktg. dir., 1985—. Mem. Direct Mktg. Assn. Detroit, Mich. Restaurant Assn., Mich. Petroleum Assn., Mich. Lodging Assn. Republican. Roman Catholic. Avocations: skiing; boating. Home: 340 Lothrop Rd Grosse Pointe Farms MI 48236 Office: MMI Distbg Inc 3910 Jonathon Dearborn MI 48126

SLAUGHTER, LURLINE EDDY, artist; b. Heidelberg, Miss., June 19, 1919; d. Gilbert Emmings and Lurline Elizabeth (Heidelberg) Eddy; B.S., Miss. U. for Women, 1939; m. James Fant Slaughter, Jan. 27, 1946; children—Beverly Lowery, Anne Towles. Tchr. high sch., Silver City, Miss., 1939-41; clk. VA, Washington, 1941-42; one-woman shows Ahda Artzt Gallery, N.Y.C., 1967, Nat. Design Center, N.Y.C., 1967, 68, Delta State U., Cleveland, Miss., 1973, 84, Gulf States Gallery, Greenville, Miss., 1973, 76, 80, 84, Southeastern La. U., Hammond, 1977, Cheekwood Fine Arts Center, Nashville, 1978, Byars Gallery, Little Rock, 1984, San Pedro Theatre, San Antonio, 1981, Cottonlandia Mus., Greenwood, Miss., 1984 exhibited in group shows U. Fla., 1969, Brooks Art Mus., Memphis, 1970, Miss. State U., 1970, Delta State U., 1971, 84; represented in permanent collection Miss. U. for Women, Miss. State U., Delta State U., Pine Bluff (Ark.) Art Ctr., Southeastern La. U., U. of South, Sewanee, Tenn., Eudora Welty Mepl. Library, Jackson, Miss.; represented in pvt. collections, Acapulco, N.Y.C., so. states. Recipient Best in Show award Acapulco Ann., Hilton Hotel, 1979. Tchr. Sunday Sch., Meth. Ch., 1953-67; pres. PTA; bd. dirs. Miss. Art Colony, 1965-85. Served as lt. USNR, 1942-45. Mem. Miss. Art Mus. Republican. Club: Humphreys Country. Address: Seldom Seen Plantation Silver City MS 39166

SLAUGHTER, SUSAN LEE BRUNDIGE, graphic designer, lecturer; b. Cin., Feb. 24, 1947; d. Jerry A. and Betty L. (Thorp) Brundige; B.F.A., Ohio State U., 1969; postgrad. U. Cin., evenings 1971-72; m. James L. Slaughter III, Sept. 16, 1972. Instr. painting Cin. Art Mus., part-time 1969-76; graphic designer Cin. Time Recorder Co., 1969-71, Hank Marowitz Advt. Agy., Cin., 1971-72; pres., graphic designer, cons. Slaughter & Slaughter, Inc., Cin., 1972—; lectr. graphics Xavier U., 1982—; painter. Chmn. spl. advt. project, designer posters, folder Radio Reading Services, 1981-82, Appreciation cert., 1981; designer posters, folder Arthritis Found. campaign, 1980—, Appreciation cert., 1979, Disting. Public Service award, 1981; designer Christmas card for fundraising Cancer Family Care, 1981; designer, dir. interior mus., permanent exhbn. African, Latin Am., S.Am. art, curator Comboni Mus. African, South Am. and Latin Am. Art and Artifacts, 1984—; co-designer program book on Nutcracker ballet for Cin. Ballet, 1985; trustee, corr. sec. in charge pub. relations, curator art gallery Unity Ctr. Cin., 1983—; treas., 1985, v.p., 1986; trustee Appalachian Community Council, Appalachian Festival, 1986—. Recipient awards Art Dirs. Club Cin., 1972-82, Am. Advt. Fedn., 1974, 80, Internat. Typographic Composition award, 1980, Bus. and Profl. Advt. Assn., 1981. Mem. Women in Communications (spl. project v.p., dir. 1981-82, recognition cert. 1981), Cin. Indsl. Advertisers (dir. 1979-81, Person of Distinction 1980, 81), Cin. Women's Network, Internat. Assn. Profl. Artists, Alliance Profl. Artists Ohio, Ky. and Ind. Office: Slaughter & Slaughter Inc 4307 Erie Ave Cincinnati OH 45227

SLAVIN, ROSANNE SINGER, textile converter; b. N.Y.C., Mar. 24, 1930; d. Lee H. and Rose (Winkler) Singer; student U. Ill.; divorced; children—Laurie Jo, Sharon Lee. Prodn. converter Doucet Fabrics, silk prints, N.Y.C., 1953-57; sales mgr., mdse. mgr. print div. Crown Fabrics, N.Y.C., 1957-65; owner Matisse Fabrics Inc., printed fabrics, N.Y.C., 1965—. Recipient Tommy award, 1978; designated ofcl. printed fabric supplier for U.S. Olympic swimteam, 1984. Office: 1457 Broadway New York NY 10036

SLAWIAK, SHEILA IAQUINTO, manufacturing corporation executive; b. Erie, Pa., Nov. 1, 1956; d. Salvatore and Carrie (Veneziano) Iaquinto; m. Thomas Arthur Slawiak, Oct. 23, 1976. Cert. lab. asst., Hamot Med. Ctr., 1975; B.S. in Chemistry, Gannon U., 1981, M.B.A., 1981. M.S. in Communications, Rensselaer Poly. Inst., 1983. Tech. rep. Hughson Chems. Co., Erie, 1976-81; sales assoc. J.C. Penney Co., Erie, 1981-82; tech. writer Allen-Bradley Corp., Highland Heights, Ohio, 1983-84, product engr., 1984—; office automation cons. First Nat. Bank, Erie, 1985—. Contbr. articles to tech. jours. Mem. Soc. Tech. Communications (research grant com.). Republican. Roman Catholic. Home: 4081 Sheffield-Monroe Rd Kingsville OH 44048 Office: Bldg 10 Allen-Bradley Corp 747 Alpha Dr Highland Heights OH 44143

SLAY, TANA SUE, psychologist, educator; b. Houston, Apr. 8, 1951; d. Thomas Benjamin and Naomi Joanne (Atwell) S. B.A. in Psychology, U. Houston, 1972, M.Ed. in Edn., 1974; Ph.D. in Psychology, Tex. A&M U., 1980. Cert. Tchr., Tex., Lic. Psychologist. Assoc. psychologist Galena Park Ind. Sch. Dist., 1974-78, lectr. Tex. A&M U., 1979-80; coordinator Houston Ind. Sch. Dist., 1980-83; psychologist CY Fair Ind. Sch. Dist., Houston, 1983—; mgmt. cons., psychologist, Houston, 1981—; mem. adj. faculty Houston Community Coll., 1983—. Contbr. numerous articles to profl. jours. Mem. Houston Hunger Project, 1982-84, Holiday Project, 1981-83. U. Houston fellow, 1972-74; Tex. A&M U. fellow, 1978-79. Mem. Am. Psychol. Assn., Nat. Assn. Sch. Psychologists, Tex. Psychol. Assn., Tex. Assn. Children with Learning Disabilities, Tex. Council for Exceptional Children. Methodist. Home: 10737 Boardwalk Houston TX 77042 Office: Cy-Fair Ind Sch Dist PO Box 44040 Houston TX 77040

SLAYDON, KATHLEEN AMELIA, lawyer; b. Fort Worth, June 1, 1951; d. A. Glynn and E. Jeanne (Miller) S. B.A., Rice U., 1973; J.D., U. Tex., 1976. Bar: Tex. 1977. Assoc. Reynolds Allen & Cook Houston, 1977-78; assoc. Ross Banks May Cron & Cavin. Houston, 1978-83, ptnr., 1983—; adv. dir. Tex. Am. Bank/Gulfway, Houston, 1985; lectr. State Bar Tex., 1983—. Pres., Owen Wister Literary Alumnae, Houston, 1983. Mem. Tex. Assn. Bank Counsel, Houston Bar Assn., Am. Mgmt. Assn. Clubs: Houston, Forum (Houston). Office: Ross Banks May Cron & Cavin Nine Greenway Plaza 20th Floor Houston TX 77046

SLAYMAKER, (CAROLYN) JANE HOYT, occupational therapist, educator; b. Detroit, Nov. 25, 1930; d. Douglas Granger and Elizabeth Carola (Wyker) Hoyt; B.A. in Art History, Wellesley Coll., 1953; cert. in interior decoration N.Y. Sch. Interior Design, 1954; cert. in occupational therapy (N.Y. State Dept. Mental Health and Hygiene scholar) N.Y.U., 1962, M.A. in Edn. (Am. Occupation Therapy Assn. scholar), 1966; postgrad. in guidance and counseling U. Ill., Urbana, 1969-70, in social change Walden U. West, 1980-83; also various seminars, workshops, insts., short courses. Recreational therapist Montefiore Hosp., Bronx, N.Y., 1958-60; staff occupational therapist Manhattan State Hosp., N.Y.C., 1962-65, Manhattan VA Hosp., N.Y.C., 1965-66; asst. prof. occupational therapy U. Fla., 1966-68, assoc. prof., 1970—, assoc. chmn., 1985—; activity therapist IV, Ill. Dept. Mental Health and Hygiene, Champaign, 1968-70; cons. gerontology, mental health; bd. dirs. North Central Fla. Community Mental Health Center, Inc., Gainesville, 1979-83, sec., 1981-82; bd. dirs. Mental Health Assn. Alachua County (Fla.), 1975-81, treas., 1976, 79, 80, 81, pres., 1978, 86. Bd. dirs. United Way Alachua County, 1976-80, Alachua County Council Child Abuse, 1978-81. Recipient Cert. of Appreciation, Mental Health Assn. Alachua County, 1975, Cert. of Commendation, 1977; Gold award United Way, 1978; Faculty Devel. award Coll. Health Related Professions, summer 1980; assoc. Center Gerontol. Studies and Programs, 1977—. Fellow Am. Occupational Therapy Assn.; mem. World Fedn. Occupational Therapy, Fla. Occupational Therapy Assn. (pres. 1971-73, rep. to Occupational Therapy Council, Bd. Med. Examiners State of Fla., 1975-83, assn. alt. rep. 1973-75, 79-82, Award of Excellence 1977, award of recognition 1983), Am. Gerontol. Soc., So. Gerontol. Assn., Pi Lambda Theta, Eta Rho Pi. Episcopalian. Contbr. articles to profl. jours. Office: Box J-164 JH Miller Health Center Gainesville FL 32610

SLEDGE, MARY PHILLIPA, advertising writer and producer; b. Memphis, Sept. 25, 1954; d. William Ruffin and Mary Jane (Pidgeon) S. Student, Mt. Holyoke Coll., South Hadley, Mass., 1972-73; cert. of studies and letters Vanderbilt-in-France, Aix-en-Provence, 1974; B.A. in Psychology and French, Duke U., 1976. Copywriter, Walker & Assocs., Memphis, 1976-78; mng. editor The Saddle Horse Report Mag., Nashville, 1979; copywriter T'NT Advt., Dallas, 1980; copywriter Rosenberg & Co., Dallas, 1981; sr. writer, producer The Sherrill Co., Dallas, 1982—. Southwest editor: Saddle & Bridle, 1983; contbr. mag. Memphis, 1978. Mem. Duke U. Alumni Assn., Dallas Soc. Visual Communications, Nat. Assn. Female Execs., Women in Communications. Office: The Sherrill Co 5115 McKinney Ave Memphis TN 75205

SLEEMAN, JANEANN CHAMNESS KING, personnel executive; b. Charleston, W.Va., July 7, 1945; d. W.E. and Maxine (Broyles) Chamness Walsh. B.S., Radford Coll., 1967. Personnel analyst, div. dir. W.Va. Civil Service System, Charleston, 1967-73; personnel officer Fin. and Adminstrn., Charleston, 1973-75; asst. dir. W.Va. Civil Service System, Charleston, 1975-78, dir., 1978-84; dir. human resources McDonough Caperton Ins. Group, 1984—; mem. Pay Equity Task Force, Charleston, 1984; ex-officio mem. W.Va. Women's Commn., Charleston, 1978—; mem. adv. curriculum com. Salem Coll., 1980—. Bd. trustees YWCA, Charleston, 1984, W.Va. Indsl. Relations Research Assn., 1984. Mem. Nat. Assn. State Personnel Execs., Internat. Personnel Mgmt. Assn. (pres. W.Va. chpt. 1977-78, bd. dirs. 1975-77), Mid-Atlantic Personnel Assessment Consortium, Am. Soc. Personnel Adminstrs., AMA. Baptist. Office: McDonough Caperton Ins Group One Hillcrest Dr Charleston WV 25326

SLEEMAN, MARY (MRS. JOHN PAUL SLEEMAN), librarian; b. Cleve., June 28, 1928; d. John and Mary Lillian (Jakub) Gerba; B.S., Kent State U., 1965, also M.L.S.; m. John Paul Sleeman, Apr. 27, 1946; children—Sandra Sleeman Swyrydenko, Robert, Gary, Linda. Supervising librarian elementary schs. Nordonia Hills Bd. Edn., Northfield, Ohio, 1965—; children's librarian Twinsburg (Ohio) Pub. Library, 1965-66. Mem. ALA, Ohio Sch. Librarians Assn., NEA, Summit County Librarians Assn., Storytellers Assn., North Eastern Ohio Tchrs. Assn. Methodist. Home: 18171 Logan Dr Walton Hills OH 44146 Office: 115 Ledge Rd Northfield OH 44067

SLEIGHT, GERALDINE MARIE, county official; b. York, Nebr., Sept. 15, 1944; d. Dennis Robert and Evelyn Rose (Prochaska) Koranda; m. Alan Wayne Sleight, Aug. 8, 1964; children—Alan M., Sheri L., William W., James A., David L. Grad. high sch., Seward, Nebr. With Nebr. Game and Parks State Agy., Lincoln, 1962-67, Peter's Moving and Storage, Lincoln, 1968-69; dep. county treas. Seward County, Nebr., 1970-78, county treas., 1978—. Sec. Assn. Retarded Citizens, Seward, 1983; v.p. St. Vincent DePaul Altar Soc., Seward, 1985. Recipient Outstanding Govt. Affairs award Seward Jayceettes, 1982. Mem. Nebr. County Treas. Assn. (pres. 1985, v.p., sec., treas. 1982-84, chmn. legis. com. 1983—), Nebr. County Ofcls. Assn. (Meritorious service award 1981), St. Vincent DePaul Altar Soc. (pres. 1985). Democrat. Roman Catholic. Avocations: sewing; gardening; reading; preparing income tax returns. Home: Box 140A Route 2 Milford NE 68405 Office: PO Box 289 Seward NE 68434

SLEITH, BARBARA ANN BALKO, educator; b. Elizabeth Twp., Pa., Jan. 29, 1946; d. Andrew and Elizabeth (Kurutz) Balko; A.A., Robert Morris Jr. Coll., 1966; B.S., California U. (Pa.), 1968, M.Ed., 1970; postgrad. U. Pitts., 1976, U. Indiana (Pa.); m. Melvin R. Sleith, Dec. 18, 1971; 1 dau., Melynda Sue. Tchr., Elizabeth (Pa.) Forward Sch. Dist., 1968-70; learning disabilities tchr. Allegheny Intermediate Unit 3, 1970-77, I.E.P. specialist, 1977-80; tchr. socially, emotionally maladjusted students, 1980—; distbr. Royal Am. Foods; cons. in field. Neighborhood chmn. Girl Scouts U.S.A., 1978-80; adult cons. ch. youth group, 1975-78; program rep., mem. liaison bd. Allegheny Intermediate Unit Edn. Assn., 1970-74; active PTA, William Penn Sch. Mem. Assn. Children with Learning Disabilities, Three Rivers Reading Council, Phi Delta Gamma (chpt. exec. officer). Democrat. Roman Catholic. Club: Confraternity of Christian Mothers (various offices) Address: RD 2 Box 115 West Newton PA 15089

SLEPAVIC, MARY ANN, advertising executive; b. Chgo., Feb. 16, 1952; d. Anthony and Mary (Kazlauskas) Slepavic. Sec., Harvard Bus. Coll., Chgo., 1969-70; collection mgr. Central Bus. Coll., Chgo., 1970-71, instr., 1971-73; sales asst. H-R/Stone Radio, Chgo., 1973-74; office mgr., exec. asst. McGavren Guild Radio, Chgo., 1974-77, Midwest research mgr., 1977—. Mem. Ill. Broadcasters Assn., Nat. Assn. Female Execs., Am. Women in Radio and TV. Democrat. Roman Catholic. Office: McGavren Guild Radio Inc 111 E Wacker Dr Chicago IL 60601

SLESAR, PAULA JEAN, communications company official; b. Milw., Feb. 8, 1955; d. Daniel L. and Louise J. (Moresco) S. B.A., Marquette U., 1977. Claims rep. Social Security Adminstrn., HEW, Waukegan, Ill., 1978-79; market adminstr. Wis. Telephone Co., Milw., 1979-80, account exec., 1980-84; sr. account exec. Wis. Bell Communications, Milw., 1984—. Vol., Italian Community Ctr. Festa Italiana, Milw., 1978-84. Mem. Am. Mktg. Assn. (chpt. sec. 1983-85), Internat. Orgn. Women in Telecommunications, Marquette U. Coll. Speech Alumni Assn. (pres. 1984, bd. dirs. 1979-85), Marquette U. Alumni Assn. (bd. dirs. 1985—). Roman Catholic. Home: 1603 S Carriage Ln New Berlin WI 53151 Office: Wis Bell Communications 200 S Executive Dr Brookfield WI 53005

SLEWITZKE, CONNIE L., government official. Brig. gen. U.S. Army; chief Army Nurse Corp. Office: Office Surgeon Gen Army Nurse Corps 5111 Leesburg Pike Fairfax VA 22041*

SLINGSBY, ANN MARY, art director; b. Bronx, N.Y., Aug. 10, 1930; d. Charles Angelo and Sarah (Smeraldi) Cimitile; m. Harry Stafford Slingsby, June 7, 1953; children—Robert, Keith, Tara. Degree in Art, Indsl. Arts Coll., N.Y.C., 1948; student Hunter Coll., N.Y.C., 1952-54. Head file dept. South African Govt., N.Y.C., 1950; salesperson, model Lord & Taylor, N.Y.C., 1950-53; art tchr. Bklyn. Archdiocese Schs., 1953-55, Archdiocese of N.Y. Schs., 1955-71; art dir. Clarkstown Recreation, New City, N.Y., 1973—; writer, producer, dir. sr. citizen annual show Town of Clarkstown, 1976—. Author: Arts and Crafts Teaching Experiences, 1975. Den mother Rockland County council Boy Scouts Am., 1962-63; vol. dir. Clarkstown Sr. Citizen Show, 1984; mem. Elmwood Playhouse, 1983—; assoc. Hudson Valley Leisure Services, 1980—. Recipient Cert. Appreciation Summit Park Hosp. Vol. Services, 1984. Roman Catholic. Avocations: Sculpture; painting; crafts; drama; dance. Home: 46 Briarwood Dr New City NY 10956

SLINGSBY, PHYLLIS LAVERNE (MRS. PERK A. SLINGSBY), journalist; b. Bakersfield, Calif., Oct. 12, 1917; d. Marion Lee and Stella Grace (Hughes) Crum; grad. high sch.; m. Perk A. Slingsby, Aug. 20, 1938; 1 dau., Sandra Lu (Mrs. Gerald Wayne Johnson). Women's editor Contra Costa Times Green Sheet, Walnut Creek, Calif., 1949-73. Charter mem. Walnut Creek Hist. Soc.; vol. Eisenhower Med. Ctr. Aux., Eisenhower and Betty Ford Ctr. Mem. Order Eastern Star, Order of White Shrine of Jerusalem (charter, past worthy high priestess). Clubs: Soroptimist (pres. 1961), Walnut Creek Profl. and Bus. Women's (pres. 1965), East Bay Women's Press (pres. 1969), Palm Springs Woman's. Home: 7 Golden State Rancho Mirage CA 92270

SLOAN, A. ELIZABETH, publishing executive, food scientist; b. Hackensack, N.J., Sept. 1, 1951; d. Kenneth Thomas Spencer and Anna Sember (Kundrat) Sloan Velebir; m. Theodore Peter Labuza, Jan. 22, 1976 (div. Jan. 1980). B.S., Rutgers State U., 1973; Ph.D., U. Minn., 1976. Communications specialist nutrition Gen. Mills, Inc., Mpls., 1976-77, mgr. nutrition edn. and communications services, 1977-79, mgr. nutrition communiction and tech. services, 1979-80; dir. sci. services Am. Assn. Cereal Chemists, St. Paul, 1980-81, also editor-in-chief Cereal foods World, Cereal Chemistry; dir. Good Housekeeping Inst., N.Y.C., 1981-85, also asst. to editor-in-chief Good Housekeeping mag., 1981-85; editor-in-chief McCall's mag., 1985—. Judge Mrs. America/Mrs. N.J. Pageant, 1984; mem. food update bd. govs. Food and Drug Law Inst., 1982-85; trustee Internat Life Scis. Inst., 1982—. Author: (with T.P. Labuza) Food for Thought, 1977; Contemporary Nutrition Controversies, 1979; coordinating editor Good Housekeeping American Family Christmas Book, 1985; contbr. articles to profl. jours. Tenneco Found. scholar, 1969-73; George H. Cook scholar, Rutgers U., 1973; Ralston Purina fellow, 1975. Mem. Inst. Food Technologists (nat. chmn. nutrition div. 1981-82), Am. Assn. Cereal Chemists, Am. Dietetic Assn., Am. Coll. Nutrition, Assn. Ofcl. Analytical Chemists, Am. Film Inst., Am. Home Econs. Assn., Home Economists in Bus., Smithsonian Instn., AAAS, Am. Soc. Prevention Cruelty to Animals, Soc. Nutrition Edn., Am. Mgmt. Assn., Soc. Consumer Affairs Profls. in Bus., Defenders of Wildlife, Am. Soc. Mag. Editors, Whitney Mus. Am. Art, Fashion Group, Womens City Club N.Y., Nat. Assn. Female Execs., N.Y. Acad. Scis., Am. Chem. Soc., Alpha Zeta, Phi Epsilon Omicron, Gamma Sigma Delta, Phi Tau Sigma, Sigma Delta Epsilon. Club: Rutgers (N.Y.C.). Avocation: golf. Office: McCall's Mag 230 Park Ave Room 721 New York NY 10169

SLOAN, BESSIE BERNICE, accountant; b. Middletown, Ohio, Apr. 17, 1949; d. Jessie and Pearlie Mae (Riley) Jemison; m. Ronald E. Sloan, Sr., Aug. 27, 1966; children—Ronald E., Natasha L. Student acctg., Miami U., Oxford, Ohio, 1986—. Operator, Ohio Bell Telephone, Dayton, 1968-76; receptionist City of Middletown, 1976-77, account clk. I, 1977-78, account clk. II, 1978-81, city acct., 1981—. Sec. Middletown City Employees Assn., 1977—; com. chair Middfest, 1980—, Elk Creek Festival, 1983—. Mem. Nat. Assn. Female Execs., Nat. Assn. Accts., Profls. in Action (sec.-treas. 1984—), Am. Payroll Assn., NAACP. Democrat. Mem. African Methodist Episcopal Ch. Club: Ebone Inc (officer 1972—) (Middletown). Avocations: golfing; reading; gardening; reupholstering furniture. Office: City of Middletown One City Centre Plaza Middletown OH 45042

SLOAN, CAROLYN JUNE, cosmetic company executive; b. Conroe, Tex., June 30, 1937; d. Hulon Jesse and Bessie Adeline (Stewart) White; m. Howard Sinclair Sloan, June 17, 1955; children—Sharon Sloan Kincannon, Kathryn Sloan Thomas, Christine D. Student Conroe pub. schs. Receivables clk. Germalene Chem. Co., Houston, 1960-61; sec. Kelly Girl Services, Houston, 1961-62; receptionist Watson Oil Co., Houston, 1962-63, Letbetter Clinic, Houston, 1963-67; sec. Parker Methodist Ch., Houston, 1967-69; owner, operator Merle Norman Cosmetic Studio, Magnolia, Tex., 1969-80, Navasota, Tex., 1976-81, Houston, 1978—. Mem. Am. Mgmt. Assn., Nat. Assn. Female Execs., Houston N.W. C. of C. (ambassador). Baptist. Home: 328 Abney Ln Magnolia TX 77355 Office: Merle Norman Cosmetics 1554 Willowbrook Mall Houston TX 77070

SLOAN, ELAINE FRANK, librarian, university dean; b. Pitts., May 20, 1938; d. Maurice and Sarah (Blecher) Frank; m. Howard R. Sloan, Aug. 30, 1959; children—Michael, Stephen, Eric. B.A., Chatham Coll., Pitts., 1959; M.A., U. Pitts., 1962; M.L.S. (Smithsonian Instn. fellow 1970-72, Outstanding Grad. award), U. Md., 1972, Ph.D., 1974. Research asst. Johns Hopkins U., 1962-66; asst. to dir. for planning and research, asst. dir. mgmt. and devel. Smithsonian Instn. Libraries, 1974-76; assoc. univ. librarian public service, lectr. Sch.

Librarianship, U. Calif., Berkeley, 1977-80; dean univ. libraries Ind. U., Bloomington, 1980—. Mem. ALA (chmn. pub. com. 1980-81). Home: 4901 E Ridgewood Dr Bloomington IN 47401 Office: Ind U Library 10th and Jordan Sts Bloomington IN 47405

SLOAN, JOAN SHAPIRO, health care executive; b. Boston, Feb. 12, 1953; d. Charles Sidney and Phyllis (Gerber) Shapiro; m. Saul Isaac Sloan, July 1, 1979; 1 son, Daniel Joshua. B.A., Brandeis U., 1975, M.A., 1978. Community health assoc. The Med. Found., Inc., Boston, 1978-79; health edn. coordinator Yale-New Haven Hosp., 1980-81, dir. health promotion services, 1981-85; mgr. contbns. program GTE, Stamford, Conn., 1985—; guest lectr. Fairfield U. (Conn.), 1983, So. Conn. State Coll., New Haven, 1981. Producer radio program Health and Lifestyle, 1982-83. Mem. planning and allocations com. United Way of Greater New Haven, 1981-85. Mem. Am. Mktg. Assn. Democrat. Jewish. Lodge: B'nai B'rith (dir. 1983—). Office: GTE 1 Stamford Forum Stamford CT 06904

SLOAN, JODY BETH, urban planner, consultant; b. Atlanta, July 16, 1953; d. Myer and Beryl (Cowan) S.; m. Joseph Raymond Crenshaw, Aug. 31, 1980. Student, U. Tenn., 1970-71; B.A., Ga. State U., 1976; M. in City Planning, Ga. Inst. Tech., 1979. Office mgr. Exec. Chairs, Atlanta, 1972-76; researcher Ga. Inst. Tech., Atlanta, 1977-79; planning cons. CMCA Cons., Atlanta, 1976-78; urban planner Jefferson County, Ala., 1978-79; transp. planner, rep. U.S. Dept. Transp.-Urban Mass. Transp. Adminstrn., Ft. Worth and Atlanta, 1979-85; cons. The Real Estate Consortium Atlanta, 1985—; co-owner The Bare Walls, Atlanta, 1981—. Contbr. articles to profl. jours.; contbr. restaurant reviews. Mem. conservation com. Sierra Club, Atlanta, 1977—; mem. fundraising com. City of Hope Hosp. and Med. Ctr., Atlanta, 1983—; v.p., bd. dirs. Westover Plantation, 1984-86. Mem. Am. Planning Assn., Women in Transp., Nat. Assn. Female Execs. (assoc. 1982—). Democrat. Home: 8 Newport Pl NW Atlanta GA 30318 Office: Real Estate Consortium 4000 DeKalb Tech Pkwy Bldg 500 Suite 550 Atlanta GA 30340

SLOAN, JUDY BECKNER, law educator; b. Cochran Field AFB, Ga., Jan. 9, 1945; d. Edward Lee and Peggy Joyce (Adkins) Beckner; m. William R. Sloan, Apr. 4, 1965; children—Anita Lee, Jacqueline H. B.A., U. Chgo., 1967; J.D., U. Md., 1975. Bar: Ohio 1976, U.S. Dist. Ct. (no. dist.) Ohio 1979. Law clk. firm Miles & Stockbridge, Balt., 1973-74; Asper fellow to R. Dorsey Watkins, Balt., 1974-75; asst. prof. law U. Toledo Coll. Law, 1975-77, assoc. prof., 1978—; Jud. fellow U.S. Supreme Ct., 1986—; cons. firm Sonnenschein, Carlin, Nath & Rosenthal, Chgo., summer 1978; auditor internat. law World Ct.-Acad. Internat. Law, The Hague, Netherlands, summer 1972. Contbr. articles to profl. jours.; composer music performed by Jewish Community Orch. Toledo, 1983, 84; performed with Toledo Opera, 1982. Trustee, Toledo Symphony Orch. 1979—, Toledo Ballet, 1977-81; mem. citizens adv. bd. N.W. Ohio Devel. Ctr., Toledo, 1979-84, chmn. pub. relations Jr. League, Toledo, 1981-84; trustee Ohio Citizens Commn. for Arts, 1980—. Recipient Toledo Arts Commn. award, 1982; NEH fellow Columbia U., summer 1981. Mem. ABA, Ohio Bar Assn., Toledo Bar Assn. (law inst. com. 1977—, med.-legal com. 1976-79), Phi Kappa Phi, Delta Theta Phi. Jewish. Club: University (pres. 1980-81) (Toledo). Home: 2138 Boshart Way Toledo OH 43606 Office: U Toledo Coll Law 2801 W Bancroft St Toledo OH 43606

SLOAN, MARY LOVE STRINGFIELD, interior designer; b. Waynesville, N.C., Aug. 7, 1947; d. Thomas and Harriet (Coburn) Stringfield; m. Hugh Johnston Sloan, III, Feb. 12, 1982; 1 stepchild, Kathleen Sloan Gebhart. B.S., U. Tenn., 1973. Staff designer Omnia Design, Inc., Charlotte, 1973-79; dir. planning and design Counterpoint, Inc., Knoxville, 1979-81; coordinator interior design Ohio State U. Hosps., Columbus, 1981—; instr. Central Piedmont Community Coll., Charlotte, 1978, U. Tenn., Knoxville, 1980. Bd. dirs., pres. ECO, Inc., Charlotte, 1977, 79; sec. Young Democrats Club, Charlotte, 1978; rep. to state bd. Women's Polit. Caucus, Knoxville, 1980; mem. Columbus Com. for UNICEF, 1982—; mem. centennial com. King Ave. United Meth. Ch., 1985—. Mem. Inst. Bus. Designers (nat. trustee 1978-79, v.p. Tenn. chpt. 1980, edn. chair Ohio regional chpt. 1985-86, Cert. of Appreciation 1980), Assn. Univ. Interior Designers (sec. 1983-85, v.p. 1985—), U. Tenn. Alumni Assn. (sec. 1984-86). Republican. Methodist. Clubs: Women's Guild Opera Columbus, World Future Soc., Sierra, Nat. Trust Hist. Preservation, Ohio Preservation Alliance. Avocations: travel; gardening; opera; theatre; philately. Home: 758 N Park St Columbus OH 43215 Office: Ohio State U Hosps 410 W 10th Ave Columbus OH 43210

SLOAN, SHERI LYNN, social worker, therapist; b. Colorado City, Tex., July 30, 1957; d. William Everd Sloan and Nedra Jane (Everitt) Kennedy. Assoc. in Psychology, Eastfield Jr., Coll., 1979; B.S.W., North Tex. State U., 1981; M.S.W., U. Tex.-Arlington, 1983. Cert. social worker. Mental health worker Timberlawn Psychiat. Hosp., Dallas, 1977-78; house parent, counselor Juliette Fowler, Dallas, 1978-79; child care worker, supr., Children's Med. Ctr.-Psychiat. Unit, Dallas, 1979-83; rehab. social worker Lighthouse for Blind, Dallas, 1983-85; family counselor/caseworker Promise House, Dallas, 1985—; caseworker Friends of the Family, Denton, Tex., 1980; caseworker, com. mem. ARC, Dallas, 1981; counselor U. Tex. Community Clinic, Arlington, 1982; social work intern Plano Ind. Sch. Dist. (Tex.), 1982-83. Author: A Self-Help Manual for Disaster Victims, 1982. Campaign asst. Democratic party hdqrs., North Central Expressway, Dallas, 1976; vol. Big Sisters' Program, Dallas, 1976-77. Recipient Social Work Outstanding Achievement award North Tex. State U., 1982. Mem. Nat. Assn. Social Workers, Phi Beta Kappa, Phi Kappa Phi, Alpha Delta Mu. Methodist. Home: 2802 Poinsettia Dr Dallas TX 75211

SLOAN, SUZANNE BARKIN, director of marketing and sales; b. N.Y.C., Aug. 20, 1959; d. Stephen Samuel and Nanette Ruth (Barkin) Sloan; m. Gary Gittelsohn. B.A., U. Rochester, 1981; M.S., Columbia U., 1983; Cert. Sign Lang., Nat. Tech. Inst. for Deaf, 1980. Cert. social worker, N.Y. Social worker Spl. Services to Children, Jamaica, N.Y., 1981-82, Pleasantville (N.Y.) Cottage Sch., 1982-83; real estate sales, devel. Stephen Sloan Realty Corp., N.Y.C., 1980—; dir. mktg. Anchorage Yacht Club, Lindenhurst, N.Y., 1983—; rep. alumni affairs Horace Mann-Barnard Sch., Bronx, 1977—. Contbr. articles to profl. jours. Bd. dirs. Citizens Com. for Urban Fishing, N.Y.C., 1979—; mem. Assoc. Humane Soc., 1980—, Am. Soc. Prevention of Cruelty to Animals, 1979—. Mem. Nat. Assn. Social Workers, Columbia U. Sch. Social Work Alumni Assn., Nat. Marine Mfrs. Assn., Nat. Maritime Assn. Home: 44 W 62d St New York NY 10023 Office: Anchorage Yacht Club 401 E Shore Rd Lindenhurst NY 11757

SLOANE, BETTY-ANN, marketing/planning executive, consultant; b. Yonkers, N.Y., Nov. 3, 1952; d. Morris and Patricia May Sloane. Student London Sch. Econs., 1972-73; B.S., Boston U., 1974; M.B.A., Northeastern U., 1979. First student mgr. Boston U. Food Service, Servomation Corp., 1974; founder, dir. elderly drug abuse program Mayors Office of Coordinating Council of Drug Abuse, Boston, 1974-77; grants obtainer, systems analyst Boston City Hosp., 1975; researcher Nat. League of Cities, U.S. Conf. Mayors, Washington, 1976; dir. bus. devel. Fred C. Hart & Assocs., N.Y.C., Washington and Denver, 1979-80; v.p. Lee Manners & Assocs., N.Y.C., 1981-82; dir. bus. devel. The Hillier Group, Princeton, N.J., 1982-83; pres. Results Plus, N.Y.C., 1983—; cons. in field. Contbr. chpt. to book. Campaign worker for Tip O'Neal, Boston, 1976, Mayor Koch, N.Y.C., 1985. Mem. Internat. Facilities Mgmt. Assn. (founder; dir. publicity 1983-84), Soc. for Mktg. Profl. Services, Women in Real Estate, Am. Mgmt. and Bus. Assn., Am. Strategic Planning Assn., Boston Jr. C. of C. Office: Results Plus 340 E 93rd New York NY 10128

SLOANE, BEVERLY LEBOV, writer; b. N.Y.C., May 26, 1936; d. Benjamin S. and Anne (Weinberg) LeBov; A.B., Vassar Coll., 1958; M.A., Claremont Grad. Sch., 1975, postgrad., 1975-76; grad. exec. program. Sch. Mgmt., UCLA, 1982; grad. pub. course Stanford U., 1982; m. Robert Malcolm Sloane, Sept. 27, 1959; 1 dau., Alison Lori. Circulation librarian Harvard Med. Library, Boston, 1958-59; social worker Conn. State Welfare, New Haven, 1960-61; tchr. English, Hebrew Day Sch., New Haven, 1961-64; instr. creative writing and English lit. Monmouth Coll., West Long Branch, N.J., 1967-69; freelance writer, Arcadia, Calif., 1970—. Mem. public relations bd. Monmouth County Mental Health Assn., 1968-69; adv. council tech. and profl. writing dept. English, Calif. State U., Long Beach, 1980-82; v.p. Council of Grad. Students, Claremont Grad. Sch., 1971-72; trustee Center for Improvement of Child Caring, 1981-83; mem. League Crippled Children, 1982—; bd. dirs. Los Angeles Commn. on Assaults Against Women, 1983-84; v.p. Temple Beth David, 1983-86; mem. community relations com. Jewish Fedn. Council Greater Los Angeles, 1985—. Coro Found. fellow, 1979. Fellow Am. Med. Writers Assn. (dir. 1980—, Pacific S.W. del. to nat. bd. 1980—, chmn. various conv. coms., chmn. nat. book awards trade category 1982-83, chmn. Nat. Conv. Networking Luncheon 1983, 84, chmn. freelance and pub. relations coms. Nat. Midyr. Conf. 1983-84, workshop leader ann. conf. 1984, 85, nat. chmn. freelance sect. 1984-85, gen. chmn. 1985 Asilomar Conf.); mem. Women in Communications (dir. 1980—, v.p. community affairs 1981-82, Northeast area rep. 1980-81, chmn. awards banquet 1982, chmn. Los Angeles chpt. 1st ann. Agnes Underwood Freedom of Info. Awards Banquet 1982, recognition award 1983, nominating com. 1982, 83), Am. Assn. for Higher Edn., AAUW (legis. chmn. Arcadia br. 1976-77, books and plays chmn. Arcadia br. 1973-74, creative writing chmn. 1969-70, 1st v.p. 1975-76, networking chmn. 1981-82), Coll. English Assn., Am. Public Health Assn., Calif. Press Women (v.p. programs Los Angeles chpt. 1982-85, pres. 1985—), AAUP, Internat. Communication Assn., N.Y. Acad. Scis., Ind. Writers So. Calif., Hastings Inst., AAAS, Am. Med. Writers Assn. (pres.-elect Pacific S.W. chpt. 1985—, nat. dir. sects. 1985—, exec. bd. dirs. 1985—), Calif. Press Women (pres. Los Angeles chpt. 1985—), AAUW (chpt. Woman of Achievement award 1986), Soc. for Tech. Communication (workshop leader, 1985, 86). Clubs: Ex-Rotary of Duarte; Vassar of So. Calif., Calif. Inst. Tech. Women's, Claremont Coll. Faculty House, Los Angeles Athletic, World Trade Greater Los Angeles, Town Hall of Calif. (vice chmn. community affairs sect. 1982—, instr. Exec. Breakfast Inst., 1985-86). Author: From Vassar to Kitchen, 1967; A Guide to Health Facilities—Personnel and Management, 1971, 2d edit., 1977; mem. adv. bd. Calif. Health Rev., 1982-83. Home and Office: 1301 N Santa Anita Ave Arcadia CA 91006

SLOANE, FAY BETH, stockbroker; b. Yonkers, N.Y., May 22, 1946; d. Morris and Helen (Kaner) Sloane; student Miami (Fla.) Dade Community Coll., 1974-75. Supr. graphic art preparation dept., Miami, 1970-80; photographer, Miami, 1974-78; account exec. G.S. Omni, Denver, 1980-82, Dean Witter Reynolds, Denver, 1982—; fin. cons. Center for Coop. Advt. Mem. pediatric devel. com. N.Y. Hosp., Cornell Med. Center; active Friends of Colo. State Ballet. Mem. Nat. Assn. for Women in Bus., Nat. Assn. for Female Execs. Jewish. Office: Dean Witter Reynolds 1125 17th St Denver CO 80202

SLOAT, JANE ROBERTS DEGRAFF, government official; b. N.Y.C., Dec. 31, 1939; d. John Wynne and Agnes (Murton) Roberts; m. Elliott Dodd DeGraff, June 28, 1959; (div.); children—Pamela DeGraff Porter, Jill Katherine; m. 2d, Jonathan Welsh Sloat, June 19, 1983. Active Hospitality and Info. Service, Washington, 1964-70, sec. bd., 1971-73; spl. asst. to ambassador-at-large for cultural affairs Dept. State, Washington, 1981, now spl. asst. to ambassador at large for refugee affairs; spl. asst. to U.S. coordinator refugee affairs, Washington, 1982-84, coordinator conf. on Ethical Issues and Moral Principles in U.S. Refugee Policy, 1983. Tour lectr. Corcoran Gallery Art, Washington, 1965-70; vice chmn. UN Concert, Washington, 1971, 50th Jubilee Nat. English Speaking Union, 1971; spl. asst. to chmn. United Givers Fund, Washington, 1971-72; chmn. ball Opera Soc. Washington, 1972; bd. dirs. Jr. League, 1970-71, Nat. Ballet Soc., 1972-74, Washington Performing Arts Soc., 1972-75; mem. D.C. Mayor's Com. on Internat. Visitors, 1972-77; trustee Hosp. for Sick Children, Washington, 1973-76; editor Washington Antiques Show Catalogue, 1972-75; mem. D.C. Republican. Fin. Com., 1972-75; trustee Meridian House Internat. Ctr., Washington, 1964-82, sec. 1974-75, vice chmn. bd., 1976-82; mem. bd. advisers D.C. Lung Assn., 1975—; active fund-raising drive for Washington Cathedral, 1976; bd. dirs. Washington Home for Incurables, 1976-84, Nat. Eye Found., 1976-78, Children's Hosp. Nat. Research Found., 1978-81, D.C. chpt. ARC, 1976-84, Travelers Aid Soc., 1976-84; chmn. Washington Antiques Show, 1976-78, Washington Cathedral Flower Mart; dir. fin. devel. YWCA of Nat. Capital Area, 1979; vice chmn. Reagan Bush Inaugural, Washington, 1981; mem. transition team for Reagan Bush for NEA, 1981; bd. dirs. Family Stress Services, 1981-84. Bd. dirs. All Hallows Guild. Republican. Episcopalian. Clubs: Sulgrave, Chevy Chase (Washington). Office: Dept State 2201 C St NW Washington DC 20520

SLOBOTZKY, LESLIE RAYE, accountant; b. New Orleans, Nov. 28, 1958; d. Joseph Emanuel and Joyce (Pollock) S.; div. 1984. B.S., La. State U., Baton Rouge, 1980. C.P.A., La. Audit staff asst. Grant Thornton Co., New Orleans, 1980-81, audit staff sr., 1981-84, audit staff supr., 1984—. Mem. Am. Inst. C.P.A.s, La. Soc. C.P.A.s, Women's Profl. Council, LWV, Assn. Sch. Bus. Ofcls., Govt. Fin. Officers Assn., Assn. Govt. Accts., Nat. Council Jewish Women. Jewish. Avocations: weight lifting; walking; swimming. Home: 212 Hollygrove St Metairie LA 70005 Office: Grant Thornton 601 Poydras St Suite 1900 New Orleans LA 70130

SLOGGETT, STEPHANIE LYNN, lawyer, airline company executive; b. Inglewood, Calif., Dec. 22, 1949; d. Bruce Carroll and Mildred May (Lynn) Sloggett; student Wichita State U., 1970-71, San Diego State U., 1971-74; B.S.L., Western State U. Coll. Law, San Diego, 1980, J.D., 1984; student Flight Attendant Safety Sch., U. So. Calif., 1979—. With Pacific S.W. Airlines, San Diego, 1973—, flight attendant, 1973-79, group supr. flight attendant dept., 1979, spl. projects supr., 1979-80, mgr. union contract adminstrn., legal dept., 1980-82, dir. labor relations, 1982-86, dir. labor relations and legal affairs, 1986—. Mem. Southwest Flight Attendants Assn. (accident investigation team party coordinator 1978-79, sec.-treas. 1977-79, negotiating team 1976-77, chairperson scheduling com. 1975-79), Indsl. Relations Research Assn., Gamma Phi Beta (pres. corp. bd.). Republican. Episcopalian. Home: 13373 Gelbourne Pl San Diego CA 92130 Office: Pacific Southwest Airlines 3225 N Harbor Dr San Diego CA 92101

SLONE, SANDI, artist; b. Boston, Oct. 1, 1939; d. Louis and Ida (Spindiak) Sudikoff; children—Erric Solomon, Jon Solomon. Student Boston Mus. Sch., 1970-73; B.A., Wellesley Coll., 1974. Mem. faculty Boston Mus. Sch., 1970—, Brandeis U., Waltham, Mass., 1976, Harvard U., Cambridge, Mass., 1982. One person shows include: Harcus Krakow Gallery, Boston, 1978, 79, 80, 82, 84, Acquavella Contemporary Art, N.Y., 1977, 79, 80, 82, 84; group shows include Mus. Fine Arts, Boston, 1977, Corcoran Gallery of Art, Washington, 1977, Hayden Gallery, MIT, 1978, New Generation Andre Emmerich Gallery, N.Y., 1980-81, Am. Ctr., Paris, 1980-81, Amerika Haus, Berlin, 1980-81, Carpenter Ctr., Harvard U., 1983, Edmonton Art Gallery, 1977, 85, Gallery One, Toronto, Ont., Can., 1981; represented in permanent collections including Mus. Modern Art, N.Y.C., Albright-Knox, Buffalo, Mus. Fine Arts, Boston, Hirshhorn Mus., Washington, Mus. Fine Arts Boston fellow, 1977, 81; Ford Found. grantee, 1979.

SLONIM, NANCY COWGER, association officer, lawyer; b. Dearborn, Mich., Jan. 25, 1946; d. William D. and Joyce Elaine (Roush) Cowger; m. Scott Slonim, Apr. 19, 1980; 1 dau., Samantha Joyce. B.J., U. Mo., 1968; J.D., Ill. Inst. Tech.-Chgo. Kent Law Sch., 1979. Bar: Ill. 1979. News reporter Evening Tribune, Hornell, N.Y., 1968-70, Paddock Publs., Arlington Heights, Ill., 1970-75; paralegal sec. Philip Maher, Esq., Chgo., 1975-76; news reporter ABA, Chgo., 1976-79, staff dir. communications div., 1979—; vol. lawyer Chgo. Bar Assn. Pro Bono Project for Battered Women, 1981-82. Contbr. articles to law jours. Contbg. mem. Brookfield Zoo (Ill.), 1976, 77; mem. ACLU, 1975—, Nat. Coalition to Ban Handguns, 1980—. Recipient book award-evidence Lawyers Coop. Pub. Co., 1978. Mem. ABA, Ill. Bar Assn., Chgo. Bar Assn., Am. Judicature Soc., NOW, Chgo. Headline Club, Sigma Delta Chi. Office: ABA 33 W Monroe St Chicago IL 60018

SLOSHBERG, LEAH PHYFER, museum director; b. New Albany, Miss., Feb. 21, 1937; d. Sisco Knox and Mary Rachel (Sandlin) Phyfer; m. Willard Sloshberg, Dec. 8, 1961; 1 son, Simeon. B.F.A., Miss. State Coll., 1959; M.A. (Woodrow Wilson fellow), Tulane U., 1961. Arts curator N.J. State Mus., Trenton, 1968-69, asst. dir., 1969-71, dir., 1971—. Home: Box 817 RFD 3 Stockton NJ 08559 Office: New Jersey State Mus Trenton NJ 08625

SLOVITER, DOLORES KORMAN, federal judge; b. Phila., Sept. 5, 1932; d. David and Tillie Korman; m. Henry A. Sloviter, Apr. 3, 1969; 1 dau., Vikki Amanda. A.B. with distinction in Econs., Temple U., 1953, L.H.D. (hon.), 1986; LL.B. magna cum laude, U. Pa., 1956; LL.D. (hon.), Dickinson Sch. Law, 1984. Bar: Pa. 1957. Assoc. firm Dilworth, Paxson, Kalish, Kohn & Levy, Phila., 1956-64, partner, 1965-69; mem. firm Harold E. Kohn, P.A., Phila., 1969-72; asso. prof. law Temple U., Phila., 1972-74, prof., 1974-79; judge U.S. Ct. Appeals, 3d Circuit, Phila., 1979—; mem. Com. of 70, 1976-79; mem. hearing panel Disciplinary Bd. Supreme Ct. Pa., 1978-79. Mem. SE region Pa. Gov.'s Council on Aging, 1976-79. Mem. Phila. Bar Assn. (gov. 1976-78), Fed. Bar Assn., Am. Bar Assn., Am. Law Inst., Fed. Judges Assn., Jewish Publ. Soc. Am. (trustee 1983—), Order of Coif (pres. U. Pa. chpt. 1975-77), Phi Beta Kappa. Office: US Courthouse Rm 18614 601 Market St Philadelphia PA 19106

SLUDER, LAURA NEAS, graphic arts firm executive; b. Lincoln, Nebr., July 30, 1943; d. Harry Clifford and Alice Pearl (Sparks) Neas; m. John Milton Sluder, Mar. 23, 1963; children—John Clifford, David Milton. Student Brevard Community Coll. Sec., Radiation, Inc., Palm Bay, Fla., 1965-66, Systex, Inc., Melbourne, Fla., 1974-75; artist/ptnr. Shoestring Gallery, Melbourne, Fla., 1975-78; freelance graphic artist, 1978-80; pres. Diversified Art, Melbourne, 1980—; cons. Brevard Symphony, Brevard Zool. Soc. Art dir. poster The Muse, 1985; artist numerous paintings, graphics. Bd. dirs. Brevard Symphony Youth Orch., Melbourne, 1986; mem. Women's Ctr., 1985-86; supporter Hacienda Girls Ranch, 1984-86; gold key contbr. Brevard Symphony Orch., 1984-86. Recipient Golden Image award, 1986. Mem. Central Fla. Advt. Fedn., South Brevard Profl. Women's Network, Nat. Assn. Female Execs., Brevard Zool. Soc. Republican. Baptist. Avocations: painting; reading; needlework. Office: Diversified Art Inc 211 E New Haven Ave Melbourne FL 32901

SLUSHER, SHIRLEY JEAN, accountant, computer specialist, consultant, financial planner; b. Battle Creek, Mich., Mar. 9, 1942; d. Ransom and Reba E. (Phillips) Parris; m. Irvon Q. Slusher, Oct. 17, 1964; children—Veronica K., Nicole J., William R. Student Washington Sch. for Secs., 1960's, income tax courses H & R Block, 1966-68; student U. Md., 1962—, Prince George Community Coll., 1983; real estate course, Calvert County Community Coll., 1983. Telephone operator Am. Tel. & Tel. Co., Battle Creek, 1959-60, clerical supr., Washington, 1960-66; tax preparer H & R Block, Bladensburg, Mich., office mgr., Landover, Mich., 1967-72; bookkeeper, receptionist, sec., office mgr. T.F. Cullen, M.D., Forestville, Md., 1974-78; owner, operator Tax Help, Inc., Dunkirk, Md., 1960—; real estate agent David Van Hoy Estate, Dunkirk, 1983—; instr. Calvert County Adult Edn., Prince Frederick, Md., 1982—; computer specialist Bay Mills Constrn. Co., Inc., 1984—; temporary mail contractor U.S. Post Office, Owings, Md., 1984. Vice pres. Bd. Edn., Calvert County, Md., 1983-84; 85— adv. bd. County Commrs., 1980-83; pres. No. High Sch. PTSA; pres., v.p. No. Middle Sch. PTSA; cert. tchr., bd. dirs. Ch. of God of Prophecy, Lanham, Md., sec. Calvert County Democrat Club., 1982. Home: 11625 Rivershore Dr Dunkirk MD 29754

SMALL, CYNTHIA CAROL, nursing educator; b. South Bend, Ind., Jan. 16, 1948; d. William Theodore and Willie Mae (Campbell) Cooper; m. Ronald Myer Small, May 23, 1971; children—Heather Lynne, Lamar Eugene, Holly Lyneise. R.N., Mercy Hosp., 1971; B.S. in Nursing, Andrews U., 1971. Staff nurse Mercy Hosp., Benton Harbor, Mich., 1971-73, 74-75, clin. coordinator open heart surg. unit II, house supr., 1973-74, 75—; instr. nursing Lake Mich. Coll., Benton Harbor, 1982—. Mem. Am. Nursing Assn., Mich. Nurses Assn., Sigma Theta Tau (Eta Zeta chpt.). Adventist. Office: Lake Mich Coll 2755 E Napier St Benton Harbor MI 49022

SMALL, HARRIETTE ROBINSON, arts administrator, author; b. Walla Walla, Wash., June 2, 1930; d. Lee Page and Harriette Watson (Livermore) Robinson; m. Harold T. Small, June 14, 1949 (div. 1972); children—Larry, Melinda, Will, Ben. Student, Denver U., 1948-50, Pikes Peak Community Coll., 1961-62. Devel. dir., finance officer Cheyenne Village, Manitou Springs, Colo., 1976-78; ticket chmn. publicity Symphony Orch. Assn., Colorado Springs, Colo., 1962-76, fin. officer, dir. youth activities, 1978—. Bd. dirs. Performing Arts for Youth Orgn., Colorado Springs, 1980-85. Minority Council for Arts, Colorado Springs, 1983—; entertainment chmn. Springspree, Colorado Springs, 1985. Author: Colorado Springs Today, 1982, rev. 2d edit., 1984. Pres. Pikes Peak Arts Council, Colorado Springs, 1982-83, mem. bd., 1985; bd. dirs. Assn. Retarded Citizens, Colorado Springs, 1985—, Arts/Bus., Edn. Com., Com., Colorado Springs, 1985. Recipient Medal of Distinction in Arts, City of Colorado Springs, 1983-84. Republican. Methodist. Advocations: gardening; furniture refinishing; bird raising. Home: 805 Pioneer Ln Colorado Springs CO 80904 Office: Colo Springs Symphony Orch Assn PO Box 1692 Colorado Springs CO 80901

SMALL, KARNA, government official; b. Wilmette, Ill. B.A. with honors, U. Mich.; postgrad. San Francisco State U., Stanford U. Newsreporter KRON-TV, San Francisco, 1968-72, news anchor KGO-TV, San Francisco, 1972-76, WTTG-TV, Washington, 1976-78; writer/moderator pub. affairs program WJLA-TV, Washington, also syndicated nationwide, 1978-81; dep. press sec. The White House, Washington, 1981, dir. media relations and planning, 1981-83; dep. asst. to pres. and sr. dir. pub. affairs Nat. Security Council, Washington, 1984—. Address: National Security Council The White House 1600 Pennsylvania Ave NW Washington DC 20500

SMALL, MARY CAROL EKLUND, lawyer; b. Pasadena, Calif., May 1, 1951; d. Fred and Helen Virginia (Spahr) Eklund; m. Michael A. Small, May 24, 1981. B.A. with distinction in gen. scholarship U. Calif.-Berkeley, 1973, J.D., U. Calif., Hasting Coll. Law, 1978. Bar: Calif. 1979, N.Y. 1980, Wash. 1982. Assoc. firm Breed, Abbott & Morgan, N.Y.C., 1979-81, Karr, Tuttle, Koch, Campbell, Mawer & Morrow, Seattle, 1981-85, Bittner & Barker, Seattle, 1985—; arbitrator Nat. Assn. Securities Dealers, Am. Arbitration Assn. Editor-in-chief Hastings Constn. Law Quar., 1977-78. U. Calif., Berkeley Alumni Assn. scholar, 1969-71. Mem. ABA, Calif. Bar Assn., N.Y. Bar Assn., Wash. Bar Assn., Seattle-King County Bar Assn., Phi Beta Kappa. Democrat. Office: 1111 3d Ave Seattle WA 98101

SMALL, MARYTHERESE, marketing research executive; b. Chgo., Nov. 5, 1932; d. Thomas and Norah (Clarke) Galligan; m. Gerald F. Small, Feb. 27, 1960; children—Andrew C., Martha D., David D. B.A. with honors, St. Xavier Coll., 1954. Research project mgr. Gen. Foods Corp., Bedford Park, Ill., 1957-62; research ops dir. Market Facts, Chgo., 1962-63; sr. adminstr. mktg. info. services Quaker Oats Co., Chgo., 1977-81; mktg. research supr. Keebler Co., Elmhurst, Ill., 1981—; cons., 1963-77. Newsletter editor Ill. Montessori Soc., 1966-77, pres. 1972-77; bd. mem., officer Ill. Adv. Com. Non-Pub. Schs., 1972-77; advisor com on standards Ill. Dept. Edn., 1976. Mem. Am. Mktg. Assn., Am. Demographics Soc., Women in Info. Processing. Republican. Roman Catholic. Club: St Ignatius Coll. Prep. Mothers (Chgo.). Home: 343 Gale Ave River Forest IL 60305 Office: Keebler Co 1 Hollow Tree Ln Elmhurst IL 60305

SMALL, REBECCA ELAINE, accountant, financial planner; b. Meridian, Tex., Apr. 5, 1946; d. James Milford and Rosa Lee Elaine (Berry) Allen; m. Jay Austin Small, Sept. 16, 1964 (div.); children—LaShawn Renee, Jay Austin Jr.; m. Jerry Leon Cooper, Dec. 10, 1983. Student Okla. Sch. Bus. and Banking, 1972; B.S. in Acctg. magna cum laude, Central State U., Edmond, Okla., 1977. Staff acct. Robert A. Mosley, C.P.A., Moore, Okla., 1972-74, Robert Stewart, C.P.A., Edmond, 1974-75, Lowder & Co., Oklahoma City, 1975-81; founder, pres. Small-Cooper, C.P.A.s, P.C., Oklahoma City, 1981—. Mem. Okla. Woman's Bus. Orgn. (chmn. 1982), Okla. Soc. C.P.A.s, Am. Inst. C.P.A.s, Am. Woman's Soc. C.P.A.s, Nat. Assn. Accts. (hon.), Alpha Lambda Delta, Alpha Chi. Democrat. Avocations: writing poetry, interior decorating, horticulture. Office: Small-Cooper CPAs PC 3022 NW Expressway Suite 212 Oklahoma City OK 73112

SMALLEY, BARBARA MARTIN, English educator; b. Connersville, Ind., Apr. 20, 1926; d. Floyd Stanley and Esther Anna (Davis) Martin; m. Donald Arthur Smalley, Sept. 8, 1952. B.S., Ind. U., 1954; M.A. in French, U. Ill., 1965, Ph.D. in Comparative Lit., 1968. Asst. prof. comparative lit. and English Lit., U. Ill., Urbana, 1968-75, assoc. prof. English and comparative lit., 1975—. Author: Flaubert and George Eliot, 1974. Editor: Ranthorpe (G.H. Lewes), 1974; (with others) Third Force Psychology and the Study of Literature, 1986; contbr. articles to profl. jours. Mem. Am. Comparative Lit. Assn., MLA, AAUP, Canadian Comparative Lit. Assn., Internat. Comparative Lit. Assn. Office: Univ of Ill English Bldg 261 608 S Wright St Urbana IL 61801

SMALLEY, HELEN DIANE, child care center administrator, consultant; b. Atlantic City, Dec. 13, 1948; d. Mortimer Canning Thompson, III and Emma Marie (Buhrman) Thompson Knight; m. Matthew Michael Previti (div. Feb. 1977); 1 child, David Russell; m. Ralph Daniel Smalley, Aug. 11, 1978. B.A. in Edn., U.S.C., 1972; postgrad. George Mason U., Fairfax, Va., 1980—. Tchr., West Side Sch., Atlantic City, 1973-78, Arlington County, Va., 1978-80; adminstr., owner Creative Play Schs., Inc., Alexandria, Va., 1980—. Pres., Abingdon Sch. PTA, Arlington, 1978-79; cons. Christ Ch., Alexandria, 1982-84; vol. Telehelp-Downtown Ministries, Alexandria, 1982—. Mem. No. Va. Assn. for Edn. Young Children, Nat. Assn. for Edn. Young Children, Alexandria C. of C. Avocations: gardening, sailing, cooking. Home: 406 Skyhill Rd Alexandria VA 22314 Office: 100 E Windsor Ave Alexandria Va 22301 also 845 N Howard St Alexandria VA 22314

SMALLWOOD, SARAH FRANCES ASHFORD, electronic manufacturing company executive; b. Dallas, Jan. 31, 1943; d. Roger F. and Rosa M. (Hancock) Ashford; m. Alford Willard Smallwood, Nov. 1, 1963; children—Sonja Mozelle Smallwood Ayers, Monica Grace Smallwood Harding. Student pub. schs., Odessa, Tex. Bookkeeper, First State Bank, Odessa, 1963-64; pres. Magnum Assembly, Inc., Austin, 1974—. Baptist. Avocations: running; water sports; dancing. Home: 7305 Bering Cove Austin TX 78759 Office: Magnum Assembly Inc 11740 Jollyville Rd Austin TX 78759

SMARIGA, LILLIAN ALLEN, accountant; b. Waco, Tex., Sept. 2, 1927; d. Homer Eugene and Lillian Louise (Smith) Allen; student U. Houston, 1964-65; m. Stanley Edward Smariga, Apr. 21, 1950; children—Robert, Melanie, Mary Hope, Russell. Bookkeeper, sec. Houston Carbide Corp., 1951-55; div. sec., bookkeeper, office mgr. Houston Carbide div. Firth Sterling, Inc., 1955-68; asst. to acctg. mgr. F. W. Gartner Co., Houston, 1968-70, asst. to acctg. mgr., office mgr., 1970-75, acctg. mgr., asst. sec.-treas., 1975—, controller, asst. sec.-treas., 1977—. Mem. Nat. Assn. Accts., Am. Soc. Women Accts. Republican. Episcopalian. Home: 1605 Alabama St Pasadena TX 77503 Office: 3805 Lamar St Houston TX 77001

SMART, DOROTHY, purchasing agent; b. Memphis, Mar. 4, 1935; d. James and Emily (Morris) Gilmore; m. Lewis Smart Jr., June 16, 1955; 4 children. Student Lincoln Corr. Sch., 1963-64 supervisory trainee Elkhart Area Career Ctr., 1980. With Clarke's Discount, Elkhart, Ind., 1963-66; billing mgr., inventory control Nat. CROP Office, Elkhart, 1966-72; asst. purchasing agt., dep. controller, mgr. Barrett Law Dept., City of Elkhart, 1972-80, dir. purchasing and materials mgmt., 1980-86. Bd. dirs. Elkhart Community Day Care, 1969-76, pres. policy and intake, 1969-75; precinct capt. Dem. Central Com., 1968-70, treas., 1970-72. Recipient Disting. Service award Elkhart Day Care Ctr., 1976; Golden Service award Ind. Black Polit. Assembly, 1975. Mem. Elkhart Urban League Guild, NAACP, LWV. Baptist. Club: Amicus Christian Guild. Home: 54657 County Road 101 N Elkhart IN 46514 Office: City of Elkhart 229 S 2d St Elkhart IN 46514

SMART, DOROTHY CAROLINE, retired social worker; b. Osborn, Mo.; d. Allen A. and Caroline (Totzke) Smart; student U. Mo., 1929-30; A.B., U. Kans., 1937, M.S.W., 1950; postgrad. U. Chgo., 1963, 65. Advt. copy writer Emery Bird Thayer, Kansas City, Mo., 1937-38; case worker Dept. Pub. Welfare, Kansas City, 1938-44, Jackson County chpt. ARC, Kansas City, 1944-49; disaster rep. Am. Nat. Red Cross, St. Louis, 1950-59, home service rep. area office, 1959-65, regional dir. service mil. families, 1965-70, asst. area dir. service to mil. families, 1970-76. Mem. Group Action Council; bd. dirs. Barnes Hosp. Aux. Mem. Nat. Assn. Social Workers, Acad. Certified Social Workers, Nat. Conf. Social Welfare, Women in Communications (pres. Kansas City alumni chpt. 1943), Am. Assn. Ret. Persons (bd. dirs.). Club: Pilot (pres. 1975-77) (St. Louis). Home: 4475 W Pine St Saint Louis MO 63108

SMART, MARRIOTT WIECKHOFF, geologist, information specialist; b. Memphis, Aug. 26, 1935; d. Gerhard Emil and Beatrice (Flanegan) Wieckhoff, m. John A. Smart, May 9, 1959; children—Denise, Holly. B.S. in Geology, U. Tex.-Austin, 1957; M.L.S., U. Pitts., 1976. Geophysicist Mobil Corp., New Orleans, 1957-59; geologist Hanson Oil Co., Roswell, N.Mex., 1959-62; info. specialist Gulf Corp., Pitts., 1977-79, library mgr., Denver, 1979-84, library cons. team, Pitts., 1984; supr. Library-Info. Ctr., Amoco Minerals Co., Englewood, Colo., 1984; dir. Library-Info. Ctr., Cyprus Minerals Co., 1985—. Dist. chmn. Am. Cancer Soc., Arapahoe County, Colo., 1981-84; mem. choir Grace Presbyn. Ch., Littleton, Colo., 1979—; block worker Republican party, Arapahoe County, 1981—. Mem. Spl. Libraries Assn. (bull. bus. mgr. 1982, treas. petroleum and energy div. 1984-86), Rocky Mountain Online Users Group, Geosci. Info. Soc., Geosci. Energy Minerals Info. Specialists, Women in Mining, Alpha Chi Omega (career network coordinator 1984). Home: 3337 E Easter Pl Littleton CO 80122 Office: Cyprus Minerals Co 7200 S Alton Way Englewood CO 80112

SMART, MARY-LEIGH CALL (MRS. J. SCOTT SMART), farm operator, civic worker; b. Springfield, Ill., Feb. 27, 1917; d. S(amuel) Leigh and Mary (Bradish) Call; jr. coll. diploma Monticello Coll., 1934; student Oxford U., 1935; B.A., Wellesley Coll., 1937; M.A., Columbia, 1939, postgrad., 1940-41; postgrad. N.Y.U., 1940-41; painting student with Bernard Karfiol, 1937-38; m. J. Scott Smart, Sept. 11, 1951 (dec. 1960). Dir. mgmt. Central Ill. grain farms, Logan County, Ill., 1939—, art collector, patron, cons., 1954—, program dir. sec. bd. Barn Gallery Assocs., Inc., Ogunquit, Maine, 1958-69, pres., 1969-70, 82—, hon. dir., 1970-78; curator Hamilton Easter Field Art Found. Collection, 1978-79, curator exhbns., 1979—; owner Lowtrek Kennel, Ogunquit, 1957-73, Cove Studio Art Gallery, Ogunquit, 1961-68. Mem. acquisition com. DeCordova Mus., Lincoln, Mass., 1966-78; mem. chancellor's council U. Tex., 1972—, U. N.H., 1977—; chmn. Outdoor-Display Bd. Perkins Cove Assn., Ogunquit, 1972; bd. dirs. Ogunquit C. of C., 1966, treas. 1966-67, hon. life mem., 1968—; bd. overseers Strawbery Banke, Inc., Portsmouth, N.H., 1971-74, 3d vice-chmn., 1972-73, 2d vice-chmn., 1973-74; bd. advisers Univ. Art Galleries, U. N.H., 1973—, v.p., 1974-81, pres., 1981—; mem. adv. com. Maine 75, Bowdoin Coll. Art Mus. Exhbn., 1975; cons. Bicentennial Exhbn. '76, Maine Artists, Maine State Mus., 1976; mem. adv. com. All Maine Biennial, Bowdoin Coll. Mus. Art, 1979; mem. York Hist. Dist. Com., 1981 ; bd. dirs. Old York Hist. and Improvement Soc., 1979-81, v.p., 1981-82; mem. nat. com. Friends of Art, Wellesley Coll., 1982—; adv. com. Maine Biennial, Colby Coll. Mus. Art, 1983; adv. trustee Portland Mus. Art, 1983—; mem. mus. panel Maine State Commn. on Arts and Humanities, 1983—; mem. jury Maine Scholarship awards Skowhegan Sch. Painting and Sculpture, 1982-84. Served to lt. (j.g.) WAVES, 1942-45. Mem. Jr. League of Springfield, Inst. Contemporary Art Boston (corporator 1965-73), Maine Coast Artists Rockport (adv. com. 1976-78). Republican. Episcopalian. Club: Western Maine Wellesley. Editor: Hamilton Easter Field Art Found. Collection Catalog, 1966; originator, dir. show, compiler of catalog Art: Ogunquit, 1967; originator exhbn. Peggy Bacon—A Celebration, Ogunquit, 1979. Address: Rural Route 2 Box 381 York ME 03909

SMEAL, ELEANOR CUTRI, organization executive; b. Ashtabula, Ohio, July 30, 1939; d. Peter Anthony and Josephine E. (Agresti) Cutri; m. Charles R. Smeal, Apr. 27, 1963; children—Tod, Lori. B.A., Duke U., 1961; M.A., U. Fla., 1963. Mem. bd. Upper St. Clair chpt. LWV, 1968-72; sec.-treas. Allegheny County council, 1971-72; mem. NOW, 1971—, convenor, 1st pres., 1971-73, 1st pres., state coordinator, Pa., 1972-75, nat. bd. dirs., 1973-75, chairwoman bd., 1975-77, pres., 1977-82, 85—; mem. 1st nominating com., founding conf. Nat. Women's Polit. Caucus, 1971; bd. dirs. Allegheny County Women's Polit. Caucus, 1971-72; co-founder, bd. dirs. South Hills NOW Day Nursery Sch., 1972—; mem. Nat. Commn., Oberservance of Internat. Women's Yr., 1977; mem. exec. com. Leadership Conf. on Civil Rights, 1979—; mem. Nat. Adv. Com. on Women, 1978. Named One of 25 Most Influential Women in U.S., World Almanac, 1978. Address: NOW Washington DC*

SMEDRESMAN, INGEBORG FREUNDLICH, artist; b. Germany; came to U.S., 1937, naturalized, 1943; d. Paul and Erna Betty (Simon) Freundlich; B.S., U. Frankfurt, Germany, 1934; postgrad. in chemistry U. Zurich, Switzerland, 1934-37, art edn. Nat. Acad. Art Students League, Queens Coll; m. Sidney Smedresman, Aug. 10, 1937; children—Ingrid Braslow, Leonard C., Paulette Mehta, Suzanne van Oers. Art lectr. Forest Hills Jewish Center, 1966-68, Guggenheim Mus., 1973-76; art tchr. Queensboro Art Soc., 1969; art dir. Temple Beth El, Great Neck, L.I., 1969-75, YM-YWHA, Little Neck, 1975. One woman shows at Fine Arts Gallery, N.Y.C., 1970, Queens Coll., N.Y.C., summer 1975, 78, 81, 85, Harrison (N.Y.) Library, 1979, 80; exhibited in group shows at ACA Gallery, 1959, Contemporary Art Gallery, 1965-66, Raymond Duncan Gallery, Paris, France, 1965-66, Ahda Arzt Gallery, N.Y.C., 1970, Ten Voorde Gallery, Amsterdam, 1973, Carrol Condit Gallery, White Plains N.Y., 1973, Westchester Art Soc., 1970-75; represented in permanent collections Godwin-Ternbach Mus. of Queens Coll., Pfizer Inc. Internat. Hdqrs., N.Y.C., City Hall, Moncton, N.B., Can., Israel Mus., Jerusalem; art instr. YM-YWHA, Flushing; lectr. Cooper-Hewitt Mus. Recipient art awards Paris Water Colors, 1965, 66, Suffolk County Artists, 1966, Queensboro Art Soc., 1975, 1st prize Westchester Art Soc., 1975. Mem. Art Students League N.Y., Artists Equity Assn., Am. Chem. Soc. Home: 147-43 77th Rd Kew Garden Hills NY 11367

SMELTER, KATHERINE VAFAKAS, psychologist, educator; b. Detroit, Dec. 30, 1941; d. Nicholas A. and Fannie D. (Pappas) Vafakas; m. Bernard Smelter, June 21, 1975; 1 dau., Christine Katherine. B.S., Eastern Mich. U., 1965; M. Ed., Wayne State U., 1967, Ed. D., 1972. Dept. chairperson counseling Oakland Community Coll., Mich., 1967-72; asst. prof. dept. psychology Northwestern State U., La., 1972-73; asst. prof. dept. counseling edn. U. Bridgeport (Conn.), 1973-75; adj. assoc. prof. C.W. Post Coll., Greenvale, N.Y., 1976, L.I. U., Westchester, N.Y., 1975; sch. psychologist Wappingers Falls (N.Y.) Central Schs., 1982—. Mem. AAUP, Am. Assn. Sch. Psychologists, A.G. Bell Assn. for Deaf. Editor profl. jours.; contbr. articles to profl. jours. Home: PO Box 231 Route 9 Garrison NY 10524

SMELTZER, SUSAN, pianist, composer; b. Sapulpa, Okla., Sept. 13, 1941; d. Frank Cecil and Mary Margaret (Robertson) S.; Mus.B. (scholar), Oklahoma City U., 1964; Mus.M. magna cum laude, U. So. Calif., 1969; postgrad. (Fulbright scholar) Akademie fur Musik, Vienna, 1969-70; master class with Gregor Piatigorsky, Los Angeles, Rosina Lhevinne, Los Angeles; m. Philip S. Snyder, June 14, 1973. Pvt. tchr. music, Sapulpa, Okla., 1956-62, Los Angeles, 1964-72; instr. piano Oklahoma City U., 1961-64, Holy Name Convent, Los Angeles, 1964-65, Valley Conservatory Music, Studio City, Calif., 1965-66, First Congl. Ch., Los Angeles, 1966-67, Mt. St. Mary's Coll., Los Angeles, 1966-69, 70-72; vis. piano faculty mem. Rice U., Houston, 1972-73; profl. accompanist U. Houston, 1972-73; artist-in-residence, instr. humanities Coll. of Mainland, Texas City, Tex., 1972-79; organist various chs., Okla., Calif., intermittently, 1957-71; profl. accompanist throughout midwest, 1961-64, Los Angeles area, 1964-72, Houston, 1972—; performed with chamber groups, Los Angeles area, 1964-69, 70-72; Carnegie Hall debut, 1975; European debut Brahmssaal, Vienna; numerous orchestral appearances; compositions include: Reverie, 1962, Kaleidescope, 1968, Twelve Mood Pictures (variations for piano on theme of Yankee Doodle and the interval sets 1-9-7-6:1-7-7-6), 1975, The Bald Eagle March, 1979, Psalm 121 (for choir and orch.), 1979, An American Tribue For A Royal Marriage, 1982. Recipient numerous awards including: Bloch Young Artist award Ladies Music Club, 1962; award Nat. Fedn. Music Clubs, 1962, Okla. Music Tchrs. Assn., 1962. Mem. Internat. League Women Composers, Am. Women Composers, Nat. Guild Piano Tchrs. (judging staff), Chamber Music Am., Broadcast Music Inc., Pi Kappa Lambda, Sigma Alpha Iota. Club: Tuesday Musica. Author: Selected Orchestrations of Poetic Expressions (book of poetry), 1982. Home and office: 8102 Tavenor St Houston TX 77075

SMETANA, E. BETH SEIDMAN, consulting company manager; b. Chgo., Nov. 23, 1941; d. Lawrence J. and Ann (Masin) Seidman; m. Gerard C. Smetana, Apr. 17, 1966; children—Susannah, Frederick. Student L'Institut des Etudes Politiques, Paris, 1961-62; B.A., Sarah Lawrence Coll., 1963; M.S. in Journalism, Northwestern U., 1965; postgrad. Loyola U., Chgo., 1974-78. C.P.A., Ill. Reporter, copy editor Hollister Publs., Wilmette, Ill., 1966-68; asst. editor The Trib, Chgo. Tribune, 1976-66; staff acct. Arthur Young & Co., Chgo., 1978-80; cash mgr. Electrographic Corp., Chgo., 1980-81; treasury mgr. A.T. Kearney, Inc., Chgo., 1981—. Rep. for Sarah Lawrence Coll., Coll. Bd. of Chgo., 1972-75; mem. alumni bd. Francis W. Parker Sch., Chgo., 1973—. Mem. Am. Inst. C.P.A.s, Ill. Soc. C.P.A.s, Women in Communications, Alliance Francaise, Beta Alpha Psi. Clubs: Chgo. Press, River, Casino. Office: A T Kearney Inc 222 S Riverside Plaza Chicago IL 60606

SMETANA, TANYA MARIE, beauty salon owner, cosmetologist; b. Karlovy Vary, Czechoslovakia, Nov. 15, 1947; came to U.S., 1968; d. Josef and Katerina (Rusecka) Sicova Stiegler; m. Jiri Jan Smetana, Sept. 5, 1970; children—Jiri Francis, Robert Brian. Hairdresser, Sch. Hairdressing, Prague, Czechoslovakia, 1965; draftsman, Mech. Engring., Prague, 1965-68; Cosmetologist, Athena Beauty Coll., Walnut Creek, Calif., 1970; Advanced Cosmetologist, Vidal Sassoon Acad., San Francisco, 1977; Esthetician, Christine Valmy Internat. Sch., N.Y.C., 1985. Owner, mgr. Hairport, Longmont, Colo., 1980—; tech. cons. Longmont Coalition for Women in Crisis, Longmont, 1980, The Palmer Drug Abuse Program, Longmont, 1981, Longmont Hosp., 1980, 81, 82, 83, Learning Ctr., Longmont, 1982, P.E.O., Longmont chpt., 1982, Perfect Image, Longmont, 1980. Mem. Nat. Hairdressers and Cosmetologist Assn., Nat. Fedn. Ind. Bus., Longmont Hairdressers and Cosmetologists Assn. (pres.), C. of C. Republican. Roman Catholic. Avocations: skiing; swimming; camping; reading; gardening; sewing. Office: Hairport 617 Coffman St Longmont CO 80501

SMIDDY, LINDA CLAIBORNE O'RIORDAN, lawyer; b. Houston, Sept. 17, 1942; d. John Eldridge and Beatrice Elma (Trudeau) O'Riordan; m. James Dallas Smiddy, Sept. 9, 1972. B.A., Northwestern U., 1964; M.A.T., Harvard U., 1965; J.D., Vt. Law Sch., 1979; LL.M., Yale U., 1983. Instr., systems engr. IBM, Chgo., 1968-74, mgr., Kingston, N.Y., 1974-75; editor Hudson Valley Mag., Pleasant Valley, N.Y., 1975-76; law clk. Hon. J.S. Holden, Fed. Dist. Ct., Vt., 1980-81; assoc. Cravath, Swaine & Moore, N.Y.C., 1981-83, Cummings & Lockwood, Stamford, Conn., 1983-86; ptnr. Smiddy & Smiddy, Greenwich, Conn., 1986—; co-chmn. Com. on Computer Crime, Hartford, Conn., 1983-84. Recipient Am. Pen Women's award Northwestern U., 1964; Learned Hand award for acad. excellence Vt. Law Sch., South Royalton, Vt., 1976. Mem. Conn. Bar Assn. (co-chmn. legis. com. computer law sect.), Phi Lambda Theta. Office: Smiddy & Smiddy Suite 100 2 Greenwich Plaza Greenwich CT 06836

SMILEY, CLEERETTA HENDERSON, educator, home economist; b. Whatley, Ala., June 20, 1930; d. Edward and Rebecca Ann (Odom) Henderson; B.S., Miles Coll., 1954; M.S., U. Md., 1971, postgrad., 1972-73; diploma esoteric sci. and psychology Am. U., 1976; children—Consuela Angelia, Robert Edward, Lisa Kay, Joan Alyssa. Correctional officer Fed. Reformatory for Women, Alderson, W.Va., 1954-55, culinary officer, 1955-56, tchr. home econs., 1956-61, asst. vocat. ednl. dir., 1959-61; tchr. gen. home econs. edn. D.C. Public Schs., 1963-80, asst. supervising dir. home econs., 1980-84, dir. Model HERO Youth Employment Tng. Program, Coolidge Sr. High Sch., 1975-80; state adv. for D.C., Future Homemakers Am./HERO, 1980-84; dir. Network of Light, Lorton Transformation Project; condr. coordr. fashion shows, model; tchr. coordinator Show Prodns. Tng. Program, 1967-80; mem. Home Econs. Adv. Council, D.C. Public Schs. and Logan Community Sch. Adv. Council; practitioner esoteric sci. Minority affairs adv. to bd. dirs. Social Services Agy., Eastern region Ch. Jesus Christ of Latter-day Saints, 1979-82, stake missionary, edn. counselor Relief Soc.; mem. hosting com. Public Communications Council, Kensington, Md., 1979-81; co-chairperson Health Commn., D.C. PUSH, 1979-80; bd. dirs. Aum Spiritual Sci. Center, Washington, 1980-82; mem. First Spiritual Leadership Conf. Network Leaders, McLean, Va., 1981; mem. family and futures bd. dirs. of FHA. Named Mrs. D.C., Mrs. America Pageant, 1968, Mrs. D.C. Savs. Bonds, 1968; Harambee Mother of Yr., Sta. WDVM-TV, 1969. Mem. Am. Vocat. Edn. Assn., D.C. Vocat. Edn. Assn., Future Homemakers Am. Home Econs. Related Occupations Youth Orgn., Nat. Assn. Black Am. Vocat. Educators (life), Nat. Collaboration of Youth Orgns., Nat. Assn. Female Execs., World Modeling Assn., Afro Am. Jubilee Commn., Am. Meta-Phys. Inst. Network Soc., Nat. Assn. Single Persons, Nat. Hist. Preservation Soc., Brigham Young U. Mgmt. Soc. Iota Phi Lambda. Democrat. Club: Circle I Am, Order Eastern Star. Home: 2209 Ross Rd Silver Spring MD 20910 Office: Ballow Sr High Sch 3401 1st St SE Washington DC 20032

SMILEY, KAREN JANE, computer software engineer; b. New Kensington, Pa., Jan. 25, 1961; d. Paul Cornelius and Maureen Frances (Gross) S. B.S. in Indsl. Engring. and Ops. Research summa cum laude, U. Pitts., 1982; postgrad. in Computer Sci., Stevens Inst. Tech., 1982—. Engring. intern Armco Inc., Butler, Pa., 1980; research asst. Health Ops. Research Group, U. Pitts., 1981-82; computer software engr. Singer Kearfott, Little Falls, N.J., 1982—. Richard King Mellon Found. scholar, 1979-82, Armco, Inc. scholar, 1979-82. Mem. Nat. Assn. Female Execs., Tau Beta Pi (pres. chpt. 1982). Avocations: reading; knitting; photography; cooking; bicycling. Office: Singer Kearfott Mail Code 1DA73 1150 McBride Ave Little Falls NJ 07424

SMILEY, KATHRYN ANNE, fundraising administrator; b. Richmond, Va., Oct. 6, 1946; d. Cabel Earl and Anne Conway (Baugh) S.; B.A., Va. Commonwealth U., 1964-69; tchr.'s cert. Montessori Internat., 1975. Tchr. public schs., Richmond, 1968; asso. dir. Va. Council on Health and Med. Care, Richmond, 1968-71; v.p. Yolton/Brown Direct Response Advt., Bethesda, Md., 1972-83, also dir.; dir. direct mail Fundraising Democratic Congl. Campaign Com.; dir. Guy L. Yolton Advt., Inc., Falls Church, Va.; cons., lectr. on media buying. Tutor, Head Start Program, Richmond; bd. dirs. L'Enfant Trust; youth counselor adminstrv. bd. Arlington United Meth. Ch. Mem. Direct Mktg. Assn. of Washington (dir.), Direct Mail Mktg. Assn., Sierra Club, NOW. Democrat. Methodist. Office: 400 N Capitol St Washington DC 20001

SMILEY, LAURA JOAN, automobile manufacturing distribution company executive; b. Peoria, Ill., Nov. 9, 1956; d. James David and Barbara Joan (McKinney) S. B.S., U. So. Colo., 1981. Keypunch operator U. So. Colo., Pueblo, 1979-81, guest lectr., 1983—; with Ford Motor Co., Denver, 1982—, spl. assignment, 1984, parts mktg. analyst 1985—. J.L. Wiggins scholar, 1981. Mem. Nat. Assn. Female Execs. Avocations: hiking; camping; skiing; tennis; softball. Office: Ford Motor Co 2650 E 40th St Denver CO 80205 also Box 5588TA Denver CO 80217

SMILEY, MARILYNN JEAN, musicologist, educator; b. Columbia City, Ind., June 5, 1932; d. Orla Raymond and Mary Jane (Bailey) S.; B.S. in Music (Ind. scholar), Ball State U., 1954; postgrad. Ind. U., 1956-60; Mus.M. in Music History and Lit., Northwestern U., 1958; cert. Ecoles d'Art Americaines, Fontainebleau, France, 1959; postgrad. U. Colo., summer 1960; Ph.D. in Musicology (Delta Kappa Gamma Soc. Internat. scholar 1964-65, Univ. fellow 1964-65), U. Ill., 1970. Tchr. music public schs., Logansport, Ind., 1954-61; instr. dept. music SUNY Coll. Arts and Sci., Oswego, 1961-64, asst. prof. music, 1964-67, asso. prof., 1967-72, prof., 1972-74, Disting. Teaching prof., 1974—, chairperson dept. music, 1976-81. Mem. Oswego County Council on Arts; bd. dirs. Oswego Opera Theatre, 1978—, Oswego Orch. Soc., 1978—. Recipient Outstanding Alumni award Music Div. Ball State U., 1969, Chancellor's award for excellence in teaching SUNY, 1973; scholarship grant named in her honor AAUW Ednl. Found., 1984; SUNY Research Found. fellow, summers 1971, 72, 74. Mem. Am. Musicological Soc. (chairperson N.Y. State chpt. 1975-77), Medieval Acad. Am., Renaissance Soc. Am., Sonneck Soc. Am., Inst. Renaissance Studies, Coll. Music Soc., Music Library Assn. AAUW (pres. Oswego br. 1984-86), Renaissance Soc. Am., Oswego County Hist. Soc., Heritage Soc., Delta Kappa Gamma, Phi Delta Kappa, Pi Kappa Lambda, Sigma Alpha Iota, Sigma Tau Delta, Kappa Delta Pi, Delta Phi Alpha. Methodist. Contbr. articles on Am. music, medieval music, local music history, chpts. to various publs.; research on Am. music, Renaissance keybd. music and theory. Home: 77 W Fifth St Oswego NY 13126 Office: Dept Music SUNY Oswego NY 13126

SMILIE, MOLLIE KAY WILLIAMS, accountant, educator; b. Bradford, Pa., Aug. 11, 1949; d. Albert Franklin and Martha Rae (Moore) Williams; m. Christopher Stephen Arthur, Sept. 11, 1969 (div. Apr. 1976); 1 child, Eric Ian; m. Michael Steven Smilie, May 9, 1980. B.S., Colo. State U., 1979. C.P.A., Colo. Staff acct. Cady & Co., Fort Collins, Colo., 1979-80, Colo. State U., Fort Collins, 1980-81, asst. to controller, 1981-83, controller, 1983—; lectr. in field; mgmt. cons. Research Inst. of Colo., Fort Collins, 1985—. Precinct chmn. Larimer County Democratic Party, Fort Collins, 1978; bd. dirs. Larimer County Boy Scouts Am., Fort Collins, 1979; bd. dirs. Colo. Com. on Acctg. Standards for Higher Edn., Denver, 1983—. Mem. Am. Inst. C.P.A.s, Colo. Soc. C.P.A.s, Nat. Assn. Coll. and Univ. Bus. Officers, Council on Govtl. Relations, Beta Alpha Psi. Republican. Unitarian. Avocations: acting; writing; horseback riding; skiing; travel. Home: 3509 N County Rd 23E LaPorte CO 80535 Office: Colo State U 202E Johnson Hall Fort Collins CO 80523

SMIRNOFF, LUCINDA (CINDY) EMILLE ROSE, travel company executive, consultant, gift shop executive; b. San Diego, Oct. 9, 1951; d. Warren Karl (Jack) and Loretta Lillian (Wiewora) Cheney; m. Steve Ross Smirnoff, Sept. 9, 1979. B.A., Marylhurst Coll., Oreg., 1973; postgrad. Lewis and Clark Coll., Portland, 1975. Cert. secondary edn. tchr. Dir., cons. TravelCtr. Internat., Anchorage, 1978—; officer Transmart Co., Anchorage, 1979—; owner, operator Things Stuff & Dodads Store, Anchorage, 1984—; instr. Alaska Pacific U., Anchorage, 1985—. Mem. Anchorage Sister Cities Commn., 1983—. Named Mgr. of Yr., Travel Ctr., 1984. Mem. Pacific Area Travel Assn. Republican. Christian Scientist. Avocations: caligraphy; water skiing; snow skiing. Home: 3581 Kachemak Circle Anchorage AK 99515 Office: TravelCtr Internat 3201 C Street 300 Anchorage AK 99503

SMITH, A(DELA) JEAN, health care organization official; b. Kewanee, Ill., Sept. 14, 1939; d. Lawrence Clarence and Grace Luron (Howell) S.; m. William Ellison Smith, June 3, 1977; children—Beverly R., Ellis, Karen L. Diploma Black Hawk Coll., 1972, Kewanee Pub. Hosp., 1972. R.N., Md. Nurse Nat. Naval Med. Ctr., Bethesda, Md., 1973-77; nurse, supr. Group Health Assocs., Rockville, Md., 1977-85, mktg. rep., Washington, 1985—. Editor prayer book. Vol. voter registration drive, Rockville, 1984, Md. Ho. of Dels. Campaign, 1986; vol. John F. Kennedy Ctr. Performing Arts, Washington, 1985. Recipient citation Gov. of Md., 1984. Mem. Rockville C. of C., Nat. Assn. Profl. Sales Women, Montgomery County Women's Fair, Nat. Assn. Female Execs., Bus. and Profl. Women (chaplain 1984-86, pres. 1985-86, Woman of Yr. award 1984). Democrat. Mem. Pentecostal Ch. Club: Toastmasters (pres. 1984-83, award 1984) (Rockville). Home: 4242 East-West Hwy Apt 405 Chevy Chase MD 20815 Office: Group Health Assn 4301 Connecticut Ave NW Washington DC 20008

SMITH, ALBERTA GRANT, production company executive, real estate consultant; b. Butler, Ga., Mar. 12, 1946; d. William and Josephine (Tripp) Blasingame; m. James Smith, Feb. 20, 1966; children—Kerry Jerome, Terry James, Jerry Darnell. B.S., Fort Valley State Coll., 1967. Cert. apt. mgr. Mgr. Hampshire House Apts., College Park, Ga., 1976-79, English Colony Apts., Atlanta, 1979-81; v.p. Southeastern Mgmt., College Park, 1979-81; mgr. Washington St. Apts., Atlanta, 1981-86, Countryside Community, Decatur, Ga., 1986—; owner Turbo Prodns., Atlanta, 1986—; cons. Housing and Phys. Devel., Atlanta, 1981—, real estate dept. AMC, Atlanta, 1981—, Merritt Realty, Atlanta, 1984. Exec. vol. Young for a Greater Atlanta, 1985; mem. dinner com. Martin Luther King, Jr., Ctr. for Non-Violent Social Change, Atlanta, 1985-86; mem. exec. com. corp. sales SCLC, Atlanta, 1986; S.E. dist. coordinator for econ. devel., 1986—. Recipient awards Apt. Owners and Mgrs. Atlanta, 1979, Nat. Coop. Housing Partnership, Washington, 1982. Mem. Nat. Assn. Bus. and Profl. Women, Nat. Bd. Realtors (accredited resident mgr.; award 1985), Nat. Assn. Female Execs., Notary Pub. Assn. Ga., Bus. and Profl. Networking Atlanta. Democrat. Baptist. Avocations: tennis; dancing; horseback riding. Office: Turbo Productions PO Box 20834 Atlanta GA 30320

SMITH, ALICE ELIZABETHSWILLEY, hospital services executive, consultant, clinical educator; b. Coral Gables, Fla., Sept. 24, 1948; d. Thomas and Alva (Zebendon) Swilley; m. Philip Edward Smith, June 26, 1971, 1 child, Eve Elizabeth. Cert. elementaire Le Cordon Bleu, Paris, 1969; B.A. in Home Econs., The Western Coll., 1970; postgrad. U. Dayton, 1972-73; dietetic intern Miami Valley Hosp., Dayton, Ohio, 1973-74; M.S. in Nutrition, No. Ill. U., 1978. Tchr. Miami Dade Jr. High, Opa Locka, Fla., 1970-71; food service coordinator Mercy Med. Ctr., Springfield, Ohio 1972-73; pub. health nutritionist Chgo. Bd. Health, 1974-78; assoc. dir. clin. dietetics Children's Meml. Hosp., Chgo., 1980-84, asst. clin. prof. U. Ill., Chgo., 1983—; dir. clin. dietetics Children's Meml. Hosp., Chgo., 1985—; liaison rep. Am. Acad. Pediatrics Com. on Nutrition, Am. Dietetic Assn., Chgo., 1981—. Contbr. articles to profl. jours. Vol. 8th Day Ctr. for Justice, Chgo., 1976-77. Grantee Mead Johnson Nutritional Co., 1983-85. Mem. Am. Dietetic Assn., AAAS, Clin. Nutrition Mgmt. Practice Group (newsletter editor, 1983-84), Chgo. Dietetic Assn., Am. Soc. Parenteral and Enteral Nutrition, Dietitians in Pediatric Practice. Avocations: Creative cookery, indoor gardening. Office: Children's Meml Hosp 2300 Children's Plaza Chicago IL 60614

SMITH, ANNIE LEE NORTHERN, school principal; b. Houston, Dec. 27, 1932; d. Lee Fletcher and Christine (Johnson) Williams; stepdau. Leamer Williams; m. Louis Northern, Dec. 23, 1956 (dec. 1965); 1 son, Eric V.; m. 2d Jules Smith, Jan 28, 1967. B.S., Tex. So. U., 1954, M.Ed., 1959, cert. mid-mgmt., 1959. Tchr. Stone Crest Nursery Sch., Houston, 1954-57, Cypress Fairbanks Ind. Sch. Dist. (Tex.), 1957-59, Houston Ind. Sch. Dist., 1959-75; instructional coordinator, 1975-77, prin., 1977—. Active Houston YWCA; reporter, announcer, St. John Bapt. Ch., 1977—. Recipient Outstanding Performance award Houston Ind. Sch. Dist., 1974, Merit award, 1978; Outstanding Leadership award Lovett Sch. and Mamie Charity Club, 1976. Mem. Parent Tchrs. Orgn., Houston Tchrs. Assn., Houston Prins. Assn., NEA, Tex. State Tchrs. Assn., Am. Legion Aux., NAACP, Sigma Gamma Rho (service award 1976-80, Outstanding Educator award 1980). Office: EO Lovett Elem Sch 8814 S Rice St Houston 77096

SMITH, BARBARA A., banker; b. Monticello, Miss., Aug. 24, 1952; d. Cephus and Lillian (Hill) Smith. Bus. cert. Draughon's Coll., 1972; B.S. in Edn., Jackson State U., 1975. Office sec. Miss. Bank, Jackson, 1975-78, adminstrv. asst., 1979-81, personnel officer, 1981—; bus. communications cons. Jackson State U. (Miss.), 1981—. Black achiever chmn. YMCA, Jackson, 1983-84. Recipient Bus. Communications award Jackson State U., 1982; Profl. Black Achiever award YMCA, Jackson, 1983. Mem. Nat. Assn. Bank Women, Capital Area Personnel Assn. (membership chmn. 1984), Am. Soc. for

Personnel Adminstrn., Zeta Phi Beta. Democrat. Mem. Ch. of God in Christ. Office: Sunburst Bank PO Box 23053 Jackson MS 39225

SMITH, BARBARA ANN, accountant, tax consultant; b. Dallas, May 6, 1935; d. George Jefferson and Ina Pearl (Nowlin) Gardner; Asso. Mid. Mgmt., Mountain View Jr. Coll., 1975; 1 dau., Cynthia Marie Dixon. Asst. cashier U.S. Rubber Co., Dallas, 1954-57; sec.-treas. Am. Graphics Co., Dallas, 1974-79; pres. Am. Way Credit Union, Dallas, 1974-76; sec.-treas. Am. Legal Printing Co., Dallas, 1964-79, Abco Inc., Dallas, 1964-79, Am. Poster & Printing Co., Dallas, 1964-79; asst. sec.-treas. Am. Equity Press Inc., Dallas, 1974-79; co-owner MS Services, Dallas, 1979—v.p. Brainstorm, Inc., Dallas, 1984—. Republican. Home: 3515 Brown St Apt 109 Dallas TX 75219 Office: 2525 Carlisle Dallas TX 75201

SMITH, BARBARA DAIL, nurse; b. Oklahoma City, July 15, 1949; d. James E. and Juanita E. (Butler) Berryhill; m. William Ben Smith, May 23, 1975; children—Rebecca Sue and James Ben. B.S. in Biology, Oklahoma City U., 1975, B.S. in Health Edn., 1984; R.N. diploma St. Anthony Hosp., 1979. Mgmt. nurse St. Anthony Hosp., Oklahoma City, 1979-83; cons. family help group cancer patients, 1981-83; nurse Oklahoma City Bd. Edn., 1983—. Author: (with others) Chemotherapy Cert. Program, 1981-82. Leader Camp Fire Orgn. Am., Oklahoma City, 1983—. Mem. Nat. Oncol. Nursing Soc., Okla. Oncol. Nursing Soc., Okla. Sch. Nurses Soc., YWCA, Beta Beta Beta. Democrat. Lodge: Fraternal Order of Police Ladies Aux.

SMITH, BARBARA GORDON, state ofcl.; b. Los Angeles, Oct. 13, 1927; d. Frank and Anna Louisa (Weidauer) Belcher; B.A., Occidental Coll., 1949; M.P.A., U. So. Calif., 1976; m. Kenneth H. Smith, Aug. 29, 1980 (dec. 1982); children—Edward Kermit, Parker, Stephen Frank Parker. Tchr., Calif. Public Schs., 1949-72; adminstrv. intern Sacramento (Calif.) Superior Ct., 1975-77; legis. aide, sr. adminstr. Calif. Assembly, Office Speaker Pro Tempore, Sacramento, 1977-80; exec. dir. Calif. Health Facilities Authority, Sacramento, 1980—. Chmn., Contra Costa County Natural Resource Commn., 1965-68; bd. dirs. Pub. Service Skills, Inc. Named Citizen of Year, Orinda, Calif., 1968. Mem. Council Hosp. Financing Authorities, Nature Conservancy, Audubon Soc. Office: 915 Capitol Mall Room 280 Sacramento CA 94814

SMITH, BARBARA JORDAN, property manager executive; b. Mathews County, Va., Apr. 5, 1936; d. Kenneth Hugh and Mary Flavia (Aldrich) Jordan; b. John Emeral White, May 4, 1954 (div. Sept. 1974); children—Mary Eileen White Smith, Shirley Ann, John Leslie; m. Robert Leonard Smith, Oct. 16, 1976. Student Richmond Bus. Coll., 1956, Va. Commonwealth U., 1974-76. Cert. property mgr., master gardner. Sec. to treas. Robertshaw Controls Co., Richmond, Va., 1968-72; sec. to pres. Concrete Structures, Inc., Richmond, 1972-75; property mgr. Terra Corp., Richmond, 1975-80, VA Realty & Devel. Co., Richmond, 1980-81; pres. Mgmt. Dimensions, Inc., Richmond, 1981—, also dir. Pres. Hamlet Condominium Homeowners Assn., Richmond, 1976-77. Recipient Designer Floral Arrangements Blue award, state level exhibits, 1978, Grower Horticulture Blue award, state level exhibits, 1978. Mem. Richmond Profl. Women's Network, Richmond Assn. Women Bus. Owners, Inst. Real Estate Mgmt. Clubs: Pamunkey Jr. Womans (pres. 1969-70), Spring Meadows Garden (pres. 1966-67). Avocations: reading, sailing. Home: 1004 Wynbrook Ln PO Box 284 Mechanicsville VA 23111 Office: Mgmt Dimensions Inc 4912 W Broad St Richmond VA 23230

SMITH, BARBARA LEE, artist; b. Camden, N.J., Apr. 1, 1938; d. John and Ruth McCandless (Cockroft) Pemberton; m. Frank Samuel Lanou, June 27, 1959 (div. 1970); children—Mark Allen, Lee Anne; m. John Melvin Smith, Mar. 22, 1970. B.S., Douglass Coll., 1959; M.F.A., No. Ill. U., 1978. Freelance artist and tchr.; owner Barbara L. Smith Designs, Glen Ellyn, Ill., 1979-83; pres. Smithworks, Inc., Oak Park, Ill., 1983—; juror Council Am. Embroiderers, 1984, Pitts. Embroiderers Guild, 1981. One-person shows: Ariel Gallery, Naperville, Ill., 1985, Kretzmann Gallery, River Forest, Ill., 1983, Art in Fiber Gallery, Washington, 1982, others; numerous commns. Mem. Oak Park Community Design Commn., 1982—, Oak Park Design Rev. Commn., 1983—. No. Ill. U. fellow, 1977. Mem. Am. Crafts Council (state rep. 1974-77), DuPage Textile Arts Guild (pres. 1974-75), Council Am. Embroiderers (faculty 1973-79, asst. editor 1972-74). Avocations: music; reading; skiing. Home: 205 N Euclid Ave Oak Park IL 60302 Office: Smithworks 205 N Euclid Ave Oak Park IL 60302

SMITH, BARBARA MARTIN, university administrator; b. Eden, N.C., Nov. 28, 1943; d. Sam Wesley and Gracie Lee (Williams) Martin; m. Michael W. Smith, Feb. 13, 1965; children—Alycia, Michael W. Jr., Marcus. B.S., N.C. A & T State U., 1974. Computer programmer, Bendix Corp., Columbia, Md., 1979; sr. programmer analyst U.S. Postal Service, Washington, 1979-81, Gordon Jewelry Corp., Houston, 1982-83, First City Services, Houston, 1983-85; dep. project mgr. Prairie View A & M U., Tex., 1985—. VIPS mem. Vols. in Pub. Schs., Houston, 1985. Mem. Nat. Assn. Female Execs., Women in Data Processing. Republican. Presbyterian. Avocations: reading; walking. Home: 3 Mayfair Grove Ct The Woodlands TX 77381 Office: Prairie View A & M Univ Prairie View TX 77446

SMITH, BARBARA SQUIRES, journalist; b. Ft. Meade, Md., Aug. 12, 1953; d. John Lester Squires and Bettye (Cost) Squires Blount; m. Don H. Smith, Apr. 7, 1973. B.A., Ga. State U., 1981. Sales mgr., dir. Lillie, Expressions in Glass, Atlanta, 1977-80; calendar editor The Atlanta Jour./Constitution, 1980-82, editorial asst., 1982—. Mem. Ga. Women's Polit. Caucus, Atlanta, 1980-84. Mem. Soc. Profl. Journalists (dir. 1983-84), Omicron Delta Kappa. Democrat. Unitarian. Home: 1910 Oak Grove Rd NE Atlanta GA 30345 Office: The Atlanta Jour and The Atlanta Constitution 72 Marietta St Atlanta GA 30302

SMITH, BETH LANEY, advertising agency executive; b. Pageland, S.C.; d. Howard Gibson and Lona Agnes (Nicholson) Laney; m. Edward Donald Smith, Apr. 28, 1956 (dec.); 1 child, Edward Laney. A.B. cum laude, U. S.C., 1944. Editor: After Hours, Am. Mission, Athens, Greece, 1948-49; editor Safari, Corps Engrs., Tripoli, Libya, 1951-52; account exec. Ayer & Gillett Advt., Charlotte, N.C., 1953-61; founder, pres. Laney-Smith, Inc., Charlotte, 1961—. Author: A Foundry, Volume I, 1977; editor, pub.: A History of the Early Years of the Roman Catholic Diocese of Charlotte, 1984. Mem. Nat. Trust Historic Preservation, Women in Communications, Victorian Soc. N.C., Historic Preservation Found. N.C., Fashion Group Charlotte, Advt. Club Charlotte (pres. 1962), Phi Beta Kappa. Republican. Mem. Unity Ch. Avocations yoga; swimming; interior design; house restoration. Home: 6114 Thornbriar Ct Matthews NC 28105 Office: Laney-Smith Inc 1370 Briar Creek Rd Charlotte NC 28105

SMITH, BETTE BELLE, banker, civic worker; b. Modesto, Calif., Jan. 17, 1921; d. James Alfred and Maysel Elizabeth (Hughes) Anderson; A.A., Modesto Jr. Coll., 1939; B.A., UCLA, 1941; m. Jean T. Smith, May 4, 1945; children—Talbott Anderson, Timothy Melton and Mary Margaret (twins). Vice pres., bank relations officer, asst. corp. sec. Modesto Banking Co., 1979—. Mem. Modesto Culture Commn., 1979-85, bd. dirs.; mem. Greater Modesto Found.; mem. Muir Trail council Girl Scouts U.S.A.; former v.p. Stanislaus County Drug Abuse Coordinating Council; bd. dirs. United Crusade, 1969-72; organizing bd., v.p. McHenry Mus. Soc.; organizing bd. pres. McHenry Mus. Guild, 1979; mem. Calif. Republican Central Com., 1970-74; v.p. Modesto Rep. Women; pres. Modesto Jr. Coll. Alumni Found., 1977-80; organizing bd. Gt. Valley Mus.; mem. Stanislaus County Hist. Soc.; past pres. PTAs, hon. service award; former leader Cub Scouts, Brownies, Jr. Girl Scouts U.S.A.; grand pres. Omega Nu, 1954; pres. 50 Plus Club of Stanislaus County; bd. dirs. Downtown Mchts. Assn., Modesto Symphony Orch., Friends of Music, Modesto Arts Adv. Council, Stanislaus County Fair Bd., 1984—; mem. Modesto City Beautification Com.; chmn. May Clean Up Month; mem. Charter Rev. Com., 1970; chmn. sr. citizen sect. Progress Greater Modesto Com.; parade chmn. All Am. City Com.; dist. rep. Stanislaus County internat. intercultural scholarship program Am. Field Service, 1961—; mem. sponsor com. Stanislaus County 4-H Club. Named Woman of Yr., Soroptimist Internat., 1958, One of 10 Outstanding Women of Yr., Stanislaus County Commn. on Women; recipient Loyalty Day award VFW, 1979, Liberty Bell award Stanislaus County Bar Assn., 1980, Calif. Parks and Recreation Soc. award, 1986. Club: Soroptimist (hon.). Home: 415 Sycamore St Modesto CA 95354 Office: 1120 11th St Modesto CA 95354

SMITH, BETTY DENNY, former county official, fashion executive, civic worker; b. Centralia, Ill., Nov. 12, 1932; d. Otto and Ferne Elizabeth (Beier) Hasenfuss; student U. Ill., 1950-52, Los Angeles City Coll., 1953-57, UCLA, 1965, U. San Francisco, 1983-84; m. Peter S. Smith, Dec. 5, 1964; children—Carla Kip, Bruce Kimball. Free-lance fashion coordinator Los Angeles and N.Y.C., 1953-58; instr. fashion Rita LeRoy Internat. Studios, 1959-60; mgr. Mo Nadler Fashions, Los Angeles, 1961-64; free-lance polit. book reviewer community newspapers, 1961-62; staff writer Valley Citizen News, 1963; showroom dir. Jean of Calif. Fashions, Los Angeles, 1966—; dir. animal care and control Los Angeles County, 1976-82; founder, pres. Bluff Investment Corp., 1982—. Bd. dirs. Pet Assistance Found., 1969-76; ind. legis. adv. for human causes, 1969-75; founder, pres., dir. Vol. Services to Animals of Los Angeles, 1972-76; mem. County Com. to Discuss Animals in Research, 1973-74; mem. blue ribbon com. on animal control Los Angeles County, 1973-74; mem. animal health tech. examining com. State of Calif., 1975-82; bd. dirs. Los Angeles Soc. for Prevention Cruelty to Animals, 1984—, So. Calif. Humane Soc., 1984—; legis. advocate Fund for Animals, 1985—. mem. Calif. Republican Central Com., 1964-72, mem. exec. com., 1971-72; mem. Rep. Central Com. Los Angeles County, 1964-70, mem. exec. com., 1966-70; active polit. campaigns Rep. candidates. Mem. Lawyers Wives San Gabriel Valley (dir. 1971-74, pres. 1972-73), Mannequins Assn. (dir. 1967-68), Internat. Platform Assn., Delta Gamma, Phi Phi Theta. Clubs: Los Angeles Athletic, Town Hall.

SMITH, BETTY LOUISE, financial group executive; b. Coplay, Pa., May 15, 1940; d. Henry Fuhlburg and Marian Alta (Ward) Schaadt; m. Robert W. Perry, Nov. 14, 1966 (div. 1971). Student Stevens Finishing Sch., Indpls., 1960-62. Asst. to pres. Snelling & Snelling, Indpls., 1966-71; adminstrv. asst. R. E. Sisk & Assocs., Indpls., 1971-72; exec. officer, v.p. Yegen Holdings Corp.-Integrity Fin. Group, Paramus, N.J., 1972—; pres. Synetics, Inc., Paramus, N.J., 1968. . Bd. dirs. Mid-Bergen Community Mental Health Ctr., Paramus, N.J. Mem. Am. Mgmt. Assn., Nat. Assn. Female Execs., Am. Soc. Personnel Adminstrs., Bergen County C. of C. Republican. Presbyterian. Office: Yegen Holdings Corp-Integrity Fin Group Mack Centre Dr Paramus NJ 07652

SMITH, BETTY MURNAN, educator; b. Indpls., Sept. 11, 1921; d. Carl J. and Helene Alice (Stephens) Murnan; B.A. cum laude in English, Butler U., 1944; M.A. in English, State U. Iowa, 1950; m. Richard Norman Smith, Oct. 21, 1951; children—Allegra Louise Smith Jrolf, Timothy and Michael (twins). Tchr. Kingsford (Mich.) High Sch., 1944-46, Bosse High Sch. Evansville, Ind., 1946-48; instr. English, Ely (Minn.) Jr. Coll., 1950-51; acting instr. English, U. Wis., Milw., 1961-66; instr. English, U. Wis. Center-Waukesha County, 1966-70, asst. prof., 1970-81, asso. prof., 1981—, senator U. Wis. Center System, 1980-81; lectr. in field. Co-prin. Hdqrs. Freedom Sch. Mil. Sch. Boycott, 1963; bd. dirs. Waukesha Symphony Orch., 1969-72; sec. Waukesha Equal Opportunity Commn., 1970-73; bd. dirs. Waukesha Civic Theatre, 1973-74; mem. Com. for Women's Issues Forum, 1979-80. Recipient award for outstanding achievement in community services U. Wis., Waukesha, 1979. Mem. AAUP (pres. chpt. 1969-70), MLA, Midwest MLA, Nat., Wis. councils tchrs. English, Am. Fedn. Tchrs. (treas. Milw. chpt. 1962-66), Assn. U. Wis. Faculties, Kappa Delta Pi, Sigma Tau Delta. Presbyterian (ruling elder). Contbr. poetry to mags. Home: 1128 Oxford Rd Waukesha WI 53186 Office: Univ Wis Waukesha County 1500 University Dr Waukesha WI 53186

SMITH, BETTY PAT (BEEPER), sales director; b. Birmingham, Ala., Jan. 24, 1933; d. Marvin Walter and Elizabeth (Patterson) Jones; m. Rodney H. Smith, June 9, 1953; children—Brad, Lee Ann. B.F.A., U. Okla., 1953. Artist, craftsman Temptation Corner, San Antonio, 1964-67; regional sales mgr. United Ch. Directories, San Antonio, 1972-81; dir. of sales, ptnr. Conv. Coordinators, San Antonio, 1981—. Mem. Republican Nat. Com., Washington, 1980—, San Antonio Conservation Soc., 1965—. Mem. San Antonio Soc. of Assn. Execs., Tex. Soc. Assn. Execs., Hotel Sales and Mktg. Assn., Meeting Planners Internat., Greater San Antonio C. of C. Methodist. Club: San Antonio Jr. Forum (pres. 1966-67). Avocations: hot air balloons. Home: 10518 Merritime Ct San Antonio TX 78217 Office: Conv Coordinators PO Box 169718 Central Park Station San Antonio TX 78280

SMITH, BETTYE DURHAM, city official; b. Margerum, Ala., Aug. 2, 1932; d. Rather Franklin and Gladys Irene (Wallece) Durham; m. Robert John Smith, Aug. 14, 1954; children—John Leon, Robert Julius, Cary Hamilton. Student U. Tenn., 1951-52; B.A. summa cum laude, U. Central Fla., 1973; M.A.T. U. Fla., 1977; postgrad. Seminole Community Coll., 1977. Cert. law enforcement officer, Fla. Dir. victim services Seminole County Sheriffs Dept., Sanford, Fla., 1977-82; adj. prof. history Seminole Community Coll., 1977—; mayor City of Sanford, 1985—. Chmn. adv. bd. Salvation Army, 1984-85; pres. Seminole Community Concert Assn., 1975-76; mem. exec. bd. Seminole County United Way, 1984-85; bd dirs. Am. Cancer Soc., 1983—. Named Woman of Yr. Kiwanis Club, 1983. Mem. Fla. Hist. Soc. (bd. dirs. 1983-85), Fla. Victim Assistance Assn. (bd. dirs. 1980-82). Democrat. Methodist. Club: Sanford Womens (1st v.p. 1984—). Home: 103 Country Pl Sanford FL 32771 Office: City of Sanford PO Box 1778 Sanford FL 32771

SMITH, BETTYE L. SEBREE, business college executive; b. Owensmouth, Calif., Feb. 25, 1926; d. Roy Albert and Thelma Hattie (Alexander) Sebree; student Brigham Young U., 1944-45, Links Sch. Bus., Boise, Idaho, 1946, Nampa (Idaho) Bus. Coll. 1956; B.S., Alaska Meth. U., 1972; cert. adminstrv. mgr.; accredited personnel diplomat; m. George R. Motschman, Feb. 26, 1948 (div. June 1959); children—Jerye Lou, Marie Louise; m. 2d, Leroy I. Smith, Mar. 13, 1961 (div. 1968). Office mgr. Intermountain Surg. Supply Co., Boise, 1945-48; sec. payroll, cost acct. Morrison-Knudsen Co., Fairbanks, Alaska and Boise, 1948-52; payroll, cost acct. Lytle, Green, Birch Contractors, Fairbanks, 1952-54; owner Fairbanks Secretarial Sch., 1956-58, Anchorage Secretarial Sch., 1958-59; pres. Alaska Bus. Coll., Inc., Anchorage, 1959—; owner City Employment Center, Anchorage, 1962-68, Western Girl Temps., Inc., 1962-68, Manpower, Inc. Bus. Services, 1969-72, Alaska Employment Agy., Anchorage, 1970-72; franchise holder Speedwriting Shorthand, 1957-76, Nancy Taylor Finishing Sch., 1960-76, ITT-Nat. Data Processing, 1968-76, Taylor Airline Careers, 1968-76; pres. Arctic Tech. Industries, 1972-76, KAVIR, Inc., Sebree, Ltd. Mem. accrediting commn. Assn. of Ind. Colls. and Schs.; bd. dirs. Eastwind Vocat. Services; mem. Gov.'s Council on Vocat. Edn., 1985—; pres. Alaska Pvt. Sch. Assn.; past pres. Horizons Unltd. Cert. adminstrv. mgr., accredited personnel diplomat. Mem. Profl. Secs. Assn. (chpt. v.p. 1962, seminar chmn. 1961, 67, 73-77, 80), Profl. secs. Internat. (Exec. of Yr. award Billikin chpt.), Alaska Vocat. Assn., Alaska Bus. Edn. Assn., Internat. Platform Assn., Nat. Assn. student Fin. Aid Officer, Nat. Bus. Edn. Assn., Adminstrv. Mgmt. Assn. Office: 5159 Old Seward Hwy Anchorage AK 99503

SMITH, BEVERLY ELAINE, educator; b. Long Branch, N.J., Aug. 2, 1935; d. Edward L. and Grace A. (Rankin) Reeves; m. Raymond Donald Smith. Student Jersey City State Coll., 1976. Pres., Smith's Inst. Cosmetology, Inc., Asbury, Park, N.J., 1979—. Recipient Achievement award Tchr. Ednl. Council, Washington, 1979, Central Jersey Club, 1984, Soroptimists Internat., 1984. Mem. N.J. Assn. Beauty Culture Schs. (Achievement award 1984), Modern Beauticians Assn., Nat. Hairdressers and Cosmetologists Assn., N.J. Beauty Culturist League, Am. Beauty Culturist League, Asbury Park C. of C. Roman Catholic. Home: 4 Williams Rd Neptune NJ 07753 Office: 717 Cookman Ave Asbury Park NJ 07712

SMITH, BILLIE NELL BRYSON, nurse; b. Linden, Tenn., May 29, 1933; d. Barney Lee and Julia Mae (Hufstedler) Bryson; grad. St. Thomas Sch. Nursing, Nashville, 1955; m. Lee Garry Smith, Aug. 20, 1960; children—Lee Garry. Office nurse for Drs. G.H. Turner and B.L. Holladay, Linden, Tenn., 1955-56; dir. nursing Perry County Hosp., Linden, 1956-80, inservice dir., 1956-80; staff nurse, charge nurse Perry Meml. Hosp., Linden, Tenn., 1980—. Vol. nurse for mass polio vaccination Pub. Health Dept., 1963, 64; vol. nurse Am. Nat. Red Cross, 1955—. Licensed Tenn. Bd. Nursing. Mem. Tenn. Hosp. Assn., Tenn. Assn. Nursing Service Dirs., St. Thomas Sch. of Nursing Alumni Assn. Home: Route 4 Box 232 Linden TN 37096 Office: Perry Meml Hosp Squirrel Hollow Dr Linden TN 37096

SMITH, CAROL ANN, lawyer; b. Birmingham, Ala., Apr. 23, 1949; d. James William and Mildred Viola (Ferguson) S. B.A., Birmingham So. Coll., 1971; J.D., U. Ala.-Tuscaloosa, 1975; LL.M., NYU, 1977. Bar: Ala. 1975, U.S. Dist. Ct. (no. dist.) Ala. 1977, U.S. Dist. Ct. (mid. dist.) Ala. 1976, U.S. Ct. Appeals (11th cir.) 1981, U.S. Ct. Appeals (5th cir.) 1979. Law clk. Ala. Supreme Ct., Montgomery, 1975-76; assoc. Lange, Simpson, Robinson & Somerville, Birmingham, 1977-81; assoc. Starnes & Atchison, Birmingham, 1981-83, ptnr., 1983—. Editorial bd. Ala. Law Rev., 1973-75. Mem. bd. mgmt. Downtown YMCA, Birmingham, 1984—, mem. exec. com., 1985—. Mem. Birmingham Bar Assn. (pres. young lawyers sect. 1984, mem. exec. com. 1986), Ala. Bar Inst. for Continuing Legal Edn. (exec. com. 1979—), Ala. Bar Assn. (editorial bd. The Ala. Lawyer 1979—, assoc. editor 1984—, exec. com. young lawyers sect. 1983-84, chmn. continuing legal edn. com. of young lawyers sect. 1984, mem. pres.'s adv. task foce 1984-85), Eleventh Cir. Jud. Conf. (alt. del. 1985), Phi Beta Kappa. Methodist. Club: Birmingham Jr. Music Bd. Home: 1511 Ridge Rd Homewood AL 35209 Office: Starnes & Atchison One Daniel Plaza Daniel Bldg Birmingham AL 35233

SMITH, CAROL ANN, nurse, univ. dean b. Waterbury, Conn., Dec. 22, 1941; d. Prosper Mark and Emma Edna (Dumschott) Zailskas; B.S. in Nursing, Boston Coll., 1965; Ph.D., 1977; M.S. in Nursing, Boston U., 1971; m. David Dennis Smith, June 19, 1965; children—Amy, Christian, Meghan. Ob-gyn assoc. Chelsea (Mass.) Naval Hosp., 1970-71; coordinator clin. nurse specialist program Boston Coll.-Harvard U. Med. Sch. 1975-78; chmn. grad. program Coll. of Our Lady of Elms, Chicopee, Mass., 1976-78, dir. B.S.N. Program, 1978-80; dean Sch. Nursing, Duquesne U., Pitts., 1980—, dissertation chmn. preceptor adminstrn. intern. Mem. Am. Nurses Assn., Nat. League for Nursing, Am. Assn. Colls. of Nursing, Nat. Assn. Women Deans, Adminstrs. and Counselors, Pa. Nurses Assn. (dir. 1982—), Western Pa. Coalition for Nurse Advancement (Pres. 1981—), Holyoke-Chicopee Mental Health Assn. (dir. 1978-80), Boston Coll. Alumnae Assn., Boston U. Alumnae Assn. Roman Catholic. Club: Boston Coll. (Pitts.). Office: Duquesne U 600 Forbes Ave Pittsburgh PA 15282

SMITH, CAROL ANN, music therapist, psychologist; b. Montgomery County, Tenn., Apr. 19, 1951; d. Carl and Ruth (Gettinger) S.; B.M.E. in Music Therapy, U. Kans., 1974; M.A. in Clin. Psychology, Middle Tenn. State U., 1977; Ed.S. in Human Service Mgmt.; Vanderbilt U., 1979. Gen. therapeutic recreation specialist VA Med. Center, Murfreesboro, Tenn., 1973-79; music therapist VA Med. Center, Marion, Ind., 1979; chief, recreation therapy service VA Med. Center, Tucson, 1979-84; chief recreation therapy VA Med Ctr., Northport, N.Y., 1984—; adj. instr. Middle Tenn. State U., part-time 1978—; guest speaker, 1975—; Mem. Am. Psychol. Assn. (asso.), Nat. Therapeutic Recreation Soc., Nat. Assn. Music Therapy (cert.), Nat. Assn. Female Execs., Pi Lambda Theta. Democrat. Methodist. Contbr. articles to profl. jours. Home: 132 Church St Apt 2A Kings Park NY 11754 Office: VA Med Center Northport NY 11768

SMITH, CAROL ANN BECHTEL, lawyer; b. Wheeling, W.Va., July 22, 1945; d. Carl Harrison Bechtel and E. LaVerne (Angelo) Hutto; m. John Anthony Smith, June 17, 1983; 1 child, Michael Anthony. B.A., Anderson (Ind.) Coll., 1967; M.A., Ohio State U., 1970; J.D., Ind. U.,-Indpls., 1978. Bar: Ind. 1978, U.S. Dist. Ct. (so. dist.) Ind. 1978. Environ. atty. to Ind. atty. gen., Indpls., 1978-79; legis. asst. U.S. Ho. of Reps., Washington, 1979-81; environ. atty. U.S. Corps Engrs., Anchorage, 1982-83; environ. cons., Anchorage, 1984—; sec.-treas., dir. Alaska Bus. Pub. Co.; adj. prof. Anchorage Community Coll., 1982; lectr. U. Alaska, Anchorage, 1982-83. Assoc. editor Ind. Law Rev., 1977-78. big sister Marion County Juvenile Ct., 1978; bd. dirs. Anchorage Symphony Orch.; corr. sec. Anchorage Symphony Women's League, 1984-86, 1st v.p. Recipient spl. performance award U.S. Army Corps Engrs., Anchorage, 1982. Mem. ABA, Ind. Bar Assn. Republican. Mem. Soc. of Friends. Home: 6861 Lovitt Circle Anchorage AK 99516 Office: 801 B St Suite 300 Anchorage AK 99501

SMITH, CAROL JEAN, family practitioner; b. Pensacola, Fla., Dec. 28, 1935; d. Lionel Alton and Marialyce (Churchill) Whidden; divorced; children—Michael, Sheila, Hans, Elizabeth, Susan, Jeannie. B.A. in Biology and English, So. Coll., Collegedale, Tenn., 1954; M.D., U. Miami, 1959; M.P.H., U. N.C., 1978. Diplomate Am. Bd. Family Practice. Intern, Tampa Gen. Hosp., Davis Islands, Fla., 1959-60; family practitioner Malin Med. Group, Hyattsville, Md., 1960-64; pvt. practice medicine specializing in family practice, Asheville, N.C., 1964-78, Woodfin, N.C., 1985—; group practice medicine specializing in family practice, Silver Spring, Md., 1984—; faculty Cecil's Coll., Ashville, N.C., 1986—. Pres. Quota Club, Asheville, 1976-77. Served as capt. USCG, 1978-84. Adventist. Avocations: sailing; volunteer organizations. Office: 14000 Castle Blvd Suite 107 Silver Spring MD 20904 also 146 Weaverville Hwy Asheville NC 28804

SMITH, CHARLENE (CHARLI) A., trust company executive; b. San Antonio, Oct. 20, 1942; d. Sydney Herbert and Pauline Mae (Rickliff) Biggs; A.A., Eastfield Coll., 1981; m. Billy R. Smith, June 7, 1958; children—Victor Lee, Sandra Lynne, Robin Rene, Charles Matthew. Adminstrv. sec. Coed, Inc., Dallas, 1975-79; sec. to indsl. relations dir. U.S. Industries, Dallas, 1979-80; adminstr. Sponsored Benefit Services, Inc., Dallas, 1979-80; v.p.;corp. sec., chief adminstrv. officer Fiduciary Trust Co. of the Southwest, Dallas, 1980—. Notary public, lic. ins. agt., Tex. Mem. Nat. Assn. Female Execs., Inst. Cert. Fin. Planners, Phi Theta Kappa. Methodist. Home: 125 Colonel Dr Garland TX 75043 Office: 12700 Hillcrest Rd Suite 175 Dallas TX 75230

SMITH, CHARLOTTE GEORGE, physiologist; b. Cin., Aug. 26, 1938; d. Karl Franklin and Thelma Alena Smith; B.S. in Zoology, U. Ill., Urbana, 1960, M.S. in Physiology, 1961. Physiologist, NASA-Johnson Space Center, 1962—; dir. Independence Inst., 1980—; cons. in rehab. physiology. Recipient NASA Apollo Achievement award, 1969; several group achievement awards; lic. pilot. Assoc. fellow Aerospace Med. Assn.; mem. AAAS, Found. Sci. and Handicapped, Assn. Women in Sci., Am. Assn. Profl. Hypnologist, Houston Profl. Hypnotists Assn. Office: NASA-Johnson Space Center Houston TX 77058

SMITH, CHARLOTTE REED, educator; b. Eubank, Ky., Sept. 15, 1921; d. Joseph Lumpkin and Cornelia Elizabeth (Spenser) Reed; m. Walter Lindsay Smith, Aug. 24, 1949; children—Walter Lindsay IV, Elizabeth Reed. B.A. in Music, Tift Coll., 1941; M.A. in Mus. Theory, Eastman Sch. of Music, 1946; postgrad. Juilliard Sch., 1949. Asst. prof. theory Okla. Bapt. U., 1944-45, Washburn U., 1946-48; prof. music Furman U., Greenville, S.C., 1948—; evaluator compositions Jr. Music Clubs of S.C., Nat. Fedn. Music Clubs, 1970-74. Editor: Seven Penitential Psalms with Two Laudate Psalms, 1983. Mem. Am. Musicol. Soc., Soc. for Music Theory, AAUP (sec.-treas. Furman chpt. 1984-85), Nat. Fedn. Music Clubs, Pi Kappa Lambda. Republican. Baptist. Office: Furman U Poinsett Hwy Greenville SC 29613

SMITH, CHERYL KIM, health care administrator; b. Newburgh, N.Y., Sept. 8, 1957; d. Gary Thomas and Joan Pamela (Eible) S. B.S.N., Vanderbilt U., 1979; M.B.A., U. Miami, 1981. Charge nurse med./surg. floor, Vanderbilt U. Med. Ctr., Nashville, 1979-80; health care mgmt. cons. Arthur Anderson & Co., Dallas, 1982-83; dept. dir. St. Paul Family Practice Ctr., Dallas, 1983-84; adminstrv. dir. satellite facilities St. Paul Med. Ctr., Dallas, 1984—. Mem. Healthcare Fin. Mgmt. Assn., Dallas/Ft. Worth Adminstrv. Jour. Club, Dallas Kappa Alpha Theta Alumni. Republican. Methodist. Office: St Paul Profl Office Bldg II 5939 Harry Hines Blvd Suite 200 Dallas TX 75235

SMITH, CHERYL LYNN, legal and financial printing company executive; b. Newark, June 20, 1958; d. Joseph and Earline Elizabeth (Gadson) S. B.S. in Journalism, Fla. A&M U., 1980; M.S. in Human Relations, Amber U., 1986. Exec. editor Capital Outlook News, Tallahassee, 1980-81; nat. prodn. coordinator TV Watch of Scripps Howard, Dallas, 1981-82; mktg. compliance assoc. J.C. Penney Ins. Co., Dallas, 1982-84; prodn. asst. Am. Equity Press, Dallas, 1984—. Author play: Sizzlin Red and the Seven Dudes, 1981. Editor newsletter Dallas Panhellenic Council, 1985—. Mem. Nat. Council Negro Women, Dallas, 1982; active Just Friends: Pregnant Teenagers Support Group; rep. Dallas chpt. Nat. Panhellenic Council, 1985—. Mem. NAACP, Fla. Black Pubs. (rep. 1980-81), Fla. A&M U. Alumni Assn. (pres. local chpt. 1985—), Soc. Profl. Journalists, Nat. Assn. Female Execs., Delta Sigma Theta (rep. local chpt. 1981—, Service award 1981, 85). Democrat. Baptist. Avocations: reading; working with children; writing; dancing. Home: Box 45331 Dallas TX 75245

SMITH, CHRISTIE LISA, radio announcer; b. San Antonio, Dec. 17, 1954; d. Walter Joseph and Barbara Alice (Bell) Smith. Student Tulane U., 1972-74, Fla. State U., 1976-77. Announcer Sta. WHBQ, Memphis, 1977-78; program dir. Sta. WICE, Providence, 1978-79; announcer Sta. WROR, Boston, 1979-80; program dir. Sta. WBGM, Tallahassee, Fla., 1981; morning announcer Sta. WOWD, Tallahassee, 1981-82; announcer Sta. WQXI, Altanta, 1982—. Author poetry: Seaside Serendipity, 1974. Vol. March of Dimes, Memphis, 1977, Leukemia Soc., Providence, 1980, Tallahassee Jaycees, 1981, Am. Cancer Soc. Atlanta, 1982. Recipient Best D.J. of Yr. award Tulane U., 1972; Pres.'s award Forward Communications, Wausau, Wis., 1981. Mem. Nat. Assn.

Female Execs. Democrat. Episcopalian. Home: 2840 Peachtree Rd NE 503 Atlanta GA 30305 Office: Sta WQXI-FM 3340 Peachtree Rd NE Atlanta GA 30026

SMITH, CLARA JEAN, former nursing home administrator; b. Berwick, Pa., Aug. 31, 1932; d. Barton Fredrick and Evelyn Miriam (Bomboy) Hough; R.N., Williamsport (Pa.) Hosp., 1953; B.S. in Nursing Edn., Wilkes Coll., Wilkes-Barre, Pa., 1960; M.S. in Edn., Temple U., Phila., 1969; m. Robert W. Smith, June 7, 1958. From staff nurse to dir. nursing Retreat State Hosp., Hunlock Creek, Pa., 1953-80; dir. long term care facility Danville (Pa.) State Hosp., 1980-82; ret., 1982; dir. accrediatation coordination and quality assurance Nursing Home Adminstrs., 1980—; speaker, instr. in field. Mem. Lake Pinecrest Sportsmen's Assn. (dir.), Pa. State Employees Retirement Assn. Methodist. Clubs: Sunshine; Town Hill Hobby Group, Town Hill Over 50 Group. Author tng. and ednl. programs. Home: Lake Pinecrest PO Box 5 Huntington Mills PA 18622

SMITH, CLARA MAE, mktg. exec.; b. Algona, Iowa., Jan. 3, 1947; d. Thees and Rachel Bernice (Becker) Schnakenberg; B.S.-A.A., Iowa State U., 1969; postgrad. in profl. selling and computers U. Wis., 1978; 1 dau., Tami Lynn. Interior designer Bank Bldg. Corp., St. Louis and Atlanta, 1969-74, Fin. Bldg. Cons., Atlanta, 1974-75, R.L. Bryan Co., Columbia, S.C., 1975-76, HBE Corp., St. Louis, 1976-79; sr. design mgr. Gresham & Smith, Nashville, 1979-80; mktg. designer McQuiddy Office Designers, Nashville, 1980—; propr. C.S. Designs Ltd., 1975—. Alumna advisor Iowa State U. Coll. Design, 1981—, Middle Tenn. State U., 1983—. Recipient awards for outstanding design Bank Bldg. Corp., 1973; Appreciation of Service award Inst. Bus. Designers, 1974. Mem. Nat. Assn. Female Execs., Inst. Bus. Designers (chpt. pres. 1981—, trustee 1974-81, nat. treas.), NOW, Nat. Assn. Profl. Sales and Mktg. Women, Delta Zeta Alumnae (province collegiate dir.). Lutheran. Home: 310 Cotton Rd Franklin TN 37064 Office: 110 7th Ave N PO Box 25290 Nashville TN 37202

SMITH, DARLENE FAITH, principal, consultant; b. Minot, N.D., Mar. 30, 1935; d. Peter Dewey Prichard and Letha Blanche (Albin) Howell; m. Sebastian Conrad Smith, Aug. 8, 1958; 1 child, Suzanne Constance. B.S., Minot State Tchr.'s Coll., 1956; M.Ed., U. Mont., 1963, Sixth Yr. Specialist, 1976. Home-econ. tchr. Whitefish Sch., Mont., 1956-57; bus. tchr., dept. head. Missoula County High Sch., Mont., 1957-66, counselor, 1967-75, asst. prin., 1975-79, prin., 1979—; cons., speaker Year Round Sch. Conv., Washington, 1975, Women in Adminstrn. seminar, Sun Valley, Idaho, 1983, Seeking Equality in Edn., Great Falls, Mont., 1984, Expanding Horizons U. Mont., Missoula, 1985. Mem. Mayor's Com., Missoula, 1979—; chairperson Title IX Bldg. Coordinator, Missoula, 1975-79. Mem. Nat. Secondary Sch. Prins. (cons. speaker New Orleans 1985), Mont. Secondary Sch. Prins., Phi Delta Kappa. Club: Am. Contract Bridge League (pres./treas. 1969—) (Missoula). Home: 2420 Glen Dr Missoula MT 59801 Office: Big Sky High Sch 3100 S Ave West Missoula MT 59801

SMITH, DAWN ELLEN, nurse; b. Youngstown, Ohio, Sept. 13, 1955; d. John Ronald and Carol Ann (Fanson) Smith. Student Barry U., 1973-75; B.S.N., Vanderbilt U., 1978; postgrad. Emory U., 1983-84. Staff nurse Ga. Bapt. Hosp., Atlanta, 1978; staff nurse Protem, Atlanta, 1978-79, dir. nursing, 1979-80; staff nurse telemetry Crawford West Long Hosp., Atlanta, 1980-81; cardiovascular staff nurse Emory U. Hosp., Atlanta, 1981-83, cardiology staff nurse, 1983-84; ICU-CCU nurse Humana Gwinnett Community Hosp., Snellville, Ga., 1984-85; customer service rep. Adler Instrument Co., Norcross, Ga., 1985—. Mem. Am. Assn. Critical Care Nurses, Gamma Phi Beta, Panhellenic Soc. (sec. Nashville 1976-77). Office: Adler Instrument Co Norcross GA 30071

SMITH, DEBORAH ANN, furniture showroom manager; b. Chgo., Feb. 14, 1953; d. James Joseph and Ann Lucille (Regan) Smith, Jr. A.A., Richard J. Daley Coll., Chgo., 1973; B.A. in Edn., Chgo. State U., 1974; diploma Harrington Inst. Interior Design, Chgo., 1980. Cert. elem. and secondary tchr., Ill. Educatable mentally handicapped tchr. Chgo. Bd. Edn., 1975-78; showroom mgr. Brickel Assocs., Inc., Chgo., 1978-81, 82—, textile sales rep., 1981-82. Mem. Art Inst. Chgo., Weaving Workshop. Roman Catholic. Home: 2300 W 99th St Chicago IL 60643 Office: Ward Bennett Designs for Brickel Assocs Inc 953 Merchandise Mart Chicago IL 60654

SMITH, DEBORAH LEE, school principal; b. Bklyn., Nov. 24, 1947; d. Harold Edward and Gloria Jean (White) Scott; m. Edwin Lowe, Aug. 2, 1969 (div. May 1972); 1 child, Brian Edwin Lowe; m. Edward G. Smith, July 21, 1984. B.S., SUNY-Buffalo, 1969, M.S. in Edn., 1982. Health and phys. edn. tchr. Waterfront Elem. Sch., Buffalo, 1976-80, Fosdick Masten High Sch., Buffalo, 1976-76; tchr. assigned to central office, coordinating 16 academy schs., Buffalo, 1980-83; asst. prin. Bennett High Sch., Buffalo, 1983-84; prin. Buffalo Traditional Sch., 1984—; phys. edn. instr. Canisius Coll., Buffalo, summers 1977-80. Choreographer, Creative Movement for Children, 1970-80; writer alcohol and drug abuse prevention program for teenagers, 1983. Bd. dirs. NAACP, Buffalo, 1983-84, Sounds and Echoes, Inc., Allentown Community Ctr., Buffalo, 1978-83, Nat. Inner Cities Youth Orgn., Buffalo, 1978-82. Mem. Buffalo Assn. Suprs. and Adminstrs., Nat. Assn. Secondary Prins., N.Y. State Assn. Health, Phys. Edn. and Recreation. Democrat. Methodist. Avocations: piano, ballet, ethnic dance. Office: Buffalo Traditional Sch 450 Masten Ave Buffalo NY 14209

SMITH, DEBORAH LEE, hospital administrator, nurse; b. Richmond, Va., Feb. 1, 1952. Staff nurse Petersburg Gen. Hosp., Va., 1973-76, 77-78; head nurse, part-time supr. Psychiat. Med. Surg. Hiram Davis Med. Ctr., Petersburg, 1976-77; staff nurse Leigh Meml. Hosp., Norfolk, Va., 1977-78; instr., part-time supr. Norfolk Gen. Hosp Sch. Profl. Nursing, 1980-82; head nurse ear, nose and throat, otolaryngology Norfolk Gen. Hosp., 1984, research coordinator, project developer, 1984—, mem. nursing mgmt. engring. com., 1982—, mem. quality rev. for home health care, 1983—, mem. mktg. red team, 1985; cons. Wren IV Therapy Ctr., Alliance Health Systems, Norfolk, 1984-85; mem. standardization com. Med. Ctr. Hosp., 1982—; mem. mgmt. cert. task force Alliance Health System, 1985; presenter seminars in field. Basic cardiac life support instr. Am. Heart Assn., 19—, advanced cardiac life support instr., 1981—; loaned exec. United Way, 1984. Mem. Am. Assn. Critical Care Nurses, Am. Nurses Assn., Va. Nurses Assn. (program com. chmn. local dist. 1981-85, del. 1983-85, mem. pub. relations com. 1984—). Home: 41 King George Quay Chesapeake VA 23325

SMITH, DEBRA ANGELA, banker; b. Phila., Mar. 6, 1954; d. Joe L. and Lucile (Cauldwell) Stephens; m. Billy J. Smith, Jan. 1, 1983; 1 child, Angela Lakisha. A.A., U. Fla., 1974; student U. South Fla., 1979-84; grad. Fla. Trust Sch., Gainesville, 1983, Nat. Trust Sch., Chgo., 1985. Teller First Nat. Bank Fla., Tampa, 1975-76; teller Flagship Bank Tampa, 1976-80, adminstrv. asst., 1980-81, trust adminstr., 1981-82; trust officer Sun Bank of Tampa Bay, 1982-84, Alaska Pacific Trust Co., Fairbanks, 1984—. Mem. Estate Planning Council, Nat. Assn. Bus. Women, Fairbanks C. of C. Democrat. Baptist. Home: PO Box 55433 North Pole AK 99705 Office: Alaska Pacific Trust Co 100 Cushman St PO Box 1230 Fairbanks AK 99707

SMITH, DEBRA LEE, underwriter; b. Miami, Fla., Mar. 24, 1957; d. Gerald Delano and Mary Kathleen (Sullivan) S. B.A. in Edn., Wake Forest U., 1979; J.D., So. Meth. U., 1982. Cert. ins. counselor. Mem. firm Childs, Fortenbach, Beck & Guyton, 1982-84; underwriting mgr. Freberg & Co., Inc., Denver, 1984—. Mem. Am. ABA, Tex. Bar Assn., Houston Young Lawyers Assn. (pub. schs. com., child abuse com.), Houston Bar Assn. Office: 1600 Broadway Suite 1790 Denver CO

SMITH, DEBRA LYNN, radio station executive; b. Los Angeles, Feb. 7, 1956; d. Dick Dan and Glennies (Pederson) S. Student S.D. Sch. Mines and Tech., Black Hills State Coll. Adminstrv. asst., weekend sports anchor KEVN-TV, Rapid City, S.D., 1976-78; sports dir. KULR-TV, Billings, Mont., 1978-79; news reporter KKLS AM & FM, Rapid City, S.D., 1980-81, news dir., 1981—. Bd. dirs. Black Hills Dance Theatre, Rapid City, 1984—, Conv. and Visitors Bur., 1985—. Recipient award for best sports feature UPI, S.D., 1984. Mem. Beta Sigma Phi. Democrat. Clubs: Zonta, Toastmasters. Avocations: skiing (water and snow); golf. Home: Box 534 Black Hawk SD 57718 Office: KKLS AM and FM Box 460 Rapid City SD 57709

SMITH, DEE ANN, government official; b. Monmouth, Ill., July 27, 1941; d. Dean Joseph Smith and Joan C. (Davis) Prendergast; m. Roger Williams Smith, Apr. 18, 1968 (div. Apr. 1976); 1 child, Curtis Hicklin. B.A., Monmouth Coll., 1963; cert. Powers Modelling Sch., Denver, 1964; lic. Dick Jones Real Estate Sch., Denver, 1978. Co-owner, City Dump & Co., Puerto Vallarta, Mex., 1972-76; fin. dir. Colo. Republicans, Denver, 1975-77; polit. cons. Rep. party, 1977-81; exec. asst. Reagan-Bush Transition Team, Washington, 1980-81, The White House, 1981; congl. liaison officer Office of Legis. Affairs, AID, Washington, 1982, dep. dir. congl. liaison, 1982-83, asso. dir. Office Legis. Affairs, 1983-86, spl. asst. to dep. adminstr., 1986—, chmn. communications rev. bd., 1986—. Mem. Arlington Hosp. Aux., Va., 1985. Recipient Superior Honor award AID, 1985. Mem. Nat. Assn. Female Execs., Am. Soc. Profl. and Exec. Women, Colo. State Soc. (treas. 1982—). Lutheran. Avocations: scuba diving; travel; reading. Home: 3228 S Utah St Arlington VA 22206 Office: AID Washington DC 20523

SMITH, DIANE, lawyer, telecommunications executive; b. Washington, Oct. 2, 1959; d. Edgar Gordon and Leona (Doherty) S.; m. David W. Pickeral, Sept. 13, 1980. B.A., George Mason U., 1981, J.D., 1986. Adminstr. Beacon Cos., Washington, 1981-83; legis. and regulatory affairs coordinator U.S. Telecom, Washington, 1983—, also treas. polit. action com.; dir. Empire-ALTEL, N.Y.C., Comptel of Colo., Denver. Mem. Nat. Assn. Female Execs., Nat. Alliance for Women in Communications, Competitive Telecommunications Assn. (state affairs com. 1984—, speaker ann. conv. 1985), Delta Theta Phi. Democrat. Avocations: playing piano; reading; antiques. Office: US Telecom 1825 I St NW Suite 1050 Washington DC 20006

SMITH, DIANNE LOUISE, lawyer; b. Orlando, Fla., Jan. 5, 1947; d. Archie Young and Olive (Lord) McMillan; m. Gary Lynn Smith, Oct. 25, 1969 (div. Feb. 1984). Student Agnes Scott Coll., 1965-67; B.A., Hendrix Coll., 1969; J.D., U. Tulsa, 1979. Bar: Okla. 1979. Clk. firm Gable & Gotwals, Tulsa, summer 1977; assoc. firm Chapel, Wilkinson, Riggs, Abney & Henson, Tulsa, 1979-82, mem., 1982—. Mem. Okla. Bar Assn., Tulsa County Bar Assn., Tulsa Women Lawyers Assn. Office: Chapel Wilkinson Riggs Abney & Henson 502 W 6th St Tulsa OK 74119

SMITH, DOLORES V(AREIKA) MASON, lawyer; b. Boston, Oct. 2, 1933; d. Michael and Annie Monica (White) Vareika; m. William Mason Smith, Apt. 21, 1963. B.A., Tulane U., 1978, J.D., 1980. Bar: La. 1980. Served in U.S. Air Force, 1955-63; advanced asst. dist. atty., New Orleans, 1980—. Notary pub., La.; mem. LWV, Ind. Women's Orgn., New Orleans. Mem. ABA, Am. Judicature Soc., La. Bar Assn., Alpha Sigma Lambda. Democrat. Roman Catholic. Home: 342 Millaudon St New Orleans LA 70118 Office: Dist Atty Office 619 S White St New Orleans LA 70119

SMITH, DONNA LILIAN, seminar executive; b. Phila., Oct. 8, 1944; d. Joseph Patrick and Mary Elizabeth (Veronica) Burke; student Calif. State U., Northridge, 1962-64; Assoc. degree, Fashion Inst. Calif., 1969. Cert. meeting profl. Fashion coordinator, 1963-68; dir. Fashion Mdsg. Inst., 1968-69; v.p. Fashion Inst. Design and Mdsg., 1969-78; pres., owner Seminars Internat., Los Angeles, 1979—; producer fashion shows, cons. in field; mem. costume council Los Angeles County Mus. Art.; mem. adv. bd. Meeting West, 1986. Mem. Costume Soc. Am., Meeting Planners Internat., Los Angeles Conv. and Visitors Bur., U.S. C. of C. Fashion Group, Am. Soc. Travel Agents, Meeting Cons. Network. Roman Catholic. Office: 15910 Ventura Blvd Suite 800 Encino CA 91436

SMITH, DONNA MCDERMOTT, county government official; b. Dubuque, Iowa, Mar. 24, 1941; d. Donald C. and Coletta A. (Hoffman) McDermott; m. Patrick Smith, May 30, 1960; children—Sheree, Shawn, Dana, Sasha. Student pub. schs., Dubuque. Lic. real estate broker, Iowa. County supr., Dubuque County, Iowa, 1978—; mem. Iowa Gov.'s Task Force on Liquor Monopoly, 1983, Iowa Dept. Health Task Force on Homemaker Health Aid, 1984, Iowa Lt. Gov.'s Tomorrow Econ. Devel. Com., 1984—. Chair, Dubuque County Democratic party, 1974-78; bd. dirs. Project Concern, Tri-State Blind Services. Recipient Gov.'s award Volunteerism in Iowa, 1985. Mem. Am. Realtors Assn., Iowa Realtors Assn., Dubuque Realtors Assn., Greater Dubuque Devel. Corp. Roman Catholic. Avocations: piano, skiing, antiques. Home: 1827 Key Way Dubuque IA 52001 Office: Dubuque County Courthouse 7th Central St Dubuque IA 52001

SMITH, DORIS HELEN, college president; b. Cleve., June 1, 1930; d. Harold Peter and Ellen Mary (Keane) S. B.S., Coll. of Mt. St. Vincent, 1952; M.A., NYU, 1957; postgrad. Fordham U., 1960-65; L.H.D., (hon.), Manhattan Coll., 1979. Joined Sisters of Charity (N.Y.), 1952. Mem. faculty Coll. of Mount St. Vincent, Bronx, N.Y., 1955-70, adminstrv. asst. to pres., 1971-72, exec. v.p., 1972-73, pres., 1973—; spl. asst. to pres. Chatham Coll., Pitts., 1970-71; dir. Hudson River Fund of Equitable Variable Life Ins., N.Y.C.; trustee Higher Edn. Service Corp., Albany, N.Y., 1980-85, Com. on Independent Colls. and Univs., Albany, 1980-83. Active Bronx Overall Econ. Devel. Corp., 1976—. Recipient Higher Edn. Leadership award Com. on Independent Colls. and Corning Glass Works, 1983, several interfaith and brotherhood awards; named Riverdalian of Yr. Riverdale Community Council, 1978; Am. Council Edn. fellow, 1970-71. Mem. Bronx C. of C. Roman Catholic. Home and Office: Coll Mount Saint Vincent Riverdale Ave Riverdale Bronx NY 10471

SMITH, DORIS JANE, nutritional consultant, retail store owner; b. Detroit, Jan. 9, 1933; d. George James and Martha (Milinski) Miller; m. Ted Carlyle Smith, Aug. 31, 1954; children—Holly, Cathy Smith Gray, Randall. B.A., U. Ark., 1977. Pres. Consol. Security Corp., Inc., Memphis, 1973-80, Sun Tree Health Foods, Inc., Fayetteville, Ark., 1977—, Sunshine Investments, Inc., Fayetteville, 1983—; nutritional cons. Hulvey Metabolic Service, Searcy, Ark., 1983—. Founder and dir. Memphis chpt. Huxley Inst. Biosocial Research, Memphis, 1975. Mem. Am. Assn. Nutritional Cons., LWV. Republican. Baptist. Avocations: water skiing, snow skiing, golf. Home: PO Box 456 Johnson AR 72741 Office: Sun Tree Health Foods Inc 1242 N College St Fayetteville AR 72703

SMITH, DORIS WILMA DUNN, educator, writer, poet, speaker; b. Greensboro, N.C., Aug. 21, 1933; d. David Harry and Wilma Gertrude (Kerns) Dunn; B.S. in Biology, Flora Macdonald Coll., 1955; M.A. in Biol. Sci. and Math., U. Calif.-Irvine, 1973; Ph.D. in Edn., U. Beverly Hills, 1980; m. Ralph Ray Smith, June 1, 1957; children—Glenn, Harriet, Marcus. Tchr. sci. St Pauls (N.C.) City Schs., 1955-57; tchr. math. Belmont (N.C.) City Schs., 1962-64, Charlotte-Mecklenburg City Schs., Charlotte, N.C., 1964-65, Newport Mesa Unified Schs., Newport Beach, Calif., 1965-67; tchr. math., sci. Anaheim (Calif.) Union High Sch., 1967-81, Fontana (Calif.) Unified Sch., 1982-84, Long Beach Unified Schs., 1984—; freelance writer, poet, 1978—; speaker various religious and civic orgns., 1979—. Mgr. Far West Anaheim Bobby Sox Softball, 1969-71, all-star mgr., 1970, all-star coach, 1969-71; leader Girl Scouts Am., 1970. E. I. du Pont de Nemours fellow, 1956. Mem. NEA, Calif. Tchrs. Assn., Anaheim Secondary Tchrs. Assn., Tchrs. Assn. Long Beach, Nat. Council Tchrs. Math., Nat. Assn. Female Execs., AAUW, Internat. Women's Writers Guild, Woman's World Internat. Democrat. Presbyterian. Club: Toastmasters. Author: A Limb of Your Tree, 1981. Home and Office: 912 Hayward St Anaheim CA 92804

SMITH, DOROTHY BYARS, music publishing and sport fishing executive; b. Charlotte, N.C., Jan. 24, 1920; d. Robert Harrison and Dovie (Lee) Byars; m. Arthur Smith, Apr. 12, 1941; children—A. Reginald, Connie Brown, R. Clayton. Student, Inst. Acad. Ikebana Art., 1968. Vice pres. Clay Music, Charlotte, 1965—. Crackerjack Enterprises, Charlotte, 1965—; sec., treas. Arthur Smith Enterprises, Charlotte, 1976—. Chmn., Mayor's Beautification Com., Charlotte, 1965. Mem. U.S. Sport Fishing Assn. (sec. 1985—), Sardlswood Garden Club (pres. 1961-62, 63, 80-82). Democrat. Baptist. Clubs: Christian Women's (area rep.) Charlotte City, Tower. (Charlotte). Avocations: china painter; flower arranging. Home: 7224 Sardis Rd Charlotte NC 28226 Office: Arthur Smith Enterprises 200 Smithfield Dr Charlotte NC 28226

SMITH, DOROTHY OTTINGER, jewelry designer, civic leader; b. Indpls.; d. Albert Ellsworth and Leona Aurelia (Waller) Ottinger; student Herron Art Sch. of Purdue U. and Ind. U., 1941-42; m. James Emory Smith, June 25, 1943 (div. 1984); children—Michael Ottinger, Sarah Anne, Theodore Arnold, Lisa Marie. Comml. artist William H. Block Co., Indpls., 1942-43, H.P. Wasson Co., 1943-44; dir. Riverside (Calif.) Art Center, 1963-64; jewelry designer, Riverside, 1970—; numerous design commns. Adviser Riverside chpt. Freedom's Found. of Valley Forge; co-chmn. fund raising com. Riverside Art Center and Mus., 1966-67, bd. dirs. Art Alliance, 1980-81; mem. Riverside City Hall sculpture selection panel Nat. Endowment Arts, 1974-75; chmn. fund raising benefit Riverside Art Center and Mus., 1973-74, trustee, 1980-84, chmn. permanent collection, 1981-84, co-chmn. fund drive, 1982-84; chmn. Riverside Mcpl. Arts Commn., 1974-76; juror Riverside Civic Center Purchase Prize Art Show, 1975; mem. pub. bldgs. and grounds subcom., gen. plan citizens com. City of Riverside, 1965-66; mem. Mayor's Commn. on Civic Beauty, Mayor's Commn. on Sister City Sendai, 1965-66; bd. dirs., chmn. spl. events Children's League of Riverside Community Hosp., 1952-53; bd. dirs. Crippled Children's Soc. of Riverside, spl. events chmn., 1952-53; bd. dirs. Jr. League of Riverside, rec. sec., 1960-61; bd. dirs. Nat. Charity League, pres. Riverside chpt., 1965-66; mem. exec. com. of bd. trustees Riverside Arts Found., 1977—, fund dr. chmn., 1978-79, project rev. chmn., 1978-79; juror Gemco Charitable and Scholarship Found., 1977-85; mem. bd. women deacons Calvary Presbyn. Ch., 1978-80; mem. incorporating bd. Inland Empire United Fund for Arts, 1980-81; bd. dirs. Hospice Orgn. Riverside County, 1982-84; Art Awareness chmn. Riverside Arts Found.; mem. Calif. Council Humanities, 1982—. Recipient cert. Riverside City Council, 1977, plaque Mayor of Riverside, 1977. Mem. Riverside Art Assn. (pres. 1961-63, 1st v.p. 1964-65, 67-68, trustee 1959-70), Art Alliance of Riverside Art Center and Museum (founder 1964, pres. 1969-70). Recipient Spl. Recognition Riverside Cultural Arts Council, 1981, Disting. Service plaque Riverside Art Ctr. and Mus. Address: 3979 Chapman Pl Riverside CA 92506

SMITH, ELASAH SCHAFF, fabric fashion designer, dancer, artist, musician, writer; b. Evanston, Ill., Oct. 14, 1953; d. Philip Haynes and Mary (Johnson) Schaff; m. Eric John Smith, Oct. 20, 1984. A.A. with honors, Bennett Jr. Coll., 1973. Apprentice Goldsholl Assocs. Film and Design Co., Northfield, Ill., 1971; fashion designer ELASAH, Honolulu, 1976-80, Chgo., 1980-84; owner, designer Elasah Designs, Inc., N.Y.C., 1983—; free-lance artist; creative dir. Sparks Multi-media, Graphic Arts Soc., Chgo., 1982-83. Avocations: dance; health movement; music composition. also PO Box 1740 Madison Sq Sta New York NY 10150

SMITH, ELIZABETH ADAMS, producer; b. Long Beach, Calif., May 21, 1944; d. Francis H. and Virginia R. (Wells) Adams; m. Richard Yeadon Smith, III, Sept. 27, 1969; children—Jason Colyer, Amanda Wells. B.S. in Broadcast Journalism, Boston U., 1966; postgrad., NYU, Sch. Visual Arts, New Sch. Copywriter Batten, Barton Durstine and Osborn, N.Y.C., 1966-71; mgr. software div. Adwell Audio-Visual Co., Bellerose, N.Y., 1971-72; freelance writer, producer, N.Y.C., 1972-76; dir. N.Y. chpt. Am. Soc. for Psychoprophylaxis in Obstetrics, 1975-76; mgr., ptnr. Adams-Smith Prodns., Rye, N.Y., 1976-83; pres. Adams-Smith Prodns. Ltd., 1983—; dir., v.p., Granlyn Farm Products, Schaticoke N.Y., 1980-84. Contbr. numerous articles to popular and profl. jours.; producer TV, audio-visual materials videos, short films. Mem. Westchester Nuclear Freeze Com. Rye Presbyn. Ch.; v.p. fundraising Rye High Sch. Parents' Assn. Mem. NOW, Westchester County C. of C., Westchester Assn. Women Bus. Owners, Women in Communications (v.p. membership), Small Bus. Council (community com.), Assn. for Multi-Image, Assn. Ind. Video and Film Makers, Assn. Visual Communicators. Club: Apawamis (Rye). Home: 127 Evergreen Ave Rye NY 10580 Office: Adams-Smith Productions Ltd Box 52 Rye NY 10580

SMITH, ELIZABETH BLOXOM, real estate broker; b. Newport News, Va., Aug. 9; d. Dennis Joseph and Elizabeth Veronica (Carter) Antinori; student Golden Gate U., 1973-74; m. Blair Eldred Smith, Aug. 30, 1968; children—Robert E., Dennis L. Salesman, half owner Bloxom Realty Co., Newport News, Va., 1962-66, broker, 1963—; owner, pres. Libby Bloxom, Inc., Newport News, 1966—. Mem. Nat. Assn. Realtors, Realtor's Nat. Mktg. Inst. (cert. residential broker), Nat. Assn. Parliamentarians (local treas. 1978, 79, pres. local unit 1981-83, pres. Va. Peninsula 1986-87), Va. Assn. Realtors (past regional v.p., Cert. of Appreciation 1979), Cert. Resdl. Brokerage Mgrs. (pres. 1986), Peninsula Retail Merchants Assn. (dir.), Newport News-Hampton Bd. Realtors (pres. 1975, plaque of appreciation 1975, Realtor of Yr. 1976), Pioneer Internat. Tng. and Communication Club (rec. sec. 1985-86). Republican. Presbyterian. Clubs: Soroptimists (corr. sec. Va. Peninsula 1985-86), Pioneer Toastmistress. Home: 924 Etna Dr Newport News VA 23602 Office: 14801 Warwick Blvd Newport News VA 23602

SMITH, ESTHER THOMAS, editor, writer; b. Jesup, Ga., Mar. 13, 1939; d. Joseph H. and Leslie (McCarthy) Thomas; B.A., Agnes Scott Coll., 1962; m. James D. Smith, June 2, 1962; children—Leslie, Amy, James Thomas. Staff writer, Sunday women's editor Atlanta Jour. Constn., 1961-62; mng. editor Bull. of U. Miami Sch. Medicine, 1965-66; corr. Atlanta Jour.-Constn. and Fla. Times-Union, 1964, 67-68; founding editor Bus. Rev. of Washington, 1978-81; ind. bus. writer, communications cons. Peat, Marwick, Mitchell & Co., Washington, 1981-82; editor Scripps-Howard Washington Bus. Jour., 1982; corp. officer, contbg. editor Washington Woman Mag., Inc., 1983-85; pres. CTR, Inc., pub. Washington Tech., 1986—; lectr. Pres., Episcopal Young Churchmen, Diocese of Ga., 1955-57; dir. pub. relations Army Community Service, Ft. Bragg, N.C., 1969-71; co-founder Army Family Symposium, 1979-80; adv. bd. bus. edn. Fairfax County Pub. Schs., 1981-82; bd. dirs. MIT Enterprise Forum of Washington/Balt., 1981-82, Women's Forum, Washington, 1981—, Nat. Mil. Family Assn., 1986-87. Republican. Episcopalian. Home: 1335 Timberly Ln McLean VA 22102 Office: 1953 Gallows Rd Suite 130 Vienna VA 22180

SMITH, EUGENIA SEWELL, funeral home executive; b. Albany, Ky., Oct. 24, 1922; d. Leo Matheny and Marjorie (Warinner) Sewell; m. James Frederick Smith, June 25, 1948; 1 child, Bryson Sewell. Student Berea Coll., 1937-41, Bowling Green Coll. Commerce, 1944-45. Owner, operator Sewell Funeral Home, Albany, 1977—. Sec. Albany Woman's Club, 1950-54; den mother Cub Scouts, Boy Scouts Am., 1958-62; pres. Clinton County Homemakers, Albany, 1968-70; mission action chmn. Missionary Baptist Ch., 1965-82. Democrat. Lodge: Order Eastern Star (former assoc. conductress). Home: Rural Route 4 Burkesville Rd Albany KY 42602 Office: Sewell Funeral Home 115 Cross St Albany KY 42602

SMITH, FAITH, educational administrator; b. Chgo. B.S., Purdue U., 1979; M.A., U. Chgo., 1982. Counselor, Clyde Warrior Inst. Am. Indians, Boulder, Colo., 1969; coordinator Am. Indian Fesitval, Field Mus. Natural History, 1968; exec. asst. Nat. Congress Am. Indians, 1966; caseworker Am. Indian Ctr., Chgo., 1966-69, exec. asst., 1968-71; coordinator Am. Indian Health Project, Am. Med. Student Assn., Rolling Meadows, Ill., 1971-76; mem. faculty Antioch U., Yellow Springs, Ohio, 1974-84; Coordinator Native Am. Ednl. Services Coll., Chgo., 1974-75, dir., 1975-78, pres., 1978—. Bd. dirs. Uptown Community Health Assn., Chgo., 1969-70, United Scholarship Service, Denver, 1969-70, Adv. Council to FTC, 1969-70, Uptown Community Health Ctr., Chgo., 1971-74, Native Am. Com., Chgo., 1971-77, Comprehensive Health Council Chgo., 1974-75, Seven Nations Indian Opportunity Program, Central YMCA Community Coll., 1974-77. trustee Robert W. Rietz Am. Indian Scholarship Fund, Chgo., 1971-78; mem. exec. com. Edgewater-Uptown Community Mental Health Ctr., Chgo., 1974-75; cons. Health Manpower Devel. Corp., Washington, 1975, numerous Ill. pub. schs., 1978-82; chmn. Ill. Adv. Council in Indian Edn., 1978-79; mem. adv. council D; Arcy McNickle Ctr. for History of Am. Indian, Newberry Library, 1978-86; mem. commn. on women's affairs Office of Mayor, Chgo., 1984-85, mem. hunger task force, 1983-84; mem., presenter Gov.'s Conf. on Human Rights, Ill., 1983; bd. dirs. Crossroads Fund, 1985—, Chgo. Access Corp., 1986—; mem. venture grants com. United Way of Met. Chgo., 1984—, mem. agy. services com., 1983—. Mem. Regional Networking for Minority Women, Am. Indian Bus. Assn. (cons., bd. dirs. tng. and devel. program 1977-78). Home: 4880 N Hermitage St Chicago IL 60640 Office: Native Am Ednl Service Coll 2838 W Peterson Chicago IL 60659

SMITH, FERN MEYERSON, lawyer; b. San Francisco, Nov. 7, 1933; d. Samuel and Sophie (Blank) Meyerson; m. Don Avery Smith, Oct. 20, 1955 (div. 1977); children—Susan Elizabeth, Julie Ann; m. F. Robert Burrows, Feb. 25, 1984. A.A., Foothill Coll., 1970; B.A., Stanford U., 1972, J.D., 1975. Bar: Calif. 1975. Assoc. firm Bronson, Bronson & McKinnon, San Francisco, 1975-82, ptnr., 1982—, mem. hiring, mgmt. and personnel coms., active recruiting various law schs. Co-author article in legal publ. Mem. ABA, Calif. Bar Assn., San Francisco Bar Assn., Downtown Women Lawyers, Def. Research Inst., Phi Beta Kappa. Office: Bronson Bronson & McKinnon 555 California St San Francisco CA 94104

SMITH, FRAN KELLOGG, lighting designer; b. Chgo., Oct. 28, 1940; d. James Hull and Jean (Defrees) Kellogg; B.A., Pomona Coll., 1966; postgrad. Claremont Grad. Sch., 1966-68; B.S. in Interior Design, Woodbury Coll., 1973;

children—Wayne E. McConnell III, Scott Kellogg McConnell, Carol Jean McConnell, Christina Louise Smith. Jr. assoc. Omnia Lighting Cons., Los Angeles, 1971-72; lighting cons. Black Swarens Okada, Los Angeles, 1972-73; lighting cons./founder Luminae Inc., Los Angeles and San Francisco, 1973—; instr. U. Calif.-Berkeley, 1981, 82, UCLA, 1982—; lectr. in field. Bd. dirs. Villa Esperanza Sch. Retarded, 1970-72; mem. Nat. Council Interior Design Qualifications, 1984—; mem. jury Halo/Am. Soc. Interior Designers Lighting competition, 1977. Recipient Designers Lighting Forum Commemorative award, 1978; Pacifica award, 1980; Halo/ASID award, 1980. Mem. Am. Soc. Interior Designers (dir. 1981, liaison to Interior Design Educators Council 1981-83), Illuminating Engring. Soc., Designers Lighting Forum (chpt. pres. 1973-75, chpt. v.p. 1976-77, dir. 1973-77, mem. nat. com. 1973-76), Interior Design Educators Council (hon. life mem.), Mensa. Republican. Episcopalian. Clubs: Calif. State Coll. Faculty Wives (v.p. 1972), Indoor Light Gardening Soc. Am. Home: 315 Orange St San Gabriel CA 91776 Office: 2015 17th St San Francisco CA 94103

SMITH, FRANCES CHERRY, funeral director; b. Williamston, N.C., June 21; d. Leo and Omenella (Riddick) Cherry; m. Alfred J. Smith, Nov. 24, 1949; children—Randy A., Trent L. Grad. McAllister Sch. Embalming, N.Y.C., 1952. Lic. funeral dir., N.J. With David D. Woody Funeral Home, Newark, 1945-49; owner, operator Smith Funeral Home, Elizabeth, N.J., 1952—; pres. N.J. Bd. Mortuary Sci. Mem. Elizabeth Bd. Edn.; mem. Elizabeth Devel. Corp.; mem. Egenolf Nursery Adv. Bd.; Recipient Key to City of Elizabeth, 1976, Appreciation and Service award Northeast region Nat. Caucus Black Sch. Bd. Mems., 1985. Mem. Union County Negro Bus. and Profl. Women (Bus. Woman award 1980), North Jersey Negro Bus. and Profl. Women's Clubs (Profl. Woman of Yr. 1959), Women's Scholarship Club (Recognition award 1980, Service award 1980), Nat. Assn. Negro Bus. and Profl. Women (treas. com. for UN). Democrat. Lodge: Soroptimists. Office: Smith Funeral Home 45 Cherry St Elizabeth NJ 07202

SMITH, FRANCES PAULINE, medical librarian; b. Long Beach, Calif., Aug. 20, 1934; d. Walter Paul and Juanita (Deskin) Downing Goodnough; m. Roy Dean Scott, July 12, 1955 (div); 1 son, Robert Downing; m. 2d, Clarence Kalani Smith, Jr., June 6, 1977; 1 child, Amanda Lani; 1 stepson, Clarence Kalani III. A.A., Leeward Community Coll., 1972, A.S., 1973; B.A., Hawaii Pacific Coll., 1979; M.L.S., U. Hawaii, 1985. Library technician med. Hawaii Med. Library, Honolulu, 1972-74; designer med. library, med. librarian Straub Cinic and Hosp. Arnold Library, Honolulu, 1974—. Mem. Med. Library Assn., Spl. Libraries Assn., ALA, Med. Library Group Hawaii. Office: Straub Clinic and Hosp Inc Arnold Library 888 S King St Honolulu HI 96813

SMITH, GLENDA, real estate broker; b. Kirbyville, Tex., July 2, 1945; d. Horace Emery and Odessal (Rodgers) Sowell; m. David Ray Smith, Aug. 1, 1974 (div. Aug. 1977); children—Robert, Tammy. Student Eastfield Coll., Dallas, 1978-80; A.A., Richland Coll., Dallas, 1981. Exec. sec. Hunt Electronics, Dallas, 1969-73; account exec. Dallas Tex. Corp., 1973-75; Realtor assoc. Realty World Case, Mesquite, Tex., 1977-79; broker assoc. Realty World Herniage, Mesquite, 1979-80; broker, owner Realty World-Glenda Smith, Mesquite, 1980—; external v.p. exec. com. Realty World, Dallas, 1982-83, pres. exec. com., 1983-84, parliamentarian exec. com., 1984—. Recipient awards North Tex. region Realty World, 1977-79. Mem. Am. Bus. Women (pres. local chpt. 1984), Nat. Assn. Realtors, Tex. Assn. Realtors, Phi Theta Kappa. Avocations: singing; dancing; acting; sports; playing organ. Office: Realty World-Glenda Smith 4126 Gus Thomasson Rd Mesquite TX 75150

SMITH, GLORIA AUNGST, nurse; b. Kendallville, Ind., Sept. 24, 1959; d. Burnell Dean and Alice Jean (Beiswanger) Aungst; m. Michael H. Smith, Oct. 6, 1984. A. in Nursing, Purdue U., 1981. R.N., Ind. Nurse's aide, nurse McCray Meml. Hosp., Kendallville, 1980-82; charge nurse Claylor-Nickel Med. Ctr., Bluffton, Ind., 1982—. Vol. blood mobile dr. ARC, Bluffton, 1982—. Tri-Kappa scholar, 1978. Avocations: gardening; camping; sewing. Home: 0371 W 1100 N Ossian IN 46777 Office: Caylor-Nickel Med Ctr Bluffton IN

SMITH, GLORIA RICHARDSON, nursing educator; b. Chgo., Sept. 29, 1934; B.S. in Nursing, Wayne State U., 1955; M.P.H., U. Mich., 1959; cert. UCLA, 1971; M.A. in Anthropology, U. Okla., 1977, Ph.D., 1979. Public health nurse Detroit Vis. Nurse Assn., 1955-56, sr. public health nurse, 1957-58, asst. dist. office supr., 1959-63; asst. prof. nursing Tuskegee Inst. Sch. Nursing, Ala., 1963-66; asst. prof. nursing Albany (N.Y.) State Coll., 1966-68; cons. nurse home health care Okla. State Health Dept., 1968-70, dist. nurse supr., 1968-70, medicare nurse cons., 1970-71; asst. prof. U. Okla. Coll. Nursing, Oklahoma City, 1971-73, asso. prof., 1975-78, prof., 1978-83, dean, 1975-83; dir. Mich. Dept. Pub. Health, 1983—; mem. adv. com. nursing Okla. State Regents for Higher Edn., from 1973; cons. VA Hosp., 1975-77, HEW, 1977-78, U. Mich. External Rev. Sch. Nursing, 1980. Mem. Mayor's Com. to Study In-Migrants, Detroit, 1963; bd. dirs. St. Peter Claver Community Credit Union, 1961-63, YMCA, Oklahoma City, 1972-76. Recipient Outstanding Service award Franklin Settlement, 1963; Disting. Alumni award Wayne State U., 1984. Mem. Nat. League Nursing (dir. from 1979), Am. Nurses Assn. (mem. commn. on nursing edn. 1978-82), Okla. League Nursing, Midwest Alliance in Nursing (dir. 1977-80), Black Personnel (exec. com. 1974-76), Am. Assn. Colls. Nursing (exec. com. from 1976), Nat. Black Nurses Assn. (dir. 1972-78), Okla. State Nurses Assn. (Named Nurse of Yr. 1972), Am. Assn. for Higher Edn., Okla. State Assn. for Black Personnel in Higher Edn. (recording sec. 1976-78), Am. Acad. Nursing (governing council 1983-85), Assn. State and Territorial Health Officers, Am. Pub. Health Assn., Okla. Public Health Assn., Sigma Gamma Rho (Named Outstanding Sigma of Yr. 1963), Sigma Theta Tau. Contbr. articles on health care and nursing edn. to profl. publs. Office: Univ Oklahoma Health Sciences Center College Nursing PO Box 26901 Oklahoma City OK 73190*

SMITH, GRACIE BERNON, dress designer; b. Hyden, Ky., Aug. 1, 1932; d. Joe and Eva Lee (Howard) Maggard; m. William Robert Smith, June 10, 1972; children by previous marriage—Donald Eugene Turpin, Jr., Daniel Edwin Turpin. Student Nat. Sch. Dress Design-Chgo., 1955-58; student in real estate Purdue U., 1973. Tailor Sovern Tailors, Lafayette, Ind., 1965-68; mgr. Millers Sportswear, Lafayette, 1968-70; with Binker Realty, Lafayette, 1973-75; service contract dept. head Montgomery Ward, Lafayette, 1975-77; alteration dept. head Montgomery Ward, 1977-80; owner, operator Bernon Custom Fashions, Lafayette, 1955—; cons. local 4-H Clubs, 1983-86; local sales rep. Leiters Designer Fabrics, Kansas City, Mo., 1982-86; local sales mgr. House of Laird Fabrics, Lexington, Ky., 1985-86. Com. mem. Tippecanoe County Fair, Lafayette, 1983-85. Fellow The Custom Tailors and Designers Assn. Am., Nat. Assn. Female Execs. Baptist. Avocations: bowling; gardening; knitting; cooking; crocheting. Home: 2350 N 23d St Lafayette IN 47904 Office: Bernon Custom Fashions 2350 N 23 St Lafayette IN 47904

SMITH, HELEN CATHARINE, author; b. Chgo., June 7, 1903; d. J. A.; B.A., U. Calif. at Los Angeles, 1926; postgrad. U. Wis., 1954-56; M.Sc., Christian Coll., 1962, Ph.D., 1965, Psy.D., 1966; Ph.D. (hon.) Free U., hon. doctorate Gt. China Arts Coll., 1969, St. Olav's Acad., Sweden, 1969, Internat. Acad. Soverign Order Alfred Gt., Eng., 1969; J.D., Ohio Christian Coll., 1969; Ph.D., U. Reno (Nigeria), 1975; m. H. C. Smith, June 7, 1932; children—Glen Dean, DeEtta Ellen (Mrs. Gerald L. Amdahl), George Dale. Tchr. 2d grade Maple Lawn Sch., Clinton, Wis.; legal sec., Janesville, Wis., Office of City Atty., Evansville, Wis., 1933—; v.p., dir. Blue Moon poetry mag., 1952-57. Recipient 1st pl. award for article Herdman Meml. Competition Brit. Press, 1957; John Francis Sims Meml. award for poetry, 1955; award of honor UN Day, Philippines, 1967; laurel wreath, gold medal Pres. Philippines, 1967; certificate recognition Nat. Poetry Day Com., 1972; Distinguished Service award Wis. Jaycees, 1975, certificate Am. Bicentennial Research Inst., 1975; named Hon. Poet Laureate (Am.-Visayan), 1967; Internat. Woman of 1975 with laureate honors by Imelda R. Marcos. Fellow Intercontinental Biog. Assn.; mem. AAUW (awards poetry, short stories 1972), Wis. Regional Writers Assn. (sec. 1949-55, 61—, hon. life dir., leadership citation 1956, Jade Ring winner for short story 1957), Am. Poetry League, Wis. Fellowship Poets, Wis. Acad. Scis. Arts and Letters, Brit. Press Assn., United Poets Laureate Internat. (Karta award), Wis. Council for Writers (life, 2d pl. award for short story 1980), Centro Studie Scambi Internazionali Roma (medal of honor 1966-67, internat. exec. bd.), Wis. Edn. Assn., Wis. Regional Artists, State Hist. Soc. Wis., Accademia Internazionale Leonardo Da Vinci (Rome; Gold medallion 1972), Accademia Internaziale Di Pontzen, Am. Lit. Assn. (life), World Poetry Soc. (hon. life), UN Assn., Phi Beta Kappa (sustaining), Alpha Psi Omega, Sigma Iota Xi. Author: Laughing Child, books I, II, III, 1945, 46, 47; Off the Record, 1949; From the Countryside, 1952; Stars in My Eyes, 1954; Wind-Falls, 1955; Chiaroscura, 1964; But Not Yet, 1973; You Can't Cry All the Time, 1975. Editor: Evansville Anthology of Verse, 1952, No. Spring, anthology, 1956; Chiaroscura, 1964; Helen's Sketch Book, 1978; contbr. articles, stories to numerous mags., newspapers, anthologies. Home: 455 S 1st St Apt 19 Evansville WI 53536 Office: 14 W Main St Evansville WI 53536

SMITH, HILDA SYKES (MISTY MORN), performing arts studio executive; b. Balt.; d. Gradie McKinley and Blanche (Hill) Sykes; m. Leroy Smith, May 9, 1952; children—Roy Sheldon, Kelli Karen. B.S. in Phys. Edn., L.I. U., 1950. Interviewer, cashier Finlay's Jewelers, Bklyn., 1947-50; social worker Bur. Child Welfare, N.Y.C., 1950-57; instr., model Scotts Beauty Sch., Newark, 1961-66; broadcaster Sta. WHBI, Newark, Sta. WNJR, Newark, WCHA, Red Bank, N.J., 1961-69; dir. modeling Mildred Thomas Studio of Music, Newark, 1964-69; co-owner, dir. Bal-zac & Misty Morn Studio, West Orange, N.J., 1969—; dir. Ctr. Stage Performing Arts Studio, Mt. Tabor, N.J.; talent cons. and mgr., 1982—. Author: E.A.S.Y., 1985. Mem. United Bodywork and Massage Practitioners Inc. Office: Bal-zac & Misty Morn Studio 263 Main St West Orange NJ 07052

SMITH, INNES ADAMS COMER (MRS. EDWARD SAMUEL SMITH), civic worker; b. Birmingham, Ala., May 10, 1920; d. Robert Thornton and May (Adams) Comer; student Birmingham So. Coll., 1937-38; A.B., Randolph-Macon Woman's Coll., 1940; m. Edward Samuel Smith, May 5, 1942; children—Edward Samuel, Innes Smith Cameron Richards. Proof clk. First Nat. Bank, 1940-41; proof trainer Birmingham Trust Nat. Bank, 1941-43; censor U.S. Postal Censorship, 1943; receptionist Textron, Inc., 1943-44; teller Union Trust Co., 1961-62; new accounts clk. Chevy Chase br. Nat. Bank Washington, 1962-64; exec. v.p., dir. Logical Products, Inc., Balt., 1968-78. Active vol. work hosps., Birmingham, Washington and Balt., various fund drives; leader Cub Scouts, Boy Scouts Am., 1952-55. Mem. Jr. League Washington (fin. bd. 1956-57; dir. 1957-58), Jr. League Balt., Nat. Soc. Colonial Dames Am. in D.C., Nat. Soc. Daus. Barons of Runnymede, Descs. of Lords of Md. Manors, Order of Crown in Am., Kappa Delta. Democrat. Episcopalian. Clubs: Homesteaders Garden. Home: 3708 Taylor St Chevy Chase MD 20815

SMITH, IOLA RAGINS (MRS. JAMES ALEXANDER SMITH), educational psychologist; b. Phila.; d. Edward and Callie (Watkins) Ragins; B.A., Pa. State U., 1956; M.A., Am. U., 1960; Ph.D., Cath. U. Am., 1966; m. James Alexander Smith, Sept. 1, 1956; children—Staci Gabrielle, Shanon Gervaise. Lectr., Cath. U. Am., 1963-67; assoc. prof. edn. Morgan State U., Balt., 1966-69, prof. edn., 1969—, acting chmn. dept., 1972, 78, also coordinator Office Contracts, Research and Ednl. Services, 1984—; lectr. Howard U., 1969—; cons., evaluation in-service tchr. workshop on desegregation Washington Pub. Schs., 1967; cons. workshop on sch. desegregation U. Md., 1967; cons. spl. planning Inst. for Center on Urban Studies, Morgan State Coll., 1968, Calvert County (Md.) Pub. Schs., 1969; alt. del. in ednl. adminstrn. Am. Council on Edn., 1977; speaker Md. Reading Assn., 1977. Recipient Distinguished Tchr. of Year award Morgan State Coll., 1969. Mem. LWV, Citizens Planning and Housing Assn., Delta Sigma Theta, Pi Lambda Theta, Pi Gamma Mu, Phi Sigma Iota. Clubs: Jack and Jill, Links (pres. Columbia chpt.), Epicureans. Co-editor: Educational Psychology and Teaching, 1968—; contbr. articles to profl. publs. Home: 11216 Green Dragon Ct Hobbits Glen Columbia MD 21044 Office: Morgan State U Coldspring Ln and Hillen Rd Baltimore MD 21239

SMITH, ISABELLE BURNS, corporate secretary; b. N.Y.C., Sept. 2, 1924; d. Robert Thomas and Catherine Dubourdieu (Neil) Burns; m. Raymond L. Smith, May 18, 1947; children—Suzanne Culin, Lynne Smith. Student Merchants & Bankers Bus. Coll., 1942. Sec., adminstrv. asst. various corps., 1942-52; adminstrv. asst. Food Concepts, Inc., Rutherford, N.J., 1969-82, corporate exec. asst., 1982-84, corporate sec., 1984—; mem. adv. bd. Bergen Community Coll. Sec. Scis., Paramus, N.J., 1978-82. Recipient TWIN award Tribute to Women in Industry, Ridgewood, N.J., 1979. Mem. Profession Secs. Internat. (pres. Bergen County chpt 1978-79, Sec. of Yr. 1979), Nat. Assn. Female Execs. Presbyterian. Avocations: travelling; dancing; photography. Office: Food Concepts Inc 290 Veterans Blvd Rutherford NJ 07070

SMITH, JANE SCHNEBERGER, city clerk; b. Chgo., Aug. 9, 1928; d. Frank R. and Marion (Durante) Schneberger; m. Z. Erol Smith, Jr., Oct. 28, 1950 (div. 1974); children—Suzan McCue, Tracy, Cameron Farley, Z. Erol III, Kimberly, Scott. B.A. in Chemistry, U. Colo., 1950; M.A. in Communication, Mich. State U., 1978, also postgrad. Chemist, Kellogg Switchboard, Chgo., 1950-51; tchr. Crab Orchard Sch., Palos Heights, Ill., 1969-70; staff advisor South Cook County Girl Scouts, Harvey, Ill., 1970-72; program and tng. dir. Mich. Capitol council Girl Scouts U.S., Lansing, 1972-75; dir. service learning ctr. Mich. State U., East Lansing, 1975-81; city clk. City of Ashland, Wis., 1981—; cons. vol. adminstrn., Mich., Wis., 1975—. Contbr. articles to profl. jours. Vice pres. South Cook County Girl Scout Council, Harvey, Ill., 1967-69 (Thanks badge 1972), Mich. Capitol Girl Scout Council, Lansing, 1976-78 (cert. appreciation 1975); bd. dirs. Lansing RSVP, 1976-81, Ashland Mus., 1985—, Ptnrs. in Recovery, 1985—, New Horizons, 1985—. Mem. Internat. Assn. Municipal Clks., Wis. Municipal Clks. Assn. (dist. dir. 1984—). Roman Catholic. Club: Am. Bus. Women's Assn. (scholarship chmn. 1985) (Ashland). Lodge: Zonta (pres. 1979-81). Avocations: stained glass, gardening. Home: 700 MacArthur St Ashland WI 54806 Office: City Ashland 601 W 2d St Ashland WI 54806

SMITH, JANET SUE, association executive; b. Chgo., Jan. 15, 1945; d. Curtis Edwin and Margaret Louise (Yost) Smith; B.A., Ind. U., 1967. Sales mgr. Marshall Field & Co., Chgo., 1968-70, programmer, 1970-72; sr. programmer, analyst Trailer Train Co., Chgo., 1972-75; data base spl. studies and systems devel. mgr. Railinc-Assn. Am. R.R.s, Washington, 1975-85, asst. v.p., 1985—. Nat. student v.p. YWCA, 1966-67, v.p. planning and fin., 1982-85; bd. dirs. Guide Internat., 1981-85, Friends of the Nat. Zoo; advisor Jr. Achievement. Mem. Ind. U. Alumni Assn. (life), Am. Council R.R. Women, Women's Transp. Seminar. Home: 2000 N St NW Washington DC 20036 Office: 20 F St NW Washington DC 20001

SMITH, JANET THOMAE, nurse, wholesale distributor; b. Fond Du Lac, Wis., July 30, 1951; d. Herbert Edward and Agnes Katherine (Stengl) Thomae; m. Patrick Charles Fletcher. Oct. 18, 1974 (div. 1980) 1 child, Alicia Ann; m. Ray R. Smith, Jr., Nov. 16, 1984. R.N. Emergency room nurse St. Elizabeth Hosp., Appleton, Wis., 1972-74; Mercy Med. Center, Oshkosh, Wis., 1974-80; v..p., pub. Benco Ltd., Viroqua, Wis., 1980-81; pres., pub. Peoples Med. Marketplace Inc., Marshfield, Wis., 1981-83; propr. Bristow Village, Marshfield, 1982—; nurse coronary care unit St. Joseph Hosp., Marshfield, 1983—. Editor, pub. Emergency Care Handbook, 1980; contbr. posters, cartoons, instr. materials in field. Fellow Nat. Assn. Female Execs., Nat. Splty. Merchandisers Assn. Republican. Roman Catholic. Home: 200 N Willow Ave Marshfield WI 54449

SMITH, JANIE WILKINS, chemical company information educator; b. Columbia, La., Apr. 5, 1930; d. James Climent and Hester (Bibb) Wilkins; B.A., La. Tech. U., 1951; postgrad. Fla. State U., 1962-70, U. Fla., 1962-63, U. South Fla., 1963-64; m. Thomas L. Smith, Nov. 3, 1950 (div.); children—Linda Karen, Thomas, Jr., Eric Andrew. English librarian Morehouse Parish Sch. Bd., Bastrop, La., 1951-52, Union Parish Sch. Bd., Farmerville, La., 1952-56, East Carroll Parish Sch. Bd., Lake Providence, La., 1957-60, Union Parish Schs., Farmerville, 1970-75, Ouachita Parish Schs., Monroe, La., 1976-79; ref. librarian Ouachita Parish Public Library, 1960-62; librarian lang. arts Brevard County Bd. Public Instrn., Titusville, Fla., 1962-70; info. specialist Columbian Chems. Co., Swartz, La., 1980—. Mem. AAUW (membership com.), Spl. Library Assn., Nat. Library Assn. Methodist. Home: 409 Birchwood Dr Monroe LA 71203 Office: PO Box 147 Marion LA 71260

SMITH, JEAN MINERVA, library educator; b. Florence, Oreg., Feb. 18, 1934; d. Theodore William and Hazel Marie (Schoenemann) Engelking; m. Harold Joseph Smith, June 2, 1957; children—Timothy William, Esther Jean, Daniel Joseph, David Harold. B.S. in English cum laude, Evangel Coll., 1967; M.L.S., U. Oreg., 1968. Asst. librarian, book store mgr. Northwest Coll. Seattle, 1956-58; asst. librarian Evangel Coll., Springfield, Mo., 1962-68, catalog librarian, 1968-72; asst. prof. library sci. Sch. of the Ozarks, Point Lookout, Mo., 1972—; chmn. faculty, 1985—, sec., 1983-85. Contbr. articles to mags. U.S. Office of Edn. fellow, 1967-68. Mem. Mo. Assn. Edn. and Communication Tech., Mo. Assn. Sch. Librarians, Mo. Library Assn., On Line Audio-Visual Catalogers Assn., AAUW. Avocations: reading, gardening, traveling. Home: Star Rt 1 Box 584 Hollister MO 65672 Office: Sch of the Ozarks Point Lookout MO 65726

SMITH, JEAN WEBB (MRS. WILLIAM FRENCH SMITH), civic worker; b. Los Angeles; d. James Ellwood and Violet (Hughes) Webb; B.A. summa cum laude, Stanford U., 1940; m. George William Vaughan, Mar. 14, 1942 (dec. Sept. 1963); children—George William, Merry; m. 2d, William French Smith, Nov. 6, 1964. Mem. Nat. Vol. Service Adv. Council (ACTION), 1973-76, vice chmn., 1974-76; dir. Beneficial Standard Corp., 1976-85. Vol., Nat Center, 1977—; bd. councillors U. So. Calif. Sch. Performing Arts, 1976—; bd. dirs. Los Angeles chpt. ARC, 1979—, Community TV So. Calif. (KCET); mem. Calif. Arts Commn., 1971-74, vice chmn., 1973-74; bd. dirs. The Founders, Music Center, Los Angeles, 1971-74; bd. dirs. costume council Los Angeles County Mus. Art, 1971-73; bd. dirs. United Way, Inc., 1973-80; trustee Calif. Hist. Soc., 1970-71; bd. dirs. Hosp. Good Samaritan, 1973-80; mem. exec. com., 1975-80; mem. nat. bd. dirs. Boys' Clubs Am., 1977-80; bd. dirs. Los Angeles chpt. NCCJ, 1977-80, Nat. Symphony Orch., 1980-85; mem. adv. bd. Salvation Army, 1979—; mem. President's Commn. on White House Fellowships, 1980—. Named Woman of Yr. for community service Los Angeles Times, 1958; recipient Citizens of Yr. award Boys Clubs Greater Los Angeles, 1982. Mem. Jr. League of Los Angeles (pres. 1954-55), Assn. Jr. Leagues of Am. (dir. Region XII, 1956-58, pres. 1958-60), Phi Beta Kappa, Kappa Kappa Gamma. Home: 1256 Oak Grove Ave San Marino CA 91108

SMITH, JEANNE, marketing research and telemarketing company executive, consultant; b. Richmond, Va., May 2, 1955; d. John Herman and Joyce (Divers) Crostic; m. Donald Wayne Smith, July 11, 1976. Nurse Richmond Pub. Schs., 1973; freelance field service worker, Richmond, 1974-80; field service worker N.Am. Mktg., Richmond, 1981-82, field service supr., 1982-83, dir. field services, 1983; owner, operator Smith Research Ctr., Richmond, 1983—. Served with U.S. Army, 1973-76. Mem. Am. Mktg. Assn., Mktg. Research Assn. Republican. Baptist. Clubs: Va. Bass'n Gals (sec., treas.), Lady Bass. Lodge: Women of Moose. Avocation: professional bass fisherwoman. Office: Smith Research Ctr PO Box 13676 Richmond VA 23225

SMITH, JENNIE BRUSILOW, accountant; b. New Orleans, Apr. 11, 1955; d. Anshel and Marilyn (Dow) Brusilow; m. Jack Timothy Smith, May 9, 1981; children—Stephen Michael, Amy Leigh. B.B.A., U. Tex., 1977. C.P.A., Tex. Tax mgr. Arthur Young & Co., Dallas, 1977-82; tax mgr., cons. Dan Krausse, Dallas, 1982-84; pvt. practice acctg., Dallas, 1984—. Mem. Am. Women's Soc. C.P.A.s, Am. Inst. C.P.A.s, Tex. Soc. C.P.A.s, North Dallas C. of C. Home and Office: 1908 Manor Ln Plano TX 75075

SMITH, JENNIFER C., city official; b. Boston, Nov. 3, 1952; d. Herman J. and Margaree L. S.; B.A. in English, Union Coll., 1974; M.A., Fairfield U., 1982. Claim rep. Travelers Ins. Co., Boston, 1974-75, supr., N.J., 1976-78, regional asst., account exec., Hartford, Conn., 1979-81, tng. adminstr., 1981, asst. dir. casualty and property depts., 1981-83, sec. casualty and property depts., 1983-85; personnel dir. City of Hartford, 1984-85, asst. city mgr., 1985—; claim rep. Sentry Ins. Co., N.J., 1975-76. Chmn. Nat. Alliance Bus. Youth Motivational Task Force; chmn. Heart Assn.; bd. dirs. Capitol region United Way. Mem. Am. Soc. Tng. and Devel., Nat. Assn. Female Execs., Project to Increase Mastery of Math., Hartford Women's Network, Travelers Forum. Contbr. articles to Conn. Bus. Times. Office: 550 Main St Hartford CT 061015

SMITH, JESSICA UDALL, Realtor; b. Thatchek, Ariz., Oct. 4, 1918; d. Jesse Addison and Lela (Lee) Udall; m. Milan Dale Smith, July 25, 1941; children—Milan Dale, Jr., Melanie, Charlotte, Gregory, Kathleen, Nicholas, Michael, Gordon, Lisa, Jessica-Ann. Student Brigham Young U., 1936-39. Realtor assoc. Tom Fannin Realty, Mesa, Ariz., 1977-78; Realtor assoc. Ariz.West Realty, Mesa, 1978-80, Realtor, 1980-81; Realtor, B.R. Brown & Co., Mesa, 1981—. Mem. Ariz. Assn. Realtors (Million Dollar Club 1979-82), Nat. Assn. Realtors. Republican. Mormon. Home: 1555 E Elmwood Circle Mesa AZ 85203 Office: BR Brown and Co 244 N Country Club St Mesa AZ 85201

SMITH, JO ANN DOKE, corporate executive, consultant; b. Gainesville, Fla., May 9, 1939; d. Lacy Doke; m. Cedrick M. Smith, Jr., 1957; children—Marty, Terri. Grad. Fla. Sch. Real Estate Law. Sec.-treas. Smith Bros., Wacahoota, Fla., 1961—; v.p. Smith Constrn. Co., Williston, Fla., 1962—; mktg. and pub. relations cons. White Meat Packers of Fla., Ocala, 1981—; chmn. bd., dir. Jacksonville br. Res. Bank of Atlanta; mem. Press Adv. Com. for Trade Negotiations, 1984—, U.S. Dept. Agr. Animal Tech. Adv. Com. on Livestock and Livestock Products, 1979-80, Meat Pricing Task Force, 1979—, Fgn. Animal Disease Adv. Com., 1979-80, Adv. Council Fla. Dept. Agr. and Consumer Services, 1983—, PRIDE bd. cattle adv. com., State of Fla. Gov. Livestock Industry Inst., Kansas City, Mo., 1981-84; mem. medicine adv. com. Coll. Vet.-U. Fla.; chmn. bd. trustees Monroe Regional Med. Ctr., Ocala, Fla., 1971-82; treas. Wacahoota Methodist Ch.; pres. McIntosh Civic League, Williston Jr. Women's Club; chmn. agrl. div., exec. com. United Way. Recipient Sioux City Stockyards and Am. Nat. CowBelles Disting. Service award, 1980; named Farm Wife of Yr., Fla. Dept. Agr., 1974; Progressive Farmer's Woman of Yr. in Agr., 1982; Woman of Yr. in Agr., Fla. Dept. Agr. and Consumer Services. Mem. Nat. Cattlemen's Assn. (exec. com. 1982—, pres. 1985; Service award Fla. Cattlemen's Assn. 1968, bd. dirs. Nat. Live Stock and Meat Bd. 1982-85), Am. Nat. CowBelles (v.p., exec. com. 1976-78). Democrat. Avocation: gardening. Home: Route 1 PO Box 350 Micanopy FL 32667 Office: Nat Cattlemen's Assn 5420 S Quebec PO Box 3469 Englewood CO 80155

SMITH, JO ANNE, journalist; b. Mpls., Mar. 18, 1930; d. Robert Bradburn and Virginia Mae S.; B.A., U. Minn., 1951, M.A., 1957. Wire and sports editor Rhinelander (Wis.) Daily News, 1951-52; staff corr., night mgr. UP, Mpls., 1952-56; interim instr. U. N.C., Chapel Hill, 1957-58; instr. U. Fla., Gainesville, 1959-65, asst. prof. journalism, communications, 1965-68, asso. prof., 1968-76, prof., 1976—, Disting. lectr., 1977; dir. Fla. Freedom of Info. Clearing House. Active, Friends of Library, Alachua County Humane Soc. Named Tchr. of Yr., U. Fla. Coll. Journalism, 1973, 74, 75, 76, 81, 86, Outstanding Tchr. Journalism Dept. U. Fla., 1973, 74, 75, 76; recipient Outstanding Prof. award Fla. Blue Key, 1976; Danforth asso.,1976-82. Mem. Women in Communication, Soc. Profl. Journalists, Assn. Edn. in Journalism, Phi Beta Kappa, Kappa Tau Alpha. Democrat. Unitarian. Author: JM409 Casebook and Study Guide, 1976; Mass Communications Law Casebook, 1980, 3d edit., 1985. Home: 208 NW 21 Terr Gainesville FL 32603 Office: 2082 Weimer Hall U Fla Gainesville FL 32611

SMITH, JOAN ANETHA, county recorder; b. Greenport, N.Y., Oct. 20, 1941; d. John Albert and Anetha Belle (Young) Litchard; m. Robert Earl Smith, Aug. 26, 1962; 1 child, David Robert. Grad. high sch., Riverhead, N.Y., 1959. Mortgage clk. Riverhead Savs. Bank, N.Y., 1959-60, sec. to bank sec., 1960-61; legal sec. Haupert, Robertson & Johnson, Marshalltown, Iowa, 1961-69; free-lance legal sec., Marshalltown, 1969-78; county recorder Marshall County, Marshalltown, 1979—. Sec., Marshall County Republican Com., 1975, credentials chmn., 1978. Mem. Marshall County Legal Secs. Assn. (pres. 1968-69), Iowa Assn. Legal Secs. (publ. editor, state conv. chmn. 1974-76), Iowa Dist. I Recorder Assn. (pres. 1979-80), Iowa Assn. County Recorders. Republican. Congregationalist. Avocations: reading; crocheting; playing cards; camping. Home: 608 W Nevada St Marshalltown IA 50158 Office: Marshall County Recorder Marshall County Courthouse Marshalltown IA 50158

SMITH, JOAN KAREN, educator; b. Oak Park, Ill., Mar. 17, 1939; d. Raymond D. and Mildred E. Johnsos; m. L. Glenn Smith, Aug. 7, 1971; 1 son, Jeffrey Robert. B.S., U. Ill., 1961; M.S., Iowa State U., 1970, Ph.D., 1976. Tchr. public schs., Champaign, Ill., 1961-64, Ames, Iowa, 1964-65; instr. Des Moines Area Community Coll., 1969-70, counselor, 1970-71; teaching asst., instr. Iowa State U., 1973-76, postdoctoral fellow, 1976-78; asst. prof. founds. of edn. Ill. State U., Normal, 1978-81; asst. prof. Loyola U., Chgo., 1981-83, assoc. prof., 1983—, assoc. dean of Grad. Sch., 1983—. Mem. Am. Ednl. Studies Assn. (mem. ex-officio exec. council 1977-81), Orgn. Am. Historians, Comparative and Internat. Edn. Soc., Council Grad. Schs. of U.S., Soc. Profs. Edn., Delta Kappa Gamma (pres. chpt. 1976-78). Club: Lakeside Country (Bloomington, Ill.). Co-Author: Lives in Education; People and Ideas in the Development of Education, 1984; editor: (with L. Glenn Smith) The Development of American Education: Selected Readings, 1976; Ellas Flagg Young: Portrait of a Leader, 1979; mng. editor Ednl. Studies, 1977-79, editor, 1979-81; mem. editorial adv.

bd. Jour. of Thought, 1982-85, Vitae Scholasticae, 1983—. Office: Loyola Univ Grad Sch and School of Education 820 N Michigan Ave Chicago IL 60611

SMITH, JOAN LEITA, school media specialist; b. Syracuse, N.Y., Sept. 17, 1938; d. James and Lucille (Fiske) Wilcox; m. Robert David Smith, July 22, 1961; children—Kenneth, Karen, B.S. in Elem. Edn., SUNY-Cortand, 1960; M.A. in Library Sci., Ind. U., 1964. Tchr., Bay Shore (N.Y.) Sch. Dist. 1960-61, Mad River Twp., Dayton, Ohio, 1962, 64; bookmobile children's librarian Dayton and Montgomery County, Ohio, 1962-63; sch. library media specialist Rome (N.Y.) Sch. Dist., 1979—; ch. librarian Bowie United Meth. Ch., Md., 1970-72. Active PTA, Rome, 1976-82; leader Girl Scouts U.S.A., Rome, 1974-81. Mem. ALA, Central N.Y. Library Assn., N.Y. Library Assn., AAUW, Beta Phi Mu, Pi Lambda Theta. Clubs: Air Force Officers Wives. Address: 18 Pleasant Dr Rome NY 13440

SMITH, JOANNE SMITH, real estate executive; b. Pine Bluff, Ark., July 3, 1927; d. Jesse Guy and Joe Alexander (Howell) Smith; m. Jack Perdue Smith, June 19, 1948; children—Jeffrey Guy, Jan Gail, Edward Howell. Student Mary Baldwin Coll., 1945-46; B.S. with honors, U. Ark., 1949. Registered real estate broker; registered apt. mgr. Nat. Assn. Homebuilders. Paralegal Coleman Ganett Ramsay and Cox, Pine Bluff, Ark., 1969-71; property mgr. Theis-Beard Realty, Pine Bluff, 1971-75; exec. v.p. Theis-Smith Property Mgmt., Pine Bluff, 1975-85; pres. First Capital Mgmt. Group. Inc., 1985—, Capstone Properties, Inc., 1985—; v.p. Mid-Am. Investment Corp., Pine Bluff, 1980-85, also Midland Corp., Smith Paper Products Co.; bd. dirs. Pine Bluff Bd. Realtors, 1981-83; pres. Ark. chpt. Inst. Real Estate Mgmt., Little Rock, 1978-79; mem. legis. affairs and research com. Nat. Inst. Real Estate Mgmt., Chgo., 1980-81. Chmn. bd. Southeast Ark. Arts and Sci. Ctr., Pine Bluff, 1982-83; co-chmn. fund drive United Way, 1983. Recipient President's award Ark. Realtors Assn., 1977-78; named Boss of Yr., Credit Women Internat., 1978, Realtor of Yr., Pine Bluff Bd. Realtors, 1982. Mem. Pine Bluff C. of C. (bd. dirs. 1978-81), Realtors Nat. Mktg. Inst. (cert. comml. investment mem.), Inst. Real Estate Mgmt. (cert. property mgr.), Internat. Coll. Real Estate Cons. Profls., Ark. Assn. Realtors (grad Realtors Inst.), Presbyterian (deacon). Club: Junior League (Pine Bluff, Ark.). Home: 17 Elm Woods Circle Pine Bluff AR 71603 Office: First Capital Mgmt Group Fin Bldg Suite 201 PO Box 8824 Pine Bluff AR 71611

SMITH, JOSEPHINE WOOLLEY, advertising executive; b. Findlay, Ohio, Mar. 15, 1934; d. Walton Douglas and Charlotte Josephine (Bente) Woolley; B.A., Sarah Lawrence Coll., 1954; m. Lawrence Sophian, June 22, 1954; children—Celia, Catherine. Advt. copywriter Batten, Barton, Durstine & Osborn, 1954-62; copy supr. Ogilvy & Mather, N.Y.C., 1962-70, v.p., 1970-73, creative dir., 1973, sr. v.p., 1974—. Office: 2 E 48th St New York City NY 10017

SMITH, JUANITA BÉRARD, lawyer; b. St. Martinville, La., Oct. 23, 1937; d. Zachary Joseph and Lucille Marie (Bourque) Bérard; m. Mark Christian Smith III, Mar. 16, 1956; children—Christian, Brett, Robyn, Tara. B.A., Loyola U., New Orleans, 1979, J.D., 1982. Bar: La. 1982. Pres., Orleans Securities, Inc., New Orleans, 1982—; sole practice, New Orleans, 1982—. Mem. ABA, Fed. Bar Assn., La. Bar Assn., Am. Trial Lawyers Assn., La. Trial Lawyers Assn. Democrat. Roman Catholic. Office: J B Smith Profl Law Corp 1539 Soniat St New Orleans LA 70115

SMITH, JUANITA (NITA), educator; b. Ionia, Mich., Sept. 10, 1928; d. Wayne H. and Ernestine M. (Green) Bradley; student Yuba Jr. Coll., Marysville, Calif., 1957-58; m. Robert L. Smith, Mar. 1, 1969 (dec. 1978); children—Suzanne Foster, Edward A. Odgen, Jr., Dawne Marie Ogden. Owner, pres. Mid-State Coll. and Secretarial Service of Stanislaus, Modesto, Calif., 1974—. Mem. Nat. Fedn. Ind. Bus., Better Bus. Bur. Modesto, Modesto C. of C., Bus. and Profl. Women's Club (v.p. Sonora, Calif. 1973). Republican. Office: Mid-State Coll 1314 H St Modesto CA 95354

SMITH, JUDITH BROOKS, marketing executive; b. Shreveport, La., Sept. 10, 1947; d. Louis Andrew and Hazel Lula (Veuleman) Brooks; m. Ronald Edward Smith, Aug. 30, 1968 (div. 1976). B.Bus. magna cum laude, Baylor U., 1969. Sales promotion asst. Success Motivation, Waco, Tex., 1969; advt. asst. Shell Chem. Co., Houston, 1970-71; bus. devel. asst. Golemon & Rolfe Architects, Houston, 1973; mktg. mgr. Drawing Bd., Dallas, 1976-80, Parker Garrick, Dallas, 1980-82; mgr. planning Heublein, Chgo., 1982-84, mktg. mgr., Hartford, Conn., 1984—. Mem. Am. Mktg. Assn. (pres. Dallas chpt. 1982) Marketer of Yr. candidate 1980), Bus. and Profl. Women, Women's Assn. Allied Beverge Industries. Theta Chi. Office: Heublein Munson Rd Farmington CT 06034

SMITH, JUDY GOLDSTEIN, lawyer; b. Chgo., June 15, 1950; d. Sidney Julius and Rose Ellen (Crane) G.; m. Willard S. Smith, Jr., Aug. 14, 1982; children—Adam David, Charles Jacob. B.A., U. Wis., 1972; J.D., Northwestern U., 1975. Bar: Ill. 1975, D.C. 1980. Staff atty. antitrust div. U.S. Dept. Justice, Washington, 1975-80, asst. U.S. atty., Phila., 1980—, chief Pres.'s drug task force and narcotics sect., 1986—. Mem. ABA (chmn. newsletter com. govt. litigation com. Litigation Sect. 1983—, RICO com. Criminal Justice Sect. 1985—), Omicron Delta Epsilon, Sigma Epsilon Sigma. Office: US Attys Office 601 Market St Philadelphia PA 19106

SMITH, JUDY YAPSUGA, stockbroker; b. Hazleton, Pa., Sept. 13, 1951; d. Leo Michael and Irene (Kanapka) Y.; B.S., Bloomsburg State Coll., 1972; M.S., U. Scranton, 1975; m. James J. Smith, Jr., Sept. 13, 1980. Tchr., Hazleton Area Sch. Dist., 1972-77; account exec. Merrill Lynch Pierce Fenner & Smith, Phila., 1977-80, coordinator estate and legal services, also money mgmt. and planning div., 1979-80; stockbroker E.F. Hutton, Strafford, Pa., 1980-81, Janney, Montgomery, Scott, Cherry Hill, N.J., 1981—; instr. Ogontz and Delaware County campuses Pa. State U., 1981—; speaker investment seminars, Phila. Bar Assn., Jewish Women's League, Paralegal Assn. Mem. Evesham Twp. Zoning Bd. Adjustment, 1984—, pres., 1985-86. Mem. NEA, PA. State (pres.-elect. dist. 5 1976-77), Hazleton Area (pres. elect 1976-77) edn. assns., Internat. Fedn. Bus. and Profl. Women (2d v.p. 1975-76, 1st v.p. 1976-77; 1st v.p. Camden County, N.J. chpt. 1983-84, program chmn. 1983-84, named Young Career Woman of Yr.), Nat. Assn. Securities Dealers Assn., Internat. Assn. Cert. Fin. Planners, N.J. Assn. Women Bus. Owners (state trustee 1983-84, fin. chmn. chpt. 1983-84), Internat. Platform Assn. Home: 302 Roberts Ln Marlton NJ 08053 Office: 1909 E Marlton Pike PO Box 5473 Cherry Hill NJ 08053

SMITH, KAREN A., marketing executive; b. Phila., Oct. 31, 1958; d. Richard A. and JoAnne E. (Heil) Smith. B.S. in Biology, Del. Valley Coll. Sci. and Agr., 1980. Tech. service rep. Nat. Can Corp., Piscataway, N.J., 1981-82; sales rep. patient care div. Johnson & Johnson, Balt., 1982-83, sr. sales rep., 1983-85, div. sales trainer, 1983-85, asst. product dir., New Brunswick, N.J., 1985-86; mktg. mgr. J & J Profl. Mktg., Piscataway, N.J., 1986—. Office: Johnson & Johnson Hosp Services PO Box 4000 New Brunswick NJ 08903

SMITH, KAREN LOUISE, communications company executive; b. Baton Rouge, Dec. 20, 1954; d. James Wilbur Smith and Carolyn (May) Carper; m. Ralph Edwin Hammond, Dec. 17, 1985. Student La. State U., 1973-75; B.S. in Journalism, U. Colo., 1978; paralegal cert. U. Tex.-Arlington, 1981. Paralegal clk. U.S. atty. for No. Dist. Tex., Dallas, 1981; news reporter Lakewood Sentinel, Colo., 1978; triex rep. Pkwy. Pontiac, Dallas, 1983—; comml. account rep. U.S. Telecom, Dallas, 1984; mktg. rep. Allnet Communications Services, Dallas, 1985—; gen. reporter DeSoto News Advt., 1979; bus. and real estate reporter Mid-Cities Daily News, 1980. Editor: Ennis Press, 1982. Vol., George McGovern for Pres., Baton Rouge, 1972; campaign mgr. for mayoral candidate, Cedar Hill, Tex., 1979; vol. Jimmy Carter for Pres., Fort Worth, 1980. Dallas Assn. Legal Assts. scholar, 1981. Mem. Soc. Profl. Journalists. Avocations: reading business magazines; photography; seeing movies. Home: 2604 Briar Glenn Ln Apt 1111 Arlington TX 76006 Office: Allnet Communications Services 2323 Bryan St Dallas TX 75201

SMITH, KATHLEEN ANN, medical technologist; b. Buffalo, Mar. 13, 1935; d. Joseph John and Rose Ann (Starke) S.; B.A., Mercyhurst Coll., 1956. From chemist to supr. hemostasis lab. Hamot Hosp., Erie, Pa., 1956-69; with Warner Lambert Co., 1969-85, supr. hemostasis ednl. services, 1972-85; with Organon Teknika Co., 1985—; adv. bd. Morris County Coll., 1980-86; presentor seminars in field. Named Med. Technologist of Yr. in N.J., 1982. Mem. Am. Soc. Med. Tech. (chmn. hemotology-hemostasis sect. 1982-84), Am. Soc. Clin. Pathology, N.J. Soc. Med. Tech. (pres. 1975), Alpha Mu Tau. Republican. Roman Catholic. Club: Morristown (N.J.) Woman's. Co-author Hemostasis Manual. Assoc. editor Clotters Corner, 1980—. Office: 201 Tabor Rd Morris Plains NJ 07950

SMITH, KATHRYN ANN, advertising executive; b. Harvey, Ill., Mar. 30, 1955; d. Kenneth Charles and Barbara Joan (Wise) S.; m. Donald Eugene Stonerock, Jr., Oct. 27, 1973 (div. Apr. 1977); m. Charles David Okoren, Oct. 31, 1980; 1 stepchild, Gwynne Marie. Student Art Inst. Chgo., 1973. Advt. salesperson Calumet Index, Inc., Riverdale, Ill., 1974-77, Towne & Country Ind., Hammond, 1977-78; owner, sales person Ad-Com, Merrillville, Ind., 1978—. Dir., producer cable TV comml., 1982. Mem. Advt. Agy. Owners Assn. (chair 1985-86). Avocations: painting, flying, outdoor activities.

SMITH, KATHRYN BAKER, educational administrator, economist; b. Atlanta, Feb. 8, 1946; d. William Martin Ross and Mildred (Walker) Ross Eatmon; m. William Hugh Baker, III, June 10, 1965 (div.); 1 child, William Hugh IV; m. R.C. Smith, Nov. 22, 1979. Student Lubbock Christian Coll., 1963-64, U. N.Mex., 1964-65, Fla. State U., 1968; B.A., U. Tex.-Austin, 1974, M.A., 1978. Research assoc. Ctr. for Study of Human Resources, Austin, Tex., 1975-76; field researcher MDC, Inc., Chapel Hill, N.C., 1976-78; research assoc. Nat. Rural Ctr., Austin, 1976-79; statewide coordinator policy, planning, and programs N.C. Dept. Nat. Resources and Community Devel., Employment and Tng., 1979-82; asst. to state pres. for policy Dept. of Community Colls., Raleigh, N.C., 1982—; dir. NC REAL Enterprises, 1985—; adv. bd. Small Bus. and Tech. Devel. Ctr., 1985—; cons. on employment and tng. Co-author: Rural Jobs from Rural Public Works, 1979; contbr. articles to profl. jours. Bd. dirs. N.C. Women's Forum, 1984-87; bd. dirs., sec. Tex. Housing Devel. Corp., 1977-79; affirmative action com. Democratic Party of Tex., 1974; exec. sec. Young Dems. of Tex., 1973-75. Office: Dept of Community Colls 116 W Edenton St Raleigh NC 27603

SMITH, KRALEEN STANFIELD, information specialist, librarian; b. Swindon, Eng., June 5, 1958; came to U.S. 1958; d. James Krahe and Marjorie Janette (King) Stanfield; m. Tolby Lynn Smith, Jan. 5, 1985. B.A. cum laude, Tex. Woman's U., 1980, M.L.S., 1981. Info. specialist Price Waterhouse, Dallas, 1981—. Mem. Spl. Libraries Assn., Dallas Soc. Acctg. Librarians (pres. 1983-85), Dallas Assn. Law Librarians (2d v.p. 1985), Beta Phi Mu. Baptist. Home: 10336 Chelmsford Dallas TX 75217 Office: Price Waterhouse 1400 First City Center Dallas TX 75201

SMITH, LAURIE KATHRYN, judge; b. Eugene, Oreg., Aug. 1, 1938; d. Laurence Edwin and Georgia Ruth (Staton) Fischer; m. Peter Evan Smith, July 27, 1962 (div. June 1969); m. 2d, William Frye, Jan. 10, 1977. B.A. in English, U. Oreg., 1961, J.D., 1973. Bar: 1973. Tchr. Sisters Sch. Dist. (Oreg.), 1962-63, Bend Sch. Dist. (Oreg.), 1963-69; ptnr. firm Frye & Smith, Eugene, 1973-81; judge Lane County Dist. Ct., Eugene, 1981—, presiding judge, 1986—; mem. Oreg. Jud. Fitness Commn., 1983-84. Chmn. bd. trustees Pub. Defender Services Lane County, 1980-81; bd. visitors U. Oreg. Law Sch., Eugene, 1980-84; pres. bd. dirs. Eugene Opera, 1982-84. Mem. Lane County Bar Assn. (pres. 1981-82), Profl. Women's Network Oreg., Nat. Assn. Women Judges; Oreg. Dist. Judges Assn. (pres. 1985-86). Office: Lane County Dist Ct 125 E 8th Ave Eugene OR 97401

SMITH, LEAH JOHNSON, economist, college official; b. Ft. Worth, Feb. 1, 1943; d. Francis Bonneau and Leah Townsend (Zeigler) Johnson; B.A., Stanford U., 1964; Ph.D., Johns Hopkins U., 1972; m. Woollcott Keston Smith, Feb. 3, 1968; children—Amelia, Keston. Instr. econs. N.C. State U., 1969-72; economist First Nat. Bank Boston, 1972-73; with Woods Hole Oceanographic Instn., 1973-82, policy asso. marine policy and ocean mgmt., 1982; asst. prof. econs. Haverford Coll., 1981-82; asst. prof. econs. Swarthmore Coll., 1982-85, asst. to pres., dir. instl. research, 1985—; mem. sci. and statis. com. New Eng. Fishery Mgmt. Council; mem. adv. bd. Dept Interior; cons. in field. Contbr. articles to profl. jours. Trustee, Woods Hole Library, 1976-81, pres., 1978-80. Research grantee Nat. Marine Fisheries Service. Mem. Am. Econ. Assn., AAAS, World Mariculture Soc. Episcopalian. Office: Swarthmore Coll Dept Econs Swarthmore PA 19081

SMITH, LENORA BURNETT, secretarial and printing company executive; b. Weakley County, Tenn., Jan. 9, 1926; d. William Horace and Cleo (Davis) Buckles; m. Frank Allen Smith, Jr., May 9, 1965 (div. 1968); children—William Gregory, Michael Glenn Arnold. Student Jones Bus. Coll., Shasta Coll. Various positions with radio stas., Memphis, Miami, Fla., Union City, Tenn., Santa Monica and Redding, Calif.; traffic mgr., program dir. Channel 7, Redding, 1956-62; exec. sec. Shasta Trinity Med. Soc., Redding, 1964—; chmn. bd., chief fin. officer House of Steno, Inc., Redding, 1962—, also v.p. Past mem. Bicentennial Com., Redding. Baptist. Democrat. Club: Soroptimist (past rec. sec.). Lodge: Eastern Star, Women of Moose. Home: PO Box 1243 Redding CA 96099 Office: House of Steno Inc 1708 Placer St Redding CA 96001

SMITH, LIBBY LEIBMAN, broadcasting executive; b. Wilkes-Barre, Pa.; m. Joseph H. Smith; children—Jason Stafford. A.A., Palmer Sch.; B.A. in Communications, Pa. State U. Artist rep. Libby Smith, Forty Fort, Pa., 1972—; dir. classical music sta. WVIA-FM, Pittston, Pa., 1972—. Host, producer various radio programs. Bd. dirs. Wilkes-Barre Fiesta, 1975—; bd. dirs. Wilkes-Barre Ballet, 1982—, Community Concert Assn., Wilkes-Barre and Scranton, Pa., 1981—; bd. advisers Dorflinger Concerts, White Mills, Pa., 1984—; bd. dirs. Mozart Club, Wilkes-Barre, 1960—; v.p. Northeast Pa. Arts Alliance, Wilkes-Barre, 1983—. Recipient awards of Merit Nat. Fedn. Music Clubs, 1975, 77, 83, 84, 85, Cultural Arts award Bucknell U., 1985. Mem. Am. Women in Radio and Television, Spectrum. Club: Northeast Opera (cert. recognition 1984); Cultural Task Force City of Wilkes-Barre, 1985. Avocations: travel; raising exotic plants; collecting cut crystal. Home: 1600 Wyoming Ave Forty Fort PA 18704 Office: WVIA-FM Pub Broadcasting Ctr Pittston PA 18640

SMITH, LILLIAN TAYLOR, county official; b. Tabb, Va., Dec. 23, 1930; d. James Wilbur and Ada Myrtle (Chandler) Taylor; m. Kirby Taylor Smith, July 10, 1948; children—Nathan Taylor, Timothy Lee, Linda Dayle Smith Morris, Nancy Lillian, James Kirby. Student Thomas Nelson Coll., 1980-82. Asst. postmaster, Tabb P.O., Va., 1945-47; sec. Newport News Law, Va., 1947-48, Noland Co., Newport News, Va., 1948-52; bookkeeper Smith's Marine Railway, Grafton, Va., 1950-80, sec.-treas., 1980—; gen. registrar County of York, Yorktown, Va., 1968—. Vice pres. York County Home Demonstration Clubs, Yorktown, 1954-55; pres. Grafton PTA, 1960-61; mem. adminstrv. bd. Providence United Methodist Ch., Grafton, 1977—, chmn. worship com., 1977-84, pres. Women, 1984-85. Mem. Voter Registrars Assn. Va. (mem. exec. com. 1980-82, sec. 1984-85). Democrat. Home: 170 Railway Rd Grafton VA 23692 Office: York County PO Box 451 1980 Alexander Hamilton Blvd Yorktown VA 23690

SMITH, LOIS MARIE (JO), publishing company executive, welcome service executive; b. Wickenburg, Ariz., Aug. 17, 1929; d. Wilbur R. and Vivian Beulah (Jenkins) McCarter; m. John Alan Smith, Nov. 4, 1950; children—Laura Brooke, Holly Marquette. Student Ariz. State Tchrs. Coll., 1948-50; B.A. in Nutrition, Mainz U., Ger., 1969. Various positions U.S. Air Force Officer Wives Clubs, U.S. and Europe, 1952-69; v.p. High Valley Enterprises, Inc., Fort Collins, Colo., 1972-75; co-owner, editor HollyBrooke House Press, Foster City, Calif., 1978—; pres. HollyBrooke House Pub., Las Vegas, 1981—; owner Western Welcome Service, Las Vegas, 1984—, personal mgr., pub. relations cons. to entertainment field. Author: Crocked, 1975; author, editor-in-chief: Las Vegas Celebrity Cookbook, 1982, The Entertainers Cookbook, 1983. Mem. Las Vegas C. of C. (mem. Women's Council), Ariz. Authors Club. Republican. Episcopalian. Avocations: running; gourmet cooking; horticulture; music; art. Home: 1674 Elaine Dr Las Vegas NV 89122 Office: HollyBrooke House 1674 Elaine Dr Las Vegas NV 89122

SMITH, LOLA SUE, medical leasing executive; b. Roanoke, Va., Feb. 8, 1943; d. Thomas William and Elsie Maxine (Hall) Brown; 1 son, Scott Thomas. Student pub. schs., Reseda, Calif. With Security Pacific Bank, Canoga Park, Calif., 1963-69; with Gen. Hosp. Leasing, 1969—, v.p., 1984—. Mem. Nat. Notary Assn., Am. Assn. Equipment Lessors, Bus. and Profl. Women's Club, Lasalle Inst. Study of Law. Home: 7403 Remmet Canoga Park CA 91303 Office: Gen Hosp Leasing 20944 Sherman Way Canoga Park CA 91303

SMITH, LORA, school librarian; b. Ava, Mo., Nov. 9, 1936, d. Maynard Lawrence Huff and Ada Mae (Davis) H.; m. Harold Richard Smith, Feb. 12, 1955; children—Bradly Clark, Curtis Ray. B.E., S.W. Mo. State U., 1961; M.L.S., Emporia State U., Kans., 1979. Cert. tchr., sch. media specialist, Mo. Tchr. pub. schs., Ellington, Mo., 1956-62, Mountain View, Mo., 1967-69; library media specialist pub. schs., West Plains, Mo., 1972-86, dist. library media coordinator, 1984—; supply instr. library and info. sci., S.W. Mo. State U., West Plains, 1986; workshop cons.; mem. Task Force to Evaluate Mo. Library Media Standards, 1986. Republican candidate for Mo. Ho. of Reps., 1982; mem. council Am. Heart Assn., Howell County, West Plains, 1985-86. Named FHA Hero, West Plains Future Homemakers Am., 1982. Mem. ALA, Mo. Assn. Sch. Librarians (pres. 1981-82), Am. Assn. Sch. Librarians (conv. del. 1980-82), Mo. Tchrs. Assn., West Plains Bus. and Profl. Women's Club (pres. 1982-83), Delta Kappa Gamma. Baptist. Club: Girl's Town (West Plains). Avocations: golf; video production; travel. Home: Route 3 Box 597 West Plains MO 65775 Office: West Plains R7 Schs Howell at Olden St West Plains MO 65775

SMITH, LORRAINE MARIE, metal fabrication company executive; b. Balt., Apr. 6, 1946; d. Albert William and Helen Cecilia (Murphy) Brazil; m. M. Gilbert Smith, Jr.; children—Sharon, Nicole, Gilbert. Acctg. sec., Balt., 1970-78; v.p. G & L Fabricators, Inc., Finksburg, Md., 1979-80; pres., 1980—, pres. bd. dirs., 1979—. Organizer, Finksburg Cedarhurst Community Action Group, 1978. Avocations: skiing; tennis; reading. Roman Catholic. Office: G & L Fabricators Inc PO Box 209 Finksburg MD 21048

SMITH, LOUISE EDWARDS, school counselor; b. Fayetteville, Ark., Sept. 12, 1926; d. William Sydney and Nora Alice (Oyler) Edwards; m. Paul Eugene Smith, Aug. 13, 1942 (div. 1972); children—Ronald Eugene, Donald Edward, Paul Eugene, Jr. B.A., U. Tulsa, 1957, M.A., 1966; cert. profl. counselor Okla. State U., 1972. Hand painter Bartlett-Collins, Sapulpa, Okla., 1951-53; counselor grades 1-12 Cleveland High Sch., Okla., 1965-66; elem. tchr. Tulsa pub. schs., 1957-64, elem. counselor, 1966—, leader Citizenship Class, 1970-84, history devel. project. Designer passive solar home, Lake Keystone, Okla., 1974. Sec. Keystone Colony Property Owners Assn., 1984; Dem. precinct chmn., Pawnee County, Okla., 1983. Mem. NEA, Okla. Edn. Assn., Tulsa Edn. Assn., Tulsa Assn. Counseling and Devel. (pres. 1984-85), Am. Assn. Counseling and Devel. (del. nat. conv. 1972-75), Okla. Assn. Counseling and Devel. (sec. 1968-69, pres. 1971-72), Nat. Bd. Cert. Counselors, Phi Alpha Theta, Pi Gamma Mu, Kappa Delta Pi. Baptist. Avocations: bridge; piano; gardening; fishing; singing. Home: Route 1 Box 130 Cleveland OK 74020 Office: Roosevelt Elem Magnet Sch 1202 W Easton St Tulsa OK 74127

SMITH, LYNDA MARIE, insurance agent; b. Ft. Wayne, Ind., Dec. 16, 1946; d. Fred Richard and Betty Jane (Shaneyfelt) Williams; m. Kenneth Lynn Smith, June 23, 1946; children—Bryan David, Brandon Daniel, Brady Dane. B.A. in Religious Edn., Central Bible Coll., Springfield, Mo., 1970. Music tchr. Jennings Music Studio, Ft. Wayne, 1972-74; office adminstr. First Assembly God, Evansville, Ind., 1974-76; music dir. Calvary Assembly, West Palm Beach, Fla., 1976-77; tchr. Ft. Wayne Christian Sch., 1977-79; ins. agt. Guarantee Mut. Ins. Co., Ft. Wayne, 1979-80; ins. agt., gen. agt. Mut. Security Life Ins. Co., Ft. Wayne, 1980-82, Houston, 1982-84, Atlanta, 1984—. Pres., Ft. Wayne Christian Sch. Aux., 1979-81. Recipient Blue Vase award Guarantee Mut. Ins. Co., 1979; Most Progressive Salesperson award Am. Heritage Ins. Co., Ft. Wayne, 1978. Mem. Gen. Agts. and Mgrs. Assn., Houston Assn. Life Underwriters. Republican. Mem. Assembly of God. Home: 1175 Old Forge Dr Roswell GA 30076

SMITH, MADELINE AMELIA MUCCIE, sculptor; b. Trenton, Jan. 10, 1920; d. Frank and Josephine (Tummillo) Muccie; student Famous Artists Schs., Westport, Conn.; m. William J. Smith, Oct. 11, 1941; 1 son, William D. One-man shows including: Phila. Mus. Art, 1974, Pennridge Art Gallery, 1979, Internat. Platform Assn., 1979, Woodmere Art Gallery, 1979, Phillips Mill, 1979, Gentle Winds Gallery, 1980; 2-man show Western Electric Corp. Edn. Center Gallery, 1981; exhibited in group shows including: Arts Alliance, 1978-79, Regional Council Community Art Centers Phila., 1978-79, Rodman House, 1980, World Trade Center-Custom House Mus., N.Y.C., 1981, Palazzo delle Manifestazioni, Accademia Italia, 1983; represented in permanent collections including: Fred Clark Mus., Carversville, Pa. Forest Ackerman Mus., Los Angeles, Pennridge High Sch., Wrightstown Twp. Bldg., also pvt. collections; creator Pearl S. Buck Women's award Pearl S. Buck Found., 1979; executed portraits of Congressman Peter Kostmayer, Dr. Selma Burke, George Trivellini, bas-relief of Pres. Ronald Reagan; writer Straight Talk column Fantasy Artists Network mag., 1979-80; dir. Bucks County Sculpture Show, 1981-84. Recipient gold medal Academia Italia della Arti e del Sadoro Italy, 1980; Effective Action award, history and arts com. Central Bucks C. of C., 1978, Excellence in Art award, 1983; Golden Centaur for art achievements Accademia Italia, 1982; gold medal for artistic merit U.S. Govt. Mem. Internat. Soc. Artists (charter), Doylestown Art League (pres. 1974-76), Allied Artists Am., Women's Caucus for Art, Yardley Art Assn. (hon. mem.), Central Bucks C. of C. (dir. 1983-84). Club: Earhart Noonan Aviation (founder, pres. 1937). Home and Studio: Dogwood Acres Box 91 Penns Park PA 18943

SMITH, MAE RIDEAU, educator; b. Palmetto, La., Dec. 4, 1937; d. Rudolph Joseph and Imelda (Simien) Rideau; m. Charles Clay Smith, Feb. 16, 1957; children—Michelle, Charles, Cherri, Anthony. B.S., U. Houston, 1971; M.Ed., Tex. State U., 1979, Ed.D., 1984. Tchr., Houston Ind. Sch. Dist., 1973-79, dept. chmn., 1975-79; adminstrv. asst. Tex. So. U., Houston, 1979-80; tchr. North Forest Ind. Sch. Dist., Houston, 1980—; tchr., chmn. dept. reading, developer computer literacy curriculum M.B. Smiley High Sch., Houston, 1983—; research chmn. Doctoral Council, Houston, 1981-82; mem. curriculum revision com. St. Piux X High Sch., Houston, 1980-81. Fin. sec. Ladies Aux. Houston, 1983-84. Mem. Greater Houston Reading Council, NEA, So. Assn. on Children, St. Monica Ct. (nat. and state del. 1983, participant state and nat. conv. 1984). Democrat. Roman Catholic. Home: 5423 Candlemist Dr Houston TX 77091 Office: MB Smiley High Sch 10725 Mesa Rd Houston TX 77091

SMITH, MARCIA JEAN, tax specialist; b. Kansas City, Mo., Oct. 19, 1947; d. Eugene Hubert and Marcella Juanita (Greene) S.; student U. Nebr., 1965-67; B.A.(Coll. Ednl. Opportunity grantee), Jersey City State Coll., 1971; M.B.A. in Taxation, Golden Gate U., 1976, postgrad., 1976-77; M.S. in Acctg., Pace U., 1982; postgrad. Canadian Tax Inst., Queen's U., Can., 1979. Resident adviser Women's Job Corps, Moses Lake, Wash., 1967-68, Jersey City, 1968-71; legal intern Port Authority N.Y., N.J., N.Y.C., 1972; legis. aide to Harrison A. Williams, U.S. Senator, Washington, 1973; internat. tax accountant Bechtel Corp., San Francisco, 1974-77; sr. tax accountant Equitable Life Assurance Soc. U.S., N.Y.C., 1977; asst. sec. Equitable Life Holding Corp., N.Y.C., 1977-79, Equico Lessors, Inc., Mpls., 1978-79, Equitable Gen. Ins. Group, Ft. Worth, 1977-79, Heritage Life Assurance Co., Toronto, Ont., Can., 1978-79, Informatics, Inc., Los Angeles, 1978-79; sec. Equico Capital Corp., N.Y.C., 1977-79, Equico Personal Credit, Inc., Colorado Springs, Colo., 1978-79, Equico Securities, Inc., N.Y.C., 1977-79, Equitable Environ. Health, Inc., Woodbury, N.Y., 1977-79; tax sr. Arthur Andersen & Co., N.Y.C., 1979-82; pres. M.J. Smith Co., 1983—; tax cons.; real estate salesperson. Human rights chmn. YWCA, Lincoln, Nebr., 1966-67; spl. advisor U.S. Congl. Adv. Bd.; nat. adv. bd. Am. Security Council. Recipient Certificate of Recognition, Central Mo. State Coll., 1965, St. Peter's Coll., 1971; Unicameral award State Neb., 1967, Mary McLeod Bethune award Jersey City State Coll., 1971. Mem. Am. Mgmt. Assn., Am. Assn. Individual Investors, Nat. Assn. Women Bus. Owners, Nat. Assn. Accts., Nat. Soc. Pub. Accts., Internat. Assn. Fin. Planners, Acad. Polit. Sci., Postal Commemorative Soc., Internat. Platform Assn., Smithsonian Assos., Am. Mus. Natural History Assos., Nat. Trust Hist. Preservation, Internat. Tax Inst., Am. Bus. Assn., Am. Econ. Assn., AAUW, N.Y. Acad. Scis., AAAS, Nat. Hist. Soc., Nat. Assn. Tax Practitioners, Assn. Managerial Economists. Club: U.S. Senatorial. Home: 300 Mercer St 23C New York NY 10003

SMITH, MARCIA SUE, government official; b. Greenfield, Mass., Feb. 22, 1951; d. Sherman K. and Shirley Fay (Schafer) S.; B.A., Syracuse U., 1972. Adminstrv. asst., corr. AIAA, Washington, 1973-75; sci. and tech. analyst Congressional Research Service, Sci. Policy Research div. Library of Congress, Washington, 1975-80, aerospace and telecommunications systems specialist, 1980-85; exec. dir. Nat. Commn. on Space, 1985—. Fellow Brit. Interplanetary Soc.; mem. AAAS, Am. Astronautical Soc. (pres., dir., exec. com.), AIAA (Disting. lectr. 1983—, pub. policy com., internat. activities com.), N.Y. Acad. Scis., Washington Acad. Scis., Internat. Acad. Astronautics, Internat. Inst. Space Law, Sigma Xi. Author or co-author numerous reports and articles.

SMITH, MARGARET, state legislator; b. Chgo.; m. Fred J. Smith; 2 sons, (dec.). Mem. Ill. Ho. of Reps., 1981-83; mem. Ill. Senate, dist. 12, 1983—. Democrat. Office: State Capitol Springfield IL 62706*

SMITH, MARILYN JOAN, educational administrator; b. Pitts., May 29, 1938; s. Joseph Edwards and Mary Elizabeth (Dolan) Lewis; B.S., U. Houston, 1959, M.A., 1962; M.S., U. Tex., Dallas, 1980; children—Joseph Lewis, Jefferson Lee, Robert Christopher. Therapist Houston Speech and Hearing Ctr., 1960-62; dir. Spl. Care Sch., Dallas, 1964-68; dir. edn. and day care service Dallas County Mental Health and Mental Retardation Ctr., 1968-70; program dir. Children, Inc., Dallas, 1970-72, Angels, Inc., Dallas, 1971-76; pres. Package Deal, Inc., 1977—; exec. dir. Creative Children's Center, 1977-82; ednl. writer Internat. House Publs. Instr. community service div. El Centro Jr. Coll., Dallas, 1968-78; faculty Richland Community Coll., 1975-78. Mem. Adv. Bd. Helping Hand Sch., Irving, Tex., 1969-78; human services adv. com. Eastfield Coll., 1975-77. Mem. Am. Assn. Mental Deficiency, Council for Exceptional Children, Gamma Phi Beta. Home: 15931 Long Vista Dallas TX 75248 Office: 14902 Preston Rd Suite 212-075 Dallas TX 75240

SMITH, MARILYN LEWIS, business executive; b. Pitts., May 29, 1938; d. Joseph Edwards and Mary Elizabeth (Dolan) Lewis; B.S., U. Houston, 1959, M.A., 1962; M.S., U. Tex., Dallas, 1979; children—Joseph Lewis, Jefferson Lee, Robert Christopher. Therapist, Houston Speech and Hearing Center, 1960-62; dir. Spl. Care Sch., Dallas, 1964-68; dir. edn. and day care service Dallas County Mental Health and Mental Retardation Center, 1968-70; program dir. Children, Inc., Dallas, 1970-72, Angels, Inc., Dallas, 1971-76; pres. Package Deal, Inc., Richardson, Tex., 1977—; exec. dir. Creative Children's Center, 1977-82; instr. community service div. El Centro Jr. Coll., Dallas, 1968-76; faculty Richland Community Coll., 1975-78. Mem. adv. bd. Helping Hand Sch., Irving, Tex., 1969-79. Mem. Am. Assn. Mental Deficiency, Council for Exceptional Children, Gamma Phi Beta. Home: 15931 Long Vista Apt 122 Dallas TX 75248 Office: 13534 Preston Rd Suite 456 Dallas TX 75240

SMITH, MARION C., educator, former health care administator; b. Catskill, N.Y., Oct. 23, 1922; d. Nathaniel and Agatha Marie (Delaney) Smith; B.A., Coll. of St. Rose, 1952; M.A., Siena Coll., 1964. Entered Order of Sisters of Mercy, Roman Catholic Ch., 1940; tchr. elem. and high schs., Albany, Troy, Cuhoes and Oneonta, N.Y., 1943-65; chmn. journalism dept. Cath. Central High Sch., Troy, 1961-65; prin. St. Mary's Sch., Oneonta, 1965-67; asso. dir. Oneonta Newman Found., 1967-76; adminstrv. asst. Stephen Smith Geriatric Center, Phila., 1977-82; faculty SUNY, Oneonta, 1976. Co-founder, chmn. Campus Ministry Com. of Oneonta, 1968-70, 74-75; co-founder, cons., counselor City Drug Crisis Center, —85—, Oneonta, 1971-75; active Human Relations Task Force, 1974-75, Family Service Com. of Oneonta, 1972-76; counselor Planned Parenthood Clinic of Otsego County, 1972-75; campus ministry com. Oneonta, 1968-76, others. Fellow Am. Coll. Nursing Home Adminstrs.; mem. Nat. Council for Basic Edn., Nat. Cath. Campus Ministry Assn., Nat. Inst. Campus Ministry, Religious Edn. Assn., Am. Acad. Religion, Hastings Center Inst. Soc., Ethics and Life Scis., Fellowship of Reconciliation, AAUW, Siena Coll. Alumni Assn., Nat. Assn. Female Execs., Nat. Assn. Profl. and Exec. Women. Contbr. articles to profl. jours.; lit. editor profl. papers and book reviews for non-English speaking profs. in higher edn.; asst. to editor Asian Thought and Soc., 1976. Home: 6119 Ellsworth St Philadelphia PA 19143

SMITH, MARJORIE ANN, college registrar; b. Seattle, May 21, 1942; d. Harold Lloyd and Irene Lucille (Lynch) Elliss; m. Forbes Denny Nichols, June 22, 1963 (div. 1970); m. 2d David DeWitt, June 9, 1975. B.S. in Bus. Adminstrn., U. Maine, 1980. Adminstrv. asst. Holy Rosary Hosp., Ontario, Oreg., 1970-72; placement service dir. Multnomah County Med. Soc., Portland, Oreg., 1972-75; asst. dir. admissions U. Tex. Med. Br., Galveston, 1981-82; registrar Galveston Coll. (Tex.), 1982-85. Mem. Tex. Assn. Collegiate Registrars and Admissions Officers, Jr. Coll. Student Personnel Assn. Tex., Nat. Assn. Fgn. Student Affairs, Tex. Jr. Coll. Tchrs. Assn., Galveston Bus. and Profl. Women, Exec. Career Women. Republican. Home: 3 Bandera Ct Pueblo CO 81005

SMITH, MARSHA ANN, government financial executive; b. Greenville, Tex., Aug. 29, 1951; d. Wilson Marshall and Henrietta Charlotte (Fritz) S. B.B.A., U. Tex., 1973. Petroleum acct. Superior Oil Co., Houston, 1974-75; mgr. fund acctg. Prudential Group, Inc., Houston, 1975-78; systems analyst AID, Washington, 1978-80, fin. analyst regional office, Abidjan, Ivory Coast, 1980-83, dep. controller regional office, Abidjan, 1983-84, controller AID Mission, Yaounde, Cameroon, 1985—; commd. fgn. service officer Dept. State, 1984. Named to Outstanding Young Women Am., U.S. Jaycees, 1973; recipient Superior Honor award AID, 1984. Mem. Nat. Assn. Female Execs. Democrat. Presbyterian. Avocations: reading about and travelling to various cultures; flying small planes.

SMITH, MARSHA ELAINE, accountant, educator; b. Portsmouth, Ohio, Apr. 21, 1949; d. A. Mac and A. Mary (Delabar) Wamsley; B.B.A. in Acctg. cum laude, Ohio U., Athens, 1974; children—David Alan, Trisha Jabrina. Asst. ops. mgr. Chase Manhattan Bank, N.A., Agana, Guam, 1971-73; dorm and dining acct. Ohio U., 1974; organized research acct. U. Akron (Ohio), 1975; owner, operator public acctg. firm, McConnelsville, Ohio, 1976; staff acct. Dorsey L. Arnold, C.P.A., Bath, 1977; supr., office mgr. Dwite A. Polos, C.P.A., Cuyahoga Falls, Ohio, 1978; pres. Smith & Assocs., C.P.A.s, 1978—; chief Fin. officer Quest Cons., Inc., 1982—; instr. acctg. Washington Tech. Coll., 1976, U. Akron, 1982—. Treas. ladies aux. Bath Fire Dept., 1979-83; Democratic precinct woman Bath Twp., 1980-82. C.P.A., Ohio, Ohio, Tenn. Mem. Am. Women's Soc. C.P.A.s, Assn. M.B.A. Execs., Nat. Assn. Accts. Am. Inst. C.P.A.s, Ohio Soc. C.P.A.s. Home: 1040 Shive Ln #E6 Bowling Green KY 42101 Office: 835 N Cleveland-Massillon Rd Bath OH 44210

SMITH, MARTHA HELEN, educator; b. Palestine, Tex., Aug. 31, 1942; d. Square Smith and Jessie (Swanson) Gladney; children—Myron, Arnissa. B.S. in English and History, Bishop Coll., Dallas, 1969; M.S. in Elem. Edn., Prairie View A&M U. (Tex.), 1975, cert. of Adminstrn., 1976. Cert. tchr., Tex. Tchr. English and History Dallas Ind. Sch. Dist., 1969—, coach basketball, 1975-76, advisor PTA, 1974-75, cheerleader sponsor, 1982-83. Mem. Am. Woodmen, Classroom Tchrs. Dallas, Tex. State Tchrs. Assn., NEA. Democrat. Baptist. Home: 1708 Trade Winds Dr Dallas TX 75241

SMITH, MARY ALBERTA HAMPTON, physician assistant; b. Hopkinsville, Ky., July 18, 1950; d. Richard H. and Bessie M. (Clardy) Hampton; B.S., Austin Peay State U., 1972; B.S., physician asst. cert., Baylor U. Coll. Medicine, 1977; cert. in CPR, Am. Heart Assn.; cert. adult reading tutor; m. Tommy R. Smith, July 19, 1981. Nursing asst. Gen. Care Convalescent Center, Clarksville, Tenn., 1971; substitute tchr. Clarksville-Montgomery County Sch. System, 1972-74; dir. nursery St. John Missionary Bapt. Ch., Clarksville, 1972-74; nursing asst. cardiovascular/ICU units St. Luke Episcopal Hosp., Houston, 1975; child care attendant for autistic children First Presbyn. Ch., Houston, 1976-77; emergency room clk. Med. Center Del Oro Hosp., Houston, 1977-81; cert. physician asst. C. R. Higgins Jr., M.D. and Assocs., Houston, 1977-81; with Iowa Vets. Home, Marshalltown, 1982-85, L'Abri Health Care, Montclair, Calif., 1986—. Resource person Concord Elem. Sch., Houston Ind. Sch. Dist., 1979-81; active Big Bros./Big Sisters Am. Mem. Am. Acad. Physician Assts., Calif. Acad. Physician Assts., AAUW, Eta Phi Beta. Baptist. Home: 2017 East Ave R-12 Palmdale CA 93550

SMITH, MARY ANN BARTHOLOMEW, speech pathologist; b. Cleve., June 22, 1943; B.F.A. in Speech and Hearing Therapy, Ohio U., 1965; M. Communicative Disorders, Calif. State U., Long Beach, 1978; 4 children. Speech pathologist Willoughby (Ohio)-East Lake Schs., 1965-66, Huron County (Ohio) Schs., 1967-68, Princeton City Schs., Cin., 1968-70; speech and lang. specialist Whittier City (Calif.) Schs., 1971—. Cert. in spl. edn., Ohio, Oreg., Calif.; specialist in speech and hearing. Home: 3627 Calmbrook Ln Diamond Bar CA 91726

SMITH, MARY ELIZABETH, company executive; b. Kansas City, Mo., Nov. 12, 1922; d. Fontaine Kincheloe and Alma Ann (Hudler) Chamber; m. Frederick Melvin Smith, Jan. 24, 1943; children: Larry Melvin, Gary Dean. A.Bus. Adminstrn., Rockhurst Coll., Kansas City, 1973, B.S. in Bus. Adminstrn., 1974. Sec. companies, Kansas City, 1941-47; founder, pres. Smith Secretarial & Office Supply Co., Inc., Kansas City, 1957—. Bd. dirs. YMCA, Kansas City, 1980; vestry woman Ch. of Epiphany, Grandview, Mo., 1964; co-chmn. fund procurement Truman Farm Found., Grandview, 1983; bd. dirs. Community Mental Health Ctr., Kansas City, Am. Cancer Soc., Kansas City; mem. Citizens Crusade Against Crime, v.p. 1980-81; hon. pres. Richards-Gebaur Base Community Council, 1983. Mem. Am. Bus. Women's Assn. (pres. Kansas City 1973, Woman of Yr. 1971), Grandview C. of C. (dir. 1972-75 super citizen award 1976), South Kansas City C. of C. (pres. 1977-79), Real Estate Bd. (affiliate mem. Kansas City), Women's Council Realtors, Rockhurst Coll. Alumni Assn., Citizens Assn. Kansas City. Republican. Club: Pres. Scholarship (Avila Coll.) (plaque award 1980). Office: Smith Secretarial & Office Supply Co 11521 Hickman Mills Dr Kansas City MO 64134

SMITH, MARY LOUISE, public affairs consultant; b. Eddyville, Iowa, Oct. 6, 1914; d. Frank and Louise Anna (Jager) Epperson; B.A., U. Iowa, 1935; L.H.D. (hon.), Drake U., 1980, Grinnell Coll., 1984; m. Elmer Milton Smith, Oct. 7, 1934; children—Robert C., Margaret L., James E. Mem. Eagle Grove (Iowa) Bd. Edn., 1955-60; Republican precinct committeewoman, Eagle Grove, 1960-62, vice-chairwoman, Wright County, Iowa, 1962-63; mem. Rep. Nat. Com., 1964-84, mem. exec. com., 1969-84, mem. conv. reforms com., 1966, vice-chairwoman Steiger com. on conv. reform, 1973, co-chmn. nat. com., 1974, chmn. Com., 1974-77; vice-chairwoman U.S. Commn. on Civil Rights, 1982-83; vice-chairwoman Midwest region Rep. Conf., 1969-71; del. Rep. Nat. Conv., 1968, 72, 76, 80, 84, alt. del., 1964; vice-chairwoman Iowa Presdl. campaign, 1964; nat. co-chmn. Physicians Com. for Presdl. Campaign, 1972; co-chairwoman Iowa Com. to Reelect the Pres., 1972; mem. Nat. Commn. on Observance Internat. Women's Year, 1975-77; vis. fellow Woodrow Wilson Fellowship Found., 1979. Mem. U.S. del. to Extraordinary Session of UNESCO Gen. Conf., Paris, 1973; mem. U.S. del. 15th session population commn. UN Econ. and Social Council, Geneva, 1969; mem. Pres.'s Commn. for Observance of 25th Anniversary of UN, 1970-71; mem. Iowa Commn. for Blind, 1961-63, chairwoman, 1963; mem. Iowa Gov.'s Commn. on Aging, 1962; trustee Robert A. Taft Inst. Govt., 1974-84, Herbert Hoover Presdl. Library Assn., Inc., 1979—. Active Planned Parenthood; pres. Eagle Grove Community Chest; bd. dirs. Mental Health Center North Iowa, 1962-63, YWCA of Greater Des Moines, 1983—, Orchard Place Resdl. Facility for Emotionally Disturbed Children, 1983—, Learning Channel, cable TV, 1984—; mem. adv. council U. Iowa Hawkeye Fund Women's Program, 1982—. Named hon. col., mil. staff Gov. Iowa, 1973; Iowa Women's Hall of Fame, 1977; recipient Disting. Alumni award U. Iowa, 1984; Cristine Wilson medal for equality and justice Iowa Commn. on Status of Women, 1984. Mem. Women's Aux. AMA, UN Assn., Nat. Women's Polit. Caucus (adv. bd. 1978—), PEO, Kappa Alpha Theta. Address: 654 59th St Des Moines IA 50312

SMITH, NANCY CLANCY, in-home child care company executive; b. New Haven, Conn., Sept. 21, 1952; d. Harold Alton and Agnes Teresa (Howe) S. A.A., Housatonic Community Coll., 1972; B.S., Eastern Conn. State U., 1975; postgrad. So. Conn. State U., 1977. Cert. tchr. Personnel mgr. Hardee's Food Systems, Atlanta, 1972-80; exec. recruiter W.B. Doolin & Assocs., Atlanta, 1981-82; profl. nanny Nanny Pop-Ins Ltd., Atlanta, 1982, mgr., 1984-85; area personnel mgr. Sambo's Restaurant, Fremont, Calif., 1982-84; owner, pres. Nanny Concepts & Service, Inc. dba Nanny Pop-Ins, Atlanta, 1985—; dir. Nanny Pop-Ins Assn., Atlanta, Atlanta Area Clin. Services; mem. certification com. Nanny Pop-Ins Assn., 1986; cons. Nanny Pop-Ins Services, 1985—. Author children's books; editor N.C.S. news newsletter; speaker various women's orgns. Mem. Nat. Orgn. Female Execs., Am. Soc. Personnel Adminstrs., Bus. and Profl. Womens Found. Roman Catholic. Avocations: travel; racquetball, reading; sailing; writing. Office: Nanny Concepts & Services Inc dba Nanny Pop-Ins Ltd 1110 Morgans Landing Dr Atlanta GA 30338

SMITH, NANCY HOWES, educator; b. Hyannis, Mass., Mar. 27, 1945; d. Harold Dudley and Dorothy (Canning) Howes; B.A., Bridgewater State Coll., 1967; M.Ed., Rivier Coll., 1981; m. Joseph W. Smith, Jr.; children by previous marriage—Eric R., David E. English tchr. Hanover (Mass.) High Sch., 1967-68; English tchr., dept. chmn. Hudson (N.H.) Meml. Sch., 1969-71, 74-85, Windham (N.H.) Ctr. Sch., 1985—; tchr. history and English, Alvirne High Sch., Hudson, N.H., 1974, Bd. dirs. Kendallwood Condominium Assn., 1977-79; troop leader Cub Scouts Am., Girl Scouts U.S.A.; merit badge counselor Troop 98, Boy Scouts Am.; ch. youth adv. Cert. prin., N.H., Mass. Mem. Nat. Council Tchrs. English, Assn. for Supervision and Curriculum Devel. Republican. Home: 26 Bowers Rd Derry NH 03038 Office: Windham Center Sch Lowell Rd Windham NH 03087

SMITH, NANCY LYNNE, journalist; b. San Antonio, July 31, 1947; d. Tillman Louis and Enid Maxine (Woolverton) Brown; m. Allan Roy Jones, Nov. 28, 1969 (div. 1975); 1 dau., Christina Elizabeth Woolverton Jones. B.A., So. Meth. U., 1968; postgrad. So. Meth. U., 1969-70, Vanderbilt U., 1964, Ecole Nouvelle de la Suisse Romande, Lausanne, Switzerland, 1962. Tchr. spl. edn. Hot Springs Sch. Dist. (Ark.), 1970-72; reporter, soc. editor Dallas Morning News, 1974-82; soc./celebrity columnist Dallas Times Herald, 1982—; stringer Washington Post, 1978; contbg. editor Ultra mag., Houston, 1981-82, Tex. Woman mag., Dallas, 1979-80, Profl. Woman mag., Dallas, 1979-80; mem. bd. advisors Ultra Mag., 1985—; appeared on TV series Jocelyn's Weekend, Sta. KDFI-TV, 1985. Bd. dirs. TACA arts support orgn., Dallas, 1980—, asst. chmn. custom auction, 1978-83; hon. mem. Dallas Opera Women's Bd., Northwood Inst. Women's Bd., Dallas Symphony League; mem. women's com. Dallas Theatre Ctr. Mem. Soc. Profl. Journalists (v.p. communications 1978-79), Nat. Press Club, Dallas Press Club, DAR, Daus. of Republic of Tex. (registrar 1972), Dallas Mus. Art League, Dallas Opera Guild. Club: Argyle (sec. 1983-84), The 500 (Dallas). Home: 4068 Lovers Ln Dallas TX 75225 Office: Dallas Times Herald 1101 Pacific Ave Dallas TX 75202

SMITH, NIKKI LEE, computer applications mgr.; b. Lansing, Mich., June 18, 1951; d. William Frederick and Thelma Margaret (Spencer) Knapp; ed. Coll. Mainland, 1980—; children—Michelle Lee Hooter, Brian Edward Hooter, Melinda Lee Smith. Programmer trainee Am. Nat. Ins. Co., Galveston, Tex., 1972-74; data analyst U.S. Auto Assn., San Antonio, 1974; with Am. Indemnity Group, Galveston, 1978—, computer applications mgr., 1981—; cons. Rollerland Skating Center, Texas City. Mem. Christian Ch. (Disciples of Christ). Office: Am Indemnity Group 2115 Winnie St Galveston TX 77553

SMITH, NORMA RUTH, nursing educator; b. N.Y.C., June 14, 1939; d. Peder and Aasta (Thompson) Askeland; m. Arthur J.S. Smith, May 20, 1966; children—Peter James Stewart, Ian Alexander Stewart. B.S.N., Columbia U., 1964, M.S., 1975. Mem. staff Vis. Nurse Assn., N.Y.C., 1964-66, N.J. Neuropsychiat. Inst., Princeton, N.J., 1967-69; instr. Helene Fuld Med. Ctr., Trenton, N.J., 1976-77; asst. prof. nursing Mercer Med. Ctr., Trenton, 1977—; postgrad. intern Family Services Agy. of Princeton, 1983-85. Recipient commendation for Princeton Peoples Yellow Pages, N.J. State Legislature, 1975. Mem. Am. Nurses Assn., N.J. Pub. Health Assn., N.J. Assn. Corrections, N.J. Mental Health Assn., Mercer Council on Alcoholism, Sigma Theta Tau, Lambda Iota Tau. Home: 4 Ober Rd Princeton NJ 08540 Office: Mercer Med Ctr Sch Nursing 446 Bellevue Ave Trenton NJ 08607

SMITH, OLIVE IRENE PERRY, realty company executive; b. nr. Shelbyville, Ill., Dec. 13; d. Joseph Luther and Pearl (Bushart) Perry; grad. Sparks Coll., 1928; student Milligan U., 1929, Northwestern U., 1934-36, UCLA, 1959-60; m. William Smith, May 11, 1942. Hosp. librarian, registrar Chgo. State Hosp., Cook County, 1929-40; dep. assessor San Diego County, Calif., 1951-52; real estate broker O.I. Smith, Hemet, Calif., 1953—; real estate investment and loan counselor. Local rep. Nat. Inst. Real Estate Bds. Active Southland Water Com., 1960-68. Mem. adv. bd. San Jacinto (Calif.) Jr. Coll., 1967-68. Mem. Nat. Inst. Real Estate Brokers, Nat. Traders, Comml., and Investment Brokers Div. (pres. 1961), Hemet-San Jacinto Bd. Realtors (sec. 1960), Calif. Real Estate Assn. (regional v.p. 1964-65), Riverside Art Assn. Republican. Club: Soroptimist (San Jacinto-Hemet, Calif.). Home: 3701 Fillmore St #180 Rancho Riverside Park Riverside CA 92505 Office: Rancho-Riverside Park Riverside CA 92505

SMITH, PAMELA JEAN, textile designer; b. Denver, Sept. 19, 1950; d. Oakley Mead and Patricia Rose (Ward) S.; children—Zim Pickens, Sophie Pickens. Diploma, Goddard Coll., 1972. Mem. faculty U. Vt., Burlington, 1972-74; tchr. Frog Hollow Craft Ctr., Middlebury, Vt., 1972-74, Weeks Sch., Vergennes, Vt., 1970-74; pres., owner Folkheart, Bristol, Vt., 1980—. Mem. Women's Bus. Assn., Weaving Guild, Vt. Handcrafters, Fiberworks. Avocations: reading, traveling, ethnic textiles, painting, writing. Office: Folkheart Rag Rugs 18 Main St Bristol VT 05443

SMITH, PAT PITTMAN, home economist, consultant; b. Mabank, Tex., Nov. 25, 1940; d. Jeff Burr and Edna Lee (Odom) Teet; m. Joel P. Pittman, Dec. 26, 1961 (div. 1975); m. 2d, William C. Smith, Jr., Nov. 21, 1976. B.S., East Tex. State U., 1962; postgrad. Cordon Bleu Cooking Sch., London, 1978, Leith's Sch. Food and Wine, London, 1979. Home economist Dallas Power & Light, 1962-69; freelance home economist, Dallas, 1969-75; home economist So. Living mag., Birmingham, Ala., 1975—, asst. dir. Cooking Schs., 1977—; freelance home economist, Houston, 1976—. Mem. Am. Home Econs. Assn., Home Economists in Bus. (nat.-internat. relations chmn. 1984-86), Houston Home Economists in Bus. (chmn. 1983-84), Home Economists in Homemaking (chmn. 1974), Chi Omega. Republican. Episcopalian. Home: PO Box 814 Bellville TX 77418

SMITH, PATRICIA ANN, lawyer; b. Charleston, W.Va., Nov. 15, 1949; d. Chester Warren and Bonnie Hazel (Moody) Smith. B.A. in Econs., U. Colo., 1971; J.D., U. Fla., 1975; LL.M., Georgetown U., 1978. Bar: Fla. 1975, D.C. 1977, Va. 1983. Atty., ICC, Washington, 1975-76, Fruit Growers Express Co., Washington, 1976-79, Assn. Am. R.R.s, Washington, 1979-83, Ferrell & Assocs., Alexandria, Va., 1983—. Contbr. articles to profl. jours. Mem. Fed. Bar Assn. (dir. young lawyers div. D.C. chpt. 1981-82 chmn. pro bono com. 1981-84), ABA (exec. council young lawyers div. 1981-83, chmn. legis. action com. 1981-83, jud. improvements 1983-85, chmn. elec. com. on r.r. law, torts and ins. practice sect. 1983-84, vice chmn. fed. practice com. 1983-84, mem. legis. action com. 1983-84), Democrat. Office: Ferrell & Assocs 1317 King St Alexandria VA 22314

SMITH, PATRICIA GRACE, government official; b. Tuskegee Institute, Ala., Nov. 10, 1947; d. Douglas and Wilhelmina (Griffin) Jones; m. J. Clay Smith, Jr., June 25, 1983; children—Eugene Douglas, Stager Clay, Michelle L., Michael L. B.A. in English, Tuskegee Inst., 1968; postgrad. Auburn U., 1969-71, Harvard U., 1974, George Washington U., 1983; sr. exec. service candidate, 1985; exec. mgmt. tng., 1986. Instr. Tuskegee Institute, Ala., 1969-71; program mgr. Curber Assocs., Washington, 1971-73; dir. placement Nat. Assn. Broadcasters, Washington, 1973-74, dir. pub. affairs, 1974-77; assoc. producer Group W Broadcasting, Balt., 1977, producer, 1977-78; dir. affiliate relations and programming Sheridan Broadcasting Network, Crystal City, Va., 1978-80; chief consumer assistance and small bus. Office Congl. and Pub. Affairs, FCC, Washington, 1980—; vice chmn. Nat. Conf. Black Lawyers Task Force on Communications, Washington, 1975—. Mem. D.C. Donor Project, Nat. Kidney Found., Washington, 1984—; trustee, mem. exec. com., nominating com., youth adv. com. Nat. Urban League, 1976-81; mem. communications com. Cancer Coordinating Council, 1977-84; mem. Braintrust Subcom. on Children's Programming, Congl. Black Caucus, 1976—; mem. adv. bd. Black Arts Celebration, 1978-83; mem. journalism and communications adv. council Auburn U., 1976-78; mem. Washington Urban League, 1985—, Ala. State Soc., Washington, 1984—. Named Outstanding Young Woman of Yr., Washington, 1975, 78; recipient Sustained Superior Performance award FCC, Washington, 1982, 83, 84, 85. Mem. Women in Communications, Inc. (mem. nat. adv. com.), NAACP, Lambda Iota Tau. Club: Broadcasters (bd. dirs. 1976-77). Democrat. Baptist. Avocations: writing; swimming. Home: 4010 16th St NW Washington DC 20011 Office: FCC 1919 M St NW Suite 254 Washington DC 20554

SMITH, PATRICIA K., educator; b. East Stroudsburg, Pa., Mar. 8, 1934; d. Joseph George and Mabel Lorraine (Repsher) Kuchinski; m. Edwin Raymond Smith, Aug. 18, 1956; children—Timothy E., Steven M., Marianne F. B.S. in Edn., East Stroudsburg State Coll., 1955; M.A., W.Va. U., 1969, D.Edn., 1975. Elem. tchr. Pleasantdale Elem. Sch., West Orange, N.J., 1955-56, Tuscarora Sch. Dist., Mercersburg, Pa., 1956-59; reading specialist Robert F. Kennedy Ctr., Morgantown, W.Va., 1970-72; asst. prof. W.Va. U., Morgantown, 1975-79, assoc. prof. reading and lang. arts, 1979—; mem. rev. bd. Prentice-Hall, Inc., Englewood Cliffs, N.J., 1979—; cons. Chpt. 1, Monongalia Pub. Schs., Morgantown, W.Va., 1983-84. Co-author: Keeping Yourself Out of Federal Court, 1980; mem. editorial bd. Reading Improvement, Chula Vista, Calif., 1983—. Postdoctoral teaching fellow Lilly Endowment, Inc., 1975-76; recipient Outstanding Tchr. award Coll. Human Resources and Edn., Morgantown, W.Va., 1978. Mem. W.Va. State Reading Council (pres. 1979-80), Human Resources and Edn. Alumni Assn. (pres. 1979-80, exec. dir. 1981-85), Kappa Delta Pi, Phi Delta Kappa. Democrat. Roman Catholic. Avocations: traveling; reading. Home: 1456 Dogwood Ave Morgantown WV 26505 Office: W Va U 506 Allen Hall Morgantown WV 26506

SMITH, PATSY JUANITA, cosmetics company executive, claims adjustor; b. Dallas, Aug. 3, 1939; d. Roland Murl and Ruby Esther (Whiteside) Stephens; m. Jerry Arlin Kerby, June 7, 1957 (div. Nov. 1971); children—Timmy Wayne, Pamela Anita; m. 2d, Charles Albert Smith, June 17, 1977. Student, Ins. Inst., Dale Carnegie Sch. Claims adjuster Crum & Forster, Dallas, 1967-77, Atlantic Mut. Co., Dallas, 1978-79, Am. States Ins. Co., Dallas, 1979-81, Trinity Adjusting Co., Dallas, 1981-83; beauty cons. Mary Kay Cosmetics, Dallas, 1980-83, sales dir., 1983—. Precinct chmn. Democratic party, Dallas, 1981, election judge, 1981, 82. Named Queen of Sales, Rachel Tarbet unit Mary Kay Cosmetics, 1982, Queen of Recruiting, 1982. Mem. Ins. Women of Dallas (Claimswoman of Year 1979, 80, pres. 1981-82), Am. Bus. Women Assn. (sec. 1980). Home: 7222 Wendell St Dallas TX 75231

SMITH, PAULINE (PAULA) VIVIAN, state administrator; b. Memphis, July 4, 1933; d. Tommie and Doveanna (Robinson) Watkins; m. James Bosman, Feb. 19, 1950 (div. 1959); children—Dwayne D. and Dwight D. (twins); m. 2d Lloyd Arthur Smith, Oct. 20, 1962; 1 dau., Cheryl D. B.S. in Econs., Washington U., St. Louis, 1972; M.B.A., St. Louis U., 1977. With TWA, 1960-81, mgr. sales and service tng., Kansas City, 1977-79, mgr. profl. tng. and devel., Kansas City, 1979-81; dir. Mo. Dept. Labor and Indsl. Relations, Jefferson City, 1981—; mem. Nat. Commn. for Employment Policy; bd. dirs. Interstate Conf. Employment Security Agys.; trustee Mo. Council Econ. Edn.; mem. Mo. Job Tng. Coordinating Council; pres. Jobs for Mo. Grads., St. Louis, 1981-84, Status of Mo. Women, 1982-84; lectr. in field, Named to Women of Achievement, Iota Phi Lambda, St. Louis, 1976; recipient Outstanding Support award Nat. Job Corps Program, Kansas City, Mo., 1981, Outstanding Achievers award Mo. Legis. Black Caucus, Jefferson City, 1983. Mem. Rep. Nat. Com., Nat. Fed. Rep. Women, Nat. Urban League, NAACP, AAUW (bd. dirs. Mo. chpt. 1983-85, Leadership award 1982), Nat. Assn. Commns. for Women (bd. dirs.). Clubs: Black Women in Bus., St. Louis Drifters (treas. 1974-76) (St. Louis). Office: Dept Labor and Indsl Relations 421 E Dunklin Jefferson City MO 65101

SMITH, PAULINE ROSALEE, educational administrator, consultant; b. Lawton, Okla., July 16, 1928; d. Robert Paul and Elsie (Tahkofper) Chaat; A.A., Cameron State U., 1948; B.S., Okla. State U., 1950, M.S., 1960; m. Clodus R. Smith, June 25, 1950; children—Martha Lynn, William Paul, Paula Diane. Tchr., public schs., Bradley, Okla., 1950-52, Booker, Tex., 1953-54, Candor, N.Y., 1957-59, Silver Spring Md., Burtonsville, Md., 1961-74; project mgr. Indian Edn. Services, Cleveland City Schs., 1977-83; vis. instr. Cleve. State U., 1978-83. Bd. dirs. Women Space, 1977-81, Council Econ. Opportunity, Cleve., 1981-83; mem. ACCESS bd. Cuyahoga Community Coll.; chmn. Lau Adv. Task Force Cleve. City Schs., 1979-80. Recipient Career Woman of Achievement award Cleve. YWCA, 1979. Mem. AAUW (pres. Cleve. 1981), Indian Edn. Assn. Ohio (pres. 1981), Nat. Indian Edn. Assn. (bd. dirs. 1983-86, 1st v.p.), Citizens League Cleve., Assn. Childhood Edn., Assn. Supervision and Curriculum Devel., Phi Delta Kappa. Democrat. Methodist. Clubs: Zonta, Womens City, Women's Law Fund (bd. dirs. 1981—). Home: Box 338 Rio Grande OH 45674

SMITH, PEGGY MARIE, government official; b. Balt., Nov. 21, 1940; d. John Weldon and Cecelia Agnes (Goddard) S. Student U. Md., 1978-79, Catonsville Community Coll., 1979-80. Various secretarial positions, until 1973; adminstrv. officer Health Care Financing Adminstrn., Balt., 1973-80; adminstrv. specialist Social Security Adminstrn., Balt., 1980-85, mgmt. analyst, 1985—. Vol. Mercy Hosp., Balt., 1960-62, Baltimore County Gen. Hosp., Balt., 1971; hotline counselor Lighthouse, Inc., Balt., 1975-77; tchr. Salem Lutheran Ch. Sch., Balt., 1962-67. Mem. Nat. Assn. Female Execs. Avocations: writing, mainly poetry; reading; psychology; parapsychology; gardening. Office: Social Security Adminstrn 6401 Security Blvd Baltimore MD 21235

SMITH, PENELOPE PENCE, advertising executive; b. Salt Lake City, Jan. 23, 1943; d. Joseph Thomas and Carol Gretchen (Hofmann) Pence; B.A., U. Wash., 1963; M.A., Annenberg Sch. Communications, U. So. Calif., 1977. Asst. media buyer J. Walter Thompson Advt., Los Angeles, 1963-64; public relations dir. John Lithen Corp., Beverly Hills, Calif., 1964-65; public service dir. Metromedia KTTV, Los Angeles, 1965-66; assoc. producer Winchell-

Mahoney Show, Metromedia KTTV, Los Angeles, 1966-67; assoc. editor Sterling Publs., Tarzana, Calif., 1967-74; spl. features corr. N.Y. Times, 1972-75; mgr. product promotion Informatics Inc., Canoga Park, Calif., 1975-79; mgr. mktg. communications Rexon Bus. Machines Corp., Culver City, Calif., 1979-80; account mgr. Keye-Donna Pearlstein Inc., Beverly Hills, Calif., 1980-81; account exec. Tycer-Fultz-Bellack, Palo Alto, Calif., 1981-82; v.p. mktg. and account services Franson & Assocs., San Jose, Calif., 1982-84; v.p. client services Doug Gotthoffer & Co., Palo Alto, Calif., 1984-85; pres. Smith & Shows, Menlo Park, Calif., 1985—. Mem. Peninsula Women in Advt. (pres. 1983), Peninsula Mktg. Assn.

SMITH, PHOEBE, state agency official; b. Irwin County, Ga., Oct. 11, 1939; d. James Cleve and Winnie Eva (Thompson) S. Student pub. schs., Atlanta. Asst. office mgr. Rich's Dept. Store, Atlanta, 1959-69; statistical analyst assoc. State of Ga., Atlanta, 1970—. Author: Phoebe, 1979; Editor: Transsexual Voice Newsletter, 1981—. Mem. Gateway Gender Alliance, Metamorphosis Found. (hon.), Internat. Friendship Force Exchange Program. Avocation: Self-help. Home: 764 North Ave Hapeville GA 30354 Office: PO Box 16314 Atlanta GA

SMITH, PHYLLIS MAE, health care consultant; educator; b. Couer d'Alene, Idaho, May 2, 1935; d. Elmer Lee Smith and Kathryn Alice (Newell) Wilson. Diploma, Lutheran Bible Inst., Seattle, 1956, Emanuel Hosp. Sch. Nursing, Portland, Oreg., 1959; student Coll. San Mateo, Calif., 1971. Staff nurse in surgery Emanuel Hosp., Portland, 1959-61, St. Vincent's Hosp., Portland, 1962-63; head nurse central service Sacred Heart Hosp., Eugene, Idaho, 1964-69; dir. central services Peninsula Hosp., Burlingame, Calif., 1969-74; pres. Phyllis Smith Assocs., Inc., Lewiston, Idaho, 1975—. Contbr. to manuals, profl. jours. Mem. Internat. Assn. Hosp. Central Service Mgmt. (dir. edn. 1973—, chmn. technician edn. and affairs com. 1978—, John Perkins award, 1977, Chesire award 1977), Assn. for Advancement Med. Instrumentation, Nat. Assn. Female Execs. Episcopalian. Lodge: Eagles Aux. Avocations: fishing; walking; photography; chess; reading. Home and office: 3730 11th St Lewiston ID 83501

SMITH, PHYLLIS MCQUEEN, newspaper publisher, artist; b. Kaslo, B.C., Can., Jan. 22, 1912; came to U.S., 1929; d. Alfred and Eleanor Margaret (McCallum) McQueen; m. Albert Glenn Smith, June 25, 1934; children—Glenn McQueen, Shelley Louise, Craig Warren. B.A., Wash. State U., 1934. Sec. to publicist Farm Credit Adminstrn., Spokane, Wash., 1934-35; publicist Boeing Aircraft Co., Seattle, 1937-39; co-pub. Whidbey Press, Oak Harbor, Wash., 1939-65; freelance writer, artist. Author, editor: The McQueen Story, 1983-84. Bd. dirs. Florence Crittenton Home, Seattle, 1966-70; publicist March of Dimes, Seattle, 1968; pres. Seattle Co-Arts; (recipient best watercolor award 1976). Recipient Cert. of award OPA, 1946; Excellence in Feature Writing award Whidbey Island Record, 1948; 1st prizes for Best Column in State Weeklies, 1961, 66. Mem. Theta Sigma Phi (Women in Communications, Inc.). Republican. Congregationalist. Home: 2314 Rosemont Pl Seattle WA 98199

SMITH, RAMONA LOUISE, word processing service co. exec.; b. Dayton, Ohio, Oct. 11, 1954; d. Frank Ray and Patricia (Mattingly) S.; m. Hardy Lee Jones, July 2, 1983. B.S., U. Mo., Columbia, 1976. Sales rep. St. Louis Mktg. Surveys, 1976-77; retail salesman Sears Roebuck & Co., Chesterfield, Mo., 1977-78; word processing composition specialist Harris Data Communication, Dallas, 1978-79; v.p. W.P. Services, Plano, Tex., 1979-81; pres., owner, Words Plus, Dallas, 1981—. Mem. state bd. Women's Polit. Caucus, 1975-76; Mo. chmn. 18-year-old voter registration drive, Parkway West High, 1972. Mem. Nat. Assn. Female Execs., Sales and Mktg. Execs. Dallas (Rookie Mem. of Yr. 1981, bd. dirs. 1982-83) N. Dallas Network of Career Women (pres. 1985), Share in Success (1st v.p. programs 1986), Farmers Branch Bus. C. of C., Dallas C. of C. Club: Toastmasters (sec. 1981, treas. 1982) (Dallas). Home: 13352 Maham Rd Apt 174 Dallas TX 75240

SMITH, RÄNDI SIGMUND, industrial psychologist, management and corporate education consultant; b. Washington, Mar. 18, 1942; d. Frederick William and Marie Rändi (Ensrud) Sigmund; m. Richard Peter Smith, Feb. 13, 1965; children—Robin Lynne, Rändi Marie. B.A. in Sociology, Coll. William and Mary, 1963, M.A. in Indsl. Psychology, Norwich U., 1985; postgrad. in adult edn. Columbia U., 1985—. Info. ctr. staff mem. Nat. Assn. Food Chains, Washington, 1963-65; asst. corp. librarian Combustion Engring., Windsor, Conn., 1965-66; telephone usage counselor So. New Eng. Telephone, Hartford, Conn., 1966; quality assurance/systems analyst Aetna Life & Casualty, Hartford, 1966-67; pres. Smith and Assocs., Inc., West Hartford, Conn., 1968—; cons. interpersonal skills, corp. edn. Aetna Life & Casualty, Hartford, 1969-84, IBM Corp., White Plains, N.Y., 1975—, Xerox Corp., Webster, N.Y., 1975-85. Author: Written Communication for Data Processing, 1976-81; also profl. articles, children's story. Active Jr. League Hartford, 1976—, Lupus Found. Am.; pres. parent council, trustee Kingswood-Oxford Sch., West Hartford, 1985-86; eucharistic minister Roman Catholic Archdiocese of Hartford, 1972. Mem. Am. Soc. Tng. and Devel., Am. Mgmt. Assn., Internat. Assn. Airline Passengers, Nat. Assn. Female Execs. Club: Hartford Golf. Avocations: scuba diving; bridge. Office: Smith and Assocs Inc 87 Westmont Hartford CT 06117

SMITH, REBECCA MCCULLOCH, educator; b. Greensboro, N.C., Feb. 29, 1928; d. David Martin and Virginia Pearl (Woodburn) McCulloch; B.S., Woman's Coll., U. N.C., 1947, M.S., 1952; Ph.D., U. N.C., Greensboro, 1967; m. George Clarence Smith, Jr., Mar. 30, 1945; 1 son, John Randolph. Tchr. public schs., N.C. and S.C., 1947-57; instr. U. N.C., Greensboro, 1958-66, asst. prof. child devel. and family relations, 1967-72, assoc. prof., 1973-78, prof., 1979—, dir. grad. program, 1975-82; ednl. cons. depts. edn. N.C., S.C., Ont.; vis. prof. N.W. La. State U., 1965, 67, U. Wash., 1970, Hood Coll., 1976, 86. Recipient Teaching Excellence award U. N.C., Greensboro, 1972, named Outstanding Alumna Sch. Home Econs., 1976; recipient Sperry award for service to families N.C. Family Life Council, 1979. Mem. Am. Home Econs. Assn., Nat. Council Family Relations (exec. com. 1974-76, Osborne award 1973), Omicron Nu. Author: Teaching About Family Relationships, 1975; Klemer's Marriage and Family Relationships, 2d edit., 1975; Resources for Teaching About Family Life Education, 1976; Family Matters: Concepts in Marriage and Personal Relationships, 1982; asso. editor Family Relations (Jour. Applied Family and Child Studies), 1980—; ednl. cons. Current Life Studies, 1977-84. Home: 1212 E Ritters Lake Rd Greensboro NC 27406 Office: Dept Child Devel and Family Relations Sch Home Economics U NC Greensboro NC 27412

SMITH, ROBBIE, oil company executive; b. Monroe, La., June 3, 1948; B.S. in English and Journalism, Roosevelt U., Chgo., 1977. With Standard Oil Co. (Ind.), Chgo., 1967—, urban affairs rep., 1977-80, coordinator urban affairs, 1980—; pres. The Right Image, Inc. Chmn. Chgo. City Wide Coll. Adv. Council, 1979—; exec. v.p. Chgo. Urban Affairs Council, 1978, now mem.; mem. task force tng. and employment Neighborhood Inst., 1978-80; bus. adv. council Westside Cluster High Schs., 1978—; mem. adv. bd. United Career Action Now, 1979-82; mem. minority profl. services com. Chgo. United; bd. dirs. Chgo. Old Town Boys Club, 1978-81, vice chmn., 1980-82; deacon Chgo. United Recipient various recognition awards. Mem. League Black Women (pres.), Cosmopolitan C. of C. (pres.), Black Pub. Relations Soc. (pres.), Blacks in Philanthropy, Nat. Assn. Media Women, Assn. Blacks in Energy, Westside Assn. Community Action, The Com. (pres.). Clubs: Chgo. City, Publicity (Chgo.). Office: 200 E Randolph Dr Room MC 4308 Chicago IL 60601

SMITH, ROBYNE MARIA, legal assistant; b. Gary, Ind., Aug. 26, 1959; d. Sylvia Maria Hill; m. Dennis Lawrence Smith, June 5, 1982. B.A., DePaul U., 1981; cert. paralegal U. So. Calif., 1982. Paralegal asst. Fields & Fields, Chgo., 1978-80; legal clk. Walzer & Gabrielson, Los Angeles, 1981-82; legal asst. Northrop Corp., Los Angeles, 1982-85; legal asst. Shea & Gould, Los Angeles, 1985—. Sec., Provisions, Inc., Los Angeles, 1984—; legal cons. Telview Communications Group, Los Angeles, 1982—. Mem. NAACP, Los Angeles Paralegal Assn., Nat. Fedn. Legal Assts., Am. Film Inst., Nat. Assn. Female Execs. Democrat. Roman Catholic. Avocations: piano; reading. Office: Shea & Gould 1800 Ave of the Stars Los Angeles CA 90067

SMITH, ROSALYN KAY, mfg. co. exec.; b. Louisville, June 21, 1950; d. Charles Edward and Katherine Estelle (Taylor) S.; M.S.W., U. Louisville, 1981. Mgr. corp. recruiting Lincoln Nat. Life, 1976-78; sr. partner Smith Hires Assos., Wilmington, Del., 1978-80; personnel cons. Control Data Corp., Phila., 1980-81; affirmative action cons. Digital, Maynard, Mass., 1981, mgr. human resources, 1981-83, orgnl. effectiveness cons., 1983—; seminar leader Minority Women in Orgns., Simmons Coll.; participant, leader innovations for women program Urban League; tng. cons. for univs.; lectr. Mem. Black Exec. Exchange Program, Nat. Assn. Female Execs., Am. Mgmt. Assn., Alpha Kappa Alpha. Democrat. Episcopalian. Office: Digital 14 Walkup Dr Westboro MA 01581

SMITH, RUBY LUCILLE, librarian; b. Nobob, Ky., Sept. 19, 1917; d. James Ira and Myrtie Olive (Crabtree) Jones; A.B., Western Ky. State Tchrs. Coll., 1943, M.A., 1966; m. Kenneth Cornelius Smith, Dec. 25, 1946; children—Kenneth Cornelius, Corma Ann. Tchr. rural schs., Barren County, Ky., 1941-42; tchr. secondary sch. English, librarian Temple Hill Consol. Sch., Glasgow, Ky., 1943-49, 49-51, 53-56, sch. librarian, 1956-83. Sec. Barren County Cancer Soc., 1968-70, Barren County Fair Bd., 1969-70; leader 4-H Club, 1957-72, mem. council Barren County. Trustee Mary Wood Weldon Meml. Library, 1964—; trustee Barren County Pub. Library, 1969—, sec., 1969—. Mem. NEA (life), Ky. Edn. Assn., Ky. Assn. Sch. Librarians (sec. 1970-71), 3d Dist. Library Assn. (pres. 1944, 66), Barren County Edn. Assn. (pres. 1960-62, treas. 1979-80), Ky. Audio Visual Assn., Ret. Tchrs. Assn. (pres. 1984—), Ky. Library Trustee Assn. (bd. dirs. 1985—), Barren County Republican Women's Club, Monroe Assn. Woman's Missionary Union (dir. 1968-72, 79-83 Monroe Assn. Baptists (library dir. 1972—), Delta Kappa Gamma. Home: Route 1 Box 65 Summer Shade KY 42166

SMITH, RUTH HODGES, city clerk; b. Roanoke, Va., Jan. 15, 1931; d. James Elpherson and Ruth Elizabeth (Morgan) Hodges; m. Leon Menaclus Smith, June 18, 1978; children—Dorothy Ruth Smith Swift, Marvis Frances Smith Mills. Student Potomac State Coll., 1949-51. Cert. mcpl. clk., Va. Legal sec. Commonwealth Atty., Woodstock, Va., 1952-54; adminstrv. asst. Nelson Oil Corp., Mt. Jackson, Va., 1954-56; exec. sec., office mgr. Tidewater Va. Devel. Co., Norfolk, Va., 1956-72; personnel mgr. Nepratex Industries, Virginia Beach, Va., 1972-77; realtor, life agt. Real Estate/Ins., 1976-78; city clk. City of Virginia Beach, 1978—. Sec.-treas. Hospice Virginia Beach, 1981—. Mem. Internat. Mcpl. Clks., Va. Mcpl. Clks. (pres. 1982-84), Clubs: Republican, Pilot (officer 1960-72). Lodges: Zonta Internat. (dir. 1983—), Order Eastern Star, Daus. of Nile, Shriners. Avocations: crafts; bicycling; skating; traveling. Home: 4504 E Honeygrove Rd Virginia Beach VA 23455 Office: City of Virginia Beach Room 281 City Hall Mcpl Ctr Virginia Beach VA 23456

SMITH, RUTH HUNTER, lawyer; b. Columbus, Ohio, Dec. 23, 1949; d. Richard F. and Bernice E. (Strawser) Hunter; m. Joel Thomas Smith, 1970 (div. 1972); 1 son, Jason C. B.S. in Edn., Ohio State U., 1973, J.D., 1977. Bar: Ohio, 1977. Tchr. English, Columbus Pub. Schs., 1973-74; cons. Franklin County Mpcl. Ct., Columbus, 1975-76; research asst. Ohio State U. Coll. Law, Columbus, 1976; law clk. Vorys, Sater, Seymour & Pease, Columbus, 1976-77; legal counsel John W. Galbreath & Co., Columbus, Ohio, Denver, 1977—; lectr. Northwest Ctr. Profl. Edn., Portland, Oreg., 1984. Milton R. Bierly scholar Ohio State U., 1972; Coll. of Law scholar Ohio State Univ. Coll. Law, 1974, 75, 76. Mem. ABA, Ohio State Bar Assn., Columbus Bar Assn., Am. Corp. Counsel Assn., Franklin County Women Lawyers Assn. Office: John W Galbreath & Co 180 E Broad St Columbus OH also 1560 Broadway Denver CO 80202

SMITH, SADIE NORMAN, nurse; b. Cedartown, Ga., Nov. 5, 1941; d. Homer Eugene and Flora Mae (Hinton) Norman; m. Joe Henry Smith, Aug. 23, 1962; children—Joe Henry, Joetta L., Jo-Carole L. Diploma in Nursing, Grady Meml Hosp. Sch. Nursing, Atlanta, 1962; Cert., Meharry Med. Coll., Nashville, 1980; student U. Tenn., Chattanooga, 1980—. R.N., Tenn. Staff nurse Erlanger Med. Ctr., Chattanooga, 1962-82; relief supr. Moccasin Bend Mental Health Inst., Chattanooga, 1967-69, supr., 1984—; health occupations instr. Kirkman Tech. High Sch., Chattanooga, 1972-74; relief supr. Met. Hosp., Chattanooga, 1983-84. Active Boy Scouts Am., 1975-76. Mem. Am. Nurses Assn. Mem. Worldwide Ch. of God. Avocations: reading, music, Bible study. Home: 5436 Winniespan Rd Chattanooga TN 37416 Office: Moccasin Bend Mental Health Inst Chattanooga TN 37405

SMITH, SALLY ANN, commercial development specialist; b. Mt. Olive, N.C., June 11, 1934; d. Leon Joseph and Ludia Irene (Montague) Simmons; B.A., Duke U., 1956; postgrad. (Rotary Found. fellow) U. Liege (Belgium), 1957, Claremont Grad. Sch., 1970-72; children—Molly, Barbara, Sara, Mary Kathryn. With Gen. Elec. Co., 1963-81, account rep. GE time-sharing, Los Angeles, 1969, br. mgr., El Monte, Calif., 1970, mgr. nat. sales support, Bethesda, Md., 1973, mgr. product programs, Rockville, Md., 1974, mgr. fed. ops., Washington, 1975, mgr. mktg. support Internat. Mktg. Dept., GE Info. Services Div., Rockville, 1977-80, mgr. operating plans Program Mgmt. Dept., 1980-81; with Electronic Data Systems Corp., 1981-84; dir. bus. planning Info. Tech. Group, Bethesda, Md., 1981-83; group v.p. planning and communications, Dallas, 1983-84; dir. comml. devel. U.S. West, Denver, 1984—; chmn. Elfun Mgmt. Orgn., Washington, D.C. chpt. Active, Montgomery County Swim League, Stedwick Swim Team, 1973-77. Mem. Phi Beta Kappa, Tau Psi Omega, Pi Mu Epsilon, Sigma Kappa. Democrat. Methodist. Club: Denver Sporting. Home: 1626 S Syracuse St Denver CO 80231 Office: 7800 E Orchard Rd Englewood CO 80111

SMITH, SARAH JANE (SALLY), state official; b. Pekin, Ill., Jan. 23, 1945; d. Claude P. and Jane (Prettyman) S.; B.S. in Music Edn., U. Ill.; postgrad. U. Alaska. Tchr. jr. high sch. Los Angels City Schs., 1968-69; adminstrv. asst. Office of Gov. of Alaska, 1971-74; project field rep Alaska Dept. Community and Regional Affairs, 1974-76; expeditor H.W. Blackstock, Inc., 1979-82; mem. Alaska Ho. of Reps. from 20th Dist., 1977-83, majority whip, 1977-79, mem. fin. com., 1979-81, chmn. rules chmn., 1981; exec. dir. Fairbanks Pvt. Industry Council, 1983-84; dir. div. pub. services Alaska Dept. Revenue, 1984—. Dir. choir Juneau Meth. and Presbyn. chs., 1972-74, 86—, Fairbanks Presbyn. Ch., 1974-75; historian Fairbanks Drama Assn., 1974-76; adv. bd. Assn. Children with Learning Disabilities, 1978-80; commr. Fairbanks Historic Preservation Commn., 1982-84; bd. dirs. Friends of U. Alaska Mus., 1983-84. Named Outstanding Freshman Legislator, 1976. Mem. Fairbanks Assn. Arts. Democrat. Club: PEO. Office: 1111 W 8th St Room 108 Juneau AK 99801

SMITH, SHARON LEE, advertising executive; b. Corpus Christi, Tex., Aug. 18, 1947; d. James Horace and Harriet Leona (McCune) Chesnutt; m. Roger John Barry, Sept. 20, 1970 (div. 1975); m. Jerry Clark Smith, Oct. 14, 1975; 1 child, Wesley Chesnutt. Student Western Wash. State U., 1965-69, Bklyn. Mus. Art Sch., 1971, Pratt Inst., 1972, Sch. Visual Arts, N.Y.C., 1973. Reservation agt. United Air Lines, N.Y.C., 1969-70; art dir. Folwell Assocs., N.Y.C., 1970-71; ptnr. Folwell & Barry Advt., N.Y.C., 1971-73; freelance graphic artist, advt. cons. Cornwallville, N.Y., 1973-75; ptnr. Hudson River Graphics, Catskill, N.Y., 1976-77; ptnr. Chesnutt & Smith, Catskill, 1977—. Instr. advt. Coxsackie Corr Inst., N.Y., 1974-75. Pres., Fedn. Block Assns., Bklyn., 1972. Republican. Lutheran. Clubs: Catskill Mountain Kennel (pres. 1981-83) (Cairo, N.Y.); Albany Schenectady Golden Retriever (pres. 1980-82). Office: Chesnutt & Smith 22 Spring St Catskill NY 12414

SMITH, SHARON LYNN, flooring company executive; b. Columbus, Ohio, Apr. 6, 1956; d. Charles Robert and Leona Marie (McMasters) Grim; m. David Gerald Smith, Sept. 8, 1973; 1 dau., Anna Marie. Sec., file clk. Victors Temporary, Columbus, 1975-77; sec., estimator W.R. Shepherd, Inc., Powell, Ohio, 1977-79, v.p., 1980-83; pres. Central and So. Interiors, Inc., Powell, 1983—. Mem. Builders Exchange of Central Ohio, Nat. Assn. Women in Constrn., Christian Motorcyclists Assn. Republican. Mem. Christian Missionary Alliance. Avocations: water skiing; motorcycling; crafts. Home: 2057 Decker Ct Worthington OH 43085 Office: Central and Southern Interiors Inc 390 W Olentangy St Powell OH 43065

SMITH, SHIRLEY ANN O'BRYAN, broadcasting executive; b. Louisville, July 28, 1949; d. Bernard Burch and Shirley Hull (Hardesty) O'Bryan; B.A. in Journalism, English and Speech, Murray (Ky.) State U., 1971; M.A. in Creative Writing, U. Louisville, 1986; m. Larry James Smith, Aug. 23, 1969; 1 child, Jessica Lauren. Writer, reporter, copy editor Enterprise Newspaper, Lexington Park, Md., 1969-70; writer Sta. WKCT, Bowling Green, Ky., 1971-74; announcer, writer Sta. WLBJ, Bowling Green, 1974; announcer, public service dir. Sta. WHEL, New Albany, Ind., 1974-75; assignment editor, newscaster, reporter, writer Sta. WKLO, Louisville, 1974-77; news dir., program dir. Sta. WNUU, Louisville, 1977-78; news dir. Ky. Network, Louisville, 1978-82; pres. Ky. UPI Internat. Adv. Bd., 1981-82; nat. correspondent, anchorperson Mut. Broadcasting System, Washington, 1982—; spl. asst., speech writer, media cons. to dep. adminstr. EPA, Washington, 1986—; speaker, tchr. in field. Recipient Louie award public affairs programming, 1979, UPI Broadcast awards, 1981; named Ky. col., 1979. Mem. Nat. Assn. Female Execs., Women in Radio and TV, Radio TV News Dirs. Assn., Nat. Assn. State Radio Network News Dirs., Murray State U. Alumni Assn., Sigma Delta Chi. Roman Catholic. Author articles, features in mags. Home: 7402 Hamilton St Annandale VA 22003 Office: Mut Broadcasting System 1755 S Jefferson Davis Hwy Arlington VA 22202

SMITH, STELLA ELIZABETH, multi-housing company executive; b. Springfield, Mo., July 6, 1931; d. Russell Lena and Oma Oble (Stockstill) Baber; m. Arthur A. Smith, May 30, 1952 (div. 1981); children—Michael A., Barbara A., James Edward, Cynthia Sue. Student St. Louis U., 1981-83. Office mgr. Consumers Warehouse Markets, Springfield, 1948-52; acctg. clk. Mathieson Chem. Corp., Little Rock, 1952-54; group leader McDonnell Aircraft Corp., St. Louis, 1954-59; office mgr. Arthur A. Smith, M.D., O'Fallon, Ill., 1968-74; pres., chief exec. officer Mantek, Inc., Springfield, 1981—. Bd. dirs. Signal Hill United Meth. Ch., Belleville, Ill., 1973—. Mem. Nat. Assn. Women Bus. Owners, Nat. Assn. Female Execs., P.E.O. (treas. 1983-84), Springfield Apt. Assn., Mo. Apt. Assn., Nat. Apt. Assn., St. Clair County LWV (bd. dirs. 1978-84), Women's Aux. Ill. Med. Soc. (bd. dirs. 1968-72), Women's Aux. St. Clair County Med. Soc. (safety chmn. 1963-69), Greater Springfield C. of C., St. Clair County Genealogy Soc. (charter 1977). Republican. Avocations: travel; theater; reading; collecting cook books. Home: 206 Country Club Ln Belleville IL 62223 Office: Mantek Inc 1010 E Elm St Springfield MO 65806

SMITH, SUE IRBY, insurance company executive; b. Dorchester, Tex., July 22, 1932; d. Titus Ardell and Daisy Mae (Adams) Irby; m. Charley William Smith, Nov. 5, 1948; 1 child, Linda S. Smith Cumming. Student math. and mgmt. Tex. Christian U., 1960-64. From clk. to mgr. World Service Life Ins. Co., Ft. Worth, 1957-80; v.p. Savers Annuity Ins. Co., Ft. Worth, 1981—. Democrat. Baptist. Home: 7224 Monterrey Dr Ft Worth TX 76112 Office: Savers Annuity Ins Co 235 NE Loop 820 Suite 500 Hurst TX 76053

SMITH, SUELLEN FANDT, communications company staff; b. Newton, N.J., June 9, 1943; d. Edward Lloyd and Mary (Boitano) Fandt; B.Mus., Westminster Coll., New Wilmington, Pa., 1965; postgrad. Trenton (N.J.) State Coll., Pace U.; m. Gary Thomas Smith, Aug. 3, 1968 (div. Sept. 1983). Tchr. elem. sch. music and reading, N.J., 1965-81; with E-Systems Co., Tampa, Fla., 1981; ops. clk. Dart Center, GTE Co., Tampa, 1981—, Bus. Phone Systems div., 1984—, GTE Communications Corp. (fully separate subs.), 1985—; lectr., Workshop presenter; cons. in field. Vol. counselor Hillsborough County Suicide and Crisis Center, 1984—. Recipient John Phillip Sousa award, 1961. Mem. NEA, Music Educators Nat. Conf., N.J. Edn. Assn., Mu Phi Epsilon. Author curriculum materials. Office: GTE Communications Corp 16107 Sagebrush Rd Tampa FL 33618

SMITH, SUSAN JOYCE, educator; b. Phila., Aug. 27, 1950; d. William and Joyce Laura (Moyer) Kodad; B.S. cum laude, Lock Haven State U., 1972; M.S., Bloomsburg State Coll., 1974; Ed.D., U. S.C., 1983; m. Jeffrey W. Smith, Aug. 5, 1972; children—Jeffrey W. II, Siri Suzanne. Tchr. severely retarded Central Susquehanna Area Intermediate Unit, Lewisburg, Pa., 1972-74; tchr. of trainable retarded Capital Area Intermediate Unit, Harrisburg, Pa., 1974-78, instructional adv. of the trainable program, 1978-79; ednl. evaluator, coordinator tutoring program Winthrop Coll., Rock Hill, S.C., 1979, asst. prof. spl. edn., 1979—. Mem. AAUW, Council Exceptional Children. Democrat. Roman Catholic. Home: 3811 High Ridge Rd Matthews NC 28105 Office: Winthrop College Withers Bldg Rock Hill SC 29733

SMITH, SUSAN KIMSEY, lawyer; b. Phoenix, Jan. 15, 1947; d. William Lewis and Margaret (Bowes) Kimsey; m. Alfred Jon Olsen, Apr. 15, 1979. Student U. Ariz., 1965-66; B.A., Principia Coll., 1969; M.A., U. Va., 1970; J.D., Ariz. State U., 1975. Bar: Ariz. 1976. Atty., Valley Nat. Bank Ariz., Phoenix, 1976-77; ptnr. Lane & Smith, Ltd., Phoenix, 1977-78; ptnr. Olsen-Smith, Ltd., Phoenix, 1979—, also pres.; lectr. Author: Estate Planning Practice Manual for the State Bar of Arizona, 1984; bd. editors Practical Tax Lawyer; contbr. articles to legal jours. Mem. 401-II Com., 1982—, Tax Study Group, 1979—, The Group (nat. pension study group), 1982—; bd. dirs. Samaritan Health Found. Recipient J.P. Walker Am. History award Principia Coll., 1969. Mem. ABA (chmn. com. econs. of tax practice 1983-84, chmn. com. liaison with other ABA sects. and coms. 1983—, com. income taxation of estates and trusts 1979—, com. D-2 formation adminstrn. and distbn. of trusts 1982—), State Bar Ariz. (chmn. sect. taxation 1985-86; Ethics award 1974), Maricopa County Bar Assn., Valley Estate Planning Council (pres. 1983-84), Central Ariz. Estate Planning Council, Alpha Lambda Delta, Phi Alpha Eta. Home: 3315 E Claremont Paradise Valley AZ 85253 Office: 301 E Virginia Ave Suite 3300 Phoenix AZ 85000

SMITH, SUSAN LEA, lawyer; b. Whittier, Calif., Oct. 31, 1953; d. Herbert Frank and Ruth Louise (Norton) Smith. B.A., Reed Coll., 1976; M.Pub. Policy, Harvard U., 1980, J.D., 1980. Bar: Colo. 1980, D.C. 1981. Assoc. firm Holland & Hart, Washington, 1980—; research assoc. Applied Social Research, Portland, Oreg., 1974-77; asst. to Sec. of State, State of Mass., Boston, 1977; asst. dir. Envion. Quality and Indsl. Fuel Use Project, Harvard Energy and Environ. Policy Ctr., Kennedy Sch., Cambridge, Mass., 1979-80. Sr. editor Harvard Environ. Law Rev., 1979-80; contbr. articles to profl. jours. Kennedy Sch. fellow, 1976-77. Mem. ABA, Colo. Bar Assn., D.C. Bar Assn., Colo. Women's Bar Assn., D.C. Women's Bar Assn. Democrat. Unitarian. Home: 1108 N Rochester St Arlington VA 22205 Office: Holland and Hart 1875 I St NW Suite 1200 Washington DC 20006

SMITH, SUSAN MAGILL, educational administrator, arts consultant; b. Denver, June 3, 1949; d. Robert Hugh and Elizabeth Nelle (Markel) Magill; m. Peter Lawrence Smith, July 29, 1972. B.A., St. Olaf Coll., 1971; postgrad. Mankato State U., 1973-75. Dir. residence life Luther Coll., Decorah, Iowa, 1975-79, asst. to pres. for programming and publs., 1979-85; dir. coll. relations Earlham Coll., Richmond, Ind., 1985—; cons. Artreach, Mpls., 1982—. Editor Luther Mag., 1979-85. Mem. regional bd. Guthrie Theatre. Mem. Univ. and Coll. Design Assn., Assn. Coll. and Univ. Arts Adminstrs., Nat. Assn. Student Personnel Adminstrs. Sigurd Olson Meml. Assn. Sierra Club, Cousteau Soc. Lutheran. Avocations: sports for fun, music, reading, travel. Home: 218 S 19th St Richmond IN Office: Earlham Coll Richmond IN 47374

SMITH, SUSAN SCHUYLER, interior designer, space planner; b. Newburgh, N.Y., Mar. 28, 1945; d. Robert Warren and Edith May (Thomas) S.; student Wheaton Coll., Norton, Mass., 1963-64; B. Design with honors, U. Fla., 1970. Interior designer Hasco, West Palm Beach, Fla., 1970-72, Robert Shaw & Assos., Palm Beach, Fla., 1972-74; partner Interior Assocs., West Palm Beach and Chgo., 1974-76, Michalaros & Smith, Palm Beach and Chgo., 1976-78; pres., owner Spectrum, Interior Design, West Palm Beach, 1978—. Mem. West Palm Beach Downtown Devel. Authority, 1981-85, sec.-treas., 1981-84; bd. dirs. West Palm Beach Downtown Assn., 1980—, pres., 1981—; bd. dirs. Palm Beach County Jr. Achievement, 1981—, Palm Beach County Devel. Bd., 1982—; bd. dirs. Big Bros./Big Sisters of Palm Beach County, 1979—, pres. 1980-81, nat. bd. dirs. 1982—; bd. dirs. United Way Palm Beach County, 1982-85; mem. Palm Beach County Econ. Council, 1983—. Mem. Am. Soc. Interior Designers, Inst. Bus. Design, AIA (affiliate), West Palm Beach C. of C. (dir. 1981—, v.p. 1981-83). Palm Beach C. of C., C. of C. of Palm Beach County (dir. 1981-84, v.p. 1981-82, pres.-elect 1983, pres. 1985). Presbyterian. Home: 3701 S Flagler Dr West Palm Beach FL 33401 Office: 325 S Olive Ave West Palm Beach FL 33401

SMITH, SUSIE IRENE, histotechnologist; b. Columbus, Ohio, Oct. 10, 1942; d. Taft and Evelyn (Samuels) Woodford; student Boston State Coll., 1975-80; m. Eugene Smith, Dec. 2, 1960; children—Regina Marie, Kimberly Denise, Teresa Yvette, Stacia Ann. Med. worker Boston City Hosp., 1970; lab. asst. Boston City Hosp., 1970-75, lab. technician hematopathology lab. Mallory Inst. Pathology, 1975-80, chief med. technologist, 1982—; lectr. and cons. in field. Sec., Com. to Elect Jesse L. Corbin for State Rep., 1981-82; treas. Whittier St. Tenants Assn., 1985-86. Mem. Am. Soc. Clin. Pathologists. Roman Catholic. Office: 784 Massachusetts Ave Boston MA 02118

SMITH, SYLVIA KAUFMAN, lawyer; b. Detroit, Nov. 10, 1945; d. Ira G. and Lillian (Farbman) Kaufman; m. Robert B. Smith, June 13, 1971 (div.); children—David, Mark, Barbara. B.A., U. Mich., 1967; J.D., Loyola U., Chgo., 1973; student U. Sheffield (Eng.), 1965-66. Bar: Ill. 1973, U.S. Dist. Ct. (no. dist.) Ill. 1980, U.S. Ct. Appeals (7th cir.) 1981, U.S. Supreme Ct. 1982. Sole practice, Flossmoor, Ill., 1975—. Author: Two Against One, 1964; Out of the Slums, 1968. Chmn. sch. bd., v.p. congregation Congregation Am Echad, Park Forest, Ill.; active Dysfunctioning Child Ctr., Chgo., Nat. Council Jewish

Women. Mem. ABA, South Suburban Bar Assn. Republican. Jewish. Home and Office: 1628 Sylvan Ct Flossmoor IL 60422

SMITH, TERESA JO, nurse, educator; b. Crawfordsville, Ind., Feb. 17, 1952; d. David L. and Jane (Taylor) Todd; m. Dennis R. Smith, June 13, 1980; children—Aaron Todd, Kyle Thomas. B.S.N., Ind. U.-Indpls., 1974, M.S. in Nursing of Children, 1981, postgrad. in nursing sci. Staff nurse Ind. U. Hosps., Indpls., 1973-76; faculty/asst. head nurse Wishard Hosp. Sch. Nursing, Indpls., 1976-78; asst. head nurse Riverview Hosp., Noblesville, Ind., 1978-79; asst. prof. nursing Ind. U.-Indpls., 1979-85, faculty sponsor Nursing Class 1982, 84; cons. Addison Wesley Pubs., 1985; reviewer Wiley Med. Books and Reston Pubs., 1983. Co-author (video teaching tapes) Basic Skills series: Taking Blood Pressure by Sphygmomanometry, 1983, Aids to Walking, 1982, Wet to Dry Dressings, 1982, Preparation for IV Therapy, 1982. Mem. Right to Life, Indpls., 1983; counselor Crisis Pregnancy Ctr., Christian Action Council, Indpls., 1983—; CPR instr. ARC, 1982. Mem. Am. Nurses Assn., Sigma Theta Tau. Mem. Ch. of the Nazarene. Home: 1525 Woodpointe Dr Indianapolis IN 46234

SMITH, VERA DAVIS, nurse; b. Wilson County, N.C., Dec. 7, 1926; d. Jessie Floyd and Addie Octavia (Lamm) Davis; m. Simon Joshua Smith, Dec. 7, 1955; children—Simon Benjamin, Jeffrey Carroll, Joseph Neil. R.N., Carolina Gen. Hosp., 1948; postgrad. Children's Hosp., Washington, 1951. Head nurse pediatrics Sampson County Meml. Hosp., Clinton, N.C., 1952; head nurse pediatrics Pitt County Meml. Hosp., Greenville, N.C., 1952-78, staff nurse ambulatory care, 1979-83, staff nurse neurology, 1983—. Democrat. Baptist. Home: Route 1 Box 90 Winterville NC 28590

SMITH, VERNA GREEN, editor; b. Oklee, Minn., Aug. 23, 1919; d. Roy Alva and Sarah Mathilda (Lindberg) Green; B.A. in Journalism (scholar), U. Mont., 1940; M.A. in Edn. Washington U., St. Louis, 1961; Ph.D. in Edn., St. Louis U., 1970; m. Alfred Nelson Smith, II, July 8, 1942 (dec.); children—Philip Roger, Alfred Nelson III, Stuart Thomas. Advt. mgr., columnist Glasgow (Mont.) Courier, 1940-41; reporter Gt. Falls (Mont.) Tribune, 1941-42; editor staff communication U.S. C.E., Ft. Peck, Mont., 1942; news editor Community News of Overland (Mo.), 1953-56; dir. public relations, tchr. English, Ritenour Sch. Dist., St. Louis County, Mo., 1956-66, adv. com. vocat. edn., 1979-80; tchr. sch. public relations St. Louis U., 1969; dir. communication services, editor CEMREL Reports, CEMREL, Inc., St. Louis, 1966-82; dir. publs. Midcontinent Regional Ednl. Lab., St. Louis, 1983-86; cons., 1986—. Pres. PTA, 1953-54; adminstrv. bd. Stephan Meml. Meth. Ch.; bd. dirs. The Learning Center, 1978-83. NDEA fellow St. Louis U., 1965; recipient ann. awards for publs. Mo. Press Women, 1967-80; 1st prize award(2), Nat. Fedn. Press Women, 1969, 2d prize, 1970; Disting. Alumnus award U. Mont. Alumni Assn., 1982. Mem. Nat. Sch. Public Relations Assn. (pres., founder Greater St. Louis chpt. 1965-66, citation of appreciation, 1973), Conf. Edn. St. Louis (charter), Met. St. Louis Press Club, Nat. Fedn. Press Women, Mo. Press Women, Ednl. Press Assn. Am., Ednl. Writers Assn., Women in Communications (pres. St. Louis chpt. 1951-52, 56-57; Regional Disting. Service award 1983) Council Ednl. Devel. and Research (exec. com. communications group 1969-73, chmn. 1981-82), Hist. Soc. Mont., U. Mont. Alumni Assn. (life), Mortar Bd., Kappa Delta Pi (chpt. pres. 1965-66), Delta Kappa Gamma, Pi Lambda Theta. Alpha Chi Omega, Contbr. articles to profl. jours. Home: 10311 Pineview Ct Saint Louis MO 63114

SMITH, VIRGINIA, television station executive; b. Billings, Mont., Mar. 28, 1931; d. Raymond A. and Emma A. (McGarvey) S. B.A. in Journalism, U. Mont., 1953; M.A. in Religious Studies, Gonzaga U., 1978. Copywriter, Sta-KBMY, Billings, 1953-55; in various positions Sta.-KGHL-Radio-TV, Billings, 1956-69; copy chief Sta.-KTVQ-TV, Billings, 1969-82, promotion dir., 1983-85. Columnist Eastern Mont. Catholic Register, 1982-83, 85—; contbr. articles to Ultreya mag., God's World Today, to nat. Cursillo lit. Active Cursillo Movement, including past mem. workshops, past nat. encounter positions; conv. del. Mont. Assn. Chs.; mem. communications com. Mont. Cath. Conf. Named TV Copywriter of Yr., Greater Mont. Found., 1975, 82; recipient First Place awards Mont. Ad Club, 1983.

SMITH, VIRGINIA DODD, congresswoman; b. Randolph, Iowa, June 30, 1911; d. Clifton Clark and Erville (Reeves) S.; A.B., U. Nebr., 1936; m. Haven N. Smith, Aug. 27, 1931. Nat. pres. Am. Country Life Assn., 1951-54; nat. chmn. Am. Farm Bur. Women, 1954-74; dir. Am. Farm Bur. Fedn., 1954-74, Country Women's Council; world dep. pres. Associated Country Women of World, 1962-68; mem. nat. home econs. research adv. com. U.S. Dept. Agr., 1960-65; mem. European inspection tour Crusade for Freedom, 1958; del. Republican Nat. Conv., 1956, 72; mem. 94th-99th congresses from 3d Nebr. Dist., mem. appropriations com., agr., energy and water subcoms., ranking mem. minority agr. appropriations com.; mem. Nat. Livestock and Meat Bd., 1955-58, Nat. Commn. Community Health Services, 1963-66, Nebr. Territorial Centennial Commn., 1953, Gov.'s Commn. on Status of Women, 1964-66; chmn. Presdl. Task Force on Rural Devel., 1969-70. Bd. govs. Agrl. Hall of Fame; v.p. Farm Film Found., 1964-74; Goodwill ambassador to Switzerland, 1950. Recipient Merit award DAR, 1956; Disting. Service award U. Nebr., 1956, 60; award Freedom Found., 1966; Eyes on Nebr. award Nebr. Optometric Assn., 1970; Internat. Service award Midwest Conf. World Affairs, 1973; Woman of Achievement award Nebr. Bus. and Profl. Women, 1971; selected as 1 of 6 U.S. women for 3-week goodwill mission to France, 1969; Outstanding 4-H Alumni award Iowa State U., 1973, 74; Farm Safety award Nat. Safety Council, 1983; Agrl. Achievement award Knights of Ak-Sar-Ben, 1983. Mem. AAUW, PEO (past pres.), Delta Kappa Gamma (state hon. mem.), Beta Sigma Phi (internat. hon. mem.), Chi Omega. Methodist. Clubs: Order Eastern Star, Bus. and Profl. Women. Office: 2202 Rayburn House Office Bldg Washington DC 20515

SMITH, WANDA JEAN, insurance salesperson; b. Atmore, Ala., July 25, 1949; d. Lloyd Scott and Edith (DuBois) Dutton; m. James A. Smith, Jr., May 29, 1970; children—Joyce A., Jeffrey A. B.A., St. Mary's U., 1970. Registered securities rep. Sec., So. Regional Edn. Bd., Atlanta, 1976-78; adminstrv. asst. Discovery Learning, Atlanta, 1978-79; sales sec. Mobay Chems., Atlanta, 1979-80; sales assoc. Lincoln Nat. Ins. Co., Atlanta, 1980-81, Am. Nat. Ins. Co., Atlanta, 1981—, Century 21 Grand South, College Park, Ga., 1984—. Pub. relations vol. East Point Track Club, 1985; mem. parents orgn. Clayton County Athletic Assn., 1986. Mem. Nat. Assn. Securities Dealers, Nat. Assn. Female Execs., Nat. Assn. Life Underwriters. Avocations: bowling; crafts. Office: WJ Smith & Assocs 1868-G W Washington Ave East Point GA 30344

SMITH, WANDA LUCILLE, realtor; b. Augusta, Ark., Nov. 1, 1923; d. Eugene Lewis and Berniece (Garrison) Billingslea; m. Claude Edgar McCreight, Jr., July 21, 1945 (div. 1962); children—William Richard, Claudia, Cindy; m. 2d, Clay Blevins Yoe, Jr., Jan. 5, 1965 (dec. 1967); m. 3d, Rex Alan Smith, Oct. 3, 1980. B.A., Henderson State U., 1945; postgrad. U. Ark., 1962-63, 1979-80. Tchr. Am. Sch. Belem, Para, Brazil, 1959-62, Fayetteville (Ark.) High Sch., 1962-65; owner, mgr. Clay Yoe Devel. Co., Fayetteville, 1967-79; co-owner, sec. Billingslea & Kirby, Inc., Nu-Tech., Inc., 1969-71; realtor Schultz & Taylor, Inc., Fayetteville, 1973-76; adminstrv. asst. to E. G. Bradberry, Fayetteville, 1977-79; sec. bd. B & B Resources, Inc., Continental Ozark, Inc., Fayetteville, Ark., 1977-79. Realtor Al Hughes Agy., Fayetteville, 1976—; editorial asst. to writers, Fayetteville, 1974—. Bd. dirs. P.T.A., Ft. Worth, 1956-58; sec. bd. Am. Sch. Belem, Para, Brazil, 1960-61. Mem. Ark. Realtors Assn., Nat. Assn. Realtors. Republican. Episcopalian. Home: 208 N East St Fayetteville AR 72701 Office: Al Hughes Agy 1765 N College Ave Fayetteville AR 72701

SMITH, WENDY HOPE, lawyer; b. N.Y.C., Jan. 19, 1957; d. Morton and Doris Smith. A.B., Smith Coll., 1978; J.D., Boston U., 1981. Bar: N.J. 1981; U.S. Dist. Ct. 1981, U.S. Ct. Appeals (3d cir.), Supreme Ct. of U.S. Law sec. to judge Superior Ct. N.J., Bergen County, 1981-82; assoc. firm Sellar, Richardson, Stuart & Chisholm, Newark, 1982—; mem. adv. com. Inst. Continuing Legal Edn., 1983—. Mem. ABA, N.J. Bar Assn., Bergen County Bar Assn., Essex County Bar Assn., Trial Attys. N.J., Mensa. Club: Smith Coll. Alumnae Assn. (fund rep. 1978-83). Home: 300 Winston Dr 2320 Cliffside Park NJ 07010 Office: Sellar Richardson Stuart & Chisholm 1180 Raymond Blvd Newark NJ 07102

SMITH, WILDA MAXINE, history educator; b. Gove, Kans., May 17, 1924; d. Corwin Leroy and Mabel Luzelle (Roberts) S. A.B. in History, Fort Hays State Coll., 1953, M.S., 1957; Ph.D., U. Ill., 1960. Elem. sch. tchr. schs. in Gove County, Kans., 1943-49; tchr. history Hays High Sch., Kans., 1953-57; asst. prof. history Fort Hays State Coll., Kans., 1960-63, assoc. prof., 1963-66, prof. history, 1966-77; prof. history Fort Hays State U., 1977—, chmn. dept., 1981—. Contbr. articles and book revs. to profl. jours. Mem. Kans. Com. for Humanities, Topeka, 1982-85; bd. dirs. Kans. State Hist. Soc., Topeka, 1983—. Univ. fellow U. Ill., Urbana-Champaign, 1958-60; recipient W.C. Wood award Fort Hays State U., 1975, Pilot award for Outstanding Faculty Woman, Srs. and Alumni Assn. Bd. Fort Hays State U., 1984. Mem. Orgn. Am. Historians, Nat. Women's Studies Assn. (nat. coordinating council 1977-80), Kans. History Tchrs. Assn. (exec. bd. 1973), ACLU, Common Cause, NOW, LWV, Delta Kappa Gamma (pres. 1974-76), Phi Delta Kappa, Phi Kappa Phi. Avocations: fishing; traveling. Home: 2924 Walnut St Hays KS 67601 Office: Fort Hays State U 600 Park St Hays KS 67601-4099

SMITH, WILMA JANICE, writer, columnist; b. Pryor, Okla., Aug. 15, 1926; d. William Henry and Mary Jo (Buffington) Bell; m. Merle Thomas Smith, Apr. 30, 1948. Student Okla. A&M Coll., 1946, Okla. Sch. Bus., 1947; continuing edn. in law, history and theology. Clk. U.S. Postal Service, Tulsa, 1945; clk.-typist Social Security Office, Tulsa, 1947-50; rec. sec. Acad. Country Music, Hollywood, Calif., 1975-78; contbg. editor Nashville Star Reporter, 1977-78; freelance writer on country music field, 1973-85; publicist U. Ill. Press, Urbana, 1975-76; profl. talent booker, Hollywood, 1975-80; record and book reviewer various pubs.; biographer, cons. to Country and Western music performers; photographer for Country and Western publs. Republican precinct worker, So. Ill. area, 1960, So. Calif. area, 1964-85. Mem. Acad. Country Music (sec. 1975-77), Greater Los Angeles Press Club, Calif. Country Music Assn. Mem. Disciples of Christ. Lodge: Rainbow Girls. Avocations: collecting celebrity and presidential autographed photos; raising and showing Boston Terriers; Indian affairs; travel; gardening. Home and Office: 503 N Platina Dr Diamond Bar CA 91765

SMITH, YVONNE SMART, advertising agency executive; b. Asheville, N.C., June 25, 1947; d. Gardner Ford and Yvonne (Boyd) Smart. B.F.A., Auburn U., 1969. Asst. art dir. Mademoiselle mag., N.Y.C., 1969-71; art dir. Cargill, Wilson & Acree Advt., Charlotte, N.C., 1971-74; art dir., creative supr. Tracy-Locke Advt., Dallas, 1974-76; v.p., assoc. creative dir., exec. art dir. Chiat/Day Advt., Los Angeles, 1976—; guest lectr. UCLA, 1980-83, Art Ctr. Coll. Design, Los Angeles, 1982. Subject of profl. articles. Recipient One Show award N.Y. Art Dirs. Club, 1974-83, Belding awards Los Angeles Advt. Club, 1976-83, Andy awards N.Y. Arts Dirs. Club, 1976-83, Art Dirs. Club award, 1976—, Steven Kelly award, 1983, 84, Clio awards, 1984, CA awards, 1976-84. Mem. Communicating Arts (sec. 1974), Los Angeles Creative Club. Club: N.Y. Jr. League (N.Y.C.). Office: Chiat/Day Advt 517 S Olive St Los Angeles CA 90013

SMITHER, SUZANNE BEALE, editor; b. Washington, Mar. 21, 1949; d. James Madison and Josephine Mary (Golemgeske) Smither; m. John Irving Stanley, Dec. 23, 1976 (div. July 1981); m. 2d Robert Gerald Miller, Oct. 24, 1983. Student St. Mary's Coll., Notre Dame, Ind., 1965-66, UniversitéCatholique de l'Ouest, Angers, France, 1966-67, St. Mary's Coll. and U. Notre Dame, 1967-68. Publs. asst. Am. Assn. on Mental Deficiency, Washington, 1968-69; assoc. editor Metro Mag., Hartford, Conn., 1970-71; area news reporter/editor Winsted Evening Citizen (Conn.), 1972-73; mgmt. cons. Curber Assocs., Washington, 1974; reporter The Evening Times, West Palm Beach, Fla., 1975-76, asst. city editor, 1976-78, features editor, 1978, asst. mng. editor, 1978-79, mng. editor, 1980—; chmn. adv. com. William S. Miller Awards for Enterprise Reporting, U. Fla./Cox Fla. Newspapers, 1980-82; ind. researcher in psychology of mgmt. Developer concept and prototype for U.S. Navy Jour. of Human Relations, 1974. chief press sect. Eugene McCarthy Presdl. Campaign, 3d Congl. Dist., Ind., 1968. Mem. Fla. Soc. Newspaper Editors (sec.-treas. 1982-83; pres. 1983-84, 1st Place award for depth reporting 1977), AP Mng. Editors, Am. Soc. Tng. and Devel. Roman Catholic. Clubs: Govs. of Palm Beaches (founding); Washington Golf and Country, The Neighbors (Arlington, Va); The Seton Guild (Washington). Office: Palm Beach Newspapers Inc 2751 S Dixie Hwy West Palm Beach FL 33405

SMITHERS, JANE BRAITMAYER, mfg. co. exec.; b. Washington, May 25, 1915; d. Otto Ernest and Kathleen (Ketcham) Braitmayer; B.A., Vassar Coll., 1937; m. William Henry Howell, Aug. 7, 1937 (dec. 1961); children—Kathleen, William David, Marian Braitmayer; m. 2d, John Abram Smithers, June 13, 1964; stepchildren—Margaret Smithers Koeniger, John A., Eleanor Smithers Blehnik, James P. Rec. sec. Children's Home, Inc., Poughkeepsie, N.Y., 1942, Dutchess County Planned Parenthood, 1941; corp. sec., dir. Smithers Tools and Machine Products, Inc., Rhinebeck, N.Y., 1965—; former dir. Bankers Trust Hudson Valley, N.A. Chmn. com. on detention Dutchess County Social Planning Council, 1949; pres. Dutchess County Soc. Mental Health, 1958-59; mem. Dutchess County Youth Bd., 1968-70; founder, pres. No. Dutchess Community Services, 1969; founder, pres. No. Dutchess Day Care Center, Inc., 1971-73, now mem. adv. bd.; bd. dirs. No. Dutchess Hosp. Republican. Episcopalian. Clubs: Sippican Tennis, Beverly Yacht (Marion, Mass.); Jr. League, Vassar (Poughkeepsie); Windermere Island (Bahamas). Home: RD 2 Box 116 Red Hook NY 12571

SMITH HARPER-NORMAN, BARBARA JEAN, government contract specialist, radio personality; b. Phillip, Miss., Feb. 14, 1945; d. Mose Reynolds and Geneva (Smith) Harper; m. Thomas S. Norman, May 4, 1963 (div. 1982); children—Richele Suzette, Christopher Thomas. Student Columbia U., 1973; B.A. in Social Work and Psychology, U. No. Iowa, 1974; postgrad. Ohio State U., 1982, U. Iowa, 1982-83. Outreach worker Jesse Cosby Neighborhood Ctr., Waterloo, Iowa, 1965-68; dir. Midtown Community Action Ctr., Waterloo, 1968-70; news reporter Sta. KWWL, NBC TV, Waterloo, 1972-74; reporter, photographer, host A.M. Quad-Cities Sta. WQAD, ABC-TV, Moline, Ill., 1974-79; sta. mgr. Sta. KUCB-FM, Des Moines, 1980; pastoral asst. Central Presbyn. Ch., Rock Island, Ill., 1982; govt. contract specialist Rock Island Arsenal, 1984—, equal opportunity employment counselor, 1985—; jazz disc jockey, radio personality Sta. KALA-FM pub. radio, Davenport, Iowa, 1984—. Pres. Quad-Cities chpt. Links, Inc., 1980-82, 85; bd. dirs. Community Mental Health of Rock Island, Mercer Counties, 1975-83, chmn. publicity com., 1976-79; bd. dirs. United Way of Quad Cities, 1976-78; mem. community relations com. Blackhawk Coll., Moline. Michele Clark journalism fellow, 1973. Mem. Friends of Des Moines Art Gallery, Friends of Davenport Art Gallery, LWV, Democrat. Presbyterian. Avocations: photography; gourmet cooking; books; art; music. Home: 1632 18th Ave Unit 6 Rock Island IL 61201 Office: Hqrs US Army Armament Munitions and Chem Command Procurement Directorate Rock Island Arsenal Rock Island IL 61299

SMITHSON, DORIS ANN, nurse; b. Greeneville, Tenn., Oct. 6, 1951; d. James Romane and Juanita (Huff) S. B.S. in Nursing, Berea Coll., 1973. R.N., Tenn., N.C., Ky. Nurse, Duke U. Med. Ctr., Durham, N.C., 1973-74, Albert B. Chandler U. Ky. Med. Ctr., Lexington, 1974—. Mem. Am. Diabetes Assn. (Ky. affiliate), Am. Assn. Diabetes Educators, Ky. Assn. Diabetes Educators (charter mem. Bluegrass region), NOW. Democrat. Methodist. Avocations: travel; theater; drama; sports; reading. Home: 385 Redding Rd Apt 77 Lexington KY 40502 Office: Albert B Chandler U KY Med Ctr Dept Medicine-Endocrinology 800 Rose St Lexington KY 40536

SMITH-WILLIAMS, MARGIE MARIAN, trailer manufacturing company executive, designer, automotive engineer; b. June 9, 1942; d. Dann Albert and Anita Pearl Smith; m. Robert E. Williams, Feb. 5, 1977. Student U. Redlands, 1960-62, San Bernardino Valley Coll., 1963-67; B.S.M.E., U. Denver, 1967; postgrad. UCLA Extension, 1970-80; student Healing Light Ctr., Glendale, Calif., 1981—. Registered engr.-in-tng., Calif. Saturday mgr. Dry Clean Agy., Novato, Calif., 1958-60; draftsman Maxwell Surveying, San Bernardino, Calif., 1961; engr. aide II, Calif. Div. Transp., San Bernardino, 1961-66; draftsman Silver Engr. Works, Denver, 1964; designer/draftsman Digmor Equipment & Engring., San Bernardino, 1966; design engr. Mattel Toys, Hawthorne, Calif., 1967-68; project mgr. Spirit of Am. Enterprises, Torrance, Calif., 1968; owner, contract engr. Internat. Racing Designs, Gardena, Calif., 1968-71; pres., chief exec. officer, design engr. IRD Trailers, South El Monte, Calif., 1971—; owner/designer Illusions, Downey, Calif., 1973—; pub. Trailer Visions, Downey, 1981—; dir. I R D, INC., South El Monte, Structural Dynamics Cons., Pacific Palisades, Calif. Author: Trailers—How to Tow and Maintain, 1982; Trailers—How To Buy and Evaluate, 1983; also tech. mail-order catalogs. Inventor, patentee (16) on trailers and toys. Engr./designer product line of weld-up kit form race car trailers, utility trailers; designer product line stuffed vehicles, decorative cork/fabric bulletin bds., metal planters. Active in effort to change dealer lic. laws and legis. of trailers in Calif., 1969, 73. Mem. Calif. Scholarship Fedn. (life), Healing Light Ctr. Republican. Spiritualist. Avocations: therapeutic touch; metaphysics; sewing; beadwork; creative designs. Office: IRD Inc 7603 E Firestone PO Box 460 Suite D-10 Downey CA 90241

SMITS, DONNA ANN, labor organizer; b. Wilmington, Del., Nov. 29, 1958; d. Edwin Joseph and Joan Dorothy (Slivocka) S. Student George Meany Ctr. for Labor Studies, Washington, 1983-84, Pa. State U., 1984-85. Vice pres. United Food and Comml. Workers Union, Wilmington, 1982, v.p., bus. rep., organizer, No. 1687, Wyoming, Pa., 1982-85, v.p., bus. agt., No. 72, Kingston, Pa., 1985—, co-dir. com. on polit. edn., 1985—. Polit. dir. Young Democrats Luzerne County, 1986—; mem. Dem. Town Com., 1985—; state committeeperson Bob Edgar for U.S. Senate, Pa., 1985-86; asst. to coordinator Mondale/Ferraro Campaign, 1983-84; mem. Pa. Pub. Interest Coalition, 1986—. Mem. Nat. Assn. Female Execs., Coalition Labor Union Women, Central Labor Council (del.). Roman Catholic. Club: Century (Washington). Office: UFCW No 72 268 Pierce St Kingston PA 19704

SMITT, JULIANN, author, photographer; b. Spokane, Wash., Apr. 19, 1955; d. John William and Gloria Elizabeth (Stauffer) S. A.A., Spokane Falls Community Coll., 1975; B.A., Wash. State U., 1977. Writer, photographer Grant County Jour., Ephrata, Wash., 1977—. Recipient 2d place news features award Wash. Newspaper Pubs. Assn., 1983, 1st pl. Comprehensive News Coverage, 1985, 2d pl. features, 1985, 3d pl. spot news, 1985. Mem. Soc. Profl. Journalists, Ephrata Bus. and Profl. Women's Club (pres. 1980-81, 82-83, Young Career Woman award 1979), Soap Lake C. of C. (dir. 1980-81, sec. 1982). Lodge: Ephrata Kiwanis (hon. mem.).

SMITTLE, DRUSILLA QUINN, weight loss company executive; b. McKeesport, Pa., May 2, 1930; d. William F. and Drucella (Howell) Quinn; m. George Bryan, Dec. 22, 1952; children—Maradee Barr, Kimberly Smittle, Rozamonde Alfonso. B.S., Edinboro State U., 1952; student Wright State U. Tchr., supr., pub. and pvt. schs., Pa., Ohio, P.R., 1952-57; owner, ptnr. The Art Gallery, Cleve., 1976-78; owner, ptnr. Quit Smoking Inc., Wilmette, Ill., 1981-83; owner, ptnr. Nutri System, Weight Loss Med. Ctr., Durham, N.C., 1982—; pres. Quinn Smittle Inc., Fayetteville, N.C., 1979—. Bd. dirs. Community Symphony Elryia, Ohio, core mem. Cleve. Womens Council, 1971-76; founder, contbr. Brunswick High Sch. Artists Recognition Scholarship Fund, 1981—; officer NOW, Elyria, Waukegan, Cleveland Heights. Mem. Better Bur. Bur. Raleigh Durham Chapel Hill (bd. dirs. 1982—), Nat. Womens Polit. Caucus. Democrat. Avocations: art; reading; beach walking.

SMOGER, MARCI-ELLEN, real estate developer, designer, builder; b. Phila., Feb. 13, 1953; d. Joseph B. and Tremayne A. (Gershenfeld) Selig; B.S. in Psychology Trinity Coll., Hartford, Conn. and U. Pa., Phila., 1974; M. Interior Design, Drexel U., Phila., 1977; m. Barry Richard Smoger, July 7, 1974; 1 son, Julian Selig. Pres., Marci-ellen Smoger Assos., Penn-Valley, Pa., 1977—; lectr. U. Pa., Nat. Assn. Women in Constrn. Mem. Pa. Builders Assn., Nat. Assn. Home Builders, Home Builders Assn. Phila. and Suburban Counties. Home and Office: 1434 Flat Rock Rd Penn-Valley PA 19072

SMRCINA, CATHERINE MARIE, nurse; b. Chgo., June 27, 1952; d. Edward Francis and Helen Marie (Smalarz) S.; B.S. in Nursing, U. Ill., 1974. Nursing asst. Columbus Hosp., Chgo., 1972-74, staff nurse, 1974-77, head nurse orthopedics, 1977-81, clin. supr., 1981-82; nurse assoc. Cabrini Hosp., Chgo., 1983-85; asst. dir. patient and staff edn. Bethany Meth. Hosp., Chgo., 1985—. Mem. Nat. Assn. Orthopedic Nurses (pres. Chgo. chpt., North Central Dist. rep.), U. Ill. Alumni Assn., Chgo. Nurses Assn., Ill. Nurses Assn., Am. Nurses Assn., Council Cath. Nurses Archdiocese Chgo., Am. Heart Assn., Am. Assn. Diabetes Educators, Am. Diabetes Assn., Chgo. Nursing Inservice Orgn. Club: Catholic Order Foresters. Home: 2335 S Westover Ave North Riverside IL 60546 Office: 5025 N Paulina St Chicago IL 60640

SMULLIN, PATRICIA CLARA, broadcasting executive; b. Eureka, Calif., Dec. 20, 1949; d. William Brothers and Patricia (Duell) S. B.S. in Communications and Psychology, Oreg. State U., 1972; postgrad. Stanford U., So. Oreg. State U. Office mgr. So. Oreg. Cable TV, Medford, 1973-74, dir. consumer relations, 1974-76, v.p., 1976-82; pres. Calif. Oreg. Broadcasting Inc., Medford, 1982—. Bd. dirs. Medford YMCA, Jackson County United Way, Rogue Valley Med. Ctr., Rogue Valley Health Found., Rogue Community Coll.; past dir. Rogue Council Camp Fire Girls. Mem. Oreg. Cable Commn. Assn. (past pres., bd. dirs.), Pacific N.W. Cable Commn. (pres.), Oreg. Pub. Broadcasting Commn., Women in Cable TV (charter mem.), Medford C. of C. (v.p., bd. dirs.), Stanford Alumni Assn. Office: Calif Oreg Broadcasting Inc 125 S Fir St Medford OR 97501

SMYTH, FRAN(CES) DALE, insurance company executive; b. N.Y.C., Sept. 6, 1941; d. Max and Aida (Heimerdinger) Goldfarb; B.S., Poly. Inst. N.Y., 1963; M.B.A., Baruch Coll. CUNY, 1973; 1 son, Kevin Jeffrey. Programmer, CIT Fin., N.Y.C., 1965-66; programmer analyst Saks Fifth Ave., N.Y.C., 1966-67; sr. programmer Sealtest Co., N.Y.C., 1967-68; mgr. Kennecott Copper Corp., N.Y.C., 1968-74; asst. v.p. Met. Life Co., N.Y.C., 1974—; assoc. adj. prof. mgmt. N.Y.U., 1969—; chmn. industry adv. bd. dept. EDP, Borough of Manhattan Community Coll., 1974—. Chmn. bd. dirs. CSC Repertory; chmn. 15th St. Block Assn. Home: 40 W 15th St Apt 1C New York NY 10011 Office: Met Life Ins Co 1 Madison Ave New York NY 10010

SMYTH, RENEE, business consultant; b. Los Angeles, Jan. 19, 1948; d. Harmon and Betty (Barrone) Hall. B.S., Glendale U., 1972; J.D., Calif. Coll. Law, 1976. Bar: Calif. Publicist Outlook and Opinion, Los Angeles, 1970-75; dir. pub. relations Richmond-Confederate Prodns., Beverly Hills, Calif., 1975-77, R. Smyth Assoc., documentary producers, Beverly Hills, 1977—; corp. planner for Maggie and Jiggs, Inc., King Features Syndicate, Inc.; cons. Budget Graphics, Los Angeles, 1980—. Assoc. del. Calif. Republican State Central Com., 1983; mem. fin. com. Calif. Rep. Party, chmn. bd. Edna Davidson Scholarship Found. Mem. Christian Legal Soc., Mary and Joseph League, Mensa. Roman Catholic. Office: Outlook & Opinion 9300 Wilshire Blvd Suite 470 Beverly Hills CA 90212

SMYTHE, MARSHA SUSAN HALLER, nurse practitioner; b. Joliet, Ill., Nov. 6, 1949; d. Eugene Keith and Margaret Evelyn (Hrebenyak) Haller; m. Bryan Edward Smythe, Nov. 15, 1969; children—Christopher, Jason. A.Arts and Scis. in Nursing, Joliet Jr. Coll., 1973; B.S. in Nursing with honors, Purdue U., 1983. R.N., cert. family nurse practitioner, Ill. Operating room nurse Silver Cross Hosp., Joliet, 1973-79; ob-gyn nurse practitioner Michael Reese Health Plan, Chgo., 1983, Joliet Med. Group, 1984-85; gynecol./pediatric nurse practitioner Kankakeeland Community Action Agy. (Ill.), 1983-84; nursing cons., Joliet, 1982-85; labor and delivery staff Trident Regional Med. Ctr., Charleston, S.C., 1985—. Mem. Am. Nurses Assn., Nurses Assn. of Am. Coll. Obstetricians and Gynecologists, Council Primary Care Nurse Practitioners, S.C. Nurses Assn., Trident Nurses Assn. Republican. Roman Catholic. Home: 103 Runnymeade Ln Summerville SC 29483

SMYTHE-GREEN, SHERRY, video cassette publishing company executive; b. Alameda, Calif., May 16, 1936; d. Lester Andrew and Alma (Farek) S.; student Brigham Young U., Atlanta Baptist Coll., Dekalb Coll., m. Wayne S. Green II; children—Abra Michelle Smith Pofelski, Roger Sunday Smith, Matthew Clinton Smith; m. 2d, Wayne Green, 1979. Exec. sec. Dairypak, Fort Worth, Tex., 1954-55; mgr. Child Care Registry, Atlanta, 1963-71; chief exec. officer Contract Carpets, Orem, Utah, 1971-73; asst. to controller Cayman Devel. Co., Rolling Hills Estates, Calif., 1973-76; exec. v.p. Wayne Green, Inc., Peterborough, N.H., 1976-83, Instant Software, Inc., 73, Inc., 1976-83; pres. Flambouyant Ltd., 1983—; pub. Butterfly Video, 1986—; pres. XL Systems; Republican. Mormon. Columnist, Kiloband Microcomputing mag., Desktop computing mag., 80 Microcomputing mag. Home: 73 Pine St Peterborough NH 03458 Office: PO Box 100 Hancock NH 03449

SNAPP, DELORES MAXINE, educator; b. Jacksonville, Ill., Apr. 12, 1936; d. Arthur Elmer and Katherine Henrietta (Koehler) Ticknor; m. Robert Lee Snapp, Aug. 3, 1958; children—Sheryl Dee Snapp Blickhan, Susan Lee Snapp Seibring. B.S.Ed., Eastern Ill. U., 1958, M.S., 1972; postgrad. Eastern Ill. U., Ill. State U., No. Ill. U., Sangamon State U. Tchr., Johns Hill Jr. High Sch., Decatur, Ill., 1958-59; tchr. home econs. Cerro Gordo High Sch., Ill., 1963-64; tchr. pub. schs. Decatur, 1964—, MacArthur High Sch., 1984—. Leader, 4-H Club, 1969-71. Chmn. church and society, council on ministries United Methodist Ch., 1984-86. Mem. Am. Home Econs. Assn., Macon County Home Economists (pres. 1982-83), NEA, Ill. Edn. Assn., Decatur Edn. Assn.

Avocations: needlework, crafts. Home: 940 Dee Lee Ln Mount Zion IL 62549 Office: MacArthur High Sch 1155 N Fairview St Decatur IL 62522

SNAPP, ELIZABETH, librarian, educator; b. Lubbock, Tex., Mar. 31, 1937; d. William James and Louise (Lanham) Mitchell; B.A. magna cum laude, North Tex. State U., Denton, 1968, M.L.S., 1969, M.A., 1977; m. Harry Franklin Snapp, June 1, 1956. Asst. to archivist Archive of New Orleans Jazz, Tulane U., 1960-63; catalog librarian Tex. Woman's U., Denton, 1969-71, head acquisitions dept., 1971-74, coordinator readers services, 1974-77, asst. to dean Grad. Sch., 1977-79, instr. library sci., 1977—, acting Univ. librarian, 1979-82, dir. libraries, 1982—, mem. adv. com. on library formula Coordinating Bd. Tex. Coll. and Univ. System, 1981—; del. OCLC Nat. Users Council, 1985-87; project dir. Nat. Endowment for Humanities consultancy grant on devel. core curriculum for women's studies, 1981-82. Co-sponsor Irish Lecture Series, Denton, 1968, 70, 73, 78. Sec. Denton County Democratic Caucus, 1970. Mem. ALA (standards com. 1983-85) Southwestern, Tex. (program com. 1978, Dist. VII chmn. 1985-86) library assns., Women's Collecting Group (chmn. ad hoc com. 1984—), AAUW (legis. br. chmn. 1973-74, br. v.p. 1975-76, br. pres. 1979—), So. Conf. Brit. Studies, AAUP, Tex. Assn. Coll. Tchrs. (pres. Tex. Woman's U. chpt. 1976-77), Woman's Shakespeare Club (pres. 1967-69), Beta Phi Mu (pres. chpt. 1976-78; sec. nat. adv. assembly 1978-79, pres. 1979-80, nat. dir. 1981—), Alpha Chi, Alpha Lambda Sigma (pres. 1970-71), Pi Delta Phi. Episcopalian (directress altar guild 1966-68, 73-76). Club: Soroptimist Internat. Asst. editor Tex. Academe, 1973-76; contbg. author: Women in Special Collections, 1984, Special Collections, 1986; book reviewer Library Resources and Tech. Services, 1973—. Contbr. articles to profl. jours. Home: 1904 N Lake Trail Denton TX 76201 Office: PO Box 24093 TWU Station Denton TX 76204

SNEATH, JUDITH MARIE, personnel executive; b. Houston, Nov. 23, 1943; d. Leonard F. and Flora Delfina (Gigliotti) Tritico; 1 dau., Alison Lea. B.S. in Elem. Edn., Tex. Tech U., 1965. Tchr., Kermit pub. schs. (Tex.), 1965-66, Garland Ind. Sch. Dist. (Tex.), 1966-67; with Crum & Forster Ins., Dallas, 1968-69, 71-73; adminstrv. mgr. Am. Internat. Group, Dallas, 1973-76; word processing mgr. Am. Internat. Group, N.Y.C., 1976-78; asst. v.p. personnel/adminstr. Constellation Reins. Co., N.Y.C., 1978-85; asst. v.p. human resources, adminstr. N.Am. Co. Property & Casualty Ins., Greenwich, Conn., 1985—. Mem. Adminstrv. Mgmt. Soc. (pres.), Ins. Human Resources Assn. Democrat. Unitarian. Office: N Am Co Property & Casualty Ins 25 Valley Dr Greenwich CT 06830

SNEDAKER, CATHERINE RAUPAGH (KIT), editor; b. Fargo, N.D., Apr. 2; d. Paul and Charity (Primmer) Raupagh; B.A., Duke U., 1943; m. William Brooks, 1943; children—Eleanor, Peter William; m. 2d, Weldon Snedaker, Sept. 17, 1950. Pub. relations exec. United Seamen's Service, 1950-57; promotion mgr. sta. WINR-TV and WNBF-TV, Binghamton, N.Y., 1957-60; TV editor, feature writer Binghamton Sun, 1960-68; mem. staff Los Angeles Herald Examiner, 1968—, food editor, 1978—, restaurant critic, 1978-80, food and travel editor, 1980-86; guest editor Mademoiselle mag., 1942. Recipient 3 awards Los Angeles Press Club, VISTA award, 1979. Mem. Newspaper Food Editors and Writers Assn., Am. Travel Editors Assn., Soc. Am. Travel Writers. Democrat. Home: 140 San Vicente Blvd Apt C Santa Monica CA 90402 Office: 1111 S Broadway Los Angeles CA 90015

SNEED, EMOGENE MILDRED, nurse; b. Kingsport, Tenn., Nov. 11, 1929; d. O.H. and Ida Theresa (King) Cox; m. John H. Sneed, Jan. 11, 1956; children—Jerry Lee, Rex Ronald, Scott Donald. R.N., Knoxville Gen. Hosp., 1953; student U. Tenn., 1952, East Tenn. State U., 1955. Staff nurse Holston Vally Hosp. Med. Ctr., Kingsport, Tenn., 1953—. Den mother Kingsport council Cub Scouts Am., 1965-66. Mem. ARC, Tenn. Nursing Assn., Am. Heart Assn., Tenn. Mental Health Assn., Am. Operating Nurses Assn. Baptist. Home: 2041 Sherwood Rd Kingsport TN 37664

SNEED, GENEVA BELL, union official; b. nr. Knoxville, Tenn., Oct. 10, 1920; d. Westly W. and Louie V. (Stallings) Fox; student U. Tenn., 1952-53; m. Luther J. Sneed, May 15, 1936; children—Mackie A., Larry K., Linda K. Sneed Holton, Martha Lou Sneed Mashburn. Officer mgr. Western Union, Sevierville, Tenn., 1936-45, operator Pub. Shirt Corp., Knoxville, 1946-49, head grievance ofcl. Local 90, AFL-CIO, Knoxville, 1948-50; pres. Knoxville CIO Council, 1951-53; dir. Women's Activities div. AFL-CIO Area Council, 1953-55; staff rep. Amalgamated Clothing Workers Am., Knoxville, 1952-69, asst. mgr. Southeastern clothing regional bd., 1969-82, mgr., 1982—; sec.-treas. Southeastern Clothing Bd. Realty Corp., 1969-82, pres., 1982—; v.p. Tenn. State Labor Council, 1959—. Co-chmn. women's div. Estes Kefauver campaign, 1956, v.p. Tenn. AFL-CIO Com. on Polit. Edn., 1959—; exec. 2d v.p. Tenn. State Labor Council AFL-CIO, 1971-81. Alderwoman, Sevierville, Tenn., 1982—. Democrat. Office: 1124 N Broadway Knoxville TN 37917

SNEED, MARIE ELEANOR WILKEY, ret. educator; b. Dahlgren, Ill., June 12, 1915; d. Charles N. and Hazel (Miller) Wilkey; student U. Ill., 1933-35; B.S., Northwestern U., 1937; postgrad. Wayne State U., 1954-60, U. Mich., 1967; m. John Sneed, Jr., Sept. 18, 1937: children—Suzanne (Mrs. Geoffrey B. Newton), John Corwin. Tchr. English, drama, creative writing Berkley (Mich.) Sch. Dist., 1952-76. Mem. Mich. Statewide Tchr. Edn. Preparation, 1968-72, regional sec. 1969-70; mem. Pleasant Ridge Arts Council, 1982—, Pleasant Ridge Parks and Recreation Commn., 1982—. Mem. NEA, Mich., Berkley (pres. 1961-62) edn. assns., Oakland Tchr. Edn. Council (exec. bd. 1973-76), Student Tchr. Planning Com. Berkley (chmn. 1971-72), Phi Alpha Chi, Pi Lambda Theta, Alpha Delta Kappa, Alpha Omicron Pi. Club: Pleasant Ridge Woman's (pres. 1980-83). Home: 21 Norwich Rd Pleasant Ridge MI 48069

SNELL, BELINDA RAE, financial services; b. Island Falls, Maine, Apr. 24, 1949; d. Keith Huggard and Madeline (Kennedy) Ingraham; B.A., U. Maine, Orono, 1971; M.Ed., U. Portland, 1974; m. Christopher D. Snell, July 31, 1977. Team leader Maine Concentrated Employment, Portland, 1972-73; coordinator Women's Reentry Ednl. Program, Bangor, Maine, 1974-76; personnel mgr. K Mart Corp., Augusta, Maine, 1977; coop. vocat. edn. coordinator Maranacook Sch., Readfield, Maine, 1978; v.p. Maine Oil Dealers Assn., Yarmouth, 1979-83; adminstrv. agt. Norton Fin. Services, Portland, Maine, 1983—. Trustee Thomas Meml. Library, Cape Elizabeth, Maine. Club: Garden. Home: 16 Orchard Rd Cape Elizabeth ME 04107 Office: 93 Exchange St Portland ME 04101

SNELL, KATHRYNE ELIZABETH, public relations executive; b. Bicknell, Ind., Dec. 16, 1922; d. Homer Hugh and Lima Blanche (Wagstaff) Cargal; student Lansing Community Coll., 1979—; m. Elwyn Snell, Apr. 4, 1944; children—Kathryne Ann Snell Nuveman, Edward Franklin. Cashier/bookkeeper, agt. Indian Trials Bus Line, Owosso, Mich., 1941-45; personnel clk. Universal Electric Co., Owosso, 1947-51, sec. to v.p./dir. indsl. relations, 1951-55, exec. sec. to chmn. bd., 1955-78, dir. public relations, 1972—; J A co. rep., 1981—. Sec., Washington Sch. P.T.A., 1958-60; sec. Shiawassee dist. exec. bd. Girl Scouts Am., 1960-61; sec. Mother's Club, troop and Post 85 Boy Scouts Am., 1963-65, co. coordinator Post 68, 1982—; bd. dirs. Com. on Alcohol and Drug Abuse, Shiawassee area, 1974-76; trustee First Bapt. Ch., 1979—, chmn., 1981; mem. Bicentennial Com., Owosso area, 1976-77; mem. indsl. com., spl. gifts com. Shiawassee Area United Way, 1974-79; mem. Shiawassee dist. Boy Scouts Am., 1976—, mem. exec. bd. Tall Pine council, 1985—, recipient Silver Beaver award, 1985; v.p. Ambassadors, 1977-80; mem. Heritage Bridge Com., City of Owosso, 1983—; chmn. bd. Christian Edn., First Bapt. Ch., 1967-69. Mem. Profl. Secretaries Internat. (Sec. of Year Shiawassee Valley chpt. 1969, pres. Mich. div. 1975-77), Pvt. Industry Council (chmn. program planning and assessment com. 1984—), Owosso-Corunna Area C. of C. (mem. exec. bd., Internat. Woman of Year in Bus. and Industry 1975, dir. 1973—, v.p. 1979-80, pres. 1981-83). Clubs: Owosso City (bd. govs., sec. 1983-84, v.p. 1984—), Zonta (dir. 1979-81, pres. 1983-85), Order Eastern Star. Home: 2509 Vandekarr Rd Owosso MI 48867 Office: 300 E Main St Owosso MI 48867

SNIBBE, PATRICIA MISCALL, advertising agency executive; b. Hackensack, N.J., June 1, 1932; d. Jack and Margaret Lois (Drake) Miscall; B.F.A., R.I. Sch. Design, 1954; postgrad. New Sch. for Social Research, 1975-80; m. Richard Wilson Snibbe, Sept. 8, 1962; stepsons—John Robinson, Paul Clor. Art dir., film producer Peckham Productions, N.Y.C., 1960-64; art dir., partner Stallman and Snibbe, N.Y.C., 1964-66; art dir. Shevlo Advt., N.Y.C., 1966-72, Bernard Hodes Advt., N.Y.C., 1972-77; owner, creative dir. Designstuff, N.Y.C., 1978—; v.p., creative dir Archtl. Film Library, N.Y.C., 1980—. Recipient Golden Circle award Affiliated Advt. Agys. Internat., 1975-77, Creativity '78 award, 1978. Mem. NOW (bd. dirs. N.Y.C. 1983-84), Graphic Artists Guild (steering com. Cartoonists Guild div. 1984-85), Nat. Acad TV and Scis. Author, artist Feminist Funnies, 1981—. Home: 139 E 18th St New York NY 10003

SNIDER, ANNE MARILYN, educator, real estate executive; b. Trenton, N.J., Dec. 20, 1945; d. Darrell Luther and Anne Mary (Brophy) S. B.A., Trenton State Coll., 1967, M.A., 1972, M.Ed., 1975. Cert. social scis. tchr., sch. counselor; lic. in real estate. Tchr., Crossroads Sch., South Brunswick Twp., N.J., 1967—; asst. v.p. Twin Trees Devel. Co., South Brunswick Twp., 1984—; pres. Marilyn Snider Co., South Brunswick Twp., 1983—; sales referral assoc. Weichert Realty, South Brunswick Twp., 1985—; adj. grad. prof. Trenton State Coll., N.J., 1978—; cons. Rider Coll., Trenton, 1978-79; dir.-trainer South Brunswick Police Juvenile Counseling Grant, 1979; tchr. and parent effectiveness trainer Effectiveness Tng. Inst., Calif., 1980; cons. elem. divs. projects Middle States Council Social Scis., 1979. Author: John Peter Zenger Rides Again, 1976. Mem. N.J. Edn. Assn., Middlesex County Edn. Assn., NEA, South Brunswick Edn. Assn., Am. Bus. Woman's Assn. (pres. Edison, N.J. 1980-81). Avocations: gourmet cooking, internat. travel. Democrat. Episcopalian. Home: 56 Fox Tail Ln Monmouth Junction NJ 08852 Office: Crossroads Sch Georges Rd Monmouth Junction NJ 08852

SNIDER, DONNA KAY, retail company official, lawyer; b. Cin., Aug. 24, 1945; d. James Benjamen and Ruby (Crowley) Battles; A.A., Coll. Mt. St. Joseph of Ohio, 1979, B.A. magna cum laude, 1980; J.D., No. Ky. U., 1984; children—Michelle Lynn, Lorrie Danielle. With Kroger Co., Cin., 1970—, legal adminstr. and asst. corp. sec. law dept., 1975—, asst. corp. sec., 1982—. Mem. mgmt. com. YMCA. Mem. Am. Bar Assn., Greater Cin. Women Lawyers, Ohio Bar Assn., Cin. Bar Assn., Assn. Trial Lawyers Am., Am. Soc. Corp. Secs., Alpha Chi, Kappa Gamma Pi. Republican. Methodist. Club: Toastmasters. Home: 2920 Pond Run Ln New Richmond OH 45157 Office: Kroger Co 1014 Vine St Cincinnati OH 45201

SNIPES, JUDIE SMITH, nursing consultant; b. Rocky Mount, Va., Feb. 28, 1947; d. Julian Oaks and Christine Edna (Foster) Smith; m. Lloyd W. Moore, Oct. 24, 1964 (div. Jan. 1973); 1 child, W. Scott; m. Lucas Arthur Snipes, Apr. 21, 1979. R.N., Roanoke Meml. Hosp., 1968; B.S., Lynchburg Coll., 1986, postgrad. in Bus. Charge nurse Roanoke Meml. Hosp., Va., 1968-69, nursing supr., intervenous nurse, asst. dir. nursing, 1975-81, nursing cons., 1985—; charge nurse Hartford Meml. Hosp., Harve de Grace, Md., 1969-70; surg. scrub nurse, office mgr. Dr. John Gardner Jr., Roanoke, 1970-75; nursing-clin. cons. Health East Inc., Roanoke, 1981—. Vol. NRC, Roanoke, 1968-80, student liaison, 1977-78; vol. Am. Heart Assn., Roanoke, 1974—, bd. dirs., 1977-78. Named Outstanding Vol., Am. Heart Assn. (Va. affiliate), 1977-80. Mem. Am. Nurses Assn., Va. Nurses Assn. (Dist. II Nurse Yr. 1977), Assn. Operating Room Nurses, Va. Hosp. Assn. Methodist. Avocations: bowling; biking; roller skating; dance. Home: 2243 Sourwood St NE Roanoke VA 24012 Office: Health East Inc 127 McClanahan St Roanoke VA 24011

SNIPES, LYNN, ballet company executive. Artistic dir. Gwinnett Ballet Theatre, Lilburn, Ga. Office: Gwinnett Ballet Theatre 4060 Five Forks Trickum Rd Lilburn GA 30247*

SNIVELY, PAMELA ANNETTE, county official; b. Columbus, Ind., Nov. 10, 1951; d. Ronald Lee and Helen Carol (Higgins) S. B.F.A., William Woods Coll., Fulton, Mo., 1974. Cert. peace officer, Calif. Paralegal. Legal Aid Soc. Lincoln, Nebr., 1974-75; family counselor Kaleidoscope, Inc., Chgo., 1975-79; office mgr. John B. Coleman & Co., Chgo., 1979-80; tchr. Peace Corps, Kenya, 1980-82; office mgr. Data Resources, Inc., Los Angeles, 1983-84; dep. sheriff Los Angeles County Sheriff's Dept., Los Angeles, 1984—. Mem. Assn. Los Angeles County Dep. Sheriffs. Avocations: needlecrafts; stained glass; snow skiing. Office: Los Angeles County Sheriffs Dept 211 W Temple St Los Angeles CA 90012

SNODDERLY, KAREN WEBSTER, university official; b. Knoxville, Tenn., July 16, 1951; d. John Arthur and Martha Elizabeth (Armstrong) Webster; B.S. in Bus. Adminstrn., Carson-Newman Coll., 1971; postgrad. U. Tenn., 1977; 1 dau., Rachel Hope. Data control clk. U. Tenn., Knoxville, 1974, research asst., 1974-75, mgr. student info., 1975-79, dir. data analysis, 1979-82, sr. systems analyst, 1983-85, asst. dir. student acad. mgmt. system, 1985—, mem. fin. aid and admission system design team, 1979-80. Vice chairperson Friends of Strawberry Plains (Tenn.) Library, 1978; vice chmn. bd. dirs. Knoxville Rape Crisis Center, 1980-82, counselor, 1980—, mem. exec. com. Mem. Am. Bus. Women's Assn. (Mem. of Month award 1981), Coll. and Univ. Machine Records Conf., Phi Chi Theta. Compiler-editor U. Tenn. Ann. Report Info. Requests, 1979-81. Office: U Tenn 4th Floor Dunford Hall Knoxville TN 37996

SNOW, EDWINA FEIGENSPAN (MRS. MACVICKER SNOW), editor, pub.; b. N.Y.C., July 14, 1927; d. Edwin Christian and Flora Marie (Russ) Feigenspan; student Barnard Coll., 1945-46, Columbia, 1946, Juilliard Sch. Music, 1943, m. David Dodge Osborn, June 1946 (div. 1951); children—Dana Dodge Osborn, Christopher Fairfield Osborn; m. 2d, MacVicker Snow, Dec. 19, 1964; children—Marina, Michael Snow. Model, John Robert Powers, N.Y.C., 1947-48, pub. relations dir. Powers cosmetics, 1948-50; model Ford Agy., N.Y.C., 1950-53, Jacques Heim, Paris, France, 1957; bilingual sec. Cofinindus, Brufina, Electrobel Belgian holding cos., 1960; co-editor, pub. Locust Valley (N.Y.) Leader, 1961-67; editor, pub. Oyster Bay (N.Y.) Guardian, 1967—; partner Locust Valley Pub. Co., Inc., 1965—; founder, pub. Glen Cove (N.Y.) Guardian, 1976—; pres. Oyster Bay Pub. Co., Inc. Bd. dirs. Nassau chpt. A.R.C.; benefit dir. Boys Town Italy, 1952-54. Mem. A.S.C.A.P., Am. Horse Protection Assn. Kiwanian (hon.). Home: Centre Island Oyster Bay NY 11771 Office: W Main St Oyster Bay NY 11771

SNOW, JUDITH ROHLETTER, jewelry store executive, gemologist, jeweler; b. Miami, Fla., May 6, 1948; d. Guy Eugene and Mary Evelyn (York) Rohletter; student Miami-Dade Community Coll., 1966-67; cert. in diamond evaluation Gemological Inst. Am., 1979, cert. in colored stones and gem indentification, 1980; student Berlitz Sch. Langs., Coral Gables, Fla., 1979—; also grad. various profl. seminars; m. Edward Hugh Snow, May 11, 1974; children—Judith Diane, Kelly Michelle, Mary Alice. Office mgr. Ross Printing Corp., Miami, 1965-74; corp. exec., gemologist Snow's Jewelers, Inc., Coral Gables, 1974—, also dir. Active Scott Kelly for Gov. of Fla. Campaign, 1965. Mem. Retail Jewelers Am., Jewelers Security Alliance, Coral Gables C. of C., Miracle Mile Mchts. Assn., Exec. Women Internat., Coral Bay Property Owner's Assn., Ferrari Club Am., Ferrari Owners Club, Zonta, Mus. Patrons. Democrat. Clubs: Ocean Reef, Coral Bay Yacht, Coral Reef Yacht, Fla. Philharm. Prelude, Noteworthy, Progress, Bimini (Bahamas) Big Game, Beach Colony. Office: 219 Miracle Mile Coral Gables FL 33134

SNOWDEN, BERNICE RIVES, former construction company executive; b. Houston, Mar. 21, 1923; d. Charles Samuel and Annie Pearl (Rorex) Rives; grad. Smalley Comml. Coll., 1941; student U. Houston, 1965; m. Walter G. Snowden; 1 dau., Bernice Ann Ogden. With Houston Pipe Line Co., 1944-45; clk.-typist Charles G. Heyne & Co., Inc., Houston, 1951-53, payroll asst., 1953-56, sec. to preys., also office mgr., 1956-62, sec. to pres., also controller, 1962-70, sec.-treas., 1970-77, chief fin. officer, also dir. Mem. Women in Constrn., Nat. Assn. Women in Constrn. (past pres.), San Leon C. of C. Methodist. Club: Lord and Ladies Dance. Home: 1638 Walton St Houston TX 77009

SNOWE, OLYMPIA J., congresswoman; b. Augusta, Maine, Feb. 21, 1947; d. George J. and Georgia (Goramites) Bouchles. B.A., U. Maine, 1969, LL.D. (hon.), 1982; LL.D. (hon.), Husson Coll., 1981. Businesswoman; mem. Maine Ho. of Reps., 1973-76; mem. Maine Senate, 1976-78, chmn. com. on health and instl. services; mem. 96th-99th Congresses from 2d Maine Dist.; corporator Mechanics Savs. Bank. Mem. Gov.'s Commn. Alcoholism, Drug Abuse and Treatment, Gov.'s Adv. Com. on U. Maine, Gov.'s Positive Action Com.; dir. Kent's Hill Sch.; mem. Bd. Voter Registration, Auburn, Maine, 1971-73. Mem. Lewiston-Auburn LWV. Republican. Greek Orthodox. Club: Philoptochos Soc. Office: 133 Cannon House Office Bldg Washington DC 20515

SNUTTJER, ANN MARIE CHAMBERS, nurse; nurse, educator; Harlan, Iowa, Sept. 11, 1941; d. Floyd V. and Phyllis Maureen (Carstensen) Chambers; R.N., Jennie Edmundson Hosp., Council Bluffs, Iowa, 1962; B.S. in Nursing, U. Nebr. Omaha, 1970; M.S. in Nursing, Creighton U.; m. Norman Snuttjer, June 8, 1963; children—Deborah, Thomas, Michael. Mem. nursing staff Jennie Edmundson Hosp., 1964-65, staff devel. instr., 1977-80, dir. community and personnel edn., 1980-82, mem. faculty Sch. Nursing, 1965-70; tchr. adult health edn. Iowa Western Community Coll., 1974-77; mem. faculty div. nursing Coll. of St. Mary, Omaha, 1982—; bd. dirs. Pottawattamie County chpt. Am. Cancer Soc., 1974-83, pres., 1976-79, mem. Iowa edn. com., 1976-77; bd. dirs. Vis. Nurses Assn. Council Bluffs, 1981-83. Mem. S.W. Iowa Health Educators (pres. 1981), Iowa Soc. Health Manpower, Edn. and Tng. Home: 3 Nall Rd Council Bluffs IA 51501 Office: Div Nursing College of St Mary Omaha NE

SNYDER, ALLEGRA FULLER, dance educator; b. Chgo., Aug. 28, 1927; d. R. Buckminster and Anne (Hewlett) Fuller; m. Robert Snyder; children—Alexandra, Jaime. B.A., Bennington Coll., 1951; M.A., UCLA, 1967. Asst. to curator, dance archives Mus. Modern Art, N.Y.C., 1945-47; dancer N.Y.C. Ballet, 1946-47; mem. staff, office and prodn. Internat. Film Found., N.Y.C., 1950-52; dance film editor Film News mag., N.Y.C., 1966-72; lectr. dance, film adviser, dept. dance UCLA, 1967-73, prof. dance and dance ethnology, 1973—, chmn. dept. dance, 1974-80, acting chmn. dept., 1985; vis. lectr. Calif. Inst. Arts, Valencia, 1972; vis. prof. performance studies NYU, N.Y.C., 1982-83; hon. vis. prof. U. Surrey, Guildford, Eng., 1983-84; mem. adv. panel on dance Nat. Endowment for Arts, 1968-72; mem. dance adv. panel Calif. Arts Commn., 1974; mem. various selection and rev. panels Nat. Endowment for Humanities, 1979, 81, 85; mem. dance-film-video selection com. Nat. Endowment for Arts, 1981—; bd. dirs. Buckminster Fuller Inst., 1983—. Bd. dirs. Council Grove Sch. III, Compton, Calif., 1976-81. Fulbright fellow, 1975, 83-84. Mem. Am. Dance Therapy Assn., Congress on Research in Dance (bd. dirs. 1970-76), Council of Dance Adminstrs., Am. Dance Guild, Soc. for Ethnomusicology, Am. Anthrop. Assn., Am. Folklore Soc., Soc. for Anthropology of Visual Communication, Soc. for the Anthrop. Study of Play, Soc. for Humanistic Anthropology, Calif. Dance Educators Assn., Los Angeles Area Dance Alliance (bd. advisers 1976-83), Fulbright Alumni Assn. Home: 15313 Whitfield Ave Pacific Palisades CA 90272 Office: Dept Dance U Calif Los Angeles CA 90024

SNYDER, ANN CATHERINE, exercise physiologist, educator; b. Lansing, Mich., July 16, 1951; d. Warren G. and Ann Catherine (Dearing) S. B.S., Western Mich. U., 1973; M.Ed., Bowling Green State U., 1975; M.A., Mich. State U., 1979; Ph.D., Purdue U., 1982. Asst. prof. exercise physiology, Ball State U., Muncie, Ind., 1982—. Contbr. articles to tech. jours. Internat. Inst. Sports Medicine research grantee, 1984-85. Mem. Am. Coll. Sports Medicine (pres. Midwest regional chpt. 1986), Am. Alliance of Health, Phys. Edn., Recreation and Dance, Muncie Jaycee Women (pres. 1984), Women Enrichment Network. Methodist. Avocations: Cross-country skiing; bicycling; running. Home: Route 9 Box 205 Muncie IN 47302 Office: Ball State Univ Human Performance Lab Muncie IN 47306

SNYDER, BARBARA IRENE, free-lance art director; b. Pittsburg, Kans., Dec. 22, 1937; d. Ian and Vera Tomasene (Jones) Pierce; m. Herman Dale Snyder, July 5, 1959 (dec. May 1967). B.F.A., Kansas City Art Inst., 1959. Visual merchandising mgr. Coach House Stores, Kansas City, Mo., 1957-59; designer Hallmark Cards, Kansas City, Mo., 1959-61; advt. mgr. Kaufman's, Colorado Springs, Colo., 1961-65, 66-67, Bain's, Colorado Springs, 1965-66; advt. mgr. Regenstein's, Atlanta, 1967-69, visual merchandising dir., 1974-76; art dir. Davison's, Atlanta, 1970-72; instr. Atlanta Sch. Fashion and Design, 1972; art dir. Case/Hout, Atlanta, 1973-74, Richway Inc., Atlanta, 1976-78, Hahne's, 1978-79, direct mail advt. mgr., Newark, 1979-83; free-lance retail catalogue art dir., South Orange, N.J., 1983—. Designer Bicentennial Exhbn. at Southeastern State Fair, Atlanta, 1979. Democrat. Avocations: fine art; painting. Home and office: 367 Vose Ave South Orange NJ 07079

SNYDER, GLADYS FLEMMER, nurse, educator; b. Napoleon, N.D., Nov. 11, 1950; d. Fred C. and Leah (Graf) Flemmer; m. Robert James Snyder, Aug. 6, 1972; children—Melissa, Brian. B.S., Union Coll., Lincoln, Nebr., 1975; M.S. Loma Linda U., Calif., 1983. R.N. Nurse Porter Mem. Hosp., Denver, 1969-70, Bryan Meml. Hosp., Lincoln, 1970-73, 75; office nurse Family Physicians Group, Lincoln, 1973-74; staff nurse Porter Meml. Hosp., Denver, 1974-75; staff nurse Hutchinson Community Hosp., Minn., 1975-76; critical care nurse Weld City Community Hosp., Greeley, Colo., 1976-80, instr. nursing Union Coll., Lincoln, 1980-84, asst. prof., 1984—; sch. nurse Greeley 7th Day Adventist Elem. Sch., Colo., 1976-80. Fellow Sigma Theta Tau; mem. Nat. Honor Soc. Nursing, Kappa Theta. Republican. Adventist. Club: Girls of Oak Park Acad. (sec. 1967-68). Office: Union Coll 3800 S 48th St Lincoln NE 68506

SNYDER, JANE LOIS, former educator; b. Greensburg, Pa., Dec. 19, 1916; d. Harry John and Alice (Keech) S.; B.Ed., Frick Tng. Sch., U. Pitts., 1937, M.Ed., U. Pitts., 1948, postgrad., 1957-58; postgrad. (scholar) Pa. State Coll., summers 1946-47; postgrad. in communications (scholar) U. Wis., summer 1955; postgrad. in communications U. Mich., summer 1948. Elem. tchr. Avonworth, Pa., 1937-47; specialist speech and lang. therapy, Pitts. Schs., 1947-79, ret., 1979. Chmn. programs for Better Films and TV Guild, 1964; speaker Kindergarten Inst., 1964; judge Optimist Oratorical Contest, 1969; mem. Allegheny County LWV, 1980-81; mem. Vets. Hosp. Radio and TV Guild, 1960-82, program dir., 1977-82; mem. YWCA; founding mem. Ft. Pitt Mus. Assocs.; dir. pet therapy programs in retirement and children's homes Animal Friends Shelter, 1984—. Recipient several awards for pub. service and volunteerism, 1983-84. Cert. supr. spl. edn. Mem. Am. Speech and Hearing Assn. (life, award, 1981), Pa. Speech and Hearing Assn. (life, co-founder), Nat. Ret. Tchrs. Assn., Frick Scholarship Alumnae Assn. (bd., 1970), Am. Assn. Ret. Persons (editor monthly newsletter, pres. 1983-84), Smithsonian Assocs., Carnegie Inst., Pitts. Poetry Club, AAUW (sec. 1963-64, chmn. ednl. funding 1979-80). Republican. Episcopalian. Clubs: Swiss-Am. Soc. of Pitts., Welsh Women's, St. David's Soc. for Welsh Ams. (sec. 1983-86), Gen. Fedn. Women's Clubs of Swissvale (Pa.) (chmn. edn. com. 1985-86). Condr. first survey on Non-English speaking students, 1969; author, participant 36 ednl. TV programs, questionnaire in ednl. field; contbr. poems to anthology. Home: 1713 Tonette St Pittsburgh PA 15218

SNYDER, JOAN, painter; b. Highland Park, N.J., Apr. 16, 1940; d. Leon D. and Edythe A. (Cohen) Snyder; A.B. in Sociology, Douglass Coll., 1962; M.F.A., Rutgers U., 1966; m. Laurence Fink, Oct. 12, 1969. One-woman exhbns. include Paley and Lowe, New Brunswick, N.J., 1971, 73, Michael Walls Gallery, San Francisco, 1971, Parker 470, Boston, 1972, Los Angeles Inst. Contemporary Art, 1976, Portland (Oreg.) Center Visual Arts, 1976, Carl Solway Gallery, N.Y.C., 1976, Neuberger Mus., Purchase, N.Y., 1978, Hamilton Gallery Contemporary Art, 1978, 79, 82, Nina Nielsen Gallery, Boston, 1981, 83, Wadsworth Atheneum, Hartford, Conn., 1981, Mus. Modern Art, 1985; travelling one-woman show San Francisco Art Inst. Grand Rapids Art Mus., Renaissance Soc., U. Chgo., Anderson Gallery, Va. Commonwealth U., Richmond, 1979-80, New Mus., N.Y.C., 1979; group exhbns. include: Whitney Ann., 1972, Whitney Bienniel, 1974, 80, Corcoran Bienniel, 1975, Mus. Modern Art, N.Y.C., 1981; mem. faculty SUNY, Stony Brook, 1967-69, Yale U., 1974, U. Calif., Irvine, 1975, San Francisco Art Inst., 1976, Princeton U., 1975-77. Grantee Nat. Endowment Art, 1974; Guggenehim fellow, 1982. Address: 105 Mulberry St New York NY 10013

SNYDER, JULIA ANN, international trade and coffee company executive; b. Springfield, Mo., May 17, 1950; d. Arthur Jennings and Catheryn Laverna (Gallion) Swain; m. Orville Edward Kelley, Dec. 29, 1968 (div. 1972); 1 child, Adam Wayne; m. Ronald Warren Synder, May 29, 1982. Cert. Graff Vocat. Tech. Ctr., 1974. Sales sec. Paul Mueller Co., Springfield, 1971-73; surg. technician Cox Med. Ctr., Springfield, 1974-76; corp. sec., dir. OR&D, Inc., Springfield, 1979—; v.p., dir. Hey Mon Coffee Ltd., Everton, Mo., 1984—. Active Nat. Republican Com., 1980, Rep. Presdl. Task Force, 1981. Recipient Medal of Merit, Rep. Presdl. Task Force, 1982. Mem. Nat. Assn. Female Execs., Am. Notary Assn., Am. Film Inst. Mem. Assembly of God Ch. Avocations: latch hooking; stitchery; writing poetry; walking; cooking. Office: Hey Mon Coffee Ltd 294A Coffee Ln Everton MO 65646

SNYDER, LOIS DE ORSEY, public relations exec.; b. Whitinsville, Mass., Aug. 12, 1929; d. Francis X. and Germaine Gagnon De Orsey; A.B., Lenoir-Rhyne Coll., 1953; postgrad. Duke U., 1953-56; m. Harry M. Snyder, Jr. (dec. 1974); children—Stephen De Orsey, Melissa Anne. French tchr. Lenoir-Rhyne Coll., 1952-53; tchr. English, speech and drama Hickory (N.C.) High Sch., 1953-54; dir. public relations Hickory Furniture Mart, 1979-81; pvt. practice public relations, Hickory, 1981—; tchr. French, Grandview Middle Sch., 1985—. Pres., Hickory Dyslexia Found., Catawba County Arts Council, Hickory Landmarks Soc., ARC, Catawba County Mental Health Assn., N.C.

Cerebral Palsy Assn.; lay reader St. Alban's Episcopal Ch., 1981—. Recipient Outstanding Service award N.C. Assn. Cerebral Palsy, 1965. Mem. Catawba County Execs., Internat. Platform Assn. Club, Catawba County C. of C. (dir.), Lenoir-Rhyne Coll. Alumni Assn. (pres.), Alpha Psi Omega. Republican. Home: 1725 5th St Dr NW Hickory NC 28601

SNYDER, LUELLA MOORE, psychology educator, counselor; b. St. Charles, Ill., July 2, 1941; d. Robert George and Maxine Eliot (Smith) S. B.A., Cornell Coll., Mount Vernon, Iowa, 1963; M.Ed., U. Ill., 1967, advanced certificate, 1968. Tchr. English lit. Palatine High Sch., Ill., 1963-66; instr. communications Parkland Coll., Champaign, Ill., 1967-72, coordinator Learning Lab., 1973-77, prof. psychology, 1978—, coordinator liberal arts, 1985—; facilitator Quality Circle Assoc., Champaign, Ill., 1984—; cons. Critical Thinking, Writing Across the Curriculum, Champaign, 1985—, Ill. Bd. Edn., 1986. Author: (plays) Praise Be: 50 Years of Prairie Quiltin, 1983, Let Them Eat Cake, 1983, Tranceformations: Women Changing & Changed, 1984. Cons., Newman Founds., Central Ill., 1970-80; founder Daughters of Pandora, Champaign, 1981; pres. A Woman's Pl. Crisis Ctr. Recipient Presentation award U. Ill. Alumni Assn., 1984; Nat. Endowment for Humanities grantee, 1982, 84, Nat. Endowment for the Arts, 1983. Mem. Nat. Inst. Staff and Orgn. Devel., Am. Assn. Counseling and Devel., Community Coll. Humanities Assn., Phi Delta Kappa. Democrat. Avocations: sailing; traveling; writing; producing plays. Office: Parkland Coll 2400 W Bradley Champaign IL 61821

SNYDER, MILDRED, weight control company executive; b. Balt., Oct. 19, 1942; d. Abraham Issac and Nettie (Pinkowitz) Weinstein; m. Harvey Martin Snyder, Oct. 31, 1967; children—Jennifer Blair, Craig Phillip. Attended schs. Balt. Vice Pres. Weight Watchers of W.Va., Charleston, 1969—; pres. Shape Shop Ltd., Charleston, 1976—; Co-author, editor: cookbook Lean and Luscious, 1984; spokesperson Weight Watchers W.Va. Home: 1881 Louden Heights Circle Charleston WV 25314 Office: Weight Watchers of WVa Inc Patrick St Plaza Charleston WV 25312

SNYDER, PHYLLIS BOPP, publishing company executive; ; b. Houston, May 1, 1945; d. Otto and Elsie Helene (Grau) Bopp; B.A., Tex. Tech U., 1967; m. Terry Eugene Snyder, June 12, 1965. Prodn. editor John Wiley & Sons, N.Y.C., 1968-71, asst. prodn. mgr., 1971-73; with Grune & Stratton, Inc., N.Y.C., 1973—, dir. editorial prodn., 1974—, v.p., 1980-84, sr. v.p., 1984—. Home: 9143 Sabal Palm Circle Windermere FL 32786 Office: Orlando FL 32887

SNYDER, RACHEL FRANCES, editor; b. Topeka, Kans., Feb. 12, 1924; d. Otis F. and Lela Gertrude (Retter) S.; A.B., Washburn U., 1945. Reporter, Topeka (Kans.) Daily Capital, 1943-45; writer Kans. Indsl. Devel. Commn., Topeka, 1946-47; asst. WTOP and Washington Post, Washington, 1948; writer FAO, Washington, 1949; reporter, mgr. Emporia (Kans.) Times, 1950-52; asst. editor Workbasket mag., Kansas City, 1952-56; editor Flower and Garden mag., Kansas City, 1957—. Recipient Profl. Writers award Am. Seed Trade Assn., 1967; Garden Writers award Am. Assn. Nurserymen, 1975. Fellow Garden Writers Assn. Am.; mem. Am. Hort. Soc., Nature Conservancy. Unitarian. Club: Sierra. Author: The Complete Book for Gardeners, 1964. Office: 4251 Pennsylvania St Kansas City MO 64111

SNYDER, RUTH COZEN, painter, sculptor; b. Montreal, Can.; d. Harry and Rachel Cozen; student UCLA, Otis Art Inst.; children—Harry M., Robert Lewis, Douglas M., Nancy J. One-woman shows include: Coos Art Mus., Coos Bay, Oreg., Riverside (Calif.) Art Center and Mus., Galerie Arcadia, Paris, Brigham Young U., Provo, Utah, HHS, Washington, Braithwaite Fine Arts Gallery, So. Utah State Coll., Cedar City, Bridge Gallery, Los Angeles City Hall, Edge Gallery, Fullerton, Calif., Merging One Gallery, Santa Monica, Calif.; group exhbns. include: Mussavi Gallery, N.Y.C., 1985, Flow Ace Gallery, Los Angeles, UN Conf., Nairobi, Mussavi Gallery, N.Y.C., Santa Barbara Contempory Arts Forum, Calif.; represented in permanent collections: Frederick S. Wight Gallery of UCLA, Textron Corp., Washington, Clorox Corp., San Francisco, Intercontinental, Singapore, Hyatt-Watertower, Chgo., U.S. Embassy Lisbon, Coos Art Mus., Smithsonian Instn., Washington, So. Utah U., Cedar City, Cedars-Sinai Med. Ctr., Los Angeles, Betty Ford Ctr., Eisenhower Hosp., Palm Springs, Calif., U.S. Embassy, Riyadh, Saudi Arabia; juror art exhibits San Diego, Long Beach and Los Angeles, Calif.; lectr., demonstrator. Recipient 6 awards Nat. Watercolor Soc.; award Scottsdale Watercolor Biennial, 1978, San Bernardino Mus. Art. Mem. Nat. Watercolor Soc., Artists Equity, Watercolor West, Women Painters West, Santa Monica C. of C. Home: 2200 Main St Santa Monica CA 90405

SNYDER, SONYA RUTH MCGINNIS, hospital personnel administrator; b. Ft. Leavenworth, Kans., Jan. 30, 1936; d. Velmer Wayne and Ruth Maxine (Babbitt) McGinnis; B.A., Northwestern U., 1957; M.S. in Indsl. Relations, Loyola U., Chgo., 1967; M. Health Sci. Adminstrn., Govs. State U., 1984; m. Daniel W. Snyder, Jr., Nov. 29, 1968. Personnel dir. Luth. Deaconess Hosp., Chgo., 1961-68; dir. personnel policies and procedures Rush Presbyn.-St. Lukes Med. Center, Chgo., 1968-71; personnel dir. Schwab Rehab. Hosp., Chgo., 1971-73, Copley Meml. Hosp., Aurora, Ill., 1973-79, Palos Community Hosp., Palos Heights, Ill., 1979—. Mem. adult edn. com. evening lay acad. Palos Park (Ill.) Presbyterian Community Ch., 1976-81, chmn., 1978—; mem. Palos Park Bicentennial Com., 1975-76. Mem. Am. Soc. Personnel Adminstrs. (accredited exec. in personnel), Am. Soc. Hosp. Personnel Adminstrs., Chgo. Hosp. Personnel Mgmt. Assn. (pres. 1975-76), Chgo. Hosp. Council. Office: Palos Community Hosp 80th Ave and McCarthy Rd Palos Heights IL 60463

SNYDER, SUSAN BROOKE, educator; b. Yonkers, N.Y., July 12, 1934; d. John Warren and Virginia Grace (Hartung) Snyder; B.A., Hunter Coll., City U.N.Y., 1955; M.A., Columbia U., 1958, Ph.D., 1963. Lectr. English, Queens Coll., City U.N.Y., 1961-63; mem. faculty Swarthmore (Pa.) Coll., 1963—, prof. English, 1975—, Eugene M. Lang research prof., 1982-86. Nat. Endowment for Humanities fellow, 1967-68; Folger Library fellow, 1972-73; Guggenheim fellow, 1980-81. Mem. MLA, Renaissance Soc. Am., Shakespeare Assn. Am. (trustee 1980-83), Spenser Soc. Mem. editorial bd. Shakespeare Quar., 1972—. Office: Dept English Swarthmore College Swarthmore PA 19081

SNYDER, SUSAN LELAND, international trade executive; b. Washington, Nov. 10, 1945; d. Arthur Leland and Jane Peters. B.A., Mt. Holyoke Coll., 1967; postgrad. SUNY-Buffalo, 1967-70. Staff adviser Institut Francais de Gestion, Paris, 1971-73; mktg. strategist Compteurs Schlumberger, Paris, 1973-76; export dir. Schlumberger Instruments & Systemes, Velizy-Villacoublay, France, 1976-78; founder, pres. Pathfinder Corp. for Internat. Trade, Washington, 1978—; mem. internat. com. Greater Washington Bd. of Trade. Sec.-treas. French-Am. Com. for the Statue of Liberty, 1981—. Mem. Washington Flute Soc. Club: City Tavern (Washington). Office: Pathfinder Corp for Internat Trade 1629 K St NW Washington DC 20006

SOAMES, CYNTHIA ELIZABETH, accountant; b. Peru, Ind., Oct. 6, 1946; d. Charles Bertrand and Elizabeth (Lee) S.; B.Mus., U. Cin., 1969; M.Mus., U. Miami (Fla.), 1973; degree acctg. Ind. U., Kokomo, 1982. C.P.A., Ind. Mem. Nashville Symphony, also mem. faculty Western Ky. U., 1969-70; mem. faculty St. Joseph's Coll., Rensselaer, Ind., 1970; instr. U. N.C.-Chapel Hill, 1971-72; grad. teaching asst. U. Miami, 1972-73; instr. U. Wis.-River Falls, 1974-75; acct. Kendall, Lechner & Co., Kokomo, 1982—. Mem. Am. Acctg. Assn., Nat. Assn. Accts. (v.p. membership), Ind. C.P.A. Soc. (continuing profl. edn. com), Bus. and Profl. Women's Club, Kokomo-Howard County C. of C., Small Bus. Council (legis. coms. retail and safety, commerce, corps. and taxation), AAUW, Leadership Kokomo. Roman Catholic. Club: Altrusa. Author articles in field of music. Address: 113 1/2 N Buckeye St Kokomo IN 46901 3071 Bentwood Circle N Drive Apt 2C Indianapolis IN 46268

SOARES, MARY ROSENQUIST, financial company executive; b. Springfield, Mass., Oct. 7, 1949; d. Jesse Woodson and Doris May (Marquette) R.; m. Earl Anthony Soares, Mar. 18, 1972 (div. 1982). Student San Domenico Sch., 1966-68, Dominican Coll., San Rafael, 1967-69, Calif., San Francisco Conservatory of Music, 1968-70; B.A., Coll. Marin, 1969. Asst. v.p. Western Travelers Life Ins. Co., San Rafael, 1970-80; v.p. Unimarc, Ltd., Novato, Calif., 1980-83, Western States Monetary Planning Services, Inc., Newhall, Calif., 1983—. Mem. exec. com. San Marin Valley Homeowners Assn., 1979-81. Mem. Internat. Assn. Fin. Planners. Democrat. Roman Catholic. Office: 22777 Lyons Ave Suite 200R Newhall CA 91321

SOBEL, SUZANNE BARBARA, clinical psychologist; b. Bklyn.; d. Albert E. and Jeannette (Schneider) S.; student Clark U., 1960-62; B.A., Adelphi U., 1964, M.A., 1966; Ph.D., U. Tenn., 1971. Psychologist, Orleans Parish Sch. Bd. (La.), 1971-72; asst. prof. Dillard U., 1972-73; clin. psychologist D.C. Children's Ctr., 1973-75; research clin. psychologist Mental Health Study Ctr., NIMH, Adelphi, Md., 1975-79; lectr. Univ. Coll., U. Md., 1975-79; pvt. practice clin. psychology, Washington, 1975-80, Indian Harbor Beach, 1980-82, Satellite Beach, Fla., 1982—; assoc. dean acad. affairs, prof. psychology Sch. Profl. Psychology, Fla. Inst. Tech., 1980-82; civil rights coordinator Alcohol, Drug Abuse and Mental Health Adminstrn., HEW, Rockville, Md., 1979-80; cons. clin. psychologist Children's Brain Research Ctr., 1976—. Public mem. D.C. Criminal Justice Coordinating Bd., 1977-78; mem. President's Commn. on Mental Health, 1977-78; mem. female offender and female juvenile offender coms. D.C. Commn. on Women, 1976. Fellow Am. Orthopsychiat. Assn., Am. Psychol. Assn. (pres. div. child and youth services 1980-81, sec. div. psychotherapy 1981-84); mem. Southeastern Psychol. Assn., Fla. Psychol. Assn., Soc. Pediatric Psychology, Am. Psychology Law Soc., Am. Soc. Correctional Psychologists, NOW, Nat. Assn. Female Execs., ORT. Mem. editorial bd. Jour. Clin. Child Psychology, 1976—, Psychotherapy and Private Practice; cons. editor Prof. Psychology, 1979—; editorial cons. Am. Psychologist, 1976—; cons. editor Psychotherapy: Theory, Research and Practice, 1980—. Contbr. articles to profl. jours. Home: 238 Harbor Dr E Indian Harbor Beach FL 32937 Office: 1680 Hwy A1A Suite 5 Satellite Beach FL 32937

SOBERANO, MERCEDES E., biochemist, researcher; b. Bacolod City, Philippines, Apr. 30, 1939; came to U.S., 1966; d. Raymundo L. and Mercedes (Esmeralda) S. B.S. in Chemistry, U. Philippines, 1961; Ph.D. in Biochemistry, Tulane U., 1970. Research technician U. Philippines Coll. Medicine, Manila, 1961-63, instr., 1963-66, asst. prof., 1970-72; assoc. research scientist NYU Med. Ctr., 1972-79, research scientist, 1979-83; research scientist Hyland Therapeutics, Los Angeles, 1983-85; dir. protein research Bion Corp., 1986—; cons. scientist Speywood Labs., Wrexham, Wales, 1979. Patentee purifying urokinase, 1978; author sci. papers., 1973—. Vice chmn. Philippine Forum, 1981-82. Rockefeller fellow, 1966-70. Mem. Assn. Women in Sci., AAAS, Am. Chem. Soc., Internat. Soc. Thrombosis and Hemostasis.

SOBERON, PRESENTACION ZABLAN, legal association administrator; b. Cabambangan, Bacolor, Pampanga, Philippines, Feb. 23, 1935; came to U.S., 1977, naturalized, 1984; d. Pioquinto Yalung and Lourdes (David) Zablan; m. Damaso Reyes Soberon, Apr. 2, 1961; children—Shirley, Sherman, Sidney, Sedwin. Office mgmt., stenography, typing cert. East Central Colls., Philippines, 1953; profl. sec. diploma, Internat. Corr. Schs., 1971; student Skyline Coll., 1979, LaSalle Extension U., 1980-82, Diablo Valley Coll., 1983—. Various clerical and secretarial positions U.S. Naval Base, Subic Bay, Philippines, 1955-73, adminstrv. asst., 1973-77; secretarial positions Mt. Zion Hosp. and Med. Center, San Francisco, 1977, Oakland City Hall (Calif.), 1978; secretarial positions gen. counsel div. State Bar of Calif., San Francisco, 1978, state bar ct. div., 1978-79, adminstrv. asst. fin. and ops. div., 1979-81, office mgr. sects. and coms. dept., profl. and pub. services div., 1981-83, adminstr. non-disciplinary standing coms. and appointment process of state bar entities, office of bar relations, 1983—; disc jockey, announcer Philippine radio stas. DZYZ, DZOR and DWHL, 1976-77. Organizer Neighborhood Alert Program, South Catamaran Circle, Pittsburg, Calif., 1979-80. Recipient numerous certs. and awards U.S. Fed. Service with USN, 1964-75, 20 Yr. pin and cert., 1975; Nat. 1st prize for community projects Inner Wheel Clubs Philippines, 1975; several plaques and award certs. for community and sch. activities, Olongapo City, Philippines. Mem. Nat. Assn. Female Execs., Subic Bay-Olongapo City Assn. No. Calif. (Pittsburg rep. 1982—). Roman Catholic. Home: 207 S Catamaran Circle Pittsburg CA 94565 Office: State Bar of Calif 555 Franklin St San Francisco CA 94102

SOBEY, FRANCINE, mental health and social work educator; b. N.Y.C., June 15, 1925; d. Louis and Esther Sandell; m. Victor M. Sobey; children—Anthony Foster, Wendy Sand. B.A., Hunter Coll., 1945; M.S., Columbia U., 1946, D.S.W., 1968. Sr. psychiat. social worker VA Mental Hygiene Clinic, Newark, 1946-49; child guidance therapist Newark Jewish Child Care Assn., 1949-51; psychiat. supr. Beth Israel Hosp., N.Y.C., 1951-54; acting dir. social service, dir. well-baby pediatric research, co-dir. child guidance services N.Y. Infirmary, N.Y.C., 1954-59; NIMH career tchr. Columbia U., N.Y.C., 1964-65, asst. prof. mental health and social work, 1968-72, assoc. prof., 1972-78, prof., 1979—, research dir. NIMH, 1966-69, project dir., 1981-82; cons. mental health to local, state nat., and internat. agys. Author: The Nonprofessional Revolution in Mental Health, 1970; Changing Roles in Social Work Practice, 1977; also monographs and articles; research on hospitalized well babies, 1956-59, prevention and utilization of paraprofls. in mental health, 1966-69, prevention in social work edn. curriculum, sexism, 1980-81, social networks for teenage mothers, 1980—. Mem. Columbia U. Commn. on Status of Women, 1974—, chairperson, 1976-78; bd. dirs. mental health assns., N.Y.C., Bronx, 1975-81, 84—. NIMH fellow, 1963-65; Kenworthy-Swift Found. grantee, 1983. Mem. Nat. Assn. Social Workers (nat. staffing task force 1971-73), Met. N.Y. Area Schs. Social Work Women's Faculty Assn. (founder), AAUP. Office: 622 W 113th St New York NY 10025

SOCHEN, JUNE, historian; b. Chgo., Nov. 26, 1937; d. Sam and Ruth (Finkelstein) S.; B.A., U. Chgo., 1958; M.A., Northwestern U., 1960, Ph.D., 1967. High sch. tchr. English and history North Shore Country Day Sch., Winnetka, Ill., 1961-64; instr. history Northeastern Ill U, 1964-67, asst. prof., 1967-69, asso. prof., 1969-72, prof., 1972—. Nat. Endowment for Humanities grantee, 1971-72. Mem. Am. Studies Assn. Author books including: The New Woman, 1971; Movers and Shakers, 1973; Herstory: A Womans View of American History, 1975, 2d edit., 1981; Consecrate Every Day: The Public Lives of Jewish American Women 1880-1980, 1981; contbr. articles on U.S. cultural and women's history to profl. jours. Office: Northeastern Ill U 5500 N Saint Louis St Chicago IL 60625

SOCOLOFSKY, IRIS KAY, lawyer; b. Davenport, Iowa, May 3, 1952; d. Forest Wesley and Josephine Jeanette (Barnett) Shaffer; 1 son, Eric Scott. B.S., Mich. State U., 1976; J.D., U. Mich., 1980. Bar: Mich. 1980, U.S. Dist. Ct. (we. and ea. dists.) Mich. 1980. Atty. Fraser, Trebilcock, Davis & Foster, P.C., Lansing., Mich., 1980—. Co-author: Michigan Usury Manual, 1982. Bd. dirs. Capital Area council Girl Scouts U.S., 1986—; mem. planning bd. Ingham County Office for Young Children, 1986—. Recipient Book award U. Mich. Law Sch., 1980. Mem. Ingham County Bar Assn., State Bar Assn. Mich., ABA, Lansing Regional C. of C. (bus. women's council 1984—), Lansing Assn. Career Women. (bd. dirs. 1983-85), Nat. Assn. Career Women (bd. dirs. 1985—). Home: 2000 Wembley Way East Lansing MI 48823 Office: Fraser Trebilcock Davis & Foster 1000 Michigan Nat Tower Lansing MI 48933

SODAWALLA, ANITA B., nurse; b. Quezon City, Philippines, Dec. 5, 1942; came to U.S., 1972, naturalized 1983; d. Jose Canete Bustamente and Esperanza Manzano Carino; m. Badruddin H. Sodawalla, Dec. 26, 1975; 1 child, Ibrahim B. Grad. in Nursing, U. Philippines, 1968, M. in Nursing, 1971; B.S. in Nursing, Philippine Women's U., 1970; postgrad. Wayne State U., 1977-80. Charge nurse neonatal and pediatric ICU, Henry Ford Hosp., Detroit, 1972-73; instr., coordinator critical care Grace Hosp., Detroit, 1973-76; sr. instr. Harper Hosp. div. Harper-Grace Hosps., 1976-79, asst. dir. nursing Grace Hosp. div., 1980; pres., exec. dir. Critical Care Unltd., Inc., Southfield, Mich., 1979-84; dir. nursing services and continuing edn. Critical Care Profl. Services, 1980-84; pres., exec. dir. Profl. Success Systems, Inc., 1982—; program coordinator/cons. Critical Care Edn. Ctr., 1984—. Named Most Outstanding Filipino Woman in Entrepreneurship, 1985. Mem. Am. Assn. Critical Care Nurses, Am. Heart Assn., Am. Soc. Health Edn. and Manpower Tng., Nat. Assn. Female Execs., Am. Soc. Profl. and Exec. Women, Am. Nurses Assn., Nat. Assn. Nurse Cons. and Entrepreneurs. (founder, pres.). Mem. Ch. of Christ. Home: 3133 Michael St Warren MI 48091 Office: Profl Success Systems Inc 17515 W Nine Mile Rd Suite 65 Southfield MI 48075

SODERBERG, JANET MARIE, insurance company executive, lawyer; b. Evanston, Ill., Dec. 10, 1955; d. John William and Georgina Marie (Navigator) S. B.A., U. Denver, 1977; J.D., John Marshall Law Sch., Chgo., 1982. Bar: Ill. 1982. Exec. v.p. Constitutional Casualty Co., Chgo., 1979—; instr. Robert Morris Coll., Chgo., 1982. Mem. Chgo. Bar Assn., Ill. Bar Assn., ABA. Republican. Episcopalian. Office: Constitutional Casualty Co 5618 N Milwaukee Ave Chicago IL 60646

SOECHTIG, JACQUELINE ELIZABETH, telecommunications executive; b. Manhasset, N.Y., Aug. 12, 1949; d. Alvin Hermann and Regina Mary (Murphy) Venzke; m. James Decatur Miller, June 28, 1976 (div. Oct. 1982); M. Clifford Jon Soechtig, Oct. 19, 1983. B.A. cum laude, Coll. of New Rochelle (N.Y.), 1974; M.A. summa cum laude, U. So. Calif., 1978. Computer operator IBM, White Plains, N.Y., 1970-72, ops. job scheduler, 1972-74, various spl. assignments, 1974-75, mktg. rep., Bethesda, Md., 1975-76, Charleston, W. Va., 1979-81, adv. regional mktg. rep. Dallas, 1981-82; dist. mgr. Am. Speedy Printing Co., Dallas, 1982-83, nat. sales devel. mgr., Detroit, 1984; regional mgr. major and nat. accounts MCI Telecommunications, Southfield, Mich., 1984—; interviewer, Sergio Segre, Bolonga, Italy, 1977, Radio Free Europe, Brussels, 1978, World Health Program, Rome, 1978, ITT, Brussels, 1977, Franz Josef Strauss, 1978. Recipient Golden Circle Achievement award IBM, 1980, Quar. Recognition award, 1980, 81; named New Bus. Pacesetter, 1980, 81. Republican. Club: German Am. Women's (v.p. Stuttgart, W.Ger. 1977-78). Home: 1809 Golf Ridge Dr Bloomfield Hills MI 48013 Office: MCI Telecommunications Corp 26913 Northwestern Hwy Southfield MI 48034

SOFFERMAN, DEBORAH ANN BLECHER, cosmetic and travel accessories company executive; b. N.Y.C., June 20, 1951; d. Jerome and Shirley (Stein) Blecher; m. Bruce Robert Sofferman, Dec. 19, 1982. A.S., Dean Jr. Coll., 1971; B.S. cum laude, Ithaca Coll., 1973. Model, Raphael Soyer, Painter, N.Y.C., 1975—; freelance photographer, N.Y.C., 1975-80; writer Intermezzo, Carnegie Hall and Town Hall program publs., 1975-78; freelance prodn. coordinator and prodn. asst. for TV commls. and feature films, 1977-81; producer, co-producer various original video tapes, N.Y.C., 1977-81; prodn. supr. TV series OMNI: The New Frontier, 1981; pres. Southport Bags, Inc., Conn., 1982—; mktg. dir. Smile Dental Ctr., Derby, Conn., 1982—; host radio show PrimeTime, Sta. WADS-AM, Conn., 1985—. Vol. Tng., Edn. and Manpower Team, Inc., Lower Naugatuck Valley, 1984- 85; co-chmn. Valley Food Bank, food collection, 1985, Toys 4 Tots, Team Inc., 1985. Name Co-Vol. of Yr., Team Inc., 1985. Avocations: writing; photography; singing; dancing; acting. Office: Southport Bags Inc PO Box 702 Southport CT 06418

SOFIOS, ANN MARIE, administrative assistant, election campaign aide; b. Indpls., Nov. 30, 1957; d. Peter Thomas and Patricia Ann (Speropoulos) Sofios. B.S. in Speech, Northwestern U., Evanston, Ill., 1980. Asst. state (Ind.) dir. Howard Baker (Rep.) for U.S. Pres., Indpls., 1980; aide constituent service U.S. Senator (Ind.) R.G. Lugar, Indpls., 1980-81; dep. campaign mgr. Friends of Dick Lugar, Indpls., 1981; fin. dir., 1981-82; personal asst. U.S. Senator Lugar, Washington, 1982-84, dep. adminstrv. asst., 1985—; participant Nat. Rep. Campaign Workshop, Indpls., 1981; pub. relations dir. Indpls. Scoliosis Assn., 1980-82. Writer Sen. Lugar campaign newsletters, 1981-82; co-editor campaign manual, 1981. Mem. Assn. Jr. Leagues, Inc., Washington, Indpls., 1981—); docent Corcoran Gallery Art, Washington, 1983—, Nat. Mus. Women in Arts, 1985—; mem. Cathedral Arts, Inc., Indpls., 1980-82; coordinator Chgo. Hellenic Ind. Day, 1978; chmn. Washington Twp. (Ind.) Bicentennial Celebration, 1975-76. Named Sagamore of Wabash, Gov. Indiana, 1982; Hoosier scholar State of Ind., 1976; Order AHEPA, Daus. Penelope scholar, 1976-79; recipient Citizenship award Soroptimist Club, Indpls. 1976. Mem. Women in Communications, Northwestern U. Alumni Assn., Mortar Bd., Kappa Kappa Gamma Alumni Assn. Greek Orthodox. Clubs: Rivera (Indpls.). Lodges: Jr. Pan Hellenic (pub. relations chmn. 1976-77), Maids of Athena, Daus. of Penelope. Home: 1071 Papermill Ct NW Washington DC 20007 Office: Office of US Senator Lugar 306 Hart Senate Bldg Washington DC 20510

SOILEAU, LOUISE BOLTS, educator; b. Hearne, Tex., Nov. 22, 1928; d. Governor Bolts and Mary Eliza (Young) Bolts Tardy; m. Samuel Williams, Sept. 1946 (dec. Jan. 1952); 1 child, Debbera Ann Williams Hayward; m. 2d, George Soileau, Aug. 21, 1977. B.S. in Edn., Tex. So. U., 1980, postgrad. in ednl. adminstrn. Cert. in early childhood edn., Tex. Case worker Tex. Dept. Human Resources, Houston, 1972-77; substitute tchr. Pasadena Ind. Sch. Dist. (Tex.), 1978-79; substitute tchr. Houston Ind. Sch. Dist., 1979-80, tchr., 1980—. Vol. worker ARC, Houston, 1978-79, Pub. Broadcasting Service Auction, Houston, 1980-81; Democratic block capt., Houston, 1979—; bd. dirs. New Directions Halfway Ho., Houston, 1975-76. Mem. LWV, Psi Chi, Phi Delta Kappa. Mem. Ch. of Christ. Home: 5503 Southwind St Houston TX 77033 Office: Lantrip Elem School 100 Telephone St Houston TX 77023

SOKOL, SUSAN, apparel company executive. Pres., Calvin Klein Ltd., N.Y.C. Office: Calvin Klein Ltd 205 W 39th St New York NY 10018*

SOKOLOWSKI, DENISE GEORGIA, librarian, university official, educator; b. Oceanside, N.Y., Nov. 2, 1951; d. Charles John and Georgia Sarah (Papadam) S.; m. Robert Harald Munoz, May 21, 1983. A.A., Modesto Jr. Coll., 1971; B.A., Calif. State Coll.-Stanislaus, 1974; M.L.I.S., U. Calif.-Berkeley, 1982. Sec. to support services officer Stanislaus State Coll., Turlock, Calif., 1973-75; vet. asst. U. Md. European Div., Heidelberg, Fed. Republic Germany, 1976-77, publs. asst., 1983-85, librarian, 1985—; tour guide, escort Great Pacific Tour Co., San Francisco, 1978-81; word processor Telegraph Ave. Geotechn. Assocs., Berkeley, 1982-83. Mem. ALA, Beta Phi Mu. Democrat. Office: U Md APO New York NY 09102

SOLDANO, CONNIE LEE, health center administrator; b. Connellsville, Pa., May 25, 1934; d. Edward James and Mary Elizabeth (Clark) Hampton; B.S., Calif. State Coll., 1980; postgrad. U. Pitts., 1980-82; m. Nick J. Soldano, May 13, 1967; children—Ken N., Terry J., Cynthia A. Sec., asst. treas. Charles F. Eggers Co., Uniontown, Pa., 1962-72; adminstrv. asst. Bauer Lumber Co., Uniontown, 1972-74; fiscal, statis. asst. Fayette County Mental Health/Mental Retardation Clinic, Inc., Uniontown, 1974-76; fiscal officer Fayette County Health Center, Uniontown, 1979-81, adminstr., 1982—. Asst. leader Girl Scouts U.S., 1949-52; pres. Dunbar Boro PTA 1961-1962; mem. Heart Fund Telethon, 1982—. Mem. Nat. Assn. Accts., Nat. Assn. Female Execs., Soc. Advancement Mgmt., AAUW (legis. chmn.), Women's Agenda, Calif. State Coll. Alumni Assn., U. Pa. Alumni Assn. Democrat. Home: 708 S Arch St Connellsville PA 15425 Office: 100 New Salem Rd Uniontown PA 15401

SOLDINGER, ELIZABETH REITZIG, advertising company executive, media director; b. N.Y.C., July 24, 1938; d. Henry Herman and Pauline (Goerse) Reitzig; m. Sydney Soldinger, July 10, 1964 (dec. 1974). B.A., Hunter Coll., 1961. Media dir. Sheldon Fredericks Advt., N.Y., 1964-71, Beckerman Roswer Wyman Advt., N.Y., 1971-75; freelance media cons. N.Y., 1975-76; v.p., media dir. Gaynor Media Corp. N.Y., 1976-85; pres. Time and Space Assos., N.Y., 1982—, E.S. Media Services, 1985—. Home: 400 E 85th St New York City NY 10028

SOLEM, MAIZIE ROGNESS, educator; b. Hendricks, Minn., Nov. 8, 1920; d. John A. and Nora Adeline (Engelstad) Rogness; m. Herman S. Solem; children—Margaret Foley, Jeffrey. B.A., Augustana Coll., 1942; postgrad. George Washington U., 1955-57, Wright State U., 1970-71; M.Ed., Miami U., Oxford, Ohio, 1970-71; Ed.D., U. S.D., 1976; postgrad U. Calif., 1978. Tchr., LeMars, Iowa, 1942-43, Internat. Children's Centre, Bangkok, Thailand, 1952-53, George Washington U., Washington, 1957, Fairfax (Va.) schs., 1956-58, Maxwell AFB Sch., Montgomery, Ala., 1963-66; tchr., librarian Central High Sch., Madison, S.D., 1943; dir., tchr., supr. remedial reading tchrs. City schs., Fairborn, Ohio, 1966-71; Title I resource tchr. L.B. Anderson Elem. Sch., Sioux Falls, S.D., 1971-73; primary coordinator Instructional Planning Center, Sioux Falls, 1973-77; curriculum coordinator Sioux Falls public schs., 1973—. Mem. adv. bd. Ret. Sr. Vol. Program, 1974-78, publicity chmn., 1975-78; mem. adv. bd. Vol. Action Center, 1976-78, mem. service com., 1974-78; chmn. exec. bd. Augustana Fellows, 1979-81; bd. regents Augustana Coll., 1984—; scholarship chmn. LaSertoma, 1979-80; active various drives including Heart Fund, Muscular Dystrophy, Cancer Fund. Recipient Gov.'s award for Volunteerism in Edn., 1983; YWCA Leader in the Professions award, 1984; Disting. Alumni award Agustana Coll, 1986. Mem. AAUW, Sch. Adminstrs. S.D. (v.p. 1977-78), Assn. Supervision Curriculum Devel. (pres. 1976-78, nat. exec. council 1979-82), Nat. Assn. Supervision Curriculum Devel. (bd. dirs. 1977-79; mem. nat. selection com. 1977-78), Assn. Childhood Edn. Internat., S.D. Assn. Elem. Prins., Elem., Kindergarten, Nursery Sch. Edn., Nat. Assn. Edn. Young Children, Sioux Land Assn. for Edn. Young Children, NEA, S.D. Edn. Assn., Nat. Council Social Studies, Internat. Reading Assn., S.D. Tchrs. Maths. Orgn., S.D. Assn. Supervision and Curriculum Devel., Orton Soc. Republican. Lutheran. Home: 1600 North Dr Box 911 Sioux Falls SD 57101 Office: 201 E 38th St Sioux Falls SD 57102

SOLER, DONA KATHERINE (FORMSMA), civic worker; b. Grand Rapids, Mich., Mar. 7, 1921; d. Melbourne and Katherine Anne (Herbst) Welch; 1 child, Suzette Maria. Student pub. and private schs., Grand Rapids, Mich. Editor, publisher, artist, counselor Psychic Exchange, 1979—. Author:

What God Hath Put Together, 1979; Our Heritage From the Angels, 1981; Expose the Dirty Devil, 1984; Contemporary Poets of America (anthology), 1984, For Love of Henry, 1985, Greyball, 1986, House of Evil Secrets, 1986. Founder, 1st pres. S. Coast Art Assn., San Clement, Calif., 1963-65, Orange Coast Catholic Christian Singles, 1970-73, Psychic Exchange, Orange County, 1979; founder, chief Lake Riverside Estates Communicators, Riverside, 1974-79. Republican. Mem. Animal Assistance League of Orange County, Animal Protection Instn. of Am., Greenpeace, People for the Ethical Treatment of Animals, Internat. Fund for Animal Welfare, World Wildlife Fund-U.S., Humane Soc. of the U.S., Am. Soc. for the Prevention of Cruelty Towards Animals, Ctr. for Environ. Edn. and Defenders of Wildlife. Home: 2604 Willo Ln Costa Mesa CA 92627

SOLER, TERRELL DIANE, dramatic soprano, real estate salesperson; b. South Bend, Ind., Apr. 26; d. Harold J. Metzler and Margaret Terrell (Whiteman) Metzler Fogarty; m. Victor M. Soler, Dec. 17, 1961 (annulled). B.A., Ithaca Coll., 1960; diploma Brown's Bus. Coll., Decatur, Ill., 1960; Nat. Assn. Securities Dealers lic. Investors Planning Corp., N.Y.C., 1961; student in real estate sales NYU Sch. Continuing Edn. Real Estate Inst., 1984. Lic. real estate salesperson, N.Y. Exec. legal asst. Carb Luria Glassner Cook & Kufeld, N.Y.C., 1962-64, Graubard Moskovitz McGoldrick Dannett & Horowitz, N.Y.C., 1964-79; free-lance opera and concert singer, N.Y.C., 1979—; real estate salesperson Rosemary Edwards Realty Corp., N.Y.C., 1985—; bd. dirs., corr. sec. Community Opera, Inc., N.Y.C., 1984—. Mem. internat. affairs com. and other coms. Women's Nat. Republican Club, N.Y.C., 1968—; active Rep. County Vols., N.Y.C., 1976—; mem. nominating com. Ivy Rep. Club, N.Y.C., 1983—; bd. dirs. Am. Landmark Festivals, 1986—. Named Female Singer of Yr., Internat. Beaux Arts, Inc., 1978; Princess Nightingale, Allied Indian Tribes N.Am. Continent-Cherokee Nation, 1985. Mem. Nat. Arts Club (music com. 1983—), Wagner Internat. Instn. (dir. pub. relations 1982-84), N.Y. Opera Club, Navy League U.S. (life, mem. N.Y. council), Assn. Former Intelligence Officers (assoc.), Friends of Spanish Opera (bd. dirs. 1982—). Avocations: tennis; swimming; dancing; travel; antiques. Home: 2 Tudor City Pl Apt 4-J South New York NY 10017

SOLES, ADA LEIGH, state legislator; b. Jacksonville, Fla., May 19, 1937; d. Albert Thomas and Dorothy (Winter) Wall; B.A., Fla. State U., 1959; m. James Ralph Soles, 1959; children—Nancy Beth, Catherine. Mem. New Castle County Library Adv. Bd., 1975-80, chmn., 1975-77; chmn. Del. State Library Adv. Bd., 1975-78; mem. Del. State Ho. Reps., 1980—. Adminstrv. asst. U. Del. Commn. on Status of Women, 1976-77; acad. advisor U. Del. Coll. Arts and Scis., 1977—. Mem. LWV (state pres. 1978-80), Phi Beta Kappa, Phi Kappa Phi, Mortar Bd., Alpha Chi Omega. Episcopalian. Office: Del Ho of Reps State Capitol Dover DE 19901

SOLIS, THERESA MARIE, nurse, educator; b. Kenmore, N.Y., Apr. 17, 1957; d. Walter Jacob and Theresa Anna (Janeczko) Preciado Freiert; m. Jesse Solis, Oct. 21, 1978, children—Stacia Marie, Michael Mathew. A.A.S. in Nursing, Niagara County Community Coll., 1977; B.S. in Nursing, U. Phoenix, 1984. Cert. in nursing adminstrn. Staff nurse San Pedro Peninsula Hosp., Calif., 1977-78; staff nurse Bay Harbor Hosp., Harbor City, Calif., 1978-80, scrub nurse catheterization lab., 1980, clin. instr., 1981-83, dir. edn., 1983—; cons. educator Nursing Ednl. Systems, Huntington Beach, Calif., 1984—. Mem. Health Care Edn. Council, So. Calif., 1983—. Recipient Outstanding Community Service award Los Angeles County, 1984. Democrat. Methodist. Avocation: music. Office: Bay Harbor Hosp Inc 1437 Lomita Blvd Harbor City CA 90710

SOLLAMI, ROSEANN, educator, administrator, politician; b. Trenton, N.J., Dec. 30, 1935; d. Joseph Thomas and Anne Esther (Lipani) Bruno; m. Paul J. Sollami, May 4, 1963; children—Paula, Maryann. B.A., Douglass Coll., 1957; student Trenton State Coll., 1964, Rutgers U. Grad. Sch. Edn., 1959-61. Tchr. history, econs. Ewing Township, Trenton, 1957-59; asst. dir. admissions Rutgers U., New Brunswick, N.J., 1959-63; ascertainment coordinator Sta. NJP-TV Channel 52, N.J., 1975-81; tchr. English Ewing Twp. High Sch., 1985—. Committeewoman Democratic Party, Trenton, 1969—; polit. fundraiser Merlino for Gov., 1982; chairwoman fundraising dinner Mercer County Dems., 1978. Mem. Douglass Coll. Alumni Assn., Ravine Club, Trenton Coll. Club, N.J. Fedn. Dem. Women. Avocations: drama; swimming; politics; photography. Home and Office: 11 Seven Oaks Ln Trenton NJ 08628

SOLLENBERGER, DONNA FITZPATRICK, administrative assistant; b. Tuscola, Ill., Jan. 13, 1949; d. Vincent Norman and Marian Louise (Mumbower) Fitzpatrick; student U. Kans., 1968-70; B.A., Sangamon State U., 1971, M.A., 1974; m. Kent Sollenberger, Dec. 30, 1984, children—Shannon, Blake, Bradley. Tchr., Springfield (Ill.) S.E. High Sch., 1971-74; public info. officer Ill. Dept. Transp., Springfield, 1974-75; exec. asst. to dir. Ill. Dept. Conservation, Springfield, 1975-76; adminstrv. asst. to chmn. dept. surgery So. Ill. U. Sch. Medicine, Springfield, 1976-80, adminstr. med. sch., 1985—; instr. communications Lincoln Land Community Coll., Springfield, part-time, 1976-77, instr. English, 1980-84. Recipient Conservation Merit award Ill. Dept. Conservation, 1976. Mem. Med. Group Mgmt. Assn. Springfield Art Assn., Delta Gamma Alumnae Assn. Mormon. Home: 1930 Whittier Springfield IL 62704 Office: 800 N Rutledge Springfield IL 62707

SOLLEY, MARY-SUE PASTORELLO, home entertainment products distributing executive; b. Chgo., Aug. 4, 1955; d. Daniel and Angela (Gatsos) Pastorello; m. Richard James Solley, Oct. 8, 1977; children—Daniel, Stephanie. Student Eastern Ill. U., 1973-76, Roosevelt U., 1980-82. Acct., office mgr. Burton's Shoes, Inc., Northbrook, Ill., 1976-80; asst. controller Sound Video Unltd., Inc., Niles, Ill., 1980-82, controller, 1982-86, chief fin. officer, 1986—, also dir.; treas., dir. JLT Films, Inc., Niles, 1983—. Mem. Nat. Assn. Accts., Bus. Planning Bd., Nat. Assn. for Female Execs., Controllers Council. Republican. Greek Orthodox. Club: St. John's Philoptochos (Des Plaines, Ill.). Avocations: piano; theatre; horseback riding; boating; swimming. Home: 811 E Appletree Ln Arlington Heights IL 60004 Office: Sound Video Unltd Inc 7000 N Austin Niles IL 60648

SOLLITT, BETTYE HERB, civic worker; b. Alton, Ill., June 4, 1911; d. Harrison Blaine Herb and Elizabeth (Green) Reticker; m. Harry Gale Nye, Jr., Dec. 4, 1935 (div. 1949); children—Julia Gale, Nancy Pogue, Sally Barbara; m. Sumner Shannon Sollitt, Nov. 30, 1949 (dec. 1964); 1 child, Bettye Martin. Student Northwestern U., 1929-31, U. Chgo., 1969-70. Acct. and circulation mgr. Barks Publs., Chgo., 1970-75; profl. fund raiser U. Mich. Coll. Engring. and Occidental Coll. Los Angeles, 1975-78. Mem. women's bd. dirs., officer Arthritis Found., Chgo., 1951—, U. Chgo. Cancer Research Found., 1958—, Henrotin Hosp., Chgo., 1964—; past mem., officer Chgo. council Girl Scouts U.S.A., 1952-68, Parents Council Latin Sch., 1959-61, 64-68; bd. dirs. English Speaking Union, Chgo., 1981—. Republican. Episcopalian. Clubs: University, Chgo. Yacht (Chgo.). Avocation: sailing.

SOLLOD, ELLEN, arts administrator, artist; b. Rockville Center, N.Y., Apr. 16, 1951; d. Norman and Phyllis Laurel (Freed) Sollod; m. Barry Michael Pierce, May 20, 1973 (div. June 1981). B.A., U. N.C., 1972; M.A., U. Md., 1975. One woman shows: Antioch Coll., 1980, Columbia Ctr. for Visual Arts (Md.), Gensler and Assocs., 1985; group shows include: Arvada Ctr. for Arts and Humanities (Colo.), 1983, Boulder Ctr. for Visual Arts (Colo.), 1984, Colo. Artists and Craftsmen, Arvada Ctr. for Arts and Humanities, 1985, Colo. Graphic Arts Ctr., 1985, Foothills Art Ctr., Golden, Colo., 1986; asst. art dir. Md.-Nat. Capital Park and Planning Commn., Riverdale, Md., 1975-78; mem. adj. faculty U. Md., College Park, 1978; policy specialist Nat. Endowment for the Arts, Washington, 1978-79, asst. dir. dance program, 1979-81; exec. dir. Colo. Council on Arts and Humanities, Denver, 1981—. Mem. adv. coms. Denver Partnership, 1983; mem. adv. council Colo. Tourism Adv. Council, Denver, 1983-84. Aspen Inst. for Humanistic Studies fellow, 1985. Mem. Western States Art Found. (chmn. bd. 1985), Am. Crafts Council, Nat. Assembly State Arts Agys. Jewish. Office: Colo Council on Arts and Humanities 770 Pennsylvania St Denver CO 80203

SOLO, GAIL DIANNE, lawyer; b. Sacramento, Calif., Aug. 29, 1950; d. Myron B. and Betty (Codron) S. A.B., UCLA, 1972, J.D., 1975. Bar: Calif. 1975, U.S. Dist. Ct. (cen. dist.) Calif. 1976, U.S. Dist. Ct. (no. dist.) Calif. 1976. Aide to Senator Robbins, Calif. State Senate, Sacramento, 1975; assoc. McKay & Byrne, Los Angeles, 1976-78, Joseph Shalant Law Corp., Los Angeles, 1978-79; prin. Solo & Baron, Los Angeles, 1979—; co-founder Women's Legal Clinic, Los Angeles, 1979—, Attys. Against Discrimination, Los Angeles, 1981—. Mem. United Jewish Welfare Fund, 1976—, Los Angeles World Affairs Council, 1980—, mem. Am. Jewish Congress Commn. on Law and Social Action. Recipient Outstanding Service award Women's Legal Clinic, 1979. Mem. Am. Judicature Soc., Affiliated Network Exec. Women, Women Lawyers Assn. Los Angeles, Los Angeles County Bar Assn., Los Angeles Trial Lawyers Assn., Beverly Hills Bar Assn. (women and law com.), NOW. Democrat. Jewish. Office: Solo & Baron Suite 3100 2049 Century Park E Los Angeles CA 90067

SOLOMON, A. MALAMA, state legislator; b. Honolulu, Mar. 3, 1961; d. Randolph Folau Solomon and Flora Beamer. B.Ed., U. Hawaii-Manoa, 1972, M.A., 1973; B.A., U. Hawaii-Hilo, 1974; Ph.D., Oreg. State U., 1980. Market and sales mgr. beef cattle Kohala Farms, from 1972; lectr. U. Hawaii-Hilo, 1973-75; program coordinator Aloha Week Festivals Inc., 1977—. Trustee, Office Hawaiian Affairs, 1980-82; mem. Hawaii Senate, Dist. 3, 1983—. Native Am. Ford fellow, 1976-80; recipient Outstanding Community Service award Hilo Coll., 1973-75; Outstanding Leadership award Council Hawaiian Civic Clubs, 1982; named Outstanding Woman of Yr., Hawaii Nat. Women's Week, 1982. Mem. Kohala Community Assn., Dist. Council Hawaiian Civic Clubs. Congregationalist. Office: Hawaii State Senate State Capitol Honolulu HI 96813*

SOLOMON, ELLEN JOAN, management analyst; b. Orange, N.J., Aug. 26, 1943; d. Abram Shrier and Mildred Elizabeth (Berger) Solomon; B.A. in Psychology, U. N.C., Chapel Hill, 1965; M.S. in Human Resource Devel., Am. U., 1985. Contract writer Conn. Gen. Life Ins. Co., Bloomfield, 1965-66; mgmt. trainee, asst. buyer G. Fox & Co., Hartford, Conn., 1966-68; account exec. WLAE-FM, Hartford, 1968; sr. analyst Travelers Ins. Co., Hartford, 1968-70; job analyst Conn. Blue Cross, New Haven, 1970-71; sr. ops. auditor Govt. Employees Ins. Co., Washington, 1972-75; employee devel. specialist Employment Standards Adminstrn., U.S. Dept. of Labor, Washington, 1975-81, mgmt. analyst, 1981-82, supervisory mgmt. analyst, 1982—; conf. speaker; workshop leader; cons. Recipient Spl. Achievement award U.S. Dept. of Labor, 1977, 78, 83, 85. Mem. Am. Soc. Tng. and Devel., OD Network, Gestalt Inst. Cleve., NOW, Alpha Gamma Delta. Democrat. Jewish. Club: U. N.C. Alumni (Washington). Home: 4977 Battery Ln #513 Bethesda MD 20814 Office: 200 Constitution Ave NW Washington DC 20210

SOLOMON, GERI ANN, lawyer; b. Chester, W.Va., June 26, 1956; d. Walter and Sarabell (Fineman) S. B.A. magna cum laude in Polit. Sci. W.Va. U., 1977, J.D., 1980. Bar: W.Va. 1980, Calif. 1983. Atty., U.S. Dept. Labor, Washington, 1980-81, IRS, Washington, 1981-82; assoc. Kray & Smith, Newport Beach, Calif., 1982-83, Voss & Cook, Newport Beach, 1983—; atty. (pro bono) Latin Am. News Service, Washington, 1980-82. Mem. ABA, W.Va. Bar Assn., Calif. Bar Assn., Orange County Bar Assn. Democrat. Jewish. Home: 104 Esplanade Ave Irvine CA 92715 Office: Voss & Cook 840 Newport Center Dr Suite 700 Newport Beach CA 92658

SOLOMON, ILENE JUDITH SINSKY, educator; b. Washington, May 24, 1944; d. Herbert Brown Sinsky and Martha (Bass) Sinsky Glukenhous; m. Marvin M. Solomon, Sept. 11, 1966; children—Jonathan Jacques, Evan Derek. B.A., U. Md., 1966; M.A., George Washington U., 1969; M.A. in Internat. Service, Am. U., 1975. Tchr. Rock Terrace High Sch. and Westland Jr. High Sch., Montgomery County Pub. Schs., Rockville, Md., 1966-69, system tchr. speech-drama, spl. edn., 1980—; with Montgomery County Day Care Assn., 1984-86; tchr. nursery sch. Adas Israel Congregation Preschool, 1985. Active Columbian Women of George Washington U., Washington, 1975—, pres., 1981-83, Quinn Casting, Silver Spring, Md., 1985; actress Cedar Lane Stage, 1985, Kennedy Ctr., De La Croix Prodns., 1985; actress in several plays and movies; tchr. Washington Hebrew congregation, 1986. Recipient award for leadership and accomplishments D.C. Bus. and Profl. Womens' Club, 1981. Mem. Council Exceptional Children, English Speaking Union, U. Md. Alumni Assn. Internat. (life), Am. U. Sch. Internat. Service Alumni Assn., Gen. Alumni Assn. George Washington U. (del. 1981-83), Pi Sigma Alpha.

SOLOMON, MOLLIE ANNA, electrical workers' union executive; b. Orange, Tex., Jan. 6, 1951; d. George Milton and Rebecca Alice (McCoppin) S. Student Lamar U. Tchr. Saint Mary's Elem. Sch., Port Arthur, Tex., 1972-74; accounts payable clk. Gulfport Shipbuilding Corp., Port Arthur, 1974-76; audit clk. Rogers Enterprises, Inc., Beaumont, Tex., 1976; office mgr. Local Union 390, Internat. Brotherhood Elec. Workers, Port Arthur, 1976—; membership officer Neches Credit Union, Port Neches, Tex., 1984—. County coordinator Jim Hightower/Agr. Commr., Tex., 1986; mem. exec. com. Muscular Dystrophy Assn., southeast Tex., 1980—; sec. Sesquicentennial Commn., Groves, Tex., 1984—; exec. com. Jefferson County Democratic Club, Tex., 1980—, precinct chmn., 1980—; sec. Jefferson County Women's Dem. Club, 1980—; mem. bd. regents Tex. State Tech Inst., 1985—. Recipient Pathfinder award Women's Commn. Southeast Tex., 1986. Mem. Am. Bus. Women's Assn. (Woman of Yr. 1979), Nat. Trust Historic Preservation, Bus. and Profl. Women Inc. (Young Careerist award 1979), Nat. Assn. Female Execs., Grove C. of C., Beta Sigma Phi. Roman Catholic. Avocations: sewing; singing; reading; embroidery; cross stitch; dancing; travel. Home: PO Box 577 Grove TX 77619 Office: Local Union 390 I B E W PO Box 3316 Port Arthur TX 77643

SOLOMON, PENNY SUE, association executive; b. Monahans, Tex., Dec. 28, 1952; d. Jean Cope S. Student U. So. Miss., 1982-85, Baylor U., 1972-73, Mid Am. Nazarene Coll., 1971-72. Mgr., Career Girl Shops, Inc., Waco, Tex., 1973-75; pvt. sec. 1st Bapt. Ch., Waco, 1975-81; exec. asst., Chattanooga, 1981-82; adminstrv. asst. 1st Bapt. Ch., Hattiesburg, Miss., 1982-85; exec. v.p. Colorado City Area C. of C., Tex., 1985—. Bd. dirs. Wallace Community Edn. Council, 1985—; actress Colorado City Playhouse, best actress award, 1985. Mem. Permian Basin Chamber Mgrs. Assn. (sec. 1986), Nat. Assn. Female Execs., C. of C. Exec. West Tex., Tex. C. of C. Execs. Baptist. Avocations; Reading; writing; physical fitness; theater.

SOLOMON, PHYLLIS, personnel firm executive; b. N.Y.C., May 9, 1935; d. Herman Aaron and Sylvia (Haymes) Kanarick; m. Harvey Charles Solomon, Feb. 5, 1955 (div. Oct. 1976); children—Deborah, William, David. Sec. Scovill Mfg., Montclair, N.J., 1955-56; co-owner, officer mgr. Bloomfield Glass Co., N.J., 1962-75; office mgr. Am. Service, Inc., Bronx, N.Y., 1975-76, PDI, Englewood Cliffs, N.J., 1976-77; pres., owner V.I.P. Exec. Personnel, Englewood Cliffs, 1977—; founder, chief exec. officer Park Ave. Faces, Inc., 1981—. Pres. Women's Am. Orgn. Rehab. Tng., Verona, N.J., 1960-61. Fellow Healthcare Businesswomen's Assn.; mem. N.J. Assn. Personnel Counsellors, Pharm. Advt. Council, Nat. Assn. Female Execs., Englewood Cliffs C. of C. Jewish. Avocations: golf; tennis; music; reading. Office: VIP Exec Personnel 701 Palisade Ave Englewood Cliffs NJ 07632

SOLOMON, TERRI MARCIA, lawyer; b. Passaic, N.J., July 22, 1955; d. Sol and Arlene (Stiskin) S.; m. Howard Michael Topaz, July 4, 1982. B.A. summa cum laude, U. Mass., 1976; J.D., U. Pa., 1979. Bar: N.Y. 1980, N.J. 1979, U.S. Dist. Ct. (so. dist.) N.Y., 1980, U.S. Dist. Ct. (ea. dist.) N.Y., 1980, U.S. Dist. Ct. N.J., 1979, U.S. Ct. Appeals (2d cir.) 1981, U.S. Ct. Appeals (3d cir.) 1981. Assoc., Simpson, Thacher & Bartlett, N.Y.C., 1979—. Mem. human resources com. UNICEF, 1983-84. Mem. ABA, N.Y. State Bar Assn., Assn. Bar City N.Y. Democrat. Jewish. Office: Simpson Thacher & Bartlett 1 Battery Park Plaza New York NY 10004

SOLON, MARCIA GOREN, consultant, author, designer; b. Houston, Apr. 9, 1943; d. Marcus and Esther Alice (Pailet) Goren; m. Emanuel Solon, June 9, 1963 (div.); children—Sara Elizabeth, Leah Katherine. Student U. Tex., 1961-63; B.A., La. State U., 1965; postgrad. Bowling Green U., 1965-66, U. Calif.-Berkeley, 1980. Program dir., exec. dir. Creative Arts San Antonio, 1973-74; art tchr. Lower Sch., St. Mary's Hall, San Antonio, 1974-76; head outreach services, dir. edn. and programs San Antonio Mus. Assn., 1976-81; dir. mktg. 1776, Inc., San Antonio, 1982-83; owner Marcia Goren Solon Creative Communications Cons., San Antonio, 1983—; art critic San Antonio Light newspaper. Author: San Antonio Mus. Assn. Look Book, 1980; contbr. articles to newspapers and jours. Vice pres., bd. dirs. Arts Council San Antonio, 1974-76; participant Greater San Antonio C. of C. Leadership San Antonio Class, 1979-80, vice chmn. steering com., 1980-81, steering com. alumni forum, 1980-83. Recipient Addy award San Antonio Advt. Fedn., 1982, 85; bronze award Art Dirs. Club Houston, 1981. Mem. Women in Communications (v.p. 1985, 86, Proliner award 1983, 84, 86), Internat. Assn. Bus. Communicators (Bronze Quill award of merit 1983), Jewish Fedn. Bus. and Profl. Women (chmn. 1982-83). Jewish. Club: B'nai B'rith Girls (internat. pres. 1961-62). Home: 116 Harmon Dr San Antonio TX 78209

SOLTER, MADELINE JONES, accounting firm executive, educator; b. N.Y.C., July 11, 1939; d. Clarence Ormsby and Helen Veronica (Kiss) Jones; m. Anthony Arthur Solter, Aug. 8, 1964 (div. June 1977). B.A., Montclair State Coll., 1961, M.A., 1964, postgrad., 1964-66; postgrad. New Sch. for Social Research, 1970-72, Hayden Planetarium, 1973-74, Am. Mus. Natural History, 1973, Hunter Coll., 1977, various adult schs. Tchr., English, Henry B. Whitehorne Jr. High Sch., Verona, N.J., 1961-62, Bloomfield (N.J.) High Sch., 1962-67; asst. prof. English, Montclair (N.J.) State Coll. 1967-70; office mgr., corp. sec., sec. to bd. dirs. Auton Computing Corp., N.Y.C., 1970-77; placement mgr. Accts. and Auditors Agy., N.Y.C., 1977-80; office mgr. Mendelsohn, Kary, Bell & Natoli, P.C., N.Y.C., 1980-86; dir. computer dept., 1986—; tchr. English, Nutley (N.J.) Adult Sch., part-time 1965, 66, Bloomfield Summer Sch., 1966, 67; adj. asst. prof. English, Coll. of Ins., N.Y.C., part-time 1980-85; ghost writer, researcher various books, 1972-85. Roman Catholic.

SOLTYSIAK, SANDRA KANTNER, automotive company executive; b. Dearborn, Mich., Aug. 19, 1948; d. John Henry and Ileine Lucille (Merz) Kantner; m. Gregory Peter Soltysiak, June 20, 1970; 1 son, John. B.A., Mich. State U., 1971, M.Labor and Indsl. Relations, 1978. Dissertation sec. U. Mich., Ann Arbor, 1970-72, research asst. Survey Research Ctr., 1972-73; placement rep., compensation rep. and labor relations rep. Ford Motor Co., Dearborn, Mich., 1973-76; compensation adminstr., mgr. compensation, dir. compensation, benefits and services Mich. Consol. Gas Co., Detroit, 1976-78; dir. compensation and benefits Mich. Nat. Bank, Lansing, 1979; supr. salaried personnel Oldsmobile div. Gen. Motors Corp., Lansing, 1979-80, adminstrv. coordinator, 1981-85; supt. materiall prodn. control Buick-Oldsmobile-Cadillac group, 1985—; instr. Lansing Community Coll, 1980-81; seminar leader Mich. State U. Bus. Sch., 1980-81. Vol. Capital Area United Way, Lansing, 1981-82, team capt., 1983, chmn. Maj. firms div., bd. dirs., 1985—; chmn. vocations com. St. Mary's Cathedral, Lansing, 1982—; adv. bd. Sch. Labor and Indsl. Relations Mich. State U. Roman Catholic. Office: Buick-Oldsmobile-Cadillac Group 920 Townsend Lansing MI 48921

SOLVANG, PAMELA JEAN, broadcast marketing executive, marketing consultant; b. Bellingham, Wash., Nov. 14, 1956; d. Merlin Nils and Phyllis Ann (Wynne) S. Student Clark Coll., Vancouver, Wash., 1975-77, Seattle U., 1977; B.A. in Communications, U. Portland, 1979. Copywriter Sugden-Freeman Advt., Portland, Oreg., 1979; writer, producer Ryan Advt., Portland, 1979-83; mktg. dir. KGON-KSGO Radio, Portland, 1983-85; corp. broadcast mktg. dir. Ackerley Communications, 1985—; video writer/producer Nat. Salon Edn. Tapes, KMS Shampoos and Research Labs., Bella Vista, Calif., 1985; writer, producer TV spl. Rose City Rock Awards, 1984, 85. Recipient Nat. Telly award Nat. Assn. TV Commls., 1982, 83, 86. Mem. Broadcast Promotion/Mktg. Execs. (outdoor advt. gold medallion awards 1984). Democrat. Methodist. Avocations: traveling; snow skiing; scuba diving. Home: 3205 E 33d St Apt 30 Vancouver WA 98661 Office: KGON/KSGO Radio 15351 SE Johnson Rd Clackamas OR 97015

SOMA, ROSE SMERALDI, broadcaster, writer, women's rights activist, TV-radio producer, reporter; b. Bronx, N.Y., Feb. 17, 1940) d. Albert and Jeanette (DiCostanzo) Smeraldi; attended NYC public schs. until 1955; m. Fraser Soma, Sept. 13, 1967; children—Michael, Carl, Paul, Steven, Nancy, Errol. Producer, interviewer, reporter WALK radio, L.I., N.Y., 1976—, producer weekly feminist radio program, 1976—; lectr., condr. workshops on women's rights; media public relations cons. feminist issues for radio and TV, 1978. Chmn. reprodn./abortion rights task force Suffolk (N.Y.) chpt. NOW, 1975—, chmn. media task force, 1975—; producer/host Women Speak Out and People Speak Out, Brookhaven Cable TV, Port Jefferson Sta., N.Y., 1979—, Women Speak Out, Sta. WYFA, Medford, N.Y., 1979—, Suffolk Cablevision, 1979—, Sta. WBLI-FM, 1980—; media coordinator, personal mgr. entertainment acts, 1981—; bd. dirs. Planned Parenthood of East Suffolk, 1977—; coordinator L.I. chpt. Nat. Coalition to Defend the Bill of Rights, 1978—; coordinator public relations and media for L.I. chpt. Internat. Women's Yr. Meeting for N.Y. State, 1977; exec. dir., co-founder Americans United to Save Legal Abortion, 1977—; founder Women Speak Out Internat., 1978; adv. bd. Women's Health Alliance L.I., 1978; chmn. abortion rights task force N.Y. State orgn. NOW, 1978; coordinator L.I. Coalition for Reproductive Rights; asso. Women's Inst. for Freedom of Press, 1976—. Mem. Am. Women in Radio and TV, Nat. Fedn. Press Women. Author: Women Speak Out About Abortion, 1978; contbr. numerous articles to profl. jours.; author monthly column for NOW newsletter, 1974—; editorial asst. and AdViews mag.; editorial asst. AdViews mag.; video editor, features editor Good Times mag. Home: PO Box AW Miller Place NY 11764 Office: UACC Brookhaven Cable TV Industrial Rd Port Jefferson Station NY 11776 also Sta WBLI 106 FM Long Island NY 11763 also AdViews Mag PO Box 268 Greenville NY 11548

SOMER, CAROL B., marketing executive; b. Bklyn., Mar. 12, 1951; d. Manny and Dorothy (Stone) S. Student, New Eng. Sch. Art and Design, Boston, Boston U., Bklyn. Coll. Editor dental affairs Boston U. Med. Ctr., 1976-82; pub. relations account exec. Fern/Hanaway Inc./Providence, R.I., 1982-85; dir. mktg. and pub. relations DiLeonardo Internat. Inc., Warwick, R.I., 1985—. Contbr. articles to profl. jours. Bd. dirs. Sojourner House Inc., Providence, 1984—; adv. bd. Bright Lights Theatre, Providence, 1986—. N.Y. Regents Scholar, 1967. Mem. Internat. Assn. Bus. Communicators, Soc. Mktg. Profl. Services, R.I. Advt. Club. Jewish. Home: 39 Thomas Olney Common Providence RI 02904 Office: DiLeonardo Internat Inc 2346 Post Rd Warwick RI 02886

SOMERICK, NANCY MARIE, communication educator, consultant; b. Barberton, Ohio, Sept. 16, 1945; d. Anthony Lawrence and Margaret Marie (Patrick) Somerick. B.S. cum laude, Ohio U., 1967, Ph.D., 1974; M.A., Kent State U., 1969. Communication dir. Kent State U. Stark Campus, Canton, Ohio, 1973-74; asst. prof. Cleve. State U., 1974-77; officer, pub. relations mgr. BancOhio/Akron Nat. Bank, Akron, 1977-78; asst. prof. U. Akron, 1978-83, assoc. prof. communication, 1983—; cons. Wadsworth Pub. Co., Belmont, Calif., 1981, 84, West Pub. Co., Mpls., 1982. Author Case Studies in Public Relations: the Profession and the Practice, 1983; contbr. articles and book revs. to profl. jours.; mem. editorial bd. Coll. Press Rev., 1980. Pub. relations cons. to community orgns., Summit County, Ohio, 1978-84; founder, adviser Pub. Relations Student Soc. Am., U. Akron, 1978-84; mem. County Bd. of Visitors, Summit County, 1980-83; judge contest for high sch. students Ohio Press Women's Assn., 1981. Recipient Merit award for teaching Cleve. State U. Dept. Communication, 1976; adviser of yearbook with 1st place rating Am. Scholastic Press Assn., 1983. Mem. Pub. Relations Soc. Am., Internat. Assn. Bus. Communicators, Internat. Communication Assn., Women in Communications, Assn. Edn. in Journalism, Akron Press Club, Akron Advt. Club, Sigma Delta Chi. Democrat. Roman Catholic. Home: 908 E Robinson Ave Barberton OH 44203 Office: Univ Akron Dept Communication Akron OH 44325

SOMERS, CARIN ALMA, librarian; b. Frankfurt, W.Ger., Mar. 18, 1934; d. Josef and Helen Josephine (Badham) Stein; B.A., Newton (Mass.) Coll. Sacred Heart, 1955; M.A., Dalhousie U., Halifax, N.S., Can., 1956; B.L.S., U. Toronto (Ont., Can.), 1961; m. Frank George Somers, Aug. 23, 1958. Registrar, lectr. French St. Mary's U., Halifax, 1956-60; with Halifax City Regional Library, 1958-64; with Halifax County Regional Library, 1964-73; with N.S. Provincial Library, Halifax, 1973—, dir. libraries, 1974—; lectr. Sch. Library Sci. Dalhousie U. Recipient Gov. Gen. medal, 1953, Queens Silver Jubilee medal, 1977. Mem. Can. Library Assn. (2d v.p. 1974-75), Atlantic Provinces Library Assn. (pres. 1969-70), N.S. Library Assn., Can. Nature Fedn., N.S. Bird Soc. Roman Catholic. Club: Royal N.S. Yacht Squadron. Contbr. articles in field. Home: Box 772 Armdale PO Halifax NS B3L 4K5 Canada Office: 6955 Bayers Rd Halifax NS B3L 4S4 Canada

SOMERSTEIN, MARIANNA, caterer; b. Hungary, Mar. 31, 1936; came to U.S., 1951; d. Steven and Lilly (Bohm) Balint; m. Howard Weitzner, June 26, 1955 (div. 1978); children—Kenneth Bruce, Cherie Ann; m. Stuart Somerstein, Jan. 7, 1979. Student schs., Hungary, Germany. Vice pres. Somerstein Caterers, Lawrence, N.Y., 1975—; caterer Water Club, N.Y.C., 1983—; owner Water's Edge Restaurant, Long Island City, N.Y. Officer Nat. Council Jewish Women, 1968-72, Sisterhood of Temple Israel, 1966-75, Hewlett Hadasseh, United Jewish Appeal, 1982-85. Republican. Jewish. Avocation: travel. Office: Somerstein Caterers 140 Central Ave Lawrence NY 11559

SOMERVILLE, EARNESTINE, business executive; b. Sawyerville, Ala., Oct. 18, 1955; d. Earnest Lee and Ella Ruth (Mims) S.; B.B.A. in Bus., Ohio U., 1978, B.S., 1978. Sales assoc. May Co., Cleveland, 1977-78, sales mgr., 1978-81, asst. mgr., 1981-84; reservations sales rep. United Airlines, 1984-85;

inventory mgmt. coordinator, 1985—; student life intern Ohio Univ., Athens, 1977-78. Mem. Ohio U. Alumni Assn., John Adams High Sch. Alumni Assn., Delta Sigma Theta (chpt. pres. 1977-78), Phi Gamma Nu. Democrat. Baptist. Lodge: Order Eastern Star (rec. sec. 1982). Home: 3929 E 120th St Cleveland OH 44105

SOMMER, JUDITH ANN, association executive; b. Rock Island, Ill., May 6, 1938; d. Ward Donald and Arline Marie (Haigh) Paley; m. Melvin Louis Sommer, July 13, 1957; children—Donald L., Cheryl L. Sommer Baudo. Student Canisius Coll., 1976, Erie Community coll., 1977-79, Millard Fillmore Coll., 1980-82. Program assoc. Amherst High Sch., N.Y., 1961-69; asst. to pres. YMCA Greater Buffalo, 1969-72, dir. personnel, 1972-84, v.p. human resources, 1984—; exec. dir. Ken-ton YMCA, Buffalo, 1982—; chmn. YMCA Life Through the Arts, Chautauqua, N.Y., 1977. Mem. Nat. Assn. Female Execs., Nat. Soc. Fundraising Execs., Assn. Profl. Dirs. (chpt. v.p. and sec. Leadership award 1984, fellow 1977), Ken-Ton C. of C., Kenmore Bus. and Profl. Women, Eta Sigma Sigma (Phi Gamma chpt.). Republican. Lutheran. Lodge: Zonta (pres. club 1986-87). Avocations: crafts; interior decorating; boating; water skiing; swimming. Home: 3100 East River Rd Grand Island NY 14072 Office: YMCA Greater Buffalo 2564 Delaware Ave Buffalo NY 14216 also 535 Belmont Ave Kenmore NY 14216

SOMMERFIELD, ELISSA BERWALD, English language educator; b. Dallas; d. Elihu Edward and Ann Shirley (Meltz) Berwald; m. Frank Edgar Sommerfield, Feb. 23, 1961; children—Frank Edgar, John. B.A. summa cum laude, Tex. U.; M.A., So. Meth. U. Instr. English, So. Meth. U., Dallas, 1956-61, Dallas Community Coll., 1968-73; tutor in English, 1961—; freelance writer, 1961—; copywriter Bloom's Advt., 1961-64; dir. Verbal and Math. Skills Seminar, SAT preparation courses, 1975—; dir. Study Skills Seminar, 1982—. Co-author: PSAT-SAT Multimedia Guide and Study Skills Guide: A Survivor's Manual. Mem. Assn. Coll. Counselors Am., Nat. Conf. Coll. English Tchrs., Phi Beta Kappa. Jewish. Home: 9636 Hollow Way Dallas TX 75220

SOMMERS, ESTELLE JOAN, retail executive; b. Balt.; d. David Isaac and Mary Agnes (Curland) Goldstein; grad. high sch.; m. Ben Sommers, Dec. 2, 1962 (dec. 1985); children—Gayle Joan, Cathy Harriet, Debbie Jane. Stylist, owner Loshins, Cin., 1948-62; mgr., owner Capezio Fashion Shop., N.Y.C., 1964-79; stylist, owner Estar Ltd., N.Y.C., 1969-79; head adminstr., joint owner Capezio Dance-Theatre Shops, N.Y.C., Boston, Chgo., Hollywood, Calif., 1970—. U.S. chmn. Dance Library of Israel, 1979—; bd. dirs. Dance Notation Bd., 1980—; mem. Am.-Israel Cultural Found., 1979-82, The Ctr. for Dance Medicine, 1983—; co-chmn. nat. adv. com. Internat Ballet Competition U.S.A., 1979-86; acting pres. Internat. Dance Alliance. Bd. dirs. New Dance Studios, 1985—, The Yard, 1986—; mem. artistic adv. com. Internat. Conf. Jews and Judaism in Dance, 1986. Office: 755 7th Ave New York NY 10019

SOMMERS, MARILYN PETERSON, law enforcement information network director; b. Phila., Nov. 12, 1946; d. William Edmund and Grace Whipple Birchall; m. Mark A. Peterson, Aug. 26, 1967 (div. 1979); 1 son, Jon Fredrik; m. Paul D. Sommers, Jr., Aug. 23, 1985. Student, Temple U., 1964-67. Freelance writer, pub. relations cons. various orgns., Phila., 1976-79; research cons. Pa. Ho. of Reps., Harrisburg, 1979-80; asst. for communications Pa. Crime Commn., St. Davids, 1980-81; mgr. Middle Atlantic-Great Lakes Organized Crime Law Enforcement Network, Malvern, Pa., 1981—. Chief co-author: 1980 Report; author and editor: 1981 Report; editor: Health Care Fraud, 1982; contbr. numerous articles to newspapers, mags. Pres., Mercer County LWV, Trenton, N.J., 1975-76, Chestnut Hill Community Assn., Phila., 1980-82; mem. Pres.'s Council, Spring Garden Coll., Phila., 1981. Mem. Internat. Assn. Law Enforcement Intelligence Analysts (dir., editor Intelscope), Police Mgmt. Assn., Nat. Assn. Female Execs. Home: 178 Benezet St Philadelphia PA 19118 Office: Middle Atlantic-Great Lakes Organized Crime Law Enforcement Network 40 Lloyd Ave Malvern PA 19355

SONCHIK, SUSAN MARIE, analytical chemist; b. Maple Heights, Ohio, Mar. 10, 1954; d. Stephen Robert and Gloria Ann (Hach) S. B.S. in Chemistry magna cum laude, John Carroll U., 1975; M.S. in Analytical Chemistry, Case Western Res. U., 1978, Ph.D. in Phys. Chemistry, 1980. Asst. chemist Horizons Research Inc., Beachwood, Ohio, 1974-75; chemist specialist Standard Oil of Ohio, Warrensville Heights, Ohio, 1975-79; organic chemistry br. mgr. Versar, Inc., Springfield, Va., 1980-83; mgr. gas chromatography program IBM Instruments Inc., Danbury, Conn., 1983—, radiation safety officer, 1985—; expert witness, cons. Martin, Craig, Chester & Sonnenschein, Chgo., 1981-83; mem. exec. com. Am. Standard for Testing and Materials E-19, Phila., 1985-87; speaker in field. Author: African Walking Safari, 1985; also articles. Editorial adv. bd. Jour. Chromatographic Sci., 1977—. Troop leader Lake Erie council Girl Scouts Am., 1972-80, Southeastern Conn. council, 1983-86; leader Explorer Post, Greater Cleve. council Boy Scouts Am., 1977-78; managerial adviser Jr. Achievement, Warrensville Heights, 1977-78; sci. fair judge Electrochem. Soc., 1977, 80, 81; asst. leader Internat. Folk Dancers, Newtown, Conn., 1985—; active Newtown Hikers Club. Recipient Overall Best Paper award Eastern Analytical Symposium, 1984, First Gas Chromatograph award IBM Instruments Inc., 1985. Mem. Am. Chem. Soc., ASTM (E-19 exec. com. 1985-87, subcom. chmn. 1986—), Nat. Assn. Female Execs., Iota Sigma Pi (pres. Northeast Ohio, 1978-79). Roman Catholic. Club: Players Racquetball (Danbury). Avocations: camping; racquetball; dancing; travel; mountain climbing. Home: 43 Bear Mountain Rd Danbury CT 06811 Office: IBM Instruments Inc Orchard Park Kenosia Rd Danbury CT 06810

SONES, KATHY DENISE, lawyer; b. Jackson, Miss., Mar. 15, 1956; d. Bob D. and Betty Jean (Mealey) Sones. A.A. summa cum laude, Hinds Jr. Coll., 1976; B.S. cum laude, Miss. State U., 1978; J.D., U. Miss., 1981. Bar: Miss. 1981, La. 1982. Gen. atty. U.S. Army Corps Engrs., Vicksburg, Miss., 1982-83, atty. advisor, 1983—. Active United Way Allocations com., Warren County, Miss., 1984—; chmn. Fed. Women's Program, Vicksburg, 1984—. Recipient Young Career Woman award Bus. and Profl. Women, Dist. IV, Miss., 1983. Mem. ABA (fed. practice com. 1982—, lawyers and arts com. 1982—), Miss. State Bar Assn., La. State Bar Assn., Miss. Trial Lawyers Assn., Am. Trial Lawyers Assn. Baptist. Home: PO Box 1758 Vicksburg MS 39180 Office: US Army Corps Engrs PO Box 60 Vicksburg MS 39180

SONGER, FRANCES VIRGINIA, counseling hypnotherapist; b. Atlanta, Feb. 13, 1957; d. Francis Harold and Lois Irene (Stringer) S.; m. Christopher Lee Clinkenbeard, Sept. 1, 1979 (div. 1980). B.A. in Exptl. Psychology magna cum laude, Ga. State U., 1982. Mgr., stores asst. Pepperidge Farm, Atlanta, 1976-82; mgr. S&A Corp., Atlanta, 1982-83; food and beverage asst. mgr., dir. meetings and banquets dir., sales dir. Guest Quarters, Atlanta, 1983—; hypnotherapist Hypnosis Motivation Inst., Atlanta, 1984—; handwriting analyst, Atlanta, 1985—. Mem. Nat. Assn. Female Execs., Am. Hypnosis Assn. (dir. chpt. steering com. 1985—), Ga. Graphological Soc., Hypnosis Union, Blue Keys, Psi Chi, Phi Kappa Phi. Republican. Avocations: writing; painting; racquetball; gardening. Home: 2508 Summerlake Dr Dunwoody GA 30338 Office: Hypnosis Motivation Inst 3700 Holcomb Bridge Rd Atlanta GA 30092

SONIES, BARBARA CAROL, speech/lang. pathologist; b. Gloversville, N.Y., Aug. 25, 1939; d. George and Eleanor S. (Kall) Myzal; B.S. with distinction, U. Minn., 1961; M.A., Stanford U., 1963; Ph.D., U. Md., 1981; m. Harvey J. Kupferberg, Jan. 5, 1975; 1 son, Mitchel H. Sonies. Speech therapist Alhambra (Calif.) Schs., 1963-65; speech pathologist U. Minn. Hosps., Mpls., 1965-67; coordinator speech diagnostic clinic Mpls. Public Schs., 1967-68; supr. speech pathology U. Minn. Health Scis. Center, Mpls., 1968-72; instr. communication disorders U. Minn., 1969-72; coordinator speech program Robbinsdale (Minn.) Public Schs., summer 1970; project mgr. sch. programs Am. Speech, Lang. and Hearing Assn., 1972-73; instr., clinic supr. dept. hearing and speech sci. U. Md., College Park, 1974-77; chief Speech-Lang. Pathology Clin. Center, NIH, Bethesda, Md., 1977—; instr. continuing edn. U. Va., Falls Church, 1975-82; research asso. prof. U. Md., College Park, 1981—; cons. Montgomery County Health Dept., Rockville, Md., 1974-79; lectr. in field. Hunt scholar, 1957-61; Rehab. Services Adminstrn. grantee, 1961-63. Mem. Am. Speech-Lang.-Hearing Assn. (chmn. augmentative communic com. 1985—, 1st place award for sci. and tech. merit 1985, Joseph H. Holmes award excellence in ultrasound research 1985), Md. Speech-Lang.-Hearing Assn. (sec. 1977-79, editor jour. 1981-83), Internat. Neuropsychol. Soc., Mortar Bd., Phi Beta Kappa, Order of Ski-U-Mah. Contbr. articles to profl. jours. Home: 8826 Tuckerman Ln Potomac MD 20854 Office: NIH Clin Center Speech Pathology Rm 5D37 Bethesda MD 20205

SONJU, SONIA TESMER, construction company executive, real estate developer; b. Milw., Jan. 31, 1939; d. Genevie Marie (Midtbo) Tesmer; m. Theodore Randolf Sonju, Oct. 9, 1959 (div. 1969); 1 child, Tonia Dedrikke; m. William Trow Bridge Dawson, July 7, 1978. B.S. in Elec. Engring., U. Wis., 1962; M.A. in Pub. Adminstrn., U. Calif.-Fullerton, 1978. Project planner Lampman & Assocs., Pomona, Calif., 1972-74; dir. planning City of Rosemead, Calif., 1974-76; pres. Mcpl. Services, Cypress, Calif., 1976-78; pres. AF COM, Seal Beach, Calif., 1978—, Sonju Constrn., Seal Beach, 1978—; lectr. in field. Mem. manpower com. County of Orange, Calif., 1978-81; chmn. Cypress Planning Commn., 1969-78; councilwoman, mayor pro tem, Cypress, 1974-78; mem. Calif. Democratic Central Com., 1976. Mem. Am. Planning Assn., NOW, So. Calif. Planning Congress. Lutheran. Avocations: dancing; painting; skiing; jogging. Office: 200 Marina Dr Suite 1 Seal Beach CA 90740

SONNE, FRANCES GRAVISH, lawyer; b. Pottsville, Pa., Aug. 26, 1951; d. Joseph Leonard and Isabel (Bulharowski) Gravish; m. Eric Steven Sonne, Oct. 20, 1973. B.A. in Social Welfare with distinction, B.A. in Psychology with distinction, Pa. State U., 1973; J.D., Temple U., 1981. Bar: Pa. 1981, U.S. Dist. Ct. (ea. dist.) Pa. 1982. Social worker Lehigh Valley Child Care, Allentown, Pa., Area Agy. on Aging, Allentown, 1974-76; jud. clk. Lehigh County, Pa., Allentown, 1981-82; sole practice, Allentown, 1982-85; ptnr. Cretsinger & Sonne, 1985—. Bd. dirs. Children's Rights of Pa., 1983—, Animals in Distress, Catasauqua, Pa., 1982-83; mem. Catasauqua Zoning Bd., 1985—. Mem. ABA, Pa. Bar Assn., Lehigh County Bar Assn., Assn. Trial Lawyers Am., Women Lawyers Lehigh Valley, Psi Chi. Home: 821 Poplar St Catasauqua PA 18032 Office: 452 Linden St Allentown PA 18102

SONNENBERG, GALE PHYLLIS, lawyer; b. Hollywood, Calif., Aug. 14, 1958; d. Bernard William and Jessica Florance (Abrahams) Sonnenberg. A.B. magna cum laude, U. So. Calif., 1979; J.D., UCLA, 1982; postgrad. in law Oxford U. (Eng.), 1980. Bar: Calif. 1982, U.S. Dist. Ct. (cen. dist.) Calif.) 1982, U.S. Dist. Ct. (so. dist.) Calif. 1982, U.S. Dist. Ct. (ea. dist.) Calif. 1982, U.S. Dist. Ct. (no. dist.) Calif. 1982, U.S. Ct. Appeals (9th cir.) 1982. Law clk. Calif. Ct. Appeals, San Diego, 1981; assoc. McLaughlin & Irvin, Los Angeles, 1981—. Mem. staff ABA Internat. Law Jour., 1981-82. Recipient U. So. Calif. Outstanding Sr. Recognition award 1979. Mem. Calif. Women Lawyers Assn., Women Lawyers Assn. of Los Angeles, Los Angeles County Bar Assn., Bar Assn. Barristers Club, Bar Assn. San Francisco, ABA, U. So. Calif. Gen. Alumni Assn., Phi Alpha Delta (sec. chpt. 1981-82, sect. rep. 1979-80), Phi Beta Kappa, Phi Kappa Phi, Pi Sigma Alpha, Phi Alpha Theta, Alpha Lambda Delta. Home: 870 Hilgard Ave #303 Los Angeles CA 90024 Office: McLaughlin and Irvin 800 W 6th St 3d Floor Los Angeles CA 90017

SONNENFELD, GRACIELA DIANA, bank manager; b. Buenos Aires, Argentina, Oct. 31, 1949; came to U.S., 1978; d. Egon Manfredo and Beatriz (Kamil) Horn; B.S., St. Catherine's Inst., 1967, London Cultural Inst., 1973; m. Peter Sonnenfeld, Oct. 28, 1978. Asst. to pres. OKS KNOS Y CIA, S.A., Buenos Aires, 1970-75; asst. to pres. Aurora S.A., Buenos Aires, 1975-78; asst. v.p. Chgo. br. Banco de la Nacion Argentina, 1979—. Pres., Gradia S.R.L., Chgo. and Buenos Aires; partner Regente S.R.L. Argentina. Mem. Women in Internat. Trade, Soc. Personnel Adminstrs. Jewish. Club: Italian Circle Buenos Aires. Home: 333 E Ontario St Apt 2301B Chicago IL 60611 Office: 135 S LaSalle Room 2240 Chicago IL 60603

SONNENFELD, JANET MARLOFF, lawyer; b. Long Branch, N.J., Feb. 9, 1948; d. Raymond James and Muriel (Goodkin) Marloff; B.A., George Washington U., 1970; J.D. cum laude, Howard U., 1973; m. Marc J. Sonnenfeld, Apr. 27, 1975. Bar: Pa. 1973, U.S. Dist. Ct. (ea. dist.) Pa. 1974, U.S. Ct. Appeals (3d cir.), 1975, U.S. Bankruptcy Ct. (ea. dist.) Pa. 1979, U.S. Supreme Ct., 1981. Assoc. firm Drinker Biddle & Reath, Phila., 1973-76; assoc. counsel consumer banking Fidelity Bank, Phila., 1976-77; owner firm, sole practice law specializing in bankruptcy, Phila., 1977—; instr. Inst. Paralegal Tng., Phila., nat. seminars, 1983—; panelist Pa. Bar Inst. Author publs. in field. Committeewoman, Democratic Com., 1974-76, 78-82, mem. policy com., 1978—. Mem. Pa. Bar Assn. (com. on alcohol and drug abuse 1979—). Home: Wanamaker House 2020 Walnut St Philadelphia PA 19103 Office: 2000 Two Mellon Bank Ctr Philadelphia PA 19102

SONTAG, SUSAN, author, film director; b. N.Y.C., Jan. 16, 1933; m. Philip Rieff, 1950 (div. 1958); 1 son, David. Student U. Calif.-Berkeley, 1948-49; B.A., U. Chgo., 1951; M.A. in English, Harvard U., 1954, M.A. in Philosophy, 1955; postgrad. St. Anne's Coll., Oxford U., 1957. Instr. English, U. Conn., Storrs, 1953-54; teaching fellow in philosophy Harvard U., Cambridge, 1955-57; editor Commentary mag., N.Y.C., 1959; lectr. in philosophy CCNY and Sarah Lawrence Coll., Bronxville, N.Y., 1959-60; instr. dept. religon Columbia U., N.Y.C., 1960-64; writer-in-residence Rutgers U., New Brunswick, 1964-65. Author: (novels) The Benefactor, 1963, Death Kit, 1967; (stories) I, etcetera, 1978; (essays) Against Interpretation, 1966; Trip to Hanoi, 1968, Styles of Radical Will, 1969, On Photography, 1977, Illness as Metaphor, 1978, Under the Sign of Saturn, 1980; (anthology) A Susan Sontag Reader, 1982; (film scripts) Duet for Cannibals, 1970; Brother Carl, 1974; editor, author introduction: Antonin Artaud: Selected Writings, 1976, A Barthes Reader, 1982; dir. film Duet for Cannibals, 1969, Brother Carl, 1971, Promised Lands, 1974, Unguided Tour, 1983. Guggenheim fellow, 1966-75; Rockefeller Found. fellow, 1965, 74; recipient Ingram Merrill Found. award in lit. in field of Am. Letters, 1976; Creative Arts award Brandeis U., 1976; Arts and Letters award Am. Acad. Arts and Letters, 1976; prize Nat. Book Critics Circle, 1978. Mem. Am. Inst. Arts and Letters. Address: care Farrar Straus & Giroux Inc 19 Union Sq W New York NY 10003

SOO, DORIS, mathematics educator; b. N.Y.C., May 22, 1953; d. Frank Edward and Ngook Ho (Tow) S.; B.A. in Math., CCNY, 1977; M.S. in Stats., Baruch Coll., 1986. Adj. lectr. Hunter Coll., N.Y.C., 1978-79, grant adminstr. to coordinator of field work Research Found., 1980-81, adminstrv. asst. to dean Sch. Social Work, 1981-82; tchr. math. William Alexander Jr. High Sch., Bklyn., 1979; adj. lectr. N.Y. City Tech. Coll., 1979-80; researcher women's bur. U.S. Dept. Labor. NSF grantee, 1979-80. Mem. Nat. Assn. Remedial Devel. Studies in Post Secondary Edn., Assn. Tchrs. Math. N.Y.C., Coalition Asian Am. Profl. Women, Asian Women United, Phi Theta Kappa.

SOPER, STACEY KIM, writer, editor; b. Corsicana, Tex., Oct. 14, 1955; d. Leigh Adelbert and Barbara Beryl (Winans) S. B.J., U. Tex., 1978; postgrad. So. Meth. U., 1983-86. Researcher Ctr. for Communication Research, Austin, Tex., 1976; mem. coll. bd. staff Mademoiselle mag., Austin, 1976-78; mem. promotion staff sta. KUT-FM, Austin, 1977; copywriter Taylor Pub. Co., Dallas, 1978-81; research asst. Tex. Oil & Gas Corp., Dallas, 1981-82; edn. writer Show Biz Pizza Place, Irving, Tex., 1982; writer, editor, analyst Future Computing, Inc., Richardson, Tex., 1983-84. Author, editor: Official Dallas Cowboys Bluebook, 1980. Mem. publicity staff Young Republicans, Austin, Tex., 1975-76; mem. Pres. Ford Com., Rep. Nat. Conv., Kansas City, Mo., 1976; host finalist So. Gov.'s Conf., San Antonio, 1977. Recipient award Printing Industry Am., 1980. DAR scholar, 1976; Journalism Faculty scholar U. Tex.-Austin, 1976; Alcoa Corp. pub. relations scholar, Austin, 1977; Cabot Journalism scholar U. Tex., Austin, 1977; 3 MLA scholarships So. Meth. U. Mem. Women in Communication, Pub. Relations Soc. Am., P.E.O. (hospitality com. 1980-84, ednl. com. 1985-86), Hist. Preservation League (feature writer, pub. relations coordinator), Alpha Xi Delta (v.p. alumnae 1983-84). Republican. Methodist. Home: 7430 W Northwest Hwy Apt 2 Dallas TX 75225 Office: Dallas Mus Art 1717 N Harwood Dallas TX 75201

SOR, YVONNE SANDA, law educator; b. Bucharest, Rumania, May 21, 1953; d. Bernard and Mina (Lazar) Sor; B.A. in French, Mundelein Coll., 1970, B.S. in Physics, 1970; M.S. in Biomed. Engring., Northwestern U., 1972; J.D., DePaul U., 1983. Registered profl. engr., Ill. Lectr. physics Mundelein Coll., Chgo., 1971-73; tech. researcher Rust-Oleum Corp., Evanston, Ill., 1973-76, group leader, 1976-77, mgr. tech. info. systems, 1977-83; instr. law DePaul U. Coll. Law, Chgo., 1983—; computer cons. various law firms, Chgo., 1982—. Author: Effect of Mercury and Lead on the Neurological Development of Newborn Children, 1975; contbr. articles to profl. jours. Ill. Bar Found. research fellow, 1982. Mem. Soc. Law and Medicine, Decalogue Soc. Lawyers, ABA, Chgo. Bar Assn., Am. Chem. Soc. Jewish. Office: DePaul Univ Coll of Law 25 E Jackson St Chicago IL 60604

SORBER, LINDA ELLEN, university administrator, lawyer; b. Wurzburg, W.Ger., July 4, 1947; came to U.S., 1948; d. John Alfred and Gaie Marie (Stone) Babcock; m. Charles Arthur Sorber, Feb. 20, 1972; children—Kimberly Ann, Kingsley Charles. A.B., Randolph-Macon Woman's Coll., 1969; J.D., U. Tex.-Austin, 1971. Bar: Md. 1973, Tex. 1977. Assoc., Semmes, Bowen & Semmes, Balt., 1973-74; assoc. Rosenstock, Burgee, Bower & Phillips, Frederick, Md., 1974-75; asst. prof. law U. Tex.-San Antonio, 1975-83; asst. dir. devel. U. Tex.-Austin, 1983—. Reader Rec. for Blind, Austin, 1982-84; trustee Westlake Meth. Ch., Austin, 1982-84; treas. T-Squares, Austin, 1982-83; solicitor United Way, Austin, 1983. Mem. ABA, Tex. Bar Assn., Am. Bus. Law Assn., Nat. Soc. Fund Raising Execs. (v.p. Austin chpt. 1983-86), Kappa Beta Pi. Clubs: Lost Creek Country, Capital, Univ. Ladies (Austin). Home: 2303 Doral Dr Austin TX 78746 Office: Devel Office U Tex PO Box 7458 Austin TX 78713

SOREL, CLAUDETTE, pianist; b. Paris; d. Michel Maximilian and Elizabeth S.; came to U.S., 1940, naturalized, 1947. B.S., Juilliard Sch. Music, 1947; student of Sigismund Stojowski, Sari Biro, Olga Samaroff Stokowski, Mieczyslaw Horszowski, Rudolf Serkin, ensemble with Felix Salmond, musicology with Dr. Robert Tangeman, music history with Marian Bauer; spl. scholar Juilliard Grad. Sch. Music, 1943; grad. Curtis Inst. Music, 1953; B.S. cum laude, Columbia U., 1954. Debut at Town Hall, N.Y.C., 1943, since appeared in leading cities U.S.; performed with N.Y. Philharmonic, N.Y. Little Symphony, Boston Symphony Orch., R.I., Reading symphony orchs., Little Orchestral Soc., NBC, Phila., New Orleans and Cin., Am. Youth Orch.; appeared at Aspen, Berkshire, Chautauqua festivals; European concert tours, 1956, 57, 58, to Eng., Sweden, Holland, Germany, Switzerland, France; appeared on various radio and TV programs; made recs. for R.C.A. Victor Rec. Co., Monitor Records, Musical Heritage; music faculty, vis. prof. Kans. U., 1961-62; asso. prof. music Ohio State U., 1962-64; prof. music, head piano dept. State U. N.Y., Fredonia, 1964—, Distinguished Univ. prof., 1969—; mem. internat. jury Van Cliburn Internat. Piano Competition, Tex., 1966, Que. and Ont. Music Festivals, 1967, 75, 81; solo appearances with 200 orchs. U.S., Europe. Author: Compendium of Piano Technique, 1970; Mind Your Musical Manners-Off and On Stage, 1972, 2d edit., 1975; The 24 Magic Keys, 3 vols., 1974; The Three Nocturnes of Rachmaninoff, 1974, 2d edit., 1975; Fifteen Smorgasbord Studies for The Piano, 1975, Arensky-Etudes, 1976. Spl. editor Music Insider, 1981—. Linguist, painter of oil portraits. Contbr. articles to profl. mags.; compiler: The Modern Music of Today, 1947; Serge Prokofieff--His Life and Works, 1947; The Ornamentations in Mozart's Music, 1948. Fulbright scholar, 1951; Ford Found. Concert grantee, 1962; recipient Harry Rosenberg Meml., Frank Damrosch prizes, 1947; winner Phila. Orch. Youth Auditions, 1950, to appear with orch. under direction Eugene Ormandy; Nat. Fedn. Music Clubs Young Artist award, 1951; citation for service to Am. music Nat. Fedn. Music Clubs, 1966; named Outstanding Young Woman in U.S.A., 1965; citation Nat. Assn. Composers and Condrs., 1967, Mu Phi Epsilon, 1968, 80. Bd. dirs. Olga Samaroff Found., jr. com. aux. bd. N.Y. Philharmonic Symphony Orch., N.Y. State Nat. Fedn. Music Clubs; mem. adv. bd. Univ. Library Soc.; chmn. music panel Presdl. Scholars in the Arts, program of Ednl. Testing Service, 1979-84; mem. bus. adv. com. U.S. Senate, 1980—. Mem. Nat. Music Council (dir. 1973—), Music Critics Assn. Pi Kappa Lambda, Mu Phi Epsilon (dir. Meml. Found., nat. chmn. Sterling Staff Concert Series, citation 1968). Home: 333 West End Ave New York NY 10023

SORENSEN, JACKI F., choreographer, dancing company executive; b. Oakland, Calif., Dec. 10, 1943; d. Roy Mills and Juanita Riley; m. Neil Sorensen, Jan. 4, 1965. B.A., U. Calif.-Berkeley, 1964; postgrad. Calif. State U.-Sacramento, Seton Hall U., Tchr. pub. schs., 1964-71; operator of dancing classes, 1964-71; chmn bd., choreographer Aerobic Dancing, Inc., Northridge, Calif., 1971—. Author: Aerobic Dancing, 1979; Jacki Sorensen's Aerobic Lifestyle Book, 1983. Editor-in-chief Aerobic Dancing Mini Mag. Clinician President's Council on Physical Fitness and Sports, 1972, cons. 1985—; adv. bd. Women's Sports Found. 1978; bd. trustees Special Olympics 1981; mem. Committee of 200; bd. dirs. Special Olympics 1983. Recipient Texas Honor award Tex. Gov's. Commn. on Physical Fitness 1971, Diamond Heart Pin Am. Heart Assn. 1978, Individual Honor award Am. Assn. Fitness Dirs. in Bus. and Ind. 1980, Spl. Olympics award 1981, Nat. Honor award for Contribution to Physical Fitness The President's Council on Physical Fitness and Sports 1982, Evelyn A. Dolan Advocacy Award The N.J. Commn. on Recreation for the Handicapped 1982. Club: Crest (Malibu, Calif.). Office: 18907 Nordhoff Northridge CA 91328

SORENSEN, JOY O'NEAL, realty agent, consultant; b. Perkinston, Miss., May 9, 1933; d. Eugene Byron and Melissa Louvenia (Bond) O'Neal; student public schs.; m. Charles Edward Sorensen, Oct. 14, 1954; children—James Andres, Cheryl Ann. Legal sec., 1951-54, 56-65; with Brenner Cine Sound, and predecessor, Washington, 1966-83, asst. v.p., 1974, exec. bus. mgr., 1974-83; cons. Ritz Audio-Visual & Cine div. Ritz Camera Center, Inc., Beltsville, Md., 1981—; agt. Llewellyn Realtors, Silver Spring, Md., 1983—; lectr. in field. Sec., Montgomery County Women's Fair, 1980, co-coordinator, 1985-86, mem. long-range planning com., 1986-87. Mem. Bethesda/Chevy Chase Bus. and Profl. Women's Club, Profl. Motion Picture Equipment Assn. Democrat. Club: Soroptimist (v.p. internat. 1980-81, dir. 1982-83). Office: 11710 Baltimore Ave Beltsville MD 20705

SORENSEN, SHERRY LYNN HAGSTETTE, nurse; b. New Orleans, Dec. 14, 1953; d. Bernard Herman and Frances (Frelich) Hagstette; m. Lawrence Lamar Sorensen, Aug. 9, 1975. Registered nurse diploma, Charity Hosp. Sch. Nursing, New Orleans, 1976; B.S. in Nursing, Loyola U., New Orleans, 1984. R.N., La. Staff nurse Hotel Dieu Hosp., New Orleans, 1976-80, head nurse, 1980-84; bone marrow transplant coordinator La. State U. Med. Ctr., New Orleans, 1984—. Mem. Am. Nurses Assn., La. State Nurses Assn., Nat. League for Nursing, New Orleans Oncology Nurse Assn., Oncology Nurses Soc., Alpha Sigma Lambda (charter), Alpha Xi Delta Alumni. Republican. Roman Catholic. Avocations: camping; boating. Office: Medical-Oncology Dept La State U Med Center 1542 Tulane Ave New Orleans LA 70112

SORENSON, MARY LOUISE, interior design firm executive; b. Wadena, Minn., Mar. 28, 1950; d. Bernard F. and Jeneva S. (Bjondal) Neuerburg; m. Mark E. Sorenson, Dec. 5, 1981; children—Shawn, Chad, Naomi, Seth, Sara. Student, U. Minn., 1974-75; cert. Nat. Assn. Credit Mgmt., 1971. Credit mgr. Homecrest Co., Wadena, 1971-73, Northland Aluminum, Mpls., 1973-75, Econs. Lab., St. Paul, 1975-77; owner, mgr. dance hall, 1977-78; salesperson Sleep Country, Dallas, 1978-80; designer Jo Mar Furniture, Duncanville, Tex., 1980-82; pres. Cedar Hill Design Ctr., Inc., Tex., 1983—; pres. Mpls.-St. Paul Credit Women's Group, 1978-79. Bd. dirs. I Am Victorious Too, Dallas, 1984—. Named Woman of Yr., Mpls.-St. Paul chpt. Nat. Assn. Credit Mgmt., 1979. Mem. Cedar Hill C. of C. (vice chmn. mchts. com.), Nat. Asssn. Builders, Cedar Hill Hist. Assn. Republican. Avocations: Bible study. Office: Cedar Hill Design Ctr Inc 115 Broad St Cedar Hill TX 75104

SORGENFRIE, BARBARA BASTIAN, hospital official; b. Hudson, Mich., May 20, 1948; d. Forrest Wilson and Willoween Elizabeth (Warner) Bastian; A.S. in Bus., Parkland Coll., 1983, Assoc. in Data Processing, 1984; B.A., Eastern Ill., U., 1982. Computer operator Bohn Aluminum & Brass Co., Adrian, Mich., 1968-69, programmer, analyst, 1969-71; programmer, analyst Second Nat. Bank, Danville, Ill., 1971-72; exec. sec., treas. Danville Sanitary Dist., 1972-77; personnel mgr. Universal Bleacher Co., Champaign, Ill., 1977-83; benefit coordinator Carle Found. Hosp., Urbana, Ill., 1983—. Mem. Am. Soc. Personnel Adminstrn., Nat. Assn. Female Execs., Nat. Sec. Assn. (cert.), Associated Photographers Internat. Address: 2313 Carlisle Dr Champaign IL 61821

SORIN, FRANNIE RUTH, image consultant; b. Cleve., Nov. 1, 1953; d. Samuel Israel and Lois (Fraiberg) Sorin; m. Betz Jungreis, Sept. 11, 1976; children—Jason, Erika. B.A. with honors in Psychology, U. Chgo., 1974. Account exec. Kaiser Broadcasting, Phila., 1975-77, Westinghouse Broadcasting, Phila., 1977-79; ptnr. Search Strategists, Wayne, Pa., 1979-81; owner Frannie Sorin Cons., Bryn Mawr, Pa., 1981—; sr. assoc. Martel & Assocs., Villanova, Pa., 1985—. Bd. dirs. Israel Aliyah Program, Phila., 1985-86; mem. Benchmark Sch. Fundraising Com., Media, Pa., 1985-86. Fedn. Exec. Recruitment and Ednl. Program scholar, 1974. Mem. Nat. Women's Polit. Caucus. Avocations: Reading; piano; weight-lifting; tennis; gardening. Home: 716 Southwinds Dr Bryn Mawr PA 19010 Office: Martel & Assoc 1 Aldwyn Ctr Villanova PA 19085

SORMANE, STEPHANIE CHARLOTTE, former ballet company executive ; b. Indpls., Aug. 20, 1938; d. Walter and Stephanie Louise (Modersohn) S.; student Northwestern U., 1959-61. Dancer, Ruth Page's Chgo. Opera Ballet, 1957-58; legal sec., Chgo. and San Francisco, 1959-71; dir. ticket sales, then asst. to pres. Ballet Theatre Found. (Am. Ballet Theatre), N.Y.C., 1971-74;

adminstrv. asst. Chgo. Ballet, 1975; acad. adminstr. Houston Ballet, 1976-77, co. mgr., 1977-86. Mem. Assn. Theatrical Press Agts. and Mgrs., Cultural Arts Council Houston.

SORRIER, ISABEL LANE, librarian; b. Statesboro, Ga., Aug. 13, 1917; d. Brooks Blitch and Caroline Viola (Moore) Sorrier; B.S., Ga. So. Coll., 1938; postgrad. U. Ga., 1940; B.S., George Peabody Coll., 1942. Intern, Warder Pub. Library, Springfield, Ohio, 1942; librarian Homerville (Ga.) High Sch., 1939-41; head librarian Waycross (Ga.) Pub. Library, 1942; librarian Newnan (Ga.) High Sch., 1943; dir. Statesboro (Ga.) Regional Library, 1944—; mem. library adv. com. bldg. constrn. Ga. Dept. Edn., mem. book selection com. Sec. chpt. ARC, 1945-48; mem. library services and constrn. Act Adv. Council, 1976—. Named Boss of Yr., Am. Bus. Women's Assn., 1980. Mem. ALA, S.E., Ga. (exec. bd. 1960, chmn. sect. 1960-62) library assns., Ga. Edn. Assn., Bus. and Profl. Women's Club (treas. 1950-52). Presbyterian. Home: 112 Park Ave Statesboro GA 30485 Office: 124 S Main St Statesboro GA 30458

SOSPENSO, ELIZABETH THERESA, stockbroker; b. Nuremburg, Ger., Nov. 22, 1936; came to U.S. 1956, naturalized 1962; d. Otto and Ida (Meyer) Laubvogel; m. Joseph P. Sospenso, Jan. 3, 1965. Grad. Hoehere Handelsschule, Nurnberg, 1955; student U. Erlangen (W.Ger.), 1955-56. Sec. to pres. Deltec Securities Corp., N.Y.C., 1959-67; account exec. Loeb Rhoades and Co., N.Y.C., 1967-77; stockbroker, v.p. Thomson McKinnon Securities, Inc., N.Y.C., 1977—, mem. pres.'s council, 1979-85. Chmn. Women in Bus. Chpt. Voice of the Electorate, N.Y. State, 1979—. Mem. Women's Stockbrokers Assn. Industry chmn. Am. Cancer Soc., 1983; com. mem. Women in Bus. Against Cancer, 1983. Lutheran. Office: Thomson McKinnon Securities Inc 1 State St Plaza New York NY 10004

SOSS, WILMA, retired association executive, former public relations consultant, and broadcaster; b. San Francisco; d. George Edison Porter and Clara Porter Weissman; student Sch. Journalism, Columbia U.; m. J. Albert Soss. (dec.). Newspaper columnist; Broadway press agt., N.Y.C.; publicity dir. Alfred Dunhill, Tailored Woman; cons. Saks Fifth Ave., N.Y.C.; publicity dir. Internat. Silk Guild; public relations counselor Evans Products Co., Detroit, Budd Co., Phila.; founder, chmn. Fedn. Women Shareholders in Am. Bus., 1949—; cons. NBC radio, 1980-82; bus. analyst, commentator Wilma Says, NBC, Radio Network, Wilma Soss, The Most Talked About Woman on Wall St. Radio and Her Pocket Book Edition of the News, 1955-80. Donor, Wilma Soss collection transcripts and broadcasts Am. Heritage Center, U. Wyo., Laramie; pioneered secret ballots for stockholders, women on corp. bds. Office: PO Box 10163 Grand Central Sta New York NY 10015

SOSTACK, LISA HILL, editor, publications consultant; b. Palo Alto, Calif., June 24, 1954; d. Francis Samuel and Norma Evelyn (Connelly) Hill; m. Gary Sostack, Jan. 17, 1981. B.A. in Polit. Sci., B.S. in Communication Arts, Calif. State Poly. U., 1976; postgrad. Tulane U., 1982—. Staff reporter Bonita Publs., Ontario, Calif., 1976; account exec. Nationwide Advt., Atlanta, 1977-78; editor Jour. of Labor, Ga. State AFL-CIO, Atlanta, 1978-79; editor Anderson & Anderson Ins. Brokers, Irvine, Calif., 1979-81; sr. editor McDermott Inc., New Orleans, 1981—; editor, cons. Fred. S. James & Co., Irvine, 1982—; cons. U.S. Dept. Energy, Washington, 1977-78. Contbr. articles to Calif. Jour. Mem. communications com. United Way of Greater New Orleans, 1982-84; campaign worker com. to elect Congressman Wyche Fowler, Atlanta, 1978. Mem. Women in Communications (v.p. 1982-83), Internat. Assn. Bus. Communicators (awards of excellence 1982), Soc. Profl. Journalists, Phi Kappa Phi. Democrat. Episcopalian. Home: 5542 Rosemary Place New Orleans LA 70124 Office: McDermott Inc 1010 Common St New Orleans LA 70112

SOSTROM, SHIRLEY ANNE, management consultant, public relations executive, educator; b. Billings, Mont., Dec. 22, 1933; d. Jack Kenneth and Edith Ester (Bates) Thompson; student U. Wyo., 1951-59; B.Sc., No. Ill. U., 1966; M.A., Central State U., 1970; Ph.D., Ohio State U., 1976; m. John Philip Sostrom, July 11, 1950; children—John David, Kristen Ingrid, Edith May. Tchr. various high schs., Ohio, Mont., 1966-74; lectr. linguistics Carroll Coll., Helena, Mont., 1972-74; lectr. linguistics Carrol Coll., lectr. communication and writing Sinclair Coll., 1976-78; program coordinator Sch. Public Adminstrn., Ohio State U., Columbus, 1978-80, lectr. English and journalism Muskingum Coll., 1980-81; pres. Sostrom Assos., Columbus, 1979—; prin. Sims Cons. Group, 1983—; prof. Grad. Sch. Adminstrn., Capital U., Columbus, 1980—. Bd. dirs. Seven Days of Creation, 1980. Mem. Women's Poetry Workshop, Am. Assn. for Tng. and Devel., Internat. Assn. Bus. Communicators, Internat. Materials Mgmt. Soc. (v.p. 1985—), Ohio State U. Alumni Assn., Phi Delta Kappa. Republican. Jewish. Club: Zonta of Central Ohio (v.p., pres.). Contbr. articles and poetry to mags.; contbg. author publs. Am. Mgmt. Assn., Internat. City Mgmt. Assn. Home: 99 E Weber St Columbus OH 43202 Office: 2199 E Main St Columbus OH 43209

SOTO, GLORIA ESTHER, lawyer; b. Aguadilla, P.R., Apr. 27, 1948; d. Santos and Milagros (Polidura) S. B.A., Douglass Coll., 1971; J.D., Rutgers U., 1974. Bar: N.J. Legis. aide, to mem. N.J. Assembly, Trenton, 1971-72; legal intern Senate Labor Com., Washington, 1973; asst. dep. pub. defender Appellate Sect. Pub. Defender, East Orange, N.J., 1975-77, Middlesex County Trial Region Pub. Defenders, New Brunswick, N.J., 1977-80; assoc. mem. N.J. State Parole Bd., Trenton, 1980-83; assoc. gen. counsel Harrah's Hotel/Casino, Atlantic City, 1983—; mem. criminal practice com. State Supreme Ct., 1983. Sec. United Way of Central Jersey, 1974-76; v.p. Puerto Rican Assn. Human Devel., Perth Amboy, 1974-79; v.p. Young Democrats, Perth Amboy, 1972-73; program hostess Community Needs radio show, New Brunswick, 1983. Mem. ABA, N.J. State Bar Assn. (young lawyers sect., prosecutor and jud. appointment com.; named Young Lawyer of Yr. 1984), Hispanic Bar Assn. (leadership and community award 1983), Middlesex County Bar Assn. (trustee 1978), N.J. Bar Found. (trustee 1983). Democrat. Roman Catholic. Home: 433 Brace Ave Perth Amboy NJ 08861 Office: Harrah's at Trump Plaza PO Box 988 Atlantic City NJ 08404

SOTO, THERESA (TERRY) JOSEPHINE, banking and financial executive; b. St. Petersburg, Fla., May 29, 1942; d. Phillip Evan and Virginia Mary (Draa) Anderson; m. Henry Dominquez Soto, Aug. 14, 1960; children—Kimberly, Patrick, Noel, Nathan, Andrew. Student Pima Community Coll., 1972-75. Cert. personnel cons. Exec. recuiter Mgmt. Recruiters, Tucson, 1976-80; corp. v.p., mgr. real estate/fin. div. Kingston & Assocs., Tucson, 1981—. Leadership tng., mem. steering com. OEO, Tucson, 1964-66; mem. community relations bd. Tucson Job Corps., 1977-79; treas. Tucson Loan Chest, 1983—. Named Outstanding Fraternalist, Ariz. Frat. Congress, 1985. Mem. Nat. Assn. Personnel Cons., Am. Mktg. Assn. (co-chairperson spl. programs 1982-83, program chairperson 1981-82, sec. chpt. 1979-80, pres. Greater Tucson chpt. 1984-85). Republican. Roman Catholic. Club: Parkwest Women's (chairperson program 1967-68, pres. 1968-69) (Tucson). Lodges: Columbiettes (K.C. aux., pres. 1982-83), Ind. Order of Foresters (chief ranger 1980-81, pub. relations officer Tucson 1983—, Ariz., N.Mex. and Nev. 1986—). Home: 2832 W Calle Carapan Tucson AZ 85745 Office: Kingston & Assocs 101 N Wilmot Suite 210 Tucson AZ 85711

SOTO, THERESE ANNE, city official; b. Tucson, July 25, 1952; d. Frank Aquirre and Julia (Corral) S. B.S. in Pub. Adminstrn., U. Ariz., 1974, also postgrad. Interviewer Model Cities program City of Tucson, 1973-75, budget analyst, 1975—; bd. mem. Ctr. Econ. Devel., Tucson, 1983—. Co-editor newsletter: Changing Tucson, 1973-75. Active Tucson Democratic Com., 1973-86. Delta Delta Delta nat. service scholar. Mem. Nat. Assn. Female Execs., U. Ariz. Hispanic Alumni. Democrat. Roman Catholic. Clubs: Image de Tucson (treas. 1979-81, Hispanic award for Outstanding Citizen 1978); Image de Ariz. (treas. 1981). Avocation: counseling and support of young students entering college. Home: 765 W Calle Garcia Tucson AZ 85706 Office: Dept Budget and Research City of Tucson Tucson AZ 85726

SOTO, YVONNE E., therapist, administrator; b. Lynwood, Calif., Jan. 26, 1951; d. William A. and Juanita A. (Tafoya) S. A.A., Los Angeles Harbor Coll., 1971; B.A., UCLA, 1973; B.A. in Music Therapy, Calif. State U.-Long Beach, 1978; M.P.A., U. San Francisco, 1987. Bd. cert. registered music therapist. Intern in music therapy Alan Short Ctr., Stockton, Calif., 1978, spl. project coordinator, 1978, performing arts instr., 1979-83, performing arts dir., 1980-81, clin. tng. dir., 1981-83, dir., 1983—. Mem. adv. bd. San Joaquin Delta Coll., 1983—. Mem. Coalition Local Area Service Providers, Dirs. Of Vol. Agys. San Joaquin County, Nat. Assn. Music Therapy (clin. chmn. 1982—), Assn. Supervision and Curriculum Devel., Music Educators Nat. Conf., Council Exceptional Children, Stockton C. of C., San Joaquin Coordinating Council. Avocations: Vocalist; guitarist. Office: Alan Short Ctr 1004 N Grant Stockton CA 95202

SOTRES, JOANNE LINK, advt. and public relations exec.; b. York, Pa., July 26, 1934; d. Fred M. and Mildred K. (Coover) Link; grad. Dwight Sch. for Girls, Englewood, N.J., 1952; m. Armando Sotres, 1955 (div. 1963); 1 son, Craig. Founder, La Fiesta Resort Wear Co., Acapulco, Mex., 1954-62; founder, mgr. Restaurant Armando's, Acapulco, 1954-62; adminstrv. asst. to Mr. and Mrs. Johhny Carson, 1962-66; mktg. cons., 1967-69; dir. mktg. Telegeneral Corp., N.Y.C., 1970, v.p., 1970-71; advt. dir. Fabric-News, N.Y.C., 1971-72; ptnr. Sotres-White Assoc., N.Y.C., 1972-73; chief exec. officer Sotres-Link Ltd., N.Y.C., 1973—; pres. Sotres-Link Mgmt., Inc., N.Y.C., 1975-80; pres. Quali-Tech Telecommunications Group, Inc., 1981—; dir., v.p. Madison Ave. Realty Corp., N.Y.C. Adv. council SBA, 1976—. Recipient numerous equestrian trophies, 1947-52; named to Ofcl. Horse Show Blue Book Hall of Fame, 1948-50. Republican.

SOULE, SALLIE THOMPSON, state official; b. Detroit, May 13, 1928; d. Hayward Stone and Elizabeth Robinson Thompson; A.B., Smith Coll., 1950; M.A., U. Vt., Burlington, 1952; m. Gardner Northup Soule, July 26, 1958; stepchildren—Gardner Northup, Nancy Soule Brown; children—Sarah Goodwin, Trumbull Dickson. Sec. trade sales dept. Macmillan Pub. Co., N.Y.C., 1952-57; tech. writer sales service div. Eastman Kodak Co., Rochester, N.Y., 1957-58; feature writer Brighton-Pittsford Post, Pittsford, N.Y., 1958-68; v.p., gen. mgr. F. H. Horsford Nursery, Inc., Charlotte, Vt., 1968-76; ptnr., pres. Bygone Books, Inc., Burlington, Vt., 1978—; mem. Vt. Ho. of Reps., 1976-80, mem. ways and means com., 1976-80; mem. Vt. Senate, 1980-84, mem. appropriation com., energy and natural resources com. 1980-84; commr. Vt. Dept. Employment and Tng., Montpelier, 1985—; chmn. Vt. Employment Security Bd., 1985—. Vice mem. governing bd. Vt. ETV; mem. Gov.'s Commn. on Higher Edn.; trustee Vt. Council on Arts; bd. dirs. Vt. Community Found., Inc. Mem. Vt. State C. of C. (bd. dirs.).

SOULLIERE, PATRICIA NELLIE, real estate broker; b. Detroit, May 12, 1949; d. Lloyd George and Bernice C. (Fons) S.; m. Marshall Eugene Ochylski, July 14, 1973; children—Kimberly Angela, Megan Lynn. B.A., U. Mich., 1971, M.B.A., 1973. Product mktg. mgr. Hallmark Card, Inc., Kansas City, Mo., 1973-75; product mgr. RCA, Indpls., 1975-78; sales assoc. ERA Realty 4, Los Osos, Calif., 1981—. Mem. Am. Mktg. Assn., South Bay Women's Network (treas. 1983—). Democrat. Roman Catholic. Home: 1458 4th St Los Osos CA 93402 Office: ERA Realty 4 1398 Los Osos Valley Rd Los Osos CA 93402

SOURWINE, KATHLEEN MARIE, office supply company executive; b. Chgo., Apr. 7, 1951; d. Robert John and Barbara Ellen (Anderson) Crorkin; m. Richard Earl Burnham, Sept. 22, 1966 (div. 1972); m. 2d. Kerry Michael Sourwine, Sept. 20, 1975; 1 dau., Karen Michelle; 1 stepdau., Evelyn Marie. Cashier, S.S. Kresge, Chgo., 1966; switchboard receptionist Churchill Cabinet, Chgo., 1967-69, bookkeeper, 1972; mgr. payroll TSC Industries, Chgo., 1972-80; mgr. payroll Wilson Jones Co., Chgo., 1981-83, mgr. distribution services, 1983—; network dir. Nat. Assn. Female Execs., N.Y.C., 1982—. Democrat. Roman Catholic. Office: Wilson Jones Co 6150 W Touhy Ave Chicago IL 60648

SOUSA, PATRICIA LOUISE, television network associate director; b. Chincoteague, Va.; d. Joseph Michael and Frances Irene (McDermont) S.; m. Lawrence Herbert Shapiro, Jan. 13, 1977. Student U. Fla., 1966-68; B.A., NYU, 1971. With Young & Rubicam, N.Y.C., 1969-70; adminstrv. asst. Home Mag., N.Y.C., 1971-74, Hughes TV Network, N.Y.C., 1974-76; adminstrv. asst., researcher, assoc. producer WNBC-TV, N.Y.C., 1976-78; assoc. dir. NBC Television Network, N.Y.C., 1979—. Vol., Jr. Army Navy Guild Orgn., Jacksonville, Fla., 1964-65. Mem. Dirs. Guild Am. (council 1984-86). Democrat. Roman Catholic. Avocation: travel. Home: 25 W 15th St New York NY 10011 Office: NBC Television Network 30 Rockefeller Plaza New York NY 10020

SOUSA, THERESA ELLEN MALONE, former govt. ofcl.; b. Frederick County, Va., Mar. 17, 1927; d. Joseph Harrison and Lillie May (Lehigh) Malone; student Strayer Bus. Coll., Columbia Tech. Inst., Washington, Oceanside-Carlsbad (Calif.) Jr. Coll., Am. U.; m. Joseph Earl Sousa, III, Oct. 20, 1946. Various adminstrv./community relations positions, 1945-50; with U.S. Geol. Survey, 1952-82, visual info. officer, Reston, Va., 1975-80, exhibits and visual info. officer, 1980-82; ret., 1982; pres. TMS Assocs., exhbn. and meeting planning, McLean, Va., 1982—. Served with USMCR, 1949-62. Recipient various achievement and service awards. Mem. Nat. Mus. Women in the Arts, Meeting Planners Internat., McLean Citizens Assn., Am. News Women's Club, Women Marines Assn. (nat. pres. 1974-76). Presbyterian. Home: 1415 Springvale Ave McLean VA 22101 Office: TMS Assocs PO Box 3302 McLean VA 22103

SOUTH, MOLLY MADSEN, real estate investment principal, shopping center management; b. Shreveport, La., June 18, 1949; d. Lawrence Edwards and Margaret Marion (Murray) Madsen; m. J. Gregory South, May 6, 1972; children—J. Madsen, J. Taylor B.A. in Journalism, U. Tex., 1971. Head copywriter Continental Advt., Dallas, 1973-74; v.p. mktg., cons. and pub. affairs, Homart Devel. Co. Chgo., 1974-1980; gen. ptnr. Moor & South, Highland Park, Ill., 1980—; v.p. Amermbass Realty Co., Highland Park, and Phila., 1980—; prin., gen. ptnr. Pier 39, San Francisco, Century City Ctr., Chgo., Ocean One, Atlantic City, numerous other comml. properties; dir. Alexanders Dept. Stores, N.Y.C.; lectr. in field. Author column Chain Store Age Mag., 1980—. Editorial bd. Shopping Ctr. World Mag., 1978-81. Contbr. articles to profl. jours. Bd. dirs. Highland Park Hosp. Jr. Bd., 1985—, also edn. chmn. Mem. Internat. Council Shopping Ctrs. (profl. standards com. 1983—, publs. com., 1984—, cert. shopping ctr. mktg. dir.), Urban Land Inst. Republican. Roman Catholic. Office: Moor and South 525 Elm Pl Highland Park IL 60035

SOUTHERN, EILEEN, musician, educator; b. Mpls., Feb. 19, 1920; d. Walter Wade and Lilla (Gibson) Jackson; B.A., U. Chgo., 1940, M.A., 1941; Ph.D., NYU, 1961; M.A. (hon.), Harvard U., 1976; D.M.A. (hon.), Columbia Coll., Chgo., 1985; m. Joseph Southern, Aug. 22, 1942; children—April, Edward. Concert pianist, 1940—; instr. Prairie View U., Hempstead, Tex., 1941-42; asst. prof. So. U., Baton Rouge, 1943-45, 49-51; tchr. N.Y.C. Bd. Edn., 1954-60; instr. Bklyn. Coll., CUNY, 1960-64, asst. prof., 1964-69; assoc. prof. York Coll., CUNY, 1969-71, prof., 1972-75; prof. music Harvard U., Cambridge, Mass., 1976—, chmn. dept. Afro-Am. studies, 1976-79. Active Girl Scouts U.S.A., 1954-63; chmn. mgmt. com. Queens Area YWCA, 1970-73. Recipient Alumni Profl. Achievement award U. Chgo., 1970, Deems Taylor award ASCAP, 1973; NEH grantee, 1979-83. Mem. Internat., Am. (dir. 1974-76) musicol. socs., Renaissance Soc., Assn. for Study Afro-Am. Life and History, NAACP, Phi Beta Kappa (hon.), Alpha Kappa Alpha. Author: The Buxheim Organ Book, 1963; The Music of Black Americans: A History, 1971, 2d edit., 1983; Readings in Black American Music, 1971, 2d edit., 1983; Anonymous Pieces in the Manuscript El Escorial, 1981; Biographical Dictionary of Afro-American and African Musicians, 1982; editor, pub. The Black Perspective in Music, 1973—; contbr. articles to profl. jours., encys. Office: Harvard U Cambridge MA 02138

SOUTHWICK, PHYLLIS CLAYTON, social worker; b. Salt Lake City, Nov. 2, 1926; d. David Hyrum and Margaret (Cannon) Clayton; B.S., U. Utah, 1949, M.S.W., 1967, D.S.W., 1976; m. A.J. Southwick, Jr., Apr. 1, 1950; children—Carolyn, Elaine, Portia Marie. Group worker, dir. Salt Lake Neighborhood House and Day Care Center, 1954-67; asso. prof. Grad. Sch. Social Work, U. Utah, 1967—, dir. continuing edn. Grad. Sch. Social Work, 1972—, mem. Univ. Publs. Council, 1982—; chmn. Utah Social Workers Lic. Bd. Mem. bd. govs. Utah Health Systems Agy. Mem. adminstrv. bd., adv. com. Utah Juvenile Ct.; mem. Bountiful City Council, 1974—; mem. Utah Constn. Revision Com., Provo/Jordan River Found., 1979—. NIMH grantee, 1974—. Mem. Nat. Assn. Social Workers (chmn. nat. com. 1976-78, pres. Utah, pres. womens state legis. council 1976-78), Acad. Certified Social Workers, Council Social Work Edn., Phi Kappa Phi, Delta Kappa Gamma. Republican. Mormon. Club: Soroptimist. Contbr. articles to profl. jours. Home: 1314 E Millbrook Way Bountiful UT 84010 Office: Grad Sch Social Work U Utah Salt Lake City UT 84112

SOUTHWORTH, LOIS GILL, educator, psychologist; b. Atoka, Okla., July 21, 1915; d. James Hugh and Lois Elizabeth (McCuiston) Gill; B.S., NE Okla. State U., 1934; Ed.S., U. Tenn., 1973; m. James Larry Southworth, Feb. 29, 1936 (dec.); children—John Scott, Bruce Alan. Tchr., Strayer Coll., Washington, 1938-39, Ballard Sch., N.Y.C., 1939-45; pvt. practice psychology, Knoxville, Tenn., 1964-68; asst. prof. dept. child and family studies, U. Tenn., Knoxville, 1967-83, researcher Appalachian Children and Families. Active Knoxville Symphony Assn., Dulin Art Gallery Assn., Women's Center of Knoxville, Children's Internat. Village, Common Cause. Lic. psychol. examiner, Tenn. Mem. AAUP, AAUW, Am. Psychol. Assn., Nat. Assn. Psychology in the Schs., Nat. Assn. of Disability Examiners, Nat. Assn. of Children with Learning Disabilities, LWV, NOW, Pi Lambda Theta, Phi Delta Kappa. Democrat. Unitarian. Club: Women's Aux. of Knoxville Acad. Medicine. Author: Screening and Evaluating the Young Child—A Handbook of Instruments to Use from Infancy to Six Years, 1980; contbr. articles in field to profl. jours. Home: 921 Kenesaw Ave Knoxville TN 37919

SOUTULLO, CATHERINE JULIA, lawyer; b. Brisbane, Queensland, Australia, Oct. 14, 1944; came to U.S., 1945; d. Joseph Anthony and Gloria Merle (Simmons) S. B.A., La. State U.-New Orleans, 1966; J.D., Loyola U., New Orleans, 1976. Bar: La. 1976, U.S. Dist. Ct. (ea. dist.) La. 1979. Tchr. high sch. English, Jefferson Parish (La.) Sch. Bd., 1966-74; assoc. firm Knight, D'Angelo & Knight, P.L.C., Gretna, La., 1976-85, sole practice, 1985—; pres. Barristers Title Agy., Inc., 1985—. Mem. Nat. Assn. Women Lawyers, ABA, Fed. Bar Assn., Assn. Women Attys., La. Bar Assn., Jefferson Bar Assn., Gretna Hist. Soc. Roman Catholic. Office: 210 Huey P Long Ave Gretna LA 70053

SOUZA, MAURENE GLORIA, toy company executive; b. Providence, July 31, 1949; d. Joseph Antonio and Georgina Irene (Matta) S. B.A. in English, U. R.I., 1973. Copywriter, Outlet Dept. Stores, Providence, 1971-73; copywriter Hasbro Industries, Pawtucket, R.I., 1973-78, product mgr., 1978-81, mktg. dir., 1981-84, assoc. v.p. mktg., 1984—. Bd. dirs. Children's Mus. of R.I., 1983-84. Mem. Nat. Assn. Female Execs. (network dir. 1985). Office: Hasbro Industries 1027 Newport Ave Pawtucket RI 02861

SOVA, DAWN BEVERLY, research consultant, lecturer, writer; b. Passaic, N.J., Oct. 6, 1949; d. Emil Jack and Violet Alice (Tomczyk) S.; B.A., Montclair State Coll., 1971; M.A. (grantee 1971-72), Ball State U., 1972; postgrad. Drew U.; 1 son, Robert. Instr., Tri-State U., Angola, Ind., 1972-74, U. W.Fla., Pensacola, 1975-76, East Carolina U., Greenville, N.C., 1977-78; owner, dir. Pro-Write Cons. Garfield, N.J., 1978—; bus. and acad. cons. Notary pub. Mem. AAUP, MLA, AAUW, Nat. Assn. Female Execs. Roman Catholic. Contbr. articles to popular mags. Home and Office; 126 Banta Ave Garfield NJ 07026

SOVIERO, DIANA BARBARA, soprano; b. Jersey City, Mar. 19, 1946; d. Amerigo and Angelina Catani; student Juilliard Sch. Music, Hunter Coll. Opera Workshop. Appearances with opera cos. including Tulsa Opera, Houston Grand Opera, San Diego Opera, Ottawa (Ont., Can.) Opera, Zurich Opera, Goldovsky Opera Theatre, Lake George Opera, New Orleans Opera, Hamburg (W.Ger.) Opera, Dallas Opera, Chgo. Opera, Rome Opera, Paris Opera, Nice Opera, Avignon Opera, San Francisco Opera, Montreal (Que., Can.) Opera, Toulouse, France, Caracas, Venezuela, Vienna Opera, Parma Opera, Italy, Munich Opera, W.Ger., Edmonton Opera, Winnipeg Opera, Calgary Opera; now leading soprano N.Y.C. Opera; instr. master classes The Faculty, sch. for actors, Los Angeles. Recipient Richard Tucker award. Mem. AFTRA, Am. Guild Musical Artists, SAG. Office: Columbia Artists 165 W 57th St New York NY 10019

SOWELL, VIRGINIA MURRAY, educator; b. Presidio, Tex., Mar. 23, 1931; d. Marshall Bishop and Mary Alice (Daniel) Murray; B.A., Sam Houston State U., 1951; M.A., Trinity U., 1957; Ph.D., U. Tex., 1975; children—John Houston, III, Paul Orin. Tchr. San Antonio (Tex.) Ind. Sch. Dist., 1951-52, 1955-58; asst. prof. San Antonio Coll., 1969-75, assoc. prof., 1976—; assoc. prof. spl. edn. Tex. Tech. U., Lubbock, 1976—, asst. v.p. acad. affairs, 1984—. Bd. govs. Tex. Sch. for Blind, v.p., 1983-86, pres., 1986-89; dir. vols. Witte Mus.; mem. research adv. com. Tex. Tech. U., 1981-82, pres. faculty senate, 1982-83, mem. acad. affairs com. faculty senate, 1978-80; bd. dirs. Developmental Edn., Birth through Two, 1977—. HEW grantee, 1977—. Mem. Council for Exceptional Children (bd. govs. 1982-85), Tex. Council Exceptional Children (treas. 1981-85), Tex. Div. Children with Learning Disabilities, Internat. Reading Assn., Assn. for Edn. and Rehab. of Blind (pres. S. Central region 1984-86), Am. Ednl. Research Assn., Assn. Edn. of Visually Handicapped (pres. South Central region 1984-86), Assn. Supervision and Curriculum Devel. (chpt. dir. 1980-83), Tex. Assn. Coll. Tchrs., AAUP, Phi Delta Kappa, Delta Kappa Gamma, Zeta Tau Alpha. Republican. Episcopalian. Home: 4610 28th St Lubbock TX 79410 Office: Office Acad Affairs Box 4609 Tex Tech U Lubbock TX 79409

SOWLES, MARCIA KAY, lawyer; b. Elkhart, Ind., Oct. 29, 1950; d. Charles H. and Maxine (Sprinkle) S. B.A., Manchester Coll., 1972; J.D., Valparaiso U., 1975; LL.M. (fellow), Yale U., 1980. Bar: D.C. 1983, Ind. 1975. Reginald H. Smith fellow Legal Service Program, South Bend, Ind., 1975-78, supervising atty., 1978-79; trial atty. U.S. Dept. Energy, Washington, 1980-84; dep. asst. gen. counsel Dept. Energy, 1984-85, asst. chief counsel, 1985—. Bd. dirs. Citizens Action Coalition Ind., Indpls., 1976-79. Luth. Laymen's League scholar, 1975; recipient award of Acad. Excellence, Manchester Coll., 1968-72; Hoosier State scholar, 1968-72. Mem. Ind. Bar Assn., D.C. Bar Assn., ABA, Delta Sigma Rho, Tau Kappa Alpha, Kappa Mu Epsilon. Ch. of Brethern. Clubs: Washington Figure Skating, No. Va. Figure Skating. Home: 2525 N 10th St Arlington VA 22201 Office: Dept Energy Econ Regulatory Adminstrn 1000 Independence Ave Washington DC 20585

SPACEK, SISSY (MARY ELIZABETH), actress; b. Quitman, Tex., Dec. 25, 1949; d. Edwin S. and Virginia S.; m. Jack Fisk, 1974; 1 dau., Schuyler Elizabeth. Student Lee Strasberg Theatrical Inst. Appeared in films: Prime Cut, 1972, Ginger in the Morning, 1972, Badlands, 1974, Carrie (Acad. award nominee Best Actress), 1976, Three Women, 1977, Welcome to L.A., 1977, Heartbeat, 1980, Coal Miner's Daughter, 1980 (Acad. award for best actress 1980), Raggedy Man, 1981, Missing, 1982; TV movies The Girls of Huntington House, 1973, The Migrants, 1973, Katherine, 1975, Verna: USO Girl, 1978; guest host Saturday Night Live, 1977. Named Best Actress by Nat. Soc. Film Critics for Carrie, 1976; Best Supporting Actress, N.Y. Film Critics, 1977. care Creative Artists Agency Inc 1888 Century Park East Suit 1400 Los Angeles CA 90067

SPADARO, CHARLOTTE, lawyer; b. N.Y.C., June 29, 1941; d. Sol and Eva (Malach) Rubinfeld; student U. Calif. at Los Angeles, 1958-60; B.A., Calif. State U., 1962; J.D., U. So. Calif., 1969; m. George Spadaro, Apr. 8, 1960; children—Michele, Jonathan. Tchr. English, Portola Jr. High Sch., Orange, Calif., 1962-63; substitute tchr. English and French, Santa Ana (Calif.) Unified and Orange (Calif.) Unified Sch. Dists., 1963-64; admitted to Calif. bar, 1970; law clk. Dist. Ct. of Appeals, Los Angeles, 1969; mem. firm Eliot B. Feldman, Los Angeles, 1970—; vice mayor City of Beverly Hills, Calif., 1986. Chmn., Beverly Hills Gen. Plan Update Study, 1979-80; mem. Nat. Com. for Citizens in Edn.; safety chmn. Beverly Hills PTA Council, 1978-79; mem. early childhood edn. adv. com., sch. improvement site council Beverly Vista Sch.; mem. Beverly Hills Unified Sch. Dist. Bd. Edn., 1979-83, pres., 1983; mem. Beverly Hills City Council, 1984. Mem. Women Lawyers Assn., Ephebian Soc., LWV (fin. chmn. Santa Ana 1965), U. So. Calif. Alumni Assn., World Affairs Council. Home: 221 S El Camino Dr Beverly Hills CA 90212 Office: 9465 Wilshire Blvd Beverly Hills CA 90212

SPADOTTO, BEVERLY THERESE, communications executive b. Syracuse, N.Y., July 11, 1951; d. Ted and Beverly Jean (Loughlin) S.; B.A. in Journalism, George Washington U., 1973; M.A., U. So. Calif., 1975. Dir. public relations D'Arcy-MacManus & Masius, advt., Los Angeles, 1976-78; editor Rangefinder mag., Santa Monica, Calif., 1978-81; communications editor CIGNA Healthplans of Calif., Glendale, Calif., 1982-85; dir. communications U.S. Adminstrs., Inc., Los Angeles, 1985—; ptnr. Flash & Class, Los Angeles, 1982—. Mem. Western Publs. Assn. Democrat. Roman Catholic. Club: Pub. of Los Angeles. Home: 410 S Hobart Blvd Los Angeles CA 90020 Office: 3540 Wilshire Blvd Los Angeles CA 90010

SPADY, CALLIE JEANETTA, social worker, human resource administrator; b. Townsend, Va., Aug. 24, 1938; d. Willie Lee and Rosie Mae (Reid) S. Student Kittrell Jr. Coll., 1956-58; B.A., Allen U., 1961. Cert. civil service investigator. Tchr. English, Marion County Sch. Bd., Ocala, Fla., 1961-62; children's counselor Human Resources Adminstrn. Bur. Child Welfare, N.Y.C., 1962-76, civil service investigator, 1976—, asst. to IRS coordinator, 1980-84; asst. tchr. Sunshine Nursery Schs., Bronx, N.Y., 1968-76. Active Met. Opera Guild, Friends of Carnegie Hall, 55th St. Dance Theater Found., Transit Riders in Pursuits, 1983—, ACLU, Archdiocese of N.Y. Cardinal's Ann. Appeal, N.Y. State Tenant and Neighborhood Coalition, 1983-84; vol. sr. citizen program St. Patrick Cathedral, N.Y.C., 1983-84; mem. Concerned Democratic Coalition No. Manhattan, Audubon Reform Dem. Club, N.Y.C., 1982—; mem. payroll deduction com. Combined Mcpl. Campaign, N.Y.C., 1982—; mem. lobby corp. LWV City N.Y., 1981—; mem. legis. com. N.Y.C. Opera Guild-Lincoln Ctr., 1983—; mem. N.Y.C. Edn. and Environ. Coms., Exec. Community Bd. No. 12, N.Y.C., 1984; charter mem. Statue of Liberty, 1985—, Ronald Reagan Trust, 1985—; mem. Rep. Nat. Com., 1985—; mem. Dem. Nat. Com., 1985—. Recipient Twenty Years Dedicated Service award Human Resources Adminstrn., 1983. Mem. Nat. Assn. Social Workers, Nat. Assn. Black Social Workers, Assn. for Study of Afro-Am. Life and History, Nat. Assn. Female Execs., AAUW, Internat. Fedn. Bus. and Profl. Women (treas. local chpt. 1981-82), NAACP (participant legal def. and ednl. fund 1983), AFL-CIO Am. Fedn. State, County and Mcpl. Employees, N.Y.C. Civil Service Ret. Employees Assn., N.Y. Urban League, Coalition of 100 Black Women, Nat. Council Negro Women, Internat. Platform Assn., Nat. Trust for Hist. Preservation, Am. Inst. for Cancer Research, Internat. Biog. Assn., N.Y. State Bus. and Profl. Women, Am. Assn. Ret. Persons (Andrus Found.), Assn. for Childhood Edn. Internat. Roman Catholic. Club: Womens (com. on status of women 1984) (N.Y.C.). Home: Washbridge Station PO Box 211 New York NY 10033 Office: Human Resources Adminstrn Bur Child Support - Central Office 6th Floor 66 Leonard St New York NY 10013

SPAGNOLA, MARY EUNICE, actress, author, educator; b. Rochester, N.Y.; d. Edward James and Maud Margaret (Westerby) Sayrahder; m. Joseph H. Spagnola, Aug. 27, 1946 (dec. 1982); 1 child, Joseph E. Student Furlong Sch. Drama, 1938-43. Dir., Mary Prodns., 1950-85; producer radio Monmouth County, N.J., 1963-78; monologuist N.Am. Martyrs Shrine, Auriesville, N.Y., Tekawitha Shrine, Fonda, N.Y., Our Lady of Fatima Shrine, Youngstown, N.Y., St. John Neumann Shrine, Phila., The Scapalar Ct., Aylesford, N.Y., Our Lady of Fatima Shrine, Blue Army, Washington, N.J., Immaculate Conception Shrine, Washington, Marian Shrine, W., Haverstraw, N.Y.; appeared throughout U.S., Can., Mexico, Italy, London. Author: Center Stage, 1972; (plays) Apostleship of Prayer, 1973. Recipient Tekakwitha award, Auriesville, N.Y., 1970, Woman of Yr. award, N.Y.C., 1983. Republican. Roman Catholic. Home: Tomaso Pl Apt 212 Oakdale Dr Middletown NJ 07748

SPAIN, JAYNE BAKER, businesswoman, educator; b. San Francisco; d. Lawrence Ian and Marguerite (Buchanan) Baker; student U. Calif. at Berkeley, 1944-47, Music U. Cin., 1947-50; LL.D., Edgecliff Coll., Cin., 1969; Dr. Pub. Service, George Washington U., 1970; LL.D., U. Cin., 1971, Dumbarton Coll., 1972, Springfield (Mass.) Coll., 1973, Gallaudet Coll., Washington, 1973; L.H.D. Bryant Coll., 1972, Russell Sage Coll., Troy, N.Y., 1973, Loyola Coll., Balt., 1975; m. John A. Spain, July 14, 1952; children—Jeffry Alan, Jon Kimberly. Pres., Alvey-Ferguson Co., Cin., 1952-66, pres. Alvey-Ferguson Operations div. Litton Industries, Inc., 1966-70, also dir. parent co., 1970—; vice chmn. CSC, 1971—; sr. v.p. Gulf Oil Corp., Pitts., from 1975; Disting. vis. prof. and exec.-in-residence George Washington U., Washington, 1979—; dir. Beatrice Foods, Chgo., Ohio Nat. Life Ins., Cin. Vice chmn. Pres.'s Com. on Employment Handicapped, 1966—; participant internat. trade fairs U.S. Depts. State, Commerce, Europe, North Africa, 1961-66, mem. trade and investment mission, India, 1965; mem. U.S. com. Internat. Council Social Welfare; mem. Internat. Soc. Rehab. Disabled; mem. adv. com. sheltered workshops U.S. sec. labor; mem. Ohio Gov.'s Commn. on Status of Women; mem. bldg. com. Children's Med. Center, Cin. Bd. dirs., past pres. Convalescent Hosp. Children, Cin., Greater Cin. Hosp. Council, Children's Neuromuscular Diagnostic Center, Cin., Cin. Sci. Center; bd. dirs. President's Commn. on Personnel Interchange; chmn. bd. trustees Fed. Women's Award; mem. dean's adv. council Coll. Bus. Adminstrn. U. Cin.; chmn. Found. of Ams. for the Handicapped; bd. dirs. Recs. for the Blind. Recipient Distinguished Service award for work overseas blind People Com., Washington, 1965; Migel medal Am. Found. Blind, N.Y., 1966; Golden Plate award industry Acad. Achievement, Dallas, 1967; Top Hat award Bus. and Profl. Women's Clubs. Am., N.Y., 1967. Mem. Conveyor Equipment Mfrs. Assn. (sec., treas., dir. 1960-63), Machinery and Allied Products Inst., Am. Mgmt. Assn. (dir.) Internat. Platform Assn. Episcopalian. Contbr. articles to profl. jours. Home: 700 New Hampshire Ave NW Washington DC 20037 Office: Sch of Govt and Bus George Washington U Washington DC 20052

SPAIN, NETTIE EDWARDS (MRS. FRANK E. SPAIN), civic worker; b. Alexandria, La., Oct. 9, 1918; d. John Henry and Sallie Tamson (Donald) Edwards; student Alexandria Bus. Coll., 1936-37, Birmingham-So. Coll., 1958-59, Nat. Tng. Inst., United Community Funds and Councils Am., 1965-66; m. Frank E. Spain, May 18, 1974. Reporter, Alexandria Daily Town Talk, 1942-45; staff writer Brimingham (Ala.) Post, 1945-49; pub. relations dir. Community Chest, Birmingham, 1949-53; dir. info. services Pa. United Fund, Phila., 1953-55; asst. exec. dir. Ala. Assn. Mental Health, Birmingham, 1956-57; pub. relations dir. United Appeal, Birmingham, 1958-68, asst. exec. dir., 1968-71; asst. to pres. for devel. U. Ala., Birmingham, 1971-74, acting dir., 1975. Mem. public relations com. Ala. Heart Assn., Birmingham, 1972-75; bd. dirs. Kate Duncan Smith DAR Sch., Grant, Ala., 1981-82; bd. dirs. Children's Aid Soc., 1971-77, 79, v.p., 1976-77; bd. dirs. Jefferson-Shelby Lung Assn., 1972-75, Vol. Bur. Greater Birmingham, 1973-77, Hale County chpt. ARC, Hale County Library; adv. com. Jr. League, 1974-75; exec. com. Historic Hale County Preservation Soc.; hon. mem. president's council U. Ala., Birmingham; bd. dirs. Norton Center Continuing Edn., Birmingham-So. Coll.; charter mem. bd. Birmingham Children's Theater. Recipient 1st Place awards Nat. Photos for Fedn., 1966-67; citation Pa. United Fund, 1955, citation for service Jefferson-Shelby Lung Assn., 1975, citation Ala. Heart Assn., 1974, Vol. Bur. Greater Birmingham, 1977; award of Merit, Ala. Hist. Commn., 1977; Rotary Found. Paul Harris fellow; Benjamin Franklin fellow Royal Soc. Arts, London, U.S.A. Mem. Nat. Public Relations Council of Health and Welfare Services (dir. 1967-69), Birmingham Women's Com. of 100, Public Relations Council Ala. (hon. life), Order of Crown in Am., Ala. Hist. Soc., Nat. Soc. Colonial Dames Am., Nat. Trust for Historic Preservation, Met. Opera Guild, Guy E. Snavely Soc. (Birmingham-So. Coll.), Colonial Dames Am., DAR, First Families of Va., Birmingham Astron. Soc. (hon.). Episcopalian. Clubs: Lakeview Country (Greensboro, Ala.); Mountain Brook Country, Relay House, The Club; Northriver Yacht (Tuscaloosa); Greensboro Study; Progress Study; Cauldron. Home: Medley Greensboro AL 36744

SPAK, MARSHA CHAIT, lawyer, educator; b. St. Louis, Aug. 2, 1942; d. Abraham Joseph and Sarah (Brownstein) Chait; m. Michael I. Spak, Aug. 29, 1965; children—Adam, Erik. B.A., City Colls. St. Louis, 1963; J.D., Ill. Inst. Tech., 1979. Bar: Ill. Tchr. St. Louis Sch. System, 1963-66; dir. testing U.S. Army, Wurzburg, W. Ger., 1966-69; sr. ptnr. Spak & Assocs., Chgo., 1979—. Author: Bar Examination Seminar, 1979; editor Bar Rev. Inst., 1979-81. Active Simon Wiesenthal Ctr., Los Angeles, 1983, Assn. Jewish Lawyers and Jurists, Washington, 1983, Blind Service Assn., Chgo., 1983, Ill. PTA, Chgo., 1983. Mem. ABA, Ill. State Bar Assn., Decalogue Soc. Lawyers, Nat. Alumni Council Ill. Inst. Tech. (dir.), Orgn. Rehab. through Tng. (v.p. 1975-76), Pioneer Women. Lodge: Hadassah (chairperson 1975-76). Office: Spak & Assocs 1143 N Smith Rd Palatine IL 60067

SPALDING, DIANA JESUROGA, computer systems company executive; b. Miami, Fla., July 22, 1960; d. Richard Steven and Cleah June (Finley) S.; m. Richard Thomas Jesuroga, Feb. 16, 1982 (div. Feb. 1986). B.A., U. Colo., 1983. Cert. paraprofl. counselor. Sales clk. Vision Ctr., Bridgewater, N.J., 1977-78; computer coder Dun & Bradstreet, N.Y.C., 1978, Parsippany, N.J., 1978-79; computer scientist NOAA/Program Regional Observing and Forecasting Services, Boulder, Colo., 1981-84; engr. NBI, Inc., Boulder, 1984—. Vol., counselor Boulder County Safehouse, 1985—; peace activist, contbr. Women's Internat. League for Peace and Freedom, Boulder, 1985—; affiliate Friendship City Project, 1985—. Avocations: hiking, bicycling, cross-country skiing. Office: NBI Inc PO Box 9001 3-2 Boulder CO 80301

SPALDING, ELAINE R., sales executive; b. Elmhurst, N.Y., June 26, 1940; d. John Arpod and Thelma (Smith) Rado; student Coll. Wooster, 1958-60; m. Larry Spalding, Dec. 24, 1966; children—Timothy A., Linda L., Med. sec. Duke U. Med. Center, Durham, N.C., 1967-70; adminstrv. sec. Tampa Heights Hosp., Tampa, Fla., 1973-74; lead distributor Seyforth Labs., Inc., Dallas, 1975-79; lead distbr. Futuron Industries, Inc., Dallas, 1979-83, dir. Futuron Distbr. Orgn., 1979—, lead distbr. Slendernow Internat., 1984—. Aide to Pinellas County Commr. Barbara Sheen Todd, 1980—; v.p. Peninsula Republican. Club, 1982—. Recipient Distbr. of Year award, 1980, Spirit of Futuron award, 1981. Mem. Women in Mgmt. Address: 1211 Brookside Dr Clearwater FL 33546

SPANDORFER, MERLE SUE, artist; b. Balt., Sept. 4, 1934; d. Simon Louis and Bernice Phyllis (Jacobson) Bank; student Syracuse U., 1952-54; B.S., U. Md., 1956; m. Lester M. Spandorfer, June 17, 1956; children—Cathy, John. One-woman exhbns. include: Phila. Print Club, 1969, Richard Feigen Gallery, N.Y.C., 1970, Marian Locks Gallery, 1973, 78, 82, U. Pa., 1974, Louis Meisel Gallery, N.Y.C., 1976, Beaver Coll., 1976, Phila. Coll. Textiles and Sci., 1977, Ericson Gallery, N.Y.C., 1978, 79, R.I. Sch. Design, 1980, Yoseido Gallery, Tokyo, 1981, Temple U., 1984, Soho South Gallery, Tampa, Fla., 1984, Tyler Sch. Art, 1985; works exhibited in 100 group shows U.S., Europe, Japan; represented in permanent collections: Met. Mus. Art, Whitney Mus. Am. Art, Mus. Modern Art, Phila. Mus. Art, Balt. Mus. Art, Library of Congress, Israel Mus., Toyoh Art Inst., Tokyo; instr. Tyler Sch. Art of Temple U., 1980-84, Phila. Coll. Textiles and Sci., 1978; instr., dir. edn. Cheltenham Art Center, 1975—; faculty Pratt Inst. Graphics Ctr., 1985-86; lectr., workshop condr. Named Outstanding Art Educator, Pa. Art Edn. Assn., 1982; recipient Balt. Mus. Art Gov.'s prize, 1970, award Md. Inst. Art, 1971. Mem. Artists Equity, Am. Color Print Soc. Jewish. Home: 8012 Ellen Ln Cheltenham PA 19012 Office: 307 E Gowen Ave Philadelphia PA 19119

SPANGLER, ANN, county official; b. Clarinda, Iowa, Apr. 29, 1947; d. Earl C. and Marian A. (Parks) Warner; m. Regan R. Spangler, Jan. 20, 1967; 1 child, Ryan Scott. A.A., Iowa Western Coll., 1967; B.A. summa cum laude, Buena Vista Coll., 1985. Sales clk. Schoenberg's Shoppe, Clarinda, 1965-66; receptionist J. B. Martin, Clarinda, 1966-67; sec. Clarinda Mental Health, 1967-76, Turner Law Firm, Clarinda, 1976-78; county recorder Page County, Iowa, 1979—. Republican precinct chmn., county sec., Page County, 1984—, chmn. platform com., 1981—, mem. state platform com., Des Moines, 1983. Mem. Assessor Edn. Commn. (vice chmn. 1984—), Iowa Recorders Assn. (legis. com. 1981—), Clarinda C. of C. (legis. com. 1984—), PEO, Beta Sigma Phi (pres. 1974-75). Mem. Disciples of Christ Christian Ch. Avocation: dir. children's church choir. Home: 410 S 18th St Clarinda IA 51632 Office: Page County Courthouse Clarinda IA 51632

SPANGLER, DAISY KIRCHOFF, (MRS. FRANCIS R. COSGROVE SPANGLER), educational consultant; b. Lancaster, Pa., Jan. 27, 1913; d. Frank Augustus and Lida Flaharty (Forewood) Kirchoff; B.S., Millersville State Coll., 1963; M.Ed., Pa. State U., 1966, Ed.D., 1972; Ph.D., Stanton U., 1974; m. Francis R. Cosgrove Spangler, June 3, 1939 (dec.); children—Stephen Russell, Michael Denis. Tchr. rural sch., Providence, Pa., 1933-35, Rapho Twp., Pa., 1935-42, Mastersonville, Pa., 1942-51; elem. sch. prin. Manheim Central, Pa., 1952-66; tchr., Manheim, Pa., 1967-68; assoc. prof. elem. edn. Millersville U., Pa., 1968-78, prof. emeritus, 1978—, advisor Kappa Delta Phi, 1968—; ednl. cons., 1978—. Dist. chmn. ARC, 1965-66; mem. Hempfield PTA, 1966-67. Mem. Pa. Edn. Assn., Pa. Elem. Prins. Assn., Assn. Pa. State Coll. and Univ. Profs., Nat., Lancaster (pres. 1963-64) prins. assns., Pa. Outdoor Edn. and Conservation Assn., Nat., Pa. councils social studies, Am. Ednl. Research Assn., Manheim Tchrs. Assn. (pres. 1964-65), Hempfield Profl. Women, Am. Assn. Ret. Persons (chpt. pres. 1983-85), Pi Lambda Theta (nat. com. 1980—, advisor Millersville U. 1968—), Delta Kappa Gamma (pres. 1976-78). Lutheran (pres. Luth. Women 1966-67, 79-81). Club: Order Eastern Star. Home and Office: Route 7 Box 238 Manheim PA 17545

SPANGLER, NANCY LEE, school psychologist; b. Peoria, Ill., Apr. 4, 1949; d. Robert L. and Lerose (Hejda) S.; student Fla. So. Coll., Lakeland, 1967-68, We. Ill. U., Macomb, 1968-71; B.S. in Psychology, Bradley U., Peoria, Ill., 1972, M.A. in Psychology, 1974. Sch. psychology intern Spl. Edn. Coop. South Cook County, Chicago Heights, Ill., 1974-75; sch. psychologist Joliet (Ill.) Pub. Schs. Dist. 86, 1975—; supr. sch. psychology interns Joliet Pub. Schs., also coordinator diagnostic and related services. Named Exceptional Educator of Yr., Joliet Pub. Schs., 1983; cert. sch. psychologist, Ill. Mem. Ill. Sch. Psychology Assn., Nat. Assn. Sch. Psychologists, Delta Kappa Gamma. Methodist. Office: 420 N Raynor St Joliet IL 60435

SPANN, CHARLOTTE BROOKS, government official; b. Washington, Jan. 15, 1932; d. Edward and Oma H. (Neverdon) Brooks; m. Kenneth Edward Spann, June 20, 1953 (div. Aug. 1958); children—Kenneth Edward II, Deborah Spann White. B.A., Howard U., 1952. Cert. assoc. contracts mgr. Supply clk. Dept. Army, Washington, 1959-63; contract adminstr. NASA, Washington, 1963-67, contract negotiator, 1967-71, contracting officer, 1971-78; chief procurement br. Dept. Interior, Washington, 1978-80, dir. office of small bus., 1980—; mem. Sr. Exec. Service, 1980—. Recipient profl. awards. Mem. Nat. Contract Mgmt. Assn., Fed. Exec. Inst. Alumni Assn. Baptist. Avocations: reading; crocheting; knitting; painting; music. Office: Dept Interior 18th and C Sts NW Room 2747 Washington DC 20240

SPANN, MARGARET ANN, banker; b. Mt. Pleasant, Tex., Feb. 16, 1930; d. Frank Minor and Clara (Arnold) C.; m. Alvin Loyd Spann, June 13, 1947; children—Karen Kay Spann Hall, Roger Caldwell, Stephen Bruce. Cert. Am. Inst. Banking; grad. Southwestern Grad. Sch. Banking-So. Meth. U., 1980. Clk.-typist Am. Liberty Oil Co., Mt. Pleasant, 1947-62, USDA-Soil Conservation, Mt. Pleasant, 1962-64; note teller credit First Nat. Bank, Mt. Pleasant, 1964-66, sec., 1966-77, asst. trust officer, 1977-80, trust officer (name changed to Inter First Bank Mt. Pleasant, N.A.), 1980—; mem. E. Tex. Estate Planning Council, Tyler, 1980—. Mem. Nat. Assn. Bank Women, Mt. Pleasant C. of C., Am. Inst. Banking (bd. dirs. E. Tex. chpt. 1978-80). Democrat. Presbyterian. Club: Pilot (Mt. Pleasant). Avocation: fishing. Office: InterFirst Bank Mt Pleasant N A PO Box 71 Mt Pleasant TX 75455

SPANN, SHERYL GENE, marketing executive; b. Baton Rouge, Apr. 14, 1955; d. Louis Grey Sr. and Emma Gene (Fleming) S. B.S. in Bus. Econs. and Fgn. Lang., La. State U., 1977; M.B.A. in Mktg. and Fin., Boston Coll., 1980. Mktg. services analyst Peter Paul Cadbury Co., Naugatuck, Conn., 1980-81; brand asst. Beecham Products Co., Pitts., 1981-82; assoc. mktg. mgr. mascara Maybelline Co., Memphis, 1982-84; mkgt. mgr. new products Webster Industries, Inc., Peabody, Mass., 1984—. Mem. Am. Mktg. Assn., Pi Sigma Epsilon, Pi Tau Pi (life), Sigma Delta Pi (life), Phi Sigma Iota (life). Presbyterian. Home: 24 Silver Ridge Common Weston CT 06883

SPARKIA, ALISA ANNE, lawyer; b. Grand Rapids, Mich., Oct. 1, 1955; d. Roy B. and Renee Anne (Nemerov) S.; m. John T. Moore, 1985. B.A., Mich. State U., 1977; J.D., U. Mich., 1981; cert. Nat. Inst. Trial Advocacy, 1983. Bar: N.Mex. 1981, U.S. Dist. Ct. 1982, U.S. Ct. Appeals (10th cir.) 1981. Assoc., Civerolo, Hansen & Wolf, Albuquerque, 1981-82, Faurot & Titus, Farmington, N.Mex., 1982-83, Ferguson & Lind, Albuquerque, 1983-84; sole practice, Albuquerque, 1984—. Precinct chmn. N.Mex. Democratic Com., 1981-82. Mem. ABA, Assn. Trial Lawyers Am., N.Mex. Trial Lawyers Assn., State Bar N. Mex., Albuquerque Bar Assn. Club: Civitan. Office: 601 Tijeras St NW Suite 200 Albuquerque NM 87102

SPARKMAN, LILA GILLIS, health care facility administrator; b. Cumby, Tex., Feb. 24, 1930; d. William Paul and Cora (Caviness) Gillis; m. Alton C. Sparkman, July 26, 1947; children—Claudia, Vivian, Alan. B.S. summa cum laude in Social Work, East Tex. State U., 1978, M.A., 1980; postgrad. U. Tex.-Tyler, 1982. Cert. social worker, mental retardation diagnostic and evaluation specialist, mental retardational profl. Prof. sociology Paris (Tex.) Jr. Coll., 1980; coordinator geriatric services Sabine Valley Regional Mental Health-Mental Retardation Ctr., Marshall, Tex., 1980-82, adminstr. Mental Retardation Residential Homes, Longview, Tex., 1983—; sec.-treas. KAM Well Service, New London, Tex., 1981—; social work cons. Forest Acres, Longview, 1983. Author: Comparison of Traditional and Non-traditional Female Students and Their Perceived Reasons for University Attendance, 1980 co-author: Day Care Centers for the Elderly: An Alternative, 1983. Mem. Am. Sociol. Assn., Nat. Assn. Social Workers, Mid South Sociol. Assn., Pub. Health Assn., Alpha Kappa Delta, Alpha Chi, Cap and Gown. Democrat. Methodist. Lodge: Rebekah. Home: Drawer 529 Winnsboro TX 75494

SPARKMAN, MYRA DUKE, advertising agency executive; b. Cooperton, Okla., Nov. 13, 1926; d. Samuel Church Scott and Mamie Hardegree; m. Joe Neal Sparkman, May 14, 1944; (div. 1964); children—Susan Melissa Sparkman Cox, Gregory Scott. Student UCLA, 1967-68. Vice pres. Elgin Davis Advt. Agy., Los Angeles, 1970-73, Graham & Sparkman, Torrance, Calif., 1973-81; pres. Sparkman Advt. Co., Palos Verdes, Calif., 1981—. Recipient numerous awards in advt. Democrat. Mem. Ch. of Religious Sci. Avocations: writing; decorating; traveling. Home: 27902 Ridgebrook Ct Rancho Palos Verdes CA 90274 Office: Sparkman Advt Inc 655 Deep Valley Dr Suite 200 Palos Verdes Peninsula CA 90274

SPARKS, MARIE ALEXANDER, real estate broker, tax service executive; b. Wetumka, Okla., Dec. 30, 1922; d. Charles Frank and Tennie Lavina (Wallace) Alexander; m. Harold Sparks, Nov. 26, 1942; children—Gordon Gerald, Bettye Sue. Student Murray State Sch. Agr., Tichominoo, Okla., 1940, Southeastern State Tchrs. Coll., Durant, Okla., 1942, Am. Banking Inst., 1962; real estate brokers lic. Northlake Coll., Irving, Tex., 1979. Tchr. LaVilla (Tex.) Pub. Schs., 1945-50; exec. sec., payroll clk. So. Plaza Express Co., Dallas, 1950-58; auditor Yeager Broker Co., El Paso, Tex., 1961; sec. asst. to pub. relations dir. State Nat. Bank, El Paso, 1962-64; tax cons. Yeager Bookkeeping Co., San Mateo, Calif., 1964-69; div. sec. Skyline Coll., San Bruno, Calif., 1969-74; sec. to dean Amarillo (Tex.) Coll., 1974-78; real estate agt., broker Century 21 Assoc. Brokers Co., Irving, Tex., 1979—; owner Sparks Tax Service, Mesquite, Tex., 1970—, cons., 1974—. Vice pres. Classified Employees Assn., Skyline Coll., 1973. Former mem. bd. dirs. Community Concert Services, Irving, 1959; former mem. Heritage Soc., Irving, 1979. Honored for Million Dollar Sales, Century 21, Irving, 1981-83, other sales awards. Mem. Am. Bus. Womens Assn. (charter Irving; corr. sec. Laurel chpt. 1960), Beta Sigma Phi (v.p., sec. 1975, various coms. 1978). Democrat. Methodist. Clubs: Toastmistree (Irving), Century 21 (Irving). Home: 1800 Ridgeview Plaza Mesquite TX 75149

SPARKS-DAVIDSON, ZOE ANN, educator, child development specialist; b. Fort Smith, Ark., Sept. 16, 1932; d. Alton A. and Dorothy M.L. (Oldham) Durden; B.S.B.A., U. Ark., 1962; M.A., 1968. Ed.D., 1977; m. Jared Sparks, Jr., Jan. 23, 1965 (dec.); 1 son, Jared Jeffrey; m. 2d Paul W. Davidson, Aug. 22, 1981. Instr. child devel. and family relationships Colo. State U., Fort Collins, 1973-74; asst. prof. family life area La. State U., Baton Rouge, 1976-82; tchr. Assumption Parish Pub. Schs. (La.), 1982-84, Concordia Parish Publ Schs. (La.), 1984—; adj. prof. curriculum and instrn. U. So. Miss., Natchez, 1984—. Contbr. articles to prof. jours. Mem. Am. Home Econs. Assn., Nat. Council Family Relations, Family Relations Council La. (pres. 1979-80). Republican. Episcopalian. Home: 127 Duster Dr Natchez MS 39120

SPARLING, REBECCA HALL, materials engineer, energy consultant; b. Memphis, June 7, 1910; d. Robert Meredith and Kate Wallace (Sampson) Hall; m. Edwin Kinmonth Smith, Oct. 30, 1935 (div. 1947); 1 child, Douglas Kinmonth; m. Joseph Sparling, July 10, 1948. B.A., Vanderbilt U., 1930, M.S., 1931. Registered profl. engr., Calif. Design specialist Gen. Dynamics Co., Pomona, Calif., 1951-68, Northrop Aircraft, Hawthorne, Calif., 1944-51; cons., 1968-85. Contbr. articles to profl. jours. Recipient Engring. Merit award Orange County Council Engrs., 1978. Fellow Soc. Women Engrs. (gold medal 1957), Inst. Advancement Engring. (Outstanding Engr. award 1978), Am. Soc. Metals; mem. Am. Soc. for Nondestructive Testing, Delta Delta Delta. Republican. Mem. Religious Sci. Ch. Address: 650 W Harrison Ave Claremont CA 91711

SPARROW, DOROTHY TALMADGE, insurance adjuster, editor; b. Balt., Mar. 7, 1943; d. Charles Edward and Margaret Elizabeth (Willis) Sparrow Jr. A.B. in Sociology, U. Balt., 1965. Social worker Dept. of Welfare, White Plains, N.Y., 1965-66; mil. dance hostess dir. YWCA West Point, White Plains, 1967-72; asst. women's editor Reporter Dispatch, White Plains, 1967-73; news bur. dir. Meth. Coll., Fayetteville, N.C., 1973-74; casualty adjuster Crawford & Co., Fayetteville, 1974-76, outside casualty, life & health adj., Newport News, Va., 1976—. Contbr. articles to profl. jours. Vol. coordinator United Service Orgn., Hampton, Va., 1985—; area rep. Youth for Understanding Fgn. Exchange, Hampton, 1979-83; bd. dirs. Fayetteville Arts Council, 1974-76, Jr. Woman's Clubs of Fayetteville and Hampton, 1973-84. Recipient cert. appreciation Yorktown Bicentennial Commn., 1981, Marjorie Branch award Va. Fedn. Women's Club, 1984, others. Mem. Nat. Assn. Female Execs., Peninsula Claims Assn. (pres. 1983, sec. 1986, Adjuster of Yr. award 1984), Am. Bus. Women's Assn. (Woman of Yr. award 1982), Alpha Xi Delta. Republican. Episcopalian. Clubs: Woman's of Hampton; Ft. Eustis Officers. Avocations: bridge; needlework; travelling; reading; literacy counseling; crafts; sports; cooking; friends. Office: Crawford & Co 11101 Warwick Blvd Newport News VA 23601

SPATARO, JANIE DEMPSEY WATTS, journalist; b. Chattanooga, May 17, 1951; d. Ray Dean and Anne America (Dempsey) Watts; m. Stephen Anthony Spataro, June 18, 1977; children—Anthony Dempsey, Stephen Jackson. B.S. in Journalism, U. Calif.-Berkeley, 1974; M.A. in Broadcast Journalism, U. So. Calif., 1982. Writer, editor McGiffin Newspapers, South Gate, Calif., 1976; news bur. mgr. Loyola Marymount U., Westchester, Calif., 1976; asst. dir. pub. relations Hawthorne (Calif.) Community Hosp. 1977-78; writer, with pub. relations dept. Moneywise, Los Angeles, 1980-81; pub. relations cons. Security Pacific Bank, Los Angeles, 1978-82; writer Cable Card, Inc., Marina del Rey, Calif., 1983; writer Reality Prodns., Huntington Beach, Calif., 1983—. Writer, producer, editor TV documentary: Who's Minding the Children?, 1983; contbr. articles to mags. and newspapers. Speaker on child care on TV, 1983-84. Beatrice E. Rice scholar U. Calif., 1973-74; Calif. State fellow, 1981-83. Mem. Women in Film, Women in Communications, Internat. Documentary Assn., DAR. Home: 2629 Arizona Ave Santa Monica CA 90404 Office: 2029 Century Park E Suite 3910 Los Angeles CA 90067

SPAULDER, JOAN ROISTACHER, publishing executive; b. N.Y.C., Jan. 5, 1939; d. Charles and Ina (Zirinsky) Roistacher; B.A., Brandeis U., 1959; M.S., Queens Coll., 1963; children—Debra Val, Mara Jill. Tchr., N.Y.C., Westfield, N.J., Scotch Plains, N.J., 1959-69; account exec. Consumer Mktg. Research Services, Inc., Hackensack, N.J., 1969-70; dir. research and edn. Allen Levis Orgn., Inc., Northfield, Ill., 1971-73; dir. mktg. research Food Fair, Inc., Phila., 1974-78; dir. mktg. W. B. Saunders div. CBS, Phila., 1978—. Pres., Women's Am. ORT, Westfield, N.J., 1968; v.p. PTA, Scotch Plains, N.J., 1969; mem. Brandeis U. Alumni Admissions Council, 1975—; mem. mktg. com. Balch Inst., 1984-86; bd. dirs. Rittenhouse Plaza, 1984-85. Mem. Forum Exec. Women (dir. 1978-80, chairperson membership 1982-85), Am. Mktg. Assn. (dir. 1977-79), Assn. Am. Pubs. (mktg. com. 1981—, chmn. mktg. com. 1986—), Direct Mktg. Assn., Phila. Direct Mktg. Club (chair Berry Awards 1986), Phila. Postal Customers Council (chmn. 1981-82), Brandeis U. Alumni Assn. (steering com. Greater Phila. chpt. 1980-85). Home: Rittenhouse Plaza Philadelphia PA 19103 Office: CBS/WB Saunders Co W Washington Sq Philadelphia PA 19105

SPEAKMAN, MARCIA LOUISE, educator; b. Columbus, Ohio, Feb. 20, 1943; d. Terence R.H. and Martha Elizabeth (Elson) Heffernan; B.S. in Edn., Ohio State U., 1965, M.A., 1968, postgrad.; m. Norman L. Speakman, Apr. 3, 1965. Tchr., Ross County (Ohio) Schs., 1965-67, Columbus Public Schs., 1967-71, Bexley Public Schs., 1971-72; tchr. Florence Crittenton Home, Adult High Sch. (Columbus Public Schs.), 1972—. Mem. Columbus Symphony Orch. Women's Assn., mem. staccato unit, mem. German village unit; mem. nat. bd. Hospitalized Vets. Writing Project. Mem. Women in Communications, Ohio Council Tchrs. English Lang. Arts, NEA, Central Ohio Tchrs. Assn., Columbus Edn. Assn., English Speaking Union, AAUW (v.p. membership), Delta Kappa Gamma (pres.). Episcopalian. Home: 733 College Ave Columbus OH 43209 Office: 1229 Sunbury Rd Columbus OH 43219

SPEAKS, DENISE DIANE, lawyer; b. Pitts., Nov. 21, 1953; d. Herbert Moody and Juanita (Waller) Speaks, B.A., Lincoln U., 1974; J.D., U. Pitts., 1978. Bar: Pa. 1978, Calif. 1980. Tchr. French, Pitts. Pub. Schs., 1975-78; tax acct. atty. Mellon Bank, Pitts., 1978-79; contract adminstr. atty. Bendix Corp., Slymar, Calif. 1979-82; staff counsel Northrop Corp., Hawthorne, Calif., 1982—; chief counsel, ptnr. Celebrity Profl. Services, Hollywood, Calif., 1983—. Vol. Los Angeles Urban League, Los Angeles, 1979—, Los Angeles NAACP, 1979—, Youth Motivation Task Force, 1979—, Black Exec. Exchange Program, N.Y., 1979—. Named Pitts. Model of Yr., 1977. Mem. Pa. Bar Assn., Calif. Bar Assn., Black Entertainment Lawyers Assn., Women Entertainment Lawyers Assn., Black Women Lawyers So. Calif., Beverly Hills Bar Assn., Century City Bar Assn., Alpha Kappa Alpha. Home: 8400 De Longpre Ave West Hollywood CA 90069 Office: Northrop Corp One Northrop Ave Hawthorne CA 90520

SPEAR, ANNE CHANDLER, county official; b. Gainesville, Ga., Mar. 22, 1942; d. Robert Henry and Virginia Lou (Stevens) Chandler; m. Jack P. Spear, June 2, 1962; children—Robert Scott, Holly Susan. Student U. Ga., 1960-63.

Service rep. So. Bell Telephone Co., Gainesville, 1960-68; tag supr. tax office Hall County, Gainesville, 1976-79, chief registrar, chmn. bd. elections, 1979—. Mem. Ga. Assn. Registrars, Fleur-de-Lis Garden Club, Beta Sigma Phi (pres. 1968). Presbyterian. Home: 228 Mountain View Dr Gainesville GA 30501 Office: Hall County Bd Registrars/Elections PO Box 1435 300 Green St Gainesville GA 30503

SPEAR, MARILYN WYMAN, editorial writer; b. Winn, Maine, Apr. 22, 1930; d. Charles Leslie and Viora Mae (Grass) Wyman; m. Matthew Spear, Apr. 1, 1955 (div. 1960). Student U. Maine, 1947-50, Clark U., 1960-63. Reporter Bangor Daily News (Maine), 1950-52; editor Back Bay Ledger, Boston, 1952-55; editor, reporter WCSH-TV, Portland, Maine, 1955-58; editor Wymann-Gordon Co., Worcester, Mass., 1960-63; reporter, editor Worcester Telegram, 1963-75, editorial writer, 1975—. Author: Worcester's Three Deckers, 1976. Bd. dirs. Worcester Foothills Theatre, 1981-84, Mass. Dance Ensemble, 1981-83; pres. Worcester Area Mental Health Assn., 1980-84; bd. dirs. Age Ctr. of Worcester, 1984—. Fellow Religious Pub. Relations Council. Episcopalian. Home: 12 Diana St Worcester MA 01605 Office: Worcester Telegram and Gazette 20 Franklin St Worcester MA 01613

SPEARMAN, PATSY CORDLE, real estate broker; b. Richmond, Va., Aug. 23, 1934; d. Lee Pierce and Kathleen Jeanette (Munn) Cordle; A.A., Coll. William and Mary, Richmond, 1952; student U. Ga., 1953-54; grad. Realtors Inst., 1979; cert. residential specialist; m. David Hagood Spearman, Dec. 18, 1954; children—Kathleen Elizabeth, David Hagood. Copywriter, Cabell Eanes Advt. Agy., Richmond, 1952; clk. athletic dept. U. Ga., Athens, 1954-55; real estate saleswoman Merrill Lynch Realty (formerly C. Dan Joyner & Co., Inc.), Greenville, S.C., 1978—. Recipient numerous awards for obtaining eye bank donors Lions Club and S.C. Eye Bank. Mem. Nat. Assn. Realtors, Real Estate Securities and Syndication Inst., S.C. Assn. Realtors, Greenville Bd. Realtors (past chair membership com.), Pickens County Bd. Realtors, Women's Council of Realtors, Million Dollar Club (charter), S.C. Vet. Aux. (treas.). Presbyterian. Club: Better Homes (Easley). Home: 505 Asbury Circle Easley SC 29640 Office: PO Box 327 Easley SC 29641

SPEARS, BRENDA SUSAN, lawyer; b. N.Y.C., Sept. 6, 1950; d. Joseph and Mattie B. (Thomas) Spears. B.A., CCNY, 1971; M.A., Rutgers U., 1972; J.D., U. Pa., 1975. Bar: N.Y. 1976. Law clk. U.S. Dist. Ct., Phila., 1975-77; assoc. Simpson, Thacher & Bartlett, N.Y.C., 1977-81; gen. counsel, 1st dep. N.Y. State Div. Housing, N.Y.C., 1981-83; sect. chief Litigation Bur., N.Y. State Atty. Gen., N.Y.C., 1983-84, dep. bur. chief Real Estate Fin. Bur., 1984—. Bd. dirs. Harlem YMCA, 1983—. Mem. Black Women Attys. Assn. (bd. dirs. 1979-80), Assn. Bar City N.Y., N.Y. State Bar Assn., ABA, Nat. Bar Assn. Democrat. Presbyterian. Office: State Atty Gen 2 World Trade Ctr 48th Floor New York NY

SPEARS, JANET E., educator; b. Chambersburg, Ill., Sept. 5, 1933; d. Enoch E. and Marguerite Irene (Riley) Downey; A.A., Black Hawk Coll., 1978; B.S. (Chris Hoerr scholar), Bradley U., 1980; postgrad. St. Ambrose Coll., 1981-84; m. Keith A. Spears, July 6, 1952; children—Bruce, Roger, Darci, Paul. Secretarial positions Kewanee Machinery Conveyor (Ill.), 1951-52, William E. Trinke, atty., Lake Geneva, Wis., 1952-53, Walworth Co., Kewanee, 1968-72; adminstrv. asst. Kewanee Pub. Hosp., 1972-75; asst. personnel dir. Davenport (Iowa) Osteo. Hosp., 1980-81; bus. mgr. Franciscan Med. Center, Rock Island, Ill., 1981; bus. prof. Black Hawk Coll., Kewanee, 1981—. Mem. Am. Mgmt. Assn., Nat. Assn. Female Execs., AAUW, Kewanee Pub. Hosp. Assn., Kewanee Art League, Phi Chi Theta. Republican. Methodist (ch. liturgist and Sunday sch. tchr., mem. adminstrv. council). Clubs: Annawan Jr. Women's (pres. 1964-65), United Fairview Women. Home: Rural Route 1 Sheffield IL 61361 Office: Black Hawk Coll East Campus PO Box 489 Kewanee IL 61443

SPEARS, JOAN, school psychologist; b. Bklyn., Dec. 9, 1938; d. Preston Vincent and Bertha (Blagrove) Spears; children—Eric Trotman, David Gaton. B.A., Bklyn. Coll.-CUNY, 1971, M.S. in Sch. Psychology, 1976; postgrad. NYU. Sch. psychologist N.Y.C. Bd. Edn., Bklyn., 1971-74; spl. edn. tchr. N.Y.C. Bd. Spl. Edn., Bklyn., 1974-81; elem. tchr. Sch.-Based Support Team, Bklyn., 1981—. Mem. Am. Psychol. Assn. (assoc.), Assn. Black Psychologists, N.Y. Assn. Sch. Psychologists, Nat. Assn. Sch. Psychologists, Internat. Sch. Psychologist Assn., United Fed. Tchrs. Democrat. Roman Catholic. Avocations; minority issues, child abuse, Apartheid, traveling. Home: 2675 W 36th St Brooklyn NY 11224 Office: PO Box 23 Brooklyn NY 11223

SPECHT, LISA, lawyer; b. Los Angeles, Dec. 5, 1945; d. Marvin Basso and Peggy (Hopkins) Shapiro; m. Ronald J. Rogers, Oct. 17, 1982. J.D., U. Laverne Los Angeles, 1976. Bar: Calif. 1976. Assoc., Manatt, Phelps, Rothenberg, Tunney & Phillips, Los Angeles, 1976—, ptnr. 1982—; legal reporter KABC-TV, Los Angeles, 1979—. Co-chmn. Women's Polit. Com. Los Angeles, 1982—; co-chmn. Dance Gallery Guild, 1983—. Mem. Los Angeles County Bar Assn., Calif. Bar Assn., Calif. Women Lawyers Assn., Los Angeles Women's Lawyers Assn. Democrat. Office: Manatt Phelps Rothenberg & Tunney 11355 W Olympic Blvd Los Angeles CA 90064

SPECTOR, JOAN, public relations executive; b. Mt. Vernon, N.Y., Oct. 19, 1929; d. Ben Harris and Helen Esther (Kest) Freedenberg; m. Ralph Spector, June 16, 1957; 1 dau., Andrea Jean Spector Anker. Student, Columbia U., Syracuse U., Tobe Coburn Sch. Fashion. Pres. Spector/Anker Assocs., Coral Gables, Fla., 1957—. Trustee North Miami Mus., 1983—. Mem. Women in Communication, Pub. Relations Soc. South Fla. Democrat. Jewish. Clubs: Jockey, Cricket, Grove Isle. Office: Spector/Anker Assocs Inc 4070 Laguna St Coral Gables FL 33146

SPECTOR, JOHANNA LICHTENBERG, musical educator; b. Libau, Latvia; d. Jacob C. and Anna (Meyer) Lichtenberg; came to U.S., 1947, naturalized, 1954; D.H.S., Hebrew Union Coll., 1950; M.A., Columbia U., 1960; m. Robert Spector, Nov. 20, 1939 (dec. 1941). Research fellow Hebrew U., Jerusalem, 1951-53; faculty Jewish Theol. Sem. Am., N.Y.C., 1954—, dir., founder dept. ethnomusicology, 1962—, assoc. prof. musicology, 1966-70, Sem. prof., 1970-85, prof. emeritus, 1985—. Fellow Am. Anthrop. Assn.; mem. Am. Musicol. Soc., Internat. Folk Music Council, World Union Jewish Studies, Asian (pres. 1973-78), African mus. socs., Soc. Ethnomusicology (sec.-treas. N.Y. chpt. 1960-64), Soc. Preservation Samaritan Culture (founder). Author: Ghetto und Kzlieder, 1947; Samaritan Chant, 1965; Musical Tradition and Innovation in Central Asia, 1966; Bridal Songs from Sana Yemen, 1960; producer documentary films: The Samaritans, 1971; Middle Eastern Music, 1973; About the Jews of India; Cochin (Cine Golden Eagle award 1979), 1976; The Shanwar Telis of India (Cine Golden Eagle award 1979), 1978; About the Jews of Yemen: A Vanishing Culture, 1985 (Cine Golden Eagle award 1986, Am. Film Festival Blue ribbon 1986). Contbr. articles to profl. jours.; editorial bd. Asian Music. Home: 400 W 119th St New York NY 10027 Office: 3080 Broadway at 122d St New York NY 10027

SPEICHER, JACQUELYN LOU, educator; b. Holdrege, Nebr., May 18, 1946; d. Jack Louis and Norma Fern (Corder) McKenzie; m. David Ross Speicher, Oct. 7, 1972; children—Jill Marie, Tracey Ann, Stepanie Jane. B.S., U. Nebr., 1969. Tchr. pub. schs., Holdrege, 1969-70; urban services worker United Meth. Ch. Bd. Global Ministries, N.Y.C., 1970-74; tchr. John F. Kennedy Sch., Berlin, 1974-77; trainer Inst. Cultural Affairs Internat., Chgo., 1977-79; instr. Central YMCA Community Coll., Chgo., 1979-80; dir., program set-up Inst. Cultural Affairs, Indpls., 1980-81; program dir. Ind. U.-Purdue U./Tng., Inc., Indpls., 1981-83; program dir. Ind. Vocat.-Tech. Coll./Tng. Inc., Indpls., 1983—. Chmn. Women's programs com. YWCA, Indpls., 1985-86, bd. dirs., 1984-86; trustee, treas. Mobile Homes Trust, 1984-86. Mem. Am. Soc. Personnel Adminstrs., Am. Soc. Tng. and Devel., Am. Vocat. Assn., Ind. Vocat. Assn., Community Service Council, Ind. Employment and Tng. Assn. (sec. 1985-86), Profl. Secs. Internat. (exec. adv. bd. 500 chpt. 1985-86), Network of Women in Bus. Republican. Methodist. Office: Training Inc 47 S Pennsylvania St Suite 801 Indianapolis IN 46204

SPEIR, BETTY SMITH, educational counselor; b. Bethel, N.C., Mar. 3, 1928; d. William Jasper and Carolyn (Pollock) Smith; A.B., Duke U., 1949; M.A., East Carolina U., 1963; m. David Ordway Speir, June 10, 1950; children—Carolyn G. Speir Brown, Christine St. Clair Speir Price. Tchr. English, Farmville (N.C.) High Sch., 1949-50, Bain High Sch., Charlotte, N.C., 1950-51, Bethel High Sch., 1961-70; cotton buyer Bethel Mfg. Co. (N.C.), 1958-60; guidance counselor North Pitt High Sch., Bethel, 1970—. Sec., N.C. Commn. on Edn. and Employment of Women, 1970-74; mem. N.C. State Bd. Edn., 1982—, N.C. Gov.'s Crime Commn., 1977-82, N.C. Commn. on Length of Sentencing, 1981-82; mem. Blue Ribbon Commn. to Study Needs of Tng. Schs.; mem. N.C. Commn. Edn. for Econ. Growth; vice chmn. N.C. Democratic Com., 1978-80, 81-84, chmn., 1980; mem. Dem. Nat. Com., 1978—; del. Dem. Nat. Conv., 1980, 84, mem. site selection com., 1984; mem. N.C. State Bd. Edn., 1982—. Named one of Winning Dem. Women of Decade, Nat. Fedn. Dem. Women, 1980. Mem. NEA, N.C. Assn. Educators, Delta Kappa Gamma. Methodist. Home: PO Box 340 Bethel NC 27812 Office: Route 1 Box 313 Bethel NC 27812

SPEIRS, CAROL LUCILLE, nurse, naval officer; b. Plainfield, N.J., Apr. 20, 1942; d. Alexander Walker and Catherine Lucille (McGovern) S.; diploma St. Peters Med. Center Sch. Nursing, New Brunswick, N.J., 1963; student Seton Hall U., 1966-72; B.A., San Diego State U., 1976; M.A., Webster Coll., 1980. Staff nurse Muhlenberg Hosp., Plainfield, N.J., 1963-64, Burdette Tomlin Meml. Hosp., Cape May Court House, N.J., 1964, 65, Georgetown U. Hosp., Washington, 1964-65; pvt. duty nurse, North Plainfield, N.J., 1965-66; staff nurse, charge nurse Raritan Valley Hosp., Greenbrook, N.J., 1966-72; commd. lt. (j.g.) U.S. Navy, 1973, advanced through grades to comdr., 1985; charge nurse Naval Regional Med. Center, San Diego, 1973-76, Iwakuni, Japan, 1977-78, Long Beach, Calif., 1978-83, Naval Hosp.; charge nurse, Bremerton, Wash., 1983-86, patient care coordinator, 1986. Mem. Founders Ball Com., City of Cypress (Calif.), 1981; bd. dirs. Kitsap County Emergency Med. Service Council. Recipient Outstanding Cath. Young Adult award Diocese of Trenton, 1970. Mem. Nat. League Nursing, Emergency Dept. Nurses Assn., Nat. Assn. Female Execs., Crocker Art Mus. Assn. Republican. Roman Catholic. Home: 3737 NW Highland Ct Silverdale WA 98383 Office: Naval Hospital Boone Rd Bremerton WA 98312-1898

SPELLMAN, MARGARET MARY, accountant; b. Chgo., Nov. 4, 1954; d. John Robert and Margaret Mary (Linnehan) S. B.S., John Carroll U., 1975. C.P.A., Tex. Nat. bank examiner Comptroller of the Currency, Dallas, 1975-84; mgr. Arthur Andersen & Co., 1984—; dir. OPEN, Inc. Vol., Little Sisters of the Poor, Chgo., 1973—; trustee Leukemia Soc. Mem. Am. Inst. C.P.A.s, Dallas C. of C. Republican. Roman Catholic (mem. budget com. 1983—). Office: Arthur Andersen & Co 1201 Elm St Suite 2200 Dallas TX 75270

SPELMAN, GRACE SUSAN, banker; b. N.Y.C., Oct. 14, 1948; d. Marco A. and Gloria (Alvino) Vale. B.S., Pa. State U., 1970; M.A., New Sch. for Social Research, 1974; cert. in mgmt. Adelphi U., 1979, M.B.A., 1980. Bus. office rep. N.Y. Telephone Co., Rockville Centre, 1971-74; social worker Children's Aid Soc., N.Y.C., 1974-75; EEO Officer Edwin Gould Services, N.Y.C., 1976-79; v.p. human resources Bankers Trust Co., N.Y.C., 1979—; instr. mgmt. Adelphi U. Grad. Sch. Bus. Adminstrn., 1981—; notary pub. State of N.Y., 1978—. Mem. Human Resource Planning Soc., Am. Compensation Assn., Wall Street Compensation and Benefits Assn., N.Y. Compensation Assn., Assn. M.B.A. Execs., Adelphi U. Businesswomen's Alumni Assn. (pres. 1980-82). Office: 16 Wall St New York NY 10015

SPENCE, JANET BLAKE CONLEY (MRS. ALEXANDER PYOTT SPENCE), civic worker; b. Upper Montclair, N.J., Aug. 17, 1915; d. Walter Abbott and Ethel Maud (Blake) Conley; student Vassar Coll., 1933-35; cert. Katharine Gibbs Sch., 1936; m. Alexander Pyott Spence, June 10, 1939; children—Janet Spence Kerr, Robert Moray, Richard Taylor. Active Jr. League, Neighborhood House, ARC, 1950-65, Girl Scouts U.S.A., 1950-60, various community drives; chmn. Darien (Conn.) Assembly, 1955-56; sec., chmn. Wilton Jr. Assembly, 1961-63; subscription chmn. Candlelight Concerts Wilton, Conn., 1963-65; rec. sec. Public Health Nursing Assn. Wilton Bd., 1964-67; corr., rec. sec. Royle Sch. Bd., Darien, 1952-55; mem. Washington Valley Community Assn., 1973—; vol. N.J. Symphony Orch., 1974—, corr. sec., 1982-85; pres. Morris county br. N.J. Symphony League, 1985-87, mem. state council, 1985—; treas. Morris County League, 1978-83, now corr. sec. Mem. Vassar (council rep. from Class of '37 1973-77, fund raiser class '37 reunion), Dobbs alumnae assns., Washington Valley Home Econs. Club (corr. sec. 1977-82, pres. 1982-84, v.p. 1984-86), Morris County Art Assn., Washington Valley Community Assn., Morris Mus. Arts and Scis. Congregationalist. Home: Washington Valley Rd Morristown NJ 07960 and 8 Evergreen Ave Kennebunk ME 04043

SPENCE, MARY OTTO, human resources executive; b. Kansas City, Mo., Mar. 9, 1948; d. Anthony John and Gertrude Louise (Allcorn) Otto; m. Hugh Curran Spence, Sept. 4, 1982. B.M., U. Mo.-Kansas City, 1971; M.A., Central Mich. U., 1981; postgrad. Nova U., Ft. Lauderdale, Fla. Personnel generalist U.S. Postal Service, Kansas City, Kans., 1973-76; labor relations specialist GSA, Kansas City, Mo., 1976-79; labor relations rep. Kansas City Power & Light Co., 1980-81; v.p. human resources Libby Corp. (formerly Libby Welding Co.), Kansas City, 1981—; dir. Mgmt. Inst., Pioneer Community Coll., Kansas City, Mo., 1983—. Mem. Am. Soc. Personnel Adminstrs., Indsl. Relations Research Assn. (bd. dirs. 1986—), Am. Compensation Assn. Club. Twin Pines Country (house com. 1983—) (Harrisonville, Mo.). Office: Libby Corp 5800 Stilwell St Kansas City MO 64120-4200

SPENCE, SUSAN CHRISTINE, data sciences writer; b. Upland, Pa., Dec. 15, 1960; d. Richard William and Sheila Mary (Carrington-Cooke)S. Student Mt. Holyoke Coll., 1978-80; cert. Computer Learning Ctr., 1983. Computer operator Digital Equipment Corp., Cherry Hill, N.J., 1983-84; asst. editor, analyst div. Ziff-Davis, Data Decisions, Cherry Hill, 1984-85; tech. writer Momentum Techs. Systems, Cherry Hill, 1985—. Author poetry: Winter Images, 1978 (Nat. Poetry Press Assn. award). Mem. Women's Nat. Book Assn., Popular Culture Assn. (panelist 1985-87), Nat. Assn. Female Execs. Libertarian. Episcopalian. Club: LIB/LIB (newsletter editor 1985) (Cherry Hill). Avocations: painting; music. Home: Kingsrow Apts 606 Lindenwold NJ 08021 Office: Momentum Techs Systems Bldg 43 2 Keystone Ave Cherry Hill NJ 08003

SPENCER, ANNIE LAURIE, realtor, genealogist; b. Spencer, La., May 10, 1914; d. James V. and Annie T. (Nabors) S.; m. William Wallace Dickinson, 1948 (dec. 1960). B.A., La. State U., 1942; student Ark. state U., Sophie Newcomb Coll. Realtor, Ark. Pres., El Dorado Real Estate Co., Inc., Ark., 1968—. Author-compilter: Marriages of Union County, 1829-1870 (Nat. award Colonial Dames 17th Century), 1962; contbr. to encys., real estate jours. Bd. dirs., sec. so. Ark. Hist. Found., 1975—; bd. dirs. Southwest Ark. Regional Archives, 1981-83; bd. dirs., sec. El Dorado council Girl Scouts U.S.A., 1955-60. Mem. Ark. Assn. Realtors (v.p. 1954, 58), Nat. Assn. Realtors (edn. com. 1952), El Dorado Bd. Realtors (sec. 1950, v.p. and pres. 1952-56), DAR (dist. dir. 1950-54), Ark. Hist. Soc. (dir. 1950-60), Ark. Geneal. Soc. (charter; past state pres.), Ark. Pioneer Assn. (past state pres.), Colonial Dames 17th Century (state pres. 1985), DAR (nat. com.). Anglican. Avocations: history, writing; painting. Office: El Dorado Real Estate 106 N Washington St El Dorado AR 71730

SPENCER, BARBARA Z., data services company executive; b. Ponce de Leon, Fla., July 21, 1939; d. J.P. and Alvesta (Simmons) Paul; student Santa Monica City Coll., 1968-70, UCLA, 1961-63; m. Walter F. Spencer, Oct. 5, 1981; children—Matthew Zuiderhof, Noah Zuiderhof, Heather Zuiderhof. Vice pres. Mgmt. Scis. Corp., Santa Monica, Calif., 1967-69; v.p. Profl. Computer Services, Anaheim, Calif., 1970-73; cons. data services, Springfield, Va., 1974; pres. Postal Data Corp., LaPlata, Md., 1976-80; pres. Mailing Data Services East, Inc., Waldorf, Md., 1980-82; pres. Pub. Data Corp., 1982—. Pres., Port Tobacco PTA, 1978; chmn. Sch. Adv. Council, 1978-79; chmn. Parent Adv. Council, 1979-80; chmn. membership Charles County LWV, 1980. Mem. Mail Advt. Services Assn. (pres. Chesapeake chpt. 1979-80), Direct Mail Mktg. Assn., Fullfillment Mgmt. Assn., Zonta Internat. (pres. chpt. 1985—). Office: Rt 5 Box 1438 Waldorf Center Bldg Waldorf MD 20601

SPENCER, CONSTANCE JANE, teacher, consultant; b. Norfolk, Va., May 23, 1917; d. Thomas Sidney and Constance Lydia (Gordon) Richter; m. Harlie S. Spencer, Jr., June 2, 1937; children—Constance Spencer Mathis, Arline Spencer Johnson, Harlie S. III, Thomas, Janice Spencer Baxter. B.S., D.C. Tchrs. Coll., 1956; M.A., NYU, 1969. Cert. tchr., Washington. Tchr. pub. schs., Washington, 1956—, tchr. trainer, 1969-75, asst. dir. reading, 1975-77, tchr., 1977—; cons. D.C. Heath Co., N.Y.C., 1974-75. Editor: Reading Skills, 1970; Advanced Reading Skills, 1971. Editor, writer curriculum guide, 1972. Mem. NEA, Research Club, Internat. Reading Assn., Coll. Reading Assn. Home: 4907 New Hampshire Ave NW Washington DC 20011 Office: DC Pub Schs 415 12th St NW Washington DC 20004

SPENCER, DIANNE LESLIE, human resources consultant; b. Detroit; d. C. Frazier and Margaret Lee (Hanvey) S. B.S., Ambassador Coll., 1978. Cert. personnel mgmt. UCLA, 1983. Fin. analyst trainee, employment rep. Capital Research & Mgmt. Co., Los Angeles, 1979-84; personnel officer Sumitomo Bank, Los Angeles, 1984-86; dir. personnel Martin, Algaze Accountancy Corp., Santa Monica, Calif., 1986—. Crisis hotline counselor Rape Hotline, YWCA, Pasadena, 1980-83. Recipient Speaker of Yr. award U. So. Calif., 1985. Mem. Personnel and Indsl. Relations Assn., Western Coll. Placement Assn., Acctg. Adminstrs. Assn., Los Angels Jr. C. of C. (project chmn. 1982). Avocations: snow skiing; tennis; reading. Office: Martin Algaze Accountancy Corp 2850 Ocena Park Blvd Santa Monica CA 90405

SPENCER, ELIZABETH, author; b. Carrollton, Miss.; d. James Luther and Mary James (McCain) S.; m. John Arthur Blackwood Rusher, Sept. 29, 1956. B.A., Belhaven Coll., 1942; M.A., Vanderbilt U., 1943; Litt. D. (hon.), Southwestern U. at Memphis, 1968. Writer-in-residence U. N.C., 1969, Hollins Coll., 1973, Concordia U., 1977-78. Recipient Women's Democratic Com. award, 1949; recognition award Nat. Inst. Arts and Letters, 1952; Guggenheim Found. fellow, 1953; Richard and Hinda Rosenthal Found. award Am. Acad. Arts and Letters, 1957; Kenyon Rev. fellow in fiction, 1957; 1st. McGraw Hill Fiction award, 1960; Bryn Mawr Coll. Donnelly fellow, 1962; Henry Bellamann award for creative writing, 1968; Award of Merit, Am. Acad.-Arts & Letters, 1983. Author: Fire in the Morning, 1948; This Crooked Way, 1952; The Voice at the Back Door, 1956; The Light in the Piazza, 1960; Knights and Dragons, 1965; No Place for an Angel, 1967; Ship Island and other Stories 1968; The Snare, 1972; The Stories of Elizabeth Spencer, 1981; Marilee, 1981; The Salt Line, 1984. Contbr. short stories to mags. and lit. collections. Mem. Am. Inst. Arts and Letters. Address: 250 S Estes Dr 50 Brookwood Chapel Hill NC 27514

SPENCER, FRANCES LOUISE, nurse anthropologist, nurse educator; b. Jamaica, W.I., Mar. 3, 1930; naturalized, 1953; d. Alexander Agustus and Elizabeth Q. (Warmington) Spencer. R.N., Bedford Gen. Hosp., South Wing, Eng., 1963; B.S., Columbia U., 1968, M.Ed., 1972, D.P.H., 1983; M.A., New Sch. for Social Research, 1977. Lab. technician dept. hosps., N.Y.C., 1955-60; staff nurse Mt. Sinai Med. Ctr., N.Y.C., 1963-64, acting head nurse, 1963-64, research asst. and pub. health nurse, 1968-70, research specialist and pub. health nurse coordinator, 1970-72; adminstr. dept. mental hygiene, State of N.Y., 1972-73; instr. Borough of Manhattan Community Coll., CUNY, 1973-76, asst. prof. 1976-79; asst. prof. nursing Jersey City State Coll, 1979—; mem. City-wide Adv. Council on Sch. Health, N.Y.C. Bd. Edn., 1973—; mem. task force Borough Pres. of Manhattan, N.Y.C., 1977—; mem. Mid-Manhattan Neighborhood Health Ctr., 1974-76; founder, chairperson Allied Disciplines for Total Health Care, Inc., 1973—; mem. internat. student program Planned Parenthood of N.Y.C., Inc., 1976—; condr. workshops, seminars. Contbr. articles to nursing jours., papers to profl. meetings; mem. adv. bd. Am. Jour. Nursing, 1973-76. Pub. Health Assn. scholar, 1964-67; NIH scholar, 1972; Dept. Pub. Health of N.Y.C./Washington scholar, 1977. Mem. Am. Nurses Assn., Nat. League for Nursing, Am. Pub. Health Assn., Am. Med. Anthropology Assn., AAAS, Phi Delta Kappa, Sigma Theta Tau. Democrat. Office: Jersey City State Coll 2039 Kennedy Blvd Jersey City NJ 07305

SPENCER, GERALDINE BRAILO, newspaper editor, journalist; b. Panama City, Panama, Nov. 8, 1943; came to U.S., 1948; d. Chester Vernon and Virginia (Dell) Sullins; m. David George Brailo, June 6, 1964 (div. June 1980); children—Christopher, Stephen; m. 2d. Riley John Spencer, Jr., Sept. 16, 1980. A.A., Los Angeles Pierce Coll., 1979. Adminstrv. asst. City of Los Angeles, 1963-67; supr. Dept. Water and Power, Los Angeles, 1967-71; reporter, bus. editor Simi Valley Enterprise (Calif.), 1979; editor-in-chief The Tolucan newspaper, Toluca Lake, Calif., 1979-81; free-lance journalist, Moorpark, Calif., 1981-83; editor-in-chief The Mirror, Simi Valley, Calif., 1983; stringer Los Angeles Times, 1984—; radio broadcaster KWNK, Simi Valley, 1986—. Editor: 1982-83 Ventura County Grand Jury Report, 1983; contbg. writer: Excellence in College Journalism, 1983. Pub. relations vol. St. Jude Children's Research Hosp., Los Angeles, 1975-78; mem. Ventura County Grand Jury, Ventura, Calif., 1982-83; commr. Area Housing Authority, Ventura, 1983-86; v.p., founding mem. Moorpark Coll. (Calif.), 1983—; trustee Los Robles Regional Med. Ctr., Thousand Oaks, Calif., 1985—. Recipient 1st place for news Journalism Assn. Community Colls., 1979; 1st place for feature San Fernando Valley Press Club, 1983, 84; Mem. Nat. Writers Club, Women in Communications, Internat. Platform Assn. Republican. Roman Catholic. Club: Valley Press (treas. 1979-82). Home: 790 Poindexter Ave Moorpark CA 93021

SPENCER, JUDITH KAY, aircraft manufacturing company administrator; b. Spokane, July 30, 1946; d. Kenneth Clair and Dolene Marianna (Hugill) S. A.A., Concordia Coll., Portland, Oreg., 1966; B.A., Concordia Coll., St. Paul, 1968; postgrad. So. Ill. U.-Edwardsville, 1971; M.A., U. Mo.-St. Louis, 1975. Tchr., Concordia Luth. Sch., Tacoma, 1968-70, Salem Luth. Sch., Florissant, Mo., 1970-73, Grace Luth. Ch., St. Louis, 1973-77; asst. to head teller Northwestern Savs. & Loan, St. Louis, 1977-79; dir. gifted program Meramec Valley Schs., Pacific, Mo., 1979-81; broker sales Century 21, Florissant, 1980—; adminstr. McDonnell Douglas Co., St. Louis, 1982—. Author: Judy's July Jaunt, 1976; September Safari, 1983. Youth dir. Immanuel Luth. Chapel, St. Louis, 1971-76, supt. Sunday sch., 1978-82, treas., 1981-82. Aid Assn. for Lutherans scholar, 1965-67; named Engr. of Week, McAir. Mem. U. Mo. St. Louis Alumni Assn. (bd. dirs. 1980-84), U. Mo. Alumni Alliance, Bach Soc. Chorus, Gifted Assn. Mo., North County Real Estate Salesmen, Assn. Midwest Disadvantaged Youth. Republican. Lutheran. Club: Golf (St. Louis). Office: McDonnell Aircraft Co PO Box 516 St Louis MO 63166

SPENCER, MARY EILEEN, biochemist, educator; b. Regina, Sask., Can., Oct. 4, 1923; d. John J. and Etta Christina (Hamren) Stapleton; m. Henry Anderson Spencer, July 3, 1946; 1 dau., Susan Mary. A.A., Regina Coll., 1942; B.A. with high honors in Chemistry, U. Sask., 1945; M.A. in Chemistry, Bryn Mawr Coll., 1946; Ph.D. in Agrl. Chemistry, U. Calif.-Berkeley, 1951. Chemist, Ayerst, McKenna and Harrison Ltd., Montreal, Que., Can., summer 1945, full time, 1946-47, Nat. Canners Assn., San Francisco, 1948; teaching fellow U. Calif.-Berkeley, 1949, instr. food chemistry, 1951; faculty U. Alta., Edmonton, Can., 1953—, instr., asst. prof., assoc. prof., acting head biochem. dept., 1960-61, plant sci. dept., 1962, prof. plant sci., 1964—, McCalla research prof., 1983-84, univ. prof., 1984—; sec.-treas. Spencer-Lemaire Industries Ltd.; mem. NRC Can., 1970, 70-73, 73-76, Task Force on Post-Secondary Edn., Alta. Govt. Commn. on Ednl. Planning, 1970-72; chmn. Nat. Adv. Com. on Biology, Nat. Research Council; adv. bd. Prairie Regional Lab.; bd. govs. U. Alta., 1976-79; chmn. ad hoc vis. com. in forestry research NRC, 1975-76; mem. Agr. Can. Cons. Com. IBT Pesticides, 1981-82; bd. dirs. Natural Scis. and Engring. Research Council Can., 1986—. Recipient Queen Elizabeth II Silver Jubilee medal. Fellow Chem. Inst. Can., Royal Soc. Can.; Mem. Can. Soc. Plant Physiologists (pres. 1971-72), Japanese Soc. Plant Physiology, Plant Growth Regulator Soc. Am., Am. Soc. Plant Physiologists, Can. Assn. Univ. Tchrs., Japanese Soc. Plant Physiologists, AAAS. Office: Univ Alberta Dept Plant Sci Faculty Agr and Forestry Edmonton AB T6G 2E3 Canada

SPENCER, MARY ELLEN, marketing research executive; b. Glen Ridge, N.J., June 18, 1957; d. Frederick Currier and Constance (Ryan) Spencer. B.S., Montclair State Coll., 1979; M.S., Cornell U., 1981. Mktg.-research asst. Child Research Services, N.Y.C., 1978-81; mktg. research supr. M & M/Mars, Hackettstown, N.J., 1982-84; mktg. research group assoc. Gen. Foods, White Plains, N.Y., 1984—. Author: (with Loretta Wiscomb) Microwave Research Bibliography, 1984. Mem. Am. Dietetic Assn. (registered dietitian), Am. Mktg. Assn., Inst. Food Technologists, Phi Kappa Phi, Omicron Nu. Club: High Life Ski (Mountain Lakes, N.J.). Avocations: skiing; racquetball; gourmet cooking. Home: 31 Burlington Rd Clifton NJ 07012 Office: Gen Foods 250 North St White Plains NY 10625

SPENCER, MARY MILLER, civic worker, club woman; b. Comanche, Tex., May 25, 1924; d. Aaron Gaynor and Alma (Grissom) Miller; B.S., North Tex. State U., 1943. 1 dau., Mara Lynn. Cafeteria dir. Mercedes (Tex.) public schs.; 1943-46; home economist coordinator All-Orange Dessert Contest, Fla. Citrus Commn., Lakeland, 1959-62, 64. Tchr. purchasing sch. lunch dept. Fla. Dept. Edn., 1960. Clothing judge Polk County (Fla.) Youth Fair, 1951-68, Polk County Federated Women's Clubs, 1964-66; pres. Dixieland Elem. Sch. PTA, 1955-57, Polk County Council PTAs, 1958-60, dist. 7. Fla. Congress Parents and Tchrs., 1961-63; chmn. public edn. com. Polk County unit Am. Cancer Soc., 1959-60, bd. dirs., 1962-70; charter mem., bd. dirs. Lakeland YMCA, 1962-72; sec. Greater Lakeland Community Nursing Council, 1965-72; trustee, vice chmn. Polk County Eye Clinic, Inc., 1962-64, pres., 1964-82; public relations chmn. Fla. Congress Parents and Tchrs., 1962-66; bd. dirs. Polk County Scholarship and Loan Fund, 1962-70; mem. exec. com. West Polk County (Fla.) Community Welfare Council, 1960-62, 65-68; mem. budget and audit com. Greater Lakeland United Fund, 1960-62, bd. dirs., 1967-70, residential chmn. fund drive, 1968; mem. adv. bd. Polk County Juvenile and Domestic Relations Ct., 1960-69; worker children's services dist. II, unit 3, Div. Family Services, Dept. Health and Rehab. Services, State of Fla., 1969-70, social worker region 7, unit 62, 1970-72, 74-82, social worker OFR unit, 1977-81, pub. assistance specialist IV, Region 6B, 1984. Mem. exec. com. Suncoast Health Council, 1968-71; mem. Polk County Home Econs. Adv. Com., 1965-71; sec. bd. dirs. Fla. West Coast Ednl. TV, 1960-81; bd. dirs. Lake Region United Way, Winter Haven, 1976-81; mem. Polk County Community Services Council, 1978—. Mem. Nat. Welfare Fraud Assn., Fla. Congress Parents and Tchrs. (hon. life), AAUW (pres. Lakeland br. 1960-61), Polk County Mental Health Assn., Fla. Health and Welfare Council, Fla. Health and Social Service Council, North Tex. State U. Alumni Assn. Democrat. Methodist. Mem. Order Eastern Star. Home: 535 W Beacon Rd Lakeland FL 33803 Mailing Address: PO Box 2161 Lakeland FL 33806

SPENCER, SHIRLEY DAWN, food packer and wholesaler, artist; b. Covina, Calif., July 5, 1957; d. Bernard McGuire and Frances C. (Coleman) S. Owner, operator The Gallery Plus, San Clemente, Calif., 1977-78; v.p. Spencer Food Co., Los Angeles, 1975—.

SPENCER, THEODORA ELAINE, marketing analyst; b. Charleston, W.Va., Sept. 9, 1954; d. Julian Lindsey and Kirsten Ruth (Manthorpe) S.; m. Robert Charles Mohl, Sept. 12, 1981 (div. Jan. 1984). B.S. in Mktg. and Mgmt. Sci., U. S.C., 1976. Sales rep. Point of Sale Systems, Inc., Dania, Fla., 1977-79; research asst. News & Sun-Sentinel Co., Fort Lauderdale, Fla., 1980-81; mktg. analyst Storer Communications, Inc., Miami, Fla., 1981—. Mem. Am. Mktg. Assn. (v.p. communications 1982-83), Mktg. Research Assn., Cable TV Adminstrn. and Mktg. Soc. Republican. Presbyterian. Avocations: golf; boating; water sports. Home: 2220 SW 43d Way Fort Lauderdale FL 33317 Office: Storer Communications Inc 12000 Biscayne Blvd Miami FL 33261

SPENCER, TRICIA JANE, limousine company executive; b. Springfield, Ill., Dec. 8, 1952; d. Frank Edward and LaWanda (Edwards) Bell; m. Mark Edward Spencer, Aug. 21, 1982. Student pub. schs. Instr., Falcons Drum & Bugle Corps, Springfield, 1969-72; concert, stage, TV, film performer, 1970-82, part-time 1982—; guest dir. Sing out Salem, Ohio, 1973; contbg. writer Saddle Tramps Wild West Revue, 1977—; legal sec. to pvt. atty., Tustin, Calif., 1980-82; owner Am. Dream Balloons & Services, Orange, Calif., 1982—; founder, corp. pres. Am. Dream Limousine Service, Inc., Orange, 1983—. Songwriter; designer greeting cards, one-of-a-kind automobile; producer, dir. mus. stage shows, 1974-82. Performer, Up With People, 1972-73; organizer Bicentennial Com. Springfield, 1976; mediator Limousine and Chauffeur Council, Orange County, 1984—; vol. Orange County Performing Arts Soc., 1985—. Recipient Appreciation, Achievement awards Muscular Dystrophy Assn., 1977-79. Mem. Am. Entrepreneurs Assn., So. Calif. Limousine Owners Assn., Nat. Assn. Female Execs., Orange County C. of C. Republican. Avocations: guitar, piano, writing. Office: Am Dream Limousine Service Inc 795 N Tustin Orange CA 92667

SPENCER-STARK, CHERRY ELLERBEE, nursing administrator, consultant; b. Atlanta, Apr. 29, 1948; d. Gerald Brooks and Kathryn Eloise (Lester) Ellerbee; m. James Thomas Spencer, Sept. 7, 1968 (div. Apr. 1977); children—G. Todd, G. Christian; m. 2d, James Edwin Stark, Apr. 5, 1981; stepchildren—David E., Thomas C. B.S. in Nursing, U. Fla., 1971; M.N., Emory U., 1982. R.N., Ga. Staff nurse Emory U. Hosp., Atlanta, 1976-77; adolescent asst. head nurse Peachtree-Parkwood, Atlanta, 1977-79, adult asst. head nurse, 1979-80; adminstrv. head nurse Ga. Bapt. Med. Ctr., Atlanta, 1980-81, nursing supr., 1981-83; dir. patient services So. Christian Home, Atlanta, 1983—; guest lectr. Nell Hodgson Woodruff Sch. Nursing, Emory U., 1982—. Co-pres. aux. Northside Youth Orgn., Atlanta, 1983-84. Mem. Am. Nurses Assn., Ga. Nurses Assn., Sigma Theta Tau. Unitarian. Office: Southern Christian Home 934 Briarcliff Rd NE Atlanta GA 30306

SPENGLER, CAROLYN SARAH, health recruiting company executive; b. Toledo, Feb. 28, 1961; d. William Frederick and Sarah Madeline (Burd) S. B.S., Northwestern U., 1983. Sales rep. American V. Mueller/AHS, McGaw Park, Ill., 1983-85; pres. Healthcare Recruiters of Chgo., Schaumburg, Ill., 1985—. Mem. Female Execs., Inc. Home: 2150 Hassell Rd Hoffman Estates IL 60195 Office: Healthcare Recruiters 1821 Walden Office Sq Schaumburg IL 60195

SPERANZO, CAROLANN MARIE, optician; b. Brookline, Mass., Mar. 2, 1954; d. Fred P. and Madeleine Elizabeth (Harrington) S.; B.A., Emmanuel Coll., 1975; postgrad Boston Coll., 1976—. Research aide, Med. Library, Harvard U., part-time 1972-75; optician, office mgr. William H. Fehrnstrom Inc., Optician, Milton, Mass., 1972-79; owner, optician Second Sight, Boston, 1979—; Mem. Mayor's Commn. on Status of Women, 1982—, chmn., 1985-86. Fellow Contact Lens Soc. Am., Nat. Acad. Opticianry; mem. New Eng. Contact Lens Soc., Mass. Assn. Registered Dispensing Opticians, New Eng. Women Bus. Owners, Am. Bd. Opticianry (charter), AAUW. Democrat. Roman Catholic. Club: Altrusa. Home: 66 Chapman St Quincy MA 02170 Office: 1147 Hancock St Quincy MA 02169

SPERLING, CATHERINE PENNY, health care professional, consultant; b. Latrobe, Pa., Mar. 24, 1939; d. Latimer and Catherine Rita (Sromko) Kooser; m. Ted D. Sperling, Nov. 21, 1962; 1 child, David Joseph. R.N., Latrobe Hosp.; B.S.N., Duquesne U., 1962; M.P.A., Calif. State U.-Lond Beach, 1980. Cert. alcoholism counselor; cert. hypho therapist. Supr. pub. health nursing Los Angeles County, Hollywood and West Los Angeles, 1962-68, substance abuse counselor, Hollywood, 1968-73; instr. U. Calif.-Irvine, 1978—, dir. outpatient nursing and clin. services, 1982—; program dir. regional alcoholism program Orange County, Westminster, Calif., 1974-79; exec. dir. Nat. Inst. Recovery, Newport Beach, Calif., 1980—; addictions cons. South Coast Med. Ctr., Laguna Beach, Calif., 1984-85; pvt. practice, Costa Mesa, Calif., 1985—. Adv. bd. Orange County W. Region Health Care Agy., Westminster, 1984—. Mem. Am. Soc. Pub. Adminstrs., Nat. Assn. Alcohol and Drug Abuse Counselors, Calif. Assn. Alcohol and Drug Abuse Counselors, Calif. Council Hypnotherapists, Calif. Assn. Alcoholism Educators. Home: 6 Goodwill Ct Newport Beach CA 92663 Office: U Calif-Irvine 101 City Dr S Orange CA 92668

SPERO, KAREN WEAVER, financial planner; b. Cleve., Sept. 8, 1943; d. Merritt W. and Naomi (Williams) Weaver; m. Keith E. Spero, Dec. 28, 1975. B.S. magna cum laude, Lake Erie Coll., 1978. Cert. fin. planner Coll. Fin. Planning, Denver. Pres., Spero Fin. Services, Inc., Cleve., 1972—; "Money Woman" on Morning Exchange, Sta. WEWS-TV, Cleve., 1980—; mem. bd. State of Ohio Econ. Devel. Financing Agy., Columbus, 1983—; mem. adv. com. Northeast Ohio region SBA, 1978—; bd. dirs. Pvt. Industry Council, Cleve., 1984—; del. White House Conf. Small Bus., 1986. Contbr. articles to fin. jours. Mem. Make-a-Wish Found. Northeast Ohio, 1984—. Mem. Internat. Assn. Fin. Planners (chpt. pres. 1983-84, chmn. bd. 1984—), Greater Cleve. Growth Assn., Council Smaller Enterprises (bd. dirs. 1981—). Office: Spero Fin Services Inc 3355 Richmond Rd Suite 231 Cleveland OH 44122

SPERRY, JEAN ELIZABETH, educator; b. Des Moines, July 30, 1951; d. Herbert J. and Helen (Anderson) S.; B.S., Drake U., 1972; M.A., Coll. St. Thomas, 1980. Tchr. spl. edn. West St. Paul Ind. Sch. Dist. 197, 1973—; mgr. concessionary St. Paul Civic Center, 1976-84; seminar leader Coll. St. Thomas, 1980-83; owner, cons. Sperry & Assocs., 1983—. Mem. task force United Handicapped Fedn. Mem. Am. Bus. Women Assn., Minn. Fedn. Tchrs., Assn. Retarded Citizens, Bus. and Profl. Women, Nat. Assn. Female Execs., Nat. Found. Ileitis and Colitis. Democrat. Presbyterian. Office: 181 W Butler Ave West Saint Paul MN 55118

SPETZ, KATHRYN FRANCES, costume design firm executive, interior decorator, landscape consultant; b. Mpls., Oct. 22, 1949; d. Glen Rudolph and Charlotte Ellen (Perks) S. B.S., Fla. State U., 1971. Corporate designer 6 Flags Over Ga., Atlanta, 1974-78; owner Spetz Prodns., Atlanta, 1978—. Publicity co-chmn. Lung Run, Am. Lung Assn. Atlanta, 1982, 83. Mem. Sales and Mktg. Execs. Internat., Nat. Assn. Female Execs., Ga. Assn. Image and Fashion Cons., Alpha Xi Delta (v.p. Atlanta 1984—). Republican. Presbyterian. Club: Atlanta Women's Rugby Football (v.p., union rep., match sec., selector 1974-81). Avocations: scuba diving, sailing, show jumping (horses), rugby. Address: 4087 Admiral Dr Atlanta GA 30341

SPICER, CHERYL ANNE, motel chain sales executive, model; b. New Bedford, Mass., Mar. 30, 1961; d. Frederick Spicer III and Karen Marie (Thomas) Spicer Tavares. A.S. in Bus. Mgmt., Bay State Jr. Coll., Boston, 1981; student in bus. mgmt. Lesley Coll., Boston, 1986—; also seminars, workshops. Telemktg. rep. Fidelity Union Life Ins. Co., Somerville, Mass., 1980-81; dir. sales Holiday Inn, Boston, 1982—; freelance fashion model, 1976-81. Mem. Sales Mgmt. Execs. Assn., Nat. Assn. Female Execs., Hotel Sales Mgmt. Assn., Boston Conv. Bur., Boston C. of C., Nat. Fedn. Republican Women. Home: 907 Pleasant St Condominium 19 East Weymouth MA 02189 Office: Holiday Inn Govt Ctr 5 Blossom St Boston MA 02114

SPIEGEL, JEANNE S., economist; b. Merion, Pa., Oct. 23, 1926; d. Stanley R. and Julia (Nusbaum) Sundheim; B.A., Wellesley Coll., 1948; postgrad. U. Pa., 1976-78; m. Walter F. Spiegel, Oct. 8, 1950; children—Walter D., Karen J., James R. Economist, Dept. Labor, Washington, 1949-50; with Walter F. Spiegel, Inc., Cons. Engrs., Jenkintown, Pa., 1963—, office mgr., 1965-78, contract adminstr., 1965-75, energy analyst, chief economist, 1975—, corp. sec., 1967—. Mem. Nat. Assn. Women in Constrn. (chpt. pres.). Home: 405 Lodges Ln Elkins Park PA 19117 Office: 309 York Rd Jenkintown PA 19446

SPIEGEL, LINDA ELLEN, diversified energy company manager; b. Phila., Aug. 6, 1953; d. Louis and Laura Widman; m. Barry S. Spiegel, Jan. 25, 1983. B.S. with highest honors, Phila. Coll. Textiles and Sci., 1975; M.B.A. with highest honors, Drexel U., 1982. Pvt. practice public acctg., Pa., 1975-78; acctg. specialist Sun Petroleum Product Co., Phila., 1978-79; mgr. internal control and adminstrn. Sun Co., Inc., Radnor, Pa., 1979-83, mgr. auditing., Phila., 1983—; speaker in field. C.P.A., Pa. Recipient Achievement award YWCA, 1983. Member Am. Inst. C.P.A.s, Pa. Inst. C.P.A.s (chmn. industry com., mem. exec. com., Scholastic award 1975), Am. Mgmt. Assn., Phila. Fin. Assn., Am. Acctg. Assn. Office: 1801 Market St Philadelphia PA 19103

SPIEGEL, MARILYN HARRIET, real estate company executive; b. Bklyn., Apr. 3, 1935; d. Harry and Sadie (Oscher) Unger; m. Murray Spiegel, June 12, 1954; children—Eric Lawrence, Dana Cheryl, Jay Barry. Grad. high sch., Bklyn. Exec. sec. S & W Paper Co., N.Y.C., 1953-54, Japan Paper Co., N.Y.C., 1954-58; salesperson Red Carpet Realtors, Los Alamitos, Calif., 1974-75, Coll. Park Realtors, Garden Grove, Calif., 1975-79; owner, broker S & S Properties, Garden Grove, 1979—. Mem. Calif. Assn. Realtors (bd. dirs. 1984—), West Orange County Bd. Realtors (bd. dirs. 1984—), Million Dollar Sales Club, Long Beach C. of C., Seal Beach C. of C. Home: 4765 Candleberry St Seal Beach CA 90740 Office: S & S Properties 5250 Lampson St Garden Grove CA 92645

SPIEGEL, MERCEDES L., public TV executive; b. Quezon, Philippines, Apr. 16, 1941; came to U.S., 1970; d. Jose and Dolores (Mendez) Lagdameo; m. Ronald Lee O'Rourke, Dec. 30, 1965 (div. May 1971); children—Renee Lee, Tanya Lee; m. William harris Spiegel, Dec. 28, 1974. Student St. Tomas U. Sec., Del Rosario Brothers, Manila, 1958-60; stewardess Philippine Airlines, Manila, 1960-65; sales coordinator PSA San Franciscan Hotel, San Francisco, 1972-73; sec. WLWT TV, Cin., 1973-74; auction mgr. WCET TV, Cin., 1975-84, assoc. dir. devel., 1984—. Recipient Devel. award Ohio Edn. Broadcasters, 1982. Avocations: Water color painting; knitting; needlepoint. Home: 811 Sabino Ct Cincinnati OH 45231

SPIEGEL, VIRGINIA ANN, nurse; b. N.Y.C., Oct. 20, 1952; d. Charles Martin and Sophie (Kuzmyn) S.; R.N., Queens Hosp., Jamaica, N.Y., 1974; B.S. in Nursing, Seton Hall U., 1978; M.S.N., Hunter Coll., 1981; doctoral student Tchr.'s Coll., Columbia U., 1982—. Staff nurse Columbia-Presbyterian Hosp., N.Y.C., 1974, Meml. Sloan-Kettering Cancer Center, N.Y.C., 1975; staff nurse Lyons (N.J.) VA Hosp., 1975-77, instr., 1977-79, nursing supr., 1979-80; nurse recruiter Bergen Pines Hosp., Paramus, N.J., 1980-83, assoc. dir. nursing, 1983, asst. exec. dir., dir. nursing, 1983—. Mem. Am. Nurses Assn., N.J. State Nurses Assn., N.J. Soc. Nursing Service Adminstrs., Sigma Theta Tau. Roman Catholic. Office: Bergen Pines County Hospital Paramus NJ 07652

SPIEGELBERG, EMMA JO, educator; b. Mountain View, Wyo., Nov. 22, 1936; d. Joseph Clyde and Dorcas (Reese) Hatch; m. James Walter Spiegelberg, June 22, 1957; children—William L., Emory Walter, Joseph John. B.A. with honors, U. Wyo., 1958, M.Ed., 1985. Tchr. bus. edn. Laramie High Sch., Wyo., 1960-61, 65—, chmn. bus. edn. dept., mgr. computer system, 1974—; cons. for VEDS program Wyo. Dept. Edn., 1980-81; guest lectr. U. Wyo., summer, 1979; chmn. Gov.'s and State Supt.'s Task Force on Vocat. Edn., 1982-83. Bd. dirs. Cathedral Home for Children, Laramie, 1967-70, 72—, now pres.; Mountain Plains Rep to Internat. Bus. Edn., 1985-86; precinct committeewoman 1964-72; pres. Beitel PTA, 1965-66; 4-H leader, 1969-75; bd. dirs. Laramie Plaines Mus., 1970-79; mem. Wyo. Telephone Consumer Panel, 1982-85. Named Wyo. Bus. Tchr. of Yr., 1982. Mem. Am. Vocat. Assn. (Region V Tchr. of Yr. award 1985), Wyo. Vocat. Assn. (exec. bd. 1978-80, pres. 1981-82, Outstanding Contbns. to Vocat. Edn. award 1983, Wyo. Vocat. Tchr. of Yr. 1985), Wyo. Bus. Edn. Assn. (pres. 1979-80), NEA, Wyo. Edn. Assn., Albany County Edn. Assn. (sec. 1970-71), U. Wyo. Alumni Assn. (bd. dirs. 1984—), Laramie C. of C. (bd. dirs. 1986—), Phi Delta Kappa, Alpha Delta Kappa (state pres. 1978-82), Chi Omega. Mem. United Ch. of Christ. Clubs: Zonta, Laramie Jr. Women's (pres. 1962-63). Home: 3301 Grays Gables Laramie WY 82070 Office: 1275 N 11th St Laramie WY 82070

SPIER, BEATRICE WALTCH, protective analysis company executive; b. N.Y.C., Dec. 17, 1930; d. Samuel Harris and Deborah (Siegel) Waltch; m. Jerome B. Spier, Dec. 23, 1951; children—Jeffrey, David, Ellen. B.S. in Edn., Boston U., 1952. Tchr. Mass., 1952-54, Ill., 1970-75; exec. dir. Bur. Protective Analysis, Chgo. Bd. dirs. Wilmette Community Concert Assn., 1972-85; sponsor Link, Unltd., Chgo., 1977—. Mem. Pi Lambda Theta. Jewish. Home: 1750 Central Ave Wilmette IL 60091

SPIGAI, FRANCES GAGE, electronic publishing consultant; b. Salina, Kans., Sept. 29, 1938; d. Frances Dana and Mina Lola (Jackson) Gage; m. Edwin B. Parker, Dec. 28, 1976. B.S., CCNY, 1960. Asst. prof. library and computer ctr. Oreg. State U., Corvallis, 1967-70; staff engr. Intrex, Cambridge, Mass., 1970-71; editor Becker & Hayes, Los Angeles, 1971-73; asst. to dir. Osshe Library Council Ashland, Oreg., 1974-76; mktg. dir. Dialog, Palo Alto, Calif., 1976-79; pres. Database Services, Los Altos, Calif., 1979—; editor, pub. Microcomputer Index, 1984—; instr. computer appreciation Linn-Benton Community Coll., Albany, Oreg., 1973. Author: (with P. Sommer) Guide to Electronic Publishing, 1982; editor series Database Search Aids, 1980-82; contbr. articles to profl. jours. Recipient disting. service cert. Nat. Micrographics Assn., 1976; cert. of appreciation Am. Soc. Info. Sci., 1976. Mem. Info. Industry Assn. (bd. dirs. 1986—), Spl. Libraries Assn. Address: Database Services 2685 Marine Way Suite 1305 Mountain View CA 94043

SPIGNER, MARLENE LAMM, consultant; b. N.Y.C., Nov. 9, 1931; d. Stanley Lamm and Esther (Deutsch) Lamm Miller; m. Philip Spigner, May 3, 1953; children—Joanne, Karen Spigner-Case. B.S., Sch. Bus., NYU, 1952; M.S., Sch. Edn., Yeshiva U., 1960. Cert. supr., adminstr., N.Y. Dept. Edn. Tchr., Lawrence Pub. Schs., N.Y. 1960-70, dir. continuing edn., 1976-81; free-lance lectr. on career-job skills, 1970-76; dir. admissions Katharine Gibbs Sch., N.Y.C., 1981-82; pres. Consultex, N.Y.C., 1982—; bd. dirs. dept. adult edn. West Side YMCA, N.Y.C., 1985—. Contbr. articles to mags.; columnist Nassau Herald newspaper, 1972-74. Reader to blind Jewish Guild for Blind, N.Y.C., 1984-85; researcher Pub. TV, N.Y.C., 1984-85. Mem. Nassau Assn. Continuing Edn. (rec. sec. and bd. dirs. 1977-81). Democrat. Avocations: photography; tennis; horticulture. Office: 170 West End Ave New York NY 10023

SPIKE, MICHELE KAHN, lawyer, editor, art researcher; b. Paterson, N.J., Oct. 1, 1951; d. Nathan and Clara (Spinella) Kahn; m. John Thomas Spike, May 26, 1973; 1 son, Nicholas Nathan. B.A. summa cum laude, Conn. Coll., 1973; J.D. cum laude, Boston U., 1976. Bar: N.Y. 1977. Assoc., Hale Russell & Gray, N.Y.C., 1976-83; sole practice, N.Y.C., 1983—. Text editor: Italian Still Life Paintings from Three Centuries (John T. Spike), 1983. Mem. ABA, Assn. Bar City N.Y., Phi Beta Kappa. Home: 85 East End Ave New York NY 10028 Office: 9 Gracie Sq New York NY 10028

SPILLANE, MARY CATHERINE, network television news producer; b. S.I., N.Y., Nov. 30, 1956; d. Joseph Bernard and Mary Catherine (Minoque) Spillane. B.A., U. Hartford, 1978. Exec. sec. CBS Evening News, N.Y.C., 1978-80, asst. to producer, 1980; weekend producer/E.N.G. coordinator KTVI-TV, St. Louis, 1981-82, spl. projects producer, 1982-83, asst. news dir., 1983-86; assoc. producer CBS News, Detroit, 1986—. Avocations: reading; travel. Home: 24484 Conifer #53107 Farmington Hills MI 48018 Office: CBS News 16550 W 9 Mile Rd Southfield MI 48075

SPILLER, MIRIAM BRITTON, fine arts appraiser; b. Reading, Pa., Sept. 4, 1926; d. William Wainwright and Katie Irene (Miller) Britton; student ceramics and sculpture Fleisher Art Meml., Phila., 1958, interior design Phila. Coll. Art, 1961; m. Raymond M. Spiller, Nov. 17, 1956. Practice interior design, 1958—; antiques cons., 1958—; officer R.M. Spiller & Assos., appraisal, conservation and restoration fine arts, Phila., 1960—; mem. Strawberry Mansion, historic preservation; slide lectr. in field. Certified fine arts appraiser, Pa. Mem. Appraisers of Fine Arts Soc. (dir., sec., treas. 1975—), Phila. Mus. Art. Republican. Address: 1025 Westview St Philadelphia PA 19119

SPILLMAN, NANCY ZOE, economics educator; b. Chgo.; d. Leo and Sarah Spillman. Student Los Angeles City Coll., 1958-61; B.S., U. So. Calif., 1963, M.B.A. magna cum laude, 1965; postgrad. Claremont U., 1966-68, UCLA, 1969-73. Mem. faculty Los Angeles Trade Tech. Coll., 1968—, assoc. prof. econs., dir. 1973-84, prof., 1984—, Ctr. for Econ. Info., 1973—; sec. Calif. State Atty. Gen.'s Subcom. Consumer Edn.; condr. radio program Consumer Mailbag Sta. KJOI, Los Angeles. Bd. dirs., chmn. edn. com. consumer credit counselors, Los Angeles. Mem. Am. Econ. Assn., U.S. Metric Assn. (former nat. sec.), Calif. Bus. Edn. Assn., Community Coll. Social Sci. Assn., Soc. Consumer Interests (editor Consumer Edn. Forum), Phi Kappa Phi. Editor: Consumers: Personal Planning Reader; contbr. articles on econs. to profl. jours. Office: Los Angeles Trade Tech Coll 400 W Washington Blvd Los Angeles CA 90015

SPININGER, CLAIRE MARIE, physician; b. Bklyn.; d. Charles John and Clara Elizabeth (Faeth) S. B.S., Fordham U., 1964; M.D., Albert Einstein Coll. Medicine, 1973. Intern, Lenox Hill (N.Y.) Hosp., 1973-74; resident in internal medicine New Rochelle Hosp. Med. Ctr., 1974-76, chief resident, 1976-77; assoc. med. dir. Equitable Life, N.Y.C., 1977-81; practice medicine, New Rochelle, N.Y., 1981—; mem. staff New Rochelle Hosp. Med. Ctr., Pelham Bay Gen. Hosp. Mem. Am. Soc. Internal Medicine, Am. Geriatrics Soc. Westchester County Med. Soc., New Rochelle Med. Soc. Office: 421 Huguenot St New Rochelle NY 10801

SPIRE, NANCY WOODSON (MRS. LYMAN SPIRE), civic worker; b. Wausau, Wis., May 6, 1917; d. Aytchmonde Perrin and Leigh (Yawkey) Woodson; B.S., Radcliffe Coll., 1939; postgrad. Syracuse U., 1957—; m. Lyman J. Spire, June 29, 1940; children—Stephen Crittenden Woodson, Abigail Lyman. Vice pres. Woodson Fiduciary Corp., Wilmington, Del. Trustee Aytchmonde Woodson Found., pres., 1963—; trustee Corinthian Found., 1958-63, 68—, Syracuse Child and Family Service, 1957-62; trustee, sec. Crouse-Irving Meml. Hosp., Syracuse; trustee Onondaga Symphony Orch.; mem. exec. com. Syracuse U. Library Assos., 1958-63, trustee, 1958—. Bd. visitors N.Y. State Tng. Sch. for Girls; v.p. bd. dirs. Leigh Yawkey Woodson Art Mus. Mem. Onondaga Symphony Guild (treas. 1958-59), U.S. Trotting Assn. Republican. Universalist (trustee). Club: Virgin Islands Game Fishing. Office: Yawkey Lumber Co Box 65 Wausau WI 55401 Lagoon Marina Red Hook St Thomas US Virgin Islands 00801

SPIRER, JUNE DALE, psychologist; b. N.Y.C., May 14, 1943; d. Leon and Gloria (Wagner) Spirer; B.A., Adelphi U., 1965; M.S., Yeshiva U., 1980, Psy.D., 1984. TV/radio buyer BBD&O, 1965-66, SSC&B, 1966-68; sr. media planner Norman, Craig & Kummel, N.Y.C., 1968-71; asso. media dir. Ted Bates Co., 1971-72; v.p., account supt. C.T. Clyne Co., N.Y.C., 1972-74; dir. advt. Am. Express, 1974-75; corporate dir. advt. Del Labs., Farmingdale, N.Y., 1975-85; pres. J. Spirer & Assos., Inc., N.Y.C., 1978—; pres., chief exec. officer Media Placement Services, Inc., 1985—. Mem. Am. Psychol. Assn., Nassau County Psychol. Assn., N.Y. State Psychol. Assn., Soc. Personality Assessment (asso.), Manhattan Inst. Office: 14 Horatio St New York NY 10014 also Media Placement Services Inc 317 W 13th St New York NY 10014

SPIRES, ELIZABETH, poet, educator; b. Lancaster, Ohio, May 28, 1952; d. Richard Clarence and Elizabeth Sue (Wagner) S. B.A., Vassar Coll., 1974; M.A., Johns Hopkins U., 1979. Vis. asst. prof. Washington Coll., Chestertown, Md., 1981; writer-in-residence Loyola Coll., Balt., 1981-82; vis. asst. prof. Johns Hopkins U., Balt., 1984-85; asst. prof. English, Goucher Coll., Towson, Md., 1985—; cons. Wesleyan U. Press, Middletown, Conn., 1981—; mem. vis. faculty Stonecoast Writers Conf., Gorham, Maine, 1982-84. Author: (children's book) The Falling Star, 1981; (book of poems) Globe, 1981, Swan's Island, 1985. Contbr. poems to various publs. including: New Yorker, Poetry, The New Republic, Am. Poetry Rev. W.K. Rose fellow Vassar Coll., 1976; Nat. Endowment Arts fellow, 1981; Md. Arts Council grantee, 1982; Amy Lowell Travelling Poetry scholar, 1986—; recipient Ingram Merrill award Ingram Merrill Found., 1982. Mem. Acad. Am. Poets, Poetry Soc. Am. Office: Dept. English Goucher Coll Dulany Valley Rd Towson MD 21204

SPIRES, LOVINA JOYCE MCLAIN, oil company executive; b. Port Arthur, Tex., July 8, 1948; d. W.M. and Ruby Mae (Jeko) McLain; m. Thomas L. Spires, Dec. 18, 1970; 1 child, Miki Jean. B.S., Lamar State Coll., 1970, M.Ed., 1979. Cert. in ednl. supervision, Tex. Tchr. Nederland Ind. Sch. Dist., Tex., 1970-81; owner ASH Petroleum, Nederland, 1981—, Airport Gulf Rental, Nederland, 1982—; distbr. Learn 21 Inc., Nederland, 1985—. Trustee Nederland Ind. Sch. Dist., 1985—, v.p. bd. trustees, 1986-87; active Juvenile Diabetes Found., 1986—, chmn. fundraiser, 1986. Mem. Nederland C. of C. Baptist. Office: ASH Petroleum PO Box 1851 Nederland TX 77627

SPITTLER, BETTY JANE, motel manager; b. Terre Haute, Ind., Nov. 12, 1922; d. John Thomas and Nellie (Brough) Jones; grad. high sch.; m. Fenton Eugene Spittler, Feb. 19, 1942 (div. July 1968); children—Robert Eugene, Karen Lynn. Mgr., Terrace Inn and Restaurant, Terre Haute, 1964-65, Hickory Manor Hotel, Crystal Lake, Ill., 1965; mgr., buyer St. Mary's Motel, Evansville, Ind., 1965-72; mgr. Donna Ct. Motel, Evansville, 1972—; mem. Evansville Conv. and Tourism Bur. Mem. Evansville C. of C. (com. mem. 1969—), Evansville Hotel-Motel Mgrs. Assn. (treas.). Republican. Lutheran (ch. council 1962-65, mem. parish bd. 1951-65, supt. Sunday sch. 1950-65). Address: 7844 Marywood Dr Newburgh IN 47630

SPITZ, CELIA SMITON, accountant; b. N.Y.C., Mar. 4, 1947; d. Meyer W. and Edna (Savitsky) Rindner; m. Stephen Michael Spitz, May 11, 1985; children—Corey Joseph Smiton, Tara Suzanne Smiton. B.A. summa cum laude, CUNY, 1977. C.P.A., Fla., N.Y. Sr. staff acct. Brout & Co., N.Y.C., 1977-79; audit mgr. Grant Thornton, Fort Lauderdale, Fla., 1979-86; controller Holy Cross Hosp., Inc., Fort Lauderdale, 1986—. Chair pub. relations com. Leadership Broward Alumni, 1985-86. Mem. Am. Inst. C.P.A.s, Fla. Soc. C.P.A.s, Am. Women's Assn. C.P.A.s, Omicron Delta Epsilon. Clubs: Women's Exec. (dir. 1984-85) (Fort Lauderdale). Avocations: racquetball; swimming. Home: 1413E NW 80 Ave Margate FL 33063 Office: Holy Cross Hosp Inc 4725 N Federal Hwy Fort Lauderdale FL 33308

SPIVACK, ELLEN SUE, writer, food company executive; b. Trenton, Dec. 2, 1937; d. Chaim David and Beatrice (Safir) Knopf; m. Roger Elliot Spivack, May 15, 1960; children—Ira, Eileen, Basha. B.S. in Edn. and Sociol. Douglass Coll., New Brunswick, N. J., 1959. Tchr., N.Y., N.J., Pa., 1959-73; tchr. nat. foods cooking, Lewisburg, Pa., 1977-80; writer articles and books, 1974—; co-owner, prin. Deep Roots Trading Co., growers, Lewisburg, 1978—. Pres., bd. dirs. Johnny Alfalfa Sprout, Inc. Author: Beginner's Guide to Meatless Casseroles, 1983; Whole Foods Experience, 1985; The Johnny Alfalfa Sprout Handbook, 1986; also others; editor newsletters in field. Vol. The Hunger Project, San Francisco Democrat. Jewish. Home: 524 Rural Ave Williamsport PA 17701 Office: 606 Market St Lewisburg PA 17837

SPIVAK, JACQUE R., consultant; b. San Francisco, Nov. 5, 1929; d. Robert Morris and Sadonia Clardine Breitstein; m. Herbert Spivak, Aug. 26, 1960; children—Susan, Donald, Joel, Sheri. B.S., U. So. Calif., 1949, M.S., 1950, M.B.A., 1959. Mgr. Internat. Escrow, Inc., Los Angeles, 1960-65, Greater Los Angeles Investment Co., 1965-75; mgr. escrow Transam. Title Ins. Co., Los Angeles, 1975-78; mgr. escrow, asst. v.p. Wells Fargo Bank, Beverly Hills, Calif., 1979-80; adminstr. escrow, v.p. 1st Pacific Bank, Beverly Hills, 1980-85; pvt. practice fin. and bus. cons., 1986—. Recipient awards PTA, Girl Scouts

U.S.A., Jewish Fedn. Los Angeles, Hadassah. Mem. Calif. Escrow Assn., Nat. Assn. Bank Women, Inst. Trustees Sales officers. Republican. Jewish.

SPIVEY, CAROLE MOYER, personnel administrator; b. Renton, Wash., June 29, 1947; d. William D. and Ellen I. (Andrews) Moyer; m. Allen P. Goldade, Apr. 29, 1971 (div. 1980); children—Shaunna M., Mathew A. B.A. in English cum laude, U. Wash., Seattle, 1969. Fashion model John Robert Powers, Seattle, 1966-72; adminstrv. asst. Bracewell & Patterson, Houston, 1973-75; personnel asst. Service Corp. Internat., Houston, 1975-77; personnel mgr. CNA Ins., Houston, 1977-80; regional personnel mgr. Stone and Webster, Denver, 1980-81; personnel dir. Holme Roberts & Owen, Denver, 1981—; mem. faculty Inst. for Continuing Legal Edn., Denver, 1983—; co-chmn. Inst. Law Office Mgmt., 1983-84. Contbr. articles to profl. jours. Mem. adv. com. Rocky Mountain Energy and Environ. Tech. and Tng. Ctr., Denver, 1982—. Mem. Am. Soc. Personnel Adminstrs., Colo. Soc. Personnel Adminstrs. (mem. various coms.), Am. Mgmt. Assn. Clubs: Internat. Travel, Profl. Women's Assn. (Denver) (sec. 1981-82). Office: Holme Roberts & Owen 1700 Broadway Denver CO 80290

SPLITT, CODY, lawyer; b. Wausau, Wis., Aug. 13, 1919; d. Anne Monahan Wendt; B.A., U. Wis., 1947, LL.B., 1949; m. Harley B. Splitt, Apr. 17, 1948; 1 dau., Leigh Rogers. Admitted to Wis. bar, 1949; individual practice, Appleton, 1949—; asst. dir. U.S. Agrl. Census, 1955; dist. dir. U.S. Census, 1960; mem. Wis. Equal Rights Commn., 1966-73, Appleton Equal Opportunities Commn., 1973-81; dir., gen. counsel Appleton Packing and Gasket, Inc., 1970-78; lectr. Law for Laymen, 1975, 79, moderator, 1980; instr. wills Fox Valley Tech. Inst., 1979-80; dir. Legal Services of Northeastern Wis., Inc., 1985—. Vice chmn. Outagamie County Republican Club, 1965; del. Wis. State Rep. Conv., 1985; pres. Outagamie County Republican Women's Club, 1951; co-pres. Appleton PTA, 1971; v.p. Appleton Big Sisters, 1974; mem. planned giving com. Fox River Area council Girl Scouts U.S.A., 1984. Served with WAVES, 1942-45. Named Woman of Yr. for Outagamie County, NOW, 1974. Mem. State Bar Wis. (sec. sect. individual rights and responsibilities 1974), Outagamie County Bar Assn. (exec. com. 1978-85, sec. 1985-86, pres. 1986-87), Fed. Bus. and Profl. Women (v.p. Wis. 1978), Appleton Northside Bus. Assn. Office: 1213 N Superior St Appleton WI 54911

SPOEHEL, JERRI HOSKINS, volunteer agency executive; b. Oak Park, Ill., Mar. 13, 1932; d. George Alex and Myrtle Jean (McBean) Hoskins; B.A. in English cum laude, Coll. Wooster; m. Edwin H. Spoehel, Apr. 16, 1955; children—Ronald Ross, Jacqueline Jean. Instr., Success-Plus, 1974; columnist Daily News, San Fernando Valley, Van Nuys, Calif., 1970-85; community relations dir. Sta. KCSN-FM, Nat. Pub. Radio, Northridge, Calif., 1975-85; exec. dir. Vol. Ctr. of San Fernando Valley, 1985—; panelist/seminar instr. Nat. Devel. Conf., Corp. Pub. Broadcasting. Recipient Nat. Abe Lincoln Merit award So. Baptist Radio and TV Commn.; named Disting. Citizen of Northridge; other awards. Mem. AAUW, Nat. Soc. Fund-Raising Execs., Calif. Women in Higher Edn., Pub. Relations Roundtable, Dirs. Vols. in Agys. Clubs: Valley Press, Soroptimists (pres.), Northridge Cultural Arts. Mem. Unity Ch. Home: 9615 Shoshone Ave Northridge CA 91325 Office: 6931 Van Nuys Blvd Suite 309 Van Nuys CA 91405

SPONSELLER, ANN ETTA NETHERY, business broker executive, realtor; b. Vernon, Tex., Mar. 2, 1950; d. Paul Fuston and Helen Louise (Mayes) Nethery; children—Jeffrey Paul, Kriiten Nicole. Realtor, owner Garland Assocs., Inc., Tex., 1976-86; broker, owner Metroplex Bus. Brokerage, Garland, 1982—. Mem. Garland Bd. Realtors (bd. dirs. 1982-86, Realtor of Yr. 1985), Garland C. of C. (bd. dirs. 1983-86). Baptist. Office: Realty World Garland Assocs 985 W Centerville Rd Garland TX 75041

SPONSLER, DIANA R., microcomputer specialist; b. Akron, Ohio, May 9, 1960; d. Philip Allen Caskey and Ruth Kathryn (Rawson) Tang; m. Michael B. Sponsler, July 17, 1982. B.S. in Computer Sci. cum laude, Bowling Green State U., 1982; M.B.A., Pepperdine U., 1985. Microcomputer specialist Arthur Young & Co., Los Angeles, 1982—. Ohio Bd. of Regents scholar, 1978. Avocations: camping; hiking; cooking; sewing; swimming.

SPONTAK, BARBARA ANN, nurse; b. Pottstown, Pa., Nov. 10, 1943; d. Wellington Farel and Mary Eleanor (Hampton) Davidheiser; A.S., Coll. DuPage (Ill.), 1974; B.S. in Nursing, U. Ill., 1978; m. Stephen John Spontak, Aug. 18, 1962; children—Stephen F., Gregory A., Mark T., Michael A. Charge nurse burn unit, then staff nurse emergency dept. Loyola U. Med. Center, 1974-77; nursing supr., asst. dir. nursing Good Samaritan Hosp., Downers Grove, Ill., 1978; asst. dir. nursing medicine U. Ill. Med. Center, 1979-81, asst. dir. nursing, coordinator nursing resources, 1981-85; div. dir. critical care I Cook County Hosp., 1985—; instr. nursing Coll. of DuPage, 1981-83, U. Ill.-Chgo., 1984-85. Sec., Park View Sch. PTA, 1975. Mem. Ill. Nurses Assn., Lombard Nurses Club. Lutheran. Club: Rams Gymnastics (pres. 1980-82). Home: 332 W Sunset Ave Lombard IL 60148 Office: 1740 Taylor St Chicago IL 60612

SPORNER, JUDITH ANN, insurance auditor; b. Chgo., Mar. 23, 1940; d. Harry William and Helen Jennie (Wengiel) Jacobs; m. Leonard Julius Sporner, Mar. 2, 1965 (div. 1984); children—Andrew J., Robert J., Helen J. Emergency med. technician, Liberty Twp., Ind., 1981-84; agrl. engr. Chester, Inc., Valparaiso, Ind., 1980; ins. agt. John M. Small Ins., Walkerton, Ind., 1983-85; ins. loss control engr. Armfelt & Assocs., Chesterland, Ohio, 1985—, auditor, 1985—. Editor: Right to Life Newspaper, 1976 (Journalism award 1977). Den mother Boy Scouts Am., 1976, recipient Silver Beaver award, 1980. Served to 1st lt. USAF, 1961-63. Mem. Ins. Auditors Am. (sec. 1984-85), Women in Ins. Assn. (v.p. 1983-84), CAP (squadron comdr.). Democrat. Lodge: Eastern Star. Avocations: Fishing; target shooting; Am. Civil War. Home: Rural Route 3 Box 202 Walkerton IN 46574

SPRACKLAND, KATHLEEN ANN, nurse; b. Portland, Maine, Sept. 3, 1957; d. Harold Matthew and Sylvia Ann (Strout) Pawlowski; m. Mark Andrew Sprackland, Aug. 13, 1977. A Sci., Westbrook Coll., 1977. Cert. in advanced cardiac life support, advanced trauma life support. Staff nurse Osteo. Hosp., Portland, Maine, 1977-82, emergency room nurse, 1982—. CPR instr. Am. Heart Assn., 1982—. Roman Catholic. Home: 30 New Rd Scarborough ME 04074 Office: Osteopathic Hosp 335 Brighton Ave Portland ME 04103

SPRAGUE, AMARIS JEANNE, real estate broker; b. Jackson, Mich., Feb. 18, 1935; d. Leslie Markham and Blanche Lorraine (Basnaw) Reed; student Mich. State U., 1952-53; B.S., Colo. State U., 1965; m. John M. Vetterling, Oct. 1985; children by previous marriage—Anthony John, James Stuart. Real estate sales Seibel and Benedict Realty, Ft. Collins, Colo., 1968-69; salesman Realty Brokers Exchange, Ft. Collins, 1969-72; broker, pres. Sprague and Assos., Inc., Realtors, Ft. Collins, 1972-80; broker assoc. Van Schaack & Co., Ft. Collins, 1980—; dir. Univ. Nat. Bank. Mem. bus. adv. council Colo. State U., 1976-84, chmn. 1979-80, mem. adv. council Coll. of Engring., 1981. Cert. real estate broker. Mem. Nat. Assn. Realtors, Colo. Assn. Realtors, Ft. Collins Bd. Realtors, Ft. Collins C. of C. (dir. 1975-78, 80-83, pres. 1982-83). Republican. Episcopalian. Home: PO Box 475 Fort Collins CO 80522 Office: 2120 S College Ave Fort Collins CO 80525

SPRAGUE, DAWN, lawyer; b. New Haven, Feb. 8, 1956; d. Seth and Anne (Hauser) S.; m. Stephen Mark Foley, 1 child, Anne Elizabeth Sprague. B.A. summa cum laude, Providence Coll., 1978; J.D. cum laude, Suffolk Law Sch., 1981. Bar: Mass. 1981, R.I. 1981. Assoc., McMahon & McMahon, Providence, 1981-82; Ptnr. Foley & Sprague, Boston, 1982—; cons. atty. Client Trust Fund Project, Dept. Mental Health, Boston, 1983-84. Recipient Am. Jurisprudence award for estate planning, 1981. Mem. ABA, R.I. Bar Assn., Mass. Bar Assn. Office: Foley and Sprague Attys at Law 726 E 8th St South Boston MA 02127

SPRAGUE, MARY G., retail exec.; b. N.Y.C., Sept. 10, 1943; d. James Joseph and Mary Catherine (Rabbett) Gribben; A.B., Sarah Lawrence Coll., 1971; M.A., N.Y. U., 1973; children—William, Jennifer. Pres., Victory Shirt Co., N.Y.C., 1974—. Arbitrator, Am. Arbitration Assn. Mem. N.Y. Assn. Women Bus. Owners. Office: 345 Madison Ave New York NY 10017

SPRAINGS, VIOLET EVELYN, psychologist; b. Omaha, Aug. 1, 1930; d. Henry Elbert and Stravnella (Hunter) S.; A.B., U. Calif., Berkeley, 1948, M.A., 1951; Ed.D., U. San Francisco, 1982; Ph.D., U. San Francisco, 1982. Tchr., Oakland (Calif.) Public Schs., 1951-58; psychologist Med. Edn. Diagnostic Center, San Francisco, 1959-62; dir. psychol. edn. and lang. services Calif. Dept. Edn., 1963-71; asst. prof. San Francisco State U., 1964-71; assoc. prof. ednl. psychology Calif. State U., Hayward, 1971-79; dir. Lang. Assocs., Orinda, Lafayette and Redwood City, 1971-79; psychologist in pvt. practice, 1962—; dir. Western Women's Bank; mem. adv. bd. Bay Area Health Systems Agy.; instr. U. Calif., Berkeley extension, 1964—; mem. Oral Bd. Ednl. Psychologists, 1972—; mem. adv. com. Foothill Jr. Coll. Dist. Recipient Phoebe Apperson Heart award San Francisco Examiner, 1968. Mem. Am. Psychol. Assn., Internat. Neuropsychol. Assn. (charter), Calif. Psychol. Assn., Calif. Assn. Sch. Psychologists and Psychometrists, Western Psychol. Assn., Nat. Council Negro Women, AAUP, Delta Sigma Theta, Psi Chi, Pi Lambda Theta. Contbr. articles to profl. jours. Home: 170 Glorietta Blvd Orinda CA 94563 Office: 3408 Deer Hill Rd Lafayette CA 94549

SPRATT, MARY JANE, industrial catering company executive; b. Ft. Worth, Feb. 17, 1949; d. Joel Orban Barnhill and Elizabeth Ann (Tannahill) Barnhill Stiles; 1 child, Samuel Adriane Spratt. B.B.A., N. Tex. State U., 1971; postgrad. in Biology Tex. Woman's U., 1972-73. Bacteriologist Oak Farms, Ft. Worth, 1973-74; ind. distbr. Supreme Catering, Houston, 1975; supr. Shaklee Corp., Cleveland, Tex., 1976-77; ind. distbr. Regal Catering, Houston, 1980-81; co-owner Road Runner Catering, Houston, 1981-85; pres. ACMS, Inc., indsl. catering, Houston, 1985—. Mem. Nat. Assn. Female Execs., Select Houston Execs. Unitarian. Avocations: restoring antiques; cooking; visiting mus. of small Tex. cities. Home: 6307 Via Espana Houston TX 77083

SPREIER, LOIS JOANNE, librarian; b. Burley, Idaho, July 27, 1932; d. Blair Howard and Gladys Lenore (Rudolph) Gochnour; m. Clifford Herman Spreier, Dec. 27, 1953; children—Annette Louise, Douglas Mark (dec.), Janet Lynne. B.A., Idaho State U., 1967. Cert. tchr., media specialist, Idaho. Sixth grade tchr. pub. schs., Buhl, Idaho, 1954-55, Filer, Idaho, 1960-61, Twin Falls, Idaho, 1962-67; Am. lit. tchr. Buhl High Sch., 1967-82, media specialist, 1982—. Mem. NEA, Idaho Edn. Assn., Buhl Edn. Assn. (sec. 1978-79, bldg. rep. several terms), Idaho Ednl. Media Assn., ALA, Idaho Library Assn., Am. Assn. Sch. Librarians; Nat. Council Tchrs. English, Alpha Delta Kappa (treas. Twin Falls 1980-82, v.p. 1982-84, pres. 1984-86). Home: 1097 Pinewood Circle Twin Falls ID 83301 Office: Buhl High Sch Buhl Sch Dist 412 Rt 4 Sawtooth Blvd Buhl ID 83316

SPRENGEL, HELEN JANE, nursing educator, administrator; b. Butte, N.D., Oct. 21, 1925; d. William and Elizabeth Ruth (Nachetilo) Tarasenko; m. Reuben A. Sprengel, June 20, 1949; children—Kaye Sprengel Whitney, Jean Sprengel Rogers. Diploma in nursing Glendale Adventist Hosp., 1947; B.S.N., Loma Linda U., 1963; M.P.H., UCLA, 1969; Ph.D., Laurence U., 1981. R.N., cert. hosp. adminstr., Calif. Dir. nursing service Bangkok Adventist Hosp., Thailand, 1958-66; adminstrn. resident Fresno Community Hosp., Calif., 1968-69, dir. allied health services, 1969-74; assoc. dir. nursing service Valley Med. Ctr., Fresno, 1974-76; asst. prof. Loma Linda U., Calif., 1976-77; assoc. prof. nursing Calif. State U., Fresno, 1978—; workshop faculty Seventh-day Adventist, Taipai, Manila, Bangkok, Tokyo. Author manual of practical nursing, 1963; speaker Nat. Orgn. Seventh-day Adventist Nurses, Los Angeles, 1984, Loma Linda, 1983. Bd. dirs. Pacific Union Coll., Angwin, Calif., 1972-77; trustee Hanford Community Hosp., 1983—; pres. Loma Linda U. Med.-Dental Women's Aux., 1965-67, 85—. Recipient Notable Ams. Bicentennial Era award Am. Biog. Inst., 1976. Mem. Nat. League Nursing, Am. Coll. Hosp. Adminstrs., Am. Hosp. Assn., Western Hosp. Assn., Calif. Hosp. Assn., Assn. for Devel. Fresno Adventist Acad. (pres. 1982-83). Republican. Club: Century (pres. 1977-79). Avocations: choir directing; sewing and making quilts; entertaining; traveling. Home: 825 S Purdue Fresno CA 93727 Office: Calif State U Cedar and Shaw St Fresno CA 93727

SPRING, WILMA BLACK, county court official; b. Tupper Lake, N.Y., Feb. 28, 1934; d. William John and Alma (Gregory) Black; children—Richard D. Peets, Karen M. Parker, Gary L. Spring, Kathleen S. Spring. Student Albany Bus. Coll., 1956. Dep. clk. Hamilton County Family and Surrogate Ct., Indian Lake, N.Y., 1957-60, chief clk., 1973—; sec. High Vacuum Equipment; Hingham, Mass., 1963-64; bookkeeper Indian Lake Garage, 1967-70, Indian Lake Sports, 1970-73. Bd. dirs. Indian Lake Central Sch., 1973-84; treas. Indian Lake Methodist Ch., 1979—. Republican. Lodge: Eastern Star (matron 1976, 83). Avocations: golf, reading. Home: Route 28 Indian Lake NY 12042 Office: PO Box 307 Indian Lake NY 12842

SPRINGER, ANN MURPHY, management consultant; b. Boston, Apr. 13, 1935; d. William James, Jr. and Katherine Mary (Danehy) Murphy; m. David Alan Springer, Nov. 27, 1971. B.S., Simmons Coll., Boston, 1956; M.S. (teaching asst.), Purdue U., 1958. Home economist, 1956-59; program developer U.S. Spl. Services, W.Ger., 1959-62; with Ford Found. project, Oakland, Calif., 1962-65; mem. staff War on Poverty, 1965-67; tng. cons. Western Community Action Tng., Oakland, 1967-69; dir. tng. Internat. Tng. Cons., Berkeley, Calif., 1969-71; ind. mgmt. cons., Bodega, Calif., 1971—; prof. mgmt. studies Sonoma (Calif.) State U., 1979—; resident, adj. faculty Nat. Fire Acad., Md., 1978—; chief Bodega Vol. Fire Dept., 1979-84; adv. com. re-entry and women's studies Santa Rosa Jr. Coll., 1977-84, mem. fire tech. adv. com., 1982-85. Co-author: The Organizational Operations Process, 1972; Management for the Fire Officer, 1981. Contbr. articles to profl. publs. First chairperson Sonoma County Commn. Status Women, 1975-76. Grantee Indian Valley Colls., Novato, Calif., 1977, 79. Mem. Internat. Assn. Fire Chiefs, Internat. Assn. Fire Service Instrs., Calif. Fire Chiefs Assn., Calif. Tng. Officers Assn., Sonoma County Fire Chiefs Assn. (past pres.). Address: 1931 Joy Rd PO Box 139 Bodega CA 94922

SPRINGER, SCOTT GLADYS LORRAINE, educator, consultant; b. N.Y.C., May 14, 1933; d. James Alexander and Gladys Isobel (Evelyn) Springer; m. George A. Scott, II, May 21, 1959; children—Celeste Lorraine, George A. III, B.A., Goddard Coll., 1972; M.S., Bank Street Coll. Edn., 1976; postgrad. U. Mass., 1984. Dir. edn. N.Y.C. Bd. Edn., Bklyn., 1972-74, ednl. adminstr., N.Y.C., 1983—; edn. dir. CUNY, Bklyn., 1976-81; exec. dir. East Harlem Community Devel. Agy., N.Y.C., 1981-83; tchr. Irvington House, Irvington, N.Y., 1956-60, Abbott House, Irvington, 1960-65; tchr., dir. East Side House Settlement, South Bronx, N.Y., 1966-72. Mem. Head Start Policy Council, N.Y.C., 1981; founder Bridge Apts. Nursery, N.Y.C., 1962. Recipient numerous awards for competitive voice concerts, 1945-47; Cary fellow Bank Street Coll. Edn., N.Y.C., 1974-76. Mem. Assn. Black Women Higher Edn., Phi Delta Kappa. Home: 276 Riverside Dr New York NY 10029 Office: New York City Bd Edn IS43 Annex 601 W 183d St New York NY 10033

SPRINGFIELD, MARY SUSAN (PANCOAST), construction management, school bond services company executive; b. Okmulgee, Okla., Feb. 25, 1944; d. Ardo Lee and Lula Mary (Matheney) Pancoast; m. Ronald Dean Springfield, Aug. 6, 1966; 1 child, Julie Lynn. B.F.A., U. Okla., 1966; M.A., Central State U., Edmond, Okla., 1974. Cert. tchr., Okla. Secondary tchr. Mid-Del Pub. Schs., Midwest City, Okla., 1966-78; gen. mgr. Redland Constrn. & Supply, Norman, Okla., 1978-80; pres. Williams-Springfield, Inc., Moore, Okla., 1980—. Mem. Statue of Liberty-Ellis Island Centennial Commn., N.Y., 1984. Mem. Nat. Wildlife Fedn., U. Okla. Alumni Assn. (life), DAR (chpt. sec.), Gamma Phi Beta (Psi chpt.). Democrat. Methodist. Avocations: flying (pvt. pilot). Home: 3636 Rolling Ln Circle Midwest City OK 73110 Office: Williams-Springfield Inc 2522 N Moore Ave PO Box 7008 Moore OK 73153

SPRINTZIN, KAREN LEE, human resource consultant; b. Washington, Jan. 6, 1949; d. Arthur and Anora (Scheer) Sprintzin; m. Mark Ellis Mausner, Aug. 17, 1980; 1 dau., Blake Arica Mausner. B.S., U. Md., 1971; M.A., George Washington U., 1978. Tng. specialist Fed. Govt., Md., 1970-76; assoc. dir. McClure Lundberg Assocs., Washington, 1976-78; pres. Sprintzin Assocs., Washington, 1978-80; asst. v.p., Citicorp., N.Y.C., 1980-84; cons. Citicorp/Choice, Towson, Md. 1984—; lectr., counselor Montgomery County Commn. for Women, Rockville, Md., 1978-80. Mem. Am. Soc. Tng. and Devel., Am. Soc. Personnel Adminstrn., AAUW.

SPRUILL, CONNIE MARIE, human resource development company executive; b. Cleveland, Tenn., Oct. 19, 1950; d. Orville Porter and Wilma Nadine (White) Porter; m. James C. Spruill, July 21, 1979; stepchildren—James C. Spruill Jr., Tina M. Spruill, Tiffeney Spruill; children by previous marriage—Heidi Marie Short, Brandy Renee Short. Student Columbus Coll. Art and Design, 1968-69; LaSalle Extension, 1966-68, A.A. in Interior Design, 1970; grad. Patricia Stevens Modeling and Finishing Sch., 1964. Owner, mgr. Viviane Woodward Cosmetic Distbrship; freelance model and comml. artist; adminstrv. asst. to purchasing agt. Columbus Wood Preserving Co., 1976-78; owner, chief exec. officer Central Ohio Forest Products, Inc., Columbus, 1979-82; co-founder Attitude Marketers Unltd., a human resource devel. co., 1982—, Entrepreneur Devel. Inst. for Tng. Coordinator, constrn. explorer post Boy Scouts Am., 1980. Named Women Bus. Advocate of Yr., Central Ohio region SBA, 1982; recipient Emily Warren Roebling award Profl. Women in Constrn., 1982, Champion of Women, 1983; Columbus Mayor's vol. service award, 1984. Mem. Assn. Bus. and Profl. Women in Constrn. (pres., founder Central Ohio, dir. Ohio region), Am. Entrepreneurs Assn., Am. Assn. Profl. Cons., Central Ohio Builders Exchange. Democrat. Club: Zonta. Office: PO Box 229 Brice OH 43109

SPURGEON, ZELMA PEARL, educator, school administrator; b. Alexandria, Mo., Nov. 15, 1936; d. James Albert and Marguerite Louise (Jones) Rennaker; m. Mirl Eugene Spurgeon, Aug. 30, 1959; children—Vicki Lynn, James Dale, Joseph Eugene. A.A., Hannibal-LaGrange Jr. Coll., 1959; B.S., Culver-Stockton Coll., 1969, postgrad., 1985—. Cert. elem. tchr., Mo. Tchr. Ballard Sch., Kahoka, Mo., 1960-63, Hermann Sch., Mo., 1963-66, Wells Carey Sch., Keokuk, Iowa, 1967-70; co-owner, bookkeeper Gene's Graphics Signs, Alexandria, 1970-79; founder, prin., tchr. Kara Baptist Acad., Alexandria, 1979—; assn. youth leader Wyaconda Bapt. Ch., LaBelle, Mo., 1970-72; vol. phys. edn. tchr. Calvary Bapt. Ch., Keokuk, 1973-75; lectr. in field. Active mem. Right to Life, Keokuk, 1980-83, Moral Majority, Lynchburg, Va., 1979—, PTO, Herman and Keokuk, 1963-70, Booster Club Kara Bapt. Acad., 1979—, Womens Missionary Assn., Wayland, 1970-80, Civic Music Assn. Mem. NEA, Assn. of Christian Edn. Democrat. Avocations: bowling, golf, reading, music, church work. Home: PO Box 68 Alexandria MO 63430 Office: Kara Bapt Acad PO Box 68 Alexandria MO 63430

SPURGIN, JUDY BARRETT, author, art curator, consultant; b. Sherman, Tex., Feb. 27, 1945; d. Hiram Hubbard and Stella (Potter) Barrett; children—Sarah Elisabeth, Jenny Rebecca. B.A., U. Tex.-Austin, 1965, M.A., 1970. Instr., U. Tex., Austin, 1966-69; freelance writer, Austin, 1971—; freelance art cons., Austin, 1974—; art curator Execucom Systems Corp., Austin, 1980-84; cons. Spicewood Gallery, Austin, Tex., 1979—, Tex. Cultural Alliance, Dallas, 1980-82, Meredith Fund, Austin, Tex., 1982-83, Second Street Gallery, Phila., 1983; ptnr. Art Mktg. Services, Austin, 1984—. Author: The Art of Cosmetic Surgery, 1979; Joys of Computer Networking, 1984; contbr. articles on art to mags. Mem. LWV, Austin, 1976; bd. dirs. Mayor's Com., Austin, 1977. Mem. Austin Writer's League (advisor 1981-84), Women in Communication, Profl. Women in the Arts. Democrat. Methodist. Office: Art Mktg Services PO Box 883 Austin TX 78767

SPURLIN, ANNIE RUTH, nurse, educator; b. Brewton, Ala., May 11, 1938; d. Perry E. and Ola Spurlin. R.N., Jackson Meml. Hosp. Sch. Nursing, Miami, Fla., 1959; B.S. in Nursing, Evangel Coll., 1963; M.Ed., Columbia U. Tchrs. Coll., 1970, Ph.D., 1981; Specialist in Clin. Nursing, Ind. U.-Purdue U., Indpls., 1978. Staff nurse Jackson Meml. Hosp., 1959-60, head nurse, 1960-61; coll. nurse Evangel Coll., Springfield, Mo., 1961-62; nursing instr. Jackson Meml. Hosp., Miami, 1963-65, instr. nursing U. Miami, 1965-66, coordinator fundamentals of nursing, 1966-67; inservice edn. instr. Baptist Hosp., Miami, summers 1967, 68; nurse researcher Nursing Resources Study, Sch. Aerospace Medicine, Brooks AFB, Tex., 1971-72; nurse researcher Office of Surgeon-Gen. U.S. Air Force, Washington, 1972-73, project dir., 1973-74; asst. prof. Seton Med. Ctr., U. Tex. System Sch. Nursing, 1974-75; assoc. prof. Sch. Nursing, U. Tex.-Austin, 1975-77; staff nurse Loeb Ctr. for Nursing and Rehab., Montefiore Hosp., Bronx, N.Y., summer 1977; fellow Robert Wood Johnson Found. Ind. U.-Purdue U., Indpls., 1977-78; assoc. prof. U. Tex., 1978-80; assoc. prof. Anna Vaughn Sch. Nursing, Oral Roberts U., 1980-81, chairperson dept. nursing for the individual 1981-83; sta. Air War Coll., Air U., 1983-84. Served with USAFR, 1964—, active duty, 1971-74, 84. Mem. Am. Nurses Assn., Ala. Nurses Assn., Res. Officers Assn., Sigma Theta Tau, Pi Lambda Theta, Am. Legion. Office: Air War College Air Univ Maxwell AFB AL 36112

SPURLING, JUDITH H. DEIST, veterinarian; b. Ketchikan, Alaska, June 25, 1941; d. William Moyer and Mildred Louisa (Willard) Hemsing; m. Gary Spurling, Sept. 1961 (div.); children—Jody, Jay; m. 2d, Harold R. Deist, Mar. 11, 1971. B.S., Colo. State U., 1962, D.V.M., 1966. Veterinarian Belleview Animal Hosp., Englewood, Colo., 1966-69; pvt. practice Centennial Vet. Clinic, Littleton, Colo., 1969—. Mem. Assn. Women Vets. (pres. 1984-86, sec. 1976-82), Denver Area Vet. Med. Soc. (treas. 1980-81), Am. Soc. Vet. Clin. Pathology, Vet. Cancer Soc., AVMA Am. Animal Hosp. Assn. (dir.), Am. Morgan Horse Assn. (youth leader). Club: Mysterious Morgan Youth (leader 1979—). Office: Judith H Spurling DVM 2731 W Belleview St Littleton CO 80123

SPURLOCK, RACHEL YVONNE, banker; b. Princeton, Ark., Sept. 16, 1937; d. Willie Roscoe and Croma Lee (Gresham) Hughes; cert. Am. Inst. Banking, 1979; grad. Southwestern Grad. of Banking, 1982; m. Burk Hobson Spurlock, Oct. 7, 1956; children—William Marcus, Gregory Morgan. Officer mgr. Salling Wiping Cloth Co., Shreveport, La., 1960-63, So. Towel, Shreveport, 1963-64; clerk Comml. Nat. Bank, Shreveport, 1964-73, mgr. ops. consumer loans, 1973—, asst. cashier, 1978-82, asst. v.p., 1982—. Mem. Am. Bus. Women's Assn., Nat. Assn. Bank Women. Democrat. Baptist. Home: Route 9 Box 850 Shreveport LA 71107 Office: 329 Texas St Shreveport LA 71152

SPYCHE, AGNES MAGDELENE (PITTNER), health services assn. exec., nurse; b. Buffalo, Oct. 27, 1936; d. Peter John and Agnes Rose (Kolasz) Pittner; diploma Sisters of Charity Hosp. Sch. Nursing, Buffalo, 1954-57; B.S. in Nursing, SUNY, Buffalo, 1961, M.S. in Health Care Planning and Mgmt., 1981; m. Gerald John Spyche, Feb. 23, 1963; children—Gerald John, Peter J., Mary A. With Sisters Hosp., Buffalo, 1957-64, 65-66, in-service coordinator, 1960-61, supr. spl. dept. emergency room, urology, out-patient dept. and ICU, 1961-64, staff nurse, 1965-66; night supr. St. Joseph's Intercommunity Hosp., Cheektowaga, N.Y., 1961-64; with Emergency Hosp., Buffalo, 1964-65; 67-78, asst. dir. nursing service, 1969-71, dir. nursing service, 1971-78; asst. dir. nursing service DeGraff Meml. Hosp., North Tonawanda, N.Y., 1979, dir. nursing service, 1979-80; dir. blood service nursing ARC, Buffalo, 1981-85; instr. obstet. nursing, acute care Sisters Hosp. Sch. Nursing, 1985—; bd. dirs. Western N.Y. High Blood Pressure Screening; cons. for developing ICUs. Mem. Erie County (N.Y.) CD Com.; mem. Erie County Disaster Com. Recipient Med. award Sisters Hosp., 1957; Hill Burton Act of 1956 trainee, 1957—. Mem. Alumni Sisters of Charity Hosp. Sch. Nursing, Alumni Sch. Nursing SUNY Buffalo, Am. Assn. Blood Banks. Roman Catholic. Home: 124 Cresthaven Dr West Seneca NY 14224 Office: 2157 Main St Buffalo NY 14214

SQUAIR, JEAN MARIE, educational administrator; b. Vancouver, B.C., Can., Jan. 19, 1925; came to U.S., 1943; d. Alfred Ernest and Bertha Edith (Bailey) Hall; student Stanford U., 1943-47, Boston U., 1964-65, U. Calif., Berkeley, 1965-68; m. Stuart Davidson Squair, Feb. 14, 1948; children—Roslyn Marie, Elizabeth Ann. Mgr., Oakland (Calif.) Symphony Chorus, 1963-70; dir. vol. services Goodwill Industries, Oakland, 1970-80; adj. prof., dir. Grad. Sch. Arts Adminstrn., Golden Gate U., San Francisco, 1976—. Bd. govs. San Francisco Symphony, 1976-81; bd. dirs. San Francisco Opera Western Opera Theater, 1970-78; trustee Calif. Hist. Soc., 1970-76; co-chmn. Piedmont Arts Festival, 1970-78; pres. San Francisco Symphony League, 1973-76. Recipient Disting. Service award Oakland Symphony, 1966; award Nat. Aux. to Goodwill Industries, 1978. Mem. Assn. Arts Adminstrn. Educators (dir.), Assn. Calif. Symphony Orchs. (founding pres.), Am. Symphony Orch. League (mem. vol. council bd.). Home: 6001 Acacia Ave Oakland CA 94618 Office: 536 Mission St San Francisco CA 94105

SQUASHIC, LAUREN MARIA, graphic designer; b. Altoona, Pa., June 30, 1957; d. Thomas Steven and Josephine Theresa (Shyrock) Squashic; m. Ralph Dennis Lewis, June 30, 1984. B.A., Pa. State U., 1979. Graphic design asst. Pa. State U., State College, 1978-79; mktg. asst. Gulf States, Inc., Freeport, Tex., 1979; graphic designer Graphics Co., Lake Jackson, Tex., 1980; art dir. Intermedics, Inc., Freeport, 1980-83; graphic designer and owner Squashic Design, Houston, 1983—; graphics judge Soc. Tech. Communication, Houston, 1982-83. Jazz dancer Linda David Dance Co., Lake Jackson, Tex., 1982. Recipient award Soc. Tech. Communication, 1982; Publ. Design award Women in Communications, 1982; Best of Show, Graphics award Soc. Tech. Communications, 1982. Mem. Am. Inst. Graphic Arts, Houston Art Dirs. Club, Phi Kappa Phi, Alpha Lambda Delta. Republican. Roman Catholic. Home: 1130 St John Dr Pearland TX 77584

SQUAZZO, MILDRED KATHERINE OETTING, business executive; b. Bklyn., Dec. 22; d. William John and Marie Margaret (Fromm) Oetting.

Student L.I. U., 1946, Am. Mgmt. Assn., intermittently, 1959-64. Sec.-treas., purchasing agt., office mgr. Kelite Corp., Berkeley Heights, N.J., 1953-59; adminstrv. asst., asst. sales mgr. electronic tube div. Burroughs Corp., Plainfield, N.J., 1960-61; sec.-treas. Stanley Engring., Inc. and v.p. Stanley Chems., Inc., Scotch Plains, N.J., 1962-68; pres., founder Chem.-Dynamics Corp., Scotch Plains, 1964-68; gen. adminstr., purchasing dir. Engring. div. Richardson Chem. Co., Metuchen, N.J., 1968-69; owner, operator Berkeley Employment Agy., Berkeley Heights, 1969—, Berkeley Temporary Help Service, Berkeley Heights, 1969—, Berkeley Employment Agy., Morristown, N.J., 1982—; pres. M.K.S. Bus. Group, Inc., Berkeley Heights, 1980—; cons. mgmt., personnel fin., lectr. in field. Served with Nurse Corps, U.S. Army, 1946-47. Mem. Nat. Bus. and Profl. Women's Club. Lutheran. Home: 721 Glenside Ave Berkeley Heights NJ 07922 Office: Profl Bldg 312 Springfield Ave Berkeley Heights NJ 07922

SQUIRE, LAURIE RUBIN, broadcasting company executive; b. N.Y.C., Jan. 30, 1953; d. Daniel and Ruth Thelma (Deutsch) Rubin; B.A. cum laude (scholar), Finch Coll., 1974; M.A., N.Y. U., 1976; postgrad. Tchrs. Coll. Columbia U., 1977—; m. Herbert E. Squire, Jr., Aug. 6, 1975; children—Amy Ruth and Julie Wynn (twins). Actress, TV commls., 1960-65; arts editor Finch/Metro N.Y.C. newspaper, 1970-74; co-editor Finch Alumnae Mag., 1971-72; intern producer WBAI-FM, N.Y.C., 1973; music prodn. coordinator WNET TV Ballet Theatre spl., 1973; Coll. Bd. writer Mademoiselle Mag., 1973; intern asst. public affairs dir. N.Y. Cultural Center, 1974; mdse. coordinator WOR-AM, N.Y.C., 1974-76, contbg. writer Bob and Ray's Mary Backstayge serial, contbr. nostalgia features Joe Franklin Show; producer Jean Shepherd Show, WOR-AM and syndicated markets, 1975-77; broadcast stage mgr. Texaco Met. Opera broadcasts, 1976—; producer Bernard Meltzer What's Your Problem, WOR-AM, 1977-80; dance critic Show Bus., theatre newspaper; dir. publicity and advt. L.I. Playhouse, 1982—; press rep. Great Neck Plaza; writer Center Island Pennysaver; publicity cons. Nassau County Mus. Fine Art, United Community Fund. Recipient commendations for Leukemia Radiothons, Peabody Broadcasting citation, 1983. Mem. Internat. Radio and TV Soc., Great Neck Hist. Soc. Home and Office: 892 Middle Neck Rd Great Neck NY 11024

SQUIRE, MATTIE LUE, educator; b. Goshen, Ala., Jan. 1, 1925; d. Brunie and Bertha M. (Smith) Sconions; m. Robert L. Squire, July 31, 1940; children—Barbara L., Madelyn C., Linda A., Robert L. A.A., Miami Dade Coll., 1970; B.S., Fla. Internat. U., 1973, M.S., 1974. Sch. lunch cashier, maid Dade County Pub. Schs., Miami, Fla., 1957-64, tchr.'s aide, 1964-69, tchr. asst., 1969-73, tchr., 1973—; mgr. New Century Reading Lab., 1975-76, mgr. Title I Reading Lab., 1976-79. Chmn. Miami Women's Com. of 100, 1980; bd. dirs. Brownsville Neighborhood Civic Assn., Miami, 1975; founder Back to Coll. Brunch, Miami, 1960; founder Israel Bethel P.B. Ch. Scholarship Fund, Miami, 1980, also Sunday Sch. tchr., 1942—. Recipient Cert. of Achievement, Fla. Internat. U., Miami, 1974. Mem. Nat. Assn. Female Execs., AAUW, Fla. Fedn. Bus. and Prof. Women's Clubs, Dade Fedn. Bus. and Profl. Women's Clubs (Woman of Yr. 1981), Fla. State Reading Council, Epsilon Tau Lambda.

SQUIRES, MARGARET ADELIA, credit manager; b. Pitts.; d. Joseph James Mowery and Felicia Irene (Stiteler) Stricklin; m. Edwin Markham Blakeslee, Apr. 10, 1937 (div. 1946); children—Russell, Karen Blakeslee Lanting, Richard; m. Bruce Glenn Squires, Nov. 23, 1957 (dec. 1981). Student pub. schs. Dearborn, Mich. Mgr. Credit Bur. Kalamazoo, Mich., 1946-75; credit mgr. Gilmore's, Kalamazoo, 1975—. Contbr. articles to profl. publs. Mem. Kalamazoo Credit Women Internat. (pres., contbr. chpt. to study manual 1985), Credit Mgrs. Assn. (pres. 1977). Republican. Baptist. Lodges: Soroptomist, Shriners, Eastern Star. Home: 4154 Standish St Kalamazoo MI 49008

SQUIRES, PATRICIA EILEEN COLEMAN, freelance journalist; b. Beaver Falls, Pa., Jan. 28, 1927; d. John Wiley and Helen Marie (Barstow) Purtell; B.A. in Journalism, Ind. U., 1949; m. Mark B. Squires, Sr., June 30, 1951; children—Sally Regan, Mark B., Susan Barstow. Staff reporter LaPorte (Ind.) Herald-Argus, 1949-51, daily columnist, 1950-51, sect. editor, 1949-51; women's news and feature writer Muskegon (Mich.) bur. Grand Rapids Herald, 1956-57; editor suburban sect. North Shore Line, Chicagoland Mag., Chgo., 1967-69; staff writer Fairpress, Westport, Conn., 1972-73; regular contbr. New Canaan (Conn.) Advertiser, 1975-78, Bridgeport (Conn.) Sunday Post, 1976-78, Soundings, Essex, Conn., 1977-78, N.Y. Times, N.Y.C., 1976—; tchr. English, journalism, social studies jr. and sr. public high schs., Jackson, Mich., 1966-67, Niles Twp., Skokie, Ill., 1967-68; vol. tutor Social Cultural Ednl. Enrichment Program, Protestant Community Center, 1979—. Public relations, promotion dir. Ella Sharp Mus., Jackson, 1964-66; publicity chmn. New Canaan Soc. for Arts, 1977-78; bd. dirs. Centennial Celebration Com., Winnetka, Ill., 1968-69; Community Council New Canaan, 1972-75; New Canaan Bicentennial Com., 1975-76; publicity chmn. parent-tchr. council Frost Jr. High Sch., Jackson, 1963-64; active Girl Scouts Am. Mem. Women in Communications, N.J. Press Women, Nat. Fedn. Press Women, AAUW, Ind. U. Alumni Assn. Presbyterian. Clubs: Cedar Point Yacht (Westport, Conn.); Lake Mohawk Golf (Sparta, N.J.). Home and Office: 688 West Shore Trail Sparta NJ 07871

SROGE, MARIAN, association executive, consultant; b. N.Y.C., Jan. 12, 1941; d. Eli and Charlotte (Radlauer) Stern; m. Marshall I. Sroge, Jan. 14, 1962; children—Rebecca, Joshua, Deborah. B.A., Queens Coll., 1962. Tchr. N.Y.C. Pub. Schs., 1964-68; community resource coordinator Mut. Aid Project, N.Y.C., 1977-79; dir. info. ref. and advt. Aging in Am., Bronx, N.Y., 1979-81; dir Empire region B'nai B'rith Women, Inc., N.Y.C., 1981-86; nat. dir. Women's Am. ORT, N.Y.C., 1986—. Author booklets: Homecare, 1980; Senior Community Information Network, 1981; co-author: Older Person's Handbook, 1978. Chairperson LWV Riverdale br., N.Y., 1975, spl. appointe to LWV, N.Y.C., 1976. Mem. N.Y. Soc. Assn. Execs., Am. Soc. Assn. Execs.

STAAS, GRETCHEN LEE, librarian; b. Dallas, Oct. 1, 1938; d. Fred Raike and Martha (Garten) Hyde; B.S., Tex. Christian U., 1961; M.S. in Library Sci., East Texas State U., 1974; doctoral candidate North Tex. State U.; m. Gene L. Staas, Aug. 29, 1959; 1 dau., Gayla Lynn. Classroom tchr. Garland (Tex.) Ind. Sch. Dist., 1967-74, librarian, 1974-78, cons. library and media services, 1978—. Mem. ALA, Tex. Library Assn., Tex. Assn. Sch. Library Adminstrs., Tex. Assn. Ednl. Tech., North Central Tex. IRA, Phi Delta Kappa, Kappa Delta Pi. Office: 720 Stadium Dr Garland TX 75040

STABILE, CAROL, banker; b. Bklyn., Mar. 1, 1951; d. Charles Joseph and Marion Theresa (Iovino) Corsentino; m. Ralph Joseph Stabile, Oct. 17, 1970 (div. Apr. 1976). A.A.S., Fashion Inst. Tech., 1970; B.B.A., Pace U., 1981. Notary pub., N.Y. Supr. check processing Anchor Savs. Bank, N.Y.C., 1973-78; asst. br. mgr. Am. Saving Bank, N.Y.C., 1978-79; group leader customer liaison Phila. Internat. Bank, N.Y.C., 1979-81, adminstrv. asst. internat. div. Tokyo desk, Phila., 1981-83, asst. treas., mgr. Asia, N.Y.C., 1983-85, asst. v.p., mgr. internat. customer service, 1986—. Active Pineapple Tenants Assn., Bklyn., 1984. Mem. Nat. Assn. Female Execs. Democrat. Roman Catholic. Avocations: collectors' plates; foreign films. Office: Phila Internat Bank 55 Broad St New York NY 10004

STABILE, ROSE TOWNE (MRS. FRED STABILE), bldg. and mgmt., public relations cons.; b. Sunderland, Eng.; d. Stephen and Amelia Bergman; student English schs., Tchrs. Coll., Columbia; m. Wilfred Kermode (dec. Feb. 1934); m. 2d, Arthur Whittlesey Towne, May 29, 1936 (dec. 1954); m. 3d, Norbert Le Veillie, June 10, 1961 (div. Feb. 1969); m. 4th, Fred Stabile, May 30, 1970. Formerly auditor Brit. Govt., Whitehall, London; activities and membership dir. N.Y. League of Girls Clubs, N.Y.C.; real estate exec., now semi-ret. bldg. mgr. State Tower Bldg., Syracuse, N.Y.; cons. public relations, office designer and decorator; lectr. real estate dept. Syracuse U. An initiator Syracuse Peace Council; mem. area sponsoring com. Assn. for Crippled Children and Adults. Mem. Syracuse Real Estate Bd., English Speaking Union (membership com.), Nat. N.Y. assns. real estate bds., Nat. Assn. Bldg. Owners and Mgrs., N.Y. Soc. Real Estate Appraisers, Syracuse C. of C., League Women Voters, Assn. UN, Women of Rotary, Bus. and Profl. Women's Clubs, Everson Mus. Art Friends of Reading, Mus. Modern Art (N.Y.C.), Internat. Center of Syracuse. Unitarian (chmn. service com. 1956-57.). Club: Corinthian. Home: 304 Malverne Dr Syracuse NY 13208 Office: State Tower Bldg Syracuse NY 13202

STACEY, PAMELA, editor, writer; b. Salt Lake City; Mar. 29, 1945; d. Jack Nordvall Freeze and Peggy (Whelan) Sherman; m. Richard C. Murphy, Feb. 22, 1981; stepchildren—Greg, Jeanne. B.A. in English, UCLA, 1968, teaching credential, 1970; M.A. in English, Calif. State U.-Long Beach, 1985. Researcher, Drew Pearson-Journalist, Washington, 1964, 66; adminstr. UNESCO, Paris, 1968-69; Rand Corp., Santa Monica, Calif., 1972-76; editor, writer Cousteau Soc., Los Angeles, 1976—. Editor, creator (mag. for children) Dolphin Log for Cousteau Soc., 1981. Avocations: scuba diving; sailing; skiing. Office: Cousteau Soc 8440 Santa Monica Los Angeles CA 90069

STACKELL, ESTHER ILANA, lawyer; b. Lvov, USSR, May 31, 1954; came to U.S. 1965, naturalized 1974; d. Joseph and Rose (Zilber) Goldstein; m. Isaac Barry Stackell, Jan. 8, 1977; 1 child, Zachary Alexander. B.A., Lehigh U., 1974; J.D., Hofstra U., 1979. Bar: N.Y. 1980. In-house counsel Jewish Hosp and Med. Ctr., Bklyn., 1979-81; assoc. gen. counsel Fedn. Jewish Philanthropies, N.Y.C., 1981; assoc. Bergner, Bergner, & Blum, N.Y.C., 1981-82; atty., cons. law offices of Esther I. Stackell, Bklyn., 1984—; cons. in field. Vice chmn. Neighborhood Tenants Assn., Bklyn., 1985; mem. Union Women's Ctr., Bklyn., 1985. Mem. New York County Lawyers, N.Y. State Bar Assn., Greater N.Y. Hosp. Assn., Med. Malpractice Com., Nat. Assn. Female Execs. Republican. Club: Lehigh Alumni Greater N.Y. Avocations: stained glass design.

STADLER, KATHERINE LOY, advertising agency executive; b. N.Y.C., Mar. 26, 1930; d. William L. and Catherine (Schmidhauser) Stadler; student St. John's U., 1948-49, Hunter Coll., 1957-59, N.Y. U. Mgmt. Inst., 1963-69. Br. mgr. Hull Travel Service, Inc., N.Y.C., 1959-63; with Loire Imports, Inc., N.Y.C., 1963-69; dist. mgr. McGraw-Hill Info. Systems Co., Sweet's Div., N.Y.C., 1969-74; nat. sales mgr. Floor Covering Weekly, N.Y.C., 1974-76; account exec. Ziff-Davis Pub. Co., Hotel & Travel Index, Los Angeles, 1976-81; founder Katherine Stadler & Assocs., 1981—; Western rep. Modern Salon, 1984—. Mem. Med. Mission Sisters, Roman Catholic Ch., 1949-57. Named Sweet's Eastern Region Salesman of Yr., 1972. Mem. Nat. Assn. Profl. Saleswomen, Nat. Home Fashions League, Early Music Ensemble Los Angeles, 1985—. Clubs: Los Angeles Ad, Toastmasters. Home: 427 S Curson Ave Los Angeles CA 90036

STADLER-COLBURN, TERESA ELLEN, ballet educator, artistic director; b. Seattle, Sept. 30, 1956; d. William J. and Elizabeth Mae (Dieckhoff) Stadler; m. Joel M. Colburn, July 21, 1984. Student Cornish Sch., 1976, First Chamber Dance Workshop, 1972-73, Joffery Workshop, 1970, McDade Ballet Sch., 1966-73. Dancer, Chgo. Ballet, 1981-82, Ballet De Marsailles, France, 1974, Milw. Ballet, 1977-79; ballet tchr., artistic dir. Seahurst Ballet Co. and Sch., Seattle, 1983—. Choreographer Seahurst Ballet, 1983—. Bd. dirs. Sea-Tac Arts Council, Seattle, 1985. Office: Seahurst Ballet 126 SW 153d St Seattle WA 98166

STADTMAN, THRESSA CAMPBELL, biochemist; b. Sterling, N.Y., Feb. 12, 1920; d. Earl and Bessie (Waldron) Campbell; m. Earl Reece Stadtman, Oct. 19, 1943. B.S., Cornell U., 1940, M.S., 1942; Ph.D., U. Calif.-Berkeley, 1949. Research assoc. U. Calif.-Berkeley, 1942-47, Harvard U. Med. Sch., Boston, 1949-50; biochemist Nat. Heart, Lung and Blood Inst., NIH, USPHS, HHS, Bethesda, Md., 1950—. Editor Jour. Biol. Chemistry, Archives Biochemistry and Biophysics, Molecular and Cellular Biochemistry; contbr. articles on amino acid metabolism, methane biosynthesis, vitamin B12 biochemistry, selenium biochemistry to profl. jours. Helen Haye Whitney fellow Oxford U. (Eng.), 1954-55; Rockefeller Found. grantee U. Munich (W.Ger.), 1959-60. Mem. Am. Soc. Microbiology, Biochem. Soc., Soc. Am. Biochemists, Am. Chem. Soc., Nat. Acad. Scis., Am. Acad. Arts and Scis. Home: 16907 Redland Rd Derwood MD 20855 Office: Nat Heart Lung and Blood Inst HHS Bethesda MD 20892

STAEBELL, SANDRA LYNNE, marketing executive; b. St. Louis, July 14, 1947; d. Louis Joseph, Jr. and Maureen (Barry) S.; B.L.S., St. Louis U., 1981. From exec. staff asst. to public relations coordinator, pub. relations dept. Seven-Up Co., St. Louis, 1972-80; dir. pub. relations Newcomb House, Inc., St. Louis, 1980, St. Mary on the Mount Hosp./Rehab. Center, St. Louis, 1981-84, Spectrum Emergency Care, Inc., St. Louis, 1984—; instr. advt. prins. and practices St. Louis U., 1981. Mem. Advt. Fedn. St. Louis (dir. 1978-80), Nat. Assn. Female Execs., Am. Soc. Profl. and Exec. Women, Am. Mktg. Assn., Bus. and Profl. Advt. Assn. LWV. Democrat. Lutheran. Home: 2829 Raritan Dr Webster Groves MO 63119 Office: 999 Executive Pkwy Saint Louis MO 63141

STAFFORD, ANITA FAYE, child therapist, author; b. Newport News, Va.; d. Sid Friend and Nina Eileen (Johnson) Rutherford; B.S., Central State U., Edmund, Okla., 1970, M.Ed., 1971; Ed.D., Okla. State U., 1975; m. J.L. Stafford; children—David Wayne, Stephen Lee. Lectr. family relations Central State U., 1971-73; asst. prof. home econs. Okla. Christian Coll., 1973-75; instr. early childhood edn. Oscar Rose Jr. Coll., Midwest City, Okla., 1975-76; asso. prof. human devel., chmn. dept. Tex. Woman's U., Denton, 1976-82; co-owner Five Senses, Inc., Denton, Tex. Mem. Nat. Assn. Edn. Young Children, Nat. Council Family Relations, AAUP, Nat. Assn. Gifted and Talented Children, Assn. Ednl. Communications and Tech., Assn. Spl. Edn. Tech., So. Assn. Children Under Six, Denton Assn. Edn. Young Children, Tex. Council Family Relations, Tex. Assn. Coll. Tchrs., Okla. Assn. Edn. Young Children (charter), Phi Delta Kappa. Republican. Baptist. Author: Human Technological Systems Series (4 vols.); also articles in field. Home: 1228 Stanley St Denton TX 76201 Office: 614 N Bell St Denton TX 76207

STAFFORD, BARBARA PRESTON, public relations specialist; b. Phila., Sept. 20, 1929; d. James Alexander and Elizabeth Marcy (Conover) Preston; m. Linley Montell Stafford, July 17, 1954 (div. June 1971); children—Preston Conover, Mary Clay. Student Wilson Coll., 1946-48; A.B., U. Ky., 1950; postgrad. in edn., Hunter Coll., 1960-62. Copywriter, Boone Advt. Agy., Louisville, 1950-51, Commonwealth Life Ins., Louisville, 1951-52; publicity asst. Rosemary Sheehan, N.Y.C., 1953-54, 55-57; pub. relations account exec. Aubrbach Agy., N.Y.C., 1957-60; elem. tchr. N.Y.C. Bd. Edn., 1962-66; copy editor Readers Digest, Chappaqua, N.Y., 1969-74, press coordinator, 1974-85, employee communications mgr., 1986—. Past officer, bd. dirs. Child Care Council Westchester. Mem. Women in Communications (v.p. Westchester). Home: 445 Broadway Hastings on Hudson NY 10706 Office: Readers Digest Chappaqua NY 10570

STAFFORD, HELEN ELIZABETH THOMSON, management consultant; b. Port Chester, N.Y., Mar. 1, 1926; d. James Ramage and Helen Cunningham (McGill) Thomson; B.S. in Psychology, Coll. William and Mary, 1948; m. Paul Tutt Stafford, Dec. 14, 1951; children—Paul Tutt, Timothy Alden, Mark Thornton, Todd Lawton. Exec. asst. commn. on worship Nat. Council Chs., N.Y.C., 1950-51; co-founder, dir., treas., sr. v.p. Paul Stafford Assos., Ltd., Mgmt. Cons., N.Y.C., 1959-82. Bd. dirs. Princeton Area YWCA, 1985—. Mem. Assn. Exec. Recruiting Cons. (dir. 1968-70), Soc. Alumni Coll. William and Mary (dir. 1984—), Mortar Board, Phi Beta Kappa, Kappa Kappa Gamma. Republican. Presbyterian. Clubs: Apawamis (Rye); Nassau (Princeton, N.J.); Hillsboro (bd. dirs. 1986—) (Pompano Beach, Fla.).

STAFFORD, REBECCA, college president; b. Topeka, July 9, 1936; d. Frank Clinton and Anna Elizabeth (Larrick) S.; B.A. magna cum laude, Radcliffe Coll., 1958; M.A., Harvard U., 1961, Ph.D., 1964; m. Willard Van Hazel, Apr. 12, 1973. Research sociologist Harvard U. Health Services, Cambridge, Mass., 1964-69, lectr. sociology Sch. Edn., 1969-70; assoc. prof. sociology U. Nev., Reno, 1970-74, prof., chmn. dept., 1974-77, dean Coll. Arts and Scis., 1977-80; pres. Bemidji (Minn.) State U., 1980-82; exec. v.p. Colo. State U., Fort Collins, 1982-84; pres. Chatham Coll., Pitts., 1984—. Bd. dirs. Urban League of Pitts., Pitts. Symphony, 1984—; trustee Presbyn.-Univ. Hosp., Pitts. Recipient McCurdy-Rinkle prize Eastern Psychiat. Assn., 1970. Mem. Am. Sociology Assn. (council sect. edn. 1971-74), Council Colls. Arts and Scis. (dir. 1977-80), Nat. Council Family Relations, Harvard U. Alumni Assn. (bd. dirs.), Phi Beta Kappa, Phi Kappa Phi. Contbr. articles on sociology to profl. jours. Home: 129 Woodland Rd Pittsburgh PA 15232 Office: Chatham Coll Woodland Rd Pittsburgh PA 15232

STAFFORD, VANESSA CAROLE, financial and management consultant; b. Norfolk, Va., Nov. 3, 1954; d. Nicholas William and Carole Anne (Barry) Flowers; m. William Allan Stafford, Oct. 10, 1972; children—Michael Augustus, Virgina Carole, Matthew Frederick. Student public and parochial schs., Balt., also Norfolk. Cert. internat. financier; accredited internat. news corr. Vice pres. United Mgmt. Group, Inc., Virginia Beach, Va., 1979-83; pres., 1983-86; sec. First City Mortgage Co., Virginia Beach, 1985—; cons. United Mgmt. Co., Virginia Beach, 1979—. Hon. girl scout Girl Scouts U.S., 1984-85. Mem. Hampton Roads C. of C., Better Bus. Bur. Southeastern Va., Nat. Assn. Female Execs., Nat. Fedn. Ind. Business, Internat. Soc. Financiers, NRA, Nat. Trust Historic Preservation, Nat. Audubon Soc., Smithsonian Instn., Republican. Roman Catholic. Avocations: boating; swimming; collecting; country crafts; travel. Home: 1256 Southfield Pl Virginia Beach VA 23452 Office: United Mgmt Group Inc 228 N Lynnhaven Rd Suite 120 Virginia Beach VA 23452

STAFFORD, VIRGINIA FRANCES, sorority administrator; b. Burlington, Iowa, Feb. 21, 1927; d. Neils Alfred and Florence Cecelia (Johansen) Rosenberg; B.A., U. Iowa, 1948; postgrad. U. Maine, 1950-51; m. Robert William Stafford, Aug. 29, 1948; children—Marcia Stafford Jorgensen, Craig William, Brian James, Maren Stafford Smith. Sub. tchr., tchr. speech Des Moines Public Schs., 1948-50; chmn. Iowa state membership Alpha Delta Pi, Ames, 1955-58, nat. chmn. membership selection, 1958-67, nat. chmn. pledge edn., 1967-73, grand sec., 1973-77, v.p. collegiate chpts., 1977-79, grand pres., 1977-83; chmn. collegiate expansion, 1983-85. Bd. dirs. Ames Internat. Festival Assn., sec., 1972-78; chmn. Ames Bicentennial Commn., 1974-76; bd. dirs. Ames Found., 1976—; bd. dirs. Mamie Eisenhower Birthplace Found., 1979—; pres. bd. dirs. Ames Community Art Council; bd. dirs. Ames Found. Mem. Assn. of Frat. Advs. (asso.), LWV, U. Iowa Alumni Assn. (com. to provide A. Craig Baird Endowment, speech dept. 1977—), Phi Beta Kappa, Delta Sigma Rho, Zeta Phi Eta. Republican. Presbyterian. Club: P.E.O. Home: 2044 Pinehurst Dr Ames IA 50010 Office: Alpha Delta Pi 1386 Ponce de Leon Ave NE Atlanta GA 30306

STAFFIN-METZ, SUSAN, college program administrator; b. Perth Amboy, N.J., Feb. 2, 1954; d. H. Kenneth and Laura (Valk) Staffin; B.A. in Psychology, Boston, U., 1976; M.A. in Individual and Group Counseling, Seton Hall U., 1978; m. Bruce Alan Metz, 1986; 1 dau., Meryl Staffin. Admissions and fin. aid counselor Stevens Inst. Tech., 1978, asst. dir. fin. aid, 1979, dir. spl. programs for women, 1980—, mem. adv. bd. tech. enrichment program, 1980—. Recipient Merit award for creative and innovative programs N.Am. Assn. Summer Sessions, 1981. Mem. AAUW, Am. Soc. Engring. Edn., Assn. Am. Colls., Nat. Assn. Women Deans, Adminstrs. and Counselors, N.J. Coll. and Univ. Coalition on Women's Edn. Office: Stevens Inst Tech Castle Point Hoboken NJ 07030

STAGER, PHYLLIS HUGO, investment executive; b. Tulsa, Nov. 16, 1937; d. Harold Arthur and Stella Josephine (Miller) Hugo; m. David R. Stager, Aug. 5, 1961 (div.); children—J. Jeff, Thomas, David, Elizabeth. R.N., St. Alexis Sch. Nursing Ohio State U., 1958; B.A. in History, So. Meth. U., 1980, postgrad. in Archaeology, 1980-81. Registered nurse, Ohio, Tex. Nurse, St. Alexis Hosp., Cleve., 1960-61; tchr. St. Christopher's Sch., Columbus, Ohio, 1962-63; head nurse Ft. Wood-Waynesville Schs. (Mo.), 1965-66; course and program asst. So. Meth. U. in Oxford, Eng., summer 1984; cons. Woodlife Ltd., Bloomingdale, Ill., 1981—; pres., owner Stager Enterprises, Dallas, 1978—; vol. archaeologist Earthwatch, Belize, 1981. Bd. dirs. Richardson Community Theater (Tex.), 1970; adv. bd. Dallas Repertory Theater, 1974; mem. advisory bd. So. Meth. U. Adult Studies in Eng., 1982; mem. arts com. Goals for Dallas, 1976. Mem. Am. Field Service (pres. 1979-80), Mensa. Inventor, disposable med. cosmetic appliance, 1978-79. Journalist (weekley column) Profiles (Willoughby News Herald), 1954-55. Office: Stager Enterprises 7619 Chattington Dallas TX 75248

STAGG, EVELYN WHEELER, educator, state legislator; b. Waterbury, Vt., Sept. 30, 1916; d. Aiton Grover and Edythe (Boyce) Wheeler; m. David Stagg, May 15, 1942; children—Christie Stagg Austin, Bonnie Stagg-Michlein, Carol Stagg Kevan. B.A., Middlebury Coll., 1939; M.A., U. Vt., 1971. Assoc. prof. Castleton State Coll., Vt., 1966-82; mem. Vt. Ho. of Reps., 1982-87; cons. communications projects, Bomoseen, Vt., 1982—. Contbr. articles to profl. jours. Chmn. Women's Legis. Caucus; pres., mem. Rutland Area Vis. Nurse Assn., 1969-75; bd. dirs. Rutland Mental Health Assn. Mem. Women's Caucus, Vt. Women's Polit. Caucus, Nat. Women's Polit. Caucus, AAUW, Inst. for Gen. Semantics, Internat. Soc. for Gen. Semantics, Am. Numismatic Soc., Am. Philatelic Soc., Castleton Hist. Soc. Democrat. Clubs: Women's, Rutland County Stamp. Avocations: stamp and coin collecting; dolls; sailing; skiing; traveling. Home: Masons Point Bomoseen VT 05732 Office: State House Montpelier VT 05602

STAHL, DULCELINA ALBANO, hospital administrator, educator, nurse; b. Bacarra, Ilocos Norte, Philippines, came to U.S., 1967, naturalized, 1978; d. Rosalino and Jovita (Acosta) Albano; m. Wendelin Walter Stahl; children—Astania, Bryan, Larraine. Cert. nurse adminstr. Dir. nursing Mary Thompson Hosp., Chgo., 1970-71; asst. dir. nursing U. Ill. Hosp., Chgo., 1971-72; faculty sch. nursing South Chgo. Community Hosp., Chgo., 1972-75; dir. nursing Bethany Hosp., Chgo., 1975-80; sr. assoc. adminstr. Olympia Fields Osteo. Med. Ctr., Ill., 1980-85; corp. adminstr. program devel., ambulatory and patient care services CCOM Hosps., 1985—; faculty nursing mgmt. nat. seminars, 1984—; faculty Prairie State Coll., Chgo., 1981—. Author: (with others) Cancer Nursing, 2d edit., 1982. Contbr. articles to profl. jours. Bd. dirs. Hospice Suburban S., Olympia Fields, 1983—; mem. adv. com. Prairie State Coll. Nursing Edn., 1981—. Recipient Disting. Alumni award DePaul U., 1985. Mem. Inst. Ethics Life Scis., Am. Mgmt. Assn., Ill. Soc. Nurse Adminstrs., League Nursing, Ill., Am. Nurses Assn., Ill. Nurses Assn., Am. Coll. Health care Execs., Am. Cath. Philos. Assn. Avocations: swimming; singing; dancing; writing poetry. Home: 2269 Post Rd Northbrook IL 60062 Office: Olympia Fields Osteo Med Ctr 20201 S Crawford Ave Olympia Fields IL 60461

STAHL, LESLEY R., journalist; b. Lynn, Mass., Dec. 16, 1941; d. Louis and Dorothy J. (Tishler) S.; m. Aaron Latham; 1 dau. B.A. cum laude, Wheaton Coll., Norton, Mass., 1963. Asst. to speechwriter Mayor Lindsay's Office, N.Y.C., 1966-67; researcher N.Y. Election unit London-Huntley Brinkley Report, NBC News, 1967-69; producer, reporter WHDH-TV, Boston, 1970-72; news corr. CBS News, Washington, from 1972; moderator Face the Nation, 1983—. Trustee Wheaton Coll. Recipient Tex. Handliners award, 1973. Office: CBS News 51 W 52d St New York NY 10019*

STAHL, MARILYN BROWN, interior designer; b. Boston, Dec. 11, 1929; d. Benjamin M. and Nettie D. (Glazer) Brown; B.S. in Art Edn., Mass. Coll. Art, 1951; m. Alvan L. Stahl, July 1, 1951; children—Robert, Barry, Kim. Instr. painting, Newton, Mass.; free-lance fabric designer, 1960-63; owner gallery, Newton, 1963-66, M.B. Stahl Interiors, Chestnut Hill, Mass., 1966; founder, pres. Maab Inc., mfrs. French furniture, 1979; pres. Decorators' Clearing House, Newton Upper Falls, Mass. Mem. Nat. Home Fashions League, Am. Soc. Interior Designers Industry Found., Nat. Home Fashions League Industry. Found. Home: 15 Manet Circle Chestnut Hill MA 02167 Office: Decorators' Clearing House 1029 Chestnut St Newton Upper Falls MA 02164

STAHL, SANDY LYNN, promotion director, advertising executive; b. Phila., Nov. 2, 1949; d. Fred Edward and Evelyn (DePolis) Barkovich; m. David Joseph Stahl, Feb. 28, 1970 (div.). B.A., U. Pa., 1970. Circulation dir. Nat. Carl Schurz Assn., Phila., 1970-71; editor Charles C Thomas Publs., Ft. Lauderdale, Fla., 1971-72; dir. advt. and promotion Sta. WRKO, Boston, 1972-77; market researcher, San Francisco, 1977-79; dir. advt. and publicity Bill Graham Presents, San Francisco, 1979-81; promotion dir. Sta. WLUP, Chgo., 1981—, photographer, 1981—; free lance publicity various pub. service orgns., Chgo., 1981—. Active Big Sisters Am., San Francisco, 1977-78. Recipient Promotion Dir. of Yr. award RKO Radio, 1975, 76. Mem. Nat. Assn. Female Execs. Democrat. Baptist. Home: 1920 N Lincoln Ave Apt 3 Chicago IL 60614

STAHLKA, WENDY TOBIN, radio executive; b. Quincy, Mass., Nov. 11, 1950; d. Joseph Henry and Eileen (Bell) Tobin; m. Clayton A. Stahlka, Sept. 18, 1975; stepchildren—Clay W., Krisann, Rachel. Diploma with honors, U. Caen (France), 1971; B.A., Newton Coll. of Sacred Heart, 1972. Asst. to editor Laser Focus Mag., Newton, Mass., 1972-73; account exec. Stahlka/Faller Advt., Buffalo, 1973-74; asst. to program dir. Sta. WBEN-AM & FM, Buffalo, 1979-83, dir. sales promotion, 1983-85; dir. mktg. and promotion Algonquin Broadcasting Corp., 1985—; freelance announcer radio commls. Mem. women's bd. Millard Fillmore Hosp., Buffalo, 1977-79. Recipient award for excellence Profl. Communicators Western N.Y., 1984. Mem. Women in Communications, Profl. Communicators of Western N.Y., Broadcast Promotion and Mktg. Execs. Home: 60 Westchester Rd Buffalo NY 14221 Office: Sta WBEN 2077 Elmwood Ave Buffalo NY 14221

STAHR, STEPHANIE ANN, lawyer; b. Lexington, Ky., Sept. 27, 1952; d. Elvis Jacob and Dorothy (Berkfield) S.; m. Jeffrey Paul Metzger, Dec. 27, 1977; 1 child, Emily Stahr Metzger. A.B. magna cum laude, Smith Coll., 1974; J.D., U. Va., 1978. Bar: D.C. 1978. Asst. editor Bur. Nat. Affairs, Washington, 1974-75; assoc. Miller & Chevalier, Washington, 1978-85, Epstein Becker Borsody & Green, Washington, 1985—. Recipient Dawes Polit. Sci. Prize, Smith Coll., 1974. Mem. D.C. Bar, Bar Assn. D.C., Women's Legal Def. Fund, Phi Beta Kappa. Democrat. Episcopalian. Office: Epstein Becker Borsody & Green 1140 19th St NW Washington DC 20005

STAKER, MARTHA DELIA, nursing educator, counselor; b. Kansas City, Mo., Jan. 30, 1945; d. William James and Mary Elizabeth (Callaghan) Leahy; m. Rodd David Staker, Sept. 6, 1969; children—David, Daniel, Bridget. B.S. in Nursing, Avila Coll., 1966; M.S. in Nursing, U. Colo., 1969; M.A. in Counseling, U. Mo., 1983. Staff nurse Bapt. Hosp. Kansas City, Mo., 1966-67, St. Joseph Hosp., Kansas City, 1967-68; instr. nursing Avila Coll., Kansas City, 1969-71, 1977-83, now mem. adj. faculty; mem. faculty St. Mary's Family Medicine Residency and Research Ctr., Kansas City, 1983—; mem. adv. bd. Kimberly Home Health Care; preceptor U. Mo.-Kansas City Sch. Nursing; cons. on psycho-social aspects of phys. illness, 1981—; speaker on pub. health, 1980—. Recipient Avila Medal of Honor, Avila Coll., 1966. Mem. Am. Nurses Assn., Mo. Nurses Assn., Am. Personnel and Guidance Assn., Mo. Personnel Guidance Assn., Sigma Theta Tau, Beta Lambda Theta. Roman Catholic. Home: 646 W 70th St Kansas City MO 64113 Office: St Mary's Family Medicine Residency and Research Center 2900 Baltimore Room 400 Kansas City MO 64113

STALEY, ELAINE MARY, administrative assistant; b. Wisconsin Rapids, Wis., Sept. 26, 1943; d. Maurice Philip and Mary Ann (Menke) S. B.S. in Communication Arts, U. Wis.-Madison, 1965. Registered profl. parliamentarian. Program specialist U. Wis. Extension, Madison, 1966-69; specialist, exec. sec. U. Wis. System-Faculty Council and Assembly, Madison, 1969-73; adminstrv. asst., exec. sec. Exec. Office, Wis. Council on Criminal Justice, Madison, 1973-75; asst. to chmn. dept. communication arts U. Wis.-Madison, 1975-80, adminstrv. asst. Sch. Social Work, 1980—; parliamentary cons. Nat. Assn. Parliamentarians, Kansas City, Mo., 1976—. Contbr. articles to profl. jours. Mem. Women's Polit. Caucus, Madison, 1973-77; mem. steering com. Dane County's Citizen Orgn., Madison, 1980-81; staff asst. Gov's Commn. on Edn., Wis., 1970-71; mem. Big Bros./Sisters Dane County, 1979—, bd. dirs., 1985-88; bd. dirs. Madison Theatre Guild, 1974-76, treas., 1974-76, cert. of merit awards 1971-72, 72-73; treas., bd. dirs. Madison Packer Backers, Inc., 1984-86; mem. Gov.'s Inaugural Ball Arrangements Com., Madison, 1979; mem. Madison Civic Opera Guild, 1977—, Madison Civic Ctr. Friends, 1983—, Friends of WHA-TV, 1977—, Friends of the Waisman Ctr., Madison, 1980—, pres., 1984-85. Recipient Exceptional Performance awards U. Wis.-State Wis., Madison, 1983, 84. Mem. Commn. on Am. Parliamentary Practice of Speech Communication Assn. (chmn. 1978-80), Am. Inst. Parliamentarians, Nat. Assn. Parliamentarians (profl. registered parliamentarian 1976—, state bd. dirs. 1977—, co-chmn. publicity and newsletter coms. 1983-85, unit treas. 1985-86), Assn. Univ. Faculty Women and Univ. Extension League, 1968-74. Democrat. Roman Catholic. Avocations: downhill and cross-country skiing; golf; swimming; crafts; reading; sailing. Home: 933 Magnolia Ln Madison WI 53713 Office: Sch Social Work U Wis-Madison 425 Henry Mall Madison WI 53706

STALEY, MARTHA MCHENRY GREEN (MRS. WALTER G. STALEY), civic worker; b. Kirkwood, Mo., Oct. 22, 1905; d. Allen Percival and Josephine (Brown) Green; A.A., Hardin Coll., 1925; postgrad. Art Student's League N.Y.C., 1925-28, 50, Acad. Julian, Paris, 1950; m. Walter Goodwin Staley, Dec. 25, 1928; children—Martha Staley Marks, Walter Goodwin, Allen Percival Green. First v.p. Mo. Assn. Mental Health, 1960-64, bd. dirs., 1958-64; v.p. East Central Mo. Mental Health Assn., 1969—; v.p. Presbyn. Home for Children Mo., 1962-63, bd. dirs., 1968-71; chmn. Audrain Fine Arts Council, 1965-70; pres. Audrain County Hist. Soc., 1965-70; mem. advisory council Mo. Arthritis Center, 1971—. Bd. dirs. Allen P. and Josephine B. Green Found; trustee Mexico-Audrain County Library, 1959-66. Life mem. St. George Village Bot. Garden of St. Croix, Landmarks Soc. of St. Croix, Island Center of St. Croix; mem. Nat. Soc. Colonial Dames Am., Nat. Soc. Magna Charta Dames, Daus. Brit. Empire, Huguenot Soc. S.C. Presbyterian. Home: 15 S Jefferson Rd Mexico MO 65265 also PO Box 397 Frederiksted St Croix VI 00840

STALKER, JOAN ELIZABETH, government official; b. St. Louis, Jan. 5, 1940; d. David Richard and Leona Margaret (Sattel) Seibert; m. Karl John Stalker, Dec. 25, 1960; children—Karl John, Karla. Student Drury Coll., 1958-59; A.S. magna cum laude, No. Va. Community Coll., Annandale, Va., 1977; B.A. in Psychology, George Mason U., 1983, cert., 1984. Cost acct. Comml. Credit, Atlanta, 1959-61; supr. First Va. Bank, Springfield, 1970-73; clk. potal adminstrn. U.S. Postal Service, Lorton, Va., 1974-81, postmaster, 1981—; also chmn. rev. bd. tng. and devel. No. Va., 1983, and mem. coms. and rev. bd., 1984. Officer PTA, Fairfax County, Va., 1969-76; leader Washington Area council Girl Scouts U.S.A., 1972-76; vol. Mt. Vernon Mental Health Ctr., Fairfax County, 1980; vol. counselor Girls Probation House, Fairfax County, 1983-84. Recipient Community Service award Nat. Capital Area Combined Fed. Campaign, 1980, Service award Am. Lung Assn. No. Va., 1981. Mem. Nat. Assn. Postmasters. Republican. Presbyterian. Avocations: boating; swimming; gardening. Home: 5917 Oak Grove St PO Box 216 Lorton VA 22079 Office: Lorton Post Office 7663 Lorton Rd Lorton VA 22079

STALLINGS, BETTY JEAN, retired army officer; b. Champaign, Ill., Jan. 16, 1935; d. Harris Dean and Harriett Louise (Pillsbury) S. B.S., Stanford U., 1957. Commd. 1st lt., U.S. Army, 1963, advanced through grades to lt. col., dir. logistics U.S. WAC Ctr. and Sch., Anniston, Ala., 1972-74; budget officer Hdqr. Dept. Army, Pentagon, Washington, 1975-79; chief food service br. Hdqr. U.S. Army Europe, Heidelberg, W. Ger., 1979-81; asst. insp. gen. Dept. Def., Alameda, Calif., 1981-84. Chmn. card and gift sales UNICEF, Alameda, 1982-83; pres. YWCA of Monterey Peninsula, 1986-87; pres. Internat. Tng. in Communication, 1986-87. Decorated Bronze Star medal, Army and Def. Meritorious Service medal. Mem. Bus. and Profl. Women (legis. chmn. 1983-84, sec. Pacific Grove 1985-86), Bay Valley Dist. Bus. and Profl. Women (legis. com. 1983-84), Am. Soc. Mil. Comptrollers (nat. sec. 1977-78), LWV (membership dir. Monterey Peninsula League 1985-86), Nat. Assn. Female Execs., Q.M. Officers Assn. Club: Toastmistress (sec. council 4, 1983-84, v.p. Alameda 1982-83, pres. Arcadames 1977-78, chmn. internat. conv. sales 1977). Office: Dept Def 316 Spruce Avenue Pacific Grove CA 93950

STALLINGS, JOYCE ELAINE, department store executive; b. East Chicago, Ind., June 24, 1956; d. William Earl and Lelia Dell (Selvie) S. B.S., Mich. State U., 1978. With Dayton's Dept. Store, Mpls., 1978—, buyer, 1981-84, sr. buyer Dayton-Hudson Dept. Store, 1984—. Named Outstanding Achiever City of East Chicago, 1982. Mem. Minn. Networking System, Turning Point, Alpha Kappa Alpha. Baptist. Avocations: aerobics; bicycling; ballet; art. Home: 4813 Cedar Lake Rd Saint Louis Park MN 55416 Office: Dayton-Hudson Dept Store Co Minneapolis MN 55402

STALSBERG, GERALDINE MARIE, accountant, systems analyst; b. Springfield, Mo., May 10, 1936; d. Gerald Earl McEwen and Marie LaVerne (Pennington) Plautz; m. Bill Eugene Bottolfson, Mar. 10, 1956 (div. 1978); children—Bill Earl, Robert Edward, Brian Everett, Michelle Marie; m. Arvid Ray Stalsberg, Sept. 21, 1979. Diploma Hastings Beauty Acad., 1955; cert. in Interior Design, Central Tech. Community Coll., 1975; student Doane Coll., 1982; cert. computer programmer Lincoln Sch. Commerce, Nebr., 1984. Cosmetologist, Marinello Beauty Shop, Hastings, 1955-57; owner Nursery Sch. for Toddlers, 1958-67; acct. grain dept. Morrison-Quirk Elevator, Hastings, Nebr., 1968-69; acct., interior decorator Uerling's Home Furnishings, Hastings, 1970-79; acct., computer programmer, Lincoln Transp., Nebr., 1980—, systems analyst, 1984—; tax cons. H&R Block, Lincoln, 1983—. Emergency radio dispatcher Adams County Civil Def., Hastings, 1973-78; active YWCA. Recipient Civic Achievement award City of Hastings, 1974. Mem. Nat. Assn. Govt. Employees, Bus. Profl. Women, Library Assn., Nat. Assn. Female Execs., Soroptimists Internat., Beta Sigma Phi. Republican. Lutheran. Avocations: reading; bowling; fishing; swimming; jogging. Office: Lincoln Transp System 710 J St Lincoln NE 68508

STAMATS, BETTE-BARRON, company executive; b. Washington, Nov. 5, 1932; d. Ernest Louis and Margaret Frances (Barron) Smith; m. Peter Owen Stamats, Aug. 31, 1957 (div.); children—Peter Spencer, William Smith. B.S., Sweet Briar Coll., 1954. Med. technician Nat. Cancer Inst., Bethesda, Md., 1954-55, Nat. Inst. Diabetes/Metabolic Diseases, Bethesda, 1955-57; asst. acting field dir. Frank Magid Assocs., Marion, Iowa, 1979-80; field dir. Hase/Schannen Research Assocs., Princeton, N.J., 1980-83; mng. dir. Greenwich Opinion Center, Old Greenwich, Conn., 1983-85, v.p. research sales, 1986—. Mem. Am. Horse Shows Assn. (judge 1970-78), Jr. League. Republican. Episcopalian. Clubs: Garden of Am., Zone (co-chairperson 1978-80). Office: Manhattan Opinion Ctr 369 Lexington Ave New York NY 10017

STAMOS, CHARLOTTE JUSTINE, court official; b. Hartford, Conn., June 18, 1943; d. Charles Joseph and Laura (Ignas) Krebs; m. Theodore William Stamos, Jan. 28, 1967. B.A., U. Conn., 1967; M.S.W., Hunter Coll., 1984. Caseworker, Conn. Welfare Dept., Hartford, 1968-70; family relations counselor Family Relations Dept., Hartford, 1970-78; family relations supr. Family Relations Div., Superior Ct., New Britain, Conn., 1978—. Avocations: cooking; reading; travel; crewel work; art history. Office: Family Services Div Superior Ct 177 Columbus Blvd New Britain CT 06051

STAMPER, CARRIE JANE, construction company executive; b. Hagerstown, Md., Oct. 28, 1960; d. Andy B. and Gladys Edith (Schwanebeck) S., Sr. B.A. magna cum laude, Shippensburg State Coll., 1982. High sch. tchr. Trust for Youth Sch., Cayman Islands, British W.I., 1978-79; optometrist asst. Allegany Optical, Hagerstown, Md., 1976-82; constrn. estimator Stamper Constrn., Hagerstown, 1982, co-owner, co-founder Milcar Constrn., Hagerstown, 1982—; co-owner, mktg. cons. TKS Properties, Hagerstown, 1984—. Author: (with others) (adv. study) Feasibility Growth Prospect of Martinsburg, W.VA., 1982. Recipient Presdl. Phys. Fitness award (7 times) 1972-78. Mem. Wash. County Softball League, YMCA, Notary Pub. Assn., Nat. Assn. Home Builders, Harrisburg Builders Exchange. Republican. Home: Milestone Garden Apt 14K Williamsport MD 21795 Office: Milcar Constrn Corp Route 6 Box 91-A Hagerstown MD 21740

STAMPER, FLORENCE LOUISE FARIS, nurse; b. Mt. Ayr, Iowa, Aug. 20, 1938; d. Wilbur Everett and Eva Faye (Sawyer) Faris; m. Doyle E. Stamper, June 17, 1962; 1 dau., Marcia Denise. Diploma Iowa Meth. Sch. Nursing, 1959. Staff nurse Ringgold County Hosp., Mt. Ayr, 1959-60, Clarke County Hosp., Osceola, Iowa, 1960-63; dir. nursing Clearview Home, Mt. Ayr, 1963—; instr. Southwestern Community Coll., Creston, Iowa. Mem. Iowa Meth. Alumni Assn., Iowa Council Gerontol. Dirs. Nursing, Am. Heart Assn. (chpt. pres. 1983-84). Republican. Mem. Christian Ch. Home: 703 W Columbus St Route 2 Box 51 Mount Ayr IA 50854

STAN, PATRICIA, savings consultant, real estate company executive; b. Chgo., Oct. 10, 1952; d. Paul and Olga (Zyluk) S.; m. Donald Ross Crabtree, Feb. 27, 1982 (div.). Student Monmouth Coll., 1964-66; B.F.A., Drake U., 1969; postgrad. U. Houston, 1974-76, Houston Coll., 1977-78. Cert. tchr., Tex.; cert. real estate broker, Tex. Tchr., Spring Branch Meml. Ind. Sch. Dist., Houston, 1976-78; cons. Sam Feldt Co., Houston, 1978-80; counselor Doyle Stuckey Homes, Houston, 1980-82; pres. Stan Internat., Houston, 1981—; counselor Am. Classic Homes, Houston, 1982-83; cons. Savs. of America, Houston, 1983—. Patron Houston Mus. Fine Arts. Mem. Mensa, Tex. Edn. Assn., Nat. Women's Council Realtors, Houston Bd. Realtors, Tex. Real Estate Commn., Archaeol. Soc. Houston, Sierra Club, Kappa Kappa Gamma.

STANAT, RUTH ELLEN, paper company executive; b. Washington, Nov. 4, 1947; d. James Frances and Wylma Ellen Corrigan; B.S. in Edn. cum laude (acad. scholar), Ohio U., 1969; M.A. in Psychology, N.Y. U., 1973, M.B.A. in Fin., 1977; m. Jon Stanat, June 24, 1972; 1 son, Scott. Regional coordinator quality control div. indsl. engring. United Airlines, 1969-74; sr. analyst market research Springs Mills, Inc., 1974-75; with Internat. Paper Co., N.Y.C., 1975—, sr. analyst market research, product coordinator reprodn. papers, product supr. electrostatic papers, product mgr. spl. markets, 1975-78, mgr. strategic planning splty. packaging group, 1979-81; sr. planning mgr. Info. Services Group, 1981—; pres., chief exec. officer Strategic Intelligence Systems, Inc. Fund raiser Am. Cancer Soc. Recipient award of merit United Airlines, 1973. Mem. Fin. Women's Assn., Women in Paper, N.Y. U. Bus. Forum, Woman's Econ. Roundtable, Beta Gamma Sigma, Pi Gamma Mu. Lutheran. Home: 875 Fifth Ave Apt 5D New York NY 10021 Office: 404 Park Ave S Room 1026 New York

STANBRIDGE, BARBARA GAYE, management consultant; b. Detroit, Aug. 4, 1940; d. Reginald and Eugenie Clara (Gold) Stanbridge; m. William T. Hickey, June 25, 1976; 1 dau., Lara Michelle Mulawka. B.A., Marygrove Coll., 1963; M.A., U. Detroit, 1970; postgrad. U. Mich., 1980; M.Human Resource Devel., Univ. Assocs., Calif., 1980. Tchr., Archdiocese of Detroit and Detroit Bd. Edn., 1963-67, 70-71; dir. religious edn. Archdiocese of Detroit, 1968-70, 71-76; instr. Wayne County Community Coll., Detroit, 1974-80; pres. Change Human Resource Devel. Corp., Detroit, 1980—. Mem. Nat. Assn. Women Bus. Owners, Am. Soc. Tng. and Devel., Orgn. Devel. Network, Am. Mgmt. Assn., Gestalt Inst. Cleve., Detroit Women's Forum. Democrat. Roman Catholic. Office: Change Human Resource Devel Corp 400 Renaissance Ctr Suite 500 Detroit MI 48243

STANBROUGH, LILLIAN BETHINE, travel agent; b. Dublin, Tex., Nov. 28, 1925; d. Dennis O. and Aubrey (Brazille) Nelson; m. Jess H. Stanbrough, Sept. 3, 1948 (div. 1971); 1 child, Gary Nelson. B.J., U. Tex., 1948. Free-lance writer, Falmouth, Mass., 1965-69; travel agt. Hoyt Tours, Fort Worth, 1969-72, Hunnicutt Travel, Fort Worth, 1972-77; owner, operator Lone Star Travel Ctr., Fort Worth, 1977—. Contbr. numerous travel articles to Boston Globe and other newspapers, 1965-75. Pres., Falmouth League Women Voters, Mass., 1967-68. Mem. Am. Soc. Travel Agts. (com. on consumer affairs 1984-85), Pacific Area Travel Assn., Cruise Lines Internat. Assn., Bus. and Profl. Women's Club, AAUW, Network Exec. Women. Democrat. Avocations: gardening; ballooning; reading; traveling; dancing. Office: Lone Star Travel Ctr 1200 Summit Suite 702 Fort Worth TX 76102

STANDARD, MARY RUSSELL, computer software company executive, consultant; b. Orange, Tex., Mar. 8, 1926; d. Junius Brownrigg and Lily Amanda (McIlroy) Russell; m. Richard Clinton Armstrong, Jan., 1952 (div.); m. Jack Standard, Nov. 1955 (dec.). B.A., Baylor U., Waco, Tex., 1947; postgrad. U. So. Calif., 1948-49, NYU, 1964-66. Sr. computer systems analyst Continental Group, Stamford, Conn., 1959-82; pvt. practice consulting, N.Y.C., 1982—; v.p. software engring. Signature Software & Services, Princeton, N.J., 1984—. Mem. Data Processing Mgmt. Assn. Democrat. Office: Signature Software & Services 601 Ewing St Suite B7 Princeton NJ 08540

STANDEFER, MALINDA KAYE, lawyer; b. Gatesville, Tex., Sept. 16, 1950; d. Jan and Gloria Inez (Cooper) Clawson; m. Eugene Richard Stanefer, Jr., Dec. 28, 1978; children—Abigail Kaye, Amelia Kaye. B.S., Tex. Tech. U., 1974, J.D., 1981. Bar: Tex. 1981, U.S. Dist. Ct. (no. dist.) Tex. 1984. Tchr. spl. edn., Lubbock Ind. Sch. Dist., Tex., 1974-75, sheltered living dir., 1975-78; sole practice, Lubbock, 1981—. Bd. dirs. Planned Parenthood Lubbock, 1976-78; bd. dirs., pres. Lubbock County Mental Retardation Assn., 1984—. Mem. ABA, Tex. Bar Assn., Lubbock County Bar Assn., Lubbock County Young Lawyers Assn., Lubbock County Womens Bar Assn., Exec. Forum. Club: Winners Group. Avocations: reading; gardening; raising horses; swimming; aerobic dancing. Home: 5421 86th St Lubbock TX 79424 Office: 6502 Slide Rd Suite 402 Lubbock TX 79424

STANDING, BEVERLEY WHITING, designer, dress manufacturing company executive; b. Balt., June 1, 1956; d. Hugo John and Jean Hope (Willis) S. B.A. in English Lit. and Fine Arts, Stanford U., 1978; Fashion Design, Otis Art Inst. of Parson's Sch. Design, Los Angeles, 1983. Fashion prodn. The Broadway Dept. Stores, Los Angeles, 1978-80; owner, designer Beverley Standing Designs, Los Angeles, 1983—; lectr. Otis Art Inst. Parson's Sch. of Design. Featured on cover The Calif. Apparel News, 1985. Mem. patron costume council Los Angeles County Mus. of Art. Home: 13525 Romany Dr Pacific Palisades CA 90292 Office: Beverley Standing Design 819 Santee St Suite 1111 Los Angeles CA 90014

STANDRIDGE, KIM DIANE, accountant; b. Santa Ana, Calif., Apr. 26, 1957; d. Howard Vernon and Mary Louise (Countryman) Horner; m. Roger Odell Standridge, Jan. 7, 1978 (div. Aug. 1983). B.S. in Bus. Adminstrn., Okla. State U., 1984. C.P.A., Okla. Acct., Kerr-McGee Corp., Oklahoma City, 1980-82, Warren Petroleum Co., Tulsa, 1983; Cities Service Oil & Gas Corp., Tulsa, 1985—; auditor Arthur Young & Co., Tulsa, 1984-85. Mem. Am. Inst. C.P.A.s, Okla. Soc. C.P.A.s, Nat. Assn. Accts., Nat. Assn. Female Execs., Phi Kappa Phi, Beta Gamma Sigma, Beta Alpha Psi. Republican. Mem. Assembly of God Ch. Club: Toastmasters. Avocations: singing and performing in musicals; snow and water skiing; sailing. Home: 1430-B E 38th Pl Tulsa OK 74105 Office: Cities Service Oil & Gas Corp PO Box 300 Tulsa OK 74102

STANEK, DONNA MARIE, lawyer; b. Coaldale, Pa., Mar. 4, 1956; d. Stanley C. and Nora M. (Zwolenik) Stanek. B.A., Allentown Coll. of St. Francis de Sales, 1978; J.D., Widener U., 1981. Bar: Pa. 1982. Jud. clk. Ct. Common Pleas, York, Pa., 1982-83; assoc. firm Anstine & Anstine, York, 1983—. Mem. ABA, Pa. Bar Assn., Assn. Trial Lawyers Am., York County Bar Assn., Moot Ct., Phi Delta Phi. Roman Catholic. Office: Anstine & Anstine 117 E Market St York PA 17401

STANFIELD, ELIZABETH POPLIN, Spanish educator, translator; b. Jacksonville, Fla., Aug. 9, 1930; d. Thomas William and Mattie Olene (Padgett) Poplin; B.A. summa cum laude, U. N.C., Greensboro, 1952; M.A., Emory U., 1966; m. William Thomas Stanfield, June 30, 1956; children—C. Freeman, William Thomas. Tchr., fgn. langs. Atlanta City Schs., 1952-57, Fulton County (Ga.) High Sch., 1963-69; instr. Spanish, Ga. State U., Atlanta, 1968-78, asst. prof., 1978—, lectr. Learning Resources Ctr., 1975—, Speakers Bur., 1979—; cons. Ga. World Congress Inst. Internat. Cons. Directory, 1984; coll. supr. student tchrs. Ga. State Dept. Edn. Author poems. Contbg. editor So. Homes Mag., 1983—; contbr. articles to profl. jours. AAUW fellow, 1964-65. Mem. Am. Assn. Tchrs. Spanish and Portuguese (pres. Ga. 1979-81), MLA, So. Conf. Lang. Teaching, Fgn. Lang. Assn. Ga., 19th Century Studies Assn., Atlanta Assn. Interpreters and Translators (bd. dirs. 1985—), Am. Translators Assn. (assoc.), AAUP, Acad. Alliances in Ga. (convenor), Phi Beta Kappa, Omicron Delta Kappa, Sigma Delta Pi, Phi Sigma Iota, Lambda Iota Tau. Mem. Ch. of Christ. Office: Dept Fgn Langs Ga State U Atlanta GA 30303

STANFILL, CHERYL KATHLEEN, real estate executive; b. Oakland, Calif., May 4, 1945; d. Morris James Engle and Virginia Margery (Estensen) Tracht; m. Edward James Wyatt (div.); 1 child, Edward James. Student, Coll. of Marin, 1971. With Eckert and Assocs., Investment Real Estate, San Rafael, Calif., 1973-75, Frank Howard Allen, Real Estate Investments, San Rafael, 1975-79; trustee Trend Coll., Vancouver, Wash., 1978—; real estate investment, property devel. and mgmt. Trend Coll. Schs., 1978—; mgmt. adv., real estate cons. Pacific Hotel & Devel., Inc., Fiji, 1980—; trustee KLRK Trust, Vancouver, 1978—; real estate con., trust adminstr., property mgr. HTW Enterprises, Inc., Trend Colls., Vancouver, 1979—, Southmark Corp., Dallas. Republican. Avocation: flying Office: Stanfill Inc 7722 N Columbia Blvd Portland OR 97203

STANFORD, PATRICIA ANN, med. technologist; b. Poplarville, Miss., Oct. 24, 1937; d. Herman Thomas and Anna M. (Lee) Holden; A.A., Pearl River Jr. Coll., 1957; B.A., Miss. So. Coll., 1959; cert. med. tech., Miss. Bapt. Hosp. Sch. Med. Tech., 1959; m. Hiram B. Stanford, July 3, 1962; children—Herman Curtis, Lawanna Lee. Med. technologist Pearl River County Hosp., Poplarville, Miss., 1959—, chief lab. and x-ray technologist, 1959—; vol. local sch. sci. dept. Active PTA; mem. Pearl River County Hosp. and Extended Care Facility Aux. Mem. Am. Soc. Clin. Pathologists (assoc. mem., cert. med. technologist), Nat. Certification Agy. for Med. Lab. Personnel (clin. lab. scientist), Miss. State Soc. for Med. Tech., Am. Soc. Med. Tech., U. So. Miss. Alumni Assn. Beta Beta Beta, Alpha Epsilon Delta. Baptist. Home: Rt 3 Box 94 Poplarville MS 39470 Office: PO Box 392 Poplarville MS 39470

STANFORD, ROSE MARY, criminal justice educator, researcher; b. Portsmouth, Va., May 12, 1942; d. Robert Marion and Ruth (Watson) S.; children—Dion C. Greenwell, Cheryl L. Greenwell. B.A. magna cum laude, U. S. Fla., 1976, M.A. in Criminal Justice, 1979; Ph.D., Fla. State U., 1984. Interviewer U. South Fla., Tampa, 1975, researcher, interviewer, 1976; adj. instr. dept. criminal justice U. South Fla., St. Petersburg, 1977; parole and probation officer Fla. Dept. Corrections, Tampa, 1977-79; researcher Arthur Young and Co., Tallahassee, 1979-80; researcher, coder Office of State Cts. Adminstrs., Fla. Supreme Ct., Tallahassee, 1980; tutor dept. athletics Fla. State U., Tallahassee, 1981, teaching asst. Sch. Criminology, 1981; planner and evaluator planning and devel. Fla. Dept. Health and Rehab. Services, Tallahassee, 1980-81; asst. prof., intern coordinator dept. criminal justice Pan Am. U., Edinburg, Tex., 1982-85; asst. prof. dept. criminal justice U. South Fla., Fort Myers, 1985—, cons. in field. Contbr. articles to profl. jours., chpts. to books. Book reviewer Criminal Justice, Rev., 1985. Mem. community rev. bd. Rio Grande State Ctr., Harlingen, Tex., 1985, Community Adv. Council, McAllen Halfway House and Parole, Tex., 1984-85, Inter-Agy. Council for Youth Services, Hidalgo County, Tex., 1983-85; mem. oral bd. for sgt. promotion, Mission Police Dept., Tex., 1982; mem. Tex. Council on Crime and Delinquency, 1982-85; active in media on child abuse. Grantee in field. Mem. Am. Soc. Criminology, Acad. Criminal Justice Scis. (program com. 1985-86), Fla. Council on Crime and Delinquency (pres. chpt. 1, 1978-79, sec. chpt. 19, 1985-86, state bd. dirs. 1978-79), Alpha Phi Sigma, Phi Kappa Phi, Phi Theta Phi. Democrat. Roman Catholic. Avocations: dancing; movies; reading. Office: U South Fla 8111 College Pkwy SW Fort Myers FL 33907

STANFORD, SHEILA, direct marketing fundraiser; b. Dublin, Ireland, Sept. 3, 1949; came to U.S., 1958; d. John Francis and Mary (Winston) S.; m. Charles Ira Gluck, Jan. 20, 1973; 1 child, Joshua David. B.A. in English, Herbert H. Lehman Coll., 1971. Assoc. dir. communications and devel. The Alan Guttmacher Inst., N.Y.C., 1971-80; dir. individual giving Am. Bible Soc., N.Y.C., 1980-84; dir. direct mktg. CARE, Inc., N.Y.C., 1984—; cons. Cancer Care, N.Y.C., 1985—. Editor TV comml.: Baby (Silver medal Internat. TV and Film awards 1985). Mem. Direct Mktg. Assn., Women in Fin. Devel., Nat. Assn. Female Execs., Direct Mail Fundraisers Assn. (pres. 1985-86, v.p. 1983-84, newsletter editor 1983-84). Democrat. Home: 22 Jefferson Ave Emerson NJ 07630 Office: Care Inc 660 1st Ave New York NY 10016

STANFORD-JONES, KATHLEEN LOUISE, computer systems consultant; b. Aiea, Hawaii, Feb. 13, 1948; d. Harold Revis and Dorothy Louise (Swedling) S.; m. Charles Edward Jones, Jr., Apr. 27, 1985; 1 child, Sterling Colin. B.A., U. Tulsa. Computer programmer Kaiser Permanente, Los Angeles, 1975-81; project leader Lockheed Corp., Burbank, Calif., 1981-83; pres. K.L. Stanford, Inc., Century City, Calif., 1983—; condr. seminars in field, 1982—. Co-author; ADF Workbook, 1984. Mem. Ind. Computer Cons. Assn. Republican. Office: 4444 Aukland Toluca Lake CA 90602

STANKEY, SUZANNE MAE, magazine executive; b. Grand Rapids, Mich., Apr. 4, 1951; d. Robert Michael and Elizabeth Mae (Rodgers) S. B.A., Ohio U., 1973; B.J., U. Mo., 1977. News asst. The Blade, Toledo, Ohio, 1977-79, feature writer, 1979-80, feature editor, 1980-82, mag. editor, 1982—. Recipient feature writing award Ohio Newspaperwomen, 1980. Mem. Sigma Delta Chi. Democrat. Avocations: billiards; swimming. Home: 2508 Kenwood Blvd Toledo OH 43606 Office: The Blade 541 Superior St Toledo OH 43660

STANLEY, AUTUMN JOY, writer; b. Vinton County, Ohio, Dec. 21, 1933; d. William Ernest and Donna Barbara (Sanders) S.; m. F. Blair Simmons, June 6, 1955 (div. 1971); children—Kathryn D. Simmons Hickinbotham, Holly, Kevin, Iris; m. John Morgan Daniel, Jan. 1, 1973 (div. 1984). A.B. with high distinction, Transylvania Coll., 1955; M.A. in English and Am. Lit., Stanford U., 1967. Sec. hepatitis research unit USPHS, Louisville, 1955-56; instr. Pacific Luth. U., Tacoma, 1957-58, Cañada Coll., Redwood City, Calif., 1969-70; editor Stanford U. Press, Calif., 1969-74; devel. editor Wadsworth Pubs., Belmont, Calif., 1974-80; affiliated scholar Ctr. for Research on Women, Stanford U., Calif., 1984—; artist-in-residence Wilbur Hot Springs, Williams, Calif., 1980, Montalvo Ctr. for Arts, Saratoga, Calif., summer 1983. Author: Asparagus: The Sparrowgrass Cookbook, 1977; 'Mainder the Buttercup, 1977; The Enchanted Quill, 1978; Mothers of Invention, 1986. Contbr. popular and scholar articles to various mags. and jours.; poetry and fiction to various mags.; contbr. articles in field of history of technology to anthologies. Mem. Inst. for Hist. Study, Nat. Women's Studies Assn. Democrat. Avocations: photography; natural history; reading; travel; ping pong. Home: 241 Bonita Los Trancos Woods Portola Valley CA 94025

STANLEY, GLORIA, office administrator; b. Augusta, Ga., Sept. 3, 1950; d. Willie Nathaniel and Verna Mae (Ealy) S.; m. Larry Deas, Aug. 10, 1974 (div. 1976). Cert. in word processing Atlanta Area Tech. Sch., 1982, also other certs. in field. Drug claim adjuster, sec. Mason Tenders Local, N.Y.C., 1967-68; key punch operator Chase Manhattan Bank, N.Y.C., 1968-72; platform sec. Bank of Commerce, Bklyn., 1972-73; drug claim adjuster Carpenter's Union, N.Y.C., 1973-76; customer service rep. Fulton Fed. Bank, Atlanta, 1976; sec. Parsons Brinckerhoff Tudor, Atlanta, 1976-79; office mgr., adminstrv. sec. Turner Assocs. Architects, Atlanta, 1979—. Vol. Mayor Young Campaign Hdqrs., 1985, tutor Literacy Action, 1986, Rich's Acad., 1986; com. mem. Southside Devel. Task Force, 1985. Mem. Nat. Assn. Female Execs., Am. Soc. Secs. Methodist. Club: Gatsby's Golden Girls. Avocations: aerobics; reading; Southern cooking; jogging; ceramics. Home: 1372 McClelland Ave East Point GA 30344 Office: Turner Assocs Architects 55 Park Pl NE Suite 600 Atlanta GA 30303

STANLEY, JOAN GLORIA, marketing and sales executive; b. Hoboken, N.J., June 14, 1939; d. Alexander John and Elfrieda Katherina (Matula) S.; student New Sch. Social Research, 1959-60, N.Y.U., 1960-63. Vice pres. N.Y. Apt. Exchange, N.Y.C., 1965-70; dir. sales promotions Zsa Zsa Internat., N.Y.C., 1970-72; v.p. mktg. Nat. Audubon Soc., N.Y.C., 1972-81; pres. Stanley-Fizer Assocs., Inc., 1981-85, J.G. Stanley Co., Inc., N.Y.C., 1985—. Mem. Lic. Industry Assn. (v.p.). Home: 35 E 35th St New York NY 10016

STANLEY, JUDITH H., civic worker; married; 4 children. B.A. in History, Smith Coll., 19—. Chmn. N.J. Hwy. Authority, 1983; pres. Monmouth County Organ. Social Services, 1976—, trustee 1966-76; chmn., chief exec. officer Monmouth County Organ. Social Services, Inc., Monmouth County Organ. Social Services Nursing Services, Monmouth County Organ. Social Services Found; founder Monmouth Conservation Found., pres. 1977—; chmn. Middletown Planning Bd., 1981—; trustee Monmouth Coll., exec. com. as head of Institutional Advancement com.; pres. Parents council of Rumson Country Day Sch.; chmn. of fund raising com. to elect Marie Muhler, 1980, 82; del. 1984 Republican Nat. Conv. Recipient 1981 Joshua Huddy Disting. Citizen award, Brotherhood award Nat. Conf. Christians and Jews, 1981, Pub. Works Improvement award Monmouth-Ocean County Devel. Council, 1984, Others award (with husband) Salvation Army, 1984.

STANLEY, JUDITH JEAN, state official; b. Neptune, N.J., Jan. 10, 1935; d. Roland Loog and Jean Chloe (Hurley) Loog Calafato; m. Anthony Huber, Aug. 8, 1955 (div. Feb. 1972); children—Lisa Huber Goodspeed, Shelley, Catherine, Andrea; m. Robert Crooks Stanley, Jr., Dec. 8, 1972 (dec. Dec. 1985). B.A., Smith Coll., 1956; D. Engring. (hon.), Steveno Inst. Tech., 1986. Pres. Monmouth County Orgn. of Social Services, Red Bank, N.J., 1976-84, chmn., chief exec. officer, 1984—, trustee, 1966—; commr. N.J. Hwy. Authority, Woodbridge, 1982-83, chmn., 1983—. Founder, pres. Monmouth Conservation Found., Middletown, N.J., 1977—; chmn. Middletown Planning Bd., 1981—, mem., 1975—; trustee Monmouth Coll., West Long Branch, N.J., 1981—, mem. exec. com., chmn. instnl. advancement com., 1983—; mem. Commn. on Future of Ind. Higher Edn. in N.J., 1986—; committeewoman Monmouth County Republican Com., 1976—; chmn. Com. to Elect Marie Muhler-Congress, 1980, 82; del. Rep. Nat. Conv., 1984. Recipient Joshua Huddy Disting. citizens award Boy Scouts Am., 1981; Brotherhood award NCCJ, 1983; Pub. Works Improvement award Monmouth-Ocean County Devel. Council, 1984; Others award Salvation Army, 1984; Virginia Apgar award March of Dimes, 1985. Mem. Internat. Bridge, Tunnel and Turnpike Assn., Monmouth County Hist. Assn. (trustee 1970—, exec. com. 1977—). Presbyterian. Club: Smith Coll. (past pres. Monmouth County). Avocations: tennis; gardening; travel; reading; skiing. Home: 578 Navesink River Rd Red Bank NJ 07701 also: Twin Brook Farm Route 82 Stanfordville NY 12581 Office: New Jersey Hwy Authority Garden State Pkwy Woodbridge NJ 07095

STANLEY, KAREN ANN ELLISON, research company official; b. Chgo., Jan. 6, 1947; d. Charles Albert and Dorothy Irene (Gallaugher) Ellison; m. Lawrence Gabriel, May 14, 1970 (div. 1972); m. Marion L. Stanley, Jan. 2, 1974. B.A., MacMurray Coll., 1968; M.Ed., Kent State U., 1970; M.B.A., U. Mich., 1981. Asst. to dean of student affairs Miss. State U., Starkville, 1970-72; assoc. dean of students Juniata Coll., Huntingdon, Pa., 1972-75; asst. dir. housing U. Toledo, 1975-79; sr. account exec. NFO Research Inc., Toledo, 1981-84, mktg. v.p., 1984—. Bd. dirs. Planned Parenthood, Huntingdon, Pa., 1973-75; mem. Toledoscape (Ohio), 1983—. Mem. Am. Mktg. Assn. Home: 2829 Barrington Dr Toledo OH 43606 Office: NFO Research Inc 2700 Oregon Rd Toledo OH 43654

STANLEY, LINDA JOYCE, community college official; b. Sault Ste. Marie, Mich., Mar. 9, 1947; d. Frank and Dorothy Elizabeth (Steele) Westover; m. Wayne Charles Stanley, Aug. 22, 1964; children—Sherri Lynn, Timothy Wayne. A.A., Longview Coll., 1982. Programmer, analyst Techmark Corp., Shawnee Mission, Kans., 1982-83; dir. systems Exxon Office Systems, Kansas City, Mo., 1983; mgr. acad. data processing Johnson County Community Coll., Overland Park, Kans., 1983—. Presbyterian. Office: Johnson County Community Coll 12345 College Blvd Overland Park KS 66210

STANLEY, MARGARET KING, performing arts administrator; b. San Antonio, Tex., Dec. 11, 1929; d. Creston Alexander and Margaret (Haymore) King; children—Torrey Margaret, Jean Cullen. Student Mary Baldwin Coll., 1948-50; B.A., U. Tex.-Austin, 1952; M.A., Incarnate Word Coll., 1959. Tchg. cert. 1953. Elem. tchr. San Antonio Ind. Sch. Dist., 1953-54, 55-56, Arlington County Schs., Tex., 1954-55, Ft. Sam Houston Schs., San Antonio, 1955-57; art, art history tchr. St. Pius X Sch., San Antonio, 1959-60; fellow Trinity U., San Antonio, 1964-66; designer-mfr., owner CrisStan Clothes, Inc., San Antonio, 1967-73; founder, exec. dir. San Antonio Performing Arts Assn., 1976—; founder Arts Council of San Antonio, 1962; founding chmn. Joffrey Workshop, San Antonio, 1979; originator, first chairwoman Student Music Fair, San Antonio, 1963; radio program host On Stage, San Antonio, 1983—. Originator of the idea for a new ballet created for the City of San Antonio Jamboree commnd. from the Joffrey Ballet, world premiere in San Antonio, 1984. Pres. San Antonio Symphony League, 1971-74; v.p. Arts Council of San Antonio, 1975; bd. govs. Artists Alliance of San Antonio, 1982. Recipient Outstanding Tchr. award Arlington County Sch. Dist., 1954, Today's Woman award San Antonio Light Newspaper, 1980, Woman of Yr. in Arts award San Antonio Express News, 1983, Emily Smith award for outstanding alumni Mary Baldwin Coll., 1973, Headliner award Women in Communications Inc., 1982; named to Women's Hall of Fame, San Antonio, 1984. Mem. Internat. Soc. Performing Arts Adminstrs. (regional rep. 1982-85), Met. Opera Nat. Council, Women in Communications, Inc., Texas Arts Alliance (bd. govs. 1983—), San Antonio Opera Guild (vice pres. 1974-76), Women in Communications (San Antonio chapter), Jr. League of San Antonio, Battle of Flowers Assn. Office: San Antonio Performing Arts Assn PO Box 12717 San Antonio TX 78212

STANLEY, MARY CAROLYN, vocational rehabilitation counselor; b. Carthage, Mo., Nov. 15, 1948; d. Ralph Eugene and Marian Jean (Van Buren) Reynolds; B.A., Marymount Coll., Salina, Kans., 1970; postgrad. Ariz. State U., Tempe, S.W. Mo. State U., Springfield. Supr. work adjustment Goodwill Industries, Phoenix, 1971-75; vocat. counselor Ariz. Found. Handicapped Maryvale, Phoenix, 1975-76, Kans. Vocat. Rehab. Center, Salina, 1977, Yuma WORC Center (Ariz.), 1977-78; project aide U. Mo. Extension Services, Springfield, 1978; case mgr. Lakes County Rehab. Center, Springfield, 1979-81; field counselor Mo. Vocat. Rehab., Springfield, 1981-83; probation and parole officer Mo. State Bd. Probation, 1983—; mem. council Region VI Adv. Council Devel. Disabilities, Springfield, 1979-81; citizen mem. Youth Services Group, Mo. State Penitentiary. Vice chmn. Ozarks Area Community Action-Family Planning Program, Springfield, 1980-81. Cert. Nat. Commn. Rehab. Counselors. Mem. Nat. Rehab. Assn. (cert.). Office: 2413 Fairlawn Dr PO Box 676 Carthage MO 64836

STANLEY, NANCY NELL, gerontologist; b. Blum, Tex., Nov. 26, 1924; d. James Harvey and Sadie Pearl (Luton) Stanley; student Southwestern Bapt. Theol. Sem., 1952-53; B.A., Mary Hardin-Baylor Coll., 1956; postgrad. in library sci. Va. Commonwealth U., 1960-61; M.A., North Tex. State U., 1982. Dir. religious edn. First Bapt. Ch., Belton, Tex., 1956-57; dir. religious edn. for youth First Bapt. Ch., Brownwood Tex., 1957-58; mgr. library and archives Fgn. Mission Bd., So. Bapt. Conv., Richmond, Va., 1958-80; long-term care adminstr., dir. staff devel. Bapt. Meml. Geriatric Center, San Angelo, Tex., 1981—. Dean women, counselor Bapt. ch. camps in Tex., 1954-58. Mem. ALA, Soc. Am. Archivists, So. Bapt. Hist. Soc., Assn. Nat. Archives, Smithsonian Instn. (asso.), Gerontol. Assn., Alpha Chi, Sigma Tau Delta. Author: Southern Baptist Involvement in Long-Term Care as Mandated by Judeo-Christian Teachings; Training Manuals in Long-Term Care. Contbr. articles to religious jours. Home: 902 N Main St Apt D 6W San Angelo TX 76902 Office: Bapt Meml Geriatric Center 902 Main St PO Box 5661 San Angelo TX 76902

STANLEY, SANDRA ORNECIA, educational researcher; b. Jersey City, July 6, 1950; d. McKinley and Thelma Louise (Newberry) S.; B.A., Ottawa (Kans.) U., 1972; M.S. in Edn., U. Kans., 1975, Ph.D. (fellow), 1980; postgrad. St. George's U. Sch. Medicine, Grenada, W.I., 1984—. Dir., head tchr. Salem Bapt. Nursery Sch., Jersey City, 1972-73; spl. ednl. instr. Joan Davis Sch. Spl. Edn., Kansas City, Mo., 1975-76; instructional media/materials trainee, then research asst. U. Kans. Med. Center, 1976-79; research asst. U. Kans., Lawrence, 1979; dir., coordinator tng. and observation Juniper Gardens Children's project Bur. Child Research, U. Kans., Kansas City, 1979-82, research assoc., 1980; lectr., speaker, cons. edn. and med. sci. Coll. Women Inc. scholar, 1977; Easter Seal grantee, 1975; recipient various certs. of recognition. Mem. Assn. Supervision and Curriculum Devel., Women's Ednl. Network, Coll. Women Inc., Nat. Assn. Female Execs. Democrat. Baptist. Author papers in field. Home: 70 Madison Ave Jersey City NJ 07304

STANLEY, WINIFRED CLAIRE, lawyer; b. N.Y.C.; d. John Francis and Mary (Gill) S. B.A. magna cum laude, U. Buffalo, 1930, J.D. (Edward Thompson Co. award), 1933. Bar: N.Y. 1934. Assoc., Finck & Huber, Buffalo, 1934-37; asst. dist. atty. Erie County (N.Y.), 1938-42; rep.-at-large U.S. Congress, 1943-44; chief counsel N.Y. State Employees' Retirement System, Albany, 1945-55; asst. atty. gen. N.Y. State Law Dept. Appeals Bur., Albany, 1955-79; pvt. practice, Albany, 1980-81, Kenmore, N.Y., 1981—. Vice-pres., Young Women's Republican Club Erie County, Buffalo, 1933-34; pres. Buffalo Bus. and Profl. Women's Club, 1938-39; bd. dirs. Buffalo YWCA, 1940-41; legis. vice-chmn. Fedn. Bus. and Profl. Women's Clubs N.Y. State, 1973-74; charter mem. Salvation Army Women's Aux., Albany, 1979; life mem. Women's Nat. Rep. Club; sustaining mem. Erie County Rep. Com., Buffalo, 1981—; mem. Crippled Children's Guild, Buffalo, Friends of Kenmore/Tonawanda Library, Friends of Buffalo/Erie County Library, Albright-Knox Art Gallery Soc. Mem. ABA, Nat. Assn. Women Lawyers, N.Y. State Bar Assn., Assn. Former Mems. Congress (charter), Bar Assn. Erie County, Grosvenor Soc., Kappa Beta Pi (life).

STANSBURY, LYNDA LUCK, public relations and political consultant; b. Richmond, Va., July 18, 1949; d. George William and Sue (Worrell) Luck; m. Warren Winn Stansbury, June 5, 1971 (div. 1981). Student Maryville Coll., 1969; B.S., East Carolina U., 1971; Library Sci. cert. Old Dominion U., 1976. Child devel. specialist pub. schs., Norfolk, Va., 1971-77; fin. cons. Republican Nat. Com., Washington, 1978; fin. dir. Nat. Fed. Republican Women, Washington, 1979-82; fin. cons. U.S. Congressman James Collins, Dallas, 1982; owner L. L. Stansbury, Dallas, 1983—. Mem. Nat. Assn. Female Execs., Nat. Fedn. Republican Women, Edn. Assn. Norfolk (bd. dirs. 1974-76). Presbyterian. Office: L L Stansbury 6443 Bordeaux Dallas TX 75209

STANSHINE, ISABEL ROCHVARG, nurse administrator; b. Phila., Feb. 14, 1952; d. Reuben Robert and Selma (Reisman) Rochvarg; m. Gerald Scott Stanshine, Aug. 17, 1975. B.S. in Nursing, Temple U., 1974; M.S. in Nursing, U. Del., 1977. Staff nurse Pa. Hosp., Phila., 1974-77; clin. specialist Jefferson Univ. Hosp., Phila., 1977-80, Episcopal Hosp., Phila., 1980-82; assoc. dir. nursing Bryn Mawr Hosp., pa., 1982—. Mem. Am. Nurses Assn., Pa. Nurses Assn. Southeastern Pa. League Nursing, Middle Atlantic Region Nurses Assn., Orgn. Nurse Execs., Nat. League Nursing, Sigma Theta Tau. Office: The Bryn Mawr Hosp Bryn Mawr Ave Bryn Mawr PA 19010

STANSHINE, SANDI TERRY, executive search company executive; b. Phila., Sept. 10, 1954; d. Bernard and Carole (Abramson) Markovitz; m. Martin Philip Stanshine (separated). B.A., Beaver Coll., 1975; M.Ed., Trenton State U., 1976; postgrad. Pa. State U., 1977. Cert. personnel cons. Personnel recruiter Edwards Employment/McFadden, Phila., 1977-79; data processing recruiter London Personnel, Phila., 1979; prin., owner Sanmar Staffing Cons., Phila., 1980—. Mem. Nat. Assn. Personnel Consultants, Pa. Assn. for Personnel Cons. (bd. dirs. 1984-85, pres. eastern chpt. 1985-86, author state newsletter 1985-86), Mid Atlantic Assn. Personnel Cons., Phila. C. of C. Jewish. Avocations: golf; tennis; theatre; scrabble; reading; traveling; piano. Office: Sanmar Staffing Cons 1211 Chestnut St Suite 200 Philadelphia PA 19107

STANTON, ELIZABETH MCCOOL, lawyer; b. Lansdale, Pa., Apr. 12, 1947; d. Leo J. and Helen M. (Gillooly) McCool; m. Robert J. Stanton, June 13, 1970; children—Jonathan R., James Alfred. B.S. in Bus. Adminstrn., Drexel U., 1969; J.D. magna cum laude, U. Houston, 1979. Bar: Tex. 1979, Ohio 1982. Sr. computer programmer Leeds & Northrup Co., North Wales, Pa., 1969-70; research computer programmer Cornell U., Ithaca, N.Y., 1970-74; law clk. Albert C. Barclay, Esq., Princeton, N.J., 1977-78; assoc. Friedman & Chaffin, Houston, 1979-80, Law Offices Elaine Brady, Houston, 1980-81, Moots, Cope & Weinberger Co., L.P.A., Columbus, Ohio, 1982—. Mem. legal com. Met. Women's Ctr., Columbus, 1983-84. Internat. Ladies Garment Workers Union scholar, 1965-69; Drexel Bd. Trustees scholar, 1965-67. Mem. ABA, Ohio Bar Assn., State Bar Tex., Columbus Bar Assn., Women Lawyers Franklin County, Barons, Phi Kappa Phi, Beta Gamma Sigma. Democrat. Roman Catholic. Clubs: University Women's Club Ohio State U., St. Agatha's Women's (Upper Arlington, Ohio). Office: Moots Cope & Weinberger Co 21 E State St Suite 1100 Columbus OH 43215

STANTON, JANE GRAHAM, advertising executive, trade association executive; b. Rice, Tex., Mar. 4, 1922; d. William Edward and Kathryn Ruth (McKay) Tidwell; student Tex. State Coll. Women, 1938-39, Abilene Christian Coll., 1939-40, N. Tex. State Coll., 1941; m. Joseph Wesley Graham, Jan. 5, 1946 (div. Aug. 1974); 1 dau., Kathryn Ann; m. 2d, Hinds Victor Thomas, Dec. 18, 1975 (div. 1977); m. 3d, Hank Stanton, June 10, 1980. Profl. singer on radio, 1941-49; producer, writer radio-TV drama, N.Y.C., 1948-56; v.p. United Nat. Films, Dallas, 1957-59; with Tracy-Locke Advt., Dallas, 1964-66; owner Jane Graham Advt., 1967—; exec. dir. S.W. Apparel Mfrs. Assn., Dallas. Active United Fund. Recipient numerous awards Dallas Advt. League. Mem. Fashion Group. Editor S.W. Advt. & Mktg., Am. Fashion mag., 1974—; contbr. articles to profl. jours.; columnist Dallas Times Herald. Home: 4727 N Central Expy Dallas TX 75205

STANTON, JEAN ELAINE, university counselor; b. Washington, Feb. 16, 1943; d. James Samuel and Helen (Kenner) Smith; m. Jimmie Lee Stanton, Sept. 4, 1965 (div. Apr. 1981); children—Derrick Austin, Letitia Antoinette. B.S. in Human Resources, U. Del., 1979; M.A., Goddard Coll., 1983. Counselor U. Del., Newark, 1979—; teen counselor Hockessin Community Ctr., Del., 1973-74; reading tutor Elem. Workshop, Wilmington, Del., 1977. Exec. adviser Jr. Achievement, 1985—. Mem. Del. Coll. Personnel Assn., Brandywine Pro Assn. (vice chmn. pro devel. com. 1984—), De Trio Orgn. (sec. 1981—), Mid-Eastern Assn. Ednl. Opportunity Program Personnel, NAACP. Avocations: creative writing; traveling. Home: Wilmington DE 19802 Office: Student Spl Services U Del 231 S College Ave Newark DE 19711

STANTON, JEANNE FRANCES, lawyer; b. Vicksburg, Miss., Jan. 22, 1920; d. John Francis and Hazel (Mitchell) Stanton; student George Washington U., 1938-39; B.A., U. Cin., 1940; J.D., Salmon P. Chase Coll. Law, 1954. Admitted to Ohio bar, 1954, U.S. Dist. Ct. (so. dist.) Ohio, 1956; chief clk. Selective Service Bd., Cin., 1940-43; instr. USAAF Tech. Schs., Biloxi, Miss., 1943-44; with Procter & Gamble, Cin., 1945-84, legal asst., 1952-54, head advt. services sect. legal div. trade practices dept., 1954-73, mgr. advt. services legal div., 1973-84. Team capt. Community Chest Cin., 1953. Mem. AAAS, Am., Ohio (chmn. uniform state laws com. 1968-70), Cin. (sec. law day com. 1965-66, chmn. com. on preservation hist. documents 1968-71) bar assns., Vicksburg and Warren County, Cin. hist. socs., Internat. Oceanographic Found., Otago Early Settlers Assn. (assoc.), Intercontinental Biog. Assn. Clubs: Cin. Lawyers (exec. com. 1978—, sec. 1980, 1st v.p. 1982, pres. 1983), Archeol. Ins. Am., Cin. Women Lawyers (treas. 1958-59), Cincinnati; Terrace Park Country. Home: 2302 Easthill Ave Cincinnati OH 45208

STANWYCK, BARBARA (RUBY STEVENS), actress; b. Bklyn., July 16, 1907; m. Frank Fay, Aug. 26, 1928; m. Robert Taylor, May 14, 1939 (div.). Ed. pub. schs., Bklyn. Began as chorus girl; later scored success in play Burlesque; motion picture appearances include: Meet John Doe, 1941, The Great Man's Lady, The Gay Sisters, 1942, Double Indemnity, 1944, My Reputations, 1945, Christmas in Connecticut, Two Mrs. Carrolls, 1946, Bride Wore Boots, Strange Love of Martha Ivers, 1947, Cry Wolf, The Other Love, B.F.'s Daughter, 1948, Sorry Wrong Number, File on Thelma Jordon, The Lady Gambles, The Lie, East-Side, West-Side, The Furies, 1949, To Please a Lady, 1950, The Man in the Cloak, 1951, Clash by Night, 1951, Jeopardy, 1952, Titanic, 1952, Executive Suite, Witness to Murder, Escape to Burma, 1955, Cattle Queen of Montana, There's Always Tomorrow, 1956, Maverick Queen, 1956, These Wilder Years, 1956, Crime of Passion, 1957, Trooper Hook, 1957, Walk on the Wild Side, 1962, Roustabout, 1964, The Night Walker, 1965; TV shows The Barbara Stanwyck Theater, NBC-TV, 1960-61, The Big Valley, ABC-TV; appeared in TV movies: The House That Would Not Die, 1970, A Taste of Evil, 1971, The Letters, 1973; TV mini-series The Thorn Birds (Emmy award 1983); guest star numerous TV shows. Recipient Emmy award, 1960-61, 66, hon. Acad. award, 1982. Address: care A Morgan Maree & Asscos Inc 6363 Wilshire Blvd Los Angeles CA 90048*

STAPLES, ELIZABETH MARIE, magazine executive; b. East Orange, N.J., Feb. 20, 1947; d. William Charles and Ellen Marie (Chaplain) Baumann; m. Kenneth T. Staples, May 15, 1971 (dec. 1976). B.A., Coll. of Wooster, 1969; M.B.A., Fairleigh-Dickinson U., 1979. Spanish lang. tchr. Carlisle Schs., Pa., 1969-71; adminstr. Drew U., Madison, N.J., 1971-78; bus. mgr. Creative Computing Mag., Morristown, N.J., 1978-79, editor, Morris Plains, N.J., 1980—. Contbr. articles to profl. jours. Mem. Christian and Missionary Alliance Ch. Avocations: linguistics; archaeology. Home: 119 Maple Ave Morristown NJ 07960 Office: Creative Computing 39 E Hanover Ave Morris Plains NJ 07950

STAPLETON, JEAN (JEANNE MURRAY), actress; b. N.Y.C.; d. Joseph E. and Marie (Stapleton) Murray; student Hunter Coll., N.Y.C.; student Am. Apprentice Theatre, Am. Actors Co., Am. Theatre Wing and with Harold Clurman; L.H.D. (hon.), Emerson Coll.; hon. degrees, Hood Coll., Monmouth Coll.; m. William H. Putch, Oct. 26, 1957; 2 children. First N.Y. stage role in The Corn is Green, Equity Library Theatre; starred as the mother in Am. Gothic, Circle-in-the-Sq.; Broadway debut with Judith Anderson in In The Summer House; also appeared on Broadway in Damn Yankees, Bells Are Ringing, Juno, Rhinoceros and Funny Girl, Arsenic and Old Lace, 1986; first major break in comic ingenue role as Myrtle Mae with Frank Fay in Harvey; played with nat. tour of Come Back, Little Sheba starring Shirley Booth; starred in tour of Morning's at Seven; appeared in motion pictures including Damn Yankees, Bells Are Ringing, Up the Down Staircase, Cold Turkey, The Buddy System; appeared in numerous TV shows including Studio One, Naked City, Armstrong Circle Theater, The Defenders, Jackie Gleason Show, with guest appearances on Laugh-In, Sonny and Cher, Mike Douglas, Dinah, The Carol Burnett Show, Tailgunner Joe; starred in the title role of Aunt Mary on Hallmark Hall of Fame, 1979; her most famous TV role was Edith Bunker on All In The Family, 1971-79; TV films include Isabel's Choice, Angel Dusted, Eleanor, First Lady of the World, A Matter of Sex; appeared the Totem Pole Playhouse, Fayetteville, Pa., starred in Daisy Mayme, 1978, The Late Christopher Bean, 1982 (both at Kennedy Center). Bd. dirs. Women's Edn. and Research Inst., Eleanor Roosevelt's Val-Kill; U.S. commr. to Internat. Woman's Year Commn. and Nat. Conf. Women, Houston, 1977. Recipient Emmy awards, 1971, 72, 78. Mem. Actors Equity, Screen Actors Guild, AFTRA. Office: care Bauman & Hiller 9220 Sunset Blvd Los Angeles CA 90069

STAPLETON, KATHARINE HALL (KATIE), food broadcaster, author; b. Kansas City, Mo., Oct. 29, 1919; d. William Mabin and Katharine (Foster) Hall; B.A., Vassar Coll., 1941; m. Benjamin Franklin Stapleton, June 20, 1942; children—Benjamin Franklin, III, Craig Roberts, Katharine Hall. Cookbook reviewer Denver Post, 1974-84; producer, writer, host On the Front Burner, daily radio program Sta. KOA-CBS, Denver, 1976-79, Sta. WGAN, Portland, Maine, 1979—, Cooking with Katie, live one-hour weekly, Sta. KOA, 1979—; guest broadcaster Geneva Radio, 1974, London Broadcasting Corp., 1981, 82; tour leader culinarys to Britain, France and Switzerland, 1978-85. Eng., 1978. Chmn. women's div. United Fund, 1955-56; founder, chmn. Denver Debutante Ball, 1956, 57; regional v.p. Nat. Travelers Aid Assn., 1952-56; commr. Denver Centennial Authority, 1958-60; trustee Washington Cathedral, regional v.p., 1967-73; mem. world service council YWCA, 1961—; trustee, Colo. Women's Coll., 1975-80. Decorated Chevalier de L'Etoile Noire (France); recipient People-to-People citation, 1960, 66, Beautiful Activist award Altrusa Club, 1972. Mem. Alliance Française (hon., pres. 1968-70). Democrat. Episcopalian. Clubs: Denver Country, Denver. Author: Denver Delicious: 150 Past and Present Recipes from the Queen City, 1980, 3d. edit., 1983; High Notes: Favorite Recipies of KOA, 1984. Home: 8 Village Rd Englewood CO 80110

STAPLETON, MAUREEN, actress; b. Troy, N.Y., June 21, 1925; d. John P. and Irene (Walsh) S.; student Siena Coll, 1943; m. Max Allentuck, July 1949 (div. Feb. 1959); children—Daniel, Katharine. Debut appearance in Playboy of the Western World, 1946; other plays include tour with Barretts of Wimpole Street, 1947, Anthony and Cleopatra, 1947, Detective Story, The Bird Cage, Rose Tatoo, 1950-51, The Sea Gull, Orpheus Descending, The Cold Wind and the Warm, 1959, Toys in the Attic, 1960-61, Plaza Suite, 1969, The Gingerbread Lady, 1970, Country Girl, 1972, Secret Affairs of Mildred Wild, 1972 The Gin Game, 1978; motion pictures include: Lonely Hearts, The Fugitive Kind, A View from the Bridge, Bye Bye Birdie, Airport, 1970, Plaza Suite, Interiors, 1978, The Fan, 1981, Reds, 1981, On the Right Track, 1981; TV drama Tell Me Where It Hurts, 1974, Cat on a Hot Tin Roof, 1976; TV films include: Little Gloria ... Happy at Last, 1982, The Electric Grandmother, 1982, Mother's Day, 1984. Recipient Nat. Inst. Arts and Letters award, 1969, Tony award for the Gingerbread Lady, 1970, Acad. Award for Best supporting actress for Reds, 1981. Address: care Internat Creative Mgmt 8899 Beverly Blvd Los Angeles CA 90048*

STARER, RUANA MAXINE, clinical psychologist; b. N.Y.C., Dec. 30, 1946; d. Emanuel and Zoe (Cibul) S.; B.A. in Psychology summa cum laude, Hunter Coll., CUNY, 1974; M.A., Calif. Sch. Profl. Psychology, 1977, Ph.D., 1980; m. Jed H. Weitzen, Oct. 27, 1979; children—Jason Seth, Mia Elyse. Psychol. asst. in pvt. practice, Upland, Calif., 1977-79; parent tng. specialist Via Avanta, Didi Hirsch Community Mental Health Center, Pacoima, Calif., 1979-80; staff clin. psychologist So. Reception Center and Clinic, Calif. Dept. Youth Authority, Norwalk, 1980-82; pvt. practice, Riverdale, N.Y., 1982—; supervising psychologist Children's Village, Dobbs Ferry, N.Y., 1985—. Mem. Am. Psychol. Assn., Psi Chi. Home: 5734 Faraday Ave Riverdale NY 10471 Office: 3640 Johnson Ave Riverdale NY 10463

STARESINA, DENISE MARIE, manufacturing company executive; b. Cleve., May 18, 1951; d. Nicholas Edward and Lucille Cecelia (Horley) S.; B.A. in Office Adminstrn., Mich. State U., 1974. With Pitney Bowes, Inc., Stamford, Conn., 1974—, bus. segment mgr. meters and mailing machines, 1981—; exec. v.p. ops. Time Sensitive Delivery Guide Inc. subs. Pitney Bowes, 1986—; program mgr. remote meter resetting system Pitney Bowes Can., Toronto, Ont., 1979-81. Mem. Nat. Assn. Female Execs., Mich. State U. Alumni Assn., Phi Gamma Mu. Home: 1941 Hudson Glen Bethel CT 06801 Office: Pitney Bowes Walter Wheeler Jr Dr Stamford CT 06926

STARFIELD, BARBARA HELEN, physician, educator; b. Bklyn., Dec. 18, 1932; d. Martin and Eva (Illions) S.; A.B., Swarthmore Coll., 1954; M.D., SUNY, 1959; M.P.H., Johns Hopkins U., 1963; m. Neil A. Holtzman, June 12, 1955; children—Robert, Jon, Steven, Deborah. Teaching asst. in anatomy Downstate Med. Center, N.Y.C., 1955-57; intern in pediatrics Johns Hopkins U., 1959-60, resident, 1960-62, dir. pediatric med. care clinic, 1963-66, dir. community staff comprehensive child care project, 1966-67, dir. pediatric clin. scholars program, 1971-76, prof., head health policy, 1973—, joint appointment in pediatrics, 1975—; cons. HEW. Recipient Dave Luckman Meml. award, 1958; HEW Career Devel. award, 1970-75. Mem. Nat. Acad. Sci. Inst. Medicine (governing council from 1981-83), Am. Pediatric Soc., Soc. Pediatric Research, Internat. Epidemiologic Assn., Ambulatory Pediatric Assn. (pres. 1980), Am. Public Health Assn., Sigma Xi, Alpha Omega Alpha, Delta Omega. Contbr. articles to profl. jours. Mem. editorial bd. Med. Care, 1977-79; Pediatrics, 1977-82, Internat. Jour. Health Services, from 1978, Med. Care Rev., 1980-85. Office: 624 N Broadway Baltimore MD 21205

STARK, JOAN SCISM, educator; b. Hudson, N.Y., Jan. 6, 1937; d. Ormonde F. and Myrtle Margaret (Kirkey) S.; B.S., Syracuse U., 1957; M.A. (Hoadly fellow), Columbia U., 1960; Ed.D., SUNY, Albany, 1971; m. William L. Stark, June 28, 1958 (dec.); children—Eugene William, Susan Elizabeth, Linda Anne, Ellen Scism; m. 2d, Malcolm A. Lowther, Jan. 31, 1981. Tchr., Ossining (N.Y.) High Sch., 1957-59; freelance editor Holt, Rinehart & Winston, Harcourt, Brace & World, 1960-70; lectr. Ulster County Community Coll., Stone Ridge, N.Y., 1968-70; asst. dean Goucher Coll., Balt., 1970-73, asso. dean, 1973-74; assoc. prof., chmn. dept. higher postsecondary edn. Syracuse (N.Y.) U., 1974-78; dean Sch. Edn. U. Mich., Ann Arbor, 1978-83, prof. higher edn., 1983—. Leader Girl Scouts U.S.A., Cub Scouts Am.; coach girls Little League;

dist. officer PTA, intermittently, 1968-80; bd. dirs. Environ. Sci. Inst.; mem. adv. com. Gerald R. Ford Library, U. Mich., 1980-82; trustee Kalamazoo Coll., 1979-85; mem. exec. com. Inst. Social Research, U. Mich., 1979-82; bd. dirs. Mich. Assn. Coll. Tchr. Edn., 1979-81. Mem. Assn. Study Higher Edn. (dir. 1977-79, pres. 1984), Soc. Coll. Univ. Planning, Assn. Innovation Higher Edn. (nat. chmn. 1974-75), Am. Assn. Higher Edn., Am. Ednl. Research Assn., Assn. Instnl. Research, Am. Conf. Acad. Deans, Am. Assn. Environ. Edn. (trustee 1979-81), Assn. Colls. and Schs. Edn. State Univs. and Land Grant Colls. (dir. 1981-83), Phi Beta Kappa, Phi Kappa Phi, Sigma Pi Sigma, Eta Pi Upsilon, Lambda Sigma Sigma, Phi Delta Kappa, Pi Lambda Theta. Contbr. numerous articles in field to profl. jours. Office: 2002 School of Education University of Michigan Ann Arbor MI 48109

STARK, MEREDITH ANNE, television executive; b. N.Y.C., Sept. 12, 1955; d. Edward Emmett and Florence Audrey (Howard) Stark. B.F.A., U. Ariz., 1977. Prodn. assoc. ABC Sports, N.Y.C., 1977; with press info. staff CBS News, N.Y.C., 1978-79, coordinator affiliate services, 1979-81, mgr. affiliate services, 1981-83, dir. affiliate services, 1983-85, dir. news services, 1985-86, assoc. producer CBS Morning News,j 1986—. Mem. Am. Women in Radio and Tev, Radio TV News Dirs. Assn., Women in Communications. Home: 1406 Manhattan Ave Union City NJ 07087 Office: CBS News 524 W 57th St New York NY 10019

STARK, PATRICIA ANN, psychologist; b. Ames, Iowa, Apr. 21, 1937; d. Keith C. and Mary L. (Johnston) Moore; m. Edward Milton Stark, June 13, 1959. B.S., So. Ill. U., Edwardsville, 1970, M.S., 1972; Ph.D., St. Louis U., 1976. Counselor to alcoholics Bapt. Rescue Mission, East St. Louis, 1969; researcher alcoholics Gateway Rehab. Center, East St. Louis, 1972; psychologist intern Henry-Stark Counties Spl. Edn. Dist. and Galesburg State Research Hosp., Ill., 1972-73; instr. Lewis and Clark Community Coll., Godfrey, Ill., 1973-76, asst. prof., 1976-84, assoc. prof., 1984—, coordinator child care services, 1974-84; mem. staff dept. psychiatry Meml. Hosp., St. Elizabeth's Hosp., 1979—; supr. various workshops in field, 1974—; dir. child and family services Collinsville Counseling Center, 1978-82; clin. dir., owner Empas-Complete Family Psychol. and Hypnosis Services, Collinsville, 1982—; cons. community agys., 1974—; mem. adv. bd. Madison County Council on Alcoholism and Drug Dependency, 1977-80. Mem. Am. Psychol. Assn., Ill. Psychol. Assn., Midwestern Psychol. Assn., Nat. Assn. Sch. Psychologists, Am. Soc. Clin. Hypnosis, Internat. Soc. Hypnosis. Home: 202 Bill Lou Dr Collinsville IL 62234 Office: 2802 Maryville Rd Collinsville IL 62234

STARKEY, JUDITH ANN, oil company executive; b. Indpls.; d. Charles Lester and Frances Lorraine (Scott) Middleton. Student Ind. U., 1955-58; Ph.B., Northwestern U., 1973; postgrad. bus. adminstrn. U. Chgo., 1978. Exec. sec., CBS, N.Y.C., 1958-63; office mgr. Radio Free Europe, Munich, 1963-65; exec. aide, cons. firm, Chgo., 1965-67, C&NW Ry. Co., Chgo., 1967-70; mgr. personnel systems, EEO, Chemetron Corp., Chgo., 1970-79; staff employee relations rep. Amoco Corp., Chgo., 1979—. Named hon. Ky. col. Mem. Human Resources Mgmt. Assn. Chgo., Am. Soc. Personnel Adminstrs., Chgo. Council Fgn. Relations, Alpha Sigma Lambda (hon. acad.). Office: Amoco Corporation Employee Relations 200 E Randolph St Chicago IL 60601

STARLING, BARBARA JOYCE, human resources consulting firm executive, consultant; b. Nashville, Jan. 4, 1935; d. William Louis and Edna Earl (Francis) Watson; m. Donal J. Starling, Sept. 21, 1957; 1 child, Karen Marie Starling Dallas. Student Kent State U., 1961, U. Tenn.-Nashville, 1965-67. In sales and promotion, various rec. cos., Nashville, 1965-74; forms clk. H.W. Black & Assocs., Inc., Nashville, 1974-76; plan adminstrn. unit supr. William M. Mercer, Inc., Nashville, 1976-81, programmer, 1981-83; plan adminstrn. unit supr. Mercer-Meidinger, Inc., Nashville, 1983-85, mng. cons., 1985—. Bible tchr. Tenn. Prison for Women, Nashville, 1983—, Met. Criminal Justice Ctr., Nashville, 1983-85. Mem. Middle Tenn. Employee Benefits Council. Mem. Church of Christ. Avocations: computing; photography; walking; reading. Home: 4905 Monterey Dr Nashville TN 37220 Office: William M Mercer-Meidinger Inc 1200 First American Ctr Nashville TN 37238

STARNES, BETTY NOBLE, special education educator; b. Colorado City, Tex., Oct. 10, 1937; d. Raymond Reagan and Rubilee (Smith) Noble; m. Mac Aubrey Starnes, Dec. 18, 1982. B.S. in Edn., Tex. Tech. U., 1980. Transitional tchr. Grand Prairie Ind. Sch. Dist. (Tex.), 1980-81; tchr. motivational adjustment program Richardson Ind. Sch. Dist., Dallas, 1981—. Vol. Cystic Fibrosis Camp, Dallas, summer 1983, Dallas Taping for Blind, 1982-83; mem. Jr. League of Dallas, 1982—. Mem. Tex. Elem. Tchrs. Assn., 500 Inc., Kappa Alpha Theta. Democrat. Presbyterian. Home: 512 Blanco St Mesquite TX 75150

STARR, ANN THERESE, electronics company executive; b. Gallup, N.Mex., Sept. 10, 1951; d. Bart Harry and Anna Mae (Daley) S.; m. Wayne Lee Ewen, Apr. 29, 1984. B.S., U. Tex., 1976; M.S.W., U. Tex.-Arlington, 1980. Cert. social worker. With Tex. Youth Commn., Crockett, 1976-78; mgr. employee assistance Motorola, Inc., Austin, Tex., 1980—; field instr. U. Tex., Austin, 1981-84; mem. Greater Austin Council on Alcoholism, 1981-84; chmn. Occupational Social Work Task Force, Tex., 1984—. Recipient Silver Quill, Motorola, Inc., 1985. Mem. Nat. Assn. Social Workers, Assn. Labor and Mgmt. Adminstrs. and Consultants on Alcoholism, Am. Soc. Personnel Adminstrn., Nat. Assn. Alcohol and Drug Abuse Counselors, Mental Health Assn. Austin. Democrat. Home: 8503 Caspian Dr Austin TX 78749 Office: Motorola Inc 3501 Ed Bluestein Blvd Austin TX 78723

STARR, JENNIE SPRING, architectural designer, building contractor, advertising executive; b. Columbus, Ohio, Jan. 7, 1935; d. Ralph Downing and Mary Alice (Gard) Spring; m. John C. Starr, June 14, 1958; children—Victoria Prince, Cynthia Knickerbocker, Teresa Gaa, Kristi Hodge, Holly Schuler, Tina Ell, Charles, Penny; foster children—Hans Jurgen Zander, Edwardo V. Rahal. Student Columbus Coll. Art and Design, 1960-62, Wittenberg U., 1962-65, Penland Sch. Crafts, 1963, Inst. Irish Studies, 1979; Cert. bldg. contractor, Fla. Art tchr. St. Patrick Sch., 1964-65; exec. sec. Madison County Continuing Med. Edn. Dept., 1967-71; owner London Internat. Travel, Inc. (Ohio), 1967-73; art dir. Madison County Schs., 1973-74; archtl. designer, art dir. Starr Studios, 1973—; advt exec., art dir Starr Mktg. & Advt., 1979—; one-woman shows sculpture and mixed media: Huntington Nat. Bank, Columbus, 1967, 74, Internat. Platform Assn., Washington, Madison County Sch Bd., 1969, 75, 76, Ohio State U., 1973; lectr. Art dir., bd. dirs. Madison County Arts Guild, 1975-76; news editor Project HOPE, 1973-74; adv. bd. dirs. Quality of Life Found., Inc., 1982-85. Recipient Spark Plug award City of London, 1967; Leadership and Edn. award Am. Heart Assn.; named Hon. Kiwanian, 1971, one of top 25 Women Execs. on the Suncoast Fla. Bus. Jour., AT&T, Woman of the Day Delta Airlines, WQSA radio; service to Women Entrepreneurs award U. South Fla. Coll. Bus., 1986. Mem. Contractors Assn. Sarasota, Manatee, Hardee and Lee Counties, Sarasota Advt. Club, Womans Owners Network Inc. (pres. 1984-85), Internat. Platform Assn. Episcopalian. Club: London County, Tips (bd. dirs. 1985-86). Contbg. editor: Madison County History, 1976; garden editor Madison Press, 1962-67; editor Florida Woman's News, 1985—, Won. Inc.; author numerous articles on Irish history, arts and crafts of Ireland, bus. jours., newspapers. Address: 3654 Dorst Ln Sarasota FL 33583

STARR, JOYCE R., foreign affairs specialist; b. Phila., Mar. 15, 1945; B.A. in History, U. Mich., Ann Arbor, 1963-67; Ph.D., Northwestern U., 1973. Program officer Drug Abuse Council, Washington, 1971-74; asst. to v.p. Nat. Urban Coalition, Washington, 1975; policy analyst U.S. Privacy Protection Commn., Washington, 1975-76; adviser to Office of Chmn., Nat. Endowment for Humanities, Washington, 1976; dep. dir. Carter-Mondale Campaign, Atlanta, 1976; asst. to counsel Carter-Mondale Transition Team, Washington, 1976-77; assoc. spl. asst. The White House, 1977-79; overseas rep. Center for Strategic and Internat. Studies, Washington, 1979—, dir. near east studies program; TV and radio appearances. Adviser, Nat. Democratic Com., 1981—; bd. dirs. Jerusalem Women's Seminar, 1980—. NIMH grantee, 1969-72; NSF award, 1971. Mem. Nat. Assn. Female Execs. Editor: (with N. Novick) Challenges in the Middle East, 1981; contbr. author Banks, Petrodollars and Sovereign Debt, 1985; author Joyce Starr Reports newsletter; Peace through Economic Security, 1983. Office: Center for Strategic & Internat Studies Suite 400 1800 K St NW Washington DC 20006

STARR, PATRICIA PLUNKETT, real estate broker; b. Birmingham, Ala., Jan. 10, 1951; d. Elmer George and Mary Martha (Sellers) Plunkett; m. James Lewis Starr, Sept. 2, 1972; 1 child, Tiffanie Joy. Student Auburn U., 1969-72. Real estate salesman Shamrock Realty, Auburn, Ala., 1975-78; real estate broker Evans Realty, Auburn, 1978-85, sales mgr., 1984; qualifying broker EquiStar Properties, Auburn, 1986—. Mem. Nat. Assn. Realtors, Nat. Assn. Securities Dealers, Ala. Assn. Realtors, Lee County Bd. Realtors (pres. 1984), Chi Omega Alumni Assn. Republican. Methodist. Club: Saugahatchee Country (Opelika, Ala.) (dir. 1982-84). Avocations: aerobics; dancing. Office: EquiStar Properties PO Box 1550 631 Stage Rd Auburn AL 36830

STARRATT, PATRICIA ELIZABETH, writer actress, composer; b. Boston, Nov. 7, 1943; d. Alfred Byron and Anna (Mazur) S.; A.B., Smith Coll., 1965; grad. prep. dept. Peabody Conservatory Music, 1961. Teaching asst. Harvard U. Grad. Sch. Bus. Aminstrn., 1965-67; mng. dir. INS Assocs., Washington, 1967-68; adminstrv. asst. George Washington U. Hosp., 1970-71; legal asst. Morgan, Lewis & Bockius, Washington, 1971-72; profl. staff energy analyst Nat. Fuels and Energy Policy Study, U.S. Senate Interior Com., 1972-74; cons., exec. asst. energy resource devel. Fed. Energy Adminstrn., Washington, 1974-75; sr. cons. energy policy Atlantic Richfield Co., 1975-76; energy cons., Alaska, 1977-78; govt. affairs assoc. Sohio Alaska Petroleum Co., Anchorage, 1978-85; mem. Econ. Devel. Commn., Municipality of Anchorage, 1981; assoc. producer TV film Then One Night I Hit Her, 1983; appeared Off-Broadway in To Be Young, Gifted and Black; performed as Blanche in A Streetcar Named Desire, Stephanie Dickinson in Cactus Flower, Angela in Papa's Wine, Elizabeth Procter in The Crucible, Candida in Candida, Zeuss in J.B., Martha in Who's Afraid of Virginia Woolf, Amy in Dinny and The Witches, as Columbina in Servant of Two Masters, as Singer in Death of Morris Biederman, as Joan in Joan of Lorraine, as Mado in Amadee, as Mrs. Rowlands in Before Breakfast, as the girl in Hello Out There, as Angela in Bedtime Story, as Hannah in Night of the Iguana, as Lavinia in Androcles and the Lion, as Catherine in Great Catherine, as Julie in Lilliom, as First Nurse in Death of Bessie Smith, as Laura in Tea and Sympathy, as Amelia Earheart in Chamber Music; appeared at Detroit Summer Theatre in Oklahoma, Guys and Dolls, Carousel, Brigadoon, Kiss Me Kate, Finnian's Rainbow; asst. to dir. Broadway plays A Cry Of Players, A Way Of Life, Off-Broadway play To Be Young, Gifted, and Black; screenwriter Challenge in Alaska, 1986. Bd. dirs. Anchorage Community Theatre; industry rep. Alaska Eskimo Whaling Commn.; mem. Alaska New Music Forum. Mem. Actors' Equity. Episcopalian. Author book. Contbr. articles on natural gas and Alaska econ. policy to profl. jours. Home: Box 2117 Aspen CO 81612

STARRETT, AGNES LYNCH (MRS C. V. STARRETT), retired educator, editor, author; b. Peru, Ind.; d. Jerome and Nancy X. (ReMine) Lynch; A.B., U. Pitts., 1920, M.A., 1925; Litt.D., Waynesburg Coll., 1960; m. Clare V. Starrett, July 29, 1923; children—Clare (Mrs. Walter L. Thompson III), David D. Tchr. Lemington Sch., 1918-22; prof. dept. English, U. Pitts. 1922-64, prof. emeritus English and humanities, 1964—, dir. Univ. Press, 1952-64, emeritus dir. and editor, 1964—, editor Pitt, 1939-59; mem. Irish Scholarship Awards Com. Free lance editor, writer, book designer, 1964—. Named Disting. Dau. of Pa. by Gov., 1954. Mem. Hist. Soc. Western Pa. (trustee 1960-82), Gaelic Art Soc., Quens, Mortar Bd., Women in Communications, Phi Beta Kappa, Phi Alpha Theta. Roman Catholic. Clubs: Faculty (U. Pitts.). Womens Press, Zonta Internat., Pitts. Bibliophiles. Author: Through One Hundred Fifty Years, 1937; Falk Foundation, A Private Fortune, A Public Trust, 1967; Henry C. Frick Educational Commission Historical Record 1909-1974, 1975. Editor, designer, coordinator, author colophon Appendix, Elena Lucrezia Conaro Piscopia 1646-1684, Prima Donna Laureata nel Mondo, 1976; co-author, editor: Pittsburgh Bibliophiles Pilgrimage to Italy, 1976; books represented in Fifty Books of Year selection, 1954, 64. Contbr. articles to jours. Address: 2233 N St James Cleveland Heights OH 44106

STASI, LINDA, author, producer; b. N.Y.C., Apr. 14, 1947; d. Anthony John and Florence (Barbera) Stasi; B.F.A., N.Y. Inst. Tech., 1970; postgrad. Hofstra U., 1971; m. John Rovello, Nov. 22, 1970 (div.); 1 dau., Jessica Stasi. Edn. editor Seventeen Mag., N.Y.C., 1970-74; freelance writer, 1974-79; producer, creator, host Good Looks Line, 1979-81; pres. Linda Stasi & Assocs., Inc., 1978—; author: Simply Beautiful, 1983, Looking Good is the Best Revenge, 1984; Impossible Dream Man, 1986; syndicated newspaper writer N.Y. Daily News and Tribune Syndicate, 1984; feature writer Redbook, Mademoiselle, Cosmopolitan, 1982—; on-camera host, producer 5-part health series Disney Channel, 1983; beauty editor New Woman mag., 1984—; syndicated writer Times of London Syndicate. Mem. Writer's Guild. Address: 20 Waterside Plaza New York NY 10010

STATES, MARY ELLEN, educator; b. Beckley, W. Va., July 24, 1940; d. Oscar Caddick and Blanche (Gilmore) Thorpe; m. Edward William States, Aug. 20, 1961; children—Michael, Michele. B.S. in Edn., Old Dominion U., 1977, M.S. in Elem. Edn., 1985. Kindergarten aide Chesapeake Pub. Schs., Va., 1973-77, 1st grade tchr., 1977—. Presbyterian. Avocations: reading; travel. Home: 452 Brockenbraugh Rd Chesapeake VA 23320 Office: Great Bridge Elem 408 Cedar Rd Chesapeake VA 23320

STATHIS, GEORGIA ANNA, astrologer, business consultant, speaker, writer; b. Chgo., Mar. 1, 1949; d. Gus and Mary (Diakomis) S.; m. Stevan Chase Kalmon, Sept. 5, 1970 (div. 1974); m. John Louis Nunes, Jr., Mar. 8, 1981; children—Alexandra Maria, Constantine John. B.S. in Speech, Northwestern U., 1970; M.B.A., Pepperdine U., 1978. Advt. staff Lester Communications, Walnut Creek, Calif., 1975-77; real estate investment staff Saxe Real Estate, Walnut Creek, 1979-81; bus. cons., Pleasant Hill, Calif., 1977—; profl. speaker Nat. Speakers Assn., San Francisco, 1983—. Author, editor of newsletter Starcycles, 1983—. Mem. Beyond War, Walnut Creek, 1984—. Recipient Am. Legion award, 1966, Elks Youth Leadership award Elks Club Am., 1966; Speakers Showcase award Nat. Speaker's Assn., 1984, Mem. Am. Fed. Astrology, Am. Fed. Astrology Network, Internat. Soc. Astrol. Research, Found. Study of Cycles, Nat. Geocosmic Research Inst. Greek Orthodox. Office: 630 Maureen Ln Pleasant Hill CA 94523

STAUBLIN, JUDITH ANN, computer co. mgr.; b. Anderson, Ind., Jan. 17, 1936; d. Leslie Fred and Esta Virginia (Ringo) Wiley; student Ball State U., 1954-55, 69-70, Savs. and Loan Inst., 1962-67, U. Ga., 1974, Wright State U., 1975; children—Juli Jackson, Scott Jackson. Teller, Anderson Fed. Savs. and Loan Assn., Anderson, 1962-64, data processing mgr., 1965-70, loan officer, 1970-72, v.p. systems, 1972-74, fin. systems mktg., 1974-76; fin. dist. mgr. data centers div. NCR Corp., Atlanta, 1977-81, nat. mgr. EFT Services data center div., Dayton, Ohio, 1981-82, fin. dist. mgr. data center div., Atlanta, 1982—. Active United Way. Mem. Am. Savs. and Loan Inst., Fin. Mgrs. Soc., Anderson C. of C. Home: 6115 Woodmont Blvd Norcross GA 30092 Office: NCR Corp 5 Executive Park Atlanta GA 30329

STAUFFER, ELIZABETH CLARE, educator, music choral director, consultant; b. Waterbury, Conn., May 15, 1948; d. Harold Henry and Minerva May (Mattoon) S. B.A., Fairleigh Dickinson U., 1970; M.S., So. Conn. State U., 1973, 6th year diploma, 1978. Cert. tchr. elem. edn., music edn., intermediate adminstrn. and supervision, Conn. Tchr. music pub. schs., Clyde, N.Y., 1970-71; tchr. Children's Corner, Inc., Stamford, Conn., 1973-79; tchr. pub. schs., Naugatuck Conn., 1972—; cons., adviser Children's Corner, Inc., Stamford, 1979-84; dir. Sweet Adelines, Inc., Waterbury, 1981—. Contbr. articles to profl. jours.; arranger songs for barbershop harmony, 1983. Mem. Republican Town Com., Seneca Falls, N.Y., 1971; edn. chmn. Town Bicentennial Com., Naugatuck, 1975-76; v.p. PTO, Naugatuck 1975-77. Mem. Naugatuck Tchrs. League (bldg. rep. 1972, 75, 78, 85), Conn. Edn. Assn., NEA, Adminstrn. and Supervision Assn., AAUW. Republican. Episcopalian. Avocations: tennis; sailing. Home: 1077 Amity Rd Bethany CT 06525 Office: Naugatuck Bd Edn Naugatuck Ct 06770

STAWASZ, CHERIE, public relations executive; b. Chgo., Apr. 10, 1946; d. Edward Paul and Louise Antoinette (Dutka) S.; m. Francis Andre Koenig, June 18, 1983. B.A., Cardinal Stritch Coll., 1968. Traffic coordinator Sta.-WPIX-TV, N.Y.C., 1969-70; prodn. assoc. Green Dolmatch Advt., N.Y.C., 1970-73; publicity assoc. Simon & Schuster, N.Y.C., 1973-75; account exec. Siesel Co., N.Y.C., 1976-78; v.p. Rowland Co., N.Y.C., 1978-84; pres. Stawasz Pub. Relations, Inc., N.Y.C., 1984—. Mem. C.G. Jung Found. Roman Catholic. Office: Stawasz Pub Relations Inc 445 Park Ave New York NY 10022

STAY, BARBARA, zoologist, educator; b. Cleve., Aug. 31, 1926; d. Theron David and Florence (Finley) Stay; A.B., Vassar Coll., 1947; M.A., Radcliffe Coll., 1949, Ph.D., 1953. Entomologist, Army Research Center, Natick, Mass., 1954-60; vis. asst. prof. Pomona Coll., 1960; asst. prof. biology U. Pa., 1961-67; asso. prof. zoology U. Iowa, Iowa City, 1967-77, prof., 1977—; Fulbright fellow to Australia, 1953; Lalor fellow Harvard U., 1960. Mem. Am. Soc. Zoologists, Am. Inst. Biol. Scis., Am. Soc. Cell Biology, Entomol. Soc. Am., Iowa Acad. Scis., Sigma Xi. Office: Dept Biology Univ Iowa Iowa City IA 52242

STEAD, FRANCESCA MANUELA LEWENSTEIN, health care consultant, massage therapist; b. Bklyn., May 2, 1949; d. Robert Gottschalk Lewenstein and Shirley Winifred (Goodman) Lewenstein Ozgen; m. Thomas David Stead, May 28, 1975; 1 child, Chandra Dharani. Student Case Western Res. U., 1967-69; B.A. in Govt. cum laude, Ohio U., 1973; Massage Therapist, Central Ohio Sch. Massage, Columbus, 1978. Lic. massage therapist. Youth service coordinator Adams-Brown Community Action Agy., Decatur, Ohio, 1973; child welfare worker Scioto Children's Services, Portsmouth, Ohio, 1975-77; project dir. youth services Scioto County Community Action Agy., Portsmouth, 1978-79; co-owner Stead Enterprises, wholesale mktg. orgn., Otway, Ohio, 1978—; self-employed massage therapist, Portsmouth, 1979—; drug and alcohol counselor Council on Alcoholism, West Union, Ohio, 1982; reimbursement officer Ohio Dept. Mental Health, Columbus, 1982—; cons. Portsmouth Police Dept., 1977, Total Health Care Consultants, Portsmouth, Ohio, 1985—; cons. drug abuse Aberdeen Sch., Ohio, 1982; Yoga instr. YMCA, Portsmouth, 1979-80, 85—. Campaign worker Ohio Democratic Party, 1968—; mem., organizer So. Ohio Taskforce on Domestic Violence, 1976—; organizer campus ministry Shawnee State Coll., Portsmouth, 1976-77; organizer Portsmouth Food Coop., 1975. Flora Stone Mather scholar Case Western Res. U., 1967. Mem. So. Ohio Mental Health Assn., Am. Massage Therapy Assn., Pi Gamma Mu. Democrat. Kagyupa Buddhist. Club: Poetry Circle (Portsmouth). Avocations: weaving, painting, skiing, gardening, ethnology. Home: 4140 Mt Unger Rd Otway OH 45657 Office: 1025 1/2 9th St Portsmouth OH 45662

STEARLEY, MILDRED SUTCLIFFE VOLANDT, foundation executive; b. Ft. Myer, Va., Aug. 3, 1905; d. William Frederick and Mabel Emma (Sutcliffe) Volandt; student George Washington U., 1923-24, 25-28; m. Ralph F. Stearley, Sept. 19, 1931. Elementary tchr. Brent Sch., Baguio, Philippines, 1929-30; staff aide vol. services ARC, also acting chmn., Charlotte, N.C., 1943, staff asst., Washington, 1943-47, Gray Lady vol., Okinawa, 1950-53, Brazil, Ind., 1954; trustee Air Force Village Found., San Antonio, 1975-78, sec. bd., 1975-77; sustaining mem. Tex. Gov.'s Com.; mem. 300 com. Bexar County Republican Com.; chmn. decoration com. St. Andrew's Episc. Ch., San Antonio Recipient commendation ARC, 1943. Mem. Army Daus., Am. Legion Aux., Army-Navy Club Aux., P.E.O. (life), Am. Security Council (nat. adv. bd.), San Antonio Mus. Assn., Pi Beta Phi. Episcopalian. Clubs: Ladies Reading (hon. mem.) (Brazil, Ind.); Lackland Officers Wives, Bright Shawl (San Antonio). Home: 4917 Ravenswood Dr San Antonio TX 78227

STEARNS, E(LIZABETH) CAROLYN, medical administrative officer; b. Mooresville, Ind., Aug. 16, 1928; d. Gale Able and Ercie Louise (Smith) Rose; grad. Mooresville public schs.; m. William Joseph Sawyers, Sept. 6, 1946, (div. May 1951); children—William Joseph, Sherry Lou; m. John Pershing Stearns, Oct. 4, 1954 (div. Mar. 1980); 1 son, Dennis Gale. Sec., Lab. Equipment Corp., Mooresville, 1946-49; sec. to chief surg. service VA Hosp., Indpls., 1950-57, sec. radiology service, 1963-64, sec. to chief med. service, 1964-66, adminstrv. asst. to chief med. service, 1966-70, adminstrv. officer med. service, 1970-72; staff asst. med. service VA Hosp., Tampa, Fla., 1972-80, adminstrv. officer, med. service, 1981—; adminstrv. officer dept. internal medicine U. So. Fla. Coll. Medicine, Tampa, 1972—. Mem. bus. edn. adv. com. J. Everett Light Career Center, Indpls., 1969-72. Mem. Adminstrs. of Internal Medicine Assn., Med. Group Mgmt. Assn., Nat. Notary Assn., Nat. Assn. Female Execs. Inc., Am. Soc. Profl. and Exec. Women, Hillsborough County Med. Assts. Assn., Fla. Med. Group Mgmt. Assn., Acad. Practice Assembly. Office: Dept Internal Medicine 12901 N 30th St Box 19 Tampa FL 33612

STEBBINS, GAIL DUFFIE, lawyer; b. Augusta, Ga., Aug. 8, 1954; d. Hubert Wallace and Eleanor (Watkins) D. B.A. with distinction and honors, Converse Coll., 1975; J.D. cum laude, U. S.C., 1978. Bar: S.C. 1978, Ga. 1978. Assoc. law firms, Darlington, S.C., 1978-82; law clk. U.S. Dist. Ct. So. Dist. Ga., Augusta, 1982; ptnr. Hull, Towill, Norman & Barrett, Augusta, 1982—. Editor S.C. Trial Lawyers Bull., 1980-82. Sponsor state handicapped olympics, state coll. scholarships and sr. citizen services fund raising Darlington Pilot Club, 1980-82; tchr. handicapped swimming Converse Coll., 1972-75; bd. dirs. Augusta chpt. ARC, 1984—, mem. exec. com., sec., 1985—; team mem. Augusta Coll. Capital Endowment Campaign, 1985; mem. exec. bd. West Lake Townhouse Assn., 1982, v.p., 1983. Recipient Most Promising Young Lawyer award Pee Dee region S.C., 1981-82. Mem. Augusta Bar Assn., Young Lawyers Assn., Ga. Bar Assn., Darlington Bar Assn. (sec.-treas. 1979-81), S.C. Bar Assn., ABA, S.C. Trial Lawyers Assn., Am. Trial Lawyers Assn., Am. Judicature Soc., Order of Wig and Robe, Pi Gamma Mu, Gamma Sigma. Republican. Baptist. Clubs: Augusta Country, Pinnacle (Augusta); Belle Meade Hunt (Thomson, Ga.). Home: 3501 Ironwood Dr Martinez GA 30907 Office: Hull Towill Norman & Barrett PO Box 1564 Augusta GA 30913

STEBER, ELEANOR, soprano; b. Wheeling, W.Va., July 17, 1914; d. William Charles and Ida A. (Nolte) Steber; Mus.B., New Eng. Conservatory Music, 1938, hon. Mus.D.; Mus.D. (hon.), Bethany Coll., U. W.Va., Fla. So. Coll., Temple U., Ithaca Coll.; L.H.D. (hon.), Wheaton Coll., 1966; A.F.D., U. Oklahoma City. Singer, 1935—; won Met. Auditions of Air, spring 1940; with Met. Opera Co., 1940-66, San Francisco Opera Co., 1945, Central City Opera Festival, 1946, Cin. Summer Opera, 5 summers; appeared with all maj. Am. opera cos., and all maj. European festivals including Glynbourne, 1948, Bayreuth, 1953, Florence (Italy), 1954, Salzburg, 1959; sang with 7 opera cos. in Yugoslavia, 1955, Vienna Staats Oper, 1956; soloist with N.Y. Philharmonic, NBC, Boston, Mpls., Chgo., Cin., Kansas City, Denver, Montreal, Phila. Symphony orchs., others; makes radio, TV appearances; star of TV's Voice of Firestone, 10 yrs. Concert tours throughout U.S., Can., Europe, Orient; head vocal dept. Cleve. Inst. Music, 1963-73; voice faculty Julliard Sch. Music, 1971—, New Eng. Conservatory Music, 1971—, Phila. Music Acad., 1975. Bd. dirs. Bklyn. Opera Co., Opera Soc. Washington; founder, pres. Eleanor Steber Music Found., 1975—. Mem. Delta Omicron, Pi Kappa Lambda. Lutheran. Home: Box 342 Port Jefferson NY 11777 Office: 2109 Broadway New York NY 10023

STECKEL, JANET LOUISE, lawyer; b. Allentown, Pa., Aug. 26, 1951; d. George William and June Louise Steckel; A.B., Smith Coll., 1973; J.D., George Washington U., 1976. Admitted to D.C. bar, 1976; law clk. D.C. Ct. Appeals, 1976-77; atty. Regulatory Litigation Sect., Office Gen. Counsel, Dept. Energy, 1977-80; asst. counsel Office Profl. Responsibility, Dept. Justice, atty. Appellate Sect., Land and Natural Resources Div., 1982—. Mem. Choral Arts Soc. Washington, 1976—. Mem. D.C. Bar Assn. Democrat. Office: Dept of Justice Land and Natural Resources Div 10th St and Constitution Ave NW Washington DC 20530

STECKER, BONNIE YANKY, employee communications specialist; b. Balt., Dec. 1, 1958; d. Arthur Emil and Bette Emma (Muhl) Yanky; m. Richard George Stecker, Sept. 29, 1984. B.A., Salisbury State Coll., 1979. Pub. relations specialist Md. Nat. Bank, Balt., 1980-83; employee communications specialist Martin Marietta Aerospace, Balt., 1983—. Mem. Internat. Assn. Bus. Communicators (treas. Balt. 1984), Phi Kappa Phi. Avocations: aerobics; needlework; sailing.

STEED, DENA BETH, musician; b. Nacogdoches, Tex., Nov. 1, 1952; d. William E. and Nora R. (Saxton) S. B.Mus., Stephen F. Austin U., 1975, M.A., 1978. Band asst. Clarksville Ind. Sch. Dist., Tex., 1975-76; bands dir. Garrison Ins. Sch. Dist., Tex., 1976-80; band asst. Humble Ind. Sch. Dist., Tex., 1980—, band asst. Humble High Sch., 1984—. Mem. Tex. Music Educators Assn., Tex. Bandmasters Assn., Tau Beta Sigma (life). Republican. Baptist. Avocations: swimming; racquetball; softball; weight training. Office: Humble High Sch 1700 Wilson Rd Humble TX 77338

STEEL, CLAUDIA WILLIAMSON, artist; b. Van Nuys, Calif., Mar. 19, 1918; d. James Gordon and Ella (Livingston) Williamson; B.A. in Art, U. Calif., Berkeley, 1939, secondary credential, 1940; M.F.A., Mills Coll., 1978; m. Lowell F. Steel, Aug. 15, 1941; children—Claudia Steel Rosen, Douglas Lowell, Roger Conant. Tchr. art Greenville Jr./Sr. High Sch., Calif., 1940-42; faculty Calif. State U., Chico, 1967-69; pvt. tchr. art, Chico; one-woman shows include: Laboudt Gallery, San Francisco, 1958, Witherspoon Bldg., Phila., 1959, traveling show with Old Bergen Guild to nat. galleries, 1971-84, Redding (Calif.) Mus., 1973, Central Wyo. Mus. Art, Casper, 1976, U. Portland 1976, U. Wis., LaCrosse, 1978, Purdue U., West Lafayette, Ind., 1979, Pratt Inst., Manhatten Gallery, N.Y.C., 1980, Creative Arts Ctr., Chico, Calif., 1980, 84;

exhibited in group shows at: Santa Barbara Art Mus., 1951, San Francisco Arts Festival (award), 1953, Oakland Art Mus., 1954, San Francisco Women Artists juried shows, 1958, 68 (award), 72, 73, 75, 76, Crocker Mus., Sacramento, 1958, 59, 60, 65, 67 (award), 73, Richmond Mus. (Calif.), 1960, DeYoung Mus. Art, San Francisco, 1960, San Francisco Mus. Art, 1959, 61 (award), Legion of Honor Mus., San Francisco, 1960, Mills Coll. Gallery, 1962, 67, 78, Berkeley Art Ctr. Gallery, 1969, San Francisco Art Commn. Gallery, 1972, Brandeis U., Mass., 1973, Ohio State U., Columbus, 1973, Brandt Gallery, Glendale, Calif., 1978, Chico State U., 1979, Fisher Gallery, Chico, Walnut Creek Art Gallery and Sonoma State U., 1979, Pratt Inst., Manhattan Gallery, N.Y.C., 1980, 1980, Calif. Soc. Printmakers traveling show, 1981, juried show, Singapore and Switzerland, 1984, Purdue U., 1982, U. Wis.-Eau Claire, 1982, others. Bd. dirs. Creative Art Ctr., Chico, 1977-81, Omni Arts, Chico, 1979-82. Recipient San Francisco Mus. of Art Serigraphy award, 1961; trustees' scholar Mills Coll., 1935, others. Mem. Calif. Soc. Printmakers (v.p., dir. 1973-77), Los Angeles Printmakers Soc., others. Republican.

STEELE, ANA MERCEDES, government official; b. Niagara Falls, N.Y., Jan. 18, 1939; d. Sydney and Mercedes (Hernandez) S.; m. John Hunter Clark, June 2, 1979. A.B. magna cum laude, Marywood Coll., 1958. Actress, 1959-64; sec. Nat. Endowment for Arts, Washington, 1965-67, dir. budget and research, 1968-75, dir. planning, 1976-78, dir. program coordination, sr. exec. service, 1979-81, assoc. dep. chmn. for programs, dir. program coordination, sr. exec. service, 1982—. Author, editor report: History of the National Council on the Arts and National Endowment for the Arts During the Johnson Administration, 1968; editor: Museums USA (Fed. Design Council award of Excellence 1975), 1974; National Endowment Arts 1965-1985: A Brief Chronology of Federal Involvement in the Arts, 1985. Former reader Rec. for the Blind, N.Y.C.; former tutor Future for Jimmy, Washington. Named Disting. Grad. in Field of Arts, Marywood Coll., 1976; recipient Sustained Superior Performance award Nat. Endowment for Arts, Washington, 1980, Disting. Service award, 1983, 84, 85. Mem. Actors' Equity Assn., Screen Actors Guild, Delta Epsilon Sigma, Kappa Gamma Pi.

STEELE, ANDREA WHITE, personnel director; b. Washington, June 1, 1955; d. Raymond Benjamin and Elizabeth Mae (Koons) White; m. Michael William Steele, Apr. 26, 1980 (div. 1984). B.A. in Behavioral Sci., U. Md., 1977; M.Bus., Central Mich. U., 1982; postgrad. in law U. Balt. Employment rep. Dart Drug Corp., Landover, Md., 1977-79; employment supr. Duron Paints and Wallcoverings, Beltsville, Md., 1979-81, dir. personnel, 1981—; guest speaker profl. assns. Mem. Am. Soc. Personnel Adminstrn., Washington Personnel Assn., Washington Retail Bd. Trade, Sigma Iota Epsilon, Kappa Kappa Gamma. Republican. Methodist. Office: Duron Paints and Wallcoverings 10406 Tucker St Beltsville MD 20705

STEELE, ELIZABETH ANN, civic counselor-advocate, community organizer; b. Indpls., Oct. 27, 1942; d. Richard Monticue and Betty (Kalleen) S. B.A., Butler U., 1965; M.Counseling, Ariz. State U., 1979. VISTA vol. OEO, Winnebago Indian Reservation, Nebr., 1966-67; community organizer-developer Bd. Global Ministries, United Meth. Ch., Cheyenne-Arapaho Tribe, Okla., 1968-70, Cherokee Tribe, N.C., 1970-73, Buffalo Creek, W.Va., 1973-76; counselor/adv. New Directions for Young Women, Tucson, 1980—; mem. Okla. Gov.'s Council on Children and Youth, 1969-70, Watonga City Planning Council, 1969-70, Buffalo Creek Citizen's Adv. Council, 1974-76, Second 40 Survival, Tucson, 1983-84, City of Tucson Rape Task Force, 1984—. Support person Take Back the Night, Tucson, 1983—, Surging Wave Womyn, Tucson, 1984. Recipient Extraordinary/Ordinary Woman award, 1984; Eli Lilly Found. scholar, 1963. Mem. Possible Human Soc., Tucson Women's Network (co-founder 1981), NOW, Tucson Networking Task Force, Am. Cetacean Soc., Pi Lambda Theta, Kappa Kappa Gamma. Democrat. Methodist. Avocations: camping; snorkeling; tidepooling; travel; writing. Home: 7335 E 28th St Tucson AZ 85710 Office: New Directions for Young Women Suite F 209 S Tucson Blvd Tucson AZ 85716

STEELE, ELLEN LIVELY, state senator; b. Fayette County, W.Va., Jan. 22, 1936; d. Alfred French and Sarah Ellen (Pritchard) L.; student N.Mex. State U., 1962-74; m. Henry Gilmer Steele, July 20, 1981; children—Gregory Benjamin Pake, Seana Ellen Pake. Civilian adminstrv. officer Dept. Army, White Sands Missile Range, N.Mex., 1962-67; mgr. Kelly Services Inc., Las Cruces, N.Mex., 1967-85; pres. Lively Enterprises, Inc., Las Cruces, 1967-76; sec., treas. Adam II, Ltd., Las Cruces, 1973-77; pres. Dr. Romero's Symposium Internat. Inc., Las Cruces, 1977-78, Asset & Resource Mgmt. Corp., Las Cruces, 1978-85; lit. agt., prin. Ellen Lively Steele & Assocs., 1979-85; pres. AVVA III, 1981-85; gen. dir. Gasco Internat., Inc., 1981-82; dir. Rosa Resources Corp.; v.p. San Augustine Pass Corp., 1981-82; mng. ptnr. Internat. Alliance Sports Ofcls., 1981—; ptnr. Steele-Lively Ventures, 1982—; dir. mktg. Las Cruces Conv. and Visitors Bur., 1984-85; senator State of N.Mex., 1985—. Mem. task force pub. relations N.Mex. Republican Party, 1977; ward chmn., mem. central com. Dona Ana County Rep. Party, 1981-85, vice chmn., 1981-83. Served with USAF, 1954-57. Mem. Internat. Assn. Fin. Planners, Sales and Mktg. Execs. Internat., Internat. Alliance Sports Ofcls. (sec.-treas. 1982—), Las Cruces C. of C. (pub. relations com. 1968-73), Am. Mgmt. Assn., D.A.R. Republican. Episcopalian. Club: Order Eastern Star; Assn. (Las Cruces). Home: Drawer 447 Organ NM 88052 Office: San Augustine Pass NM

STEELE, EVELYN JANE, public relations and advt. agy. exec.; b. Berkeley, Calif., Feb. 14, 1911; d. Carlos Louis and Jane Catherine (Jensen) de Clairmont; student Munson Bus. Coll., San Francisco, 1929-30; m. Donald Dickinson Steele, May 8, 1932; 1 son, Donald de Clairmont. Pvt. sec., 1930-32; engaged in public relations, publicity and advt., 1940—; v.p., dir. Steele Group, San Francisco, 1977—; sec.-treas. Internat. Pub. Relations Co., Ltd., San Francisco; sec.-treas. Internat. Bus. Interface, Inc., Don Steele Advt. Pres. Ladies Aid Retarded Children, San Francisco, 1977-78, bd. dirs., 1978-86. Mem. Fashion Group (regional dir. 1965-67). Republican. Unitarian. Clubs: Metropolitan (dir. 1961-68), Order Rainbow Girls. Office: 703 Market St San Francisco CA 94103

STEELE, HILDA HODGSON, retired home economist, educator; b. Wilmington, Ohio, Mar. 24, 1911; d. George and Mary Jane (Rolston) Hodgson; certificate Wilmington Coll., 1931, B.S., 1935; M.A. in Home Econs. Edn., Ohio State U., 1941; postgrad. Ohio U., 1954, Miami U., 1959; m. John C. Steele (dec. Jan. 1973). Tchr., Brookville (Ohio) Elementary Sch., 1932-37; tchr. home econs., Lincoln Jr. High Sch., Dayton Public Schs. (Ohio), 1937-40, coordinator home econs. dept., travelling exptl. home econs. tchr., 1940-45, supr. home econs., 1945-81. Mem. Ohio Farm Electrification Com., 1964-66. Jr. adv. com. Montgomery County chpt. ARC, 1940-70; mem. town and country br. career com. Miami Valley br. YMCA, 1948-59; adv. bd. Dayton Sch. Practical Nursing, 1951—; adv. com. Dayton Miami Valley Hosp. Sch. Nursing, 1951-67; mem. child care adv. com. Central State U., 1973—; bd. dirs. mem. for youth group FHA-HERO of Ohio, 1979—; mem. legis. network com. Dept. Vocat. Home Econs., State of Ohio, 1979-81; mem. adv. com. community and home service Sinclair Community Coll. Mem. Montgomery County Nutrition Council (Dayton area. 1st vice-chmn. 1967), Am. Home Econs. Assn. (del. 1961-76, chmn. found. com. 1979-81), Ohio (chmn. elementary and secondary edn. com. 1947-51, co-chmn. ann. conv. 1961-77, mem. housing, equip. com. 1965-68), Dayton Met. (pres. 1949-50, 60-61) home econ. assns., Am. (life mem.), Ohio (Supr. Home Econs. award 1981), Western Ohio (sec. 1977) vocational assns., Am. Vocat. Home Econs. Assn., Nat., Ohio edn. assns., Dayton Sch. Adminstrs. Assn., Dayton Sch. Mgmt. Assn. (program com. 1971), Elec. Women's Round Table, Ohio Assn. Childhood Edn., Phi Upsilon Omicron (hon. mem. Alpha Omega chpt.). Mem. Ch. of Christ. Mem. Order Eastern Star. Club: Zonta (pres. Dayton 1950-52). Research in public sch. food habits, 1957. Home: 1443 State Route 380 Xenia OH 45385

STEELE, LYNETTE JOYCE, economist, consultant; b. Rio, Claro, Trinidad, June 24, 1942; came to U.S., 1970; d. Wilfred Isaac and Edna Winifred (Saunders) Jackson; m. Alexander Steele, Mar. 19, 1960; children—Gary, Sharon. B.A. magna cum laude, Howard U., 1972, M.A. with honors, 1974, Ph.D., 1980. Research asst. Nat. Acad. Sci., Washington, 1973-75; fellow Howard U., 1974-76; professorial lectr. Am. U., Washington, 1975-83; economist JRB Assoc., McLean, Va., 1976-80; research analyst Chessie System R.R., Balt., 1980—. Recipient Statis. award Am. Statis. Soc., 1974; Meritorious award Grad. Sch. Howard U., 1975. Mem. Phi Beta Kappa. Avocations: cooking; sewing; traveling. Home: 316 Serena St Upper Marlboro MD 20772 Office: Chessie System Railroads 1 Charles Ctr Baltimore MD 21201

STEELEYSMITH, DEBORAH LYGIA, educational administrator; b. N.Y.C., Oct. 6, 1951; d. Ellis Robert and Deressa Doris (Moultrie) Steeley; m. Allan David Smith, Oct. 14, 1978. B.A. in Psychology, Coll. Mt. St. Vincent, 1974; M.S.Ed., Fordham U., 1981. Cert. trainer group and Orgnl. Devel. Mental health counselor Harlem Hosp., N.Y.C., 1973-74, Project Create, N.Y.C., 1974-77; tng. specialist N.Y. State Bur. Tng. and Resource Devel., N.Y.C., 1978-82; dir. tng. and staff devel. Manhattan Psychiat. Center, N.Y. State Office Mental Health, 1982-85, 86—; Kirby Forensic Psychiat. Ctr., 1985; trainer Gov.'s Office Employee Relations, State of N.Y. Cons. Nat. Inst. Drug Abuse, Adelphi U. Nat. Tng. Inst., Native N.Am. Drug and Alcohol Program, Yellowknife, N.W.T., Can., Native N.Am. Tng. and Support System, Winnipeg, Alta., Can., 1984, others, 1977—; active PBS-Channel 13, N.Y.C., 1971—. Cert. trainer Nat. Drug Abuse Tng. Center. Mem. N.Y. Zool. Soc., Orgn. Mgmt. Confidential Employees State of N.Y. Democrat. Office: Ward's Island New York NY 10035

STEEN, BARBARA JEAN, educational administrator; b. Greenville, S.C., July 23, 1941; d. Larry Lester and Katie Lula (Jones) Erwin; m. Frederick R. Steen, Aug. 15, 1964; children—Bryan Frederick, Roland Erwin Nathaniel. Assoc., Mars Hill Coll., 1961; B.S. in Home Econs., Carson Newman Coll., 1963; postgrad. So. Baptist Sem., 1963-64, New Orleans Bapt. Sem., 1965-66. Tchr., Spring Creek High Sch., Hot Springs, N.C., 1964-66, Mid City High Sch., New Orleans, 1966-67, Borgemouth Sch., New Orleans, 1967-69, Mountain View Elem. Sch., Taylors, S.C., 1971-74; presch. children's dir. First Bapt. Ch., Chattanooga, 1981—. Mem. Ministers Religious Edn. Hamilton County Assn. (pres. 1984-85). Avocations: gardening, piano, organ, reading. Home: 3122 Rose Terr Chattanooga TN 37404 Office: First Baptist Ch 401 Gateway St Chattanooga TN 37401

STEENBURGEN, MARY, actress; b. Newport, Ark., 1953; m. Malcolm McDowell; children—Lily, Charlie. Films: Goin' South (film debut), 1978, Time After Time, 1979, Melvin and Howard (Academy award for best supporting actress), 1980, Ragtime, 1981, A Midsummer Night's Sex Comedy, 1982, Cross Creek, 1983, Romantic Comedy, 1983, One Magic Christmas, 1985; TV miniseries, Tender Is The Night, 1985; Showtime TV Faerie Tale Theater prodn. Little Red Riding Hood, 1983. Address: care International Creative Management 8899 Beverly Blvd Los Angeles CA 90048

STEEPLES, MARIAN MILLS, quality and productivity resource developer; b. Akron, Ohio, Jan. 6, 1940; d. Herbert Asa and Marjorie Josephine (Joy) Mills; m. Douglas Wayne Steeples; children—John Mills Powell, Victoria Joy Powell. B.A., Earlham Coll., 1962; M.Ed. in Adminstrn. and Curriculum Devel., Miami U., Oxford, Ohio, 1976; Ph.D. in Bus. Mgmt., Columbia Pacific U., 1985. Tchr. Delaware City Schs., Ohio, 1970-72, Richmond Sch. Corp., Ind., 1972-79; adminstr. Comprehensive Energy Mgmt., Richmond, 1979-80; sr. analyst Aerospace div. Hercules, Magna, Utah, 1980-83; dir. quality program Utah Tech. Coll., Salt Lake City, 1983-85; pres. Steeples & Assoc., Salt Lake City, 1985—; adj. prof. Taylor U., Upland, Ind., 1976-77, Ind. U., Richmond, 1976-78; lectr. U. Utah, Salt Lake City, 1983-84; mem. faculty U. Phoenix, Salt Lake City, 1985; trustee Utah Math-Sci. Network, Salt Lake City, 1982—; bd. mem. Westminster Coll. Profl. Studies, Salt Lake City, 1983—. Author: Approaches to Natural Science, 1977, Productive Mathmatics, 1978; Systematic Writing, 1979; Quality and Productivity Improvement, 1985. Assoc. campaign chmn. United Way, Salt Lake City, 1981—. Recipient Instructional Achievement award Gov. and Dept. Pub. Instrn., Ind., 1976, U.S. Presdl. award Dept. Interior, 1978. Mem. AAUW, Am. Soc. Quality Control, Am. Soc. Tng. and Devel. (program com., orgn. devel. com.), Internat. Assn. Quality Circles, Salt Lake City C. of C. (program chmn. 1982-85, projects chmn. 1982-85), DAR, Delta Kappa Gamma, Delta Gamma.

STEEVES, HARRIET CORBIN, town official; b. Boston, Aug. 20, 1927; d. Leander frost and Marion Palmer (Bonney) Corbin; m. Robert Wesley Steeves, Nov. 28, 1948; children—Ellen Marsha, Robert Allen, Donald Evan. B.S. in Chemistry, Tufts Coll., 1948. Lab. technician Polaroid Corp., Cambridge, Mass., 1948-50; dog officer Town of Nahant, Mass., 1960-74, town clk., 1974—, Sec., Pub. Recreation Commn., Nahant, 1956-68; pres., treas. Nahant Republican Women's Club, 1964—. Named Vol. of Yr. Lynn Daily Evening Item for Nahant, 1966. Mem. Internat. Inst. Mcpl. Clks., New Engl. Town Clks. Assn., North Shore City and Town Clks (sec. 1978-84), Mass. Town Clks. Assn., Nahant Garden Club (treas. 1980-83), Nahant Dory Club (sec. 1984—). Universalist. Avocations: gardening; sailing; sewing and needlework; choir singing; flute playing. Home: 51 Fox Hill Rd Nahant MA 01908-1199 Office: Town Hall 334 Nahant Rd Nahant MA 01908-0175

STEFAN, PEGGY SEHLIN, marketing communications executive; b. Mpls., Feb. 19, 1960; d. Arthur Andrew and Zana (Windahl) Sehlin; m. Scott L. Stefan, July 23, 1983. B.S. in Bus. Fin., Mont. State U., 1981. Lic. stockbroker. Registered rep. Investors Diversified Services, Mpls., 1981-83; mktg. rep., tng. cons. Golle & Holmes Fin. Learning, Mpls. and N.Y.C., 1983-84; dir. mktg. communications Integrated Resources Equity Corp., N.Y.C., 1984—; owner Equinox, Inc., East Rutherford, N.J., 1985—. Recipient sales achievement awards Investors Diversified Services, 1982. Mem. Internat. Assn. Fin. Planners, Nat. Assn. Female Execs., Mont. State U. Alumni Assn., Pi Beta Phi. Avocations: skiing; travel. Office: Integrated Resources Equity Corp 733 3d Ave New York NY 10017

STEFANATOS, JOANNE, veterinarian; b. N.Y.C., Aug. 26, 1945; d. Fotios and Adele (Zaferatos) Stefanatos; m. David Ross Hetzel, June 26, 1983. B.S. in Zoology, U. Nev., 1967; D.V.M., U. Mo., 1972; postgrad. (fellow) St. Louis U., 1967-68. Vet. surgeon Paradise Pet Clinic, Las Vegas, 1972-73; vet. surgeon, bird specialist Angel Nev. Pet Clinic, Las Vegas, 1973-74; owner, veterinarian, hosp. dir. Animal Kingdom Vet. Hosp., Las Vegas, 1974—; Nev. wildlife veterinarian, 1972—; Nev. commr. of fish and game, 1977-80; co-owner Animal Emergency Clinic, Las Vegas, 1978-80, Animal Birth Control Clinic; Patentee in field; contbr. articles to profl. jours. Bd. dirs. Animal Rescue Found., 1979-83; chmn. CCVMA Ethics Com., 1975-77. Mem. Am. Animal Hosp. Assn., Holistic Vet. Med. Soc., Am. Assn. Zoo Veterinarians, Soc. Ultramolecular Medicine (bd. dirs.), Am. Radiologists Soc., Clark County Vet. Assn., Tri Penta, Phi Zeta. Democrat. Greek Orthodox. Home: 379 Desert Palm Dr Las Vegas NV 89124 Office: Animal Kingdom Vet Hosp 1325 Vegas Valley Dr Las Vegas NV 89109

STEFFEY, LELA, state legislator, banker; b. Idaho Falls, Idaho, Aug. 8, 1928; d. Orawell and Mary Ethel (Owen) Gardner; m. Carl A. Hendershott, Jr., Apr. 16, 1949 (div. 1961); children—Barry G., Bradley Carl, Barton P.; m. 2d Warren D. Steffey, July 13, 1973; children—Dean, Wayne, Luann, Scott, Susan. Grad. Am. Inst. Banking, 1972. With Pacific Tel. & Tel., San Diego, 1949-58, Bank of Am., San Diego, 1949-52, Gen. Dynamics/Astro, San Diego, 1960-61; escrow officer, mgr. consumer loans Bank of Am., San Diego, 1961-73; real estate agt. Steffey Realty, Mesa, Ariz., 1978—; mem. Ariz. Ho. of Reps, Phoenix, 1982—, vice chmn. banking and ins. com., 1982—, mem. house appropriations, judiciary, counties and municipalities coms., 1982—, chmn. appropriations sub-com. Founder, Citizens Com. Against Domestic Abuse; precinct com. Legis. Dist. 29, 1978—, dep. registrar, 1978—; pres. Mesa Republican Women, 1980; chmn. Mesa Mus. Adv. bd., 1981-83; del. to conv. Nat. Fedn. Rep. Women, Colo., 1981; del. to Rep. Nat. Conv., Dallas, 1984. Bd. dirs. Mesa Community Council, 1985-88. Mem. Nat. Order Women Legislators (sec.), Am. Mothers Assn., Nat. Fedn. Republican Women, Ariz. Fedn. Republican Women (dir.), Ariz. Assn. of Women (dir.), Am. Legis. Exchange Council, Pi Beta Phi. Mem. Ch. of Jesus Christ of Latter-Day Saints. Home: 1439 E Ivyglen St Mesa AZ 85203 Office: Ariz House of Representatives 1700 W Washington Phoenix AZ 85007

STEFFY, MARION NANCY, state official; b. Fairport Harbor, Ohio, Sept 23, 1937; d. Felix and Anna (Kosaber) Jackopin; m. Donald H. Steffy, Apr. 15, 1961; 1 son, Christopher C. B.A., Ohio State U., 1959; postgrad. Butler U., 1962-65, Ind. U., 1983. Exec. sec. Franklin County Mental Health Assn., Columbus, Ohio, 1959-61; caseworker Marion County Dept. Pub. Welfare, Indpls., 1961-63, supr., 1963-66, asst. chief supr., 1966-73; dir. div. pub. assistance, Ind. Dept. Pub. Welfare, Indpls., 1973-77, asst. adminstr., 1977—; lectr. Ball State U., Lockyear Coll., Ind. U. Grad. Sch. Social Work; mem. Ind. Devel. Disabilities Council, 1979-81, Ind. Community Services Adv. Council, 1978-81; Ind. Child Support Adv. Council, 1976-82, Welfare Service League, 1968—; chmn. rules com. Ind. Health Facilities Council, 1974-81. Chmn. Lawrence Republican Roundtable, 1983—. Mem. Nat. Assn. State Pub. Welfare Adminstrs., Am. Pub. Welfare Assn., Network of Women in Bus. Roman Catholic. Home: 6846 E 65th St Indianapolis IN 46220 Office: Ind Dept Pub Welfare 701 State Office Bldg Indianapolis IN 46204

STEGEMOELLER, SUSAN WARNER, financial planner; b. Rochester, N.Y., July 20, 1956; d. Harold J. and Jeannette (Nichols) Warner; m. James Fred Stegemoeller, July 28, 1979. B.A., Miami U., Oxford, Ohio, 1978; postgrad. Xavier U. Loan specialist HUD, Columbus, Ohio, 1978-79, Cin., 1979-83; fin. planner IDS Fin. Services, Inc., Cin., 1983—; housing cons., Cin., 1985—. Author: Community Land Coop. Residents' Handbook, 1986. Adv., Cin. Tech. Coll., 1984—; mem. fin. com. Community Land Coop., Cin., 1985—; exhibits chair Conf. Cin. Women, 1985, corp. patrons chair, 1986, conf. coordinator, 1987—; vol. Am. Cancer Soc., 1981-84. Recipient profl. awards; Mercury award IDS, Cin., 1984. Mem. Nat. Assn. Female Execs. Republican. Roman Catholic. Avocations: reading; gardening; making teddy bears; softball; theatre. Home: 2598 Queen City Ave Cincinnati OH 45238 Office: IDS Fin Services 4823 N Bend Rd Cincinnati OH 45211

STEIGER, JANET DEMPSEY, government official; b. Oshkosh, Wis., June 10, 1939; 1 son, William Raymond. B.A., Lawrence Coll., 1961; postgrad. U. Reading (Eng.), 1961-62, U. Wis., 1962-63. Legis. corr. Office of Gov. Wis., 1965; v.p. The Work Place, 1975-80; commr. Postal Rate Commn., Washington, 1980—, acting chmn., 1981-82, chmn., 1982—. Author: Law Enforcement and Juvenile Justice in Wisconsin, 1965; co-author: To Light One Candle, a Handbook on Organizing, Funding and Maintaining Public Service Projects, 1978, 2d edit., 1980. Woodrow Wilson scholar; Fulbright scholar, 1954. Address: Postal Rate Commn Room 1333 H St NW Suite 300 Washington DC 20268*

STEIN, ADLYN ROBINSON (MRS. HERBERT ALFRED STEIN), jewelery co. exec.; b. Pitts., May 8, 1908; d. Robert Stewart and Pearl (Geiger) Robinson; Mus.B., Pitts. Mus. Inst., U. Pitts., 1928; m. J. Francis Hollearn, 1929 (dec.); children—Adlyn (Mrs. Brandon J. Hickey), Frances (Mrs. Ralph A. Gleim); m. 2d, Allen Burnett Williams, Dec. 5, 1955 (dec.); m. 3d, Herbert Alfred Stein, Nov. 28, 1963; 1 adopted dau., Rachel Lynn (Mrs. Stephen M. Kampfer). Treas., R.S. Robinson, Inc., Pitts., 1947—. Mem. Pitts. Symphony Soc., Tuesday Musical Club, Pitts.; mem. women's com. Cleve. Symphony. Mem. D.A.R. Republican. Anglican. Clubs: Duquesne, University, Lakewood Country; Clifton; South Hills Country. Home: 22200 Lake Rd Cleveland OH 44116 Office: Clark Bldg Pittsburgh PA 15222

STEIN, BARBARA LAMBERT, marriage and family therapist; b. Detroit, Feb. 10, 1945; d. Joseph J. and Sylvia (Siegel) Lambert; m. David Joel Stein, Jan. 1, 1967; children—Craig Andrew, Todd Alexander. Student psychology Mich. State U., 1962-64; B.A. in Sociology, Wayne State U., 1966, postgrad. in psychiat. social work, 1972-74; M.S. in Counseling Psychology, Nova U., 1980; student, Art Inst. Ft. Lauderdale, 1985. Vol. abuse and neglect dept. Wayne County Juvenile Ct., Detroit, 1964-65; vol. D.J. Healy Shelter for Children, 1965-67; med. social worker Hutzel Hosp., Detroit, 1967-68; developer neighborhood teen drug program City of West Bloomfield (Mich.), 1970-71; med. social worker Extended Care Facilities Inc., Birmingham, Mich., 1972-73; vol. group and occupational therapist Henderson Psychiat. Clinic Day Treatment Ctr., Ft. Lauderdale, Fla., 1977-78; pvt. practice family and marital therapy, Deerfield Beach, Fla., 1980-85. Mem. Temple Beth El of Boca Raton (Fla.) Sch. Edn. Bd., until 1985; founding mem. Levis Jewish Community Ctr., Boca Raton. Recipient cert. of Meritorious Achievement, Henderson Psychiat. Clinic Day Treatment Ctr. Mem. Am. Assn. Marriage and Family Therapy (assoc.), Am. Psychol. Assn. (assoc.), Am. Assn. Counseling and Devel., Wayne State U. Alumni Assn., Nova U. Alumni Assn., Photogroup Miami, Friends of Photography of Cornel (Calif.), Camera Club of Boca Raton, Boca Raton Mus. Art, Nat. Trust Historic Preservation, Opera Soc. Ft. Lauderdale, Zool. Soc. Fla., Orton Dyslexia Soc., Assn. Children and Adults with Learning Disabilities, South County Jewish Fedn. (bd. dirs. until 1986, chmn. community relations council 1984-85, chmn. speakers bur. 1985-86).

STEIN, DEBORA SUSAN, magazine executive; b. Detroit, June 7, 1953. B.A., U. Colo., 1975; M.A., U. Denver, 1978. Prodn. dir. 4M Advt. Agy., Albuquerque, 1975-76; mktg. dir. Mktg./Media Enterprises, 1976-77; copy writer Marketplace Cons., Denver, 1978; account coordinator Mefford Weir Advt., 1978-79; account exec. Baker Publs., Aurora, Colo., 1979—. Mem. Home Builders Assn., Sales and Mktg. Council, Denver Advt. Fedn., Housing Research Council, Denver C. of C.

STEIN, ELEANOR BANKOFF, judge; b. N.Y.C., Jan. 24, 1923; d. Jacob and Sarah (Rashkin) Bankoff; m. Frank S. Stein, May 27, 1947; children—Robert B., Joan Jenkins, William M. Student, Barnard Coll., 1940-42; B.S. in Econs., Columbia U., 1944; LL.B., NYU, 1949. Bar: N.Y. 1950, Ind. 1976, U.S. Supreme Ct. 1980. Atty. Hillis & Button, Kokomo, Ind., 1975-76, Paul Hillis, Kokomo, 1976-78, Bayliff, Harrigan, Kokomo, 1978-80; judge Howard County Ct., Kokomo, 1980—; co-juvenile referee Howard County Juvenile Ct., 1976-78. Mem. Republicans Women's Assn. Kokomo, 1980—; bd. dirs. Howard County Legal Aid Soc., 1976-80; commn. mem. Kokomo Bd. Human Relations, 1967-70. Mem. law rev. bd. NYU Law Rev., 1947-48. Mem. Am. Judicature Soc., Ind. Jud. Assn., Nat. Assn. Women Judges, ABA, Ind. Bar Assn., Howard County Bar Assn. Jewish. Clubs: Kokomo Country, Altrusa. Home: 3204 Tally Ho Dr Kokomo IN 49602 Office: Howard County Ct Howard County Courthouse Kokomo IN 49601

STEIN, ELLEN GAIL, urban planner; b. N.Y.C., May 19, 1951; d. Manuel W. and Bella (Skutel) Stein; B.A., SUNY-Stony Brook, 1972; M.U.P., Hunter Coll., 1976. Sr. research assoc. Nassau Suffolk (N.Y.) Regional Med. Program, 1976-77; sr. planner N.Y.C. Dept. Correction, 1977-79; group leader criminal justice Mayor's Office Ops., N.Y.C., 1979-81, dep. asst. dir. citywide spl. projects, 1981, dir. citywide audit implementaion, 1981-84; adminstr. Bur. Supplies, N.Y.C. Bd. Edn., 1984—. Mem. Assn. Sch. Bus. Ofcls., Nat. Inst. Govt. Purchasing Agts., Am. Soc. for Pub. Adminstrn., Am. Planning Assn. Home: 67 Park Terr E New York NY 10034 Office: 44-36 Vernon Blvd Long Island City NY 11101*

STEIN, GERTRUDE EMILIE, educator, soprano, pianist; b. Ironton, Ohio; d. S.A. and Emilie M. (Pollach) Stein; Mus.B., Capitol Coll., 1927; B.A., Wittenberg Coll., 1929, M.A., 1931, B.S. in Edn., 1945; Ph.D., U. Mich., 1948; piano and voice student Cin. Coll. Conservatory Music. Music supr. Centralized County Schs. Ohio, Williamsburg, 1932-37; dir. jr. high sch. music, 1937-68; mem. faculty Adult Evening Sch. Springfield (Ohio) Pub. Schs., 1951-68; head dept. music, assoc. prof. piano and music edn. Tex. Luth. Coll., Seguin, 1948-49. Donor, founder Rev. Dr. and Mrs. S.A. Stein Meml. Funds, 1955—. Mem. Am. Symphony Orch. League, AAUW, Nat., Ohio edn. assn., Ohio Assn. Adult Edn., Council Exceptional Children, Asso. Council Arts, Met. Opera Guild, Assn. Tchr. Educators, Am. Film Inst., Nat. Music Tchrs. Assn., Ohio Music Tchrs. Assn., Nat. Story League, Music Tchrs. Nat. Assn., Music Educators Nat. Conf., Nat. Assn. Schs. Music, Nat. Fedn. Music Clubs (spl. mem. Ohio, Tex.), Amateur Chamber Music Players, Nat. Fedn. Bus. and Profl. Women, Zonta Internat., Phi Kappa Phi, Pi Lambda Theta. Lutheran. Contbr. articles to profl. jours. Home: 133 N Lowry Ave Springfield OH 45504

STEIN, HEATHER LYNN, writer, public relations specialist; b. Pitts., Mar. 13, 1945; d. Aron and Sophia (Markowitz) Harris; m. Melvin P. Stein, Aug. 11, 1968; children—Matthew Scott, Paula Rachel. B.A., U. Pitts., 1967. Editorial asst. Westinghouse, Large, Pa., 1967; editor Duquesne Light Co., Pitts., 1968-70; pub.'s asst. Basic Products, Pitts., 1980, 81; staff asst. Mayor's Task Force on Women in Renaissance II, Pitts.; free-lance pub. relations specialist, Pitts. City chmn. Women's Plea for Human Rights for Soviet Jewry, Pitts., 1976; pres. Pitts. council Pioneer Women/Náa mat, 1977-79, mem. Midwest bd., Chgo., 1979-83, nat. bd. dirs., N.Y.C., 1983-85, 85-87, Israel seminarist, N.Y.C., 1981. Recipient 2d pl. award Assoc. Editors Soc., Pitts., 1969. Mem. Women in Communications. Home: 2928 Fernwald Rd Pittsburgh PA 15217

STEIN, LOUISE SHARON, civic worker; b. Milw., May 2, 1938; d. David Samuel and Bessie (Kaplan) Mendelson; m. Gerald Marvin H. Stein, Sept. 6, 1959; children—Debra, Leslie, Leigh. Student U. Wis.-Milw., 1956-58. Intern in med. tech. St. Joseph's Hosp., Milw., 1958-59, research med. technologist, 1959-62; active B'Nai B'rith Women, 1950s, 60s; sec., v.p. women's div. Milw. Jewish Fedn., 1982-85; sec. bd. trustees, centennial chmn. Congregation Beth Israel, Milw., 1980-85; v.p. Milw. Assn. Jewish Edn., 1981-83, pres., 1983-86. Recipient Young Leadership award women's div. Mil. Jewish. Fedn., 1983.

Mem. Am. Soc. Clin. Pathologists (registered med. technologist). Avocations: tennis; reading; cooking; gardening; travel. Office: Milw Assn Jewish Edn 4650 N Port Wash Rd Milwaukee WI 53212

STEIN, SUSAN JANE, travel executive; b. Mineola, N.Y., Dec. 12, 1955; d. Richard and Jane Sue (Parrott) S.; m. Richard P. Wisniewski, May 24, 1980 (div. Oct. 1983). B.S. magna cum laude, Barry U., 1986; cert. Taylor Bus. Inst., 1974. Pres., Gallant Voyages Ltd., Fort Lee, N.H., 1986—; asst. to v.p., exec. sec. Trade Wind Tours, Great Neck, N.Y., 1974-86; group sales coordinator Arthur Frommer Charters, Inc., N.Y.C., 1977-78; dir. sales Great Escape Travel, Inc., Miami, Fla., 1978-79; asst. mgr./service cons So. Bell Telephone Co., Miami, 1979-82; adminstrv. supr. AT&T Info. Systems, Fort Lauderdale, Fla., 1983; sales mgr. Pulsar Components Internat., Inc., Los Gatos, Calif., 1983-84; staff mgr. AT&T Info. Systems, Morristown, N.J., 1984-85. Mem. Nat. Assn. Female Execs., Gateway Assn., Internat. Assn. Exec. Communication. Club: Lioness. Avocations: skiing; swimming; yachting; reading; hiking. Office: 1550 Lemoine Ave Fort Lee NJ 07024

STEINBACH, ALICE, writer. Student U. London. Formerly dir. pub. info. Balt. Mus. Art; freelance writer; mem. staff The Balt. Sun, 1981—. Recipient Pulitzer Prize for feature writing, 1985. Office: The Balt Sun Abell Pub Co Calvert and Centre Sts Baltimore MD 21278

STEINBAUER, MARTHA JUNE, nurse; b. Niles, Mich., Aug. 21, 1955; d. Robert Andrus and June Louise (Young) S. Student Kans. State U., 1973-75; B.S.N., U. Kans., 1977. Cert. in advanced cardiac life support. Staff nurse ICU, Presbyn. Hosp., Dallas, 1977-79, head nurse ICU, 1979—, chmn. incident report com., 1982—, resource person nursing seminars, unit dir. thoracic ICU, 1985—. Mem. Am. Assn. Critical Care Nurses (sec. 1980-81), Music Service Guild Kans. State U., U. Kans. Alumni Assn., Sigma Theta Tau, Kappa Alpha Theta. Presbyterian. Office: Presbyn Hosp Dallas 8200 Walnut Hill Ln Dallas TX 75231

STEINBERG, JANET DEBERRY, optometrist, educator researcher; b. Phila., July 28, 1940; d. Bill and Florence (Kurtz) DeBerry; m. J. Arthur Steinberg, June 17, 1962; 1 child by previous marriage, J. Douglas Milner. Student Rider Coll., 1975-77; B.S., Pa. Coll. Optometry, 1978, O.D., 1981. Assoc. Ophthalmic Eye Assocs., 1982-85; dir. Hopewell Valley Eye Assocs., Hopewell, N.J., 1982—; chief Low Vision Ctr., Scheie Eye Inst. dept. ophthalmology U. Pa., Phila., 1984—, also clin. assoc., 1985—; asst. adj. prof. Pa. Coll. Optometry, Phila., 1983-85, mem. adj. faculty, 1986—; mem. N.J. Low Vision Panel, 1981—. Mem. Am. Optometric Assn. (optometric recognition award 1983, 84, 85, 86), N.J. Optometric Assn., Central N.J. Optometric Assn., Beta Beta Beta. Avocations: sailing; snorkeling. Office: Hopewell Valley Eye Assocs 84 E Broad St Hopewell NJ 08525 also Low Vision Ctr Scheie Eye Inst 51 N 39th St Philadelphia PA 19104

STEINBERG, JANET ECKSTEIN, journalist; b. Cin.; d. Charles and Adele (Ehrenfeld) Eckstein; m. Marvin B. Steinberg, June 24, 1951 (dec.); children—Susan Carole Steinberg Somerstein, Jody Lynn Steinberg Lazarow. B.S., U. Cin., 1964. Free-lance writer; guest appearances Braun and Co., Sta.-WLW-TV. Contbr. numerous articles to newspapers, mags. and books, U.S., Can., Singapore, Australia, N.Z.; weekly travel columnist Cin. Post, 1978-86, Ky. Post, 1978-86; contbg. editor Singles Scene and Cin. Mag., 1980—; cons. editor Travel Agt., 1986—, Entree, 1986—; columnist N.E. mag., 1986—, South Fla. Single Living, 1984—. Recipient Lowell Thomas travel journalism award, 1985, 86. Mem. Am. Soc. Journalists and Authors, Soc. Am. Travel Writers (1st place award for best newspaper story 1981, 3d place award for best mag. story 1981, 1st place award for best newspaper article award 1984, best mag. article 1985), Midwest Travel Writers Assn. (Best Mag. Story award 1981, Best Series award 1981, 84 Cipriani award 1981 2d place award for best article 1982, 83, 84), Pacific Area Travel Assn. Club: Losantiville Country. Home: 2676 Fair Oaks Ln Cincinnati OH 45237

STEINBERG, JANET KAY, real estate leasing company executive; b. Dallas, Mar. 4, 1959; d. Morris and Dorothy Jean (Walen) S. Student, U. Tex., 1977-80; cert. real estate Dallas Comml. Coll., 1980. Real estate agt. Henry S. Miller, Dallas, 1980-82; mgr. div. Realty Resources, Dallas, 1982-83; pres., owner Property Pursuits, Inc., Dallas, 1983—. Vol., Reagan campaign, Dallas, 1985. Active Better Bus. Bur., 1985—, Jewish Fedn. Dallas, 1982—. Mem. Dallas Apt. Assn., Greater Dallas Bd. Realtors, Dallas C. of C. Home: 10650 Steppington Dallas TX 75230 Office: Property Pursuits Inc Suite 207 5440 Harvest Hill Rd Dallas TX 75230

STEINBERG, JILL ENID, computer sales executive; b. Jersey City, Oct. 27, 1955; d. Edwin Jay and Renee Ruth (Kaufman) S. B.A., U. Miami (Fla.), 1979. Salesperson luggage Burdine's, Miami, Fla., 1979-80, asst. mgr. area, 1980-81, commn. sales advanced consumer electronics, 1981-83, asst. mgr. computer sales, 1983—; participant Apple seminar, 1983. Named outstanding salesperson So. Region, Hartmann Luggage, 1980; mem. Burdine's B Club. Mem. AAUW (com.), Nat. Assn. Female Execs., Alpha Kappa Delta, Delta Phi Epsilon. Lodge: Hadassah (life). Home: 15725 SW 88th Ct Miami FL 33157 Office: Burdines Computer Depot 7303 N Kendall Dr Miami FL 33156

STEINBERG, MARGERY S., marketing educator, consultant; b. N.Y.C., Oct. 11, 1948; d. Noah and Janet (Horowitz) Greenstein; m. Lewis J. Steinberg, Aug. 20, 1978. B.A., Boston U., 1970; M.A., U. Conn., 1972, M.B.A., 1979, Ph.D., 1984. Tchr. Manchester pub. schs. (Conn.), 1970-71, Regional Sch. Dist. 13, Durham, Conn., 1971-74; book club editor Xerox Edn. Publs., Middletown, Conn., 1974-77; lectr. Asnuntuck Community Coll., Enfield, Conn., 1976-79; asst. prof. Post Coll., Waterbury, Conn., 1979-80; asst. prof. mktg. U. Hartford, West Hartford, Conn., 1980—, seminar leader Div. Adult Ednl. Services, 1982—; cons. Coleco Industries Inc., West Hartford, 1983—, Soc. for Savs., Hartford, 1978; cons. trainer Westfarms Mall Mgmt., Farmington, Conn., 1983—. Author: Animalympics Guide to the Olympics, 1980; Christopher Reeve Scrapbook, 1980; author series of children's books. Mem. Bd. Edn., Cromwell, Conn., 1971-74; mem. Dem. Town Com., Cromwell, 1970-75; bd. dirs. Greater Hartford Chamber Orch., 1983-85. Inst. Ednl. Leadership edn. policy fellow, 1976. Mem. Am. Mktg. Assn. (pres. Conn. 1984-85, internat. v.p. collegiate div. 1986—), Coll. and Univ. Bus. Instrs. Conn. (bd. dirs. 1976-82). Home: Terry Rd Hartford CT 06105 Office: U Hartford 200 Bloomfield Ave West Hartford CT 06117

STEINBERG, MONICA NORA, cosmetics company executive; b. Santiago, Chile, May 17, 1952; came to U.S., 1973; naturalized, 1980; d. Cesar de la Guadra and Maria Teresa Eysaguirre; m. Wolfgang W. Steinberg, Mar. 13, 1979; children—Monica Vanessa, Tatiana Marie. B.S., U. Chile, 1971; student NYU, 1979, 1982. Sec., Chilean Mission to UN, N.Y.C., 1973; apprentice Chilean Line, N.Y.C., 1973-74; export and sales mgr. Allcargoes Mercantile, N.Y.C., 1974-76; documentation adminstr. Rhode & Liesenfeld, N.Y.C., 1976-78; br. mgr. United Intermodal Line, N.Y.C., 1978-79; pres., dir. Amcorp., N.Y.C., 1980-85; chmn. bd. Monique Cosmetics & Fashions Inc., Chappaqua, N.Y., 1985—, Globex Internat. Inc., 1985—. Mem. Sales Execs. Am. Roman Catholic. Club: Jefferson Valley (Westchester, N.Y.). Avocations: reading; music; photography; scuba diving. Office: Monique Cosmetics & Fashions Inc 29 King St Chappaqua NY 10514

STEINECKE, MAUREEN KANE, assn. exec.; b. Boston, Dec. 18, 1932; d. Martin and Helen (Leonard) Kane; A.B. in Am. Lit., Middlebury Coll., 1954; M.S. in L.S., Pratt Inst., 1956; m. Charles Steinecke, July 7, 1956; children—John, Ann, Patricia. Asst. to coordinator children's services D.C. Pub. Library, Washington, 1956-59; free-lance indexer, 1959-65; exec. dir. Md. Assn. Bds. of Edn., Annapolis, 1978—. Vice pres. LWV of Prince George's County, 1971-73; mem. Prince George's County Bd. Edn., 1973-78; bd. mgmt. Prince George's County YMCA, 1979-82. Named Prince Georgian of yr., Sentinel Newspapers, 1977. Mem. Am. Soc. Assn. Execs., Md. Soc. Assn. Execs., Md. Congress Parents and Tchrs. (hon. life). Democrat. Episcopalian. Office: 130 Holiday Ct Suite 105 Annapolis MD 21401

STEINEM, GLORIA, writer, editor, lecturer; b. Toledo, Mar. 25, 1934; d. Leo and Ruth (Nuneviller) Steinem; B.A., Smith Coll., 1956; postgrad. (Chester Bowles Asian fellow), India, 1957-58; D. Human Justice, Simmons Coll., 1973. Co-dir., dir., ednl. found. Ind. Research Service, Cambridge, Mass. and N.Y.C., 1959-60; editorial asst., editorial cons., contbg. editor, free-lance writer various nat. and N.Y.C. publs., 1960—; co-founder, contbg. editor New York mag., from 1968; feminist lectr., 1969—; co-founder, Ms. mag., 1971, editor, from 1971, columnist, 1980—. Active various civil rights and peace campaigns including United Farmworkers, Vietnam War Tax Protest, Com. for the Legal Def. of Angela Davis (treas., 1971-72); active polit. campaigns of Adlai Stevenson, Robert Kennedy, Eugene McCarthy, Shirley Chisholm, George McGovern. Co-founder, chairperson bd. Women's Action Alliance, from 1970; convenor, mem. nat. advisory com. Nat. Women's Polit. Caucus, 1971—; co-founder, mem. bd. Ms. Found. for Women, 1972—; founding mem. Coalition of Labor Union Women, 1974; mem. Internat. Women's Yr. Commn., 1977. Recipient Penney-Missouri Journalism award, 1970; Ohio Gov.'s award for Journalism, 1972; Bill of Rights award ACLU of So. Calif., 1975; named Woman of Yr. McCall's mag., 1972; fellow Woodrow Wilson Internat Center for Scholars, 1977. Mem. Nat. Orgn. for Women, AFTRA, Nat. Press Club, Soc. Mag. Writers, Authors' Guild, P.E.N., Phi Beta Kappa. Author: The Thousand Indias, 1957; The Beach Book, 1963; Outrageous Acts and Everyday Rebellions, 1983. Contbr. to various anthologies. Address: Ms Mag 119 W 40th St New York NY 10018

STEINER, DIANA, concert violinist; b. Portland, Oreg., July 17, 1932; d. Ferenz and Elizabeth (Levy) Steiner; diploma Curtis Inst. Music, Phila., 1949, Mus.B., 1957; M.M., U. So. Calif., 1970; m. Edward R. Dickstein, Dec. 13, 1956; children—Sallie, Marcia. Concert violinist, tchr. Columbia Artists Mgmt., 1953-56; violin soloist at festivals, including Tanglewood, Marlboro, Hollywood Bowl, others, 1950-75, with maj. symphony orchs., including N.Y. Philharmonic, Phila. Orch., others, 1943—; rec. artist Orion Records, 1974—; mem. Steiner-Berfield Trio, 1966—; faculty Loyola Marymount U., Los Angeles, Calif. State U.-Dominguez Hills; tchr.; writer ednl. books for performing students; books include: Violin Classics, Books I and II, 1972; String Orchestra Classics, Book I, 1975, Book II, 1979; string editor Music Tchrs. Assn. Calif. mag., 1982—; condr. master classes and workshops; host, producer radio show Air for Strings. Nat. violin editor Am. String Tchr., 1985—. Bd. dirs. Curtis Inst. Music, 1981—. Recipient W.W. Naumburg Found. award, 1952, Young Artists award Nat. Fedn. Music Clubs, 1959. Mem. Curtis Alumni Assn. S.W., Curtis Alumni Assn. (nat. v.p.), Nat. Assn. Composers U.S.A. (nat. dir.), Nat. Fedn. Music Clubs, Music Tchrs. Nat. Assn., Am. String Tchrs. Assn., Am. Fedn. Musicians, Music Tchrs. Assn. Calif., Calif. Profl. Music Tchrs. Assn., Mu Phi Epsilon. office: 223 S Bundy Dr Los Angeles CA 90049

STEINFELD, NAOMI BERTON, editor, writer; b. N.Y.C., Nov. 12, 1945; d. Max and Lillian (Makofsky) Berton; m. Richard George Steinfeld, Dec. 14, 1968; 1 son, Gabriel. Student Hunter Coll., 1962-63; B.A. Cum laude, City Coll., CUNY, 1966; M.A., U. Conn., 1970; postgrad. John F. Kennedy U., 1983-85. Editor Real Estate Ctr., U. Conn., Storrs, 1969-70; editor editcetera, Berkeley, 1972—, coordinator, 1982-84; publs. cons. to pubs. and writers. Author, editor: The New Holistic Health Handbook, 1985. Editor: The Last Meal On Earth (Owen Spann), 1979; MBO II: A System of Managerial Leadership for the 80s (George S. Odiorne), 1979; Energy-Saving Projects, 1980, The Ecology of Freedom (Murray Bookchin), 1982; The Human Element (Will Schutz), 1984; Writing, 2d edit., 1986; High Level Wellness, 2d edit., 1986; contbr. chpt. to At Your Fingertips: Making the Most of the Micro, 1984. Mem. Assn. for Transpersonal Psychology, Assn. for Humanistic Psychology, Nat. Assn. Female Execs. Home: 262 40th St Way Oakland CA 94611

STEINGART, LISA JILL, lawyer; b. Milw., Sept. 18, 1954; d. Rona Schapiro Steingart. B.S., U. Wis., 1976; J.D., U. Santa Clara, 1981. Bar: Calif. 1981. Tchr. pub. schs., Modesto, Calif., 1976-77, Milw., 1977-78; mem. firm Gould, Sayre & Chavez, San Jose, Calif., 1981-82, Jane Slenkovich, San Jose, 1982-83; tchr. pub. schs., San Jose, 1982—; sole practice, Campbell, Calif., 1983—; legal counselor Assoc. Students Union, San Jose State U., 1983-84; adv. com. mem. dept. edn. U. Santa Clara, 1983-84. Editor: Special Education Case Law, 1983-84. Recipient Service award Santa Clara County, 1979; named Outstanding Vol., U. Wis., 1975. Mem. Santa Clara County Bar Assn. (exec. com.), ABA, Calif. State Bar, Council Exceptional Children (pres. 1976). Democrat. Club: Barristers. Office: 1475 S Bascom Ave Suite 107 Campbell CA 95008

STEINHARDT, DORIS EDITH, state official; b. N.Y.C., Mar. 7, 1949; d. Herbert Harold and Blanche Edith (Gormann) S. B.S., SUNY-Albany, 1971, M.S.W., 1976; J.D., Albany Law Sch., 1979; LL.M. in Taxation, NYU, 1986. Bar: N.Y. 1980, U.S. Dist. Ct. (no. dist.) N.Y. 1980, U.S. Tax Ct. 1983. Social worker, community organizer SUNY, Albany, 1975-76; student atty. Prisoners' Legal Services, Albany, 1977-79; atty. Mental Health Info. Service, Valhalla, N.Y., 1979-80; adminstrv. law judge N.Y. State Tax Commn., Albany, 1980-85; asst. sec. N.Y. State Tax Commn., 1985—; mem. N.Y. Dept. Taxation and Finance Affirmative Action Subcom. for Women, 1980-83, statewide activities dir., 1983-85, counsel, 1985—. Sec., Albany County chpt. Liberal party, 1983—. Bus. and Profl. Women's Assn. scholar, 1967. Mem. ACLU, N.Y. State Bar Assn., N.Y. Women's Bar Assn. Home: 101 Grove Ave Albany NY 12208 Office: State Tax Commn State Office Campus Albany NY 12227

STEINKAMP, CHERYL DUNLOP, college development officer; b. Chadron, Nebr., Mar. 28, 1944; d. Ralph William and Mariana Mildred (Cunningham) Dunlop; m. Robert Theodore Steinkamp, Aug. 19, 1967; children—Theodore Bewick, Rebecca Anne. Student Stephens Coll., 1962-63; B.A., William Jewell Coll., Liberty, Mo., 1965-67. Speech therapist Headstart Program, Hutchinson, Kans., 1967; speech instr. William Chrisman Jr. High Sch., Independence Mo., 1967-69; dist. dir. Sunflower council Campfire Girls, Inc., 1969-73; dir. alumni services William Jewell Coll., Liberty, 1979-83, dir. devel. and alumni relations, 1984-85, chief devel. officer, 1985—; past officer, bd. dirs. Liberty Symphony, Mo., 1982—; mem. staff. parrish relations com. United Methodist. Ch., 1983, trustee, 1986—; mem. Liberty Fall Festival Com., 1979-83; bd. dirs. Jr. Women's Philharmonic Assn., Kansas City, 1974-77; mem. exec. bd. North Suburban Swim Conf. Mem. Council Advancement and Support Edn. Republican. Meth. Clubs: Kansas City, Central Exchange; Liberty Hills Country. Avocations: writing poetry, songs; traveling. Office: William Jewell Coll Liberty MO 64068

STEINMAN, JOAN ELLEN, lawyer, educator; b. Bklyn., June 19, 1947; d. Jack and Edith Ruth (Shapiro) S.; m. Douglass Watts Cassel, Jr., June 1, 1974; children—Jennifer Lynn, Amanda Hilary. Student U. Birmingham, Eng., 1968; A.B. with high distinction, U. Rochester, 1969; J.D. cum laude, Harvard U., 1973. Bar: Ill. 1973. Assoc., Schiff, Hardin & Waite, Chgo., 1973-77; asst. prof. Ill. Inst. Tech. Chgo.-Kent. Coll. Law, 1977-82, assoc. prof., 1982-86, prof., 1986—; cons. in atty. promotions Met. San. Dist. Greater Chgo., 1981, 85. Coop. atty. ACLU Ill., Chgo., 1974, Leadership Council for Met. Open Communities, Chgo., 1975, Better Govt. Assn., 1975; arbitrator Better Bus. Bur. Met. Chgo., 1984. Mem. Chgo. Council Lawyers, Phi Beta Kappa. Democrat. Jewish. Office: ITT Chgo Kent Coll Law 77 S Wacker Dr Chicago IL 60606

STEINMETZ, DEBORAH SUSAN, interior designer; b. New Orleans, Nov. 29, 1951; d. Donald Frederick and Estelle Margaret (Ulmer) Tossell; B.F.A., La. State U., 1973; m. Robert Steinmetz, Dec. 29, 1973. Interior designer David Grinnell Architect, 1973-75; interior design cons., Columbus, Ga., 1975-77; designer Dameron-Pierson, New Orleans, 1977-79; v.p. interior design Interior Environments, Inc., New Orleans, 1979-83; pres., owner Steinmetz & Assocs., 1983—; mem. interior design curriculum com. Dominican Coll., New Orleans, 1981-82; mem. interior design adv. com. Delgado Community Coll., New Orleans, 1982—. Mem. visual arts com. Contemporary Art Center, 1980-81. Mem. Am. Soc. Interior Designers (Presdl. citation; chmn. New Orleans assn. 1980-81, dir. La. chpt. 1982—, newsletter editor La. Chpt. 1982, chain membership/admissions La. chpt. 1984), Nat. Trust Hist. Preservation, La. Landmarks Soc. Roman Catholic. Home: 2850 Annunciation St New Orleans LA 70115 Office: 225 Baronne St Suite 207 New Orleans LA 70112

STEINMILLER, ANITA MARY, nurse; b. Pitts., Feb. 4, 1951; d. Henry James and Ann Frances S., diploma Ohio Valley Gen. Hosp. Sch. Nursing, 1972; B.S.N. magna cum laude LaRoche Coll., 1981, B.A., 1979; M.Nursing Adminstrn., U. Pitts., 1984. Cert. in nursing adminstrn. Am. Nurses Assn. Staff nurse Ohio Valley Gen. Hosp., McKees Rocks Pa., 1972-75, patient care coordinator infection control, audit inservice edn., 1975-81, asst. dir. nursing, 1981—; vol. instr. nursing service ARC; vol. lectr. Am. Cancer Soc. Mem. Ohio Valley Nurses Alumni Assn., Sigma Theta Tau. Roman Catholic. Home: 334 Bascom Ave Pittsburgh PA 15214 Office: Ohio Valley Hosp Heckel Rd McKees Rocks PA 15136

STEINMULLER, KAREN ANNE, accountant; b. Washington, Nov. 15, 1954; d. Herbert M. and Edith Frieda (Bley) S. B.B.A., Coll. William and Mary, 1977. C.P.A., Va. Staff acct. Aaron Roesen & Co., Newport News, Va., 1977-80; sr. staff acct. Hart Adams & Scollin, P.C., Hampton, Va., 1980-83; sr. to mgr. Hart Adams & Toney, P.C., Hampton, 1983-85; shareholder John T. Hart & Assocs., P.C., Hampton, 1985—. Mem. Am. Inst. C.P.A.s, Va. Soc. C.P.A.s, Am. Woman's Soc. C.P.A.s, Nat. Assn. Female Execs. Luthern. Avocations: music; reading; sewing; aerobics. Office: John T Hart & Assocs 2101 Executive Dr Tower Box 30 Hampton VA 23666

STEINTHAL, LOIS NANCY, stockbroker; b. Hackensack, N.J., Jan. 23, 1943; d. Julius and Doris Y. (Wagner) Stein; m. Arthur Donald Steinthal, Aug. 21, 1965; 1 dau., Susan Judy. B.A., Hunter Coll., 1977. Asst. to chancellor CUNY, 1965-68; dir. pub. relations, Nat. Bur. Econ. Research, N.Y.C., 1968-77; asst. v.p., asst. mgr. E.F. Hutton & Co., N.Y.C., 1979—. Mem. Women Investment Brokers (v.p.). Democrat. Jewish. Contbr. articles to profl. jours. Home: 445 East 80th St New York NY 10021 Office: EF Hutton & Co 1 State Street Plaza New York NY 10004

STEKLIS, ELAINE JEANNE, personnel manager; b. East Chicago, Ind., Feb. 10, 1945; d. Emil George and Josephine (Gregory) De Henes; m. Detlev Kurt Steklis, Oct. 8, 1982; 1 dau., Heidi Marie; children by previous marriage—Cristine Elaine, Adrienne Michele. A.A. in Bus. Adminstrn., Chabot Coll., 1980; B.A. in Bus. Adminstrn., Calif. State U., 1984. Pharmacy technician Hoosier Drugs, Whiting, Ind., 1972-74, Walgreens Chgo., 1974-77; lab. technician Barnes Hinds Pharms., Sunnyvale, Calif., 1977-79; personnel coordinator West Coast Fed. Savs. & Loan, San Mateo, Calif., 1979-81; personnel mgr. Cetus Corp., Emeryville, Calif., 1981—; lectr. Chmn., No. Calif. Human Resource Council, Berkeley, 1979—; v.p. bd. dirs. Raiders Drum & Bugle Corps, San Jose, 1979-82; pub. relations dir. Sports Car Club Am., 1965-75, St. John Community Theater, Whiting, 1965-73. Mem. Bay Area Savs. and Loan Personnel Officers (sec. 1978-80), Am. Soc. Personnel Adminstrs., No. Calif. Human Resources Council, Am. Compensation Assn., No. Calif. Pharm. Group. Democrat. Roman Catholic. Club: Daughters of Mary (v.p. 1963). Home: 648 Via Pacheco San Lorenzo CA 94580

STELLMAN, JEANNE MAGER, public health educator; b. Bensheim, W.Ger., May 27, 1947; came to U.S., 1948, citizen, 1951; d. Abraham and Rosalie (Shapiro) Mager; m. Steven D. Stellman, Sept. 10, 1967; children—Andrew Benjamin, Emma Deborah. B.S. in Chemistry, CCNY, 1968; Ph.D. in Phys. Chemistry, CUNY, 1972. Adj. prof. Labor Edn. Ctr., Rutgers U., 1971-76; asst. to pres. for health and safety Oil, Chem. and Atomic Workers Internat. Union, Denver, 1972-75; chief div. occupational health and toxicology Am. Health Found., N.Y.C., 1977-80; exec. dir. Women's Occupational Health Resource Ctr., N.Y.C., 1978—; clin. asso. prof. research medicine Sch. Medicine, U. Pa., 1975-80; assoc. prof. Sch. Pub. Health, Columbia U., N.Y.C., 1980—, asst. dir. cancer control Comprehensive Cancer Ctr., 1981-85; cons. Am. Occupational Health Nurses Assn., 1983—, Port Authority N.Y. and N.J., 1983—, TVA Office Safety and Health, 1980-82, N.Y. State Dept. Health, 1982—, Coalition Labor Union Women, 1975-80, Nat. Union Hosp. and Health Care Workers, 1975—; chmn. task force on reproductive hazards in workplace March of Dimes, 1980-84; mem. merit peer rev. com.-cancer control Nat. Cancer Inst., 1979-81; mem. expert panel for guidelines on pregnant working women Am. Coll. Ob-Gyn, 1978; mem. environ. health task force Am. Lung Assn., 1976-80; mem. task force on preventing disease, workgroup on occupational health U.S. Surgeon Gen.'s Office, 1979; mem. adv. com. for 14 chem. carcinogens to U.S. Sec. Labor, 1972; mem. tech. rev. coms. for criteria documents on cadmium, mercury, sulfur dioxide and benzene Nat. Inst. Occupational Safety and Health; speaker on occupational health hazards, U.S. and Can. Author: (with S.M. Daum) Work Is Dangerous to Your Health, 1973 (transl. into Italian, Portuguese, French); Women's Work, Women's Health: Mayth and Realities, 1978 (transl. into Italian, French, Japanese); (with Mary Sue Henifin) Office Work Can Be Dangerous to Your Health, 1984; also govt. reports, chpts. in books, articles in profl. jours. Contbg. editor Environment, 1975-76; editorial bd. Jour. Women and Health, 1983-85, editor, 1985—; editorial bd. Indsl. Hygiene Safety News, 1982—. Recipient Preventive Oncology Acad. award Nat. Cancer Inst., 1980-85; named one of 80 Women to Watch in 80's, Ms mag., 1980; NASA trainee, 1968-69; NSF grad. trainee, 1969-70; N.Y. State Regents fellow, 1970-72. Mem. Am. Pub. Health Assn. (governing council 1981-83), Am. Chem. Soc. (chmn. task force on benzene 1978-79, mem. com. chem. safety 1973-79, taskforce safe lab. practices 1978-79), Am. Phys. Soc., AAAS, Soc. Occupational and Environ. Health, N.Y. Acad. Scis., Am. Indsl. Hygiene Assn., Sigma Xi. Democrat. Jewish. Office: Sch Public Health Columbia U 21 Audubon Ave New York NY 10032

STELLMAN, L. MANDY, lawyer; b. Toronto, Ont., Can., Aug. 22, 1922; came to U.S., 1946, naturalized, 1948; d. Abraham and Rose (Rubinoff) Mandlsohn; m. Samuel David Stellman, July 11, 1943; children—Steven D., Leslie Robert. B.Sc. summa cum laude, Ohio State U., 1966; J.D., Marquette U., 1970. Bar: Wis. 1971. Tchr., Toronto Pub. Schs., 1943-46; recreation specialist, Toronto, 1942-46; educator, social worker Columbus Jewish Ctr., Ohio, 1951-64; instr. U. Wis. Extension-Milw., 1970-76; sole practice, Milw., 1971—. Bd. dirs. Women's Crisis Line, Women's Coalition, Milw. Jewish Home for Aged. Recipient Disting. Alumni award Ohio State U., 1976, Hannah G. Solomon award Nat. Council Jewish Women, 1984. Mem. Assn. Trial Lawyers Am., Lawyers Assn. for Women, Wis. Assn. Trial Lawyers, Nat. Council Jewish Women (life), Women's Polit. Caucus, Common Cause, NOW (Milw. Woman of Yr. award 1977). Jewish. Home: 1545 W Fairfield Ct Glendale WI 53209 Office: 606 W Wisconsin Ave Suite 308 Milwaukee WI 53203

STEMEN, SUE ELLEN, lawyer; b. Noblesville, Ind., Feb. 6, 1958; d. Daryl Dean and Joan Frances (Perkey) S.; m. Mark J. R. Merkle, Apr. 12, 1986. B.A., DePauw U., 1980; J.D., Ind. U.-Indpls., 1983. Bar: Ind. 1983. Law clk. Castor, Richards, Adams & Boje, Noblesville, Ind., 1980; law clk., mayor's intern City-County Legal Div., Indpls., 1981; law clk. Forbes, Kias & Pennamped, Indpls., 1982-83; intern Senator Richard G. Lugar, Washington, 1979; dep. securities commr. securities div., Ind. Sec. of State, Indpls., 1983-85, acting dep. of state, 1985, legal counsel, 1985—. Fund raiser Ind. Sec. of State, 1983. Mem. Indpls. Bar Assn., ABA, N.Am. Securities Adminstrs. Assn. (abusive tax shelter com.), Alpha Chi Omega, Phi Sigma Alpha, Phi Delta Phi. Republican. Methodist. Home: 6248 N Meridian St Indianapolis IN 46260 Office: Office of Sec of State 201 State House Indianapolis IN 46204

STENBORG, CAROL ANN, technical writing consultant; b. Columbus, Ohio, Oct. 22, 1956; d. Frank Batista and Caroline (Fata) Decaminada; m. Frederic J. Stenborg, June 24, 1978; children—Eric John, Karl Joseph. B.A. in Journalism, Ohio State U., 1977; postgrad. U. Wis., 1977-78; M.A. in Tech. Communication, U. Minn., 1986. Reporter, wire editor Ohio State Daily Lantern, Columbus, 1977; grad. asst. U. Wis., Madison, 1977-78; free-lance writing cons., St. Paul, 1980—; adminstrv. asst. ACM-SIGGRAPH, St. Paul, 1984-8; mem. faculty Mpls. Coll. Art and Design, 1984—. Membership chmn. Minn. Women's Polit. Caucus, St. Paul, 1982, newsletter editor, 1981; neighborhood rep. Neighborhood Press Assn., St. Paul, 1983. Women in Communications, Inc. scholar, 1974, 77. Mem. Women in Communications, (pres. Ohio State U. chpt. 1976-77, v.p. for membership Twin Cities St. Paul 1981-82), Soc. for Tech. Communicators. Democrat. Roman Catholic.

STENBORG, MARGARET ANN, music educator; b. Bellville, Tex., Sept. 28, 1940; d. Lawrence Jerome and Arminda Pascual (Gomez) Schwender; m. Rodney Eugene Stenborg, Dec. 19, 1967; children—Jeanne Alicia, Derek Vincent, Julia Christine. Student Juilliard Sch. Music, 1965-66; B.A. in Music Edn., Sacred Heart Dominican Coll., 1962. Music tchr. Alcott Sch., 1962-65, St. Peter's Sch., Houston, 1974-75, St. Christopher Sch., Houston, 1973, 75-78, Mahanay Sch., Alief, Tex., 1980-82, Cornelius Sci. and Math. Acad., Houston, 1982—, Gregg Elem. Sch., Houston, 1982—; profl. chorister Amor Artists Chorale, N.Y.C., Camerata Singers, N.Y.C., 1966-68, Robert Shaw Chorale, N.Y.C., 1965-66; opera chorister Oberhausen City Theater (W. Ger.), 1970-73, Houston Grand Opera, 1959-65, 76—. Choir dir. St. Christopher's Cath. Ch., Houston, 1975-81, 83—. Named 2d Place Finalist Met. Opera Southwest Auditions, San Antonio, 1964, Tchr. of Yr., Gregg Elem. Sch., 1984; study grantee Tuesday Music Club, 1964, Phi Beta, 1965. Mem. Am. Guild Mus. Artists (bd. govs. Tex. 1982—), Tex. Music Educators' Assn., Gulfcoast Orff Assn., Houston Music Educators Assn., Orgn. Am. Kodaly Educators. Roman Catholic. Lodge: Sons of Norway. Home: 5403 Oriole St Houston TX 77017 Office: Gregg Elem Sch 6701 Roxbury St Houston TX 77087

STEPHAN, INEZ VALLS, secretarial service company executive; b. Columbus, Ohio, Nov. 22, 1911; d. Rafael W. and Euphemia (Lloyd) Valls; 2 children.

Student pub. schs., Cleveland Heights. Sec. Harlow Co., Coral Gables, Fla., 1959-63, U. Miami, Coral Gables, 1963-75; pres., owner Stephan Secretarial Coral Gables, 1975—; real estate salesperson Wirth Realty, Coral Gables, 1975—. Mem. Nat. Assn. Female Execs., Notary Pub. Assn., Coral Gables Bd. Realtors, Coral Gables C. of C. Republican. Roman Catholic. Avocations: swimming; playing bridge. Home: 6051 SW 27th St Miami FL 33155 Office: Stephan Secretarial Service 3132-B Ponce de Leon Blvd Coral Gables FL 33134

STEPHENS, DORYCE MARIE, tax accountant; b. Houston, Nov. 21, 1950; d. Thomas Barcklay and Doris Francis (Belcher) S.; m. Kenneth James Ellen, June 28, 1980; children—Jill Denise, Christina Marie. B.B.A. with honors, U. Houston, 1976; M.Acctg., Rice U., 1978. C.P.A., Tex. Tax cons. Price Waterhouse, Houston, 1978-80; sr. tax acct. Hughes Tool Co., Houston, 1980-82; sr. mgr. tax compliance Global Marine Inc., Houston, 1982—. Adviser, Santa Maria Hostel Galveston-Houston Diocese, 1979; vol. Friends of Houston Pub. Library, 1979; sponsor North Atlantic Cultural Exchange League Cultural Exchanges, Tours, France, 1983. Mem. Am. Inst. C.P.A.s, Tex. Soc. C.P.A.s, Am. Women's Soc. C.P.A.s, Phi Kappa Phi, Beta Alpha Psi, Beta Gamma Sigma, Phi Gamma Nu (v.p. 1974-75). Club: Internat. Toastmasters (v.p. 1978-79) (Houston). Home: 4207 Yupon Ridge Houston TX 77072 Office: Global Marine Inc 777 Eldridge Rd Houston TX 77079

STEPHENS, ESME MCDERMOT, social worker, consultant; b. Kingston, Jamaica, W.I., Oct. 14, 1923; came to U.S., 1945, naturalized, 1956; d. Clifford Constantine and Vera Annabelle (Baraham) DePass; m. Basil El'strande Stephens, Aug. 20, 1949; children—JoAnn and Michele (twins), Basil J. B.A., U. W.I., 1945. With customer relations dept. R.H. Macy & Co., N.Y.C., 1945-46; analyst Reuben H. Donnelley Corp., 1946-49; dept. head Posner Labs., Inc., 1965-69; dir. A.B.C. Youth Program, Corona/East Elmhurst, N.Y., 1968-70; sr. caseworker Office of Congressman Herman Badillo, Bronx, N.Y., 1970-77, asst. to dep. mayor Herman Badillo, N.Y.C., 1978-79; sr. caseworker Office of Congressman Robert Garcia, Bronx, 1979-81; dir. mgmt. and tng. Holiday Inns, Inc., N.Y.C. and Los Angeles, 1981—. Pub. relations officer East-Elmhurst Civic Assn., N.Y., 1968-81; mem. Nat. Council Negro Women, Inc., N.Y.C., 1968-82; civic worker and youth council mem. Crestview-Greentree East Assn., Victorville, Calif., 1983—. Recipient plaque N.Y. State Female Correction Officers, 1974. Mem. Coalition of 100 Black Women, NAACP (life), Nat. Assn. Negro Bus. and Profl. Women, Nat. Urban League. Democrat. Roman Catholic. Avocations: swimming; aerobics. Home: 14126 Montecito Ln Victorville CA 92392

STEPHENS, PATRICIA LOVE, oil and gas executive; b. Columbus, Miss., Mar. 23, 1935; d. Charles Sherrod and Louise (Miller) L.; m. Walter Harold Stephens, Dec. 5, 1961; children—Sutton Elizabeth, Heather Love; 1 stepdau., Sheryl Stephens Jones. Student U. Ala., 1952-54, Miss. State Coll., 1954-55. Regent, James Campbell DAR, Dallas, 1978-80; pres. Charles Taylor Daus. Republic of Tex., Dallas, 1982-85; sr. pres. James Haynes Children Am. Revolution, Dallas, 1981-83; pres. Pub. Affairs Luncheon Club, Dallas, 1983-85; pres. Metroplex unit Nat. Assn. Parlimentarians, Dallas, 1981-83; nat. vice-chmn. nat. def. com. Nat. Soc. DAR, Washington, 1983-86, nat. vice-chmn. Am. heritage, 1980-83, nat. resolution com., 1984, 85; sr. theme chmn. Tex. Soc. Children Am. Revolution, Dallas, 1983-85, sr. librarian-curator, 1981-83. Editor The Roundup, 1979-83 (Best Nat. 1981, 83), Haynes Herald, 1981-83 (Best Regional 1982, 83). Vice-pres. projects Freedoms Found./Valley Forge, Pa., 1980-82, v.p. edn., 1982-84; bd. dirs. PTA, Dallas Met. Ballet. Mem. Colonial Dames (sec. 1982-84), Daus. Am. Colonists (treas. 1983-84), Colonial Dames Am. (rec. sec. 1982-84), Nat. Geneal. Soc. (life), New Eng. Hist. and Geneal. Soc., Old Tryon County Geneal. Soc. N.C. (life), S.C. Geneal. Soc., Miss. Geneal. Soc., Dallas Geneal. Soc. (life), Va. Hist. and Geneal. Soc., Park Cities Hist. League, Jamestowne Soc., Dallas So. Meml. Assn. (life). Republican. Presbyterian. Clubs: Jr. Matheon (treas. 1983-84) (Dallas); Beverly Drive Book. Home: 3919 Beverly Dr Dallas TX 75205

STEPHENSON, BETTE M., Canadian provincial official, physician; b. Aurora, Ont., Can., July 31, 1924; d. Carl Melvin and Clara Mildred (Draper) S.; grad. Earl Haig Coll. Inst.; M.D., U. Toronto, 1946; m. Gordon Allan Pengelly, 1948; children—J. Stephen A., Elizabeth Anne A., C. Christopher A., J. Michael A., P. Timothy A., Mary Katharine A. Mem. med. staff Women's Coll. Hosp., 1950—, chief dept. gen. practice, dir. outpatient dept., 1956-64; mem. med. staff N.Y. Gen. Hosp., 1967—; elected Ont. Legislature for York Mills, 1975, 77, 81, 85; minister labor, 1975-78; minister edn., minister colls. and univs., 1978-85, treas. and dep. premier, 1985. Fellow Coll. Family Physicians Can. (chmn. nat. coordinating com. on edn. 1961-64, chmn. confs. on edn. for gen. practice 1961, 63), Acad. Med. Toronto; mem. Ont. Med. Assn. (dir. 1964-72, pres. 1970-71), Can. Med. Assn. (dir. 1968-75, pres. 1974-75), Art Gallery Ont., Royal Ont. Mus. Office: Parliament Bldgs Toronto ON M7A 1A1 Canada

STEPHENSON, DOROTHY (DOTTY) GRIFFITH, journalist, speaker; b. Terrell, Tex., Nov. 4, 1949; d. Edward Morrill and Dorothy (Koch) Griffith; m. Thomas Lee Stephenson, June 4, 1977; children—Kelly Griffith, Caitlin Lee. B.J., U. Tex., 1972; M.L.A., So. Methodist U., 1980. Gen. assignment reporter Dallas Morning News, 1972-73, edn. writer, 1973-74, gen. assignment reporter, 1974-76, polit. writer, 1976-78, food editor, 1978—; guest host Warner-Amex, Qube Cable TV, Dallas, 1982-83. Mem. nutrition task Am. Heart Assn., Dallas, 1981—. Author: Wild about Chili, 1985. Mem. Newspaper Food Editor's and Writer's Assn. (v.p. 1984-86, pres. 1986-88), Les Dames d'Escoffier (founding mem. Dallas chpt.), Internat. Assn. Cooking Profls., Am. Inst. Wine and Food.

STEPHENSON, HELEN ROSE, writer; b. Pitts.; d. Charles E. and Ruth L. (Bowers) Gibson; B.A., U. Pitts.; m. George M. Stephenson, June 10, 1961; children—Rosalind, Karen. Account supr. Ketchum, MacLeod & Grove, Inc., Pitts., 1955-61; editor-supr. printed materials Gen. Foods Corp., White Plains, N.Y., 1964-73; free-lance writer, 1973—, contbr. articles to various pubs., including N.Y. Times, Wall St. Jour., Ladies Home Jour., Town & Country. Recipient Golden Quill award Sigma Delta Chi, 1960. Mem. Conn. Press Women, Nat. League Am. PEN. Editor, author various cookbooks Gen. Foods Corp., 1964-73. Home and Office: 190 Chestnut Ridge Rd Bethel CT 06801

STEPHENSON, IRENE HAMLEN, biorhythm analyst, consultant, editor, teacher; b. Chgo., Oct. 7, 1923; d. Charles Martin and Carolyn Hilda (Hilgers) Hamlin; m. Edgar B. Stephenson, Sr., Aug. 16, 1941 (div. 1946); 1 child, Edgar B. Author biorhythm compatibilities column Nat. Singles Register, Norwalk, Calif., 1979-81; instr. biorhythm Learning Tree Open U., Canoga Park, Calif., 1982-83; instr. biorhythm character analysis 1980—; instr. biorhythm compatibility, 1982—; owner, pres. matchmaking service Pen Pals Using Biorhythm, Chatsworth, Calif., 1979—; editor newsletter The Truth-Biorhythm, Chatsworth, 1979—. Author: Learn Biorhythm Character Analysis, 1980; Do-It-Yourself Biorhythm Compatibilities, 1982. Contbr. numerous articles to mags. Office: Irene Hamlen Stephenson PO Box 3893 Chatsworth CA 91313

STEPHENSON, LINDA SUE, cosmetic company executive; b. Monroeville, Ind., June 30, 1939; d. LeRoy Lloyd and Edith Lillian (Marquardt) Koehlinger; m. Jack Lynn Stephenson, Dec. 31, 1961. Student modeling Ft. Wayne Finishing Sch., 1959, instr. cert., 1961. Bus. mgr. Ft. Wayne Finishing Sch., Ind., 1960-64; dir., tchr. Cameo Finishing Sch., Ft. Wayne, 1964-65; assoc. dir. Fashion Two Twenty, Decatur, Ind., 1969-71; dir. Marjo Cosmetics, Ft. Wayne, 1971-81; founder, dir. Cozme Cosmetics. Ft. Wayne, 1981—; founder, tchr. Image Projection Workshops, Ft. Wayne, 1981—; dir. The Body Parlour, Ft. Wayne, Author: New Dimensions, 1982; Eyes on Ft. Wayne, 1983, also articles. 4-H leader 4-H Horse and Pony Club, Monroeville, Ind., 1962-75; foster parent Adams County Welfare, Decatur, Ind., 1969-73, Indian Program, Ft. Wayne, 1970-72; choral dir. Community Youth Choir, Monroeville, 1967-80, Methodist Men's Chorus, 1980—. Named Equity Queen, Nat. Farmers Equity, 1960. Mem. Ft. Wayne Better Bus. Bur., Ft. Wayne Women's Bur., Women Bus. Owner's Assn., Nat. Hairdressers and Cosmetologists Assn., Ft. Wayne C. of C. Avocations: physical fitness; music; bird watching; flower gardening. Home: Rural Route 2 Monroeville IN 46773 Office: Cozme Cosmetics 5821 Decatur Rd Fort Wayne IN 46816

STEPHENSON, TONI EDWARDS, publisher, banker; b. Bastrop, La., July 23, 1945; d. Sidney Crawford and Grace Erleene (Shipman) Little; m. Arthur Emmet Stephenson, June 17, 1967; 1 dau., Tessa Lyn. B.S., La. State U., 1967. Co-pub. Denver Bus. mag., 1978—, Denver mag., 1982—, Vail mag., (Colo.), 1980—, Devel. Sales Catalog, Denver, 1980—; dir. Charter Bank and Trust, Englewood, Colo., 1983—; sr. v.p. Gen. Communications, Inc., Denver, 1978—; ptnr. Stephenson and Co., Denver, 1971—, Stephenson Ventures, 1981—; dir., founder Charter Bank and Trust Co., 1980—, Gen. Communications, Inc., 1978—; dir. Globescope Corp., Denver, 1976—. Bd. dirs. Children's Hosp. Mem. Mag. Pubs. Assn., Colo. Bankers Assn., Assn. Area Bus. Publs., Colo. Press Assn., Denver Advt. Fedn., DAR. Clubs: Petroleum (Denver); Annabel's (London); Thunderbird (Rancho Mirage, Calif.). Home: 11102 E Harvard Dr Aurora CO 80014 Office: Stephenson and Co 100 Garfield St Denver CO 80206

STEPHENS-BASSI, KAREN ANITA, manufacturing executive; b. Pasadena, Tex., Apr. 4, 1945; d. Patrick Kitchener and Francena (Ryan) McPearson; m. Phillip Von Stephens, Dec. 28, 1968 (div. Apr. 1981); m. Marco Vinicio Bassi, Dec. 3, 1984. B.S., West Tex. State U., 1969, M.F.A., 1970. Cert. comml. investment mem. Tchr. Houston Ind. Sch. Dist., 1969-73, North Harris County Jr. Coll., Spring, Tex., 1973-76; instr. Market of Tex. Inc., Houston, 1976-79; v.p. Tecnomatic, Inc., Houston, 1979-81, chmn. bd., 1981-85; v.p., sec. bd. dirs. Mfrs. Group, Inc., Houston, 1981—. Bd. dirs. Cultural Art Council of Houston, 1978-83. Mem. Instrument Soc. Am. Home: 3217 Iola Houston TX 77017 Office: Manufacturer's Group Inc 4611 Berrydale Houston TX 77017

STEPKE, KRYSTEN MARIE, personnel company executive, personnel psychologist-psychometrist; b. West Allis, Wis., Sept. 17, 1952; d. Gerald Floyd and Diana Gertrude (Branski) S. B.S. in German and French, U. Wis.-Whitewater, 1974, M.S. in Psychology and Counseling, 1978. Cert. in edn., counseling psychology, Wis. Tchr. German, Kewaskum High Sch., Wis., 1974-76; grad. asst. U. Wis.-Whitewater, 1977, instr. career edn., summer 1978; counselor, psychologist Burlington Schs., Wis., 1978-80; analyst temperament index Manpower Inc., Milw., 1980-81, test program adminstrs., 1981-83, mgr. office automation test devel., 1983—; chairperson adv. com. Milw. Area Tech. Schs., 1985—; mem. info. processing com. Gateway Tech. Schs., Elkhorn and Racine, Wis., 1985—; speaker Am. Soc. Personnel Adminstrs. Conf., Holland, Mich., 1984. Named Outstanding Young Alumni, U. Wis.-Whitewater, 1978. Mem. Office Tech. Mgmt. Assn. (editor newsletter 1983—), Adminstrv. Mgmt. Soc., Nat. Assn. Female Execs., Personnel Testing Council, Office Systems Research Assn., NOW, Humane Animal Welfare Soc., Nat. Humane Edn. Soc., Tri Sigma (sec. alumnae chpt. 1982-83, pres. chpt. 1983-84, Outstanding Alumnae 1985), Sigma Sigma Sigma (chpt. adviser 1979—), Phi Kappa Phi. Club: Waukesha Athletic. Avocations: racquetball; soccer; softball. Office: Manpower Inc 5301 N Ironwood Milwaukee WI 53217

STERBENZ, JOANNE RUTH, accountant; b. New Orleans, June 16, 1947; d. Joseph Roch and Merlin (Prieto) S.; B.S., U. Southwestern La., 1969; M.B.A., Tulane U., 1971. With Arthur Young & Co., Los Angeles, 1971-83, mgr., 1976-80, coordinator computer auditing, 1976-79, prin., 1980-83, office dir. edn., 1979; controller Met. Theatres, Los Angeles, 1985—. Assoc. v.p. for ticketing Los Angeles Olympic Organizing Com., 1984. C.P.A., Calif.; Tulane U. fellow, 1969-71. Mem. Am. Inst. C.P.A.s, Nat. Assn. Female Execs., Am. Women's Soc. C.P.A.s, EDP Auditors Assn., NOW, Tulane Assn. Bus. Alumni, Greater Los Angeles Zoo Assn., Smithsonian Assos. Democrat. Roman Catholic. Home: 222 7th St Apt 107 Santa Monica CA 90402 Office: Metropolitan Theatres Corp 8727 W 3d St Los Angeles CA 90048

STERETT, NANCY, interior designer; b. Portsmouth, Va., Sept. 2, 1944; d. William L. and Alene (Park) S.; m. Rex Howard Brumley, June 26, 1962 (div. 1975); m. 2d, Aiken Montague Lord, Apr. 8, 1978 (div. 1984); children—Todd, Keith. Student, Chgo. Sch. Interior Design, Mundelein, Ill., 1973-74, U. Dayton Profl. Sch. Designers. Accountant, bookkeeper Sterett Constrn. Co., Owensboro, Ky., 1961-64; interior designer Lord Interiors, Owensboro, 1968—; cons. Fiber-Seal, Inc., Owensboro, 1981-84. Named Ky. Col., 1970. Mem. Am. Soc. Interior Designers. Republican. Baptist. Clubs: Spring Bank Assocs., Zonta. Home: 4100 Mason Woods Ln Owensboro KY 42301

STERLING, CAROL OLIVIA, music educator, church musician; b. Frankfurt, W.Ger., Apr. 11, 1959; came to U.S., 1959; d. Harry William and Mercedes Delores (Morgan) Sterling; m. Michael Ward Mills, June 19, 1984. Mus. B. with high distinction, U. Mich., 1982; postgrad. U. Southwestern La., 1984—. Cert. tchr. music, Tex. Hist. guide Henry Ford's Greenfield Village and Mus., Dearborn, Mich., summer, 1979; contract specialist U.S. Dept. Army, Warren, Mich., summer, 1980; orientation leader U. Mich., Ann Arbor, summer, fall, 1981; pianist, soloist Geneva Presbyn. Ch., Canton, Mich., 1980-82; elem. sch. music specialist Spring Branch Schs., Houston, 1982—; violinist North Houston Symphony, 1982; pianist, organist Spring Branch Community Ch., Houston, 1982—; choral condr. Cornerstone, Houston, 1982—; pvt. violin tchr., Houston, 1982—; opera coach, accompanist U. Southwestern La., Lafayette, 1984—; violinist Acadiana Symphony, Lafayette, 1984—; coordinator children's choirs. Recipient Scuyler award U. Mich. Music Sch., 1981, cert. of Achievement Dept. Army, 1980; monetary award Mich. Found. for Arts, 1982; Angell scholar, 1980-81. Mem. Am. Choral Dirs. Assn., Tex. Music Educators Assn., NEA, Gulf Coast Christian Edn. Assn. (clinician 1983 conv.), Phi Beta Kappa, Mu Phi Epsilon (corr. sec. 1981-82, scholastic award 1981, 82), Pi Kappa Lambda (honor award 1985). Home: 12219 Nathaline Redford MI 48239 Office: Spring Branch Ind Sch Dist 11202 Smithdale Houston TX 77024

STERMER, NANCY LOUISE, information systems coordinator; b. Canandaigua, N.Y., Dec. 19, 1952; d. Gordon Ernest and Elaine Louise (Jones) Stermer. B.A., Mich. State U., 1975; M.A., U. Mich., 1979. Cert. tchr. continuing edn., Mich. Teaching asst. Mich. State U., East Lansing, 1974-75; tchr. adult edn. Flint Community Schs., Mich., 1976; tchr. elem. edn., jr. high sch. Waterford Sch. Dist., Pontiac, Mich., 1976-80; tng. specialist Fed.-Mogul Corp., Southfield, Mich., 1981-83, office systems analyst and tng. specialist, 1983-86, info. systems coordinator, 1986—. Bd. dirs. Mich. chpt. Am. Lupus Soc. Named Outstanding Sr., Class of '75, Mich. State U., 1975. Mem. Nat. Assn. Female Execs., Detroit Area Trainers Assn., Office Automation Mgmt. Assn., NOW, U. Mich. Alumnae, Kappa Delta Pi. Home: Birmingham MI 48010 Office: Fed-Mogul Corp PO Box 1966 Detroit MI 48235

STERN, ARLENE HELEN, human resources administrator; b. Bklyn., Nov. 7, 1950; d. Irving and Shirley Judith (Koretz) Stern. B.S. in Labor Relations, U. Bridgeport, 1971; postgrad. Pace U., 1972-75. Personnel asst. Pathmark, Woodbridge, N.J., 1971-72, regional personnel mgr., 1972-75, dir. human resource planning, 1975-77, dir. personnel and labor relations, Phila., 1977-81; v.p. human resources Howland-Steinbach-Hochschild's, White Plains, N.Y., 1981-85; sr. v.p. human resources P.A. Bergner & Co., Milw., 1985—; mem. Frederick Atkins Personnel Adv. Bd., N.Y.C., 1981—, chmn., 1984. Mem. bus. and profl. div. Jewish Fedn. Mem. Am. Soc. Personnel Adminstrs., Am. Soc. Tng. and Devel. Home: 4800 N Lake Drive Whitefish Bay WI 53217

STERN, CYNTHIA JO, management consultant; b. St. Louis, Oct. 30, 1957; s. Bernard M. Stern and Gloria Sue (Goffstein) Ellis. A.B., U. Mo., 1979, M.B.A., 1981. Staff cons. Arthur Andersen & Co., St. Louis, 1981-83; sr. cons. Price Waterhouse, St. Louis, 1983-85, mgr. mgmt. cons., 1985—. Cons., Project Bus./Jr. Achievement, 1984-85. Mem. St. Louis Women's Commerce Assn., Nat. Assn. Female Execs., Am. Mgmt. Assn. Jewish. Avocations: gardening; racquetball; aerobics; boating. Home: 10415 Willowdale Saint Louis MO 63146 Office: Price Waterhouse One Centerre Plaza Saint Louis MO 63101

STERN, ELIZABETH MARY, graphic design executive; b. Milw., July 28, 1959; d. Robert Malcom and Mary Della (Mayer) S. A.A., Columbia Coll., Mo., 1979; B.A., Bradley U., 1981. Box office mgr. Stardate Prodns., Ltd., Milw., 1981-82, pub. relations dir., 1982-83; pres. Promo Nova, Inc., Milw., 1983—; chmn. bd. Quantum Mgmt., Milw., 1985—, also dir. Com. mem. Hands Across Am./Milw. Effort, 1986. Mem. Nat. Assn. Female Execs., Women in Communications, Nat. Assn. Rec. Arts and Scis., Council Small Bus. Execs., Milw. Assn. Commerce, Milw. Ad Club. Unitarian. Avocations: antique collecting; sports; travel; silk screening. Home: 2413 W Bonniwell Rd Mequon WI 53092 Office: Promo Nova Inc 210 E Michigan St Suite 210 Milwaukee WI 53202

STERN, JOANNE SUE, television station executive; b. Cleve., June 17, 1953; d. Sterling and Shirley Minette (Scragg) S. B.A., Ohio State U., 1975. Continuity clerk Sta. WJKW-TV (now WJW-TV), Cleve., 1976, continuity writer, 1976-77, publicity dir., 1977-79, on-air promotion dir., 1979-80, asst. dir. creative services, 1980-81, dir. creative services, 1981—; mem. CBS promotion mgrs. caucus CBS Network, N.Y.C., 1984-85. Exec. producer comml.: B-Movie (Distinctive Merit award 1982), 1981, Bootcamp: The New Secret Weapon (Monitor award 1983), 1982; producer comml.: You Sure Look Like a Winner (Twyla M. Conway award 1983), 1983, Managers Tape (Graphic Excellence award 1984), 1983. Vol. Easter Seal Soc. Greater Cleve., 1983. Recipient 3 Bronze/3 Silver awards Internat. Film and TV Festival N.Y., 1980-84; Cleve. Communicators awards Women in Communications, Inc., 1982 through 85; Broadcast Media award San Francisco State U., 1983; Bronze Telly awards Local/Regional TV Commls. Festival, Cin., 1983, 84, 85; Spl. Recog. award Cleve. Advt. Club, 1983; 2 Fifth Dist. Addy awards Am. Advt. Fedn., 1982-83, Nat. Addy award, 1983; Finalist award Clio Awards, 1983; Finalist award Internat. Radio Festival N.Y., 1984. Mem. Nat. Acad. TV Arts and Scis. (bd. govs. 1981-85, 2d v.p. 1985, 5 Emmys 1980-81-82-83), Broadcast Promotion and Mktg. Execs. Assn. (Gold Medallion finalist-2), Am. Women in Radio and TV. Office: Sta WJW-TV 5800 S Marginal Rd Cleveland OH 44103

STERN, MYRA, health care consultant; b. Phila., Sept. 25, 1939; d. Israel Abraham and Freda (Sanders) S.; R.N., Albert Einstein Med. Center, 1964; B.A., Temple U., 1961; M.S., Nat. Coll., 1984. Head nurse Michael Reese Hosp., Chgo., 1965-68, clin. coordinator nephrology program, 1968-73; clin. adminstr. North Central Dialysis Centers, Chgo., 1973-79, dir. adminstrv. devel., 1979-83; founder Myra Stern & Assocs., health care mgmt. cons., 1984—; lectr. health systems Northwestern U. Bd. dirs. Nat. Kidney Found. Ill., 1971-79. Mem. Am. Mgmt. Assn., Women in Health Care, Am. Bus. Women's Assn., Am. Hosp. Assn., Am. Nurses Assn., Am. Assn. Nephrology Nurses and Technicians. Home: 2200 Benjamin Franklin Pkwy West-605 Philadelphia PA 19130

STERN, PAULA, government official; b. Chgo., Mar. 31, 1945; d. Lloyd and Fan (Wener) S.; B.A., Goucher Coll., 1967; M.A. (Nat. Def. Fgn. Lang. fellow), Harvard U., 1969; M.A. (scholar), Tufts U., 1970, Ph.D., 1976; m. Paul A. London, Dec. 28, 1971; children—Gabriel Stern London, Genevieve Stern London. Staff writer New Republic mag., 1969; legis. asst. to U.S. Senator Gaylord Nelson, 1972-74, 76; guest scholar Brookings Instn., 1975-76; mem. Carter-Mondale transition team, 1976-77; internat. affairs fellow Council Fgn. Relations, 1977-78; commr., chairwoman U.S. Internat. Trade Commn., Washington, 1978—; adj. asso. prof. urban and policy scis. program Averill Harriman Sch., SUNY, Stony Brook, 1974-75. Bd. dirs. Inter-Am. Found., 1980-81; bd. visitors U. Md. Sch. Pub. Affairs; corp. bd. Babson Coll. Recipient Alicia Patterson Found. award, 1970-71; U.S. Dept. State fellow Arabic Lang. Study, Am. U., Cairo, 1968. Mem. Nat. Women's Polit. Caucus, Council on Fgn. Relations. Democrat. Jewish. Author: Water's Edge: Domestic Politics and the Making of American Policy, 1979; contbr. articles to Atlantic Monthly, New Republic, Washington Post, Washington Star-News, Middle East Jour., New York Times, others. Office: 701 E St NW Washington DC 20436

STERN, REBECCA ANNE MILLER, food company executive; b. N.Y.C., Aug. 5, 1958; d. Joseph Carl and Sarah (Lew) Miller; m. Lawrence David Stern, May 24, 1981. Cert., Universite de Paris, Sorbonne, 1979; B.S., Boston U., 1980. Cert. in bus. and spl. edn., Mass. Br. mgr. Te Corp., Boston, 1980-81; pres., chief exec. officer Legendary Foods Inc., Broomall, Pa., 1981—; presenter workshop Women in Bus. Conf., 1983. Contbr. articles to newspapers. Exec. bd. Abbott Ctr. Condominium, Broomall, 1983—. Mem. Pa. Restaurant Assn., Del. County C. of C. (speakers bur.). Home: 210 Summit House West Chester PA 19380 Office: Legendary Foods Inc 510 C Abbott Dr Broomall PA 19008

STERN, RONDA JANICE BRAND, nurse; b. Corpus Christi, Tex., June 13, 1952; d. Morris and Sylvia (Blair) Brand; m. Howard W. Stern, Mar. 1, 1981; 1 child, Mathew Scott. A.D.N., Galveston Coll., 1973; B.S.N., Tex. A & I U., 1978. Coronary care charge nurse Bellaire Gen. Hosp., Houston, Univ. Community Hosp., Tamarac, Fla. and St. Luke's Episc. Hosp., Houston, 1973-75; cardiovasular nurse specialist program Meth. Hosp., Houston, 1975-76; charge nurse coronary ICU and post coronary care units Spohn Hosp., Corpus Christi, 1976-78; cardiovascular nurse specialist Med. Nursing Service, assoc. lectr. Nurse Cons., Inc. and peripheral vascular lab. and staff nurse surg. service Meth. Hosp., Houston, 1978—. Author: EKG Interpretation-Level I, 1985. Bd. dirs. Infertility Network, 1985—; bd. dirs. Shoestring Tennis, Inc., 1984—. Jewish. Address: 1543 Locke Ln Sugarland TX 77478

STERN, SANDRA SILVERSTONE, television actress; b. London, Eng.; d. Arthur Joseph and Pearl (Finkelstein) Silverstone; A.B., Vassar Coll., 1955; m. Robert Lowell Stern, June 19, 1955; children—Antony Ian, Michael Keith, Wendy Joy, Peter Jonathan, Valery Jennifer. Summer stock actress, Ogunquit, Maine, 1954; apprentice actress, 1955-56; writer, performer children's TV program Jr. Clubhouse, Sta. CHCT-TV, Calgary, Alta., Can., 1957-59, Romper Room hostess, 1959-60, writer, producer, performer Teddy Bear Quiz and 12 and Under, 1960-61; writer, producer, performer children's TV program TV Partytime, CFCN-TV, Calgary, 1962-65, writer, producer, hostess Rocket IV Club, 1965-67; sec. R.L. Stern Mgmt. Co. Ltd., Calgary, 1967—; co-owner Court Stars, active sportswear boutiques, West Vancouver and Vancouver, 1978-84; co-owner, ptnr. Dr. Tomorrow's Toy Galaxy, 1986—. Mem. Jr. League Calgary and Vancouver; bd. dirs. Calgary Dance Theatre, 1974, Festival Calgary, 1975; pres. West Vancouver Newcomers Club, 1977, Can't Wait Tennis Assn., 1981—; mem. Amnesty Internat. Club Author: (ballet play) The Absent-Minded Sorcerbird. Home: 889 Farmleigh Rd West Vancouver BC V7S 1Z8 Canada

STERN, SHIRLEY, lawyer, author; b. Bklyn., Aug. 16, 1929; d. Bernard and Bessie (Tasgal) Gartenstein; m. Leonard W. Stern, Dec. 24, 1949; children—Erwin Samuel, Elana Debra, Gil Avram. B.A., CUNY, 1950, M.A., 1956; J.D., St. John's U., 1982. Bar: N.Y. 1983. Freelance writer, New Hyde Park, N.Y., 1972—; sole practice, New Hyde Park, 1983—. Author: Exploring Jewish History, 1979; Exploring Jewish Wisdom, 1980; Exploring Jewish Holidays, 1981; Exploring the Prayerbook, 1982; Exploring the Torah, 1984. Mem. Nat. Assn. Temple Educators, ABA, N.Y. Bar Assn., Nassau County Bar Assn., Nassau/Suffolk Women's Bar Assn. Democrat. Jewish. Office: 26 Birchwood Dr New Hyde Park NY 11040

STERN, SONIA WYNTREE, editorial services company executive; b. N.Y.C.; d. Mark Efimovitch and Rose (Goldenberg) Weinbaum; m. Charles Stern, Nov. 3, 1955 (div. 1981); 1 son, Adam Richard. Student Columbia U., Art Students League; cert. Winona Sch. Photography, 1959. Mgr., Louelle Photographers, Inc., N.Y.C., 1960-73; contbg. editor PTN Publs., L.I., N.Y., 1972-75; pub. relations account exec. Gilbert, Felix & Sharf, Inc., N.Y.C., 1975-77; sr. product publicist GAF Corp., N.Y.C., 1977-81; pres. Prism Internat. Co., N.Y.C., 1981—. Contbr. articles on photography to profl. jours. Fellow Am. Photographic Hist. Soc. (pres. 1977-78); mem. Photographic Adminstrs., Inc., N.Y. Women in Communications, Profl. Photographers N.Y. State (Bronze medal 1970). Office: Prism Internat Co 322 W 57th St Apt 16R New York NY 10019

STERNBERG, CORA N., physician; b. Phila., Oct. 21, 1951; d. Samuel and Barbara S.; B.A. summa cum laude, U.Pa., 1973, M.D., 1977. Resident, Stanford (Calif.) Hosp., 1979-80, Mt. Sinai Hosp., N.Y.C., 1980-81; research and clin. fellow in hematology and oncology Sloan-Kettering Cancer Center, N.Y.C., 1981-85, clin. asst. physician Solid Tumor Service, 1986—; clin. instr. Cornell-N.Y. Hosp., N.Y.C., 1981—. Mem. AMA, N.Y. Acad. Scis. Jewish. Office: Sloan-Kettering Cancer Center 1275 York Ave New York NY 10021

STERNBERG, DONNA UDIN, lawyer; b. Phila., May 3, 1951; d. Jack and Frances (Osner) U.; m. Harvey Jay Sternberg; 1 child, Zachary Samuel. Student Tel Aviv U., 1971; B.A., Northwestern U., 1973; J.D., Loyola U., Chgo., 1976. Bar: Ill. 1976, Pa. 1979. Profl. actress, dancer, model, 1961-76; dancer Boishoi Ballet Co., 1965, 66, 67, Leningrad Kirov Ballet Co., 1966; actress Broadway prodn., 1966; appeared stage plays, TV and film roles, 1961-77; model nat. fashion mags. and publs., 1961-77; assoc. firm Ronald H. Balson & Assocs., Chgo., 1976-79, Mesirov, Gelman, Jaffe, Cramer & Jamieson, Phila., 1979-81, Blank, Rome, Comisky & McCauley, Phila., 1981—. Active young leadership council Fedn. Allied Jewish Appeal, 1982-84; mem. Israel Bonds New Leadership Cabinet, 1982-84. Mem. ABA, Pa. Bar Assn., Phila. Bar Assn., Chgo. Bar Assn. Jewish. Club: Locust (Phila.). Office: Blank Rome Comisky & McCauley Four Penn Center Plaza Philadelphia PA 19103

STERNBERG, SIMONE ELSA, psychoanalyst, educator; b. Newark, Nov. 18, 1933; d. Norman and Anita (Chivian) S.; B.A., Antioch Coll., 1955; postgrad. Inst. de Phonetique Sorbonne, Inst. des Hautes Etudes, 1960-68; M.A., New Sch. Social Research, 1971; Ed.D., Columbia U., 1976; cert. New Hope Guild Therapist Tng. Program, 1976, N.Y. Ctr. for Psychoanalytic Tng., 1978; m. Robert Morris Feinstein, Nov. 1972; 1 child, Noah Carl. Actress/

mime, Theatre de la Mandragore, France, 1958-68; research assoc. psychol. cons. Teaching and Learning Research Corp., N.Y.C., 1971-73; coordinator, instr. Inst. Study for Older Adults, N.Y.C., 1973-79; prof. Brookdale Center, Hunter Coll., N.Y.C., 1976-77, New Sch., N.Y.C., 1977-78; pvt. practice psychoanalysis and psychotherapy, N.Y.C. and Elmwood Park, N.J., 1978—; adj. assoc. prof. Fordham U. Sch. Social Service; clin. supr. Ctr. for Creative Living; dean students, bd. dirs. N.Y. Ctr. Psychoanalytic Tng.; clin. instr., supr. New Hope Guild, N.Y. Center Psychoanalytic Tng.; cons. Met. Inst. Lic. psychologist, N.J., Pa.; cert. sch. psychologist, N.Y. State; HEW grantee, 1975. Mem. Soc. Psychoanalytic Tng. (v.p.), Am. Psychol. Assn., Council Psychoanalytic Psychotherapists, N.Y. Soc. Clin. Psychologists, Nat. Psychol. Assn. for Psychoanalysis. Author: She Must Have Been a Beautiful Woman Once, 1975; An Exploration of the Cognitive and Personality Functioning of Older Adults, 1976; co-author: Fear of Flying High: Fear of Success in Women, 1978; How Blank is the Blank Screen?, 1979; The Mother Tongue and Mother's Tongue, 1984; The Forgotten Man Remembered, 1986. Office: 300 West 72d St Suite 2F New York NY 10023 also 131A River Dr Elmwood Park NY 07407

STEAN-SOLIS, DEBRA-LYNNE ANN, marketing executive; b. Toms River, N.J., Mar. 12, 1954; d. Samuel Robert and Sylvia Dorothy (Bushing) Stean; B.A., Gettysburg Coll., 1976; postgrad. in bus. adminstrn. U. So. Calif., 1981-83; m. Carlos Solis, Aug. 15, 1981. Real property analyst, La Jolla, Calif., 1976-77; comml. loan officer/analyst Union Bank, Los Angeles, 1977-80; bus. devel. officer First Los Angeles Bank, 1980-81; profl. evaluation cons. Seven-Up Bottlers div. Westinghouse Beverage, Los Angeles, 1981-82; mktg. devel. cons. Sav-On Drugs Inc. div. Jewel Corp., Anaheim, Calif., 1982-84; advt. and promotions mgr. Sav-On Drugs div. Am. Stores Corp., 1984-85; mktg. dir. Coast Fed., Pasadena, Calif., 1985—. Chmn. mgmt. devel. com. Los Angeles Jr. C. of C., 1980-81, chmn. exec. devel. program, 1980-81, bd. dirs., 1981-83, Century of Pacific del., 1982, v.p. pub. relations, 1983-84, v.p. leadership, 1984-85, pres., 1985-86; trustee Los Angeles Open Golf Found., 1983-84, pres., 1986; trustee Century of Pacific Found., 1984-85; mem. U. So. Calif. Student Adv. Council. Named to Career Bd., Mademoiselle Mag., 1976-83. Mem. Am. Mktg. Assn., Entertainment Mgmt. Assn., Am. Fin. Assn., Los Angeles Credit Assn., Univ. and Profl. and Businesswomen's Assn., Los Angeles Area C. of C. (bd. dirs. 1986—), Alpha Xi Delta. Clubs: Los Angeles Athletic, Westside Young Profls. (pres. 1979-81). Home: 590 Bradford Pasadena CA 91105 Office: 70 S Lake Ave Pasadena CA 91101

STETSON, PATRICIA ANN, nursing director; b. Santa Maria, Calif., Dec. 12, 1945; d. Rodney Alexis and Claire W. (Goedinghaus) S. Diploma in nursing, Mercy Coll., 1966. Pediatric nurse Mercy Hosp., San Diego, 1966-67, operating room nurse, 1967; operating room nurse Little Company of Mary Hosp., Torrance, Calif., 1968; flight nurse United Air Lines, 1969; operating nurse Cottage Hosp., Santa Barbara, Calif., 1970-71, inservice instr., 1972, nursing supr. out-patient surgery, 1974-81, dept. head out-patient surgery, 1981—. Contbr. articles to profl. jours., chpt. to book. Mem. Assn. Operating Room Nurses. Republican. Office: Cottage Hosp Out-Patient Surgery Pueblo at Bath Santa Barbara CA 93102

STETTNER, FRANN MARY, public relations firm executive; b. Bklyn., Mar. 3, 1945; d. Samuel Joseph and Ruth Estelle (Rifkin) Lobenfeld; 1 dau., Jessica Daryll. Student Bklyn. Coll., 1961-64, Katherine Gibbs Sch., 1964-65. Asst. to chmn. Computer Horizons, N.Y.C., 1972-75; asst. to sr. ptnr. Parker, Chapin, Flattau & Klimpl, N.Y.C., 1975-78; asst. to chmn. bd. Arlen Realty & Devel. Co., N.Y.C., 1978-81; v.p., gen. mgr. Ecom/DDB Inc., N.Y.C., 1981—. Mem. Am. Mgmt. Assn. Office: Ecom/DDB Inc 444 Madison Ave New York NY 10022

STEUER, KATHLEEN ANNE, architect; b. Bedford, Ohio, Aug. 14, 1953; d. Ralph and Evelyn May (Ryan) Steuer. B.Arch., Kent State U., 1978; student Rosary Coll., Florence, Italy, 1977. Registered architect, Ohio. Architect, Richard Jencen Assocs., Cleve., 1978-79, Koerper Blatchford, Cleve., 1979-82, Technicare Corp., Solon, Ohio, 1982—. Mem. AIA (com. on architecture for health), Archtl. Soc. Ohio, Am. Bus. Women's Assn. (pres. 1985-86, mem. ways and means com. 1984, nat. conv. del. 1984), Kent State U. Alumni Assn., Kappa Omicron Phi. Christian Ch. Avocations: travel; walking; theatre; reading; woodworking. Home: 1511 Aurora-Hudson Rd Aurora OH 44202 Office: Technicare Corp A Johnson & Johnson Co 29100 Aurora Rd Solon OH 44139

STEVENS, ANNE HAWLEY, executive search firm executive, consultant; b. Altoona, Pa., May 30, 1956; d. John King McClanahan and Carol (Bradford) S. B.A., Boston U., 1978, M.Ed., 1981. Workshop/residential coordinator Task Oriented Communities, Waltham, Mass., 1978-80; clin. intern Counseling Services, Inc., Boston, 1980-81; dir. human resources, assoc. dir. Fee Mail Couriers, Boston, 1981-84; pres. A. H. Stevens Assocs., Inc., Boston, 1984—; housing renovator. Mem. Mass. Assn. Personnel Cons. (regional bd. dirs. 1984—), Assn. Women in Psychology, Thespian Soc., Nat Mus. of Women in Arts (charter), Nat. Assn. Female Execs. Democrat. Episcopalian. Avocations: water skiing; cooking.

STEVENS, ANNETTE MARIE, librarian; b. Dallas, May 19, 1936; d. Alexander C. and Catherine Ann (Redmond) Zeck; m. Harrell Stevens, June 8, 1957 (div. 1973); children—Catherine, Caryn. B.A., North Tex. State U., 1957; M.Ed., East Tex. State U., 1976. Cert. tchr., librarian Tex. Librarian, Dallas Ind. Sch. Dist., 1958—. Vice pres. PTA, Dallas, 1978, 83; campaign worker Dallas Democratic Com., 1982, 84. Mem. Dallas Assn. Sch. Librarians, Classroom Tchrs. Dallas, Tex. Tchrs. Assn., NEA, Delta Kappa Gamma (sec. 1980-82), Zeta Tau Alpha. Roman Catholic. Home: 3840 Treeline Dr Dallas TX 75224 Office: Dallas Ind Sch Dist 1303 Reynoldston Ln Dallas TX 75232

STEVENS, CHRISTINA LEA, film director, writer; b. Sydney, N.S.W., Australia, Apr. 9, 1948; came to U.S., 1971; d. William James and Margaret Diana (Young) Stevens. Sr. writer, Young & Rubicam, Inc., N.Y.C., Sydney, Hong Kong, Paris, 1971-76; cons. N.Y.C., 1979-81; sr. writer Wells Rich Green, Los Angeles, 1977-79; sr. v.p. creative dir. Ogilvy & Mather, Los Angeles, 1981-84; pres. Blue Sky Prodns., Inc., Santa Paula, Calif., 1984—; creative dir., cons. Ogilvy & Mather, Inc., 1984—. Author: Vic the Viking, 1968; Illuminations, 1984. Founder, pres. Angel Found., Inc., Los Angeles, 1983. Recipient Gold Lion, Cannes Film Festival 1975; Lulu award Los Angeles Advt. Women, 1977, 80; Clio awards, 1978, 79; IBA awards Internat. Advt. Bur., 1978, 81, 82. Mem. Dirs. Guild Am., Screen Actors Guild Am. Spiritualist. Home: 16812 S Mountain Rd Santa Paula CA 93060

STEVENS, DEBORAH JANE, company executive; b. Winona, Miss., Oct. 3, 1956; d. Earl and Doris Lee (Cox) Bailey; m. Perry Barton Stevens, July 28, 1979. Grad. high sch., Duck Hill, Miss. Sec., Telecor, Inc., Houston, 1979; sec., mgr., exec. sec. Allied TV Rental, Columbia, S.C., 1979-81; sec. Curtis Mathis, Columbia, 1981-82, Ace TV Rental, Columbia, 1982; owner, pres. Stevens Enterprises, Inc., Newberry, S.C., 1983—. Sponsor, Newberry Recreational Basketball Team, 1984-85. Mem. S.C. C. of C. Republican. Baptist. Home: Route 3 Box 376 Chapin SC 29036 Office: Stevens Enterprises Inc 1530 Main St Newberry SC 29108

STEVENS, ELAINE BURR, marketing executive; b. Coshocton, Ohio, Jan. 11, 1942; d. Earl Radcliffe and Jeanette Isbelle (Spies) S.; student Northwestern U., 1960-63 Harvard Grad. Sch. Bus., 1968-70, Case Western Res. Sch. Mgmt., 1975; children—Steven Burr Erikson, Michael Brandt Erikson. Sales rep. Hilton Hotels, Chgo., 1963-64; div. mgr. Maxwell Sroge, Chgo., 1964-68; cons. Store Front Learning Center, Boston, 1968-70; product mgr. Disston, Inc., Pitts., 1975-78; exec. dir. Health Maintenance Orgn., Akron, Ohio, 1978-80; v.p. strategic mktg. team Bus. Support Group, Hudson Ohio, 1980-82; pres. Home Mgmt. Technologies Inc., 1982-83; chmn. Renaissance Techs., Inc., 1983—. Mem chief exec. officers roundtable Council Small Enterprise, 1980—; bd. dirs. Chamber Music Soc., 1976-78, vice-chmn. bd. 1978-79; bd. dirs. Jr. League Akron, 1981-82, exec. bd., 1981-82; mem. health maintenance orgn. adv. council Case Western Res. U., 1978-79. Health Maintenance Orgn. Devel. grantee, 1978. Mem. Direct Mail Advt. Assn. (dir. 1966-69), Council Small Enterprise, Woman's Network Speakers Bur., Greater Cleve. Growth Assn. Mem. Christian Ch. Patentee in field. Office: PO Box 669 186 N Main St Hudson OH 44236

STEVENS, ELEANOR SANDRA, professional service executive; b. Oklahoma City, Nov. 1, 1932; d. Benjamin F. and Mary L. (Smith) Williams; m. Clifton Wilson; m. Rufus Stevens; 4 children. A.S. in Medicine, Fresno State U., 1954; student Los Angeles Trade Tech. Sch., 1972-73. Radio disc jockey, Fresno, Calif., 1954-55; bookkeeper Los Angeles County, 1961-69; clerical supr. Holzman-Begue Real Estate Co., Los Angeles, 1969-73; dist. mgr. United Systems Inc., Los Angeles, 1973-77; pub. relations cons. H.G. Simon & Assocs., Vernon, Calif., 1977-81; owner, mgr. Stevens Personalized Services, Los Angeles, 1982—. Active mem. Women's Referral Service, Good Neighbor Council. Recipient various awards. Mem. Nat. Assn. Female Execs., Bus. Mgmt. Assn. Methodist. Avocations: creative art work; creative cooking. Office: 4614 S Western Ave #B Los Angeles CA 90062

STEVENS, ELISABETH GOSS (MRS. ROBERT SCHLEUSSNER, JR.), author, journalist; b. Rome, N.Y., Aug. 11, 1929; d. George May and Elisabeth (Stryker) Stevens; B.A., Wellesley Coll., 1951; M.A. with high honors, Columbia U., 1956; m. Robert Schleussner, Jr., Mar. 12, 1966 (dec. 1977); 1 dau., Laura Stevens. Editorial assoc. Art News Mag., 1964-65; art critic and reporter Washington Post, Washington, 1965-66; freelance art critic and reporter, 1966—; contbr. art critic The Wall Street Jour., N.Y.C., 1969-72; art critic Trenton (N.J.) Times, 1974-77; art and architecture critic Balt. Sun, 1978—. Recipient art critics' fellowship Nat. Endowment for the Arts, 1973-74; A.D. Emmart award for Journalism, 1980; citation for critical writing Balt.-Washington Newspaper Guild, 1980; McDowell Colony fellow, 1981; Va. Ctr. for Creative Arts fellow, 1982, 84, 85; Ragdale Found. fellow, 1984; Balt. City Arts grantee for book illustration, 1986. Mem. Coll. Art Assn. Am., Am. Soc. Journalists and Authors, Authors Guild, MLA, Internat. Assn. Art Critics, Balt. Writers Alliance, Am. Studies Assn., Soc. Archtl. Historians, Popular Culture Assn., Balt. Bibliophiles, Md. Writers Council. Author: Elisabeth Stevens's Guide to Baltimore's Inner Harbor, 1981; Fire and Water: Six Short Stories, 1982; Children of Dust: Portraits and Preludes, 1985. Contbr. articles, poetry and short stories to jours., nat. newspapers and popular mags. Home: 6604 Walnutwood Circle Baltimore MD 21212

STEVENS, ELIZABETH DREW, lawyer; b. Syracuse, N.Y., Dec. 19, 1946; d. Phil Franklin Blum and Helen Marie (Yarwood) Drew; B.A. cum laude, (Nat. Merit scholar), U. No. Iowa, 1973; postgrad. Schoitz Hosp. Sch. Med. Tech., 1973-74; J.D. (research scholar), Washburn U., 1981; children—Denise Anne Beving, Cynthia Marie Beving. Quality supr. U.S. Gypsum Co., Ft. Dodge, Iowa, 1974-75, employment supr., 1975-77; realtor assoc. Toothaker Real Estate Co., Manhattan, Kans., 1978, Anderson Realty Agy., Manhattan, 1978-79; research asst. Washburn U. Sch. Law, Topeka, 1979-80; law clk. Kans. Corp. Commn., Topeka, 1980-81; bar: Kans. 1981, U.S. Dist. Ct. Kans. 1981; individual practice law, Manhattan, 1981-83; atty. Myers & Pottroff, Manhattan, 1983—; mgr. personnel K-State Union, Manhattan, 1981-83, mem. univ. staff devel. task force, 1981-83, mem. univ. appeal and rev. com., 1982-83. Active LWV, 1977-80; mem. adv. bd. 4-H Club, 1981-84, chmn., 1983-84; solicitor United Way, 1981, 82, bd. dirs., 1984—; solicitor Cancer Crusade, 1975. Mem. ABA (sects. on corps., bus., banking, real property, probate, trust, taxation, econs.), Kans. Bar Assn. (coms. on legal malpractice prevention, continuing legal edn., sects. on corp. banking, bus. law), Riley County Bar Assn. (chmn. Law Day 1984), Am. Trial Lawyers Assn., Kans. Trial Lawyers Assn., North Central Iowa Personnel Assn. (sec. 1976-77), Manhattan Personnel Assn., Bus. and Profl. Women, Washburn Women's Legal Forum (v.p. and pres. 1979-80), Manhattan C. of C. (various coms. Leadership award 1983), Manhattan Arts Council, Am. Legion Aux., Phi Delta Phi. Republican. Methodist. Club: Pilot. Home: PO Box 1511 Manhattan KS 66502

STEVENS, GWENDOLYN RUTH, psychologist; b. Los Angeles Feb. 29, 1944; d. Oscar and Alice (Whalen) Stevens; B.A., Calif. State U., Los Angeles, 1973, M.A., 1974; Ph.D., U. Calif., Riverside, 1978; m. Sheldon Gardner, Oct. 27, 1972; children—Lorin Ann, Stephen Forrest. Research asst. Los Amigos Hosp., Downey, Calif., 1973-75; research dir. Client Assistance Program, Downey 1975-77; psychotherapist, psychodiagnostician Luth. Family and Children's Services, Cape Girardeau, Mo., 1978-82; assoc. prof. humanities U.S. Coast Guard Acad., New London, Conn., 1982—; mem. faculty East Los Angeles Community Coll., 1975, Cypress (Calif.) Community Coll., 1975, Whittier (Calif.) Coll., 1976; mem. psychology faculty S.E. Mo. State U., 1978-82. Mem. Am. Psychol. Assn., Nat. Women's Studies Assn., Cherion, Mo. Psychology Assn., Eastern Psychol. Assn., Assn. Women Psychologists, Eastern Ednl. Research Assn., Internat. Council Psychologists. Author: Care and Cultivation of Parents, 1979; Women of Psychology: Pioneers and Innovators, 1981; Women of Psychology: Refinement and Elaboration, 1981; A Feminist Bibliography; 1979; Hyperkinesis: A Parent Guide, 1979; contbr. articles to profl. jours. Home: 29 Denison Ave Mystic CT 06355 Office: Dept Humanities US Coast Guard Acad New London CT 06320

STEVENS, JILL WINIFRED, control systems technologist, training supervisor; b. Southampton, Eng., June 29, 1939; came to U.S., 1964; d. William Horace Routledge and Winifred Mabel (Richards) S. Asst. to producer BBC, London, 1961-64; governess pvt. home, Hillsboro, Calif., 1964-65; adminstrv. asst. Cambridge U. (Eng.), 1965-66; expediter, buyer, technician Bechtel Petroleum Inc., San Francisco, 1966-77, control systems technologist, Houston, 1978-83; control systems technologist Bechtel Power Corp., Houston, 1983—. Recipient awards in English lang. and English lit. with honors, Royal Soc. Arts and Scis., City of London, 1956. Mem. Instrument Soc. Am., Soc. Women Engrs. (assoc.). Roman Catholic. Home: 2121 Fountainview E81 Houston TX 77057 Office: Bechtel Constrn Inc Limerick Nuclear Generating Sta Evergreen Rd Sanatoga PA 19464

STEVENS, MARCIA ELISSA, lawyer; b. Washington, Feb. 3, 1954; d. Howell Edward and Irena Marcia (Nowak) Stevens; 1 son, Brandon Gabriel. B.A., U. Ala., 1978, M.A., 1978; J.D., St. Mary's U., 1980. Bar: Ala. 1982. Mem. firm Brown, Hudgens, Richardson, Whitfield & Gillion, Mobile, Ala., 1981; sole practice law, Huntsville, Ala., 1982-83; ptnr. Smith & Stevens, 1983—. Instr. law U. Ala., Huntsville, 1983—. Mem. ABA, Ala. Bar Assn., Ala. Trial Lawyers Assn., Huntsville-Madison County Bar Assn., Assn. Trial Lawyers Am., Madison County Trial Lawyers Assn., Huntsville-Madison County Young Lawyers Assn. Office: Smith & Stevens 108 S Side Sq Huntsville AL 35801

STEVENS, MARGOT DUBOSE SEMPLE, mortgage company executive; b. Waco, Tex., Nov. 18, 1929; d. John Dick and Maryliza (Figuers) DuBose; student U. Houston, 1948-49, Howard Payne U., 1963-65, Pa. State U., 1965-66, 73-74; m. William Stilwell Semple, Apr. 17, 1948; children—Toni, Jock Stilwell (dec.) Todd Bertrand, Robin Scot; m. 2d, Keith Frederick Stevens, Oct. 19, 1974. Prodn. mgr. Sta. KEAN, Brownwood, Tex., 1963-65; bus. mgr. Sta. WMAJ, State College, Pa., 1965-67; rental agt. Federated Home & Mortgage Co., Inc., State College, 1967-68, rental mgr., 1968-70, asst. v.p., 1970-76, v.p. rental div., 1976-86; v.p. S&G Apt. Mgmt. Co., 1985-86; property mgr. Toftrees Planned Community in Pa., 1986—; mem. housing adv. panel McGraw Hill Publs. Bd. dirs. Skills Inc., Vacationland Coll. Lic. real estate salesman, Pa.; cert. property mgr. Mem. Inst. Real Estate Mgmt., State College Area C. of C. (dir., mem. exec. bd.). Republican. Presbyterian. Club: Square Dance. Home: 16 High Meadow Ln State College PA 16803 Office: 808 Cricklewood Dr State College PA 16803

STEVENS, MARILYN RUTH, publishing co. exec.; b. Wooster, Ohio, May 30, 1943; d. Glenn Willard and Gretchen Elizabeth (Ihrig) Amstutz; B.A., Coll. Wooster (Ohio), 1965; M.A.T., Harvard U., 1966; J.D., Suffolk U., 1975; m. Bryan J. Stevens, Oct. 11, 1969; children—Jennifer Marie, Gretchen Anna. Tchr., Lexington (Mass.) Public Schs., 1966-69; in various editorial positions Houghton Mifflin Co., Boston, 1969—, editorial dir. sch. depts., 1978-81, editorial dir. math. and scis. Sch. Div., 1981-84, mng. editor, 1984—; admitted to Mass. bar, 1975. Mem. Mass. Bar Assn., Am. Bar Assn. Office: One Beacon St Boston MA 02106

STEVENS, MARLA JEAN, veterinarian; b. Scranton, Pa., May 28, 1953; d. Glen W. and Valeda R. (Kinney) S. Student U. Pa., Pa. State U.; V.M.D., Phila Sch. Vet. Medicine, U. Pa. Equine practitioner Reisterstown Vet. Ctr. (Md.), 1980—. Mem. AVMA, Am. Assn. Equine Practitioners. Home: 1301 Wesley Rd Finksburg MD 21048 Office: Reisterstown Vet Ctr 13030 Hanover Rd Reisterstown MD 21136

STEVENS, MARRE DANGAR, marketing consultant; b. Atlanta, Mar. 21, 1943; d. Paul Adonaldson and Catherine Eveline (Merritt) Dangar; m. Elmer Cominceola Cowley, June 30, 1968 (div. Jan. 1973); m. 2d John Chenoweth Stevens, Jan. 26, 1973; 1 son, James Chenoweth. Student Oglethorpe U., 1961-63, 73, U. Calif.-San Francisco, 1965. Head directory div. W.R.C. Smith Publs., Atlanta, 1974-75; customer service rep. Visual Graphics Corp., Atlanta, 1974-75; editor Terminus Media, Inc., Atlanta, 1975-76; mktg. mgr. Tech. Analysis Corp., Atlanta, 1976-80; owner Indsl. Mktg. Strategy, Atlanta, 1980-86. Chmn. pub. relation com. Salvation Army Youth Clubs, Atlanta, 1986—. Mem. Am. Mktg. Assn. (bd. dirs., chmn. employee referral com. 1979-80), Southeast Brit. Olympic Assn. (coordinator 1984), atlanta Hist Soc. Democrat. Home and Office: 4093 N Ivy Rd Atlanta GA 30342

STEVENS, MARY ANN, state official; b. Frankfort, Ky., Oct. 17, 1941; d. Howard William and Madelyn Frances (Pauly) Pogue; m. James Thaddeus Stevens, May 25, 1963; children—James Thaddeus, Martha Frances, William E. Jr. clk., typist Ky. Personnel Dept., Frankfort, 1960-61; clk.-typist Ky. Labor Dept., Frankfort, 1961-64; sr. clk., typist Ky. Transp. Dept., Frankfort, 1964-66, adminstrv. sec., 1975-83; exec. sec. Office of Gov of Ky., Frankfort, 1983—. Corr. sec. Democratic Woman's Club; co-leader Wilderness Road council Girl Scouts U.S.A., 1972; cub scout leader Bluegrass council Boy Scouts Am., 1971; sec. Good Shepherd PTO; former vol. ARC Bloodmobile, Franklin County unit Am. Cancer Soc. Mem. Phi Beta Psi (Pres.'s award 1975). Roman Catholic. Club: Western Hills Booster (sec., v.p., pres.). Avocations: bowling; reading; golf. Home: 108 Pinehurst Dr Frankfort KY 40601 Office: Office of Gov Capitol Bldg Room 157 Frankfort KY 40601

STEVENS, PATRICIA CAROL, univ. adminstr.; b. St. Louis, Jan. 11, 1946; d. Carroll and Juanita Donohue; A.B., Duke U., 1966; M.A., U. Mo., Kansas City, 1974, Ph.D., 1982; m. James H. Stevens, Jr., Aug. 27, 1966; children—James H. III, Carol Janet. Tchr. math, secondary schs., Balt., St. Louis, Shawnee Mission, Kans., 1966-71; lectr. U. Mo., Kansas City, 1975-76, research asst. affirmative action, 1976-79, coordinator affirmative action, 1979-81, instl. research assoc., 1981-84; dir. instl. research Lakeland Community Coll., Mentor, Ohio, 1984-86; asst. dean acad. affairs math, engring. & techs. Harrisburg Area Community Coll., 1986—. Bd. dirs., v.p. Am. Cancer Soc. Jackson County, 1973-80, 82-84; bd. dirs. PTA, 1975-77. Recipient Outstanding Service and Achievement award U. Mo. Kansas City, 1976; Jack C. Coffey grantee, 1978; Cream Rose Outstanding Service award Delta Gamma, 1970. Mem. Nat. Council Tchrs. Math, Assn. Supervision and Curriculum Devel., Women's Equity Project, Nat. Assn. Student Personnel Adminstrs., Assn. Instl. Research, Am. Ednl. Research Assn., Women's Network, Phi Delta Kappa, (pres.), Phi Kappa Phi, Delta Gamma (v.p.). Home: 925 PA Ave Harrisburg PA 17112 Office: Harrisburg Area Community Coll 3300 Cameron St Rd Harrisburg PA 17110

STEVENS, ROSEMARY ANNE, health services educator, consultant; b. Bourne, Eng.; d. William Edward and Mary Agnes (Tricks) Wallace; B.A., Oxford (Eng.) U., 1957; Diploma in Social Adminstrn., Manchester (Eng.) U., 1959; M.P.H., Yale U., 1963, Ph.D., 1968; m. Robert B. Stevens, 1961 (div. 1983); children—Carey, Richard. Came to U.S., 1961, naturalized, 1968. Various hosp. and adminstrv. positions, Eng., 1959-61; research assoc. Yale Med. Sch., 1962-68, asst. prof., 1968-71, assoc. prof., 1971-74, master Jonathan Edwards Coll., 1974-75, prof. pub. health, 1974-76; prof. health systems mgmt., Sch. Public Health and Tropical Medicine, Tulane U., 1976-79, prof. history and sociology of sci. U. Pa., 1979—, chmn. dept., 1980-83, 86—; vis. lectr. Johns Hopkins U., 1967-68; guest scholar Brookings Instn., Washington, 1967-68; acad. visitor London Sch. Econs., 1962-64, 1973-74. Bd. dirs. Presbyn. Hosp., Phila., Mem. Inst. Medicine, Nat. Acad. Sci., Sigma Xi. Author: Medical Practice in Modern England: The Impact of Specialization and State Medicine, 1966; American Medicine and the Public Interest, 1971; Foreign Trained Physicians and American Medicine, 1972; Welfare Medicine in America, 1974; Alien Doctors: Foreign Medical Graduates in American Hospitals, 1978. Contbr. articles to profl. jours. Address: Dept History and Sociology of Science U Penn D6 Philadelphia PA 19104

STEVENSON, BARBARA JEAN, sales executive; b. Tucson, Apr. 3, 1955; d. Carl Glenn and Barbara Patricia (Fritz) Stevenson; student U. Ariz., 1972-74; B.S. in Animal Sci., Wash. State U., 1976. Area sales rep. Syntex Animal Health, Inc., Wash., Oreg., Idaho, 1977-78, area sales cons. for Tex. Panhandle and N.Mex., 1980-84, nat. accounts coordinator, 1982-84, mgr. advt. and sales promotion, 1984-85, mgr. advt. and pub. relations, 1985-86, western region sales mgr., 1986—; office mgr. Red Rock Feeding Co. (Ariz.), 1978-79. Vice pres. Cattle Capital Cowbelles, 1981, pres., 1982; mem. Pres.'s Council, 1981, 82, 83, 84. Quotamaster, Syntex, 1980. Mem. Am Nat. Cattlewomen, Ariz. Cattle Feeders' Assn. Republican. Home: PO Box 440455 Aurora CO 80044 Office: 4800 Western Pkwy Suite 200 West Des Moines IA 50265

STEVENSON, DENISE L., business executive, consultant; b. Washington, Sept. 18, 1946; d. Pierre and Alice (Mardrus) D'Auga; m. Walter Henry Stevenson, Oct. 17, 1970. A.A., Montgomery Coll., 1967; B.A. in Econs./Bus. Mgmt., N.C. State U., 1983. Lic. ins. agt. Savs. counselor Perpetual Am. Fed., Washington, 1968-70; regional asst. v.p. 1st Fed. Savs., Raleigh, N.C., 1971-83; pres., owner Diversified Learning Services, Raleigh, 1983—; instr. Inst. Fin. Edn., Raleigh, 1983—, Am. Inst. Banking, 1986. Mem. Inst. Fin. Edn. (2d v.p. 1982-83), Am. Bus. Women's Assn. (woman of yr. award 1982), Nat. Assn. Female Execs., Nat. Assn. Bank Women, Am. Soc. Tng. and Devel., Omicron Delta Epsilon. Clubs: Laurel Hills Women's (pres. 1974-75) (Raleigh). Avocation: fishing. Office: Diversified Learning Services PO Box 33231 Raleigh NC 27606

STEVENSON, NORMA ETZEL DOLLY, association administrator, nurse; b. Phila., Oct. 10, 1929; d. Herbert John and Florence Olive (Eisele) Etzel; divorced; children—Janet, Jane Patricia, Dorothy Louise. Diploma St. Luke's Hosp. Sch. Nursing, St. Louis, 1950; B.S., Am. Tech U.; M.Edn., Tex. A&I U., 1985. R.N., Va., Mo., Tex. Supr. operating room Pontiac Gen. Hosp., Mich., 1955-57; field exec. Bluebonnet council Girl Scouts U.S.A., Waco, Tex., 1974-82, exec. dir. Tip of Tex. council, Weslaco, Tex., 1982-86, assoc. exec. staff, mem. referral com., Tex., Okla., Ark., N.Mex., 1981-84, trainer Girl Scouts U.S.A., Tex., 1969—, devel.-mktg. dir. Totem council, 1986—; instr. Am. Camping Assn., Tex., 1980-84, Outdoor Biol. Instructional Strategies, Tex., 1978—. Mem. Woodley Hills PTA, Mount Vernon, Va., state rep., 1960's; mem. Am. humanics bd. Pan Am. U., 1982—; bd. dirs. Am. Heart Assn., 1978-82. Recipient Thanks Badge award Council of Nation's Capital, Girl Scouts U.S.A., 1971. Mem. AAUW. Episcopalian. Club: Sulgrave Garden (Alexandria, Va.) (sec., program chmn. 1960's). Office: Totem Girl Scout Council 3611 Woodland Park Ave N Seattle WA 98103

STEVENSON, RUTH CARTER, civic worker; b. Ft. Worth, Tex. B.A., Sarah Lawrence Coll.; Hum.D., Tex. Wesleyan Coll., 1972; D.H.L., Tex. Christian U., 1973. Pres., Ft. Worth Jr. League, 1954-55; pres., trustee Amon Carter Mus. Western Art, Ft. Worth, 1961—; pres. Arts Council Greater Ft. Worth, 1963-64; bd. regents U. Tex.-Austin, 1963-69; v.p. internat. council Mus. Modern Art, 1965-72; bd. dirs. Nat. Trust Hist. Preservation, Nat. Collection Fine Arts, Smithsonian Instn., 1966-70, Nat. Gallery of Art, 1979—; mem. Council Fgn. Relations, 1983—; pres. bd. dirs. Amon G. Carter Found., 1982—. Address: Amon Carter Museum PO Box 2365 Fort Worth TX 76113

STEVER, MARGO TAFT, poet; b. Cin., Mar. 4, 1950; d. David Gibson and Katharine Longworth (Whittaker) Taft; m. Donald Winfred Stever, Jr., July 31, 1976; children—; David Whittaker, James Taft. A.B., Radcliffe Coll., 1972; Ed.M., Harvard U., 1974. Asst. dir. N.H. Civil Liberties Union, Concord, 1976-77, dir. women's rights project, 1976-77; classroom tchr. learning disabled children The Krebs Sch., Lexington, Mass., 1975-76; staff asst. Senator Ted Stevens, U.S. Senate, Washington, 1974-75; dir. Sleepy Hollow Poetry Series, Warner Library, Tarrytown, N.Y., 1983. Author: (teacher's manual) Behavior Influence and Personality, 1973; A Psychological Approach to Abnormal Behavior, 1975. Contbr. poetry to profl. jours. Bd. dirs., sec. N.H. Pro Bono Referral System, N.H. Bar Assn., Concord, 1977-78; bd. dirs. Tarrytown Coop. Nursery Sch., N.Y., 1983-84, Sleepy Hollow Nursery Sch., Scarborough, N.Y., 1984-85. Mem. Poets and Writers, Acad. Am. Poets. Democrat. Episcopalian. Clubs: Adirondacks League; Abenakee (Biddeford Pool, Maine). Avocations: riding; tennis. Home: 157 Millard Ave North Tarrytown NY 10591

STEVENS-TARWATER, LYNDA SUE, public relations executive; b. Ypsilanti, Mich., Nov. 9, 1947; d. Elmer Eric and Mary (Moore) Weatherford; m. Steven Stevens (div. 1977); 1 child, Emily K.; m. William O. Tarwater, June 25, 1983; children—Adam S., Maggie E. B.A., U. Tex.-Arlington, 1981. Stockbroker Prudential Bache, Fort Worth, 1982-84, Dean Witter, Fort Worth, 1984-85; pub. relations account exec. Witherspoon Co., Fort Worth, 1985—. Am. Bus. Women grantee, 1980; Grace Gee Thornton Found. grantee, 1981. Mem. Nat. Assn. Female Execs., Fort Worth Ad Club, Fort Worth C. of C., Internat. Assn. Bus. Communicators, Women in Communications, Soc. Profl.

Journalists, U. Tex. Arlington Alumni. Republican. Baptist. Avocations: windsurfing; waterskiing; diving; photography. Home: 6808 Riverridge Rd Fort Worth TX 76116

STEWARD, LINDA SUSAN, accountant; b. Columbus, Ohio, Oct. 26, 1956; d. James B. and Josephine (Johnson) S. Student Lake Forest Coll., 1974-76; B.S. in Acctg. and Fin., Franklin U., 1979. Cert. fin. planner; econ. devel. profl. Acct. Nationwide Ins. Co., Columbus, 1976-79; acct. Kinnear Mfg. Co., Columbus, 1979-80; investment analyst dept. devel. State of Ohio, Columbus, 1980—. Mem. Am. Mgmt. Assn., Am. Soc. Exec. and Profl. Women, Nat. Assn. Accts., Assn. Bus. and Profl. Women in Constrn., Ohio Soc. C.P.A.s, Am. Mktg. Assn., Am. Women's Soc. C.P.A.s, Tech. Alliance Central Ohio, Columbus C. of C., Franklin U. Alumni Assn. Researcher in field. Office: 65 E State St Suite 200 Columbus OH 43215

STEWARD, PATRICIA ANN RUPERT, real estate consultant; b. Panama City, Panama, Apr. 20, 1945 (parents Am. citizens); d. Paul S. and Ernestina M. (Ward) Rupert; grad. Sch. of Mortgage Banking, Grad. Sch. of Mgmt., Northwestern U., 1979; m. Robert M. Levine, Oct. 28, 1978; children by previous marriage—Donald F. Steward III, Christine Marie Steward. Lic. mortgage broker, Ariz. Vice pres. Assoc. Mortgage & Investment Co., Phoenix, 1969-71; v.p., br. mgr. Sun Country Funding Corp., Phoenix, 1971-72, Freese Mortgage Co., Phoenix, 1972-74, Utah Mortgage Loan Corp., Phoenix, 1974-81; pres. Elles Corp., 1982—, pres., 1983—; condr. numerous seminars on mortgage fin. Author: A Realtors Guide to Mortgage Lenders, 1972. State chmn. Ariz. Leukemia Dr., 1977-78, mem. exec. com., 1979-80; troop leader Cactus Pine council Girl Scouts U.S.A., 1979-80; bd. dirs. Mental Health Assn. Maricopa County, 1984—, treas., 1984-85, v.p., 1985-86, pres., 1986-87; pres. Ariz. Mental Health Assn., 1986-87; bd. dirs. Nat. Mental Health Assn., 1985—; mem. Ariz. Foster Care Rev. Bd., 1984—. Recipient cert. of appreciation Multiple Listing Service, Phoenix Bd. Realtors, 1975, Multiple Listing Service, Glendale Bd. Realtors, 1977. Mem. Mortgage Bankers Assn. Am., Ariz. Mortgage Bankers Assn. (dir., chmn. edn. com. 1981-82), Young Mortgage Bankers Assn. (chmn. exec. com. 1980-81), Central Ariz. Homebuilders Assn. Republican. Office: 4041 North Central Suite 405 Phoenix AZ 85012

STEWART, ARLENE JEAN GOLDEN, designer, stylist; b. Chgo., Nov. 26, 1943; d. Alexander Emerald and Nettie (Rosen) Golden; B.F.A. (Ill. state scholar), Sch. of Art Inst. Chgo., 1966; postgrad. Ox Bow Summer Sch. Painting, Saugatuck, Mich., 1966; m. Randall Edward Stewart, Nov. 6, 1970; 1 child, Alexis Anne. Designer, stylist Formica Corp., Cin., 1966-68; with Armstrong World Industries, Lancaster, Pa., 1968—, interior furnishings analyst, 1974-76, internat. staff project stylist, 1976-78, sr. stylist Corlon flooring, 1979-80, sr. exptl. project stylist, 1980—; exhibited textiles Art Inst. Chgo., 1966, Ox-Bow Gallery, Saugatuck, Mich., 1966. Home: 141 E Marion St Lancaster PA 17602 Office: Armstrong Tech Center 2500 Columbia Ave Lancaster PA 17604

STEWART, AUDREY JOY, design engineer; b. N.Y.C., Nov. 9, 1956; d. Leslie Owen and Ruby Violet (Bucknor) Stewart. A.A.S., Fashion Inst. Tech., 1979; B.S. in Indsl. Engring., Pratt Inst., 1982. Design engr. N.Y. Telephone, Portchester, 1982—. Recipient Engring. scholarship Minority Engring. Assn., 1979-82. Mem. Nat. Assn. Female Execs., Soc. Women Engrs., Inst. Indsl. Engrs. Democrat. Office: New York Telephone 375 Pearl St Room 1711 New York NY 10038

STEWART, BARBARA DEAN, writer, musician, educational consultant; b. Rochester, N.Y., Sept. 17, 1941; d. George Adgate and Louise (Griswold) Dean; B.A., Cornell U., 1962; M.S., Simmons Coll., 1964; diploma with honors in flute, Eastman Sch. Music, 1958; children—Allison, Whitney. Asst. law librarian Cornell U., 1963-64; writer/performer Kazoophony, Rochester, N.Y., 1972—; pres. Stewart Assocs. Ednl. Systems Group, Rochester, 1979-85; pres. Smart Writers, Inc., 1985—; flutist La Jolla Civic Orch., 1966-68. Dir. jr. devel. U.S. Squash Racquets Assn.; pres. bd. dirs. Rochester Chamber Orch.; bd. dirs. Rochester chpt. English Speaking Union, 1982-85. Recipient Achievement Bowl U.S. Squash Racquets Assn., 1981. Mem. Am. Fedn. Musicians, ASCAP. Author: How to Kazoo. Home and Office: 292 Wintergreen Way Rochester NY 14618

STEWART, BONNIE L., state legislator. Mem. R.I. State Senate, 1985—. Republican. Office: State Capitol Providence RI 02903*

STEWART, CLARA WOODARD, advertising agency executive; b. Mineola, N.Y., May 1, 1952; d. Samuel Woodard and Irene Colm Stewart. B.A. in Broadcasting and Psychology, Mich. State U., 1974; M.A. in Journalism and Communications, U. Fla., 1975. Sales rep. Sta. WSBR, Boca Raton, Fla., 1976-77; media dir. Fred Wagenvoord Assocs., Boca Raton, 1977-81; v.p., account exec., media dir. Birkenes & Foreman Co., Boca Raton, 1981—; cons. on mktg. Computer Advantage, West Palm Beach, Fla., 1981—; instr. effective media Fla. Atlantic U., Boca Raton, 1984-85. Bd. dirs., chmn. communications United Way of Greater Boca Raton, 1979—; bd. dirs. Friends of Boca Raton Pub. Library, 1981—, pres., 1983-84; treas. bd. dirs. Friends of Caldwell Playhouse, Boca Raton, 1985—; young pres.' council Norton Gallery, West Palm Beach, 1983—; mem. adv. bd. Boca Raton Symphony Orch., 1983—. Mem. Bus. and Profl. Advt. Assn. (treas. S.E. Fla. chpt. 1985—), Am. Mktg. Assn. (exec. bd. Gold Coast chpt. 1982-83), Advt. Fedn. Greater Fort Lauderdale, Palm Beach Hist. Soc. (newsletter editor 1980-81), Mensa, Phi Kappa Phi. Avocations: science fiction; geneology; computers; BMW's. Home: 1755 Forest Hill Blvd Apt 4 West Palm Beach FL 33406 Office: Birkenes & Foreman Inc 1388 NW 2d Ave Boca Raton FL 33432

STEWART, DEBRA GAYLE, dentist; b. Bryan, Tex., Nov. 22, 1952; d. Louis Alvin and Della Polly (Laqua) Stewart; m. Donald Ray Tamplen, June 21, 1980. B.S., Southwest Tex. State U., 1974; D.D.S., U. Tex.-Houston, 1980. Instr. biology lab. Southwest Tex. State U., San Marcos, 1973-74, instr. chemistry lab., 1974; gen. practice, dentistry, Stafford, Tex., 1981—; mem. staff Fort Bend Community Hosp., 1984—. Mem. Houston Dist. Dental Soc., Tex. Dental Assn., ADA, Xi Psi Phi (best sec. award 1977), Sigma Kappa. Home: 5711 Sanford Houston TX 77096 Office: 435 FM 1092 Suite E Stafford TX 77477

STEWART, DEBRA (JANE) FENZAU, accounting executive; b. Hillsboro, Ill., Nov. 1, 1950; d. Clarence John and Helen Thelma (Olson) Fenzau; m. Jeffrey Kim Lyons, June 20, 1970 (div. 1971); m. 2d John Edward Stewart, May 3, 1981. B.S. with distinction in Indsl. Mgmt., Purdue U., 1973. C.P.A., Ill. Audit sr. Arthur Andersen & Co., Chgo., 1973-77; audit mgr. CNA Ins., Chgo., 1977-79; owner acctg. practice Debra Stewart, C.P.A., Chgo., 1979—. Speaker in field to profl. groups, Chgo.; appeared on Lee Phillip Show, Sta. WBBM-TV, Chgo., 1983. Mem. Am. Inst. C.P.A.s, Ill. C.P.A. Soc., Am. Woman's Soc. C.P.A.s, Chgo. Soc. Women C.P.A.s (bd. dirs. 1977-82, pres. 1980-81), Nat. Assn. Women Bus. Owners (bd. dirs. Chgo. 1981-83), Alpha Lambda Delta, Beta Gamma Sigma. Home and Office: 1560 N Sandburg Terr Chicago IL 60610

STEWART, DOROTHY ANNE, research physicist; b. Beach Grove, Ind., June 2, 1937; d. Thomas Edward and Dorothy Anne (Browne) S.; B.S., U. Tampa, 1958; M.S., Fla. State U., 1961, Ph.D., 1966. Tchr. math, sci., high sch., Live Oak, Fla., 1958-59; research physicist U.S. Army Missile Command, Redstone Arsenal, Ala., 1966—. Mem. Am. Meteorol. Soc., Am. Geophys. Union, AAAS, Ala. Acad. Scis., Sigma Xi. Contbr. articles to profl. jours. Home: 5204 Whitesburg Dr Huntsville AL 35802 Office: US Army Missile Command Attn AMSMI-RD-RE-AP Redstone Arsenal AL 35898

STEWART, ELIZABETH JASON, lawyer; b. Boston, Sept. 3, 1936; d. Richard Eliot and Elizabeth Harding (McClure) Jason; m. Robert B. Stewart, July 2, 1960 (div.); children—Eleanor Anne, Robert Jason, Lee Bamford. B.A. in History, U. Mass., 1958; M.Ed., U. Hartford, 1969; J.D., Western New Eng. Coll., Springfield, Mass., 1977. Bar: Mass. 1977, U.S. Dist. Ct. Mass. 1978, Va. 1981, U.S. Dist. Ct. (ea. dist.) Va. 1981, U.S. Dist. Ct. D.C. 1981, U.S. Dist. Ct. (we. dist.) Va. 1982, U.S. Ct. Appeals (4th cir.) 1982, U.S. Supreme Ct. 1984. Ptnr. firm Thompson & Stewart, Ludlow, Mass., 1977-80; adminstr. Office Atty. Gen., Commonwealth of Va., Richmond, 1980-82, asst. atty. gen., 1982-84; dep. Commr. Indsl. Commn. Va., 1984—. Trustee Ludlow Hosp., 1979-80. Mem. ABA, Richmond Bar Assn., Va. Bar Assn., Ludlow C. of C. (pres. 1980). Episcopalian. Home: 5606 Matoaka Rd Richmond VA 23226 Office: Office of Attorney General 101 N 8th St Richmond VA 23219

STEWART, JENNIFER, advertising executive; b. Sutton Coldfield, Eng., May 30, 1940; d. Eric Laughlan and Rita Joan (Taylor) S.; B.A. with honors in Philosophy and Econs., Univ. Coll., U. London, 1961. With Cement Mktg. Co., London, 1961-63, ICI Fibres Ltd., London, 1963-65, Research Services Ltd., London, 1965-68, Barton, Barton, Durstine & Osborne, Inc., N.Y.C., 1968-69; with Ogilvy & Mather Inc., N.Y.C., 1969—, now sr. v.p., head planning and research dept., U.S. dir., mem. N.Y. operating bd. Mem. Am. Mktg. Assn. (past dir. N.Y., past chmn. Effie awards com.), Am. Assn. Advt. Agencies (research com.), Market Research Council, Copy Research Council (past pres.), Conf. Board (trustee). Home: 130 W 67th St New York NY 10023 Office: 2 E 48th St New York NY 10017

STEWART, KAREN MARIE, public relations executive; b. Detroit, Apr. 18, 1954; d. Donald James and Margot Ann (Waters) Stewart; m. Paul Michael Stern, June 30, 1979; stepchildren—Rebecca, Michael, William. B.A. in Journalism and Bus., Central Mich. U., 1976. Various reporting and photography positions Suburban News, Southfield, Mich. and Central Mich. Life, Mt. Pleasant, early 1970's; pub. relations intern Dow Chem. Co., Midland, Mich., 1976; pub. relations assoc. Met. Detroit Conv. and Visitors Bur., 1976-78; publs. asst. Mich. Credit Union League, Southfield, 1978-79, pub. relations coordinator, 1979-84, dir. pub. relations, 1985-86; mgr. news relations Chrysler Corp., Detroit, 1986—; charter mem. bd. dirs. Mich. Services Credit Union, Southfield, 1980-86, pres. bd., 1983-85. Dir. pub. relations Detroit Bud Light U.S. Triathlon Series, Pontiac, 1985, Detroit, 1986; mem. pub. relations com. YMCA Met. Detroit, 1984—; mem. publicity com. Detroit-Windsor Internat. Freedom Festival, 1976-79; publicity and/or fundraising dir. Farmington Founders Festival, Mich., 1972-82. Mem. Pub. Relations Soc. Am. (accredited), bd. dirs. Detroit chpt. 1981—, pres. bd. 1986—), Women in Communications (bd. dirs. 1980-86, pres. bd. Detroit profl. chpt. 1984-85, Outstanding Profl. Chpt. award 1984-85), Internat. Assn. Bus. Communicators, Sigma Delta Chi, NOW, Detroit Press. Presbyterian. Avocations: volleyball; water and snow skiing; triathlons. Home: 1500 Seminole St Detroit MI 48214 Office: Chrysler Corp PO Box 1919 Detroit MI 48288

STEWART, KAREN RUTH, medical technologist, nutritional consultant; b. Houston, Oct. 30, 1955; d. Jacob Thomas and Ruth Ella (Caldwell) S. B.S. in Med. Technology, La. Tech. U., 1976; cert. med. technology St. Francis Med. Ctr., 1979. Histology technician U. South Ala. Med. Ctr., Mobile, 1977-78; med. technologist U. Tex. Med. Br., Galveston, 1979—; pres. Visions Unltd., Galveston, 1984—, SW Enterprises, 1986—. Mem. survey com. Galveston Women's Council, 1985-86. Mem. Nat. Assn. Female Execs., Am. Assn. Nutrition Cons., Alpha Kappa Alpha (pub. relations chmn. 1986). Home: 320 Ferry Rd Apt 1206 Galveston TX 77550

STEWART, MARY AGNES, music critic, journalist; b. Battle Creek, Mich., Feb. 25, 1899; d. William Ray and Mary Ann (Hays) Simpson; ed. Pacific Union Coll., U. Wash., U. Md., Am. U., Southeastern U., Washington, San Diego State U.; m. William Robert Stewart, May 4, 1918; children—William Robert, Ray Simpson, Stanley Hays. Asso. editor Calif. Hawaii Hotel-Life and Ocean Travel, 1925-36; impresario L. E. Behymer, Honolulu, 1926-29, La Jolla, Calif., 1941-44; San Diego rep. Pacific Coast Musician, 1945-54; La Jolla corr. Los Angeles Times, 1952-60; interior decorator Mary Stewart Interiors, La Jolla, 1942-86; researcher books The Spanish West, 1976, San Diego County Pioneer Families, 1976; free-lance writer, La Jolla, 1982—; contbr. Opera News, San Diego Union, San Francisco Chronicle. Historian, San Diego Opera Guild; chmn. San Diego Woman's Philharm. Com., La Jolla, Los Angeles Philharm. Orch., 1975-78. Recipient Letter of Commendation, USN, 1972; Agnes Ave. (North Hollywood) named in her honor. Mem. Nat. League Am. Pen Women (br. pres. 1960-62), DAR (chpt. registrar 1966-67), Women in Communications, Nat. Geneal. Soc., Nat. Soc. Colonial Dames Am., First Families Va., San Diego Geneal. Soc., Social Service League La Jolla (life), Library Assn. La Jolla (life), Scottish Record Soc., Friends of Glasgow Cathedral (life), Magna Charta Soc., Owsley Family Hist. Sigma Alpha Iota. Clubs: Woman's (La Jolla); Clan Hay (life). Home: 7118 Olivetas Ave La Jolla CA 92037

STEWART, MARY CATHERINE, psychologist; b. Sault Ste. Marie, Mich.; d. Alexander Pringle and Marguerite Louise (Mc Carron) S.; A.B., U. Miami, 1941, M.S., 1960; m. Charles William Marker, Nov. 14, 1942 (div.); 1 son, Kevin Charles Stewart Marker. Human engring. analyst Boeing Co., Seattle, 1960-69; cons., Seattle, 1969-71, MITRE Corp., McLean, Va., 1971-74; research contract mgr. U.S. Dept. Transp., Washington, 1974-76; supervisory auditor psychologist GAO, Washington, 1976-78; established human factors group Idaho Nat. Engring. Lab. EG&G Idaho, Inc., Idaho Falls, 1978, mgr., 1978-82; profl. staff TRW Ballistic Missile Div., Norton AFB, Calif., 1982—. Mem. Human Factors Soc. (founder, 1st pres. chpt.), Assn. Women in Sci., Evaluation Research Soc., Audubon Soc., LWV. Office: TRW Ballistic Missile Division Norton AFB CA 92409

STEWART, MYRNA LOUISE, educator; b. San Angelo, Tex., June 11, 1939; d. Grady Cleo Huckaby and Anna Florene (Shawn) Gibson; m. Jerry Ray Stewart, Dec. 27, 1957; children—Deborah Anne, Jerry Ray II, Randy Scott. B.S., East Tex. State U., 1980, M.S., 1983. Life cert. tchr., Tex. Dir., Nat. Child Care, Dallas, 1974-78; tchr. Dallas Ind. Sch. Dist., 1980-81, 84—, Allen (Tex.) Ind. Sch. Dist., 1981-84. Mem. Assn. Tex. Profl. Educators, Kappa Delta Pi, Alpha Chi. Republican. Mem. Ch. of Christ. Home: 10403 Robindale Dr Dallas TX 75238

STEWART, ORO ROZELLA, retail executive; b. Pendleton, Oreg., July 8, 1917; d. Joseph Allen and Oro Rozella (Overholtzer) Holaday; B.E., Oreg. State Coll., 1940; postgrad. Wash. State Coll., 1940-42; m. Ivan Stewart, Apr. 4, 1943. Owner, mgr. Stewart's Photo Shop, Anchorage, 1943—; co-owner Stewarts Jewel Jade Mine, 1970—; instr. TV Sch. Photograhpy. Mem. Anchorage Centennial Com., 1967, organizer time capsule to be buried in Juneau; lectr. on Alaskan movies. Recipient various awards, gem and mineral shows. Mem. Anchorage C. of C., Chugach Gem and Mineral Soc. (pres. 1967, chmn. field trips 1965-78, internat. chmn. 1967-82), Master Photo Dealers Assn., Profl. Photographers Alaska, Alaska Miners Assn., Am. Fedn. Lapidary Socs. (internat. relations com. 1977-80), Pioneers of Alaska, Nat. Businessmens Assn., Alaska Geol. Soc., Riflemans Assn., N.W. Fedn. Mineral Socs., Anchorage Downtown Assn., Fairview Homeowners Assn., Tropical Fish Club. Democrat. Mem. Soc. Friends. Clubs: Zonta (v.p. 1971), Scottish. Writer Alaskan directory on rockhound and internat. locations. Home: 840 W 10th Anchorage AK 99501 Office: 531 4th Ave Anchorage AK 99501

STEWART, PATRICIA ANN, forest industries company executive; b. Phoenix, Nov. 3, 1953; d. Travis Delano and Ann Helen (Lopez) Hill; B.S., Ariz. State U., 1975. Programmer, analyst Victor Comptometer Corp., Phoenix, 1975-77, Lewis & Roca, Attys., Phoenix, 1977-79; data processing mgr. Central Mgmt. Corp., Phoenix, 1979-80; corp. systems cons. S.W. Forest Industries, Phoenix, 1981—; partner Abacus Group, 1981-83. Mem. Data Processing Mgmt. Assn. (pres. Phoenix chpt. 1982). Home: 15849 N 20th Pl Phoenix AZ 85022 Office: SW Forest Industries Co 6225 N 24th St Phoenix AZ 85011

STEWART, PATRICIA CARRY, foundation administrator; b. Bklyn., May 19, 1928; d. William J. and Eleanor (Murphy) Carry; student U. Paris, 1948-49; B.A., Cornell U., 1950; m. Charles Thorp Stewart, May 30, 1976. Fgn. corr. Irving Trust Co., N.Y.C., 1950-51; with Janeway Research Co., N.Y.C., 1951-60, sec., treas., 1955-60; dir. Galt Malleable Iron Ltd., 1958-60; with Buckner & Co., N.Y.C., 1961-71, partner, 1962-71; pres., treas. Knight, Carry, Bliss & Co., Inc., N.Y.C., 1971-73; pres., treas. G. Tsai & Co., Inc., 1973; v.p. Edna McConnell Clark Found. Inc., 1974—; dir. Trans World Corp., Borden Inc., Continental Corp., Bankers Trust Co.; allied mem. N.Y. Stock Exchange, 1962-73; past mem. nominating com. Am. Stock Exchange, N.Y. Stock Exchange; past chmn., dir. Investor Responsibility Research Center. Trustee Cornell U., bd. overseers Med. Coll.; vis. com. Grad. Sch. Bus., Harvard U., 1974-80; dir. Women's Forum, Women in Founds./Corp. Philanthropy 1980-86; vice chmn. CUNY, 1976-80; bd. dirs. United Way of Tri-State, 1977-81, Inst. for Edn. and Research on Women and Work; voting mem. Blue Cross and Blue Shield Greater N.Y., 1975-82; trustee N.Y. State 4-H Found., 1970-76, Internat. Inst. Rural Reconstruction, 1974-79; mem. N.Y.C. panel White House Fellows, 1976-78. Recipient Elizabeth Cutter Morrow award, 1977; Catalyst award, 1978; Wings Club N.Y. award, 1984. Mem. Council Fgn. Relations, Pi Beta Phi. Clubs: Cosmopolitan, (N.Y.C.); Gullane Golf (Scotland). Home: 135 E 71st St New York NY 10021 Office: 250 Park Ave New York NY 10017

STEWART, PATRICIA LUCILLE, nurse, army officer; b. Terre Haute, Ind., Dec. 31, 1946; d. Etzell L. and Virginia Pearl (Ripple) S.; diploma, St. Anthony Hosp. Sch. Nursing, 1967; B.S.N., Loretta Heights Coll., 1972; M.Hosp. Adminstrn., Baylor U., 1977. Commd. 2d lt. Nurse Corps, U.S. Army, 1967, advanced through grades to lt. col., 1985; staff nurse Ft. Bragg Hosp., N.C., 1967-68, Vietnam, 1968-69, resigned, 1969, rejoined service, 1970; head nurse, supr. dept. clinics W. Ger., 1972-74, spl. projects officer dept. nursing Brooke Army Med. Center, Ft. Sam Houston, Tex., 1974-75; nursing methods analyst, computer project officer William Beaumont Army Med. Center, El Paso, Tex., 1977-81; asst. chief dept. nursing Redstone Arsenal, Ala., 1981-82; chief functional br. and computer project contracting office Health Services Command, Ft. Sam Houston, Tex., 1982—. Evening charge nurse Porter Meml. Hosp., Denver, 1969-70. Decorated Army Achievement medal, Army Commendation medal with two oak leaf clusters, Meritorious Service medal. mem. Tex. Hosp. Assn., Am. Hosp. Assn. Republican. Baptist. Home: 5837 Archwood San Antonio TX 78239 Office: Hdqrs Health Services Command HSHS-U Fort Sam Houston TX 78234

STEWART, PEGGY IRENE, automobile warranty company executive; b. Hayward, Calif., May 18, 1954; d. Emory and Atha Mae (Cole) Pettigrew; m. Michael Stephen Stewart, Nov. 16, 1972. Student Chabot Coll., Calif., Scottsdale Community Coll., Ariz., Western Internat. Coll., Phoenix; student ins. course Ford Sch., Phoenix. Adminstrv. asst. Great Expectations, Phoenix, 1979-81; controller UDG, Phoenix, 1981-84; dist. sales mgr. NSCC Corp., Bridgeport, Conn., 1984-85; pres. Total Concept Dealer Service, Fremont, Calif., 1985—; treas. Fleet 42 Bus. Group, Phoenix, 1983-84; pres. S & G Cons., Los Gatos, Calif., 1985—. Photographer numerous mag. articles. Named Coach of Yr., Gym Kids Gymnastics Team, Lufkin, Tex., 1977. Mem. Nat. Assn. Female Execs., Nat. Automobile Dealers Assn., Nat. Automobile Vehicle Leasing Assn., No. Calif. Motor Dealers Assn. Clubs: G-Cat Fleet 42 (treas. 1983-84) (Phoenix); MHRA (Monterey, Calif.). Avocations: sailing; photography; gymnastics; automobile-motorcycle racing. Home: Star Route 2 Box 918 Cave Creek AZ 85331 Office: Total Concept Dealer Services Inc 4074 Eggers Suite 1 Fremont CA 94536

STEWART, PHYLLIS ANN, automobile company manager; b. Hampton, Va., Nov. 13, 1952; d. Lawrence George and Mary (George) S. B.A. in Econs. and Fin., Douglass Coll., 1974; postgrad. Gen. Motors Sch. Merchandising and Mgmt. Adminstrv. asst. Trust Co. of N.J., Jersey City, 1973-75; materials control supr. Gen. Motors, Linden, N.J., 1978-83, dist. sales mgr. Chevrolet Motor div., Purchase, N.Y., 1983—. Mem. Rockland County Negro Scholarship Fund, N.Y., 1984—; mem. exec. bd. N.Y. State Minority Careers Expo, 1984-85. Mem. Nat. Orgn. Bus. and Profl. Women, Female Automotive Execs. (pres. 1984—), Nat. Coalition of 100 Black Women, Alpha Kappa Alpha. Baptist. Avocations: sailing; tennis. Home: 85 N Middletown Rd Nanuet NY Office: Chevrolet Motor Div Gen Motors 2500 Westchester Ave Purchase NY 10590

STEWART, PRISCILLA ANN MABIE, art educator; b. Iowa City, Sept. 21, 1926; d. Edward Charles and Grace Frances (Chase) Mabie; m. Thomas Wilson Stewart, Aug. 28, 1949. B.A., State U. Iowa, 1948; M.A., U. South Fla., 1971; Ed.S., Fla. Atlantic U., 1983. Coordinator elem. art Manatee County, Fla., 1953-59; tchr. art Manatee Community Coll., Bradenton, Fla., 1959—; organizer, dir. Pelican Perch Wild Bird Hosp., Bradenton, 1953—. Mem. Mensa, Intertel Soc., Nat. Art Edn. Assn., Fla. Art Edn. Assn., Fla. Ornithol. Soc., Phi Beta Kappa (pres. Sarasota-Manatee chpt. 1984-86), Alpha Xi Delta, Phi Kappa Phi. Republican. Episcopalian. Home: 2705 Riverview Blvd W Bradenton FL 33505 Office: Dept Art Manatee Community Coll Bradenton FL 33507

STEWART, SUE STERN, lawyer; b. Casper, Wyo., Oct. 9, 1942; d. Fraizer McVale and Carolyn Eliabeth (Hunt) Stewart; B.A., Wellesley Coll., 1964; postgrad. Harvard U. Law Sch., 1964-65; J.D., Georgetown U., 1967; m. Arthur L. Stern, III, July 31, 1965 (div.); children—Anne Stewart, Mark Alan; m. John A. Ciampa, Sept. 1, 1985. Admitted to N.Y. bar, 1968; clk. to Judges Juvenile Ct., Washington, 1967-68; mem. firm Nixon, Hargrave, Devans & Doyle, Rochester, N.Y., 1968-74, partner, 1975—; lectr. in field; trustee Found. of Monroe County (N.Y.) Bar, 1976-78. Sec., dir. United Community Chest of Greater Rochester, 1977—; trustee, sec. Internat. Museum Photography at George Eastman House, Rochester, 1974—, Genesee Country Mus., Mumford, N.Y., 1976—; bd. dirs. Ctr. for Govtal. Research. Mem. Am. (chmn. task force on charitable giving, exempt orgns. com. tax sect. 1981—), N.Y. State (exec. com. tax sect., 1974-76, chmn. com. exempt orgns. 1975-76), Monroe County (trustee 1974-75) bar assns. Author: Charitable Giving and Solicitation. Office: Nixon Hargrave Devans & Doyle Lincoln First Tower Rochester NY 14603

STEWART, SUZANNE, pension consultant; b. Schenectady, June 3, 1948; d. George Curtis and Janet (Gurney) S.; B.A., U. Pa., 1970, M.S. in Cardiovascular Physiology (teaching fellow), 1978. Plan adminstr. Todd Service Corp., Greenwich, Conn., 1978-80; spl. agt. Northwestern Mut. Life Ins. Co., Milw., 1980-82; sec.-treas. John O. Todd Orgn., Stamford, Conn., 1980-82; service co. exec., ins. agt. Servestate Corp., Stamford, 1980-82; Todd Service Corp., Stamford, 1980-82; sr. assoc. John O. Todd Orgn., 1980-82; pension cons. Future Planning Assocs., Inc., Burlington, Vt., 1983—. Office: 1150 Airport Dr South Burlington VT 05401

STICH, DEBRA JEAN, health care executive; b. Holton, Kans., July 1, 1954; d. Eugene P. and Joan (Hedrick) Stich. A.A., Labette Community Coll., 1974; B.A., Southwestern Okla. State U., 1977, B.S., 1979; M.Health Care Adminstrn., Tex. Woman's U., 1986. Adminstrv. intern Dallas/Ft. Worth Med. Ctr., Grand Prairie, Tex., 1979; asst. support service mgr. Baylor Med. Ctr., Dallas, 1979; support service mgr. Baylor Med. Ctr., Dallas, 1980-83; staff exec. George S. May Internat. Co., Park Ridge, Ill., 1984-86; mgmt. engr. Parkland Med. Ctr., Dallas, 1986—; mgmt. cons. George S. May Internat., Park Ridge, 1984-86. Mem. Am. Coll. Health Care Execs., Nat. Assn. Female Execs., Am. Mgmt. Assn. Avocations: tennis; photography. Home: 7929 Hunnicut Apt B Dallas TX 75228

STICKLE, MARGARET ALICE, controller; b. Russell, Ky., Oct. 3, 1934; d. Russell De Atley and Lorah Ellen (Ferrell) Kegley; B.A., Marshall Coll., 1956; postgrad. UCLA 1973-75; 1 child, David Brent. Asst. controller R & B Devel., Los Angeles, 1973-78; pres. Evergreen Realty Corp., and Evergreen Realty Corp., Tex., Los Angeles, 1978-80; v.p., controller Consol. First Nat. Corp., Los Angeles, 1980-83; treas., controller Western Cons. Group, Inc., real estate syndicators, 1983—; controller western div. Niagara Cyclo Massage, 1968-70; sec. various corps. Treas., Boy Scouts Am., 1965-68; mem. election bd. Republican Party, 1968-71. Mem. Nat. Acctg. Assn., Nat. Notary Assn. Presbyterian. Club: Northridge Woman's (sec. 1967). Home: 8338 Woodley Pl Unit #41 Sepulveda CA 91343 Office: 8718 Woodley Ave Sepulveda CA 91343

STICKLE, MARILYN GREGER, clinical social worker; b. Johnson City, N.Y., Jan. 20, 1947; d. George William Beers and Mary (Breckner) Thomas; B.A., George Washington U., 1968; M.Ed., Am. U., 1971; M.S.W., Ind. U., 1974; m. Warren E. Stickle, III, Aug. 15, 1970. Tchr.-counselor Todd County High Sch., Mission, S.D., 1969-70; social worker Logansport (Ind.) State Hosp., 1971-73; clin. social worker Guidance Center, Logansport, 1973-75, Arlington (Va.) Guidance Assn., 1976-78; clin. social worker, dir. services Arlington Counseling Center, 1978—. Active polit. campaigns for Dem. candidates, 1972, 81. Lic. clin. social worker. Mem. Greater Washington Soc. Clin. Social Work (pres. 1983-85, dir.), Nat. Assn. Social Workers (chmn. Va. Pace com. 1981-84). Home: 7311 Hooking Rd McLean VA 22101 Office: 5319 Lee Hwy Arlington VA 22207

STICKLES, BONNIE JEAN, nurse; b. Waukesha, Wis., Nov. 24, 1944; d. Donald William and Betty Jane S.; B.S. in Nursing, U. Wis., 1967; M.S. in Nursing, Midwifery, Columbia U., 1974. Mem. nursing staff Grace Hosp., Detroit, 1970-73; mem. faculty and staff U. Minn. Sch. Nursing and Nurse-Midwifery Service, Mpls., 1974-76; chief nurse-midwife, clin. instr. St. Paul-Ramsey Med. Center, 1976-84; midwifery supr. IHS/PHS Chinle Hosp., 1984-85; program mgr. maternal health sect. N.Mex. Dept. Health and Environ., 1985—; mem. consumer adv. pool FDA; adv. bd. Childbirth Edn. Assn., 1980—. Served with USNR, 1965-70. Decorated Letter of Commendation. Mem. Am. Coll. Nurse-Midwives (chmn. profl. affairs com. 1975-80),

Nurses Assn. Am. Coll. Obstetricians and Gynecologists (charter), Aircraft Owners and Pilots Assn., Gt. Plains Perinatal Orgn., Alpha Tau Delta. Author articles in field; patentee teaching model.

STICKNEY, CECELIA CATHERINE, nurse; b. Elizabeth, N.J., Dec. 13, 1944; d. Thomas Kenneth and Lottie Theresa (Kociolek) S. Diploma, Johns Hopkins Hosp. Sch. Nursing, 1965; B.S., St. Francis Coll., 1979; M.P.A., NYU, 1982. Supr. CCU, Doctors Hosp., N.Y.C., 1968-69; adminstrv. supr., dir. staff edn. Gracie Sq. Hosp., N.Y.C., 1969-71; asst. dir. nursing Park East Hosp., N.Y.C., 1971-73; adminstrv. supr., dir. to staff edn. Gracie Sq. Hosp., 1973-76; med. surg. supr. N.Y. Infirmary, N.Y.C., 1976-77, asst. dir. nursing, 1977-80; dir. nursing Morningside House Nursing Home, Bronx, 1981-84, asst. adminstr. patient care services, 1984—; mem. faculty Aging in Am., Inc.; mem. adv. council grad. nursing studies Herbert H. Lehman Coll.; cons. grid matrix project N.Y. Dept. Health Systems Mgmt. Mem. Nursing Service Council (sec.), N.Y. Assn. Homes for the Aging, N.Y. Assn. Homes Aging, Coalition of Institutionalized Aged and Disabled, Am. Nurses Assn., Am. Nurses Found., Am. Pub. Health Assn., Am. Soc. Pub. Adminstrn., Nat. Assn. Female Execs. Republican. Club: Century. Office: 1000 Pelham Pky S Bronx NY 10461

STIDGER, RUTH WILLMAN, editor; b. Rodney, Iowa, Sept. 20, 1939; d. Kenneth Wilbur and Eileen Lucille (Walton) Willman; student U. Iowa, State Coll. Iowa, Northwestern U.; M.Sc., Columbia Pacific U., 1984; m. 2d, Howe C. Stidger; children by previous marriage—Ellen Joyce, Susan Grace. Constrn. field mgr. Saul Cohen Realty, Gary Ind., 1965-67; editor house mag. Dilts Equitable Life Assurance Agy., Gary, 1967-68; staff editor Instns., Chgo., 1968-70; features editor Nation's Schs., Chgo., 1970-71; editorial dir. internat. group Tech. Pub. Co., N.Y.C., 1975—. Recipient Jesse H. Neal Editorial award, 1969, 83; cert. merit, 1978 80; Nat. Merit scholar, 1957. Mem Am. Bus. Press (past chmn., editorial bd.), N.Y. Bus. Press Editors (past pres.), Mensa. Author: Cost Reduction From A to Z, 1975; Inflation Management, 1976; Mining Equipment Handbook, 1982; The Compentence Game, 1981; Automation and Robotics Handbook 1982; 187 Ways to Amuse a Bored Cat, 1983; Business Basic: English-Deutsch, English-Français, English-Español. Editor Mining Equipment Internat., 1977-78; asso. editor World Constrn. 1975-77. Office: 875 3d Ave New York NY 10022

STIEFEL, BETTY KRAEUCHE, nurse, clothing co. exec.; b. Hartford, Wis., May 24, 1941; d. George Roland and Delores (Horst) Kraeuche; R.N., Mt. Sinai Hosp. Sch. Nursing, 1962; grad. Patricia Stevens Sch., 1963; student U. Wis., 1962-63, 69—; m. William James Stiefel, May 20, 1964; children—John Benjamin, James Gottfried, Elisabeth Kraeuche, William George. Model various firms, Milw., Chgo. and Green Bay, Wis., 1962-78; staff nurse med. surg. floor to asst. head nurse Mt. Sinai Med. Center, Milw., 1962-64; weekend night nurse Ivanhoe Sanitarium, Milw., 1962-64; vol. research asst. Marquette U., Milw., 1962; occupational nurse Stiefel Clothing Co., Green Bay, 1965-79, office/personnel mgr., 1976-79, dir., 1969—, v.p., 1976—; pres., owner Betty K Stiefel & Assos., Green Bay, 1980—; librarian Green Bay Montessori Soc., 1970-78; librarian Brown County Library, chmn. taping for blind and handicapped, 1973-79, cons., 1981—. Vol., Blood Donor Center, ARC, Green Bay, 1965-75; tres. Cnesses Israel Sisterhood, 1981—; pres. Green Bay Symphony Orch. Women's Guild, 1980—, also bd. dirs.; pres., bd. dirs. City of Hope; mem. adv. bd. Green Bay Symphony Orch. Assn., bd. dirs., 1980—; bd. dirs. YWCA; bd. dirs., sec. Service League Green Bay; pres., bd. dirs. Green Bay Montessori Soc.; bd. dirs. Brown County Civic Music Assn., also mem. adv. bd.; mem. sustaining com. Peninsula Music Festival; trustee Peninsula Arts Assn., 1980—. Served to 2d lt., Nurse Corps, U.S. Army, to 1964. Recipient Jaycettes Community Appreciation award, 1969; others. Mem. Beta Sigma Phi.

STIEGHORST, JUNANN JORDAN, seed company executive; b. Hydro, Okla., June 8, 1923; d. John Wallace and Myrtle Mae (Harrison) Jordan; student Southwestern Coll., Weatherford, Okla., 1940-41; B.A. in L.S., U. Okla., 1944, B.A. in English, 1947, postgrad., 1959-60; postgrad. So. Meth. U., 1945; m. Guenther Paul Stieghorst, Aug. 13, 1955; 1 son, Theodore Mark. Stewardess, Braniff Airways, 1944-45; advt. copywriter, model Neiman-Marcus, Dallas, Tex., 1945-46, dir. clientele and charge account promotion, 1947-55; advt. copywriter Wilhelm-Laughlin-Wilson, Dallas, 1946; dir. pub. relations and clientele Lichensteins, Corpus Christi, Tex., 1955-56; clientele dir. Joskes of Tex., San Antonio, 1957-58; children's librarian Jefferson County Public Library, Golden, Colo., 1967-69; co-owner Stieghorst Seed Co., Golden, 1973—. Recipient award for outstanding book U. Okla., 1966. Mem. AAUW, Colo. Archaeol. Soc., Internat. Platform Assn., DAR (nat. chairman's award 1975; nat. vice-chmn. public relations, state chmn., chpt. regent), Alpha Chi Omega. Republican. Lutheran. Clubs: Soroptimist, Braniff Clipped B's. Author: Bay City and Matagorda County: A History, 1965; Colorado Historical Markers, 1978; History of Mt. Lookout Chapter DAR, 1923-83; contbr. articles on retail bus. to various mags. Home and Office: Golden CO 80401

STIEREN, PATRICIA MAGDALENA, direct marketing executive; b. Springfield, Ill., Dec. 4, 1957; d. George Edward and Maria de la Paz Enriqueta (Hernandez) S. B.A. in French, U. Ill., 1980; M. Internat. Mgmt., Am. Grad. Sch. of Internat. Mgmt., Glendale, Ariz., 1982. Asst. mgr. Zorba's Greek Restaurant, Champaign, Ill., 1977-81; account rep. M & T Pub. Co., Palo Alto, Calif., 1984-85; account coordinator Grey Advt. Agy., San Francisco, 1985; asst. account exec. Grey Direct Mktg. Group, Inc., San Francisco, 1985-86; account exec. Grey Direct Internat., Frankfurt, Germany, 1986—. Recipient Internat. Advt. award Ariz. Republic, Phoenix, 1982. Mem. Summit Orgn., Mensa. Democrat. Roman Catholic. Club: Toastmasters. Avocations: skiing; travel; reading; biking; writing. Office: Grey Direct Internat Eysseneckstrasse 34 6000 Frankfurt am Main West Germany

STILES, CAROLYN HOGAN, personnel consultant; b. Little Rock, Feb. 28, 1937; d. George Donaghey and Thelma (Williams) Hogan; m. Charles Merrill Stiles, Aug. 22, 1958; children—Steven Merrill, Sherri Suzanne. Student Baylor U., 1955-57; B.A., U. Kans., 1959. Research asst. U. Kans., Lawrence, 1959-61; claims authorizer Social Security Adminstn., HEW, Kansas City, Mo., 1961-64; sales mgr. Coastal Employment Services, Galveston, Tex., 1980-81; pres. Carolyn H. Stiles, Inc., Galveston, 1981—. Pres. Galveston Arts, 1975-76; mem. Galveston Planning Commn., 1977-78, chmn., 1978-82; v.p. League Women Voters, Galveston, 1978-81; mem. exec. com. United Way, Galveston, 1981—. Named to Galveston Hall of Fame for Women, Tex. Gov.'s Women's Council, 1984. Mem. Nat. Assn. Personnel Cons. (cert. personnel cons.), Tex. Assn. Personnel Cons., Jr. League (bd. dirs. Galveston County chpt. 1975-77), Galveston C. of C. (bd. dirs. 1981—), Chi Omega. Republican. Episcopalian. Avocations: traveling; reading; volunteer work. Office: Carolyn H Stiles Inc 1617 Tremont St Galveston TX 77551

STILL, PATRICIA ADELENE, paramedic, ambulance service executive; b. Atmore, Ala., Dec. 7, 1937; d. John Alfred King Trudeau and MargaretLouise (Cheatham) Allen; m. Merrill Harlan Still, Jan. 1, 1956; children—Terrell Harlan, Kathy Ann, Louie Bryan, Jon Braden. Grad. Emergency Med. Technician Sch., Atmore, 1972, U. South Ala. Paramedic Sch., 1975. Lic. paramedic, Ala., Fla. Office mgr. Dr. S.N. Rumpanos, Mobile, Ala., 1962-75; owner, paramedic Atmore Ambulance, Inc., Ala., 1975—; owner, mgr. Western Auto Assoc. Store, Atmore, 1979—; CPR instr. Am. Heart Assn., Mobile, 1973—, mem. state affiliate faculty, 1978—, advanced cardiac life support instr., 1984—; instr. emergency med. technicians Ala. Health Dept., 1976—; instr. first aid, CPR, emergency med. technician classes. Recipient Paramedic Class award Mobile County, 1975; named 1st Paramedic in Escambia County, Ala., 1975, Emergency Med. Technician Instr. of Yr., 1984. Democrat. Baptist. Home: Star Route A Box 124 Atmore AL 36502 Office: Atmore Ambulance Inc 120 Ashley St Atmore AL 36502

STILLER, SHARON PAULA, lawyer; b. Rochester, N.Y., Mar. 31, 1951; d. Alfred Stiller and Hilda (Silver) Ring; m. John F. Everett, Nov. 21, 1981; stepchildren—Sarah, Sean, Liam. B.A. magna cum laude, SUNY-Albany, 1972; J.D., Albany Law Sch., 1975. Bar: N.Y. 1976, U.S. Supreme Ct. 1979. Asst. dist. atty. Monroe County Dist. Atty. Office, Rochester, 1976-83, spl. asst. dist. atty., 1983; asst. adj. prof. Monroe Community Coll., Rochester, 1981—; assoc. Goldstein, Goldman, Kessler & Underberg, Rochester, 1983—; lectr., cons. in med.-legal issues U. Rochester Med. Sch., 1980—; cons. Women's Career Ctr., Rochester, 1984—; lectr., cons. GRO Displaced Homemakers Program, Rochester, 1984—. Co-author: Handling Drunk Driving Cases, 1985. Editor law rev. Albany Law Sch., 1974-75. Contbr. articles to profl. jours. Bd. dirs. Community Ptnrs. for Youth, Rochester, 1980-84, v.p., 1984—; bd dirs. Monroe County Legal Assistance Corp., Rochester, 1981—, v.p., 1982-84. Recipient Outstanding Service award Community Ptnrs. for Youth, 1983. Mem. Greater Rochester Assn. Women Attys. (bd. dirs., chmn. legis. com. 1984-85), Monroe County Bar Assn. (mem. judiciary com. 1980-83), N.Y. State Bar Assn., N.Y. State Trial Lawyers Assn., Zonta (pres. 1982-84, area dir. 1984—). Avocations: art; theater productions; playing penny whistle and flute. Office: Goldstein Goldman Kessler & Underberg 1800 Lincoln First Tower Rochester NY 14607

STILLMAN, ANNE WALKER, fashion designer; b. Amsterdam, Apr. 15, 1951; came to U.S., 1953; d. Edmund and Mary (Gwathmey) S. Student Barnard Coll., 1968-72. Owner, designer Sofia & Anne, Bethel, Conn. and N.Y.C., 1978—, Sofia & Anne Sportknit, Bethel and N.Y.C., 1983—, Sofie & Annie (Children's Wear), Bethel and N.Y.C., 1985—. Office: Sofia & Anne 37 W 39th St New York NY 10018

STILLMAN, DOREAN, hotel executive; b. N.Y.C., June 27, 1935; d. Meyer Eli and Dolores Letica (Blauvelt) Lefkowitz; m. John Leonard Adams, Mar. 2, 1985; children—Doug Soren, Rhonda Soren Mona. Student Adelphi U., Hunter Coll., U. Nev.-Las Vegas. Asst. dir. sales and mktg. Ambassador Inns, Las Vegas, Nev., 1976-78; sales mgr. Flamingo Hilton Hotel, Las Vegas, 1978-79; dir. mktg. Mini Price Inns, Las Vegas, 1979-82, v.p., 1982—; mem. Tourism Council, Las Vegas, 1983—. Named Mgr. of Yr. for Hotels, Hotel Sales and Mktg. Assn., 1985. Mem. Nev. Hotel Mktg. Assn. (sec. 1979), Nev. Hotel Motel Assn. (bd. dirs. 1982—), Las Vegas C. of C. (press com. 1984—). Office: Mini Price Inns 4155 Koval Ln Las Vegas NV 89121

STILLMAN, GINGER HAYNES, policy analyst; b. Mount Airy, N.C., Jan. 9, 1955; d. William John and Lillie Mae (Bond) Haynes; m. John Arthur Stillman, Mar. 30, 1975; children—William Arthur, Jennifer Lee. B.S., Wake Forest U., 1977; postgrad. Fairleigh Dickinson U. Installation foreman Plant dept. So. Bell, Charlotte, N.C., 1977-79; asst. staff mgr. network dept. N.J. Bell, Newark, 1979-80, service costs dept., 1980-82; staff mgr. docket mgmt. AT&T, N.Y.C., 1982-83, in mktg., Basking Ridge, N.J., 1983—. Mem. Nat. Assn. Female Execs., Sounding Board Network. Republican. Methodist. Home: Randolph NJ Office: AT&T Communications 295 N Maple Ave Basking Ridge NJ 07920

STILLMAN, MARY ELIZABETH, librarian, educator; b. Phila., Oct. 31, 1929; d. Ernest E. and Rosalie (Burhans) Stillman; B.A., Wilson Coll., Chambersburg, Pa., 1950; M.S., Drexel U., Phila., 1952; Ph.D. (fellow), U. Ill., 1966. Librarian, USAF, 1953-63, Export-Import Bank U.S., 1965-68; asst. prof. Drexel U., 1968-72; mem. faculty Albright Coll., Reading, Pa., 1972—, prof., librarian, 1975—; editor Drexel Library Quar., 1969-72; cons. research info. system Social and Rehab. Service, 1972-74; del. Pa. Gov.'s Conf. on Libraries, 1977; chmn. Pa. Library Week, 1978, 79; shareholder Reading Library Co., 1980—; mem. long-range planning com. Reading Pub. Library, 1982—, trustee, 1985—; pres. Reading Library, 1985—. Bd. dirs. Reading YWCA, 1981-83. Mem. ALA (reviewer Subscription Books Bull. 1969—), Pa. Library Assn. (dir. pub. relations task force 1974-79, editor bull. 1973-79, treas. colloquium on info. retrieval 1978-79), AAUP. Contbr. articles to profl. jours. Home: 1375 Pershing Blvd Apt 102 Reading PA 19607 Office: Albright Coll Reading PA 19604

STILLMAN, STEPHANIE MATUSZ, computer contract company executive; b. Middlesex County, N.J., July 16, 1946; d. William Stephan Matusz and Mary Jane (Van Horn) Falger; m. Dennis Edison DeMercer, Aug. 22, 1970 (div. 1977); m. Richard Alan Stillman, May 10, 1980; 1 child, Taylor Edison. B.A., Morarian Coll., 1968. Tchr., Hawaii Edn. Dept., Kohala, 1968-71; acct. exec. with various ins. agys., N.J., 1975-79; div. mgr. E.T. Lyons Y Assoc., New Brunswick, N.J., 1979-80; sr. personnel adminstr. Systemp, Inc., New Brunswick, 1980-84; br. mgr. Officeforce, Inc., Cedar Knolls, N.J., 1984; pres., mktg. dir. The Resource Group, Inc., Cambridge, Mass., 1985—. Bd. dirs., pres. Rutgers-Livingston Day Care Ctr., Piscataway, N.J., 1978-80. Mem. Cambridge C. of C., Smaller Bus. Assn. New Eng., Data Processing Mgmt. Assn., Assn. Women in Computing. Republican. Avocations: skiing; travel. Office: The Resource Group Inc 124 Mt Auburn St Cambridge MA 02138

STIMPSON, CATHARINE ROSLYN, university dean, educator, writer, editor; b. Bellingham, Wash., June 4, 1936; d. Edward Keown and Catharine Charlotte (Watts) S. A.B., Bryn Mawr Coll., 1958; B.A. (Fulbright fellow), Cambridge (Eng.) U., 1960, M.A., 1965; Ph.D., Columbia U., 1967. Mem. faculty English dept. Barnard Coll., N.Y.C., 1963-80; prof. English, Douglass Coll., Rutgers U., New Brunswick, N.J., 1980—, dean grad. sch., 1986—; cons. Nat. Inst. Edn., 1978—, UNESCO, 1979, various colls. and univs. on women's studies, 1972—. Founding editor Signs: Jour. of Women in Culture and Society, 1974-80. Author: Class Notes, 1979; (novel) J.R.R. Tolkien, 1969. Editor book series on women and culture U. Chgo. Press, 1981—. Mem. nat. adv. bd. Southwest Inst. for Research on Women, 1979—; mem. nominating com. Nat. Medal for Lit., 1980; mem. nat. com. Emergency Civil Liberties Com., 1975—; mem. com. on status of women U.S. Commn. on UNESCO, 1979—; chmn. N.Y. State Council for Humanities, 1984—; chmn. Nat. Council for Research in Women, 1985—. Nat. Humanities Inst. fellow, 1975-76; Rockefeller Humanities Inst. fellow, 1983-84. Mem. Nat. Abortion Rights Action League, NOW, MLA. Democrat. Office: Office Grad Dean Rutgers U New Brunswick NJ 08903

STIMPSON, CYNTHIA CHATMAN, photographic/graphic presentations company executive; b. Odessa, Tex., Feb. 3, 1935; d. Cecil Lamar Chatman and Roberta Belle (Coffin) Merillat; m. Irving E. Stimpson, Nov. 7, 1970. B.A., North Tex. State U., 1955; M.S.W., Denver U., 1960. Dist. dir. Dallas council Girl Scouts U.S.A., Dallas, 1955-58, dir. programs and pub. relations Mile Hi council, Denver, 1960-64, western regional program dir., 1966-68; project dir. San Francisco Sr. Ctr., 1964-66; planning cons. United Way, King County, Wash., 1968-72; dir. spl. projects Region IV Wash. State Dept. Social and Health Services, 1972-73; exec. dir. United Community Services, Seattle, 1973-74; founder, pres. Chroma Copy West, Inc., Seattle, 1981—; mem. adj. faculty Denver U., 1962-64, U. Wash., Seattle, 1969-72; mem. faculty Edmonds Community Coll., 1973. Author, editor: Avesta, 1955. Pres. Totem council Girl Scouts U.S.A., Seattle, 1974-79; exec. com. Council of Planning Affiliates, King County, Wash., 1977-80; state v.p. Wash. Council on Crime and Delinquency, 1978-79; v.p. Cardio-Pulmonary Research Inst., King County, 1981-83; chmn. citizens adv. com. King County Dept. Youth Services, 1982-84; vol. trainer United Way Am.; mem. corp. task force City of Seattle Kidsplace. Named Social Worker of Yr., Nat. Assn. Social Workers, 1975; recipient Mayor's Small. Bus. award City of Seattle, 1985. Mem. Seattle C. of C., Regrade Property Assn. (bd. dirs. 1984-85), Women's Managerial and Profl. Network, Women in Communication, NOW. Clubs: City, Wash. Athletic (Seattle). Avocations: continuing edn.; travel; writing. Home: 8611 Inverness Dr NE Seattle WA 98115 Office: Chroma Copy West Inc 2720 3d Ave Seattle WA 98121

STIMPSON, VIOLA KATES, dancer, actress, educator; b. N.Y.C., Oct. 25, 1906; d. Abraham Jacob and Helena (Yezierska) Katz; m. H Tevis Wilson, 1938 (div. 1941); m. Paul McIntosero Derby, June 1943 (div. 1951); 1 child, Helena Edin Derby Leiner; m. Robert P. Stimpson, Oct. 23, 1953 (div. 1968). B.S., NYU, 1935; grad. Daykarhanova Sch. for Stage, 1941. Dancer Lillian Shapero Graham Dance Group, Greenwich Village Follies, N.Y.C., 1925-26, Top Hole, N.Y.C., 1927, Making Mary, N.Y.C., 1928, Fox Movietone Follies, Hollywood, Calif., 1929-30; Show of Shows, Hollywood, 1929-30, Garrick Gaieties Theatre Guild, 1931; stage performances include Murder Is Announced-Miss Marple, Uncommon Women, Los Angeles Stage Co., Summer and Smoke, Coronet Theater, Picnic, The Silver Sword, Seattle Cirque Dinner Theatre; TV shows include Mama's Family, Fall Guy, Too Close for Comfort, General Hospital, All in the Family, Chips, Bionic Woman, Magruder and Loud, E.R., St. Elsewhere, Simon and Simon, Trapper John, Capitol, Still the Beaver; films include Lies, Alchemist, Woman in Red, Into the Night, When a Stranger Calls, Valentine, Sweater Girl, Stewardess School, The Deacon Street Deer; mem. Am. Actors Co., N.Y.C., Ensemble Studio West-Los Angeles Theatre Co. Mem. Screen Actors Guild, Actors Equity Assn., AFTRA, AFI Writers Workshop Alumni Assn. Club: Zeigfeld. Home: 522 N Rossmore Los Angeles CA 90004 Office: Amaral-Murphy Agy 10000 Riverside Dr Toluca Lake CA 91602

STIMSON, DOROTHY BRICKWEDDE, stockbroker; b. Cin., Dec. 31, 1917; d. Harry Joseph and Marie (Ihlendorf) Brickwedde; m. Harry Poyner Stimson, Aug. 12, 1943 (dec.); children—Harry Richard, Jane Stimson Schweitzer, Cynthia Stimson Howe, Denise Stimson Anderson, Scott R., Jeffrey D.; m. Robert W. Duffield, Oct. 16, 1970. Ph.B., Marygrove Coll., Detroit, 1940; postgrad. U. Mich., N.Y. Inst. Fin., U. Pa. Wharton Sch. Fin., U. Detroit, Oakland U. Mem. Signal Corps Ground Signal Service, 1941-44; stockbroker Bache & Co., 1960-65; asst. mgr. Paine Webber Jackson & Curtis, Detroit, 1965-70, v.p., 1970—; lectr. Pres. Detroit Osteo. Hosp. Aux; trustee Marygrove Coll., also charter mem. president's council; trustee Providence Hosp. Found. Recipient Outstanding Vol. award Mich. chpt. Nat. Soc. Fundraising Execs., 1984. Mem. Mich. Women's Osteo. Assn. (pres.), Women in Fin., N.Y. Stock Exchange, Mich. Security Dealers, Mich. Ins. Underwriters Nat. Assn. Republican. Roman Catholic. Clubs: Zonta, Recess, Detroit Golf. Home: 161 Hendrie Blvd Royal Oak MI 48067

STIMSON, MIRIAM MICHAEL, educational administrator; b. Chgo., Dec. 24, 1913; d. Frank Sharpe and Mary Frances (Holland) S.; B.S., Siena Heights Coll., 1936; M.S., Instn. Divi Thomae, Cin., 1939, Ph.D., 1948. Joined Adrian Dominican Sisters, Roman Catholic Ch., 1935; mem. faculty Siena Heights Coll., Adrian, Mich., 1939-68, chmn. chemistry dept., 1948-68, dir. grad. studies, 1978—; research assoc. Fla. State U., Tallahassee, 1969; prof. Keuka Coll., Keuka Park, N.Y., 1969-78; lectr. Canisius Coll., 1961; mem. screening panel NSF, 1963. Speaker Ch. Women United, Penn Yan, N.Y., v.p., 1973-74, pres., 1974-76; chmn. pub. events com. Keuka Coll. Campaign 1970, Penn Yan, 1970-72; mem. Lenawee County Profl. Devel. Policy Bd., 1976—, chmn., 1979-80; mem. Lenawee County Home Health Care Adv. Bd., 1981—, chmn., 1982-86; exec. com., bd. dirs. Mich. Consortium of Substance Abuse Edn., 1984-87. Mem. Am. Chem. Soc., Nat. Assn. Women Deans, Mich. Assn. Women Deans, AAUW. Home: 1126 E Siena Heights Dr Adrian MI 49221 Office: 1247 E Siena Heights Dr Adrian MI 49221

STINNETT, SUSAN SMITH, nurse; b. Detroit, Sept. 14, 1955; d. Herman Colvin Smith and Hazel Manoka (Lyons) Janke; B.S. in Nursing, U. Ariz., 1984. Postgrad. Northwestern U., Shreveport, La. R.N., Ariz., Nev. Dental lab. technician Lessner Dental Lab., Tucson, 1973-77; nursing med. asst. Nursefinders, Tucson, 1979-82, 83, 84; nurse So. Nev. Meml. Hosp., Las Vegas, 1984; care unit nurse Hosp. Nev., Las Vegas, 1984-86; nurse Schumpert Med. Ctr., Shreveport, 1986—. Editor jour. Dental Capacity. Served with U.S. Army, 1973-76. Mem. Vietnam Vets. Las Vegas. Mem. Ch. of Christ. Avocations: cycling; embroidery; knitting; film making; creative writing. Home: 8500 Jackson Sq 4-H Shreveport LA 71115 Office: Schumpert Med Ctr 915 Margaret Pl Shreveport LA

STINSON, MARY FLORENCE, nursing educator; b. Wheeling, W.Va., Feb. 11, 1931; d. Rolland Francis and Mary Angela (Voellinger) Kellogg; m. Charles Walter Stinson, Feb. 12, 1955; children—Kenneth Charles, Karen Marie, Kathryn Anne. B.S. in Nursing, Coll. Mt. St. Joseph, 1953, postgrad., 1983; M.Ed., Xavier U., Cin., 1967; postgrad. U. Cin., 1981. Staff nurse contagious disease ward Cin. Gen. Hosp., 1953-54, asst. head nurse med. and polio wards, 1955, acting head nurse, clin. instr., 1955-56; instr. St. Francis Hosp. Sch. Practical Nursing, Cin., 1956-57; instr. Good Samaritan Hosp. Sch. Nursing, Cin., 1957-65; instr. refresher courses for nurses Cin. Bd. Edn. and Ohio State Nurses Assn. Dist. 8, 1967-70; coordinator sch. health office Coll. Mt. St. Joseph (Ohio), 1969-72, instr. dept. nursing, 1975-79, asst. prof., 1979—. Charter mem. Adoptive Parents Assn. St. Joseph Infant and Maternity Home; active Women's Com. for Performing Arts Series, Coll. Mt. St. Joseph; mem. St. Antoninus Rosary Altar Rosary and Sch. Soc., St. Antoninus Athletic Club, com. chmn., 1969-70; bd. dirs. Coll. Mt. St. Joseph Alumnae Assn., sec., 1968-69, v.p., 1969-70, pres., 1970-71, chmn. revision of constn., 1976-77; homecoming chmn. Coll. Mt. St. Joseph, 1970, co-chmn., 1977; mem. Gamble Nippert YMCA. Mem. Am. Nurses Assn., Ohio Nurses Assn., Southwestern Ohio Nurses Assn., AAUP. Democrat. Roman Catholic. Club: River Squares (v.p. 1967). Home: 5549 Cleander Dr Cincinnati OH 45238 Office: College Mount Saint Joseph 5701 Delhi Mount Saint Joseph OH 45051

STIP, CATHERINE ANN, contracts administrator, interior designer; b. Canton, Ohio, Mar. 10, 1943; d. Joseph, Jr., and Anna Catherine (Wiley) Sekely; m. Arthur Wayne Stip, Feb. 15, 1975; 1 child, Arthur Wayne. Student interior design Parsons Sch. Design, Los Angeles, 1984—; student bus. adminstrn. and interior design Orange Coast Coll., 1983—. Sec. to various execs. Los Angeles area, 1962-70; contracts coordinator Murdock, Inc., Carson, Calif., 1974-75; contracts adminstr. AHF-Ducommun, Gardena, Calif., 1970-74, 78—, owner Catherine Ann Interiors, Huntington Beach, Calif., 1985—; cons. Artistic Interiors, Fountain Valley, 1984, Trans Designs, Ga., 1984-85. Mem. Nat. Assn. Female Execs., Huntington Beach C. of C., Nat. Secs. Assn. (sec. 1974-75), Childrens Home Soc. Orange County. Democrat. Avocations: art; cooking; sewing; jogging; sailing. Home: 16391 Fairway Ln Huntington Beach CA 92649 Office: AHF-Ducommun 131 E Gardena Blvd Gardena CA 90247

STIPE, JEAN ELIZABETH, nurse; b. Easton, Pa., Sept. 23, 1933; d. Charles and Margaret (Schnell) Boyer; diploma St. Lukes Hosp. Sch. Nursing, 1954; m. Edwin Stipe, Aug. 14, 1954; children—Daniel, Kelly. Staff nurse community hosps., Easton, Pa., 1957-59, Phillipsburg, N.J., 1961-62, Mt. Kisco, N.Y., 1964-66, Needham, Mass., 1969-71; head nurse neurology unit Lyons (N.J.) VA Hosp., 1971-85, utilization rev. coordinator, 1985—. Mem. Nurses Orgn. VA (chpt. officer). Contbr. article to profl. jour. Home: 70 Queen Ann Dr Basking Ridge NJ 07920 Office: Lyons VA Hospital Lyons NJ 07939

STIRLING, ANNE ADAMS, marketing and public relations executive; b. Shaw AFB, S.C., Mar. 7, 1944; d. John Adrian and Mary Margaret (Rogers) Butler; B.A. in Edn. and Bus. Edn., La. State U., 1965, M.B.A., 1970; M.A. in Journalism, U. Nev.-Reno, 1982; m. Evan M. Stirling, Dec. 9, 1977. Tchr. public high schs., La., Ga., N.C., 1965-69; loan officer City State Bank, Honolulu, 1969-72; asst. credit mgr. Trailmobile Inc., Dallas, 1972-74; credit and collections mgr. Lear Corp., Reno, 1974-75; gaming supr. Del Webb's, Reno, 1976-77; gaming supr. Summa Corp., Reno, 1977-80; editor Bus. Monitor/Vigen Publs., Sparks, Nev., 1980-81; founder Kamerus Labs., Reno, 1982; dir. Mansfield Bank & Trust Co. (La.). Mem. Pub. Relations Soc. Am., Internat. Assn. Bus. Communicators, Am. Mktg. Assn., Acad. Health Services Mktg., Market Research Assn., Nat. Assn. Female Execs. Republican. Methodist. Club: Mansfield Country, Hidden Valley Country. Office: PO Box 6317 Reno NV 89513

STITH, KATE, legal educator; b. St. Louis, Mar. 16, 1951; d. Richard Taylor and Ann Carter (See) Stith; m. José A. Cabranes, Sept. 15, 1984. B.A., Dartmouth Coll., 1973; M.P.P., Kennedy Sch. Govt., Harvard U., 1977, J.D., 1977. Bar: D.C. Law clk. U.S. Supreme Ct., Washington, 1978-79; economist, Dept. Justice, Washington, 1979-80, spl. asst., 1980-81; asst. U.S. atty., U.S. Atty. So. Dist. N.Y., N.Y.C., 1981-84; assoc. prof. Yale U. Law Sch., New Haven, 1984—. Contbr. chpt. to book, articles to legal rev. Mem. Phi Beta Kappa. Roman Catholic. Home: 65 Sperry Rd Bethany CT 06525 Office: Yale Law School New Haven CT

STITH, ROBIN SUZAN, lawyer, educator; b. Ft. Wayne, Ind., Jan. 16, 1956; d. Harold and Hana Lee (Bryant) S.; m. Kenneth James, Sept. 7, 1980. B.A., Northwestern U., 1977; J.D., Georgetown U., 1980. Bar: Ohio 1980. Legal intern EPA, Washington, 1977-79; educator high sch. law, Street Law Inst., Washington, 1978-79, adults, 1979-80; mem. Beatty & Stith, Columbus, Ohio, 1980—; educator Am. Paralegal Inst., Columbus, 1983—; spl. counsel Ohio atty gen., Columbus, 1983—; hearing officer Ohio Dept. Adminstrv. Services, 1984. Guest editor Columbus Call and Post, 1984. Trustee Nat. Urban League, 1981; v.p. Alliance of Black Women, 1983—; pres. Met. Community Services, 1984—; trustee Century Found., Columbus, 1984—; chmn., treas. Beatty for State Rep. Campaign, Columbus, 1982, 84; mem. speakers bur. Met. Women's Club, 1983—. Mem. ABA, Ohio State Bar Assn., Columbus Bar Assn. (speakers bur.), Assn. Trial Lawyers Am., Women Lawyers Franklin County. Methodist. Home: 7623 Coronado Blvd S Reynoldsburg OH 43068 Office: Beatty & Stith 233 S High St Suite 300 Columbus OH 43215

STITT, SUSAN MARGARET, museum administrator; b. East Liverpool, Ohio, Jan. 24, 1942; d. Wilson Montgomery and Cora Blanche (Link) S.; B.A. in Am. History, Coll. William and Mary, 1964; M.A. in Am. Civilization, U. Pa., 1966. Asst. to dir. Hist. Soc. of Pa., Phila., 1966; dir. Mus. of Albemarle, Elizabeth City, N.C., 1967-68; adminstr. Mus. of Early So. Decorative Arts, Winston-Salem, N.C., 1969-71; asst. to dir. Bklyn. Mus., 1971-72; project dir. survey of placement and tng. Nat. Endowment for Humanities, Old Sturbridge Village, Sturbridge, Mass., 1972-74; dir. Museums at Stony Brook (N.Y.), 1974—; adj. asso. prof. dept. art SUNY, Stony Brook, 1975-78. Mem. Am.

Assn. Mus., N.Y. State Assn. (pres.), Am. Assn. State and Local History, L.I. Mus. Assn., N.Y. State Assn. Mus. (v.p.). Office: The Museums at Stony Brook 1208 Route 25A Stony Brook NY 11790

STIVERS, ANN EVELYN, delivery co. exec.; b. Casper, Wyo., Oct. 26, 1948; d. Winthrop Newcomb and Merva (Culver) S.; B.S., Tex. Woman's U., 1970. Tchr., Dallas, 1971-75; with United Parcel Service, 1975—, mgr., Little Rock, 1978—. Republican. Presbyterian. Office: UPS 8121 Distribution Dr Little Rock AR 72209

STNALEY, JEAN AGATHA FULLER, chemistry educator; b. White Hall, St. Thomas, Jamaica, Sept. 17, 1951; came to U.S., 1978; d. Clifford Alexander and Lovina Rebecca (Wilson) Fuller; m. Ernie Stanley, Oct. 4, 1976; children—Sofia, Nadia. B.Sc. with honors, U. London, 1976; M.S. in Chemistry, U. Nebr., 1980, Ph.D. in Organic Chemistry, 1984. Teaching asst. U. Nebr., Lincoln, 1978-84; asst. prof. chemistry Wellesley Coll., Mass., 1984—. Mem. Am. Chem. Soc., Royal Soc. Chemistry, Am. Inst. Chemistry, Phi Lambda Upsilon, Sigma Xi. Avocations: sports; music; dancing; reading; sewing. Office: Wellesley Coll Science Ctr Wellesley MA 02181

STOCK, BARBARA M., psychologist; b. Pitts., May 4, 1943; d. Samuel M. and Hilda (Marmins) Morris; B.A., Chatham Coll., 1964; Ph.D., U. Mich., 1972; div.; children—Aric, Adam, Michael. Cons., Ky. Infant Presch. Project, Dept. Econ. Security, Frankfort, 1972; asst. prof. dept. spl. edn. Eastern Ky. U., Richmond, 1972-74; instr. parent courses, Lexington, Ky., London, Eng., 1972-75; stringer, feature writer Suburban Tribune, Hinsdale, Ill., 1977-81; pvt. practice clin. psychology, Wilmette, Ill., 1980—; staff psychologist One to One Learning Center, Wilmette, 1980-83; psychologist Lake County Mental Health, Round Lake Park, Ill., 1983-85, Mt. Sinai hosp., Chgo., 1985—. Mem. Ky. Gov.'s Ad Hoc Com. for Programs for Children with Behavioral Disorders, 1972; mem. Lake County Task Force for Sexual Abuse. Mem. Am. Psychol. Assn., Ill. Psychol. Assn., Internat. Transactional Analysis Assn., Phi Beta Kappa. Home: 930 Linden Ave Wilmette IL 60091 Office: Pediatric Ecology Program Mt Sinai Hosp 15th and California Chicago IL

STOCKANES, HARRIET PRICE, publishing executive, consultant; b. Crawford, Nebr., Oct. 31, 1923; d. Joseph Hartwell and Lyda Marie (Chadderdon) Price; m. Robert Ward O'Brien, Dec. 28, 1946 (div. Aug. 1964); children—Nan O'Brien Beman, Julia O'Brien Domingue, Lewis W.; m. 2d, Anthony Edward Stockanes, Jan. 7, 1966. Student Carleton Coll., 1941-43; A.B., U. Wis., 1945. Sec., Bitker & Marshall, Milw., 1945-46, Hale & Dorr, Boston, 1946-47; underwriter Standard Annuity & Life Ins. Co., Champaign, Ill., 1964-67; sec. U. Ill., Champaign, 1967-75; rights mgr. U. Ill. Press, Champaign, 1975—. Village clk., Park Forest, Ill., 1950-54. Republican. Home: 2201 E Vermont Ave Urbana IL 61801 Office: U Ill Press 54 E Gregory Dr Champaign IL 61820

STOCKDALE, GAYLE SUE, wholesale florist, ornamental horticulturalist; b. Crawfordsville, Ind., July 3, 1955; d. Robert Lavern and Faye Louise (Ball) S. Student St. Joseph's Coll., 1973-74, Purdue U., 1974; B.S. in Tech. Horticulture, Eastern Ky. U., 1977. Reclamation foreman South East Coal Co., Irvine, Ky., 1977-79; asst. mgr., landscape designer Evergreen Garden Ctr., Lexington, Ky., 1979-80; asst. mgr., landscape designer, head grower South Trail Garden Ctr., Ft. Myers, Fla., 1980-82; floral designer Flowers by Jean, Cape Coral, Fla., 1982-83; floral designer, landscape designer Bev's Greenhouse, Owenton, Ky., 1983-84; co-owner Royalty Wholesale, Lexington, 1984—. Contbr. poetry to anthologies. Sponsor, Save the Children, Korea, 1986. Moose lodge scholar, 1973, band scholar St. Joseph's Coll., 1974. Mem. Nat. Assn. Female Execs. Avocations: reading; movies; exercise. Democrat. Roman Catholic. Office: Royalty Wholesale 322 W 3d St Lexington KY 40508

STOCKDALE, SALLY BOYD, artist; b. Coral Gables, Fla., Apr. 20, 1941; d. Edward Grant Stockdale and Alice Boyd (Magruder) Proudfoot; m. David Michael deWilde, Dec. 21, 1968 (div. 1978); children—Holland Stockdale, Christian duCroix; m. Mariano Eduardo Munoz-Lopez, Mar. 26, 1981. A.A., Bennett Coll., Millbrook, N.Y., 1961; postgrad. Trinity Coll., Dublin, Ireland, 1962; B.F.A., Am. U., 1980; postgrad. Corcoran Sch. Art, Washington, 1980—. Painter, one-woman shows include: Tahiti Gallery, Marbella, Spain, 1978, Dumbarton Series, Washington, 1982; commd. murals include Children's Hosp., Washington; represented in permanent collection Folger Library, Washington; portrait artist state and fed. legislators, others; illustrator Holiday Mag., 1963-68, Spanien Jour., 1979; book illustrator: The Dreadful Day, 1981, Patrick, 16 Centuries, 1983. Work featured in Washington Evening Star, 1971, Washington Post, 1984. Mem. Artists Equity, NOW, Nat. Mus. Women in Arts. Democrat. Episcopalian. Home: 4719 Chesapeake St NW Washington DC 20016

STOCKMAN, JUDITH FAE, manufacturing company executive, nurse; b. Pratt, Kans., Sept. 15, 1939; d. Forrest Muir and Eva Mae (Bradley) Doan; m. Earl D. Stockman, May 30, 1959 (div. 1977); children—Travis, Terry, Tamara. R.N., U. So. Calif., 1960, postgrad. in orthopedics, 1961; B.S., Chapman Coll., 1978; postgrad U. Calif.-Long Beach, 1979. Cert. adult nurse practitioner, occupational health nurse, workers' compensation adminstr. Nursing supr., orthopedic clinician Gallatin Med. Group, Downey, Calif., 1961-65; office mgr., clinician Dr. William Nelson, Lynwood, Calif., 1965-70; mgr. med. services and worker's compensation Weiser Co. div. NI Industries Corp., Huntington Beach, Calif., 1973-78, mgr. div. loss control, 1978—; instr. U. Calif.-Irvine, 1980—. Editor, contbr. Protocol Guide for Occupational Health Nurses, 1980. Co-chmn. occupational health com. Am. Lung Assn., Los Angeles; v.p. spl. projects Whittier Union Sch. Dist. PTA, 1971-74. Mem. Assn. Occupational Health Nurses Calif. (pres. 1983-85), Calif. Assn. Occupational Health Nurses (pres. 1983—), Am. Heart Assn. (high blood pressure control council), Calif. Mfrs. Assn., Workers' Compensation Def. Forum, Workers' Compensation Claims Assn., Chi Rho. Republican. Baptist. Home: 14736 Dunton Dr Whittier CA 90604 Office: NI Industries 5555 McFadden Ave Huntington Beach CA 92649

STODDARD, LINDA GANDRUD, veterinarian; b. Owatonna, Minn., Apr. 28, 1944; d. Ebenhard S. and Edith M. (Christensen) G.; m. Hannis L. Stoddard, Jr., July 10, 1973; children—Ebenhard C., Ryan M., Dahlen Ross. B.S. in Edn., U. Minn., 1966, B.S. in Vet. Medicine, 1968, D.V.M., 1970. Veterinarian, Dueland Animal Clinic, S.I., N.Y., 1970-72; dir. advt. Gandy Co., Owatonna, 1972-74, corp. dir., 1962—; owner Branford Vet. Clinic, Inc., Fla., 1974-83, Shamrock Vet. Clinic and Fisheries, fish diseases and aquaculture mgmt., Cross City, Fla., 1984—; guest lectr. U. Fla. Coll. Vet. Medicine, 1978-82; tchr. physics Branford High Sch., 1984. Grant writer Branford Sch. Adv. Council, 1982-84. State of Fla. grantee, 1983. 84. Mem. AVMA, Suwannee Valley Vet. Med. Assn. (pres. 1980—), Am. Animal Hosp. Assn., Fla. Vet. Med. Assn., Am. Heartworm Soc., Alpha Delta Kappa. Avocations: reading; music; architecture.

STODGHILL, RUTH LAUNA, real estate executive; b. Beaumont, Tex., Apr. 2, 1944; d. Hayward Olin and Hazel Lee (Alford) S. B.A., Lamar U., 1966. Free-lance appraiser; staff appraiser Suburban Coastal Mortgage, Houston, 1981; pres. Stodghill & Assos., Houston, 1982—. mem. fee panel VA, Houston, 1983—. Chmn. ecology com. Young Republicans, Houston, 1970. Fellow Internat. Inst. Valuers, Assn. Profl. Mortgage Women; mem. Soc. Real Estate Appraisers (speakers bur.). Republican. Home: 4253 Albans St Houston TX 77005 Office: Stodghill and Associates 6633 Hillcroft Suite 212 Houston TX 70018

STOECKMANN, ETHEL DOLORES, fin. exec.; b. N.Y.C., July 4, 1922; d. Albert Lewis and Ethel Carol (Wade) Infantas; student public schs., N.Y.C.; m. Sept. 17, 1944; 1 son, Robert W. Sec./treas. Stoeckmann Land Co., Inc., Baudette, Minn., 1972—, Stoeckmann Ranches, Inc., Red Bluff, Calif., 1976—, Stoeckmann Farms, Inc., Pecos Tex., 1977—, dir., 1951—; partner Stoeckmann & Co., 1972—, S & S Enterprises, Baudette, 1976—, Stoeckmann Investment Co., Red Bluff, 1976—. Democrat. Home: PO Box 2017 Pecos TX 79772 Office: Route 2 PO Box 24 Red Bluff CA 96080

STOERKER, HOLLY EILEEN, association executive, water resources analyst; b. Oak Park, Ill., May 24, 1953; d. Theodor Frederick and Joyce Clair (Thomson) S. B.A., Macalester Coll., 1975; M. Planning, U. Minn. Hubert H. Humphrey Inst. Pub. Affairs, 1979. Clk. supr. Minn. Dept. transp. St. Paul, 1975-76; water resources planner Upper Mississippi River Basin Commn., Bloomington, Minn., 1977-82; program dir. Upper Mississippi River Basin Assn., Bloomington, 1982-83, exec. dir., St. Paul, 1983—; teaching asst. Macalester Coll., St. Paul, 1974; research asst. Hubert H. Humphrey Inst. Mpls., 1976-77. Vol. Minn. Civil Liberties Union, Mpls., 1972, Legal Assistance of Ramsey County (Minn.), 1973. Recipient Disting. Service award Upper Mississippi River Basin Commn., 1981. Mem. Phi Beta Kappa. Office: Upper Mississippi River Basin Assn 408 Saint Peter St St Paul MN 55102

STOFER, PATRICIA ANNE, land development executive; b. Gregory, S.D., Aug. 6, 1950; d. Charles Blaine and Theresa Kathryn (Janak) Show; m. John Lind Stofer, Jan. 27, 1973 (div. June 1979); children—Nicole E., John M. Student, U. Colo., 1968-69, U. Houston, 1977-78. Stewardess, Frontier Airlines, Dallas, 1970-73; property mgr. Maxwell-Cottrell, Houston, 1978-78; mktg. dir. Ashford Properties, Houston, 1978-79; program dir. West Houston Assn., 1979-83; v.p. Landar Corp., Houston, 1984—; dir. Harris County Mcpl. Utility Dist. #225, Houston, 1983—. Mem. West Houston C. of C. (dir.). Republican. Baptist. Club: Houston Christian Women's (chmn. 1975-77). Lodge: Women of Rotary.

STOIK, MARY ELIZABETH, corporate administrator, risk mgr.; b. Clinton, Iowa, Oct. 31, 1952; d. Lloyd P. and Mary (Johnson) Stoik. B.A., U. S.D., Vermillion, 1975. Paralegal firm Ross Hardies, Chgo., 1975-77, firm Calkins & Kramer, Denver, 1977-79, firm Holland and Hart, Denver, 1979-81; corp. affairs adminstr., risk mgr. asst. sec. Axem Resources, Denver, 1981—; asst. sec. Laser Oil Co., Axroyalty Inc.; corp. sec. Axem Found. Active Denver Sym. Orch., 1982-85, choreographer for local dance co., 1982-85. Mem. Risk Ins. Mgrs. Soc., Delta Phi Alpha, Phi Alpha Theta, Pi Beta Phi (v.p., 1974-75). Home: 1616 S Grant St Denver CO 80810 Office: Axem Resources Inc 7800 East Union Ave Suite 1100 Denver CO 80237

STOKES, CELESTE TYRRELL, lawyer; b. Bremerton, Wash., Apr. 11, 1955; d. Gale and Diane (Wilcox) Stokes. B.A., U. Wash., 1977; J.D. cum laude, Gonzaga U., 1981. Bar: Wash. 1981, Alaska 1982, U.S. Dist. Ct. Alaska, U.S. Dist. Ct. (we. dist. Wash.). Law clk. to judge Superior Ct., Anchorage, Alaska, 1981-82; law clk. to judge Alaska Ct. Appeals, Anchorage, 1982-83; instr. law U. Alaska, Eagle River Correctional Facility, Alaska, 1982-83; dep. pros. atty. King County, Seattle, 1984—. Mem. ABA, Wash. State Bar Assn., Alaska State Bar Assn. Methodist.

STOKES, DEBRA LYNN, educational administrator, business educator; b. Cin., Sept. 26, 1959; d. Wesley Wright and Annie (Stokes) O'Neille. B.S. in Bus. Edn., Fla. A&M U., 1980. Cert. secondary tchr., Fla. Sec., Leon County Schs., Tallahassee, 1981-84; instr. Century Coll., Tallahassee, 1984—, dir. edn., 1985—; curriculum cons. Orr-iginals Fashion Inst., Tallahassee, 1985. Co-writer: Decision, 1980. Researcher, Jesse Jackson for Pres. Campaign, Fla., 1984. Recipient Outstanding Service award Helena Barrington Crusades, 1981. Mem. Tallahassee Urban League, Nat. Black Voters Assn., Fla. Assn. Private Schs., Tallahassee Area C. of C., Phi Beta Lambda, Pi Omega Pi. Democrat. Avocations: singing; reading; acting; travel. Home: 3102 Parkridge Dr Tallahassee FL 32304 Office: Century Coll 2520 N Monroe St Suite 260 Tallahassee FL 32303

STOKES, GAIL ELIZABETH, advertising executive; b. Cambridge, Mass., Sept. 14, 1949; d. John Francis and Margaret Cecilia (MacDonnell) Stokes; children—Sarah Chardo, Alex Chardo. B.A. in English, Salem State Coll., 1972. Advt. exec. Jordan Marsh, Boston, 1972-75; advt. dir. James Bliss Marine, Dedham, Mass., 1975-78; freelance writer, designer, Concord, Mass., 1978-84; catalog and direct mail mgr. Dennison Mfg., Framingham, Mass., 1985-86; account exec. Concord Mail Mktg., Mass., 1986—. Bookbuilders of Boston scholar, 1984. Mem. New Eng. Direct Mail Assn., Women in Communications, Nat. Assn. Female Execs. Democrat. Roman Catholic. Club: White Pond Garden (publicity chmn. 1978-84). Avocations: swimming; gardening; raising bulldogs. Home: 62 Eaton St Concord MA 01742

STOKKE, DIANE REES, lawyer; b. Kansas City, Mo., Jan. 29, 1951; d. William James and MaryBeth (Smith) Rees; m. Larry Ernst Stokke, June 9, 1973; children—Michelle, Megan. A.B. magna cum laude, Gonzaga U., 1972; J.D. with high honors, U. Wash., 1976. Bar: Wash. 1976. Assoc. firm Preston, Thorgrimson, Ellis & Holman, Seattle, 1976—; ptnr. 1983—. Mem. law rev. staff U. Wash. Law Rev., 1974-76, notes editor, 1975-76, author, 1976. Atty. Seattle Ctr. Found., 1977—. Acad. scholar Gonzaga U., 1968. Mem. ABA, Seattle-King County Bar Assn., Wash. State Bar Assn., Wash. Women Lawyers. Roman Catholic. Home: 2608 10th Ave E Seattle WA 98102 Office: Preston Thorgrimson Ellis & Holman 5400 Columbia Sea First Ctr 701 Fifth Ave Seattle WA 98111

STOKLOSA, JANIS HELENA, psychologist, air safety investigator; b. Panama C.Z., Oct. 13, 1946; d. Joseph Francis and Helena Ann (Wolosz) S. A.B., Emmanuel Coll., 1968; Ph.D., Harvard U., 1976. Teaching fellow, lectr. Harvard U., 1970-77; psychol. cons. spl. edn. program Basics, Inc., Charlestown, Mass., 1977-78; project asst. dir. MIT, 1978-80; engring. psychologist Transp. Systems Ctr., Cambridge, Mass., 1978-80; air. safety investigator Nat. Transp. Safety Bd., Washington, 1980-85; aircraft ops. specialist NASA Hdqrs., Washington, 1985—; lectr. Armed Forces Inst. Pathology, 1984; guest lectr. MIT, 1980; mem. human factors adv. com. Office of Sec., Dept. Transp., 1983. Contbg. mem. Smithsonian Mus., Washington; vol. Boston Symphony Orch., 1980. Recipient spl. service award Nat. Transp. Safety Bd., 1981, 82, 83, 84; New Eng. Psychol. Assn. undergrad. fellow. Mem. Am. Psychol. Assn., Human Factors Soc., Aerospace Med. Assn., Assn. Aviation Psychologists, Women's Transp. Seminar, Boston Mus. Fine Arts, Mass. Fedn. Polish Women, Sigma Xi, Psi Chi, Kappa Gamma Pi. Clubs: Harvard, FAA Flying. Home: 2801 Park Ctr Dr Alexandria VA 22302 Office: NASA Hdqrs NF 400 Maryland Ave SW Washington DC 20546

STOLL, PATRICIA ANN, office services manager; b. Corpus Christi, Tex., Oct. 4, 1954; d. Edward and Mable (Davis) Sheridan; m. Merritt Russell Stoll., Nov. 25, 1978; 1 dau., Michelle Lynn. Student Del Mar Coll., 1972-75. Compensation asst. Riviana Foods, Houston, 1980-81, personnel adminstr., 1981-82, office services mgr., 1983—. Mem. Assn. Personnel Adminstrn., Southwest Communications. Roman Catholic. Address: Riviana Foods Inc 2777 Allen Pkwy Houston TX 77252

STOLLER, IRENE DAVIS, librarian; b. Edinburgh, Scotland; d. Ellis and Alice (Davis) Stoller; m. Irving Gitomer, Dec. 23, 1944 (div. 1975); children—David, Jonathan, Philip, Ellen, Daniel. B.A., Rutgers Univ., 1961; M.S. in L.S., Drexel U., 1962. Adminstrv. asst. to dean Drexel Grad. Sch. Library Sci., Phila., 1960, dir. pub. relations, 1961, instr., 1965; dir. Cherry Hill (N.J.) Free Pub Library, 1962-70; library cons., 1970-71; dir. Oldbridge (N.J.) Free Pub. Library, 1971-75; head Central Library, Contra Costa County Library, 1976-79; head Extension Services, Phoenix Pub. Library, 1980; asst. dir. Madison (Wis.) Pub. Library, 1980-84; dir. Paramus (N.J.) Pub. Library, 1984—; instr. Drexel U., Phila. Community Coll., 1968-69, Glassboro State Coll., 1969. Author: The Trustee and Personnel, 1970, rev., 1983. Mem., Burlington County Human Relations Commn.; bd. dirs. Drexel U. Alumni, 1974-76. Mem. ALA, Am. Trustee Assn., N.J. Trustee Assn., SLA, Library Pub. Relations Council, Catholic Library Assn., Jewish Library Assn., N.J. Library Assn. (mem. at large exec. bd. 1972-75), Camden County Library Assn. (pres. 1968-69), ACLU (exec. bd. So. Jersey), League Women Voters, Women's Polit. Caucus, Beta Phi Mu, Phi Kappa Phi, Club: Zonta (chmn. service project 1965). Address: 119 Lafayette Ave Hawthorne NJ 07506

STOLP, LOUISE VAUGHN, personnel administrator, counselor; b. Nashville, Aug. 31, 1934; d. Shurley L. and Lena (George) Vaughn; m. James A. Stolp, Apr. 3, 1953; children—Phyllis, Patrick, Stephen. A.A. in Mgmt., Belmont Coll., 1983, B.S. in Psychology, 1986. Exec. asst. Tenn. Baptist Conv., Brentwood, Tenn., 1967-76; personnel adminstr. ITT Automotive Distbrs., Nashville, 1977-79; adminstrv. asst. Vanderbilt U. Sch. Engring., Nashville, 1981-82, asst. to human resources dir. med. ctr., 1982-85, counselor admitting, 1985—. Vol., Action Auction, 1974-75, Am. Assn. Retarded Persons, 1985-86. Belmont Coll. grantee, 1985-86. Mem. Nat. Assn. Female Execs., Am. Soc. Personnel Adminstrs., Profl. Secs. Internat. Baptist. Avocations: amber glass collector; stamp collector; square dancing. Home: 824 Heritage Trail Hermitage TN 37076 Office: Vanderbilt U Med Ctr Admitting Office 21st and Garland Nashville TN 37235

STOLTZ, NORMA LOUISE MEHRHOFF, travel company executive, lecturer, consultant; b. St. Louis, Apr. 30, 1947; d. Louis James and Melba Katherine (Weber) Mehrhoff; m. James Clark Stoltz, Apr. 26, 1980. Student Washington U., St. Louis, 1967-69. Adminstrv. asst. Govt. Resarch Inst., St. Louis, 1965-67; asst. to chmn. dept. psychology Washington U., 1967-82; exec. dir. Horizon Seminars, St. Louis, 1982—; v.p. Service Travel Co.; cons. in career devel. and exec. etiquette; dir. Service Horizons, Inc. Instr., Thomas Dunn Memorials Adult Edn. Program, St. Louis, 1974—. Mem. com. Carousel Restoration Com., St. Louis, 1984—. Mem. Nat. Soc. Tole and Decorative Painters (pres. St. Louis, 1976), Travel Trust Internat., Nat. Assn. Female Execs. Republican. Presbyterian. Avocations: painting; travel; creative writing; calligraphy; needlework. Home: 13320 Woodlake Village Ct Saint Louis MO 63141 Office: Horizon Seminars 6421 Hampton Ave Saint Louis MO 63109

STONE, BARBARA FROST, speech pathologist; b. Robinson, Ill., Feb. 13, 1929; d. Virgil Elsworth and Nancy Brittimer (Sutfin) Frost; B.S., Eastern Ill. State Coll., 1951; M.A., St. Louis U., 1965; m. Neville Stone, Feb. 2, 1974; children—Nancy, Michael. Instr., St.-Mary of-the-Woods (Ind.) Coll., 1953-55; speech clinician Spl. Sch. Dist. St. Louis County (Mo.), 1958-63; instr. St. Louis U. Sch. Medicine, 1963-65; cons. Mo. Crippled Children's Service, St. Louis, 1967-74; instr., exec. dir. cleft palate div. Washington U. Sch. Medicine, 1974-75; cons. speech pathology, Chesterfield, Mo., 1981—. Asst. to dep. dir. George Bush Nat. Polit. Campaign, Alexandria, Va., 1980. Mem. Am. Speech, Hearing, Lang. Assn., Am. Cleft Palate Assn. Republican. Presbyterian. Clubs: Forest Hills Country, Clayton. Home: 14928 Manor Lake Dr Chesterfield MO 63017

STONE, BETTY RUTH BOYLS, editor; b. West Point, Miss., Mar. 3, 1930; d. Gaston Dean and Mary Frances (Yeates) Boyls; A.B., Miss. U. Women, 1951, M.S., 1972; m. Douglas Clyde Stone, July 8, 1951; children—Nora Frances Stone McRae, Kate Terrell Stone Rogers, Diana Gaston Futrell Stone. Med. lab. technologist, 1951-53; recruiting counselor Miss U. Women, Columbus, 1965-67, instr. physiology lab., 1972-74; editor Showcase publ. Columbus Civic Arts Council, 1981—. Pres., Columbus Jr. Aux, 1963, Demonstration PTA, 1966, Les Amis Club, Four Seasons Club, Lawyers Wives Club. Mem. Beta Beta Beta, Gamma Sigma Epsilon, Pi Kappa Delta. Methodist.

STONE, DEBORAH ANN, lawyer; b. New Castle, Pa., Oct. 6, 1949; d. Martin Albert and Ilona Jean (Stevenson) Holtzapple; m. Richard Courtney Stone, Aug. 22, 1970; 1 son, Thomas Martin. B.S. in Edn., Bowling Green State U., 1972; J.D., Woodrow Wilson Coll. Law, 1981. Bar: Ga. 1981. Routing clk. Kent State U., Ohio, 1970-71; reader/advisor Bookmobile, State of Ohio Library, Napoleon, 1971-72; tchr. history Gwinnett County Schs., Lawrenceville, Ga., 1973-80; ptnr. firm Davis Kirsch & Stone, Atlanta, 1983—; lectr. in field. Precinct chmn. Gwinnett County Republican Com., 1979, alt. del. Rep. State Conv., Atlanta, 1979. Mem. ABA, Ga. Bar Assn., Atlanta Bar Assn., Gwinnett Bar Assn. Republican. Home: 3042 Meadow Wood Ct Lawrenceville GA 30245 Office: Davis Kirsch & Stone 1458 Atlanta Center 250 Piedmont Ave NW Atlanta GA 30308

STONE, DENISE MAUREEN, petroleum exploration geologist; b. Summit, N.J., Sept. 2, 1957; d. Joseph J. and Clara (Vandenberg) Stone. B.S. in Geology, Tex. Christian U., 1979; M.S. in Geology, Memphis State U., 1981. Asst. geologist Union Oil Calif., Houston, summers 1978-80; petroleum geologist Superior Oil Internat., Houston, 1981-84, Mobil Exploration and Producing Services Inc., 1985, Amoco Prodn. Co., 1985—. Alumni admissions counselor Tex. Christian U., Ft. Worth, 1980—. Mem. Am. Assn. Petroleum Geologists, Houston Geol. Soc. Home: 1201 Bering Dr Unit 94 Houston TX 77057 Office: Amoco Prodn Co PO Box 3092 Houston TX 77253

STONE, DOROTHY CAROL, lawyer; b. Inglewood, Calif., Apr. 13, 1951; d. John Richard and Mary Ruth (McCoy) Stone; m. Richard Bolado Holloway, July 1, 1972 (div. Oct. 1975); m. Joseph Stephen Broz, May 27, 1978 (div. June 1986). B.A. in Psychology summa cum laude, Calif. State U.-Long Beach, 1974; M.A. in Devel. Psychology, U. Colo., 1977; J.D., Boston U., 1981. Bar: D.C. 1981, Colo. 1983. Teaching asst. U. Colo., Boulder, 1974-77; law clk. Rio Blanco Oil Shale Co., Denver, 1980-81, Sisk, Foley, Hultin & Driver, Washington, 1981; law clk. Tilly & Graves, P.C., Denver, 1982-83, assoc., 1983—. Bd. dirs. Juvenile Offenders in Need, Denver, 1984. Phi Kappa Phi scholar, 1973. Mem. ABA, D.C. Bar Assn., Colo. Bar Assn., Denver Bar Assn., Colo. Women's Bar Assn., Mortar Bd., Phi Alpha Delta. Home: 552 High St Denver CO 80218 Office: Tilly & Graves PC 3773 Cherry Creek North Dr Denver CO 80209

STONE, ELIZABETH WENGER, emeritus dean; b. Dayton, Ohio, June 21, 1918; d. Ezra and Anna Bess (Markey) S.; m. Thomas A. Stone, Sept. 14, 1939; children—John Howard, Anne Elizabeth, James Alexander. A.B., Stanford U., 1937, M.A., 1938; M.L.S., Catholic U. Am., 1961; Ph.D., Am. U., 1968. Tchr. pub. schs., Fontana, Calif., 1938-39; asst. state statistician State of Conn., 1939-40; librarian New Haven Pub. Libraries, 1940-42; dir. pub. relations, asst. to pres. U. Dubuque, Iowa, 1942-46; substitute librarian Pasadena (Calif. Pub. Library System), 1953-60; instr. Cath. U. Am., 1962-63, asst. prof., asst. to chmn. dept. library sci., 1963-67, asso. prof., asst. to chmn., 1967-71, prof., asst. to chmn., 1971-72, prof., chmn. dept., 1972-80, dean Sch. Library and Info. Scis., 1981-83, prof. and dean emeritus, 1983—; exec. dir. Continuing Library Edn. Network and Exchange, 1975-79. Author: Factors Related to the Professional Development of Librarians, 1969; (with James J. Kortendick) Job Dimensions and Educational Needs in Librarianship, 1971; (with R. Patrick and B. Conroy) Continuing Library and Information Science Education, 1974; Continuing Library Education as Viewed in Relation to Other Continuing Professional Movements, 1975; (with F. Peterson and M. Chobot) Motivation: A Vital Force in the Organization, 1977; American Library Development 1600-1899, 1977; (with others) Model Continuing Education Recognition System in Library and Information Science, 1979; (with M.J. Young) A Program for Quality in Continuing Education for Information, Library and Media Personnel, 1980. Editor: D.C. Libraries, 1964-66. Contbr. articles to profl. jours. Program mgr. Nat. Rehab. Center, 1977-83; mem. Pres.'s Com. on Employment of Handicapped, 1972—; pres. D.C. chpt. Am. Mothers, Inc., 1984-85. Mem. ALA (council 1976-83, v.p. 1980-81, pres. 1981-82, chmn. Nat. Library Week 1983-85), D.C. Library Assn. (pres. 1966-67), Spl. Libraries Assn. (pres. D.C. chpt. 1973-74), Assn. Am. Library Schs. (pres. 1974), Am. Soc. Info. Sci., Cath. Library Assn. (hon. life), Am. Soc. Assn. Execs., Phi Sigma Alpha, Beta Phi Mu, Phi Lambda Theta. Presbyterian. Club: Washington. Home: 4000 Cathedral Ave NW Washington DC 20016 Office: Catholic U Am Washington DC 20064

STONE, HELENA, publisher; b. Swanlin Bar, County Cavan, Ireland, July 26, 1942; came to U.S., 1960; d. James Joseph and Margaret Tuohey) McManus; 1 child. Sinead Flattly. Operator N.Y. Telephone Co., N.Y.C., 1960-63; sales mgr. Holiday Inn, Mount Kisco, N.Y., 1966-72; salesman Hudson Pharm., N.J., 1973-75; v.p. V.I.P. Guide-Pubs., Mount Kisco, 1976-82; pres. pub., owner Graphic Art Works Ltd., Quaker Hill, Pawling, N.Y., 1982—. Home: PO Box 48 Quacker Hill Pawling NY 12564

STONE, JOAN KIRKLEY, computer systems consultant; b. Norfolk, Va., Sept. 27, 1947; m. 2 children. B.A. in Math., Coll. of William and Mary, 1969; M.S. in Tech. of Mgmt., Am. U., 1976. Tchr. secondary math. Newport News City Schs., Va., 1969-70; tchr. and chmn. dept. secondary math. York County Pub. Schs., Yorktown, Va., 1970-72; analyst, designer and programmer for redesign of Consumer Price Index System, Bur. Labor Stats., Dept. Labor, Washington, 1972-73, analyst of info. flows and reviewer of data requirements for statis. surveys, 1973-75, project mgr., 1975-79; systems programmer Hercules Inc., Wilmington, Del., 1979-81, sr. tech. support analyst, 1982-85; computer systems cons., Elkton, Md., 1985—; part-time instr. Goldey Beacom Coll., Wilmington, Widener U., Wilmington, U. Del.-Newark. Vice pres. Civic Assn. of Tara, 1983-85; tchr. Sunday Sch., Christiana Presbyterian Ch., 1984-86; mem. com. on women in Ch. of Synod of Piedmont, 1985—; leader Brownie Scouts, Girl Scouts U.S.A., 1985—. Mem. Am. Mgmt. Assn., Brandywine Bus. and Profl. Women (2d v.p. 1981-82, 1st v.p. 1982-83, pres. 1983-84), Soc. for Mgmt. Info. Systems (treas. 1978-79), Phila. Computer Measurement Group (sec.-treas. 1985—). Home and office: 105 Rhett Ct Tara Elkton MD 21921

STONE, JULIE ROSE, real estate developer, investment consultant; b. Los Angeles, July 20, 1941; d. Arthur N. and Julie (Lacknitt) Massaro; m. John B. Stone, Jan. 23, 1969 (div. Oct. 1982); children—Corinne Leann, Jon Douglas Rockwell. A.A., Victor Valley Jr. Coll., 1965; B.A., U. Calif.-Riverside, 1967; postgrad. U. No. Colo., Greeley, 1976. Instr. communications San Bernardino

Valley Jr. Coll., Calif., 1967-69; instr. adult edn. Arapahoe Community Coll., 1970-85; pres., owner Stone/Buckles Real Estate Assocs., Denver, 1976-83; pres., owner Julie Stone Investments, Inc., Denver, 1983—, Cherry Creek Real Estate Ctr., Denver, 1983—; cons. in field. Mem. Nat. Assn. Female Execs., Denver Bd. Realtors, Colo. Assn. Commerce and Industry. Club: Sporting of Cherry Creek. Office: Julie Stone Investments Inc 3773 Cherry Creek N Dr #240 Denver CO 80209

STONE, KATHRYN DOLORES, credit union executive; b. Pontiac, Mich., June 12, 1929; d. Durward South and Betty Marie (LaVelle) Young; student public schs.; m. James Macklin Stone, Oct. 19, 1946; children—James Durward, David Allan. With T&C Fed. Credit Union, Pontiac, 1955—, asst. gen. mgr., teller mgr., acctg. mgr., 1972-77, chief fin. officer, 1977—, treas. bd. dirs., exec. gen. mgr., 1977-83, pres., chief exec. officer, 1977—, exec. com. Credit Union Data Acctg. Council, 1972-74, mem. exec. com. Oakland County (Mich.), chpt. Credit Unions, 1980—; exec. bd. Credit Union Met. Area Advt. Council, Detroit, chmn., 1983; dir. Joint Advt. Bd., Flint, Mich., v.p., 1983. Chmn. community div. Pontiac United Way, 1972; fin./treas. 125th anniversary celebration City of Pontiac, also chmn. fundraising and promotion. Recipient various service awards, certs. appreciation. Mem. Credit Union Execs. Soc., Jayno Heights Women's Assn., Epsilon Sigma Alpha (chpt. pres. 1966, 76-77, pres. Mich. council 1968-69). Episcopalian. Author manuals, policy books in field. Office: 939 S Woodward Ave Pontiac MI 48056

STONE, LESLIE JUNE, publisher, graphic designer; b. Oxnard, Calif., Nov. 2, 1953; d. Jay Edlin and Carole Louise (Zimet) S. B.A., UCLA, 1976. Pub., editor Women's Yellow Pages, Los Angeles, 1981—. Bd. dirs. Woman's Bldg, Los Angeles. Recipient award Calif. Design Show, Pacific Design Ctr., Los Angeles, 1976. Mem. Calif. Women Bus. Owners, Women's Referral Service, Nat. Assn. Women's Yellow Page Pubs., Women in Design, Nat. Council Jewish Women, NOW. Democrat. Avocations: skiing; tennis; ceramics; piano; guitar. Office: Women's Yellow Pages 3942 Sawtelle Blvd Los Angeles CA 90066

STONE, M. BEVERLEY, university dean emeritus, city official; b. Norfolk, Va., June 10, 1916; d. James Leland and Clara Mae (Thompson) Stone. A.B., Randolph-Macon Woman's Coll., Lynchburg, Va., 1936; M.A., Columbia U., 1940, Dean of Students Diploma, 1956; L.H.D. (hon.), Purdue U., 1986. . Tchr., math. and chemistry, Norfolk, Va., 1936-41; counselor, asst. prof. chemistry Tusculum Coll., 1941-43; asst. dean women U. Ark., 1946-50, assoc. dean, 1952-55, acting dean women, 1955; asst. dean women Purdue U., West Lafayette, Ind., 1956-67, assoc. dean women, 1967-68, dean women, prof., 1968-74, dean students, prof., 1974-80, emeritus, 1980—; mem. council-at-large West Lafayette City Council, 1984—; cons. and lectr. in field. Author: (with Barbara Cook) (monograph) Counseling Women, 1973. Contbr. articles to profl. jours. Mem. community adv. com. Sch. Nursing Purdue U., 1985—. Served to lt. comdr. U.S. Navy Res., 1943-46, 1950-52. Recipient Disting. Alumnus award Purdue U., 1980; Sagamore of the Wabash, Gov. of Ind., 1980, 1985. Mem. Nat. Assn. Women Deans Adminstrs. and Counselors (treas. exec. bd. 1973-75, bd. dirs. found. 1978-83, v.p. nat. council.), Ind. Assn. Women Deans, Phi Beta Kappa, Alpha Lambda Delta (v.p. nat. council 1974-79). Democrat. Methodist. Clubs: Parlor (v.p. 1974), Lafayette Country (Lafayette). . Home: 1807 Western Dr West Lafayette IN 47906

STONE, MARSHA, courier company executive; b. Queens, N.Y., Aug. 6, 1953; d. Andrew and Ruth (Strissof) Storti. Student pub. schs. Mgr. Archer Courier, N.Y.C., 1978-83; dir. ops. Concord Courier, N.Y.C., 1983-85; owner All-Star Courier Systems, Inc., 1986—. Sec., trumpet player, drum major Big Apple Corps Marching Band, v.p. Big Apple Corps Mem. Nat. Assn. for Female Execs., Greater Gotham Bus. Council.

STONE, MINNIE STRANGE, retired automotive service company executive; b. Palatka, Fla., Mar. 10, 1919; d. James Arrious and Pansy (Thomas) Strange; student Massey Bus. Coll., 1938-39; m. Fred Albion Stone, Nov. 30, 1939; children—Fred Albion, James Thomas, Thomas Demere. Sec., bookkeeper Sears, Roebuck & Co., Jacksonville, Fla., 1939-41; financial sec. U.S. Army, Macon, Ga., 1941, Atlanta, 1942; sec., bookkeeper Raleigh Spring & Brake Service, Inc. (name changed to Stone Heavy Vehicle Specialist) (N.C.), 1953-84, sec.-treas. corp., 1960-84, now dir., sec. Pres., YWCA, Wake County, 1973-76, bd. dirs., 1966-76; bd. dirs. Urban Ministry Center, Raleigh, 1983—. Mem. N.C. Mus. of History Assocs., Raleigh Council Smaller Garden Clubs (pres. 1960-61), N.C. Art Soc., Vol. Wake County Mental Health Assn., Monthly Investors Club, Coley Forest Garden Club. Republican. Baptist. Home: 920 Runnymede Rd Raleigh NC 27607 Office: 2200 Hwy 70 E Garner NC 27529

STONE, PAULA LENORE, lawyer, medical consultant; b. N.Y.C., Nov. 1, 1942; d. Milton H. and Pauline (Smith) Stone; m. Richard J. Chodoff, July 29, 1969 (dec. 1983). A.B. in Biology, Muhlenberg Coll., 1961; student Lehigh U., 1960, Jefferson Med. Sch., 1961-63; J.D., Temple U., 1981. Bar: Pa. 1982. Med. cons. to trial lawyers Bala Cynwyd, Pa., 1963-85, N.Y.C. and Norristown, Pa., 1985—; sole practice, N.Y.C. and Norristown, 1985—; of counsel firm Turrey Kepler, Norristown, 1985—; assoc. firm Murray Sams, P.C., Miami, Fla., 1982—. Editor Psychopharmacology Abstracts, Cancer Chemotherapy Abstracts; author: (with R.J. Chodoff) Doctor for the Prosecution, 1983. Mem. Assn. Trial Lawyers Am., Coll. of Physicians, ABA, N.Y. Acad. Sci., Pa. Bar Assn., Phila. Bar Assn., ACLU. Democrat. Jewish. Address: Suite 8-B 870 UN Plaza New York NY 10017

STONE, ROSE MARIE, physician's assistant, nurse; b. Vicenza, Italy, Dec. 2, 1957; came to U.S., 1958; d. Richard Douglas and Helen Grace (Kolaja) S. B.S. in Nursing, Tex. Woman's U.; B.S., Physician's Asst., U. Tex. Med. Br.-Galveston. Sales mgr., Mr. Hardware, Houston, 1974-80; health dir., nurse Campfire, Rosebud, Tex., 1980; nursing supr. evening shift Austin State Sch. (Tex.), 1981-82; physician's asst. U. Tex. Med. Br., Galveston, 1982-84, now with MacGregor Med. Assn., Houston. Author patient pamphlets. Nurse, Spl. Olympics basketball tourney, Austin, 1982-83. Mem. Am. Acad. Physician Assts. (student del. to ho. of dels. 1982, 83), Tex. Acad. Physician Assts., Tex. Nurses Assn., U. Tex. Med. Br. Alumni. Republican. Roman Catholic. Club: Young Adults (Galveston). Home: 4910 Laurel Bellaire TX 77401 Office: Mac Gregor Med Assn 8100 Greenbriar St Houston TX 77054

STONE, RUTH SHELTON, escrow company executive; b. Purdy, Okla., Aug. 13, 1926; d. Joseph Curtis and Mollie Lou (Graham) Shelton; m. Russell E. Stone, Apr. 17, 1954 (dec. June 1984); 1 child, Cheryl Stone Ohrt. Chief teller Bank of Am., Montebello, Pasadena, 1950-57; chief teller loan dept. Security Pacific Nat. Bank, Pasadena, 1960-63; escrow officer Lockwood Escrow, Pasadena, 1963-68, pres., owner, 1968—; founder, dir. Crown Valley Fed. Savs. and Loan, Brookside Savs. and Loan Assn., 1982-84. Mem. Escrow Inst. Calif. (bd. dirs. 1974—), Calif. Escrow Assn., San Gabriel Valley Escrow Assn., Pasadena Bd. Realtors (Affiliate of Yr. 1984), Pasadena C. of C. Republican. Club: Zonta (Pasadena) (bd. dirs., officer 1974—). Avocations: golf; fishing. Office: Lockwood Escrow Corp PO Box 60544 Pasadena CA 91106

STONER, CHRISTINA WILLIAMS, automotive leasing company executive; b. Atlantic City, Sept. 1, 1952; d. Joseph John and Mary Ann (Weyand) Williams; m. H. Robert Stoner, Oct. 28, 1978 (div. 1985); 1 stepson, Jan Erik. B.Mus., U. Del.-Newark, 1974; postgrad. Sch. Music Temple U., 1974-75. Leasing mgr. Brown Auto Rental & Leasing, Hatboro, Pa., 1975-77; account rep. Hertz Corp., Phila., 1977-79; sales mgr. Pa. Leasing Corp., Harrisburg, 1979-81; v.p. Titus Leasing Co., Harrisburg, 1981—; pres. Alternatives in Action Cons. Services, Carlisle, Pa., 1979-84; mem., speaker Doering Nat. Leasing 30 Group, Hartland, Wis., 1984—. Sr. bd. mem. Delancey Ct. Condominium Assn., Wormleysburg, Pa., 1984—. Recipient Fellowship/Scholarship awarde Temple U. Music Inst., summer 1970. Mem. Alternatives in Action for Women (founding pres. 1980-82). Republican. Roman Catholic. Club: Carlisle Country. Avocations: Classical and contemporary piano; interior decorating; gourmet cooking; entertaining. Home: 479 Delancey Ct Mechanicsburg PA 17055 Office: Titus Leasing Co 2222 Paxton St Harrisburg PA 17111

STONER, FRANCES WYNETTE, city official, city secretary; b. Lake City, Fla., Oct. 2, 1943; d. Monroe Mattox Neveils and Freda Bryan (Mobley) Neveils Hollingsworth; m. Jerry Kay Stoner, Dec. 16, 1962; 1 child, Wynette Renae. Diploma Massey Bus. Coll., Jacksonville, Fla., 1962; student Alvin Community Coll., Tex., 1980-81. Legal sec. Crofton Holland & Starling, Titusville, Fla., 1962-63, Davis & Katz, Lebanon, Pa., 1963; dep. city clk. City of Titusville, 1964-68, sec., 1968-72; city clk. City of Alvin, Tex., 1974—. Recipient Cert. of Excellence award U.S. Dept. Labor, Washington, 1980. Mem. Assn. City Clks. and Secs., of Tex. (Salt Grass chpt. sec., treas., 1975, pres. 1978), Internat. Inst. Mcpl. Clks., Nat. Purchasing Inst., Alvin C. of C. Club: Soroptimist Internat. of Alvin (sec. 1984-85, v.p. 1985-86). Home: 113 S Jane St Alvin TX 77511 Office: City of Alvin 216 W Sealy St Alvin TX 77511

STONER, SUE BURKHART, travel consultant; b. Seminole, Okla., June 8, 1942; d. E.D. and Atha Miriah (Brown) Burkhart; m. George M. Stoner, Jr., Sept. 5, 1964; children—Shelby Lynn, Steven Laird. B.A., Howard Payne Coll., 1964. Pres., Travel World, Inc., Gig Harbor, Wash., 1965—; sec.-treas. Travel Stamps, Inc., Gig Harbor, 1978—; dir. admissions Profl. Tng. Sch., Gig Harbor, 1984—. Mem. distributive edn. com. Peninsula Sch. Dist., Gig Harbor. Mem. Am. Soc. Travel Agts. (com. chmn.), Inst. Cert. Travel Agts. (cert. travel cons., nat. rep.), Assn. Retail Travel Agts. (com. chmn.), Dist. Assn. Gig Harbor Lady Mchts. (v.p.), Gig Harbor C. of C. (tourism com.). Republican. Baptist. Club: Dover AFB Officers' Wives (v.p.) (Gig Harbor). Avocations: reading, travel, painting. Home: 15018 Sherman Dr NW Gig Harbor WA 98335 Office: PO Box 427 3116 Judson St Gig Harbor WA 98335

STOOKEY, PEGGY ANN, cabinet manufacturing company sales and marketing executive; b. Rising Sun, Md., Apr. 11, 1941; d. Herman Carroll Reynolds and Evelyn May (Benjamin) Reynolds Griffith; m. Laurence Hull Stookey, June 8, 1963; children—Laura Ann, Sarah Elizabeth. B.S., Western Md. Coll., 1963; postgrad. Cecil Community Coll., 1971-72, Wesley Theol. Sem., 1974-75; cert. bus. mgmt. Hofstra U., 1984. Tchr., Cecil County Schs., Elkton, Md., 1963-65; designer M. Saunders Kitchens, Bethesda, Md., 1976-78; sales mgr. Custom Crafters, Kensington, Md., 1978-80; dir. sales and mktg. Roseline Products, Farmingdale, N.Y., 1980-86; nat. sales mgr. CLB Bath & Kitchen Corp., 1986—. Mem. Am. Inst. Kitchen Dealers (v.p. Balt.-Washington chpt. 1978, pres. 1979), Nat. Council Mfrs. Democrat. Methodist. Home: 223 Waldo St Copiague NY 11726 Office: Roseline Products Inc 120 Schmitt Blvd Farmingdale NY 11735

STOOP, NORMA MCLAIN, editor, author, photographer; b. Panama, C.Z., July 20, 1910; b. Harry Edward and Gladys (Brandon) McLain; student Penn Hall Jr. Coll., Carnegie Inst. Tech., New Sch., N.Y. U.; m. William J. Stoop, Jr., Sept. 20, 1932. Contbg. editor Dance Mag., N.Y.C., 1969-71, asso. editor, 1971-79, sr. editor, 1979—; sr. editor After Dark, 1978-82, also feature writer; also photographer, theater, ballet and film critic; entertainment editor sr. edit. WNYC-AM, 1980-83; chief film critic Manhattan Arts, 1983—; mem. nat. adv. bd. TV Arts Studio, Inc. Mem. Poetry Soc. Am., Acad. Am. Poets, Dance Masters Am., Dance Critics Assn., TV Acad. Arts and Scis., Sigma Delta Chi. Club: Overseas Press. Contbr. poems to Tex. Quar., Chgo. Rev., N.Y. Times, Arts in Society, Quest, Atlantic Monthly, Christian Sci. Monitor, others, 1958—, essays to Book Week in N.Y. Herald Tribune; represented in Best Poems of 1973, Exhibit of Dance Photography, Harvard U., Tufts Coll., 1975. Recipient award Dance Tchrs. Club Boston, 1977. Office: 33 W 60th St New York NY 10023

STOPKEY, LINDA JOHANNA, electronics company official; b. Chgo., Mar. 3, 1960; d. Waldemar Dmitro and Lorraine (Bielenberg) S. B.S. in Mgmt. summa cum laude, Tulane U., 1981; M.B.A., U. Tex., 1984. Cost engr. IBM, Austin, 1981-84, cost engrng. mgr., 1984-86, pricer, 1986. Mem. Am. Soc. Women Accts., Am. Mgmt. Assn., Nat. Assn. Female Execs., Beta Alpha Psi, Phi Chi Theta. Office: IBM 11400 Burnet Rd Austin TX 78758

STORAASLI, MARIE ELIZABETH, med. technologist, educator; b. Milw., June 26, 1945; d. Tollef Bardolf and Ruth Elizabeth (Storvick) S.; B.S. in Med. Tech., Northwestern U., 1967; M.S. in Clin. Sci., San Francisco State U., 1978; m. Jörn Olaf Thomas von Ramm, July 12, 1981; children—Olaf, Karl. Chemist, Rikshospital Sentrallaboratoriet, Oslo, 1967-68; med. technologist Clinic Internal Medicine, Wauwatosa, Wis., 1968-69; med. technologist U. Minn., Mpls., 1969-71; supervisory med. technologist Hoag Hosp., Newport Beach, Calif., 1971-73; supr. hematology Project HOPE, Maceio, Brazil, 1973; staff research asso. dept. medicine U. Calif., San Diego, 1974-77; instr. hematology San Francisco State U., 1977-78; edn. coordinator Sch. Med. Tech., Scripps Clinic and Research Found., LaJolla, Calif., 1978-80; asst. prof. med. tech. U. N.C., Chapel Hill, 1980—. Mem. Durham (N.C.) Arts Council, Project HOPE Alumni Assn. Mem. AAUP, Am. Soc. Clin. Pathology (asso.), Am. Soc. Med. Tech., N.C. Soc. Med. Tech., Triangle Weavers Guild. Republican. Lutheran. Club: Univ. Women's (U. N.C.), Univ. Women's (Duke U.). Home: 3433 Dover Rd Durham NC 27707 Office: U NC Med Sch Wing B113 207-H Chapel Hill NC 27514

STOREY, J. JAYNELL SAYLOR, compensation specialist, human resources developer; b. Kingsport, Tenn., May 6, 1939; d. J.C. and Jessie Lee (Little) Saylor; m. Phillip Reed Storey, Aug. 5, 1961 (div.). Student Milligan Coll., Tenn., 1957-60, Furman U., Greenville, S.C., 1977, Limestone Coll., Gaffney, S.C., 1981-83. Mgr. Western Girl, Inc., Sacramento, 1965-67; personnel counselor Livingston Co., Sacramento, 1968-70; counselor, office mgr. McNabb Mental Health Ctr., Knoxville, Tenn., 1971-74; exec. legal sec. Daniel Constrn. Co., Greenville, 1974-77; compensation analyst, 1977-79, adminstrv. exec. compensation, 1979-84; staff Ashley Acad., Johnson City, Tenn., 1984—. Vol. Am. Cancer Soc., 1979; adv. Vol. Action Com., Greenville Mental Health Ctr., 1982; coordinator United Way Campaign, 1980-81, capt. corp. campaign, 1983, all Greenville. Named Family of Yr., Farm Bur., Jonesboro, 1958. Mem. Internat. Assn. Staff Mgrs. (v.p. 1980-81, mem. dir. 1979-81), Am. Bus. Women's Assn. (Bus. Woman of Yr. 1980, sec. 1981-82, pres. 1983-84), Foothills Area Counsel (planning com. 1983), Women's Network (Greenville, steering com. 1981-82). Republican. Mem. Ch. Christ. Home: 4204 Navaho Dr Apt 2 Johnson City TN 37601 Office: Ashley Acad Knob Creek Rd Johnson City TN 37601

STORSETH, JEANNIE PEARCE, insurance administrator; b. Casa Grande, Ariz., Sept. 24, 1948; d. Johnnie E. and Barbra (Dismukes) Pearce; m. Bryce Hallice Storseth, Aug. 15, 1981; 1 child, Michael Scott. B.S., U. Ariz., 1979. Mktg. rep. Group Health Coop., Seattle, 1981-83; dist. mgr. Health Plus/Blue Cross, Seattle, 1983-84; mktg. dir. Personal Health, Seattle, 1984-85; sales dir. Cigna Health Plan, Seattle, 1985—. Mem. Wash. Assn. Health Underwriters (v.p.), Am. Coll. Healthcare Mktg., Nat. Assn. Female Execs. Republican. Mem. Christian Ch. Club: Quota (Tacoma). Avocations: oil painting; writing. Office: Cigna Health Plan 701 5th Ave Seattle WA 98104

STORSTEEN, LINDA LEE, librarian; b. Pasadena, Jan. 26, 1948; d. Oliver Matthew and Susan (Smock) Storsteen. A.B. cum laude in History, UCLA, 1970, M.A. in Ancient History, 1972, M.L.S., 1973. Librarian, Los Angeles Pub. Library, 1974-79; city librarian Palmdale City Library (Calif.), 1979—. Adv. bd. So. Calif. Inter-Library Loan Network, Los Angeles, 1979-80; commr. So. Calif. Film Circuit, Los Angeles, 1980—; council South State Coop. Library System, 1981—, chmn., 1982-83, 85-86; pres. So. Calif. Film Circuit, 1985-86; rec. sec. So. Antelope Valley Coordinating Council, Palmdale, 1983-84. Mem. ALA, Calif. Library Assn., Pub. Libraries Exec. Assn. So. Calif., Am. Saddle Horse Assn., Pacific Saddlebred Assn., So. Calif. Saddle Bred Horse Assn. (bd. dirs.). Home: PO Box 129 Palmdale CA 93550 Office: Palmdale City Library 700 E Palmdale Blvd Palmdale CA 93550

STORY, CYNTHIA STINSON, government official; ofcl.; b. Siler City, N.C., July 28, 1956; d. Benner H. and Evangeline D. Stinson; A.A., Elon Coll., 1976; m. Douglas T. Story, June 27, 1981; 1 child, Amber Brittany. With Faison M. Hicks, atty., Raleigh, N.C., 1976-77; regional audit team mem., asst. del. team E.F. Hutton & Co., Inc., Raleigh, 1977-82; spl. asst. to U.S. Sen. John P. East, Greenville, N.C., 1982—. Dist. dir. N.C. Fedn. Young Republicans, 1976-77, exec. sec., 1977-79, nat. committeewoman, 1979—, Woman of Yr., 1980; chmn. N.C. Fedn. Young Republicans, 1983-84. Named Woman of Yr., Young Reps. Nat. Fedn., 1981. Baptist. Club: Toastmasters. Home: 200 Staffordshire Rd Greenville NC 27834 Office: PO Box 8087 Greenville NC 27834

STORY, NANCY LOUISE, association executive; b. Kansas City, Kans., Aug. 18, 1944; d. Elmer Myron and Frances Louise (Hendrickson) Swengel; m. Marvin L. Story, Nov. 9, 1961; 1 child, Christine L. Story-Hadley. Grad. high sch. Spl. teller Brotherhood Bank, Kansas City, 1964-65; claims advisor Boilermakers Trust, Kansas City, 1965-67; asst. bus. mgr. Radiology Chartered, Kansas City, 1969-75; bus. mgr. Allen Radiology, Kansas City, 1976-82; exec. dir. Radiologists Bus. Mgrs. Assn., Kansas City, 1983—. Mem. Am. Soc. Assn. Execs., Mid-Am. Soc. Assn. Execs., Radiol. Bus. Mgrs. Assn. (regional dir. 1980-81), Am. Assn. Med. Assts. (pres. local chpt. 1977-78), Exptl. Aircraft Assn. Avocations: aviation; high-country camping; back packing; cross-country skiing. Office: Radiologists Bus Mgrs Assn 8047 Parallel Pkwy Suite 7 Kansas City KS 66112-1155

STOSUR, APRIL MARIE, stockbroker; b. Chgo., Dec. 2, 1955; d. Donald Eugene and Marie Annette (Thilmont) S.; B.A. in Polit. Sci., No. Ill. U., DeKalb, 1977, M.P.A., 1979; m. Perry Martin Bassett, Feb. 14, 1981. Evaluation and planning project asso. N.W. Criminal Justice Commn., Dixon, Ill., 1977-78; circuit ct. dep. Ogle County Circuit Ct., Oregon, Ill., 1977-78; uniform crime report field rep. Wash. Assn. Sheriffs and Police Chiefs, Olympia, Wash., 1979-82; stockbroker Foster-Marshall/Am. Express, Bellevue, Wash., 1983—. Mem. ednl. policies com. Shimer Coll., Mt. Carroll, Ill., 1975. Title IX Public Service Edn. fellow 1978. Mem. Am. Soc. Public Adminstrn., Nat. Assn. Female Execs., Bus. and Profl. Women's Club, Pi Sigma Alpha, Pi Alpha Alpha. Club: Toastmasters. Office: One Bellevue Ctr 411 108th Ave NE Suite 2100 Bellevue WA 98004

STOTHART, ROBERTA BATES, bookstore manager; b. Long Beach, Calif., Mar. 29, 1934; d. Morley DaCosta and Dorothy Clarice (Graham) Bates; children—Lisa Camille, Anna, Elizabeth. Student U. Ariz., 1952-53. Library asst. Am Sch. Switzerland, Lugano, 1967-70; mus. bookstore mgr. J. Paul Getty Mus., Malibu, Calif., 1974—. Mem. Mus. Stores Assn. (dir.). Home: 1472 Palisades Dr Pacific Palisades CA 90272 Office: 17985 Pacific Coast Hwy Malibu CA 90265

STOTLER, ALICEMARIE H., federal judge; b. Alhambra, Calif., May 29, 1942; d. James R. and Loretta M. Huber; m. James A. Stotler, Sept. 11, 1971. B.A., U. So. Calif., 1964, J.D., 1967. Dep., Orange County Dist. Atty.'s Office, 1967-73; mem. Stotler & Stotler, Santa Ana, Calif., 1973-76, 83-84; judge Orange County Mcpl. Ct., 1976-78, Orange County Superior Ct., 1978-83, U.S. Dist. Ct. (cen. dist.) Calif., Los Angeles, 1984—. Mem. ABA, Orange County Bar Assn., Calif. Judges Assn. Office: US Courthouse 312 N Spring St Los Angeles CA 90012

STOTT, MARY LOU, real estate broker; b. Washington, Mar. 2, 1933; d. Martin Anthony and Mary Louise (Berberich) Dempf; B.S. in Edn., D.C. Tchrs. Coll., 1955; M.S.W., U. Hawaii, 1972; m. George W. Stott, Jr., Aug. 4, 1956; children—Michael, Helen, Tracey Anne. Tchr. public schs., 1955-69; family therapist Catholic Social Service, Honolulu, 1972-74; public relations dir. Sheraton Hotel Disco, 1975; dir. counseling Chaminade U., 1975-76, dir. women's programs, 1976-77; v.p. Stott Real Estate, Inc., Kailua, Hawaii, 1978—; guidance dir. St. Anthony Sch.; condr. U. Hawaii Career Seminar; mem. Gov.'s Com. on Children and Youth, 1974-75. Recipient Fed. grant for services to women re-entering career world, 1976. Mem. Am. Bus. Women's Assn., Acad. Cert. Social Workers, Nat. Assn. Social Workers, Am. Assn. Sex Educators and Counselors, Nat. Assn. Realtors, Hawaii Assn. Realtors, Honolulu Bd. Realtors. Republican. Roman Catholic. Club: Cath. Daus. Home: 360 Dune Circle Kailua HI 96734

STOTTLEMYRE, DONNA MAE, jewelry store executive; b. Mystic, Iowa, Nov. 11, 1928; d. Clarence William and Nina Allene (Millizer) Clark; m. Robert Arthur Stottlemyre, May 8, 1946; children—Roger Dale, Amber Anita, Tamra Collette. Owner, operator Donna's Dress Shop, Unionville, Mo., 1973-76, Donna's Jewelry Box and Bridal Boutique, Unionville, 1978—. Sunday sch. tchr. First Baptist Ch., Unionville, Bible sch. tchr.; 4H Club judge County Fair, Unionville. Mem. C. of C. Baptist. Avocations: sewing; flower arranging. Home: 217 N 14th Unionville MO 63565 Office: Donna's Jewelry and Bridal 1610 Main Unionville MO 63565

STOTZ, NATALIE HAMER, business official; b. Great Falls, Mont., Oct. 22, 1921; d. Arthur C. Hamer and Gertrude H. (Kaufmann) Wallace; m. Theodore Philip Stotz, June 9, 1956. Student Great Falls Comml. Coll., 1939. C.L.U. Br. office cashier Occidental Life Ins. Co., Great Falls, 1939-44; sec. to underwriter, San Francisco, 1944-47; head claims dept. Friedman & Co., San Francisco, 1947-62; adminstrv. asst. to underwriter, San Jose, Calif., 1962—. Mem. Am. Soc. C.L.U.s. Sec.-treas. West Bay Opera Guild, Palo Alto, Calif., 1965-67. Republican. Christian Scientist. Avocation: ballet. Home: 988 N California Ave Palo Alto CA 94303 Office: 333 W Santa Clara St Suite 712 San Jose CA 95113

STOUFF, FAYE, craft association executive; b. Kirkland, Tex., June 27, 1908; d. George Lee and Eliza Ann (Smith) Rogers; m. Emile Anatol Stouff, Mar. 5, 1925 (dec. 1978); 1 child, Nicholas Leonard. Student pub. schs., Fort Worth. Tchr. cane basketry Chetimacha Indian Reservation, Charenton, La., 1953-84, tchr. beadwork, 1969; mgr. Chetimacha Craft Assn., 1970—. Author: Chetimacha Beliefs, 1970; (booklet) History of Indians, 1975. Baptist. Home: Rural Route 2 Box 224 Jeanerette LA 70544

STOUGH, TERA DIANE, educator, reading specialist; b. Okarche, Okla., Sept. 18, 1958; d. Thomas Ross Stough and Evelyn Carol (Swaggart) Stough Holman. B.S. in Edn., U. Okla., 1980; M.S., reading specialist, 1985. Cert. tchr., Okla. Tchr. Moore Pub. Schs., Okla., 1980-84; mem. faculty U. Okla., Norman, 1984-85; tchr. Mid-Del Schs., Midwest City, Okla., 1985—; faculty adviser Student Okla. Edn. Assn., Norman, 1984-85. Organizer Nancy Virtue election to House campaign, Norman, 1984; del. Democratic Conv., Norman, 1984. Recipient Tchr. of Yr. award Moore Pub. Schs., 1983. Mem. Mid-Del Assn. Classroom Tchrs. (mem. steering com. of polit. action com. 1985-86), Internat. Reading Council, Okla. Reading Council, Okla. Edn. Assn., NEA. Methodist. Avocations: flying; karate; gardening.

STOUT, DONNA KARY, manufacturing company sales executive; b. Balt., Aug. 16, 1954; d. Donald Angelo and Anna May (Vollenweider) Kary; B.Biology, Western Md. Coll., 1976; M.S., George Washington U., 1980; m. David M. Stout, Aug. 13, 1977. Microbiologist, McCormick & Co., Balt., 1976-79, specifications coordinator, Hunt Valley, Md., 1979-80, supr. tech. services, indsl. bus., Balt., 1980-83, tech. sales services mgr., Hunt Valley, 1984, sales service mgr., 1984-85, product mgr., 1985, sales and mktg. services mgr., 1985—. Mem. Inst. Food Technologists.

STOUT, HELEN LOUISE, nursing home administrator; b. Maryville, Mo., Mar. 2, 1927; d. Frank Gordon and Jenny Helene (VanCouvering) Tebow; m. William Jerold Stout, June 24, 1949; children—Janet Louise Stout Boyer, William Jerold Jr. B.A., Bob Jones U., 1949; B.S., U. Tenn., 1960, M.S., 1961. Lic. nursing home adminstr., Tenn. Tchr., Knox County Schs., Knoxville, Tenn., 1952-58; minister of music First Bapt. Ch., Paris, Tenn., 1958-62; tchr. supr. Stafford Schs., Stafford Springs, Pa., 1963-69; prof. music LeTourneau Coll., Longview, Tex., 1962-63; Realtor Main Line Bd. Realtors, Phila., 1970-75; owner, pres., adminstr. Royal Care, Inc., Cleveland Tenn. and Erin, Tenn., 1977—; owner Royal Care of Jackson, Royal Care of Lawrenceburg, Stonehenge Health Care Ctr., Shadescrest Health Care Ctr., 1978—, Lo-Ra Motel, Coleman Laundermat, Erin, Tenn., 1983—; cons. Life Care Ctrs., Cleveland, Tenn., 1976-78; concert pianist McDowell Club, Chattanooga, 1978—; organist, pianist First Bapt. Ch., Cleveland, 1978—. Composer and arranger of piano and choral works, 1961—. Mem. Tenn. Health Care Assn., Am. Health Care Assn., Am. Coll. Health Care Adminstrs. Home: 2105 Hickory Dr Cleveland TN 37311 Office: Royal Care Inc 147 Inman St PO Box 1051 Cleveland TN 37311

STOUT, JUANITA KIDD, judge; b. Wewoka, Okla., Mar. 7, 1919; d. Henry Maynard and Mary Alice (Chandler) Kidd; m. Charles Otis Stout, June 23, 1942. B.A., U. Iowa, 1939; J.D., Ind. U., 1948, LL.M., 1954; LL.D. (hon.) Ursinus Coll., 1965, Ind. U., 1966, Lebanon Valley Coll., 1969, Drexel U., 1972, Rockford Coll. (Ill.), 1974, Roger Williams Coll., 1984, Morgan State U., Balt., 1985; U. Md.-Eastern Shore, 1980; D.H.L., Russell Sage Coll., 1966. Bar: D.C. 1950, Pa. 1954. Tchr. pub. schs., Seminole and Sand Springs, Okla., 1939-42; tchr. Fla. A&M U., Tallahassee, 1949, Tex. So. U., Houston, 1949; adminstrv. asst. to judge U.S. Ct. Appeals (3d circuit), Phila., 1949-55; asst. dist. atty., Phila., 1955-59; judge Ct. of Common Pleas, Phila., 1959—. Recipient Jane Addams medal Rockford Coll., 1966, Disting. Service award U. Iowa, 1974; named to Hall of Fame of Okla., Okla. Heritage Soc., 1981. Mem. ABA, Nat. Assn. Women Judges, Nat. Assn. Women Lawyers, Pa. Bar Assn., Phila. Bar Assn. Democrat. Episcopalian. Home: 1919 Chestnut St Apt 2805 Philadelphia PA 19103 Office: Ct of Common Pleas Room 536 City Hall Philadelphia PA 19107

STOUTE, MARGUERITE ALLYN, nurse, consultant; b. Bklyn., Aug. 27, 1949; d. Allan Humphrey and Ina Gertrude (Ricketts) S. B.A., Manhattanville

Coll., 1973; B.S. in Nursing Edn., NYU-Washington Square, 1981, M.A. in Nursing Edn., 1983. R.N. Researcher Mt. Sinai Hosp., N.Y.C., 1973, Columbia U., N.Y.U., 1973-74; staff/charge nurse Kings County Hosp., Bklyn., 1983—; coordinator inservice edn. Bklyn. Hosp., 1986—; cons. Ina Mag Assn., Bklyn., 1984—; adj. prof. N.Y.C. Tech. Community Coll., 1985—. Pres. Scholarship Fund, Nazarene Ch., Bklyn., 1983—; assoc. mem. Bedford Stuyvesant Alcoholic Treatment Ctr., Bedford, Monroe, Bklyn., 1980—; class agt. class of '73, Manhattanville Coll. Mem. Am. Nurses Assn., Nat. Assn. Female Execs., NYU Alumni Assn. Club: Manhattanville (Purchase, N.Y.). Avocations: writing; singing; speaking; teaching. Home: 1158 Bedford Ave Brooklyn NY 11216

STOVALL, ANN ELIZABETH, medical technologist, administrator; b. Oak Park, Ill., Apr. 16, 1942; d. William Buell and Cleo Ann (Crews) Gardner; m. Michael Edward Swords, Feb. 4, 1966 (div. 1980); m. Wallace Russell Stovall, Sept. 11, 1982. Diploma Am. Acad. Med. Tech., 1962; student Northwestern U., 1962-64. Cert. med. technologist, Ill., Okla., Nev. Immunology supr. Meml. Hosp., Elmhurst, Ill., 1970-81; lab. mgr. St. Joseph Med. Ctr., Ponca City, Okla., 1981-83; asst. chief technologist Duncan Regional Hosp., Okla., 1983-85; clin. lab. supr. So. Nev. Meml. Hosp., Las Vegas, 1985—; guest faculty Beckman Inst., Chgo., 1980; cons. in field. Gen. chmn. Meml. Hosp. Guild, Elmhurst, 1980; pres. Elmhurst Community Theatre, 1980-81; organizer Friends of Library, Marlow, Okla., 1985. Mem. Am. Med. Technologist Assn., Am. Soc. for Med. Tech., Am. Soc. for Microbiology, Nat. Cert. Agy. (clin. lab. scientist). Republican. Club: Bus. and Profl. Women. Avocations: theater; traveling. Home: 6255 W Tropicana Las Vegas NV 89103 Office: So Nev Meml Hosp Las Vegas NV

STOVALL, BETTY MARILYN, freight and warehousing company executive; b. Houston, May 16, 1942; d. William Lynwood and Wilma Ether (Davis) Hill; m. Raymond P. Stovall, Feb. 24, 1963; children—Ernest Brazil, Mary Elizabeth, Carol Janette. Student East Tex. State U., Commerce, 1960-61. Sec., Huey-Philips, Dallas, 1962-63; bookkeeper Tex. & Pacific Employees Fed. Credit Union, Dallas, 1973-74; v.p., sec., treas. Trans Tex Terminal, Inc., Dallas, 1974—. Methodist. Office: Trans Tex Terminal Inc 3025 Oak Ln Dallas TX 75226

STOVALL, CATHERINE LOUISE, wholesale giftware co. exec., restaurateur; b. Phoenix, Oct. 31, 1955; d. Jack Kerwin Stovall and Noyla Gayle (Jamison) Augspurger; B.A., Calif. State U., Long Beach, 1979; m. Daniel De La Rosa, Jan. 31, 1976 (div. 1983); 2 daus., Cara Marie, Jennifer Lauren. Owner, operator De La Rosa's Indian Jewelry, Anaheim, Calif., 1975-77; sales and banquet mgr. Stovall Motor Hotels, Anaheim, 1976-82; pres. Delcourval, Inc., Anaheim, 1980—; owner, operator Kingdom Gifts, Anaheim, 1981—; gen. mgr. Spaghetti Sta. Restaurant, Anaheim, 1982—; Leader Girl Scouts U.S.A.; active Anaheim Visitor and Conv. Bur. Mem. Nat. Assn. Female Execs., Anaheim C. of C., AAUW. Republican. Roman Catholic. Home: 5 Cornwallis St Irvine CA 92714 Office: 999 Ball Rd Anaheim CA 92802

STRACENER, CAROL ELIZABETH, lawyer; b. Baton Rouge, La., Mar. 28, 1951; d. Nealon and Mary Helen (Langlois) S.; m. John J. Nicholson, June 2, 1973; 1 dau., Courtney Elizabeth. B.S., La. State U., 1973; J.D., So. U., Baton Rouge, 1977. Bar: La. 1977. Ptnr., Stracener, Stracener & Stracener, Attys., Baton Rouge, La., 1977—; loan closing atty. Guaranty Fed. Savs. & Loan Assn., Baton Rouge, 1977-81. Mem. ABA, La. Bar Assn., East Baton Rouge Bar Assn., Baton Rouge Assn. Women Attys., Am. Trial Lawyers Assn., Am. Judicature Soc. Republican. Baptist. Home: 3695 Ridgemont Dr Baton Rouge LA 70814 Office: Stracener Stracener & Stracener 3155 Wller Ave Baton Rouge LA 70805

STRADER, MARCIA D., technical writer, trainer; b. Myrtle Point, Oreg., Nov. 12, 1955; d. G. Howard and Durelle (Hill) S.; m. D.S. Crawford, Sept. 10, 1982. Student Skagit Valley Coll., Mount Vernon, Wash., 1972-73; B.S., Oreg. State U., 1978, M.Ed., 1979. Grad. teaching asst. dept. English, Oreg. State U., Corvallis, 1978-79, asst. dir. Oreg. State U. Found., 1979-80; documentation specialist Spartin Systems, Houston, 1980-82; owner, mgr., writer TekniKraft, Houston, 1982—; cons. Rice U., Houston, 1981-82. Author numerous tech. manuals on data processing, 1980—; Editor-in-chief: Introducing Indonesia, 1986. Treas. Jakarta Am. Women's Assn., Indonesia, 1985—; active Jakarta Internat. Community Activity Ctr., 1985—. Mem. Soc. Tech. Communication, Nat. Assn. Female Execs. Avocation: camping. Office: care Marathon Internat-Jakarta PO Box 3128 Houston TX 77253

STRAHLER, VIOLET RUTH, educational consultant, writer; b. Dayton, Ohio, Sept. 30, 1918; d. Ezra F. and Bertha (Daniels) S. A.B. magna cum laude, Wittenberg U., 1944, L.H.D. (hon.), 1986; M.A., Miami U., Ohio, 1959; Ed.D., Ind. U., 1972. Cert. tchr., supt., Ohio. Tchr. Miamisburg Pub. Schs., Ohio, 1944-51; tchr., counselor Dayton Pub. Schs., 1952-66, supr. sci. and math. curriculum, 1967-72, acting asst. supt. curriculum, 1972-73, exec. dir. curriculum services, 1973-85; tchr. U. Dayton, 1985—; ednl. cons., writer, 1985—; instr. U. Dayton, Miami U., 1959-74. Author and co-author numerous textbooks, lab. guides. Editor newsletter Ohio Jr. Acad. Sci., 1950-52. Contbr. articles to profl. jours. Mem. Dayton/Montgomery County Arson Task Force; trustee Dayton Mus. Natural History; sec. staff/parish relations com. South Park United Meth. Ch., 1984—. Ford Found. fellow, 1952-53. Mem. NOW, Am. Assn. Sch. Adminstrs., Buckeye Assn. Sch. Adminstrs. (life), Assn. Supervision and Curriculum Devel., Am. Chem. Soc., Nat. Sci. Tchrs. Assn. (life), Ohio Acad. Sci., Phi Delta Kappa, Delta Kappa Gamma (pres. Pi Chpt. 1984-86). Clubs: Altrusa (pres. 1982-84) (Dayton), Pres.'s of Dayton (v.p. 1985-86). Home: 5340 Brendonwood Ln Dayton OH 45415 Office: 213 Chaminade Hall U Dayton 300 College Park Dayton OH 045469

STRAIGHT, BEATRICE WHITNEY (MRS. PETER COOKSON), actress; b. Old Westbury, L.I., N.Y.; d. Willard Dickerman and Dorothy (Whitney) S.; student pvt. schs.; m. Peter Cookson, June 2, 1949; children—Gary, Tony, stepchildren—Peter, Brookse. Appeared in Broadway prodns. The Crucible, Eastward in Eden, The Innocents, Twelfth Night, The Heiress, Macbeth, Sing Me No Lullaby, Everything in the Garden; appeared in off-Broadway prodn. Phedre, All My Sons, 1974; toured with Streetcar Named Desire, 1969-70; motion picture appearances include Phone Call From A Stranger, Patterns, The Silken Affair, The Nun's Story, The Promise, Bloodline, Endless Love, 1981, Poltergeist, 1982; appeared TV series Beacon Hill, 1975, Kings Crossing, 1982; appeared as Rose Kennedy in mini series Robert Kennedy and His Times, 1984; founder Michael Chekov Studio, N.Y.C., 1982—, Eng., U.S.; co-founder Theatre, Inc., 1946. Recipient Antionette Perry award for role in The Crucible, 1953, Acad. award for supporting actress in Network, 1977. Address: 156 E 62d St New York NY 10021

STRAKOSCH, KATHERINE WENTON, executive recruiter; b. N.Y.C., Oct. 4, 1933; d. William J. and Elsie G. (Sullivan) Wenton; m. Raymond D. Strakosch, Nov. 10, 1956 (div. May 1977); children—Joanne, Mark, Gregory, Karen. B.A. cum laude, Coll. Mt. St. Vincent, 1955. Cert. personnel cons. Vice pres. Dunhill of Greater Stamford, Inc., Wilton, Conn., 1976-80, pres., 1980—; mem. Town of Wilton Personnel Policies Com., 1983—. Pres. bd. dirs. Wilton Playshop, 1971-73, vice chmn. bd. trustees, 1982—; mem. Democratic Town Com., Wilton, 1976-79. Mem. Conn. Assn. Personnel Consultants (sec. 1979, mem. ethics com. 1981—, newsletter editor 1980), Nat. Assn. Personnel Consultants. Roman Catholic. Avocations: tennis; travel; reading. Home: 28 Glen Ridge St Wilton CT 06897 Office: Dunhill 213 Danbury Rd Wilton CT 06897

STRAND, NANCY MARIE, nurse; b. Phila., Dec. 27, 1926; d. Edward Joseph and Ella Frances (Waldron) McNelis; student in Nursing, Coll. St. Rose, 1944-47; B.S., N.Y.U., 1951, M.A. in Counseling, 1954; m. Bart Strand, Jan. 15, 1955; children—Deirdre, Maureen, Sheila. Staff nurse, relief supr. VA Hosp., Bronx, N.Y., 1947-59; staff nurse Children's Hosp., Buffalo, 1959-61, VA Hosp., Buffalo, 1961-62; with U. Ark. Hosp., 1962-77, asso. dir. nursing, 1966-73, dir. nursing, 1973-77; clin. coordinator nursing VA Hosp., Little Rock, 1977—; mem. nursing curriculum project So. Regional Edn. Bd.; mem. faculty research workshop U. N.C. R.N. Mem. Am. Nurses Assn. (cert. nursing adminstr.), Ark. State Nurses Assn., Nat. League Nursing, Ark. League Nursing (Ann. award of Merit 1971), AAUW. Roman Catholic. Home: 464 Midland Ave Little Rock AR 72205

STRANG, SANDRA LEE, airline official; b. Greensboro, N.C., Apr. 22, 1936; d. Charles Edward and Lobelia Mae (Squires) S.; B.A. in English, U. N.C., 1960; M.B.A., U. Dallas, 1970. With American Airlines, Inc., 1960—, mgr. career devel. for women, N.Y.C., 1972-73, dir. selection and tng., 1974-75, sr. dir. selection, tng. and affirmative action, 1975-79, sr. dir. compensation and benefits, Grand Prairie, Tex., 1979-84, dir. passenger sales tng. and devel., 1984—. Mem. Am. Mgmt. Assn., Assn. Advancement of Women into Mgmt., Am. Soc. Tng. and Devel., Am. Compensation Assn. Home: 4521 Rawlins St Dallas TX 75219 Office: 4200 American Blvd Euless TX 76039

STRANGE, DOUGLAS HART MCKOY, civic worker; b. Wilmington, N.C., Mar. 16, 1929; d. Adair Morey and Katie Reston (Grainger) McKoy; student Hollins Coll., 1946-48; m. Robert Strange, July 16, 1949; children—Robert VI, John Allan, Elizabeth Adair, Katherine Grainger. Fin. chmn. and provisional co-chmn. Knoxville Jr. League; former tchr. Bible class, vestrywoman, pres. ch. women Fox Chapel Episcopal Ch.; former chmn. Fox Chapel House Tour; former chmn. altar guild, mem. worship com. bd. dirs. ch. women, St. John's Episcopal Ch.; altar chmn. Episcopal Diocese of Tenn.; bd. dirs. Dulin Com., Dulin Gallery Art; invitation coordinator Heart Gala Ball, 1985. Recipient cert. of merit Pitts. Heart Fund, 1975, engraved plate Fox Chapel Episcopal Ch., 1976. Mem. Assn. Jr. Leagues Am., Nat. Soc. Colonial Dames Am. (asst. to editor and bus. mgr. newsletter, 1978-79), Knoxville Civic Opera. Republican. Clubs: Cherokee Garden, Nine-o-clock Cotillion, Cherokee Country. Home: 1126 Bordeaux Circle Knoxville TN 37919

STRATFORD, CAROL ANN DEERING, occupational therapist; b. Columbus, Ohio, Dec. 17, 1946; d. Earl Brent and Gladys May (Wade) Deering; A.A., Brevard Jr. Coll., 1966; B.S., U. Fla., 1968; m. Francis A. Stratford, Jr., Aug. 4, 1973. Staff occupational therapist Hosp. Albert Einstein Coll. Medicine, Bronx, N.Y., 1968-74; sr. research therapist Inst. Rehab. Medicine N.Y. U. Med. Center, N.Y.C., 1975-81, mem. developmental team voice recognition, wheel chair and environ. control system; supr. dept. occupational therapy Danbury (Conn.) Hosp., 1982-84; tech. aids cons., 1984—. Registered occupational therapist. Mem. Am. Occupational Therapy Assn. (resource person in rehab. engring.), Conn. Occupational Therapy Assn., Rehab. Engring. Soc. N. Am. Co-author, editor: (monograph) Environmental Control Systems and Vocational Aids for Persons with High Level Quadriplegia, 1979; contbr. articles to profl. jours. Methodist. Home: Shady Knolls Danbury CT 06811

STRATMAN, MAXINE THEOBALD, banker; b. Brigham, Wis., May 22, 1938; d. Max L. and Gladys B. (Olson) Theobald; student Barneveld (Wis.) public schs.; children—Julie Lynn, Jodie Lynn. With Barneveld State Bank, Ridgeway, Wis., 1956—, beginning in bookkeeping dept., successively teller, asst. br. mgr., mgr. and asst. cashier 1956-80, asst. v.p., br. office mgr., 1980—. Chair Meml. Hosp. Campaign Fund 1980, Ridgeway Salvation Army, 1981—; treas. Methodist Ch. Mem. Iowa County Bankers Assn. (pres. 1984-86), Nat. Assn. Bank Women. Republican. Home: Rt 1 Box 170 Barneveld WI 53507 Office: Barneveld State Bank Main St Ridgeway WI 53582

STRATOULY, PAULA ELAINE, mechanical engineer; b. Chelsea, Mass., May 10, 1954; d. Dean Constantine and Elaine (DeClerico) S. B.S. in Mech. Engring., Worcester Poly. Inst. (Mass.), 1976; M.S. in Fin. Tex. A&M U., 1985. Indsl. sales rep. Exxon Co. U.S.A., Pitts., 1976-79; sales engr. Gulf Oil Co. U.S., Boston, 1980-81; mech. engr. Fluor Engrs., Inc., Houston, 1981-83, R.L. Allen & Assocs., Houston, 1983-84; dir. ops. Dawn Co., Dallas, 1986—; cons. real estate, 1985-86. Probation officer Worcester Juvenile Ct., 1975. Mem. Houston Alumni Orgn. (pres. 1982-85), Beta Sigma Gamma. Home: 5626 Preston Cars #38B Dallas TX 75240

STRATTON, EVELYN JOYCE, lawyer; b. Bangkok, Thailand, Feb. 25, 1953; came to U.S., 1971; d. Elmer John and Corrine Sylvia (Henricksen) Sahlberg; m. R. Stephen Stratton, June 16, 1973; 1 son: Luke Andrew. A.A., U. Fla., 1973; B.A., Akron U., 1975; J.D., Ohio State U., 1978. Bar: Ohio 1979, U.S. Dist. Ct. (so. dist.) Ohio 1979. Teaching asst. history LeTourneau Coll., Longview, Tex., 1973-74; sales clk. Higbees, Canton, Ohio, 1974-76; sales clk. Lazarus, Columbus, Ohio, 1976-78; law clk. Knepper, White, Columbus, 1978-79, Crabbe & Brown, Columbus, 1977-79; assoc. Hamilton, Kramer, Myers & Cheek, Columbus, 1980-85; ptnr. Hopple, Wesp, Osterkamp, Columbus, 1985—; trustee Linc Resources, Columbus, 1980—; speaker legal seminars. Worker Republic Party Campaign, Columbus, 1983-84; vice chmn. fund drive United Way Columbus, 1984; fundraiser Easter Seal Telethon, 1986, Columbus Mus. Art, 1986. Recipient Gold Key award LeTourneau Coll., Gainesville, Fla., 1974; service commendation Ohio Ho. of Reps., 1984. Mem. Columbus Bar Assn. (com. chmn. 1982-84, bd. govs. 1984—), Ohio Bar Assn., ABA, Ohio Assn. Civil Trial Attys., Columbus Def. Assn., Columbus Bar Found. (trustee 1985—), Am. Arbitration Assn., Phi Delta Phi (pres. 1982-83). Clubs: Civitan (trustee 1982-83), Exec. of Columbus (bd. dirs. 1986—). Office: Hopple Wesp Osterkamp 42 E Gay St Suite 812 Columbus OH 43215

STRATTON, LOIS JEAN, state legislator; b. Springdale, Wash., Jan. 5, 1927; d. Charles B. and Ann B. (Hill) Brunton; m. Allen F. Stratton, 1946; children—Alan Edward, Kathleen Prater, Mark Charles, Scott D., Karen Jeanne. Student Kinman Bus. U., 1944-45. Democratic precinct committeewoman, Spokane County, Wash., from 1958; mem. Spokane County Dem. Exec. Bd.; alt. del. Dem. Nat. Conv., 1976; co-chmn. Gov. Dixy Lee Ray Com., 1976; committeewoman Wash. State Dem. Com., from 1977; now mem. Wash. Senate, Dist. 3; exec. sec. pub. affairs Kaiser Aluminum & Chem. Corp., Spokane, from 1963; adminstrv. asst., exec. sec. to pres. Expo 74 World's Fair, Spokane. Recipient World's Fair Expo 74 Vol. Service citations Gov. of Wash. and Wash. State Commn., 1974. Mem. Spokane County Dem. Club (sec.), Jane Jefferson Dem. Club (1st v.p.). Roman Catholic. Office: State Capitol Olympia WA 98504*

STRATTON-MONROE, CHRISTINA MARIA, nurse; b. Monticello, N.Y., Oct. 19, 1948; d. Ludington Burdell and Louise Barbara (Tiffinger) Stratton; m. J. Nelson Monroe, Oct. 11, 1969; children—James Ludington, Katharine Elizabeth-Hamilton. A.A.S., Orange County Community Coll., 1972. Head nurse Loomis Hosp., Liberty, N.Y., 1972-74; charge nurse Monticello Hosp., 1974-75; operating room nurse Hamilton Ave. Hosp., Monticello, 1976-77; jail nurse Sullivan County Jail, Monticello, 1979-82; med. dir. Hebrew Acad. for Spl. Children Residential Sch., Parksville, N.Y., 1979-81; supervising nurse Sullivan County ARC/Bennett Residence, Liberty, N.Y., 1981—; chmn. Bennett Residence Utilization Rev. Com., Liberty, N.Y., 1982—; cons. on Sexuality Policy Sullivan County Assn. for Retarded Children Fallsburg. N.Y., 1983. Author: Bennett Drug Formulary, 1981; (with Gershon J. Weiss) Sexuality Awareness Program, 1983. N.Y. State Bd. Regents nursing scholar, 1966. Democrat. Episcopalian. Office: Sullivan County ARC/Bennett Residence Lake and Carrier Liberty NY 12754

STRAUBER, GRACE FRANCES, hospital administrator; b. N.Y.C., Oct. 24, 1927; d. Jerome James and Grace Frances (Martin) S.; B.B.A., Siena Coll., Loudonville, N.Y., 1963; M.H.A., St. Louis U., 1968. Joined Order Franciscan Sisters of Poor, Roman Catholic Ch., 1947; bus. mgr. St. Francis Hosp., Bronx, N.Y., 1954-56; asst. adminstr. St. Clare Hosp., Schenectady, 1956-59, St. Michael's Med. Center, Newark, 1960-61; asst. adminstr. St. Clare Hosp., Schenectady, 1961-65; provincial treas. Province of St. Anthony, Franciscan Sisters of the Poor, 1966-68; gen. treas. Franciscan Sisters of Poor, 1968-70; exec. dir. St. Mary Hosp., Hoboken, N.J., 1971-80, pres., 1980-85, cons., 1986—, bd. dirs., 1970-85; bd. dirs. St. Anthony Community Hosp., Warwick, N.Y., 1966—, pres. bd., 1980-83; bd. dirs. St. Francis Community Health Center, 1981-85, Hudson Health Systems Agy., 1976-82; dir. Hudson United Bank, 1979—. Named to Hudson County Health Hall of Fame, 1975; named Hudson County Woman of Achievement, 1976. Mem. N.J. Hosp. Assn. (dir. 1977-79), Am. Coll. Hosp. Adminstrs., Am. Hosp. Assn., Cath. Hosp. Assn., Hosp. Fin. Mgmt. Assn., Hosp. Trustees N.Y. State, Nat. Assn. Female Execs., Hudson Hosp. Council, Met. N.Y. Hosp. Fin. Assn., Acad. for Cath. Health Care Leadership, Internat. Health Econs. and Mgmt. Inst. Office: 308 Willow Ave Hoboken NJ 07030

STRAUS, ELLEN SULZBERGER, radio station executive; b. N.Y.C., Mar. 11, 1925; d. David Hays and Louise (Blumenthal) S.; m. R. Peter Straus, Feb. 6, 1950; children—Diane Straus Tucker, Katherine Straus Caple, Jeanne Straus Tofel, Eric. B.A., Smith Coll., 1945; D.C.S. (hon.), St. John's U., 1985; D.H.L. (hon.), Franklin Pierce Coll., 1985. Program sec. LWV, N.Y.C., 1945-48; asst. dir. pub. info. U.S. AEC, 1948-49; campaign mgr. Herbert Lehman for Senate, 1949; fgn. corr. No. N.Y. Newspapers, 1950-55; editor McCall's mag., 1972-74; dir. spl. projects Sta. WMCA, N.Y.C., 1973-76, v.p., 1976-77, pres. 1976—; co-pub. Cranford (N.J.) Citizen & Chronicle, 1976-77. Author: A Smith College Mosaic, 1974; A Survival Kit for New Yorkers, 1973; The Volunteer Professional: What You Need To Know, 1972; Women's Almanac, 1976; monthly column McCall's mag., 1972-74. Pres., chairperson Nat. Call for Action Inc., 1969-75; founder Vol. Profl. Inc., N.Y.C., 1970; aux. policeperson Mounted, Central Park, N.Y.C., 1974-77; mem. nat. steering com. Election of Carter-Mondale, 1976; co-chairperson Women United for N.Y., 1976—; chair communications com. Pres.' Task Force on Pvt. Sector, 1982; Pres., Women's Forum, 1982-83; chair Pub. Safety Com., N.Y.C. partnership, 1981—; mem. State-City Commn. on Integrity in Govt., 1986. Recipient Nat. Council of Women of Conscience award, 1970; Am. Jewish Congress Louise Waterman Wise award, 1971. Smith Coll. medal of honor, 1971; Nat. Council Jewish Women Hannah G. Solomon award, 1972; Olive award Council of Chs. City N.Y., 1983; named Ladies Home Jour Woman of Yr., 1973; Woman of Outstanding Achievement, Women's Equity League, 1984; Am. Inst. Pub. Service award, 1974; B'nai B'rith Women Dist. award, 1976; Caveat Emptor Mag. Consumer Crusader award, 1978; Abram L. Sachar award Brandeis U., 1980; Amita Golden Lady achievement award, 1981; Radio award Am. Women in Radio and TV, 1984; Caring New Yorker award Community Council Greater N.Y., 1986. Democrat. Jewish. Office: WMCA Radio 888 7th Ave New York NY 10019

STRAUS, JEANNE H., broadcaster; b. Washington, Mar. 19, 1957; d. R. Peter and Ellen (Sulzberger) Straus; m. Richard Jeffrey Tofel, Feb. 26, 1983. B.A., Dartmouth Coll., 1979. Staff asst. Spl. Trade Rep., Washington, 1979; editorial asst. White House News Summary, Washington, 1979-80; stringer AP, Jerusalem, Israel, 1980; v.p., program dir. WMCA Radio, N.Y.C., 1980-85, v.p. ops., 1985—; dir. Straus Communications, N.Y.C., 1982—. Trustee, Riverdale Country Sch., N.Y., 1984; co-chair, mem. com. N.Y. chpt. Am. Jewish Com., 1985—. Konrad Adenauer Found. fellow, Fed. Republic Germany, 1985. Democrat. Jewish. Office: WMCA Radio 888 7th Ave New York NY 10019

STRAUSS, DEBORAH E., hotel company executive; b. Buffalo, Aug. 22, 1956; d. Curt L. and Alice Agatha (Klavzer) S.; m. John A. Droney, Oct. 21, 1979 (div. Aug. 1984). B.A. in Sociology, Ithaca Coll., 1978. Personnel clk. Broadway Southwest, Tucson, 1980-81; asst. mgr. Cranberry Inn, Chatham, Mass., 1981-83; asst. personnel dir. Arrowwood, Rye Brook, N.Y., 1983-84, dir. personnel, 1984—. Editor Whispers, 1984—. Rep. March of Dimes, Westchester, N.Y., 1985—, United Way, Westchester, 1985—; coordinator Adopt-A-School Program, Rye, N.Y., 1985—; mem. Job Service Employers' Com., White Plains, N.Y., 1984—. Mem. Am. Soc. Personnel Adminstrs., Nat. Assn. Female Execs., Westchester C. of C. Avocations: sailing; public speaking; nautilus; travel. Home: 55 N Broadway Apt 8 White Plains NY 10601 Office: Arrowwood of Westchester Anderson Hill Rd Rye Brook NY 10573

STRAVATO, CLAUDIA DELAUGHTER, state official; b. Dallas, May 25, 1942; d. Arman Dale and Nina Marie (Bear) DeLaughter; student U. Mo., 1967-70, Tex. Womans U., 1959-60, U. Tex., Arlington, 1961-66; B.S., W. Tex. State U., 1974, M.A., 1977; children by previous marriage—Michael Armand, Anna Teresa. Adminstrv. asst. to pres. AMA, Dallas, 1961-67; dir. Panhandle div. Arthritis Found., Amarillo, Tex., 1971-73; enforcement fieldmgr. Tex. Comptroller of Public Accts., Amarillo, 1976-84, Pres., Amarillo Republican Womens Club, 1974-75; bd. dirs. Amarillo LWV, 1973; chmn. High Plains Womens Polit. Caucus, 1974, 79; founder, co-chmn. Amarillo Rape Crisis Service, 1975; state polit. action chmn. Tex. Womens Polit. Caucus, 1977; bd. dirs. Tex. Abortion Rights Action League, 1978—, Tex. Women's Advocacy Project, 1982-85; founder, 1st pres. Amarillo Women's Network, 1980-81. Named Woman of Yr., Amarillo NOW, 1977, Mem. Tex. Press Women (dir. 1984-85), Exec. Women in Tex. Govt. (founder, pres. 1985), NAACP, ACLU (state dir. 1984—, pres. High Plains chpt. 1982—). Unitarian. Home: 210 S Avondale Amarillo TX 79106 Office: LBJ Office Bldg Austin TX 78701

STRAW, BARBARA CURTIS, management analyst; b. Phila., Nov. 22, 1950; d. James Robert and Marie Lily (Phillips) Curtis; B.S. with distinction, Pa. State U., 1973; M.S., Drexel U., 1978; m. Ronald Charles Straw, June 29, 1974; 1 son, Jonathan David. Mgmt. analyst mgmt. analysis br. Navy Ships Parts Control Center, Mechanicsburg, Pa., 1973-78, orgn. and manpower devel. sect., 1978-80, supr. orgn. and position mgmt. sect., 1980-82, head orgn. planning br., 1982—; mem. fed. women's program subcom., 1975-79; career counselor, 1979—. Mem. Federally Employed Women (program chairperson Almech chpt. 1978-79, pres. 1979-81, treas. 1982-83, mem. nat. awards com. 1982-83, chmn. scholarship and tng. com. 1983-84, chmn. nominating com. 1984-85), Exec. Assn. Central Pa. Nat. Ichthyosis Found., Nat. Assn. Female Execs., Psi Chi. Roman Catholic. Home: 3615 Dwayne Ave Mechanicsburg PA 17055 Office: PO Box 2020 Code 0731 5450 Carlisle Pike Mechanicsburg PA 17055

STRAWINSKY, ELIZABETH ROWE, psychiatrist; b. Gainesville, Fla., Aug. 31, 1925; d. Albert Reed and Elizabeth Ellen (Rowe) Caro; B.S., Coll. William and Mary, 1948; M.D., Med. Coll. Va., 1948; m. Albert Strawinsky, Dec. 28, 1957. Intern, St. Elizabeths Hosp., Washington, 1948-49, resident in psychiatry, 1949-52, clin. dir., 1962-69, dir. forensic programs, 1969-73; psychiatrist No. Va. Mental Health Inst., Falls Church, 1974—. Recipient Superior Performance award, HEW, 1962. Diplomate Am. Bd. Psychiatry and Neurology. Fellow Am. Psychiat. Assn.; mem. AMA, Med. Soc. Va., Washington Psychiat. Soc., Am. Acad. Psychiatry and Law, Am. Group Psychotherapy Assn., Am. Med. Women's Assn., N.Y. Acad. Scis. Democrat. Home: 16000 Bealle Hill Rd Accokeek MD 20607 Office: 3302 Gallows Rd Falls Church VA 22042

STRAWN, FRANCES FREELAND, Realtor, broker, real estate executive; b. Waynesville, N.C., Nov. 18, 1946; d. Thomas M. and Jimmie (Smith) Freeland; m. David Updegraff Strawn, Aug. 31, 1974; children—Laurel, Kirk, Trisha. A.A., Brevard Community Coll., Cocoa, Fla., 1975; postgrad. U. Central Fla., 1979. Acting sr. buyer Brevard County Purchasing Bd. of County Commns., Titusville, Fla., 1971-75; asst. to v.p. Brevard Community Coll., Cocoa, Fla., 1975-76; realtor assoc. Area One, Inc., Orlando, Fla., 1979-83; pres., realtor Advance Am., Inc., Orlando, 1983—. Contbr. articles to profl. publs. Gen. worker campaigns for Fla. Senate, Fla. Ho. of Reps., gubernatorial campaigns, Titusville, 1975-83; program chmn. Young Republican Women, Orlando, 1983; mem. Rep. Womens Orgn., Orlando, 1983. Mem. Orlando Bd. Realtors (grievance com. 1985), Fla. Assn. Govt. Purchasing (asst. membership chmn. 1971-75), Orlando Area Bd. Realtors (membership com. 1980-84, profl. standards com. 1983-84). Club: Horizan (bd. govs. 1985). Avocations: cooking; traveling; needle point; embroidery; cross-stitch. Home: 8338 Caracas Ave Orlando FL 32825 Office: Advance Am Inc 100 W Lucerne Circle Suite 602 Orlando FL 32801

STRAWN, SARAH CATHERINE, veterinarian; b. Bloomington, Ind., Apr. 28, 1951; d. Richard R. and Doris M. (Turner) S. B.A., Earlham Coll., 1975; D.V.M., Purdue U., 1975. Gen. practice vet. medicine Hafner Vet. Clinic, Huntington, Ind., 1975-76, Crawfordsville, (Ind.) Vet. Clinic, 1976-78; owner, veterinarian Brookville (Ind.) Vet. Clinic, 1978-85; small animal vet. practitioner Green Valley Vet. Clinic, Yucaipa, Calif., 1985—. Mem. AVMA, Calif. Vet. Med. Assn., Ind. Vet. Med. Assn., Phi Zeta. Democrat. Office: Green Valley Vet Clinic 35037 Ave B Yucaipa CA 92399

STREBEIGH, BARBARA, organization administrator, editor; b. Rye, N.Y., July 29, 1902; d. Harold Strebeigh and Blanche (Pierce) Bonaparte. Student Sargent Sch. Phys. Edn. (now Boston U.), 1923; sculpture student of Alexander Archipenko, 1940-41; student U. Calif.-San Diego Extension, 1924-25. Mem. phys. therapy staff U.S. Marine Hosp., San Francisco, 1923-24; head dept. field hockey Sargent Coll. Camp, N.H., 20 yrs.; dir. Firefly Diabetic Camp for Children, Pa., 1949; from sec. to v.p. to pres. Airedale Terrier Club Am., 1948-85, hon. pres., dir. 1985—; dog show judge, 1950—; bd. dirs. Animal Rescue League, Phila., 1975—. Author: Pet Airedale Terrier, 1960; Your Airedale. Editor newsletters for Airedale Terrier Club Am., 1948-85; contbr. to field hockey guides; columnist for various dog mags. Exhibitor terracotta sculpture in galleries. Mem. All-Am. Hockey Team, 1928-40. Mem. U.S. Field Hockey Assn. (sec. 1937-40, originator former editor Eagle). Republican. Episcopalian. Home: Beaver Hill Rd Birchrunville PA 19421

STRECKER, FRANCES IRENE BROWN, civic worker; b. Denver, Aug. 28, 1896; d. Edward Newton and Frances Evelyn (Hittson) Brown; student Colo. Woman's Coll., 1917; m. George O. Strecker, Oct. 21, 1922 (dec. May 1962); children—Muriel Frances, Roger William. Pres. women's aux. Highland Park (Ill.) Hosp., 1956-60, Northwestern U. Settlement, 1960-64; pres. Glencoe (Ill.) Sr. Aux. Infant Welfare Soc. Chgo., 1968-71; corr. sec. Eng. women HEW, 1978-80, chaplain, 1980-82. Mem. Colonial Dames Am. (pres. chpt. 1965-71),

Women's Descs. Ancient and Hon. Arty. Co. (pres. Ill. chpt. 1968-71, v.p. Conn. chpt. 1977-80, dep. 1980-83), Greenwich New Eng. Women (librarian 1982—), Ill. Soc. Daus. Colonial Wars (rec. sec. 1968-71, chaplain 1974-77, corr. sec. Conn. 1977-80), Nat. Soc. Daus. Founders and Patriots Am. (pres. Ill. chpt. 1964-67, council Conn. chpt. 1975-78, 81—), Conn. Soc. Genealogists, Colo., Stamford (pres. 1975-77) geneal. socs., Colo. Hist. Soc., Conn. Hist. Soc., Stamford Hist. Soc., Conn. Daus. Am. Colonists (v.p. 1976-78, 82-84, pres. 1978-80, librarian 1984-86), DAR (N. Shore regent 1946-48, 53-54, chaplain Stamford chpt. 1975-77, librarian 1977-79, chmn. manuals 1979-85), Pilgrims, Colo. Hist. Soc. Episcopalian. Clubs: Stamford Woman's; Denver Athletic; New Eng. Women (chaplain 1984-86). Republican. Home: 39 Tannery Ln Weston CT 06883

STRECKER, SUSAN LINNEA, editor, association executive; b. Aurora, Ill., Aug. 22, 1941; d. John Anthony and Doris (Connery) S.; student Coll. of St. Teresa, 1959-61; B.A. in English, So. Meth. U., 1963. Area supr. Am. Field Service, N.Y.C., 1964-66; adminstrv. sec. B.D./M.T.S. com. Harvard U. Div. Sch., Cambridge, Mass., 1967-68; tchr. Boston Public Schs., 1968-73, Albert Inst. and Am. Sch., Madrid, 1973-75; office mgr. Allende & Brea, N.Y.C., 1975-77; analytic asst. Citibank, N.Y.C., 1977-78; v.p. publs., editor Exec. Female and More Money mags., Nat. Assn. Female Execs., 1978—; start-up cons. mags.; freelance editor, writer; feature stories pub. The Exec. Female, Collector Editions Quar. Mem. Women in Communications (roundtable chmn. N.Y. chpt.). Home: 324 E 77th St New York NY 10021 Office: 1041 3d Ave New York NY 10021

STREEP, MERYL (MARY LOUISE STREEP), actress; b. Summit, N.J.; d. Harry Jr. and Mary W. Streep; B.A., Vassar Coll., 1971; M.A. in Fine Arts, Yale U., 1975; D.Arts (hon.), Dartmouth Coll., 1981; m. Donald J. Gummer, 1978; children—Henry, Mary Willa, Grace. Appeared with Green Mountain Guild, Woodstock, Vt.; debut at Lincoln Center Beaumont Theater in Trelawny of the Wells, 1975; N.Y.C. theatrical appearances include: 27 Wagons Full of Cotton (Theatre World award), A Memory of Two Mondays, Henry V, Secret Service, The Taming of the Shrew, Measure for Measure, The Cherry Orchard, Happy End, Wonderland, Taken in Marriage, Alice in Concert; movie appearances include: Julia, 1977, The Deer Hunter (Best Supporting Actress award Nat. Soc. Film Critics), 1978, Manhattan, 1979, The Seduction of Joe Tynan, 1979, Kramer vs. Kramer (N.Y. Film Critics' award and Los Angeles Film Critics' award for best actress, Acad. Motion Picture Arts and Scis. award for best supporting actress), 1980, The French Lieutenant's Woman (Brit. Motion Picture Acad. award for best actress), 1981, Still of the Night, 1982, Sophie's Choice (Acad. Motion Picture Arts and Scis. award for best actress), 1982, Silkwood, 1983, Falling in Love, 1984, Plenty, 1985, Out of Africa, 1985; TV film: The Deadliest Season, 1977; TV mini-series: Holocaust (Emmy award), 1978; TV dramatic spls.: Secret Service, 1977, Uncommon Women and Others, 1978. Recipient Mademoiselle award, 1976; Woman of Yr. award B'nai Brith, 1979, Hasty Pudding Soc., Harvard U., 1980; People's Choice award, 1983. Office: care Internat Creative Mgmt 40 W 57th St New York NY 10019

STREEPER, MARY SUE, librarian, consultant; b. Cleve., Feb. 11, 1949; d. Nicholas Thomas and Mary (Popa) Daramus; m. Steven Michael Streeper, Oct. 7, 1978. Diplome superieur d'etudes Francaise, U. Strasbourg (France), 1970; B.A., Denison U., 1971; M.A., U. Denver, 1976. Cataloging asst. U. Wyo., Laramie, 1973-75; reference librarian Wyo. State Library, Cheyenne, 1976-78, collection devel. automation officer, 1978-79, head bibliographic services/automation, 1979-83, head tech. services, 1983—; library automation cons. Cin. Electronics Corp., 1982. Editor Wyoming Union List of Periodicals, 1978; contbr. articles to profl. jours. Active Zonta Club Cheyenne, 1982—; Library of Congress name authority liaison from Wyo., 1985—. Mem. ALA, Mountain Plains Library Assn., Wyo. Library Assn. (sec. 1984-85). Home: 404 Hacker Ct Cheyenne WY 82009 Office: Wyo State Library Supreme Ct Bldg Cheyenne WY 82002

STREEKY-GENET, HEIDI MARIE, lawyer; b. Zel am See, Saalfelden, Austria, Apr. 8, 1954; came to U.S., 1955; d. John Mitchell and Katherine (Pfendt) Streeky; m. Nico Gerard Genet, Oct. 29, 1983. B.A. with honors in English and Polit. Sci., Elmhurst Coll., 1976; J.D., John Marshall Law Sch., 1980. Bar: Ill. 1980, U.S. Dist. Ct. (no. dist.) Ill. 1980. Research asst. to Prof. Arthur Sabin, Chgo., 1978-80; assoc. firm Holstein, Mack & Assocs., Chgo., 1980—; arbitrator Am. Arbitration Assn., Chgo., 1980—. Author and editor course materials Ill. Trial Lawyers Assn., 1980; editor: Product Liability Law, 1978. Mem. ABA, Ill. Bar Assn., Chgo. Bar Assn., Assn. Trial Lawyers Am., Ill. Trial Lawyers Assn. Democrat. Office: Holstein Mack and Assocs 30 N LaSalle St Suite 3220 Chicago IL 60602

STREET, JULIA MONTGOMERY (MRS. CLAUDIUS AUGUSTUS STREET), writer; b. Concord, N.C., Jan. 19, 1898; d. Samuel Lewis and Elizabeth Blanche (Norris) Montgomery; A.B., U. N.C., Greensboro, 1923; m. Claudius Augustus Street, Sept. 13, 1924; children—Carol Street McMillian, Claudius Augustus. Tchr. public schs., N.C., 1918-20, 23-24; field worker N.C. Children's Home Soc., Greensboro, 1924; faculty U. N.C., Greensboro, summer 1922; cons. N.C. History-in-Sch. Radio, 1970—; script writer N.C. History (radio) State of N.C., 1970—. Mem. Winston-Salem (N.C.) Radio Council, 1940—. Recipient award AAUW, 1956, 63, 66; Alumni Service award U. N.C., Greensboro, 1967. Mem. N.C. Poetry Soc., N.C. Writers Conf., N.C. Folklore Soc., N.C. Lit. and Hist. Assn. Author: Fiddler's Fancy, 1955; Moccasin Tracks, 1958; Candle Love Feast, 1959; Drovers' Gold, 1961; Dulcie's Whale, 1963; (with Richard Walser) North Carolina Parade, 1966, 2d edit., 1972, paperback edit., 1984; (poetry) Street Lights, 1949; Salem Christmas Eve, 1955; Judaculla's Handprint, and Other Mysteries from North Carolina, 1975; book reviewer Suburbanite. Contbr. articles to various mags. Home: 545 Oaklawn Ave Winston-Salem NC 27104

STREET, NANCY HACKNEY, accountant; b. Springfield, Tenn., Sept. 8, 1958; d. Brooks Hall and Margaret Anne (Adams) Hackney; m. Don Street, July 30, 1982. B.B.A., Belmont Coll., 1980. Corp. acct. Am. Retirement Corp. Nashville, 1980—.

STREETER, ANNE PAUL, state senator; b. Phila., July 21, 1926; d. Henry Neill and Marianne Frazer (Harris) Paul; B.A., Smith Coll., 1948; m. Ronald Mather Streeter, June 18, 1949; children—Jean M., Deborah H., Stephen M., Richard H., Jonathan P. Mem. town council Town of West Hartford (Conn.), 1973-81, mayor, 1975-81; chmn. Capitol Region Council of Govts., 1979-81; pres. West Hartford Community TV, Inc., 1979-84; mem. Conn. Senate, 1983—, dep. majority leader, 1984-86; v.p. Environ. Ctr., Inc., 1983—. Named Man of Yr., West Hartford C. of C., 1979. Mem. LWV (pres. Central San Mateo, Calif. 1966-67, pres. West Hartford 1970-73). Republican. Congregationalist.

STREHLAU, BETTY GENE, educator; b. Seattle; d. John A. and Clara (Wabraushek) S.; B.A., U. Wash., 1944, M.A., 1954. Asst. advt. and asst. sales promotion dir. The Bon Marche, Seattle; sales promotion dir. Western Hotels Internat., Seattle; propr., dir. Strehlau Publicity and Advt. Services, Seattle; co-pub. West Woodland-Fremont News, Seattle; prof. journalism and mass media Highline Coll., Midway, Wash., 1962-80; propr. Strehlau Pub. Relations, Advt. and Mktg., 1981—. Mem. Wash. Press Women (Superior Performance award 1965, Torchbearer award 1979), Community Coll. Journalism Assn. (nat. pres. 1979—), Pacific N.W. Assn. Journalism Educators (regional pres. 1979-80), Am. Women in Radio and TV (Wash. State pres. 1979), Nat. Council Coll. Publ. Advisors (Nat. Disting. Advisor 1977), Nat. Press Women Assn., Women in Communications (Founders' award for leading communicator 1980), Pi Lambda Theta, Alpha Delta Pi. Club: Wash. Athletic. Office: Strehlau Pub Relations Advt Mktg 835 Securities Bldg Seattle WA 98101

STREISAND, BARBRA JOAN, singer, actress; b. Bklyn., Apr. 24, 1942; d. Emanuel and Diana (Rosen) S.; student Yeshiva of Bklyn.; m. Elliott Gould, Mar. 1963 (div.); 1 son, Jason Emanuel. N.Y. theatre debut Another Evening with Harry Stoones, 1961; appeared Broadway musical I Can Get It for You Wholesale, 1962, Funny Girl, 1964-65; rec. artist Columbia Records; motion pictures include: Funny Girl, 1968, Hello Dolly, 1969, On a Clear Day You Can See Forever, 1970, The Owl and the Pussy Cat, 1970, What's Up Doc?, 1972, Up the Sandbox, 1972, The Way We Were, 1973, For Pete's Sake, 1974, Funny Lady, 1975, The Main Event, 1979, All Night Long, 1981; star, producer film A Star is Born, 1976; dir., co-author screenplay, star Yentl, 1983; TV spls. include: My Name is Barbra (5 Emmy awards), 1965, Color Me Barbra, 1966, Putting it Together, HBO, 1986; record albums include: People, 1965, My Name is Barbra, 1965, Color Me Barbra, 1966, Stoney End, 1971, Barbra Joan Streisand, 1972, The Way We Were, 1974, A Star is Born, 1976, Superman, 1977, The Stars Salute Israel at 30, 1978, Wet, 1979, (with Barry Gibb) Guilty, 1980, The Broadway Album, 1985. Recipient Acad. award as best actress of 1968 (Funny Girl); Georgie award AGVA, 1977; Grammy awards for best female vocalist, 1964, 65, 78, for best song writer (with Paul Williams), 1978, for album of yr., 1963. Address: William Morris Agy care Stan Kamen 151 El Camino Beverly Hills CA 90212

STRETCH, SHIRLEY MARIE, marketing educator; b. Wauneta, Nebr., May 6, 1949; d. Lloyd Ray and Roberta Marie (Schroeder) S.; B.S., U. Nebr., 1971; M.S., Kans. State U., 1972; M.B.A., Ohio State U., 1977, Ph.D., 1982. Instr. clothing and textiles Bowling Green (Ohio) State U., 1972-75; grad. adminstrv. asso. Univ. Coll., Ohio State U., 1976-78, 80; asso. mgr. direct mktg. div. Ashland Petroleum Co. (Ky.), 1979-80; asst. prof. clothing and textiles Tex. Tech U., Lubbock, 1980-85; assoc. prof. mktg. Valdosta State Coll., Ga., 1985—. Pres., mem. bd. adminstrn. Sunport Condominium. Ednl. Profl. Devel. fellow, 1971-73. Mem. Am. Mktg. Assn., Lubbock Assn. M.B.A. Execs., Nat. Assn. Female Execs., Am. Home Econs. Assn., So. Mktg. Assn., Southwestern Mktg. Assn., Am. Collegiate Retailing Assn., Omicron Nu, Phi Upsilon Omicron. Republican. Methodist. Home: 1614 Williams St Apt V-6 Valdosta GA 31601 Office: Dept Mktg Valdosta State Coll Valdosta GA 31698

STRICH, GABRIELLE LYONS, lawyer; b. Haifa, Israel, Aug. 11, 1951; came to U.S., 1957; d. Werner Eli and Ruth Joy (Lyons) S.; m. Robert S. Kivetz, Aug. 20, 1972 (div. 1976); m. Andrew C. Lipka, Aug. 19, 1984. A.A., Miami U.-Oxford, Ohio, 1972; B.A. with honors, U. South Fla., 1974; J.D., Rutgers U.-Camden, 1980. Bar: Pa. Personnel mgmt. trainee Exchange Nat. Bank of Tampa, Fla., 1973-74; employee relations assoc. Am. Can Co., Tampa, 1974-75, adminstr. employment and benefits, Tampa, 1975-76, coordinator employee relations, Edison, N.J., 1976-77, coordinator satellite employee relations, Oakland, Calif., 1977-78, gen. supr. employee relations, Phila., 1978-79; assoc. labor relations counsel ARA Services, Inc., Phila. 1980-81; atty. litigation and labor depts. Pepper, Hamilton and Scheetz, Phila., 1981-82; corp. counsel Phila. Gas Works, 1982-84, mgr. claims and ins., 1984—. Mem. Am. Soc. Personnel Adminstrs. (regional dir. student chpts. 1975-76), Pi Beta Phi. Democrat. Jewish. Home: 1631 Country Mill Dr Cranbury NJ 08512 Office: Philadelphia Gas Works 1800 N 9th St Philadelphia PA 19122

STRICK, DOLLY JEAN, nurse practitioner, hypnotherapist, consultant; b. Los Angeles, Mar. 15, 1949; d. Richard Melvin and Faye Louise (Smith) Mack; m. Walter George Strick, June 15, 1968; children—Leanette, Tanya, Jeanelle, Denise, Thi. Student Met. State U., 1969-71, 83—; grad. nurse practitioner St. Joseph Hosp., 1969. Team leader Colo. Gen. Hosp., Denver, 1971-72; foster care team mem. Evergreen Devel. Ctr., Denver, 1972-83; clin. specialist Gardner-Denver, Denver, 1974-75; med. dir. Personal Arts, Golden, Colo., 1975-76; med. instr. Parks Coll., Denver, 1976-78; health coordinator Notre Dame Sch., Denver, 1981-84; pvt. cons., Denver, 1981-86; dir. Stop Taking Our Children, 1984-86, v.p., 1986; child advocate, 1985-86; guardian ad litem vol., Colo. Bd. dirs. Notre Dame Church and Sch., Denver, 1981-84; ACS grantee, Denver, 1971. Mem. Colo. Foster Parent Assn., Denver County Foster Parent Assn. Democrat. Roman Catholic. Home: 3904 W Quigley Dr Denver CO 80236

STRICKLAND, BUNNY JUMP, caterer, accountant, bridal consultant; b. Athens, Ga., Apr. 12, 1925; d. Claude Arthur and Myrtle Florence (Barnwell) Jump; m. Warren Davis Strickland, Dec. 22, 1945; children—Warren David, Jacque Bonita Niles. A.A., Mercer U., 1969. Bookkeeper Firestone Tires, Jesup, Ga., 1950-61, Rural Electric Assn., Jesup, 1964-67, Jones Ford, Jesup, 1967-69, Wayne TV, Jesup, 1969-82; cosmetologist Laurie's, Jesup, 1961-64; contract caterer ITT-Rayonier, Jesup, 1980—; caterer, food service cons., Jesup, 1982—; bridal cons., floral designer, cake designer, gown seamstress, Jesup, 1962—. Asst. chmn. Bloodmobile Procurement Team, 1958; chmn. fund raising com. PTA, 1958; campaign aide Jones for Ga. Ho. Reps., 1955; hostess Thomas for U.S. Congress, 1982; pres. Band Boosters, 1961; chmn. benevolent com. 1st Bapt. Ch., 1968-75, dir. Sunday Schs., 1956- 68, tchr., 1978—; active Hosp. Aux., Jesup. Winner 1st place in class, Body Building Competition, Dalton, Ga., 1983, 3rd place overall, 1983; placed 2nd Paper Chase Mile Run, 1983. Mem. AAU. Democrat. Club: Jesup Garden (sec. 1974-78, pres. 1977-81). Lodge: Eastern Star. Avocations: oil painting; cooking; sewing; running; body building.

STRICKLAND, CAROL ANNE, trust company executive; b. Cold Spring, N.Y., Dec. 21, 1949; d. David J., Jr., and Katharine J. (Daly) S.; m. Thomas C. McGinnis, Jr., Sept. 1, 1979; 1 dau., Ashley Katharine. B.A., Skidmore Coll., 1972; Trusts and Estates cert. Inst. Paralegal Tng., Phila., 1972; M.P.A., NYU, 1978. Paralegal, Sherman & Sterling, N.Y.C., 1972-74; estate planner Chem. Bank, N.Y.C., 1974-76; asst. sec. U.S. Trust Co. N.Y., N.Y.C., 1976-78, corp. sec., 1979-80, v.p. and sec., 1980—; cons. Arts and Bus. Council, Inc., N.Y.C., 1974-80. Bd. dirs. Counterpoint Theatre Co., N.Y.C., 1974-80. Mem. Am. Soc. Corp. Secs. (sec. N.Y. regional group 1982-83, treas. 1983-84, v.p. and program chair 1984-85, pres. 1985-86, dir. 1986—). Episcopalian. Home: 6 Olde English Ct Woodcliff Lake NJ 07675 Office: US Trust Corp 45 Wall St New York NY 10005

STRICKLAND, CHARLOTTE ROZIER, mortgage banker; b. West Palm Beach, Fla., Dec. 21, 1953; d. Ralph R. and Rebecca (Tromp) Rozier; m. J. Ray Strickland, May 23, 1986. Grad. high sch. Customer service rep. SCN Bank, Columbia, S.C., 1972-74; loan processor Collateral Investment Co., Columbia, 1974-78; br. mgr. Mortgage Corp. of South, Columbia, 1978-82; asst. v.p. Colonial Mortgage Co., Columbia, 1982—; fee examiner HUD, Columbia, 1983—. Named an Outstanding Woman of Yr., Heritage World, Columbia, 1981. Mem. Mortgage Bankers Carolinas, Greater Columbia Mortgage Bankers (pres. 1982). Home: 1200 Princeton St Columbia SC 29205 Office: 712 Calhoun St Columbia SC 29201

STRICKLAND, DEBRA LYNN, publisher; b. Denver, Apr. 27, 1958; d. William Edward and Carol Lynn (Schlotterback) S. Student Colo. State U., 1976-78, U. No. Colo., 1978-79. Research coordinator Moore & Co. Realtors, Denver, 1979-80; regional pub. Black's Guide, Englewood, Colo., 1980—; v.p. Blacks Research Inc., Englewood, 1980—; founder, pres. Women's Real Estate Network, Denver, 1983—. Mem. Nat. Assn. Female Execs., Denver Advt. Fedn., Denver C. of C., Centennial C. of C., Womens Real Estate Network (pres. 1983), Bldg. Owners, Mgrs. Assn., Internat. Real Estate Mgmt. Republican. Home: 960 Pennsylvania #12 Denver CO 80203 Office: Black's Guide 5680 S Syracuse St Suite 300 Englewood CO 80110

STRICKLAND, MARGARET CHAPPELL, gerontologist; b. Harlan, Ky., Apr. 22, 1941; d. Clarence Delmer and Edna O. (Collins) Pyle; m. Raymond L. Tassinari, Sept. 1966 (div. Feb. 1979); children—Michael Joseph, David Anthony; m. James Clyde Strickland, Feb. 14, 1980 (div Dec. 1982). A.A., Pasco-Hernando Community Coll., 1974; B.A., St. Leo Coll., 1976; postgrad. U. South Fla., 1982—. Recreational therapist Sr. Guidance Ctr., New Port Richey, Fla., 1976-78; activity coordinator John Knox Village of Tampa Bay Med Ctr., Tampa, Fla., 1979—; mem. adv. bd. dirs. Anclote Manor Hosp., 1977-79, Paseo Mental Health Assn., 1976-79; bd. dirs. Peoples Pharmacy Continuing Edn. Adv. Council, Tampa, 1986; participant Fla. Gov.'s Challenge Program, 1982, 83, 84. Vol. Tampa Bay Performing Arts Ctr., 1985—. Mem. So. Gerontol. Soc., Fla. Health Care Activity Coordinators Assn. (dist. pres. 1980-81, state v.p. 1981-82), Fla. Folk Dance Council, Fla. Blue Key, Sigma Phi Omega. Club: Friends of Fla. Folk (pres. 1982-83). Avocations: folk dancing; scuba diving; hot air ballooning; traveling. Home: 1801 Morrison Ave Tampa FL 33606 Office: John Knox Village of Tampa Bay Med Ctr 4100 Fletcher Ave Tampa FL 33613

STRICKLAND, SHERRY ANN, lawyer; b. Houston, July 18, 1956; d. Shelby Clark and Doris Jean (Brown) S. B.A. in Sociology, Baylor U., 1977; J.D., South Tex. Coll. Law, 1980. Bar: Tex. 1980. Assoc. firm Margraves, Schueler, Parker and Montgomery, Houston, 1980-81; atty. Columbia Gas Devel. Corp., Houston, 1981—. Mem. ABA, Tex. Bar Assn., Houston Bar Assn., Tex. Young Lawyers Assn., Houston Young Lawyers Assn., Delta Delta Delta, Gamma Phi Beta, Delta Theta Phi. Presbyterian. Home: 6633 W Airport Apt 805 Houston TX 77035 Office: Columbia Gas Devel 1700 West Loop South Houston TX 77027

STRICKLER, DIANA HOLE, investment banker; b. N.Y.C., July 25, 1951; d. Richard Witherspoon and Tacey (Belden) Hole; student Wellesley Coll., 1969-71; B.A., magna cum laude, Williams Coll., 1973; M.B.A., Columbia U., 1979; m. Richard Stoner Strickler, Jr., June 11, 1977; children—Margaret Evans Hennen, William Belden. Comml. officer First Pa. Bank, Phila., 1974-77; cons. Booz Allen & Hamilton, N.Y.C., 1978; v.p. corp. fin. dept. First Boston Corp., N.Y.C., 1979—. Trustee Williams Coll., 1977-81; bd. dirs. Columbia Bus. Sch. Alumni Assn. Mem. Phi Beta Kappa, Beta Gamma Sigma. Republican. Episcopalian. Clubs: Siwanoy Country (Bronxville, N.Y.); Madison Beach. Home: 10 The Byway Bronxville NY 10708 Office: Park Avenue Plaza New York NY 10055

STRICKLIN, ELIZABETH RAY, real estate manager; b. Vallejo, Calif., June 20, 1945; d. T.C. and Viva (Ellison) Stricklin; children—Kimberly Deanne, Brandi Ray, Chance E. Noble. B.B.A., So. Meth. U. Hosp. adminstr. Green Clinic Hosp., Dallas, 1968-73; leasing mgr. Keystone Park, Dallas, 1973-80; real estate mgr. Henry S. Miller Co., Dallas, 1983—; mem. Tex. Real Estate Commn., 1978; instr. Brookhaven Community Coll. Mem. Dallas Bd. Realtors, Inst. Real Estate Mgmt. Republican. Episcopalian. Home: 3840 Mockingbird Ln Dallas TX 75205 Office: Henry S Miller Co 2001 Bryan Tower 30th Floor Dallas TX 75201

STRIGENZ, DEBORAH ANN, lawyer, educator; b. Stuttgart, W.Ger., Mar. 8, 1956; came to U.S., 1958; d. Anthony and Elizabeth A. (Walker) S. B.S. in Elem. Edn., U. Wis.-Oshkosh, 1978, M.S. in Ednl. Adminstrn., U. Wis.-Madison, 1980, J.D., 1981. Bar: Wis. 1981, U.S. Dist. Ct. (we. dist.) Wis. 1981. Coordinator law-related edn. Drake U., Des Moines, 1981—, dir. law sch. placement, 1983—; instr. Des Moines Area Community Coll., Ankeny, Iowa, 1982—. Contbr. articles to profl. publs. Student selection coordinator Am. Field Service, Des Moines, 1983. Named regional finalist client counseling competition U. Wis. Law Sch., 1981. Mem. State Bar Assn. Wis., ABA, Polk County Bar Assn., Iowa State Bar Assn. (law day com.), Polk County Women Attys. Assn. (bd. govs., chairperson community edn. com. 1983-84). Home: 2011 40th Pl Des Moines IA 50310 Office: Drake U Law Sch Drake U Des Moines IA 50311

STRINGHAM, JUDITH MITCHELL, equipment sales exec.; b. Hartford, Conn., May 9, 1939; d. William Joseph and Irene Elizabeth (Campion) Mitchell; A.A.S., Fashion Inst. Tech., 1959; B.S., Cornell U., 1961; M.S., SUNY, New Paltz, 1964; m. Varick Van Wyck Stringham, Jr., June 15, 1963; children—Amanda, Pamela, Varick Van Wyck III, Rebecca. Tchr., Fishill (N.Y.) Elem. Sch., Lamar Elem. Sch. and Presbyn. High Sch., Kingsville, Tex., 1961-65; sec.-treas. North Atlantic Equipment Sales, Inc., Wappingers Falls, N.Y., 1972—. Former bd. dirs. Jr. League Poughkeepsie; former bd. dirs. LWV; past treas., bd. dirs. and pres. Community Children's Theatre; pres., past sec. Community Exptl. Repertory Theatre; former sec., mem. bd. dirs., former sec. adv. com. Dutchess County Arts Council Adv. Com.; sec., charter bd. dirs. Cunneen-Hackett Cultural Complex; former crew Hudson River Sloop Clearwater; former mem. bd. dirs. PTA; mem. Cornell Secondary Schs. Com.; Paul Harris sustaining mem. Rotary Found. of Rotary Internat. Mem. Nat. Assn. Female Execs., NOW, Cornell U. Alumni Assn., Cornell Coll. Human Ecology Alumni, Cornell Chorus Soc., Dutchess County Hist. Soc., Fishkill Hist. Soc., Bardavon 1869 Opera House, Hudson Valley Philharm., County Players, Dutchess County Landmarks, Mt. Gulian Soc., Mental Health Assn. Dutchess County, Century Circle of Vassar Bros. Hosp. Assn., Dutchess County Soc. for Prevention Cruelty to Animals. Mem. Reformed Ch. in Am. Club: Mid-Hudson Cornell. Home: Dogwood Hill Rd Wappingers Falls NY 12590 Office: PO Box 619 Route 376 Wappingers Falls NY 12590

STRO, MARY ANNE, educational administrator; b. Chgo., Jan. 19, 1943; d. James Vicent and Edna Marica (O'Connell) Routson; m. Jack Hugh Stro, June 21, 1969 (div. 1979). B.A., Northeastern Ill. State U., 1968; postgrad. U. Calif.-San Diego, 1969-74; M.S., San Diego State U., 1976; Ed.D., U.S. Internat., 1982. Counselor, Montgomery Jr. High Sch., San Diego, 1971-75, asst. prin., 1975-77, prin., 1982-84; asst. prin. Southwest High, San Diego, 1977-82; dir. curriculum and instrn. Sweetwater Union High Sch., Chula Vista, Calif., 1985—; mem. Western Assn. Schs. and Colls. Accredation Team, San Diego, 1982, 83, 84, 86; assessor, dir., trainer San Diego County Leadership Assessment Ctr., 1984—; mem. San Diego Council Adminstrv. Women Edn., 1984—. Active City Chula Vista Human Relation Commn., 1974; treas. South Bay Community Services, Inc., 1985—. Recipient Susan B. Anthony award NOW, 1983; twin honoree YWCA, 1986; named Woman of Achievement, Pres.'s Council 1983 01; Exec. Educator 100, 1985. Mem. Am. Bus. Women's Assn. (exec. bd. 1984—, NOW, Assn. Supervision and Curriculum Devel., Assn. Calif. Sch. Adminstrs., Southwest Adminstrn. Assn. (v.p. 1983-84), Mgmt. Assn. Sweetwater Dist. (pres.-elect 1985), Nat. Council Adminstrv. Women Edn. Office: Sweetwater Union High Sch Dist 1130 5th Ave Chula Vista CA 92011

STROBEL, BARBARA LOUISE, accountant, taxation specialist; Apr. 6, 1955; d. Arthur H. and Margaret (Hanlon) S. B.B.A. summa cum laude, U. Houston, 1976. C.P.A., 1978. Staff Deloitte Haskins & Sells, Houston, 1976-81, mgr., 1981-83; ptnr. Strobel Tate & Co., 1983—; cons. DD Rental & Supply, Houston, 1981—, Drilling and Prodn. Engrs., Houston, 1977—; instr. U. Houston, 1979. Active Salem Luth. Ch., local politics. Mem. Am. Women's Soc. C.P.A.s, Tex. Soc. C.P.A.s, Tax Forum 77, Am. Inst. C.P.A.s, Internat. Assn. Drilling Contractors, Mortar Board Alumni Assn., Chi Omega Alumni. Club: Seabreeze Sailing (LaPorte, Tex.). Office: Strobel Tate & Co 4545 Post Oak Pl Suite 102 Houston TX 77027

STROH, PATRICIA ANN BARBIER, child care executive; b. Muncie, Ind., June 30, 1946; d. Carl John Barbier and Syble Leola (Rhodes) Barbier Smith; m. David Leroy Stroh, Aug. 6, 1967; children—Todd, Andrea, Nick. B.S., Ball State U., 1967; M.A., 1969. Tchr., Castleton Pre-Sch., Indpls., 1970-71, Collier County Schs., Naples, Fla., 1973-74; owner Castle Pre-Sch., Naples, 1974-77; owner Trinity Schs., Plano, Tex., 1977—; sec., dir. Trinity Pre-Schs., Inc.; adult educator Collier County Schs., Naples, 1977. Contbr. articles to profl. jours. Chmn. pub. relations Bicentennial Com., Naples, Fla., 1974-76; mem. Collier County Conservancy, Naples, 1976; bd. dirs. Big Cypress Nature Center, Naples, 1974-76; pres. PTO, Plano, 1980-81; leader Boy Scouts Am., Naples, 1974-77; trustee United Meth. Ch., 1984—. Mem. Nat. Assn. for Edn. of Young Children, Tex. Lic. Child Care Assn., Tex. Assn. for Edn. Young Children, Dallas Assn. Edn. Young Children, Assn. for Gifted Students, Home Econs. and Co-op Edn. Assn. (pres. 1983-84), Plano Heritage Assn. Clubs: Jr. Women's of Naples, Naples Players.

STROHM, LILLIAN ANN, home economist; b. South Bend, Ind, Oct. 17, 1914; d. John and Sadie (Kelley) Murphy; B.S., Purdue U., 1938; M.A., George Washington U., 1941; m. John Strohm, Sept. 8, 1941; children—Terry, Karen, Robert, Cheryl, Dave, Colleen. Head home econs. dept. USDA, Bainbridge, Ind., 1938-39, home demonstration agt., Vigo County, Ind., 1938-41; homemaking editor Ford Almanac, Woodstock, Ill., 1954—; cons. Nat. Wildlife Mag., 1984-85. Exec. sec., then pres. Woodstock Opera House Community Center, Inc., 1970-80. Purdue U. scholar, 1928-32; USDA fellow, 1939-40. Mem. AAUW, Omicron Nu, Kappa Delta Pi, Alpha Lambda Delta. Roman Catholic. Clubs: Garden (pres. 1985-86), Book (v.p.), Investment (pres. 1984). Address: 515 W Jackson St Woodstock IL 60098

STROMAN, JOANN, nurse, consultant; b. Orangeburg, S.C., Apr. 27, 1959; d. Jessie and Martha Ann (Hart) S.; 1 child, Kwakiutt Marie. B.S.N., U. S.C., 1982. R.N., S.C. Charge nurse Orangeburg Regional Hosp., 1982—; cons. Princess House, North Deighton, Mass., 1984—. Home: Route 2 Box 115 Neeses SC 29107

STROMAN, PATRICIA ANN HARRIS, systems analyst; b. Charleston, W.Va., Dec. 2, 1953; d. Paul Frederick and Faye Virginia (Shafer) Harris; m. Harry Jackson Stroman Oct. 23, 1980; children—James Harris, Virginia Louise. A.S., W.Va. Inst. Tech., 1973. Programmer, Carlton Industries, Richmond, Va., 1974-76; cons. SIS Inc., Richmond, 1976-77; team leader State of Va., Richmond, 1977-80, Airline Tariff Co., Dulles Airport, Washington, 1980-82; WITCO Chem. co., Woodcliffe Lake, N.J., 1982-84. Mem. Nat. Assn. Female Execs. Republican. Presbyterian. Home: 1022 Winfield Ct Lansdale PA 19446

STROMBERG, LISEN HOEM, fundraiser, consultant; b. Palo Alto, Calif., Aug. 9, 1962; d. Jackson Clafflin and Elizabeth (Hoem) S. B.A. in Poli. Sci., Dartmouth Coll., 1984. Mktg. rep. Outline, Inc., N.Y.C., 1984-85; coordinator planning and devel. NOW Legal Def. and Edn. Fund, N.Y.C., 1985—; cons. Planned Parenthood Fedn. of Am., N.Y.C., 1984-85. Chmn. jr. com. of friends Ensemble Studio Theatre, N.Y.C., 1985—. Clubs: Meadowwood (Napa,

Calif.); Mill Valley Tennis (Calif.). Democrat. Avocations: skiing; tennis; running. Home: 666 West End Ave #6S New York NY 10025 Office: NOW Legal Def and Edn Fund 99 Hudson St New York NY 10013

STROMME, DELORIS ANN, Realtor; b. Fargo, N.D., Oct. 19, 1919, d. Jacob William and Alma (Sievers) Heldman; m. Floyd M. Stromme, Nov. 13, 1937; children—Dianne, Larry (dec.), Bonnie, Ronald. Student Interstate Bus. Coll., Fargo, 1937; grad. Realtors Inst. Ptnr., Justrom & Stromme Realtors, Coos Bay, Oreg., 1957—; pres. Timber Park Devel. Corp., Coos Bay, 1968-69; property mgr. VA, North Bend, Oreg., 1965-84, also HUD; owner Coos County Escrow Co., 1974-81, Mountain Title Co., 1979-82; sec. Blossom Gulch Properties, 1972-84, Broadway Suites, 1979-84.Trustee, United Meth. Ch. Named Realtor of Yr., Southwestern Oreg. Bd. Realtors, 1967. Mem. Oreg. Assn. Realtors (exec. com. 1975-76, v.p. 1976), Coos County Bd. Realtors (past pres. 1968, Realtor of Yr. 1977), Internat. Inst. Valuers, Bus. and Profl. Women's Club (pres. 1956). Republican. Clubs: Toastmistress (pres. 1981), Zonta (treas.). Lodge: Elks. Home: 3029 Sheridan Rd North Bend OR 97459 Office: Coldwell Banker Justrom & Stromme 543 S 4th St Coos Bay OR 97420

STROMP, PHOEBE A., township official; b. Wyandotte, Mich., July 23, 1932; d. Frank A. and Elizabeth M. (Rushlow) Beaker; student Wayne County Community Coll., 1974—; m. William J. Stromp, Sept. 22, 1951; children—Elizabeth, Christine, John, Francis, Phoebe M., Renee, William J. Mgmt. info. coordinator Detroit Edison Co.; trustee Brownstown Twp., 1976-84; supr. Charter Twp. of Brownstown, 1984—. Mem. Engring. Soc. Detroit. Democrat. Roman Catholic.

STRONG, ALDA (MRS. LAVERN STRONG), community service volunteer, realtor; b. Menan, Idaho, Sept. 22, 1911; d. William D. and Margaret (Hunting) Watson; grad. high school; nat. grad. Realestate Inst., 1977; m. LaVern Strong, June 14, 1930; children—Nalda (Mrs. Richard C. Powell), Harvey, Deanna (Mrs. Douglas Vollmer). Active Internat. Toastmistress Clubs, 1951—, organizer 4 local clubs, pres. council number 9, No. region, 1959-60, parliamentarian No. region, 1960-61; legislative chmn. Idaho Bus. and Profl. Women's Clubs, 1958-59, chmn. pub. relations, 1959-61, pres.; safety chmn. Idaho Gen. Fedn. Women's Clubs, 1960-61, Idaho chmn., 1964, state safety chmn.; sec. dist. South Central Bus. and Profl. Clubs, 1967; pres. 20th Century, Twin Falls, Idaho, 1962-63; bd. dirs. Twin Falls Salvation Army, chmn., 1975-78, life mem. Salvation Army; state rep. to President's Safety Conf. Mich. State U. Organizer 5 safety clubs Nat. Safety Council; safety chmn. So. Idaho Citizens Safety Council; regional dir. Idaho Women's Hwy. Safety Leaders, 1971-74; bd. dirs. Twin Falls Civic Auditorium, 1959-61; chmn. Twin Falls County chpt. Nat. Found.; sec. Idaho Hosp. Auxiliaries, 1959-60; pres. Twin Falls YWCA; sponsor Sigma chpt. Beta Sigma Phi; sec.-treas. Twin Falls County Civil Def.; past pres. Gem. State Writers Guild, editor Gem State News Letter, 1970-71; mem. Nat. Assn. Parliamentarians (Idaho pres. 1977-80). Democratic candidate Idaho Ho. of Reps., 1960. Recipient Certificate of Merit award Nat. Safety Council, 1959; named Woman of Year, Bus. and Profl. Women's Clubs, 1960, Magic Toastmistress Club, Number 1002, No. region, 1959; Disting. Service award Jr. C. of C., 1960, merit award Idaho Safety Council; registered parliamentarian. Mem. Idaho Bd. Realtors (parliamentarian 1976—). Clubs: Altrusa (internat. chmn.); 20th Century Federated (fine arts chmn. 2d v.p.), Ladies of Elks (past pres.). Home: 2016 Stadium Blvd Twin Falls ID 83301

STRONG, BETHANY JUNE, novelist, publisher, editor; b. Oklahoma City, June 13, 1906; d. Nicholas Henry and Anna Augusta (Spuhler) McLaughlin; m. John Donovan Strong, Sept. 2, 1928; children—Patricia, Virginia. B.S. in History of Ideas, Johns Hopkins U., 1966. Novelist, freelance writer, pub., editor Parable Press, Amherst, Mass., 1978—; cons. in field. Author: The King's Generalissima, 1976, First Love, 1978, Murder in the Mirror, 1985; also articles. Mem. Nat. Writers Club, Nat. League Am. Pen Women (pres. Conn. Valley br.). Roman Catholic. Avocation: photography.

STRONG, CAROLYN RAY, electronics company official; b. Pasadena, Calif., Jan. 9, 1951; d. Albert Charles and Juliana (Ray) Strong; B.A. in Math., Whitworth Coll., 1973; postgrad. DeVry Inst. Tech., 1975-77. Math. and aerospace demonstrator Pacific Sci. Center, Seattle, 1970, 71; component info. specialist Tektronix, Inc., Beaverton, Oreg., 1973-75, tech. writer, 1975-76, tech. publs. group mgr., 1976-79, tech. communications mgr., 1979-85; tech. publs. and computer tng. mgr., 1985—; cons. Portland Community Coll., Chemeketa Community Coll. Bd. dirs. Tektronix Fed. Credit Union, 1984—, sec., 1985-86, vice chmn., 1986—. Mem. Soc. Tech. Communications (sr. mem., sec. Willamette Valley chpt. 1978, treas. 1979, pres. 1979-80). Home: 1325 NW 92d St Portland OR 97229 Office: PO Box 500 Beaverton OR 97077

STRONG, CATHERINE ELLIS, lawyer; b. Albuquerque, July 12, 1950; d. William Henry and Bernadette (Fitzgerald) Ellis; m. Richard Willis Strong, Aug. 5, 1972; 1 child, Andrew Ellis. B.A., Northwestern U., 1972; J.D., Creighton U., 1976. Bar: Nebr. 1976, Wis. 1977, U.S. Dist. Ct. Wis. 1977. Atty., Strong & Strong, Green Bay, Wis., 1978-82, 83—, Condon, Hanaway, Wickert Fenwick & Strong, Ltd., Green Bay, 1982-83; mem. adv. bd. Juvenile Ct., Green Bay, 1978-80; chmn., organizer Juvenile Restitution Project Fundraising campaign, 1981-82, bd. dirs., 1978-81. Bd. dirs. LacBaie council Girl Scouts U.S., 1978-80; bd. dirs. YWCA, 1980-82, mem. membership/mktg. com., 1985—; mem. resource devel. div. United Way, 1981—; pres., bd. dirs. Family Service Assn., Green Bay, 1982—, Family Service Properties, 1982—; mem. accreditation task force Family Service Assn., 1986—. Recipient Appreciation award Ashwaubenon Assn. Spl. Children's Needs, 1980. Mem. ABA, Nebr. Bar Assn., Wis. Bar Assn., Brown County Bar Assn. (mem. Liberty Bell award selection com. 1983), Alpha Phi. Roman Catholic. Office: Strong and Strong Attys 2301 Riverside Dr Green Bay WI 54301

STRONG, FRANCES, state legislator. Mem. Ala. Senate, dist. 22, 1985—. Democrat. Office: Ala State Senate State Capitol Montgomery AL 36130*

STRONG, GAY, industrial relations executive; b. Santa Monica, Calif., Jan. 13, 1930; d. Claude Roderick and Katherine Anna (Brown) Riley; student UCLA, 1947-49; A.A., Pierce Coll., Los Angeles, 1969; B.A. in English, Calif. State U.-Northridge, 1973; m. Duane Gordon Strong, Aug. 20, 1949; children—Philip, Katherine, Patricia, Barbara. With credit office, store ops., then asst. personnel mgr. Builders Emporium, Van Nuys, Calif., 1969-74, personnel mgr., 1974-78; dir. indsl. relations GC Internat., Hawthorne, Calif., 1978-81; personnel mgr. Lok Products Co., Fullerton, Calif., 1981-82; chief exec. officer Asset Recovery, Santa Monica, Calif., 1982-83; dir. human resources Targeted Coverage, Inc., Pomona, Calif., 1983—. Mem. Am. Mgmt. Assn., Am. Soc. Personnel Adminstrs., Personnel and Indsl. Relations Assn. Republican. Editor Builders Emporium house organ, 1972-78, Targeted Coverage house organ, 1984—. Home: 14456 Foothill Blvd #32 Sylmar CA 91342 Office: 3200 A Pomona Blvd Pomona CA 91768

STRONG, HELEN FRANCINE, lawyer; b. Detroit, Mar. 22, 1947; d. Lonia and Nancy Lula (Proctor) Lanier; m. Douglas Donald Strong, Oct. 26, 1974; 1 son, Douglas Donald. A.B., U. Detroit, 1969, J.D., 1972. Bar: Mich. 1972. Asst. atty. gen. Office of Atty. Gen., Lansing, Mich., 1972-83; staff atty. Detroit Edison Co., 1973-80; assoc. William C. Gage, P.C., Detroit, 1980-81; sr. assoc. Lewis, White & Clay, P.C., Detroit, 1981—. Bd. dirs. Detroit Inst. Arts, Founders Jr. Council, 1979—, Founders Soc., 1977—, mem. adv. com. Centennial Com., 1983—; mem. adv. com. Your Heritage House, Inc., Detroit, 1983—; com. mem. exhbns. Detroit Hist. Mus., 1984. Recipient Cert. for Outstanding Service to Univ. of Detroit Sch. Law, 1972. Mem. ABA, Fed. Bar Assn., Mich. Bar Assn., Detroit Bar Assn., Wolverine Bar Assn., Nat. Bar Assn., Assn. Trial Lawyers Am., Delta Sigma Theta, NAACP. Roman Catholic. Office: 1300 1st Nat Bldg Detroit MI 48226

STRONG, JILL ADAMS, food company executive; b. Waukesha, Wis., Apr. 14, 1949; d. Paul Ingham and Thelma Margaret (Inman) S. B.A., Parsons Coll., 1971. Tchr., Green Bay Sch. System, Wis., 1971-73; pres., treas. Old Tavern Food Products, Inc., Waukesha, 1973—. Area chmn. PBS Auction, Milw., 1973—; bd. dirs., treas. Waukesha YWCA, 1980-84; bd. dirs. Humane Animal Welfare Soc., Waukesha, 1982—, pres., 1986—; vol. Am. Lung Assn., Milw., 1982—; bd. dirs. Kern Found., Waukesha, 1985—. Named Woman of Yr., Milw. Panhellenic, 1981. Mem. Wis. Gift Cheese Assn. (bd. dirs. 1984—, sec.-treas. 1986—), Waukesha C. of C. (bd. dirs. 1980-83), Nat. Assn. Female Execs., Alpha Xi Delta (pres. 1976-78; Outstanding Alumnae award 1981; jour. corr. 1985—). Republican. Episcopalian. Club: Fox River Saddle (sec. 1978, pres. 1982-83) (Waukesha). Avocations: horseback riding; needlepoint. Home: S40 W22760 Sommers Hills Dr Waukesha WI 53186 Office: Old Tavern Food Products Inc PO Box 438 Waukesha WI 53187

STRONG, JOYCE ELIZABETH, pianist, educator; b. Kansas City, Mo., May 26, 1933; d. Melvin Witzel and Lucy Mae (Adams) S. Student U. Pitts. 1951, Eastman Sch. Mus., Rochester, N.Y. 1951-53; B.S., Juilliard Sch. Music, 1957, M.S., 1959. Piano debut, Pitts., 1952; recitalist primarily in So. and Eastern U.S., also Lincoln Center for Performing Arts, N.Y.C., Hartford, Conn., Columbus, Ohio, Dallas, Austin, Tex., U. Mich. Internat. Conf. on Women in Arts, 1982; tchr. Kent Place Sch., Summit, N.J. 1959-60; asst. prof. Huntingdon Coll., 1961-63; instr. U. Ala., 1963-67; assoc. prof. Tex. Woman's U., Denton, 1967—. Recipient Alta. Symphony Assn. award 1948, Pitts. Concert Soc. award 1952, award of merit Nat. Fedn. Music Clubs 1977. Mem. Women in Arts, Coll. Music Soc., Am. Music Scholarship Assn., Tex. Assn. Coll. Tchrs., Music Tchrs. Nat. Assn., Pi Kappa Lambda. Home: 514 E Windsor Dr Denton TX 76201 Office: Music Department Texas Woman's University Denton TX 76204

STRONG, JUDITH ANN, chemist, educator; b. Van Hornesville, N.Y., June 19, 1941; d. Philip Furnald and Hilda Bernice (Hulbert) S.; B.S. cum laude (N.Y. State regents scholar), SUNY, Albany, 1963; M.A., Brandeis U., 1966, Ph.D., 1970. Asst. prof. chemistry Moorhead State U. (Minn.), 1969-73, acting chmn. chemistry dept., 1976, assoc. prof., 1973-81, prof., 1981—, chmn. dept., 1984-86, dean natural and social scis., 1986—. Recipient Tietzen Meml. award SUNY, Albany, 1963; NSF fellow, 1965-67. Mem. Am. Chem. Soc., NEA, Minn. Edn. Assn., Minn. Acad. Sci., Sigma Xi. Home: 1209 12th St S Moorhead MN 56560 Office: Academic Affairs Moorhead State U Moorhead MN 56560

STRONG, MAYDA NEL, psychologist, educator; b. Albuquerque, May 6, 1942; d. Floyd Samuel and Wanda Christmas (Martin) Strong; B.A. cum laude, Tex. Western Coll., 1963; M.Ed., U. Tex., Austin, 1972, Ph.D. in Counseling Psychology (AAUW fellow), 1978; 1 son. Asst. instr. in ednl. psychology U. Tex., Austin, 1974-78; instr.psychology Austin Community Coll., 1974-78, Otero Jr. Coll., La Junta, Colo., 1979—; dir. outpatient and emergency services S.E. Colo. Family Guidance and Mental Health Center, Inc., La Junta, 1978-81; pvt. practice psychol. therapy, La Junta, 1981—. Co-star The Good Doctor, Picketwire Theatre, La Junta, 1980, On Golden Pond, 1981. Mem. Bus. and Profl. People (legis. chairperson 1982-83), Colo. Psychol. Assn. Contrbr. articles in field to profl. publs. Author poems in Chinnok, Paths through the Puzzle, Decisions, Passion. Home: 1 Opera House Apts La Junta CO 81050 Office: 208 Santa Fe Ave La Junta CO 81050

STRONG, STEPHANIE LYNN, financial auditor; b. High Point, N.C., June 19, 1956; d. William and Minnie (Moose) Strong. B.S. in B.A., N.C. Central U., 1978; M.B.A., Atlanta U., 1980. Summer intern Lincoln Health Ctr., Durham, N.C., 1978, IRS, Washington, 1979; internal auditor Greyhound Corp., Phoenix, 1980-81; budget asst. Dept. Gen. Services, Washington, 1982-83; internal auditor First Nat. Bank of Atlanta, 1983-84; fin. auditor Harris/Lanier, Atlanta, 1984—. Mem. Nat. Assn. Female Execs., Am. Soc. Tng. and Devel. Bus. and Profl. Women's Club of Atlanta (chmn. fellowship com., treas. 1986—). Democrat. Methodist. Avocations: aerobics; sewing; jogging; traveling. Home: 3379 Valley Brok Pl Decatur GA 30033

STROPUS, JUDITH VICTORIA (JURA), public relations consultant, race driver; b. Kaunas, Lithuania, Oct. 7, 1943; came to U.S., 1949, naturalized, 1963; d. Algirdas and Malvina Brucas (Bubelevicius) S.; student public and parochial schs., N.Y.C. Public relations sec. Western Electric Co., N.Y.C., 1960-64; legal sec. Bucknum & Archer, N.Y.C., 1964-67, Dills & Schelker, N.Y.C., 1967-70; public relations rep. Fred Opert Racing, N.J., 1971, Mobility Systems Co., N.Y.C., 1971-75; founder, owner JVS Enterprises, Ridgefield, Conn., 1976—; pub. relations rep. various automative mfg. cos. and auto racing groups; profl. timer and scorer for U.S. auto racing teams including Lincoln-Mercury's Cougar Team, Am. Motors Javelin Team, Penske Racing Team, Peter Gregg's Brumos Racing Team, BMW Motorsports Team, Toyota Factory Team, Bob Akin Motor Racing, Holbert Racing, Ford Motorsports Team, B.F. Goodrich Racing Team, Group 44 Jaguar Team, 1967—; profl. race driver, 1973—, sponsored by Dunlop Tire Co., 1975-80; asst. to author Karl Ludvigsen, 1968-73. Mem. Internat. Motor Press Assn. (dir., editor Arrow 1985—), Auto Racing Writers and Broadcasters Assn., Internat. Motor Sports Assn. (editor Arrow), Sports Car Club Am., Madison Ave. Sports Car Driving and Chowder Soc., Motor Racing Safety Soc., Vintage Sports Car Club Am. Author: The Stropus Guide to Auto Race Timing & Scoring, 1975; mem. cross country contingent demonstrating Run-Flat tire, Dunlop Tire Co., 1980; star in dealer promotional film for Volvo, 1981, for Volkswagen, 1985; East Coast rep. Vista Group, 1983-84. Home and Office: 170 Old Sib Rd Ridgefield CT 06877

STRONG-TIDMAN, VIRGINIA ADELE, marketing and advertising executive; b. Englewood, N.J., July 26, 1947; d. Alan Ballentine and Virginia Leona (Harris) Strong; m. John Fletcher Tidman, Sept. 23, 1978. B.S., Albright Coll., Reading, Pa., 1969; postgrad. U. Pitts., 1970-73, U. Louisville, 1975-76. Exec. trainee Pomeroy's div. Allied Stores, Reading, 1969-70; mktg. research analyst Heinz U.S.A., Pitts., 1970-74; new products mktg. mgr. Ky. Fried Chicken, Louisville, 1974-76; dir. Pitts. office M/A/R/C, 1976-79; assoc. research dir. Henderson Advt., Inc., Greenville, S.C., 1979-81; sr. v.p., dir. research Bozell, Jacobs, Kenyon & Eckhardt, Inc., Irving, Tex., 1981—; cons. mktg. research Greenville Zool. Soc., 1981. Mem. Am. Mktg. Assn., Population Assn. Am. Episcopalian. Home: 2816 Silverspring Rd Carrollton TX 75006 Office: Bozell Jacobs Kenyon & Eckhardt Inc 201 E Carpenter Freeway Irving TX 75038

STROTHER, PAT WALLACE, author; b. Birmingham, Ala., Mar. 11, 1929; d. Claude Hunter and Gladys Eleanor (English) Wallace; student U. Tenn., Knoxville, 1947-51; m. Lee Levitt, 1951 (div. 1957); m. 2d, David G. Latner, 1958 (div. 1968); m. 3d, Robert A. Strother, 1980. Dir. women's programs WGNS Radio, Murfreesboro, Tenn., 1951-52; continuity dir. WMAK Radio, Nashville, 1952-54; asst. editor Civil Service Leader, N.Y.C., 1955-57; adminstrv. sec. Local 237 Teamsters, N.Y.C., 1957-76; works include: House of Scorpio, 1975, This Willing Passion, 1978, The Wand and the Star, 1978; Traitor in My Arms, 1979; The Voyagers, 1980; Once More the Sun, Silver Fire, 1982; My Loving Enemy, Summer Kingdom, 1983; Sweetheart Contract, Shining Hour, Objections Overruled, 1984; Love Scene, Star Rise, Unyielding Fire, 1985, Under the Sign of Scorpio, The Constant Star, A Wife for Ransom, 1986. Mem. Authors Guild. Democrat.

STROTHER, SHERRIE KAYE CARTER, county official; b. Charleroy, Pa., July 2, 1948; d. Thomas Earl Jordan and Mary Anne (Fair) Lightner; m. Ronald O. Strother, Feb. 14, 1982; m. Phillip E. Carter, June 6, 1967 (dec. Sept. 1975); 1 child, Staci Dione. B.A., La. State U., 1979; postgrad. Tex. A&M U., 1984, FBI Nat. Acad., 1984. Lic. polygraph examiner; lic. pilot. Sec., Aetna Life & Casualty Co., Shreveport, La., 1967-68; investigator Fed. Civil Service, Ariz., Okla., La., 1969-75; supr. pub. relations, crime prevention and internal affairs divs. Caddo Sheriff's Dept., Shreveport, La., 1979—; editor The Caddo Star, 1981—. Bd. dirs. dept. Bossier Community Coll., 1985-86; adviser Law Enforcement Explorers Group, 1980-85. Mem. La. Sheriff's Assn., La. Polygraph Assn., La. Peace Officers Assn., Nat. Sheriff's Task Force, Am. Bus. Womens Assn., La. State U. Shreveport Alumni Assn. (alumni bd. dirs. 1981-83), Women in Law Enforcement Assn. (merit award 1983). Republican. Baptist. Avocations: flying; motor cycling; bowling; reading; karate. Home: 263 Pomeroy Dr Shreveport LA 71115 Office: Caddo Sheriff's Dept 501 Texas St Shreveport LA 71101

STROUP, MARY A., title company executive; b. Rock Island, Ill., Jan. 15, 1947; d. Oscar Louis and Margaret Elizabeth (McGuire) Lorenz; 1 child, Lisa Ann. Student, Robert Morris Coll., 1965-68. Exec. v.p. Commerce Title Co., Dallas, 1982—. Republican. Roman Catholic. Office: Commerce Title Co Suite 100 5400 LBJ Freeway Dallas TX 75240

STROUSE, CAROL LOUISE KIRCHMAN, vocational educator; b. Bloomsburg, Pa., Sept. 14, 1947; d. George and Jessie Helen (Kitchen) Kirchman; m. William Earle Strouse, June 21, 1965; 1 child, Matthew Alexander. B.S. in Health and Phys. Edn., Lock Haven U., Pa., 1970; M.S. in Phys. Edn., Ind. State U.-Terre Haute, 1976. Cert. tchr. health, phys. edn. and spl. edn., Md. Tchr. phys. edn., Charles County Bd. Edn., LaPlata, Md., 1970-78, tchr. spl. edn., 1978-85, vocat. tchr., 1978-85, work domain coordinator, 1983—, team leader, 1981-84, cons. elementary career edn., 1986—; gymnastics instr., coach Charles County Dept. Parks and Recreation, La Plata, 1973-79. Area coordinator Charles County Spl. Olympics, 1976-78, 82-83; coach soccer St. Mary's County Recreation and Parks, Mechanicsville, Md., 1982-84; mem. Charles County Bd. Elections, 1986. Recipient Outstanding Coach award Saint Gymnastics Club, Waldorf, Md., 1982; Recognition for Vocat. Guidance Project, Charles County Bd. Edn., 1982. Mem. United Teaching Assns. (faculty rep. 1983-86), Nat. Assn. Female Execs. Democrat. Methodist. Avocations: reading; swimming; cycling; arts and crafts. Home: Route 2 Box 174 Charlotte Hall MD 20622 Office: Charles County Bd Edn Star Route 5 Box 536 LaPlata MD 20646

STRUTHERS, DEBORAH MARY, medical corporation executive; b. Sydney, N.S.W., Australia, Feb. 4, 1952; came to U.S., 1973; d. Anthony Eric and Mary Patricia (O'Mullane) Gray; m. Theodore Ralph Culbertson, July 31, 1971 (div. 1979); m. Scott Cameron Struthers, Jan. 31, 1981. Student St. Petersburg Jr. Coll., 1978—. Fin. counselor Wuesthoff Meml. Hosp., Rockledge, Fla., 1973-75; adminstrv. dir. Dresden & Ticktin, M.D.s, P.A., St. Petersburg, Fla., 1976-80; exec. dir., v.p. Am. Med. Mgmt., Inc., Clearwater, Fla., 1980—; pres., dir. All Women's Health Ctr., Inc., St. Petersburg, 1980—, All Women's Health Ctr. North Tampa, Inc., Fla., 1980—, All Women's Health Ctr. Tampa, Inc., 1980—, Women's Ob-Gyn Ctr. Countryside, Inc., 1984—, All Women's Health Ctr. Sarasota, Fla., 1980—, All Women's Health Ctr. Ocala, Fla., 1980—, All Women's Health Ctr. Gainesville, Fla., 1981—, Lakeland Women's Health Ctr., Fla., 1980—, Ft. Myers Womens Health Ctr., Fla., 1980—, All Women's Health Ctr. Jacksonville, Fla., 1980—, Nat. Women's Health Services, Inc., Clearwater, Fla., 1983—, D.M.S. of Ft. Myers, Inc., 1985—. Roman Catholic. Avocations: skiing; scuba diving; photography; pursuing an education.

STUARK, BARBARA IRENE, retail management executive; b. Chgo., Mar. 19, 1948; d. Frank R. and Irene Julia (Wojnicki) S. Ph.B., Northwestern U., 1973, postgrad. in computer sci.; C.B.A., Keller Grad. Sch. Mgmt., Chgo., 1978. Buyer, Goldblatts, Chgo., 1974-79; outside sales rep. Raymor/Moreddi, Ridgefield, N.J., 1979-80; div. mgr. Lord & Taylor-Water Tower Place, Chgo., 1980-83; dir. pub. merchandising Field Mus. of Natural History, Chgo., 1983—. Mem. Nat. Assn. Female Execs. Roman Catholic. Club: Northwestern of Chgo. Office: Mus Stores Field Mus Natural History Roosevelt Rd and Lake Shore Dr Chicago IL 60605

STUART, ALICE MELISSA, lawyer; b. N.Y.C., Apr. 7, 1957; d. John Marberger and Marjorie Louise (Browne) Stuart. B.A., Ohio State U., 1977; J.D., U. Chgo., 1980; L.L.M., NYU, 1982. Bar: N.Y. 1981, Ohio 1982, U.S. Dist. Ct. (so. dist.) Ohio 1983, U.S. Dist. Ct. (so. and ea. dist.) N.Y. 1985. Teaching fellow DePaul Coll. Law, Chgo., 1980-81; assoc. firm Schwartz, Shapiro, Kelm & Warren, Columbus, Ohio, 1982-84, Paul, Weiss, Rifkind, Wharton & Garrison, N.Y.C., 1984-85, Kassel, Neurith & Geiger, 1985—. Vol. Reagan-Bush Commitment '80, N.Y.C., surrogate Speakers' Bur., Reagan-Bush campaign, 1984. jr. counsel Columbus Mus. Art, 1983-84. Mem. ABA, N.Y. State Bar Assn., Columbus Bar Assn., Women Lawyers of Franklin County, D.A.R. Phi Beta Kappa, Phi Kappa Phi, Alpha Lambda Delta. Republican. Presbyterian. Clubs: Soc. Mayflower Descs., Women's Nat. Republican.

STUART, ANNE PASLEY, hospital executive; b. Caldwell, Idaho, Nov. 25, 1944; d. Robert Laverne and Jane Elizabeth (Pasley) Alexanderson; B.S.; m. Thomas R. Stuart III, Apr. 14, 1978; 1 dau., Lisa. Health adminstr. Dept. Health & Welfare, 1973-76; mgmt. cons., 1976-79; dir. personnel Provident Fed. Savs. & Loan Assn., Boise, Idaho, 1979-83; dir. personnel Mercy Med. Center, Nampa, Idaho, 1983—; spl. lectr. Coll. Idaho, 1982—, U. Wash., 1982. Chmn., Idaho Commn. on Womens Programs, 1979-81; mem. Idaho Personnel Commn., 1981—; bd. dirs. YWCA, Treasure Valley Better Bus. Bur., Ada County United Way; mem. Ada County Central Com. Democratic Party; bd. dirs. Citizens Alliance for Polit. Action, Treasure Valley Health Care Cost Containment Coalition. Mem. Am. Affirmitive Action Assn., Am. Soc. Personnel Adminstrs., Nat. Assn. Commns. for Women, Am. Soc. for Hosp. Personnel Adminstrn., Idaho Assn. Affirmative Action (bd. dirs.), Am. Compensation Assn., Am. Soc. for Tng. and Devel., Am. Mgmt. Assn., AAUW, NOW. Democrat. Unitarian. Office: Mercy Medical Center 1512 12th Ave Rd Nampa ID 83651

STUART, COLBY, marketing company executive; b. Phila., July 12, 1951; d. Clinton and Margo (Lujan) S.; m. Barron Wallace Chandler, Jr., Jan. 25, 1971 (div. Oct. 1974); 1 child, Joshua Sebastian. B.S., Villanova U., 1971; grad. studies in bus. Pa. State U., 1973-74; M.B.A., U. Pitts., 1976. Mktg. asst. Ketchum, McLeod & Grove, Pitts., 1975-76; owner Mountain Mktg. and Design, Taos, Santa Fe and Albuquerque, 1977-80; pres. St. Louis Mktg. and Design, 1981-82; corp. dir. mktg. and advtg. Breckenridge Hotels Corp., St. Louis, 1982-84; pres. WAVES, Inc., St. Louis, 1983—; interior design cons. Renaissance Devel. Co., St. Louis, 1983—. Vice pres., exec. bd. dirs. Young Variety Club, St. Louis, 1983-84, charter mem., 1984-86; vol. writer Victim Witness Assistance Program, St. Louis, 1983; cons. P.B.S., Washington, 1985. Recipient Advt. Fedn. and Print awards for designs, posters and menus. Mem. Am. Mktg. Assn. Republican. Roman Catholic. Avocations: painting; golf; skiing; chess; sailing. Home: 4264 Arsenal St Saint Louis MO 63116 Office: WAVES Inc 8212 Exchange Way PO Box 20022 Saint Louis MO 63144

STUART, COLLEEN MURRAY, manufacturing company executive; b. Wheeling, W.Va., Oct. 8, 1945; d. Edward James and Margaret Hanna (Parker) M.; B.A., W. Liberty State Coll., 1964; postgrad. CCNY, 1969-70; m. Walter Tomasulo, Jr., Sept. 4, 1980; 1 son, Thomas Beecher Stuart. Tchr., Coop. Nursery Sch., Ringwood, N.J., 1968-69; mgr. R & R Printing Co., Wayne, N.J., 1976-78; sales mgr. Technicorp, Wayne, 1978-79, v.p., 1979—; freelance graphic artist. Vice pres. Ringwood Manor Arts Assn., 1974-75; sec. Ringwood Jayceettes, 1968-69. Mem. Am. Soc. Quality Control, Am. Soc. Metals, ASTM, Instrument Soc. Am., Nat. Audubon Soc., The Planetary Soc. Democrat. Presbyterian. Club: PEO. Contbr. to trade publs. Home: 16 Knox Terr Wayne NJ 07470 Office: 153 Orchard St East Rutherford NJ 07073

STUART, JOAN MARTHA, association administrator; b. Huntington, N.Y., June 2, 1945; d. Ervin Wencil and Flora Janet (Applebaum) Stuart; student Boston U., 1963-67. Prodn. asst. Random House, N.Y.C., 1968-69; book designer Simon & Schuster, N.Y.C., 1969-71; feature writer Palm Beach Post, West Palm Beach, Fla., 1971-72; co-founder, communications dir. Stuart, Gleimer & Assocs., West Palm Beach, 1973-84, pres., 1982—; fin. devel. dir. YWCA Greater Atlanta, 1984—. Mem. crusade com. Am. Cancer Soc. Bd., 1981—; bd. dirs. Theatre Arts Co., 1980-81; community services chmn., bd. dirs. B'nai B'rith Women, 1980-82; chmn. publicity Leukemia Soc. Atlanta Polo Benefit, 1983; com. chmn. Atlanta Zool. Beastly Feast Benefit, 1984; mem. Atlanta Symphony Assocs. Recipient Nat. award B'nai B'rith Women, 1978, Regional award, 1979; cert. of merit Big Bros./Big Sisters, 1976. Mem. Nat. Soc. Fund Raising Execs., Ga. Exec. Women's Network, Atlanta Women's Network, B'nai B'rith Women. Republican. Jewish. Contbr. articles to profl. jours. Office: 100 Edgewood Ave NE Suite 806 Atlanta GA 30303

STUART, KATHERINE J., research laboratory administrator; b. Dennis, Ky., June 8, 1929; d. Fred and Ida May (Hutchinson) Stuart; m. App Russell, July 28, 1962 (div. 1974). Cert. in stenography Ashland Bus. Coll., 1947; student cosmotology Crown Beauty Acad., Ironton, Ohio, 1958; A.A. in Engring., Chabot Coll., Hayward, Calif., 1969; B.S. in Bus. Adminstrn., U. San Francisco, 1978. Stenographer Ky. Employee Dept.; sec. Ky. Hwy. Dept., Ashland, 1947-48; head bookkeeper Jack's Auto & Appliance, Ashland, 1948-52, credit mgr., 1956-62; head bookkeeper sta. WCMI, Ashland, 1952-54; office mgr. sta. WTCR, Ashland, 1954-55; piping clk. United Engrs. & Constrn., Phila., 1955-56; resource mgr. Lawrence Livermore Nat. Lab., U. Calif.-Livermore, 1962—. Vol. VA, Livermore, 1985—. Mem. Am. Bus. Women's Assn. (v.p. 1983-84, pres. 1984-85, Woman of Yr. 1984), Sci. Investments (pres. 1982—), Lawrence Livermore Lab. Women's Assn. (pres. 1981-83, treas. 1984-85), IBM Personal Computer Valley Blue, U. San Francisco Alumni Assn. Avocations: arts; dancing; gardening; theatre; gourmet cooking. Home: 1849 Elm St Livermore CA 94550 Office: Lawrence Livermore Nat Lab PO Box 808 L-198 Livermore CA 94550

STUART, LISA USHER, advertising agency executive; b. Royal Oak, Mich., Nov. 22, 1955; d. Alan Douglas and Lois Ann (Hayes) Stuart; m. Arthur James Usher, June 3, 1978 (div. 1986). Student Kendall Sch. Design, 1975-78. Art dir. Jack Luce Advt., Albuquerque, 1978-80, Adland Corp., Albuquerque, 1980-81, DBG&H Advt., Albuquerque, 1981; owner Usher & Co. Design Studio, Albuquerque, 1981-82; pres. Usher Stuart Advt., Albuquerque, 1982—.

Recipient Best of Show award Zia Airlines, 1979, First place award N.Mex. Mortgage Fin. Authority, 1980, 2d place awards Am. Cancer Soc., 1980, World Balloon Corp., 1982, Usher & Co., Inc., 1983, Award of Merit, Usher & Co., Inc., 1983. Mem. Nat. Assn. Female Execs. Inc., N.Mex. Advt. Fedn. (bd. mem. 1983-84). Roman Catholic. Office: Usher Stuart Advt 1209 Mountain Rd Pl NE Albuquerque NM 87110

STUART-O'SHEA, MARY TERESA, nursing education director; b. Dublin, Ireland, May 26, 1926; d. Cornelius and Sarah (Burke) O'Shea; came to U.S., 1952, naturalized, 1958; M.A. Ed., U. San Francisco, 1977; m. William Stuart, June 4, 1966. Instr. nursing Los Angeles Community Coll., 1965-69; dir. nursing edn. Berkeley Sch. Nursing Art, Santa Monica, 1970-79, dir. nursing continuing edn. Stuart Enterprises, Santa Monica, 1979—; cons. nursing edn. Nat. Assn. Practical Nurse & Service Inc., N.Y.C., 1979—; ednl. cons. Surgeon Gen. USAF, 1980. Disaster nurse, disaster health services Am. Nat. Red Cross, Los Angeles, 1978-82. Served with USAF, 1960-63, to col. USAFR, 1963—. Mem. Am. Nurses Assn., Calif. Nurses Assn., Am. Nurses' Found., Inc. Air Force Assn., Res. Officers Assn. Home: 235 15th St Santa Monica CA 90402 Office: 2021 Arizona Ave Santa Monica CA 90404

STUBAUS, KAREN RUTH, university dean; b. Englewood, N.J., June 12, 1950; d. Kenneth L. and Margaret S. (Dunning) S.; B.A. cum laude, Douglass Coll., 1972; M.A., Rutgers U., 1975, Ph.D., 1984; m. Stephen M. Goldfarb, May 6, 1978. Teaching asst. history dept. Douglass Coll., 1973-76; adminstrv. asst. to v.p. univ. personnel Rutgers U., 1976-77; program devel. specialist Bur. Research, N.J. Div. Youth and Family Services, 1977-78; asst. to dean, dir. continuing edn. Coll. Allied Health Scis., Thomas Jefferson U., Phila., 1978-81; exec. asst. Office Vice Chancellor, N.J. Dept. Higher Edn., 1981-82; acad. planning assoc. Rutgers U., New Brunswick, N.J., 1982-84, asst. dean, 1984—. Mem. Am. Hist. Assn., Orgn. Am. Historians, Nat. Coordinating Com. Promotion History (pres. N.J. chpt. 1982), Phi Beta Kappa. Co-editor: The American Revolution: Whose Revolution?, 1977. Home: 20 Aldrich Ave Metuchen NJ 08840 Office: Rutgers U New Brunswick NJ 08903

STUBBEN, DOLUS JANE (D.J.), advertising executive; b. Clovis, N.Mex., Sept. 12, 1951; d. Joseph P. Harmon and Maurine Yvonne (Simmons) McDonald; m. Ronald Patrick Day, Apr. 11, 1970 (div.); m. 2d, John David Stubben, Sept. 23, 1979 (div.); 1 dau., Patricia Joan. Student West Tex. State U., 1969-70. Instr. Amarillo (Tex.) Coll., 1971-73; advt. cons., Amarillo, 1976-78; advt. mgr. Montgomery Ward, Amarillo, 1978-80; musician Furr's Cafeteria, Amarillo, 1978-80; piano bar musician, comedienne Quigley's Restaurant, Eugene, Oreg., 1980-81; owner, mgr. Welcome Pardner!, Amarillo, 1981—; arbitrator Better Bus. Bur., Amarillo, 1978-79. Author: #555 Death Row, 1981 (Nat. Press Women 2d place award, 1981), Dog Pause ..., 1981 (Nat. Press Women 2d place award 1982); It's a Secret, I Can't Tell You, 1984. Media chmn. Am. Cancer Soc., Amarillo, 1978-79; media dir. Bralley's 4th of July Picnic, Amarillo, 1977-78; media relations com. St. Jude's Hosp. Tex. Com., Amarillo, 1983; Mem. Tex. Press Women (v.p. 1982, state treas. 1986, membership chmn. 1986), Amarillo C. of C. (membership com. 1983). Office: Welcome Pardner PO Box 30926 Amarillo TX 79120

STUBBLEFIELD, JENNYE LEE WASHINGTON, home economist; b. Jacksonville, Fla., Mar. 6, 1925; d. Marion and Ira (McCombs) Washington; B.A. in Instn. Mgmt., Tuskegee (Ala.) Inst., 1946; M.S. in Nutrition, Rutgers U., 1966; m. Charles Stubblefield, June 26, 1954. Dietitian, Lincoln Hosp., Durham, N.J., 1946-48; instr. vets. cooking and baking schs., 1948-50; tchr. vocat. foods, cafeteria mgr. William Jason High Sch., Georgetown, Del., 1950-56; asst. dietitian Mercer Hosp., Trenton, N.J., 1957; instr. nutrition St. Francis Hosp. Sch. Nursing, Trenton, 1957-64, Helene Fulde Hosp. Sch. Nursing, Trenton, part-time 1965-71; dir. food service Middlesex County Head Start, New Brunswick, N.J., 1965-66; tchr. foods and nutrition Nottingham Jr. High Sch., Trenton, 1966-71; dir. dept. health, recreation and welfare City of Trenton, 1971-74; dir. Aid to Low Income Alcoholics Mercer County, Trenton, 1974-76; supr. consumer and homemaking edn. Trenton Bd. Edn., 1976—; co-adj. instr. Douglass Coll., 1964-65; adv. council Sch. Vocat. Edn., Rutgers U., 1977—. Chmn. bd. dirs. United Progress, Inc., Trenton, 1974-76; mem. Trenton City Council, 1976—, Black Women for Democratic Action, 1976—; vice chmn. Mercer County Dem. Com., 1981-83, chmn., 1983; bd. dirs. Trenton chpt. ARC, 1972-77, chmn., 1976-77. Mem. Am. Dietetic Assn., Am. Home Econs. Assn., Home Econs. Edn. Assn., Vocat. Edn. Assn., Am. Vocat. Assn., N.J. Assn. Secondary Sch. Prins. and Suprs., Women's Polit. Caucus, NAACP. Home: 21 Alden Ave Trenton NJ 08616 Office: 108 N Clinton Ave Trenton NJ 08609

STUBBS, FRANCES EVELYN, banker; b. N.Y.C., Dec. 7, 1926; d. Cyrilo Juan and Madeline Orenina (Bowman) Lima; student public schs.; diploma Am. Inst. Banking, 1963; m. Andrew Stubbs, Nov. 25, 1946; children—Steven, Andrea. With Home owners Loan Corp., 1944-47, Kay Jewelers, N.Y.C., 1948-58; with Chase Manhattan Bank, N.A., N.Y.C., 1959—, asst. v.p., mgr. comml. loan ops., 1981-83, asst. v.p., mgr. lockbox, 1983-85, tng. coordinator, 1985—. Vice pres. Family Services Westchester, 1983—. Mem. Nat. Assn. Bank Women (chpt. chmn. 1979-80), Westchester County Bankers Assn. (treas. 1979-85), Bus. and Profl. Women New Rochelle (pres. 1983-85), Negro Bus. and Profl. Women New Rochelle (fin. sec. 1980-85). Presbyterian. Office: 1 New York Plaza New York NY 10081

STUBBS, JUDY MARIE, physician; b. Dayton, Ohio, Oct. 1, 1950. B.S., U. N.Mex, 1972, M.D., 1977. Resident in family practice Good Samaritan Hosp., Dayton, 1977-80; gen. practice medicine, Peoria, Ill., 1980—; assoc. dir. impatient care dept. family practice, U. Ill.-Peoria, 1981—, also instr. head coordinator single group 1st Assembly of God Ch., 1981—, also Sunday sch. tchr. Mem. Peoria Med. Soc., Ill. Med. Soc., AMA, Active Med. and Dental Staff Meth. Med. Ctr. Ill. Office: Glen Oak Assocs SC 120 NE Glen Oak Suite 100 Peoria IL 61603

STUBBS, SUSAN LEE, mental health services administrator, psychotherapist; b. Boston, Oct. 23, 1946; d. Harold LeRoy and Lucille F. (Benedetti) S.; m. Barry Stuart Goldstein, Apr. 29, 1971; children—Robin Stubbs Goldstein, Rosemary Stubbs Goldstein. B.A., Northeastern U., 1986; M.S.W., Fordham U., 1972. Lic. ind. clin. social worker. Social worker N.Y.C. Housing Authority, 1972-73; dir. learning ctr. Children's Aid Soc., N.Y.C., 1974-78; clin. supr. Gandara Mental Health Ctr., Springfield, Mass., 1978-80; asst. dir. Hampshire Assn. Mental Health, Northampton, Mass., 1980-81, exec. dir., 1982; exec. dir. Valley Programs, Northampton, 1983—; psychotherapist, Northampton, 1978—. Mem. Gov.'s Adv. Bd. Homelessness, 1984—, Mayor's Task Force Deinstitutionalization, 1982—. Mem. Nat. Assn. Social Workers, Mass. Council Human Service Providers, Mass. Coalition on Homelessness. Democrat. Home: 13 Trumbull Rd Northampton MA 01060 Office: Valley Programs 98 Main St Northampton MA 01060

STUBITS, DORIS JUNE, fund raising executive; b. St. Louis, Dec. 11, 1934; d. Robert Lavern and Frances Lucille (Klemme) Welch; m. John Leonard Stubits, June 25, 1954 (div.); children—John, James, Jerome. Student Sanford Brown Bus. Sch., 1953. Dir. devel. St. Louis Christian Home, 1972-82; dir. found. and ann. giving Nat. Benevolent Assn., St. Louis, 1982-85; dir. devel. Fla. Christian Ctr., Jacksonville, 1985—. Mem. Nat. Assn. Fund Raising Execs., Nat. Assn. Hosp. Devel. Republican. Club: Altrusa (Jacksonville). Home: 6747 Periwinkle Dr Jacksonville FL 32244 Office: Fla Christian Ctr 1071 S Edgewood Ave Jacksonville FL 32205

STUCKEY, REGENA NICHOLS, telephone company executive; b. Shreveport, La., Jan. 15, 1955; d. Ernest and Pinkey Lee (Tillman) Nichols; m. John Stuckey, Jr., Aug. 14, 1982. B.F.A., U. Cin., 1977, M.A., 1978. Producer, Sta. WGUC, Cin., 1974-75, Sta. WLW, Cin., 1975-76; news intern Sta. WDTN-TV, Dayton, Ohio, 1975; prop technician Sta. WCPO-TV, Cin., 1976; pub. relations assoc. Cin. Bell Telephone Co., 1978—; sr. cons. Pulse Communications, Cin., 1982—; trustee, pres. Cin. Cable Access Corp., 1983—. Bd. dirs. program policy com. Sta. WCET-TV, Cin., 1983—; v.p. Martin Luther King, Jr. Coalition, Cin., 1980—; mem. disabilities com. Community Chest, Cin., 1981—, chmn. Recipient Outstanding Civic Leader award Bloom Jr. High Sch., Cin., 1984. Mem. Women in Communications, Nat. Assn. Female Execs., Delta Sigma Theta (advisor 1980-83, v.p. 1981-83, Advisor of Yr. award 1982, Excellence award 1983). Baptist. Home: 1531 Northwood Dr Cincinnati OH 45237 Office: Cincinnati Bell Telephone Co 201 E 4th St Cincinnati OH 45202

STUDLEY, DEBRA LYNN, office automation executive; b. Milton, Mass., Sept. 24, 1958; d. Melvin Raymond and Eunice Estelle (Forsberg) Studley; m. Steven D. Brown, Sept. 5, 1981. A.S., N.H. Coll., 1982; postgrad. U. Tenn.-Knoxville, 1981—. Reservation mgr. 1982 World's Fair, Knoxville, 1981-82; account rep. Tex. Instruments, Knoxville, 1982-83, System Source, 1983-84; office automation mgr. Olsten Services, Knoxville, 1984—; cons. in field. Fund raiser Arts Council of East Tenn., Knoxville, 1986, Jr. Achievement, Knoxville, 1986. Mem. Assn. Info. Systems Profls. (v.p. pub. relations), Nat. Assn. Female Execs., Greater Knoxville C. of C. (diplomat 1983—, award of appreciation 1985). Republican. Congregationalist. Avocations: wine collecting; tennis; counted crosstitch. Home: 625A Idlewood Ln Knoxville TN 37923 Office: Olsten Services 1900 Winston Rd Suite 402 Knoxville TN 37919

STUDY, MARY MARGARET (TELLER), small business owner; b. Oklahoma City, Dec. 3, 1945; d. Ernest Leonard and Mary Ann Teller; B.A., U. No. Colo., 1967; M.A. in Public Relations, M.A. in Journalism, Ball State U., 1970; m. Larry Lee Study, Jan. 3, 1970; 1 son, Darren Boyd. Report specialist, adminstrv. specialist, Avionics Research, Ohio U., Athens, 1971-73, exec. sec. dean Coll. Engring. and Tech., 1973-74; instr.-lectr. public relations Sch. Mass Communications, Mara Inst. Tech., Shah Alam, Malaysia, 1974-76; owner-mgr. Alpha Graphics Ltd., Print Media Service Center, Muncie, 1976—; cons. advt. spltys., 1980—; freelance public relations writer, cons., Athens, 1970-74; free lance writer, pub. periodicals on small bus., graphics, advt. Chmn., Oktoberfest, 1979—; mem. Downtown Bus. Council Retail Promotions and Spl. Events Com., 1978-81, chmn., 1979-81; mem. Try Muncie First Com.; mem. Public Relations Task Force, 1972. Mem. Women in Communications (advisor Ball State U. chpt. 1969), C. of C. Muncie-Delaware County (small bus. council 1979), Alpha Gamma Delta. Editor, pub. Muncie Marketeer, 1978. Office: 111 E Adams Muncie IN 47305

STUEHR, GAIL ANNE, journalist; b. Cleve.; d. Lee R. and Isabel M. (McCaa) Featheringham; children—Laura Lee, David John, Eric William, Andrea Lynne. Student Muskingum Coll., U. Mich.; B.S. in Edn., Kent State U., 1961; postgrad. Case Western Res. U. Corr., Plain Dealer, Cleve., 1971-81, Sun Newspapers, 1971-76; free-lance writer, pub. relations cons., 1971—; editor, writer Case Western Res. U., Cleve., 1979-80, sr. editor, 1980, dir. media relations, 1980-81, dir. pub. relations Sch. Medicine, 1981—. Contbr. articles to profl. jours. and newspapers. Bd. dirs. Greater Cleve. Counseling Service of Greater Cleve. Interch. Council. Recipient Communicators award Women in Communications, Inc., 1982; Amateur Photography Contest winner Cleve. Press, 1978, 79. Mem. Women in Communications, Inc., Press Club of Cleve. (awards com. 1983—), Internat. Assn. Bus. Communicators, Am. Assn. Med. Colls. Avocations: swimming; fiction writing; travel; photography. Home: 2183 Demington Dr Cleveland Heights OH 44106 Office: Case Western Res U Room T505 Sch of Medicine Cleveland OH 44106

STUMBO, ANITA YVONNE, investment industry publishing company executive, stockbroker; b. Dallas, Dec. 9, 1948; d. Earnest Eugene Randall and Edna Maureen (Dill) Randall Dill; m. Allen Stumbo, May 20, 1972; children—John Allen, Kelli Cathleen, James Michael. Student North Tex. State U., 1967-69. Mut. fund clk. Republic Nat. Bank, Dallas, 1969-72; asst. sec.-treas. Fund Mgmt. Co., Dallas, 1972-75; v.p., broker Schneider Bernet & Hickman, Dallas, 1975-83; br. mgr. mcpl. bond dept. Bateman Eichler Hill Richards, Dallas, 1983-84; pres. RR Publ. & Prodn. Co., Inc., Dallas, 1984—; stockbroker W.S. Griffith & Co. Inc., Dallas, 1986—; trustee Walnut Hill UMC Found., Dallas, 1984—; registered rep. N.Y. Stock Exchange, Am. Stock Exchange, Chgo. Bd. Options Exchange; assoc. Commodity Futures Trading Commn. Author, pub. book and study course: Winning Big with UIT Commissions, 1984; author, editor, pub.: The UIT Directory, 1984—; author, pub.: Wall Street Minder, 1985—. Contbr. articles to local newspapers, mags. Creator Parent to Parent, Dallas, 1980-84; active Edna Gladney Aux., Dallas; bd. dirs. Assn. Retarded Citizens Dallas, Walnut Hill UMC Creative Sch., Dallas, 1985—. Named Miss Denton, Denton Jr. C. of C., Tex., 1968. Mem. Nat. Assn. Security Dealers (registered rep. 1972—, registered prin. 1979—), Exec. Women Dallas, Dallas Women's C. of C. (bd. dirs. 1982-83). Methodist. Avocations: organ; piano. Office: RR Publication & Prodn Co Inc 2639 Walnut Hill Ln Suite 123A Dallas TX 75229

STUMBO, DIANE MARIE, accountant; b. Pulaski, Va., Jan. 4, 1956; d. Marvin Davis and Edna Marie (Boothe) Moles; m. John Lewis Stumbo, Jr., May 7, 1978 (div. 1986); 1 child, Heather Beth. B.S., Radford U., Va., 1977. Staff acct. A.J. Smith, C.P.A., Pulaski, 1977-79; staff acct. Hubbell Lighting Div., Christiansburg, Va., 1979-81, gen. acctg. mgr., 1981—. Fundraiser Am. Arthritis Assn., Pulaski, 1982, 83; adviser Pentecostal Young Peoples Assn.; bd. suprs. Hubbell Lighting Div. Credit Union, 1982-84, bd. dirs., 1985—. Recipient mgmt. cert., Hubbell Lighting Div., 1983. Mem. Nat. Assn. Accts., Nat. Assn. Female Execs., Am. Mgmt. Assn. (cert. acctg. mgmt., 1981, cert. report systems, 1984), Pulaski Republican Assn. Methodist. Club: Positive Christian Singles (Pulaski). Avocations: woodworking; sewing; cooking; aerobics. Home: PO Box 1957 Pulaski VA 24301 Office: Hubbell Lighting Div 2000 Electric Way Christiansburg VA 24073

STUMP, SANDRA SUE, medical technologist; b. Ft. Wayne, Ind., Feb. 11, 1936; d. Hubert A. and D'Maris A. (Smith) S.; B.A., DePauw U., 1958; M.T., Borgess Hosp., Kalamazoo, Mich., 1959. Clin. microbiologist Borgess Hosp., Kalamazoo, Mich., 1960-63; chief med. technologist Luth. Hosp., Ft. Wayne, 1964-65, clin. microbiologist, 1965-74, program dir., 1975—. Mem. Am. Soc. Clin. Pathologists, Am. Soc. Microbiology, South Central Assn. Microbiology, Consortium Ind. Med. Lab. Educators (pres. 1984-85). Methodist. Office: 3024 Fairfield Ave Fort Wayne IN 46807

STUMPF, NANCY LYNN, human resources consultant; b. Peoria, Ill., June 15, 1957; d. Howard Eugene and Mary Elaine (Morris) Moreland; m. Francis Jerome Stumpf, Sept. 17, 1977. B.S. in Communications, Bradley U., M.A. in Human Resources and Counseling. Coll. recruiter Milton (Wis.) Coll., 1980-81; with advt. recruitment dept. Energy Publs., Pasadena, Calif., 1981-83; cons., owner The Moreland Co., Pasadena, 1981—; cons. various small cos., Los Angeles, 1982-83. Author: The Perfect Job Search, 1983; editor: Human Resources Index, 1982. Mem. Am. Soc. Personnel Adminstrn., Am. Soc. Tng. and Devel., Nat. Assn. Female Execs., Am. Mgmt. Assn. Roman Catholic. Home: 536 S Euclid Apt 8 Pasadena CA 91100

STUNKEL, CLARE FRANCES, lawyer; b. Chgo., Dec. 7, 1953; d. Joseph Peter and Clare Natalie (Andros) Bell; m. Werner L. Stunkel, Man. 14, 1978. B.A., Lake Forest Coll.; J.D., Northwestern U. Bar: Ill. Assoc., Walter E. Heller & Co., Chgo., 1978-81; v.p. and atty. Exchange Nat. Bank of Chgo., 1981—. Lincoln scholar, Lake Forest Coll., 1975, recipient Emma O. Haas scholarship award, 1972, 73, 74, 75. Mem. ABA, Ill. State Bar Assn., Chgo. Bar Assn., Phi Beta Kappa. Republican. Home: 347 Cherokee Rd Lake Forest IL 60045 Office: Exchange Nat Bank of Chgo LaSalle & Monroe Sts Chicago IL 60603

STURDIVANT-THACKER, JILL CRAMER, singer, songwriter, football player; b. Raleigh, N.C., Nov. 16, 1956; d. Rom DeVan and Joyce Wiggs Sturdivant; m. Douglas B. Thacker, Sept. 6, 1981. B.S., U. Miami, 1976; A.D. in Acctg., Roanoke Valley Coll., 1979. Singer, N.Y.C., 1976-79; loan officer Kroger Credit Union, Salem, Va., 1979; actress, bartender Barn Dinner Theatre, Roanoke, Va., 1979; pres., player L.A. Scandals Women's Pro-Football, North Hollywood, Calif., 1985—; singer, session artist Warner Records, North Hollywood, 1984—. Mem. Nat. Acad. Recording Arts and Scis. Office: Warner Records PO Box 9753 North Hollywood CA 91609

STURGEON, PAULINE RUTH, editor; b. Centralia, Mo., Sept. 4, 1907; d. William Arthur and Ruth Jane (Cook) Sturgeon. B.J., U. Mo.-Columbia, 1929, B.A., 1977. Staff, Centralia Fireside Guard, 1956-60; feature writer Columbia Daily Tribune (Mo.), 1960-64; editor The Russell Record, (Kans.), 1967—. Mem. Kans. Press Women, Fedn. Press Women, DAR, Sigma Delta Chi. Club: Bus. and Profl. Women's. Address: The Russell Record 802 N Maple St Russell KS 67665

STURGES, FLORENCE MARGARET, librarian; b. Boston, July 2, 1908; d. Edgar Saxon and Charlotte Jane (Case) Stanley; student New Eng. Conservatory, 1928-30; student Boston Public Library Tng. Sch., 1931-33; diploma Curry Coll., 1940; m. Dwight Richard Sturges, Oct. 12, 1935. Children's librarian Boston Public Library, 1932-41; children's librarian Wellesley (Mass.) Free Library, 1943-70, reference librarian, 1943-70; children's librarian, asst. librarian Skidompha Library, Damariscotta, Maine, 1970—; cons. in establishment of library at Children's Hosp., Boston, 1956-60; pres. New Eng. Round Table of Children's Librarians, 1960-62; mem. Sci. Mus. Book Com., Boston, 1962-68; Caroline M. Hewins lectr., Boston, 1959. Mem. Bronte Soc. of Eng., Nat. Book League, Am. Pen Women (book rev. editor 1968-70). Club: Women's Club. Author: Elizabeth Coatsworth Beston, A Brontë Tapestry, History of Newcastle-Damariscotta Area, History of the Skidompha Library, History of the First and Second Congregational Churches in Newcastle, Maine. Author: Our Memorial Windows, 1985; Five Years of Inspiration, 1986. Contbr. articles to lit. publs. Home: Old County Rd Damariscotta ME 04543 Office: Skidompha Library Damariscotta ME 04543

STURGES, GLORIA JUNE, learning disabilities educator; b. Ingallas, Kans., Nov. 10, 1937; d. Donald Nathan and Dorothy Ellen (Whaley) Kitch; m. W.G. Bray, Jan. 22, 1960 (div. Apr. 1978); children—Lori Lynn, William Don; m. Sidney James Sturges. B.S. in Edn., Southeastern State U., 1959; M.A. in Edn., Webster U., 1975; postgrad. U. Kans., 1978-84, cert. learning disabilities specialty, 1984. Cert. tchr. elem. edn., Colo., Mo., reading and learning disabilities specialist, Mo. Tchr., Jefferson County Schs., Denver, 1959-60, Briggsdale, Colo., 1960-63, Colo. Sch. for Deaf and Blind, Colorado Springs, 1963-66, Bertha Heid Sch., Thornton, Colo., 1966-70; reading specialist Center Sch. Dist., Kansas City, Mo., 1970-78, learning disabilities specialist, 1985—; bus. exec. Sturges Co., Independence, Mo., 1982—. Active ARC, 1984—, Nat. Polit. Action, Kansas City, Mo., 1970—. Recipient Excellence in Edn. award ARC, 1984-85; Outstanding Achievement award Colo. for Deaf and Blind, 1963. Mem. Nat. Assn. Females Execs., NEA, Kappa Delta Pi. Republican. Baptist. Avocations: gourmet cooking; tennis; swimming; antiques. Home: 16805 Cogan Rd Independence MO 64055 Office: Red Bridge Sch 418 E 106th Terr Kansas City MO 64131

STURGIS, JANE PHILBECK, federal official; b. St. Louis, May 3, 1936; d. Robert Hoyle and Ruby Lillian (Glawe) Philbeck; student Am. U., 1976-80; children by previous marriage—Gene Mark, Donna Susan, Christopher Drew; m. 2d, Ralph M. Sturgis, Jan. 12, 1980. Sec., Dept. Agr., 1954-58, IRS, Dept. Treasury, Washington, 1971-72; sec. Nat. Library Medicine, NIH, Bethesda, Md., 1972-74, adminstrv. intern, 1974-76, contract specialist, 1976-84; contract specialist USDA, 1984-85; contracting officer Social Security Adminstrn., 1985—. Mem. Am. Contract Bridge League, Smithsonian Assocs. Methodist. Home: 4806 Davron St Laurel MD 20707 Office: Social Security Adminstrn 1848 Gwynn Oak Ave Baltimore Md 21207

STURGIS, JOSEPHINE GARDNER, retail management executive; b. Boston, Sept. 20, 1961; d. Nathaniel Russell and Ecaterini (Satolias) S. Mgr. Store 24, Inc., Waltham, Mass., 1981-84; mgr. Mrs. Fields Cookies, Boston, 1984-85, tng. ctr. mgr., 1985, regional ops. dir., 1985—. Avocations: tennis; skiing; running. Home: 33 Pond Ave #413 Brookline MA 02146 Office: Mrs Fields Cookies 278 Harvard St Brookline MA 02146

STURGIS, ROSLYN POPE, sales executive; b. Atlanta, Oct. 29, 1938; d. Rogers William and Ruth Pauline (Singleton) Pope; m. John W. Walker, May 17, 1960 (div. 1969); children—Rhonda Lynn, Donna Walker Belle; m. John Lawrence Sturgis, Sept. 30, 1978. Certificat de Musique, L'Ecole Normale de Musique, Paris, 1959; B.A. in Music, Spelman Coll., 1960; M.A. in English Lit., Ga. State U., 1968; Ph.D. in Humanities, Syracuse U., 1974. Asst. prof. religious studies Pa. State U., State College, 1974-76; chairperson div. humanities Bishop Coll., Dallas, 1976-79; dir. ethnic and intercultural relations U. Tex.-Arlington, 1979-81; advt. sales exec. Southwestern Bell Publs., Fort Worth, 1982—. Merrill scholar Spelman Coll., 1958-59, Kent fellow Danforth Found., Syracuse U., 1970-74, Univ. fellow Syracuse U., 1969-70. Democrat. Nichiren Shoshu Buddhist. Home: 7821 Acapulco Rd Fort Worth TX 76112

STURGULEWSKI, ARLISS, state legislator; b. Blaine, Wash., Sept. 27, 1927. B.A. in Econs. and Bus. Adminstrn., U. Wash. Formerly vice-chmn. New Capital Site Planning Commn., mem. Anchorage Mcpl. Assembly, chmn. legis. com. Alaska Mcpl. League, mem. Capital Site Selection Commn.; mem. Greater Anchorage Area Planning and Zoning Commn., 1975-76; mem. Anchorage Mcpl. Assembly, 1976-78; mem. Alaska Senate, 1978—. Office: State Capitol Juneau AK 99811

STURM, RUTH FOSTER, lawyer; b. Bklyn., Jan. 3, 1911; d. Ernest and L. Elsie (Foster) Sturm; B.A., Vassar Coll., 1932; LL.B., Columbia, 1935; summer study U. Lausanne (Switzerland), 1929, U. Berlin, 1931. Admitted to N.Y. bar, 1936, pvt. practice N.Y.C., 1936-42, assoc. with Walter F. O'Malley, Esq.; law asst. Ct. of Appeals State N.Y., 1942-44; U.S. Customs Ct., 1944-76. Mem. Gov.'s Com. Edn. and Employment Women, 1964-65, adv. com. Hudson River Valley Commn., 1965-66. Mem. N.Y. County Lawyer's Assn., Fed. Bar Assn., Bus. and Profl. Women's Club Tarrytowns (pres. 1948-50, N.Y. State safety chmn. 1950-52, by-laws chmn. 1953-58, 2d v.p. 1958-60, 1st v.p. 1960-62, pres. 1962-64, parliamentarian 1972-76), Nat. Council Women, Phi Beta Kappa, Kappa Beta Pi. Republican. Presbyn. Author: A Manual of Customs Law, 1974, supplement, 1976; Customs Law and Administration, 1980, 3d edit. 1982, rev. edits., 1983, 84, 85, 86. Home: Hudson House Ardsley-on-Hudson NY 10503

STURNICK, JUDITH A., university president. Pres., U. Maine at Farmington. Office: Office of Pres Univ of Maine at Farmington 86 Main St Farmington ME 04938*

STUTHRIDGE, LINDY-LOU, advertising executive; b. Durban, Natal, South Africa, Apr. 8, 1960; d. William Travelle and Miranda (Maritz) S. B.S., Lee Coll., 1983. Announcer, copywriter WQNE AM, Cleve., 1981-82; news desk asst. WTVC TV, Chattanooga, 1983; media dir. Calvary Temple, Allentown, Pa., 1983-85; account exec. Don Mann Advt., Stockton, 1985—. Producer, dir. musical To Russia With Love, Russia and Romania, 1983. Mem. Nat. Assn. Female Execs., Lodi C. of C., Stockton C. of C. Republican. Club: Exec. Lead. Avocations: Writing; snow skiing; tennis; racquetball. Office: Don Man Advt 4600 N Pershing Ave Suite B Stockton CA 95207

STUTMAN, NANCY, calligrapher, graphic designer, educator; b. Detroit, Feb. 26, 1938; d. Albert E. and Pearl P. (Liebovich) Cook; m. William N. Stutman, Oct. 20, 1963; children—Michael, David. Student U. Ill., 1956-58; cert., grad. with honors Tobe Coburn Sch. for Fashion Careers, N.Y.C., 1959. Asst. buyer millinery R.H. Macy Co. Herald Sq., N.Y.C., 1959-60; exec. asst. Doris Weston, N.Y.C., 1960-64; account exec. Promotion Council Am., N.Y.C., 1965; v.p., co-owner Stutman Assocs., Inc., N.Y.C., 1965-83; prin. Nancy Stutman Calligraphics, Chappaqua, N.Y., 1982—; workshop instr. for calligraphic socs. The Bus. of Calligraphy, 1984—. Group show Master Eagle Gallery, N.Y.C., 1982, 85. Coordinator bus. services-donations for auction to send local baseball team to Cuba, 1982; chairperson fundraising tag sale Blythedale Children's Hosp., Valhalla, N.Y., 1983; vol. Am. Cancer Soc., White Plains, 1985-86, New Westchester Orch., 1985; vol. calligrapher Temple Beth El of No. Westchester, Chappaqua, 1978—, also active sisterhood and brotherhood. Recipient Service award Temple Beth El of No. Westchester, 1982, 85. Mem. Advt. Club Westchester (hon. mem. 1984—, bd. dirs. 1985—, sec. 1986—, Gold design award 1984, 85, 86, 2 Bronze awards 1986, Hall of Fame award 1985), N.Y. Soc. Scribes, (conf. chairperson promotional gifts/lit. 1986), Westchester Assn. Women Bus. Owners (bd. dirs. 1981—, Pres.'s award 1983), Women in Communications, Westchester County C. of C. (vol. Small Bus. Week, chairperson support network 1985). Democrat. Home and Office: 22 Chatham Rd Chappaqua NY 10514

STUTT, MARILYN JEAN, publisher; b. St. Croix Falls, Wis., Aug. 25, 1927; d. Myron Lawrence and Margaret Julia (O'Neil) Heebink; student Stout Inst., Menomonie, Wis., 1945-46; divorced; children—Dena Margaret Heston, David Michael Stutt, Scott Patrick Anderson. Musician, arranger, vocalist with all girl orch. Sweethearts of Swing, 1947-53; music dir., disc jockey sta. KNIT, Abilene, Tex., 1958-59, writer sta. KRBC-TV, Abilene, also sta. KOAT-TV, Albuquerque, 1959-61; writer, editor U.S. Civil Service, Sandia Base, N.Mex., 1962-63; advt. dir. Roger Cox & Assocs. Enterprises, Albuquerque, 1974-77; owner Marilyn Stutt Advt. Agy., Albuquerque, also pres. Marilyn Stutt Enterprises, Inc., Albuquerque, 1977—; founder, 1979, since publisher Albuquerque Singles Scene mag.; pres. Singles Scene, Inc., nat. licensing network, 1981—; founder, pres. Unicorn Publs., Inc., 1984—. Mem. Mag. Pubs. Assn., N.Mex. Advt. Fedn., Albuquerque Women in Bus. Democrat. Club: N.Mex. Press. Office: 8421 Osuna NE Suite H Albuquerque NM 87111

STYLES, MARGRETTA MADDEN, nursing educator, university dean; b. Mount Union, Pa., Mar. 19, 1930; d. Russell B. and Agnes (Wilson) Madden; B.S., Juniata Coll., 1950; M. in Nursing, Yale U., 1954; Ed.D., U. Fla., 1968;

m. Douglas F. Styles, Sept. 4, 1954; children—Patrick, Michael, Megan. Staff nurse VA Hosp., West Haven, Conn., 1954-55; instr. Bklyn. Hosp. Sch. Nursing, 1955-58; supr. North Dist. Hosp., Pompano Beach, Fla., 1961-63; dir. nursing edn. Broward Community Coll., Ft. Lauderdale, Fla., 1963-67; asso. prof. Sch. Nursing, Duke U., Durham, N.C., 1967-69, dir. undergrad. studies, 1967-69; prof., dean Sch. Nursing, U. Tex., San Antonio, 1969-73, Wayne State U., Detroit, 1973-77; cons. doctoral program U. Minn., 1977, U. Wis., Madison, 1978; chairperson Com. for Study of Credentializing in Nursing, 1976-79; mem. adv. group div. nursing HEW, 1977; prof., dean Sch. Nursing, U. Calif., San Francisco, 1977—; mem. accreditation team Western Assn. Schs. and Colls.; bd. dirs. Am. Jours Nurses, Nurses House Inc.; spl. asst. to pres. for health affairs U. Calif. Systemwide, 1979; assoc. dir. nursing services U. Calif. Hosps. and Clinics, 1978-83; mem. Nat. Commn. Nursing, 1980-83; mem. tech. adv. com. on nursing edn. Calif. Postsecondary Edn. Commn., Sacramento, 1978-79. Mem. health personnel task force Gov.'s Office of Health and Med. Affairs, 1974-76; mem. adv. com. nursing home project Citizens for Better Care, Detroit, 1974-76; bd. dirs. Wayne State U. Clinics, 1973-76, mem. planning com., 1973-76, fin. com., 1973-76; mem. Calif. Gov.'s Bd. Registered Nursing, 1985—. Recipient Disting. Alumna award Yale U. Sch. Nursing, 1979. Fellow Am. Acad. Nursing; mem. Am. Nurses Assn. (Disting. scholar 1984-85), Nat. Acad. Sci./Inst. Medicine, Sigma Theta Tau. Contbr. articles on nursing edn. to profl. publs.; editorial bd. Nursing Leadership, 1977-83, Cancer Nursing, 1977. Office: Univ California School Nursing Dean's Office San Francisco CA 94143

STYNES, BARBARA BILELLO, wellness program marketing executive; b. N.Y.C., Apr. 24, 1951; d. Sylvester Francis and Jacqueline Marie (Giardelli) Bilello; m. Frank Joseph Stynes, Aug. 24, 1969; children—Christopher Francis, Jeremy Scott. B.A., Rutgers U., 1976. Supr. Sav-On Foods, Perth Amboy, N.J., 1978-79; mktg. rep. McNeil Consumer Products Co., Fort Washington, Pa., 1979-82, Met Path Inc., Des Plaines, Ill., 1982-85; mktg. coordinator Life program Meml. Hosp. and YMCA, Chattanooga, 1986—; mem. providor council Chattanooga Wellness Council, 1986—; fiber sculptor, 1975-77; weaver, 1976-79. Vol. Am. Heart Assn., 1972-86, Spl. Olympics, Chgo., 1982-84; chairperson fundraising, trustee Pine Grove Coop. Sch., New Brunswick, N.J., 1977-78; bd. dirs. Signal Mountain Newcomers Assn., Tenn., 1985-86. Fellow Nat. Assn. Female Execs., Fiber Arts Guild. Roman Catholic. Avocations: ballet; piano; aerobics. Home: 914 Dunsinane Rd Signal Mountain TN 37377 Office: Meml Hosp 2500 Citico Ave Chattanooga TN 37404

SUAO, ADRIANA CARTAYA, magazine publisher; b. Havana, Cuba, Jan. 20, 1946, came to U.S., 1962; d. Moises Gregorio and Acela Maria (Latour) Cartaya; m. Luis Suao, May 20, 1967; children—Tania Maria, Adriana Elena, Luisa Maria. Student Am. Dominican Acad., Cuba, 1962. Pub. relations staff Kenyon Wiles Advt. Agy., Miami, Fla., 1965, copy editor, 1965-69; gen. mgr., prodn. mgr. Internat. Constrn. Pub. Co., Inc., Miami, 1972—; pres. Cieco, Miami, 1977—; adminstr. BYS Tunnel Forms Co., Miami, 1983—. Republican. Roman Catholic. Avocations: yachting, fishing, cooking. Home: 1401 Lugo Ave Coral Gables FL 33156 Office: Internat Constrn Pub Inc Suite 110 9200 S Dadeland Blvd Miami FL 33156

SUAREZ, YOLANDA QUINTERO, military association executive; b. San Antonio, May 20, 1949; d. Bonifacio P. Quintero and Maria Louisa (Valdez) Quintero Flores; m. Lawrence Anthony Suarez, Sept. 17, 1968 (div. Sept. 1980); children—Lori Ann, David Anthony. A.A. in Mid-Mgmt., San Antonio Coll., 1986. Notary pub., Tex. Tchr.'s aide Region 20, Edn. Service Ctr., San Antonio, 1975-78; with Am. GI Forum, San Antonio, 1978—, personnel/account mgr., 1981-85, adminstrn. coordinator nat. vets. outreach program, 1985—. Recipient Spl. award MDA Cake Decorating Show, 1980, 2d Place award, 1980; First Place award J. C. Penney Advanced Show, 1981; Outstanding Servcie award Nat. Vets. Outreach Program, 1982. Mem. Nat. Assn. Female Execs., Ms. Found. For Women, Am. GI Forum (award 1983, Nat. Queen Pageant Appreciation award 1985, Ednl. Fund scholar 1984, chairperson Miguel Women's chpt. 1981-83, 84-85), Profl. Cake Decorators (treas. 1980-81). Roman Catholic. Avocations: tennis; aerobics. Office: Am GI Forum 1017 N Main Suite 200 San Antonio TX 78212

SUBY, CHRYS MARIE, nurse practitioner; b. Buffalo, Minn., Mar. 11, 1952; d. Howard William and Evelyn Dorothy Sophia (Gunnerson) Holland; m. Terry Lane Suby, Feb. 25, 1983; 1 child, Jason William. A.S.N., Met. State Coll., Mpls., 1972; cert. nurse pracittioner adult medicine U. Minn., 1981. Charge nurse surgery United Hosp. St. Lukes, St. Paul, 1972-73; head nurse med. unit Methodist Hosp., Mpls., 1973-77; nurse practitioner Endocrinology Assocs., Mpls., 1977-82; v.p. Telescan Corp., Mpls., 1982—; chief operating officer Nursing Mgmtm. Services Inc., Mpls., 1984—. Cons., speaker on heart and respiration monitoring, 1984—. Bd. dirs. Methodist Hosp. Found., Mpls., 1986, Am. Diabetes Assn. Minn., 1982—. St. Lukes Hosp. scholar, 1971. Mem. Am. Nurses Assn., Nurse Practitioner Council, Am. Diabetes Assn. Republican. Congregationalist. Avocations: Needlepoint; singing; guitar; piano; travel. Office: Telescan Corp 6490 Excelsior Blvd #E109 Minneapolis MN 55426

SUDBRINK, JANE MARIE, financial consultant; b. Sandusky, Ohio, Jan. 14, 1942. B.S., Bowling Green State U., 1964; student in cytogenetics Kinderspital-Zurich, Switzerland, 1965. Field rep. Random House and Alfred A. Knopf Inc., Mpls., 1969-72, Ann Arbor, Mich., 1973, regional mgr., Midwest and Can., 1974-79, Canadian rep., mgr., 1980-81; psychology and ednl. psychology adminstrv. editor Charles E. Merrill Pub. Co. div. Bell & Howell Corp., Columbus, Ohio, 1982-84; sales and mktg. mgr. trade products Wilson Learning Corp., Eden Prairie, Minn., 1984-85; fin. cons. Merrill Lynch, Pierce, Fenner & Smith Inc., Edina, Minn., 1985—. Mem. Am. Ednl. Research Assn., Nat. Assn. Female Execs. Lutheran. Avocations: Volunteer United Way, Mpls. Home: 6730 Vernon Ave Edina MN 55436 Office: Merrill Lynch 3400 W 66th St Southdale Place Edina MN 55435

SUDDUTH, MARY HOSSLEY, operations supervisor; b. Vicksburg, Miss., Sept. 18, 1947; d. Earl Secil and Elsie Jane (Tucker) Hossley; m. James A. Sudduth, Mar. 7, 1986; stepchildren—Shawn, Bradley. B.S. in Edn., Miss. State U., 1970. Tchr., Columbus pub. schs., Miss., 1972; sec. to pres. Columbus Marble Works, 1972-76; sec. Miss. State U., Miss., 1976-77; sec. J.L. Teel Co., Columbus, 1977; sec. to v.p. Northrup King Co., Columbus, 1977-82; ops. supr. Yellow Freight System, Columbus, 1982—. Republican. Roman Catholic. Avocations: needlework; sewing; reading; fishing. Home: PO Box 2643 Columbus MS 39704 Office: Yellow Freight System PO Drawer 2188 Columbus MS 39704

SUDERMAN, INEZ ALDENE, real estate broker; b. Bessie, Okla., July 10, 1938; d. Adolph B. and Lea (Wedel) Javorsky; m. Emery Lowell Suderman, July 29, 1960; children—James, Carol, Timothy. B.S. in Edn., Southwestern U., 1960; B.S., Pan Am. U., 1964. Cert. tchr., Okla., Tex. Tchr. various schs., Kansas City, Kans., 1960-61, Grand Junction, Colo., 1961-62, Pharr, Tex., 1962-64; realtor Century 21 Homefinders, McAllen, Tex., 1978-80, Action Realty, McAllen, 1980—; pres. Women's Council Realtors, McAllen, 1983—; dir. McAllen Bd. Realtors; exec. sec., dir. Lone Star Nat. Bank, Pharr, 1986—. Chmn. phone ctr. Clements for Gov. campaign, 1982; bd. dirs. South Tex. Symphony Assn., 1986. Named Outstanding Woman, McAllen C. of C., 1979. Mem. Tex. Assn. Realtors, McAllen Bd. Realtors (treas. 1985), Tex. Agri-Woman (1st v.p.), Tex. State Garden Clubs (life, state trustee 1983-89). Am. Osteo. Assn. Aux. (dir. various coms.), Tex. Osteo. Assn. Aux. (pres. 1980). Mennonite. Clubs: Vesta Study (McAllen) (pres. 1983-84), McAllen Fedn. Women's Clubs (pres. 1978-79). Office: Action Realty 2415 N 10th St McAllen TX 78501

SUDIA, MARY EILEEN, nurse; b. Denver, Oct. 18, 1922; d. Joseph and Perenella (McDonald) Tenhaeff; R.N., Mercy Hosp. Sch. Nursing, 1944; B.S. in Nursing Edn., Colo. U., 1950; m. Andrew T. Sudia, Dec. 30, 1949; children—Thomas M., Joseph A., Patricia Sudia Bittner. Nurse, VA Hosp., Ft. Lyons, Colo., 1946-50; instr. San Antonio Jr. Coll., 1951-53, Union Meml. Hosp., Balt., 1961-66; asso. dir., dir. nursing Pickersgill Inc., Balt., 1971-83; night supr. Ft. Howard (Md.) VA Med. Ctr., 1983-84. Served with U.S. Army, 1944-46. Mem. Am. Nurses Assn., Nat. League Nursing. Club: Am. Nurses Found. Century (founding mem. 1981). Home: 1556 Putty Hill Ave Baltimore MD 21204 Office: Fort Howard VA Med Ctr Fort Howard MD

SUDOL, VALERIE JEANNE, dance critic; b. Passaic, N.J., Aug. 28, 1951; d. Theodore Valentine and Jeanne (Bastek) Sudol. A.A. cum laude, Ocean County Coll., 1972. Staff writer Daily Observer, Toms River, N.J., 1970-71; staff writer Asbury Park Press (N.J.), 1971-77; freelance writer, 1972—; administrv. asst. Burklyn Ballet Theatre, East Burke, Vt., 1978-79; dance critic Star Ledger, Newark, 1978—. Mem. Dance Critics Assn. (fellow Durham, N.C. 1979). Home: 5206 Asbury Ave Tinton Falls NJ 07753 Office: Star-Ledger Ledger Plaza Newark NJ 07101

SUEHR, SUSAN LYNN, chemical engineer; b. Pitts., Feb. 19, 1952; d. Robert L. and Betsy (DeMello) S., m. William L. Smallwood, Jr., Oct. 11, 1980; 1 child, Leigha Christine. B.S. in Chem. Engring., U. Pitts., 1974. Engr., Proctor & Gamble, Cin., 1974-75, Green Bay, Wis., 1975-77, project engr., Cin., 1977-81; sr. engr. Johnson & Johnson, North Brunswick, N.J., 1981-85, project mgr., engr., 1985—. Mem. Republican Nat. Com., 1981—; bd dirs. Huntington Park Homeowners Assn., 1983-86, head budget and fin. com., 1983-86, mem. archtl. com., 1983—. Mem. Soc. Women Engrs. (sr.; chpt. pres. 1979-80), Nat. Assn. Female Execs. Republican. Roman Catholic. Club: Sweet Adelines (chpt. historian 1984-86). Avocations: singing women's barbershop; stained glass design; tennis; swimming; aerobics. Office: Johnson & Johnson E1149 501 George St New Brunswick NJ 08903

SUELTENFUSS, SISTER ELIZABETH ANNE, university president; b. San Antonio, Apr. 14, 1921; d. Edward L. and Elizabeth (Amrein) S.; B.A. in Botany and Zoology, Our Lady of the Lake Coll., 1944; M.S. in Biology, U. Notre Dame, 1961, Ph.D. in Biology, 1963. Joined Sisters of Divine Providence, 1939; tchr. high schs., Okla. and La., 1942-49, Our Lady of the Lake Coll., San Antonio, 1949-59, chmn. biology dept., 1963-73, pres., 1978—; adminstrv. staff Superior Gen. of Congregation of Divine Providence, 1973-77; sec. Tex. Ind. Coll. Fund. Bd. dirs. Sta. KLRN Public TV, S.W. Research Found., San Antonio Air Force Community Council, Friends of Library, Inst. for Ednl. Leadership, 1981—. Recipient award of yr. for achievement and leadership U. Notre Dame, 1978-79, Headliner award for profl. achievement Women in Communications, 1980; Outstanding Woman in Career-Service, San Antonio Express, 1983; named to San Antonio Women's Hall of Fame, 1985. Atomic Energy grantee. Mem. AAAS, Am. Soc. Microbiology, AAUP, AAUW, Nat. Assn. Women Religious, Tex. Acad. Sci. Club: Zonta (past pres. San Antonio). Office: 411 SW 24th St San Antonio TX 78285

SUERTH, NANCY HINES, cleaning company executive; b. Boston, Nov. 22, 1931; d. Theodore Jay and Daisy Eleanor (White) Hines; children—Monica Read Gudaitis, Candice Ann Sullivan, William J. Sullivan III, Kimberly Ann Suerth. B.S. in Mass Communications, U. Bridgeport, 1953; postgrad. Catonsville Community Coll., Md., 1975, Johns Hopkins U., 1977; Mgmt. degree Service Master Industries, Downers Grove, Ill., 1976. Sales mgr. interior design Standard Interiors, Balt., 1971-72; gen. mgr. Service Master Service, Balt., 1972-74; owner, pres. Accurate Cleaning Co., Edgewood, Md., 1974—; dir. Rollin Jubilee, roller skating extravaganza, 1976-86. Chmn. New Directions for Women, Balt., 1978; campaign mgr. G.P. Mahoney for U.S. Senate, Balt., 1968; v.p. Dundalk Community Theatre, 1985-86, also bd. dirs.; active Operation Human Survival. Mem. Bldg. Owners and Mgrs. Assn. (pres. 1976), Nat. Assn. Women Bus. Owners. Democrat. Lutheran. Club: Susquehanna Skating. Avocations: stage acting; dancing; skating; swimming; skiing. Home: 1889 Grempler Way Edgewood MD 21040 Office: Accurate Cleaning Co PO Box 743 Edgewood MD 21040

SUGGS, MARILYN MARGARET, human services administrator; b. Washington, Dec. 20, 1955; d. Frederick Joseph and Barbara Kathryn (Pope) Adler; B.S., Mercy Coll., 1977; M.Ed., Plymouth State Coll., 1979; Ed.D., Va. Tech. Inst., 1983. Tchr., Hardin No. Elem. Sch., Dola, Ohio, 1977; counselor, vocat. specialist Androscoggin Valley Mental Health Center, Berlin, N.H., 1977-79; primary counselor Fairfax Falls Ch. Community Services, Vienna, Va., 1979-81, asst. dir. Community residences, group homes, 1981-85; dir. rehab. therapy and adolescent program Briarwood Hosp., Alexandria, La., 1985—. Mem. Council Exceptional Children, Am. Assn. Mental Deficiency, Am. Assn. for Counseling and Devel. Roman Catholic. Home: 3617 Royce Dr Alexandria LA 71303 Office: Briarwood Hosp PO Box 12960 Alexandria LA 71315

SUGHRUE, KATHRYN EILEEN, state legislator; b. Oketo, Kans., May 2, 1913; d. John and Charlotte Peterman; B.S. in Home Econs., Kans. State U., 1937; M.S. in Adminstrn., Colo. State U., 1962; m. Herbert Sughrue, May 3, 1941; children—Kathleen, Margaret, Patricia, John, Tim. Extension home economist, Ford County, Kans., 1937-41, Dodge City, Kans., 1949-61; dist. supt., asso. state leader Kans. State U., 1962-69; adv. Home Econs. Coll., Andra Pradesh U., Hyderabad, India, 1969; state leader N.D. State U., Fargo, 1969-73; freelance profl. speaker, 1973-76; mem. Kans. Ho. of Reps., 1976—. Vice pres., sec. Ford County Democratic Party. Recipient Top award Kans. 4-H Club Program, Finney County, 1958; Disting. Service award Kans. State U., 1981. Mem. Home Econs. Extension (pres. state chpt. 1957-58), Nat. Home Econs. Assn. (pres. state chpt. 1956-57), Kans. Home Econs. Assn. (pres. 1976-77), Home Econs. Club, Arts Council Speakers Guild, AAUW, Delta Kappa Gamma, Epsilon Sigma Phi (pres. state chpt. 1959-60). Roman Catholic. Clubs: Bus. and Profl. Women's, Women's Democratic. Philomat, PEO. Contbr. articles to mags. Office: 1809 La Mesa Dodge City KS 67801

SUIDA, BETTY J., air pollution control official; b. Harbor Beach, Mich.; d. David Frank and Suzanne (Olshove) Suida. A.A. in Bus., Eastern Mich. Coll. Commerce; A.A. in Liberal Arts, Macomb Coll.; B.A. in Polit. Sci., Wayne State U., later postgrad.; postgrad. U. Detroit, Cranbrook U.; grad. Congl. Sch., Washington, 1980; M.B.A., Central Mich. U. With product design office Chrysler Corp.; commr. Mich. Air Pollution Control Commn., 1982—; speaker to women's groups. Congl. candidate 18th Congl. Dist., 1980; mem. Mich. State budget com., 1982, state issues com., 1972; mem. Oakland County Exec. Com., 17th Congl. exec. com.; bd. dirs. Lincoln Republican Club; nat. del., Kansas City, 1976; nat. hon. sgt.-at-arms, Miami Beach, Fla., 1972; Rep. precinct delt.; mem. Oakland County campaign com.; mem. Mich. State com., 1980—; past v.p. Royal Oak Area Rep. Com. (Mich.); sponsor Mich. Opera Theatre; mem. Project Hope, Founders' Soc., Detroit Art Inst. Recipient Women to Watch award Cobo Hall, 1980. Mem. Bus. Women's and Profl. Assn. (legis. liaison), Women of Wayne, Jr. League (past pres.), Internat. Platform Assn., Rep. Women's Forum—Bus. and Profl., Gold Key, Beta Sigma Phi, Pi Sigma Alpha, Sigma Iota Epsilon. Clubs: Detroit Yacht, Women's Econ. (publicity com.), Economic (Detroit). Address: 1841 Wickham Rd Royal Oak MI 48073

SUITER, PATRICIA ALICE, school administrator, writer; b. Portland, Mar. 25, 1922; d. Patrick Thomas and Eleanor Alice (Cringle) Silvester; m. Jack D. Suiter, Dec. 14, 1948 (div. Mar. 1973); 1 child, Wendy Lee. A.B. cum laude, U. Miami, 1952; M.A., U. Fla., 1953; M.Ed., U. Miami, 1967. Cert. tchr., Fla. Tchr., Dade County Pub. Schs., Miami, 1960-65, Alexander Sch., Miami, 1965-67, McGlannon Sch., Miami, 1967-68; asst. prof. edn. U. Miami, Coral Gables, 1968-70; dir., owner House of Learning, Miami, 1970—. Author: Handbook on Diagnostic Teaching, 1974; Behavior Resource Guide I, 1975, Guide II, 1976; Handbook in Diagnostic-Prescriptive Teaching, 1979. V.P. environ. edn. Tropical Audubon Soc., Miami, 1982—. Served with WACS, 1943-48; China. Recipient Conservation award Tropical Audubon Soc., 1983. Mem. Fla. Council Ind. Schs., Assn. Ind. Schs. (v.p. 1978-81, Disting. Educator award 1981), Council Exceptional Children, Assn. Children with Learning Disabilities, Sierra Club (nat. chmn. environ. edn. com. 1982—). Democrat. Unitarian. Office: House of Learning 10545 SW 97th Ave Miami FL 33176

SUITERS, DOLORIS FAE, realtor, real estate company executive; b. Veedersburg, Ind., Feb. 5, 1929; d. Virgil L. and Anna E. (Wolfe) Warrick; m. Gordon L. Suiters, May 3, 1947; children—Phyllis Jean Suiters Salts, Patricia Ann Suiters Donald. Student in real estate Ind. State U., 1974; grad. Realtors Inst., 1983. Salesperson World Book Ency., Covington, Ind., 1961-64; sales clk. Roysters Jewelers, Danville, Ill., 1967-68; real estate salesperson West Central Ind. Realty, Covington, 1975-77; broker, owner, mgr. Suiters Real Estate, Covington, 1978—; mem. bldg. trades bd. Covington High Sch., 1982-84. Mem. Fountain Warren County Bd. Realtors (pres. 1980-82, v.p. 1984-85). Republican. Mem. Ch. of Christ. Home: Rural Route 3 Box 276 Veedersburg IN 47987 Office: 522 3d St Covington IN 47932

SUITS, DIANE STEWART, librarian; b. Norwich, N.Y., Dec. 9, 1939; d. Clarence Eugene and Margaret Alice (Carr) Stewart; B.S. in Child Devel. and Family Relationships, Cornell U., 1962; m. Allen P. Suits, Nov. 29, 1968; children—Brian, Andrew; stepchildren—Catherine, Valerie, Stephen, Jeanne. Lic. real estate broker, Mass. Kindergarten and elem. sch. tchr., N.Y. and Mass., 1962-70; asst. librarian Brookline (Mass.) schs., 1970-72; tchr. 2d grade, Salem, N.H., 1972-73; sch. librarian, Windham, N.H., 1973-80; librarian Meml. High Sch., Manchester, N.H., 1980—. Mem. NEA, N.H. Edn. Assn., Manchester Edn. Assn., N.H. Ednl. Media Assn., Cornell U. Alumni Secondary Schs. Com. Home: 38 Bedard Ave Derry NH 03038 Office: Memorial High Sch S Porter St Manchester NH 03103

SUJANSKY, JOANNE GENOVA, management consultant; b. Freedom, Pa., Mar. 21, 1950; d. John W. and Mary Ellen (Mandarino) Genova; m. R. Charles Sujansky, Jr., Apr. 22, 1977; children—Cara, Justin. B.S., Slippery Rock State Coll. 1972, M.Ed., 1974; Ph.D., U. Pitts., 1980. Grad. asst. Slippery Rock (Pa.) State Coll., 1972-74; dir. tng., employee counselor Presbyn.-Univ. Hosp., Pitts., 1974-78; dir. edn. Mercy Hosp., Pitts., 1978-80; pres. JGS Assocs., Pitts., 1980—. Past bd. dirs. Job Adv. Service of Pitts. Mem. Am. Soc. Tng. and Devel. (Nat. pres.-elect, nat. bd. mem.; past pres. Pitts. chpt., Torch award 1983, Outstanding Leadership award, Pitts. 1980), Pitts. Personnel Assn., Exec. Women's Council. Home: 6 Rushmore Dr Pittsburgh PA 15235 Office: SU 870 Kossman Bldg Pittsburgh PA 15222

SUJECKI, JOY MARY, medical technologist; b. Milw., Nov. 29, 1935; d. John Henry and Helen Eleanor (Bronikowski) Jakubowski; B.S. in Med. Tech., Marquette U., Milw., 1957; M.A. in Health Adminstrn., Central Mich. U., 1979; divorced; children—Ellen, Michael, Laura, Paul, Carol, Nancy, Thomas. Med. technologist for physicians and hosps., Milw., 1957-59; med. technologist Trinity Meml. Hosp., Cudahy, Wis., 1969—, adminstrv. technologist, lab. mgr., 1975—; mem. insp. team Coll. Am. Pathology. Bd. dirs. South div. Am. Cancer Soc., 1975-79; assoc. editor news Our Lady of Lourdes Roman Cath. Ch., Milw., 1974-75; pres. Trinity Meml. Hosp. Aux., 1982-85. Mem. Clin. Lab. Mgmt. Assn. (pres. Wis. chpt. 1986—), Nat. Assn. Female Execs., Wis. Assn. Med. Technologists (chmn. edn. com. 1976). Editorial bd. Med. Lab. Observer. Office: care Trinity Memorial Hospital 5900 S Lake Dr Cudahy WI 53110

SUKET, JUDITH ANN, nurse anesthetist, consultant; b. Milton, Mass., Oct. 28, 1942; d. Ralph Eugene and Mary Jane (Hall) S. B.S., St. Joseph Coll., Standish, Maine, 1975; M.S., Lesley Coll., 1986; R.N., Lynn Hosp. Sch. Nursing, 1964. Cert. nurse anesthetist. Staff anesthetist Quincy City Hosp., Mass., 1967-69, clin. instr. sch. nurse anesthesia, 1969-74, asst. dir., 1975-76; staff anesthetist New Eng. Bapt. Hosp., Boston, 1976-82, Met. Anesthesia Assn., Braintree, Mass., 1982—; cons. Cosgrove & Eisenberg, Quincy, 1974—. Mem. Am. Assn. Nurse Anesthetists, Am. Soc. Law and Medicine, New Eng. Assembly Nurse Anesthetists (bd. dirs. 1979-85, chmn. 1985—), Mass. Anesthesia Council Edn. (sec. 1978-80), Mass. Assn. Nurse Anesthetists (bd. dirs. 1984—, continuing edn. coordinator 1984—). Clubs: Altrusa Internat. (treas. 1982-83) (Quincy); Yankee Golden Retriever (sec. 1985—) (Andover, Mass.). Avocations: camping; gardening; cross country skiing; golden retrievers. Home: 76 Bicknell St Quincy MA 02169 Office: Met Anesthesia Assn 400 Washington St Braintree MA 02184

SUKOL, SHERRY MERLE, psychologist; b. Phila., June 29, 1951; d. Austin Lewis and Elvera (Promisloff) S.; B.A., Carnegie-Mellon U., 1973; M.S., Ohio U., 1975, Ph.D. in Clin. Psychology, 1978. Clin. fellow psychology Harvard Med. Sch., 1977-78; clin. intern Children's Hosp. Med. Center, Boston, 1977-78; asst. prof. counseling psychologist West Chester (Pa.) State Coll., 1978-79; fellow Counseling Assos., Paoli, Pa., 1979-81; consulting psychologist Interac Community Mental Health Center, Phila., 1979-81; pvt. practice psychology, Wayne, Pa., 1980—; asst. prof. Grad. program in counseling and human relations Villanova (Pa.) U., 1980-84. Advisor Women Against Rape, Athens, Ohio, 1977. Lic. psychologist, Pa.; cert. sch. psychologist, Pa. Mem. Am. Psychol. Assn., Phila. Soc. Clin. Psychologist, Phi Kappa Phi. Editor: Consumer's Guide to Psychotherapy, 1980. Office: 400 E Lancaster Ave, Ave 8 Wayne PA 19087

SUKONECK, HARRIET, psychologist, computer scientist; b. Newark, Jan. 30, 1945; d. Edward and Mae S.; B.A., Rutgers U., 1966; M.A., U. So. Calif., 1968, Ph.D. (NIMH fellow), 1971. Lectr., Calif. State U., Los Angeles, 1971-76; mem. research faculty Calif. Sch. Profl. Psychology, 1973-76; NIH postdoctoral fellow Childrens Hosp. of Los Angeles, 1971-73; vis. asst. prof. Loyola Marymount U., Los Angeles, 1976-78; research asso. Neuropsychiat. Inst., UCLA, 1978-80; sr. mem. tech. staff, project leader Computer Scis. Corp., El Segundo, Calif., 1980-81; project mgr. 1st Interstate Services Co., El Segundo, 1981-83; dir. research and product planning Data Line Service Co., Covina, Calif., 1983-84; project mgr. Xerox, El Segundo, Calif., 1984—; cons., sr. faculty U. Phoenix, 1982—; dir. Brainstorms, Los Angeles, 1985—. Lic. psychologist, Calif. Mem. Assn. Computing Machinery, Am. Psychol. Assn., AAAS. Contbr. articles to profl. jours. Editor et. al, social sci. jour., 1971-76. Office: 830 S Nash St El Segundo CA 90245

SULERZYSKI, MARGARET DOROTHY, accountant; b. N.Y.C., Mar. 14, 1951; d. Thomas Edward and Margaret Dorothy (Quinlan) Sulerzyski; student Skidmore Coll., 1969-71; B.A., Barnard Coll., 1973; M.B.A., U. Pa., 1975; certificate in profl. accountancy with honors Northwestern U. Grad. Sch. Bus., 1976. Jr. acct. Arthur Young & Co., N.Y.C., 1975-76; sr. acct. Arthur Young & Co., 1977-79, audit mgr., 1980-83; mgr. audits Merrill Lynch & Co., Inc., 1983-85, v.p., assoc. dir. internal auditing, 1985—; lectr. in field. C.P.A., N.Y.; cert. internal auditor; registered rep. Nat. Assn. Securities Dealers. Mem. Am. Women's Soc. C.P.A.s, N.Y. State Soc. C.P.A.s, Am. Inst. C.P.A.s. Clubs: Wharton Bus. Sch., Barnard Coll. Home: 7 W 14th St #21 PS New York NY 10011 Office: 1 Liberty Plaza New York NY 10080

SULFARO, JOYCE A., school principal; b. Bklyn., Oct. 23, 1948; d. John Joseph and Mildred Ann (Credidio) Carvelli; m. Guy Sulfaro, Aug. 1, 1971; children—Jacqueline A., Kristin Lynn. B.A., Molloy Coll., 1970; postgrad. Fla. Atlantic U., 1979-80; M.S. in Adminstrn. and Supervision, Nova U., 1982. Tutor reading Our Lady of Loretto, Rockville Centre, N.Y., 1969-70; tchr. lang. arts and math. Resurrection Sch., Bklyn., 1970-73; tchr. Annunciation Sch., Hollywood, Fla., 1976-80, prin., 1980-84; tchr. St. Thomas More Sch., 1984—; writer English curriculum for Jr. High for Archdiocese of Miami, 1979. Travel coordinator/sec. Rego Park (N.Y.) Met. Youth Orgn., 1969-70. Mem. Nat. Council Tchrs. Math., Fla. League Middle Schs., Cath. Educators Guild Archdiocese of Miami, Nat. Cath. Ednl. Assn., Am. Mus. Natural History. Author: (with M. Sue Timmins) The Basket, 1980. Home: 5626 Centennial Dr Durham NC 27712 Office: 900 Carmichael Dr Chapel Hill NC

SULLIVAN, A(NNA) MANNEVILLETTE, metallurgist, editor; b. Washington, Aug. 18, 1913; d. Francis Paul and Villette (Anderson) Sullivan; student Wellesley Coll., 1931-33; A.B., George Washington U., 1935; postgrad. Cath. U., 1935-36, M.S., U. Md., 1955. Asst. metallurgist, Geophys. Lab., Carnegie Inst. Washington, 1942-45; metallurgist Nat. Bur. Standards, Washington, 1945-46, U.S. Naval Research Lab., Washington, 1947-78; dep. tech. editor ASME Trans., Jour. Engring. Materials and Tech., 1978-81, cons., 1982—. Mem. Am. Soc. Metals ASTM, ASME, Mensa, Sigma Xi, Alpha Delta Pi. Iota Sigma Pi. Clubs: Toastmasters, Altrusa Internat. Research in fracture of metals with spl. reference to fracture mechanics. Home: 4000 Massachusetts Ave NW Washington DC 20016

SULLIVAN, BERNICE, nurse, county health department official; m. Amherstdale, W.Va.; d. Louis and Mary (Finn) Dubanowich; m. Stewart M. Sullivan, Dec. 30, 1950; children—Deborah Ann, Patrick Joseph, Maureen Adele. B.S. in Nursing, Avila Coll., 1975. R.N., Kans. Staff nurse Johnson County Health Dept., Mission, Kans., 1967-75, nursing dir., 1975-77, health dir., 1977—. Bd. dirs. Mission Am. Heart Assn., 1975—; mem. adv. bd. nursing Johnson County Community Coll., Overland Park, 1976—. Mem. Kans. Pub. Health Assn. (bd. dirs. 1983—, pres. 1984-85), Am. Pub. Health Assn., Kans. Nurses Assn. (chmn. nursing interest group 1971-72), Am. Nurses Assn., Am. Legion Aux., Sigma Theta Tau. Roman Catholic. Lodge: Zonta Internat. Avocations: dancing, reading, gardening. Home: 6008 Halsey St Shawnee KS 66216 Office: Johnson County Health Dept 6000 Lamar St Mission KS 66202

SULLIVAN, CARLEY HAYDEN, political party executive; b. Elko, Nev.; student U. Oreg., 1945-47; m. Will Sullivan; children—Blaine Sullivan Rose, Valerie Sullivan Mitchell, Dan, Peggy Sullivan Hagen. Mgmt. asst. State of Nev., Elko, 1967—; sec. Elko County (Nev.) Democratic Central Com., 1972—; treas. Nev. Dem. Com., 1980-82, co-chmn. state conv., 1980, mem. state cons. planning com., 1982; mem. state hosp. adv. bd., 1964-66, adv. council on children and youth, 1970-80; mem. gov.'s State Sch. Survey Com., 1975-77, Gov.'s Drug Abuse Adv. Bd., 1974-76; gov.'s del. to Nev. Library Conf., 1981; alt. del. White House Conf. on Libraries, 1982; Nev. del. to Presdl. White House Conf. on Children and Youth, 1970; life mem. Gov.'s Youth Traffic Safety Assn.; exec. sec., interim mgr. Elko C. of C., 1961-68. Pres. Elko

Dem. Women, 1970; bd. dirs. Elko Dem. Club, 1970-82; chmn. Rural Nev. Mental Health Adv. Bd., 1973-78; bd. Nev. PTA, 1962-72, pres., 1972-74; v.p. Am. Lung Assn. of Nev., 1972-82, pres.-elect, 1982-84, pres., 1984—; coordinator Youth Traffic Safety Confs., 1968-78; bd. mgrs. Nat. Com. Health and Welfare, PTA, 1972-74; adv. bd. Nat. Council Juvenile Ct. Judges, 1972-74; mem. 8 state project Designing Edn. for the Future, 1965-68; Nev. rep. to nat. ALA conv., 1981; vol. Elko Hosp. Aux.; co-chmn. 1st Rural Nev. Women's Conf., 1980; mem. Nev. Adv. Council for Vocat. Tech. Edn., 1982—; mem., Nev. commr./Nat. Council, Future of Women In The Workplace, 1983-1985; Nev. rep. to Nat. Commn. for Eleanor Roosevelt Centennial, 1984-85; del. to Dem. Nat. Conv., 1984; sec./treas. Elko County Dem. Central Com., 1984-86; mem. Nev. State Dem. Central Com. Recipient honors Am. Lung Assn. Nev., C. of C., Nev. Dept. Edn., Gov.'s Office State of Nev.; Citizen of Year Elko County Mental Health Assn., 1985. Mem. Elko Bus. and Profl. Women (state legis. chmn., scholarship award com.), Sigma Kappa.

SULLIVAN, CLAIRE FERGUSON, marketing educator, marketing consultant; b. Pittsburg, Tex., Sept. 28, 1937; d. Almon Lafayette and Mabel Clara (Williams) Potter; m. Richard Wayne Ferguson, Jan. 31, 1959 (div. Jan. 1980); 1 child, Mark Jeffrey Ferguson; m. David Edward Sullivan, Nov. 2, 1984. B.B.A., U. Tex., 1958, M.B.A., 1961; Ph.D., North Tex. State U., 1973. Instr. So. Meth. U., Dallas, 1965-70; asst. prof. U. Utah, Salt Lake City, 1972-74; assoc. prof. U. Ark., Little Rock, 1974-77, U. Tex.-Arlington, 1977-80, Ill. State U., Normal, 1980-84; prof., chmn. mktg. Bentley Coll., Waltham, Mass., 1984—; cons. Gen. Telephone Co., Irving, Tex., 1983, McKnight Pub. Co., Bloomington, Ill., 1983, Dental Practitioner, Bloomington, 1982-83, Olympic Fed., Berwyn, Ill., 1982. Contbr. mktg. articles to profl. jours. Named Outstanding Prof., So. Meth. U., 1969-70; Direct Mktg. Inst. fellow, 1981, Ill. State U. research grantee, 1981-83. Mem. Am. Mktg. Assn. (faculty fellow 1984-85), So. Mktg. Assn., Southwestern Mktg. Assn., Sales and Mktg. Execs. Boston, Beta Gamma Sigma. Republican. Presbyterian. Home: 9 Potter Rd Lexington MA 02173 Office: Mktg Dept Bentley Coll Waltham MA 02554

SULLIVAN, CONSTANCE ROSE, hair designer, author, consultant, lecturer; b. Boston, Jan. 23, 1940; d. Nicholas Pecora and Rosalie (Santaniello) Devoines; m. Robert Patrick Sullivan, Aug. 20, 1967; 1 child, Robert Christopher. Degree in Cosmetology Mansfield Beauty Acad. Lic. for advanced tng. ctr., Mass. Pres. Constance Cora, Inc., Newton, Mass., 1966—; v.p. Geneses-Faneuil Hall, Boston, 1981—, pres., 1983—, artistic dir., 1985—; nat. spokesperson Clairol, Inc., N.Y.C., 1985—, presdl. council, 1983—; founder Geneses Internat. Advanced Tng. Ctr.; lectr. Hair Club, Paris, 1985, Americoif, Detroit, 1984, The Phila. Group, 1984; spl. guest of honor Paris Mondial, 1985. Author: The Art of Designing Hair, 1984; producer video: The Gene-Metre Method, 1985. Bd. dirs. Speech and Hearing Found., Boston, 1979, Ileitus and Colitis Found., Boston, 1983. Named Hairstylist of Yr., Service Publs., 1983; Bostons Best, Boston Mag., 1983; Who's Who: USA Harper's Bazaar, 1984; Best of Boston, 1985. Mem. Intercoiffure Am./Can., Nat. Hairdressers/Cosmetologists Assn. Democrat. Roman Catholic. Office: Geneses 51 Boylston St Chestnut Hill MA 02167

SULLIVAN, DONNA SIMONNE, education research and development company director; b. Potomac, Md., June 25, 1943; d. James Brendan and Anita Laura (Cousineau) Sullivan; m. Michael D. Bass, Dec. 14, 1975; children—Lindsay Rebecca Bass, James William, Israel Bass. B.A. in Chemistry, Notre Dame Coll., Manchester, N.H., 1965; M.S. in Tech. of Mgmt., Am. U., Washington, 1973; Cert. AFL-CIO Labor Studies, Washington, 1971. Chemistry tchr. Manchester pub. sch., N.H., 1965-67, cons., 1969; assoc. ednl. specialist Westinghouse Learn, Syracuse, N.Y., Manchester, 1968-70; curriculum specialist, educator Washington Tech. U. D.C., Washington, 1970-71, dir., research and devel. div., 1971-73, program coordinator, 1973-74; dir. edn. research and devel. Progressive Learning Systems, Potomac, Md., 1974—; cons. Mid-Atlantic AMIDS Washington, 1970-72. Organizer Dem. Party, Manchester, 1965. Mem. IEEE (Computer Soc., Communications Soc.). Home: 6 Deborah Ct Potomac MD 20854 Office: Progressive Learning Systems 11325 Seven Locks Rd Potomac MD 20854

SULLIVAN, ELEANOR ELIZABETH, management consultant; b. Detroit, Aug. 9, 1958; d. Daniel William and Mary (Morse) S. B.B.A. in Mktg., Western Mich. U., 1980. Field sales mgr. Lone Star Life Ins., Dallas, 1980-81; mgmt. cons. Ernst & Whinney, Dallas, 1981—. Mem. Am. Mktg. Assn., Women in Bus., Nat. Assn. Female Execs., Am. Soc. Tng. and Devel. Roman Catholic. Home: 7407 Fair Oaks Apt 247 Dallas TX 75231

SULLIVAN, ELEANOR REGIS, editor; b. Cambridge, Mass., Oct. 19, 1928; d. Timothy Joseph and Katherine Irene (Dowd) S. B.S. in Edn., Salem State Coll., 1950. Tchr., Clinton Grammar Sch., Conn., 1950-53, Russell Sch., Cambridge, Mass., 1953-57, George Washington Sch., White Plains, N.Y., 1957-60; editorial asst. Pocket Books, Inc., N.Y.C., 1960-62; editor Charles Scribner's Sons, N.Y.C., 1962-69, Ellery Queen's Mystery Mag., N.Y.C., 1970—; instr. writers' workshops, 1972—. Author: Whodunit: A Biblio-Bio-Anecdotal Memoir of Frederic Dannay (Ellery Queen), 1984. Contbr. articles and stories to mags., newspapers and books. Vol., ARC, St. Alban's Naval Hosp., Queens, N.Y.C., 1968-70, Euphrasian Residence, Sisters of the Good Shepherd, N.Y.C., 1970-71. Mem. Mystery Writers of Am. (sec. 1974-76, bd. dirs. 1974-77, 82—), Dramatists Guild, Am. Film Inst. Democrat. Roman Catholic. Office: Davis Pub Inc 380 Lexington Ave New York NY 10017

SULLIVAN, KAREN HARRIS, retail chain executive; b. St. Louis, Dec. 12, 1954; d. William Clinton and Elsie (Jackson) Harris; B.F.A., S.W. Mo. State U., 1976; 1 dau., Lauren Marie. Dept. mgr. Famous-Barr, St. Louis, 1976-77, dept. mgr. budget store, 1977, asst. buyer designer sportswear and accessories, 1977-78, dept. mgr. designer sportswear, dresses, furs, coats, FB Ltd., Frontenac, Mo., 1978-79, dept. mgr., 1979-80, sr. asst. buyer, 1980-81; dist. mgr. Libson's, Inc., St. Louis, 1981, dir. store supervision, 1981-82, asso. gen. mdse. mgr., 1982, gen. mdse. mgr., 1982-83; dist. mgr. J. Riggins Corp., 1983; buyer, mdse. mgr. S. Mizrahi Sons, 1983—. Mem. Alpha Delta Pi. Roman Catholic. Office: 1540 University Blvd W Jacksonville FL 32217

SULLIVAN, KATHERINE MCGURK, law association executive; b. Holyoke, Mass., Oct. 2, 1949; d. John Joseph and Mary Helen (Knightly) McGurk; m. Thomas Christopher Sullivan, Aug. 18, 1973. B.A., Regis Coll., Weston, Mass., 1971. Aide to Rep. Silvio O. Conte, U.S. Congress, Washington, 1973-74; adminstrv. asst. ABA, Washington, 1974-76, asst. staff dir., 1976-79, dir. pub. service div., 1979-81, dir. pub. service group, 1981-83, asst. exec. dir., 1983—; spl. asst. to pres. U.S. Synthetic Fuels Corp., Washington, 1980-81. Contbr. in field. Mem. Women's Legal Def. Fund, U.S. Sup. Ct. Hist. Soc., Assn. Female Execs. Democrat. Roman Catholic. Office: ABA 1800 M St NW Washington DC 20036*

SULLIVAN, KATHRYN, lecturer, writer, educator; b. Buffalo, Mar. 21, 1918; d. Florence and Ann (Gallagher) S.; m. Edward Otto Solomon, June 27, 1940 (dec. Oct. 1950); m. William O. Hagstotz, May 7, 1951 (div. Oct. 1976); 1 child, Linda Ann Solomon Sullivan. A.A., Villa Maria Coll., Buffalo, 1971; B.S. in Edn., Medille Coll., Buffalo, 1973; M.S. in Edn., State Tchr. Coll., Buffalo, 1976; Ph.D. Candidate SUNY-Buffalo, 1985—. Lic. tchr. Travel bur. mgr. Am. Express, Buffalo, 1947-51; tchr. Queen of Heaven Sch., Buffalo, 1952-76; with Erie County Sheriff's Dept., Buffalo, 1977-79; substitute tchr. City of Buffalo, 1982—; cons., 1976—. Republican committeewoman, West Seneca, N.Y., 1977-81; 2d v.p. West Seneca Rep. Club, 1978; active juvenile ct. Recipient numerous awards; Rosary Hill Coll. grantee, 1965; Edith Macy Tng. Acad. scholar, 1966. Mem. Am. Ednl. Research Assn., State Tchrs. Coll. Alumni Assn., SUNY-Buffalo Alumni Assn., Bus. and Profl. Women. Lodge: Order Eastern Star (Historian 1983-84). Avocations: organ; travel; painting; doll houses; reading. Home: 23 Southwood Dr West Seneca NY 14224

SULLIVAN, MARGARET DONNA, dental hygienist; b. Fairfax, Okla., Mar. 4, 1957; d. Robert Joseph and Mary (Hutsko) S. A.A., Dental Sch., U. Tex. Houston, 1977. Cert. dental hygienist, Tex. Dental hygienist M.D. Anderson Cancer Hosp. and Tumor Inst., Houston, 1977—; clin. inst. Dental br. U. Tex., Houston, 1977—; lectr. in field. Recipient Clinic award Dallas County Dental Soc., 1978; Table Clinic award Houston Dist. Dental Soc., 1978; Cert. of Merit, Am. Prosthodontic Soc., 1979; Outstanding Employee award M.D. Anderson Hosp. and Tumor Inst., 1980; Jack Winston award for grad. hygienist, 1984. Mem. Jr. Dental Hygienist Assn., Am. Dental Hygienist Assn. Roman Catholic. Office: MD Anderson Hosp & Tumor Inst 6723 Bertner Ave Houston TX 77030

SULLIVAN, MARILYN MCWILLIAMS, state justice; b. Portsmouth, N.H., Sept. 19, 1923; d. Joseph and Mary (McWilliams) S. A.B. magna cum laude, Radcliffe Coll., 1945; J.D., Columbia U., 1949. Bar: Mass. 1949. Law clk. Mass. Supreme Ct., 1949-51; assoc. Ropes & Gray, Boston, 1951-73; justice land ct. dept. Mass. Trial Ct., Boston, 1973—, chief justice, 1985—. Served to lt. (j.g.) USNR, 1944-46. Mem. Nat. Assn. Women Judges (dir. dist. 1, 1980-82), Abstract Club, Mass. Conveyancers Assn., Mass. Assn. Women Lawyers, Mass. Bar Assn., Boston Bar Assn., Phi Beta Kappa (past pres.). Roman Catholic. Clubs: Radcliffe, Harvard (gov. 1983—) (Boston); Emma Forbes Cary Guild (Cambridge, Mass.), Guild of Our Lady of Ranson. Office: Land Ct Room 408 Old Courthouse Boston MA 02108

SULLIVAN, MARILYN OCASEK, college administrator; b. Evergreen Park, Ill., Nov. 14, 1936; d. Joseph William and Myrtle (Hill) Ocasek; m. Daniel H. Sullivan (dec.); children—Paul, Katherine, Hugh, Margaret. B.S., U. Wis.-LaCrosse, 1958; M.A., Mich. State U., 1961. Tchr. high sch., Rhinelander, Wis., 1958-60; counselor Lake Park High Sch., Roselle, Ill., 1961-64, Kaiserslautern High Sch., Germany, 1964-65; personnel asst. U. Wis.-River Falls, 1965-66; counselor jr. high sch., East Irondequoit, N.Y., 1966-67; dir. placement Colo. Tech. Coll., Colorado Springs, 1980-82, pres., 1982—. Mem. Exec. Women Internat., AAUW, Am. Soc. Engring. Educators, Tau Alpha Pi. Office: Colo Tech Coll Colorado Springs CO 80907

SULLIVAN, PAMELA GRACE, engineer, research specialist; b. Rio de Janeiro, Brazil, Apr. 11, 1945 (parents Am. citizens); d. Lloyd Charles and Helen Postill Hawken; A.S., Long Beach (Calif.) City Coll., 1968; B.S.M.E., Calif. State U., Long Beach, 1971, M.S.M.E., 1978; m. Charles J. Sullivan, Feb. 22, 1962 (div.); 1 dau., Catherine Anne. Engr., Nevada Engring. & Tech. Corp., Long Beach, 1971-79, also sec.; staff engr. Lockheed Missles & Space Co., Sunnyvale, Calif., 1979—. Mem. ASTM, ASME, AIME, Am. Ceramic Soc., Soc. Women Engrs. Contbr. articles to profl. publs. Home: 544 W Latimer Campbell CA 95008 Office: Lockheed Missles & Space Co 30-20 B/559 1 PO Box 3504 Sunnyvale CA 94086

SULLIVAN, PATRICIA, recreation therapist; b. N.Y.C., Feb. 10, 1948; d. John Joseph and Emilie (O'Mara) Sullivan. B.A., SUNY, 1970; M.A., NYU, 1980. Recreation therapist Letchworth Devel. Services, Thiells, N.Y., 1972-76, sr. recreation therapist, 1976-80, head, 1980-85, chief, 1985—; stage mgr. wardrobe supr. Penquin Repertory Co., Stony Point, 1981—; counselor Vol. Counseling Service, New York City, N.Y., 1984—. Fellow N.Y. State Recreation and Park Soc. (bd. dirs. 1982-84, sec., treas. 1984-86; Disting. Service award 1984, 1986); mem. Nat. Recreation and Park Assn., Nat. Therapeutic Recreation Soc., Nat. Assn. Female Execs. Office: Letchworth Devel Services Thiells NY 10984

SULLIVAN, PATRICIA LANCE, writer, editor; b. Austin, Tex., Feb. 15, 1950; d. Frederick Lee and Betty Ellen (Leonard) Stead; m. John Edward Sullivan, Jan. 1, 1978. Student U. N.Mex., 1967-70; B.A. in English Lit., Calif. State U.-Northridge, 1978. Clk., typist Adamson Co., Santa Monica, Calif., 1970-71; graphic artist Hughes Research Labs., Malibu, Calif., 1971-79; sales rep. In This Issue Mag., Costa Mesa, Calif., 1979-80; pub. relations rep. C.E.C., Newport Beach, Calif., 1980-81; freelance writer, Atlanta, 1981—; writer, editor The Preferred Press, Atlanta, 1984-86, The Newsletter, Atlanta, Occupational Medicine, 1985—. Author: Just Perfect Meeting Planning, 1986. Editor: Atlanta Professional Women's Directory, 1982-83. Contbr. articles to profl. jours. Pub. relations staff Nat. MS Soc., Atlanta, 1982. Mem. AAUW, Nat. League Am. Pen Women, Soc. Profl. Journalists, Village Writers Group, Kappa Kappa Gamma. Republican. Presbyterian. Avocations: reading, computing, travel, writing. Home and office: 3746 Wieuca Rd NE Atlanta GA 30342

SULLIVAN, PATRICIA MAUREEN, psychologist; b. Des Moines, June 24, 1946; d. Paul John and Maureen (Tighe) S.; B.A., Marycrest Coll., 1968; Ed.S., U. Iowa, 1977, Ph.D., 1978. Secondary sch. tchr., Mo., 1969-70; coordinator dormitory counselors Pa. Sch. Deaf, Phila., 1970-74; tchr. autistic and emotionally disturbed children, supr. spl. edn. student tchrs., pediatric psychology grad. asst. U. Iowa Grad. Sch. Employment, 1974-78, coordinator psychoednl. services for hearing-impaired Boys Town Inst. Communication Disorders in Children, Omaha, 1978—; sec. Nebr. Commn. Hearing Impaired, 1979-82, chmn., 1982-84; adv. council edn. and welfare of deaf Nebr. Bd. Edn., 1981. Mem. Am. Psychol. Assn., Nat. Assn. Sch. Psychologists, Internat. Neuropsychol. Assn., Nebr. Psychol. Assn., NOW, Delta Epsilon Sigma. Democrat. Roman Catholic. Author articles, films in field. Office: Boys Town 555 N 30th St Omaha NE 68131

SULLIVAN, RITA PAYNE, oil and marketing company executive; b. Memphis, Feb. 3, 1942; d. Fred G. and Mignon (Shinault) P.; m. Richard Russell Sullivan, Oct. 18, 1974; stepchildren—Stacy, Russell. B.A., U. Tulsa, 1964. Placement asst. coordinator Skelly Oil Co., Tulsa, 1964-73, assoc. personnel rep., 1973-74, personnel rep., 1974-75; employment and coll. relations rep. Getty Refining & Mktg. Co., Tulsa, 1975-77, wage and salary adminstr., 1977-78, compensation, employment mgr., 1978—. Mem. bus. adv. bd. Okla. State Tech. Sch., Okmulgee, 1978—; mem. adv. council Tulsa Pub. Schs., 1978-81. Mem. Am. Compensation Assn., Coll. Placement Council, Southwest Placement Assn. (officer 1973—), Am. Soc. Personnel Adminstrn., U. Tulsa Alumni Assn. (bd. dirs. 1972), Kappa Kappa Gamma. Republican. Episcopalian. Club: U. Tulsa Hurricane (bd. dirs. 1984). Office: Getty Refining and Mktg Co PO Box 1650 Tulsa OK 74102

SULLIVAN, SALLY ANN, highway construction company executive; b. Elma, Iowa, Oct. 19, 1942; d. Dale Joseph and Inez B. (Evans) Clark; m. James Thomas Sullivan, Aug. 18, 1962 (div. Mar. 1981); children—John Thomas, Kelly Ann. Student Gates Bus. Sch., 1960-61, U. No. Iowa, 1982-84. Lic. contractor for asbestos removal. Treas. Dale Clark Contracting Co., Waterloo, Iowa, 1976-83; pres. Rose Corp. of Iowa, Cedar Falls, 1983—. Mem. Associated Gen. Contractors, Minority Bus. Assn. (sec. 1984). Roman Catholic. Avocation: reading. Home: 2202 Yorkshire Dr Cedar Falls IA 50613 Office: Rose Corp of Iowa PO Box 632 Cedar Falls IA 50613

SULLIVAN, SANDRA JONES, designer, design company executive; b. Fredericksburg, Va., Jan. 26, 1948; d. Carle Hamilton and Lily Mae (Rose) Jones; m. Lehmer Kent Sullivan, July 11, 1970; children—Lehmer Cameron, Catherine Hollis. B.S. in Bus. Edn., Longwood, Coll., 1970. Tchr. James Monroe High Sch., Fredericksburg, 1970, Stafford High Sch., Va., 1971-72, 74-76; pres., designer Homespun Elegance Ltd., Fredericksburg, 1980—. Author, designer numerous needlework leaflets including Elegant Ducks, 1981, A Christmas Sampler, 1981, Wedding Folk Art, 1982, Candlewicking for Christmas, 1982, Tea Dyeing, 1982, Willow Tree Sampler, 1984, Antique Flowers, 1984, Cinnamon Stick Christmas, 1985, The Amish, 1985. Mem. jr. bd. Historic Fredericksburg, 1977—. Mem. Needlework Markets Inc., Nat. Needlework Assn., Am. Ind. Designers Assn., Embroiders Guild, Fredericksburg C. of C. Republican. Methodist. Avocations: antiques; gardening. Home: 104 Holly Circle Fredericksburg VA 22405 Office: Homespun Elegance Ltd 1006 Princess Anne St Fredericksburg VA 22401

SULLIVAN, SHEILA EILEEN, magazine editor; b. L.I., N.Y., July 23, 1953; d. Thomas James and Anne Clark S.; m. Anderson Jonas, May 30, 1981; 1 child, Anderson Sullivan Jones. B.A. in English, UCLA. Editorial coordinator Bon Appetit mag. Knapp Communications, Inc., Los Angeles, 1982—. Vol. worker Sta. KPFK, nat. public radio, Los Angeles. Mem. Women in Communications. Democrat. Roman Catholic. Home: 7803 Torreyson Dr Los Angeles CA 90046 Office: Knapp Communications Inc 5900 Wilshire Blvd Los Angeles CA 90036

SULLIVANT-KAHN, KATHERINE, social worker, family planning clinic administrator; b. Beaumont, Tex., Dec. 27, 1951; d. George Andrew and Ann (Petty) Sullivant; m. Michael Adrien Kahn, May 29, 1983. B.A., U. Tex., 1976. Social worker Brackenridge Hosp. unit U. Tex. Sch. Social Work, Austin, 1976; family planning counselor S.W. Women's Ctr., Houston, 1977-78, exec. dir., 1978—; mem. speakers bur. Planned Parenthood, 1971—; facilitator women's share group YWCA, Houston, 1977-81; dir. Tex. Abortion Rights Action League, 1978-83; del. Women's Lobby Alliance, Houston, 1980-83. Del. Tex. Democratic Conv., 1980; vol. Nat. Women's Conf., Houston, 1977; fund raising chmn. Choice PAC Night at Comedy Workshop, 1980; fund raiser ACLU, Houston, 1977-82. Recipient award for outstanding service YWCA, 1980. Mem. Nat. Abortion Fedn. (board nominee 1983), Nat. Abortion Rights Action League, Harris County Women's Polit. Caucus. Democrat. Jewish. Office: Southwest Women's Center 6565 DeMoss St Suite 117 Houston TX 77074

SULLO, ROSE ANN, sculptor, artist; b. N.Y.C., Mar. 27, 1919; d. Saverio and Rosina (Palumbo) Pesce; student Leonardi DaVinci Cultural Center, N.Y., 1934-37, Poppenhusen Inst., N.Y., 1936-37, Delphic Studios, N.Y., 1937, Cooper Union Inst., N.Y., 1937-39; m. Joseph A. Sullo, Oct. 12, 1947; children—Susan Ann, Donna Rose, Peter Adam. Free-lance profl. sculptor and artist; one woman shows include: Halifax Hist. Soc., Daytona Beach, Fla., 1978, Ormond Meml. Art Gallery, Ormond Beach, Fla., 1979; group shows: Brockton (Mass.) Art Center, 1972, United Fedn. Doll Clubs, Detroit, 1970, Los Angeles, 1971, Omaha, 1972, Louisville, 1973, Miami, 1974, San Francisco, 1976, San Diego, 1977, Hartford, Conn., 1973, 77, Seattle, 1972, Denver, 1978, N.Y.C., 1979, Akron, Ohio, 1979, Washington-Balt., 1980, St. Louis, 1981, Bedford, N.H., 1982, Kansas City, Kans., 1982, Patchogue, N.Y., 1982, Harrisburg, Pa., 1983, Ormond Beach, Fla., 1983, Flushing (N.Y.) Council Women's Clubs, 1977, 78, Nat. League Am. Pen Women, 1974, 75, 76, 77, 78, Daytona Automobile Conf. (Fla.), 1983, Daytona Community Coll., 1983, Daytona Mus. Arts and Scis., 1983; represented in permanent collections: Wee Lassie Doll Mus., Homstead, Fla., Mus. City N.Y., Strong Mus., Pittsford, N.Y., Morristown (N.J.) Mus. Arts and Scis.; presented work to Pres. Nixon, 1972. Del., art chmn. Flushing Council Women's Clubs, 1975—. Recipient many awards for art works and sculpture; Internat. Women's Year award, 1975; award of distinction for sculptural portraiture Deland Mus. (Fla.), 1983. Mem. Nat. Inst. Am. Doll Artist, Inc. (award of excellence 1970), Nat. League Am. Pen Women, (spl. award 1974), Sculpture, United Fedn. Doll Clubs, Dollology Club Washington, Doll Collector's Guild N.Y., Flushing Art League, Internat. Doll Clubs, Dutchess Art Assn. Home: RD 3 Box 72 Bria Hill Rd Route 52 Hopewell Junction NY 12533

SULTANA, NAJMA, psychiatrist; b. Nirmal, Andhra, India; July 22, 1948; came to U.S. 1973; d. Khaja Moinuddin and Mujib (Unnisa) Begum; m. Khaja Mohiuddin, July 8, 1971 (div. 1978); m. M. Rashid Chaudhry, Oct. 16, 1981. M.B.B.S. Gandhi Med. Coll., Hyderaba, India, 1973. Resident in psychiatry SUNY/Kings County Hosp. Ctr., Bklyn., 1976-78, fellow child psychiatry, 1978-80; asst. clin. physician S. Beach Psychiat. Ctr., S.I., N.Y., 1980-81; clin. instr. SUNY Downstate Med. Ctr., N.Y.C., 1981—; attending psychiatrist King's County Hosp., Bklyn., 1981—. Mem. Am. Psychiat. Assn. Democrat. Muslim.

SULZBY, ELIZABETH FAY, educator; b. Walker County, Ala., Feb. 25, 1942; d. Phillip Glen and Ophelia Sulzby; B.A., Birmingham-So. Coll., 1963; M.Ed., Coll. William and Mary, 1969; Ph.D., U. Va., 1977; m. Mitchell Frank Rouzie, July 8, 1980; 1 dau., Kiran Elizabeth. Tchr. public schs., 1966-75; instr. Jacksonville (Fla.) U., 1970-71, R.I. Coll., Providence, 1973-74, U. Va., Charlottesville, 1975-77; asst. prof. edn. Northwestern U., Evanston, Ill., 1977-83, assoc. prof., 1983-86; assoc. prof. edn. U. Mich., Ann Arbor, 1986—, also Ctr. for Learning and Schooling, 1986—; cons. in field. Mem. adv. bd. One-To-One Learning Center, Wilmette, Ill., 1980-82, Solomon Schecter Schs., 1986—. Woodrow Wilson fellow, 1963-64; Nat. Council of Tchrs. of English grantee, 1980-81; Nat. Inst. Edn. grantee, 1980-82; Spencer Found. grantee, 1981-82, 84—. Mem. Am. Ednl. Research Assn., Am. Psychol. Assn., Internat. Reading Assn., Nat. Council of Tchrs. of English, Nat. Reading Conf., Soc. Research in Child Devel. Author: Emergent Writing and Reading in 5-6 Year Olds: A Longitudinal Study, 1986; Emergent Literacy: Writing and Reading, 1986; contbr. articles to profl. publs. Home: 1555 Scio Church Rd Ann Arbor MI 48103 Office: U Mich Sch Edn Ann Arbor MI 48109

SUMMER, DONNA (LA DONNA ANDREA GAINES), singer, actress, songwriter; b. Boston, Dec. 31, 1948; d. Andrew Gaines; m. Helmut Sommer (div.); 1 child, Mimi; m. Bruce Sudano; children—Brooklyn, Amanda Grace. Profl. singer, 1967—; appeared in German prodn. of Hair, also in Vienna Folk Opera prodns. of Porgy and Bess; TV show Donna Summer Spl., 1980; rec. artist; platinum albums: Live and More, 1978, Bad Girls, 1979, On The Radio-Greatest Hits, vols. 1 and 2, 1979, She Works Hard for the Money, 1983; numerous gold albums, gold and platinum singles; forerunner of disco style. Named best rhythm and blues female vocalist Nat. Acad. Rec. Arts and Scis., 1978, best female rock vocalist, 1979, best inspirational record (He's a Rebel), 1984, (Forgive Me), 1985; favorite female pop vocalist Am. Music Awards, 1979, favorite soule music female vocalist, 1979; Ampex Golden Reel award for single On the Radio, 1980, for album On the Radio, 1979, for album Bad Girls, 1979; Soul Artist of Yr., Rolling Stone mag., 1979; Best of Las Vegas Jimmy award, 1980. Has sold over 20 million records. Office: care Susan Munao Mgmt 1224 N Vine St Los Angeles CA 90038

SUMMERS, LORETTA MAE, labor relations executive; b. Cin., Oct. 14, 1952; d. Stoughton and Lorena (Bass) Summers. B.S. in Office Adminstrn., Ind. State U., 1973. Customer service supr. Gen. Telephone Co., Richmond, Ind., 1974-75, affirmative action coordinator, Ft. Wayne, Ind., 1975-77; personnel supr. Allis-Chalmers, Matteson, Ill., 1977-81; employment/benefits mgr. Armour Dial Inc., Montgomery, Ill., 1981-84, labor relations mgr., 1984—. Mem. Pvt. Industry Council, Aurora, Ill., 1982-84; bd. dirs. Aurora Area Urban League, 1982-84. Mem. Valley Personnel Assn., Nat. Assn. Female Execs., Am. Soc. Personnel Adminstrn. Democrat. Baptist. Home: 1058 Amherst Ln University Park IL 60466 Office: Armour-Dial Inc 2000 Aucutt Rd Montgomery IL 60538

SUMMERS, LORRAINE DEY SCHAEFFER, librarian, association official; b. Phila., Dec. 14, 1946; d. Joseph William and Hilda Lorraine (Ritchey) Dey; m. F. William Summers, Jan. 28, 1984. B.A., Fla. State U., 1968, M.S., 1969. Extension dir. Santa Fe Regional Library, Gainesville, 1969-71; pub. library cons. State Library of Fla., Tallahassee, 1971-78, asst. state librarian, 1978-84; dir. adminstrv. services Nat. Assn. for Campus Activities, Columbia, S.C., 1984-85; asst. state librarian State Library of Fla., Tallahassee, 1985—; cons. in field. Del. Pres.'s Com. on Mental Retardation Regional Forum, Atlanta. 1975; del. Fla. Gov.'s Conf. on Library and Info. Services, 1978. Mem. ALA (orgn. com. 1979-83, council 1982-84, resolutions com. 1983-85), Assn. Specialized and Coop. Library Agys. (dir. 1976-82, chmn. planning and orgn. com. 1976-80, chmn. nominating com., 1980-81, chmn. by laws com. 1985—, exec. bd. state library agy sect. 1983-86), Southeastern Library Assn. (exec. bd. 1976-80), Fla. Library Assn. (sec. 1978-79, dir., 1976-80), Am. Soc. Pub. Adminstrn. Democrat. Methodist. Contbr. articles in field. Office: State Library Fla RA Gray Bldg Tallahassee FL 32301

SUMMERS, MARSHA JOY, university official; b. San Francisco, Dec. 24, 1953; d. James Benton and Berniece Glendora (Bernard) Summers. B.A., San Francisco State U., 1976, M.A., 1985. Receptionist Mary's Help Hosp., Daly City, Calif., 1972-77; ECE tchr. Jefferson Elem. Sch. Dist., Daly City, 1978; adminstrv. supr. San Francisco State U., 1979—; tchr. Recipient Achievement award Bank of Am., 1971; award Modern Music Masters, 1971. Mem. Assn. Supervision and Curriculum Devel., Basic Edn. Assn., Student Calif. Teachers Assn. (awards 1979, 80), Internat. Platform Assn., Phi Delta Kappa. Republican. Roman Catholic. Contbr. articles to profl. jours. Home: 438 Skyline Dr Daly City CA 94015

SUMMERS, PATTI PRATT, human ecology consultant; b. Uniontown, Pa., Jan. 14, 1938; d. M. Wayne and Helen J. (Burke) Pratt; R.N., Presbyn. Hosp.-U. Pitts. Sch. Nursing, 1958; B.A., Marietta (Ohio) Coll., 1976; postgrad. W.Va. U., 1976-78; M.A., U. N.C., 1986, postgrad., 1986—; m. James C. Summers, June 14, 1977; children—William W., Marian L., Douglas L. Med.-surg. clin. instr. Presbyn.-U. Pitts. Sch. Nursing, 1960-64; instr. staff devel., human resources dept. Camden-Clark Hosp., Parkersburg, W.Va., 1976-78; dir. public relations Greensboro (N.C.) Hosp., 1980; mktg. and human ecology cons. Farr Assocs. Behavioral Sci. Cons., Greensboro, 1982—; past bd. dirs. Mid-Ohio Valley chpt. ARC, Greensboro Drug Action Council, 1984. Mem. Pitts. Symphony Women's Aux., 1970-72, Parkersburg Art Center, 1974-77; mem. alumni council Marietta Coll., 1978-81, 1st v.p., 1979-80, mem. parents' council, 1985—. Recipient commendation Freedoms Found. Mem. Women's Profl. Forum (chmn. internal relations), Nat. Council Family Relations Republican. Presbyterian. Address: 3617 Gramercy Rd Greensboro NC 27410

SUMMERSELL, FRANCES SHARPLEY, club woman; b. Birmingham, Ala.; d. Arthur Croft and Thomas O. (Stone) Sharpley; student U. Montevallo, Peabody Coll., Nashville; m. Charles Grayson Summersell, Nov. 10, 1934. Partner, artist, writer Asso. Educators, 1959—. Mem. D.A.R., Magna Charta Dames, U. Women's Club (pres. 1957-58), U.D.C. (state historian 1956-58, pres. Robert Emmet Rodes chpt. Tuscaloosa 1953-55), Daus. Am. Colonists (organizing regent Tuscaloosa 1956-63), English Speaking Union, Marquis Biog. Library Soc. (adv. mem.). Vice-chmn. Ft. Morgan Hist. Commn., 1959-63. Mem. Tuscaloosa County Preservation Soc. (trustee 1965-78, service award 1975), W. Ala. Art Assn., Nat. Trust Historic Preservation, Birmingham-Jefferson Hist. Soc. Clubs: Country, University (Tuscaloosa). Co-author: Alabama History Filmstrips, 1961; Viewing Alabama History Filmstrips, 1961; Florida History Filmstrips, 1963; Texas History Filmstrips, 1965-66; Ohio History Filmstrips, 1967 (Merit award Am. Assn. State and Local History 1968); California History Filmstrips, 1968; Illinois History Filmstrips, 1970. Home: 1411 Caplewood Tuscaloosa AL 35401

SUMMY, ANNE TUNIS, artist; b. Balt.; d. Archer Carlton and Ethel Cleveland (Farlow) Tunis; student Pa. Acad. Fine Arts, 1933-36, Edison Community Coll., 1975-78; further studies at Inst. Allende (Mex.), Millersville (Pa.) Coll., Franklin and Marshall Coll; m. C. Frank Summy, Jr., Jan. 21, 1939. One-woman shows include: York Mus., 1968, William Penn Mus., Harrisburg, Pa., 1970, Goethaen Gallery Art, Lancaster, Pa., 1970, Millersville State Coll., 1980, Bradley Gallery, Naples, Fla., 1982; group shows include Edison Community Coll., Ft. Myers, Fla., 1977; represented in permanent collections: William Penn Meml. Mus., Court Art Trust, Washington, Bloomsburg (Pa.) Coll., Franklin and Marshall Coll., Millersville Coll., Armstrong Cork Co., Rehoboth (Del.) Art League, Landscape Painters Pa.; pres. Art Encounter, Inc.; juried shows include: Pa. Acad. Fine Art, 1969-70, Balt. Mus. Art, 1969-74, Butler Inst. Am. Art, 1968, Soc. Four Arts, Palm Beach, Fla., 1975-78, Sarasota Arvida Show, 1979-82, Jacksonville Art Mus., 1976, Met. Mus. and Art Center, Miami, Fla., 1977. Recipient Neuman medal Nat. Soc. Painters in Casein, 1968; Lorne medal, 1969; 1st award Cape Coral Nat., 1974; 1st award Naples Art Assn., 1979; 1st award Fla. Artists Group Area VII, 1977; awards Bloomsburg Coll., 1970, Harmon Gallery Major Fla. Artists Show, 1976, 80-86, Hamel award Fla. Artists Group Statewide Show, 1980. Mem. Fla. Artist Group, Inc. (pres. area VII), Club: Naples Yacht. Home: 2885 Gulf Shore Blvd N Apt 501 Naples FL 33940

SUMRALL, HELEN RUTH, supermarket chain executive; b. Ancon, Canal Zone, Panama, Aug. 5, 1929 (parents Am. citizens); d. Jose Maria and Maria Luisa (Grimaldo) Llopis; m. David Victor Sumrall, Aug. 30, 1947 (div. 1954); children—Hesper Lynn Sumrall Hall, Rosa Leigh Sumrall Brooks, Darlene Frances Sumrall Marshall. A.A., Fla. Jr. Coll., 1975; B.A., U. North Fla., 1978. Sec. Food Fair Stores, Inc., Jacksonville, Fla., 1960-73; asst. buyer Pantry Pride Stores, Inc., Jacksonville, 1973-81, dairy-deli buyer, 1981-84; dairy-frozen food buyer Super Valu Stores, Inc., Jacksonville, 1984—. Mem. Navy League U.S., Lupus Erythematosus Found., Inc. (Atlanta chpt.), Phi Theta Kappa. Democrat. Roman Catholic. Avocations: writing fiction; gourmet cooking; reading; collecting art and wine; tennis. Home: 7900 Baymeadows Circle E Apt 87 Jacksonville FL 32216 Office: Super Valu Retail Support Ctr 5233 Commonwealth Ave Jacksonville FL 32205

SUN, COSSETTE TSUNG-HUNG WU, library administrator; b. Taipei, Taiwan, July 14, 1937; came to U.S., 1960, naturalized, 1972; d. Lin Tuang Hsieh and Chiu Chin Wu; LL.B., Nat. Taiwan U., 1960; M.A., U. Houston, 1963; M.S., Simmons Coll., 1965; m. Stanley Siann-Shyang Sun, Nov. 23, 1961; children—Louise Caroline, Marina Sheree, Olivia Cossette. Asst. prof. law, assoc. librarian St. Louis U., 1965-73; reference librarian U. Calif., Berkeley, 1974-75; br. librarian Alameda County (Calif.) Law Library, Hayward, 1975-77, law library dir., Oakland, 1977—. W.H. Anderson scholar, 1966; Matthew Bender scholar, 1971. Mem. Am. Assn. Law Libraries (cert. law librarian, vice chmn. pub. relations com. 1983—), Bay Area Library Info. Network (exec. com. 1983—), ALA, Spl. Library Assn., Asian/Pacific Librarians Assn., Council Calif. County Law Librarians (pres. 1981—), No. Calif. Assn. Law Libraries (chmn. edn. com. 1980) Editor State Ct. County Law Libraries Newsletter, 1979; chmn. Law Library Services to Instl. Residents, 1979-80; contbr. article to legal review. Office: 1225 Fallon St Oakland CA 94612

SUNA, MICHELLE KAREN, artist, fashion designer; b. N.Y.C., Feb. 7, 1959; d. Harry and Bernice (Gross) S. Student Newhouse Sch. Communication and Art, Syracuse U., 1976-78; student Fashion Inst. Tech., N.Y.C. 1979-80. Asst. to prin. Richard Meier Architect, N.Y.C., 1978-79; owner, designer, Diversified Designs, N.Y.C., 1980—, Michelle Karon Ltd., N.Y.C., 1980—; creative cons. Silvercup Studios, Long Island City, N.Y., 1981—; events dir. Palladium, N.Y.C., 1985. Painter, group shows include: Ward-Nasse Gallery, Soho, N.Y., 1981-82, April Fools Show, Bklyn., 1983, Nassau County Village Exhibits, 1983, 84 represented in permanent pvt. collections. Jewish. Avocations: snow skiing, horseback riding, car racing. Home: Apt 10A 145 E 27th St New York NY 10016 Office: Silvercup Studios 42-25 21st St Long Island City NY 11101 also Palladium 126 E 14th St New York NY 10003

SUNDBERG, NORMA ELIZABETH JOHNSON (MRS. COLLINS Y. SUNDBERG), funeral dir.; b. Rockford, Ill.; d. Conrad Walfred and Olga (Pierson) Johnson; student Brown's Bus. Coll., 1928-30; m. Collins Y. Sundberg, June 20, 1942. Partner Sundberg Funeral Home, Rockford, 1952—. Sec.-treas. Col-Nor Corp., Rockford, 1961—. Mem. Winnebago County Women's Republican Club, 1948—, v.p., 1956, 57. Mem. Nat., Ill. funeral dirs. assns., Rockford Humane Soc. Aux. (v.p.). Lutheran. Clubs: Zonta (dir.), Rockford Woman's, Ostende, Forest Hills Country, Am. Legion Aux., Women of Moose, Daus. of Nile, Order Eastern Star, Order White Shrine of Jerusalem. Home: 5431 Einor Ave Rockford IL 61108 Office: 215 N 6th St Rockford IL 61107

SUNDEEN, MARCIA HENNINGER, lawyer; b. Cleve., Nov. 5, 1954; d. John George and Emily (Stochmal) Henninger; m. James Thomas Sundeen, Aug. 20, 1977. B.S. in Chemistry, Marquette U., 1976; J.D., Case Western Res. U., 1981. Bar: Ohio 1981, D.C. 1983, U.S. Dist. Ct. (no. dist.) Ohio 1981, U.S. Patent and Trademark Office, 1983. Synthetic chemist Standard Oil Co., Cleve., 1977-78; patent atty. Watts, Hoffman et al, Cleve., 1981-82; patent atty. Finnegan, Henderson et al, Washington, 1982—. Contbr. articles to profl. jours.; patentee in field. Mem. Am. Patent Law Assn., ABA, D.C. Bar Assn., Am. Chem. Soc., D.C. Women's Bar Assn., Sierra Club. Democrat. Roman Catholic. Home: 1921 Park Rd NW Washington DC 20010 Office: Finnegan Henderson Farabow et al 1775 K St NW Washington DC 20006

SUNDERLAND, BARBARA ANNE, international marketing company executive, fund raising executive; b. Providence, R.I., Mar. 7, 1948; d. Everett Swan and Marica Anne (Galgas) S. B.A., Brown U., 1977; postgrad. U. Houston, 1978; M.P.H., U. Tex., 1984. Cert. fund raising exec. Owner, Barbara Enterprises, Inc., Providence, 1962-78; exec. dir. Houston Area Parkinsonism Soc., 1979-82; pres. Sunderland Assocs., Internat. Mktg., Houston, 1982—; v.p. Van Dyke Travel Agy., Houston, 1983—; cons. dept. neurology U. Tex. Med. Sch., 1982. Bd. dirs. R.I. Better Bus. Bur., 1975-78. bd. dirs. Am. Epilepsy Found., Houston chpt., 1983—; mem. edn. com. Houston Area Health Care Coalition, 1983; mem. Patient Edn. and Exchange Group, Health Meeting Planners; bd. dirs. Parkinsonism Support Groups Am., Washington, 1981—; founder, pres. Stroke Found. of Tex., 1984. Recipient Jewish Vets. Brotherhood award, 1965; John Philip Sousa Music award, 1966; award J. Arthur Trudeau Center for Retarded, 1975; recognized as Outstanding Female Bus. Owner, Dept. Labor, 1976. Mem. Nat. Soc. Fund Raising Execs. (spl. event award Houston chpt. 1982, bd. dirs. S.W. chpt., 1980-83, sec. 1982), Internat. Assn. Bus. Communicators, Nat. Assn. Female Execs., Women's Profl. Assn. (bd. dirs. 1980—) Clubs: Brown U. (pres., newsletter editor) (Houston); Forum; Combined Sch. Alumni (bd. dirs. 1978—). Home and Office: PO Box 56754 Houston TX 77256

SUNDERMAN, MAY MURRAY, retired nurse; b. Niles, Ohio, Apr. 7, 1924; d. George and Euphemia (Sterling) Murray; R.N., Warren City Hosp. Sch. Nursing, 1945; B.S.P.A., St. Joseph's Coll., 1981; 1 son, Kurt Vaughn. Staff nurse Warren (Ohio) City Hosp., 1945, Fed. Machine & Welding, Warren, 1945-47; office nurse, Warren, 1947-57; pvt. duty nurse, Warren, 1957-62; head nurse Packard Electric div., GMC, Warren, 1962-75, staff nurse, biol. testing OSHA standards, 1975-79, head nurse, 1979-85. Cert. occupational health nurse. Mem. NOW, Sierra Club, ACLU, Handgun Control, Inc., Equal Rights Am., Nat. Abortion Rights Action League, Am. Assn. Occupational Health Nurse, Am. Pub. Health Assn., Nat. Assn. Female Execs. Home: 3073D Ivy Hill Circle Cortland OH 44410

SUNDICK, SHERRY SMALL, author, journalist, poet; b. Washington, July 17, 1946; d. Charles Haskell and Ruth (Behrend) Small; B.A., Am. U., 1970; m. Gary Norman Sundick, Aug. 3, 1969; children—Amy Beth, Suzanne Faye. Columnist, Today Newspapers, Rockville, Md., 1973-75; journalist The Jour. Newspapers, Chevy Chase, Md., 1975—, The Potomac Almanac, 1976-80. Recipient N.Am. Mentor Mag. Ann. Mentor Poetry award, 1973. Mem. Nat. League Am. Pen Women, Writers Center, World Poetry Soc. Jewish. Author: Celebration, 1977; (with Ruth Small) Potpourri, 1978; contbr. articles to various mags. and jours. including Md. Mag., No. Va. Mag. Design, Maine Life, others. Address: 11809 Hunting Ridge Ct Potomac MD 20854

SUNDQUIST, BARBARA LOUISE, personnel executive; b. Grand Forks, N.D., Feb. 10, 1934; d. Elmer Ferdinand and Carolyn Johanna (Schmidt) Anderson; student Northwestern U., 1952-53; B.A. cum laude, U. Minn., 1956; m. John Lewis Sundquist, Oct. 13, 1956. Civil service technician Minn. Civil Service Dept., St. Paul, 1956-58; personnel officer Minn. Dept. Hwys., St. Paul, 1959; personnel dir. Minn. State Prison, Stillwater, 1959-67; suggestion system adminstr. Minn. Dept. Adminstrn., St. Paul, 1970-71; dir. Minn. merit system Minn. Dept. Human Services, St. Paul, 1967-77, personnel dir., 1977-79; commr. Minn. Dept. Employee Relations, St. Paul, 1979-82; personnel dir. Minn. Dept. Human Services, St. Paul, 1983—. Recipient cert. of appreciation Internat. Personnel Mgmt. Assn., citation of honor Office of Gov., State of Minn. Mem. Internat. Personnel Mgmt. Assn., Am. Soc. Personnel Adminstrn., Twin City Personnel Assn., Nat. Pub. Employer Labor Relations Assn., St. Paul Personnel Dirs., Alpha Omicron Pi. Republican. Lutheran. Home: 2750 Dale #50 Roseville MN 55113 Office: 654 Cedar St Saint Paul MN 55155

SUNIER, KATHERINE JOHNSON, nurse; b. Chgo., Mar. 16, 1952; d. Frank Richard and Mary Elizabeth (Pierce) J.; m. Richard Joseph Sunier, Oct. 15, 1983; 1 child, Jessica Michelle. B.S. in Nursing, Iowa Wesleyan Coll., 1975; postgrad. Rush U. Staff nurse Rush-Presbyn.-St. Luke's Hosp., Chgo., 1975-78, head nurse cardiovascular thoracic surgeries, 1979-82; staff nurse operating room Lake Forest Hosp., Ill., 1982—. Mem. Assn. Operating Room Nurses, Am. Endurance Ride Conf., Riding for the Handicapped Orgn., Upper Midwest Endurance and Competitive Riding Assn. Avocations: horseback riding; running; aerobics; handcrafts; computers. Home: 6618 88th Ave Kenosha WI 53140

SUNLIGHT, CAROLE, psychologist; b. DuBois, Pa., Aug. 19; d. Andy and Mary Ann Gaborick. Med. Technologist, Carnegie Inst., 1959; B.A., Cleve. State U., 1971; M.A., Pepperdine U., 1973; Ph.D. in Profl. Psychology, U.S. Internat. U., 1980. Med. technologist, Cleve., 1959-67; chief technologist med. dept. U.S. Steel Corp., Lorain, Ohio, 1967-69; office mgr. dept. philosophy and religious studies Cleve. State U., 1969-70; counselor Gardena (Calif.) Valley Counseling Service, 1971-72; testing technician Norco-Corona (Calif.) Sch. Dist., 1973; dir. treatment services Unfinished Symphony Ranch Inc., Agoura, Calif., 1973-77; staff Kaiser Permanente Mental Health Center, Los Angeles, 1977—; pvt. practice clin. psychology, Torrance, Calif., 1980—, also Cypress, Calif., 1986—; speaker in field. Bd. dirs. COMOSI Mental Health, Thousand Oaks, 1977-78. Registered med. technologist; lic. psychologist, Calif.; recipient pub. award Ohio soc. A.M.T., 1972. Mem. Am. Psychol. Assn., Calif. Psychol. Assn., Western Psychol. Assn., Los Angeles County Psychol. Assn. (editor newsletter 1982-84)), NOW, Am. Med. Technologists, Calif. Neuropsychol. Soc., Assn. for Women in Sci., Psi Chi. Office: 765 W College St Los Angeles CA 90012 also 3250 W Lomita Blvd Suite 305 Torrance CA 90505 also 5400 Orange Ave Suite 114 Cypress CA 90630

SUNSTEIN, CAROLYN RUTH NETTER, antique dealer; b. Phila., Jan. 5, 1922; d. Morton Angelo and Dorothy G. (Goldsmith) Netter; B.S. in Edn., Temple U., Phila., 1942; m. Charles Gerstley Sunstein, Aug. 22, 1941; children—Florence Gertsley Sunstein Begun, Lynn Carol, Charles Gerstley, Jr. Antique miniature collector, 1942—; dealer, show coordinator Phila. Miniature Show, 1972—; lectr., appraiser, 1977—; adv. bd. Warmans Antique Guild, 1981. Sec., Adoption Center Del. Valley, 1982—; bd. dirs. Samuel Paley Day Care Center, 1942—, Albert Einstein Med. Center, 1975—. Mem. Pa. Antique Assn., Nat. Assn. Miniature Enthusiasts. Republican. Jewish. Office: PO Box 26734 Elkins Park PA 19117

SUPALLA, SHERYL K., restaurant owner, educator; b. Fairfield, Iowa, July 15, 1944; d. Glen Edward and Erma Eileen (Smutz) Dimmitt; m. Gary J. Supalla, July 31, 1967; children—Laura, Julia. B.S. in Elem. Edn. cum laude, Mo. Western State Coll., 1973. Life teaching cert., Mo. Elem. tchr. St. Joseph Sch. Dist., Mo., 1973-78, tchr. Buchanan County Children's Home, 1985—; elem. tchr. Park Hill Sch. Dist., Mo., 1978-80; owner Miller's Grill, St. Joseph, 1980—; owner Atchison Inn Family Restaurant, Kans., 1984—. Fellow Mo. Restaurant Assn., Nat. Assn. Female Execs. Republican. Roman Catholic. Avocations: reading; travel; gardening. Office: Miller's Grill 3110 S 169 Hwy Saint Joseph MO 64503

SUPINSKI, CATHERINE JOSEPHINE CURRAN (MRS. EDMUND SUPINSKI), ret. librarian; b. N.Y.C., Aug. 27, 1915; d. Francis Joseph and Mary (Jordan) Curran; B.A., Hunter Coll., 1936; M.A., Columbia, 1937, B.S. in Library Sci., 1943; m. Edmund Supinski, June 2, 1951. Asst. librarian Nat. Indsl. Conf. Bd., N.Y.C., 1943-48; librarian N.Y. C. of C., N.Y.C., 1948-64, Dumont (N.J.) High Sch., 1964-80. Mem. Spl. Libraries Assn. (N.Y. pres. 1950-51, internat. 2d v.p. 1953-54), ALA, NEA, N.J., Bergen County, Dumont edn. assns., N.J., Bergen County (rec. sec. 1967-68) sch. librarians assns., N.J. Secondary Tchrs. Assn. Home: 30 Kinderkamack Rd Woodcliff Lake NJ 07675

SURAN, SANDRA ANNE, accountant; b. Appleton, Wis., Apr. 12, 1944; d. Robert Joseph and Joyce Cameron (Jones) Van Handel; m. Keith F. Wernli, Aug. 7, 1965 (div. 1972) children—Lisa, Cameron; m. Dale William Suran, May 31, 1974. C.P.A., Oreg. Staff acct. George E. Mack, C.P.A., Portland, Oreg., 1967-69, Dant, Suran & Co., Portland, 1970-74; owner, operator Sandra Suran, C.P.A., Portland, 1974-77; sr. ptnr. Suran & Co., Portland, Beaverton, Oreg., 1977-85, ptnr.-in-charge Peat, Marwick, Mitchell & Co., Beaverton, 1985—. Vice chmn. adv. council small bus. and agrl. Fed. Res. Bank San Francisco, 1985—, dir. Fed. Res. Bank San Francisco, Portland Br., 1985—; bd. dirs. Nat. Assn. State Bds. Accountancy, 1980—, pres., 1984-85; bd. dirs. Oreg. State Bd. Accountancy, 1977-82, chmn., 1980-81. Bd. dirs. Tualatin Valley Econ. Devel. Corp., Oreg., 1984—, chmn., 1984-85; bd. dirs. St. Vincent's Hosp., Portland, 1985—; mem. com. Regional Conv., Trade and Spectator Facilities, Portland, 1985—; mem. adv. bd. St. Mary's Home for Boys, Beaverton, 1983—; bd. dirs. Oreg. Fair Access to Ins. Requirements Plan, Salem, Portland, 1976-81, chmn. 1980-81; mem. The Assocs. of Good Samaritan Hosp., Portland, 1982-85, Washington County Budget Com., Oreg., 1978-81. Named Nat. Acct. Advocate of Yr., Small Bus. Adminstrn., 1983. Mem. Am. Inst. C.P.A.s (council 1982-85), Beaverton C. of C. (bd. dirs. 1977—, pres. 1979-80; Named Bus. Leader of Yr., 1981), U. Portland Nat. Alumni Council (chmn. bd. dirs. 1982-85), Inst. Bus. Profl. Women (adv. bd. dirs. 1986—), Beta Alpha Psi (nat. adv. bd.). Club: Multnomah Athletic. Office: Peat Marwick Mitchell & Co 4800 SW Griffith Dr 301 Beaverton OR 97005

SURBER, ELLEN ELIZABETH, veterinarian; b. Nashville, Oct. 20, 1954; d. Wilmer C. and Ann B. (Chambliss) S. B.S., Middle Tenn. State U., 1976; D.V.M., Auburn U., 1979. Staff veterinarian The Animal Clinic, Hendersonville, Tenn., 1979-80, Metro Emergency Clinic, Jonesboro, Ga., 1980; owner, veterinarian Atlanta Area Animal Clinic, College Park, Ga., 1980—. Active Meadows Bapt. Ch., Coll. Park, Ga., 1982—. Mem. AVMA, Nat. Wildlife Fedn. Contbr. article to profl. jour.

SURILLO, THEODOSIA VAZQUEZ, educator; b. Yabucoa, P.R., Mar. 19, 1950; d. Rogelio and Agustina (Solis) Surillo. B.A., John Carroll U., 1973; M.Ed., Baldwin Wallace Coll., 1979. Cert. in Spanish, reading, adminstrn. and supervision. Day care dir. Spanish Am. Com. Day Care Ctr., Cleve., 1975-77; tchr. corps intern Cleve. Pub. Schs., 1977-79, resource cons., tchr., 1980-82, tchr. Spanish, 1979-80, 82—. Active Hispanic Community Devel. Task Force, 1980—. Recipient Secondary Bilingual Program service award, 1982. Democrat. Methodist. Home: 2863 Avondale Cleveland Heights OH 44118 Office: Joseph McGallagher Jr High School 6601 Franklin Blvd Cleveland OH 44102

SUSANK, WENDY DAWN, music, biology educator; b. Las Vegas, Sept. 27, 1955; d. Robert Louis and Phyllis Elsie (Wells) Ellis; m. Michael Kevin Susank, July 19, 1975. Student, Mt. St. Mary's Coll., 1976; B.A. in Music Edn., credential in music edn., Calif. State U.-Northridge, 1979, also postgrad. in conducting. Student tchr. Hamilton High Sch., Los Angeles, 1976, Pasteur Jr. High Sch., Los Angeles, 1976; tchr. music, biology Baldwin Park Unified Sch. Dist., Baldwin Park, Calif., 1976-79, Notre Dame Acad., Los Angeles, 1979—; tchr. music and biology Daniel Murphy High Sch., Los Angeles, 1982—. Singer, St. Charles/St. Basils Ch. Choirs, North Hollywood, Calif., 1973-84, Ex Indigo Singers, Los Angeles, 1984-85. Mem. So. Calif. Vocal Assn. (area rep. 1983-84; dir. rep. 1984—; choral judge 1983—), Calif. Music Educators Assn. (pub. relations rep. 1984), Marina Del Rey Columbia 22 Sailing Assn. (sec. 1978), Am. Choral Dirs. Assn. Avocations: Sailing; guitar; sewing; gardening; painting; writing. Home: 344 Salem St Glendale CA 91203 Office: Notre Dame Acad High Sch 2851 Overland Ave Los Angeles CA 90064

SUSE, RUTH E., data processor; b. Jackson, Mich., Jan. 11, 1910; d. Howard A. and Bessie (Oliver) Matthews; student MacMurray Coll., Jacksonville, Ill., 1928-29, U. Mich., 1929-33; A.B., U. So. Calif., 1942; certificate Los Angeles Sch. Lab. Tech., 1946; postgrad. Am. U.; m. Edmund T. Suse, July 20, 1935 (div. Sept. 1940); 1 dau., Barbara J. Tchr., Am. Sch., Colombia, 1933-35, schs. in Guatemala, 1939-40; geodesist U.S. Govt., 1942-44, 54-57, 58-61; clin. pathologist Pasadena (Calif.) Hosps., 1945-54; med. technologist, tchr. Am. Hosp., La Paz, Bolivia, 1957-58; math. linguistics U.S. Govt. and Gen. Elect., 1961-62; educator langs. U.S. Army Okinawa, 1962-64; tech. asst., dept. dir. biomed. div. Documentation, Inc., Bethesda, Md., 1964-66; systems analyst U.S. Army, Washington, 1966; tech. dir. edn. resources br. Nat. Naval Med. Sch., Bethesda, Md., 1967-68; computer systems analyst Naval Air Systems Div. Integrated Logistics Support Center, 1968-70; computer specialist U.S. Army Computer Systems Support and Evaluation Command, Washington, 1970-72, computer systems br. U.S. Forest Service, 1972-73, now cons. data processing mgmt.; bus. adv. bd. for data processing Woodrow Wilson Rehab. Ctr., 1980—; exec. dir. Pacific Grove Art Center (Calif.), 1974-75; project coordinator Vols. Intervening for Equity of Jr. Leagues; tchr. data processing; substitute tchr. Va. Schs. Fairfax County. 1966. Bd. govs. U. Mich. Alumni Club, Alumni Devel. Council; active Girl Scouts U.S.A.; mem. adv. bd. Vol. Service Bur., Human Services Planning Council; mem. Linguistic U. Mich. Alumni Club, devel. council U. Mich.; commr. Va. Commonwealth Health Regulatory Bds., 1980-84. Recipient citation for meritorious service Dept. Army; Ruth Suse award established in her honor U. Mich., 1973. Mem. Linguistic Soc. Am., Am. Documentation Inst., Am. Fedn. Information Processing, Data Processing Mgmt. Assn. (chpt. award Outstanding Service in Edn. 1978, v.p. edn. Richmond chpt. 1982-83), Federally Employed Women, Soc. for Applied Learning Tech., U. Mich. Alumni Assn. (bd. govs.), C. of C. of Winter Park, Sigma Kappa, Phi Delta Gamma. Club: Univ. Mich. Alumni of Washington (bd. govs. 1967-73, pres. Richmond chpt. 1982). Home: care Capt BJ Suse USN NAVAD MINCOM NTC Great Lakes IL 60088

SUSMAN, KAREN LEE, lawyer; b. Austin, Tex., Oct. 26, 1942; d. Paul and Dorothy (Goudchaux) Hyman; m. Stephen D. Susman, Dec. 26, 1965; children—Stacy M., Harry P. B.A., U. Tex., 1964; J.D., U. Houston, 1981. Bar: Tex. 1981. Tchr. English pub. high schs., Houston and Washington, 1964-68; real estate broker Susman Realty, Houston, 1968-78; assoc. Saccomanno, Clegg, Martin & Kipple, Houston, 1981-83, Marian S.Rosen & Assocs., Houston, 1983-86; sole practice, Houston, 1986—; of counsel Webb, Zimmerman, Flaum & Svetlik, Houston, 1986—. Author outlines on law. Pres. Downtown YWCA, 1974, bd. dirs., 1969-74; chmn. PBS TV Art Auction, Houston, 1975; bd. dirs. Tex. Arts Alliance, Houston, 1975-78, Antidefamation League of B'nai B'rith, Houston, 1983—; mem. fin. council Tex. State Democratic Party, 1983—, chmn.' council Harris County Dem. Party, 1984-86, mem. candidate selection com., 1986. Editor Internat. Law Jour., 1980-81. Fellow Houston Bar Found.; mem. Houston Bar Assn., ABA, Tex. Bar Assn., A.A. White Soc., Vol. Lawyers and Accts. for the Arts (bd. dirs. 1985—), U. Houston Law Alumni (v.p., sec., bd. dirs. 1983, 84, 85, 86, chmn. ann. dinner 1986). Jewish. Club: Houstonian. Avocations: marathon running; snow skiing; modern art collecting. Home: 10 Shadder Way Houston TX 77019 Office: Post Oak Central Suite 2000 1990 S Post Oak Blvd Houston TX 77056

SUSMAN, VIRGINIA LEHMANN, psychiatrist, medical educator; b. Bronxville, N.Y., Nov. 30, 1949; d. Arthur Edwin and Jeanne Anne (Uebelacker) Lehmann; m. William Mark Susman, June 24, 1973; 1 child, Julianne Marie. B.A., Fordham U., 1971; M.D., U. Rochester, 1975. Diplomate Am. Bd. Psychiatry and Neurology. Resident Bronx (N.Y.) Mcpl. Hosp. Ctr., 1975-78, asst. dir. psychiat. outpatient dept., 1978-79, assoc. dir. psychiat. outpatient dept., 1979-80, unit chief inpatient dept., 1980-81; unit chief Westchester div. N.Y. Hosp., White Plains, 1981—, acting. dir. med. student edn., 1984—; asst. prof. psychiatry Albert Einstein Coll. Medicine, Bronx, 1979-81, Cornell U. Med. Coll., White Plains, 1981—; practice medicine specializing in psychiatry, White Plains, 1978—. Contbr. articles to profl. jours. Research grantee Cornell U. Med. Coll., 1982-85; Picker Found. grantee, 1986—. Mem. Am. Psychiat. Assn., Am. Med. Womens Assn., Physicians for Social Responsibility (acting chmn. Westchester County br. 1982). Office: NY Hosp Westchester Div 21 Bloomingdale Rd White Plains NY 10605

SUSSMAN, DEBORAH EVELYN, designe company executive; b. N.Y.C., May 26, 1931; d. Irving and Ruth (Golomb) S.; m. Paul Prejza, June 28, 1972. Student Bard Coll., 1948-50, Inst. Design, Chgo., 1950-53, Black Mountain Coll., 1950, Hochschule fur Gestaltung Ulm (Fulbright grantee), W.Ger., 1957-58. Art dir. Office of Charles and Ray Eames, Venice, Calif., 1953-57, 61-67; graphic designer Galeries Lafayette, Paris, 1959-60; prin. Deborah Sussman and Co., Santa Monica, Calif., 1968—; founder, pres. Sussman-Prejza and Co., Inc., Santa Monica, 1980—; speaker, lectr. UCLA Sch. Architecture, Archtl. League N.Y.C., Smithsonian Inst., Stanford Conf. on Design, Am. Inst. Graphic Arts Nat. Conf. at MIT, Design Mgmt. Inst. Conf., Mass.; spl. guest Internat. Design Conf., Aspen, Colo., Fulbright lectr., India, 1976. Mem. editorial adv. bd. Arts and Architecture Mag., 1981—. Recipient numerous awards AIA Nat. Inst. Honors, Am. Inst. Graphic Arts, Calif. Council AIA, Communications Arts Soc., Los Angeles County Bd. Suprs, Vesta award Women's Bldg. Los Angeles. Mem. Am. Inst. Graphic Arts (bd. dirs. 1982-85, founder Los Angeles chpt., chmn., 1983-84, numerous awards), Los Angeles Art Dirs. Club (bd. dirs., numerous awards), Alliance Graphique Internat., Architects, Designers and Planners Social Responsibility. Democrat. Jewish. Avocations: Photography. Office: Sussman-Prejza & Co Inc 1651 18th St Santa Monica CA 90404

SUSSMAN, VALERIE JOY, librarian; b. Bklyn., Oct. 4, 1946; d. Morris and Beatrice (Rifkin) S. B.A., Queens Coll., 1967, M.L.S., 1970. Tchr. of library Peter Rouget Intermediate Sch. 88, Bklyn., 1970-82, Bronx High Sch. Sci. (N.Y.), 1982—; conv. presenter L.I. Library Assn., 1984. Co-author sci. curriculum guide, 1982; author math. and sci. bibliography, 1981. Bd. dirs. Jeffrey P. Cohen Found., Queens, N.Y. 1973-82; active Adlai E. Stevenson Regular Democratic Club, Queens, 1969-82; mem. adv. com. N.Y. State Senator Gary Ackerman, N.Y. State Assemblyman David Cohen, 1980-82. U.S. Dept. Edn. grantee, 1979. Mem. N.Y.C. Sch. Librarians Assn. (conv. presentor 1982, rec. sec. 1978-80, pres. 1982-84 past pres. 1984-86), ALA, N.Y. Library Assn. (conv. presentor 1982, vitality com. 1984—), Queens Coll. Library Sci. Alumni Assn. (treas. 1979—), N.Y. Sci. Fiction Soc. (exec. bd. 1984—, chmn. 1986 conv.), Queens Coll. Choral Soc., Masterwork Chorus, Harmony Singers. Jewish. Home: 39 Madison St Pequannock NJ 07440 Office: Bronx High Sch Sci Library 75 W 205th St Bronx NY 10468

SUSTENDAL, DIANE MARIE, fashion consultant; b. New Orleans, Aug. 30, 1944; d. George and Mary (Anderson) S.; student La. State U., 1963-64; certificate John McCrady Sch. Fine Arts, 1966; Asst. art critic Times-Picayune, New Orleans, 1966-68; asst. mng. editor spl. studies div. Frederick A. Praeger, N.Y.C., 1969; fashion and beauty editor Times-Picayune, New Orleans, 1970-82; assoc. editor M & Men's Wear Mags., Fairchild Publs., N.Y.C., 1982-83; cons. Men's Fashions of the Times, N.Y. Times, N.Y.C., 1983—; freelance writer, editor, stylist. Bd. dirs. New Orleans Ballet, 1971-73. Recipient award La. Press Anns., 1972; Lulu award Men's Fashion Assn. Am., 1985. Mem. Fashion Group (dir. New Orleans chpt. 1973-74), New Orleans Symphony (women's com.), New Orleans Mus. Art, La. Council Music and Performing Arts, Art Assn. New Orleans. Republican.

SUTCLIFFE, MARILYN CASE, research technician; b. New Haven, Apr. 20, 1936; d. Warren Evans and Esther Mary (Snow) Case; B.A. summa cum laude, U. Bridgeport, 1957; postgrad. Sorbonne, Paris, 1957-58, Duke U., 1958-59; m. William Manchester Sutcliffe, Dec. 27, 1958; children—Stacy Ellen, James Sheldon. Substitute tchr. Broward County, Fla., 1966-67; tchr. chemistry Nova Sr. High Sch., Ft. Lauderdale, Fla., 1967-68; research technician dept. infectious diseases VA Med. Center, Nashville, 1968—. Fulbright scholar, 1957-58; James B. Duke fellow, 1958. Mem. Am. Soc. Microbiology. Republican. Contbr. articles to profl. jours. Home: 6824 Highland Park Dr Nashville TN 37205 Office: 1310 24th Ave S Nashville TN 37203

SUTER, PATSY JEAN, nurse, pediatric educational coordinator; b. Perrysburg, Ohio, Nov. 18, 1941; d. William Arnett and Elsie Pearl (Cooper) McGhee; m. Jan Waggoner Suter, Feb. 14, 1960 (div. Feb. 1976); children—Ammon Waggoner, Anna Arminta, Cooper William. Assoc. Health Scis./Nursing, U. Toledo, 1974. Cert. child and adolescent nurse. Float nurse Toledo Hosp., Ohio, 1974, team leader psychiatry, 1974-77, team leader pediatrics, 1977-81, staff nurse pediatric intensive care, 1981-82, asst. clin. mgr. pediatrics, 1982-85; pediatric ednl. coordinator Riverside Hosp., Toledo, 1985—. Field worker Am. Friends Service Com., Toledo, 1972. Mem. Assn. for Care of Children's Health, Toledo Area Pediatric Mgrs. Orgn. Democrat. Mem. Soc. of Friends. Club: Toastmasters (Oregon, Ohio). Avocations: writing; sewing; swimming; education volunteer at Toledo Zoo. Home: 25 Van Buren Ave Toledo OH 43605 Office: Riverside Hosp 1600 N Superior St Toledo OH 43604

SUTHERLAND, JESSICA LOUISE, financial executive; b. Ketchikan, Alaska, May 21, 1946; d. William Edward and Evelyn E. (Dick) Cogo; student Edmonds Community Coll., 1979-80; children—Angelica, Jennifer. Model, Bon Marche, Seattle, 1964-65; with Boeing Comml. Airplane Div., Seattle, Everett, Wash., 1965-69; with J.P. Wilder Co., Inc., Portland, Oreg., 1972-74; accounts payable clk. Sky Chief div. Am. Airlines, Portland, 1974-76; N.W. regional mgr. Sealaska Corp., Seattle, 1976-86; ptnr. G.R.&J. Enterprises, Travel Chair Co.; treas. Rumor Productions. Mem. Seattle Mayor Royer's campaign fin. com., 1981—; notary public, 1976—; past mem. adv. bd. Seattle Center. Mem. Nat. Assn. Female Execs., Alaska Native Sisterhood, N.W. Mining Assn., Seattle C. of C., China Relations Council Washington. Democrat. Club: Alaska Airlines Bd. Room. Home: 14727 60 Ave W Edmonds WA 98020

SUTHERLAND, MARY LOUISE WADDELL, communication consultant, counselor; b. St. Clairsville, Ohio, Feb. 6, 1930; d. Paul V. and Grace (Robinson) Waddell; B.S., Ohio State U., 1952; M.A., Mich. State U., 1975; m. Dale E. Sutherland, Dec. 28, 1951 (dec.); children—Timothy, Paul, Patricia, Robert, Matthew, Michael. Health edn. dir. YWCA, Lansing, Mich., 1952-55, adult activities dir. N.W. br., Detroit, 1956; tchr. pre-sch., elem., secondary, adult edn. Ednl. Instns., Mich., 1957-73, free-lance writer, 1968-73; communications cons., Traverse City, Mich., 1976—; co-owner, dir. Retreat for Growth, Glen Arbor, Mich., 1981—; profl. public speaker; instr. Northwestern Mich. Coll., Traverse City. Author: Claim Your Self; The Mommy and Daddy's Book of Finger Plays, Games and Rhymes. Campaign mgr. Leelanau County Probate Judge, 1974. Mem. Nat. Speakers Assn., Mich. Woman's Studies Assn., NOW (v.p. Traverse City chpt. 1979-80). Club: Glen Arbor Woman's. Home: 5685 Manitou View Blvd Glen Arbor MI 49636 Office: 230 Brooks St Traverse City MI 49684

SUTHERLAND, ZENA BAILEY, library school educator, columnist; b. Winthrop, Mass., Sept. 17, 1915; d. Jack Karras and Lena (Cohen) Baum; m. Roland Bailey, Dec. 19, 1937 (div. 1962); children—Stephen, Thomas, Katherine Bailey Linehan; m. 2d, Alec Sutherland, July 30, 1964. B.A., U. Chgo., 1937, M.A., 1966. Editor, Rev. Bull., U. Chgo., 1958—; contbg. editor Saturday Rev., N.Y.C., 1966-72; editor children's books, Chgo. Tribune, 1972—; prof. emeritus Grad. Library Sch., U. Chgo., 1977—; cons. NBC, Chgo., 1968-71. Co-author reference book: Children and Books, (Pi Lambda Theta award 1974); editor: Children and Libraries, 1981; author 11 other books, various articles. Active U. Chgo. Service League, Neighborhood Club, Hosp. Vol. group, First Unitarian Ch. Recipient Children's Reading Round Table award, 1978; Sutherland Lectureship established U. Chgo., 1981. Mem. ALA (Grolier award 1983, bd. dirs., jury pres.), Internat. Bd. on Books for Young People, Internat. Reading Assn., Internat. Research Soc., Nat. Council Tchrs. English, Internat. Soc. for Research in Children's Lit., Mensa. Beta Phi Mu. Democrat. Clubs: University Women's (London), Quadrangle (Chgo.), Colony (Chgo.). Home: 1418 E 57th St Chicago IL 60637 Office: Grad Library Sch 1100 E 57th St Chicago IL 60637

SUTPHIN, JANICE S., accountant; b. Columbus, Nebr., July 30, 1942; d. William Albert and Barbara Schwader; m. Allen Lee Sutphin, Dec. 17, 1962 (dec. 1984); children—Allen, Janene. B.S. cum laude, High Point Coll., 1980. C.P.A., N.C. Sr. acct. Witherington, Wells & Goble, C.P.A.s, Statesville, N.C., 1983-85, Cherry, Bekaert & Holland, Charlotte, N.C., 1985, Jones Group, Inc., Charlotte, 1985—; staff acct. Cherry, Bekaert & Holland, Raleigh, 1981-82. Judge, Republican Party Precinct, Thomasville, N.C., 1978, 79; active Girl Scouts U.S.A., 1975-78; treas. Indian Ridge Assn., Statesville, 1984-85; pres. PTA, High Point, N.C., 1970. Mem. N.C. Soc. C.P.A.s (state continuing edn. com.), Soc. Advancement Mgmt. (sec. 1978-79), Nat. Assn. Accts., Am. Inst. C.P.A.s, Delta Mu Delta, Alpha Chi. Presbyterian. Avocations: swimming; piano; cross stitch. Home: 349 Goodman Rd Concord NC 28025 Office: Jones Group Inc 6060 St Albans St Charlotte NC 28287

SUTPHIN, SUSAN COCKRELL, librarian; b. San Antonio, July 26, 1947; d. Alford R. and Eunice (Thigpen) Cockrell. B.A., Huntingdon Coll., 1968; M.L.S., U. N.C.-Chapel Hill, 1969; A.S., Amarillo Coll., 1983; M.A. in Polit. Sci., W. Tex. State U., 1984. Asst. librarian Davidson County Community Coll., 1969-71; acquisitions librarian Central Piedmont Community Coll., 1971-76; tech. librarian Mason & Hanger-Silas Mason Co., Inc., Amarillo, Tex., 1977—. Republican. Home: 4515 Virginia St Apt 123F Amarillo TX 79109 Office: PO Box 30020 Amarillo TX 79177

SUTTER, CAROLYN OPTHOFF, city official; b. Kalamazoo, Oct. 9, 1942; d. John Martin and Lorraine Eleanor (Kloosterman) Opthoff; B.S., Calvin Coll., 1964; M.S., Western Mich. U., 1972; M.P.A., Calif. State U.-Long Beach, 1982; children—Chandra, Stephan. Dir., Library System of Southwestern Mich., 1974-76; asso. dir. Long Beach (Calif.) Public Library, 1977-79; dir. library and mus. services, City of Long Beach, 1979-81, dir. telecommunications, 1981-82, now gen. mgr. Tidelands Agy. Chairwoman Mich. 4th Dist. Tricounty Women's Polit. Caucus, 1972-76; mem. adv. bd. Sch. Bus., Calif. State U.-Long Beach. Mem. Long Beach C. of C. (dir. women's council), Calif. State U.-Long Beach Alumni Bd. (bd. dirs.), Urban Land Inst., Waterford Ctr., Council Urban Econ. Devel. Office: Tidelands Agy Long Beach City Hall 333 W Ocean Blvd Long Beach CA 90802

SUTTER, ELIZABETH HENBY (MRS. RICHARD A. SUTTER), civic leader, management company executive; b. St. Louis, May 15, 1912; d. William Hastings and Alvina (Steinbreder) Henby; A.B., Washington U., St. Louis, 1931; m. Richard A. Sutter, June 15, 1935; children—John Richard, Jane Elizabeth, Judith Ann (Mrs. William Hinrichs). Sec.-treas. Sutter Mgmt. Co., St. Louis, Sutter Clinic, St. Louis; v.p. Downtown Med. Bldg., Inc., St. Louis, until 1985. Chmn. com. on mental health AMA Aux., 1960-62, v.p., 1962-63, 64-64, pres. 1965-66, editor Direct Line newsletter, 1967-74; assoc. editor MD's Wife, 1973-80; mem. adv. bd. Deaconess Hosp. Sch. of Nursing, St. Louis; trustee John Burroughs Sch., 1958-61, v.p. 1959, devel. commn., 1960-61; mem. Historic Bldgs. Commn. St. Louis County, 1957—, chmn., 1973—; chmn. Com. for Preservation Children's Teeth; mem. planning bd. Health, Hosp. Health, Welfare Council Met. St. Louis, 1955-64; pres. Aux. Central States Soc. Indsl. Medicine and Surgery, 1960-61; pres. St. Louis County Med. Soc. Aux., 1948-49, Mo. Med. Soc. Aux., 1952-53; sec. St. Louis County Health and Hosp. Bd., 1956-61, chmn., 1961; bd. dirs. Am. Lung Assn. Eastern Mo., exec. com., 1956-85, v.p., 1960-61; pres. Tb and Health Soc. of St. Louis, 1962-65; adv. council vol. services Nat. Assn. Mental Health, 1962-64; bd. dirs. Am. Cancer Soc., St. Louis, exec. com., 1954-64; bd. dirs. Mental Health Assn. St. Louis, 1960-61; mem. Practical Nursing Edn. Council, chmn. exec. com., 1959-60; mem. AMA Council on Mental Health Planning for Nat. Conf. on Mental Health, 1961; mem. adv. com. on women in services Dept. Def., 1969-72, vice chmn., 1971; participant 24th ann. global strategy discussion U.S. Naval War Coll., 1972; bd. govs. Washington U. Alumni, 1970-71, 75—, vice chmn. 1979-80, chmn., 1980-81; trustee Washington U., 1979-81; pres. Washington U. Arts and Scis. Century Club, 1970-71; bd. dirs. St. Louis Conv. and Tourist Bur., 1975-83, sec., 1980-82; bd. dirs. Health Services Agy., 1975-82; mem. East West Gateway Coordinating Council Task Force on Historic Preservation, 1975-81, University City Historic Preservation Commn., 1977; bd. dirs. Whitney Beach III Assn., Longboat Key, Fla., 1984-87; del. Mo. Republican Conv., 1972, 76, 80, 84, del. Nat. Rep. Conv., 1984. Named 1 of 10 Women of Achievement in good citizen category St. Louis Globe-Democrat, 1961; Alumna of Yr., Gamma Phi Beta, St. Louis, 1966; recipient St. Louis County Med. Soc. award of merit, 1964; Disting. Alumni citation Washington U., 1968, Disting. Alumni Service citation, 1977; Life Style award Eastern Mo. chpt. Am. Lung Assn., 1982; Meritorious Service award Am. Park and Recreation Soc., 1985. Mem. Mo. Hist. Soc., St. Louis Symphony Soc., AMA Aux. (hon. life), Mo. Med. Aux. (hon. life), Met. St. Louis Med. Aux. (hon. life). Presbyterian. Home: 7215 Greenway Dr Saint Louis MO 63130

SUTTIN, DORIS BETH, real estate broker and developer, mortgage broker, business owner; b. Chgo., July 5, 1940; d. Saul S. and Pearl (Goldberg) Siegal; m. Eugene N. Suttin, Feb. 1, 1961 (div. 1968); m. Myron J. Sponder, July 5, 1976 (div. 1977). B.S., U. Ill.-Urbana, 1961. Lic. real estate broker, Fla. Advt. mgr. Goldblatt Bros. Inc., Urbana, 1961-62; real estate salesperson Grand Bahama Devel. Co., Freeport, Grand Bahamas, 1963-65; asst. sales mgr. Coral Beach Ltd., Freeport, 1968-70; owner-mgr. Saul S. Siegal Co., Miami, Fla., 1970-82; developer DLM Partnership, Miami, 1978—; owner, comml. real estate broker Doris B. Suttin Realty, Inc., Miami, 1981—. Vice pres. corporate devel Lowe Art Mus., Friends of Art, U. Miami. Mem. Women in Communication, S. Fla. Poetry Inst., Mensa. Home: 1063 NE 204 Terr North Miami Beach FL 33179 Office: Doris B Suttin Realty Inc 4784 NW 167th St Miami FL 33014

SUTTLES, VIRGINIA GRANT, advertising executive; b. Urbana, Ill., June 13, 1931; d. William Henry and Lenora (Fitzsimmons) Grant; student pub. schs., Mahomet, Ill.; m. John Henry Suttles, Sept. 24, 1977; step-children—Linda Suttles, Peg Suttles Hanly, Pamela Suttles Diaz, Randall. Media estimator and Procter & Gamble budget control Tatham-Laird, Inc., Chgo., 1955-60; media planner, supr. Tracy-Locke Co., Inc., Dallas and Denver, 1961-68; media dir., account exec. Lorie-Lotito, Inc., 1968-72; v.p., media dir. Sam Lusky Assos., Inc., Denver, 1972—; ind. media buyer, 1984—; part-time mktg. dept. Del E. Webb Devel. Co., Sun City West, Ariz., 1985—; lectr. sr. journalism class U. Colo., Boulder, 1975-80; condr. class in media seminars Denver Advt. Fedn., 1974, 77; Colo. State U. panelist Broadcast Day, 1978, High Sch. Inst., 1979, 80, 81, 82, 83. Mem. Denver Advt. Fedn. (dir. 1973-75, 80-82, exec. bd., v.p. ops. 1980-81, chmn. Alfie awards com. 1980-81, advt. profl. of yr. 1981-82), Denver Advt. Golf Assn. (v.p. 1976-77, pres. 1977-78), Colo. Broadcasters Assn., Sun City West Bowling Assn., Sun City West Women's Social Club. Republican. Congregationalist. Club: Denver Broncos Quarterback. Home: 21022 Sunglow Dr Sun City West AZ 85375 Office: Suite 1616 First of Denver Plaza Bldg 633 17th St Denver CO 80202

SUTTON, DOROTHY LOUISE, educator; b. Cherry Tree, Pa., Nov. 18, 1929; d. Paul and Viola Trudell (Leamer) S.; B.S. in Bus. Edn., Ind. State Coll., 1952; M.Ed., Pa. State U., 1956; postgrad. U. Colo., 1958, Pa. State U., 1964-65, Temple U., 1968, U. Pitts., 1970-72; m. William R. Ferencz, Dec. 28, 1946; 1 dau., Lucinda Kay Rollin. Tchr., Clarion-Limestone Joint High Sch., Strattonville, Pa., 1952-54; faculty Allegheny Coll., Meadville, Pa., 1954-61, Mohawk Valley Community Coll., Utica, N.Y., 1961-64; prof. secretarial sci. Harrisburg (Pa.) Area Community Coll., 1964—, pres. faculty orgn., 1985-86. Sec. bd. dirs. ARC, Meadville, 1956-61; mem. Harrisburg Nursing and Health Services Com., 1977-82. Mem. Exec. Women internat. (v.p. 1979-81, pres. 1981), Assn. Info. Systems Personnel (treas. 1981-82), Delta Pi Epsilon. Republican. Roman Catholic. Club: Soroptimist (pres. 1979-81). Home: 4301 Beaufort Hunt Dr Harrisburg PA 17110 Office: 3300 Cameron St Rd Harrisburg PA 17110

SUTTON, GLORIA JEAN, health sciences counselor; b. Salisbury, Md., Oct. 2, 1948; d. Paul Weldon and Doris Mabel (Tribeck) S.; B.S., Towson State U., 1971; M.Ed., Western Md. Coll., 1977. Lic. profl. counselor, Tex.; nat. cert. counselor. Tchr., counselor Carroll County Bd. Edn., Westminster, Md., 1971-77; vocat. evaluator Goodwill Industries, Austin, Tex., 1977-78; vocat. rehab. counselor Tex. Rehab. Commn., Austin, 1978-81; health scis. counselor Austin Community Coll. (Tex.), 1981—, also part-time instr. allied health scis.; pres. Taysa Video. Mem. Nat. Vocat. Guidance Assn., Am. Assn. Counseling and Devel., Jr. Coll. Personnel Assn. of Tex., Tex. Assn. Counseling and Devel., Internat. Arabian Horse Assn., Am. Horse Shows Assn., Central Tex. Arabian Horse Club. Home: Route 1 Box 150 C43 Paige TX 78659 Office: Austin Community Coll Riverside Campus 5712 E Riverside DrAustin TX 78741

SUTTON, KAREN MARIE, architect, consultant; b. Santa Monica, Calif., June 17, 1943; d. D. Philip and Eva Margaret (Christianson) Johnson; m. Jonathan Stone Sutton, May 21, 1970; children—Eva Marie, Theodora Stone, Karen Amelia. B.A., U. Wash., 1965; M.Arch., U. Pa., 1969. Registered architect, Pa. Draftsperson Vincent Kling, Phila., 1966-69; designer Thomas Hseih, San Francisco, 1969-70; designer, architect GBQC, Phila., 1970-75; architect Rhett Jones Assocs., Phila., 1975-78; architect, gen. ptnr. Adaptive Design, Phila., 1979—; owner Growth Properties, Phila., 1980—. Bd. dirs. Community Art Ctr., Wallingford, Pa., 1978—, pres., 1979-81; bd. dirs. Nursery Day Sch., Swarthmore, Pa., 1976-78; mem. Found. for Architecture, Phila., Phila. Mus. Art. Mem. Am. Soc. Registered Architects, Nat. Assn. Home Builders, Delaware County C. of C. Presbyterian. Club: Rose Tree Garden. Avocations: painting; gardening; flower arranging. Home: 335A Plush Mill Rd Wallingford PA 19086 Office: Adaptive Design 125 S 9th St Suite 801 Philadelphia PA 19107

SUTTON, LORI ANN KOSIOR, financial planning company executive; b. Beaver Falls, Pa., May 12, 1955; d. Joseph Anthony and Angela Marie (Santelli) Kosior; m. Kevin Roger Sutton, Aug. 20, 1977. A.B. in Communications and Edn., Grove City Coll., 1977; postgrad. Pa. State U., 1978, 79. Tchr. Lincoln High Sch., Ellwood City, Pa., 1978-81; personnel counselor Champion, Cleve., 1981; assoc. planner Bolanis & Assocs., Cleve., 1981-83; v.p. Carroll Fin. Planning, Charlotte, N.C., 1983-85; v.p., gen. mgr. Pacific Fin. Group, Bellevue, Wash., 1985—. Mem. Jr. Women's Club, Wampum, Pa., 1977-81, Civitans, Charlotte, 1985. Mem. Internat. Assn. Fin. Planning, Inst. Cert. Fin. Planners, Nat. Assn. Female Execs. Republican. Roman Catholic. Avocation: reading.

SUTTON, MARILYN ROBERTA, insurance company executive; b. Marion, Ohio, May 20, 1947; d. Ralph Edward and Ida Loree (Walker) Hill; m. Joseph Sutton, May 28, 1982; 1 child, Carmen Michelle Lauderdale. B.S. in Bus. Adminstrn., Franklin U., Columbus, Ohio, 1981. Successively claims examiner, lead examiner, unit supr. claims and customer service, div. mgr. Nationwide Ins. Co., Columbus, 1968-84; dir. instl. claims Blue Cross & Blue Shield, Cleve., 1984-85, v.p. claims and customer service, 1985—. Mem. Nat. Assn. Female Execs., Greater Cleve. Growth Assn., Cleve. Playhouse Club, Black Profls. Assn. Democrat. Avocation: golf. Home: 2930 North Bay Dr L-5 Westlake OH 44145 Office: Blue Cross & Blue Shield of No Ohio 2060 E 9th St Cleveland OH 44115

SUTTON, MICHELE MARIE, printing company executive; b. Hermosa Beach, Calif., Sept. 30, 1945; d. Richard Prentice and Melva Marie (Jensen) Prentice Jenkins; m. Darel Lee Sutton, May 25, 1968; 1 child, Joshua James. Paralegal, City's Atty.'s Office, Santa Monica, Calif., 1970-77; owner, pres. Kwik-Kopy Printing, Grand Junction, Colo., 1981—. Trustee Western Colo. Ctr. for Arts, Grand Junction, 1985—. Mem. Nat. Assn. Quick Printers, Nat. Assn. Female Execs., Grand Junction C. of C. (v.p. and mem. bd. dirs. women's div. 1984). Democrat. Avocation: photography. Home: 556 Rio Oso Ln Grand Junction CO 81501 Office: Kwik-Kopy Printing 904 N 7th St Grand Junction CO 81501

SUTTON, NORMA JEAN, lawyer, educator; b. Chgo., June 11, 1952; d. Harry and Beatrice (Ross) Sams; 1 son, Edward Michael. B.A., Loyola U., Chgo., 1974, J.D., 1980; M.A., Gov.'s State U., Park Forest, Ill., 1976. Bar: Ill. 1980, U.S. Dist. Ct. (no. dist.) Ill. 1980, U.S. Ct. Appeals (7th cir.) 1980. Tchr., Tri-County Head-Start, Benton Harbor, Mich., 1974; research assoc. CEMREL, Inc., Chgo., 1975-77; law clk. NACOLAH, Chgo., 1977-80; jud. clk. Ill. Jud. System, Chgo., 1980-82; corp. counsel Soft Sheen Products, Inc., Chgo., 1982-85; regional atty. Digital Equipment Corp., 1985—. Mem. Tuley Park Players Theater Group, Richard B. Harrison Little Theatre Group. Am. Polit. Sci. Assn. fellow, 1974-75; Fred Hampton Meml. scholar, 1977; Loyola U. Alumni scholar, 1977. Mem. ABA, Ill. Bar Assn. (young lawyers div. council), Chgo. Bar Assn., Pi Sigma Alpha. Roman Catholic. Office: Digital Equipment Corp 1155 W Dundee Rd Arlington Heights IL 60004

SUTTON, SUSAN LOUISE, lawyer, journalist; b. Charlotte, N.C., Mar. 30, 1950; d. Robert Thomas Sutton and Edith Louise (Smith) Brennan; m. James Jay Mitchell, May 21, 1977. Cert. Alliance Française, Paris, 1972; B.A. in French, U. N.C.-Charlotte, 1972; postgrad. U. Santa Clara, 1978-79; J.D., U. San Diego, 1979. Bar: Calif. 1979. Reporter, Sanford Herald (N.C.), 1972-73, Evening Herald, Rock Hill, S.C., 1973-75; publicity coordinator Home Fed. Savs., San Diego, 1975-77; assoc. Carey & Carey, Palo Alto, Calif., 1979-80; ptnr. Moran, Rogers & Sutton, Palo Alto, 1980-82; sole practice, Palo Alto, from 1982; now mng. atty. Law Office of Susan L. Sutton; dir. Com. on Women Lawyers Santa Clara County, 1980—; trustee Santa Clara County Bar, 1984-86, exec. com., 1986—. Contbr. news articles to Electronic Bus., 1979. Recipient award Nat. Youth in Achievement, 1980, Pub. Service award for winning series S.C. AP, 1974. Mem. ABA (assoc. editor quar. Affiliate), Santa Clara Bar Assn. (chmn. pub. affairs 1982-84, chmn. debtor/creditor bankruptcy 1986), Palo Alto Bar Assn. (legislation chair 1981-84, chmn. women lawyers com. 1986), Santa Clara Trial Lawyers, Sigma Delta Chi, Phi Delta Phi. Democrat. Presbyterian. Address: 123 Fremont Ave Los Altos CA 94022

SUTTY, BETTY RAE, association executive; b. Columbus, Ga., May 31, 1948; d. Ralph Lanier and Elizabeth Inez (Simpson) Davis; m. Randall Wayne Young, Apr. 2, 1967 (div.); children—Sean, Alicia, Matthew; m. Arthur P. Sutty, July 7, 1984. Grad. Inst. Orgn. in Mgmt., 1986. Asst. exec. v.p. Greater Lafayette C. of C., Ind., 1979-84; program dir. Aurora C. of C., Ill., 1984-85; asst. dir. Naperville C. of C., Ill., 1985; exec. dir. N.W. Suburban Assn. Commerce and Industry, Schaumburg, Ill., 1985—; discussion facilitator Inst. Orgn. Mgmt., 1984, 85. Contbr. articles to profl. jours. Bd. advisor Boy Scouts Am. and Girl Scouts U.S.A., White County, Ind., 1970-74; chmn. Young People to Re-elect Nixon, White County, 1972; v.p. Women's Republican Club, White County, 1972-74; dir. state and local Am. Diabetes Assn., Ind., 1977-80. Recipient Designated Resource Person award Sch. Career Bank, 1983, 84. Mem. Am. C. of C. Execs., Ill. Assn. C. of C. Execs. Baptist. Club: Women's Forum (chmn. 1985). Avocations: reading; golf; needlepoint; travel. Home: 2025 Springside Dr Naperville IL 60565 Office: NW Suburban Assn Commerce and Industry 1375 E Woodfield Rd Schaumburg IL 60195

SUYETSUGU, GRACE TAMIKO, nurse; b. San Mateo, Calif., Feb. 16, 1957; d. Frank Takiji and Mitsuka (Shimizu) S. B.S. magna cum laude in Nursing, San Francisco State U., 1979. R.N., Calif. Charge nurse med./surg. unit Peninsula Hosp. and Med. Ctr., Burlingame, Calif., 1979-84; staff nurse ICU, 1984—. Mem. Calif. Nurses Assn., Am. Assn. Critical Care Nurses. Democrat. Buddhist. Avocations: traveling; photography; cooking; needlework; sports. Home: 1274 40th Ave San Francisco CA 94122 Office: Peninsula Hosp and Med Ctr 1783 El Camino Real Burlingame CA 94010

SUZOR, MARGARET ANN, lobbying firm executive; b. Springfield, Mass., Feb. 19, 1955; d. Lester George and Mary Margaret (McCarthy) Suzor. B.A., Trinity Coll., Washington, 1976. Asst. researcher Republican Nat. Com., Washington, 1976; mgmt. trainee Mass. Mut. Life Ins. Co., Springfield, 1977; exec. asst. Honorable Philip M. Crane, Washington, 1978-81; confidential asst. Honorable David A. Stockman, Washington, 1981-85; exec. asst. Timmon's Co., Washington, 1985—. Vol., Folger Shakespeare Library, Washington. Mem. Trinity Coll. Alumni Assn. (dir. regional chpt. 1980-81), Republican Women's Fed. Forum. Republican. Roman Catholic. Club: Jr. League (com. chmn. 1982-84) (Washington). Avocations: swimming; tennis. Home: 2643 41st St NW Apt 4 Washington DC 20007 Office: Timmons & Co 1850 K St NW Suite 850 Washington DC 20006

SVEC, CYNTHIA LILLIAN, business services administrator, building manager; b. Chgo., Jan. 20, 1941; d. George Mitchell Smith and Lillian (Mottl) Smith Trousil; m. 1964 (div. 1975); children—Victoria Lynn, Jacqueline Paige, Alison E. Student public schs., Cicero, Ill. Office mgr. Belmont Industries, Cicero, Ill., 1958-67; pres., exec., owner August Bus. Service, Inc., LaGrange, Ill., 1975—; v.p. Stewart's Indsl. Services Inc., LaGrange, 1979-83; owner, mgr. LaGrange Profl. Bldg., LaGrange, 1981—. Recipient Beautification award West Suburban C. of C., LaGrange, 1981. Mem. West Suburban C. of C., Midwest Assn. Commerce and Industry. Republican. Roman Catholic. Avocations: interior decoration and design; international travel; astrology; reading. Office: August Bus Services Inc 110 N LaGrange Rd LaGrange IL 60525

SVEC, JANICE LYNN, navy enlistedwoman; b. Santa Anna, Calif., May 14, 1948; d. Leonard August Svec and Wanda Marcelle (Richards) McMillon; m. Lewis Eugene Humphrey, May 24, 1974 (div. 1977); 1 child, Jeromy Starbuck Svec. A.A. in Adminstrn. of Justice, Los Angeles Met. Community Coll., 1982; student criminal justice Thomas Edison State Coll., Trenton, 1985—. Adminstrv. supporter Naval Investigative Service, Subic Bay, Philippines, 1979-81; office supr. Naval Communication Ctr., Yokosuka, Japan, 1981-82; chief master at arms Naval Support Facility Security Dept., Diego Garcia, Brit. Indian Ocean Ter., 1982-83, U.S. Navy Drug Rehab. Ctr., San Diego, 1983-85; instr. U.S. Navy, Lakehurst, N.J., 1985—. Roman Catholic. Avocations: body building; horseback riding. Home: PO Box 578 Lakehurst NJ 08733

SVEINSSON, LINDA RODGERS, computer scientist; b. Tuscaloosa, Ala., July 1, 1938; d. Eric and Sarah Ella (Haughton) Rodgers; B.A. in Math., Birmingham-So. Coll., 1960; M.S. in Indsl. Engring. (NSF trainee 1970-72), U. Ala., 1972; m. Hjalmar Sveinsson, May 29, 1971; children—Martha M. Reed, Stephen R.M. Moreno, III. Systems analyst U. Ala. Med. Center, Birmingham, 1967-69; systems mgr. Internat. Data Systems, New Orleans, 1969-70; computer scientist Computer Scis. Corp., Silver Spring, Md., 1973-76; computer systems specialist System Devel. Corp., McLean, Va., 1976-78; mem. tech. staff Bell Labs., Columbus, Ohio, 1978-85, tech. supr., 1979-85; mgr. bus. devel. No. Telecom, Inc., Research Triangle Park, N.C., 1985—. Mem. Assn. Computing Machinery, Phi Beta Kappa, Alpha Pi Mu. Republican. Methodist. Home: 10409 Byrum Woods Dr Raleigh NC 27612 Office: PO Box 13010 Research Triangle Park NC 27709

SVETLOVA, MARINA, choreographer, ballerina, educator; b. Paris, France, May 3, 1922; d. Max and Tamara (Andreieff) Hartman; came to U.S., 1940, naturalized, 1946; student Vera Trefilova, Paris, 1930-36, L. Egorova and M. Kschessinska, Paris, 1936-39, A. Vilzak, N.Y.C., 1940-57. Debut Paris Opera, 1932; baby ballerina, original Ballet Russe de Monte Carlo, 1939-41; guest ballerina Ballet Theatre, Met. Opera tour, 1942; prima ballerina Met. Opera Co., N.Y.C., 1943-50, N.Y.C. Opera, 1950-52; appeared Jacob's Pillow Summer Festival, 1949; own concert group under mgmt. Columbia Artists Mgmt., 1944-58, Nat. Artists Corp., 1958-69; ballet tours in U.S., 1944—, Far East, 1953, Middle East, 1954, Europe, 1955, 59, S. Am., 1962; guest ballerina London's Festival Ballet, 1953, Teatro dell Opera, Rome, 1953. Nat. Opera, Stockholm, 1955, Suomi Opera, Helsinki, Finland, 1956, Het Nederland Ballet, Holland, 1954, Cork Irish Ballet, 1955, Paris Opera Comique, 1958, London Palladium, 1959-60; appeared in Les Sylphides, 1943, Bluebeard, 1943, Balustrade, 1940, Giselle, 1953, Pas de Quatre, 1943, Swan Lake, 1941, Graduation Ball, 1940, also various classical ballets, 1939-69; choreographer Dallas Civic Opera, 1964-67, Seattle Opera, 1961-62, Houston Opera, 1965, Kansas City Performing Arts Found., 1965-67, Ft. Worth Opera, 1967-83, San Antonio Opera, 1983—; ballet dir. So. Vt. Art Center, Manchester, 1959-65; dir. Svetlova Dance Center, Dorset, Vt., 1963—; prof. ballet Ind. U., Bloomington, 1969—. Mem. Am. Guild Mus. Artists (dir. 1943), Nat. Soc. Arts and Letters (nat. dance chmn.). Contbr. articles on theatre, choreography and ballet works to newspapers and various mags. Home: Dorset VT 05251 Office: 2100 Maxwell Ln Bloomington IN 47401 also 25 W 54th St New York NY 10019

SVEZIA, VERA TISHEFF, concert pianist, educator; b. Alliance, Ohio, Sept. 5, 1937; d. Thomas and Anna (Tarpov) Tisheff; m. Rudolph Svezia, Mar. 14, 1970; children—Alexander, Alexandria. Student Yale U., Julliard Sch. Music, Eastman Sch. Music, Mich. State U. Founder, dir. Vera Tisheff Sch. of Music, N.Y. and N.J., 1971—. Concert performances with leading orchs. in U.S. and Europe; solo concerts, U.S. and European cities. McDowell Colony scholar, 1964; Martha Baird Rockefeller award, 1966. Fellow AAUW, Phi Omega. Home: 130 E Hamilton Ave Englewood NJ 07631 Office: Vera Tisheff Sch Music 138 W 25th St New York NY 10001

SVILAR, CYNTHIA A. DAVIS, pharmaceutical representative; b. Knoxville, Tenn., Feb. 19, 1953; d. James C. and Margaret L. (Rucker) Davis; m. Dennis Michael Svilar, June 28, 1975; children—Kyle M.D. Svilar, Drew S.D. Svilar, Colin M.D. Svilar. B.A., Ind. U., 1978, Cert. in Computers, 1984. Pharm. rep. Merrell Dow, Cin., 1979—; cons. Aspen Transp., Hobart, Ind., 1984—; cons. in computers Combined Transport Systems, Chgo., 1984—; pres. SRB Transp., Hammond, Ind., 1985—. Recipient Pres.'s Pin, Merrell Dow Pharm., 1980, 81, Century Club, 1985. Mem. Nat. Assn. Female Execs., Bus. and Profl. Women. Home: 875 Luther Dr Hobart IN 46342 Office: 875 Luther Dr Hobart IN 46342

SVOBODA, JOANNE DZITKO, artist, educator; b. Jersey City, Dec. 24, 1948; d. John Richard and Joanna Frances (Rygiel) Dzitko; student Parsons Sch. Design, 1966, Kean Coll., 1970; B.A., Jersey City State Coll., 1970, M.A.,

1975; postgrad. Tchrs. Coll., Columbia U., 1972; m. Peter W. Svoboda, Sept. 3, 1972; children—Kimberly Anne, Lauren Anne. Art tchr. YMCA, Jersey City, 1966-70, Henry Snyder High Sch., Jersey City, 1970-80; propr., craftsman, instr. Mountain Designers and Craftsmen, Long Valley, N.J., 1977-80; partner, craftsman, instr. Four Seasons Crafts, Chester and Long Valley, 1978-85; designer, estimator, v.p. Estate Contracting Inc., Long Valley, 1978—; tng. specialist Johnson & Johnson Baby Products, Skillman, N.J., 1984—; instr. interior design Jersey City Bd. Continuing Edn., 1974. Trustee, Jersey City Mus. Assn., 1973-79, chmn. fine arts dept., 1972-79; mem. curriculum revision com. Jersey City Bd. Edn., 1976; judge Distributive Edn. Clubs N.J., 1976, 77, 78; mem. Washington Twp. Shade Tree Commn., 1979-81, chmn., 1981; mem. Washington Twp. Hist. Heritage Commn., 1981-85, Washington Twp. Friends of the Library; publicity chmn. Washington Twp. Hist. Soc., 1980-81; mem. choir Our Lady of the Mountain Cath. Ch. Grantee, N.J. State Dept. Edn., 1973; awards N.J. Fedn. Jr. Woman's Clubs: black and white photography, 1979, crafts, 1979, 1st place color photography, 1980, free form, 1981. Mem. Am. Soc. Interior Designers (affiliate), Federated Art Assn. N.J., Art Educators N.J., N.J. Designer Craftsmen. Democrat. Exhibited Courtney Gallery, Jersey City State Coll., 1970, 74, Long Valley, 1979-80; active encouraging establishment of hist. zone Long Valley, landmarks, Jersey City and Washington Twp.; contbr. articles in field to various publs. Home and Office: 143 W Springtown Rd Long Valley NJ 07853

SWAILS-MORAH, TANYA MARIA, univ. ofcl.; b. Cleve., Jan. 7, 1954; d. Nathaniel and Jane (Lane) Swails; B.A., Ohio State U., Columbus, 1974, M.A. in Black Lit., 1976, M.A. in Journalism, 1976; m. Emeka Ogbogu Morah, July 9, 1981. Moderator, producer talk show sta, WVKO, Columbus, 1976; communicative skills instr. Ohio State U., 1976; mng. editor Columbus Onyx News, 1975-77; asst. to news dir. sta. WTVN-TV, Columbus, 1977; news reporter sta. WBIE/WCOB, Marietta, Ga., 1977, Atlanta Daily World, 1977; newscaster sta. WCSU, Wilberforce, Ohio, 1979; staff writer Dayton (Ohio) Black Press, 1979-80; news corr. Daily Gazette, Xenia, Ohio, 1980; instr. English, Wilberforce U., 1977-78, dir. mass media communications program, also asst. prof. English, 1978-81; instr. dance Central State U., Wilberforce, 1978-81, adj. prof. English, 1981—, coordinator publs., 1981—. Mem. exec. bd. Universal Liberty in Christ Truth Kingdom, 1981—. Recipient Outstanding faculty award Wilberforce U., 1980, Disting. Service award, 1981. Mem. Nat. Council Tchrs. English, AAUP, Black Women Academicians, Delta Sigma Theta. Democrat. Office: Office Univ Relations Central State U Wilberforce OH 45384

SWAIN, ANNA CHAMBLEE, marketing consultant; b. N.Y.C., Mar. 31, 1954; B.B.A. in Internat. Mktg., Bernard M. Baruch U., 1981. Sec. to pres. Bleuette, Inc., N.Y.C., 1970-73; asst. to dir. classified advt. Fairchild Publs., N.Y.C., 1974-75, asst. mgr. real estate advt., 1976-77; asst. to publs. dir. and nat. sales mgr. Lebhar-Friedman Pub., N.Y.C., 1975; asst. account exec. Gaynor & Lucas Advt., N.Y.C., 1976; research analyst, asso. client service rep. Time, Inc., N.Y.C., 1977-80; mktg. cons., N.Y.C., 1980—. Pub. relations liaison Black Liberation Thru Action, Collectiveness and Knowledge, 1979-80. Mem. Am. Soc. Personnel Adminstrn. (pres. Baruch U. chpt. 1980-81; Harry M. Sherman award 1981), Baruch Arts and Letters Soc. (founder), Women for Racial and Econ. Equality, Nat. Council Culture and Art, Nat. Bus. League, Internat. Arts Forum (founder), Smithsonian Instn., Mark Twain Assn., N.Y. Poetry Forum. Club: Beaux Arts (N.Y.C.). Office: PO Box 1142 Ansonia Station New York NY 10023

SWAIN, CLAUDIA JONES, reading demonstration educator, writer; b. Ft. Worth, Dec. 15, 1937; d. Vidal Leonard and Wynona (Dews) Jones; m. Richard E. Swain, Jr., Apr. 28, 1973. B.S., East Tex. Baptist Coll., 1962; M.Ed., North Tex. State U., 1980, Ph.D., 1985. Classroom tchr. several sch. dists., Northeast Houston, Dencanville, Tex., and Dallas, 1962-69; asst. dean students East Tex. Bapt. Coll., Marshall, 1969-70; presch./children's cons. Bapt. Gen. Conv. Tex.-Womans Missionary Union, Dallas, 1970-77; primary classroom tchr. B.F. Darrell Sch., Dallas, 1977-80, 82-83, title I-primary, 1980-82; reading demonstration tchr. Dallas Ind. Sch. Dist. at B.F. Darrell Sch., Dallas, 1983-85, Charles Rice Sch., Dallas, 1985—. Author: God Leads His Children, 1979; author curriculum Womans Missionary Union, So. Bapt. Conv., Birmingham, 1970-80. Mem. Assn. Supervision and Curriculum Devel., Assn. Childhood Edn. Internat., Assn. Tex. Profl. Educators, Internat. Reading Assn., Delta Kappa Gamma (Alpha state scholar 1982), Phi Delta Kappa. Baptist.

SWAIN, KATHLEEN BUCK, government official; b. Wilmington, Del., Dec. 18; d. Shelburne Taylor and Edith Winona (Bruce) Buck. B.A., Va. Poly. and State U., 1970; postgrad. Coll. William and Mary, 1970-71. Homebound tchr. Muscogee County Sch. Dist., Columbus, Ga., 1972; property mgmt. dir. urban renewal Columbus Housing Authority, 1972-74; head cashier Target Stores, Dallas, 1974; case analyst Tex. Dept. Human Resources, Dallas, 1974—; dept. regional rep. Wage Report Work Group, 1983; speaker, lectr. Active polit. campaigns. Recipient 3 Idea awards Tex. Dept. Human Resources; named Actress of Yr., Va. Poly. Inst. and State U., 1970. Mem. Tex. Pub. Employees Assn. (past chpt. pres.; Top Head award 1984), Audubon Soc., Smithsonian Assocs. Democrat. Presbyterian. Home: 2525 Maverick St Dallas TX 75228 Office: Texas Dept of Human Resources 230A Lancaster-Kiest Dallas TX 75216

SWAIN, NANCY JANE COX (MRS. JAMES OBED SWAIN), former educator; b. Elwood, Ind., Dec. 19, 1901; d. Alfred Thomas and Emma (Allen) Cox; A.B. with high distinction, Ind. U., 1923, postgrad., 1928; M.A., U. Tenn., 1951, postgrad., 1953; m. James Obed Swain, June 24, 1923; children—J. Maurice, J. Robert. Teaching missionary M.E. Ch., Costa Rica, 1923-28; instr. U. Tenn., Knoxville, 1943, 45, non-resident instr. corr. Extension Div., 1959-71; tchr. Oak Ridge High Sch., 1943-67, Hollins Coll., 1967. Mem. Am. Assn. Tchrs. Spanish and Portuguese, E. Tenn. Edn. Assn., S. Atlantic Modern Lang, Assn., Phi Beta Kappa, Phi Kappa Phi, Sigma Delta Pi, Pi Delta Phi, Pi Lambda Theta. Republican. Methodist. Mem. P.E.O. Home: 414 Forest Park Blvd Apt 622 Knoxville TN 37919

SWAIN, NANCY JAYNE, statistician; b. Dallas, Jan. 13, 1950; d. Jack Curtis and Jayne (Earnest) S. B.A. in Sociology, U. Tex.-Dallas, 1978; M.A. in Sociology, U. Tex.-Arlington, 1979; postgrad. in sociology U. Tex.-Austin. Interviewer Behavioral Research Inst., Denver, 1978; research asst., then teaching asst. U. Tex. System, 1978-81; forecasting asst. econ. forecasting and planning GTE, Texarkana, Tex., 1981-82; quality control statistician Dallas County Appraisal Dist., Dallas, 1983-84. Mem. Tex. Assn. Assessing Officers, Alpha Kappa Delta. Office: Dallas County Appraisal Dist 2601 Live Oak Dallas TX 75219

SWAIN, NOLA V., real estate appraiser; b. Tacoma, Wash., Mar. 10, 1942; d. Arthur and Viola Mafalda (Sirianni) De Caro; m. Lloyd E. Montgomery, Dec. 8, 1961 (div. 1971); children—Gina N. Montgomery, Melissa R. Montgomery; m. Walter B. Swain, Mar. 11, 1977. Student, U. Puget Sound, 1959-62. Cert. real estate appraiser Colo. Appraiser, assessor Pierce Co. Assessors Office, Tacoma, 1971-77; chief appraiser Otero Savs. & Loan, Colorado Springs, 1977-78; pvt. fee appraiser N.W.S. & Assocs., Colorado Springs, 1978—; pres., designer N.V.S. Enterprises, Colorado Springs, 1980—. Designer numerous gift items. Recipient Women at Work award Council on Working Women, 1985; Pub. Service award Colorado Springs Assn. Life Underwriters, 1985. Mem. Soc. Real Estate Appraisers (treas. 1978, bd. dirs. 1982-84). Democrat. Roman Catholic. Avocations: skiing; traveling; crafts. Office: NWS & Assocs NVS Enterprises 3028 N El Paso St Colorado Springs CO 80907

SWALES, SUZANNE UHRMANN, sales representative; b. Chgo., June 4, 1936; d. Carl John and Olive E. (Addie) Uhrmann; m. Donald G. Swales, Apr. 30, 1955; children—Kimberly, Kelly, Kevin. Student U. Chgo., 1951-53; B.Sc., Ohio State U., 1954. Mgr., buyer Sabbatini Sport, Aspen, Colo., 1978-81; sales rep. Geiger of Austria, Middlebury, Vt., 1981—. Pres. Aspen Valley Hosp. Blue Ladies, 1978. Republican. Club: Aspen Ski (sec. 1975). Avocations: tennis, skiing, gardening. Home and office: Box 1596 Aspen CO 81612

SWAN, GLADYS, writer, literature educator; b. N.Y.C., Oct. 15, 1934; d. R.J. and Sarah (Taub) Rubenstein; m. Richard B. Swan., Sept. 9, 1955; children—Andrea, Leah. B.A., Western New Mex. U., 1954; M.A., Claremont U., 1955. Mem. faculty dept. English, Franklin Coll., 1961—; disting. vis. writer in residence U. Tex.-El Paso, 1984—; mem. faculty Vt. Coll., Montpelier, 1981—. Author: On the Edge of the Desert, 1979. Carnival for The Gods, 1986. Contbr. articles to profl. jours. Lilly Endowment fellow, 1975; recipient Disting. Service award Western N.Mex., 1985. Mem. Assoc. Writing Programs. Home: 450 E Madison St Franklin IN 46131

SWANSON, BARBARA JEAN, writer; b. Englewood, N.J., Aug. 8, 1947; d. John and Rose Marie (Elkas) Mardinly; m. Robert Ernest Swanson, Apr. 13, 1968; children—John Halladay, Jeffery Robert, Matthew Elias. B.A., Smith Coll., 1969. Author: Careers in Health Care, 1984; co-author: (with Robert Swanson) Tax Shelters: A Guide for Investors and Advisors, 1983, 3d edit., 1985.

SWANSON, BERNICE MARIAN OLSON, psychologist; b. Taft, Calif., Jan. 30, 1924; d. Albert B. and Bertha G. (Jacobsen) Olson; B.S., U. Oreg., 1951; M.Ed. (Tex. Soc. Crippled Children scholar, Midland Council Retarded Children scholar), Tex. Wesleyan U., 1956; Ph.D. (Will Rogers Service scholar), U. Okla., 1969; m. Louis M. Swanson, Dec. 23, 1943; 1 son, Gregory K. Tchr. exceptional children, Ft. Worth, 1953-55, Midland, Tex., 1955-61; prin., dir. spl. edn., Midland, 1961-66; clin. coordinator Muskogee (Okla.) Guidance Center, 1969-70; prof. psychology Northeastern State U., Tahlequah, Okla., 1970—; cons. psychologist Cherokee County Guidance Center. Mem. adv. bd. Okla. Assn. Citizens with Learning Disabilities, 1972—; bd. dirs. Muskogee Sheltered Workshop Activity Program, 1979—. Recipient Disting. Internat. award for noble achievement Epsilon Sigma Alpha, 1972. Mem. Okla. Psychol. Assn., Am. Psychol. Assn., Council Exceptional Children, Okla. Assn. Citizens with Learning Disabilities, Nat. Health Register, Delta Kappa Gamma, Phi Delta Kappa. Author: The Instructor, 1965; Ginger and The Little Lost Kitten, 1974; Understanding Exceptional Children and Youth—An Introduction to Special Education, 1979, rev. edit., 1985; contbg. author: Handbook of Child Psychopathology, 1984. Home: 311 Gawf Rd Muskogee OK 74403 Office: College Ave Northeastern State University Tahlequah OK 74464

SWANSON, DENISE ELAINE, hotel chain executive; b. Atlanta, Feb. 12, 1957; d. Anderson Bart and Betty Jean (Evans) S.; m. Thomas A. Shackleford, May 21, 1984 (div. 1985). Cert., P. Stevens Career Coll., 1976; B.S., Ga. State U., 1984. Dir. mktg. Lodging Unltd., Atlanta, 1981-83; dist. sales mgr. Day Co., Atlanta, 1983-84; internat. tour mgr. Victor Mgmt. Co., Newport News, Va., 1984; v.p. sales, mktg. K&I Tours, Atlanta, 1986; nat. sales mgr. Howard Johnson Co., Atlanta, 1984—. Vocalist for State of Ga., World's Fair, 1982. Mem. Calvary Ladies Union, Powder Springs, Ga., 1986, Calvary Choir, Powder Springs, 1986. Stpehen Styron scholar Ga. State U., 1977, Omni scholar, 1978, Ga. Hospitality Travel Assn. scholar, 1980-81. Mem. Hotel, Sales, Mktg. Assn., Nat. Assn. Female Execs., Atlanta Women's C. of C., Am. Bus. Women's Assn. Democrat. Baptist. Club: Midtown Bus. (Atlanta). Lodge: Austell (worthy adviser 1972-73, grand rep. to Can 1973-74). Avocations: bowling; singing; reading; gymnastics. Home: 5195 Cherry Ln Powder Springs GA 30073 Office: Howard Johnson Co 1901 Powers Ferry Rd Suite 190 Marietta GA 30076

SWANSON, FERN ROSE, former educator; b. Kalmar Twp., Minn.; d. Henry E. and Susie (Hastings) Rose; student Winona (Minn.) Normal Coll., 1918-20; B.S., St. Cloud (Minn.) State Coll., 1955, M.S., 1958; m. Walter E. Swanson, June 24, 1928. Tchr. high sch. English, Latin, Eyota, Minn., 1920-21; tchr. jr. high sch. English, Appleton, Minn., 1921-22; tchr. elementary schs., Harmony, Minn., 1922-23; tchr. high sch. English, Latin, Augusta, Wis., 1923-24, South Haven, Minn., 1924-26; tchr. elementary and high sch. dramatics, Waterville, 1926-27; tchr. elementary schs., South Haven, 1927-41, 43-51, Silver Creek, Minn., 1941-43; tchr. elementary schs., Annandale, Minn., 1951-53, prin., 1953-67; tchr. elementary reading, Belgrade, Minn., 1967-71. Organizer, South Haven council Girl Scouts U.S.A., 1927, leader, 1927-30. Mem. Minn. Elementary Sch. Prins. Assn. (charter mem. 25 Year Club), NEA, Nat. Assn. Elem. Sch. Prins., Ret. Educators Assn. Minn., Minn. Edn. Assn., Nat. Council Tchrs. English, Central Minn. Reading Council (past dir.), Internat., Minn. reading assns., DAR, Ladies of Grand Army Republic (registrar Lookout Circle, dept. pres. Minn. 1974-77, nat. pres. Betsy Ross Club 1978, nat. patriotic instr. 1981-84, nat. jr. v.p. 1984-85, nat. council adminstrn. 1985—), Minn. Hist. Soc., Rebekah, Delta Kappa Gamma (past chpt. pres., Minn. Woman of Achievement award 1982). Episcopalian. Home: 541 Fairhaven Av South Haven MN 55382 Office: South Haven MN 55382

SWANSON, HOLLY ANN, advertising and public relations agency executive; b. Encino, Calif., Aug. 10, 1954; d. Howard Alfred and Catherine Elnor (Hacker) S.; m. C.W. Bottorff, Oct. 10, 1980. Student So. Oreg. State Coll., 1972-76; diploma Italian U. for Foreigners, Perugia, 1974. Teller, Cascade Fed. Savs., Eugene, Oreg., 1976; mgr. sales Kendall Ford Rent-a-Car, Eugene, 1976-79; exec. v.p. Profl. Mgmt. Systems, San Francisco, 1979-80; nat. promotion dir. Medi-Grafix Corp., Scottsdale, Ariz., 1980-81; pres., Calif. First Editions, San Francisco, 1981-83; owner First Editions, Medford, Oreg., 1984—. Creator stationery supplies items and sch. study sheets. Vol. art tchr. Medford/Jackson County Detention Ctr., 1972-76; active Big Sister program Eugene Juvenile Ct. System/Detention Ctr., 1979; coach softball Eugene Sports Program, 1979; spirit advisor Fremont High Sch. Spiritleaders/Spirit Club, Sunnyvale, Calif., 1981-83. Mem. Medford C. of C., Women Entrepreneurs of Oreg., Nat. Assn. Female Execs. Republican. Roman Catholic. Avocations: art; music; writing; child psychology; summer sports. Office: First Editions 38 N Central Plaza Suite M-5 Medford OR 97520

SWANSON, JENNIE ELIZABETH, educator; b. Atlanta, Aug. 5, 1932; d. Chester Arthur and Cleo Annie (McEachern) Williams; B.S., Northwestern U., 1954; M.S., No. Ill. U., 1972, Ed.D., 1976; m. Richard Edward Swanson, Apr. 24, 1954; children—Laurel Dee, Jeffrey Richard, Scott Edward. Public sch. tchr., 1954-69; psycho-ednl. diagnostician, 1969-72; mem. faculty Loyola U., Chgo., 1976-82, asst. prof. ob-gyn and pediatrics, 1979-82, dir. pre-start project depts. ob-gyn and pediatrics Stritch Sch. Medicine, 1978-82; dir. spl. services Community Unit Sch. Dist. 220, 1982—; mem. Gov. Ill. Com. Preventive Services, 1979-80; chmn. B-3 subcom. First Chance Consortium, 1978-80; chmn. INTER-ACT, 1979-80; cons. in field. Grantee HEW, 1973-76, 78-82. Mem. Council Exceptional Children, Assn. Maternal and Child Health, Nat. Perinatal Assn., Nat. Assn. Edn. Young Child, Northwestern U. Alumni Assn., Delta Delta Delta, Delta Kappa Gamma (scholar 1974). Lutheran. Author: (with others) Partners in Child Development, 1978. Office: 310 E James St Barrington IL 60010

SWANSON, JUDITH ANNE, probate paralegal, legal office procedures educator; b. Loma Linda, Calif., June 24, 1941; d. Edward Henry and Gertrude Louella (Ary) Gable; m. Dennis Elroy Swanson, Dec. 30, 1966; children—Shellie Jean, Kimberly Anne, Cynthia Lynn. Cert. paralegal, Calif. State U., 1977. Legal sec. Superior Ct., San Bernardino, Calif., 1958-65; King & Mussell, Attys., San Bernardino, 1965-71, George Starr, Atty., Yucaipa, Calif., 1971-74; probate paralegal William J. Brunick, Atty., Redlands, Calif., 1975—; instr. legal office procedures Crafton Community Coll., Yucaipa, 1977—. Mem. Yucaipa Little Theater, 1973-80. Mem. Nat. Paralegal Assn. (charter). Republican Lutheran. Clubs: Yucaipa Art Assn., Fontana Art Assn., Arlington Art Assn. Avocations: oil painting; hiking; camping. Home: 34033 Nebraska Ln Yucaipa CA 92399 Office: Brunick Pyle Ludvigsen & Murray Attys 215 Cajon Redland CA 92373

SWANSON, MARILYN TOWNSON, retail buyer; b. Fort Oglethorpe, Ga., Jan. 25, 1959; d. Hurshel Milford and Treva Anne (Finch) Townson; m. Charles Strickland Swanson, Apr. 20, 1985. A.A., Am. Coll. Applied Arts, Atlanta, 1979; B.S., U. Tenn., 1983. Sales rep. Lily of France, Atlanta, 1978-79, Givenchy, Atlanta, 1978-79; sales clk. Neiman-Marcus, Atlanta, 1979-80; mgr. Sakowitz, Houston, 1982-83; buyer for mail order Neiman-Marcus, Dallas, 1983—; cons. and lectr. in field. Republican. Episcopalian. Home: 5539 McCommas Blvd Dallas TX 75206 Office: Neiman-Marcus Main at Ervay Dallas TX 75201

SWANSON, MARY CAMILLE STEWART, editor, writer; b. Mpls., Apr. 11, 1933; d. James Jewell and Camille Beatrice (Madden) Stewart; m. Roger Whitten Swanson, Sept. 11, 1954 (div. Apr. 1976); children—Paul Stewart, Susan Marie; m. 2d, John Elbert Zelenka, June 30, 1978. B.A., U. Minn.-Mpls., 1954, M.A., 1970, Ph.D. in English, 1977; postgrad. Oxford U. (Eng.), summer 1976. Editor, Sun Newspapers, Mpls., 1976-77; teaching assoc. U. Minn.-Mpls., 1977-79; sr. editor Golle & Holmes Fin. Learning Inc., Minnetonka, Minn., 1979-84; freelance editor, writer, Washington, 1984-85. Author: FLS Financial Writing Guide: A Manual of Style for the Securities Industry, 1982; also articles; editor: Securities Basic Study Course, 30 vols., 1979-83; FLS Blue-Sky Guide, 1979; Securities Selling Skills, 1980; Financial Planning Skills, 1981; Securities Prospecting, 1981; Operations Certification, 1983; Series 6 Plus, 1983, Series 22 Plus, 1983. Home: 1 East Pleasant Lake Rd North Oaks MN 55110

SWANSON, NORMA LEE, quality assurance administrator; b. Kokomo, Ind., May 10, 1934; adopted d. Roy and Lora E. (Ewer) Hupp; m. Ray A. Swanson, Nov. 1, 1952 (div. Nov. 1972); children—Michael, Patrick, Lisa, Kelly. B.S. in Mgmt., St. Mary-of-the-Woods Coll., 1987. Nursing staff hosps. in Ill., 1952, 54, med. records adminstr., Ill., Iowa, 1964-77; med. records adminstr. and instrs. hosps. in Saudi Arabia, 1977-80; quality assurance coordinator VA, Murfreesboro, Tenn., 1980-83, hosps. in Tabuk, Saudi Arabia, 1983-84; health systems specialist VA Med. Ctr., Marion, Ind., 1984—; cons. Author: Adventures of Lee Kelly, 1976; profl. articles. Mem. Am. Med. Record Assn., Illowa Med. Record Assn. (pres. 1975-77), Iowa Med. Record Assn. (program chair 1975-76), Nat. Assn. Quality Assurance Profls., Nat. Assn. Female Execs. Club: Altrusa. Office: VA Med Ctr 38th St Marion IN 46952

SWANSON, ROCHELLE ANITA, recreation coordinator; b. Kenmare, N.D., Apr. 16, 1949; d. Arthur Reuben and Verna Waneta (Nederbo) S.; student Phoenix Coll., 1968-69; B.S. in Public Adminstrn., U. Ariz., 1971; postgrad. U. So. Calif., 1972. Recreation specialist Los Angeles County Parks and Recreation, 1974-82; program coordinator ARCO Jesse Owens Games, Los Angeles, 1982-84; pres. Promotional Cons. Services, Glendale, Calif., 1984—; lectr. Calif. State U., Northridge, 1981; cons. Fountain Valley Parks and Recreation, 1979; coordinator, computer specialist Calif. Spl. Olympics Gymnastics, 1972-82, tng. coordinator Orange County Spl. Olympics, 1983-85, track and field coordinator, 1983-86, gymnastics coordinator, 1986. Calif. bowling state handicapper Assn. for Retarded Citizens, 1979-82, dist. IX bowling chmn., 1978—; youth adv. com. Nat. Youth Sports Program, U. So. Calif., 1977—; pres. bd. 1st Luth. Day Sch., 1983-84; mem. council 1st Luth. Glendale Ch., pres., 1986. Registered recreation therapist. Mem. Calif. Parks and Recreation Soc. (dist. XIII sec., therapeutic sect., awards chmn., dep. dir., ways and means chmn.), Chi Kappa Rho (scholarship chmn. Alpha chpt.). Republican. Lutheran. Clubs: Wildcat (U. Ariz.), Sons of Norway (cultural dir. Edvard Grieg Lodge), Vasa Lodge. Contbr. article in field to publ. Home and office: 1756 N Verdugo Rd Apt 22 Glendale CA 91208

SWANSON, SHARON LOUISE, school nurse; b. Erie, Kans., Dec. 5, 1942; d. Otis Benton and Ruth Louise (George) Brasier; m. Larry Virgil Swanson, June 6, 1965; children—Larry Albert Benton, Todd Allen, Sharese Louise. Student Chanute Jr. Coll., 1960-61; B.S.N., U. Kans., 1964. Staff nurse Kans. U. Med. Ctr., Kansas City, 1964-65, 75-81, practical nurse instr., 1966-68; coordinator mothers day out Overland Park Christian Ch., Overland Park, Kans., 1973-74; office nurse Benjamin F. Hard, Prairie Villae, Kans., 1974-79; sch. nurse Shawnee Mission Public Schs. #512, Kans., 1979—. Pres., PTA West Antioch, Merriam, Kans., 1975-76, 76-77; den mother Cub Scouts, 1976; pres. Antioch Presch. PTA, 1973-74, Milburn Jr. High Sch., 1981-82, Shawnee Mission North Patrons Art Gallery, Mission, Kans., 1985—. Am. Legion scholar, 1960. Mem. Nat. Assn. Sch. Nurses, Kans. Assn. Sch. Nurses, Kans. Assn. Sch. Health, U. Kans. Alumni, Kans. U. Nursing Alumni (bd. dirs. 1976-77), Phi Kappa Phi. Democrat. Avocations: Boating; reading; gardening; bridge; travel. Home: 10112 W 70th St Merriam KS 66203 Office: Flint Elemn Sch 5705 Flint St Shawnee KS 66203

SWANSTROM, KATHRYN RAYMOND, convention management executive; b. Milw., Sept. 5, 1907; d. William Hyland and Jessie Viola (Bliss) Raymond; student Bryant and Stratton Bus. Coll., 1927-28; m. Luther D. Swanstrom, Aug. 27, 1937; 1 son, William Hyland Raymond. Caterer, Racine, Wis., 1926; field rep., asst. mgr. Master Reporting Co., 1936-52; dir., sec. Diesel-Ritter Corp., 1942-46; pres. Kay C. Raymond Assos., 1952—; v.p., treas. Kenneth G. Mackenzie Assos., 1954—. Asst. sec. nat. com. U.S.A. 3d World Petroleum Congress, 1950-51. Sec. Ridge Civic Council, 1940-69, Police Traffic Safety Com.; state chmn. legislation Ill. Congress Parents and Tchrs. Rep. Ill. Central Republican party committeewoman, 1938-44; asst. ofcl. reporter Rep. Nat. Conv., 1940-48. Mem. Anti-Cruelty Soc., AIM, Soc. Mayflower Descs. (dep. gov.-gen.), DAR, Nat. Geog. Soc., ASTM, Ladies Oriental Shrine N.Am. Founders, Patriots and Aux. Ancient Honorable Arty. Co. of Boston (nat. treas. 1971-77, nat. pres. 1977-80), John Alden Kindred, Colonial Dames Am., Daus. of Colonial War (organizing sec. 1983—), Magna Charta Dames, Internat. Platform Assn., Hugenot Soc. (1st v.p. gen. 1975-79, pres. gen. 1979-83), Sons and Daus. of Pilgrims (organizing sec. gen. 1975—), Ams. of Armorial Ancestry (1st v.p.), Pi Omicron (nat. pres. 1950-54). Episcopalian. Clubs: Beverly Hills, Woman's Crescendo. Address: 9027 S Damen Ave Chicago IL 60620 also 3 Old Hill Farms Rd Westport CT 06880

SWANT, JOSANNE GLASS, employee relations manager; b. Bangor, Maine, Feb. 4, 1956; d. William Howard and Beatriz Alicia (Ruiz de Zuniga) Glass; m. Mark Allen Swant, Aug. 25, 1979. A.A., DeAnza Community Coll., 1975; B.A. in Sociology, Calif. State U.-Chico, 1978, B.A. in Psychology, 1978. Youth counselor Alum Rock Sch. Dist., San Jose, Calif., 1978, Teen Enrichment, Inc., Milpitas, Calif., 1978-79; mgmt. rep. McKellard & Assocs., Menlo Park, Calif., 1979; benefits coordinator Utah Bancorp., Salt Lake City, 1979-80; employee relations mgr. Nat. Semiconductor Corp., West Jordan, Utah, 1980—; counselor Social Advocates for Youth, Mountain View, Calif., 1978-79, Suicide and Crisis Intervention, San Jose, Calif., 1977-79; advisor, cons. Sandy City (Utah) Personnel Bd., 1981-83. Mem. Am. Soc. Personnel Adminstrn., Utah Personnel Assn., Utah Assn. Employee Assistance Programs. Office: Nat Semiconductor Corp 3333 W 9000 S West Jordan UT 84084

SWART, SALLY ANN, insurance company executive; b. Jackson, Mich., July 9, 1947; d. Edwin Jay and Betty Mary (Elmer) Lane; m. Jay P. Lepert, Aug. 16, 1969 (div. Aug. 1970); m. Kenneth D. Swart, Apr. 25, 1981. Cert. gen. ins. Ins. Inst. Am., 1972; B.A., Western Mich. U., 1969; postgrad. Aquinas Coll., Grand Rapids, Mich., 1985—. Claims rep. Md. Casualty Co., Bloomfield Hills, Mich., 1970-76; comml. lines rep. Campbell Agy., Grand Rapids, Mich., 1976-80, Poggi Harrison Agy., Grand Rapids, 1980-82; property-casualty underwriting supr. Benson Ins. Co., Naples, Fla., 1981-82; rate, issue supr. Am. Bankers Ins. Co., Miami, Fla., 1982-84; bus. analyst Foremost Inst. Co., Grand Rapids, 1984-86; comml. rating supr. Foremost Ins. Co., 1986—. Writer newsletters DeKoven Found., 1980. Intake counselor Women's Resource Ctr., Grand Rapids, 1977-80; assoc. mem. Community of St. Mary, Racine, Wis., 1979—. Episcopalian. Avocation: reading. Home: 2620 Ridgecroft SE Grand Rapids MI 49506 Office: Foremost Ins Co PO Box 3333 Grand Rapids MI 49501

SWARTOUT, JEAN ANN, travel agency executive; b. Catskill, N.Y., Feb. 28, 1945; d. Charles Richard and Vera Mildred (Bower) S. Cert. travel cons. Inst. Cert. Travel Agts. Clk., W.T. Grant Co., Albany, N.Y., 1962-63; mail clk. Mchts. Mut. Ins. Co., Albany, 1963-65; bookkeeper Mountain View Coachline, West Coxsackie, N.Y., 1965-73; mgr. Argus Travel, Inc., West Coxsackie, 1973-84; owner, mgr. CountrySide Travel, West Coxsackie, 1984—. Mem. Women In Travel Services, Town and Country Bus. and Profl. Women's Club (2d v.p. Coxsackie 1985—). Roman Catholic. Avocations: music; reading; theatre. Home: 33 Appleblossom Ln West Coxsackie NY 12192 Office: Country Side Travel Route 9-W West Coxsackie NY 12192

SWARTZ, CAROLE BARBARA, travel agent; b. Boston, June 20, 1945; d. William and Bella (Berstein) S. Pres. Great Internat. Travel, Winthrop, Mass., 1975—. Mem. Am. Soc. Travel Agts., Pacific Area Travel Assn. Jewish. Clubs: Women in Travel, (sec. 1981-83), Boston Athletic. Avocations: ski, raquetball, jog. Home: 22 Chestnut Pl Unit 303 Brookline MA 02146 Office: Great Internat Travel 484 Shirley St Winthrop MA 02152

SWARTZ, TERESA ANNE, marketing educator, marketing researcher; b. Port Alleghany, Pa., May 3, 1953; d. Robert Wilson and Geraldine Elizabeth (Hess) S. B.S. in Edn., Clarion State Coll., 1974, M.B.A., 1977; Ph.D. in Bus. Adminstrn., Ohio State U., 1981. Cert. secondary tchr., Pa., High sch. tchr. Bradford Area Schs., Bradford, Pa., 1975-76; grad. asst. Clarion State Coll., Pa., 1976-77; research, teaching assoc., Ohio State U., Columbus, 1977-80; lectr. Ariz. State U., Tempe, 1980-81, asst. prof., 1981—. Mem. Am. Mktg. Assn. (mem. Phoenix bd. dirs. 1982-85, nat. bd. dirs., v.p. elect western region 1985—), Assn. Consumer Research, Am. Acad. Advt., Am. Psychol. Assn. Republican. Avocations: golf; tennis; travel Office: Dept Mktg Ariz State U Tempe AZ 85287

SWARTZBECK, EDNA MARGARET, clinical nurse specialist; b. Greenville, Pa., Oct. 28, 1933; d. Daniel and Helen (Simpson), S. Diploma in Nursing,

Sharon Gen. Hosp., 1954; B.S. in Nursing, U.S.C., 1963, M. Nursing, 1974. Emergency Room nurse Sharon Gen. Hosp., Pa., 1954-56; commd. 2d lt., U.S. Army Nurse Corps, 1956, advanced through grades to col., 1977; staff nurse, head nurse U.S. Army Nurse Corps., Tex., N.Y., S.C., 1956-59; staff nurse VA Med. Ctr., Columbia, S.C., 1960-65, supr. ambulatory care, 1965-74, clin. nurse specialist, 1974—; staff nurse, asst. chief nurse U.S. Army Reserve, Ft. Jackson, S.C., 1960-77; chief nurse U.S. Army Hosp. Reserve Unit, Ft. Jackson, 1977—. Contbr. articles to profl. jours. U.S.C. Edn. Found. fellow, 1974—. Recipient Excellence in Communication award, VA Med. Ctr., 1970, nominated Fed. Employee of Yr., 1979. Mem. Am. Nurses Assn. (cert. geriatric nursing), S.C. Nurses Assn. (Excellence in Practice award 1982), Res. Officers Assn., U.S.C. Alumni Assn., Sigma Theta Tau. Lutheran. Lodge: Order Eastern Star. Avocations: golf, fishing, gardening, travel. Home: 19 Churchill Circle Columbia SC 29206 Office: VA Med Ctr Columbia SC 29201

SWAYNE, MARGARET MARY, nurse; b. N.Y.C., May 19, 1960; d. Ronald Anthony Swayne and Mary Patricia (Fallon) Giorlando. B.S. in Nursing summa cum laude, Hunter-Bellevue Sch. Nursing; postgrad. Wagner Coll. Lic. R.N., N.Y.; cert. in med.-surg. nursing. Youth worker U.S. Youth Corps, S.I., N.Y., 1975-76; bookkeeper J.B. Jackway, P.C., S.I., 1976-78; computer operator Caltex, Inc., N.Y.C., 1982-83; nurse's aid USPHS Hosp., S.I., 1980-82; registered nurse S.I. Hosp., 1982—, mem. utilization rev. com., 1982-83, preceptor for students, 1983—, mem. DRG com., 1985. Mem. Am. Nurses Assn., Am. Nurses Found., Student Nurses Assn. (v.p. 1981-82), Sigma Theta Tau. Republican. Roman Catholic. Avocations: Writing; running; sewing; designing and making furniture. Home: 455 Stobe Ave Staten Island NY 10306 Office: Staten Island Hosp 475 Seaview Ave Staten Island NY 10306

SWAZEY, JUDITH POUND, institute president; b. Bronxville, N.Y., Apr. 21, 1939; d. Robert Earl and Louise Titus (Hanson) Pound; A.B. (scholar), Wellesley Coll., 1961; Ph.D. (Wellesley Coll. Alumnae fellow, NIH predoctoral fellow, Radcliffe Coll. grad. fellow), Harvard U., 1966; m. Peter Woodman Swazey, Nov. 28, 1964; children—Elizabeth, Peter. Research assoc. Harvard U., 1966-71, lectr., 1969-71, research fellow, 1971-72; cons. com. brain scis. Nat. Research Council, 1971-73; staff scientist MIT Neuroscis. Research Program, 1973-74; prof. history Boston U., 1974-80, assoc. prof. dept. socio-med. scis. and community medicine, 1974-77, prof., 1977-80, adj. prof., 1980—; exec. dir. Medicine in the Public Interest, Inc., Boston and Washington, 1979-82, now mem. bd. dirs.; pres. Coll. of the Atlantic, Bar Harbor, Maine, 1982-84; pres. Acadia Inst., Bar Harbor, 1984—; dir. Center for Drug Devel. Fellow Inst. Soc., Ethics and Life Scis. (v.p. 1980); mem. Inst. Medicine, Nat. Acad. Scis., AAAS, Sherrington Soc., Soc. Health and Human Values, Phi Beta Kappa, Sigma Xi (bd. dirs.). Author: Reflexes and Motor Integration, the Development of Sherrington's Integrative Action Concept, 1969; (with others) Human Aspects of Biomedical Innovation, 1971; (with R.C. Fox) The Courage to Fail, a Social View of Organ Transplants and Hemodialysis (hon. mention Am. Med. Writers Assn. 1975, C. Wright Mills award Am. Sociol. Assn. 1975), rev. edit., 1978; Chlorpromazine in Psychiatry, a Study of Therapeutic Innovation, 1974; (with K. Reeds) Today's Medicine, Tomorrow's Science, Essays on Paths of Discovery in the Biomedical Sciences, 1978; with Hignsom, Scotch, Sorenson) In Sickness and in Health: Social Dimensions of Medical Care, 1981; (with Sorenson and Scotch) Reproductive Past, Reproductive Futures: Genetic Counseling and Its Effectiveness, 1982; editor: (with C. Wong) Dilemmas of Dying, Policies and Procedures for Decisions Not to Treat, 1981; (with F. Worden and G. Adelman) The Neurosciences: Paths of Discovery, 1975; (with A. Doudera) Refusing Treatment in Mental Health Institutions; (with S. Scher) Whistleblowing in Biomedical Research, 1982, Social Controls and the Medical Profession, 1984; contbr. articles to profl. jours.; asso. editor IRB: A Jour. of Human Subjects Research, 1979—; editorial bd. Bioethics Quar., 1981-83. Office: The Acadia Institute 118 West St Bar Harbor ME 04609

SWEARINGEN, CAROL CANFIELD, accountant; b. Wichita, Sept. 1, 1944; d. Charles Calvin and Arlee Jeanne (Featherston) Canfield; children—Gretchen Christine, Jeffrey Blair; m. Robert Goodwin Swearingen, Sept. 13, 1980; 1 dau., Ashley Brooks; stepchildren—Andrew McCraw, Benjamin Patrick. Student U. Ottawa (Ont.), 1961 63, Cambridge (Eng.) U., 1968 70; B.S., 1971; postgrad. Tex. Tech. U., 1978, Rice U., 1984. Lic. pvt. pilot. Analyst, Seiscom-Delta Co., 1974-75; research asst. Alaska Interstate, 1975-76; asst. controller Dan-Tex Internat., 1977-79; controller Levering & Reid, 1980-81; pres. Canfield-Swearingen, 1982—, (all Houston); pres. Canfield Aviation, Inc. Mem. Nat. Women's Conf., Houston, 1977; violinist The Chamber Group, The Houston Symphonetta; mem. Bd. Adjustment, Hedwig Village. Republican. Episcopalian. Home: 11774 Duart St Houston TX 77024 Office: 800 Gessner Suite 170 Houston TX 77024

SWECKER, ELIZABETH HINER, educational administrator, county official; b. Monterey, Va., Dec. 14, 1933; d. Gideon Jesse and Eunice Brown (Lightner) Hiner; m. Robert T. Swecker, Oct. 26, 1957 (div. Oct. 1978); children—Kimberly Brown, Jesse Jennings. Student William and Mary Coll., 1952-53, Strayer Bus. Coll., Washington, 1953-54; B.S. in Edn., James Madison U., Harrisonburg, Va., 1965, M.S. in Edn., 1969. Lic. profl. tchr., Va. Asst. registrar Madison Coll., Harrisonburg, 1969-72; counselor, tchr. Elkton High Sch., Va., 1974-77; counselor, tchr. Highland High Sch., Monterey, 1977-84, prin., 1984—. County supr. Highland County, Monterey, 1979—; mem., sec. Central Shenandoah Valley Planning Commn., Staunton, Va., 1983—. Mem. Va. Assn. of Counties, Va. Assn. Secondary Sch. Prins., Central Valley Counselors Assn. Methodist. Home: Star Route C Box 5 Monterey VA 24465 Office: Highland High Sch PO Box 430 Monterey VA 24465

SWEEN, JOYCE ANN, sociologist, psychologist; b. N.Y.C.; d. Sigfried Joseph and Julie (Hollins) Ellmer; B.S. in Math., Antioch Coll., 1960; M.S. in Exptl. Psychology, Northwestern U., 1965, Ph.D. in Social Psychology/Evaluation Research, 1971; children—Terri Lynn, James Michael. Univ. fellow Northwestern U., Evanston, Ill., 1960-63, dir. computer ops. Inst. Met. Studies, Northwestern U., 1965-70; asst. prof. sociology DePaul U., Chgo., 1971-74, assoc. prof., 1974-80, prof., 1980-83, prof. sociology and pub. service, 1983—; cons. Nat. Commn. on Violence, 1968; cons. in field. NIH grantee, 1971-75, 78-81; NSF grantee, 1979-82. Mem. Internat. Sociol. Assn., Am. Sociol. Assn., Am. Psychol. Assn., Midwest Sociol. Soc., Sociologists for Women in Soc., AAAS, Sigma Xi. Research, publs. on fertility, African polygyny, childlessness, urbanization, social effects of assassination, evaluation methodology, bilingual education. Office: Dept Sociology DePaul U 2323 N Seminary Ave Chicago IL 60614

SWEENEY, EMILY MARGARET, lawyer; b. Cleve., May 2, 1948; d. Mark Elliot and Neydra (Ginsburg) Mirsky; m. Patrick Anthony Sweeney, Dec. 30, 1983; 1 child, Maryanne Anne. B.A., Case Western Res. U., 1970; J.D., Cleve. Marshall Coll. Law, 1981. Bar: Ohio 1981. Tchr. English, Cleve. Pub. Schs., 1970; plant mgr. Union Gospel Press Pub. Co., Cleve., 1971-73; publ. specialist Cleve. State U., 1973-82; asst. U.S. atty. Dept. Justice, Cleve., 1982—. Precinct committeeman, Woodmere, Ohio, 1978; mem. candidates scanning com. Citizens League Greater Cleve., 1982; subcom. chmn. St. Vincent Charity Hosp. Benefit, 1983; com. mem. Gourmet Gala of March of Dimes, Cleve., 1983. Recipient Eddy award for graphic design, 1977; Spl. Achievement award U.S. Dept. Justice, 1985. Mem. Fed. Bar Assn., ABA, Ohio Bar Assn. Democrat. Office: US Attorneys Office 1404 E 9th St Suite 500 Cleveland OH 44114

SWEENEY, ERMENGARDE COLLINS, horse breeder; b. Falfurrias, Tex., Nov. 3, 1922; d. John and Ophelia (Fant) Sweeney; m. William Wallace Walton, Jr., Nov. 8, 1940 (div. 1972); children—William Walton III, Ermengarde Walton, Julia Walton. Student, Tex. Sch. Fine Arts, 1939-40. Horse breeder, exhibitor, Corpus Christi and Helotes, Tex., 1956—; pres. Paws Gulf Coast Humane Soc., Corpus Christi, 1978-86; lectr. in field. Bd. dirs., dir. region 5 of Tex. Human Info. Network, 1978-81. Mem. Arabian Horse Club of Am. Republican. Club: Corpus Christi Town. Contbr. to Arabian Horse Jour. in Eng. Address: 3461 Floyd St Corpus Christi TX 78411

SWEENEY, ERNESTINE KAY, nurse; b. Savannah, Ga., Oct. 26, 1959; d. James William and Jane Catherine (Brewer) S.; m. John Earl Foshee, Feb. 12, 1983. A.D. in Nursing Sci., Northwestern State U., Shreveport, La., 1982. R.N., La. Dental asst. Barksdale AFB, Bossier City, La., 1978-79; nurse Bossier Med. Ctr., 1982—. State officer Internat. Order Rainbow for Girls, 1977-80; vol. La. State Spl. Olympics, Bossier City, 1977-78. Mem. NOW. Democrat. Roman Catholic. Home: 3314 Schuler Dr Bossier City LA 71111 Office: Bossier Med Ctr 200 E 2105 Airline Dr Bossier City LA 71111

SWEENEY, JOYCE KAY, writer; b. Dayton, Ohio, Nov. 9, 1955; d. Paul Harris and Emma Catharine (Spoon) Hegenbarth; m. Jay S. Sweeney, Sept. 20, 1979. B.A. summa cum laude, Wright State U., 1977; postgrad. Ohio U., 1978. Teaching asst. Ohio U., Athens, 1978; copywriter Philip Office & Assocs., Dayton, 1978, Rikes Dept. Store, Dayton, 1978-80; workshop leader Cultural Affairs Dept., Ormond Beach, Fla., 1985. Author: (novel) Center Line, 1984 (Delacorte Press prize for outstanding first young adult novel 1983); also short stories, including Raindance (Playgirl's first ann. coll. fiction competition winner 1976). Office: care Marcia Amsterdam 41 W 82d St New York NY 10024

SWEENEY, JULIA, public relations executive; b. Ladonia, Tex., Feb. 2, 1927; d. Albert Earle and Julia (Nunn) S. Grad. Am. Acad., N.Y.C., 1946; student So. Meth. U., 1958-59. Asst. mgr. Ambrosia House, Milw., 1951-56; sec. Neiman-Marcus, Dallas, 1956-70, publicity dir., 1970-74; columnist, feature writer Dallas Times Herald, 1974-81; pres. Callas, Foster & Sweeney, Dallas, 1982—. Bd. dirs. TACA, Dallas Opera Women's Bd., Susan G. Koman Found. for Cancer Research, Boys' Clubs Dallas, Inc.; bd. dirs., 1st v.p. Friends of Dallas Pub. Library; trustee Protection of Animal World Soc.; mem. March of Dimes Women's Aux., Dallas Theater Ctr. Women's Com.; mem. Southwestern hospitality bd. Met. Opera; mem. Dallas Ballet Women's Com. Mem. Dallas C. of C., Dallas Symphony Orch. League, Dallas Mus. Art League, Dallas County Heritage Soc., Charter 100. Episcopalian. Home: Terrace House 3131 Maple Ave Apt 11B Dallas TX 75201 Office: Callas Foster & Sweeney 2515 McKinney Ave Dallas TX 75201

SWEET, DEE (MRS. HERBERT A. SWEET), business executive; b. Muskogee, Okla., June 3, 1913; d. Walter Oliver and Lola R. (Morris) McDaniel; student Butler U., 1931, 33, summer sch. Oxford U.; m. Herbert A. Sweet, Aug. 28, 1935; children—Judee Lo, Jill B. Sweet Bowles. Asst. to interior decorator L.S. Ayres & Co., Indpls., 1930-33; co-dir. Acorn Farm Camp, Carmel, Ind., 1933-77; owner Acorn Farm Antiques, Carmel, 1960—, Acorn Farm Workshops, 1972—; dir. TV programs WFBM, Indpls., 1949-54, WISH, Indpls., 1955-60; lectr. adult edn. Ind. U., Purdue U. Co-author 2 Try It books for children. Mem. Appraisers Assn. Am. (sr.), Appraisers Soc. Am. (sr.), Antique Dealers Am., Am. Camping Assn., Am. Women in Radio and TV, Ind. Hist. Soc., C. of C., Asso. Antique Dealers Am. Author newspaper column Ind. Soc. Auctioneers. Home: 15466 Oak Rd Carmel IN 46032

SWEET, MARTHA HERBERT, management consultant; b. San Francisco, Oct. 21, 1949; d. Charles Aldrich and Elizabeth (Herbert) S.; student U. Calif.-Davis, 1967-69; B.S. in Bus. Mgmt., Pepperdine U., 1979. Personnel supr. Calif. Canners & Growers, San Francisco, 1971-74; employee relations and compensation mgr. Xerox Corp., El Segundo, Calif., 1974-84; human resource mgmt. cons., 1984—. Republican. Episcopalian. Home and Office: 2603 Dove Creek Ln Carrollton TX 75006

SWEET, PATRICIA MAYER, small business executive, consultant; b. Paris, Tex., Sept. 3, 1944; d. Edward and Claire Dorothy (Gade) Mayer; m. David Charles Sweet, July 3, 1965; children—Britton David, Melissa Mayer, Marc Edward, Kathryn Patricia. B.A., U. Okla., 1968. Field coordinator Franklin County Democratic Party, Columbus, Ohio, 1976-77, exec. dir., 1977-78; exec. dir. Ednl. Fund LWV of Cleve., 1980—, pres. SPD, Inc., Cleveland Heights, Ohio, 1983—; caseworker Franklin County Children's Services, 1966-67. Mng. editor: The Youth Vote: The Registration and Voting Patterns of Youth Since the Passage of the 26th Admendment, 1984; New Voters Guide to Practical Politics, 1982; project mgr.: A Citizen's Guide to Cleveland, 1984. Mem. WomenSpace, Cleve., 1981-86, Heights Community Congress, 1979-86, Citizens' League, Cleve., 1986; campaign coordinator Metzenbaum for Senate, Columbus, 1976; vol. coordinator Rosemond for Mayor, Columbus, 1974, Ohioans for Gov. Gilligan, Columbus, 1974. Mem. Alpha Gamma Delta (Arc of Epsilon Pi). Lutheran. Clubs: City (Cleve.); Severance Athletic (Cleveland Heights). Home: 1210 Oakridge Dr Cleveland Heights OH 44121

SWEETING, LECIA G., marketing analyst, programmer, speech writer; b. Seattle, Nov. 6, 1953; d. Fester Richard Thurston and Lucille Frances (Smith) Cole; m. Stephen Gregory Sweeting, July 3, 1974; children—Stephen Gregory, Christina Marie. Student U. Mich., 1971-73. Statistician, U. Mich. Basketball, Ann Arbor, 1972-74; dance instr. King High Sch., Detroit, 1972; tech. rep. Xerox, Southfield, Mich., 1974-79; data systems analyst Michigan Bell, Southfield, 1979-85, mktg. analyst, 1985—; news broadcaster sta. WDET-FM, 1979—. Author editor newsletter: News for Liberty, 1983; author ednl. game: Bible Pyramid, 1978. Lectr. Am. Cancer Soc., Southfield, 1980—; sign lang. interpreter Bethlehem Temple Ch., Brightmoor Tabernacle, 1982-85; vice chmn. bd. dirs. Nat. Amyotrophic Lateral Sclerosis Assn., Mich., 1985. Recipient Good Citizens award, Mich. Bell Telephone, 1984, Scruggs-Patrick Trailblazer award, 1985. Mem. Engring. Soc. Detroit (sci. fair mgr. West Side Schs., 1980, co-dir. judging sci. fair 1985—, civic affairs com. 1985—). Democrat. Avocation: reading. Office: Michigan Bell Telephone 16025 Northland Dr Room 150 Southfield MI 48075

SWEETING, LINDA MARIE, chemistry educator; b. Toronto, Ont., Can., Dec. 11, 1941; came to U.S., 1965, naturalized, 1979; d. Stanley H. and Mary (Robertson) S.; B.Sc., U. Toronto, 1964, M.A., 1965; Ph.D., UCLA, 1969. Asst. prof. chemistry Occidental Coll., Los Angeles, 1969-70; asst. prof. chemistry Towson (Md.) State U., 1970-75, assoc. prof., 1975-85, prof., 1985—; guest worker NIH, 1976-77; program dir. chem. instrumentation NSF, 1981-82; vis. scholar Harvard U., 1984-85. Bd. dirs. Chamber Music Soc. Balt. Mem. Md. Acad. Scis. (mem. sci. council 1975-83), Assn. for Women in Sci. (treas. 1977-78), Am. Chem. Soc. (mem. women chemists Com. 1983—), AAAS, Sierra Club, Wilderness Soc., Sigma Xi (sec. TSU Club 1979-81). Office: Dept Chemistry Towson State U Baltimore MD 21204

SWEETLAND, KAREN ELIZABETH, marketing consultant, editor; b. Portland, Oreg., July 31, 1941; d. Earle E. and Daisy E. (Cline) S.; 1 son, Craig. Student, Shreveport (La.) pub. schs. Stewardess Eastern Airlines, N.Y.C., 1963-65; aide Congressman R.J. Corbett, Washington, 1965-66; sales promotion staff 3M Co., Los Angeles, 1968-69; dir. mil. sales Prince Matchabelli Co., Los Angeles, N.Y.C., 1969-71; membership mgr., news dir. San Francisco Conv. and Visitors Bur., 1971-73; dir. pub. relations Fairmont Hotel Corp., San Francisco, 1974-75; owner, mgr. Southwick Agy., San Francisco, 1975-76; pres. Creative Concepts Unlimited, San Francisco, 1979-83; editor-in-chief Bohn & Bland Pubs. Inc., Burlingame, Calif., 1983—; mktg. cons., writer. Recipient Appreciation awards Big Bros. of San Francisco, Jr. C. of C., 1982. Clubs: San Francisco Ad, Commonwealth, San Francisco. Republican. Contbr. articles to profl. and popular mags.

SWEGEL, DOROTHY, personnel service executive; b. Forest City, Pa., Dec. 23, 1932; d. John J. and Anna T. (Loush) S.; student Chestnut Hill Coll., Phila., 1950-51. Periodicals librarian Charles M. Schwab Meml. Library, Bethlehem (Pa.) Steel Co., 1952-55; with spl. sales Nat. Airlines, Miami, Fla., 1955-58; sr. supr. TWA Ambassadors Club, Kennedy Airport, Jamaica, N.Y., 1959-66; pres. CoverTemp Inc., Gateway Careers, Inc., Word Pro Center, White Plains, N.Y., 1969—; dir. Gerber Life Ins. Co.; del. White House Conf. on Small Bus., 1986. Bd. dirs. United Way of Westchester, Pvt. Industry Council; pres. Westchester Council for Arts; assoc. dir. White Plains Beautification Found.; del. White House Conf. on Small Bus., 1986. Mem. Adminstrv. Mgmt. Soc. (dir.), New Rochelle C. of C., Westchester Women Bus. Owners Assn., County C. of C. (dir.), Westchester County Assn. (dir.), Sales and Mktg. Execs. of Westchester (dir., v.p.), Soroptimist Internat. (dir. Central Westchester). Republican. Roman Catholic. Office: 235 Main St White Plains NY 10601

SWENSON, GAY LEAH, consulting psychologist, educator; b. St. Paul, Jan. 21, 1936; d. Robert and Sarah Winifred (Gridley) Fisher; Diplôme Supérieure avec honneurs, Sorbonne, Paris, 1960; B.A. cum laude, U. Calif., Berkeley, 1958; M.A., San Francisco State U., 1966; Ph.D., Union Grad. Sch., 1977. Tchr., Aragon High Sch., San Mateo, Calif., 1966-73; human relations trainer/facilitator Coll. of San Mateo, 1971-73; founder Women's Center, La Jolla, Calif., 1973-77; founder, dir. Living Now Inst. of Center for Studies of the Person, La Jolla, 1977—, Inst. Person-Centered Approaches to Peace, 1984—; internat. cons. in field; lectr. in field. Mem. Belmont City Fair Housing Commn., 1965-69, San Mateo County Human Rights Commn., 1967-69; mem. Community Congress of San Diego, 1978, San Diego County Regional Consortium on Aging, 1975-77, Common Cause, 1980—. Mem. ACLU, AAUW, NOW, Psychologists for Social Responsibility, Podium, Assn. for Humanistic Psychology, Alpha Omicron Pi. Democrat. Club: Charter 100. Contbr. articles to profl. jours. Office: 1125 Torrey Pines Rd La Jolla CA 92037

SWENSON, MAY, poet; b. Logan, Utah, May 28, 1919; d. Dan Arthur and Margaret (Hellberg) S.; B.S., Utah State U. Editor New Directions Press, 1959-66; poet-in-residence Purdue U., Lafayette, Ind., 1966-67, U. N.C., Greensboro, 1968-69, 75, Lethbridge U., Alta., Can., 1970, U. Calif., Riverside, 1973; Phi Beta Kappa poet Harvard U., 1982; Hurst prof. Washington U., St. Louis, 1982; mem. staff Breadloaf Writers Conf., 1976. Author: Another Animal, 1954; A Cage of Spines, 1958; To Mix with Time, 1963; Poems to Solve, 1966; Half Sun Half Sleep, 1967; Iconographs, 1970; More Poems to Solve, 1971; (translated from Swedish) Windows & Stones (Tomas Tranströmer), 1972; The Guess and Spell Coloring Book, 1976; New and Selected Things Taking Place, 1978. Recipient Nat. Inst. Arts and Letters award, 1960; Brandeis U. award, 1967; Disting. Service Gold medal Utah State U., 1967; Shelley Meml. award Poetry Soc. Am., 1968; Bollingen prize in poetry Yale U., 1981; Golden Rose award New Eng. Poetry Club, 1984; Guggenheim fellow, 1959; Amy Lowell Travelling scholar, 1960; Ford Found. fellow, 1965; Rockefeller Found. fellow, 1967-68, Lucy Martin Donnally fellow Bryn Mawr Coll., 1968-69; Nat. Endowment for Arts grantee, 1974. Fellow Acad. Am. Poets (chancellor 1980); mem. Am. Acad. and Inst. Arts and Letters. Home: 73 Boulevard Sea Cliff NY 11579

SWENT, MARGARET PAGE, community and health nurse; b. Stickney, S.D., Jan. 3, 1922; d. Charles and Marie (Dittman) Page; m. Johnnie Swent, Aug. 21, 1948; children—Cheryl, Milce, Lisa. Diploma, Presentation Order of Nursing, Mitchell, S.D., 1946; workshops, Denver, Kansas City, Kans.; cert. community health nurse, S.D. Nurse, Doctor's Hosp., Seattle, 1946-48, Utah County Hosp., Provo, 1948-49, Utah County Infirmary, 1950, Deaconess Hosp., Spokane, Wash., 1950-52, St. Joseph Hosp., Mitchell, S.D., 1952, Douglas County Meml. Hosp., Armour, S.D., 1953-70; head nurse Farmers State Bank, Stickney, S.D., 1968-70; community health nurse Aurora County, S.D., 1971—; initiator program Tri-County Health Inc., 1975-83, bd. dirs. Dist. III Planning Bd., 1979-83. Mem. Am. Nurses Assn. Office: County Courthouse Box 502 Plankinton SD 57368

SWERGOLD, MARCELLE MIRIAM, sculptor; b. Antwerp, Belgium, Sept. 6, 1927; came to U.S., 1939, naturalized, 1947; d. Gillel and Sarah (Matuzewitz) Elfenbein; student NYU, Art Students League, Sculptors Workshop; m. Maurice Swergold, June 12, 1949; children—Diane Botnick, Henry, Gary Swergold, Paul Kogan, George Kogan. Sculptor, 1965—; one-woman exhbns. include: Studio 12, N.Y.C., 1980, 82, Nat. Fedn. Temple Sisterhoods, 1984; group exhbns. include Farleigh Dickinson U., Teaneck, N.J., 1972, Audubon Artist Ann., N.Y.C., 1978-86, Internat. Treasury Fine Arts, Plainview, N.Y., 1979, New Britain (Conn.) Mus., 1980, also Cork Gallery, Lincoln Center, N.Y.C., Allied Artists Nat. Acad. Galleries, N.Y.C., U.S. Custom House, N.Y.C., others; represented in permanent collection New Britain Mus. Am. Art. Recipient Best in Show award for Tetons, Women's Art Gallery, N.Y.C., 1977; 1st prize S.L. Richter Assn. for Arts, Danbury, Conn., 1985; Vincent Glinsky meml. award Audubon Artists, 1986. Mem. N.Y. Soc. Women Artists (pres. 1979-81, exec. v.p. 1981—), Artists Equity, Contemporary Artists Guild. Jewish. Home: 450 West End Ave New York NY 10024 Studio: 246 W 80th St New York NY 10024

SWIBOLD, GRETCHEN ANN, librarian, author; b. Holland, Mich., May 3, 1933; d. Jan D. and Margaret Ann (Raak) Vanderploeg; m. Richard Edward Swibold, Aug. 15, 1955; children—Katharine Margaret, Edward Jan. A.B., Bryn Mawr Coll., 1955; postgrad. U. Ill.-Urbana, 1958-59; M.S., So. Conn. State Coll., 1970; postgrad. Central Conn. State Coll., 1973-82. Editorial asst. Our Wonderful World, Urbana, Ill., 1955-57; editor Spencer Press, Urbana, 1957-58; research asst. U. Ill.-Urbana, 1958-59; librarian Yale U. Polit. Sci. Research Library, New Haven, 1967-71; librarian Canton Elem. Schs. (Conn.), 1971—. Editor: Animals in Action, 1958; Rolling Wheels, 1959; contbr. articles to profl. jours. Bd. dirs. Creative Arts Workshop, New Haven, 1967-71; mem. women's com. Yale U. Art Gallery, New Haven, 1967-71; active Democratic Town Com., Canton, Conn., 1973—, Charter Commn., Canton, 1983-84, Canton Creative Arts Council, 1980—; chmn., sec. Bd. Assessors, Canton, 1975-79. Mem. ALA, Conn. Ednl. Media Assn., Nat. Council Tchrs. English, Conn. Edn. Assn., Delta Kappa Gamma. Democrat. Home: 731 Cherry Brook Rd North Canton CT 06059 Office: Canton Middle Sch Dyer Ave Collinsville CT 06022

SWICK, MYRA AGNES, accountant; b. Chgo., Dec. 5, 1945; d. Arthur T. and Marcella M. (Pankiewicz) Swick. B.B.A. cum laude, Loyola U.-Chgo., 1967. C.P.A., Ill. Mem. audit staff Ernst & Ernst, Chgo., 1967-72; controller Shorr Paper Products, Aurora, Ill., 1972-73; audit mgr. Otto Hillsman & Co., Ltd., Chgo., 1973-81; audit mgr. Walton, Joplin, Langer & Co., Chgo., 1981-82, ptnr., 1982—; mem. audit com. Loyola U., Chgo., 1977—. Contbr. articles to profl. jours. Mem. Am. Woman's Soc. C.P.A.s (hon., pres. 1976-77), Chgo. Soc. Women C.P.A.s (founder, dir. 1977-80), Am. Soc. Women Accts. (chpt. pres. 1974-75), Chgo. Fin. Exchange (dir. 1984—), Ill. C.P.A. Soc. (com. mem. 1982-86, task force chair 1985-86, dir. 1986—), Am. Inst. C.P.A.s, Nat. Assn. Accts. (chpt. dir. 1972-74), Nat. Assn. Women Bus. Owners, Beta Alpha Psi, Beta Gamma Sigma. Avocations: travel; reading; crafts. Office: Walton Joplin Langer & Co 55 E Jackson Blvd Chicago IL 60604

SWIFT, EVANGELINE WILSON, lawyer; b. San Antonio, May 2, 1939; d. Raymond E. and Josephine (Woods) Wilson; student So. Methodist U., 1956-59, UCLA, 1959; LL.B., St. Mary's U., 1963; 1 son, Justin Lee. Bar: Tex. 1963, U.S. Ct. Appeals (5th cir.) 1972, D.C. 1976, U.S. Supreme Ct. 1980, U.S. Ct. Appeals (11th cir.) 1981, U.S. Ct. Appeals (10th and D.C. cirs.) 1982, U.S. Ct. Appeals (fed. cir.) 1983. Atty., advisor ICC, 1964-65; staff atty. headstart program OEO, 1965; exec. legal asst. to chmn. and spl. asst. to vice chmn. EEOC, 1965-71, chief decisions div., 1971-75, asst. gen. csl., 1975-76; cons. to sec. Employment Standards Adminstrn., Dept. Labor, Washington, 1977-79; ptnr. firm Swift & Swift, P.C., Washington, 1976-79; gen. counsel Merit Systems Protection Bd., Washington, 1979-86, mng. dir., 1986—; guest lectr. Drake U., U. Pa., M.I.T.; mem. U.S. del. 23d Session of UN Econ. and Social Council Commn. Status of Women, Geneva, 1970. Recipient Fed. Govt. Meritorious Service award, 1967; Fed. Women's award, 1975; Performance award Merit Systems Protection Bd., 1981, 82, 83, 84, 85. Methodist. Office: 1120 Vermont Ave NW Washington DC 20419

SWIFT, RHONDA LOUISE, high school educator, small business consultant; b. Houston, July 21, 1952; d. Archie Swift and Dorothy Nell (Fitzpatrick) Johnson. B.A., Tex. So. U., Houston, 1974, M.A., 1977. Cert. tchr., Tex. Tchr., Aldine Sch. Dist., Houston, 1974—, gifted and talented curriculum developer, 1982, sponsor Literary mag. Nimitz High Sch., 1980—, speech coach Carver High Sch., 1975. Vol., campaign to elect Rodney Ellis to City Council Houston, 1983; orientation coordinator Holman St. Baptist Ch., Houston, 1983—; vol. campaign to elect Anthony Hall for city Council Houston, 1983. Named Tchr. of Month, Aldine Sch. Dist., 1977. Mem. NEA, Tex. State Tchrs. Assn., Nat. Council Tchrs. English. Democrat. Clubs: Houston Urban League, Young Democrats. Office: Nimitz High Sch 2005 W W Thorne St Houston TX 77073

SWIFT, VIRGINIA MAE, electronic cash register and computer company executive; b. Indpls., Feb. 28, 1950; d. Leighton Simieon and Ola Mae (Ray) S. Student DeKalb Coll., 1972-74. Sales mgr. Anker Data Co., Atlanta, 1980-81, Victor Bus. Products Co., Atlanta, 1978-79, 81-82; programmer, mgr. Kingtron Co., Atlanta, 1983-85; programmer, installer TEC Am. Inc., Atlanta, 1985—. Author: Dial Success. Counselor, Long Beach Task Force on Battered Women, NOW, 1976-77, DeKalb County Youth Assistance Program, 1981—, Nat. Com. Prevention Child Abuse, Atlanta, 1983—. Mem. Masters Club, Victor Bus. Products Co., 1978, 79, Sales Support award Kingtron Co., 1982. Mem. Am. Bus. Women's Assn., Nat. Assn. Female Execs. Avocations: photography. Home: 1903 Summerbrook Dr Dunwoody GA 30338 Office: TEC Am Inc 4401-A Bankers Circle Atlanta GA 30360

SWINGLE, ARTICE MAY, educational administrator, special education educator; b. Schenectady, Jan. 28, 1939; d. Arto Webster and Ida Elzada (Gosnell) S.; m. Richard Henry Burke, July 29, 1961 (div. 1973); children—Richard Robert, Daniel Douglas; m. John Joseph Wordin, Dec. 31, 1974. B.S. cum laude, Syracuse U., 1961, M.S., 1963; cert. adminstr. spl. edn. Calif. State U.-Los Angeles, 1976. Lic. marriage, family and child guidance counselor, Calif.; cert. tchr., adminstr., coll.-level instr., Calif.; cert. elem. tchr., spl. edn. tchr., N.Y. Tchr. educable mentally retarded children, chmn. dept. Tully Central Sch., N.Y., 1961-65; therapist, dir. ednl. services Los Angeles Child Achievement Ctr., 1967-70; diagnostic clinic tchr. Diagnostic Sch. for Neurologically Impaired Children So. Calif., Los Angeles, 1970-78; mem. faculty Calif. State U.-Los Angeles, 1974, 77; coordinator spl. services Idaho Falls Sch.

Dist. 91, Idaho, 1977—; regional coordinator spl. needs low-incidence programs, Idaho Falls Sch. Dists. 91, 59, 60, 93, 1982-86; lectr. to various profl. and community groups. Co-author: Development of Ordinal Scales of Non-Culturally Biased Development Diagnostic Instrument, 1976. Chmn. bd. dirs. 1st Congl. Ch., Idaho Falls, 1983-84, moderator, 1984—; cons. Human Relations Ctr., Woodland Hills Congl. Ch., also former trustee; den leader Great Western council Boy Scouts Am., 1961. N.Y. Regents scholar, 1957-61; research grantee U.S. Dept. Edn. and ESEA. Mem. Idaho Falls Weavers and Spinners Guild (chmn. spinning study group 1983-86), Pi Lambda Theta. Republican. Avocations: spinning; fly tying. Home: Route 2 Box 139 Shelley ID 83274 Office: Idaho Falls Sch Dist 91 690 John Adams Pkwy Idaho Falls ID 83401

SWINK, RHONDA LYNN, data processing consultant, software company executive; b. Ft. Dodge, Iowa, Mar. 15, 1954; d. Robert Leo and Donna Jean (Nordstrom) S.; student Calif. State U.-Fresno, 1972-73, Rio Hondo Community Coll., 1973-77, Calif. State U.-Pomona, 1984—; cert. in programming Basic Four Corp., 1975. With Nev. Meats Inc., Las Vegas, 1973; computer operator, collections Monfort Food Distbg. Co., Long Beach, Calif., 1973-75; computer operator, programmer accounts receivable Rod's Food Products, Inc., Los Angeles, 1975-77; data processing mgr., statistician Wilcour Food Products, Inc., Los Angeles, 1977-80; systems analyst Monogram Aerospace Fasteners, City of Commerce, Calif., 1980; pres. owner Basic 4 Software and Ops. Cons., Hacienda Heights, Calif., 1980-83; sr. systems analyst CFS Continental Foodservice, 1983-84; data processing mgr. Transducers, Inc., 1984—. Mem. Data Processing Mgmt. Assn., Nat. Assn. Female Execs., Am. Entrepreneurs Assn., Library Computer and Info. Scis., Am. Mgmt. Assn., Western Basic Four Users Group. Republican. Roman Catholic. Home: 2310 S Stimson Hacienda Heights CA 91745 Office: Cerritos CA 90701

SWINTON, PATRICIA ANN WATERFORD, clinical psychologist; b. Washington, Feb. 19, 1953; d. James Raleigh and Nathalie (Wardy) S. B.S., U. D.C., 1967-70; M.A., Howard U., 1973, Ph.D., 1981; postdoctoral in health services UCLA, 1984—. Counselor, educator D.C. Pub. Sch. System, Washington, 1970-80, sch. psychologist, 1980-82; research and evaluation specialist Howard U., Washington, 1977-80, acad. counselor, 1979-80, research and evaluation specialist, 1981-82; psychology therapist D.C. Gen. Hosp., Washington, 1979-81; clin. staff psychologist Augustus F. Hawkins Mental Health Ctr., Los Angeles, 1983—, asst. ward chief, 1985—; cons. Charles R. Drew Postgrad. Med. Sch., Los Angeles, 1982-84, Child, Youth and Family Services, Los Angeles, 1983-84; curriculum research specialist Computer Assisted Instructional Resources, Carson, Calif., 1983—. Mem. Compton Community Services, Compton Community Coll., Calif., 1983—, Los Angeles Union PTA, 1983—, Long Beach Mental Health Assn., Calif., 1984—. Recipient Recognition award Los Angeles Sentinel, 1983. Mem. Am. Ednl. Research Assn., Am. Personnel and Guidance Assn., Nat. Assn. for Mental Health Specialists, Long Beach Psychol. Assn., Careers in Health, Kappa Delta Pi, Alpha Kappa Alpha (corr. sec. 1968-70). Democrat. Congregationalist. Club: Carson's Women's (Calif.). Avocations: skiing; painting; classical dance; boating; flying. Office: Augustus F Hawkins Mental Health Ctr Martin Luther King Gen Hosp 1720 E 120th St Los Angeles CA 90059

SWISHER, MARILYN THORNE, animal welfare administrator; b. Tampa, Fla.; d. Rufus Allen and Alice Lauretta (Seibold) T.; m. Carl Craik Swisher, July 2, 1954; children—Patricia Alice, Barbara Sue. A.S.N., Orange Meml. Hosp., 1941. 1st pres. bd. Boulder Valley Spay Clinic, Boulder, Colo., 1973-74; exec. dir. Queen City Spay Clinic, Denver, 1976—, Capitol Hill Spay/Neuter Clinic, 1978—, Boulder Spay/Neuter Clinic, 1980—; adviser, Humane Fedn. Wyo., Laramie, 1973—, Hamlett Spay Clinic, Colorado Springs, 1974-78, Colo. Humane Soc., Henderson, 1979—, Pueblo Animal Welfare and Protection Service, 1983—. Mem. Colo. Humane Soc., Animal Rescue and Adoption Service. Republican. Presbyterian. Office: Queen City Spay Clinic 4170 Tennyson St Denver CO 80212

SWISHER, VERNA LOUISE, nursing educator; b. Ridgeway, Pa., July 14, 1937; d. Clifford and Josephine (Hollabaugh) Beck; m. William E. Swisher, May 18, 1957; children—Sharon Louise Cooney, Traci Lynn. R.N., Clearfield Hosp. Sch. Nursing (Pa.), 1960; B.S.N., Pa. State U., 1967; M.Sc. in Nursing, Indiana U. of Pa., 1986. Nurse, Clearfield Hosp., 1960-63, acting head nurse, 1964, asst. instr., 1964-67, med.-surg. instr., 1967-69; med.-surg. instr. Philipsburg State Gen. Hosp. Sch. Nursing (Pa.), 1969-82; med.-surg. instr. Central Pa. Sch. Nursing, 1982—, mem. admissions com., 1982-83, chmn. inservice com., 1982-83, 85-86. Tchr., Sunday Sch., Presbyn. Ch., Clearfield, 1970-73; deacon 1st United Presbyn. Ch., 1970-72. Mem. Am. Nurses Assn., Pa. Nurses Assn., Dist. 5 Nurses Assn. (nominating com.), Philipsburg Nurses Alumnae Assn., Clearfield Nurses Alumnae Assn. (pres. 1982), Nat. League Nursing, Clearfield Bus. and Profl. Womens Club (pres. 1971-72). Republican. Home: 204 Spruce St Clearfield PA 16800 Office: Central Pa Sch Nursing 110 Lock Lomond Rd Philipsburg PA 16866

SWIT, LORETTA, actress; b. N.J., Nov. 4; student Am. Acad. Dramatic Arts, Gene Frankel Repertoire Theatre, N.Y.C. Stage appearances include: Any Wednesday, The Odd Couple, Mame, The Apple Tree, Same Time Next Year; films include: Stand Up and Be Counted, 1972, Freebie and the Bean, 1974, Race with the Devil, 1975, S.O.B., 1980; star TV series MASH, 1972-83; TV movies: Shirts/Skin, Hostage Heart, Coffeeville, Superman, The Loveboat Movie, Mirror, Mirror, Valentine, The Walls Came Tumbling Down, The Love Tapes, The Kid From Nowhere, Games Mother Never Taught You, First Affair; appeared TV series: Gunsmoke, Mannix, Hawaii Five-O, Mission Impossible, The Doctors, Cade's County, Love, American Style, Bonanza, Cagney and Lacey; star on maj. dramatic shows and musical variety shows, including The Muppet Show, Bob Hope Christmas Spl. Mem. AFTRA, Screen Actors Guild, Actors Equity. Office: care William Morris Agency 151 El Camino Ave Beverly Hills CA 90212*

SWITZ, MARY ANN, funeral home executive; b. Massillon, Ohio, July 1, 1944; d. Harold Homer and Margaret Ann (Abel) Hartel; m. David Lee Switz, Oct. 13, 1962 (div. 1970); children—Bethany Lynne, Philip David. Student Cleve. Inst. Music, 1974-75, Cuyahoga Community Coll., Cleve., 1976—. Sec., Calvin Woodward, Atty., Warren, Ohio, 1969-73, Univ. Circle Research Center, Cleve., 1973-74; program coordinator Univ. Circle Center Community Programs, Cleve., 1974-77; bus. office mgr. Johnson-Romito Funeral Homes, Bedford, Ohio, 1977—; dir. music Luth. Ch. of Covenant, Maple Heights, Ohio, 1982-86. Mem. bd., accompanist, keyboard prin. Chagrin Valley Choral Union, and Orch., Cleve., 1981—, soloist, 1986; accompanist, concertmistress Solon Players Community Theatre and Orch. (Ohio), 1981-83. Mem. Nat. Assn. Female Execs., Chagrin Valley Choral Union, Am. Guild Organists. Lutheran. Home: 17304 Mapleboro Ave Maple Heights OH 44137 Office: Johnson-Romito Funeral Homes 521 Broadway Ave Bedford OH 44146

SWITZER, KATHRINE VIRGINIA, TV sports commentator, sports marketing executive; b. Amberg, Ger., Jan. 5, 1947; d. Homer and Virginia Irene (Miller) S. B.A., Syracuse U., 1968, M.A., 1972. Indsl. editor Bristol Myers Corp., Syracuse, N.Y., 1968-72; pub. relations coordinator AMF Inc., White Plains, N.Y., 1973-77; mgr. spl. promotions Avon Products, Inc., N.Y.C., 1977-80, dir. media affairs and sports programs, 1980-85, also dir. sports program pub. relations, lectr. in field. Trustee Women's Sports Found.; spl. advisor Pres.'s Council on Phys. Fitness and Sports. Recipient outstanding individual contbn. award Womens Sports Found., 1982; honor fellow award Nat. Assn. for Girls and Women in Sports, 1983; nat. honor award President's Council on Phys. Fitness and Sports, 1984. Mem. Assn. of Internat. Marathons, Am. Running and Fitness Assn. Club: Road Runners of N.Y. Office: 211 W 56th St New York NY 10019

SWOLL, MARUTH JEAN, graphic arts company executive, artist; b. Madison, Tenn., Oct. 22, 1946; d. Roy Kenneth and Wilma Jean (Christian) Pace; m. Ronald Lee Swoll, July 3, 1981. B.S., Austin Peay State U., 1970; M.B.A., U. North Fla., 1982. Kitchen designer, Gen. Electric Co., Louisville, 1970-74; tchr. phys. edn. Richmond County Bd. Edn., Augusta, Ga., 1974-75; art dir. A.A. Friedman Co., Inc., Augusta, 1975-77; asst. project mgr. design Seaboard System R.R., Louisville and Jacksonville, Fla., 1978-83, mgr. reprographics, 1983-85; owner Marographics, Jacksonville, 1985—. Recipient Gracey award for jewelry art, 1976. Mem. In-Plant Printing Mgrs. Assn., Nat. Assn. Purchasing Mgrs. Republican. Roman Catholic. Clubs: Civitan Internat. (newsletter pub. 1985—), Internat. Aerobatic (sec. 1986—, newsletter editor 1986—), 99's, Women Pilots Assn. Avocations: flying; scuba diving; painting; golf. Home and Office: 4732 Beauchamp Ct Jacksonville FL 32217

SWOPE, SUZANNE, speech educator; b. Lakewood, Ohio, Nov. 7, 1941; d. Armstead Miller and Diana (Waits) Swope; B.S. in Edn., Ohio State U., 1963, M.A., 1964; Ed.D., Boston U., 1974; m. Carlyle D. Eckstein, May 21, 1977; children—Diana Caryl Eckstein, Max Swope Eckstein. Pub. sch. speech/hearing therapist Groton (Conn.) Pub. Schs., 1964-65, Burlington (Mass.) Pub. Schs., 1965-67; instr. Emerson Coll., Boston, 1967-70, asst. prof., 1970-73, assoc. prof., 1973-79, prof., 1979—, asst. to pres., 1980, assoc. dean, 1980-82, v.p. adminstrn. and student services, 1982-84; lang. cons. Behavioral Devel. Center, 1978-86; cons. Zenker Assocs., 1973-79. VA rehab. trainee/fellow, 1964-65; Am. Council Edn. fellow, 1981—. Mem. AAUP (v.p. 1972-73, 78-79), Mass. Speech Assn., Am. Speech and Hearing Assn., Internat. Assn. Logopedics and Phoniatrics, Pi Lambda Theta, Sigma Alpha Eta. Unitarian. Contbr. articles to profl. jours. Home: 55 Fiske Rd Wellesley MA 02181 Office: 100 Beacon St Boston MA 02116

SYKES, GRACE BROWN, nurse; b. Sneads, Fla., Sept. 30, 1929; d. Ulysses Seab and Mettie Isabelle (Conely) Brown; m. Roy Sykes, Jr., June 20, 1951; children—Reginald Leroy, Manuel LeVette, Darryl Keith. R.N., Brewster Hosp. Sch. Nursing, 1951; student Edward Waters Coll., 1965-66, Fla. Jr. Coll., 1976. Staff and head nurse Brewster Hosp., Jacksonville, Fla., 1951-66; clin. nurse U.S. Naval Hosp., Jacksonville, 1966-68; asst. head nurse St. Vincent Med. Ctr., Jacksonville, 1968-70; occupational nurse U.S. Post Office, Jacksonville, 1970—; staff nurse City of Jacksonville, 1969. Home nursing instr. ARC, Jacksonville, 1980—. Mem. Am. Nurses Assn., Brewster and Community Nurses Alumni Assn. (sec. 1953-56, treas. 1975-80), Nat. Postal Profl. Nurses (shop steward 1980—); Nurses Guild (pres. Jacksonville unit 1980—). Democrat. Mem. Pentecostal Ch. Home: 5832 Iris Blvd Jacksonville FL 32209

SYKORA, JANE MONICA, library executive; b. Prague, Czechoslovakia, Mar. 20, 1930; came to U.S., 1964, naturalized 1970; d. Vaclav and Olga (Surovsky) Gregr; m. George Sykora, Sept. 28, 1954. M.L.S., Rutgers U., 1975; Ph.D., Charles U., Prague, 1954. Asst. curator U. Mich., Ann Arbor, 1966-68; head Order div. Princeton U. Library, 1968-77; dir. Ednl. Testing Service Test Library, Princeton, 1977—. Vol., Med. Ctr. Princeton, 1983. Mem. ALA. Clubs: Rutgers Alumni Assn., Alumni Resource Bank. Office: Educational Testing Service Rosedale Rd Princeton NJ 08541

SYLVAN, RITA, painter, printmaker, photographer; b. Mpls., 1928; children—Paul, Judy, Carolyn. B.A. in Fine Arts magna cum laude, U. Minn., 1948; postgrad. NYU, 1951, 52-53, Bennington Coll., 1983-84; M.A. in Fine Arts and Fine Arts Edn., Columbia U., 1967. Teaching asst. in art history U. Minn., Mpls., 1948-49, guest lectr. dept. humanities, 1948; asst. curator to Edward Steichen for The Family of Man exhbn. and book Mus. Modern Art, N.Y.C., 1951-53; asst. curator photography, asst. to John I. H. Baur exhbn. and book Revolution and Tradition in Am. Art Bklyn. Mus., 1951; tchr., art cons. Tenafly Adult Community Edn. (N.J.), 1966-77; tchr. art Tenafly Pub. Schs., 1966-78; a founder, tchr. Art Ctr. No. N.J., Englewood, 1957-62, dir. faculty, 1961, tchr., 1957-62, developer speakers bur., 1957; lectr., discussion leader in field; spl. ednl. projects. One-woman shows include: Columbia U., N.Y.C., 1963 Bergen Mus., Paramus, N.J., 1977, Nat. Endowment for Arts; group shows include: N.J. State Mus., 1970, Newark Mus., 1958, 59, 60, Audubon Artists, N.Y.C., 1962, 67, 84, Broward Art Guild, Ft. Lauderdale, Fla., 1981-86, Boca Raton Mus. Art (Fla.), 1984, Norton Gallery Art, Palm Beach, Fla., Hollywood Art and Culture Center, Thomas Ctr. Biennial, Gainesville-Tallahassee, 1986, Boca Raton Mus., Fla. Internat. U., others; represented in permanent collections: Rose Mus., Brandeis U.; work subject of profl. publs. Recipient Purchase award Columbia U., 1962, First award for painting Midwest Regional Exhbn., Mpls. Inst. Art, 1949, Nat. Assn. Women Artists award, 1966, Seasoned Eye, Modern Maturity Mag., 1986, award Boca Raton Profl. Artists, numerous others. Mem. Modern Artists Guild Inc. (a founder, trustee), Phi Beta Kappa, Kappa Delta Pi. Home and Studio: 23385 Barlake Dr Boca Raton FL 33433

SYLVESTER, HAZEL ANN, educational consultant; b. Lubbock, Tex., Mar. 18, 1931; d. John W. and Bula M. (Hatridge) Harrison; B.S. in Edn., Tex. Tech. U., 1953, M.S. in Edn., 1971; m. Charles A. Sylvester, Aug. 23, 1951; children—Mary Ann, Laurie Lynn, Julie Kay. Tchr. lang. arts grades 6-8 Ropesville (Tex.) Public Schs., 1951-52; part-time English instr. South Plains Jr. Coll., Levelland, Tex., 1961-63; tchr. grade 5 Levelland (Tex.) Public Schs., 1965-71, dir. elem. edn., 1971-74; Title I reading tchr. leader Round Rock (Tex.) Public Schs., 1975-76, supr. elem. edn., 1976-79, dir. elem. edn., 1979-85, ind. cons., 1985—, mem. state com. on nutrition Tex. Assessment of Basic Skills, 1979-81; mem. Tex. Right to Read Com.; trainer New Adventures in Learning, 1980; speaker various ednl. projects. Sunday sch. pres. South Plains Coll. Faculty Wives, 1959-61. Mem. Nat. Assn. Edn. Young Children, Tex. Assn. Edn. Young Children, Assn. Childhood Edn., So. Assn. Colls. and Schs. (state area chmn. 1983-84), Delta Kappa Gamma (various chpt. coms.), Alpha Chi, Phi Kappa Phi, Phi Delta Kappa. Author staff devel. and curricular materials. Contbr. articles to edn. jours.

SYMONDS, ELSA ORNELAS (BONNIE), lawyer; b. Mexico City, Mexico, Dec. 15, 1939; came to U.S., 1946 naturalized, 1970; d. Jaime Josue and Esther Barber Ornelas; m. Michael F. Symonds, Sept. 5, 1964; children—Bonnie Michael, Joshua Michael. A.A. (valedictorian), San Antonio Coll., 1960; B.A. summa cum laude, St. Mary's U., 1967, J.D., 1980. Bar: Tex. 1980. Sec., Mexicana Airlines, San Antonio, 1960-65; translator R. F. Barnes Customhouse Brokers, San Antonio, 1969-72; instr. GT Program, Ft. Sam Houston, San Antonio, 1972-77; instr. San Antonio Coll., 1972—; sole practice law, San Antonio, 1981—. Exhibited one-man show Branch Savs. Assn., San Antonio, 1973. Mem., Hispanic Women's Com. San Antonio, 1983—; mem. Alternatives to Juvenile Delinquency Arrest Program, 1981—; mem. Guardianship Adv. Bd., San Antonio, 1983—; mem. Bexar County Women's Polit. Caucus, 1982—; lector, former mem. parish council Holy Spirit Roman Catholic Ch., San Antonio; bd. dirs. San Antonio YWCA. Mem. San Antonio Bar Assn., Tex. Trial Lawyers Assn., Assn. Trial Lawyers Am., ABA, Democrat. Office: 515 S Main St San Antonio TX 78204

SYMONDS, GENEVIEVE ELLEN, leather goods bus. exec.; b. Wilson Boro, Pa., Mar. 1, 1931; d. Jacob Rush and Ellen Maria (Brackmann) Twining; student Mercer County Coll., 1974, 76; m. Howard Eugene Symonds, May 21, 1950; children—Jess Howard, Bryce Dale. Acct., Miller's Chrysler Plymouth, Glen Gardner, N.J., 1950-55; officer mgr. Centrum Constrn. Corp., Clinton, N.J., 1969-76; owner, mgr. S & S Bus. Services, Clinton, 1976-81, Gen's Shop for Pappagallo, Clinton, 1982-85; owner, mgr. Gen's/Acctg., 1982—; corp. sec. Nat. Sporting Frat. Ltd. Pres., Lebanon Twp. (N.J.) Vol. Fire Co. Aux., 1960-64, treas., 1964-68; pres. Lebanon Twp. PTA, 1965-69; committeeperson Hunterdon County Republican Party, 1968—, vice chmn., 1974-77; state committeeperson Rep. Party N.J., 1977-81; mem. com. George Washington council Boy Scouts Am., 1974-78; bd. dirs. Hunterdon County Learning Ctr., Califon, N.J., 1984—. Recipient Service award PTA, 1969, Spl. Service award Boy Scouts Am., 1974. Methodist. Clubs: Hunterdon County Women's Rep. (pres. 1970-74, treas. 1978-82), African Safari of N.Y. Weekly columnist Star newspaper, Washington, N.J., 1964-68; monthly columnist What's In The Pot, Today In Hunterdon Mag., 1977-80. Home: Mountain Top Rd RD #3 Glen Gardner NJ 08826 Office: #1 Main St Clinton NJ 08809

SYMONDS, JOHNNIE PIRKLE, retired psychologist; b. Wynnewood, Okla., Apr. 5, 1900; d. John Thomas and Lillie Belle (Driver) Pirkle; B.A., U. Tex., 1920, M.A., 1921; postgrad. Columbia U. Tchrs. Coll., 1921-22, 26-27, 28-29, 30-31, NYU, 1975; m. Percival Mallon Symonds, Dec. 25, 1922. Research asst. dept. psychology U. Tex., Austin, 1919-21; research assoc. Inst. Ednl. Research Tchrs. Coll. Columbia U., N.Y.C., 1921-22; psychologist Family Service Soc., Yonkers, N.Y., 1937-47; ret., 1960. Mem. Columbia Com. for Community Service, 1972—; active English in Action Program, English Speaking Union, Riverside Ch., N.Y.C., 1974-75, honored 50th anniversary mem., 1981. Mem. Am., N.Y. State psychol. assns., Am. Assn. Applied Psychology, AAAS, Ednl. Press Assn., World Fedn. Mental Health, AAUW, Pi Lambda Theta, Kappa Delta Pi. Club: Appalachian Mountain (hon. award 50th anniversary mem. 1980). Editor, Jour. Cons. Psychology, 1937-47; contbr. articles to psychol. jours. Home: 106 Morningside Dr Apt 71 New York NY 10027

SYMONETTE, LYS, foundation executive, musician, writer; b. Mainz, Germany, Dec. 21, 1920; came to U.S., 1936; d. Max Weinschenk and Gertrude (Metzger) Honheisser; m. Randolph Symonette, Sept. 1, 1949; 1 child, Victor. Student Curtis Inst., Phila., 1937-39. Piano accompanist to internat. singers, 1940—; musical asst. to Kurt Weill and L. Lenya, 1945-81; tchr. Curtis Inst., Phila., 1976—; musical exec., v.p. Kurt Weill Found., N.Y.C., 1981—. Translator operas from English to German and German to English, 1945—. Mem. Am. Fedn. Musicians, Alumni Assn. Curtis Inst. Music. Home: 160 W 73d St New York NY 10023 Office: Kurt Weill Found for Music 142 West End Ave New York NY 10023

SYPHER, ELEANOR KRAMER, educator; b. Kansas City, Mo., Feb. 3, 1941; d. Ambrose Nelson and Bernice (Cole) Kramer; m. Francis J. Sypher, July 11, 1970 (div. 1983); 1 child, Eleanor Holbrook. B.A., Smith Coll., 1963; M.A., Columbia U., 1966, Ph.D., 1973. Tchr. classics Calhoun & Spence Schs., N.Y.C., 1963-69; editor SUNY Press, Albany, 1973-75, Praeger & Rockefeller Found., N.Y.C., 1975-77; instr. Latin, U. Mo., Kansas City, 1978-79; tchr. classics Chapin Sch., N.Y.C., 1979—. Author: Ysengrimus, 1980. Mem. Am. Philol. Assn. Club: Daughters of Cin. (N.Y.C.). Home: 515 E 89th St New York NY 10128 Office: Chapin Sch 100 East End Ave New York NY 10028

SYRING, ANN FRITTS, steel company executive; b. Orange, N.J., Apr. 19, 1946; d. Harry Donald and Ruth Doris (Holmes) Fritts; m. Edward M. Syring, Jr., Apr. 24, 1983. B.A., Jackson Coll. for Women, Tufts U., 1968. Sales analyst Polaroid Corp., Cambridge, Mass., 1969-70; sales exec. Dead River Co., Kingfield, Maine, 1971-72; free-lance pub. relations consultant, Athens, Greece, 1972-73; assoc. in internat. corp. fin. White Weld & Co. Inc. (now Merrill Lynch White Weld), N.Y.C., 1974-78; dir. corp. devel. Armco Inc., N.Y.C., 1978—. Mem. N.Am. Soc. Corp. Planning, Women's Econ. Roundtable. Republican. Episcopalian. Clubs: Sleepy Hollow Country (Scarborough, N.Y.); Doubles (N.Y.C.). Office: Armco Inc 375 Park Ave New York NY 10152

SYVERSEN, JUDITH SAWYER, nurse educator, nurse; b. Watertown, N.Y., Sept. 21, 1941; d. Arthur Joseph and Florence Pearl (Hockey) Sawyer; m. David Eugene Alhart, June 10, 1961 (div. 1972); children—Randi Lynne, Scott David, Mark David, Janee J.; m. 2d, Robert Gerald Syversen, July 12, 1975; 1 dau., Ellen Lorraine. Lic. Practical Nurse, Rochester Gen. Hosp., 1962; R.N., Monroe Community Coll., 1972; B.S., Alfred U., 1979; M.S., SUNY-Buffalo, 1983. R.N., N.Y. Surg. nurse U. Rochester Med. Ctr. (N.Y.), 1972-73; operating room nurse Genesee Hosp., Rochester, 1973-75, inservice instr. operating room, 1975-79; operating room nurse Rochester Gen. Hosp., 1979-81; asst. prof. nursing Alfred U., Rochester, 1981; asst. prof. nursing Monroe Community Coll., Rochester, 1982—, sec. faculty governance bd., 1983—, program advisor, 1983, sec. curriculum com. nursing dept., 1982-84, student nurse clin. advisor, 1981—, coordinator course, 1983; assoc. prof. nursing Keuka Coll., Keuka Park, N.Y. Mem. Genesee Valley Nurses Assn., N.Y. State Nurses Assn., AAUP, Grad. Student Nurse Assn. (pres. SUNY-Buffalo 1981-82), Student Nurse Assn. (Monroe Community Coll.), Sigma Theta Tau. Democrat. Club: Sodus Bay Yacht (trustee 1982-83, 85—). Home: 10 White Briar Pittsford NY 14534 Office: Keuka Coll Nursing Div Keuka Park NY 14478

SZATALOWICZ, VICTORIA LYNN, physician; b. Manhattan, Kans., June 19, 1948; d. Marion Thomas and Helen Maureen (Freb) Szatalowicz. B.S., U. Wis., 1970; M.D., U. Okla., 1974. Internal medicine intern Duke U., Durham, N.C., 1974-75, jr. asst. resident, 1975-76, sr. asst. resident, 1976-77; clin. fellow nephrology, U. Colo., Denver, 1977-78, research fellow nephrology, 1978-80; physician emergency dept. Encino Hosp. (Calif.), Beverly Hosp., Montebello, Calif., Washington Hosp., Culver City, Calif., med. dir. La Palma Office Am. Emergicenters, Inc., 1984—. Mgr. Pacific region Hunger Project Briefing Leaders, Internat., 1983-84; mem. Wash. Hosp. Infectious Disease Com., Culver City, 1982-84. Recipient Mrs. Fay Lester award U. Okla. Med. Sch., 1974; Anesthesiology Directorship scholar Am. Soc. Anesthesiologists, 1972—. Mem. Am. Med. Women's Assn., ACP, Am. Soc. Internal Medicine, Am. Soc. Emergency Physicians, Student Am. Med. Assn., Delta Zeta (v.p. 1969-70). Office: 5959 La Palma Ave La Palma CA 90623

SZCZEPKOWSKI, LORI ANN, art consultant; b. Naugatuck, Conn., Dec. 15, 1960. Student Chatham Coll., 1978-80, Ariz. State U., 1980-81; B.A. in Anthropology, Salve Regina Coll., 1986. Account exec. Task Force, Phoenix, 1981; system cons. Sentinel Communications, Phoenix, 1981; dir. corp. sales Malke-Sage Galleries, Santa Clara, Calif., 1981-84; environ. cons. Signatures Unltd., Santa Clara, 1983-84; mgr. Le Select, Newport, 1985—. Author: Academic Integrity, 1986. Avocations: dancing; oil painting; poetry; running; weight training. Home: 12 Underwood Ct Newport RI 02840

SZEKELY-SHELLEY, MARIA MAGDALENA, chem. engr.; b. Timisoara, Romania, Apr. 21, 1931; came to U.S., 1974; d. Sigmund and Maria (Konnerth) Kohn; M.S. in Chem. Engring., Kazan (USSR) Inst. Chem. Tech., 1955; m. John Szekely, Sept. 2, 1954; 1 son, Attila. Project engr., Iprochim Central Project Inst. Chem. Industry, Bucharest, Romania, 1955-62, project mgr., 1962-74; project mgr. E.R. Squibb Co., Princeton, N.J., 1975-81; plant engr. Hoffmann La Roche, Belvidere, N.J., 1981-84; sr. project engr. John Brown Crawford and Russel Inc., Stamford, Conn., 1984—. Recipient Romanian Govt. decoration for starting of Romanian synthetic fiber plant, 1962. Mem. Am. Inst. Chem. Engrs. Home: 47 Barberry Ct Lawrenceville NJ 08648 Office: PO Box 1432 Stamford CT 06904

SZOLD, RUTH, modeling agy., cosmetic co. and sch. exec.; b. Bronx, N.Y., Oct. 14, 1929; d. Albert and Margaret (Karl) Nussbacher; student Hunter Coll., N.Y.C., 1947; m. Martin Szold, Apr. 10, 1949 (div. Sept. 1978); children—Lauren, Terry; m. James C. Stern, Aug. 22, 1982. Exec. legal sec. to sr. partner firm Paul, Weiss, Rifkind, Wharton & Garrison, N.Y.C., 1958-62; asst. to pres. M.E. Green & Co., brokerage co., N.Y.C., 1962-65; demonstrator and cons. for various cosmetic cos., 1965—; founder, pres. Ruth Szold Promotional Models, N.Y.C., 1968-84, Cosmetic Art, Inc., cosmetic and theatrical workshops, N.Y.C., 1979—; founder, pres., designer, promoter cosmetic line Cosmetic Art, 1979—; demonstrator-lectr. for TV, also video tapes; condr. cosmetic workshops for N.Y. Salute to Fashion Industries, 1981; cons. in field. Mem. council Girl Scouts U.S.A., 1964-69; bd. dirs. Bleecker Tower Tenants Corp., N.Y.C., 1979-80, chmn. architecture and design com., 1979-80, chmn. maintenance, 1980—, pres., 1981-82; mem. Hunger Project, Financial Family; lectr., mem. panel Am. Women's Econ. Devel. Corp., 1981. Recipient Gold medal Deborah Fund Raising Dinner, 1955. Mem. Foragers of Am., Nat. Retail Mchts. Assn., Fragrance Found., Cosmetic Exec. Women. Clubs: Brandeis U., Hadassah. Home and Office: 644 Broadway New York NY 10012

SZPREJDA, EVELYN, marketing executive; b. Green Bay, Wis., Nov. 30, 1944; d. John Otto and Pearl Helen (Cwiak) S. Student U. Wis., 1962-63, 67-68, U. Minn., 1975-77; B.B.A., Coll. St. Thomas, 1980, postgrad., 1984—. Mktg. adminstrn. specialist Medtronic Inc., Mpls., 1978-79, mgr. internat. market planning and adminstrn., 1979-80, mgr. market info. and research, 1980-81; dir. market planning and research Gibsongroup, Mpls., 1981-82; trade ops. devel. mgr. Control Data Mpls., 1982-83, mktg. mgr. health care products, 1983—1983-84; dir. planning and new program devel. 1st Internat. Corp., Mpls., 1984—; ptnr. Intermar Group, Mpls.; dir. IXI World Trade Corp. Bd. dirs. Minn. World Trade Assn., Mpls., 1980-84, pres., 1983-84, 1st v.p., 1982-83, sec.-treas., 1981-82; sec.-treas. Japan-Am. Soc. Minn., 1981-82; mem. Minn. Gov.'s Task Force Internat. Bus. Edn., 1983-84. Recipient Bus. Woman Leader award YMCA Mpls., 1980. Mem. Am. Mktg. Assn., Internat. Advt. Assn., Internat. Platform Assn., Mpls. C. of C. (world trade com. 1982—). Roman Catholic. Club: Greenway Athletic (Mpls.). Home: 121 S Washington Ave Apt 1310 Minneapolis MN 55401 Office: IXI World Trade Corp 11551 K-Tel Dr Minneapolis MN 55343

SZUMANSKI, DEBRA LYNN, computer programmer; b. Detroit, Mar. 12, 1957; d. Stanley and Anneliese Szumanski. A.A.S. in Computer Sci., Wayne County Coll., 1982. Computer lab. asst. Wayne County Coll., Taylor, Mich., 1980-82; computer operator Ford Aerospace, Newport Beach, Calif., 1982-83, computer programmer, 1983-85; computer programmer Hughes Aircraft Co., Long Beach, 1985—; cons. in field.

SZWAJER, KATHRYN EDNA, nurse; b. S.I., N.Y., Apr. 16, 1951; d. Thaddeus Xavier and Georgene Margret (Denis) S. A.A.S. in Nursing, Brookdale Community Coll., 1975; postgrad. Georgian Ct. Coll., 1981—. R.N., N.J. Staff nurse St. Barnabas Hosp., Livingston, N.J., 1976, Jersey Shore Med. Ctr., Neptune, N.J., 1976-77; pvt. duty nurse, 1977-78; staff nurse Freehold Area Hosp. (N.J.), 1978, Green Grove Convalescent Ctr., Neptune, 1978; charge nurse Heritage Hall Nursing Home, Tinton Falls, N.J., 1978-80; staff nurse Eatontown Convalescent Ctr. (N.J.), 1982, The Lodge, Neptune,

1980, Tower Lodge, Wall, N.J., 1980—. Republican. Home: 1318 Walnut Ave Wanamassa NJ 07712 Office: Tower Lodge 1506 Gully Rd Wall NJ

SZYMKOWICZ, KATHERINE CALLAWAY, contract specialist; b. Atlanta, Jan. 4, 1956; d. William H. and Juanita (Warren) Callaway; m. Paul James Szymkowicz, July 31, 1983. B.A., Oglethorpe U., 1977; M.B.A. candidate San Francisco State U. Contract specialist Dept. Def., San Bueno, Calif., St. Louis and White Sands, N.Mex., 1977-84; contract negotiator Pacific Bell, San Francisco, 1984-86; small co. specialist Fed. Res. Bank San Francisco, 1986—; cons. Urban Contract Cons., San Francisco, 1985—. Mem. Nat. Assn. Female Execs. Democrat. Home: 3877 21st St San Francisco CA 94114 Office: Fed Res Bank 101 Market St San Francisco CA 94105

TABACHUK, EMELIA, banker; b. Passaic, N.J., Aug. 3, 1926; d. Michael and Fannie (Stefanyk) T.; student Drake Bus. Coll., 1956, N.Y. Inst. Credit, 1978-80. With Marine Midland Bank, N.Y.C., 1946—, adminstrv. asst., 1975-76, ops. asst., 1976-78, comml. banking officer, 1978-82, asst. v.p., 1982-85, ret., 1985. Mem. Nat. Assn. Bank Women, Am. Soc. Profl. and Exec. Women, Nat. Assn. Female Execs. Home: 78 Stadtmauer Dr Clifton NJ 07013 Office: 140 Broadway New York NY 10015

TABAKIN, LORAINE SMITH, lawyer; b. Cambridge, Mass., July 2, 1940; d. Albert Frances Smith and Eileen (Mullett) Boynton; m. Frank Tabakin, Sept. 1, 1963; children—Jennifer, Steven. B.S., Simmons Coll., 1962; M.S.W., Columbia U., 1964; J.D., U. Pitts., 1976. Bar: Pa. 1976, U.S. Supreme Ct. 1980. Psychiat. social worker Altro Health Rehab. Service, N.Y.C., 1964-65, Pitts. Child Guidance Center, 1965-67; asst. county solicitor Allegheny County Law Dept., Pitts., 1976-80; assoc. atty. Strassburger, McKenna, Pitts., 1980-83; ptnr. Tabakin, Carroll & Curtin, Pitts., 1984—. Mem. exec. bd. 14th Ward Democratic Club, Pitts., 1972-73, 80—; bd. dirs. ACLU, Pitts., 1978-82. Mem. ABA, Pa. Bar Assn., Allegheny County Bar Assn. (council family law sect.), Assn. Trial Lawyers Am. Office: Tabakin Carroll& Curtin 1430 Grant Bldg Pittsburgh PA 15219

TABBERT, RONDI JO, accountant; b. Dallas, Mar. 14, 1953; d. Jack H. and June F. (Williams) Russell; m. William Henry Tabbert, Nov. 16, 1979. A.A., Tarrant County Jr. Coll., 1975; B.S. in Bus., U. Tex.-Dallas, 1980; M.B.A., U. Dallas, 1984. C.P.A., Tex. Bookkeeper, Kelly-Moore Paint, Dallas, 1976-78; corp. acct. Gen. Portland, Dallas, 1978-80; chief acct. W.R. Grace & Co., Dallas, 1980-83; controller Little & Assocs., Dallas, 1983-85; prin. Rondi J. Tabbert, C.P.A., Desoto, Tex., 1985—. Mem. Tex. Soc. C.P.A.s, Nat. Assn. Female Execs., Dallas Soc. C.P.A.s (tax edn. com. 1985-86), Am. Women's Soc. C.P.A.s, DeSoto C. of C. Mem. Libertarian party. Home: 1055 Turner Ave Dallas TX 75208 Office: 500 N Hampton B-6 DeSoto TX 75115

TABEN, EVA MARX, librarian, genetic counselor; b. Munich, Germany, Oct. 1, 1937; came to U.S., 1939; d. Karl Jacob and Ruth (Hirschland) Marx; m. Stanley Taben, Aug. 25, 1957; children—Peter, Charles, Elizabeth, B.A., Sarah Lawrence Coll., 1970, M.S., 1971; M.L.S., Columbia U., 1980. Genetic counselor Albert Einstein Coll. Medicine, Bronx, N.Y., 1971-79; outreach services coordinator Westchester Library System, Elmsford, N.Y., 1981—. Chairperson bd. dirs. Westchester Ind. Living Ctr., Inc., White Plains, N.Y., 1983—. Mem. adv. council Westchester Community Coll. Retirement Inst. Mem. ALA, N.Y. Library Assn., Westchester Library Assn., Westchester Assn. Continuing Edn. Democrat. Jewish. Home: 36 Paddington Rd Scarsdale NY 10583 Office: Westchester Library System 8 Westchester Plaza Elmsford NY 10523

TABER, CATHERINE ALDEN CHAPMAN, public affairs specialist; b. Washington, Jan. 10, 1945; d. John Phillips and Suzanne (Fidel) Chapman; m. Edward A. Taber, Dec. 19, 1970 (div.). B.A. in Polit. Sci., Ripon Coll., 1967; M.A. in Legis. Affairs, George Wash. U., 1977. Staff asst. Vice-Pres. Mondale, Washington, 1974-78; editor U.S. Dept. Commerce, Washington, 1978-81; constituency action coordinator Presdl. Task Force, Washington, 1981-82; pub. affairs specialist U.S. Dept. Commerce, Washington, 1982—. Recipient cert. of Achievement, U.S. Dept. Commerce, 1982-83. Mem. AAUW, Pub. Relations Soc. Am., Internat. Assn. Bus. Communicators, Nat. Assn. Female Execs. Episcopalian.

TABER, JUDITH ANN SPAIN, sales representative, consultant; b. Cohoes, N.Y., Sept. 5, 1931; d. Edward Howard, Jr. and Marie Magdeline (Montmarquet) Spain; m. Erik Rodney Taber, Aug. 23, 1952 (div. Oct. 1974); children—Erik Rodney, Jr., Diane Marie Taber VanWert. B.S., Russell Sage Coll., 1953; M.B.A., U. Houston, 1984. Asst. dir., math. fellowship program Rensselaer Poly. Inst., Troy, N.Y., 1953-54; tchr., bus. St. Anne Inst., Albany, N.Y., 1960-73; researcher Boyden Assocs., Houston, 1974; sr. profl. field sales rep. McNeil Pharm. Co., Spring House, Pa., 1975—, field sales trainer Southwest region, 1981, mem., rep. Nat. Pharm. Council, Washington, D.C., 1981-82. Com. woman Woodway Bend Townhome Assn., Houston, 1978-79; vol. George Bush for Pres. Campaign, Houston, 1980; bd. dirs. Greater Houston Skating Council, 1982-83. Named Houston Businesswoman of Year YWCA, 1979; co-recipient Nat. Silver Medal in Ice-Dancing, Ice-Skating Inst. America, 1983, 84. Mem. Bus. and Profl. Women, Assn. M.B.A. Execs. Republican. Episcopalian. Clubs: Iceland Figure Skating (dir.), Elan (Houston). April Sound Country (Conroe, Tex.); Hertford (London).

TABER, LINDA PERRIN, public relations exec.; b. Marshalltown, Iowa, Dec. 30, 1941; d. Burr H. and Luella M. (Memler) Perrin; m. Roy H. Pollack, Oct. 1983. B.A., U. Iowa, 1964; M.A., Syracuse U., 1969. Women's editor Cedar Rapids (Iowa) Gazette, 1964-67; writer Inst. Life Ins., N.Y.C., 1969-70; account supr., v.p. Carol Moberg Communications, N.Y.C., 1970-78; dir., sr. v.p. Ketchum Public Relations, N.Y.C., 1978—. Mem. Public Relations Soc. Am., Fashion Group, Nat. Home Fashions League, Women in Communications, Nat. Acad. TV Arts and Scis., Women Execs. in Pub. Relations. Home: 160 West End Ave New York NY 10023 Office: 1133 Ave of Americas New York NY 10036

TABOR, MILA VILLASOR, computer programmer; b. Bacolod City, Philippines, May 5, 1954; came to U.S., 1975; d. Guillermo Piccio and Milagros (Araneta) Villasor; m. Raymond J. Tabor, Dec. 16, 1982. B. in Bus. and Econs., Lewis U., Lockport, Ill., 1977; postgrad. DePaul U., 1983, Nat. Coll. Edn., Evanston, Ill. Dir. Rural Bank of San Fernando, Inc., Cebu, Philippines, 1974—; asst. to prof. Lewis U., 1975-77; pres. Tabor Industries, Chgo., 1978-84; programmer Sears Merchandise Group, Chgo., 1984—; project mgr. Primary Cons. Services, N.Y.C., 1980-81; group benefit analyst Bankers Life & Casualty, Chgo., 1981-83. Editor, Systems Project, Users Manual Documentation, 1983. Guide Girl Scouts of Philippines, Manila, 1973. Recipient Nat. Observer award Dow Jones/Lewis U., 1977. Mem. Assn. Info. Mgrs., Nat. Assn. Female Execs., Assn. Women in Computing, Phi Gamma Nu (co-editor newsletter 1975-77). Lodge: Soroptimist of Philippines (organizer, dir. 1973).

TACKOVICH, JO ANN, tire company executive, fashion and image consultant; b. Hampton, Tenn., May 4, 1938; d. John Paul and Lena Jane (Cooke) Greer; m. Sidney Clayton Jones, Dec. 22, 1956 (div. Apr. 1959); 1 child, Randall Jones Tackovich; m. Martin David Tackovich, June 18, 1966. Student U. Arkon, 1974-75. Cert. profl. sec. Tech.-chem. sec. Goodyear Tire & Rubber Co., Akron, 1959-69, corp. law sec., 1969-75, corp. law paralegal, 1975-81, consumer relations profl., 1981—; owner, pres. Exclusively Jo Ann, fashion image and wardrobing cons., Akron, 1986—. Mem. Akron Women's Network (founder 1978, mem. bd. 1978-81, sec.-treas. 1978-80). Republican. Avocations: fashion, running, aerobics, weight lifting, reading. Home: 1052 N Portage Path Akron OH 44313 Office: Goodyear Tire & Rubber Co 1144 E Market St Akron OH 44316

TADDEO, LINDA FOCER, librarian; b. Pitts., Oct. 24, 1935; d. Samuel Walter and Mary Isabelle (Haworth) Focer; m. Daniel Taddeo, Aug. 6, 1956 (div. 1984); children—Laurie Yarbrough, Dana Belkot, Christian Daniel. B.A., Geneva Coll., Beaver Falls, Pa., 1958; M.L.S., U. Pitts., 1982. Elem. tchr. Avon (Ohio) Bd. Edn., 1966-71; pre-sch. dir. Presbyn. Nursery Sch., Sewickley, Pa., 1973-75; asst. librarian Beaver County Bookmobile, Aliquippa, Pa., 1975-77; children's librarian Beaver (Pa.) Meml. Library, 1977-79, Carnegie Library, Beaver Falls, Pa., 1979-81; dir. Carnegie Free Library, Beaver Falls, 1983—. Contbr. poetry to various publs. Mem. Pa. Library Assn. (legis. liaison rep. Beaver Falls chpt. 1983—), ALA, AAUW. Club: Ctr. Civic Women's (chmn. edn. com. 1977) (Monaca, Pa.). Home: 123 Temple Rd Monaca PA 15061 Office: Carnegie Free Library 1301 7th Ave Beaver Falls PA 15010

TAFF, JULIA EDITH, medical technologist; b. Ft. Bragg, N.C., Apr. 16, 1927; d. John Baskerville and Elmer Lucille (Myers) Joyner; B.S., U. Tulsa, 1971; M.A., Central Mich. U., Mt. Pleasant, 1977; m. Francis Malcolm Taff, Aug. 18, 1946; children—David Malcolm, Sheila Marie, Randall Martin. Med. technologist microbiology St. John Med. Center, Tulsa, 1961-73, program dir. Sch. Med. Tech., 1973-83, mgr. materials mgmt., 1983-84, mgr. spl. projects, 1984—; adv. bd. Tulsa Jr. Coll.; cons., lectr. in field. Named Med. Technologist of Yr. in Okla., 1978. Mem. Am. Soc. Microbiologists, Am. Soc. Med. Technologists, Am. Soc. Clin. Pathologists, Okla. Soc. Med. Tech. Educators (scholarship 1980), Alpha Sigma Alpha. Democrat. Methodist. Office: 1923 S Utica St Tulsa OK 74104

TAFFET, ELIZABETH ROSE, national fund raising consultant; b. Bklyn., July 10, 1934; d. Morris and Sylvia (Samovitz) Gropper; m. Arthur S. Taffet, June 11, 1953 (div. Dec. 1982); children—George, Allen, Mimi. Student Adelphi U., 1979-84, Clark U., Worcester, Mass., 1952-53, Philanthropy Tax Inst., N.Y.C., 1981, 84. Research dir. Douglas Lawson, Inc., N.Y.C., 1979-80; dir. planned giving Jewish Nat. Fund, N.Y.C., 1980-81, nat. dir. major gifts and bequests, 1981-85, Deferred Planning Concepts, 1985—, Planned Giving Concepts, 1986—; asst. coordinator Found. Caucus White House Conf. Library and Info. Services, 1979; account exec. Juvenile Diabetes Research, Miami, 1979; preparer planned giving instruments Care, Inc., N.Y.C., 1979. Research editor Foundation 500, 1979. Vice pres. Hadassah, Oceanside, N.Y., 1975, also editor newspaper; community rep. Middle States Evaluation Com., Oceanside, 1976; pres. Oceanside council PTA, 1977, also editor newsletter; mem. Adult Edn. Adv. Com., Oceanside, 1978. Mem. Nat. Soc. Fund-Raising Execs., N.Y. League of Bus. and Profl. Women, Nat. Speakers Assn., Internat. Assn. Fin. Planning, Women in Fin. Devel., Am. Women's Econ. Devel. Assn., Women's Econ. Devel. Assn. Corp., N.Y. Planned Giving Assn., Nat. Assn. Female Execs. Democrat. Home: 135 Irma Dr Oceanside NY 11572

TAGGART, MOLLYE SUE, communications industry executive; b. Greenville, Tex., Feb. 23, 1949; d. William Jennings Bryan and Anna Pearl (McConnell) Taggart. Student Kilgore Coll., 1966-67. Directory compilation clk. Southwestern Bell, Dallas, 1967-69, service rep., 1969-74, employment interviewer, 1974-75, bus. office supr., 1975-77, staff supr. tng., 1977-82; asst. mgr. consumer mktg., AT&T Communications, Houston, 1982-83, asst. staff mgr., 1983-85, asst. sales mgr., mktg., 1985—. Named to Circle of Excellence, AT&T Communications, 1985. Mem. NOW, Bus. and Profl. Women's Clubs, Nat. Assn. Female Execs. Democrat. Methodist. Avocations: swimming; walking; volleyball; reading. Home: 1505 Winrock #10501 Houston TX 77057 Office: AT&T Communications 1360 Post Oak #300 Houston TX 77057

TAGGART, VALERIE MANNING, judge; b. Cranbrook, B.C., Can., Aug. 9, 1926; d. Viril Zenis and Jessie Manson (Burgess) Manning; m. Kenneth Elliot Meredith, Sept. 7, 1949 (div. 1976); children—Deborah, Guy, Daphne; m. John David Taggart, June 18, 1981. LL.B., U. B.C. Cert. barrister, solicitor. Assoc. Meredith & Co., Vancouver, 1949-50; research assoc. Fulton Cumming & Co., Vancouver, 1972-74; acting dir. Continuing Legal Edn., Vancouver, 1974-76; exec. dir. Law Found., Vancouver, 1976-80; judge, Vancouver, 1980—; chmn. Family Court Com., Vancouver. Pres. Jr. League, Vancouver; v.p. B.C. Cancer Found., Vancouver; bd. dirs. United Way, Vancouver. Served as wren W.R.C.N.S., 1944-45. Mem. Provincial Judges Assn., Gamma Phi Beta. Avocations: golf; skiing; gardening; fishing. Office: Provincial Court 814 Richards Vancouver BC V6J 2K3 Canada

TAGRIN, EDITH SWEEDER (MRS. MARVIN S. KAPLAN), medical illustrator; b. Boston; d. David and Anna (Morillo) Sweeder; m. Ralph Tagrin, Nov. 14, 1948 (dec. July 1958); m. Marvin S. Kaplan, Oct. 23, 1966. Student Mus. Fine Arts, Boston, 1942-46, Boston U., 1945-46, Sch. Med. Illustration, Mass. Gen. Hosp., 1946-49. Free-lance med. artist, Boston, 1949-58; staff artist Mass. Gen. Hosp., Boston, 1958-60, dir. med. art unit, 1960—, dir. Sch. Med. Illustration, 1966—. Illustrator: Violence and the Brain, 1970; Gynecology, Principles and Practice, 1971; Human Design, 1971; Surgery of Upper Respiratory System, 1971; Fundamentals of Colon Surgery, 1974; Altas of Infertility Surgery, 1975; Textbook of Emergency Medicine, 1978; Manual of Lower Intestinal Surgery, 1980; Surgical Management of Cerebrovascular Disease, 1983; also numerous other med. books, jours. Mem. Soc. Tech. Writers and Pubs., Assn. Med. Illustrators (editor directory, chmn. fin., bd. govs.; v.p. 1969, chmn. scholarship, chmn. archives), Art Dirs. Club Boston. Office: Med Art Dept Mass Gen Hosp Boston MA 02114

TAIT, FELICIA HELEN, collectibles shop executive, insurance agent; b. Detroit, Sept. 22, 1938; d. Stephen Stanley and Ann Eleanore (Patyk) Cyrek; m. David Alexander Tait, July 12, 1958; children—Karen Lynn, Laurie Ann, David Gerard, Stephen Michael. Cert. jr. acct., Pontiac Bus. Inst., 1976; lic. ins. agt., Mich. State U., 1978. Service asst. mgr. Crowley Milner, Detroit, 1955-57; service rep. Plymouth Motor Car Co., Detroit, 1957-59; acctg. clk. Prestolite Inc., Port Huron, Mich., 1976-77; ptnr., owner, agt. Tait Ins. Agy., Port Huron, 1978—; owner, pres. Curio Cabinet Collectibles & Gift Shoppe, Port Huron, 1983—. Personal appearance leader 4-H, North Street, Mich., 1970-77; bd. dirs., treas. Clyde Twp. Baseball League, 1975-76; active St. Stephen's Caring Com., Port Huron, 1980—; bd. dirs., treas. Wadhams Council Commerce, Port Huron, 1984—. Mem. Nat. Fedn. Ind. Bus. Roman Catholic. Avocations: photography, knitting, interior/exterior decorating. Home: 4191 Vincent Rd North Street MI 48049 Office: Curio Cabinet Collectibles & Gift Shoppe 5005 Lapeer Port Huron MI 48060

TAIT, LYNETTE MARIE, merchandising executive; b. Cleve., Jan. 30, 1949; d. John James and Laura Marie (Zore) Sedlak; m. Newton Dewit Tait, Jan. 20, 1973; 1 child, Shawn Michael. B.S., Kent State U., 1971. Clk., Lawson Co., Cuyahoga Falls, Ohio, 1969-71, store mgr., 1971-75, group mgr., 1975-78, div. supr., 1978-83, regional sales mgr., 1983-85, mdse. mgr., 1985, sr. mdse. mgr., head buyer, 1985—. Tchr., St. Ambrose Parish Sch. Religion, Brunswick, Ohio, 1981—. Mem. Nat. Assn. Female Execs. Democrat. Roman Catholic. Lodge: Am. Slovenian Catholic Union. Avocations: racquetball; golf; bowling; basketball; reading. Office: Lawson Co 210 Broadway E Cuyahoga Falls OH 44222

TAITANO, MAGDALENA SANTOS, librarian; d. Jose S. and Josefa (Ignacio) Santos; B.A., Mt. Mary Coll., 1955; M.L.S., Tex. Woman's U., 1959; m. Richard F. Taitano, June 20, 1959; children—Taling Maria, Richard, John Joseph, Carmen Teresita. Reference librarian Office Tech. Services, Dept. Commerce, Washington, 1962-64; chief librarian U. Guam, Mangilao, 1964-66; territorial librarian Guam Public Library, Agana, 1966—. Sec., Guam council Girl Scouts U.S.A. Mem. Guam Library Assn., ALA. Clubs: Guam Women's, Soroptimist. Address: Nieves M Flores Memorial Library Box 652 Agana Guam 96910

TAKACH, MARY HUDCOVIC, mus. dir.; b. N.Y.C., Sept. 22, 1932; d. Gabriel and Mary (Sudjak) Hudcovic; B.A., Harpur Coll., Binghamton, N.Y., 1967; M.A. (Jennie F. Snapp scholar) in Art History, SUNY, Binghamton, 1973; m. Michael T. Takach, Jan. 31, 1953; 1 son, David T. Asst. art dept. SUNY, Binghamton, 1966-67; art tchr. Endicott (N.Y.) Public Schs., 1967-74; asst. prof. art history Syracuse U., 1974-77; curator, asst. dir. Joe and Emily Lowe Art Gallery, Syracuse U., 1974-77; cons. Nat. Endowment Humanities, 1978; ind. exhbn. cons. U.S. Ho. of Reps., 1978-79; cons. N.Y. State Council on Arts, 1980; dir. Pensacola (Fla.) Mus. Art, 1980—; small mus. com. N.E. Regional Conf. Mus., 1974-77; reader Nat. Endowment Humanities, 1981—; guest lectr. colls., hist. socs. Bd. dirs. Pensacola People to People, 1981—; mem. regional library bd. Friends of W. Fla. Regional Library Bd., 1981—; commr. Galvez Celebration, Pensacola, 1980. Ruth Frazer scholar, 1974. Mem. Am. Assn. Mus., Coll. Art Assn., S.E. Mus. Conf., LWV, Delta Kappa Gamma. Democrat. Roman Catholic. Club: Altrusa. Author: The Mural Art of Ben Shahn, 1977; contbr. chpt. in book. Research on letters of Benjamin West. Home: PO Box 641 Pensacola FL 32593 Office: Pensacola Museum of Art 407 S Jefferson St Pensacola FL 32501

TALAB, ROSEMARY STURDEVANT, library/media specialist; b. Rochester Minn., Oct. 6, 1948; d. Raymond C. and Inga E. (Sattre) Sturdevant; m. Dan H. Talab, July 9, 1980. B.A., Wichita State U., 1971; M.A. in Library Sci. Edn., M.A. in Audio Visual Edn., Ariz. State U., 1975; Ph.D., U. So. Calif., Los Angeles, 1979. Tchr. Smith Ctr. (Kans.) schs., 1971-73; intern, then asst. Mesa Community Coll., Sacaton, Ariz., 1975-76; sr. researcher, U. So. Calif., 1977-79; asst. prof. Portland (Oreg.) State U., 1980-81, audiovisual coordinator Hollywood Presbyn. Med. Ctr., Los Angeles, 1981-84; asst. prof. Coll. Edn., Kans. State U., 1984—; cons., com. mem. Med. Audiovisual Consortium, Los Angeles, 1982-84. Recipient award U. So. Calif. Alumni Assn., 1977, plaque of appreciation, Faculty Senate Gila River (Ariz.) Career Ctr., 1976; Educare scholar, 1977-79. Mem. Calif. Media Library Educators, Computer Users in Edn., Health Scis. Communicators Assn., ALA, Mid-Continental Med. Library Assn., Med. Library Group So. Calif. and Ariz., Assn. Ednl. Communications and Tech. (Kans. cert. Appreciation 1985), Am. Film Inst., Calif. Med. and Library Edn. Assn., Pi Lambda Theta, Kappa Delta Pi, Alpha Phi. Author: Commonsense Copyright, 1986. Contbr. articles to profl. jours., books. Office: Hollywood Presbyterian Medical Ctr 1300 N Vermont Ave Los Angeles CA 90027

TALAN, CAROLE SMITHERS KERNS, educational administrator; b. Lafollette, Tenn., May 8, 1945; d. G. Ray Smithers and Olive Y. (Bolinger) Smithers Bible; m. Tony L. Kerns, Apr. 15, 1966 (div. 1976); 1 child, David Ray; m. Jack R. Talan, Mar. 30, 1979. B.S., East Tenn. State U., 1968, M.A.A., 1970; Ed.D., U. Tenn., 1980. Cert. elem. and secondary tchr., specialist, Tenn.; cert. community coll. and multiple subject tchr., Calif. Elem. tchr. Unicoi County Schs., Erwin, Tenn., 1968-70; instr. East Tenn. State U., Johnson City, 1970-71; asst. prof. Tusculum Coll., Greeneville, Tenn., 1971-78; pubs. cons. Economy Co. No. Calif., 1980-82; cons. Calif. Dept. Corrections, Tracy, 1982-84; dir. Project 2d Chance, Contra Costa County Library, Pleasant Hill, Calif., 1984—; sec. Reading Council, Johnson City, 1970-71; cons. Right to Read, Morristown, Tenn., 1972-73; cons., coordinator Upward Bound, Greenville, 1972-75; reading cons. Arista, Pleasant Hill, Calif., 1979-82; v.p. JT's Barbeque Heaven, Concord, Calif., 1984—; part owner JT's Am. Food & Bar, Walnut Creek, Calif., 1985—. Recipient Disting. Service award in adult literacy U.S. Dept. Edn., 1985, Vol. Orgn. of Yr. award Contra Cost County Bd. Suprs., 1985. Mem. Internat. Reading Assn., Correctional Educators Assn. (social chmn. 1982-83), Bay Area Literacy Coop., Laubach Literacy Internat., U. Tenn. Alumni No. Calif., Kappa Delta Pi, AAUW, Alpha Xi Delta (local pres. 1966). Avocations: travel, Alpine skiing, reading. Home: 912 Mohr Ln Concord CA 94518 Office: Project Second Chance 1750 Oak Park Blvd Pleasant Hill CA 94523

TALBERT, DOROTHY GEORGIE BURKETT, social worker; b. Rison, Ark.; d. Booker T. and Dorothy (Ragan) Burkett; m. Ernest Talbert, May 14, 1949; children—Ernest George, Dorothy Ernette. A.B., Ark. State A. M. and N. Coll., 1946; M.S.W., Atlanta U., 1948; postgrad. U. Pa., 1962, Tulane U., 1965. Caseworker child welfare services Miss. Dept. Pub. Welfare, 1948-49, Ill. Pub. Aid Commn., Chgo., 1951-53; probation counselor Family Ct. Del., 1956-58; with Del. State Dept. Pub. Welfare, Dover, 1958-71, unit supr., 1962-64, supr. licensing and day care services, 1964-67, chief program devel. Child Welfare Services, 1967-68, chief services to families and children, 1968-71; asst. dir. family services, div. social services Del. Dept. Health and Social Services, 1971-78, dep. dir. adult and spl. services, 1978-82, adult crisis intervention coordinator, Newark, 1982—, staff tng./resource developer, 1985—; instr. continuing edn. program U. Del., part time 1968—; mem. social services adv. com. Del. Adolescent Program, 1969-75, bd. dirs., 1969-75; mem. State Adv. Council on Alcoholism, 1972-76; mem. Del. Devel. Disabilities Planning Council, Del. Adv. Council for Coordination of Services to Handicapped; social work edn. adv. com. Del. State Coll., 1978—. Bd. dirs. United Way of Del., 1979. Mem. Nat. Assn. Social Workers, Am. Pub. Welfare Assn., Nat. Council Pub. Welfare Adminstrs., Black Profl. Forum (sec. 1979), Nat. Caucus Black Aged, NAACP, Delta Sigma Theta. Home: 3007 W 3d St Wilmington DE 19805 Office: Div State Service Ctrs 501 Ogletown Rd Newark DE 19711

TALBERT, KATHRYN YORK, personnel executive; b. Statesville, N.C., Jan. 4, 1949; d. Robert Anderson and Kathryn Leona (Poole) York; m. William Steven Talbert, June 21, 1971 (div. Dec. 1984); 1 child, Bradley Steven. B.S. in French and B.A. in Psychology, Appalachian State U., 1970. Office mgr., receptionist Dr. Gerald Turner, D.D.S., Statesville, N.C., 1972-75; prodn. controller Grenadier Knitwear Ltd., Statesville, 1975-78; substitute tchr. West Iredell Middle Sch., Statesville, 1978-79; personnel asst. Davis Community Hosp., Statesville, 1979-83; personnel dir. Lowrance Hosp., Mooresville, N.C., 1983-85, Armitage Shanks Inc., Mooresville, 1985—; mem. indsl. relations com. Mooresville/South Iredell C. of C., 1984-85; orientation facilitator Armitage Shanks N.C. Inc., Mooresville, 1985—. Profl. chmn. Mooresville/South Iredell United Fund, 1985; adult mem. Tiger Cub Pack Boy Scouts Am., Statesville, N.C., 1985—; Smithsonian assoc. Smithsonian Inst., Washington, 1986. Recipient Profl. Chmn. Plaque, Mooresville/South Iredell United Fund, Mooresville, N.C., 1985. Mem. Nat. Assn. Female Execs., Mooresville Personnel Assn. Democrat. Baptist. Avocations: reading; bowling; camping; needlecraft. Home: 415 Bristol Dr Statesville NC 28677 Office: Armitage Shanks NC Inc PO Box 390 Mooresville NC 28115

TALBOT, MARY LEE, clergywoman; b. Cleve., Apr. 18, 1953; d. Richard William and Mary Helen (Jacobs) T. B.A., Coll. Wooster, 1975; M.Div., Andover-Newton Theol. Sch., 1979. Ordained to ministry Presbyterian Ch. (U.S.A.), 1981. Asst. in ministry Grace Congl. Ch., Framingham, Mass., 1975-78; resources coordinator Women's Theol. Coalition, Boston, 1977-79; assoc. editor Youth Mag., Phila., 1979-80; assoc. youth and young adult program Presbyn. Ch. (U.S.A.), N.Y.C., 1981—; bd. dirs. Christian Assn., U. Pa., 1979-81. Author, editor: Suicide and Youth, 1981; editor: Racism and Anti-Racism, 1982; One Fantastic Book, 1982; contbr. articles to Youth mag. Mem. Bread for the World, N.Y.C., 1980-83. Recipient English award Bus. and Profl. Women, 1971. Mem. Assn. Presbyn. Ch. Educators, Religous Edn. Assn. (bd. dirs. 1986—), ACLU, NOW, Nat. Assn. Female Execs. Republican. Presbyterian. Office: Room 1164 Youth and Young Adult Program Presbyn Ch (USA) 475 Riverside Dr New York NY 10115

TALBOT, NORMA MORRIS, broadcasting executive; b. Elisabeth City, N.C., May 9, 1922; d. Paul Monroe and Mary Elizabeth (Boseman) Morris; m. Thomas William Talbot Oct. 1, 1943 (dec. Dec. 1976); children—Mary Patricia Talbot Broda, Thomas Paul. Student Elon Coll., 1940-41. Pres. Niagara Frontier Broadcasting Corp., Niagara Falls, N.Y., 1976-83, chmn., 1983—. Bd. dirs. Mt. St. Mary's Hosp. Aux., Lewiston, N.Y., 1980-83; sec. Niagara Council on Arts, 1982-83; bd. dirs. Niagara County council Girl Scouts U.S.A., 1983. Mem. Nat. Assn. Broadcasters, Am. Women in Radio and TV. Republican. Roman Catholic. Clubs: Lioness (pres. 1961-62), Niagara Falls Country, Zonta. Avocations: golf; bridge. Home: 920 Mohawk St Lewiston NY 14092 Office: Niagara Frontier Broadcasting Corp 1224 Main St Niagara Falls NY 14301

TALBOTT, EUNICE TILLMAN, clubwoman; b. Springfield, Mo., Jan. 25, 1911; d. Sidney Ellis and Nancy Elizabeth (Denney) Tillman; B.S. (Ed.), U. Tampa, 1947; postgrad. U. Fla., 1959-61; m. William W. Talbott, June 23, 1933; 1 dau., Sharon Lynn Webb. Tchr., Hillsborough County, Fla., 1947-68; lectr. table settings; poet. Recipient awards flower shows, 1968—. Mem. NEA, Fla. Edn. Assn., English Council (program chmn. Hillsborough County 1963-65), DAR (regent 1970-72), Colonial Dames (pres. 1977-79), Magna Charta Dames, Tampa and Fla. Fedn. Garden Clubs, Plantagnet Soc., Tri Sigma. Democrat. Methodist. Clubs: Sundial Garden (pres. 1970-72), State Jr. Garden (chmn. 1945-47), Tampa Woman's (librarian 1979-80), Jasmine Garden Circle, Order of Crown. Home: 2810 Parkland Blvd Tampa FL 33609

TALBOTT, LINDA HOOD, educator, foundation executive, communications executive; b. Kansas City, Mo., Dec. 29, 1941; d. Henry H. and Helen E. (Hamrick) Hood; B.A. with highest distinction, U. Mo., 1962, M.A. (grad. fellow), 1964, Ph.D., 1973; postgrad. (postdoctoral fellow) Harvard U. Inst. Ednl. Mgmt., 1974; m. Thomas H. Talbott, Mar. 5, 1965. Prof. English, Met. Jr. Coll., Kansas City, Mo., 1963-67; prof. English, Queensborough Community Coll., Bayside, N.Y., 1967-68; prof. English, editor Nassau Rev., Nassau Community Coll., Garden City, N.Y., 1968-69; prof. English, adminstr. Lesley Coll., Cambridge, Mass., 1969; founding editor Tempo mag. and devel. officer U. Mo., Kansas City, 1969-76, dir. spl. projects Office of Chancellor, 1976—, adj. prof. edn., 1975—; pres. Talbott & Assocs., Kansas City, 1975—; exec. dir. Clearinghouse for Midcontinent Founds., Kansas City, 1975-85, pres., 1985—; dir. Kansas City Power and Light Co., 1983; lectr., cons. in field. Bd. Exchange Programming Corp., 1984—, mem. exec. N.Y.C., 1976-79, United Community Services/Heart of Am. United Way, 1974-82; mem. exec. com. The Central Exchange, 1978-85; bd. dirs. The Central Exchange Programming Corp., 1984—, Women's Employment Network, Kansas City, 1985—; mem. exec. com. Dimensions Unltd., Kansas City, 1973-77; commr. Kansas City Commn. on Status of Women, 1978-82; adminstrv. dir. Mid-Am. Assembly on Future of Performing Arts, 1979; chmn. Internat. Women's Yr. in Mid-Am. Symposium, 1975; del. Nat. Women's Conf., Houston, 1977; bd. advisors Center for

Mgmt. Assistance, Kansas City, 1979—, bd. advs. Kansas City Arts council, 1980-85, Long Term Care Project for Elderly Nat. Demonstration, Mid-Am. Regional Council, 1981—, Women's Resource Service, U. Mo., Kansas City, 1971-85; hon. dir. Rockhurst Coll., 1977—; hon. trustee Truman Med. Center Found., 1980—; bd. dirs. Greater Kansas City Mental Health Found., 1980-85, Starlight Theatre Assn., 1980—; bd. advisors Greater Kansas City Community Found., 1980-85; cons. R.A. Long Found., 1982—; mem. Community Care Funding Partners Council, 1982—. Named Kansas City Tomorrow Leader, 1978; Chi Omega Pub. Service award, 1962; Outstanding Young Woman of Mo., 1967; Woman of the Yr. award, VFW, 1972; Outstanding Achievement award, U. Mo., Kansas City Sch. Edn., 1973; publ. awards, Nat. and Regional Council for Advancement and Support of Edn., 1971, 72, 73; Regional Citizen of Yr. award Mid Am. Regional Council, 1982; Am. Inst. for Public Service award, 1982; Outstanding Career Achiever in Greater Kansas City, Mo. Gen. Assembly citation, 1985; Harvard U. fellow, 1974, others. Mem. Am. Assn. Higher Edn. (coordinator 1973-75), AAUW, Council for Advancement and Support of Edn., Council on Founds., Women and Founds./Corp. Philanthropy, Soroptimist Internat., Mortar Bd., Phi Kappa Phi, Phi Theta Kappa, Phi Delta Kappa, Pi Lambda Theta, Delta Kappa Gamma, Chi Omega. Presbyterian. Clubs: Univ. Women's, Woodside Racquet, Kansas City, Central Exchange. Author: The Community College in Community Service, 1973; Grantmaking in Greater Kansas City: The Philanthropic Impact of Foundations, 1976-80; editor: The Foundation Exchange, 1976—; A History of the University of Kansas City: Prologue to a Public University, 1976; A Brief History of Philanthropy in Kansas City, 1980; The Case for the Community Foundation, 1981; Perspectives on Trusteeship for the 80s, 1981; contbr. articles to profl. jours. Office: PO Box 7215 Kansas City MO 64113

TALLCHIEF, MARIA, ballerina; b. Fairfax, Okla., Jan. 24, 1925; d. Alexander Joseph and Ruth Mary (Porter) T.; student public schs., Calif.; A.F.D. (hon.), Lake Forest Coll. (Ill.), Colby Coll., Maine, 1968, Ripon Coll., 1973, Boston Coll., Smith Coll., 1981; hon. degree Northwestern U., 1982, Yale U., 1984, St. Mary's of the Woods, 1984; m. Henry Paschen, Jr., June 3, 1957; 1 dau., Elise. Joined Ballet Russe de Monte Carlo, 1942; prima ballerina N.Y.C. Ballet, 1947-60; guest star Paris Opera, 1947; prima ballerina Am. Ballet Theater, 1960; with N.Y.C. Ballet Co. until 1965; now artistic dir. Chgo. City Ballet. Recipient Achievement award Women's Nat. Press Club, 1953; Dance mag. award, 1960; Capezio award, 1965; named Hon. Princess-Osage Indian Tribe, 1953; Disting. Service award U. Okla., 1972; Jane Addams Humanitarian award Rockford Coll., 1973; award Dance Educators Am., 1956. Mem. Nat. Soc. Arts and Letters. Office: care Chgo City Ballet 223 W Erie St Chicago IL 60610

TALLEY, CAROLYN CORBIN, physician's office official; b. Greenville, S.C., June 14, 1940; d. Macie (Emory) Corbin; m. James C. Odom, Mar. 13, 1958 (div.); children—Alonda C. Rollison, Vicky A. Walton, Richard J.; m. 2d, Frank H. Talley, May 6, 1978. Student Draughons Bus. Coll., 1962-64. Vice pres. Talley Industries, Greenville, 1978-83; v.p., cons. Talley, Corbin, Jones & Assocs., Greenville, 1982-83; office mgr. adminstrn. Orthopedic Assocs., Greenville, 1960—. Mem. Christian Children's Fund, Worldwide, 1979-83; mem. Abused Children Fund, 1980-83; chmn. Am. Cancer Soc., Greenville, 1976—, Am. Heart Fund, Greenville, 1977. Mem. S.C. Assn. Med. Mgrs. (charter), Greenville C. of C. Baptist. Office: Orthopedic Assocs Greenville 901 W Faris Rd Greenville SC 29605

TALLEY, ELIZABETH ANN KEYS, editor; b. Stillwater, Okla., Jan. 20, 1958; d. Howard Newton and Jacquelyn (Holland) Keys; m. Kevin Dean Talley, Dec. 23, 1979. B.S., Okla. State U., 1980. Asst. editor PennWell Pub., Houston, 1981; editor Drilco div. Smith Internat., Houston, 1982-83; editor: research product coordinator Underwood, Neuhaus & Co., Inc., Houston, 1984—. Scripps-Howard Found. journalism scholar Okla. State U., 1977-78, 79-80, Lahoma Faculty Wives acad. scholar, 1979; Oklahoma City Profl. Advt. Assn. scholar, 1980. Mem. Internat. Assn. Bus. Communicators, Women in Communications, Mortar Bd., Omicron Delta Kappa, Sigma Delta Chi, Alpha Chi Omega. Methodist. Office: Underwood Neuhaus & Co Inc 724 Travis St at Rusk Ave Houston TX 77002

TALLEY, JANET LEE, electronics manufacturing company executive; b. Ironton, Ohio, Aug. 23, 1946; d. Richard Gordon and Mabel Louise (Markel) Hackworth; m. Jerold Charles Burch, Aug. 23, 1969 (div. Jan. 1974); m. Walter Reese Talley, Feb. 14, 1975; children—Garrett Lawton, Ryan Zachary. Student U. Del., 1964-66. Clk. typist Am. Life Ins. Co., Wilmington, Del., 1966-67, policy issue supr., 1968-70, life underwriter, 1971-73; office mgr. Infinetics, Inc., Wilmington, 1973-77, mgr. adminstrv. services, 1978—, asst. treas., 1981—. Vol. VA Hosp., Elsmere, Del., 1980-81; mem. Senator Joseph Biden's Adv. Commn., Wilmington, 1980—; pres. Wellington Woods Civic Assn., Newark, Del., 1983-84. Mem. Nat. Assn. Female Execs. Democrat. Methodist. Avocations: reading; travel. Office: Infinetics Inc 201 Vandever Ave Wilmington DE 19802

TALLEY, RONDA CAROL, educational administrator; b. Glasgow, Ky., Nov. 21, 1951; d. Jack Howard and Ronda Mae (McCoy) T.; B.S., Western Ky. U., 1973; M.Ed., U. Louisville, 1974, Ed.S., 1976; Ph.D., Ind. U., 1979. Spl. edn. tchr. Jefferson County Public Schs., Louisville, 1973-76; research assoc. U. Calif., Riverside, 1977, Ind. U., Bloomington, 1977; adminstrv. intern Bur. Edn. Handicapped, HEW, Washington, 1978-81; adj. prof. dept. spl. edn. U. Louisville, 1981-83; adj. prof. Spalding U., 1984-86; coordinator assessment/placement services exceptional child edn. Jefferson County Public Schs., Louisville, 1981—; founder, pres. Tri-T Assocs., 1982—. Sta. WHAS Crusade for Children grantee, 1974-76; Bur. Edn. for Handicapped student research grantee, 1978; cert. sch. psychologist. Mem. Am. Psychol. Assn. (chmn. adminstrs. sch. psychol. services), Am. Ednl. Research Assn., Nat. Assn. Sch. Psychologists, Women in Sch. Adminstrn., Ky. Assn. Sch. Adminstrs., Ky. Assn. Psychology in the Schs. (pres.), Council Exceptional Children, AAUP, Phi Delta Kappa, Kappa Delta. Republican. Methodist. Editor: Special Education in Transition: Administrator's Handbook on Integrating America's Mildly Handicapped Students, 1982. Home: 9104 Hurstwood Ct Louisville KY 40222 Office: 4409 Preston Hwy Louisville KY 40213

TALLMAN, BONNIE GOLDMAN, lawyer; b. Trenton, N.J., Feb. 11, 1950; d. Norman and Sylvia (Azarchi) Goldman; m. Irving W. Tallman, Jr., Jan. 10, 1982. B.A. magna cum laude, Boston U., 1972; J.D., New Eng. Sch. Law, Boston, 1976. Bar: N.J. 1977, U.S. Dist. Ct. N.J. 1977, U.S. Supreme Ct. Law clk. Superior Ct., Mt. Holly, N.J., 1976-77; asst. county prosecutor Burlington County, Mt. Holly, 1977-82, chief trial atty., 1981-82; ptnr. Goldman and Goldman, Robbinsville, N.J., 1982—; police instr. Burlington County Pub. Safety Ctr. (N.J.), 1977-82 lectr. seminars on juvenile and criminal justice, 1978-81. Speaker Community Vols. in Edn., 1979-81; mem. Bordentown 300th Com. Recipient award of appreciation for instrn. Burlington County Fire Acad., 1980; cert of appreciation Legal Secs. Assn., 1980; cert of achievement Pemberton Twp. Police Dept. (N.J.), 1982. Mem. Burlington County Bar Assn. (Robert Criscuolo Lawyer of Yr. award 1982, trustee, 1981), N.J. Bar Assn., Mercer County Bar Assn., ABA, Assn. Trial Lawyers Am., Am. Arbitration Assn. (arbitrator), Bordentown Hist. Soc. (exec. com.) rec. sec. 1981), Sarah Seidel Sisterhood. Jewish. Office: Goldman and Goldman Route 526 PO Box 174 Robbinsville NJ 08691

TALLMAN, MARILYN MARIE, radio consulting firm executive; b. Atlanta, Feb. 6, 1954; d. Benjamin Snow and Marjorie Alice (Murphy) Hand; m. Donald Spencer Tallman, Sept. 10, 1972 (div.). Student W.Va. State Coll., 1971-72, Valley Coll., North Hollywood, Calif., 1973-75. With McKee Baking Co., Collegedale, Tenn., 1971-72; product devel. coordinator Superscope/Marantz, Northridge, Calif., 1972-74; office mgr. Drake-Chenault, Inc., Canoga Park, Calif., 1974-79; music dir. Sta. KIQQ Radio, Los Angeles, 1979-80; traffic dir. Watermark, Inc., North Hollywood, Calif., 1980-81; v.p. ops. Jeff Pollack Communications, Inc., Pacific Palisades, Calif., 1981—, seminar coordinator, music dir., 1982—. Vol. big sister Big Sisters Am., 1977—, recipient Proficiency and Leadership award, 1978. Mem. Meeting Planners Internat. Republican. Episcopalian. Home: 14945 Moorpark St Apt 103 Sherman Oaks CA 91403 Office: Jeff Pollack Communications Inc 984 Monument St Suite 204 Pacific Palisades CA 90272

TALLMAN, RUTH MARCHAK (MRS. FRANK G. TALLMAN III), aviation exec.; b. Scranton, Pa., July 18, 1929; d. Michael and Mary (Hosko) Marchak; student Seton Hall Coll., 1948; m. Frank Gifford Tallman, III, Feb. 18, 1968. Fashion model Blue Book Modeling, Hollywood, Calif., 1944-48; sec. to controller, personnel mgr Sta. KTLA-TV, Hollywood, 1955-63; owner Tallmantz Aviation Inc. Frank Tallman's Movieland of the Air Aircraft Mus., John Wayne Airport, Santa Ana, 1968—. Mem. Soc. Exptl. Test Pilots, Newport Harbor Art Mus., Ladies Aux. Whirly Girls. Roman Catholic. Clubs: Balboa Bay, Indian Wells Racquet. Home: 1973 Vista Caudal Newport Beach CA 92660 Office: 19711 Airport Way S John Wayne Airport Santa Ana CA 92707

TALLY, LURA SELF, state legislator; b. Statesville, N.C., Dec. 9, 1921; d. Robert Ottis and Sara (Cowles) Self; A.B., Duke U., 1942; M.A., N.C. State U., Raleigh, 1970; m. J.O. Tally, Jr., Jan. 30, 1943 (div. 1970); children—Robert Taylor, John Cowles. Tchr., former guidance counselor Fayetteville (N.C.) city schs.; mem. N.C. Ho. of Reps. from 20th Dist., 1971-83, chmn. com. higher edn., from 1975, also 1980-83, vice chmn. com. appropriations for edn., 1973-86; state senator from 12th Dist. N.C., 1983—. Past pres. Cumberland County Mental Health Assn., N.C. Historic Preservation Soc.; trustee Fayetteville Tech. Inst., 1981-86. Mem. Am. Personnel and Guidance Assn., Fayetteville Bus. and Profl. Women's Club, Kappa Delta, Delta Kappa Gamma. Methodist. Club: Fayetteville Woman's (past pres.). Office: NC Legis Bldg W Jones St Raleigh NC 27611

TALTY, LORRAINE CAGUIOA, manufacturer's representative; b. Makati, Manila, Philippines, July 3, 1957; came to U.S., 1973, naturalized, 1983; d. Leon Perez and Asuncion (Rodriguez) Caguioa; m. Kevin Michael Talty, Jan. 23, 1982. B.B.A. in Acctg. magna cum laude, Chaminade U., Honolulu, 1979. Office mgr., comptroller Caro of Honolulu, 1976-82; acct. David Schenkein, C.P.A., Latham, N.Y., 1984—; sales rep. Caromat Corp., Torrance, Calif., 1985—; owner Kevlor Internat., mfrs. rep. agy., Clifton Park, N.Y., 1985—. Newsletter editor Country Knolls West Civic Assn., Clifton Park, 1984-85, civic com. rep., 1985-86. Home: 8 Firestone Ln Clifton Park NY 12065

TAMA, PHYLLIS ELAINE, executive search consultant; b. Bklyn., Sept. 23, 1938; d. Louis and Fritzi (Perschetz) T. A.A.S., Bklyn Coll., 1961. Fashion coordinator V.F. Corp., N.Y.C., 1962-73; v.p., dir. corp. exec. placement May Dept. Stores, N.Y.C., 1973-78, Saks Fifth Ave., N.Y.C., 1978-80; div. v.p., exec. placement Associated Merchandising Corp., N.Y.C., 1980-82; exec. search cons. Thorndike Deland Assocs., N.Y.C., 1982—. Mem. The Fashion Group, Nat. Assn. Female Execs., Networks Unlimited, Inc. Contbr. article to profl. jours. Home: 150 West End Ave New York NY 10023 Office: Thorndike Deland Assocs 1440 Broadway New York NY 10018

TAMBURO, CONSTANCE DOLORES, sales representative; b. Englewood, N.J., Oct. 6, 1940; d. Anthony M. and Carmella (Masci) Merlino; m. Vincent A. Tamburo, Aug. 4, 1962; children—Robert M., Theodore V. A.B., Chatham Coll., 1962. Cert. tchr. Tchr., Fox Chapel and Penn Hills, Pa., 1962-64, 73-76; real estate agt. Koenig & Strey, Lake Forest, Ill., 1977-79; sales rep. Commerce Clearing House, Chgo., 1980—. Docent, Midwest Mus. Am. Art, Elkhart, Ind., 1980-84; pres. Pitts. Opera Guild, 1972-76; mem. Pitts. Opera Aux., 1986—. Andrew Smalley scholar, 1960, 61, 62. Mem. Nat. Orgn. Female Execs., AAUW (v.p. Lake Forest 1976-79), Chatham Coll. Alumnae Assn. (exec. bd. 1986—), Mortar Board. Roman Catholic. Avocation: Tennis. Home: 119 Pheasant Dr Pittsburgh PA 15238 Office: Suite 1175 Chatham Two Pittsburgh PA 15219

TAMEN, HARRIET, lawyer; b. Yonkers, N.Y., May 17, 1947; d. Saul and Lily (Balglau) Tamen. A.B., Bryn Mawr Coll., 1969; J.D., George Washington U., Washington, 1973. Bar: N.Y. 1974, U.S. Dist. Ct. (so. dist.) N.Y. 1975. Atty., W.T. Grant, N.Y.C., 1974-76; atty. City of N.Y. Office Econ. Devel., Div. Real Property, N.Y.C., 1977-81; atty. Credit Lyonnais Bank, N.Y.C., 1981-86, Chase Manhattan Bank, 1986—. Bd. dirs. Dromenon Theatre, N.Y., 1980—; bd. dirs. Nat. Dance Inst., N.Y., 1982, chmn. bd. dirs., 1984—; mem. campaign staff Ed Koch for Mayor, N.Y.C., 1977. Mem. ABA, Bar Assn. City of N.Y.

TAMERIN, BARBARA JACOBS, corporate art consultant; b. N.Y.C., Dec. 6, 1939; d. Robert Alan Jacobs and Frances Nathan (Cullman) Boas; m. John S. Tamerin, July 25, 1962 (div.); children—Elizabeth Nathan, John S. B.A., NYU, 1963; postgrad., Yale U., 1965-66, Bank Street Grad. Sch., N.Y.C., 1966-67. Dir. art exhibits, U. Va., Charlottesville, 1968-69; head children's art workshops, Corcoran Mus., Washington, 1969-70; sr. assoc., cons. Art Placement Internat., N.Y.C., 1980-81; pres. Barbara J. Tamerin Fine Arts, N.Y.C., 1980—; Campaign worker Mondale for pres., N.Y.C., 1980; mem. Central Synagogue, N.Y.C. Mem. N.Y. Assn. Women Bus. Owners. Democrat. Club: Century Country (Purchase, N.Y.). Address: 120 E 81st St New York NY 10028

TAMKIN, PRISCILLA MARTIN, investment management company executive; b. San Francisco, June 1, 1949; d. Francis Augustus, Jr., and Consuelo (Tobin) Martin; m. Curtis Sloane Tamkin, Oct. 18, 1975; 1 son, Curtis Sloane. B.A. in Communications, Stanford U., 1971; J.D., Hastings Coll. Law, U. Calif.-San Francisco, 1974. Bar: Calif. 1975. Staff counsel Pacific Lighting Corp., Los Angeles, 1974-76, Times Mirror Co., Los Angeles, 1977-82; ptnr. Mariposa Investors, Pasadena, Calif., 1982—; v.p. sec., Tamkin Co., 1983—. Bd. dirs. Santa Fe Festival Theatre (N.Mex.), 1980—; mem. Blue Ribbon Four Hundred Music Ctr., Los Angeles, 1975—. Mem. ABA, Calif. State Bar. Republican. Roman Catholic. Office: Mariposa Investors 650 Sierra Madre Villa Ave Pasadena CA 91107

TAMM, JUDY ELIZABETH, banker; b. Gordonsville, Va., Nov. 21, 1946; d. John R. and Martha W. (Willis) T.; B.S. in Edn., Bucknell U., Lewisburg, Pa., 1968; postgrad. N.Y.U. Security analyst Keefe Bruyette & Woods, Inc., N.Y.C., 1968-72; with Chase Manhattan Bank, N.Y.C., 1972—, v.p., mcpl. trader, 1980—. Mem. jr. exec. com. Women's Nat. Republican Club, 1976-79. Mem. Investment Assn. N.Y., Women's Mcpl. Bond Club (sec. 1983-84), Jr. League City N.Y. Republican. Mem. Reformed Ch. Home: 46 Dale Ave Wyckoff NJ 07481 Office: 1 Chase Manhattan Plaza New York NY 10081

TAN, JULIA, cardiologist, internist; b. Kunming, China, Mar. 1, 1943; came to U.S., 1949, naturalized, 1961; d. Pia Chu and Alice (Wong) Tan; A.B., Wilson Coll., 1965; M.D., Med. Coll. Pa., 1969. Intern, resident Med. Coll. Va., Richmond, 1969-71; resident N.Y. Med. Coll. Hosps., 1971-73; resident in cardiology Case-Western Res.-Cleve. Met. Gen. Hosp., 1973-75; practice medicine specializing in internal medicine and cardiology, Visalia, Calif., 1975—, pres. Julia Tan, M.D., Inc.; dir. CCU Visalia Community Hosp., 1975—; mem. staffs Kaweah Delta Dist. Hosp., Visalia Community Hosp.; cons. staff Exeter Meml. Hosp., Tulare Dist. Hosp.; mem. Calif. 9th Dist. Med. Quality Rev. Com., 1976-83. Diplomate Am. Bd. Internat. Medicine. Fellow Am. Coll. Cardiology (assoc.); mem. Am. Heart Assn. (dir. Central Valley chpt. 1975-80), Calif. Med. Assn., AMA, Tulare County Med. Soc. Office: 1827 S Court St Suite C Visalia CA 93277

TANA, ALICE MCFADDEN, business services firm executive; b. Freeland, Pa., Oct. 17, 1935; d. Adrian W. and Alice T. (Campbell) Carr; student Georgetown U., 1968-70, Catholic U. Am., 1967-69, U. Mich., 1963-67, Eastern Mich. U., 1963-67, U. Calif., San Diego, 1977-79; also numerous workshops, symposiums; m. Yasuto Tana, Oct. 13, 1973. Supr. order dept. Gallant Inc., Washington, 1954-58; tchr. Mary Anne Baldwin Sch., Pitts., 1958-60; dir. sr. citizen and women City of Ypsilanti (Mich.), 1961-67; regional dir. Nat. Council on Aging, Washington, 1967-70; liaison officer congl./pvt. sector Exec. Office of Pres., Washington, 1971-72; dir. Pres.'s Task Force on Aging, Washington, 1972-73; tng. specialist Japanese Self Def. Force/Sumitomo Corp., Taura, Japan, 1973-76; econ. devel. specialist County San Diego (Calif.), 1977-80, project dir. transp. research and mktg. study, 1980, budget analyst, 1981-82; founder Ask Alice, bus. and personal services for profls., San Diego, 1982—; mem. adv. bd. Women and Mgmt., Georgetown U.; mem. women in politics and govt. Rutgers U., 1980-81. Founder, pres. Diversified Bus. Women, ednl. orgn., San Diego; trustee World Family Living, San Diego, Internat. Student Exchange Program TZ Assos., San Diego. Recipient B-MAC award Mich. Recreation and Parks Assn., 1967, Disting. Service in Disaster Ops. award Pres. U.S., 1972, cert. appreciation Japanese Self-Def. Force, 1975. Mem. Calif. Women in Govt. (pres. 1980-81), San Diego C. of C. (Econ. Research Council), Am. Soc. Public Adminstrs., Nat. Assn. Female Execs., San Diego Women Execs. Network GROW (dir.), Republican Bus. and Profl. Women, Eastern Mich. U. Alumni Assn. (condr. ann. events 1967—), Econ. Research Bur. Clubs: Exchange (Outstanding award 1967), Optimists (Outstanding award 1963). Contbr. articles to profl. jours. Home and office: 3114 E Fox Run Way San Diego CA 92111

TANCZAK-DYCIO, MARY, physician; b. Rybnyky, Ukraine, July 10, 1922; came to U.S., 1950, naturalized, 1955; d. Basil and Helen (Cisyk) Tanczak; student U. Lviv, 1940-41, Med. Sch., 1942-44, U. Erlangen (Germany), 1945-49; m. George Dycio, Nov. 11, 1949; children—George Myron, Mark Roman. Resident, Contagious Disease Hosp., Belleville, N.J., 1951-52; intern Mercy Hosp., Canton, Ohio, 1952-53, resident anesthesia, 1952-55; practice medicine specializing in anesthesiology, 1955-58; mem. staff Irvington (N.J.) Gen. Hosp., 1955-58; staff St. Mary's Gen. Hosp., Lewiston, Maine, 1958—, chief anesthesia dept., 1960—, also dir. Sch. Nurse Anesthetists. Fellow Am. Coll. Anesthesiologist; mem. AMA, Am.-Ukrainian, Maine. Androscoggin County med. socs. Office: 300 Pine St Lewiston ME 04240 also 3 Bayberry Ln Lewiston ME 04240

TANDY, JESSICA, actress; b. London, June 7, 1909; d. Harry and Jessie Helen (Horspool) Tandy; student Dame Alice Owens Girls Sch., also Ben Greet Acad. Acting, 1924-27; LL.D. (hon.), U. Western Ont., 1974; m. Jack Hawkins, 1932 (div. 1940); 1 dau., Susan (Mrs. John Tettemer); m. Hume Cronyn, 1942; children—Christopher Hume, Tandy. First profl. acting role in Manderson Girls, later appeared in Comedy of Good and Evil, Alice Sit-by-the-Fire, Yellow Sands: London debut in The Rumor, 1929, other theatre appearances in Twelfth Night, 1930, Man Who Pays the Piper, Autumn Crocus, Port Said, 1931; various engagements Old Vic, London, including Midsummer Night's Dream, Hamlet, King Lear, 1933-40; first stage appearance U.S., 1930, on Broadway in Time and Conways, 1938, White Steed, 1939, Yesterday's Magic, 1942, Streetcar Named Desire, 1947, Four Poster, 1951-53, Madame Will You Walk, 1953, The Honeys, 1955, A Day by the Sea, 1955, The Man in the Dog Suit, 1958, Five Finger Exercise, 1959, The Physicists, 1964, Noel Coward in Two Keys, 1974, Salonika, 1985, The Petition, 1986; played in Mpls. in Hamlet, Three Sisters, Death of a Salesman, 1963, in Way of the World, The Cherry Orchard, The Caucasian Chalk Circle, 1965; summer theatre prodns., 1950-55; appeared Triple Play, 1958-59, Big Fish, Little Fish, London, 1962; reading tour U.S. (with husband), Face to Face, 1954, A Delicate Balance, 1966-67, The Miser, 1968, Heartbreak House, Shaw Festival, 1968; Tchin-Tchin, Chgo., 1969, Camino Real, Lincoln Center, N.Y.C., 1970, Home, Morosco, N.Y., 1971, All Over, N.Y.C., 1971; appeared (with husband) in Samuel Beckett festival, Lincoln Center, N.Y.C., 1972; tour of Promenade All, 1972-73, Tour Not I, 1973; limited concert recital tour Many Faces of Love, 1974, 75, 76, also Seattle Repertory theatre; tour Noel Coward in Two Keys, 1975; tour The Gin Game, U.S., Toronto, London, USSR, 1978-79; appeared (with husband) in Foxfire, Stratford (Ont.) Festival, 1980, Guthrie Theatre, Mpls., 1981, Long Day's Journey into Night, also in Rose, N.Y.C., 1981, Glass Menagerie, N.Y.C., 1983, 84; appeared in The Way of the World, A Midsummer Night's Dream, Eve, Stratford (Ont.) Festival, 1976, Long Day's Journey Into Night, London, Ont., 1977, The Gin Game, New Haven, 1977, N.Y.C., 1978; motion pictures include Valley of Decision, Green Years, Desert Fox, A Light in the Forest, 1958, The Birds, 1962, Butley, 1973, Honky Tonk Freeway, 1980, Still of the Night, 1981, Best Friends, 1982, The Bostonians, 1983; TV prodns., Portrait of a Madonna, 1948, Christmas 'Till Closing, 1955, Marriage, series, 1954, The Fallen Idol, 1959, The Moon and Sixpence, 1959, Cocoon, 1985. Dramatic adv. Goddard Neighborhood Center, N.Y.C., 1948. Recipient ann. Antoinette Perry award for performance Streetcar Named Desire, 1948; Twelfth Night Club award for performance Streetcar Named Desire; Della Austria Medal from the Drama League N.Y.; bronze medallion (with husband) for performance The Four Poster, Comedia Matinee Club, 1952; Obie award for Not I, 1973; Drama Desk award for Happy Days and Not I, Drama Desk award, Tony award for best actress in The Gin Game, 1978; Los Angeles Critics award, 1979; Sarah Siddons award, 1979; Theater Arts medal for lifetime of disting. achievement Brandeis U.; Tony award for best actress in FoxFire, Drama Desk award, Outer Circle Critics award, 1983; Commonwealth award for disting. service to dramatic arts, 1983; elected to Theatre Hall of Fame, 1979. Office: care Hesseltine Baker & Assocs Ltd 165 W 46th St New York NY 10036

TANENBAUM, TERESA (TERRI) ANN, educational service executive; b. Primghar, Iowa, Jan. 1, 1952; d. Owen Edward and Mildred Anna (Livezey) Crosbie; m. Steven Claire Waugh, June 15, 1974 (div. 1979); m. Joseph Israel Tanenbaum, Aug. 26, 1979. B.S. in Child Devel., Iowa State U., 1974. Vice prin., tchr. Bishop Helmsing Early Childhood Ctr., Kansas City, Mo., 1974-77; seminar leader Tanenbaum & Assocs., Marina Del Rey, Calif., 1979—; owner In Care of Women, cons., 1984—; mem. Couples Consortium (group sponsor confs. U.S. and Europe dealing with human relationships), Los Angeles, 1983—; pub. speaker, also radio and TV appearances, Denver, Houston, Aspen (Colo.), Los Angeles. Mem. Women's Referral Service, Women's Ednl. Service Assn., Nat. Assn. Female Execs. Democrat. Quaker. Home and Office: 14108 W Tahiti Way #624 Marina Del Rey CA 90292

TANG, ANNE, physician; b. Hong Kong, Feb. 2, 1950; d. Kwok-Ying and Moo-Ching (Chan) T.; m. Kin H. Luk; 1 child, Joseph Kent. A.B. in Bacteriology, U. Calif.-Berkeley, 1970, M.D., U. Calif.-San Francisco, 1974. Diplomate Am. Bd. Internal Medicine. Intern, resident Kaiser Found. Hosp., San Francisco, 1975-77; staff internist Kaiser-Permanente Med. Group, San Francisco, 1977—, pres. med. staff Kaiser Found. Hosp., San Francisco, 1982—, sec., 1980-82; clin. instr. dept. medicine Stanford U. Sch. Medicine, 1980—. Bd. dirs. Lay Acad. Episcopal Diocese Calif., San Francisco, 1982—; choirmaster True Sunshine Episc. Parish, San Francisco, 1981-83, vestry mem., 1978-81. Recipient Osgood Research award Western sect. Am. Fedn. Clin. Research, 1972; Kraft prize U. Calif.-Berkeley, 1967; Dean's prize in Research, U. Calif.-San Francisco, 1974. Mem. Phi Beta Kappa.

TANGUAY, ANITA WALBURGA, real estate broker; b. Oberndorf, Germany, July 31, 1936; came to U.S., 1958, naturalized, 1968; d. Karl W. and Luise (Roescheisen) Ederle; m. Donald M. Tanguay, Jan. 21, 1958; children—Elizabeth Ivy, Aimee Marie. Student schs. Oberndorf, Heidelberg; grad. Real Estate Inst. Middlesex Coll., N.J., 1981. Sales assoc. Lois Schneider Co., Summit, N.J., 1978-82; pres. Tanguay Assocs. Inc., Millburn, N.J., 1982—. Co-founder Hospice Overlook Hosp., Summit, 1978—, bd. dirs., 1980-84. Mem. Bd. Realtors Maplewood Oranges (trustee), N.J. Assn. Realtors, Nat. Assn. Realtors, Comml. Indsl. Real Estate Women (exec. bd., treas. 1983—). Republican. Roman Catholic. Avocations: gardening; classical music. Home: 26 Crescent Pl Short Hill NJ 07078 Office: The Courtyard 343 Millburn Ave Millburn NJ 07041

TANKERSLEY, VICTORIA RISS, university official; b. Kansas City, Mo., May 13, 1954; d. Richard Roland Riss II and Freda Gale (Hunt) Riss Middaugh; m. Herbert Wayner Tankersley, Mar. 17, 1982. Real estate salesman's lic., Colo. Sr. data controller Bayly Corp., Englewood, Colo., 1976-79, computer operator, 1979-81; computer operator Mid-Continent Computer Services, Englewood, 1981; sr. operator Energetics, Inc., Englewood, 1981-82; computer room supr. U. Denver, 1982-84, ops. mgr., 1984—. Home: 2351 S Gaylord Denver CO 80210 Office: U Denver 2020 S Race St Room BA367 Denver CO 80208

TANKOOS, SANDRA MAXINE, court reporting executive; b. Bklyn., Nov. 12, 1936; d. Samuel J. and Ethel (Seltzer) Rich; m. Kenneth Robert Tankoos, Mar. 17, 1957; children—Robert Ian, Gary Russell, Jenine Sheryl. A.A., Stenotype Inst., 1957; B.A., Queens Coll., 1969; M.A., C.W. Post Coll., 1973. Cert. stenotype reporter, 1959. Ct. reporter free lance, N.Y.C., 1957-70; tchr. Spanish, various high schs., L.I., 1970-76; pres. Tankoos Reporting, N.Y.C., 1976—, Ar-Ti Recording, Mineola, N.Y., 1977—. Contbr. articles to profl. jours. Bd. dirs. Temple Sinai, Roslyn Hts., N.Y., 1979—, Liberal Jewish Day Sch., W. Hempstead, 1984—, LWV, Roslyn, 1969-75, NOW, Nassau County, 1975-77. Mem. Nat. Assn. Shorthand Reporters, Principal's Assn. Democrat. Club: Numismatic (pres. 1973-78). Avocations: writing; piano. Home: 77 Shepherd Ln Roslyn Heights NY 11577 Office: Ar-Ti Recording Inc 223 Jericho Turnpike Mineola NY 11501 also Tankoos Reporting Co 150 Nassau St New York NY 10038

TANNEN, RICKI LEWIS, lawyer, writer; b. N.Y.C., Apr. 29, 1952; d. Paul and Lillian (Singer) Lewis; m. Marc Jay Tannen, Aug. 25, 1972; children—Laine Amy, Adam Jesse. B.A. in History U. Fla., 1975, M.Ed. in Linguistics, 1981, J.D. with honors, 1981. Bar: Fla. 1982. Tchr. Oak Hall Pvt. Sch., Gainesville, Fla., 1976-79; atty., jud. clk. U.S. Dist. Cts., Miami, Fla., 1981-82; assoc., representing Ft. Lauderdale News and Sun-Sentinel newspaper Ferrero, Middlebrooks, Strickland & Fischer, Ft. Lauderdale, Fla., 1982—; co-chmn. 1986 Fla. Bar Media Law Conf.; research coordinator Ctr. for Govtl. Responsibility, Gainesville, 1979-81. Editor: Elderly Law in Florida, 1982. Contbr. articles to profl. jours. Mem. ABA, Fla. Bar Assn., Am. Fedn. Trial

Laws, Fla. Assn. Women Lawyers. Office: Ferrero Middlebrooks Strickland & Fischer 707 SE 3d Ave Fort Lauderdale FL 33316

TANNENBAUM, ALICE SUSAN, pathologist; b. Washington, Sept. 30, 1942; d. Hyman and Ida (Grodensky) T.; m. Douglas E. Nemens, Feb. 23, 1974; children—Katherine, Deborah. B.S. cum laude, U. Md., 1964, M.D., 1968. Diplomate Am. Bd. Pathology. Intern and resident NYU-Bellevue Med. Ctr., N.Y.C., 1968-70, resident in pathology and research fellow in electron microscopy, 1970-71; lectr. pathology St. Thomas Hosp. Med. Sch., London, 1972; research fellow in clin. immunology dept. pediatrics Mt. Sinai Hosp., N.Y.C., 1972-73; research fellow and assoc. in allergy and immunology Meml.-Sloan Kettering Cancer Ctr., N.Y.C., 1973-76; resident in clin. pathology Bryn Mawr Hosp., Pa., 1976-78; asst. pathologist St. Lukes-Roosevelt Med. Ctr., N.Y.C., 1978-80; assoc. pathologist Luth. Med. Ctr., N.Y.C., 1980-81; blood bank dir. trainee N.Y. Blood Ctr., N.Y.C., 1981-82; asst., then assoc. dir. clin. pharmacology Revlon Health Care Group, Tuckahoe, N.Y., 1982—. Contbr. articles to profl. jours. NIH fellow Marine Biol. Lab., summers 1965, 66; Physician's Recognition award in continuing med. edn. AMA, 1984. Fellow Am. Soc. Clin. Pathologists, Coll. Am. Pathologists; mem. Am. Soc. for Clin. Pharmacology and Therapeutics, AAAS, Am. Assn. Blood Banks, N.Y. Med. Women's Assn., N.Y. Acad. Scis. Avocations: running, gardening, art. Home: 338 W 72d St New York NY 10023

TANNENBAUM, BERNICE SALPETER, association executive; b. N.Y.C.; d. Isidore and May Franklin; B.A., Bklyn. Coll.; m. Nathan Tannenbaum; 1 son, Richard Salpeter. Mem. exec. bd. Nat. Conf. Soviet Jewry; mem. exec. bd. Am. sect. World Jewish Congress, chmn. internat. affairs com.; mem. Zionist Gen. Council; chmn. Am. sect. World Zionist Orgn.; bd. govs., mem. gen. assembly Jewish Agy.; bd. dirs., v.p. United Israel Appeal, Jewish Nat. Fund; mem. exec. com. Am. Zionist Fedn.; mem. Conf. of Pres. of Maj. Jewish Orgns.; nat. pres. Hadassah, N.Y.C., 1976-80, immediate past pres., 1980—; nat. chmn. Hadassah Med. Relief Assn.; mem. Jewish Telegraphic Agy.; bd. govs. Hebrew U. Office: 50 W 58th St New York NY 10019

TANNENBAUM, ELIZABETH GINSBERG, lawyer; b. Phila., Jan. 24, 1956; d. Norman William and Diane (Budwig) Ginsberg; m. Jerome S. Tannenbaum, June 4, 1977. Student Emory U., 1973-75; B.S., Vanderbilt U., 1977; J.D., magna cum laude, St. Louis U., 1981. Bar: Mo. 1981, Tex. 1983. Staff acct. McNeilly Day Home, Nashville, 1977-78; summer assoc. Husch, Eppenberger, Donohue, Elson & Cornfeld, St. Louis, 1980, assoc., 1981-83; assoc. Johnson & Swanson, Dallas, 1983-85; pres. HyperScan Dallas, Inc., 1985—; dir. KinCare, Inc., Dallas. Mem. ABA (joint exec. com. ABA/Am. Land Inst. 1980-81), Dallas Bar Assn., State Bar Tex., Alpha Sigma Nu. Republican. Jewish. Office: HyperScan Dallas Inc 4809 Cole Ave Suite 330 Dallas TX 75205 also HyperScan Nashville 4515 Harding Rd Suite 308 Nashville TN 37205

TANNER, DONNA SUE, office systems company executive, word processing trainer; b. Plant City, Fla., Dec. 27, 1957; d. Albert Roy and Francis Laverne (Copeland) Neal; m. Michael George Tanner, June 9, 1979; 1 child, Samantha. A.A., Bauder Coll., 1978; Assoc. Bus., Coastal Carolina Community Coll., 1983. Sec., bookkeeper Marine Gun & Lock, Jacksonville, N.C., 1981-82; office mgr. Ch. of Christ, Jacksonville, 1982-84; mktg. service rep. South Office systems, Pensacola, Fla., 1985—, office mgr., 1984—; software cons. South Office Systems, Pensacola, 1985—. Mem. Nat. Assn. Female Execs. Republican. Mem. Ch. of Christ. Clubs: Nat. Rifle Assn. (instr. 1982-84), Onslow Ladies Gun (pres. 1982). Avocations: rock climbing; sailing; racquetball. Office: South Office Systems 4400 Bayou Blvd Suite 39B Pensacola FL 32503

TANNER, HELEN HORNBECK, historian; b. Northfield, Minn., July 5, 1916; d. John Wesley and Frances Cornelia (Wolfe) Hornbeck; A.B. with honors, Swarthmore Coll., 1937; M.A., U. Fla., 1949; Ph.D. (AAUW fellow), U. Mich., 1961; m. Wilson P. Tanner, Jr., Nov. 22, 1940 (dec. 1977); children—Frances, Margaret Tanner Tewson, Wilson P., Robert (dec. 1983). Asst. to dir. public relations Public Schs. Kalamazoo, 1937-39; with sales dept. Am. Airlines, Inc., N.Y.C., 1940-43; teaching fellow, then teaching asst. U. Mich., 1949-53, 57-60, lectr. extension service, 1961-72, asst. dir. Center Continuing Edn. Women, 1964-68, project dir. Newberry Library, Chgo., 1976-81, research assoc., 1981—; dir. D'Arcy McNickle Ctr. for Indian History, 1984-85; cons., expert witness Indian treaties; mem. Mich. Commn. Indian Affairs, 1966-70. Grantee NEH, 1976. Mem. Am. Soc. Ethnohistory (pres. 1982-83), Am. Hist. Assn., Western Hist. Assn., Conf. Latin Am. History, Soc. History Discoveries, Can. Cartographic Assn., Fla. Hist. Soc., Hist. Soc. Mich. Author: Zespedes in East Florida, 1784-1790, 1963; General Green Visits St. Augustine, 1964; The Greeneville Treaty, 1974; The Territory of the Caddo Tribe of Oklahoma, 1974; editor: Atlas of Great Lakes Indian History, 1986. Home: 1319 Brooklyn Ave Ann Arbor MI 48104 Office: 60 W Walton St Chicago IL 60610

TANNER, JANET WITTE, corporate executive; b. Buffalo, Dec. 21, 1944; d. Michael and Louise (Wujek) T. Student, Paris, 1965; B.A. in Econs., Mt. Holyoke Coll., 1966; M.B.A. in Fin. and Acctg., Columbia U., 1971. Security analyst Am. Security and Trust, Washington, 1967-69; mgr. common stock analysis Aetna Life and Casualty Co., Hartford, Conn., 1971-73, dir. fin. analysis, 1974-76, asst. v.p. bond investment dept., 1977-82; pres. Tanner Capital Corp. (investment banking), Boston, 1982—. Chmn. fin. com. YWCA, Hartford, 1981-82; exec. com. bd. dirs. Hartford Ballet, 1977-81. Mem. Boston Soc. Security Analysts, Hartford Soc. Fin. Analysts (assoc.). Club: Sky (Boston). Home: 5 Spruce Ct Boston MA 02108

TANNER, PENNY LEAH, nurse, hypnotherapist; b. Lubbock, Tex., May 7, 1951; d. William Douglas and Alma Jeanne (Sprawls) Tanner; 1 child, Morghan Laine Austin. Diploma, N.W. Tex. Hosp. Sch. Nursing, 1976; B.S.N. with highest honors, U. Tex. Med. Br., Galveston, 1979; M.P.H., U. Tex.-Houston, 1985; M.S., Tex. Woman's U., 1985. R.N., Tex. Emergency room staff nurse Methodist Hosp., Houston, 1976-79; staff nurse ICU Hermann Hosp., Houston, 1977; head nurse intensive care-coronary care Northshore Med. Plaza, Houston, 1977-78; staff relief nurse intensive care-coronary care, Nursefinders, Houston, 1978-80; hosp. supr. West Oaks Hosp., Houston, 1982—; pvt. practice hypnotherapy, Houston, 1984—. Designer and stitcher Yellow Rose of Tex. piece, Am. Needlepoint Guild, 1982. Vol. Hospice of Vis. Nurses Assn., Houston, 1980—, Am. Cancer Soc., Houston, 1982—; vol. speaker, Am. Heart Assn., Houston, 1978—; vol. children's psychiatry dept. Tex. Children's Hosp., Houston, 1981-82. Recipient cert. of appreciation Hospice of Vis. Nurses Assn., 1981, 82. Mem. Am. Nurses Assn., Am. Group Psychotherapy Assn. (student mem.), Houston Group Psychotherapy Assn., Houston Area Psychiatric Nurse Mgrs. Assn., Sigma Theta Tau. Embroiderer's Guild, Needlepoint Guild, Smocking Arts Guild. Republican. Baptist. Office: Hypnotherapy Ctr 5555 W Loop S Suite 409 Bellaire TX 77401

TANNER, SHARON MARIE, hospital administrator; b. Fort Wayne, Ind., May 8, 1949; d. Robert Milton and Marie Anna (Mullen) Tanner; B.S. in Advt., U. Fla., 1971; M.S.A., George Washington U., 1980; m. B. J. Sherwin. Mgr. tng. and devel. Am. Auto Assn., Falls Church, Va., 1976-78; dir. personnel Chestnut Lodge, Hosp., Rockville, Md., 1978-80; dir. personnel Suburban Hosp., Bethesda, Md., 1980-83, asst. adminstr., 1983-85; v.p. research Hosp. Council Nat. Capital Area, 1983—; v.p. Med. Ctr. Hosps., Norflok, Va. Mem. Am. Coll. Healthcare Execs., C. of C. of Hampton Roads, Tidewater Bus. and Profl. Women, Women's Network, NOW. Office: 600 Gresham Dr Norfolk VA 23507

TANNER, TERRIE LEE, accountant; b. Battle Creek, Mich., Apr. 1, 1955; d. Wilfrid and Donna Tanner. A.A., Los Angeles Harbor Coll., 1976; B.A., Calif. State U.-Long Beach, 1978; M.A. in Mgmt., U. Redlands, 1986. Ops. mgr. One Day Foto Inc., Rolling Hills, Calif., 1973-78; teller, notes and collections loan clk., bank service rep. Crocker Nat. Bank, Torrance, Calif., 1978-83; jr. fin. analyst Mattel Toys, Inc., Hawthorne, Calif., 1983-85, assoc. acct., 1985—. Tchrs. aide in ceramics Rolling Hills High Sch., 1976. Recipient Cash award for suggestion Crocker Nat. Bank, 1982. Mem. Nat. Assn. Female Execs. Avocation: art. Home: 5 Cypress Way Rolling Hills Estates CA 90274

TANOUS, EVELYNE NAJLA, lawyer; b. Zanesville Ohio, Feb. 11, 1947; d. Joseph and Rose (Mokarzel) Tanous; B.A., U. Tex., 1961-65; J.D., South Tex. Coll. Law, 1972; 1 dau., Chantal. Admitted to Tex. bar, 1973; pros. trial atty. Dist. Atty's Office, Houston, 1973-75; asst. dist. atty. U.S. Small Bus. Adminstrn., N.Y.C. and Houston, 1977-81; mem. legal staff Union Oil Co. Calif., Houston, 1981—. Recipient French Lit. award U. Tex., 1962. Mem. Am., Tex., Houston bar assns., Nat. Assn. Dist. Attys., Tex. Dist. Atty. Assn., Sigma Delta Pi, Pi Delta Phi, Iota Tau Tau. Maronite Catholic. Clubs: World Wing Internation; Metropolitan Racquet. Office: 4635 Southwest Freeway 900 Executive Plaza West Houston TX 77027

TANOUS, HELENE MARY, physician; b. Zanesville, Ohio, Oct. 22, 1939; d. Joseph Carrington and Rose Marie (Mokarzel) Tanous; B.A., Marymount Coll., 1961; M.D., U. Tex., 1967. Intern, County Hosp., Los Angeles, 1967-68; resident in radiology U. So. Calif. Hosp., Los Angeles, 1969-71; practice medicine specializing in radiology, Los Angeles, 1972-73; instr. radiology U. So. Calif. Med. Sch., Los Angeles, 1971-72; asst. prof. diagnostic radiology Baylor Med. Sch., Houston, 1973-75; dir. med. student elective in diagnostic radiology Ben Taub Hosp., Houston, 1973-75; pvt. practice diagnostic radiology, Largo, Fla., 1975—; asst. prof. diagnostic radiology U. South Fla. Med. Sch., 1980—. Pres., founder Children's Advocates, Inc.; bd. dirs. Fla. Endowment for Humanities, 1979-83. Diplomate Am. Bd. Radiology. Mem. AMA, So. Med. Assn., Am. Med. Women's Assn., L'Alliance Francaise of Tampa (bd. dirs. 1984—, pres. 1985-86). Office: Dept Radiology U South Fla Med Sch Box 17 12901 N 30th St Tampa FL 33612

TANSEY, IVA LEE MARIE, state legislator; b. Elyria, Ohio, Jan. 6, 1930; d. Edwin Jacob and Fern L. (McKee) Law; student Lorain Bus. Coll., 1965; m. Charles J. Tansey, Sept. 7, 1948; children—Mark, Dennis, Richard. Sec., Vermilion (Ohio) High Sch., 1959-64; exec. sec. Vermilion C. of C., 1964-67; br. sec., asst. mgr. Cardinal Fed. Savs. & Loan Assn., 1967-76; mem. Ohio Ho. of Reps., 1977; Republican. Congregationalist. Office: State House Columbus OH 43215

TAPP, ELISE MARIE, software training company executive; b. Detroit, Feb. 10, 1950; d. George M. and Simonne Marie (Auger) Bergeron; m. Darrell Owen Tapp, Jan. 23, 1983. B.A., U. Mich.; M.A. in Adminstrn., Eastern Mich. U. Cert. tchr., Mich., Tex. With Xerox Corp., Dallas, 1979-81; program instr. Digital Switch Corp., Dallas, 1981-83; software instr. Businessland, Houston, 1983-84;, pres. BusinessWare Learning Ctrs., Inc., Houston, 1985—; with Bus. Software Support, Houston, 1984—; cons. Compaq Computer Co., Houston, 1984—, Tenneco Inc., Houston, 1985—, Exxon, Houston, 1986. Mem. Info. Ctrs. Mgmt. Assn., Ind. Computer Cons., Assn. Profl. Educators. Republican. Roman Catholic. Office: BusinessWare Learning Ctrs Inc 6700 West Loop S Suite 110 Bellaire TX 77401

TAPPAN, NANCY MACK, editor, publisher; b. Los Angeles, Feb. 9, 1939; d. Augustus Frederick and Edith (Staples) Mack; m. Mel Tappan, May 8, 1958 (dec. 1980). Student Stanford U., 1956-58. Owner Janus Press, Rogue River, Oreg., 1980—, editor, 1975—; co-owner, editor and pub. Survival Tomorrow, Rogue River, 1981—; also free lance editor. Address: PO Box 1050 Rogue River OR 97537

TAPPAN, SANDRA HAZEN, counselor, dance school executive; b. Burlington, Vt., Sept. 25, 1940; d. Joseph and Elaine (Hazen) Rogow; B.A., Trinity Coll., 1979; M.S., U. Vt., 1983; cert. elem. tchr. and counselor, Vt.; m. Walter House Tappan, Dec. 27, 1958; children—Suzanne E., Heidi L. Tchr. pre-sch., Enosburg Falls, Vt., 1967; owner, choreographer, tchr. Sandra Tappan Profl. Sch. Dance, St. Albans, Vt., 1968—; counselor CRASH, 1977-79; counselor Planned Parenthood of Vt., 1979-80; cons. staff Northwestern Med. Ctr., 1985—. Mem. Franklin County Planning Commn., 1974-76; exec. bd. United Way, 1984-85. Mem. Am. Assn. Counseling and Devel., Vt. Personnel and Guidance Assn., Am. Psychol. Assn. (assoc.), AAUW. Republican. Home: 22 Rugg St Saint Albans VT 05478

TARASI, ROSE STATTI, nursing home administrator; b. Pitts., June 1, 1912; d. Peter Anthony and Emilia (Aiello) Statti; m. Rocco F. Tarasi, Nov. 24, 1938 (dec. 1954); children—Linda, August, Rocco F. II, Louis. B.A., U. Pitts., 1930, M.S. in Hygiene, 1965; B.S. in L.S., Carnegie Inst. Tech., 1931. Cert. tchr., Pa. Tchr., librarian Pitts. Pub. Schs., 1932-36; librarian Westinghouse Electric Corp., 1936-40; research assoc. U. Pitts., 1965-69; adminstr. Angelus Convalescent Ctr., Pitts., 1970-80, cons., 1980—, pres., 1970—. Fellow Am. Coll. Health Care Adminstrs.; mem. Am. Coll. Hosp. Adminstrs., Am. Pub. Health Assn., Pitts. Opera Assn., Met. Opera, Pitts. Symphony Assn., Chautauqua Symphony Assn., Buhl Sci. Ctr., Carnegie Inst., Western Pa. Conservancy, Pitts. History and Landmarks Found., LWV. Democrat. Roman Catholic. Clubs: Pitts. Garden, Italian Cultural. Avocations: symphony; ballet; theatre; quilting; gardening. Home: 12 James Ross Pl Pittsburgh PA 15215 Office: Angelus Convalescent Ctr 200 Amber St Pittsburgh PA 15206

TARBELL, JOY ELAINE, marketing executive; b. Providence, June 21, 1947; d. Robert Stone and Helen (Pilkington) Tarbell; m. Joseph L. Berry; 1 child, Alexander S. Tarberry. Student, Boston U., 1965-66. Lic. real estate broker, N.H., Ill., Mich. Sales assoc. Rohter & Co., Chgo., 1975-78, Byron W. Trerice Co., Southfield, Mich., 1978-79; broker, sales assoc. The Wilcox Co., Chgo., 1979-81; dir. sales mktg. Eastern Slope Inn Resort, N. Conway, N.H., 1981—, Attitash Mt. Village, Bartlett, N.H., 1981—. Editor Investors' Newsletter, 1978. Mem. Nat. Fedn. Bus. and Profl. Women's Clubs, NOW, Nat. Assn. Female Execs., Am. Resort and Residential Devel. Assn. (Excellence Sales Mgmt. award 1983). Avocations: skiing; sailing; tennis; horseback riding. Office: Eastern Slope Inn Resort PO Box 1070 Main St North Conway NH 03860

TARDY, JUDITH L., government official; b. Carlisle, Pa., Feb. 7, 1944; B.A., U. Hawaii, 1966. Tchr. public schs., Hawaii, 1967-68, Fairfax County, Va., 1968-69; personnel mgmt. specialist Dept. Transp., Washington, 1969-71; personnel mgmt. specialist Dept. Labor, 1971-72; spl. asst. to dep. dir. Cost of Living Council, Washington, 1972-74; spl. asst. to adminstr. Fed. Energy Adminstrn., Washington, 1974-75; dir. for mgmt. Commodity Futures Trading Commn., Washington, 1975-76; dir. exec. secretariat Dept. Labor, 1976-79, dir. adminstrv. services Dept. Labor, Washington, 1979-80; asst. sec. HUD, Washington, 1981—. Office: HUD 451 7th St SW Washington DC 20410*

TARGOW, JEANETTE GOLDFIELD, clinical social worker; b. Chgo., May 21, 1910; d. Isadore and Rebecca Covici Goldfield; children—Patricia Skinner, Richard Targow. Ph.B., U. Chgo., 1930; M.S.W., UCLA, 1953. Social worker U. So. Calif. Psychology Clinic, Los Angeles, 1953-55; clin. social worker Psychol. Service Center, Los Angeles, 1955-60; pvt. practice clin. social work, Los Angeles, 1960—; instr. Calif. Sch. Profl. Psychology; mem. faculty dept. psychology Loyola-Marymount Coll., 1981-83; supr. Didi Hirsch Mental Health Center, Culver City, Calif., 1977-81. Fellow Am. Group Psychotherapy Assn. (chmn. task force on womens' issues 1983-86), Soc. for Clin. Social Work; mem. Los Angeles Group Psychotherapy Soc., Nat. Assn. Social Workers, Nat. Acad. Practice in Social Work, ACLU. Democrat. Jewish. Home: 1835 N Doheny Dr Los Angeles CA 90069 Office: 648 N Doheny Dr Los Angeles CA 90069

TARLTON, SHIRLEY MARIE, coll. dean; b. Raleigh, N.C., Aug. 8, 1937; d. Lloyd E. and Mary O. (Suycott) Tarlton; diploma Peace Coll., Raleigh, N.C., 1957; B.A. in French, Queens Coll., Charlotte, N.C., 1960; M.S.L.S., U. N.C., Chapel Hill, 1966. Head tech. services div. U. N.C., Charlotte, 1961-68, asst. librarian, 1961-63; asso. dir. tech. services Winthrop Coll. Library, 1968-73, acting dir., 1971, 73-74, dean library services, 1974—; mem. bd. Southeastern Library Network; mem. council Online Computer Library Center. Mem. ALA, Southeastern N.C., S.C., Metrolina, Mecklenburg library assns., Am. Soc. Info. Sci., Rock Hill C. of C., Sigma Pi Alpha, Phi Theta Kappa, Beta Phi Mu, Phi Kappa Phi. Home: 7406 Windyrush Rd Matthews NC 28105 Office: Winthrop College Rock Hill SC 29733

TARNOSKI, LORI M., clothing company executive; b. 1940. With V F Corp., Wyomissing, Pa., 1961—, adminstrv. asst. to v.p., 1970-73, asst. sec., 1973-74, sec., 1974-79, v.p., 1979. Address: VF Corp 1047 N Park Rd Wyomissing PA 19610

TARRANT-FITZGERALD, MAUREEN, hospital marketing director; b. N.Y.C., Mar. 18, 1955; d. Kevin Barry and Alberta Ann (Manitt) Tarrant; m. John Patrick Fitzgerald, June 23, 1979. B.A., SUNY, 1977; M.B.A., Boston U., 1981. Info. asst. Blue Cross-Blue Shield, Washington, 1977-78; service coordinator Kelly Health Care, Boston, 1978-81; dir. Am. Med. Personnel Services, Denver, 1981-82; dir. clinics Rocky Mountain Hosp., Denver, 1982-83, adminstrv. officer Rocky Mountain Hosp., 1983-85; dir. mktg. Porter Meml. Hosp., Denver, 1985—; cons. Arapahoe Med. Found., Englewood, Colo., 1983-84. Site coordinator 9 Health Fair, Denver, 1982-83. Mem. Am. Mktg. Assn., Am. Coll. Health Care Marketers, Am. Hosp. Assn., Soc. for Planning and Mktg., Soc. for Pub. Relations Mktg., Denver C. of C. (ambassador 1982-84). Democrat. Roman Catholic. Office: Porter Meml Hosp 2525 S Downing Denver CO 80210

TARSELL, THOMASINE MISSOURI, insurance agency executive, financial advisor; b. Shamokin, Pa., Sept. 27, 1941; d. Walter Thomas and Missouri Elizabeth (Haas) T.; m. David Charles Cohen, Aug. 13, 1969 (div. Jan. 1982). Grad. Phoenixville Area High Sch., Pa. Cert. ins. counselor. Mfrs. rep. Ardlee Assocs., Phila., 1963-66; v.p. mktg., nat. sales mgr. Marlee Creations, Phila., 1965-66; owner Schneider, Hill & Spangler, 1966-68; account exec., ins. broker Schaprio-Shadline & Balser, Inc., Balt., 1968-71; gen. mgr., ins. broker Bruce Ins. Corp., Balt., 1971-77; founder, chief exec. officer Tomco Ins. Corp. and Tomco Money Mgmt. Corp., Towson, Md., 1977—; dir. Care First Health Maintenance Orgn., Balt., now advisor; founder, exec. First Comprehensive Directory of Women Owned Businesses in State Md., 1983—, First Women in Exporting Trade Mission, 1985—. Bd. dirs. Md. Woman's Campaign Fund, Inc., Balt., 1983-84; founder, treas. Pulling of Women Entrepreneurial Resources Polit. Action Com., 1984—. Named Woman of Yr., Nat. Assn. Women Bus. Owners, 1981, Woman Bus. Advocate of Yr., SBA, 1984. Mem. Ind. Ins. Agts. Assn., Cert. Fin. Planners Assn., Nat. Assn. Women Bus. Owners, Minority Bus. Council Md. (bd. advisors). Republican. Lutheran. Club: Woodholme Country (Balt.). Avocations: golf; racquetball; reading; sailing; boating. Office: Tomco Ins Corp 660 Kenilworth Dr Suite 101 Towson MD 21204

TARTAGLIA, JANICE TRANTHAM, consultant, social service administrator; b. San Diego, Feb. 4, 1943; d. William H. and Geneva L. (Vogler) Funk; m. Robert E. Trantham, June 17, 1961 (div. 1970); children—Joseph R., David R.; m. Louis M. Tartaglia, Mar. 21, 1980. Student San Diego Mesa Coll., 1969-71; B.A. in Liberal Arts with honors, San Diego State U., 1971-73, M. Rehab. Counseling, 1979; M.B.A. candidate Nat. U., 1984. Coordinator, counselor, instr. LaVerne Coll., San Diego, 1973-75; counselor Chadwick Employment Agy., San Diego, 1975-76; dep. dir. Project J.O.V.E. Inc., San Diego, 1976-85; pres. Profl. Research and Tng., Inc., San Diego, 1985—; counselor Comprehensive Therapy Ctr., San Diego, 1984-85. Rep. Neighborhood Alert Program, San Diego, 1980-85; vol. San Diego Mayoral Re-election Campaign, San Diego, 1984; mem. Republican Nat. Com., Washington, 1984-85. Mem. Job Tng. Assn. (mem. fin. com. 1984-85). Republican. Methodist. Avocations: snow skiing; quilt making; flower arranging; gardening. Home: 4514 LaCuenta Dr San Diego CA 92124 Office: Profl Research and Tng Inc 10615 G Tierrasanta Blvd Suite 102 San Diego CA 92124

TARVER, MAE-GOODWIN, statistical and quality control consultant b. Selma, Ala., Aug. 9, 1916; d. Hartwell Hill and R. Louise (Wilkins) T.; B.S. in Chemistry, U. Ala., 1939, M.S., 1940. Project supr. container shelflife Continental Can Co., Inc., Chgo., 1941-48, project engr. stats., 1948-54, quality control cons., research statistician, 1954-77; pres., prin cons. Quest Assocs., Ltd., Park Forest, Ill., 1978—; adj. assoc. prof. biology dept. Ill. Inst. Tech., Chgo., 1957-81. Bd. dirs. Ash St. Coop., Park Forest, Ill., 1976-85. Fellow Am. Soc. Quality Control (Joe Lisy award 1961, Edward J. Oakley award 1973, E.L. Grant award 1983); mem. Inst. Food Technologists, Soc. Women Engrs., Am. Statis. Assn., Sigma Xi. Home: 130 26th St Park Forest IL 60466 Office: PO Box 156 Park Forest IL 60466

TASHJIAN, JULIA HARRIET, state official; b. Pawtucket, R.I., June 8, 1938; d. Harry and Eliza Kaffeian Zakarian; m. James Samuel Tashjian, 1959; children—Sherri L., James E., Lisa H., Charles H. Student Greater Hartford Community Coll., Pres., Windsor (Conn.) Democratic Women's Club, 1967-69; sec. Windsor Jury Com., 1969-72, chmn., 1972-79; dep. registrar of voters, Windsor, 1969—; legis. clk. Conn. Gen. Assembly, 1969-78, spl. asst. fin. com., 1978—; exec. bd. mem. Hartford County Fedn. Dem. Women's Clubs, 1971-81; treas. 7th Senatorial Dist. Orgn., 1972-74, vice chmn., 1974-80; com.woman Conn. State Central Com., 1977—; del. Dem. Nat. Conv., 1980, 84, Nat. Party Conf., 1981, 82; Mem. Dem. Platform Com., 1984; mem. adv. com. Eleanor Roosevelt Centennial, 1984; mem. Nat. Dem. Com. Ethnic Ams.; sec. of state, Conn., numerous other civic groups. Recipient Dem. of Yr. award Windsor Dem. Town Com., 1979. Mem. Civitan Club, Conn. Registrars Assn., Nat. Bus. Women's Assn., Daus. of Vartan. Address: Office of Sec of State State Capitol Hartford CT 06106

TASSIS, DEBORAH ANN, environmental planning company executive; b. Bonne Terre, Mo., Dec. 11, 1956; d. Costas Charles and Hazel Ruth (Cox) T. B.S., Calif. State U.-Fresno, 1978. Activities coordinator Bel Haven Convalescent Hosp., Fresno, Calif., 1976; urban studies researcher U. Louisville, 1977; contract writer Dept. Transp., City of Fresno, 1978; group mgr. operators Pacific Telephone, San Francisco, 1978-79; word processing supr. Edgar, Dunn & Conover, Inc., mgmt. cons., San Francisco, 1979-81; mgr. info. support systems EDAW, Inc., San Francisco, 1981—; word processing cons. McCutchen, Doyle, Brown & Enersen, San Francisco, 1982-83. Tokalon's Ina Gregg Thomas Meml. scholar, 1977. Mem. Nat. Assn. Female Execs., Golden Gate Wordprocessing Exchange, Phi Chi Theta (scholar 1977). Home: 237 Picnic Ave Apt 19 San Rafael CA 94901 Office: EDAW Inc 1725 Montgomery St San Francisco CA 94111

TATA, TRACY BURT, administrative assistant; b. Eufaula, Ala., June 10, 1958; d. Barney Mitchell Burt and Frances (Olliff) Wiley; m. Anthony Jean Tata, July 16, 1983. A.A., Columbus Coll., 1976; postgrad., 1982; B.S., Auburn U., 1980. Teaching cert., Ala., Ga., Hawaii; lic. realtor, Hawaii. Tchr. Warren County, Ga., Warrenton, 1980-81, Muscogee County, Columbus, Ga., 1981-83; adminstrv. asst. to v.p. Petty Corp., Honolulu, 1983-85, also seminar dir.; adminstrv. asst. to pres. Dolman Assocs., Inc., 1985—. Mem. Kappa Delta Pi, Phi Mu. Methodist. Home: 92-1300 Kikaha St 82 Palehua Hillside Ewa Beach HI 96707

TATE, CAROL FAY, social worker; b. Mitchell, Nebr., Apr. 5, 1937; d. Laurence and Vivian Joan (Powell) T.; B.S., Sioux Falls (S.D.) Coll., 1959; postgrad. Kent State U., 1961-64; M.S.W., Fla. State U., 1969. Asst. dir. health, phys. edn. YWCA, Akron, Ohio, 1959-61; home vis. tchr. Summit County Assn. Retarded Children, Akron, 1961-62, Summit County Child Welfare Bd., Akron, 1962-63; instr. Youngstown (Ohio) U., 1964-65; dir. sch. for trainable mentally retarded Scotts Bluff County (Nebr.) Assn. Retarded Children, 1964-65; tchr. Scotts Bluff County Sch. Bd., 1965-66; with Fla. Dept. Health and Rehab. Services, Tampa, 1966-69; pvt. practice social work, Tampa, 1970-75; dir. social work Hope Haven Children's Hosp., Jacksonville, Fla., 1975; dir. Gulf County Activity Center for Retarded Adults, Port St. Joe, Fla., 1976-77; pvt. practice med. social services, St. Petersburg, Fla., 1977-78; staff social worker Bay Area Home Health Services, St. Petersburg, 1978-79; dir. social services Global Home Health Services, Inc., Treasure Island, Fla., 1979—; supr. developmental disabilities, Clearwater, Fla., 1980; adminstr. Omni Home Health Services, Cleveland, Tenn., 1982-84; with research div. Am. Health Enterprises, Chattanooga, 1984—. Mem. Nat. Assn. Social Workers, Acad. Cert. Social Workers, Fla. Assn. Health and Social Services. Democrat. Home: 2341 Gale Ln Chattanooga TN 37421

TATE, EVELYN RUTH, real estate broker; b. Ottumwa, Iowa, Sept. 21; d. Frank Edward and Ella Belle (Smith) Ross; student public schs., Huntington Park, Calif.; m. William Tate (dec.); 1 son, William. Owner, mgr. Evelyn R. Tate Realty Co., Sherman Oaks, Calif., 1943-53, Beverly Hills, Calif., 1942—; owner, mgr. Evelyn Tate Fine Arts, San Francisco, 1976—; mgr. Beverly Hills Galleries, Hyatt Regency Hotel, San Francisco, 1979—; mgr. art gallery Fairmont Hotel; owner, mgr. Tate Gallery, Cathedral Hill Hotel, San Francisco, Hyatt Regency Hotel San Francisco, Fairmont Hotel, Dallas. Mem. Nat. Assn. Female Execs., The Exec. Female. Home: 999 Green St Apt 1003 San Francisco CA 94133

TATE, MERZE, educator; b. Blanchard, Mich., Feb. 6, 1905; d. Charles H. and Myrtle Katora (Lett) T.; B.A. Western Mich. U. 1927; M.A. Columbia U. 1930, B.Litt. Oxford U. 1935, Ph.D. Harvard U. 1941; LL.D. (hon.) Morgan State U., Bowie State Coll. 1977, Lincoln U. 1978; D.H.L., Havard U., 1986. Tchr., Crispus Attucks High Sch., Indpls. 1927-32, Barber Scotia Coll. Concord, N.C. 1935-36, Bennett Coll. 1936-41, Morgan State U. 1941-42; faculty Howard U. 1942-74, now prof. emeritus; Fulbright prof. India 1950-51. Fellow and grantee in field; recipient Nat. Urban League Disting. Achievement award 1948; Western Mich. U. Disting. Alumna award 1970; Mayor of Detroit award 1978; Am. Black Artist's Pioneer award 1978; award The Prometheans, Inc., 1980; Am. Assn. State Colls. and Univs. award, 1982. Mem. Am. Hist. Assn., Assn. Study Afro-Am. History, AAUW (Disting. Mem. award D.C. chpt. 1983), Phi Beta Kappa, Alpha Kappa Alpha (3d fgn. fellow), Pi Gamma Mu. Roman Catholic. Clubs: Radcliffe of Washington, Harvard of Washington, Writers, Howard U. Women's, Howard U. Retirees, Bridge Builders, Bridge Eights. Author: The Disarmament Illusion—The Movement for a Limitation of Armaments to 1907; The United States and Armaments 1948, The United State and the Hawaiian Kingdom 1965, Hawaii: Reciprocity or Annexation 1968, Diplomacy in the Pacific, 1973; contbr. numerous articles to profl. jours.

TATE, SHEILA BURKE, public relations executive, former press secretary to First Lady U.S.; b. Washington, Mar. 3, 1942; d. Eugene L. and Mary J. (Doherty) Burke; B.A. in Journalism, Duquesne U., 1964; postgrad. U. Denver, 1975-76; m. William J. Tate, May 2, 1981; children—Hager Patton, Courtney Patton. Research asst. Westinghouse Air Brake Co., Pitts., 1964-65; copywriter Ketchum, MacLeod & Grove, Pitts., 1965; asst. account exec. Fahlgren & Assocs., Parkersburg, W.Va., 1966; account exec. Burson-Marsteller Assocs., Pitts., 1967, sr. v.p., Washington, 1985—; public relations mgr. Colo. Nat. Bank, Denver, 1967-70; v.p. Hill and Knowlton, Houston and Washington, 1977-81; press sec. to First Lady Nancy Reagan, Washington, 1981-85. Mem. Public Relations Soc. Am., Nat. Press Club. Republican. Presbyterian. Club: Duquesne U. Century. Office: 1850 M St NW #900 Washington DC 20006

TATEM, NANCY GAUER, nursing services director, surgical assistant; b. Newark, N.J., Aug. 16, 1942; d. Harry and Jean (Hill) Gauer; m. H. Randolph Tatem, 3d, Sept. 14, 1963 (div. 1979); children—Jeffrey Randolph, Kyra Elizabeth. R.N., Hahnemann U., 1963; B.S. in Nursing, Gwynedd-Mercy Coll., Gwynedd, Pa., 1984. Cert. gerontol. nurse Am. Nurses Assn., 1985. Med.-surg. nurse Hahnemann U., Phila., 1963-65; health info. coordinator Nat. Found. March of Dimes, Bucks County, Pa., 1977-78; nurse/instr. Upjohn, Doylestown, Pa., 1978-80; head nurse Doylestown Manor (Pa.), 1980-82; surg. asst. AJL Simoes Assocs., Lansdale, Pa., 1982-84; dir. nursing Doylestown Manor, 1984-85; co-founder, dir. nursing Services The Respite, alternative adult day program, Mechanicsville, Pa., 1986—; vol. nurse ARC, Bucks County, 1977-80. Com. mem. Bucks County Hist. Soc., 1972-78; founding mem. PAK Teen Drug and Alcohol Program, 1976-78; bd. dirs. Bucks County chpt. March of Dimes, 1979-80. Mem. Bucks County Registered Nurses Assn. (sec. 1980-84), Pa. Nurses Assn., Forum for Advancement Nursing Excellence, 1984—, Am. Nurses Found, Pa. Adult Day Care Assn. Republican. Presbyterian. Club: PEO. Home: 54 Spring Dr Doylestown PA 18901 Office: The Respite Route 413 PO Box 294 Mechanicsville PA 18934

TATE-RAMIREZ, FRAN M., small business owner; b. Auburn, Wash., Oct. 5, 1929; dau. Frank Joseph and Theresa Mary (Bingesar) Pfulg; m. Rory Tate, Sept. 30, 1970 (div.); children—Michael C., Joseph M.; m. 2d, Juan Ramon Ramirez, Sept. 6, 1981. Student U. Wash. Gen. mgr., Sorensen Heating Co., Auburn, 1952-70; cons. Success Motivation Inst., Bellevue, Wash., 1970-72; field engr., draftsman, J. Dalton and Assocs., Point Barrow, Alaska, 1973-75; pres., owner Inupiat Water Delivery Co., Barrow, Alaska, 1977—; pres., owner Elephant Pot Sewage Haulers, Barrow, 1977—; pres., owner, operator Pepe's North of the Border Restaurant, Barrow, 1978—, Burger Barn, Barrow, 1984—; disc jockey, Sta. KBRW, Barrow. Recipient Boss of Yr. award Credit Women Internat., 1969; Outstanding Service award Barrow PTA; Alaska's Outstanding Women State Comm. for Status of Women, 1984; featured on Johnny Carson Show and in Wall St. Jour., Time mag. Mem. Barrow C. of C., Nat. Geog. Soc., Smithsonian Instn., Jazz Heritage Found. Roman Catholic. Club: Las Vegas Jazz.

TATLIAN, ENID WETZLER, communications agency executive; b. Bklyn., June 24, 1945; d. Jerome and Bertha (Abramson) Wetzler; m. Edward Anthony Tatlian, June 18, 1978. Student Am. Acad. Dramatic Arts, 1965-66, U. Miami, 1968, St. John's U., 1983. Buyer in tng., garment industry, N.Y.C., 1972-78; adminstrv. asst. Tracer Offset Co., Inc., N.Y.C., 1978-81; media asst., traffic coordinator Laddin & Co. Inc., N.Y.C., 1981-84, field worker, 1981—; office adminstr. Home Buyers Assistance Corp., N.Y.C., 1984—. Jewish. Home: 246 Town Line Rd West Nyack NY 10994

TATRO, BRENDA LOUISE, association executive; b. Denver, Dec. 15, 1948; d. Jack Roald and Violet Leona (Stensrud) White; m. Steven Robert Tatro, Sept. 24, 1985. B.S., U. No. Colo., 1970; postgrad., 1973-78. Cert. tchr., Colo. Tchr. Harrison Sch. Dist., Colorado Springs, Colo., 1971-80; Uni Serv dir. Okla. Edn. Assn., Tulsa, 1980-83; dir. field services Ala. Edn. Assn., Montgomery, 1983—. Author, editor: El Carro, 1978; La Tortuga, 1978. Telethon vol. Muscular Dystrophy Assn., Tulsa, 1980-83, pub. relations chair, 1982-83. Recipient Outstanding Achievement in Pub. Relations award NEA, 1979-80; Spl. Membership Achievement award Colo. Edn. Assn., 1979-80; Outstanding Achievement award Tulsa Pub. Schs., 1983. Mem. Ala. Edn. Assn. (lobbyist 1983—), NEA, Smithsonian Instn., Assn. Supervision and Curriculum, Nat. Assn. Female Execs. Avocations: golf, cards, bowling, crafts, cooking. Office: Ala Edn Assn 422 Dexter Ave Montgomery AL 36195

TATUM, BARBARA WILSON, advertising executive; b. Houston, May 27, 1958; d. Dean Maxwell and Charlotte Bonnie (Richards) W.; m. Lawrence Glenn Tatum, June 27, 1981. B.S. in Advt., U. Tex.-Austin, 1980. Sect. editor Tex. Student Publs., Austin, 1979-80; copywriter, intern Lee Tilford Advt., Austin, 1980; account exec. Bernard Hodes Advt. subs. Doyle Dane Bernbach Inc., Houston, 1980—; freelance writer, Houston, 1983—. Vol. adolescent unit Tex. State Hosp., Austin, 1980. Roman Catholic. Office: Bernard Hodes Advt 7676 Hillmont St #290 Houston TX 77063

TATUM, GLORIA JEAN, social worker; b. Colbert, Ga., Aug. 20, 1948; d. John Henry and Rosa Lee (Hitchcock) Curry; m. William Robert Tatum, Nov. 21, 1972; children—William Robert III, Alonzo Delarrence. B.A., Spelman Coll., 1971; M.S.S.W., U. Louisville, 1979. Accounts receivable clk. Gold Kist, Inc., Athens, Ga., 1971-72; U.S. pub. health rep. Dept. Pub. Health, Chgo., Atlanta, 1972-73; field researcher U.S. Census Bur., Chgo., and so. Ind., 1975-76; social worker Jefferson County Fiscal Ct., Louisville, 1978—; active community outreach services Jefferson County Dept. Human Services, Louisville, 1985—. Group work leader Up Black Emphasis on Adoptions, Inc., Louisville, 1982—; mem. vis. com. U. Louisville Bd. Overseers, 1985—; adoptive parents support group worker Floyd County Dept. Welfare, New Albany, Ind., 1985—. Mem. Nat. Assn. Social Workers, Nat. Assn. Female Execs., Acad. Cert. Social Workers, Spelman Coll. Alumni Assn., U. Louisville, Alumni Assn. Democrat. Baptist. Avocations: fishing; cycling; reading, especially economic and medical writings. Home: 21 W Robin Rd New Albany IN 47150 Office: Jefferson County Fiscal Ct 216 S 5th St Louisville KY 40202

TAUB, DIANA LYNN, school administrator, artist, designer, actress; b. Houston, May 16, 1950; d. Howard Edward and Alice Laverne (Clayton) Taub. B.F.A., Pratt Inst., 1972; M.S., Nova U., 1981. Cert. tchr., adminstr., Fla. Costume designer Isracine Prodns., N.Y.C., 1968; freelance artist, designer, actress, Miami, Fla., 1972—; prof. Bauder Fashion Coll., Miami, 1972; tchr. Dade County Pub. Schs., Miami, 1974-83; asst. prin. Howard D. McMillan Jr. High Sch., Miami, 1983—; sch. rep. South Area Adv. Com., Miami, 1980-83; participant Citizens' Oversight Com., Miami, Citizens' Task Force on Drugs, Miami, 1983—. Pub. relations campaign worker, John Connally for Pres., Miami, 1980; v.p., treas. Glades Jr. High Sch. PTSA, Miami, 1980-83; active Big Sisters of Dade County, Miami, 1980-82; organizer Chem. People Task Force, Miami, 1983. Recipient 1st place art award Brandeis U. Women's Alumni, Hollywood, Fla., 1968, 1st place design award Trevira Fabrics, N.Y.C., 1972, Asst. Prin. Honor award, Kappa Delta Pi, Miami, 1983, Merit award, Dade County PTSA, Miami, 1983. Mem. Screen Actors Guild, Nat. Assn. Secondary Sch. Prins., Fla. Assn. Sch. Adminstrs., Dade County Adminstrs. Assn., Dade Assn. Secondary Sch. Prins., Phi Delta Kappa, Am. Soc. Interior Designers. Home: Miami FL Office: Howard D McMillan Jr High School 13100 SW 59th St Miami FL 33183

TAUBENBLATT, RENEE STARR, nurses' registry executive; b. N.Y.C., July 15, 1924; d. Harry and Melanie (Krauss) Starr; m. Leonard Taubenblatt, July 4, 1948; children—Lucie Taubenblatt Lapovsky, Peter, Ellen Taubenblatt Harmon. B.S. in Edn., NYU, 1946, M.A. in Edn., 1948; M.A. in Polit. Sci., New Sch. Social Research, 1972. Tchr. N.Y.C. Bd. Edn., 1947-51; with Star Registry for Nurses, Bklyn., 1954-75; head of reservations Windows on the World, N.Y.C., 1976-77; owner, exec. Star Registry, Bklyn., 1978—. Mem. Community Bd. 6, Bklyn., 1979-83, Community Com. Bklyn. Mus., 1970-80; pres. Dena Group of Hadassah, Bklyn., 1972-74. Home: 150 E 69th St New York NY 10021 Office: Star Registry 47 Plaza St Brooklyn NJ 11217

TAUBER, INGRID DIANE, clinical psychologist; b. Washington, Jan. 30, 1952; d. Laszlo Nandor and Lilly Katherine (Manovill) T.; B.A., Boston U., 1973; M.A., U. Md., 1976; Ph.D., Calif. Sch. Profl. Psychology, 1980. Counselor youth services Area B Community Mental Health Center, Washington, 1974-76; psychology intern Gladman Meml. Hosp., Oakland, Calif., 1976-77, San Francisco Gen. Hosp., 1976-77; pre- and post-doctoral trainee VA Med. Center, San Francisco, 1977-81; pvt. practice clin. psychology, San Francisco, 1977—; tchr. psychol. testing VA Med. Center. Bd. overseers Tauber Inst. Holocaust Studies, Brandeis U. Lic. psychologist, Calif. Mem. Am. Psychol. Assn., Calif. Psychol. Assn., Am. Orthopsychiat. Assn., Assn. Mental Health Affiliation with Israel. Home: 2090 Green St 26 San Francisco CA 94123 Office: 348 Spruce St San Francisco CA 94118

TAUFEN, JUDITH JOHANNA, shuttle service executive, chamber of commerce executive; b. St. Cloud, Minn., Feb. 7, 1948; d. Ervin J. and Marie C. (Zabinski) Skaja; m. Ronald M. Taufen, Apr. 15, 1967; children—Tamara B., Curt R., Jennifer M., Tessa R. Interior designer Taufen Builders, Minn. and Colo., 1972-82; mktg. dir. Summit County C. of C., Colo., 1984—; owner, mgr. Resort Express Airport Shuttle, Frisco, Colo. Mem. Breckenridge C. of C. (mktg. com. 1984—). Roman Catholic. Avocations: skiing; camping; hiking; reading. Office: Resort Express PO Box 1269 761 Ten Mile Dr Frisco CO 80443

TAUNTON, WANDA CARDA, govt. agy. ofcl.; b. Pickstown, S.D., Aug. 24, 1949; d. Lloyd Louis and Viola Vera (Thaler) Carda; B.S. in Bus. Mgmt. magna cum laude, Met. State Coll., 1971; M.P.A., U. Colo., 1983; m. Richard Way Taunton, Jan. 31, 1976; stepchildren—Victoria, Wayne, Jennifer, David. Bus. tchr. Woodland Park (Colo.) High Sch., 1971-72; tchr. bus. and adult edn. Basseterre (St. Kitts, B.W.I.) as Peace Corps vol., 1972-74; clk.-typist Denver Public Schs. and Channel 6 Public TV, 1974-75; sec. EPA, Denver, 1975-76, environ. protection specialist, 1976-80, staff asst. to div. dir. budget, fin. and program analysis, 1980-83; budget dir. Community Coll. Denver, 1984-85; fiscal services officer Colo. Commn. Higher Edn., 1985—; co-chair Fed. Women's Program Region VIII, 1982—. Recipient Bronze medal for commendable service EPA, 1979. Mem. Am. Soc. Public Adminstrn., Colo. Fiscal Mgrs. Assn., Nat. Assn. Female Execs., Nat. Wildlife Fedn. Methodist. Home: 2368 S Holland Ct Lakewood CO 80227 Office: 1300 Broadway Denver CO 80203

TAVARES, MARIANNE CYNTHIA, marketing company executive; b. Cambridge, Mass., Aug. 29, 1956; d. Manuel Simoes and Dorothy Mary (Martin) T. B.S., Framingham State Coll., 1978. Telemarketing rep. Waters Assocs., Milford, Mass., 1977-82, mktg. research analyst, 1982-84; mktg. info. services mgr. Millipore Corp., Bedford, Mass., 1984-85, communications mgr., 1986—. Trustee, Yankee Village Condominiums, Acton, Mass., 1985-86; vol., group leader CODE Hotline, 1984—. Mem. Am. Mktg. Assn., Am. Mgmt. Assn., Earthwatch. Republican. Roman Catholic. Avocations: Photography; travel. Home: 1 Townhouse Ln Unit 3 Acton MA 01720 Office: Millipore Corp 80 Ashby Rd Bedford MA 01730

TAVARES, PHYLLIS CLAIRE, health care administrator; b. N.Y.C., June 9, 1937; d. John Resto and Martha Joanna (Herdeman) Shiller; m. David Wrathall Johnson, Dec. 3, 1958 (dec. 1971); 1 child, Rebecca; m. Gordon Tavares, Mar. 3, 1973; 1 child, Kevin. A.A., Valley Community Coll., 1957, El Camino Community Coll., 1969; B.A., St. Mary's U., Moraga, Calif., 1979. Dept. dir. Centinela Hosp. Med. Ctr., Inglewood, Calif., 1969—; lectr. Resource Applications, Balt., 1982-85. Author: Organizing and Managing a Gastroenterology Department, 1981; Soc. Gastrointestinal Assts. Manual of Gastrointestinal Procedures, 1985. Contbr. articles to profl. jour. Mem. Am. Med. Writers Assn., Women in Mgmt., Nat. Assn. Female Execs., So. Calif. Gastrointestinal Assts. (pres. 1985—), Soc. Gastrointestinal Assts. (mem. numerous coms., mem. editorial bd.; Outstanding Paper award 1980), Mensa. Roman Catholic. Avocations: travel; swimming; horseback riding; dance. Home: 6332 W 85th Pl Westchester CA 90045 Office: Centinela Hosp Med Ctr Gastroenterology Dept 555 E Hardy St Inglewood CA 90301

TAVERNA, ROSE CHRISTINE, advertising executive; b. Riverdale, N.Y., Jan. 22, 1923; d. Salvatore J. and Mary S. Taverna; student Bergen (N.J.) Jr. Coll., CCNY. With Nat. Wage Stblzn. Bd., Washington, 1948, Standard Brands Inc., N.Y.C., 1949; with Dancer Fitzgerald Sample Inc., N.Y.C., 1950—, asst. treas., 1965—, v.p., 1972-81, sr. v.p., 1981—, sec. of corp., 1977—; dir. Program Syndication Services, Inc. Office: Dancer Fitzgerald Sample 405 Lexington Ave New York NY 10174

TAYLER, JOAN MCLELLAN, real estate company executive; b. San Francisco, Apr. 11, 1928; d. Roderick McLellan and Vivian (Goddard) Irwin; B.A., Sarah Lawrence Coll., 1950; children—James D., Wendy Tayler Clarke, Roderick T., Garratt M. Dir., costume designer various TV stas., 1950-53; real estate sales assoc. William Wright & Co., Burlingame, Calif., 1966-69; v.p., mgr. Wright & Co., 1974-76; sales assoc. Grubb & Ellis, Burlingame, 1969-74; adminstr., pres. Joan M. Tayler Inc., Burlingame, 1976—; dir. McLellan Estate Co., Rod McLellan Co. Mem. San Mateo County Devel. Assn. Mem. Pvt. Industry Council, Burlingame C. of C. Republican. Episcopalian. Clubs: Commonwealth, Town and Country. Home: 49 Florence St San Francisco CA 94133 Office: Joan M Tayler & Co 100 El Camino Real Burlingame CA 94010

TAYLOR, ANN RENÉE, sales consultant; b. Algona, Iowa, Mar. 19, 1953; d. Gerald Dean and Patricia Ann (Matzener) T. B.S., St. Louis U., 1975. Sales mgr. Swank. Motion Pictures, St. Louis, 1975-81, Dalls, 1983-84; sales mgr. Aldershot Inc., Dallas, 1984-85; sales mgr. Allnet Communication, Inc., Dallas, 1985—. telemarking cons. MCCA, Dallas, 1982-83. Worthy adviser Rainbow Girls, 1970. Mem. Am. Mgmt. Assn., Am.Assn. Female Execs., Nat. Assn. Female Execs. Democrat. Methodist. Avocations: swimming; golf. Office: Allnet Communications Inc Suite 1950 2323 Bryan St Dallas TX 75201

TAYLOR, ANNA DIGGS, federal judge; b. Washington, Dec. 9, 1932; d. Virginius Douglass and Hazel (Bramlette) Johnston; B.A., Barnard Coll., 1954; LL.B., Yale U., 1957; m. S. Martin Taylor, May 22, 1976; children—Douglass Johnston Diggs, Carla Cecile Diggs. Bar: D.C. 1957, Mich. 1961. Atty. Office Solicitor, Dept. Labor, Washington, 1957-60; asst. prosecutor Wayne County (Mich.), 1961-62; asst. U.S. atty. Eastern Dist. Mich., 1966; ptnr. firm Zwerdling, Maurer, Diggs & Papp, Detroit, 1970-75; asst. corp. csl. City of Detroit, 1975-79; U.S. dist. judge Eastern Dist. Mich., Detroit, 1979—; adj. prof. law Wayne State U., Detroit, 1976. Trustee, Det. Receiving Hosp., Met. Hosp., Detroit, Health Alliance Plan, Detroit, Detroit Sci. Center, Planned Parenthood League Detroit, Community Found. Southeastern Mich., United Found., Mich. Cancer Found., Detroit Symphony Orch., Episcopal Diocese of Mich., Sinai Hosp. Detroit, Neighborhood Service Orgn. Mem. Fed. Bar Assn., Nat. Lawyers Guild, State Bar Mich., Wolverine Bar Assn., Women Lawyers Assn. Mich. Democrat. Episcopalian. Office: 235 Federal Courthouse Detroit MI 48226

TAYLOR, BARBARA ALDEN, public relations executive; b. Dallas, Aug. 21, 1943; d. Harold Earl and Sally Alden (Howard) T.; B.A., Smith Coll., 1965; M.A., Antioch Coll., 1971. Vol., Peace Corps, India, 1966-68; tchr. Upper Merion Sch. Dist., King of Prussia, Pa., 1969-70; tchr. Cheltenham Sch. Dist., Elkins Park, Pa., 1970-74; pub. relations dir. Princess Hotels Internat., N.Y.C., 1974-75; chmn. Taylor & Hammond Ltd., N.Y.C., 1975-84; pres. Doremus/Marketshare, 1984—. Bd. dirs. Madison Square Boys' Club N.Y., also mem. women's bd. Boys' Club N.Y. Mem. Women in Communications, Pub. Relations Soc. Am., Soc. Am. Travel Writers. Clubs: Doubles Internat., Smith Coll. Club N.Y., Jr. League City N.Y. Office: 120 Broadway New York NY 10271

TAYLOR, BARBARA JEAN, insurance industry association executive; b. White Plains, N.Y., Feb. 3, 1933; d. Charles George and Gladys Isobel (Winch) Watkins; B.A. in English, SUNY, New Paltz, 1974; m. Richard Taylor, Apr. 10, 1955 (div. 1977); children—Mark Evan, Linda Elizabeth, Janice Barbara, Nancy Jane. Advt. copywriter McCann-Erickson, N.Y.C., 1953-55; newspaper reporter Patent Trader, Mt. Kisco, N.Y., 1962-63, Evening Star, Peekskill, N.Y., 1963-65; founding editor The Yorktowner (N.Y.), 1965-66; gen. news reporter Westchester/Rockland (N.Y.) newspapers, 1966-70, bur. chief, editor No. Westchester Bur., 1970-72; communications specialist fed. Community Devel. Program, Yorktown, 1975-77; asso. dir. N.Y. State Petroleum Council (arm of Am. Petroleum Inst. trade assn.), N.Y.C., 1977-85; dir. consumer affairs and edn. Ins. Info. Inst., 1985—; founder, mgr. speakers bur. in field; freelance writer for New Dawn, Feminist Bull., The Entertainer; tchr. creative writing adult edn. classes; speaker civic and edn. groups. Bd. dirs. Food for the Hungry; adv. Citizens Commn. on Urban Renewal. Mem. Nat. Assn. Female Execs., NOW, Soc. Consumer Affairs Profls., Home Economists in Bus., Nat. Assn. Ins. Women, Ins. Consumer Affairs Exchange, Nat. Bus. Edn. Assn., Women in Communication, Am. Council on Consumer Interests, Publicity Club of N.Y., Bus. and Profl. Women. Presbyterian. Office: 110 William St New York NY 10038

TAYLOR, BARBARA JO ANNE HARRIS (MRS. RICHARD POWELL TAYLOR), educator, government official, civic and political worker; b. Providence, Sept. 9, 1936; d. Ross Cameron and Anita (Coia) Harris; student Tex. Christian U., 1952, Salve Regina Coll., 1952-53, Our Lady of the Lake Coll. and Convent, 1953-54, St. Mary's U., summer 1954, Incarnate Word Coll., 1954-55; student, Georgetown U., 1956-59, 62-63, B.S., 1963; m. Richard Powell Taylor, Dec. 19, 1959; 1 son, Douglas Howard. Adminstrv. asst. profl. devel. and welfare NEA, Washington, 1956-59; asst. to dir. Georgetown U., Washington, 1956-59; exec. asst. All Am. Conf. to Combat Communism, Washington, 1960; spl. legis. asst. for. mil. affairs to chmn. mil. research and devel. subcom. U.S. Senate Armed Services Com., 1971-72; apptd. U.S. nat. commr. to UNESCO, 1982—; mem. U.S. Nat. Commn. Libraries and Info. Sci., 1985—; mem. exec. bd. Salvation Army Aux., D.C., 1967—, chmn. fund-raising, 1968, co-chmn. fundraising, 1972, 74, chmn. membership com., 1969-70, co-chmn., 1972-74, mem. exec. com. of exec. bd., 1970—, treas., mem. fin. com., 1970-71, v.p., 1971-72, historian, 1972-73, editor Our Watchword Newsletter, 1968-69, chmn. Christmas Toycenter com., 1972—; mem. exec. bd. Welcome to Washington Internat., 1969-72, bd. advs., 1969-72, dir. workshop, 1969—, tchr. English and Spanish lit., 1970—; exec. bd. Am. Opera Sch. Soc., Washington, 1970—, v.p., program chmn., 1973—; exec. bd. Women's Aux., St. David's Episcopal Ch., Washington, 1970-75, v.p., 1970-71, 73-74, chmn. program com., 1970-71, 73-74; exec. bd. Women's Aux. Episcopal Center for Emotionally Disturbed Children, Washington, 1970—, Women's Aux. Episcopal Ch. Home for Aged, 1970—. Mem. exec. bd. League Republican Women D.C., 1964-67, 75-77, treas., 1964-67; mem. nat. council Womens Nat. Rep. Club, N.Y.C., 1969—; mem. Nat. Fedn. Rep. Women, 1964—; mem. Md. Fedn. Rep. Women, 1969—, state regents chmn., 1981; mem. Nat. Reagan for Pres. Fin. Com., 1979-80, chmn. Md. Reagan Bush Effort Com., 1980; coordinator for Md., Reagan-Bush Inaugural Com., 1980-81; Md. Rep. State fin. chmn., 1980. trustee, vice chmn. Crossnore Sch., Inc., N.C.; trustee Kate Duncan Smith Sch., Inc., Grant, Ala.; adviser Bacone Am. Indian Sch., Inc., Muscogee, Okla., Berry Coll., Rome, Ga., Hillside Sch., Inc., Marlborough, Mass., Hindman Settlement Sch., Ky. Recipient spl. award for vol. Salvation Army, 1969, 72. Mem. Internat. Platform Assn., Spanish-Portuguese Study Group (dir. 1969-74, treas. 1970-73, fin. chmn. 1972), DAR (nat. vice chmn. mus. docent com. 1974-77, nat. vice chmn. meml. service com. 1977—, chmn. nat. resolutions com., 1980—, mem. state bd. mgmt. 1973-80, state exec. com. 1978-80, state historian 1978-80, other offices, nat. campaign chmn.), Nat. Capital Law League, Nat. Assn. Parliamentarians, Nat. Soc. Children of the Am. Revolution, Sr. Nat. Bd. Mgmt. Clubs: Internat., Nat. Lawyers Wives, Capitol Hill, Capital Speakers, Congressional Country, Washington (internat. com. 1971-75), Am. News women's. Editor, Museum Newsletter, 1978-79; sr. editor, sr. publs. chmn. D.C. Children of the Am. Revolution, 1978-79. Home: 8801 Belmart Rd Potomac MD 20854

TAYLOR, BERNICE JONES, laboratory technologist; b. Mobile, Ala., Mar. 20, 1929; d. Ike and Robirta (Lankster) J.; m. Leo Taylor, June 8, 1955; 1 child, Patricia Ferguson. Student Springhill Coll., 1981-84. Presser, Chins Dry Cleaners, Mobile, 1955-68; lab. technologist Mobile Branch Lab., 1968—. Election law commr. State of Ala., 1980; dep. register Bd. Registration, Mobile, 1985—; dir. youth Met. A.M.E. Ch., Mobile, 1975-85; mem. pub. relations staff Women's Missionary Soc. Conf., Mobile, 1984-85, A.M.E. Ch., Mobile., 1975-85; exec. mem. Ala. President's Club. Mem. Ala. State Employees Assn. (pres. Bay Area 1984-85), Sister City Federated, Ala. Pub. Health Assn., Urban League, Profl. Golfers Assn. Inner Circle. Club: Pres.'s (Washington). Avocations: golf; music; dancing; reading; international travel. Home: 1059 Summerville St Mobile AL 36617 Office: Mobile Branch Lab Museum Dr Mobile AL

TAYLOR, BETTY ANN, American Red Cross administrator; b. Greentown, Ohio, May 26, 1929; d. Ivan Ronald and Ruth Marie (Martin) Daily; 1 child, K. Dean. A.A., Walsh Coll., 1973; student Aultman Hosp., Canton, Ohio, 1949, 50-51; B.A., Malone Coll., 1979; postgrad. other colls., univs. Casework-er ARC, Canton, 1968-73, asst. exec. dir., 1978-80, exec. dir., 1980—, family service officer ARC Nat., Washington, 1979—. Service in numerous disasters in Vietnamese Refugees-Indiantown Gap, Pa., W.Va., Md., Ala., Tex. P.R., N.C., Miss., Ohio; 1st dir. of Canton Red Cross Rape Crisis Ctr., 1975. Recipient award for Community Action, Gov. State of Ohio, 1973; Vice Pres.'s award Nat. ARC, 1985; Vol. Service award Rotary Club of Canton, 1985. Mem. Ohio Citizens Council, Nat. Assn. Social Workers, Nat. Assn. Female Execs. Republican. Office: ARC Canton chpt 618 Second St NW Canton OH 44703

TAYLOR, BETTY JO, film executive, producer, writer, director; b. Dallas, Feb. 10, 1933; d. William Samuel and Donna Mazie (Lester) Taylor. B.Journalism, U. Tex., 1955. Reporter Dallas Times Herald newspaper, 1955-56; editor Republic Nat. Life, Dallas, 1956-59; dir. media Presbyn. Ch. U.S., Nashville, Atlanta, 1959-70; mgr. communications Coca-Cola USA, Atlanta 1970-81; creative dir. The Bloom Cos., Dallas, 1981-82; pres. The Communications Dept., Inc., Dallas, 1982—; founding bd. dirs. IMAGE Media Ctr., Atlanta, 1978-80; pres., bd. dirs. Women in Film, Atlanta, 1979-81. Author: Where The Clock Walks, 1963; writer, producer, dir. corp. and ednl. films, 1970—; screenings at nat., internat. festivals. Former bd. dirs. Religion in Am. Life, N.Y.C., 1970. Recipient ADDY award for best black-white consumer advt. campaign, Am. Advt. Fedn., 1967; spl. award for film, for Juvenile Diabetes Found, 1980, nat. award for film for United Ways Am, 1980; 3 CINE Golden Eagles for best Am. nontheatrical films; awards from N.Y., Am., Chgo., San Francisco, and other film festivals, 1970—. Mem. Dallas Communications Council, Women in Communications, Pub. Relations Soc. Am. Democrat. Presbyterian. Home: 7603 Bryn Mawr Dallas TX 75225

TAYLOR, BETTY LOUISE, nurse; b. San Augustine, Tex., Jan. 18, 1953; d. Aruessie and Gertrude (Garrett) Taylor. A.A., Tyler Jr. Coll., 1975; B.S., Tex. Woman's U., 1982. R.N. Surg. nurse Ben Taub Gen. Hosp., Houston, 1982—. Mem. Alpha Delta Sigma. Democrat. Baptist.

TAYLOR, BETTY THOMAS, nurse; b. Asheville, N.C., May 10, 1936; d. Horace Cleo and Jessie Lee (Burnett) Thomas; m. Grady Daniel Taylor, Sept. 29, 1956; children—Pamela Marie Taylor Mintz, Elizabeth Susan Taylor Decker. R.N. diploma Meml. Mission Sch. Nursing, Asheville, 1957; cert. family nurse practitioner U. N.C. Mt. Area Health Edn. Ctr., Asheville, 1980. Lic. R.N., N.C. Head nurse ob-gyn Meml. Mission Hosp., Asheville, 1957-64; gen. duty nurse Skyland Med. Assn. P.A., (N.C.), 1964-79, family nurse practitioner, 1980—. Mem. N.C. Nurses Assn. Democrat. Mem. Assembly of God Ch. Home: 115 Pine Ridge Dr Fairview NC 28730

TAYLOR, BEVERLY LOY, management and training executive; b. Pitts., Dec. 4, 1943; d. Jack Glenn and Marie Crissy (Kennedy) Loy; m. James Arthur Taylor, Jan. 13, 1967 (div. Mar. 1972). B.A. (scholar), U. Pitts., 1968; Ph.D., 1974. Writer, editor Van Trump, Ziegler & Shane, Pitts., 1968-70; case mgr., interviewer Dept. Pub. Welfare, Pitts., 1970-71; instructional developer Research for Better Schs. Phila., 1974-76; project mgr. Ctr. Policy Research, N.Y.C., 1976-80; sr. program mgr. Xerox Learning Systems, Stamford, Conn., 1980-83; dir. program devel. Jack Morton Prodns., N.Y.C., 1983—; cons., 1975—; research assoc. Ctr. Policy Research, N.Y.C., 1978—. Adminstr., Pitts. Ballet Theatre, 1968-71; bd. dirs. Cambium Assn., Ithaca, N.Y., 1972-74. U.S. Office Edn. fellow, 1971-74; cert. N.Y. Marathon Com., 1980, 83. Bd. dirs. internat. rev. bd. Protection Rights of Human Subjects, 1978-80. Mem. Am. Ednl. Research Assn., Am. Soc. Tng. and Devel., Friends of N.Y. Pub. Library, Women's Campaign Fund N.Y.C. Club: N.Y. Road Runners. Office: Jack Morton Prodns 830 3d Ave New York NY 10022

TAYLOR, CAROL ANN, food service exec.; b. Phila., Nov. 11, 1938; d. Isaac Earl and Theresa Mary (Fitzpatrick) T.; student Drexel Inst. Tech., 1956-58; B.S. in Home Econs., Pa. State U., 1960. Home economist Acme Markets, Inc., Phila., 1961-63; homeservice rep. Phila. Gas Works, 1963-68; home economist

SCM Proctor Silex, Inc., Phila., 1968-71; sr. project mgr. ARA Food Services Co., Phila., 1971-81; dir. staff resources The Freshie Co., Phila., 1981—. Mem. Am. (registered), Phila. dietetic assns., Nat. Assn. Female Execs. Home: 4980 State Rd 1 607 Drexel Hill PA 19026 Office: 200 Pattison Ave Philadelphia PA 19148

TAYLOR, CLAIRE MCKECHNIE, radio station executive; b. Palermo, Maine, Mar. 29, 1927; d. Everett Harold and Annabelle (Tobey) McKechnie; m. Alcott Elwin Taylor, Aug. 17, 1946; one child, Nancy Taylor Ibarguen. Student pub. schs., Augusta, Maine. Mgr. Sta.-WKTJ, Farmington, Maine, 1974—.

TAYLOR, CORA HODGE, social worker; b. Fayetteville, N.C., Nov. 25, 1942; d. John Marlin and Cora Louise (Mitchell) Hodge; B.S., N.C. Coll., Durham, 1963; M.S.W., U. N.C., Chapel Hill, 1965; m. Charles L. Taylor, June 26, 1965; children—Charles L., John M. Clin. social worker VA Hosp., Bedford, Mass., 1965-68, 73-79; chief social worker Regional Health Center, Wilmington, Mass., 1978-79; clin. social worker VA Hosp., Bedford, Mass., 1979—; field instr. Boston U. Sch. Social Work, 1979—; instr., cons. primary care residents Tufts U. Med. Sch., Regional Health Center, Wilmington, Mass., 1978-79. Mem. Town Meeting, Billerica, Mass., 1981—; precinct clk., 1981, 82, precinct chmn., 1984, 85; deacon First Congl. Ch., 1986—. Recipient Superior Performance award VA Hosp., Bedford, 1966, 84. Mem. LWV (dir. 1970-73), Acad. Cert. Social Workers, Nat. Assn. Social Workers. Home: 35 Wildwood Rd Pinehurst MA 01866 Office: 200 Springs Rd Bedford MA 01730

TAYLOR, DEBORAH ARLENE, information systems director, consultant; b. Norfolk, Va., Jan. 25, 1954; d. Floyd Harold and Maybelline (Buck) Davenport; m. Raymond Alan Newlon, Aug. 19, 1972 (div. 1979); 1 child, Christine Autumn; m. George Richard Taylor, Apr. 24, 1981; 1 child, Zachary Lee. Assoc. Data Processing, Tidewater Community Coll., 1986; cert. Data Processing Chesapeake Vocat. Sch., 1972. Cert. systems profl. Computer operator Stewart Sandwiches, Norfolk, Va., 1971-75, communications programmer, 1975-76; programmer analyst Citizens Trust Bank, Portsmouth, Va., 1976-77; ops. mgr. Eastern Va. Med. Authority, Norfolk, 1977-80, systems analyst, 1977-80, dir. info. systems, 1980—; pvt. practice cons., Chesapeake, Va., 1977—; mem. EDP planning com. Virginia Beach Gen. Hosp., Va., 1981-82. Author articles in field. Active YWCA, Norfolk; mem. College Park PTA. Mem. Nat. Assn. Female Execs., Data Processing Mgmt. Assn., Am. Mgmt. Assn., IEEE, IBM Small Systems Users (dir. 1977-84, pres. 1980-81). Democrat. Mem. Ch. of Christ. Home: 5952 Appleton Ct Virginia Beach VA 23464 Office: Eastern Va Medical Authority 358 Mowbray Arch Norfolk VA 23510

TAYLOR, DEBRA HONEYCUTT, technical engineer; b. Gastonia, N.C., Nov. 15, 1955; d. John Fred and Evelyn Eletha (Connell) Honeycutt; m. Bill R. Taylor, Mar. 20, 1986. A.A.S. in Chem. Engring. Tech., Central Piedmont Community Coll., 1976; B.S. magna cum laude in Textile Chemistry, N.C. State U., 1979. Research technician Collins & Aikman, Charlotte, N.C., 1976-77, corp. research chemist, 1980-85; tech. engr. Salem Carpet Mills, Ringgold, Ga., 1985—. Mem. Am. Assn. Textile Chemists and Colorists, Nat. Assn. for Female Execs., Kappa Tau Beta, Sigma Tau Sigma, Phi Theta Kappa. Republican. Lutheran. Home: Route 6 27 Clay Ct Ringgold GA 30736 Office: PO Box 10 Ringgold GA 30736

TAYLOR, DELLA MAE, registered nurse; b. Johnson City, Tenn., Apr. 15, 1932; d. Lee Roy and Honolulu Cornelia (Holley) Brewer; m. John R. Taylor, Jr., Feb. 12, 1955; children—Aliesa Benea Taylor Meade, Celeste Taylor Eversole. R.N., Meml. Hosp., 1953; B.S., Steed Coll., 1978; postgrad. Milligan Coll., 1986. R.N., Tenn. Head nurse polio Meml. Hosp., Johnson City, Tenn., 1953-54; staff nurse VA Ctr., Mountain Home, Tenn., 1954-55, Meml. Hosp., Clarksville, Tenn., 1954-55; staff nurse pediatrics U.S. Army Hosp., Augsburg, Fed. Republic Germany, 1957-59; staff nurse VA Ctr., Mountain Home, 1959-62; part-time pvt. duty nurse, Jonesboro, Tenn., 1962-78, Life Exams Farm Bur., Washington and Unicol Counties, Tenn., 1978—. Contbr. articles to mags. Precinct chmn. Washington County Democrats, Jonesborough, 1975-85; mem. Washington County Dem. Women's Club, 1970-85; del. Dem. Conv., Nashville, 1975; co-chmn. campaign Lloyd Blevins for Congress, Jonesborough, 1975; chmn. Morthers March of Dimes; youth chmn. Washington County Heart Assn.; dir., coordinator Miss Teen Bd. Scholarship Orgn., Jonesborough, 1980-85; coordinator Dr. Charles T.R. Underwood Scholarship Meml. Fund, 1984; chmn. youth Neighborhood Heart Fund; judge Christmas Parade, Greenville, Tenn., 1978-86, other towns, cities, 1980-86. Mem. Nat. Assn. Female Execs., Bus. Profl. Women's Club, Steed Coll. Alumni Assn., Nurses Christian Fellowship. Baptist. Avocation: rose growing. Home: RFD #8 Taylor Rd Jonesborough TN 37658

TAYLOR, DIANA LYNN PRENTISS, giftware manufacturing company executive, designer; b. Lafayette, Ind., Mar. 25, 1951; d. Paul Homer and Bonny Rose (Oswalt) Prentiss; m. Charles Bernard Taylor, Feb. 27, 1970; children—Natalie, Cecily, Abraham, Nicholas. Pvt. practice as artisan, Columbus, Miss., Fayetteville, Ark., 1978-82; resident artisan Ozark Bazaar, Fayetteville, 1982-83; pres., owner Granny's Fan, Inc., Fayetteville, 1983—. Avocations: travel; music. Home: 734 E Lakeside Dr Fayetteville AR 72701 Office: Granny's Fan Inc 734 E Lakeside Dr Fayetteville AR 72701

TAYLOR, DOROTHY HARRIS, real estate broker; b. Richmond, Va., Nov. 3, 1931; d. Edgar Alan and Sadie (Wheeler) Harris; m. Gethsemane Jess Taylor (dec. Nov. 1964); children—Marlene J., Eric M., Andre E. Student L.I. U., 1959, John J. Criminal Coll., 1974, Queen's Coll., 1983, St. John's U., 1984, 86. Lic. real estate broker. Toll collector Port of N.Y. Authority, N.Y.C., 1967-80, tolls dispatcher, 1967; real estate salesperson Parkfield Realty, Queens Village, N.Y., 1982-83, Arro of Queens, 1983-84; real estate broker Arro of Queens, Queens Village, 1984-85, residential appraiser, N.Y.C., 1986—. Mem. Nat. Assn. Female Execs. (network dir. 1983-84), Am. Assn. Ret. Persons. Democrat. Club: Dorcas Soc. (pres. 1957-58) (Bklyn.). Lodges: Order Eastern Star, Heralds of Jericho. Avocations: gardening; crocheting; reading; contesting; interior decoration; travel.

TAYLOR, ELAINE CLAIRE NELSON, experimental psychologist; b. Meadville, Pa., Dec. 2, 1927; d. John David and Martha Margaret (Zurfluh) Nelson; B.S., Pa. State U., 1949; M.A., Bowling Green (Ohio) State U., 1951; Ph.D., State U. Iowa, 1954; divorced; children—Jenny, Jess. With Human Resources Research Orgn., 1954-84, sr. scientist, sr. staff scientist, Monterey, Calif., 1968-80, sr. staff scientist, Louisville, 1980-82, Carmel, Calif., 1983; pvt. cons., 1984—; with Woodside Summit Group, Inc., Mountainview Calif., 1985-86. Fellow Am. Psychol. Assn. (pres. div. mil. psychology 1978-79), mem. Human Factors Soc., AAAS, Sigma Xi. Republican. Author reports in field, chpts. in books; contbr. to popular mags. Home and Office: 18 Meadow Pl Carmel Valley CA 93924

TAYLOR, ELIZABETH, actress; b. London, Feb. 27, 1932 (parents Am. citizens); d. Francis and Sara (Southern) T.; ed. Byron House, Hawthorne Sch., Metro-Goldwyn-Mayer Sch.; 4 children. Motion pictures include: There's One Born Every Minute, Lassie Come Home, The White Cliffs of Dover, Jane Eyre, National Velvet, Life With Father, Courage of Lassie, Cynthia, A Date With Judy, Julia Misbehaves, Litte Women, Conspirator, The Big Hangover, Father of the Bride, Father's Little Dividend, A Place in the Sun, Love is Better Than Ever, Ivanhoe, Elephant Walk, Rhapsody, Beau Brummel, The Last Time I Saw Paris, Giant, Raintree County, Cat on a Hot Tin Roof, Butterfield 8 (Acad. award best actress), Cleopatra, The V.I.P.'s, Sandpiper, Who's Afraid of Virginia Woolf?(Acad. award 1966), Taming of the Shrew, The Comedians, Reflections in a Golden Eye, Dr. Faustus, Boom, Secret Ceremony, The Only Game in Town, X, Y and Zee, Under Milk Wood, Hammersmith is Out, Night Watch, Ash Wednesday, The Driver's Seat, The Blue Bird, A Little Night Music, Victory at Entebbe, Return Engagement, The Mirror Crack'd; narrator (with Orson Welles) Genocide; Broadway stage appearances include: The Little Foxes, Private Lives, 1983; (films for TV) Between Friends, Hotel, Malice in Wonderland, North/South, There Must Be a Pony. Author: Nibbles and Me; (with Richard Burton) World Enough and Time (poetry reading), 1964; Elizabeth Taylor, 1965. Fundraiser Chaim Sheba Hosp., Variety Clubs Internat., Martha Graham Dance Co., Alvin Ailey Dance Co., NAACP, Gaulladet Coll., Wolf Trap Farm Pk. for the Performing Arts; founder health clinics Botswana, Africa, 1976—; Elizabeth Taylor Fund for the Children of the Negev, Ben Gurion U., Israel; nat. chmn. Am. Found. for AIDS Research, 1985—. Office: care Chen Sam & Assocs 315 E 72d St Suite 19 G New York NY 10021

TAYLOR, ELIZABETH JANE, investment consultant, real estate company executive; b. Tiffin, Ohio, Oct. 27, 1941; d. Albert Joseph Lucas and Mary Jane Siebenaller-Swander; m. Gaylen Lloyd Taylor, July 11, 1977. Student, Heidelberg Coll., 1961, Austin Community Coll., Tex., 1983-84. Cons., Hypnosis Conn., Ohio and Tex., 1967—; dir. regional mktg. Sibrow, Inc., Ottawa, Can., 1981-83; rep. Aquilon Interests, Austin, 1985—; realtor assoc. Alliance Sales, Austin, 1985—. Author: profl. column Austin Women Mag., 1984—; (poetry) Letters from Home, 1986. Vice pres. Am. Congress on Real Estate, 1982-83; arbitrator Better Bus. Bur., 1984—; mem. speakers bur. Austin Woman's Ctr., 1985—; v.p. Austin World Affairs Council, 1984—; mem. adv. panel Austin Woman Mag., 1984—. Nominated to Tex. Womens Hall of Fame, 1984. Mem. Nat. Assn. Female Execs. (network dir. 1980—). Avocations: writing; behavior research. Home: 3406 Danville Dr Cedar Park TX 78613

TAYLOR, ELLEN BORDEN BROADHURST, civic worker; b. Goldsboro, N.C., Jan. 18, 1913; d. Jack Johnson and Mabel Moran (Borden) Broadhurst; student Converse Coll., 1930-32; m. Marvin Edward Taylor, June 13, 1936; children—Marvin Edward, Jack Borden, William Lambert. Bd. govs. Elizabethan Garden, Manteo, N.C., 1964-74; mem. Gov. Robert Scott's Adv. Com. on Beautification, N.C., 1971-73; mem. ACE nat. action com. for environ. Nat. Council State Garden Clubs, 1973-75; bd. dirs. Keep N.C. Beautiful, 1973-85; mem. steering com., charter mem. bd. dirs. Keep Johnston County (N.C.) Beautiful, 1977-85; life judge roses Am. Rose Soc.; chmn. local com. that published jointly with N.C. Dept. Cultural Resources: An Inventory of Historic Architecture, Smithfield, N.C., 1977; co-chmn. local com. to survey and publish jointly with N.C. Div. Archives and History: Historical Resources of Johnston County, 1980-86. Mem. Nat. Council State Garden Clubs (life; master judge flower shows), Johnston County Hist. Soc. (charter), N.C. Geneal. Soc. (charter), Johnson County Geneal. Soc. (charter), Hist. Preservation Soc. N.C. (life), N.C. Art Soc. (life). Democrat. Episcopalian. Clubs: Smithfield (N.C.) Garden (charter; pres. 1969-71), Smithfield Woman's (v.p. 1976), DAR (organizing vice-regent chpt. 1976), Gen. Soc. Mayflower Descs. (life), Descs. of Richard Warren, Nat. Soc. New Eng. Women (charter mem. Carolina Capital chpt.), Colonial Dames Am. (life), Magna Charta Dames, Nat. Soc. Daus. of Founders and Patriots Am. Home: 616 Hancock St Smithfield NC 27577

TAYLOR, FANNIE TURNBULL, educator; b. Kansas City, Mo., Sept. 11, 1913; d. Henry King and Fannie Elizabeth (Sills) Turnbull; B.A., U. Wis., Madison, 1938; L.H.D. (hon.), Buena Vista Coll., Storm Lake, Iowa, 1975; m. Robert Taylor, Dec. 2, 1938 (div. 1974); children—Kathleen Muir Taylor Isaacs, Anne Kingston Taylor Wadsack. Mem. faculty U. Wis., Madison, 1941—, prof. social edn., 1949—, emeritus, 1979—, dir. Wis. Union Theatre, 1946-66, coordinator univ. systems arts council, 1967-70, assoc. dir. Center Arts Adminstrn., 1970-72, coordinator Consortium Arts, 1976-84; program dir. music Nat. Endowment Arts, 1966-67, program info. dir., 1972-76; bd. dirs. Wis. Arts Council, 1964-72, Wis. Found. Arts, 1976—, Madison Civic Music Assn., 1976-84; Madison Children's Mus., 1983—; council chair Elvehjem Mus. Art, 1976—; mem. grant rev. panel Madison Civic Center, 1981-86, Madison Civic Ctr. Found., 1985—; cons. in field. Bd. dirs. Wis. chpt. Nature Conservancy, 1963-84, chmn., 1976-77; bd. dirs. Shorewood Hills Found., 1976—, pres., 1976-81. Recipient Oak Leaf award Nature Conservancy, 1981. Mem. Assn. Coll., Univ. and Community Arts Adminstrs. (exec. dir. 1970-72; Fannie Taylor award 1972), Am. Assn. Dance Cos. (dir. 1967-72), Nat. Assn. Regional Ballet (dir. 1975-77), Nat. Guild Community Schs. Arts (dir. 1977-80), Women in Communications (Writers' Cup 1980), U. Wis. Alumni Assn. (Disting. Service award 1979), Mortar Bd. Clubs: Madison Civics (pres. 1969-70), Madison, University (pres. 1982-85). Author articles in field, (handbook). The Arts at a New Frontier. Home: 1213 Sweet Briar Rd Madison WI 53705 Office: 5525 Humanities U Wis Madison WI 53706

TAYLOR, GINGER GAY OHLENBUSCH, interior designer; b. Lubbock, Tex., Apr. 21, 1947; d. Albert Bernhardt and Wilma (Limmer) Ohlenbusch; m. Howard Edward Taylor, Dec. 18, 1971 (div. June 1980); children—Julie Elizabeth, Leslie Ann. B.F.A., U. Denver, 1969. Cert. tchr., Colo. Tchr. elem. art Jefferson County Pub. Schs., Lakewood, Colo., 1971-74; owner, interior designer Taylor'd Designs, Denver, 1974-80, 84—; interior designer Spectrum III, Inc., Littleton, Colo., 1980-81; exec. adminstr. Overthrust Resources, Ltd., Denver, 1981-82; interior designer Davis & Shaw, Denver, 1982-84; instr. interior design Denver YWCA Programs, 1977-79. Mem. Interior Design Soc. (assoc.), Am. Soc. Interior Design (assoc.). Republican. Lutheran. Avocations: skiing; tennis; floral designing. Home: 3655 S Verbena St F-302 Denver CO 80237 Office: Taylor'd Designs 2785 N Speer Blvd Suite 200 Denver CO 80211

TAYLOR, GRACE ELIZABETH WOODALL, law librarian, educator; b. Butler, N.J., June 14, 1926; d. Frank E. and Grace (Carlyon) Woodall; A.B. with honors (Lewis scholar), Fla. State U., 1949, M.A., 1950; J.D., U. Fla., 1962; m. Edwin S. Taylor, Feb. 4, 1951 (dec.); children—Carol Lynn Taylor Crespo, Nancy Ann. Asst. in library U. Fla., Gainesville, 1950-56, asst. law librarian, 1956-62, assoc. law librarian, 1962-66, librarian, 1966-73, dir. Legal Info. Center, 1962—, prof. law, 1976—; hearing officer Career Service Grievance Hearings; speaker in field. Bd. dirs. SOLINET, 1981-84, chmn., 1983-84; chmn. LAWNET Com. NEH grantee, 1980-81, 85-86; Council Library Resources grantee, 1985-86. Mem. Am. Assn. Law Libraries (exec. bd. 1981-84), Assn. Am. Law Schs., ABA, ALA, Am. Soc. Info. Sci., Fla. Library Assn., OCLC Users Council (v.p. 1984-85, pres. 1985-86), Order of Coif, Phi Beta Kappa, Beta Phi Mu. Contbr. articles to profl. jours. Home: 2116 NE 7th Terr Gainesville FL 32609 Office: Legal Info Center U Fla Gainesville FL 32611

TAYLOR, JACQUELINE, human resources manager; b. Martinsville, Va., July 21, 1955; d. William Archie and Cornelia (Cobler) Taylor. A.A., Patrick Henry Community Coll., 1975; B.S.B.A., Va. Commonwealth U., 1977, M.S. in Mgmt., 1978. Personnel mgr. Coburn Optical/REVLON, Colonial Heights, Va., 1978-80; employment mgr. Med. Coll. Va., Richmond, 1980-81; personnel mgr. ROLM Mid-Atlantic, Tysons Corner, Va., 1981-83; mgr. human resources Nixdorf Computer Software Co., Richmond, Va., 1983—; adj. faculty mem. J. Sargeant Reynolds Community Coll., Richmond, 1978—, John Tyler Community Coll., Richmond, 1979-82. Mem. adv. bd. Va. Employment Commn., Petersburg, 1979. Named Outstanding Student Sch. Bus. Va. Commonwealth U., 1977. Mem. Am. Soc. Personnel Administrators, Am. Mgmt. Assn., Am. Soc. Tng. Devel., Nat. Assn. Female Execs. Republican. Baptist. Office: Nixdorf Computer Software Co 6517 Everglades Dr Richmond VA 23225

TAYLOR, JILL OLSEN, lawyer, artist; b. Logan, Utah, June 1, 1955; d. Keith Conrad and Norma Elveda (Correll) Olsen; m. Bruce T. Taylor, July 3, 1979; children—Jenny, Benjamin, Christina. B.A. summa cum laude, Brigham Young U., 1977; J.D., Brigham Young U., 1980. Bar: Utah, 1980. Dep. county atty., Emery County, Utah, 1980-81; corp. atty. Physicians Emergency Service, Price, Utah, 1981—. Bd. dirs., pres. Covered Bridge Canyon Homeowners Assn., 1983—. Mem. Utah State Bar Assn., ABA, Order of Barristers (mem. nat. bd. govs.), Phi Kappa Phi. Republican. Mormon.

TAYLOR, JILL RENEE, radio station executive; b. Buffalo, Oct. 3, 1956; d. Carl William and Marjorie Jean (Harmon) T. B.A., Pa. State U., 1977. Announcer, Sta. WOTR, Corry, Pa., 1970-74; counselor On Drugs Inc., State College, Pa., 1975-77; news dir. WWRN Radio, West Palm Beach, Fla., 1977-78; reporter Beacon News, Jupiter, Fla., 1978-80; news dir. Sta. WRIT, Stuart, Fla., 1978—. Mem. Fla. Assoc. Press Broadcasters (pres. 1984—), SAA (bd. dirs. 1982-84), Martin County Press Club (founder, pres. 1983-85). Avocations: reading; skin diving; writing; gardening. Office: WRIT Radio PO Drawer 359 Stuart FL 33495

TAYLOR, JUANITA EDNA, educator, antique dealer; b. Pueblo, Colo., Apr. 22, 1922; d. Mike and Myrtle (Chavalia) Joseph; children—Michael Frank, Peter Adrian. B.A., Adams State Coll., 1952, M.A., 1961; postgrad. U. Calif.-Riverside, 1955-59, U. Okla., 1966. Psychiat. nurse Pueblo State Hosp., Colo., 1940-42; tchr. pub. schs., Colo. and Calif., 1949-59; supt. schs. Costilla County, Colo., 1959-62; supr. resident relations Denver Housing Authority, 1962-66; ednl. advisor Dept. State, Montevideo, Uruguay, 1967-69; program rev. and resources officer HEW, 1969-73, children's services specialist Denver, 1973-76; cons. Office Econ. Opportunity, State of Colo., 1968; asst. dir. Planning for Vocat. Rehab., Colo., 1966-67; treas. Fulbright Commn., Montevideo, 1968-69; owner Queen Bee Antiques, Denver, 1973—. Recipient Doll Artist award, 1984, 85. Served with USAAF, 1942-44, USN, 1944-46. Mem. NEA, Colo. Edn. Assn., Colo. Assn. County Supts. (sec. 1958-59), Calif. Edn. Assembly (rep.), DHA Employees Assn., Am. Legion. Roman Catholic. Club: Catharis Theatre. Home: 922 W 101st Ave Northglenn CO 80221 Office: 2727 W 27th Ave Denver CO 80211

TAYLOR, JUNE ANN, association executive; b. London, May 28, 1939; came to U.S., 1959, naturalized, 1968; d. William Alfred and Doris (Chambers) Cook; m. Karl W. Taylor, Dec. 15, 1956; children—Susan, Dennis, Julie. A.A., Pratt Jr. Coll., 1968. Pres., Mothers Against Drunk Driving, Ohio, 1982-85, state co-ordinator, 1983—, vol. exec. dir., 1985—; cons. for media P.M. Mag., Can. Film Industry, various others. Named Women of the Year Cin. Enquirer, 1982. Republican. Methodist. Home and Office: Box 194 Ross OH 45061

TAYLOR, KATHARINE, personnel and executive recruiting executive; b. Tarrytown, N.Y., Aug. 8, 1936; d. Frank Alba and Katharine Margaret (Koch) Foley; m. Richard Paul Taylor, Aug. 26, 1978 (div. 1982); children—Sharon, Susan, Elizabeth, Margaret. Student Brenau Coll., 1954-55; cert. Katharine Gibbs Sch., N.Y.C., 1956. Personnel asst. Warwick & Legler Advt. Agy., N.Y.C., 1956-60; dir. Colegio Whitman, Guatemala City, Guatemala, 1966-69; owner, dir. Colegio Gibbs, Guatemala City, 1970-77; mgr. Meade Services, Beverly Hills, Calif., 1977-79; v.p., div. mgr. Bus. Women of Dallas div. Jean West Assocs., Inc., 1980-85; owner Taylor Burrell & Assocs., 1985—. Dir. fundraising Guatemala Symphony Orch., Guatemala City, 1975-77; sponsor Girls Club of Dallas. Mem. Assn. Women Execs. (1st v.p. 1983-84, membership dir. 1982-83, North Dallas C. of C.). Republican. Club: Zonta. Home: 7985 Fallmeadow Ln Dallas TX 75248 Office: Bus Taylor Burrell & Assoc Inc 12200 Park Central Dr Suite 180 Dallas TX 75251

TAYLOR, KATHLEEN OWEN, nurse; b. Milw., Mar. 22, 1935; d. Thomas Jackson and Frieda Anna (Kamin) Wilson; diploma vocat. nursing Houston adult edn. program Meml. Bapt. Hosp., 1959; children—Judith Ann, Donald Eugene, Carolyn Ruth, Wanda Kay; m. Bruce F. Taylor, June 28, 1982. Staff nurse Meml. Bapt. Hosp., Houston, 1959-60; emergency room nurse Height Hosp., Houston, 1960-72; emergency room nurse Twelve Oaks Hosp., Houston, 1972-77, orthopedics staff nurse, 1977-79, outpatient dept. coordinator, 1979-84; owner Taylor Hosp. Cost Audit and Ins. Filing Inc., 1985—. Mem. Tex. Lic. Vocat. Nurses Assns., Emergency Dept. Nurses Assn., Harris County Vocat. Nurses Assn., Am. Heart Assn. Mem. Assembly of God. Home: 6730 Acorn Houston TX 77092

TAYLOR, KENDALL FRANCES, arts administrator, educator; b. N.Y.C., May 9; d. Alexander and Sophie (Tannenbaum) Finne; m. David R. Garner, Nov. 23, 1979. Cert. of Achievement, U. Oslo, 1960; B.A., Fairleigh Dickinson U., Rutherford, N.J., 1962; M.A., Vanderbilt U., 1963, M.A.T., 1964; M.A., Syracuse U., 1977, Ph.D., 1979. Lectr., U. Md., 1964-71; writer, producer Stas. KNBC-TV, KTTV-TV, KPIX-TV, 1971-73; dir. Brainerd Art Gallery SUNY, Potsdam, 1979-80, chmn. Council of SUNY Gallery and Exhibit Dirs., 1979-80; asst. prof. Grad. Sch. George Washington U., 1980—; dir. traveling exhbn. program Library of Congress, 1980-84; dir. Arts Mgmt. Assocs., Washington, 1984—Nat. Speaker represented by Ross Assocs. Speakers Bur., N.Y.C. Author: (with Lila Weingarten) Arts and Crafts in Los Angeles, 1974; Never Separate from the Heart: The Life and Work of Philip Evergood, 1986; contbr. articles to profl. jours. Field rep. N.Y. State Council on the Arts, N.Y.C., 1980—; mem. steering com. Women Adminstrs. in Higher Edn. Adminstrn., Washington, 1983-84. Ford Found. fellow, 1963-64, Syracuse U. Florence fellow (Italy), 1974-75; Smithsonian fellow, 1977-78. Mem. Am. Assn. Mus. (mem. accreditation com. 1983—, chmn. Women Mus. Dirs. Caucus 1983-84, reviewer Mus. Assessment program 1984), Coll. Art Assn., Nat. Assn. Women Deans & Adminstrs. (presider Conf. 1984), Writers Guild Am. Democrat. Jewish. Home: 1841 Columbia Rd NW Washington DC 20009

TAYLOR, LESLIE ANN, lawyer; b. Honolulu, May 22, 1948; d. Jerry Hampton and Geraldine (Samples) Taylor; m. Stuart D. Rick, May 1, 1976; children—Evan Louise, Adam Taylor. B.A. with honors, U. South Fla., 1969; J.D., George Washington U., 1973. Bar: D.C. 1974. Gen. atty. Pvt. Radio Br., FCC, Washington, 1974-76, atty.-advisor Common Carrier Br., 1976-79, chief internat. and satellite br. Common Carrier Bur., 1979-80; policy specialist Nat. Tel. and Info. Adminstrn., Dept. Commerce, 1980-81; legal advisor to Commr. Dawson, FCC, Washington, 1981-82; legal advisor to Ambassador Washburn, U.S. Del. 1983 Region 2 Conf. for Broadcasting Satellite Services, 1982-83; dir. govt. affairs GTE Spacenet Corp., McLean, Va., 1983—. Mem. ABA. Office: GTE Spacenet Corp 1700 Old Meadow Rd McLean VA 22102

TAYLOR, LILA MAELAWSON, nurse; b. Pauline, S.C., May 24, 1935; d. Robert Edward and Jessie Carrie (Cathcart) Lawson; m. Rex Adams Taylor, Dec. 22, 1957; children—Elizabeth Taylor Davison, Robert Adams. R.N., York Gen. Hosp., 1955. Office nurse Johnson, Elemore & Adams, Spartanburg, S.C., 1952-53, Hastings & Hanna M.D., Spartanburg, 1953-58; staff nurse Petersburg Gen. Hosp. (Va.), 1958-59, Hillcrest Hosp., Simpsonville, S.C., 1962-63; dir. nurses Palmetto Nursing Home, Simpsonville, 1968-76; staff nurse Dan River Inc., Fountain Inn, S.C., 1976—. Recipient cert. of Merit ARC, 1984. Mem. Am. Assn. Occupational Health Nurses, Council Accredition Occupational Hearing Conservation, S.C. Assn. Occupational Health Nurses. Methodist.

TAYLOR, LINDA JEAN, financial services manager; b. Buffalo, May 30, 1959; d. Alfred James and Ileane (Kunold) Taylor. B.A., Kalamazoo Coll., 1980; M.Internat. Bus. Studies, U. S.C., 1982. Fin. analyst Gen. Motors Co., Detroit, 1978-79; researcher Traverse Bay Regional Planning Commn., Traverse City, Mich., 1979-80; intern OCFIBRAS subs. Owens Corning Fiberglas, São Paulo, Brazil, 1981-82; internal auditor Monsanto Co., St. Louis, 1982-85, fin. services mgr., 1985—. Mem. presdl. adv. com. on coll. investment in South Africa, Kalamazoo Coll., 1980. Mem. Nat. Networking, St. Louis Assn. Credit mgmt. Home: 507 E Sarah Ln Creve Coeur MO 63141 Office: Monsanto Co 800 N Lindbergh Blvd Saint Louis MO 63167

TAYLOR, LINDA T(HORNTON), information systems executive, educator, speaker, writer; b. Cambridge, Mass., Apr. 16, 1942; d. Ferdinand and Hazel Irene (Towne) Karamanoukian; m. John Robert Thornton, Jan. 21, 1961 (div. 1966); 1 son, John Robert; m. 2d F. Jason Gaskell, Nov. 30, 1978. A.A. in Bus. Adminstrn., West Los Angeles Coll., 1976; B.S. in Bus. and Info. Sci., West Coast U., 1980, M.S. in Bus. and Info. Sci., 1980. Adminstrv. asst. to credit mgr., accounts receivable clk. Pitts. Plate Glass Co., Boston, 1960-61; adminstrv. asst. to chief indsl. engr. Holtzer Cabot Corp., Boston, 1962-64; adminstrv. mgr. and asst. to br. dirs. Fin. Collection Agys., Ltd., Boston, 1964-67; corp. sec., gen. mgr. Bankers Fin. Equity Corp. (subs. Seaboard Corp.), Boston and Los Angeles, 1967-72, mem. adminstrv. com. and internal ops. auditor Seaboard Corp.; owner, operator Tay-Kara Mgmt. and Systems, Los Angeles, 1972-74; fin. and adminstrv. systems devel. mgr. Transaction Tech., Inc., Santa Monica, Calif., 1974-77; mgr. software engring. mgmt. control center, mgr. tech. audits software engring. div., mgr. software devel. electronic publ. div. System Devel. Corp., Santa Monica, 1977-81; corp. dir. info. and mgmt. systems Filmways, Inc. (Orion Pictures, Inc.), Los Angeles, 1981-82; v.p. Gaskell & Taylor Engring., Inc., Los Angeles, 1982—; faculty grad. sch. bus. West Coast U., 1980—; vis. lectr. Calif. Polytech. U., San Diego State U. Editorial bd. Data Processing Quality Assurance Jour. Fiscal adv. com. Santa Monica Unified Sch. Dist., 1979-81; chmn. Republican State

Central Com., Bus. and Profl. Women's Cm., 1974; participant White House Commn. on Workers Compensation, 1976. Recipient Pub. Service award West Los Angeles C. of C., 1974, honorable mention Woman of Yr. YWCA, Los Angeles, 1980. Mem. Assn. for Women in Computing (nat. pres. 1980-84, chpt. v.p. 1979-80), Nat. Computer Conf. (vice chmn. 1980), Data Processing Mgmt. Assn. (chpt. v.p. 1979-80, chpt. dir., speaker, panelist profl., civic, ednl. groups), Internat. Fedn. Info. Processing, IEEE Software Engring. Task Force, Assn. Systems Mgmt. (chpt. sec. 1974-75), EDP Auditor Assn., Assn. Computing Machinery, Nat. Assn. Women Bus. Owners, Ind. Computer Cons. Assn., Women in Mgmt., System Devel. Corp. Mgmt. Assn. (sec. 1979). Office: Gaskell & Taylor Engrs Inc 3572 Greenfield Ave Los Angeles CA 90034-6102

TAYLOR, LINN KAY, city government recreation official; b. Algona, Iowa, Jan. 18, 1948; d. Mitch Jacob and Lorraine Inez (Willrett) T.; m. John A. Templeton, May 25, 1971 (div. May 1981). Student Ariz. State U., 1966-67; B.S., Central Mo. State U., 1970. Recreation supr. City of Omaha, 1970-80; club mgr. Lakes Community Assn., Tempe, Ariz., 1980-84; dir. recreation Silveridge R.V. Resort, Mesa, Ariz., 1984—. Mem. allocations com. Tempe United Way, 1984—, chmn. small bus., nominations coms., 1985—; fund raiser Tempe YMCA, 1985-86. Recipient Highest in Div. award Tempe United Way, 1986. Mem. Ariz. Park and Recreation Assn. (chmn. comml. com. 1984-85), Resort and Comml Recreation Assn. (resort S.W. rep. 1984-85, sec. 1986), Alpha Omicron Pi Alumni Assn. (sec. Phoenix 1984-86). Avocations: racquetball, aerobics. Home: 6409-D S Kenneth Pl Tempe AZ 85283

TAYLOR, LISA SUTER, museum director; b. N.Y.C., Jan. 8, 1933; d. Theo and Martina (Weincerl) von Bergen-Maier; m. Bertrand L. Taylor III, Oct. 30, 1968; children—Lauren, Lindsay, Student Corcoran Sch. Art, 1958-65, Georgetown U., 1958-62, Johns Hopkins U., 1956-58; D.F.A. (hon.), Parsons Sch. Design, 1977, Cooper Union for Advancement Sci. and Art, 1984. Adminstrv. asst. President's Fine Arts Com., 1958-62; membership dir. Corcoran Gallery Art, 1962-66; program dir. Smithsonian Instn., 1966-69; dir. Cooper-Hewitt Mus. Decorative Arts and Design, Smithsonian Instn., 1969—. Mem. adv. bd. Mayor's Adv. Com. Design, Fashion Inst. Tech., N.Y., Art Deco Soc., Documents of Am. Design, Living Stage, Washington; mem. vis. com. Bank St. Coll., Moore Coll. Art, Phila. Recipient Thomas Jefferson award, 1976; Bronze plaque Johns Hopkins YMCA, 1958; medal of honor Am. Legion, 1951; Bronze Apple award Am. Soc. Indsl. Designers, 1977; named Trailblazer of Yr., Nat. Home Fashion League, 1981, Dame of Honour, Order of St. John of Jerusalem. Mem. Art Mus. Dirs. Assn., Am. Mus. Assn., Am. Craftsmans Council, Archtl. League, N.Y. State Mus. Assn., N.Y.C. Mus. Assn., Mcpl. Arts Soc., Central Parks Conservancy, Ceramics Circle, Needle and Bobbin Club, Smithsonian Instn. (Exceptional Service award 1969, Gold medal 1972, Hon. women's council award 1979), AIA (hon.), Am. Soc. Interior Designers (hon.). Co-dir. (film) A Living Museum, 1968; editor: Urban Open Spaces, 1979; Cities, 1981; The Phenomenon of Change, 1984. Office: 2 E 91st St New York NY 10028

TAYLOR, MABEL RUTH, educator; b. McPherson, Kans., Dec. 15, 1924; d. Oscar A. H. and Mildred Marie (Johnson) Larson; B.A., U. Kans., 1948; M.T., Central State Coll. Okla., 1965; Ed.D., U. Okla., 1971; m. John Taylor, Jr., Sept. 7, 1947; children—John Larson, Susan Louise Taylor Painter, Robert Lewis. Tchr. public schs., 1959-61; counselor, psychometrist Oklahoma City Public Schs., 1961-70; mem. faculty Central State U., Edmond, Okla., 1970-74, 1980—, also program dir. tng. sch. psychologist and sch. psychometrists; dir. diagnostic prescriptive learning center Tulsa Jr. Coll., 1976-80. Mem. Okla. Sch. Psychol. Assn. (state sec. 1976-78, Fay G. Catlett award 1981), Okla. Psychol. Assn. (pres. div. edn. and sch. psychology 1983), Nat. Assn. Sch. Psychologists, Okla. Assn. Gifted Creative Talented Inc., Delta Kappa Gamma (state scholarship chmn. 1981-83). Author: (with N. Ferguson and M. Scott) New Discoveries in Early Education, 1968. Home: 2604 NW 58th Pl Oklahoma City OK 73112 Office: Dept Psychology and Personnel Services Central State U Edmond OK 73034

TAYLOR, MAGGIE HENRIETTA PRICE, govt. ofcl.; b. La Grange, Ga., Feb. 18, 1936; d. Nathan and Maggie (Lee) Price; B.S., D.C. Tchrs. Coll., 1969; M.Ed., Fed. City Coll., Washington, 1974; Ed.D., George Washington U., 1978; m. James Taylor, Jr., Jan. 29, 1956 (dec.); 1 dau., Constance Marie. Grants adminstrn. specialist NSF, 1970-71; grants mgmr. officer Dept. Commerce, 1971-73; contract specialist Nat. Inst. Edn., 1973-75; contract and grant specialist U.S. Office Edn., 1975-78; bus. liaison specialist Dept. Energy, 1978-79; dir. community services div. Office Procurement and Contracts, HUD, 1979—; workshop leader, speaker in field. Recipient Outstanding Performance award NSF, 1971, HUD, 1980; named Am. Businessperson of yr. in D.C., Future Bus. Leaders, 1978. Mem. Am. Bus. Women's Assn. (corr. sec. 1978-79; Woman of Year award D.C. chpt. 1979), D.C. Bus. Edn. Assn. (pres. 1977-78, 79-82, dir. 1981—), Nat. Assn. Female Execs., Nat. Contracts Mgmt. Assn., Nat. Council Career Women, Nat. Bus. Edn. Assn., Nat. Assistance Mgmt. Assn., Phi Delta Kappa, Delta Pi Epsilon. Republican. Roman Catholic. Author career booklets. Office: HUD 451 7th St SW Washington DC 20410

TAYLOR, MARGARET TURNER, clothing designer, economist; b. Wilmington, N.C., May 7, 1944. A.B. in Econs., Smith Coll., 1966; M.A. in Econ. History, U. Pa., 1970, now Ph.D. candidate in City and Regionel Planning. Tchr. Jefferson Jr. High Sch., New Orleans, 1966-69; instr. econs. U. Tex.-El Paso, 1974-75; adj. prof. econs., Salisbury State Coll., (Md.), 1976-78; prin. mgr., designer Margaret Norriss, women's clothing, Salisbury, Md., 1980—; planner at Wharton Ctr. Applied Research, Phila., 1985-86.

TAYLOR, MARGARET UHRICH, college official consultant; b. Lebanon, Pa., Nov. 27, 1952; d. William Murray and Anne (Shultz) Uhrich; m. Timothy Norman Taylor, Sept. 29, 1979; 1 child, Walter Marshall. B.A., Shippeensburg U., 1974. Adminstrv. asst. Patriot-News Co., Harrisburg, Pa., 1974; reporter Pub. Opinion, Chambersburg, Pa., 1975-78; assoc. editor, Miami bur. chief OAG, Inc., N.Y.C., 1978-79; pub. affairs dir. Wilson Coll., Chambersburg, 1980—, co-founder women in transition program, 1985; mem. adj. faculty Shippensburg U., Pa., 1981—. Founding mem. Commonwealth Assn. Students, 1972; charter mem. Friends of Fulton County Library, McConnellsburg, 1975; founder Unforgettable Charity Ball, Chambersburg, 1983—; active Gotemba Sister-City Com., Borough of Chambersburg, 1981—; cons. dir. Straight Love Franklin County, Chambersburg, 1982-83; founder Women's Network Franklin County, 1982—. Mem. Soc. Profl. Journalists (treas. Central Pa. chpt. 1981-82, v.p. 1982-83, pres. 1983-84, chmn. freedom of info. com. 1980-81, chpt. del. nat. conv. 1977), Women in Communications, Pa. Pub. Relations Soc. Home: PO Box 552 Hustontown PA 17229 Office: Pub Affairs Office Wilson College Chambersburg PA 17201

TAYLOR, MARSHA HARVEY, construction company executive, trucking company executive; b. Concord, N.C., July 22, 1948; d. Robert Perry and Elzena (Widenhouse) Harvey; m. William Forrest Taylor, Sept. 16, 1982; stepchildren—Forrest, Gina, Bobby; children by previous marriage—Heather, Angelette, Vance. Student Wingate Coll., 1966-67, N.Y. Sch. Interior Design; computer degree Automation Inst., Charlotte, N.C. Mgr. AC Widenhouse, Inc., Wilmington, N.C.; sec.-treas. T & T Devel., Inc., Shallotte, N.C., 1971—; ptnr. TMT Properties, Shallotte, 1981—, MHT Ventures, Shallotte, 1984—; pres. Wilderness, Inc., Rockingham, N.C., 1981—; dir. Barefoot Oil Co., Concord, N.C., Carolina Oil Co., Concord, Widenhouse Service Co., Concord, HTS Corp., Long Beach, N.C. Mem. N.C. Bd. Realtors, South Brunswick Home Builders Assn. Avocations: single-engine flying; water skiing; handmade crafts; horseback riding. Office: T & T Devel Co Inc Route 5 Box 107 Unit 4 Shallotte NC 28459

TAYLOR, MARY JAN LIPTHRATT, public relations specialist; b. Brunswick, Ga., Mar. 14, 1955; d. C. Donald and Virginia Dare (Browher) Lipthratt; m. Kevin Patrick Taylor, Oct. 16, 1982. A.B.J. magna cum laude, U. Ga., 1977. Asst. editor Coastal Media, Inc., St. Simons Island, Ga., 1977-81; dir. research Glover Printing Co., Brunswick, Ga., 1982-83; dir. pub. relations Joseph Citron, M.D., P.C., Atlanta, 1984-85; dir. mktg. and pub. relations Cob Gen. Hosp., Austell, Ga., 1985—. Mem. communications com., newsletter editor Brunswick-Glynn County Clean Community Commn., Brunswick, 1983. Mem. Women in Communications, Am. Soc. Hosp. Mktg. and Pub. Relations, Pub. Relations Soc. Am. Phi Kappa Phi, Kappa Tau Alpha. Home: 887 Regal Path Ln DecaturAtlanta GA 30030 Office: Cobb Gen Hosp 3950 Austell Rd Austell GA 30001

TAYLOR, MARY JOAN (MRS. EDWARD MCKINLEY TAYLOR JR.), lawyer; b. Kenton, Ohio, Dec. 24, 1926; d. Maurice A. and Martina (Dolan) McMahon; student St. Mary Springs Coll., 1944-45; Asso. Degree in Bus. Administrn. Franklin U., 1946-49; J.D. with high distinction, Ohio No. U., 1951; postgrad., U. Wyo., 1954-56; m. Edward McKinley Taylor, Jr., Apr. 23, 1952; 1 dau., Mary Margaret. Admitted to Ohio bar, 1951; gen. practice law, Kenton, 1951-52, Wichita Falls, Tex., 1953—; mem. law firm Taylor and Taylor, Dayton, Ohio, 1957—; law librarian Franklin U., 1948-49. Trustee, Harrison Twp., 1980—. Mem. Ohio Bar Assn., Montgomery County Law Library Assn., Ohio No. U. Alumni Assn. (sec. Miami Valley 1958-60), Iota Tau Lambda, Kappa Beta Pi. Club: Soroptimist. Address: 7417 N Main St Dayton OH 45415

TAYLOR, MARY MCCAIN, educator, genealogy researcher; b. Tippo, Miss., Mar. 3, 1927; d. Joseph Samuel and Vennia Pearl (Nerren) McCain; m. Cecil William Taylor, Dec. 25, 1943 (div. Oct. 1984); 1 child, Daniel Joseph. B.S. in Social Sci., Delta State U., 1976. Payroll clk., sec. Itzig Wholesale Grocery, Inc., Greenville, Miss., 1962-64; payroll clk. Burdine & Ross, Inc., Greenville, 1964-69; eligibility worker Food Stamp Office Welfare Dept., Greenville, 1977-79; acct. Rosella's, Inc., Greenville, 1980-82; substitute tchr. Greenville Pub. schs., 1982—; free-lance genealogy researcher, 1968—. Candidate for Miss. Ho. of Reps., 1971; col. on staff Miss. gov., 1976. Recipient short fiction writing award Writer's Digest Sch., 1970. Mem. Humane Soc. Democrat. Mem. Ch. of Christ. Avocations: painting; ceramics; gardening; camping; courthouse records. Home: PO Box 695 Greenville MS 38701

TAYLOR, MARY ROSE, television anchor, reporter; b. Denver, May 26, 1945; d. Walter Gorringe and Marylynn (Eusterman) King; m. Charles Peete Rose, Aug. 10, 1968 (div.); m. 2d, Charles McKenzie Taylor, Feb. 26, 1983; stepchildren—Andrew McKenzie, Camille Williams. B.A. in Polit. Sci., U. N.C., 1967. Researcher, CBS-TV News, N.Y.C., 1968-71; assoc. producer BBC-TV Documentaries, N.Y.C., London, 1971-73; assigment editor Sta. WNEW-TV Metromedia, N.Y.C., 1973-74; documentary producer PBS, N.Y.C., Washington, 1974-76; producer, assigment editor Sta. WTOP-TV Post-Newsweek, Washington, 1976-77; anchor, reporter KTUL-TV News, Tulsa, 1978-79; anchor, reporter Gannett Broadcasting Sta. WXIA-TV, Atlanta, 1980-84; cons. producer documentary film Pumping Iron, N.Y.C., 1975-76; cons. producer Marshall McLuhan-the Man and his Message, N.Y.C., Toronto, 1982—. Trustee Atlanta Arts Alliance; mem. com. Gannett Community Service Awards. Recipient 1st place State UPI award, Ga., 1982. Mem. Am. Women in Radio TV, Nat. Acad. TV Arts & Scis., Sigma Delta Chi. Roman Catholic. Researcher: File on the Tsar, 1980-81; researcher on cities European Economic Community, German Marshall Fund, 1976. Office: Suite 217 375 Pharr Rd Atlanta GA 30305

TAYLOR, MAUREEN EUGENIA, hospital administrator; b. N.Y.C., Feb. 16, 1947; d. Samuel Goodwin and Genevieve (Scott) Taylor; 1 child, Jamal. B.S. in Criminal Justice, Mercy Coll., 1980; M.P.A., NYU, 1984; postgrad. N.Y. Inst. Tech., 1983—. Adminstrv. sec., asst. Mt. Sinai Hosp., N.Y.C., 1973-77; adminstrv. asst. Transit Police Acad., N.Y.C., 1978-79; bus. instr. PRC Metronamics, Corona, N.Y., 1979-80; clerical skills instr. ICD Rehab. Ctr., N.Y.C., 1980-81; adj. instr. Monroe Bus. Inst., N.Y.C., 1981-82; exec. asst. Dept. Juvenile Justice, N.Y.C., 1981-84; hosp. adminstr. Health & Hosp. Corp., 1984—; co-owner, pres. TPC Cons. Services, N.Y.C., 1982—. Recipient Criminal Justice Departmental award Mercy Coll., 1980; Mayor's Grad. scholar N.Y. Inst. Tech., 1983. Mem. Am. Soc. Pub. Adminstrn., Adminstrv. Mgmt. Soc., Am. Correctional Assn., Correctional Edn. Assn., Nat. Assn. Female Execs. Democrat. Roman Catholic. Office: Health and Hosps Corp Harlem Hosp Ctr Sydenham Neighborhood Family Clinic 215 W 125th St New York NY 10027

TAYLOR, MERRILY ELLEN, university librarian; b. Winchester, Mass., May 24, 1945; d. Philip Forbes and Ruth Ellen (Piper) T. A.A., St. Petersburg Jr. Coll., 1965; B.A., U. South Fla., 1967, M.A., 1973; M.L.S., Fla. State U., 1968. Reference librarian U. South Fla. Library, Tampa, 1968-69, head circulation dept., 1969-74, head collection devel., 1974-77; asst. to univ. librarian Yale U. Library, New Haven, 1977-78; dir. services group Columbia U. Libraries, N.Y.C., 1978-82; univ. librarian Brown U., Providence, 1982—. Author: The Yale University Library 1901-1978, 1978; author, editor: Remembering P.D. Ouspensky (exhbn. catalog), 1978. Acad. Library Mgmt. intern Council on Library Resources, Washington, 1976. Mem. ALA, R.I. Library Assn., Research Libraries Group (bd. govs. 1982—), Assn. Research Libraries (com. on library edn., adv. com. pub. services self study program 1982—), NOW, Nat. Trust Hist. Preservation, Providence Preservation Soc. Democrat. Methodist. Office: Brown U Library Box A Rockefeller Library Providence RI 02912

TAYLOR, MILDRED HENDERSON, recreation specialist; b. Newberry, S.C., May 15, 1925; d. John and Rachel Elizabeth (Reeder) Henderson; ed. Howard U., 1944-46, N.Y. U., 1948-53, Am. U., 1960, Md. U., 1962-64, Catholic U. Am., 1976, 79; m. Dec. 11, 1949; 1 dau., Brenda Christina Taylor Kellogg. Clk., GAO, Washington, 1943-44; with D.C. Dept. Recreation 1945-82, recreation supr., 1945-73, recreation adminstr., asst. dir. Before/After Sch. Care Program, 1974-82; tutor; counselor. Vol. Reading Is Fundamental; bd. dirs. Georgetown Children's House; v.p. Georgetown Community Parents Council, Washington, 1957-60, Block Community Orgn., Washington, 1960-62; pres. Ladies Usher Bd., Vermont Ave. Baptist Ch., Washington, 1972—, dir. Children's Worship Hour, 1962—; block capt. D.C. Neighborhood Watch; 2d v.p. Georgetown Neighborhood House; instr. needlework sr. citizens Vt. Ave Bapt. Ch. Recipient Kennedy Found. award, 1964; Disting. Service award Kiwanis Internat., 1970; Beautification award White House, 1973; Outstanding Performance award D.C. Dept. Recreation, Thirty Yr. Service in Govt. award 1975. Mem. Nat. Recreation and Park Assn., D.C. Recreation and Parks Soc. (life), Smithsonian Assos., AAPHER, Friends Nat. Zoo. Better Edn. for Children, Nat. Assn. Edn. Young Children. Clubs: Ladies Needlework, Brooks Meml. (fin. sec.). Home: 6109 7th Pl NW Washington DC 20011

TAYLOR, MILDRED LOIS, nursing home adminstr.; b. Conroe, Tex., July 23, 1927; d. George Carl and Bertha Elizabeth (Swift) Ferguson; student Hunter Coll., 1944, U.S. Navy Hosp. Corps Sch., Bethesda, Md., 1944, corr course Am. Sch., Chgo., 1971, Central Tex. Coll., 1971, U. Tex., Austin, 1975; m. Thomas Nielsen Taylor, Dec. 1, 1945; children—Linda Sue, Thomas Grant, Charles Nielsen. Nurse aide St. David's Hosp., Austin, Tex., 1965-67; adminstr.-in-tng. North Lamar Nursing Home, Austin, 1971-72, adminstr., 1973-75; adminstr. Austin Nursing & Convalescent Center, 1976—, sec., treas., 1976—. Pres. Episcopal Women of the Ch., Austin, 1966; mem. Tex. Nursing Home Adminstrs. Polit. Action Com., 1976—. Served with WAVE, USNR, 1944-45. Lic. nursing home adminstr., Tex. Mem. Tex. Nursing Home Assn., Am. Health Care Assn., Austin C. of C., U.S. C. of C. Clubs: Lost Creek Country, Order Eastern Star, St. David's Hosp. Women's Aux. (Austin). Home: 1909 Glencliff Dr Austin TX 78704 Office: 110 E Live Oak Austin TX 78704

TAYLOR, NANCY CLAIRE, insurance executive; b. Orange, Tex., Jan. 12, 1952; d. Larry Lee and Betty Ruth (Estes) Duhon; m. James Tunney Taylor, Jr., Apr. 22, 1972; children—Avy Heather, Holly-Nan. Program dir. YMCA, Orange, Tex., 1977-79; personnel sec. Baptist Hosp., Beaumont, Tex., 1979-83, adminstrv. sec. for human resources, 1983-85; exec. sales rep. Colonial Life & Accident Ins. Co., Beaumont, 1985, sales dir., 1985—. Mem. Jaycees, Proudest Crowd. Republican. Mem. Ch. of Christ. Avocations: singing; dancing; exercise; decorating. Home: 2325 Monterrey St Orange TX 77630 Office: Colonial Life & Accident Ins Co 1495 N 7th St Suite 4 Beaumont TX 77702

TAYLOR, PATRICIA BLOCKETT, civil engineer; b. Merigold, Miss., May 15, 1959; d. McKinley and Annie Lee (Daughtrity) B.; m. James Justin Taylor, Dec. 27, 1983. B.S. in Civil Engring., Tenn. State U., 1983. Engring. aide Blockett Constrn. Co., Cleveland, Miss., 1975-80; civil engr. trainee Dept. Transp., State Ga., Atlanta, 1981; civil engr. U.S. Army C.E., Omaha, 1984—. Mem. Soc. Women Engrs. (v.p. 1984-86), Nat. Assn. Female Execs., NAACP (advisor youth council 1986). Democrat. Baptist. Avocations: music; musical instruments; softball; basketball; volleyball. Home: 6805 B Plaza Apt 201 Omaha NE 68106 Office: US Army CE 6014 USPO and Courthouse Omaha NE 68102

TAYLOR, PATRICIA LLOYD, nurse, educator; b. Franklyn, Ky., May 19, 1931; d. Samuel A. and Ina Mae (Wade-Goldman) Taylor. R.N., Washington U. St. Louis, 1954; B.S. in Nursing, U. Evansville (Ind.), 1955; M.S. in Nursing, Duke U., 1963; Ph.D., U. Pitts., 1978. Staff nurse St. Louis Children's Hosp., 1955-58; instr. nursing Iowa Meth. Sch. Nursing, Des Moines, 1958-60, Bapt. Hosp. Sch. Nursing, Nashville, 1960-61; asst. prof. nursing Catholic U., 1963-67; assoc. prof. nursing U. Okla.-Oklahoma City, 1973-78, Vanderbilt U., 1978-79, Med. U. S.C., Charleston, 1979-82, Oreg. Health Scis. U. at Eastern Oreg. State Coll., La Grande, 1982—; cons. Oklahoma City-County Health Dept., 1976-82, pediatrics nursing com. children Grande Rhonde Hosp., 1983-84. Editor research news U. Okla. Coll. Nursing, 1976-78; contbr. articles to profl. jours. Bd. dirs. Parents Anonymous (dir., treas.); mem. adv. bd. Head Start, 1982—, Foster Grand Parents, Charleston, S.C., 1979-82. Mem. Am. Nurses Assn., Nat. League Nursing, Assn. Care of Children's Health, ARC, Am. Nurses Found., Sigma Theta Tau. Club: American Contract Bridge League (dir. 1983-84). Home: 2108 Aries Ln La Grande OR 97850 Office: Eastern Oreg State Coll La Grande OR 97850

TAYLOR, PEGGY LYNN, naval officer; b. St. Paul, Dec. 10, 1955; d. Charles Curtis Taylor and Ruth Marilyn (Walstad) Kranz. B.A., Calif. Baptist Coll., 1981. Commd. ensign U.S. Navy, 1983, advanced through grades to lt. (j.g.), 1985; retention officer, officer recruiter Naval Res. Readiness Command, Region 20, San Francisco, 1983-86; with Surface Warfare Officer Sch., San Diego, 1986—. Mem. Calif. Bapt. Coll. Alumni Assn. (mem. steering com., chmn. publicity com.), Res. Officers Assn., Nat. Assn. Female Execs., Naval Res. Assn., Navy League U.S. Republican. Baptist.

TAYLOR, RAMONA G., financial services company executive; b. Dallas, 1930. Student So. Meth. U. Sec. Lomas and Nettleton Fin. Corp., Dallas, Lomas and Nettleton Mortgage Investors, Affiliates of Lomas and Nettleton Fin. Corp., L&N Housing Corp. Address: Lomas and Nettleton Fin Corp PO Box 225644 Dallas TX 75265*

TAYLOR, RENATE HILDE, legal rights activist; b. Stuttgart, Germany, May 10, 1933; came to U.S., 1951; d. Ernest and Elsa Maria (Rossi) Quastler; m. David Wilson Taylor, Aug. 17, 1957. A.A., U. Calif.-Berkeley, 1953; B.S. in Phys. Therapy, U. Mich., 1956; M.S. in Justice, Am. U., 1980. Investigator on campaign fin. of Senator Magnuson, Congress Project, Ralph Nader, Washington, 1972; bd. mem. Ohio Citizens Coalition on Criminal Justice, Columbus, 1972-73; bd. mem. Ct. Watching Project Inc., Columbus, 1974-75; research asst. Ohio Shock Parole Statute, Ohio State U. Program on Crime and Delinquency, Columbus, 1975; mem. jud. process subcom. Criminal Justice Coordinating Council, Columbus-Franklin County Regional Planning Unit, 1975; indexer Educación Liberadora newsletter, Info. and Resources Ctr. for Education Liberadora, Reston, Va., 1983. Sec. Capital area ACLU, Olympia, Wash., 1968-70, mem. legis. com. Wash. State, Seattle, 1970-72; mem. justice com. League Women Voters-Ohio, Columbus, 1973-75. Mem. Nat. Lawyers Guild, AAUW (mem. legis. liaison com. state div. 1971-72), Pi Alpha Alpha. Home: 11420 Links Dr Reston VA 22090

TAYLOR, ROSANNE CAPPIELLO, training consultants executive; b. Darby, Pa., June 14, 1945; d. Frank S. and Louise Ann (Moreschi) Cappiello; m. Frank Moffa, Sept. 16, 1967 (div. 1984); m. A. Jeffrey Taylor, Apr. 27, 1984; stepdau., Jackie. A.B., Immaculate Coll., 1967; Cert. Bus., Villanova U., 1977; postgrad. in Bus. Adminstrn., Wilmington Grad. Sch., 1980-81. Clk. typist AMP Products Corp., Valley Forge, Pa., 1975-76, sales corr., 1976-77, tng. coordinator, 1977-78, supr. and trainer, 1978-80, sales rep., 1980-83, asst. product mgr., 1983-85; dir. mktg. Spitz Space Systems, Chadds Ford, Pa., 1985-86; pres., owner R.C. Taylor & Assocs. Tng. Cons., West Chester, Pa., 1986—. Chmn. Friends for Maggie Found., West Chester, 1984-85. Mem. Nat. Assn. Female Execs. (area dir. 1982—), Women in Electronics. Republican. Roman Catholic. Avocations: racquetball; bicycling; reading; cooking. Home: 20 Cannon Hill Rd West Chester PA 19382 Office: R C Taylor & Assocs 20 Cannon Hill Rd West Chester PA 19382

TAYLOR, ROSE MARY, chamber of commerce executive; b. Alton, Ill., July 12, 1913; d. Frank A. and Rosa Ann (Eisler) Price; m. Courtney Page Taylor, Jan. 23, 1937. Mgr., operator services Ill. Bell Telephone Co., Alton, Ill., 30-78; membership dir. Greater Alton Twin Rivers Growth Assn., Alton, 1979—. Sec., Am. Cancer Soc., Alton, 1950—; mem. St. Anthony's Aux., Alton, St. Ambrose Alter Soc., Easter Seal Soc. Ursuline Convent, Animal Protection Inst. of Am., Alton Area Aid Assn. Mem. Delta Council of the Telephone Pioneers (program chmn. 1978). Roman Catholic. Club: Soroptimists (del. 1949). Avocations: animal lover; collector antique glass; organ. Home: 1501 Glen Vista Godfrey IL 62002 Office: Greater Alton Twin Rivers Growth Assn 200 Piasa Alton IL 62002

TAYLOR, RUTH ADAMS, clinical social work administrator; b. Houston, Dec. 3, 1949; d. John Beverly and Minerva (Young) Adams; 1 dau., Ann. B.A., Prairie View A&M U., 1970; M.A., U. Toledo, 1972; M.S.W., U. Houston, 1975; J.D., So. Tex. Coll. of Law, 1984. Cert. social worker-advanced clin. practitioner, Tex. Adj. clin. social worker Baylor Coll., Houston, 1976; social worker Ben Taub Hosp., Houston, 1975-76; clins. supr. Dept. Mental Health-Mental Retardation, Houston, 1976—. Mem. Nat. Bar Assn. (student div.), Tex. Bar (student div.), NAACP, Delta Sigma Theta. Democrat. Baptist. Office: Mental Health Mental Retardation 1400 N Loop W Suite 200 Houston TX 77091

TAYLOR, RUTH ELINOR HOSTETTER, logistics management specialist; b. Portland, Maine, June 12, 1929; d. Paul Eugene Hostetter and Ethel Emily (Butler) Alden; m. David E. Taylor, Apr. 9, 1949 (div. June 1978); children—Anna Christine Slifkin, Laura Jean Myers, Steven Albert. B.S. in Bus. Mgmt., Evans-Carolina Coll., Charlotte, N.C., 1949; postgrad. N.C. State U., 1958; spl. courses U.S. Army. Program analyst U.S. Army, Ft. Bragg, N.C., 1968-78, Ft. Sheridan, Ill., 1979-79, chief mgmt. div., 1979-80, chief supply and services div., 1980-81, asst. chief of logistics, 1981-84, logistics mgmt. specialist, Ft. Lee, Va., 1984—. Author: Symbolism, 1983. Vol. worker leper colony, P.R., 1961-63; leader Girl Scouts U.S.A., 1963-77; pres. woman's guild Lutheran Ch., Fayetteville, 1970. Recipient Teamwork award U.S. Army, 1980, Civilian of Yr. nomination, 1981, Exceptional Performance awards, 1978-83, 85, commendation cert., 1985. Mem. Nat. Assn. Female Execs., Art Inst. Chgo., Art Council Waukegan, LWV, Assn. U.S. Army, Luth. Ch. Women. Democrat. Club: Waukegan Newcomers. Lodge: Eastern Star (worthy matron 1977, 83, personal page to grand officer 1983). Home: 16101 Tri-Gate Rd Chester VA 23831 Office: US Army Logistics Ctr Concepts and Doctrine Fort Lee VA 23801

TAYLOR, SANDRA ANDERSON, car rental company executive, consultant; b. Richmond, Va., Sept. 10, 1946; d. William Fitzhugh Lee and Mary (Toney) A.; m. James Edward Taylor, Aug. 26, 1963; children—Tamarro Lynn, James Edward, Troy David. B.S., Va. Union U., 1972; M.S. with honors, Johns Hopkins U., 1974. Instr., Balt. Pub. Sch., 1972-74, curriculum specialist, 1972-74; coordinating prin. Los Angeles Met. Colls., Okinawa, Japan, 1975-79, asst. dir., 1975-79; instr. chemistry Richmond Pub. Sch., 1979-80; instr. U. Md., Okinawa, 1978-79, also prof. English, Kyuku U.; pres. Manhattan for Hire Car Corp., Richmond, 1981—; pres. SATCo Constrn., Richmond, 1985—; Japanese culture and lang. cons. Richmond Pub. Sch., 1984—; fin. cons. Kayhan Enterprises, Richmond, 1984-85; dir. Anderson Enterprises, Richmond, 1981—. Author: Genetic Continuity, 1973; Essentials of Mathematics, 1978; An Individualized Approach to Chemistry, 1980. Contbr. articles to profl. jours. Mem. NAACP, Met. Bus. League, Va. Taxicab Assn. (bd. dirs. 1985-86). Democrat. Baptist. Clubs: Gordon Black Ski (Richmond) (pres. 1982-85); Toastmasters (Okinawa); Daus of Iris (corr. sec. 1978-79). Avocations: skiing; swimming; cooking; entertaining; Japanese flower arranging. Home: 4228 Knob Rd Richmond VA 23235 Office: Manhattan for Hire Car Corp 1615 Brook Rd Richmond VA 23220

TAYLOR, SANDRA LOUISE, nurse; b. Jacksonville, Fla., Jan. 27, 1960; d. Lonnie James and Inez (Sands) Taylor. A.D.N., Fla. Jr. Coll. Sch. Nursing, 1981. R.N., Fla. Nursing service technician Bapt. Med. Ctr., Jacksonville, 1980-81, staff nurse, 1981—, staff nurse rep. staff nurse com. Democrat. Baptist. Home: Route 2 PO Box 542-A Macclenny FL 32063 Office: Bapt Med Ctr 800 Prudential Dr Jacksonville FL 32207

TAYLOR, SHIRLEY DARLENE BURNS, paralegal; b. Decatur, Ill., Oct. 30, 1938; d. Robert and Sylvia Faye (Cowger) Belke; grad. Decatur Public Schs., 1956; m. Richard Lee Burns, Nov. 24, 1956 (div. July 1980); children—Cindi Lynn (Mrs. Thomas A. Diprima), Richard Todd, Scotti Lee, Kristin Annette; m. Edward C. Taylor, June 24, 1983; stepchildren—Krista Dawn, Russell Joseph. With C. N. Gorham & Sons, Decatur, 1956-57, Burger,

Geisler, Fombelle & Wheeler, Decatur, 1961-74; legal sec. Geisler, Waks & Geisler, Decatur, 1974—; rec. and corr. sec. Macon C. of C., 1974-80; sec.-treas. South Macon Twp. Library Bd., 1975-80. Cert. profl. legal sec. Mem. Macon-Moultrie Counties Legal Secs. Assn., Ill. Assn. Legal secs. (pres. 1982-83, legal edn. chmn. 1985—, Legal Sec. of Yr. 1977), Nat. Assn. Legal Secs. (Area 5 membership dir. 1980-82 scholarship chair 1983-85), Macon C. of C., Winning as Single Adults (sec. 1980-83), Parents Without Partners (newsletter editor 1980-82, membership dir. 1982-83, regional council sec. 1981-83). Democrat. Methodist. Home: RR #1 Box 129 Sullivan IL 61951 Office: 241 S Main St PO Box 1147 Decatur IL 62525

TAYLOR, SHIRLEY FAE, nurse; b. Blackshear, Ga., Sept. 20, 1936; d. John Gordon and Thelma (Johnson) Thrift; m. Charles Neil Farrell, Sept. 27, 1958 (div. 1976); children—Pamela Cheree, Brenda Susan Desser; m. 2d Lawton Garnis Taylor, July 26, 1980. Student Armstrong Coll., 1954-55, Boston Coll., 1961-63, U. Ga.-Waycross, 1967-69, Mass. Gen. Hosp.-Harvard U. Seminars, 1966-82, U. N. Fla., 1976-82; R.N., Candler Sch. Nursing, 1958. Clinician, IV therapist Beverly (Mass.) Hosp., 1964-66; night supr. Pierce County Hosp., Blackshear, Ga., 1966-69; dir. nurses Unicare-Milwaukee, Jacksonville, Fla., 1972-75; inservice instr. Univ. Hosp., Jacksonville, Fla., 1975-76; dir. nurses Ora Industries, Jacksonville, Fla., 1976-77; plant nurse, employee guidance program coordinator Maxwell House, Jacksonville, Fla., 1977—; instr. Jacksonville chpt. ARC; mem. utilization rev. com. Duval Med. Soc., 1972-77; v.p. Jacksonville Nursing Instrs., 1975-77. Author: Emergency/Disaster Nursing, 1965; Catheter Care, 1975. Dist. supr. Arlington chpt. Am. Cancer Soc., 1972-82; dist. supr. Arlington chpt. Am. Lung Assn., 1972-80; hon. med. librarian Univ. Hosp., Jacksonville, 1975—. Mem. Am. Nurses Assn., Fla. Nurses Assn., Fla. Occupational Nurses Assn., Am. Occupational Nurses Assn., Internat. Rehab. Inst. Roman Catholic. Club: Jacksonville Women's (past sec.). Home: 6604 Gamewell Rd Jacksonville FL 32211

TAYLOR, SUSAN CAROL HAYMAN, publishing and advertising executive; b. Rockville Centre, N.Y., Aug. 10, 1948; d. Robert Charles and Carol Hope (Wyman) Hayman; cert. Cambridge (Eng.) U., 1969; B.S., U. Kans., 1970; postgrad. Eastern Mich. U., 1971, Pace U., 1977-78; m. F. M. Taylor, Jr., Oct. 28, 1979; stepchildren—Pamela Suzanne, John Nelson. Tchr., Fauldhouse (Scotland) Jr. Secondary Sch., 1970; corr. Playboy Internat., Chgo., 1971-72; with Reader's Digest, Pleasantville, N.Y., 1972-85, mgr. special sales, 1974-78, mgr. trade sales, 1975-78, dir. market devel., 1978-85; v.p. Denhard & Stewart Advt., 1985—. Mem. Nat. Assn. Female Execs., Am. Mgmt. Assn., Am. Booksellers Assn., ALA, Assn. Am. Pubs., Pub. Advt. Club, Christian Booksellers Assn., U. Kans. Alumni Assn., Religious Pubs. Club, Alpha Chi Omega. Republican. Methodist. Home: 21-6 Croton Lake Rd Katonah NY 10536 Office: Denhard & Stewart 240 Madison Ave New York NY 10016

TAYLOR, TERRI LEE, lawyer; b. Salisbury, Md., Dec. 16, 1956; d. Orlando Washington and Jeanette Louise (Messick) T.; B.S., Washington Coll., Chestertown, Md., 1978; J.D., U. Balt., 1981. Bar: U.S. Ct. Appeals (4th cir.) U.S. Dist. Ct. Md. Assoc. Law Offices of Jay S. Engerman, Balt., 1981—; cons. for low-income Md. Vol. Lawyers, Balt., 1982—; atty. Frat. Order Eagles. Youth champaign chmn. Wicomico County Republican Central Com., 1974-75; vol. social worker Dept. Social Services, Kent County, Md., 1977-78. Mem. ABA, Am. Trial Lawyers Assn., Women's Bar Assn. Md. Trial Lawyers Assn., Bar Assn. Balt. City, William James Soc. (sec. Chestertown 1975-76). Democrat. Episcopalian. Home: 7003 York Rd Baltimore MD 21202 Office: Equitable Towson Bldg Suite 406 401 Washington Ave MD 21204

TAYLOR, THELMA JEAN, bus. records mgmt. co. exec.; b. Memphis, Aug. 21, 1932; d. Athey Howard and Elva Orean (Thomas) Doyle; student Memphis State U., 1975-78; student Mary Baldwin Coll., 1978-79; m. Myron B. Taylor, June 10, 1954 (div. Oct. 1977); children—Myra Gail, Jerry Cam, Timothy Thomas; m. 2d, Robert L. Hillenbrand, Apr. 17, 1982. Founder, pres. Archives, Inc., Memphis, 1979—; dir. R.H. Data Services, Microfilm Group; cons. Total Info. Exec. Support. Mem. Sales and Mktg. Execs. (Most Profl. Exhibit award 1980), Planning Execs. Inst., Data Processing Mgrs., Assn. Records Mgrs. and Assos., Assn. Comml. Record Centers. Republican. Presbyterian. Club: Toastmasters. Office: 1675 Shelby Oaks Dr N Memphis TN 38134

TAYLOR, VINITA JACKSON, commercial artist; b. Dallas, Apr. 18, 1954; d. O.C., Sr. and Pearlie Mae (Jones) Jackson; married. B.S., E. Tex. State U., 1977; postgrad. in comml. arts U. Tex.-Arlington, 1980-82. Data processing clk. Southwestern Bell Telephone Co., Dallas, 1979-82; directory artist Ad/Vent Craft, Dallas, 1982—; freelance designer, 1981—. Active in career devel. tng. Dallas Urban League, 1981. Democrat. Baptist. Home: 2720 Bowling Green St Dallas TX 75216

TAYLOR, WINNIFRED JANE, psychologist; b. Akron, Ohio, Aug. 27, 1925; d. Edwin Dain and Jessie Pearl (Keeran) Fletcher; B.S., U. Akron, 1962, M.S., 1965, Ph.D., 1971; m. John Idris Taylor, June 22, 1943; children—John Frederick Taylor, Timothy David Taylor, Kathryn Sue Taylor Cline. Tchr., Akron and Barberton, Ohio, 1959-65; sch. psychologist Akron Pub. Sch., 1965-74; pvt. practice family counseling and psychology, Clinton, Ohio, 1969-74; assoc. prof. and coordinator counseling programs U. Wis., Superior, 1974—; pvt. practice counseling psychology and family therapy, 1982—. Recipient Freedom Found. award for Teaching, 1965-66. Mem. Nat. Assn. Sch. Psychologists, Am., Wis. personnel and guidance assns., Am. Soc. Adlerian Psychology, Am. Edn. Research Assn., Am. Sch. Counselors Assn., Assn. Humanistic Psychology, Douglas County Mental Health Assn., Am. Soc. Indiviual Psychology. Contbr. articles to profl. jours.; syndicated columnist. Home: 1421 E 6th St Superior WI 54880 Office: U Wis Div Edn-Counseling Superior WI 54880

TAYLOR-LITTLE, CAROL J(OYCE), state legislator, real estate agent; b. Berkeley, Calif., Aug. 13, 1941; d. Harold Robert and Marjorie Evelyn (Strawn) Hochmuth; m. Nicholas G. Kappas, Aug. 29, 1959 (div. Sept. 1980); children—Anthony N., Katherine M.; m. Donald L. Little, June 19, 1982. Student in real estate Red Rocks Community Coll., 1978; cert. degree adminstrn. non-profit agys. Met. State Coll., Denver, 1981, postgrad. in urban studies and polit. sci., 1981—. Lic. in real estate, Colo. Recreation instr. North Jefferson County (Colo.), 1970-82; real estate sales agt. Crown Realty/Better Homes & Gardens, Arvada, Colo., 1979—; pub. relations coordinator Woman Sch. Network, Lakewood, Colo., 1980-81; mem. Colo. Ho. of Reps., Denver, 1982-84, 84-86, House majority whip, 1984-86; mem. Colo. Commn. on Women, Denver, 1979-80; legis. intern U.S. Senator William Armstrong, Washington, 1982, Senator Al Meiklejohn, Denver, 1982. Bd. dirs. Spouse Abuse Services and Research Jefferson County, 1980-82; mem. Merit Appeals Bd., Arvada, 1980-82. Named Woman of Yr., Beta Chi chpt. Beta Sigma Phi, 1968; recipient Outstanding Service award Jefferson County Bd. Realtors, 1978. Mem. Nat. Conf. State Legislators, Nat. Fedn. Bus. and Profl. Women's Clubs, Inc., Nat. Fedn. Republican Women, Colo. Hist. Soc., Arvada C. of C. (Image award 1980), Arvada Ctr. for Arts and Humanities. Club: Arvada Rep. Office: Colo State Ho of Reps State Capitol Denver CO 80203

TAYLOR-NASH, RITA CONSTANCE, equal opportunity specialist, sociology educator; b. Chgo., Nov. 26, 1949; d. James and Minnie Mary (Lucas) Taylor; m. Anderson Renee Nash, Aug. 26, 1978. B.A. in Sociology, U. Chgo., 1971; M.A. in Sociology, U. Mich., 1972. Claims adjustor Social Security Adminstrn. Chgo., 1973-74; instr. sociology Ill. Central Coll., East Peoria, 1974-75; equal opportunity specialist EEOC, Chgo., 1977-78; EEO adminstr. IIT Research Inst., Chgo., 1978-81; sr. EEO-affirmative action specialist, Health Care Service Corp., Chgo., 1981—. Ill. State scholar, 1967-71; Opportunity scholar, U. Chgo., 1967-71; scholar Transitional Yr. Program Yale U., 1966; Rackham fellow, U. Mich., 1971-72. Mem. Affirmative Action Assn. (1st v.p. 1980—, dir. 1980—), Chgo. Area Assn. for Affirmative Action and Compliance. Democrat. Baptist. Club: Ruth Circle. Office: Health Care Service Corp 233 N Michigan Ave Chicago IL 60601

TAYLOR-SMITH, ELLEN LOUISE, financial journalist; b. Montclair, N.J., Feb. 24, 1950; d. Samuel Perry and Estelle Gerda (Hagberg) Taylor; m. John Lewis Smith, May 19, 1979. Student U. N.C., 1968-70; B.A. cum laude, U. N.H., 1972. Registered security dealer Nat. Assn. Security Dealers. Fin. mgr. Morgan Stanley & Co., N.Y.C., 1977-81; money desk mgr., repo trader Refco Ptnrs., N.Y.C., 1981-83; fin. reporter Knight-Ridder Fin. News Service, N.Y.C., 1984—; corporate bond/mcpl. bond sales asst. G. H. Walker & Co., N.Y.C., 1972; money market adv. Chase Manhattan Bank, N.Y.C., 1973-76; govt. bond salesperson, CD trader Second Dist. Securities, N.Y.C., 1976-77. Author, co-editor: Money Market Manual, 1975. Bd. dirs. 139-94 Corp., N.Y.C., 1981-83. Presbyterian. Avocations: singing; rock and roll; travel; swimming; writing poetry; theatre; cooking. Home: 8 Pennoyer St Rowayton CT 06853 Office: Knight-Ridder Fin News 55 Broadway One Exchange Plaza New York NY 10006

TEAL, DOROTHY EILEEN, textiles company executive; b. Hot Springs, Ark., Feb. 21, 1946; d. Woodrow Wilson and Dorothy Vernice (Henley) T. B.S. in Edn., U. Central Ark., 1967, M.S. in Edn., 1969. Cert. jr. coll. tchr., Calif., high sch. tchr., Ark., Fla., Calif. Tchr. bus. Little Rock Central High Sch., 1969-71, Cocoa Beach High Sch., Fla., 1971-74, Santa Maria High Sch., Calif., 1975-79; auditor market services div. Continental Arilines, Los Angeles, 1979-82; mktg. liaison, export adminstr. Informer Computer Terminals, Garden Grove, Calif., 1982-84; sales mgr. western states, nat. sales rep. Opelika Mfg. Corp., Chgo., 1984—; former part-time instr. Allan Hancock Coll., Santa Maria, Golden Gate Coll., LaVerne Coll., Vandenberg AFB, Calif. Named Outstanding Tchr., Cocoa Beach High Sch., 1974. Mem. Inst. Environ. Scis., Delta Zeta. Democrat. Presbyterian. Avocations: tennis, reading, weaving, pottery making, beach recreation. Home: 7600 W Manchester St Apt 1307 Playa del Rey CA 90293 Office: Opelika Mfg Corp 5855 W Centinela Ave Los Angeles CA 90045

TEARE, MARALYN LOIS, marriage, family, and child counselor; b. Montclair, N.J., Sept. 2, 1937; d. Malcolm and Dolores (Griffin) T.; B.S., Fla. State U., 1959, M.S., 1978; m. William E. Jacobs, Jan. 30, 1959 (div. 1974); children—Cheri Kay, Shanna Lynn. Intern, Parent Tng. Clinic, Neuropsychiat. Inst., UCLA, 1977-79; pvt. practice counseling, specializing in treatment of anxiety and phobias, especially environ. phobias, Beverly Hills, Calif., 1980—; clin. instr. psychiatry U. So. Calif. Med. Sch.; lectr. to state, nat. orgns., on TV. Fellow Menninger Found.; mem. Mental Research Inst. Palo Alto, Phobia Soc. Am. (charter), Assn. Humanistic Psychology (clin.), Calif. Assn. Marriage and Family Therapists (clin.). Episcopalian. Office: 383 S Robertson Blvd Suite A Beverly Hills CA 90211

TEBAY, LEE NELL WHARTON, accountant; b. Vernon, Tex., Apr. 11, 1929; d. Walter Lee and Clida Catherine (Richardson) Wharton; m. Charles A. Norman, Jan. 27, 1950 (div. Aug. 1961); children—Vicki, Kathryn, Elizabeth, Lisa Cynthia; m. 2d, Ernest A. Tebay, Mar. 6, 1970. B.B.A., U. Colo., 1949; M.B.A., U. Tex., 1951. C.P.A., Tex. Payroll officer USAF, U.S. Army, Loring AFB, White Sands Missile Range, Maine and N.Mex., 1951-60; staff acct. Alton L. Smith, Dallas, 1960-68; tax acct. Recognition Equipment, Dallas, 1968-70; pvt. practice acctg., Dallas, 1970-83; corporate acct. supr. Ebby Halliday, Inc., Dallas, 1983—; pres. Transp. Specialist Inc., Dallas, 1986—; chmn. bd. Tax, Acctg., Bus. Services, Inc., Dallas, 1970—. Mem. Ch. of Christ. Home: 5740 Marview Ln Dallas TX 75227 Office: Tax Acctg Bus Service 100 Glass St Dallas TX 75207

TEBBETTS, DIANE RUTH, librarian, educator; b. Buffalo, N.Y., May 3, 1943; d. Bernard John and Ruth Amy (Arlin) T.; B.A. cum laude, U. N.H., 1965; M.L.S., Simmons Coll., 1972, D.A., 1985; M.L.A., Boston U., 1978. Cataloging library asst. U. N.H., 1965-71, asst. reference librarian, 1971-81, asst. dir., 1981—; asst. prof., 1971-78, assoc. prof., 1978—; reviewer Nat. Endowment for the Humanities, 1982—. N.H. Council Humanities grantee, 1979-81. Mem. New Eng. Library Assn. (dir. 1981-83, v.p. 1985-86), Assn. Coll. and Research Libraries, NEC (pres. 1984-85), N.H. Library Assn. (v.p. 1977-78, pres., 1978-79), ALA, N.H. Conf. on Library and Info. Services. Contbr. in field. Home: 2 Anita St Rochester NH 03867 Office: Adminstrn Office U NH Library Durham NH 03824

TECKEMEYER, IRENE CHARLOTTE, chemist; b. Oceanside, N.Y., Dec. 10, 1956; d. Herbert John and Helen (Boutis) T. B.A., U. Western Australia, 1973; postgrad. U. Louisville, 1974-75; B.S. in Physics, De La Salle U., Manila, 1977; B.S. in Chemistry, Ga. Inst. Tech., 1980. Research chemist M.D. Anderson Hosp. and Tumor Inst., Houston, 1980—. Mem. Am. Chem. Soc., Soc. Nuclear Medicine. Democrat. Lutheran. Club: Alliance Francaise (Houston). Home: 2402 S Voss Rd Apt B312 Houston TX 77057

TEDDLIE, KATHY BOWER, coagulation specialist; b. San Juan, P.R., May 5, 1944; d. David William and Gladys Marie (Tollinche) Bower; m. M. B. Teddlie, May 27, 1970 (div. May 1976); 1 dau., Andrea Lee. B.S. in Chemistry and Med. Tech., U. Tex.-Arlington, 1966. Staff endocrinology Baylor U. Med. Ctr., Dallas, 1966-68; supr. spl. chemistry Presbyn. Hosp., Dallas, 1968-75; mktg. rep. Curtin Mathison Sci., Dallas, 1975-78; coagulation specialist Gen. Diagnostics div. Warner Lambert, Morris Plains, N.J., 1978-81, Organon Teknika, Morris Plains, 1981—. Mem. Assn. Women Execs., AAUW. Republican. Episcopalian. Club: 500, Inc.

TEDESCO, REBECCA SMITH, temporary help service company executive; b. Gulfport, Miss., Jan. 17, 1946; d. Benjamin Edwin and Marguerite (Moore) Smith; m. Anthony Joseph Tedesco, Mar. 11, 1979; m. George Paul Shaw, Jr., Dec. 30, 1967 (div. Oct. 1972); 1 child, Heather Chi. B.A., Maryville Coll., Tenn., 1967; B.Ed., U. Tenn.-Chattanooga, 1968. Sales rep. Xerox Corp., Richmond, Va., 1973-75; stockbroker Moseley, Hallgarten, Washington, 1975-77; DC mgr. Tele Sec. Temporary Personnel, Washington, 1977-79; sales mgr. SelecTemps, Inc., Washington, 1980-81; gen. mgr. MBA Office Temps, Vienna, Va., 1981-82; owner, pres. Ameritemps, Inc., Washington, 1982—. Mem. Met. Washington Temporary Services Assn. (pres. 1986—), Nat. Assn. Temporary Service (ethics com.), Greater Washington Bd. Trade, D.C. Conv. Visitors Bur. Democrat. Presbyterian. Avocation: writing. Home: 6315 Chaucer Ln Alexandria VA 22304 Office: Ameritemps Inc 1100 17th St NW #607 Washington DC 22036

TEED, CYNTHIA CASON, author, art educator; b. Dallas, Mar. 9, 1941; d. Jack Charles and Gladys (Swope) Cason; m. Michael Joseph Pizzitola, Aug. 1, 1982; children by previous marriage—Bayard Swope and Bret Cason (twins). B.A., Newcomb Coll., 1962; M.A., Middlebury Coll., 1963; diploma Sorbonne, Paris, 1964, U. Dijon (France), 1967. Lectr. lang. and art U. Houston, 1965-66 79-82; tour guide Mus. Fine Arts, Houston, 1975-81. Author: Guidebook for American Bar Association; Walking Tour of Museum of Fine Arts, Houston, 1981; Conversational Spanish for Medical and Allied Health Personnel, 1983. Vol. translator Ben Taub Hosp., 1968-70. Govt. of Spain travel stipend, 1962. Mem. AAUP, Soc. Profl. Journalists, Kappa Kappa Gamma. Episcopalian.

TEED, PATRICIA JONES, university administrator; b. Pampa, Tex., Nov. 29, 1940; d. Clifford Frank and Mary (Abbott) Jones; m. John Edson Teed, Oct. 8, 1966 (div. 1971); 1 son, Arthur Mayo. B.A. cum laude, Rice U., 1962; Ph.D., 1971; M.A. Emory U., 1963. Asst. to pres. The Crispin Co., Houston, 1970-75; research assoc. Solar Lab., U. Houston, 1975-76, coordinator Half Century Program, 1976-78, dir. camp/community relations, 1978-79, exec., dir., 1979-82, asst. chancellor, 1982-84; v.p. univ. affairs SUNY, Stony Brook, 1984—. Dir., v.p. Alliance Francaise de Houston, Inc., 1973-76; vice chmn. Nice-Houston Sister Assn., 1975-77; dir. CrimeStoppers, Inc., 1980-82. Fulbright scholar, U.S. Govt., 1963; decorated Palmes Academiques, French Govt., 1979. Mem. Council for Aid and Support Edn., Cultural Arts Council Houston, Fulbright Alumni Assn., Phi Kappa Phi, Pi Delta Phi. Office: Vice Pres Univ Affairs SUNY Stony Brook NY 11794

TEER, LOIS MCCALL, public relations executive, civic worker; b. Camden, N.J., July 16, 1933; d. Elmer Joseph and Evelyn Doris (Chard) McCall; m. Ronald M. Teer, June 28, 1952 (div. June 1977); children—Robert, Michael, Kathleen, Jane, Ronald, Kevin. Student Thomas Edison U., Princeton, N.J., 1975-79. Reporter, columnist Atlantic City Press, Vineland (N.J.) Times Jour., Hammonton (N.J.) News and Williamstown Plain Dealer, 1963-69; asst. dir. Operation Concern, Haddon Heights, N.J., 1969-72; exec. dir. Nat. Multiple Sclerosis Soc., Collingswood, N.J., 1972-76; dir. pub. relations Rancocas Valley Hosp., Willingboro, N.J., and Garden State Community Hosp., Marlton, N.J., 1976-78, Inst. Med. Research, Camden, N.J., 1978-82; dir. pub. affairs U. Medicine and Dentistry of N.J.-Sch. Osteo. Medicine, Camden, 1982—. Pres. Cooper Plaza Neighborhood Assn., 1982-84; coordinator Camden Neighborhood Promotion Campaign; mem. Camden City Hist. Rev. Com. Recipient Nat. Pub. Edn. award Multiple Sclerosis Soc., 1976, 77; commendation Pres. Reagan, 1984, N.J. Pride award, 1986. Mem. Women in Communications (Sarah award 1980, 83, Clarion award 1983, pres. 1986—), Am. Med. Writers Assn., Pub. Relations Soc. Am. Silver Anvil award 1983, Pepper Pot award 1983), N.J. Hosp. Pub. Relations Assn. (award 1978, 79, 80, 81), Del. Valley Health Pub. Relations Assn. Democrat. Roman Catholic. Home: 582 Auburn St Camden NJ 08103 Office: University of Medicine and Dentistry New Jersey-School Osteopathic Medicine 300 Broadway Camden NJ 08103

TEETERS, LINDA MARIE, educator; b. Cin., Aug. 22, 1945; d. Irvin Louis and Shirley H. (Huenefeld) T.; cert. dental asst. U. N.C., 1973. Pharmacy intern Edward W. Wolff Pharmacy, 1963-67; dental asst. to dentists, 1967-73; coordinator, dental asst. clinics Hamilton County (Ohio) Bd. Health, 1973-76; dental coordinator Western Hills Vocat. High Sch., Cin., 1976—, chmn. adv. bd. for dental program, 1976—; mem. Ohio Commn. Dental Assisting Cert., 1981—. Mem. Am. Dental Assts. Assn. (3d dist. trustee 1984-86), Ohio Dental Assts. Assn. (pres. 1982-83, editor newsletter 1979-84), Cin. Dental Assts. Assn. (pres. 1971-72, 77-78). Democrat. Roman Catholic. Club: Internationally Yours (pres. 1985—). Home: 1828 Sunset Ave Apt 32 Cincinnati OH 45238 Office: 2144 Ferguson Rd Cincinnati OH 45238

TEETERS, NANCY HAYS, economist, business executive; b. Marion, Ind., July 29, 1930; d. S. Edgar and Mabel (Drake) Hays; A.B. in Econs., Oberlin (Ohio) Coll., 1952, LL.D. (hon.), 1979; M.A., U. Mich., 1954, postgrad., 1956-57, LL.D., 1984; LL.D., Bates Coll., 1981, Mount Holyoke Coll., 1984; m. Robert Duane Teeters, June 7, 1952; children—Ann, James, John. Staff economist govt. fin. sect. FRS, 1957-66, bd. govs., 1978-84; economist on loan Council Econ. Advs., 1962-63; fiscal economist planning and analysis staff Office Mgmt. and Budget, 1966-70; sr. fellow Brookings Instn., 1970-73; sr. specialist Congressional Research Service, Library of Congress, 1973-74; asst. staff dir., chief economist com. budget U.S. Ho. of Reps., 1974-78; instr. U. Md., overseas, 1955-56, U. Mich., 1956-57. Recipient Disting. Alumni award U. Mich., 1980. Mem. Nat. Economists Club (past pres.), Am. Fin. Assn. (dir. 1969-71), Am. Econ. Assn., Nat. Assn. Bank Women, Women in Mgmt. Democrat. Author articles in field. Office: IBM Corporation Old Orchard Rd Armonk NY 10504

TEFFERTELLER, RUTH SINOVOY (MRS. RALPH B. TEFFERTELLER), social worker; b. Albany, N.Y., Aug. 28, 1917; d. Samuel and Jennie (Katz) Sinovoy; B.A., N.Y. State Coll. for Tchrs., 1939; postgrad. Iowa U., 1939-40; M.S.W., Columbia, 1955; m. Ralph B. Tefferteller, Sept. 5, 1941. Social worker A.R.C., St. Louis, Denver, Roswell, N.Mex., Ft. Bragg, N.C., 1942-46; dir. Children's div., camp dir., program dir., dir. spl. project for delinquency prevention and control Henry Street Settlement, N.Y.C., 1946-68; asst. chief Unitarian-Universalist Service Com. Project in Vietnam, in cooperation with U.S. AID Mission, 1968-71; asso. area dir. Danvers-Salem area Mass. Dept. Mental Health, 1971-78, area dir., 1978—; cons. Astor Project, 1961-62. Recipient Florence Luscomb award for outstanding achievement, 1980; Edward C. O'Keefe award, 1986. Mem. Nat. Assn. Social Workers, Nat. Acad. Social Workers. Contbr. articles to profl. jours. Address: 127 Front St Marblehead MA 01945

TEGTMEIER, DELORES ANN HOLBEN, educator; b. Woodbine, Iowa, Sept. 16, 1940; d. Wilson Edwin and Reva Eldora (Boyd) Holben; m. Dennis Harvey Tegtmeier, Sept. 6, 1964; children—John Wilson, DeAnne Malia, Jason Harvey. Student U. Iowa, 1958-59; B.S.N., U. Nebr.-Omaha, 1962; M.S.N., U. Wash., 1965; postgrad. U. Nebr.-Lincoln, 1981—. R.N., Nebr. Nursing instr. St. John's Sch. Nursing, Springfield, Ill., 1965-66, U. Hawaii, Honolulu, 1966-68, 72-73, San Joaquin Delta Jr. Coll., Stockton, Calif., 1970-72; asst. prof. Midland Luth. Coll., Fremont, Nebr., 1975-79; asst. prof., clin. nurse specialist U. Nebr., Omaha, 1980—; family-centered care course coordinator Midland Luth. Coll., Fremont, Nebr., 1975-77. Contbr. articles to profl. jours. USPHS grantee, 1963-64. Mem. Am. Nurses Assn., Nat. Council on Family Relations, D.A.R., U. Nebr. Alumni Assn., Sigma Theta Tau, Delta Zeta. Republican. Lutheran. Home: 805 Oakridge Rd Omaha NE 68128 Office: U Nebr Med Center Meyer Children's Rehab Inst 4111 Dewey Ave Omaha NE 68105

TEICHER, MARCIA HARRIET, personnel consultant company executive; b. Bklyn., Mar. 31, 1947; d. Max and Bettina (Koerner) Fleschner; m. Arthur Mace Teicher, Nov. 23, 1974; 1 child, Craig Morgan. B.A., Queens Coll.-City U. N.Y., 1967. Sr. v.p., owner Smith's 5th Ave Agy., Inc., N.Y.C., 1965—; lectr. in field. Mem. Orgn. for Rehab. and Tng., Scarsdale, N.Y. Recipient Cert. Service award Lions Club, 1983. Mem. Advertising Women of N.Y., Assn. Personnel Cons. of N.Y. (cert., bd. dirs. 1979-80), N.Y. Chpt. of Am. Mktg. Assn. (bd. dirs. 1973—, Cert. award 1982, Cert. award 1984, publs. dir. 1984-85), Nat. Assn. Personnel Cons. Club: Castaways Yacht (New Rochelle). Avocations: boating; reading. Office: Smith's Fifth Ave Agy Inc 17 E 45th St New York NY 10017

TEICHMANN, DIETRA DUFFALA, psychologist; b. Cleve., Sept. 9, 1946; d. Stephen Harold and Mary (Hrivnak) Duffala; B.A. in Math., Valparaiso U., 1969; B.S. in Psychology, Mills Coll., 1974; M.S. in Counseling and Sch. Psychology, Calif. State U., Hayward, 1976; Ph.D. in Psychology, Calif. Sch. Profl. Psychology, 1978; m. Nelson E. Teichmann, Aug. 30, 1980; 1 dau., Natalie Dyann. Staff psychologist, head injury treatment program Santa Clara Valley Med. Center, San Jose, Calif., 1976-79; psychol. asst. Behaviordyne, Inc., Palo Alto, Calif., 1978-79; staff psychologist, coordinator Neuropsychol. Ctr. for Evaluation and Tng.; supr. Inst. Phys. Medicine and Rehab., Peoria, Ill., 1979—; speaker; tchr. neuropsychology Bradley U., 1979-82; resource person rehab. centers. Mem. Am. Psychol. Assn., Ill. Psychol. Assn., Internat. Neuropsychol. Soc. Lutheran. Home: 6501 N Sheridan Rd Peoria IL 61614

TEILHET, HILDEGARDE TOLMAN, author; b. Tucson, Nov. 22, 1906; d. Cyrus Fisher and Hannah Marthe (van Steen) Tolman; B.A., Stanford U., 1926, postgrad., 1926-27; postgrad. U. Heidelberg (Ger.), 1927-28; m. Darwin L. Teilhet, Oct. 28, 1927; children—Marta, Saral, Jehanne. Manuscript editor Center for Advanced Study of Behavioral Scis., Stanford, Calif., 1964-72. Mem. Pen and Brush, Authors Guild, Mystery Writers Am., Nat. Soc. Lit. and Arts, Internat. Bibl. Centre, IPA, World Affairs Council, Assos. of Stanford U. Libraries (dir. 1976—, chmn. 1979-81, chmn. pub. Imprint 1976-79, 81—), Alpha Phi. Democrat. Episcopalian. Author: (with Darwin L. Teilhet) The Ticking Terror Murders, 1935, The Crimson Hair Murders, 1936, The Feather Cloak Murders, 1938, The Broken Face Murders, 1940; sole author: Hero by Proxy, 1941; The Double Agent, 1945; The Assassins, 1946; The Terrified Society, 1947; The Rim of Terror, 1950; A Private Undertaking, 1953; Trouble Shooters, 1958. Address: 14141 Miranda Rd Los Altos Hills CA 94022

TEITZ, BETTY BEATRICE GOLDSTEIN, interior designer; b. Rochester, N.Y., Mar. 10, 1914; d. Albert Stanley and Dora (Finestone) Gould; m. Milton A. Nusbaum, Apr. 10, 1943 (dec. Nov. 1956); 1 dau., Alberta Joyce Nusbaum Duckman; m. 2d, Harry Teitz, Dec. 28, 1959. Student Rochester Bus. Inst., 1932-34, Rochester Inst. Tech., 1950-51, Columbia U., 1957-58. Owner design studio, Rochester, 1957; trainee W.J. Sloane, 1958; head design dept. Mason Furniture Co., Fall River, Mass., 1959; pvt. practice interior design, Providence, 1961-65; pres. Indesign Inc., Newport, R.I., 1974—; designer guest house U.S. War Coll., Newport, 1969-70; lectr. Navy Wives U.S.A. Staff asst. Motor Corps Grey Lady Rochester chpt. ARC, 1941-46, active Newport chpt.; Gray Lady vol. Genesee Hosp., Rochester, 1945-55, mem. Rochester Planned Parenthood, 1945-48; active Mental Health Clinic Newport; mem. Citizens Adv. Com., Newport, 1967-78; mem. yachting com. Am.'s Cup Race, summer 1950. Recipient Centennial Pageant Scenic award Rochester, 1948; ARC awards, 1943-53, 10 yr. service pin Genesee Hosp., 1955, Blue Ribbon awards for flower show arrangements, 1950, 52, 55. Mem. Am. Inst. Interior Designers, Constrn. Specifications Inst. R.I. (sec.), Preservation Soc. Newport County, Newport C. of C. (bldg. com.). Club: Flower City Garden (past v.p. Rochester). Home and studio: 29 Rovensky Ave Newport RI 02840 Office: 10 Long Wharf Mall Newport RI 02840

TEKIELI, DELORES LORETTA TOCCO, municipal official; b. Youngstown, Ohio; d. Dominic and Annette Pauline (Naples) Tocco; m. Edward Thomas Tekieli, Sr., July 2, 1966; children—Edward Thomas, Michele, Tiffany. B.S. in Bus. Edn. and Bus. Adminstrn., Youngstown State U., 1963; postgrad. Kent State U., 1964, Northwestern U., 1965, Lakeland Coll., 1980, John Carroll U., 1981. Instr. bus. edn. Euclid (Ohio) Sr. High Sch., 1963-67; instr. TRW, Inc., 1967-69; bus. instr. Cuyahoga Community Coll., 1967-70; instr. Lakeland Community Coll., 1975-78; owner, pres. Custom Cover Leasing, 1976-78; coordinator Downtown Euclid Assn., 1979-80; comml. affairs coordinator City of Euclid, also dir. community festival, 1980—; cons. to mchts. assns., festival sponsors, coms. Co-founder Euclid Women's Caucus, dir., 1978-81, now v.p.; publicity dir. Shore Civic Ctr.; trustee Euclid Devel. Corp., Euclid Coalition Club, Democratic Caucus; mem. adv. bd. site com. Euclid Day Care Center; co-founder Euclid Conservation Assn.; founder, prin., mem. staff St. Robert's Catholic Pres-Sch.; mem. Euclid Cultural Council. Named Outstanding Citizen of Yr., Euclid post Am. Legion, 1976; cert. Devel. Council. Mem. Realtors Assn., Euclid C. of C. (dir., treas. 1985—), Sigma

Sigma Sigma. Editor City of Euclid Bus. Quar., 1983—. Columnist Ecology Corner for Euclid News Jour., 1971-73. Home: 5 E 221st St Euclid OH 44123 Office: Euclid City Hall Annex 21331 Wilmore Ave Euclid OH 44123

TELEGA, MILDRED C, sales executive; b. Sewickley, Pa., Sept. 16, 1953; d. Mitchell Richard and Ruth (Decker) Telega. B.S. in Edn., Calif. U., Pa., 1975, M.Ed., 1976. Speech pathologist Community Devel. Ctrs.-Highland Park Ctr., Pitts., 1975-78, supr. program services, 1978-79, program dir., 1979-81, asst. dir. for program services, 1981-83; sales rep. Adaptive Communication Systems, Coraopolis, Pa., 1983—. Mem. Am. Speech & Hearing Assn., Assn. for Persons with Severe Handicaps. Avocations: reading; painting. Home: 309 Colony W Dr Caraopolis PA 15108 Office: Adaptive Communication Systems 994 Broadhead Rd Coraopolis PA 15108

TELEGO, TACY COOK, government public affairs officer; b. Orono, Maine, Nov. 5, 1946; d. Charles T. and Virginia Louise (Totman) Cook; m. Dean Jeffery Telego, May 21, 1983; m. Glenn Allen Yachachak, Sept. 1965 (div. Sept. 1968). B.A., Douglass Coll., Rutgers U., 1968; M.S., Am. U., Washington, 1972. Writer, editor USAF Research and Analysis, Pentagon, Washington, 1968-69; editor Challenge mag. HUD, Washington, 1969-74, pub. info. officer, San Francisco, 1974-75; pub. affairs officer Treasury Bur. Alcohol, Tobacco and Firearms, Chgo., 1975-76, Washington, 1976-78; pub. affairs officer Def. Mapping Agy., Washington, 1978-80; dir. legis. and pub. affairs Mil. Sealift Command, U.S. Navy, Washington, 1980—; owner, mgr. Peacock Internat. Enterprises, Bethesda, Md., 1981—; cons. The Support Ctr., Washington, 1980—. Mem. adv. publicity bd. YWCA Nat. Capital Area, Washington, 1983-84. N.J. Soc. Indsl. Editors scholar, 1968. Mem. Federally Employed Women (editor News & Views; recipient Barbara B. Tennant award 1983), Pub. Relations Soc. Am. (accredited; chpt. v.p. 1981-82; service awards 1978-83), Washington Women in Pub. Relations (founder), Nat. Def. Transp. Assn. (publ. adv. bd.), Navy League. Republican. Episcopalian. Clubs: Nat. Press, Propeller (Washington). Home: 4 Sangamore Ct Bethesda MD 20816 Office: Mil Sealift Command US Navy 4228 Wisconsin Ave NW Washington DC 20016

TELFORD, VIRGINIA LYNN, nursing administrator; b. Salem, Ill., Dec. 3, 1941; d. John Clyde and Mabel Lovell (Booher) Ray; m. David Eugene Telford, Sr., May 30, 1959; children—David, Jr., Douglas E., Daniel. Assoc. degree in Nursing, Rend Lake Coll., Ina, Ill., 1978; B.S. in Nursing, McKendree Coll., Lebanon, Ill., 1981; M.A., Webster U., Webster Grove, Mo., 1985. R.N., Ill. Lic. practical nurse St. Mary's Hosp., Centralia, Ill., 1970-78, registered nurse, 1978-81, dir. nursing service, 1981—; sch. nurse Central City Schs., Centralia, 1980-81. Blood drive coordinator ARC and St. Mary's Hosp., 1983—. Mem. Ill. Soc. Nurse Adminstrs. Republican. Avocations: bicycling, down-hill skiing. Home: Rural Route 2 Box 143 Salem IL 62881 Office: St Mary's Hosp 400 N Pleasant Centralia IL 62801

TELL, KATHLEEN ELLEN, manufacturing company executive; b. Detroit, Oct. 28, 1956; d. George and Patricia Ellen (St. Onge) Ziehr; m. Gregory Francis Tell, Oct. 3, 1981. A.A. in Langs., Marygrove Coll., also B.A. in Langs. and Bus.; M.B.A. in Mktg. and Fin., U. Detroit. Sales rep. Burroughs Corp., Detroit, 1978-83; product mgr. worldwide mktg., 1983-85; mgr. planning and research Wickes Mfg. Co., Southfield, Mich., 1985—; cons. Marygrove Coll., Detroit, 1978-86; career cons. U. Mich.-Dearborn, 1985-86. Active Sister City Assn., 1972-86. Recipient Overseas China Study Program award, 1978. Mem. Industry Mktg. Group, Motor Equipment Mfrs. Assn., Nat. Assn. Female Execs., Detroit Econ. Club.; vis. mem. Automotive Mktg. Research Council. Republican. Roman Catholic. Club: Ford Sea Lancers (v.p., bd. dirs. 1981-84); Spirit of Detroit. Office: Wickes Mfg Co Box 999 Southfield MI 48037

TELLEZ, DIANE MARIE, television station official; b. Johnson City, N.Y., Aug. 10, 1959; d. William Robert and Phyllis Christine (Rudenauer) Bryan; m. Gabriel Escalante Tellez, Sept. 4, 1982. B.A., Calif. State U.-Fullerton, 1982. Writer, reporter Century Cable, Brea, Calif., 1980-81, Sta. KEZY-AM-FM and Sta. KIKF-FM, Anaheim, Calif., 1981; TV reporter, news writer cameraperson Sta. KOLO-TV, ABC affiliate, Reno, 1981; talk show host Storer & Group Cable TV, Anaheim, 1980-82; intern Donrey Media, KOLO-TV, Reno, 1982; TV prodn. asst., talk show host Community Cablevision, Newport Beach, Calif., 1982-84; community cablevision programming coordinator Channel 3, Irvine, Tustin and Newport Beach, Calif., 1984—. Mem. Women in Communications, Radio, TV and Film Soc. (v.p. 1981-82), Nat. Fedn. Local Cable Programmers, Orange County Cable Assn. (bd. dirs.). Office: Community Cablevision Co 1061 Camelback St Newport Beach CA 92660

TEMIN, DAVIA BETH, marketing executive; b. Cleve., June 5, 1952; d. J.T. and Sylvia (Black) Temin. B.A., Swarthmore Pa./Coll., 1974; M.A., Columbia U., 1976. Community services specialist Commonwealth Mass., Boston, 1975; editor-in-chief, founder Hermes mag. Columbia U. Bus. Sch., N.Y.C., 1976-79, dir. publ. affairs, 1979-83; v.p., dir. marketing Citicorp Global Investment Bank, N.Y.C., 1983—; cons. pub. relations, N.Y.C., 1980-83. Bd. dirs. Motio Dance Found., N.Y.C., 1982—; Recipient Nat. Sch. Pub. Relations award, 1978, numerous Printing Industries of N.Y. awards, 1979—, Meritorious Service award Commonwealth of Mass, 1976. Mem. Internat. Assn. Bus. Communicators, Women in Communications, Council Fgn. Relations. Clubs: Princeton (N.Y.), Swarthmore (N.Y.) Layman's (St. John the Divine Cathedral N.Y.C.), Sand Bar (Quoque, N.Y.) Home: 1755 York Ave 24F New York NY 10028 Office: Citicorp Investment Bank 120 Wall St New York NY 10043

TEMKIN, MAIRLYN LISA, cardiologist, educator; b. Bklyn., June 8, 1954; d. Max Temkin and Sarah (Braun) T. B.A., Johns Hopkins U., 1975; M.D., med. Coll. Pa., 1979. Diplomate Am. Bd. Internal Medicine. Intern internal medicine Nassau County Med. Ctr., East Meadow, N.Y., 1979-80; resident internal medicine, 1980-82, cardiology fellow, 1982-84; research asst. Johns Hopkins U., Balt., 1973-74; clin. supr. SUNY-Stony Brook Med. Sch., 1981-82, asst. clin. instr., 1984—; asst. dir. cardiology Brookhaven Meml. Hosp Med Ctr Patchogue, N.Y., 1984—; jr. attending div. cardiology dept. medicine Nassau County Med. Ctr., East Meadow, 1985—. Chmn. physician's edn. com. Suffolk County chpt. Am. Heart Assn., 1984—, bd. dirs., 1985—. Mem. ACP Am. Heart Assn., AMA, Am. Coll. Cardiology. Office: Dept Cardiology Brookhaven Meml Hosp Med Ctr Patchogue NY 11772

TEMPLE, JOAN CHRISTINE, power boat component manufacturing executive; b. Detroit, Jan. 18, 1941; d. Charles H. and Jane (Robertson) Bennett; m. Wendell C. Koester (dec. Sept. 1978), May 15, 1965 (div. Aug. 1975), Harry Earl Temple, Mar. 8, 1980. Student Wheaton Coll., 1959-61, Eastern Mich. U., 1972-74, Walsh Coll., Troy, Mich., 1975. Order clk. Gen. Motors, Dearborn and Southfield, Mich., 1961-69; sec. Ford Motor Co., Dearborn, 1972-75; v.p. Bennett Marine, Inc., Deerfield Beach, Fla., 1975—. Mem. Broward County Republican Exec. Com., Ft. Lauderdale, Fla., 1985; bd. dirs. Youth for Christ, Ft. Lauderdale, 1985. Presbyterian. Avocations: cooking, boating, skiing, traveling. Home: 3701 NE 28th Ave Lighthouse Point FL 33064 Office: Bennett Marine Inc 550 NW 12th Ave Deerfield Beach FL 33441

TEMPLE, THERESA MARIE GRENIER, government official; b. Buffalo, Oct. 2, 1929; d. Thomas Joseph Henry and Mary Alice (Tehan) Grenier; m. Frederick Blake Temple, Dec. 16, 1950 (dec. Jan. 1980); children—Frederick Blake, Marie Jeanne, Sally Anne. Student U. Md., 1980-82. Instr. dance and piano accompanist Lola Beaver Sch. Dance, Washington, 1946-47; bus. office toll biller C & P Telephone Co., Washington, 1947-50; adminstr. processing overseas civilian personnel U.S. Army, Washington, 1950-51; sec. San Diego City Schs., 1952-53; substitute tchr. elem. sch., Hillcrest Heights, Md., 1960-70; instr. dance, choreographer Amendolair Sch. Dance, Hillcrest Heights, 1968; sec. U.S. Navy, Washington, 1979-82, adminstrv. technician, 1982—; pres. Grenier Temple Services, Temple Hills, Md., 1979—; facilitator workshops and seminars, 1982—. Mem. Women's Center and Referral Service, Adelphi, Md., 1979—. Recipient Community Service award Prince Georges Recreation Dept. (Md.), 1965. Mem. Nat. Capital Speakers Assn., Federally Employed Women, Washington Area Writers Assn., Navy Speech Club, Am. Bowl Congresswomen's Internat. Bowling Congress (acting capt.). Republican. Presbyterian. Club: Toastmasters. Home: 2606 Berkley St Temple Hills MD 20748 Office: Dept Navy Naval Air Systems Command Washington DC 20361

TEMPLES, PAMELA R., interior designer; b. Columbia, S.C., Mar. 27, 1949; d. Marvin C. and Margaret E. (Berry) Reames; m. Samuel E., Feb. 6, 1971 (div. 1981); children—Stephanie Dawn, Melissa Gayle. B.F.A., U.S.C., 1971. Designer, Stig Sjoberg Interiors, Columbia, S.C., 1970-73; designer, sales R.L. Bryan Co., Columbia. 1973-75, Arch. Interiors, Columbia, 1976-78; pres. Pamela Temples Interiors, 1979-84; pres. PTI Assocs. Inc., 1984—. Contng. author to mags. and book reviews; contbg. editor: Law of Bus. and Resort Devel., 1986. Mem., Women's Symphony Assn., Columbia, 1984—; fundraiser March of Dimes, 1986. Mem. Am. Land Devel. Assn. (1st place design award 1984), Am. Residential/Resort Devel. Assn. (bd. dirs. 1985—, 1st place design award 1985), Am. Soc. Interior Design, Constrn. Specifications Inst., Nat. Timeshare Council (bd. dirs., sec. 1984—), Columbia C. of C., Urban Land Inst., Zeta Tau Alpha. Republican. Baptist. Avocations: racquetball; snow skiing; water skiing. Home: 2212 Quail Hollow Ct West Columbia SC 29169

TEMPLETON, ARLETTE JEANETTE, nurse; b. Kingston, Tenn., Sept. 3, 1941; d. Archie Floyd and Mildred Agnes (Burnette) Roberts; m. David Elmer Templeton, Dec. 1, 1961; children—Sonya, Ronald, Floyd. L.P.N., Harriman (Tenn.) Vocat. Sch., 1974; A.S., Roane State Coll., Harriman, 1983. R.N. Sewer, Roane Hosiery, Harriman, 1959-62; meat packer Oscar Meyer, Chgo., 1964-67; cashier Harrell's IGA Store, Harriman, 1969-70; with security and payrole dept. Big K, Harriman, 1970-73; nurse Chamberlain Meml. Hosp., Rockwood, Tenn., 1974-83, nurse mgr., 1983—; also mem. various coms. Named Employee of Quarter, Chamberlain Meml. Hosp., 1980; recipient letter of commendation Chamberlain Meml. Hosp. Med. Staff, 1983. Democrat. Baptist. Home: 608 S Ridge Ave Rockwood TN 37854

TEMPLIN, ETHELYN MERLE, nurse; b. Giltner, Nebr., Nov. 2, 1928; d. John Pearson and Odessa Merle (Hendrickson) Anderson; student Hastings Coll., 1947-48; R.N., Mary Lanning Meml. Hosp., 1950; B.S. in Psychology, Kearney State Coll., 1976; m. William Samuel Templin, Nov. 3, 1951 (dec.); children—Samuel Ray, Daniel Caye (dec.), Roger Lee. Head nurse, clin. instr. Hastings (Nebr.) Regional Center, 1956-59; staff nurse VA Med. Center, Grand Island, Nebr., 1952-55, head nurse, 1960-74, staff nurse intensive care, 1975-76, staff, supr., 1976—, nurse mental hygiene clinic, 1986—, clin. privileges in chemotherapy. Cert. Reach to Recovery vol. Am. Cancer Soc., 1974—; Nebr. civil def. nurse, 1963-65. Recipient Cert. of Recognition, Nebr. Nurses Assn. Commn. on Edn., 1976, 78, 80, Disting. Service award, 1977. Mem. Nat. Assn. Orthopedic Nurses, Assn. Operating Room Nurses, Nebr. Nurse Assn., Mary Lanning Meml. Hosp. Alumnae Assn., Prospectors Investment Lodge: Republican. Methodist. Club: Order Eastern Star. Home: 1335 W 5th St Hastings NE 68901 Office: 2201 N Broadwell St Grand Island NE 68801

TEMPLIN, MARY ANNE, title company executive; b. Nagodoches, Tex., July 4, 1944; d. Melvin L. Hansen and Kathleen Ann (Orr) Hansen Pyle; m. Timothy James Templin, Dec. 19, 1964 (div.); 1 son, James Kirk. Student U. Houston, 1962-64. With Houston Title Co., 1966-72; sec., escrow officer Guardian Title Co., Houston, 1972-73; escrow officer, mktg. rep. So. Title Co., Houston, 1973-74; mktg. rep. 1st Am. Title, Houston, 1974-75; v.p., mktg. dir. Capital Title Co., Houston, 1975—; lectr. cable TV, real estate schs., corps. Active Young Republican Women, Houston, 1979-82; nominating com. West Univ. Party city elections, Houston, 1979. Mem. Houston Bd. Realtors (membership chairperson 1982-83), Greater Houston Builders Assn., Tex. Land Title Assn. Republican. Methodist. Home: 4114 Marlowe Ave Houston TX 77005 Office: Capital Title Co 2929 Allen Pkwy Suite 200 Houston TX 77019

TENGLER, JOAN MARIE, accountant; b. Freeport, Tex., Aug. 5, 1953; d. Jerry Fred and Angeline Josephine (Hollas) Tengler; m. Randal Lee Cade, Feb. 14, 1976 (div. 1980); 1 child, Daniel. A.S., Brazosport Coll., Tex., 1973; B.S., Tex. Women's U., 1975; postgrad. U. Tex., 1978-79. Cost. acct. Drawing Bd. Greeting Cards Inc., Dallas, 1977-78; corp. acct. CoreLab Inc., Dallas, 1978-80; supr. acctg. Rowbotham Tankships Ltd., London, Eng., 1980-82; audit mgr. Thompson, Gratzer & Clem C.P.A.s, Angleton, Tex., 1983—. Community planner Angleton C. of C., Tex., 1983, seminars com., 1984, ambassador, 1985-86, fin. com. advisor, 1985-86. Mem. Am. Inst. C.P.A.s, Nat. Assn. Female Execs. Roman Catholic. Club: Angleton Bus. and Profl. Women (pres. 1985-86). Avocations: reading; child development. Home: 208 Swift Angleton TX 77515 Office: Thompson Gratzer & Clem CPA's 2801 N Hwy 288 Suite C Angleton TX 77515

TENNANT, MARY JO, educator; b. Tacoma, Jan. 6, 1938; d. Glenn Everett and Adelia Maurine (Converse) Sigler; m. Charles Edward Tennant, June 27, 1959; children—Stephen Victor, Catherine J. Ziarnowski, Susan M., Willigam G. A.B., Cornell U., 1959; M.T., U. Ariz., 1976. Tchr. Yuma Dist. 1, Ariz., 1975-77, Children's Way Sch., Fairfax, Va., 1977-78, St. Michael Sch., Annandale, Va., 1978-84; substitute tchr. Conejo Valley Unified Dist., Thousand Oaks, Calif., 1985—; tchr. English Newbury Park High Sch., 1986—. Mem. secondary schs. com. Cornell U., Cornell Club of Washington, 1979-84, Cornell Club So. Calif., 1984—; v.p. sch. bd. Am. Sch. Vientiane, Laos, 1973-74, sec. sch. bd., 1972-73; neighborhood chmn. Ariz. Cactus-Pine council Girl Scouts U.S.A., 1974-77, bd. dirs., 1976-77. Recipient Service award Lao Mil. Wives, 1974. Mem. Alpha Phi (dist. alumnae chmn. 1985—). Republican. Roman Catholic. Avocations: reading; sewing; walking. Home: 1317 Breckford Ct Westlake Village CA 91361 Office: Newbury Park High Sch 456 Reino Rd Newbury Park CA 91320

TENNEY, DELLA WOOTEN, court reporter, writer; b. Chattanooga, May 5, 1930; d. Charles Madison Wooten and Belle (Davis) Knight; m. Gene William Ailor, Aug. 2, 1948 (div. May 1959); children—Linda Hughie, Sandra Barnwell, Angela Ailor; m. Frank Leonard Stilin, Feb. 21, 1964 (div. Apr. 1971); 1 child, Andrew; m. Edward Jewett Tenney, II, Feb. 17, 1983; stepchildren—Cyndra Fontaine, Edward B. II, Jill. Grad. Gregory Bus. Coll., Knoxville, Tenn., 1950-52; student U. S.C., 1958-59, Stenotype Inst., Jacksonville Beach, Fla., 1972-74, Lippert Sch. Ct. Reporting, Plainview, Tex., 1974. Cert. court reporter, Ga., Fla., Tenn., Guam, N.H. Former personal sec. to lt. gov. of Ga., Atlanta; legal sec. Witt-Gaither-Abernathy, Chattanooga, 1971-72; pres. Accurate Reporting Service, Chattanooga, 1975-78; dean, chief exec. officer The Stenotype Ctr., Chattanooga, 1978-79; ofcl. ct. reporter Guam Superior Ct., 1979-80, N.H. Superior Ct., Concord, 1980—. Author, editor, pub. Basic Stenotype Manual, 1979. Sec., Am. Cancer Soc., Aiken, S.C., 1952-53; campaign mgr. election com. for supt. edn., Aiken, 1954. Mem. N.H. Shorthand Reporters Assn. (sec., v.p.), Nat. Shorthand Reporters Assn., Nat. Assn. Female Execs. Republican. Roman Catholic. Club: Kaypro Users Group. Avocations: traveling; reading; book collecting; motorcycling; photography. Home: PO Box 322 River Rd Claremont NH 03743 Office: NH Superior Ct 163 N Main St Concord NH 03743

TENNEY, ROBERTA EDWINA COUGHLIN, educator; b. Lowell, Mass., Jan. 19, 1945; d. Robert Edward and M. Geraldine (Barry) Couglin; m. Rodney Emerson Tenney, Dec. 26, 1968; children—Catherine, Thomas. B.A., U. N.H., 1968; A.M., Dartmouth Coll., 1974; cert. advanced studies Harvard U., 1982. History tchr. St. Pauls Sch., Concord, N.H., 1970, adminstr., history tchr. 1970-83, dept. chmn., 1977-78, coll. admissions adviser, 1984—. Bd. dirs. N.H. Council World Affairs, 1976; vol. United Way, 1970; vice chairperson Bicentennial Com., 1975-76; dir. advanced studies program state wide gifted children, 1979; v.p. Child and Family Services, N.H., 1979. Mem. Nat. Assn. Coll. Admissions Counselors, Coll. Bd. Assn., Nat. Assn. Ind. Schs. Avocations: skiing; sailing; tennis; squash. Home: St Paul's Sch Concord NH 03301 Office: St Paul's Sch 325 Pleasant St Concord NH 03301

TENNYSON, MARJORIE LEIGH, exercise physiologist; b. Youngstown, Ohio, May 7, 1953; d. Edson Leigh and Shirley Lou (Forward) T.; B.S., Pa. State U., 1974, M.Ed., 1977; M.S., U. Pitts., 1980; m. Stephen John Podgajny, 1980. Geol. field asst. U. Wash., Seattle, 1972, 73; student personnel asst. Coll. Edn., Pa. State U., 1974-77; asst. to dean student life services Clarion State Coll. (Pa.), 1977-78, dir. assn. women students, 1977-78. Exercise physiologist Alcoa Preventive Med. Program, Am. Corp. Health Programs Inc., 1980-81 exercise specialist, Lifeline program U. So. Maine, 1982—. Bd. dirs. Maine affiliate Am. Heart Assn. Mem. Am. Coll. Sports Medicine, Am. Assn. Fitness Dirs. in Bus. and Industry, Phi Delta Kappa. Club: Moving Comfort Racing Team. Set record in women's marathon, Maine, 1981. Home: 45 Cleveland St Saco ME 04072 Office: U So Maine Lifeline 93 Falmouth St Portland ME 04103

TENOPYR, MARY LOUISE WELSH (MRS. JOSEPH TENOPYR), psychologist; b. Youngstown, Ohio, Oct. 18, 1929; d. Roy Henry and Olive (Donegan) Welsh; A.B., Ohio U., 1951, M.A., 1951; Ph.D., U. So. Calif., 1966; m. Joseph Tenopyr, Oct. 30, 1955. Psychometrist, Ohio U., Athens, 1951-52, also housemother Sigma Kappa; personnel technician to research psychologist USAF, 1953-55, Dayton, Ohio, 1952-53, Hempstead, N.Y.; indsl. research analyst to mgr. employee evaluation N.Am. Rockwell Corp., El Segundo, Calif., 1956-70; asso. prof. Calif. State Coll.-Los Angeles, 1966-70; asso. research educationist UCLA, 1970-71; program dir. U.S. CSC, 1971-72; mgr. human resources research AT&T, N.Y.C., 1972—; lectr. U. So. Calif., Los Angeles, 1967-70; vice chmn. research com. Tech. Adv. Com. on Testing, Fair Employment Practice Commn. Calif., 1966-70; adviser on testing Office Fed. Contract Compliance, U.S. Dept. Labor, Washington, 1967-73. Pres., ASPA Found.; mem. Army Sci. Bd. Recipient Profl. Practice award Soc. Indsl. and Organizational Psychology, 1984. Fellow Am. Psychol. Assn. (bd. profl. affairs, pres. div. indsl. organizational psychology, mem. employment and human resources com.); mem. Eastern Psychol. Assn., Nat. Council Measurement in Edn., Psychomatic Soc., Met. N.Y. Assn. Applied Psychology, Am. Ednl. Research Assn., Sigma Xi, Sigma Kappa, Psi Chi, Alpha Lambda Delta, Kappa Phi. Editorial bd. Jour. Applied Psychology; contbr. articles to profl. jours. Home: 557 Lyme Rock Rd Bridgewater NJ 08807 Office: 550 Madison Ave New York NY 10022

TEPPER, BLOSSOM WEISS, clinical psychologist; b. Bklyn., Oct. 15, 1921; d. Meyer and Anna (Lax) Weiss; B.A., Bklyn. Coll., 1942; M.Ed., Lehigh U., 1962, Ed.D. in Clin. and Counseling Psychology, 1967; m. Louis Tepper, Apr. 17, 1942 (dec. August 1978); children—Irene Tepper Homa, Allan M. Tchr. sci., guidance counselor Blue Mountain Sch. Dist., Schuylkill Haven, Pa., 1958-64; successively grad. asst., instr., asst. prof. Lehigh U., Bethlehem, Pa., 1964-71; dir. home and sch. visitor project Luzerne County Schs., Wilkes-Barre, Pa., 1968-71, also adj. prof. Wilkes Coll., Wilkes-Barre, 1969-71; clin. psychologist base service unit, dir. Schuylkill County Mental Health/Mental Retardation, Pottsville, Pa., 1971-72; clin. psychologist Northampton County Mental Health/Mental Retardation, Easton, Pa., 1972-75; clin. psychologist, mental retardation and devel. disabilities specialist, cons. community living program for mental retardation Northampton County Mental Health/Mental Retardation, Bethlehem and Easton, 1975—. Lic. psychologist, Pa.; cert. sch. psychologist, Pa. Fellow Pa. Psychol. Assn.; mem. Am. Personnel and Guidance Assn., Pa. Personnel and Guidance Assn., Am. Psychol. Assn., Eastern Psychol. Assn., Am. Assn. Mental Deficiency, Am. Assn. Psychiat. Services for Children, Pa. Assn. Sch. Psychologists (charter), Nat. Register Mental Health Providers in Psychology, Am. Assn. Higher Edn. (charter, life), Hadassah (life). Developer exptl. program tng. sch. social workers. Home: Bridle Path Woods Apt C12 Bethlehem PA 18017 Office: Northampton County Mental Health Mental Retardation 2009 Lehigh St Easton PA

TERBORG-PENN, ROSALYN MARIAN, historian, educator; b. Bklyn., Oct. 22, 1941; d. Jacques Arnold Sr. and Jeanne (Van Horn) Terborg; 1 dau., Jeanna Penn. B.A. in History, Queens Coll., CUNY, 1963; M.A. in History, George Washington U., 1967; Ph.D. in Afro-Am. History, Howard U., 1978. Day care tchr. Friendship House Assn., Washington, 1964-66; program dir. Southwest House Assn., Washington, 1966-69; adj. prof. U. Md.-Balt. County, Catonsville, 1977-78, Howard Community Coll., Columbia, Md., 1970-74; prof. history Morgan State U., Balt., 1969—, project dir. oral history project, 1978-79; project dir. Assn. Black Women Hist. Research Conf., Washington, 1982-83. Author: (with Thomas Holt and Cassandra Smith-Parker) A Special Mission: the Story of Freedmen's Hospital, 1862-1962, 1975. Editor (with Sharon Harley) The Afro-American Woman: Struggles and Images, 1978, 81. History editor Feminist Studies, 1984—. Founding mem. Howard County Commn. for Women. Ford Found. fellow, 1980-81, Smithsonian Instn. fellow, 1982; Howard U. grad. fellow in history, 1973-74, recipient Rayford W. Logan Grad. Essay award Howard U., 1973. Mem. Assn. Black Women Historians (co-founder, 1st nat. dir. 1980-82, nat. treas. 1982-84, cert. outstanding achievement 1981), Am. Hist. Assn. (mem. com. on women historians 1978-81), Orgn. Am. Historians (mem. black women's history project adv. com. 1980-81), Alpha Kappa Alpha. Office: Morgan State U Baltimore MD 21239

TERMINI, CHRISTINE, artist; b. Bklyn., Sept. 30, 1947; d. Thomas and Josephine (Sara) T.; B.F.A., Pratt Inst., 1969; M.A., Hunter Coll., 1973. Dir. Circle Gallery, N.Y.C., 1975-76, Jack Gallery, N.Y.C., 1976-77, Gallerie La Grande Illusion, N.Y.C., 1977-78, Neill Gallery, N.Y.C., 1978-79, Atelier Royce, N.Y.C., 1980-81; mng. dir. Hanover Fine Arts Pub. Co., 1983-84; one-woman shows: N.Y.C., 1975, U. Pa. Gallery, 1982, Emrose Art Corp., N.Y., 1986; group shows include: Nat. Acad. Galleries, N.Y., 1977, Heckscher Mus., Huntington, N.Y., 1978, 80, Long Beach Mus., 1981, 84, Los Angeles Artcorc Ctr., 1984, Newport Harbor Art Mus., Newport Beach, Calif., 1984, Laguna Beach Mus. (Calif.), 1984; lectr. Found. for Community Artists, community schs. Recipient prize Internat. Art Competition, Los Angeles. Mem. Found. for Community Artists, Artists Equity Assn. N.Y.; assoc. mem. Audubon Artists, Women in the Arts, Nat. Soc. Painters in Casein and Acrylic. Home: 243 E 78th St New York NY 10021

TERMINI, DEANNE LANOIX, research company executive; b. New Orleans, May 2, 1943; d. Albert Oliver and Freida (Fisher) Lanoix; m. Raymond Joseph Termini, Sept. 4, 1965; 1 dau., Andrea. B.A., Tulane U., 1964; M.A., U. Tex., Austin, 1968. Research analyst Belden Assocs., Dallas, 1968-70, research assoc., 1970-75, v.p., 1975-79, sr. v.p., 1979—, dir., 1979—; discussion leader Am. Press Inst., Reston, Va., 1983—. Author research reports. Active Greenhill Parents Assn., 1979-85, rec. sec., 1982-83, mem. math. subcom. bd. trustees, 1983-84; Mem. Women in Communications, Am. Mktg. Assn., Internat. Newspaper Advt. and Mktg. Execs., Nat. Assn. Women Bus. Owners, Tulane U. Alumni Assn. Home: 13641 Far Hills Ln Dallas TX 75240 Office: Belden Assocs 2900 Turtle Creek Plaza Dallas TX 75219

TERPENING, VIRGINIA ANN, artist; b. Lewistown, Mo., July 17, 1917; d. Floyd Raymond and Bertha Edda (Rodifer) Shoup; studied with William Woods, Fulton, Mo., 1936-37; student Washington U. Sch. Fine Arts, St. Louis, 1937-40; m. Charles W. Terpening, July 5, 1951; 1 dau. by previous marriage, V'Ann Baltzelle Dlatrick. Exhibited in one-man shows at Culver-Stockton Coll., Canton, Mo., 1956, Creative Gallery, N.Y.C., 1968, The Breakers, Palm Beach, Fla., 1976; others; exhibited in group shows, including Mo. Annual, City Art Mus., St. Louis, 1956, 65, Madison Gallery, N.Y.C., 1960; Ligoa Duncan Gallery, N.Y.C., 1964, 78, 74, Two Flags Festival of Art, Douglas, Ariz., 1975, 78-79, Internat. Art Exhibit, El Centro, Calif., 1977, 78, Salon des Nations, Paris, 1985; lectr. on art; jurist for selection of art for exhibits Labelle (Mo.) Centennial, 1972; chmn. Centennial Art Show, Lewiston, 1971, Bicentennial, 1976; dir. exhibit high sch. students for N.E. Mo. State U., 1974; supt. ann. art show Lewis County (Mo.) Fair; executed Mississippi RiverBoat, oil painting presented to Pres. Carter by Lewis County Dem. Com., Canton, 1979. Mem. Lewistown Bicentennial Hist. Soc. Recipient certificate of merit Latham Found., 1960-63, Mo. Women's Festival Art, 1974, Bertrand Russell Peace Found., 1973; gold medallion award Two Flags Festival Art, 1975; Safeco purchase award El Centro (Calif.) Internat. Art exhibit, 1977; 1st pl. award LaJunta (Colo.) Fine Arts League, 1981; diploma Universita Delle Arti, Parma, Italy, 1981; Purchase award Two Flags Art Festival, 1981; award Assn. Conservation and Mo. Dept. Conservation Art Exhbt., 1982; paintings selected for Competition '84 Guide by Nat. Art Appreciation Soc., 1984. Mem. Artist Equity Assn., Inc., Internat. Soc. Artists, Internat. Platform Assn., Animal Protection Inst. Mem. Disciples of Christ Ch. Address: Lewistown MO 63452

TERRAS, AUDREY ANNE, mathematics educator; b. Washington, Sept. 10, 1942; d. Stephen Decatur and Maude Mae (Murphy) Bowdoin. B.S. with high honors in Math., U. Md., 1964; M.A., Yale U, 1966, Ph.D., 1970. Instr. U. Ill., Urbana, 1968-70; asst. prof. U. P.R., Mayaguez, 1970-71; asst. prof. Bklyn. Coll., CUNY, 1971-72; asst. prof. math. U. Calif.-San Diego, La Jolla, 1972-76, assoc. prof., 1976-83, prof., 1983—, vis. positions MIT, fall 1977, 83, U. Bonn (W.Ger.), spring 1977, Inst. Mittag-Leffler, Stockholm, winter, 1978, MIT, fall 1983, Inst. for Advanced Study, spring 1984; dir. West Coast Number Theory Conf., U. Calif.-San Diego, 1976; lectr. in field. Author: Harmonic Analysis on Symmetric Spaces and Applications, Vol. I, 1985. Contbr. articles and chpts. to profl. publs. Woodrow Wilson fellow, 1964; NSF fellow, 1964-68; NSF grantee Summer Inst. in Number Theory, Ann Arbor, Mich., 1973; prin. investigator NSF, 1974—. Fellow AAAS; mem. AAAS (nominating com. math. sect.), Am. Math. Soc. (council), Math. Assn. Am., Soc. Indsl. and Applied Math., Assn. for Women in Math., Assn. for Women in Sci. Research in harmonic analysis on symmetric spaces and number theory. Office: Dept Math CC-012 U Calif-San Diego La Jolla CA 92093

TERREBONNE, ANNIE MARIE, medical technologist, educator; b. Isola, Miss., Mar. 17, 1932; d. Tommy Wiley and Alpha Cora (Whitfield) P.; m. Frank Paul Terrebonne, May 7, 1960. A.A., Co-Lin Jr. Coll., 1950; B.S., Miss.

State U., 1952; grad. Knoxville Gen. Hosp. Sch. Med. Tech., 1953. Cert. Nat. Cert. Agy. Med. Lab. Personnel. Med., x-ray and EKG technician Layman-Saffold Clinic, Knoxville, Tenn., 1952-55; med. technologist in bacteriology St. Dominic's Hosp., Jackson, Miss., 1956-58; parasitologist Oschner's Clinic and Hosp., New Orleans, 1959-65; sr. med. technician II spl. hematology dept. U. Tex. Med. Br., Galveston, 1969—, mem. research and devel. staff, 1974—, instr. med. technologists, 1981—. Contbr. articles to profl. jours. Mem. Am. Assn. Med. Technologists, Galveston Dist. Soc. Med. Technologists, Tex. Soc. Med. Technologists, Am. Soc. Clin. Pathologists (cert.), Bayou Vista Fireman's Aux., Mental Health Assn. Galveston County, Miss. State U. Alumni. Democrat. Methodist. Clubs: Loyalty, Found. for Christian Living, Miss. State U. Bulldog, Positive Thinkers'. Lodge: Order of Eastern Star. Home: 353 Ling Dr Hitchcock TX 77563 Office: Special Hematology Dept U Tex Med Br 425 Clin Sci Bldg 300 University Blvd Galveston TX 77550

TERRELL, CAROL DIANE, real estate investment company executive; b. Levelland, Tex., Feb. 16, 1957; d. Milton Leon and Lois Leona (Cook) Terrell. Student Cisco Jr. Coll., 1975-76, Ranger Jr. Coll., 1979-80. Registered prin. Nat. Assn. Securities Dealers. Office mgr., bookkeeper M.L. Terrell Real Estate, Eastland, Tex., 1976-79; mgr. Eastland Mchts. Credit Assn., 1978-79; office mgr., bookkeeper West Tex. Legal Services, Eastland, 1979-80; legal sec. Murray Fin. Corp., Dallas, 1980; dir. investor services Murray Realty Investors, Inc., Dallas, 1980-84; dir. investor ops. Watson & Taylor Cos., Dallas, 1984—; v.p. ops Watson & Taylor Investments, Dallas, 1986—. Eastland County area chmn. Am. Heart Assn., 1977. Recipient Ben Little scholarship, 1975, Good Citizenship award Tex. Farm Bur., 1975. Mem. Internat. Assn. Fin. Planning, Nat. Assn. Female Execs., Nat. Beta Club. Republican. Baptist.

TERRELL, RUTH ANN, nurse, educator; b. Guthrie, Okla, July 20, 1951; d. Ramon Richard and Juanita Ruth (McKenzie) McNulty; m. Stephen John Terrell, July 22, 1977 (div. 1979). B.S. in Health Edn., Central State U., Edmond, Okla., 1982, M.Ed. of Adult Edn., 1985; A.S. in Nursing, Okla. State U. Tech. Inst., Oklahoma City, 1976. R.N., Okla., Nebr. Staff nurse Okla. Teaching Hosp., Oklahoma City, 1976-77; dir. nurses Beatrice Manor (Nebr.), 1977-78, Good Samaritan Ctr., Wymore, Nebr., 1978-79; house supr. Logan County Health Ctr., Guthrie, Okla., 1979-82, Bapt. Med. Ctr., Oklahoma City, 1982-83; practical nurse instr. Francis Tuttle Vocat.-Tech. Ctr. Oklahoma City, 1983—; cons. Guthrie Nursing Ctr., 1979-80. Author: Team Teaching in Nursing Education, 1983; Computer Medical Terminology. Democrat. Roman Catholic. Home: 1717 Cleveland St Guthrie OK 73044 Office: Francis Tuttle Vocat-Tech Ctr 12777 N Rockwell St Oklahoma City OK 73034

TERRELL, SALLIE FRANCES, association executive; b. Mount Sterling, Ky., Apr. 2, 1938; d. Roy and Iva Mae (Fanning) Spencer; m. Lucien Hart Terrell, Aug. 10, 1957; children—Hart Spencer, Lu Anne. Student, U. Ky., 1955-56. Sec. W.O. Laslie C.P.A.s, Lexington, Ky., 1958-63; bookkeeper Kaufman Clothing Co., Lexington, 1963-64; credit investigator Retail Credit Co., Lexington, 1965-66; clerical worker County Sheriff's Office, Lexington, 1966-67; exec. officer Lexington Apt. Assn., 1981—; instr. Weikel Real Estate Sch., Lexington, 1984—, Fugazzi Bus. Coll., Lexington, 1986—. Active local PTAs, Lexington, 1969-71; bd. dirs., officer Fayette County PTA Council, Lexington, 1970-80; cand. County Sch. Bd., Lexington, 1974; treas. Bluegrass Regional Birth Planning Council, Lexington, 1975-80; county chmn. Democratic Gubernatorial Race, Lexington, 1976, mem. steering com., 1979, 82; treas. Sch. Bd. Race Lexington, 1978; bd. dirs. Mental Health Assn. of Central Ky., 1978-81, Emergency Housing Coalition, Lexington, 1983—; sec. State Polit. Coalition, Frankfort, Ky., 1983—. Mem. Ky. Soc. Assn. Execs., Am. Soc. Assn. Execs., Assn. Execs. Council of Nat. Apartment Assn. (pres.-elect 1986). Club: Woman's of Central Ky. (Lexington). Avocations: needlework; reading; houseboating. Home: 1761 Hawthorne Ln Lexington KY 40505 Office: Lexington Apt Assn 465 E High St Suite 104 Lexington KY 40508

TERRIS, LILLIAN DICK, psychologist, association executive; b. Bloomfield, N.J., May 5, 1914; d. Alexander Blaikie and Herminia (Doscher) Dick; B.A., Barnard Coll., 1935; Ph.D., Columbia U., 1941; m. Louis Long, Apr. 22, 1935 (dec. Sept. 11, 1968), 1 son, Alexander Blaikie Long; m. Milton Terris, Feb. 6, 1971. Instr. psychology Sara Lawrence Coll., Bronxville, N.Y., 1937-40; jr. personnel tech. SSA, Washington, 1941; sr. personnel clk. OWI, N.Y.C., 1941-43; dir. profl. examination service Am. Public Health Assn., N.Y.C., 1943-70, pres., 1970-79, pres. emeritus, 1979—, assoc. editor Jour. Public Health Policy, 1979—; bd. dirs. Profl. Exam. Service, Vis. Nurse Assn., Chittenden County, Vt. Recipient Nat. Environ. Health Assn. award, 1976; Cert. of Service award Am. Bd. Preventive Medicine, 1979. diplomate Am. Bd. Examiners in Profl. Psychology. Fellow Am. Psychol. Assn.; mem. Am. Public Health Assn., N.Y. State Psychol. Assn., Am. Coll. Hosp. Adminstrs. (hon. fellow), Phi Beta Kappa, Sigma Xi. Contbr. articles in field to profl. jours. Home: 208 Meadowood Dr South Burlington VT 05401 Office: 475 Riverside Dr New York City 10027

TERRY, ELLEN COLEMAN, real estate executive; b. Paris, Tex., June 11, 1939; d. Rodgers G. and Brown (Dodson) Coleman; children—Todd, Amy. A.A., Christian Coll.-Columbia, Mo., 1959; B.A., So. Meth. U., 1961. Tchr. Cooper High Sch., Abilene, Tex., 1961-63, Hockaday Sch., Dallas, 1963-66; travel cons. 1975-76; real estate agt. Coldwell-Banker, Dallas, 1976-79; pres., ptnr. Terry, Abio & Adleta, Realtors, Dallas, 1981; owner, pres. Ellen Terry, Realtors, Inc., Dallas, 1981—; bd. dirs. Tex. Commerce Bank Dallas. Bds. dirs. So. Meth. U. Mustang Club, Swiss Ave. Counseling Center, Dallas Challenge, Dallas Epilepsy Assn., Dallas Soc. Crippled Children, Susan G. Komen Found., Suicide Crisis Ctr.; mem. adv. com. Crystal Charity Ball. Recipient Disting. Alumni award So. Meth. U., 1985, Disting. Alumnae award Columbia Coll., 1986. Mem. Nat. Assn. Realtors Tex. Assn. Realtors Greater Dallas Bd. Realtors (Eastwood cup for outstanding realtor). Dallas Women's Council of Realtors, Leadership Tex., Leadership Dallas, Nat. Women's Econ. Alliance (bd. govs.), Pi Beta Phi (Community service award 1985-86, sr. alumnae group); Motivational speaker. Office: 5401 N Central Suite 225 Dallas TX 75205

TERRY, LINDA MALCZYK, lawyer; b. Buffalo, Feb. 18, 1949; s. Leo Charles and Estelle (Dziak) M.; m. Kenneth Walter Merz, Aug. 23, 1969 (div. Sept. 1975); m. 2d, William James Terry II, Dec. 5, 1975; 1 son, Christian Danforth. Student Cornell U., 1967-69; B.S., U. Hartford, 1971; J.D., U. Conn., 1979. Bar: Conn. 1979; C.L.U. Programmer, systems analyst Conn. Gen. Life Ins. Co., Bloomfield, Conn., 1971-75, pension research analyst, mgr., 1975-79; mgmt. asst. Congen Realty Adv. Co., Bloomfield, 1979-80; atty. CIGNA Corp., Bloomfield, 1980—. Sec. Granby Democratic Town Com., 1980-82, mem. 1982-84; mem. Granby Econ. Devel. Commn., 1981. Mem. ABA, Conn. Bar Assn., Hartford County Bar Assn. Lutheran. Home: 5 Roundhill Rd Granby CT 06035 Office: CIGNA Corp Hartford CT 06152

TERRY, MARY SUE, state attorney general; b. Martinsville, Va., Sept. 28, 1947; d. N.C. and Nannie Ruth T. B.A. in Polit. Sci., Westhampton Coll., Richmond, 1969; M.A. in Govt., U. Va., 1970, J.D., 1973. Bar: Va. 1973. Asst. Commonwealth's Atty., Patrick County, Va., 1973-77; rep. Ho. of Dels., Va., 1977-85; ptnr. Terry and Rogers, Stuart, Va., 1978—, B.H. Cooper Farm Inc., Stuart, 1978—; atty. gen. Va., 1986—; bd. dirs. First Nat. Bank, Stuart, 1978—, chmn., 1981—. Bd. dirs. Va. YMCA, 1980—; chair Gov.'s Task Force to Combat Drunk Driving, Va., 1982. Recipient Service to Youth award Va. YMCA, 1981; Disting. Alumna award U. Richmond, 1984. Mem. ABA, Va. Trial Lawyers Assn. Democrat. Am. Baptist. Office: Atty Gen's Office 101 N 8th St Richmond VA 23219

TERRY, MICHELE, biotechnology company executive; b. Detroit, Feb. 13, 1952; d. Philip Charles and Vicki (Makres) Terry. B.S. in Med. Tech., U. Mich., 1974. Med. technologist William Beaumont Hosp., Royal Oak, Mich., 1974-79; mktg. rep. Bio-Sci. Lab. div. Am. Hosp. Supply, Farmington Hills, Mich., 1979-82; product mgr. Am. Biosci. Co. div. Am. Hosp. Supply, Van Nuys, Calif., 1982-84; dir. mktg. Lifecodes Corp., Elmsford, N.Y., 1984—. Mem. Am. Soc. Human Genetics, Clin. Lab. Mgrs. Assn., Nat. Child Support Enforcement Assn., Am. Mktg. Assn. Avocations: tennis; golf; real estate investing. Office: Lifecodes Corp 4 Westchester Plaza Elmsford NY 10523

TERWISKE, MARY ELIZABETH, insurance company service specialist; b. Leominster, Mass., July 14, 1957; d. Cletus Albert and Eleanor Mae (Andrews) T. Student Bentley Coll., Waltham, Mass., 1979-83. Head teller The Fed. Savs. Bank, Waltham, 1977-79, br. mgr., 1979-81, asst. v.p., 1981-83; sr. funding technician New Eng. Mut. Life Ins. Co., Boston, 1983-85, sr. service specialist, 1985—. Mem. Nat. Assn. Female Execs. Democrat. Roman Catholic. Office: New England Mutual Life Ins Co 399 Boylston St Boston MA 02117

TESA, TANYA K(OVACH), law firm executive; b. N.Y.C., June 24, 1947; d. Stephen P. and Tessie R. Kovach. B.A., Bernard M. Baruch Coll., 1974; postgrad. CUNY, 1976-79. Owner, Mint Condition, Inc., antiques, N.Y.C., 1969-72; disbursing agt. U.S. Bankruptcy Ct., So. Dist. N.Y., 1976—; exec. asst. to sr. mng. partner firm Burns Summit Rovins & Feldesman, N.Y.C., 1972—, spl. projects mgr., 1980—; dir. communications summit Rovins & Feldesman, N.Y.C., 1986—; exec. asst. to nat. chmn. Union Coll. 64th and 65th Ann. Funds, 1976-77; exec. asst. to chmn. Union Coll. Terr. Council, Schenectady, 1977-78; exec. asst. to chmn. Cornell U. Law Sch. Met. Campaign for Funds, 1979-83; exec. asst. to chmn. bd. Freedoms Found., Valley Forge, Pa., 1983-85; mem. Defender of Freedoms program, 1983-85; exec. asst. to nat. asso. and v.p., fundraiser Boys Clubs Am., 1980-85; exec. asst. to mem. bd. dirs. and fundraiser I Love A Clean New York, Inc., N.Y.C., 1981-83; exec. asst. to chmn. bd. trustees Union Coll. Schenectady, 1982-86. First v.p. Ocean Bay Park Assn., Inc., Fire Island, N.Y., 1980—; mem. bd. Fire Island Assn., Inc., 1981—; bd. dirs. Ocean Bay Park Water Corp., 1985—. Home: 20 Park Ave New York NY 10016 also 19 Champlain Ocean Bay Park Fire Island NY 11770 Office: 445 Park Ave New York NY 10022

TESAURO, MICHELE BLANCHE, bilingual educator, translator; b. N.Y.C., Mar. 20, 1948; d. Adrian Michael and Delia Wilfreda (Rivera) Romero; m. John Albert Tesauro, Aug. 14, 1982; children—Aletheia, Zoe. B.A., Interm. U., P.R., 1969; M.Ed., Boston U., 1978; postgrad. Calif. State U.-Long Beach, 1980-83. Bilingual tchr. pub. schs. Bronx, N.Y., 1970-71, 73-75, Newark, 1973, Bklyn., 1976-77, Winter Gardens Elem. Sch., Montebello Unified Sch. Dist. East Los Angeles, Calif., 1979-83; instr. English, Interm. U., San German, P.R., 1971-72; Spanish tchr. trainer, N.Y.C. Bd. Edn., 1975; bilingual tchr. Drug Abuse Control Commn., N.Y. Dept. Correctional Services, Bronx, 1975-76; testing asst. ESAA Bilingual Testing and Measurement Component, Boston, 1977-78; cons. Bilingual Resource Ctr., Boston U., 1977-78; bilingual reader, cons. Scott, Foresman and Co., Glenview, Ill., 1983-84; Spanish translator, ednl. cons., 1984—. Tutor Neighborhood Youth Corps, N.Y.C., 1966, 67, Martin Luther King Ctr., Boston U., 1977; mem. tng. unit P.R. Traveling Theater, N.Y.C., 1973-75; recruiter, fund sponsor Kennedy-King Scholarship Fund, Interm. U. Mem. Boston U. Alumni Assn. Avocation: gardening. Address: 2266 Argonne Ave Long Beach CA 90815

TESMER, NANCY ANN STUTLER, librarian; b. Akron, Ohio, Aug. 25, 1934; d. Ernest Lynn and Sophrona Rebecca (Pepper) Stutler; student U. Akron, 1952-54; B.A., Kent State U., 1956; m. Clifford Frank Haines, Aug. 20, 1960 (div.); m. 2d, John A. Tesmer, Sept. 10, 1980. Jr. asst. librarian E. Br. Library, Akron, 1956-59; hosp. librarian VA Hosp., Northampton, Mass., 1959-61; med. librarian VA Hosp., Brecksville, Ohio, 1961-65, chief librarian, 1965-73; asso. chief librarian Cleve. VA Hosp., 1973-75, chief librarian, 1975—. Mem. Med. Library Assn., N.E. Ohio Med. Library Assn., Zeta Tau Alpha. Home: 603 Tollis Pkwy Broadview Heights OH 44147 Office: 10000 Brecksville Rd Brecksville OH 44141

TESSER (DIAMOND), JACQUELINE, physician billing company executive, consultant; b. N.Y.C., Mar. 29, 1941; d. Louis and Rebecca (Smith) Tesser; m. Mitchell E. Diamond, June 19, 1960; children—Lisa, Rebecca, Benjamin. B.A. in History and Secondary Edn., Queen's Coll., 1961; M.A. in Social Sci., 1964; M.B.A. in Mgmt., C.W. Post Coll., 1974. Tchr., N.Y.C. Schs., 1961-64, East Meadow Schs., N.Y., 1965; mgr. Health Providers, N.Y.C., 1974-76; sales person ITEL, L.I., N.Y., 1976-78; pres. DX Systems for Health Inc., East Meadow, 1979-84; regional dir. N.Y. div. Cycare, 1984—. Mem. Healthcare Fin. Mgmt. Assn. Jewish. Home: 1446 Mark Dr East Meadow NY 11554 Office: DX System for Health 1900 Hempstead Turnpike East Meadow NY 11554

TESTA, ELAINE SILVA, educator, civic worker; b. Watsonville, Calif., Oct. 21, 1942; d. Julius Raymond and Mary Dolores (Fuller) Silva; B.A. in Edn. and Psychology (Rotary scholar), San Jose State U., 1965; m. John Vincent Testa, Feb. 6, 1965; children—Laura Marie, Linda Antoinette, John Peter. Elem. tchr. Gilroy (Calif.) Sch. Dist., 1966-68. Chair environ. exec. com. South Lake Tahoe, Calif., 1972-73; mem. state and local environ. coms. AAUW, 1970-80; mem. Lake Tahoe Unified Sch. Dist. Bd. Edn., 1979-83; realtor; vol. tchr. local schs. Recipient Bank of Am. award, 1960, cert. parent adv. com. Lake Tahoe Community Coll., 1972; hon. lt. col. U.S. Army Pershing Rifles, 1964. Mem. AAUW, Calif. Sch. Bds. Assn., South Lake Tahoe Bd. Realtors. Republican. Roman Catholic. Author: Our Environment—No Deposit, No Return, 1973; author environ. and recycling lessons, environ. radio spot announcements. Home: PO Box 13274 South Lake Tahoe CA 95702

TETERYCZ, BARBARA ANN, advertising executive; b. Chgo., Jan. 23, 1952; d. Sylvester and Anne (Deutsch) T.; m. Robert Nathan Estes, Oct. 13, 1984. B.A., U. Ill., 1974; postgrad. Parkland Coll., 1975-76, U. Ill., 1976-77. Teller, First Fed. of Champaign, Ill., 1974-75; cashier Korger Co., Champaign, 1975-77; merchandise rep. RustCraft Greeting Cards, Champaign, 1977-78; sales rep. Hockenberg-Rubin, Champaign, 1978, John Morrell & Co., Champaign, 1978-80; account exec. WICD TV, Champaign, 1981—; owner Left-Handed Compliments, Champaign. Contbg. editor mag. Champaign County Bus. Reports, 1986. Vol. Am. Cancer Soc., 1985, U. Ill. Alumni Assn., 1985, Com. to Elect Beth Beauchamp to City Council, Champaign, 1984. Ill. State scholar, 1970-74. Mem. Ad Club of Champaign, Women's Bus. Council Urbana C. of C., Champaign C. of C. (pub. relations com.), Nat. Assn. Female Execs. (network dir.), Alpha Omega. Roman Catholic. Avocations: reading; writing; bicycling; bodybuilding. Home: 1615 Harbor Point Dr PO Box 873 Champaign IL 61820 Office: WICD TV 250 Country Fair Dr PO Box 3750 Champaign IL 61821

TETI, CATHERINE POWER, lawyer; b. Charleston, W.Va., Nov. 17, 1954; d. Francis Ray and Mary Jo (Crozier) P; m. John Joshua Teti, Jr., Aug. 27, 1966; children—John Joshua III, Sarah Margaret. A.B., W.Va., U., 1967; J.D., U. Richmond, 1979. Bar: Va. 1979, Fla. 1980. Social worker Preston County Dept. Welfare, Kingwood, W.Va., 1967-68; mng. editor King George (Va.) News, 1972-74; sole practice law, Clearwater, Fla., 1980-82; legal counsel Hillsborough County Office of Child Support Enforcement, Tampa, Fla., 1982—. Chmn., King George Bicentennial Commn., 1974-76; mem. Germana Community Coll. Citizen's Adv. Panel, King George, 1974-76, King George Planning Commn., 1978-79, King George Democratic Com., 1978-79; del. Va. Dem. Conv., 1978. Mem. ABA, Va. Bar Assn., Fla. Bar, Fla. Assn. Women Lawyers, LWV, Sigma Sigma Sigma. Office: Office of Child Support Enforcement Suite 401 505 Twigg St Tampa FL 33601

TEUNISSEN-MYERS, JACQUELINE, family physician; b. Amsterdam, Netherlands, Mar. 20, 1952; came to U.S., 1978; d. Jacobus and Dirkje Hendrika (Polman Tuin) Teunissen; m. James Arthur Myers, Mar. 18, 1977. M.D., Vrije U., Amsterdam, 1979. Resident, U. Minn.-Mpls., 1979-82; owner, family physician Rockford FamilyCare Ctr., Minn., 1982—; clin. instr. dept. family practice U. Minn., 1983—. Fellow Am. Acad. Family Practice; mem. AMA. Avocations: tennis, golf, skiing, photography, travel. Office: Rockford FamilyCare Ctr PO Box 39 Rockford MN 55373

TEWS, EVE LYNN, insurance adjuster; b. Berea, Ohio, Aug. 11, 1956; d. Clee Clifton Leatherman and Marlene J. (Shepard) Findlay; m. James Edward Tews, May 24, 1975 (div.); children—James Wesley. Grad. high sch. Sec., Toensmeier Adjustment, Allentown, Pa., 1974-78, adjuster, 1978-81; resident adjuster Gemmill Adjustment, Reading, Pa., 1981-84; ins. adjuster/owner E.L. Tews Adjustment, Allentown, 1984—. Mem. Lehigh Valley Claims Assn. (pres. 1986—), Nat. Assn. Self-Employed, Nat. Assn. Female Execs., Reading Claims Assn. Democrat. Avocations: aerobics; reading; crocheting. Office: PO Box 294 Allentown PA 18105

TEXTER, ETHEL E., projects director; b. Trauger, Pa., Apr. 6, 1932; d. Theodoius Myron and Elvera E. (Boruch) Volkay; m. William M. Schofield, Jan. 24, 1954 (div. 1980); children—Deborah, Michele, Roseanne, David; m. Walter F. Texter, Dec. 7, 1980. Student Felt & Tauant Bus. Sch., Newark. Lic. food mgr. Acct., Levenger's Inc., Allentown, Pa., 1962-71; dir. services Miller Meml. Blood Ctr., Bethlehem, Pa., 1971-72; sec.-treas. ABC Automotive, Allentown, 1972-73; projects dir. Lehigh County Sr. Citizens, Inc., Allentown, 1973—; dir., treas. Endeavor, Inc., Bethlehem, 1982—, Rape Crisis Council, Allentown, 1976-79. Mem. Women's Adv. Bd. Lehigh County, 1985—. Mem. Pa. Assn. Notaries, Nat. Assn. Female Execs. Democrat. Byzantine Catholic. Avocations: music; gourmet cooking. Home: 41 S 13th St Allentown PA 18102 Office: SW 28th St and Arcadia Ave Allentown PA 18103

THAGARD, SHIRLEY STAFFORD, sales and marketing executive; b. Detroit, Nov. 29, 1940; d. Walter Jay Stafford and Marjorie Gertrude (LaRa) Stafford Goode; m. Charles Wendell Thagard, Sept. 21, 1963; children—Grayson Jay, Devon Charles. Assoc. Bus., Webber Coll., 1961; cert. Pierce Coll., 1973. Dir. pub. relations Miami Herald, Fla., 1963-67; pres. Thagard Enterprises, Woodland Hills, Calif., 1980—; v.p. mktg. R.T. Durable Med. Products, Inc., Miami, also Woodland Hills, 1983-85; investment cons., lectr. investments Palisades Fin. Services, Sherman Oaks, Calif., 1985—; ind. lectr. women's issues and children's health care, 1980—. Editor, pub. Pediatric Network, 1980-85. Contbr. articles to various jours. Creator Med. Moppets healthcare teaching tools, 1983. Chairperson Los Angeles County Mental Health (Expressing Feelings), 1985-86; ind. lobbyist for child abuse legislation Calif. Legislature, 1985—. Recipient commendation Los Angeles City Council, 1983, Calif. Congresswoman Bobbi Fiedler, 1984. Mem. Nat. Assn. Female Execs., Assn. Care of Children's Health, Am. Bus. Women's Assn., Pilot Internat. (pub. relations com. 1985-86, San Fernando Valley club commendation 1985), Nat. Assn. Edn. Young Children, Direct Mktg. Council Los Angeles. Avocations: travel, writing. Office: PO Box 8396 Calabasas CA 91302

THAL, ANNE ELISE, psychotherapist, consultant; b. Toledo, Aug. 3, 1945; d. William S. and Florence Marian (Salzman) T.; m. Bruce Andich, 1968 (div. 1970); m. Stephen H. Soboroff, Sept. 2, 1972 (div. Aug. 1974). A.B., U. Chgo., 1966, A.M., 1968; postgrad. in bus. adminstrn. U. South Fla., 1982-83. Lic. clin. social worker, Ill., Fla. Research assoc. Hills County Schs., Tampa, Fla., 1972-73; exec. dir. Suicide/and Crisis Ctr., Tampa, 1973-74, bd. dirs., 1972-81, v.p., 1977-79; exec. dir. Tampa Jewish Social Service, 1974-83; pvt. practice psychotherapy, Tampa, 1977—; founder, pres. The Playmakers, Inc., Tampa, 1981-83, dir. mgmt./devel., 1983-85; lectr. Field Inst., U. South Fla., Tampa, 1975-83; cons. in fields; profl. actress, 1962-82. Chmn. Hills County Crisis Council, Tampa, 1975-77; campaign worker People For George Sheldon, Tampa, 1975-83; mem. adv. bd. Sr. Resource Ctr., Tampa, 1976-82, Hillsborough Info. Line, Tampa, 1978-82. Named Outstanding Bd. Mem., Suicide and Crisis Ctr., Tampa, 1978; One of 33 Women to Watch, Tampa Tribune, 1982; NIMH fellow, 1967-68. Fellow Acad. Cert. Social Workers; mem. Nat. Assn. Social Workers, Network Exec. Women, NOW. Office: 3802 Bay to Bay Blvd Suite 12 Tampa FL 33629

THALER, ANDREA JASPER, health care administrator, social work administrator; b. N.Y.C., Sept. 9, 1951; d. Milton I. and Sylvia (Rockwerk) Jasper; m. Gregory H. Moser, Aug. 1, 1970 (div. 1976); m. Ted N. Thaler, Dec. 29, 1985. Student Radford Coll., 1968-70, 73-75; B.A., U. Tenn.-Nashville, 1979; M.S. in Social Work, U. Tenn.-Knoxville, 1980. Eligibility counselor Va. Dept. Social Services, Christiansburg, 1972-75; policy specialist state office Tenn. Dept. Human Services, Nashville, 1976-83; dir. mktg. and member services Tenn. Primary Care Network, Inc., Nashville, 1983—. Treas., mem. exec. bd. Social Action Group on Aging, Nashville, 1980—; del. Dem. Nat. Platform Com. Hart Campaign, Tenn., 1984-85; mem. health care com. LWV, Nashville, 1984—; active mem. Peace Links, Tenn., 1984-85, Women's Political Caucas, Nashville, 1984—. Named nominee Chancellor's award for outstanding community service work U. Tenn., 1980. Mem. Tenn. Conf. on Social Welfare. Jewish. Avocations: swimming, volunteer work. Home: 6501 Harding Rd Nashville TN 37205 Office: Tenn Primary Care Network 205 Reidhurst Ave Nashville TN 37203

THALL, LETTY DERMAN, social services administrator; b. New Orleans, Jan. 6, 1947; d. Herbert and Mary Virginia (Coughlin) Derman; m. Bruce Louis Thall, June 23, 1968; 1 son, Gregory Coughlin. B.A., Skidmore Coll., 1968; M.S.S., Bryn Mawr Coll., 1974. Trainer, cons. Bell Telephone Co., Phila., 1968-71; policewoman Phila. Police Dept., 1971; planning cons. Health and Welfare Council, Phila., 1974-75; dir. WOAR, Phila., 1975-77; program coordinator Hall-Mercer Ctr., Phila., 1978-80; dir. and planner Community Services Planning Council, Phila., 1980-85; exec. dir. Delaware Valley Child Care Council, 1986—; pres. bd. CHOICE, 1977-80; alumni com. mem. Community Leadership Seminars, Phila., 1978-83. Coordinator Shirley Chisholm for Pres., Miami, Fla., 1972; fin. dir. Bill Gray for Congress Com., Phila., 1978; co-chairperson Marion Tasco for City Commr., Phila., 1983; mem. Phila. Mayor's Commn. for Women, 1980-85, vice-chair., 1983-85. Mem. Mid Atlantic Assn. for Tng. and Counseling (trainer, group facilitator 1979—), Women's Way (co-founder; bd. dirs. 1975-81), Delaware Valley Assn. for Edn. Young Children, Nat. Assn. Social Workers, Assn. for Creative Change. Democrat. Office: 121 N Broad St 5th Floor Philadelphia PA 19107

THARP, TWYLA, dancer, choreographer; b. Portland, Ind., July 1, 1941; student Pomona Coll., Am. Ballet Theatre Sch.; grad. Barnard Coll.; D. Performing Arts (hon.), Calif. Inst. Arts, 1978; hon. degrees Brown U., 1981, Bard Coll., 1981; student Richard Thomas, Merce Cunningham, Igor Schwezoff, Louis Mattox, Paul Taylor, Margaet Craske, Erick Hawkins; m. Robert Huot (div.); 1 son, Jesse. With Paul Taylor Dance Co., 1963-65; freelance choreographer with own modern dance troupe and various other cos. including Joffrey Ballet and Am. Ballet Theatre, 1965—; teaching residencies various colls. and univs. including U. Mass., Oberlin Coll., Walker Art Center, Boston U.; major works choreographed: Tank Dive, 1965; Re-Moves, 1966; Forevermore, 1967; Generation, 1968; Medley, 1969; Fugue, 1970; Eight Jelly Rolls, 1971; The Raggedy Dances, 1972; As Time Goes By, 1974; Sue's Leg, 1975; Push Comes to Shove, 1976; Once More Frank, 1976; Mud, 1977; Baker's Dozen, 1979; When We Were Very Young, 1980; film Hair, 1979; videotape Making Television Dance, 1977, CBS Cable Confessions of a Corner Maker, 1980. Recipient Creative Arts award Brandeis U., 1972; Dance Mag. Annual award, 1981. Office: Twyla Tharp Dance 30 Lafayette Ave Brooklyn NY 11217

THATCHER, MARY JO, television producer; b. Des Moines, Dec. 24, 1951; d. Ben and Barbara Jean (Ward) Thatcher; student Citrus Coll., 1970-72. Actress, various parts, incl. part in Helter Skelter, 1975; with Denny Harris Inc. of Calif., Los Angeles, 1977—, exec. producer TV commls., 1979—. Mem. Screen Actors Guild, Am. Film Inst., Assn. Ind. Comml. Producers (bd. dirs.), Women in Film, NOW. Office: 12166 Olympic Blvd Los Angeles CA 90064

THAXTER, MARY LYNNE, lawyer; b. Sangley Point, Philippines, Oct. 26, 1956; came to U.S., 1957; d. Clinton Ewart Jr. and Jo Anne (Keyes) Thaxter. B.A. magna cum laude in Polit. Sci., UCLA, 1978; J.D. cum laude, U. Santa Clara, 1982. Bar: Calif. 1982; U.S. Dist. Ct. (no. dist.) Calif. 1982. Assoc. Hoge, Fenton, Jones & Appel, Inc., San Jose, Calif., 1982—. Comments editor Santa Clara Law Rev., Vol. 22, 1981-82. Mem. Santa Clara County Bar Assn., ABA, State Bar Calif., UCLA Polit. Sci. Honor Soc., Pi Sigma Alpha, Pi Gamma Mu. Republican. Home: 517 Troy Dr No 4 San Jose CA 95117 Office: Hoge Fenton Jones & Appel Inc 4 N 2d St Suite 1300 San Jose CA 95113

THAXTON, VERA, home economics educator; b. Wenatchee, Wash., Aug. 15, 1933; d. Charles Clay and Ruth Ellen (Parsons) T. A.A., Mt. San Antonio Coll., 1954; B.A., San Diego State U., 1956; M.S., U. Ill.-Urbana, 1958. Cert. secondary tchr., Calif. Child welfare worker I, Lucas County (Ohio) Child Welfare, Toledo, 1958-60; home econs. instr. Bridgewater (Va.) Coll., 1960-62; licensing caseworker I, Los Angeles County Dept. Charities, Bur. Licensing, 1962-63; home econs. tchr. Pomona (Calif.) Unified Sch. Dist., 1963-69, Sonora (Calif.) High Sch., 1969-71, Banning (Calif.) High Sch., 1971-73, Coachella High Sch., Thermal, Calif., 1974—. Sec., La Quinta Property Owners Assn., 1979-82, 83-84. Mem. Assn. Supervision and Curriculum Devel., AAUW, Am. Home Econs. Assn., Calif. Home Econs. Assn. (dist. past pres., treas.), Nat. Assn. Edn. Young Children, Calif. Assn. Edn. Young Children, Future Homemakers Am. (sponsor), Fgn. Affairs Council. Republican. Presbyterian. Club: U. Ill. Alumni (past treas.). Home: PO Box 85 La Quinta CA 92253 Office: 83-800 Airport Blvd Thermal CA 92274

THAYER, EDNA ISABELLE, nurse; b. Manchester, N.H., July 25, 1923; d. Charles Everett and Maude Isabelle (Messenger) Trask; R.N., Elliott Community Hosp., 1944; B.S.N., UCLA, 1953; m. Charles Albert Thayer, Feb. 18, 1946; 1 dau., Linda Louise. Supr., Meriden (Conn.) Hosp., 1950-53, Inst. Living, Hartford, Conn., 1954-59; vol. tchr. educationally handicapped Brockton Sch., West Los Angeles, 1972-78; dir. nurses Canoga Terr., Canoga Park, Calif., 1979-80; dir. nurses Corbin Convalescent Hosp., Reseda, Calif., 1981-82; dir. nurses Sun Air Convalescent Hosp., 1982—. Served with Nurse Corp, AUS, 1945-46. Recipient Golden Apple award Los Angeles Unified Sch. Dist., 1976. Mem. Am., Calif. nurses assns., Nat. League Nursing Edn., Calif. Congress Parents and Tchrs., Bus. and Profl. Womens Club, Am. Legion.

Republican. Baptist. Club: Emblem. Office: Sun Air Hosp 7120 Corbin Ave Reseda CA 91335

THAYER, STEFANIE REITER, educational psychologist; b. Washington, Aug. 23, 1946; d. Alfred William and Frances Louise (Stiffman) Reiter; m. Gregory Keith Thayer, Aug. 24, 1980. A.A., Montgomery Coll., 1966; B. Gen. Studies, U. Iowa, 1972, M.A., 1974. Staff Georgetown Dental Sch., Washington, 1966-68; faculty Ferris State Coll., Big Rapids, Mich., 1969-70; research asst. U. Iowa, Iowa City, 1973-74, ednl. psychologist I, 1974-76, ednl. psychologist II, 1976-82; v.p. for profl. edn. Arthritis Found., Atlanta, 1982—; ednl. cons. Ohio State U., Columbus, 1977; ednl. cons. U. Man. (Can.), 1976, Acad. of Pediatrics, Iowa City, 1980. Contbr. articles to profl. jours. Kellog fellow, 1968-69; USPHS grantee, 1970-72, 72-73. Mem. Nat. Soc. for Performance and Instrn., Am. Soc. for Tng. and Devel.

THAYER, SUSAN BERMAN, cable television executive; b. Bayonne, N.J., July 11, 1941; d. Arthur Milton and Beatrice (Goldklang) Kaufman; m. Jack G. Thayer, Nov. 28, 1978; children—Jennifer, Rachel. B.A., Oberlin Coll., 1962; postgrad. Queens Coll., 1967-68, Baruch Coll., 1975-76. Editor, writer Ms. Mag. Corp., N.Y.C., 1972-77; pres. Susan K. Berman Assocs., N.Y.C., 1977-78; dir. mktg. Met. Transp. Authority, N.Y.C., 1978-81; account exec. Lifetime Network, N.Y.C., 1981—. Author published articles. Bd. dirs. Women's Action Alliance, N.Y.C., 1982-84. Mem. Internat. Radio and TV Soc., Women in Communications, Women in Cable. Jewish. Office: Lifetime Network 1211 Avenue of Americas New York NY 10036

THAYER, WANDA E., business owner; b. Tuscaloosa, Ala., July 27, 1943; d. Herman Springer and Anita (Rogers) Parker; m. Cameron Jones, (div. 1976); children—Bryan Keith, Kimberly Ann. Student Foothills Jr. Coll., Palm Beach Jr. Coll. Co-owner Aluma Loc Awning, San Jose, Calif., 1964-67; sec.-treas. A&A Air Conditioning, Boca Raton, Fla., 1968-76; pres. Personalized Air Conditioning, Inc., Boca Raton, 1978—. Chmn. BACPAC, 1979-81; bd. dirs. SAFEPAC, 1983—, Boca Raton United Way, 1984—; mem. bd. of rules and appeals City of Boca Raton. Mem. Boca Raton C. of C. (dir.), Fla. Atlantic Builders Assn. (past 2d v.p., past sec.; Assoc. of Yr. 1983), Nat. Fedn. Ind. Bus., Fla. Air Conditioning Contractors Assn., Better Bus. Bur. Democrat. Lutheran. Avocations: tennis; travel; reading. Home: 149 NW 70th St #205 Boca Raton FL 33432 Office: 121 NW 11th St Boca Raton FL 33432

THEBERGE, VIRGINIA RICE, media company executive; b. Worcester, Mass., July 18, 1936; d. Harvey Reginald Rice and Grace Beatrice (Bennett) Chamberlain; m. Leonard Joseph Theberge, Aug. 1, 1963 (dec. 1983); children—Michele Elizabeth, Christine Grace Anne, Valerie Bennett. B.A., Wellesley Coll., 1958. Field supr. Procter & Gamble Co., Cin., 1960-62; field dir. Interpub. Group of Cos., Inc., N.Y.C., 1962-64; dir. Kalamazoo Research Assocs., Mich., 1970-72; editor Media Inst., Washington, 1979-82; dir. Transnational Communications Ctr., Media Inst., Washington, 1982-84; pres. Internat. Info. Services, Inc., Washington, 1984—; cons. Rowan & Blewitt, Inc., Washington, 1984—. Editor: Glossary for International Communications, 1983; The Press and Policymaking in the U.S., 1983; Terrorism and the Media in the 1980's, 1984. Pres. St. Peter's Coll. Oxford Found., Washington, 1983—. Presbyterian. Club: University (Washington). Avocations: travel; swimming; skin diving. Home: 4333 Westover Pl NW Washington DC 20016

THELEEN, KIM DOROTHY, lawyer; b. Bklyn., Dec. 20, 1958; d. Charles William and Jeanne (Stagg) Schroeder; m. Ronald James Theleen, Sept. 3, 1983. B.A. summa cum laude, Washington and Jefferson Coll., 1980; J.D., Del. Law Sch., Wilmington, 1983. Bar: N.J., 1983, Pa., 1983. Assoc. Spevack & Cameron, Edison, N.J., 1983—. Birch scholar, 1980. Mem. ABA, Pa. Bar Assn., Middlesex Bar Assn., Phi Beta Kappa. Republican. Methodist. Home: 125-B N Randolphville Rd Piscataway NJ 08854 Office: Spevack & Cameron 2060 Oak Tree Rd Edison NJ 08820

THEODORE, CRYSTAL, artist, retired educator; b. Greenville, S.C., July 27, 1917; d. James Voutsas and Florence Gertrude (Bell) T.; A.B. magna cum laude, Winthrop Coll., 1938; M.A., Columbia U., 1942, Ed.D., 1953; postgrad. U. Ga., 1947. Instr. art Winthrop Coll., 1938-43; prof. art, head dept. Huntingdon (Ala.) Coll., 1946-52; prof. art, head dept. E. Tenn. State U., 1953-57; prof. art, head dept. Madison Coll., 1957-68; vis. prof. art World Campus Afloat, Chapman Coll., Calif., 1967; prof. art James Madison U., Harrisonburg, Va., 1968-83, ret. Bd. dirs. Rockingham Fine Arts Assn., 1980—, Women's Coop. Council Harrisonburg and Rockingham County, 1976-79; cons. Valley Program for Aging Services, 1976. Served with USMC, 1944-46. Gen. Edn. Bd. of Rockefeller Found. fellow, 1952-53; award Carnegie Found. Advancement of Teaching, 1947, 48, 49, 50; Ednl. Found. Program grantee AAUW, 1981-82. Mem. AAUW (cultural interests rep., dir. 1980-82, dir. Va. div. 1985—) Coll. Art Assn., Southeastern Coll. Art Conf., Mensa, Kappa Delta Pi, Kappa Pi, Delta Kappa Gamma, Sigma Phi, Pi Lambda Theta. Democrat. Lutheran. Contbr. articles to profl. jours.; paintings in regional and nat. exhbns. Home: Route 5 Box 202 Harrisonburg VA 22801

THEODORE, JASMINA ALEXANDRA, lawyer, economist; b. Kenosha, Wis., June 2, 1955; d. Sima Vladimir and Maria Therese (Churamowicz) Todorovic. B.A. U. Wis.-Parkside, 1973, M.S. in Econs., U. Wis.-Madison, 1975, J.D., 1979. Bar: Calif. 1980, Wis. 1980, U.S. Ct. Appeals (9th cir.) 1980. Intern (vis. economist) Bd. Govs. FRS, Washington, 1977; lectr. econs. U. So. Calif., Los Angeles, 1977-78; assoc. Latham & Watkins, Los Angeles, 1980-83; asst. counsel Union Oil Co. of Calif., Los Angeles, 1983—; journal referee Jour. Econ. Behavior and Orgn., Los Angeles, 1982—; guest lectr. law, econs. Claremont (Calif.), McKenna Coll. 1982—. Bd. dirs. Jazz-Tapp Ensemble, Inc., Los Angeles, 1984-86. Recipient Spl. Recognition as Youngest U. Grad., U. Wis., 1973, Faculty Innovation award U. So. Calif., 1978; Pro Bono Legal Work award State Bar Assn. Calif., 1982-83; national finalist White House Fellowship, 1983. Mem. State Bar Calif., Wis. Bar Assn., Town Hall of Calif., ABA.

THEVENET, SUSAN MARIE, lawyer; b. San Antonio, Apr. 6, 1950; d. Stanley Edward and Marie Therese (Hulsebosch) Thevenet; m. Paul Steven Casamassimo, June 28, 1975 (div. 1981). B.A., Pa. State U., 1971; M.A., Georgetown U., 1973; J.D., U. Iowa, 1978. Bar: Colo. 1979, U.S. Dist. Ct. Colo. 1979. Legis. asst. Am. Assn. Dental Schs., Washington, 1973-74; civil rights investigator Cedar Rapids Human Rights Commn., 1974-75; assoc. Shoemaker & Wham, Denver, 1979; vis. prof. U. Colo. Coll. Law, Boulder, 1980; assoc. Smart, DeFurio & McClure, Denver, 1979-85, ptnr., 1985—. Co-author; Iowa Law Rev., 1977, editor-in-chief, 1977-78. Mem., officer Iowa Women's Polit. Caucus, 1974. Mem. ABA, Colo. Bar Assn. (mem. grievance policy com. 1982—), Denver Bar Assn. Republican. Roman Catholic. Office: Smart DeFurio & McClure 1120 Lincoln St Suite 1600 Denver CO 80203

THIEL, RUTH ELEANOR, real estate broker; b. Chgo., June 11, 1930; d. Frank A. and Lucille L. (Bromm) Dell; m. Joseph Donald Thiel, Sept. 30, 1950; children—Michael F., Jeffrey D., Patti Thiel Fricks, Mary Beth Thiel Cramer, Tracy J. Thiel Carroll. A.A., Evanston Twp. Community Coll., 1950; grad. Realtors Inst., 1972. Sales assoc. Indian Hill Realty, Winnetka, Ill., 1967; v.p., mgr. Mitchell Bros. Realtors, Northbrook, Ill., 1972-75; exec. v.p., gen. mgr. Century 21 Mitchell Bros., Evanston, Ill., 1975-82; v.p. Koenig & Strey Realtors, 1982—. Mem. State of Ill. Real Estate Examining Com., 1977—, Evanston Econ. Devel. Com., 1979; treas. North Shore Assn. Retarded, 1977-79; mem. instl. rev. com. St. Francis Hosp., 1981—; mem. Evanston Zoning Bd., 1983-85; pres. Evanston Library Friends, 1984—; alderman 2d Ward, City of Evanston, 1985—. Recipient Ill. Women's Council of Realtors Woman of the Year award, 1979; Service award City of Hope, North Shore Assn. for Retarded, 1977. Mem. Nat. Assn. Realtors (bd. dirs. 1978—), Ill. Assn. Realtors (exec. com. 1979, bd. dirs. 1977—, Realtor of Yr. award 1984), North Shore Bd. Realtors (dir. 1970-80), Evanston North Shore Bd. Realtors (pres. 1978), Women's Council Realtors (state pres. 1977), Evanston Bus. and Profl. Women, Women in Real Estate (award 1980). Clubs: Woman of Evanston, Univ., YWCA, Million Dollar, Zonta Internat. Home: 1221 Greenwood St Evanston IL 60201 Office: 165 Green Bay Rd Evanston IL 60091

THIELE, GLORIA DAY, retired librarian; b. Los Angeles, Sept. 4, 1931; d. Russell Day Plummer and Dorothy Ruby (Day) Th.; m. Donald Edward Cools, June 13, 1953 (div.); children—Michael, Ramona, Naomi, Lawrence, Nancy, Rebecca, Eugene, Maria, Charles. B.Mus., Mt. St. Mary's Coll., Los Angeles, 1953. Library asst. Anaheim (Calif.) Pub. Library, 1970-73, head Biblioteca de la Comunidad, 1973-74, children's library asst., 1974-76, children's br. specialist, 1976-78, children's librarian, 1978-81; children's librarian Santa Maria (Calif.) Pub. Library, 1981-85; cons. Literature Continuum, Santa Maria Sch. Dist., 1981-85; cons. Organizational Ch.-Sch. Library, Los Angeles, 1980; guest lectr. children's lit. Allan Hancock Coll., Santa Maria, 1981-85. Library liaison Casa Amistad Community Service Group, Anaheim, 1973-74; mem. outreach com. Santiago Library System, Orange County, 1973-74, mem. children's services com., 1971-81; mem. Community Services Coordinating Council, Santa Maria, 1982-85; chairperson children's services com. Black Gold Library System, 1983-84. Mem. ALA, Calif. Library Assn., So. Calif. Council Lit. for Children and Young People, Women's Network, Delta Epsilon Sigma. Republican. Roman Catholic. Club: Minerva (Santa Maria).

THIELS, ELIZABETH LOUISE, public relations executive; b. Lecompte, La., Aug. 3, 1944; d. Frank Alphonse and Marguerite Magdalen (Dekeyzer) T.; m. Edward John Kollis, Feb. 29, 1970 (div. 1973). Student U. So. La., 1963-65. Reporter, Town Talk, Alexandria, La., 1966; press sec. Rep. S.O. Long from La., Washington, 1966-67; v.p. Exit/In, Nashville, 1972-75; dir. pub. relations Sound Seventy Corp., Nashville, 1975-79; pres. Network Ink, Inc., Nashville, 1979—. Mem. Country Music Assn., Nashville Music Assn., Nashville Acad. Rec. Arts and Scis. (assoc.). Avocations: music, gardening, reading. Office: Network Ink Inc 2012 21st Ave S Nashville TN 37212

THIEM, DOLLY IRENE, child development center administrator; b. Galveston, Tex., Apr. 23, 1945; d. Richard Joseph and Dolly Irene (Culbertson) T.; m. Bobby John Jones, July 16, 1983. B.S. in Home Econs., Lamar U., 1967; M.S. in Child Devel., Tex. Woman's U., 1977, Ph.D. in Child Devel., 1980. Cert. provisional home econs. tchr. Tchr. homemaking High Island Ind. Sch. Dist., Tex., 1967-71, Dallas Ind. Sch. Dist., 1971-72, Galveston Ind. Sch. Dist., Tex., 1972-75; teaching, research, adminstrv. asst. Tex. Woman's U., Denton, 1975-78; editor EPD Consortium-N.E. Tex., Richardson, 1978-79; dept. head Tarleton State U., Stephenville, Tex., 1979-83; asst. prof. Tarleton State U., Stephenville, 1983-84; owner, dir. Rolling Hills Child Devel. Ctr., Cedar Hill, Tex., 1984—. Co-author: Planning Day Care, 1975. Pres. Erath County Women's Polit. Caucus, Stephenville, Tex., 1982. EDP fellow U.S. Dept. Edn., Washington, 1976-78, state doctoral fellow Tex. Woman's U., Denton, 1978. Mem. Dallas Assn. Edn. Young Children (asst. v.p. 1984-85). Democrat. Lutheran. Avocations: antiques; traveling; photography. Home: 703 Long Ct Cedar Hill TX 75104 Office: Rolling Hills Child Devel Ctr 717 N Hwy 67 Box 923 Cedar Hill TX 75104

THIERSTEIN, EMMA JOAN, lawyer, technical information specialist; b. Newton, Kans., Oct. 5, 1937; d. William and Emma Voth; m. Eldred A. Thierstein, May 16, 1959; children—Joel, Gretchen. A.B. in Chemistry, Bethel Coll., North Newton, Kans., 1958; grad. Kans. U., 1958; J.D., U. Ky., 1976. Bar: Ky. 1976, D.C. 1979, Mich. 1979, U.S. Patent Office 1979. Pub. sch. tchr., Woodstock, Nfld., Can., 1960-61; lab. technician Procter & Gamble, Cin., 1966, tech. info. specialist, mgr., Cin. and Brussels, 1967-72, summer 1974; patent examiner U.S. Govt., Washington, 1976-78; patent atty. Upjohn Co., Kalamazoo, 1978-84, Parke Davis div. Warner Lambert, Ann Arbor, Mich., 1984—. Mem. Mich. bd. SSS. Mem. Ky. Bar Assn., D.C. Bar Assn., Mich. Bar Assn., Am. Patent Lawyers Assn., Women Lawyers Assn. S.W. Mich., Phi Alpha Delta Internat. (sec.-treas. 1973-74). Home: 2636 Lakeshore Dr Hillsdale MI 49242 Office: Warner Lambert 2800 Plymouth Rd Ann Arbor MI 49105

THOM, LILIAN ELIZABETH, remedial educator; b. Georgetown, Guyana, July 11, 1937; came to U.S., 1976; d. William Buller and Venus Henrietta (Albert) Thom. M.S., Adelphi U., 1983. Tchr. home econs. St. Philip's Govt. Sch., Georgetown, 1960-62, tchr. elem. edn. St. Philip's Govt. Sch., Georgetown, 1962-75; sr. mistress, tchr., St. Barnabas Govt., Georgetown, 1975-77; day care edn. asst. Community Sponsors, Bklyn., 1978; tchr., supr. edn. St. Mark's Sch., Bklyn., 1978-82; instr. resource room Jr. High Sch. #44, N.Y.C., 1982—; tutor dressmaking Carnegie Sch. Home Econs., Georgetown, 1960, tutor St. Barnabas Govt., Georgetown, 1975-76, evening class Taylor Bus. Sch., Manhattan, N.Y., 1983. Sec., mem. Friends St. George's Cathedral, Georgetown, 1958—. Mem. United Fedn. Tchrs., Nat. Assn. Female Execs., Guyana Tchrs. Assn. Anglican.

THOMA, JANET HOOVER, editor, writer; b. Pitts., Apr. 17, 1937; d. Wayne George and Elizabeth (Coopernail) Hoover; m. John Barry Thoma, Nov. 25, 1961; children—Christine Lynne, Janet Elizabeth, Heidi Ann. B.A. in English, Ohio U., 1959, M.S. in Journalism, 1983. Asst. editor David C. Cook Pub., Elgin, Ill., 1977-78, assoc. editor, 1978-79, editor Chariot Books, 1979-80, mng. editor, 1980-84; acquisitions editor Thomas Nelson Pubs., Nashville, 1984—; cons. children's books, 1983; speaker in field. Author: (with Maggie Mason) Esther, 1978; author series: Buddy Books, 1978; contbr. articles to Christian Herald Mag., Moody Monthly, Bookstore Jour. Bd. dirs. Jr. League Kansas City (Mo.), 1975-76; mem. mayor's com. Alt. Futures for Kansas City, 1976; mem. adv. bd. Elgin Community Coll., 1983. Mem. Mortar Bd. Republican. Episcopalian. Home and Office: 1307 Little John Dr Elgin IL 60120

THOMAS, ADELE CHAIKIN, psychological counselor; b. N.Y.C., June 25, 1926; d. Morris A. and Sarah (Kunin) Chaikin; B.A., Syracuse (N.Y.) U., 1947; M.S., Bank St. Coll. Edn., N.Y.C., 1972; M.S.W., Adelphi U., Garden City, N.Y., 1982; m. Reuben Thomas, May 29, 1949; children—Martin Jay, Gael, Eileen. Counselor psychol. services Ramapo Coll., Mahwah, N.J., 1973—. Cert. social worker N.Y.; lic. marriage counselor, N.Y. Mem. N.Am. Soc. Adlerian Psychology, Am. Assn. Counseling and Devel., N.J. State Soc. Clin. Social Workers, Nat. Assn. Advancement Psychoanalysis, Met. Coll. Mental Health Assn., Psi Chi. Author papers in field. Home: 47 Hidden Ledge Rd Englewood NJ 07631 Office: 505 Ramapo Valley Rd Mahwah NJ 07430

THOMAS, ANN LOUISE, personnel services administrator; b. West Green, Ga., Sept. 5, 1930; d. Alpheus Albert and Martha Josephine (Williams) Hazard; div.; children—Rodney, Michael, Karen. Student Wayne State U., 1948-50, Harlem Sch. Nursing, N.Y.C., 1951, Wayne County Community Coll., 1969, Henry Ford Community Coll., 1970. Nat. recruiting dir. Internat. Personnel, Detroit, 1962-69; EEO recruiting specialist Blue Cross/Blue Shield Mich., Detroit, 1969-72; assoc. dir. Detroit Indsl. Mission, 1972-76; personnel adminstr. Parke-Davis div. Warner & Lambert Co., Detroit, 1976-79; adminstr. Comprehensive Health Services Detroit, 1979—. Organizer, planner Focus Hope, Detroit, 1970, bd. dirs., 1970—; advisor-cons. Mich. Inter-Collegiate Black Bus. Students Assn., Detroit, 1970-74; co-founder, mem. Detroit Metro EEO Forum, 1973—; chair bd. dirs. Eastwood Clinics, Detroit, 1986—; active in civil rights movement, 1970's—. Named one of 10 Outstanding Detroit Women, Detroit News, 1972. Democrat. Avocations: travel; gourmet cooking; reading; stamp collecting; classical and jazz music. Home: 17334 Santa Rosa Dr Detroit MI 48221

THOMAS, ANNE CAVANAUGH, lawyer; b. Louisville, July 13, 1950; d. Harry Edward and Martha Mae (Marks) Cavanaugh; m. Andrew Dennis Thomas, Aug. 16, 1975; 1 dau. by previous marriage, Shelley Anne. B.A. with honors, Ind. U. Southeast, Jeffersonville, 1973; J.D., Ind. U., Bloomington, 1976. Bar: Ind. 1976. Staff counsel Teamsters Local 215, Evansville, Ind., 1976-81; pvt. practice, Evansville, 1981—; instr. U. Evansville, 1976-77; hearing mem. Indsl. Bd. Ind., 1984—. Bd. dirs. Big Bros./Big Sisters of Southwestern Ind., Inc., Evansville, 1977—, v.p., 1982-84; mediator City of Evansville and Fraternal Order Police, 1982. Mem. ABA, Ind. State Bar Assn. (mem. council young lawyers sect. 1981-84, author column Res Gestae 1983-84), Evansville Bar Assn. (co-chmn. young lawyers sect. 1983, dir. 1984-85, 86-87, chmn. Lawyers Assistance Program 1985—). Democrat. Office: 222 Court Bldg 123 NW 4th St Evansville IN 47708

THOMAS, BARBARA CECILIA, corporate course developer; b. Atlantic City, Sept. 9, 1952; d. David Henry and Anniebelle (Daniels) Miller; m. Ronald Edward Thomas, Aug. 31, 1974; 1 child, Ebony Danielle. B.A., Livingston Coll., 1973; Ed.M., Rutgers U., 1974; postgrad. Kean Coll. of N.J., 1975-78, Trenton State Coll., 1975-76. Cert. elem. and spl. edn. tchr., prin., N.J. Tchr. New Brunswick pub. schs., N.J., 1974-77; learning disabilities tchr., cons. Hillside pub. schs., N.J., 1977-79, Plainfield pub. schs., N.J., 1979-81; vice prin. Damon High Sch., Paterson, N.J., 1981-82; staff asst. AT&T, Piscataway, N.J., 1982-84, assoc. mgr., 1984—; editor, assoc. editor co. news mag., also feature writer co. news letter. Mem. Nat. Assn. Negro Bus. and Profl. Women's Clubs (pres. Union County Club 1985—), Nat. Assn. Univ. Women (pres. Plainfield-Brunswick br. 1985—), Nat. Soc. Performance and Instrn., Nat. Assn. Female Execs. Democrat. Baptist. Avocations: jogging; reading; writing; cooking. Home: 1451 W 4th St Piscataway NJ 08854 Office: AT&T 140 Centennial Ave Room 9B140 Piscataway NJ 08854

THOMAS, BARBARA MCCALL, federal probation officer; b. Montgomery, Ala., Aug. 4, 1939; d. Edward Cornelius and Bertha Lee (Robinson) McCall; m. Charles William Thomas, Apr. 10, 1969 (div. May 1970); 1 child, Michael Edward M. B.A., Spelman Coll., 1961; M.Ed., Ala. State U., 1972. Ordained to ministry African Meth. Episcopal Ch., 1985. Tchr. pub. schs., Dalton, Ga., 1961-62, Greensboro, Ga., 1963-64, Montgomery, Ala., 1964-66; social worker N.Y.C. Dept. Social Service, Bklyn., 1967-69; probation officer Montgomery County, Ala., 1973-74, U.S. Dist. Ct. (mid. dist.) Ala., Montgomery, 1974—; assoc. dir. Christian edn. Montgomery dist. African Meth. Episcopal Ch., 1986—. Mem. Human Rights Com. for Mentally Retarded, Tuscaloosa, Ala., 1976-79; pres. Crusaders Federated Club, Montgomery, 1980-84; bd. dirs. Family Guidance, Montgomery, 1976-79; v.p. bd. dirs. Brantwood Children's Home, Montgomery, 1978-80. Recipient Service award Brantwood Children's Home, 1980, Outstanding Community Service award Gov. Ala., 1984, Outstanding Community Service award Montgomery County Commrs., 1984. Mem. Fed. Probation Officers Assn. (Ezra Nash S.E. Regional award 1983), Ala. Council Crime and Delinquency, Ala. Fedn. Women and Youth Clubs, Nat. Fedn. Women and Youth Clubs, Delta Sigma Theta. Methodist. Home: 35 N Anton Dr Montgomery AL 36105 Office: US Probation 301 Lee St PO Box 39 Montgomery AL

THOMAS, BARBARA SINGER, merchant banker, former commissioner SEC, lawyer; b. N.Y.C., Dec. 28, 1946; d. Jules and Marcia Singer; B.A. cum laude, U. Pa., 1966; J.D. cum laude, N.Y. U., 1969; m. Allen L. Thomas, Mar. 12, 1978. Admitted to N.Y. bar, 1969, D.C. bar, 1981; asso. firm Paul Weiss Rifkind Wharton & Garrison, N.Y.C., 1969-73; asso. firm Kaye Scholer Fierman Hays & Handler, N.Y.C., 1973-77, partner, 1978-80; commr. SEC, Washington, 1980-83; pres. Samuel Montagu Holdings, Inc., 1983—; Asia-Pacific regional dir. Samuel Montagu & Co., Ltd., 1983—. Bd. overseers Wharton Sch. Fin., U. Pa.; trustee Inst. East-West Securities Studies, Youth for Understanding, Washington Opera; mem. secondary sch. com. U. Pa. John Norton Pomeroy scholar; recipient Am. Jurisprudence prizes, 1964-66. Mem. Internat. Bar Assn., Am. Bar Assn. (com. fed. regulation of securities, ad hock task force internat. aspects of U.S. law), N.Y. State Bar Assn. (securities regulation com.), Fin. Women's Assn. N.Y., Assn. Bar City N.Y. (chmn. corp. law com. 1969-80), Council Fgn. Relations, U. Pa. Alumni Assn. N.Y.C. (trustee), N.Y. U. Law Alumni Assn., N.Y. U. Law Rev. Alumni Assn., Order of Coif. Club: Economic (N.Y.C.). Contbr. articles to profl. jours. Home: 35 Sutton Pl New York NY 10022 Office: 535 Madison Ave New York NY 10022

THOMAS, BETH EILEEN WOOD (MRS. RAYMOND O. THOMAS), editor; b. North Vernon, Ind., May 12, 1916; d. Fayette J. and Emma J. (Ream) Wood; m. Raymond O. Thomas, Feb. 28, 1941; 1 son, Stephen W. Comml. diploma, Bedford High Sch., 1934; student, Lockyear Bus. Coll., 1936. Sec. WPA, Vincennes, Ind., 1935-36, Evansville, Ind., 1937-38, Indpls., 1939-41; sec. to adj. AAF Storage Depot, Indpls., 1941-44; sec. Coll. Life Ins., Indpls., 1957-58, Indpls. Sch. Bd., 1958-59; classified office mgr. North Side Topics Newspaper, Indpls., 1960-67. Editor: Child Life Mag. Indpls., 1967-71, Brownie Reader, 1971-73, Children's Playmate mag. Indpls., 1968—; editorial assoc. Saturday Evening Post, Indpls., 1971; exec. editorial dir.: Jack and Jill mag., 1971—, Young World mag. 1971-79, Child Life mag. 1971—, Design mag. 1977-80, Turtle Mag. for Presch. Kids, 1979—, Humpty Dumpty's mag. 1980—, Children's Digest, 1980—. Mem. Women in Communications, Indpls. Press Club. Club: Thetis. Home: 6172 Compton B Indianapolis IN 46220 Office: 1100 Waterway Blvd Indianapolis IN 46202

THOMAS, BETTY, actress; b. St. Louis. B.F.A., Ohio U. Former sch. tchr.; with Second City improvisational troupe, Chgo., comedy ensemble player Fun Factory; with TV series Hill Street Blues, 1981—; films for TV include Nashville Grab, 1981, When Your Lover Leaves, 1983. Emmy nominee for best supporting actress in a drama series. Office: Hill St Blues Set care MTM Enterprises 4024 Radford Ave Studio City CA 91604

THOMAS, CAROL MARIE, hotel executive; b. Cadillac, Mich., Apr. 8, 1940; d. Robert David and Lorane Rosena (Flory) Olson; m. Frank William Gloistein, June 25, 1960 (div. 1968); children—Michael William, Mark David; m. 2d, Sherman Michael Thomas, Oct. 6, 1973. Student Central Mich. U., 1958-59, Mt. Diablo Coll., Pleasant Hill, Calif., 1977-78. Catering mgr. Sheraton Inn, Concord, Calif., 1976-78, dir. sales, 1978-82; dir. sales Hilton Inn, Oxnard, Calif., 1982-83, gen. mgr., 1983—; lectr. Oxnard Coll. Hotel Sch., 1983-84. Bd. dirs. Oxnard Conv. and Visitor Bur., 1983—, chmn., 1986—; adv. bd. Oxnard Coll. Hotel and Restaurant Sch. Recipient Merit award U.S. Naval Mobile Constrn. Bn. Mem. No. Calif. Soc. Assn. Execs., Ventura County Profl. Women's Network, Hotel Sales Mktg. Assn., Delta Zeta. Republican. Home: 1234 Via Montoya Camarillo CA 93010 Office: Oxnard Hilton Inn 600 Esplanade Dr Oxnard CA 93030

THOMAS, CAROLYN ELISE, educator; b. Mt. Clemens, Mich., Mar. 8, 1943; d. Jack W. and Agnes E. (Anderson) T.; B.A., Western Mich. U.; M.S., U. Wash.; Ph.D., Ohio State U. Instr., U.Idaho, 1966-70; asst. prof. phys. edn. Denison U., Brockport State U., 1972-73; asst. prof. SUNY, Buffalo, 1973-76, asso. prof., 1976—, chmn. dept. phys. edn., 1976-83, chmn. dept. phys. therapy and exercise sci., 1983—. Mem. Philosophic Soc. for Study Sport, Nat. Assn. Sport and Phys. Edn., Soc. Health and Human Values, Nat. Assn. Phys. Edn. in Higher Edn. Author: Sport in a Philosophic Context, 1983; editor: Aesthetics and Dance, 1980. Office: 405 Kimball Tower SUNY Buffalo NY 14214

THOMAS, CATHY DAWNELLE, nurse; b. Baton Rouge, Apr. 17, 1960; d. George C. and Martha (Patterson) T. B.S. in Nursing, Southeastern La. U., 1982; M.N. in Nursing, La. State U., 1985. Cert. chemotherapist, Ala.; lic. R.N., La. Staff R.N. oncology Baton Rouge Gen. Med. Ctr., 1982, oncology charge nurse, 1982-83, team leader oncology, 1983-84, head nurse hematology-oncology, 1984—, developer out-patient chemotherapy and transfusion services, 1985—. East Baton Rouge Parish Med. Aux. scholar, 1981-82; La. State U. Med. Ctr. grantee, 1984. Mem. Oncology Nursing Soc. (presented papers nat. congress 1986), Internat. Soc. Nurses Cancer Care, Baton Rouge Oncology Nurses Soc. (pres.), New Orleans Oncology Nurses Assn. Republican. Baptist. Avocation: snow skiing. Home: 11011 Cal Rd 114 Baton Rouge LA 70809 Office: Baton Rouge Gen Med Ctr 3600 Florida Blvd Baton Rouge LA 70806

THOMAS, CHARLOTTE W(ILLIAMSON), accounting firm executive, consultant; b. Atlanta, June 15, 1941; d. James Otis and Katie Gold (Hobbs) Williamson; m. Jesse E. Thomas, Feb. 28, 1965; children—Angel Ann Thomas Fannin, Jesse Andre. Student Ga. State U., 1968, Edison Coll., 1983. Cost ascertainment ofcl. Post Office Dept., Atlanta, 1963-67; auditor IRS, Chamblee, Ga., 1968-78; pres. Cons. Acctg. Services, Ltd., Atlanta, 1979—, franchiser, 1983. Editor Acctg. Services, 1983; editor tax preparation tng. program, 1983; creator Five Dollars Research Program, 1983. Bd. dirs. SWAYBO, Atlanta, 1979. Mem. Nat. Assn. Accts., Nat. Assn. Female Execs., Nat. Inst. Accts. Democrat. Baptist. Club: Old Nat. Garden (College Park, Ga.). Home: 5570 Scofield Rd College Park GA 30349 Office: Cons Acctg Services Ltd 100 Galleria Pkwy Suite 400 Atlanta GA 30339

THOMAS, CHERYL YVETTE, nurse; b. Chgo., June 12, 1960; d. Varner Lee and Beverly JoAnn (Hall) T. B.S. in Nursing, Dillard U., 1983, cert. in chemotherapy adminstrn. U. Ala.-Birmingham; postgrad. La. State U., 1985—. Charge, staff nurse VA Med. Ctr., Birmingham, mem. recruitment and retention com., 1983-84; charge, staff nurse Ala., 1983-85, New Orleans, 1985—, mem. quality assurance com., 1985—. Campaign rep. Richard Arrington Campaign Com. for Mayor of Birmingham, 1983. Mem. Nat. Black Nurses Assn. (v.p. New Orleans chpt.), Alpha Kappa Alpha (v.p. 1981-82), Chi Eta Phi. Democrat. Home: 6881 Parc Brittany Blvd Apt A 204 New Orleans LA 70126

THOMAS, CLAUDIA LYNN, orthopaedic surgeon; b. N.Y.C., Feb. 28, 1950; d. Charles Mitchell and Daisy Mae T.; m. Maxwell Delaine Carty, Aug. 24, 1985. B.A., Vassar Coll., 1971; M.D., Johns Hopkins U., 1975. Diplomate Am. Bd. Orthopedic Surgery. Intern, Yale-New Haven Hosp., 1975-76, resident in surgery, 1976-77, resident in orthopaedic surgery, 1977-80; orthopaedic trauma fellow Md. Inst. Emergency Med. Services Systems, Balt., 1980; asst. prof. orthopaedic surgery Johns Hopkins Hosp., 1981-85, Balt. City Hosp., 1981-85; mem. staff Children's Hosp., Provident Hosp. (both Balt.). Mem. AMA, Eastern Orthopaedic Assn., Yale Orthopaedic Assn., Newington Alumni Assn., Nat. Med. Assn., Monumental Med. Assn. (v.p. 1983-85), Johns

Hopkins Minority Faculty Assn. (pres. 1983-85). Democrat. Author: (with A.A. White, M.M. Panjabi) Clinical Biomechanics of the Spine, 1978; (with P. Leppert, E. Siff, C. Thomas) Being a Woman: Your Body and Birth Control, 1979. First black female orthopedic surgeon; contbr. articles to profl. jours. Office: St Thomas Hosp Saint Thomas VI 00801

THOMAS, DOROTHY, indexing consultant; b. N.Y.C., Mar. 3, 1923; d. Hyman and Clara (Lond) Fisch; student Hunter Coll., 1940-43; cert. N.Y. U. Sch. Bus., 1944; m. Sidney Thomashower, Sept. 2, 1944; children—William Jay, James Evan. Personnel troubleshooter W.P.B., 1943; employment mgr. Emerson Radio & Phonograph Corp., 1943-47; editor, author, 1947—; indexer, cons., N.Y.C., 1960—; biographer, lectr., radio producer and moderator; specialist in history of women in legal profession; dir. spl. projects Found. Continuing Legal Edn.; dir. Documentation Abstracts Inc., lectr. colls., clubs, orgns. Active legis. reform and women's movement; mem. Nat. Women's Polit. Caucus, NOW. Mem. AFTRA, Am. Soc. Indexers (pres. elect 1982-83, pres. 1983-84, dir.), Coalition of Labor Union Women, Friends of Columbia Libraries, Friends of Schlesinger Library of Harvard U., N.Y. Hist. Soc. Ind. Democrat. Club: Women's City (N.Y.C.). Author: Women Lawyers in the U.S., 1957; Women, The Bench and The Bar, in preparation; contbr. articles and biographies to Notable American Women, 1607-1950, 1971, Law Book Indexing, 1983; author: Wigmore on Evidence, Vol. XI, 1985, also other indexes and tables. Home and Office: 123 W 74th St New York NY 10023

THOMAS, DOROTHY BRADFORD, educator; b. Huntsville, Tex., Feb. 18, 1947; d. Robert and Irene (Wynne) Bradford; m. Roy Jerry Thomas, July 6, 1974; children—Sean Trevor, Tamia Sherelle, Timothy Andre. B.S., Sam Houston State U., 1969; M.S., LaVerne Coll., Calif., 1976; Ed.D., U.S. Internat. U., 1985. Journalist, Huntsville Item, 1965-67; insp. Tex. Instruments, Dallas, 1967-68; elem. tchr. Santa Ana Unified Sch. Dist., Calif., 1969-80, counselor, 1984, intermediate tchr., 1980—; adult educator Santa Ana Coll., 1984. Leader Camp Fire, Inc., Santa Ana, 1982-83; mem. steering com. Youth Dept., Los Angeles, 1986; bd. dirs. Pride Devel. Council, Santa Ana, 1980—. Recipient cert. appreciation RCA, 1985; Santa Ana Unified Sch. Dist. classroom tchr. instructional improvement grantee, 1985, 85-86. Mem. Assn. Calif. Sch. Adminstrs., Nat. Assn. Female Execs., Santa Ana Educators Assn., Calif. Tchrs. Assn., Bus. and Profl. Women, Democrat. Baptist. Lodge: Zonta (v.p. 1986—). Avocations: computers; travel; baking; writing; photography. Home: 2521 W Rowland Ave Santa Ana CA 92704 Office: Santa Ana Unified Sch Dist 1405 French St Santa Ana CA 92704

THOMAS, DOROTHY LOUISE, textiles company executive; b. Union, S.C., July 23, 1949; d. Henry Oliver and Sarah Florence (Gibbs) T.; m. Donald Hemmings Duff, May 31, 1980. B.S. in Bus. Adminstrn., Washington U., St. Louis, 1979. File clk., Milliken & Co., Union, 1968-71, sec., 1971-73, sec., St. Louis, 1973-78, sales rep., 1978-82, sr. account exec., 1982—. Avocations: running; camping; hiking. Office: Milliken & Co 1750 S Brentwood Blvd Saint Louis MO 63144

THOMAS, DOROTHY NELL, home health care company administrator; b. Wiggins, Miss., Aug. 20, 1935; d. Chester and Alma (Smith) Rouse; m. Richard L. Thomas, Oct. 6, 1957; 1 dau., Deborah. Diploma, Mather Sch. Nursing, New Orleans, 1956; student William Carey Sch. Nursing, 1972-73, U. N.C. Sch. Pub. Health, 1974-75. Staff nurse So. Bap. Hosp., New Orleans, 1956-57, asst. head nurse, 1957; clin. dir. Mather Sch. Nursing, New Orleans, 1957-59; pub. health nurse New Orleans Health Dept., 1960-64, asst. supr., 1964-68; aide supr. Home Health Services La., Inc. (subs. Hillhaven Corp.), New Orleans, 1968-71, nursing supr., 1971-72, assoc. dir. patient care services, 1972-81, adminstr./dir. patient care services, 1981—; regional dir. Nat. Med. Home Care, New Orleans, 1983—; preceptor Community Health Nursing sect. Dept. Applied Health Scis., Tulane U. Sch. Pub. Health and Tropical Medicine, 1980-81. Mem. La. Assn. Home Health Agys. (dir. 1982-83, pres. 1981-82); Nat. League for Nursing, South La. League for Nursing (bd. dirs. 1979-82). Baptist. Home: 8401 Palm St New Orleans LA 70118 Office: Home Health Services of LA 2001 Canal St Suite 211 New Orleans LA 70112

THOMAS, ELLEN DILLON, advertising executive; b. Nashville, Oct. 29, 1958; d. William Wesley and Ellen Wallace (White) Dillon; m. James Anderson Thomas, June 20, 1981. B.S., Vanderbilt U., 1980; M.B.A., 1981. Mktg. dir. corr. banking div. U.S. Bank, Nashville, 1981-83; advt. dir. Jacques-Miller, Inc., Nashville, 1983—; sec., treas. Silver Lining, Inc., 1982—; mktg. cons. Second Harvest Food Bank Inc., 1985—. Mem. Am. Mktg. Assn. (treas. Nashville), Pi Beta Phi. Mem. Christian Ch. Avocations: gardening; skiing; travel. Home: 716 Cantrell Ave Nashville TN 37215 Office: Jacques Miller Inc 211 7th Ave N Nashville TN 37219

THOMAS, EMMA JOAHANNE, educator; b. Jacksonville, Fla., Feb. 8, 1944; d. Titus Leonard and Abbie (Benn) Moody; B.S., Tuskegee Inst., 1965; M.A., N.Mex. Highlands U., 1966; Ed.D., Wash. State U., 1976. Tchr., Radford High Sch., Honolulu, 1966-67; Shadle Park High Sch., Spokane, 1967-68; instr. Prairie View (Tex.) A. and M. U., 1968-70, asst. to dean, instr., 1970-73, head dept. English, 1976-78, v.p. academic affairs, 1978—. Mem. Nat. Assn. Women Deans, Counselors and Adminstrs., Nat. Council Tchrs. English, Tex. Assn. Coll. Tchrs., Wash. Assn. Adult Edn., AAUP, Zeta Phi Beta. Methodist. Home: PO Box 2109 Prairie View TX 77446

THOMAS, ETHEL COLVIN NICHOLS (MRS. LEWIS VICTOR THOMAS), educator; b. Cranston, R.I., Mar. 31, 1913; d. Charles Russell and Mabel Maria (Colvin) Nichols; Ph.B., Pembroke Coll. in Brown U., 1934; M.A., Brown U., 1938; Ed.D., Rutgers U., 1979; m. Lewis Victor Thomas, July 26, 1945 (dec. Oct. 1965); 1 child, Glenn Nichols. Tchr. English, Cranston High Sch., 1934-39; social dir. and adviser to freshmen, Fox Hall, Boston U., 1939-40; instr. to asst. prof. English Am. Coll. for Girls, Istanbul, Turkey, 1940-44; dean freshman, dir. admission Women's Coll. of Middlebury, Vt., 1944-45; tchr. English, Robert Coll., Istanbul, 1945-46; instr. English, Rider Coll., Trenton, N.J., 1950-51; tchr. English, Princeton (N.J.) High Sch., 1951-61, counselor, 1960-62, 72-83, coll. counselor, 1962-72. Mem. NEA, AAUW, Nat. Assn. Women Deans Adminstrs. and Counselors, Am. Assn. Counseling and Devel., Bus. and Profl. Women's Club (named Woman of Yr., Princeton chpt. 1977), Met. Mus. Art, Phi Delta Kappa, Kappa Delta Pi. Presbyn. Clubs: Brown University (N.Y.C.); Nassau. Home: 900 E Harrison Ave B-11 Pomona CA 91767

THOMAS, FLORENCE KATHLEEN, army officer; b. Torrington, Conn., June 20, 1945; d. James Dudley and Nova Lee (Campbell) T. B.A. in Mass Communications, U. Tex.-El Paso, 1970; M.A. in Adminstrn. of Justice, Wichita State U., 1984. Commd. 2d lt. U.S. Army, 1969, advanced through grades to lt. col., 1986; chief ops. tng. devels. U.S. Mil. Police Sch., Ft. McClellan, Ala., 1979-80; exec. officer criminal investigation div. Kaiserslautern, Germany, 1980-82; comdr. criminal investigation div. Nuernberg Field Office, Fed. Republic Germany, 1982-83; corrections officer Forces Command, Provost Marshal, Ft. McPherson, Ga., 1985; chief law enforcement mgmt. div., 1985—; mil. cons. law enforcement activities, 1977—. Mem. Assn. U.S. Army, Nat. Assn. Female Execs., U.S. Golf Assn., Am. Correctional Assn. Avocation: running; golf; fishing. Home: 9466 Cypress Ln Jonesboro GA 30236 Office: Forscom Provost Marshal Bldg 246 Fort McPherson GA 30330

THOMAS, GEORGIE A., state official; B.A. (Nat. Merit Scholar), Cornell U., 1965; M.B.A. in Fin., Columbia U., 1973. Asst. portfolio mgr. R. W. Pressprich & Co., Inc., N.Y.C., 1968-71; portfolio analyst pension and welfare fund dept. Bache & Co., N.Y.C., 1971-72; mgr. employee thrift fund portfolio, investment div. Exxon Corp., N.Y.C., after 1973, external mgrs. monitor pension fund, to 1975, fin. analyst, treas.'s dept., 1975, consolidation analyst, 1976; treas. Penntech Papers, Inc., N.Y.C., 1976-79; budget dir. Yankee Pub. Inc., Dublin, N.H., 1982-84; treas. State of N.H., Concord, 1984—; mem. econ. growth com. and productivity and tech. com. of bus. research adv. council Bur. Labor Stats., 1978-79; bd. govs., v.p.-research Ripon Soc. N.Y., 1978-79. Editor Jour. World Bus. Mem. Columbia Bus. Sch. Alumni Counseling bd., 1973-79; v.p. Cornell Club Fairfield County, Conn., 1974-76. Mem. Beta Gamma Sigma. Office: NH State House Annex Room 121 Concord NH 03301

THOMAS, GRACE FERN, physician, psychiatrist; b. Gothenburg, Nebr., Sept. 23, 1897; d. George William and Martha C. (Johnson) Thomas; B.S., U. Nebr., 1924; M.A., Creighton U., 1926; M.D., U. So. Calif., 1935; postgrad. U. Colo., 1942-43, Inst. of Living, 1943, U. So. Calif., 1946, UCLA, Angeles, 1947-50, Columbia U., 1953; M.A. in Religion, U. So. Calif., 1968. Instr. chemistry, biology Duchesne Coll., 1924-27; lab. technician various hosps., 1927-32; intern Los Angeles County Hosp., 1934-35; resident physician Riverside County Hosp., 1935-36; resident psychiatrist Los Angeles County Psychopathic Hosp., 1936-37; staff psychiatrist Calif. State Hosp. System, 1937-42, Glenside San., 1943-44; pvt. practice neuropsychiatry, Long Beach, Calif., 1946-51; chief mental hygiene clinic VA, Albuquerque, 1951-54; dir. psychiat. edn. Miss. State Hosp., Jackson, 1955; dir. Stark County Guidance Center, Canton, Ohio, 1956-58; dir. Huron County Guidance Center, Norwalk, Ohio, 1958-61, Arrowhead Mental Health Center, San Bernardino, Calif., 1962-64; dir. Mendocino County Mental Health Services, Ukiah, Calif., 1964-65; chief psychiat. edn. Porterville (Calif.) State Hosp., 1965-66; dir. Tuolumne County Mental Health Services, Sonora, Calif., 1966-70; psychiatrist-cons. Emanuel Hosp. Mental Health Center, Turlock, Calif., 1970-71; pvt. practice psychiatry, Turlock, 1970-73, Modesto, Calif., 1973—; cons. psychiatrist Stanislaus County Mental Health Dept., Modesto, 1972-73; alienist to Stanislaus County Superior Ct., Modesto, 1972—; psychiatrist-cons. Cath. Social Service Agency, 1974-78. Ordained to ministry United Meth. Ch., 1968. Served as capt. M.C., AUS, 1944-46. Diplomate Am. Bd. Psychiatry and Neurology. Fellow Am. Psychiat. Assn.; mem. AMA, Stanislaus Med. Soc., Central Calif. Psychiat. Assn., Inst. Religion and Health, Am. Med. Women's Assn. Am. Legion, AAUW, Soroptimists, Phi Delta Gamma, Phi Beta Kappa, Sigma Xi, Phi Kappa Phi, Nu Sigma Phi. Methodist. Home: 2001 LaJolla Ct Modesto CA 95350 Office: 1130 Coffee Rd Suite 8B Modesto CA 95355

THOMAS, JACQUELYN MAY, librarian; b. Mechanicsburg, Pa., Jan. 26, 1932; d. William John and Gladys Elizabeth (Warren) Harvey; m. David Edward Thomas, Aug. 28, 1954; children—Lesley J., Courtenay J., Hilary A. B.A. summa cum laude, Gettysburg Coll., 1954; student U. N.C., 1969; M.Ed., U. N.H., 1971. Librarian, Phillips Exeter Acad., Exeter, N.H., 1971-77, acad. librarian, 1977—; chair Com. to Enhance Status of Women, Exeter, 1981-84; dir. Loewenstein Com., Exeter, 1982—; pres. Cum Laude Soc., Exeter, 1984—. Editor, The Design of the Library: A Guide to Sources of Information, 1981. Trustee, treas. Exeter Day Sch., 1965-69; mem. bd. Exeter Hosp. Vols., 1954-59; mem. Exeter Hosp. Corp., 1978—; mem. bldg. com. Exeter Pub. Library, 1986—; chair No. New Eng., Council for Women in Ind. Schs., 1985—; Chmn. Lamont Poetry Program, Exeter, 1984—. N.H. Council for Humanities grantee, 1981-82; Nat. Endowment Humanities grantee, 1982. Mem. ALA, New Eng. Library Assn., N.H. Ednl. Media Assn., New Eng. Assn. Ind. Sch. Librarians, Am. Assn. Sch. Librarians (program com. for non-pub. sch. sect. 1985—), Phi Beta Kappa. Home: 16 Elm St Exeter NH 03833 Office: The Library Phillips Exeter Acad Exeter NH 03833

THOMAS, JANICE LINDA, communication executive; b. Brockton, Mass., Oct. 25, 1949; d. George Sidney and Jean Louise (Currier) McLean, Jr.; B.A. magna cum laude, Framingham State Coll., 1976; student Boston State Coll., 1967-68; children—Michelle, Kristin. Public info. officer Mass. Dept. Edn., Bur. Fire Tng., Sudbury, Mass., 1976-77, dir. info., 1977-78; public info. officer Internat. Soc. Fire Service Instrs., Hopkinton, Mass., 1976-79; asst. editor Internat. Assn. Fire Chiefs, Washington, 1979-80; mgr. Fire Edn. Resource Network, 1980-82, Fed. Emergency Mgmt. Agy., Office of Planning and Edn., U.S. Fire Adminstrn.; cons. Paradigm, Inc., Potomac, Md., 1981-82; cons. Energy, Mgmt. and Mktg. div. IMR Corp., Falls Church, Va., 1982-84; ind. cons. Thomas Communication Services, 1984—; lectr. in field. Precinct leader for local, congressional campaigns, 1970-74. Recipient Spl. award, 7th Annual Public Fire Educators Conf., 1981; Ark. Traveler award, 1982; Ill. Spark Plug award, 1982. Mem. NOW, Am. Mgmt. Assn., Internat. Assn. Bus. Communicators, Nat. Assn. Female Execs., Washington Women in Public Relations, Women in Communications. Unitarian Universalist. Contbr. articles to profl. jours. Office: 20667 Highland Hall Dr Gaithersburg MD 20879

THOMAS, JOYCE CAROL, author; b. Ponca City, Okla., May 25, 1938; children—Monica, Gregory, Michael, Roy. B.A., San Jose State U., 1966; M.A., Stanford U., 1967. Former asst. prof., later prof. San Jose State U.; vis. prof. English, Purdue U., 1984. Author: (poetry) Bittersweet, 1973, Black Child, 1981, Inside the Rainbow, 1982; (novels) Marked by Fire (Am. Book award), 1982, Bright Shadow, 1983, Water Girl, 1986, The Golden Pasture, 1986. Office; care Internat Creative Mgmt Inc 40 W 57th St New York NY 10019

THOMAS, JUDY DIANNE, lawyer; b. Blountsville, Ala., July 17, 1953; d. Richard M. and M.L. (Meade) T.; m. Thomas L. Davis, Mar. 11, 1978. B.S. in Math., U. Ala.-Birmingham, 1977; J.D., U. Ala.-Tuscaloosa, 1980. Bar: Ala. 1980. Sole practice law, Oneonta, Ala., 1981—. Vice pres. Ala. Young Democrats, 1983-84; pres. Blount County Young Democrats, 1981-83. Mem. ABA, Ala. State Bar, Blount County Bar Assn. (v.p. 1983-84), Assn. Trial Lawyers Am. Baptist. Home: Route 1 Box 214 Cleveland AL 35049 Office: PO Box 1056 1208 2nd Ave E Oneonta AL 35121

THOMAS, KATHLEEN ANNETTE, city official; b. Bronx, N.Y., Nov. 17, 1959; d. Cornelius Hudson and Anne Camille (Griffin) Walker. B.S., St. Augustine's Coll., Raleigh, N.C., 1981. Cashier, Kansas Fried Chicken, Bronx, 1979; sec.-chmn. phys. edn. St. Augustine's Coll., 1979-80, sec. acctg. dept., 1980, sec. chmn. bus., 1980-81; office assoc. N.Y.C. Dept. Parks and Recreation, Bronx, 1981—; shop stewardess dist. council 37 local 1549, N.Y.C., 1982—, sec.-treas. local chpt. 1549, 1984—. Editor: Recreation, 1982. Mem. V.I.P. Pub. Employees Organize to Promote Legis. Equality-Local 1549, N.Y.C., 1984—, com. mem. Employee Asst. Program, 1984—, Employee Recognition Program, 1984—, Worksite, 1984—; panelist United Negro Coll. Fund, Lou Rawls Parade of Stars. Mem. Quality of Worklife, Precious Pearls, Groose Phi Honey, Soc. Advancement Mgmt. Democrat. Baptist. Avocations: shorthand; typing; swimming; ice skating; writing. Home: 1515 Grand Concourse Apt 1C Bronx NY 10452 Office: NYC Dept Parks and Recreation 1 Bronx River Pkwy Bronx NY 10462

THOMAS, LEONA MARLENE, medical records educator; b. Rock Springs, Wyo., Jan. 15, 1933; d. Leonard H. and Opal (Wright) Francis; m. Craig L. Thomas, Feb. 22, 1955; (div. Sept. 1978); children—Peter, Paul, Patrick, Alexis. B.A., Govs. State U., 1982, also postgrad.; cert. med. records adminstrn. U. Colo., 1954. Dir. med. records dept. Meml. Hosp. Sweetwater County, Rock Springs, 1954-57; staff assoc. Am. Med. Records Assn., Chgo., 1972-77, asst. editor, 1979-81; instr. Chgo. State U., 1984—; statistician Westlake Hosp., Melrose Park, Ill., 1982-84. Co. pres. Ill. Dist. 60 PTA, Westmont, Ill., 1972. Mem. Am. Med. Records Assn., Ill. Med. Records Assn., Chgo. and Vicinity Med. Records Assn. Democrat. Methodist. Home: 6340 F Americana Dr Apt 1101 Clarendon Hills IL 60514 Office: Coll Allied Health Chicago State Univ 95th at King Dr Chicago IL 60608

THOMAS, LORENE E., director nursing services; b. Creek County, Okla., Jan. 5, 1928; d. Roy and Ozie Viola (Gaines) Washington; m. Aaron Stockstill, Mar. 2, 1948 (div. 1978); children—Ella M., Brenda D., Sarah, Roger A., Kenneth M., Kevin A., Cynthia L.; m. Jeremiah Thomas, July 7, 1979. A.S. in Life Sci., Imperial Valley Coll., 1977, A.S. in Nursing, 1978; B.A., St. Mary's Coll., 1982. Lic. vocat. nurse. Charge nurse, Pioneers Meml. Hosp., Brawley, Calif., 1976-78; staff nurse Sierra Health Care Convalescent Hosp., Davis, Calif., 1978-79, Woodland Skilled Nursing Facility, Calif., 1979-80, supr. nursing, asst. to dir. nursing services, 1980-82; dir. nursing services Valley Skilled Nursing Facility, Sacramento, 1982-84, Driftwood Convalescent Hosp., Yuba City, Calif., 1984—. Calif. State Bd. Nursing scholar, 1977; recipient awards including: Pioneers Meml. Hosp. Aux., 1976, 75; Soroptomist Internat. of the Ams., 1976; Dist. award, Los Angeles, 1975; Regional award, Los Angeles, 1975; Local Award, El Centro, Calif., 1975. Mem. Alpha Gamma Sigma. Democrat. Club: Ebonyte Civic and Social Women's (pres. 1968-69). Lodge: Order Eastern Star (matron chpt. 41 1968-70). Avocations: Sewing; travel; baseball. Office: Driftwood Convalescent Hosp 1220 Plumas St Yuba City CA 95991

THOMAS, LUCIA THEODOSIA, judge; b. Cheyenne, Wyo., Mar. 10, 1917; d. Benjamin Franklin Thomas and Dottie Mae (Sears) McKinney. B.A. magna cum laude, Xavier U., New Orleans, 1936; postgrad. U. Mich., 1936-38; LL.B., Robert Terrell Law Sch., 1940; LL.M., John Marshall Law Sch., Chgo., 1942, M.P.L., 1943, J.D., 1969. Bar: D.C. 1940, Ill. 1942, U.S. Supreme Ct. 1944. Assoc. Benjamin H. Crockett, Chgo., 1948-56; asst. state's atty. Cook County (Ill.), Chgo., 1957-61, 65-69; atty. legal dept. Juvenile Ct., Chgo., 1969-73; law clk. to justice Appellate Ct., Chgo., 1973-74; asst. corp. counsel City of Chgo., 1974-77; judge Marriage Ct., Circuit Ct. Cook County (Ill.), Chgo., 1977—; moot ct. judge Ill. Inst. Continuing Legal Edn., Chgo., 1983, Juvenile div. Ill. State Bar Assn., Chgo., 1983, Mem. NAACP Legal Def. Fund, Chgo., 1945-84; mem. Chgo. Urban League, 1970-86. Mem. Cook County Bar Assn. (Jud. award 1978), Nat. Bar Assn. (pres. award 1982, Ill. Jud. Council 1978-86), Women's Bar Assn. Ill., Chgo. Bar Assn. (Com. award 1975), Ill. State Bar Assn., ABA, Ill. Judge's Assn., World Assn. Judges, Fed. Bar Assn., Nat. Assn. Women Lawyers, Cath. Lawyers Guild, Nat. Assn. Women Judges. Lodge: Knights and Ladies of St. Peter Claver (Silver medal 1971, Gold medal 1984). Office: Room 1407 Circuit Ct Cook County Daley Center Chicago IL 60602

THOMAS, LUCILLE COLE, librarian; b. Dunn, N.C., Oct. 1, 1921; d. Collie and Minnie (Lee) Cole; m. George Browne Thomas, May 24, 1943; children—Ronald C., Beverly G. Effatt. B.A., Bennett Coll., 1941; M.A., N.Y.U., 1955; M.S., Columbia U., 1957. Tchr., Bibb County Bd. Edn., Macon, Ga., 1947-55; librarian Bklyn. Pub. Library, 1955-56; librarian N.Y.C. Bd. Edn., Bklyn., 1956-68, supr. libraries, 1968-77, dir. elem. sch. libraries, 1977-83; program dir. Weston Woods Inst., Weston, Conn., 1984-85; founder Sch. Library Media Day, N.Y. State, 1973; cons. Putnam Pub. Group, N.Y.C., 1983; dir. Am. Reading Council, N.Y.C., 1976—; mem. adv. bd. Regents' Adv. Council on Learning Tech., Albany, N.Y., 1982—; trustee N.Y. Met. Reference and Research Library Agy., N.Y.C., 1979-83. Editor: Insight, 1974. Contbr. articles to profl. publs. Treas., Bklyn. Home for Aged Commn., 1967—. Recipient Disting. Alumna award Bennett Coll., 1981; Edn. award Bus. and Profl. Women's Club, Bklyn., 1983; Merit award Bklyn. Council Suprs., 1983. Mem. ALA (councilor 1980—, exec. bd. 1985—), N.Y. Library Assn. (pres. 1977-78, Appreciation cert. 1983, pres. sch. library media sect. 1973-74, Outstanding Achievement award 1984), N.Y. Library Club (pres. 1977-78), N.Y.C. Sch. Librarians Assn. (pres. 1970-72), Bklyn. Hist. Soc. Democrat. Episcopalian. Club: Women's City (bd. dirs. 1986—) (N.Y.C.). Home: 1184 Union St Brooklyn NY 11225

THOMAS, LUCINDA ELLEN, psychologist; b. Ft. Collins, Colo., May 21, 1932; d. Glen Vincent Swearingen; B.S. in Psychology, Colo. State U., 1953, M.Ed. in Coll. Student Personnel Adminstrn., 1968; cert. Am. Inst. for Fgn. Trade, 1957; children—Nicholas Paul Thomas, Terence Philip. Tchr., Agana Jr. High Sch., Guam, Marianas Islands, 1953-54; dir. guidance services Am. Community Sch., Buenos Aires, Argentina, 1962-64; dir. testing center and staff psychologist Univ. Counseling Center, Colo. State U., Ft. Collins, 1968—; mem. Larimer County (Colo.) Mental Health Bd., 1979-84, pres., 1981, 82. Mem. City of Ft. Collins Personnel Bd., 1973-79, chmn., 1979. Mem. Am. Psychol. Assn., Rocky Mountain Psychol. Assn., Am. Coll. Personnel Assn., Nat. Vocat. Guidance Assn., Colo. Personnel and Guidance Assn., Colo. Coll. Personnel Assn., Assn. of Women Psychologists, Phi Delta Kappa. Contbr. articles in field to profl. jours. Home: 104 N Roosevelt St Fort Collins CO 80521 Office: Univ Testing Service C-81 Clark Bldg Colo State U Fort Collins CO 80523

THOMAS, MARGARET JEAN, clergywoman; b. Detroit, Dec. 24, 1943; d. Robert Elcana and Purcella Margaret (Hartness) Thomas. B.S., Mich. State U., 1964; M.Div., Union Theol. Sem. Va., 1971. Ordained to ministry, United Presbyn. Ch. U.S.A., 1971. Dir. research Bd. Christian Edn., Presbyn. Ch. U.S., Richmond, Va., 1965-71, Gen. Council, Atlanta, 1972-73; mng. dir. research div. Support Agy., United Presbyn. Ch., U.S.A., N.Y.C., 1974-76; dep. exec. dir. United Presbyn. Ch. U.S.A., N.Y.C., 1977-83, dir. N.Y. coordination, 1983-85; exec. dir. Minn. Council Chs., Mpls., 1985—; mem. permanent judicial commn. Presbyn. Ch., 1985—; mem. Com. on Ministry, Mpls., 1985—; dir. Joint Religious Legis. Coalition, Mpls., 1985—. Contbr. articles to profl. jours. and religious pubs. Bd. dirs. Minn. Foodshare, Mpls., 1985—; mem. Crime Victim/Witness Adv. Panel, Hennepin County Atty.'s Office, Mpls., 1985-86. Named Outstanding Woman of Minn., Minn. NOW, 1986. Mem. Nat. Assn. Ecumenical Staff, NOW, Religious Edn. Assn., People for The Am. Way, Amnesty Internat., ACLU. Democratic/Farm Labor. Avocation: archaeology. Office: Minn Council Churches 122 W Franklin Ave #230 Minneapolis MN 55404

THOMAS, MARGARET MISKELLY, educational administrator, writer; b. Chgo., Feb. 2, 1943; d. Robert Andrew and Margaret O. (Higgins) Miskelly; m. William Hoffman Thomas, Jan. 3, 1975; children—Katherine, Eric, Megan. B.A. in English, George Washington U., 1965; M.A., Mills Coll., 1967, postgrad. Loyola U., Chgo., 1963, U. Calif.-Berkeley, 1968-70. Registrar, Mills Coll., Oakland, Calif., 1972-79, mem. faculty English, 1972-75, asst. to dean faculty, 1978-79, exec. dir. Alumnae Assn., 1979—. Contbr. articles to profl. jours. DAR scholar, 1963-64; teaching fellow Mills Coll., 1965-67. Mem. Council for Advancement and Support of Edn., Alumnae Dirs. and Pres. (facilitator-coordinator 1984-85), AAUW. Democrat. Avocations: backpacking; travel; writing. Home: 6878 Colton Blvd Oakland CA 94611 Office: Alumnae Assn Mills Coll PO Box 9998 Oakland CA 94613

THOMAS, MARJORIE KINNEY, marketing executive; b. Gary, Ind., Jan. 11, 1940; d. David Harrison and Florence Clara Dunning; student El Camino Coll., 1957-58; L.H.D., West Coast U., 1982; m. Daniel Dean Kinney, Dec. 31, 1958 (div. 1973); children—Steven Daniel, Michael Alan, Gregory Lincoln, Bradford David; m. Bradley Morris Thomas, 1985. Partner, Kinney Advt., Inc., Inglewood, Calif., 1958-68; chmn. bd. Person to Person, Inc., Cleve., 1969-72; pres. Kinney Mktg. Corp., Encino, Calif., 1972-80; sr. v.p. Beverly Hills Savs. and Loan Assn., 1980-84; chmn., pres. Kinney Corp., 1985—; dir. Safeway Stores Inc., Chubb/Pacific Indemnity Co.; adv. bd. Marine Nat. Bank; lectr. profl. groups, univs. Bd. dirs. ARC, 1976-81, United Way, 1979-81; trustee West Coast U., 1981-86; adv. bd. U.S. Human Resources. Republican. Presbyterian. Office: Kinney Corporation 340 E Berger St PO Box 4098 Santa Fe NM 87502-4098

THOMAS, MARJORIE OLIVIENE, health care administrator; b. Spaldings, Jamaica, Sept. 5; came to U.S., 1971; d. Cedrick Milo and Avis Clair (Morgan) West; m. Carol Oswald Thomas, Sept. 10, 1977; children—Chandra, Brian. A.A., Kendall Coll., 1973; B.S., U. Ill.-Chgo., 1975; M.P.A., Roosevelt U., 1977. Asst. to dir. utilization rev. Bellevue Hosp., N.Y.C., 1977-81, risk mgr., 1981-83, assoc. dir./dir. quality assurance, 1983-85; risk mgr. Adminstrs. for the Professions, Inc., Manhasset, N.Y., 1985—. Mem. Am. Soc. Hosp. Risk Mgmt., Assn. Hosp. Risk Mgmt. N.Y., Nat. Assn. Female Execs. Mem. Christ Temple. Avocations: cooking; reading; writing.

THOMAS, MARTHA ANN, program analyst; b. Meridian, Miss., Apr. 26, 1945; d. Sandy and Duffie D. (Cannon) Thomas. B.A. in Pub. Mgmt., U. D.C., 1983, M.A. in Pub. Adminstrn., 1984. Flexiwriter operator HHS, Washington, 1964-67, clk.-typist, 1967-68, sec., 1968-71, sec.-stenographer, 1971-81, mgmt. asst., 1981-84; program analyst Dept. Treasury, Washington, 1984—. Recipient letters of commendation, CPT Corp., Rosslyn, Va., 1983, HHS, Washington, 1983. Democrat. Baptist. Club: The Natural Women, Ltd. (Washington) (sec. 1975—). Avocations: travel; writing; dancing; theatre; school; social activities. Home: 1234 Massachusetts Ave NW Apt 515 Washington DC 20005

THOMAS, MARTHA WETTERHALL, advertising agency executive; b. Ann Arbor, Mich., Aug. 23, 1949; d. Roy Christner and Doreen (Armstrong) Wetterhall; m. James William Thomas, May 22, 1982. B.A. cum laude, U. Mich., 1971. Copywriter, McCaffrey & McCall, N.Y.C., 1972-76, Cunningham & Walsh, N.Y.C., 1976-78; sr. copywriter Grey/2 Advt., N.Y.C., 1978-79, Symon, Thomas & Hilliard, N.Y.C., 1979-82; exec. v.p., creative dir. Thomas & Thomas Advt., N.Y.C., 1983—; writer, producer first paid TV advt. campaign for nonprofit instn., 1985. Mem. Advt. Women of N.Y., Am. Women's Econ. Devel. Corp., Ad.Net. Office: 61 E 77th St New York NY 10021

THOMAS, MARY BARTON, marriage and family counselor; b. Sherman, Tex., Nov. 4, 1954; B.S. in Social Sci. and Elem. Edn., Southeastern Okla. State U., 1976; M.Ed. in Ednl. Diagnosis and Psychology, Abilene Christian U., 1979; m. William M. Thomas, 1978. Lic. profl. counselor, Tex.; basic, intermediate, advance and instrs. certs. Tex. Commn. on Law Enforcement Officer Standards and Edn. Tchr. Durant (Okla.) Middle Sch., 1976; substitute tchr. Sunset Elem. Sch., Healdton, Okla., 1976; asst. ednl. diagnostician spl. edn. dept. Abilene Ind. Sch. Dist., 1978; police officer Dallas Police Dept., 1979—, staff counselor, investigator, 1981—. Recipient Life Saving award Dallas Police Dept., 1983, Safe Driving award, 1985. Delta Kappa Epsilon scholar, 1973; Red River Valley Hist. scholar, 1975-76. Mem. Internat. Law Enforcement Stress Assn., Dallas Psychol. Assn., Am. Assn. Counseling and Devel., Tex. Mcpl. Police Assn., Dallas Police Assn., Nat. Assn. Female Execs., Dallas Mus. Art., Historic Preservation League of Dallas, Nat. Trust Historic Preservation, Dallas County Heritage Soc., Tex. Hist. Found., Smithsonian Inst. Nat. Assn., Friends of Kennedy Ctr., Young Republican Nat. Fedn.,

Dallas County Rep. Assembly, Nat. Rep. Senatorial Com., Nat. Rep. Congl. Com., Kappa Delta Pi, Phi Alpha Theta. Home: 16208 Fallkirk Dr Dallas TX 75248 Office: 8700 Stemmons Freeway Suite 352 Dallas TX 75247

THOMAS, MARY LEE, social agency administrator; b. Eutan, Ala., Mar. 23, 1918; d. Junious and Alice (Meriweather) Anderson; m. Issac D. Thomas, Nov. 29, 1935 (dec.); children—Issac D., William E., Mary Anderson, Woody R. B.S. in Spl. Edn., Eastern Mich. U., 1965. With Children's Ctr. for Social Change, Inkster, Mich., 1977-84; dir. Better Living Ctr., Detroit, 1984—. Office: Better Living Ctr 3240 Puritan Detroit MI 48238

THOMAS, MARY LYNN, nurse; b. Monongahela, Pa., Jan. 19, 1948; d. Clarence A. and Sally Ann (Hannan) Sterner; L.P.N., Indian River Jr. Coll., Ft. Pierce, Fla., 1971; A.S. in Nursing Sci., Indian River Community Coll., 1975; m. Ronald Allen Thomas, Dec. 16, 1965; 1 son, Ronald Allen. Mem. staff hosps. in Fla., 1971-73; nurse Indian River Community Mental Health Center, 1977-81; mem. part-time staff Easter Manor Nursing Home, Ft. Pierce, 1976-81; dir. nursing services Hardee Manor Nursing Home, Wauchula, Fla., 1981-84; relief supr. Hardee Meml. Hosp., 1984-85, 86—; dir. nursing Lakeland Convalescent Ctr., 1985. Mem. Fla. Nurses Assn. Democrat. Baptist. Home: 345 Willow Ave Bowling Green FL 33834 Office: Carlton St Wauchula FL 33873

THOMAS, MARYELLEN, public relations executive; b. Chgo., Mar. 31, 1943; d. Thomas Ward and Lillian (Henton) Ward/Vesely; m. Kenneth Thomas, Apr. 20, 1963; children—Maria, Crystal. Diploma in nursing Ill. Research Coll., 1959; B.A., Columbia Coll., Chgo., 1962. Nurse, Chgo. Bd. Health, 1965-69; copywriter N.W. Ayer, Chgo., 1969-70; with pub. affairs dept. Blue Cross/Blue Shield, Chgo., 1970-75; pub. relations rep. Proctor and Gardner Co., Chgo., 1975—. Chmn. com. Pvt. Industry Council, Chgo. Mem. Publicity Club of Chgo., Women in Communications, League of Black Women (asst. to pres. 1979-81). Democrat. Roman Catholic. Office: Proctor and Gardner Advt Agy 111 E Wacker Dr Chicago IL 60601

THOMAS, MELANIE ANN, writer; b. Santa Monica, Calif., Sept. 11, 1957; d. Erving Robert and Vertis Lee (Sample) T. B.S., U. Bridgeport, 1979. Utility clk. Bank of Am., Santa Monica, Calif., 1979-82; tchr. English, Los Angeles Unified Sch., 1982-83; instr. computers Tex. Instruments, San Diego, 1982-83; adminstrv. exec. Mobile Telephone Am., Los Angeles, 1983-84. Author: During the Day I See, 1983; New England, 1983; Waiting for December, 1984. Mem. Los Angeles Police Dept. Aux., 1984; mem. Burbage Theatre Ensemble, 1984. Mem. Nat. Assn. Female Execs., Nat. Soc. Pub. Accts., Nat. Writers Club. Democrat.

THOMAS, MILDRED REINWALD (MRS. LLEWYN U. THOMAS), retired educator; b. Galeton, Pa., Apr. 11, 1912; d. Walter J. and Nora (Woodhouse) Reinwald; B.S., Mansfield State Tchrs. Coll., 1933; M.S., Syracuse U., 1954; postgrad. Alfred U., 1947-48, Buffalo State U., 1947; m. Llewyn U. Thomas, June 3, 1936; 1 son, Llewyn Walter. Tchr., Potter County Schs. (Pa.), 1933-42, N.Y. State Pub. Schs., 1942-63; asst. prof. and primary edn. supr. SUNY-Cortland, 1963-74, emeritus, 1974—. Leader Girl Scouts, 1942-63; active YWCA; mem. Animal Welfare League Charlotte County; pres. Cortland County Women's Republican Club, 1969, 70; mem. exec. com. N.Y. State Fedn. Rep. Women; del.-at-large Nat. Fedn. Rep. Women Conv., 1971; sec. Charlotte County Rep. Club, 1980-81; pres. Federated Rep. Women's Club, 1982; Rep. precinct committeewoman, 1984—; mem. Spl. Persons Advocacy League Charlotte County; deacon, ordained elder Presbyterian Ch.; mem. exec. com. Susquehanna Valley Presbyterial, 1975-77; ch. sch. supt. First Presbyn. Ch. of Port Charlotte, 1980-81, now mem. bd. elders. Mem. DAR (past regent Tioughnioga chpt.), NEA, Assn. Higher Edn., Internat. Reading Assn., Retarded Children's Assn. Cortland County, Cortland County Hist. Soc., AAUW (pres.; chmn. resolutions com. state div. bd.), Yates-Ontawa Tchrs. Assn. (pres. 1961), LWV. Lodge: Order Eastern Star. Home: 338 Lasayette Dr Port Charlotte FL 33952

THOMAS, MITZY CASSANDRA, systems software engineer; b. Tupelo, Miss., Aug. 9, 1962; d. Jo Ann Thomas. B.S. in Computer Sci., Jackson State U., 1984. Apprentice database mgr. Lawrence Berkeley Lab., Calif., 1981-82; graphics programmer Nat. Ctr. Atmospheric Research, Boulder, Colo., 1982-83; systems software engr. Bell No. Research, Richardson, Tex., 1984—. Author: Graphical Overlays on Two Dimensional Grids, 1983. Mem. NAACP, Nat. Assn. Female Execs., Phi Gamma Nu. Democrat. Baptist. Club: Jackson State U. Karate (sec. 1982-84) (Miss.). Avocations: basketball; softball; martial arts; reading; music; dancing; sketching. Home: 4905 Oak Bluff Mesquite TX 75150

THOMAS, NANCY NOBLE, former councilwoman; b. Pitts., Aug. 18, 1928; d. Albert Garfield and Neva (Loomis) Noble; student Md. Coll. for Women, 1946-47, Curry Coll., 1947-48; m. Donald Bartlett Thomas, June 11, 1949; children—Douglas, Cynthia, Cathryn, Gregory. Mem. Town Bd. of Webster (N.Y.), 1976-83, dep. town supr.; cons. Rochester Women's Career Devel. Center. Bd. dirs. Webster Community Chest, 1979-88; town co-chmn. ARC Blood Drive, 1978-80; chmn. Bicentennial Ball, 1976; parade chmn. Independence Day, 1978-80; memls. chmn. Ch. of the Good Shepherd, 1978-86; Monroe County committeewoman, 1975-86; 4th v.p. N.Y. State Fedn. Women's Clubs, 1986—. Mem. Webster Mus. and Hist. Soc. (bd. dirs. 1984-86), Webster C. of C. (chmn. planning 1978-80, Webster Woman of Yr. 1986). Republican. Episcopalian. Clubs: Webster Bus. and Profl. Women, Guardians, Women's of Webster (founding mem.). Home: 402 Bittersweet Ln Webster NY 14580

THOMAS, PAMELA RAE, marketing consultant, freelance journalist-copywriter; b. La Crosse, Wis., July 30, 1955; d. Dale Richard and Betty Jean (Clark) T. B.A. in Journalism, Marquette U., 1977. Copywriter J. Gillette & Assocs., La Crosse, 1978-79; dir. publs. Century Telephone Co., Monroe, La., 1980-82; pres. Visual Concepts, Ltd., La Crosse, 1982-85, TCF Publs., Inc., La Crosse, 1982-84; mktg. cons. Thomas & Assocs. Mktg., La Crosse, 1985—; freelance journalist-copywriter, 1985—; advt. cons. Republican Party, La Crosse, 1982—. Author: From My Pallet of Winter Let Me Paint You Spring, 1978. Editor: Bridal Guide, 1984. Mem. Com. on Aging, La Crosse, 1985. Recipient 1st place award, mag. advt. Ad Club, La Crosse, 1984, 3d place award, mag. advt., Ad Club, La Crosse, 1984. Mem. Pub. Relations Soc. Am., C. of C., Ad Club, Sigma Delta Chi. Republican. Lutheran. Lodge: Eagles. Avocations: writing; skiing; music. Home: 426 S 9th St La Crosse WI 54601 Office: Bridal Guide Ltd PO Box 2091 La Crosse WI 54601

THOMAS, PATRICIA ANNE, law librarian; b. Cleve., Aug. 21, 1927; d. Richard Joseph and Marietta Bernadette (Teevans) T.; B.A., Case Western Res. U., 1949, J.D., 1951. Admitted to Ohio bar, 1951, U.S. Supreme Ct. bar, 1980; librarian Arter & Hadden, Cleve., 1951-62; asst. librarian, then librarian IRS, Washington, 1962-78; library dir. Adminstrv. Office, U.S. Cts., 1978—. Mem. Am. Assn. Law Libraries, Law Librarians Soc. D.C. (pres. 1967-69). Office: Adminstrv Office US Cts Washington DC 20544

THOMAS, PATRICIA GRAFTON (MRS. LEWIS EDWARD THOMAS), educator; b. Michigan City, Ind., Sept. 30, 1921; d. Robert Wadsworth and Elinda (Oppermann) Grafton; student Stephens Coll., 1936-39, Purdue U., summer 1938; B.Ed. magna cum laude, U. Toledo, 1966; postgrad. (fellow) Bowling Green U., 1968; m. Lewis Edward Thomas, Dec. 21, 1939; children—Linda L. (Mrs. John R. Collins), Stephanie A. (Mrs. Andrew M. Pawuk), I. Kathryn (Mrs. James N. Ramsey), Deborah (Mrs. James E. Masker). Tchr., Toledo Bd. Edn., 1959—, tchr. lang. arts Byrnedale Sch., 1976-81. Exhibited in group shows Spectrum, Toledo Artists Club, Flower Hosp. Dist. capt. Planned Parenthood, 1952-53, ARC, 1954-55; mem. lang. arts curriculum com. Toledo Bd. Edn., 1969, mem. grammar curriculum com., 1974; bd. dirs. Anthony Wayne Nursery Sch., 1981—; sec., bd. dirs. Toledo Women's Symphony League, 1982—. Mem. Toledo Soc. Profl. Engrs. Aux., Helen Kreps Guild, AAUW, Spectrum, Friends of Arts, Phi Kappa Phi, Phi Delta Kappa, Kappa Delta Pi, Pi Lambda Theta (chpt. pres. 1978—), Delta Kappa Gamma (chpt. pres. 1976-78, area membership chmn. 1978-82). Republican. Episcopalian. Club: Toledo Artists. Home: 4148 Deepwood Lane Toledo OH 43614 Office: 3645 Glendale St Toledo OH 43614

THOMAS, PEARLIE M., school principal; b. Paige, Tex., Jan. 14, 1935; d. Early and Ophelia (Ridge) Brown; m. Willie R. Thomas, Jan. 15, 1955; 1 child, Willie R., II. B.S., Prairie View Coll., 1956; M.Ed., Va. State U., 1974. Cert. tchr., adminstr., Va. Tchr. Verdun Mil. Sch., France, 1958-60, Verdun Am. Sch., 1960-61, Grand St. Sch., Newburgh, N.Y., 1963-68, Woodlawn Elem. Sch., Hopewell, Va., 1968-74; prin. Arlington Elem. Sch., Hopewell, 1974—; craft tchr. and dir. Recreation Ctr., Manhattan, Kans., 1956-58; chmn. bd. dirs. Tabernacle Day Care Ctr., Petersburg, Va., 1984—. Named Most Outstanding Women Petersburg's Girl Scouts U.S.A., 1984-85. Mem. Va. Assn. Elem. Sch. Prins. (area rep. 1980-84), Nat. Assn. Elem. Sch. Prins., Kappa Delta Pi, Zeta Phi Beta (chmn. voter registration 1984, Haitian project 1983, 1st anti basilus Alpha Omega chpt. 1985). Democrat. Baptist. Clubs: Las Amigas (pres. 1981-83) (Petersburg/Hopewell); Adult Fellowship (pres. 1980-82) (Petersburg). Avocations: cross-stitching; bowling. Home: 3317 Dupuy Rd Ettrick VA 23803

THOMAS, RUBY BELL, educator; b. Van Buren, Ark., Sept. 2, 1916; d. Oscar Isaac and Ollie Pearl (Flanagan) Gulley; m. Foster Oliver Thomas, July 3, 1943; children—Candetta Kay, Catrena Renee. Student Okla. State U., 1969. Tchr. Ark. Bd. Edn., Van Buren, 1936-41; electric engr. Lockheed Aircraft, Maywood, Calif., 1942-44; owner Lady Kay Beauty Salon, Tulsa, 1951-78; sales and info. specialist Airport Ins., Tulsa, 1979-82; ins. agt., Tulsa, 1983-85; owner Lady Kay Beauty Salon, 1985—. Club: Sweet Adelines. Lodge: Eastern Star. Avocations: fishing; boating; hiking; singing; sewing. Home: 6131 E Admiral Pl Tulsa OK 74115

THOMAS, SHARON MAUREEN, geography educator; b. Steubenville, Ohio, Apr. 3, 1945; d. Lincoln George and Lillian Marcella (Virden) T. A.A., Phoenix Coll., 1966; B.A., Ariz. State U., 1968, M.A., 1975, Ph.D., 1980. Teaching asst. dept. geography Ariz. State U., Tempe, from 1971, teaching assoc., grad. research asst., to 1978; environ. planner Dalton Dalton Newport, Shaker Heights, Ohio, 1979-80; asst. prof. geography Central Mich. U., Mt. Pleasant, 1981-84, 85—; asst. prof. geography U. Central Ark., Conway, 1984-85. Assn. Am. Geographers premier display grantee, 1982, 83, research grantee, 1983. Mem. Assn. Am. Geographers, Mich. acad. Sci., Arts and Letters. Office: Dept Geography Central Mich U Mount Pleasant MI 48859*

THOMAS, SHIRLEY CAROLE, government official; b. Mobile, Ala., Dec. 22, 1943; d. John Mark and Leona Margaret (Carleton) Shaw; m. Dewey Thomas, Aug. 20, 1964; children—Pamela Renee, John Derek. A.A., Ala. State U., 1964. File clk. Naval Tng. Ctr., San Diego, 1966-67; supply asst. Naval Ordnance, San Diego, 1969-72; social ins. rep. Social Security Adminstrn., San Diego, 1977-81; mgr. Social Security Hearings and Appeals, San Diego, 1981-82; adminstrv. officer U.S. Dept. HUD, San Diego, 1984—; career counselor Vol. Basis, San Diego, 1980—. Recipient Superior Achievement award Social Security Adminstrn., 1979. Democrat. Baptist. Avocations: sewing; crafts. Home: 7010 Jackson Dr San Diego CA 92119 Office: US Dept HUD 880 Front St San Diego CA 92188

THOMAS, SUSAN JANE, marketing executive; b. Omaha, Sept. 20, 1953; d. Earl Wayne and Helen Marie (Muller) T.; m. Robert Spalding Winborne, May 19, 1984. A.B., Vassar Coll., 1975; M.B.A., Harvard U., 1980; student Macalester Coll., 1971-73. Asst. treas. Morgan Guaranty Trust Co., N.Y.C., 1975-78; cons. The Boston Cons. Group, 1979; asso. Booz, Allen & Hamilton, Inc., N.Y.C., 1980-82; mktg. mgr. Merrill, Lynch Pierce Fenner & Smith, N.Y.C., 1982-85; v.p. mktg. Merrill Lynch Capital Markets, N.Y.C., 1985—. N.Y.C. div. head Macalester Coll. Campaign for the 1980's, 1981-82, mem. president's alumni adv. council, 1984—. Mem. Fin. Women's Assn. N.Y., Women's Econ. Roundtable, Nat. Abortion Rights Action League, NOW. Democrat. Clubs: Harvard of N.Y., Harvard Bus. Sch. N.Y., Vassar of N.Y., Macalester of N.Y. (pres. 1984—); Macalester of N.J. and Conn. Home: 438 W 23d St New York NY 10011 Office: 165 Broadway New York NY 10080

THOMAS, SUZANNE LOUISE, nurse; b. Des Moines, Sept. 23, 1956; d. Harold Raymond Thomas and Patricia Ann Belding. B.S.N., Grand View Coll., 1980. R.N., Tex. Staff nurse Broadlawns Med. Ctr., Des Moines, 1980-81, Dallas County Mental Health/Mental Retardation Ctr., Dallas, 1981—. Mem. Am. Nurses Assn., Tex. Nurses Assn. Republican. Evangelical. Club: Fellowship Bible Ch. of Park Cities. Office: Dallas County Mental Health/Mental Retardation 329 Centre St Dallas TX 75208

THOMAS, TERESA ANN, biologist, educator; b. Wilkes-Barre, Pa., Oct. 17, 1939; d. Sam Charles and Edna Grace Thomas; B.S. cum laude, Coll. Misericordia, 1961; M.S. in Biology, Am. U. Beirut, 1965; M.S. in Microbiology, U. So. Calif., 1973. Tchr., sci. supr., curriculum coordinator Meyers High Sch., Wilkes-Barre, 1962-64, Wilkes-Barre Area Public Schs., 1961-66; research asso. Proctor Found. for Research in Ophthalmology U. Calif. Med. Center, San Francisco, 1966-68; instr. Robert Coll. of Istanbul (Turkey), 1968-71, Am. Edn. in Luxembourg, 1971-72, Bosco Tech. Inst., Rosemead, Calif., 1973-74, San Diego Community Coll. Dist., 1974-80; instr. math.-sci. div. Southwestern Coll., Chula Vista, Calif., 1980—; adj. asst. prof. Chapman Coll., San Diego, 1974-83; asst. prof. San Diego State U., 1977-79; chmn. Am. Colls. Istanbul Sci. Week, 1969-71; mem. adv. bd. Chapman Coll. Community Center, 1979-80. Pres. Internat. Relations Club 1959-61; mem. San Francisco World Affairs Council, 1966-68; mem. exec. bd. U.S. Orgn. Med. and Ednl. Needs No. Calif., 1967-68; v.p. Palomar Palace Estates Homeowners Assn., 1983-84. NSF fellow, 1965; USPHS fellow, 1972-73; Pa. Heart Assn. research grantee, 1962. Mem. Am. Soc. Microbiology, Nat. Sci. Tchrs. Assn., Nat. Assn. Biology Tchrs. San Diego Natural History Mus., S.D. Zool. Soc., Calif. Tchrs. Assn., NEA, Soc. Coll. Sci. Tchrs., MENSA, Arab Am. Med. Assn., Am.-Lebanese Assn. San Diego (chmn. scholarship com.), Defenders of Wildlife, Kappa Gamma Pi, Sigma Phi Sigma. Club: Am. Lebanese Syrian Ladies (pres. 1982-84). Office: Southwestern College 900 Otay Lakes Rd Chula Vista CA 92010

THOMAS, VERONICA MCCULLION, furniture company executive; b. Darby, Pa., Nov. 18, 1956; d. Thomas Aquinas and Anna Marie (Green) McCullion; m. Kevin Joseph Thomas, June 7, 1984. A.A., Atlantic Community Coll., 1979; B.A., Upsala Coll., 1981. With pub. relations dept. Metro Rehab. Inc., Bethesda, Md., 1981-82; sales cons. Englewood Furnishings, Englewood, Fla., 1982; sales mgr. Diet Ctr., Bradenton, Fla., 1982; sales mgr. Jansen Furniture, Naples, Fla., 1982—; interior accessory designer Trans Designs, Atlanta, 1986. Author basic sales manual, 1983. Named Salesperson of Yr. Jansen Furniture, 1984, 85. Mem. AAUW, Nat. Assn. Female Execs., Upsala Coll. Alumni Assn. Avocations: home decorating; travel; antique collecting; scuba diving. Office: Ed Jansen Furniture 3030 V Horseshoe Dr Naples FL 33942

THOMAS, VICKI ANN, communications co. exec.; b. Chgo., Jan. 7, 1946; d. Charles K. and Lillian T. (Chuckwins) Pazar; B.S., U. Wis., Stevens Point, 1968; m. Stephen J. Thomas, Sept. 19, 1970. Feature editor Credit Union Nat. Assn., Madison, Wis., 1971-75, dir. advt., 1975-77, v.p. mktg. and advt., 1971-80; account exec. ABC, Chgo., 1980—; tchr. Madison Area Tech. Sch., 1979-80. Mem. Profl. Communicators Wis. (v.p. 1979-80). Republican. Roman Catholic. Club: Chgo. Ad. Author: How to Make Advertising Work for Your Financial Institution, 1977. Office: ABC 233 N Michigan Ave Suite 1923 Chicago IL 60601

THOMAS, VIRGINIA LEE, microscopist; b. Traer, Iowa, Sept. 22, 1916; d. Paul and Zenaide Vonhesion (Kahler) T.; grad. Gates Coll., 1939, U. Mich., 1943. Spectrographer Rock Island (Ill.) Arsenal, 1943-45; electron microscopist U.S. Rubber Research Labs., Passaic, N.J., 1945-54; group leader Interchem. Research Labs., N.Y.C., 1954-62; research scientist Am. Standard Research Lab., Piscataway, N.J., 1962-68; lectr., supr. microscopy U. Medicine and Dentistry, Rutgers U. Med. Sch., Piscataway, 1968-84. Active Westfield Human Rights, Plainfield Joint Def., Rainbow Food Coop, ACLU. Fellow N.Y. Microscopical Soc. (pres. 1960-61, Ashby award 1962); mem. Electron Microscopical Soc. Am., N.Y. Soc. Electron Microscopists. Clubs: Sierra, Porsche Club Am., Nat. Wildlife Assn., Nature Conservancy. Contbr. chpts. to books in field, articles to profl. jours. Home: 2369 Whittier Ave Westfield NJ 07090

THOMAS, VIRGINIA M ROBINSON, contract administrator; b. Lumberton, N.C., Sept. 13, 1950; d. James Edward and Cora Lee (Hunt) Robinson; m. Joseph Terry Thomas, Sept. 27, 1969; 1 child, Joey. B.A. in Psychology-Sociology, Bellevue Coll., Nebr., 1980, B.A. in Bus. Adminstrn., 1981. Info. specialist U.S. Air Force, 1968-70; sales staff Sears, Charleston, S.C., 1971-72; mgr. Charles Furniture Co., Okinawa City, Japan, 1975-76; buyer City of Greenville, Tex., 1982-85; contract adminstr. Def. Logistics Agy., Greenville, Tex., 1985—. Served with USAF, 1968-70. Mem. Nat. Assn. Female Execs., Greenville Bus. and Profl. Women (chmn. young careerist 1984-85), Alpha Kappa Psi. Republican. Roman Catholic. Avocations: golfing; reading.

THOMAS, WILMA JEAN, city official; b. Dill City, Okla., Aug. 25, 1931; d. Joel Peter and Grace Ethel (Williams) Clark; m. James Logan Thomas, Aug. 27, 1954; children—Philip Arlen, David Alan. B.S. in Edn., Southeastern Okla. State U., 1953. Registered profl. mcpl. clerk, Tex. Sec. Okla. Edn. Assn., Oklahoma City, 1953-54, Dept. Air Force, Enid, Okla., 1954-55; sec. City of Wichita Falls, Tex., 1963-64, city clk., 1964—; mem. adv. com. for election code revision Tex. Legis. Council, Austin, 1984-85. Mem. Assn. City Clks. and Secs. Tex. (pres. Red River Chpt. 1978-80, v.p. 1984-85, pres. 1985-86, City Clk. of Yr. award 1980; River chpt. 1978-80), Internat. Inst. Mcpl. Clks. (cert.), Acad. for Advanced Edn. Mem. Ch. of Christ. Office: City of Wichita Falls 1300 7th St Wichita Falls TX 76301

THOMAS-BUCKLE, SUZANN REMINGTON, public policy and planning educator; b. Elizabeth City, N.C., Jan. 22, 1945; d. James Ernest Thomas and Marion (Blackwell) Dodson; m. Leonard Gould Buckle, June 4, 1966. B.A. in English Lit., Wellesley Coll., 1962-66; Ph.D. in Urban Studies and Planning, MIT, 1974. Instr. pub. policy and planning MIT, Cambridge, 1970-74, asst. prof., 1974-78, assoc. prof., 1978-85; community and environ. mediator, 1984—; assoc. prof., dir. law, policy and soc. programs Northeastern U., Boston, 1985—; research assoc. John F. Kennedy Sch. Govt., Harvard U., Cambridge, 1979-81; cons. U.S. Dept. Labor, Nat. League of Cities, 1971-76, Mus. Fine Arts, Boston, 1972-75; reporter ABA, Washington, 1973-77; research cons. U.S. Dept. Justice, Washington, 1975-76; mem. Forum on Negotiation, Harvard Law Sch., also adv. bd. specialization in negotiation Program on Negotiation. Author: Bargaining for Justice, 1977; Standards Related to Planning for Juvenile Justice, 1980; mem. editorial bd. Law and Society Rev., 1985—; contbr. articles to profl. jours. Trustee Mass. Council for Pub. Justice, Boston, 1982—. Recipient Everett Moore Baker award MIT, 1972; Eli Lilly postdoctoral fellow, 1974; German Marshall fellow, 1979. Mem. Am. Sociol. Assn., Soc. Profls. in Dispute Resolution, Law and Soc. Assn., Soc. for Study of Social Problems. Office: Programs in Law Policy and Soc Northeastern U Boston MA 02115

THOMASON, CINDY L., broadcasting executive; b. Morristown, N.J., Oct. 28, 1956; d. Marvin Lincoln and Lois Jean (Neal) T. B.S. in Communications, Ithaca Coll., 1978. Account exec. Sta.-WTKO, Ithaca, N.Y., 1977-78, Sta.-WFBL, Syracuse, N.Y., 1978-80; promotion dir. stas.-WHEN/WRRB, Syracuse, 1980—; mem. Sta.-WCNY TV Auction Promotion Com., 1983—. Sec. March of Dimes, Syracuse, 1983-84, vice chmn., 1984—. Recipient Vol. award Cystic Fibrosis Found., Syracuse, 1984. Mem. Syracuse Advt. Club. Presbyterian. Office: Stas-WHEN/WRRB PO Box 6975 Syracuse NY 13217

THOMASON, EVELYN BETTS, lawyer; b. Sioux City, Iowa, Nov. 9, 1942; d. Claude Alfred and Sibyl Winifred (Syverson) Betts; m. Laird Allan Thomason, June 23, 1963; children—Andrew Allan, Jon Claude. B.S., B.A., Drake U., 1966; J.D., Am. U., 1980. Bar: D.C. 1980, Md. 1981. Budget analyst Ford Motor Co., Dearborn, Mich., 1966-71; self employed bus., tax. cons., lectr., Bethesda, Md., 1971-81; assoc. Miller, Miller & Canby, Rockville, Md., 1981-83; sole practice, Bethesda, 1983-84; assoc. McChesney, Pyne & Duncan, Washington, 1984—. Bd. dirs. Christian Ch. Found, Indpls., 1984—, trustee Christian Ch., Capital Area, Chevy Chase, Md., 1984; treas. E. Bethesda Citizens Assn., 1980—. Mem. D.C. Bar Assn., Md. Bar Assn., ABA, Women's Bar Assn. Md. Democrat. Mem. Disciples of Christ. Home: 4503 Sleaford Rd Bethesda MD 20814 Office: McChesney Pyne & Duncan 1000 Connecticut Ave NW Washington DC 20036

THOMASSEN, JANE, educator; b. Tracy, Iowa, July 28, 1932; d. Gerrit Edward and Bertha Ethel (Davis) Thomassen; B.S. cum laude SUNY, New Paltz, 1965, M.S. summa cum laude, 1973; m. Sylvester D. Van Oort, Sept. 3, 1950 (div. 1968); children—Janis K., Kathleen V.O. Davis, Marcus K. Tchr., South Orangetown Public Schs., 1965-66; tchr., union rep. Ramapo Public Schs., Suffern, N.Y., 1966-71; tchr. Clarkstown Public Schs., 1971—; radio announcer, 1975-76; instr., cons. Evelyn Wood Reading Dynamics, 1967-71. Pres. bd. mgrs. Bon Aire Three Condominium, 1978-81; choir dir. Reformed Ch., Beacon and Glenham, N.Y., 1958-62; mem. human relations com. Clarkstown Schs., 1982-84; Mem. United Fedn. Tchrs., AFL-CIO, N.Y. State United Tchrs., Clarkstown Tchrs. Assn., Rockland County Tchrs. Assn., Kappa Delta Pi. Democrat. Home: 16 Somerset Dr Suffern NY 10901 Office: 661 W Nyack Rd West Nyack NY 10994

THOMPKINS, ANNETTE, product marketing engineer; b. Shreveport, La., Oct. 3, 1957; d. Walter Lee and Louise (Scott) Thompkins. B.S. in Mktg. and Mgmt., So. U., 1978. Mktg. rep. Honeywell, Inc., Houston, 1978-79; installation supr. Lifemark Corp., Houston, 1979-82; mgr. hosp. installations Am. Med. Internat., Houston, 1982-84; product mktg. engr. Tex. Instruments, Houston, 1984—. Recipient Nat. Mktg. cert. Honeywell, Inc., Boston, 1978; Data Processing cert. Data Gen., Los Angeles, 1982. Mem. Nat. Mktg. Assn. (sec. 1977-78, cert. 1978), Alpha Kappa Alpha. Democrat. Baptist. Home: 7575 Cambridge Apt 1605 Houston TX 77054 Office: Tex Instruments 4000 Greenbriar Houston TX 77251

THOMPSEN, GAYLE SUSAN, accountant, C.P.A.; b. Albuquerque, Sept. 29, 1953; d. Anderson Hassell and Sally Suzanne (Eckhart) Norton; m. Steven Roy Thompsen, June 25, 1978 (div. Oct. 1983); 1 child, Lisa Leigh. B.B.A. in Acctg., Tex. Tech. U., 1975. C.P.A., Colo. Acct. Atlantic Richfield, Dallas, 1975-80; sr. cons. acct. Anaconda Minerals, Denver, 1980-81; supr. revenue Petro-Lewis Corp., Denver, 1981-85; mgr. acctg. U.S. West Info. Systems, Denver, 1985—. Home: 4181 S Fraser Ct #E Aurora CO 80015 Office: US West Info Systems 6200 S Quebec Suite 250 Englewood CO 80111

THOMPSON, A LEIGH, tape company executive; b. St. Louis, Nov. 9, 1954; d. Bill Cleveland and Lois Ann (Hough) Thompson; m. Francis Thomas Campos, May 26, 1980 (div. Apr. 1986). A.A. in English, St. Louis Community Coll., 1975; B.S. in Psychology magna cum laude, Lawrence U., 1977. Cert. tchr. spl. edn. Caterer, St. Louis, Appleton, Wis., 1973-77; tchr., therapist The Day Sch., Chgo., 1977-78; mktg. service supv. Market Facts, Inc., Washington, 1978-80; sales promotion mgr. Gentec/Foremost-McKesson, San Francisco, 1981-82; sales trainer, specialist Profl. Tape, Burr Ridge, Ill., 1982—; trainer Dimensions of Profl. Selling, 1984—; speaker in field. Softball coach Police Activities League, San Francisco, 1986. Recipient Take-Me-Along Winner award Profl. Tape, 1984; Lawrence U. grantee, 1976, 77. Mem. Nat. Assn. Profl. Salespersons (pub. relations com. 1985—), Nat. Assn. Female Execs., Lawrence Univ. Alumni (recruiter 1985—), Mortar Bd. Alumni (treas. 1975-77), Phi Theta Kappa. Roman Catholic. Club: Telegraph Hill. Avocations: skiing; modern dance; hiking; racquetball; running; reading; writing. Home: 2601 Chestnut St #1 San Francisco CA 94123 Office: Profl Tape/Time Products 144 Tower Dr Chicago IL 60521

THOMPSON, ANNE ELISE, judge; b. Phila., July 8, 1934; d. Leroy H. and Mary E. (Jackson) Jenkins; B.A., Howard U., 1955, LL.B., 1964; M.A., Temple U., 1957; m. William H. Thompson, June 19, 1965; children—William H., Sharon A. Admitted to N.J. bar, 1966; judge Mcpl. Ct., 1972-75, U.S. Dist. Ct., Trenton, N.J., 1979—; Mercer County prosecutor, 1975-79. Recipient Disting. Service award Nat. Dist. Attys. Assn., 1979. Mem. Am. Bar Assn., N.J. Bar Assn., Mercer County Bar Assn. Democrat. Office: PO Box 401 Trenton NJ 08618

THOMPSON, BARBARA EDITH, machines and machine shop supplies distributor; b. Jamaica, N.Y., Mar. 25, 1946; d. Lloyd Frederick and Helen Olga (Kolmodin) T. Student SUNY-Oneonta, 1963-68, SUNY-Farmingdale, Suffolk Community Coll., Notary pub., N.Y. Acctg. mgr. Iverson Cycle, Medford, N.Y., 1974-77; payroll and accounts payable mgr. Venus Sci., Farmingdale, N.Y., 1977-80; accounts payable mgr. Audiovox, Hauppauge, N.Y., 1980-82; acctg. mgr. Video Data Systems, Hauppauge, 1982-85; asst. ops. mgr. MSC Indsl., Central Islip, N.Y., 1985—. Mem. Nat. Assn. Female Execs., NOW (pres. South Shore chpt. 1981-83, v.p. membership 1980-81). Lutheran. Avocations: arts; crafts; bowling; tennis; painting.

THOMPSON, CAROL JEAN, realty executive; b. Rock Island, Ill., June 23, 1941; d. J. Deane and Doris Darlene (Jean) Fisher. Ed., Catalina High Sch., Tucson. Asst. v.p. First Am. Title, Tucson, 1969-84, Fidelity Nat. Title, Tucson, 1984—; asst. v.p., escrow mgr. USLife Title (name now Title USA), Tucson, 1985—; instr. escrow Pima Community Coll., Tucson, 1979—, also escrow supr., tng. dir. Escrow Tng. Manuals. Mem. Am. Escrow Assn. (bd. dirs. 1981-86, 1st v.p. 1985-86, 2d v.p. 1986-87), Ariz. State Escrow Assn. (cert. sr. escrow officer; pres. 1982-83, 85-86), So. Ariz. Escrow Assn. (pres. 1981-82). Lodge: Jobs Daus. Address: 9945 E War Bonnet Ln Tucson AZ 85749

THOMPSON, CAROLYN BELL, rehabilitation administrator; b. Cleve., Apr. 20, 1959; d. Peter and Letitia (Bell) T. B.A., Northwestern U., 1981; M.S., Ill. Inst. Tech., 1985. Cert. rehab. counselor. Unit coordinator rehab. counselor Chgo. Assn. Retarded Citizens, 1981-82; child life therapist Shriner's Hosp., Chgo., 1982; placement specialist Chgo. Assn. Retarded Citizens, 1982-83; dir. placement services, 1983—. Mem. adv. Ill. Jobs Com. for Handicapped, 1985; chmn. planning council vocat. edn. curriculum Ill. Dept. Rehab. Services, 1985—. Mem. Nat. Rehab. Assn., Ill. Rehab. Assn. (pres.), Nat. Job Placement Div. (membership chmn.), Ill. Job Placement Div. (bd. dirs.), Am. Assn. Counseling and Devel., Delta Zeta. Republican. Episcopalian. Avocations: swimming; skiing; aerobics; reading; cooking. Office: CARC Placement Services 8562 S Vincennes St Chicago IL 60620

THOMPSON, CAROLYN SUE, advertising agency executive, artist; b. Oakland, Calif., Mar. 21, 1952; d. Rufus Lee and Jacqueline (Queen) T. B.S. in Art Edn., S.W. Tex. State U., 1974. Cert. art tchr., Tex. Tax examiner IRS, Austin, Tex., 1977-79; art dir. William Lacy Co., Austin, 1979-80, Ind. Automotive Service Assocs., Bedford, Tex., 1980-81; comml. artist Moore Paper Co., Houston, 1981, Ogilvy & Mather, Houston, 1982-83; pres., artist Thompson Arts Inc., Houston, 1983—. Acting pres. assocs. group Scottish Heritage Found. Inc., 1986—. Mem. Westside Jaycees (charter 1985—). Avocations: scuba diving; bicycling. Home and Office: 2901 Elmside 192 Houston TX 77042

THOMPSON, CHRISTINE EPPS, librarian; b. Ft. Worth, Nov. 1, 1940; d. John Robert Epps and Eva May (Taylor) Epps McKee; m. Robert Edgar Thompson, Jr., Sept. 28, 1957; children—Thomas Len, Robert Kearn. B.A., North Tex. State U., 1964, M.A., 1966, M.L.S., 1970. Teaching asst. North Tex. State U., Denton, 1964-65, library clk., 1968-70; librarian Tarleton State U., Stephenville, 1970-83; teaching asst. Tex. Woman's U., Denton, 1983-84; head original cataloging dept. Tex. A&M U. Library, College Station, 1984-85, acting head processing div., 1985—. Author: The Works of Zbigniew K. Brzezinski; Management Information Systems Bibliography; Decision Support Systems: A Bibliography, 1980-84. Mem. ALA, Assn. Coll. Research Libraries, Tex. Library Assn. (chmn. scholarship com. 1980-81, chmn. intellectual freedom com. 1983-84), Tex. Assn. Coll. Tchrs. (exec. bd. 1980-81, nomination com. 1983-84), Am. Mgmt. Assn., Library Adminstrn. and Mgmt. Assn. Democrat. Baptist.

THOMPSON, DANIELA NICOLE, educator, administrator; b. Fuerth, W. Ger., June 8, 1958; came to U.S., 1975, naturalized, 1983; d. B. Forster and Helga Forster-Howell; m. Daniel O. Thomspson, III, Nov. 26, 1982. B.A. in Psychology, Southwestern U., 1981. Owner, dir. Forster Holz Sch., Austin, Tex., 1983—. Avocations: flying; singing; home economics; opera; travel. Home: 3109 Wheeler St Austin TX 78705 Office: Forster Holz Sch 1400 Lorrain St Austin TX 78707

THOMPSON, DIANA ROSEBUD, poet, history exhibit coordinator, marketing consultant; b. N.Y.C., Dec. 25, 1957; d. Samuel Joseph Daniels and Anna Louise (Thompson). B.A. in Psychology, Barnard Coll., 1979; A.A.S. cum laude in Cosmetics Mktg., Fashion Inst. Tech., N.Y.C., 1981. Prin. exhibit coordinator, mktg. cons. D.R. Thompson Enterprises, N.Y.C., 1980—, mktg. cons. 127th Street Repertory Ensemble, 1982-83, 20 West Theatre, Cultural Events Comm., Bassinova Inc. (all N.Y.C.). 1983—, Art Against Apartheid, N.Y.C., 1984. Judge math. NAACP Acad., Cultural, Technol. and Sci. Olympics Competition II, Corona N.Y., 1980. Recipient cert. of merit Nat. Council Negro Women, N.Y.C., 1981; poetry Soc. Am. scholar, fall 1985. Mem. Fashion Inst. Tech. (life), AAUW (publicity chmn. Queens br. 1980-81), Metamorphosis Writers Collective, MLA, Zeta Phi Beta (fin. sec. L.I. br. 1980-81). Congregationalist. Office: 34-20 112th St New York NY 11368

THOMPSON, DIDI (MARY BENNETT) CASTLE, writer, editor; b. Terre Haute, Ind., Feb. 7, 1918; d. Robert Langley Bennett and Marjorie Rose (Tyler) Bennett Castle; student U. Ill., Champaign, 1935-36, U. Ky., 1936-39; m. Jamie Campbell Thompson, Jr., June 24, 1939; children—Jamie III, Julia King, Marjorie Castle Stewart. News editor Glen-Echoes, Glencoe, Ill., 1930; columnist Ky. Kernel, U. Ky., Lexington, 1937-39; radio script writer Modern Am. Music, 1940-42; asst. pub. relations dir. Salem Coll., Winston-Salem, N.C., 1945; pub. relations chmn. Barrington (Ill.) Horse Show, 1959-67; staff writer, columnist Barrington Press Newspapers, 1958-84; editor ECHO, Defenders of the Fox River, Inc. newsletter, 1970—; travel editor Barrington Press Newspapers, 1973-84; columnist The Daily Herald, Paddock Publs., 1984—; freelance writer, 1943—. Past bd. mem. Barrington chpt. Lyric Opera Guild Chgo., Barrington Sr. Center, Infant Welfare Soc. Chgo., Art Inst. Chgo., Barrington Assos.; elected trustee Village of Barrington Hills, 1969-73, health, pub. relations chmn., 1969-73; mem. Barrington Hills Plan Commn., 1986—. Mem. Women in Communications (past dir.), Citizens for Conservation (past dir.), Barrington Countryside Assn. (past dir.), Barrington Hist. Soc., Spring Creek Basset Hounds Club, Barrington Hills Riding Club (past dir.), Pan Hellenic Council, DAR, Chgo. Press Club, Chi Omega. Episcopalian. Address: 94 Otis Rd Barrington IL 60010

THOMPSON, DOROTHY BROWN, writer, poet; b. Springfield, Ill., May 14, 1896; d. William Joseph and Harriet (Gardner) Brown; A.B., U. Kans., 1919; m. Dale Moore Thompson, July 2, 1921; 1 son, William Brown Began writing professionally, 1931; contbr. verse to nat. mags. and newspapers including Saturday Rev., Sat. Evening Post, Va. Quar. Rev., Poetry (Chgo.), Commonweal, Good Housekeeping; author research articles for hist. jours.; poems pub. in numerous collections and textbooks, mags. and textbooks in Eng., Can., Australia, Sweden, N.Z., 26 in Braille; poems selected for art exhbt. Contemporary Gallery, Jewish Community Center, Kansas City, Mo., 1976, 77, 78, 79, 80; 10 poems pub. as songs; leader poetry sect. Writers' Conf., U. Kans., 1953-55, McKendree Coll., 1961, 63, Creighton U., 1966, Central Mo. State U., 1974, Am. Poets Series, Kansas City, Mo., 1972-73; residency Mo. Council Arts, 1975; workshop leader U. Mo. at Kansas City, 1975. Recipient Mo. Writers Guild award, 1941, awards poetry socs. Ga., 1955, Va., 1956, La., 1958, also Poetry Soc. Am. and various local awards, including Kansas City Star award, 1975, Order First Families of Va., 1607-22. Mem. Diversifiers, Poetry Soc. Am., Nat. Soc. Colonial Dames. Mem. Christian Ch. Clubs: Woman's City, Filson. Author: (poetry) Subject to Change, 1973. Address: 221 W 48th St Apt 1402 Kansas City MO 64112

THOMPSON, ELIZABETH REES, transit administrator; b. Columbus, Ind., Aug. 23, 1954; d. Myron D. and Marian Louise (Ray) Rees; m. Mark Thompson, May 31, 1980. B.S. with distinction in Recreation, Ind. U., 1976. Supr., Bloomington Parks and Recreation, Ind., 1976-77; exec. dir. Morgan County Sr. Ctrs., Inc., Martinsville, Ind., 1977-79, Hamilton County Sr. Citizens Services, Inc., Noblesville, Ind., 1979-80; community planner North Iowa Area Council of Govts., Mason City, Iowa, 1981-82, transit adminstr., 1983—. Liturgy com. St. Joseph's Catholic Ch., Mason City, 1984, tchr. Cath. edn., 1984—. Cummins Diesel scholar, 1972-76; State of Ind. hon. scholar, 1972; Ind. U. merit scholar, 1973-76. Mem. Iowa Pub. Transit Assn., Am. Pub. Transit Assn. Club: Wa-tan-ye. Avocations: swimming; running; crafts. Home: 302 E Lake St Ventura IA 50482 Office: North Iowa Area Council Govts 121 3d St Mason City IA 50401

THOMPSON, FRANCES ANN, ESL educator; b. Havre, Mont., Nov. 2, 1945; d. William Compton and Bess Irene (Harrison) T. B.A. in English, U. Tex.-Arlington, 1967; M.A. in English, East Tex. State U., 1973, Ed.D. in Elem. Edn., 1983. Cert. tchr. all levels and ESL, Tex. Kindergarten tchr. Mrs. Schaeffer's Sch., Arlington, 1967-68; tchr. English, Crystal City Ind. Sch. Dist., Tex., 1969-71; elem. and English tchr. Mirando City Ind. Sch. Dist., Tex., 1974-81; ESL tchr. Como-Pickton Ind. Sch. Dist., Como, Tex., 1981—. Contbr. articles to profl. jours., also poetry to Poor Richard's Poetry, 1968 (1st Pl. award). Mem. Tex. State Tchrs. Assn., Phi Kappa Theta. Republican. Baptist. Avocations: crochet; reading; crafts; needlework. Office: Como-Pickton Ind Sch Dist PO Box 18 Como TX 75431

THOMPSON, FREDA ALFORD, corporate executive; b. Manchester, Ga., May 28, 1939; d. Frederick Napoleon and Sabra Irene (Venable) Alford; m. 2d, Theodore James Thompson, July 18, 1981; m. LeRoy Christopher Delatorre, Feb. 8, 1963 (div. 1977), 1 dau., Linda Elaine. Student Montreat (N.C.) Coll., 1958-59. Co-founder, v.p. Panex Corp., Houston, 1974—. Vol. Pub. Schs., Spring, Houston, 1969-74, Mensa, Houston, 1978; coordinator Republican Party Coffees, spring, 1971. Greek Orthodox. Club: Neighborhood Swim (Spring) (social chmn. 1970). Home: 10006 Olympia Houston TX 77042 Office: Panex Corp 12823 Park One Dr Sugar Land TX 77478

THOMPSON, GERALDINE JUDITH, institute administrator; b. London, Apr. 27, 1942; d. Thomas John and Edyth Margaret (Walker) Bray; came to U.S., 1960; B.A. magna cum laude, Smith Coll., 1963; M.A., U. London, 1974; m. Kenneth Stuart Thompson, Mar. 20, 1965; 1 dau., Kirsten Deborah. Asst. to pres. Internat. Schs. Services, N.Y.C., 1963-66; program dir. Noise Abatement Soc., London, 1972-73; asst. dir. African Imprint Library Services, Mt. Kisco, N.Y., 1974-77; sr. v.p., dir. coll. programs Am. Inst. for Fgn. Study, Greenwich, Conn., 1977—; contbr. Coutry Index, Los Angeles, 1982—. Trustee Richmond Coll., 1982—. Mem. Nat. Assn. Fgn. Student Affairs. Club: Smith of Westchester County. Contbr. New Horizons in Education, 1965. Home: Holly Hill Ln Katonah NY 10536 Office: Am Inst Fgn Study 102 Greenwich CT 06830

THOMPSON, HAZEL PAULISON (RUSTY), sch. dist. adminstr.; b. Passaic, N.J., Feb. 4, 1928; B.S. in Edn., Glassboro Coll., 1949; M.A. in Adminstrn. and Supervision, Columbia U., 1960; m. W. Stuart Thompson; 3 children. Tchr., Ridgewood (N.J.) Bd. Edn., 1949-61; tchr. Bloomfield (N.J.) Bd. Edn., 1964-66, reading specialist, 1966-70, adminstrv. asst. in curriculum and instrn., 1970-82, asst. to supt. and dir. personnel, 1982—, also coordinator recruitment, affirmative action officer for hiring policies and procedures; TV coordinator between sch. dist. and N.J. Public TV. Elder, Ref. Ch. in Am. Mem. N.J. Assn. Curriculum Devel., Am. Assn. Curriculum and Supervision, Am. Assn. Sch. Personnel Adminstrs., Mid-Atlantic Assn. Sch. Coll. Univ. Staffing, NEA N.J. Edn. Assn., Internat. Reading Assn., N.J. Reading Tchrs. Assn. Co-author numerous curriculum guides and writings for title funds. Certified as prin., supr., N.J.; specialist in reading, lang. arts, kindergarten through 12th grades, curriculum devel., kindergarten through 12th grades, adminstrv. supervision for classroom instruction, kindergarten through 12th grades, elementary and secondary libraries coordination. Home: Jacquelin Ave Ho-Ho-Kus NJ 07423 Office: 155 Broad St Bloomfield NJ 07003

THOMPSON, JACQUELINE DALE, property management business owner; b. Fargo, N.D., Dec. 27, 1950; d. John Seth and Mary Ellen (Pentecost) Thompson; children—Nicholas, Samantha. B.S., N.D. State U., 1973. With music dept. Nels Vogel, Moorhead, Minn., 1973-75; owner Dale Mgmt., Fargo, 1975—. Bd. dirs. Rape and Abuse Crisis Ctr., Fargo, 1984—, Dakota Montesori Sch., 1980-82; mem., past officer Fargo-Moorhead Chamber Chorale, 1980—; mem. Citizens for a Real Choice, Fargo, 1982—. Mem. Women's Network Red River Valley, NOW, Nat. Assn. Female Execs., Fargo/Moorhead Apt. Assn. (bd. dirs., pres. 1983-84, sec.-treas. 1982-83, lobbyist 1983, 85), N.D. Apt. Assn. (bd. dirs. 1982—, sec.-treas. 1982-85), AAUW, LWV. Methodist. Avocations: jazzercise; biking; singing; performing. Home: 411 Lindenwood Dr Fargo ND 58103 Office: Dale Management PO Box 7303 Fargo ND 58103

THOMPSON, JAYNE AUDREY, lawyer; b. Albert Lea, Minn., Aug. 19, 1939; d. John Blain and Harriet Ordella (Blume) Roberts; children—Theresa Brown, Laura, Jennifer Thompson. B.A., Hamline U., 1961; M.Ed., U. Minn., 1965; J.D., No. Ky. U., 1979. Bar: Ohio 1979. Tchr., U.S. Army Mil. Schs., Wuerzburg, W.Ger., 1962-63, St. Paul Pub. Schs., 1961-62, 63-65, Parkway Sch. Dist., St. Louis, 1965-66; tchr.'s aide U. Cin., Cin. Pub. Schs.; tchr. Wyoming (Ohio) Pub. Schs., 1966-68; substitute tchr. Lockland, Greenhills and Finneytown, Ohio, 1968-70; corp. atty. Eagle Savs. Assn., Cin., 1979; sole practice, Cin., 1980—. Author: Changing Attitudes through Literature, 1965; editor: (TV tape) Around the World with Literature, 1964. Reader, Clovernook Home for Blind; trustee No. Hills Unitarian Ch.; pres. Cin. Unitarian Universalist Council; v.p. UN Info. Com.; mem. Met. Area Religions Coalition Council; co-leader Girl Scouts U.S.A.; mem. Finneytown PTA; mem. Citizens Com. on Justice and Corrections; mem. allocations bd. children's services United Appeal; bd. dirs. Mental Health Services N.W. Mem. ABA, Ohio Bar Assn., Cin. Bar Assn., Assn. Trial Lawyers Am., LWV. Republican. Clubs: Singletons, Cingles (treas.), Zonta. Home: 8393 Sailboat Ln Maineville OH 45039

THOMPSON, JAYNE CARR, lawyer; b. Oak Park, Ill., Apr. 7, 1946; d. Robert Edward and Laurette Marie (Rentner) Carr; B.A., U. Ill., 1967; J.D., Northwestern U., 1970; m. James Robert Thompson, Jr., June 19, 1976; 1 dau., Samantha Jayne. Admitted to Ill. bar, 1970; assoc. McDermott, Will & Emery, Chgo., 1970; asst. atty., office of atty. gen. of Ill., Criminal Justice Div., Chgo., 1970-77, dep. chief prosecution assistance bur., 1974-76, dep. chief criminal justice div., 1976-77; of counsel firm Brown, Hay & Stephens, Springfield, Ill., 1977. assoc. Silets & Martin Ltd., Chgo., 1983—. Recipient Atty. Gen.'s award for Outstanding Pub. Service, 1976. mem. Fed. Bar Assn., Ill. State Bar Assn. Republican. Presbyterian. Co-author articles in field. Office: 140 S Dearborn St Suite 1510 Chicago IL 60603

THOMPSON, JENENNE MARIE, dietitian; b. Trinidad, Colo., July 7, 1947; d. Edward Eli and Cecilia Josephine (Castor) Jenkins; m. G. Neal Thompson, July 31, 1964; (div. 1972); 1 child, Shawn Eric. B.S., U. N.Mex., 1975. Dietary dir. San Juan Regional Med. Ctr., Farmington, N.Mex., 1976-78, Meml. Gen. Hosp., Las Cruces, 1978-80; asst. dietary dir. Presbyn. Hosp., Denver, 1980-82; dietary dir. Parkview Hosp., Pueblo, Colo., 1983-85; pres. Cons. in Health and Healing, Denver, 1982—; cons. food service mgmt. St. Joseph's Hosp., Del Norte, Colo., 1984—, Alamosa Hosp., Colo., 1985—, Sangre de Cristo Nursing Facility, Monte Vista, Colo., 1984—, Sanhaven Nursing Facility, Lamar, Colo., 1984—. Mem. Am. Dietetic Assn., Colo. Dietetic Assn., Am. Hosp. Assn., Hosp. Food Service Adminstrn., Am. Diabetes Assn. Democrat. Roman Catholic. Avocations: Skiing; gourmet cooking. Home: 4113 Grove St Denver CO 80211 Office: Consultants in Health and Healing 1818 Vine St Denver CO 80206

THOMPSON, JOANNE, artist, porcelain mfg. co. exec.; b. Chgo., Nov. 2, 1922; d. George A. and Mary Louise Thompson; student U. Colo., Boulder, 1940-42; divorced; children—Barrett, Marc, Stacy. Exhibited group shows Nat. Arts Club Gallery, N.Y.C., 1965-69; Mus. Fine Arts, Springfield, Mass., 1965-70; Am. Artists Profl. League Grand Nat., N.Y.C., 1966-70; Hammond Mus., Westchester, N.Y., 1968; owner, artist, tchr. Joanne Thompson Studio, Scottsdale, Ariz., 1979—. Mem. Am. Artists Profl. League, Artists Guild Chgo., Acad. Artists. Author, illustrator: Fun to Sketch With Pencil and Crayon, 1973; illustrator Love Circles, 1978. Office: PO Box 4042 Scottsdale AZ 85261

THOMPSON, LEONA POLINER, social worker, educator; b. Ogden, Utah, June 22, 1911; d. Joseph and Freda (Muldavin) Poliner; B.S., N.Y. U., 1932, M.A., 1933; M.S.W., Columbia, 1959; m. Robert George Thompson, Oct. 13, 1939 (div. Nov. 1961); children—Ellen, James. Psychotherapist, Wiltwyck Sch. for Boys, N.Y.C., 1958-60; dir. social service Knickerbocker Hosp., N.Y.C., 1960-80; psychotherapist Morningside Mental Hygiene Clinic, N.Y.C., 1960-66; asst. prof., then asso. prof. sociology dept. Lehman Coll., N.Y.C., 1968-80, dir. social work program, 1973-80; cons. Sr. Citizen Peer Counseling Tng. Program, East Harlem, N.Y.C., 1976-77. Mental health cons. Caribbean Fedn. Mental Health, from 1965; mem. adv. bd. Manhattanville Community Health Service Center, 1968-69, Manhattanville Head Start, from 1969; mem. dean's steering com. Council Teaching Agys. N.Y.U. Grad. Sch. Social Work. Mem. Am. Soc. Dirs. Social Service, Am. Hosp. Assn., Nat. Assn. Social Workers, Nat. Council Social Work Edn., Nat. Welfare Assn. Office: Lehman Coll Bedford Park Blvd W Bronx NY 10468

THOMPSON, LIBBIE MOODY (MRS. CLARK W. THOMPSON), civic worker; b. Galveston, Tex., Nov. 22, 1897; d. William Lewis and Libbie Rice (Shearn) Moody; student Holton-Arms, Washington, 1915; m. Clark W. Thompson, Nov. 16, 1918 (dec.); children—Clark W., Libbie (Mrs. James I. Stansell) (dec.). Past dir. YWCA, ARC, Galveston; bd. dirs. Nat. Eye Found.; mem. nat. bd. Med. Coll. Pa.; mem. fine arts com. State Dept., Washington; mem. chancellor's council U. Tex.; mem. pres.'s club U. Tex. Med. Br.; founding mem. Jr. Welfare; bd. dirs. Meridian House Internat.; Mem. Plantagenet Soc., Colonial Dames Am., Daus. Republic of Tex., Am. Legion Aux., Am. Newspaper Women's Club, LWV (past dir.), Huguenot Soc., U.D.C., Soc. Sponsors USN (life), Magna Charta Dames, Smithsonian Soc. of Assocs. (life, mem. James Smithson Soc.), Order of Washington, Descs. Most Noble Order of Garter, Salvation Army Aux. Washington, Friends of Kennedy Center, Friends of Rosenberg Library, Galveston, Jr. League (hon.), Friends of LBJ Library, Fine Arts Soc. Tex (dir.), Presidents Assocs. of Med. Coll. Pa., Friends of Am. Philos. Soc., Nat. Preservation Hist. Internat. Fund Monuments, Com. Ireland (charter), Hubert H. Humphrey Leadership Fund, ARC Aux., UN Assn. U.S.A. Clubs: Women's Nat. Democratic, Sulgrave, 1925 F Street (Washington); Georgetown; Galveston Artillery. Home: 1616 Driftwood Ln Galveston TX 77551 also 3301 Massachusetts Ave NW Washington DC 20008

THOMPSON, LINDA PARRETT, mailing service company executive; b. Sylacauga, Ala., Nov. 30, 1941; d. Henry Whit and Robbie Eliene (King) Parrett; m. Gerald Clifford Thompson, Dec. 29, 1962; children—Lisa Eliene, Clifford Alan. Grad. high sch. Sylacauga, Teletype operator South Central Bell, Atlanta, 1960-61, stenographer, Birmingham, Ala., 1961-64; sales rep. Mail Sort, Inc., Birmingham, 1980-81, owner, operator, 1981—. Membership chmn. Gresham Jr. High Sch. PTO, Birmingham, 1979-80; publicity chmn. Shades Valley High Sch. PTO, Birmingham, 1981-82; co-commr. Cahaba Heights Athletic Assn. girls softball, Birmingham, 1973-75, asst. coach girls softball, 1970-71. Mem. Birmingham C. of C., Postal Customer Council of Birmingham, Beta Sigma Phi (former pres., v.p., corr. sec., extension officer). Baptist. Home: 3152 Valley Park Pl Birmingham AL 35243 Office: Mail Sort Birmingham 620 24th St S Birmingham AL 35233

THOMPSON, LINDA RUTH, psychiatrist; b. Bristol, Va., May 17, 1941; d. Eugene Cassidy and Kitty Ruth (Corum) T.; A.B., King Coll., 1962; M.D., U. Va., 1966; children—Ethan Eugene, Daniel Richard. Diplomate Am. Bd. Psychiatry and Neurology. Intern, State U. of Iowa Hosp., Iowa City, 1966-67; resident in psychiatry U. Va. Hosp., Charlottesville, 1967-71; practice medicine specializing in psychiatry, Bristol, Va. Mem. Am. Psychiat. Assn., Tenn. Psychiat. Assn., Am. Psychoanalytic Assn., Washington Psychoanalytic Soc. Office: 1909 Euclid Ave Bristol VA 24201

THOMPSON, MARGUERITE MYRTLE GRAMING (MRS. RALPH B. THOMPSON), librarian; b. Orangeburg, S.C., Apr. 23, 1912; d. Thomas Laurie and Rosa Lee (Stroman) Graming; B.A. in English cum laude, U. S.C., 1932, postgrad., 1937; B.L.S., Emory U., 1943; m. Ralph B. Thompson, Sept. 17, 1949 (dec. Oct. 1960). Tchr. English public high schs., S.C., 1932-43; librarian Rockingham (N.C.) High Sch., 1943-45, Randolph County (N.C.) Library, Asheboro, 1945-48, Colleton County (S.C.) Library, Walterboro, 1948-61; dir. Florence (S.C.) County Library, 1961-78. Sec. com. community facilities, services and instns. Florence County Resources Devel. Com., 1964-67; vice chmn. Florence County Council on Aging, 1968-70, exec. bd. 1968-82, bd. treas., 1973-75, bd. sec., 1976-77, bd. v.p., 1979; mem. Florence County Bicentennial Planning Com., 1975-76; mem. relations and allocations com. United Way, 1979-80. Named Boss of Year Nat. Secs. Assn., 1971. Mem. ALA (council 1964-72), Southeastern, S.C. (pres. 1960, chmn. assn. handbook revision com. 1967-69, 80, sect. co-chmn. com. standards for S.C. public libraries 1966-73, fed. relations coordinator 1972-73, planning com. 1976-78) library assns., Greater Florence C. of C. (women's div. chmn. 1969-70, dir. 1975-77), Southeast Regional Conf. Women in Chambers Commerce (dir. 1970-71), Florence, Bus. and Profl. Women's Club (2d v.p. 1975-76, Career Woman of Year 1974, parliamentarian 1980-81, chmn. scholarship com. 1981-82), Delta Kappa Gamma (county chpt. charter pres. 1963-65, treas. 1966-70, chmn. com. on expansion 1977-80, 82—, state chpt. chmn. state scholarship com. 1967-73, state 2d v.p. 1971-73, state 1st v.p. 1973-75, state pres. 1975-77, chmn. policy manual 1977-81, chmn. adv. council 1978—, chmn. fin. com. 1981 , dir. SE Region 1978-80, coordinator SE Regional Golden Anniversary Conf. 1979, internat. scholarship com. 1970-74, internat. exec. bd. 1975-77, 78-80, internat. adminstrv. bd. 1978-80, internat. constn. com. 1980-82) Methodist (chmn. ch. library com. 1965-71, chmn. com. ch. history, 1968-69, sec. adminstrv. bd. 1979-82). Club: Florence Literary (sec. 1964-66, 79-82, pres. 1970-72). Home: Route 2 Box 1000 Apt 8B Orangeburg SC 29115

THOMPSON, MARY CATHERINE, state auditor; b. Troy, N.Y., Nov. 11, 1942; d. Milford and Mary (Normandin) T. B.Acctg., Russell Sage Coll., 1967, M.Pub.Adminstrn., 1979. C.P.A., cert. internal auditor. Assoc. state accounts auditor State of N.Y., Albany, from 1967, sr. state accounts auditor, now state accounts auditor. Mem. Assn. Govt. Accts. (v.p. membership 1984-85, treas. 1985-86), Inst. Internal Auditors (pres. Albany chpt. 1983-85, mem. internat. com., bd. dirs. 1984-86, Martin Ives award 1985), AAUW (chpt. treas. 1984—). Avocations: crafts, bowling, swimming, reading. Home: 139 Middletown Rd Waterford NY 12188

THOMPSON, MARY EMMA, school administrator; b. Paris, Ill.; d. Fred Mascher and Velma Cleo (Britton) Gillson; m. George Elmer Thompson, Aug. 6, 1950 (dec. Aug. 1959); children—Anthony Eugene, Mary Roberta, Gary Alan. A.A., Palm Beach Jr. Coll., 1965; B.S. in Elem. Edn., Fla. Atlantic U., 1966; M.S., Eastern Ill. U., 1975; postgrad. So. Ill. U., 1969-71, Western Ill. U., 1975, 76, 78; Ed.S. in Ednl. Adminstrn., Eastern Ill. U., 1978; Ph.D., Ind. State U., 1985. Cert. tchr., ednl. adminstr., Ill. Tchr. Monroe County Schs., Key West, Fla., 1967-68; tchr. Pittsfield Sch. Dist., Ill., 1968-78; prin. Westfield Dist. #105, Ill., 1978—, Westfield Dist. #201, 1984—; mem. com. North Central Assn. Evaluation Team, Covington, Ind., 1983, Sch. Evaluation Teams Ind. State, Terre Haute, 1983-84. Mem. Clark County Mental Health Bd., Marshall, Ill., 1981—, treas., 1983—. Mem. Assn. Supervision and Curriculum Devel., Delta Kappa Gamma. Republican. Baptist. Avocations: reading; sewing; crocheting. Home: RR 1 Box 85 Westfield IL 62474 Office: Westfield Pub Schs 412 S Madison St Westfield IL 62474

THOMPSON, MARY KRUSE, artist, educator; b. Mankato, Minn., Oct. 22, 1931; d. Cyril Frederic and Ramona (Shepherd) Kruse; B.A., U. Minn., 1954, M.A., 1957; m. Russell A. Thompson, Sept. 12, 1975; children—Julie Ann, Peter Joseph, Mary Susan. Tchr. art Taylors Falls (Minn.) High Sch., Blake Sch. for Boys, Hopkins, Minn., Richfield (Minn.) High Sch.; instr. Gustavus Adolphus Coll., St. Peter, Minn., U. Minn., Mpls., 1970-75; mem. faculty Willmar (Minn.) Community Coll., 1958—; one woman shows include Gustavus Adolphus Coll. Gallery, Gallery 401, Willmar; group shows include: Willmar Community Coll., Women in Art, Marshall (Minn.) State U., U. Wis., Edina Art Ctr., White Bear Lake Community Coll. Bd. dirs. Women's Assn. Mpls. Symphony Orch., Mpls. Women's Club, Kandiyohi Art Assn. Mem. Southwestern Minn. Art and Humanities Council, Minn. Edn. Assn., Nat. Art Edn. Assn., AAUP, U. Minn. Alumnae Assn., Mpls. Woman's Club, Minn. State Med. Aux., Midwest Pastel Soc., Wis. Women in Arts, Delta Phi Delta, Club: Minneapolis Woman's. Home: 1000 SW 14th St Willmar MN 56201 Office: Fine Arts Bldg Willmar Community Coll Willmar MN 56201

THOMPSON, MARY LASCHELLE, healthcare executive, nurse, consultant; b. Jourdanton, Tex., Aug. 27, 1940; d. Earl Fredrick and Mary Eddie (Kaiser) T. B.A., Southwestern U., Georgetown, Tex., 1962; M.A., Incarnate Word Coll., San Antonio, 1968; Assoc. in Nursing, San Antonio Coll., 1976. Educator, San Antonio Sch. Dist., 1962-70; cons. San Antonio Metro Health Dept., 1970-77; patient care coordinator San Antonio Community Hosp., 1977-79; nursing adminstr. St. Luke's Luth. Hosp., San Antonio, 1979-84; corp. dir. nursing Am. Healthcare Mgmt., Dallas, 1984—; mem. governing body Community of North Las Vegas Hosp., Nev., 1984-85, Doctors Hosp. of Jackson, Miss., 1985-86. Mem. Am. Nurses Assn., Am. Hosp. Assn., Tex. Nurses Assn., Assn. Nurse Execs., Tex. Soc. Hosp. Nursing Services Adminstrn. Republican. Methodist. Avocations: reading, tennis, gardening. Home: 5222 Timber Trace San Antonio TX 78250 Office: Sharpstown Gen Hosp PO Box 740389 Houston TX 77274

THOMPSON, MATTIE, city official; b. Jacksonville, Tex., June 3, 1943; d. Merrion and Sylvia (Spencer) Johnson; children—Tarey, Todd, Travis. Student Jarvis Christian Coll., 1960-63, Tex. Coll., 1963-64; B.S. in Acctg., Calumet Coll., 1979. Research asst. Chgo. Child Care Soc., 1973-75; asst. to gen. mgr. St. Paul Fin. Devel. Corp., Chgo., 1975-76; mgr. budget City of Chgo., 1978-80, asst. budget dir., 1980-81, dep. budget dir., 1981-83; dep. commr. City of Chgo. Dept. Streets and Sanitation, 1983—. Active South Shore Women's Workshop, League of Black Women; treas. Chgo. Health Systems Agy., 1981—; bd. dirs. YWCA Met. Chgo. Jarvis Christian Coll. Scholar, 1960-61. Mem. Exec. Women in Mcpl. Govt. Democrat. Home: 9723 S Oglesby St Chicago IL 60617 Office: City of Chicago Streets and Sanitation 121 N LaSalle St Room 700 Chicago IL 60617

THOMPSON, MAVIS SARAH, physician; b. Newark, June 22, 1927; d. Nathaniel Albert and Mavis Carolyn (Smart) T.; B.A., Hunter Coll., N.Y.C., 1947; M.D., Howard U., 1953; m. James Blaize, Apr. 17, 1955; children—

Clayton, Marcia, Sidney, Ronald, Kevin. Intern, then resident in internal medicine Kings County Hosp., Bklyn., 1953-57; practice medicine specializing in internal medicine, Bklyn., 1957-76; med. dir. Lyndon B. Johnson Health Complex, Inc., Bklyn., 1970-71, 74-76; sch. med. insp. N.Y.C. Bd. Edn., Bklyn., 1962—; family physician Kingsboro Med. Group, Bklyn., 1976—; tchr. dept. nursing Medgar Evers Coll., 1975-76; mem. adv. com. Gerontol. Services Adminstrn. program New Sch. Social Research, N.Y.C.; cons. in field. Bd. dirs. Camp Minisink, 1973—; active local Boy Scouts Am.; lic. lay reader St. George's Eplsc. Ch., Bklyn. Recipient Community Service award St. Mark's Meth. Ch., N.Y.C., 1973; Alberta T. Kline service award Camp Minisink, 1980. Mem. Am. Public Health Assn. (pres. Black caucus health workers 1976-77), Nat. Med. Assn., Am. Mgmt. Assn., Am. Geriatrics Soc., Am. Med. Women's Assn., Kings County Med. Soc., Delta Sigma Theta. Episcopalian. Contbr. articles to med. jours. Office: 1000 Church Ave Brooklyn NY 11218

THOMPSON, MELISSA ANN, entrepreneur; b. Astoria, Oreg., Sept. 14, 1950; d. Bernard Eugene and Evelyn Elaine (May) T.; m. William Leslie Harrington, June 3, 1972; children—Elaine Leslie Ione, Thomas Jefferson Eugene. B.A., U. Wash., 1972. Legis. dir. NOW, Washington, 1976-77; Wash. rep. Population Resource Ctr., Washington, 1977-78; mgr. Feminist Fed. Credit Union, Seattle, 1979-81; exec. dir. Associated Women Contractors, Seattle, 1981-82; ops. mgr. KAPA, Inc., Seattle, 1983; pres. MTA Services, Seattle, 1984—. Treas. Northwest Women's Law Ctr., Seattle, 1981-83; endorsement chmn. Wash. State Women Polit. Caucus, Seattle, 1981; chmn. King County Women's Polit. Caucus, Seattle, 1982-84. Mem. Associated Builders and Contractors (bd. dirs. 1985), Associated Women Contractors (treas. 1985), Wash. Assn. Temporary Service (sec. 1985), Women Constrn. Owners and Execs., Women's Managerial and Profl. Network, Sea-First Bus. and Profl. Women (treas. 1982-83). Avocations: reading; women's rights; politics. Office: MTA Services Inc PO Box 9634 Seattle WA 98109

THOMPSON, PAULA ANN, restaurant executive; b. Floral Park, N.Y., Sept. 10, 1940; d. Chester H. and Emma P. (Sternberg) Jordan; 1 child, Julie Ann. B.A. in Math., Hofstra U., Hempstead, N.Y., 1962. Research analyst Carter Wallace, N.Y.C., 1964-68; mgr., market research Grey Advt., Los Angeles, 1970-77; v.p., research dir. Larson, Bateman Inc., Santa Barbara, Calif., 1977-80; dir. market research and strategic planning Vicorp Specialty Restaurants, San Diego, 1980—. Recipient Twin award San Diego YWCA, 1985. Mem. Am. Mktg. Assn. Home: 334 S Granados Ave Solana Beach CA 92075 Office: Vicorp Specialty Restaurants 6610 Convoy Ct PO Box 121513 San Diego CA 92112

THOMPSON, PAULINE CARMEN, real estate company executive; b. Lewiston, Maine, Sept. 1, 1941; d. Ralph O. and Yvonne Blanche (Gousse) Labbe; divorced. Student U. Va., George Washington U. Founder, pres. chief exec. officer Tysons Realty, Inc., McLean, Va., 1971—; tchr. Realtor Assocs., McLean. Founding mem. McLean Savs. and Loan Assn.; membership chmn. No. Va. Mental Health Assn.; mem. Commn. for Dulles Internat. Airport. Mem. No. Va. Bd. Realtors (chmn. various coms.), Nat. Assn. Realtors, No. Va. Apt. Assn., Internat. Real Estate Fedn., Inst. Real Estate Mgmt., Nat. Assn. Indsl. Office Bldg. Assn., Community Assn. Inst., McLean Bus. and Profl. Assn., Fairfax Hosp. Assn., Smithsonian Inst., Corcoran Art Gallery, Am. Film Inst., Fairfax Symphony. Washington Met. Exchangors, Internat. Platform Assn., Nat. Geog. Soc., Maine State Soc., Fairfax County C. of C., Arlington County C. of C., English Speaking Union. Clubs: Soroptimist, Potomac River Jazz, Regency Racquet, Nat. Press. Office: Tysons Realty Inc 1984 Chain Bridge Rd McLean VA 22102

THOMPSON, PHEBE KIRSTEN, physician; b. Glace Bay, N.S., Can., Sept. 5, 1897; came to U.S., 1923, naturalized, 1937; d. Peter and Catherine (McKeigan) Christianson; M.D., C.M., Dalhousie U., Halifax, N.S., 1923; m. Willard Owen Thompson, M.D., June 21, 1923 (dec. Mar. 1954); children—Willard Owen, Frederic, Nancy, Donald. Intern, Children's Hosp., Halifax, N.S., 1922-23; asst. biochemistry, dept. applied physiology Harvard Sch. Public Health, 1924-26; research fellow in medicine, thyroid clinic Mass. Gen. Hosp., Boston, 1926-29; asst. in metabolism dept., endocrinology Rush Med. Coll. U. Chgo. and The Central Free Dispensary, Chgo., 1930-46; asso. with husband in pvt. practice medicine, Chgo., 1947-54; mng. editor Jour. Clin. Endocrinology and Metabolism, 1954-61, cons. editor, 1961-65; cons. editor Endocrinology, 1961-65; editor Jour. Am. Geriatrics Soc., 1954-82; freelance editor and writer, 1961—. Recipient Appreciation cert. Am. Thyroid Assn., 1966. Fellow Am. Geriatrics Soc. (Thewlis award 1966), Gerontol. Soc., Am. Med. Writers Assn. (adv. com. 1958-61, v.p. Chgo. 1962-63); mem. Endocrine Soc., AAAS, Am. Genetic Assn., Am. Public Health Assn., Ill. Acad. Scis., Ill. Public Health Assn., Chgo. Hist. Soc. (life), Art Inst. (life). Clubs: Harvard, University (Chgo.); Canadian (Chgo. corr. sec. 1968-73, dir. 1973-76). Address: 2300 Lincoln Park W Chicago IL 60614

THOMPSON, ROSEMAE MURPHY, hospital executive; b. Hannibal, Mo., Apr. 17, 1923; d. Raina and Mallie Elizabeth (Dickerson) Murphy; m. Albert F. Schenck, July 26, 1942 (dec.); children—Loretta Schenck Grunden, Elizabeth Schenck Barnes; m. 2d, Herbert J. Thompson, Dec. 24, 1983. Instr. airplanes Curtiss Wright Aircraft Co., 1942-45; credit mgr. Montgomery Ward, 1947-51; bookkeeper Internat. Shoe Co., Hannibal, Mo., 1951-65; purchasing agt. Levering Hosp., Hannibal, 1967—. Mem. Am. Legion Aux. (past aux. pres.); Assn. Hosp. Purchasing Materials Mgmt. Greater St. Louis, N.E. Mo. Med. and Dental Soc. (past pres.), Bus. and Profl. Women (past pres.), Epsilon Sigma Alpha (past pres. Loveland, Colo.). Club: Bowling Assn. Monday Night Hannibal Ladies League (pres. 1969-81). Home: Ideal Villa Subdiv Hwy 61 S 158 Janapas Dr Hannibal MO 63401 Office: 1734 Market St Hannibal MO 63401

THOMPSON, SHARON UNDERHILE, county treasurer; b. Sublette, Ill., Jan. 7, 1942; d. Elmer C. and Ruth (Reid) Underhile; children—Angela, Bob. Grad. Sauk Valley Coll., 1985. Various positions in ins., 1960-74; mem. County Bd., Lee County, Dixon, Ill., 1972-74, treas. Lee County, 1974—. Mem. Lee County Hist. Soc., Lee County Assn. for Handicapped, Sauk Valley Humane Soc., Dixon Booster Club; co-chmn. Govt. Div. for the United Fund; active in cancer drives, Heart Fund drives; vol. Reach to Recovery, Am. Cancer Soc. Mem. Nat. Assn. County Treas. and Fin. Officers, Ill. Assn. County Ofcls. (6th v.p. 1985—), Lee County Dem. Women's Assn. (co-chmn. legis. com. 1984—), Dem. Action for the 16th Congressional Dist. (exec. com., steering com.), Lee County Young Dems., Internat. Assn. Clks., Recorders, Election Officers and Treasurers, Ill. County Treasurers Assn. (pres. 1982-83, legis. chmn. for Zone 4 1985—), Sauk Valley Alumni Assn., Dixon C. of C. (v.p. Ambassadors Club 1985). Baptist. Home: 321 E Bradshaw St Dixon IL 61021 Office: Lee County PO Box 328 Dixon IL 61021

THOMPSON, SUSAN PROBASCO, acctg. co. exec.; b. Bloomington, Ill., Aug. 8, 1946; d. Lewis William and Barbara Claire (Welles) Probasco; student U. Wis., 1965; B.A. in English, Rollins Coll., 1968; m. Thomas Miller Thompson, Aug. 22, 1967; 1 dau., Ruth Helen. Research assoc. Heidrick and Struggles, Chgo., 1969-70, assoc., Houston, 1981-82; v.p. mktg. L. N. Smith, Inc., Houston, 1976-78; pres., owner, cons. Suzy Thompson Personnel Service, Inc., and Susan P. Thompson and Assocs., Houston, 1977-82; mgr. Peat, Marwick, Mitchell and Co., Houston, 1982—. Mem. grievance com. State Bar Tex., 1979-82; bd. dirs. Mental Health Assn. Houston and Harris County, 1979—, v.p., 1980-82; trustee Rollins Coll., 1980—. Mem. Houston Bus. Exchange Club, Profl. Women Execs., Exec. Forum. Episcopalian. Office: Peat Marwick Mitchell 4300 One Shell Plaza Houston TX 77002

THOMPSON, SYLVIA A. DAVIS, government official; b. Crystal Springs, Miss.; d. Morris C. and Mary Joe (Solomon) D.; m. Bernard E. Thompson. B.S., Tougaloo Coll., 1964; M.S.W., U. Ill., 1970; postgrad. U. Calif., Berkeley, 1973, 76. Ill. Legis. Internship fellow, 1969-70; accounts receivable clk. Tougaloo Coll., 1964-68; contractual services State of Ill., 1970; legis. staff asst. Ill. Senate, 1971-77, asst. staff dir. to pres., 1977-81; legis asst. to Senator Dixon of Ill., U.S. Senate, Washington, 1981—. Mem. Nat. Assn. Black Social Workers, NAACP, Springfield Urban League, U. Ill. Alumni Assn., Lupus Erythematosis Soc. Ill., Tougaloo Alumni Assn. Baptist. Office: Room 316 Hart Senate Bldg Washington DC 20510

THOMPSON, THELMA GUNN, publishing company executive; b. Meridian, Miss., July 20, 1928; d. Richard Harvey and Thelma Lee (Covington) G.; m. Harold Fredrick Thompson, Aug. 23, 1950 (div. July 1974); children—Jena, Steve, Tracy, Robert, Cindy. Grad. Ponta High Sch., Meridian, Miss., 1946. Telephone operator South Central Bell, Meridian, Miss., 1946-60; ptnr. So. Horseman mag., Meridian, 1962-74; owner, pub., editor So. Horseman mag., Meridian, 1974—; pres., owner So. Pub. Inc., Meridian, 1974—. Presbyterian. Home: 3042 Hwy 45 N Meridian MS 39301 Office: So Pub Co Inc PO Box 71 Meridian MS 39302

THOMPSON, VIRGINIA ELIZABETH, city official; b. Greensburg, Pa., July 18, 1919; d. Michael Rocco and Louise Margaret (Occhiuzzi) Santoro; m. Murrell Robert Thompson, Apr. 7, 1942 (dec.); children—Sharon Virginia, Murrell Robert Jr. Cert. mcpl. clk. Office mgr. Thomas Drug Store, Greensburg, Pa., 1937-46, O'Malley Builders Hardware, Phoenix, Pa., 1961-68; co-owner The Triangle, Latrobe, Pa., 1946-59; clk. City of Tempe, Ariz., 1968-78, 82—. Author: City of Tempe Records Management Manual, 1984. Mem. adv. bd. Tempe Salvation Army, 1975-78, ARC, 1982—; mem. exec. bd. Theodore Roosevelt council Boy Scouts Am., 1975-78; mem. Tempe Hist. Soc., 1975—; charter mem. Fine Arts Ctr. of Tempe, 1982—; sec. Tempe Sister City Corp., 1969-78, historian, 1982—. Recipient spl. award Bob Finch Post Am. Legion, Tempe, 1972. Mem. Internat. Inst. Mcpl. Clks. (bd. dirs. 1978), Ariz. Mcpl. Clks. Assn. (pres. 1974-76), Am. Bus. Women's Assn. (sec. 1974-75, v.p. 1976-77; Woman of Yr. 1972). Roman Catholic. Club: Ladies Sodality. Lodges: Zonta (v.p. 1985-86), Ladies Aux. Elks. Avocations: genealogy; reading; music; antiques collecting. Office: City of Tempe 31 E 5th St PO Box 5002 Tempe AZ 85281

THOMPSON, VIVIAN OPAL, nurse; b. Lebanon, Va., Nov. 30, 1925; d. Luther Smith and Cora Belle (Baugh) Thompson; R.N., Knoxville (Tenn.) Gen. Hosp., 1947. Supr. obstetrical dept. Knoxville Gen. Hosp., 1947-48; gen. duty nurse Clinch Valley Clinic Hosp., Richlands, Va., 1948-52, supr., 1957-61, 68-78, 78—; indsl. nurse, Morocco, Africa, 1952-56; charge nurse Bluefield Sanitarium, W.Va., 1961-65, Rochingham Meml. Hosp., Harrisonburg, Va., 1965-68. Democrat. Presbyterian. Home: 205 Pennsylvania Ave Richlands VA 24641

THOMPSON, YVONNE ELIZABETH, business executive; b. Charleston, S.C., Jan. 10, 1948; d. Lurie Darwin and Constance (Morrison) Thompson. B.A. in Polit. Sci., Fisk U., 1969; M.B.A., U. Calif.-Berkeley, 1975. Gen. mgr. Ventures Mgmt. Co., San Francisco, 1974-75; pres. The Venture Group, Inc., San Francisco, 1975-80; pres. Puget Sound Pet Supply Co., Oakland, Calif., 1976-80; v.p. Fulcrum Venture Capital Co., Washington, 1980-81; v.p. mktg. Gen. R.R. Equipment & Services, Inc., East St. Louis, Ill., 1981—; participant Career Pathfinders, St. Louis pub. schs. 1986—. Mem. Gov.'s Club, Springfield, Ill., 1984—; bd. dirs. Arthritis Found., St. Louis, 1985—; mem. adv. council U.S. SBA, 1979-80; vice chmn. Minority and Female Bus. Enterprise Council, Chgo., 1984-86; mem. small bus. com. Minority Bus. Brain Trust, Ho. of Reps., Washington, 1979—. Mem. Nat. Assn. Female Execs., Profl. Women in Constrn., NAACP, Alpha Kappa Alpha. Club: Citizens for Thompson. Avocations: art collecting; travel; skiing; tennis. Home: 4501 Lindell Blvd Saint Louis MO 63108 Office: Gen RR Equipment & Services Inc PO Box 159 East Saint Louis IL 62202

THOMPSON-LICCKETTO, DEBRAH, naval officer; b. Claremore, Okla., Aug. 29, 1954; d. Lee Monroe and Jessie (Maxine) Cain Thompson; m. Keith Raymond Liccketto, Nov. 5, 1983; 1 child, Aubrey-Tyler. B.S., Northeastern Okla. U., 1975; M.A., in Computer Systems Mgmt., Webster U., St. Louis, 1986. Commnd. lt. U.S. Navy, 1978, legal officer, Washington, 1979-81, recruiter, 1981-83, head fiscal div., 1983—, computer systems security mgr., 1984—, internal control program coordinator, 1984—, pub. affairs officer, 1979-81, area recruiting dir., 1983. Editor: (newspaper) NAF Flyer, 1980; (pamphlet) Advanced Pay Grades, 1980. Named Outstanding Recruiter, USN, 1982, 83. Mem. Nat. Assn. Female Execs., Women Officers Profl. Network. Republican. Am. Baptist. Avocations: ballroom dancing; weightlifting; cooking. Office: Fiscal Officer Recruit Tng Command Bldg 1212 NTC Great Lakes IL 60088

THOMSEN, JEAN LOUISE, real estate agent, artist, writer; b. Williamsport, Pa., June 9, 1931; d. Alfred Robert and Ivy Mariam (Middleton) Miller; m. Stephen John Thomsen, Dec. 27, 1970; children—Denise Raymond Barnes, Suzette Raymond stepchildren—Kari Thomsen, Elizabeth Thomsen. B.A., Vassar Coll., 1976; M.A., State Coll. New Paltz, 1980. Tchr. art City of Poughkeepsie Sch., N.Y., 1977-78; manpower program coordinator Dutchess County Office Human Resources, 1978-83; pub. assistance examiner Dutchess County Dept. Social Services, 1983-84; real estate sales/agt. N.J. Anderson Assocs., Fountain Hills, Ariz., 1985-86; writer, acquisitions Eleanor Roosevelt's Val Kill, Hyde Park, N.Y., 1981-85. Rep. Com. on Handicapping and Affirmative Action, 1978-84; mem. Vassar Coll. Friends of Art Gallery, Poughkeepsie, 1975—; sec. Rural Dutchess Econ. Devel. Corp., Poughkeepsie, 1983—. Mem. N.Y. State Bd. Realtors, Scottsdale Artists League, Fountain Hills Art League, Dutchess County Art Assn. (past bd. dirs.), Nat. Writers Club. Republican. Club: Pol Area Vassar (Poughkeepsie) (area rep.). Home: 15609 Mustang Dr Fountain Hills AZ 85268

THOMSEN, PEGGY JEAN, educator, civic worker; b. St. Louis, Feb. 28, 1940; d. Harold Herman and Crystal Mary (Margolf) Levora; m. John Henry Thomsen, Dec. 1, 1961; children—Dianna, James, Robert. B.A., Calif. State U.-Fresno, 1961, M.A. with honors, 1968. Gen. secondary credential, Calif. Instr., Central Tex. Coll., 1980-83, City Colls. of Chgo., 1983-86. Mem. sch. bd. Albany Unified Sch. Dist., Calif., 1978—, pres. sch. bd., 1980-81, 85-86; pres. PTA, Albany, 1976-78, 69-71; leader Girl Scouts U.S.A., Albany, 1970-82; mem. fund-raising team YMCA, Albany, 1981-85; bd. dirs., sec. Bay Area chpt. March of Dimes, San Francisco, 1979-85, chmn., 1985-86; mem. adminstrv. code Rev. com. Calif. Dept. Edn., 1981-83, chmn. sch. improvement program selection panel, 1981, mem. fin. com. 1982 state budget, 1982; Elm Br. Assoc. Children's Hosp., Oakland. Recipient service award Jaycees, Albany, 1970; service awards Calif. PTA, 1971, 78; Vol. of Yr. award March of Dimes, Alameda County, 1984; Sta. KABL Citizen of Day, 1984. Mem. NEA, Nat. Sch. Bds. Assn., Calif. Sch. Bds. Assn., Pi Gamma Mu. Democrat. Avocations: needlework; editing; reading. Home: 757 Pierce St Albany CA 94706 Office: Albany Unified Sch Dist 904 Talbot St Albany CA 94706

THOMSON, BARBARA JEANNE, purchasing executive; b. Cardiff, Calif., Feb. 10, 1929; d. Zack Rowden and Zula Mae (Tuckness) Taylor; m. Robert Allyn San Clemente, Feb. 8, 1946 (div. Aug. 1954); children—Robert Allyn Jr., Frances Irene, Michael George; m. Seeth Lyle Thomson, Aug. 7, 1954; 1 child, David Seeth. Grad. high sch., Encinitas, Calif. Various positions Gen. Dynamics Convair, San Diego, 1957-73; purchasing agt. Systems, Sci. & Software, San Diego, 1973-78; sr. buyer Gen. Dynamics Electronics, San Diego, 1978-80; sr. buyer LSI Products div. TRW, San Diego, 1980-84, purchasing mgr., 1984—. Named Employee of Yr., Gen. Dynamics Electronics, San Diego, 1978. Mem. Ry. Hist. Soc. (sec. San Diego 1957-60), Pacific Beach Model R.R. Club (sec. 1955-65). Democrat. Avocations: model railroading; photography; baseball; football. Home: 3204 McGraw St San Diego CA 92117 Office: TRW LSI Products Div 4243 Campus Point Ct San Diego CA 92121

THOMSON, GRACE MARIE, nurse, minister; b. Pecos, Tex., Mar. 30, 1932; d. William McKinley and Elzora (Wilson) Olliff; m. Radford Chaplin, Nov. 3, 1952; children—Deborah C. Thomson Meshirer, William Earnest. Assoc. Applied Sci., Odessa Coll., 1965; extension student U. Pa. Sch. Nursing, U. Calif.-Irvine, Golden West Coll. Dir. nursing Grays Nursing Home, Odessa, Tex., 1965; supr. nursing Med. Hill, Oakland, Calif.; charge nurse pediatrics Med. Ctr., Odessa; dir. nursing Elmwood Extended Care, Berkeley, Calif.; surg. nurse Childrens Hosp., Berkeley; med-surg. charge nurse Merritt Hosp., Oakland, Calif.; active Watchtower and Bible Tract Soc.; evangelist for Jehovah's Witnesses, 1954—.

THOMSON, JOY, educational administrator; b. Gleason, Tenn., Nov. 14, 1930; d. Fairraughrr Charles and Ellen May (Grogan) Prince; m. Oliver Russell Thomson, June 15, 1956; children—Russell, LaWanda, Kenneth, Ellen. B.A., Tenn. Temple U., 1956. Cert. ednl. adminstr. ch. schs. Tchr. Park Ave. Day Sch., Corpus Christi, Tex., 1962-63, Westwood Christian Schs., Miami, Fla., 1964-67; 1st tchr., prin. Grace Baptist Kindergarten, Decatur, Ala., 1969-72; founder, prin. Bethel Bapt. Schs., Hartselle, Ala., 1972-77, Hartselle Christian Acad., grades K-12, 1978—; co-founder, prin. Hartselle Christian Acad., 1978—. Soprano on albums The Riches of Live, 1967, Be Still and Know, 1973, Amazing Grace, 1976. Recipient 1st Christian Sch. Tchr. in Area plaque Parents and Students Bethel Bapt. Schs., 1977; Appreciation cert. Morgan County Water and Soil Conservation Dist., 1984. Republican. Baptist. Avocations: arranging and directing plays for students. Home: PO Box 1234 Hartselle AL 35640 Office: Hartselle Christian Acad PO Box 1234 Hartselle AL 35640

THOMSON, LINDA RECKHOW, nurse, consultant; b. Binghamton, N.Y., Sept. 7, 1948; d. George Adelbert and Lillian (Walker) Reckhow; m. George Ora Thomson, June 24, 1972; children—Amanda, Marshall, Brenton. B.S., Hartwick Coll., 1972; M.S., U. Mass., 1977; nurse practitioner Northeastern U., 1975. Cert. pediatric nurse practitioner. Sch. nurse tchr. Eagle Hill Sch., Hardwick, Mass., 1972-73; teaching asst. U. Mass., Amherst, 1973-74; health coordinator PAGE Infant and Toddler, Springfield, Mass., 1978-80, Headstart Program, Springfield, 1978-80; health cons. Early Childhood Ctrs., Springfield, 1979-81, 83—; pediatric nurse practitioner Pioneer Valley Pediatrics, Longmeadow, Mass., 1975—; health cons., bd. dirs. Hardwick Preschool, 1979—; mem. adv. panel Am. Jour. Nursing, N.Y.C., 1972-75; bd. dirs. Am. Cancer Soc., Worcester, Mass., 1972-75. Author: (collaborative) Current Practice in Pediatric Nursing, 1980. Contbr. articles to profl. jours. Charter mem., sec. Inner Wheel, Ware, Mass., 1981—; v.p. Tri Parish Women's Fellowship, Hardwick, 1983-84, pres., 1984-85. John Christopher Hartwick scholar, 1971-72; named Outstanding Young Alumna, Hartwick Coll., 1974. Fellow Nat. Assn. Pediatric Nurse Assocs. and Practitioners (treas. 1983—), Childbirth Edn. Assn., Am. Nurses Assn., Hartwick Coll. Alumni Assn. (dir. 1974-83), Sigma Theta Tau. Congregationalist. Home: Eagle Hill Hardwick MA 01037 Office: Pioneer Valley Pediatrics 123 Dwight Rd Longmeadow MA 01106

THOMSON, THYRA GODFREY, state official; b. Florence, Colo., July 30, 1916; d. John and Rosalie (Altman) Godfrey; B.A. cum laude, U. Wyo., 1939; m. Keith Thomson, Aug. 6, 1939 (dec. Dec. 1960); children—William John II, Bruce Godfrey, Keith Coffey. With dept. agronomy and agrl. econs. U. Wyo., 1938-39; writer weekly column Watching Washington pub. in 14 papers, Wyo., 1955-60; planning chmn. Nat. Fedn. Republican Women, Washington, 1961; sec. state State of Wyo., Cheyenne, 1962—; mem. exec. com. Nat. Conf. Lt. Govs., 1976, 81. Mem. Marshall Scholarships Com. for Pacific Region, 1964-68; del. 72d Wilton Park Conf., Eng., 1965, Nat. Women's Conf., 1977; mem. youth commn. UNESCO, 1970-71, Allied Health Professions Council HEW, 1971-72. Recipient Disting. Alumni award U. Wyo., 1969; named internat. woman of distinction Alpha Delta Kappa; recipient citation Omicron Delta Epsilon, 1965, Beta Gamma Sigma, 1968, Delta Kappa Gamma, 1973; Internat. Women's Yr. guest Fed. Republic Germany. 1975. Mem. N.Am. Securities Adminstrs. (pres. 1973-74), Nat. Assn. Secs. of State, Council State Govts. (chmn. natural resources com. Western States 1966-68), AAUW, Wyo. Press Women, Spurs, PEO, Pi Beta Phi, Alpha Kappa Psi, Psi Chi. Office: Office of Sec State State Capitol Bldg Cheyenne WY 82002

THOMSON, VIRGINIA WINBOURN, history educator, author; b. Oakland, Calif., Aug. 6, 1930; d. Harry Linn and Jennie Cook (Vineyard) T. A.A., San Mateo Coll., 1948; B.A., San Jose State Coll., 1951; M.A., U. Calif.-Berkeley, 1952. Cert. secondary tchr., Calif. Social sci. tchr. Capuchino High Sch., San Bruno, Calif., 1952-54, Watsonville High Sch., Calif., 1954—; saleswoman and storyteller Home Interiors, San Mateo, 1963-64. Author: The Lion Desk, 1965; Short Talks Around The Lord's Table, 1985. Recipient Silver Pitcher award Home Interiors, 1964. Mem. Nat. Geog. Soc. (life), AAUW (life), Calif. Alumni Assn. (life), Am. Fedn. Tchrs. Phi Alpha Theta. Republican.

THOMSON-KEITH, ELAINE AUDREY, nurse, hospital administrator; b. Portage la Prairie, Man., Can., Oct. 2, 1939; came to U.S., 1961; d. Melvin George and Iverna Mary (Hall) T.; m. Samuel Roddey Keith, July 2, 1983. Diploma in nursing Children's Hosp., Winnipeg, Man.; B.S. in Nursing, Tex. Woman's U.-Houston. R.N., Man., Mo., Mich., Tex. Staff nurse Children's Hosp., Winnipeg, 1960-61; supr. operating room and recovery room Children's Mercy Hosp., Kansas City, Mo., 1961-62, asst. dir. nursing, 1967-72; asst. head nurse Baylor U. Med. Ctr., Dallas, 1962-63; head nurse Univ. Hosp., Ann Arbor, Mich., 1965-67; adminstrv. supr. Methodist Hosp., Houston, 1977—, coordinator and tchr. cert. classes for nurses, 1979; presentations in field. Vol. for blood pressure screening and teaching Greater Houston area Am. Heart Assn., 1976—; CPR instr. and trainer, Houston, 1979—. Named Outstanding Houston Profl. Woman, Fedn. Houston Profl. Women, 1983. Mem. Am. Nurses Assn. (council nursing adminstrn. 1983—), Assn. Operating Room Nurses (cert.; charter mem. and chmn. Southfield chpt. 1965-67, com. chmn. Greater Kansas City chpt. 1963-64, dir. Greater Kansas City chpt. 1967-73, com. chmn. Greater Houston chpt. 1974-76, 77-78, 80-81, 83-84, pres. Greater Houston chpt. 1982-83, chmn. nat. com. on edn. 1981-82, chmn. nat. congress planning com. 1983, nat. dir. 1984—), Am. Nurses Found. Century Club, Lion's Eye Bank (life). Republican. Presbyterian. Home: 702 Woodhorn Ct Houston TX 77062 Office: Meth Hosp 6565 Fannin Houston TX 77030

THORBIN, PATRICIA ANN, home care executive; b. Bronx, N.Y., July 30, 1946; d. Robert George and Anita Marie (Bally) Thoubburon; m. Robert Murphy, Mar. 5, 1965 (div. 1973); children—Heather Gail, Doreen Leanora. A.A.S. in Nursing, Stuffolk Community Coll., 1971; B.S. in Health Adminstrn., St. Joseph's Coll., 1984; postgrad. Baruch Coll., 1985—. R.N., N.Y.; cert. utilization rev. coordinator. Staff nurse Southside Hosp., Bay Shore, N.Y., 1975-78; nat. sales coordinator Polyshell Chem., St. James, N.Y., 1978-80; indsl. nurse Abraham & Straus, Huntington, N.Y., 1980-81; supr. nurse Patchogue Nursing Ctr., N.Y., 1981-82; utilization rev., D.R.G. coordinator VA, Northport, N.Y., 1982-85; adminstr. Unlimited Care, Inc., Hicksville, N.Y., 1985—; cons. Chalet Home Care, Port Jefferson, Midland Career Ins., Hempstead, N.Y., 1985—. Mem. Medford Taxpayers Assn., Medford, 1984—, CB'ers for Cerebral Palsy, Smithtown, N.Y., 1983—. Mem. L.I. Council Utilization Rev. Nurses (sec. 1986), N.Y. State Public Health Assn., Nurse Adv. Bd. Myasthenia Gravis, Assn. of Home Care Profls., Nat. League for Nursing, Am. Bd. Utilization Rev. Profls. Republican. Roman Catholic. Avocations: canoeing; horseback riding; bowling; drives in mountains. Office: Unlimited Care Inc 76 N Broadway Hicksville NY 11801

THORBURN, KIM MARIE, prison internist, educator; b. San Francisco, May 11, 1950; d. Jack Donald and Margaret Marie (Carpenter) T. B.A., Stanford U., 1971; M.D., U. Calif.-San Francisco, 1976. Diplomate Am. Bd. Internal Medicine. Intern Highland Gen. Hosp., Oakland, Calif., 1976-77, resident in internal medicine, 1977-78; resident in internal medicine U. Calif.-San Francisco, 1978-79, asst. clin. prof., 1979-84; asst. clin. prof. U. Calif.-Irvine, 1984—; physician Jail Med. Services, San Francisco, 1979-80; staff physician Calif. State Prison, San Quentin, 1980-83, Calif. Instn. for Men, Chino, 1983-84; chief med. officer Calif. Rehab. Ctr., Norco, 1985, Calif. Instn. for Men, Chino, 1986—; cons. Task Force Licensure of Correctional Med. Facilities, Calif. Bd. Corrections, 1983, panel on irritant chems. Nat. Acad. Scis., Washington, 1983; chmn. plenary session panel World Congress Prison Health Services, 1983. Contbr. articles on prison medicine and riot control methods to profl. jours. Advisor Amnesty Internat., 1982—. Recipient cert. of appreciation Men's Adv. Council of San Quentin Prison, 1982; winner awards in surfing; Kellogg Nat. Leadership fellow, 1983—. Mem. ACP, Calif. Med. Assn. (chmn. task force on health care standards for juvenile detention ctrs., chmn. corrections and detentions health care com.), Am. Correctional Health Services Assn. (pres. Calif. chpt. 1984, nat. treas. 1985-86), Internat. Council Prison Med. Services (treas.), San Bernardino County Med. Soc., San Francisco Med. Soc. (del. to Calif. Med. Assn. 1983). Democrat. Office: California Institution for Men PO Box 128 Chino CA 91710

THORELL, SHARILYN HANSON, educational administrator; b. Los Angeles, Feb. 17, 1944; d. Albert and Madelyne (Pobanz) Hanson; m. Robert C. Thorell, Jan. 29, 1965; children—Keith Robert, Kirk Alan. B.S., U. So. Calif., 1965; student U. Hawaii, 1961, Cambridge U., 1963. Dir. univ. events U. So. Calif., Los Angeles, 1965-68, dir. spl. programs, 1968-71, dir. devel. and pub. relations Andrus Gerontology Ctr., 1975-82; exec. dir. Gen. Alumni Assn., 1982-84, assoc. v.p. univ. relations, 1984—; cons. Los Angeles Olympic Organizing Com., 1983-84; cons. Hanson Olson, Pasadena, 1976—, ST & Assocs., Los Angeles, 1980—. Mem. Jr. League of Los Angeles, 1974—. Mem. Council for Advancement and Support of Edn., Orgn. Women Execs., Phi Beta Kappa, Phi Kappa Phi, Alpha Delta Pi. Republican. Presbyterian. Clubs: Calif., Univ. Address: U So Calif Alumni House 0461 Los Angeles CA 90089

THORELLI, IRENE MARGARETA, marketing educator; b. Stockholm, Sweden, July 12, 1950 (parents U.S. citizens), came to U.S., 1956; d. Hans Birger and Sarah Virginia (Scott) T. A.B., Ind. U., 1970; M.A., U. Tex., 1978, Ph.D., 1983. Lic. psychologist, Wis. Research assoc. U. Tex., Austin, 1979-81; cons. Tex. Adult Probation Commn., Austin, 1981, Orgn. and Human

Resource Devel. Assocs., Austin, 1982; prof. psychology Ball State U., Muncie, Ind., 1983-84, prof. mktg., 1984-85; prof. mktg. U. Wis.-La Crosse, 1985—; cons. Big Brothers/Big Sisters Am., Phila., 1984-85, Big Brothers Can., Toronto, 1985—; lectr. in field. Contbr. articles to profl. jours.; presenter, lectr. numerous profl. seminars in psychology, edn. and mktg. Charter mem., vol. Muncie Children's Mus. Guild, 1983-85; mem. mktg. com. Assn. for Retarded Citizens/Ind., Indpls., 1985. U. Tex. travel scholar, 1978; named Outstanding Young Woman Am., 1983; Ball State U. research grantee, 1984-85; U. Wis.-La Crosse grantee, 1986. Fellow Acad. Mktg. Sci.; mem. Am. Psychol. Assn., Am. Ednl. Research Assn., Am. Mktg. Assn., Acad. Mgmt., Nat. Assn. Female Execs., Mensa, Midwest Bus. Adminstrn. Assn. (Outstanding paper award 1986), Sigma Xi. Avocations: entertaining; literature; music; traveling. Home: PO Box 7407 Austin TX 78713 Office: U Wis Dept Mktg Coll Bus Adminstrn La Crosse WI 54601

THORESEN, WENDY ANN, architect; b. Boston, July 6, 1953; d. Philip Benjamin and Eleanor F. (Jackson) T.; m. Horace Harrison Beaven, Jr., Nov. 21, 1979. B.F.A., U. Colo., 1977, B.A., 1978; M.Arch., U. Colo., Denver, 1980. Designer Robert C. McHugh Inc., Steamboat Springs, Colo., 1979; Midyette/Seieroe, Boulder, Colo., 1981-84; pvt. practice designing, Louisville, Colo., 1984, NBI, Inc., Boulder, 1984—. Mem. Nat. Trust for Historic Preservation, AIA (bd. dirs. Colo. North chpt., assoc. dir. 1984-85, bd. dirs. 1986). Democrat.

THORN, SUSAN HOWE, interior designer; b. Washington, Apr. 22, 1941; d. James Bennett Cowdin and Lois (Fiesinger) Howe; A.B. cum laude, Syracuse U., 1962; postgrad. N.Y. Sch. Interior Design, 1965, lighting design Parsons Sch. Design, 1975-77; m. William D. Thorn, June 22, 1963; children—Melissa Ann, William David. Owner, designer Susan Thorn Interiors, Inc., Cross River, N.Y., 1965—; designer total bldg. Cooper Labs, Bedford Hills, N.Y., 1973, total redesign Nycrest Corp., Cold Spring, N.Y., 1973-75, showrooms, model rooms stylist and coordinator France Voiles Co. Inc., N.Y.C., 1976, total design new corp. hdqrs. in Gen. Dynamics Bldg. (with Marjorie Borradaile Helsel), Robert E. Eastman Co., N.Y.C., 1967, Cummin & Friedland Capital Corp., 1982; designer offices, stores, employee areas comml., public, residential clients, including Waccabuc (N.Y.) Country Club, 1969, S. Salem (N.Y.) Library; instr. adult edn. dept. John Jay High Sch., Jr. League No. Westchester, Caramoor Mus.; speaker civic orgns. Mem. Am. Soc. Interior Designers (profl.), Internat. Assn. Lighting Designers (asso.). Episcopalian. Club: Waccabuc Country. Writer weekly decorating column in The Patent Trader, 1965-66; contbr. articles to newspapers. Home: Route 121 Cross River NY 10518

THORNBURY, BETTY WARD, pharmaceutical company sales executive; b. Okmulgee, Okla., June 15, 1946; d. Harold Banaugh and Vetrus (Tennison) Ward; m. Robert Allen Thornbury, June 16, 1967 (div. Jan. 1969). A.S., Bacone Coll., Muskogee, Okla., 1967; B.S., Northeastern State U., Tahlequah, Okla., 1969; postgrad. in geology Okla. State U., 1970-71. Tchr. sci., coach basketball and track Broken Arrow Pub. Schs. System, Okla., 1969-76; sr. profl. med. rep. Roerig div. Pfizer Pharms., Broken Arrow, 1976—; in-service educator nursing homes, Tulsa, 1976—; cons. to retail and hosps. pharmacists, Tulsa, 1976—; drug cons. Okla. Osteo. State Conv., Afton, 1976—, Okla. Med. Assn., Tulsa, 1986. Bd. dirs. Broken Arrow Youth Basketball Assn., 1982—, v.p., 1986. Recipient various awards Roerig, 1979-82; Muskogee Women's Bus. Assn. scholar Bacone Coll., 1967, Northeastern State U., 1967-69; NSF grantee, 1970-71. Mem. Nat. Diabetes Assn., Tulsa Diabetes Educators Assn., Tulsa Med. Service Assn., Nat. Assn. Female Execs., Phi Theta Kappa. Democrat. Baptist. Avocations: coaching; reading. Home and Office: 2705 E Knoxville Broken Arrow OK 74014

THORNHILL, LOIS, photographer; b. Boston, Apr. 7, 1945; d. Fred S. and Mary (Evans) Thornhill; B.A., Middlebury Coll., 1966; postgrad. U. St. Thomas, Houston, 1967-69; M.A., N.Y. U., 1971; cert. in graphic design U. Calif.-Santa Cruz, 1983; m. Edward J. McCluskey, Feb. 14, 1981. Research technician dept. virology Baylor Sch. Medicine, Houston, 1966-68; with Kelly Girls, Palo Alto, 1971-72; slide curator dept. art Stanford (Calif.) U., 1972-80; founder, pres. Stanford Design Assocs., Palo Alto, 1981—; cons. copy and museum photography; designer, producer custom slide lectures. Mem. Smithsonian Assos., Coll. Art Assn. Am. Home: 895 Northampton Dr Palo Alto CA 94303 Office: PO Box 60451 A Palo Alto CA 94306

THORNLOW, CAROLYN, law firm administrator, consultant; b. Kew Gardens, N.Y., May 25, 1954. B.B.A. magna cum laude, Bernard M. Baruch Coll., 1982. Gen. mgr. Richard A. Ramm Assocs., Levittown, N.Y., 1972-78; adminstr. Tunstead Schechter & Torre, N.Y.C., 1978-82, Cowan Liebowitz & Latman, P.C., N.Y.C., 1982-84, Rosenberg & Estis, P.C., N.Y.C., 1984-85; controller Finkelstein, Borah, Schwartz, Altschuler & Goldstein, P.C., N.Y.C., 1986—; pres. Concinnity Services, Hastings, N.Y., 1984—; instr. introduction to law office mgmt. seminars Assn. Legal Adminstrs., N.Y.C., 1984. Contbr. numerous articles to profl. jours. Mem. N.Y. Assn. Legal Adminstrs. (v.p. 1982-83), Internat. Assn. Legal Adminstrs. (asst. regional v.p. 1983-84, regional v.p. 1984-85), ABA, Mensa, Beta Gamma Sigma, Sigma Iota Epsilon.

THORNTON, BEVERLY ANN, sales executive; b. McDonald, Pa., Oct. 9, 1951; d. William Franklin and Roma Louise (Fullum) T. B.S., Calif. State Coll., 1973; postgrad. U. Pitts., 1975-76. Secondary English tchr. Penn Hills Sch. Dist. (Pa.), 1973-76; sales trainee PPG Industries, Pitts., 1976-77, sales rep., Houston, 1977-78, Dallas, 1978-80, resident sales rep., 1980-82, br. sales mgr., 1982—, mem. PPG Bus. Council-Tex., 1983. Mem. Tex. Assn. Bus., Soc. Plastics Industry, Fiberglass Fabricators Assn., Assn. Exec. Saleswomen. Baptist. Democrat. Office: PPG Industries 14001 Goldmark St Suite 141 Dallas TX 75240

THORNTON, FLORENCE EMMA (MRS. LAURANCE C. THORNTON), freelance writer and lecturer; b. Boston, May 9, 1897; d. August L. and Emma (Ericson) Tobin; student Emerson Coll, Boston, 1917-18; m. Laurance C. Thornton, Oct. 19, 1946 (dec. 1952). With U.S. Govt. in Alaska, 1921-53; sec. Bethlehem Shipbuilding Corp., 1917-19l bookkeeper Granite Trust Co., Quincy, Mass., 1920-21; chief civilian personnel USCG, 1940-51; acting mgr. OPS, Fairbanks, Alaska, 1952-53; pvt. tchr. of violin 1921-30; co-founder Orthopedic and Tech. Center, Kottayam, Kerala, India, 1963-64; lectr. on her extensive world travels, also art and religion, U.S., Alaska, 1953—; humorist. Pres., Alaska Fedn. Music Clubs, 1928-34. Mem. Dept. of Alaska Am. Legion Aux. (life, pres. 1935-36), W.C.T.U. (sec. Alaska 1950-53), Nat. Assn. Ret. Fed. Employees (past pres.), World War I Vets. Aux. Republican. Methodist (cert. lay speaker 1983—). Clubs: Writers, Alaska (Woodburn, also Salem). Home: 1291 Princeton Rd Woodburn OR 97071

THORNTON, JUDY CARRUTH, printing company executive; b. Andrews, Tex., Sept. 19, 1950; d. Odis O. and Edith Jessie (Clem) Carruth; student U. Tex., Arlington; m. James W. Thornton, Nov. 22, 1969; children—Michael Paul, Elisa Jennifer, Formerly with City Dallas, Tex., Metroplex Nat. Bank, Arlington; now owner Stockton Printing and Equipment Co., Xerox authorized sales agt., Fort Stockton, Tex., 1980—. Den leaders coach Cub Scouts Am., 1981—. Mem. Nat. Assn. Printers and Lithographers, Nat. Office Products Assn., Nat. Office Machine Dealers Assn., Printing Industries Am., Fort Stockton C. of C. (dir.), Xi Zeta Lambda (v.p., sec.). Methodist. Office: 109 N Nelson St Fort Stockton TX 79735

THORNTON, LINDA, lawyer; b. Salt Lake City, Sept. 16, 1951; d. Bruce G. and Betty (Junker) Thornton; m. Steven A. Broiles, Aug. 29, 1982. B.A., U. Calif.-Irvine, 1972; J.D., Loyola U., Los Angeles, 1976. Bar: Calif. 1977. Dep. dist. counsel South Coast Air Quality Mgmt. Dist., El Monte, Calif., 1977-79; atty. So. Calif. Edison Co., Rosemead, Calif., 1979-80; assoc. firm Best, Best & Krieger, Los Angeles, 1981-83; ptnr. firm Dunne, Phelps, Mills, Stall & McCord, Los Angeles, 1983; assoc. Law Offices Robert L. Baker, Pasadena, Calif., 1983—. Mem. ABA, AAUW, Air Pollution Control Assn. Office: Law Offices Robert L Baker 1115 Hudson Ave Suite A Pasadena CA 91101

THORNTON, MARY JANE, editor, writer; b. Honolulu, July 26, 1923; d. Harvey John and Mable Wilma (Lane) Thornton. Student Nat. U. Mex., 1944-45; B.A. in English, U. Vt., 1946; M.Litt., San Francisco State U., 1979. Reporter, columnist Fairchild Pubs., N.Y.C., 1948-49; editor N.Y. State Pharmacist, N.Y.C., 1949-53; editor, mgr. Med. Pubs., N.Y.C., 1953-57; editor, writer Liquidometer Corp., L.I., 1958-67, graphics cons., 1958-67; mng. editor Am. Thoracic Soc., N.Y.C., 1967—; editor, artist ATS News, N.Y.C., San Francisco, Balt., 1974—; cons. Com. to Research TV Programming, N.Y.C., 1970-71. Mem. NOW, Mortar Bd. Mem. Soc. Tech. Writers and Editors, Am. Med. Writer's Assn., House Mag. Inst. (cited for excellence of pub. 1953). Author: Down Memory Lane: Connections with the DC-8, 1960. Office: Am Rev Am Thoracic Soc 1740 Broadway New York NY 10019

THORNTON, ROSALYN SHIRLEEN, nurse; b. Waynesville, Ga., Feb. 8, 1935; d. William Henderson and Marguerite Elizabeth (Mattox) Jacobs; m. Redick Aaron Thornton, Jr., Aug. 4, 1951; children—Redick Aaron III, Robert O., Sinda, Joel, Susan, Rose, Allen. R.N. A.A. in Nursing, Brunswick Jr. Coll., 1982. Telephone operator Brantley Telephone Co., Nahunta, Ga., 1950-51; shoe factory worker Rubin Bros./Spatola, Waycross, Ga., 1951-59; sleever Brunswick Mfg., Ga., 1965-78; ward clk. Glynn Brunswick Meml. Hosp., 1978-82, nurse, 1982—. Baptist. Home: PO Box 96 Waynesville GA 31566

THORNTON, YVONNE SHIRLEY, physician, musician; b. N.Y.C., Nov. 21, 1947; d. Donald E. and Itasker F. (Edmonds) T.; B.S. in Biology, Monmouth Coll., 1969; M.D., Columbia U., 1973; m. Shearwood McClelland, June 8, 1974; children—Shearwood III, Kimberly Itaska. Resident in ob-gyn Roosevelt Hosp., N.Y.C., 1973-77; fellow maternal-fetal medicine Columbia-Presbyn. Med. Center, N.Y.C., 1977-79; commd. lt. comdr. M.C., USN, 1979; asst. prof. ob-gyn Uniformed Services U. Health Scis., 1979-82, Cornell U. Med. Coll., N.Y.C., 1982—; dir. clin. services dept. ob-gyn N.Y. Hosp.-Cornell Med. Center, 1982—; asst. attending N.Y. Lying-In Hosp., 1982—; staff Nat. Naval Med. Center, Bethesda, Md.; saxophonist Thornton Sisters ensemble, 1955-76. Diplomate Am. Bd. Ob-Gyn, Nat. Bd. Med. Examiners. Fellow Am. Coll. Obstetricians and Gynecologists; mem. AMA, N.Y. Acad. Medicine, Am. Fertility Soc., Soc. Perinatal Obstetricians, Am. Fedn. Musicians. Lambda Sigma Tau. Democrat. Baptist. Office: 525 E 68th St New York NY 10021

THORNTON-CARTER, MARGARET ALICIA JOAN, management company executive; retail executive; b. Gt. Brit., Dec. 23, 1937; d. James and Doris (Bajana) C.; came to U.S., 1961; Royal Soc. Arts degree, 1954. Real estate broker, Providence, 1970—; registered apt. mgr., Providence, 1969-70; foreman constrn. site; owner, operator mgmt. co., Providence, 1973—. Mem. Pvt. Industry Council R.I., 1983—. Mem. C. of C. U.S., Johnston (R.I.) C. of C. (pres. 1981—), Nat. Assn. Home Builders, Nat., R.I. builders assns., SBA. Episcopalian. Home: 1145 Hartford Ave Johnston RI 02919 Office: 1145 Hartford Ave Johnston RI 02919

THORP, PAMELA LYN, oil field equipment manufacturing company executive; b. Vienna, Austria, Mar. 6, 1949; came to U.S., 1951; d. Joseph William and Winifred Johanna (Van Kuelan) Jogl; m. Stephen K. Thorp, Dec. 22, 1967; children—Tracy Elizabeth, Stephen K. Student Palmer Inst. Profl. Writers, 1968-70. Clk., NL Shaffer, Houston, 1978-80, capacity planner, 1980-82, credit rep., 1982—. Sec., Greenridge North Civic Club, 1975-84, pres., 1985—. Mem. Nat. Assn. Credit Mgmt., Houston Assn. Credit Mgmt., Petroleum Equipment Suppliers Assn., Houston Credit Womens Assn. Republican. Mem. Christian Ch. Home: 15026 Kirkfield Ln Houston TX 77060 Office: NL Shaffer PO Box 1473 Houston TX 77251

THORPE, JANET CLAIRE, lawyer; b. Bklyn., Dec. 8, 1953; d. Burton Walter and Phyllis Claire (Read) T.; m. David Frank Palmer, Aug. 26, 1978; children—Katherine Elaine, Jennifer Claire. Student, Boston U., 1972-74; A.B. in Polit. Sci. and History, Union Coll., 1975; postgrad. Western New Eng. Sch. Law, 1975-76; J.D., Emory U., 1978. Bar: Ga. 1978, U.S. Ct. Appeals (5th and 11th cirs.) 1978, 80, U.S. Dist. Ct. (no. dist.) Ga. 1978. Comptroller's asst. Boston U., 1974-75; law librarian Western New Eng. Coll., Springfield, Mass., 1976; law clk. to judge U.S. Dist. Ct., Atlanta, 1978; regional atty. Comptroller of Currency, Atlanta, 1978-80; assoc. corp. counsel Trust Co. Ga., Atlanta, 1980—; dir. Trusco Properties, Inc., Atlanta; mng. ptnr. PROP, a Ga. Gen. Partnership, Atlanta, 1984—. Mem. Council on Battered Women, Atlanta, 1983—, bd. dirs., 1986. Mem. Ga. Bar Assn. (banking and corp. sect.), Assn. Bank Holding Cos. (lawyers com. 1983—), Am. Corp. Counsel Assn. Atlanta Arts Alliance, 1985—. Democrat. Episcopalian. Avocations: gardening; child rearing; house renovation; photography. Office: Trust Co Ga One Park Pl Atlanta GA 30303

THORPE, MARY WILLA, nurse; b. Phila., Sept. 22, 1948; d. Willie and Emma Louise (Thorpe) Thorpe. A.S.A., Community Coll. Phila., 1969; B.A., Lincoln U., 1973; B.S., LaSalle U., 1985; postgrad. Coll. Textile and Sci., Phila. Head surg. nurse Guiffre Hosp., Phila., 1969; staff nurse ARC, Phila., 1969-75; nursing supr. Dept. Public Health, Phila., 1975-86; nurse mgr. Ambulatory Health Ctrs., Osteo. Med. Ctr., Phila., 1986—. Senator Hankins scholar, 1970, 71; Phila. Public Sch. Bd. scholar, 1966-69. Mem. Assn. MBA Execs., Nat. Assn. Female Execs., Zeta Phi Beta, Chi Eta Phi. Democrat. Mem. Ch. Christ. Home: 8067 Temple Rd Philadelphia PA 19150

THORPE, PATRICIA ANN, nursing educator and administrator; b. Lakin, Kans., Feb. 9, 1933; d. Everett Gareth and Helen Elizabeth (Hinden) Wilson; m. John Norman Thorpe, Apr. 15, 1955; children—Glenn Richard, Barbara Lynn, Roger Gary. Student Idaho State U., 1951-54; B.S.Nursing, U. Utah, 1957; postgrad. La. State U., 1981, Northwestern State U., Shreveport, La., 1982-83. Nursc St. Anthony Community Hosp., Pocatello, Idaho, 1957-58; staff and adminstrv. nurse Southeastern Dist. Health, Pocatello, 1958-68; asst. supr., then supr. Mont. Dept. Health and Environ. Scis., Butte, 1969-73; instr. Sch. Nursing, Mont. State U., Butte, 1973-77; dir. Home Health Agy., Butte, 1977-78; dir. sch. health St. Charles Paris Pub. Schs., Luling, La., 1979-81; nurse coordinator La. Dept. Edn., Baton Rouge, 1981-82; instr. Coll. Nursing, Northwestern State U., Shreveport, 1982-83; supr. pediatrics Med. Coll., U. Okla., Tulsa, 1983—. Author: School Health Manual, 1981; also articles. Active vol. in numerous community welfare, health and edn. projects; former bd. dirs. Mont. Health System Agy., Mont. Com. Child Abuse and Neglect, Community Day Care Center, Butte; mem. adv. bd. PEP Community Edn. Vols., Tulsa, 1983—. Mem. Am. Nurses Assn., Nat. Sch. Health Assn., Nat. Sch. Nurse Assn. Mont. Home Health Assn. (state treas. 1978). Episcopalian. Home: 625 S 278th E Catoosa OK 74015 Office: U Okla Tulsa Med Coll 2815 S Sheridan St Tulsa OK 74129

THORSEN, NANCY DAIN, real estate broker; b. Edwardsville, Ill., June 23, 1944; d. Clifford Earl and Suzanne Eleanor (Kribs) Dain; m. David Massie, 1968 (div. 1975); i dau., Suzanne Dain Massie; m. James Hugh Thorsen, May 30, 1980. B.Sc. in Mktg., So. Ill. U., 1968, M.Sc. in Bus. Edn., 1975; grad. Realtor Inst., Idaho, 1983. Cert. resdl. and investment specialist. Personnel officer J.H. Little & Co. Ltd., London, 1969-72; instr. in bus. edn. Spl. Sch. Dist. St. Louis, 1974-77; mgr. mktg./ops. Isis Foods, Inc., St. Louis, 1978-80; asst. mgr. store Stix, Baer & Fuller, St. Louis, 1980; assoc. broker Century 21 Sayer Realty, Inc., Idaho Falls, Idaho, 1981—. Bd. dirs. Idaho Vol., Boise, 1981-84, Idaho Falls Symphony, 1982; pres. Friends of Idaho Falls Library, 1981-83; chmn. Idaho Falls Mayor's Com. for Vol. Coordination, 1981-84. Recipient Idaho Gov.'s award, 1982, cert. appreciation City of Idaho Falls/Mayor Campbell, 1982; named to Two Million Dollar Club; named Top Investment Sales Person for Eastern Idaho, 1985. Mem. Idaho Falls Bd. Realtors (chmn. orientation 1982-83, chmn. edn. 1983), So. Ill. U. Alumni Assn. Clubs: Newcomers, Civitan (Idaho Falls). Office: Century 21 Sayer Realty Inc 403 First St PO Box 1606 Idaho Falls ID 83403

THOYER, JUDITH REINHARDT, lawyer; b. Mt. Vernon, N.Y., July 29, 1940; d. Edgar Allen and Florence (Mayer) Reinhardt; m. Michael Edward Thoyer, June 30, 1963; children—Erinn, Michael John. B.A., U. Mich., 1961; LL.B. summa cum laude, Columbia U., 1966. Bar: N.Y. Law librarian U. Ghana, Accra, 1963-64; assoc. Paul, Weiss, Rifkind, Wharton & Garrison, N.Y.C., 1966-74, ptnr., 1975—. Contbr. articles to profl. jours. Bd. dirs. Women's Action Alliance, N.Y.C., 1977—; active Am. Cancer Soc., N.Y.C., 1982—; Women in Bus. Against Cancer. Mem. Assn. Bar City of N.Y. (com. on recruitment of lawyers 1981-83, com. securities regulation 1976-79), N.Y. County Lawyers' Assn. (com. on securities and exchanges 1982—). Home: 1115 Fifth Ave New York NY 10128

THRALL, MARY ANNA HULL, veterinarian; b. Montreal, Que., Can., July 4, 1944; d. John Floyd and Mariella (Godfrey) Hull; B.A., U. Evansville, 1966; D.V.M., Purdue U., 1970; M.S., Colo. State U., 1977; m. F.G. Freemyer, Mar. 21, 1975; children—Joseph Paul, Anna Marie, Sarah Elizabeth. Pvt. vet. practitioner Eldred Animal Hosp., Greeley, Colo., 1970-74; resident in clin. pathology Colo. State U., Fort Collins, 1974-77; asst. prof. clin. pathology, 1978-84, assoc. prof., 1984—, dir. lab., 1981-84. Mem. Am. Coll. Vet. Pathologists, AVMA, Colo. Vet. Med. Assn., Am. Animal Hosp. Assn., Colo. Vet. Med. Assn., Am. Animal Hosp. Assn., Am. Soc. Vet. Clin. Pathology, Womens Vet. Med. Assn., Colo. Soc. Cytology, Colo. Assn. Continuing Med. Lab. Edn., Am. Soc. Cytotechnology, Assn. Am. Vet. Med. Colls., Phi Kappa Phi, Phi Zeta. Office: Dept Pathology Colo State U Fort Collins CO

THRASH, DORA ANN, nursing educator; b. Georgetown, Tex., Aug. 28, 1945; d. Honley and Florence Lee (Gadison) Jefferson; m. William Albert Thrash, Dec. 13, 1969; 1 son, Lester. B.S. in Nursing, Prairie View A&M U., 1968; M.S. in Nursing, Tex. Woman's U., 1979. Staff nurse M.D. Anderson Hosp., Houston, 1968-69, Kings Dau. Hosp., Temple, Tex., 1970, Darnall Army Hosp., Ft. Hood, Tex., 1970-73; assoc. instr. Central Tex. Coll., Killeen, 1974—. Treas. Fowler Elem. PTA, Killeen, 1980-84; den leader Boy Scouts Am., Killeen, 1982-83. Mem. Am. Nurses Assn., Tex. Nurses Assn., Delta Sigma Theta. Democrat. Baptist. Lodge: Daus. of Isis (asst. marshal 1982-83). Home: 1308 Brock Dr Killeen TX 76541 Office: Central Texas College W Hwy 190 Killeen TX 76541

THROCKMORTON, KAREN PETERSON, lawyer; b. Miami Beach, Fla., Oct. 9, 1954; d. Robert Arthur and Virginia Bertha (Clements) Peterson; m. Charles Withers Throckmorton, IV, June 16, 1979. B.A. in History, Duke U., 1976; J.D., U. Miami, 1981. Bar: Fla. 1981. Paralegal McGuire, Woods & Battle, Richmond, Va., 1976-78; law clk. U.S. Dist. Ct., Miami, Fla., 1981-83; assoc. Mershon, Sawyer, Johnston Dunwody & Cole, Miami, 1983—. Lobbyist Jr. League Miami, Fla., 1982—, mem. governing bd., 1984—. Mem. Ransom-Everglades Alumni Assn. (pres. 1983-84), Fla. Bar, Dade County Bar Assn. Democrat. Episcopalian. Club: The Bath (Miami Beach, Fla.). Home: 9940 SW 59th Ave Miami FL 33156 Office: Mershon Sawyer Johnston Dunwody and Cole Southeast Fin Ctr 200 S Biscayne Blvd Miami FL 33131

THROOP, BEATRICE TERRY, educator; b. Raymond, Ill.; d. John Charles and Therese (Mathis) Terry; B.E., Ill. State U., 1930; M.S. (fellow), U. Chgo., 1938; postgrad. U. Oreg., summer 1939, Oreg. State U., summer 1953, Colo. U., summers 1955-56, U. Caen (France), summers 1965-66, U. Md., summer 1963, 65-66; m. Vincent Medville Throop, May 29, 1940 (dec. Oct. 1968); children—Medville Jay, Alice Milberry, David Edmund, Annette Beatrice, Julian. Tchr., Lima (Peru) High Sch., Women's Fgn. Missionary Soc. of Meth. Ch., 1930-36; instr. Stephens Coll., 1938-40; tchr. public schs., Portland (Oreg.) Air Base, 1941; bibliographer Library of Congress, Washington, 1960-61; tchr. Prince George's County Schs., Brandywine, Md., 1961-77; George Washington U., summers 1967-69, 73-74. Bd. dirs. Suitland Manor Owners Assn., 1981—, sec., 1984—. Mem. AAUW, Assn. Am. Geographers, NEA, Md. Edn. Assn., Prince George's County Tchrs. Assn., Am. Assn. Tchrs. Spanish and Portuguese, Alliance Francaise, Sigma Delta Epsilon. Contbr. articles to local publs. Home: 6100 Westchester Park Dr #1104 College Park MD 20740

THRYFT, ANN R., corporate communications manager; b. San Francisco, Dec. 22, 1950; d. William Boyd and Margaret Evelyn (Wilson) T.; m. Alfred Stephens Nelson, May 15, 1971 (div. 1983). B.A. in Anthropology, Stanford U., 1976. Cert. bus. communicator U.S.A. Mktg. communications specialist Franklin Electric, Sunnyvale, Calif., 1981-82; advt. specialist Lear Siegler Inc., Menlo Park, Calif., 1982-83; mktg. communications mgr. Buscom Systems, Santa Clara, Calif., 1983-84; corp. communications mgr. Nat. Tech. Systems, Calabasas, Calif., 1985—; cons. in field. Contbr. article to profl. jour. Mem. Bus.-Profl. Advt. Assn., Stanford Alumni Assn., Publicity Club of Los Angeles. Avocations: historical research; history of religious research; painting. Office: Nat Tech Systems 24007 Ventura Blvd Calabasas CA 91302

THULIN, ADELAIDE ANN, design company executive, interior designer; b. Chgo., Nov. 15, 1925; d. Martin Evold and Kathleen Marie (Glennon) Peterson; m. Frederick Adolph Thulin, Jr., Aug. 18, 1945; children—Frederick, Kristin, Mary, Margaret, Francis, Peter, Andrea, Charles, Joseph, Kathleen, James, Suzanne, Patricia. Student Northwestern U., 1943-46; A.A. in Interior Design, Harper Coll., 1977. Asst. production mgr. Cruttenden & Eger, Chgo., 1946; editor Mt. Prospect Independent, Ill., 1960; real estate salesperson Homefinders, Northwest Chgo. suburbs, 1965-67; asst. v.p. advt. Littelfuse, DesPlaines, Ill., 1965-67; owner, pres. Applied Design Assocs., Mt. Prospect, 1977—; profl. affiliate Am. Inst. Architects. Author, editor monthly newsletter Women's Archtl. League, 1983-85, The Binnacle, CYC, 1979-81. Organizer, Mother's March of Dimes, Mt. Prospect, 1953-54; orgaizer Vols. for Stevenson, 1952, 56, Citizens for Douglas, 1954, Citizens for Kennedy, 1960, mem. Fair Review Council, Chgo., 1983-84; mem. 13th Congl. Dist. Democratic Women's Club, publicity chmn. 1957-58; mem. Chgo. Symphony Orchestra Chorus, 1972; del. Ill. Statehouse Conf. on Small Bus., 1984, 85, mem. Dist. 214 Continuing Edn. Bd.; mem. social service com. Arts Council of Mt. Prospect. Mem. Ill. Devel. Council, Ind. Bus. Assns. Ill., Women's Archtl. League (publicity chmn. 1964-65), Mt. Prospect C. of C. Roman Catholic. Avocations: reading for print-handicapped on CRIS radio; choral singing. Home: 4 S Owen St Mt Prospect IL 60056 Office: Applied Design Assocs Ltd 200 E Evergreen Ave Mount Prospect IL 60056

THUMLER, BARBARA BELLE, educational adminstrator; b. Jersey City, Feb. 11, 1936; d. Albert A. and Cecelia E. (Wilking) T. B.S. in Edn., Temple U., 1958, M.S. in Edn., 1961. Tchr. Sch. Dist. Phila., 1958-72, dept. head, 1972-74, asst. dir., 1974—. Chairperson ARC Youth Services Program, Phila., 1975-76; mem. YWCA Task Force for Health, Phys. Edn. and Recreation, Phila., 1976-77; mem. Mayor's Commn. for Women Edn. Task Force, Phila., 1981-82. Recipient William A. Stecher award Sch. Dist. Phila., 1973, Disting. Service award Lincoln High Sch., Phila., 1977, Cert. of Honor, Gen. Alumni Assn. Temple U., Phila., 1984. Mem. AAHPER and Dance, Nat. Council Adminstrv. Women in Edn., NOW, Pa. Assn. Health, Phys. Edn. and Recreation (conv. mgr. 1979, State Honor award 1973), Phila. Assn. Health, Phys. Edn. and Recreation (pres. 1973-74), Phila. Assn. Sch. Adminstrs., Temple U. Coll. Health, Phys. Edn., Recreation and Dance Alumni Assn. (pres. 1976-77). Avocations: skiing; golf; gardening. Office: Sch Dist Phila Div Phys And Health Edn Stevens Adminstrv Ctr 13th and Spring Garden Sts Philadelphia PA 19123

THURMAN, JUDITH, writer; b. N.Y.C., Oct. 28, 1946; d. William A. and Alice (Meisner) T. B.A., Brandeis U., 1967. Author: Isak Dinesen: The Life of a Storyteller, 1982 (Am. Book award 1983); others. Contbr. articles to profl. jours.

THURMAN, KAREN, state senator; b. Rapid City, S.D., Jan. 12, 1951; d. Lee Searle and Donna (Altfillisch) Loveland; m. John Patrick Thurman, 1973; children—McLin Searl and Liberty Lee. B.A., U. Fla., 1973. Mem. Dunnellon City Council (Fla.), 1974-82; mayor of Dunnellon, 1979-81; mem. Monroe Regional Med. Ctr. Governancy Com.; mem. Comprehensive Plan Tech. Adv. Com.; del. Fla. Democratic Conv.; Dem. Nat. Conv., 1980; mem. Regional Energy Action com.; mem. Fla. State Senate, 1982—. Recipient Service Above Self award Dunnellon C. of C., 1980; Regional Planning Council Appreciation for Service award. Mem. Dunnellon C. of C. (dir.), Fla. Horseman's Children's Soc. (charter). Episcopalian. Office: Fla Senate State Capitol Tallahassee FL 32301*

THURMAN, NORMA JEAN, nurse; b. Hannibal, Mo., Feb. 24, 1927; d. David Robert and Sylvia Martha (Sonner) Shuck; R.N., Hillcrest Med. Center, Tulsa, 1955; B.S., St. Mary-of-the-Woods Coll., 1978; M.Liberal Studies, U. Okla., 1983; m. Andrew Frank Thurman, July 11, 1959. Head nurse emergency room Hillcrest Med. Center, 1957-63; surg. nurse to Herman Flanigan, M.D., Tulsa, 1956-57, to Robert Spencer, M.D., Tulsa, 1958-59; public health nurse Tulsa City and County Health Dept., 1963; adminstr. med. services Rockwell Internat., Tulsa, 1963-86; ret., 1986. Named Employee of Month, Rockwell Internat., 1966; R.N., Okla.; cert. occupational health nurse. Mem. Am. Assn. Occupational Health Nurses, Am. Nurses Assn. (chmn. Okla. occupational nurse sect. 1966), Okla. Nurses Assn., Rockwell Internat. Mgmt. Assn. Tulsa, Nat. Mgmt. Assn., Alumnae Assn. U. Okla., Alumnae Assn. St. Mary-of-the-Woods Coll.

THURMAN, THEODORA (TEDI), broadcasting personality; b. Midville, Ga., June 23, 1932; d. John Benjamin and Para Zona (Roughton) Thurman. Student U. Ga., 1948-50, Corcoran Mus. Art, 1950. Photographer's fashion model, Vogue Mag. and all fashion publs., N.Y.C., Paris, 1951-55; commentator, actress NBC, N.Y.C., 1955-63; actress Metro Goldwyn Mayer, Hollywood, Calif., 1958; films include Ten Thousand Bedrooms and Jail Bait, 1954. Named Woman of the Year, Nat. Radio and TV Daily, 1960, Most Promising New Talent, 1959. Address: 8375 Fountain Ave Los Angeles CA 90069

THURN, VICKIE RHODES, electronics corp. ofcl.; b. Long Beach, Calif., Oct. 20, 1953; d. Marlan B. and Carole Ann Rhodes; B.A. in Communication, U. Central Fla., 1975; postgrad. in bus. mgmt. and psychology, U. South Fla.; m. Walt Thurn, Apr. 11, 1981. Communications specialist Fla. Power Corp., St. Petersburg, 1975-80; mgr. tng. and devel. E-Systems, Inc., St. Petersburg, 1980—; public relations adv. council U. Fla. Mem. Internat. Assn. Bus. Communicators (pres., dir.), Am. Soc. Tng. and Devel., AAUW, Suncoast Mgmt. Inst. (dir.), Women in Communication, Internat. Assn. Quality Circles (pres.). Republican. Methodist. 1247 Murok Way S Saint Petersburg FL 33705 Office: PO Box 12248 Saint Petersburg FL 33733

TIBERIO, FAITH KUHRA, metal stamping company executive; b. St. Augustine, Fla., Jan. 23, 1926; d. Raymond Theodore and Marguerita (Phillips) Kurt; student John B. Stetson U., 1944-45; B.A., Boston U., 1965, M.A., 1967; m. Joseph William Tiberio, May 18, 1945; children—Frederick Morris, Faith Phillips. With Western Union, Phila., 1943-44, So. Bell Telephone Co., St. Augustine, 1944-45; co-founder, mgr. Ty-Car Mfg. Co., Holliston, Mass., 1946-49; partner Century Mfg. Co., Holliston, 1949—, dir., 1970—; v.p. Ty-Wood Corp., Holliston, 1965—. Trustee, Hillside Sch., 1977-80. Mem. Bus. and Profl. Women's Club, DAR (state regent 1977-80, nat. curator gen. 1980-83). Club: Framingham Women's Republican (pres. 1983-84). Office: Ty-Wood Corp 383 Fiske St Holliston MA 01746

TIBURZI, ANITA M(ARIE), marketing and public relations firm executive, consultant; b. Englewood, N.J., Aug. 14, 1944; d. August Robert and Gunvor Inga Britt (Dahlberg) T.; m. Stephen F. Johnson, Aug. 3, 1973; 1 child, James Wood. B.A., U. Stockholm, 1966; postgrad. Centre Universitaire Mediterrannee, Nice, France, 1967. Dir. corp. communications Kenton Corp., N.Y.C., 1968-72; dir. bus. devel. L.M. Rosenthal, N.Y.C., 1972-73; cons. Monsanto Corp., Simplicity Corp., Helena Rubenstein, N.Y.C., 1973-78; v.p. Perrier Group, Greenwich, Conn., 1978-83; pres. Atwood Internat. Inc., N.Y.C., 1983—; cons. mktg./pub. relations and creative spl. events; dir. Salt-Free Gourmet Corp., N.Y.C.; trustee Philharmonia Virtuosi, N.Y.C., 1985—. Patentee ednl. toy. Com. mem. Am. Cancer Soc., N.Y.C., 1975—, Millay Colony for Arts, N.Y.C., 1977—, Just One Break, Inc., N.Y.C., 1978—; mem. Inner Circle Republican Com., Washington, 1984—. Episcopalian. Avocations: art and antique collecting; historical preservation and conservation; riding; tennis. Office: Atwood Internat Inc 22 E 72d St New York NY 10021

TIBUS, CHERYL ANN, quality improvement program facilitator; b. Detroit, Jan. 18, 1953; d. Joseph Edmund and Barbara Dawn (Derkis) T. B.A., Mich. State U., 1975; M.B.A., Nova U., 1983. Communications dir. Realtek Real Estate, Jupiter, Fla., 1976-78; continuity dir. Sta. WJNO, West Palm Beach, Fla., 1978-79; tech. writer Butler/Pratt & Whitney Aerospace, West Palm Beach, 1979-82, media communications specialist, 1982; mktg. analyst Fla. Power and Light Co., Miami, 1982—. Bd. dirs. Miami's For Me, 1982, 83, 84; judge Miami Herald Silver Knight awards, 1983, Optimist Oratorial Contest, Hialeah, Fla., 1983; active Greater Miami Host Com., 1982. Mem. South Fla. Internat. Assn. Bus. Communicators (bd. dirs. 1983, 84), Am. Mktg. Assn. (bd. dirs. 1985-87). Office: Fla Power and Light Co PO Box 029311 Miami FL 33102

TICE, DIANA KOTLAR, steel company manager; b. N.Y.C., Dec. 13, 1955; d. Albert and Elisabeth Barbara (Specht) Kotlar; m. Edward Thomas Tice, Feb. 10, 1979. B.A. in French, Fordham U., 1977. Optometric technician E & V Lapidus, O.D., Little Neck, N.Y., 1972-77; product mgr. Usinor Steel Corp., N.Y.C., 1977—. Mem. Am. Mus. Natural History, WNET-TV (both N.Y.C.), Com. to Re-elect Pres. Reagon, Washington. Mem. Am. Soc. Metals, Am. Iron and Steel Soc., Assn. Iron and Steel Engrs., Assn. Women in Metals Industry. Republican. Roman Catholic. Office: Usinor Steel Corp 600 3d Ave New York NY 10016

TICHENOR, CAROLYN JEAN, business development executive; b. Indpls., Sept. 16, 1943; d. Edsel Ralph and Tracy Mae (Byrdsong) Ford; 1 child, DeLynn Michelle Hayes. B.B.A., U. Tex.-Arlington, 1977; postgrad. U. Minn., 1980, U. Wash., 1981, Ind. U.-Purdue U., Indpls., 1984, U. Ill.-Chgo., 1985, Wilberforce U., 1985. Account clk. Civil Rights Commn., Indpls., 1971-74; acctg. asst. U. Tex.-Arlington, 1974-77; fiscal trainee Community Addiction Services Agy., Indpls., 1978; chief acct. Goodwill Industries, 1978-79; bus. devel. cons. Minority Bus. Devel. Ctr., Indpls., 1979—; instr. Lockyear Coll., Indpls., 1985—. Mem. U. Tex.-Arlington Alumni Assn., Flanner House Track and Field Com., Black Adoption Com. Democrat. Mem. Disciples of Christ Ch. Avocations: camping; sewing; reading; music. Office: Minority Bus Devel Ctr 3921 N Meridian St Indianapolis IN 46208

TICHENOR, LESLIE MILLS, interior design and retail executive; b. Louisville, Ky., Dec. 10, 1945; d. Arthur Wilbur and Mable Lucile (Davidson) M.; m. Everett Scott Tichenor, Aug. 19, 1967. Student U. Cin., 1964-67, U. Louisville, 1967-78. Ch. organist Suburban Christian Ch., Louisville, Ky., 1962-64; mem. sales staff Stewart Dept. Store, Louisville, 1962-66; life guard, camp counselor Tall Trees Camp, Louisville, 1964-65; archtl. draftsman Design Environment Group Architects, Louisville, 1966-67; owner, sec., treas. ES Tichenor Co., Louisville, 1968—. Com. head ch. art and architecture Diocese of Ky. Episcopal Ch., Louisville, 1972—; trustee Thomas Edison House, Butchertown House, Louisville, 1980—. Mem. Delta Delta Delta. Republican. Home: 1426 E Washington St Louisville KY 40206 Office: ES Tichenor Co 122 N Adams St Louisville KY 40206

TICHMAN, NADYA ERICA, violinist; b. Freeport, N.Y., June 12, 1958; d. Herbert L. and Ruth (Budnevich) T.; B.Mus., Curtis Inst. Music, 1980. Violinist, Aspen Music Festival 1975, 76, Opera Co. Phila. 1978, 79, Concerto Soloists of Phila. 1979-80, Santa Fe Opera Orch. 1979-81, San Francisco Symphony 1980—, Grand Teton Music Festival 1982—; numerous solo and chamber music recitals; co-dir. Chamber Music Sundaes, San Francisco.

TICKETT, DEBORAH LANEY, insurance company executive; b. Jacksonville, Fla., May 18, 1951; d. Charles T. and Isabelle E. (Capers) Laney; m. Kenneth Tickett, Mar. 15, 1969; children—Kenneth II, Steven Lee. Student Pinellas Vocat. Tech. Inst., Tampa U., Lic. ins. agent. Sec. Laney & Assocs., Clearwater, Fla., 1974-75, bookkeeper, 1975-77, ins. agent, 1977—, asst. mgr., 1977-82, v.p., mgr., 1979-85, pres., owner, 1973-80. Tchr. Episc. Ch. of Good Samaritan, 1972-79. Mem. Ins. Women St. Petersburg, Nat. Assn. Female Execs., Clearwater C. of C., Beta Sigma Phi (v.p.). Democrat. Episcopalian. Avocations: design, decorating. Office: Laney & Assocs 514 N Ft Harrison Rd PO Box 1508 Clearwater FL 33517

TICKI, LUCY ELIZABETH, township official, volleyball coach; b. Puerto Alegre, Brazil, June 11, 1959; came to U.S., 1961; d. Michael and Maria Josephine (Festleitner) T. Student Montclair State Coll., 1977-78, Temple U., 1978-79; B.A. magna cum laude, Kean Coll., 1981. Parks and recreation supr. Twp. of Irvington (N.J.), 1981—; women's head volleyball coach Seton Hall U., South Orange, N.J., 1981—; mem. Mayor's Adv. Com. on Recreation, Irvington, 1981—, Friends of the Park Com., Irvington, 1983—; div. rep. Big East Volleyball Com., Nat. Collegiate Athletic Assn., Providence, 1983—; head coach Garden Empire Volleyball Assn., Region II, 1983. Chmn. March of Dimes, Essex County, N.J., 1982—; sec. Irvington Parades Com., 1981—, Keep Irvington Clean Com., 1982. Mem. U.S. Volleyball Assn., Women's Sports Found., N.J. Recreation and Park Assn. Republican. Roman Catholic. Club: Bayern-Verein (Newark). Home: 19 Essex St Irvington NJ 07111 Office: Parks and Recreation Department Town Hall Civic Square Irvington NJ 07111

TICKNER, ELLEN MINDY, lawyer, law educator; b. Phila., May 30, 1951; d. Arnold Charles Tickner and Priscilla Francis (Wertlieb) Klomparens. B.S., Northwestern U., 1973; postgrad. Sch. Law, U. Miami, 1973-74; J.D., De Paul U., 1976. Bar: Ill., 1977, Mich. 1977, U.S. Dist. Ct. (ea. dist.) Mich., 1979. Legal research, writing instr. writing Sch. Law, U. Detroit, 1976-77; staff atty. Juvenile Defender's Office, Detroit, 1977-79; litigation atty., Inst. Gerontology U. Mich. Law Sch., Ann Arbor, 1980, clin. instr. law Law Sch., 1980-82, clin. asst. prof. law, 1982-83; assoc. Raymond, Rupp, Wienberg, Stone & Zuckerman, P.C., Troy, Mich., 1984—; lectr. seminars and tng. programs. Editorial assoc. De Paul Law Rev., 1974-76. Contbr. articles to profl. pubs. Mem. Women Lawyers Assn. Mich. (bd. dirs. 1981-82), Family Law Project (bd. dirs. 1980-83), Nat. Com. for Prevention Child Abuse (dir. Mich. chpt. 1980-82), ABA (litigation sect.), Fed. Bar Assn., 13th Nat. Conf. on Women and the Law (steering com. 1981-82), Assn. Trial Lawyers Am., State Bar Mich., Oakland County Bar Assn. (continuing legal edn. com.), Mich. Trial Lawyers Assn. Democrat. Jewish. Office: 755 W Big Beaver Rd Suite 1900 Troy MI 48084

TICKTIN, STEPHANIE, lawyer; b. Los Angeles, Feb. 20, 1955; d. Theodore J. and Eleanor Carol (Kopin) Ticktin. B.A. cum laude, UCLA, 1979; J.D., Southwestern U. Sch. Law, 1982. Bar: Calif. 1982; lic. FCC gen. radiotelephone with radar endorsement. Editor-at-large The Commentator, 1981-82. Mem. elections com. Southwestern Student Bar Assn., Los Angeles, 1980. Byron Holland hon. scholar, 1977.

TIDBALL, M. ELIZABETH PETERS, physiologist, educator; b. Anderson, Ind., Oct. 15, 1929; d. John Winton and Beatrice (Ryan) Peters; B.A., Mt. Holyoke Coll., 1951, L.H.D., 1976; M.S., U. Wis., 1955, Ph.D., 1959; Sc.D., Wilson Coll., 1973; D.Sc., Trinity Coll., 1974, Cedar Crest Coll., 1977, U. of South, 1978, Goucher Coll., 1979, St. Mary-of-Woods Coll., 1986; H.H.D., St. Mary's Coll., 1977; Litt.D., Regis Coll., 1980; D.Litt., Coll. St. Catherine, 1980; H.H.D., Hood Coll., 1982; L.L.D., St. Joseph Coll., 1983; L.H.D., Skidmore Coll., 1984, Marymount Coll., Tarrytown, N.Y., 1985, Converse Coll., 1985; m. Charles S. Tidball, Oct. 25, 1952. Teaching asst. physiology dept. U. Wis., 1952-55, 58-59; research asst. anatomy dept. U. Chgo., 1955-56, research asst. physiology dept., 1956-58; USPHS postdoctoral fellow NIH, Bethesda, Md., 1959-61; staff pharmacologist Hazleton Labs, Falls Church, Va., 1961, cons. 1962; asst. research prof. dept. pharmacology George Washington U. Med. Center, 1962-64, asso. research prof. dept. physiology, 1964-70, research prof., 1970-71, prof., 1971—; disting. vis. trustee prof. natural scis. Mills Coll., 1980; vis. scholar Coll of Preachers, 1984; disting. scholar in residence So. Meth. U., 1985; scholar in residence Salem Coll., 1985; cons. FDA, 1966-67, asso. sci. coordinator sci. assos. tng. program, 1966-67; mem. com. on NIH tng. programs and fellowships Nat. Acad. Scis., 1972-75; lectr. on edn. of women, dual career marriage; faculty summer confs. Am. Youth Found., 1967-78; cons. for instrl. research Wellesley Col., 1974-75; exec. sec. com. on edn. and employment women in sci. and engring. Commn. on Human Resources, NRC/Nat. Acad. Scis., 1974-75, vice chmn, 1977-82; cons., staff officer NRC/Nat. Acad. Scis., 1974-75; cons. Woodrow Wilson Nat. Fellowship Found., 1975—, NSF, 1974—. Rep. to D.C. Commn. on Status of Women, 1972-75. Trustee Mt. Holyoke Coll., 1968-73, vice chmn., 1972-73; trustee Hood Coll., 1972-84, 86—, exec. com., 1974-84, 86—; overseer Sweet Briar Coll., 1978-85; councillor Coll. of Preachers, Washington Cathedral Found., 1979-85, chmn. council, 1983-85, mem. exec. com., 1983-85; trustee Cathedral Choral Soc., 1976—, pres., 1982-84. Nat. Panelist, Am. Council on Edn., 1983—; center assoc. Girls Clubs of Am., 1983—; trustee Washington Cathedral Found., 1983-85, mem. exec. com., 1983-85. Shattuck fellow, 1955-56; Mary E. Wooley fellow Mt. Holyoke Coll., 1958-59; USPHS postdoctoral fellow, 1959-61; recipient Alumnae Medal of Honor, Mt. Holyoke Coll., 1971. Mem. AAAS, Am. Physiol. Soc. (chmn. task force on women in physiology 1973-80, com. on coms. 1977-80), Am. Assn. Higher Edn., Mt. Holyoke Alumnae Assn. (dir. 1966-70, 76-77), Histamine Club, Sigma Delta Epsilon, Sigma Xi. Episcopalian. Editorial bd. Religion and Intellectual Life, 1983—. Contbr. sci. articles and research on edn. of women to profl. jours.; mem. editorial bd. Jour. Higher Edn., 1979-83, cons. editor, 1984—. Home: 4100 Cathedral Ave NW Washington DC 20016 Office: Dept Physiology George Washington U Med Ctr 2300 I St NW Washington DC 20037

TIEFENWERTH, ELEANOR GERTRUDE, foundation executive; b. Bayonne, N.J.; m. William J. Tiefenwerth, Apr. 27, 1947; 1 child, William J. B.A. in Edn., Jersey City State Coll., 1946; student in parliamentary law Jersey City State Coll., 1964-66; student in pub. speaking Douglass Coll., 1966-68. Exec. dir. Bayonne Econ. Opportunity Found., N.J., 1976—; mem. exec. bd. Community Action Programs Exec. Dirs. Assn., Trenton, 1982—. Editor: Learning Together At Project HeadStart, 1984. Parliamentarian, Pavonia council Girl Scouts U.S., 1978-84; pres. Hudson County council PTA, N.J., 1978-80; sec. Bayonne Mayor's Adv. Com., 1981-83; chairperson Ambulance Study for City of Bayonne, 1982; site chairperson Holocaust Com. Meml., Bayonne, 1985-86. Mem. Community Action Dirs. Assn. State of N.J. (by-laws chairperson 1985-86), Headstart Dirs. Assn., Nat. Assn. Female Execs., Am. Legion Aux. Lodge: Women of Moose (sr. regent, Red Stole Collegiate award 1981). Avocations: reading; baking; travel. Office: Bayonne Econ Opportunity Found 555 Kennedy Blvd Box 1032 Bayonne NJ 07002

TIEGEN, ELAINE MALIN, accounting company executive; b. Elizabeth, N.J., May 22, 1944; d. Bernard Edwin and Estelle (Radin) Malin; m. Robert A. Tiegen, Feb. 2, 1973 (div. Nov. 1975); 1 child, Heike-Ann M. B.S. in Acctg., Fairleigh Dickinson U., Madison, N.J., 1966. C.P.A., Fla. Staff auditor Peat, Marwick, Mitchell and Co., Miami, 1968-69; sr. staff auditor J.H. Cohn and Co., C.P.A.s, Newark, N.J., 1969-71; with Clarence Rainess and Co., C.P.A.s, N.Y.C., 1971-73; spl. asst. to sr. ptnr. Wiener, Stern and Hantman, C.P.A.s, Miami, 1973-74; sr. specialist Laventhol & Horwath, Coral Gables, Fla., 1974-78, supr. dept. total acctg. services, 1978-79, mgr., 1979, head dept., 1980-83; prin. Elaine Tiegen & Co., C.P.A.s, Miami, 1983—; mem. adv. council Fed. Res. Bank of Atlanta, 1986—; v.p. So. Fla. Interprofl. Council, 1984-85, pres., 1985—. Mem. Am. Women's Soc. C.P.A.s, Am. Soc. Women Accts (chpt. pres. 1975-76; Fla. Acct. of Yr. award 1976), Am. Inst. C.P.A.s (small bus. council 1984-86), Fla. Inst. C.P.A.s (recipient Disting. Service award Dade County chpt. 1980, 81, 82, gov. 1983-85, pres. chpt. 1984-85, bd. dirs. chpt. 1985-86), Am. Arbitration Assn., Nat. Assn. Women Bus. Owners (bd. dirs. and fin. chmn. 1985-86), Mensa, Zonta (fin. chmn. Miami Lakes chpt. 1984-85). Office: Elaine Tiegen & Co CPAs 7220 NW 36th St Suite 520 Miami FL 33166

TIEGS, CHERYL, model; b. Calif.; d. Theodore and Phyllis Tiegs; student Calif. State U., Los Angeles. Profl. model, appearing in mags. including Bazaar, Glamour, Time, Life, Seventeen, Sports Illustrated; also appearing in TV commls. Cover Girl; producer Cheryl Tiegs women's apparel, shoes, accessories for Sears, Roebuck and Co., Cheryl Tiegs Eyewear, distributed nationally. Author: The Way to Natural Beauty, 1980. Address: 1036 Park Ave New York NY 10028

TIEMEYER, HOPE ELIZABETH JOHNSON, advertising company executive, club woman; b. Ft. Wayne, Ind., May 20, 1908; d. Edward Tibbens and Burton (Meyers) Johnson; B.A., U. Cin., 1932; m. Edwin H. Tiemeyer, Oct. 30, 1929 (dec. Apr. 1955); children—Ann Elizabeth (Mrs. G. L. Lewin, Jr.), Edwin Houghton (dec.). Pres., owner Mail-Way Advt. Co., Cin., pres., 1955—. Regent, Cin. chpt. D.A.R., 1956-58, chmn. nat. sch. survey com., 1961-62, nat. vice chmn. Americanism Manual for Citizenship, 1962-65, Continental Congress program com., 1962-65, Congress Marshall Com., 1966-68, mem. Congress hostess com., 1969-77; rec. sec. Nat. Chmn.'s Assn., 1969-71, pres. Ohio State Officers Club, 1975-77; sr. nat. membership chmn. Children Am. Revolution, 1958-60, sr. nat. rec. sec., 1960-62, nat. chmn. Mountain Sch., 1962-64, hon. sr. nat. v.p., 1963-64, sr. nat. 1st v.p. 1964-66, sr. nat. pres., 1966-68, hon. nat. life pres., 1970—, 1st v.p. Nat. Officers Club, 1965-69, pres., 1970-73, hon. sr. life pres. Ohio soc.; hon. life mem. Ohio Congress PTA, treas., 1957-62, v.p., dir. dept. health, 1962-63; hon. life mem. Nat. Congress PTA; life mem. Kappa Alpha Theta Mothers Club, pres., 1958-59; v.p. women's com. Cin. Symphony Orch., 1964-65; pres. U. Cin. Parents Club, 1959-61, v.p., 1963-64; area chmn. State House Conf. on Edn., 1953; dir. Am. Assn. U. Women, 1963-64; mem. Cin. Social Health Bd., 1950—, exec. com., 1965-70, v.p., 1973-75, treas., 1975-78, life trustee, 1978—; pres. Singleton's of Cin. Club, 1969-71, 73-76, mem. travel bd., 1973—, pres., 1973-74, art com., 1971—, mem. membership com., 1973-78; pres. Newtown Garden Club, 1947-49, City Panhellenic Assn., 1951-52, Ohio Hobby Club, 1958-59, Sigma Nu Mothers Club, 1963-65, pres. Alumnae chpt. Alpha Omicron Pi, 1930-32, nat. admissions com., 1933-35; life mem. Craftshops for Handicapped; chmn. Amelia Earhart Fellowship com. Zonta Club, Cin., 1963-64, program chmn., 1964-65, orientation chmn., 1965-67, internat. relations chmn., 1967-68, dir., 1969-74, mem. exec. com., 1969-74, mem. nat. nominating com., 1970-74, v.p., 1971-73; mem. music com., mem. tea room com. Cin. Woman's Club, 1969—; treas. Queen City chpt. Nat. Assn. Parliamentarians, 1965-69; v.p. Greater Cin. area women's chpt. Freedoms Found. at Valley Forge, 1975-77, sec. 1977-79, pres., 1978-80. Mem. Nat. Platform Assn., Nat. Gavel Assn., English Speaking Union. Recipient Jonathon Moore citation and award Ind. Soc. S.A.R., 1967; Good Citizenship medal Nat. Soc., 1967; named Ky. col. Club: Town. Home: 2786 Little Dry Run Rd Cincinnati OH 45244 Office: 229 426-30 Plum St Cincinnati OH 45202

TIENDA, MARTA, demographer, educator; b. Tex. Ph.D. in Sociology, U. Tex., 1976. From asst. prof. to prof. rural sociology U. Wis., Madison, 1976—. Co-author: Hispanics in the U.S. Economy, 1985. Contbr. articles to profl. jours. Mem. Nat. Council on Employment Policy, Population Assn. Am. (adv. com.). Office: U Wis Rural Sociology Dept Madison WI 53706*

TIERNEY, NANCY SUE, health services administrator, lawyer; b. Brookline, Mass., Jan. 7, 1954; d. Irving and Gertrude (Goldfarb) Sternberg; m. Christopher Tierney, Aug. 15, 1979. B.A., Wellesley Coll., 1975; J.D., Suffolk U., 1978; M.B.A., Cornell U., 1980. Bar: Mass., 1978. Records technician Melrose-Wakefield Hosp., Melrose, Mass., 1972-76; records technician N.E. Meml. Hosp., Stoneham, Mass., 1978-79; grad. teaching asst. Cornell U., Ithaca, N.Y., 1978-80; assoc. v.p. Cape Cod Hosp., Hyannis, Mass., 1980-82; atty. Nancy S. Tierney, Wakefield, Mass., 1978—; health services adminstr. Laconia State Sch. and Tng. Ctr., Laconia, N.H., 1982—. Trustee Laconia (N.H.) Pub. Library, 1983-85. Mem. ABA. Democrat. Office: Laconia State Sch and Tng Center PO Box 370 Laconia NH 03247

TIERNO, KAREN JONES, business executive; b. Stillwater, Okla., June 4, 1950; d. Dale Elmer and Floretta (Frank) Jones; m. Robert F. Tierno, Oct. 20, 1972. B.A., U. Okla., 1972. Agt., Travelers Ins., Denver, 1975-76; salesman John Poppell-Toyota, Denver, 1974-75, Mercedez-Benz-Old Hickory Motors, Durham, N.C., 1976-77; regional mgr. sales Glaser Bros., Los Angeles, 1977-83; dist. mgr. sales Phototron, San Jose, Calif., 1983—. Mem. NOW, AAUW (networking chmn. 1982), Nat. Assn. Female Execs. Home: 1103 Nottingham Ct Roseville CA 95678

TIKELLIS, PAMELA SUZANNE, lawyer; b. Lawrence, Kans., Aug. 9, 1952; d. Ignatius James and Elizabeth (Deery) Tikellis; m. John Heggie Small, Mar. 5, 1982. B.A. in Psychology, Manhattanville Coll., 1974; M.A. in Psychology, New Sch. for Social Research, 1976; J.D., Del. Law Sch., 1982. Bar: Del. 1982, U.S. Dist. Ct. Del. 1983. Law clk. Prickett, Jones, Elliott, Kristol & Schnee, Wilmington, Del., 1981-82; jud. law clk. Ct. of Chancery, Wilmington, 1982-83; assoc. Biggs & Battaglia, Wilmington, 1983—. Mng. editor Del. Law Sch. Law Rev., Wilmington, 1981-82. Mem. Jr. League of Wilmington, 1982—. Mem. ABA, Del. State Bar Assn. Republican. Roman Catholic. Home: 209 Edgewood Rd Wilmington DE 19803

TILIPKO, LAURA, nursing administrator, educator, consultant; b. N.Y.C., Mar. 16, 1953; d. Peter and Alfreda (Jankowski) T. B.A. in Polit. Sci., Lebanon Valley Coll., 1975; M.S., Pace U./N.Y. Med. Coll., 1979, cert. nurse practitioner, 1979; M.P.A., Baruch Coll., 1986. R.N., N.Y. Staff nurse ICU New York Hosp., N.Y.C., 1979-80; family nurse practitioner Roosevelt Hosp., N.Y.C., 1980-81; adult nurse practitioner Bellevue Hosp., N.Y.C., 1981-82; nursing supr. St. Barnabas Hosp., N.Y.C., 1982-84; asst. dir., project dir. Met. Hosp., N.Y.C., 1984-85; asst. adminstr., dir. nurses No. Dutchess Hosp., Rhinebeck, N.Y., 1985—; advisor nursing curriculum Dutchess Community Coll., Poughkeepsie, N.Y., 1985, 85; advisor Ulster Community Coll., Stone Ridge, N.Y., 1985; advisor econs. com. SUNY-New Paltz, 1986. Mem. com., faculty Am. Heart Assn., Poughkeepsie, 1985-86. Mem. Am. Nursing Assn. (cert. family nursing practice), Sigma Theta Tau, Pi Gamma Mu. Avocations: scuba diving; skiing; swimming. Home: RD #3 PO Box 149 Rhinebeck NY 12572

TILLERY, LINDA ANN, nurse; b. Wichita, Kans., Dec. 9, 1951; d. J.B. and Letha Ann (Summerhill) Belk; m. Maurice Odell Tillery, May 29, 1969; children—Kevin Bartlett, Angela Wynelle. B.S.N. with honors in Nursing, Ark. Tech. U., Russellville, 1981. R.N., Ark. Staff nurse St. Mary's Hosp., Roswell, N.Mex., 1981-82; nursing dir. Lane's Rest Home, Caraway, Ark., 1982-83; charge nurse Hillhaven Nursing Home, Little Rock, 1983; staff devel. instr. Benton Services Ctr. (Ark.), 1983—. Mem. Am. Guild Organists. Democrat. Baptist. Home: PO Box 1485 Benton AR 72015 Office: Benton Services Center Benton AR 72015

TILLEY, ELIZABETH ROBERTS CORNWALL (MRS. THOMAS CLARK TILLEY), astronomer, civic worker; b. New Haven, Sept. 23, 1914; d. Charles Edward and Millicent (Johnson) Cornwall; B.A., Vassar Coll., 1935; postgrad. Yale U., 1935-36; M.A., Wellesley Coll., 1939; Ph.D., U. Mich., 1942; m. Thomas Clark Tilley, Oct. 31, 1942; children—Thomas Clark III, Anne Bradford. Computer, Mt. Wilson Obs., Pasadena, Calif., 1936-37; asst. tchr. Wellesley (Mass.) Coll., 1937-40, U. Mich., Ann Arbor, 1940-42; editor, supr. computers OSRD Rocket Project, Calif. Inst. Tech., Pasadena, 1943-44; tchr. St. John's Prep. Sch., San Juan, P.R., 1958-60; supr. lab. tests Analysts, Inc., San Juan, 1961-63; mem. altar guild St. John's Cathedral (Episcopal), San Juan, 1964-80, pres., 1968-69, mem. vestry, 1974-80, mem. cathedral chpt., 1974-80, parish treas., 1974-80; mem. bishop's council advice Diocese P.R., 1968-69; vice chmn. St. Cecilia Guild All Saints Ch., Winter Park, Fla., 1982-83, chmn., 1983-85. Bd. dirs. Ladies Aux. Presbyn. Hosp., San Juan, 1964-79, pres., 1966-70, treas., 1972-79, trustee hosp., 1970-80. Mem. Am. Astron. Soc., Phi Beta Kappa. Club: Vassar Central Fla. (pres. 1982—). Home: 360 Sylvan Blvd Winter Park FL 32789

TILLINGHAST, META IONE, civic worker; b. Newark, Nov. 14; d. Ralph Vincent and Florence Virginia (MacDonald) Muldoon; student Leland Powers Sch. of Spoken Word, Boston; m. Frederick William Tillinghast, Apr. 20; children—Anne (Mrs. Robert Riley), Patricia (Mrs. Charles McLaughlin). Bd. dirs. Balt. chpt. ARC, 1955-58, chmn. Queen Anne's chpt. 1964-66, nat. bd. govs., 1966-69, Md. state fund chmn., 1969-71, Delmarva div. chmn. mems., funds, 1971-73, vols., 1971-74, coordinator community relations Eastern area, 1975-76; chmn. vols. nat. field office (now Eastern field office) ARC, Alexandria, Va., 1976-83, regional chmn. Eastern ops., 1983—; dir. ch. plays; chmn. United Fund Baltimore County (Md.) Women's div., 1950. Named vol. of year Md., ARC, 1965; recipient award Gen. Fedn. Women's Clubs, 1952. Mem. Md. No. Dist. Fedn. Women's Clubs (pres. 1953-55). Clubs: Women's Glyndon (pres. 1949-51), Talbot County Women's (pres. 1962-64), Women's Ten Hills (pres. 1940-42). Home: Queenstown MD 21658 Office: 615 N St Asaph Alexandria VA 22314

TILLMAN, CAROL SCHILLER, financial consultant; b. Marshfield, Wis., Jan. 31, 1934; d. Otto and Caroline (Wundrow) Schiller; m. Roderick W. Tillman, Feb. 3, 1957 (div. Nov. 1973); children—Jefferson Marc, Frederic George; m. George Robert Hanks, Aug. 26, 1978. B.S., U. Wis., 1956. Journalist, Norfolk Virginian Pilot (Va.), 1957-58; tchr. Tulsa Pub. Schs., 1970-76; asst. v.p. Merrill Lynch, Tulsa, 1976—. Mem. Am. Bus. Women's Assn., Women in Communications, Older Women's League, Audubon Soc. Unitarian. Office: Merrill Lynch 3960 One Williams Ctr Tulsa OK 74172

TILLMAN, CHRISTINE THOMPSON, medical technologist; b. Los Angeles, Sept. 13, 1952; d. George Irwin Thompson and Willita Albertina (Glover) Thompson Reagan; m. Jackie Williams Tillman, Oct. 11, 1975; children—James Christopher, Kimberly Michelle. A.S., Southwestern Jr. Coll., Chula Vista, Calif., 1972; B.S., Salve Regina Coll., Newport, R.I., 1975; cert. med. technologist Norwalk Hosp., Conn., 1974-75. Staff med. technologist Mercy Hosp., San Diego, 1975-83, supr. blood bank, 1983—; faculty Mercy Hosp. Sch. Med. Technology, 1982-85. Mem. Am. Soc. Clin. Pathologists, Am. Soc. Med. Technology, Calif. Assn. Med. Lab. Technology (dir. 1979-81, del. to conv. 1979) activities chairperson 1979-80), Calif. Blood Bank System, Nat. Cert. Agy. Med. Lab. Personnel, Tau Omicron Phi. Democrat. Episcopalian. Avocations: oriental art; genealogy. Office: Mercy Hosp Med Ctr 4077 5th Ave San Diego CA 92103

TILLMAN, DONNA, marketing educator; b. Linn, Mo., Dec. 23, 1940; d. Clarence A. and Josephine (Balkenbush) T.; m. Leo Iven, June 8, 1957 (div. 1970); children—Monica, Greg; m. Mahmood Qureshi, July 13, 1977 (div. 1983). B.S., Lincoln U., 1966; M.A. in Research, St. Louis U., 1967, Ph.D., 1970; M.B.A., DePaul U., 1980. Instr. Parks Coll. Aero. Engring. of St. Louis U., 1968-70; asst. prof. Western Ill. U., Macomb, 1970-71; vis. research fellow Birmingham U., Eng., 1977-78; prof. Northeastern Ill. U., Chgo., 1971-81; chmn. bus. dept. Barat Coll., Lake Forest, Ill., 1980-81; prof. Calif. State Poly. U., Pomona, 1981—; guest lectr. Claremont Grad. Sch., Calif., U. Calif.-Riverside. Contbr. articles to profl. jours. St. Louis U. fellow, 1966-68. Mem. Am. Mktg. Assn., So. Calif. Mktg. Assn., Acad. Mktg. Sci. Avocations: flying; sailing. Home: 12064 Roswell Ave Chino CA 91710 Office: Calif State Poly U 3801 W Temple Ave Pomona CA 91768

TILLMAN, HOPE NELSON, librarian; b. Balt., Sept. 8, 1941; d. Richard Nelson and Hope (Sturtevant) T.; m. Gregory E. Nagy, Dec. 11, 1962 (div.); children—Ilona Kimberly, Paul Gregory; m. 2d, William W. Buckley, Nov. 18, 1977 (div.). Student Goucher Coll., 1959-60, Middlebury Coll., 1960-62; A.B., U. Pa., 1964; M.L.S., Rutgers U., 1966; M.B.A., Rider Coll., 1979. Library trainee Free Library Phila., 1965; jr. librarian Trenton Pub. Library (N.J.), 1968, br. librarian, 1968-69; reference librarian Rider Coll., Lawrenceville, N.J., 1970-82, coordinator info. services, 1982—. Editor: Education Libraries,

1986—. Mem. Spl. Libraries Assn. (Princeton-Trenton chpt. bus. mgr. 1981-82, pres. 1984-85), AAUP (Rider Coll. chpt. corr. sec. 1974-75, 85-86, treas. 1982-85, fin. sec. 1986-87), N.J. Library Assn., ALA, Govt. Documents Assn. N.J. Unitarian. Home: 16 Alyce Ct Lawrenceville NJ 08648 Office: Rider Coll Library 2083 Lawrenceville Rd Lawrenceville NJ 08648

TILLMAN, MARY ANNE TUGGLE, pediatrician; b. Bristow, Okla., Sept. 4, 1935; d. Thomas Gus and Ruthie (English) Tuggle; B.S., Howard U., 1956, M.D., 1960; postgrad. Harvard Grad. Med. Sch., 1965; m. Daniel Tillman, Apr. 20, 1957; children—Dana, Daniel. Intern, Homer G. Phillips Hosp., St. Louis, 1960-61, resident pediatrics, 1961-63; practice medicine, specializing in pediatrics, St. Louis, 1963—; dir. nurseries Homer G. Phillips Hosp., St. Louis, 1964-79, St. Louis City Hosp., 1979-85; mem. staffs St. Louis Children's, Deaconess, Barnes, Jewish hosps.; asst. prof. Washington U. Sch. Medicine, St. Louis, 1963—, pediatric cons. Project Head Start, 1969—. Recipient Woman of Year award Zeta Phi Beta, 1970; Woman of Achievement, St. Louis Globe Democrat, 1982. Diplomate Am. Bd. Pediatrics. Fellow Am. Acad. Pediatrics (nat. com. adoptions 1969—); mem. Am., Nat. med. assns., Am. Med. Women's Assn. Presbyterian. Contbr. articles to profl. publs. Home: 26 Washington Terr Saint Louis MO 63112 Office: Northland Office Bldg 330 W Florissant at Lucas Hunt Saint Louis MO 63136

TILLMAN, MARY NORMAN, urban affairs consultant; b. Atlanta, Jan. 31, 1926; d. Mary Nellie Shehee; B.A., Morris Brown Coll., 1947; postgrad. U. Minn., 1964, Old Dominion U., 1975—; m. James A. Tillman, Jr., Apr. 11, 1952; children—James A., Gina G. Asst. bus. mgr. Morris Brown Coll., Atlanta, 1947-53; race relations and urban affairs cons. Tillman Assos. Cons. Social Engrs., Atlanta and Syracuse, N.Y., 1963—, sr. partner, treas., from 1965, now pres.; clin. prof. United Theol. Sem., New Brighton, Minn.; adj. prof. Gordon-Conwell Theol. Sem., South Hamilton, Mass. Mem. adv. council to urban ministries dept. So. Bapt. Conv.; bd. dirs. Christian Council Met. Atlanta, Tillman Inst. Human Relations. Mem. Tidewater Assn. Public Adminstrs. (dir.), Am. Acad. Consultants, Nat. Black Writers Consortium (v.p.). Author: What is Your Racism Quotient?, 1964; (with James A. Tillman, Jr.) Why America Needs Racism and Poverty, 1972; (with J.A. Tillman, Jr.) Black Intellectuals, White Liberals and Race Relations: An Analytic Overview, 1973. Office: 1765 Glenview Dr SW Atlanta GA 30331

TILLMAN, MAYRE LUTHA, political consultant; b. Dover, Fla., Aug. 24, 1928; d. Luther E. and Marietta T. Wheeler; student Fla. State U., 1945-46, Aladin Bus. Coll., 1963-64; m. Paul D. Tillman, Apr. 7, 1947 (div.); children—Daniel Paul, Shayla Denise Tillman Nail. Credit investigator Maas Bros., Tampa, 1946-47; sec.-bookkeeper Dover Sch., 1950-53; adminstrv. asst. Dave Gordon Enterprises, Tampa, 1965-68; office mgr. Bumby & Stimpson, Inc., Plant City, Fla., 1968-70; tax clk., clk. of circuit ct. Hillsborough County (Fla.) Courthouse, 1970-73; adminstr. property mgmt. Tampa-Hillsborough County Expressway Authority, 1973-74; exec. asst. Fla. Democratic Party, Tallahassee, 1976-78; adminstrv. asst., office mgr. E. F. Hutton & Co., Tampa, 1979-80; cons. politics, meeting planning, Dover, 1980—; consumer advocate Fla. Dept. Ins., Tampa, 1982-84; real estate devel. specialist Dept. Bus. Regulations, Div. Land Sales, Condominiums and Mobile Homes, 1985—. Precinct 67 committeewoman Hillsborough County Dem. Exec. Com., 1964—, sec., 1965-68, state committeewoman, 1974-77, 80-84, state liaison for county conv., 1979; pres. Dem. Women's Clubs Fla., 1979-81, bd. dirs., 1969—, chmn. polit. action com., 1985-87, chmn. campaign com., 1985-87; Fla. coordinator for ERA, Dem. Nat. Com., 1982; active Dem. Exec. Com. Fla., 1974-84, vice chmn. 7th Congl. Dist. on Central Com., 1974-76, 80-84, nat. committeewoman for Fla., 1980-84; chmn. So. region Nat. Fedn. Dem. Women, 1981-82, mem. nat. credential com., 1980; mem. Duke U. Forum on Presdl. Nominations; candidate Fla. Ho. of Reps., 1980; participant Fla. Gov.'s Challenge Conf., Fla. Endowment for Humanities, 1981; mem. hon. bd. Dr. Martin Luther King, Jr. Commemoration and Black History Month Celebration, 1986. Named Hon. Col., State Miss., 1980, State Ky., 1981. Mem. Fla. Fedn. Bus. and Profl. Women's Clubs (pres. Plant City club 1967-69, dist. com. chmn. 1969-71, organizer chmn. talent bank 1970, state chmn. legis. 1970-73, chmn. state conv. 1982), East Hillsborough County Hist. Soc., Plant City Women's Club (parliamentarian 1980-82). Home: PO Box 97 Dover FL 33527

TILSON, KATHERINE ANNE, home health agency executive; b. Cin., Mar. 21, 1951; d. Paul Joseph Walter and Anne Elizabeth (Kleemann) Centner; m. Dennis Bascombe Tilson, II, June 8, 1974. B.S. in Nursing, Med. Ctr. U. Kans.-Kansas City, 1973; M.B.A., Avila Coll., 1983. R.N., Kans., Mo. Staff nurse U. Kans. Med. Ctr., Kansas City, 1973-76, Menorah Med. Ctr., Kansas City, 1976-78; nursing coordinator Kelly Health Care, Inc., Kansas City, 1978, nursing supr., 1978-79, br. mgr., service dir., 1979-83; mgr. ServiceMaster Home Health Care Services, Kansas City, 1983, adminstr., 1983-84; cons. Am. Nursing Resources, Inc., Kansas City, 1984, adminstr. Am. Nursing Resources Home Health Agy., Inc., 1985—, exec. dir. Am. Nursing Resources, Inc., 1984—; jr. faculty liaison for home health nursing practice residency tng. program S.S.M. Family Practice, Kansas City, 1982-83; mem. in-home services com. Johnson County Area Agy. on Aging, 1982-83. Mem. Challinor Guild, St. Andrew's Episcopal Ch., 1981—, choir, 1980—, Scola Cantorum, 1984-85, Metro Discharge Planners Group, 1985—, Mayor's Corps of Progress for Greater Kansas City, 1980-83. Mem. Broadway Bus. Assn., Mid-Am. Regional Council (in-home services task force 1980—, in-home services com. 1979—), Kansas City Regional Home Health Assn. (bd. dirs. 1979-83, mem., chmn. coms.), Kansas City C. of C. Republican. Avocations: piano; singing; sailing; swimming; sports; sewing; gardening. Home: 4600 W 66th St Prairie Village KS 66208 Office: American Nursing Resources Inc 3100 Broadway Suite 118 Kansas City KS 64111

TILTON, BERNICE ELIZABETH SHEPPARD (MRS. EARLE BARTON TILTON), civic worker; b. Chgo.; d. Samuel Charles and Elizabeth (Keith) Sheppard; Mus.B., Wis. Coll. Music, 1954; m. Earle Barton Tilton, Mar. 12, 1940. Performed as soloist and two-piano team for orgns., Ill., Wis., Fla., 1947—. Pres., Symphony Club, Clearwater, Fla., 1958-60; founder Mus. Arts Soc., Clearwater, 1960, pres., 1960-62, 81-83; chpt. pres. Delta Omicron, 1964-66, Fla. chmn. alumnae-at-large, 1965-67, internat. v.p. alumnae, internat. bd. dirs., 1967-71; pres. Fla. West Coast Panhellenic Assn., 1967-68, chpt. adv. bd., 1968—. Bd. dirs. Clearwater Community Concert Assn., 1963-74. Recipient Gold Star Delta Omicron, 1967, Recognition award, 1971. Mem. Nat. Soc. Arts and Letters (local sec., v.p. 1972-73), Henry Solomon Lehr Soc. (life), Delta Omicron (alumnae chpt. pres. 1973-74, 81-84, rec. sec. 1985—). Home: 6 Belleview Blvd Apt 608 Belleair FL 33516

TILTON, TERRI LYNN, artist manager, career development consultant; b. Milw., Sept. 25, 1954; d. Aaron Lionel and Anita Jane (Willens) T. B.F.A., U. Ariz., 1978. Cert. tchr. speech and drama. Dir., coordinator Free To Be Theatre, Tucson, 1976-78; tchr. acting schs. and theatres, Tucson and Los Angeles, 1976-82; v.p. sales and distbn. Wheel Records, Los Angeles, 1980-82; dealer, mktg. and sales Biotone Internat./Bloomex Internat., Los Angeles, 1982-84; ptnr., exec. Group Royal Prodns., Los Angeles, 1984—; artist mgr. Terri Tilton Mgmt., Los Angeles, 1984—; bd. dirs. Jazz for Life Project, Ann Arbor, Mich., 1985—; membership dir. Nat. Acad. Jazz, Van Nuys, Calif., 1985—. Mem. Am. Soc. Profl. and Exec. Women, AFTRA, Nat. Acad. Recording Arts and Scis., Nat. Assn. Jazz Educators, Nat. Assn. Female Execs. Avocations: horseback riding; decorating; tennis; cooking; entertaining. Office: Terri Tilton Management 7135 Hollywood Blvd Suite 601 Los Angeles CA 90046

TIMBERLAKE, LOIS PAULINE, educational administrator; b. Brookston, Ind., Dec. 6, 1935; d. Everett L. and Veda M. (Craig) Richardson; m. Reece Devon Hobby, Mar. 13, 1955 (div. Mar. 1970); children—Valerie, Reece; m. Ted Sán Stuart Timberlake, Mar. 14, 1970; children—Sally, Beau, TedSán. B.S.E., U. Houston, 1958; M.S.E., Ark. State Tchrs. Coll., 1965; Ed.D., U. Ga., 1972. Cert. tchr., adminstr. Romper Room tchr. Sta. KATV, Little Rock, 1959; women's dir. Sta. KTHV-KTHS/Radio and TV, Little Rock, 1960-62; instr. State Coll. Ark., Conway, 1965-70; tchr. sociology Hickman High Sch., Columbia, Mo., 1971-72; head dept. social studies Cypress High Sch., Fort Myers, Fla., 1972-77; asst. prin., 1977-79; prin. Caloosa Middle Sch., Cape Coral, Fla., 1979-82, Gulf Middle Sch., Cape Coral, 1982—; adj. prof. U. South Fla., Fort Myers, 1974—; mem. faculty Nat. Seminar Latin Am. Studies, summer 1974; speaker. Author articles in field. Named Mrs. Ark., 1962; Nat. Endowment Arts grantee, 1967. Mem. AAUW (chpt. charter mem.; chpt. pres. 1975-77, state bd. dirs. 1985—, chpt. issues chmn. 1984-85), Latin Am. Studies Assn., Fla. Assn. Sch. Adminstrs., Assn. Advancement Internat. Edn., Nat. Council Social Studies (ethics com. 1980-81), Nat. Assn. Secondary Sch. Prins., Assn. Supervision and Curriculum Devel., Am. Assn. Sch. Adminstrs., Phi Delta Kappa (chmn. spl. projects 1983-84), Delta Kappa Gamma. Avocations: travel; photography; languages. Home: 5936 SW 1st Ave Cape Coral FL 33914 Office: 1809 SW 36th Terr Cape Coral FL 33914

TIMBERLIN, BEVERLY JEAN, industrial supply company executive, business executive; b. Alvarado, Ind., Feb. 10, 1935; d. Lyle Spangler and Helen Juanita (Mason) Leas; m. David John Timberlin, Dec. 19, 1954; children—Michelle Renea, David Douglas. Student Ball State U., 1953-54; A.A., Jackson Community Coll., 1968; B.A. in Edn., Mich. State U., 1970, postgrad., 1970-73. Spl. edn. tchr. Jackson County Pub. Schs., Mich., 1970-73; spl. edn. tchr. Wichita Falls Pub. Schs., Tex., 1973-81; owner Sun Valley Distbrs., Phoenix, 1981—; corp. sec.-treas. Cupp's Indsl. Supply, Inc., Phoenix, 1981—. Republican. Methodist. Avocations: swimming; gardening; golf; skiing. Home: 13431 N 68th Dr Peoria AZ 85345 Office: Cupp's Indsl Supply Inc 3418 W Flower St Phoenix AZ 85017

TIMES, MISBREW LOUISE, educator; b. Sumter, S.C., Sept. 14, 1950; d. Adam and Edna (Lowery) T.; B.S., S.C. State Coll., 1972; M.Ed., U. S.C., 1976. Music dir. Lee County (S.C.) Schs., 1972-75; fine arts dir., tchr. Clarendon Sch. Dist., Summerton, S.C., 1975-82; cons. ch. choral music, time mgmt. Del., N.Y. Nat. Democratic Com., 1980; mem. S.C. State Dem. Exec. Com.; exec. 1st v.p. Sumter County (S.C.) Dem. Com., 1978-82, mem. council, 1982; bd. dirs. P.D. Regional Health Systems Agy., exec. com., chmn. project rev. com., 1981, 82. Mem. S.C. Edn. Assn., NEA, S.C. Assn. Supervision and Curriculum Devel., Nat. Assn. Supervision and Curriculum Devel., Internat. Platform Assn. Democrat. Mem. African Methodist Episcopal Ch. Office: PO Box 2691 Sumter SC 29150

TIMM, CHRISTINE ANNA, credit union executive; b. Milw., Feb. 24, 1946; d. Elmer J. and Regina F. (Rewolinski) Zielinski; m. Jeffrey A. Timm, Apr. 21, 1969; children—Dawn, Lynn. Student U. Wis.-Milw., 1964. Clk.-teller Milw. Mcpl. Credit Union, 1964-73, v.p., 1973-83, pres., 1984—. Mem. Credit Union Execs. Soc., Woman to Woman (bookkeeper 1975—, bd. dirs., treas. 1985, Woman of the Yr. 1984), Credit Grantors of Wis., Credit Grantors of Milw. Avocations: nature appreciation; reading. Office: Milw Mcpl Credit Union 200 E State St Milwaukee WI 53202

TIMM, JEANNE ANDERSON, musician; b. Sioux City, Iowa, Aug. 15, 1918; d. Milton Earnest and Hazel Fern (Cunningham) Anderson; B.Mus., Morningside Coll., Sioux City, 1940; postgrad. Eastman Sch. Music, La. State U.; m. Everett L. Timm, Aug. 5, 1940; children—Gary Everett, Laurance Milo. Prof. woodwind instruments Morningside Coll., 1943-45, 48—; staff flutist Sta. KSCJ, Sioux City, 1941; prin. flutist Sioux City Symphony, 1943-45; vis. flutist New Orleans Philharm., New Orleans Opera Orch; prof. flute and chamber music La. State U., 1968—; cons., clinician flute cos.; editor Armstrong Edu-tainment Co., 1976—; flutist Baton Rouge Little Theater, summers 1965-81. Mem. Nat. Assn. Wind and Percussion Players, Nat. Flute Assn., Music Educators Nat. Conf., Music Tchrs. Nat. Assn., La. Music Educators Assn., Baton Rouge Music Club, Pi Kappa Lambda, Mu Phi Epsilon. Roman Catholic. Home: 465 Magnolia Woods Baton Rouge LA 70708 Office: 269 Music and Dramatic Arts Bldg La State U Baton Rouge LA 70803

TIMMER, SHARON PHYLLIS, marketing communications company executive, novelist; b. Detroit, July 7, 1934; d. Manuel M. and Evelyn (Goldis) Nidorf; m. Jerome L. Vedborg, July 12, 1959 (div. 1963); m. John J. Timmer, Apr. 9, 1965; 1 child, Stacy A. Vice pres. Madison Ave. Advt. Agy., N.Y.C., 1955-58; acct. exec., v.p. Nides-Cini Advt., Los Angeles, 1958-67; founder, owner operator Timmerco, Los Angeles, 1967-73, corp. v.p., pres., chief exec. officer Santa Monica, 1981—; dir. worldwide sales promotion Max Factor, Los Angeles, 1973-77; v.p. spl. events Vidal Sassoon, Los Angeles, 1978-79, pres. of internat., 1979-80, corporate v.p., 1980-81; lectr. various colls. and univs. Contbr. articles to popular mags. Bd. dir. Los Angeles Arts Council. Awards of Merit, Advt. and Editorial Art in the West, Indsl. Graphics Internat., Arts Dirs. Club. of Los Angeles; Outstanding Contbn. award YWCA. Mem. Nat. Womens Forum (Los Angeles chpt., bd. dirs. Jewish.

TIMMERMANN, MARIE JOSEPHINE, county official; b. St. Louis, Feb. 13, 1926; d. Lester and Frieda M. (Young) VonGerichten; m. Erbin George Timmermann, Apr. 17, 1951 (dec. Nov. 1963); children—Dale, Jerry, Karen, Kevin. Grad. high sch., Breese, Ill. Circuit clk. Clinton County, Carlyle, Ill., 1968—. Leader 4-H Club, Breese, 1967-72; active Breese Republican Com. Mem. St. Dominic Altar Soc. Roman Catholic. Lodge: Daus. of Isabella (trustee 1984—). Home: Crestview Apts 9 Rural Route 1 Breese IL 62230 Office: Clinton County Courthouse Carlyle IL 62231

TIMMERMANN, SANDRA, educational gerontologist, communications specialist; b. Orange, N.J., Mar. 25, 1941; d. Bernhard and Matilda (Schaaf) T.; m. George W. Bonham. B.A. with honors, U. Colo., 1963; M.A., Columbia U., 1967; Ed.D., 1979. Account exec. Rowland Co., N.Y.C., 1964-67; dir. pub. info. The N.Y. TV Network. SUNY, N.Y.C., 1967-72; asso. Hoefer/Amidei Pub. Relations/Mktg., 1972-74; asso. dean Inst. Lifetime Learning, Am. Assn. Ret. Persons, Washington, 1974-76, dir. Inst., 1976-84, dir. geriatric edn., 1984—; edn. and tng. cons. Western Gerontol. Soc.; mem. tng. com. Nat. Ctr. for Black Aged; mgr. older adults sect. HEW Lifelong Learning Project; cons. Brookdale Ctr. on Aging, Hunter Coll.; cons. to bus. and industry; adv. com. nat. project on counseling older people Am. Personnel and Guidance Assn.; nat. adv. com. vocat. edn. and older adults U.S. Dept. Edn. Trustee, chmn. adv. com. on later years Am. Found. for the Blind. Kellogg fellow. Mem. Am. Assn. Adult and Continuing Edn. (editor Edn. and Aging newsletter, chmn. commn. on aging, bd. dirs.), Coalition Adult Edn. Orgns. (dir., pres. 1984-85), Pi Beta Phi, Pi Lambda Theta, Kappa Delta Pi, Phi Delta Kappa. Club: Capital Speakers. Contbr. articles to profl. jours. Home: 371 Cypress Point Rd Half Moon Bay CA 94019

TIMMERMANS, DEANNA D., pharmacist, advertising executive; b. Rapid City, S.D., Feb. 5, 1939; d. Bernard Briggs and Luella (Olson) Dodds; B.S., State U. Iowa, 1961; m. John J. Timmermans, June 24, 1961 (dec. Oct. 1978); 1 son, Jeffrey Jay. Pharmacist, Race Drug, Ketchikan, Alaska, 1961-63, St. Vincent's Hosp., N.Y.C., 1965-66, S.I. Hosp., 1966-71; pharm. market research analyst William Douglas Mc Adams, N.Y.C., 1980-82; account exec. pharm. advt. Dorritie & Lyons, N.Y.C., 1982-84, account supr., 1984—. Mem. Jr. Guild S.I., 1970—; treas. Women's Guild S.I. Mental Health Assn., 1970-71; toy chmn. Christ Ch. Day Sch. Fair, N.Y.C., 1971. Mem. Women for Rockefeller, S.I., 1970; mem. com. Republican party, Richmond County, 1970-71; chmn. credentials com. Women's Rep. Conf., Phila., 1972; mem. Met. Rep. Club, 1972—; bd. dirs. Women's Aux. N.Y. U. Coll. Dentistry, sec., 1974, treas., 1974-76, v.p., 1976—; bd. dirs. Yorkville Civic Council, 1977-78, Knickerbocker Greys; bd. dirs., mem. exec. com. Burden Center for Aging, 1977—; coordinator congl. life St. Peter's Luth. Ch., 1976-77, dir. vols., 1977-78, ch. council, 1979-81; active Muscular Dystrophy Assn. Telethon Fund, 1978—. Mem. Pharm. Soc. State N.Y., Assn. Hosp. Pharmacists, Am. Pharm. Assn., Iowa Pharm. Assn., Pharm. Advt. Council, Acad. Pharm. Scis., Fgn. Policy Assn., Parents League N.Y., Aircraft Owners and Pilots Assn., Jr. League City N.Y. (bd. mgrs., exec. com.), Kappa Alpha Theta Alumni Assn., Kappa Alpha Theta (past v.p.), Kappa Epsilon. Home: 400 E 56th St New York NY 10022 Office: Dorritie & Lyons 655 3d Ave New York NY 10017

TIMMINS, LOIS FAHS, professional speaker, writer, consultant; b. N.Y.C., July 3, 1914; d. Charles Harvey and Sophia (Lyon) Fahs; m. James W. Timmins, Aug. 12, 1942 (div.); children—Nancy Timmins Kirk, Kathy. B.S. in Edn., Northwestern U., 1935; M.A., Columbia U., 1936, Ed.D., 1941. Instr., Mt. Allison U., Sackville, N.B., Can., 1936-39; asst. prof. Willimantic (Conn.) State Tchrs. Coll., 1941-43; social dir. UNESCO, Mondsee, Austria, summer, 1950; asst. prof. Tex. Woman's U., Denton, 1953-57; prof. staff Timberlawn Psychiat. Hosp., Dallas, 1957-80; dir. Communication Studies, Dallas, 1972—; profl. speaker, Dallas, 1980—. Author: Swing Your Partner, 1939; Understanding Through Communication, 1972; Life Time Chart, 1978, Cassettes Making Friends with All Your Feelings, 1984, The Mirrors Inside You, 1984, Ambivalance, 1985; booklet Finding Words for Your Feeling, 1985; contbr. articles to profl. jours. Recipient citation Nat. Therapeutic Recreation Soc., 1976; Top Rating Profl. Showcase, Internat. Platform Assn., 1982. Mem. Nat. Speakers Assn. Unitarian. Home: 6145 Anita St Dallas TX 75214

TIMMONS, BESS SPIVA, foundation executive, education advocate; b. Galena, Kans., Oct. 12, 1901; d. George Newton and Bess (Tamblyn) Spiva; m. Leroy Kittrell Timmons, Sept. 2, 1922 (dec. 1954); children—Robert L., George S., Judith Ann Timmons Spears. Grad. Monticello Coll., 1921. Mem. George N. Spiva scholarship com. Pittsburg State U., Kans., 1951—; pres. Bess Spiva Timmons Found., Pittsburg, 1967—; donor Univ. Scholarship Trusts in Kans., Mo., Wyo., 1967—; mem. Timmons Chapel Com., Pittsburg, 1966—. Author: Yesterday, 1976. Life mem., past pres. Salvation Army Adv. Bd., Pittsburg, 1930's—; charter mem., past pres. Pittsburg State U. Endowment Assn., 1951—; sec. Mt. Carmel Found., Pittsburg, 1984-86. Mem. Mt. Carmel Found. (charter). Club: Altrusa (hon.). Republican. Presbyterian.

TIMMONS, EVELYN DEERING, pharmacist; b. Durango, Colo., Sept. 29, 1926; d. Claude Elliot and Evelyn Allen (Gooch) Deering; B.S. cum laude in Chemistry and Pharmacy, U. Colo., 1948; children—Roderick D., Steven P. Chief pharmacist Meml. Hosp., Phoenix, 1950-54; med. lit. research librarian Hoffman-LaRoche, Nutley, N.J., 1956-57; mgr. Profl. Pharmacies Inc., Phoenix, Airz., 1968-72; owner, mgr. Mt. View Pharmacy, Phoenix, 1972—; pres. Ariz. Apothecaries, Inc., 1976—; mem. profl. adv. bd. Hospice of Valley, 1984—; APHA appointee Am. Council Pharm. Edn., 1986—. Mem. platform com. State of Ariz., Nat. Rep. Conv., 1964; asst. sec. Young Rep. Nat. Fedn., 1963-65; active county and state Rep. coms. Named Outstanding Young Rep. of Yr., Nat. Fedn. Young Reps., 1965; recipient Disting. Public Service award Maricopa County Med. Soc., 1966, 67; Disting. Alumni award Wasatch Acad., 1982. Fellow Am. Coll. of Apothecaries (edn. com. 1979-80, pres. Ariz. chpt. 1979-81, Ariz. state dir. 1981-83, nat. 1st v.p. 1982-83, nat. pres.-elect 1983-84, nat. pres. 1984-85, nat. chmn. bd. 1985-86, Victor H. Morganroth award 1985); mem. Ariz. Soc. of Hosp. Pharmacists, Am., Ariz. (service to Pharmacy award 1976, Pharmacist of Yr. 1981), Maricopa County (pres. 1977, service to Pharmacy award 1977) pharmacy assns., Am. Soc. of Hosp. Pharmacists, Aux. to County Med. Soc. (pres. 1967-68), Am. Aircraft Owners and Pilots Assn., Nat. Assn. of Registered Parliamentarians. Contbr. articles to profl. jours. Office: 10565 N Tatum Blvd Paradise Valley AZ 85253

TIMMONS, JOYCE TERRELL, lawyer; b. West Middleton, Ind., July 2, 1930; d. Charles Joseph and H. Elizabeth (Johnson) Terrell; m. Lewis E. Bigelow, Mar. 3, 1949 (div.); children—Rodney A., Ray E., Mona J.; m. 2d, Chester L. Timmons, Sept. 7, 1963 (div. 1978); 1 son, Chester L. Student Huntington Coll., 1955-56, Ball State U., 1969, Wright State U., 1976; B.S., Manchester Coll., 1969; M.S. in Edn., St. Francis Coll., 1970; J.D., Stetson Coll., 1981. Bar: Fla. 1981, Ohio 1981. Operator, supr. Ind. Bell Telephone Co., Huntington, 1948-66; tchr. Huntington County Community Schs., 1968-79; staff atty. Gulfcoast Legal Services, Bradenton, Fla., 1981-83; ptnr. Thompson & Timmons, Eastpoint, Fla., 1983-84; sole practice Joyce Terrell Timmons, Atty.-at-Law, 1984—; dir. Washington Aluminum Castings Co., 1978-84, treas., 1983-84. Mem. ABA, Fla. Bar, Ohio Bar Assn., Franklin County Bar Assn. (pres. 1985—), Apalachicola Bay C. of C. (dir. 1985—). Unitarian-Universalist. Club: Eastpoint Women's. Office: Joyce Terrell & Timmons PO Box 726 Eastpoint FL 32328

TINDAL, CAROLYN LEE, nurse consultant; b. Balt., Dec. 5, 1946; d. Henry Whitfield and Ola Mae (Hilton) Tindal; R.N., Luth. Hosp. Sch. Nursing, 1967; B.S.N., Hampton Inst., 1975; M.S., U. Md., 1976; postgrad. Am. U. Head nurse, U. Md., Balt., 1968-75; staff asst. for edn. Johns Hopkins Hosp., Balt., 1976-77; edn. specialist Howard U. Hosp., Washington, 1977-79; dir. continuing edn. Walter Reed Army Med. Center, Washington, 1979-81, nurse cons. Tri-Service Med. Info. Systems, 1981—; cons. continuing edn. Resource Applications, Inc., 1981—. Served as maj. USAR, 1981—. Recipient Luth. Mission Soc. of Md. honor award, 1967; Purdue-Fredericks Co. scholarship, 1975. Mem. Am. Nurses Assn., Am. Soc. for Training & Devel., Md. League for Nursing, Alpha Kappa Mu, Sigma Theta Tau. Mem. 1st Ch. of Faith, Power and Deliverance. Contbr. articles to profl. jours. Home: 3401 Yataruba Dr Baltimore MD 21207 Office: Trimis Army Bldg T 60A Walter Reed Army Med Center Washington DC 20012

TINDALL, CHARLA HINDLEY, lawyer; b. Long Beach, Calif., Aug. 1, 1945; d. Charles Thompson and Frances Jean (Combs) Hindley Heckman; m. Richard Steven Archer Tindall, Dec. 19, 1970; children—Lora Kimberlin Archer, Heather Combs Archer, Ashley Jean Archer. A.B., U. So. Calif., 1967; M.A., Columbia U., 1969; postgrad. U. Tex. Health Sci. Ctr., 1974-75, J.D., So. Meth. U., 1978. Bar: Tex. 1978, U.S. Dist. Ct. (no. dist.) Tex. 1979. Tchr., N.Y.C. Sch. Dist., 1969-70; counselor, lectr. U. Minn., Mpls., 1970-71; tchr., counselor San Dieguito Union High Sch. Dist., San Diego, 1972-74; atty. Law Offices of Patricia A. Hill, Dallas, 1978-81; sole practice Charla J. H. Tindall, A Profl. Corp., Dallas, 1982—. Bd. dirs. Am. Social Health Assn., Palo Alto, Calif., 1981—, Mental Health Assn. Dallas County, 1982—, Exec. Women of Dallas, 1981-82, Promise House; mem. adv. com. Dallas County Mental Health and Mental Retardation, 1981—. Fellow Tex. Bar Found.; mem. ABA, Am. Trial Lawyers Assn., Am. Soc. Law and Medicine, State Bar Tex. (vice chmn. health law sect.), Tex. Trial Lawyers, Dallas Bar Assn., Dallas Women Lawyers Assn. (pres. 1981-82). Office: Charla JH Tindall Profl Corp 8300 Douglas Ave Suite 805 Dallas TX 75225

TINGEY, CAROL, psychologist, educator; b. St. James, Mo., Sept. 24, 1933; d. Willis Alma and Lola (Madsen) Tingey; B.S. magna cum laude, U. Utah, 1970, M.Ed., 1971, Ph.D., 1976; children—Richard, Blaine, James, Neil, Trish. Tchr. public schs., Salt Lake City, 1970, spl. edn. tchr., 1971-72; clin. instr. spl. edn. U. Utah, Salt Lake City, 1972-74; dir. staff devel. Utah State Tng. Sch., American Fork, Utah, 1974-75; asst. prof. spl. edn. U. No. Iowa, Cedar Falls, 1975-77; asst. prof. spl. edn. Trinity Coll., Washington, 1977-78; asst. prof. spl. edn. of severely handicapped George Mason U., Fairfax, Va., 1978-79; assoc. prof. edn. and tng. physically and multi-handicapped Northwestern State U. of La., Natchitoches, 1979-81; assoc. prof. spl. edn. Ill. State U., Normal, also coordinator program for physically handicapped, 1981-83; assoc. prof. psychology Utah State U., Logan, 1983—; cons. in field. Fellow Am. Assn. on Mental Deficiency (sec. Utah chpt. 1975, ednl. chmn. region VIII 1976-77, treas. edn. div. 1979-80), mem. Assn. for Severely Handicapped, Council for Exceptional Children (pres. Utah chpt. 1974-75), Assn. for Retarded Citizens, Phi Delta Kappa, Phi Kappa Phi. Author: Home and School Partnerships in Exceptional Education; Handicapped Infants and Children: Handbook for Parents and Professionals; New Perspectives on Down Syndrome; contbr. articles to profl. jours.; recorded albums: Self Help Skills, Adaptive Behavior; Socialization Skills; Adaptive Behavior; Daily Living Tasks, Housekeeping Skills, Vocational Awareness, Community Helpers; editorial adv. bd. Exceptional Parent mag. Home: 1565 Rose Orchard Circle Logan UT 84321 Office: 174 Developmental Ctr for Handicapped Persons Utah State Univ Logan UT 84322

TINKHAM, JUDY MAY, real estate executive; b. Putnam, Conn., June 26, 1943; d. Fred S. and Lydia W. Tinkham. Cert. in fed. income taxes Nat. Tax Tng. Sch., 1964, tax cons., 1982; cert. in real estate brokerage Lee Inst., 1967; diploma in complete real estate tng. LaSalle U., 1972, student archtl. drafting and law, 1974—, Assoc. in Bus. in Gen. Acctg., 1976, B.S. in Bus. Mgmt., 1977, Assoc. in Bus. in Banking and Fin., 1977; cert. Grad. Real Estate Inst. Tri-State Inst., 1979; cert. in bus. mgmt. Dale Carnegie, 1980. Lic. realtor, N.H., Mass.; lic. justice of peace, N.H. Treas. family owned corp. contracting bus., 1963-67; co-owner, mgr. Tinkham Realty, Inc., Londonderry, N.H., 1967—. Mem. Nat. Apt. Mgmt. Council, 1977; team capt. Nutfield United Way, 1978; mem. ordinance com. Londonderry Comml. Indsl. Zoning Dists., 1980; mem. Republican Senate Legis. Adv. Bd., 1983; mem. Nat. Rep. Senatorial Com., 1983; mem. Rep. Presdl. Task Force, 1984; mem. N.H. Rep. Com., 1984; state advisor U.S. Congl. Adv. Bd., 1984; mem. Nat. Conservative Polit. Action Com., 1985. Mem. Greater Salem Area Bd. Realtors (bd. dirs., lock box com., study com. for forms, Realtor of Yr. award 1984, other coms.), Greater Manchester Bd. Realtors, N.H. Assn. Realtors (bd. dirs.), Nat. Assn. Realtors, Women's Council Realtors, N.H. Realtor Polit. Action Com., So. N.H. Homebuilders Assn., U.S. Senatorial Club, Londonderry C. of C. (subcom.). Avocations: photography; gardening; home designing. Office: Tinkham Realty Co Route 102 Londonderry NH 03053

TINKHAM, MYRA CELESTE MELTON, nurse; b. Galesburg, Ill., Oct. 9, 1954; d. Roy Ray and Junella (Wilson) Melton; Asso. in Sci., Carl Sandburg Coll., 1977; m. Todd Tinkham, June 19, 1982; 1 son, Jason Elvin. With Belscot Dept. Store and Bonanza Sirloin Pit, Galesburg, 1972-73; nurse's aide Americana Health Care Center, Galesburg, 1975-77, R.N., night supr., 1980; now supr. nursing Golden Age Leisure Gardens, Vista, Calif.; nurse Cottage Hosp. and pvt. care, 1978-80. Mem. Pres. Council for Phys. Fitness and Health in Am., 1970-73. Baptist. Address: 1451 Lindsey Ln Galesburg IL 61401 Office: 304 N Melrose Vista CA 92083

TINO, CARMELA MARY, librarian; b. Meriden, Conn., May 24, 1933; d. Pasquale John and Josephine Mary (Cotrona) Nesci; m. Richard Louis Tino, July 4, 1959; children—Carla, Laura. B.A. in French, Coll. of New Rochelle, 1955; M.L.S., So. Conn. U., 1975; M.S. in Edn., U. Bridgeport, 1982. Tchr., Meriden Bd. Edn., 1955-60; instr. Housatonic Community Coll., Bridgeport, Conn., part-time 1975-78; librarian Fairfield Library Br., Fairfield, Conn., part-time 1976-77; periodicals librarian U. Bridgeport, 1978—. Mem. Stratford, (Conn.) Gen. and Sch. Bldg. Needs Com., 1978-80. Mem. ALA, Assn. Coll. and Research Libraries, Southwestern Conn. Library Council (trustee), AAUP. Democrat. Roman Catholic. Home: 55 Maple St Stratford CT 06497 Office: Wahlstrom Library U Bridgeport 126 Park Ave Bridgeport CT 06601

TIPPETT, DEBRA LYNN, health services company marketing executive; b. Casper, Wyo., Oct. 29, 1954; d. Robert L. and Evelyn J. (Andrews) T. B.B.A., So. Meth. U., 1976, M.B.A., 1977. Banking officer Interfirst Bank N.A., Dallas, 1977-79; mktg. analyst Pearle Health Services, Inc., Dallas, 1979-81, mgr. mktg. and display merchandising, 1981—. Mem. Am. Mktg. Assn., Dallas Soc. Crippled Children, Kappa Alpha Theta. Republican. Presbyterian. Home: 8443 Barnaby Dallas TX 75243 Office: Pearle Health Services Inc 2534 Royal Ln Dallas TX 75229

TIPPIT, ANN TOMPKINS PEARCE, stenography service exec., investment co. exec., counselor; b. Lake City, Fla., Oct. 26, 1934; d. Zack Brown and Lelia Iva (Langford) Tompkins; m. M.E. (Gene) Tippit; 1 stepson, George A. Pearce. Ph.D., Neotarian Coll. Philosophy, Kansas City, Mo., 1979. Ct. reporter, Fla. and La., 1950-70; owner, operator telephone answering service, Jacksonville, Fla., 1951-53; corp. officer A to Z Driving Schs., Tampa, Fla., 1951-53; com. sec. Fla. Legislature, 1960; engrossing clk. Ala. Legislature, 1963; co-owner Globe Tank Constrns., Houston, 1962-65; owner, operator Ann Tompkins Services, public stenography service, New Orleans, 1970-72, Tampa, 1972—, Lantom Properties, Odessa, Fla., 1979—, co-owner Inst. Balanced Individuality, Odessa, 1983—; owner MTP Prodns., entertainment bur., 1979—; co-owner Custom Services Unltd., Specialized Personal Services. Roads chmn. Keystone Civic Assn., Odessa, 1979-81; bd. dirs. Gunn Hwy. Vol. Fire Dept., Odessa, 1979-81; mem. adv. com. N.W. Hillsborough Expy. Authority; hon. county commr. Hillsborough County, 1981—. Mem. Internat. Enterpreneurs Assn., Nat. Assn. Female Execs. (charter), Am. Soc. Profl. and Exec. Women, Internat. New Thought Alliance, Alcoholism and Drug Addiction Profls'. Assn., Internat. Clergy Assn., Parapsychology Research Assn., Assn. Research and Enlightenment, LWV, Hillsboro County Mental Health Assn., Fla. Sheriffs Assn. Mem. Unity Ch. Clubs: Lutz-Lake Fern Garden, Keystone Homemakers Extension.

TIPPS, LISA JEAN, graphics company executive; b. Dallas, Aug. 2, 1955; d. Gene A. Tipps and E. Ruth (Breazeale) Barrett. Student U. Tex., 1974—. Bookkeeper Dynamic Reprographics, Austin, Tex., 1978-79, printer, 1979-80, mgr., 1980-82, pres., co-owner, 1982—; cons. on pin graphics, 1983—. Fundraiser Women's Advocacy Project, 1984; mem. Austin Women's Polit. Caucus, 1983-85, J. Lassen Boysen scholar U. Tex., 1983-84. Mem. Internat. Reprographics Assn., Delta Phi Alpha, Phi Kappa Phi. Democrat. Avocations: reading; writing poetry; walking; boating.

TIPTON, JENNIFER, lighting designer; b. Columbus, Ohio, Sept. 11, 1937; d. Samuel Ridley and Isabel (Hanson) Tipton; B.A., Cornell U., 1958; m. William F. Beaton, Aug. 29, 1976. Lighting designer Paul Taylor Dance Co., Twyla Tharp and Dancers, 1965, Pa. Ballet Co., 1966, Macbeth, Am. Shakespeare Festival, Stratford, Conn., Harkness Ballet Co., 1967, Dan Wagoner Dancers, Richard II, Love's Labour's Lost, Am. Shakespeare Festival, HB Studios N.Y., 1968, Horseman Pass By, Fortune Theatre, Les Grands Ballet Canadiens, Yvonne Rainer Co., City Center Joffrey Ballet, Our Town Anta Theatre, 1969, Anta Theatre Dance Series, 1971, 72, Eliot Feld Ballet Co., Am. Ballet Theatre, 1971, Kazuko Hirabayashi Dance Co., A Ballet Behind the Bridge, Negro Ensemble Co., Delacorte Dance Festival, Houston Ballet Co., 1972, Nat. Ballet Co., Hartford Ballet Co., Celebration: The Art of Pas de Deux, Jerome Robbins, Jose Limon Dance Co., 1973, Tempest, Macbeth, Midsummer Night's Dream, N.Y. Shakespeare Festival-Newhouse Theatre, The Killdeer, Newman Theatre, Jerome Robbins' The Dybbuk, N.Y.C. Ballet, Dreyfus in Rehearsal, Barrymore Theatre, 1974, San Francisco Ballet Co., Anthony Tudor's The Leaves Are Fading, Am. Ballet Theatre, Habeas Corpus, Martin Beck Theatre, Murder Among Friends, Biltmore Theatre, 1975, Rex, Lunt-Fontanne Theatre, For Colored Girls Who Consider Suicide When the Rainbow is Enuf, Booth Theatre, Cleve. Ballet Co., Mikhail Baryshuikov's The Nutcracker, Am. Ballet Theatre, 1976, The Landscape of the Body, Newman Theatre, The Cherry Orchard, Agamemnon, Beaumont Theatre, Happy End, Martin Beck Theatre, Agamemnon, Delacorte Theatre, 1977, Museum, Public Theatre; Runaways, Public Theatre and Plymouth Theatre, All's Well That Ends Well, Taming of the Shrew, Delacorte Theatre, After the Season, Academy Festival Theatre, A Month in the Country, Williamstown Theatre Festival, Mikhail Baryshnikov's Don Quixote, Am. Ballet Theatre, The Goodbye People, Westport Playhouse, Funny Face, Buffalo Studio Arena, Drinks Before Dinner, Public Theatre, Alice in Wonderland, Public Theatre, 1978. Recipient Drama Desk award for For Colored Girls, The Cherry Orchard, 1977; Tony award for the Cherry Orchard, 1977; Joseph Jefferson award for the Landscape of the Body, 1977; Creative Arts award Brandeis U., 1981. Office: Yale Drama School Yale Univ 1903A Yale Station New Haven CT 06520

TIPTON, MARY DAVISON, banker; b. Atlanta, Jan. 11, 1947; d. W. Kay and M. Estelle (Reynolds) T. M.A. in History, Emory U., 1969, postgrad. in fin., 1978, M.B.A., 1986. Asst. bank examiner Fed. Res., Atlanta, 1969-72; credit officer 1st Nat. Bank, Atlanta, 1975-77; asst. treas. Bankers Trust, N.Y.C., 1979-81, asst. v.p., 1982; asst. v.p. Amro Bank, N.Y.C., 1983-84; fin. mgr. Reynolds Properties, 1984-86. Author essay: The Analysis of Foreign Banks (Robert Morris Assocs. Contest Southeastern winner 1977), 1977. Vol. tutor basic bus. Martin Luther King Assn., Atlanta, 1975-79. Mem. Nat. Assn. Female Execs., Emory Alumni Club of N.Y.C., Phi Beta Kappa, Phi Kappa Phi. Office: 188 Triumph Dr NW Atlanta GA 30342

TISCHER, MAE MARION, state legislator, businesswoman; b. Sleepy Eye, Minn., Oct. 16, 1928; d. Paul Fredrick and Frieda (Macho) Lowinske; children—Brad, Becky, Mark, Daniel, Kathleen, Julie. Farmer, Meeker County, Minn., 1949-60; homesteader, Susitna Valley, Alaska, 1961-64; ptnr., owner Mobile Home Movers, Anchorage, 1963-72, Tischer's Burner Service, Anchorage, 1963-72; dist. dir. Muscular Dystrophy Assn. Alaska, 1974-82; mem. Alaska Ho. of Reps., 1982—, chmn. health, edn. and social services com., 1983-84, mem. rules com., 1983-84, fin. subcom. budget oversite and corrections, 1983-84. Organizer Alaska Mobile Home Dealers Assn., Anchorage, 1967; organizer, chmn. Montana Mothers' Club, Montana Creek, Mich., 1962; organizer, bd. chmn. Barrier-Free Recreation, Inc., Anchorage, 1977; organizer Youth against Dystrophy, Anchorage, 1975. Recipient Regional Spl. Events award Muscular Dystrophy Assn., Anchorage, 1978-79, 80; Humanitarian Recognition award Sta. KIMO-TV, Anchorage, 1982; Humanitarian Dedication award Internat. Firefighters Assn., Anchorage, 1981; citation for Humanitarian Efforts, Alaska State Legislature, 1981. Mem. Commn. Opportunities for Handicapped, Anchorage Republican Women's Club. Lodges: W.O.O.M., Am. Legion Aux. Office Alaska Ho of Reps Pouch V Juneau AK 99811*

TISINGER, CATHERINE ANNE, college president; b. Winchester, Va., Apr. 6, 1936; d. Richard Martin and Irma Regina (Ohl) T. B.A., Coll. Wooster, 1958; M.A., U. Pa., 1962, Ph.D., 1970; LL.D. (hon.), Coll. of Elms, 1985. Provost Callison Coll., U. of Pacific, Stockton, Calif., 1971-72; v.p. Met. State U., St. Paul, 1972-75; interim pres. Southwest State U., Marshall, Minn., 1975-77; dir. Ctr. for Econ. Edn., R.I. Coll., Providence, 1979-80; v.p. acad. affairs Central Mo. State U., Warrensburg, Mo., 1980-84; pres. North Adams State Coll., Mass., 1984—; cons. North Central Assn. Colls. and Schs., 1980-84, New England Assn. Schs. and Colls., 1978-79, 85—, Minn. Acad. Family Physicians, 1973-77; mem. adv. bd. First Agrl. Bank, North Adams, 1985—; pres. No. Berkshire Cooperating Colls., 1986—. Vice pres. Med. Simulation Found., 1986—. Mem. No. Berkshire C. of C. (bd. dirs. 1984—). Avocations: fiber/textile arts; photography; choral and instrumental music. Office: North Adams State Coll Church St North Adams MA 01247

TITRAN, COLETTE GAIL, manufacturing company executive, medical careers consultant; b. Detroit, Sept. 12, 1958; d. Pierre Joseph and Jean (Fisk) T. R.N., St. Elizabeth Sch. Nursing, Youngstown, Ohio, 1979; B.A., St. Mary's Coll., Moraga, Calif., 1983; M.B.A., U. Phoenix, 1986. Nurse, Swedish Med. Ctr., Denver, 1979-80; med. sales rep. Abbott Labs., San Francisco, 1980-83; med. sales rep. USCI Internat. div. C.R. Bard Co., San Francisco, 1983-85, surg. product mgr., Boston, 1985—; med. career cons., Boston, 1985—. Author: How To Get Out of Nursing, 1986. Mem. Radiological Nurses Assn., Nat. Assn. Female Execs. Republican. Roman Catholic. Avocations: skiing; tennis; jogging; real estate investing. Office: USCI Internat 129 Concord Rd Billerica MA 01821

TITUS, DOROTHY ELLEN, postmaster; b. Arcade, N.Y., Sept. 20, 1935; d. Lawrence Earl Stevens and Mary Amanda (Sullivan) Stevens Haggerty; m. Harold Jay Titus, July 31, 1954; children—Deborah, Lawrence, Brian, Pamela. Grad. high sch., Machias, N.Y. Clk. carrier U.S. Postal Service, Arcade, 1971-77, postmaster, Sardinia, N.Y., 1977-79, Delevan, N.Y., 1979—; tng. postmaster, Delevan, 1983—, leader rural seminars, Buffalo, 1983. Mem. Cattaraugus County Assn. Postmasters, Erie County Postmasters (treas. 1983), Nat. Assn. Postmasters, Nat. League Postmasters. Address: 11719 Grove St Rural Route 2 Box 2604 Delevan NY 14042

TITUS, PAMELA LOUISE, real estate broker; b. Ft. Wayne, Ind., Aug. 15, 1953; d. Gene Wesley and Louise (George) Eby. B.S. in Speech and Hearing, Purdue U., 1975, M.S. in Speech Pathology, 1976. Speech pathologist Speech Pathology Assocs., Houston, 1977-80; profl. recruiter Diversified Human Resources Group, Houston, 1980-81, Key Personnel Pty., Ltd., Sydney, Australia, 1981-82; computer sales rep. ComputerLand, Houston, 1982-84; broker Coldwell Banker Comml. Real Estate Services, 1985—. Com. chmn. Houston Area Assn. for Communication Disorders, 1978-80; campaign worker Hill for Gov., Houston, 1978. Republican. Presbyterian. Home: 2001 Bering Dr Houston TX 77057 Office: Coldwell Bankers 2500 West Loop S Houston TX 77027

TOBE, SUSAN BRING, lawyer; b. N.Y.C., 1949; d. Ira and Sylvia (Stevelman) Bring; m. Richard M. Tobe, 1980. B.A., State U. Coll., Buffalo, 1971; J.D., SUNY-Buffalo, 1974. Bar: N.Y. 1975. Asst. gen. counsel Carborundum Co., Niagara Falls, N.Y., 1974-75; asst. corp. counsel City of Buffalo, 1975-78; atty.-advisor U.S. Dept. HUD, Buffalo, 1978-81; asst. atty. gen. State of N.Y., Buffalo, 1981—; supervising atty. Pub. Interest Law Clinic, 1982; program lectr. St. Law Inst., N.Y., 1978; guest lectr. various high schs., colls., 1975—; dir. State U. Coll. at Buffalo Alumni Assn., 1984—; dir. SUNY Sch. Law Alumni Assn., Buffalo, 1979-82. Vol. Leukemia Soc., Buffalo, 1981—, United Way Campaign, Buffalo, 1977, Friends Community Music. Sch., Buffalo, 1984—; com. person Democratic Party, Buffalo, 1976-78. Mem. N.Y. State Bar Assn. (com. profl. ethics 1984—), Erie County Bar Assn., N.Y. Civil Liberties Union, ABA, Women Lawyers of Western N.Y. Office: NY State Atty Gen's Office Dept Law 125 Main St Buffalo NY 14203

TOBER, BARBARA MAUD, magazine editor; b. Summit, N.J., Aug. 19, 1934; d. Rodney and Maude (Grebbin Starkey) Fielding; m. Donald Gibbs Tober, Apr. 5, 1973. Student Traphagen Sch. Fashion, N.Y.C., 1954-56, Fashion Inst. of Tech., 1956-58, N.Y. Sch. Interior Design, N.Y.C., 1964. Copy editor Vogue Pattern Book, N.Y.C., 1958-60; beauty editor Vogue Mag., N.Y.C., 1961; dir. women's services Bartell Media Corp., N.Y.C., 1961-66; editor-in-chief Bride's Mag., N.Y.C., 1966—; mem. home furnishing com. Fashion Group, N.Y.C., 1978-79, mem. career com., 1982—; dir. Gen. Brands, N.Y.C.; bd. dirs. N.Y. chpt. Confrerie de la Chaine des Rotisseurs. Author: The ABC's of Beauty, 1963; The Bride, 1984; contbr. articles to profl. jours. Mem. adv. bd. Traphagen Sch. Fashion, N.Y.C.; nat. pres. Pan Pacific Southeast Asia Women's Assn., N.Y.C., 1982-83; mus. assoc. Am. Crafts Council, N.Y.C., 1983—. Recipient Alumni award Traphagen Sch. Fashion, 1975, Diamond Jubilee award, 1983; Great Cook award Bon Appetit, 1981. Mem. Soc. Profl. Journalists, Am. Soc. Mag. Editors, Wine & Food Soc. (chief protocol 1981), Nat. Home Fashions League (chmn. program 1975, 83, Intercorporate Group, Women in Communication, Women in Food Service. Office: Bride's Mag 350 Madison Ave New York NY 10017

TOBEY, LOUISE S., contractor, hairdresser; b. Galax, Va., Mar. 5, 1929; d. Henry Harrison and Carrie Virginia (Horne) Sawyers; m. James F. Tobey, Oct. 3, 1981; children by previous marriage—Pamela L. Moore, Keven F. Moore, Karen L. Moore. Student Nat. Bus. Coll., 1949, Va. Western Community Coll., 1975; diploma Alice's Beauty Culture Sch., 1962. Sec., Eaton Yale & Towne, Salem, Va., 1948-49; sec. Valleydale Pakcers, Salem, 1949-52; owner Beverly Hts. Beauty Shop, Salem, 1962-65; pres., owner Salem Curb & Gutter, Inc., Salem, Va., 1976—. Mem. Roanoke Valley Home Builders Assn., Am. Bus. Women's Assn., Women of the Moose. Republican. Christian Ch. Avocations: art; crafts; sewing; tennis; cooking. Address: 365 Keesling Ave Salem VA 24153

TOBEY-HAMPSON, RUTH, city official; b. Laconia, N.H., Aug. 21, 1919; d. Fred Charles and Susan Lucretia (Colby) Tobey; m. Arthur Hampson, May 24, 1943; 1 child, Arthur Hampson. Student Plymouth State Coll., U. Hawaii. Mem. N.H. Ho. of Reps., 1962-63; real estate broker, East Hebron, N.H., 1963-73; adminstrv. asst. Nat. Spiritual Assembly of the Baha'is of U.S., Wilmette, Ill., 1971-73; clk. City of Canon City, Colo., 1977—. Speaker UN Orgn. of Colo., Denver, 1981—; lectr. on Baha: Faith. Mem. Internat. Inst. Mcpl. Clks., Colo. Mcpl. Clks., Women for Internat. Peace and Arbitration. Club: Toastmistress. Avocations: gardening; biking; skiing; public speaking. Address: 1228 Grand Ave Canon City CO 81212

TOBIAS, JUDY, university development executive; b. Pitts.; d. Saul Albert Landau and Bess (Previn) Kurzman; m. Seth Tobias (dec. May 1983); children—Stephen Frederic, Andrew Previn. Student Silvermine Artists Guild, 1951-55. Art cons. Westchester Mental Health Assn., White Plains, N.Y., 1968-69; cons. sch. social work NYU, 1973-74, devel. exec. 1976—; conf. coordinator Today's Family: Implications for the Future, N.Y.C., 1974-75; cons. Playschools, Inc., N.Y.C., 1975. Mem. Gov.'s Commn. on Continuing Edn., Albany, N.Y., 1968-70, Nat. Council on Children and Youth, Washington, 1974-75, Manhattan Inter-Hosp. Group on Child Abuse, 1975-76; chmn. N.Y. met. com. for UNICEF, 1976-77; mem. exec. com. Town Hall Found., N.Y.C., 1979—; founder, bd. dirs. N.Y. chpt. WAIF, Inc., 1961—, nat. pres., 1978-82; bd. dirs., v.p. Citizen's Com. for Children, City of N.Y., 1975—, Am. br. Internat. Social Service; bd. dirs. Andrew Glover Youth Program, 1986—, Goddard Riverside Community Services, 1985—, Dance Mag. Found., 1986—. Mem. Nat. Assn. Female Execs., Child Study Assn. Am. (bd. dirs. 1963-71, pres. 1969-71), Child Study Assn./Wel-Met, Inc. (bd. dirs. 1981-85). Democrat.

TOBIAS, ROSE MARY BOMBELA, state official, journalist; b. East Chicago, Ind., May 2, 1950; d. Leonardo and Haydee (Martinez) Bombela; m. Domingo Tobias, Jr., May 26, 1985. B.A., U. Tex.-El Paso, 1972. Asst. dir. Revenue Sharing Project, East Chicago, 1972-74; news reporter WJOB, Hammond, Ind., 1972-74; adminstrv. asst. Metro Corps, Inc., Gary, Ind., 1975; news reporter WLTH, Gary, 1974-77, WTAX-WDBR, Springfield, Ill., 1977-78; asst. press sec. Office of Ill. Gov., Chgo., 1978-79; spl. asst. to gov. Gov.'s Office on Interagy. Coop., Chgo., 1979-81; asst. dir. Ill. Dept. Personnel, Chgo., 1981-82, Ill. Dept. Central Mgmt. Services, Springfield, 1982—. Chairperson, Ill. Hispanic Women's Conf., Chgo., 1981; YWCA bd. dirs. Land of Lincoln council Girl Scouts U.S., Springfield, Ill., 1983-84; bd. dirs. YWCA of Sangamon County, Springfield, 1983-84, 3d v.p. bd. dirs., 1985; trustee Citizens Info. Service, Chgo., 1984—; mem. Hispanic Alliance for Career Enhancement, Chgo., 1983-84; mem. Nat. Republican Hispanic Assembly, Chgo., 1983—, Midwest Women's Agenda, Chgo., 1984—, minority women's com. Ill. Commn. on Status of Women, Springfield, 1982-85. Recipient cert. of appreciation Chgo. Fed. Exchange Bd., 1980; Pub. Service award Region V, U.S. Dept. Labor, 1981, citation of honor Fedn. Bus. and Profl. Women's Clubs, 1981, recognition award Latin Am. Police Assn., Chgo., 1984; named Contemporary Woman of Yr., Mexican-Am. Bus. and Profl. Women's Club, Chgo., 1984. Nat. Council Hispanic Women, 1986. Republican. Roman Catholic. Office: Dept Central Mgmt Services 100 W Randolph 4th Floor Chicago IL 60601

TOBIN, ILONA L., psychologist, marriage/family counselor, sex educator and counselor, consultant; b. Trenton, Mich., Apr. 15, 1943; d. Frank John and Marjorie Cathalean (Lines) Kotyuk; m. Roger Lee Tobin, Aug. 20, 1966. B.A., Eastern Mich. U., 1965; M.A., 1968; M.A., Mich. State U., 1975; Ed.D., Wayne State U., 1978. Tchr., counselor Willow Run Pub. Schs., Ypsilanti, Mich., 1966-72; prof. Macomb County Community Coll., Mt. Clemens, Mich., 1974-79; psychotherapist Identity Center, Inc., Mt. Clemens, 1974-79; dir. treatment Alternative Lifestyles, Inc., Orchard Lake, Mich., 1979-80; psychologist Profl. Psychotherapy and Counseling Ctr., Farmington Hills, Mich., 1980-83; pvt. practice clin. psychology, Birmingham, Mich., 1983—; lectr. Wayne State U., Detroit, 1977—; recruitment dir. Upward Bound Eastern Mich. U., Ypsilanti, 1969-72. Co-chmn. Birmingham Families in Action, 1982-83; bd. dirs. HAVEN-Oakland County's Physical and Sexual Abuse Ctr. and Oakland Area Counselors Assn., 1984-85; mem. exec. bd., v.p. personnel Birmingham Community Women's Ctr., 1984-85, also dir.; mem. adv. bd. Woodside Med. Ctr. for Chemically Dependent Women, 1984-85. NIMH fellow, 1976; Wayne State U. scholar, 1976-78. Creator, mfgr. Doc's Dolls. Mem. Am. Psychol. Assn., Mich. Psychol. Assn., Am. Assn. Sex Educators, Counselors and Therapists, Am. Assn. for Counseling and Devel., Pi Lambda Theta, Phi Delta Kappa. Unitarian. Clubs: Birmingham Bus. Womens.

TOBOLOWSKY, SARAH, retired librarian; b. Dallas; d. A.B. and Lena (Skibell) T. B.A., So. Meth. U., 1934, M.A., 1938; M.S. in Library Sci., Columbia U., 1952; postgrad. U. So. Calif., Northwestern U., U. Hawaii, Boston U. Sch. tchr. Dallas Ind. Sch. Dist., 1935-80, ret. 1980; sch. librarian Benjamin Franklin Jr. High Sch., Dallas, 1957-80, ret. 1980; instr. North Tex. State U., 1966-70. Honors Day speaker Tex. Woman's U., Denton, 1981. Mem. NEA (life), ALA (joint com. mem. with NEA), Am. Assn. Sch. Librarians (regional bd. dirs.), Dallas Classroom Tchrs. Assn. (pres. 1952-54), Tex. Classroom Tchrs. Assn. (legis. chmn. 1952-53, adv. bd. 1953-55), Tex. State Tchrs. Assn. (life), Tex. Library Assn., Dallas Sch. Librarians (pres. 1947-49), Delta Kappa Gamma (chpt. pres. 1956-58, state pres. 1963-65, State Achievement award 1963, Internat. Achievement award 1984; internat. pres. 1980-82), Kappa Kappa Iota. Home: 6838 Orchid Ln Dallas TX 75230

TOCKLIN, ADRIAN MARTHA, insurance company executive; b. Miami, Fla., Aug. 4, 1951; d. Kelso Hampton and Patricia Jane (Crook) Cook Atkins; m. Gary Michael Tocklin, Nov. 23, 1974. B.A., George Washington U., 1972. Regional claim examiner Interstate Nat. Corp., St. Petersburg, Fla., 1973-74; branch supr. Underwriter's Adjusting Co. subs. Continental Corp., Tampa, Fla., 1974-77, asst. dir. edn. tng. adminstrn., N.Y.C., 1977, asst. regional mgr. adminstrn. ops., Livingston, N.J., 1977-78, br. mgr., Paramus, N.J., 1978-80, sr. v.p. mktg., N.Y.C., Piscataway, N.J., 1980-85, regional v.p., mgr., Livingston, N.J., 1985—, also dir.; pres. U.S. Protection Indemnity Agy., Inc., N.Y.C., 1983-85, also dir.; v.p. Continental Risk Services, Inc., Hamilton, Bermuda, 1983—; editor-in-chief Profl. Ins. Bulletin Update, N.Y.C., 1977-79. Mem. Nat. Assn. Ins. Women (Outstanding Ins. Woman in N.Y.C.), NOW. Democrat. Lutheran. Office: Underwriters Adjusting Co 2 Peachtree Hill Rd Livingston NJ 07659

TODD, BARBARA SHEEN, county commissioner; b. Phila., Mar. 10, 1942; d. Milton Roy and Jeanette (Brown) Sheen; m. Thomas C. Todd, May 18, 1973; children—Kimberly, Tamara, Tiffany. Student Instituto Tecnologico, Monterrey, Mexico, 1962; B.A. in Spanish and Sociology, Fla. State U., 1963, M.A. in Fgn. Lang. Edn., 1964. Personnel mgr. State of Fla. and pvt. industry, 1965-75; state adminstr. for spl. programs, Fla. Bd. of Regents, 1973-75; acting asst. sec. for adminstrn. Office of Sec. of Edn. and Cultural Affairs, S.D., 1975; owner, mgr. cons. firm, Pierre, S.D., 1975-79; county commr. Pinellas County, Fla., 1980—, chmn., 1983. Chmn. Met. Planning Orgn., Pinellas County Property Appraisal and Adjustment Bd., 1984—, Tourist Devel. Council, 1983, Child Safety Task Force, 1985, Leon County Sch. Bd., 1973, State Task Force on Elem. Guidance, 1972, State Adv. Panel on Differentiated Staffing; bd. dirs. League of Cities, 1985-86, Juvenile Welfare Bd., 1982-83, Mental Health Bd., 1981-86; mem. Pinellas Arts Council, Pinellas County Day Care Licensing Bd., 1985-86, Pinellas Planning Council, 1980-86; mem. steering com. Nat. Assn. of Counties, 1985-86, also men. nat. health and edn. com., 1984-85, also task force on refugees, aliens and migrants; mem. Fla. State Commn. on Child Support, 1985-86; sec., treas. State Assn. of County Commrs., 1984, v.p., 1985-86; mem. Gov.'s Growth Mgmt. Adv. Com., 1985-86; state legis. chmn. S.D. PTA, 1977-79; pres. Women's Fellowship, Congl. Ch. of Pierre, 1974-75; vice chmn. Leon County Sch. Bd., 1972. Mem. Am. Assn. of Sch. Adminstrs., Nat. U. Extension Assn., Beta Sigma Phi (past pres.), Sigma Delta Pi, Kappa Delta Pi. Recipient Outstanding Service award Pinellas County Extension Hort. Adv. Com., 1984, Award for Patriotic Services Rendered to the Community, VFW, 1984; named Outstanding Elected Ofcl. for 1983, Greater Seminole Republican Club. Club: Pilot. Home: 1934 Arrowhead Dr NE St Petersburg FL 33703 Office: Pinellas County Courthouse 315 Court St Clearwater FL 33516

TODD, JOYCE ANDERSON, social service agency director; b. Lumberton, N.C., June 2, 1940; d. Irvin L. and Esther (Huggins) Anderson; m. William H. Strickland, Dec. 9, 1960 (div. Oct. 1976); 1 child, William (dec.); m. John Wendell Todd, July 6, 1979; 1 stepchild, Stephanie Leigh. B.A., Coker Coll., 1960. Social worker Horry County Dept. Social Services, Conway, S.C., 1962-66, casework supr., 1966-73, county dir., 1973—. Mem. S.C. Assn. County Human Service Adminstrs., S.C. County Dirs. and Suprs. Assn., Am. Pub. Welfare Assn., Child Welfare League Am. Democrat. Baptist. Avocations: cooking; snow skiing; golf. Office: Horry County Dept Social Services PO Drawer 1465 Conway SC 29526

TODD, JUANITA JUNE, business executive; b. Tamms, Ill., Dec. 6, 1926; d. Elbert and Emma Grace (Mossberger) Fulkerson; m. Harold E. Todd, June 11, 1948, Nov. 11, 1983 (div. 1976, div. 1986). B.S. in Edn. summa cum laude, So. Ill. U., 1948, M.A., 1954; postgrad. Oxford U., DePauw U., Northwestern U., Bucknell U., Rosary Coll., River Forest, Ill. Instr. English, So. Ill. U., Carbondale, 1948-50, dir. admissions, 1951-52; tchr. English and math. Hurst Bush High Sch., Ill., 1950-51; tchr. English and French, Athens Consol. High Sch., Ill., 1952-55; tchr. English and history Thacker Jr. High Sch., Des Plaines, Ill., 1955-56; tchr. English, Niles Twp. High Sch., Skokie, Ill., 1956-67, mem. adv. bd. to supt., 1959-64; tchr. English, New Trier Twp. High Sch., Winnetka, Ill., 1969-83; owner, mgr. All Things Small & Beautiful, Inc., Skokie, 1986—. Patron Chgo. Opera Theatre; Sforzando mem. Bel Canto Found., Chgo.; friend Athanaeum Players; mem. com. of 1000 Am. Humanist. Named Outstanding High Sch. Educator of Region, U. Chgo., 1976, 78, 79, 81, So. Ill. U. scholar, 1944-48, 54; Coe fellow DePauw U., 1958. Mem. Nat. Assn. Female Execs., Am. Fedn. Tchrs. (past mem. exec. bd.), Friends of Animals, North Shore Animal League, Nat. Humane Edn. Soc., I-Kare Wildlife Assn., Am. Soc. for Prevention Cruelty to Animals, Greenpeace, Save-A-Pet, Defenders Animal Rights, Chgo. Council Fgn. Relations, Lyric Opera, Met. Mus. Art, Mus. Art (Boston), Skokie Valley Lyric Opera Guild, People United to Serve Humanity, Citizens Opposed to Rising Utility Bills, People for the Way, Physicians for Social Responsibility, State Univs. Annuitants Assn., Stratford Shakespeare Fund, Ams. for Religious Liberty, ACLU, Animal Protection Inst. Am., Andrus Found., Smithsonian Assocs., Art Inst. Chgo. Sphinx Club (So. Ill. U.), Delta Rho, Mu Tau Pi, Sigma Tau Delta. Democrat. Avocations: reading; playing piano; camping; collecting primitive art; interior decorating. Home: 8101 N Keating Skokie IL 60076 Office: Winnetka IL

TODD, MARGARET BISHOP, artist; b. Sycamore, Ala., Apr. 1, 1940; d. Aldun Alvist and Louise J. (Gamel) Bishop; m. Slater H. Wilson, Oct. 21, 1964 (div. Mar. 1973); m. Donnie Douglas Todd, Sr., Dec. 3, 1977; stepchildren—Donnie Todd, Selisa Todd Turnbull. Student U. Ala., 1975-76. Owner-operator Margaret's Ceramics, Tuscaloosa, Ala., 1971-73; stenographer Equifax Corp., Tuscaloosa and Birmingham, Ala., 1973-76; purchasing agt. Diesel Equipment Co., Birmingham, 1976-78; ptnr., bookkeeper Ala. Saw Co., Birmingham and Pell City, 1978—; owner-operator Chula Vista Art Gallery, Pell City, 1984—; ptnr. Todd Farms, Pell City, 1980—. Mem. Jaycettes Tuscaloosa (publicity chair 1971-72), Ceramic Hobb Guild (v.p. 1972-73). Baptist. Lodge: Order Eastern Star (Pell City). Avocations: piano; crocheting; knitting; water skiing; iceskating. Office: Chula Vista Art Gallery Rt 3 Box 539-A Pell City AL 35125

TODD, NORMA JEAN ROSS, retired government official; b. Butler, Pa., Oct. 3, 1920; d. William Bryson and Doris Mae (Ferguson) Ross; student spl. courses Pa. State U., 1944-46, Yale U., 1954-57; m. Alden Frank Miller, Jr., Apr. 16, 1940 (dec. Feb. 1975); 1 son, Alden Frank III; m. 2d, Jack R. Todd, Dec. 23, 1977. Exec. mgr. Donora (Pa.) C. of C., 1950-57, Donora Community Chest, 1950-57; office mgr. Donora Golden Jubilee, 1951; staff writer Herald-Am., Donora, 1957, city editor, 1957-70; asso. editor Daily Herald, Donora, 1970-73; service rep. Pitts. Teleservice Center, Social Security Adminstrn., HHS, 1977-83. Mem. Mayor's Adv. Council, Donora, 1965-69, Citizens' Adv. Council, Donora, 1965-69; mem. Donora Bd. Edn., 1954-60, pres., 1960; mem. Donora Borough Council, 1970-72; bd. dirs. Mon Valley chpt. ARC, 1964—, sec. bd., 1966—; bd. dirs. Washington County Tourism Agy., 1970—, sec., 1972—; bd. dirs. Washington County History and Landmarks Found. 1971-80, sec., 1975-80; bd. dirs. Mon Valley council Camp Fire Girls, 1965-79, Mon Valley Drug and Alcoholism Council, 1971-78; bd.

dirs. United Way Mon Valley, 1973-82, chmn. pub. relations, 1973-74. Mem. Pa. Soc. Newspaper Editors, Pitts. Press Club, Donora C. of C. (pres. 1971-72), DAR (regent Monongahela Valley chpt. 1974-77), Washington County Poetry Soc. (pres. 1967-69), Washington County Fedn. Women's Clubs (rec. sec. 1964-66). Clubs: Order Eastern Star (worthy matron 1966-67), White Shrine of Jerusalem (high priestess 1973-74), Order of Amaranth (royal matron 1966, dist. dep., grand rep. W.Va. 1979-80), Donora Forecast (pres. 1962-63), Donora Unidon (pres. 1965-66, 56-57). Home: Overlook Terr Donora PA 15033

TODD, SANDRA BEAN, public relations specialist; b. Brainard, Minn., Jan. 14, 1945; d. Roger Allan and Sara Jeann (Hinde) Bean; m. H. Hottell, 1965 (div.); 1 son, Kevin Witt Todd; m. Mark Todd, Dec. 23, 1978; 1 son, Richard Jaeger. A.B. in Journalism, U. Ga., 1967. Cert. French tchr., Ga. Editorial asst. Am. Physical Therapy Assn., Washington, 1975-78; pub. relations dir. Chesapeake Bay GSC, Wilmington, Del., 1978-80; editor Am. Life Ins. Co., Wilmington, 1980-82, mgr. publs., 1982—; media cons. Baha'is of Del. Valley, Phila., 1982-83. Pub. coordinator Race Unity Festival, Wilmington, 1982-84. Mem. Internat. Assn. Bus. Communicators, Wilmington Women in Bus., Phi Kappa Phi. Office: Am Life Ins Co 12th and Market Wilmington DE 19806

TODD-SPRING, DEBORAH ANN, engineering consultant; b. Long Island City, N.Y., June 18, 1955; d. Ralph and Mae Williams (Milligan) Todd; m. Stephen Spring; 1 child, Stephanie Forbes Spring. B.S.M.E. summa cum laude, Union Coll., 1976; M.S.M.E., Rensselaer Poly. Inst., 1978; M.B.A., Harvard Bus. Sch., 1985. Mech. design engr. large steam turbine div. Gen. Electric Co., Schenectady, N.Y., 1976-78, mech. engr. projects engring. ops., 1978-79; mech. job engr. Gibbs & Hill, Inc., N.Y.C., 1979-80; project engr. internat. projects dept. Gen. Electric Co., N.Y.C., 1980-83; instr. profl. engring. rev. course, 1980—, mgr. engring. Visy Bd. Engring., Reservoir, Victoria, Australia, 1986—. Recipient Top Young Engr. award Gen. Electric Power Systems Sector; registered profl. engr., N.Y. Mem. Nat. Soc. Profl. Engrs., ASME, Tau Beta Pi. Republican. Clubs: Appalachian Mountain, Appalachian Trail Conf., N.Y./N.J. Trail Conf. Home: 10 Para St Balwyn Victoria 3103 Australia Office: Visy Bd Engring 25 Plateau Rd Reservoir Victoria 3073 Australia

TODOROFF, LINDA SUE, educational program adminstrator, consultant; b. Granite City, Ill., Apr. 28, 1952; d. Theodore and Margaret (Hollo) T. B.A., So. Ill. U.-Edwardsville, 1977; M.S., 1980. Counselor, Hope Clinic for Women, Granite City, 1975-78; asst. dir., program counselor Vets. Upward Bound program So. Ill. U., Edwardsville, 1978-82; project dir. Upward Bound Talent Search Program, Emporia State U. (Kans.), 1983—. Mem. Mid.-Am. Assn. Ednl. Opportunity Program Personnel (state rep., pres.-elect Mo.-Kans.-Nebr.). Home: 2604 Jules St Saint Joseph MO 64501 Office: Project Focus Upward Bound Emporia State U 902 Edmond St Saint Joseph MO 64501

TOEDTMAN, MELISSA JEAN, music teacher; b. Boston, June 11, 1947; d. William Harold and Doris Jean (Gilman) Holbrook; m. John Kumler Toedtman, Dec. 29, 1973; children—William Frederick, John Charles. B.Music, U. Cin., 1969, postgrad., 1969-70; tchrs. cert. in Orff method U. Toronto, 1975. Tchr. music Southwest Sch. Dist., Harrison, Ohio, 1971-72, Sycamore County Schs., Montgomery, Ohio, 1972-76, Lotspeich Sch., Cin., 1976-77, Mercy Montessori Sch., Cin., 1979-82; pvt. piano tchr. Cin., 1968—; co-dir. Toedtman Sch. Music, Sharonville, 1974-85; presenter workshops; Orff cons. Cathedral Child Devel. Ctr., Covington, Ky., 1982-84. Composer music Pub. TV program Measure-Up, 1975. Vice-pres. Dumont PTA, Madeira, Ohio, 1984-85, sec., 1985-86. Mem. Ohio Music Tchrs. Assn. (county pres. 1983-85, state Buckeye audition chairperson 1985—), Am. Orff Schulwerk Assn. (county pres. 1973-75), Euterpe Music Club Cin. (pres. 1985—). Mu Phi Epsilon. Republican. Episcopalian. Avocations: walking, swimming, reading. Home: 6530 Shawnee Run Rd Cincinnati OH 45243 Office: Toedtman Sch Music 12171 Mosteller Rd Cincinnati OH 45241

TOENJES, SALLY ANN, vocational educator; b. Detroit, Jan. 20, 1935; d. Robert Clarence and Frances May (Koenig) Hull; m. Richard Gerhard Toenjes, Jan. 25, 1958; children—Sandra Therese, Timothy Richard. B.S. in Biology, U. Detroit, 1957; M.A. in Counselor Edn. and Personal Devel., Central Mich. U., 1982. Registered med. technologist; cert. med. asst. Med. technologist St John's Hosp., Detroit, 1958-73; instr. Macomb Community Coll., Mt. Clemens, Mich., 1974—. Mem. Am. Assn. Med. Assts. (pres. 1982-83), Gamma Pi Epsilon. Roman Catholic. Avocations: sailing, swimming, tennis, sewing, knitting. Office: Macomb Community Coll 44575 Garfield St Mount Clemens MI 48044

TOENSING, VICTORIA, lawyer; b. Colon, Panama, Oct. 16, 1941; d. Philip William and Victoria (Brady) Long; m. Trent David Toensing, Oct. 29, 1962 (div. 1976); children—Todd Robert, Brady Cronon, Amy Victoriana; m. Joseph E. di Genova, June 27, 1981. B.S. Edn., Ind. U., 1962; J.D. cum laude, U. Detroit, 1975. Bar: Mich. 1976, D.C. 1978. Tchr. English, Milw., 1965-66; law clk. to pres. justice U.S. Ct. Apls., Detroit, 1975-76; asst. U.S. atty., U.S. Attys Office, Detroit, 1976-81; chief counsel U.S. Senate Intelligence Com., Washington, 1981-84; dep. asst. atty. gen. criminal div. Dept. Justice, Washington, 1984—. Contbr. articles to profl. jours. Founder, chmn. Women's Orgn. to Meet Existing Needs, Mich., 1975-79; chmn. Republican Women's Task Force, 1979-81; bd. dirs. Project on Equal Edn. Rights, Mich., 1980-81. Recipient Spl. commendation award Atty. Gen. U.S., 1980. Mem. ABA (standing com. on law and nat. security, adv. bd. com. complex crimes and litigation, vice chmn. white collar crime com.), State Bar Mich. (constl. law com. 1978-82), U. Detroit Law Sch. Alumni Assn. (bd. dirs. 1984—), Alpha Chi Omega. Office: Dept Justice 10th and Constitution Ave NW Washington DC 20530

TOEPFER, SUSAN JILL, editor; b. Rochester, Minn., Mar. 9, 1948; d. John Bernard and Helen Esther (Chapple) T.; m. Lorenzo Gabriel Carcaterra, May 16, 1981; 1 dau., Katherine Marie. B.A., Bennington Coll., 1970. Mng. editor Photoplay Mag., N.Y.C., 1971-72; free-lance writer, N.Y.C., 1972-78; TV week editor N.Y. Daily News, N.Y.C., 1978-79, leisure editor, 1979-82, features editor, 1982-84, book editor, 1984-85, arts and entertainment editor, 1985—. Mem. Nat. Book Critics Circle. Democrat. Presbyterian. Office: NY Daily News 220 E 42d St New York NY 10017

TOFANI, LORETTA, journalist; b. N.Y.C., Feb. 5, 1953. B.A., Fordham U., 1975; M.S. in Journalism, U. Calif.-Berkeley. Reporter, Knoxville News-Sentinel (Tenn.), Democrat. and Chronicle, Rochester, N.Y., UPI, Portland, Oreg., N.Y.C., and Los Angeles, The Washington Post, 1978—. Recipient AP Mark Twain award, 1982; Washington-Balt. Newspaper Guild's Front-Page award, 1982; Washington Monthly Nat. Journalism award, 1982; Sigma Delta Chi award for gen. reporting, 1983; Pulitzer prize for spl. local reporting, 1983. Address: The Washington Post 1150 15th St NW Washington DC 20071*

TOFSRUD, LOREEN ANN, lawyer; b. Devils Lake, N.D., Nov. 6, 1953; d. Roy Geoffrey and Irene Mae (Hedine) Mercer; m. Robert D. Tofsrud, Dec. 23, 1971 (div. 1973); 1 dau., Michelle Lea. B.S. in Bus., N.D. State U., 1976; J.D., U. Wis., 1983. Bar: Wis. 1983, U.S. Dist. Ct. (we. dist.) Wis. 1983, U.S. Dist. Ct. N.D. 1984. Mgmt. trainee First Bank System, Fargo, N.D., 1976-77, credit analyst, 1977, indirect lending, 1978, personal banking loan officer, 1978-79, asst. mgr. Br. Bank, 1979-80; staff atty. Ind. Law Unit, Legal Assn. N.D., Devils Lake, 1983-84; tribal atty., tax commr. Devils Lake Sioux Tribe, Ft. Totten, N.D., 1984—; tchr. fed. Indian law Little Hoop Community Coll., Ft. Totten, 1984; advisor Devils Lake Sioux Tribal Council, Devils Lake Sioux Tribe, Ft. Totten, 1984. Campfire leader Campfire Girls, West Fargo, 1978-80; leader Girl Scouts Am., Madison, Wis., 1982-83. Reginald Heuber Smith fellow Howard U. Sch. Law, Washington, 1983-84. Mem. State Bar Assn. Wis., ABA. Democrat. Home: 820 4th Ave Devils Lake ND 58301

TOKAR, MAUREEN TANSEY, architect; b. Cin., Mar. 4, 1933; d. Bernard Joseph and Cecile Marie (Sunman) Tansey; B.S. in Architecture, U. Cin., 1955; m. Edward Tokar, June 29, 1974. Job capt. Hixson, Tarter & Merkel, Cin., 1964-68; dir. interior architecture Ferry & Henderson, Springfield, Ill., 1968-72; project coordinator Skidmore, Owings & Merrill, Chgo., 1972-76; rev. architect Ill. Capital Devel. Bd., Chgo., 1977-82; v.p. Planning and Design Cons., 1975—. Mem. AIA, Chgo. Women in Architecture, Art Inst. Chgo., Field Mus., Alpha Omicron Pi. Home: 4951 W Melrose St Chicago IL 60641

TOKARCIK, ANDREA, banking executive; b. Houtzdale, Pa., Jan. 29, 1940; d. Andrew Paul and Antonia (Mekis) Bezilla; (div.); children—Diane M., Steven J. B.S. in Social Sci., U. Md., 1973, M.A. in Adminstrn., 1977. Staff liaison, tchr. Prince George County Bd. of Edn., Upper Marlboro, Md., 1973-78; assoc. cons. Potomac Tng. (Md.), 1978-79; tng. specialist Am. Security Bank, Washington, 1979-81; asst. cashier, mgr. 1st Am. Bank, Washington, 1981-85; asst. v.p., mgr. human resources First Am. Data Services, Inc., Reston, Va., 1985—; co-chmn. Nat. Am. Inst. Banking Conf., Washington, 1983; mem. faculty Am. Inst. Banking, 1980—, U. Va., Regional Ctr. Falls Ch., Va., 1982—. Mem. President's Membership Council Bd. Trade, Washington, 1983—. Mem. D.C. Banker's Assn., Am. Soc. Tng. and Devel., Reston C. of C. (large employers com.). Democrat. Office: 1880 Campus Commons Dr Restongton VA 22091

TOKUNAGA, KAZUKO, banker; b. Hoolehua, Molokai, Hawaii, June 24, 1938; d. Torao and Yukie (Taniguchi) Matsuda; student pub. schs., Honolulu; children—Eric Yukio, Kent Ken. Bookkeeper, Central Pacific Bank, Honolulu, 1957; bookkeeper Bank of Hawaii, Honolulu, 1958-65, clk., 1965, supr., 1965-73, group mgr., 1973-81, asst. cashier, 1974-81, asst. v.p., 1981-84, v.p., mgr., 1984—. Office: PO Box 2900 Honolulu HI 96846

TOLAND, FLORENCE WINIFRED, printing co. exec.; b. Paola, Kans., Aug. 6, 1906; d. Frederick W. and Bertha G. (Cartwright) Arzberger; B.A., U. Ariz., 1935, M.S. in Bus. Adminstrn., 1946; m. Jess William Toland, Dec. 23, 1934 (dec. 1954); 1 son, Ronald William. Tchr. grade sch., Dos Cabezos, Willcox and Mascot, Ariz., 1925-32, jr. high and high sch., 1934-36, 38-42; asst. prof. U. Ariz., Tucson, 1942-71, asst. prof. emeritus, 1971—; owner, mgr., pres. Pima Printing Co., Tucson, 1954—. Mem. Ariz. Bus. Educators Assn. (life), Nat. Bus. Educators Assn., Western Bus. Educators Assn., Pi Omega Pi. Democrat. Club: Order Eastern Star. Co-author: Transcription Method Shorthand, 1946. Home: 5461 N Paseo Espejo Tucson AZ 85718 Office: 110 S Park Ave Tucson AZ 85719

TOLAND, MARY EVONNE, hospital executive; b. Waverly, Tenn., Dec. 25, 1935; d. Ernest Aubrey and Annie Pezola (Petty) T.; B.A., Bethel Coll., 1959; M.A., Vanderbilt U., 1961. Tchr. bus. adminstrn. Obion County Bd. Edn., Union City, Tenn., 1956-64; sec. Founders Security Life Ins. Co., Memphis, 1965-67; adminstrv. asst. to pres., exec. v.p. Pace Corp., Memphis, 1967-72; adminstrv. asst. to exec. dir. United Way of Greater Memphis, 1972-82; dir. devel. Brooks Meml. Art Gallery, 1982-83; exec. asst. to dir. St. Jude Children's Research Hosp., 1983—. Mem. Am. Soc. Personnel Adminstrn., Exec. Women Internat. (pres. 1977), Memphis Personnel Assn. (sec., treas. 1979), Am. Legion. Republican. Baptist. Home: 5549 Hinton Cove Memphis TN 38119 Office: St Jude Children's Research Hosp 332 N Lauderdale PO Box 318 Memphis TN 38101

TOLCHIN, SUSAN JANE, public administration educator, writer; b. N.Y.C., Jan. 14, 1941; d. Jacob Nathan and Dorothy Ann (Markowitz) Goldsmith; m. Martin Tolchin, Dec. 23, 1965; children—Charles Peter, Karen Rebecca. B.A., Bryn Mawr Coll., 1961; M.A., U. Chgo., 1962; Ph.D., N.Y.U., 1968. Lectr. in polit. sci. City Coll., N.Y.C., 1963-65, Bklyn. Coll., 1965-71; adj. asst. prof. polit. sci. Seton Hall U., South Orange, N.J., 1971-73; assoc. prof. polit. sci., dir. Inst. for Women and Politics, Mt. Vernon Coll., Washington, 1975-78; prof. pub. adminstrn. George Washington U., Washington, 1978—; editorial bd. mem. Policy Studies Rev., Tempe, Ariz., 1982—. Co-author (with Martin Tolchin): To The Victor: Political Patronage from the Clubhouse to the White House, 1971; Clout-Womanpower and Politics, 1974; Dismantling America-The Rush to Deregulate, 1983. Pres. Wyngate Elem. Sch. PTA, Bethesda, Md., 1981-82; county committeewoman Democratic Party, Montclair, N.J., 1969-73. Dilthey fellow George Washington U., 1983, Aspen Inst. fellow, 1979; named Tchr. of Yr., Mt. Vernon Coll., 1978; recipient Founder's Day award NYU, 1968. Mem. Am. Polit. Sci. Assn. (pres. Women's Caucus for Polit. Sci. 1977-78), Am. Soc. Pub. Adminstrn. (chairperson sect. Natural Resources and Environ. Adminstrn. 1982-83). Democrat. Jewish. Office: George Washington Univ Dept Pub Adminstrn Washington DC 20052

TOLEDO-SANTA, HERMINIA, personnel administrator; b. Santurce, P.R., Dec. 24, 1929; d. Vicente Toledo and Maria Santa; m. Miguel Rodriguez, Feb. 22, 1956; children; Ivelisse, Marisabel. Adminstrv. asst. Gonzalez Padin Co., Inc., San Juan, P.R., 1949-69, personnel dir., 1969—. Mem. Am. Soc. Personnel Adminstrs. Roman Catholic. Office: Gonzalez Padin Co Inc Fortaleza & Cruz San Juan PR 00903

TOLER, MELISSA ANN, health organization executive; b. Carrolltohn, Mo., Nov. 18, 1953; d. Billy Gene and Sarah Ann (Schnell) T.; m. Garry Stuart Mueller, Mar. 11, 1978 (div. 1983); Diploma in nursing Newman Hosp. Sch. Nursing, 1974; student Christopher Newport Coll., 1979-80; B.A. in BMus. Mgmt., U. South Fla., 1983; postgrad. Fla. Inst. Tech., 1985—. With U.S. Navy Nurse Corps, Orlando, Fla., 1974-76, Portsmouth, Va., 1976-78; adminstr. Wooten, Honeywell, Kest and Mratinez, Orlando, 1983-84; dir. physician recruitment CIGNA Health Plan of Fla., Inc., Orlando, 1984—. Served to lt. USNR, 1978. Mem. Phi Kappa Phi, Beta Gamma Sigma, Sigma Iota Epsilon. Republican. Avocations: reading; swimming; scuba diving; travel. Office: Cigna Health Plan of Fla Inc 2603 Maitland Ctr Pkwy Maitland FL 32715

TOLIVER, C. R., fashion coordinator; b. Chgo., Aug. 4, 1952; d. William Saunders and Amo B. (McWhorter)-Evans; m. Steve N. Toliver, July 2, 1969 (div. July 1980); 1 dau., Stephanie Monique. Telephone operator Ill. Bell Telephone Co., Chgo., 1979-82; owner, pres. Ceci, fashion coordinating, Chgo., 1979—; chmn. Adaptations, entertainment service and cons. firm, not-for-profit, 1984—. Mem. Cosmopolitan C. of C., Am. Mus. Natural History, Am. Film Inst., Nat. Assn. Female Execs. Democrat. Roman Catholic.

TOLL, JACQUELINE JOY, accountant; b. Iola, Kans., Mar. 23, 1947; d. Clarence Leslie and Marie Irene (Pearman) Robinson; m. Benjamin Thomas Toll, Nov. 24, 1967; children—Dacia Ianthe, Thaddeus Nathaniel, Allegra Alexandra. A.A., Kansas City Community Coll. Kans., 1973; B.S., Avila Coll., 1979, M.B.A., 1981. Cert. mgmt. acct. Assoc. adminstr. Clinicare, Kansas City, 1979-82; chief fin. officer Alexian Bros. Health Mgmt., St. Joseph Home, Kansas City, 1982—. Mem. Soc. Advancement Mgmt., Am. Mktg. Assn., Nat. Assn. Accts., Dimensions Unlimited. Baptist. Avocations: cooking; sightseeing; computer operations.

TOLL, ROBERTA DARLENE (MRS. SHELDON S. TOLL), social worker; b. Detroit, May 14, 1944; d. David and Blanche (Fischer) Pollack; B.A., U. Mich., 1966; M.S.W., U. Pa., 1971; m. Aug. 11, 1968; children—Candice, John, Kevin. Dir. counselors Phila. Family Planning, Inc., 1971-72; psychologist Lafayette Clinic, Detroit, 1972-73; social worker Project Headline, Detroit, 1973-75; pvt. practice social work, Bloomfield Hills, Mich., 1975—; adj. prof. U. Detroit, Oakland Community Coll. Bd. dirs. Detroit chpt. Nat. Council on Alcoholism. Cert. social worker, Mich. Fellow Masters and Johnson Inst.; mem. Nat. Assn. Social Workers. Democrat. Club: Franklin Hills Country. Home and office: 640 Lone Pine Hill Rd Bloomfield Hills MI 48013

TOLLERIS, M. ANGELA, lawyer; b. Nassau County, N.Y., July 9, 1939; d. Harold Tolleris and Patricia Ruth (Goodstein) Tolleris Kurz; m. Theodore Schneider, Aug. 7, 1955 (div.); children—Adam, John, David, Nancy. A.G.S. summa cum laude, Montgomery County Community Coll., Blue Bell, Pa., 1971; B.A. magna cum laude, Beaver Coll., Glenside, Pa., 1973; J.D., Rutgers U.-Camden, 1976; grad. teacher tng. program Nat. Inst. Trial Advocacy 1983. Bar: N.J. 1977, U.S. Dist. Ct. N.J. 1977. Nat. Reginald Heber Smith fellow in community law Camden Regional Legal Services, Gloucester County Office, Woodbury, N.J., 1976-78; asst. dep. pub. defender N.J. Office Pub. Defender, Vineland, N.J., 1978-81, sr. trial counsel, 1981-85; sole practice, Bridgeton, N.J., 1986—; adj. prof. Cumberland County Coll., Vineland, 1980; guest lectr. N.J. criminal def. practice Del. Law Sch., Wilmington, 1982, 83; Moot Ct. judge, 1982, 83, 84; Moot Ct. judge Rutgers-Camden Law Sch., 1985. Founding dir. Headstart, Monmouth County, N.J., 1963-64; twp. committeewoman, Matawan, N.J., 1965; founding mem. Pa. Women's Polit. Caucus, 1973; founding trustee, legal counsel Cumberland County Women's Ctr.; gov.'s appointee Montgomery County Welfare Bd., Pa., 1976; bd. dirs. Camden Regional Legal Services. Davison-Foreman Found. fellow, 1973-76. Mem. ABA (criminal justice sect.), N.J. State Bar Assn. (criminal justice sect.), Nat. Assn. Criminal Def. Lawyers (regional dir. speakers bur. 1984—), Cumberland County Bar Assn. (jud. selection com. 1983—, chmn. speakers bur. 1982—, trustee 1983-85, 85-87), Nat. Assn. Women Lawyers, Assn. Criminal Def. Lawyers N.J. Office: 230 E Commerce St Bridgeton NJ

TOLLETT, EILEEN RICE, business owner; b. Little Rock, Mar. 28, 1947; d. Charles J. and Mary Lois (Carroll) Rice; B.S.E., U. Central Ark., 1969; M.L.A., So. Meth. U., 1972; Ph.D., U. Tex., Dallas, 1981; m. Billy E. Tollett, Aug. 16, 1969; 1 dau., Casey Elaine. Pub. relations field cons. Ark. Lung Assn., Little Rock, 1969; instr. McKinney (Tex.) Job Corps Center for Women, 1970-75; staff U. Tex., Dallas, 1976-77, research asst., 1978, 78-79, 79, teaching asst., 1979, research asst., 1980, teaching asst., 1980, 81; owner, operator Tollett Typing & Cons., Allen, Tex., 1977—; copy editor Developmental Learning Materials, Allen, 1981-84; staff editor Population Inst., So. Meth. U., 1984. Vice pres. Allen Pub. Library Bd., 1980-82, sec., 1983-86; guest lectr. Heard Mus., 1985; advisor to bd. dirs. Country Day Montessori Sch., Allen, 1980-81, bd. dirs., 1979-80; treas. Montessori Parents Assn., Allen, 1979-80; bd. dirs. Inspired Tchrs. Studio, Inc., Dallas, 1979-80; advisor Allen Pub. Library regarding ref. materials collection on Am. Indians, 1979-80; mem. Allen City Council, 1976-78; underwriter Heard Natural Sci. Mus. Biology Camp, 1983, 84. UN and Population Inst. scholar, Europe, 1973. Mem. Am. Bus. Women's Assn., Alpha Chi. Democrat. Address: PO Box 235 Allen TX 75002

TOLLEY, CAROLYN JACKSON, audiologist, audiometric service executive; b. DeQueen, Ark., Aug. 27, 1953; d. Carlton Conway and Charlie Mae (Chaney) Jackson; m. Philip Austin Tolley, June 25, 1977. B.S.E., U. Ark., 1975; M.S. (grantee), So. Methodist U., 1979. Tchr. of deaf Mo. State Sch. for the Deaf, Fulton, 1975-76, Tex. Regional Day Sch. for the Deaf, Kenedy, 1976-77; clin. audiologist E.N.T. Surg. Assn., Richardson, Tex., 1979-81; indsl. audiologist, pres. Audiometric Services, Inc., Dallas, 1982—. Mem. Tex. Safety Assn. (dir. 1983—), Nat. Hearing Conservation Assn. (bd. dirs. 1985—), Am. Speech Lang. Hearing Assn. (cert. clin. competence in audiology), Tex. Speech Hearing Assn., Am. Soc. Safety Engrs., Am. Indsl. Hygiene Assn. Avocations: sailing, travel. Office: Audiometric Services Inc 2718 Hollandale Suite 200 Dallas TX 75234

TOLLIVER, BRENDA JOY, real estate broker; b. Chattanooga, Sept. 18, 1951; d. Noble Edward and Elizabeth (Loisteen (Wheeler) T. A.B., Clark Coll., 1972; M.A., Atlanta U., 1973. Lic. real estate broker, Ga. Asst. dir. alumni affairs Clark Coll., Atlanta, 1973-74; real estate sales assoc. Sanford Realty, Atlanta, 1974-80, real estate assoc. broker, 1980-85; real estate assoc. broker Re/Max Real Estate, Stone Mountain, Ga., 1985—. Mrm. Rosewood Park Community Orgn., Decatur, Ga., 1983—; v.p. Friendship In-Betweeners, Atlanta, 1986. Recipient 10Yr. Service award Sanford Realty Co., 1984; named Salesperson of Yr., 1984, to Century 21 Million Dollar Club, 1981, Pres.'s Club Re/Max of Ga., 1985. Mem. DeKalb Bd. Realtors, Nat. Assn. Female Execs., Clark Coll. Alumni Assn. (sec. 1984—). Democrat. Baptist. Avocations: playing piano and organ; bowling; reading; bridge. Home: 2312 Shamrock Dr Decatur GA 30032

TOLLIVER, LENNIE-MARIE P., government official; b. Cleve., Dec. 1, 1928; B.S., Hampton Inst., 1950; A.M., U. Chgo., 1952; Pd.M., 1961; m. Alonzo H. Cent. Psychiat. social worker N.J. Mental Hygiene Clinic, 1952-55; psychiat. social worker, instr. Duke U. Med. Center, Durham, N.C., 1956-58; acting dir. social work Johnstone Tng. and Research Center, Bordentown, N.J., 1959; instr. field work U. Sch. Social Work, 1957-58; asst. prof. Sch. Social Service, U. Chgo., 1961-64; prof., supr. field work U. Okla., 1964-81; commr. Adminstrn. on Aging, Washington, 1981—; cons. Oklahoma City-County Mental Health Clinic, 1965-66, LaHuman Rehab. Center, 1968. Vice-pres., chairperson health and welfare com. Urban League, Oklahoma City, 1969-71; bd. dirs. United Appeal of Greater Oklahoma City; mem. budget and fin. com. Avery Chapel AME Ch. Mem. Nat. Assn. Social Workers, Acad. Certified Social Workers, Council on Social Work Edn., Okla. Health and Welfare Assn., Okla. Assn. Black Personnel in Higher Edn., Am. Gerontol. Soc., Delta Sigma Theta (nat. sec. 1967-71). Club: Links (past chpt. pres.). Office: Adminstrn on Aging 330 Independence Ave SW Washington DC 20201*

TOLLIVER, NILA MOZINGO, pastoral care educator, chaplain; b. Charleston, W. Va., Aug. 7, 1928; d. Samuel Franklin and Lulu Myrtle (Foster) Mozingo; m. Robert Fulton Tolliver, July 29, 1944; children—Trulafaye, Samuel Robert, Dorothy Charlene. Cert. clin. pastoral educator, chaplain; ordained minister Ch. of God, 1972. A.A., Gulf-Coast Bible Coll., Houston, 1969; B.A., Houston Baptist U., 1971; M.A., Anderson (Ind.) Sch. Tehology, 1978. Adminstr. Houston Christian Mission, 1967-70; adminstr. group home Roanoke City Welfare Dept. (Va.), 1971-73; tchr. Nicholas County Schs., Summersville, W.Va., 1973-76; adminstr. Group Home, Hillcrest Girls Home, Anderson, Ind., 1976-78; instr. Gulf-Coast Bible Coll., Houston, 1979-83; prof., Houston Baptist Grad. Sch. Theology, 1983—; cons. chaplaincy Harris County (Tex.) Hosp. Dist., Houston, 1979—; chaplain Tex. Inst. Rehab. Research, 1979—part time, Ben Taub Gen. Hosp., 1978—, San Jacinto Bus. and Profl. Women, 1979-82 (all Houston). Contbr. articles to religious publs. Mem. state com. Am. Cancer Soc., 1983. Named Tchr. of Yr., Bay Ridge Christian Coll., Kendalton, Tex., 1980. Mem. Assn. Clin. Pastoral Edn., Coll. Chaplains (nominating com. 1983), SE Texa Assn. Chaplains (sec.-treas. 1982, pres. 1984), Christian Assn. Psychol. Studies, Hosp. Christian Fellowship. Clubs: Women of Ch. of God (sec. 1964-66) (Anderson). Home: 8252 White Oak Pl Houston TX 77040 Office: Houston Grad Sch Theology 1129 Wilkins St Suite 200 Houston TX 77030

TOM, BARBARA JEAN, real estate executive, financial consultant; b. Warren, Pa., Jan. 20, 1946; d. Roy Jim and Margorie Lois (McCurty) Baker; m. Ping Hon Tom, Feb. 7, 1969; children—Chong-Kee, Hsiu-Yen, Hsiu-Ann, Hsui-Ming. A.A., DeAnza Coll., 1970; B.S., San Jose State U., 1972, M.B.A. magna cum laude, 1973; J.D., Lincoln Law Sch., 1980; real estate assoc., Anthony Sch., 1976; real estate broker, Chamberlain Sch., 1978. Lic. real estate broker, tchr. jr. coll., Calif. Account rep. Control Data Corp., Palo Alto, Calif., 1973-75; mktg. rep. N.C.S.S., Sunnyvale, Calif., 1975-76; pres. Bell Realtors, Los Altos, Calif., 1977—; guest speaker investment analysis seminar, 1983; lectr. Grad. Realtors Inst., 1981. Author pamphlet and manuals. Coordinator Children's Community Theatre, Los Altos, 1981, designer costumes, 1983; resource liaison Community Services Agy., 1982; chmn. City Planning Commn., Los Altos, 1979. Winner 1st prize sales contest Control Data Corp., 1974; mem. Million Dollar Club, Sunnyvale Real Estate Bd., 1977. Mem. Nat. Assn. Realtors, Calif. Assn. Realtors, Women's Council Realtors (speaker), Soc. for Advancement of Women in Mgmt., San Jose State Alumni Assn. (pres. 1974-75), Phi Beta Kappa. Republican. Clubs: Los Altos Golf and Country, Nat. Ballroom Dancers Mountain View. Home: 14965 Page Mill Rd Los Altos CA 94022 Office: Bell Co 241 S San Antonio Rd Los Altos CA 94022

TOMANIO, PATRICIA ANN, printing company executive, reading specialist; b. Westchester, Pa., Feb. 25, 1936; d. James Minds and Mildred (Ellison) Jones; m. John Joseph Tomanio, Oct. 22, 1955; children—Sharon Louise, Patricia Ann, John Joseph. B.S. in Elem. Edn. and Psychology, East Stroudsburg State Coll., 1974, M.Ed., magna cum laude, 1977. Reading lab. supr. East Stroudsburg (Pa.) State Coll., 1970-73; tchr. Stroudsburg and East Stroudsburg Pub. Schs., 1973-74; substitute tchr., Stroudsburg, 1974-75; reading tchr., supr. cert. individual prescribed instrn. East Stroudsburg Coll., 1975-82; reading specialist Pocono Mountain Sch. Dist., 1975—, mem. faculty adv. bd., 1980-83; pres. Latch String Co., Stroudsburg, Pa., 1982—; owner, pres. Printmaster, Stroudsburg, 1983—. Mem. Pocono Mountain Edn. Assn. (exec. council 1981-82). Republican. Lutheran. Home: RD 2 Box 2011 Stroudsburg PA 18360

TOMARKIN, PEGGY FREED, advertising executive; b. Cleve., Apr. 27, 1942; d. Bernard H. and Gyta Elinor (Arsham) Freed; m. Gary Tomarkin, Aug. 7, 1966 (div. 1981); children—Craig William, Eric Lawrence. B.S., Simmons Coll., 1964. Asst. account exec. Howard Marks/Norman, Craig & Kummel, Inc., N.Y.C., 1964-66; account exec. Shaw Bros. Advt. Co., N.Y.C., 1966-67; copywriter Claire Advt. Co., N.Y.C., 1967; ptnr. Copywriters Coop., Hartsdale, N.Y., 1970-73; copy chief Howard Marks Advt., N.Y.C., 1973-80; sr. copywriter Wunderman, Ricotta & Kline, N.Y.C., 1980-82; v.p., assoc. creative dir. Ayer-Direct (N.W. Ayer), N.Y.C., 1982-84; sr. v.p., creative dir. D'Arcy Direct (D'Arcy, MacManus & Masius), N.Y.C., 1984—; judge various advt. awards. Author: Kiss, The Real Story, 1980. Mem. The One Club, Direct Mktg. Creative Guild, Direct Mktg. Assn. Office: D'Arcy Direct 909 3d Ave New York NY 10022

TOMAS, WANDA BRICE, corporate executive; b. Nagogodoches, Tex., Mar. 3, 1942; d. James Ernest and Sally Rebekah (Sommerville) Brice; m. Paul Elliot Pitt; 1 child, Jon Fitzgerald Pitt; m. Michael S. Tomas, Nov. 2, 1973; children—Michael Joseph, Michele. B.A. in Polit. Sci., Rutgers U., 1976. Data processing mgr. Modern Am. Co., Dallas, 1966-73; v.p. adminstrn. Exec. Fringe Benefits, Freehold, N.J., 1974-76; exec. staff Carterfone Communications, Dallas, 1976-77; client services mgr. Mobil Oil Corp., Dallas, 1977-78; pres. Legal Documentation, Dallas, 1978—; dir. Tex-Sun Realty, Dallas, 1982—, Integrated Electric Supply Inc., Dallas, 1985—; alt. del. White House Conf. Small Bus., 1985, del., 1986. Campaigner, Democratic Party, Dallas, 1973-86; mem. com. ladies aux. March of Dimes, Dallas, 1984-86. Mem. Mortgage Bankers Assn., Nat. Assn. Women Bus. Owners (bd. dirs. 1985-86, v.p. 1986-87), Assn. Women Entrepreneurs, Exec. Women Dallas (mem. chair, bd. dirs. 1980-86, v.p. 1986-87). Democrat. Methodist. Clubs: Univ., 2001 (Dallas); Literary (Freehold, N.J., pres. 1975). Avocations: Golf; racquetball; reading; creative writing. Home: 2420 Cedar Elm Ln Plano TX 75075 Office: Legal Documentation Systems Inc 2001 Bryan Dallas TX 75201

TOMASI, MARILYN JOAN, state official; b. Bowling Green, Ohio, Sept. 14, 1952; d. David Kenneth and Lillian Elizabeth (Roos) Garno. Student Owens Tech. Coll., 1970-72; B.A., Bowling Green State U., 1973-75; postgrad. U. Toledo, 1978. Counselor coordinator Lucas County, Toledo, 1975-79; recruiter-mktg. cons. Aim Exec., Toledo, 1980-82; conv. mgr. Toledo C. of C., 1982-83; tourism dir. State of Ohio, Columbus, 1983—; hon. dir. Ohio Festival and Events Assn., 1983—; mem. nat. domestic mktg. task force Travel Industry Assn., 1985; mem. program adv. council U.S. Travel Data Ctr., Washington, 1985. Chmn. Task Force on Women in Labor and Employment, Toledo, 1980-82; trustee V.I.P. Fundraiser, Easter Seals N.W. Ohio, Toledo, 1982-83; trustee Ctr. for Adult Learning of Ex-Offenders, Toledo, 1983; mem. Ohio Historic Site Preservation Bd., 1985. Recipient cert. of appreciation Ohio Basic Econ. Devel. Course, 1985, Ctr. of Sci. and Industry, 1985. Mem. Travel Industry Am., Nat. Council State Travel Dirs., Gt. Lakes Council State Travel Dirs., Ohio Travel Assn., Ohio Campground Owners and Operators Assn., Ohio Hotel Assn., Ohio State Restaurant Assn., Ohio Downtown Assn., Ohio Parks and Recreation Assn., NOW (v.p. Toledo 1981-82). Democrat. Roman Catholic. Avocations: reading; arts. Home: 638B City Park St Columbus OH 43208 Office: State of Ohio Office of Travel and Tourism 30 E Broad St Columbus OH 43215

TOMASZ, MARIA, chemist; b. Szeged, Hungary, Oct. 18, 1932; came to U.S., 1956, naturalized, 1963; d. Ivan and Margit Okalyi; diploma chemistry, Eotvos U., Budapest, 1956; Ph.D., Columbia U., 1962; m. Alexander Tomasz, 1956; children—Martin, Julie. Research assoc. Rockefeller U., N.Y.C., 1962, NYU, 1962-66; vis. research assoc. N.Y. Blood Ctr., 1966; asst. prof., then assoc. prof. Hunter Coll., CUNY, N.Y.C., 1966-79, prof., 1979—. Grantee NSF, USPHS. Mem. Am. Chem. Soc., Fedn. Am. Biol. Socs., Biophys. Soc., N.Y. Acad. Scis., Sigma. Author papers in field. Office: Hunter Coll 695 Park Ave New York NY 10021

TOMBLIN, ELIZABETH ALENE, educational administrator; b. Beaumont, Tex., Feb. 25, 1947; d. Hollis David and Mary Risinger; B.A., U. Tex., 1969; M.S., U. Colo., 1972; Ph.D., 1976; m. Douglas Tomblin, Feb. 18, 1970. Tchr., counselor, asst. to dir. eval. Northglenn (Colo.) Schs., 1971-77; asso. dir. eval. research No. Colo. Bd. Coop. Services, 1977-78; program developer, evaluator and presenter NW Regional Edn. Lab., 1978-80; prin. investigator, psychologist Navy Personnel Research and Devel. Center, San Diego, 1980; dir. program gifted Escondido (Calif.) Public Schs., 1982; assoc. dir. eval. dept. San Diego City Schs., 1982—; cons. in field. Bd. dirs. Bonita Pet Hosp. Mem. Calif. Assn. Elected Women, Am. Ednl. Research Assn., Evaluation Network, Assn. Calif. Sch. Adminstrs., Calif. Ednl. Research Assn., San Diego Council Adminstrv. Women in Edn., Am. Soc. Tng. and Devel. Contbr. articles to profl. jours. Office: 4100 Normal St Room 3150 San Diego CA 92103

TOMISKA, CORA LORENA, civic worker; b. Fontana, Calif., July 30, 1928; d. Riley Royston and Winifred Lillian (Humphry) Green; A.A., Chaffey Jr. Coll., 1948; B.A., Calif. State Coll., San Bernardino, 1976, postgrad., 1976—; m. Joseph Frank Tomiska, June 19, 1950; children—Jo Ann, William Joseph, Robert Royston, Charity Lillianne, Angelina Kathleen. Owner Tomiska Aviaries, Fontana, 1963—. Pres. Redwood PTA, 1976, Sequoia Jr. High PTA, 1969-70, Fontana Council PTA, 1972-74; mem. exec. bd. 5th Dist. PTA, 1972-83, historian, 1976-79, v.p., dir. health, 1979-81, v.p., dir. parent edn., 1981-83; mem. Redwood PTA; sec. consol. projects adv. com. Fontana Unified Sch. Dist., 1972-81, sec. family life edn. project, 1982-86; mem. Mayoral Candidacy Com., 1978: counselor jr. gardening Fontana Redwood Blue Jays, 1964-83; pres. Fontana Garden Club, 1974-77; vol. Fontana Youth Service Center, Am. Heart Fund, Am. Cancer Soc., Christian Youth Edn., Valley Bible Ch., Fontana United Way; scholarship chmn. San Bernardino Valley dist. Calif. Garden Clubs, 1974-83; sec.-treas. Fontana Family Service Agy., 1976-79, pres., 1980-82; mem. Arthritis Found. Recipient 1st place award Calif. Jr. Flower Shows, 1969-73. Mem. ARC, San Bernardino County Mus. Assn., Fontana Hist. Soc., AAUW (edn. chmn. 1981-82), Am. Fedn. Aviculture. Address: 8365 Redwood Ave Fontana CA 92335

TOMKO, CAROLE W., manufacturing company official; b. Columbus, Ohio, Dec. 3, 1954; d. Paul Arthur and Nancy Anne (McGinnis) Wherry; m. Michael Paul Tomko, Jr., May 9, 1981. B.A. in Sociology, U. Cin., 1977; J.D., Ohio State U., 1980. Bar: Ohio 1981. Legal intern State of Ohio, Columbus, 1979-81; employment supr. Federated Dept. Stores, Columbus, 1981-83; mgr. employee relations Standard Register Co., Newark, Ohio, 1983—. Mem. Newark Area Safety Council, 1983—, v.p., 1984, pres., 1985; mem. Pvt. Industry Council. Recipient Mortar Bd. award U. Cin., 1976. Mem. Central Ohio Personnel Assn., Personnel Mgmt. Assn. Home: 153 Clinton Heights Columbus OH 43202 Office: Standard Register Co PO Box 400 Newark OH 43055

TOMLIN, ANNE RITCHIE, educator; b. Washington, Sept. 6, 1937; d. Albert Lawrence and Beatrice (West) Ritchie; m. Paul H. Tomlin, Oct. 14, 1961; 1 child, Brent. B.A., Am. U., 1959; M.S., Gallaudet Coll., 1961. Tchr. pub. elem. schs., Washington, 1959-60, 61-62; tchr. deaf, White Plains, N.Y., 1962-65; tchr. pub. elem. schs., West Nyack, N.Y., 1966—; tutor Jewish League, Mt. Vernon, N.Y., 1965-66. Editor video show: Tomlin's Talking Zoo, 1984; International Fashion Show, 1985. Active YWCA, Nuclear Freeze, Westchester County, 1985—, Community Devel., Mt. Vernon, N.Y., 1981-82. Mem. NEA, United Fedn. Tchrs., Kappa Delta Epsilon. Democrat. Clubs: Quarterback (sec.-treas. 1980-83), Eastchester Blue Devils. Avocations: knitting; crafts; decorating; art; dancing. Address: 415 Gramatan Ave Fleetwood NY 10552

TOMLINSON, DOROTHY MONTGOMERY, special education teacher, consultant; b. St. Paul, Sept. 30, 1946; d. Eugene Martin and Mary Ellen (Hunt) Montgomery; m. Ronnie Warren Tomlinson, Jan. 30, 1970; children—Jonathan Hunt, Matthew Reeves. B.A., North Tex. State, 1969, M.A., 1970; Ph.D., Tex. Women's U., 1983. Cert. speech and hearing therapist, spl. edn. tchr. Tchr., speech therapist, adminstrv. asst. Helping Hand Sch., Irving, Tex., 1970-72; tchr., programmer adult vocat. ctr., adminstrv. asst., paraprofl. supr. Angels, Inc., Dallas, 1972-77; tchr. Dallas Ind. Sch. Dist., 1977—, supervising tchr., 1978—, mem. program rev. task force, 1979—; mem. task force govt. project SPICY, Dallas, 1978-80; mem. so. regional task force Inst. Career and Leisure Devel., Dallas, 1979-81; supervising tchr. Dallas C. of C., 1981. Author: Curriculum Guide, 1979; contbr. articles to profl. publs. Vol. Spl. Olympics, Dallas, 1975-76, Southeast YMCA, 1977—; adviser Boy Scouts Am., Dallas, 1974-76. Mem. Am. Assn. Retarded Children, Tex. Classroom Tchrs. Assn., Council for Exceptional Children. Methodist. Home: 2550 N St Augustine Dallas TX 75227

TOMLINSON, MINNIE ALLISON, nurse administrator; b. Detroit, May 13; d. Elijah and Callie (Guthrie) Allison; m. Arthur Feagin, Feb. 15, 1952 (div. 1956); m. Christopher Tommie Tomlinson, Mar. 7, 1957; children—Lisa Louise, Kimberly Kay, Christopher Marvin. R.N., Harlem Hosp. Sch. Nursing, 1952; B.S. in Nursing Adminstrn., Wayne State U., 1956, M.S., 1978, Ph.D., 1981. Hosp. adminstr. Edythe K. Thomas Hosp., Detroit, 1952-56; hosp. adminstr., dir. nursing St. Agatha Hosp., Detroit, 1957-61, North Detroit Gen. Hosp., 1965-67; asst. dir. nursing Hutzel Hosp., Detroit, 1969-79; nursing adminstr. VA Med. Ctr., Allen Park, Mich., 1979—; nurse clinician State of Mich., Detroit, 1977-82; adminstr., dir. nursing Americana Nursing Ctr., Detroit, 1968-69; dir. nursing Law Den Nursing Ctr., Detroit, 1967-68; adminstr. supr. Boulevard Gen. Hosp., Detroit, 1961-63. Contbr. articles to profl. jours. Activities dir. United Ch. of God in Christ, Detroit, 1972-82; bd. dirs. Wayne State U. Women of Wayne, Detroit, 1985—; pres. adv. bd. dirs. Highland Park Community Coll. of Nursing, Mich., 1981—; del. Luther High Sch. Assn., East Detroit, 1980—. Served to 1st lt. U.S. Air Force Nurses Corp, 1956-57. Recipient Profl. Scholarship award Wayne State U., 1978, Hands and Heart award Adminstrs. Office-VA, 1982, Fed. Employee's Adminstrv. and Supervisory award Fed. Exec. Bd., U.S. Govt.; named Nurse of Yr., Detroit Free Press, 1984, 85. Mem. Am. Nurses Assn. (cert. nursing adminstr.), Am. Acad. Med. Adminstrs., Assn.'s Panel of Arbitrators for Mich. Med. Arbitration Program, Harlem Hosp. Sch. Nursing Council (pres. Detroit chpt.). Avocations: photography; music; art. Home: 1785 Meadow Lane Inkster MI 48141

TOMLINSON, ROXANNE NORTON, civil design engineer; b. Concord, N.H., Jan. 13, 1957; d. James Bernard and Sigrun Ursala (Groger) Norton; m. Larry Curtis Tomlinson, Sept. 3, 1983. B.S.C.E., Va. Poly. Inst. and State U., 1980. Registered profl. engr., Tex. Civil and elec. estimator Brown & Root, Inc., Houston, 1980-82; design engr. Harris County Engring. Dept., Houston, 1982—. Ct. vol. Juvenile Ct. Vols., Houston, 1980—; bd. dirs., treas. River Stone Homeowners Assn., 1980—. Mem. Soc. Women Engrs., Nat. Soc. Profl. Engrs. (assoc.), Va. Tech. Alumni Assn. (v.p. chpt. 1984). Republican. Roman Catholic. Office: Harris County Engring Dept 1001 Preston Ave 7th Floor Houston TX 77002

TOMMASO, ANNE KATHRYN, health care consultant; b. Bklyn., July 25, 1960; d. Nicholas and Vincenza Jean (DiGiovanna) T. B.S. in Mgmt., St. John's U., Jamaica, N.Y., 1982; M.P.A., Columbia U., 1986. Adminstr. Boulevard Hosp., Long Island City, N.Y. 1982-84; health care cons. Healthscope Mgmt. Services Corp., Mount Vernon, N.Y., 1985—. Treas. 33d AD Democratic Club, Queens, N.Y., 1979. Mem. N.Y. Soc. Health Planning, Nat. Assn. Female Execs. Roman Catholic. Avocations: skiing; flying; reading. Home: 91-10 68th Ave Forest Hills NY 11375 Office: Healthscope Mgmt Services Corp 100 Stevens Ave Mount Vernon NY 15505

TOMPANE, MARY BETH, organization administrator, management consultant; b. Hollywood, Calif., Sept. 27, 1928; d. Richard Earl and Mary Elizabeth (McGregor) Goss; A.A., Phoenix Coll., 1948; postgrad. No. Ariz. U., Ariz. State U., 1946-55; M.Banking Mgmt., U. Calif., Riverside, 1973; m. Eugene F. Tompane, Nov. 4, 1950; children—Michael, Richard, Donald, John. Mgmt. analyst, 1955-69; dept. head Boswell Hosp., Sun City, Ariz., 1969-72; non profit orgn. cons., Phoenix, 1972-80; travel agt., Phoenix and Tempe, Ariz., 1972-81; interim exec. dir. Girl Scouts U.S.A., 1981—; mgmt. cons., 1981—; mem. nat. women's bd. Northwood Inst., 1980—. Pres. Maricopa County YWCA, 1962-65, Phoenix Day Nursery, 1965-67, Friends of Thunderbird, 1975-77; pres. Family Service Phoenix, 1980; Horizons chmn. Bicentennial City of Phoenix, 1974-76; bd. dirs. Tempe United Way, 1983—. Named Woman of Year, Phoenix, 1965. Mem. Internat. Assn. Vol. Edn., Dirs. of Vols., Am. Assn. Assn. Execs. Republican. Episcopalian. Address: Tempe AZ

TOMPKINS, A. KATHLEEN KELLY, civic worker; b. St. Johns, Mich., Jan. 15, 1903; d. William Thomas and Harriet A. (Wright) Kelly; grad. U. Cin. Conservatory of Music, 1926; m. Neil Wright (dec.); children—Neil, Ross; m. 2d, Raymond McLaughlin, June 1961 (dec.); m. 3d, Lawrence E. Tompkins, June 5, 1976 (dec. Apr. 1985). Concert pianist, 1932-37; social dir. Lakeside Hotel, Eaglesmere, Pa., 1938-47; publicity dir. Pocono Manor, 1947-49; resident mgr. Gulf Winds Apts., St. Petersburg, Fla., 1949-50; social dir. Marshall House, York Harbor, Maine, 1951. Bd. dirs. Sarasota Music Club, 1964—, pres., 1966-68, parliamentarian, 1976-81; bd. dirs. Fla. Fedn. Music Clubs, 1968—; piano chmn., mem. artists selection com. Community Concerts Bd., 1971—; pres. Golden Gate Point Assn., 1962—, cons., 1977-81, also bd. dirs. Named Realtor of Yr., Sarasota Realtors Assn., 1960. Mem. Delta Omicron (nat. pres. 1931-37). Episcopalian. Club: Intercity Bridge. Home: 350 Golden Gate Point Sarasota FL 33577

TOMPKINS, BONNIE BALES, accountant; b. Walterboro, S.C., Dec. 10, 1955; d. Grady Marvin and Doris E. (Smoak) Bales; m. James B. Tompkins, June 26, 1982. A.S. in Real Estate, Midlands Tech. Coll., Columbia, S.C., 1977, A.S. in Bus. Mgmt., 1976; B.S. in Acctg., Baptist Coll. at Charleston, 1981. Acct., Hawthorne Aviation Co., Charleston, 1981-82, Eastwood Hosp., Memphis, 1982—. Jack Page Meml. scholar Nat. Assn. Accts., Charleston, 1980. Baptist. Avocations: swimming, traveling. Home: 3344 Kirby Trees St Memphis TN 38115 Office: Eastwood Hosp 3000 Getwell Rd Memphis TN 38118

TOMPKINS, FRANCES FISH, investment company executive; b. Logan, W.Va., Apr. 13, 1939; d. Joseph Theodore (J.T.) and Charlotte (Blackman) Fish; m. Harold Tompkins, June 28, 1959; 1 child, Laurence Alan Fish. A.A., Finch Coll., 1957; grad. Tobe Coburn Sch. for Fashion Careers, 1959. Pres. Raven Mining Equipment Co., Logan, 1961-74; v.p. Nationwide Mining Equipment Co., Logan, 1960-70; pres., ptnr. Mining Equipment Exchange, Logan, 1965—; dir. Mialla Realty Co., Logan, 1972—; dir. J.T. and C.B. Fish Found., Logan, 1970—. Mem. Women's div. bd. dirs. Jewish Guild for the Blind, N.Y.C., 1964—, chmn. ann. luncheon, 1971, 81, bd. dirs., 1979—, chmn. ann. jour., 1979, chmn. ERTE 90th Birthday Celebration and Art Auction, 1983; mem. various fund raising coms. and chmn. various functions Park Ave. Synagogue, N.Y.C., 1959—, mem. ann. art sale com., 1960-72, chmn. 1st ann. ball, 1977; mem. fund raising com. Juvenile Diabetes Found. N.Y. chpt., 1980—, benefit com. Mt. Sinai Med. Ctr., 1982—, Council for Beautiful Israel, 1985; active Am. Cancer Soc., 1962—; del. to N.Y. County Democratic Com., 1982—; asst. campaign mgr. N.Y. State Supreme Ct. jud. candidate, 1966; active various campaigns for Congress, state and city offices; campaign mgr. for jud. candidate, 1981; advisor to 6 jud. candidates, 1982—. Democrat. Jewish. Clubs: Finch (various offices 1960-70), Tobe Coburn Alumni (various offices 1960—, chmn. archives com. 1985) (N.Y.C.). Avocations: foreign travel; theater; interior design; theatrical productions investing. Home: 205 E 78th St New York NY 10021

TOMPKINS, JANET STARIHA, nursing researcher; b. Muskegon, Mich., June 18, 1942; d. Frank R. and Anne Elizabeth (Agnich) Stariha; m. Davis W. Tompkins, Apr. 30, 1967; children—Matthew, Elizabeth (dec.), Benjamin. B.S., Marquette U., 1964; M.S., Fla. Internat. U., 1973. R.N., Fla. Staff nurse Jackson Meml. Hosp., Miami, Fla., 1967-70; instr. Miami Dade Community Coll., 1971-82; research assoc. U. Miami Sch. Medicine, 1982—. Biog. compiler, proofreader Intradiseal Therapy (Mark D. Brown, M.D.), 1983. Den leader Cub Scouts, 1978-79; developer Sex Edn. in Religious Edn. program Ch. of St. Hugh, 1980-83. Served to lt. U.S. Navy, 1964-67. Mem. Am. Nurses Assn., Nat. Assn. Orthopedic Nurses, Alpha Tau Delta. Democrat. Roman Catholic. Club: Stanford of South Fla. (pres. 1974), Coconut Grove (Fla.) Sailing. Home: 810 Pinecrest Dr Miami Springs FL 33166 Office: U Miami Sch Medicine 1600 NW 12th Ave R2 Miami FL 33101

TOMS, KATHLEEN MOORE, nurse; b. San Francisco, Dec. 31, 1943; d. William Moore and Phyllis Josephine (Barry) Stewart; R.N., A.A., City Coll. San Francisco, 1963; B.P.S. in Nursing Edn., Elizabethtown (Pa.) Coll., 1973; M.S. in Edn., Temple U., 1977; postgrad. Gwynedd Mercy Coll.; children—Kathleen Marie Toms, Kelly Terese Toms. Med.-surg. nurse St. Joseph Hosp., Fairbanks, Alaska, 1963-65; emergency room nurse St. Joseph Hosp., Lancaster, Pa., 1965-69, blood, plasm and components nurse, 1969-71; pres. F.E. Barry Co., Lancaster, 1971—; dir. inservice edn. Lancaster Osteo. Hosp., 1971-75; coordinator practical nursing program Vocat. Tech. Sch., Coatesville, Pa., 1976-77; dir. nursing Pocopson Home, West Chester, Pa., 1978-80, Riverside Hosp., Wilmington, Del., 1980-83; assoc. Coatesville VA Hosp., 1983—; chief Nurse, 1984—; mem. Pa. Gov.'s Council on Alcoholism and Drug Abuse, 1974-76; mem. Del. Health Council Med.-Surg. Task Force, 1981—; dir. Lancaster Community Health Center, 1973-76; lectr. in field. Served to maj. Nurse Corps, USAR, 1973—. Decorated Army Commendation medal; recipient Community Service award Citizens United for Better Public Relations, 1974; award Sertoma, Lancaster, 1974; Outstanding Citizen award Sta. WGAL-TV, 1975; U.S. Army Achievement award, 1983. Mem. Elizabethtown, Temple U. alumni assns., Pa. Nurses' Assn. (dir.). Inventor auto-infuser for blood or blood components, 1971. Home: 400 Summit House 1450 West Chester Pike West Chester PA 19380 Office: Coatesville VA Med Center Black Horse Pike Coatesville PA

TOMSICK, MARY JO, rehabilitation organization executive; b. Pueblo, Colo., Nov. 8, 1950; d. Aldridge Boyd and Rose Marie (Coffee) O'Quin. B.S., U. So. Colo., 1972; M.A. in Rehab. Adminstrn., U. San Francisco, 1981. Line foreman Pueblo Diversified Industries, Pueblo, 1972-74, work adjustment specialist, 1974-75, case worker, 1975-77, program dir., 1977-80; dir. adult services devel. Pathways, Denver, 1981—; sec. Colo. Rehab. Enterprises, 1984, chmn., 1986—. Coach, vol. Colo. Spl. Olympics, Pueblo, 1973-79; mem. com. Mayors Com. to Promote Employment of Handicapped, Pueblo, 1977-79, White House Comf. Com. for Handicapped, Pueblo, 1977; mem. Assn. Retarded Citizens, Pueblo, 1975-80, Arapahoe County, 1985—. Mem. Nat. Rehab. Assn. (adminstrv. div.), Colo. Rehab. Assn., Am. Assn. Mental Deficiency, Assn. for Severely Handicapped, Nat. Assn. Female Execs. Democrat. Roman Catholic. Avocations: softball, skiing; fishing. Office: Devel Pathways 2000 S Quebec Denver CO 80231

TONDREAU, BEVERLY FRANCIS, computerized teleprompting service executive; b. Los Angeles, Dec. 2, 1945; d. Thomas Francis and Beverly Green (Goodrich) Hanley; m. William P. Tondreau, Oct. 26, 1968 (div. Feb. 1971). B.A. in Art, Immaculate Heart Coll., 1967. Dir. rental promotions Compu-Prompt, Hollywood, Calif., 1984, v.p. ops., 1984—; reporter Nat. Pub. Radio, Washington; ind. producer various prodns., Hollywood, 1985—. Mem. Internat. Documentary Assn., Nat. Assn. Female Execs., Women in Film, Assn. Entertainment Industry Computer Profls. Democrat. Avocations: hiking; writing. Home: 152 N Irving Blvd Los Angeles CA 90004

TONELLI, EDITH ANN, art gallery director, art historian; b. Westfield, Mass., May 20, 1949; d. Albert Robert and Pearl (Grubert) T. B.A., Vassar Coll., 1971; M.A., Hunter Coll., 1974; Ph.D., Boston U., 1981; grad., Mus. Mgmt. Inst.-U. Calif.-Berkeley, 1981. Arts curriculum coordinator Project SEARCH, Millbrook, N.Y., 1972-74; curator DeCordova Mus., Lincoln, Mass., 1976-78; dir. art gallery, asst. prof. art U. Md., College Park, 1979-82; dir. Frederick S. Wight Art Gallery, 1982—; adj. asst. prof. art UCLA, 1982—; reviewer pub. programs Nat. Endowment Humanities, 1977—; dir. mus. studies program U. Md., College Park, 1979-82; project dir. Summer Inst. Artists (U. Md.), 1981-82. Author exhbn. catalogs. Fellow Nat. Endowment Arts, 1981; predoctoral fellow Smithsonian Instn., 1979; doctoral and teaching fellow Boston U., 1974-76; mem. Helen Squire Townsend fellow, Vassar College, 1971-72; recipient dissertation award Boston U. Vis. Com., 1979. Mem. Am. Assn. Museums, Coll. Art Assn., Women's Caucus for Art, Art Mus. Assn. Am. (advisor profl. tng.), Assn. Art Mus. Dirs., Am. Studies Assn., Art Table Inc. Office: Frederick S Wight Art Gallery UCLA 405 Hilgard Ave Los Angeles CA 90024

TONEY, DONNA JEAN, manufacturing company executive; b. Bartlesville, Okla., Oct. 28, 1947; d. Troy Herbert and Ruth Amanda (Baker) Main; m. Fred E. Toney, Apr. 6, 1972 (div. Aug. 1983); 1 dau., Shelli Ann. Student, Wesleyan Coll., Bartlesville, 1978—. Clk., TRW Reda Pump Co., Bartlesville, 1966-75, mgr. adminstrv. services, 1975-82, supr. labor relations, 1982—. Co. div. chmn. United Fund, Bartlesville, 1980-83, town div. chmn., Copan, Okla., 1981-82, mem. budget rev. com., Bartlesville, 1982-83; 1st vice chmn. Mayor's Commn. on Employment of Handicapped, Bartlesville, 1982-83. Recipient Funder Finder award United Fund, 1980, 81, 82, 83. Fellow Am. Soc. Personnel Assocs. Republican. Club: Civitan (Bartlesville) (pres. 1980-81, lt. gov. 1981-82). Office: TRW Reda Pump PO Box 1181 Bartlesville OK 74003

TONEY, EDNA, playwright, actress; b. N.Y.C., Mar. 22, 1914; d. Henry and Frieda (Berger) Greenfield; m. Anthony Toney, Apr. 8, 1947; children—Anita Karen, Adele Susan. Student New Theatre Sch., 1936; Columbia U., 1953-55, New Sch. Social Research, 1975. Actress WPA Theatre Project, N.Y.C., 1937; writer Kraft Music Hall, N.Y.C., 1946; writer, producer, actress schs., community ctrs., colls., libraries, etc., 1972-82; playwright Baby Brother Prodn., Mid-Hudson Arts and Sci. Ctr., Poughkeepsie, N.Y., 1980; writer, dir., actress, producer Katonah Community Theatre, N.Y., 1984; columnist Queries and Theories. Author: Once Told Tales, 1967. Benefit performance Meet Miss Lucy Stone, North Westchester-Putnam County Women's Resource Ctr., Mahopac, N.Y., 1986. Recipient acting awards 10th Annual Arts Festival, 1976. Mem. NOW, Women's Internat. League Peace and Freedom, SANE, Katonah Gallery. Democrat. Avocations: swimming. Home: 16 Hampton Pl Katonah NY 10536

TONIETTE, SALLYE JEAN, physician; b. Sulphur, La.; d. Eugene Augusta and Sallye (Tanner) Toniette; student John McNeese Jr. Coll., 1946-47; B.S., La. State U., 1949; tchrs. certificate La. State U., 1950, M.D., 1955. Intern, Crawford W. Long Meml. Hosp., Emory U., Atlanta, 1955-56, resident in ob-gyn., jr., sr., chief residencies, 1956-59; practice ob-gyn, Sulphur, La., 1959—; bd. dirs. Holly Hill Nursing Home; mem. med. staff West Calcasieu Cameron Hosp., 1959—. Dir. Calcasieu Parish Cancer Soc. 1963-67. Named Woman of Dinstinction, Calcasieu Parish Police Jurors, also Bus. and Profl. Women's Club of West Calcesieu, 1969; Queen of Krewe of Cosmos, 1963 Mardi Gras. Fellow Am. Coll. Ob-Gyn; mem. AMA, So. Med. Assn., La., Calcasieu Parish med. socs., La. Wildlife Fedn., Am. Quarter Horse Assn., Assn. Am. Physicians and Surgeons, Am., La. Paint horse assns., Alpha Chi Omega, Beta Tau Mu, Iota Sigma Pi, Phi Theta Kappa, Beta Sigma Phi. Democrat. Methodist. Clubs: Quota, Bus. and Profl. Women's, Lake Charles Country, Bayou Oaks Country (v.p. bd. dirs. 1974-82), Krewe de La Bon Vie. Contbr. articles to profl. jours. Home: 301 W Verdine St Sulphur LA 70663 Office: 521 Cypress St Sulphur LA 70663

TOOKE, MERIBETH KOVAR, marketing executive; b. Chgo., Aug. 30, 1944; d. Harold James and Bessie Ann (Kuchar) Kovar; m. John W. Tooke, June 4, 1966; 1 child, Jon Wenceslaus. A.S., Lyons Twp. Jr. Coll., 1965; B.S., Okla. State U., 1966; M.S. in Edn., No. Ill. U., 1974; M.B.A., Rosary Coll., 1985. Buyer Ben Franklin, Pella, Iowa, 1966, Margie's Bridal, Niles, Ill., 1966-67; home economist Club Aluminum Cookware, LaGrange, Ill., 1967-68; home service economist No. Ill. Gas, Aurora, Ill., 1968-74, market planner, 1974-80, sr. market adminstr., 1980—. Mem. vocat. bd. Wheaton High Sch., Ill., 1985—, Lyons Twp. High Sch., 1978-85, Elmwood Park High Sch., Ill., 1974-85. Mem. Ill. Home Econs. Assn. (pres. 1978-79), Lakeshore Home Econs. Assn. (pres. 1974-75), Textile, Clothing and Related Arts Assn. (pres. 1972-73), Home Economists in Bus. (newsletter contbr.), Am. Gas Assn. (vice chmn. mktg. sect. consumer info. com.), Ill. Assn. Sch. Bds. (mem. service assn. exec. bd. 1976—), Phi Delta Kappa, Sigma Kappa. Home: 740 N Brainard Ave LaGrange Park IL 60525 Office: No Ill Gas Co East West Tollway at Route 59 Aurora IL 60507

TOOTE, GLORIA E. A., lawyer, writer, government official, housing developer; b. N.Y.C., Nov. 8, 1931; d. Frederick A. and Lillie M. (Tooks) T. Student Howard U., 1949-51, J.D., 1954; student NYU, 1951; LL.M., Columbia U., 1956. Bar: N.Y. 1955, U.S. Dist. Cts. (so. and ea. dists.) N.Y. 1956, U.S. Supreme Ct. 1956. Assoc. Greenbaum, Wolff & Ernst, 1957, mem. editorial staff TIME mag., 1957-58; asst. gen. counsel N.Y. State Workmen's Compensation Bd., 1958-64; pres. Toote Town Pub. Co. and Town Sound Studios, Inc., 1966-70; asst. dir. ACTION Agy., 1971-73; asst. sec. Dept. HUD, 1973-75; vice chmn. Pres.'s Adv. Council on Pvt. Sector Initiatives, 1983-85; pres. Trea Estates and Enterprises, Inc., 1976—. Newspaper columnist Nat. Newspaper Pub. Assn. Past bd. dirs. Citizens for the Republic, Nat. Black United Fund, Exec. Women in Govt., Am. Arbitration Assn., Consumer Alert; past mem. Council Econ. Affairs, Republican Nat. Com.; pres. N.Y.C. Black Rep. Council; bd. overseers Hoover Instn.; 2d vice chmn. Nat. Polit. Congress of Black Women. Recipient numerous citations from assns., councils. Address: 282 W 137th St New York NY 10030

TOPFER, SUE ACE, librarian; b. Media, Pa., Mar. 30, 1925; d. Percy Henry and Dorothy Austin (Redheffer) Ace; B.S., Ursinus Coll., 1946; M.S., Syracuse U., 1951; m. Alvin Richard Topfer, Nov. 27, 1952; children—Edward Henry, Dorothy Sue, Keith Ace, Kurt Alan. Asst. chem. lab. Am. Viscose Corp., Marcus Hook, Pa., 1946-50; librarian electronics and elec. lab. U.S. Naval Air Devel. Center, Johnsville, Pa., 1951-53; asso. librarian Luzerne County Community Coll., Nanticoke, Pa., 1967-78; serials Librarian Wilkes Coll., Wilkes-Barre, Pa., 1979—. Mem. exec. bd. Glen Summit Community Club, Mountaintop, Pa., 1971-72. Mem. Pa. Library Assn., Am. Coll. and Research Libraries, Wilkes Faculty Women, N. Am. Serials Interest Group. Home: Box 387 Rural Delivery #3 Loop Rd Mountaintop PA 18707 Office: Eugene Shedden Farley Library Franklin at South St Wilkes-Barre PA 18766

TOPHAM, SALLY JANE, ballet educator; b. N.Y.C., June 2, 1933; d. William Holroyd Topham and Marian Phyllis (Thomas) Topham Halligan; m. Joseph Vincent Ferrara, Dec. 27, 1958 (div. 1977); children—Gregory Paul, Mark Edward. Student Ballet Theatre Sch., Royal Acad. Dancing, London; trained in Europe. Free-lance profl. dancer ballet, opera ballet, summer stock, 1956-59; founder, dir. Monmouth Sch. Ballet, N.J., 1963-83; founder Central Jersey Acad. Ballet, Red Bank, N.J., 1983—, also dir.; dir. Westfield sch. Ballet, N.J., 1976-77; tchr., dir. Mount Allison U. Summer Sch., New Brunswick, Can., 1973-77; prof. ballet Monmouth Coll., West Long Branch, N.J., 1981-83. Choreographer (ballet) Coppelia, 1981, 83; Shubert Songs, 1980; Homage to

Bouroonville, 1977; Nutcracker, 1985; staged many ballets and opera ballets. Bd. dirs. Monmouth Arts Found., Red Bank, 1972—, Shore Ballet Co., Red Bank, 1976—; founder, bd. dirs. Monmouth Civic Ballet, Red Bank, 1972-75. Mem. Royal Acad. Dancing (advanced tchr's. cert. 1979), English Speaking Union. Avocations: sailing; theatre; music; books. Office: Central Jersey Acad Ballet 8 Monmouth St Red Bank NJ 07701

TOPINKA, JUDY BAAR, state legislator; b. Riverside, Ill., Jan. 16, 1944; d. William Daniel and Lillian Mary (Shuss) Baar; B.S., Northwestern U., 1966; 1 son, Joseph Baar. Features editor, reporter, columnist Life Newspapers, Berwyn and LaGrange, Ill., 1966-77; with Forest Park (Ill.) Review and Westchester News, 1976-77; coordinator spl. events Dept. Fedn. Communications, AMA, 1978-80; research analyst Senator Leonard Becker, 1978-79; mem. Ill. Ho. of Reps., 1981-84; mem. Ill. Senate, 1985—; former mem. minority bus. resource ctr. adv. com. U.S. Dept. Transp.; mem. adv. bd. Nat. Inst. Justice. Founder, pres., bd. dirs. West Suburban Exec. Breakfast Club, from 1976; Republican candidate Ill. Senate, 1984; chmn. Ill. Ethnics for Reagan-Bush, 1984; mem. Ill. Gov.'s Task Force on Horse Racing. Office: 6924 W Cermak Rd Berwyn IL 60402

TOPJIAN, MENA ROSE, educator; b. Cambridge, Mass., Sept. 7, 1936; d. Daniel and Siran T. B.S. in Edn., Boston U., 1958, M.Ed. in Sch. Librarianship, 1966. Tchr., Deep River Elem. Sch., Conn., 1958, Prospect Sch., Beverly, Mass., 1959, Oak Grove Sch., North Miami Beach, Fla., 1960, Franklin Sch., Lexington, Mass., 1961-83, Bowman Sch., Lexington, 1983—. Author articles and reports in field of Native Am. studies. Mem. Nat. Council Social Studies Tchrs., Mass. Council Social Studies Tchrs., NEA, Mass. Tchrs. Assn., Lexington Tchrs. Assn., Pan Am. Soc., Cultural Survival Soc. Club: Victorian, World Affairs Council (Boston); Peabody Mus. (Cambridge, Mass.). Home: 36 F Jacqueline Rd Waltham MA 02154 Office: Bowman Sch Lexington MA 02154

TOPPEL, HEIDI JEAN, lawyer; b. Ridgewood, N.J., Dec. 11, 1955; d. Donald R. and Jean (Schultze) T. Student Lafayette Coll., Easton, Pa., 1973-75; B.S., U. Pa., 1977; J.D., Seton Hall U., Newark, N.J., 1982. Bar: N.J. 1982; C.P.A., N.J. Staff acct. Rayfield & Co., East Orange, N.J., 1977-79; acct. Frankel & Co., Ft. Lee, N.J., 1980-81; tax atty. Brach, Eichler, Roseland, N.J., 1981-83; compensation research mgr. The Wyatt Co., Ft. Lee, 1983—; pvt. practice tax cons. Mahwah, N.J., 1979—. Sr. editor: Stock-based Compensation, 1984. Recipient citation of honor in young career woman program, Bus. and Profl. Women's Club, 1983. Fellow N.J. Soc. C.P.A.s; mem. ABA, N.J. Bar Assn., Am. Inst. C.P.A.s. Republican. Mem. Dutch Reformed Ch.

TORANO-PANTIN, MARIA ELENA, public relations consultant; b. Havana, Cuba, Feb. 13, 1938; came to U.S., 1960; d. Julio Diez-Rousselot and Sira M. (Vidal) D.-R.; m. Arturo Torano, Feb. 9, 1958 (div. 1979); children—Arthur, Eric; m. Leslie P. Pantin, Sept. 28, 1980. B.A. in Langs., U. Havana, 1958. Tchr. home econs. Demonstration Sch., U. Havana, 1958-60; orientation tchr. Dade County Pub. Schs., Miami, Fla., 1962-63; caseworker family and children services Fla. Dept. Pub. Welfare, 1965-68; with Eastern Airlines, 1968-76, program mgr. Latin Am. Affairs, Miami, 1974-76; dir. Latin Am. affairs Jackson Meml. Med. Center, Miami, 1976-77; assoc. dir. pub. affairs U.S. Community Services Adminstrn., Washington, 1977-79; pres. and founder Nat. Assn. Spanish Broadcasters, Washington, 1978-80; pres. META, Inc., Miami, 1980—; cons. Miami Dolphins, 1980—, Rouse Co., Colombia, M.D., 1983—; dir. Date Ptnrs.-Pub. Sch. System, Miami, 1982—; chmn. Nat. Leaders Forum, Miami, 1982—. Chmn. Hispanic Heritage Festival, 1975; mem. task force Gov.'s Health Care Cost Containment, Tallahassee, 1982—; exec. com. Fla. Arts Council, 1981—; adv. Fla. Power and Light, Miami, 1983—; mem. Dade County Community Relations Bd.; chmn. Internat. Health Com. Greater Miami. Recipient various commendations, certs. of appreciation; nominee Nat. Wonder Woman award, 1983. Mem. Coalition Hispanic Am. Women, AAUW, Nat. Assn. Latino Elected and Apptd. Ofcls. (dir. 1978—), Greater Miami C. of C. Democrat. Roman Catholic. Club: Cuban Women's. Home: 150 SE 25th Rd 14-M Miami FL 33129 Office: META Inc 800 Douglas Rd Coral Gables FL 33134

TORBERG, VIRGINIA HUBBARD, wood carver, soap manufacturer; b. Mpls., May 8, 1922; d. Albert Jerry and Thaaline (Hauge) Hubbard; student pub. schs., Mpls., U. Minn.; m. Bernie R. Torberg, Sept. 18, 1948; children—Steven M., Richard L., Robin S., Peter L., Daniel J. Propr., North Country Soap, Lyndale, Minn., 1973—, partner Country Woodcraft, Lyndale, 1964—; demonstrator soapmaking, wood carving; designer, producer Woodcraft Carving Kit, 1971—; carvings exhibited: Sons of Norway, Mpls., Lutheran Brotherhood Gallery, Mpls., 1975. Pres. local PTA, 1968; mem. Independence (Minn.) Bicentennial Commn. Mem. Minn., Minnetonka (charter) hist. assns., Minn. Valley Restoration Project, Nat., Minn. woodcarvers assns., Nat. Carvers Museum, Smithsonian Assocs., Mus. Store Assn. (assoc.), Am. Heritage Assn., Audubon Soc., Weaver's Guild, Internat. Platform Assn., LWV. Christian Scientist. Clubs: Garden, Lit., Spinner's, Order Eastern Star. Author: Why Carve Just One?, 1970; Country Pattern Book for Woodcarving, 1972; Something About Soap, 1973; also articles. Address: 7888 County Rd 6 Maple Plain MN 55359

TORBET, LAURA, graphic designer, author; b. Paterson, N.J., Aug. 23, 1942; d. Earl Buchanan and Ruth Claire (Ehlers) Robbins; B.A., B.F.A., Ohio Wesleyan U., 1964; m. Bruce J. Torbet, Sept. 9, 1967 (div. 1971); m. Peter H. Morrison, June 19, 1983. Mng. editor Suburban Life mag., East Orange, N.J., 1964-65; asst. public relations dir. United Funds N.J., Newark, 1965-67; art dir. Alitalia Airlines, N.Y.C., 1967-69; propr. Laura Torbet Studio, N.Y.C., 1969—; author: Macrame You Can Wear, 1972, Clothing Liberation, 1973, Leathercraft You Can Wear, 1975, The T-Shirt Book, 1976, The Complete Book of Skateboarding, 1976, How To Do Everything With Markers, 1977; Squash: How to Play, How to Win, 1977; How to Fight Fair With Your Kids...and Win!, 1980; editor: The Encyclopedia of Crafts, 1980; Helena Rubenstein's Book of the Sun, 1979; (with George Bach) The Inner Enemy, 1982, A Time for Caring, 1982; (with Hap Hatton) Helpful Hints for Hard Times, 1982, The Virgin Homeowners Handbook, 1984, Helpful Hints for Better Living, 1984, (with James Braly) Dr. Brady's Optimum Health Program, 1985; (with Bernard Gittelson) Intangible Evidence; editor, co-author books. Mem. Am. Crafts Council, Am. Women's Econ. Devel. Corp. Home and Office: 225 E 73d St New York NY 10021

TORKELSON, NATALIE GAIL, nurse; b. Manchester, N.H., Feb. 27, 1949; d. Einar Oliver and Ruby Hilma (Swanson) Peterson; m. Bruce Emil Torkelson, June 27, 1970; children—Kristen Emily, Katie Olivia. B.A. in Nursing, Gustavus Adolphus Coll., 1971; M.S. in Nursing, U. Okla., 1984. Nurses' aide Elliott Hosp., Manchester, 1965-69; nursing asst. Bethesda Lutheran Hosp., St. Paul, 1969-71; St. Francis Hosp., Tulsa, 1970; staff nurse Hillcrest Med. Center, Tulsa, 1971-75, head nurse, 1975-86, dir. profl. nursing, critical care, 1986—; cons. primary nursing program devel. Creative Specialists, Inc., Tulsa, 1979. Co-author: Heart Disease/Rehabilitation, 1979. Staffing coordinator Neighbor for Neighbor free health clinic, Tulsa, 1972—. Mem. Am. Heart Assn. (bd. dirs. NE Okla. chpt. 1984—), Am. Assn. Critical Care Nurses (treas. 1974-76, v.p. 1976-77, pres. 1977-78), Am. Nurses Assn., Okla. Nurses Assn. (dist. dir. 1980-81), Sigma Theta Tau. Republican. Lutheran. Office: Hillcrest Medical Center Utica on the Park Tulsa OK 74104

TORME, MARGARET ANNE, public relations agency executive; b. Indpls., Apr. 5, 1943; d. Ira G. and Margaret Joy (Wright) Barker; Coll. San Mateo, 1960-66; children—Karen Anne, Leah Vanessa. With Hoefer, Dieterich & Brown, San Francisco, 1964-73; co-founder, v.p., creative dir. Lowry & Partners, San Francisco, 1975-82; founder, pres., creative dir. Torme & Co., San Francisco, 1982—. Office: Torme & Co 414 Jackson St San Francisco CA 94111

TOROK, HELEN ELIZABETH, information resources automation company executive, computer systems analyst; b. Sylvania, Ga., May 1, 1942; d. Walter Owen and Alma (Corley) Odum; m. Tibor Torok, July 4, 1967; children—Andrea, Derek, Marika. Student IBM programming Am. Computer Inst., 1965-67; student Combination Bus., 1966-67; student BASIC/COBOL programs Pace U., 1978-80. Service mgr. Valtronic Corp., Bronx, N.Y., 1962-67; EDP supr. Marine Midland Bank, N.Y.C., 1968-72; EDP mgr. Electronic Data System, N.Y.C., 1972-73; EDP supr. Nat. State Bank, Linden, N.J., 1973-77, Blyth Eastman Dillon, N.Y.C., 1977-80; pres. Stored Info. Systems, Hazlet, N.J., 1979—; adj. prof. Office Personnel Mgmt., Ctr. Info. Mgmt. and Automation, Washington, 1979—. Author: Magnetic Media Tape Library series, 1979; Mini/Microcomputer Applications, 1980. Vol. tchr. computers, Hazlet, 1983—. Mem. Data Processing Librarians and Documentation Mgrs. Nat. Assn. (nat. speaker 1978, 82, 83, nat. bd. dirs. 1979—, nat. sec. 1979-81, nat. treas. 1982—), Ind. Computer Cons. Assn. (nat. speaker 1982), N.J. Assn. Women Bus. Owners. Avocations: music; dance; skiing; antiques; stamp collecting. Office: Stored Info Systems Inc PO Box 37 Hazlet NJ 07730

TORRE, ELIZABETH LASSITER, social worker, educator; b. Winston-Salem, N.C., June 17, 1931; d. Vernon Clark and Mary (Pfohl) Lassiter; student Wellesley (Mass.) Coll., 1948-49; B.A., Duke U., 1952; M.R.E., Union Theol. Sem., 1957; M.S.W., Tulane U., 1966, Ph.D., 1972; cert. social worker, La. m. Mottram Peter Torre, Apr. 13, 1957. Field dir. undergrad. admissions Duke U., Durham, N.C., 1952-53; head tchr. primary dept. Riverside Ch., N.Y.C., 1957-60; instr. Sch. Social Work, Tulane U., New Orleans, 1966-72, assoc. prof., 1972—, coordinator Indsl. Social Work Program, 1982—; non-govtl. orgn. rep. UNICEF, World Fedn. Mental Health, 1957-61; cons. to v.p. community affairs WETA, Washington, 1979; cons. Office Spl. Symposia and Seminars, Smithsonian Instn., Washington, 1979—. Treas., N.Y. Jr. League, 1961-62, v.p., 1962-63; bd. dirs. Community Vol. Services, New Orleans, 1965-68; mem. profl. adv. com. Project Pre-Kindergarten, Orleans Parish Sch. Bd., New Orleans, 1967-69; mem. adv. bd. DePaul Community Mental Health Center, New Orleans, 1971-72; mem. citizens adv. com. Orleans Parish Juvenile Ct., New Orleans, 1970-73; mem. Council on Social Work Edn. Task Force on Prevention, 1981—; mem. New Orleans Women's Coalition Task Force on Employers and Working Parents, 1985-86. NIMH grantee; Summer Inst. grantee Nat. Endowment Humanities, 1982. Mem. Council Social Work Edn., Nat. Assn. Social Workers, Am. Orthopsychiat. Assn., AAUP, World Future Soc., Phi Beta Kappa. Office: Sch Social Work Tulane U New Orleans LA 70118

TORRES, BARBARA JANE, food company executive; b. San Diego, July 24, 1954; d. Leonard and Barbara Jane (Walker) Torres. A.A., Grossmont Coll., 1974; B.S., San Diego State U., 1977; postgrad. U. Calif.-San Diego, 1978-80; M.S., Boston U., 1982. Cashier, sales F.W. Woolworth Co., El Cajon, Calif., 1974-76; delivery cook Gatekeeper Restaurant, San Diego, 1975-77; dietetic intern U. Mpls. Hosp., Mpls., 1977-78; dir. nutrition Bay Gen. Hosp., Chula Vista, Calif., 1978-81; pub. relations intern Gov. King., Mass. State House, Boston, 1981-82; editorial publicist Sunkist Growers, Inc., Los Angeles, 1982—. Contbr. articles to numerous newspapers and mags. Mem. Am. Dietetic Assn., Calif. Nutrition Council, Soc. Nutrition Edn., Home Economists in Bus., Phi Upsilon Omicron. Democrat. Office: Sunkist Growers Inc 14130 Riverside Dr Sherman Oaks CA 91423

TORRES, ERIKA VOGEL, college administrator; b. Fulda, Hessen, W. Ger., Mar. 22, 1939; came to U.S. 1962, naturalized, 1966; d. Hermann Josef and Ella Mathilde (Schneider) Vogel; m. Angelo Torres, Jr., Mar. 2, 1974; children—Karen Doris, Christopher Hans, Alexandra Eran. B.S., U. Bridgeport, 1973, M.S., 1975, Diploma 6th Year Profl., 1977; Ph.D., Columbia Pacific U., 1982. Instr., U.S. Army Edn. Ctr., W.Germany, 1966-71, mil. test proctor, 1969-71; exec. sec., adminstrv. asst. U. Bridgeport, Conn., 1972-76, admissions counselor, 1976-77, dir. grad. admissions, 1977-79; dean records and registrar Post Coll., Waterbury, Conn., 1979—, instr. German, 1983-84; tchr. German, Ind. German Lang. Schs. of Conn., Westport, 1983—. Editor: Post College Catalog, 1980—, Admissions Viewbook, 1981-83. Mem. Am. Assn. Collegiate Registrars and Admissions Officers, Nat. Assn. Female Execs., Am. Personnel Guidance Assn., Am. Assn. Tchrs. German, Nat. Assn. Vets. Program Adminstrs. Avocations: reading; travel. Home: 97 Wilson St Bridgeport CT 06605

TORRES, LORETTA RUBY, automotive company executive; b. Hopkinsville, Ky., July 5, 1946; d. James Vincent and Joan Wilma (Wilson) Dennett Fiore; m. George Joseph Torres, June 1, 1963; children—Georginna Jo, Daniel Andrew, Tammara Lyn. Student, Whatcom Community Coll., U. N.Mex., U. Wis.; Cert. in Service Mgmt., Calif. Poly. U.-Gen. Motors, 1986. Cert. emergency med. technician, Wash. Mem. retail staff Ben's Dept. Store, 1973-74, mgr. supr. The Hawthornes', Pt. Roberts, Wash., 1975-76; mem. staff warranty claims Lee Galles Oldsmobile, Albuquerque, 1978-82, service advisor, 1982-85. Service, part dir. Baca Motors Inc., Belen, N.Mex., 1983—. Pres., PTA, Acoma Elem. Sch., Albuquerque, 1970-72; emergency med. technician Pt. Roberts Community Fire Dept., Wash., 1975-76; mem. Blaine Boosters Assn., Wash., 1976-77. Republican. Roman Catholic. Avocations: Reading; gardening; yoga; art, dancing. Office: Baca Motors Inc 101 Rio Communites Bellen NM 87002

TORRES DE WALSH, LUCILLE, marketing executive; b. Bklyn., Nov. 21, 1952; d. Alberto Luis and Vene (Santos) Torres; m. Alberto Jose Walsh, Dec. 23, 1977; children—Luciann, Alberto Jose III. B.A., Keuka Coll., 1974. Mktg. asst. Colgate Palmolive Co., San Juan, P.R., 1977-78, asst. product mgr., 1978-79, product mgr., 1979-80; sr. brand mgr. Tylenol, Johnson & Johnson Hemisferica, S.A., Hato Rey, P.R., 1980—. Mem. Sales and Mktg. Execs. Assn., Am. Mktg. Assn., Kappa Pi, Pi Delta Epsilon. Democrat. Roman Catholic. Home: X-19 Calle Arizona Parkville Guaynabo PR 00657 Office: Johnson & Johnson Hemisferica SA 269 Ponce de Leon Ave Hato Rey PR 00919

TORRINGTON, MARY CHRISTINE, international training consultant executive; b. Denver, July 20, 1949; d. Warren Rene and Inez Marie (Alexander) T. B.S. in Zoology, Duke U., 1971; M.A., U.S. Internat. U., 1973, Ph.D. in Clin. Psychology, 1976. Psychology postdoctoral fellow Devereux Found., Santa Barbara, Calif., 1976-77; psychol. cons. Alysan Center, Santa Clara, Calif., 1979; counselor, cons. Employee Assistance Program, Wells Fargo Bank, San Francisco. 1980; participant, intern, The Johnston Inst., Mpls., 1980; internat. tng. cons. spl. health services Standard Oil of Calif., San Francisco, 1980-81; pres. M.C. Torrington & Assocs., San Francisco, 1981—. Mem. Am. Psychol. Assn., Calif. State Psychol. Assn., Alameda County Psychol. Assn., San Francisco Bay Area Psychol. Assn., World Affairs Council, Soc. for Intercultural Edn., Tng., and Research, World Trade Assn., Internat. Trade Council, Calif. Council for Internat. Trade, Sell Overseas America, U.S.-Arab C. of C., San Francisco C. of C., Japan Soc. No. Calif., Pan Am. Soc., Internat. Mgrs. Assn. (dir.), Internat. Visitors Ctr. Club: Commonwealth Club of No. Calif. Office: M C Torrington & Assocs 211 Sutter St Suite 318 San Francisco CA 94108

TOSH, JUANITA PRILLAMAN, tire company executive; b. Axton, Va., Jan. 13, 1930; d. Stuart Owen and Ann Halvorsen (Jamison) Prillaman; student public schs. Bassett, Va.; m. James Cleavon Tosh, June 5, 1961; children—Rebecca Ann Craze, Cheryl Sue Tuggle, Mark Cleavon. Owner, Russ Auto Service Co., Norfolk, Va., 1954-59; v.p. Russ & Prillaman Auto Service Inc., Collinsville, Va., 1959-68; co-owner John Allen Estates, Collinsville, 1975—, Town Gun Shop, Collinsville, 1983—; owner Tosh Tire Town, Collinsville, 1969—; sec.-treas. Cash Oil Sales Inc., Collinsville, Va., 1982—. Mem. Retail Mchts. Assn., Va. Tire Dealers and Retreaders Assn., Nat. Tire Dealers and Retreaders Assn. Baptist. Home: 208 Ferndale Dr Collinsville VA 24078

TOSH, NANCY PECKHAM, magazine editor; b. Clinton, Iowa, May 5, 1932; d. George Taylor and Mildred Amelia (Smallfeldt) Peckham III; m. David Warren Tosh, July 5, 1958 (div. 1978); children—Murray, Warren, Amy. Student Sullins Coll., 1950-52; B.A., U. Iowa, 1954. Copywriter Sears, Roebuck and Co., Chgo., 1954-58; copywriter, staff writer Clapper Pub. Co., Inc., Park Ridge, Ill., 1973-76, copy editor Crafts 'N Things Mag., 1976-77, asst. editor, 1977-79, editor, 1979—; weekly rep. Bright Ideas segment Crafts 'n Things (SPN Cable TV), 1984—. Mem. P.E.O., Gamma Alpha Chi. Republican. Home: 1804 S Prospect St Park Ridge IL 60068 Office: Crafts 'N Things Mag 14 Main St Park Ridge IL 60068

TOSINI, PAULA ANN, government economist; b. Balt., May 20, 1938; d. Paul Joseph and Ruth (Callahan) Wiegard; m. Peter Charles Tosini, May 23, 1964; children—Stephen, Suzanne, Jennifer. B.S. summa cum laude, Georgetown U., 1960; cert. U. Brussels, Belgium, 1961; M.S., Georgetown U., 1964; Ph.D., U. Md., 1976. Economist U.S. AID, Washington, 1961-63, 64-66; fgn. service officer U.S. Dept. of State, Washington, 1964; asst. prof. econs. U. Md., College Park, 1976-77; economist U.S. Commodity Futures Trading Commn., Washington, 1977-80, research dir., 1980-84, dir. div. of econ. analysis, 1984—. Author: (monograph) Princeton Essay Series, 1977. Contbr. articles to profl. jours. Fulbright scholar, 1960-61, Brookings Instn. research fellow, 1974-75. Avocations: swimming; tennis. Home: 7808 Hamilton Spring Rd Bethesda MD 20817 Office: Div Econ Analysis Commodity Futures Trading Commn 2033 K St NW Washington DC 20581

TOTH, ANNE PATTEN, convalescent center executive; b. Bridgeport, Conn., Dec. 14, 1947; d. Albert Allen and Harriet Ellen (Leib) Garofalo; m. Kevin Randall Meyer, July 29, 1967 (div. June 1972); 1 child, Nicole Marie; m. Michael Edward Toth, Oct. 6, 1978; children—Alexis Patten, Aaron Michael. Student Quinnipiac Coll., Wharton Sch., Harvard Bus. Sch. Programmer, Save the Children, Westport, Conn., 1966-69; systems analyst Burndy Corp., Norwalk, Conn., 1969-70; pvt. practice systems analyst cons., Fairfield, Conn., 1970—; adminstrv. asst. Southport Manor, Conn., 1974-75, adminstr., chief exec. officer, 1975—. Chpt. pres. Am. Field Service, Greens Farms, Conn., 1984-86; chairwoman Daffodil Festival, Am. Cancer Soc., Fairfield, 1984; chairwoman Gourmet Gala March of Dimes, Stamford, Conn., 1985. Mem. Young Pres. Orgn., Fairfield C. of C. (treas. 1986), Am. Coll. Health Adminstrs. (cert.), Concerned Women's Colleagues, Am. Mgmt. Assn. Democrat. Roman Catholic. Club: YWCA-100 Com. (bd. dirs. 1982—). Avocations: scuba diving; skiing; swimming; horseback riding; traveling. Home: 160 Farmstead Hill Rd Fairfield CT 06430 Office: Southport Manor Convalescent Ctr Inc 930 Mill Hill Terr Southport CT 06490

TOTH, JUDITH COGGESHALL, state legislator; b. Rochelle, Ill., Oct. 21, 1937; d. Dr. and Mrs. R.J. Coggeshall; children—Christina, Adriana. Student Mexico City Coll. (U. of Americas), 1956-57; B.A. in Latin Am. Studies, Northwestern U., 1959; postgrad. Georgetown U., 1960-61, U. Andes, Bogota, Colombia, 1965-66, Montgomery Coll., 1980-81, U. Md., 1981-83; M.P.H., Johns Hopkins U., 1984. Bookkeeper, salesperson, professional model, dental asst. and sec., 1955-64; instr. polit. sci. and history U. of the Andes, 1964-66; legis. liaison and office mgr. Emergency Com. for Gun Control, 1968-69; cons. to Internat. Study Ctr., 1968, Pres.'s Commn. on the Causes and Prevention of Violence, 1969; researcher Assoc., Ideas, Inc., 1970-71; v.p. Polit-Econ, Inc., 1971-74; mem. Md. Gen. Assembly, Annapolis, 1975—, mem. various coms., Gov.'s Commn. on Hispanic Affairs, 1979—, chmn. Joint Com. on Medicaid, 1980-82; mem. Task Force to Rev. Hosp. Regulations, 1980-82; cons. in field; mem. adv. com. to NASA, 1976-82; mem. Md. Hist. Trust, 1982—; appointee Washington Met. Council of Govts., 1975—, mem. pub. safety policy com., 1985—. Bd. dirs. Md. Assn. of the Deaf, 1979-82, Citizens Transp. Coalition, 1971-73; pres. Montgomery County Civic Fedn., 1973-74, Washington Met. Congress of Citizens, 1971-73, Cabin John Park Citizens Assn., 1970-72, founding editor Cabin John Village News; founder, co-chmn. Montgomery County Coalition of Pres.'s, 1973-74; mem. adv. com. on the Potomac River, Montgomery County Council, 1970-71; bd. govs. ACLU of Md., 1970-73; mem. environ. groups; bd. dirs. Nat. Consumer Orgn. for Hearing Impaired, 1979-80; active numerous Democratic campaigns in local, state and nat. elections, 1956—; founding mem. Alliance for Dem. Reform, Montgomery County, 1968; Dem. precinct chairperson Cabin John-Bannockburn Estates, 1969-74; mem. Dem. polit. orgns. Recipient numerous award from assns., fedns., socs., Washington Star Cup for Civic Activity, 1974. Mem. Nat. Conf. of State Legislatures (state-fed. assembly, com. on transp. and communication), Nat. Orgn. Women Legislators, Women's Legis. Caucus, Am. Pub. Health Assn., Kappa Kappa Gamma. Office: Lowe House Office Bldg Annapolis MD 21401

TOURETZ, LILLIAN CAROLE CONRAD, psychotherapist; b. N.Y.C., Oct. 17, 1923; d. Philip and Rose Helen Stetsky; B.A., Hunter Coll., 1944; M.S.W., N.Y.U., 1968; m. Martin Conrad, June 3, 1944; children—David, Donna; m. 2d, Arthur Touretz, May 28, 1977. Asst. mgr. N.Y.C. Housing Authority, 1946-49; pres. Profl. Workers AFL-CIO, 1947-49; lectr., cons. in field, 1952-78; psychotherapist Pelham (N.Y.) Family Service, 1968-77; pvt. practice psychotherapy, Hartsdale, N.Y., 1977—; field instr. Adelphi U., 1972-77. Chmn. United Jewish Appeal; v.p. regional bd. B'nai B'rith, chpt. pres. B'nai B'rith, 1981-84, v.p. Council of Pres. Mem. Nat. Assn. Social Workers, Soc. Clin. Social Work Psychotherapists, O.R.T., Hunter Coll., N.Y.U. alumni assns. Democrat. Address: 55 Edgewood RD Hartsdale NY 10530

TOUS FERNOS, LUZ M., banker; b. San Juan, P.R., Apr. 23, 1944; d. Rafael Tous Cortes and Iris Fernos; B.B.A., U. P.R., 1965; M.B.A., Interam. U., 1976, also P.R. Sch. Banking, 1976; children—Rosa Iris, Lara Sofia. With Banco Popular, San Juan, 1965—, employee relations dir., 1969-85, v.p., asst. to pres., 1986—. Co-founder P.R. Indsl. Editors Assn., pres., 1970-72; dir. bank's blood program for ARC, 1972—, dir. bank's personnel donors program United Fund, 1981—. Recipient Outstanding Acad. Achievement award Interam. U., 1976. Mem. Am. Soc. Personnel Adminstrs. (accredited personnel mgr.), Am. Mgmt. Assn., Internat. Assn. Bus. Communicators, Labor Relations Practitioners Assn. Office: GPO Box 2708 San Juan PR 00936

TOUSIGNANT, DOROTHY WILTAMUTH (MRS. LEONARD A. TOUSIGNANT), management executive; b. East Moline, Ill., Jan. 7, 1920; d. Edward W. and Eleonora (Struss) Wiltamuth; B.S., U. Ill., 1941; M.E., State Tchrs. Coll., Fitchburg, Mass., 1951; postgrad. Am. U., 1959-61; m. Leonard A. Tousignant, June 11, 1949; 1 dau., Carmen Louise. Chief dietitian U.S. Army Hosps., CBI, 1942-45; served to capt.; food service tng. supr. Air Transport Command Hdqrs., Washington, 1946-47; cons. Office Surgeon Gen., Washington, 1948, Inflight Feeding Manual Air Quartermaster, 1948, Office Quartermaster Gen.; ednl. promotion, sales work Basic Vegetable Products, Inc., San Francisco, 1947-49; dietitian resident halls State Tchrs. Coll., Fitchburg, Mass., 1950; ednl. promotion work Dehydrated Food Industries, San Francisco, also Washington, 1950-53; instr. home econs. U. Md., College Park, 1954; nutritional cons., Washington, 1955; asst. prof. nutrition Cath. U. Am., Washington 1954-55; dist. mgr. United Food Mgmt. Services, Inc., Washington, 1955-64, v.p. Hosp. Dietetics, Inc. div. Interstate United Corp., Washington, 1964-67; pres. D.W. Tousignant & Assos., Inc., Washington, 1967—. Served with AUS, 1942-45. Decorated Bronze Star. Mem. Am. Home Econs. Assn. (pres. Washington 1958), Am. Dietetics Assn., Nat. Restaurant Assn., English-speaking Union. Contbr. articles to profl. jours. Research in dehydrated foods. Address: 3919 Watson Pl Washington DC 20016 also Bollingbrook Upperville VA 22176

TOVAR, ELIZABETH, economist; b. Caracas, Venezuela, Mar. 13, 1950; came to U.S., 1982; d. Silvestre A. Tovar and Elizabeth (Degwitz) T.; children—Cristina, Andres. Student Escuela Nacional Agrotecnica, 1980; D.Agronomy, Florence U., 1968. Dir., gen. mgr. Trassa S.A., Puerto La Cruz, Venezuela, 1978-82; pres. Trassa Internat., Miami, Fla., 1982—; v.p. 60 Magic Minutes, Miami, 1982—; v.p. Ultra Internat., Miami, 1984—; dir. Trans 28 Corp., Curacao, N.A. Founder Orquesta Nacional Juvenil de Venezuela, Caracas, 1967-68, Airclubs Barcelona, Zaraza, Caroni, Venezuela, 1979-80. Served with 1st Res. Force, Venezuelan Air Force, 1980-82. Named Person of Yr., Venezuelan Fedn. Gen. Aviation/Transport Minister, 1981. Mem. Internat. Bottled Water Assn., Nat. Assn. Female Execs., Coral Gables C. of C., Greater Miami C. of C. Roman Catholic. Avocations: pilot; sailing; reading; golf; tennis. Home: 10050 NW 4th Ln Miami FL 33172 Office: 60 Magic Minutes 6907 Red Rd Coral Gables FL 33143

TOVSEN, JOAN ESTHER, relocation and welcome service executive; b. Chgo., Dec. 3, 1950; d. Oliver Kermit and Josephine Esther (Daleo) T.; student Anchorage Community Coll., U. Alaska, 1969-72, night classes, 1973-78; m. Ralph Jones, May 1976 (div. 1977). Procurement and legal clk. Bur. Land Mgmt., Anchorage, 1973-78; pres. Anchorage Welcome Service, 1978—, pres., relocation cons. subs. Anchorage Relocation Center, 1980—, editor Anchorage Blue Book: A Guide to Public Services and Resources and The Anchorage Economic Compass: A Socio Economic Profile, 1980—; pres. Alaskan Hospitality and Relocation Services, 1984—; pub. Community Blue Book Map & Guide; Anchorage, Eagle River; pub. other maps; relocation cons.; guest speaker community groups. Municipality of Anchorage grantee, 1981-82. Mem. City Hostess Internat. Assn. (pres. 1982-83), Advt. Fedn. Alaska (sec. 1982, dir.), Anchorage C. of C. (co-chmn. hospitality com.), Anchorage Conv. and Visitors Bur. Mem. Worldwide Ch. of God. Home: PO Box 9-1975 Anchorage AK 99509 Office: 4141 Ingra St Anchorage AK 99503

TOWE, NANCY ELLEN CARPENTER, electronics manufacturing company executive; b. Kildav, Ky., July 28, 1941; d. John Henry and Nora Jenny (Snyder) Carpenter; m. Marshall Towe, Sr., Dec. 1, 1958 (div. 1981); children—Marshall, Jr., Michael Lee; m. John Edward Lescher, July 26, 1986. A.A.S. in Mktg. Mid-Mgmt., McHenry Community Coll., 1981; B.A. in Orgnl. Psychology, Nat. Coll. Edn., 1982. Switchboard operator Malibu Answering Service, Chgo., 1964-71; corr. Seaboard Life Ins. Co., Chgo., 1972-74; sales corr. Chgo. Miniature div. Gen Instrument Co., Chgo., 1975-77; product mgr. Oak Industries, Crystal Lake, Ill., 1978-82; pres., chief exec. officer Lamptronix Co., Ltd., Crystal Lake, 1982—; speaker in field. Den mother Chgo Area council Boy Scouts Am., 1970-75; active Pierce Sch. PTA, Chgo., 1973; mem. Lake in the Hills Property Owners Assn., 1978-82; founder Woodstock Ctr. for Women, Ill., 1982. Recipient Disting. Service scroll Ill. Congress PTA, 1973. Mem. Women in Electronics, Nat. Network of Women in Sales, Aerospace Lighting Inst., Crystal Lake C. of C. (bd. dirs.). Congregationalist. Home: 2412 N Orchard Beach McHenry IL 60050 Office: Lamptronix Co Ltd 85 N Williams Crystal Lake IL 60102

TOWER, JOAN PEABODY, composer, educator; b. New Rochelle, N.Y., Sept. 6, 1938. B.A., Bennington Coll., 1961; M.A., Columbia U., 1964, D.M.A., 1978. Pianist, Da Capo Chamber Players, 1969-84, compositions include: Amazon II (premiered by Hudson Valley Philharmonic), Sequoia (premiered by Am. Composers Orch.); Breakfast Rhythms, Black Topaz, Amazon (original scoring for quintet), Fantasy (cello concerto), Fantasy (clarinet and piano), Cello Concerto, Piano Concerto; works recorded; commns.: Contemporary Music Soc., Jerome Found., Mass. State Arts Council, Schubert Club St. Paul, Richard Stoltzman, St. Louis Symphony, Fromm Found., Nat. Endowment Arts; assoc. prof. Bard Coll., N.Y.C., 1972—; composer-in-residence St. Louis Symphony, 1985-87. Recipient N.Y. State Council for Arts award, 1980; award in music Am. Acad. and Inst. Arts and Letters, 1983; Guggenheim fellow, 1976; Nat. Endowment Arts fellow, 1974, 75, 80, 84, Koussevitzky Found. grantee, 1982.

TOWEY, MARIE ELIZABETH, nurse administrator, educator; b. Salem, Mass., Jan. 13, 1934; d. Daniel and Mary Catherine (Buckley) Linehan; m. Carroll Francis Towey, Aug. 24, 1957; children—Mary Ellen Towey Roth, Michael Carroll, Kevin James. Diploma Burdett Coll., 1952; R.N., Salem Hosp. Sch. Nursing, 1955; postgrad. Boston Coll. Sch. Nursing, 1956-61; B.S., Salem State Coll., 1975, M.Ed. in Health Counseling and Guidance, 1978. R.N., Mass., Va., D.C. Staff nurse Salem Hosp. and Mass. Gen. Hosp., 1955; nursing instr. Salem Hosp. (Mass.), 1955-59, med. nursing supr., 1960-61; staff nurse Twin Oaks Nursing Home, Danvers, Mass., 1961-71, Mt. Pleasant Hosp., Lynn, Mass., 1971; social worker, nurse NIMH Tng. Grant, Malden Ct. Clinic (Mass.), 1972-73; region IV coordinator North Shore Council on Alcoholism, Danvers, 1973-74; community mental health nurse Danvers-Salem Community Mental Health Resources Unit, Salem, 1974-78; nurse instr. Med. Aid Tng. Sch., Washington, 1978-79, Fairfax County Div. Continuing Edn. med. div., Woodson High Sch. (Va.), 1979-80; dir. nursing and health services ARC, Alexandria, 1980-81; dir. nursing services Med. Personnel Pool, Alexandria, 1981-82, adminstr., 1982-84; adminstr. ambulatory care ctr. Medic 24-Ltd., Baileys Crossroads, Va., 1984—; adminstr. Am. Med. Services, Springfield, Va., 1984-85; dir. nursing service Camelot Hall Nursing Facility, Arlington, Va., 1985-86, Clinton Convalescent Ctr., Md., 1986—; lectr. in field. Co-author planning grant in mental health and mental retardation, 1978. Area chmn. Burke Centre Conservancy (Va.), 1981—; mem. town meeting Danvers Town Govt., 1971-78; pres. Mass. Region IV Mental Health and Mental Retardation Adv. Council, 1977-78; sec., treas. Mass. Area Bd. Coalition, 1977-78; trustee Danvers State Hosp., 1977-82; community mental health resources devel. unit com. chmn. Danvers-Salem Area Mental Health Retardation Bd., 1973-78, pres., 1975-77; chmn. emergency med. services com. North Shore Council on Alcoholism, 1972-76; mem. adv. com. for adult edn. North Shore Region, 1974-75; mem. Danvers Task Force on Deinstitutionalization, 1975-76; bd. dirs. Archdiocesan Council Cath. Nurses, 1969-72. Recipient Merit and Appreciation certs. various agys., socs. and hosps. Mem. Am. Nurses Assn. (membership com. 1983—), Va. Nurses Assn. (hospitality com. 1983), Va. Assn. Home Health Agys. (chmn. region I legis., rep. 1984—), D.C. Nurses Assn. (conf. com. 1982), Health Adminstrs. Assn. of Nat. Capitol Area, Salem Hosp. Alumnae Assn. (past treas. and chmn. program 1956-58, 60-64), Alexandria C. of C. Republican. Club: Danvers Garden (pres., chmn. civic beautification 1972-77). Home: 10711 Oakenshaw Ct Burke VA 22015 Office: Clinton Convalescent Ctr 9211 Stuart Ln Clinton MD 20735

TOWNE, CLAUDIA CIACCO, data processor; b. N.Y.C., Apr. 6, 1945; d. Francesco and Angelina (Gaultieri) Ciacco; B.A., Hunter Coll., N.Y.C., 1966; m. Gene Leonard Towne, Dec. 23, 1967. Graphics systems analyst Mergenthaler Linotype Co., N.Y.C., 1966-68; systems analyst Service Bur. Corp., Honolulu, 1968-71; systems and programming mgr. Automatic Data Processing, Inc., N.Y.C., 1971-79; info. systems mgr. Berol USA, Danbury, 1979-84; corp. dir. mgmt. info. systems IPCO Corp., White Plains, N.Y., 1985—. Bd. dirs. Greater Danbury Area Jr. Achievement, 1980-83. Mem. Data Processing Mgmt. Assn.

TOWNE, DOROTHEA ALICE, III, chiropractor; b. Easton, Ill., Feb. 1, 1910; d. Elnathan and Fairy Alice (Downey) T. D.C., Cleveland Chiropractic Coll., Los Angeles, 1954, Ph.C., 1955, B.S., 1977; student U. Wash., 1928-30; B.A. magna cum laude, U. So. Calif., 1946. Indsl. relations dir. Standard Paper Box Corp., Los Angeles, 1943-54; assoc. dean acad. affairs Cleveland Chiropractic Coll., 1956-75, tchr., 1976-82, dir. clin. scis., 1972-78, emerita, 1981—; lectr. in field; numerous radio and TV appearances. Composer: (with L. Mayberry) The Presidents Parade. Contbr. to poetry anthologies. Recipient numerous awards including appreciation award San Francisco Bay Research Assn., C.S. Cleveland, Sr., award for outstanding service, 1984. Fellow Internat. Chiropractors Assn., Gamma Phi Beta, Psi Chi, Sigma Chi Psi. Address: E 508 Eaton Ave Spokane WA 99218

TOWNER, NAOMI WHITING, fiber artist, educator; b. Providence, May 8, 1940; d. Basil J. and Nellie (Woolhouse) Whiting; B.F.A. in Textile Design, R.I. Sch. Design, 1962; postgrad. (Textron fellow) Foreningen Handarbetets Vanner, Stockholm, 1962-63; M.F.A. in Textile Design, Rochester Inst. Tech., 1965. Teaching grad. asst. Sch. Am. Craftsmen, Rochester (N.Y.) Inst. Tech., 1963-65, instr. textile design, summer 1964; instr. Ill. State U., Normal, 1965-68, asst. prof., 1968-72, asso. prof., 1972-76, prof. art, 1976—; lectr. various art guilds and schs., 1967—; dir. workshops on weaving and textile design, 1964—; one person shows art fabrics include: Fox Valley Art League, St. Charles, Ill., 1968, Fine Arts Center Clinton (Ill.), 1971, Old Town Gallery, St. Charles, Mo., 1973, Lincoln Coll., Lincoln, Ill., 1974, Craft Alliance Gallery, St. Louis, 1974, Unitarian Ch., Bloomington, Ill., 1975, The Art-In, Riverton, Wyo., 1975; numerous group shows including: Mus. Contemporary Crafts Fabrics Internat. travelling exhibit, 1961-62, Security Trust Co., Rochester, N.Y., 1965, Ill. State U., Normal, 1965-68, 71, 73-84, Old Town Art Center, Chgo., 1967, Brooks Meml. Art Gallery, Memphis, 1967, Lakeview Center for Arts, Peoria, Ill., 1967-68, Ill. State Mus., 1968, Wis. State U., Oshkosh, 1969, Art Inst. Chgo., 1971, No. Ill. U., DeKalb, 1971, U. Mass. Art Gallery, Amherst, 1972, Evansville (Ind.) Mus. Arts and Scis., 1973, Eureka Coll. (Ill.), 1973, Mills Coll., Oakland, Calif., 1974, Columbus (Ga.) Mus. Arts and Crafts, 1974, Wright Art Center, Beloit (Wis.) Coll., 1975, Lowe Art Mus., U. Miami (Fla.) Goldstein Gallery, 1976, U. Minn., St. Paul, 1977, Paul Sargent Gallery, Eastern Ill. U., Charlestown, 1977, Boise (Idaho) State U., 1978, Cin. Art Mus., 1978, Kearney (Nebr.) State Coll. Art Gallery, 1979, Coll. Art Gallery, 1979, Rahr-West Mus., Manitowoc, Wis., 1979, Ill. State Mus., Springfield, 1979, No. Calif. Handweavers, Inc., San Mateo, 1979, Ill. Arts Council Gallery, Chgo., 1979, Tex. Tech. U., Lubbock, 1980, Caterpillar Internat., Peoria, Ill., 1980, No. Ill. U., Midwest Constructed Fibers, 1940-80, travelling exhibit, 1980-82, Loveland (Colo.) Mus., 1981, Ft. Collins (Colo.) Mus., 1981, Fiber Art Trends, 1982, Pyramid Arts Center, Rochester, N.Y., 1983, U. Wis.-Green Bay travelling exhibit, 1984-85, Ariel Gallery, Naperville, Ill., 1984, Premonitions, Nashville, 1985; represented in permanent collections Ill. State Mus., Springfield, Washington U., St. Louis, Eureka (Ill.) Coll., pvt. collections; juror exhbns. Recipient numerous awards including Silver Shuttle award U. Rochester, 1964, Owens-Corning Fiberglas competition, 1964, award of excellence Ill. Craftsmen's Council Invitational, 1967, Merit award Springfield Art Assn., 1976; grantee Handweavers Guild Am. and Ill. Arts Council, 1975-78. Mem. Am. Crafts Council, Midwest Weavers Conf., Am. Fedn. Tchrs., AFL-CIO, Handweavers Guild Am. (rep. 1973-77, bd. dirs. 1978-80), ACLU, Surface Design Assn. Contbr. articles on textile design and weaving to profl. publs.; editor Fiber News, 1975-85. Home: 610 E Taylor St Bloomington IL 61701 Office: Art Dept Illinois State Univ Normal IL 61761

TOWNSEND, ALAIR ANE, city official; b. Rochester, N.Y., Feb. 15, 1942; d. Harold Eugene and Dorothy (Sharpe) T.; B.S., Elmira Coll., 1962; M.S., U. Wis., 1964; postgrad. Columbia U., 1970-71; m. Robert Harris, Dec. 31, 1970. Asso. dir. budget priorities Com. on Budget, U.S. Ho. of Reps., Washington, 1975-79; dep. asst. sec. for budget HEW, Washington, 1979-80, asst. sec. for mgmt. and budget, 1980-81; dir. N.Y.C. Office Mgmt. and Budget, 1981-85; dep. mayor for fin. and econ. devel. City of N.Y., 1985—. Mem. Am. Public Welfare Assn., Am. Soc. Public Adminstrn., Mcpl. Fin. Officers Assn., Nat. Acad. Pub. Adminstrn., Fin. Women's Assn. N.Y.

TOWNSEND, JANE KALTENBACH, zoologist, educator; b. Chgo., Dec. 21, 1922; B.S., Beloit Coll., 1944; M.A., U. Wis., 1946; Ph.D., U. Iowa, 1950; m. 1966. Asst. in zoology U. Wis., 1944-47; asst., instr. U. Iowa, 1948-50; asst., project assoc. in pathology U. Wis., 1950-53; Am. Cancer Soc. research fellow Wenner-Grens Inst., Stockholm, 1953-56; asst. prof. zoology Northwestern U., 1956-58; asst. prof. to assoc. prof. zoology Mt. Holyoke Coll., South Hadley, Mass., 1958-70, prof., 1970—, chmn. biol. scis., 1980-86. Fellow AAAS (sec. sect. biol. sci. 1974-78); mem. Am. Assn. Anatomists, Am. Inst. Biol. Scis., Am. Soc. Zoologists, Sigma Xi. Office: Dept of Biology Mount Holyoke College South Hadley MA 01075

TOWNSEND, MARILYN MORAN, video production company executive; b. Seminole, Okla., Sept. 12, 1954; d. Melvin R. and Jasmine L. (Birchell) Moran; m. Bill Dean Townsend, July 31, 1976; children—Allison, Julie. B.A., Purdue U., 1976. Announcer Sta. KWSH, Seminole, Okla., 1973; news/weather anchorwoman Sta. WLFI TV, West Lafayette, Ind., 1973-76, Sta. WBBH, Ft. Myers, Fla., 1976-77, Sta. WKJG-TV Ft. Wayne, Ind., 1977-81; owner, mgr. Custom Video Corp., Ft. Wayne, 1981—; dir. Pvt. Industry Council Ft. Wayne, 1983—, vice chmn., 1986; chmn. Small Bus. Council, Ft. Wayne, 1983—; TV producer, series Heartbeat, 1982-84. Active Ft. Wayne Fine Arts Found., Parkview Hospice, 1978-80. Recipient 1st place award for news documentary AP, Ind., 1979, for med. documentary Ind. Med. Assn., 1978-79; Named Ind. Women Bus. Owners Advocate of Yr., SBA, 1985. Mem. Women in Communications (past pres.; numerous awards), Women Bus. Owners Assn. (founding mem.), Nat. Assn. Female Execs., Ft. Wayne C. of C. (dir. 1983—). Home: 5131 Binford Ln Fort Wayne IN 46804 Office: Custom Video Corp PO Box 11723 Fort Wayne IN 46860

TOWNSEND, PAMELA GWIN, business educator; b. Dallas, Aug. 24, 1945; d. William Thomas and Doris (Gwin) T.; B.A. with distinction in Econs. (Univ. scholar), U. Mo., Kansas City, 1977, M.B.A. (Outstanding Acctg. Grad.), 1980. Real estate sales assoc. KEW Realtors, Austin, Tex., 1967-70; staff mktg. asst. Lincoln Property Co., Dallas, 1970-72; dir. mktg. Commonwealth Devel. Co., Dallas, 1972-73; v.p. market analysis Fin. Corp. N.Am., Kansas City, 1973-75; asst. prof., dir. dept. acctg. Park Coll., Parkville, Mo., 1980—, on leave to U. Kans. Ph.D. program. Mem. Friends of Art, Nelson Gallery; Underwriter Folly Theater. C.P.A., Kans.; lic. real estate broker, Tex., Mo., Kans. Mem. Am. Inst. C.P.A.s (tax div.), Kans. Soc. C.P.A.s, Mo. Soc. C.P.A.s, Am. Acctg. Assn., Nat. Assn. Accts., Beta Alpha Psi Alumnae (pres. 1982), Beta Gamma Sigma, Phi Kappa Phi, Omicron Delta Epsilon, Alpha Chi Omega, Mortar Bd. Episcopalian. Columnist, Tax Tips, Platte County Gazette, 1981. Home: 2604 University Lawrence KS 66044 Office: Summerfield Hall U Kans Lawrence KS 66045

TOWNSEND, PHYLLIS FRENEA, lawyer; b. Temple, Tex., Mar. 30, 1955; d. Elder D. Townsend and Glenoria Lorraine (Butler) Banks. B.A., Wellesley Coll., 1977; J.D., Hastings Coll. Law, San Francisco, 1980. Bar: Calif. 1980. Asst. chief law clk. U.S. Atty.'s Office, San Francisco, 1979; spl. asst. Mervyn Dymakly for Congress, Los Angeles, 1980; legal cons. to city mgr. Compton (Calif.), 1980-81; sole practice, Inglewood, Calif., 1981—. Mem. central com. Los Angeles County Democratic party; del. and exec. bd. rep. Dem. State Party, Los Angeles. Mem. ABA, Los Angeles County Bar Assn., Black Women Lawyers Assn., S. Central Bar Assn., Wellesley Club Los Angeles. Mem. Ch. of Christ. Office: 111 N La Brea Ave Suite 614 Inglewood CA 90301

TOWNSEND, ROBERTA SUSAN, computer center administrator; b. Belzoni, Miss., Apr. 20, 1956; d. Robert Love and Ruby Carolyn (Oakes) T. B.S., U. So. Miss., 1977; M.S., Purdue U., 1979. Quality assurance specialist Gen. Electric Info. Services, Rockville, Md., 1979-81, sr. tech. services rep., Dallas, 1981-82; mgr. service ops. VMX, Inc., Richardson, Tex., 1982—. Mem. Women in Computing. Office: VMX Inc 1241 Columbia Dr Richardson TX 75081

TOWNSEND, RUTH MARIE, nurse; b. West Grove, Pa., Nov. 25, 1957; d. Robert Malcolm and Hazel Ruth (McDowell) T. B.S. in Biology, Geneva Coll., 1981; diploma in profl. nursing Union Meml. Hosp., 1981. Charge night nurse Wilmington Med. Ctr., Del., 1981-83; staff night nurse Burdette Tomlin Hosp., Cape May Court House, N.J., 1983-84; dir. nursing Rapp Health Facilities, Hayward, Calif., 1984-85; staff rehab. nurse Mills Hosp., San Mateo, Calif., 1985—; camp nurse O.P. Ch., French Creek, Pa., 1983. Vol. ARC, Brandywine Chpt., Pa., 1981-83. Active Orthodox Presbyn. Ch.; staff developer Oaktree Convalescent Hosp., Oakland, Calif., 1985. Mem. Calif. Assn. Nurses, Rehab. Nursing Assn. Republican. Avocations: knitting; handcrafts; vocalist; piano music. Home: 226 Carlton #2 San Bruno CA 94066 Office: Mills Hosp 2d St San Mateo CA 94401

TOWNSEND, TERRY, publisher; b. Camden, N.J., Dec. 14, 1920; d. Anthony and Rose DeMarco; B.A., Duke U., 1942; m. Paul Brorstrom Townsend, Dec. 8, 1961; 1 son, Kim. Public relations dir. North Shore Univ. Hosp., Manhasset, N.Y., 1955-68; pres. Theatre Soc. L.I., 1968-70; pres. Townsend Communications Bur., Ronkonkoma, N.Y., 1970—, L.I. Communicating Service, Ronkonkoma, 1977—; columnist, writer L.I./Bus., Ronkonkoma, 1970-75, pub., 1978—; pub. L.I. Bus. Newsweekly, 1978—; v.p. Parr Meadows Racetrack, Yaphank, N.Y., 1977. Assoc. trustee North Shore U. Hosp., 1968—; bd. govs. Adelphi U. Friends Fin. Edn., 1978-85; chmn. ann. archtl. awards competition N.Y. Inst. Tech., 1970-83; trustee Dowling Coll., 1984—, L.I. Fine Arts Mus., 1984-85; bd. dirs. Family Service Assn. Nassau County, 1982—. Recipient Media award 110 Center Bus. and Profl. Women, 1977; named First Lady of L.I., L.I. Public Relations Assn., 1973; Enterprise award Friends of Fin. Edn., 1981; L.I. Loves Bus. Showcase Salute, 1982; Community Service award N.Y. Diabetes Assn., 1983; Disting. Long Islander in Communications award L.I. United Epilepsy Assn., 1984. Mem. Public Relations Soc. Am. (pres. L.I. chpt. 1979). Office: 2150 Smithtown Ave Ronkonkoma NY 11779

TOWNSEND, VERLENE, educator; b. Starkville, Miss., Jan. 15, 1944; d. Adolphus Vick and Beulah (Childs) Skinner-Vick; m. Roy C. Townsend (div. May 1985); children—Nisha, Andre. B.S., Cameron U., Lawton, Okla., 1975; M.Ed. magna cum laude, Southwestern State U., Weatherford, Okla., 1982. Tchr., Lawton Schs., 1975-78, counselor, 1979-80, asst. prin., 1980. Sec. St. Mary Number 88 Club, Lawton, 1971-75. Mem. NEA (del. 1977, 84), Vallejo Edn. Assn., Lawton Edn. Assn. (com. mem. 1984-85), Phi Delta Kappa, Zeta Phi Beta (pres. 1984-85). Democrat. Baptist. Avocations: cooking; sewing; reading. Office: Penny Cook Elem Sch 3620 Fernwood Vallejo CA 94591

TOWNSON, MONICA JANE, economist; b. Docking, Eng.; d. Terence Rowland and Dorothy (Batchelor) Wagg; came to Can., 1956, naturalized, 1968; B.S., London Sch. Econs., 1954; children—Diana, David, Rachel, Michael. Econs. editor Fin. Times of Can., Montreal, Que., 1972-75; economist, writer Royal Bank Can., Montreal, 1975-77; v.p. Can. Adv. Council on Status of Women, Ottawa, Ont., 1977-78; sr. econ. adviser Centre Study Inflation and Productivity, Econ. Council Can., 1978-79; sr. adviser communications, 1979-81; pres. Monica Townson Assos. Inc., Ottawa, 1982—. Asst. treas., bd. dirs., exec. com. YWCA, Montreal, 1975-77; bd. dirs. Ottawa Women's Credit Union, 1978-80; mem. research com. Can. Research Inst. Advancement of Women, 1979-80; mem. Can. Human Rights Commn. Task Force on Equal Pay for Work of Equal Value, 1978; coordinator women and pensions workshops Nat. Pensions Conf., 1981. Mem. Ottawa Assn. Applied Econs. (exec. com. 1978-81), Can. Assn. Bus. Econs., London Sch. Econs. Soc. Producer TV programs on women in labour force. Author: The Canadian Woman's Guide To Money, 1982; regular contbr. to Report/Money of Ottawa Citizen, Your Money of Fin. Post, Take Thirty, CBC-TV; research on fully-paid parental leave, pensions for part-time workers, impact of recession on affirmative action programs. Home: 168 Sunnyside Ave Ottawa ON K1S 0R3 Canada

TOWZEY, PAMELA ANN, neurosurgery registered nurse; b. Butler, Pa., Oct. 23, 1958; d. Earl Master Jr. and Peggy Ann (Irwin) T. Assoc. Degree Nursing, Butler County Community Coll., 1982. Lic. practical nurse in charge Sunnyview Nursing Home, Butler, 1978-81; med./surg. nurse Armstrong County Hosp., Kittaning, Pa., 1982-83; neurosci., neurosurgery nurse Shadyside Hosp., Pitts., 1983-85; nurse Neurol. ICU, Norfolk Gen. Hosp., Va., 1985—; vol. med. cons. Spl. Olympics, Butler, 1984-85. Patentee teaching aid, postoperative report guidelines. Avocations: bicycling; reading; dancing. Home: 749 Maury Ct #8 Norfolk VA 23517 Office: Norfolk Gen Hosp 600 Gresham Dr Norfolk VA 23517

TOY, DONNA, biology educator, software consultant; b. Hawthorne, Calif., Mar. 30, 1957; d. Wong Wing and May Gill (Yee) Toy. B.A. cum laude, in Biology Calif. State U.-Dominguez Hill, 1979, M.A. in Biology, 1981. Mem. faculty Calif. State U.-Dominguez Hill, Carson, 1981—, El Camino Coll., Torrance, Calif., 1982—, Cerritos Coll., Calif., 1983—; coordinator Los Angeles Software Ctr., med. and ednl. software evaluator, cons., Commodore Internat., West Chester, Pa., 1983—. Editor lab. manual and instr.'s guide, 1983. Eva Murdock Tchr. scholar El Camino Coll., 1977. Mem. Orgn. Chinese Am. Women, United Chinese Am. League, Chinese Scientists and Engrs. So. Calif. (scholarship com. 1982—), Am. Pub. Health Assn., United Profs. Calif. Clubs: Culture (Carson, Calif.) (founder, pres.); Culture (Orange County). Home: 23505 Archibald Ave Carson CA 90745 Office: Calif State U Dominguez Hills Biology Dept 1000 E Victoria St Carson CA 90747

TOYSER, FRANCINE, home remodeling equipment company executive; b. Chgo., Feb. 13, 1946; d. Angelo Ralph and Gilda (Stellato) Trozzolo; m. Frank J. Amabile, Apr. 12, 1970 (div. Sept. 1977); 1 child, Laura Rose; m. Richard Walter Toyser, Aug. 26, 1978; step-children—Tammy J., Wendy J. A.A., Coll. of St. Francis, Joliet, Ill., 1967. Tech. writer GTE, Northlake, Ill., 1976-78; dir. services Lion-Hearted Remodeling, Inc., Elmhurst, Ill., 1978-85, corp. sec., 1978—; pres., chief exec. officer Pride Kitchens & Baths, Inc., Villa Park, Ill., 1985—. Mem. Nat. Assn. Remodeling Industry, Nat. Kitchen and Bath Assn., Nat. Assn. Female Execs. Republican. Roman Catholic. Avocation: sailing. Office: Pride Kitchens & Baths Inc 22 S Villa Ave Villa Park IL 60181

TRACEY, JOAN ABBOTT, telecommunications company executive, consultant; b. Orange, N.J., Aug. 29, 1935; d. James Thomas and Mary (Scalley) Abbott; m. Clifford James Tracey, May 10, 1958 (dec. Sept. 1969); children—Noreen, Michael, Daniel, Timothy, Gerard, Patricia. B.A. in Psychology, Caldwell Coll., 1978. Sales, Quigley's, West Caldwell, N.J., 1972-79; after care coordinator Turning Point, Verona, N.J., 1978-80; pres., cons. TLC Assocs., Caldwell, N.J., 1980—; employee asst. counselor ATT Communications, Piscataway, N.J., 1984—; mem. adv. com. N.J. div. Alcoholism, Trenton, N.J., 1983, Turning Point, 1980-81; mem. N.J. Task Force on Women and Alcohol, 1980—. Mem. county com. Essex County Democratic Party, Caldwell, 1976-85. Mem. Assn. Labor, Mgmt., Adminstrs. and Cons. on Alcoholism (pres. N.J. chpt. 1982-83). Democrat. Roman Catholic. Home: 204 Berger St Somerset NJ 08873 Office: ATT Communications 30 Knightsbridge Rd Piscataway NJ 08854

TRACHTENBERG, SELMA HARRIS, educator; b. Troy, N.Y., Nov. 7, 1924; d. Hyman and Rose (Kutler) Harris; m. David Trachtenberg, May 27, 1945; children—Carl Harris, Bruce Sheldon. B.E., State U. Coll., Oneonta, N.Y., 1945, postgrad. State U. Coll., New Paltz, N.Y., 1968-77. Jr. high sch. tchr., Dolgeville, N.Y., 1945-46, Ravena, N.Y., 1946-49; intermediate tchr. Acad. Ave. Sch., Middletown, N.Y., 1963-80. Pres., Sisterhood Temple Sinai, 1956-57; voters service chmn. LWV, 1956-58; sec. Middletown chpt. Hadassah, 1958-61, HMO chmn., Gainesville, Fla. chpt., 1980-83; pres. Sisterhood Temple B'nai Israel, Gainesville, 1982-83; v.p. U. Fla. Law Wives, 1980-81. Mem. Delta Kappa Gamma (membership chmn. Middletown chpt. 1972-78, coordinating com. Gainesville chpt. 1981-83). Club; Women's U. of Middletown (pres. 1967). Address: 3154 Via Poinciana 101 Lake Worth FL 33467

TRACY, FRANCES LEE, cleaning service exec., steel co. rep.; b. Denison, Tex., May 1, 1926; d. Raymond Evan and Mary Florence (Bock) Tilger; student U. Mexico de San Antonio, San Antonio, 1972, Acad. Real Estate, 1978; m. John L. Tracy, May 6, 1944; children—Thomas Lee, Cynthia A. Tracy Walter, Diane Tracy Richardson, Steven D. Personnel clk., Kelly AFB, San Antonio, 1943-44; sec. Corp. Engrs., Los Angeles, 1955; legal clk. Indsl. Accident Commn., Long Beach, Calif., 1956-58; interviewer Dist. Atty., Santa Ana, Calif., 1959-61; owner, mgr. Tracy Cleaning Service, San Antonio, 1961—; dealer Tri-Steel Structures, Inc., San Antonio, 1981—. Mem. Greater San Antonio Builders Assn., San Antonio Better Bus. Bur., S.W. Tex. Assn. Bldg. Contractors. Democrat. Roman Catholic. Home: PO Box 9251 San Antonio TX 78204 Office: 1011 S Main San Antonio TX 78204

TRACY, GRACE CAROL, nurse; b. Clark Field, Minn., Apr. 30, 1931; d. Clifford Harold and Gerda Emelia (Dregseth) Falmoe; student Lutheran Bible Inst., Mpls., 1950-51, Sioux Valley Hosp., 1952; m. Richard Paul Tracy, Mar. 1, 1958 (div. 1965); children—Robert Allan, Bemgecha Marie, Bonnie Kay. Mem. staff Canton Inwood Hosp., Canton, S.D., 1952-54; staff nurse St. Joseph Hosp., Mitchell, S.D., 1955-57, 58-60, Methodist Hosp., Mitchell, 1959-64; nurse, head nurse obstetrics St. Mary's Hosp., Rochester, Minn., 1965-71, nurse coordinator, 1971-82, surg. nurse, 1971-82; obstetrics staff nurse Waterman Meml. Hosp., Eustis, Fla., 1982—; distbr. Amway Corp., Rochester, 1979-82, Eustis, 1982—; Mary Kay beauty cons. Pres., Luther League. Mem. Christian Nurse Assn., Christian Nurses Fellowship (pres.). Lutheran. Office: Waterman Meml Hosp Eustis FL 32726

TRACY, LAURIE KATHLEEN, mortgage company executive; b. Watertown, S.D., Nov. 10, 1954; d. Charles Richard and Kathleen Rae (Quinn) Steinmetz; m. Michael L. Tracy, Aug. 14, 1972 (div. Apr. 1983); 1 child, Matthew L. Student pub. schs., Sioux Falls, S.D. Comml. banker Frontier Bank, Denver, 1974-76; asst. v.p. Reliance Mortgage, Englewood, Colo., 1976-82; v.p. Reliance Equities, Englewood, 1982—, also dir. Mem. Dam West-Archtl. Control, Aurora, Colo., 1983—; chmn. Dam West Homeowners-Welcoming, Aurora, 1984—; active Gourmet club, Aurora. Mem. Homebuilders Assn. of Met Denver, (sales and mktg. council 1984-86), Am. Mgmt. Assn., Assn. Profl. Mortgage Women, Million A Month Club (assoc.). Republican. Club: Pinery Country (Parker, Colo.). Home: 7885 Windfont Packer CO 80131 Office: Reliance Equities Inc 84 Inverness Circle E Englewood CO 80112

TRACY, MARY ELIZABETH, librarian; b. Joliet, Ill., Aug. 18, 1922; d. Charles Joseph and Catherine (Fay) Tracy; B.A. cum laude, Coll. St. Francis, 1944; M.A. in L.S., Rosary Coll., River Forest, Ill., 1958. Tchr., Joliet grade schs., 1944-52, 54-61, Am. schs., Bremerhaven, Frankfurt, Ger., 1952-54; librarian Joliet Twp. Central High Sch., 1961—, dist. dir., 1972-73; instr. library tech. Joliet Jr. Coll., 1973—. Pres., Joliet Jr. Catholic Woman's League, 1950-51. Mem. Am., Ill. library assns., Library and Media Assn. Will County (pres. 1976), Ill. Assn. Media in Edn., Ill. Assn. Ednl. Communication and Tech., Chgo. Suburban Audiovisual Roundtable, Alumnae Assn. Coll. St. Francis (sec. 1946-48, v.p. 1957-59, bd. advisers 1965-67, Dist. 204 archives com. 1975—, chmn. 1980—). Home: 1010 Glenwood Ave Joliet IL 60435 Office: 201 E Jefferson St Joliet IL 60432

TRADEWELL-VEGA, CAREY, mental health, alcohol and drug educator; b. Antigo, Wis., June 4, 1948; d. James Bennett and Rosemary (Wall) Tradewell; m. William H. Frackelton, Jan. 27, 1968 (div. 1974); children—Bill, Damion Clayton; m. Daniel Paul Vega, Feb. 15, 1986. B.S.W., U. Wis.-Milw., 1974, postgrad. in social work, 1978—. Cert. alcohol and other drug abuse counselor. Social worker Planned Parenthood, Milw., 1974-77, coordinator social services, 1977-82; family program coordinator Kettle Moraine Hosp., Oconomowoc, Wis., 1982-84, dir. tng. and edn., 1984—; therapist Catalyst Counseling, Milw., part-time 1984—; field instr. U. Wis.-Milw., 1982—; field advisor, bd. dirs. U. Wis.-Whitewater, 1985—; cons. woman and family psychotherapy services, Waukesha, Wis., 1986—; mem. subcom. on sexual abuse and assault Wis. Ho. of Reps., 1980-81. Vol. Parents Anonymous, Milw., 1977-82; vol. speaker Alcoholics Anonymous and Alanon, Milw., Waukesha, 1982—; vol. cons. Mental Health Clinic, Milw., 1977—. Mem. Am. Assn. for Marriage and Family Therapy, Nat. Assn. Social Workers, Wis. Family Relations Council, Wis. Alcohol and Other Drug Abuse Council. Democrat. Mem. United Ch. of Christ. Avocations: travel; reading; family activities. Home: 4313 N Maryland Ave Shorewood WI 53211 Office: Kettle Moraine Hospital 4839 N Hewitts Point Rd Oconomowoc WI 53086

TRAEGER, BARBARA SHIELDS, public relations executive; b. Pitts., Oct. 19, 1932; d. Marshall Charles and Margaret Helen (Ward) Shields; B.A., Ripon Coll., 1954; cert. mgmt. U. Chgo., 1965; cert. mktg. Northwestern U., 1978; m. John E. Traeger, Apr. 30, 1971; children—Cynthia Langston, Charles R. Carner, Jr., Henry M. Carner (by previous marriage). Dir. public relations Chgo. unit Am. Cancer Soc., 1964-65; public relations asso., exec. sec. Am. Soc. Hosp. Public Relations of Am. Hosp. Assn., Chgo., 1966-68; dir. public relations U. Chgo. Hosps., 1968-72, Evanston Hosp., Ill., 1972-84; asst. v.p. pub. relations Evanston Hosp. Corp., 1985—. Recipient 45 profl. awards. Mem. Am. Soc. Hosp. Pub. Relations and mktg., Internat. Assn. Bus. Communications, Pub. Relations So. Am. Clubs: Publicity, Suburban Press. Office: 1301 Central St Evanston IL 60201

TRAHAN, MARGARET ANN, manufacturing company executive; b. Houston, Nov. 15, 1935; d. Joseph A. and Mary Lou (Guillory) Whalen; m. Leonard A. Trahan, Apr. 27, 1957; children—Monica Trahan Knighton, Leonard A., Steven G., Cheryl. Student Houston Community Coll., 1968-70. Cert. quality engr. Electronic assembler Schlumberger Well Service, Houston, 1966-70, electronic technician, 1970-77, mfg. supr., 1977-80, quality control supr., 1980—; chmn. bd. Schlumberger Employees Credit Union, 1980-81. Mem. Am. Soc. for Quality Control. Office: Schlumberger Well Services 5000 Gulf Freeway Houston TX 77210

TRAHAN, MARGARET FRITCHEY, owner wholesale food distributing company; b. Harrisburg, Pa., May 3, 1934; d. John Augustus and Dorotha Amy (Warren) Fritchey; m. Henry Voltaire Trahan, Jr., Sept. 29, 1956; children—Henry Voltaire III, Randall Scott. B.S. in Bus. Edn., Cedar Crest Coll., 1955; B.S. in Edn., Fla. Atlantic U., 1971. Corr. course writer Acad. Health Scis., U.S. Army, San Antonio, 1976-77, team chief, individual analysis and design. br., 1977-80, dep. chief individual tng. analysis and design br., 1980-81; satellite TV program dir. U.S. Army Health Services Command, San Antonio, 1981-84; chief individual tng. in forces bd. Acad. of Health Scis., U.S. Army, San Antonio, 1984-85; owner, operator Circle T Farms, San Antonio, 1985—. Vol. worker Army Community Services, 1966-67, ARC, 1966-74; pres. sr. state officer club, sr. 1st v.p. Tex. soc. Children of the Am. Revolution, 1979-81, sr. nat. v.p. south central region, 1978-80, sr. nat. historian, nat. conv. vice chmn., 1980-82, hon. sr. nat. v.p. nat. soc., 1982-85. Recipient Outstanding Performance award Acad. of Health Scis. and Sec. of Army, 1958, 79, 80; commendation cert. ARC, 1967, U.S. Army Community Services, 1974, Nat. Soc. Children Am. Revolution, 1980; Exceptional Performance award U.S. Army Health Services Command and Acad. of Health Scis., 1981, 83, 84; Comdr.'s award for civilian service Dept. Army, 1985. Mem. AAUW, Fed. Ednl. Tech. Assn., Assn. Edn. and Communication Tech., Armed Forces Pub. Affairs Council, Nat. Assn. Female Execs., Am. Mgmt. Assn., DAR (rec. sec. Alamo chpt. 1975-76). Republican. Lutheran. Club: U.S. Army Theater Support Communications Officers Wives (pres. 1968-69). Lodge: Ladies of the Shrine. Avocations: tennis; seashells; swimming; knitting; latchhook. Home: 9322 Oak Downs San Antonio TX 78230 also PO Box 2576 Hilton Sea Island Tower South Padre Island TX 78597 Office: Circle T Farms 9322 Oak Downs San Antonio TX 78230

TRAINOR, AGNES MARIE, aviation economist; b. Washington, Nov. 14; d. William Ernest and Agnes Rose (Drew) T.; B.A., Trinity Coll., Washington, 1973. With FAA, U.S. Dept. Transp., Washington, 1973-75, CAB, Washington, 1975-82; sr. air transport ofcl. Internat. Civil Aviation Orgn., Montreal, Que., Can., 1982-86, U.S. Dept. Transp., 1986—; expert witness on air carrier selection and airline mergers; pvt. pilot. asso. transp. research bd. Nat. Acad. Scis. Mem. Internat. Aviation Club, Aero Club Internat. (pres. 1983-86). Roman Catholic. Home: 2904 Upton St NW Washington DC 20008 Office: 400 7th St SW Washington DC 20590

TRAINOR, LILLIAN (MIDGE), elections official; b. Norma, N.J., Oct. 30, 1936; d. Loenell Lesley and Lillie Ara (Kenyon) Barber; m. Leroy Jarboe, July 17, 1952 (div. 1956); 1 child, Michael Lesley; m. Arthur James Trainor, Mar. 9, 1959; children—Arthur, Lynn Marie. Student pub. schs., Pleasantville, N.J. Chmn. Burlington County Bd. Elections, Mount Holly, N.J., 1978-81, commr. of registration, 1981-83, chmn., 1983—. Vice chmn. Burlington County Democratic County Com., 1977—, exec. bd., 1977—; chmn. Bd. County Convassers, Mount Holly, 1978—; del. Dem. Nat. Conv., 1984; chmn. Southampton Twp. Dem. County Com., 1976-79; v.p. Southeastern Dem. Coalition, 1977—; campaign mgr. Florio for Gov., N.J., 1980; campaign mgr. Carter for Pres., Burlington County Area, 1980. Served with WAC, 1955-57. Mem. N.J. State Assn. Election Ofcls. Clubs: VFW Aux., Big Six (pres. 1973-79). Avocations: accordian; piano; reading. Home: 20 Pleasant St Vincentown NJ 08088 Office: Bd Elections 49 Rancocas Rd Mount Holly NJ 08060

TRAINOR, VIRGINIA CECILE, university center administrator; b. Brighton, Mass., Jan. 25, 1952; d. Philip Montague and Virginia Marie (Flynn) Trainor. B.S. in Bus. Adminstrn., Boston U., 1986. Mgr. cold type dept. Citizen Groups Publs., Brookline, Mass., 1968-74; adminstrv. asst. Harvard Med. Sch., Boston, 1974-78, adminstrv. asst. Boston U. Sch. Medicine, Boston, 1978-80, mgr. mktg., 1980. Contbr. articles to various newspapers. Mem. Newmarket Bus. Assn. (mem. membership com. 1983—), Am. Mktg. Assn. (mem. organizing and membership coms. health services group Boston chpt.), South End Bus. Assn. (bd. dirs.). Democrat. Roman Catholic. Advocations: Art; Gardening. Home: 46 Jamaica Rd Brookline MA 02146

TRAMBLE, RENEE, accounting firm executive; b. Cleve., June 30, 1954; d. William Pedro and Louise Ellen (McGugan) T.; B.B.A., Kent State U., 1976; M.B.A., Cleve. State U., 1981; postgrad. Cleve. Marshall Coll. Law. Fin. instns. examiner State of Ohio Div. Banks, Columbus, 1976-78; acct. Watson, Rice & Co., Cleve., 1978—, mgr. acctg. staff, 1980—, ptnr., 1985—. Treas. bd. dirs. Am. Sickle Cell Anemia Soc., 1980-82; mem. allocations panel United Way Services, 1980-82, mem. audit com., 1980-82; mem. Citizens League of Greater Cleve., 1979-82; treas. bd. Lee Rd. Bapt. Ch., 1984. C.P.A. Mem. Am. Inst. C.P.A.s, Ohio Soc. Public Accts., Nat. Assn. Black Accts. Home: 3826 Silsby Rd University Heights OH 44118 Office: Watson Rice & Co Suite 1200 Citizens Federal Tower Cleveland OH 44114

TRAMMELL, CAROLYN JANE, aerospace company executive, consultant; b. Seattle, Aug. 26, 1945; d. Robert Hugo and Edna Margurite (Williams) Klamer; m. Daniel Stewart Trammell, Nov. 25, 1966 (div. Dec. 1973); children—Michelle Dyan, Marcee Lynn. A.A., Yuba Coll., Marysville, Calif., 1966; tchr.'s cert. U. Calif.-Berkeley, 1976; postgrad. U. San Francisco, 1978. Vocat. tchr.'s engring. credential, Calif. Draftsman Lockheed Missiles and Space Co., Sunnyvale, Calif., 1966-70, 74-76, mgmt. trainee, 1976-78, subcontract coordinator, 1978-86, procurement specialist, 1986—; instr. San Jose and Foothill Coll. dists., 1974-85; travel agt. Mission Park, Santa Clara, Calif., 1982—; cons., co-founder LMSC Women's Seminars, 1975—. Recipient Pres.'s award Lockheed Mgmt. Assn., 1984, 85. Mem. Nat. Mgmt. Assn. (exec. bd. 1975-86, exec. v.p. 1983-84), Nat. Contract Mgmt. Assn. (exec. v.p. 1986-87). Republican. Episcopalian. Avocations: travel; photography. Home: 6105 Castleknoll San Jose CA 95129 Office: Lockheed Missiles and Space Co 1111 Lockheed Way Sunnyvale CA

TRAN, NGOC-BICH, economist, electric utility planner; b. Gia-Dinh, Vietnam, Aug. 10, 1946; came to U.S., 1973, naturalized, 1981; d. Hoan Van and Loi Thi (Do) T.; m. Kho Huu Nguyen, June 4, 1983; 1 child, Carling Tran Nguyen. B.Comm., U. Canterbury, Christchurch, N.Z., 1969, M.Comm., 1970; M.A. in Econs., SUNY-Binghamton, 1975, Ph.D. in Econs., 1978. Mgmt. trainee Res. Bank N.Z., Wellington, 1970; fin. analyst Esso Eastern Inc., Saigon, Vietnam, 1970-72; customer service rep. Citibank (N.Y.), Saigon, 1972-73; assoc. sr. research economist Gen. Motors Research Labs., Warren, Mich., 1976-80, chmn. inter-departmental seminar program, 1978; project dir. in mktg. Gen. Electric Co., Bridgeport, Conn., 1980-82; sr. staff planner Houston Lighting & Power Co., 1982—; instr. Wayne State U., Detroit, 1978; adj. asst. prof. U. Mich.-Dearborn, 1979-80. N.Z. Govt. Colombo Plan scholar U. Canterbury, 1966-69; N.Z. Govt. Colombo Plan tng. grantee, 1970; Fulbright-Hayes grantee, 1973-76. Mem. Nat. Assn. Bus. Economists, Internat. Energy Economist Assn., SUNY-Binghamton Alumni Assn., Fulbright-Hayes Alumni Assn., Omicron Delta Epsilon. Avocations: reading; aerobics exercise. Office: Houston Lighting & Power Co 611 Walker St Houston TX 77001

TRANELLI, ANNE, principal, nun; b. Villa Santo Stefano, Fosinone, Italy, Feb. 24, 1929; d. Luigi F. and Antonia (Iorio) Tranelli. Cert. Spanish tchr., sch. adminstr. and supr. Joined Sisters of St. Joseph of Carondelet. Tchr., St. Brigid's Sch., Watervliet, N.Y., 1957-60, St. Mary's Inst., Amsterdam, N.Y., 1960-65; tchr. Spanish, Cardinal McCloskey High Sch., Albany, N.Y., 1966-69; tchr. Spanish, Bishop Scully High Sch., Amsterdam, 1969-75, prin., 1978—, drama dir., 1969-75; instr. elem. Spanish Coll. St. Rose, Albany, N.Y., 1976, bd. trustees, 1985—; dir. Cath. Youth Orgn. of Amsterdam, 1974—; modern language coordinator Diocese of Albany, 1967-70. Bd. dirs. Catholic Family Services, Amsterdam, 1975-76, Peace and Justice Commn. Diocese of Albany, 1984—. Mem. Cath. Sch. Adminstrs. Assn. N.Y. State (exec. bd. 1981—), Alpha Mu Gamma. Democrat. Avocations: travel, music, hiking, oil painting. Home: Bishop Scully Convent Upper Church St Amsterdam NY 12010 Office: Bishop Scully High Sch Upper Church St Amsterdam NY 12010

TRANSOU, LYNDA LEW, advertising art administrator; b. Atlanta, Dec. 11, 1949; d. Lewis Cole Transou and Ann Lynette (Taylor) Putnam. B.F.A. cum laude, U. Tex.-Austin, 1971. Art dir., The Pitluk Group, San Antonio, 1971, Campbell, McQuien & Lawson, Dallas, 1973-74, Bozell & Jacobs, Dallas, 1974-75; art dir., ptnr. The Assocs., Dallas, 1974-77; art dir. Belo Broadcasting, Dallas, 1977-80; creative dir., v.p. Allday & Assocs., Dallas, 1980-85; owner Lynda Transou Advt. & Design, 1986—. Recipient Merit award N.Y. Art Dirs. Show, 1980; Gold award Dallas Ad League, 1980, Silver award, 1980, Bronze award, 1981, 82, Merit awards, 1978-86; Merit award Broadcast Designers Assn., 1980, 82; Gold award Tex. Pub. Relations Assn., 1982, 85; Gold award N.Y. One Show, 1982, others. Mem. Dallas Soc. Visual Communications (Bronze award 1980, Merit awards, 1978-86), Delta Gamma (historian 1969-70).

TRASK, BETTY M., journalist; b. Laconia, N.H., Jan. 28, 1928; d. James Edwin and Clemency (Anstey) Burbank; m. Allison Keith Trask, June 28, 1947; children—Frank Edwin, Michael Thomas, Rory Scott, Allison Keith, Jr. Women's editor Laconia Evening Citizen, 1966-70, county editor, 1970—; mem. adv. bd. N.Y. Vocat.-Tech. Coll., Laconia, 1972-78; treas. N.H. Commn. on Status of Women, Concord, 1974-76; mem. state adv. bd. N.H. Vocat.-Tech. Coll. and Inst., Concord, 1981-84. Bd. dirs. Laconia Salvation Army, 1973—, Belknap Easter Seals, 1980—; trustee Gilford Village Knolls, Inc., N.H., 1985—; mem. task force on alcohol and drug abuse N.H. Gov.'s Commn. on Criminal Adminstrn. and Juvenile Delinquency, 1969-71. Recipient Recognition award Laconia Lions Club, 1977, Lakes Region Citizenship award N.H. Bocat. Tech. Coll., 1978. Mem. New Eng. Women's Press Assn. Republican. Avocations: travel, photography. Home: RFD 6 Box 408 Laconia NH 03246 Office: Evening Citizen 171 Fair St Laconia NH 03247

TRATNIK, FRANCES ELIZABETH, press clipping bureau executive; b. Nashville, Nov. 18, 1924; d. Louis Willson and Ella Lucille (Johnson) Royster; m. Joseph Steven Tratnik, Oct. 3, 1941 (dec. June 1947); children—Joseph Steven, Louis Henry. Supr., Ohio News Bur., Cleve., 1947-79, pres., 1979—. Mem. Fedn. Internat. Press Services, Conf. Press Services (pres. 1958—), Mich. Press Services (pres. 1979—), Fedn. Press Clipping Burs., N. Am. Press Clipping Burs. (pres. 1983—), Mich. Press Club (pres. 1979). Republican. Baptist. Office: Ohio News Bur Inc 1900 Euclid Ave Cleveland OH 44115

TRAUNFELD, LINDA BARBARA, temporary employment agency executive; b. Clewiston, Fla., Dec. 4, 1942; d. Samuel Schneider and Edna Helen (Koster) Schneider Brown; m. Joel Chanin, Mar. 21, 1964 (div. Dec. 1974); children—Lisa, Susan, Debra; m. Milton Robert Traunfeld, Dec. 23, 1976; children—Faith, Dana. A.A.S., Fashion Inst. Tech., 1963. Adminstrv. asst. to v.p. Leviton Mfg., Little Neck, N.Y., 1977-79; adminstrv. asst. to pres. Olsten Corp., Westbury, N.Y., 1979-81; field mgr. Dunhill Personnel, Carle Place, N.Y., 1981-83; dist. mgr. Kelly Services, N.Y.C., 1983—. Mem. adv. bd. Kingsborough Community Coll., Bklyn., 1984—; co-chairperson adv. bd. N.Y.C. Partnership/Bd. Edn.-Summer Tchrs. Program, 1985-86. Mem. Am. Soc. Personnel Adminstrs., N.Y. Assn. Temporary Services (legis. com.). Office: Kelly Services 420 Lexington Ave New York NY 10017

TRAURIG, LEONA, researcher, therapist in orthomolecular medicine; b. Chgo., Aug. 14, 1934; d. Daniel and Sonia (Lemson) Leviton; m. Walter Bernard Traurig, Nov. 6, 1955; children—Marcia, William, Donald. R.N., Jackson Meml. Hosp., Miami, Fla., 1955. Asst. charge nurse labor and delivery Jackson Meml. Hosp., 1955-56; dir. employee health services Larkin Gen. Hosp., Miami, 1972-73; med. examiner, Miami, 1973-82; pres. Miami Med. Assocs., 1982—; cons. Life Extension Found., Hollywood, Fla., 1982—; organizer-vol. Sch. Systems Clinics, Dade County, Fla., 1970-79; cons. Girl Scouts Am., 1968-74, Home for Aged, 1979— (both Miami). Contbr. articles to profl. jours. Vol. examiner Am. Cancer Soc., Miami, 1982—; vol. counselor health fairs Am. Heart Assn., Miami, 1980-83; vol. coordinator summer camp clinics clinics Girl Scouts U.S.A., Miami, 1971-73. Recipient Best All Round Nurse award Alumnae Assn. Jackson Meml. Hosp., 1955; Appreciation award Dade County (Fla.) Sch. Bd., 1979. Mem. Am. Heart Assn., Am. Nurses Assn., Nat. Bus.-Profl. Assn., Ctr. Chinese Medicine, Life Extension Found. Democrat. Jewish. Address: 13149 SW 91 Ct Miami FL 33176

TRAVAGLINI, BARBARA CARLSON (MRS. ALFONSO FREDERICK TRAVAGLINI), steel co. exec.; b. Easton, Pa., Nov. 4, 1925; d. Gunard Oscar and Margaret Bailey (Berry) Carlson; Bryn Mawr Coll., 1943-44, Moore Coll. Art, 1944-48; m. Alfonso Frederick Travaglini, June 15, 1946; children—Gunard Carlson, Frederick Carlson, Mark Carlson. Vice chmn., sec., dir. G.O. Carlson, Inc., Thorndale, Pa., 1956—. Pres. Coatesville Hosp. Aux., 1967-72, 1st v.p., 1972—; sec. Chester County Airport Authority. Exec. dir., sec., treas. Gunard Berry Carlson Meml. Found.; trustee Saint Francis Coll., Lafayette Coll. Republican. Roman Catholic. Author: The Kelly Green Cow, 1949; Henry Hippo, 1972; columnist A Woman's Pen and As I See It. Home: 4000 Hazelwood Ave Thorndale PA 19372 Office: G O Carlson Inc Thorndale PA 19372

TRAVER, DOROTHY ALICE, librarian; b. Highmore, S.D., Sept. 20, 1909; d. Eugene Clifton and Mabel Vivian (Miller) T. B.A., Pomona Coll., 1931; cert. Sch. Librarianship, U. Calif.-Berkeley, 1933. Cert. county librarian, Calif. Librarian, sec. Elsinore Unigh High Sch., Lake Elsinore, Calif., 1933-36; with sch. dept. with San Bernardino County Library, Calif., 1936-50, head br. dept., 1950-57, county librarian, 1957-74; ret., 1974. Author: (with Art Miller) Growing Oranges, 1958; (with Lucy Moore and Maxine Kahuda) History of the San Bernardino County Free Library, 1914-64, sole author, 1964-75. Pres. LWV, San Bernardino, 1983-85; chmn. Katharine K. Murray Meml. Scholarship Fund, 1965—, Inland Counties Health Systems Agy., San Bernardino Task Force, 1982—. Mem. ALA, Calif. Library Assn., San Bernardino County Ret. Employees Assn. (pres. 1979-80), Audubon Soc. Democrat. Presbyterian. Clubs: Sierra, Friends of San Bernardino Pub. Library. Avocations: traveling; gardening; reading. Home: 3052 Genevieve St San Bernardino CA 92405

TRAVERS, TRACYANNE, electrical products distributor; b. Bklyn., Oct. 10, 1960; d. John Raymond and Jane Robertshaw (Hirst) T. B.S., Coll. of S.I., 1983. With contract sales dept. East Coast Lighting, Inc., S.I., N.Y., 1983-85; customer rep., inventory mgr. Wiedenbach-Brown, Inc., N.Y.C., 1985—. Avocation: needlepoint. Home: 473 Doane Ave Staten Island NY 10308 Office: Widenbach-Brown Inc 435 Hudson St New York NY 10014

TRAVIESO, CHARLOTTE B., computer systems analyst; b. New Orleans, Sept. 11, 1942; d. Harry Frederick and Magda Helen (Janssen) Barkerding; m. John Joseph Travieso, May 27, 1977 (div. 1984); m. Raymond Henry Marcotte, Apr. 23, 1966 (div. 1972). B.S. in Math., Newcomb Coll., 1964; student Sorbonne, Paris, 1962-63; M.S. with distinction, Am. U., 1984. Mathematician Nat. Security, Washington, 1964-68; mem. tech. staff Lambda Corp., Washington, 1968-71; sr. assoc. Hendrickson Corp., Washington, 1971-80; supr. computer systems analyst USDA, Washington, 1980—; chmn. Resource Exchange Program, Washington, 1983—; pres. Mgmt. Transformation Inc., 1986—. Pres. Tulane Alumni Council, Washington, 1978-85. Mem. Assn. Computing Machinery, Nat. Assn. Female Execs., Assn. Women in Computing, Tulane U. Alumni Assn. (mem.-at-large bd. dirs. 1986—). Clubs: Potomac Valley Sr. Track (Washington). Office: USDA Extension Service 14th and Independence Ave SW Room 3331 Washington DC 20250

TRAVIS, ANN, veterinarian; b. Orange, Calif., Apr. 15, 1943; d. Coleman and Dorothy (Borchert) T. B.S., U. Calif.-Davis, 1966, D.V.M., 1968. Veterinarian, McBride Animal Hosp., Pasadena, Calif., 1966-69, Miraloma Veterinary Hosp., Anaheim, Calif., 1969-70, Dr. Brown Equine Practice, Norco, Calif., 1970-75, Dept. Health, Downey, Calif., 1975-76, Animal Birth Control, Chino, Calif., 1975-83, Humane Soc. San Bernardino (Calif.), 1983-84, 85—, Arlanza Pet Hosp., Riverside, Calif., 1984-85. Recipient Large Animal award Merck Co., 1968. Mem So. Calif. Vet. Med. Assn. (pres. pub. health 1975), Calif. Veterinary Med. Assn., AVMA, Am. Assn. Equine Practitioners. Democrat. Roman Catholic. Club: Calif. Dressage Soc. Home: 3812 California Ave Norco CA 91760 Office: Humane Soc San Bernadino 763 W Highland St San Bernadino CA

TRAVIS, JOAN FAYE SCHILLER, lawyer; b. Chgo., Mar. 15, 1939; d. Jack and Betty (From) Schiller; Ph.B. in Psychology, Northwestern U., 1969; J.D., John Marshall Law Sch., Chgo., 1981; m. Maurice Travis, May 31, 1959; children—Jeffrey Bernard, Leonard Edwin, Elizabeth Sue. Elem. sch. tchr., Chgo., 1970-72; admitted to Ill. bar, 1981, U.S. Ct. Appeals, 1981, U.S. Dist. Ct. bar, 1981, U.S. Ct. Mil. Appeals, 1982, Wis. bar, 1986; sole gen. practice, Park Ridge, Ill.; freelance writer, 1971-77; speaker, lectr. in field. Chmn. Consumer Affairs Commn., Skokie, Ill.; Niles Twp. collector. Mem. ABA, Ill. Bar Assn., Chgo. Bar Assn., Def. of Prisoners Com., N.W. Suburban Bar Assn. (parliamentarian), North Suburban Bar Assn. (2d v.p.), Women's Bar Assn., Nat. Acad. TV Arts and Scis., Delta Theta Phi. Jewish. Author numerous articles in field. Office: 1550 N Northwest Hwy Suite 308 Park Ridge IL 60068

TRAVIS, LYNN MICHELLE, lawyer; b. Cedar Falls, Iowa, July 18, 1957; d. Ray Martin and Judith Ann (Huyck) T. A.A., Ill. Central Coll., 1977; B.A., U. Ill., 1979; J.D., Washington U., St. Louis, 1982. Bar: Mo. 1982, Ill. 1983, U.S. Dist. Ct. (central dist.) Ill. 1984. Assoc. firm Clem & Triggs, P.C., Peoria, Ill., 1982—. Notes and comments editor Urban Law Ann., 1981. Campaign worker Com. to Re-Elect H. Woods, 1980. James scholar U. Ill., 1977. Mem. ABA, Ill. Bar Assn., Mo. Bar Assn., Peoria County Bar Assn., Phi Alpha Theta, Phi Delta Phi, Phi Theta Kappa. Lutheran. Home: 50-V Georgetown Rd Washington IL 61571 Office: Clem & Triggs PC 300 NE Perry Ave Peoria IL 61603

TRAVIS, SHARON KAY, credit corp. exec.; b. Buchanan, Mich., Mar. 2, 1946; d. Galen A. and Dorothy J. (Harroff) Weaver; A.A., Lake Mich. Coll., 1965; student Marywood Coll., 1978-81. Personnel adminstr. Clark Equipment Co., Buchanan, 1974, personnel rep., 1975; employee relations supr. Clark Equipment Credit Corp., Buchanan, 1976-79, employee relations mgr., 1979—, v.p., human resources mgr., 1980-85. Past bd. dirs., treas., chmn. fin. com. Unity Hosp. Named Woman of Year, YWCA, 1981. Mem. Internat. Assn. Bus. Communicators, Am. Soc. Personnel Adminstrn., Adminstrv. Mgmt. Soc.

TRAYLING, KAREN J(EANNETTE) (HAHLBECK), librarian; b. Chgo., Dec. 22, 1950; d. Dallas E. and Vera B. (Linka) Hahlbeck; m. Arthur R. Trayling, Apr. 15, 1977; children—Barbara Jean (dec.), Kenneth Scott. B.A., Nat. Coll. Edn., 1972, M.Ed., 1974; M.A. in Library Sci., Rosary Coll., 1977. Head children's services Dolton Pub. Library Dist. (Ill.), 1975-79, Acorn Pub. Library Dist., Oak Forest, Ill., 1979-82; reference-adult services librarian Alsip-Merrionette Park Library Dist. (Ill.), 1982-84, dir. youth services, 1984—. Co-author: Illinois Legislative Handbook for Students, 1970. Mem. Berkeley 50th Anniversary Com. (Ill.), 1974; co-chair bicycle race Northlake Community Theatre (Ill.) 1973-75; mem. adv. council Cook County Sch. Dist. 87 (Ill.), 1972-74; bd. deacons Berkeley Hillside Presbyterian Ch., 1975-79; commr. Country Club Hills Zoning Bd. Appeals, 1982-87; trustee Grand Prairie Library Dist., 1983—. Mem. Reference Assn. of South Suburban Librarians, ALA, Ill. Library Assn. (youth services sect.), Heartland Story League (charterr, v.p. 1985-86), Ill. Library Trustees Assn., Children's Librarians Assn. of South Suburbs (v.p. and program chairperson 1977-78, pres. 1980-81), Student Ill. Edn. Assn. (state chairperson membership 1970-71), Student Ill. Edn. Assn. (founder and pres. Nat. Coll. Edn. chpt. 1971)

TRAYLOR, CHERYL LEE, psychiatric social worker; b. Oswego, N.Y., June 20, 1944; d. Donald Elton and Harriette (Lee) Gais; B.A., State U. N.Y., Buffalo, 1966, M.S.W., 1972; m. Jean LaRue Traylor, Jr., Nov. 11, 1965 (div. Dec. 1970). With Psychiat. Clinic, Buffalo, 1967-70; psychiat. social worker Hillcrest Childrens Center, Washington, 1972-74; asst. dir. outpatient services Comprehensive Community Mental Health Center #2, Seat Pleasant, Md., 1974-77; psychiat. social worker Arlington (Va.) Mental Health Center, 1977-78, So. Calif. Permanente Med. Group, San Diego, 1978—. NIMH fellow, 1970-72. Mem. Nat. Assn. Social Workers, Nat. Assn. Black Social Workers, Acad. Certified Social Workers. Club: Foxtrappe (Washington).

TREADWELL, MARY MAUDE (LONE STAR), construction worker; b. L.I., N.Y., Oct. 11, 1945; d. Walter Clinton (Chief Wild Pigeon) and Julia Loise (Viet) Treadwell; A.A.S., Suffolk County Community Coll., 1979; children—Robin Yellow Dawn Lee, James Strong Bow Lee, Robert Spotted Pony Lee. Communications operator Suffolk County Police Dept., Hauppauge, N.Y., 1975; adminstrv. asst., student personnel div. Suffolk County Community Coll., 1977-80; adminstrn. analyst Equitable Life Assurance Soc., Melville, N.Y., 1980; native Am. field rep. Affirmative Action Program, Melville, 1980-81; constrn. worker Dravo Utility Constructors Inc., Wading River, N.Y., 1981—; founder, chmn. bd. Paumanok Algonquin Found. Inc. Suffolk chmn. L.I. Women's Equal Opportunity Council, 1980; treas. Brookhaven Town Minority Bus. Council, 1980. Contbr. articles in field to profl. jours. Office: Dravo Utility Constructors Inc Shoreham Power Sta Box 606 Wading River NY 11792

TREBILCOT, JOYCE, feminist philosopher, educator; b. San Diego, Feb. 15, 1933; d. Earl and Angela (Dameral) T. B.A. in Philosophy, U. Calif.-Berkeley, 1957; M.A., U. Calif.-Santa Barbara, 1966, Ph.D., 1970. NEH teaching fellow Bryn Mawr Coll., 1967-69; vis. scholar/tchr. women studies U. N.Mex., Albuquerque, 1977-78; assoc. prof. philosophy Washington U., St. Louis, 1977—, coordinator women's studies, 1980—; vis. prof. feminist thought Wheaton Coll., Norton, Mass., 1979-80. Author: (pamphlet) Taking Responsibility for Sexuality, 1983; editor: Mothering: Essays in Feminist Theory, 1984; mem. editorial bd. Hypatia: Jour. Feminist Philosophy, 1977—, Social Theory and Practice, 1979—, Jour. Social Philosophy, 1981—; contbr. essays to jours. NEH fellow, 1974-75; Washington U. grantee. Mem. Soc. for Women in Philosophy, Nat. Women's Studies Assn., Am. Philos. Assn., Am. Soc. Social Philosophy (dir. 1982), NOW. Office: Campus Box 1073 Washington Univ Saint Louis MO 63130

TRECIOKAS, ALODIA DICIUTE, mezzo-soprano, educator; b. Kaunas, Lithuania, Sept. 15, 1905; d. John and Eugenia (Rinkevich) Dicius; came to U.S., 1947, naturalized, 1953; diploma Lithuanian State Sch. of Music, 1930; student of Mme. Gladkaja, Paris, France, 1928-30, Mme. Edwige Ghibaude, Rome, Italy, 1937-38; m. Joseph Treciokes, Oct. 10, 1925; 1 son, Leopold John. Debut in opera as Zibeland Marta in Faust, Lithuanian State Opera, 1930, debut as Carmen, 1935, debut as Delilah in Samson and Delilah, 1938; mem. Lithuanian (Kaunas) State Opera, 1930-44, leading roles in Samson and Delilah, Carmen, Tiefland, Boris Godunov, Prince Igor, Pericola, Faust; appeared as concert soloist numerous concerts Lithuania, Estonia, Germany, U.S.A. including Lithuania Radio Symphony, Lithuania State Opera Orch., Chgo. Symphony Orch.; appeared as soloist in various radio programs in Lithuania, 1923-44, Estonia, 1936—, Germany, 1946-47, U.S., 1949-75; Am. debut as Carmen in Carmen-Bizet, 1949; soloist in recital, Kimball Hall, Chgo., 1951; debut as Catherine in Joan of Arc at the Stake, Orchestra Hall, Chgo., 1952; concert soloist with Nordic Philharmonic Orch., Chgo., 1959; pvt. tchr. voice and opera, Chgo., 1950-65, Tinley Park, Ill., 1963—; dir. opera theatre class Am. Conservatory of Music, Chgo., 1957; recording artist Webb Recording Co., RCA records. Mem. Nat. Assn. Tchrs. of Singing, Nat. Ret. Tchrs. Assn., Musician Club of Women in Chgo. Roman Catholic. Address: 332 26th St Santa Monica CA 90402

TREE, MARIETTA, city planner; b. Lawrence, Mass.; d. Malcolm E. and Mary (Parkman) P.; B.A., U. Pa.; postgrad. Columbia U. Sch. Urban Planning; numerous hon. degrees; m. Desmond FitzGerald, 1939; m. Ronald Tree, July 28, 1947; children—Penelope Tree, Frances FitzGerald. Commr. human rights City of N.Y., 1958-61; ambassador U.S. Mission to UN, N.Y.C., 1961-65; personal staff of sec.-gen. UN Secretariat, N.Y.C., 1965-67; dir. Llewelyn-Davies, Sahni, Inc., city planners and architects; dir. CBS, Internat. Income Properties, Pan Am. Airways, Lend-Lease Corp. (Australia); trustee U.S. Trust Co. Bd. dirs. Am. Ditchley Found.; mem. vis. com. Sch. Architecture and Planning, M.I.T.; chmn. Citizens Com. for N.Y.C., Inc.; mem. Cooper Hewitt Council; bd. dirs. Churchill Found. Mem. Council Fgn. Relations, Pilgrim Soc. Home: 1 Sutton Pl S New York NY 10022

TREECE, MALRA CLIFFT, educator, author; b. Oxford, Ark., Nov. 19, 1923; d. Joseph A. and Ruth (Thompson) Clifft; B.S., Ark. State U., 1947; M.A., Memphis State U., 1956; Ph.D., U. Miss., 1971; m. Guy Treece, Jan. 18, 1946; children—Diana, Mark David. Prof. bus. communication Memphis State U., 1957—. Recipient Nat., State, Mid-South Poetry awards. Mem. Am. Bus. Communication Assn., Nat. Bus. Edn. Assn., Nat. League Am. Pen Women, Tenn. Poetry Soc., Phi Kappa Phi, Delta Pi Epsilon. Methodist. Author: Communication for Business and the Professions, 1978; 2d edit., 1982, 3d edit., 1986; Successful Business Communication, 1980, 2d edit., 1984, 3d edit., 1987; Effective Reports, 1982, 2d edit., 1985; contbr. articles to profl. jours. Home: 1064 Estate Memphis TN 38119 Office: 317 Bus Adminstrn Bldg Memphis State U Memphis TN 38152

TREFTS, DOROTHY ELEANORE, consultant; b. Ithaca, N.Y., Apr. 24, 1953; d. Albert Sharpe and Joan (Landenberger) T.; B.A. cum laude (Coll.

scholar), Wellesley Coll., 1975; M.B.A., Harvard U., Boston, 1978. Intern, Wellesley-M.I.T. Urban Legal Studies Project, summer 1973; Washington intern Wellesley Coll., summer 1974; cons. Data Resources, Inc., San Francisco, 1975-76; fin. analyst IBM, Manassas, Va., 1978-79; trainee mgmt. tng. program First Nat. Bank Boston, 1979-80; product mgr. Saddlebrook Corp., Cambridge, Mass., 1980-85; cons. McKinsey and Co., Inc., N.Y.C., 1985-86; v.p. Chem. Technologies Corp., 1986—. Vol., Frontier Nursing Service, Wendover, Ky., spring, 1971, mem. Boston exec. com., recruiting coordinator, 1979-85. Mem. Boston Wellesley Career Assos. Republican. Presbyterian. Clubs: DAR, Nat. Soc. Dames XVII Century (charter mem. chpt.) (Cleve.); Harvard Bus. Sch., Wellesley Coll., Harvard (Boston). Office: 52 Broadway 18th floor New York NY 10022

TREGELLAS, PATRICIA, musical director, composer; b. Kans., Feb. 22, 1936; d. Clarence and Lena T.; B.Mus. in Edn., U. Denver, 1959; scholar, Trossingen, Germany, 1960-61; M.A. in Teaching Music, CUNY, 1985. Concert artist, chamber musician, condr.; music supr. Prowers County (Colo.) High Sch. Band and Chorus, 1962-65; accordionist and orch. leader USO tours abroad, 1966-69; mem. orch., asst. condr. Hal Prince musicals on nat. tours, 1969-71; freelance musician, N.Y.C., 1972—; mus. dir., condr. N.Y. Concerto Orch., 1979—; condr. workshops, Tokyo, London, N.Y.C.; performed in premier performances of new music. Recipient cert. appreciation Gen. Westmoreland and others for work in Vietnam with USO. Mem. Chamber Music Am., Am. Accordion Assn., AAUW, Sigma Epsilon Chi, Kappa Delta, Mu Phi Epsilon. Methodist. Home: 817 West End Ave New York NY 10025

TREI, ALICE ROSALIE, ret. occupational therapist; b. Estonia, Oct. 17, 1909; d. Prüdu and Müna (Kraun) Roost; came to U.S., 1929, naturalized, 1938; certificate occupational therapy, Columbia U., 1948; B.S., N.Y. U., 1954; m. Peter Trei, Sept. 20, 1928 (dec. Jan. 1962); children—Astra (Mrs. Felix Bottenhorn), Alan. Occupational therapist N.Y. State Psychiat. Inst., N.Y.C., 1948-53, head occupational therapist, 1953-79; clin. instr. occupational therapy Columbia U., 1966-79. Recipient Outstanding Employee award N.Y. State Dept. Mental Hygiene, 1975. Mem. Am., N.Y. State (treas. 1959-62, 69-73) occupational therapy assns., Met. N.Y. Dist., World Fedn. Occupational Therapists. Home: 15 Sickles St New York NY 10040

TREIMAN, JOYCE WAHL (MRS. KENNETH TREIMAN), artist; b. Evanston, Ill., May 29, 1922; d. Rene and Rose (Doppelt) Wahl; A.A., Stephens Coll., 1941; B.F.A. (Grad. fellow 1943), State U. Iowa, 1943; m. Kenneth Treiman, Apr. 25, 1945; 1 son, Donald. One-man shows include Paul Theobald Gallery, Chgo., 1942, John Snowden Gallery, Chgo., 1945, Art Inst. Chgo., 1947, North Shore Country Day Sch., Winnetka, Ill., 1947, Fairweather-Garnett Gallery, Evanston, 1950, Edwin Hewitt Gallery, N.Y.C., 1950, Palmer House Galleries, Chgo., 1952, Glencoe (Ill.) Library, 1953, Elizabeth Nelson Gallery, Chgo., 1953, Charles Feingarten Gallery, Chgo., 1955, 58, Marian Willard Gallery, N.Y.C., 1960, Felix Landau Gallery, Los Angeles, 1961, 64, Adele Bednarz Gallery, Los Angeles, 1969, 74, Forum Gallery, N.Y.C., 1970, La Jolla (Calif.) Mus. 10 year retrospective, 1971; retrospective exhibit Municipal Art Gallery, Los Angeles, 1947-78; exhibited group shows at Met. Mus., 1950, Carnegie Internat., 1955, 57, Whitney Mus., 1951, 52, 53, 58, John Herron Art Inst., 1953, Art Inst. Chgo., 1954-59, Library of Congress, 1954, Corcoran Gallery, 1957, Pa. Acad. Fine Art, 1958, Mus. Modern Art, 1962, Whitney Mus., 1962, Penelope Gallery, Rome, 1964, numerous others; represented in permanent collections Denver Mus. Art, State U. Iowa, Ill. State Mus., Tupperware Art Mus., Orlando, Fla., Art Inst. Chgo., Utah State U., Abbott Labs., Oberlin Allen Art Mus., Internat. Mineral Corp., Pasadena Art Mus., U. Oreg., Whitney Mus. Am. Art, Long Beach Mus. Art; also pvt. collections; artist in residence San Fernando Valley State Coll., 1968; vis. artist Art Center Sch., Los Angeles, summer 1968; vis. prof. San Fernando Valley State Coll., Northridge, Calif., 1969; vis. lectr. U. Calif. at Los Angeles, 1969-70; vis. artist Calif. State U., Long Beach, 1976. Recipient numerous awards including Logan prize and purchase prize Art Inst. Chgo., 1951; Martin B. Cahn prize, 1959, 60; Pauline Palmer prize, 1953; Saratosa Am. Painting Exhbn. award, Ford Found. purchase prize, 1960; Ball State Coll. purchase prize, 1961; La Jolla Art Mus. prize, 1961; Pasadena Art Mus. purchase prize, 1961; named Woman of Year for Arts, Los Angeles Times, 1965. Tiffany fellow, 1947, Tupperware Art Fund fellow, 1955, Tamerino Lithography fellow, 1961. Home: 712 Amalfi Dr Pacific Palisades CA 90272

TREINZVICZ, KATHRYN MARY, programmer analyst, computer consultant; b. Brockton, Mass., Nov. 25, 1957; d. Ralph Clement and Frances Elizabeth (O'Leary) T. B.S., Salem State Coll., Mass., 1980. Tchr., Brockton Pub. Schs., 1980-81; instr. Quicy CETA Inc., Mass., 1981-82; programmer systems Architects Inc., Randolph, Mass., 1982, programmer analyst, Dayton, Ohio, 1982-84; sr. programmer analyst System Devel. Corp., Dayton, 1984—. Mem. Nat. Assn. Female Execs. Democrat. Roman Catholic. Avocations: Steven King novels; needlepoint; knitting; crocheting.

TREITLER, RHODA CHAPRACK, artist; b. N.Y.C., Apr. 18, 1937; d. Arthur A. and Lillian (Feinberg) Chaprack; m. Byron M. Treitler, May 15, 1960; children—Michael Eric, Betsy Dale. Student Artists in Am., 1954-58; A.B., Bennington Coll., 1958; studied with Paul Feeley; student Artists in Am., 1973-78. Editorial asst. McCalls mag., N.Y.C., 1958-60; artist, N.Y., 1970—; pres. Aquarelle, Port Washington, N.Y., 1984—. Exhibited in group shows at Coe Hall, Locust Valley, N.Y., 1976, Firehouse Gallery, Nassau Community Coll., Garden City, N.Y., 1977, 78, 80, 81, Plandome Gallery, Manhasset, N.Y., 1980, 85, Bryant Library, Roslyn, N.Y., 1981, Seamans Bank, Manhasset, 1981, Adelphi U., Garden City, N.Y., 1983, Fed. Bldg. N.Y.C., 1982-85, Hempstead Harbor Gallery, Glen Cove, N.Y., 1983, Post Coll., Brookville, N.Y., 1983-84, Nassau County Mus. Fine Art, Roslyn, 1982, 83. Pres. Parents Assn., Roslyn Elem. Sch., 1970-72, Parents Assn. Roslyn High Sch. 1977-79, budget advisor, 1974-76; mem. coordinating council Parents Assn. liaison with Sch. Bd., 1970-82. Mem. Aquarelle, Nat. Assn. Women Artists, Huntington Twp. Art League, Nassau County Fine Art Mus. (council for celebration of arts). Clubs: Racquet at Old Westbury (N.Y.); Hunters Run Racquet (Boynton Beach, Fla.). Avocations: tennis; music; travel.

TRELA, VIRGINIA MAY, publications specialist, writer, publicist; b. Grand Rapids, Mich., Feb. 15, 1925; d. Clair and Sally Jousma; A.A., Green Mountain Coll., 1945; postgrad. U. Calif., Irvine, 1965-66, UCLA, 1978-79; B.A., U. Redlands, 1983; m. Joseph C. Trela, Sept. 11, 1954; children—Christopher Alan, Brian Philip. Profl. actress, 1945-51; exec. adminstrv. asst. McCann Erickson, Inc., 1954-55; sec. Arabian Am. Oil Co., Dhahran, Saudi Arabia, 1951-53; service rep., public relations Champagne Temporary Help, Newport Beach, Calif., 1965-75; publicity coordinator Knott's Berry Farm, Buena Park, Calif., 1975-76; publicity mgr. Five Star Mktg. Services, Santa Ana, Calif., 1976-83; pub. coordinator/newsletter editor Pickard, Lowe & Garrick, Inc., Newport Beach, 1983—; founding mem. weCan Women's Network. Bd. dirs. U. Redlands, 1984-87. Recipient award of excellence for nat. pub. campaign Los Angeles Advt. Women. Mem. Calif. Press Women 1st place writing award for press releases, 3d place writing award for brochures), Nat. Fedn. Press Women (past pres. Orange County dist., 1st place writing award for press releases), Orange County Press Club, Women in Communications. Home: 8832 Dolphin Dr Huntington Beach CA 92646 Office: 555 Parkcenter Dr Santa Ana CA 92705

TREMULIS, ELIZABETH PICKETT, social worker; b. N.Y.C., June 3, 1928; d. Ralph Edgar and Helen Margaret (Richardson) Pickett; B.A., Stanford U., 1950; M.A., U. Chgo., 1951; m. Demosthenes Tremulis, Dec. 22, 1951; children—Michael Sarantos (dec.), Andrea, Peter Alexander, William Stephen. Caseworker, Family Service Bur., United Charities of Chgo., 1951-54; social worker North Suburban Spl. Edn. Dist., Highland Park, Ill., 1970-72, Sch. Dist. 28, Northbrook, Ill., 1969-70, 72—; cons. St. David's Nursery Sch., 1968, Highland Park Community Nursery Sch., 1969-70, Ravinia Nursery Sch., 1970. Mem. Highland Park Caucus Com., 1977-79; mem. Highland Park Landmark Preservation Com., 1979-80; bd. dirs. Highland Park Community Nursery Sch., 1964-65, Northbrook YMCA, 1961-63. Mem. Acad. Cert. Social Workers, Nat. Assn. Social Workers, Nat., Ill. assns. sch. social workers, Ill. Soc. Clin. Social Work, Council for Exceptional Children. Mem. staff Sch. Social Work Jour., 1979-81. Home: 466 Laurel Ave Highland Park IL 60035 Office: 1600 Walters Ave Northbrook IL 60062

TRENT, NELLIE JANE, psychologist; b. St. Louis, July 5, 1921; d. Richard Wesley and Helen Elizabeth (Kuhn) Mellow; A.B., Wellesley Coll., 1943; M.A., Washington U., St. Louis, 1944; m. John Brabson Trent, Apr. 9, 1946; children—Elizabeth Mellow (Mrs. Peter D.W. Heberling), John Brabson. Lic. psychologist, Mo. Tchr., Mary Inst., St. Louis, 1944-46; grad. asst. psychology dept. Washington U., 1963-65; psychologist Kirkwood (Mo.) Sch. Dist., 1965-75; psychologist, chmn. spl. services Ladue Jr. High Sch., St. Louis. 1975-83; pvt. practice psychology specializing in gerontology, counseling elderly and aging, 1983—; instr. psychology Meramec Community Coll., St. Louis, 1969-70; instr. spl. edn. St. Louis U., 1970. Founder, pres. Greater St. Louis Women's Assn. of Freedoms Found. at Valley Forge, 1968; residential chmn. St. Louis and St. Louis County United Fund, 1968; v.p. Wellesley Coll. Class of '43, 1973-78. Founder, pres. bd. Ladue Chapel Nursery Sch., 1957-59, bd. dirs., 1985-87, chmn. pictorial directory of Ladue Chapel, 1984, ordained elder/trustee, chmn. lay visitors com., 1985-87; mem., sec. long-range planning com. Ladue Chapel, 1976-79; bd. dirs. Campbell House, Girls Home, Multiple Sclerosis Soc. St. Louis, Internat. Inst. Advanced Studies, YMCA/YWCA of Washington U; mem. Council on Aging, Presbytery of Elijah Parish Lovejoy. Recipient Wellesley Coll. award of year, 1968; Liberty Bowl, Freedoms Found., 1968. Lic. psychologist, Mo. Mem. Am. Psychol. Assn., Mo. Psychol. Assn., Nat. Assn. Sch. Psychologists (charter), Mo. Assn. Sch. Psychologists (charter), Soc. St. Louis Psychologists, Assn. Children with Learning Disabilities, Council Exceptional Children, Am. Personnel and Guidance Assn., St. Louis Jr. League (dir. 1950-53), Mo. Hist. Soc. (pres. women's assn. 1964-66, trustee soc. 1968-71), Kirkwood Community Tchrs. Assn. (dir. 1970-75), Mo. State Tchr. Assn., Ladue Community Tchr. Assn.. Home: 70 Fair Oaks Saint Louis MO 63124 Office: Ladue Jr High Sch 9701 Conway Rd Saint Louis MO 63124

TREPPLER, IRENE ESTHER, state senator; b. St. Louis County, Mo., Oct. 13, 1926; d. Martin H. and Julia C. (Bender) Hagemann; student Meramec Community Coll., 1972; m. Walter J. Treppler, Aug. 18, 1950; children—John M., Steven A., Diane V., Walter W. Payroll chief USAF Aero. Chart Plant, 1943-51; enumerator U.S. Census Bur., St. Louis, 1960, crew leader, 1970; mem. Mo. Ho. of Reps., Jefferson City, 1972-84; mem. Mo. Senate, Jefferson City, 1985—. Mem. Oak-Le-Mehl Republican Club, Concord Twp. Rep. Club; alt. del. Rep. Nat. Conv., 1976, 84; charter mem., bd. dirs. Windsor Community Ctr. Mem. Nat. Order Women Legislators (rec. sec. 1981-82, pres. 1985), Nat. Fedn. Rep. Women. Republican. Mem. Ch. of Christ. Office: Room 424 Mo State Senate State Capitol Bldg Jefferson City MO 65101

TRESMONTAN, OLYMPIA DAVIS, psychotherapist, marriage and family counselor; b. Boston, Nov. 27, 1925; d. Peter Konstantin and Mary (Hazimanolis) Davis; B.S., Simmons Coll., 1946; M.A., Wayne State U., 1960; Ph.D. (Schaefer Found. grantee), U. Calif., Berkeley, 1971; m. Dion Marc Tresmontan, Sept. 15, 1957 (dec. Mar. 1961); m. 2d, Robert Baker Stitt, Mar. 21, 1974. Child welfare worker San Francisco Dept. Social Service, 1964-66; sensitivity tng. NSF Sci. Curriculum Improvement Study, U. Calif., Berkeley, 1967-68; individual practice psychol. counseling, San Francisco, 1970—; dir. Studio Ten Services, San Francisco, Promise for Children, San Francisco, 1981—, tchr. U. Calif. extension at San Francisco, 1971-72, Chapman Coll. Grad. Program in Counseling, Travis AFB, 1971-74; clin. cons. Childworth Learning Ctr., San Francisco, 1976-80; cons. project rape response Queen's Bench Found., San Francisco, 1977. Active Friends San Francisco Pub. Library, Internat. Hospitality Com. Bay Area; bd. dirs. Childworth Learning Center, 1976-80. Mem. Am. Psychol. Assn., Am. Orthopsychiat. Assn., Am. Assn. Marriage Counselors, Calif. Assn. Marriage, Family and Child Therapists. AAUW. Club: Commonwealth. Author: (with J. Morris) The Evaluation of A Compensatory Education Program, 1967; (Karplus edit.) What is Curriculum Evaluation, Six Answers, 1968. Home: 2611 Lake St San Francisco CA 94121

TRIBBLE, DAGMAR HAGGSTROM (MRS. ELSTON J. TRIBBLE), artist; b. N.Y.C.; d. Olaf Albin and Ida (Sabini) Haggstrom; student Parsons Sch. Design, N.Y. and Paris, 1928, Art Students League, 1930-32, Farnsworth Sch. Painting, 1949-50; m. Elston J. Tribble, July 15, 1933; 1 dau., Martha Watkins (Mrs. James Malcolm McKinnon). Tchr. fashion illustration Parsons Sch. Design, 1929-32; designer sportswear and beachwear Travelo Corp., N.Y.C., 1933-45. One-man shows at Beard Sch., Orange, N.J., Monmouth Coll., West Long Branch, The Present Day Club, Princeton, N.J., 1968, 71, 73-75, 77-78, 82, M.S. Kungsholm, 1971-74, M.S. Sagafjord, 1971, United Nat. Bank, Fenwood, N.J., 1972, others; exhibited in group shows at Cape Cod Art Assn., 1963, Knickerbocker Artists Ann. Exhbn., 1963, Westfield Art Assn. State Show, 1963, 64, Hunterdon County Art Center Ann., 1963, 64, Catherine Lorillard Wolfe Art Show, 1964, Nat. Arts Club shows, also Met. Mus. Art, Nat. Acad., N.Y.C., Am. Water Color Soc. Ann., 1978, Nat. Assn. Women Artists Ann., 1967—, Nat. Assn. Women Artists Internat., Paris, 1969, Am. Watercolor Soc. anns., 1967—, Garden State Watercolor Soc. anns., 1970—, Am. Watercolor Soc. Ann. Traveling Exhbn., 1972, N.J. State Cultural Center, Trenton, 1977; represented in pvt. collections. Recipient Agnes B. Noyes award, 1962; Windsor Newton award, 1963; Captain's Barn award for Watercolor Westfield Art Assn. State Show, 1964; Steinback Co. award for watercolor Festival of Fine Art Exhbn., 1964; Am. Artist medal merit, Am. Watercolor Soc., 1965; Jane C. Stanley Meml. prize, Nat. Assn. Women Artists, 1966. Mem. Fashion Group, Am. Watercolor Soc., Garden State Watercolor Soc. (pres. 1970—; Squibb award 1973), Nat. Assn. Women Artists, Princeton Art Assn. (pres. 1968-69), Salmagundi Club. Club: Nat. Arts (N.Y.C.). Home: 12 Battle Rd Princeton NJ 08540

TRIBBLE, LAVIECE EDITH, guidance administrator; b. Campbell, Mo., Nov. 7, 1925; d. James Herman and Grace Elizabeth (Grimes) Anders; A.B., George Washington U., 1960; M.S., U. Hawaii, 1965; m. Cecil Wayne Tribble, July 7, 1945; children—Suzanne Beth, Jana Kay. Tchr., pub. schs., Mo., 1954-57, Guantanamo Bay, Cuba, 1955-58, Arlington, Va., 1960-64, Kamehameha Schs., Honolulu, 1964-67; resource tchr. Custis Elementary Sch., Arlington, Va., 1967-68; dir. guidance Swanson Jr. High Sch., Arlington, Va., 1968—. Ward chmn. Polit. Action Com., 1977. Mem. NEA, Va., Arlington edn. assns., Am., Va. personnel and guidance assns., Northern Va. Guidance Assn., Am. Sch. Counselors Assn., Delta Kappa Gamma. Democrat. Methodist. Home: 2924 S Grant St Arlington VA 22202 Office: 5800 Washington Blvd Arlington VA 22205

TRICARICO, LINDA MARIE, fashion designer; b. Bklyn., June 8, 1961; d. John William and Phyllis Jean (D'Addario) Tricarico. Student Fashion Inst. Tech., 1979-80. Sales and design coordinator Sure Snap Corp., N.Y.C., 1983-84; asst. designer E.S. Sutton Inc., N.Y.C., 1984-86; designer Good N Plenty Inc., N.Y.C., 1986—; free lance illustrator, designer. Mem. Fashion Soc., Nat. Assn. Female Execs., Am. Millionaires. Democrat. Roman Catholic. Avocations; fashion design; illustration; travel. Home: 322 E 82nd St Apt GC New York NY 10028

TRICKEL, MARY E., chemical company executive, educator; b. Elizabeth, N.J., Aug. 4, 1940; d. James Franklin and Helen Mary (McGuire) Marken; m. Francis William Trickel, Aug. 20, 1960; children—Debra, Anne, Mary, Ellen. A.A.S. in Acctg., Middlesex Coll., 1977; B.S. in Acctg., Rutgers U., 1979; M.B.A., Fairleigh Dickinson U., 1982. Sec. Cities Service Research and Devel., Cranbury, N.J., 1969-70; with Essex Chem. Corp., Clifton, N.J., 1970-84, controller to 1984; acctg. mgr. Econs. Lab., Woodbridge, N.J., 1984—; bus. cons. Rutgers U., New Brunswick, N.J., 1979—; adj. prof. Middlesex Coll., Edison, N.J., 1980—; career cons. Mem. exec. bd. Middlesex Coll. Found., 1982—. Mem. Nat. Assn. Accts. (ednl. dir. 1980-83), Nat. Assn. Female Execs., N.J. Assn. Notary Pubs., Quill & Ink, Middlesex Coll. Alumni Assn. (founding pres.), Delta Mu Delta. Roman Catholic. Avocations: gourmet cooking; writing; word games. Home: 37 Hillside Ave Sayreville NJ 08872 Office: Econs Lab Inc 255 Blair Rd Avenel NJ 07001

TRIGG, SHARI JENELL, sales account executive; b. Lawton, Okla., Sept. 21, 1957; d. Jasper Alphonso and Aurora Lou (Cooke) T. B.S., Northwestern U., 1978. Asst. mgr. The Ltd., Chgo., 1978; advt. asst. Bentley, Barnes & Lynn Advt., Chgo., 1978-79; account mgmt. trainee Leo Burnett Advt., Chgo., 1979-80; sales account exec. WMAQ-TV NBC Channel 5, Chgo., 1980—; spl. events com. mem. Broadcast Advt. Club Chgo., 1981—. Mem. Chgo. Urban League, 1982-84; mem. employer adv. bd. Project Skil-Disadvantaged Youth Employment Service, Chgo., 1982-83, chair adv. bd., 1983-84; co-chmn. Friends of the El-Commuter Grop, Chgo., 1978; chmn. prize com. BAC Christmas program, 1985—; chmn. employee aux. bd. Project Skill Disadvantaged Youth Vocat. Service, Chgo., 1982—. Recipient Outstanding Leadership award YWCA Met. Chgo., 1982, named Outstanding Achiever of Industry, 1983. Mem. Nat. Assn. Female Execs., Delta Sigma Theta, Club: NBC Variety Soc. (com. chmn. 1983). Democrat. Unitarian. Office: WMAQ-TV NBC Chgo Merchandise Mart Plaza Chicago IL 60654

TRIGO, LOUISE ARROTA, elementary educator; b. Bklyn., Mar. 9, 1949; d. Jose DaCruz Fernandes z and Marie (Horta) A.; m. Antonio Jose Trigo, Aug. 1, 1970; 1 child, Christina Arrota. A.A., Staten Island Coll., 1968; B.S. in Edn., Bklyn. Coll., 1970, M.S. in Edn., 1973; postgrad. L.I. U., 1985—. Transitional program staff Pub. Sch. 107 N.Y.C. Bd. Edn., Bklyn., 1980-81, mem. Gates program, 1981-82, tchr. 4th and 5th grade, 1970—. Roman Catholic. Club: Luso-Am. Social (dir. Portuguese Sch. Escola Florbela Espanca 1982—, treas. 1975-78) (Bklyn.). Avocation: arts and crafts. Home: 388 Hoyt St Brooklyn NY 11231

TRIMBLE, CELIA DENISE, lawyer; b. Clovis, N.Mex., Mar. 3, 1953; d. George Harold and Barbara Ruth (Foster) T.; m. Grady Brian Jolley, Aug. 9, 1980. B.S., Eastern N.Mex. U., 1976, M.A., 1977; J.D., St. Mary's U., San Antonio, 1982. Bar: Tex. 1982, U.S. Dist. Ct. (no. dist.) Tex. 1983, U.S. Ct. Appeals (5th cir.) 1985, U.S. Supreme Ct. 1986. Instr. English, Eastern N.Mex. U., Portales, 1977-78; editor Curry County Times, Clovis, 1978-79; assoc. Schulz & Robertson, Abilene, Tex., 1982-85, Scarborough, Black, Tarpley & Scarborough, 1985—; instr. legal research and writing St. Mary's Sch. Law, 1981-82. Legal adv. to bd. dirs. Abilene Kennel Club, 1983-85. Mem. ABA, State Bar Tex., Am. Trial Lawyers Assn., Tex. Trial Lawyers Assn., Tex. Criminal Def. Lawyers Assn., Abilene Bar Assn. (bd. dirs. 1985-86, sec./treas. 1985-86), Abilene Young Lawyers Assn. (bd. dirs. 1984-85, treas. 1984-85, pres.-elect 1986-87), NOW, ACLU, Phi Alpha Delta. Office: Scarborough Black Tarpley & Scarborough 500 Alexander Bldg 104 Pine St Abilene TX 79604

TRIMBLE, JANA DENMAN, training official; b. Houston, Mar. 9, 1955; d. Peyton Linwood and Paula Gene (Wilroy) Denman; m. Dale L. Trimble, May 25, 1985. B.A., U. Houston, 1981, M.Ed., 1984, postgrad. in instrnl. tech., 1985—. Cert. social sci. tchr., Tex. With Highlands Ins. Co., Houston, 1976-78, Cowen, Rowles, Winston, brokerage firm, Houston, 1978; high sch. tchr. Alief Ind. Sch. Dist., Houston, 1981-83; internal tng. coordinator Community Health Computing, Houston, 1983—Republican. Home: 9407 Roos Houston TX 77036 Office: Community Health Computing 4242 Southwest Freeway Houston TX 77027

TRIMBLE, LORA NELLE GARRETSON (MRS. JAMES CURTIS TRIMBLE), writer; b. Wichita Falls, Tex., Aug. 12, 1935; d. Jesse Columbus and Alma Geneva (Higgenbottom) Garretson; student Sul Ross State Tchrs. Coll., 1954, Midwestern U., 1956; B.A., So. Meth. U., 1961; m. James Curtis Trimble, Sept. 4, 1954; children—James Curtis, Mary Christiana. Free lance writer, 1961-67; dir. Royal Lane Lang. Ctr., Dallas, 1969-77; English lang. tchr. to fgn. adults, 1969-77. Mem. Theta Sigma Phi. Address: Dallas TX 75229

TRIMMER, DOROTHY ANN, nurse; b. Newark, Jan. 28, 1951; d. Robert Stanley and Jane Melissa (Cone) T.; B.S. in Nursing (state scholar), Seton Hall U., 1973; M. Nursing magna cum laude, City U. N.Y., 1976. Staff nurse United Hosp. Med. Center, Newark, 1973-74, St. Barnabas Med. Center, Livingston, N.J., 1974-75; instr. Passaic County Community Coll., Paterson, N.J., 1976-77; dir. staff devel. Riverside Gen. Hosp., Secaucus, N.J., 1977-81; instr. U. Fla., Gainesville, 1981-82, U. Ariz. Coll. Nursing, Tempe, 1982—. Lectr. to civic groups; instr. CPR, Am. Heart Assn.; active Am. Lung Assn. and Am. Cancer Soc. T.J. Kavanagh grantee, 1972; Seton Hall U. grantee, 1973. Mem. Am. Nurses Assn., Am. Assn. Critical Care Nurses, Hudson County Cancer Soc., Am. Soc. Health Edn. and Tng., Hudson County Council Inservice Educators (chmn. 1978-81). Presbyterian (past Sunday sch. tchr.). Office: Arizona State Univ Dept of Nursing Tempe AZ 85287

TRIPOLI, DONNA THOMPSON, horticulturist; b. Waco, Tex., Mar. 2, 1954; d. Louis Aerl and Janie Ruth (Blevins) Thompson; m. Richard Edwin Barnes, July 20, 1974 (div. Mar. 1982); m. Thomas Joseph Tripoli, June 24, 1984; children—JoAnn Barnes, Thomas Joseph Jr. B.B.A., U. Tex.-Arlington, 1981. Pres., founder Innerscape Designs, Inc., Arlington, 1979—. Mem. North Tex. Interiorscape Assn. (v.p. 1984-85). Home: 5501 Forest Bend Dr Arlington TX 76017 Office: Innerscape Designs Inc 3008 Pleasant Valley Ln Arlington TX 76015

TRISTANO, SANDRA, lawyer; b. Chgo., Aug. 30, 1951; d. Elias and Shirley (Wood) Snitzer; m. Michael Tristano, Sept. 29, 1979. B.A. in Psychology, Cornell U., 1973; J.D., Washington U., St. Louis, 1977. Bar: Ill. 1977. Staff atty. Ill. Dept. Pub. Aid, Springfield, 1977-80; gen. counsel Ill. Dept. Energy and Natural Resources, Springfield, 1980—; atty. Vols. for Justice, Springfield, 1982—. Mem. ABA, Ill. Bar Assn., Sangamon County Bar Assn., Jr. League. Home: 39 Inverness Rd Springfield IL 62704 Office: Ill Dept Energy and Natural Resources 325 W Adams Springfield IL 62706

TRIVISON, MARGARET ANN, librarian; b. Cleve., Aug. 9, 1942; d. Amilio S. and Louise (Zaccagnini) Trivison. B.A., Notre Dame Coll. (Ohio), 1964; postgrad. Columbia U., 1965; M.S. in Library Sci., Case Western Res. U., 1969. Instr., Cath. Bd. Edn., Cleve., 1964-66; sch. librarian Cleve. Bd. Edn., 1966-69; reference librarian Cuyahoga County Library, Cleve., 1969-71; librarian III, San Diego County Library, San Diego, 1971—; dir. adult literacy project Outreach Services, San Diego Mem. Calif. Library Services Bd., Sacramento, 1977-81. Mem. Calif. Library Assn., ALA, UN Assn. Democrat. Roman Catholic. Club: San Diego Mus. Art. Address: 6216 Agee St Apt 115 San Diego CA 92122

TROISE, AUDREY HELENA, lumber co. exec.; b. Schenectady, Sept. 22, 1934; d. George H. and Emma (Relyea) Flavin; student pub. schs., Mechanicsville, N.Y.; m. Frank Troise, Aug. 1, 1964. Steno-sec. Gen. Electric Co., Waterford, N.Y., 1951-52; sec. Taft Hotel and Republic Pictures, N.Y.C., 1952-54; sec. Walter Schneider Assocs., Inc., N.Y.C., 1954-57; sec. William G. Moore & Son Inc. of Del., N.Y.C., 1957-64, corp. sec., dir., 1965-69, v.p., dir., 1969-76, pres., owner, 1976—. Mem. Am. Wood Preservers Assn., Soc. Am. Mil. Engrs., Assn. Bus. and Profl. Women in Constrn., Assn. of Women Bus. Owners.

TROISI, BARBARA DAVIES, reading specialist; b. Rahway, N.J., June 16, 1937; d. Thomas Edward and Ruth Marie (Ohlott) Davies; B.S., N.Y.U., 1959, postgrad., 1981—; (dissertation in progress); M.A., Fairleigh Dickinson U., 1979; m. Frank X. Troisi, Aug. 22, 1959; children—Pamela Ann, Morgan Andrew. Tchr. English, Cliffside Park (N.J.) Sr. High Sch., 1959-62; reading tchr. Pascack Valley Regional High Sch., Hillsdale, N.J., 1976-78, reading specialist, 1979—; cons. in field. N.Y.U. Alumni Scholar, 1955-59; Alcoa scholar, 1955-59; recipient Founders Day award N.Y.U., 1959. Mem. N.J. Assn. Learning Cons., N.J. Reading Assn., Nat. Council Tchrs. English, Internat. Reading Assn., Assn. for Supervision & Curriculum Devel., Kappa Delta Epsilon. Republican. Roman Catholic. Clubs: Jr. Women's of Upper Saddle River, Women's of Upper Saddle River. Contbr. articles to profl. jours. Office: Pascack Valley Regional High Sch Piermont Rd Hillsdale NJ 07642

TROOP, VIOLA STASIO, cosmetic company executive; b. N.Y.C.; d. Joseph and Rose Stasio; student St. John's U., 1965; m. Roger Joseph Troop, Sept. 12, 1970; stepchildren—Roger, Rawlins, Jessica, Claudia. Sr. market research analyst Colgate-Palmolive Co., N.Y.C., 1965-68; asst. product mgr. Yardley of

London, N.Y.C., 1968-69; product counselor Avon Products Inc., N.Y.C., 1969-71; franchise mgr. Revlon Internat. Inc., N.Y.C., 1971-72, mktg. dir., 1975-80, group mktg. dir., 1980-81, v.p., group mktg. dir., 1981-83; sr. product mgr. Menley & James, N.Y.C., 1972-75; v.p. mktg. Warner Cosmetics Inc., N.Y.C., 1983-85; sr. v.p. fragrances selection, 1985-86. Mem. Fashion Group, Cosmetic Career Women's Assn., Soc. Cosmetic Chemists, Am. Mktg. Assn., Advt. Women of N.Y. (past officer). Home: 211 E 77th St New York NY 10021 Office: V&R Assocs Inc 211 E 77th St New York NY 10021

TROPP, LOUISE CONSTANCE VELARDI, aircraft spare parts co. exec.; b. Phillipsburg, N.J., Apr. 30, 1942; d. John Francis and Julia Cecilia (Pisaniello) Velardi; B.A., New Sch. Social Research, 1976; m. Howard S. Tropp, June 6, 1964; children—Josephine, Philip. Elem. sch. tchr., Princeton, N.J., 1962-64; owner MPT Enterprises div. Aero. Procurement and Tech. Inc., N.Y.C., 1976—; dir. Jefferson Towers Inc., N.Y.C., 1976—, chmn., 1979-81, v.p., 1982-83, sec., 1983-84; dir. Tall Timbers, Sussex, N.J., 1980-83, chmn., 1981-83, cons. ex-officio, 1983—. Mem. bd. Parents Assn. of Columbia Prep. Sch., 1981-83. Mem. Am. Women's Econ. Devel. Corp., Women Bus. Owners N.Y., N.Y. Chamber Commerce and Industry, La Leche League (chpt. treas. 1970—). Address: 700 Columbus Ave Apt 7C New York NY 10025

TROSTLE, MARY PAT, lawyer; b. Wilmington, Del., Dec. 15, 1951; d. Robert Eyer and Loretta Carolyn (Grane) Albert; m. Keith Allen Trostle, Aug. 16, 1974. B.S., Miami U., Oxford, Ohio, 1972; J.D., Ohio No. U., 1975; postgrad. Temple Sch. Law, 1979-80. Bar: Del. 1976. Assoc., Biggs & Battaglia, Wilmington, Del., 1975—; mem. Superior Ct. Adv. Com. on Med. Malpractice, Wilmington, 1979—; seminar lectr. Palmer Assocs., Aurora, Ill., 1981-85. Mem. ABA, Del. State Bar Assn. (treas. 1979-81, chmn. med.-legal, dental-legal com. 1985-87), Wilmington Women in Bus. (co-editor WWB News 1985-86). Republican. Roman Catholic. Home: 321 Hampton Rd Wilmington DE 19803 Office: Biggs and Battaglia 1206 Mellon Bank Ctr Wilmington DE 19801

TROTTER, CHRISTINE DENISE, business systems company executive; b. Tulsa, July 5, 1953; d. William and Barbara Jean (Allen) Briggs; m. Benjamin Lynn horne, Aug. 2, 1971 (div. Dec. 1983); m. Mark Anderson Trotter, Feb. 14, 1985; children—Marlon, Ashley, Megan. B.S., Okla. U., 1976. Computer programmer Mich. Bell Tel. Co., Grand Rapids, 1978-80; programmer analyst Okla. U. Health Sci. Ctr., Tulsa, 1980-82; systems analyst Dept. Army, Fort Hood, 1983-85; sr. bus. systems designer Martin Marietta Data Systems, San Antonio, 1985—. Mem. Nat. Assn. Female Execs. Republican. Baptist. Home: 3521 Wimbledon Dr Cibolo TX 78108 Office: Martin Marietta Data Systems 6100 Bandera Rd Suite 900 San Antonio TX 78238

TROUBETZKOY-LEWIS, DARIA SERGEIVNA, communications company executive, technical writer, consultant; b. N.Y.C., Dec. 15, 1944; d. Sergei Sergeivich and Dorothy Livingston (Ulrich) Troubetzkoy; m. Robert Matthew Lewis, Jan. 15, 1968 (div. 1974); 1 dau., Sorrell Zenaide. B.A., U. Hartford, 1971, M.A., 1973; postgrad. CUNY, 1975-79, Bridgeport Engring. Inst., 1979-81, Sacred Heart U., Bridgeport, Conn., 1982—. Instr. English, Queens Coll., 1974-78; tech. writer Moore Spl. Tool Co., Inc., Bridgeport, 1978-79; sr. tech. writer Perkin-Elmer Corp., Norwalk, Conn., 1979-81; mgr. engring. communications TIE/Communications, Inc., Shelton, Conn., 1981—; freelance tech. writer, 1977-82. Mem. Women in Communications, Soc. Tech. Communication, Women in Telecommunications, Mensa (editor So. Conn. chpt. 1982-83, Conn. and Western Mass. chpt. 1981-82, Firebird award 1982). Russian Orthodox. Home: 203 Samp Mortar Dr Fairfield CT 06430 Office: TIE/ Communications Inc 5 Research Dr Shelton CT 06484

TROUPE, MARILYN KAY, cosmetologist, educator; b. Tulsa, Sept. 30, 1945; d. Ernest Robinson and Lucille (Andrew) Troupe. B.A. in Social Sci., Langston U., Okla., 1967; M.A. in History, Okla. State U., 1976; D. in Beauty, Nat. Inst., Nat. Beauty Culturists League, Washington, 1978; Lic. in Cosmetology, Troupe's Beauty Sch., 1970. Cert. tchr. Okla. Tchr. social studies Margaret Hudson Program, Tulsa, 1969-81, tutor Tulsa Indian Youth, 1971-72; instr. cosmetology McLain-Tulsa Pub. Schs., 1982—; owner Troupe's Salon of Beauty, Tulsa; vis. lectr. Okla. State U., 1980-81; cons., lectr. cosmetology. Mem., Foster Care Rev. Bd., Tulsa, 1985-86; registrar Osage County Election Bd., Tulsa, 1985-86; pres. Minority Polit. Women, Tulsa, 1986; pres. Holy Family Sch. Bd., Tulsa, 1985-86; mem. Tulsa Ballet Guild, 1985-86, Gilcrease Mus., 1986, N. Tulsa Heritage Found. Inc., vol. numerous other civic orgns. including Youth Services, Tulsa; gov. bd., chmn. Community Action Com., Roman Catholic Ch., Tulsa, 1985-86. Recipient numerous awards for profl. and civic contbns. including Woman of Yr., Zeta Phi Beta, 1985; Salute award Gov. Okla., 1985; Outstanding Community Service Cert., WomenFest, 1985. Mem. Vocat. Indsl. Clubs Am. (dist. advisor 1985-86, Appreciation award 1985), Am. Vocat. Assn., Okla. Vocat. Assn., Okla. State Beauty Culturalists League (pres. 1979-85, Outstanding Service award 1985), Phi Alpha Theta, Theta Nu Sigma (fin. sec. 1985-86), Alpha Kappa Alpha. Democrat. Roman Catholic. Clubs: Tulsa Links, Cath. Daus. Am. (treas. 1986). Avocations: travel; ballet; opera; Broadway plays; collecting stamps and coins. Home: PO Box 27583 Tulsa OK 74149 Office: McLain High Sch 4929 N Peoria Tulsa OK 74126

TROUT, MARGIE MARIE MUELLER, civic worker; b. Wellston, Mo., Apr. 27, 1923; d. Albert Sylvester and Pearl Elizabeth (Jose) Mueller; student Webster Coll., 1944-45; cert. genealogist Bd. Cert. Genealogy; m. Maurice Elmore Trout, Aug. 24, 1943; children—Richard Willis, Babette Yvonne. Sec. offices Robertson Aircraft Corp., St. Louis, 1942; speed lathe and drill press operator Busch-Selzer Diesel Engine Co., St. Louis, 1942-43; Cub Scout den mother, Vienna, Austria, 1953-55, Mt. Pleasant, Mich., 1955, London, 1956-57; leader Nat. Capitol council Girl Scouts U.S.A., Bethesda, Md., 1963-65; co-chmn. Am. Booth YWCA and Red Cross Annual Bazaars, Bangkok, Thailand, 1970-72; worker ARC, Vientiane, Laos, 1959-60, Bangkok, 1970-72; activities co-chmn., exec. bd. mem. Women's Club Armed Forces Staff Coll., Norfolk, Va., 1975-77; mem. Am. Women's Clubs, Embassy Clubs, Internat. Women's Clubs Vienna, 1952-55, London, 1956-59, Vientiane, 1959-61, Bangkok, 1969-72, Munich, Germany, 1965-69, Norfolk, 1975-77. Crochet articles exhibited Exhibition of Works of Art by the Corps Diplomatique, London, Eng., 1958. Home: 6203 Hardy Dr McLean VA 22101

TROUTWINE, CHARLOTTE TEMPERLEY, psychologist, medical executive, educator, clergyman; b. Newton, Mass., Nov. 27, 1906; d. Joseph and Libbie (Kempton) Temperley; B.S., Simmons Coll., 1927; grad. student Boston U., 1947-49; M.A., Northeastern U., 1966; m. Arklay S. Richards, Nov. 28, 1928 (div. 1942); children—Whitman Albin, Lincoln Kempton, Sylvia Caroline; m. Harry Troutwine, May 3, 1945 (div. 1954); m. Charles McCrum, 1961 (div. 1966); m. Lester Lewis Walsh, Feb. 16, 1968 (div. 1972); m. George Braun, Feb. 6, 1975 (dec. Oct. 1975). Pvt. sec. to pres. Hygrade Sylvania Electric Corp., Salem, Mass., 1927-28; pvt. and dept. exec. sec. Dr. Stanley Cobb, Bullard prof. neuropathology Harvard Med. Sch., 1928-31; part-time work, various positions, 1931-51; exec. dir. Postgrad. Med. Inst., 1951-57; mgr. Postgrad. Info. Service, Lederle Labs. div. Am. Cyanamid Co., Pearl River, N.Y., 1957-61; exec. sec. postgrad. med. edn. Hahnemann Med. Coll. and Hosp., also exec. dir. Mary Bailey Inst. Cardiovascular Research, Phila., 1961; high sch. counselor; instr. psychology Holliston High Sch., 1965-66, Falmouth (Mass.) High Sch., 1966-74; psychotherapist Hallgarth Assocs., 1974-75, Friends of Framingham Reformatory; pastor Internat. Ch. Ageless Wisdom, 1982-86; speaker for Am. Epilepsy League. Mem. Simmons Coll. Alumnae Assn., Mass. Psychol. Assn., Am. Assn. Psychical Research, Spiritual Frontiers Fellowship (life), NEA (life), States Med. Postgrad. Assn. (past sec.), Am. Assn. Med. Soc. Execs. (emeritus), Mass. Tchrs. Assn. (life), Nat. Ret. Tchrs. Assn. (life), Nat. Sch. Counselors Assn. (life and charter), Soc. Mayflower Descs. (life), Assn. Research and Enlightenment, World Fedn. Healing, Interface, North Falmouth Village Civic Assn. (life), Am. Spiritual Healing Assn. (adv. bd.) Mass. Healing Assn. Mem. Soc. of Friends. Author articles in field. Home: 83 Falmouth Ct Bedford MA 01730

TROVER, ELLEN LLOYD, lawyer; b. Richmond, Va., Nov. 23, 1947; d. Robert Van Buren and Hazel (Urban) Lloyd; m. Denis William Trover, June 12, 1971; 1 dau., Florence Emma. A.B., Vassar Coll., 1969; J.D., Coll. William and Mary, 1972. Asst. editor Bancroft-Whitney, San Francisco, 1973-74; owner Ellen Lloyd Trover Atty.-at-Law, Thousand Oaks, Calif., 1974-82; ptnr. Trover & Fisher, Thousand Oaks, 1982—; dir. Burco Mfg., Los Angeles, 1981—. Editor: Handbooks of State Chronologies, 1972. Trustee, Conejo Future Found., Thousand Oaks, 1978—, vice chmn., 1982-84, chmn., 1984—; pres. Zonta Club Conejo Valley Area, 1978-79; trustee Hydro Help for the Handicapped, 1980-85. Mem. Conejo Simi Bar Assn. (pres. 1979-80, dir. 1983-86), Ventura County Bar Assn. (state del. 1984), State Bar Calif., Va. State Bar, Phi Alpha Delta. Democrat. Presbyterian. Home: 11355 Presilla Rd Camarillo CA 93010 Office: Trover and Fisher 1107E Thousand Oaks Blvd Thousand Oaks CA 91362

TROWNSELL, GAIL KAYE, jewelry importer, educator; b. Bagley, Minn., Apr. 27, 1945; d. Burdette Francis and Stella Marie (Horner) Bushman; m. Michael Vickers Trownsell, July 2, 1982; dau. by previous marriage, Melissa Gail Anderson. B.A. with honors, U. Calif.-Berkeley, 1963-69. Cert. tchr., reading specialist, Calif. Tchr. elem. schs., Antioch, Calif., 1969-78, reading specialist, 1978-81; reading cons. elem. schs., Modesto, Calif., 1981-84; owner, mgr. Jewelry of the Rich and Famous, Modesto and Redondo Beach, Calif., 1984—; hist. jewelry cons., 1985—. Creator ednl. game. Chmn. Antioch Sch. Improvement Program, 1975-77; chmn. Modesto PTA, 1982-86; troop leader John Muir council Girl Scouts U.S.A., 1982—. Mem. Calif. Reading Assn., AAW, Nat. Assn. Female Execs. Republican. Avocations: travel, historical research.

TROY, JANE CAROLYN, government official; b. Washington, Nov. 11, 1935; d. John and Allene (Parry) T.; With Overseas Pvt. Investment Corp., Washington, 1966—, dep. dir., now regional mgr. Europe/Middle East/Africa Internat. div. Office: 1615 M St NW Washington DC 20527

TROYKA, LYNN QUITMAN, educator; b. Phila., Feb. 21, 1938; d. Sidney L. and Belle (Furman) Q.; B.A., Brandeis U., 1959; M.A., N.Y. U., 1960, Ph.D., 1973; m. David Troyka, Aug. 13, 1965. Tchr., Hastings-on-Hudson (N.Y.) Public Schs., 1960-63; tchr., head jr. high div. Baldwin Sch., N.Y.C., 1963-67; instr. dept. basic ednl. skills Queensborough Community Coll., City U. N.Y., 1967-69, asst. prof., 1969-72, asso. prof., 1972-76, prof., 1976-83, supr. writing skills program, dep. dept. chmn., 1967-75; prof. Center for Advanced Study in Edn., City U. N.Y., 1975-78, research assoc. Office Acad. Affairs, Bd. Higher Edn., 1980-84, research assoc. Instructional Resource Ctr., 1984—; cons. The Coll. Bd., 1972-79, N.Y. State Regents, 1978-80, Nat. Endowment Humanities, 1980-81, Nat. Inst. Edn., 1978-82, Nat. Assessment of Ednl. Progress, 1980—; chmn. N.E. Regional Conf. on English in 2-Year Coll., 1974-76. Accredited writing program evaluator. Mem. Nat. Council Tchrs. English (dir. 1979—, exec. com. 1980—, coll. sect. chair 1985—), MLA (exec. com. div. on teaching of writing 1983—, chair 1986—), Conf. Coll. Composition and Communication (chmn. 1979-82), N.Y. State English Council, Internat. Reading Assn. Author: Steps in Composition, 1970, 5th edit., 1982; An A Posteriori Study of the Writing Assessment Test, CUNY, 1982; Taking Action: Writing, Reading, Speaking, and Listening Through Simulation-Games, 1975; A Strategy for Coping with High School and College Remedial English Problems, 1977; Structured Reading, 1978, 2d edit., 1984; A Checklist and Guide for Reviewing Departments of English, 1985; Simon and Schuster Handbook for Writers, 1986; Simon and Schuster Workbook for Writers, 1986; editor: Guide to Writing, 1974; two-year coll. editor Freshman English News, 1973-75; editorial bd. Teaching English in the Two-Year College, 1978-83; Simulation/Gaming: Jour. of Experiential Learning, 1977-79; College Composition and Communication, 1983-87; editor Jour. Basic Writing; columnist English in the Two-Yr. Coll., 1982—. Home: 166-25 Powells Cove Blvd Beechhurst NY 11357

TRUAX, SUZY, office complex and secretarial service executive; b. Reno, Dec. 10, 1939; d. James A. and J. Sue (Hawkins) Smith; A.A. in Bus., Truckee Meadows Community Coll., 1977; div.; children—Coleen Sue, Kevin Todd. Asst. sales mgr. Western div. Baker & Taylor Co., 1968-70; spl. edn. tchrs. asst. Washoe County Sch. Dist., Reno, 1970-75; exec. sec. Heppner & Crofoot, C.P.A.s, 1975-79; sec. to mng. partner Alexander Grant Co., Reno, 1980; owner, operator The Exec. Center, Reno, 1980—. Mem. Reno-Sparks C. of C., Am. Bus. Women's Assn. (past pres. Washoe Zephyrs chpt.), Profl. Assn. Secretarial Services, Bricklin Internat., Nor-Cal Bricklin Owners Assn. Democrat. Home: 2300 Harvard Way #126E Reno NV 89502 Office: 1105 Terminal Way Suite 202 Reno NV 89502

TRUBEK, JOSEPHINE SUSAN, lawyer; b. Uniontownship, N.J., Oct. 16, 1942; d. Herbert and Elizabeth (Throckmorton) T.; m. Barry W. Crouse, Sept. 2, 1967; 1 child, Elizabeth Trubek Crouse. B.A. in Econs., Skidmore Coll., 1964, M.A. in Econs., New Sch. Social Research, 1967; J.D., SUNY-Buffalo, 1975. Bar: N.Y. 1976, U.S. Dist. Ct. (we. dist.) N.Y. 1976. Research positions, 1964-69; regional planning specialist N.C. State U., Raleigh, 1970-72; assoc. Emmelyn Logan-Baldwin, Rochester, N.Y., 1975-76; staff atty. Rochester Telephone Corp., 1977-79, mgr. corp. law, 1979-82, corp. counsel. asst. sec., 1982—. Bd. dirs. Women's Career Ctr., Rochester, 1981—, chmn. bd., 1985—. Mem. ABA, N.Y. State Bar Assn., Monroe County Bar Assn. Home: 4950 Oak Orchard Rd Albion NY 14411 Office: Rochester Telephone Corp 100 Midtown Plaza Rochester NY 14646

TRUE, CLAUDIA, oil company executive, geologist; b. Kingsville, Tex., Sept. 15, 1948; d. Elmer Conrad and Gift Jeanette (Haralson) T.; m. Michael Frank Driggs, Mar. 31, 1983. B.A. in Geology, Trinity U., 1971; M.S. in Geology, Pa. State U., 1978. Research aide Tex. Bur. Econ. Geology, Austin, 1972-73; coal petrologist coal research sect. Pa. State U., University Park, 1974-77; cons. in coal petrology, University Park, 1975-77; coal geologist U.S. Geol. Survey, Denver, 1977-80; profn., exploration geologist Mobil Alternative Energy, Inc., Denver, 1980-85; prodn. geologist Mobil Oil Corp., Denver, 1986—; art cons.; speaker in field. Contbr. articles to profl. publs. Mem. Am. Inst. Profl. Geologists, AIME, Denver Coal Club (program chmn. 1984-85, bd. dirs. 1985—), Soc. Organic Petrolgists, Women in Mining (scholarship awards chmn., tech. adviser 1986-87). Republican. Methodist. Avocations: arts; music; travel. Home: 3284 Newton Denver CO 80211 Office: Mobil Oil Corp PO Box 5444 Denver CO 80217

TRUE, JEAN DURLAND, business executive; b. Olney, Ill., Nov. 27, 1915; d. Clyde Earl and Harriet Louise (Brayton) Durland; student Mont. State U., 1935-36; m. Henry Alfonso True, Jr., Mar. 20, 1938; children—Tamma Jean (Mrs. Donald G. Hatten), Henry Alfonso III, Diemer Durland, David Lanmon. Partner, True Drilling Co., Casper, Wyo., 1951—, True Oil Co., Casper, 1951—, Eighty-Eight Oil Co., 1955—, True Geothermal Energy Co., 1980—, True Ranches, 1981—; officer, dir. True Service Co., Casper, Toolpushers Supply Co., Casper, White Stallion Ranch, Inc., Tucson; dir. Belle Fourche Pipeline Co., Casper, Black Hills Trucking, Smoky Oil Co., True Geothermal Drilling Co.; dir. White Stallion Ranch, Tucson. Mem. steering com. YMCA, Casper, 1954-55, bd. dirs., 1956-58; mem. exec. bd. trustees Gottsche Rehab. Center, Thermopolis, Wyo., 1966—, v.p., 1973—; mem. adv. bd. for adult edn. U. Wyo., 1966-68; mem. Ft. Casper Commn., Casper, 1973—; bd. dirs. Mus. of Rockies, Bozeman, Mont., 1983—. Mem. Nat. Fedn. Republican Women's Clubs; del. Rep. nat. conv., 1972. Mem. Rocky Mountain Oil and Gas Industry, Casper Area C. of C., Alpha Gamma Delta. Episcopalian. Club: Casper Country; Petroleum Women's (Casper). Home: 6000 S Poplar St Casper WY 82601 Office: Rivercross Rd PO Box 2360 Casper WY 82602

TRUESDELL, CAROLYN GILMOUR, lawyer; b. Oak Park, Ill., July 15, 1939; d. William Bonney and Gladys (Chapman) Gilmour; m. J. Richard Cheney, June 26, 1982; children by previous marriage—Kelly Elizabeth, Robin Suzanne. Student Stanford U., 1957-59; B.A., Case Western Res. U., 1961; J.D., U. Houston, 1975. Bar: Tex. 1975. Law clk. Chief Judge John R. Brown, U.S. Ct. Appeals, 5th Cir., Houston, 1975-76; assoc. Vinson & Elkins, Houston, 1976-83, ptnr., 1983—. Mem. ABA, Nat. Assn. Bond Attys. Office: Vinson & Elkins 2700 First City Tower Houston TX 77002

TRUITT, EVELYN MACK, corporate executive; b. Los Angeles, July 2, 1931; d. Everett E. and Celeste (Pratt) Mack; m. Edwin A. Truitt, (div.). Student Los Angeles City Coll., UCLA, Sawyer Sch. Bus. Sec., United Calif. Bank, Los Angeles, 1951-57; group tour coordinator Gray Line Tours, Los Angeles, 1957-60; corp. exec. sec. Signal Cos., Inc., LaJolla, Calif., 1960-78, v.p., 1978—. Author: Who Was Who on Screen, 1974, 76, 83. Bd. dirs. Old Globe Theatre, San Diego, 1981, Girl Scouts U.S.A., San Diego, 1983. Republican. Office: Signal Cos Inc 11255 N Torrey Pines Rd LaJolla CA 92037

TRUJILLO, LINDA ANN, computerized adminstrv. services exec.; b. Tulsa, Dec. 28, 1947; d. William C. Lagoni and Mildred A. (Campbell) Wasson; student Coll. Marin, 1965-66, Calif. State U., Long Beach, 1978-82, Calif. State U., Dominiquez Hills, 1978-81; m. Allen H. Trujillo, Jan. 25, 1976; children—Rand B., Allison J., Shawn A., Curtis G. Adminstrv. asst. Kaiser Hosp., Bellflower, Calif., 1976-78; emergency services coordinator City of Long Beach, 1978, supr., 1978-79, mgr./adminstr. Emergency Communications Center, 1979-81; owner, mgr. Exec. Word Systems, Santa Ana, Calif., 1981-83; mgmt. cons. Planning Research Corp., 1982-83; communications mgr. Codex Corp., 1983—. Mem. Nat. Assn. Female Execs., WeCan Women's Network, Nat. Notary Assn. Republican. Adventist. Club: Racquetball World Health. Office: 920 W 17th St Suite C Santa Ana CA 92706 also 18700 Beach Blvd Suite 230 Huntington Beach CA 92648

TRUMAN, RUTH, administrator, writer, lecturer, consultant; b. Ashland, Ky., Oct. 5, 1931; d. Rexford Maitland and Allene G. (Barber) Dixon; B.S., Taylor U., 1952; M.S., Calif. State U., 1967; Ph.D. in Higher Edn., UCLA, 1978; m. Wallace Lee Truman, June 5, 1952; children—Mark, Rebecca, Timothy, Nathan. Tchr. Atco (N.J.) Elem. Sch., 1954; tchr. home econs. Chatham (N.J.) High Sch., 1955; counselor, instr. Citrus Coll., Azusa, Calif., 1967-70; dir. counseling Calif. Luth. Coll., Thousand Oaks, Calif., 1971-74; cons. Women's Ednl. Improvement Program, Los Angeles, 1978-80; women's center facilitator Mt. San Antonio Coll., Walnut, Calif., 1981-82; free-lance writer, lectr., cons., 1982-83; coordinator Cancer Mgmt. Network, U. So. Calif., 1983, assoc. dir. office cancer communications Comprehensive Cancer Ctr., 1984—; dir. Cancer Info. Service Calif., U. So. Calif., 1985-86; dir. cert. programs Calif. State U., Fullerton, 1986—. Trustee Baker Home for Ret. Ministers, Rowland Heights, Calif., 1982—; chmn. Com. Status and Role of Women, Pacific and Southwest Conf., United Meth. Ch., 1980-82, mem. Bd. Higher Edn., 1983-84; mem. exec. com. Ventura County Council Drug Abuse, 1972-73. Mem. UCLA Doctoral Assn., U. So. Calif. Women in Mgmt., Phi Delta Kappa. Democrat. Methodist. Author: How To Be A Liberated Christian, 1981; Spaghetti From the Chandelier, 1984; Mission of the Church College, 1978; Underground Manual for Ministers' Wives and Other Bewildered Women, 1974. Home: 2814 E Roberta Dr Orange CA 92669

TRUMM, NORMA MARIE, nurse, public relations representative, educator; b. Marion, S.D., Sept. 25, 1924; d. Francis Edward and Ruth Melinda (Carlson) Bittner; m. Dean Arba Trumm, June 12, 1954 (dec. 1982); children—Michael John, Bruce Douglas, David Wayne. Diploma in Nursing, Presentation Sch. Nursing, Aberdeen, S.D., 1945; postgrad. No. State Coll., 1942, U. Nebr.-Omaha, 1953, Linn-Benton Community Coll., 1982, Oreg. State U., 1981-82; Polio workshops, U. Mich., 1951, Mich. State U., 1952. R.N. Staff nurse Pontiac Gen. Hosp., Mich., 1945-47; pediatrics supr. Little Traverse Hosp., Petoskey, Mich., 1947-53; clin. instr. Children's Meml. Hosp., Omaha, 1953-55; med. student assignment Univ. Hosp. Clinic, Omaha, 1955-57; part time nurse Emanual Hosp., Omaha, 1957-59, Chamberlain Clinic, S.D., 1971-73; vol. home extension agt. Oreg. State U. Extension Service, Albany, 1983-84; pub. relations rep. Linn County Extension Service, Albany, Oreg., 1978—, ednl. programs, 1978—; pres. Linn County Homemakers Council, Albany, 1983-85. Area disaster chmn. Polio Found., Petoskey, 1950-53, del. nat. conv. March of Dimes, Polio Found., 1952; condr. legis. workshops Oreg. State U. Extension Service, Lebanon, 1981, 83, capitol tours, Salem, 1981, 83; mem. adminstrv. bd., council ministries, youth council Methodist Ch.; adminstrv. bd. United Methodist Women, 1986. Served with Cadet Nursing Corps., 1943-45. Mem. Extension Homemakers Council (pres. Linn County 1982-85, pin award 1985), Oreg. Extension Homemakers Council (cert. of appreciation 1984, pub. relations award 1984), Am. Country Women of World, Nat. Assn. Female Execs., Oreg. Tourism. Republican. Clubs: Sweet Home Extension (pres. 1981-83), Foster Scouter Club (advisor 1978-86), Kibitzer Bridge (pres. Sweet Home 1984-86). Lodge: Elks. Avocations: crochet; knitting; skiing; reading; politics. Home: 27630 Riggs Rd Foster OR 97345

TRUXILLO, BETTY DAVID, educator; b. Erwinville, La., Nov. 27, 1943; d. Willie and Lucia (Bizette) David; m. Russell J. Truxillo, Jr., Apr. 25, 1975; children—Lisa, Moira, Huber, Leslie, Dionne Wilkinson. Student Spencer Bus. Coll., 1962. Mgr. Brumfield Attys., Baton Rouge, 1974-76; dir. fin. aid Computer Bus. Mgmt., Baton Rouge, 1976-79; pres., dir. Baton Rouge Sch. of Computers, 1979—. Bd. dirs. La. Proprietary Commn., Baton Rouge, 1984—; col. of staff of Gov. Dave Treen, Baton Rouge, 1982-83. Named Boss of Yr., Am. Bus. Women's Assn., 1984. Mem. Baton Rouge C. of C., Nat. Assn. Fin. Aid, La. Assn. Fin. Aid, Better Bus. Bur., La. Proprietary Sch. Assn. (bd. dirs.), Nat. Assn. Trade and Tech. Schs. (adminstrv. adv. com.). Republican. Roman Catholic. Avocations: tennis; reading; traveling. Home: 7738 Don Budge Dr Baton Rouge LA 70809 Office: Baton Rouge Sch of Computers 9255 Interline Ave Baton Rouge LA 70809

TRZYNA, CHRISTINE ANN, physical education teacher; b. Chgo., Mar. 2, 1954; d. Edward J. and Helen J. (Partyka) T. B.S. in Edn., No. Ill. U., 1976, M.S., 1983. Cert. tchr., Ill., 1976. Tchr., Libertyville (Ill.) High Sch., 1976—. Mem. AAHPERD, Ill. Assn. Health, Phys. Edn. Recreation and Dance, Delta Psi Kappa (v.p. 1975-76). Democrat. Roman Catholic. Office: Libertyville High School 708 W Park Ave Libertyville IL 60048

TSAI, ELIZABETH TAN, lawyer; b. Roxas City, Philippines, Nov. 6, 1940; naturalized U.S. citizen, 1973; d. Vicente Robles and Rosario (Gonzaga) Tan; A.A. with honors, U. Philippines, Iloilo City, 1958; B.S. in Jurisprudence, LL.B. (Coll. of Law Golden Jubilee scholar), 1962; LL.M. (Univ. fellow), Yale U., 1965; m. Nien-Tszr Tsai, Dec. 2, 1967; children—Pearl Tan, Andrew Tan. Admitted to Philippine bar, 1963, Calif. bar, 1973, D.C. bar, 1974; assoc. firm SyCip, Salazar, Luna & Assocs., Manila, 1963-64; editor Lawyers Coop. Pub. Co., Rochester, N.Y., 1965-71; individual practice law, San Diego, 1973-74; atty.-adv. Div. Investment Mgmt., SEC, Washington, 1977-81, spl. counsel, 1981—. Mem. U. Philippines Alumni Assn. of Met. Washington Area (1st v.p. 1986-87). Democrat. Mem. Chinese Christian Ch. Recent decisions editor Philippine Law Jour., 1961-62; assoc. editor Philippine Internat. Law Jour., 1963-64. Office: 450 5th St Washington DC 20549

TSCHINKEL, VICTORIA JEAN, state official; b. Mt. Vernon, N.Y., Oct. 30, 1947; d. William Aaron and Edith (Meyerson) Nierenberg; m. Walter Rheinhardt Tschinkel, June 15, 1968. A.B. in Zoology, U. Calif.-Berkeley, 1968. Biologist, librarian Tall Timbers Research Sta., Tallahassee, 1970-74; field insp. Trustees for Internal Improvement Trust Fund, Tallahassee, 1974-76; environ. specialist Dept. Environ. Regulations, Tallahassee, 1976; asst. to sec. Dept. Environ. Regulations, 1976-77, asst. sec., 1977-81, sec., 1981—; mem. energy research adv. bd. Dept. Energy, 1979—; mem. adminstrv. toxic substances adv. council EPA, 1982-84; dir. Environ. and Energy Inst., Washington, 1984—; mem. Gas Research Adv. Council, Chgo., 1983—, NRC, Washington, 1983—, Space Applications Bd., 1983-85; mem. adv. panel on energy in city bldgs. Office Tech. Assessement, 1980-81; mem. adv. bd. Solar Energy Inst., 1985. Mem. Capital Womens Network, Tallahassee, 1983-84, Community Adv. Bd., Ctr. for Profl. Devel., 1983-84. Named North Fla. Pub. Aminstr. of Yr., Am. Soc. Pub. Adminstrs., 1984. Mem. Women Execs. in State Govt., Nat. Acad. Pub. Adminstrn. Office: Fla Dept Environ Regulation 2600 Blairstone Rd Tallahassee FL 32301

TSCHUDIN, GENEVIE NAOMI, former nurse, anesthetist, writer; b. Shelley, Idaho, Feb. 28, 1906; d. Willard Joseph and Naomi Elzada (Lawrence) Goff; m. Paul Tschudin (dec. Nov. 1973). R.N., Latter Day Saints Nurses Tng. Sch., 1923. Sch. nurse, Salt Lake City, 1923-24; nurse for children's orphanage, Salt Lake City, 1924-25; head nurse supt. Hull Hosp., Ypsilanti, Mich., 1930-36; founder unit for contagious diseases Latter Day Saints Hosp., Salt Lake City, 1936-39; chief nurse, anesthetist ob-gyn Jamaica Hosp., N.Y., 1936-39, nurse anesthetist in operating room, 1941; anesthetist ob-gyn Lenox Hill Hosp., N.Y.C., 1939, 41-71; nurse anesthetist operating room Queens Gen. Hosp., Jamaica, 1940. Author (poetry): U.S. Nurses Poetry, 1940 (1st prize). Mem. Fla. State Poets Assn. Republican. Mormon. Club: Poetry Appreciation (Ocala, Fla.). Avocation: writing. Home: 1130 NE 12th Ave Ocala FL 32670

TSE, DAPHNE CHIU-FUN, biochemist; b. Hong Kong, Mar. 11, 1939; came to U.S., 1958, naturalized, 1971; d. Kwong Chiu and Yee Wan (Choy) Hui; B.S., UCLA, 1962; m. Tim Tse, Feb. 1, 1964; children—Anthony, Eric. With Hyland Therapeutics div. Travenol Labs., Inc., Glendale, Calif., 1963—, sr. research scientist, 1979-81, research mgr., 1981—. Recipient Inventor's award Baxter Travenol Co., 1979, 84, 85. Mem. Am. Chem. Soc., Internat. Soc. Thrombosis and Hematology, Am. Heart Assn., AAAS. Methodist. Author articles in field; patentee in field. Office: 444 W Glenoaks Blvd Glendale CA 91202

TSENG, JOAN LIU, librarian; b. Chengtu, China, Jan. 5, 1939; came to U.S., 1963, naturalized, 1973; d. Yi-chiang and Chin-feen (Chou) Liu; m. Gan-tai Tseng, Sept. 5, 1965; children—Carol, Michelle. B.A., Nat. Taiwan U., Taipei, 1961; M.L.S., Tex. Woman's U., 1965. Children's librarian San Mateo County (Calif.) Library, 1965-66; periodical librarian Loyola Maymount U., Los Angeles, 1966-70, cataloging librarian, 1977-80; catalog librarian Palos Verdes (Calif.) Library Dist., 1980-84, asst. supr. tech. services, 1984—. Vol., Maurice Hawks Sch., Princeton Junction, N.J., 1975-77, Montemalaga Elem. Sch., Palos Verdes Estates, Calif., 1977. Scholar Nat. Taiwan U., 1957-61. Mem. ALA, Calif. Library Assn. (councilor 1983-85), Chinese-Am. Librarians Assn. Office: Palos Verdes Library Dist 650 Deep Valley Rd Palos Verdes Peninsula CA 90274

TSENG, SALLY CHENG, librarian, researcher; b. Chan-An, Kwang-tung, China, July 10, 1937; d. Yun-hsiang and Chin-han (Chen) Cheng; m. Joseph C. Tseng, May 25, 1969; children—David, Linda. B.A., Soochow U., 1962; M.L.S., U. Oreg., 1968. Cataloger U. Nebr., Lincoln, 1968-77, head serials cataloging, 1977-81; prin. serials cataloger U. Calif.-Irvine, 1981—, acting head serials dept., 1984—; workshop leader Nebr. Library Commn., Lincoln, 1980-81, OCLC Pacific Network, Claremont, Calif., 1981—, Calif. Library Assn., Sacramento, 1982, Nat. Central Library, Taipei, Taiwan, 1983—. Author: (with Christa F.B. Hoffman) Getting Ready for AACR2, 1980; editor Jour. Ednl. Media and Library Scis., 1981. Recipient Career Devel. award U. Calif., 1983. Scholar U. Oreg., 1966-68. Mem. ALA, Asian/Pacific Am. Librarians Assn. (pres. 1982-83), Chinese-Am. Librarians Assn. (pres. 1984—), Calif. Library Services, Calif. Library Assn., Pacific Rim Library and Information Service Com. Office: Univ Library Univ of Calif Irvine CA 92713

TUBRIDY, GENEVIEVE ROSE, writer; b. St. Paul, Dec. 2; d. Michael Joseph and Rose Florence (Urbanski) Ledo; m. Martin Paul Tubridy, June 2, 1956; children—Peggy Marie Tubridy Ery, Polly Maureen Tubridy. A.A. in Journalism, Riverside Coll., 1977; student pub. relations Calif. State U.-Long Beach, 1978; student journalism U. Toledo, 1979. Editor, reporter, supr. Travelers Aid, Los Angeles Internat. Airport, 1970-73; editor, bd. dirs. Parapsychology Assn. Riverside (Calif.), 1973-75; contbg. editor, reporter Connections and Consumer Guide Newspapers, Toledo, 1979-81; pub. service coordinator, promotion asst. Sta. WDHO-TV, Toledo, 1979-81; asst. pub. info. dir. Sta. WGTE-TV, Toledo, 1981; asst. exec. producer The Jeffersons, Embassy TV, Los Angeles, 1983-84; community liaison cons. Van Nuys C. of C., 1984-85; mem. communications staff Am. Cancer Soc., Van Nuys, Calif., 1985—. editor-in-chief Viewpoints Newspaper, Riverside, 1975-77. Contbr. article to jour., poetry to anthology. Coordinator Riverside Coll. Bicentennial Com., 1976; sec. World Affairs Council Club, Riverside, 1977; 1st v.p. San Fernando Valley Republican Women's Club, 1985-86; alt. del. Nat. Federated Rep. Women Biennial Conv., Phoenix, 1985. Recipient 2d place on-spot editorial award JACC Conv., 1975; 1st place rev. award U. So. Calif., 1976; Woman of Distinction award Riverside Coll., 1976, 77; Outstanding Service award Area Office on Aging, Northwestern Ohio, 1981. Mem. Profl. Women's Club (publicity and newsletter com. 1980), Women in Communications (sec. 1981), Advt. Club Toledo (pub. service com. 1980-81, silver award 1981), Alpha Gamma Sigma (publicity com. 1977; service award 1977), Sigma Delta Chi. Republican. Home: 4144 Woodman Sherman Oaks CA 91423

TUCEI, RENEE LYNN NICHOLS, savings association executive; b. Akron, July 15, 1956; d. Richard Gene and Dolores Evelyn (DePaul) Nichols; m. Alan Louis Tucei, Aug. 17, 1979; children—Brian Matthew Nichols, Linda Gabrielle. B.B.A. with honors, U. Tex., Austin, 1977. C.P.A., Tex. Staff auditor Arthur Anderson & Co., Houston, 1978-79; audit mgr. Peat Marwick Mitchell & Co., Houston, 1979-83; v.p., audit mgr. Home Savs. Assn., Houston, 1983-85, v.p., treas., 1985—; instr. Tex. Soc. C.P.A.s, Dallas, 1982. Docent, Harris County Heritage Soc., Houston, 1981-83; controller Southdown Village Community Assn., Houston, 1981-83; vol. Houston Jr. Achievement, Tex. Children's Hosp., Crisis Hotline of Houston. Mem. Fin. Mgrs. Soc., Galveston Hist. Found.; Am. Inst. C.P.A.s, Tex. Soc. C.P.A.s. Roman Catholic. Home: 7714 River Garden Dr Houston TX 77095 Office: Home Savings Assn PO Box 908 Houston TX 77001

TUCKER, BARBARA (BEBE LOU MUEHLE) (MRS. RICHARD WALTER TUCKER), arts patron, fashion cons.; b. Des Moines; d. Louis John and Harriett (Shilke) Muehle; student Drake U. Music Sch., Acad. Nvart, Detroit, Center Creative Studies, Detroit, Birmingham-Bloomfield Art Assn.; B.S., Iowa State U.; m. Richard Walter Tucker; 1 dau., Pamela Helen. Fashion writer W.T. Grant, N.Y.C., 1946-47, Kresge Newark, Newark, 1947-50, Best & Co., N.Y.C., 1950-51; millinery designer Chez Nous, Detroit, 1954-57; instr. fashion design Detroit Bd. Edn., 1960-63; fashion lectr. John Robert Powers Sch., Detroit, 1965-68; fashion coordinator Armo Co. of N.Y., 1968-72, Hoechst Fibers, 1972-75; v.p. Richard Tucker & Co., Detroit, 1969—; pres. Barbara Tucker Assos., 1967—. Mem. Met. Opera Com., Detroit, 1962—; charter mem. Am. Symphony Orch. League Vol. Council, nat. pres., 1971-73, instr. vol. mgmt., 1975—; pres. Detroit Symphony League, 1957—, hon. mem. Women's Assn. Detroit Symphony Orch., 1960—, pres., 1963, bd. dirs. Detroit Symphony, 1969—; bd. dirs. Women's com. Am. Lung Assn., 1967—, Women's Com. for Project Hope, 1966—; trustee Nat. Guild Community Schs. Arts, 1976—; mem. nat. women's bd. Northwood Inst., 1972—; bd. dirs. Am. Symphony Orch. League, 1971-73, 84—, nat. conf. chmn., 1986; bd. dirs. Mich. Orch. Assn., 1976, state pres., 1977—; bd. dirs. Oakland County Cultural Council. Mem. Am., Mich. home econs. assns., Founders Soc. Detroit Inst. Arts, Fashion Group Detroit (sec. 1973—), Internat. Platform Assn., Alpha Gamma Delta. Home: 3335 Burning Bush Rd Birmingham MI 48010

TUCKER, BETHANIE HAMLETT, educator of gifted and talented; b. Pittslvania, Va., Nov. 13, 1949; d. Warner H. and Estelle Joy (Hundley) H.; m. William L. Tucker, July 26, 1978. B.S., Averett Coll., 1972; M.Edn., U. Va., 1977. Cert. elem. edn. tchr. Tchr. Pittslvania County Schs., Chatham, Va., 1972-75, resource person, 1975-81; gifted and talented specialist, tchr. Halifax County Schs., Halifax, Va., 1981—, workshop dir., 1985; developer of regional creative competitions. Co-author: Curriculum--Primary Gifted/Talented. Contbr. activities to edn. mags. Mem. Parson's Bruce Art Assn., South Boston, Va., 1983—. Named Alumnae of Yr., Averett Coll., 1982. Mem. Va. Assn. Edn. of Gifted, Phi Delta Kappa. Avocations: water skiing, beekeeping, traveling, canoeing, archaeology. Home: Route 1 Box 204-A Alton VA 24520 Office: Project IDEA PO Box 838 South Boston VA 24592

TUCKER, DALE CAROLYN, obstetrician, gynecologist; b. Phila., July 6, 1951; d. Robert Benjamin and Kay (Bernstein) T. B.S., Drexel U., 1974; M.D., Jefferson Med. Coll., 1978. Intern, Mount Sinai Hosp., Toronto, Ont., Can., 1978-79; resident ob-gyn Thomas Jefferson U. Hosp., Phila., 1979-82; practice medicine specializing in ob-gyn Permanente Med. Group, Walnut Creek, Calif., 1982—. Fellow Am. Coll. Ob-Gyn; mem. Calif. Med. Assn., Am. Med. Women's Assn., Phi Kappa Phi. Home: 53 Sereno Circle Oakland CA 94619 Office: Permanente Med Group 1425 S Main St Walnut Creek CA 94596

TUCKER, DENISE JOYCE, marketing executive; b. N.Y.C., Mar. 25, 1948; d. Jeffrey James and Jeannine (Dutka) Joyce; m. Thomas C. Tucker, Dec. 24, 1983. B.A., Trinity Coll., Conn., 1972. Mktg. services coordinator Wilson Haight & Welch, Inc., Hartford, Conn., 1972-76; sr. mktg. analyst Travelers Ins. Co., Hartford, 1976-81; 2d v.p. mktg. Covenant Ins. Co., Hartford, 1981—. Arts bus. cons. Greater Hartford Arts Council, 1982—; bd. dirs. Conn. Opera, 1983-85; mem. Leadership Greater Hartford, 1985. Recipient Friends of Art award Trinity Coll., 1972. Mem. Aerobics and Fitness Assn. Am., Internat. Dance Exercise Assn., Greater Hartford C. of C. (sports and recreation com., women execs. task force). Avocations: aerobics; weight training; bicycling; skiing; reading. Office: Covenant Ins Co 95 Woodland St Hartford CT 06101

TUCKER, FLORENCE DENSLOW, government official; b. Greenville, Miss., Nov. 12, 1925; d. Victor Amos and Martha Buchannan (Binkley) Denslow; diploma piano (scholarship 1943), Ward-Belmont Coll., Nashville, 1945; piano pupil of Michael Field, N.Y.C., 1945-46; B.Mus.Edn. (Dean's scholar 1958-60), Delta State U., Cleveland, Miss., 1960; M.S. in Counseling, U. So. Miss., 1971; Hattiesburg; Ed.D., George Washington U., 1982; m. Joseph Nathaniel Tucker, Jr., Nov. 9, 1946 (dec.); children—Joseph Nathaniel, III, Frederick Steven, James Denslow; m. 2d, Noel Francis Parrish, June 25, 1983. Tchr. music Gulfport (Miss.) public schs., 1959-63; recreation therapist VA Hosp., Gulfport, 1964-70; edn. counselor USAF, Miss. and Japan, 1971-74, edn. services officer, Korea, 1974-75, asst. dir. sr. tng. CAP nat. hdqrs., 1975-77; EEO officer D.C. Dept. Labor, 1977-80; bur. chief complaints processing and adjudication Office EEO, U.S. Geol. Survey, Reston, Va., 1980-82, employee devel. specialist, Dept. Interior, 1982-84; internat. forum coordinator Pres.'s Com. on Employment of Handicapped, 1985; mem. Alexandria Commn. on Aging, Va., 1985—, chmn. edn. and cultural affairs com.; dir. Wake Assocs., Ltd., mgmt. cons., Washington, 1980-84; vis. prof. Kunsan (Korea) Tchrs. Coll., also Kunsan Jr. Coll., 1974-75; workshop leader, cons. in field. Organizer, pres. Gulfport chpt. Parents-Without-Partners, 1962-64; charter mem. Westminster Presbyn. Ch., Gulfport, 1961; mem. Nat. Council on Aging. Recipient Outstanding Vis. Prof. award Kunsan Tchrs. Coll., 1974, award promoting tchr. exchange program Kunsan Jr. Coll., 1975, also certs. commendation. Mem. AAAS, Am. Soc. Tng. and Devel., Women in Communication, Am. Soc. Pub. Adminstrn., Nat. Assn. Female Execs., Adult Edn. Assn., Am. Soc. Profl. and Exec. Women, Soc. Internat. Devel., Phi Delta Kappa. Clubs: Gulfport Yacht, Bayou View Country (Gulfport). Contbr. articles to profl. jours. Home: 4701 Kenmore Ave Apt 1310 Alexandria VA 22304

TUCKER, FRANCES GAITHER, marketing educator, researcher; b. Pittsburg, Mass., June 7, 1947; d. William Brian and Elizabeth (Walker) Gaither; m. James Burke Tucker, June 14, 1969; 1 child, Lauren Jessica. B.A., Wellesley Coll., 1969; M.B.A. with honors, Boston U., 1974; Ph.D., Ohio State U., 1980. Adminstrv. asst. Bolt Beranek & Newman, Cambridge, Mass., 1969-72; research assoc. Ohio State U., Columbus, 1974-79; asst. prof. Syracuse U. (N.Y.), 1979—; sr. cons. partner Bus. Research and Cons., Syracuse, N.Y., 1982—. Reviewer, contbr. articles profl. jours. Named Outstanding Young Women in Am., 1983; doctoral fellow Richard D. Irwin Found, 1978. Mem. Am. Mktg. Assn. (local officer 1979-83), Council Logistics Mgmt. (various coms. 1978—, doctoral research fellow 1978), Women's Transp. Seminar. Club: Syracuse Wellesley (career coordinator 1981—). Office: Syracuse U Sch Mgmt Syracuse NY 13244

TUCKER, FRANCES LAUGHRIDGE, civic worker; b. Anderson, S.C., Dec. 4, 1916; d. John Franklin and Sallie V. (Cowart) Laughridge; m. Russell Hatch Tucker, Aug. 30, 1946 (dec. Aug. 1977); children—Russell Hatch, Pamela H. Student U. Conn., 1970, Sacred Heart U., Fairfield, Conn., 1977, 79, Fairfield U., 1978, U. S.C., 1984. Sec. to atty., Asheville, N.C., 1935-37; sec. to gen. mgr. Ga. Talc Mining & Mfg., Asheville, 1937-42; sec. engring. dept. E.I. duPont de Nemours, Wilmington, Del., 1942-46. Chmn. radio com. D.C. chpt. ARC, 1947-48, bd. dirs., Beaufort County chpt., 1982—, chmn. pub. relations, Hilton Head Island, S.C., 1980—; mem. pub. relations com. United Fund, Westport-Weston, Conn., 1968-69; bd. dirs., communications media St. Luke's Episcopal Ch., Hilton Head Island, 1980—; media pub. relations Bloodmobile Hilton Head Hosp. Aux., 1984—. Clubs: Sea Pines Golf; Princeton of N.Y.C. Home: 13 Willow Oak Rd Hilton Head Island SC 29928

TUCKER, GEORGINIA MAY PETHERAM (MRS. RALPH J. TUCKER), home economics consultant, author; b. Hanford, Wash., Jan. 14, 1911; d. George Thomas and Emily (Russett) Petheram; B.S., Wash. State U., 1933; m. Ralph J. Tucker, Sept. 22, 1940 (div. Apr. 1954). Trainee, Cascadian Hotel, Wenatchee, Wash., 1933-35; food mgr. Roosevelt Hotel, Seattle, 1936-40, Rhodes Dept. Store Seattle, 1940-43; with U.S. Govt. survey Affect of Food on the Aging, 1951; food mgr. Boise Hotel (Idaho), 1953-57; food research Western Internat. Hotels, Seattle, 1957-59, asst. dir. food and beverage, 1959-66; dir. housekeeping Century Plaza Hotel, Los Angeles, 1966-75, ret., 1975; now cons.; instr. exec. housekeeping Pepperdine U.; instr. Golden Gate U. Hotel and Restaurant Sch., career devel. program Cornell U. Hotel and Restaurant Sch. Bd. mem. Com. of Profl. Women Los Angeles Symphony, 1971-72; docent, mem. bd. Filoli nat. trust. Recipient Disting. Home Econs. Alumnus award Wash. State U., 1978. Mem. Nat. Exec. Housekeepers Assn. (chpt. bd. mem. 1969-72, sec. 1969-70), Nat. Assistance League (mem. nat. bd. 1963-64), Home Economists in Bus. (nat. directory chmn. 1965), Am. Home Economists Assn., Wash. State Home Economists Assn., Alpha Delta Pi. Episcopalian. Club: Soroptimist (1st v.p. 1967-71, pres. 1971-72) (Beverly Hills, Calif.). Author: The Science of Housekeeping, 1970; The Professional Housekeeper, 1975. Home and Office: 25 Arroyo Ct #3 San Mateo CA 94402

TUCKER, GLORIAN DAILE, publishing company executive; b. Haleyville, Ala., July 11, 1948; d. Roy Lee and Doris Jean (Pierce) Buchanan; m. Stanton Tucker, June 30, 1964; 1 child, Nathan Pierce. Student NW Ala. State Jr. Coll., 1971-73, U. North Ala., 1980. Typesetter layout NW Alabamian, Haleyville, Ala., 1967-72, Daniels Golden Rule Press, Birmingham, Ala., 1977-78; owner, operator Typographics, Birmingham, 1977-81; v.p. The Drawing Board, Inc., Birmingham, 1981-84; exec. asst. Central Pub. Co., Inc., Birmingham, 1984—. Contbr. poems to poetry anthologies. Active P.T.A. Democrat. Baptist. Avocations: reading; poetry; hiking; travel. Home: 1020 Capri Circle Hueytown AL 35023 Office: Central Pub Co Inc 2708 Republic Blvd Birmingham AL 35214

TUCKER, HAZEL LEE, civic worker; b. Greenville, S.C., Jan. 28, 1930; d. Dean Wellington and Ruth Irene (Batson) Stepp; m. Jake William Hollingsworth, Mar. 12, 1947 (dec. Sept. 1975); children—Phyllis, Pamela; m. Lewis Gerald Tucker, Nov. 14, 1976. Bookkeeper, Batson Oil Co., Travelers Rest, S.C., 1953-75; owner, mgr. Colonial Oaks Mobile Manor, Travelers Rest, 1972-85. Pres. North Greenville Hosp. Aux., Travelers Rest, 1985—; mem. exec. com. Greenville Hosp. System Aux., 1985—; counselor Help Line, Emergency Ctr., Greenville, 1985—; mem. exec. council Piedmont Council for Prevention of Child Abuse, Greenville, S.C., 1985—; vol. Dept. Social Services, Greenville, 1985—; pres. Circle #5 parisview Ch., Greenville, 1985—. Named Vol. of Yr., North Greenville Hosp., Travelers Rest, 1985. Baptist. Home: 18 Quail Trail Route 9 Greenville SC 29609

TUCKER, HELEN WELCH, writer; b. Raleigh, N.C., Nov. 1, 1926; d. William Blair and Helen (Welch) T.; B.A., Wake Forest Coll., 1946; postgrad. Columbia U., 1957-58; m. William T. Beckwith, Jan. 9, 1971. Reporter, Burlington (N.C.) Times-News, 1946-47, Twin Falls (Idaho) Times-News, 1948-49, reporter Idaho Statesman, Boise, 1950-51; copy writer Sta. KDYL, Salt Lake City, 1952-53; copy supr. Sta. WPTF, Raleigh, 1953-55; reporter Raleigh Times, 1955-57; editorial asst. Columbia U. Press, 1959-60; dir. publicity and publications N.C. Mus. Art, Raleigh, 1967-70; author books: The Sound of Summer Voices, 1969, The Guilt of August Fielding, 1971, No Need of Glory, 1972, The Virgin of Lontano, 1973, A Strange and Ill-Starred Marriage, 1978, A Reason for Rivalry, 1979, A Mistress to the Regent, 1980, An Infamous Attachment, 1980, The Halverton Scandal, 1980, A Wedding Day Deception, 1981, The Double Dealers, 1982, Season of Dishonor, 1982, Ardent Vows, 1983; Bound by Honor, 1984; contbr. short stories to nat. mags. Recipient Disting. Alumni award in Journalism, Wake Forest U., 1971. Episcopalian. Home: 2930 Hostetler St Raleigh NC 27609

TUCKER, JOYCE ELAINE, lawyer, state human rights administrator; b. Chgo., Sept. 21, 1948; d. George M. and Vivian Louise T. B.S., U. Ill., 1970; J.D., John Marshall Law Sch., 1978. Bar: Ill. 1978. Substitute tchr. Chgo. Public Schs., 1970-71; mental health specialist Tinley Park (Ill.) Dept. Mental Health, 1970-74; coordinator Title VII Program, Ill. Dept. Mental Health, Chgo., 1974-76, chief mental health equal employment opportunity officer, 1976-79; acting dir. Ill. Dept. Equal Employment Opportunity, Chgo., 1979-80; dir. Ill. Dept. Human Rights, Chgo., 1980—. Mem. Nat. Bar Assn., Cook County Bar Assn. (Spl. Achievement award 1980), Am. Bar Assn., Chgo. Bar Assn. Mem. African Methodist Episcopal Ch. Chicago IL 60601 also 619 Stratton Office Bldg Springfield IL

TUCKER, LEIGH ANNE, microbiologist; b. Montgomery, Ala., Oct. 8, 1961; d. Frank Gordon Tucker and Mary Allen (Hargrove) Tucker Payne. B.S. in Microbiology, U. Ala., 1984; postgrad., Auburn U. Preparations supr. dept. microbiology, U. Ala., Tuscaloosa, 1984-85; pub. health rep. State of Ala., Montgomery, 1985—. Mem. Ala. Pub. Health Assn., Ala. State Employees Assn., State Employees Assn. (Polit. Action Com.), U. Ala. Nat. Alumni Assn., Nat. Assn. Female Execs. Republican. Methodist. Avocations: rafting; camping; swimming; singing; aerobics. Office: State of Alabama Dept Health 501 Dexter Ave Montgomery AL 36130

TUCKER, MARCIA, museum director, curator; b. N.Y.C., Apr. 11, 1940; d. Emanuel and Dorothy (Wald) Silverman; student Ecole du Louvre, Paris, 1959-60; B.A., Conn. Coll., New London, 1961; M.A., Inst. Fine Arts, N.Y. U., 1969; hon. doctorate San Francisco Art Inst. Curator, William N. Copley Collection, N.Y.C., 1963-66; editorial asso. Art News mag., N.Y.C., 1965-69; collection cataloger Alfred H. Barr, Jr., N.Y.C., 1966-67, catalog raisonée Howald Collection Am. Art, Ford Found., Columbus (Ohio) Gallery Fine Arts, 1966-69; curator painting and drawing Whitney Mus. Am. Art, N.Y.C., 1969-77; dir./founder The New Museum, N.Y.C., 1977—; faculty U. R.I., Kingston, 1966-68, City U. N.Y., 1967-68, Sch. Visual Arts, 1969-73, Columbia U. Sch. Arts and Scis., N.Y.C., 1977; guest lectr. San Francisco Art Inst., Yale U., Balt. Mus. Art, Art Inst. Chgo., Smithsonian Instn., Princeton U.; U.S. commr. 1984 Venice Biennale Mem. Coll. Art Assn., Am. Assn. Mus. (dir.), Phi Beta Kappa. Author: Anti-Illusion: Procedures/Materials, 1969; Catalogue of Ferdinand Howald Collection, 1969; Robert Morris, 1970; The Structure of Color, 1971; James Rosenquist, 1972; Bruce Nauman, 1973; Al Held, 1974; Richard Tuttle, 1975; Early Work by 5 Contemporary Artists, 1977; Bad Painting, 1978; Barry Le Va, 1979; John Baldessari, 1981; Not Just For Laughs: The Art of Subversion, 1981; Earl Staley: 1973-83, 1984; Paradise Lost/Paradise Regained, 1984; Choices: Making An Art Out of Everyday Life, 1986; catalog for Am. exhbn. at Venice Biennale; also articles. Office: New Museum Contemporary Art 583 Broadway New York NY 10012

TUCKER, MELODY SUE, planning analyst; b. Louisville, Nov. 9, 1947; B.S., Ind. U., 1970; M.P.A., Ariz. State U., 1985. Trainer, U.S. Office Edn. Alcohol and Drug Abuse Prevention Program, Chgo., 1974-77; coordinator prevention activities for alcohol, drug abuse, and mental health prevention activities Ariz. Dept. Health Services, Phoenix, 1978-83, contracts coordinator, 1983-84, trainer, 1984-85; planning analyst Community Hosps. of Central Calif., 1985—; staff Ariz. Gov.'s Task Force on Alcohol and Hwy. Safety, 1982; cons. human services, 1976—. Bd. dirs. Ariz. Right to Choose, 1982-83. Home: 5458 N Fresno St 102 Fresno CA 93710 Office: PO Box 1232 Fresno CA 93715

TUCKER, MICHELLE HEIDI, lawyer, certified public accountant; b. Gross Point Farms, Mich., Mar. 22, 1955; d. Edward Anthony and Rosemarie (Lendenmann) T. B.A. in Bus. Adminstrn. with high honors in Acctg., U. Hawaii, 1977; J.D., Richardson Sch. Law, 1981. C.P.A., Hawaii, Wash.; bar: Hawaii, Wash. Asst. real estate appraiser No Ka Oi Realty, Honolulu, summer 1975; acct., legal researcher Atty. Kwan Hi Lim, Honolulu, 1972-79; with Arthur Andersen & Co., Seattle, 1981-84. Pres. Hawaii Friends of the Library, 1986. Recipient Arthur Lyman Dean award U. Hawaii, 1977; J. Watamull scholar, 1977. Mem. ABA, Wash. Bar Assn., Hawaii Bar Assn., Am. Inst. C.P.A.s, Hawaii Soc. C.P.A.s, Bus. and Profl. Women. Democrat. Home: 1450 Aala St #2204 Honolulu HI 96817 Office: 820 Mililani St Suite 505 Honolulu HI 96813

TUCKER, NELDA JOY, school principal; b. Elk City, Okla., Nov. 14, 1950; d. Kenneth Dale and Nelona (Barnes) Campbell; m. Thomas Lee Tucker, July 12, 1969; children—Lisa Lenel, Monte Earl. B.S., Southwestern Okla. State Coll., 1973, M.S., 1983. Tchr., Sweetwater Sch., Okla., 1975-79, prin., 1979—. Mem. Okla. Coop. Sch. Adminstrs., Nat. Math. Tchrs., Nat. Sci. Tchrs. Democrat. Mem. Ch. of Christ. Avocations: reading, gardening. Home: Route 1 Box 146 Sweetwater OK 73666 Office: Sweetwater Sch Route 1 Box 6 Sweetwater OK 73666

TUCKER, REBECCA PERDUE, county official; b. Columbus, Ga., May 17, 1947; d. Joseph Bradley and Kathleen Jewette (Newsome) Perdue; children by previous marriage—Mary Kathleen Lucas, JaDon Lucille Lucas; m. Elton Glenn Tucker, Oct. 8, 1977; children—James Kirt, Karl Monroe, Kyle Watson. Dep. register of deeds New Hanover County, Wilmington, N.C., 1970-73, registrar of deeds, 1980—; paralegal Robert Calder, Wilmington, N.C., 1973-76, Elton G. Tucker, Wilmington, 1976-80; mem. Land Records Com. N.C., 1983-85. Pres. New Hanover County Democratic Women, 1985-86; 1st vice chmn. Dem. Precinct-Harnet 3, New Hanover County, 1985—. Mem. Wilmington Legal Secs. (pres. 1977, 78, Legal Sec. of Yr. award 1979, 83), Am. Bus. Women Assn. (Cape Fear Charter chpt.), Register of Deeds Assn. N.C. (pres. 1984-85), LWV. Club: Zonta. Lodges: Shriners Ladies (lodge pres. 1986), Order Eastern Star. Avocations: fishing; needlework; reading. Home: 5707 Park Ave Wilmington NC 28403 Office: Office Register of Deeds 314 Princess St Wilmington NC 28401

TUCKER, SALLY (SARAH ANN), art appraiser; b. Austin, Tex., Dec. 24, 1934; d. Jim and Lorena Leah (Kinsey) Tucker; m. Peter S. Solito, Aug. 31, 1978; 1 son, Keny Jim. B.A., U. St. Thomas, 1975; postgrad. S.W. Tex. State U., Ind. U. Ins. agt., Houston, 1952—; legal sec., 1960-70; real estate broker, owner Sally Tucker Investments, 1970—; fine arts appraiser, owner Tucker Appraisal Assocs., 1975—. Docent, Houston Mus. Fine Arts. Fellow Valuers Consortium Internat. (Founding); mem. Internat. Soc. Fine Arts Appraisers (charter), Internat. Soc. Appraisers, (ethics com., chmn. dist. fine arts rev. com.), Drawing Soc. N.Y., Houston Watercolor Soc., Artists Equity, Mensa, Am. Soc. Appraisers (cert.), Phi Alpha. Democrat. Methodist. Clubs: Houston, Riv-O-Lon Garden (pres. 1981). Home: 3219 Ella Lee Ln Houston TX 77019 Office: Tucker Appraisal Assocs River Oaks Shopping Center 1310 McDuffie Suite 31 Houston TX 77019

TUCKER, SHERRY ELIZABETH, lawyer; b. Guilford County, N.C., July 25, 1947; d. Raymond Jacob and Irma (Davis) T.; B.A. in Sociology, U. N.C., Asheville, 1973; M.A. in Sociology, Appalachian State U., 1974; J.D., N.C. Central U., 1977; m. James D. Coble, Dec. 19, 1979. Admitted to N.C. bar, 1978; individual practice law, Chapel Hill, N.C. 1978—; mem. N.C. Lawyer Referral Service. Mem. Am. Bar Assn., N.C. State Bar, N.C. Bar Assn. Office: PO Box 2504 Chapel Hill NC 27514

TUITE, KATHLEEN, communications company executive; b. Ottawa, Ill., Mar. 28, 1954; d. Robert Thomas and Barbara (Mills) T.; m. Jocques Kris Plothow, Mar. 22, 1986. B.S., Ball State U., 1977. Mgr. Estee Lauder, Ball Stores, Muncie, Ind., 1977-79; customer service AVCO Corp., Muncie, 1979-81; account exec. Ocala Broadcasting Co., Fla., 1981-82, Metromedia, Inc., St. Petersburg, Fla., 1982—. Mem. Nat. Assn. Profl. Sales Women (assoc.), Kappa Alpha Theta. Republican. Presbyterian. Home: Apt 1206 9100 9th St N Saint Petersburg FL 33702

TUITE, KATHY PATRICIA, photographer; b. Mpls., Nov. 2, 1954; d. John Francis and Camille Miriam (Maloof) T.; B.A. in Film Studies, Purdue U., 1976, M.S. in Ednl. Media, 1978. Grad. teaching asst. Purdue U., West Lafayette, Ind., 1977-78, visual aids specialist, audio-visual prodn. dept., 1978-81; staff photographer, writer Lafayette (Ind.) Sport Spirit, 1979-81; cinematographer Central Catholic High Sch., Lafayette, 1978-81; photography editor Natural Bodybuilding mag., 1982—; product photographer Shamrock Labs., Dublin Calif., 1982—; staff photographer: Body Power Mag., Iron Man, Woman and Strength, Lady Athlete, Muscular Development, SPA News; freelance photographer for publs. including NBC SportsWorld, Muscular Development, Powerlifting USA, Muscle Mag., 1979—; participant shows, including Hist. Wabash Valley Photo Contest, Lafayette, 1976, Invitational Diana Show, Berea (Ky.) Coll., 1977, Campus Arts to Community Grant Program, 1977, Open Wall Show, Chgo., 1977, Me-Understanding Myself and Others, Peoria, Ill., 1977, Women See Men, shows N.Y.C. and Boston, 1977, Magic Silver Show, Murray (Ky.) State U., 1978 (award). Named Ind. Hoosier Scholar, 1980; recipient Salute to Women sports award, AAUW and Lafayette Bus. and Profl. Women, 1980; named most valuable player Purdue Powerlifting Team, 1980, 81, 82 named Ms. Natural Calif., 1981, Ms. Ironwoman, 1981, Ms. Central U.S.A., 1981, YMCA Nat. Physique Champion, 1980; best lifter Memphis Open, 1980; No. Calif. Women's Powerlifting Champion, 1983, honorable mention Indsl. Photography Ann. Awards, 1983. Mem. Communications and Tech., Univ. Press Photographers Assn., Women in Communications, U.S. Powerlifting Fedn. (nat. powerlifting referee, mem. women's exec. com.), Purdue Powerlifting Team. Democrat. Roman Catholic. Editorial adviser The Steel Tip. Contbr. photographs to books, mags. Home: 563 Rica Ln Woodmere NY 11598

TULECKE, ROSE OSBORNE, writer, educator; b. Newton, Kans., Dec. 3, 1942; d. Donald A. and Helen M. (Hartman) Osborne; B.S., U. Kans., 1964; m. Jerome B. Tulecke, June 7, 1965; children—Mark, Linda. Free-lance writer Fort Worth Mag., 1973-77, asso. editor, 1980-81, editor, 1981-84; free-lance writer, 1984—; instr. media communications Tex. Christian U., Ft. Worth, 1984-85; publs. coordinator, editor United Way Met. Tarrant County, 1985—; asso. editor Tarrant County Med. Soc. Physician, Ft. Worth, 1977-79; editor Focus, Harris Hosp. mag., Ft. Worth, 1979-80. Leader, Girl Scouts U.S.A., 1978-81. Recipient Anson Jones award for excellence in coverage of health industry Tex. Med. Assn., 1984. Mem. Advt. Club Ft. Worth, Women in Communications, Tarrant County Med. Soc. Aux. Club: Fort Worth Woman's.

Home: 5201 South Dr Fort Worth TX 76132 Office: United Way Met Tarrant County 210 E 9th St Fort Worth TX 76102

TULL, THERESA ANNE, foreign service officer; b. Runnemede, N.J., Oct. 2, 1936; d. John James and Anna Cecelia (Paull) T. B.A., U. Md., 1972; M.A., U. Mich., 1973; postgrad. Nat. War Coll., Washington, 1980. Fgn. service officer Dept. State, Washington, 1963—, dep. prin. officer, Brussels, Saigon, Danang, 1973-75; prin. officer Cebu, Philippines, 1977-79; dir. office human rights, 1980-83; charge d'affaires, Am. Embassy, Vientiane, Laos, 1983—. Recipient Civilian Service award Dept. of State, 1970, Meritorious Honor award, 1977. Mem. Am. Fgn. Service Assn. Club: Cathedral Choral Soc. (Washington). Home: care Waldis 416 N Washington Ave Moorestown NJ 08057 Office: Am Embassy Box V APO San Francisco CA 96346

TULLER, WENDY JUDGE, petroleum company executive; b. Cranston, R.I., Dec. 17, 1943; d. Alfred Carman and Anna Louise (Waterman) Judge; A.B., Brown U., 1965; M.L.S., U. R.I., 1969. Elem. sch. librarian Providence Public Sch. System, 1965-69; mgr. Xerox Corp., various locations, 1969-75; mgr. Carter Hawley Hale Stores, Inc., Los Angeles, 1976; cons. Sibson & Co. Inc., Princeton, N.J., 1976-78; cons. equal opportunity affairs Atlantic Richfield Co., Los Angeles, 1978-84, cons. coll. relations, 1984—. Named Woman of Yr., YWCA, Stamford, Conn., 1974. Mem. Am. Soc. Personnel Adminstrs., Am. Soc. Tng. and Devel., Internat. Assn. Personnel Women, AAUW. Club: Los Angeles Athletic. Home: 222 S Figueroa St Los Angeles CA 90012 Office: 515 S Flower St Los Angeles CA 90071

TULLMAN, MARCIA, business executive; b. N.Y.C., Dec. 25, 1927; d. Irving Fierstein and Gertrude (Muschel) Laban; m. Irwin Ress, 1947 (div. 1961); children—Erica, Michal, Douglas; m. Milton Tullman, May 31, 1965. B.A., Bklyn. Coll., 1947; postgrad. Queens Coll., 1961-65. Substitute tchr., N.Y.C., 1961-65; pres. Milmar Washroom Service Co., Woodside, N.Y., 1982, Milmar Chem. Co., Woodside, 1982—. Co-author: Tiger, Tiger, 1965; contbr. to in-house newsletter. Democrat. Jewish. Avocations: writing; theater; cooking; swimming; singing. Home: 85-15 Main St Briarwood NY 11435 Office: Milmar Chem Co Inc 37-14 55th St Woodside NY 11377

TULLOCH-REID, ELMA DEEN, consultant; b. Erie, Pa., June 27, 1938; d. Theodore and Roberta (Hicks) Carlisle; B.S., N.C. Agrl. and Tech. State U., 1960; M.A., Calif. State U., 1977; Ed.D., Nova U., 1981; children—Robynne and Stacey (twins). Staff nurse Michael Reese Hosp., Chgo., 1960-62; instr. Cook County Sch. Nursing, Chgo., 1962-64; tchr. St. Joseph Convent, Trinidad, West Indies, 1964-66; med.-surg. coordinator St. Vincent Coll. Nursing, Los Angeles, 1967-69, me.-surg. coordinator, 1967-69; charge nurse Century City Hosp., Los Angeles, 1971-72; tchr. Los Angeles Unified Schs., 1972-75; instr. inservice dept. St. Vincent Med. Center, Los Angeles, 1972-75; dir. edn. and tng. Imperial Hosp., Inglewood, Calif., 1977-79; pres. Elma Tulloch-Reid Assocs., Los Angeles, 1981—; asst. prof. dept. continuing edn. Calif. State U., Long Beach, 1977-81, asso. prof., 1982—; instr. Pilot Program in Health Occupations, Culver City Unified Sch. Dist., 1985—; provider Advanced Life Support in Cardiopulmonary Resuscitation, Am. Heart Assn., 1982-84. Community instr. certified basic life support Los Angeles Cardio-Pulmonary Resuscitation Consortium, 1981-82. Recipient commendation City of Los Angeles, 1984. Mem. Nat. Orgn. Mothers of Twins, Am. Nurses Found., Nat. Assn. Female Execs., N.C. Agrl. and Tech. State U. Alumni Assn., AAUW, Phi Kappa Phi. Club: Westside Mothers Twins (pres. 1971-73) (Los Angeles). Home: 1056 Cochran Ave Los Angeles CA 90019 Office: Wilshire Blvd 36A47 Los Angeles CA 90036

TULP, GAYE G. K., oil and gas company executive, artist; b. Bismarck, N.D., Aug. 26, 1947; d. Virgil Ralph and Violet Flora (Burg) T.; grad. Famous Artist Sch., 1975; student in bus. mgmt. Houston Community Coll., 19 , also profl. seminars; 1 son, Travor Will Rogers. Sec., Thomas W. Moore, Atty., Houston, 1969-70; underwriter Gt. So. Life Ins. Co., Houston, 1970-71; temporary sec. Top Girls, Houston, 1972-73; sec. to v.p. Rex Supply Co., Houston, 1973; office mgr. John L. Skalla Agy., Houston, 1973-74; traffic coordinator Nat. Supply Co. div. Armco Inc., Houston; owner G&T Art Studio; cons. Internat. Transp. Mgmt. Assn. Served with USN, 1965-68, Vietnam. Mem. Internat. Transp. Mgmt. Assn., Nat. Assn. Female Execs. (network dir.), Houston Women's Bus. Club. Home: 3407 westhampton Houston TX 77045 Office: NSCo PO Box 4638 Houston TX 77210-4638

TUNG, BETTY WONG, ski apparel company executive; b. Shanghai, China, Feb. 23, 1944; d. Foo Yuan and Joanna (Chen) Wong; came to U.S., 1962; m. Michael Hong-nien Tung, Dec. 23, 1967; children—Patricia J., Eric M. B.S. in Chemistry, U. Calif.-Berkeley, 1966; M.S. in Phys. Chemistry, U. So. Calif., 1967. Research engr. NCR Corp., El Segundo, Calif., 1967-73; engring. specialist Northrop Corp., Hawthorne, Calif., 1973-78; pres. Fera Internat. Corp., Torrance, Calif., 1978—; dir. F.Y. Garments Ltd., Singapore, Ski Industries Am., 1985—. Contbr. article to profl. jour.; patentee electroless plating bath. Mem. Electrochem. Soc., Ski Industries Am. (bd. dirs.), Ski Fedn. Office: Fera Internat Corp 20603 Earl St Torrance CA 90503

TUNG, ROSALIE SUET-YING, educator; b. Shanghai, China, Dec. 2, 1948; came to U.S., 1975; d. Andrew Yan-Fu and Pauline Wai-Kam (Cheung) Lam; B.A. (Univ. scholar), York U., 1972; M.B.A., U. B.C., 1974, Ph.D. in Bus. Adminstrn. (Univ. fellow, Seagram Bus. fellow, H.R. MacMillan Family fellow), 1977; m. Byron Poon-Yan Tung, June 17, 1972; 1 dau., Michele Christine. Lectr., diploma div. U. B.C., 1975, lectr. exec. devel. program, 1975; prof. mgmt. Grad. Sch. Mgmt., U. Oreg., Eugene, 1977-80; vis. scholar U. Manchester (Eng.) Inst. Sci. and Tech., fall 1980; vis. prof. UCLA, spring 1981; prof. mgmt. Wharton Sch. Fin., U. Pa., Phila., 1981-85; prof. bus. adminstrn., dir. internat. bus. ctr. U. Wis., Milw., 1985—. Mem. Acad. Internat. Bus. (treas.), Acad. Mgmt., Am. Psychol. Assn., Am. Inst. Decision Scis., Am. Mgmt. Assn., Am. Econ. Assn., Internat. Assn. Applied Psychology, Am. Arbitration Assn. (comml. panel arbitrators). Roman Catholic. Author 6 books; contbr. articles to profl. jours. Office: U Wis-Milw Sch Business PO Box 742 Milwaukee WI 53201

TUNGATE, SUSAN SUMNER, lawyer; b. Watseka, Ill., July 25, 1947; d. Edward Culver and Theresa Eagle Sumner; m. James L. Tungate, Aug. 25, 1973; 1 child, Edward Earnest. B.S., B.A., Ill. Wesleyan U., 1970; postgrad. John Marshall Law Sch., Chgo., 1970-73; J.D., Loyola Sch. Law, New Orleans, 1975. Bar: Ill. 1976, La. 1986, U.S. Supreme Ct. 1981. Asst. pub. defender Iroquois County, Ill., 1978-82; sole practice, Watseka, Ill., 1976-79; ptnr. Tungate & Tungate, Watseka, 1979—. Republican candidate States Atty., Iroquois County, Ill., 1984. Mem. Iroquois County Bar Assn. (v.p. 1981-82), Ill. Bar Assn., Chgo. Bar Assn., Women's Bar Assn., Bus. and Profl. Women (pres. 1983), Ill. Assn. Trial Lawyers, ABA, Ill. Pub. Defender Assn., La. Bar Assn., Women's Law Club, DAR, Phi Alpha Delta, Phi Kappa Delta. Episcopalian. Club: Home Extension Assn. (pres. 1983). Home: PO Box 285 Milford IL 60953 Office: Tungate & Tungate 535 Walnut St E Watseka IL 60953

TUNKIEICZ, MARY URSULA, farm company executive, clown; b. Chgo., Sept. 28, 1937; d. Gunnar and Jennie Adella (Howe) Gram; student public schs., Mich. and Ill.; m. Charles Tunkieicz, Feb. 23, 1957; children—Charlene, John, Jennie, Robert. Vice pres. Charles Tunkieicz Farms, Inc., Kenosha, Wis., 1972—, sec., 1972-80, sec.-treas., 1980—, v.p., sec., 1982-86, chmn. bd., 1985-86; clown Kenosha Unified Sch. Dist., 1979—; dir. I Am Sorry God, Somers Clowns Circus film, Alpha Film Corp.; clown ambassador Cousin Otto's Alley #22, Franzen Bros. Traveling Circus, Delavan, Wis. Leader for cooking Somers 4-H Club, 1974-75, clown project leader, 1976-80; chairperson Kenosha Farm Bur., 1975-78, pres. women's group, 1982-84; pres. Homemakers Club, 1986. Mem. Somers Clowns Clubs (dir.), Soc. Am. Magicians, Wis. Magical Entertainers Club. Democrat. Roman Catholic. Lodges: Moose, Eagles. Contbr. poetry to various publs. Home: 8410 W 60th St Kenosha WI 53142 Office: 8418 38th St Kenosha WI 53142

TUNSKY, PATRICIA A., designer, executive; b. Manchester, Conn., Sept. 18, 1943; d. William R. and Catherine Tunsky; Cert. Tobe-Colburn Sch., N.Y.C., 1964; 1 dau., Arianna Deyan Tunsky Brashich. Dept. mgr. Saks Fifth Ave., N.Y.C., 1964-67; fashion coordinator Bobbie Brooks, 1967-68; fashion dir. Monsanto Textiles, 1969-71; v.p. Grey Advt., 1972; pres., chief exec. officer Pat Tunsky, Inc., N.Y.C., 1972—, Interior Colors, Inc., 1972—, Color Projections, Inc., 1972—; ptnr. The Report for Accessories, Inc., 1983—; lectr. in field. Recipient Mehitabel award Tobe Coburn Sch., 1981. Mem. Fashion Group, Inner Circle, Fashion Inst. Tech. Author articles in field. Home: 343 E 30th St New York NY 10016 Office: 80 W 40th St New York NY 10018

TUPAS, NENITA SERVAS, health services company executive, nurse; b. Dau, Pampanga, Philippines, June 24, 1952; came to U.S. 1976, naturalized 1982; d. Marcelino Valdez and Flaviana (Serafica) Servas; m. Manuel Villareal Tupas II, Mar. 3, 1975; children—Sharon, Manuel IV, Shelly. R.N., St. Louis U. Baguio Gen. Hosp. Sch. Nursing, Baguio City, Philippines, 1974. Nurse, U. Santo Tomas, Manila, Philippines, U. of East, Ramon Magsaysay Meml. Med. Ctr., Manila, 1975-76, Harbor-UCLA Hosp., Torrance, 1982; v.p. Paramed Health Services, Carson, Calif., 1982—, Systematic Ins. Review, Inc., Carson, 1976—. Republican. Roman Catholic. Avocations: playing chess, outing, traveling, fishing. Office: SIR Inc 18813 S Avalon Blvd PO Box 4511 Carson CA 90749

TUPPER, TERESA LEE, oil co. acctg. mgr.; b. Batavia, N.Y., Feb. 13, 1949; d. Lyle Franklin and Gwen Jane (Day) T.; B.A. in Math., Hastings Coll., 1971; M.B.A., Pa. State U., 1973. With Exxon Co. U.S.A., 1973—, budget analyst, Los Angeles, 1979-80, dist. acctg. supr., Harvey, La., 1980-81, div. mgr. oil and gas acctg., New Orleans, 1981—. Adv., Explorer Post, Houston council Boy Scouts Am., 1974-76. Recipient Good Citizen award DAR, 1967. Mem. Am. Mgmt. Assn., Petroleum Accts. Soc. (council), Nat. Assn. Female Execs. Republican. Presbyterian. Office: PO Box 60626 New Orleans LA 70160

TURCHUK, JULIA GRACE, multi-media director, artist; b. Yonkers, N.Y., Apr. 24, 1945; d. Elsie Riley; 1 dau., Felicia Eve. Student Sch. Visual Arts, 1964, 74, 81, 83, Am. Art Sch., 1962. Artist, Burt Wenk Studio, N.Y.C., 1966, Metro Seliger, N.Y.C., 1967; Freelance artist, art dir. 1492 Prodns., N.Y.C., 1967-70; art dir. Laser, Aniforms Prodns., N.Y.C., 1970-71, Aniforms, Melandrea, Prodns., N.Y.C., 1972-73; owner, dir. Coopdesign Studio, N.Y.C., 1974—; dir. co-producer various ednl./sci. confs., internat. showings, 1976—. Group show: Para Art, 1977; contbg. artist to mags.; photographer video works. Recipient Bronze medal Internat. Film and TV Festival, 1978, Info. Film Producers of Am., 1978; Silver medal Info. Film Producers Am., 1980; Presdl. Sports award Roller Skate, 1982. Mem. Nat. Assn. Female Execs. Club: Roxy Roller Skate (instr. N.Y.C. 1983-85). Home: 313 E 10th St New York NY 10009

TURCK, KATHRYN MARY, casualty insurance specialist; b. N.Y.C., June 28, 1950; d. John James and Gladys Lucy (Campkin) Delaney; m. Thomas Herbert Turck, July 11, 1970 (div. Mar. 1983). B.B.A., Baruch Coll., 1978; M.B.A., NYU, 1985. C.P.C.U. Asst. underwriter INA, N.Y.C., 1970-71; underwriting agt. Huntington T.Block Ins., Washington, 1971-73; account exec. Herbert L. Jamison & Co., N.Y.C., 1973-80; casualty ins. mgr. ITT Corp., N.Y.C., 1980—. Active Food and Justice Program-Riverside, N.Y.C., 1986—. Mem. C.P.C.U. Soc. (v.p. N.Y. chpt. 1985-86), Risk and Ins. Mgmt. Soc., Nat. Assn. Female Execs. Home: 345 E 80th St New York NY 10021 Office: ITT Corp 320 Park Ave New York NY 10021

TURCO, EILEEN, assn. exec.; b. Jersey City, Apr. 29, 1949; d. Arthur and Eileen (Warwick) Kaehler; student public schs.; m. Richard S. Turco, July 18, 1977; children—Robert Turco, Richard Sam II. Legal sec. Deeba, DeStefano, Sauter & Herd, St. Louis, 1976-77; exec. sec., asst. dir. devel. YMCA Greater St. Louis, 1978-80; dir. devel. YWCA, St. Louis, 1980—. Bd. dirs. Indsl. Aid. Mem. Regional Commerce and Growth Assn. (membership leader 1977-81), Nat. Soc. Fund-Raising Execs., Women's Info. Network. Clubs: Direct Mktg. of Am., Elks Ladies Aux., Ad Club of Mo. Office: YWCA Metro St Louis 1015 Locust St Suite 310 Saint Louis MO 63101

TURCO, MIMI, real estate executive, health club administrator; b. Newark, June 6, 1958; d. Jerry Carlo and Dolores Joanne (Scacco) T. Student in bus. adminstrn. U. Miami (Fla.), 1976-77. Adviser to pres. Jeryl Industries, Inc., Kearny, N.J., 1974-80, Road Bldg. and Constrn. Co., Kearny, 1976—; dir., gen. mgr. King's Court Health and Racquetball Club, Lyndhurst, N.J., 1979—; dir., gen. mgr., fin. adviser King's License, Inc., Lyndhurst, 1980—, dir. gen. mgr. DCT Yacht Charter Corp., Lyndhurst, 1981—; dir. fin. adviser Carla Devel. Corp., Lyndhurst, 1979—, Pond View Town Houses, Inc., Lyndhurst, 1979—, Mimi Urban Renewal Devel., Lyndhurst, 1980—, Lincoln Park Nursing Home (N.J.), 1980—. Active Passaic River Coalition, Lyndhurst, 1980-82. Recipient award Congressman Hollenback, 1982, USMC award Toys for Tots Campaign, 1982, Easter Seals benefit award, 1981, Lyndhurst Good Citizen award, Lyndhurst Twp., 1982. Mem. C. of C. Greater Newark, Chamber Commerce and Industry of Bergan County, Assn. for Fitness in Bus. and Industry, Nat. Assn. Geocosmic Research, Nat. Assn. Female Execs. Republican. Roman Catholic. Office: King's Ct Racquetball Club 525 Riverside Ave Lyndhurst NJ 07071

TURCOTTE, MARGARET JANE, nurse; Stow, Ohio, May 17, 1927; d. Edward Carlton and Florence Margaret (Hanson) McCauley; R.N., St. Thomas Hosp., Arkon, Ohio, 1949; m. Rene Turcotte, Nov. 24, 1961 (div. 1967); 1 son, Michael Lawrence. Gen. duty nurse, central supply staff St. Thomas Hosp., 1949-50; pvt. duty nurse, 1950-57; polio nurse Akron Children's Hosp., 1953-54; operating room, recovery room, emergency room nurse Robinson Meml. Hosp., Ravenna, Ohio, 1961-67, head nurse, 1966-67; staff nurse med. surg. service, head nurse central service Brentwood Hosp., Warrensville Heights, Ohio, 1967—, infections control officer, 1982—. Democrat. Roman Catholic. Home: 6037 Highview St Lot 14F Ravenna OH 44266 Office: 4110 Warrensville Center Rd Warrensville Heights OH 44122

TURECK, ROSALYN, pianist, harpsichordist, conductor, author, educator; b. Chgo., Dec. 14, 1914; d. Samuel and Monya (Lipson) T.; student of Sophia Brilliant-Liven, Jan Chiapusso, Olga Samaroff, Theremin; grad. cum laude Juilliard Sch. Music; m. George Wallingford Downs, Sept. 1, 1964. Concert pianist since age of 9, debut N.Y. Phila. Orch., Carnegie Hall, solo recitals with Chgo. Symphony Orch., at Carnegie Hall, Town Hall, Phila. Orch.; European debut, Copenhagen, 1947; conert tours of U.S., Europe, South Africa, S.Am., Israel, Hong King, India, Australia, and with orchs. throughout world; condr./soloist with London Philharmonia, 1958, N.Y. Philharm., 1958, Collegium Musicum, Copenhagen, 1958, Scottish Nat. Symphony, 1963, Israel Philharm., 1963, Internat. Bach Soc. Orch., 1967, 69, 70, Washington Nat. Symphony, 1970, others; with Tureck Bach Players, London, 1958—; TV appearances include Today Show, Camera 3, also in Eng.; mem. faculty Phila. Conservatory of Music, 1935-42, Mannes Coll. Music, 1940-44, Juilliard Sch. Music, 1943-55, Columbia U., 1953-55; vis. prof. Washington U., St. Louis, 1963-64; prof. music U. Calif., San Diego, 1967-72, U. Md., 1982-84; Regents lectr. U. Calif., San Diego, 1966, prof. music 1967-76; Corbett lectr. U. Cin.; lectr. various other colls. and univs.; vis. fellow St. Hilda's Coll., Oxford (Eng.) U., 1974, Wolfson Coll., 1975—; hon. life fellow St. Hilda's Coll.; founder/dir. Composers of Today, 1951-55, Tureck Bach Players, London, 1957—, Internat. Bach Soc., 1966, Inst. Bach Studies, 1968, Tureck Bach Inst., 1981; rec. artist. Recipient 1st prize Greater Chgo. Piano Playing Tournament, 1928; Schubert Meml. Contest, 1935, Nat. Fedn. Music Clubs Competition, 1935; Phi Beta award for Excellence; First Town Hall Endowment award, 1938; MacDowell Colony fellow, 1978; decorated officer Order of Merit (W.Ger.), 1979; nominee Grammy award, 1980; Mus.D. (hon.), Colby Coll., 1964, Roosevelt U., Chgo., 1968, Wilson Coll., 1968, Oxford U., 1977. Mem. Am. Music Scholarship Assn. (pres.), Societe Johann Sebastian Bach de Belgique (hon.), Royal Mus. Assn. (London), Royal Philharm. Soc. (London), Oxford Soc., Inc. Soc. Musicians (London), Am. Musicol. Soc., New Bach Soc. Clubs: Cosmopolitan, Bohemians (hon. life) (N.Y.C.). Author/editor: An Introduction to the Performance of Bach, 3 vols., 1959-60, Japanese edit., 1966, Spanish edit., 1975; Tureck Bach Urtext Series, 1981, 82; Tureck Bach Urtext Series, 1983—; also transcriptions, articles. Office: care Columbia Artists Mgmt Inc 165 W 57th St New York NY 10019

TURK, BLOSSOM MICHELE, educational administrator, educational consultant, counselor; b. N.Y.C., July 3, 1934; d. Joseph Jacob and Ann (Resnick) T.; m. Arthur Jacob Schlanger, July 4, 1954 (div. 1973); children—Jed Seth, Gregg Alex. B.S., CUNY, 1956; M.A., San Francisco State U., 1968; Ed.D., U. Idaho, 1978. Cert. tchr. counselor, prin. supt., Calif., Ida., N.Y. Tchr. Boise Schs., Idaho, 1968-72, counselor, 1972-77, adminstrv. intern, 1977-79, asst. prin., 1979-82, prin., 1982—; cons., speaker Mind Action Inc., Boise, 1981—. Active in Am. Ballet Aux., Boise, 1985; bd. dirs. YWCA, Boise, 1985. Recipient Woman Helping Women award Soroptomists of Idaho 1984. Mem. AAUW, N.W. Women in Edn., Nat. Assn. Secondary Prins., Am. Soc. Trainers, Idaho Assn. Sch. Adminstrs., Phi Delta Kappa. Avocations: swimming; cooking; travel. Home: 1433 E Woodvine Ct Boise ID 83706

TURKNETT, MARILYN JEAN, engineer; b. Houston, Aug. 15, 1960; d. Leo and Dorothy (Glover) Frank; m. Jerry Ciaid Turknett Jr.; 1 child, Tishun Nikco Turknett. B.S. in Civil Engring. cum laude, Prairie View A&M U., 1981. Sect. asst. Shell Oil Co., Houston, 1977-78; asst. engr. Phila. Electric Co., 1978-79; engr. onshore gas pipeline design div. Transco Energy, Houston, 1982-84. Author: Water Resources for 21st Century, 1982. Mem. ASCE, Tau Beta Phi. Baptist. Home: 5626 Ashburn Houston TX 77033 Office: PO Box 1396 2700 S Post Oak Houston TX 77029

TURLEY, ANN MARIE, graphic designer, painter; b. Los Angeles, May 28, 1947; d. Wilson Walter and Lillian Margaret (Hughes) T. B.A., Emmanuel Coll., 1969. Tchr. art Boston Pub. Schs., 1969-73; mural artist fed. grant, Somerville, Mass., 1973-76; tchr. art Somerville Pub. Schs., 1976-77, Boston Pub. Schs., 1978-79; designer D.C. Heath & Co., Lexington, Mass., 1979-83, design supr. DCH Ednl. Software div., 1983—. Artist, designer, painter mural paintings in pub. bldgs., 1973-76. Mem. Women in Communications, Inc., Networking for Emmanuel Women. Roman Catholic. Home: 141 Aldrich St Roslindale MA 02131 Office: Ednl Software Div DC Heath & Co 125 Spring St Lexington MA 02178

TURNBULL, DOREEN JOYCE, EDP consultant; b. Evanston, Ill., Jan. 10, 1938; d. Dale M. and Juliet L. (Van Buskirk) T.; m. Larry Russell, Apr. 13, 1984. B.S. in Bus. Mgmt., Calif. State Poly., Pomona, 1969; M.A. in Mgmt., Claremont Grad. Sch., 1984. Sr. systems analyst Sunkist Growers Inc., Sherman Oaks, Calif., 1968-74; EDP systems analyst Ralphs Grocery Co., Compton, Calif., 1974-77; propr. DJT Cons., 1977-80; project mgr., sr. systems analyst, Xerox Corp., Pasadena, Calif., 1980-84; project mgr. DHL Corp., San Bruno, Calif., 1984-86; propr. DJT Cons., 1986—. Mem. Data Processing Mgmt. Assn. (chpt. dir., sec.), Am. Mgmt. Assn., Nat. Assn. Female Execs., Women in Mgmt., IS/DP Alumni Assn. (dir.). Club: Altrusa (treas., past sec.) (Arcadia, Calif.). Home and Office: 760 Edgemar Ave Apt 307 Pacifica CA 94044 Office: 1000 Cherry Ave San Bruno CA 94066

TURNBULL, MARY EDITH, painter, art educator; b. Surrey, B.C., Can., Oct. 24, 1927; came to U.S., 1943, naturalized, 1952; d. Henry Harvey and May Lavina (Winter) T.; m. Dudley Charles Ambrose, July 16, 1949 (div. Apr. 1977); children—Peter Charles, Janet Mary, Antoinette Carmen Theresa. B.S., U. Calif.-Berkeley, 1949, teaching credential Calif. Poly. State U., 1979; postgrad. UCLA, 1984. Contract art instr. San Luis Obispo Art Assn., Calif., 1978-82, Paso Robles Art Assn., Calif., 1977-85, Cuesta Coll., San Luis Obispo, 1976-82; art therapist Riverview Vol. Assn., New Westminster, B.C., summer 1985; art co-ordinator Culver City Unified Sch. Dist., Calif., 1985—. Painter in oils and watercolor; one-woman shows include: Western Orchid Congress, Anaheim, Calif., 1975, Calif. Poly. State U., San Luis Obispo, 1977, Santa Barbara Mus. Natural History, 1981, Descanso Gardens Hospitality House Gallery, 1986; exhibited group shows including: Fresno Arts Ctr., 1978, Art Ctr., San Luis Obispo, 1980, Mid-State Fair (1st prize for watercolor) 1980, San Bernardino County Mus., 1985. Leader 4-H Club, Atascadero, Calif., 1950-54, 70-75; condr. art tours San Luis Obispo Civic Assn., 1978; fund raiser Monday Club, San Luis Obispo, 1974-80, chmn. art com., 1973-82. Mem. Nat. Watercolor Soc., San Luis Obispo Art Assn. (chmn. bus. exhibits 1973-78), Women in Design, Artists Equity Assn. (chmn. programs, sec. 1983-86), Exec. Female. Democrat. Avocations: reading; writing; traveling. Home: 4309 Radford Ave Suite A Studio City CA 91604 Office: Farragut Sch 10820 Farragut Dr Culver City CA 90230

TURNER, BENITA, beauty salon executive; b. Tyler, Tex., Aug. 12, 1949; d. Erroll Wesley McFarland and Jimmie Louise (Riddle) Blackburn; m. Robert Michael Turner, June 5, 1969; children—Kristi Michelle, Troy Neal, Jason Adam. Cosmetologist diploma Barrow Beauty Sch.; Color cons. diploma Beauty for All Seasons; student Sebastian Internat. Operator, S.E. Plaza Beauty, Salon, Tyler, 1968-69, Dillards Beauty Salon, Austin, Tex., 1969-71; legal sec. Pye, Dobbs, Johnson, Tyler, 1979-80; oil and gas sec. Black Hawk Oil Co., 1980-83; owner, stylist Casa Benita Beauty Salon, Tyler, 1983—. Active East Tex. Crisis Ctr., Tyler, 1984—. Mem. Tex. Hairdressers and Cosmetologists Assn. (pres. 1983—), Am. Bus. Women Assn., Tyler C. of C. (com. 1985—), Nat. Hairdressers and Cosmetologists Assn., S.E. Crossing Mchts. Assn. (sec. 1983-85), Beta Sigma Phi (pres. 1975, 77-78, 80-82, Area Girl of Yr. award 1980), Chi Xi Sigma (corr. sec. 1985). Democrat. Baptist. Avocations: sewing; reading. Home: 2327 Devine St Tyler TX 75701 Office: Casa Benita Hair Designs 3320 Troup Hwy Suite 115 Tyler TX 75701

TURNER, CATHY, retail manager; b. Denison, Iowa, June 1, 1951; d. Teddy Junior and Ruth F. (Paulsen) Cornelius; m. Billy Don Turner, July 3, 1975 (div. Dec. 1979); 1 child, Michelle Suzanne. B.A., U. Iowa, 1973. Asst. store mgr. Casual Corner, Houston, 1975-77, store mgr., 1977-80, dist. mgr., Tampa, Fla., 1980-81, regional mgr., Boca Raton, Fla., 1981—; bd. dirs., sec. Galleria Mall, Houston, 1979-80. Mem. Nat. Assn. Female Execs., Gamma Phi Beta. Methodist. Avocations: water skiing; skiing; softball. Office: Casual Corner 9353 W Atlantic Blvd Coral Springs FL 33065

TURNER, CHERI ANNE, financial paraplanner, securities agent, real estate agent, musician; b. Spring City, Pa., Apr. 7, 1949; d. Harold William and Evelyn Virginia (Wagner) T. Student Syracuse U., 1967-69; Cert. Fin. Paraplanner, Coll. Fin. Planning, Denver, 1985, student Fin. Planning. Pub. relations mediator Don Poindexter & Assocs., St. Petersburg, Fla., 1969-72; exec. sec. Honeywell Inc., Largo, Fla., 1972-75; sec., design coordinator SCM Design Ctr., Syracuse, N.Y., 1975-76; personnel dir. Jay Galbraith's Penthouse, St. Petersburg, 1977-79; cert. fin. paraplanner R. A. Siebern & Assocs., St. Petersburg, 1982—; real estate sales rep. McCormack/Terwilliger Assocs., St. Petersburg, 1984—; registered rep. gen. securities Mut. Benefit Fin. Service Co. Inc., Tampa, Fla., 1985—; music dir. Capt. Anderson Cruises, Clearwater, Fla., 1982—; pvt. practice music tchr., Largo, 1964—. Composer, illustrator children's music book: Ditties for Kiddies, 1980. Mem. Internat. Assn. Fin. Planners, Nat. Assn. Female Execs., Nat. Assn. Security Dealers, Internat. Cert. Fin. Planners (provisional). Democrat. Clubs: U.S. Figure Skating Assn. (preliminary test judge 1975—), Sun Coast Figure Skating Club. Avocations: figure skating; music; fishing; gemology; rock hounding. Home: 1213 Markley Dr Largo FL 33540 Office: RA Siebern & Assocs 7901 4th St N Suite 213 Saint Petersburg FL 33702

TURNER, CONSTANCE BRIDGES, psychologist; b. Sanford, Maine, Jan. 23, 1943; d. Cecil Foster and Ellen Lavinia (Hannaford) Bridges; m. C. William Turner, June 13, 1964; children—Tracey Jane, Joel Bridges. R.N., Maine Med. Ctr., 1964; B.A., Roger Williams Coll., 1978; M.A., U. Houston, 1980, Ph.D., 1982. R.N., Tex., R.I.; lic. psychologist, Tex. Charge nurse R.I. Med. Ctr., Cranston, 1964-65; nurse R.I. Hosp., Providence, 1965-72; research asst. U. Houston, 1978-80, teaching fellow, 1980-82; research assoc. Tex. Children's Hosp., Houston, 1982, psychologist, psychol. nursing cons., 1983—; adj. asst. prof. psychiatry Baylor Coll. Medicine, 1984—; mem. faculty Cardiovascular Seminar, Houston, 1984; pvt. practice psychology, Houston, 1984—; presenter at conf. S.W. Soc. for Research in Human Devel., Galveston, 1982. Reviewer Jour. Clin. Child Psychology, 1983-84. Vol., Tex. Children's Hosp. Aux., 1982. Mem. Am. Psychol. Assn., Soc. for Research in Child Devel., S.W. Soc. for Research in Human Devel. Episcopalian. Office: Dept Pediatric Psychiatry Tex Childrens Hosp PO Box 20269 Houston TX 77225 also Northwoods Park 4606 FM 1960 Suite 620 Houston TX 77069

TURNER, CURLEY B., auditor; b. Mansfield, La., Apr. 13, 1951; d. Coy and Iona (Howard) Green; m. Wilbert Louis Turner, May 8, 1971; 1 child, Terri Curtrice. B.S., So. U., 1972. Internal auditor Houston Natural Gas Co., Houston, 1972-76, staff acct., 1976-79; tax specialist Southwestern Bell Telephone Co., St. Louis, 1979-81, internal auditor, Dallas, 1981—. Bus., tax cons. WCT Bus. Cons., Dallas, 1982—. Mem. Nat. Assn. Black Accts., Nat. Assn. Female Execs., AAUW, NAACP. Democrat. Baptist. Avocations: reading; fashion; tennis. Office: Southwestern Bell Tel Co 311 S Akard St #1602 Dallas TX 75202

TURNER, DELORIS BACK, nurse; b. Paintsville, Ky., Dec. 22, 1951; d. Freman and Barbara Leigh (Howard) B.; m. James Turner, Jr., July 20, 1968; children—Heather Sue, Richard Freman. B.S. in Nursing, U. Ky., 1975. R.N., Ky. Staff nurse St. Joseph Hosp., Lexington, Ky., 1975-77; staff nurse VA Med. Ctr., Lexington, 1977-78, nurse coordinator, 1978—; instr. critical care course, Lexington, 1985. Recipient Hands and Heart award VA Med. Ctr., 1985. Mem. Am. Assn. Neurosci. Nursing (acting chmn. Bluegrass chpt. 1984). Lodge: Order Eastern Star. Avocations: knitting; reading. Home: 3544 Sundart Dr Lexington KY 40502 Office: VA Med Ctr Cooper Dr Lexington KY 40511

TURNER, ELAINE HELGA SWANSON, physician; b. Glen Cove, N.Y., Feb. 19, 1947; d. Elston Hubert and Helga (Thompsen) Swanson; m. David Benjamin Turner, May 11, 1974; children—Petra Elaine, Paul David. B.A., Wheaton Coll., 1968; postgrad. U. Pa., 1968-69; M.D., Med. Coll. Pa., 1974. Diplomate Am. Bd. Internal Medicine, Am. Bd. Allergy and Clin. Immunology. Intern Michael Reese Hosp., Chgo., 1974-75; resident in internal medicine Cleve. Clinic, 1976-78; fellow in allergy and clin. immunology Northwestern U., Chgo., 1975-76, 78-80, clin. instr. internal medicine Northwestern U. Med. Sch., 1978-79; attending physician Inst. Allergy and Immunology, Grant Hosp., Chgo., 1980-82; clin. instr. medicine and allergy/immunology Rush Med. Sch., Chgo., 1981-82; allergy and immunology cons. Mile Square Ctr. and Anchor Health Maintenance Orgn., 1981-82; practice medicine specializing in allergy and immunology, L.I., N.Y., 1982—; mem. staff Community Hosp. at Glen Cove (N.Y.), 1982—, North Shore Univ. Hosp., Manhasset, N.Y.; cons. staff Syosset Community Hosp., 1985—. Contbr. articles to profl. jours. Mem. ACP, Am. Acad. Allergy, Nassau-Suffolk Allergy Soc. Office: 4 Medical Plaza Glen Cove NY 11542

TURNER, ELIZABETH ADAMS NOBLE, realty co. exec.; b. Yonkers, N.Y., May 18, 1931; d. James Kendrick and Orrel (Baldwin) Noble; B.A., Vassar Coll., 1953; M.A., Tex. A&I U., 1964; m. Jack Rice Turner, July 11, 1953; children—Jay Kendrick, Randall Ray. Ednl. cons. Noble & Noble Pub. Co., N.Y.C., 1956-67; psychometrist Corpus Christi Guidance Center, 1967-70; psychologist Corpus Christi State Sch., 1970-72, dir. programs, 1972, dir. vol. service, 1972-76; program cons. Tex. Dept. Mental Health and Mental Retardation and Corpus Christi State U., 1976—; dir. staff devel. Corpus Christi State Sch., 1978-79; coordinator vols. Summer Head Start Program, Corpus Christi, 1967. Mem. allocations com. United Fund, Corpus Christi, 1970; mem. Corpus Christi City Council, 1979-81; mayor pro tem Corpus Christi, 1981—; co-owner Turner, Whittle & Tate, Inc., Realtors. Leadership Corpus Christi, Com. of 100—Goals for Corpus Christi; mem. adv. bd. U. Tex.; bd. dirs. Coastal Bends Council Govts., Conv. and Tourist Bur., Big Bros., YWCA, Corpus Christi Hearing and Speech, C. of C., Coastal Bend Mental Health Assn., Suicide Prevention Inc., Tb Assn. (all Corpus Christi), Corpus Christi Mus., Art Mus. S. Tex., Corpus Christi. Recipient Love award YWCA, 1970. Mem. Tex. Psychol. Assn. (pres., mem. exec. bd.), Psychol. Assos. (pres.), Jr. League Corpus Christi, Tex. Bookman's Assn., C. of C. (dir.), Tex. Assn. Realtors, Kappa Kappa Gamma. Clubs: Corpus Christi Country, Corpus Christi Yacht, Junior Cotillion, Corpus Christi Press. Home: 4466 Ocean Dr Corpus Christi TX 78404

TURNER, ELIZAPETH ANN, insurance agent, risk management consultant; b. Vancouver, Wash., July 27, 1951; d. Wallace L. and Pearl (Burk) T.; m. Franklin R. Fulkerson, May 16, 1982. B.A., Whittier Coll., 1973; postgrad. UCLA, 1975, 76. Account exec. Albert G. Ruben & Co., Beverly Hills, Calif., 1973-77, Alexander & Alexander, Los Angeles, 1977-78; mktg. specialist Continental Ins. Co., Newport Beach, Calif., 1978-79; account exec. John Burnham & Co., Newport Beach, 1979-82; pres. Atherton Assocs., Santa Ana, Calif., 1982—; dir. Vortex Industries, Inc., Los Angeles, 1978—. Mem. Nat. Assn. Women Bus. Owners (v.p. membership 1983-85, bd. dirs. 1983—, v.p. programs 1985—), Contacts Orange County (bd. dirs. 1984—), Wome in Bus., Connections. Republican. Club: Lido Sailing (Newport Beach, Calif.). Avocations: sailing; travel; fine wine and Gourmet foods. Office: Atherton Assocs 534 W 17th St Santa Ana CA 92706

TURNER, GARNETTE MARIE, lawyer, management trainer; b. Columbus, Ohio, Aug. 21, 1938; d. Rufus Harris and Hazel Garnet (Christian) Harris Hays; m. Ronald William Turner, June 19, 1965; children—Ronald William, Michelle Elaine, Lloyd Keith. B.A., U. Detroit, 1977, J.D., 1980. Bar: Mich. 1982. Adminstrv. asst. U.S. Govt., Kerner Commn., Washington, 1967-68, U. Md., College Park, 1969; program asst. Nat. Tng. Lab., Washington, 1969; program coordinator NEA, Washington, 1969-71; grants mgr. City of Detroit, 1971-73, tng. coordinator, 1973-75; ptnr. Turner and Assocs., Birmingham, Mich., 1980—; instr. Detroit Inst. Tech., 1980. Author: Management Training, 1974; editor: National Advisory Commission Civil Disorders, 1967. Vice pres. Civic Citizens Southfield (Mich.), 1980; treas. Citizens for Coleman, Southfield, 1981; chairperson Pray Breakfast, Detroit, 1978; cons. Wellness Group, Birmingham, 1983-84; bd. dirs. Met. Detroit Youth Found., 1978-80, Westside Youth Inc., Detroit, 1972-74. Mem. Mich. Bar Assn., Mich. Trial Lawyers Assn., ABA, Assn. Trial Lawyers Am., Nat. Bar Assn. Democrat. Baptist. Home: 23471 Lake Ravines Southfield MI 48034 Office: Turner and Assocs 6785 Telegraph Rd Rd Birmingham MI 48010

TURNER, GLENNA SUE, accountant; b. Hutchinson, Kans., Jan. 8, 1956; d. William Glynne and Norma Lee (Montford) S.; m. Robert Eugene Turner, June 19, 1976; children—Matthew Robert, Michelle Renee. A.A., Hutchinson Community Jr. Coll., 1976; B.B.A., Wichita State U., 1979. Acct., Koch Industries, Wichita, 1979; controller D.G. Calhoun Inc., Hutchinson, Kans., 1979-85; pvt. acct., Hutchinson, 1985—. Mem. Nat. Assn. Female Execs., Phi Theta Kappa. Methodist. Avocations: swimming; aerobics; biking; softball. Home: 1616 W 22d St Hutchinson KS 67502

TURNER, JANET E., artist, educator; b. Kansas City, Mo., 1914; d. James Ernest and Hortense (Taylor) T.; A.B., Stanford U., 1936; diploma, postgrad. Kansas City Art Inst. (under Thomas H. Benton, John de Martelly), 5 years; student art Claremont Grad. Sch. (Millard Sheets, Henry McFee), 2 years, M.F.A., 1947; student serigraphy, Edward Landon; Ed.D., Columbia U., 1960. Faculty, Girls Collegiate Sch., Claremont, Calif., 1942-47; asst. prof. art Stephen F. Austin State Coll., Nacogdoches, Tex., 1947-56; asst. prof. Chico State U., 1959-63, asso. prof., 1963-68, prof., 1968-80, emeritus, 1980—. Works have been shown in painting, water color and print exhbns. throughout U.S.; exhibited over 200 one-woman shows in U.S., Israel, Japan; exhibited in Internat. Biannual of Graphics, Krakow, Poland, Internat. Exchange Exhbn., Seoul, Korea; represented in permanent collections in U.S., fgn. countries; illustrator The Yazoo. F. Smith. Guggenheim fellow, 1952; Tupperware fellow, 1956—; recipient prizes including: (painting) 1st prize Tex. Fine Arts Assn., 1948; Dealey purchase prize and Comini popular prize 11th Tex. Gen. Exhbn.; R.D. Straus prize 13th Tex. Gen. Exhbn.; 3 prize oils 50th Anniversary Exhbn. Art Assn. New Orleans; S. Karasick prize 59th Ann. Nat. Assn. Women Artists; (water colors) purchase prize 2d Tex. Water Color Soc.; Sun Carnival prize 3d Ann. Southwestern Sun Carnival Fine Arts Exhbn., El Paso; purchase prize Smith Coll. Mus. Art, 37th Ann. Exhbn. Western Art, Denver; Marcia Tucker prize Nat. Assn. Women Artists; (prints) Nat. Assn. Women Artists 1950; (graphics) 1st prize Painters and Sculptors Soc. N.J., 32d Ann. Springfield (Mass.) Art League, Pen and Brush Black and White Exhbn., N.Y.C.; purchase prize Soc. Am. Graphic Artists 36th Ann. A.N.A., 2d prize, Springfield Art League, Mass., 1955, 1st prize, Pen and Brush, 1956, 8th ann. Boston Printmakers purchase prize; 6th Southwestern Dallas Mus. Fine Arts, 1st prize graphics, Painters Sculptors Soc. of N.J., Tupperware Art Fund Fellowship award for painting, Los Angeles County Nat. purchase prize, purchase prize Calif. State Fair, 1960, Cannon prize N.A.D., 1961; Medal of Honor and Alice S. Buell Meml. prize Nat. Assn. Women Artists, 1963, Katheryn Colton prize, Medal of Honor and Mabel M. Garner award, 1967; A.P. Hankins Meml. prize Print Club Pa., 1972; award Assoc. Am. Artists, 1982; award NAD, 1985; co-recipient Outstanding Prof. award Calif. State U. and Colls., 1975. Mem. League Am. Pen Women, Los Angeles Printmaking Soc. (Purchase prize 1971), Nat. Assn. Women Artists (award 1983), Audubon Artists (Horizdorsky award 1981), Am. Color Print Soc., Soc. Am. Graphic Artists, NAD (academician), Nat. Art Edn. Assn., AAUW, Calif. Soc. Printmakers, San Francisco Women Artists, Internat. Arts Guild, Centro Studie Scambi Internazionale, Delta Kappa Gamma, Alpha Omicron Pi, Kappa Delta Pi, Pi Lambda Theta. Home: 567 E Lassen St Sp 701 Chico CA 95926

TURNER, JANICE MARGARET, advertising agency executive; b. Chester, Pa., Feb. 7, 1953; d. Percy Franklin Shadwell and Joyce A. (Buxo) Blevins; m. Thomas L. Myers, Aug. 6, 1975 (div. 1981); m. Stephen Edward Turner, Nov. 27, 1982; 1 child, Justin Edward. B.A., Fla. State U., 1975. Comml. artist Graphic Design Ad Group, Inc., Chattanooga, Tenn., 1978-80; pres., owner The Lead Banana, Inc., Chattanooga, 1980-81; advt. and pub. relations dir. Paul Walker mgmt. Co., Chattanooga, 1980-81; mktg. dir. CBL & Assocs., Inc., Chattanooga, 1981-82; creative dir., gen. mgr. Brady, Goode & Aiken Advt., Inc., Chattanooga, 1982-83; promotion mgr. Sta. WTVC TV ABC affiliate, Chattanooga, 1983-85; account exec. Interchange Communications, Atlanta, 1985—. Mem. Big Bros.-Big Sisters, Dalton, Ga., 1981; youth dir. Trinity Luth. Ch., Chattanooga, 1983-85; bd. dirs. Chattanooga Psychiat. Clinic, 1984-85. Recipient Chad award Local Advt. Fedn., 1981, 82, IABC award, 1981. Mem. Am. Advt. Fedn. (dist. liaison 1980, mem. com. 1985), Mensa, Ad II (eastern regional chmn. to nat. bd. 1981, pres. 1979). Republican. Lutheran. Avocations: tennis; softball; fencing. Home: 765 Waterbrook Terr Roswell GA 30076

TURNER, JEAN-LOUISE, public relations executive; b. Washington, Sept. 29, 1942; d. Fletcher Wood and Mary Louise (Gant) T.; student Howard U., 1959-62; B.A., Fed. City Coll., 1970; M.A., 1972; children—Nathaniel Anthony Landry, Mark Andrew Landry. Coordinator public relations Sta. WRC-TV, Washington, 1969; adminstr. prodn., 1970-72; mgmt. trainee NBC, Washington, 1972; producer spls. Sta. WRC-TV, 1972-76, asso. producer documentaries, 1972-76; mgr. community affairs and public affairs, host Sta. WRC/WKYS, Washington, 1976-78, producer WRC 1978-79; media rep. PEPCO, Washington, 1979-81; press aide D.C. City Council, 1981-82; dir. pub. relations LaMancha, Inc., 1983-84; v.p. Talisman Assocs., 1984—. Judge Gabriel awards; mem. media panel D.C. Arts and Humanities Commn.; bd. dirs. Anchor Mental Health Assn., Epilepsy Found. Am.; career role model St. Anthony's High Sch. Recipient Hallmark award Jr. Achievement, 1976, Public Service award Washington Area Council Alcoholism and Drug Abuse, 1977; Public Interest award Council Better Bus. Burs. Inc., 1977. Mem. Capital Press Club, Washington Assn. Black Journalists, Nat. Acad. TV Arts and Scis., Nat. Assn. Public Continuing Adult Edn., Washington Women's Forum (charter), Alpha Kappa Alpha. Roman Catholic. Editorial bd. NAPCAE Exchange, 1979-81. Home: 2715 31st Pl NE Washington DC 20018 Office: 4005 20th St NE Washington DC 20018

TURNER, JUDY SHARON, residential construction company owner; b. Champaign, Ill., May 5, 1945; d. Clarence Otto and Jennie Margaret (Dunn) Reinhart; m. Robert Eugene McCall, Nov. 8, 1961 (div. May 1975); children—Kathy, Sherry, Amy; m. James Harold Turner, May 14, 1976; stepchildren—Vickie, Anita, Symphoney. Student Parkland Jr. Coll., 1976, Bert Rogers Sch. Real Estate, 1983-84. Receptionist, bookkeeper Thomas, Hamer, Haughy, Champaign, Ill., 1975-76; bookkeeper Goggin Electronics, Champaign, 1976-78; acct. Am. Quotation Systems, Champaign, 1978-79; sec., bookkeeper J. Pat Corrigan Ranch, Vero Beach, Fla., 1980-81; adminstr., co-owner Turner Builders Vero Beach, Inc., 1981—; broker, owner Turner Realty, Vero Beach, 1984—. Interim treas. Indian River Spouse Abuse, Vero Beach, Fla., 1981; dir. Beach Bus. Bur., Vero Beach, 1983, pres., 1984. Recipient 2d in Nat., Com., Nat. Bd. Realtors, 1985, 1st Pl. Com., Fla. State Bd. Realtors, 1985. Mem. Nat. Assn. Female Execs., Treasure Coast Builders Assn., Indian River County-Vero Beach Bd. Realtors, Vero Beach-Indian River County C. of C. (dir. 1986, chmn. legis. adv. com. 1985—). Republican. Lutheran. Clubs: Exchange, Treasure Coast Pilot (pres. 1985—), Welcome Wagon Jr. (v.p. 1980), Encore (Vero Beach). Home: 405 20th Ave Vero Beach FL 32965 Office: Turner Builders Vero Beach Inc PO Box 65-0236 Vero Beach FL 32965

TURNER, KAREN M., media management intern; b. Trenton, N.J., May 23, 1954; d. Arthur H. and Gloria (Scott) Turner. A.B., Dartmouth Coll., 1976; J.D., Northwestern U., 1979; M.S., Columbia U., 1985. Staff dir. ABA, Chgo., 1980-84; intern Manhattan Community Bd. #7, N.Y.C., 1984-85, Newsweek Mag., 1985, Greater Media, Inc., East Brunswick, N.J., 1985-86. Bd. dirs. Hyde Park-Kenwood Community Health Ctr., Chgo., 1983-84, NIA Comprehensive Ctr. for Devel. Disabilities, Chgo., 1982-84. Mem. Cook County Bar Assn., Dartmouth Alumni Council (exec. commn. Hanover, N.H. 1982-85), Dartmouth Black Alumni Assn. (sec. Hanover 1979-85), Phi Alpha Delta. Author, editor: Model Lawyers Guide to Legal Services, 1983; author: The Father of Black Aviation; Legal Self-Help is on the Way; editor: Lawyers See Yourselves as Others See You: Feasibility Study on Institutional Advertising, 1984. Office: Greater Media Inc PO Box 859 East Brunswick NJ 08816

TURNER, KAREN YOUNG, construction company executive; b. Columbus, Ohio, Sept. 20, 1955; d. Lynn Elmer and Elizabeth Jane (Albough) Young; m. Joseph M. Turner, July 1, 1984; 1 child, Christy Lynn. A. in Bus. Adminstrn., Franklin U., 1980. Bookkeeper, sec. M-B Bldg. Cons., Columbus, Ohio, 1973-82; acct. Systems Mech. Constrn., Inc., Westerville, Ohio, 1982-85; pres. Westerville Plumbing and Heating, Inc., 1985—. Mem. Nat. Assn. Women in Constrn. (trustee Ohio chpt. 1985—). Republican. Avocation: boating. Office: Westerville Plumbing and Heating Inc 6270 Frost Rd Westerville OH 43081

TURNER, LOIS LOUISE, college service administrator; b. Peoria, Ill., Feb. 24, 1931; d. William Henry and Dorothy Louise (Binns) Suter; m. Harold Eugene Turner, June 24, 1950; children—Linda S. Turner Oliver, Michael E. Student pub. schs., Peoria. Dir. ops. student ctr., Bradley U., Peoria, 1980—, producer dinner theaters, 1981-85; producer Madrigal Dinner, Peoria, 1985-86. Mem. Assn. Coll. Unions Internat., Nat. Assn. Female Execs., Bowling Propr.'s Assn. Am., Peoria Bowling Assn., Republican. Methodist. Club: Quail Meadow Country. Lodge: Moose. Avocations: golf, bowling, camping. Home: 502 W Gift St Peoria IL 61604 Office: Bradley U Student Ctr 915 Elmwood St Peoria IL 61625

TURNER, MARY LOUISE, librarian, educator; b. Quincy, Ill., Oct. 13, 1925; d. Thelbert R. and Ellen E. (Tucker) T.; A.B., U. Mo., 1967, A.M. (Mo. State Library scholar), 1968, Ph.D. in Ednl. Media, 1978; postgrad. U. Tex., 1973-74, 74-75, U. Nebr., 1976, St. Cloud State U., 1979. Library asst. Little Dixie Regional Library, Moberly, Mo., 1959-62, U. Mo., Columbia, 1962-67; cons. for instl. library services Mo. State Library, Jefferson City, 1968-69; librarian Mo. Tng. Sch. for Boys, Boonville, 1969-71, Parkway N. Sr. High Sch., Creve Coeur, Mo., 1971-73; reference librarian Meramec Community Coll., St. Louis, summer, 1972; head librarian El Paso (Tex.) Community Coll., 1973-74; audiovisual ednl. specialist Grad. Sch. Library Sci., U. Tex., Austin, 1974-75; instr. library sci. Coll. Edn., U. Nebr., Omaha, 1975-76, dir. Ednl. Tech. Center, Coll. Edn., 1976-77; div. leader for instrn. Learning Resource Services, St. Cloud (Minn.) State U., 1978-79; chief edn. and info. Med. Coll. Ga. Library, Augusta, 1979—, asso. prof. library sci., 1979—. Sec. career planning and counseling Huntsville (Mo.) Meth. Ch., 1978. Recipient cert. of recognition Mid-Mo. Mental Health Center, 1967. Mem. ALA, Assn. Ednl. Communication and Tech., Internat. Visual Literacy Assn., Am. Soc. Info. Sci., Assn. for Computing Machinery, NEA, Ga. Health Sci. Library Assn., Mo. Assn. Sch. Librarians, Mo. Library Assn., Ga. Library Assn., Ga. Assn. Instrnl. Tech., Central Savannah Regional Assn., Med. Library Assn., Internat. Platform Assn., AAUW, Bus. and Profl. Women, U. Mo. Alumni Assn., Kappa Delta Pi, Beta Phi Mu. Contbr. articles on ednl. communications and instructional materials to profl. publs. Office: Medical College of Georgia Dept of Library Science 1120 15th St Augusta GA 30912

TURNER, MARY PAULINE CURTIS (MRS. JAMES CASTLE TURNER), artist; b. Lincoln, Nebr., Feb. 14, 1916; d. William Clapp and Nellie (Lee) Curtis; student Wilson Tchrs. Coll., 1940, Corcoran Sch. Art, 1950-54, Am. U., 1955; m. James Castle Turner, Apr. 14, 1934; children—Vivian Lee Turner Polak, Daniel Castle, Brian, Lisa, Lauran. Exhibited at Corcoran Gallery, 1951, Rockville Art Center, 1968, bronze sculpture of Esther Peterson, asst. sec. labor under Kennedy and Johnson at Rehoboth Beach Art League, 1968; retrospective one-man show Labor Tng. Center, Washington, 1978; art tchr. for ret. persons Sargent House Project, 1965-69. Housing chmn. LWV, 1950; U.S del. Trade Union Conf., Blackpool, Eng., 1977; mem. budget com. D.C. Schs., 1969; mem. D.C. Council Arts and Humanities, 1974; membership chmn. Mus. African Art, 1974—; bd. dirs. Washington Ballet, 1976-82. Recipient Ronshein award, 1951, prizes Corcoran Sch., 1951, Washington Area award, 1952. Episcopalian (vestry 1969-71, pres. all women's activities 1969, mem. ch. centennial com.). Home: 15101 Interlachen Dr Apt 317 Silver Spring MD 20906

TURNER, MIKKI, life insurance agent, real estate agent; b. Oakland, Calif., Jan. 9, 1947; d. James John and Anna Sue (Gober) Tornow; 1 child, Kevin. A.A., Coll. of Sequoias, 1967. Lic. real estate, life, disability, fire, casualty ins. Caseworker Tulare County, Visalia, Calif., 1968-69, probation officer, 1970-71; Wanda Shields Realty agt., Farmersville, Calif., 1978-80; agt. Combined Ins., Chgo., 1984-85; agt. Lee's Real Estate, Exeter, Calif., 1980-86; agt. United Ins., Visalia, 1985—. Past pres. Women of the Moose; mem. Nat. Audubon Soc., Am. Mus. Natural History, Smithsonian Instn. Mem. Nat. Assn. Exec. Women, Life Underwriter Assn. Republican. Home: PO Box 1007 Exeter CA 93221 Office: United Insurance 2150 S Mooney Visalia CA 93277

TURNER, NATALIE MURRAY, librarian; b. Kingston, N.Y., Jan. 11, 1930; d. Francis Thomas and Marion (Kelly) Murray; m. John Paul Turner, July 26, 1952; children—Peter, Nancy, Jennifer. B.A., SUNY-Albany, 1950; M.L.S., So. Conn. State U., 1969. Librarian Rocky Hill High Sch., Conn., 1964-68; head librarian Nicolet High Sch., Glendale, Wis., 1969-73; dir. learning resources Nicolet High Sch. Dist., Glendale, 1973—. Vice pres. Mequon-Thiensville Library Bd., Wis., 1977—; v.p., bd. dirs. Weyenberg Found., Mequon, 1983—; pres. Library Council Met. Milw., 1976, bd. dirs., 1983—. Fulbright grantee, India, 1975. Mem. Research Clearinghouse, Wis. Library Assn. Home: 4101 W Freistadt Rd Mequon WI 53092 Office: Nicolet High Sch Dist 6701 N Jean Nicolet Rd Glendale WI 53217

TURNER, PAMELA JAYNE, Presdl. staff ofcl.; b. Newport, R.I., Oct. 29, 1944; d. Fontaine Stoughton and Irene (Langstaff) T.; B.A., Ind. U., 1966. Legis. asst. to Senator Edward J. Gurney, 1967-75; chief legis. asst. to Senator John G. Tower, 1975-81; dep. asst. to Pres. for legis. affairs, Washington, 1981—. Home: 2126 Connecticut Ave NW Washington DC 20008 Office: The White House Washington DC 20500

TURNER, PAMELA WALKER, former educational administrator; b. Montgomery, Ala., July 28, 1943; d. Frederick J. and Yvonne L.B. (Chaplin) Walker; B.A. in Econs., Wellesley Coll., 1965; S.M. in Mgmt., Sloan Sch., MIT, 1971; m. F. Cort Turner, III, Oct. 19, 1968; children—Frederica Chaplin, F. Cort, IV. Cons. energy econs. Arthur D. Little, Inc., Cambridge, 1965-67; mem. corp. orgn.-info. staff, dept. mgr. mktg. div. Soc. Nationale de Siderurgie, Algiers, Algeria, 1970-72; dir. recruitment and placement, Sloan Sch. Mgmt., M.I.T., 1975-79, mgr. accelerated master's program, 1978-79, dir. external relations, 1979-82, lectr. in mgmt., 1978-82; cons. in field. Treas., Buckingham, Browne & Nichols Parents Assn., P.A., 1984-86; treas., bd. dirs. Ten Ten Meml. Dr. Corp., 1984—. Clubs: Wellesley Coll. (Boston); Longwood Cricket, Cambridge Skating (pres. 1983—), Badminton and Tennis. Address: 1010 Memorial Dr Cambridge MA 02138

TURNER, SHIRLEY SUE, med. technologist, lab. adminstr.; b. Danbury, Iowa, Nov. 17, 1935; d. Wilmer and Aleva Alice (Diment) Earnest; cert. med. tech. St. Joseph Mercy Hosp. Sch. Med. Tech., 1956; student Nebr. State Tchrs. Coll., 1953-55; m. Edmund Bruce Turner, Sept. 30, 1965; 1 dau., Lisa Kay. Gen. lab. technician Magic Valley Meml. Hosp., Twin Falls, Idaho, 1956-57, Buena Vista County Hosp., Storm Lake, Iowa, 1957-59, Rockwood Clinic, Spokane, Wash., 1969-60; lab., x-ray technician Greene County Hosp., Jefferson, Iowa, 1961-65; chief technologist Gt. S.W. Gen. Hosp., Grand Prairie, Tex., 1965-71; technologist spl. chemistry dept., electrophoresis and autoanalyzers, Internat. Clin. Labs., Fort Worth, 1971-73; supr. chemistry dept. Pathology Assos. of Tex., Fort Worth, 1973-75; chief technologist Dallas-Ft. Worth Med. Center, Grand Prairie, Tex., 1975—; mem. med. lab. technician adv. bd. El Centrol Community Coll., Dallas. Mem. Am. Soc. Clin. Pathologists (affiliate mem., cert. med. technologist), Am. Soc. Med. Technologists. Republican. Methodist. Address: 3544 Granada Fort Worth TX 76118

TURNER, SUZANNE, state ofcl.; b. Hollywood, Fla., July 29, 1943; d. John F. and Lucille D. Turner; B.S., Ind. State U., 1964, M.S., 1972; postgrad. Ind. U. Sch. Law, 1964-66; postgrad. John Hopkins U., Mich. State U., Tex. Tech U., Ky. State U. Disability adjudicator Ind. Dept. Public Instrn., 1964-65, vocat. rehab. counselor, 1965-67; counselor women's prison Ind. Dept. Corrections, 1967-68; field cons. Ind. Dept. Health, 1968-69; exec. dir. Johnson County (Ind.) Assn. for Retarded Citizens, 1969-70; asso. dir. Ind. Mental Retardation Planning Project, 1970-72; evaluator Marion County (Ind.) Health and Hosp. Corp., 1972-73; dir. residential services Ohio Devel. Disabilities, Inc., Columbus 1973-76; grants coordinator Epilepsy Found. Am., Washington, 1976-77, dir. tech. assistance, 1977-78; dir. tech. assistance Nat. Assn. Mental Retardation Program Dirs., Arlington, Va., 1978-79; intergovtl. liaison for handicapped HUD, Washington, 1979; spl. asst. to dep. asst. sec. for legislation Dept. Health and Human Services, Washington 1979-81; commr. Dept. Social Services, Commonwealth of Ky., Frankfort, 1981—; mem. Ky. Council on Developmental Disabilities, Ky. Juvenile Justice Commn. Chmn. human resources com. LWV, Arlington County, Va., 1978, chmn. womens rights com., 1979-81; mem. Arlington County Community Block Grant Adv. Bd., 1978-79, 80-81, Arlington County Criminal Justice Com., 1980-81; mem. exec. com. Arlingtonians for a Better County, 1980-81. Named Ind.'s Outstanding Young Woman, 1972; recipient award for outstanding service Ohio Assn. Retarded Citizens, 1974; honored by Ohio Gen. Assembly, 1976; recipient Disting. Alumni award Ind. State U., 1981. Mem. Am. Correctional Assn., Nat. Assn. Juvenile Correctional Agys., Nat. Assn. Retarded Citizens, Ky. Council on Crime and Delinquency, Ky. Assn. Retarded Citizens, Johnson County Assn. Retarded Citizens, Am. Pub. Welfare Assn., Ind. State U. Alumni Assn., AAUW. Democrat. Baptist. Clubs: Badoura Temple, Daus. of Nile. Co-author: Community Living for Ohio Developmentally Disabled Citizens, Vols. I and II; Guide to Epilepsy Services; Housing for Developmentally Disabled Citizens; Our Human Resources; author: Guidelines for the Establishment of a Group Home; Resource Guide for Persons with a Developmental Disability. Office: Dept Social Services 275 E Main St Frankfort KY 40624

TURNER, TAMARA ADELE, medical librarian; b. Seattle, Mar. 27, 1940; d. Fredrick Patrick and Florence Elfreda (Puntenney) T. B.A., U. Wash., 1972, M.L.S., 1974. Staff librarian Rainier Sch., Wash. State Library, Buckley, 1974-77; dir. med. library Children's Hosp. and Med. Ctr., Seattle, 1977—. U.S. OEO fellow, 1973-74. Mem. Wash. Med. Librarians Assn., Seattle Area Hosp. Library Consortium (pres. 1981), Med. Library Assn., Am. Soc. Info. Sci. Assn. Spl. Libraries. Home: 1931 E Calhoun Seattle WA 98112 Office: Childrens Hosp and Med Ctr PO Box 5371 Seattle WA 98105

TURNER, TINA (ANNIE MAE TURNER), singer; b. Brownsville, Tenn., Nov. 25, 1941; m. Ike Turner, 1956 (div. 1978); children—Craig, Ike, Michael, Ronald. Sang with Ike Turner Kings of Rhythm and Ike and Tina Turner Revue; appeared in films Gimme Shelter, 1970, Soul to Soul, 1971, Tommy, 1975, Mad Max, Beyond Thunderdome, 1985; participated in USA for Africa song We Are the World, 1985, Live Aid Concert, 1985; concert tours of Europe, 1966, Japan and Africa, 1971, solo tour of Europe, 1983-84. Rec. artist albums including: (with Ike Turner) Hunter, 1970, Ike & Tina Show, 1966, Bad Dreams, 1973; (solo) Let Me Touch Your Mind, 1972, Tina Turns the Country On, 1974, Rough, 1978, Airwaves, 1979, Private Dancer, 1984. Recipient Grammy award for Proud Mary, 1972, 2 Grammy awards for What's Love Got to Do With It, 1985, Grammy award for vocal Better Be Good to Me, 1985. Mailing address: care Capitol Records 1370 Ave of Americas New York NY 10019*

TURNER-RICHARDS, MARY DEAN, publisher; b. Augusta, Ga., Dec. 22, 1938; d. John Dean and Mary Pierce (Wade) Turner; m. Robert Lee Richards, Oct. 15, 1967; children—Jeanette Richards Savant, Dean Turner Richards, Lee Andrew Richards. B.A. in French, Coll. of Charleston, 1985. Vice pres. The Richards Co. Inc., Johns Island, S.C., 1967—; pres., pub. The Charleston Gateway Inc., S.C., 1975—; owner, Reflections Inc., Kiawah, S.C., 1975-81; pres., owner Gateway to Historic Charleston mag., 1978—; pub. The Charleston Coloring Book, 1983—; asst. dir. Internat. Studies Program, Coll. of Charleston, 1985—. Dir. daytime activities Spoleto Festival U.S.A., 1977; bd. dirs. Charleston Travel Council, 1977-83, chmn., 1979; bd. dirs. Young Charleston Theater Co., 1984-85. Mem. Charleston Trident C. of C., Charleston Hotel-Motel Assn., Omicron Delta Kappa. Episcopalian. Avocations: reading; collecting antiques and prints; swimming; riding; traveling. Office: The Charleston Gateway Inc PO Box 803 Charleston SC 29402

TURNER-WALLS, VALERIE, criminal investigator, urban planner; b. Chgo., June 12, 1957; d. Clifford Turner and Eliza (Kaywood) Turner; m. Lucious Gerald Walls, Jr., Nov. 17, 1984. B.S., Ill. State U., 1979; M.Urban Planning and Policy, U. Ill.-Chgo., 1983; postgrad. John Marshall Law Sch., Chgo., 1985—. Cert. tchr., Ill. Tchr., Chgo. Bd. Edn., 1979-84; ops. mgr. Allstate Ins. Co., Skokie, Ill., 1980; research asst U. Ill.-Chgo., 1981-83; urban planner/cons. Village of Robbins, Ill., 1981-83; auditor Leadership Council, Chgo., 1982-83; criminal investigator Dept. Justice, Chgo., 1984—; tchr., cons.

Bryant & Stratton Coll., Chgo., 1983. Mem. legal com. Chgo. Urban League, 1983; chairperson juvenile advocacy unit Robbins Econs. Devel. Corm., 1983. Ill. Govs. summer fellow, 1978. Mem. Fed. Law Enforcement Officers Assn., Fed. Criminal Investigators Assn., Am. Planning Assn., Alpha Kappa Alpha. Avocations: tennis; reading; traveling.

TURNEY, EMMA LEE PRESLAR, publisher, show producer; b. Van Buren, Ark., Sept. 27, 1928; d. Wray Preslar and Ann Lorraine (Faulkner) Preslar Rutherford. Student Tusla U., 1945. Owner Antiques Prodns., Houston and Round Top, Tex., 1963—, Creative Press, Houston and Round Top, 1978—, S.W. Antiques News/SWAN, Houston and Round Top, 1983—. Author: Antiques Business as a Lifestyle, 1978; contbr. articles to jours. in field. Active Friends of Winedale, Friends of Festival Inst., Round Top. Home PO Box 66402 Houston TX 77006

TURNEY, VIRGINIA LEE, land investment company executive; b. Raton, N.Mex., Oct. 15, 1933; d. Otto Olson and Lillian (Olson) Olson Molter; m. Eugene T. Turney, July 17, 1955 (dec. Oct. 1979); children—Dianne, D'Jinnee, Jeffree, Nils Tore and Tore Nils (twins). Student UCLA, 1950; degree in Liberal Arts, U. Miami, 1966. Lic. psychologist, Calif., Fla. Food and liquor controller Diplomat Hotels, Hollywood, Fla., 1951-55; v.p. sales Anodyne, Inc., North Miami Beach, Fla., 1957-75; pres. E.T. Turney, Inc., Hollywood, Fla., 1975—, chmn., 1979—; pres., chmn. Ginni Lee All Sports, Hollywood and Lower Matecumbe, Fla., 1975—; v.p., dir. D.O.T.F., Inc., San Diego, 1983—; owner shop ToysCrafts Gms, Islamorada, Fla.; dir. L&M Land Corp., Hollywood, Fla. Author: Cuban American Spy For Freedom, 1981; Operation Truth. Lectr. on sports to handicapped groups; chmn. Hire the Handicapped, Miami, 1960; co-chmn. Big Bros. and Big Sisters, Miami, 1968. Mem. Internat. Gamefish Assn., Rolls Royce Owners Club Am., Rolls Royce Enthusiasts Club, Islamorada Fishing Club, Mercedes Benz Club Am., Fla. C. of C., Women's Doubles Tennis League (pres. 1978). Republican. Roman Catholic. Clubs: Yacht (Marathon, Fla.); Jockey, Palm Bay (Miami); Cheeca (Islamorada, Fla.); West Palm Beach Fish; Catskill Fly Fishing; Roscoe Golf. Avocations: fishing; tennis; skiing; swimming; golfing. Home: 75050 Overseas Hwy Lower Matecumbe FL 33036

TURNIPSEED, DENISE TREMBLY, mktg. exec.; b. San Francisco, June 3, 1950; d. Jean Evan and Mary Frances (O'Connor) Tremley; B.S., Ill. State U., 1973; 1 son, Eric Brading. Customer service/sales rep. StarData, Crystal Lake, Ill., 1976-77; mktg. rep. Datacorp, Chgo., 1977-79, Anacomp Micrographics, Los Angeles, 1978-80, Honeywell, Los Angeles, 1980-81, Automated Concepts, Inc., Century City, Calif., 1981-82; sr. mktg. rep. ICS Group, Inc., Torrance, Calif., 1982—. Pres., Camelot Primary Sch. PTA, Chgo., 1977-78. Mem. Exec. Females, Nat. Assn. Bus. and Indsl. Saleswomen, Data Processing Mgmt. Assn. (dir.). Office: ICS Group 3848 Carson St Suite 320 Torrance CA 90503

TUROCK, BETTY JANE, information scientist, educator; b. Scranton, Pa., June 12; d. David and Ruth Carolyn (Sweetser) Argust; B.A. magna cum laude (Charles Weston scholar), Syracuse U., 1955; postgrad. (scholar) U. Pa., 1956; M.L.S., Rutgers U., 1970, Ph.D., 1981; m. Frank M. Turock, June 16, 1956; children—David L., B. Drew. Library and materials coordinator Holmdel (N.J.) Public Schs., 1963-65; story-teller Wheaton (Ill.) Public Library, 1965-67; ednl. media specialist Alhambra Public Sch., Phoenix, 1967-70; br. librarian, area librarian, head extension service Forsyth County Public Library System, Winston-Salem, N.C., 1970-73; asst. dir. Montclair (N.J.) Public Library, 1973-75, dir., 1975-77; asst. dir. Monroe County Library System, Rochester, N.Y., 1978-81; asst. prof. Rutgers U. Grad. Sch. Communications, Info. and Library Studies, 1981—; dir. Grass Roots, Inc., Montclair, 1974—; vis. prof. Rutgers U. Grad. Sch. Library and Info. Studies, 1980-81. Trustee, Raritan Twp. (N.J.) Public Library, 1961-62; mem. Bd. Edn. Raritan Twp., 1962-66; mem. Title VII Adv. Bd., Montclair Public Schs., 1975-77; ALA mem. coordinating council Task Force on Women, 1978—; treas. Social Responsibilities Round Table, 1978—. Named Woman of Yr., Raritan-Holmdel Woman's Club, 1975. Mem. ALA (councilor 1984—), Public Library Assn., NOW, Rutgers U. Grad. Sch. Library and Info. Studies Alumni Assn. (pres. 1977-78), Phi Theta Kappa, Psi Chi, Beta Phi Mu, Pi Beta Phi. Unitarian. Author: Serving Older Adults, 1983; editor: Money and Management for Libraries, 1984—; contbr. articles to profl. jours. Home: 11 Undercliff Rd Montclair NJ 07042 Office: Rutgers U 185 College Ave New Brunswick NJ 08903

TURPIN, MARY FRANCES, language development specialist; b. Hartford, Ky., Nov. 5, 1949; d. Overt Hurt and Gleema Pearl (Stearns) Tallent; m. James Thomas Turpin, June 18, 1971; 1 child, James Thomas, Jr. B.S., Eastern Ky. U., 1971, M.S., 1974. Cert. tchr., Ky. Mental health assoc. Bluegrass Comprehensive Care, Richmond, Ky., 1973; sci. tchr. Hart County Bd. Mental Retardation and Devel. Disabilities, Munfordville, Ky., 1973-74; speech therapist Clinton County Schs., Albany, Ky., 1977-81; lang. devel. specialist Montgomery County Bd. Mental Retardation and Devel. Disabilities, Dayton, Ohio, 1983—. Tchrs. aide Englewood United Methodist Ch., Ohio, 1985, Maple Heights Baptist Ch., Fairborn, Ohio, 1983. Republican. Avocations: redecorating old home; nature; crafts. Home: 204 Valley View Dr Englewood OH 45322 Office: Adult Services Bd Mental Retardation and Devel Disabilities 1507 Kuntz Rd Dayton OH 45404

TURTON, DOROTHY LOUISE, dietitian, hospital food service administrator, consultant; b. Waterloo, Ill., Feb. 13, 1919; d. Friedrich Wilhelm and Bertha Emilia (Schmitt) Braun; m. Roger Charles Dale, Dec. 8, 1944 (dec. Oct. 11, 1964); children—Barbara, Diane; m. 2d, Robert Allen Turton, Feb. 13, 1970; children by previous marriage: Beth, Andrew, Roberta. B.S., Sam Houston State U., 1940. Cert. permanent high sch. tchr., dietary cons., vocat. tchr., Tex. Tchr. homemaking League City High Sch. (Tex.), 1940-43; intern Deaconess Hosp., St. Louis, 1943-44, teaching dietitian, 1943-46; tchr. sci. Belville High Sch. (Tex.), 1946-49; food service dir. Heights Hosp., Houston, 1949-53, San Jacinto Hosp., Baytown, Tex., 1955-59, Spring Br. Hosp., Houston, 1959-64; therapeutic dietitian Meml. Baptist Hosp., Houston, 1953-55, chief dietitian, 1964-71; freelance cons. to several hosps. and nursing homes, Houston, 1971-74; area cons. Cantex Nursing Homes, Houston, 1974-81; dir. Dietitics Belt Way Community Hosp., Pasadena, 1981—; cons. adv. staff San Jacinto Coll. Mem. Phi Theta Kappa. Republican. Mem. United Ch. Christ. Clubs: C.P.A. Aux., St. Peters Womens Guild (Houston) (pres. 1971-75, 80-83); Spring Woods Townhouse (aux. pres. 1980-81). Home: 2938 Gessner St Houston TX 77080 Office: Belt Way Community Hosp 4040 Red Bluff Rd Pasadena TX 77503

TURZINSKI-CLASON, PATRICIA ANN, business consultant; b. Milw., Nov. 11, 1950; d. Richard James and Doris Lorene (Smith) Turzinski; student U. Wis., Milw., 1968-69; m. Steven W. Clason, June 1, 1986. Supr. mortgage servicing A.L. Grootemaat & Sons., Milw., 1969-72; legal sec., 1973; exec. sec. Plastronics Inc., Milw., 1974; mgr. mortgage servicing Universal Mortgage Co., Milw., 1975; mgr. Outpost Natural Foods Coop., Milw., 1975-76; owner Genesis, Milw., 1976-79; owner Manifestation Mgmt. Inc., Milw., 1979—, Great Ideas! Speakers Bur. and Meeting Planning Cons., 1983—; owner Dreikurs Relationship Ctr. Milw.; founder Women's Resource Network Milw.; pres., bd. dirs. Woman to Woman Inc., 1983—, conf. coordinator, 1984; bd. dirs. Save-A-Farm, Inc.; co-founder, bd. dirs. Tai Chi Chuan Center, Milw.; instr. Cardinal Stritch Coll., Marquette U., Waukesha County Tech. Coll., Mt. Mary Coll. Mem. Wis. Profl. Speakers Assn. (bd. dirs. 1984—), Nat. Speakers Assn., Meeting Planners Internat. Author articles, cassette tapes in field. Address: 2437 N Booth St Milwaukee WI 53212

TUTSCH, DEBORAH E(LIZABETH) HUSCH, insurance company executive; b. Washington, Aug 4, 1960; d. Jakob and Ingrid (Fischer) Husch; m. Lonnie L. Tutsch, Jan. 21, 1984. B.S. in Mktg., U. Md., 1982. Food and beverage mgr. Washington Boat Lines, 1982-84; dist. rep. Aid Assn. for Lutherans, Appleton, Wis., 1984—. Mem. Nat. Assn. Life Underwriters, Women's Life Underwriters Conf., D.C. Life Underwriters Assn., Nat. Assn. Female Execs., Million Dollar Round Table. Republican. Lutheran. Avocations: aerobics; running; reading; hiking; camping. Home: 6301 Sandy St Laurel MD 20707 Office: Aid Assn for Lutherans 6301 Sandy St Laurel MD 20707

TUTTLE, DONNA FRAME, government official; m. Robert Tuttle. Former tchr. Los Angeles sch. system; undersec. Dept. Commerce, head U.S. Travel and Tourism Adminstrn., Washington, 1984—. Office: Dept Commerce US Travel and Tourism Adminstrn 15th and Constitution Ave NW Washington DC 20230

TUTTLE, DOROTHY EDITH LORNE, writer, communications consultant; b. Seattle, Dec. 7, 1916; d. William Henry and Maude alice (Fuller) T. Student U. Wash., 1936-37, U. Richmond, 1946, Stanford U., 1945-46; Banking/Econs. grad. Am. Inst. Banking, 1941; B.A., Am. U., Washington, 1955; postgrad. Mich. State U., 1960-61; grad. nat. security mgmt. Indls. Coll. Armed Forces, 1969. Pub. relations dir. Mich. Council State Coll. Pres., Lansing, 1961; pub. relations dir. woman's div., dir. weekly press and small dailies Republican Nat. Com., Washington, 1962-64; pub. info. officer, div. dir., br. chief Dept. Navy, Washington, 1965-71; info. and editorial specialist Assn. Am. R.R.s, Washington, 1973-75; writer, communications cons. DELT Communications Serives, Washington, Ithaca, Mich., 1976-84; internat. press corr. and editor USIA, 1948-59; freelance writer and communications cons., Ithaca, 1984—. Editor USA Life, 1950, Navy Mgmt. Rev., 1965-69; contbr. articles to nat. to nat. periodicals and govt. publs. Mem. pres.'s circle Am. U.; mem. Republican Congl. Com. Served with USN-USCG, 1942-46. Am. Inst. Banking fellow, 1936-42; recipient Outstanding Performance award Navy Bur. Supplies and Accounts, 1966; Superior Accomplishment award and Cash award Dept. Navy, Washington, 1967, Fed. Civilian Service award, 1969, Civilian Meritorious Service award, 1971. Mem. Nat. Press Club, Am. Newspaper Women's Club (1st v.p., dir.), AAUW, Am. Legion, Res. Officers Assn., Internat. Fedn. Univ. Women, Washington Press Club (officer, com. mem.), Am. U. Alumni Assn., Stanford U. Alumni Assn., Mich. State U. Alumni Assn., Women in Communications, Inc. Republican. Episcopalian. Home: 636 N Baldwin Rd Ithaca MI 48847

TUTTLE, ELSIE ELEANOR, religious organization executive; b. Springfield, Ill., Feb. 15, 1927; d. Percy Bayard and Anna Gertrude (Veail) Smith; m. Daniel Webster Tuttle, Jr., June 28, 1947; children—Kay Tuttle Hancock, Daniel Webster III, David Bayard Hampton. A.B., Ill. Coll., 1948; postgrad. U. Minn., 1948; M.A., U. Wyo., 1950. Prof. Spanish, Honolulu Christian Coll., 1953-60; lectr. Spanish, U. Hawaii, part-time, 1960-62; interim exec. sec. Woman's Bd. of Missions for Pacific Island, United Ch. of Christ, Honolulu, 1984—; pres. Woman's Bd. of Missions, Honolulu, 1982-84; bd. dirs. Oahu Assn. United Ch. of Christ, 1980—, Hawaii Conf. United Ch. of Christ, 1980—. Editor Morning Star newsletter, 1984-85. Vice pres. YWCA of Oahu, 1968-72; bd. dirs. PTA, Honolulu, 1968-70, Laryngectomee Assn., 1960-64; sec. Friends of Library of Hawaii, 1974-80; trustee Central Union Ch., Honolulu, 1976-80; panel mem. Aloha United Way, 1980-85; dist. chmn. Am. Cancer Soc., 1983-85. Mem. Phi Kappa Phi, Psi Chi, Phi Sigma Iota. Home: 14 Akilolo St Honolulu HI 96821 Office: Woman's Bd of Missions for Pacific Islands Hawaii Conf United Ch of Christ 15 Craigside Pl Honolulu HI 96817

TUTTLE, KATHLEEN J., lawyer; b. Lynwood, Calif., Apr. 15, 1953; d. Burt Joseph and Dolores Elaine (Feipel) Tuttle. A.B. summa cum laude, U. Calif.-Santa Barbara, 1975; J.D., U. Calif.-Berkeley, 1978; postgrad. Cambridge U. (Eng.), 1984. Bar: D.C. 1983, U.S. Ct. Appeals (D.C. cir.) 1983, U.S. Dist. Ct. D.C. 1983. Assoc. firm Wald, Harkrader & Ross, Washington, 1978-80; nat. fundraiser Democratic Nat. Com., Washington, 1980; staff asst. to Vice Pres. U.S., 1980; counsel Com. on Rules and Dem. Caucus, U.S. Ho. of Reps., 1981-83; minority counsel Com. on Govtl. Affairs, U.S. Senate, 1983—. Assoc. editor Calif. Law Rev. Mem. staff Dem. Nat. Conv., N.Y.C., 1980; staff Dem. Nat. Conf., Phila., 1982. Mem. ABA, Bar Assn. D.C., Women's Bar Assn. D.C., Washington Council Lawyers, World Affairs Council Washington, Counselor's Table (Boalt Hall). Lutheran. Office: Com on Govtl Affairs US Senate 346 Dirksen Senate Bldg Washington DC 20510

TUTTLE, TONI BRODAX, swimming pool company executive; b. Bklyn., July 19, 1952; d. Abraham Paul and Marilyn (Monte) Brodax; m. Roy Lee, May 21, 1978; 1 son, Sean Monte. student Lesley Coll., 1972; B.A. in Journalism, U. R.I., 1974. Reporter Mexico City Daily News, 1972; freelance photographer/writer N.Y. Yankees, Communications Group, Ft. Lauderdale, Fla., 1974-78; editorial asst. Boating Mag., N.Y.C., 1974-76; pub. relations cons. B. Altmans Dept. Store, N.Y.C., 1975-76; dir. pub. relations Windjammer Barefoot Cruises, Miami, Fla., 1976-78; account exec. Art Jacobson Advt., Miami, 1978-79; v.p. Tuttle's Pool Co., Inc., Miami, 1979—. Jewish. Home: 6740 SW 94th St Miami FL 33156

TUTTRUP, JOAN MAXINE, microelectronics company executive; b. Middlebury, Ind., Apr. 8, 1932; d. Oliver J. and Verna (Hershburger) Bontrager; m. Bertram Jean Tuttrup, Aug. 4, 1956 (div. 1985); children—Devon and Dale Miller, Bonnie and Barry Tuttrup. Student, Marciopa Community Coll., 1961, Ariz. State U., 1963-66, Austin Community Coll., 1973. Pilot line operator Motorola Inc., Phoenix, 1963-64, engring. asst., 1964-70, engring. technician, 1970-75, product engring. supr., Austin, Tex., 1975-81; process control supr. Inmos Corp., Colorado Springs, Colo., 1981—. Mem. Going Concern, Colorado Springs, 1985—. Mem. Women's Network, Nat. Assn. Female Execs. Avocations: singing; reading; flowers, gardening. Office: Inmos Corp PO Box 16000 Colorado Springs CO 80935

TUTWILER, MARGARET D., presidential assistant; b. Birmingham, Ala., Dec. 28, 1950; B.A., U. Ala. Office mgr., sec. Office of Ala. Republican Chmn., 1973; surrogate scheduler Pres. Ford Com., 1975-76, exec. dir. Ala., 1976; pub. affairs rep. N.Am. for Ala. and Miss., 1976-78; scheduling dir. for George Bush, 1980; exec. asst. to chief of staff White House, Washington, 1981—, spl. asst. to the Pres., 1983—. Address: Dept of The Treasury 15th and Pennsylvania Ave Washington DC 20220*

TUTWILER, MYRA SMITH, personnel consultant; b. Johnson City, Tenn., Oct. 16, 1942; d. Lynn Bachman and Trula Blanche (Irwin) Smith; student East Tenn. State U., 1960-62; Radiologic Technician, Holston Valley Meml. Hosp., 1963; m. Tommy R. Baker, Oct. 13, 1961; children—Kristi Lynn, Laura Marie; m. 2d, Richard G. Tutwiler, June 8, 1979. Radiol. technologist Radiology Cons., Knoxville, 1963-64, Moses H. Cone Meml. Hosp., Greensboro, N.C., 1964; office mgr. Albany Advt. Assos. (Ga.), 1966-68; adminstrv. asst. Don Richard Assos., Inc., Bethesda, Md., 1976, cons. personnel, 1977—. Vice pres. Sherwood Elem. Sch. PTA, 1970-71; corr. sec. Ayrlawn Elem. Sch. PTA, 1976-78; leader Brownies, 1970-72; mem. Albany Community Council, 1971-72; bd. dirs. Albany Community Drug Abuse Council, 1972-73; pres. Jr. Woman's Club Albany (Ga.), 1971-72, Chevy Chase (Md.), 1976-77; bd. dirs. Montgomery County Fedn. Women's Clubs, 1976—, Ga. Fedn., 1968-73, Md. Fedn. Women's Clubs, 1973—; hdqrs. coordinator, women vols. coordinator Jimmy Carter for Gov. Campaign, Dougherty County, Ga., 1968-70. Recipient Georgia Allie Bates Jolly Poetry Cup, 1972; Community Improvement award Jr. Woman's Club Chevy Chase, 1978; named Md. Jr. Clubwoman of Yr., 1979. Democrat. Episcopalian. Clubs: Bryce Resort (tennis com. chmn.) (Basye, Va.); Montgomery County (Md.) Young Woman's (treas. 1979-80). Home: PO Box 355 Bryce Resort Basye VA 22810

TUZIL, TERESA JORDAN, clinical social worker, psychotherapist; b. N.Y.C., May 13, 1948; d. Lester Francis and Kathleen Geraldine (Brady) Jordan; B.A., St. John's U., 1970; M.S.W., Hunter Coll., 1973, certified in gerontology, 1977; m. Joseph Stephen Tuzil, Jan. 15, 1972; children—Joseph IV, Brian Joseph. Social worker Salvation Army Foster Care and Adoption Services, N.Y.C., 1971-72; sr. caseworker Jewish Assn. for Services to the Aged, N.Y.C., 1973-78; program cons. Community Council of Greater N.Y., N.Y.C., 1978-79; pvt. practice individual and family psychotherapy, Seaford, N.Y., 1976—; caseworker Nassau County Dept. Social Services Children's Protective Service, 1983—; adj. clin. instr. Hunter Grad. Sch. Social Work, 1975-78; field instr. Grad. Sch. Social Work, Rutgers U., 1975-77; program cons. Assn. for Services to Aged, Bklyn., 1981—. Certified, registered clin. social worker, N.Y. Mem. Nat. Assn. Social Workers, Acad. Certified Social Workers. Editor: Jour. of Gerontological Social Work, 1977—; contbr. articles to profl. publs. in field. Home and Office: 3859 Tiana St Seaford NY 11783

TWA, INEZ LOUISA ARBUTHNOT, writer; b. Boulder County, Colo., Nov. 9, 1905; d. George John and Nancy Louisa (Brammeier) Arbuthnot; student Coll. Commerce, Stockton, Calif., 1929; m. Norman Osbert Twa, Nov. 7, 1929 (dec.); children—Lois, Gordon, Audrey. Office positions, U.S. and Can., 1929-57; with FAA, 1957-75, sec. CAA, Grand Junction, Colo., 1957-63; adminstrv. asst. to dist. chief FAA, Reno, 1963-65, mgmt. tech./specialist area office, Salt Lake City, 1965-68; mgmt. specialist, asst. motor fleet mgr. Dept. Transp., Los Angeles, 1968-72, regional motor fleet mgr. Rocky Mountain Region, Denver, 1972-75, ret., 1975; author short stories pub. 1977—; editor Buckingham Gardens News and Revs. newsletter, 1984-86; contbr. stories to Colo. Old Times Mag., Denver Post newspaper. Active Mental Health Assn., 1958-63, Republican Party. Recipient award C. of C., 1963; service citation CSC, 1975. Mem. Profl. Secs. Internat., Arbuthnot Family International Assn. Aurora Geneal. Soc. Presbyterian. Home: 800 S Ironton St #95 Aurora CO 80012

TWANMOH, CATHERINE MARIE, sales and marketing official; b. Bklyn., Apr. 4, 1952; d. Thomas Twanmoh and Mary Vivian (Fu) Wells; m. Jeffrey D. Charney, Aug. 23, 1980; 1 son, James R. Charney. B.A., Beloit Coll., 1974; M.Art Edn., R.I. Sch. Design, 1978; M.B.A., Rutgers U., 1979. Tchr. art Fair Haven (N.J.) Bd. Edn., 1974-78; mktg. services mgr. Oden Inc., Phillipsburg, N.J., 1980-81; mktg. cons. Southard Research Assocs., North Brunswick, N.J., 1981; sales rep. Air Products & Chems., Iselin, N.J., 1981—; ptnr. Rocket Enterprises, Flemington, N.J., 1980—. One person show Monmouth County (N.J.) Library, 1976; 2 person show Guild Creative Art, Shrewsbury, N.J., 1978; 3 person show Studio Gallery, Red Bank, N.J., 1976; exhibited in group shows Wright Art Ctr., Beloit, Wis., 1973, Guild Creative Art, Shrewsbury, N.J., 1974. Recipient 1st place for sculpture award Red Bank Festival Arts, 1975. Vice pres. Monmouth County Young Democrats, 1977-79, sec., 1976; committeewoman Monmouth Beach Dem. City Com., 1977; treas. Hist. Soc. Clinton, 1982-84. Mem. Am. Mktg. Assn. (v.p. N.J. chpt. membership 1982-84 v.p. communication 1984-86), Guild Creative Art, Hunterdon Art Ctr. Home: 12 Kirkbride Rd Flemington NJ 08822 Office: Air Products & Chemicals Inc 1680 Oak Tree Rd PO Box 170 Iselin NJ 08830

TWISS, ENA LUCILLE WAHL, real estate broker, former educator and educational administrator; b. Kewanee, Ill., Dec. 3, 1906; d. Henry John and Marie Adelaide (Heise) Wahl; m. Wesley Edwin Sharer, Aug. 5, 1933 (dec.); children—Jon Wesley, Judd Wahl; m. William Albert Twiss, July 25, 1966. B.E., Chgo. Tchrs. Coll., 1926; Ph.B., U. Chgo., 1932; M.E., Loyola U., Chgo., 1954, postgrad., 1955-65. Tchr. then prin. pub. sch., Chgo., 1928-54; art tchr. pub. sch., Miami, Fla., 1954-55; music tchr. pub. sch., Miami, 1955-57; prin. pub. sch., Manattee County, Fla., 1957-60; tchr. high sch., Key West, Fla., 1960-66; real estate broker, Miami, 1955—. Contbr. articles to profl. jours. Rep. World War I vets. VA Hosps., Bay Pines, Fla., 1970; chaplain Belleair Republican Club, 1968-70. Mem. Vets. World War I Ladies Aux. (aux. pres. 1979-80, 81-85, state pres. 1983-84, nat. pub. TV and radio chmn. 1979-80, nat. photographer 1984-85, pres. dist. 5, 1985-86, state pub. TV radio chmn. 1977-83), NEA Chgo. Edn. Assn., Fla. Edn. Assn. AAUW, Am. Legion Ladies Aux. Club: Clearwater Women's (pub. chmn.). Lodges: Eastern Star, White Shrine. Avocations: painting; church organist; swimming; ice hockey; tennis. Home: 220 Belleview Blvd Apt 311 Belleair FL 33516

TWISS, MAURINE CHRISTMAN, consultant, public relations, author's editor; b. Westervelt, Ill., July 4, 1919; d. Paul and Leota Madge (Jenkins) Christman; student Ill. Wesleyan U., 1937-39; m. Armin Russel Twiss, Oct. 16, 1937; 1 child, Belinda Sue Twiss Allison. Copywriter, Montgomery Ward Corp., Chgo., 1939-41; editorial copy desk Chgo. Tribune, 1948-49; women's editor Jackson (Miss.) Daily News, 1950-54, feature editor, 1954-55; dir. public info. U. Miss. Med. Center, Jackson, 1955-73, dir. spl. services, 1973-78; cons. public relations, author's editor, Jackson, 1978—. Publicist, Miss. Heart Assn., 1953-70, bd. dirs., 1972-78, mem. So. regional evaluation subcom. Am. Heart Assn., 1970-74, chmn., 1973-74; mem. City of Jackson Planning Bd., 1974—; mem. City of Jackson Zoning Bd., 1976-79, 81-86, chmn., 1978-79, 85-86, chmn. comprehensive plan, 1982-86; mem. adv. council Miss. Employment Security Commn., 1978-79, Southeastern Regional Med. Library Program, 1970-72; pres. Miss. Women's Cabinet of Public Affairs, 1963-64; bd. dirs. New Stage, 1965—, pres., 1974-78; bd. dirs. Jackson Arts Alliance, 1979-83, pres., 1981-82. Recipient citation Miss. Assn. Mental Health, 1956, Service to Field award Public Relations Assn. Miss., 1981, numerous state, nat. awards for excellence in writing; named Woman of Achievement, Miss. Press. Women, 1973. Mem. Assn. Am. Med. Colls. Group on Public Relations (chmn. 1967-68, Disting. Service award 1978), Nat. Fedn. Press Women (regional chmn. 1961-65), Miss. Press Women (pres. 1958-60). Democrat. Club: Country of Jackson. Home: 1738 Douglass Dr Jackson MS 39211

TWISTOL, JOYCE ANN, city official; b. St. Paul, Apr. 19, 1941; d. Willard Edward Wolf and Ann Eleanora (Engmark) Wolf Boyer; m. Theodore Twistol, Oct. 10, 1963 (div. Dec. 1980); 1 child, Roxanne. Student U. Minn., 1980. Cert. municipal clk. Adminstrv. sec. Sch. Dist. 1, McGregor, Minn., 1961-63; office mgr. H&R Block, Fridley, Minn., 1974-75, city clk. City of Blaine, Minn., 1976—, city clk., dir. personnel, 1979—; advisor election laws Sec. of State's Office, Minn., 1980—. Chair of pastor, parish Blaine Methodist Ch., 1978-80, bd. chmn., 1980; mem. Blaine Community Theatre, 1983—, mem. local govt. adv. bd. 6th Congressional Dist., 1983. Mem. Mem. Internat. Personnel Mgrs. Assn., Assn. Record Mgrs. and Adminstrs., Internat. Inst. Municipal Clks. (vice chmn. acad. 1985), Municipal Clks. and Fin. Officers (pres., v.p., sec. treas. 1976—), Nat. Pub. Employers Labor Relations Assn., Minn. Pub. Employers Labor Relations Assn. (treas. 1985), Met. Area Urban Mgmt. Assts. (parlimentarian 1982—). Club: North Metro Bus. and Profl. Women's (Woman of Achievement award 1979). Office: City of Blaine 9150 Central Ave NE Blaine MN 55434

TWYMAN, GENEVA MAE, school administrator; b. Fayette, Pa., Mar. 2, 1928; d. George W. and Ionia (Davis) Potts; m. Arthur W. Twyman, June 28, 1950; children—Karen, Marvin, Kevin. Cert. in bus. Bus. Tng. Coll. Pitts., 1948; bus. mgmt. cert. Duquesne U., 1976. Sec. to exec. dir., YMCA, Pitts., 1949; receptionist Montefiore Hosp., Pitts., 1959-63, Roth Rug Co., Pitts., 1963-68; dir. vol. services El Gar Rehab. Ctr., Pitts., 1968-70; asst. for parent reps. Pitts. Bd. Edn., 1970—. Bd. dirs. Sta. WQED-TV, Pitts, 1983, Princess Wilborne Sickle Cell Found., 1983, Mayor's Task Force For Women, 1983, Alma Illery Med. Ctr., 1983; v.p. Pa. Elected Women's Assn., Women in Urban Crisis; bd. dirs. Juvenile Ct. Children's Fund. Com., 1980-83; state rep. Nat. Women's Polit. Caucus; mem. Chadwick Civic League. Recipient Community Service award Pitts YWCA, 1974, George Washington Carver Com. award, 1976; Community Service award Allegheny Community Coll., 1974. Democrat. Baptist. Home: 1225 Lincoln Ave Pittsburgh PA 15206 Office: Board of Education 341 S Bellefield Ave Pittsburgh PA 15213

TWYNER, ALEXIS CHERYLE, special education educator; b. Iowa City, Iowa, Sept. 19, 1946; d. Lafayette James and Rosemary Lucille (Roberts) T.; B.A. in Edn. and History, U. Iowa, 1964-68, Ph.D. in Adminstrn., 1975-78; M.A. in Reading and Learning Disabilities, Marycrest Coll., 1971; Ph.D. in Adminstrn., U. Iowa, 1978. Tchr. Pleasant Valley Community Sch. Dist., LeClaire, Iowa, 1968-73; reading specialist Lincoln Elem. Sch., 1973-75; specific learning disability tchr. North High Sch., Davenport, 1975—; adult edn. instr. Davenport Community Sch. Dist., 1980-83. Mem. NEA, Iowa State Edn. Assn., Davenport Edn. Assn., Internat. Reading Assn., Assn. for Children with Learning Disabilities, Pi Lambda Theta. Republican. Office: 626 W 53d St Davenport IA 52804

TYLER, ANNE (MRS. TAGHI M. MODARRESSI), author; b. Mpls., Oct. 25, 1941; d. Lloyd Parry and Phyllis (Mahon) T.; B.A.; Duke U., 1961; postgrad. Columbia U., 1962; m. Taghi M. Modarressi, May 3, 1963; children—Tezh, Mitra. Author: (novels) If Morning Ever Comes, 1964; The Tin Can Tree, 1965; A Slipping-Down Life, 1970; The Clock Winder, 1972; Celestial Navigation, 1974; Searching for Caleb, 1976; Earthly Possessions, 1977; Morgan's Passing, 1980; Dinner at the Homesick Restaurant, 1982; The Accidental Tourist, 1985. Editor: (with Shannon Ravenel) Best American Short Stories, 1983. Contbr. short stories to nat. mags. Recipient Janet Heidinger Kafka prize, 1981; PEN/Faulkner award for fiction, 1983. Mem. Am. Acad. and Inst. Arts and Letters (award for lit. 1977), Phi Beta Kappa. Mem. Soc. of Friends. Office: care Alfred A Knopf Inc 201 E 50th St New York NY 10022*

TYLER, AUDREY ELAYNE, library administrator; b. Norfolk, Va., Aug. 24, 1944; d. Oscar Simpson and Geneva Evangeline (Shokes) Quick; m. Eugene Wilson Tyler, June 8, 1968; children—Gregory Eugene, Jennifer Elayne, Daniel Edward. B.S. in Biology, S.C. State Coll., 1965; postgrad. U. Okla., 1965, John Carroll U., 1965-66; M.S. in L.S., Atlanta U., 1968. Caseworker N.Y.C. Dept. Social Services, Bronx, 1966-67; research librarian Bristol Myers Research Labs., East Syracuse, N.Y., 1968-70; asst. dept. head, dept. head Atlanta Pub. Library, 1972-74; br. head Atlanta Pub. Library, 1977-78, br. services adminstr., 1978-83; personnel and staff devel. officer Atlanta-Fulton Pub. Library, 1983—. Bd. dirs. Atlanta Council Internat. Programs, 1980—. Presdl. scholar Atlanta U., 1967-68. Mem. ALA, Pub. Library Assn., Library Adminstrn. and Mgmt. Assn., Black Caucus ALA (chmn. coms.), Met. Atlanta Library Assn., S.C. State Coll. Nat. Alumni Assn. (nat. recording sec. 1983-87), S.C. State Coll. Alumni Assn. (past pres., corr. sec.), Delta Sigma Theta. Democrat. Methodist. Avocations: needlecrafts; traveling; cookbook of fruitcake recipes. Home: 1421 S Gordon St SW Atlanta GA 30310 Office: Atlanta-Fulton Pub Library 1 Margaret Mitchell Square Atlanta GA 30303

TYLER, DARLENE JASMER, dietitian; b. Watford City, N.D., Jan. 26, 1939; d. Edwin Arthur and Leola Irene (Walker) Jasmer; B.S., Oreg. State U., 1961; m. Richard G. Tyler, Aug. 26, 1977; children—Ronald, Eric, Scott. Clin. dietitian Salem (Oreg.) Hosp., 1965-73; sales supr. Sysco Northwest, Tigard, Oreg., 1975-77; clin. dietitian Physicians & Surgeons Hosp., Portland, Oreg., 1977-79; food service dir. Meridian Park Hosp., Tualatin, Oreg., 1979—. Registered dietitian. Mem. Am. Dietetic Assn., Oreg. Dietetic Assn., Portland Dietetic Assn., Am. Soc. Hosp. Food Service Adminstrs. Episcopalian. Home: 12800 SE Nixon Ave Milwaukie OR 97222 Office: 19300 SW 65th St Tualatin OR 97062

TYLER, GAIL MADELEINE, nurse; b. Dhahran, Saudi Arabia, Nov. 21, 1953 (parents Am. citizens); d. Louis Rogers and Nona Jean (Henderson) T. A.Sc., Front Range Community Coll., Westminster, Colo., 1979. R.N., Colo. Ward sec. Valley View Hosp., Thornton, Colo., 1975-79; nurse Scott and White Hosp., Temple, Tex., 1979-83, Meml. Hosp. Laramie County, Cheyenne, Wyo., 1983—. Mem. Critical Care Assn. Avocations: collecting international dolls; sewing; reading; traveling.

TYLER, JOANNA ARMIGER, research and counseling psychologist; b. Balt., Jan. 23, 1943; d. William James Armiger and Marie Eileen (Edmonds) Lowery; A.A., Coll. San Mateo, 1968; B.A. cum laude in Psychology, San Jose State U., 1971, M.A. in Psychology, 1973; Ph.D. in Human Devel. Psychology (grad. fellow), U. Md., 1977; 1 son, Christopher Blair. Research asst., instr. U. Md., 1973-77; adj. asst. prof. Catonsville (Md.) Community Coll., 1973-78; sr. research analyst Teledyne Brown Engring., Rockville, Md., 1976-78; tech. mgr. Applied Mgmt. Scis., Silver Spring, Md., 1978-82; research project mgr. Arbitron Co., Laurel, Md., 1982-83; pvt. practice psychology, Columbia, Md., 1978—; conf. presenter; coordinator review panel VA grant proposals rev. NIH, 1983—; coordinator/moderator psychology lecture series. Smithsonian Inst.; cons. Mem. Howard County Drug Abuse Adv. Council, 1980-83, Howard County Mental Health Adv. Council, 1983-85. Cert. community coll. tchr. and counselor, Calif.; lic. psychologist, Md. Mem. Md. Psychol. Assn., Am. Psychol. Assn., Phi Kappa Phi. Democrat. Roman Catholic. Contbg. editor to Md. Psychol. Assn. newsletter, 1980-85; contbr. articles to profl. jours. and newspapers. Office: 5525 Twin Knolls Rd Suite 321 Columbia MD 21045

TYLER, MARGO HILLS (MRS. CONVERSE TYLER), retired foundation communications executive, free lance writer; b. Salt Lake City, Sept. 4, 1921; d. Harold Haven and Mary Edith (Roberts) Hills; B.A., U. Utah, 1942; m. Converse Tyler, Sept. 30, 1950. Asst. city editor Salt Lake Telegram, Salt Lake City, 1942-45; adminstrv. asst. safety service ARC, Washington, 1945-55; dir. public relations Am. Cancer Soc., Washington, 1957-65, Am. Assn. Motor Vehicle Adminstrs., Washington, 1966-68; dir. public info. Coll. V.I., St. Thomas, 1968-70; asst. dir. communications div. Nat. 4-H Council. Washington, 1970-86, mng. editor 4-H Leader mag., 1983-86. Mem. adv. council nat. orgns. Corp. Public Broadcasting, Washington, 1971-77, exec. com., 1973-75, 77; co-founder Public Info. Assn. St. Thomas, V.I., 1969, sec., 1969. Mem. Public Relations Soc. Am. (chpt. bd. 1962-64, 1967, 72-73, 81, v.p. 1980), Mortar Bd., Phi Beta Kappa, Phi Kappa Phi, Delta Gamma. Clubs: Nat. Press. (Silver Spring, Md.). Home: 13516 Middlevale Ln Silver Spring MD 20906

TYLER, PHYLLIS STEPHANIE, monument company executive; b. Johnstown, N.Y., Dec. 16, 1943; d. Emerson Stevens and Doris Christina (Busse) T.; Student SUNY, Cortland, 1962-63, Syracuse U., 1981. Foreperson, Letter Memls., Johnstown, N.Y., 1963-67, mgr. alternate days Cherry Valley Memls., 1965-67; salesperson Castle Monument Co., Waltham, Mass., 1967-69, mgr. retail br., 1968; owner, mgr., carver Kellogg Memls., Mexico, N.Y., 1969—. Mem. Vol. Ambulance Corps; trustee Village of Mexico, 1971-77, dep. mayor, 1976-78; mem. Mexico Acad. and Central Sch. Occupational Adv. Council, 1983—; deacon 1st Presbyterian Ch., 1971-72, trustee, 1973-74, ruling elder, 1975-79, 82—; Republican committeeperson Town of Mexico. Recipient various Skiing medals and trophies; named Unsung Heroine, Central N.Y. chpt. NOW, 1982. Mem. Monument Builders N. Am., N.Y. Monument Builders Assn. (dir. 1984—), Greater Mexico C. of C., Assn. Profl., Managerial and Exec. Women. Club: Order Eastern Star. Designer and creator memls. and cast bronze art pieces. Home and Office: 5358 Academy St Mexico NY 13114

TYNDALL, CONNIE BRITT, soft drink bottling company executive; b. Clinton, N.C., Feb. 13, 1949; d. Colonel Ashford and Eunice (Bryant) Britt; student in home econs. Campbell Coll., 1967-70; profl. devel. courses Clemson U., 1977-81; m. Jimmie L. Tyndall, Aug. 29, 1970; 1 son, Stuart Harrison. With Wilmington Coca-Cola Bottling Works (N.C.), 1970—, acctg. auditor, 1973-80, adminstrv. officer, 1981—, asst. to pres. in labor negotiations, 1981—, chief fin. officer, dir. 1985—; sec., dir. Kelford Coca-Cola Bottling Co., Inc., Coca-Cola Bottling Co. of Rocky Mount, Inc., 1983—. Mem. human relations task force com. New Hanover County (N.C.); treas. Ch. Circle Group, Wesley Meml. United Methodist Ch., Wilmington, 1979-80; co-chairperson Human Relation Month (Songfest), Wilmington, 1980. Mem. N.C. Coca-Cola Bottlers Council, N.C. Softdrink Assn., Wilmington C. of C. (edn. liaison com. 1985-86). Democrat. Home: 2325 Camellia Dr Wilmington NC 28403 Office: 921 Princess St Wilmington NC 28401

TYNDALL, KAREN MARIE, nurse; b. Norwich, Conn., Mar. 24, 1959; d. Thaddeus Peter and Constance Joan (Iskripski) T. Diploma in Nursing, St. Francis Hosp., 1980; B.S. in Nursing, Western Conn. State U., 1985. R.N., St. Francis Hosp. and Med. Ctr., Hartford, Conn., 1980-82, William W. Backus Hosp., Norwich, 1982—. Photographer: Morning on the Beach, 1980, Deserted Station, 1983. Bd. dirs. Griswold Pub. Health Nursing Orgn., 1984—. Mem. Nat. League Nursing, Conn. League Nursing (Student Writing award 1984). Roman Catholic. Avocation: photography.

TYNDALL, SYBIL MARIE, nurse; b. Durham, N.C., July 7, 1943; d. Carlos Furman and Margaret Virginia (Overton) Powell; m. Alton Ross Tyndall, Aug. 12, 1959; children—Angela Marie, Alton Jr. L.P.N., Durham Tech. Inst., 1981; R.N., Watts Sch. Nursing, 1984. With Burlington Industries, Durham, N.C., 1961-71, Liggett Myers Tobacco Co., 1971-79; nurse Durham County Hosp., 1981-84; nurse Durham County Gen. Hosp., 1984—. Recipient Sharon Sawyer Meml. award Durham Tech. Inst., 1981. Democrat. Baptist. Avocations: genealogy; photography; cross-stiching. Home: 219 Chateau Rd Durham NC 27704 Office: Durham County Gen Hosp 3643 Roxboro Rd Durham NC 27704

TYNES, H. ELIZABETH, educator; b. Tampa, Fla., Oct. 5, 1926; d. John B. and Alberta (Brown) Loude; m. Arnold Reginald Tynes; children—Lisa Renee, Patrice Arnee. B.S., Oakwood Coll., 1954; M.A., U. S.Fla., 1968; postgrad. Nova U., since 1984—. Tchr. Central States Conf., Kansas City, Mo., 1954-60, Hillsborough County, Tampa, Fla., 1961-67; reading coordinator Dade County Pub. Schs., Miami, Fla., 1968-82, prin., 1982—. Communication sec. Bethany Seventh-day Adventist Ch., Miami, 1983-84; recruiter YWCA, Miami, 1968—; leader Suncoast council Girl Scouts U.S.A., 1961-70. Recipient Tchr. of Yr. plaque Parkway Jr. High Sch., Miami, 1975; Workshop Instr. plaque Bethany Seventh-day Adventist Ch. Mem. Dade County Adminstrs. Assn., Urban League, King's Daus. (pres. Miami 1970-85). Democrat. Avocations: piano; singing; reading; writing stories and poetry. Office: Dade County Adminstrn Assn U Miami PO Box 1605 Miami FL 33165

TYNG, ANNE GRISWOLD, architect; b. Kuling, Kiangsi, China, July 14, 1920; d. Walworth and Ethel Atkinson (Arens) T. (parents Am. citizens); 1 dau., Alexandra Stevens. A.B., Radcliffe Coll., 1942; M.Arch., Harvard U., 1944; Ph.D., U. Pa., 1975. Asso. Stonorov & Kahn (Architects), 1945-47, Louis I. Kahn (Architect), 1947-73; pvt. practice architecture, Phila., 1973—; adj. asso. prof. architecture U. Pa. Grad. Sch. Fine Arts, 1968—; asso. cons. architect Phila. Planning Commn. and; Phila. Redevel. Authority, 1952-54, Mill Creek Redevel. Plan, 1954; vis. disting. prof. Pratt Inst., 1979-81, vis. critic architecture, 1969, Rensselaer Poly. Inst., 1969, 78, Carnegie Mellon U., 1970, Drexel U., 1972-73, Cooper Union, 1974-75, U. Tex., Austin, 1976; lectr. Archtl. Assn., London, also numerous univs. throughout U.S. and Can.; asst. leader People to People Archtl. del. to China, 1983. Subject of: films Anne G. Tyng at Parsons School of Design, 1972, Anne G. Tyng at University of Minnesota, 1974, Connecting, 1976, Forming the Future, 1977; work included in, Smithsonian Travelling Exhbt., 1979-81, 82; Contbr. articles to profl. publs.; Prin. works include: Walworth Tyng Farmhouse (Hon. mention award Phila. chpt. AIA 1953). Fellow Graham Found. for Advanced Study in Fine Arts, 1965, 79, 80, 81. Fellow AIA (Brunner grantee N.Y. chpt. 1964, 83, dir., mem. exec. bd. Phila. chpt., 1976-78); mem. NAD (asso.), Nat. Assn. Archtl. Historians, C.G. Jung Center Phila. (planning com. 1979—), Form Forum (co-founder, mem. planning com. 1978—). Democrat. Episcopalian. Patentee Tyng Toy. Office: Dept Architecture Grad Sch Fine Arts U Pa Philadelphia PA 19104

TYRRELL, KARINE, technical writer; b. Saarbrucken, Germany, Nov. 4, 1940; came to U.S., 1968, naturalized, 1978; d. Eduard and Charlotte (Faber) Ambrosius; B.A., McMaster U., Can., 1964; M.A., So. Ill. U., 1972, Ph.D., 1984; m. James Tyrrell, Aug. 27, 1964 (div. 1979); 1 child, Dalton. Tchr., Hamilton (Ont., Can.) Sch. Bd., 1964-65, Ottawa (Ont., Can.) Sch. Bd., 1966-68; research asst. U.S. Grant Assocs., So. Ill. U., Carbondale, 1973-74, teaching asst. 1974-77, dissertation fellow, 1977-78; tech. writer Action Data Services, St. Louis, 1979-80, Boeing Computer Services, Wichita, Kans., 1980—. Home: 9459 E Skinner Ave Wichita KS 67207 Office: BMAC M/S K79-51 PO Box 7730 Wichita KS 67277-7730

TYSON, CHARLOTTE ROSE, electrical engineer; b. San Mateo, Calif., Aug. 14, 1954; d. Herbert Parry and Rose (Goldner) T.; m. Edward Philip Sejud, Aug. 11, 1979; children—Laura Rose, Elizabeth Ann. A.A. in Physics, DeAnza Coll., 1974; B.S. in Elec. Engring., U. Calif.-Berkeley, 1976. Jr. engr. IBM, Boulder, Colo., 1976-77, assoc. engr., 1977-80, sr. assoc. engr., 1980-82, project engr., 1982-84, devel. engr., 1984—, first line mgr., 1982—. Mem. Soc. Women Engrs. (life), IEEE (Debt of Gratitude award 1981, 82, 83, chmn. Denver sect. 1982-83, bd. dirs. 1985—). Avocations: gardening; reading; sewing. Home: 1231 Martin Rd Longmont CO 80501 Office: IBM PO Box 1900 Boulder CO 80302

TYSON, CICELY, actress; b. N.Y.C.; d. William and Theodosia Tyson; m. Miles Davis. Student N.Y. U., Actors Studio; hon. doctorates Atlanta U., Loyola U., Lincoln U. Former sec., model; stage appearances include The Blacks, 1961-63, Off-Broadway, 1961-63, Moon on a Rainbow Shaw, 1962-63, Tiger, Tiger, Burning Bright, Broadway; star film Sounder, 1972, Bustin' Loose, 1981; other film appearances include: Twelve Angry Men, 1957, Odds Against Tomorrow, 1959, The Last Angry Man, 1959, A Man Called Adam, 1966, The Comedians, 1967, The Heart is a Lonely Hunter, 1968, The Blue Bird, 1976, The River Niger, 1976, A Hero Ain't Nothin' but a Sandwich, 1978, The Concorde-Airport '79, 1979; TV appearances include series East Side, West Side, 1963, spl. TV plays, The Autobiography of Miss Jane Pittman, 1973, 74, A Woman Called Moses, 1978; series Roots, 1977, King, 1978, TV movie Just An Old Sweet Song, 1976, Benny's Place, 1982, Marva Collins Story. Co-founder Dance Theatre of Harlem; bd. dirs. Urban Gateways; trustee Human Family Inst., Am. Film Inst. Recipient Vernon Price award, 1962; named best actress for Sounder, Atlanta Film Festival, 1972; Nat. Soc. Film Critics, 1972; nominee best actress for Sounder, Acad. awards, 1972; Emmy award for best actress in a spl., 1973; also awards NAACP, Nat. Council Negro Women; Capitol Press award. care Creative Artists Agency Inc 1888 Century Park East Suite 1400 Los Angeles CA 90067

TYSON, HELEN FLYNN, civic leader; b. Wilmington, N.C.; d. Walter Thomas and Fannie Elizabeth (Smith) Flynn; Student Guilford Coll., Am. U., Washington; m. James Franklin Tyson, Dec. 25, 1940. Auditor, Disbursing Office, U.S. Civil Service, AUS, Ft. Bragg, N.C., 1935-46, chief clerical asst. Disbursing Office, Pope AFB, N.C., 1946-49, asst. budget and acctg. officer, 1949-55, supervisory budget officer hdqrs. Mil. Transport Command, USAF, 1955-57, budget analyst Hdqrs. USAF, Washington, 1957-74, ret. Active, Arlington Com. 100, Alexandria City Hosp. Corp., Ft. Belvoir, U.S. Army Engr. Center, Civilian-Mil. Adv. Council, Salvation Army Women's Aux., Inter-Service Club Council of Arlington; pres. Operation Check-Mate Council of Arlington, 1981-83; charter asso. Alexandria City Hosp. Found. Recipient awards U.S. Treasury, 1945, 46, U.S. State Dept., 1970; Good Neighbor award Ft. Belvoir Civilian-Mil. Adv. Council, 1978; awards U.S. First Army, 1973, ARC, 1977; named Inter-Service Club Council Woman of Yr., 1975, Cert. of Recognition, 1981, Vol. Activists awards. Mem. Nat. Fedn. Bus. and Profl. Women's Clubs, Am. Assn. Ret. Fed. Employees, Am. Soc. Mil. Comptrollers, Am. Inst. Parliamentarians, Guilford Coll. Alumni Assn., N.C. Soc. Washington. Club: Altrusa Internat., Friends of Kennedy Ctr., Friends of Arlington County Library, Arlington Hosp. Found. Home: 4900 N Old Dominion Dr Arlington VA 22207

TYSON, MARY (MRS. KENNETH W. THOMPSON), artist; b. Sewanee, Tenn., Nov. 2, 1909; d. Stuart L. and Katherine Tyson; student Grand Central Sch. Art, 1928-30, Eastport Sch. Art, 1928, New Sch. Social Research, 1975-76; m. Kenneth W. Thompson, Oct. 1, 1931; children—Kenneth Stuart, Loran Tyson. Exhibited one-man shows: Montross Gallery, N.Y.C., Bruce Mus., Greenwich, Conn., Present Day Club, Princeton, N.J., Pen and Brush Club, N.Y.C., Bodley Gallery, N.Y.C.; exhibited group shows: Balt. Water Color Club, Phila. Watercolor Club, Addison Gallery, Andover, Mass., Bklyn. Mus., Coll. Arts Assn., Morton Gallery, N.Y.C., St. Louis Mus. Contemporary Art, Government House, Nassau, Pen and Brush Club, N.Y.C. (19 awards), New Rochelle (N.Y.) Art Assn., Allied Artists, Knickerbocker Artists, Katherine Lorillard Wolfe, Nat. Arts Club, Lobster Pot Gallery, Nantucket, Am. Watercolor Soc., Easthampton Guild Hall (award), Nantucket Artists Assn.; represented in permanent collections: Guild Hall Mus., Easthampton, Monterey (Calif.) Peninsula Mus., Nantucket Artists Assn., Harrison Meml. Library, Carmel, Calif. Mem. Am. Watercolor Soc., Pen and Brush Club, Nat. Arts Club. Address: 20 W 11th St New York NY 10011

TYSON, PHOEBE WHATLEY, painter; b. Wichita Falls, Tex., May 5, 1926; d. Mertic Boyd and Susie Phoebe (Creath) Whatley; student Abilene Christian U., 1943-45; B.A., North Tex. State U., 1946, M.A., 1951; m. Josiah William Tyson, Jr., Dec. 20, 1946; children—Josiah William III, Phoebe Creath Tyson McDavid. Elem. art tchr. Ft. Worth Ind. Sch. Dist., 1946-47; pvt. tchr. art, Haskell, Tex., 1948-50; painter watercolors, acrylics, Seabrook, Tex., 1971-79; exhibitor Biennial Exhbn., Nat. League Am. Pen Women, Kennedy Center, Washington (award of distinction), 1976, Rocky Mountain Nat. Watermedia Exhbn., Golden, Colo., 1977, 82, 85. Recipient purchase prize San Antonio McNay Art Mus., 1985. Mem. Tex. Fine Arts Assn., McLean (Va.) Art Club (pres. 1970-71), Nat. League Am. Pen Women (nat. art bd. 1972-74, Tex. v.p. 1972-74, Meml. br. pres. 1976-78), Art League Houston, AAUW (v.p. Austin 1955-56), Clear Creek Art League, Watercolor Art Soc. Houston, San Antonio Watercolor Group, Waterloo Watercolor Group, Tex. Watercolor Soc. Mem. Church of Christ. Home: 8600 Appalachian Austin TX 78759

TYSON, SARAH CONDON, interior design company executive; b. Corning, N.Y., July 11, 1940; d. Reginald Lovell and Martha Elizabeth (Hale) Howell; m. William Frederick Condon, Apr. 13, 1963 (div. Oct. 1974); children—James Richard, Jeanine Elizabeth; m. Michael Mark Tyson, Dec. 24, 1983. B.F.A., Syracuse U., 1962. Dir. design Hurbson Office Equipment Co., Syracuse, N.Y., 1961-68; designer S. Condon Design, Cheshire, Conn., 1970-75; dir. design BKM, East Hartford, Conn., 1975-81; pres. Advent Design Inc., Hartford, Conn., 1981—. Recipient award for renovation Conn. Soc. Architects, 1974. Mem. Inst. Bus. Designers (v.p. program 1976-82, nat. trustee 1980-82), Soc. for Mktg. Profl. Services (sec. Conn. 1985—), Conn. Soc. Architects/AIA (edn. com. 1984—). Congregationalist. Avocations: running; tennis. Home: 34 Charter Oak Pl Hartford CT 06106 Office: Advent Design Inc 56 Arbor St Hartford CT 06106

TYTELL, PEARL LILY (MRS. MARTIN KENNETH TYTELL), examiner disputed documents; b. N.Y.C., Aug. 29, 1918; d. Harry and Yetta (Feigenbaum) Kessler; student St. John's U., 1941-43; B.S., N.Y. U., 1962, M.A., 1968; m. Martin Kenneth Tytell, May 23, 1943; children—Peter, Pamela. Examiner disputed documents, N.Y.C., 1950—; lectr. on handwriting, typewriter identification, detection forgery colls., univs., 1955—; lectr. N.Y. U., 1955-57; mem. faculty N.Y. Inst. Criminology, N.Y.C., 1958; cons. govtl. agys., law firms; expert witness in city, state, fed. cts., U.S. and Commonwealth P.R. Sec. Along The Hudson Home Owners Assn., 1960—. Mem. AAAS, Internat. Assn. Chiefs of Police (asso.), Eastern Bus. Tchrs. Assn. Club: N.Y. Univ. Co-author: The Confrontation of Anonymous Letter Writers. Home: 3031 Scenic Pl Riverdale NY 10463 Office: 116 Fulton St New York NY 10038

TYTLER, LINDA JEAN, marketing executive, state legislator; b. Rochester, N.Y., Aug. 31, 1947; d. Frederick Easton and Marian Elizabeth (Allen) Tytler; m. George Stephen Dragnich, May 2, 1970 (div. July 1976). A.S., So. Sem., Buena Vista, Va., 1967; student U. Va., 1973; student in pub. adminstrn. U. N. Mex., 1981-82. Spl. asst. to Congressman John Buchanan, Washington, 1971-75; legis. analyst U.S. Senator Robert Griffin, Washington, 1975-77; ops. supr. Pres. Ford Com., Washington, 1976; office mgr. U.S. Senator Pete Domenici Re-election, Albuquerque, 1977; pub. info. officer S.W. Community Health Service, Albuquerque, 1978-83; cons. pub. relations and mktg., Albuquerque, 1983-84; account exec. Rick Johnson & Co., Inc., Albuquerque, 1983-84; dir. mktg. St. Joseph Healthcare Corp., 1984—; mem. N.Mex. Ho. of Reps., Santa Fe, 1983—, vice chmn. appropriations and fin. com., interim com. on children and youth, mem. voters and election com., chmn. Republican caucus, 1985—; mem. hosp. cost containment task force Nat. Conf. State Legislatures. Bd. dirs. N. Mex. chpt. ARC, Albuquerque, 1984. Recipient 2d place award N.Mex. Advt. Fedn., Albuquerque, 1981, 82, 85, 86, hon. mention award, 1982. Mem. Am. Soc. Hosp. Pub. Relations (cert.). Republican. Baptist. Office: 400 Walter NE Albuquerque NM 87102

TZENG, MARIAN C., pediatrician; b. Taipei, Taiwan, Aug. 23, 1949; came to U.S., 1974; d. Muran and Onai Chen; m. Stephen S. Tzeng, Aug. 28, 1973; children—Grace Alice, Christine. M.D., Taipei Med. Coll., 1974. Diplomate Am. Bd. Pediatrics. Resident in pediatrics Coll. Medicine and Dentistry of N.J., Newark, 1976-79; fellow in pediatric infections Newark Beth Israel Hosp., 1978-79, mem. staff, 1979-81; Care for Handicapped Children fellow Cleve. Met. Gen. Hosp., 1981-82; clin. instr. St. Luke's Hosp., Cleve., 1982-83, Case Western Res. U. Sch. Medicine, 1982-83; practice medicine specializing in pediatrics, Monterey Park, Calif., 1983—; mem. staffs Garfield Med. Ctr., Beverly Hosp., Valley Vista Hosp. Mem. Am. Acad. Pediatrics. Office: Suite 8 206 E Las Tunas Dr San Gabriel CA 91776 also 1900 S Atlantic Blvd Monterey Park CA 91754

UBELL, SHIRLEY LEITMAN, dance educator, therapist, choreographer, dancer; b. Flushing, L.I., N.Y., Mar. 26, 1928; d. Morris Leitman and Esther (Steckler) Sobel; m. Earl Ubell, Feb. 12, 1949; children—Lori Ellen, Michael Charles. B.A. in Psychology, Hunter Coll., 1948, M.S. in Dance Movement Therapy, 1984. Tchr. dance, Paramus, N.J., 1952-62; founder, artistic dir. Ctr. for Modern Dance, Hackensack, N.J., 1962—; founder Repertory Dancers (profl. modern dance), 1969-74; choreographer 25 solos in N.Y. Loft, 1977—. Recipient numerous grants. Mem. Creative Arts Rehab. Ctr. of N.Y.C. (sec. 1975—). Avocations: reading; swimming; traveling; poetry writing. Office: Ctr for Modern Dance Edn 84 Euclid Ave Hackensack NJ 07602

UBOSI, ANGIE NONYGLUM, nutrition center executive, consultant; b. Enugu, Nigeria, Aug. 12, 1952; came to U.S., 1978, naturalized, 1978; d. Thomas and Nwaobonne (Ukagi) U.; m. Williams Clearame, Nov. 8, 1984. B.S., U. Ark., 1982; B.A. in Bus., McNeese State U., 1983; candidate M. Psychology and Counseling, Donsbech U., 1984—. Registered nutrition cons. Officer, Dept. Customs, Nigeria, 1973-78; mgr. Nutrition, Little Rock, 1978-82; pres. Angie Internat. Nutrition Ctr., Inc., Lake Charles, La., 1982-86, Nutritional Motivation, Lake Charles, 1983—. Author poetry, Pres. Lake Charles chpt. Am. Cancer Soc., 1982—; vol. Edn. Therapy Ctr., Lake Charles, 1986. Mem. Am. Nutritional Med. Assn., Nat. Assn. Female Execs. (network dir. 1983-85), Internat. Trade Orgn., Nat. Health Assn. (pres. Lake Charles chpt. 1983—). Office: Angie Internat Nutrition Ctr Inc PO Box 7223 Lake Charles LA 70606

UDRIS, MONICA ALANE, nurse; b. Balt., Nov. 9, 1958; d. Albert Joseph and Gloria Jean (Manning) U. A.A., Community Coll. Balt., 1978; student Essex Community Coll. R.N., Md. Nurse, Mercy Hosp., Balt., 1978—, mentor, 1984—. Campaign vol. for candidate Md. Ho. of Dels., 1982—. Roman Catholic. Avocations: sewing; reading; interior design; ethnic cooking; aerobics. Home: 2810 Parkview Terr Baltimore MD 21214

UECKERT, AUDREY ANN, news photographer; b. Laredo, Tex., May 4, 1956. B.Journalism, U. Tex.-Austin, 1980. News photographer UPI, Houston, 1979-82, Houston Post, 1982-84, Tampa Tribune, 1985; freelance, Houston, 1986—. Mem. Nat. Press Photographers Assn., ACLU. Democrat. Office: Houston Post 4747 Southwest Freeway Houston TX 77001

UEHLING, BARBARA STANER, university chancellor; b. Wichita, Kans., June 12, 1932; d. Roy W. and Mary Elizabeth (Hilt) Staner; B.A. in Psychology, U. Wichita, 1954; M.A. in Exptl. Psychology, 1956, Ph.D., 1958; L.H.D. (hon.), Drury Coll., Springfield, Mo., 1978; LL.D. (hon.), Ohio State U., 1980; m. Stanley Johnson; children by previous marriage—Jeff, David. Mem. faculty Oglethorpe U., Atlanta, 1959-64, Emory U., Atlanta, 1966-69; adj. prof. psychology U. R.I., 1970-72; mem. faculty, then acad. dean Roger Williams Coll., Providence, 1972-74; dean arts and scis. Ill. State U., 1974-76; provost U. Okla., 1976-78; chancellor U. Mo., Columbia, 1978—; mem. Nat. Council Ednl. Research; dir. Mercantile Bancorp., Inc.; adv. dir. Merc. Trust Co., St. Louis, Meredith Corp., Des Moines. Bd. dirs. United Way Columbia; trustee Carnegie Found. Advancement of Teaching; mem. adv. com. Nat. Ctr. for Food and Agrl. Policy; bd. dirs. Resources for the Future; mem. NCAA Pres.'s Commn.; bd. visitors Air U., 1984—. Recipient Alumnae award Northwestern U., 1985. NIHM fellow, 1966-69. Mem. Am. Assn. Higher Edn. (past pres.), Am. Council on Edn. (dir. 1979-82), Columbia C. of C. (dir.), Sigma Xi. Author monograph, chpt. in book. Office: 105 Jesse Hall U Mo Columbia MO 65211

UELAND, ERICA, make-up artist, flight instructor; b. Longview, Wash., June 9, 1949; d. Arnulf and Rebecca Prentiss (Lucas) U.; m. Denis Roy Whitaker Harrap, Sept. 24, 1973 (div.). B.A. in English Lit., Beloit Coll., 1971; student Dartmouth Coll., 1968, 69. Cert. aircraft dispatcher, comml. pilot, flight instr., advanced ground instr., flight engr. Chief make-up artist for films and numerous TV commls., London, 1973-76, Hollywood, Calif., 1976—; flight instr., Burbank, Calif., 1983—; guest speaker CBS PM Mag., 1980, AM Los Angeles, 1980, Nat. Women in Communication, Internat. Audio Visual Assn. Mem. Nat. Wildlife Assn., Internat. Wildlife Assn., NOW, Audubon Soc., Nat. Assn. Female Execs. Home: 4339 Clarissa Ave Los Angeles CA 90027 Office: 1888 Century Park E Suite 10 Los Angeles CA 90067

UGAI, SUSAN M., lawyer; b. North Platte, Nebr., Jan. 4, 1956; d. Norman F. and Alice T. (Nakada) U. B.A., U. Nebr., 1978, J.D., 1981. Bar: Nebr. 1981. City atty. City of North Platte (Nebr.), 1981—. Adv. bd. Salvation Army, North Platte, 1982—, Women in Transition/Displaced Homemaker, North Platte, 1983—; chmn. edn. and prevention com. Sexual Assault Task Force, North Platte, 1983—. Mem. Nat. Inst. Mcpl. Law Officers (state chairperson Nebr. 1983-84), ABA (young lawyers div. com. delivery legal services to elderly, exec. com. 1983—), Nebr. State Bar Assn. (young lawyers sect. com. delivery legal services to elderly, co-vice chmn. 1983—), Lincoln County Bar Assn., Nat. Fedn. Bus. and Profl. Women, AAUW. Republican. Episcopalian. Club: Altrusa Internat. Home: PO Box 1993 North Platte NE 69103 Office: City of North Platte 211 W 3d St North Platte NE 69101

UGISS-ALTIERI, CAROLYN, real estate consulting and development company executive, broker; b. Scott Field, Ill., Nov. 19, 1947; d. Philip Patrick and Marcia (Truxton) U.; m. Donald R. Altieri, Dec. 12, 1982. B.S., Cornell U., 1969. Lic. real estate broker, N.Y., Colo.; lic. real estate salesperson, Calif. Pub. relations dir. Smoke Watchers Internat., N.Y.C., 1969-73; mktg. dir. Environ. Research & Devel., N.Y.C., 1973-76; exec. v.p. CPC/Corp. Planners and Coordinators, Inc., N.Y.C., 1976—, dir. subs. cos.; dir. Beri, Inc., Salem, Oreg. Mem. Real Estate Bd. N.Y. Club: Cornell of Fairfield County (Conn.). Office: CPC Corp Planners and Coordinators 130 E 35th St New York NY 10016

UHL, PATRICIA SANDRA, software company executive; b. Bayonne, N.J., July 10, 1950; d. George Joseph and Veronia (Lukaszewich) U.; m. Michael De Rubertis, 1986. B.S., U. Md., 1972. Account rep. Gen. Electric Co., San Francisco, 1975-77; tech. rep. Computer Scis. Corp., San Francisco, 1977-78; cons., pres. Uhl Assocs., Tiburon, Calif., 1978-81; cons. mgr. Ross Systems, Palo Alto, Calif., 1981-83; v.p. Distributed Planning Systems, Calabasas, Calif., 1983—. Troop leader San Francisco council Girl Scouts U.S., 1974; participant Women On Water, Marina Del Rey, Calif., 1983. Mem. Nat. Assn. Female Execs., Dalta Delta Delta. Democrat. Club: San Fernando Valley Yacht (Marina Del Rey, Calif.). Office: Distributed Planning Systems 23632 Calabasas Rd Calabasas CA 91302

UHLAND, RUTH ELLEN, educator; b. Escondido, Calif., May 4, 1925; d. William and Ruth (Rooker) U.; A.A., Mira Costa Coll., 1945; B.A., San Diego State Coll., 1947, postgrad., 1948-49, 61, 62, 64, 70-72; postgrad. San Jose State

Coll., 1966-67, Fresno State Coll., 1956-57, U. San Diego, 1969, Internat. U., 1971—. Tchr. jr. high sch. Brawley (Calif.) Elem. Sch. Dist., 1947-50, 53-54, 56-64, elem. tchr., 1950-53, 55, 65—, chmn. health-phys. edn. dept., 1960. Active various community drives; adv. bd. Rainbow Girls, 1972—. Mem. Internat. Reading Assn. (sch. rep. 1969-72), Calif., Brawley tchrs. assns., Imperial Valley Girls Phys. Edn. Assn. (sch. rep. 1967-68), Brawley Bus. and Profl. Women's Club (v.p. desert sect. 1968-69, pres.'s ecology citation 1972), Desert Protective Council (life), Nat. Audubon Soc., Cooper Ornithol. Soc. (life), Wilson Ornithol. Soc., Am. Ornithologists Union, Nat. Ret. Tchrs. Assn., Calif. Ret. Tchrs. Assn., Internat. Platform Assn., AAUW, Delta Kappa Gamma. Clubs: Order Eastern Star, Venture (pres. 1954-55) (Brawley); Sierra (San Diego). Home: 158 G St Brawley CA 92227

UHLER, JANIE RUSSELL, retail men's clothing store executive; b. Warrensburg, Mo., Aug. 31, 1927; d. Henry Hagan and Ida Mae (Wolf) Russell; m. Earl D. Uhler, Sept. 4, 1949; children—Jill Uhler Buford, Bruce D. B.S. in Edn., U. Mo., 1948. Tchr. Warrensburg High Sch., 1949; sec. alcohol tax unit IRS, Washington, 1949-50; bookkeeper, sales clk. Russell Bros. Clothing, Warrensburg, 1950-52, sales clk., asst. mgr., 1959-81; broker, owner Century 21 Blackwater Real Estate, Warrensburg, 1978—; pres., buyer, mgr., owner Russell Bros. Clothing Co., 1981—; sec., owner Qualitech Computer Ctrs., S.E. and Mid-Atlantic regions, Camp Hill, Pa., 1984—; founder, pres. Sta. KLUK-FM, Knob Noster, Mo., 1982—; dir. Citizens Bank, Warrensburg. Bd. dirs. Arrow Rock Lyceum Theater, Mo., 1970—; bd. dirs., officer United Fund, Warrensburg, 1973-80; bd. dirs. Distributive Edn. Clubs of Am., 1974-80; sec., bd. dirs. Warrensburg Planning and Zoning Commn., 1962-65; mem. Warrensburg Traffic Commn., 1979—; drive ward chmn. Johnson County Mercy Hosp., 1963; den mother Cub Scouts Am., 1963-66; leader Girl Scouts U.S.A., 1950-51. Mem. Mo. Retailers Assn. (bd. dirs.), Menswear Retailers Am., Mo. Broadcasters Assn., Mo. Real Estate Assn., DAR, Kappa Kappa Gamma. Mem. Christian Ch. Club: Secunda Study. Avocations: canoeing; sailing; camping. Home: 512 Christopher St Warrensburg MO 64093 Office: Russell Brothers Clothing Co PO Box 1038 Warrensburg MO 64093

UHLER, SHIRLEY KAY, nursery and landscaping company executive; b. Riverton, Wyo., June 9, 1949; d. Julius Herbert and Mary Ellen (Thompson) Keil; m. Terrance Michael Uhler, Dec. 7, 1974; children—Jennifer Lee, Joseph Michael. B.S., U. Wyo., 1971. Sec. U.S. Senate, Washington, 1971-73; legal sec. Texaco Inc., Denver, 1973-74; mem. advt. staff Bowman County Pioneer, Bowman, N.D., 1975-77; co-owner Green Acres Nursery, Gillette, Wyo., 1980—. Leader Girls Scouts U.S.A., Gillette, 1983-85. Mem. Am. Nurserymen's Assn., Colo. Nurserymen's Assn., Am. Bus. Women's Assn. (pres. Gillette 1984-85), Am. Legion Aux. Republican. Methodist. Lodge: Order of Eastern Star. Avocations: reading; piano; camping. Home: 1206 W 5th Ave Gillette WY 82716 Office: Green Acres Nursery 3204 E 2d St Gillette WY 82716

UHRMAN, CELIA, artist, poet; b. New London, Conn., May 14, 1927; d. David Aaron and Pauline (Schwartz) U.; B.A., Bklyn. Coll., 1948, M.A., 1953; Ph.D., U. Danzig, 1977; postgrad. Tchrs. Coll., Columbia U., 1961, City U. N.Y., 1966, Bklyn. Mus. Art Sch., 1956-57, Ph.D. (hon.), Litt.D., 1973; cert. Koret Living Library U. of San Francisco, 1982. One-woman shows: Leffert Jr. High Sch., Bklyn., 1958, Flatbush C. of C., N.Y.C., 1963, Conn. C. of C., New London, 1962; exhibited in group shows: Smithsonian Instn., Washington, 1958, Springfield (Mass.) Mus. Fine Arts, 1959, Bklyn. Mus., 1959, Old Mystic (Conn.) Art Center, 1959, Carnegie Endowment Internat. Center, N.Y.C., 1959, Lyman Allyn Mus., New London, 1960, Palacio de La Virrelna, Barcelona, Spain, 1961, YMCA, Bklyn., 1962, UFT Art Exhibit, N.Y.C., 1963, Soc. of 4 Arts, Palm Beach, Fla., 1964, Perspective 68, Monte-Carlo, Monaco, 1968, George W. Wingate High sch., Bklyn., 1967, Premier Salon Internat., Charleroi, Belgium, 1968, Palme d'or Beaux Arts, Monte-Carlo, 1970, 72, Dibuix-Joan Miro Premi Internacional, Barcelona, 1970; N.Y. Art Festival, 1970, Internat. Platform Assn. Art Show, Washington, 1971, 73, Ovar Mus., Portugal, 1974, others; represented in permanent collections: Bklyn. Coll., Ch. of Evangel, Bklyn.; tchr. N.Y.C. Sch. System, 1948-82; partner Uhrman Studio, 1973-83; hon. rep. U.S., Centro Studi E Scambi Internazionali, Rome, mem. Internat. com., 1969. Hon. life mem. World Poetry Day Com., Inc. and Nat. Poetry Day Com., 1977. Recipient award Freedoms Found., George Washington medal of honor, 1964; Diplome d'Honneur Palme d'Or des Beaux Arts Exhbn., Monaco, 1969, 72, Diploma and Gold medal, Certro Studi E Scambi Internazionali, 1972; decorated Order of Gandhi Award of Honour, Knight Grand Cross, 1972, personal poetry certificate WEFG stereo, 1970; Gold Laurel award Esposizione Internazionale D'Art Contemporain, Paris, 1974; named Poetry Translator Laureate World Acad. Lang. and Lit., 1972; Poet of Mankind Acad. Philosophy, 1972; cert. of appreciation Bd. Edn. of N.Y.C., 1982. Fellow World Lit. Academy Eng.; mem. Internat. Arts Guild (comdr. 1966—), World Poetry Soc. Intercontinental (rep. at large 1969—), Internat. Acad. Poets (founding fellow), N.Y. Artists Equity. Author: Poetic Ponderances, 1969; A Pause for Poetry, 1970; Poetic Love Fancies, 1970. A Pause for Poetry for Children, 1973; The Chimps Are Coming, 1975; also poems. Home: 1655 Flatbush Ave Apt and Studio C106 Brooklyn NY 11210

UITERMARK, HELEN JOAN, computing services executive; b. Zandvoort, Netherlands, May 4, 1941; came to U.S., 1968, naturalized, 1977; d. Peter Theodore and Maria Francisca (Castien) U.; ed. London, Ont., Can. With Drug Trading Co., London, 1957-59, Richard-Wilcox, London, 1959-62, Friden Bus. Machines, Toronto, Ont., 1962-68, Permatex, West Palm Beach, Fla., 1968-70, Singer Bus. Machines, London, Ont., Can., 1970-72, Los Angeles, 1972-74; with Safariland Leather Co., Monrovia, Calif., 1974-81, v.p. adminstrn., 1975-81; ind. systems analyst, Los Angeles, 1981-83; owner Timor Computing Services, Azusa, Calif., 1983—; exec. dir. Forum Internat., 1983—. Mem. Forum Internat., Aircraft Owners and Pilots Assn.

ULBRICH, DIANE L., accountant; b. Chgo., Jan. 26, 1953; d. Norbert T. and Phyllis L. (Shelton) U. B.B.A, N. Tex. State U., 1981. Acctg. services staff Hankins Powers, Fergerson & Co., Denton, Tex., 1977-81; tax staff Fox & Co., Dallas, 1981, Mem. Am. Soc. Women Accts. (treas. 1984, co-chair student seminar 1983), Tex. Soc. C.P.A.s (chpt. entertainment com.), Nat. Assn. Accts., Dallas Estate Planning Council, Am. Women's Soc. C.P.A.s, Am. Inst. C.P.A.s.

ULBRICH, JANET LYNN, food service company administrator; b. Cleve., Feb. 3, 1962; d. Emmet Charles and Patricia Sue (Ferrell) Ulbrich. B.B.A., Cleve. State U., 1983. Data entry staff Facs, Inc., Mayfield, Ohio, 1979-84; asst. mgr. Pizza Hut, Inc., Rocky River, Ohio, 1984-85; regional tng. mgr. Food Service Enterprise, Rocky River, 1985-86, area supr. Multi-unit mgmt., 1986—. Mem. Nat. Assn. Female Execs. Republican. Baptist. Avocations: golf; racquetball. Home: 2167 W 45th St Cleveland OH 44102 Office: Food Service Enterprise Zone A Tng Ctr 34263 Center Ridge Rd North Ridgeville OH 44039

ULICHNY, BARBARA L., state legislator; b. Milw., June 10, 1947; d. Clarence and Karmen Egge Seybold; married. B.A. in Econs., Northwestern U., 1969. Former high sch. tchr., YWCA program dir.; mem. Wis. Assembly, 1978-84; mem. Wis. Senate, 4th Dist., 1984—. Democrat. Office: State Capitol Madison WI 53702*

ULITT, LILLY ROSE, dietitian; b. Charleston, W.Va., June 11, 1936; d. Elias and Georgette Haddad; B.S. in Foods and Nutrition, W.Va. State U., 1960; B.B.A. in Mgmt., Ariz. State U., 1975; M.B.A., Pepperdine U., 1980; m. Carl Ulitt, Sept. 16, 1967; 1 dau., Karen Marie. Dietitian, Bethesda Hosp., Cin., 1962-64; food service mgr. U. Ariz., Tucson, 1968-70, Long Beach (Calif.) Unified Sch. Dist., 1977-78; food service dir. Chino (Calif.) Community Hosp., 1978-80, San Diego Naval Regional Med. Center, 1981—; vol. nutritionist ARC, Okinawa, Japan, 1971-72; nutrition cons. Title VII Sr. Nutrition Program, 1977-78; instr. instl. food service program Palomar Coll., San Marcos, Calif. Active Meals-On-Wheels, Chino. Served to capt. USAF, 1964-68. Recipient cert. of achievement U.S. Army Med. Center, Okinawa. Mem. Am. Dietetic Assn., Calif. Sch. Food Service Assn., Calif. Dietetic Assn., Am. Soc. Hosp. Food Service Adminstrs., Aircraft Owners and Pilots Assn., Civil Air Patrol. Home: PO Box 351 Coronado CA 92118 Office: Food Mgmt Services Naval Regional Med Center San Diego CA 92134

ULLMAN, MARIE, mfg. co. exec.; b. Linlithgo, N.Y., Mar. 19, 1914; d. Max and Sarah (Jaffe) Michaelson; R.N., Bklyn. Hosp., 1935; m. Robert Ullman, Aug. 15, 1935. Pres., sec.-treas. Ullman Devices Corp., Ridgefield, Conn., 1938—; dir. State Nat. Bank Conn., Ridgefield. Mem. C. of C. Ridgefield, Bklyn. Hosp. Nurses Alumnae. Home: 43 Chestnut Hill Rd Wilton CT 06897 Office: PO Box 398 Ridgefield CT 06877

ULLMAN, ROSANNE MARIE, editor; b. Harrisburg, Pa., May 7, 1953; d. Robert and Bertha (Pollack) U.; m. Keevan David Morgan, Sept. 4, 1977; children—Rebecca, Jaina. B.A., Hofstra U., 1975; M.S. in Journalism, Northwestern U., 1977. Sec. Proprietary Assn., Washington, 1975-76; news editor Modern Salon, Chgo., 1978-79, mng. editor, 1979, local editor, 1981—; mng. editor Pub. Trade, Northfield, Ill., 1983-84, editor, 1984-85; founder greeting card co. Wimminotes, Inc., 1976. Advisor girls' chpt. B'nai B'rith, Northbrook, 1981—. Mem. Kappa Tau Alpha. Office: Pub Trade mag 464 Central Ave Northfield IL 60093

ULMER, HARRIET GLASS, health care administrator; b. St. Louis, June 7, 1940; d. Melvin G. and Deenie (Laskowitz) Shcolnik; m. Raymond A. Ulmer, Feb. 26, 1980; children by previous marriage—Bonnie Glass Neilson, Bernard J., Laura L. B.A. in English, UCLA, 1976; M.P.A. in Health Services Adminstrn., U. So. Calif., 1980. Membership mgr. Santa Barbara County Med. Assn., Calif., 1971-73; regional project coordinator Kaiser Found. Health Plan, Los Angeles, 1978-80; cons. Humana, Inc., Newport Beach, Calif., 1980; health systems planner/cons. Los Angeles Health Planning and Devel. Agy., 1981; dir. planning and mktg. Hosp. of Good Samaritan, Los Angeles, 1981—; instr. strategic health planning and mktg. Calif. State U.-Long Beach. Mem. Calif. Senate health promotion task force, 1984-85; bd. dirs. U. So. Calif. Health Services Adminstrn. Alumni Assn., 1980—; mem., subcom. chmn. Pub. Policy Com., Greater Los Angeles affiliate, Am. Heart Assn., 1981—; mem. Coro Assocs., Los Angeles, 1982—. Mem. Am. Mktg. Assn. (bd. dirs. So. Calif. 1983, pres. health care div. 1984-85, editorial rev. bd. Jour. Health Services Mktg.), Am. Coll. Health Care Execs., Health Care Execs. So. Calif., Soc. Hosp. Planning and Mktg. (editor jour. 1983-84), Women in Health Adminstrn. Avocations: travel; jogging; reading; dancing. Office: The Hosp of Good Samaritan 616 S Witmer St Los Angeles CA 90017

ULRICH, GERTRUDE ANNA, nurse; b. Steinauer, Nebr., Oct. 19, 1922; d. Fred, Jr. and Matilda (Rinne) U.; R.N., Lincoln (Nebr.) Gen. Hosp., 1960; postgrad. Wesleyan U., Lincoln, 1960-61, B.S. in Natural Scis., 1972; postgrad. U. Nebr., 1967-68, Omaha U., 1966. Instr. Lincoln (Nebr.) Gen. Hosp. Sch. Nursing, 1960-61, 66-67; staff nurse Lincoln Gen. Hosp., 1961-62, 68-71; missionary nurse to Turkey, United Ch. Bd. World Ministries, N.Y.C., 1963-64; camp nurse Girl Scouts U.S.A., Nebraska City, Nebr., summer 1964; staff nurse Homestead Nursing Home, 1964-66; nursing supr. Tabitha Home, Lincoln, 1972-80, med. record supr., 1975-80; evening nursing supr. Homestead Nursing Home, Lincoln, 1980—. Lincoln Found. ednl. grantee, 1971; named Nurse of Week, Sta. KFOR, 1973, 76. Mem. Am. Nurses Assn. Mem. Reformed Ch. Am. Home: 410 S 41 Lincoln NE 68510

UMBER, NOVALINE PIERCE, pharmacist; b. nr. Mangum, Okla., Nov. 13, 1924; d. John Carlton and Anna Lue (Whitmire) Pierce; B.A. in English and Music Edn., Southwestern State U. Okla., 1946, B.S. in Pharmacy (scholar), 1959; m. Herbert Umber, May 29, 1956 (div. 1977). Tchr. Okla. schs., 1943-56; pharmacist Umber Drug, Apache, Okla., 1959-72, Phil's Discount Drug, Carnegie, Okla., 1977, TGY, Wichita, Kans., 1977-78, Tom's Profl. Pharmacy, Andarko, Okla., 1978-79, United Drug, Purcell, Okla., 1980-81; relief pharmacist Marshall Drug, Cyril, 1979-82, Osco Drug, Lawton, 1980-82. Mem. Okla. Pharm. Assn., Mensa, Okla. Poetry Soc., Am. Pharm. Assn., Alpha Phi Sigma. Methodist. Clubs: Apache Study, Rebekahs. Author: Star Dust and Sand Dunes, 1968; Excelsior, 1975. Home: 2204 Northfield Coffeyville KS 67337

UMBRO, SALLY MARIE, oncology nurse; b. New Rochelle, N.Y., May 20, 1955; d. Vincent John and Laura Nadine (Sclafani) Razionale; m. Frank Joseph Umbro, Dec. 3, 1977; children—Jessica Anne, Matthew Vincent. B.S.N., Keuka Coll., 1977. Staff nurse oncology Montefiore Hosp., Bronx, 1977-79, head nurse oncology, 1979-81; staff nurse oncology Lawrence Hosp., Bronxville, N.Y., 1982—. Recipient Miss Hope N.Y. State award Am. Cancer Soc., 1975. Mem. Oncology Nursing Soc., N.Y. State Nurses Assn. Republican. Roman Catholic. Home: 62 Pershing Ave New Rochelle NY 10801 Office: Lawrence Hosp 55 Palmer Rd Bronxville NY 10708

UMPHRESS, AGNES ELLEN, clin. therapist; b. Ashland, Oreg., June 27, 1925; d. Charles Albert and Mabel (Rice) White; B.A., Willamette U., 1947; M.S.W., U. Wash., 1961; m. Rupert Hampton Umphress, Jan. 20, 1962. Supr., Harry & David, Medford, Oreg., 1947-56; med. social worker Oreg. Welfare Commn., 1956-59; clin. therapist U. Wash., 1961-68; chief therapist Children's Home Soc. Wash., Tacoma, 1968-78; co-owner, therapist Counseling Resource Center, Inc., Chehalis, Wash., 1979—; adv. bd. Child Abuse Program, 1974-78, Sexual Assault Program, 1977-78, Family Planning Assn., 1975-80. Cert. Acad. Cert. Social Workers. Mem. Nat. Assn. Social Workers, Nat. Assn. Clin. Social Workers, Am. Assn. Psychiat. Services for Children, Am. Orthopsychiat. Assn. Republican. Club: Sertoma. Contbr. articles to profl. jours. Research on therapeutic programs in technologically advanced and Third World nations. Home: 625 Tauscher Rd Chehalis WA 98532 Office: 118 N Market Blvd Chehalis WA 98532

UMSHLER, SUE ELAINE, petroleum engineer, consulting firm executive; b. Tucumcari, N.Mex., May 25, 1953; d. Raymond Roy and Frances Gertrude (Brewer) Gibson; m. Dennis Bryan Umshler, Aug. 12, 1972. B.S. in Environ. Engring., N.Mex. Inst. Mining and Tech., 1975; M.S. in Civil Engring., U. N.Mex., 1980. Registered profl. engr., N.Mex. Petroleum engr. U.S. Geol. Survey, Roswell, N.Mex., 1975-76, environ. scientist, Albuquerque, 1976-77; civil engr. Boyle/Bohannon-Huston, Albuquerque, 1978-79; petroleum engr., supr. U.S. Geol. Survey, Albuquerque, 1979-83; fluids br. chief U.S. Bur. Land Mgmt., Albuquerque, 1983-85; pres., founder, chief engr. GULRAM, Inc., Albuquerque, 1985—. Contbg. author study on use of uranium wastewater for mcpl. supply, Gallup, N.Mex., 1980. Recipient Kennecott scholarship award Kennecott Mines, N.Mex., 1974-75; Spl. Achievement award for natural gas policy act procedures establishment U.S. Geol. Survey, Albuquerque, 1979. Mem. Soc. Petroleum Engrs., N.Mex. Geol. Soc., Nat. Soc. Profl. Engrs., N.M. Landman's Assn., N.Mex. Oil and Gas Assn., Albuquerque Petroleum Assn. Republican. Lutheran. Avocations: gardening; reading; sewing. Office: GULRAM Inc PO Box 6548 Albuquerque NM 87197

UNCAPHER, BARBARA WIDLITZ, educator; b. Cleve., Sept. 9, 1940; d. William F. and Virginia Widlitz; B.A., Denison U., 1962; M.A., W.Va. U., 1965; Ph.D., U. Pitts., 1983; m. Andrew G. Uncapher, Jr., Aug. 26, 1961; children—Leslie, Daniel. Speech therapist Marion County Bd. Edn., Fairmont, W.Va., 1963-65; pvt. practice speech pathology, 1965-67; instr. speech Pa. State U., 1967-71; asst. prof. speech communication Pa. State U., New Kensington campus, 1971—; lectr. in field; sec., treas., dir. Indigo Inc., New Kensington, 1980—. Past bd. dirs. Kiski Valley Vis. Nurse Assn., Kiski Valley Civic League, YMCA; mem. Westmoreland County Republican Com., 1969-72; mem. William Bell's Clown Troop; past leader Girls Scouts U.S.A.. Mem. Eastern Communication Assn., Speech Communication Assn. Pa. (exec. council, vice chmn. interpersonal organizational council). Episcopalian. Club: Order Eastern Star. Contbr. articles to profl. jours. Office: Dept Speech Pa State U New Kensington PA 15068

UNDERWOOD, JACQUELINE MARTIN, advisory internal auditor; b. Knoxville, Tenn., Mar. 23, 1934; d. Ralph Henry and Anna Lou (McMahan) Martin; children—Paul, Carla. B.S., Knoxville Coll., 1955; M.S., U. Tenn., 1962, M.M., 1964, Ed.D., 1976. Tchr. Schutz Sch., Alexandria, Egypt, 1955-58, Vine Jr. High Sch., Knoxville, 1961-65; assoc. prof. Knoxville Coll., 1958-60, 65-78; part-time instr. Walters State Community Coll., Morristown, Tenn, 1975-76; computer programmer IBM, Rochester, Minn., 1978-79, asst. to systems assurance lab. mgr., 1979-80, mgr. equal opportunity programs, 1980-83, adv. internal auditor, Purchase, N.Y., 1983—; instr. Rochester Community Coll., 1978-83. Bd. dirs. Rochester Better Chance, 1979-82, pres., 1980-81; vol. Rapeline, 1979-83, Recreation for Mentally Retarded Adults, 1979-80; mem. Rochester Human Rights Commn., 1980-83, pres., 1982-83; mem. affirmative action and instrnl. adv. com. Rochester Sch. Bd.; v.p. Rochester United Way Campaign, 1983. Grantee NSF, 1963-64, U.S. Office Edn., 1969, 74-76. Mem. Nat. Council Tchrs. Math., Research Council on Diagnostic and Prescriptive Math., AAUW (bd. dirs. Rochester chpt. 1979-81), LWV (bd. dirs. Rochester chpt. 1979-80), Rochester Ebon Sisters, Jack and Jill of Am., (founder Knoxville chpt.) NAACP (life), Waterbury Links Inc., Danbury Pride Inc., Alpha Kappa Alpha. Democrat. Mem. African Methodist Episcopal Zion Ch. Home: 95-14 Park Ave Danbury CT 06810 Office: IBM 2000 Purchase St LA-09 Purchase NY 10577

UNDERWOOD, MARY ELIZABETH, antique dealer, real estate buyer; b. Bethesda, Md., Mar. 2, 1945; d. William Arthur and Mary (Cochrane) Hallett; m. Dennis Francis Underwood, July 12, 1980. B.S. in Edn., Towson State U., Md. Early childhood edn. tchr. St. Pius X Sch., Balt. City Schs., 1968-70; office mgr., bookkeeper Arlen Realty Mgmt., Bethesda, 1970-75, area supr., 1975-78; dir. of housing Johns Hopkins U., Balt., 1978-80; purchaser, mgr. real estate, Md., N.Y., Pa., Del., Ga., 1980—; owner, operator Homespun Antiques, Atlanta, Wilmington, Del., 1983—. Real estate licensesure, Balt., 1974-80; notary pub., Md., 1975-80, N.Y., 1980-85; bd. dirs. Cliff House Condominium Council, 1984-85. Republican. Roman Catholic. Club: Md. Boxer (bd. dirs. 1974-80). Avocations: sewing; antiquing; interior decorating. Home: PO Box 550 104 Atlanta GA 30355

UNDERWOOD, NANCY MAE, occupational health and safety cons.; b. Vancouver, Wash., Dec. 29, 1944; d. Robert Izea and Jennie Mae (McWhorter) Espie; B.S. in Occupational Health and Safety, Calif. State U., 1974, now post grad.; cert. of proficiency-engring./occupational safety and health, Travelers Ins. Co., 1975, Textron, Inc., 1977; postgrad. U. San Francisco, 1978-81; 1 dau., Apryl. Safety engr. Travelers Ins. Co., Los Angeles, 1975-76; tchr. Los Angeles City Unified Sch. System, 1976; mgr. safety Hydraulic research subs. Textron, Inc., Valencia, Calif., 1977-78; mgr. safety Northrop Aircraft Group, Hawthorne, Calif., 1978—; operator Nancy's Safety Tng. and Cons. firm. Recipient Performance —78— Monthly Cost Reduction/Recognition award, Northrop Aircraft Corp., 1978. Mem. Nat. Safety Council, Am. Soc. Safety Engrs., Am. Indsl. Hygiene Assn., Intersafe Safety Soc., Nat. Assn. Female Execs., Am. Soc. Profl. and Exec. Women, Calif. State Univ. Alumni Assn., Am. Mgmt. Assn. Christian Scientist; Clubs: Wilshire; Tiffanys Social; Eastern Star; Daughters of Isis Court. Office: Northrop Aircraft Group 3516 E Century Blvd Lynwood CA 90262

UNDERWOOD, WINIFRED LEIGH, lawyer; b. Beckley, W.Va., Oct. 1, 1948; d. James Fredrick and Waughilla E. (Lilly) Bucy; m. Woodrow Franklin Underwood, June 9, 1972; 1 dau., Samantha Lilly. A.A., Beckley Coll., 1971; B.A. (John Taylor award), Morris Harvey Coll., 1978; J.D., W.Va. U., 1982. Bar: W.Va. 1982. Sec., Raleigh Bd. Edn., Beckley, 1969; tchr.'s aide Raleigh Bd. Edn., 1969-71; bookkeeper Beckley Nat. Bank, 1971-73; key-punch operator Vecellio & Grogan, Beckley, 1973-75; with W.Va. Dept. Welfare, Beckley, 1975-79; practice law, Beckley, 1982—; intern W.Va. Senate, 1978, Raleigh County Prosecutor, 1981; law clk. Raleigh County Circuit, 1980. Pres. Raleigh County Correctional Officers Civil Service Commn., 1984—; deaconess, First Christian Ch., Beckley, 1984, asst. organist, 1977-85. Mem. ABA, W.Va. Bar Assn., Raleigh County Bar Assn., Assn. Trial Lawyers Am., W.Va. Trial Lawyers Assn. Democrat. Lodge: Women of Moose. Office: 106 1/2 S Fayette St Beckley WV 25801

UNFRIED, DONA LEE, clergywoman, realty saleswoman; b. Los Angeles, Oct. 11, 1928; d. Howard Peter and Helyn Grace (Howson) Wraith; student Santa Monica State Coll., 1948; grad. Unity Sem., 1973, D.D., 1981; diploma in hypnotherapy Ft. Worth Inst., 1970; m. Sept. 1, 1950 (div. 1969); children—Robert F., Teri Lynn. Mgmt. personnel Pacific Telephone, Sacramento, 1947-68; mgr. Match-O-Mates, Ft. Worth, 1968-70; ordained to ministry Unity Ch., 1973; minister Unity Village Chapel, Kansas City, Mo., 1972-75; sr. minister Unity Ch., Overland Park, Kans., 1975-76; sr. minister, chmn. bd. Unity Ch. of Light, Longview, Tex., 1976-83; realty mgr. Realty World, Longview, 1976-83; v.p. Century C-21, 1982; owner employment agy., La Jolla, Calif., 1984—; tchr. in field; condr. workshops; counselor. Mem. Indsl. relations com., public relations com. Longview C. of C., 1981; bd. dirs. Gateway Found., Sacramento. Mem. Internat. New Thought Alliance, Nat. Assn. Realtors, Tex. Assn. Realtors, Million Dollar Club, Nat. Assn. Female Execs., Assn. Unity Chs., Longview Assn. Realtors, Longview Bd. Realtors (chmn. edn. com. 1982). Club: Toasmistresses (pres. Limerick club 1967; numerous speaking awards 1966-72. Office: Unity Church of Light PO Box 16857 San Diego CA 92116 Home: 4350 Executive Dr #212 San Diego CA 92109

UNGASHICK, ANDREA LYNN, U.S. Air Force officer; b. Kansas City, Mo., May 24, 1958; d. William Frederick and Mary Margaret (Whisler) U. B.S., U.S. Air Force Acad., 1980; M.S., U. So. Calif., 1984. Commnd. lt. U.S. Air Force, 1976, Soviet analyst, HQ SAC, Omaha, 1980-81, command briefer, 1981-82, exec., 1982-84, command analyst, briefer HQ UN Command, Seoul, 1984—, now capt. Decorated numerous medals USAF. Roman Catholic. Avocations: Sky diving; backpacking; mountain climbing; cooking; swimming. Home: 1305 Fairway Cir Blue Springs MO 64015

UNGER, BARBARA FRANKEL, educator, poet; b. N.Y.C., Oct. 2, 1932; d. David and Florence (Schuchalter) Frankel; B.A., CCNY, 1955, M.A., 1957; advanced cert. NYU, 1970; children—Deborah, Suzanne. Grad. asst. Yeshiva U., 1962-63; edn. editor County Citizen, Rockland County, N.Y., 1960-63; tchr. English, N.Y.C. Pub. Schs., 1955-58, Nyack (N.Y.) High Sch., 1963-67; guidance counselor Ardsley (N.Y.) High Sch., 1967-69; assoc. prof. English, Rockland Community Coll., Suffern, N.Y., 1969—; poetry fellow Squaw Valley Community of Writers, 1980; writer-in-residence Rockland Ctr. for Arts, 1986; contbr. poetry to over 40 lit. mags., including: Kans. Quar., Beloit Poetry Jour., Minn. Rev., Poet and Critic, The Nation, Poetry Now, Invisible City, Thirteenth Moon, So. Poetry Rev., Mass. Rev., Nebr. Rev., Wis. Rev.; Anniversary Issue, Disenchantments. Nat. Endowment for Humanities 1975; The Man Who Burned Money, 1981; contbr. to Anthology Mag. Verse, Yearbook Am. Poetry, 1984; Ragdale Found. fellow, 1985; Va. Colony Anniversary Issue. Nat. Endowment for Humanities grantee, 1975; SUNY Creative Writing fellow, 1981-82; Edna St. Vincent Millay Colony fellow, 1983; Ragdale Found. fellow, 1984; Va. Colony Creative Arts fellow, 1985; N.Y. State Council Arts grantee, 1986; finalist W.Va. Writing Competition, 1982. Mem. Poets and Writers, Poetry Soc. Am., Assoc. Writing Programs, Women in Media, Writers' Community. Office: Rockland Community Coll 145 Coll Rd Suffern NY 10901

UNGER, MARY ANN, artist, sculptor. B.A. magna cum laude, Mt. Holyoke Coll., 1967; postgrad. U. Calif.-Berkeley, 1968; M.F.A., Columbia U., 1975. Tchr. elem. art Adirondack Central Sch. (N.Y.), 1970-71; tchr. art therapy program, children Columbia Presbyn. Med. Ctr., 1974; instr. intaglio techniques Printmaking Workshop, N.Y.C., 1974-75; instr. ceramics, children Third St. Music Settlement, N.Y.C., 1976-77; instr. ceramic sculpture Coll. Mt. St. Vincent, N.Y.C., 1977; instr. etching, studio founds. Montclair State Coll. (N.J.), 1977-78; instr. sculpture, 3-D design Kutztown State Coll. (Pa.), 1979; mem. faculty, adult degree program Goddard Coll. (Vt.), 1979-80; vis. artist, lectr., various schs., 1979-81. One-woman shows: Mt. Holyoke Coll., South Hadley, Mass., 1967, Columbia U., 1975; 10 Downtown, N.Y.C., 1977, CUNY Grad. Ctr., N.Y.C., 1982, 55 Mercer, N.Y.C., 1983, John Jay Coll., N.Y.C., 1984, Tweed Courthouse, N.Y.C., 1985, Sculpture Ctr., N.Y.C., 1986; group shows include: Aldrich Mus. Contemporary Art, Ridgefield, Conn., 1977, Boulder Arts Center, 1979, Hudson River Mus., Yonkers, N.Y., 1981; Bronx River Restoration Center, N.Y.C., 1983, Sculpture Center, N.Y.C., 1983; represented in permanent collections: E. F. Hutton, Inc., Best & Co., Columbia U., N.Y.C., Mt. Holyoke Coll., Printmaking Workshop; also pvt. collections. Subject of profl. publs.

UNION, VELMA RAMSEY, accounting company executive; b. Chattanooga, Aug. 15, 1948; d. Billy and Norma (Porter) Ramsey; m. Richard Union, July 7, 1977; children—Juan, Andress. B.S., Tenn. State U., 1971; postgrad. in fin. West Coast U., 1979—. Acct., Bratton/Smith C.P.A.s, Los Angeles, 1971-73, I.N.A. Ins. Co., Los Angeles, 1973-76; team auditor IRS, Los Angeles, 1974-79; pres., acct. Accent on Taxes, Inc., Los Angeles, 1979—. Sec. Republica, Los Angeles, 1984. Recipient Superior Performance award IRS, 1978. Mem. Nat. Soc. Pub. Accts., Nat. Assn. Black Accts., Black M.B.A.s Assn. (speaker 1983), Jr. All Am. Cheerleader Dirs. (bd. dirs. 1977-78), Delta Sigma Theta. Republican. Mem. Victory Bible Ch. Avocations: reading; working with youth. Home: 2485 N Santa Rosa Ave Altadena CA 91001 Office: Accent on Taxes Inc 3850 Wilshire Blvd Suite 203 Los Angeles CA 90010

UNREIN, MARGARET JOAN, preschool administrator; b. N.Y.C., Apr. 3, 1929; d. Francis Carroll Pickett and Ruth Elizabeth (Newpher) Murray; m. Raymond Frank, Oct. 15, 1965 (div. Oct. 1981); children—Shawn Mahoney, Erin Mahoney, Maureen Mahoney, Keith Mahoney; m. 2d, Harry Alvin Hook, May 17, 1985. B.A., SUNY-Old Westbury, 1977; M.S., Adelphi U., 1979. Cert. tchr., N.Y. Tchr., Central Islip State Hosp., N.Y., 1967-69; rehab. dir., edn. supr. Sagamore Children's Ctr., Melville, N.Y., 1969-82; program dir. Melville

House, 1980-82; owner, dir. Learning Seeds Pre-Sch., Holbrook, N.Y., 1982—. Contbr. articles to profl. jours. Mem. Holbrook C. of C., Unified Pvt. Schs. of N.Y. Avocations: golf; travel; dancing. Office: Learning Seeds Pre Sch 900 Main St Holbrook NY 11741

UNRUH, JOLENE, business executive; b. Colby, Kans., Feb. 1, 1943; d. Irvin A. and Goldie M. (Kornelsen) U. B.A., U. Denver, 1964; S.T.B., Boston U., 1967; postgrad. U. Tex., 1972-75. Ordained to ministry United Methodist Ch., 1968. Minister, United Meth. Ch., Wilmore, Kans., 1967; bill collector Credit Bur., Chgo., 1968; missionary United Meth. Ch., Kuala Lumpur, Malaysia, 1969-71, minister, N.Y.C., 1972-75; owner, operator Typing Unltd., Tucson, 1979—. Dep. registrar Pima County, Ariz., 1984—. Democrat. Office: Typing Unlimited 906 E University Blvd Tucson AZ 85719

UNTERBERGER, BETTY MILLER, historian, educator; b. Glasgow, Scotland, Dec. 27, 1923; d. Joseph and Leah Miller; A.B., Syracuse U., 1943; M.A., Harvard U., 1946; Ph.D., Duke U., 1950; m. Robert R. Unterberger, July 27, 1944; children—Glen, Gail Lynn, Gregg Russell. Asst. prof. history E. Carolina U., Greenville, N.C., 1948-50; lectr. Whittier (Calif.) Coll., summers 1950-54; asso. prof., dir. Liberal Arts Center for Adults, 1954-61; asso. prof. Calif. State U., Fulleton, 1961-65, prof., chmn. grad. studies, 1965-68; prof. history Tex. A&M U., College Station, 1968—; vis. prof. U. Hawaii, summer 1967; mem. hist. adv. com. U.S. Dept. Army, 1980-82; mem. adv. com. hist. diplomatic documentation U.S. Dept. State, 1977-81, chairperson, 1981; mem. Nat. Hist. Publs. and Records Commn. Chairperson acad. council Tex. A&M U., 1976. Ford Found. grantee, 1959; Am. Philos. Soc. grantee, 1960-61, 62; Woodrow Wilson Found. fellow, 1979; recipient Disting. Teaching award Calif. State U., 1966, Tex. A&M U., 1975. Mem. Am. Hist. Assn., Orgn. Am. Historians, NOW, Soc. Historians Am. Fgn. Relations (pres. 1986), Coordinating Com. on Women in the Hist. Profession, Assn. Pakistan and Indic-Islamic Studies, Conf. on Peace Research in History, Am. Inst. for Pakistan Studies (trustee). Author: America's Siberian Expedition, 1918-1920: A Study of National Policy (Pacific Coast award Am. Hist. Assn.), 1956, 2d edit., 1969; American Intervention in the Russian Civil War, 1969; Woodrow Wilson and the Russian Revolution, 1982; also articles. Editorial bd. Diplomatic History, Red River Valley Hist. Rev., Humboldt Jour. Social Relations, Papers of Woodrow Wilson. Home: Route 3 Box 314 College Station TX 77840 Office: Tex A&M U College Station TX 77843

UNTERMEYER, SALLE PODOS, lawyer; b. Bklyn., Oct. 1, 1938; d. David Meyer and Rose (Ifshin) Garber; m. Steven Maurice Podos, June 20, 1959 (div. Dec. 1978); children—Richard Lance Podos, Lisa Beth Podos; m. Walter Untermeyer, Jr., May 2, 1982. B.A., Vassar Coll., 1959; M.A., Brandeis U., 1960; J.D., Columbia U., 1977. Bar: N.Y. 1978. Assoc., Paul, Weiss, Rifkind, Wharton & Garrison, N.Y.C., 1977-79; gen. counsel v.p., sec. MacAndrews & Forbes Group, Inc., N.Y.C., 1979-81; sr. assoc. Sage Gray Todd & Sims, N.Y.C., 1981-84, Proskauer Rose Goetz & Mendelsohn, N.Y.C., 1984—. Class fund-raising chmn. Vassar Coll., 1977-80; bd. dirs. Vassar Club N.Y., 1978-80; chmn. women's div. U.S. Senate Campaign, 1970; regional chmn. U.S. Presdl. Campaign, 1972; chmn. State Rep.'s Campaign, 1973; del.-elect Interim Democratic Conv., 1974, Lawyers Com. for Gov. Carey, 1978; chmn. Mo. state legis. Nat. Council Jewish Women, 1969-75, mem. nat. affairs com., 1969-77, chmn. Mo. juvenile justice project, 1970-75, mem. legis. coordinating com. Midwestern region, 1971-75, mem. nat. task force on constl. rights, 1974-77; v.p., bd. dirs. St. Louis Jewish Community Relations Counsel, 1970-75, chmn. ch.-state and Black Jack Amicus Curiae coms.; v.p., bd. dirs. St. Louis chpt. Am. Jewish Com., 1969-75, chmn. urban affairs and placement for ex-offenders coms., mem. com. on status of women, 1974-77; mem. legis. liaison Coalition for Environment, St. Louis, 1970-74; bd. dirs. St. Louis Jewish Community Ctrs. Assn., 1970-74, chmn. urban affairs and legis. affairs coms.; bd. dirs. St. Louis Jewish Family and Children's Service, 1972-74, chmn. welfare rights and health services coms.; vol. coordinator Poor People's Campaign, 1968; founder, bd. dirs. Consumer's Assn., 1967-69; founder, chmn. Urban Corps program St. Louis Mayor's Com. on Youth, 1969-72; panelist White House Conf. on Children and Youth, 1970, 72, White House Conf. on Aging, 1974; founder, bd. dirs. Mo. chpt. PEARL (Pub. Edn. and Religious Liberty), 1972-75. Woodrow Wilson Found. fellow, 1959; NDEA fellow, 1959. Mem. Assn. Bar City N.Y., ABA, N.Y. State Bar Assn. Home: 950 Park Ave New York NY 10028 Office: Proskauer Rose Goetz & Mendelsohn 300 Park Ave New York NY 10022

UPDIKE, HELEN HILL, economist, educator; b. N.Y.C., Mar. 27, 1941; d. Benjamin Harvey and Helen (Gray) Hill; B.A., Hood Coll., 1962; Ph.D., SUNY, Stony Brook, 1978; m. Charles Bruce Updike, Sept. 9, 1963; children—Edith Hill, Nancy Lamar. Asst. prof. Suffolk U., Boston, 1965-67; lectr. SUNY, Stony Brook, 1969-75, vis. asst. prof., 1977-78; asst. prof. U. Mass., 1975-77; asst. prof. econs. Hofstra U., Hempstead, N.Y. 1978-85, assoc. prof., 1985—, chmn. dept. econs. and geography, 1981-84, assoc. dean planning and budgeting, 1984—; dir. Rapid-Am Corp.; cons. in environ. econs., 1973-78; econs. cons. Trustee, v.p. L.I. Forum for Tech., 1979-85; trustee Madeira Sch., 1985—; bd. advisors Outward Bound USA, 1985—; trustee Planned Parenthood of Suffolk County, 1980. H.B. Earhart fellow, 1962-63; Georgetown U. fellow, 1963-64. Mem. AAAS, Am. Econ. Devel. Assn. Author: The National Banks and American Economics Development, 1870-1900. Office: Hofstra University Hempstead NY 11550

UPJOHN, MARY KIRBY, educator; b. Kansas City, Mo., Sept. 30, 1948; d. William Bryant and Mary Analaura (Harrington) U.; B.A., Pomona Coll., 1970; M.S., Boston U., 1977; m. Dean Robert LaCoe, May 23, 1981. Dir. product devel. and promotion Urban Systems, Inc., Cambridge, Mass., 1970-73; pres., co-founder Funktions, Inc., Watertown, Mass., 1973-75; mng. editor Decade Mag., Boston, 1978-79; assoc. prof. Boston U. Coll. Communication, 1978—; cons. Urban Systems Research and Engring., 1975—, bd. dirs., 1982—; cons. Economica, Inc., Goodmeasure, Inc. Recipient awards of merit New Eng. Newspaper Execs., 1978, 79, 80, 81, 82, 83, 85, Women Grad. award Boston U., 1981. Mem. Women in Communications, Inc. (Nat. Outstanding Adviser award 1980, 81, 83 v.p. Boston chpt. 1981-82, pres. 1983, nat. v.p. 1986—), Informational Film Producers Assn., Pomona Coll. Alumni Assn. (bd. mem. New Eng. chpt.). Author: Urban Homsteading: A Guide for Local Officials, 1978; (with Kathleen Heintz) Neighborhood Planning Primer, 1979; (with others) Television Literacy, 1981; prin. author Case Study of the Alaska National Communication Program. Home: 39 Marion Rd Watertown MA 02172 Office: 640 Commonwealth Ave Boston MA 02215

UPPLEGER, RUTH SIMPSON, magazine and newspaper controller; b. Grand Ridge, Fla., Dec. 1, 1943; d. Chester Leon and Nellie Ada (Middleton) Jeter; m. James Bernard Simpson, Sept. 16, 1962 (div. 1984); children—Tonya Ruth, Michael James; m. Lawrence Frank Uppleger, Jan. 25, 1986. Student Chipola Jr. Coll., 1961-62, Canal Zone Coll., 1971-73; B.B.A., Austin Peay State U., 1985. Bookkeeper, Leaf Chronicle, Clarksville, Tenn., 1976-78, office mgr., 1978-81, asst. controller, 1981-84; controller Music City News (Gallatin News Examiner, Nashville Record, Hendersonville Star News), Nashville, 1984—. Mem. Nat. Assn. Female Execs. Democrat. Baptist. Club: Civitan. Avocations: Hiking; dancing; reading; horticulture. Home: Route 5 Box 190 Clarksville TN 37042 Office: Music City News PO Box 22975 Nashville TN 37202

UPSHAW, ANNE MOSES, real estate salesman; b. Dallas, Mar. 12, 1935; d. Harry Bowman and Carolyn (Holmes) Moses; m. Banks Upshaw, Feb. 25, 1960; children—Garth, Banks, Gregg, Lauren. B.A., North Tex. State U., 1956; postgrad. U. Tex., 1957-58. Sec. Archtl. Assn., Eugene, Oreg., 1967-71; legis. asst. Oreg. Legislature, Salem, 1971; adminstrv. asst. Cosanti Found., Scottsdale, Ariz., 1975-78; real estate sales agt. Ben Brooks Assocs., Phoenix, 1978—; dir. services Scottsdale House, 1980—. Pres. Lane County Democratic Women, Eugene, Oreg., 1966; sec. Lane County Dem. Central Com., Eugene, 1972; chmn. Nancie Fadeley for Legislature, Eugene, 1970; v.p. bd. trustees First Unitarian Ch., Phoenix, 1984, pres., 1985. Club: Toastmasters (Scottsdale). Home: 6902 E Chaparral Rd Scottsdale AZ 85253 Office: Ben Brooks & Assocs 4402 E Camelback St Phoenix AZ 85018

UPSHUR, CAROLE CHRISTOFK, community psychologist, educator; b. Des Moines, Oct. 18, 1948; d. Robert Richard and Margaret (Davis) Christofk; A.B., U. So. Calif., 1969; Ed.M., Harvard U., 1970, Ed.D. (NIMH fellow), 1975; m. Robert Wesley Upshur, July 18, 1970; 1 dau., Emily. Planner, Mass. Com. on Criminal Justice, Boston, 1970-73; licensing specialist, planner, policy specialist Mass. Office for Children, Boston, 1973-76; asst. prof. Coll. Public and Community Service, U. Mass., Boston, 1976-81, assoc. prof., 1982—, chmn. Center for Community Planning, 1979-81, 84-86; cons. to govt. and community agys. on mental health and social service policy and mgmt., 1970—; cons. Harvard Family Research Project, 1983-86; sr. research assoc. U. Mass. Med. Sch., 1983—; adj. prof. Heller Sch. Social Welfare, Branders U., 1985-87. Lic. psychologist, Mass. Mem. Am. Psychol. Assn., Am. Assn. Mental Deficiency, New Eng. Child Care Assn. Author: How to Set Up and Operate a Non-profit Organization, 1982; cons. editor Mental Retardation. Office: Coll Public and Community Service U Mass Boston 02125

UPTON, LUCILE MORRIS, writer; b. Dadeville, Mo., July 22, 1898; d. Albert G. and Veda (Wilson) Morris; student Drury Coll., 1915-16, S.W. Mo. State Coll., 1917-20; m. Eugene V. Upton, July 22, 1936 (dec. July 1947). Public sch. tchr., Dadeville, Mo., 1917-19, Everton, Mo., 1920-22, Roswell, N.Mex., 1921-23; tchr. creative writing Adult Edn. div. Drury Coll., 1947-52; reporter Denver Express, 1923-24, El Paso (Tex.) Times, 1924-25, Springfield (Mo.) Newspapers, Inc., 1926-64, writer weekly hist. column, 1942-82; ofcl. historian of Greene County, Mo., 1983—. Mem. Springfield City Council, 1967-71, Springfield Hist. Sites Bd., 1972-78. Named Woman of Achievement Woman's div. Springfield C. of C., 1967; named to Greater Ozarks Hall of Fame, Ralph Foster Mus., Point Lookout, 1980; recipient Ozark Heritage award Mus. of Ozarks, 1978. Mem. Mo. Writers Guild (past pres.), State Hist. Soc. Mo. (life), Greene County (Mo.), White River Valley hist. socs. Congregationalist. Club: Springfield Soroptomist (hon.). Author: Bald Knobbers, 1939; (booklet) Battle of Wilson's Creek, 1950. Collaborator: Nathan Boone, A Neglected Hero. Contbr. short stories, articles to mags., newspapers. Home: 1305 S Kimbrough Springfield MO 65807

URAGO, GAIL MIEKO, university librarian; b. Honolulu, Sept. 8, 1954; d. Kenneth Keichi and Fusayo T. Urago. B.A., U. Hawaii, 1976, M.L.S., 1978. Intern univ. archives U. Hawaii, Honolulu, 1978, resource ctr. specialist Sea Grant Marine Adv. Program, 1979, librarian Western Curriculum Coordination Ctr., 1979—, cons., 1978; vol. Kaimuki Regional Library, Honolulu, 1978, Sinclair Library, Honolulu, 1977-78; cons. Newman Ctr. Library, Honolulu, 1982—. Editor: Computers and Computer-Assisted Instruction: an annotated bibliography, 1983; Dialcom Handbook: EDREG AND ADVOCNET, 1984. State of Hawaii scholar, 1977-78. Mem. Spl. Libraries Assn., Hawaii Library Assn., Am. Vocat. Assn. (vocat. instructional materials sect.), Hawaii Vocational Assn. Club: Hui Dui (Honolulu) (sec. 1978). Office: Western Curriculum Coordination Ctr U Hawaii 1776 University Ave Wist 216 Honolulu HI 96822

URBAN, JO ANN REBECCA, transp. co. exec.; b. Allentown, Pa., Aug. 24, 1936; d. Joseph Leo and Anna Roslyn (Loftus) McLaughlin; student Drakes Secretarial Sch., 1952-54; m. Victor John Urban, Oct. 3, 1959; 1 son, Victor John. With Armstrong Trucking, Westinghouse Electric, N.Y.C., 1955-58, various trucking cos. including Long Transp., Jersey Truck Center, South Kearny, N.J., 1958-73; terminal mgr. Midwest Seaboard Transp. div. Midwest Emery, Dana Transport, Perth Amboy, N.J., 1973-76; pres. Food Products Refrigerated Express, Inc. South Kearny 1979—; cons. women in transp. field. Active cub scout com. Hazlet chpt. Boy Scouts Am., 1974-75. Mem. Nat. Assn. Female Execs., Delta Nu Alpha. Office: Jersey Truck Center Room 15 South Kearny NJ 07032

URBELIS, KATHLEEN, software company executive; b. Amsterdam, N.Y., May 20, 1946; d. Henry and Armida M. (Casline) Flesh; m. Joel G. Summers; 1 child. B.S. in Mgmt. Sci., U. Rochester (N.Y.), 1968, M.B.A., 1972. Programmer, IAI, Rochester, N.Y., 1971-72; co-founder Integral Systems, Inc., Walnut Creek, Calif., 1972, v.p. product devel., 1977-83, v.p. system architecture, 1983-84, corp. sec., 1972-83, v.p. product mgmt., 1984—. Home: PO Box 583 Diablo CA 94528 Office: 165 Lennon Ln Walnut Creek CA 94598

URBINA, OTILIA (TELA), educational administrator; b. Port Arthur, Tex., Aug. 27, 1946; d. Ellis and Bertha (Orena) U. B.S., East Tex. Bapt. Coll., 1964; M.Ed., Sam Houston State U., 1976; Ed.D., U. Houston, 1980. Cert. tchr., Tex. Elem. sch. tchr. Houston Ind. Sch. Dist., 1964-67, supr. Head Start, 1967-69; primary cons. Galveston-Houston Diocese, 1969-72; project assoc. Tchr. Corps, U. Houston, 1972-74; cons. Houston Ind. Sch. Dist., 1974-76, elem. sch. prin., 1976—. Bapt. Gen. Conv. Tex. scholar, 1960. Mem. Phi Delta Kappa (chpt. historian 1974-75). Republican. Roman Catholic. Office: Houston Schools 3248 6th Ave Port Arthur TX 77640

URDANG, NICOLE SEVERYNA, psychotherapist; b. N.Y.C.; b. May 16, 1953; d. Laurence and Irena Urdang; B.A. in Psychology, U. Conn., 1974; M.S. in Marriage and Family Counseling, So. Conn. State Coll., 1980; m. Mark Alan Criden, Mar. 1, 1980; 1 child, Madelaine. Co-mng. editor CBS Almanac, Essex, Conn., 1975; psychiat. aide Inst. of Living, Hartford, Conn., 1975-76; supr. Alcohol Aftercare Center, Middletown, Conn., 1977-78; interim dir. Alcoholism Services Orgn., New Haven, 1978; alcoholism program coordinator Yale-New Haven Hosp., 1978-80; pvt. practice psychotherapy, New Haven, 1980-81, Buffalo, 1981—; radio psychotherapist Sta. WKBW, Buffalo, 1982-84; weekly columnist Metro Community News, 1985; vol. counselor Norwich State Hosp., 1973-74, Planned Parenthood, 1975, Wesleyan U. Women's Center, 1977-78, New Haven Women's Center, 1979; guest speaker community groups. Mem. Am. Assn. for Counseling and Devel., Nat. Assn. Anorexia Nervosa and Associated Disorders, Am. Assn. Sex Educators, Counselors and Therapists, NOW, Inst. Rational-Emotive Therapy (assoc. fellow, supr.), Am. Mental Health Counselors Assn., Planned Parenthood, Am. Anorexia/Bulimia Assn., Soc. Sexuality Profls. Home and Office: 650 Lafayette Ave Buffalo NY 14222

URDANG, STEPHANIE MILLER, training center executive; b. N.Y.C., Mar. 24, 1937; d. Samuel Charles and Mae R. (Rodgers) Miller; student N.Y. U.; children—Scott C. Nevins, Kent S. Nevins. Mgr., dir. Thinking People, Forest Hills, N.Y., 1970-72; adminstrv. dir., v.p. Leisure Learning Center, Greenwich, Conn., 1972-80; dir., pres., creator The Self Paced Learning Center, Stamford, Norwalk and Greenwich, Conn., 1980-86; dir., mgr. Self Paced Learning Ctr. div. HippWaters Inc., Greenwich, 1986—. Mem. Am. Soc. Tng. and Devel., Nat. Audio Visual Assn., Southeastern Area Commerce and Industry Assn. Office: 209 Bedford St Stamford CT 06901

UREEL, PATRICIA LOIS, retired manufacturing company executive; b. Detroit, Nov. 29, 1923; d. Peter Walter and Ethel Estelle (Stewart) Murphy; grad. Detroit Bus. Inst., 1941; student Wayne State U., 1942, U. Detroit, 1943, U. Miami, 1945-46; m. Joseph Ralph Ureel, Jan. 4, 1947; children—Mary Patricia, Ronald Joseph. Exec. sec. to chmn. bd. and pres. Detroit Ball Bearing Co. of Mich., 1965-67; exec. sec. to partner charge Mich. dist. Ernst & Ernst, Detroit, 1967-71, Clubs of Inverrary, Lauderhill, Fla., 1971-72, partner charge of group Coopers & Lybrand, Miami, Fla., 1972-74; corp. sec., personnel mgr. Sanford Industries, Inc. and 4 subsidiaries, Pompano Beach, Fla., 1974-81; corp. sec., asso. Asphalt Assos., Ft. Lauderdale, 1982-86. Named Sec. of Yr. for City of Detroit, 1966; cert. profl. sec. Mem. Nat. Secs. Assn., Women's Econ. Club Detroit. Republican. Roman Catholic. Club: Moose. Home: 5375 SW 40th Ave 101 Fort Lauderdale FL 33314

URMER, DIANE HEDDA, management firm executive, financial officer; b. Bklyn., Dec. 15, 1934; d. Leo and Helen Sarah (Perlman) Leverant; m. Albert Heinz Urmer, Sept. 2, 1952; children—Michelle, Cynthia, Carl. Student U. Tex., 1951-52, Washington U., St. Louis, 1962-63; B.A. in Psychology, Calif. State U.-Northridge, 1969. Asst. auditor Tex. State Bank, Austin, 1952-55; v.p., controller Enki Corp., Sepulveda, Calif., 1966-70, also dir.; v.p., fin. Cambia Way Hosp., Walnut Creek, Calif., 1973-78; v.p., controller Enki Health & Research Systems, Inc., Reseda, Calif., 1978—, also dir. Contbr. articles to profl. jours. Pres. Northridge PTA, 1971; chmn. Northridge Citizens Adv. Council, 1972-73. Mem. Women in Mgmt. Club: Tex. Execs. Avocations: bowling; sailing; handcrafts; golf. Office: Enki Health and Research Systems Inc 6660 Reseda Blvd #203 Reseda CA 91335

URSINI, JOSEPHINE LUCILLE, lawyer; b. N.Y.C., Sept. 17, 1952; d. Edilio R. and Lucille V. (Ciufo) Ursini; m. Kenneth A. Krantz. B.S., Boston Coll., 1974; J.D., NYU, 1977. Bar: D.C. 1978. Law clk. trial div. U.S. Ct. Claims, Washington, 1977-78; assoc. firm Fried, Frank, Harris, Shriver, Kampelman, Washington, 1978-83; prin. firm Dickstein, Shapiro & Morin, Washington, 1983-85; sole practice, 1985—. Contbr. articles to profl. jours. Mem. ABA, D.C. Bar Assn., Fed. Bar Assn. Roman Catholic. Georgetown Gilbert and Sullivan Soc. (dir.). Home: 4523 Pickett Rd Fairfax VA 22032 Office: 600 New Hampshire Ave NW Washington DC 20037

USHER, ESTHER, librarian; b. Lynn, Mass., Oct. 10, 1917; d. Arthur Lester and Ada Josephine (Nichols) Usher. B.S., Simmons Coll., 1938. Cataloger, assoc. librarian Essex Inst., Salem, Mass., 1938-56, asst. editor Hist. Coll., 1943-55; cataloger Jackson & Moreland Library, Boston, 1956-57; librarian Jackson & Moreland Library, 1957-72, United Engrs. & Constructors, Inc. Library, Boston, 1972-81. Treas., Danvers Council Chs., 1958-82. Recipient Simmons Coll. Alumnae Service award, 1977. Mem. ALA, Mass. Library Assn., Spl. Libraries Assn. Congregationalist. Club: North Shore Simmons. (tres. 1970-82, 85—). Home: 22 Centre St Danvers MA 01923

USHER, PHYLLIS LAND, state official; b. Winona, Miss., Aug. 29, 1944; d. Sandy Kenneth and Ruth (Cottingham) L.; m. William A. Usher. B.S., U. So. Miss., Hattiesburg, 1967; M.S. (Title II-B fellow 1968-69), U. Tenn., Knoxville, 1969; postgrad. Purdue U., Ind. U., Utah State U. Librarian, Natchez (Miss.)-Adams County schs., 1967-68; materials specialist Fulton County Bd. Edn., Atlanta, 1969-71; cons. div. instructional media Ind. Dept. Public Instrn., Indpls., 1971-74, dir. div., 1974—, dir. fed. resources and sch. improvement, 1982-85; acting assoc. supt. Ind. Dept. Edn., 1985—; sr. officer Ctr. for Sch. Improvement, Ind. Dept. Edn.; pres. bd. dirs. INCOLSA, mcpl. corp., 1980-82; sec.-treas. Usher Funeral Home, Inc.; mem. task force sch. Libraries Nat. Commn. Libraries and Info. Sci.; dir. NU Realty Corp.; cons. in field. Mem. Gov. Inst. Conf. Children and Youth Task Force. Recipient citation Internat. Reading Assn., 1975. Mem. ALA, Nat. Assn. State Ednl. Media Profls., Delta Kappa Gamma. Adv. bd. Booklist. Office: Room 229 State House Indianapolis IN 46204

USHIJIMA, JEAN MIYOKO, city official; b. San Francisco, Feb. 14, 1933; d. Toyoharu George and Frances Fujiko (Misumi) Miwa; m. Tad E. Ushijima, Dec. 30, 1951; 1 child, Carol M. B.S., U. San Francisco, 1981. City clk. City of Beverly Hills, Calif., 1973—. Bd. dirs. West Los Angels Japanese Am. Citizens League, 1979—. Mem. City Clks. Assn. Calif. (pres. 1986), Calif. Women in Govt. (program chmn. 1978-79), League Calif. Cities (adminstrv. services com. 1982-86). Avocations: reading; Japanese dancing. Office: City Clerk 450 N Crescent Dr #102 Beverly Hills CA 90210

USSELMAN, DARETIA MARY, chemical engineer, management consultant; b. Breese, Ill., Nov. 8, 1953; d. Raymond Andrew and Florence Irene (Hilmes) U. B.S. in Chem. Enging., U. Ill., Champaign-Urbana, 1976; M.B.A., U. Chgo., 1982. Research chemist Amoco Chems. Corp., Naperville, Ill., 1974; research engr. Amoco Oil Co., Naperville, 1975; with domestic and internat. mktg., mgmt. dept. Standard Oil Co. (Ind.) Amoco Chems. Corp., Chgo., 1976-81; sr. mgmt. cons. Coopers & Lybrand, Inc., Houston, 1983—. Mem. fin. com. Hollywood Towers Condominium Assn., Chgo., 1979-80; staff vol. Ill. Primaries 1980 Presdl. Campaign, 1980. B.M. Compton Chem. Engring scholar, 1971; U. Ill. Assn. scholar, 1971; Ill. Benedictine Coll. Acad. Achievement scholar, 1971; Ill. State Scholarship Commn. grantee, 1971-75. Mem. Bus. and Profl. Women's Soc., Soc. Women Engrs., Am. Inst. Chem Engrs., Am. Chem. Soc., Internat. Assn. Energy Economists. Office: Coopers & Lybrand Inc 1100 Louisiana St Suite 4100 Houston TX 77002

USSERY, LUANNE, insurance company executive, business communicator; b. Kershaw, S.C., Feb. 20, 1938; d. Ralph Thurston and Mary Elizabeth (Haile) U. B.A., Winthrop Coll., 1959. Assoc. editor Kershaw News-Era, 1959-61; advt. saleswoman Nonpareil newspaper, Council Bluffs, Iowa, 1961-67; mag. editor Mutual of Omaha-United of Omaha Life Ins. Co., 1968-78, asst. v.p., 1977-82, 2d v.p., 1982—. Editor: The Presbyterian, Presbytery of Missouri River Valley, Omaha, 1984—. Elder, clk. of session First Presbyn. Ch. U.S.A., Council Bluffs; chair communications com. Presbytery of Missouri River Valley, 1985—; trustee Christian Home Assn., Council Bluffs, 1985—. Mem. Internat. Assn. Bus. Communicators (sec. chpt. 1971, pres. 1972, Communicator of Yr. 1973), Ins. Consumer Affairs Exchange. Office: Mutual of Omaha Mutual of Omaha Plaza Omaha NE 68175

UTLEY, DONNA LAVELLE, hospital personnel administrator; b. Tulare, Calif., June 30, 1948; d. Donald Raymond and Vivian Lee (Baber) Rogers; B.S., Calif. State U., Fresno, 1970; M.P.A., U. So. Calif., 1985; m. July 23, 1970. Resources and devel. asst. Concentrated Employment Program, Fresno, Calif., 1970-72; personnel analyst Fresno County Personnel Dept., 1972-74; personnel mgr. Fresno County Health Dept., 1974-79; personnel dir. Merced (Calif.) Community Med. Center, 1979-81; dir. human resources Bay Area Hosp., Coos Bay, Oreg., 1981-85; dir. human resources St. Elizabeth Med. Ctr., Yakima, Wash., 1985—. Mem. Am. Soc. Hosp. Personnel Adminstrn., Nat. Assn. Female Execs., Pacific N.W. Personnel Mgmt. Assn. Republican. Methodist. Club: Soroptimist (chmn. chpt. edn./leadership com.). Office: 110 S 9th Ave Yakima WA 98902

UTT, SANDRA HELENE, journalism educator; b. West Palm Beach, Fla., Feb. 18, 1946; d. Alan Ray and Clara Margaret (Shuman) Englebright; m. David Wilson Utt, Aug. 31, 1968 (div. 1976); 1 dau., Rebecca Margaret. B.S.J., W.Va. U., 1968; M.S.J., 1974; Ph.D. in Mass Communication, Ohio U., 1983. Tchr., Morgantown (W.Va.) High Sch., 1968-70, Eastern Acad., Norfolk, Va., 1970-75; instr. Norfolk State U., 1975-78; grad. asst. Ohio U., Athens, 1978-81; asst. prof. communications Tex. A&M U., College Station, 1981-84; asst. prof. journalism Memphis State U., 1984—; freelance graphics designer; cons. graphics design, 1981—; dir. High Sch. Communication Workshop, College Station, 1981-84. Editor: The Newsletter, Memphis State U. Ctr. for Research on Women, 1985—; contbr. articles in jours. Named Outstanding Grad. Student, Ohio U., 1979; Bd. Regents scholar, 1968. Mem. Women in Communications (chmn. ind. adv. nat. task force 1983-84, Outstanding Faculty Advisor 1983), Assn. Edn. in Journalism and Mass Communication (2d vice chair visual communications div. 1985-86, adv. div., editorial bd. Newspaper Research Jour. 1985), AAUW (v.p. programming 1982-83), Kappa Tau Alpha. Unitarian. Home: 1268 Sessions Ct Memphis TN 38119 Office: Dept Journalism Memphis State Memphis TN 38152

UTTERBACK, ALICE SKILTON, real estate broker; b. Phila., Mar. 3, 1921; d. Frank Redmond and Mary Ann Verner (Corder) Skilton; student Real Estate Coll., Washington, 1957-58, No. Va. Community Coll., 1971; m. Fred Dailey Utterback, June 15, 1940; 1 dau., Mary Ann Utterback Burritt. With Fairfax County (Va.) Health Dept., 1938, Woodward & Lothrop, Washington, 1939, F. W. Woolworth, Washington, 1940-41, Capital Transit, Washington, 1942-43; with J. H. and O. V. Carper, McLean, Va., 1943-63, office mgr., adminstrv. asst., 1958-63; owner Great Falls (Va.) Realty Assocs., 1958—. Pres., PTA, Great Falls, 1950-52, Fire Dept. Ladies Aux., Great Falls, 1945-47, Meth. Women, 1956-78; bd. dirs. Great Falls Grange; pres. Altar Guild. Mem. Nat. Assn. Realtors, Va. Assn. Realtors, No. Bd. Realtors, Great Falls Hist. Soc. Great Falls Bus. and Profl. Women (charter; parlimentarian 1984, chmn. fin. com. 1985). Clubs: Great Falls Lioness (pres.), Forestville Home and Community. Home and Office: 11007 Georgetown Pike Great Falls VA 22066

UTZ, LOIS MARIE, day care center executive; b. Paterson, N.J., Jan. 4, 1932; d. Ralph August and Maria Margaret (Schumacher) Cook; 1 child, Heidi Utz. B.A. in Psychology, Caldwell Coll., 1982; M.Counseling, Human Services and Guidance, Montclair State Coll., 1984; student Berkeley Sch., 1950-51. Adminstrv. asst. Gen. Precision, Inc., Little Falls, N.J., 1951-57; freelance writer, illustrator, Little Falls, 1957-78; asst. editor Children's World Mag., Cedar Grove, N.J., 1978-79; owner, operator Lois Utz Originals, Little Falls, N.J., 1979-83; dir. recreation Daus. of Miriam Day Care Ctr., Clifton, N.J., 1983—; bd. dirs. Spl. Friends, Cedar Grove, N.J., 1976-82; intern art therapist Essex County Hosp., Cedar Grove, N.J., 1976-83; mental health worker Bloomfield Child Devel. Ctr., N.J., 1981-82; intern for Essex County Employee Assistance Program, Cedar Grove, 1985—; communications group leader Turning Point, Verona, N.J., 1982—; pvt. practice counseling, Little Falls, 1984—; v.p. Donald Utz Engring., Inc., Clifton, N.J., 1976-78; pub. relations dir. Mt. St. Dominic Acad., Caldwell, N.J., 1977-79; pub. relations dir. Lacordaire Acad., Montclair, 1980-82. Author/illustrator: The Pineapple Duck with the Peppermint Bill, 1968; The Simple Pink Bubble That Ended the Trouble with Jonathan Hubble, 1972; The Houdstooth Check, 1972; A Delightful Day with Bella Ballet, 1972; The King, The Queen and the Lima Bean, 1974. Recipient 1st Poetry award, This Singing Earth World Anthology, 1954. Mem. Phi Kappa Phi. Republican. Roman Catholic. Avocations: art; writing; dancing; acting; bowling. Address: 64 Stevens Ave Little Falls NJ 07424

UTZ, SARAH WINIFRED, nursing educator; b. San Diego, Nov. 2, 1921; d. Frederick R. and Margaret M. (Gibbons) U.; B.S., U. Portland, 1943, Ed.M., 1958; M.S., UCLA, 1970; Ph.D., U. So. Calif., 1979. Clin. instr. Providence

Sch. Nursing, Portland, Oreg., 1946-50, edn. dir., 1950-62; edn. dir. Sacred Heart Sch. Nursing, Eugene, Oreg., 1963-67; asst. prof. nursing Calif. State U., Los Angeles, 1969-74, assoc. prof., 1974-81, prof., 1981—, assoc. chmn. dept. nursing, 1982—; cons. in nursing curriculum, 1978—; past chmn. ednl. adminstrs., cons., tchrs. sect. Oreg. Nurses Assn., past pres. Oreg. State Bd. Nursing; mem. research program Western Interstate Commn. on Higher Edn. in Nursing; chmn. liaison com. nursing edn. Articulation Council Calif. Served with Nurse Corps, USN, 1944-46. HEW grantee, 1970-74, Kellogg Found. grantee, 1974-76; R.N., Calif., Oreg. Mem. Am. Nurses Assn., Calif. Nurses Assn. Am. Ednl. Research Assn., AAUP, Town Hall Calif., Phi Delta Kappa, Sigma Theta Tau. Formerly editor Oreg. Nurse; reviewer Western Jour. Nursing Research. Home: 1409 Midvale Ave Los Angeles CA 90024 Office: 5151 State University Dr Los Angeles CA 90032

VACHER, CAROLE DOUGHTON, psychologist; b. Rocky Mount, Va., Dec. 31, 1937; d. John Harold and Mamie Katherine (Frith) Doughton; B.A., W.Va. Wesleyan U., 1960; M.A., Ohio U., 1962; Ph.D., N.C. State U., 1973; m. A. Ray Mayberry, Sept. 2, 1978; 1 child, Elizabeth Michele Vacher. Birth defects coordinator W.Va. U. Med. Sch., Morgantown, 1962-63; research assoc. U. N.C. Med. Sch., Chapel Hill, 1965-70; intern in clin. psychology Vanderbilt U. Med. Sch., 1972-73; psychology research cons. N.C. Dept. Mental Health, Raleigh, 1971-73, research psychologist, 1973-75; asst. prof. psychology family practice residency program East Tenn. U. Med. Sch., Johnson City, 1975-77; psychol. cons. Overlook Mental Health Center, Knoxville, 1977—; pvt. practice clin. psychology Maryville (Tenn.) Psychiat. Service, 1974—; cons. Knox County Child Abuse Rev. Team, Knoxville, 1977—; asst. prof. psychology U. Tenn., Knoxville, 1976—. Organizer, Community Psychology Task Force, Knoxville, 1977, Mental Health Assns. in Sevier and Monroe Counties, Tenn., 1978, also clinics, workshops; vol. Knoxville Med. Assn. Aux., 1979—, bd. dirs., 1980—; vol. Methodist Ch., 1979, mem. Maryville Dist. Council of Ministries, 1983—; bd. dirs. Orange County Mental Assn., Chapel Hill, 1967-68, Contact Teleministries Knox County, 1981-83, Blount County Contact Teleministries, 1984—. Recipient Wesleyan Key award, 1960; Outstanding Vol. Service award Tenn. Dept. Human Services, 1978; N.C. Dept. Mental Health scholar, 1970-71; lic. clin. psychologist, Tenn. Mem. Am. Psychol. Assn., Tenn. Psychol. Assn., Knoxville Area Psychol. Assn., Phi Kappa Phi, Psi Chi, Alpha Psi Omega. Democrat. Methodist. Author: Consultation-Education: Research and Evaluation, 1976. Researcher, compiler: Self-Help Directory: Knox County and Surrounding Area, 1981, Health and Mental Health Mutual Aid/Self-Help Groups in Knox County and East Tennessee, 1985. Contbr. articles to profl. jours. Home: Route 23 Topside Rd Knoxville TN 37920 Office: 822 Tuckaleechee Pike Maryville TN 37801

VACHON, MARILYN A(NN), insurance executive; b. Ft. Wayne, Ind., Dec. 12, 1924; d. Robert J. and Maude (Shaffer) V. Student pub. schs., Ft. Wayne. Asst. treas. Lincoln Nat. Life Ins. Co., Ft. Wayne, 1961—, asst. v.p., 1973—, asst. sec., 1980, sec., 1980—; asst. treas. Lincoln Nat. Corp., Ft. Wayne, 1968—, asst. sec., 1977-80, sec., 1980—; v.p., sec., dir. Lincoln Nat. Life Found., Inc.; v.p., sec. Lincoln Nat. Corp. Bond Fund, Inc., Lincoln Nat. Growth Fund, Inc., Lincoln Nat. Managed Fund, Inc., Lincoln Nat. Money Market Fund, Inc., Lincoln Nat. Spl. Opportunities Fund, Inc.; sec. The Insurers' Fund, Inc., Lincoln Nat. Adminstrv. Services Corp., Lincoln Nat. Health & Casualty Ins. Co., Lincoln Nat. Info. Services, Inc., Lincoln Nat. Intermediaries, Inc., Lincoln Nat. Investment Mgmt. Co., Lincoln Nat. Life Reins. Co., Lincoln Nat. Pension Ins. Co., Lincoln Nat. Realty Corp., Modern Portfolio Theory Assocs., Inc., Lincoln Nat. Sales Corp., Lincoln Nat. Variable Annuity Fund A, Lincoln Nat. Variable Annuity Fund B, Reliance Life Ins. Co. Pitts. Mem. Ft. Wayne c. of C. (cultural arts Com. 1984). Roman Catholic. Office: Lincoln Nat Corp 1301 S Clinton Fort Wayne IN 46801

VAETH, NANCY ANN, sales executive; b. Mineola, N.Y., Oct. 21, 1954; d. Jerome Marcus and Mary Teresa (MacStoker) V. B.A., Syracuse U., 1976. Advt. salesperson Sta. WEZG/WSOQ, Syracuse, N.Y., 1976-78, KMJQ, Houston, 1978-80; advt. salesperson Sta. WPLX/KLIF, Dallas, 1980-81, nat. sales mgr., 1981-82, gen. sales mgr., 1982—. Republican. Roman Catholic. Office: Sta KPLX/KLIF 411 Ryan Plaza Dr Arlington TX 76011

VAIL, ANNE WARRINER, fuel oil company executive; b. Clayville, Va., July 12, 1920; d. John Taylor and Bettie Oscar (Fowlkes) Warriner; m. William Arthur Vail, Mar. 12, 1941; children—John Taylor, Anne Vail Thomas, William Mathews. Student Va. Commonwealth U., 1937-39, William and Mary Coll., 1939. Sec. So. Fuel Oils, Inc., Richmond, Va., 1973-78; chmn. So. Fuel Oils, Inc. & Owen Transport, 1978—. Mem. women's council Va. Mus. Fine Arts, Richmond; bd. dirs. Va. Home for Boys, Richmond, 1978—. Mem. Va. Oilmen's Assn., Tuckahoe Woman's Club, The Woman's Club, Windsor Farms Civic Assn., West Hampton Civic Assn. Republican. Episcopalian. Clubs: Country Club Va.; Deep Run Hunt (Sabot, Va.), Farmington Country (Charlottesville); 2300 Club (Richmond). Home: 323 Clovelly Rd Richmond VA 23221 Office: So Fuel Oils Inc Owen Transport Richmond VA 23230

VAIL, IRIS JENNINGS, civic worker; b. N.Y.C., July 2, 1928; d. Lawrence K. and Beatrice (Black) Jennings; grad. Miss Porters Sch., Farmington, Conn.; m. Thomas V.H. Vail, Sept. 15, 1951; children—Siri J., Thomas V.H. Jr., Lawrence J.W. Mem. women's council Western Res. Hist. Soc., 1960—; mem. jr. council Cleve. Mus. Art, 1953—; chmn. Childrens Garden Fair, 1966-75, Public Square Dinner, 1975; bd. dirs. Garden Center Greater Cleve., 1963-77, Garden Club Cleve., 1981—; trustee Cleve. Zool. Soc., 1971—; mem. Ohio Arts Council, 1974-76, public sq. com. Cleve. Area Devel. Corp. Recipient Amy Angell Collier Montague medal Garden Club Am., 1976, Ohio Gov.'s award, 1977, Margaret Ireland award Women's City Club of Cleve. (trustee, hist. sites com.). Episcopalian. Clubs: Chagrin Valley Hunt, Cypress Point, Kirtland Country, Union, Women's City of Cleve. Home: Hunting Valley Chagrin Falls OH 44022

VAIL, LOIS MAE, nurse; b. Arcata, Calif., July 5, 1924; d. William A. and Marie Ruby (Peters) Reeves; A.A., Sacramento Coll., 1944; R.N., Sacramento Sch. Nursing, 1945; m. Ronald A. Vail, Mar. 27, 1948; children—Phyllis and Pamela (twins), Cheron, David, Beckey, Bonnie. Dir. nurses Kahuku (Oahu) Hosp., Hawaii, 1945-48; supr. surgery Wahiawa (Oahu) Hosp., Hawaii, 1948-49; dir. nurses Alpine (Calif.) Convalescent Center, 1968-70, Alvarado Convalescent Rehab. Center, San Diego, 1970-71; staff nurse Foothills Hosp., El Cajon, Calif., 1971-72; supr. intensive care unit El Cajon Valley Hosp., 1972—. Bd. dirs. United Cerebral Palsy, 1954. Mem. Assn. Critical Care Nurses. Home: 1301 Bobcat Ln Alpine CA 92001

VAIL, MARY, lawyer; b. Hollywood, Calif., Mar. 25, 1949; d. Granville Barrere and Christine (Flack) V. B.A. in Polit. Sci. with honors, U. Calif.-Santa Barbara, 1971; J.D., U. Pacific, 1974. Bar: Calif. 1974. VISTA atty. San Francisco Neighborhood Legal Assistance Found., 1974-76; dir. Women's Research Ctr., San Francisco Sheriff's Dept., 1977; staff atty. sects. and coms. State Bar Calif., San Francisco, 1978-80, sr. staff atty. Office Legal Services, 1980—; writer, researcher Hastings Coll. Law, 1977-78; instr. sex discrimination and law Golden Gate U. Law Sch., 1978. Mem. San Francisco Democratic County Central Com., 1978-85; mem. Calif. Dem. Exec. Bd., 1979-85; alt. del. Nat. Dem. Midterm Conf., 1982; del. Dem. Nat. Conv., 1984. Recipient Cert. of Merit, San Francisco Bd. Suprs., 1978. Mem. Service Employees Internat. Union (negotiating com. 1982—), ACLU, Calif. Women Lawyers (founding com. 1974-75), San Francisco Barristers Club (pres. 1978), Bar Assn. San Francisco (bd. dirs. 1976-78). Avocations: backgammon; needlepoint; vacationing in Hawaii; reading. Home: 4406 Park Blvd Oakland CA 94602 Office: State Bar Calif 555 Franklin St San Francisco CA 94102

VAIL, SUSAN MARIE, social work adminstr.; b. Portland, Oreg., Feb. 17, 1943; d. Ralph Orville and Perla Cora Elisabeth (Dobberstein) Clave; B.A., Portland State U., 1965, M.S.W., 1972; children—Catherine Anastasia, Juliana Elisabeth. Caseworker, Multnomah County Welfare, Portland, 1968-69, 69-70; service worker Multnomah County Childrens Services, Portland, 1971; social worker Bess Kaiser Hosp., Portland, 1972; med. social worker Emanuel Hosp., Portland, 1972-73; dir. social work St. Vincent Hosp. and Med. Center, Portland, 1974—. Bd. dirs. Regional Conf. for Managerial and Profl. Women, 1978, N.E. Portland Mental Health Planning Council, 1973-74; mem. Washington County Home Health Adv. Bd., 1974-77; chmn. Washington County Child Abuse Council, 1975-76; adv. com. St. Vincent Hosp. Home Care, 1978—; dir. St. Vincent Portland Fed. Credit Union, 1984-86. Mem. Nat. Assn. Social Workers (Oreg. chpt. pres. 1980-81), Soc. Hosp. Social Work Dirs. (sec.-treas. Oreg. chpt. 1980-81), Acad. Cert. Social Workers, Am. Pub. Health Assn., Nat. Assn. Female Execs., World Affairs Council Oreg., Oreg. Women's Polit. Caucus, LWV, Alpha Chi Omega. Democrat. Roman Catholic. Club: City of Portland. Home: 3226 NE 19th Ave Portland OR 97212 Office: 9205 SW Barnes Rd Portland OR 97225

VAILE, JEAN ELIZABETH, association executive; b. Cut Bank, Mont., July 18, 1938; d. Leo M. and Evelyn A. (Hensrude) Baker; m. Alvin L. Vaile (div.); children—Arthur Henry, Sheila Jean, Leo Michael. Student Kinman Bus. Sch., 1956-57, Fresno City Coll., 1975-76, U. San Francisco, 1980, State Center Community Coll., Fresno, Calif., 1981-82. Lic. life disability ins. agt., real estate agt., Calif.; notary pub., Calif. Mgr., Glacier Drug, Browning, Mont., 1958-60, Club Cafe, Browning, 1960-67; office mgr. J.C. Penny Co., Mont., 1967-69, Bob Ward & Sons, Inc., Missoula, Mont., 1970-73; acct. Sun Fruit, Ltd., Fresno, 1973-76; bus. adminstr. Assn. for Retarded Citizens, 1976-82; adminstrv. asst. to sr. v.p. Guarantee Savs., Fresno, 1985—; Amway distbr., 1975—; owner part-time income diversification and 2d income devel. bus. Chmn. supervisory com. Fresno Consumers Credit Union, 1979; voting mem. two social service health orgns., 1979—. Mem. Republican Presdl. Task Force. Lutheran. Club: Toastmasters. Home: 2007 E Austin Fresno CA 93726

VAINA, JENNIE CAROLINE, nurse; b. Arnold, Pa., Aug. 23, 1918; d. Joseph and Anna (Szulinski) Plaszczynski; R.N., Allegheny Valley Sch. Nursing, Tarentum, Pa., 1940; postgrad. U. Pitts.; m. Casimer Charles Vaina, Aug. 23, 1941. Mem. staff Citizens Gen. Hosp., New Kensington, Pa., 1943—, supr., 1945-77, asst. dir. nursing service, 1977—. Roman Catholic. Address: 522 Charles Ave New Kensington PA 15068

VAKIL, VIRGIE MAY, lawyer; b. Hershey, Pa., Oct. 4, 1943; d. John Henry and Mary Dorothy (Phillips) Tshudy; m. Hassan C. Vakil, Mar. 9, 1967; children—Jeffrey Jahan, Mark Mehdi. Diploma in nursing Harrisburg Hosp. (Pa.), 1964, Ga. State U., Atlanta, 1970; B.A. summa cum laude, West Chester State U., 1976; J.D., Temple U., 1981. R.N., Pa., Ga. Nurse, Allegheny Gen. Hosp., Pitts., 1964-66; nurse Piedmont Hosp., Atlanta, 1966-67, instr. nursing, 1968; utilization rev. analyst Blue Cross/Blue Shield Del., Wilmington, 1971; sole practice, Media, Pa., 1982—. Contbg. author: Practices, 1983, Nurses Legal Handbook, 1985. Bd. dirs. women in bus. com. Delaware County C. of C., 1981-85; Republican committeewoman Upper Providence Twp. (Pa.), 1982—; bd. dirs. Community Care Programs, 1986—. Mem. ABA, Am. Assn. Nurse-Attys., Assn. Trial Lawyers Am., Delaware County Bar Assn. (chmn. med./dental law com. 1985—), LWV, Psi Chi, Pi Gamma Mu, Phi Alpha Delta. Republican. Home: 690 Meadowbrook Ln Moylan PA 19065 Office: 113 N Olive St Media PA 19063

VALAD, PAULA TOLTESY, international organization executive; b. Bklyn., Sept. 17, 1938; d. Paul Joseph and Hattie Wood Toltesy; B.A., Goucher Coll., 1960; cert. of accomplishment in editorial practices U.S. Dept. Agr. Grad. Sch., 1972; postgrad. George Washington U., Am. U., 1960—; 1 son, Hossain M. Sec., IBRD, Washington, 1960-70, tech. editor, 1970-74, evaluation officer, 1975-83, loan officer Eastern Africa Country Programs Dept., 1983—, vice-chmn., coordinator career devel. and day care coms., consultation com. Staff Assn., 1973-74. Chmn. subcom. on mobility of status of women working group Personnel Classification Rev. Panel, vice chmn. task force on legal aspects of taxation and pensions, 1981-82, alt. chmn. job grading rev. panel, 1986-88. Mem. Soc. Internat. Devel., Assn. Women in Devel. Clubs: Toastmasters; Georgetown Women's. Home: 5221 Marlyn Dr Bethesda MD 20816 Office: 1818 H St NW Washington DC 20433

VALANCE, MARSHA JEANNE, library director, story teller; b. Evanston, Ill., Aug. 2, 1946; d. Edward James, Jr. and Jeanne Lois (Skinner) Leonard; m. William George Valance, Dec. 27, 1966 (div. 1976); 1 dau., Marguerite Jeanne. Student Northwestern U., 1964-66; A.B., UCLA, 1968; M.L.S., U. R.I., 1973. Children's librarian trainee N.Y. Pub. Library, N.Y.C., 1968-69; reference librarian Action Meml. Pub. Library (Mass.), 1969-70; mgr. The Footnote, Cedar Rapids, Iowa, 1976-78; assoc. editor William C. Brown, Dubuque, Iowa, 1978-79; library dir. Dubuque County Library, Dubuque, 1979-81; library dir. G.B. Dedrick Pub. Library, Geneseo, Ill., 1981-84; library dir. Grand Rapids Pub. Library, Minn., 1984—; workshop coordinator, participant, featured speaker, panelist, sect. chmn. profl. confs. Co-author: Mystery, Value and Awareness, 1979; Pluralism, Similarities and Contrast, 1979; contbr. articles to publs. Troop leader Mississippi Valley Council Girl Scouts U.S.A., Cedar Rapids, 1976-78; mem. liturgy com. St. Malachy's Roman Catholic Ch., Geneseo, 1983; com. judging clinic 4-H, Moline, Ill., 1984; trustee KAXE Northern Community Radio, Grand Rapids, 1986—; chair County 4-H Horse Bowl, 1986—. chair Itasca County Project Survive Task Force, 1985-86; sec. Grand Rapids Community Services Council, 1985-86. Iowa Humanities Bd. grantee, 1981, Blandin Found., grantee, 1984, Minn. Library Found. grantee, 1985. Mem. ALA, Minn. Library Assn. (pub. library div. com. to rev. Minn. plan for pub. libraries in Minn. 1985-86, meeting planning com. 1987), Iowa Libraries of Medium Size (sec. 1981), Northlands Storytelling Network, Alliance Info. and Referral Services, DAR (constn. chmn. 1983-84), Am. Morgan Horse Assn., Mississippi Valley Morgan Horse Club, North Central Morgan Assn., Alpha Gamma Delta. Club: Geneseo Jr. Women's (internat. chmn. 1983-84). Home: 227 Robinson Rd Grand Rapids MN 55744 Grand Rapids Pub Library 21 E 5th St Grand Rapids MN 55744

VALDES, DIANE GRACE, marketing and sales executive; b. Maspeth, N.Y., Apr. 20, 1948; d. Alfred Otto and Charlotte Florence (Bronnenkant) Bruggeman; m. Julius Valdes, Apr. 4, 1971. A.A.S., Queensborough Community Coll., 1967; B.S., Nova U., 1979. Jr. acct. Exxon, N.Y.C., 1967-69; acct. BRM Assos., N.Y.C., 1969, Texaco, N.Y.C., 1969-74; supr. Eutectic, Flushing, N.Y., 1974-76; regional industry dir. Am. Express, N.Y.C., 1976-83; v.p. Eastern Exclusives, Boston, 1983—; pres. The Mktg. Dept., 1985—. Author tng. manual, Travel newsletter, 1982. Active Murray Hill Community, 1982, 7 E. 35th Coop, 1983. Recipient VISTA award Am. Express, 1983. Mem. Am. Soc. Travel Agts (tour relations com. 1983), Am. Hotel and Motel Assn., Am. Film Assn., Am. Mgmt. Assn., Sigma Mu Omega (pres. Bayside, N.Y. 1966-67). Home: 7 E 35th St New York NY 10016

VALDES-DAPENA, MARIE AGNES, pathologist; b. Pottsville, Pa., July 14, 1921; d. Edgar Daniel and Marie Agnes (Rettig) Brown; B.S., Immaculata Coll., 1941; M.D., Temple U., 1944; m. Antonio M. Valdes-Dapena, Apr. 6, 1945 (div. Oct. 1980); children—Victoria Maria Valdes-Dapena Hiltebeitel, Deborah Anne Malle, Maria Cristina Valdes-Dapena, Andres Antonio, Antonio Edgardo, Carlos Roberto, Marcos Antonio, Ricardo Daniel, Carmen Patricia, Catalina Inez, Pedro Pablo. Intern, Phila. Gen. Hosp., 1944-45, resident in pathology, 1945-49; asst. pathologist Fitzgerald Mercy Hosp., Darby, Pa., 1949-51; dir. labs. Woman's Med. Coll. Pa., Phila., 1951-55, instr. pathology, 1947-51, asst. prof., 1951-55, asso. prof., 1955-59; asso. pathologist St. Christopher's Hosp. for Children, Phila., 1959-76; dir. div. pediatric pathology Jackson Meml. Hosp., Miami, 1976-81, pediatric pathologist, 1981—; dir. div. edn. dept. pathology U. Miami-Jackson Meml. Med. Ctr., 1982—; cons., lectr. U.S. Naval Hosp., Phila., 1972-76; instr. pathology Sch. Medicine U. Pa., 1945-49, instr. Sch. Dentistry, 1947, instr. Grad. Sch. Medicine, 1948-55, vis. lectr., 1960-62; asst. prof. Temple U. Med. Sch., 1959-63, asso. prof., 1963-67, prof., 1967-76, prof. pediatrics, 1967-76, prof. pathology and pediatrics, 1981—; prof. pathology and pediatrics U. Miami, 1976—; cons. pediatric pathology div. med. examiner Dept. Pub. Health Phila., 1967-70; mem. perinatal biology and infant mortality research and tng. com. Nat. Inst. Child Health and Human Devel., NIH, 1971-73; mem. sci. adv. bd. Armed Forces Inst. Pathology, 1976-82; assoc. med. examiner, Dade County, Fla., 1976—; chmn. med. bd. Nat. Sudden Infant Death Syndrome Found., 1961-81, nat. pres., 1984—, chmn. bd. trustees, 1985—. NIH grantee. Diplomate Am. Bd. Pathology. Mem. Internat. Acad. Pathology, Soc. Pediatric Pathology (pres. 1980-81), Coll. Physicians Phila., Internat. Assn. Pediatric Pathology, Alpha Omega Alpha. Roman Catholic. Contbr. articles to profl. jours. Office: Dept Path Univ of Miami Sch Med PO Box 016960 Miami FL 33101

VALENSTEIN, KAREN, investment company executive; Ed. Conn. Coll., Hawthorne Coll., postgrad. NYU; m. John V. Valenstein; 2 children. Former mcpl. analyst Bank of N.Y., Citibank; with Lehman Bros. Kuhn Loeb Inc., v.p., to 1983; v.p. E.F. Hutton Group, Inc., N.Y.C., 1983—. Office: E F Hutton Group Inc 1 Battery Park Plaza New York NY 10004

VALENTI, PAULA JO ZIMMERMAN, health care facility administrator; b. Defiance, Ohio, Feb. 16, 1940; d. Harry Paul and Dorothy Evelyn (Habeggar) Zimmerman; m. Salvatore Nathan Valenti, July 4, 1962; children—Paul Darryl, Dawn Elise. Grad. nurse Hinsdale Sanitarium and Hosp., Ill., 1961. R.N., Pa. Founder, co-adminstr., dir. nursing services Valenti Alzheimer Care Ctr., Inc., Columbia, Pa., 1982—. Home: PO Box 159 Hopeland PA 17533 Office: Valenti Alzheimer Care Ctr Inc 225 Cherry St Columbia PA 17512

VALENTINE, ANNETTE DILDINE, restaurant company executive; b. Big Flats, N.Y., Mar. 28, 1939; d. Leo Willard and Mary (Sopp) Dildine; m. James Charles Valentine, Aug. 31, 1959. Student pub. schs. Various positions Thatcher Glass Co., N.Y.C., 1956-62, asst. to chmn., 1962-72; asst. to pres. Bristol Devel. Co., N.Y.C., 1972-77; asst. to pres. Restaurant Assocs., N.Y.C., 1977-80, asst. to chmn., 1980—, asst. corp. sec., 1982—. Mem. Ivy Republican Club, N.Y.C., 1984—. Mem. Am. Soc. Corp. Secs. (nat. conf. com. 1984—), Roundtable for Women in Foodservice (sec. N.Y. Met. chpt. 1986—). Episcopalian. Avocations: jogging; photography. Office: Restaurant Assocs Industries Inc 1540 Broadway New York NY 10036

VALENTINE, KAREN MOEN, advertising agency executive; b Roswell, N.Mex., July 20, 1945; d. Norman R. and Dorothy E. (Sebens) Moen; m. William L. Valentine III, May 13, 1972 (div. 1985) 1 child, Craig E. B.A., Drake U., 1972. Advt. mgr. Internat. Travel Assocs., Des Moines, Iowa, 1974-77; writer, account coordinator Doty, Phillips and Laing, Battle Creek, Mich., 1977-81; account exec. Beardsley and Co., Richland, Mich., 1981-82; sr. account exec. Target Mktg. (now Valentine, Bear, and Woodruff, Inc.), Kalamazoo, 1982-84, pres., 1984—. Bd. dirs. Kalamazoo Sr. Citizens Fund, 1984—, Kalamazoo Vis. Nurse Assn., 1984—; judge Chgo. Advt. Club Addy awards, 1983, 84. Mem. Am. Mktg. Assn., Mktg. Advt. Rountable of Southwestern Mich. (pres. 1982-83). Avocations: painting; drawing; photography; music; bicycle touring. Home: 10462 N 44th St Augusta MI 49012 Office: Valentine Bear and Woodruff 151 S Rose St Kalamazoo MI 49007

VALENTINE, LINDA JEANNE KROES, apparel manufacturing company executive; b. Kalamazoo, Mar. 9, 1950; d. Keith Edward and Delores June (Burpee) Kroes; student Mich. State U., 1969-70; B.B.A., Western Mich U., 1974; M.B.A., Loyola U. Chgo., 1980; m. Clark McCray Valentine, Jr., Apr. 17, 1971. Sr. tng. specialist Montgomery Ward & Co., Chgo., 1976-79, salary adminstrn. specialist, 1979-80; compensation analyst Hart Schaffner & Marx, Chgo., 1980-81, corp. compensation mgr., 1981-83, corp. compensation and human resource systems mgr., 1983—. Mem. Am. Compensation Assn., Chgo. Compensation Assn., Human Resource Systems Profls., Internat. Assn. Personnel Women, Human Resource Planning Soc., Nat. Assn. Female Execs., M.B.A. Network, Loyola Grad Sch. Bus. Alumni Assn., NOW. Office: 101 N Wacker Dr Chicago IL 60606

VALENTINE, LINDA WEAVER, lawyer; b. Indpls., Sept. 15, 1956; d. Charles Allen and Lenora Weaver. A.B. in Journalism magna cum laude, Ind. U., 1980, J.D. magna cum laude, 1982. Bar: Ind. 1983, U.S. Dist. Ct. (so. dist.) Ind. 1983, U.S. Ct. Claims 1983, U.S. Tax Ct. 1983, U.S. Ct. Mil. Appeals 1983, U.S. Ct. Appeals (7th cir.) 1983. Assoc. Bose McKinney & Evans, Indpls., 1983—. Mem. Soc. Profl. Journalists, ABA, Ind. Bar Assn., Indpls. Bar Assn. Pi Beta Phi. Republican. Baptist. Office: Bose McKinney & Evans 11 N Pennsylvania St Indianapolis IN 46204

VALENTINE, MARJORIE PARKS, psychologist; b. Chattanooga, Apr. 20, 1928; d. Leon C. and Marjorie (Atlee) Parks; m. Andrew J. Valentine, July 20, 1949; children—Rawson J., Atlee Ann, Sarah. B.A., U. Tenn.-Chattanooga, 1949; M.A., George Washington U., 1954; Ph.D., Am. U., 1976. Lic. psychologist, D.C. Sch. psychologist, Pensacola, Fla., 1962-65, dir. Headstart Program, 1965; sch. psychologist Arlington (Va.) Pub. Schs., 1966-79; instr. U. Va. Regional Ctr., 1975-76; research affiliate Program on Women, Northwestern U., Evanston, Ill., 1979-82; assoc. Casse, Rath & Stoyanoff, Ltd., Winnetka, Ill., 1981-84; mem. adj. faculty Seabury-Western Sem., 1984—. Bd. dirs., mem. exec. com. Chgo. Commons, 1980—, pres., 1986—; bd. dirs. Inst. for Living, Winnnetka, mem. exec. com., 1980-83. Mem. Am. Psychol. Assn., D.C. Psychol. Assn., Ill. Psychol. Assn., Jr. League Evanston. Republican. Episcopalian. Home and office: 1091 Sheridan Rd Winnetka IL 60093

VALENTINO, CECILIA GLORIA, career development consultant; b. Chgo., Apr. 10, 1940; d. Vito and Antonietta (Lauro) V. Student Mundelein Coll., 1979—. Sec. Motorola Inc., Chgo., 1963-76; owner Pepnique Enterprises, Chgo., 1976—; mktg. dir. Leigh Communications Inc., Chgo., 1981-83; career cons. Control Data Inst., Chgo., 1983—; speaker Women's Career Conv., also various schs. and orgns. Active women's aux. Salvation Army, Chgo., 1982—. Named Vol. of Yr., Salvation Army, 1982. Democrat. Roman Catholic.

VALENTINO, LINDA ANNE, administrator court reporters, court reporter; b. Chgo., Nov. 28, 1945; d. Charles Peter Paul and Theresa Josephine (Oskvarek) Mitlevic; m. Frank Michael Valentino, July 27, 1968 (div. 1974); 1 child, Franco Michelangelo. Student Spencerian Coll., 1964; A.S., Kenosha Tech. Inst., 1966; student Triton Coll., 1973, 74. Registered profl. reporter; cert. shorthand reporter, Ill. Pvt. practice ct. reporter, Chgo. and Wheaton, Ill., 1966-68; offcl. ct. reporter State of Ill., Chgo., 1968—; adminstrv. asst. of Offcl. Ct. Reporters Cook County, Chgo., 1980—; chmn. Cert. Shorthand Reporters Bd. Examiners, Springfield, Ill., 1981-86. Active Democratic Party, Oak Park, Ill., 1979-86; adv. bd. Triton Coll., 1986; mgr. coordinator Eagles Hockey, Squirt AA PeeWee A., Oak Park, 1983-85; coordinator Jets Hockey Squirt A Div., Franklin Park, Ill., 1982. Mem. Nat. Shorthand Reporters Assn. (membership com. 1984-86), Ill. Shorthand Reporters (membership chmn. 1984-85), Cook County Ofcl. Ct. Reporter Assn., Ill. Ofcl. Ct. Reporters Assn., Nat. Assn. Female Execs. Roman Catholic. Club: St. Guiles Guild. Avocations: Aerobics; politics. Home: 1123 N Kenilworth Oak Park IL 60302 Office: Official Court Reporters 1500 Maybrook Dr Room 019 Maywood IL 60153

VALERIO, HELEN JOSEPHINE, restaurant company executive; b. Chelsea, Mass., Nov. 23, 1938; d. William P. and Helen (Hoffman) Kazukonis; m. Michael A. Valerio, Oct. 6, 1957; children—Michael A., Laura L., Linda M. Acct., Piece O Pizza, of Am. Inc., Arlington, Mass., 1958-63; treas. Papa Gino's of Am., Inc., Needham Heights, Mass., 1963—, sr. v.p., 1980-81, exec. v.p., 1981—; chmn. bd. Helen Broadcasting. Bd. dirs. Cath. Charitable Bur. Boston, Family Counseling Service Boston; chmn. Nat. Adv. Council Women's Ednl. Programs; trustee Nichols Coll., Dudley, Mass. Mem. Nat., Mass. restaurant assns., Fin. Execs. Inst. Roman Catholic. Clubs: Weston Community League, St. Julia's Women's (pres. 1977-78). Home: 1064 Grove St Framingham MA 01701 Office: 600 Providence Hwy Dedham MA 02026

VALERIO, KAREN THERESA, telecommunications manager; b. Calgary, Alta., Can., Oct. 24, 1955; came to U.S., 1958; d. Eugene Frank and Anne (Kuri) V. Student U. Minn.-Mpls., 1974-77, Loyola U., Chgo., 1981-82. Word processor IDS, Mpls., 1973-76; sec. MCI Telecommunications, Mpls., 1977-79, coordinator, Chgo., 1979-81, supr., 1981-83, ops. mgr., Los Angeles, 1983-85, customer service mgr., 1985—. Mem. NOW, Nat. Assn. Female Execs. Roman Catholic. Club: Am. Millionnaires (Los Angeles). Avocations: bicycling; reading; cooking. Home: 3539 Sawtelle Los Angeles CA 90066 Office: MCI Telecommunications 6101 W Centinella Culver City CA 90230

VALETTE, REBECCA MARIANNE, foreign languages educator; b. N.Y.C., Dec. 21, 1938; d. Gerhard and Ruth Adelgunde (Bischoff) Loose; B.A., Mt. Holyoke Coll., 1959, L.H.D. (hon.), 1974; Ph.D., U. Colo., 1963; m. Jean-Paul Valette, Aug. 6, 1959; children—Jean-Michel, Nathalie, Pierre. Instr., examiner in French and German, U. So. Fla., 1961-63; instr. NATO Def. Coll., Paris, 1963-64, Wellesley Coll., 1964-65; asst. prof. Romance langs. Boston Coll., 1965-68, asso. prof., 1968-73, prof., 1973—; lectr., cons. fgn. lang. pedagogy; Fulbright sr. lectr., Germany, 1974. Am. Council on Edn. fellow in acad. adminstrn., 1976-77. Mem. MLA (task force on commonly taught langs.), Am. Council on Teaching Fgn. Langs., Am. Assn. Tchrs. French (v.p. 1980-86), Am. Assn. Tchrs. German, Phi Beta Kappa, Alpha Sigma Nu. Author books, including: Modern Language Testing, 1967, rev. edit., 1977; French for Mastery, 1975, rev. edit., 1982; Contacts, 1976, 3d edit., 1985; C'est comme ça, 1978; Spanish for Mastery, 1980, rev. edit., 1984; Con Mucho Gusto, 1980, 2d edit., 1984; Nouvelles Lectures Libres, 1982; Album, 1984; Rencontres, 1985; contbr. numerous articles to fgn. lang. pedagogy and lit. publs. Home: 16 Mount Alvernia Rd Chestnut Hill MA 02167 Office: Lyons 311D Boston Coll Chestnut Hill MA 02167

VALIAVEEDAN, ROSE ANTHONY, pediatrician; b. Palai, Kerala, India, Feb. 19, 1944; came to U.S., 1979; d. Thomas Purayidom and Mary (Thekekutt) Purayidom; m. Anthony Valiaveedan, Sept. 3, 1978 (dec. June

1981). B.S., Assumption Coll. Changanacherry, Kerala, India, 1965; M.D., U. Padova (Italy), 1971. Jr. dr. Ospedale Civile, Conegliano, Italy, 1971-76; med. asst. Pius XII Hosp. Marian Ctr. Marygirl, Kalaketty, Palai, Bharananghanah, India, 1977-79; pediatric resident Jewish Hosp. Ctr., Bklyn., 1979-80, Monmouth Med. Ctr., Long Branch, N.J., 1980-82; fellow Downstate Med. Ctr., Bklyn., 1982—. Jr. fellow Am. Acad. Pediatrics; mem. AMA. Roman Catholic. Home: 441 Clarkson Ave Brooklyn NY 11203

VALKEMA, KAREN SUE, marketing agency executive; b. Freeport, Ill., Aug. 23, 1956; d. Donald Francis and Norma Jean (Gusloff) V. Grad. tng. program Ctr. for Health Scis., U. Wis.-Madison, 1977; B.S. in Mktg. with high honors, Northeastern Ill. U., 1984. Cert. radiologic technologist. Research asst. Univ. Hosp., Madison, Wis., 1975-77; surg. radiologic technologist Alexian Bros. Med. Ctr., Elk Grove Village, Ill., 1977-79; promotions mgr. Universal X-Ray, Inc. div. Allegheny Internat., Chgo., 1979-83; mktg. communications mgr. Allied Imaging div. Allegheny Internat., Bensenville, Ill., 1983-86; account exec. Fleishman Communications, Inc., Palatine, Ill., 1986—. Mem. Am. Mktg. Assn., Am. Mktg. Assn. (Chgo. chpt.). Avocations: biking; guitar; tennis; yoga. Office: Fleishman Communications Inc 2401 Plum Grove Rd Palatine IL 60067

VALKO, CINDY YVONNE, insurance company official; b. Williamsport, Pa., Dec. 15, 1954; d. Bruce Richard and Sharon (Secules) Hill; m. George Paul Valko, July 16, 1977. B.S., Juniata Coll., Huntingdon, Pa., 1976. Underwriter, Aetna Life & Casualty Co., Phila., 1976-78, underwriting supr., 1978-79, unit mgr., 1979-82, personal lines mgr., 1982-83, underwriting mgr. personal fin. security div., 1983—, cons. Women's Task Force, 1983—. Mem. Women's Ins. Soc. Phila. (pres. 1982-83). Democrat. Lutheran. Home: 43304 Delaire Landing Philadelphia PA 19114 Office: Aetna Life & Casualty Co 1 Logan Sq Philadelphia PA 19103

VALLANCOURT, SHEILA ANN, real estate broker; b. Brockton, Mass., May 21, 1945; d. A. Roland Benoit and Ella R. (Lauzon) Benoit; m. Lawrence R. Vallancourt, Dec. 14, 1963; children—Kimberly A., Aimée M. Grad. Realtors Inst., 1979. Owner, mgr. Vallancourt Realty, Brockton, Mass., 1981—. Trustee Brockton Christian Regional High Sch. Fellow Nat. Assn. Female Execs., Brockton C. of C., Realtors Inst. Baptist. Avocations: deer hunting; camping; fishing; travel. Home: 4 Kimberley Dr North Easton MA 02356 Office: Vallancourt Realty 810 Belmont St Brockton MA 02401

VALLBONA, RIMA-GRETEL ROTHE, Spanish educator, writer; b. San José, Costa Rica, Mar. 15, 1931; d. Ferdinand Hermann and Emilia (Strassburger) Rothe; B.A./B.S., Colegio Superior de Señoritas, San José, 1948; diploma U. Paris, 1953; diploma in Spanish Philology, U. Salamanca, Spain, 1954; M.A., U. Costa Rica, 1962; D.M.L., Middlebury Coll., 1981; m. Carlos Vallbona, Dec. 26, 1956; children—Rima-Nuri, Carlos-Fernando, María-Teresa, María-Luisa. Tchr., Liceo J.J. Vargas Calvo, Costa Rica, 1955-56; faculty U. St. Thomas, Houston, 1964—, prof. Spanish, 1978—, head dept. Spanish, 1966-71, chmn. dept. modern fgn. lang., 1978-80; vis. prof. U. Houston, 1975-76, Rice U., 1980-81, U. St. Thomas, Argentina, summer 1972, Rice U. program in Spain, summer 1974. Mem. scholarship com. Inst. Hispanic Culture, 1978-79, chmn., 1979, bd. dirs., 1974-76, chmn. cultural activities, 1979, 80, 85; bd. dirs. Houston Pub. Library, 1984—. Recipient Aquileo J. Echeverria Novel prize, 1968; Agripina Montes del Valle Novel prize, 1978; Jorge Luis Borges Short Story prize, Argentina, 1977; lit. award Southwest Conf. Latin Am. Studies, 1982; Constantin Found. grantee for research U. St. Thomas, 1981; Ancora lit. award, Costa Rica, 1984. Mem. Am. Assn. Tchrs. Spanish and Portuguese, Houston Area Tchrs. of Fgn. Langs., S. Central MLA, S. Central Orgn. Latin Am. Studies, Latin Am. Studies Assn., Latin Am. Writers Assn. of Costa Rica, Inst. Hispanic Culture of Houston, Casa Argentina de Houston, Instituto Literario y Cultural Hispanico, MLA, Phi Sigma Iota, Sigma Delta Pi (hon.). Roman Catholic. Club: Nat. Writers. Author: Noche en vela, 1968; Polvo de camino (short stories), 1971; Yolanda Oreamuno, 1972; La Salamandra rosada (short stories), 1979; La obra en prosa de Eunice Odio, 1981; Mujeres y agonias (short stories), 1982; Las Sombras que perseguimos, 1983; Baraja de Soledades, 1983; mem. editorial bd. Letras Femeninas, U.S.; co-dir. Foro Literario, Uruguay, Alba de América; contbr. numerous short stories to lit. mags. Home: 3002 Ann Arbor St Houston TX 77063 Office: 3812 Montrose Blvd Houston TX 77006

VALLEAU, NORMA KATHRYN SASS, lawyer; b. Dearborn, Mich., Mar. 9, 1933; d. Norman Ralph and Dorothy Lorraine (Mullreed) Sass; m. Kenneth William Valleau, Sept. 2, 1953 (div. 1956); children—Bobbee Leota Kovar, Carla Renee Margolis; m. 2d John Henry Metz, July 15, 1983. A.S., Henry Ford Coll., 1974; B.S., Western State Coll., Fullerton, Calif. 1980, J.D., 1980. Bar: Ind. 1981. Actress, singer, dancer Kennedy Artists, N.Y.C., 1960-78; actress Eastside/Westside Repertory, N.Y.C., 1960-63, Herbert Berghof Studios, N.Y.C., 1963-64; legal intern Screen Actors Guild, Hollywood, Calif., 1978-80; ptnr. Metz & Valleau, Indpls., 1981-82; law clk. U.S. Bankruptcy Ct., Indpls., 1982-85; atty. legal div., bankruptcy specialist FDIC, 1985—; program dir. Lawyers in the Classroom project, N.Y. State Bar Assn., 1977; outstanding dir. Fullerton Children's Theatre, 1979. Mem. Friends of Benjamin Harrison House, Indpls., 1983—, Indpls. Hist. Soc., 1983—; instr. Free U., Indpls., 1983; v.p. Women's Caucus, Fullerton, Calif., 1978-81. Women's Caucus Book scholar, 1978-80. Mem. ABA, Ind. Bar Assn., Indpls. Bar Assn., Screen Actors Guild, Actors Equity Assn., Am. Guild Variety Artists, AFTRA, DAR (Caroline Scott Harrison chpt.). Lutheran. Home: 3663 N Pennsylvania Indianapolis IN 46205 Office: FDIC Dept Head Bankruptcy Sect Indianapolis IN 46200

VALLERY, JANET ALANE, industrial hygienist; b. Lincoln, Nebr., Apr. 4, 1948; d. Gerald William and Lois Florence (Robertson) V.; B.S., U. Nebr., Lincoln, 1970; diploma Bryan Meml. Sch. Med. Tech., Lincoln, 1971. Med. technologist Lincoln Gen. Hosp., 1971-72; congressional sec., 1973; lab. scientist Nebr. Dept. Health, 1973-79; sr. safety indsl. hygienist Nebr. Dept. Labor, 1979-85; indsl. hygienist U.S. Dept. Labor OSHA, 1985—; cons. in field. Mem. Am. Conf. Govt. Indsl. Hygienists, Am. Soc. Clin. Pathologists (assoc.), Arabian Horse Assn. Nebr., Nebr. Dressage Assn., Am. Indsl. Hygiene Assn., Am. Legion Aux. Republican. Methodist. Home: 4900 S 30th St Lincoln NE 68516 Office: 6910 Pacific St Rm 100 Omaha NE 68106

VALLETTE, LOVELL IRENE, college administrator; b. Bridgeport, Ill., Dec. 5, 1937; d. Arthur Albert and Ruth Pauline (Phillips) Leib; m. Gary Ray Vallette, Apr. 20, 1956; children—Toni Lynn Vallette Satterfield, Kelley Ray Vallette. Student in Nursing, Wabash Valley Coll., Ill., 1973-74; A.D. in Nursing, Olney Central Coll., Ill., 1977; B.S.N., So. Ill. U., 1983, M.S.N., 1986. Supr., staff nurse Fairfield Meml. Hosp., Ill., 1974-75, 1977-79; dir. nursing Meadowood Health Care, Grayville, Ill., 1979-80; instr. nursing, CPR Ill. Eastern Community Colls., Fairfield, 1980-85, dir. Assoc. Degree Nursing, 1986—; cons. in field. Collector data for Cancer Research, 1986—. Mem., Republican Women Assn., Albion, 1973-86. Recipient Nursing award Olney Central Coll., 1977; So. Ill. U.-Edwardsville Trainee, 1985. Mem. Am. Nurses Assn., Am. Cancer Soc., NEA, Profl. Women's Orgn. of Albion, Sigma Theta Tau. Republican. Methodist. Home: RR 3 Albion IL 62806 Office: Ill Eastern Community Colls Dist 529 300

VALLEY, IVA LESLIE SIMS, realtor; b. Lakewood, Ohio, Aug. 10, 1913; d. Edwin Willis Leslie and Carrie Edith (Uber) L.; m. Vernon Elbert Sims, Nov. 7, 1936; children—Barbara Jean, Judith Eileen Sims Knight; m. Harry Raymond Valley, Feb. 29, 1976. Student Spencerian Coll., 1932-34, Fenn coll., 1964. Sec.-clerk Wellsted, Macklin & Co., 1934; exec. sec., cashier Gordon S. Macklin & Co., 1935-39; dir. city-wide day camps, bd. dirs. Greater Cleve. Girl Scouts U.S.A., 1953-60; realtor HGM-Hilltop, Inc., Rocky River, Ohio, President's council 1972-83. Pres. Rocky River PTA-Beach Sch., 1952. Named Profl. of Yr. HGM-Hilltop, Inc. 1983. Mem. Cleve. Bd. Realtors, Ohio State Bd. Realtors, Nat. Assn. Realtors, West Shore Round Table. Republican.

VALMY, CHRISTINE, cosmetic co. exec.; b. Bucharest, Romania, Oct. 25, 1926; came to U.S., 1961, naturalized, 1966; d. Cristofor J. and Florika (Zamfiratos) Xantopol; cosmetology degree U. Medicine, Bucharest, 1949; student Law Sch., Bucharest, 1946-50; m. Henry D. Sterian, June 23, 1972; 1 dau. by previous marriage, Marina Valmy. Founder, pres. Christine Valmy, Inc., N.Y.C., 1965—; dir. Christine Valmy Internat. Sch. for Skin Care, 1966—. Named Small Bus. Person of Yr. for State of N.J., SBA, 1976. Mem. Am. Assn. Esthetics (pres.), Cosmetic Career Women. Republican. Author: Esthetics, The Keystone Guide to Skin Care, 1978; Christine Valmy's Skin Care and Makeup Book, 1982. Office: Christine Valmy Inc 767 Fifth Ave New York NY 10153

VALO, CAROLYN ROSE, hospital medical records director; b. Mpls., Dec. 29, 1952; d. Pierson John and Dancia (Bubalo) Kirk; m. David Allen Valo, Oct. 12, 1985. A.A.S., St. Mary's Jr. Coll., 1977; B.A., Metro State U., 1982. Cert. Am. Med. Record Assn. Sec. Nat. Assn. Ind. Businessmen, Mpls., 1969-70; clk., typist, data clk. Mpls. Health Dept., 1970-75, health info. mgr., 1977-84; faculty asst. St. Mary's Jr. Coll., Mpls., 1976-77, adj. faculty, 1978—; client service rep. Code 3 Health Info. Systems 3M, Mpls., 1984-85; asst. dir. med. records Fairview-Southdale Hosp., Mpls., 1985, dir. med. records, 1985—; adj. faculty Moorhead Area Vocat. Tech. Inst., 1986—; pvt. practice cons. Ambulatory Care, Mpls., 1983; speaker profl. groups in field. Contbr. articles to profl. jours. Mem. Am. Med. Record Assn. (appeals panel), Minn. Med. Record Assn. (pres. 1984-85, award, dir.), Twin Cities Women in Computing, Assn. Record Mgrs. and Adminstrs., Nat. Assn. Female Execs. Home: 1897 Carroll Ave Saint Paul MN 55104 Office: Fairview-Southdale & Ridges 6401 France Ave S Minneapolis MN 55435

VALO, MARTHA ANN, hospital dietary official; consultant; b. West Aliquippa, Pa., Apr. 6, 1938; d. George and Susan Helen (Pollak) V.; m. John Daniel Dempsey, Dec. 17, 1974. B.S., Carlow Coll., 1960; postgrad. U. Pa. Registered dietitian. Food service mgr. Stouffer's Mgmt. Co., Phila., 1960-76; restaurant mgr. Strawbridge & Clothier, Phila., 1976-78; food service dir. Saunders House, Phila., 1978-80; dir. dietary services Kennedy Meml. Hosp., U. Med. Ctr., Stratford, N.J., 1980—; cons. dietitian Pinecrest Nursing Home, Sewell, N.J., 1980—; chmn. N.J. Hosp. Assn. Dietary Group Purchasing, Princeton, 1980—; adj. faculty Camden County Coll., Blackwood, N.J., 1985—. Mem. Am. Dietetic Assn., N.J. Dietetic Assn., Phila. Dietetic Assn., So. N.J. Nutritional Council, Am. Soc. for Hosp. Food Service Adminstrs. Home: 43 Harwood Ln Clementon NJ 08021 Office: Kennedy Meml Hosps Univ Med Ctr 18 E Laurel Rd Stratford NJ 08084

VALONE, MELISSA BRIANA, audio-visual company executive; b. Austin, Tex., Dec. 10, 1950; d. James Floyd and Elizabeth (Emerson) V. m. Don Shuwarger, Oct. 31, 1981. B.A., U. Colo., 1974. Studio mgr. United Audio Rec., San Antonio, 1974-76; co-owner Cat Tracks, San Antonio, 1976-78, Houston, 1978-82, v.p. Cat Tracks, Inc., Houston, 1982-83, pres., 1983—. Recipient 1st, 2d and 3d place awards for audio-visual prodn. Internat. Assn. Bus. Communicators, Houston, 1983, merit award, 1984; 1st place Addy award San Antonio Advt. Fedn., 1978, 79, 2 awards of excellence, 1977, others. Mem. Audio Engring. Soc., Houston Advt. Fedn., Assn. for Multi-Image, Women in Communications (1st place Matrix award Houston chpt. 1984, 85), Baylor Coll. Medicine Housestaff Aux. Home: 16325 Brook Forest Dr Houston TX 77059 Office: Cat Tracks Inc 602 Sawyer St Suite 206 Houston TX 77007

VAMBERY, MARIE JOSEPHE, drug company executive, consultant; b. Oran, Algeria, Aug. 3, 1950; d. Jean and Santina (Linteris) Radenac; m. Robert George Vambery, Mar. 5, 1976. Lic. in English, U. Paris, 1969; M.B.A., Ecole de Haut Enseignement Commercial, Paris, 1971, Columbia U., 1973. Brand supr. Procter & Gamble Co., Paris, 1973-76; product mgr. L'Oreal Co., N.Y.C., 1976-77; sr. product mgr. Block Drug Co., Inc., Jersey City, 1979-81, dir. new products, 1981—; sr. product mgr. CPC Internat. Best Foods, Englewood Cliffs, N.J., 1979-81. Author: Marketing in the French Tire Industry, 1971. Fulbright Found. scholar, 1971; Johnson Wax Found. fellow, 1971, French Govt. Fgn. Office fellow, 1972. Mem. Am. Mgmt. Assn., Am. Mktg. Assn. Club: Essex County Country (West Orange, N.J.). Home: Wildwood Ave Llewelyn Park West Orange NJ 07052 Office: Block Drug Co Inc 257 Cornelison Ave Jersey City NJ 07302

VAN, CHERYL MAXINE, organization development consultant; b. San Francisco, July 13, 1958; d. Clyde Everett and Maxine (Roper) Hollie; m. Steven Anthony Van, Aug. 8, 1981; 1 son, Steven Anthony. B.A., U. Calif.-Santa Barbara, 1979; postgrad. U. San Francisco. Student counselor U. Calif.-Santa Barbara, 1977-78, student recruiter, 1978-79; personnel coordinator First Data Resources, San Mateo, Calif., 1979-80; personnel asst. Kaiser Hosp., San Francisco, 1980-82, asst. personnel dir., 1982-85, orgn. devel. cons., 1985—. Mem. Bay Area O.D. Network, Am. Soc. Personnel Adminstrs., Delta Sigma Theta (v.p. 1978-79), Democrat. Baptist. Office: Kaiser Hosp 2425 Geary Blvd San Francisco CA 94115

VAN AMAN, CONSTANCE SUE, data processing mgr.; b. South Bend, Ind., Oct. 5, 1953; d. Jack Vernon and Phyllis Henrietta (Smith) Hess; m. Dale Patrick Vanaman, Oct. 15, 1976; (div. 1985); children—Troy Alan, Chad James. ADP, Ind. Vocat. Tech. Coll., 1981. Programmer, Triad-Utrad, Huntington, Ind., 1980-81; project mgr. K-Mart Corp., Fort Wayne, 1981—; prof. Ind. Vocat. Tech. Coll., Fort Wayne, 1981—. Bd. dirs. SCAN (Suspected Child Abuse and Neglect), Fort Wayne, 1985-86. Mem. Soc. to Advance Total User Systems (sec. bd. dirs. 1985-86), Nat. Assn. Female Execs. (fellow). Democrat. Methodist. Avocations: piano; music; interior decorating; tennis. Home: 123 N Indiana Ave Auburn IN 46706 Office: K-Mart Corp Ferguson Rd Box 359 Fort Wayne IN 46801

VAN ANDEL, BETTY JEAN, household products company executive; b. Mich., Dec. 14, 1921; d. Anthony and Daisy (Van Dyk) Hoekstra; A.B., Calvin Coll., 1943; m. Jay Van Andel, Aug. 16, 1952; children—Nan Elizabeth, Stephen Alan, David Lee, Barbara Ann. Elementary sch. tchr., Grand Rapids, Mich., 1943-45; service rep. and supr. Mich. Bell Telephone Co., Grand Rapids, 1945-52; dir.-stockholder Amway Corp., Grand Rapids, 1972—. Treas., LWV, 1957-60; chmn. Eagle Forum, Mich., 1975—; bd. dirs. Christian Sch. Ednl. Found., Pine Rest Christian Hosp., Mem. Nat. Trust Hist. Preservation, St. Cecelia Music Soc., Smithsonian Assos. Republican. Club: Women's City of Grand Rapids. Home: 7186 Windy Hill Rd SE Grand Rapids MI 49506 Office: PO Box 172 Ada MI 49301

VAN ARK, JOAN, actress; b. N.Y.C.; d. Carroll and Dorothy Jean (Hemenway) Van A.; m. John Marshall, Feb. 1, 1966; 1 child, Vanessa Jeanne. Student Yale U. Sch. Drama. Appeared at Tyrone Guthrie Theatre, Washington Arena Stage, in London, on Broadway; appeared in plays Barefoot in the Park, School for Wives, Rules of the Game, As You Like It, Cyrano de Bergerac, Ring Round the Moon, others; TV series: Temperatures Rising, 1972-74, We've Got Each other, 1977-78, Dallas, 1978, Knots Landing, 1979—. Films: Frogs, 1972; films for TV: Big Rose, 1974, Shell Game, 1975, The Last Dinosaur, 1977, Red Flag, 1981; TV miniseries: Testimony of Two Men, 1978. Office: care William Morris Agy Inc 151 El Camino Beverly Hills CA 90212

VAN BRONKHORST, ERIN MARIE, journalist, educator; b. Seattle, June 24, 1949; d. John and Edna Marie (de la Torre) Van B.; B.A. in History, U. Wash., 1971, M.Bus. and Econs. Journalism (Bus. and Econs. Reporting fellow), 1982. News writer Sta. KIRO-TV, Seattle, 1970-71; newswoman AP, Seattle and Olympia, Wash., 1971-73; editor, co-pub. Pandora Women's News Jour., Seattle, 1973-76; polit. writer Fairbanks (Alaska) Daily News-Miner, 1976-77; reporter Seattle Post-Intelligencer, 1977-79, copy editor, 1979-83; vis. asst. prof. communication arts Gonzaga U., Spokane, Wash., 1983-84; copy editor Tacoma News Tribune, 1984-86; writer Seattle Bus. Jour.; tchr. news writing YWCA, 1974. Recipient Hearst monthly award for spot news, 1977; 1st place for page layout Nat. Fedn. Press Women, 1984. Mem. Wash. Press Assn., Phi Beta Kappa. Roman Catholic. Author: (with Cara Peters) How to Stop Sexual Harassment: Strategies for Women on the Job, 1980. Home: 620 W Mercer Pl #1A Seattle WA 98119

VAN BRUNT, MARCIA ADELE, social worker; b. Chgo., Oct. 21, 1937; d. Dean Fredrick and Faye Lila (Greim) Slauson; student Moline (Ill.) Pub. Hosp. Sch. Nursing, 1955-57; B.A. with distinguished scholastic record, U. Wis., Madison, 1972, M.S.W. (Fed. tng. grantee), 1973; M.O.E. Bartholomew; children—Suzanne, Christine, David. Social worker div. community services Wis. Dept. Health Social Services, Rhinelander, 1973-79, regional adoption coordinator, 1979-83, chief adoption and permanent planning no. region, 1983-84, asst. chief direct services and regulation no. region, 1984—; adminstr., clin. social worker No. Family Services, Inc.; counselor, public speaker, cons. in field of clin. social work. Home: 5264 Forest Ln Route 1 Box 2262 Rhinelander WI 54501 Office: Box 697 Rhinelander WI 54501

VANCE, CARRIE TEMPLE, nurse; b. Jackson, Miss., Nov. 20, 1944. A.A. in Nursing, San Joaquin Delta Coll., Stockton, Calif., 1974; B.A. in Health Service Adminstrn., St. Mary's Coll., Moraga, Calif., 1978; M.S. in Nursing Adminstrn. and Music, Ph.D. in Music Performance, Columbia Pacific U., 1985. Lic. nurse, Calif. Staff nurse Dameron Hosp., Stockton, Calif., 1976-77, charge nurse, 1977-80, supr. nursery, 1980—. Mem. San Joaquin Gen. Hosp. Delta Coll. Nurse Alumni Assn., Soc. Nursing Service Adminstrs., Nat. Assn. Female Execs., Columbia Pacific U. Alumni Assn., Nat. Assn. Neonatal Nurses, St. Mary's Coll. Alumni Assn., The Smithsonian Assocs. Seventh-day Adventist. Office: Dameron Hosp Assn 525 W Acacia St Stockton CA 95208

VANCE, DONNA KAY, home builders company executive, dental hygienist; b. Bethesda, Md., May 6, 1954; d. Harold Joseph and Marion (Plum) Baird; m. Gary Craig Vance, Dec. 17, 1977; children—Derek Adam, Marcus Trevor. B.E., Ohio State U., 1975. Cert. dental hygiene. Dental hygienist James Cook D.D.S., Columbus, Ohio, 1976-78, Joseph Mitchel, D.D.S., Columbus, 1976-78, David Bone D.D.S., Vandalia, Ohio, 1978-81, Jack Perkins D.D.S., Dayton, Ohio, 1978-82, Michael Hall D.D.S., Vandalia, Ohio, 1982-85; v.p. Precision Home Builders, Inc., Vandalia, 1981—; dir. Precision Home Builders, Inc., Vandalia, Bd. dirs. County Manor Condominium Assn., Tipp City, Ohio, 1983—. Mem. Am. Dental Hygiene Assn., Delta Zeta. Republican. Methodist. Avocations: sewing; swimming; crafts. Home: 7530 Winding Way Tipp City OH 45371 Office: Precision Home Builders Inc PO Box 425 Vandalia OH 45377

VANCE, JUDITH GILES, judicial executive; b. Wickliffe, Ky., July 16, 1939; d. Raymond Franklin and Mary Kathleen (Horn) Giles; m. Herby Gene Vance, June 8, 1957; children—Darrell Gene, Raymond David, Jill, Nick Tod. Circuit Ct. clk. Ballard County Seat Courthouse, Wickliffe, 1976—. Mem. Circuit Clks. Assn. (v.p. 1978-85, clks. edn. com. 1976-79, clks. exec. com. 1982-84, clks. retirement com. 1984—). Democrat. Baptist. Home: PO Box 265 Wickliffe KY 42087

VANCE, KATHERINE MCCORMICK, lawyer; b. Missoula, Mont., Nov. 30, 1953; d. John Thomas and Camilla (McCormick) V.; m. G. Bruce Sewell, May 1, 1982. B.A., St. Lawrence U., 1976; J.D., Tulsa U., 1979. Bar: Okla. 1979. Pvt. practice, Tulsa, 1979-84; estate adminstr. U.S. Bankruptcy Ct. Eastern Dist. Okla., 1984—. Mem. Women's Concerns Forum, Tulsa, 1981-84; mem. Task Force on Domestic Violence, Tulsa, 1981-84; pres. Democratic Women's Action Group, Tulsa, 1983-84; mem. Okla. Dem. Task Force on Women, 1984. Mem. ABA, Okla. Bar Assn. (dir. Tulsa County young lawyers 1983, 84, 85, dir.-at-large 1986), Okla. Trial Lawyers Assn. (membership com. 1984), Tulsa County Bar Assn., Tulsa Women Lawyers Assn. (exec. com. 1984). Democrat. Episcopalian. Office: US Bankruptcy Ct PO Box 1347 Okmulgee OK

VANCE, TERRY, interior designer; b. Cleve., Sept. 22, 1929; d. Toby and Edith (Zulli) Gesualdo; m. Edward Francis Vance, May 26, 1951; children—Victoria, Deborah, David, Rebecca, Sarah, Barbara. B.A., Case Western Res. U., 1951. Interior designer Bonhard Interiors, Cleve., 1968-80; pres., interior designer Terry Vance, Inc., Shaker Hts., Ohio, 1980—. Mem. Am. Soc. Interior Designers. Office: Terry Vance Inc 18740 Chagrin Blvd Shaker Heights OH 44122

VAN CLEAVE, KAY VIVIAN, educator; b. Fort Worth, Nov. 14, 1937; d. Henry S. and Lola Kate (Wimberly) Van Cleave. B.A., N. Tex. State U., 1959; M.Ed. in Psychology, U. Houston, 1982. Tchr., Houston Ind. Sch. Dist., 1959—; tchr. High Sch. for Law Enforcement and Criminal Justice, Houston, 1981—. Contbr. articles to newspaper. NDEA grantee, 1960. Mem. Tex. Assn. Alcoholism Counselors. Republican. Mem. Unity Ch.

VAN CLEAVE, KIRSTIN (KIT) DEAN, writer, educator, publishing executive; b. Ft. Worth, Jan. 9, 1940; d. Henry Shibley and Lola Kathryn (Wimberly) van C. B.A. in Journalism, N. Tex. State U., 1961; M.A. in English, U. Houston, 1972; D.L. in English, London Inst., 1973. Reporter, Associated Gen. Contractors News Service, Houston, 1961-62; dir. pub. relations Diboll Advt. Agy. (Tex.), 1963-64; writer Goodwin, Dannenbaum, Littman and Wingfield advt. agy., Houston, 1964-65; reporter Houston Tribune, 1965-68; copywriter sales promotion dept. Gulf Publishing Co., 1968-70; Houston editor, then mng. editor Metrobeat, Dallas, 1970; editor publs., dir. pub. relations, press rep. Baroid div. NL Industries, Inc., Houston, 1973-74; presdl. speechwriter Gulf Oil Co., 1974-76; chief exec. officer Inner-View Publishing Co., Houston, 1980—; past mem. faculty St. Agnes Acad., Houston; mem. faculty U. Houston, Coll. of Mainland, Texas City, Tex. Author: They Still Do, 1973, Folklore of Texas Cultures, 1975; (poetry) Day of Love (set into a song cycle which was nominated for Pulitzer prize in Mus. Composition), 1978, Amourette, 1979, Laurels, 1980; librettist: Four Songs (composer Thomas Pasatieri), 1980; editor Inner-View mag., Houston; columnist: Houston Home & Garden, Houston Guide, Scene mag., In Houston, Billboard; contbr. articles to mags. Mem. S.W. C. of C., Houston C. of C., AAUP, Music Critics Assn., Internat. Assn. Bus. Communicators, Am. Soc. Authors and Journalists, World Tae Kwon Do Fedn., Tex. Press Assn., Houston Press Club, Houston Guardian Angels (asst. chpt. leader). Home: PO Box 66156 Houston TX 77266

VAN CLEVE, RUTH GILL, government official; b. Mpls., July 28, 1925; d. Raymond S. and Ruth (Sevon) Gill; student U. Minn., 1943; A.B. magna cum laude, Mt. Holyoke Coll., 1946, LL.D., 1976; LL.B., Yale, 1950; m. Harry R. Van Cleve, Jr., May 16, 1952; children—John Gill, Elizabeth Webster, David Hamilton Livingston. Intern Nat. Inst. Pub. Affairs, 1946-47; admitted to D.C. and Minn. bars, 1950; atty. Dept. Interior, 1950-54, asst. solicitor, 1954-64, dir. Office Territories, 1964-69, dir. Office Territorial Affairs, 1977-80, dep. asst. sec., 1980-81, atty. Solicitor's Office, 1981—; atty. FPC, 1969-75, asst. gen. counsel, 1975-77. Trustee, Mt. Holyoke Coll. Recipient Fed. Woman's award, 1966, Disting. Service award Dept. Interior, 1968. Mem. Phi Beta Kappa. Unitarian. Author: The Office of Territorial Affairs, 1974. Home: 4400 Emory St Alexandria VA 22312 Office: Dept Interior Washington DC 20240

VAN DAM, DORIS MAY, water treatment plant executive; b. Grand Rapids, Mich., Jan. 27, 1924; d. John Henry and Alice (Small) De Vries; m. Lloyd Arie Voshel, Oct. 30, 1946 (div. 1969); children—David, Anne Voshel Nudo; m. Ernest D. Van Dam, Jan. 27, 1971. B.A. in Edn., Sherwood Acad., Chgo., 1942; postgrad. Calvin Coll., 1942-44. Chief chemist, engr. City of Grand Rapids, 1944-73; gen. mgr. Grand Haven/Spring Lake Wastewater Treatment Plant, Grand Haven, Mich., 1973—; mem. mgmt. adv. group to EPA, Washington, 1977-79. Contbr. articles to profl. jours. Chmn. bd. trustees North Ottawa Community Hosp., Grand Haven, 1982—; mem. exec. bd. West Central Mich. Hosp. Council, 1983—; gen. campaign chmn. Tri-Cities United Fund, Grand Haven, 1977, 82; trustee Grand Haven Area Community Found., 1983—. Recipient Arthur Sydney Bedell award, William D. Hatfield award, Philip F. Morgan award, James R. Rumsey award, others. Mem. Counterpart (Woman of Yr. 1980), Mich. Water Pollution Control Assn. (pres. 1979), Water Pollution Control Fedn. (bd. dirs. 1981-84, exec. bd. 1981). Republican. Mem. Reformed Ch. Am. Clubs: Spring Lake Country (Mich.); Century (Muskegon, Mich.). Avocation: music (perform and instruct piano and organ). Home: 10975 Lakeshore Dr West Olive MI 49460 Office: Grand Haven-Spring Lake Wastewater Plant 1525 Washington St Grand Haven MI 49417

VANDAME, LYNN MICINSKI, food manufacturing company executive; b. South Bend, Ind., May 23, 1954; d. Harry Patrick and Shirley Ann (Kaysen) Micinski; m. Danny Lee VanDame, Nov. 27, 1982; children—Helen Michele, Katrina Ann. A.Applied Sci., Tex. State Tech. Inst., 1974; completion cert. McLennan Community Coll., 1978; B.S., Purdue U., 1982. Lic. practical nurse; registered animal technician. Personnel mgr. Mott's, Inc., Waco, Tex., 1974-76; sr. quality assurance operator M & M Mars Candy, Waco, 1976-77; research asst. Purdue U., West Lafayette, Inc., 1980, 82-84; quality assurance supr. Gen. Foods Mfg. Corp., Lafayette, Ind., 1985—. Contbr. articles to various publs. Mem. Inst. Food Technologists, Leather Artisans Internat., Lafayette Kennel Club, Alpha Zeta. Democrat. Roman Catholic. Avocations: leathercraft; raising, training, and breeding Appaloosa horses and Siberian Huskies. Home: Box 5215 Lafayette IN 47903 Office: General Foods Mfg Corp Box 7678 Lafayette IN 47903

VAN DE BOVENKAMP, SUE ERPF, charitable organization executive; b. N.Y.C.; d. George Norton and Bettina Lions (Hearst) Mortimore; student Gardner Sch., Art Students League, Cooper Union; m. Armand Grover Erpf, 1965; children—Cornelia Aurelia, Armand Bartholomew; m. Gerrit Pieter Van de Bovenkamp, Aug. 11, 1973. Chmn. Armand G. Erpf Fund, N.Y.C., 1971—; founder, hon. chmn. Erpf Catskill Cultural Ctr., 1972—. Bd. advisors, founder N.Y. Zool. Soc., 1971—, William Beebe fellow, 1983—; fellow in perpetuity Met. Mus. Art, 1977; life fellow Pierpont Morgan Library, 1974—; mem. council of friends Whitney Mus. Am. Art, 1971-77; mem. Whitney Circle, 1978—; bd. dirs. Catskill Ctr. for Conservation and Devel., 1983-86; mem. adv. council, dept. art history and archaeology Columbia U., 1972—, established univ. seminar on uses of oceans, 1977, mem. adv. council Translation Ctr., 1986; life conservator N.Y. Pub. Library, 1980; fellow Frick Collection; 1971—; mem. council Agribus. Council, Inc., 1979—; Bot. Gardens, 1980—; founder, life mem. World Wildlife Fund, 1973—, bd. dirs., 1984—; mem. pres.'s council Columbia U., 1973-78. Life mem. Mus. City N.Y., 1972—, mem. pres.'s council; mem. Asia Soc. (benefactor, mem. pres.'s council 1983—), Nathaniel Lord Britton Soc. (charter 1983—), N.Y. Acad. Scis., The Planetary Soc., The Nat. Audubon Soc., The Am. Scottish Found. Office: The Armand G Erpf Fund 640 Park Ave New York NY 10021

VAN DEMARK, RUTH ELAINE, lawyer; b. Santa Fe, N. Mex., May 16, 1944; d. Robert Eugene and Bertha Marie (Thompson) Van D.; m. Leland Wilkinson, June 23, 1967; children—Anne Marie, Caroline Cook. A.B., Vassar Coll., 1966; M.T.S., Harvard U., 1969; J.D. with honors, U. Conn., 1976. Bar: Conn. 1976, U.S. Dist. Ct. Conn. 1976, Ill. 1977, U.S. Dist. Ct. (no. dist.) Ill. 1977, U.S. Ct. Appeals (7th cir.) 1984, U.S. Supreme Ct. 1983. Instr. legal research and writing Loyola U. Sch. Law, Chgo., 1976-79; assoc. Wildman, Harrold, Allen & Dixon, Chgo., 1977-84, ptnr., 1984—. Assoc. editor Conn. Law Rev., 1975-76. Mem. adv. bd. Horizon Hospice, Chgo., 1978-84; del.-at-large White House Conf. on Families, Los Angeles, 1980; adv. bd. YWCA Battered Women's Shelter, Evanston, Ill., 1984—; bd. dirs. Friends of Battered Women and Their Children, 1986—; vol. atty. Pro Bono Advocates, Chgo., 1982—. Mem. ABA, Ill. Bar Assn., Conn. Bar Assn., Chgo. Bar Assn., Chgo. Council Lawyers, 7th Circuit Bar Assn., Appellate Lawyers Assn. Ill. (bd. dirs. 1985—), Women's Bar Assn. Ill., AAUW, Jr. League Evanston (Vol. of Year award 1983-84). Clubs: Chgo. Vassar (pres. 1979-81), Cosmopolitan (N.Y.C.). Home: 1127 Asbury Ave Evanston IL 60202 Office: Wildman Harrold Allen & Dixon 1 IBM Plaza Chicago IL 60611

VANDERBILT, GLORIA MORGAN, artist, actress, fashion designer; b. N.Y.C., Feb. 20, 1924; d. Reginald Claypoole and Gloria (Morgan) Vanderbilt; attended Mary C. Wheeler, Miss Porter's schs.; studied acting with dir. Sanford Meisner, beginning 1955; m. Pasquale di Cicco (div.); m. Leopold Stokowski, 1945 (div. 1955); children—Stanislaus, Christopher; m. Sidney Lumet, 1956 (div.); m. Wyatt Emory Cooper, 1963; children—Carter V., Anderson H. Exhibited in one-man shows at Rabun Studio, N.Y.C., 1948, Bertha Shaeffer Gallery, N.Y.C., 1954, Juster Gallery, N.Y.C., 1956, Hammer Gallery, N.Y.C., 1966, 68, Cord Gallery, N.Y.C., 1966, Washington Gallery Art, 1968, Neiman-Marcus, Dallas, 1968, Vestart Gallery, N.Y.C., 1969, Parish Museum, Southampton, N.Y., also in Nantucket, Mass., Houston, Reading, Pa., Monterey, Calif., Nashville; exhibited in group shows Washington Gallery Art, 1967, Hoover Gallery, San Francisco, 1971; acted in summer stock prodn. The Swan; made Broadway debut in The Time of Your Life, 1955; other stage appearances include Picnic, 1955, The Spa, 1956, Peter Pan, 1958, The Green Hat; made TV debut in Tonight At 8:30; other TV appearances include Colgate Comedy Hour, 1955, Flint and Fire on U.S. Steel Hour, 1958, Family Happiness on U.S. Steel Hour, 1959, Very Important People; appeared in film Johnny Concho, 1955; dir. design Riegel Textile Corp., N.Y.C., 1970—; designer stationary and greeting cards Hallmark Co.; designer fabrics Bloomcraft Co. designer bed linens Martex Co., table linens Leacock Co., Gloria Vanderbilt jeans, also china, glassware, scarves. Recipient Sylvania award, 1959, Fashion award Neiman-Marcus, 1969. Mem. Actors Equity, Screen Actors Guild, AFTRA, Authors League Am., Am. Fedn. Arts Author: Love Poems, 1955: (with Alfred Allen Lewis) Gloria Vanderbilt Book of Collage, 1970; Woman to Woman, 1979; Once Upon a Time, 1985. author play: Three by Two, early 1960's, poems and short stories. Office: 1411 Broadway New York NY 10018*

VAN DER MEER, GRETA, indsl. cons.; b. Chgo., Jan. 15, 1949; d. Walter Henry and Virginia Mae (Olson) Van der M.; Ph.B. in Psychology, Northwestern U., 1974. With Leo Burnett Co., Chgo., 1969-72; personnel asst. Inst. Psychiatry, Northwestern Meml. Hosp., Chgo., 1972-77, coordinator perinatal addiction program, 1975-77; mgr. prodn. and adminstrn., nat. orgnl. surveys Sears, Roebuck & Co., Chgo., 1977-81; nat. sec.-treas. Mayflower Group, 1980-81, nat. vice chmn., 1981-82, nat. chmn., 1982-83; indsl. cons. Harbridge House, Inc., 1981—; v.p. CDS. Grantee, Ill. Dangerous Drugs Commn., 1975. Mem. Am. Assn. Public Opinion Research, Ill. Group Psychotherapy Soc. Office: 150 N Wacker Chicago IL 60606

VANDERSANDEN, SUZANNE, life insurance company executive; b. Seattle, June 7, 1957; d. William Garrett VanderSanden and Linda Anne (Mitchell) Archer. Student Wash. State U., 1975-77. Sr. title technician Chgo. Title Ins. Co., Seattle, 1977-80; field underwriter Mut. of N.Y., 1980-83, agy. supr., 1983—. Mem. campaign to elect Norman Maling, Seattle, 1978, campaign to elect George Bush, 1979. Mem. Nat. Assn. Profl. Saleswomen (founder N.Y.C. chpt., pres. 1982, Merit award 1982), Nat. Assn. Female Execs. Home: 240 E 32d St Apt 30 New York NY 10016

VANDERSLICE-BELLER, SUELLYN, psychologist, air force officer b. Baytown, Tex., Oct. 10, 1948; d. Thomas J. Vanderslice Jr. and Teodosia E. (Bevers) Loerwald; student Brevard Community Coll., 1966-67; B.A. in Sociology, La. State U., 1970; M.S. in Recreation Therapy, Calif. State U., 1975; Ph.D. in Psychology, U. Hawaii, 1986; m. John Walter Patrick Jr., May 30, 1970 (div. 1975); m. James Edward Beller, Dec. 18, 1983; stepchildren—Steven Kevin, Jeffrey Earl. Community social worker City of Pensacola (Fla.), 1970-71; therapeutic recreation supr. Salvation Army, Honolulu, 1973-74; community social worker Girl Scout Council of the Pacific, Honolulu, 1974-75; psychiat. social worker Mental Health Div., State of Hawaii, summer 1977; lectr. dept. psychology U. Hawaii, Honolulu, 1978-82; state mental health program dir. for women, dir. alternatives for women Dept. Health, State of Hawaii, 1979; pvt. practice marriage and family counseling, Honolulu, 1977-82; resident in clin. psychology USAF, Wilford Hall, Lackland AFB, Tex., 1982-83; chief psychol. services USAF Hosp., Tyndall AFB, Fla., 1983—; adj. faculty Gulf Coast Community Coll., Panama City, Fla., 1983—, Fla. State U., Panama City, 1984—. Mem. Lt. Gov.'s Com. on Women and Family, State of Hawaii, 1979-82; mem. Gov.'s Com. on Children; bd. dirs. Panhandle Alcohol Council. Mem. Am. Psychol. Assn., Western Regional Psychol. Assn., Hawaii Psychol. Assn., Hawaii Assn. for Humanistic Psychology (v.p. 1976-77, sec.-treas. 1977-78), Nat. Assn. Parks and Recreation, Am. Personnel and Guidance Assn., AAUW, Network of Mktg. Women, Gamma Phi Beta. Democrat. Baptist. Contbr. articles to jours. in psychology. Home: 601 S Berthe Ave Panama City FL 32404 Office: SGHMA/USAF Hosp Tyndall AFB FL 32403

VANDERSLUYS, CORA, med. technologist; b. Chester, Pa., Aug. 27, 1923; d. Edward and Florence C. (Murtaugh) Vandersluys; B.S., Fairleigh Dickinson U., 1960. Med. technologist St. Joseph Hosp., Paterson, N.J., 1955-60, asst. chief technologist, head hematology dept., 1960-66; research asst. N.J. Coll. Medicine, Jersey City, 1966-67; mgr. tech. resources Ortho Diagnostic Systems Inc., Raritan, N.J., 1967—; adj. asst. prof. Rutgers Med. Sch., Piscataway, N.J. Mem. Am. Soc. Clin. Pathologists, Am. Soc. for Med. Tech., N.J. Soc. for Med. Tech. (sec. 1958-60) pres. 1960-61). Mem. Christian Reformed Ch. Office: Rt 202 Raritan NJ 08869

VAN DERWEELE, MARY AMANDA, reporter, editor; b. Lansing, Mich., Jan. 11, 1930; d. Elon Samuel and Helen (Andreas) Bolton; student Western Mich. U., 1956-57; m. Denton Dexter Van DerWeele, May 1, 1970; children by previous marriage—Robert Clarke, Craig Clarke; stepchildren—Sandra Groat, K.S. Van DerWeele. Writer, Sta. WKZO-AM-TV, Kalamazoo, 1958-64, publications coordinator radio and TV, 1968-71; freelance writer Ford Times, Trailer Life, Health, Ladies Home Companion, Golden Mag. for Boys and Girls, 1964-68, also Battle Creek Enquirer and News, The Kalamazoo Gazette; partner, mgr. Van the Printer, Vicksburg Broadcast, Trading Post, Vicksburg, Mich., 1971-77; editor, writer Richland (Mich.) Jour. weekly, 1979-85. Author: A Pocket Full of Dreams, 1986. Area rep. Youth for Understanding, 1978—; spl. rep. World Radio Missionary Fellowship Inc., 1984—; St. Joseph County del. State and County Republican Convs., 1974-76; vice chmn. Womens Rep. Com., St. Joseph County, 1975-77; bd. dirs. Constatine Library, 1976. Mem. Mich. Press Assn. Home and Office: 2538 Norris St Hickory Corners MI 49060

VANDEVENTER, JANICE LEIGH, cartographer, flight instructor; b. Long Beach, Calif., Aug. 10, 1944; d. Owen Jerome and Laurence Elizabeth (Monninger) V.; B.A. in Geography, UCLA, 1966. Cartographer, Automobile Club So. Calif., Los Angeles, 1966-70, sr. cartographer, 1970-72, research coordinator, 1972-74, chief cartographer, 1974—; flight instr. Falcon Air, Long Beach, 1975—. Recipient FAA Safety Pin, 1974. Mem. Am. Congress Surveying and Mapping, Nat. Computer Graphics Assn., Los Angeles Area C. of C., Aircraft Owners and Pilots Assn., Sweet Adelines, Goldenaires Quartet (lead singer, group named novice quartet champions 1982), UCLA Alumni Assn., Alpha Xi Delta. Home: 5141 E Burnett St Long Beach CA 90815 Office: 2601 S Figueroa St Los Angeles CA 90007

VANDEVER, LOIS ARLENE LAYCOCK, nurse; b. Milw., Apr. 17, 1931; d. Russell Dana and Thelma Elizabeth (Strodthoff) Laycock; B.S., U. Denver, 1959; pediatric nurse practitioner U. Colo., 1970; m. Mar. 1957 (div. 1981); 1 son, Vincent James. Staff nurse Denver Public Schs., 1959-64; coordinator health services Cherry Creek Schs., Englewood, Colo., 1970-73; cons. U. Colo. Sch. Nursing, Colo. Bd. Nursing, Denver, 1975-79; seminar developer, presenter Invest in Yourself, Arapahoe Community Coll., 1980, pres. bd., 1981—; instr. various colls.; cons. in field; monitor, mem. rewrite com. nurse practice act com. Colo. Bd. Nursing; chmn. fund raiser event Colo. Woman's Coll.; lay minister Stephen Series. Mem. Nat. Assn. Female Execs., U. Denver Alumni Club, Non-Practicing and Part-Time Nurses Assn. (lobbyist), Nat. Assn. Pediatric Nurse Practitioners and Assos., Am. Nurses Assn., Colo. Nurses Assn., Friends U. Denver Sch. Nursing (dir.), Centennial C. of C., Instr. Noetic Scis. Republican. Episcopalian. Clubs: Colo. Columbine Dollogy, Rocky Mountain Standard Schnauzer, Denver Minikins, Zonta (dir. Englewood-Littleton). Editorial bd. Nursing, 1970-75; pioneer nurse practitioner program in public schs.; co-author: Invest in Yourself, 1982. Home: 835 W Geddes Circle Littleton CO 80120 Office: PO Box 3493 Littleton CO 80161

VAN DE WALLE, ANNA TAYLOR, county official; b. Hondo, Tex., Ja. 9, 1942; d. Tony Travis and Lorine Anna (Zinsmeyer) T.; m. Robert Henry Van De Walle, June 18, 1960; children—Brian, Curt, Steven, Stacie, Robert, Jr., Tony, Tom. Grad. high sch., Hondo, Sales clk. Fashion Key, Hondo, 1979-83; county clk. Medina County, Tex., 1983—. Mem. County and Dist. Clks. Assn. (legis. com.), Sigma Tau. Democrat. Roman Catholic. Avocations: dancing; sewing; crocheting. Office: Medina County Courthouse Room 100 Hondo TX 78861

VAN DE ZILVER, VALERIE JEAN, sales executive; b. Michigan City, Ind., Feb. 28, 1949; d. William Manny and Alice Pearl (Wright) Dieckilman; m. Peter Antonie Leonardus van de Zilver, Sept. 10, 1977; 1 son, Eric. Student Lincoln Christian Coll., 1967-70, Orange Coast Coll., 1970-73. Salesperson Nat. Community Builders, San Diego, 1972-74, Walker & Lee, Inc., Santa Ana, Calif., 1974-78; regional sales mgr. Walker & Lee, Inc., 1978-81; gen. sales mgr. Ponderosa Homes, Irvine, Calif., 1982-84; sales mgr. J.M. Peters Co., Newport Beach, Calif., 1984—. Producer, author multi-media motivational presentation Making of a No. 1 Team, 1984. Named Rookie Mgr. of Year, Walker & Lee, 1978. Mem. Sales and Mktg. Council So. Calif. (2nd v.p. 1983-84, Salesperson of Yr. award 1976, Sales Mgr. of Yr. 1983), Sales and Mktg. Execs. Republican. Mem. Christian Ch. Home: 19512 Surfdale Ln Huntington Beach CA 92648 Office: JM Peters Co Inc 1601 Dove St Suite 190 Newport Beach CA 92660

VAN DINE, HOLLY, steel co. corp. communications mgr.; b. Pitts., Jan. 1, 1943; d. Paul and Elaine (Kinder) Long; B.A., Bennington Coll., 1964; m. Alan Van Dine, Apr. 24, 1977; children—Laura, Alexander. Asst. dir. pub. relations ARC, Allegheny County, 1973-75; asst. mgr. advt. L.B. Foster Co., Pitts., 1975-76, mgr. pub. relations, 1976-77, mgr. advt. and pub. relations, 1977-81, mgr. corp. communications, 1981—. Mem. steering com. Pitts. Children's Mus., 1969-71. Mem. Bus. and Profl. Advt. Assn., Bus. Publ. Audit Assn. Office: 415 Holiday Dr Pittsburgh PA 15220

VANDIVER, COLEENE SAVAGE, credit union executive; b. Hollis, Okla., Nov. 18, 1932; d. Lee Austin and Effie Sarah (Kizer) Savage; m. Billy J. Vandiver, Apr. 10, 1950; children—Jay Lynn, Letitia Vandiver Bell. Student Amarillo Coll., 1961-62. Personnel clk. City of Amarillo, Tex., 1962-66; asst. mgr. Amarillo City Fed. Credit Union, 1966-68, State Farm Fed. Credit Union, Dallas, 1968-69; pres. Trailways Credit Union, Dallas, 1969—; chmn. bd. Users Inc., Valley Forge, Pa., 1982—. Pres. Oakdale PTA, Amarillo, 1960-62. Mem. Dallas Dist. Tex. Credit Union League (adv. dir. 1975—), Credit Union Execs. Soc., Tex. Council Credit Union Execs. (v.p. 1984). Republican. Mem. Ch. of Christ. Office: Trailways Credit Union 1500 Jackson St Suite 518 Dallas TX 75201

VAN DOREN, DEBRA LYNN, nutritionist; b. East Orange, N.J., Aug. 9, 1954; d. Richard Merrill and Desiree Beryl (Joerger) Van Doren. B.S. in Food and Nutrition, U. Houston, 1980. Nutrition surveyor System Devel. Corp., Santa Monica, Calif., 1980; food service supr. St. Luke's Hosp., Houston, 1981—. Democrat. Episcopalian. Home: 6919 Indian Falls Dr Missouri TX 77489 Office: St Luke's Hosp 6720 Bertner St Houston TX 77020

VAN DOREN, META WESTFALL, music educator; b. Atkinson, Nebr., Sept. 26, 1902; d. George Elbert and Myrtle AnnaLee (Mackrill) Westfall; m. Paul VanDoren, June 24, 1926; 1 child, Meta Joan Gay. Teaching and music credential San Diego State Coll.; student piano and organ U. Hawaii; organ student U. Calif.-San Diego. Tchr. music pub. schs. Los Angeles, Pasadena, Chula Vista, Oceanside, Calif.; tchr. piano, organ, Calif.; chmn. auditions Nat. Piano Tchrs.; organist, choir dir. various chs. Co-author: Folk Songs of the United States, Calif. State Series. Music scholar Inst. Nat. Bellas Artes, Mexico City, 1956, Royal Acad. Music, London, 1960, Vienna Music Acad., 1962, Nazionale di Cecilia, Rome, 1966, Konserratorium, Lucerne, Switzerland, 1970, Royal Music Conservatory, Brussels, 1971. Mem. Am. Coll. Musicians (cert.), Nat. Guild Mus Tchrs. (Hall of Fame). Lodge: Daus. of Nile. Home: 602 S Nevada St Oceanside CA 92054

VAN DUSSELDORP, MARY ELLEN, conference center manager; b. Newton, Iowa, Sept. 10, 1930; d. Swan Theodore and Ellen Isabelle (Stevenson) Goss; m. Melvin Dwane Van Dusseldorp, Mar. 19, 1949; children—Rodney, Rhonda, Reginald. Student pub. schs., Colfax, Iowa. Dir., Colfax InterFaith Ctr., Iowa, 1975—. Pres., Jasper County Republican Women, 1986. Recipient Citizens award Colfax Kiwanis Club, 1984. Mem. Am. Bus. Women Assn., Nat. Assn. Female Execs. Republican. Disciple of Christ. Clubs: LaFemme Fed. Women's Club (pres. 1972-74), Colfax Contract Bridge (pres. 1982). Avocations: hunting; fishing; traveling. Home: 901 N League Rd Colfax IA 50054

VAN DUYN, MONA JANE, poet; b. Waterloo, Iowa, May 9, 1921; d. Earl George and Lora G. (Kramer) Van Duyn; B.A., U. No. Iowa, 1942; M.A., U. Iowa, 1943; D.Litt. (hon.), Washington U., St. Louis, 1971, Cornell Coll., Iowa, 1972; m. Jarvis A. Thurston, Aug. 31, 1943. Instr. English, U. Iowa, 1943-46, U. Louisville, 1946-50; lectr. English, Univ. Coll., Washington U., 1950-67; adj. prof. Grad. Poetry Workshop, Washington U., St. Louis, 1983, 85; poetry readings, 1970—; poetry editor, co-pub. Perspective, A Quar. of Lit., 1947-67; lectr. Salzburg (Austria) Seminar Am. Studies, 1973; poet-in-residence Breadloaf Writing Conf., Mass., 1974, 76. Recipient Bollingen prize, 1970, Nat. Book award, 1971; Eunice Tietjens award, 1956; Helen Bullis prize, 1964, 76; Harriet Monroe award, 1968; Hart Grane Meml. award, 1968; Borestone Mountains 1st prize, 1968; grantee Nat. Council Arts, 1967; Guggenheim fellow, 1972; fellow Acad. Am. Poets, 1980; recipient Carl Sandburg prize Cornell Coll., 1982; Lit. award Mo. Library Assn., 1984; Nat. Endowment Arts fellow, 1985. Mem. Nat. Inst. Arts and Letters (Loines prize 1976), Acad. Am. Poets (chancellor 1985). Author: Valentines to the Wide World, 1959; A Time of Bees, 1964; To See, To Take, 1970, Bedtime Stories, 1972; Merciful Disguises, 1973; Letters from a Father and Other Poems, 1982. Address: 7505 Teasdale Ave Saint Louis MO 63130

VAN DYKE, PAMELA JEAN, nurse; b. Madison, Wis., July 4, 1949; d. David Edward and Shirley Gene (Fields) Haase; m. Kenneth John Van Dyke, Sr., Aug. 6, 1972; children—Kenneth John, Jr., Ryan Everett. B.S. in Nursing, Alverno Coll., Milw., 1972. Staff nurse Lakeland Hosp., Elkhorn, Wis., 1972-75, Columbia Hosp., Milw., 1975-76, Lakeland Hosp., Elkhorn, 1978-79; nursing mgr. Riverside Hosp., Waupaca, Wis., 1982-85, nurse outpatient surgery, 1985—. Active PTA. Avocations: cooking; gardening; biking; camping; cross-country skiing. Home: Route 1 Box 621 Scandinavia WI 54977

VAN DYKE-COOPER, ANNY MARION, financial company executive; b. Howard, Ont., Can., Sept. 30, 1928; d. Anthony and Anna (Koolen) Van D.; m. John Arnold Cooper, Apr. 9, 1983. C.F.A., U. Va., 1969; B.A., Sir George Williams U., 1959. Tchr., Lanoraie Sch. Bd., 1946-47; sec. Can. Nat. Rys., Montreal, Que., Can., 1947-51; sec. Sorel Industries Ltd., Sorel, Que., Can., 1952-53; with Bell Investment Mgmt. Corp. and BIMCUR, Inc. subs. Bell Canada, Montreal, 1953-83; portfolio mgr. U.S. Equities, 1953-83; v.p. investments, dir. Cooper, Van Dyke Assocs. Inc., Birmingham, Mich., 1983—. Mem. Inst. Chartered Fin. Analysts (trustee 1979-80), Fin. Analysts Soc. Detroit, Montreal Soc. Fin. Analysts (program chmn., pres. 1974-75), Can. Council Fin. Analysts (vice-chmn. 1976-77), Fin. Analysts Fedn. (treas. 1977-78, vice chmn. 1978-79, chmn. 1979-80). Home: 1660 Apple Ln Bloomfield Hills MI 48013 Office: 1100 N Woodward Ave Birmingham MI 48011

VANE, SYLVIA BRAKKE, anthropologist, cultural resource management company executive; b. Fillmore County, Minn., Feb. 28, 1918; d. John T. and Hulda Christina (Marburger) Brakke; m. Arthur Bayard Vane, May 17, 1942; children—Ronald Arthur, Linda, Laura Vane Spooner. A.A., Rochester Jr. Coll., 1937; B.S. with distinction, U. Minn., 1939; student Radcliffe Coll., 1944; M.A., Calif. State U.-Hayward, 1975. Med. technologist Dr. Frost and Hodapp, Willmar, Minn., 1939-41; head labs. Corvallis Gen. Hosp., Oreg., 1941-42; dir. lab. Cambridge Gen. Hosp., Mass., 1942-43, Peninsula Clinic, Redwood City, Calif., 1947-49; v.p. Cultural Systems Research, Inc., Menlo Park, Calif., 1978—; pres. Ballena Press, Menlo Park, 1981—; cons. cultural resource mgmt. So. Calif. Edison Co., Rosemead, 1978-81, San Diego Gas and Elec. Co., 1980-83, Pacific Gas and Elec. Co., San Francisco, 1982-83, Wender, Murase & White, Washington, 1983—, Yosemite Indians, Mariposa, Calif., 1982-84. Author: (with L.J. Bean), California Indians, Primary Resources, 1977, The Cahuilla and the Santa Rosa Mountains, 1981. Contbr. chpts. to several books. Bd. dirs. Sequoia Area council Girl Scouts U.S., 1954-61; bd. dirs., v.p., pres. LWV, S. San Mateo County, Calif., 1960-65, cons. San Francisco council Girl Scouts U.S., 1962-69. Fellow Soc. Applied Anthropology; mem. Southwestern Anthrop. Assn. (program chmn. 1976-78, newsletter editor 1976-79), Am. Anthropology Assn., Soc. for Am. Archaeology. Mem. United Ch. of Christ. Office: Ballena Press 823 Valparaiso Ave Menlo Park CA 94025

VAN EERDE, KATHERINE S(OMMERLATTE), history educator and administrator; b. Terre Haute, Ind., June 17, 1920; d. Ewald and Flora Lillian (Hoff) Sommerlatte; m. John A. Van Eerde, July 23, 1946; 1 dau., Elizabeth Marie. B.A., Coll. of Wooster, 1941; M.A., Yale U., 1942, Ph.D., 1945. Instr. Scripps Coll., Claremont, Calif., 1944-46, Smith Coll., Northampton, Mass., 1946-48, Johns Hopkins U., Balt., 1948-51; reviewing officer Dept. of State, Intelligence, Washington, 1951-55; asst. prof. U. R.I., 1955-61; assoc. prof., prof. Muhlenberg Coll., Allentown, Pa., 1961—, head history dept., 1978-84. Author: John Ogilby, 1976; Wenceslaus Hollar, 1970; contbr. articles to publs. Com. mem. synodical United Ch. of Christ. Guggenheim fellow, 1971; Huntington Library fellow, 1979; grantee Am. Philos. Soc., 1974, Ford Found. (3); recipient Lindback teaching award, 1968. Mem. Am. Hist. Assn., Renaissance Soc. Am., Conf. on Brit. Studies, Lehigh County Hist. Soc., AAUP, Am. Printing History Assn., Phi Beta Kappa. Democrat. Mem. United Ch. of Christ. Home: 2423 Washington St Allentown PA 18104 Office: Dept History Muhlenberg Coll Allentown PA 18104

VANEK, EUGENIA POPORAD, community dentistry educator ednl. cons.; b. Cleve., June 23, 1949; d. George and Anna P. (Dumitru) Poporad; B.S., Case-Western Res. U., 1970; M.A. (fellow), Boston U., 1972; Ed.D., U. Rochester, 1974; m. John Albert Vanek, Aug. 28, 1971; children—Matthew Dumitru, Jessica Petera. Tchr. Cleveland Heights (Ohio) High Sch., 1970; instr. Monroe Community Coll., Rochester (N.Y.) Inst. Tech., 1972-74; asst. prof. med. edn. research Case-Western Res. U., Cleve., 1974-80, asst. prof. family medicine, 1979-80, asst. clin. prof. community dentistry, 1978—; adj. prof. Goddard Coll., Plainfield, Vt., 1980-81; ednl. cons. 1980—. Chmn. Northeastern Ohio alumni scholarship admissions com. U. Rochester, 1974-76, 1979-80; active N.E. Ohio affiliate Am. Heart Assn., 1977; mem. Task Force on Heart Disease in Young; trustee Oberlin (Ohio) Early Childhood Center, 1980-83, Oberlin Friends of Pub. Library, 1982-84. Ednl. cons. study fellow, 1977. Mem. Am. Ednl. Research Assn., Am. Assn. Higher Edn., Assn. Supervision and Curriculum Devel., Assn. Tchr. Educators. Author: In Piagetian Research: Compilation and Commentary, Vol. 4, 1976; contbr. numerous articles to various publs. Home and Office: 46 Stewart Ct Oberlin OH 44074

VANELL, JANET SUSAN, advertising/public relations agency executive, consultant; b. Toledo, Feb. 11, 1952; d. Melvin Clair and Mary Jane (Jozwiak) V.; m. Daniel David Flavin, Oct. 23, 1983. B.S., Miami U., Oxford, Ohio, 1974. Asst. promotion dir. Sta.-WTOL-TV, Toledo, 1974-76; promotion dir. Sta.-WBRC-TV, Birmingham, Ala., 1976-79; owner, v.p. Creative People, Inc., Chgo., 1979-82, Clay Vanell, Inc., Chgo., 1982-83, Vanell, Inc., Chgo., 1983-86; v.p. creative services Conway/Milliken & Assocs., Chgo., 1986—. Mem. Pacific Area Travel Assn., Am. Soc. Travel Agts. (allied), African Travel Assn., Kappa Delta Alumnae. Office: Conway/Milliken & Assocs 875 N Michigan Ave Chicago IL 60611

VANESS, MARGARET HELEN, artist, consultant; b. Seattle; d. Paul Edward and Alma Magdalena Lauch; B.F.A., U. Wash., Seattle, 1970, 71, M.F.A., 1973; cert. bus. Drexel U., Phila., 1975; m. Gerard Vaness; children—Bette, Bruce, Barbara, Helen-Cathleen. Teaching asst. Sch. Art, U. Wash., 1971-73; illustrator DuPont Co., Wilmington, Del., 1973-74, Boeing Vertol Co., Phila., 1974-75; illustrator, program mgr. Boeing Co., Seattle, 1978-84; judge art shows, 1969—; executed mural for Dr. L. Mellon-Boeing Vertol Med. Center, 1974; commd. by USIA, 1973. Mem. Coll. Art Assn., Soc. for Tech. Communication, Photog. Soc. Am. (area rep. 1985—), U. Wash. Alumni Assn. (life), U. Wash. Arboretum Found. (unit pres. 1981-83), Lambda Rho (past pres.). Address: 17128 2d St SW Seattle WA 98166

VAN ETTEN, MARGUERITE RUBY, dietitian; b. Sayre, Okla., July 2, 1921; d. Monroe Clarence and Susie Estella (Larkey) Baggett; B.S. in Home Econs. and Dietetics, U. Okla., 1945; M S. in Behavioral Sci. and Human Services, Nova U., 1981; m. George Douglas Van Etten, June 9, 1945; children—Karen Lynette, Janel Anne, Vicki Tina. Dietitian Montgomery County (Md.) Jewish Day Camp, Bethesda, 1949; clin. dietitian and relief dietitian Chestnut Lodge Mental Health Facility, Rockville, Mo., 1949-50; relief clin. and adminstrv. dietician, dir. dietary balance, dir. dietary service Suburban Hosp., Bethesda, 1954-64; dir. dietary services; cons. dietitian Althea Nursing Home, Silver Spring, Md., 1964-65; adminstrv. and clin. dietitian Holy Cross Hosp., Silver Spring, 1964-72; clin. dietitian St. Michael's Hosp., nr. Stevens Point, Wis., 1972-73; dietitian, preceptor dietetic assts., preceptor coordinated undergrad. dietetic program U. Wis., Stevens Point, 1972-73; cons. dietitian St. Jude's Nursing Home, Wis., 1972; clin. and adminstrv. dir. dietary services South Fla. Bapt. Hosp., Plant City, 1973-74; pub. health nutrition cons. Fla. State Health and Rehab. Services Office of Licensure and Cert., Miami, 1974—. Mem. Am. Dietetic Assn., Broward County Dietetic Assn. (pres.-elect, acting pres. 1983, plaque 1985), Fla. Council on Aging, Cons. Dietitians of Health Care Facilities of Am. Dietetic Assn., Broward County Geneal. Soc. (life mem.; v.p. 1982, pres. 1983), U. Okla. Alumni Assn. (life), Okla. Hist. Assn., Madison County Geneal. Assn. (Ill.), AAUW, LWV, Ellis County Geneal Soc. (Tex.), Ill. State Geneal. Assn., Holston Geneal. Soc. (Va.), New Eng. Hist. Geneal. Soc., DAR (life, 1st vice regent Cypress Chpt. 1982, regent 1984), Cherokee Hist. Soc. Congregationalist. Lodge: Order Eastern Star (past matron Rockville, Md. 1964, dep. grand lectr. 1965, 66, 67). Author: Masters Practicum-Cons. Dietitians Handbook, 1980. . Home: 460 SW 131st Ave Ft Lauderdale FL 33325 Office: 5190 NW 167th St Miami FL 33014

VAN GILDER, BARBARA JANE DIXON, interior designer, cons.; b. South Bend, Ind., Dec. 6, 1933; d. Vincent Alan and Wanda Anita (Rapell) Dixon; student Mich. State U., 1951-55; postgrad. St. Mary's Coll., 1956-57, N.Y. Sch. Design, 1956-58; m. Erwin Dalton VanGilder, May 25, 1959; children—Eric Dalton, Marc David. Factory color cons. Smith-Alsop Paint Co., Terre Haute, Ind., 1955-56; archtl. design cons., Mishawaka, Ind., 1956-58; residential-comml. designer, South Bend, Chgo., 1958-63; designer industrialized housing industry, Ga., Fla., Ind., Mich., 1962—; design cons. Skyline Corp., Ind., Calif., Pa., 1962-66; v.p. design Treasure Chest Corp., Sturgis, Mich., 1969, also dir.; pres., dir. Sandpiper Art, Inc.; v.p. T.C.I. Ltd.; design cons. C.O. Smith Ind. Peachtree Housing, Moultrie, Ga., Nobility Homes, Ocala, Fla.; head merchandising and design Sandpiper Originals, clothing boutique, 1978—; currently pub. relations ofcl. Am. Mktg. Assn., adj. tchr. Lakeshore Sch. System. also coordinator trade show displays; nat. advt. rep. Studebaker-Packard Corp., Mercedes Benz, Clark Equipment, 1959-63; writer series on decorating for 2 Mich. newspapers, 1961-63; participant TV show Know Your Decorator, Calif. and Maine, 1962, 77. Officer, Shoreham Village (Mich.) Bd. Zoning, 1960-63. Named Woman of Year, Profl. Model's Club, 1952; recipient 1st pl. furniture design hardwoods Nat. Hardwoods Assn., 1956; 1st pl. Best in Show award, Louisville, Atlanta, 1964-65, 66, 69, 70-74, 76; others. Mem. Design Council Industrialized Housing (award 1974), Nat. Soc. Interior Designers, Mich. State U. Alumni Assn., Internat. Platform Assn., Internat. Biog. Assn. Contbg. editor Skyliner mag., 1962-66; permanent guest editor, contbr. Today's Home mag., 1974—. Home: 3630 S Lakeshore Dr St Joseph MI 49085 Office: PO Box 244 Stevensville MI 49127 also PO Box 1100 Dunedin FL 33528

VAN GUNDY, SUZANNE S., craft kits manufacturing company executive, consultant; b. Weehawken, N.J., Jan. 15, 1945; d. John George and Madeline Barbara (Fritchie) Schweigart; m. Dorwin James Van Gundy, Sept. 20, 1967; children—Douglas James, Christine. B.S., Miami Dade Jr. Coll., 1965; student U. Fla.-Gainesville, 1966-67. Pres. Country Quickies, Inc., Clemmons, N.C.; cons. Craft and Art Market, Miss. U. for Women, Columbus, 1985-86. Chmn. Bi-centennial Com. Biscayne Park, Miami, Fla., 1976. Mem. Assn. Crafts and Creative Industries, S.W. Craft and Hobby Assn., Hobby Industry Am., Sdc. Craft Designers, Mid-Atlantic Craft and Hobby Assn. Republican. Presbyterian. Lodge: Rainbow Girls. Avocations: tennis; reading; water skiing; snow skiing. Office: Country Quickies Inc PO Box 337 Lewisville NC 27023

VAN HEMERT, JUDY, electronic manufacturing company executive, educator; b. Dallas, Feb. 8, 1947; d. Marion Everett and Thelma Rhea (Robinson) VanH.; m. Milton Martin Dusek, Aug. 29, 1970 (div. Sept. 1981); children—Christopher Martin, Matthew Everett. B.A., Vanderbilt U., Nashville, 1969; cert. lang. therapist Scottish Rite Hosp., Dallas, 1971. Cert. secondary tchr., Tex., cert. Lang. therapist. Lang. therapist Scottish Rite Hosp., Dallas, 1970-72, The Winston Sch., Dallas, 1975-82; mktg., purchasing S.V. Mfg., Richardson, Tex., 1982-84; pres. Bullet Electronics, Rockwall, Tex., 1984—; co-owner The Nikao Co.; owner C-Power, Inc. Mem. Assn. Women Entrepreneurs of Dallas, Nat. Assn. Women Bus. Owners, Small Bus. Owners. Republican. Presbyterian. Avocations: golf; tennis. Home: 1135 Ridge Rd W Rockwall TX 75087 Office: C-Power Products Inc 2001 B Industrial Ln Rockwall TX 75087

VANHOOZER, JEAN ELIZABETH, auditor, credit union exec.; b. Marlow, Okla., May 4, 1932; d. Thomas Osa and Gladys Mamie (Sample) McCarley; student Okla. Baptist U., Shawanee, 1951-52; B.S. in Bus Adminstrn., Cameron U., Lawton, Okla., 1978; m. Teddy Gene VanHoozer, Sept 2, 1952; children—Dewayne, David, Nancy. With Lawton (Okla.) Public Schs., 1952-68, bus. office mgr., 1960-68, auditor, 1968—; mgr. Lawton Tchrs. Fed. Credit Union, Lawton, 1968—. Mem. Nat. Edn. Credit Union Council, Data Processing Mgmt. Assn., Okla. Public Acct. Democrat. Baptist. Club: Altrusa. Office: 1806 Liberty St Lawton OK 73501

VAN HORN, ELAINE CLAUDER, ins. agt.; b. Houston, Nov. 11, 1936; d. Samuel H. and Margaret F. (Hall) Clauder; student Southwestern Jr. Coll., Waxahachie, Tex., 1955-56, U. Houston, 1956-57; completed bus. course, Massey Bus. Coll., 1955; m. Richard W. Van Horn, June 21, 1957 (div., 1968); children—Wesley W., Alex C., Richard A.; m. 2d. George E. Veo, Nov. 13, 1969 (div. 1980). Exec. sec. to officers Sakowitz, Inc., Houston, various years 1957-68; exec. sec. to owner boat co., Houston, 1968-69; agt. Union Central Life Ins. Co., Houston, 1970-75; agt. Sun Life Ins. Co., 1975-77; gen. agt. Gen. Am. Life Ins. Co., Houston, 1977-80; brokerage supr. Union Mut. Life Ins. Co., Houston, 1980—. Dir. secretarial duties Hofheinz for Mayor campaign, 1971. Mem. President's Club, Union Central, 1973-75, Centurian Club, 1972, qualified nat. quality award, 1973-77, Health Ins. quality award, 1974-77; named to Tex. Leaders Roundtable, 1972; recipient nat. sales achievement, 1973-74; named to Women Leaders Roundtable, 1972-74; qualified conf. of champions, Gen. Am. Life, 1977, conv. speaker, 1977. Mem. Nat. Assn. Life Underwriters (program Women's Leaders Roundtable, conv., 1974), Tex. Assn. Life Underwriters, Houston Assn. Life Underwriters (public service award for work with Houston Epilepsy Assn., 1974), Gulf Coast Conservation Assn., Bus. and Profl. Womens Assn. Houston. Pianist, organist, vibraharpist, play various other instruments. Office: Union Mutual Life Insurance Co 3100 Eastside Houston TX 77098

VAN HOWE, ANNETTE EVELYN, real estate agent; b. Chgo., Feb. 16, 1921; d. Frank and Susan (Linstra) Van Howe; B.A. in History magna cum laude, Hofstra U., 1952; M.A. in Am. History, SUNY-Binghamton, 1966; m. Edward L. Nezelek, Apr. 3, 1961. Editorial asst. Salute Mag., N.Y.C., 1946-48; asso. editor Med. Econs., Oradell, N.J., 1952-56; nat. mag. publicist Nat. Mental Health Assn., N.Y.C., 1956-60; exec. dir. Diabetes Assn. So. Calif., Los Angeles, 1960-61; corporate sec., v.p., editor, public relations dir. Edward L. Nezelek, Inc., Johnson City, N.Y., 1961-82; mgr. condominium, Fort Lauderdale, Fla., 1982-83; dir. Sky Harbour East Condo, 1983—; substitute tchr. high schs., Binghamton, N.Y., 1961-63. Bd. dirs. Broome County Mental Health Assn., 1961-65, Fine Arts Soc., Roberson Center for Arts and Scis., 1968-70, Found. Wilson Meml. Hosp., Johnson City, 1972-81, Found. SUNY, Binghamton; trustee Broome Community Coll., 1973-78; v.p. Broward County Commn. on Status of Women, 1982—; grad. Leadership Broward Class III, 1985; trustee Unitarian-Universalist Ch. of Ft. Lauderdale, 1982—. Mem. AAUW, Am. Med. Writers Assn., LWV (dir. Broome County 1969-70), Alumni Assn. SUNY Binghamton (dir. 1970-73), Am. Acad. Polit. and Social Sci., Nat. Assn. Female Execs., Am. Heritage Soc., Nature Conservancy, Nat. Hist. Soc., Alpha Theta Beta, Phi Alpha Theta, Phi Gamma Mu. Clubs: Binghamton Garden, Binghamton Monday Afternoon, Acacia Garden (pres.). Editor newsletter Mental Health Assn., 1965-68, newsletter Unitarian-Universalist Ch., weekly 1967-71, History of Broome County Meml. Arena, 1972. Home: 2100 S Ocean Dr Fort Lauderdale FL 33316 Office: 2230 SE 17th St Fort Lauderdale FL 33361

VANIDES, ALEXIA, marketing consulting executive; b. Los Angeles, Mar. 11, 1951; d. Thanos Demitrious and Constance (Trigonis) V.; B.A. in English cum laude, Calif. State U., Long Beach, 1973; M.B.A., Pepperdine U., 1980. Vice pres., creative dir. Thanos Vanides & Co., West Los Angeles, 1973-75, Chgo., 1975-77; mktg. communications mgr. Tubular group Hydril Co., Los Angeles, 1977; mktg. communications specialist Hughes Helicopters, Los Angeles, 1977-79; advt. mgr. Electron Device group Varian Assos., Palo Alto, Calif., 1979-85; pres. Vanides Mktg. Communications, San Carlos, Calif., 1985—. Recipient 1st Pl. award Nat. Agrl. Advertisers Assn., 1978. Mem. Bus./Profl. Advt. Assn. (sec. bd. dirs. 1978-79, 2d v.p. bd. dirs. Los Angeles chpt. 1979-80; sec. bd. dirs. No. Calif. chpt. 1980-81, v.p. programs 1981-82, dir. 1982-83, chpt. pres. 1983-84), Am. Mktg. Assn., Am. Helicopter Assn. Writer award-winning ads for indsl. cos., 1977-79, 80-81. Office: 1010 McCue Ave San Carlos CA 94070

VAN LAAR, MYRTLE JUNE, children's librarian; b. Leota, Minn.; d. Lambertus and Sadie (Boermans) Van L. B.A. in Edn., Calvin Coll., 1949; A.M. in Art Edn., U. Mich., 1955, A.M. in L.S., 1965. Cert. tchr. and librarian, Md. Elem. tchr. Christian Schs., Grand Rapids, Mich., 1949-60; tchr. Washington Christian Sch., Silver Spring, Md., 1960-63; library assoc. Silver Spring Pub. Library, 1963-64; curriculum ctr. dir. Calvin Coll., Grand Rapids, 1965-68; children's age-level specialist Hyattsville br. Prince George's County Meml. Library System, 1968—; library chmn. Washington Christian Reformed Ch., Washington, 1983-86. Sec. Washington Christian Sch. Bd., Silver Spring, 1978-79, mem. edn. com., 1976-78. Mem. ALA. Mem. Christian Reformed Ch. Club: Laurel Art Guild.

VANLEEUWEN, LIZ SUSAN (ELIZABETH), farmer, state legislator; b. Lakeview, Oreg., Nov. 5, 1925; d. Charles Arthur and Mary Delphia (Hartzog) Nelson; B.S., Oreg. State U., 1947; m. George VanLeeuwen, June 15, 1947; children—Charles, Mary, James, Timothy. Secondary sch. and adult tchr., 1947-70; news reporter, feature writer The Times, Brownsville, Oreg., 1949—; co-mgr. VanLeeuwen Farm, Halsey, Oreg.; mem. Oreg. Ho. of Reps., 1981—; weekly radio commentator, 1973-81. Active E.R. Jackman Bd., PTA, sch. adv. com.; precinct committeewoman. Recipient Outstanding service award Oreg. Farm Bur., 1975, Oreg. Farm Family of Yr. award, 1983; Chevron Agrl. Spokesman of Yr. award, 1975. Mem. Oreg. Women for Agr. (pres.), Oreg. Women for Timber, Linn-Benton Women for Agr. (pres.), Linn County Farm Bur., Linn County Econ. Devel. Com., Grange, Am. Agri-Women, Nat. Conf. State Legislature's Agr. and Food Policy Com. Republican. Office: Capitol Bldg H382 Salem OR 97310

VAN LEUVEN, HOLLY GOODHUE, social scientist, consultant, researcher; b. Salem, Mass., Dec. 2, 1935; d. Nathaniel William and Elizabeth VanClowes (Crowley) Goodhue; m. John Jamison Porter, II, Oct. 16, 1954 (div. 1974); children—Donald J. II, Nathaniel G., Alison A. Dionne, Erin E.; m. Robert Joseph VanLeuven, Dec. 31, 1976. B.A. with honors, Western Mich. U., 1971, M.A. with honors, 1975. Exec. dir. Community Confrontation and Communication Assocs., Grand Rapids, Mich., 1969-73; coordinator tng., research Nat. Ctr. for Dispute Settlement, Washington, 1973; tng. dir. Forest View Psychiat. Hosp., Grand Rapids, 1974; case coordinator Libner, Van Leuven, & Kortering, P.C., Muskegon, Mich., 1982—; talk show host Sta. WTRU-TV, Muskegon, 1985; cons. U.S. Dept. Justice, Washington, 1969-73, No. Ireland Dept. Community Relations, Belfast, 1971; jury selection cons. various law firms in Midwest, 1975—. Contbr. articles to profl. jours. Bd. dirs. Planned Parenthood Western Mich., Grand Rapids, 1964-72, Jr. League Grand Rapids, 1955—, YFCA, Muskegon, 1981-83; chmn. Student Showcase, Inc., Muskegon, 1983—; candidate for Mich. State Rep. 97th Dist., Muskegon, 1978; pres. Planned Parenthood Assn., Muskegon, 1980. Mem. Am. Sociol. Assn. Clubs: Muskegon Country, Century; Women's City (Grand Rapids). Lodges: Zonta, Compass. Home: 966 Mona Brook Rd Muskegon MI 49441 Office: Libner VanLeuven & Kortering PC 400 Comerica Hackley Bank Bldg Box 450 Muskegon MI 49443

VAN LOAN, MARY KIRKWOOD (MARY K. TWIDDY), personal financial counseling officer, educator, author; b. Mitchell, S.D., Dec. 18, 1934; d. Robert Campbell and Virginia Viola (Bates) Kirkwood; m. Richard Rodman Van Loan, July 11, 1959 (div. 1977); children—Richard Rodman, Lynn Virginia, Robert Edward; m. John William Twiddy, Aug. 23, 1980; stepchildren—John Peter, Susan Twiddy Slink. B.A. in English, Mt. Holyoke Coll., 1956; postgrad. in Secondary Edn., Boston U., 1957-58. Cert. fin. planner, tax preparer. English tchr. Castilleja Sch. for Girls, Palo Alto, Calif., 1956-57, Andrew Warde High Sch., Fairfield, Conn., 1958-60; substitute tchr. Town of Greenwich, Conn., 1974-79; co-owner, developer Assoc. Budget Cons., Greenwich, 1979-80; personal fin. counseling officer Union Trust Co., Greenwich, 1980—; instr. fin. planning adult edn., Greenwich, 1983—. Author various articles. Officer, Young Republicans, Greenwich, 1961-62; mem. Greenwich council Boy Scouts Am., 1968—, exec. bd., 1985—, asst. treas. 1986—. Recipient awards Boy Scouts Am., 1974. Mem. Internat. Assn. Fin. Planning (chmn. S. Conn. Chpt. 1986—, pres. 1985-86), Inst. Cert. Fin. Planners, Nat. Assn. Bank Women, Conn. Estate and Tax Planning Council, Lower Fairfield County Estate Planning Council, AAUW, Mt. Holyoke Fairfield Villages Alumnae Assn., Nat. Assn. Female Execs. Mormon. Avocations: handcrafts; sports; travel. Home: 12 Old Forge Rd Greenwich CT 06830 Office: Union Trust Co 1 Lafayette Pl Greenwich CT 06830

VANMEER, MARY ANN, publisher, writer, researcher; b. Mt. Clemens, Mich., Nov. 22, 1947; d. Leo Harold and Rose Emma (Gulden) VanM.; stepdau. Ruth (Meek) VanM. Student Mich. State U., 1965-66, 67-68, Sorbonne U., Paris, 1968; B.A. in Edn., U. Fla., 1970. Pres. VanMeer Tutoring and Translating, N.Y.C., 1970-72; freelance writer, 1973-79; pres. VanMeer Publs., Inc., Clearwater, Fla., 1980—, VanMeer Media Advt., Inc., Clearwater, 1980—; exec. dir., co-founder Assn. for Med. and Health Alternatives, Inc., Clearwater, 1982—. Author: Traveling with Your Dog, U.S.A., 1976; How to Set Up A Home Typing Business, 1978; Freelance Photographer's Handbook, 1979; See America Free, 1981; Free Campgrounds, U.S.A., 1982; (with Michael Pasquarelli) Free Attractions, U.S.A., 1982; VanMeer's Guide to Free Attractions, U.S.A., 1984; VanMeer's Guide to Free Campgrounds, 1984. Pub. info. chairperson, bd. dirs. Pinellas County chpt. Am. Cancer Soc., Clearwater, 1983-84. Mem. Am. Booksellers Assn., Author's Guild. Republican. Club: RAND Real Estate Investment (Tampa, Fla.). Office: VanMeer Publs Inc PO Box 1289 Clearwater FL 33517

VAN METER, CHRISTINE MARY, nursing educator; b. Paterson, N.J., Dec. 29, 1951; d. Joseph Charles and Marion Elizabeth (Tacq) Babcock; m. Robert Allen Van Meter, Mar. 16, 1974 (div. 1985); 1 son, Daniel Joseph. B.S. in Phys. Edn., U. Oreg., 1973; B.S. in Nursing, Russell Sage Coll., Troy, N.Y., 1980; postgrad. in nursing U. Portland, 1984—. R.N., N.Y., Wash. Nurse, Albany (N.Y.) Med. Ctr. Hosp., 1979-80, Kadlec Med. Ctr., Richland, Wash., 1980—; instr. nursing Columbia Basin Coll., Pasco, Wash., 1982—, coordinator paramedic program, 1983—, instr. advanced cardiac life support, 1982, 83—. Kellas scholar, 1980; W.K. Kellogg fellow, 1985-86. Mem. Am. Nurses Assn., Wash. Edn. Assn., Sigma Theta Tau. Home: 1845-D Peachtree Ln Richland WA 99352 Office: Columbia Basin College 2600 N 20th St Pasco WA 99301

VANN, ROBERTA JEANNE, educator; b. Indpls., Dec. 17, 1947; d. John Robert and Viola Mae (Bannon) V.; m. Frederick Lorenz. B.A., Ind. U., 1970, M.S., 1973, Ph.D., 1978. Vol., Peace Corps, Haile Salaissie U., Gondar, Ethiopia, 1970-71; Fulbright lectr. U. Gdansk (Poland), 1974-76; assoc. prof. English, Iowa State U., Ames, 1978—, dir. intensive English and orientation program, 1980—; lang. cons. USICA, Yugoslavia, Poland, Syria, Czechoslavakia, 1975-84. Mem. Nat. Council Tchrs. English, TESOL, Phi Delta Kappa. Democrat. Author: (with V. Hefley) Viewpoints USA: A Basic ESL Reader, 1984. Editor: (with B. Kroll) Exploring Speaking-Writing Relationships: Connections and Contrasts, 1981. Office: Dept English Iowa State U Ames IA 50011

VAN NAME, JUDITH ANN, consumer economist, educator; b. Cin., July 14, 1945; d. Glen Albert and Lena Anna (Woerner) Beyring; B.S., Miami U., Oxford, Ohio, 1967; M.S., Ohio State U., 1968. Instr. home econs. U. Del., Newark, 1968-71, asst. prof., 1971-77, assoc. prof. Coll. Human Resources, 1977—, chmn. textiles, design and consumer econs., 1978-83; dir. Computer Input Services, Inc. Pres., White Haven Poconos Homeowners Assn., 1975-76, dir., 1976-79. HEW grantee, 1974-76. Mem. Am. Home Econs. Assn., Am. Council Consumer Interests, Assn. for Fin. Counseling and Planning Edn., Phi Upsilon Omicron. Author: (with James D. Culley and Barbara H. Settles) Understanding and Measuring the Cost of Foster Family Care, 1975; contbr. articles and revs. to profl. jours. Home: 125 Dallam Rd Newark DE 19711 Office: Textiles Design and Consumer Econs U Del Newark DE 19711

VAN NATTA, ELEANOR SUE POUNDSTONE, nurse, educator; b. Decatur, Ill., Nov. 22, 1932; d. Herbert Lloyd and Blanche Cleo (Zink) Poundstone; diploma nursing, Washington U., St. Louis, 1953; B.S. in Nursing, U. Mo., 1956; M.S. in Nursing, Washington U., 1961; M.S.Ed., Purdue U., 1970; m. Charles R. Van Natta, Jr., June 12, 1971 (div. 1977); children—Laura, Sue. Staff nurse Barnes Hosp., St. Louis, 1953-54; staff nurse, then head nurse U. Mo. Med. Center, Columbia, 1954-58; instr. Decatur (Ill.) and Macon County Hosp. Sch. Nursing, 1958-60; instr. U. Colo., Denver, 1961-63; asst. prof. U. Mo., Columbia, 1964-66; asst. prof. Forest Park Community Coll., St. Louis, 1967-69; high sch. counselor, Decatur, 1970-71; coordinator diagnostic and evaluation project Comprehensive Devel. Centers, Monticello, Ind., 1975-77; asst. prof. Purdue U. Sch. Nursing, 1980-84; program supr. Ind. Vocat. Tech. Coll., Lafayette, 1984—; pres. White County Registered Nurses Orgn., 1975-76. Vol., Twin Lakes Contact, crisis hotline, Monticello, 1975-76; ednl. coordinator Matrix Lifeline, 1981-82; bd. dirs. Tippecanoe County affiliate Am. Heart Assn. Mem. Ind. League for Nursing (bd. dirs.), Am. Nurses Assn., Ind. Nurses Assn., Sigma Theta Tau, Phi Delta Kappa, Kappa Kappa Kappa. Club: Order Eastern Star. Home: 1137 Hillcrest Rd West Lafayette IN 47906 Office: 3208 Ross Rd Lafayette IN 47903

VAN NORTWICK, BARBARA LOUISE, administrator, librarian; b. Johnson City, N.Y., Jan. 3, 1940; d. Joseph John and Mary Louise (Hamzik) Goodwin; B.A., Harpur Coll., 1961; M.L.S., State U. N.Y. at Albany, 1976; D.A. Info./Library Adminstrn. (U.S. Govt. Title II B fellow in library adminstrn.), Simmons Coll., Boston, 1986; m. David Harry Van Nortwick, Nov. 17, 1962; children—Kimberly Lynn, Craig Michael. Coordinator ednl. facilities Maine-Endwell High Sch., Endwell, N.Y., 1961-64; tchr. English, Guilderland High Sch. (N.Y.), 1965-66; audiovisual librarian So. Colonie (N.Y.) High Sch., 1974-76; head librarian Westfield (Mass.) High Sch., 1976-78, Columbia High Sch., East Greenbush, N.Y., 1978-79; library dir. N.Y. State Nurses Assn., 1979-84; dir. Com. Aging and Subcom. libraries N.Y. State Senate, 1983-84, dir. Select Com. Interstate Coop., 1985—; del. Mass. Gov.'s Conf. Libraries and Info. Services, 1978-79; cons. HEW grant on self-directed continuing edn. for nurses; prof. Sch. Library and Info. Sci., SUNY-Albany, 1983-84. Mem. ALA, N.Y. Library Assn., Med. Library Assn., Assn. Bus. and Profl. Women. Methodist. Home: Rural Delivery 1 Box 292 Nassau NY 12123 Office: Room 706 LOB Albany NY 12247

VAN NOY, LINDA INEZ, personnel management specialist; b. Neptune, N.J., Oct. 25, 1949; d. Roy and Isabelle Maime (Lawrence) Williams; m. George Ingram, Oct. 11, 1969 (div. 1973); m. Irving Van Noy, Dec. 10, 1982. A.A., Brookdale Coll., N.J., 1978; B.S., U. Md., 1985. Sec., Dept. of Army, Ft. Monmouth, N.J., 1967-78, exec. sec., 1978-79, intern, 1979-81, equal opportunity mgr., Adelphi, Md., 1981-85, personnel mgmt. specialist, 1985—. Named Outstanding Young Woman of Am., 1984. Mem. Federally Employed Women, Nat. Assn. Female Execs., Occupational Services Inc. (bd. dirs. 1980-81). Democrat. Am. Baptist. Avocation: Bowling. Home: 3927 Blackburn Ln Burtonsville MD 20866 Office: Lab Command 2800 Powder Mill Rd Adelphi MD 20783

VAN OST, LORETTA BAILEY, real estate broker; b. Abilene, Tex., Oct. 12, 1925; d. Julian F. and Lora (Wooten) Bailey; m. Sanford Lansing Van Ost, Aug. 27, 1946 (dec. Nov. 1983); children—Katharine Van Ost Jones, Sanford Lansing, Susan Van Ost Wulz, Dirck Romeyn. Student UCLA, 1943-45, U. Calif.-Berkley, 1946. Lic. real estate broker. Acct. exec. Crosson & Dewey Advt., Newport Beach, Calif., 1964-66; sales mgr. San Vista Bldg. Co., Costa Mesa, Calif., 1966-69; v.p., gen. mgr. John D. Lusk Realty Co., Newport Beach, 1969-82; owner, operator Loretta Van Ost & Assocs., Newport Beach, 1982—. Contbr. articles to real estate mag. Mem. Friends of So. Coast Repertory, Irvine, Calif. Mem. Newport Harbor-Costa Mesa Bd. Realtors (mem. multiple listing com. 1978, ethics com. 1979-81), Nat. Assn. Home Builders (Million Dollar Circle; mem. sales and mktg. council), Kappa Alpha Theta Alumni. Avocations: crafts; sailing; travel; painting. Home: 4351 Rafael St Irvine CA 92714 Office: Loretta Van Ost & Assocs 11 Canyon Island Newport Beach CA 92663

VANOVER-BREWER, THELDA OLLIE, computer hardware and software sales executive; b. Miami, Fla., Apr. 13, 1951; d. Lee Alan and Thelda Frances (Stone) Vanover; m. Steven D. Rasbach, Jan. 15, 1977 (div. Sept. 1979); m. Darrell Steven Brewer, Apr. 13, 1985; 1 child, Travis Cristian. Student bus. Miami-Dade Community Coll., 1969-71; Notary public, lic. real estate broker, mortgage broker, Fla. Sales mgr. All-Am. Properties, North Miami, Fla., 1978-80; ptnr. H.V.L.L., Inc., Miami, Fla., 1980-82; v.p. Action Title Co., Miami, 1982-85; owner Unltd. Connections, Miami, 1984—; systems cons., computer sales and services Login Systems, Ft. Lauderdale, Fla., 1985—; cons. to new small businesses, Miami, 1984—. Writer Unltd. Connections News, 1985. Democrat. Avocations: painting; sewing; tennis; country cooking. Office: Unltd Connections 12555 Biscayne Blvd #812 North Miami FL 33181

VAN PATTEN, ELIZABETH, communications and marketing consultant; b. Schenectady, N.Y., Aug. 25, 1945; d. Eben Ellsworth and Agnes Frances (O'Connell) Van Patten. B.F.A., Ithaca Coll., 1967; postgrad. Baruch Coll., New Sch. Social Research, NYU, 1978-80. Research analyst Gene Reilly Group, N.Y.C., 1970-71; v.p. Child Research Service, N.Y.C., 1972-81; pres. Van Patten Research, N.Y.C., 1981-85; v.p. Nova Research Inc., 1986—; producer, dir. film and video prodns. Mem. Am. Mktg. Assn., Quality Research Cons. Assn., NOW (hon. mem. Staten Island, N.Y. chpt.). Producer films on women's rights and achievements.

VAN RAALTE, POLLY ANN, educator; b. N.Y.C., Sept. 22, 1951; d. Byron Emmanuel and Enid (Godnick) Van R.; student U. London, 1972; B.A., Beaver Coll., 1973; M.S. in Edn., U. Pa., 1974, postgrad. in edn., 1975—; postgrad. in spl. edn. West Chester State Coll., 1975-77. Title I reading tchr. Oakview Sch., West Deptford Twp. Sch. Dist., Woodbury, N.J., 1974-75, Title I reading supr., summer 1975; lang. arts coordinator Main Line Day Sch., Mitchell Sch., Haverford, Pa., 1975-76; reading supr. Salvation Army, Phila., summer 1976; reading Huntingdon Jr. High Sch., Abington (Pa.) Sch. Dist., 1976-78; reading specialist No. 2 Sch., Lawrence Pub. Sch., Inwood, N.Y., 1978—; instr. reading and spl. edn. dept. Adelphi U., 1979—; cons. to sch. dists.; speaker at reading convs. Coordinator, Five Towns Young Voter Registration, Hewlett, N.Y., summer, 1971; chmn. class fund Beaver Coll., also mem. internat. relations com. U. Pa. scholar, 1977-78. Mem. Internat. Reading Assn., Nat. Council Tchrs. English, Nassau Reading Council, N.Y. Reading Assn., Council Exceptional Children, Nat. Assn. Gifted Children, Assn. of the Gifted, Assn. Curriculum Devel., Cooper-Hewitt Mus., Mus. Modern Art, Met. Mus. Art, Whitney Mus., Friends of Carnegie Hall, Friends of Am. Ballet Theatre, Pi Lambda Theta, Kappa Delta Pi (sec.). Club: Human Relations (sec.). Home: 26 Meadow Ln Lawrence NY 11559 Office: Number 2 School Donahue Ave Inwood NY 11696

VANREENAN, GLENDA, radio executive; b. Marlinton, W.Va., Dec. 24, 1952; d. Leonard Francis and Jenny Marie (Sharp) Cutlip; m. Alfred Roger VanReenan, Dec. 4, 1970; children—Jessica, Michael. B.A., Salisbury State U., Md., 1979; postgrad. W.Va. Coll. Grad. Studies, Institute, 1980—. Lic. tchr., W.Va. Teen dir. Dept. Recreation, Ocean City, Md., 1975; mgr. Schwartz Theatre, Newark, Del., 1976-79; coordinator Pcoahontas County Health Dept., Marlington, 1980; news dir. WVMR Radio, Dunmore, W.Va., 1981-84, sta. mgr., 1984-85; tchr. Poca County Bd. Edn., Marlinton, 1983-84; vol. com. Pocahontas Communications, Dunmore, 1980; personnel com. Poca Communications, Dunmore, 1980; teaching asst. Sch. Telecommunications, Ohio U., Athens. Author and editor tng., policy and procedure manuals in field. Editor lay-out: Radio Waves. Pres., state dir., treas. Jaycettes, Marlinton, 1982-85. Mem. Friends Pub. TV. Republican. Methodist. Avocations: Reading; bicycling; tennis; camping. Home: Route 1 Box 199 Marlinton WV 24954 Office: News Dir Sta WVMR Dunmore Frost WV 24934

VAN SICKLE, BETSY DOLORES, university sports information official; b. Pitts., Nov. 26, 1952; d. Francis Anthony and Betty Dolores (Varhol) Bjalobok; m. Gary Alyn Van Sickle, Sept. 1, 1984. B.S., Edinboro U., 1973. Tchr. English and journalism Canon McMillan Schs., Canonsburg, Pa., 1974-75, Sto-Rox High Sch., McKees Rocks, Pa., 1975-76; asst. sports info. dir. Duquesne U., Pitts., 1976-78; acting sports info. dir. Old Dominion U., Norfolk, Va., 1978-79; sports info. dir. Marquette U., Milw., 1979—; press officer U.S. Olympic Com. for Pan Am. Games, Caracas, Venezuela, 1983, for Nat. Sports Festival, Indpls., 1982. Editor: Basketball Media Guide (Best in Nation award Coll. Sports Info. Dirs. Am.), 1981, also other press guides on athletics. Mem. pub. relations com. Wis. Spl. Olympics, Madison, 1983—. Mem. Coll. Sports Info. Dirs. Am. (numerous publ. awards 1980—), Women in Communications (co-editor newsletter 1982-84), U.S. Basketball Writers Assn., Women's Sports Found., Milw. Pen and Mike Club, Milw. Advt. Club.

VANSICKLER, LINDA ANN, postal service official; b. Bklyn., Oct. 3, 1951; d. Anthony Alfonse and Lillian Bruno; A.A. in Elem. Edn., Nassau Community Coll., 1971; B.S. in Elem. Edn., SUNY Coll., Oneonta, 1973; postgrad. in liberal studies SUNY-Stony Brook, 1973-75; postgrad. in bus. adminstrn. Suffolk U., 1980, George Mason U., 1983. With U.S. Postal Service, 1973—, supr. of mails Postal Inspection Service, 1979-80, postal insp., 1980-81, postal insp.-audit specialist level 23, Boston, 1981—, postal insp.-project coordinator level 24, Washington, 1982—; Mem. Mensa. Democrat. Roman Catholic. Home: 8138 Carrleigh Pkwy Springfield VA 22152 Office: 475 L'Enfant Plaza Washington DC 20260

VAN SLETT, KAREN ANN, researcher, nurse; b. Milw., Sept. 13, 1950; d. Theodore Ernst and Regina Viola (Orlikowski) Voss; m. Gene Francis Van Slett, Nov. 6, 1971. B.S., U. Wis.-Milw., 1972. R.N., Wis., Calif. Nursing instr. County Hosp. Sch. Nursing, Milw., 1973-75; nursing supr. Project INvolve, Milw., 1976-77; pub. health nurse Home Kare, Inc., San Jose, Calif., 1977-78; br. mgr. Quality Care, Inc., San Jose, 1978-79; ops. mgr. Cardiodyne Gen., Los Gatos, Calif., 1979-83; clin. research assoc. Barnes-Hind, Inc., Sunnyvale, Calif., 1983-86, Genetech, Inc., 1986—. Mem. Assocs. Clin. Pharmacology, Nat. Assn. Female Execs., Assn. Research in Vision and Ophthalmology. Democrat. Mem. Friends of Berkeley Shakespeare Festival. Home: 44467 Arapaho Ave Fremont CA 94539

VANSTON, MARY MARGARET, realtor; b. Scranton, Pa., Apr. 13, 1934; d. John Anthony and Rose C. (Rooney) Kane; m. Eugene Louis Vanston, Sept. 14, 1957; children—Timothy, Robert, Michael. Student Lacka Bus. Coll., Scranton, 1953, U. Scranton, 1954, 71-72, Pa. State U., 1972-74. Clk., Internat. Correspondance Schs., Scranton, 1952-57; waitress Catskill Mountains, N.Y., 1964-67, Scranton Country Club, 1967-70; bookkeeper Romart, Dickson City, Pa., 1970-73; realtor Vanston Real Estate, Scranton, 1973—; instr. Pa. State U., Scranton, 1985; appraiser 3d Nat. Bank, Scranton, 1983—. Mem. Govt. Study Commn., Lackawanna County, Pa., 1972-74. Mem. Greater Scranton Bd. Realtors (v.p. 1985), Pa. Assn. Realtors (Grad. Realtors Inst. 1978, Million Dollar award 1978), Nat. Assn. Realtors. Internat. Orgn. Real Estate Appraisers, LWV. Democrat. Roman Catholic. Club: Mid Valley Woman's. Avocations: reading; walking/jogging. Home: RD 4 Oak Ln Box 394 Jefferson Heights Lake Ariel PA 18436 Office: Vanston Real Estate 1511 N Main Ave Scranton PA 18508

VAN TASSEL, JANET SUE, business consultant; b. Bloomfield Hills, Mich., Apr. 4, 1941; d. Edward Stanley and Isabel Marie (Hollway) Van T. B.A., Hillsdale Coll., 1963; postgrad. Eastern Mich. U., 1969-70, Western Mich. U., 1984. Tchr. deaf edn. Bloomfield Hills schs., 1970-71; indsl. engr. Chrysler Corp., Highland Park, Mich., 1972-77; owner Baskin-Robbins Ice Cream Store, Kalamazoo, Mich., 1977-79; pres. Van Tassel & Co., Kalamazoo, 1979—. Mem. Nat. Assn. Securities Dealers, Nat. Assn. Life Underwriters. Republican. Club: Zonta Internat. Address: 101 North St Vicksburg MI 49097

VANTREASE, ALICE TWIGGS, marketing executive; b. Augusta, Ga., Mar. 29, 1943; d. Samuel Warren and Harriett Alice (Wright) Twiggs; m. James David Vantrease, May 9, 1980; m. John Mulford Marks, July 8, 1964 (div. Oct. 1972); children—John Mulford, Sarah Elizabeth. Student Winthrop Coll., 1961-62, Augusta Coll., 1962-64. Sales staff Chalker Publ. Co., Waynesboro, Ga., 1972-74; with Creative Displays, Inc., Tuscaloosa, Ala., 1974-78; sales mgr. GMC Bdcasting, Chattanooga, 1978-80; corporate sales, mktg. dir. Creative Displays Inc., Augusta, 1980-83; pres. Creative Mktg. Services, Augusta, 1983—. Mem. Outdoor Advt. Suppliers Assn. (v.p.), Am. Mgmt. Assn., Am. Assn. Coop Advt. Profls., Outdoor Advt. Assn. Am., Outdoor Advt. Suppliers Assn. (v.p. 1984-86; editor newspaper 1985-86). Instr., Small Bus. Devel. Council, Augusta, 1985-86. Episcopalian. Club: Jr. League. Avocations: Painting; writing. Home: 2927 Lake Forest Dr Augusta GA 30909 Office: Creative Mktg 825 Russell St Augusta GA 30904

VAN VLACK, MELVA BULLINGTON (MRS. WILLIAM CLARK VAN VLACK), retired home economist; b. Vesta Community, Charleston, Ark., Apr. 3, 1909; d. Baxter Lee and Ella Emma (McConnell) Bullington; B.S., U. Ark., 1932, M.S., 1965; postgrad. U. Calif. at Berkeley, 1939, U. Ala., 1948, Jacksonville State U., 1949; m. William Clark Van Vlack, Aug. 9, 1946. Home econs. instr., Prairie Grove, Ark., 1932-33; elementary tchr., Liberty-Tulsa County, Okla., 1933-34; home demonstration agt., Magnolia, Ark., 1934-36, Hope, Ark., 1936-39, Pine Bluff, Ark., 1939-47; jr. high sch. home econs. instr., Atalla, Ala., 1949-57; extension home economist, Ft. Smith, Ark., 1957-75. Ofcl. home econs. div. Ark.-Okla. Livestock Show and Fair, Ft. Smith U., 1958-72. Recipient Distinguished Service award Nat. Assn. Extension Home Economists, 1970. Mem. Am. Home Econs. Assn., Ark. Assn. Extension Home Economists (dist. counselor), Bus. and Profl. Women Pine Bluff and Ft. Smith, Sebastian County 4-H Club Found. (life), Epsilon Sigma Phi, Delta Gamma Sigma. Methodist. Clubs: Sorosis (Magnolia); Soroptimist, Altrusa. Home: 11 Salome St Fort Smith AR 72901

VAN VLIET-HILL, JACQUELINE, broadcasting company executive; b. Sioux City, Iowa, Dec. 10, 1943; d. John Huff and Miriam (Samelson) Van Vliet; B.A., Hastings Coll., 1965; postgrad. U. Iowa, 1968-69. Tchr. pub. schs., Omaha, 1965-66, Houston, 1966-67, Iowa City, 1967-71; with communications dept., chmn. bd. Sta. WMFE-TV, Orlando, Fla., 1979—. Vice pres. Human Services Planning Council, 1973-80; mem. Fla. Environ. Regulation Commn., 1981-86; mem. Orange County Pollution Control Bd., 1979-80. Mem. LWV, Pub. Broadcasting Service, Sierra Club, Nat. Audubon Soc. Republican. Episcopalian. Home: PO Box 18 Windermere FL 32786

VAN VOORHIS, LINDA LYON, poet; b. Rochester, N.Y., May 7, 1902; d. Edmund and Carolyn H. (Talcott) Lyon; student Masters Sch., Dobbs Ferry; m. John Van Voorhis, June 2, 1928; children—Emily (Mrs. Edward Ridgway Harris), June Allis (Mrs. Louis D'Amanda), Eugene. Mem. Women's com. Rochester (N.Y.) Art Gallery, Bausch Meml. Mus. (now Rochester Mus. and Sci. Center), Japan Internat. Christian U. Found., Inc., N.Y.C., Rochester (N.Y.) Civic Music Assn. Bd. dirs. Rochester Sch. for Deaf. Recipient citation for book of poetry St. Lawrence U., 1979. Fellow Rochester Acad. Medicine (hon. life); mem. Poetry Soc. Am., Rochester Poetry Soc., Rochester Jr. League, English Speaking Union, Sigma Alpha Iota. Republican. Episcopalian. Clubs: Century, Chatterbox. Author: June's Verses, 1924, More June's Verses, 1935; June in September, 1973, also numerous poems pub. in popular anthologies, including The Golden Book of Catholic Poetry (by Alfred Noyes), 1946. Home: 714 Rock Beach Rd Rochester NY 14617

VAN WAZER, MARY, educator; b. Chgo., June 11, 1936; d. William Ortman and Anna (Kunz) Ortman; m. Thomas Philip Van Wazer, July 3, 1958; children—Thomas, Mary Kay, Barbara Jean. B.S., Coll. St. Francis, 1958; postgrad. Nat. Coll. Edn., 1984—. Sec., sr. ptnr., sales mgr. Kidder, Peabody Investment Brokers, 1958-62; tchr. St. Zachary Sch., Mt. Prospect, Ill., 1964—. Vol., Talkline, Elk Grove Village, 1979-81; pres. Mt. Prospect Midget Football Assn. Aux., 1969-71; leader Girl Scouts; den mother Cub Scouts; lector of communion trainer Roman Catholic Ch., 1978—, tchr. trainer CCD, 1977, 80—. Mem. Chgo. Archdiocesan Tchr. Assn. (pres.), Call to Action, Nat. Assn. Cath. Sch. Tchrs., Chgo. Council Fgn. Relations, Nat. Assn. Personal Rights, Nat. Assn. Female Execs., Chgo. Assn. Cath. Sch. Tchrs., Coll. St. Francis Alumni Assn. Democrat. Home: 633 S Albert St Mount Prospect IL 60056 Office: PO Box 15 Mount Prospect IL 60056

VAREJCKA, JANET FAYE, educational administrator; b. Columbus, Nebr., June 23, 1944; d. John and Blanche (Aringdale) V. B.A. in Edn., Wayne State Coll., 1966; M.A. in History, U.. Nebr.-Omaha, 1977, 30 hr. Endorsement, 1979. Tchr. Lo-Ma Schs., Logan, Iowa, 1967-80; prin. Bennett County High Sch., Martin, S.C., 1980—. Author Czech Hist. Nebr. Hist. Jour., 1985. Mem. S.D. Assn. Secondary Sch. Prins., (pres. elect 1985—), Sch. Adminstrs. S.D. (exec. bd.), Nat. Assn. Secondary Sch. Prins. (standing com. small secondary schs.), S.D. Future Homemakers Am., Beta Iota (pres. 1985—). Democrat, Methodist. Avocations: reading, sports. Office: Bennett County Sch Dist 3-1 Box 580 Martin SD 57551

VARELLAS, SANDRA MOTTE, lawyer, judge; b. Anderson, S.C., Oct. 17, 1946; d. James E. Jr. and Helen Lucille (Gilliam) Motte; m. James J. Varellas, July 3, 1971; children—James J., David Todd. B.A., Winthrop Coll., 1968; M.A., U. Ky., 1970, J.D., 1975. Bar: Ky. 1975, Fla. 1976. Mem. faculty Midway Coll., Ky., 1970-72; adj. prof. Coll. Law U. Ky., Lexington, 1976-78, instr. dept. bus. adminstrn., 1976-78; mem. firm Varellas, Pratt & Cooley, Lexington, 1975—; judge-exec. Fayette County, Ky., 1980—. Contbr. articles to legal jours. Bd. dirs. Philharmonic Womens Guild, Lexington, 1979-81; grad. Leadership Lexington, 1981. Mem. ABA, Ky. Bar Assn. (treas. young lawyers div. 1978-79), Fla. Bar Assn., Fayette County Bar Assn. (treas. 1977-78, bd. govs. 1978-80), Fayette County Young Democrats (pres. 1977), Ky. Young Democrats (nat. com. 1977-80, named Outstanding Young Dem. Woman. 1977), Ky. Dem. Women's Club (bd. dirs. 1980—), Lexington Profl. Women's Forum (membership chmn. 1984). Presbyterian. Office: Varellas Pratt & Cooley 134 N Limestone St Lexington KY 40507

VARGAS, LENA BESSETTE, nursing administrator; b. Hardwick, Vt., Dec. 26, 1922; d. Leon Alphonse and Dorilla Leah (Boudreau) Bessette; m. Jose Enilio Vargas, Sept. 3, 1949; children—Jose Emilio, Maria del Carmen, J. Ramon, Vicente Andres, Yolanda Teresa. B.S. in Nursing Edn., U. Vt., 1949. Instr. basic nursing Mary Fletcher Hosp., Burlington, Vt., 1947-49; clin. instr. St. Francis Hosp., Evanston, Ill., 1949-50; nurse participant streptomycin therapy research H.M. Biggs Meml. Hosp., Ithaca, N.Y., 1950-51; supr. ancillary personnel Providence Hosp., Washington, 1953-55, asst. dir. nursing, 1965—. Mem. council, del. cooperative congress Greenbelt Coop., Savage, Md., 1983—; bd. dirs. Providence Hosp. Fed. Credit Union, Washington, 1977-80, v.p. bd. dirs., 1983-85. Mem. AAUW (chmn. various coms.), Nat. League for Nursing, Christ Child Soc. Roman Catholic. Avocations: bridge; archery; fencing; horseback riding. Home: 10706 Keswick St Garrett Park MD 20896 Office: Providence Hosp 1150 Varnum St Washington DC 20017

VARKONY, PAMELA DOYLE, advertising company executive; b. Quakertown, Pa., June 9, 1946; d. Clyde Irvin and Gladys Rhea (Doyle) Feist; m. Theodore T. Stepanoff, Nov. 4, 1967 (div. 1978); children—Bridget Anne, Sean Alexander; m. Zsolt Ferenc Varkony, Apr. 17, 1982. Student, Temple U., 1963, Am. Acad. Dramatic Art, 1964, Hillsboro Community Coll., 1977. Dir. co-op. advt. Sta. WFLA AM/FM, Tampa, 1978-79; exec. v.p., Co-op Advt. Bur., Tampa, 1979-80; pres. Media Resources, Inc., Allentown, Pa., 1981—; cons. Radio Advt. Bur., N.Y.C., 1978-81. Contbg. author: How to Profit from Radio Co-op, 1979. Mem. exec. com. Hillsboro County Republican Party, Tampa, 1979; del. to straw vote Rep. Party Conv., Orlando, Fla., 1980. Recipient Disting. Service award Brandon C. of C., 1978, Disting. Service award Am. Cancer Soc., 1979. Mem. Allentown/Lehigh County C. of C. (chmn. pub. relations com. 1984—). Avocations: travel; gardening. Home: Zsoltana Farm RD #1 Hellertown PA 18055 Office: Media Resources Inc 114 N Madison St Allentown PA 18102

VARLEY, AUDREY MARGARET, food company executive; b. Bklyn., June 15, 1935; d. John Andrew Spreitzer and Charlotte Johanna (Schmidt) Spreitzer Poydasheff; m. Maximilian B. Kollwitz, June 25, 1955 (div. Mar. 1970); children—Michael John, Kenneth Robert, Cynthia Audrey; m. Robert Dean Varley, Apr. 18, 1970. Grad. high sch., Elmhurst, N.Y. Comptometer operator A & P Tea Co., Elmhurst, 1954-55, adminstrv. sec., 1955-57; clk. Nabisco Brands, Inc., Riverside, Calif., 1965-79, ops. mgr., Oxnard, Calif., 1979—. Pres., Sandpiper Village, Point Hueneme, Calif., 1983-85. Recipient Suggestion award Nabisco Brands, Inc., 1984. Mem. Bus. and Profl. Women Oxnard (treas. 1981-83, 2d v.p. 1983-84, pres. 1984-85). Avocations: swimming; cooking; fishing; crocheting; reading. Office: Nabisco Brands Inc PO Box 5445 Oxnard CA 93010

VARMECKY, BETTY JO, electronic instrumentation executive; b. Tulsa, Jan. 22, 1927; d. Walter Jonathon and LaVinia (Clear) Eyestone; m. Joseph Dean Varmecky, Jan. 11, 1947; children—Joseph Dean Jr., Diane Louise, David Charles. Student U. Tulsa, 1945, Okla. State U., 1946. Sec. Tri-State Instrument Lab. Inc., Tulsa, 1959-75, pres., 1975—. Mem. Instrument Soc. Am. Democrat. Christian Scientist. Avocations: travel; exercise; reading. Office: Tri-State Instrument Lab Inc 6801 E 15th St Tulsa OK 74112

VARNEDOE, BARBARA SPOHR, marketing executive; b. Chgo., July 1, 1941; d. George B. and Patricia (Malloy) Spohr; m. T. Victor Varnedoe, Oct. 17, 1964; children—Laura Jean, Paul David. Freelance artist, Ft. Lauderdale, Fla., 1970-74; mktg. officer Sun Banks of Broward County, Ft. Lauderdale, 1977-79; dir. mktg. Peat, Marwick, Mitchell & Co., Atlanta, 1980—. Mem. Internat. Assn. Bus. Communicators (exec. a bd.), Women in Communications, Pub. Relations Soc. Am. Episcopalian. Office: Peat Marwick Mitchell & Co 245 Peachtree Center Ave NE Atlanta GA 30043

VARNER, CHARLEEN LAVERNE MCCLANAHAN (MRS. ROBERT B. VARNER), educator, adminstr., nutritionist; b. Alba, Mo., Aug. 28, 1931; d. Roy Calvin and Lela Ruhama (Smith) McClanahan; student Joplin (Mo.) Jr. Coll., 1949-51; B.S. in Edn., Kans. State Coll. Pittsburg, 1953; M.S., U. Ark., 1958; Ph.D., Tex. Woman's U. 1966; postgrad. Mich. State U., summer 1955, U. Mo., summers 1952, 62; m. Robert Bernard Varner, July 4, 1953. Apprentice county home agt. U. Mo., summer 1952; tchr. Ferry Pass. Sch., Escambia County, Fla., 1953-54; tchr. biology, home econs. Joplin Sr. High Sch., 1954-59; instr. home econs. Kans. State Coll., Pittsburg, 1959-63; lectr. foods, nutrition Coll. Household Arts and Scis., Tex. Woman's U., 1963-64, research asst. NASA grant, 1964-66; asso. prof. home econs. Central Mo. State U., Warrensburg, 1966-70, adviser to Colhecon, 1966-70, adviser to Alpha Sigma Alpha, 1967-70, 72, mem. bd. advisers Honors Group, 1967-70; prof., head dept. home econs. Kans. State Tchrs. Coll., Emporia, 1970-73; prof., chmn. dept. home econs. Benedictine Coll., Atchison, Kans., 1973-74; prof., chmn. dept. home econs. Baker U., Baldwin City, Kans., 1974-75; owner, operator Diet-Con Dietary Cons. Enterprises, cons. dietitian, 1973—. Mem. Joplin Little Theater, 1956-60. Mem. NEA, Mo., Kans. state tchrs. assns., AAUW, Am., Mo., Kans. dietetics assns., Am., Mo., Kans. home econs. assns., Mo. Acad. Scis., AAUP, U. Ark. Alumni Assn., Alumni Assn. Kans. State Coll. of Pittsburg, Am. Vocat. Assn., Assn. Edn. Young Children, Sigma Xi, Beta Sigma Phi, Beta Beta Beta, Alpha Sigma Alpha, Delta Kappa Gamma, Kappa Kappa Iota, Phi Upsilon Omicron. Methodist (organist). Home: Main PO Box 1009 Topeka KS 66601

VARNER, CLARETTA JANE, lawyer; b. Oklahoma City, Mar. 25, 1945; d. Daniel George and Claretta (Scott) Sampson; m. Lee Homer Varner, Aug. 27, 1967; children—Daniel Scott, Teri Lynn. B.A., Spelman Coll., 1966; M.A., U. Mich., 1967; M.A., Coll. V.I., 1976, J.D., Wayne State U., 1984. Bar: Mich. 1984, U.S. Ct. Appeals (6th cir.). English instr. Bd. Edn., Detroit, 1967-77, St. Croix Central High Sch., V.I., 1971-73, St. Croix Country Day Sch., 1973-76; lit., communications instr. Lincoln Trail Coll., Robinson, Ill., 1976-79; English instr. Region Five Middle Sch., Detroit, 1979-80; lawyer, counselor Hall & James P.C., Detroit, 1984-85, Office of Juvenile Defender, Detroit, 1985—. Mem. Detroit Bar Assn., Wolverine Bar Assn., Mich. Trial Lawyers Assn. Democrat. Roman Catholic. Office: Juvenile Defender Office 51 W Warren St Detroit MI 48201

VARNER, VICKI LEE, utility company official; b. Alton, Ill., July 21, 1953; d. James Rutherford and Betty Helen (Shaw) V. B.S., U. Ill., 1976. Counselor, Cath. Charities, New Orleans, 1976-77; personnel dir. Edgewater-Uptown Community Mental Health Center, Chgo., 1977-80; group personnel mgr. Burns Internat. Security Services subs. Baker Industries, Chgo., 1980-82, mgr. div. human resources, 1982—. Named Support Staff Person of Year, Baker Industries, 1983. Mem. Women in Mgmt., Am. Soc. Personnel Adminstrn., Am. Soc. Tng. and Devel., AAUW. Home: 5118 Fairview Ave #411 Downers Grove IL 60515 Office: Burns Internat Security Services 1980 University Ln Lisle IL 60532

VASS, JOAN, fashion designer; b. N.Y.C., May 19, 1925; d. Max S. and Rose K.; children by previous marriage—Richard, Sara, Jason. Student Vassar Coll., 1941; B.A., U. Wis., 1946. Pres., Joan Vass Inc., N.Y.C., 1977—. Recipient Prix de Cachet, Prince Machiabelli, 1980; Coty award, 1979; Disting. Woman in Fashion award Smithsonian Instn., 1980. Office: Joan Vass Inc 418 W 25th St New York NY 10001

VASSALLO, HELEN GUILLETTE, management and biology educator, management consulting executive; b. Attleboro, Mass., Nov. 21, 1931; d. Louis Joseph and Rosella Mary (Farrell) Guillette; m. Charles Vassallo, June 9, 1956; children—Susan, Patricia, Charles M., Vincent, Kathleen, Virginia, Elizabeth, Rosemary, Steven, Michael. B.S. summa cum laude, Tufts U., 1953, M.S., Sch. Medicine, 1955; Ph.D., Clark U., 1967; M.B.A., Worcester Poly. Inst., 1982. Asst. prof. biology Clark U., Worcester, Mass., 1967-73; head data evaluation Astra Pharm., Worcester, 1974-77, cons., 1982—, assoc. dir. clin. research, 1977-79, dir. clin. research, 1979-81, dir. sci. info., 1981-82; assoc. prof. mgmt. and biology Worcester Poly. Inst., 1982—; speaker anesthesia socs., 1974—. Sr. co-author: Bupivacaine, 1982; jr. co-author: Local Anesthetics: Mechanisms of Action, 1976; contbr. articles in field to publs. Instl. rev. bd. St. Vincent Hosp., Worcester; mem. Diocesan Sch. Bd., 1967-74, Edn. Bd., 1974-76; trainer leaders Girl Scouts U.S.A.; bd. dirs. Guild of Our Lady of Providence, St. Vincent Hosp.; sorority advisor to women engring. students. Appearances on Good Morning America, 1984, Today Show, 1985. Mem. Soc. Mfg. Engrs., Am. Inst. Indsl. Engrs. (local bd. dirs.), Am. Soc. Anesthesiology, Am. Soc. Regional Anesthesia, Am. Med. Writers Assn., Am. Bus. Women's Assn. (Nat. Woman of Yr. 1981), Phi Beta Kappa, Phi Sigma Sigma. Roman Catholic. Avocations: sewing; knitting; karate; scuba diving. Office: Management Dept Worcester Polytechnic Inst 100 Institute Rd Worcester MA 01609

VASSALLO, WANDA JO, former educational communications administrator, educator, clergywoman; b. Dallas, Aug. 9, 1930; d. Lawrence Odom and Mary Irene (Hearon) Ballard; m. Julius Vassallo, Dec. 27, 1954; children—Richard Dale, Laurie Lynn. B.A., Baylor U., 1953; M.Ed., East Tex. State U., 1968, postgrad. Ordained Christian minister, 1985. Tchr., Sour Lake Ind. Schs. (Tex.), 1953-54, Liberty Ind. Schs. (Tex.), 1954-57, 60-61; coordinator-ITV Mesquite Ind. Schs. (Tex.), 1965-69; dir. communications Dallas Ind. Schs., 1969-85; leader workshops; lectr. in field. Contbr. articles to profl. jours. Deaconess, Lighthouse Christian Ctr., Dallas, 1982-84, dir. communications, 1980-84, dir. Christian Art Players, 1982-84, pianist, 1980-84; dir. Mesquite Teen Theatre, 1963-64; life mem. Samuell High Sch. PTA, 1981. Mem. Dallas Sch. Adminstrs. Assn., Nat. Sch. Pub. Relations Assn. Republican. Home: 8940 Shorelark Dr Dallas TX 75217

VASSAR, TINA MARRIE, nurse; b. Port Norfolk, Va., Oct. 29, 1956; d. John Dixie and Hazell (Barr) V. B.S. in Nursing, Radford U., 1979; M.S. in Nursing, U. Va., 1983. Staff nurse U. Va. Hosp., Charlottesville, 1979-80, head nurse, 1980-83; cardiothoracic surgery clin. nurse specialist N.C. Meml. Hosp., Chapel Hill, 1983—; adj. instr. U. N.C. Sch. Nursing, Chapel Hill, 1986—. Bd. dirs. ARC, Chapel Hill. Mem. Am. Nurses Assn. (bd. dirs., research chmn. Dist. II 1984—), Am. Assn. Critical Care Nurses (bd. dirs., workshop chmn. Triangle chpt. 1984-85, chpt. treas.-elect 1985-86, treas. 1986-87), Alpha Delta Pi. Republican. Baptist. Avocations: swimming; music. Office: NC Meml Hosp Manning Dr Chapel Hill NC 27514

VATANDOOST, NOSSI MALEK, art school administrator; b. Teheran, Iran, May 22, 1935; d. Abdullah Goodar and Mahtaban (Goodar) Malek; B.A., Western Ky. U., 1970; m. Ira Vatandoost, May 31, 1964; children—Debbie, Cyrus. Art tchr. Met.-Davidson County Sch. System, Nashville, 1970-71; dir., owner Nossi Sch. Art, Madison, Tenn., 1973—; treas. Malek & Assos. Inc., 1976; dir. EXCEL Edn. Corp., 1980—; vis. lectr., cons. EXCEL Bus. Inst., 1980—. Mem. Hendersonville Art Council, Hendersonville Art Guild (com. chmn.). Club: Soroptimists (Upper Cumberland Valley, Tenn.). Home: 105 Country Club Dr Hendersonville TN 37075 Office: 620 Gallatin Rd S Madison TN 37115

VATHIS, ALMA CHRISTINE, educator, librarian; b. Phila., Oct. 24, 1948; d. James and Joyce Crouthamel (Beer) V. B.S. in Edn., Shippensburg State U., 1970; M.A. in Librarianship, U. Denver, 1972; cert. in advanced studies Drexel U., 1982. Tchr., librarian Bensalem Sch. Dist. (Pa.), 1970-71, 72—, K-12 library coordinator, 1984—. Editor Learning and Media Jour., 1982—; contbr. articles to profl. jours. Mem. Bucks County Sch. Librarians Assn. (v.p. 1981-82), Pa. Sch. Librarians Assn. (editor 1982—), Am. Assn. Sch. Librarians, ALA, Bensalem Twp. Edn. Assn. (treas. 1981, 82), NEA, Pa. State Edn. Assn. Club: Liberty Divers (pres. 1976) (Levittown, Pa.). Home: 1455 Neshaminy Valley Dr Bensalem PA 19020 Office: C Snyder Middle Sch 3330 Hulmesville Rd Bensalem PA 19020

VAUGHAN, BRENDA BEATRICE, interior designer; b. Honey Grove, Tex., Nov. 19, 1953; d. Dillard and Lydia L. (Boles) Sisco; m. George Edwin Vaughan, Aug. 25, 1975. B.S., East Tex. State U., 1975. Interior designer Pope & Turner Co., Tyler, Tex., 1976-77; ptnr. Sabine River Studios, Hawkins, Tex., 1977-78, interior designer Draperies and Interiors, Longview, Tex., 1978-79, Metroplex Furnishings Co., Dallas, 1979-81; dir. interior design Talmadge Tinsley Interiors, Dallas, 1981-82; pres. Haven Interior Designs, Inc., Dallas, 1982—. Mem. Am. Soc. Interior Designers, Dallas C. of C. Home: 3865 Wemdon St Dallas TX 75220

VAUGHAN, MARILOU TAYLOR, magazine editor; b. Detroit; d. Robert Adams and Dorothea (Trauffer) Taylor; B.A., Eastern Mich. U., 1958; postgrad. Stanford U., 1959; m. David Rodman Vaughan, Jan. 2, 1960. Asst. editor Smithsonian mag., Washington, 1974-76; assoc. editor New West mag., Beverly Hills, Calif., 1976-77, Archtl. Digest, Los Angeles, 1977-79; editor Bon Appetit mag., Los Angeles, 1979-85; sr. editor Los Angeles Times Mag., 1985—. Mem. Am. Assn. Mag. Editors. Office: Times Mirror Sq Los Angeles CA 90053

VAUGHAN, SALLY SEDLAK, farm owner; b. Springfield, Ill., Jan. 25, 1942; d. Frank A. and Lorraine (Watts) Sedlak. A.A., Gulf Park Coll., 1961; B.A., MacMurray Coll., 1965; M.A., Sangamon State U., 1973. Tchr. remedial reading and English, Pana Jr. High Sch., Ill., 1966-67, Springfield High Sch., 1967-70; coordinator community service ctr. Lincoln Land Community Coll., 1974-77; tng. officer Ill. Dept. Aging, Springfield, 1977-85; farm owner, Elkhart, Ill. 1981, Springfield, 1985—; chmn. health and human services Region V Tng. and Edn. Consortium, 1979. Contbr. to Gerontology in Higher Education, 1979. Chmn. Know Your Springfield Com., 1977-78, 79-80; mem. Vols. in Probation, Sangamon County Juvenile Ct. Services, 1977-79; mem. Springfield Mental Health Fund Raising Com., 1976; mem. steering com. to establish Epilepsy Assn., 1975-76; mem. pres.'s adv. com. Lincoln Land Community Coll., 1975-77, mem. Capitol Bicentennial Commn. Speakers Bur., 1975-76; spl. gifts chmn. Sangamon County Heart Fund Drive, 1975; corr. sec. Sangamon County Young Republicans, 1968-70, 73-74, rec. sec. 1968-69; treas. Sangamon County Republican Women's Club, 1975-77. Recipient Good Citizenship award SAR, 1959, cert. of appreciation Springfield Noonday Lions Club, Sangamon County Juvenile Ct. Services. Mem. Am. Soc. for Tng. and Devel., DAR (chaplain 1968-70, 5th div. Jr. membership com. regional rep., 1968-70), AAUW, Springfield Art Assn., Jr. League Springfield (placement com. chmn. for provisionals 1980-81, community research chmn. 1979-80, bd. dirs. 1979-80, mgmt. by objective trainer 1978-79), Children of Am. Revolution (Ill. pres. 1959-60, numerous state and local offices), Sangamon State U. Alumni Assn., Friends of Old State Capitol, Sangamon County Farm Bur., Ill. Farmers Union, Animal Protective League, St. John's Hosp. Guild. Republican. Methodist. Lodge: Zonta (chmn. pub. relations com. 1977-79). Office: 1422 W Ash St Springfield IL 62704

VAUGHAN, SANDRA MARIA ADAIR, lawyer, securities trader; b. Trenton, N.J., Sept. 26, 1948; d. Franklin McKinley and Emma (Smith) Crews; m. Stephen Frederick Vaughan, Aug. 12, 1978; children—Emma Fredericka Adair, Stephen. B.A., Howard U., 1972; J.D., Georgetown U., 1977. Bar: D.C. 1978; registered rep. Nat. Assn. Securities Dealers 1983. Researcher, HEW and Commn. for Protection of Human Subjects, Bethesda, Md., 1976; asst. dir. admissions Georgetown U. Law Ctr., Washington, 1974-77; atty. FTC, Washington, 1977-79; instr. Va. State U., Ettrick, 1980; registered rep. Anderson & Strudwick, Petersburg, Va., 1983—; mem. White House Task Force on Minorities and Communications, 1972-79; cons. Beaux 20, Debutantes, Petersburg, 1980—, Career Day, Va. State U., 1982—. Mem. Women's Com. to Support Symphony, Petersburg, 1983—, Petersburg Sch. Bd., 1983—. Recipient Meritorious Service award FTC, 1978. Mem. ABA, Nat. Conf. Black Lawyers, AAUW (chmn. internat. affairs 1983—), Va. Sch. Bd. Assn., Links, Inc., Delta Sigma Theta. Democrat. Baptist. Clubs: Beaux 20 Wives, Jack & Jill, Inc. Home: 2017 Dodson Rd Petersburg VA 23805 Office: Anderson & Strudwick 19 Bollingbrook St Petersburg VA 23803

VAUGHN, CAROLYN SUE, social worker; b. Centralia, Ill., Apr. 12, 1943; d. Robert Vaughn and Frances Vaughn Bradford; B.A., So. Ill. U., 1965; M.S., Case Western Res. U., 1974. Social worker Cuyahoga County Welfare Dept., Cleve., 1965-67; counseling coordinator Neighborhood Youth Corps, City of Cleve., 1967-73; caseworker Children's Services, Cleve., 1974-76; case mgr., vocat. rehab. specialist Panta Rhei Inc., Cleve., 1976-77; lectr. Cuyahoga Community Coll., 1974—; mental health planner Cuyahoga County Community Mental Health and Retardation Bd., Cleve., 1980—; pres. Vaughn & Assocs. Cons. Mem. Hough Community Council, 1977—; trustee Hough Area Devel. Corp. Ill. State scholar, 1961; NIMH grantee, 1972-74. Mem. LWV (dir. 1979—, 2d v.p. 1981-83), Acad. Cert. Social Workers, Child Welfare Assn., Nat. Assn. Social Workers, Alpha Kappa Alpha. Baptist. Home: 949 Helmsdale Cleveland Heights OH 44112 Office: 2900 Community College Ave Cleveland OH 44115

VAUGHN, LESLEY MILLER MEHRAN, lawyer; b. Eng., Aug. 24, 1944; came to U.S., 1952; d. Victor Raymond and Daphne T. Miller; m. G. Mehran, June 29, 1966 (div. 1979); children—Diana, Mark, Rawley, Peter; m. 2d, John Spencer Vaughn, Aug. 6, 1983. Cert., U. Paris, 1965, U. Geneva, 1966; B.A., U. Calif.-Berkeley, 1967; J.D., Loyola U., Los Angeles, 1982. Bar: Calif. 1982. Assoc. Finley, Kumble, Wagner, Heiner, Underberg, Manley & Casey, Beverly Hills, Calif., 1982-83, Smith & Holland, Los Angeles, 1983—. Articles editor Loyola of Los Angeles Law Rev., Internat. Law Jours.; contbr. articles to legal jours. Recipient Jessup honors in internat. law Loyola U., Los Angeles. Mem. ABA, Calif. Bar Assn., Phi Alpha Delta. Republican. Presbyterian. Office: Smith & Holland 333 S Grand Ave Los Angeles CA 90071

VAUGHN, MARY, health care facilities exec.; b. Trafford, Ala., Apr. 20, 1930; d. Grover Webster and Vivian Lenora (Dorman) V.; student Birmingham Bus.

Coll., 1952, Howard Coll., 1959, U. Ala., 1960, 62, Balboa Intermediate Care Facility, San Diego, 1969-76; certificate in therapeutic activities tng. Grossmont Adult Sch., 1975; m. James T. Lovvorn, Mar. 1952 (div. 1959). Owner, pres., treas. Balboa Manor Inc. and Balboa lManor Health Facility, San Diego, 1969-79. Charter pres. Quota Club of Birmingham (Ala.), 1967-68; lt. gov. 8th dist. Quota Internat., 1968-69; supr. adv. com. to Jim Bates, 4th Dist. Supr. San Diego County, 1973—; mem. San Diego County Com. on the Handicapped, 1979—; mem. support com. Community Video Center, pub. access TV, 1979—. Recipient Safety award Indsl. Indemnity, 1973, 75, certificate of appreciation Jim Bates, 1975; notary pub., cert. nursing home adminstr., Calif. Mem. Am. Health Care Assn., Am. Coll. Nursing Home Adminstrs., Am., Calif. nursing home assns., Com. of 100 of San Diego Klee Wyk Soc., San Diego Opera, Bus. and Profl. Women's Club (pres. Birmingham chpt. 1967-69), San Diego Mus. Natural History, San Diego Mus. of Man, Nat. Notary Assn. Republican. Methodist. Author: Exploring Mental Therapy. Home: 2804 C St San Diego CA 92102

VAUGHN, MARY EDITH, land developer; b. Macon, Ga., Nov. 21, 1955; d. Albe Lee and Edith Laura (Dungan) V. Student Middle Ga. Jr. Coll., 1973-75; B.S. in Mcpl. Recreation, Ga. Coll., 1978. Cert. recreation supr., Ga. Asst. office mgr. Vaughn Lumber Co., Forsyth, Ga., 1978—; co-owner Triple Crown Devel. and Montpelier Devel., 1982—. Mem. Ga. Recreation and Park Soc., Inc. Democrat. Baptist. Avocations: Photography; needlecrafts; owning and showing quarter horses; collecting depression glass. Home: 28 Hickory Pl PO Box 735 Forsyth GA 31029 Office: Vaughn Lumber Co 96 Berner Ave PO Box 31 Forsyth GA 31029

VAUGHN, NOEL WYANDT, lawyer; b. Chgo., Dec. 15, 1937; d. Owen Heaton and Harriet Christy (Smith) Wyandt; m. David Victor Koch, July 18, 1959 (div.); 1 child, John David; m. Charles George Vaughn, July 9, 1971. B.A., DePauw U., 1959; M.A., So. Ill. U., 1963; J.D., U. Dayton, 1979. Bar: Ohio 1979, U.S. Dist. Ct. (so. dist.) Ohio 1979. Lectr. Wright State U., Dayton, 1965-67; communications specialist Charles F. Kettering Found., Dayton, 1968-71; tchr. English, Miami Valley Sch., Dayton, 1971-76; clk. to judge Dayton Mcpl. Ct., 1978-79; coordinator Montgomery County Fair Housing Ctr., Dayton, 1979-81; atty. Henley Vaughn Becker & Wald, Dayton, 1981—. Chmn. Dayton Playhouse, Inc., 1981—; pres. Freedom of Choice Miami Valley, Dayton, 1980-83; bd. dirs. ACLU, Dayton, 1982—; com. mem. Battered Woman Project-YWCA, Dayton, 1983-84; pres. Legal Aid Soc. Dayton, 1983-84; chmn. Artemis House, Inc., 1985—; bd. dirs. Miami Valley Arts Council, 1985—. Recipient Order of Barristers award U. Dayton, 1979. Mem. ABA, Dayton Bar Assn. (chmn. delivery legal services com. 1983-84). Democrat. Home: 3700 Wales Dr Dayton OH 45405 Office: Henley Vaughn Becker & Wald 200 Talbott Tower Dayton OH 45402

VAUGHN, (OLIVE) RUTH, author, playwright; b. Wellington, Tex., Aug. 31, 1935; d. S.L. and Nora Norris (Knowles) Wood; B.A., M.A., U. Kans.; Ph.D., Am. U.; children—Billy, Ron. Author 40 books, including: Fun for Christian Youth, 1960, Dreams Can Come True, 1964, Portrait in a Nursery, 1965, What I Will Tell My Children About God, 1966, Skits that Win, 1967, No Matter the Weather, 1968, Hey! Have You Heard?, 1969, Playlets and Skits, 1970, Baby's Album, 1973, Even When I Cry, 1975, Proclaiming Christ in the Caribbean, 1976, More Skits that Win, 1977, Celebrate with Words, 1979, What's a Mother to Say?, 1980, Write to Discover Yourself, 1980, To Be a Girl—To Be a Woman, 1982, My God! My God!, 1982; author 46 plays, including: The Living Last Supper, The Man on the Center Cross, Behold a New World!, Lions Can't Eat Truth, Morning Comes at Sunrise, Catherine Marshall's Christy, Eugenia Price's The Beloved Invader; musical stageplays include: God's Dream, To Touch a Rainbow, Once Upon a Hill: The Coward and the Cut-Throat, Please Be King!, Shadow of the Almighty; prof. drama/creative writing Bethany Nazarene Coll., 1968-76; pvt. practice counseling; resident playwright Denver First Nazarene Ch., 1976-83; pres. Ruth Vaughn Incorporated, 1983—; author numerous short stories and articles. Mem. Women in Communication Internat., Internat. Platform Assn., Pi Lambda Theta, Theta Sigma Phi. Republican. Nazarene. Home: 3801 N Rockwell #222 Bethany OK 73008

VAUGHN, RUBY WENTWORTH, artist, real estate executive; b. Ringwood, Okla., Dec. 18, 1909; d. John Logan and Roberta L. (Courtney) Wentworth; student Ind. U., U. Baffalo, Allegheny Sch. Natural History; m. Thomas H. Vaughn, Sept. 13, 1930; children—Jolan Adele, Vicki Lee, Trudy Gail. Artist, comml. craft designer, 1960—; pres. Splty. Designs Studio, Waretown, N.J., 1970—, Vaughn Realty Corp., Chgo., 1971-82; flower arranger, creator artistic and craft designs, 1958—. Mem. women's adv. council U. Notre Dame, 1968—. Recipient numerous awards in art, craft and flower shows. Mem. Soc. Craft Designers, Hackensack (N.J.) Art Club, Bergen Artists Guild, Ridgefield (N.J.) Art Club, Pine Shore Art Assn. (N.J.), Boynton Beach Art Assn. (Fla.), DAR. Mem. Christian Ch. (Disciples of Christ). Address: 13 Jolly Roger Way Waretown NJ 08758

VAUGHNS, BERTHA, government official, community relations specialist; b. Cloutierville, La., June 7, 1944; d. Iris Jenkins and Beatrice (Solitaire) Jones; m. Henry C. Jones, Apr. 26, 1966 (div.); children—Yolanda Yvette, Lynette Carroll; m. Horace Vaughns, Sept. 4, 1981. B.S., So. U., 1966; M.S., Va. Commonwealth U., 1972. Recreation supr. City of Richmond (Va.) 1966-70; community relations specialist City of Houston, 1973-82; occupational therapist supr. Dept. Mental Health and Hygiene, Petersburg, Va., 1972-73; revenue officer IRS, Houston, 1982—; chmn. Ann. Recreation Conf., Houston, 1982; chmn. workshops Va. Occupational Therapy Soc., Petersburg, 1972-73. Active Girl Scouts U.S.A., Houston, 1977-80; founder Houston Area Parks and Recreation Booster Club, 1980-82; pres. Woodglen Civic Assn., Houston, 1980-82. Recipient cert. of appreciation, City of Houston, 1980; Dept. Mental Health and Mental Retardation fellow, 1970-72. Mem. Nat. Recreation and Park Soc., Tex. Recreation and Park Soc. (pub. relations officer 1980-81, booster club chmn. 1980-82), Va. Recreation and Park Soc., Delta Sigma Theta. Democrat. Baptist. Home: 9815 Denning Dr Houston TX 77078 Office: IRS 3223 Briarpark St Houston TX 77042

VAUGHT, JANET MAUREEN BURGER, city official; b. Indpls., Jan. 23, 1952; d. Clifford Robert and Opal June (McKinnon) Burger; m. Charles H. Vaught, Jr., Sept. 15, 1977; children—Patricia Lynn, Jennifer Leigh. B.S. in Edn., So. Ill. U., 1974, M.S. in Edn., 1984. Registered mcpl. clk.; cert. mcpl. clk. Research asst. So. Ill. U., Carbondale, 1974, sec., 1974-75, researcher, 1976; sec. City of Carbondale, 1976-77, dep. city clk., 1977-79, city clk., 1979—. Ill. tchr. edn. scholar State of Ill., 1970. Mem. Internat. Inst. Mcpl. Clks., Nat. Bus. Edn. Assn. (award of merit 1974), Ill. Bus. Edn. Assn. (scholar 1973), So. Ill. Bus. Edn. Assn., Mcpl. Clks. Ill. (pres. 1987), Delta Pi Epsilon, Pi Omega Pi, Pi Lambda Theta, Kappa Delta Pi. Methodist. Avocations: traveling; reading; being with children. Home: 620 Glenview Dr Carbondale IL 62901 Office: City of Carbondale PO Box 2047 Carbondale IL 62902-2047

VAUTIER, ALICE FORSHA, nurse, administrator; b. Camden, N.J., Mar. 20, 1940; d. George Oilver and Elna Margaret (Nordberg) Forsha; m. Robert Arthur Vautier, Oct. 5, 1968; children—Robert Arthur, Charlene Elisabeth. Diploma in Nursing Cooper Hosp., Camden, N.J., 1961; B.S. in Nursing, U. Pa., Phila., 1981: M.S. in Nursing, Villanova U., Pa., 1983; postgrad. Tchrs. Coll., Columbia U. Nursing educator St. Christopher's Hosp. for Children, Phila., 1963-75, coordinator nursing edn., 1975-77, asst. v.p. nursing, 1977-81; assoc. dir. nursing Mercy Cath. Med Ctr., Phila., 1983-84; sr. nursing cons. O'Leary and Assocs., Inc., Wayne, Pa., 1983-85; v.p. patient services Cabell Huntington Med. Ctr., Huntington, W.Va., 1985—; coordinator CPR, Camden County Heart Assn., N.J., 1973-74. HEW grantee, 1977-81. Mem. Nat. League Nursing, Phi Kappa Phi, Sigma Theta Tau. Episcopalian. Home: RD 2 Box 99A Ona WV 25545 Office: Cabell Huntington Med Ctr 1300 Hal Greer Blvd Huntington WV

VEA, M. VIRGINIA YULO, educator; b. Aparni, Cagayan, Philippines, July 21, 1936; d. Fausto M. and Ursula (Alcaraz) Yulo; m. Pepito D.W. Vea, Dec. 2, 1965; children—M. Elaine Y., M. Elizabeth Y., Rosemarie Virginia. B.A., Nat. U.-Philippines, 1954, B.A. in Edn., 1955; M.A., U. Philippines, 1960; M.A. in Adult Edn., Ball State U., 1982. Instr. Nat. Heroes Coll., Manila, Philippines, 1954-55; chief librarian, instr. Roxas Meml. Colls., Manila, 1955-56; prof. Nat. U., Manila, 1957-67; press writer Citizens for Yulo for Pres., Manila, 1957-58, coordinator, 1957-58; instr. and advisor Capitol City Coll., Quezon City, Philippines, 1958-60; exec. asst. Nat. U. Alumni Assn., 1960-63; tech. asst. Office of Pres., Malacanang Palace, Manila, 1963-64; substitute tchr. Indpls. pub. schs., 1975-79; edn. specialist U.S. Army Adminstrn. Ctr., Ft. Benjamin Harrison, Indpls., 1979-80, U.S. Army Inf. Sch. and Ctr., Columbus, Ga., 1981-82, U.S. Army Engr. Sch. and Ctr., Ft. Belvoir, Alexandria, Va., 1983; edn. specialist/internal cons. U.S. Coast Guard Res. Tng. Ctr., Yorktown, Va., 1983—. Assoc. editor The Nationalist, 1953-54; contbr. articles to profl. jours. Coordinator Citizens for Yulo for President, Manila, 1957-58, press writer, 1957-58; campaign mgr. Nat. U. Faculty Club, 1960-61. Voted Most Outstanding Student, Nat. U. Faculty Bd. Trustees, 1954. Mem. Nat. Assn. Female Execs., Nat. Soc. for Performance and Instruction, Philippine Am. Nat. Assn. Democrat. Roman Catholic. Office: US Coast Guard Res Tng Center Yorktown VA 23690

VEATCH, ROBERTA ANN, marketing executive, perfume company executive; b. Holdredge, Nebr., Oct. 10, 1955; d. Robert Wesley and Mildred Lillian (Pavelka) Hull; m. Thomas Dale Veatch, May 23, 1973; 1 child, Kyna Harmony. Student Ariz. State U., Scientia Coll. Make up artist, Houston, 1975-78; cosmetic trainer Dynige Internat., Phoenix, 1978-80; nat. tng. dir. Chem. Assocs., Phoenix, 1980-81; nat. cosmetic dir. d'Saison Cre Creative Color, Houston, 1981-82; exec. v.p., 1982-84; pres. Entourage Perfumery, Houston, 1984—. Author: Mirror Image, 1981. Recipient top sales awards Home Care Internat., 1982, Dynique Internat., 1979. Mem. Nat. Female Execs., Delta Delta Delta. Avocations: hot air ballooning; painting; writing. Home: 1918 E Myrna Ln Tempe AZ 85284 Office: Entourage Internat Inc PO Box 19934 Houston TX 77024

VEAZIE, EVA L(UCILLE), insurance agency owner; b. Ft. Wayne, Ind., Dec. 15, 1941; d. Daniel Roy McKinney and Versa L. (Gibson) Cook; m. Richard R. Niehus, Sept. 5, 1959 (div. 1970); children—Douglas R., Janette Marie; m. 2d Donald E. Veazie, May 26, 1971. Student Marylhurst Coll. Various positions Oreg. Mut. Ins. Co., McMinnville, 1959-71; account exec. Alexander & Alexander, Portland, Oreg., 1971-73; owner Eva Veazie Ins., Portland, 1973—. Bd. dirs. Boys' Club of Portland, 1983-84; com. chmn. City Club of Portland, 1980-82; active polit. campaigns. Mem. Ind. Inst. Agts. Oreg. (bd. 1980-83), Ind. Ins. Agts. Portland (pres. 1983-84), Ins. Women of Portland (pres. 1979, Woman of Yr. 1983). Republican. Methodist. Home: 3825 SW 52nd Pl Portland OR 97221 Office: Eva Veazie Ins 6406 SW Beaverton Hillsdale Hwy Portland OR 97221

VECCHIOTTI, MARIA LOUISE, lawyer; b. Newark, June 3, 1955; d. Frank John and Inez Joan (Colarusso) V. B.A. summa cum laude in Econs., Fordham U., 1977; J.D., 1980. Bar: N.J. 1980, U.S. Dist. Ct. N.J. 1980. Assoc. Lum, Hoens, Abeles, Conant & Danzis and predecessor firm, Newark, 1980—. Editor Fordham Urban Law Jour., 1979-80. Mem. Essex County Bar Assn., N.J. Bar Assn., Phi Beta Kappa, Alpha Mu Gamma. Republican. Roman Catholic. Home: 275 W 96th St Apt 9-O New York NY 10025 Office: Lum Hoens Abeles Conant & Danzis 550 Broad St Newark NJ 07002

VEDDER, MARION GRIFFIN, elementary sch. prin.; b. Oswego, N.Y., June 11, 1914; d. James John and Helen Frances (LaGoe) Griffin; B.S. in Edn., Oswego State Tchrs. Coll., 1938; M.A., N.Y. U., 1945; m. Ross John Vedder, Dec. 9, 1949. Spl. edn. tchr. schs. in N.Y. State, 1936-54; prin. schs. in North Babylon, N.Y., 1954—, prin. Deer Park Ave. Elementary Sch., 1959—; cons. in field. Chmn. N. Babylon Sch. Dist. Bicentennial, 1975-76. Recipient Am. Edn. award, Babylon, 1964; Disting. Alumnus award SUNY, Oswego; 1982. Mem. Suffolk County, N. Babylon adminstrs. assns., PTA (hon. life), Catholic Daus. Am. Democrat. Club: Arethusa. Author tchrs. guides, articles. Home: 108 Ketewamoke Ave Babylon NY 11702 Office: 794 Deer Park Ave North Babylon NY 11703

VELA, CELIA TOMACITA, federal agent; b. Bremerton, Wash., Mar. 29, 1953; d. Jesse and Maria Juana (Lujan) Ramirez; m. Pedro Vela, Jr., Oct. 6, 1979 (dec. 1983). B.S. in Criminal Justice, San Diego, 1975, postgrad., 1976-78. Cert. explosive instr. Fed. agt. Alcohol, Tobacco & Firearms, Treasury Dept., Phoenix, 1978-82, San Diego, 1982—, vault custodian, 1982—, destruction officer, 1982—, recruiter, 1984—, explosive instr., 1986—, arson investigator, 1985—. Author recruitment manual: How to Fill Out 171, 1985. Local Bd. Selective Service System, Chula Vista, Calif., 1985—. Served with USAR, 1976-78. Recipient Outstanding Performance award Treasury Dept., 1981. Mem. Nat. Assn. Arson Investigators, Nat. Assn. Treasury Agts., Internat. Assn. Bomb Technicians and Investigators, Nat. Assn. Female Execs. Roman Catholic. Club: St. Mary's Women Choir (National City). Avocations: violin; running; swimming; bicycling. Office: Alcohol Tobacco and Firearms 880 Front St Room 6N16 San Diego CA 92188

VELAQUEZ, NYDIA M., political science educator; b.Yabucoa, P.R., Mar. 28, 1953; d. Benito and Carmen (Luisa) Velaquez. B.A. in Polit. Sci., U. P.R., 1974; M.A., NYU, 1976. Dir. social sci. dept. U. P.R., 1977-79, instr., 1976-81; instr. Hunter Coll., CUNY, 1981-83; spl. asst. Congressman Ed Towns, N.Y., 1983-84; mem. City Council, City of N.Y., 1984-85; owner Quick Stop Emporium, Bklyn., 1985—; nat. dir. migration div. Dept. Labor and Human Resources, Commonwealth of P.R.; columnist El Diario/La Prensa, 1984-85. Bd. dirs. Caribbean Action Lobby, Washington, 1983, Boringuen Sr. Citizen Ctr., Bklyn., 1984-86; mem. community adv. bd. Woodhull Hosp., Bklyn., 1984-86. Named Outstanding Citizen of Yabucoa, P.R., 1983; U. P.R. scholar, 1974-76. Mem. Nat. Assn. Female Execs., Bklyn. Women's Polit. Caucus, Caribbean Action Lobby (N.Y. chpt.), Nat. Conf. P.R. Women. Democrat. Roman Catholic. Avocations: jogging; tennis; dance; reading. Home: 676 Grand St #6 Brooklyn NY 11211

VELARDE, MARGARITA BERNARDO, physician; b. Manila, Feb. 22, 1936; came to U.S., 1966; m. Augusto B. Velarde, June 1, 1974; 1 dau., Cecilia; 1 stepdau., Aura. M.D., Far Eastern U., Manila, 1963. Pediatric staff St. Anne's Hosp., Manila, 1964-66; intern Queen of Angels Hosp., Los Angeles, 1967-68; assoc. Calif. Lutheran Hosp., Los Angeles, 1969, U. So. Calif. Med. Ctr. and Los Angeles County Hosp., 1971-72; pediatrics staff Cedars of Lebanon Hosp., Los Angeles, 1972-73; child psychiatry dept. UCLA Hosp. and San Fernado Child Guidance Clinic, 1973-74; practice medicine, specializing in pediatrics, Los Angeles, 1974, Florence Western Med. Group, Los Angeles, 1974-75, Los Angeles County Dept. Health Services, 1975; physician specialist Paramount Health Ctr., Los Angeles, 1975-76; dep. health officer Compton Health Dist., 1977-79, acting dist. health officer, 1979-80, dist. health officer, 1980. Contbr. article to profl. jour. Mem Am. Pub. Health Assn., So. Calif. Pub. Health Assn., Philippine Med. Soc. So. Calif., Philippine Am. Soc. West Orange County. Roman Catholic. Home: 17392 Wildrose Ln Huntington Beach CA 92649 Office: 300 E Rosencrans Ave Los Angeles CA 90220

VELAZQUEZ, SUSAN NOGRADY, lawyer, development executive, real estate investor; b. Lancaster, Calif., Feb. 23, 1953; d. Leslie John Nogrady and Martha (Sipos) Feher; m. David Velazquez, Feb. 14, 1985; 1 child, Nicole Suzanne. A.A., Los Angeles Valley Coll., 1974; B.A., Pepperdine U., 1976; J.D., Western State U., 1982; M.A. (hon.) U. Rome, 1976. Exec. asst. Congressman R.K. Dornan, Washington, 1976-77; dir. adv. councils Republican Nat. Com., Washington, 1977-78; campaign mgr. Goedeke for Congress, Santa Ana, Calif., 1978; v.p. Meridian Land, Malibu, Calif., 1980-82, pres. Meridian Land Devel., Inc., 1982—; pres. Lenders Processing Services, Inc.; sr. ptnr. Golden Earth Investment Co., Granada Hills, Calif.; ptnr. Golden Vale Properties, Malibu; legal cons. Network & Telephone Systems, Inc., Laguna Niguel, Calif., 1983—. Fundraiser Com. to Reelect Pres. Ford, Los Angeles, 1976, Citizens for Republic, Santa Monica, Calif., 1978, Reagan for Pres., Santa Monica 1980. Recipient Am. Jurisprudence award West Pub. Co., 1981. Roman Catholic. Home: 21771 Regal Way Lake Forest CA 92630

VELEZ, DOLORES, management consultant; b. Jacksonville, Fla., Mar. 26, 1926; d. Fred Gomez and Deonecia (Herrera) V.; m. David Seeley Selden (div. 1953); 1 dau., Denise Dolores; m. James Conklin, (dec. 1964); 1 dau., Lisa Velez. Student N.Y. Tutoring Sch., N.Y.C. Adminstrv. asst. Denimex Devel. Corp., Ossining, N.Y., 1962-64; mgmt. asst. Lescarboura Advt., Inc., Ossining, 1964-65; engring. planner McDonnell Douglas Aircraft, Lakewood, Calif., 1965-76; chmn., chief exec. officer Planning Systems Internat., Inc., Boston, 1976-83, Diversifed Designs Inc., Boston, 1983—; mem. adv. bd. George Washington U., 1982—, lectr., 1982—; cons. fed. contracting, Boston and Washington, 1981—. Mem. Nat. Bus. League, Nat. Contract Mgmt. Assn., Armed Forces Communications and Electronics Assn. Roman Catholic. Office: Diversified Designs Inc 2127 Newport Pl Washington DC 20037

VELLEMAN, RUTH ANN, librarian; b. N.Y.C., Apr. 12, 1921; d. Joseph C. and Celia (Applebaum) Saltman; m. Moritz Velleman, June 11, 1944; children—Paul Flor, J. David, Daniel Jon. B.A., Smith Coll., 1942; M.S., C.W. Post Coll., 1965. Dir. library and info. services Human Resources Ctr. and Sch., Albertson, N.Y., 1963—; adj. prof. Palmer Grad. Library Sch., C.W. Post Coll., 1977—; cons. Harold Russell Assocs., 1981; nationwide lectr., leader workshops, 1974—; mem. outreach com. Nassau Library System. Author: Serving Physically Disabled People, 1979 (Ralph R. Shaw award, 1981); mem. editorial bd. Rehab. Lit. mag.; contbr. articles to profl. jours. Mem. ALA, Med. Library Assn., N.Y. Library Assn. (award for service to disabled 1983), Beta Phi Mu. Home: 15 Cliffway Port Washington NY 11050 Office: Human Resources Ctr and Sch Albertson NY 11507

VELLER, MARGARET PAXTON, physician; b. Beaver Dam, Ky., Dec. 14, 1925; d. Darrell K. and Gladys (Myers) V.; B.A., Vanderbilt U., 1947, M.D., 1950. Intern, resident Vanderbilt U. Hosp., Nashville, 1950-54; practice medicine, 1954—. Mem. Am., Miss. (com. maternal and child care 1956-72), Homochilto Valley med. assns., Miss. Obstet. and Gynecol. Soc., Phi Beta Kappa, Alpha Omega Alpha. Baptist. Club: Pilgrimage Garden. Home: 28 S Circle Dr Natchez MS 39120 Office: Natchez Med Clinic 49 Sgt S Prentiss Dr Natchez MS 39120

VELTHOUSE, BETTY ANN, management consultant, nurse; b. Holland, Mich., July 11, 1943; d. Egbert and Anna (Bouwman) Velthouse. R.N., Henry Ford Hosp., Detroit, 1964; B.S., Ball State U., Muncie, Ind., 1972; M.S.N., U. Wis.-Milw., 1979; postgrad. U. Pitts., 1983—. Care coordinator Rainbow Mental Health Ctr., Kansas City, Kans., 1973-76; care coordinator Wood VA Center, Milw., 1976-77; asst. dir. nursing Northview County Home, Waukesha, Wis., 1977-78; mgmt. cons. Vogt-Velthouse Assocs., Pitts., 1978—; adj. instr. Marquette U., Milw., 1976—; vis. asst. Prof. U. West Fla., Pensacola, 1981-83; mem. adv. bd. Nursing Life mag.; lectr. tng. programs. Author: (with Vogt, Cox, Thames) Retaining Professional Nurses: A Planned Approach, 1983; contbg. Author: Practices; contbr. articles to publs. Home: 6805 Penn Ave Pittsburgh PA 15208 Office: U Pittsburgh Coll Bus Pittsburgh PA 15260

VELTMAN, HENRIETTA, social worker; b. Muskegon, Mich., May 17, 1928; d. Douglas and Minnie (Achterhof) V. Student Chgo. Sch. Nursing, Hope Coll., Holland, Mich., Milw. Bible Inst. (now Grace Bible Coll.). Social worker Salvation Army, Holland, Mich., 1961—. Mem. Nat. Assn. Female Execs. Republican. Avocations: photography; reading. Home: 148 W 16th St Holland MI 49423 Office: The Salvation Army 4 E 9th St Holland MI 49423

VELUSWAMY, ANGAMMAL NANJAPPASARI, psychiatrist; b. Coimbatore, India, Feb. 22, 1940; came to U.S., 1964, naturalized, 1976; s. P. and Parvathi (Krishnaswamy) Nanjappasari; M.D., U. Madras (India), 1963; m. V. P. Veluswamy, Apr. 23, 1965; children—Murali, Asha. Intern, Troy, N.Y., 1964-65; resident in psychiatry Clinton Valley Center, Pontiac, Mich., 1966-69; staff psychiatrist Clinton Valley Center, Pontiac, 1969-76; chief substance abuse program VA Hosp., Allen Park, Mich., 1976-78; pvt. practice psychiatry, Southfield, Mich., Mount Clemens, Mich., 1978—; mem. staff Kingswood Hosp., Ferndale, Mich., St. Joseph Hosp., Mount Clemens. Mem. Am. Psychiat. Assn., Mich. Psychiat. Assn., Mich. Neuropsychiat. Hosp. and Clin. Physicians (pres. 1978-79). Home: 2150 Shore Hill West Bloomfield MI 48033 Office: 30161 Southfield Rd Southfield MI 48076

VENDITTI-HASTIE, ANITA MARIE, special education educator; b. Schenectady, N.Y., Oct. 22, 1956; d. Felix George and Maria Dominica (Iovinelli) Venditti; m. Michael Simpson Hastie, May 18, 1985. B.S., Coll. St. Rose, Albany, N.Y., 1978; M.Ed., U. Tex. magna cum laude, 1982. Cert. elem. and spl. edn. tchr., N.Y., Tex. Spl. edn. tchr. Washington County Boces, Hudson Falls, N.Y., 1978, Oswego County Boces, Mexico, N.Y., 1978-81, Tex. Sch. for Deaf, Austin, 1981-82, Austin Independent Sch. Dist., 1982-83; caseworker II, supr. Community Living Autism Support Program Austin Travis County Mental Health Mental Retardation, 1983-85; spl. edn. tchr. Eanes Independent Sch. Dist., Austin, 1985—. Co-author: What Do I Do Now? Let's Try Behavior Management, 1981. Speaker, State Conf. Mental Health Mental Retardation, Beaumont, Tex., 1984, Conf. on Emotional Disturbance, Austin, 1985, nat. conf. Nat. Soc. Autistic Citizens, 1984. U. Tex.-Austin fellow, 1981. Mem. Capital Area Nat. Soc. for Autistic Citizens (v.p. 1984- 85), Phi Beta Kappa. Roman Catholic. Avocations: hiking; camping; reading. Home: 8421 Spring Valley Dr Austin TX 78736 Office: Eanes Independent Sch Dist 1203 Loop 360 S Austin TX 78746

VENDLER, HELEN HENNESSY, educator; b. Boston, Apr. 30, 1933; d. George and Helen (Conway) Hennessy; A.B., Emmanuel Coll., 1954; Ph.D., Harvard, 1960; Ph.D. (hon.), U. Oslo; D.Litt. (hon.), Smith Coll., Kenyon Coll., U. Hartford, Union Coll.; 1 son, David. Instr., Cornell U., Ithaca, N.Y., 1960-63; lectr. Swarthmore (Pa.) Coll. and Haverford (Pa.) Coll., 1963-64; asst. prof. Smith Coll., Northampton, Mass., 1964-66; assoc. prof. Boston U., 1966-68, prof., 1968-85; Fulbright lectr. U. Bordeaux (France), 1968-69; vis. prof. Harvard U., 1981-85, prof., 1985—; reviewer N.Y. Times Book Review, 1968—; poetry critic New Yorker, 1978—. Fulbright fellow, 1954; Guggenheim fellow, 1971-72; Am. Council Learned Socs. fellow, 1971-72; AAUW fellow, 1959; Nat. Endowment Humanities fellow, 1980, 86; Overseas fellow Churchill Coll., Cambridge, 1980; recipient Lowell prize, 1969, Explicator prize, 1969, award Nat. Inst. Arts and Letters, 1975; Nat. Book Critics Circle award, 1980. Mem. MLA (exec. council 1972-75, pres. 1980), English Inst. (trustee 1977-85), Am. Acad. Arts and Scis., Phi Beta Kappa. Author: Yeats's Vision and the Later Plays, 1963; On Extended Wings: Wallace Stevens' Longer Poems, 1969; The Poetry of George Herbert, 1975; Part of Nature, Part of Us, 1980; The Odes of John Keats, 1983; Wallace Stevens: Words Chosen Out of Desire, 1984; editor: Poems of Wallace Stevens, 1985, The Harvard Book of Contemporary American Poetry, 1985; Voices and Visions: Essays on American Poetry, 1986. Home: 16 A Still St Brookline MA 02146 Office: Warren House Harvard U Cambridge MA 02138

VENDRELY, NANCY JO, newspaper features editor; b. Monroe, Mich., July 31, 1935; d. Erving Roy and Dorothy May (Hursh) Vendrely; children—Randall L. Romero, Scott A. Romero. Student Ind. U., 1953-55. Staff writer The News-Sentinel, Ft. Wayne, Ind., 1954-57, 71-73, accent editor, 1973-82, features editor, 1982—; staff writer, food editor The Lima News (Ohio), 1970-71. Recipient Best Family Sect. award Hossier State Press Assn., 1980, 82, Third Features Sect. award Penney-Mo. Nat. Contest, 1983. Mem. Women in Communications Inc. Office: The News-Sentinel 600 W Main PO Box 102 Fort Wayne IN 46801

VENEZIA, DEBORAH JANE, lawyer; b. Woodbridge, N.J., Feb. 6, 1956; d. G. Nicholas and Dorothy Diane (Hospodar) Venezia. B.A. in History, Fairfield U., 1978; J.D., St. Mary's U., San Antonio, 1981. Cert. secondary sch. tchr., Conn. Assoc. firm Venezia & Nolan, Woodbridge, 1981—; mcpl. prosecutor Borough of Jamesburg (N.J.), 1982-83; mcpl. judge, 1983—, Old Bridge, 1986—. Editor casenotes and comments St. Mary's Law Jour., 1980-81; contbr. article to law jour. Mem. ABA, Middlesex County Bar Assn., N.J. Bar Assn., Tex. Bar Assn., Phi Delta Phi. Roman Catholic. Office: Venezia & Nolan 306 Main St Woodbridge NJ 07095

VENNE, PAMELA E., personnel manager; b. Alton, Ill., Dec. 25, 1948; d. Everett C. and Flossie E. (Maynard) Auer; m. Jim Venne, May 1, 1971 (div. 1975); m. W. David Snyder, Feb. 13, 1982; 1 dau., Amissa Lynn. B.S., North Central Coll., 1971; postgrad. U. Wis., 1974, St. Louis U., 1975, U. Utah, 1978. Credit and collection mgr. Ziegler Candy Co., Milw., 1972-73; personnel asst. Erie Mfg. Co., Milw., 1973-75; personnel mgr. Foods Service Mgmt., St. Louis, 1975-77; personnel dir. Ireco Chems., Salt Lake City, 1978-79; supr. Kelly Services, Salt Lake City, 1979; div. personnel mgr. Southland Corp., Dallas, 1979—. Chmn. Polit. Action Com., Dallas, 1982—. Mem. Dallas Personnel Assn. (exhibits dir. 1982-83, v.p. 1984-85, treas. 1985-86), Am. Soc. Personnel Adminstrs., Nat. Assn. Female Execs. Office: The Southland Corp Box 719 Dallas TX 75221

VENNING, ELEANOR HILL, ret. biochemist; b. Montreal, Que., Can., Mar. 16, 1900; d. George William and Elsie Annette (Kent) Hill; B.A., McGill U., Montreal, 1920, M.S.C., 1921, Ph.D. in Exptl. Medicine, 1933; m. E. A. Venning, June 29, 1929. Assoc. prof. exptl. medicine McGill U., 1950-60, prof., 1960-65; dir. endocrine labs. Royal Victoria Hosp., Montreal, 1950-65. Fellow Royal Soc. Can.; emeritus mem. Can. Soc. Biochemistry, Can. Soc. Physiology, Endocrine Soc. U.S. (Fred Comad Koch award 1962), N.Y. Acad. Scis., Can.

Soc. Endocrinology and Metabolism. Contbr. chpts., numerous articles to profl. publs.

VENNING, JACQUELINE LOUISE, educational administrator; b. Charleston, S.C., May 3, 1948; d. James M. and Nathalie E. (Williams) V. B.A., Winthrop Coll., 1970, M.Ed., 1973. Social worker Winthrop Coll., Rock Hill, S.C., 1970-73; tchr. York Sch. Dist. # 1, S.C., 1973-76, Fairfield County Schs., Winnsboro, S.C., 1976-77; counselor Benedict Coll., Columbia, S.C., 1977-80, dir. housing, 1980—, dir. student affairs and housing, 1982—. Mem. voter registration staff Democratic Party, Columbia, 1984. Named Disting. Staff mem. Benedict Coll., 1985. Roman Catholic. Avocations: listening to jazz; arts and crafts; aerobics; reading Office: Benedict Coll Harden & Blanding Sts Columbia SC 29204

VENNOCHI, JOAN LOBIONDO, journalist; b. N.Y.C., Jan. 27, 1953; d. John Joseph and Martha Diane (Homick) LoBiondo; m. Thomas Michael Vennochi, Feb. 19, 1977. B.S., Boston U., 1975; student law, Suffolk U., from 1980. Editor Thomaston (Conn.) Express, 1975; staff reporter Danbury (Conn.) News-Times, 1975-77; mem. Spotlight Team Boston Globe, 1977—, staff reporter, gen. assignment Spotlight Team, 1981-83, polit. reporter City Hall bur., 1983—. Recipient Pulitzer prize for local investigative reporting, 1980. Office: care The Boston Globe 135 Morrissey Blvd Boston MA 02107

VENTRICE, MARIE PAULETTE BUSCK, mechanical engineering educator, researcher; b. Allentown, Pa., Oct. 17, 1940; d. Poul Gunni and Edith Marie (Petersen) Busck; m. Carl A. Ventrice, Jan. 25, 1960; children—Ruth, Carl, James. Student Pa. State U., 1958-61; B.S., Tenn. Tech. U., 1966, Ph.D., 1974; M.S., Auburn U., 1968. Registered profl. engr., Tenn. Instr. mech. engring. Tenn. Tech. U., Cookeville, 1969-70, asst. prof., 1974-79, assoc. prof., 1979—; interim dir. Ctr. Electric Power, Modeling, Simulation and Control, 1985—. Contbr. articles to profl. jours. Recipient Outstanding Faculty award Tenn. Tech. U., 1979, 84. Mem. AAUP, AIAA, Am. Soc. Engring. Edn., ASME, Am. Solar Energy Soc., Internat. Solar Energy Soc., Assn. Energy Engrs., Nat. Soc. Profl. Engrs., Soc. Women Engrs., Sigma Xi, others. Avocation: racquetball. Home: 183 Paris St Cookeville TN 38501 Office: Tenn Tech Univ Dept Mech Engring Cookeville TN 38505

VEON, DOROTHY HELENE, educator; b. Oxford, Nebr., May 31, 1914; d. John B. and Ella V. (Robertson) V.; B.Sc., U. Nebr., 1935; M.A., George Washington U., 1939; Ed.D., Columbia U., 1947; M. Med. Sci. (fellow), Tulane U., 1969. Asst. prof. edn. dept. George Washington U., Washington, 1941-50; prof. edn. Pa. State U., Phila., 1950-66; asst. dir. Sch. of Nursing, Thomas Jefferson U., Phila., 1966-68; vis. prof. Ariz. State U., 1959-60, Drexel U., Phila., 1973-74, Temple U., Phila., 1974-75; ednl. and bus. cons., Phila., 1972—; prof., dir. div. econs. and bus. adminstrn. Community Coll. Phila., 1976-86; vis. prof. U. Vt., summer 1966, Bradley U., summers 1956-58, U. Oreg., summer 1964. Bd. dirs. Va. Guildersleeve Internat. Found. for Univ. Women, 1982—. Recipient Nat. Research award Delta Pi Epsilon, 1949; Internat. Disting. Service award for Status of Women, 1986; Radcliffe research scholar, 1986—. Mem. AAUW (v.p. Pa. div. 1964-66, pres. Phila. br. 1983-85), Am. Acad. Natural Scis., Am. Mgmt. Assn., Am. Mktg. Assn., Am. Bus. Communications Assn. (v.p. 1962-65, nat. fellow 1970), Internat. Soc. Bus. Edn. (pres. 1958-60), Am. Econ. Assn., World Affairs Council Phila., Phila. Mus. Art, Kappa Delta (province pres. 1948-50, 62-64, 70-72), Phi Delta Gamma, Pi Omega Pi, Am. Acctg. Assn. Republican. Episcopalian. Editor Am. Bus. Edn. Home: 2200 Benjamin Franklin Pkwy Philadelphia PA 19130 Office: 249 S 18th Philadelphia PA 19103

VERANO, BEVERLY JO, lawyer, accountant, financial planner; b. Lafayette, Ind., Nov. 7, 1950; d. John Peter and Josephine Annetta (Horney) Speicher; m. Roger Wayne Huffer, June 28, 1969 (div. 1977); m. Hugh Tabor Verano, Jr., Dec. 20, 1981. B.S. magna cum laude, San Diego State U., 1974; J.D., U. San Diego, 1980; LL.M. in Taxation Boston U., 1981. Bar: Calif. 1981, Mass. 1982; C.P.A., Calif. Hon. acctg. intern Price Waterhouse & Co., San Diego, 1973, tax acct., 1974-77; law clk. firm Ball, Hunt, Hart Brown & Baerwitz, Beverly Hills, Calif., 1979; tax research asst. to Boris I. Bittker, Yale U. Law Sch., New Haven, 1979-80; assoc. firm Holzwarth & Schoellerman, Newport Beach, Calif., 1981-83; tax planning cons. CIGNA Corp., Newport Beach, 1983-84; acting tax mgr. Arthur Anderson & Co., Costa Mesa, Calif., 1984—; pres. CFG Planning Group, Irvine, Calif., 1985—. Mng. research editor U. San Diego Law Rev., 1979-80; author audio recs., mag. article. Mem. ABA (tax sect.), Calif. Bar Assn. (com. on taxation), Orange County Bar Assn. (estate planning and probate com., taxation com.), Orange County Women Lawyers, Calif. Soc. C.P.A.s, Am. Assn. Personal Fin. Planners, Women in Bus. (fin. com.), Beta Alpha Psi, Phi Kappa Psi. Republican. Baptist. Home: 24 Springwood Irvine CA 92714 Office: CFG Planning Group 18201 Von Karman Suite 210 Irvine CA 92715

VERBOFSKY, MARNIE ROSALYN, clinical laboratory executive, industrial film producer; b. Pitts., Aug. 14, 1946; D. Isadore and Ethelee (Rosenberg) Verbofsky; Student, U. Ill., 1964-65, Roosevelt U., 1965-66. Payroll adminstr. Cushman Belmont, Chgo., 1966-68; asst. credit mgr. Bailey Beauty Supply, Chgo., 1968-73; corp. asst. sec. Med. Analytics, Inc., Chgo., 1973-74; nat. satellite field coordinator Metpath, Inc., Hackensack, N.J., 1974-77; area dir., regional sales mgr. Nat. Health Labs. div. Revlon, Inc., San Mateo, Calif., 1977-78; v.p., ptnr. COMUTEC, Agoura, Calif., 1978—; pres. Abused Drugs Lab., Inc., Canoga Park, Calif., 1983—; trainer Small Bus. Adminstrn. Legis. appointee to Calif. State Conf. on Small Bus., 1980, 81. Recipient Award of Merit, SBA, 1982; Cert. of Appreciation, Pierce Coll., 1982, Western Regional Los Angeles C. of C., 1983, others. Mem. Clin. Lab. Mgmt. Assn., Sales and Mktg. Execs., Los Angeles Mayor's Adv. Council, Nat. Speakers Assn. Republican. Home: 22111 Calvert St Apt 108 Woodland Hills CA 91367 Office: 21822 Sherman Way Suite 203 Canoga Park CA 91303

VERBRUGGE, BETTY LOU, county official; b. Dakota City, Iowa, Jan. 15, 1927; d. Myron and Bernice Sarah (Soppeland) Doty; m. Durand Daniel Verbrugge, Oct. 25, 1945; children—Judy, Gary. B.A. in Polit. Sci., Ft. Wright Coll., 1978. Chief dep. Pend Oreille County, Newport, Wash., 1964-73, treas., 1973—. Mem. Nat. Assn. County Treas. (bd. dirs. 1978—), Wash. State Treasurers Assn. (pres. 1977-78), Wash. Assn. County Ofcls. (pres. 1982-83). Club: Soroptimist (pres. 1968-70, sec. Dist. 3, 1970-72, bd. dirs. 1972-78, treas. Northwestern region 1974-78). Lodge: Noble Grange. Avocations: music; reading; bird watching; hiking; gardening.

VERBURG, PEGGY PROBASCO, lawyer; b. Ogden, Utah, Aug. 13, 1952; d. Robert Vere and Dorleen Elfrieda (Oppliger) Probasco; m. John Matthias Verburg, Dec. 18, 1972. Student Weber State Coll., 1971-72, Utah State U., 1972-74, U. Utah, 1977-79; B.A. in Philosophy, U. Mont., 1980, J.D., 1983. Bar: Mont. 1983. Unit mgr. Univ. Med. Ctr., Salt Lake City, 1975-81; inventory controller U. Mont., Missoula, 1981-82, research asst. Sch. Law, 1981-82; legal intern Petersen & Berndt, Missoula, 1982, Robinson, Doyle & Bell, Hamilton, Mont., 1982-83; assoc. Law Office of Gerald D. Schultz, Hamilton, 1983-86; staff atty. Dist. XI Human Resource Council, Inc., Missoula, 1985—; dep. county atty. Ravalli County, 1986—; city judge, Stevensville, 1985—; rep. Women's Law Caucus, Missoula, 1980-83; researcher Rocky Mountain Natural Resource Clinic, Missoula, 1981-83. Del. Utah Democratic Conv., Salt Lake City, 1972; candidate Mont. Ho. of Reps., 1984. Mem. ABA, Mont. Bar Assn., Assn. Trial Lawyers Am., Am. Judicature Soc., Mont. Magistrates Assn. (dist. chmn.), LWV, Phi Delta Phi. Club: Soroptimists (1st v.p.). Home: 310 8th St Stevensville MT 59870 Office: Ravalli County Atty's Office Courthouse Box 5008 Hamilton MT 59840

VERDESI, ELIZABETH HOWELL, religious educator, historian; b. Elmira, N.Y., Feb. 5, 1922; d. Everts Howe and Gladys Mae (Shaw) Howell; m. Alan G. Gripe, 1951 (div.); children—Stephen Howell, David Alan; m. Ariel E. Verdesi. B.A. magna cum laude; Elmira Coll., 1944; M.A., Union Theol. Sem., N.Y.C. and Tchrs. Coll., Columbia U., 1952, Ed.D., 1975. Traveling fellow Bd. Christian Edn., Presbyterian Ch. U.S., sec. youth work Bd. Nat. Missions, 1946-51; dir. Christian edn. 1st Presbyn. Ch., Westfield, N.Y., 1962-64; cons. Crisis in Nation Project, United Presbyn. Ch. U.S., N.Y.C., 1968, assoc. Council on Women and Ch., 1977—; dir. cultivation Ch. Women United in U.S., 1971-77; ruling elder 1st Presbyn. Ch., Congers, N.Y.; mem. ministerial relations com. Hudson River Presbytery. Pres., Westfield PTA, 1960-62; organizer, bd. dirs. Westfield Counseling Service, 1963-64; treas. Women's Club, West Point, N.Y., 1954-55; pres. Div. Dames Western N.Y. Presbytery, 1960; organizer, dir. Choral Speaking Group, West Point and Westfield, 1953-64. Mem. AAUW, Phi Beta Kappa. Democrat. Author: In But Still Out: Women in the Church, 1976; (play) Straight Furrow (with Hilda Benson), 1948; contbr. articles to mags. Office: 475 Riverside Dr New York NY 10115

VERDUIN, BERT M., real estate executive; b. Benton, Ark., Feb. 9, 1947; d. Elvis Lee and Helen Lee (McBride) Moses; m. Michael Hankins, May 23, 1970; children—Valerie Ann, Clinton Logan. A.A.S., Brookhaven Coll., 1982. Acct., Realty Devel. Corp., Dallas, 1970-77; owner, mgr. Tax Service, Dallas, 1977-83; sr. v.p., controller Realty Devel. Corp., Dallas, 1983—. Republican. Mem. Ch. of Christ. Avocations: reading; crafts. Office: Realty Devel Corp 8214 Westchester Suite 800 Dallas TX 75225

VERDUIN, BETTY RUTH, nurse, karate school administrator; b. Muskegon, Mich., Feb. 6, 1938; d. Clarence Earl and Melba Lanea (Hallman) Monticue; m. Robert Visscher Verduin, July 28, 1962; children—Mark, Scott, Kurt. Diploma Augustana Hosp. Sch. Nursing, Chgo., 1958; student U. Mich., 1977-81. Registered profl. sch. nurse, 1976. Nurse, Meml./Mercy Hosp., St. Joseph, Mich., 1958-73; dir. health services Lakeshore Schs., Stevensville, Mich., 1974-81; dir. nurses Shoreham Terrace Nursing Home, St. Joseph, 1981-82; dir. Beverly Home Health of St. Joseph, 1982-85; clinic dir. MARCHA (Migrant & Rural Community Health Assn.), Benton Harbor, Mich., 1986—; owner, chief black belt instr. The Unicorn Acad. of Traditional Tae Kwondo Karate, St. Joseph, 1984—. Sec. Berrien County Heart Unit, 1978-80. Named Foster Parent of the Yr. Dept. Social Services, Benton Harbor, 1975; Certificate of Appreciation Mich. Heart Assn., 1979. Mem. Nat. Assn. Female Execs., Universal Tae kwondo Assn. Republican. Avocations: oil painting; horse back riding. Home: 1574 Oak Terr Saint Joseph MI 49085 Office: Unicorn Acad Traditional Taekwondo Karate 1055 Main St Saint Joseph MI 49085

VEREEKE-HUTT, JUNE MARIE, publisher, consultant; b. Bklyn.; d. Robert Mathews and Edith Marie (Mount) Mathews Bradshaw; m. Edwin W. Vereeke, Oct. 11, 1973 (dec.); m. Martin C. Hutt, May 17, 1981; children—Jill, Lee, Kim. Student Urbana Coll., 1976. Mktg. dir. Marriott/Holiday Inns, Cleve., 1970-73; pres., cons. Orgn. Resource Assocs., Cleve., 1975—; pub. New Cleve. Women Jour., Inc., 1983—. Mem. adv. bd. Cuyahoga Community Coll., 1975-77, mem. women's focus program, 1983-84. Recipient Cleve. mag. award, 1979, Cleve. Gazette award, 1983; Career Woman of Achievement, YWCA. Mem. Am. Soc. Tng. and Devel., Women's Career Network Assn. (nat. keynote speaker), Women Bus. Owners Assn., Cleve. Ad Club. Republican. Club: Cleve. Press. Home: 19961 Idlewood Trail Stronsville OH 44136 Office: New Cleve Women Jour Inc 106 E Bridge Berea OH 44017

VEREEN, EMASUE ALFORD, financial consultant; b. Atlanta, May 31, 1936; d. Helion Giles and Sara Margaret (Smith) Alford; m. Carl Harry Vereen, June 7, 1957; children—Susan Elizabeth, Douglas Helion. B.A. in Music, Agnes Scott Coll., 1958. Buyer, part owner Alford Stores, Fayetteville, Ga., 1958-68; minister music Fayetteville Bapt. Ch., 1965-69; sales coordinator Vereen & Connell, Atlanta, 1972-74, Con-Tech, Doraville, Ga., 1974-76; fin. cons. MerrillLynch, Nashville, 1976—. Mem. gen. bd. Vine St. Christian Ch., Nashville, 1984—. Home: 12 Foxhall Close Nashville TN 37215 Office: Merrill Lynch Pierce Fenner & Smith 4th Ave N and Church St Nashville TN 37219

VEREEN, JO ANNE POPE, social services director; b. Hickory, N.C., Jan. 22, 1931; d. Jesse Lee and Edith Marie (Whitener) Pope; m. Jack Guy Vereen, July 21, 1957; children—Steven Jack, Leigh Anne Vereen Cook. A.A., Mars Hill Jr. Coll., 1951; B.A. cum laude, Wake Forest Coll., 1953. Minister of youth edn. First Baptist Ch., Whiteville, N.C., 1953-57; bookkeeper United Caroline Bank, Whiteville, 1957-58; case work asst. Columbus County Dept. Social Services, Whiteville, 1958-62, social worker II, 1962-76, dir. II, 1976-80, dir. III, 1980—. Mem. Bus. and Profl. Women, Whiteville, 1954-58. Mem. N.C. Assn. County Dirs., N.C. Social Services Assn. Democrat. Baptist. Avocation: handcrafts. Home: Route 7 Box C-53 Whiteville NC 28472 Office: Columbus County Dept Social Services PO Box 397 Whiteville NC 28472

VERGUSON-RUSSO, JUDITH MAE, educational administrator; b. Lockport, N.Y., Dec. 4, 1945; d. Elmer William and Phyllis Mae (Glenn) Verguson; m. Christopher Russo, Sept. 2, 1978; children—Sandra Phyllese, Andrew Elmer. B.A. in Lit., Roberts Wesleyan Coll., 1975; M.Ed., SUNY-Brockport, 1981. Cert. elem. tchr., N.Y. Electrologist, Kree Internat. N.Y.C., 1969-70; asst. mgr. Naum Bros. Rochester, N.Y., 1970-72; cosmetics mgr. B. Forman Co., Rochester, 1972-74; employment counselor Snelling and Snelling, Rochester, 1978-79, tchr. Rochester Christian Acad., 1975-76, prin., 1976-78, 79—. Mem. Assn. for Supervision and Curriculum Devel., Am. Mus. Natural History. Republican. Methodist. Avocations: painting; sculpture. Home: 4 Twin Oak Dr Rochester NY 14606

VER HULST, FREDERIKA MARIE, translator, interpretor; b. Versailles, France, Aug. 21, 1953; d. George Mitchell and Elieanne Marie (De Kergorlay) Ver H. B.A. in Fashion Merchandising, J. Byrs Internat. Sch., Paris. Interpretor, asst. tchr. J. Byrs, Paris, 1974; tchr. adminstrn. Berlitz, Houston, 1975-78; supervising lang. specialist Fluor E & C, Houston, 1978—. Home: 5247 Arboles St Houston TX 77035 Office: Fluor Engrs & Constructors One Fluor Dr Sugarland TX 77478

VERMETTE, CARLOTTA ROSE (MRS. JOSEPH SERGE VERMETTE), business executive; b. Detroit, Nov. 30, 1944; d. Dario D. and Rosa Gertrude (Shortt) Bautista; student St. Petersburg Jr. Coll., 1972-82; m. Joseph Serge Vermette, June 20, 1964; children—Joseph Paul, Matthew Allen. Vol., Rehab. Inst. Detroit, 1959-60; with Grace Hosp., 1963-64, with St. Joseph Mercy Hosp., 1964-66; med.-surg. asst. Dr. Jaime Florez, 1972-73; med.-surg. asst. Dr. David Hill, St. Petersburg, Fla., 1973-77; med. asst. Dr. David Hubbell, St. Petersburg, 1977-78; med.-surg. asst. Drs. Bell & Bell, P.A., St. Petersburg, 1978-81; exec. sec. Park Bank of Fla., St. Petersburg, 1982-83; pres., owner C.R. & Co., St. Petersburg, 1983—. Bd. dirs. St. Petersburg chpt. Am. Cancer Soc., 1970—, sec., chmn. public edn., 1970-74. Mem. Assn. Surg. Technologists, St. Petersburg Preservation Inc., Preserve our Waterfront, Inc. Home: 729 18th Ave N Saint Petersburg FL 33704

VERMEULE, EMILY DICKINSON TOWNSEND, classicist, educator; b. N.Y.C., Aug. 11, 1928; d. Clinton Blake and Eleanor Mary (Meneely) Townsend; A.B., Bryn Mawr Coll., 1950, Ph.D., 1956; M.A., Radcliffe Coll., 1954; D.Litt., Douglass Coll., 1968; D.F.A., U. Mass., 1970; LL.D., Regis Coll., 1970, Tufts U., 1980; D.Litt., Smith Coll., 1971, Wheaton Coll., 1973, U. Pitts., 1983, Bates Coll., 1983; L.H.D., Trinity Coll., 1974, Emmanuel Coll., 1980; m. Cornelius Clarkson Vermeule III, Feb. 2, 1957; children—Emily Dickinson Blake, Cornelius Adrian Comstock. Instr. Greek, Bryn Mawr Coll., 1956-57, Wellesley Coll., 1957-58; asst. prof. classics Boston U., 1958-61, asso. prof., 1961-64; prof. Greek and fine arts Wellesley Coll., 1965-70; fellow for research mus. Fine Arts, Boston, 1965—; James C. Loeb vis. prof. classics Harvard U., Cambridge, Mass., 1969, Samuel E. Zemurray and Doris Zemurray Stone-Radcliffe prof., 1970—; Sather prof. classical lit. U. Calif., Berkeley, 1975; Geddes-Harrower prof. Greek art and archaeology U. Aberdeen (Scotland), 1980; Bernhard vis. prof. Williams Coll., 1986; Jefferson lectr. Nat. Endowment for Humanities, 1982. Alumnae dir. Bryn Mawr Coll., 1965-70; trustee Radcliffe Coll., 1974-82. Recipient Gold medal Radcliffe Grad. Soc., 1968; Fulbright scholar, 1950-51, Catherwood fellow, 1953-54, Guggenheim fellow, 1964-65; Am. Council Learned Socs. grantee, 1963. Fellow Brit. Acad., Soc. Antiquaries; mem. Am. Philos. Soc. (grantee 1959, 71, v.p. humanities div. 1978-81), Am. Acad. Arts and Scis., Archaeol. Inst. Am., Am. Philol. Assn., Soc. Promotion Hellenic Studies, Deutsches Archaeologisches Instituts. Republican. Episcopalian. Club: Cosmopolitan (N.Y.C.). Author: Euripides V, Electra, Complete Greek Tragedies, 1959; Greece in the Bronze Age, 1964; The Trojan War in Greek Art, 1964; The Mound of Darkness, 1974; Götterkult, 1974; Death in Early Greek Art and Poetry, 1979; (with V. Kara-georghis) Mycenaean Pictorial Vase-Painting, 1982; contbr. articles to profl. jours. Home: 47 Coolidge Hill Rd Cambridge MA 02138 Office: Dept Classics 319 Boylston Hall Harvard U Cambridge MA 02138

VERMILYEA, GAIL DIANNA, computer software company executive, information systems consultant; b. Poughkeepsie, N.Y., Mar. 13, 1942; d. George Smith and Sarah Eustice (Dugan) V. B.A., Seton Hill Coll., 1964; postgrad. Am. U., Washington, 1966-71. Programmer/analyst Dept. Defense, Washington, 1964-67; cons., mgr. Control Data Corp., Rockville, Md., 1967-71, 72-82, The Netherlands, 1971-72, Mpls., 1982-84; cons., officer Vertek Assocs., Washington, 1984-86; v.p. QTNT Database System Corp., Washington, 1986—; com. mem. Initial Graphics Exchange Specification Standards Com., Nat. Bur. Standards, Gaithersburg, Md., 1985—; vice-chmn. Common Data System Lang./End User Facility Com., Washington, 1978-82; research assoc. Nat. Bur. Standards, Gaithersburg, 1986—. Bd. dirs. Bethesda Overlook Condo Bd., Bethesda, Md., 1985-87, Seton Hill Coll. Alumnae, Greensburg, Pa., 1978-84; trustee Seton Hill Coll., 1986—. Recipient Profl. Services Outstanding Achievement award Control Data Corp., Mpls., 1976, 78. Mem. Assn. Computing Machinery, IEEE., Nat. Assn. Female Execs. Roman Catholic. Avocations: tennis; skiing; travel. Home: 5300 Pooks Hill Rd Bethesda MD 20814 Office: QTNT Database Systems Corp 1100 17th St NW Suite 330 Washington DC 20036

VERNICK, ANDREA MERRILL, cosmetic company advertising executive; b. Newark, Nov. 18, 1949; d. Harold David and Ada Beatrice (Lipnik) V.; B.A., Sch. Communications, Am. U., 1971. Clerical Asst. promotion dept. Estee Lauder, Inc., N.Y.C., 1971-72, dir. promotions, 1975-82, dir. promotions and coop. print advt., 1982-83, exec. dir. promotions and coop. print advertising, 1983—. Mem. Nat. Assn. Female Execs., Am. U. Alumni Assn. Home: 311 E 71st St New York NY 10021 Office: 767 Fifth Ave New York NY 10153

VERNICK, SHEILA K., clinical psychologist; b. Boston, Nov. 23, 1939; d. David and Bertha (Ruby) Kunian; B.A. cum laude, Wheaton Coll., 1961; M.A., Harvard U., 1963; M.Ed., Salem State Coll., 1975; Ph.D., U. Fla., 1979; children—Robyn, David. Psychotherapist Behavioral Devel. Assos., Boston, 1978-79; mem. staff psychol. testing New Center for Psychotherapies, Boston, 1979-80; psychotherapist Bay Area Psychiat. Assos., Lowell, Mass., 1980-81; pvt. practice clin. psychology, Lexington, Mass., 1979—; instr. Framingham (Mass.) State Coll., 1979—; psychotherapist, psychol. tester F. Khajavi, M.D., Mass., 1981-83; psychologist Counseling and Psychiat. Assocs., Lowell, Mass., 1983-85. Mem. Am. Psychol. Assn., Mass. Psychol. Assn., Am. Orthopsychiat. Assn., Mensa, Pi Lambda Theta. Home and Office: 502 Tumbling Hawk Acton MA 01718

VERRILLO, EUGENIE DIERINGER, lawyer; b. Far Rockaway, N.Y., Mar. 4, 1953; d. Eugene Michael and Marian (French) Dieringer; m. James Glenn Verrillo, June 23, 1979. B.A., Duke U., 1974; J.D., U. Conn., 1977. Assoc., Senie, Stock & LaChance, Westport, Conn., 1977-82, ptnr., 1982—. Dist. leader Am. Cancer Soc., Fairfield, Conn., 1982—; Duke U. Fairfield County Alumni Adv. Com., 1985—. Mem. ABA, Conn. Bar Assn., Westport Bar Assn. Roman Catholic. Club: Fairfield Jr. Woman's (co-chmn. ways and means com. 1985—). Avocation: swimming. Home: 610 Fairfield Beach Rd Fairfield CT 06430 Office: PO Box 750 125 Main St Westport CT 06881

VER STEEG, DONNA FRANK, nurse-sociologist, educator; b. Minot, N.D., Sept. 23, 1929; d. John Jonas and Pearl H. (Denlinger) Frank; B.S. in Nursing, Stanford, 1951; M.S. in Nursing, U. Calif. at San Francisco, 1967; M.A. in Sociology, UCLA, 1969, Ph.D. in Sociology, 1973; m. Richard W. Ver Steeg, Nov. 22, 1950; children—Juliana, Anne, Richard B. Clin. instr. U. N.D. Sch. Nursing, 1962-63; USPHS nurse research fellow U. Cal. Los Angeles, 1969-72; spl. cons., adv. com. on physicians' assts. and nurse practitioner programs Calif. State Bd. Med. Examiners, 1972-73; asst. prof. UCLA Sch. Nursing, 1973-79, assoc. prof., 1979—, asst. dean, 1981-83, chmn. primary ambulatory care, assoc. dean, 1983-86; co-prin. investigator PRIMEX Project, Family Nurse Practitioners, UCLA Extension, 1974-76; assoc. cons. Calif. Postsecondary Edn. Commn., 1975-76; spl. cons. Calif. Dept. Consumer Affairs, 1978; accredited visitor Western Assn. Schs. and Colls., 1985—; mem. Calif. State Legis. Health Policy Forum, 1980-81. Named Outstanding Faculty Mem., UCLA Sch. Nursing, 1982. Fellow Am. Acad. Nursing; mem. AAAS, Am. Pub. Health Assn., Am. Soc. Law and Medicine, Nat League Nursing, Calif. League Nursing, Soc. Study Social Problems, Assn. Health Services Research, Am., Calif. (pres. 1979-81) nurses assns., Am. Sociol. Assn., Stanford Nurses Club, Sigma Theta Tau. Contbr. articles to profl. jours., chpts. to books. Home: 708 Swarthmore Ave Pacific Palisades CA 90272 Office: UCLA Sch Nursing Los Angeles CA 90024

VERT, COLLEEN MARY, food service manager; b. Traverse City, Mich., Mar. 11, 1954; d. John Amos and Audrey Irene (Minch) Zoulek; m. Donald Wayne Vert, Oct. 28, 1972; children—Eric Scott, Christopher Robin. Cert. in Dietary Mgmt., U. Fla., 1985. Loan bookkeeper Mich. Nat. Bank, Traverse City, 1975-77; office clk. dietary Occana County, Hart, Mich., 1977-79; bookkeeper Kwik Print, Traverse City, 1979-80; kitchen supr. YMCA Storer Camps, Jackson, Mich., 1980-84; food service mgr. Fairlawn Haven, Archbold, Ohio, 1984-85; food service dir. Hillsdale County Med. Care Facility, Mich., 1985—. Sec., Napoleon Music Boosters, Mich., 1985—. Mem. Dietary Mgrs. Assn. (cert. 1985), Nat. Orgn. Women, Nat. Assn. Female Execs. Democrat. Roman Catholic. Avocations: Swimming; skiing. Home: 7631 Napoleon Rd Jackson MI 49201 Office: Hillsdale County Med Care Facility 140 W Mechanic Hillsdale MI 49242

VER VYNCK-POTTER, VIRGINIA MARY, general contractor, builder, designer; b. Chgo., Sept. 30, 1940; d. Anthony James and Virginia Ann (O'Day) DePadro; student Rosary Coll., 1958-60, Loyola U., Chgo., 1960-62, Coll. of DuPage, 1969-72; m. Ronald Lloyd Potter, May 7, 1977; children—Elizabeth Marie, Michael Anthony, John Patrick. Constrn. apprentice, draftsman Utility Engring Co., Oak Park, Ill., 1956-61; draftsman, 1960-66; color coordinator Hoffman Rossner, Lombard, Ill., 1966-67; constrn. supr., draftsman, designer De Pado Engring. Co., Woodridge, Ill., 1967-70; interior designer Brady Wyte Furniture, Lombard, Ill., 1967-68, Carson Pirie Scott & Co., Downers Grove, 1967-70; head interior designer, head dept. rehab. and remodeling House of Woods and Wovens, Lisle, Ill., 1970-74; pres., owner Archtl. Designers & Assocs., Lisle, 1974—; leader seminars. Recipient Silver Key Award, 1982, Cert. of Merit Home Builders Assn. Greater Chgo., 1981, key awards, 1982, only women builder-owner to recieve key awards for Excellence in Housing Design from Home Builders Assn. of Greater Chgo. for the categories of Remodeling/Rehab./conversions; recipient grand prize for best builder exhibit Home Show, 1982, award for most informative exhibit, 1984, 4 awards Parade of Homes, 1984; named Builder of Month, Builder-Architect Mag., June 1984. Mem. Nat. Assn. Women in Constrn. (pres. Oakbrook chpt.), Nat. Assn. Women Bus. No. Ill. Home Builders Assn., Home Builders Assn. Ill., Profl. Remodelers Assn. Ill., Nat. Assn. Female Execs.

VESPERI, MARIA DAVOREN, anthropologist, educator, journalist, gerontology specialist; b. Worcester, Mass., June 24, 1951; d. Arthur Ernest and Mary Elizabeth (Davoren) V.; 1 dau., Corinna Aline Calagione. B.A., U. Mass.-Amherst, 1973; M.A., Princeton U., 1975, Ph.D., 1978. Vis. asst. prof. anthropology, U. South Fla., Tampa, 1978-81, adj. asst. prof. anthropology, 1981—; vis. asst. prof. anthropology New Coll., Sarasota, 1985-86; cons., writer St. Petersburg Times (Fla.), 1980, staff writer, 1981—; project dir. folk arts documentary supported by Nat. Endowment for Arts; cons. hist. photo exhibit Mus. Fla. History. Active Gray Panthers. Commonwealth scholar, U. Mass., 1969-73; Princeton U. fellow, 1973-75; NIH Pub. Health Service research fellow, 1976-78; doctoral dissertation grantee NSF, 1975-76; grantee Adminstrn. on Aging, 1975-76, Nat. Endowment for Arts, 1983. Mem. AAAS, Am. Anthropol. Assn., Gerontol. Soc. Am., N.Y. Acad. Scis., Assn. for Anthropology and Gerontology (newsletter editor), Nat. Council on Aging, Fla. Press Club, Phi Beta Kappa, Alpha Lambda Delta. Author: City of Green Benches: Growing Old in a New Downtown, 1985. Contbr. articles to publs. in field. Home: 1209 Alcazar Way S Saint Petersburg FL 33705 Office: PO Box 1121 Saint Petersburg FL 33731

VESSEL, RUTH ONEAL, auditor; b. New Orleans, July 1, 1956; d. Lawrence and Mary Lee (Patterson) Vessel. B.S., So. U. A & M, 1977; M.B.A., U.Wis., 1978. C.P.A., Tex. Student worker Southern U. A & M, Baton Rouge, 1975-76; intern, auditor RCA Internal Audit, N.Y.C., summer, 1976, Arthur Anderson & Co., C.P.A., Cin., summer, 1978; auditor Alexander Grant & Co. C.P.A., Houston, 1979-81, Baker Internat. Audit Dept., Houston, 1981—. Mem. Yale Street Bapt. Ch. Mission, Houston, 1983. Fellow, U. Wis., 1978; Scholar, So. U. A & M, Baton Rouge, 1975. Mem. Nat. Assn. Accts., Nat. Assn. Women C.P.A.s. Democrat. Baptist. Home: 11963 Medicine Bow Circle Houston TX 77067 Office: Baker Internat Audit Dept 3920 Essex Box 22111 Houston TX 77027

VEST, MARLYN MARIE, activity and rehabilitation therapy administrator, consultant; b. Pensacola, Fla., July 29, 1947; d. Arthur Frederick and Marlyn (Shaw) Farwell; m. Bill Robert Vest, Oct. 25, 1969; 1 child, Scott Brian. B.S. in Recreation Adminstrn., U. Fla., 1969; M.S. in Continuing and Vocat. Edn., U. Wis., 1976. Recreation supr. Beloit Recreation Dept., Wis., 1969-70; recreation therapist Mendota Mental Health Inst., Madison, Wis., 1970-75; acting unit chief Mendota Deaf Treatment Ctr., Madison, 1976; instr. U. Wis.,

Madison, 1977; dir. activity and rehab. therapy Mendota Mental Health Inst., Madison, 1976—; therapies cons. Dept. Health and Social Services, Madison, 1976—; preceptor U. Wis., Madison, 1984—; clin. asst. prof. U. Wis., Milw., 1983—; lectr. state and nat., 1973—; dir. tourism and recreation adv. com. Madison Area Tech. Coll., 1982—. Contbr. articles to profl. jours. Instr., advocate Tourette Syndrome Assn., Wis. chpt., 1981—. Recipient Gov.'s Merit award State Wis. Dept. Health and Social Service, Madison, 1982. Mem. Wis. Parks and Recreation Assn. Therapeutic Soc. (chmn. 1970—, outstanding contbns. to field award 1979), Wis. Parks and Recreation Assn. (service recognition award 1985), Dane County Recreation Coordinating Council (chmn. 1974). Methodist. Avocations: travel; cross-country skiing; wind surfing; gardening; canning. Home: 21 Aarback Rd Cambridge WI 53523 Office: Mendota Mental Health Inst 301 Troy Dr Madison WI 53704

VEST, MARY ELIZABETH, transportation company official; b. Roanoke, Va., Nov. 19, 1954; d. Robert Ellsworth and Margaret (Taylor) V.; student St. Andrew's Coll., Laurinburg, N.C., 1972-74, Coll. of Journalism, U. S.C., 1976. Mng. editor Richlands (Va.) News-Press, 1976-78, Delmarva News, Millsboro, Del., 1979-83; ops. mgr. Mer-Lou Transp. Inc., 1983—; part-time journalism tchr. Del. Tech. and Community Coll., 1981-83; profl. cons. sch. publs.; dir. Millsboro Hut, Inc. Recipient awards for spot news, series, and photo story, Va. Press Assn., 1977; award for layout, design, photo series, feature series, and editorials Md.-Del.-D.C. Press Assn., 1980, 81, 82. Mem. Sigma Delta Chi. Roman Catholic. Home: 41 C Blue Teal Rd Selbyville DE 19975 Office: Box 247 Millsboro DE 19966

VETCHER, ALICIA, benefits consultant; b. Bklyn., Oct. 2, 1948; d. John and Irene Veronica (Gerus) V.; B.A. in English and Speech, Montclair (N.J.) State Coll., 1970. Sales rep. L'Eggs Products Co., 1973, 3M Co., 1973-76; group sales rep. Hartford Ins. Co., 1977-79; internat. benefits cons. Am. Internat. Group, N.Y.C., 1979-81; asst. v.p. Alexander & Alexander, Inc., N.Y.C., 1981—. Mem. Nat. Assn. Female Execs., Group Ins. Assn. Greater N.Y., Screen Actors Guild, Actors Equity Assn. Methodist. Clubs: Toastmistress, Sales Execs. of N.Y. Office: 1185 Ave of Americas New York NY 10036

VETERAN, JANICE LYNN, semiconductor engineer, researcher; b. San Jose, Calif., July 24, 1958; d. David Robert and Ruth Ann (Harryman) Veteran. B.S. in Physics, U. Calif.-Santa Barbara, 1980; M.S.E.E., U. Calif.-San Diego, 1984. Scientist, Hewlett Packard, Palo Alto, Calif., 1980; scientist Naval Ocean Systems Ctr., San Diego, 1980-83, engr., 1983-85; mem. tech. staff Bell Labs., Holmdel, N.J., 1983; engr. Hughes Aircraft Co., Carlsbad, Calif., 1985—. Contbr. articles to profl. jours. Mem. Am. Phys. Soc., IEEE. Avocations: tennis; running; karate; golf; camping. Home: 484 Summer View Circle Encinitas CA 92024 Office: Hughes MS-102 6155 El Camino Real Carlsbad CA 92008

VETO, JANINE MARIE, arts administrator, fund raiser, poet, author; b. Chgo., May 14, 1949; d. Emil and Marie Hermine (Walton) V. B.S., Northwestern U., 1971. Continuity dir. Sta. WTTW-TV, Chgo., 1974-77; dir. of info. Chgo. Council on Fine Arts, 1978-81; devel. dir. Poets & Writers, Inc., N.Y.C., 1982—; writer Stagebill Mag., N.Y.C., 1980—. Author: (poem) Cedar Rock, 1980; (novel) Iris, 1983; (anthology) The Dream Book, 1985. Prodn. grantee Nat. Endowment for the Arts, Chgo., 1979; Screenplay Devel. grantee Columbia Coll., Chgo., 1980-81. Mem. Authors Guild Am. Democrat. Home: 151 E 83d St 8B New York NY 10028 Office: Poets & Writers Inc 201 W 54th St New York NY 10019

VETTER, BETTY MCGEE, non-profit organization official; b. Center, Colo., Oct. 25, 1924; d. William Allen and Bonnie (Hunsaker) McGee; m. Richard C. Vetter, Sept. 4, 1951; children—David Bruce, Richard Dean, Robert Alan. B.A., U. Colo., 1944; M.A., Stanford U., 1948. Chemist Shell Devel. Co., Emeryville, Calif., 1944-45; instr. Fresno State Coll., Calif., 1948-50, Far Eastern div. U. Calif., 1950-51; adj. prof. Am. U., Washington, 1952-64; part-time instr. U. Va., Arlington, 1952-64, U. Med. extension div., College Park, 1960-61; exec. dir. Commn. on Profls. in Sci. and Tech., Washington, 1964—. Editor Sci., Engring., Tech. Manpower Comments, 1965—. Served with U.S. Naval Women's Res., 1944-45. Mem. Manpower Analysis and Planning Soc., AAAS. Office: 1500 Massachusetts Ave NW Suite 831 Washington DC 20005

VETTER, ELAINE, advertising agency executive; b. Freeport, N.Y., Oct. 23, 1938; d. Otto and Lillian (Pedersen) Buhler; m. William Vetter, Aug. 31, 1957 (div.); 1 child, Robert. A.A.S., SUNY-Farmingdale, 1958. Traffic mgr. Campbell-Ewald Advt., N.Y.C., 1962-68; traffic mgr. A C & R Advt., Inc., N.Y.C., 1968-78, asst. account exec., 1978-79, account exec., 1979-84, v.p., creative coordinator, 1984—. Office: A C & R Advt Inc 16 E 32d St New York NY 10016

VETTER, MARY MARGARET (PEGGY), investment manager, financial consultant; b. Richmond, Va., June 7, 1945; d. Robert Joseph and Miriam Thomas V.; B.A., Cath. U. Am., 1967; M.B.A. with distinction, N.Y.U., 1978; m. Dimitri Yannacopoulos, May 24, 1980. Asst. to controller N.C. Trading Co., N.Y.C., 1972-74; asst. controller Shaheen Natural Resources Inc., N.Y.C., 1974-76; fin. coordinator mining div. Nat. Bulk Carriers, Inc., N.Y.C., 1976-77; corp. cons. mktg. and strategic planning Gen. Electric Co., Bridgeport, Conn., 1978-80; v.p., internat. mktg. strategy Bankers Trust Co., N.Y.C., 1980-83; fin. cons. Shearson Lehman/Am. Express, Stamford, Conn., 1984—; mgmt. cons. Urban Bus. Assistance Corp., N.Y.C. Bd. dirs. South Central Conn. Emergency Med. Services Council. Named Woman of Yr., N.Y.U. Alumnae Assn., 1978. Mem. Fin. Women's Assn. N.Y., Women in Mgmt., Beta Gamma Sigma. Republican. Roman Catholic. Home: 11 Don Bob Rd Stamford CT 06903 Office: 5 High Ridge Stamford Park Stamford CT 06905

VETTER-CAMPION, DAWN MUNRO, administrator; b. Gary, Ind., Jan. 1, 1947; d. Erwin E. and Isabelle M. (Munro) Vetter; m. William Henry Campion, Dec. 18, 1982. B.A., St. Xavier Coll., Chgo., 1972; M.A. Andrews U., Berrien Springs, Mich., 1975, now postdoctoral. Cert. elem. tchr. Ill, Mich.; cert. high sch. art tchr. Mich., Ill; cert. social worker, Mich.; cert. counselor, Mich., Ill. Tchr., Lourdes High Sch., Chgo, 1972-73, Bangor, Mich., schs., 1973-74; dir. Southwestern Mich. Substance Abuse Services, Berrien Springs, Mich., 1980-83, cons., 1983—; dir. Heritage Homes, Holland, Mich. Vol., Ill. Sch. for Blind, Jacksonville, Ill., 1968. State of Ill. grantee, 1968, 1970-75. Mem. Mich. Counselor Assn., Women in Psychology, Am. Personnel and Guidance Assn., Republican. Presbyterian. Home: PO Box 937 Saugatuck MI 49453

VEZEAU, SISTER JEANNETTE EVA, former college president; b. Rochester, N.H., May 11, 1913; d. Edward U. and Laura Ann (Richey) Vezeau; B.S., Boston U., 1948, M.Ed., 1955, Ed.D., 1960. Joined Sisters of Holy Cross, 1933; tchr. high sch., Manchester, N.H., 1937-45, North Grosvenordale, Conn., 1945-49, New Bedford, Mass., 1949-57; prin. St. George High Sch., Manchester, N.H., 1960-64; supr. schs. for Sisters of Holy Cross in New Eng., Pittsfield, N.H., 1964-67; pres. Notre Dame Coll., Manchester, 1967-84; bd. corporators Amoskeag Savs. Bank, 1981-84. Mem. Christian Unity Commn., 1965-71, Diocesan Sch. Bd., Manchester, 1965-71, adv. bd. Elliott Sch. Nursing, Manchester, 1968-71; exec. bd. N.H. Coll. and Univ. Council, 1967-84, Council for Better Schs. in N.H., 1975-80; mem. Gov.'s Commn. on Post Secondary Edn., 1973-84; bd. incorporators Cath. Med. Center, 1979—, Amoskeag Savs. Bank; bd. dirs. NE Regional Exchange, 1981-84. Recipient Woman of Achievement award N.Y. Fedn. Bus. and Profl. Women's Clubs, Inc., 1974. Mem. Am. Council Edn. Author: (with others) 10,000 Legal Words, 1971. Address: 181 Hall St Manchester NH 03103

VÉZINA, MONIQUE, Canadian government official; b. Rimouski, Que., Can., July 13, 1935; d. André-Albert and Eliane Levesque Vezina; m. Jean-Yves, Oct. 26, 1957; children—Marie Andrée, Marc, Mireille, Marie Claire. Mem. House of Commons, Ottawa, Ont., Can., 1984—, minister Ministry of State for External Relations, 1984—. Bd. dirs. Fedn. du Qué. des Caisse Pop. Desjardins, sec. bd. dirs., 1977—; pres. Fondation Girardin-Vaillancourt, 1981-84; pres. bd. dirs. Inst. coopératif Desjardins, 1981-84; bd. dirs. Que. Real Estate Bd., 1984. Mem. Rimouski C. of C. (bd. dirs. 1982-84). Mem. Progressive Conservative. Office: Ministry State for External Relations Lester B Pearson Bldg 125 Sussex Dr Ottawa K1A 0G2 ON Canada*

VIACAVA, LILLIAN D., librarian; b. Bklyn.; d. Frank and Camille (Raffetto) V. B.A., Coll. New Rochelle, 1951; M.S. in Library Service, Columbia U., 1954. Reference librarian Iona Coll., New Rochelle, 1954-59, asst. librarian, 1960-75, assoc. librarian, 1976—. Mem. ALA, AAUP, Cath. Library Assn. Westchester Library Assn. (chair coll. sect. 1978-79), Am. Soc. Info. Sci. Office: Ryan Library Iona Coll New Rochelle NY 10801

VIATOR, GRACE M. STECK, nurse; b. Port Arthur, Tex., Oct. 2, 1926; s. Edward William and Clarissa Eliza (Scott) Steck; m. Dallas Joseph Viator, Sept. 17, 1950; children—Ralph Edwrd, Charels Raymond, Glenn Paul, Kathryn Marie, Anita Louise, Bentley Joseph. Diploma in nursing St. Mary Sch. Nursing, Port Arthur, Tex., 1948, LaMar Jr. Coll., 1948. Charge nurse St. Mary Hosp., Port Arthur, 1948-49, 59-70, 83—, night supr., 1965-66; office nurse H.B. Eisenstadt M.D., Port Arthur, 1949-51; office nurse H.B. Eisenstadt, 1970-75, A.J. Espiritu, E. Tansiongco, Port Arthur, 1975-83. Pres., St. Paul Roman Catholic Altar Soc., 1985—. Mem. Tex. registered Nurses Assn., Beta Sigma Phi. Democrat. Home: 4647 Redbird St Port Arthur TX 77642 Office: St Mary Hosp 3600 Gates Blvd Port Arthur TX 77642

VICARS, MARGARET ELAINE, municipal finance officer; b. Poplar Bluff, Mo., Dec. 3, 1947; d. Jeffrey Clifford and Velma Jean Louise (Davis) Dearing; B.A. in Econs., U. Mich., 1970; M.P.A., Golden Gate U., 1973; student extension cert. program in contract adminstrn. U.Calif.-Berkeley, 1981—. Bookkeeper/mgr. Feiner's Inc., Ann Arbor, Mich., 1971-72; acctg. asst. Lee Wilson, C.P.A., Oakland, Calif., 1974; grant programs coordinator Calif. Coll. Podiatric Medicine, San Francisco, 1974-78; controller Inst. for Research in Social Behavior, Oakland, 1978-83; fin. mgr. City of Pismo Beach (Calif.), 1983—. Mem. speakers bur. Planned Parenthood, Oakland, 1973-74; founder, coordinator Bed and Breakfast Program, San Francisco League Women Voters, 1977-80; bd. dirs. Vernon Villa Homeowners Assn., Oakland, 1979-81, pres., 1980-81; fin. dr. coordinator Oakland LWV, 1981-83; mem. Hearst Castle Citizens Com., 1982-84; treas. Friends of Hearst Castle, 1984—. Mem. Am. Soc. Public Adminstrn., Am. Bus. Women's Assn., San Luis Obispo LWV. Democrat. Office: 1000 Bello St Pismo Beach CA 93449

VICK, MARIE, ret. educator; b. Saltillo, Tex., Jan. 22, 1922; d. Alphy Edgar and Mollie (Cowser) Pitts; B.S., Tex. Woman's U., Denton, 1942, M.A., 1949; m. Joe Edward Vick, Apr. 5, 1942; children—Mona Marie, Rex Edward. Instr., Tex. Woman's U., Denton, 1948-50; tchr. Harlingen (Tex.) High Sch., 1959-62, Harlingen Bonham Elem. Sch., 1958-59, San Angelo (Tex.) Sr. High Sch., 1957-58, San Angelo (Tex.) Jr. High Sch., 1950-52, Monroe Jr. High Sch., Omaha, 1947-48, Crozier Tech. High Sch., Dallas, 1946-47, Santa Rita Elem. Sch., San Angelo, 1943-45, Coahoma (Tex.) High Sch., 1942-43; prof. health sci. Coll. Edn., U. Houston, 1962-80, prof. emeritus, 1980—. artist in oil, watercolor and acrylic. Chmn., Council V, Sch. and Coll. Task Force, Am. Heart Assn.; Reach to Recovery vol. Am. Cancer Soc.; active Houston Planned Parenthood. Recipient Cert. of Achievement, Tex. Commn. Intercollegiate Athletics for Women, 1972, Research Service award Tex. Cancer Control Program, 1978-79, Plaudit award Nat. Dance Assn., 1982, Disting. Service award Pan Am. U., 1983, Service citation Am. Cancer Soc., Cert. of Appreciation, Tex. div. Am. Cancer Soc., 1980; Favorite Prof. honoree Cap and Gown Mortar Bd., U. Houston, 1974. Mem. AAHPER (dance editor 1971-74), Am. Sch. Health Assn., AAHPERD, NEA, So. Assn. Health, Phys. Edn. Coll. Women (sec. dance sect. 1970-73), Tex. State Tchrs. Assn. (sect. chmn. 1964-65), Tex. Assn. Health, Phys. Edn. and Recreation (chmn. dance sect. 1968-69), Tex. Assn. Coll. Tchrs., Tex. Women's U. Nat. Alumnae Assn. (life), Tex. Women's Pioneer Club, Am. Assn. Ret. Persons, Nat. Ret. Tchrs. Assn., Tex. Assn. Ret. Tchrs., Pasadena Assn. Ret. Tchrs., Univ. Houston Assn. Ret. Profs., Tex. Women's Univ. Alumnae Assn. Democrat. Baptist. Author: A Collection of Dances for Children, 1970; Health Science in the Elementary School, 1979; contbr. articles to profl. jours. Home: 238 Ravenhead St Houston TX 77034

VICK, VIRGINIA, education consultant; b. Abilene, Tex., Mar. 8, 1948; d. Vaiden and Clara Mae (Brooks) Hiner; m. Richard S. Fancovic, Dec. 28, 1967 (div. May 1980); m. James D. Vick, Jan. 1, 1982; stepchildren—James Jr., Vicki Brady. B.A. summa cum laude, McMurry Coll., 1969; M.Ed. summa cum laude, Abilene Christian U., 1979. Cert. edn. supr., Tex., spl. edn., Tex., secondary tchr., Tex., vocat. eval. specialist, Tex. Tchr. homebound Abilene Ind. Sch. Dist., 1969-70, 71-75, tchr. classroom, 1970-71, vocat. coordinator, 1975-82; owner, operator Educative/Motivative Services, Abilene, 1982—; cons. in field, 1974—; lectr. in field, 1975-80. Author: Vocat. Assessment Battery, 1976, Vick Study Method, 1983. Editor gen., profl., spl. interest newsletters. Contbr. articles to popular magazines and profl. jours. Mem. Heath User's Group, Commodore User's Group. Mem. Ch. of Christ. Club: Good Sam (asst. state dir. 1976-77). Avocations: computer skills; music; needlework; reading; camping; water sports. Home: Route 12 Box 345 Abilene TX 79601 Office: Educative/Motivative Services 3041 S 7th St Abilene TX 79605

VICKERS, NAOMI R., manager; b. Anderson, Ind., Mar. 25, 1917; d. Floyd Leroy and Gertrude Marie (Richards) Stamm; m. Robert Ross Vickers (dec.); children—Robert Vernon, Richard Ross, Philip Leroy, Denise Healey. Sec., treas. Vickers Fine Homes, Anderson, 1951—, Vickers Apts., 1956—; sec., treas. Comml. Bldgs., 1958—. Mem. Order Eastern Star, White Shrine, Madison County Shrine. Home: 2003 E 7th St Anderson IN 46012

VICKERY, BYRDEAN EYVONNE HUGHES (MRS. CHARLES EVERETT VICKERY, JR.), library services administrator; b. Belleview, Mo., Apr. 18, 1928; d. Roy Franklin and Margaret Cordelia (Wood) Hughes; m. Charles Everett Vickery, Jr., Nov. 5, 1948; 1 dau., Camille. Student Flat River (Mo.) Jr. Coll., 1946-48; B.S. in Edn., S.E. Mo. State Coll., 1954; M.L.S., U. Wash., 1964; postgrad. Wash. State U., 1969-70. Tchr., Ironton (Mo.) Pub. Schs., 1948-56; elem. tchr. Pasco (Wash.) Sch. Dist. 1, 1956-61, jr. high sch. librarian, 1961-68, coordinator libraries, 1968-69; asst. librarian Columbia Basin Community Coll., Pasco, 1969-70, head librarian, dir. Instructional Resources Center, 1970-78, dir. library services, 1979—; chmn. S.E. Wash. Library Service Area, 1977-78. Bd. dirs. Pasco-Kennewick Community Concerts, 1977—, pres., 1980-81; bd. dirs. Mid-Columbia Symphony Orch., 1983—; trustee Wash. Commn. Humanities, 1982-85. Author, editor: Library and Research Skills Curriculum Guides for the Pasco School District, 1967; author (with Jean Thompson), also editor Learning Resources Handbook for Teachers, 1969. Recipient Woman of Achievement award Pasco Bus. and Profl. Women's Club, 1976. Mem. AAUW (2d v.p. 1966-68, corr. sec. 1969), Wash. Dept. Audio-Visual Instrn., ALA, Wash. Library Assn., Am., Wash. assns. higher edn., Wash. State Assn. Sch. Librarians (state conf. chmn. 1971-72), Tri-Cities Librarians Assn., Wash. Library Media Assn. (community coll. levels chmn. 1986-87), Am. Assn. Research Libraries, Soroptimist Internat. Assn. (rec. sec. Pasco-Kennewick chpt. 1971-72, treas. 1973-74, pres. 1978-80), Columbia Basin Coll. Adminstrs. Assn. (sec.-treas. 1973-74), Pacific N.W. Assn. Ch. Libraries, Women in Communications, Pasco Bus. and Profl. Women's Club, P.E.O. Beta Sigma Phi, Delta Kappa Gamma, Phi Delta Kappa (sec. 1981-82, Outstanding Educator award 1983). Home: 4016 W Park St Pasco WA 99301 Office: 2600 N 20th Ave Pasco WA 99301

VICKERY, MILLIE MARGARET, photographer, journalist; b. Clinton County, Ind., Apr. 29, 1920; d. Walter L. and Opal M. (Small) Cox; m. Eugene Livingstone Vickery, Dec. 21, 1941; children—Douglas Eugene, Constance Michelle Suski, Anita Sue Ramsey, Jon Livingstone. Student Ind. U., 1938-42, U. Toledo, 1944. Writer, Sheridan News (Ind.), 1937-38; floor mgr. Lamsons Dept. Store, Toledo, 1943-45; receptionist, bookkeeper Office E.L. Vickery, M.D., Lena, Ill., 1946—; freelance writer-photographer, Lena, 1964—. Author: P.S. I Love You, 1983; editor Pulse of the Doctor's Wife mag., 1966-78; contbg. editor MD's Wife mag., 1964-74; contbr. articles and photographs to various newspapers and mags. Bd. dirs. Highland Coll. Found., Freeport, Ill., 1970-87. Recipient Pacesetter award Highland Community Coll., Freeport, 1978; Sweepstake award, several 1st trophies Rockford Cooking Contests (Ill.), 1979-81; Disting. Alumnae award Marion-Adams High Sch., Sheridan, Ind., 1981. Mem. Ill. Woman's Press Assn. (pres. 1971-73, over 40 writing awards, Woman of Achievement award 1984), Nat. Fedn. Press Women (dir. 1971-73), Ill. State Med. Soc. Aux. (state pres. 1975-76), Ill. Acad. Family Physicians Aux. (state pres. 1976-77), Ill. Press Photographers Assn., Women in Communications, Mortar Board, Delta Delta Delta, Beta Sigma Phi (pres. chpt. 1950, 72, Order of Rose award 1981, internat. award of Distinction 1982, photography award 1982-84). Republican. Mem. Evangel. Free Church. Clubs: Lena Women's, Lena Golf. Lodges: Order Eastern Star, PEO. Home: 602 Oak St Lena IL 61048

VICTOR, JUDITH MAY, advertising agency executive; b. Tucson, Apr. 12, 1949; d. Hubert R. and Ruby M. (Buehrer) James; m. Lindsay Copeland, 1970 (div. 1977); m. 2d, David Victor, June 16, 1979; children—David, Laurie, Andrew. B.F.A., U. Ariz., 1970. Columnist, Tucson Newspapers, Inc., 1970-71; copywriter Broadway Hale, Inc., 1971-72; copy dir. Diamond's, 1972-73; pres. Way Out West Prodns., 1973-77; owner pres., The Producers, Inc., Phoenix, 1977—. Active, Charter 100, Phoenix, 1981—; (bd. dirs. Park Found. Phoenix, 1981-82) Mem. Nat. Assn. Women Bus. Owners, Women in Communications (pres., 1976-77, S.W. region Woman of Achievement award 1977). Democrat. Club: Phoenix Country. Home: 3835 East Sahuaro Blvd Phoenix AZ 85028

VICTORY, LUANN JEANETTE, health care official; b. Mpls., May 3, 1955; d. John F., Jr., Theresa A. Victory; A.A., North Hennepin Community Coll., 1975; B.A. (scholar), St. Cloud State U., 1976; M.A. with high honors, S.W. Mo. State U., 1978. Grad asst. S.W. Mo. State U., Springfield, 1976-77; dir. public relations Park Central Hosp., Springfield, 1977-79; dir. community relations and devel. Mt. Carmel Med. Center, Pittsburg, Kans., 1980-82; dir. med. staff devel. Coordinated Services, Wichita, Kans., 1982-85; mgr. profl. relations Republic Health Corp., Dallas, 1985—; public relations cons. Am. Diabetes Assn.; instr. creative dramatics; TV and radio host weekly program. Bd. dirs. ARC, Pittsburg Community Theatre, 1980, 81; coordinator CPR community cert. program. Recipient cert. for contbn. to field of oral interpretation; cert. of excellence for informative speaking. Mem. Am. Soc. Hosp. Public Relations, Mo. Assn. Hosp. Public Relations, Internat. Assn. Bus. Communicators, Pittsburg C. of C. (dir.), Press Women, Pub. Relations Soc. Am. Editor Inner View, 1977-78, Spectrum, 1980-82, Hints for Health, 1980-82, Community, 1981-82. Home: 18200 Gallery Dr Apt 522 Dallas TX 75252 Office: Republic Health Corp 14951 Dallas Pkwy Suite 1100 Dallas TX 75240

VIDOVIC, AGNES ANN, physical education educator; b. Chgo., Jan. 28, 1929; d. Joseph and Mary (Kirincic) Radich; m. Martin P. Vidovic, Sept. 14, 1957; children—Janice Geralyn, Christopher Martin. A.A., Wilson Jr. Coll., 1949; B.S., U. Ill.-Urbana, 1951; M.S., W.Va. U., 1952; postgrad. numerous univs. Instr., ARC, 1947-49, YMCA, Chgo., 1953-55, YWCA, Chgo., 1956-57, Chgo. Park Dist., 1951; waterfront dir. Clearwater Camp for Girls, Minocqua, Wis., 1955; instr. U. Chgo. Lab. Sch., 1952-54, Lindblom High Sch., Chgo., 1954-62; chair girls' dept. phys. edn. Hubbard High Sch., Chgo., 1962-63, Morgan Park Acad., Chgo., 1965-67; prof. phys. edn. Truman Coll., Chgo., 1967—; judge/referee Ill. High Sch. Assn., 1969-74; ednl. film distbr. U.S. Gymnastics Fedn. Women's Com., 1969-72; timer/scorer Midwest Open Gymnastics Championship for Women, 1969-70; vol. lectr. Mayfair Coll. Adult Edn., 1968-74, cons. 1968-73; voting rep. Chgo. City Colls. Faculty Council, 1983-85; mem. Nat. Bd. Women Athletics, 1974-80. Bd. dirs. Mothers Assn. U. Ill., 1977—, chair fall conf., 1983, 2d v.p., 1984-85; mem. choir Assumption Cath. Ch., Chgo., 1953-59, St. Monica Cath. Ch., Chgo., 1968-71; mem. 41st Ward Women's Democratic Orgn.; faculty rep. Truman Coll. Community Council, 1981-83. State of Ill. scholar, 1949-51; Oscar Mayer scholar, 1962; recipient 25-Yr. Service award ARC, 1984. Mem. AAHPER and Dance (life; charter 500, Nat Intramural Sports Council 1967-71), Nat. Dance Assn. (higher edn. div.), Ill. Assn. Health, Phys. Edn., Recreation and Dance. Democrat. Club: St. Monica Women's (Chgo.). Office: Truman Coll 1145 W Wilson Ave Chicago IL 60656

VIEREGG, VIRGINIA ANDERSON (MRS. JAMES WILBUR VIEREGG), civic worker; b. Aurora, Nebr., Sept. 14, 1916; d. Charles Olaf and Minnie Marie (Isaacson) Anderson; student U. Omaha, 1934-35; B.A., U. Nebr., 1938; m. James Wilbur Vieregg, Sept. 21, 1940; children—Anne Vieregg Urick, James, William, Gretchen Vieregg Olenberger, John. Chmn., State Adv. Council Vocat. Edn., 1970—; mem. Nebr. Council for Tchr. Preparation, U. Nebr., 1969-70; mem. State Manpower Council, 1971-72; mem. Gov.'s Block Grant Adv. Council, 1981. Mem. Grand Island Bd. of Edn., 1958-84, pres., 1961-68, 73; trustee Mid-continent Regional Ednl. Lab., 1971—; trustee Nebr. State Drug Abuse Found., dir. 1971—; mem. external adv. bd. Tchrs. Coll., U. Nebr. Mem. State Sch. Bd. Assn. (pres. 1969-70), AAUW, PEO, Theta Sigma Phi, Kappa Alpha Theta, Delta Kappa Gamma (hon.). Presbyterian. Home: 1016 W Division St Grand Island NE 68801

VIGIL, CAROL JEAN, lawyer; b. Sante Fe, Oct. 24, 1947; d. Martin Elias and Evelyn (Abeita) V.; m. Phillip David Palmer, Dec. 16, 1977; 1 child, Erika Lee; B.Univ. Studies, U. N.Mex., 1974, J.D., 1978. Bar: N.Mex. 1979. Regional Heber Smith fellow, staff atty. Indian Pueblo Legal Services, Santa Ana Pueblo, N.Mex., 1978-80; asst. atty. gen. Office Atty. Gen., Santa Fe, 1980-84; sole practice law, Santa Fe, 1984—. Mem. Women's Vote '84 Task Force for N.Mex., 1984; mem. econ. devel. com. Pueblo Tesuque; chmn. No. N.Mex. Legal Services, Santa Fe, 1980—; bd. dirs. Southwestern Assn. on Indian N.Mex. Affairs, 1983—. Mem. State Bar N.Mex. (dir. womens legal rights sect. 1984—), Am. Indian Lawyers Assn. (dir. 1981—). Democrat. Roman Catholic. Home: 214 McKenzie Santa Fe NM 87501 Office: PO Box 6100 Tesuque NM 87574

VIGIL, TERRY ANNE, college official; b. Detroit, July 25, 1946; d. Charles Howard and Margo (Carroll) Peake; A.B., Brown U., 1968; M.R.P., Syracuse U., 1970; m. Roy Max Vigil, June 27, 1970; children—Kiara Maria, Ryan Howard. Planner, Mass. Dept. Community Affairs, Boston, 1970-72; regional planner Bur. Transp. Planning and Devel., Mass. Dept. Public Works, Boston, 1972-79; supr. State Transp. Plan Staff for Bur. Transp. Planning and Devel. in cooperation with Exec. Office Transp. and Constrn., Boston, 1979-81; pres., chmn. bd. Kidpool, Inc., 1982-83; planning cons., freelance writer, 1982; grants dir. Bridgewater (Mass.) State Coll., 1982—. Sec.-treas. Brookline Council for Planning and Renewal, 1980-82, vice chmn., 1979-80; founder, treas. Friends of Lost Pond, Chestnut Hill, Mass., 1981—; pres. Chestnut Hill Village Assos., 1974-76. Mem. AAUW, Assn. Women Deans, Adminstrs. and Counselors, Women's Transp. Seminar Greater Boston. Christian Scientist. Author: Citizen's Transportation Handbook, 1975; Regional Transportation Plan Guidelines, 1978; I-93 Joint Transportation Study, 1980. Home: 10 Craftsland Rd Chestnut Hill MA 02167

VILA, ESTELLE V., financial institution official; b. N.Y.C., Dec. 24, 1922; d. Diego and Mercedes Encarnation (Lopez) Villar; m. Carlos A. Vila, Oct. 4, 1942; children—Sonja V. John, Henry L. Vila, Darlene V. Varona, Charles D. Vila. A.A., CCNY, 1943. Bookkeeper Dade Nat. Bank, Miami, Fla., 1956-58; teller Comml. Bank, Miami, 1958-61; teller, with pub. relations dept. Bank of Kendall, Miami, 1961-72. Bd. dirs. Puerto Rican Democrats Orgn., Miami, 1980—, Federacion Puertoriquena, Miami, 1980—. Mem. Nat. Orgn. Puerto Rican Women. Roman Catholic. Avocation: political activities. Home: 943 W 64th Pl Hialeah FL 33012

VILIMAS, JACQUELINE SMITH, counselor, educator; b. Chgo., Jan. 22, 1931; d. James Leo and Catherine Ann (Schaack) Smith; B.A., DePaul U., 1954; M.Ed., Boston Coll., 1972, postgrad., 1972—; m. Joseph Vilimas, Sept. 6, 1952; 1 dau., Joanna Marie. Asst. dir. Office Student Devel., Bentley Coll., Waltham, Mass., 1972-74; treatment/process cons. Community Alcoholism Services, Portland, Maine, 1972-74; program devel. specialist Alcoholism Research and Tng. Center, Framingham, Mass., 1974-77; psychol. asst. Assoc. Psychologists Inc., 1976—, Therapeutic Tutors and Counseling, Westford, Mass., 1982-83; curriculum devel. specialist Boston State Coll., 1977-83, adj. assoc. prof. psychology, 1977-83; adj. lectr. U. Mass., 1983—; clin. dir. Brighton Ct. Alcoholism Program, 1984—; cons. J.F. Kennedy Multi-Service Center, Hope House, Inc., Steppingstone, Inc.; speaker Emmanuel Coll., U. Maine, 1975, Boston Coll., 1976—. Program leader Great Books Program, 1967-70; mem. Watertown (Mass.) Town Meeting, 1965-67. Recipient Disting. Columnist award DePaul U., 1952, 53, 54. Mem. Am. Psychol. Assn., Am. Personnel and Guidance Assn., Assn. for Advancement Behavior Therapy. Home: 67 Marlboro St Newton MA 02158 Office: 625 Huntington Ave Boston MA 02111

VILINSKY, MURIEL, data collection services executive; b. N.Y.C., Aug. 9, 1923; d. Joseph and Rose (Migdal) Putterman; m. Abraham Jack Vilinsky, Jan. 25, 1945; children—Robert Paul, Jeffrey Steven. Student Fairleigh Dickenson U., New Sch. Social Research, 1968—. Sec., bookeeper Stickless Printing Co. and Whitely Tailleurs Corp., N.Y.C., 1940-48, mktg. research interviewer, Fair Lawn, N.J., 1962-63; ptnr., owner No. Jersey Market Surveyors, Fair Lawn, 1963-73; pres. Interviewers for Research Inc., Fair Lawn and Edison, N.J., 1973—. Sec., trustee Sisterhood Congregation B'nai Israel, 1952-65; mem. edn., fin. and budget coms. LWV, 1965-67. Mem. Mktg. Research Assn., Democrat. Avocations: Playwriting; piano; theatre. Home: 25-06 Berkshire Rd Fair Lawn

NJ 07410 Office: Interviewers for Research Menlo Park Mall Parsonage Rd Edison NJ 08837

VILLA, JOAN, management consultant, writer, poet, educator; b. San Mateo, Calif., June 14, 1949; d. Leonard Charles and Angeline Josephine (Arena) Calabrese; m. Anthony Q. Villa, Jan. 20, 1973. B.S. in Exceptional Child Edn., State U. Coll. at Buffalo, 1973; M.S. in Edn., Nova U., 1978. Cert. tchr. pre-sch., elem., N.Y., emotionally handicapped, jr. coll. adminstrn., supr., Fla. Tchr. emotionally disturbed Sch. Bd. Broward County, Ft. Lauderdale, Fla., 1974-79; adj. prof. U. La Verne, Calif., 1979, 80; sr. coordinator Personal Dynamics Inst. Minn., 1978-85; adj. prof. Nova U., Davie, Fla., 1981—; resident mgr. Personal Dynamics Inst., 1985; pres., owner Personal & Profl. Devel. Ctr., Coral Springs, Fla., 1979—; sponsor continuing profl. edn. program Fla. State Bd. Accountancy, Gainesville, 1982—; apptd. Fla. teaching profl.-NEA Women's Leadership Tng. Cadre, 1980. Contbr. articles to profl. jours. Mem. edn. task force Ft. Lauderdale/Broward County C. of C., 1985, mem. small bus. coalition, 1984; recipient Outstanding Young Woman of Am. award, 1984; coordinator Exceptional Child week Council for Exceptional Children, 1979, communications chmn., 1977-78, sec., 1976-77. Recipient Appreciation award Am. Soc. Tng. and Devel., Broward-Palm Beach chpt., 1983, Dedicated Service award, 1983, regional chpt. excellence award, 1983, chpt. of the yr. award, 1983, Nat. Profl. Contbn. award, 1983, Outstanding Leadership award, 1982, Outstanding Service award, 1981, others. Mem. Am. Soc. Tng. and Devel. (region IX conf. strategic planning chmn., 1984, strategic planning chmn., nat. issues chmn. 1985), (Broward-Palm Beach chpt. exec. bd., 1984, pres. 1983, mem.ship chmn., 1981) Classroom Tchrs. Assn. (bldg. chmn., 1976-79), Fla. Freelance Writers Assn., Pompano Beach C. of C., Ft. Lauderdale C. of C., Assn. Profl. Saleswomen, Network Connection, Women in Sales Assoc., NEA. Clubs: Coral Springs Exec., Women's Exec. Avocations: bicycling; reading; rug hooking; leather craft; dancing. Home: 8811 NW 21st St Coral Springs FL 33065 Office: Personal and Profl Devel Center 1439 S Pompano Pkwy Suites 301 303 Pompano Beach FL 33069

VILLA, ROSA OLIVIA, banker; b. Mexico City, Mexico, June 17, 1944; d. Roberto and Delia (Martinez) Villa; 1 child, Maria Fernanda. M. Econs., National Autonomous U. Mex., 1965; postgrad. Inst. Social Studies, The Hague, Holland, 1967. Prof. Nat. Autonomous U., Mex., 1968-73; dep. mgr. fin. programming Nacional Financiera, Mexico, 1976-77; chief advisor Treasury Dept., Mexico, 1979-81; chief compensation and benefits div. Inter-Am. Devel. Bank, Washington, 1985—; mem. editoral bd. dirs. Investigación Económica mag., Mexico, 1969-70; mem. presdl. commn. on fin. Pres.'s Office, Mex., 1978-81. Author: Nacional Financiera: Development Bank for the Economic Improvement of Mexico, 1976. Nat. Autonomous U. grantee, 1967; hon. mem. "Juan Loyola Prize", Economists Nat. Assn. Mexico, 1978-81. Avocations: music; reading; movies. Home: 11002 Wickshire Way Rockville MD 20852 Office: Inter-Am Devel Bank 1300 New York Ave Washington DC 20577

VILLAFUERTE, CECILIA CRUZ, savings and loan executive; b. Baguio City, Philippines, Jan. 7, 1945; came to U.S. 1971, naturalized 1976; d. Ricardo Lipana and Cresencia (Beltran) Cruz; m. Abelardo Torrano Villafuerte, Aug. 20, 1965; children—Celia Lourdes, Elix, Olivia Christine. B.S. in Civil Engring., Baguio Coll. Found., 1966; Cert. of Achievement, Inst. Fin. Edn., Honolulu, 1973-82; Diploma in Mgmt., Hawaii Ednl. Council, 1979. With Internat. Savs., Honolulu, 1972-83; mktg. research dir. Internat. Savs. & Loan Assn., Honolulu, 1983; v.p. ATV Engring. Co., Inc., Honolulu, 1984—; asst. v.p. New People's Savs., Honolulu, 1983—; treas. Community Instant Printing, Honolulu, 1985—. Commr. Honolulu Planning Commn., 1983—; treas. United Filipino Council of Hawaii, 1985—; precinct officer Dem. Party of Hawaii, Honolulu, 1978-86; bd. govs. United Filipino Council of Hawaii, 1984-85; mem. Hawaii Ednl. Council, 1983. Recipient Outstanding Service award Oahu Filipino Jaycees, 1983, 84; Leadership award YWCA, Honolulu, 1978; named Most Outstanding Mem., Filipino C. of C., 1985; Cert. of Appreciation, Gov. George Ariyoshi, Hawaii, 1983, Mayor Eileen Anderson, Honolulu, 1984; Disting. Service award United Filipino Council of Hawaii, 1985. Mem. Women's Community Action League (bd. dirs.), Hawaii Filipino Contractors Assn. (bd. dirs.), Filipino C. of C. Hawaii (v.p. and editor newsletter 1986). Democrat. Roman Catholic. Clubs: Zonta, Hawaii Filipino Civic (auditor), Filipino Women's (pres. 1985). Avocations: sewing; machine embroidery. Home: 1203 Wanaka St Honolulu HI 96818 Office: New Peoples Savings and Loan Assn 1188 Fort Street Mall Honolulu HI 96813

VILLAMIL, YOLANDA ISABEL, real estate developer, lawyer; b. San Juan, P.R., July 29, 1957; d. Joaquin A. Villamil and Yolanda Passalacqua Freiria. B.A., Tufts U., 1978; J.D., Yale U., 1981. Bar: P.R. 1982, Fla. 1983. Real estate atty. Greenberg, Traurig, Askew, Hoffman, Lipoff, Rosen & Quentel, P.A., Miami, Fla., 1982-83; real estate developer, 1983—. Home: 598 Sandpiper Way Sanctuary Boca Raton FL 33431 Office: care M&E Investors 340 Clematis St West Palm Beach FL 33401

VILLANI, SUSAN, sch. adminstr.; b. Bklyn., July 4, 1950; d. Jerry C. and Helen (Hartzman) V.; B.A., Harpur Coll., SUNY, Binghamton, 1970; M.Ed., Tufts U., 1971; C.A.G.S., Northeastern U., 1979, Ed.D., 1983; m. Harvey T. Buford, Aug. 3, 1980; 1 son, Evan. With Havils Jewelers, Riverhead, N.Y., 1958-71, Meenan Oil Co., Hicksville, N.Y., 1967; substitute tchr. Somerville (Mass.) Public Schs., 1971; tchr., cons. to adminstrs. Batchelder Sch., North Reading, Mass., 1971-78; prin. Hazard Elementary Sch., Wakefield, R.I., 1978—; cert. instr. Parent Effectiveness Tng., 1977. Mem. Bus. and Profl. Women and Young Career Women of R.I. (Young Career Woman of R.I. 1979), North East Coalition of Ednl. Leaders (pres. 1981-83), R.I. Assn. Sch. Prins., Nat. Assn. Elem. Sch. Prins., Assn. Supervision and Curriculum Devel., Am. Assn. Sch. Adminstrs., Am. Ednl. Research Assn. So. R.I., Kappa Delta Pi, Phi Delta Kappa. Home: Route 1 Box 681 Ashaway RI 02804 Office: 67 Columbia St Wakefield RI 02879

VILLAROSA, LESLIE BUGARIN, market information executive; b. Calapan, Philippines, Oct. 30, 1948; came to U.S., 1971; d. Enrico M. and Isabel (Mendoza) Bugarin; m. Oscar Tambunting Villarosa, Aug. 13, 1979. B.S. in Psychology, U. St. Thomas, Manila, 1968. Instr. St. Joseph's Coll., Quezon City, Philippines, 1970-71; guidance counselor La Consolacion Coll., Manila, Philippines, 1970-71; clk.-typist Hanover Ins., Chgo., 1971-72; centrex operator U. Chgo., 1972-74; adminstrv. asst. Chgo. Bd. Trade, 1974-80, mgr. mktg. info., 1980—. Editor: Statis. Ann., 1980-83; coordinator: 10 Year Soybean Book, 1978-79. Mem. Chgo. Agrl. Economist Club, Nat. Assn. Farm Broadcasters, Nat. Agrl. Mktg. Assn. Roman Catholic. Home: 1351 W Touhy Ave Apt 1N Chicago IL 60626 Office: Chicago Bd Trade 141 W Jackson St Chicago IL 60604

VILLARREAL, LINDA PYLE, manufacturing executive; b. Houston, Aug. 4, 1948; d. Johnnie A. and Iola (McKnight) P.; m. Charles Clayton McNatt, May 23, 1970 (div. July 1972); m. Joe David Villarreal, Mar. 8, 1986. Student S. Tex. Jr. Coll., U. Houston. Sec., buyer B&B Engring. & Supply Co., Inc., Houston, 1964-70; owner/mgr. A Touch of Talent, Houston, 1970-72; spl. asst. continuing edn. U. Houston, 1972-74; real estate sales, Houston, 1974-80; gen. mgr. Lion's Gallery, Houston, 1981-85; gen. mgr. Silk Jungle Warehouse Inc., 1985—. Fellow Nat. Home Fashions League, Young Women of the Arts, Gift Assn. Am., Greater Houston Builders Assn.; mem. Spring Branch Meml. C. of C. (ambassador 1984-85). Republican. Episcopalian. Avocations: reading; needlework; painting; sports; gourmet cooking. Home: 10310 Londonderry Houston TX 77043 Office: Silk Jungle Warehouse 1085 Gessner Suite R Houston TX 77055

VILLARREAL, LORA JEAN, printing and mailing company personnel executive, consultant; b. Los Angeles, Mar. 14, 1944; d. Carlos L. and Estella M. (Marquez) Licon; m. Lorenzo Villarreal II; children—Michelle Villarreal Price, Christopher J. A.A. in Interior Design and Bus. Adminstrn., East Los Angeles Coll., 1973; student in bus. adminstrn. Bellevue Coll., 1979-82. Personnel mgr. Omaha World-Herald, 1977-81; personnel specialist Youth for Understanding, Washington, 1981-82; spl. asst. EEO Commn., Washington, 1982-83; asst. to dir. EEO, Legal Services Corp., Washington, 1983; employment mgr. United Hosp., Grand Forks, N.D., 1984-85; personnel mgr. Rapid Printing & Mailing, Omaha, 1985—; cons. human resources; adviser Women in Edn., Bellevue, Nebr., Hispanics in Edn., Omaha, 1985, Women of 80's, Omaha, 1985. Active Republican Nat. Hispanic, Washington, 1985. Named to Outstanding Young Women Am., U.S. Jaycees, 1975; recipient Mil. Wife of Yr. award Bd. of Base Leaders, Whiteman AFB, Mo., 1976. Mem. Personnel Assn. of Midlands, Am. Soc. Personnel Adminstrs., Am. Soc. Tng. and Devel., Hispanic Women's Council, Nat. Assn. Female Execs. Roman Catholic. Club: Officers' Wives (Offutt AFB, Nebr.). Avocations: jogging; reading; Jazzercise. Home: 3726 Burr Oak Dr Omaha NE 68123 Office: Rapid Printing & Mailing Inc 9320 J St Omaha NE 68127

VILLINES, DONNA JEAN, paralegal; b. Wilson, Okla., Sept. 20, 1945; d. Jack and Corine (Culbreth) Greenwood; m. (div. Feb. 1986); children—Jackie Don Trotter, Travis Chad Morgan, Zaundra Rene Morgan, Judith Lin Morgan, Toni Dawn Adams. Cert. legal asst., U. Okla., 1982; student Oklahoma City U., 1981—. Cert. legal asst. Asst. cashier Texoma Bank, Kingston, Okla., 1974-76; adminstrv. legal asst. Jack T. Crabtree & Assocs., P.C., Oklahoma City, 1976-83; v.p. adminstrn. Kempton Co., Oklahoma City, 1983-85; paralegal Legal Support Group, Inc., Oklahoma City, 1985—, Planned Staffing, Inc., Oklahoma City. Mem. Okla. Paralegal Assn. (pres.-elect 1985—), Central Okla. Assn. Legal Assts., Nat. Assn. Legal Adminstrs. (past pres.). Lodge: Altrusa (treas. 1982, editor 1982). Home: 8105 Curtis Terr Oklahoma City OK 73116 Office: Legal Support Group Inc 6600 N Meridian Suite 230 Oklahoma City OK 73116

VINCE, JANET MARIE, accountant; b. Bridgeport, Conn., Feb. 11, 1951; d. Raymond Herbert and Ethel Helen (Halapin) V. B.S., Sacred Heart U., 1979. C.P.A., Conn. Sr. acct. J. Gabriel C.P.A., Bridgeport, Conn., 1982-86; freelance acct., Milford, Conn., 1986—. Mem. Conn. Soc. C.P.A.s, Nat. Assn. Female Execs., Am. Inst. C.P.A.s, Roman Catholic. Office: 23A Monroe St Milford CT 06460

VINCENT, BARBARA HATHCOCK, banker; b. Dundee, Fla., Nov. 3, 1938; d. Milton Augusta and Trummie (Mattox) Hathcock; m. Tommy G. Smith, Dec. 8, 1962 (div. 1978); children—Vicki Smith Allman, Timothy M.; m. Charles L. Vincent, Nov. 3, 1979 (div. 1982). Student Winter Haven Bus. Coll., 1959-61, St. Leo Jr. Coll., 1976-78. Exec. sec. circuit court judge, Bartow, Fla., 1960-64; paralegal Nelson, Hesse, et. al., Sarasota, Fla., 1968-76; v.p. First Am. Bank and Trust, Palm Beach, Fla., 1980—. Officer, dir. Jr. Woman's Club, Sarasota, 1968-74; leader Girl Scouts Am., Sarasota, 1966-69. Mem. Homebuilders Contractors Auzilliary, Beta Sigma Phi. Democrat. Office: First Am Bank and Trust Co 701 U S Hwy 1 North Palm Beach FL 33408

VINCENT, CLARE, museum curator; b. Jersey City, Aug. 30, 1935; d. Harold and Lorena (Cole) V.; A.B., Coll. William and Mary, 1958; M.A. Inst. Fine Arts, N.Y. U., 1963; cert. mus. tng. Met. Mus. Art and Inst. Fine Arts, 1963. Cataloguer slides Cooper Union Sch. Architecture, 1959-60; asst. to curator decorative arts Cooper Union Mus. Arts of Decoration, 1960-61; curatorial asst. western European arts Met. Mus. Art, N.Y.C., 1962-67, asst. curator, 1967-72, asso. curator European sculpture and decorative arts, 1972—; cons. to cataloguer of antique sci. instruments Adler Planetarium, Chgo., 1984—. Mem. Antiquarian Horological Soc. (v.p. Am. sect. 1977—), N.Y. Acad. Sci., Furniture History Soc., Société Internationale de l'Astrolabe, Internat. Union History and Philosophy of Sci. (sci. instrument commn.), History Sci. Soc., Renaissance Soc. Am., Coll. Art Assn. Author: European Clocks in New York Collections, 1972; Rodin at the Metropolitan Museum Art, 1981; contbr. in field. Home: 326 E 85th St New York NY 10028 Office: Metropolitan Museum of Art 5th Ave and 82d St New York NY 10028

VINCENT, HELEN, editor; b. Elizabeth, N.J.; d. James Burlin and Eva Harriet (Winter) V. B.A. with honors, Elmira Coll. Mng. editor: True Confessions, Macfadden-Bartell Corp., N.Y.C., 1954-73; editor, 1973-75, True Story, 1975—. Home: 10 Mohawk Trail Westfield NJ 07090 Office: 215 Lexington Ave New York NY 10016

VINCENT, M. DIANE, mental health administrator; b. Sandusky, Mich., Jan. 20, 1943; d. Frank Sherman and Ethyl Marie (Paige) Reiner; Ph.B., Wayne State U., 1965; M.A., Oakland U., 1978; m. Gerald Vincent, 1963 (div. 1978); children—Melissa, Michael, Geoffrey; m. Ronald W. Marr, 1985. Caseworker, State of Mich., 1965-66; therapist Project Fresh Start, Dept. Labor Spl. Project, Detroit, 1966-68; probation officer Recorders Ct., Detroit, 1968; dir. Hotline, Birmingham, Mich., 1971-75; adminstrv. dir., v.p., bd. dirs. Square Lake Mental Health Center, P.C., Birmingham, from 1975, now chief exec. officer; dir. Common Ground, Inc., 1975-80; pres. Whethersfield Assocs., consultants, 1980-84; mem. coordinators council Oakland County Office of Substance Abuse Services, 1972-80; sec.-treas. EAP, Inc., 1985—; cons. employability programming for women, 1979—, Booth Communications, 1982-84; mem. Oakland County Prosecutor's Task Force on Child Molesters, 1978; bd. dirs. Community Action Council. Trainer, empathy trainers; mem. Gov.'s Task Force Substance Abuse Prevention, 1972; sec. bd. dirs. Mich. Assn. Crisis Centers, 1972-75; mem. Substance Abuse Adv. Council, 1980-85; mem. adv. bd. Woodside Hosp., 1984—, Common Ground, 1980—; sec. bd. dirs. Madrigal Chorale. Cert. social worker, Mich. Mem. Mich. Assn. Substance Abuse Program Dirs., Am. Assn., Counseling and Devel. Mich. Assn. Program Dirs. Mich. Alcohol and Addiction Assn., Assn. Labor Mgmt. Adminstrs. and Cons. on Alcoholism. Co-author: Prosecuters Handbook To Prevent Child Molesting; A Guide to Public Access in Cable Television. Home: 1727 Washington St Birmingham MI 48009 Office: 2550 S Telegraph St Bloomfield Hills MI 48013

VINE, JANET DIANA, educator, author; b. Albany, N.Y., Apr. 6, 1937; d. Harold Arthur and Dora Mary (Meyer) Vine; B.A., Syracuse U., 1959; M.A., SUNY, 1964. Tchr. English, Herbert Hoover Jr. High Sch., Kenmore, N.Y., 1959-66; tchr. Kenmore East Sr. High Sch., 1966—, chmn. dept. English, 1970-83; cheerleading coach, 1959-77; sr. asso. Write Assos., 1982—. Mem. Am. Fedn. Tchrs., N.Y. State United Tchrs., Kenmore Tchrs. Assn., NEA, Nat. Council Tchrs. English, Authors Guild, Nat. League of Am. Pen Women (pres. Western N.Y. br. 1984-86), Assn. Profl. Women Writers, The Write People, Nat. Council Tchrs. English, AAUW, Pi Lambda Theta, Eta Pi Upsilon, Sigma Kappa. Methodist. Club: Kenmore Women Tchrs. Bowling Assn. (pres. 1983-84). Author: English: A Comprehensive Review, 1982; Discovering Literature, Reading Guide and Review Tests, 1968; Exploring Literature, Reading Guide and Review Tests, 1968; contbr. articles to newspapers and mags. Office: 350 Fries Rd Tonawanda NY 14150

VINECOUR, ONEIDA AGNES, nurse; b. Port Arthur, Tex., Oct. 15, 1917; d. Ernest Eugene and Gertrude Mary (Wooldridge) Thorn; m. Seymour Vinecour, Jan. 14, 1943 (dec. 1976); children—Seymour Jacob, Rebecca Leah. Diploma, St. Mary's Hosp. Sch. Nursing, Port Arthur, 1939; postgrad., cert. Surg. Tech., Anesthesia, Cook County Hosp., 1939-40; postgrad. U. Chgo., 1939-40, Tex. Coll. Mines, 1943. R.N. Operating room supr., instr. Schumpert Meml. Hosp., Shreveport, La., 1940-41; anesthetist St. Joseph Hosp., Albuquerque, 1941-42; operating room supr., instr. Lynn City Hosp. (Mass.), 1946-48; staff anesthetist St. Mary's Hosp., Port Arthur, Tex., 1951-53, in service dir., 1971-73; dept. head, supr. Park Pl. Hosp., Port Arthur, 1965-71; operating room supr. Mid-County Hosp., Nederland, Tex., 1973-81; staff nurse Baptist Meml. Hosp., Beaumont, Tex., 1973-81; part time staff Health Care Services, Port Arthur, 1983—; indsl. nurse Synpol Inc., 1984-86. Served as officer U.S. Army Nurse Corps, 1942-46. Mem. Am. Nurses Assn., Mass. Nurses Assn., Tex. State Nurses Assn. Republican. Methodist. Home: 2502 Glenwood Port Arthur TX 77642

VINELLI, MONIQUE FOREST, agribusiness executive, financial consultant; b. Montreal, Que., Can., Dec. 16, 1941; came to U.S., 1950; d. Joseph and Anita (Babin) Forest; m. Jose Luis Vinelli, Aug. 17, 1968; 1 son, Peter. A.A., Ottawa U., 1965; B.S., Fla. State U., 1978, M.B.A. summa cum laude, 1979. Bus. instr. Fgn. High Sch., Montevideo, Uruguay, Ottawa, Can., 1963-72; adminstrv. aide Dept. Health and Rehab. Services, Tallahassee, Fla., 1972-75; bus. cons., Tallahassee, 1976-79; cons. Fla. State U./SBA program; internat. lending officer C & S Nat. Bank, Atlanta, 1979-82; exec. v.p. Internat. Stock Food Corp., Waverly, N.Y., 1982—, cons., 1976-82; treas. bd. dirs. ISF Corp., Waverly, N.Y., 1983—. Mem. Beta Gamma Sigma. Roman Catholic. Home: Internat Stock Food Corp 533 Broad St Waverly NY 14892

VINES, DIANE WELCH, psychotherapist, educator; b. Rochester, Minn., Apr. 3, 1945; d. Howard Henshel and Edna (Steck) Welch; B.A., St. Petersburg Jr. Coll., 1964; B.S. magna cum laude, Vanderbilt U., 1967; M.A. with honors, N.Y.U., 1973; postgrad. Boston U.; 1 son, Juan Antonio. Coordinator emotionally disturbed children unit state hosp., Phila., 1967-68; instr. nursing Mt. Sinai Hosp. Sch. Nursing, N.Y.C., 1968-69; asst. dir. nursing Vista Hill Psychiat. Hosp., Chula Vista, Calif., 1969-70; chmn. dept. New Rochelle (N.Y.) Hosp. Sch. Nursing, 1970-71; part-time staff nurse Manhattan Bowery Project, N.Y.C., 1971-72; evening supr. state hosp. for emotionally disturbed children and adolescents, 1972-73; psychotherapist Albert Einstein Med. Center, Bronx, 1973-74; instr. Faulkner Hosp. Sch. Nursing, Boston, 1974-75; instr. students preparing for licensure exam. Mass., Boston, 1974-75; pvt. practice psychotherapy, co-founder Beacon Assos., Brookline, Mass., 1976—; dir. ambulatory nursing Boston Children's Hosp. Med. Center, 1975-78; asst. prof. grad. program psychiat. community mental health nursing, Boston, 1978—; White House fellow, spl. asst. to sec. edn., Washington, 1982-83; dir. Nat. Adult Literacy Initiative, U.S. Dept. Edn., 1983-85; dir. spl. programs Calif. State U., 1985—; adv. com. Mass. Bd. Registration in Nursing; co-founder sexual abuse program Children's Hosp. Med. Center, Boston, 1977, cons., 1978; psychiat. nurse cons. Criminal Victimology Cons., Inc., Boston, 1978. Active, YMCA, Germantown, Pa.; vol. activities dir. Boys' Club, National City, Calif. Recipient Nat. Research Service award, 1981; cert. psychiat. nurse, psychotherapist, Mass.; cert. secondary sch. tchr., Pa. Mem. Am. Nurses Assn., Am. Orthopsychiat. Assn., Nurses United for Reimbursement of Services, Advanced Council on Psychiat. Mental Health Nursing (Am. Nurses Assn.), AAUW, Advocates for Child Psychiat. Nursing, Am. Sociol. Assn., Sigma Theta Tau (treas. 1966-67), Contbr. articles to profl. jours. Home: 2606 Purdue Ave Los Angeles CA 90064 Office: Calif State U 400 Golden Shore Long Beach CA 90802

VINEYARD, GERRY LYNN LESTER, educator; b. Monroe, La., Aug. 28, 1938; d. A.J. and Mattie Lou (Oliver) Lester; B.A., NE La. U., 1959, M.A., 1963; student Saltillo Tchrs. Coll., Mex., Southwestern Theol. Sem., Ft. Worth; m. Percy Ray Vineyard, July 7, 1962; children—William Webster, Margaret Loraine, Elizabeth. Tchr. West Monroe (La.) Jr. High Sch., 1959-61, Crosley Elementary Sch., West Monroe, 1961-62, Ouachita (La.) Parish Jr. High Sch., 1963-65, Ponchatoula (La.) High Sch., 1968-69, Natalbany (La.) Bapt. Sch., 1970-74, Madisonville (La.) Jr. High Sch., 1975-80, Covington (La.) High Sch., 1980—. Nat. Def. Act grantee, 1960. Mem. Council Exceptional Children, Assn. Children with Learning Disabilities, La. Edn. Assn., NEA, DAR (state chmn. 1972-75, librarian 1976-78). Democrat. Baptist. Clubs: Les Medames, Womans Missionary Union. Office: PO Box 838 Covington LA 70440

VINEYARD, PHYLLIS SMITH, maternal and child health cons.; b. Ridgefield, Conn., Nov. 22, 1923; student Simmons Coll., Boston U., 1941-44, U. Mo., 1945, SUNY, Empire State Coll., 1982; m. George Vineyard, Feb. 3, 1946; children—John, Barbara. Chmn., Suffolk (N.Y.) Community Council, 1977-79, Nassau-Suffolk Health Systems Agy., 1979-80; mem. council Coll. of Old Westbury, SUNY; former chmn. N.Y. Statewide Health Coordinating Council; dir. L.I. Lighting Co.; lectr. and analyst on health policy UN Conf. for Women, Copenhagen, 1980, White House Conf. on Families, 1980, UN Conf. on Population, Geneva, 1983; leader in China for family planning workers, 1977, 78, 81. Recipient Humanitarian award ARC, L.I. Profl. Women's award, 1981. Mem. Am. Pub. Health Assn., Nat. Assn. Corp. Dirs., NOW.

VINSON, JENNIE ANN, business executive, consultant; b. Pasadena, Tex., Apr. 25, 1946; d. Charles Eugene and Iva (Vaughn) V.; m. Bruce Elliott Hlavacek, Sept. 27, 1980. B.B.A, Lamar U., 1968. Acctg. office supr. Southwestern Bell Telephone Co., Houston, 1973-75, phone power specialist, 1975-76, sales mgr., 1976-77, dist. mgr., St. Louis, 1977-79, div. mgr., Dallas, 1979-82; br. mgr. AT&T, Dallas, 1982-83; owner, chief exec. officer Exec. Compensation Systems, Inc., Dallas, 1983—; sec., dir. C & I Devel. Corp., Houston, 1979—. Mem. Tex. Women's Polit. Caucus, Dallas, 1983-84; sponsor Dallas Pub. Opera, 1983-84; bd. dirs. Recovery Assn., 1984. Mem. Nat. Speakers Assn., NOW, Club: University (Dallas). Home: 14933 Oaks N Dr Addison TX 75240 Office: Exec Compensation Systems Inc 14800 Quorum Dr Suite 200 Dallas TX 75240

VINSON, JULIA ANN (JUDD), accounting/consulting company executive; b. Memphis, Sept. 10, 1940; d. John Ervin Shelby and Mary Erlene (Gregory) Creekmur. B.S. No. Ill. U., 1975. Asst. to dir. mgmt. info. services Michael Reese Hosp., Chgo., 1976-79; v.p. mgmt. info. services Nat. Bus. Lists, Chgo., 1979-82; sr. v.p. mgmt. info. services and long-range planning Allnet Communication Services Inc., Chgo., 1982-86; owner Casady & Assocs., Lacey, Wash., 1986—, dir. Philon Inc., N.Y.C. Mem. Assn. Systems Mgmt., Data Processing Mgmt. Assn., Nat. Assn. Female Execs. Republican. Office: Casady & Assocs 4412 Pacific Ave Lacey WA 98503

VINSON, MARGARET CAROLYN, petroleum properties broker; b. Waco, Tex., May 29, 1942; d. Presley Ewing and Margaret Helen (Pond) V.; m. Robert C. L. Robertson II, Aug. 27, 1960 (div. July 1964); children—Lisa Lee Robertson Williamson, Laura Ellen. Student U. Tex., 1960-61, Art Ctr. Sch., Los Angeles, 1962-63, Massey Bus. Coll., 1964, Inst. Energy Devel., Houston, 1980. Sec., chmn. bd. Continental Oil Co., Houston, 1964-68; exec. asst. Reading & Bates, Houston, 1969-71; prodn. coordinator King Resources Co., Denver, 1974-75; adminstrv. asst. Astrodamain Corp., Houston, 1976-78; exec. asst. Lucey Products Co., Houston, 1978-80; self-employed as petroleum properties broker, Houston, 1980—. Instr., Jefferson and Weld County 4-H, Colo., Denver, 1972-74; precinct chmn. Macey for Mayor Campaign, Houston, 1981; mem. steering com. Tim Hearns Benefit, Houston, 1982; vol. Am. Heart Assn., Houston, 1983. Mem. Am. Assn. Petroleum Landmen, Houston Assn. Petroleum Landmen. Presbyterian.

VINTON, DOLORES (DEE) ANNE, corporation executive, consultant; b. Chgo., Oct. 8, 1930; d. Roy A. and Hattie Anne (Younger) Berg; m. Charles J. Vinton, Sept. 29, 1951 (div. 1968); children—Sharon Anne, Charles Daniel. Student Ariz. State U., 1967, Ednl. Inst. Am. Motel and Hotel Assn., 1977; diploma Wine Inst., San Francisco, 1974. Cert. in food service sanitation. Actress, Bobbie Ball Agy., Scottsdale, Ariz., 1966-77; recreation supr. pub. relations dept. City of Tempe (Ariz.), 1966-68; mgr. pub. facilities Sky Chefs, Tulsa and Phoenix, 1970-78; sr. food service dir. Saga Corp., San Francisco, 1978—, also job bank dir. for hiring handicapped, 1982—. Bd. dirs. Ariz. Cactus Pine council Girl Scouts U.S.A., 1961-64, dist. chmn., 1964; mem. com. Scottsdale Town Enrichment Program, 1965; mem. Mayor's Com. Hiring of Handicapped, San Francisco, 1983. Recipient Disting. Pub. Service award City of Scottsdale, 1965; Life Saving award City of Phoenix, 1970; cert. of merit Gov.'s Com. Hiring of Handicapped, 1979, 81; cert. of appreciation Careers Abound, 1982, award for support employment of disabled youth, 1983; named Calif. Small Employer of Yr., Calif. Gov.'s Com., 1982; named Employer of Yr., Goodwill Industries, 1982. Mem. AFTRA, Nat. Assn. Female Execs., Nat. Assn. Bus. and Profl. Women. Clubs: Commonwealth, Golden Gate Tennis (San Francisco). Home: 550 Battery Apt 2003 San Francisco CA 94111

VINTON, KAREN LYNN, management educator; b. Evanston, Ill., Dec. 21, 1949; d. Robert Eugene and Frances Irene (Shields) Edwards; m. Richard Otto Vinton, Sept. 25, 1976. A.B., Ind. U., 1971, M.B.A., 1974; Ph.D., U. Utah, 1983. Switching services supr. Ind. Bell Telephone Co., Indpls., 1971-76, asst. facilities supr., 1976, mgmt. employment coordinator, 1976-77; state employment mgr. Mountain Bell Telephone Co., Salt Lake City, 1977-79; research asst. U. Utah, 1979-82; asst. prof. mgmt. Mont. State U., Bozeman, 1983—; cons., dir. Roy M. Moffitt Co., Schiller Park, Ill., 1981—; co-owner MMC, Belgrade, Mont., 1983—. Sec. Friends of Gallatin Library, Bozeman, 1983-84, pres., 1985; trustee Bozeman Pub. Library, 1986; mem. Utah Commn. on Employment and Careers for Women, Salt Lake City, 1977-79; vice chmn. Voting Dist., Salt Lake City, 1978-80; adv. bd. Rapline, Indpls., 1971-73. Recipient Excellence award Bozeman C. of C., 1983. Mem. Acad. Mgmt., Am. Soc. for Personnel Adminstrn., Internat. Council for Small Bus., Am. Inst. for Decision Scis., Soc. for Applied Anthropology, Bozeman Assn. Personnel Adminstrs. (pres. 1985-86), Zeta Tau Alpha (alumni sec. Indpls. 1976-77, alumni pres. Salt Lake City 1977-82, Dist. Service award 1983). Home: 2915 Secor St Bozeman MT 59715 Office: Montana State U Sch of Business Bozeman MT 59717

VINTON, KENDRA JO, medical technologist, microbiologist, b. Takoma Park, Md., Oct. 20, 1955; d. Kenneth Watrous and Margaret May (Lustig) V. B.S. in Animal Sci., U. Md., 1977, B.S. in Med. Tech., 1978; M.A. in Mgmt. and Supervision, Central Mich. U., 1983. Adminstr., bookeeper, cons. Lynn Animal Hosp., Riverdale, Md., 1974—; med. technologist VA Med. Ctr., Washington, 1979-81; sr. med. technologist Walter Reed Army Med. Ctr., Washington, 1981—. Mem. Friends of Nat. Zoo, Washington, 1979—. Recipient Letter of Appreciation for Dedication to Duty VA, 1980. Mem. Nat. Assn. Female Execs., Am. Soc. Clin. Pathologists, Am. Soc. Med. Technologists, Am. Soc. Microbiology, U. Md. Alumni Assn., Phi Sigma, Alpha Phi Zeta, Alpha Omicron Pi. Republican. Lutheran. Avocations: antiques; photography;

water sports; needlework. Home: 14726 Valiant Terr Laurel MD 20707 Office: Walter Reed Army Med Ctr Dept Pathology Washington DC

VIOLET, ARLENE, attorney general Rhode Island; b. Providence, Aug. 19, 1943; d. Henry and Alice (Duffy) V. B.A., Salve Regina Coll., 1966; J.D., Boston Coll., 1974. Legal intern R.I. Legal Service, 1971-73; jud. asst. Supreme Ct., 1974-75; chief legal counsel, office consumer affairs R.I. Atty. Gen.'s Office, 1975-76; pub. interest atty. State of R.I., 1976-84; atty. gen. R.I., Providence, 1985—. Mem. R.I. Bar Assn., NOW. Office: RI Atty Gen 72 Pine St Providence RI 02903*

VIPPERMAN, CAROL FAYE, consultant; b. Renton, Wash., Feb. 24, 1948; d. James Riley and Lydia Bobbyette (Caldwell) V.; m. Jerry Lee Price, Mar. 10, 1979. B.A., U. Wash., 1970. Service rep. Liberty Mut. Ins. Co., Seattle, 1970-72; group sales mgr. John A. Tetley Co., Seattle, 1972-76; regional sales mgr. Harrison Hotel, Seattle, 1976-78; pres. Carol Vipperman Inc., Seattle, 1978—; bd. advisers No. Sun, Inc., Lynnwood, Wash., 1983-84, W.I.S.E., Bellevue, Wash., 1984—; mem. mktg. adv. bd. Seattle office Deloitte Haskins & Sells. Author: Solution to Sales Problems, 1983; contbr. articles to profl. jours. Bd. dirs. Alki Found., Seattle, 1984; advocate Seattle Children's Home, 1984; chmn. Wash. State Small Bus. Improvement Council, 1984-86; participant White House Conf. on Small Bus., 1986. Mem. Travellarians (pres. 1974-75), Sales and Mktg. Execs. (pres. 1980-81), Internat. Transactional Analysis Assn. (spl. fields mem. 1982—), Women Bus. Owners (co-founder 1979-80), Greater Seattle C. of C. (vice chmn. 1984-86). Democrat. Club: Seattle. Office: Carol Vipperman Inc 1932 1st Ave Suite 609 Seattle WA 98101

VIRGA, KAREN FAYE, physical therapist; b. San Jose, Calif., Apr. 14, 1951; d. Nicholas and Edna Faye (Bishop) Chimento; m. Richard Virga, June 22, 1975; children—Jason, Justin. B.S., NYU, 1975; M.A., Columbia U. Lic. phys. therapist, N.Y., Conn. Phys. therapist Burke Rehab. Ctr., White Plains, N.Y., 1975-79, Danbury Ortho. Assocs., Conn., 1980—; lab instr. neurobiology NYU, 1978-79; lectr. Danbury Orthopedic Assocs., 1983—; pvt. practice phys. therapy, N.Y. and Conn., 1975—; dir. Back Sch., Danbury Orthopedic Assocs., 1985—. Contbr. articles to profl. jours. Mem. Am. Phys. Therapy Assn., Arthritis Found., Paraplegic Found. Democrat. Home: 12 Kilian Dr Danbury CT 06811 Office: Danbury Orthopedic Assocs 73 Sandpit Rd Danbury CT 06811

VIRNICH, S. JOYCE, mktg. exec.; b. Ft. Lauderdale, Fla., Apr. 15, 1941; d. James Barney Wetherington and Bonnie Maxine (Hull) Wetherington Murphy; B.S., U. Tulsa, 1963; postgrad. Northwestern U., 1964, DePaul U., 1966; 1 son, Patrick Eugene. Leasing mgr. Apeco Corp., Des Plaines, Ill., 1963-70; regional credit mgr. Bell & Howell Corp., Chgo., 1971; adminstrv. sales mgr. Oce-Industries, Inc., Chgo., 1971-73, product mgr. design and engring. div., 1977-83; dir. mktg. communications CPT Corp., Mpls., 1983—; pres. Genesis Group, Inc., Waukegan, Ill., 1973-77. Treas., Lake Forest Condominium Assn. Mem. Am. Mgmt. Assn., Internat. Entrepreneur's Assn., Nat. Computer Graphics Assn., Nat. Microfilm Assn., Nat. Assn. Female Execs. Republican. Home: 14199 Valley View Rd Eden Prairie MN 55344 Office: 8100 Mitchell Rd Eden Prairie MN 55344

VIROSTKO, JOAN, educator; b. Jackson Heights, N.Y., Feb. 6; d. John and Dorothy Veronica (Eckert) Virostko. Cert. of Studies, Oxford U., 1972; B.S., St. John's U., 1968, M.S., 1970, P.D., 1972, 85, M.B.A., 1980, Ph.D., 1983. Cert. elem. tchr., N.Y.; cert. sch. bldg. adminstr., sch. dist. adminstr., N.Y. Educator Half Hollow Hills Paumanok Sch., Dix Hills, N.Y.; instr. Oxford U., England, summer 1985, 86. Contbr. Ellis Island Found, 1984-86; sustaining mem. Rep. Nat. Com., 1980—. Recipient Disting. Dissertation award, 1983; named Educator of Yr., N.Y. State Assn. Tchrs., 1985. Mem. N.Y. State United Tchrs. Assn., Kappa Delta Pi, Phi Delta Kappa, Alpha Sigma Alpha, Delta Sigma Chi. Republican. Roman Catholic. Avocations: traveling; music; stamp and coin collecting; skiing; water sports. Office: Paumanok Sch 1 Seaman Neck Road Dix Hills NY 11746

VISCONTI, JANNA PEARL, lawyer, artist; b. N.Y.C., Dec. 17, 1952; d. Stanley Schwartz and Marion Sue (Wasserman) Goldstein; m. Richard D. Visconti, Dec. 31, 1985. B.F.A., Pratt Inst., 1975; J.D., St. John's U., 1979. Bar: N.Y. 1979, Ariz. 1982. Assoc. firm Rogers & Wells, N.Y.C., 1979-82, Snell & Wilmer, Phoenix, 1982-85, Cummings & Lockwood, Stamford, Conn., 1985—. Mem. Friends of Vol. Bur., Phoenix, 1983-84. Mem. ABA, N.Y. State Bar Assn., Nat. Assn. Bond Lawyers, State Bar Ariz., Maricopa County Bar Assn., Ariz. Women Lawyers Assn. Episcopalian. Club: Phoenix Fencer's. Office: Cummings & Lockwood 10 Stamford Forum Stamford CT 06904

VISCUSO, SHARON LYNNE, manufacturing company manager; b. Long Beach, Calif., Dec. 14, 1944; d. Harvey Wyrill and Doris June (Henneberry) Kenworthy; m. Jeffrey Richard Viscuso, Feb. 28, 1970. B.A. in Psychology cum laude, Upsala Coll., 1966. Vol. U.S. Peace Corps, Philippines, 1966-68; mgmt. devel. and tng. assoc./specialist Western Electric Co., N.Y.C., 1968-71, sect. chief manpower devel., 1971-72, buyer, East Orange, N.J., 1972-76; mgr. contract adminstrn. Wallace Computer Services, Hillside, Ill., 1976-85, mgr. price and contract adminstrn., 1985—. Mem. Nat. Assn. Female Execs., Upsala Coll. Alumni Assn. (alumni council 1974-76). Republican. Episcopalian. Avocations: singing; reading; photography. Home: 303 Norton Ln Bloomingdale IL 60108 Office: Wallace Computer Services Inc 4600 W Roosevelt Rd Hillside IL 60162

VISTA, ANICETA ABOBO, nurse; b. San Jose, Philippines, July 16, 1947; came to U.S., 1972, naturalized, 1978; d. Rufo Pragata and Maria Marzo Abobo; m. Denis Bueta Vista, Jan. 23, 1971; children—Diane, Anne Marie. Student nursing Philippines Statesmen Coll., Cabanatuan City, 1965; degree in nursing Martinez Sch. Nursing, Caloocan City, Philippines, 1968; B.S. in Nursing, Philippines Womens' U., Manila, 1970; postgrad. Columbia Pacific U., 1985—. R.N., Mich., N.Y., W.Va. Charge nurse Nagcarlan Hosp. Laguna, Philippines, 1968-69; staff nurse, charge San Lazaro Hosp., Manila, 1970-72; pvt. duty nurse, Weirton, W.Va., 1972-73; staff-charge-asst. head nurse Detroit Osteo. Hosp., 1973-79; supr., clin. nurse specialist, pres., dir. Vista Nursing Services, Troy, Mich., 1980—; v.p., adminstr. PRN Nurse Specialists, Inc., Southfield, Mich., 1982-85, also dir.; v.p. Expanded Health Specialists, Ltd., Southfield, 1985—, also dir.; v.p. Di-Ann Corp., 1983—; dir. PNAM Corp., Southfield. Author: Cardiac Rehabilitation, 1979. Treas. Kiwanis Cosmo Cheerleaders, Southfield, 1982-83; mem. Philippines Health and Med. Campaign, Southfield, 1985—, Novo Ecijanos, Mich., 1985—. Mem. Philippine Nurses Assn. of Mich. (pres.; bd. dirs., Outstanding Woman award 1985), Nat. Orgn. Philippine Nurses in U.S., Mich. Nurses Assn. Roman Catholic. Club: Willowood Assn. Avocations: tennis; golf; volleyball; reading. Home: 1676 Black Maple Dr Rochester Hills MI 48063

VITA, DIANA, aerobics instructor; b. N.Y.C., Aug. 22, 1955; d. Michael Joseph and Lillian Diana (Mandracchia) V. B.A., Hunter Coll., 1978. Instr. aerobics and slimnastics YMCA, Bklyn., 1981-83; owner, mgr. Diana Vita's Aerobic Dance Studio, Bklyn., 1983—. Instr., Sch. Settlement, Bklyn., 1982-83, 85, Mut. of N.Y. (MONY), N.Y.C., 1983, ITT, N.Y.C., 1983—, Pratt Inst., Bklyn., 1985—. Mem. Aerobics and Fitness Assn. Am. Office: Diana Vita's Aerobic Dance Studio 776A Manhattan Ave Brooklyn NY 11222

VITAGLIANO, MARIA TERESA, real estate broker, investor, lawyer; b. N.Y.C., Dec. 26, 1946; d. Giuseppe and Kathryn Eleanor Vitagliano. Student Smith Coll., 1964-66; B.A., Barnard Coll., 1969; M.A., Middlebury Coll., 1971; J.D., Pace U., 1979. Bar: Fla. 1980, N.Y. 1980. Saleswoman, mem. mgmt. G. Vitagliano Real Estate Agy., N.Y.C., 1969-83; owner, 1983—. Mem. Com. to Oppose Sale of St. Bartholomew's Ch., N.Y.C., 1984. Mem. Palm Beach County Bar Assn., N.Y. Bar Assn., ABA, N.Y. Bd. Real Estate. Republican. Clubs: N.Y. Jr. League; Belle Haven (Greenwich, Conn.). Office: M Vitagliano Real Estate Agy 403 E 58th St New York NY 10022

VITAL, TINA JEAN, chemical engineer; b. Atlantic City, Dec. 22, 1953; d. Andrew and Dorothy (Clark) Vital; B.S., U. Pitts., 1976; M.S. in Chem. Engring., Lehigh U., 1979; postgrad. U. Mass., 1985—. Engring. intern Hoffman LaRoche, Inc., Nutley, N.J., summer, 1980; control engr. Exxon Chem. Ams., Baytown, Tex., 1980-83; applications engr. combustion engring. Simcon, Bloomfield, N.J., 1983-85. Mem. Soc. Women Engrs., Am. Inst. Chem. Engrs., Am. Chem. Soc., Nat. Soc. Profl. Engrs. Contbr. articles to profl. jours.

VITALE, ANNE THERESE, lawyer; b. N.Y.C., Sept. 27, 1947; d. Ventura John and Flora Rose (Cerrato) Vitale. B.A., Fordham U., 1970; M.Ed., Boston Coll., 1974; J.D., Fordham U., 1981. Bar: N.Y. 1982, U.S. Dist. Ct. (so. dist.) N.Y. 1982. Tchr. St. Vito Sch., Mamaroneck, N.Y., 1970-73, St. Helena Comml. High Sch., Bronx, N.Y., 1973-78; law clk. U.S. Dist. Ct., N.Y.C., 1981-82; assoc. Andrew M. Lawler, P.C., N.Y.C., 1983; asst. U.S. atty., N.Y.C., 1983—. Editor Fordham Law Rev., 1980-81. Recipient William Hughes Mullican Moot Ct. award Fordham Law Sch., 1979, Sutherland Moot Ct. award Catholic U., 1980. Mem. N.Y. State Bar Assn., ABA, N.Y. State Women's Bar Assn., Fordham Law Rev. Alumni Assn. of N.Y.C. (bd. govs. 1981—). Democrat. Roman Catholic. Home: Apt 5A 7 W 73d St New York NY 10023 Office: US Attorney's Office 1 St Andrews Plaza New York NY 10007

VITALE, CONCETTA, educational administrator, nurse; b. New Kensington, Pa., May 21; d. Theodore R. and Anna Marie (Pecoraro) V.; m. Joseph Lewis Hlafcsak, Mar. 19, 1983; children—Susan, Judith. Diploma in Nursing, Mercy Hosp. Sch. Nursing, 1960; B.S., U. Pitts., 1973, M.S. in Nursing, 1975, postgrad., 1985. Staff nurse Mercy Hosp., Pitts., 1960-61, 67-68, VA Hosp., Butler, Pa., 1961-62, VA Hosp., Pitts., 1962-67; faculty Catherine McAuley Sch. Practical Nursing, Pitts., 1968-73; pvt. duty nurse Mercy Hosp., Pitts., 1973-75; faculty U. Pitts., 1975-77; clin. specialist John J. Kane, Hosp., 1977-78; nurse clinician Western Psychiat. Inst. and Clinic, U. Pitts., 1978-81; dir. nursing Community Coll. Allegheny County-Boyce Campus, Monroeville, Pa., 1981—; mem. craft adv. com. Forbes Rd. E. Area Vocat. Tech. Sch., Monroeville, 1981. Vol. Pitts. Action Against Rape, 1977, 78. Mem. Am. Nurses Assn., Pa. Assn. Assoc. Degree Nurse Educators (sec. 1983-87), Sigma Theta Tau (sec. Eta chpt. 1984-86). Roman Catholic. Avocations: skiing; hiking; biking. Home: 5421 Kentucky Ave Pittsburgh PA 15232 Office: Community Coll Allegheny County-Boyce Campus 595 Beatty Rd Monroeville PA 15146

VITALE, LINDA BEIER, advertising agency executive; b. Dover, N.J., Oct. 27, 1944; d. Helmuth and Frieda (Griesbach) Beier; m. Lawrence C. Vitale, Aug. 27, 1972; 1 dau., Leslie. B.A., Roanoke Coll., 1966. Jr. copywriter Leber, Katz, Paccione, N.Y.C., 1967-69; promotional writer Doyle Dane Bernbach, N.Y.C., 1969-73, 75-76; copywriter DKG Advt., N.Y.C., 1973-75; promotional writer Wells, Rich, Greene Advt., N.Y.C., 1976-78, v.p., 1979—; sr. copywriter Batton, Barton, Durstein & Osborne, N.Y.C., 1978-79. Recipient several awards N.Y. Art Dirs. Club. Republican. Lutheran. Home: One Kitchell Rd Convent Station NJ 07961 Office: Greene Advt 9 W 57th St New York NY 10019

VITENAS, BIRUTE KAZLAUSKAS, systems engineer; b. Los Angeles, Feb. 12, 1949; d. Vincent and Valeria (Dambrauskaite) Kazlauskas; B.S. in Stats., Stanford U., 1970; M.S. in Ops. Research, Columbia U., 1972; postgrad. Rutgers U., 1976; m. Almis T. Vitenas, July 4, 1970; 1 son, Aleksas Joseph. Mem. of tech. staff-switching maintenance Bell Labs., Holmdel, N.J., 1970-71, mem. tech. staff PAR Radar Evaluation, Whippany, N.J., 1971-74, mem. tech. staff, operator services planning, Holmdel, 1974-77, supr. operator services planning, 1977-81, dept. head network project planning, 1981-83; asst. to v.p. customer systems AT&T Info. Systems, Lincroft, N.J., 1983-85; dir. tech. program analysis AT&T Bell Labs, 1985—. Mem. Ops. Research Soc. Am., Am. Statis. Assn. Republican. Roman Catholic. Office: AT&T Bell Labs Holmdel NJ

VITILLO, REBECCA ANNE, nursing executive; b. Newark, Jan. 23, 1946; d. Ralph and Helen Jacqualyn (Naturale) V. B.S.N., Seton Hall U., 1971. R.N.; cert. nurse adminstr. Staff nurse Morristown Meml. Hosp., N.J., 1971-72; staff nurse, operating room nurse Columbus Hosp., Newark, 1972-76, supr. operating room, 1976-80, assoc. dir. nursing, 1980—. Sch. nurse, Villa Walsh Acad., Morristown, 1972-76, tchr. health, biology, sci., 1972-76. Mem. Assn. Operating Room Nurses, ARC, Am. Nurses Assn., N.J. Soc. Nursing Adminstrs., N.J. Nurses Assn., Nat. League Nurses. Republican. Roman Catholic. Avocations: organ; piano; guitar; reading; dancing. Home: 111 Passaic Ave Apt C2 Nutley NJ 07110 Office: Columbus Hosp 495 N 13th St Newark NJ 07107

VITLE, ANNA M., construction company executive, real estate management executive; b. Newark, July 17, 1942; d. Andrew and Pearl (Chelak) Franchak; m. Frederick R. Vitale, May 7, 1961; children—F. Richard, J. Steven, J. Christipher. Student Trenton State Coll., 1967-68. Vice pres. Vitran, Inc., Allentown, N.J., 1972-80, pres., 1980—, also dir.; mgr., owner LaChez Salon, Allentown, 1966-76, Colonial Manor Salon, Jacobstown, N.J., 1977—. Mem. U.S. Trotting Assn., N.J. and Pa. Racing Commn., Am. Soc. Noteries. Home: RD 1 Box 111-5 Wrightstown NJ 08562

VITTER, PATRICIA BUTLER, lawyer; b. Gainesville, Fla., Dec. 31, 1951; d. Robert Hardy and Charleton (Galloway) Butler; m. William R. Vitter, Dec. 2, 1978; 1 son, Robert S. B.S.Ed., Fla. State U., 1973, J.D., 1975. Bar: Fla. 1976. Jud. asst. 2d Dist. Ct. Apls., Lakeland, Fla., 1976-77; atty. Charles Mixon, Tampa, 1977-79; sole practice, Inverness, Fla., 1979—. Bd. dirs. Withlacochee Area Legal Services, Ocala, Fla., 1980-82; trustee Central Fla. Community Coll., Ocala, 1984; mem. regional citizens adv. council Withlacochee Regional Planning Council, 1982—. Mem. Fla. Bar Assn., ABA, Citrus County Bar Assn., Tri County Bar Assn., Citrus County C. of C., Beta Sigma Phi. Democrat. Methodist. Club: Altrusa. Home: 1215 E Bucknell St Inverness Fl 32650 Office: 405 Grace St PO Box 881 Inverness FL 32651

VITTI, MADELYN MARIE, accounting service company executive; b. Stamford, Conn., Jan. 17, 1960; d. Nazzareno James and Anna Marie (Forlenzo) V. B.B.A. in Acctg., U. No. Fla., 1982. Acctg. mgr. Shawnee Airlines, Miami, Fla., 1978-80; night auditor Inn at Baymeadows, Jacksonville, Fla., 1981-83; asst. cashier Capital Bank, Miami, 1983-85; pres. Acctg. for Small Bus., Inc., Jacksonville, 1985—, chmn. bd., 1985, treas., 1985-86. Mem. Nat. Assn. Female Execs. Republican. Lutheran. Avocations: racquetball; knitting. Office: Acctg for Small Bus Inc One San Jose Pl 14-H Jacksonville FL 32217

VITTORI, WENDY DOREEN, software company executive; b. Washington, Sept. 9, 1951; d. Francis and Doreen (Possnett) V. A.B. cum laude, Radcliffe Coll., 1973; M.B.A., Northeastern U., 1977; postgrad. Harvard Bus. Sch., 1977-80. Corp. programmer, analyst Med. Info. Tech., Inc., Cambridge, Mass., 1973-74; systems mgr. Ctr. for Med Manpower Studies, Northeastern U., Boston, 1974-77; cons. pvt. practice, Boston, 1977-80; group mgr. med. info. systems Digital Equipment Corp., Marlboro, Mass., 1980-83; pres., chief exec. officer Computers in Medicine, Cambridge, 1983—; founder EMERGE, Inc., Boston, 1985—. Contbr. articles to profl. jours. Recipient Merit award Beta Gamma Sigma, 1977; named Ten Outstanding Young Leaders Boston Jaycees, 1985; Arthur D. Little Found. fellow, 1979, Harvard Bus. Sch. admissions fellow, 1977. Mem. Bus. Assocs. Club. Clubs: Harvard, Ten (Boston). Office: Computers in Medicine Inc 124 Mt Auburn St Cambridge MA 02138

VITZ, EVELYN BIRGE, foreign language educator, writer; b. Indpls., Oct. 16, 1941; m. 1969; 5 children. B.A., Smith Coll., 1963; Ph.D. in French, Yale U., 1968. From instr. to asst. prof. NYU, 1968-74, assoc. prof. French, 1974—, co-dir. Medieval and Renaissance studies, 1983—. NEH fellow, 1974-75. Mem. MLA, Medieval Acad. Am., Société Rencesvals. Author: The Crossroad of Intentions: A Study of Symbolic Expression in the Poetry of François Villon, 1974; A Continual Feast: A Cookbook to Celebrate the Joys of Family and Faith Throughout the Christian Year, 1985. Contbr. articles to profl. jours. Address: Dept French NYU New York NY 10003

VIZNER, TATJANA, psychiatrist; b. Zrenjanin, Yugoslavia, Nov. 2, 1944; came to U.S., 1963, naturalized, 1982; d. Radoslav and Helen (Jassarewsky) Vukanovich; m. Nikola Vizner, Mar. 8, 1971; children—Vladimir, Julius. Student Vassar Coll. 1963-66; M.D., Belgrade Med. Sch. (Yugoslavia), 1973. Diplomate Am. Bd. Psychiatry and Neurology. Intern, Belgrade Clinic Hosp., 1973-74; resident ob-gyn St. Francis Gen. Hosp., Pitts., 1977-80; fellow psychosomatic and liaison medicine SUNY Downstate Med. Center, Bklyn., 1980-81; cons., liaison psychiatrist Goldwater Meml. Hosp., NYU Med. Center, N.Y.C., 1982-84; practice medicine specializing in psychiatry, Bklyn., 1982—. Mem. Am. Psychiat. Assn., Am. Assn. for Advancement Liaison Psychiatry. Contbr. articles to profl. jours. Home: 5223 9th Ave Brooklyn NY 11220 Office: 9920 4th Ave Brooklyn NY 11209

VLACHOS, CAROL GLISSMAN, lawyer; b. Denver, July 15, 1957; d. Richard Lee and Jean Audrey (Riggs) Glissman; m. Stacey Daniel Vlachos, Aug. 15, 1981. B.S. with high honors in Psychology and Criminal Justice, Mich. State U., 1979; J.D., Wayne State U., 1982. Bar: Mich. 1983, N.J. 1983. Sole practice, Southgate, Mich., 1983—. Active Big Sister, Big Bros., East Lansing, Mich., 1979. Mem. ABA, Bar Assn., Women's Lawyers Assn. Mich., Dearborn Bar Assn., Downriver Bar Assn., Phi Kappa Phi, Tau Sigma, Alpha Phi, Delta Theta Phi, Lambda Chi, Sigma Chi. Greek Orthodox. Club: Soroptimist Internat. Home: 22351 Cherryhill Dearborn MI 48180

VLACHOS, ESTELLA MARIA, construction company executive; b. Santa Monica, Calif., Oct. 24, 1939; d. Rudolph John and Estelle Smith (Scott) Carlson; A.A., Long Beach City Coll., 1959; student Long Beach State Coll., 1959-60; m. Emanuel James Vlachos, Feb. 19, 1966. Acct. Smith & Smith, public accts. Long Beach, 1959-65; auditor, tax acct. Lyons, Bandell & Bryant C.P.A.s, Santa Ana, Calif., 1965-67, Diehl, Evans & Co., Santa Ana, 1967-69; controller, C.R.S. Inc., Mikkelson Enterprises Inc., and San Bernardino Bus. Men's Assn., computerized credit reporting and collection, 1969-73; controller Griffith Bros., constrn., farming and fruit packing houses, Orange Calif., 1973—; comptroller Trans Western Airlines of Utah, 1978-81. Mem. parish council Greek Orthodox Ch., also ch. treas. Mary E. Baker Meml. scholar, 1957; Am. Soc. Women Accountants scholar, 1959. Lic. collector, tax preparer. Mem. Am. Soc. Women Accts. (pres. chpt.), Nat. Notary Assn., Taxpreparers Assn. Calif. (charter), Soc. Calif. Accts., Nat. Soc. Public Accts. Smithsonian Assos. Designer computerized acctg. program for collection agys. Home: PO Box 6094 Anaheim CA 92807 Office: 1421 N Wanda Rd 200 Orange CA 92667

VLAHAC, MARY ANN RITA, market research consultant; small business owner; b. Bridgeport, Conn., June 11, 1954; d. John S. and Catherine R. (Landor) V.; m. James Thomas Westerman, May 13, 1978; 1 child, Christopher James. A.S., Housatonic Community Coll., 1974; B.S., U. Conn., 1976; M.B.A., U. Bridgeport, 1980. Market research Remington Arms/duPont, Bridgeport, 1976-79; sr. market research staff Pitney Bowes, Stamford, Conn., 1979—; v.p. mktg. Mar-Kris Trading Co., Stratford, Conn., 1985—; owner Gewgaw, Stratford, 1980—; ptnr. Glass & Crafts, Bridgeport, 1980—. Stained glass artist. Adv., Housatonic Community Coll., 19—; mktg. cons. Stamford YWCA, 1982—. Mem. U. Conn. Alumni Assn., U. Bridgeport Alumni Assn., Housatonic Community Coll. Alumni Assn., Conn. Crafts Guild, Stratford Hist. Soc. Avocations: art; classic film; mystery writing. Home: 545 Windsor Ave Stratford CT 06497

VLAICH, MILDRED ANN, judge; b. Detroit, Oct. 16, 1922; d. Michael Stephan and Anna Louise (Drazich) Jovanovich; m. George Vlaich, June 22, 1947; children—Kristine A. Vlaich, Melanie G. Flessner, Natalie Louise Worthy, Michelle Georgette Lee, Jacqueline Kimberly Wood. A.B., Wayne State U., 1944, L.L.B., 1946, J.D., 1946. Bar: Mich. 1946. Asst. prosecutor Macomb County, Mt. Clemens, Mich., 1949-52; ptnr. Vlaich & Orris, Attys. at Law, Center Line, Mich., 1952-74; dist. judge State of Mich., Oakland County, Rochester, 1974-80, vis. dist. judge, 1980—; pres. Wolverine Holding, Mt. Clemens, 1984—; legal cons. Order Eastern Star, Rochester, 1979—; Macomb County supr., 1963-64. Mem. Rochester Bar Assn. (pres. 1979-80), Macomb County Bar Assn. (dir. 1960-67), Oakland County Bar Assn., St. Clair County Bar Assn., ABA, Mich. Bar Assn., Women's Lawyers Assn., Rochester Bus. and Profl. Club (pres. 1981-82). Democrat. Mem. Serbian Eastern Orthodox Ch. Lodge: Order Eastern Star. Home: 643 Fieldstone Dr S Rochester MI 48063 Office: Dist Judge 643 Fieldstone Dr S Rochester MI 48063

VLASSARA, HELEN, physician, educator, researcher; b. Athens, Greece, July 3, 1947; came to U.S., 1974; d. Vassilios and Asteria (Petropoulou) V.; m. Anthony Cerami, May 1, 1981. M.D., Med. Sch. Athens, 1973. Postdoctoral fellow Rockefeller U., N.Y.C., 1974-76, research assoc., 1980-82, asst. prof., 1983—; intern, resident in internal medicine Columbia U. Coll. Physicians and Surgeons, N.Y.C., 1976-79; endocrinology fellow N.Y. Med. Ctr., N.Y.C., 1980-82; physician assoc. Rockefeller U. Hosp., N.Y.C., 1981—; attending physician Cornell U. Med. Sch., N.Y.C., 1984—. Author research papers. Mem. Am. Coll. Physicians and Surgeons, Am. Diabetes Assn., N.Y. Clin. Diabetes Assn., European Assn. for Study of Diabetes. Office: Rockefeller U 1230 York Ave New York NY 10021

VOCKINS, KATHERINE LYNN, international marketing services consultant; b. Los Angeles, Sept. 22, 1943; d. Stan Lee and Emily Ann Boyd; student Westchester Community Coll., 1961-63, Mercy Coll., 1978. Adminstrv. asst. Dansk Internat. Designs, Mt. Kisco, N.Y., 1965-71, coordinator sales services, 1971-76; freelance mktg. services, Tokyo and N.Y.C., 1976-78; owner, pres. KV Mktg. Inc., Katonah, N.Y., and br. office, N.Y.C., 1978—. Mem. Nat. Assn. Female Execs., Ind. Cons.'s Am. (dir.). Club: Tokyo Am. Office: The Courtyard Box K Katonah NY 10536 also 41 Madison Ave New York NY 10010

VODENOS, ARNA SUSAN, television production company executive; b. Balt., May 21, 1959; d. Phillip and Stella Eve (Seltzer) Vodenos. B.S., Boston U., 1981. Prodn. asst., newswriter Sta. WCVB-TV, Boston, 1980; producer P.M. Mag. Sta. WDVS-TV, Washington, 1981; freelance producer, Los Angeles, Balt., 1981-83; dir. audio visual dept. Phillip Willen Assocs., Balt., 1983-84; pres., exec. producer A.V.P., Inc., Rockville, Md., 1984—. Author video 100 TV productions "For Our Children", Boston, Balt., 1981. Bd. dirs. People Encouraging People, Balt., 1984—. Recipient 1st prize Md. Council on Arts, Balt., 1980; 1st prize John B. Muir Med. Film awards, San Francisco, 1986. Republican. Jewish. Avocations: oil painting; classical piano and violin.

VOEKS, VIRGINIA WILNA, educator; b. Champaign, Ill., May 9, 1921; d. B. Forrest and Dorothy (Wade) V.; B.S. summa cum laude, U. Wash., 1943, M.S., 1944; Ph.D., Yale U., 1947; m. William McBlair IV. Research asso. Yale U., New Haven, 1944-45; asst. prof. U. Wash., 1947-49; asst. prof. San Diego State U., 1949-55, asso. prof., 1955-58, prof., 1958-71, prof. emeritus, 1971—. Recipient Pres. medal U. Wash., 1943; Sterling award Yale, 1945. Fellow N.Y. Acad. Scis., Am. Psychol. Assn. (sec.-treas. div. I 1965-77, editor Newsletter); mem. Western Psychol. Assn., AAUP, AAAS, Nat. Geog. Soc., Psychonomic Soc. (charter), UN Assn. San Diego, U.S. Olympic Soc., San Diego Ballet Assn. (charter), Jacques Cousteau Soc., Am. Bible Soc., Nat. Wildlife Fedn., Asso. Council Arts, Phi Beta Kappa, Sigma Xi, Psi Chi (pres. U. Wash. chpt. 1942-44), Phi Kappa Phi, Sigma Epsilon Sigma, Alpha Lambda Delta. Episcopalian. Club: Heritage. Author: On Becoming an Educated Person, 1957, 64, 70, 79; contbr. article to Internat. Ency. Social Scis., 1971; contbr. articles to profl. jours. Editorial bd. Teaching Psychology. Home: PO Box 877 4319 Explorer Rd La Mesa CA 92041 Office: Dept Psychology San Diego State U San Diego CA 92182

VOELKER, MARY VAN BECK, gas company training official; b. Milw., Sept. 30, 1944; d. Raymond W. and Josephine H. (Beyer) Van Beck; m. Robert J. Voelker, Jan. 31, 1981; children—Margaret Mary, Rose Elizabeth. B.A., Cardinal Stritch Coll., 1966; M.A., U. Mich., 1970; M.B.A., U. Wis.-Milw., 1978. Cert. tchr. Math. instr. Cardinal Stritch Coll., Milw., 1977-79; math. tchr. Nicolet High Sch., Milw., 1966-79; systems analyst Wis. Gas Co., Milw., 1979-81, mgr. tng., 1981-82, mgr. corp. tng. and devel., 1982-85, mgr. mgmt. devel. and safety, 1985—. Co-author: Basic Technical Mathematics, 1979; Introduction to Algebra, 1977; contbr. articles to publs. Mem. Am. Soc. Tng. and Devel., Wis. Math. Council (editor 1977-79, v.p. 1975-77).

VOGEL, DONNA MARIE, management consultant; b. Monroe, Wis., Aug. 14, 1954; d. Robert John and Delores Kathleen V.; B.A. in Econs., U. Wis., Madison, 1975. With unit buying control div. Sears Roebuck, Madison, 1974-75; research analyst Pres.'s Commn. on Marihuana and Drug Abuse, HEW, U. Wis., Madison, 1975; area mgr., asst. buyer H.C. Prange Co., Green Bay, Wis., 1975-78; sr. mgmt. cons. SYCOM, Madison, 1978-83; sr. cons. Accelerated Practice Concepts, North Oaks, Minn., 1983—; mem. practice mgmt. faculty Loyola U. Sch. Dentistry, Chgo. Named Mktg. Support Rep. of Year, SYCOM, 1981. Mem. Am. Mgmt. Assn., Am. Soc. Profl. Cons., Nat. Soc. Practice Mgmt. Cons.

VOGEL, MARY STALGAITIS, dentist, dental educator; b. Hazleton, Pa., Aug. 2, 1949; d. Joseph George and Sylvia (Nicholas) Stalgaitis. B.S., Pa. State. U., 1974; D.M.D., U. Pitts., 1974. Dental extern Home for Crippled Children, Pitts., 1973-75; pres. Mary Vogel, D.M.D., P.C., Pitts., 1976—; asst. clin. prof. Sch. Dental Medicine U. Pitts., 1974—; panel discussant on Women's Careers, Pa. Sect. Edn., Indiana U. Pa. Demonstrator dental procedures TV, 1981.

Troop leader Girls Scouts U.S.A., Forrest Hills, P.A., 1983; active health fair booth Women's Task Force on Alcoholism, Pitts., 1982; keynote speaker Marian High., Tamaqua, Pa., 1981. Mem. Am. Assn. Women Dentists (v.p. Pitts. br. 1982-83), ADA, Pa. Dental Assn. (del. 1980), East End Pitts. Odontol. Soc. (pres. 1978-79), Acad. Oral Medicine, (Sr. Dental Student award 1974), U. Pitts. Dental Alumni (exec. com. 1977—). Roman Catholic. Club: Equicess. Home and Office: Suite 340 Gateway Towers Pittsburgh PA 15222

VOGELGESANG, LAURA JANE, lawyer; b. Cin., July 9, 1951; d. John Marshall and Elizabeth Jane (Carter) V. B.A., U. Denver, 1973, J.D., 1976. Bar: Colo. 1976. Assoc. firm Canges & Shaver, Denver, 1976-78, Thomas & Esperti, Denver, 1978-79, Sherman & Howard, 1979-83, Hutchins & Assocs., Denver, 1983-84; Bradley, Campbell & Carney, P.C., Golden, Colo., 1984—; mem. editorial com. Colorado Estate Planning Forms, 1982-83. Contbr. articles to profl. jours. Bd. dirs. Community Coll. of Denver System Found., 1984—. Mem. ABA, Colo. Bar Assn., Denver Bar Assn. Republican. Home: 550 E 12th Ave Apt 1406 Denver CO 80203 Office: Bradley Campbell & Carney PC 1717 Washington Ave Golden CO 80401

VOGES-RUGGLES, PAMELA, city official; b. Van Nuys, Calif., June 10, 1949; d. Emil Charles Voges and Margaret (Remington) Williams; m. Larry C. Ruggles, Sept. 7, 1984; 1 child, Sierra. Cert. mcpl. clk. Santa Cruz U., 1985. Sec. Universal Studios, Universal City, Calif., 1967-70; exec. sec. San Luis Bay Club, Avila Beach, Calif., 1970-74; owner, operator Secretarial Services, San Luis Obispo, Calif., 1974-75; dep. clk. City of San Luis Obispo, 1975-81, city clk., 1981—; pres. Mid-Coast Devel., San Luis Obispo, 1985—. Chmn. Mgmt. Info. Com. San Luis Obispo, 1981-85. Mem. City Clks. Assn. Calif., Internat. Inst. Mcpl. Clks., Tri-Counties City Clk. Assn. (co-founder). Club: Quota. Republican. Lutheran. Office: City of San Luis Obispo 990 Palm St San Luis Obispo CA 93401

VOGT, JUDITH CLARA, microbiologist; b. Hutchinson, Kans., Oct. 2, 1939; d. Albert and Leona Helena (Reimer) V.; registered med. technologist, Methodist Hosp., Houston, 1960; B.S., Kans. State U., 1961; M.S., Wash. State U., 1966; Ph.D., Oreg. State U., 1975. Vol., Peace Corps, Togo, 1962-64; sales rep. Pfizer Diagnoitics Co., Los Angeles, 1966-67; food chemist Petersville Pty. Ltd., Melbourne, Australia, 1967-68; tchr. chemistry and sci. Convent of Sacre Coer, Melbourne, 1968; lectr. chemistry Taylor's Coll., Kuala Lumpur, Malaysia, 1969-71; asst. prof. biology St. Francis Coll., Biddeford, Maine, 1974-75, Ft. Hays (Kans.) State U., 1975—; chmn. Kans. Med. Tech. Edn. Conf., 1978-80. USPHS fellow, 1965; research trainee N.W. Coll. and Univ. Assn., 1973-74. Mem. Am. Soc. Clin. Pathologists, Am. Soc. Mircobiology, Am. Soc. Med. Tech., Kans. Acad. Sci., LWV, Earthwatch, Sigma Xi, Phi Delta Kappa, Phi Kappa Phi. Methodist. Office: Biology Dept Fort Hays State U 600 Park St Hays KS 67601

VOIGHT, ELIZABETH ANNE, lawyer; b. Sapulpa, Okla., Aug. 6, 1944; d. Robert Guy and Garnetta Ruth (Bell) Voight; m. Bodo Barske, Feb. 22, 1985. B.A., U. Ark.-Fayetteville, 1967, M.A., 1969; postgrad. U. Hamburg (W.Ger.), 1966-67; J.D., Georgetown U., 1978. Bar: N.Y. 1979. Lectr. German, Oral Roberts U., Tulsa, 1968-69; tchr. German, D.C. pub. schs., 1971-73; instr. German, Georgetown U., Washington, 1973-74, adminstrv. asst. to dean Sch. Fgn. Service, 1974-77; law clk. Cole & Corette, Washington, 1977-78; atty. Walter, Conston & Schurtman, N.Y.C., 1978—. Translator articles for profl. jours. Chmn. regional screening Am. Field Service, N.Y.C., 1981-86. German Acad. Exchange Program fellow, 1966-67. Mem. Assn. Bar City N.Y., ABA, Internat. Fiscal Assn., Phi Beta Kappa, Kappa Kappa Gamma. Office: Walter Conston & Schurtman 90 Park Ave New York NY 10016

VOIGHT, NANCY LEE (MRS. JAY VAN HOVEN), psychologist; b. Kansas City, Mo., Nov. 24, 1945; d. Paul and Leona Alvina (Schultz) V.; B.A., Wittenberg U., 1967; M.A., Ball State U., 1971; Ph.D., Mich. State U., 1975; m. Jay Van Hoven, June 27, 1975; children—Joshua, Janna, Lydia. Tchr. lang. arts Ashland (Ohio) City Schs., 1967-68; tchr. English, Speedway (Ind.) City Schs., 1969; basic literacy instr. Army Edn. Center, Gelnhausen, Germany, 1969-70; individual assistance Bethel Home for Boys, Gaston, Ind., 1970-71; counselor Wittenberg U. Ohio, 1971-72; staff psychologist Ingham County Probate Ct., Lansing, Mich., 1972-74; asst. prof. U. N.C., Chapel Hill, 1975-79, counseling psychologist, 1976-79, psychologist for employee devel. Gen. Telephone Electronics, No. Region Hdqrs., Indpls., 1979-80; behavioral sci. coordinator Family Practice Center Community Hosp., Indpls., 1980-82; psychologist PME Ctr. of Indpls. Inc., Alternatives to Expulsion Program, Indpls.; counselor Alternatives for Runaways, Marion County Prosecutor's office, 1984—; media talk show psychologist Sta. WIFE, Indpls., 1982-83; v.p. Westlake Profl. Services, 1981—; treas. Med. Splty. Disability Ins. Corp., 1982—; media psychologist Sta. WISH-TV, Indpls., 1982-83. Chmn. housing bd. U. N.C., 1976-79; dir. Behavior Therapy Center, Indpls., 1982—. Diplomate Acad. Behavioral Medicine; cert. sex educator; cert. sex therapist. Office Edn. grantee, 1977-78, 78-80; Spencer Found. young scholars grantee. Mem. Am. Psychol. Assn., Ind. Psychol. Assn., Assn. Advancement Behavior Therapy, Am. Assn. Marriage and Family Therapists. Lutheran. Author: Becoming, 1978; Becoming: Leader's Guide, 1978; Becoming Aware, 1979; Becoming Informed, 1979; Becoming Strong, 1979; also articles. Home: 600 N High School Rd Indianapolis IN 46224 Office: 6357 W Rockville Rd Indianapolis IN 46224

VOLID, RUTH, art gallery owner; b. Chgo.; d. Ben and Ida (Saykowitch) Volid; ed. Art Inst. Chgo., U. Chgo., Chouinard Art Sch., Otis Art Inst., Am. Acad. Art; 2 daus. Art tchr., Chgo., 1950-52; owner, designer Fashion Hat Bus., 1945-47; interior designer, graphic designer, copy chief Meyer Both Co., 1939-45; owner, designer Dude Ranch, 1947-50; creative dir. King Korn Stamp Co., Chgo., 1962-70; public relations staff Merchandising Group, N.Y.C., 1970-72; owner Ruth Volid Gallery, Ltd., Chgo., 1970—; judge art shows; speaker in field. Mem. U.S. affiliated bd. Mus. Contemporary Art, 1976; mem. exec. bd. Sinfonia Orch. Chgo. Mem. Archives Am. Art, Am., Soc. Interior Designers Industry Found. Bd., Soc. Archtl. Historians, North Shore Art League, Arts Club Chgo. Club: President's. Author: The Designer; Investor Collector; Executive 40; contbr. Crain's Chgo. Bus. Office: 225 W Illinois St Chicago IL 60610

VOLK, HELEN D(OHRAU), lawyer; b. Cornwall, N.Y., Sept. 18, 1947; d. Francis Robert, Sr., and Marion (Mitchell) Dohrau. B.S. cum laude, SUNY-Potsdam, 1969; J.D., Albany Law Sch., 1973. Bar: N.Y. U.S. Dist. Ct. (no. dist.) N.Y., U.S. Supreme Ct. Tchr., Greece Central Sch. Dist., N.Y., 1969-70; atty. mcpl. affairs N.Y. State Dept. Audit and Control, Albany, 1973-75, sr. atty., 1979-81, legis. liaison, 1981; counsel N.Y. State Emergency Control Bd. for City of Yonkers, Albany, 1975-79; asst. counsel N.Y. State Edn. Dept., Albany, 1981—; mem. com. on character and fitness, 3d Jud. Dept., Albany, 1980—; adj. prof. Russell Sage Coll., Troy, N.Y., 1978-80. Contbr. article to legal publ. Vol. March of Dimes, Latham, N.Y., 1980-84, pub. TV Sta. WMHT-TV, Schenectady, 1979—. Featured alumna SUNY-Potsdam Alumni Assn., 1983. Mem. ABA (urban, state and local govt. sect.), N.Y. State Bar Assn. (mcpl. law sect. chmn. 1983-85, ho. of dels. 1985—, 1st vice chair and fiscal officer 1981-83, 2d vice chair 1979-81, sec. 1978-79, exec. com. 1976—), Women's Bar Assn. State of N.Y. (chpt. organizer 1977, v.p. 1983-84, legis. chair 1982-83, dir. 1977-82), Am. Soc. Pub. Adminstrn., Exec. Women in Govt. Democrat. Mem. Reformed Ch. Am. Clubs: Zonta (bd. dirs. Albany 1980-82, 83-85), Bus. and Profl. Women, Kripalu Yoga Fellowship. Office: NY State Education Dept 138 EB Albany NY 12234

VOLKERT, DORIS CAMPBELL, microbiologist; b. Youngstown, Ohio, Apr. 1, 1923; d. Frank Dickson and Frances Fitzgerald (Baker) Campbell; B.S., Pa. State U., 1944; M.S. in Bacteriology, U. Pitts., 1950; m. Charles Fredric Volkert, Oct. 11, 1947; children—Fredric Campbell, Christy Campbell. Research asst. N.Y. State Dept. Health, Albany, 1944-48; research fellow West Penn Hosp., Pitts., 1948-50; office mgr. West Penn Dairies, Gibsonia, 1960-64; assoc. prof. biology Monmouth Coll., West Long Branch, N.J., 1965—; microbiologist Paul Kimball Hosp., Lakewood, N.J., 1970—. Pres., North Suburban Fine Arts League, Richland, Pa., 1958-59. NASA grantee, 1960-61. Mem. Am. Soc. Med. Tech., AAUP, N.Y. Acad. Sci., Am. Soc. Microbiology, Am. Women in Sci., Theobald Smith Soc., Phi Sigma, Beta Beta Beta. Clubs: Monmouth College Faculty, Zonta. Home: 2031 New Bedford Rd Spring Lake Heights NJ 07762 Office: Biology Dept Cedar Ave Monmouth College West Long Branch NJ 07764

VOLKIN, HILDA APPEL, artist, educator. B.S., Mass. Coll. Art; M.A.T., Radcliffe Coll.; postgrad. UCLA, Tamarind Inst., Albuquerque. One-and two-person shows: Mass. Coll. Art, Boston, Aldridge Gallery, Albuquerque, Munson Gallery, Santa Fe, Gallery A., Taos, Governor's Gallery, Santa Fe, Weninnger Graphics Gallery, Boston, Mayville State Coll., N.D., U. Portland, Oreg.; group shows include: Cleve. Mus. Art, Santa Festival of the Arts, N.Mex., Bergen Community Mus., Paramus, N.J., Amarillo Competition (Tex.), Mus. Albuquerque, Governor's Gallery, State Capitol, N.Mex., Contemporary Am. Graphics, N.J., N.Mex. State U. Biennial, Mus. Fine Arts, Santa Fe, Printmakers, SPAR Nat., Shreveport, La., Contemporary Arts and Crafts, Palm Beach, Fla., Cleve. Mus. Art Travel Exhibit, Baldwin Wallace Coll., Berea, Ohio, Ohio Print Shows; represented in permanent collections: Cleve. Mus. Art, Mus. Albuquerque, U. N.Mex. Art Mus., Massillon Mus. (Ohio), Beth Israel-West Temple, Cleve., Los Alamos High Sch., Los Alamos Nat. Lab., Pub. Service Co. N.Mex., Sunwest Bank, Albuquerque, Moncor Bank, Albuquerque, Albuquerque Fed. Savs. and Loan Co., Massillon Mus., Cleve. Playhouse Gallery, also pvt. collections: dir. Fuller Lodge Art Ctr., Los Alamos; instr. art U. N.Mex.-Los Alamos, Cuyahoga Community Coll., Cleve. Recipient awards Nat. Assn. Women Artists, Cleve. Mus. Art, Canton Art Inst. (Ohio), Massillon Mus.; Purchase award, Ann. N.Y. in Graphics. Mem. Albuquerque Mus. Soc. Layerists-Multi Media.

VOLLAND, CAROL TASCHER, financial services company executive; b. Morris, Ill., Mar. 23, 1935; s. Murl Elvyn and Helen Marie (Lindquist) Tascher; m. George William Volland, Aug. 12, 1978. Student Monmouth Coll., 1953-55; B.S. in Interior Design, U. Ill., 1957; postgrad. Art Inst. Chgo. Evening Sch., 1959-62. Lic. real estate broker, ins. and securities broker, Colo., Ill. Archtl. and interior designer Peoples Gas Light & Coke Co., Chgo., 1957-65, consumer lectr., corp. architect and interior designer, 1965-70, dir. home planning bur., 1970-74; corp. fashion coordinator Ozite Corp. div. Brunswick Corp., Libertyville, Ill., 1974-75, dir. pub. relations, 1975-77, contract sales mgr., 1977-78; pres. Volland & Assocs., Lakewood, Colo., 1982—; mem. corp. responsibilities bd. Brunswick Corp. Internat., 1976-77. Author: Creative Moneystretchers for the Home, 1973. Mem. Nat. Home Fashions League (exec. v.p. 1977-78), Am. Soc. Interior Designers, Women in Communications, LWV, Nat. Trust Hist. Preservation, Genesee Found. Republican. Methodist. Club: Altrusa of Jefferson County. Home: 1962 Montane Dr E Golden CO 80401 Office: Volland and Assocs 165 S Union Blvd Suite 718 Union Tower Lakewood CO 80228

VOLLRATH, MARILYN ANNE, public relations executive; b. Milw., July 20, 1949; d. Norman C. and Anne (Buschmann) Lemke; m. Philip K. Vollrath, May 25, 1979; 1 child, Jessica. B.A., U. Wis.-Milw., 1970. Accredited in pub. relations. Reporter, Grand Forks Herald, N.D., 1970-71; various pub. relations positions ending as v.p. pub. relations NN Corp., Milw., 1971-79; founder, pres. Vollrath Assocs., Inc., Cedarburg, Wis., 1979—. Active Republican polit. campaigns, Wis., 1970—, Ozaukee Rep. Women, Cedarburg, 1979—; bd. dirs. YMCA, Milw., 1976—. Mem. Tempo (past pres.), Pub. Relations Soc. Am. (bd. dirs.), Nat. Investor Relations Inst. Congregationalist. Office: Vollrath Assocs Inc N62 W248 Washington Ave Cedarburg WI 53012

VOLLRATH, SANDRA JENKINS KING, aviation company official, pilot, ins. co. exec.; b. Jackson, Ga., Mar. 23, 1946; d. Richard Lamar and Margaret Lucille (Pugh) Jenkins; student Jackson public schs. Sec., salesperson Spencer Ins. Agy., Jackson, 1964-66; sec., dispatcher, office mgr. Atlanta Air Taxi, 1966-69; mgr. office and ops., pilot Mobley Aviation, Inc., Atlanta, 1969—; real estate sales rep., asso. broker Thompson Group Realtors, Mableton, Ga.; v.p. Thompson Group Insurors. Mem. Aircraft Owners and Pilots Assn. Baptist. Home: 463 Landmark Way Austell GA 30001

VOLPE, LORETTA ANN, advertising agency executive, lecturer; b. N.Y.C., Feb. 27, 1954; d. Eugene Francis and Marie Antoinette (Pati) Volpe. A.S., S.I. Coll., 1974; B.B.A., Bernard Baruch Coll., 1976, M.B.A., 1982. Media planner Ted Bates, N.Y.C., 1975-77; media supr. Foote, Cone & Belding Advt. Agy., N.Y.C., 1977-81; dir. planning and media ops. SSC&B Advt. Agy., N.Y.C., 1981—; adj. lectr. Bernard Baruch Coll., N.Y.C., 1978-83. Mem. Bernard Baruch Coll. Alumni Assn. of N.Y.C. (bd. dirs. 1979—). Democrat. Roman Catholic. Office: SSC&B Advt 1 Dag Hammerschold Plaza New York NY 10017

VOLTZ, JEANNE APPLETON, magazine editor, writer, food consultant; b. Collinsville, Ala., Nov. 12, 1920; d. James Lamar and Marie (Sewell) Appleton; m. Luther Manship Voltz, July 31, 1943 (dec. Aug. 1976); children—Luther Manship, Jeanne Marie. A.B., U. Montevallo, Ala., 1942. Corr., The Birmingham News (Ala.), 1939-42; reporter The Press-Register, Mobile, Ala., 1942-45; reporter, feature writer The Miami Herald, 1947-53, food editor, 1953-60; food editor Los Angeles Times, 1960-73, Woman's Day, N.Y.C., 1973-84; editor Food News Update, 1984—; instr. wine and food in civilization UCLA, 1972-73; expert witness Senate Com. on Nutrition and Health, Ft. Lauderdale, Fla., 1980. Author: The California Cookbook, 1970 (Tastemaker award 1970); The Los Angeles Times Natural Foods Cookbook, 1974; The Flavor of the South, 1976 (Tastemaker award 1976), An Apple A Day, 1983; Barbecued Ribs and Other Great Feeds, 1985. Mem. Met. Mus. Art, N.Y.C., 1975. Recipient Vesta award Am. Meat Inst., 1962-72; Alumni of Yr. award U. Montevallo, 1981. Mem. Les Dames d'Escoffier (dir. 1976, pres. 1985-86), Inst. Food Technologists, Soc. Nutrition Edn., Women in Communication, Soc. Women Geographers, Internat. Assn. Cooking Profls., N.Y. Acad. Scis., Phi Tau Sigma. Democrat. Methodist.

VOLZ, ELIZABETH BEEBE, lawyer, educator; b. Oneonta, N.Y., Feb. 10, 1954; d. James Judson and Carolyn Joan Hayward; m. Dennis Michael Volz, Aug. 25, 1979. B.A., Hartwick Coll., 1976; J.D., Albany Law Sch., 1979. Bar: N.Y. 1980, S.C. 1980. Staff asst. Prisoners' Legal Services, Albany, N.Y., 1977-79; asst. pub. defender Charleston (S.C.) Pub. Defender, 1980-83; instr. legal studies U. Guam, 1984—; asst. atty. gen. Ter. of Guam, 1984-85, dep. atty. gen., chief prosecution div., 1986—; com. mem. Charleston (S.C.) Family Ct. Liason Com., 1980; intern Congressman D. Mitchell, Washington, 1975. Mem. election com. Family Ct. Judge Election for Judy Bridges, Charleston, S.C., 1983; chmn. Guam Task Force on Child Sexual Abuse, 1986. Saxton fellow Hartwick Coll., 1975, Richard K. Meeker fellow, 1976. Mem. ABA, N.Y. Bar Assn., S.C. Bar Assn. Republican. Presbyterian. Home: 10 Poinciana Circle S Finegayan FPO San Francisco CA 96630

VON DER EMBSE, MARIE ANNETTE, lawyer; b. Lima, Ohio, Jan. 3, 1947; d. James Vincent and Marie Catherine (Niese) Von der Embse; m. Clyde M. Simon, June 29, 1974 (div. 1975). B.Ed., Ohio State U.-Columbus, 1968; M.Ed., U. Dayton, 1979; J.D., Ohio No. U., 1982. Bar: Ohio 1983. Vol., Peace Corps, Mukah, Sarawak, Malaysia, 1968-71; tchr. Lima and Ft. Jennings Schs. (Ohio), 1971-74; tchr.-librarian U. Mindanao, Philippines, 1974-75; tchr. Mizpah Community Ctr., Lima, 1975-76, Lima City Schs., 1976-80; assoc. firm Lawson & Smith, Lima, 1983—. Mem. Lima City Council, 1982-84, chmn. tree com. 1982-85; alt. mem. Regional Planning Commn., Lima, 1981-85, Joint Planning Commn., Delphos, Ohio, 1981-85; chmn. citizen adv. bd. Oakwood Forensic Ctr., Lima, 1985. Mem. Ohio State Bar Assn., Allen County Bar Assn., Lima Edn. Assn., Jennings Edn. Assn. Democrat. Roman Catholic. Home: 1091 N Main St Lima OH 45801 Office: Lawson & Smith Attys at Law 115 W North St Lima OH 45801

VON DER HEYDE, JANE COWAN, lawyer; b. N.Y.C., Apr. 3, 1949; d. Matthew Jennings and Camilla (Cowan) von der H.; m. David Morrison Lindley, June 12, 1971; children—Camilla, Carolyn. B.A., Barnard Coll., 1971; J.D., Boston U., 1974. Bar: N.Y., 1975. Assoc., Skadden Arps Slate Meagher & Flom, N.Y.C., 1974-80; v.p. and gen. counsel Gen. Occidental Inc. and related cos., N.Y.C., 1980-84; sr. v.p., gen. counsel G.O. Holdings, Mgmt. Inc. and related cos., N.Y.C., 1984—; dir. Grand Union Co., Elmwood Park, N.J., 1982—. Editor Boston U. Law Rev., 1973-74. Mem. ABA, Assn. Bar City N.Y. Office: GO Holdings Mgmt Inc 650 Fifth Ave New York NY 10019

VON FURSTENBERG, DIANE SIMONE MICHELLE, fashion designer, clothing and cosmetics executive b. Brussels, Dec. 31, 1946; came to U.S., 1969; d. Leon L. and Liliane L. (Nahmias) Halfin; student U. Madird, 1965-66, U. Geneva, 1966-68; m. Eduard Egon von Furstenberg, July 16, 1969; children—Alexandre, Tatiana. Founder, pres. Diane Von Furstenberg, Ltd., mfr. ladies clothing, N.Y.C., 1970—, Diane Von Furstenberg Cosmetics div. Diane Von Furstenberg, Inc., N.Y.C., 1974—, also chmn. Diane Von Furstenberg Studio div. Office: Diane Von Furstenberg Ltd 745 Fifth Ave New York NY 10151*

VON HOLT, LAEL POWERS, psychotherapist, psychiatric social worker; b. Boston, Apr. 9, 1927; d. Merritt Adams and Rea Francisca (Hunt) Powers; B.A., U. Mass., 1950; M.S.W., U. Mo., 1972, postgrad., 1978; postgrad. Menninger Found., Topeka, 1977-85; m. Henry William Von Holt, Jr., Sept. 18, 1954; children—Gardner, Dudley, Edward. Psychiat. social worker N.Y. Dept. Mental Hygiene, Wingdale, 1950-51, Mass. Dept. Mental Health, Worcester, 1951-54; instr., social worker U. Oreg., Eugene, 1954-59; psychiat. social worker Mo. Dept. Mental Health, Fulton State Hosp., 1973-81, Columbia (Mo.) Regional Hosp. Psychiat. Services, Inc., 1977-82, Family Mental Health Ctr., Jefferson City, Mo., 1982—. Bd. dirs. PTA, 1970-74, 77-78; mem. health com. Boone County Community Services Council, 1975-76; vol. Meals on Wheels, 1972-73, 76-79; den mother Boy Scouts Am., 1968-69, 71-72; mem. by-laws com. Springdale Neighborhood Assn., 1977. Diplomate Internat. Acad. Profl. Counseling and Psychotherapy; named Social Worker of Yr. Central Mo., 1986. Mem. Nat. Assn. Social Workers, Acad. Cert. Social Workers, Registry Clin. Social Workers, Boone County Assn. Mental Health, LWV (city council observor 1976-82, chmn. local action com. 1979-80, sec. 1974-77, chmn. Observer Corps 1981-83), Kappa Kappa Gamma. Republican. Methodist. Club: Stephens Coll. Faculty Wives (pres. 1979-80). Home: 378 Crown Point Columbia MO 65203 Office: Family Mental Health Center 1905 Stadium Jefferson City MO 65101

VONNOH, GIGI L(ICHTENSTEIN), newspaper editor; b. N.Y.C., Mar. 8, 1936; d. Alfred Boyd and Ilai (Bingham) Lichtenstein; m. Pen W. Reed, Nov. 30, 1957 (div. 1963); children—Pen W., Kent B.; m. 2d, George E. Vonnoh, Apr. 8, 1965. Student schs. Summit, N.J. Photo-journalist The Reporter, Florida Keys, Fla., 1965-70; reporter Free Press, Key Largo, Fla., 1970-74; reporter Keynoter, Marathon, Fla., 1974-79; photographer Sundial, Marathon, 1974-79; editor The Graham Star, Robbinsville, N.C., 1979—; dir. journalism class Stecoah, N.C., 1982; cons. Keys News, Marathon, 1970-79, Beta Club, Robbinsville, 1982-84, The Robin, Robbinsville, 1980-83. Trustee Graham County Mus. History, Robbinsville, 1982-83; bd. dirs. Graham County United Way, 1979-84; chmn. Am. Heart Assn., Robbinsville, 1979-84. Mem. Fla. Press Assn., N.C. Press Assn., Graham County C. of C. (dir. 1982-83). Republican. Lutheran-Episcopal. Clubs: Women's (pres. Marathon 1970-78), Hosp. Aux. (pres. Marathon 1972-76), Graham County Woman's. Home: Route 3 Box 234C Robbinsville NC 28771 Office: Graham Star 129 By Pass Robbinsville NC 28771

VON RAFFLER-ENGEL, WALBURGA, linguist, educator; b. Munich, Germany, Sept. 25, 1920; came to U.S., 1949, naturalized, 1955; d. Friedrich J. and Gertrud E. (Kiefer) von Raffler; m. A. Ferdinand Engel, June 2, 1957; children—Lea Maxine, Eric Robert von Raffler. D.Litt., U. Turin, Italy, 1947; M.S., Columbia U., 1951; Ph.D., Ind. U., 1953. Freelance journalist, 1949-58; mem. faculty Bennett Coll., Greensboro, N.C., 1953-55, Morris Harvey Coll., Charleston, W.Va., 1955-57, Adelphi U., CUNY, 1957-58, NYU, 1957-59, U. Florence, Italy, 1959-60, Istituto Post Universitario Organizzazione Aziendale, Italy, 1960-61, Bologna Center of Johns Hopkins U., 1964; mem. faculty Vanderbilt U., Nashville, 1965—, assoc. prof. linguistics, 1966-77, prof., 1977—, dir. linguistics program, 1978—; sr. research assoc. Inst. for Public Policy Studies, 1986—; chmn. com. on linguistics Nashville Univ. Center, 1974-79; vis. prof. U. Ottawa, 1971-72, Inst. for Lang. Scis., Tokyo, 1976, faculty devel. program Shanxi U., Peoples' Republic of China, 1985; grant evaluator NSF, NEH, Can. Council; manuscript reader Ind. U. Press, U. Ill. Press, Prentice-Hall; cons. Trinity U., Simon Frazer U. Author: Il prelinguaggio infantile, 1964; The Perception of Nonverbal Behavior in the Career Interview, 1983; co-author: Language Intervention Programs 1960-74, 1975. Editor, co-editor 10 books. Author film and videotape. Contbr. over 250 articles to profl. and popular publs. Grantee Am Council Learned Socs., NSF, Can. Council, Ford Found., Kenan Venture Fund, Japanese Ministry Edn., NATO, Finnish Acad., Meharry Med. Coll., Internat. Sociol. Assn., Internat. Council Linguists, Tex. A&M U., Vanderbilt U., also others. Mem. AAUP, Internat. Linguistics Assn., Linguistic Soc. Am. (chmn. golden anniversary film com. 1974. Internat. Assn. Applied Linguistics (com. on discourse analyses, sessions chmn. 1978), Internat. Sociol. Assn. (research com. on sociolinguistics, session co-chmn. profl. conf. 1983), Inst. Nonverbal Communication Research (workshop leader 1980, 81), Tenn. Conf. on Linguistics (pres. 1976), Semiotic Soc. Am. (organizing com. Internat. Semiotics Inst. 1981), Internat. Assn. for Study of Child Lang. (chmn. internat. conf. 1972, v.p. 1975-78). Office: Vanderbilt U Nashville TN 37235

VON SELDENECK, JUDITH CROWELL, educator, interior designer; b. New Rochelle, N.Y., Feb. 12, 1945; d. Robert Kenyon and Susan Ann (Mitchell) Crowell; B.A., U. Richmond (Va.), 1967; cert. N.Y. Sch. Interior Design, 1971; m. Roger Dean von Seldeneck, June 24, 1967; 1 son, Jeffrey Dean. Tchr. English, Augusta County (Va.), 1967-69; asst. to designers Young Assos., Staunton, Va., 1969-70; self-employed interior designer, Lynchburg, Va., 1971-74; tchr. design Balt. County Adult Edn., 1976-78; tchr. bus. English and interior design Patricia Stevens Career Coll., Balt., 1979; substitute tchr. Harrisonburg City and Rockingham County (Va.), 1981-83. Instr., Harrisonburg Recreation Dept., 1980-83; interior designer, sales/showroom mgr. Va. Craftsmen, Inc., 1983-85; owner von S Interiors, 1985—. Mem. DAR (chpt. 2d vice regent 1981-83, chpt. regent 1983-86, asst. to state treas. 1983-86, nat. vice chmn. pages 1983-86), U. Richmond-Westhampton Coll. Alumnae Assn. (nat. v.p. 1975-77). Republican. Clubs: Lynchburg Jr. Woman's (rec. sec. 1973-74); Valley Intermediate Pacesetters (sec. 1980-82) (Harrisonburg); Harrisonburg Jr. Woman's Club (co-chmn. hospitality com. 1982-83). Address: 88 Maplehurst Ave Harrisonburg VA 22801

VON SELDENECK, JUDITH METCALFE, search firm executive; b. High Point, N.C., June 6, 1940; d. Frederick and Harriet C. (Metcalfe) Metcalfe; B.A., U. N.C., 1962, A.A., St. Mary's Coll., 1960; postgrad. Am. U. Coll. Law, 1963-64; m. G. Clay von Seldeneck, Apr. 8, 1972; children—Rodman C., Kevin Clay. Exec. asst. to Senator Walter F. Mondale, Washington, 1963-73; with Diversified Search, Inc., Phila., 1973—, pres., 1980—; dir. Central Pa. Nat. Bank, Meridian Corp. Bd. dirs. Greater Phila. Partnership, 1980—, Pvt. Industry Council, WHYY-TV, Greater Phila. C. of C., Phila. Econ. Devel. Coalition, Zool. Bd.; mem. Mayors Small Bus Adv. Council, 1978—; trustee St. Mary's Coll., Raleigh, N.C., 1980—. Mem. Nat. Assn. Personnel Adminstrn., Forum of Exec. Women, Com. of 200. Democrat. Episcopalian. Clubs: Phila. Cricket, Country, Phila. Racquet, Sea Pines Country, Cosmopolitan. Home: 8124 Saint Martins Ln Philadelphia PA 19118 Office: 2 Mellon Bank Ctr Suite 2600 Philadelphia PA 19102

VON WEBER, DANA LYNN, lawyer, author; b. Columbus, Ohio, Nov. 12, 1955; d. Donald Arthur and Norma Jean (Cowgill) Weber. B.A., Mich. State U., 1979; J.D., Wayne State U., 1982. Bar: Mich. 1982. Legal asst. Charfoos, Christensen, Gilbert & Archer, P.C., Detroit, 1979-81; ct. clk. Oakland County Cir. Ct., Pontiac, Mich., 1981-82; staff atty. Mich. Nat. Corp. Banks Southeastern Mich. Legal Div., Clawson, 1982-83; assoc. Roth & Dean, P.C., Southfield, Mich., 1983—; co-host A Single Touch, Omnicom Cable Co., Plymouth, Mich., 1984—; co-author: A Woman's Guide to the Men of Michigan, 1983. Exec. com., Com. to Elect Edward Sosnick, 48th Dist. Judge, Birmingham, Mich., 1984; mem. Oakland County Young Republicans, Pontiac, 1972—, Kirk in the Hills Ch., Bloomfield Hills. Recipient Gold Key, Detroit News, 1974, award editorial writing; mem. Wayne Law Rev., 1980-82. Mem. ABA, State Bar Mich., Oakland County Bar Assn., Detroit Bar Assn., Nat. Assn. Women Lawyers. Presbyterian. Home: 4383 Oakgrove Dr Bloomfield Hills MI 48013

VON WINCKLER, BEVERLY ANN, personnel consultant; b. Joliet, Ill., Feb. 16, 1935; d. Edwin Dodd and Viola U. (Nelson) Purnell; m. David F. von Winckler, Sr., Oct. 26, 1957 (div. Aug. 1985); 1 child, David Franz. Student Joliet Jr. Coll., 1953-55, Brenau Coll., Ga., 1956-57. Sec., Govt. P.R., Chgo., 1973-76; sales rep. Standard Register Co., Schiller Park, Ill., 1976-77; dir. devel. Irish Found., Chgo., 1978-79; pres. Beverly von Winckler & Assocs., Chgo., 1980—; lectr. Northwestern U. Program on Women, 1983—; prin. Hispanic-Am. Film Festival, Chgo., 1979; panelist Mundelein Coll., Chgo., 1985; lectr. Midwest Women's Ctr., 1985; guest TV shows. Vol., Sta. WTTW Pb. TV, 1966-72, Chgo. Internat. Film Festival, 1964-85; pub. relations dir. Democratic mayoral campaign, Evanston, Ill., 1981. Recipient Service award Chgo. Internat. Film Festival, 1964. Mem. Evanston Jr. Women's Club, Alpha Delta Pi. Avocation: wall crafts. Home: 1018 Lee St Evanston IL 60202 Office: 105 W Madison St #1600 Chicago IL 60602

VOORHEES, ELIZABETH C. KAY, writer, director, producer media materials; b. San Jose, Calif.; d. Edwin Lee and Helen (Boyd) Camp; student Whittier Coll., 1928-29; B.A., U. So. Calif., 1933; M.A., 1965; children—Sharon, Debriana; m. Joseph Vernor Voorhees, II, Sept. 4, 1982. Tchr., Los

Angeles City Sch. Dist., 1958-73; writer, dir., producer film-multi-media prodns. Mich. State U., 1973-78; ind. film-media prodns., 1978-80; writer, 1980—; writer, dir., producer Lizbeth Camp Communications, La Canada, Calif., 1965—. Mem. Am. Soc. Profl. and Exec. Women, AAUW, Women in Communications, Nat. Assn. Edn. Young Children, Edn. Assn. Alumni U. So. Calif., Pi Lambda Theta, Delta Kappa Gamma. Republican. Presbyn. Home: PO Box 577 La Canada CA 91011

VOORHIS, BRENDA HEATH JACOBSEN, psychiatrist; b. Buffalo, Feb. 22, 1930; d. Alfred Wilmot and Evelyn (Heath) Jacobsen; B.A., Wellesley Coll., 1951; M.D., Johns Hopkins U., 1955; children—Catherine, Mary Jo, Brenda, Ann, Edward, Karin. Intern in pediatrics Johns Hopkins Hosp., Balt., 1955-56, fellow in pediatric cardiology, 1957; resident in psychiatry Erie County Med. Ctr. and Gowanda Psychiat. Center, Helmuth, N.Y., 1967-69, 82-83, mem. staff, 1969—, unit chief, 1979, dep. program dir., 1980, with community services, 1983-84; practice medicine specializing in psychiatry, Gowanda, N.Y.; mem. staff Tri County Hosp., Gowanda. Bd. dirs. Cattaraugus County Council on Alcoholism and Substance Abuse, 1979—. Mem. Cattaraugus County Mental Health Assn. Democrat. Roman Catholic. Home: 45 Memorial Dr Gowanda NY 14070 Office: Gowanda Psychiat Center Helmut NY 14079 also 148 W Main St Gowanda NY 14070

VOORLAS, LANAY LUSSIER, systems control specialist; b. Racine, Wis., Aug. 17, 1952; d. Lawrence Joseph and Evelyn Marie (Howe) Lussier; m. Peter Gust Voorlas, Sept. 7, 1975. Student pub. schs., Racine. Records clk. Wis. Natural Gas Co., Racine, 1972-74, systems control specialist, 1974—. Home: 3171 Lathrop Ave Racine WI 53405 Office: Wis Natural Gas Co 233 Lake Ave Racine WI 53401

VOPNFORD, BARBARA LOU, resort company executive; b. Everett, Wash., May 30, 1952; d. Daniel Arthur Martin and Lucille (Thoemke) Martin Angeloff; m. Alan W. Young, May 12, 1973 (div. June 1980); children—Matthew, Treena, Joshua; m. David Thor Vopnford, Sr., Apr. 29, 1981; children—Kelda, Leif. Grad. high sch., Snohomish, Wash., 1970. Office coordinator Roberts Constrn. Co., Marysville, Wash., 1977-79; corp. sec., mem. pub. relations staff Thousand Adventures Inc., Blair, Nebr., 1982—. Mem. Am. Land Devel. Assn., Camp Coast to Coast (affiliate). Republican. Lutheran. Avocations: writing poetry; reading.

VORBACH, RENEE LENA RELYEA, freelance journalist; b. Bklyn., Sept 28, 1946; d. Ford S. and Jeanne (Magill) Relyea. A.A. in English, Orange County Community Coll., Middletown, N.Y., 1967; B.A. in English, SUNY, New Paltz, 1969; m. Joseph R. Vorbach; 2 daus., Cassie Ebba, Vanna Jeanne. Gen. assignment reporter Help columnist Newburgh (N.Y.) Evening News, 1969-74, food columnist, editor, 1974-83, asst. editor family and food, 1974-83; freelance writer, photographer, editor, associated with Hersh Communications Inc., 1983-84. Publicist, United Fund, 1979-81. Recipient 2d place award N.Y. State Dental Soc. contest, 1977; Cert. of Appreciation, U.S. Navy, 1981. Mem. Newspaper Food Editors and Writers Assn. (charter). Republican.

VOREIS, MARILYN LOUISE, retail merchandise manager; b. Plymouth, Ind., Aug. 10, 1941; d. Orville Jacob and Nita Louise (Leland) V.; B.S. in Home Econs., Purdue U., 1963. Home economist, 4-H Club agt. U.S. Dept. Agr., U. Ariz., 1963-65; trainee, dept mgr., asst. buyer, buyer L.S. Ayres, Indpls., 1965-76; with Liberty House Calif., 1976, buyer, 1976-77, br. divisional mdse. mgr., 1977-79, buyer cosmetics, Oakland, 1981, divisional mdse. mgr. fashion accessories and cosmetics, 1981-83, divisional mdse. mgr. fashion accessories and intimate apparel Liberty House Hawaii, Honolulu, 1983—, div. mdse. mgr. fashion accessories and children's apparel, 1985-86; buyer R.H. Macy, San Francisco, 1979-81; bd. dirs. Luggage and Leathergoods Mag., 1973-76. Home: 444 Lunalilo Home Rd #216 Honolulu HI 96825 Office: PO Box 2690 Honolulu HI 96845

VORWERK, E. CHARLSIE, artist; b. Tennga, Ga., Jan. 28, 1934; d. James A. and Hester L. (Davis) Pritchett; A.B., Ga. State Coll. for Women, 1955; m. Norman T. Vorwerk, Feb. 9, 1956; children—Karl, Lauren, Michael. Billboard design artist Vanesco Poster, Chattanooga, 1955; cartographic draftsman TVA, Chattanooga, 1955; fashion illustrator Loveman's, Chattanooga, 1956; freelance comml. artist, 1957—; pvt. art instr. children and adults, all media, 1966—; art instr. continuing edn. Bapt. Coll. Charleston, S.C., 1979-82. Mem. Bd. Archtl. Rev., Summerville, 1976—; chmn. YMCA Flowertown Festival Art Exhibit, 1972-86; mem. women's bd. St. Paul's Episcopal Ch. 1968-84; active Boy Scouts Am., Girl Scouts U.S.A.; vol. Mental Health Clinic, 1972-74, others; coordinator Washington Park Picolo-Spoleto Art Exhibit, 1983-86, also exhibit chmn. for low country artists. Mem. Charleston Artists Guild, League of Charleston Artists, Minature Art Soc. Fla., Beaufort Art Assn., Am. Art Soc., Italian Art Acad. Illustrator: Tales and Taradidales; St. Paul's Epitahs; Captain Tom, others. Address: 315 W Carolina Ave Summerville SC 29483

VOSBURGH, SANDRA JOAN, mfg. co. personnel exec.; b. Cleve., July 31, 1939; d. Courtland Jackson and Margaret Esther (Regal) V.; student Hiram Coll., 1957-60, Baldwin Wallace/Western Res. U., 1977-79; cert. employee benefit specialist Wharton Sch., U. Pa., 1981. Asst. to comptroller Clark Reliance Corp., 1963-65; adminstrv. mgr. firm Goldfarb & Reznick, Cleve., 1970-74; adminstrv. mgr. firm Persky, Marken, Konigsberg & Shapiro, Cleve., 1974-79; corp. dir. human resources Work Wear Corp., Inc., Cleve., 1980—. Mem. adv. council Gt. Lakes Assn. Industry and Rehab.; mem. exec. bd. Hiram Coll. Recipient Vol. Service award United Services, 1980-81. Mem. Citizens League, Council World Affairs, Jobs Council Greater Cleve., Beck Center Cultural Arts, Am. Mgmt. Assn., Am. Soc. Personnel Adminstrn., Am. Bus. Women's Assn., Resource. Republican. Club: Women's City of Cleve. Recipient Journalism award Ohio State U., 1957; contbr. articles to profl. jours. Home: PO Box 263 San Rafael CA 94915 Office: Work Wear Corp 1768 E 25th St Cleveland OH 44113

VOSS, CAROLYN JEAN, nursing educator; b. Battle Creek, Mich., Dec. 28, 1937; d. Melvin O. and Ruth A. (Armantrout) Buck; m. Calvin W. Voss, Sept. 17, 1978. B.S. in Nursing, Walla Walla Coll., 1973; M.A. in Nursing, Ball State U., 1975; Ph.D. in Nursing Adminstrn. and Health Edn., Columbia Pacific U., 1983. ICU staff relief charge nurse Portland Adventist Hosp., 1971-72; ICU charge nurse, staff nurse Kettering Med. Ctr., 1973-74; instr. Andrews U., Berrien Springs, Mich., 1975-77; asst. dir. nursing Hinsdale Hosp. (Ill.), 1977-78; instr. nursing St. Luke's Sch. Nursing, Racine, Wis., 1978-86; cons. VNA, Racine, 1986—; instr. Mifton Coll., 1979-82, Mt. Sinai Coll., Ladysmith, Wis., 1983. Author: Poetry for High School Studies, 1955. Bd. dirs. Racine chpt. Am. Cancer Soc., 1980; instr. CPR ARC, Racine, 1980—. Mem. Nat. League Nursing, Assn. Seventh-Day Adventist Nurses. Home: Franksville WI 53126

VOUGHT, KATHRYN DEBAUN, editor; b. Ridgewood, N.J., Feb. 19, 1952; d. Norman and Harriet (Davison) Vought; B.A. with honors, Skidmore Coll., 1974. Proofreader, Data Communications, Parsippany, N.J., 1975; editorial asst. Avon Books, N.Y.C., 1976-77, asso. editor, 1977-80, mng. editor, 1981—. Mem. NOW. Clubs: Mt. Lakes Badminton (sec. 1980-81), Glenburnie Cottager's Assn. (sec. 1981—). Editor: Nan, Sarah & Clare: Letters Between Friends, 1980. Office: care Avon Books 1790 Broadway New York NY 10019

VOURNAS, ANASTASIA PETROW, marketing executive; b. Washington, Aug. 28, 1946; d. George Christian and Helen Jean (Petrow) V.; B.A., U. Denver, 1969, M.B.A., 1970. From account coordinator to account exec. Young & Rubicam, Inc., N.Y.C., 1971-77; account mgr. Compton Advt., Inc., N.Y.C., 1977-78; account supr. SSC&B, Inc., N.Y.C., 1978-80; v.p., account supr. Benton & Bowles, Inc., N.Y.C., 1980-82; mktg. cons. Phoenix House Found., Inc., Warner Communications Inc., N.Y.C., 1982-84; v.p. Am. Express Travel Related Services Co., Inc., N.Y.C., 1984—. Democrat. Home: 230 E 50th St New York NY 10022 Office: 200 Vesey St New York NY 10285

VOWELL, EVELENE C., real estate broker; b. Hickman, Ky., May 11, 1940; d. Haughty Chester and Lottie Bell (Williams) Craddock; m. Darrell Odine, Dec. 27, 1959; children—Amy Darlene, Kerry Don, Dai Keith. Student Memphis State U., 1976-85. Lic. real estate affiliate broker. County agrl. sec. Extension Service, Hickman, Ky., 1957-59; payroll sec. Roper Pecan Co., Hickman, 1961-63; PR3 inspector Gen. Electric Co., Memphis, 1969-71; sec. Swift and Co., Memphis, 1971-73; affiliate broker John R. Thompson Realtors, Memphis, 1976-83, Crye Leike Realtors, Memphis, 1983—. Named Million Dollar Seller, Crye Leike Realtors, Memphis, 1984, 85. Mem. Memphis Bd. Realtors. Club: Ind. Order Foresters (Memphis). Home: 5714 Blackwell St Bartlett TN 38134

VOWELS, ELEANOR ELAINE, speech pathologist; b. Pitts., Mar. 10, 1937; d. Arnett Lloyd and Amanda (Anthony) Wooding; B.S. in Psychology, Howard U., 1962; M.A. in Speech Pathology and Audiology (Vocat. Rehab. fellow 1965-67), Catholic U. Am., 1967; postgrad. U. Md.; m. Aug. 27, 1960; 1 son, David Scott. Speech pathologist Prince George County (Md.) Diagnostic Teaching Center, 1967-70; speech pathologist Dept. Human Resources D.C., 1970-72, dir. speech pathology and audiology, 1972—; dir. speech pathology and audiology children and youth project D.C. Gen. Hosp., 1972—, dir. handicapped infant intervention project, 1977—, dir. tng. grant, 1980—; v.p. D.C. Consortium Handicapped Children's Programs, 1979, pres., 1980. Pres., D.C. Area chpt. Children Internat. Summer Villages, Inc., 1981, 82-83, mem. expansion com., trustee-at-large Nat. Children's Internat. Summer Villages, Inc. 1982—, also mem. long range planning com.; chmn. com. on handicapped Commn. Pub. Health, 1982. HEW Bur. Edn. grantee, 1977—. Mem. Am. Speech and Hearing Assn. (cert. clin. competence), D.C. Assn. Retarded Citizens (dir. 1972—), D.C. Speech and Hearing Assn., Md. Speech and Hearing Assn., Nat. Assn. Retarded Citizens, Zeta Phi Beta. Democrat. Baptist. Producer audio visual slide presentations on handicapped children, 1962, 70. Home: 7718 Jaffrey Rd Fort Washington MD 20744 Office: 1900 Massachusetts Ave SE Washington DC 20003

VRANA, MAULFREY STEWART, public relations and advertising agency executive; b. Omaha, Mar. 11, 1933; d. Roland Augustus and Marian Youel (Thompson) Stewart; B.Sc. in Edn., U. Nebr., Omaha, 1953; m. Laird B. Fisher, Aug. 7, 1958; children—Stephen Laird, Andrew Scott, Pamela Jane; m. 2nd Theodore W. Vrana, Nov. 27, 1982. Editor Exec. mag., Omaha, 1978-81; communications dir. Century 21, 1976-78; public relations exec. Easter Seal Soc., 1981-82; owner Muffy Fisher Assos., Omaha, 1976—; editor, pub. Time Manager, 1982—. Co-author Alive and Writing in Nebraska, 1986. Recipient merit mother award Nebr. Mothers Assn., 1985. Mem. S.E. Nebr. Library System Bd. Mem. Nat. League Am. Pen Women (Nebr. state pres.), Public Relations Soc. Am., Am. Soc. Tng. and Devel., Nat. Assn. Female Execs., Profl. Women's Assn., Bus. and Profl. Women's Assn., Nat. Assn. Women Bus. Owners, Nebr. Travel Industry Task Force, Nat. Speakers Assn. Lodge: Altrusa. PEO. Republican. Episcopalian. Address: 3260 Van Dorn Lincoln NE 68502

VRBA, MARY KAY, county official; b. Fremont, Nebr., Dec. 28, 1951; d. Frank S. and Angie (Wisnieski) V. B.A., Coll. St. Mary, Omaha, 1973; M.S., George Williams Coll., 1983. Recreational therapist Uta Halee Home for Girls, Omaha, 1973-74; recreation supr. Romeoville Recreation, Ill., 1974; supr. recreation Bolingbrook Park Dist., Ill., 1974-77; recreation and parks dir. Town of Pawling, N.Y., 1977-80; commr. Dutchess County Parks, Recreation and Conservation, Poughkeepsie, N.Y., 1980—; mem. adv. bd. Dutchess Community Coll., Poughkeepsie, 1977—; campaign leader Dutchess County Art Fund, Poughkeepsie, 1980—; community mem. Exec. Task force on Tourism, Poughkeepsie, 1983-84; pres. Dutchess/Dominica Partnership, Poughkeepsie, 1985; lectr. in field. Pres. Vida Nueva, Poughkeepsie, 1984-85; team div. mgr. United Way Poughkeepsie, 1985; bd. dirs. Dutchess County council Boy Scouts Am., 1982-83. Mem. Nat. Recreation and Parks Assn. (profl.), N.Y. State Parks and Recreation (profl., chmn. mcpl. sect. 1985—), Nat. Heritage Trust Assn., Coll. St. Mary's Alumni Assn. Roman Catholic. Home: 24 Spring St Pawling NY 12526

VREELAND, DIANA DALZIEL, magazine editor, fashion consultant; b. Paris, France; d. Frederick Y. and Emily Key (Hoffman) Dalziel; m. Thomas Reed Vreeland, Mar. 1, 1924; children—Thomas Reed, Frederick D. D.F.A. (hon.), Parsons Sch. Design, 1977. Brit. subject, until 1925. Fashion editor Harper's Bazaar, 1937-62; with Vogue mag., 1962—, editor-in-chief, 1962-71, cons. editor, 1971—. Author: (with Irving Penn) Inventive Paris Clothes, 1909-1930, A Photographic Essay, 1977; Allure, 1980; DV, 1984. Cons. Costume Inst., Met. Mus. Art, 1972—. Decorated Legion of Honor; chevalier L'Ordre des Arts et Lettres (France); recipient numerous awards. Office: Metropolitan Museum Art 1000 Fifth Ave New York NY 10028

VROOMAN, JOAN JEFFERSON, community living editor, freelance writer; b. Toronto, Ont., Can., Oct. 6, 1929; came to U.S., 1951, naturalized, 1962; d. Arthur Richard and Ivy Lillian (Umpleby) Jefferson; m. Gerald Willard Ames, Aug. 11, 1951 (div. 1962); children—Susan D., Michael G., Dianne E., Kathleen E.; m. William Chester Vrooman, Aug. 24, 1963; 4 stepchildren. ARCT, Royal Conservatory Music,-Toronto, 1946; student Victoria Coll. of Toronto U., 1947-51. Women's community living editor Cortland Standard Printing Co., (N.Y.), 1962—; bd. dirs., pres. County Communications Council, Cortland, 1970-80; lectr. in field. Bd. dirs. Cortland County C. of C., 1976-8; adv. bd. Aid to Women Victims of Violence, Cortland, 1978; counselor Finger Lakes Assn., Penn Yan, N.Y., 1980—; bd. dirs. 1980 House Mus., Cortland, 1984—. Club: Zonta (bd. dirs. 1978—; Cortland County Woman of Achievement, 1985). Republican. Episcopalian. Home: 721 Lime Hollow Rd Cortland NY 13045 Office: Cortland Standard Printing Co 110 Main St Cortland NY 13045

VUCANOVICH, BARBARA FARRELL, congresswoman; b. Camp Dix, N.J., June 22, 1921; d. Thomas F. and Ynez (White) Farrell; m. George J. Vucanovich, 1965; 5 children. Student Manhattan Coll. Sacred Heart, 1939. Owner franchise Evelyn Wood Reading Dynamics, 1968-71; owner, operator Welcome Aboard Vacation Ctr., 1970-74; dist. rep. for Senator Paul Laxalt for No. Nev., 1974-82; mem. 98th and 99th Congresses, mem. House Adminstrn., Interior and Insular Affairs coms. Mem. Nev. Fedn. Republican Women, Rep. Women's Club Reno, St. Mary's Hosp. Guild, CAP, Washoe Med. Center Women's League. Roman Catholic. Club: Emblem. Address: 507 Cannon House Office Bldg Washington DC 20515*

VUICH, ROSE ANN, state legislator. Mem. Calif. Senate from 15th dist. Democrat. Office: Calif State Senate State Capitol Sacramento CA 95814*

WACHNER, LINDA JOY, company executive; b. N.Y.C., Feb. 3, 1946; d. Herman and Shirley Wachner; widowed. B.S. in Econs. and Bus., U. Buffalo, 1966. Buyer Foley's Federated Dept. Store, Houston, 1968-69; sr. buyer R.H. Macy's, N.Y.C., 1969-74; v.p. Warner div. Warnaco, Bridgeport, Conn., 1974-77; v.p. corp. mktg. Caron Internat., N.Y.C., 1977-79; pres. U.S. div. Max Factor & Co., Hollywood, Calif., 1979-82; pres. Missoni Profumi S.p.A. subs. Max Factor, 1980—; pres. Max Factor Worldwide, 1982—; pres. Almay Inc., 1983—; mng. dir. Adler & Shaykin Leverage Buyout Firm. Active Chancellor's Assocs. UCLA, trustee found.; council U. So. Calif. Soc. Bus. Adminstrn.; mem. bus adv. council City of Los Angeles; mem. mktg. adv. bd. U. So. Calif.; trustee UCLA Found.; Presdl. appointment to U.S. Adv. Council for Trade Negotiations. Recipient Outstanding Woman in Bus. award Women's Equity Action League, 1980; Silver Achievement award for corp. bus. YWCA of Los Angeles, 1984. Mem. Young Pres.'s Orgn. (U.S. and internat.), Am. Mgmt. Assn., Fragrance Found. (bd. dirs.), Los Angeles C. of C. (bd. dirs.). Republican. Jewish. Office: 10790 Wilshire Blvd Suite 1701 Los Angeles CA 90024

WACHSMAN, KATHRYN MARY, lawyer; b. Providence, Oct. 27, 1949; d. Anthony and Mayme D'Agostino; m. Harvey F. Wachsman, Jan. 31, 1976; children—Dara Nicole, David Winston. B.A. in Math., Avail Coll., 1971; J.D., Washburn U., 1974. Bar: Conn., N.Y., Fla., D.C., Kans. Ptnr. Wachsman & Wachsman, Newtown, Conn., 1976—; assoc. firm Pegalis & Wachsman, Great Neck, N.Y., 1978—. Mem. ABA, N.Y. State Bar Assn., Conn. Bar Assn., Fla. Bar Assn., D.C. Bar Assn., N.Y. State Trial Lawyers Assn., Nassau-Suffolk Trial Lawyers Assn., Nassau County Bar Assn., Kans. Bar Assn., Kans. Trial Lawyers Assn., Am. Soc. Law and Medicine, Am. Coll. Legal Medicine (assoc. in law), Assn. Trial Lawyers Am. Office: Pegalis & Wachsman PC 175 East Shore Rd Great Neck NY 11023

WACHTELL, ESTHER, music center executive; b. N.Y.C., June 30, 1935; d. Victor and Rnoda (Wolin) Pickard; m. Thomas Wachtell, Jan. 27, 1957; children—Roger Bruce, Wendy Anne, Peter James. B.A., Conn. Coll., 1956; M.A., Cornell U., 1957. Exec. dir. Performing Tree, Los Angeles, 1978-79; dir. tech. assistance Calif. Arts Council, Los Angeles and Orange Counties, 1979-81; coordinator vol. activities Music Ctr. Los Angeles, 1974-83, coordinator spl. projects, 1980-84; dir. devel. Music Ctr. Unified Fund, Los Angeles, 1984—; arts mgmt. cons., lectr. So. Calif., 1975-82. Bd. dirs. Los Angeles, Philharmonic, 1973-75; bd. govs. Performing Arts Council, Los Angeles, 1975—; vice. chmn. Am. Council for Arts, 1979—; mem. fin. com. Com. to Reelect Tom Bradley, Los Angeles, 1978; trustee Coro Found., 1979-85, Orthopaedic Hosp., Los Angeles, 1980—, Claremont McKenna Coll., 1983—; commr. Calif. Council for Humanities, 1984—; mem. adv. bd. May Co., 1985. Recipient Eve award Assistance League Los Angeles, 1978, Activist award Broadway Dept. Stores, 1980, Recognition award Big Sisters Los Angeles, 1982, Presdl. citation Music Ctr., 1982, 84, Portfolio award Exec. Women, 1985. Mem. Phi Beta Kappa. Republican. Club: Regency (Los Angeles). Home: 35 Crest Rd E Rolling Hills CA 90274 Office: Performing Arts Council 135 N Grand Ave Los Angeles CA 90012

WACHTER, SUSAN MELINDA, finance educator, consultant; b. Newark, June 22, 1943; d. Nathaniel and Edith (Dubow) Jaffe; m. Michael Lawrence Wachter, June 23, 1968; children—Jessica, Jonathan. B.A., Radcliffe Coll., 1965; Ph.D., Boston Coll. Grad. Sch. Arts and Sci., 1974; M.A. (hon.), U. Pa., 1978. Lectr., Bryn Mawr Coll. (Pa.), 1969-72; lectr. Wharton Sch., U. Pa., Phila., 1972-74, asst. prof. fin., 1974-78, assoc. prof., 1978—; mem. exec. council Savs. Forum, Phila., 1983; dir. Beneficial Corp. Author: Latin American Inflation: The Structuralist-Monetarist Debate, 1976; co-author: Redlining and Public Policy, 1980; co-editor: Towards a New U.S. Industrial Policy?, 1981; Removing Obstacles to Economic Growth, 1984; Savings and Capital Formation: The Policy Options: assoc. editor Housing Fin. Rev., Phila.; bd. editors: Jour Real Estate Research. Recipient Lindbach award for disting. teaching Lindbach Soc., U. Pa., 1974-75; Wharton Grad. Anvil award for teaching excellence Wharton Sch., U. Pa., 1973-74; research fellow Ctr. for Internat. Affairs, Harvard U., 1966. Mem. Am. Econ. Assn., Am. Fin. Assn., Econometric Soc., Am. Real Estate and Urban Econs. Assn. (dir. 1984—), Lambda Alpha. Home: 355 Margo Ln Berwyn PA 19312 Office: Fin Dept Wharton Sch U Pa Philadelphia PA 19104

WACHTER, WANDA VALERIE, accountant; b. Enda, Okla., Dec. 5, 1952; d. Robert J. and Jean M. (Debold) W.; B.B.A. with honors, George Washington U., 1978. With Telesec Temporaries, Falls Church, Va., 1972; mgmt. accountant Am. Assn. Coll. Registrars and Adminstrs., Washington, 1973; accountant technician Am. Council on Edn., Washington, 1973-74, Naval Regional Med. Center, Washington, 1974-77, Immigration and Naturalization Service, Washington, 1978; staff accountant Assn. Advancement of Med. Instrumentation, Roslyn, Va., 1978-79, Honeywell Info. Systems, Inc., McLean, Va., 1979-80; asst. controller Fairmac Realty Corp., Arlington, Va., 1980-82; prin. D.J. Wachter, Inc., Arlington, 1983—.

WADDELL, MARY DUGGAN (MIKKI), social worker; b. Columbus, N.J., July 11, 1929; d. James J. and Edna M. Duggan; B.A., Marshall U., 1950; M.S.S.W. in Social Work, U. Louisville, 1960; postgrad. U. Wis.-Madison, 1972; m. Thomas K. Waddell, Jan. 2, 1954; children—Sue Ann, Nancy, Joan. Psychiat. social worker VA, Wadsworth, Kans., Temple, Tex., 1964; lectr. sociology U. Md., Camp Zama, Japan, 1965-68; chief psychiat. social worker Harriet Cohn Mental Health Center, Clarksville, Tenn., 1970-71; acting dir. Cochise County Family Guidance Center, Bisbee, Ariz., 1972-73; instr. sociology Cochise Coll., Sierra Vista, Ariz., 1972—; dir. social services Geriatric Center, Louisville, 1962; social work advisor Army Community Services, Camp Zama, Japan, 1965-68; social work cons. Cochise County Health Depts. Pres. bd. dirs. Awareness House and Southeast Ariz. Drug Abuse Council, 1971-74; mem. Planning and Zoning and Beautification Commn., 1974-75; mem. city council City of Sierra Vista, 1975-79; chmn. exec. bd. Southeast Ariz. Govt. and Orgn., 1977-79; mem. Balance of State and Manpower Council, 1977-79; mem. Foster Home Care Rev. Bd. 1979—; Cochise County, Ariz. State Employment and Tng. Council; chmn. Water Quality Control Adv. Bd. Ariz., 1979-82; mem. adv. council Sch. Social Work, Ariz. State U., Tempe, 1980-82; chmn. bd. dirs. Cochise Community Counseling Soc., 1981-84, Southeastern Ariz. Behavioral Health Service, 1981-84; precinct Committeewoman Democratic Party, 1981—; treas. Greater Huachuca Area Dem. Club, 1982-85; mem. Gov.'s Council Children Youth and Families, 1984-86; bd. dirs. Parents Anonymous. NIMH grantee, 1959-60. Mem. Nat. Assn. Social Workers (chmn. council of inquiry 1980—), Acad. Cert. Social Workers, Alpha Xi Delta, Phi Delta Kappa. Home: 265 Cochise Ct Sierra Vista AZ 85635

WADDINGTON, BETTE HOPE (STAGE NAME ELIZABETH CROWDER), violinist; b. San Francisco, July 27, 1921; d. John and Marguerite (Crowder) Waddington; A.B., U. Calif. at Berkeley, 1945, postgrad.; postgrad. (scholarship) Juilliard Sch. Music, 1950, San Jose State Coll., 1955; M.A., San Francisco State Coll., 1953; student of Joseph Fuchs, Melvin Ritter, Frank Gittelson, Felix Khuner, Daniel Bonsack; life cert. music and art Calif. Jr. Coll. Violinist, St. Louis Symphony, 1958—. Cert. gen. elem. and secondary tchr., Calif.; cert. jr. high sch. librarian. Mem. U. Calif., San Francisco State Coll., San Jose State U. alumnae assns., Sierra Club, Alpha Beta Alpha. Home: 2800 Olive St Saint Louis MO 63103 Office: St Louis Symphony Orch Powell Hall Grand Ave and Delmar Blvd Saint Louis MO 63103

WADDINGTON, EDWINA ELIZABETH, nursing administrator; b. Boardcamp, Ark., June 9, 1939; d. Nathan Edwin Bates and Maude Maxine (Titsworth) Bates Gipson; m. Ralph Read Waddington, Sept. 10, 1960; children—Kelly Jean, Ralph Read Jr. Diploma in Nursing, Sparks Meml. Hosp. Sch. Nursing, 1960; B. Health Scis., Coll. St. Francis, 1981. Head nurse pediatric clinic Reynolds Army Hosp., Fort Sill, Okla., 1966-68; charge nurse obstetrics/gynecology clinic Bernalillo County Med. Ctr., Albuquerque, 1970-74; clin. supr. Cancer Research and Treatment Ctr., Albuquerque, 1974-76; head nurse oncology unit St. Joseph Hosp., Albuquerque, 1978-82; dir. nursing Quality Care, Inc., Albuquerque, 1983—; lectr. in field. Bd. dirs. Bernalillo County Unit div. Am. Cancer Soc., 1974—, pres. bd. dirs., 1981-82; bd. dirs. N. Mex. div. Am. Cancer Com., 1974—, pres. bd. dirs., 1980-81, chmn. bd., 1984- 86; nursing adv. com. Nat. Am. Cancer Soc., 1984, 85. Recipient Annual Nat. Div. Outstanding Vol. award Am. Cancer Soc., 1982. Mem. N. Mex. Oncology Nurses Assn., N. Mex. Assn. Continuity Care. Republican. Avocations: reading; camping; hiking. Home: 10513 Santa Susana Rd NE Albuquerque NM 87111 Office: Quality Care Inc 1100 Eubank NE Albuquerque NM 87112

WADDLE, AUDREY STERLING, nurse; b. Gloucester County, Va., June 20, 1932; d. James Edward and Ethel Hayden (Williams) Sterling; R.N., Riverside Sch. Profl. Nursing, 1952; student Hampton Inst., 1971-72, Thomas Nelson Community Coll., 1973; B.S. in Health Adminstrn., St. Joseph's Coll., 1980; m. Travis Gene Waddle, May 4, 1952; children—Pamela Gayle Waddle Furr, Anita Darlene Smith. Head nurse Riverside Hosp., Newport News, 1953, Onslow County Hosp., Jacksonville, N.C., 1954; pvt. duty, relief dir. Gray's Clinic & Hosp., Springhill, La., 1955-57; gen. duty nurse Eastern State Hosp., Williamsburg, Va., 1957-58, head nurse, 1958-59, nurse supr., 1959-65, mental health nurse instr. and tng. coordinator, 1982—, chmn. ward manual com., 1967-81, others. Adv. bd. and selection com. Lafayette Practical Nurse Program, Williamsburg, 1972-82; mem. State of Va. Dept. Mental Health/Mental Retardation Individualized Treatment Planning Com., 1979-80; chmn. Eastern State Hosp. United Fund drive, 1978-79. Registered profl. nurse, Va.; U. Md. grantee, 1964. Mem. Va. Govt. Employees Assn., Nat. Soc. Registered Nurses. Presbyterian. Developer psychiat. practical nurse program Eastern State Hosp., 1967; co-author manuals. Home: 108 Underwood Rd Williamsburg VA 23185 Office: Drawer A Williamsburg VA 23187

WADE, BARBARA LOUISE, county official; b. Choctaw, Ala., Aug. 14, 1938; d. Joe Siah and Fannie Mae Rodgers; B.S., Roosevelt U., 1971; M.A. Governor's State U., 1977; m. Thomas Robert Wade, Dec. 24, 1974; children—Diann, Tyree, Kim, Carolyn. Co-chmn. housing, chmn., youth community organizer TWO, Chgo., 1960-72; planning intern City of Chgo.; probation officer Juvenile Ct., Cook County, Ill., 1971-75; clin. supr., Jacksonville, Fla., 1976-77, juvenile ct. unit supr. post arrest unit, domestic intervention Dade State's Atty. Office (Fla.), 1977-78, 78-80, dir. pretrial diversion, Miami, Fla., after 1980; youth gang Coordinator Miami Police Dept.; cons. Miami chpt. SCLC of Dade County, Urban League of Jacksonville. Pres. AO Sexton Sch. Council; bd. dirs. Harris YWCA. Cert. social worker, Ill. Mem. Urban League, Women in Criminal Justice, Probation and Parole, Am. Probation and Parole Assn., Nat. Assn. Female Execs., AAUW, Black Social Workers, Roosevelt U. Alumni Assn., Governor's State U. Alumni Assn. Address: 11125 SW 156th Terr Miami FL 33157

WADE, ELIZABETH BARTLETT, geodesist; b. Washington, Dec. 6, 1950; d. Victor E. and Elizabeth B. (Denham) Bieber; m. Dennis L. Wade, June 24,

1972; 1 child, Deborah L. B.S., U. Md., 1972. Geodesist, Nat. Geodetic Survey, NOAA, Rockville, Md., 1972-77, supervisory geodesist, chief new datum, 1977-78, geodesist, new datum mgr., 1978-84, EEO coordinator, 1979—, supervisory geodesist project mgr. N.Am. Datum of 1983, 1984—. Author papers in field. Recipient Spl. Achievement award NOAA, 1976, 77, 82, 83, 84, 85. Mem. Am. Congress Surveying and Mapping, Am. Shetland Sheepdog Assn. Methodist. Avocations: raising and showing Shetland Sheepdogs. Home: 6711 Sage Ct Adamstown MD 21710 Office: Dept Commerce Nat Geodetic Survey NOAA N-CG12 Rockville MD 20852

WADE, GAIL LORETTA, wine import company executive, computer consultant; b. Richmond, Va., Apr. 3, 1954; d. Joseph Louis Thompson and Mae Frances (Fries) McCoy; m. Leon Wade, Dec. 27, 1975; children—Chrystyna, Galadriel, Sara. Student Fayetteville State U., 1976-80; B.S. in Natural Sci., Edison State Coll., 1985. Lab. technician Am. Hoescht Corp., Branchburg, N.J., 1980-83; asst. mgr. Atlas Door Corp., Edisn, N.J., 1984-86; chief of staff Winebow, Inc., Hohokus, N.J., 1986—; pres. GDN Data Systems, New Brunswick, 1985—. Contbr. poetry to mags. Mem. Nat. Assn. Female Execs., Black Women's Network Assn. (exec. bd. dirs.), N.J. Bus. Women's Assn. Democrat. Roman Catholic. Home: 260 Delavan St New Brunswick NJ 08901

WADE, JENNY, industrial market communications executive, consultant; b. Rome, N.Y., Mar. 12, 1952; d. Clyde LeRoy and Faye (Moses) W.; m. Stephen DeLano Gillett, July 18, 1980 (div. 1983). B.A. cum laude, Tex. Christian U., 1974. Exec. sec. News, Inc., Houston, 1974-75; sales promotion supr. Dresser Industries, Inc., Dallas, 1975-79; mgr. market services and planning Harris Graphics Corp., Dallas, 1979—; cons. Designs Under Glass, Dallas, 1977—. Author, editor trade jour. articles. Recipient Silver Echo award Direct Mktg. Assn., 1983, various advt. awards. Mem. Graphic Arts Mktg. Info. Service, Printing Industries Am. (chmn. geog. market potentials com. 1979-80, 83-84). Episcopalian. Club: Maledicta. Home: 3911-F Fairmount Dallas TX 75219 Office: Harris Graphics Corp Comml Press Div PO Box 61485 Dallas Fort Worth Airport TX 75261

WADE, JUDITH LYNN, stockbroker; b. Richmond, Va., Dec. 1, 1947; d. Frank Alton and Evelyn H. (Clark) Wade. B.A. in Math., Mary Baldwin Coll., 1969; M.P.A., Ga. State U., 1976. Asst. to dir. spl. projects Govs. Office, Atlanta, 1971-72; asst. to commr. human resources Ga. Dept. Human Resources, Atlanta, 1972-76; So. desk person Jimmy Carter Campaign for Pres., Atlanta, 1976; asst. to sec. Cecil Andrus, U.S. Dept. Interior, Washington, 1977-79; dir. assoc. dep. sec.'s office U.S. Dept. Commerce, Washington, 1980-81; account exec. Merrill, Lynch, Pierce, Fenner & Smith, Atlanta, 1983—; cons. Am. Pioneer Life Ins., Orlando, Fla., 1983, Albers, Cronin & Garrity, Washington, 1983. Mem. nat. alumni bd. Mary Baldwin Coll., Staunton, Va., 1977-79, chmn. Washington chpt., 1977-79, chmn. Atlanta chpt., 1986—; vol. fundraiser Atlanta Arts Alliance, 1983-86. Democrat. Presbyterian.

WADE, JULIA HOWARD, interior designer; b. Alexandria, La., Dec. 2, 1928; d. Samuel Eugene and Louis D'Or (Moore) Howard; B.A., Baylor U., 1948; student La. Coll., 1946; m. Nelsyn Ernest Brooks Wade, June 29, 1948; children—Sylvia Laureen, Lisa Frances, William Alan, David Eugene. Organizer, dir. Children's Theatre, San Augustine, Tex., 1948-52; tchr. English San Augustine High Sch., 1948; partner, decorator, advt. mgr., buyer Nelsyns Furniture Store, San Augustine, 1958—; lectr. in field. Hist. chmn. 8-County Deep East Tex. Devel. Assn., 1975; bd. dirs. San Augustine Public Library, 1980-82; bd. devel. E. Tex. Bapt. Coll., 1978-82. Named Outstanding Small Retailer, S.W. Home Furnishings Assn., 1979; Pres.'s award, C. of C., 1973; Rotary award, 1980, Outstanding Dealer, Kirsch, 1985. Mem. C. of C. (v.p. 1972-77), S.W. Home Furnishings Assn. (cert.), Nat. Assn. Retail Dealers of Am., Nat. Assn. Female Execs., Tex. Old Missions and Forts Restoration Assn., Nat. Trust Hist. Preservation, Baylor U. Alumni Assn., Tex. Forestry Assn., DAR, San Augustine County Hist. Soc., Internat. Platform Assn. Republican. Baptist. Clubs: Heritage (pres. 1963), Bible (pres. 1953, 57). Home: 412 Baxter Ln San Augustine TX 75972 Office: 128 E Columbia St San Augustine TX 75972

WADE, LINDA MARLENE, airline executive; b. Long Beach, Calif., Aug. 30, 1944; d. Charles Thurston and Roberta Grace (Howe) Davis; m. Joseph Donald Wade, Sept. 16, 1977; m. Louis William Leopold, Feb. 25, 1964; (div. Feb. 1972), 1 dau., Tracey Jo. Reservation agt. Los Angeles Airways, 1962-64; service rep. Pacific Telephone, Fullerton, Calif., 1965-66; reservation agt. AirCal, Newport Beach, Calif., 1966-68, from instr. to asst. mgr. tng. to mgr. tng., 1968-81; dir. reservations and telecommunications Jet Am., Long Beach, 1981-83, v.p. passenger service, 1983—. Mem. Internat. Orgn. Women in Telecommunications, Women in Mgmt. (scholarship com.), Am. Bus. Women's Assn., Nat. Assn. Female Execs., Women's Profl. Network, Long Beach C. of C. (women's council). Republican. Mormon. Club: Zonta (bd. dirs.). Office: 3521 E Spring St Long Beach CA 90806

WADE, MARY CARROLL, pyschologist, educator, government official; b. Rome, Ga., Sept. 1, 1909; d. Seaborn Rosa and Dollie Savannah (Hill) Carroll; student Maryville Coll., 1926-28, B.A., 1931; postgrad. U. of the South, summer, 1938; M.A., George Washington U., 1948; Ed.D., Am. U., 1970; lic. psychologist, Washington; m. Richard Rudolph Wade, Apr. 1, 1967 (dec.). Tchr., Hawkins County, Tenn., 1934-36, Pittman Center, Tenn., 1937-38, Chattanooga, 1938-42, Meigs County, Tenn., 1936-37; with War Dept., Washington, 1942-43; library asst. Library of Congress, Washington, 1943-44; planner, U.S. Govt. Printing Office, Washington, 1944-67, planner-in-charge, 1967-72, chief marginally forms continuous forms sect., Specifications Div., 1972-80, chmn. Fed. Women's Program, 1972-73; cons. psychologist Va. Vocational Rehab. Dept., 1954-57; lectr. Montgomery Coll., Rockville, Md., 1981-82; freelance writer and lectr., 1982—; lectr. Fed. Office Systems Expo, 1982, No. Va. Community Coll., 1984. Active Girls Scouts U.S.A.; bd. dirs. United Cerebral Palsy, D.C., 1970-82; active ARC; hon. staff mem. Tenn. State Senator Annabelle Clement O'Brien, 1982. Recipient United Service Orgn. award, 1946; Superior Service award, U.S. Govt. Printing Office, 1963, 66, 67, 68, Spl. Achievement award, 1971-72, others. Mem. Am. Psychol. Assn., Va. Psychol. Assn., D.C. Psychol. Assn., Soc. for Personnel Adminstrn., Nat. Vocat. Guidance Assn., Am. Personnel and Guidance Assn., Pub. Personnel Assn., Franklin Tech. Soc., Bus. Forms Mgmt. Assn. (rec. sec. 1980-81), Am. U. Alumni Assn., George Washington U. Alumni Assn., Maryville Coll. Alumni Assn., Nat. Trust Historic Preservation, Poetry Soc. Va., Va., Nat. Assn. Ret. Fed. Employees (rec. sec. 1984-85), Kappa Delta Epsilon, Psi Chi, Phi Delta Gamma (pres. Beta chpt., nat. council rep.). Presbyterian. Clubs: Wash. Club of Printing House Craftsmen, Wash. Litho, George Washington Univ., Americana, Toastmistress, Altrusa, (corr. sec. 1982-84, rec. sec. 1984-85), Columbian Women, (corr. sec. 1984-85), 1983-85), Club Council of Alexandria (rec. 1981), Fairfax County Bus. and profl. Women's (pres. 1975-76). Contbr. articles to profl. jours.

WADE, MARY LOUISE POWELL, counselor; b. Springfield, Ohio, Sept. 25, 1932; d. Gamaliel Wyatte Holmes and Lucy Maxwell (Sloan) Powell; A.A., Meridian Jr. Coll., 1951; B.A., U. So. Miss., 1953, M.A., 1954; counselor cert. U. So. Ala., 1979; student Columbia Theol. Sem., Decatur, Ga., 1984-85, St. Paul Theol. Sem., Kansas City, Mo., 1985—; m. Walter B. Wade, Aug. 25, 1956 (div. July 1980); children—Susan Sloan Wade Massey, Holly Bibb Wade Crane, Walter Wyatte. Speech therapist Moultrie Ga. Speech Clinic, 1954-55, U. Tenn. Speech and Hearing Center, 1955-56, Jackson County Exceptional Sch., 1957-58; vending machine sales Morrisons Co., Pascagoula, 1974; newspaper dealer, Clarion Ledger, Jackson, Miss., 1974-75; audiologist, hearing aid salesman Beltone Co., Hattiesburg, Miss., 1975-77; receptionist Singing River Mental Health Services, Pascagoula, 1977; youth services counselor Jackson County Youth Ct., Miss. Dept. Youth Services, Pascagoula, 1977-84, also chief counselor, probation officer; night mgr. N.E.W.S. Shelter for Battered Women, 1985—; youth minister Grace Presbyn. Ch., Kansas City, 1985—. Neighborhood chmn. Girl Scouts, 1958-68; trombonist Gulf Coast Symphony, 1981-84; asst. coach Aquatic Club swim team, 1960-70; dir. youth choir 1st Presbyn. Ch., Pascagoula; elder 1st Presbyn. Ch., Ocean Springs, Miss., 1982—; instr. water safety ARC; rape crisis counselor Gulfcoast Women's Center, Biloxi, Miss.; mem. Pas-Point Singers. Mem. Miss. Assn. Clin. Counselors, State Employees Assn. Miss. Democrat. Presbyterian. Home: 811 Benton Blvd Kansas City MO 64124

WADE, MELISSA ANN MARQUART, architect; b. Crestline, Ohio, Aug. 26, 1952; d. Paul Frederick and Anna Marie (Perito) Marquart; B.Design-Interior Design with high honors, U. Fla., 1974, B. Design-Architecture with honors, 1975, M.A. in Architecture, 1976; m. Raymond John Wade, Jr., May 2, 1981; children—Raymond John III, Jason Paul. Design draftsman Schweizer Assos., Inc., Orlando, Fla., 1977-78; job capt. Catalyst, Inc., Orlando, 1978-79; project coordinator Lynn M. Teneyck Architect, Inc., Orlando, 1979-80; architect, project coordinator Duer & Assos. Architects, Inc., Winter Park, Fla., 1980-82. Cert. class A gen. contractor, Fla.; registered architect, Fla. Mem. AIA. Lutheran. Home and Office: 428 Wilderness Dr Longwood FL 32779

WADE, NANCY ANN, pediatrician, allergist; b. Boston, Aug. 7, 1950; d. Roger J. and Dorothy (Errington) Wade; m. John Parkhurst Leary, Jan. 27, 1979. B.A., Fitchburg State Coll., 1972; B.Med. Sci. (scholar), Dartmouth Coll., 1974; M.D., Tufts U., 1975. Diplomate Am. Bd. Allergy and Immunology. Resident in pediatrics Albany Med. Ctr. (N.Y.), 1975-77, chief resident in pediatrics, 1977-78; practice medicine specializing in pediatrics Hudson Headwaters Health Network, Warrensburg, N.Y., 1978-80; asst. prof. pediatrics Albany Med. Coll., 1980—, fellow in allergy and immunology, 1982-84; pvt. practice pediatric immunology, 1984—. AAUW fellow, 1974-75; Fuller Jr. research fellow, 1971. Fellow Am. Acad. Pediatrics; mem. Am. Acad. Allergy and Immunology. Office: 77 Van Dam St Saratoga Springs NY 12866

WADE, SARA THOMASON, health care executive, real estate broker; b. New Albany, Miss., Jan. 30, 1936; d. James Henderson and Rosabel (Purvis) Thomason; m. John Smith Wade, Sr., Dec. 23, 1956 (div. Oct. 1968); children—John Smith, Kimberly Rose. B.S., Blue Mountain Coll., Miss., 1957; M.Ed., U. Miss., 1973; M.A., Central Mich. U., 1976. Cert. med. technologist, cytotechnologist. Cytotechnologist, Huntsville (Ala.) Hosp., 1958; bench technologist North Miss. Med Ctr., Tupelo, 1960-61, ednl. coordinator Sch. Med. Technology, 1961-70, adminstrv. dir., 1970—; med. technologist S.J. McDuffie, M.D., Nettleton, Miss., 1970—; cons. med. tech. Miss. State U., Starkville, 1973—, Clay County Hosp., West Point, Miss., 1983; lectr. workshops. Author: Management, 1983; Quality Circles Training Manual, 1983. Mem. Miss. Soc. Med. Tech. (state pres. 1979-80, dist. pres. 1977, dir. 1970-72, 76-78), Am. Soc. Med. Tech. (del. 1976-80), Am. Soc. Cytotechnologists (state rep.). Republican. Baptist. Clubs: Tupelo Running (dir. 1982-83), Miss. Magnolia Quality Circles (dir. 1983-84), Tupelo Soroptimist (sec. 1982-84, dir. 1981-82), Alpha Mu Tau. Home: 3 Songbird Ln Tupelo MS 38801 Office: North Mississippi Medical Center 830 S Gloster St Tupelo MS 38801

WADLOW, JOAN KRUEGER, university administrator; b. LeMars, Iowa, Aug. 21, 1932; d. R. John and Norma I. (Ihle) Krueger; m. Richard Wadlow, July 27, 1958; children—Dawn, Kit. B.A., U. Nebr., 1953; M.A., Fletcher Sch. Law, 1956; Ph.D., U. Nebr., 1963. Prof., asst. U. Nebr., Lincoln, 1959-79, assoc. dean coll. arts and scis., 1972-79; dean coll. arts and scis. U. Wyo., Laramie, 1979-84, v.p. acad. affairs, 1984—; asst. pub. relations U. Nebr., 1958-59; reporter Lincoln Star, Nebr., 1953. Editor: International Studies Notes. Trustee Bryan Meml. Hosp., Lincoln, 1978-79; bd. dirs. Jr. League, Lincoln, 1985; research dir. Gubernatorial Campaign, Lincoln, 1985; pres. YWCA Adv. Bd., Lincoln, 1970-71. Recipient Seacrest Journalism award 1953-54, Mortar Bd. Teaching award 1976, Disting. Teaching award U. Nebr. 1979. Rotary fellow 1956-57. Mem. Consortium Internat. Devel. (exec. com., trustee 1984—), Council Colls. of Arts and Scis. (pres. 1984-85), Internat. Studies Assn. (gov. council 1977-84), Laramie C. of C. (bd. dirs. 1983-84), Nat. Assn. State Univs. and Land Grant Colls. (chmn. steering com. 1985-86). Republican. Home: 4630 Meadowlark Ln Laramie WY 82070 Office: U Wyo Acad Affairs PO Box 3302 University Sta Laramie WY 82071

WADSWORTH, DOROTHY BUCKNAM, retired civic worker; b. Geneseo, N.Y., July 23, 1920; d. Roland Franklin and Julia Anne (Krotts) Bucknam; m. Robert Hume Wadsworth, Oct. 17, 1943; children—Ann Hunter, Barbara Jane. B.A. in Econs., Mt. Holyoke Coll., 1941. Dir. devel. Rochester Inst. Tech., N.Y., 1972-75; commr. N.Y. State Spl. Commn. on Attica, 1971-72; bd. dirs. Rochester Telephone Corp., 1972-76; commr. N.Y. State Moreland Act Commn. on Nursing Homes, N.Y.C., 1975-76, N.Y. State Commn. of Correction, Albany, 1975-79; Western N.Y. Rep., N.Y. State Senate Select Com. of Crime, Rochester and Albany, 1979-82. Active Jr. Guild for Crippled Children, Rochester Philharm. Orch. Study, 1959-60, Rochester Regional Research Library Council, 1968-72; vice chmn. N.Y. State del. White House Conf. on Libraries, 1977-79; rep. 7th Jud. Dist. Grievance Com., 1979-84; mem. Planned Parenthood Rochester and Monroe Counties, 1982-84; chmn. Monroe County Citizens for Family Planning, 1983, pres. Planned Parenthood-Monroe County, 1953-55, Meml. Art Gallery Women's Council, U. Rochester, 1957-59, Genesee Valley Mt. Holyoke Club, 1950-52, Rochester Jr. League, 1954-55; trustee Rochester Inst. Tech., 1960-72, Sta. WXXI-Pub. TV, 1968-72; founder Neighborhood Health Ctr. Rochester and Monroe Counties, 1968-72; bd. dirs. Blue Cross, 1968-75, Arts Council Monroe County, 1971-72, York State Craftsman, 1960-63, Community Chest-United Way, 1970-72; spl. asst. to chmn. Monroe County Republican Com., 1983-84; Rep. candidate for N.Y. Senate, 1984. Recipient Helen Stone Jones award, 1968; B. Forman Flair award, 1969; Mt. Holyoke Coll. Medal of Honor, 1970; Rochester C. of C. Civic medal, 1971; Alpha Phi Omega Outstanding Service award, 1972; Anthony Jordan Health Ctr. award, 1973; UN Internat. Women's Yr. citation Rochester Assn. for UN, 1974; N.Y. State Sheriff's Assn. Friend of Law Enforcement award, 1979. Mem. Mt. Holyoke Coll. Alumni Assn. Presbyterian. Home: 147 Chelmsford Rd Rochester NY 14618

WADZINSKI, DIANE, radio station sales executive; b. Manitowoc, Wis., Apr. 28, 1952; d. Ralph William and Marcella Erna (Luebke) Pleuss; B.S., U. Wis.-Stevens Point, 1974; M.B.A., U. Wis.-Oshkosh, 1986. Electric living rep. Wis. Electric Power Co., Milw., 1974-75; office service mgr. Sentry Ins., Stevens Point, Wis., 1975-76; account exec. Circa 1946 Advt. Agy., Green Bay, Wis., 1976-78; mktg. dir. Port Plaza Mall, Green Bay, 1978-81; sales rep. Sta. WIXX, Green Bay, 1981-83, sales mgr., 1983—. Bd. dirs. United Way, Green Bay, 1985, campaign communications chmn., 1982-83. Mem. Green Bay Advt. Fedn. (pres. 1983-84, v.p., 1982-83, Addy awards chmn. 1981-82, sec. 1979-81). Avocations: running; racquetball. Home: 2922 Waubenoor Dr Green Bay WI 54301 Office: WIXX Radio 115 S Jefferson St Green Bay WI 54301

WAELTY, BEATRYCE ANN, rubber and tire company executive; b. Mpls., Aug. 25, 1938; d. Paul Peter and Marion Ann (Hopkins) Heltemes Jerome; m. Thomas K. Hallcock, June 21, 1963 (div. 1977); m. Waldo G. Waelty, Apr. 7, 1979; children—Thomas J.P., Shawn M. (dec.), Kimberley A., Scott E. A.A., Stephens Coll., 1958; B.S., U. San Francisco, 1986. Mgr., Shasta Valley Realty, Weed, Calif., 1978-79; sec., account clk. Area Agy. on Aging, Weed, Calif., 1980-81; data reductionist Aerojet Tactical Co./Aerojet Strategic Propulsion Co., Sacramento, 1982-84; documentation coordinator, 1984, documentation supr., 1984—. Lodge: Order Eastern Star (worthy matron). Avocations: Gardening; needlepoint; carpentry. Home: 1806 Sheffield Way Roseville CA 95678 Office: Aerojet Strategic Propulsion Co Hwy 50 and Hazel Ave Sacramento CA 95813

WAGENER, MARGUERITE MARY, free lance writer, advertising sales consultant; b. North Kingston, R.I., Feb. 12, 1954; d. Richard V. and Lucille M. Wagener; B.A. in English and Communication Arts, St. Mary's Coll., Winona, Minn., 1975. Reporter, photographer, anchorperson Sta.-WKBT-TV, La Crosse, Wis., 1975-78; salesperson Anything Groes Corp., La Crosse, 1978-79; audio-visual scriptwriter Trane Co., La Crosse, 1979-81, mgr. dept. tech. lit., 1981-82; freelance writer, advt. sales, cons., 1982-83; asst. sales mgr. WISQ-FM, La Crosse, 1983-85; co-owner Peregrine Marine. Vice pres. alumni bd. dirs. St. Mary's Coll., 1980-86.

WAGENHOFFER, RUTH ALMA, nurse, educator; b. Boise, Idaho, Apr. 12, 1936; d. Hilding Algot Verner and Maxine Mabel (Foren) Anderson; m. Gustave Victor Wagenhoffer, June 14, 1958; children—Mark, Janet, Teresa, Karl. A.A., Coll. of Sequoias, Visalia, Calif., 1956; B.S. in Nursing, U. Calif.-San Francisco, 1959, M. Health Sci., Davis, 1976. Cert. nursing instr., Calif. Staff nurse U. Calif.-San Francisco, 1959-60, Pioneer Hosp., Escalon, Calif., 1962-63, Lodi Meml. Hosp. (Calif.), 1964-67; instr. nursing San Joaquin Delta Coll., Stockton, Calif., 1967—; family nurse practitioner Vinewood Family Practice, Lodi, 1975—. Democrat. Roman Catholic. Home: Acampo CA Office: San Joaquin Delta Coll 5151 Pacific St Stockton CA 95207

WAGNER, ALLISON JEAN, vocational nurse; b. Los Angeles, Calif., Dec. 14, 1960; d. Kurt Joseph and Casilda Kathleen (Kelley) Wagner. A.A./B.A., U. of the Pacific, 1979-83; L.V.N., Maric Coll., 1984-85. Lic. vocat. nurse. Editor/distbr. Winning Images, Beverly Hills, Calif., 1985—; med. cons. Ctr. for Spl. Surgery, Los Angeles, 1985—; publicist Your'e Becoming, Los Angeles, 1986. Mem. Calif. Theatre Council, Los Angeles, 1986. Recipient Multiple Athletic awards, scholastic awards, The Buckley Sch. Mem. Nat. Assn. Female Execs., Alpha Chi Omega. Methodist. Club: Mary Duque Guild. Avocations: tennis; weight training; scuba diving; racquetball; golf. Office: Center for Spl Surgery 1125 S Beverly Dr Suite 505 Los Angeles CA 90035

WAGNER, DOROTHY MARIE, court reporter, service executive; b. Milw., June 8, 1924; d. Theodore Anthony and Leona Helen (Ullrich) Wagner; grad. Milw. Bus. U., 1944; student Marquette U., U. Wis., Milw. Stenographer, legal sec., Milw., 1942-44; hearing reporter Wis. Workmen's Compensation Dept., 1944-48; ofcl. reporter to judge Circuit Ct., Milw., 1952-53; owner, operator ct. reporting service Dorothy M. Wagner & Assos., Milw., 1948—; guest lectr. ct. reporting Madison Area Tech. Coll., 1981—. Recipient Gregg Diamond medal Gregg Pub. Co., 1950. Mem. Nat. (registered profl. reporter, certificate of proficiency), Wis. shorthand reporters assns., Am. Legion Aux. Roman Catholic. Home: 214 Williamsburg Dr Thiensville WI 53092 Office: 135 Wells St Suite 400 Milwaukee WI 53203

WAGNER, ELLEN CAROL, funds manager; b. New Britain, Conn., Oct. 11; d. Paul and Charlotte Helen (Gloersen) Wagner; B.F.A., Boston U., 1960; M.B.A., Fordham U., 1975. Adminstrv. and prodn. asst. Hurok Concerts Inc., 1960-70; funds mgr. pension and health funds Am. Guild Mus. Artists, N.Y.C., 1971—. Mem. nat. alumni council Boston U., 1981—, chmn. Theatre Network, 1980-81; active Vol. Services for Children. Mem. Am. Mgmt. Assn., Fordham U. Alumni Assn. (Fedn. dir. 1976-80), Assn. M.B.A. Execs., Am. Soc. Profl. and Exec. Women, Scandinavian Am. Found., Vol. Services for Children. Office: care AGMA Pension & Health Funds 1841 Broadway Room 507 New York NY 10023

WAGNER, ELLEN MARIE, government official, publicist, lecturer; b. Washington, Mar. 30, 1946; d. Paul Henry and Edna Lorraine (McKenny) W. A.A., Immaculata Coll., Washington, 1966; cert. in communications George Washington U., 1982. Adminstrv. asst. Dept. Def., Washington, 1966-70; program officer Export/Import Bank, Washington, 1970-72; program coordinator Com. Re-election of the Pres., Washington, 1972-73; pub. and internat. affairs officer Dept. of Commerce, Washington, 1973—; freelance in pub. relations, Washington, 1981—. Chmn. pub. relations Federally Employed Women No. Va., 1983, Commerce Com. for Women, 1983. Mem. Washington Women in Pub. Relations. Roman Catholic. Clubs: Nat Press, Networking (Washington). Home: 2727 29th St NW Apt 223 Washington DC 20008 Office: Dept of Commerce 14th St and Constitution Ave NW Room 3800 Washington DC 20230

WAGNER, ELLEN PAYNE, telephone company executive; b. Rome, Ga., June 15, 1945; d. Richard William and Helen (Hatch) Payne; B.A., Shorter Coll., Rome, 1966; M.S. (Belle Baruch fellow 1966-68), Clemson U., 1968; postgrad. Auburn U.; m. Conrad John Wagner, Oct. 21, 1978; 1 adopted son, Conrad John, II; 3 stepchildren. Scientist Ga. State Crime Lab., 1973-74; mgr. network design So. Bell Telephone Co., Atlanta, 1974-78, staff assoc. minicomputer support, 1978-82, minicomputer project mgr., 1982-83; FACS project mgr. BellSouth Services Inc., Atlanta, 1983—; cons., speaker in field. Organizer, vol. rape crisis center Grady Hosp., Atlanta, 1974; alt. del. Ga. Democratic Conv., 1975; mem. Internat. Women's Yr. task force Ga. Commn. Status Women, 1977; mem. steering com. Atlanta Dogwood Festival, 1983-86; mem. transp. adv. bd. Atlanta Regional Commn., 1985-86. Recipient Outstanding Leadership award Atlanta chpt. AAUW, 1976; lic. real estate broker. Mem. Bus. and Profl. Women (pres. Atlanta chpt. 1978-79), Atlanta Women's C. of C. (editor newsletter 1982-83, bd. dirs. 1983-85, 2d v.p. 1985-86). Unitarian. Clubs: Quota (2d v.p. Northside 1981-82, pres. 1983-84), Women's Commerce (Atlanta). Home: Route 5 Box 5311 Dawsonville GA 30534 Office: 10E61 675 W Peachtree St Atlanta GA 30375

WAGNER, FLORENCE, telecommunications executive; b. McKeesport, Pa., Sept. 23, 1926; d. George and Sophia (Petros) Zeleznik; B.A. magna cum laude, U. Pitts., 1977, M.P.A., 1981; m. Francis Xavier Wagner, June 18, 1946; children—Deborah Elaine Wagner Franke, Rebecca Susan Wagner Schroettinger, Melissa Catherine Wagner Good, Francis Xavier, Robert Francis. Sec. to pres. Tube City Iron & Metal Co., Glassport, Pa., 1944-50; cons. Raw Materials, Inc., Pitts., 1955; gen. mgr. Carson Compressed Steel Products, Pitts., 1967-69; partner Universal Steel Products, Pitts., 1970-71; gen. mgr. Josh Steel Co., Braddock, Pa., 1971-78; owner Wagner's Candy Box, Mt. Lebanon, Pa., 1979-80; borough sec./treas. Borough of Pennsbury Village, Allegheny County, Pa., 1980—; ptnr. Tele-Communications of Am., Burgettstown, Pa., 1984—; trustee Profit-Sharing trust, Pension trust; mem. Foster Parents; vol. St. Peters' Child Devel. Ctrs., Inc., Pitts. Mem. Pitts. Symphony Soc., Pitts. Ballet Theater Guild. Mem. Soc. Pub. Adminstrn. (founder U. Pitts. br.), Acad. Polit. Sci., U.S. Strategic Inst., Southwestern Pa. Sec. Assn., AAUW, Alpha Sigma Lambda (past pres., sec., pres.) Republican. Roman Catholic. Home: RD 2 Box 105 Lee Rd Burgettstown PA 15021 Office: 6 Pennsbery Blvd Pittsburgh PA 15205

WAGNER, JACQUELINE ANN, city planner; b. N.Y.C., B.S. magna cum laude in Bus. Adminstrn., N.Y. Inst. Tech., 1974; M.B.A., Nova U., 1976, D.B.A., 1981. Asst. to v.p. sales Giannini Sci. Corp., N.Y.C., 1964-67; planning analyst City of Hollywood (Fla.), 1968-72, zoning adminstr., 1973-77, city planner, 1977-80, prin. planner, 1980—; staff adv. Planning and Zoning Bd., City Commn. adj. prof. mgmt. Boward County (Fla.) Community Coll., 1981—; adj. prof. bus. policy M.B.A. program Nova U., Ft. Lauderdale, Fla., 1982. Youth adv., counselor St. John's Episcopal Ch., Hollywood, 1973-75. Mem. Acad. Mgmt., Am. Inst. Planners, Fla. Planning and Zoning Assn., Am. Soc. Public Adminstrs., Internat. Platform Assn. Club: Zonta. Home: 2822 Monroe St Hollywood FL 33020 Office: 2600 Hollywood Blvd Hollywood FL 33020

WAGNER, JUDITH BUCK, investment counselor, banker; b. Altoona, Pa., Sept. 25, 1943; d. Harry Bud and Mary Elizabeth (Rhodes) Buck; m. Joseph E. Wagner, Mar. 15, 1980; 1 child, Elizabeth Buck. B.A., U. Wash., 1965; grad. N.Y. Inst. Fin., N.Y.C., 1968; chartered fin. analyst I, Inst. Chartered Fin. Analysts, U. Va., 1972. Security analyst Morgan, Olmstead, Kennedy & Gardner, Los Angeles, 1968-71, research cons., St. Louis, 1971-72; security analyst Boettcher & Co. Denver, 1972-75; chmn., dir. Women's Bank, Denver, 1980—. Women's Bank N.Am., Denver, 1977—; chmn. Wagner & Hamil, Inc., Denver, 1983—; pres. Wagner Inverstment Counsel, Inc., Denver, 1975—; chmn. Equitable Bankshares of Colo., Inc., Denver, 1980—; pres. Organizational Group for Women's Banks, Denver, 1975-77. Bd. dirs. Big Sisters Colo., Inc., Denver, 1973-84, pres. 1977-82; mem. Women's Forum Colo., Denver, 1977—, pres., 1979. Mem. Colo. Growth Capital (1979-82), Denver Soc. Security Analysts (v.p. 1980, pres. 1981), Fin. Analysts Fedn., Pi Beta Phi. Office: Wagner & Hamil Inc Investment Counsel 410 17th St Suite 840 Denver CO 80202

WAGNER, JUDITH L., government official; b. Washington, Feb. 26, 1947; d. Henry C. and Pauline O. (Woodruff) W.; B.S., Madison Coll., 1968; M.S.A., George Washington U., 1970. Mgmt. analyst Office Sec. Army, Washington, 1968-73, U.S. Secret Service, Washington, 1973-74, chief mgmt. programs and studies br., mgmt. and orgn. div., 1974-77, chief paperwork mgmt. br., 1977-78; chief mgmt. and orgn. div. U.S. Mint, Washington, 1978-79, asst. dir. mgmt. services, 1979—. Collegiate profl. teaching cert., Va. Mem. Am. Soc. Public Adminstrn., Am. Mgmt. Assn., Am. Assn. Budget and Program Analysis, Fed. Exec. Inst. Alumni Assn. Office: 633 3d St NW Washington DC 20220

WAGNER, JULIA A(NNE), editor; b. Alexandria, Va., Feb. 15, 1924; d. Luigi and Domenica (Di Giammarino) Coppa; Widowed. B.A., George Washington U., 1948, M.A., 1950. With U.S. Govt., Washington, 1941-55, publs. editor, 1951-55; editorial asst. Dell Pub. Co., N.Y.C., 1956-59, mng. editor, 1959-72, editor-in-chief, 1973—. Mem. Am. Fedn. Astrologers. Democrat. Roman Catholic. Office: Dell Pub Co Inc 245 E 47th St New York NY 10017

WAGNER, LOUISE HEMINGWAY BENTON, educational company executive; b. Chgo., July 29, 1937; d. William and Helen (Hemingway) Benton; student Skidmore Coll., 1955-57; B.A. in English, Finch Coll., 1960; m. Ralph C. Wagner, May 23, 1979. Pub. relations asst. Look mag., N.Y.C., 1960-62, Compton Ency., Chgo., 1962-63; mktg. services Ency. Brit. Press, Chgo., 1963-66; dir. exhibits Ency. Brit. Ednl. Corp., Chgo., 1966-70, v.p. mktg. services, 1970-83, chmn. bd. dirs., 1983—, also dir. Bd. dirs. Chgo. Lying-In Hosp., Columbia Coll., Chgo., Cradle Soc., Evanston, Ill., Reading is

FUNdamental, Chgo.; mem. women's bd. U. Chgo.; governing mem. Orchestral Assn. Chgo., Art Inst. Chgo. Mem. Publicity Club Chgo., ALA, Assn. for Edn. Communication Tech. Episcopalian. Clubs: Racquet, Mid-Am., Arts (Chgo.); Country of Fairfield (Conn.); Thorngate Country (Deerfield, Ill.). Home: Southport CT and Chicago IL Office: Ency Brit Edn Corp 425 N Michigan Ave Chicago IL 60611

WAGNER, MARJORIE COOGAN DOWNING, educator; b. N.Y.C., Mar. 16, 1917; d. Charles A. and Marguerite C. (Ohland) Coogan; B.A., Coll. Mt. St. Vincent, 1938; M.A., Cath. U. Am., 1939; Ph.D., Yale U., 1942; LL.D., Chapman Coll., 1975; m. M. John Wagner, June 6, 1974; children—Francis, Margaret, Nicholas. Dean, Sarah Lawrence Coll., Bronxville, N.Y., 1961-65; dean of faculty Scripps Coll., Claremont, Calif., 1965-71, Frederick Hard prof. English Lit., 1971-74; pres. Calif. State Coll. Sonoma, Rohnert Park, 1974-76; vice chancellor faculty-staff affairs Calif. State U., Long Beach, 1976-80; dir. Insts. for Chief Acad. Officers, Am. Council Edn., 1980-82; cons. Ednl. Inst. Bd. dirs. United Way, 1975; trustee Mt. St. Mary's Coll., Los Angeles, 1979—; mem. Sr. Commn. Commn. on Future of State Colls. and Univs., 1986. Mem. Western Coll. Assn. (dir. 1969-71), Western Assn. Schs. and Colls. (sr. commn. 1968-71, 76-82), Am. Council Edn. (dir. 1977-79, commn. on leadership).

WAGNER, MARYFRANCES ELIZABETH CUSUMANO, educator, poet; b. Kansas City, Mo., Oct. 22, 1947; d. Samuel Salvadore and Margaret Elizabeth (Passiglia) Cusumano; m. Gale E. Wagner, June 13, 1970 (div. 1978). B.A. in English, U. Mo.-Kansas City, 1969, M.A., 1974. Lic. tchr., Mo. Profl. model Monza Models, Kansas City, Mo., 1966-69; tchr. English, Raytown High Sch., Mo., 1969—; workshop leader, cons. Author: Bandaged Watermelons and Other Rusty Ducks, 1978; Tonight Cicadas Sing, 1981. Editor: Missouri Poets: An Anthology, 1983. Contbr. poems to various lit. mags. Recipient Excellence in Teaching award C. of C., Kansas City, 1984. Mem. Poets and Writers, Inc., Nat. Council Tchrs. English, Mo. Council Tchrs. English. Presbyterian. Avocations: travel; photography; reading; hiking. Home: 5907 Northern St Raytown MO 64133 Office: Raytown High Sch 6019 Blue Ridge St Raytown MO 64133

WAGNER, SUE ELLEN, state legislator; b. Portland, Maine, Jan. 6, 1940; d. Raymond A. and Kathryn (Hooper) Pooler; m. Peter B. Wagner, 1964; children—Kirk, Kristina. B.A. in Polit. Sci., U. Ariz., 1962; M.A. in History, Northwestern U., 1964. Asst. dean women Ohio State U., 1963-64; tchr. history and Am. govt. Catalina High Sch., Tucson, 1964-65; reporter Tucson Daily Citizen, 1965-68; mem. Nev. Assembly, 1975-83; now mem. Nev. Senate from 3d dist. Author: Diary of a Candidate, On People and Things, 1974. Mem. Reno Mayor's Adv. Com., 1973-84; chmn. Blue Ribbon Task Force on Housing, 1974-75; mem. Washoe County Republican Central Com., 1974-84, Nev. State Rep. Central Com., 1975-84; mem. Nev. Legis. Commn., 1976-77; del. social service com. Council State Govts.; v.p. Am. Field Service, 1973, family liaison, 1974, mem.-at-large, 1975. Kappa Alpha Theta Nat. Grad. scholar, also Phelps-Dodge postgrad. fellow, 1962; named Outstanding Legislator, Nev. Young Republicans, 1976, One of 10 Outstanding Young Women in Am. Mem. AAUW (legis. chmn. 1974), Bus. and Profl. Women, Kappa Alpha Theta. Episcopalian. Office: Nevada State Senate State Capitol Carson City NV 89710*

WAGNER, SYLVIA RAE, personnel executive; b. Mitchell, S.D., Feb. 14, 1949; d. Robert Henry and Rose Ann (Heiter) W. B.A., U. S.D., 1971; M.A., Okla. State U., 1974. Tchr., Ft. Riley Jr. High Sch., Junction City, Kans., 1971-72; instr. Okla. State U., Stillwater, 1972-74; communications specialist St. Paul Cos., 1974-76, mgmt. tng. supr., 1976-80, asst. to v.p. human relations, 1981-82; personnel officer Western Life Ins. Co., 1982-85, sr. personnel officer, 1985—; cons. Mgmt. Assistance Project, Mpls., 1980-86; instr. Nat. Coll. Bus., St. Paul, 1974-75. Bd. dirs. KOPE, St. Paul, 1980-85; mem. Nat. Women's Polit. Caucus, Mpls., 1982—. U. S.D. scholar, 1967-71. Mem. Am. Soc. Personnel Adminstrn., Am. Soc. Tng. and Devel., Mortar Bd., Phi Beta Kappa, Alpha Lambda Delta. Home: 1116 James Ave Saint Paul MN 55105 Office: Western Life Ins Co PO Box 64271 Saint Paul MN 55164

WAGONER, GERALDINE CAROL, music educator; b. Kankakee, Ill., Sept. 16, 1931; d. Ralph and Josie (Mieras) VanderPol; B.A., Central U. of Iowa, 1954; M.A., Montclair State Coll., 1968; postgrad. Juilliard Sch. Music, 1955, 56, 66, 67, NYU, Royal Conservatory, Toronto, 1971, Mozarteum, Salzburg, Austria, 1972; children—Joel Timothy, Stephanie Anne. Music coach, piano pedagog, cons. Bd. Edn., Edison, N.J., Englewood and Ridgewood, N.J., 1954-74; music specialist, Ridgewood, 1975—; cons. NYU spl. project; cons. Project Impact. Trustee, Hudson Symphony Orch., 1965-71; mem. Met. Mus. of Art. Mem. Profl. Music Tchrs. Guild (cert. for highest goals and achievements 1966), Music Educators Assn., Nat. Music Tchrs. Assn., N.J. Music Tchrs. Assn., Am. Orff Schulwerk Assn., N.J. Edn. Assn., NEA, Music Educators Assn. Am., Bergen County Music Educators Assn., Choristers Guild, Theater Devel. Found., Met. Opera Guild. Club: Les Amis du Vin. Composer sequential tonal and rhythm curriculum for children.

WAGONER, GRACE WILLIAMS, university administrator; b. Winston-Salem, N.C., Nov. 10, 1927; d. Samuel Carter and Grace Belle (Redmond) Williams; m. Leo Wayne Wagoner, June 4, 1949; children—Deborah Wagoner Miller, Leo Wayne, Katharine Wagoner Willis, Suzanne. Cert. in bus. U. N.C.-Greensboro, 1945, B.S. in Home Econs., 1949; cert. in mgmt. devel. U. N.C., Chapel Hill, 1981. High sch. tchr. N.C. Sch. System, Pleasant Garden, 1949-50, Yadkinville, 1951-52, Mt. Airy, 1954-55; adminstrv. sec. to vice chancellor for bus. affairs U. N.C., Chapel Hill, 1960-65, adminstrv. asst. to vice chancellor for bus. affairs, 1965-71, univ. property officer, 1971—; v.p., chmn. bd. Orange Fed. Savs. and Loan, Chapel Hill, 1978—. Mem. diaconate Binkley Baptist Ch., Chapel Hill; mem. Chapel Hill Appearance Commn., 1979—; bd. dirs. Ruth Faison Shaw Meml. Com., Chapel Hill, Chapel Hill Preservation Soc., Horace Williams House Com., Chapel Hill; mem. budget com. United Fund, Chapel Hill, 1975-81, mem. admissions com., 1979-81. Fellow Am. Assn. Real Estate, State Employees Assn. Republican. Club: Altrusa (sec. 1977, bd. dirs. 1977-78, 80-82, pres. 1980-81) (Chapel Hill). Home: 744 Shady Lawn Rd Chapel Hill NC 27514 Office: U NC Chapel Hill NC 27514

WAGONER, SUELLYN, nursing administrator; b. Vincennes, Ind., Aug. 6, 1954; d. John Frank and Delores Mae (Robold) W. A.A.S. in Nursing, Vincennes U., 1974. R.N., Ind. Charge nurse Good Samaritan Hosp., Vincennes, 1974-75; staff nurse Comprehensive Community Mental Health Ctr., 1976-81; asst. dir. nursing, 1981—. Recipient Resouer in Basic Life Support award Am. Heart Assn., 1980-85. Mem. Mental Health Assn. (contributor). Democrat. Avocations: fishing; crocheting; reading; playing piano. Home: RR1 Box 190 Vincennes IN 47591

WAHL, BONNIE RAE, telephone company executive; b. Beardstown, Ill., Dec. 1, 1940; d. Raymond George and Melba Maureen (Lobb) Brocksieck; grad. high sch.; 1 dau., Marsha Kay Cox; m. David L. Wahl, Mar. 30, 1984; 3 stepchildren. Cashier, bookkeeper Gen. Fin. Co., Springfield, Ill., 1960-62, Orlando, Fla., 1963-64; head cashier Beneficial Fin. Co., Orlando, 1962-63, 65-71; with Assocs. Fin. Services, Orlando, 1971-85, div. auditor, Atlanta, 1976-85, auditor, 1978-85, credit counselor in charge of woman's loan program, 1978-85, also sr. asst. mgr., until 1985. Named Credit Woman of Orlando, Fla. Credit Women Internat., 1974-75. Lic. real estate salesperson, Ga. Mem. Internat. Consumer Credit Assn. (credit edn. chmn., bd. dirs.), Credit Women Internat. (pres. Orlando 1974-75, pres. Atlanta 1979-80, chmn. bd. 1980-81; Credit Woman of Year Atlanta 1980, also Ga. and Dist. 3 and 4, v.p. Dixie council, conf. chmn. Ga. chpt.), Vols. in Bus. Edn. DeKalb County, Soc. Cert. Consumer Credit Execs., Conyers/Rockdale C. of C. (Adopt a Sch. program), Homebuilders Assn. Met. Atlanta, Ga. Interconnect Assn. Women's C. of C. Atlanta (bus. resource com.), Am. Bus. Women of Conyers. Club: Leads of Conyers (coordinator). Office: care Wahl Phone Company Inc PO Box 504 Conyers GA 30207 Home: 3604 Sand Hill Dr Conyers GA 30208

WAHL, JOAN CONSTANCE, tech. writer, editor; b. Phila., Dec. 23, 1921; d. Frank L. and Sara E. (Timoney) O'Brien; B.A., Rosemont Coll., 1943; postgrad UCLA, 1960-61; m. John Carl Wahl, Jr., Dec. 31, 1943 (div. 1959); children—John, Mark, David, Lawrence, Thomas, Jeanne Wahl Pearring, Madeleine Sophie, Eugene. Substitute tchr. Los Angeles City Bd. Edn., 1961; editor, proofreader Renner/Cal-Data Corp., Los Angeles, 1962-63; editor, tech. writer Volt Tech. Corp., 1964-66; sr. tech. writer, sr. project editor Aerospace Corp., El Segundo, Calif., 1966—. Sect. chmn. United Way, Los Angeles, 1963-64; mem. communications com. St. Paul the Apostle Roman Cath. Ch., Westwood, Calif., 1976-78. Recipient Outstanding Service award United Way, 1964. Mem. Soc. Tech. Communications (sr. mem.), Aerospace Women's Com., Mental Health Assn. Los Angeles County, Kistler Honor Soc. Contbr. articles to profl. jours. Office: Aerospace Corp 2350 El Segundo Blvd El Segundo CA 90245

WAHL, ROSALIE, associate justice Supreme Court Minnesota; b. Gordon, Kans., Aug. 27, 1924; B.A., U. Kans., 1946; J.D., William Mitchell Coll. Law, 1967; children—Christopher Roswell, Sara Emilie, Timothy Eldon, Mark Patterson, Jenny Caroline. Admitted to Minn. bar, 1967; practice law, Mpls., from 1967; adj. prof. criminal law U. Minn., 1972-73; clin. prof. law William Mitchell Coll. Law, 1973-77; assoc. justice Minn. Supreme Ct., 1977—. Fellow Am. Bar. Found.; mem. ABA (accreditation com., council sect. legal edn. and bar admissions, criminal justice sect.), Minn. Bar Assn., Am. Judicature Soc., Nat. Assn. Women Lawyers, Nat. Assn. Women Judges, Minn. Assn. Women Lawyers. Office: State Supreme Ct 230 State Capitol Saint Paul MN 55155

WAHL, ROSEMARY, data processing consultant; b. Grand Rapids, Mich., Apr. 26, 1952; d. Burdette Fred and Marian Lou (Wiseman) Scobey; m. Ronald Wahl, June 19, 1971 (div. Apr. 1980); children—Dennis Ryan, Darin Christopher. B.A. cum laude, Golden Gate U., 1975. With Gen. Electric Co., Phoenix, 1970-71; programmer Marcona Corp., San Francisco, 1971-75; data processing cons. Wahl Computing, San Francisco, 1975-82, Telca, Inc., San Francisco, 1982-83; v.p., dir. programming Computer Systems Design, San Francisco, 1983-85; data processing cons., pres. Telca, Inc., 1985—. Republican. Roman Catholic. Avocations: soccer; reading. Home: 373 85th St Brooklyn NY 11209

WAHLIG, CYNTHIA DECK, accounts receivable manager; b. Trenton, N.J., Apr. 15, 1954; d. Carlton Laquay and Norma Mae (Shelton Deck); m. Bruce Cameron Wahlig, Jan. 12, 1985. A.A. in Elem. Edn., Bucks County Community Coll., 1974; B.S. in Early Childhood Edn., Trenton State Coll., 1976. Cert. elem. tchr., N.J. Bursar, Rider Coll., Lawrenceville, N.J., 1977-83; credit adminstr. SEI Corp., Wayne, Pa., 1983-85; accts. receivable mgr. Scotfoam Corp., Eddystone, Pa., 1985—. Republican. Avocations: photography; skiing; antique collecting.

WAHONICK, NANCY ANNE, communications consultant and educator; b. Baldwin, Fla., Aug. 20, 1935; d. Herbert A. and Jeannette (Rainer) Pope; m. Donald R. Wahonick July 3, 1955 (div. 1975); children—Donald R., Bobbie Ruth. B.A., Cleve. State U., 1976; M.A., St. Louis U., 1980. Vice pres. communications Nat. Benevolent Assn., St. Louis, 1976-85; adj. prof. communications dept. Maryville Coll., St. Louis, 1984—. Editor mag. Family Talk, 1976-84; contbg. author: Religious Public Relations Handbook, 1983; contbr. articles to profl. jours.; contbg. author: All God's Children, 1979. Media liaison Reagon/Bush Innagural Com., Washington, 1981; religious press rep. Carter/Ford Debates, 1976; trustee W. Shore Chorale, Lakewood, Ohio, 1972-76; mem. Lakewood Ohio Civil Service Commn., 1973-74, Arts and Edn. Com. and Mo. Arts Council, 1979-81; pub. relations dir. Crestwood Children's Theatre, 1980-83; mem. long range planning com. Webster Groves Christian Ch., St. Louis; bd. dirs., ch. sch. dir. Lakewood Christian Ch., Cleve., 1959-76. Recipient Hinkhouse-DeRose award for exhibits and displays, 1982, for Film Caring Changes, 1984; award Women in Communication, 1984; Outstanding Alumnae award, Cleve. State U., 1976; Bus. and Profl. Women scholarship award, 1975; Lakewood Coll. Club Career Advancement scholar, 1975; State of Ohio Career Advancement grantee, 1975; Cleve. State U. Literary award, 1974. Mem. Religious Pub. Relations Council (treas. 1980-82), Assoc. Ch. Press (dir. 1980-82), Pub. Relations Soc. Am., Women in Communications. Mem. Christian Ch. Club: St. Louis Press. Office: Maryville College 13550 Conway Rd Saint Louis MO 63141

WAINWRIGHT, HILDA ALEXANDER, high tech component manufacturing company executive; b. Teheran, Iran, June 18; came to U.S., 1945, naturalized 1947; d. Mamikon and Balasan (Carapetyan) Ohanian; m. Boris Alexander, May 27, 1945 (dec. Aug. 1961); children—Ronald Boris, Douglas Haig; m. Richard A. Wainwright, Feb. 18, 1977. Student Ecole Jean D'Arc, Teheran, 1945, Brown Bus. Sch., 1947, Gemological Inst. Am., 1959, Banford Acad. Styling, 1950. Design stylist Elizabeth Arden, N.Y.C., 1949-52; owner, mgr. Randough, N.Y.C., 1960; sales rep. Roux Labs., Jacksonville, Fla., also N.Y.C., 1968-71, Mackey Internat. Airline, Ft. Lauderdale, Fla., 1971-73; owner, mgr. CIR-Q-TEL Inc., Kensington, Md., 1980—, exec. v.p., pres., 1982-84, treas., 1980—. Mem. Armenian Gen. Benevolent Union, N.Y.C. and Fla., 1945—. Clubs: Washington Speakers, Black Tie, Chevy Chase Women's, Columbia Country. Avocations: tennis; golf; swimming; gardening; painting in oil and acrylic; backgammon; bridge; languages. Home: 3333 University Blvd W Kensington MD 20895 Office: Cir-Q-Tel Inc 10504 Wheatley St Kensington MD 20895

WAITE, GLORIA E., optometrist; b. Rochester, N.Y., May 12, 1943; d. Warren Henry and Frieda (Plapp) Horn; B.S., U. Calif., Berkeley, 1965, O.D., 1966; m. Ray L. Waite, Aug. 20, 1966. Pvt. practice optometry, Pinole, Calif., 1977—; asst. clin. prof. Sch. Optometry, U. Calif.-Berkeley, 1983—. Recipient Cert. of Appreciation Richmond Unified Sch. Dist., 1978-81. Mem. Alameda-Contra Costa Counties Optometric Soc. (dir. 1975-83, pres. 1981-82), Calif. Optometric Assn. membership div. exec. com. 1978-83, Speaker award 1979-82), Pinole-Hercules C. of C. (dir. 1977-83), AAUW (mem. Richmond-El Cerrito chpt. hosting com. 1978, treas. 1979), Am. Optometric Assn., Calif. Optometric Assn. Republican. Lutheran. Club: Soroptimists (chmn. El Pinablo nominating com. 1980, Woman of Achievement award 1977). Contbr. articles in field to profl. publs. Office: 635 Tennent Ave Pinole CA 94564

WAITE, SALLY GRIFFITH, lawyer; b. Newark, Ohio, July 20, 1946; d. John Gerald and Mildred Marie (Shorts) Griffith; m. David R. Middleton, June 4, 1967 (div. Jan. 4, 1977; 1 son, Brock David. B.A., Berea Coll., 1968; J.D., Stetson U., 1978. Bar: Ind. 1979. Tchr., Troy Public Schs. (Ohio), 1968-70; labor relations atty. Bethlehem Steel Co., Chesterton, Ind., 1978-79; union relations atty. Gen. Electric Co., Cin., 1979-81, mgr. employee relations, 1981-83, mgr. employee relations, community relations, Tiffin, Ohio, 1983-85, mgr. profl. relations Aerospace Electronics Systems dept., 1985-86, mgr. employee relations electronics lab., 1986—. Mem. ABA, Ind. Bar Assn., Seneca County Personnel Assn., Indsl. Mgmt. Council Tiffin, Phi Delta Phi. Republican. Methodist. Home: 102 Old Lyme Rd Syracuse NY Office: Gen Electric Electronics Parkway Syracuse NY

WAITE, SCOTIA BALLARD KNOUFF, criminal justice specialist; b. Willis Wharf, Va., Apr. 8, 1909; d. Warren Alan and Lotta Mondora (Chard) Ballard; B.L.I., Emerson Coll., 1931; M.Ed., Boston U., 1933; diploma Sch. Social Work, Columbia U., 1939; m. William Francis Knouff, Oct. 9, 1943 (dec. Jan. 1968); children—Mary Francis Knouff Linn, Warren Irving Knouff; m. 2d Frederick Waite, Jan. 3, 1976. Dir., Mathews County (Va.) Relief Office, 1932-35, Rappahanock County Relief Office, 1935-36, dir. relief offices Norfolk County and City of S. Norfolk (Va.), 1936-37, case worker Henry Watson Children's Aid Soc., Balt., 1937, with New Orleans Council Social Agys., 1938-40, dir. Council Social Agencies, Syracuse, NY, 1940-44, asst. dir. Detroit Council Social Agys., 1944-45, tech. cons. juvenile delinquency Dept. Justice, Washington, 1948-50, instr., dir. Sociology Research Lab. CCNY, 1950-55, faculty dept. Sociology Adelphi U., 1955-63; dir. research and staff devel. Nassau County (N.Y.) Probation Dept., 1963-78; co-dir. Improving Victim Services Through Probation project Am. Probation and Parole Assn. of Aberdeen (N.C.) and Blackstone Inst. of Washington, 1978-80; cons. criminal justice, Pinehurst, N.C., 1980—; examiner Nat. Commn. on Accreditation for Corrections, 1979—; adj. asso. prof. Sch. Criminal Justice, C.W. Post Coll., L.I.U., 1967—; tech. cons. Nat. Inst. Corrections, 1983; mem. Child Placement Rev. Com. Moore County, N.C.; chmn. Youth Services Commn. Moore County. Mem. Nat. Republican Com. Recipient Outstanding Achievement award C.W. Post Coll. Sch. Criminal Justice, 1977, Spl. award Nassau County Probation Dept., 1978. Mem. Am. Probation and Parole Assn. (Walter Dunbar award 1977), Am. Correctional Assn., Northeastern Assn. Correctional Educators, Tex. Correctional Assn., AAUW. Episcopalian. Clubs: Pinehurst Country. Author numerous reports in corrections, victim services. Home: PO Box 456 McDonald Rd Pinehurst NC 28374

WAITE, SHIRLEY ELEANOR, nurse, nursing administrator; b. Gloucester, Mass., Jan. 4, 1925; d. Walter Dunlap and Ida Estelle (Robinson) Collins; R.N., Truesdale Hosp. Sch. Nursing, Fall River, Mass., 1946; student Miami Dade Community Coll., 1963-68, Fla. Internat. U., Miami, 1974-77; cert. in nursing adminstr., 1980; m. Horatio Simmons Waite, Feb. 15, 1946; children—Bruce F., Cheryl J. Waite Kapit, Charles W., David W., Gayle I. Staff nurse, St. Luke's Hosp., New Bedford, Mass., 1946; nurse premature and new born nursery Union Hosp., Fall River, Mass., 1947-48; supr. Newport (R.I.) Hosp., 1951-52; staff nurse, supr. Jackson Meml. Hosp., 1953-63; supr. Meml. Hosp., Hollywood, Fla., 1964-65; supr., asst. dir. nursing, dir. nurse recruitment Cedars of Lebanon Health Care Center, Miami, Fla., 1966-77; head nurse North Miami Gen. Hosp., 1978; v.p. nursing service DeSoto Meml. Hosp., Arcadia, Fla., 1978—; mem. adv. com. South Fla. Community Coll.; Charlotte Vo-Tech. Sch., DeSoto LPN Sch.; 2d v.p. Cedars of Lebanon Credit Union. Notary pub., Fla. Mem. Nat. League Nursing, Fla. League Nursing, Fla. Orgn. Nursing Execs., Charsoto Council Continuing Edn. for Nurses (pres. 1981-82), Dade County Practitioners in Infection Control (past v.p.). Home: Route 1 Box 411 Herbert Rd Arcadia FL 33821 Office: PO Box 2180 Arcadia FL 33821

WAITES, CANDY YAGHJIAN, county official; b. N.Y.C., Feb. 21, 1943; d. Edmund Kirken and Dorothy Joanne (Candy) Yaghjian; m. Robert Geddings Waites, Sept. 4, 1965; children—Jennifer Lisa, Robin Shelley. B.A., Wheaton Coll., Mass., 1965. Elected county councilwoman Richland County, S.C., 1976—; legal adminstr. firm Adams, Quackenbush, Herring & Stuart; vice chmn. Adv. Commn. on Intergovtl. Relations, S.C., 1977—; bd. dirs. Interagy. Council on Pub. Transp., S.C., 1977—, Central Midlands Regional Planning Council, Columbia, S.C., 1977-84; dir. S.C. Nat. Bank. Vice pres. bd. dirs. United Way of Midlands, 1977-89; trustee Columbia Mus. Art, 1982-88; bd. dirs. Rape Crisis Network, Columbia U., 1984-87. Named Outstanding Young Career Woman, Columbia YWCA, 1980; Outstanding Young Woman of Yr., Columbia Jaycees, 1975; Pub. Citizen of Yr. Nat. Assn. Social Workers. Mem. S.C. Women in Govt. (vice chmn. 1984—), S.C. Assn. Counties (bd. dirs. 1982—, Pres's award 1983), Network Female Execs., LWV (pres. 1973-76). Democrat. Episcopalian. Club: Univ. Assocs. (Columbia). Avocations: exercising; drawing; walking. Home: 818 Gregg St Columbia SC 29201 Office: Richland County Council 1701 Main St Columbia SC 29201

WAITS, CLAUDIA BESS, administrative nurse; b. Tyler, Tex., Sept. 22, 1943; d. Tommie Houston and Alma (Olive) McKay; student Tyler Jr. Coll., 1962-64; R.N., Tex. Eastern Sch. Nursing, 1965; grad. Park Coll., 1984; m. Buford Benjamin Waits, Mar. 17, 1978; children—Jason Fortenberry, Joel Fortenberry, Amy Fortenberry. Lic. nursing home adminstr. Dir. nursing service Med. Surg. Clinic, Tyler, 1965-66; dir. nursing service So. Heritage Retirement Home, Palestine, Tex., 1967-68; relief supr. ICU, Med. Center Hosp., Tyler, 1969-70; in-service edn. Augusta, Ga., 1971; dir. nursing service Rikard Nursing Home, Lexington, S.C., 1976-81; dir. inservice edn., relief adminstr. Forest Hills Nursing Center, Columbia, S.C., 1981-83; dir. nursing services Capitol Convalescent Ctr., Columbia, 1983-86; adminstr. Richland Convalescent Ctr., Columbia, 1986—; owner/operator So. Heritage, Inc., 1983—. Cub Scout den mother council Boy Scouts Am., 1971-74. Mem. Am. Nurses Assn., Central Council Nurses in Long-Term Care (pres. 1979-80, 84-85, state v.p. 1980-81, mem. exec. bd. 1979—), S.C. Nurses Assn., S.C. Forum of Nursing Orgns., Am. Health Edn. Council. Democrat. Methodist. Home: 114 Laurel Bluff Dr Lexington SC 29072 Office: PO Box 1364 Lexington SC 29072

WAITZ, MARY LOUISE, educator; b. Telluride, Colo., Feb. 8, 1940; d. John Wesley and Kathrine Rose (Penasa) Dabney; B.S., Colo. State U., 1963, M.Ed., 1969; m. Edward K. Waitz, Jan. 25, 1964. Tchr. home econs. Tehachapi (Calif.) Jr. High Sch., 1962-63, Frederick (Colo.) Jr. High Sch., 1964-67, Lyons (Colo.) Jr.-Sr. High Sch., 1967—, acting home econs. coordinator St. Vrain Valley Sch. Dist., Longmont, Colo., 1975-77. Named Home Econs. Tchr. of Year for State of Colo., Am. Home Econs. Assn.-Family Circle Mag., 1980. Mem. NEA, Colo. Edn. Assn., St. Vrain Valley Edn. Assn., Am. Home Econs. Assn., Colo. Home Econs. Assn. (now co-chairperson pub. relations), Home Econs. Tchrs. Assn., Am. Vocat. Assn., Colo. Vocat. Assn., Colo. Assn. Vocat. Home Econs. Tchrs., (chairperson pub. relations), Delta Kappa Gamma (pres.). republican. Methodist. Home: PO Box 677 Lyons CO 80540 Office: PO Box 619 Lyons CO 80540

WAITZ-HALPERIN, ESTHER, sportswear manufacturing company executive; b. Allentown, Pa., Aug. 17, 1925; d. Abraham and Sadie (Ostrow) Waitz; m. Bernard Halperin, June 15, 1963 (dec. 1964); children—Richard Goldberg, Jonathan Halperin; m. Abe Krantz, June 19, 1974 (div. dec. 1985). B.A., Moravian coll., 1948; M.S., Temple U., 1962. Pre-sch. tchr. Jewish Community Ctr., Allentown, 1955-63, summer camp tchr. 1955-63; kindergarten tchr. Jewish Day Sch., Allentown, 1962; pres. Halsen Products, Inc., Slatington, Pa., 1964—. Chmn. Allentown United Way, 1966-81; subscriber Met. Opera, N.Y.C., 1974—. Mem. Atlantic Apparel Assn., Lehigh Valley Needle Trades (bd. dirs. 1964-80, chmn. Pa. apparel week 1969), Pi Delta Epsilon. Republican. Clubs: Hadassah, ORT (Allentown). Lodge: Shriners. Avocations: opera; ballet; dancing; horseback riding; travel. Home: 3717 Congress St Allentown PA 18104 Office: Halsen Products Inc 216 Cherry St Slatington PA 18080

WAITZMAN, TERESA ANN, data processing company manager; b. Dayton, Ohio, Nov. 17, 1950; d. Charels Arthur and Bertha Margaret (Trimbach) W. B.S., U. Dayton, 1973, M.S., Kans. State U., 1977; Ph.D., Miami U., 1983. Tchr. sci. West Carrollton Schs., Ohio, 1979-81; vis. instr. Miami U., Oxford, Ohio, 1982-83; health educator, adminstr. Children's Med. Ctr., Dayton, 1983-85; program control adminstr. Battelle Meml. Inst., Columbus, Ohio, 1985; mgr. fin. and adminstrn. Electronic Data Systems, Dayton, Ohio, 1985—; adj. instr. Sinclair Community Coll., Dayton, 1982—. Mem. Housing Bd. Appeals, Oxford, 1982. Miami U. fellow, 1981; U. Dayton Meml. scholar, 1971; PTA Ohio Assn. scholar, 1969. Mem. Nat. Assn. Female Execs., U. Dayton Alumni Assn., Miami U. Alumni Assn., Phi Delta Kappa, Ohio Perinatal Assn. Avocations: skiing; travel; swimming; dancing. Office: Electronic Data Systems 2701 Home Ave Dayton OH 45417

WAKELEE, ADAH MAE, microbiologist; b. Conneaut, Ohio, Apr. 6, 1935; d. Walter Ivan and Arleen Louise (Beach) Terrill; B.S. in Med. Tech., Wittenberg U., 1960; m. Robert L. Wakelee, Jr., May 23, 1963; children—Kieth Robert, Kent Walter. Staff technologist, Mercy Hosp. Lab., Springfield, Ohio, 1959-63, Grant Hosp. Lab., Columbus, Ohio, 1963-64, J. Mark Handley, M.D., Santa Maria, Calif., 1965-69; microbiologist Rome (N.Y.) City Hosp. Lab., 1972-79; chief technologist MDS Health Systems Inc. (formerly Lorkim Labs.), Rome, 1980-85; asst. lab. supr. Slocum Dickson Med. Group, 1985—; cons. in microbiology Rose Hosp., Rome, Slocum-Dickson Med. Group, Utica, N.Y. Mem. Oneida County Profl. Adv. Council, 1977, 78; trustee Rome Acad. Scis., 1978—, pres., 1979-81; mem. Rome Mayor's Water Com., 1983-85; Cert., registered Am. Soc. Clin. Pathologists; lic. clin. med. technologist, Calif. Mem. Am. Soc. Clin. Pathology, Am. Soc. Microbiology, N.Y. State Assn. Public Health Labs., Mohawk Valley Engrs. Exec. Council (chmn. 1981-82, sec. 1983-84), AAUW (pres. Rome br. 1980-82). Republican. Congregationalist. Clubs: Order Eastern Star, Daus. of the Nile. Determined causes of illnesses, Rome, 1975, Holland Patent (N.Y.) area, 1976; co-author article in field for profl. jour. Home: 123 Glen Road S Rome NY 13440

WAKLEY, BARBARA, utility company project manager; b. Spokane, Wash., Sept. 3, 1938; d. Daniel I. and Marie G. (Hennen) Donovan; children—Cheryl Wakley Tschirhart, James Richard. B.A. cum laude, U. Wash., 1974, postgrad., 1974-75; cert. Pub. Adminstrn. and Mgmt. Tech., S. Seattle Community Coll., 1986. Adminstrv., orgn. analyst Boeing Co., Seattle, 1958-70; counselor, teaching asst. psychology dept. U. Wash., Seattle, 1971-72, communications dir., teaching asst. Indian Tchr. Edn. Program, conf. coordinator Advs. for Indian Tchr. Edn., part-time 1974-75; instr. German, Seattle, 1973-74; tutor algebra, Russian, lang. arts, 1973-75; various positions City of Seattle, 1980-83; mgmt. systems analyst, project mgr. for human resource mgmt. system Seattle City Light, 1983—. Composer: song I Will Dance and Sing, 1980. Vol., Mt. St. Vincent Nursing Home, Seattle, 1974-75. Scholar: Boeing Co., 1968-70, Seattle German Assn. Continental Club, 1972, Nez Perce Indian Tribe, 1974-75. Mem. Am. Mgmt. Assn., Mortar Board, Phi Beta Kappa, Pi Lambda Theta. Clubs: Swedish (life), Seattle Toastmistress (membership chmn. 1960-62). Avocations: playing piano; solving logic puzzles; reading; travel; language study. Office: Seattle City Light 1015 3d Ave Seattle WA 98104

WALAS, CYNTHIA CAROLYN, graphic arts buyer; b. Chgo., Apr. 1, 1954; d. Bruno Stanley and Julia (Cholodnicki) Brozowski; m. Anthony Michael Walas, May 19, 1979. B.Mus., Am. Conservatory of Music, 1976. Group asst. N.W. Ayer, Chgo., 1976-77, print traffic coordinator, 1977-80; print traffic supr. Campbell-Mithun, Chgo., 1980-82; graphic arts buyer/mgr. The John Volk Co., Chgo., 1982—. Mem. Gravure Tech. Assn., Advt. Print Prodn. Club of Chgo., Art Inst. Chgo., Wilderness Soc., Sierra Club. Roman Catholic. Office: The John Volk Co 676 Saint Clair St Chicago IL 60611

WALBERT, VIRGINIA HOLLIS, insurance company executive; b. Manchester, Conn., July 19, 1948; d. Thomas and Alcester (Weare) Hollis; m. Peter Charles Walbert, Aug. 19, 1972; 1 child, Katherine Hollis. B.A., Allegheny Coll., 1970. With Aetna Life & Casualty Co., Hartford, 1970-78, asst. adminstr., 1975-76, adminstr., 1976-78; mgr. Conn. Gen. Life Ins. Co., Bloomfield, Conn., 1978-79, asst. dir., 1979-82, dir., 1982-84, asst. v.p., 1984—. Republican. Congregationalist. Office: Conn Gen Life Ins Co Hartford CT 06152

WALBRAN, BONNIE (JANE) BREAUX, psychologist; b. Little Rock, Feb. 23, 1938; d. Bertin Joseph and Jeanne Rita (LaNasa) Breaux; A.B. cum laude, Vassar Coll., 1960; Ph.D., Washington U., 1975; postgrad. St. Louis U.; m. Jon A. Newell, July 21, 1984; children by previous marriage—Stephanie Jane, Alexa Suzanne. Research asst. Milbank Meml. Fund, Hudson River St. Hosp., Poughkeepsie, N.Y., 1960-61, Tufts U. Med. Sch., Boston, 1961-62, Harvard U. Sch. Public Health dept. epidemiology, Boston, 1962-64; research asst. Washington U. Sch. Medicine dept. psychiatry, St. Louis, 1965-69, 75-77, research asso., 1978-79; dir. New Hope Learning Center, St. Louis U., 1979-81; unit psychologist, coordinator psychol. services St. Louis Developmental Disabilities Treatment Center; instr. Webster Coll. Mem. Am. Psychol. Assn., Am. Assn. Mental Deficiency, Valley Sailing Assn., Sigma Xi. Democrat. Contbr. articles in field to profl. jours. Home: 215 Jefferson Rd Webster Groves MO 63119 Office: MS 429 5400 Arsenal St St Louis MO 63139

WALCOTT, CYNTHIA ANN, nurse, marketing manager; b. Troy, N.Y., Sept. 16, 1948; d. Walter William and Anna (Tanchak) Wilsnack; R.N., New England Bapt. Hosp., 1969. Operating room specialist Columbus (Ga.) Med. Center, 1970-71, Meml. Hosp., Albany, N.Y., 1971-73, Holyoke (Mass.) Hosp., 1974-77; asst. head nurse operating room Noble Hosp., Westfield, Mass., 1973-74; nurse operating room, product evaluation specialist Newton (Mass.) Wellesley Hosp., 1977-78; nurse specialist Davol, Inc., Cranston, R.I., 1978-79, area sales mgr., 1979-80, profl. edn. dir., 1980-82; mgr. profl. services surg. products USCI Internat. div. C.R. Bard, Inc., Billerica, Mass., 1982-83, product mgr. surg. products, 1983-84; product mgr. cardio thoracic products Bard Cardiosurgery div. C.R. Bard, Inc., 1984—; cons. in field. Mem. Assn. Operating Room Nurses, Assn. Advancement of Med. Instrumentation. Home: 72 Prescott Dr North Chelmsford MA 01863 Office: 129 Concord Rd PO Box M Billerica MA 01821

WALCZER, IRENE ANNA, real estate executive; b. Bethlehem, Pa., Mar. 8, 1929; d. John and Anna Horvath Vitez; student Bethlehem Bus. Coll., 1947-48, Pa. State U., Extension, 1962, 66; grad. Pa. Realtors Inst., 1975; m. Michael John Walczer, Nov. 12, 1949; children—Frank, Michele, Teller, Keystone Savs. & Loan Assn., Bethlehem, 1957-59, head teller, 1959-61; sales rep., assoc. broker Merritt Miller Real Estate, Allentown, Pa., 1962-67; assoc. broker Terry Realty Co., Whitehall, Pa., 1967-72; prin. Irene A. Walczer Agy., Allentown, 1972—. Mem. Allentown Bd. Realtors, Pa. Assn. Realtors, Nat. Assn. Realtors, Allentown Bus. Women's Assn., Nazareth High Sch. Alumni, Allentown Bus. and Profl. Women's Club. Democrat. Lutheran. Home: 1250 Wynnewood Dr Bethlehem PA 18017 Office: 823 Turner St Allentown PA 18102

WALD, DONNA G(ENE), advertising agency executive; b. Peekskill, N.Y., July 24, 1947; d. David and Blossom (Karlin) W. B.A., Rider Coll., 1969, M.A., Hunter Coll., 1974. Supr. broadcast traffic SSC&B Inc., N.Y.C., 1969-74; broadcast buyer J. Walter Thompson U.S.A., Inc., N.Y.C., 1974-78, regional broadcast supr., v.p. Dallas, 1978-81, Los Angeles, 1981—; instr. bus. and mgmt. UCLA, extension program, spring 1984. Mem. Advt. Industry Emergency Fund, Hollywood Radio and TV Soc. Office: J Walter Thompson USA Inc 10100 Santa Monica Blvd Los Angeles CA 90067

WALD, FRANCINE JOY WEINTRAUB (MRS. BERNARD J. WALD), physicist; b. Bklyn., Jan. 13, 1938; d. Irving and Minnie (Reisig) Weintraub; student Bklyn. Coll., 1955-57; B.E.E., CCNY, 1960; M.S., Poly. Inst. Bklyn., 1962, Ph.D., 1969; m. Bernard J. Wald, Feb. 2, 1964; children—David Evan, Kevin Mitchell. Engr., Remington Rand Univac div. Sperry Rand Corp., Phila., 1960; instr. Poly. Inst. Bklyn., 1962-64, adj. research asso., 1969-70; lectr. N.Y. Community Coll., Bklyn., 1969-70; instr. sci. Friends Sem., N.Y.C., 1975-76, chmn. dept. sci., 1976—. NDEA fellow, 1962-64. Mem. Am. Phys. Soc., Am. Assn. Physics Tchrs., Assn. Tchrs. in Ind. Schs., N.Y. Acad. Scis., Nat. Sci. Tchrs. Assn., AAAS, Sigma Xi, Tau Beta Pi, Eta Kappa Nu. Home: 520 LaGuardia Pl New York NY 10012

WALD, PATRICIA M., judge; b. Torrington, Conn., Sept. 16, 1928; d. Joseph F. and Margaret (O'Keefe) McGowan; B.A., Conn. Coll., 1948; LL.B., Yale, 1951; m. Robert L. Wald, June 22, 1952; children—Sarah, Douglas, Johanna, Frederica, Thomas. Admitted to D.C. bar, 1952; clk. U.S. Ct. Appeals judge, 1951-52; asso. firm Arnold, Fortas & Porter, Washington, 1952-53; mem. D.C. Crime Commn., 1964-65, Dept. Justice, 1967, Neighborhood Legal Service, D.C., 1968-70; co-dir. Ford Found. Project Drug Abuse, 1970, Center for Law and Social Policy, 1971-72, Mental Health Law Project, from 1972; asst. atty. gen. legis. affairs Dept. Justice, 1977-79; judge U.S. Ct. Appeals for D.C., 1979—. Trustee Ford Found., 1972-77, Conn. Coll., 1975-77, Exeter Acad., 1976-77. mem. Carnegie Council Children. Mem. Am., D.C. (dir.) bar assns., Inst. Medicine, Am. Law Inst. (council). Author: Law and Poverty, 1965; co-author: Bail in the United States, 1964; Dealing with Drug Abuse, 1973. Mem. bd. editors Am. Bar Assn. Jour., 1978-84. Office: US Courthouse John Marshall Pl Washington DC 20001

WALD, SYLVIA, artist; b. Phila., Oct. 30, 1915; d. H.F. and T. (Weiner) W.; m. Po Kim, 1969. Grad., Moore Inst., Phila. Cert. fine arts, N.Y. Artist, printmaker, sculptor, N.Y.C. Represented in permanent collection Worcester Mus., Mass., Mus. Modern Art, N.Y.C., Whitney Mus., N.Y.C., Guggenheim Mus., N.Y.C., Bklyn. Mus., Victoria and Albert Mus., London, others. Avocation: raising birds. Home and Studio: 417 Lafayette St New York NY 10003

WALDAU, HELEN FRANCES, educator; b. Torrington, Conn., Mar. 21, 1925; d. Teofil and Michaelena (Plaga) Budney; B.A., U. Conn., 1953, 6th yr. cert., 1968; M.A., U. Hartford; divorced; children—Geoffrey, Christopher, Peter, Sandra. Tchr., Hopewell Sch., Glastonbury, Conn., 1966—, tchr. academically talented, 1982-85, supr. U. Conn. open edn. interns, 1971-75, Task Force Gifted Edn., 1976-81. Fellow U. Conn., 1967-68. Mem. NEA, Conn., Glastonbury edn. assns., Greater Conn. Council for Open Edn. (charter), Conn. Tchr. Center for Humanistic Edn., Psi Upsilon Omicron. Home: 1808 Main St Glastonbury CT 06033

WALDAUER, KAREN, publisher; b. N.Y.C., Jan. 13, 1938; d. Max and Sylvia Gordon; student CCNY, 1955-58; m. Charles Waldauer, May 8, 1958; children—Jan, Kim. Head art dept. Bohanon Printing, Syracuse, N.Y., 1960-64, A.S. Barnes Co., 1964-65; prodn. dir., regional editor, mng. editor Rutgers U. Press, 1965-68; pres. Middle Atlantic Press, Wallingford, Pa., 1968-84; pub. Valley Del Publs., 1984—; pub. cons. Wilmington (Del.) News Jour., Corp. Service Co. Bd. dirs. Sch. in Rose Valley. Mem. Pubs. Alliance, Phila. Pubs. Group, Small Mag. Pubs. Group, Brandywine Valley Press Assn. Clubs: Phila. Skating, Skating of Radnor (past pres.). Office: 840 E St Rd PO Box 31 Westtown PA 19395

WALDECK, EMMA DEAN, travel agency executive; b. Centertown, Ky., Mar. 30, 1923; d. John H. and Irene (Ford) Bradshaw; children—Sharon A. Goldsmith, Jackie C., Robbin Lynn. Student U. Louisville. Timekeeper, Curtis Wright Airplane Div., Louisville, 1943-45; owner Boone Laundry & Dry Cleaners, Louisville, 1945-47, Town Resturant, Bonneville, Ky., 1947-51, E'Town Travel Agy., Elizabethtown, Ky., 1965—, World Wide Christian Tours, Elizabethtown; travel agt. Fort Knox Travel Agy., 1951-65; owner, mgr. Downtown Apartment & Offices, Elizabethtown, 1978—. Author, pub. World Wide Adventures newsletter. Fundraiser, Bonneville Vol. Fire Dept.; chmn. Membership and Evangelism Camp; mem. Pastor Parish Com. Mem. Soc. Travel Agts. Republican. Methodist. Clubs: Christian Women's (Elizabethtown); Woman's (Bonneville) (pres. 1948-49). Lodge: Order Eastern Star. Avocations: travel; quilting; interior decorating; walking. Office: E'Town Travel Agy 114 W Dixie Ave PO Box 506 Elizabethtown KY 42701

WALDEN, AMELIA ELIZABETH, author; b. N.Y.C.; d. William A. and Elizabeth (Wanner) Walden; B.S., Columbia, 1934; certificate Am. Acad. Dramatic Arts; m. John William Harmon, Feb. 9, 1946 (dec. 1950). Author: Gateway, 1946; Waverly, 1947; Sunnycove, 1948; Skymountain, 1950; A Girl Called Hank, 1951; Marsha, On-Stage, 1952; Victory for Jill, 1953; All My Love, 1954; Daystar, 1955; Three Loves Has Sandy, 1955; The Bradford Story, 1956; I Found My Love, 1956; My Sister Mike, 1956; Palomino Girl, 1957; Flight Into Morning, 1957; Today is Mine, 1958; Queen of the Courts, 1959; (duo of novels) An American Teacher: Where is My Heart?, 1960, How Bright the Dawn, 1962; A Boy to Remember, 1960; Shadow on Devils Peak, 1961; (trilogy) The American Shakespeare Festival: When Love Speaks, 1961, So Near the Heart, 1962, My World's the Stage, 1964; My Dreams Ride High, 1963; To Catch A Spy, 1964; The Spy on Danger Island, 1965; Race the Wild Wind, 1965; The Spy with Five Faces, 1966; In Search of Ophelia, 1966; A Spy Called Michel-E, 1967; A Name for Himself, 1967; The Spy Who Talked Too Much, 1968; Walk In A Tall Shadow, 1968; A Spycase Built For Two, 1969; Same Scene, Different Place, 1969; The Case of the Diamond Eye, 1969; Basketball Girl of the Year, 1970; What Happened to Candy Carmichael?, 1970; Valerie Valentine is Missing, 1971; Stay to Win, 1971; Play Ball, McGill, 1972; Where was Everyone when Sabrina Screamed?, 1973; Go, Phillips, Go, 1974; Escape on Skis, 1975; Heartbreak Tennis, 1977. Amelia Walden collection personal, profl. papers, original manuscripts, research data established at U. Oreg., Eugene, 1982; pioneer young adult novel. Home: 89 N Compo Rd Westport CT 06880

WALDEN, OMI GAIL, public affairs and government relations specialist; b. Alma, Ga., Dec. 25, 1945; d. Banner H. and Naomi (Thomas) Lee; A.B. in Journalism, U. Ga., 1967; exec. mktg. mgmt. program Stanford U., 1981; m. Ralph Edward Walden, Apr. 27, 1968. Asst. dir. pub. relations Ga. Ports Authority, Savannah, 1968-69; dir. pub. relations U.S. HUD Model Cities Program, Alma, 1970-73, citizens participation coordinator, 1970, dir. research and evaluation, 1971-72; fed. and state relations coordinator, policy advisor on energy and environ. issues Former Gov. Jimmy Carter and Gov. George Busbee, Atlanta, 1973-76; dir. Ga. Office Energy Resources, Atlanta, 1976-78; asst. sec. conservation and solar applications U.S. Dept. Energy, Washington, 1978-79, adv. to sec. for conservation and solar mktg., 1979-80; now pres. Omi Walden & Assocs., pub. affairs and govt. relations cons. firm; exec. dir. Nat. Energy Mgmt. Inst., Washington; gov. rep. to Pres. Intergovernmental Sci., Engring. and Technology Advisory Panel, 1978. Democrat. Baptist. Contbr. articles in field to profl. jours. Home: 829 Colony House E 145 15th St Atlanta GA 30361 Office: 1150 17th St NW Suite 300 Washington DC 20036

WALDER, DEBBY JEAN, nursing service administrator, nurse, educator; b. Watertown, S.D., Nov. 25, 1947; d. James Russell and Gladys Elizabeth (Owen) W. B.S. in Nursing with honors, S.D. State U., 1970; M.S. in Nursing, U. Minn., 1977. Staff nurse VA Med. Ctr., Mpls., 1970-71, instr., 1971-75, coordinator, 1976-77, trainee-assoc. chief nursing service for edn., 1977; assoc. chief nursing service for edn. VA Med. Ctr., Wilmington, Del., 1977-80; assoc. Chief nursing service for edn. VA Med. Ctr., Richmond, Va., 1980-83; chief nursing service VA Med. Ctr., Huntington, W.Va., 1983-85, VA Med. Ctr., Cin., 1985—; adj. faculty Med. Coll. Va., Richmond, 1980-82; basic cardiac life support instr.-trainer Am. Heart Assn., Richmond, 1980-83; clin. prof. Marshall U. Sch. Nursing, Huntington, 1983. Mem. task force Richmond Area chpt. Am. Heart Assn. Recipient Outstanding Cardio-pulmonary Resuscitation Instr. award Richmond Area chpt. Am. Heart Assn., 1982, Achievement award VA Med. Ctr., Richmond, 1983, recognition award for excellence in mgmt. VA Med. Ctr., Huntington, 1983; Bush Found. fellow, 1975-76. Mem. Nat. League for Nursing, Am. Hosp. Assn., Am. Soc. Nursing Service Adminstrs., Phi Kappa Phi, Sigma Theta Tau (Phi chpt. scholar 1969-70), Pi Lambda Theta. Roman Catholic. Office: VA Med Ctr 3200 Vine St Cincinnati OH 45220

WALDMAN, JUDITH L., clinical psychologist; b. N.Y.C., Aug. 28, 1942; d. Abraham and Adele Pauline (Wolitzer) W. B.S., SUNY-New Paltz, 1964; M.A., Hofstra U., 1975, M.A., 1980, Ph.D., 1983. Cert. tchr., psychologist. Tchr. North Babylon, N.Y., 1964-79; asst. psychologist United Cerebral Palsy, Commack, N.Y., 1982-83; psychologist, Schwartz & Assocs., Brightwaters, N.Y., 1982—, N.Y. Mental Health Services, Brightwaters and Bethpage, N.Y., 1985—. Mem. Am. Acad. Psychotherapists, Am. Psychol. Assn., N.Y. State Psychol. Assn., Suffolk County Psychol. Assn. Home: 9 Hiawatha Rd Babylon NY 11702 Office: NY Mental Health Services 140 S Windsor Ave Brightwaters NY 11718

WALDMAN, REBECCA, art dealer; b. Phila., July 11, 1947; d. Frank Cooper and Bernice Silverstein Lewis; m. Michael J. Waldman, June 27, 1982. B.A., NYU 1969, M.A., 1971, now doctoral candidate; Owner, operator Gallery Rebecca Cooper, Washington and N.Y.C., 1974-80; pres. Rebecca Cooper, Inc., N.Y.C., 1980—; N.Y. Mayor's Adv. Com. on Interior Furnishings and Design Industry, 1981-82; mem. N.Y. Assn. Woman Bus. Owners-Artsroundtable, 1980; mem. exec. bd., sec. assocs. Am. Craft. Mus.; lectr. Collectors Circle. Program com. Women's Campaign Fund; mem. Whitney Mus. Circle of Friends, Guggenheim Mus. Assocs. Com., N.Y.C. Ballet Guild, Am. Fedn. Art (nat. patron). Address: 929 Park Ave New York NY 10028

WALDO, CAROL DUNN, government financial administrator; b. Springfield, Tenn., Mar. 30; d. W.J. and Mildred (Blakemore) Dunn; m. Steiner L. Waldo, Aug. 12, 1972; children—Sean, Candice. B.S.B.A., Tenn. State U., 1970; M.B.A., Atlanta U., 1973; postdoctoral U. S.C., 1981. Econ. analyst Exxon Co., USA, Houston, 1973-76; sr. fin. analyst R.J. Reynolds-Aminoil, USA, Houston, 1976-79; dir. budgeting Health and Human Services Fin. Commn., Columbia, S.C., 1979—; instr. U. S.C., 1980; research assoc. Irons & Assocs. Cons., Atlanta, 1972-73. Bd. dirs. Columbia Urban League, 1983—; mem. Les. Amis des Enfants, Columbia, 1985—. Recipient cert. of appreciation Jr. Achievement, 1975. Mem. Nat. Govt. Fin. Officers Assn. (agy. rep.), State Govt. Fin. Officers Assn., Assn. Govt. Accts., Nat. Assn. State Budget Officers (assoc.), Nat. Assn. Female Execs., LWV (edn. com. 1982-85). Avocations: tennis; travel. Home: 2125 Beaver Ln West Columbia SC 29169 Office: PO Box 8206 Columbia SC 29202

WALDO, SALLY (MRS. CLAUDE A. WALDO), insurance and real estate broker; b. Seattle, Jan. 8, 1903; d. Hyman and Lena (Kaplan) Rosenstein; student Modesto Jr. Coll., 1930; m. Claude A. Waldo, Nov. 6, 1925 (dec. 1969). Exec. sec., co-owner firm Claude A. Waldo, land surveyor, Martinez, Calif., 1945-69, bus. opportunity broker, real estate broker, 1949-83, ins. broker, 1950-83. Mem. Calif. 50-50 Bill Com., 1937; mem. constn. revision com. nat. conv. Young Democratic Clubs Am., 1937, nat. committeewoman, 1937-39, 1st v.p., 1936-37, chmn. woman's activities, 1936; Calif. chmn. circulation Nat. Young Dem. Paper, 1937; adv. bd. women's div. Calif. Dem. Central Com., 1936-38; organizer three young Dem. clubs in Stanislaus County, 1935; mem. Calif. Dem. Campaign Com., 1936; v.p. San Joaquin dist. Fed. Dem. Women's Study Clubs, 1940; mem. Civic Arts League, Walnut Creek, Calif. Mem. AIM (assoc.), San Joaquin Dist. Conv. Fedn. Women's Clubs (pub. chmn. 1935, legislation chmn. Stanislaus County 1934), Women's Improvement Club, Modesto, Calif. (sec. 1933), Women's Progressive Club (charter), Modesto (sec. 1933), Tres Artes (organizer 1935), Modesto Art League (charter), Martinez Grange, Town Hall Forum Los Angeles, Irish-Israeli-Italian Soc. San Francisco, Civic Arts League Walnut Creek, Internat. Platform Assn., Nat. Women's Polit. Caucus. Clubs: Toastmistress (charter mem. Modesto); Order Eastern Star; San Francisco Press (hon.) (San Francisco); Berkeley, City Commons, Polit. Sci. (Berkeley, Calif.). Address: Box 1023 Lafayette CA 94549

WALDORF, JEAN MOSELEY, newspaper executive; b. Montgomery, Ala., Mar. 15, 1942; d. Max Houston and Lillian (Campbell) Moseley; m. Ronald Clarence Waldorf, May 7, 1983; children by previous marriage—Kathleen, Michael, Patrick. Student U. Ala.-Montgomery, U. Ill., Troy State U. With Montgomery Advertiser (Ala.), 1959; mgr. promotion Champ-Urbana Courier (Ill.), 1960-68; mgr. promotion Sta. WRIL-FM, Grenada, Miss., 1971; mgr. Daily Sentinel Star, Grenada, 1971-74; owner, pub., editor The Copper Era, Clifton, Ariz., 1977—; pres. New Horizon Pub. Co.-Az. Corp., Clifton, 1982—. Bd. dirs. Job Tng. Partnership Act, Clifton, 1983. Mem. Ariz. Newspaper Assn., Nat. Press Assn., Ala. Fedn. Women's Clubs, Greenlee County C. of C. (dir. 1978), Prescott Bus. Assn. (dir. 1981). Republican. Roman Catholic. Club: Soroptimist. Home: 55 Coronado Blvd PO Box 1357 Clifton AZ 85533 Office: New Horizon Pub Co 20 Chase Creek Clifton AZ 85533

WALDRON, BARBARA PHYLLIS, holistic medical research executive, public relation consultant; b. Boston, Oct. 11, 1932; d. Charles and Rose (Salzburg) Waldron; m. Melvin Shulman, July 31, 1952 (div.); children—Bonita Waldron, H. Michael Waldron. Psychodrama therapist, Los Angeles, 1972-79; prin. Designs by Barbara, Marina del Rey, Calif., 1975-80; owner, editor, graphics designer Graphic Coordinates, Los Angeles, 1978-80; holistic med. cons., Los Angeles, 1977-80; exec. dir. Holmes Ctr. for Research in Holistic Healing, Los Angeles, 1980-84; founding dir. Bo-Jian Research Lab., Los Angeles, 1984—; lectr. on holistic health; bd. dirs. Chinese health scis. Am. U., Los Angeles, 1980-85; cons. Health-data Internat., Inc., Westport, Conn., 1983-84. Designer photographic process, 1981. Tchr. Joint Venture, Van Nuys, Calif., 1969-71. Mem. Nat. Council Internat. Health, Nat. Assn. Female Execs., Woman's Am. ORT, Assn. Humanistic Psychology. Democrat. Jewish. Office: 743 S Ogden Dr Los Angeles CA 90036

WALDRON, GAILYN LEE, architect; b. Bradford, Pa., Oct. 10, 1951; d. Jerome and Joan (Isroff) Weinberg. B.A., Stephens Coll., Columbia, Mo., 1972; M.A. in Architecture, U. Colo., 1973, in Solar Architecture, Ariz. State U., 1976. Jr. planner Beardsley David Assocs., Inc., Denver, 1972; land planner, landscape architect David Clinger Assocs., Lakewood, Colo., 1973; land planner Benedict Assocs., Inc., Aspen, Colo., 1973-75; co-founder, ednl. dir. Roaring Fork Resource Ctr., Aspen, 1973-79; design guidelines coordinator Green Valley Rancy, Denver, 1981; with Skidmore, Owings & Merrill, 1981-83; prin. archtl. planner, designer GW Designs, Aspen and Denver, 1981—; cons. to gov.'s office State of Calif., 1979; energy cons. Pitkin County, 19 . Author: Solar Architecture, 1975. Editor Sun Jour., 1973-78. Mem. Downtown Denver, Ind. Mem. AIA, Am. Planning Ctr., Internat. Solar Soc., Colo. Solar Energy Soc. Jewish. Avocations: triathletics.

WALDSMITH, MARY LOUISE, lawyer; b. Chgo., Feb. 22, 1956; d. Herman Waldsmith. B.S., Ariz. State U., Tempe, 1977, J.D., 1980. Bar: Ariz. 1980. Reporter, editor Phoenix Gazette, 1973-78; atty. U.S. Navy San Diego, 1983-85; counsel Naval Weapons Ctr., China Lake, Calif., 1985—. Served to capt. JAGC, U.S. Army, 1980-83. Recipient cert. of achievement U.S. Army, 1983. Dean's award Ariz. State U., 1980, Sustained Superior Performance award Naval Regional Contracting Ctr., 1985; Phoenix Gazette scholar, 1973. Mem. ABA, Phi Alpha Delta, Sigma Delta Chi (pres. 1976-77, scholar award, 1975-77).

WALK, CYNTHIA DIANE, broadcasting executive; b. Balt., Jan. 6, 1958; d. Walter Martin and Irene (Wanchisen) W. Student Broadcasting Inst. of Md. Traffic dir. United Broadcasting Co., Balt., 1977-79, television producer, Manchester, N.H., 1979-80, research dir., Washington and Balt., 1980-81, program dir., Balt., 1981—, prodn. dir., Balt., 1984—. Assoc. editor United Broadcasting Co. News, 1984—. Named Employee of Month, United Broadcasting, 1984. Roman Catholic. Avocations: skiing; photography; scuba diving. Home: 12501 Greenspring Ave Owings Mills MD 21117 Office: WYST 1111 Park Ave Penthouse Baltimore MD 21117

WALKE, JEAN HOLLAND, software systems engineer, computer systems consultant; b. Detroit, May 16, 1950; d. Harold Ferguson and Anne (Kostrick) Holland; m. Le Verne Douglas Rizor, June 19, 1971 (div. Aug. 1977); 1 child, James Delbert; m. Sanford E. Walke, III, Aug. 23, 1980. Student U. Mich., 1968-71; B.B.A., Eastern Mich. U., 1980. Office mgr. Mich. Testing Engrs., Inc., Ann Arbor, 1972-75, Constrn., Testing & Inspection, Inc., Ann Arbor, 1977-78; pvt. practice word processor, Ann Arbor, 1978-81; systems analyst ADP Network Services, Dearborn and Ann Arbor, 1981-84; tech. mgr. ADP Dealer Services, Southfield, Mich., 1984-85; engring. supr. Applicon-Schlumberger, Ann Arbor, 1985-86; pvt. practice computer systems cons., 1986—; v.p., dir. Bay & Tool Rental, Inc., Ann Arbor, 1977-83; v.p., dir., cons. Am. Lender Services, Inc., Ann Arbor, 1984—. Named Steward of the Meet, Criterium du Quebec, 1977; recipient award of appreciation City of Grayling, Mich., 1978; 6th Overall Nat. Championship for Co-Drivers, Sports Car Club Am., 1979; named tech. cons. ofyr. Mich. region ADP Network Services, Ann Arbor, 1982. Mem. Nat. Assn. Female Execs., Sports Car Club Ann Arbor (pres. 1973-74). Republican. Presbyterian. Club: Ralligators (treas. 1973-74) (Dearborn, Mich.). Avocations: contract bridge; sports car rallying. Home: 3509 Hillside Dr Ypsilanti MI 48197 Office: J H Walke Cons 2010 Hogback Rd Suite 2 Ann Arbor MI 48105

WALKER, ALICE MALSENIOR, author; b. Eatonton, Ga., Feb. 9, 1944; d. Willie Lee and Minnie (Grant) W.; m. Melvyn R. Leventhal, Mar. 17, 1967 (div. 1977), 1 dau., Rebecca Walker Leventhal. B.A., Sarah Lawrence Coll., 1966; Ph.D. (hon.), Russell Sage U., 1972, D.H.L., U. Mass., 1983. Author: Once, 1968, The Third Life of George Copeland, 1970, In Love and Trouble, 1973, Langston Hughes, American Poet, 1973, Meridian, 1976, I Love Myself When I Am Laughing, 1979, You Can't keep a Good Woman Down, 1981, The Color Purple, 1982, In Search of Our Mothers' Gardens, 1983, Good Night, Willie Lee, I'll See You in the Morning, 1979, Revolutionary Petunias, 1974, Horses Make a Landscape Look More Beautiful, 1984. Recipient Lillian Smith award, 1979, Rosenthal award Nat. Inst. Arts and Letters, 1973, Guggenheim Found. award, 1979, Am. Book award, 1983, Pulitzer prize, 1983. Office: care Harcourt Brace Jovanovitch Inc 757 3d Ave New York NY 10017

WALKER, ANITA MARIE RANSDELL, educator; b. Dallas, Feb. 13, 1957; d. Palmer Norman and Shirley Ann (Harding) Ransdell; student Marquette U., Ger., 1976; B.A. summa cum laude, So. Meth. U., 1978, B.S. summa cum laude, 1978; postgrad. Goethe-Inst., Freiburg in Breisgau, W. Ger., 1978, Johannes Gutenberg-Universität, Mainz, W. Ger., 1978-79; M.A. in Math., U. Okla., Norman, 1980, Ph.D., 1983; m. Billy Kenneth Walker, Mar. 8, 1980. Pvt. practice tutoring, 1976-78; grader dept. math. So. Meth. U., 1976-78, tutor, 1977, summer orientation leader, 1977-78, registration clk., 1977-78; grader dept. math. U. Okla., 1979-80, tutor, 1980-82, instr. math. Am. Indian Bus. and Engring. Edn. Center, 1981, Karcher grad. teaching fellow, 1979-83; with dept. math. East Central U., Ada, Okla., 1983—. Nat. Indian seminar instr. Boy Scouts Am. Order of the Arrow; mem. Okla. Masters Swim Team, 1981—; coach Greater Ada Swim Club, 1983—. Mem. Am. Math. Soc., Am. Indian Sci. and Engring. Soc., Math. Assn. Am., Phi Beta Kappa. Republican. Presbyterian. Clubs: German Tex. Heritage Soc., Dallas Goethe Center (dir. 1977-81), Order Eastern Star, Soroptimists, Internat. Order Rainbow Girls (adv.). Home: PO Box 2107 Ada OK 74820 Office: Department of Mathematics East Central U Ada OK 74820

WALKER, ANN MARTINA, lawyer, educator; b. Anniston, Ala., Aug. 1, 1940; d. Stanley Denton and Cornelia Moore (Brewster) W. B.S., Auburn U., 1962; M.A., La. State U., 1968; J.D. summa cum laude, Birmingham Sch. Law, 1982. Bar: Ala. 1982. Instr. math. Therrell High Sch., Atlanta, 1962-67, Northside High Sch., Atlanta, 1968-70, Mountain Brook Bd. Edn. (Ala.), 1970—; sole practice law, Birmingham, Ala., 1982—. Recipient Am. Jurisprudence Book award; Outstanding Jr. award, 1981. Mem. Ala. State Bar Assn., ABA, Birmingham Bar Assn., Phi Delta Kappa. Democrat. Baptist. Home: 3100-H Napoleon Ct Birmingham AL 35243 Office: Mountain Brook High Sch 3650 Bethune Dr Mountain Brook AL 35223

WALKER, ANN YVONNE, lawyer; b. San Francisco, Sept. 26, 1954; d. C. Richard and Athene (Henderson) Walker. B.S. with distinction in Math., Stanford U., 1976, J.D., 1979. Bar: Calif. 1979. Assoc. Wilson, Sonsini, Goodrich & Rosati, Palo Alto, Calif., 1979—. Corp. sec., atty. Primarius Ensemble Found., Menlo Park, Calif., 1983; violinist Stanford U. Symphony Orch., 1972—, mem. cast Stanford Gilbert & Sullivan group, 1979—. Mem. ABA, Calif. State Bar Assn., Santa Clara County Bar Assn., Phi Beta Kappa. Office: Wilson Sonsini Goodrich & Rosati 2 Palo Alto Sq Palo Alto CA 94306

WALKER, BEATRICE MCRAE, retired medical technologist, retired teacher, consultant; b. Maxton, N.C., Feb. 7, 1918; d. John and Sarah Jane (McRae) McRae; m. Eugene Howell, Jan. 29, 1940 (dec. 1943); m. Lawrence Jarvis Walker, Sr., Aug. 27, 1950 (dec. 1975); children—Beverly Jean Crumley, Lawrence Jarvis, Jr., John McRae. B.S., Bethune-Cookman, 1945; Diploma in Med. Tech. Franklin Sch. Sci. Arts, 1946; Diploma in Voc. Tech. Edn. U. So. Fla., 1969. Lic. med. technologist, Fla.; cert. tchr., Fla. Tchr. Marion County Schs. and Gilchrist County Schs., Fla., 1940-49; med. technologist, dir. Fla. A&M U. Hosp., Talla, 1949-54; asst. sci. dir. sci. dept. Fla. A&M U., 1954-56; prin. Mathew-Scippio Acad., Ocala, Fla., 1964-65; social worker Health and Rehab. Services, Ocala, 1965-68; tchr., med. technologist Div. Youth Services and Fla. Correctional Inst., 1968-82; chief lab. and missionaries advisor Seventh Adventist Hosp., Addis Ababa, Ethiopia; tchr. Am. Sch. Missionaries (Presbyterian), Iran; vol. in mental and pub. health. Active Am. Cancer Assn., mem. Fla. Farmers and Migrate Workers Bd. State of Fla.; chartered mem. West Side Devel. Corp., pres. 1981; past bd. dirs. LWV; past pres. Womans Federated Club., Ocala. Established first bloodbank Leon County, Talla, Fla., 1950, Ethiopia, 1960, Tehran, Iran, 1961; recipient Outstanding Contributions award Ambassador of Theran, Iran, 1964; honored by U.S. Info. Service and

Am. Embassy in Iran. Mem. Fla. State Med. Technologists, Retired Tchrs. Assn., U.S. Correctional Inst., Am. Legion Aux. (pres. Ocala unit). Democrat. Methodist. Club: Pacesetters. Avocations: Speaking; travel films; vol. services in social and health field. Home: 2323 SW 3rd St Ocala FL 32674

WALKER, BETSY ELLEN, computer services company executive; b. Atlanta, Sept. 14, 1953; d. John Franklin and Betty Louise (Brown) Walker. B.A., Duke U., 1974; M.B.A., Harvard U., 1978. Officer, First Atlanta, 1974-76; analyst Coca Cola, Atlanta, 1977; v.p. Am. Mgmt. Systems, Inc., N.Y.C., 1978—. J. Spenser Love fellow Harvard U., 1976. Mem. Phi Beta Kappa. Office: Am Mgmt Sys Inc 2 Rector St New York NY 10006

WALKER, CAROLINE ANN, utility manager; b. Seattle, Nov. 16, 1944; d. Charles Leonard and Ann Phyllis (Dziedzic) W.; B.A. in Econs., U. Wash., 1966; M.A. in Econs., UCLA, 1968; m. James C. Sudduth, Mar., 1971 (div. Mar. 1978). Regional economist U.S. Army C.E., Los Angeles, 1969-70, Seattle, 1971-73, 78-79; econ. analyst Library of Congress, Congl. Research Service, Washington, 1970-71; project coordinator Pierce County (Wash.) Wash., Alaska Regional Med. Program, 1974-75; market adminstr. Pacific N.W. Bell Telephone Co., Seattle, 1979, staff specialist, 1979-83, project mgr., 1983, mgr. internal auditor, 1983—; staff specialist AT&T, 1983; lectr. 13th Ann. Pacific N.W. Regional Econ. Conf., 1979. Campaigner mem. Republican Nat. Com. Cert. info. systems auditor. Mem. Inst. Internal Auditors Alumni Assn. U. Wash., EDP Auditors Assn., Soc. Info. Mgmt., Internat. Platform Assn. Clubs: Wash. Athletic, Women's University. Won appeal against Sec. of Wash. State on anti-fluoridation measure, 1976. Home: 24645 8th Ave S Kent WA 98032 Office: 2509 Bell Plaza Seattle WA 98191

WALKER, CAROLYN ANN, telephone company official; b. Lynchburg, Va., July 24, 1945; d. Charlie Stencil and Virginia May (Scruggs) W.; student No. Va. Community Coll., 1972—. Long distance operator C & P Telephone, Arlington, Va., 1966-69, employment interviewer, 1969-75, supr. service order typists, 1975-76, govt. liaison, Washington, 1976-78, staff supr., Silver Spring, Md., 1978-82, Washington, 1982-83; staff supr. Bell Atlantic Network Services, Inc., Silver Spring, 1984—. Adv., exec. adv. Jr. Achievement. Mem. Nat. Assn. Female Execs. Office: 13100 Columbia Pike Chesapeake Complex Silver Spring MD 20904

WALKER, CAROLYN PEYTON, English educator; b. Charlottesville, Va., Sept. 15, 1942; d. Clay M. and Ruth (Newman) Peyton; B.A. in Am. History and Lit., Sweet Briar Coll., 1965; cert. in French, Alliance Francaise, Paris, 1966; Ed.M., Tufts U., 1970; M.A. in English and Am. Lit., Stanford U., 1974, Ph.D. in English Edn., 1977. Tchr. Elem. and jr. high schs. in Switzerland, 1967-69; tchr. elem. grades Boston Sch. System, 1969-70, Newark (Calif.) Unified Sch. System, 1970-72; instr. div. humanities Canada Coll., Redwood City, Calif., 1973, 76-78; instr. Sch. Bus., U. San Francisco, 1973-74; evaluation cons. Inst. Profl. Devel., San Jose, Calif., 1975-76; asst. dir. Learning Assistance Ctr., Stanford U., Calif., 1972-77, dir., 1977-84, lectr. Sch. Edn., 1975—, dept. English, 1977-84, supr. counselors, tutors and tchrs., 1972-84; assoc. prof. dept. English, San Jose State U., Calif., 1984—, head cons. to pres. to evaluate coll.'s writing program, 1985-87; pres. Waverley Assocs., ednl. cons., 1980—; condr. reading and writing workshops, 1972—; reviewer Random House Books, 1978—, Research in the Teaching of English, 1983—; cons. Basic Skills Task Force, U.S. Office Edn., 1977-79, Right to Read, Calif. State Dept. Edn., 1977—, Program for Gifted and Talented, Freemont (Calif.) Unified Sch. Dist., 1981-82; bd. dirs. proposed high tech. sci. ctr., San Francisco, 1983-84. Recipient award ASPIRE (federally funded program), 1985. Mem. MLA, Calif. Profs. of Reading, Western Coll. Reading Assn. (treas. 1982-84), Nat. Council Tchrs. English, No. Calif. Coll. Reading Assn. (sec.-treas. 1976-78), Jr. League Palo Alto (bd. dirs. 1977-78, 83-84). Author: (with Patricia Killen) Handbook for Teaching Assistants at Stanford University, 1977; How to Succeed As a New Teacher: A Handbook for Teaching Assistants, 1977; (with others) Academic Tutoring at the Learning Assistance Center, 1980; also articles. Home: 2350 Waverley St Palo Alto CA 94301 Office: English Dept San Jose State U San Jose CA 95192

WALKER, CONSTANCE MAXFIELD, management consultant; b. Washington, Mar. 16, 1949; d. Orville Eldred and Rose Mary (Stiarwalt) Maxfield; m. Robert Charles Kneip, III, Aug. 21, 1971 (div. Apr. 1981); 1 dau., Stephanie Alexandra; m. Richard Howard Cowles, May 16, 1981 (dec.); m. Phillip Walker, July 25, 1985. Clk.-typist HEW, Social Security Adminstrn., New Orleans, 1971-72, service rep., 1972-73; mgmt. analyst Office Comptroller of Currency, Treasury Dept., Washington, 1974-77; dir. mgmt. analysis div. U.S. Customs, New Orleans, 1978-80, mgmt. analyst, Houston, 1980-81, program analyst, 1981-82, chief data processing br., 1982-83, chief mgmt. analysis br., 1983-85; pres. Constance Walker Assocs., Inc., 1985—. Author: MBO Handbook, 1979; (with others) Program Management Handbook, 1983; Introduction to Employee Involvement, 1985; contbr. numerous articles to profl. jours. Mem. Friends of Stehlin Found., 1982—, Friends of the Cabildo, 1978-80. Named Customs Woman of Yr., U.S. Customs, 1979, recipient Outstanding Performance award, 1979, 80, 81, 82, 83, 84, 85; named Fed. Exec. Bd. Woman of Yr., 1979; recipient Outstanding Service award Office of Sec. of Treasury, 1976; Cora Bell Wesley scholar, UDC, 1969. Mem. Internat. Assn. Quality Circles, Treasury Hist. Assn., DAR, Daus. Rep. of Tex., Daus. 1812, UDC, Va. Tech. Alumni Assn., Delta Zeta. Episcopalian. Home: 12218 Gladewick St Houston TX 77077 Office: Constance Walker Assocs Inc 1500 S Dairy Ashford Suite 215 Houston TX 77077

WALKER, CYNTHIA, clin. psychologist; b. Barre, Vt., Aug. 16, 1936; d. Joseph Francis and Catherine Clark (Cousins) W.; B.A., Pomona Coll., 1962; M.A., Pepperdine U., 1974; Ph.D., Calif. Sch. Profl. Psychology, 1977; 1 son, Adrian. Exec. dir. San Diego (Calif.) Hospice, 1977; pvt. practice clin. psychology, San Diego, 1977-79, Costa Mesa, Calif., 1980—; staff oncology psychologist St. Jude Hosp., Fullerton, Calif., 1980. Mem. Am. Psychol. Assn., Orange County Psychol. Assn. (dir.). Democrat. Office: 1533 W Baker St Costa Mesa CA 92626

WALKER, DARCY LYNN, banker; b. Chgo., June 29, 1949; d. Blake Mitchell and Dorothy Virginia (Schlickan) Walker. B.A., Yale U., 1971; M.B.A., Wharton Sch., U. Pa., 1973. Lending officer Citibank N.Y., N.Y.C., 1973-75, Citibank Houston, 1975-79, v.p., dir. corp. tng. Citibank N.Y., 1979-82, v.p., dir. Bankcard credit policy Citicorp Credit Services Inc., N.Y.C., 1982-84, v.p., dir. nat. collections, 1984—. Bd. advisor Girl Scout Council Greater N.Y., 1982-84. Mem. Fin. Women's Assn. Republican. Methodist. Clubs: Tuxedo (N.Y.); Jr. League, Yale (N.Y.C.). Office: Citibank 399 Park Ave New York NY 10042

WALKER, DONNA HENRY, securities executive; b. Atlanta, Feb. 9, 1954; d. Robert Edward and Evelyn Pauline (Smith) Henry; m. Robert Martin Walker, May 20, 1977; children—Robert Brandon and Matthew Lee (twins). B.A., So. Methodist U., 1976, M.B.A., 1977. Asst. securities officer Southwestern Life Ins. Co., Dallas, 1977-80; convertible securities trader Bass Bros., Ft. Worth, 1980-84; v.p. convertible arbitrage Paine Webber, Inc., N.Y.C., 1984—. Sponsor, The 500 Inc. Mem. Fin. Analysts Fedn., Jr. League of Stanford-Norwalk, Inst. Chartered Fin. Analysts. Republican. Methodist. Home: 76 Noroton Ave Darien CT 06820 Office: Paine Webber 1285 Ave of Americas New York NY 10019

WALKER, EDNA GROVEY, educator; b. Camilla, Tex., July 5, 1923; d. George W. and Margery (Willis) McGowan; m. William G. Grovey, Aug. 29, 1948; 1 son, Godwyn R.; m. 2d James S. Walker; stepchildren—Donn R., Deborah Walker Bibbs. B.S., Houston Coll. for Negroes, 1945; M.A., Tex. So. U., 1954; cert. U. Brazil, 1962, Nat. Tax Tng. Sch., 1973. Tchr. history Pickard High Sch., Brenham, Tex., 1945-50; tchr. E.O. Smith Jr. High Sch., Houston, 1950-68; tchr. Lamar Fleming Jr. High Sch., Houston, 1968—; resident tchr., trainer Tchr. Trainer's Program Tex. So. U., Houston, 1970-72; owner, asst. mgr. Grovey's Bus. Service, Houston, 1948-69; owner, asst. mgr. Roy's Bar-B-Q, Houston, 1972—; lectr., cons. State dir. young people's dept. A.M.E. Ch., 1967-75; pres. Women's Missionary Soc. Wesley Chapel, A.M.E. Ch., Houston, 1975—; promotion missionary edn. chmn. Tex. Conf. Women's Missionary Soc., 1976—. Recipient Outstanding Service award Harris County Tb Assn., Houston, 1962; Fulbright grantee, 1962. Mem. NEA, Tex. Edn. Assn., Houston Tchr's. Assn., Zeta Phi Beta, Houston Citizens C. of C., Assn. Am. Overseas Educators Orgn., Nat. Social Studies Tchrs. Assn., Tex. Social Studies Tchrs. Assn., Houston Social Studies Tchrs. Assn., Phi Beta Sigma, Zeta Phi Beta. Club: Shadows. Contbr. articles to profl. jours. Home: 5027 Briscoe Houston TX 77033 Office: 7441 Calhoun Houston TX 77033

WALKER, ELIZABETH KAY, broadcasting executive; b. Minot, N.D., Sept. 8, 1948; d. Ernest Hartwell and Glennis Irene (Simmons) W.; m. Richard Curtis Ulsh, Aug. 15, 1971 (div. 1977). B.A., Berea Coll., 1970; M.A., Ind. U., 1971; postgrad Ind. U., 1971-76, Pa. State U., 1974-76. Utilization coordinator Sta. WITF TV/FM, Harrisburg, Pa., 1973-76, mgr. ednl. services 1976-78, TV program mgr., 1978-79; dir program adminstr. PBS, Washington, 1982-83; mgr. program services Sta. KTEH TV, San Jose, 1979-82, 83-85; chief operating officer Sta. KTEH-TV Found., 1985—; cons. CPB Sta. Adv. Service, Washington, 1984—; guest lectr. Stanford U., Calif. State U., Hayward, San Jose State U., San Jose City Coll. 1980—. Mem. PBS Program Adv. Com., 1984—, Interregional Program Service Adv. Com., 1980-82, 84—. Mem. Santa Clara County Broadcasters Assn. (v.p. 1979-81), Nat. Assn. TV Arts and Scis. (bd. govs. No. Calif. chpt. 1984—), Assn. Calif. Pub. TV Sta. (chmn. programming subcom. 1981-82). Democrat. Mem. Ch. Brethren. Avocations: running; bicycling; singing; reading; sewing. Office: KTEH 100 Skyport Dr San Jose CA 95115

WALKER, ELJANA M. DU VALL, civic worker; b. France, Jan. 18, 1924; came to U.S., 1948, naturalized, 1954; student Med. Inst., U. Paris, 1942-47; m. John S. Walker, Jr., Dec. 31, 1947; children—John, Peter, Barbara. Pres., Loyola Sch. PTA, 1958-59; bd. dirs. Santa Claus shop, 1959-73; treas. Archdiocese Denver Cath. Women, 1962-64; rep. Cath. Parent-Tchr League, 1962-65; pres. Aux. Denver Gen. Hosp., 1966-69; precinct committeewoman Arapahoe County Republican Women's Com., 1973-74; mem. re-election com. Arapahoe County Rep. Com., 1973-78; pres. Denver U. Art Conservation Center, 1980-82; blockworker Am. Heart Assn., 1980-86, Leukemia Soc., 1980-86, Nat. Multiple Sclerosis Soc., 1980-86. Recipient Disting. Service award Am.-by-choice, 1966; named to Honor Roll, ARC, 1971. Mem. Cherry Hills Symphony (life), Lyric Opera Guild, Alliance Française (life mem.), ARC, Civic Ballet Guild (life mem.), Needlework Guild Am. (v.p. 1980-82), Kidney Found. (life), Denver Art Mus., U. Denver Art and Conservation Assns. (pres. 1980-82), Chancellors Soc. U. Denver, U. Denver Women's Library Assn., Childrens Diabetes Found. Denver, Internat. Club Welcome to Colo., Nat. Jewish Hosp. Aux., Beth Israel Hosp. Aux., Central City Assn. Guild, Cancer Aux. Colo. Roman Catholic. Clubs: Union (Chgo.); 26, Denver Athletic (Denver). Address: 6185 S Columbine Way Littleton CO 80121

WALKER, ETHEL GORDON, medical technologist; b. Chgo., Apr. 25, 1939; d. Edward and Sophia Mildred (Siegel) Gordon; m. Howard Walker, Jan. 28, 1962; children—Dina, Gordon. B.S., U. Ill., 1960; postgrad. in med. tech. Northwestern U., 1961. Registered med. technologist. Standards technologist Coll. Am. Pathologists, Chgo., 1964-65; med. technologist Western Electric Co., Chgo., 1965-66; mgr. North Shore Travel Shop, Winnetka, Ill., 1978-81; with sales and mktg. dept. Xonics Med. Systems, Des Plaines, Ill., 1981-82; v.p. Ctr. for Mammography, Inc., Northfield, Ill., 1983-85; ptnr. SK Cons., Cary, Ill., 1985—. Active Nat. Abortion Rights Action League, 1974—; bd. dirs. LWV, 1975; mem. nat. women's com. Brandeis U., 1980—. Mem. Soc. Study Breast Disease. Democrat. Jewish. Office: SK Cons PO Box 247 Cary IL 60013

WALKER, EUNICE MIRIAM ARNAUD, writer; b. Monett, Mo.; d. Emile and Pauline (Barriquand) Arnaud; student S.W. Mo. State U.; B.A., U. Ark.; postgrad. George Washington U., 1956; m. Joseph Edward Walker (div.); children—Diane Leigh Walker Smith, Carole Cecile Walker Baker; m. 2d, William Roy Little. Reporter, feature writer Monett Times, Kansas City (Mo.) Star; publs. writer Woodrow Wilson Centennial Celebration Commn., Washington, 1957; pub. relations writer Senator Joseph S. Clark, Washington, 1958-59; asst. pub. relations Ho. of Reps. Com. on Sci. and Astronautics, 1959-61; info. specialist ACDA, Washington, 1961-65, policy reports officer, 1965-70; pub. info. officer U.S. Dept. Agr., Washington, 1970-76; free lance writer, 1976—. Mem. LWV, Nat. League Am. Penwomen, Nat. Fedn. Press Women, Nat. Press Club, Assn. Agr. Coll. Editors, Nat. Hist. Soc., Am. Hist. Soc., Nat. Archives, Smithsonian Assos., Nat. Trust Historic Preservation, Nat. Cathedral Assn., Huguenot Soc., Am. Hort. Soc., Kappa Delta Pi, Lambda Tau. Episcopalian. Club: City Tavern (Washington). Author: Woodrow Wilson, 1958; contbr. articles to various publs. Home: 205 James Thurber Ct Falls Church VA 22046

WALKER, EVELYN, former educational radio-TV broadcasting exec.; b. Birmingham, Ala.; d. Preston Lucas and Mattie (Williams) W.; A.B., Huntingdon Coll., 1927, L.H.D. (hon.), 1974; postgrad. Cornell U., 1927-29; M.A., U. Ala., 1963, postgrad., 1965-75; spl. TV course U. Ill., summer 1953. Tchr. speech Phillips High Sch., Birmingham, 1930-34; head speech dept. Ramsay High Sch., Birmingham, 1934-52; chmn. schs. radio, TV, 1944-75, producer, coordinator TV-radio Birmingham Pub. Schs., 1952-69; head instrnl. TV programming services, 1969-75; broadcaster daily children's program, Birmingham, 1946-57; staff producer Birmingham Ednl. TV Studio for Ala. Pub. TV Network, 1954-75. Mem. Def. Adv. Com. on Women in Services, 1958-60; chmn. TV and radio competition Festival of Arts, 1962-65; bd. dirs. Women's Com. of 100 for Birmingham, 1968—, Ala. Humane Soc.; TV radio co-chmn. Gov.'s Adv. Bd. to State Safety Com., 1965-68; nat. del. Asian-Am. Women Broadcaster's Conf. 1966; mem. Salvation Army Aux.; audio visual chmn. Birmingham Council PTA, 1966-75; mem. acad. jurors Obelisk Awards, 1978-83; media Chmn. Gov.'s Commn. on Ala. Yr. of Child; bd. dirs. Women's Army Corps Found. Recipient Educator's Medal award Freedoms Found., 1963; Spl. award for Arts Birmingham Festival of Arts, 1962; Red Cross TV award, 1964; Nat. Headliner award Women in Communications, 1965; Key to City of Birmingham, 1966; Ala. service award Nat. Exchange Club, 1969; named Tops in Our Town, Birmingham News, 1957, Ala. Woman of Achievement, 1964, Birmingham Woman of Yr., 1965; Ala. Woman of Yr., Progressive Farmer mag., 1966; named hon. col. Ala. militia, hon. lt. a.d.c.; 20-Year Service award Ala. Ednl. TV Commn.; Obelisk award Children's Theatre, 1976. Mem. Nat. League Am. Pen Women, Nat. Eagle Forum, Am. Women in Radio and TV (local pres. 1959-60; past trustee area ednl. found.; dir.), Marquis Biog. Library Soc., Ala. Hist. Assn., Colonial Dames XVII Century, DAR (state program chmn.), Daus. Am. Colonists (state TV chmn. 1966-76), Noble Order of Crown, Colonial Order of Crown, Am. United Daus. 1812, Huntingdon Coll. Alumnae Bd. (achievement award, 1958, 1st nat. v.p. 1959-60, internat. pres. 1961-63, 2d v.p. 1973-76), Ams. Royal Descent, Royal Order Garter, Magna Charta Dames (sec.-treas. 1963-64), UDC, Ret. Tchrs. Assn. (past state chmn. internat. travel), Plantagenet Soc., Freedom Ednl. Found. (dir.), Ala. Congress PTA (audio visual chmn. 1966-75), Arlington Hist. Assn. (pres. 1981-83), (dir. 1969—), Greater Birmingham Arts Alliance, English Speaking Union, Nat. Trust for Historic Preservation (Arlington adv. bd.), Ala. Dist. Exchange Clubs (hon. life, bronze plaque award 1969), Internat. Platform Assn., Birmingham-Jefferson Hist. Assn. (trustee), Art Assn., Art Mus., Bot. Soc., Symphony Women, Golden Circle, Delta Delta Delta Alumna. Methodist. Clubs: Press, The Club, Downtown, Birmingham Country (mem. Ladies Golf Assn.). Home: 744 Euclid Ave Mountain Brook Birmingham AL 35213

WALKER, GAIL JUANICE, electrologist; b. Bosque County, Tex., Sept. 3, 1937; d. Hiram Otis and Hazel Ruth (Carmichael) Gunter; cert. Shults Inst. Electrolysis, 1971; children—Lillian Ruth, Deborah Lynn. In quality control Johnson & Johnson, San Angelo, Tex., 1962-70; with Electrolysis of Scottsdale (Ariz.), 1970-80; owner, pres., electrologist Ariz. Inst. Electrolysis, Scottsdale, 1979—. Mem. Ariz. Assn. Electrologists (pres. 1980—), Am. Electrolysis Assn. (editor Electrolysis World), Internat. Guild Profl. Electrologists, Nat. Fedn. Ind. Businessmen, Ariz. Assn. Electrologists (organizer 1980), Nat. Electrology Educators (sec.). Republican. Baptist. Club: Order of Eastern Star. Area corr. Hair Route mag. Office: 7033 E Indian Sch Rd 2 Scottsdale AZ 85251

WALKER, GAIL MARIE, marketing programs manager; b. San Antonio, June 24, 1957; d. Neilson P. and Martha L. (Yeargan) W. B.B.A., Baylor U., 1978. Systems engr. Computer Lang. Research Inc., Carrollton, Tex., 1979-82, sr. systems engr., 1982-83, mktg. analyst, 1983-85, mktg. programs mgr., 1985—. Pres., Dallas Baylor Alumni Assn., 1985-86; com. chmn. HPPC Bridges Class, Sunday Sch., Dallas, 1985-86. Mem. Internat. Exhibitors Assn., Meeting Planners Internat., Alpha Kappa Psi (treas. 1984-85). Republican. Presbyterian. Avocations: singing; tennis; travel. Home: 6054 McAfee The Colony TX 75056 Office: Computer Lang Research Inc 2395 Midway Rd Carrollton TX 75006

WALKER, HELEN ELIZABETH, travel agency executive; b. Athens, Tenn., Nov. 30, 1940; d. H. Maynard and Mary Ruth (Dake) Ellis; m. John Davis Walker, Jan. 21, 1961 (div. July 1977); children: John Jeffrey, Sharon Ruth; m. Cleo Waters, Apr. 13, 1984. B.S., Tenn. Wesleyan Coll., 1971. Cert. tchr., Tenn., Ga., Ala. Owner, mgr. Johnny Walker Tours, Nashville, 1975-77, Stardust Tours, Nashville, 1977—. Mem. Am. Bus. Assn., Nat. Tour Brokers, Women in Travel Services (pres. Nashville 1983), Nashville Assn. Tour Operators (pres. 1985), Nashville Area C. of C. Democrat. Home: 1107 17th Ave S Nashville TN 37212 Office: Stardust Tours Inc 1504 Demonbreun St Nashville TN 37203

WALKER, IMOGENE, acountant; b. Branford, Fla., Nov. 20, 1929; d. John Quincey and Helen Katie (Clemons) W. R.N., Riverside Hosp., 1951; B.B.A., N. Tex. State U., 1966. C.P.A., Tex. Sec.-treas. M.D. Labs., Inc., Dallas, 1977—; pres. Trinity Title, Waxahachie, Tex., 1965—, J.M.I. Mfg. Co., Dallas, 1976—; controller, chief fin. officer Safeco Land Title, Dallas, 1979—; sec.-treas. N. Tex. Title, Hunt Co., Greenville, Tex., 1980—, Rockwall (Tex.), 1980—; controller Metro Title Co., Ft. Worth, 1981—; dir. Tex. Am. Bank. Richardson Bd. dirs. Multiple Sclerosis, Dallas, 1976; regent Nat. Fedn. Republican Women, Washington, 1983. Mem. Am. Inst. C.P.A.s, Tex. Soc. C.P.A.s, Dallas Soc. C.P.A.s. Republican. Home: 7233 Lupton Circle Dallas TX 75225 Office: Safeco Land Title of Dallas 1510 Pacific Ave Dallas TX 75201

WALKER, IMOGENE LORETTO, lawyer; b. Little Rock, Apr. 10, 1943; d. Arthur J. and Joe Willie (Criswell) W. A.A., San Francisco City Coll., 1963; B.A., San Francisco State U., 1975; J.D., U. Calif.-San Francisco, 1978. Clk., Crocker Bank, San Francisco, 1964-66; teller Golden Gate Bank, San Francisco, 1966-68; data clk. Bank of Calif., San Francisco, 1968-74; asst. tchr. Acad. Stenographic Arts, San Francisco, 1975-76; asst. coordinator Hastings Coll. Advocacy, San Francisco, 1977-78; staff atty. Ga. Legal Services, Douglasville, 1978-83, mng. atty., Valdosta, 1983-86, chair affirmative action com., 1985-86; new lawyer trainer Reginald Heber Smith Community fellow, Washington, 1979, 81, 85. Housing discrimination checker Stanford Urban Coalition, Palo Alto, Calif., 1977; precinct insp. City-County San Francisco, 1975-78; mem. bd. Southside Recreation Ctr., Valdosta, 1985-86, Dist. 11 Child Welfare Adv. Bd., Ga., 1984—. Reginald Heber Smity Community lawyer fellow Howard U., 1978-80; Law Wives scholar Hastings Coll. Law, 1977; Denman scholar City Coll. San Francisco, 1962. Mem. State Bar Ga. (mem. legal aid com. 1982-83, v.p. individual rights sect. 1985-86), Valdosta Bar Assn., Ga. Assn. Black Women Attys. (historian-journalist 1986, R. Pruden Herndon award 1985), Nat. Legal Aid and Defender Assn., Phi Alpha Delta. Democrat. Baptist. Office: Ga Legal Services Program 114 N Toombs St Valdosta GA 31601

WALKER, JACQUELINE CLARKE, state govt. ofcl.; b. Summit, N.J., May 7, 1926; d. Allen Hillyer and Evelyn (Cook) Clarke; R.N., Buffalo Children's Hosp., 1951; B.A., U. Conn., 1972, M.S.W., 1975; m. James Walker, Dec. 29, 1951 (div.); children—Michael Clarke, John Howland, Naomi Silliman. Pediatric nurse Buffalo Children's Hosp., 1951-52; charge nurse local nursing home, 1973-75; state ombudsman Conn. Dept. Aging, Hartford, 1975—; cons. Greater Hartford Process Community Life Assn., 1975. Founder, pres. Glastonbury Human Rights Council, 1968; mem. Glastonbury Citizens Adv. Council, 1964, Glastonbury Charter Revision Comn., 1965. Mem. LWV (chpt. pres. 1961-63), Nat. Caucus of Black Aged (dir. 1976-80), Am. Gerontol. Assn., Northeastern Gerontol. Soc., Nat. Assn. Ombudsman/Advocates (dir. 1978—). Democrat. Contbr. chpt.: Victimization of the Elderly: Causes and Intervention, 1982. Home: 119 Springbrook Dr Glastonbury CT 06033 Office: 175 Main St Hartford CT 06106

WALKER, JESSICA LEE, portrait painter; b. Kansas City, Mo., May 22, 1930; d. Jesse Boone and Mildred (Trueblood) Walker; student San Jose State Coll., 1947-49, Dallas Mus. Fine Arts Sch., 1949-51. Asst. to portrait painter Matteo Sandona, San Francisco, 1952-54; free lance portrait painter, San Jose, Calif., 1955-59, Chgo., 1964—; med. illustrator Consol. Lithograph Co., San Jose, 1960-63; instr. adult art classes, Dallas, 1950-52; painter portraits James Boccardo and family, 1959, Melvin Belli, 1960; represented in collections U.S. and abroad. Winner scholarship Dallas Mus. Fine Arts Sch., 1946. Mem. Am. Soc. Artists. Home: 1730 N McVicker Ave Chicago IL 60639

WALKER, JESSIE, writer, photographer; b. Milw.; d. Stuart Richard and Loraine (Freuler) Walker; m. Arthur W. Griggs, Feb. 5, 1984; B.S., Medill Sch. Journalism, Northwestern U., also M.S. First major feature article appeared in The Am. Home mag.; contbr. numerous articles to nat. mags. including Am. Heritage's Americana, Better Homes and Gardens, McCall's, House and Garden, Good Housekeeping, others; midwest editor Am. Home mag.; contbg. editor Better Homes & Gardens; cover photographer Country Living, 1984, 85. Recipient Dorothy Dawes award for distinguished journalistic coverage in home furnishing, 1976, 77. Mem. Am. Soc. Interior Designers (press mem.), Women in Communications. Author: How to Plan a Trend Setting Kitchen, 1962; How to Make Window Decorating Easy, 1969; Shaker Design-150-year-old Modern, 1972; Good Design—What Makes It Last?, 1973; Junking Made Easy, 1974; Poster Power, 1976; For Collectors Only, 1977; Bishop Hill-Utopian Community 1978; also articles. Photographer cover photo Better Homes & Gardens, Sept. 1982, Oct. 1980, House Beautiful, Dec. 1981, Country Living, Jan., Feb., Sept., Nov., 1983, Jan., 1984, Dec., 1985, May, 1986. Address: 241 Fairview Rd Glencoe IL 60022

WALKER, JO ANN HOOVER, nurse anesthetist; b. St. George, Kans., Dec. 20, 1931; d. Joel Louis and Juanita Fern (Shelton) Hoover; R.N., Stormont-Vail Sch. Nursing, 1952; cert. registered nurse anesthetist Charity Hosp. Sch. Anesthesia for Nurses, 1969; m. Rankin T. Walker, Jr., Nov. 27, 1955; 1 dau., Victoria Ann. Office nurse, med. sec., asst. office mgr. Manuel De J. Castillo, M.D., Los Angeles, 1952-60; office nurse, med. sec., David Brobeck, M.D., Inglewood, Calif., 1959-60; emergency rm. nurse Centinela Hosp., Los Angeles, 1963-64; staff nurse Bd. Nat. Missions, United Presbyn. Ch., Ganado Mission, Ganado, Ariz., 1964-67; surg. intensive care nurse VA Hosp., Albuquerque, 1969; staff cert. registered nurse anesthetist U., N.Mex. Hosp., Albuquerque, 1969—. Mem. N.Mex. Assn. Nurse Anesthetists (pres.), Am. Assn. Nurse Anesthetists, Am. Bus. Women's Assn. (treas. 1983-84). Republican. Presbyterian. Home: 225 Sycamore St NE Albuquerque NM 87106 Office: 2211 Lomas Blvd NE Albuquerque NM 87106

WALKER, JOAN LOBIANCO, lawyer; b. St. Petersburg, Fla., July 27, 1942; d. John Andrew and Edna (DaSylva) LoBianco; m. David Seth Walker, Aug. 26, 1962; children—Stacy, Jason, Alexandra. Student Fla. State U., 1960-62; B.A., U. South Fla., 1964; J.D., Stetson U., 1971. Bar: Fla. 1971. Tchr., Pinellas County Sch. System, St. Petersburg, 1964-67; sole practice, St. Petersburg, 1971-78; ptnr. Walker and Azdell, St. Petersburg, 1978-82; ptnr. Fisher & Sauls, P.A., St. Petersburg, 1982—. Contbr. articles to profl. jours. Trustee Bayfront Med. Ctr., St. Petersburg, 1977-83, Fla. Orch.; liaison com. U. South Fla., Pinellas County. Mem. Fla. Bar Assn., St. Petersburg Bar Assn. (sec. 1976), Legal Aid Soc. (pres. 1974-75), Fla. Acad. Trial Lawyers, Fla. Assn. Women Lawyers, St. Petersburg C. of C., Kappa Delta. Republican. Roman Catholic. Home: 300 Park St S Saint Petersburg FL 33707 Office: Fisher & Sauls PA 501 Florida Nat Bank Bldg Saint Petersburg FL 33701

WALKER, JOSEPHINE GREGORY, postal service administrator; b. Staten Island, N.Y., Nov. 13, 1936; d. Joseph and Tommie (Gregory) Snoddy; m. Theodore Walker, July 4, 1954 (div. 1962); children—Ted Vance, Tony Vincent. Student Kent State, Cuyahoga Community Coll. Supr. East Cleve. br. U.S. Postal Service, 1980-82, supt. Beachwood br., 1982-84, acting mgr. Garfield Hgts. br., 1984-85, mgr. Bay Village br., 1985—; assoc. editor Women's Newsletter U.S. Postal Service, 1978-79. Recipient Spl. Achievement award U.S. Postal Service, 1982, Women's Program award, 1979. Democrat. Roman Catholic. Avocations: bowling; reading. Home: 23755 Banbury Cir #12 Warrensville Heights OH 44128 Office: U S Postal Service Bay Village Branch 27106 E Oviatt Bay Village OH 44140

WALKER, JOYCE JULIA, writer; b. Windsor, Colo., Feb. 16, 1941; d. Robert Harrison and Katherine Eunice (Frye) W. B.A. with honors in Edn. (Boettcher scholar), U. No. Colo., 1963; M.P.A., U. Colo., 1965. Tchr. East Jr. High Sch., Colorado Springs, Colo., 1963-64; mgmt. analyst Bur. Labor Stats., AID, Washington, 1965-68; adminstrv. officer Devel. and Resources Corp., N.Y.C., 1968-70; asst. chief budget preparation br. Exec. Office of the Pres., Office of Mgmt. and Budget, Washington, 1971-73, chief budget preparation br., 1973-76, dep. assoc. dir. transp., commerce and housing, 1976-85; mem. program for sr. mgrs. in govt. Grad. Sch. Bus., Harvard U., Cambridge, Mass., 1979; mem. adv. panel on pub. mgmt. edn. John F. Kennedy Sch. Govt., Harvard U., Cambridge, 1980-82. Recipient Fed. Woman's award CSC, 1976, Roger W. Jones award Am. U., 1983; Pub. Service award Presdl. Mgmt. Intern Alumni Group, 1984; named Meritorious Exec.,

Sr. Exec. Service, Pres. of U.S., 1980. Mem. Exec. Women in Govt. Home and Office: 3465 Lochwood Dr F27 Fort Collins CO 80525

WALKER, JOYCE LEHMAN, mag. exec.; b. Georgetown, Tex., May 9, 1947; d. Wilfred Paul and Pauline Anne (Cell) Lehman; student Alvin Community Coll., 1965-66, Fordham U., 1978, N.Y. U., 1980—; m. Russell L. Walker, Nov. 29, 1969 (div.). Asst. to dir. recruiting DuPont Glore Forgan, Dallas, 1973-74; sales rep., Southwest mgr. Cathy Corp., Dallas, 1974-77, Eastern regional mgr., N.Y.C., 1977; advt. sales rep. Instl. Investor mag., N.Y.C., 1978-79; nat. sales mgr. Registered Representative mag., N.Y.C., 1979-80; advt. sales N.Y. Times, 1980-81; corp. advt. mgr., assoc. N.Y. mgr. Omni mag., N.Y.C., 1981-83; pres. First Step Prodns., Inc., N.Y.C., 1983-84; advt. sales rep. MS mag., N.Y.C., 1984—; lectr. in field. Mem. Advt. Women N.Y. Democrat. Office: MS Mag 119 W 40th St New York NY 10022

WALKER, LAURA JEANNE, designer, author, consultant; b. Leadville, Colo., Jan. 21, 1953; d. Harold Ralph and Uretta Claire (Johnson) Walker. A.S. in Mfg. Design Tech., Comml. Coll. of Ft. Worth, 1976; B.A. in Journalism, Adams State U., 1974; postgrad. women's labor studies Shoreline Community Coll., 1978-82. Designer, tech. writer Boeing Corp., Seattle, 1977-82; cons. on research and writing, Washington, 1982—. Contbr. articles to profl. jours. Exec. dir. Coalition Labor Union Women Ctr. for Edn. and Research; bd. dirs. Nat. Com. on Pay Equity. Mem. Coalition of Labor Union Women (chmn. tng. and edn., co-chmn. nat. task force on new tech. 1982—, dir. women's edn. and resource ctr. 1980-82), NOW, Seattle Profl. Engring. Employees Assn. (rep. sec. 177-82, Outstanding Service award 1981, 82, chmn. affirmative action women's com. 1979-82), Nat. Assn. Working Women. Democrat. Methodist. Home: 1700 17th St NW Apt 404 Washington DC 20009

WALKER, LAURICE CAMPFIELD, social worker; b. Tuskegee, Institute, Ala., Sept. 25, 1922; s. Charles Gary and Isabella (Kent) Campfield; m. William Walker, Jr., July 3, 1944; children—Lynn L. Casper, Michael W., Craig V. B.S., Tuskegee Inst., 1943; M.S.W., Rutgers U., 1964. Cert. social worker. Substitute tchr. Pub. Schs. Atlantic City, 1952-55; social case worker Div. Youth and Family Services, Atlantic City, 1955-64, asst. supr., 1964-66; social worker Greater Egg Harbor Regional High Sch. Dist., Mays Landing, N.J., 1966—. Vice chmn. Atlantic City Housing Authority, 1977-83; trustee Atlantic Mental Health Center, 1981-83, Elliott House, Inc. (sr. citizens), 1981—; bd. dirs. United Way, 1972-77; charter mem. Child Rev. Bd. Atlantic County, 1978-80. Mem. Acad. Cert. Social Workers, Nat. Assn. Social Workers, Register Clin. Social Workers, NEA, N.J. Edn. Assn. Democrat. Presbyterian. Home: 306 Beach Ave Atlantic City NJ 08401

WALKER, LINDA KAREN, insurance executive; b. Bridgeport, Conn., Dec. 27, 1944; d. Otto Erick and Lilly Marie (Carlson) Sorensen; children—Allison Marie, Lawrence Douglas Clarke. B.S. in Edn., Northwestern U., 1966. Lic. gen. ins. broker Am. Mut. Ins. Alliance; C.P.C.U. Agt. service rep. Allstate Ins. Co., Skokie, Ill., 1967-69; underwriter Brummel Bros., Inc., Chgo., 1969-72; adjuster Unigard Ins., Arlington Heights, Ill., 1972-75; reclaim supr. Aetna Ins. Co., Chgo., 1975-81; mgr. Firestone Ins., Chgo., 1983—; risk mgmt. cons., 1977—. Author: Prison Poetry: An Insight Into Man (poetry anthology), 1983. Vice pres. U.S. Jaycee Women and Transylvania Jayceettes, 1983. Named Keywoman, Jaycees, 1983, Spl. Lady, 1983. Mem. Ins. Women Suburban Chgo. (dir. 1977-78) Nat. Assn. Female Execs. Republican. Methodist. Home: 522 E Algonqurn Rd Schaumburg IL 60195

WALKER, LYNN JONES, lawyer, found. adminstr.; b. Ft. Lee, Va., Jan. 24, 1948; d. Lawrence Neal and Mary Ellen Jones; student Fisk U., 1963-65; A.B. in Sociology, Barnard Coll., 1967; J.D. cum laude, Columbia U., 1970. Admitted to N.Y. bar, 1971; law clk. to Chief Judge U.S. Dist. Ct. of So. Dist. N.Y., 1970; atty. NAACP Legal Def. and Ednl. Fund, Inc., N.Y.C., 1971-73, 75-78; gen. counsel N.Y.C. Commn. on Human Rights, 1973-75; sect. chief, dep. asst. atty. gen. Civil Rights div. U.S. Dept. Justice, Washington, 1978-82; program officer Ford Found., N.Y.C., 1982—. Recipient Outstanding Performance rating Dept. Justice, 1980, 81, 82, Spl. Commendation award, 1980. Mem. Nat. Bar Assn., Assn. Black Found. Execs., N.Y.C. Legal Aid Soc. Office: Ford Found 320 E 43d St New York NY 10017

WALKER, LYNN LOUISE, lawyer, women's health activist; b. Orange, Calif., July 20, 1951; d. James Ross and Velma Louise (Koontz) W.; B.A., Calif. State U., Fullerton, 1973; secondary edn. cert. Chapman Coll., 1975; J.D., Western State U., 1984; 1 son, Tru. Health staff Feminist Women's Health Center of Orange County (Calif.), 1974-76, dir., 1976-82. Community organizer Women Against Violence Against Women, Orange County, 1975-76; bd. dirs. Nat. Abortion Fedn., 1978-79, Anaheim Free Clinic, 1984, Feminist Women's Health Center of Orange County. Recipient Margret Sanger award Fedn. of Feminist Women's Health Centers, 1976. Mem. Internat. Law Soc., NOW, Internat. Childbirth Edn. Assn., Am. Public Health Assn., Nat. Assn. Parents and Profls. for Safe Alternatives in Childbirth, Assn. for Childbirth at Home Internat., Abortion Rights Movement. Home: 601 N Clementine Anaheim CA 92805

WALKER, MARION FRANCIS, lawyer; b. Tuscaloosa, Ala., Jan. 19, 1950; d. Audiss Marion and Mildred (Newton) Walker. A.B., Sweet Briar Coll., 1972; J.D., Cumberland Sch. Law, 1976. Bar: Ala. 1976, Ga. 1980. Investment clk. Fed. Home Loan Bank Bd., Washington, 1972-73; law clk. McDaniel, Hall, Birmingham, Ala., summers 1974, 75; assoc. Charles Tartar, Birmingham, 1977; sole practice, Birmingham, 1977—. Mem. Jr. League Birmingham, 1978; bd. dirs. YWCA, Birmingham, 1984—. Mem. Ala. Bar Assn., ABA, Birmingham Bar Assn., PEO, Republican. Presbyterian. Club: Birmingham Backpaddlers. Home: 424 Glenwood Rd Birmingham AL 35216 Office: 608 N 21st St Birmingham AL 35203

WALKER, MARY ALEXANDER, author; b. Beaumont, Tex., Sept. 24, 1927; d. James Cosper Alexander and Mary Helen (Johnson) Alexander Shelley; m. Tommy Ross Walker, Dec. 23, 1952; children—Timothy Ross, Mark Thomas, Miles Stephen. A.A., Lamar Inst. Tech., 1945; B.S., Tex. Women's U., 1950; M.A., San Francisco State U., 1981. Cert. community coll. tchr., Calif. Instr., Dominican Coll., San Rafael, Calif., 1972-80, coordinator writers conf., 1979-80, cons. writing program, 1984; lectr. U. San Francisco, 1983-84; cons. bus. writing Marriott Hotels, Santa Clara, 1983. Author: Year of the Cafeteria (Breadloaf Writers' Conf. fellow for disting. book for young people 1972), 1971; To Catch a Zombi, 1979; Maggot, 1980; also short stories, articles, revs. Recipient 1st prize for short story Pacific N.W. Writers' Conf., 1976, 79, award for play adaptation Actor's Workshop, Santa Rosa, Calif., 1978; Lilly Endowment fellow, 1977. Mem. Soc. Children's Book Writers, Mystery Writers Am. Democrat. Unitarian. Home: 22 Corte Lodato Greenbrae CA 94904

WALKER, MARY ALICE, educator; b. Warrenton, Ga., Feb. 5, 1941; d. Pierce and Bessie (Pitts) Hill; B.S., Brockport State U., 1963; M.Ed., Nazareth Coll., Rochester, N.Y., 1975; cert. sch. adminstrn. Brockport State U., 1984; m. James Walker, June 29, 1963. Tchr., Jonathan Child Sch., Rochester, N.Y., 1963-66; dir. Work Edn. Teaching Center, Rochester, 1966-68; tchr. Project Follow Through, John Williams Sch., Rochester, 1968-77, tchr. reading, 1977—. Treas., United Ch. Ministry, Rochester; chmn. bd. Rochester Opportunities Industrialization Center; chairperson fin. com. N.Y.-Wash. Missionary Soc. Mem. N.Y. State Tchrs. Assn., Rochester Tchrs. Assn., Reading Tchrs. Assn. Methodist-Episcopal. Address: 797 Arnett Blvd Rochester NY 14619

WALKER, MARY CUNNINGHAM, lawyer; b. Cleve., Sept. 4, 1944; d. Geoffrey Everett and Katherine E. (Danforth) Cunningham; J.D., U. Tenn., 1975; B.A., Smith Coll., 1966; M.A.T. in French, Wesleyan U., 1967; m. John Albert Walker, Jr., Nov. 26, 1977; children—Christopher Danforth Swann, John Albert III. Admitted to Tenn. bar, 1975; atty. fin. div. Office Procs., ICC, Washington, 1975-76, Office Gen. Counsel, 1976-77; atty. U.S. Dept. Energy, Oak Ridge, 1977-78; mem. firm Fowler & Rowntree, Knoxville, Tenn., 1979-83, Walker & Walker, P.C., Knoxville, 1983—. Bd. dirs. Children's Center, Inc., Knoxville, 1980—; regional dir. Am. Field Service, N.Y.C., 1974—. Mem. Am. Bar Assn., Tenn. Bar Assn., Knoxville Bar Assn., Phi Delta Phi. Clubs: LeConte, Knoxville Symphony League. Home: 800 Blows Ferry Rd Knoxville TN 37919 Office: 700 First Tennessee Bank Bldg Knoxville TN 37902

WALKER, MARY ELLA, nurse; b. St. Louis, Aug. 23, 1945; d. Earl Earnest and Mrytle Emma (Agnew) W.; B.S. in Nursing, Tex. Christian U., 1967; M.S. in Nursing, U. Tex., 1972, Ph.D., 1976. Staff nurse, asst. head nurse, head nurse Barnes Hosp., St. Louis, 1967-71; staff nurse Brackenridge Hosp., Austin, Tex., 1972; research asso. U. Tex. System, 1973-74; research asso. Center Study of Human Resources, Austin, 1975-76, So. Regional Council, Inc., Atlanta, 1975-76; nurse cons. Tex. Med. Found., Austin, 1976-77; vis. lectr. U. Wis., Oshkosh, 1977-78; program dir. S.W. Rural Health Field Services Program Nat. Rural Center, Austin, 1977-78; program dir. Tex. Rural Health Field Services Program, 1979-85; health care cons., 1986—; lectr. U. Tex., 1979-85. Mary Gibbs Jones scholar, 1976; Meadows fellow, 1983-85. Fellow Am. Acad. Nursing; mem. Am. Nurses Assn., Am. Rural Health Assn., Sigma Theta Tau, Phi Kappa Phi. Contbr. in field. Office: 701 Jessie St Austin TX 78704

WALKER, MICHELLE JEANINNE, network controller; b. Chgo., Feb. 6, 1956; d. Macio and Mary Frances (Brooks) Brown; m. Gregory Dion Walker, Aug. 14, 1982; children—Mikeisha, Genesse. Student, U. Ill. Supr. data ops. Pullman Inc., Chgo., 1975-81; hardware and tech. specialist Ryan Ins. Group, Chgo., 1981-85; network control analyst, network controller Central States Pension Fund, Chgo., 1985—. Mem. Nat. Assn. Female Execs., Black Data Processing Assocs. (charter mem., chmn. 1986-88). Democrat. Baptist. Home: 10441 S Hoxie Ave Chicago IL 60617

WALKER, NORMA ELIZABETH PEDEN, educator; b. Grove City, Pa., Sept. 26, 1921; d. David Stanton and Mary Louella (Giebner) Peden; B.S., Indiana U. of Pa., 1958; M.S., Pa. State U., 1961, Ph.D., 1968; m. Charles Linn Walker, May 14, 1940 (dec.); children—Edward Erdman, Charles Linn, Rebecca Walker Mihelcic, Ellen Walker Torrey (dec.), Esther Walker Habla, Charlotte Walker Whatley; m. 2d, Russell Gras, Sept. 17, 1983. Homemaking tchr. Marion Center (Pa.) Area High Sch., 1958-60, tchr., head homemaking dept., 1961-63; grad. research asst. Pa. State U., 1960-61, instr., 1963-68; assoc. prof. clothing and textiles Tex. Tech. U., 1968-69, asso. prof., chmn. clothing and textiles, 1969-70, prof., chmn., 1970-75, Margaret W. Weeks prof., 1975-77; prof. consumer services Indiana U. of Pa., 1977-83. Mem. AAUW, Am. Cancer Soc., Am. Assn. Textile Chemists and Colorists (council for profl. devel. 1973-75), Am. Home Econs. Assn. (ofcl. bd. 1973-75, state adv. student membership sect. 1979-83), ASTM, Assn. Coll. Profs. Textiles and Clothing (sec. 1977, rep. central region 1976-78), Indiana County Hist. Soc. (curator of costume), Pierian Sorosis Study Club (pres. 1986-87), Kappa Delta Pi, Kappa Omicron Phi, Delta Kappa Gamma, Phi Delta Kappa. Republican. Methodist (bd. edn. Western Pa, lay del. ann. conf. Western Pa., mem. Council of Ministries, various bds. and coms., Martas Circle, commn. missions and benevolence). Club: Current Events (pres.). Home: 3007 55th St Lubbock TX 79413

WALKER, OLIVIA GRANDA, law educator; b. Tacloban, Philippines, Dec. 5, 1943; came to U.S., Jan. 21, 1971; d. Rafael Hugo Neri and Aurora (Ratcliffe) Granda; m. G. Daniel Walker, Sept. 12, 1965; children—Aurora, Drew, John, Ophelia. B.S. in Nutrition, Philippine Women's U., 1962; LL.B., Magna Carta U., 1978; LL.D., Bates U., 1983; D., U. Philippines, 1983. Dietitian, Food Dimensions, Inc., San Francisco, 1971-75; dietitian Nat. Health Enterprises, San Pablo, 1975-78; investigator Dist. Atty., Martinez, Calif., 1978-79; prof. law Magna Carta U., San Francisco, 1978-81, dean, 1981-83; dean Bates U. Law Sch., Vacaville, Calif., 1983—, pres. Bates Law Sch. Found., 1983—; cons. dietitian Nat. Health Enterprises, Oakland, Calif., 1976-81; trustee Irene H. Walker Trust, Waverly, Ohio, 1980—; dir. Investigator Paralegal Services, Vacaville, 1978—. Legal asst. VAC/PAC, Folsom, Calif., 1982; investigator Consumer Fraud. Sect., Martinez, Calif., 1981-82; campaigner Re-election Com., Sacramento, 1983-84. Fellowship candidate White House, Washington, 1984; recipient Award of Service Asean Research Legal Group, Vacaville, 1983; Award of Appreciation Calif. Legis., Sacramento, 1982. Mem. Calif. Trial Lawyers Assn., Assn. Trial Lawyers Am., ABA, Los Angeles Paralegal Assn., Office of Postsecondary Edn. Republican. Roman Catholic. Contbr. numerous articles to profl. jours.

WALKER, PAMELA DREXEL, arts executive; b. Providence, Jan. 14, 1943; d. John Rozet and Noreen (Stonor) Drexel; children—Andrew B.H., James Drexel. B.A., Sarah Lawrence Coll., 1964; M.A., New Sch. Social Research, 1967. Psychotherapist, Pacific Psychotherapy, San Francisco, 1970-77; pres. Western Opera Theater, San Francisco, 1975-77; sr. adviser Trans Century Found., Washington, 1977-79; dir. cultural programs Ptnrs. of the Americas, Washington, 1979-80; pres. PDW Assocs., Washington, 1980—; exec. dir. Arts Internat., Washington, 1983-86, N.Y. Internat. Festival of Arts, Inc., N.Y.C., 1980—, evaluator Nat. Endowment Arts, 1978—. Bd. dirs. The House Found., N.Y.C., Acad. London. Office: NY Internat Festival of Arts Inc 127 E 73d St New York NY 10021

WALKER, PATRICIA ANN, lawyer; b. Latrobe, Pa., Nov. 13, 1953; d. William J. and Sylvia (Fradel) Walker; m. Ralph E. Jocke, Oct. 8, 1982. A.B. in History and Polit. Sci., Grove City Coll., 1975; J.D., Cleve.-Marshall Coll. Law, 1981. Bar: Ohio 1981, U.S. Dist. Ct. (no. dist.) Ohio, 1981, U.S. Ct. Appeals (6th cir.) 1982, U.S. Supreme Ct., 1985. City clk. City of Broadview Heights (Ohio), 1975-77; claims rep. Social Security Adminstrn., Cleve., 1977-81; assoc. Law Offices of Ellis B. Brannon, Sharon Center, Ohio, 1981-85. Sec. Am. Bicentennial Com., Broadview Heights, 1975-76; sec. 50th Anniversary Com., City of Broadview Heights, 1976-77; adviser Divorce Equity, Inc., Medina, Ohio, 1981—. Mem. ABA, Assn. Trial Lawyers Am., Fed. Bar Assn., Nat. Orgn. Social Security Claimants Reps., Ohio Bar Assn., Ohio Acad. Trial Lawyers, Medina County Bar Assn., Akron Bar Assn., Cuyahoga County Bar Assn., Bar Assn. Greater Cleve., Cleve. Women Lawyers Assn. Democrat. Mem. United Ch. of Christ. Lodge: Slovenian Nat. Benefit Soc. Office: 225 E Liberty St Medina OH 44256

WALKER, PATRICIA BARNES, educational publishing executive; b. Salisbury, Md., Dec. 28, 1943; d. Herman Noel and Elnor Frances (Gibbons) Dykes; m. John Gordon Barnes, June 13, 1961 (div. Jan. 1976); children—Carol Kimberly, Christine Kelly; m. Kent Walker, Feb. 27, 1976. B.S. in Elem. Edn., Salisbury State Coll., 1967; M.Ed. in Reading, U. Mont., 1974; Ph.D. in Urban Services, Va. Commonwealth U., 1985. Cert. tchr., administr., Va. Tchr. Accomack County Schs., Va., 1967-77, asst. prin., Melfa, Va., 1977-78, middle sch. prin, Parksley, Va., 1978-81; state supr. Va. Dept. Edn., Richmond, 1981-85; pres. Peopleworks Publs., Richmond, 1985—; mem. adj. faculty Va. Commonwealth U., Richmond, 1984, U. Va., Charlottesville, 1986; cons., trainer Allied Corp., Petersburg, Va., 1984, 85, Va. Dept. Gen. Services, Richmond, 1984. Bd. dirs. Accomack County Players, Accomac, 1980; vol. March of Dimes, Richmond, 1986. Mem. Nat. Assn. Female Execs., Phi Delta Kappa, Phi Kappa Phi. Avocation: writing historical novel. Home: 936 St John's Wood Dr Richmond VA 23225 Office: Peopleworks Publs PO Box 13766 Richmond VA 23225

WALKER, PATRICIA LILLIAN, editor; b. Chgo., Jan. 2, 1943: d. Robert Warren and Virginia Margaret Walker; B.A., U. Ill., 1965; M.S. in Communications, Mich. State U., 1967; m. Peter Klaus Jeziorski, Aug. 28, 1971; 1 son, Peter. Reporter, Chgo. Tribune, 1967-69, Metalworking News, Chgo., 1969-71; mng. editor Am. Metal Market and Metalworking News, N.Y.C., 1971-74, editor-in-chief, 1974—; pres. Exec. Press Inc., 1981-84; trustee Inst. Archeo-Metall. Studies; bd. dirs. Copper Club. Office: 7 E 12th St New York NY 10003

WALKER, PATRICIA SEARS CHALLENDER, government contracts official; b. Sunfield, Mich., Apr. 7, 1934; d. Verle Eugene and Rhoda Leora (Sweet) Sears; B.A., Golden Gate U., 1976, M.B.A., 1978; m. Wilford J. Challender, Apr. 13, 1952 (dec. Oct. 1960); children—Wilford, Patricia; m. 2d, Russell E. Walker, Sept. 28, 1963 (dec. May 1971); 1 son, Russell. Contract specialist U.S. Army, Presidio of San Francisco, 1956-63; contracting officer Naval Supply Center, U.S. Navy, Oakland, Calif., 1964—, now dir. contracts. Mem. Nat. Contract Mgmt. Assn. (pres. Golden Gate chpt., 1978, dir. 1979, 80, v.p. N.W. region 1981-83, nat. v.p., sec. 1983-84), Federally Employed Women, NOW, AAUW, ACLU, Nat. Women's Polit. Caucus. Democrat. Unitarian. Club: Am. Contract Bridge League. Home: 14 Cheyenne Way Corte Madera CA 94925 Office: Code 201 A Naval Supply Center Oakland CA 94625

WALKER, PEGGY JEAN, social work agency administrator; b. Carbondale, Ill., Aug. 9, 1940; d. George William and Lola Almeda (Black) Robinson; children—Edith Nell and Keith Alan. B.A., So. Ill. U., 1962, Ph.D., 1986; M.S.W., Washington U., St. Louis, 1967. Caseworker, casework supr. Ill. Dept. Public Aid, 1964-71; child welfare adminstr. Ill. Dept. Children and Family Service, 1971-75; mem. faculty social work program So. Ill. U., 1975-79; adminstrv. dir. Western div. Children's Home Soc. of Fla., Pensacola, 1979—; appointed to Ill. Juvenile Justice and Delinquency Prevention Adv. Council, 1978-79; adj. adv. bd. dept. social work U. West Fla., 1982—. Bd. dirs. Hoyleton (Ill.) Children's Home, 1975-79. Mem. Nat. Assn. Social Workers, Acad. Cert. Social Workers, Council Social Work Edn., Fla. Assn. Health and Social Services. Presbyterian. Club: Pensacola Yacht. Home: 107 Florida Ave Gulf Breeze FL 32561 Office: 5375 N 9th Ave Pensacola FL 32504

WALKER, SALLY BARBARA, glass company executive; b. Bellerose, N.Y., Nov. 21, 1921; d. Lambert Roger and Edith Demerest (Parkhouse) W.; diploma Cathedral Sch. St. Mary, 1939; A., Finch Jr. Coll., 1941. Tchr. interior design Finch Coll., 1941-42; draftsman AT &T, 1942-43; with Steuben Glass Co., N.Y.C., 1943—, exec. v.p., 1959-62, exec. v.p. ops., 1962-78, exec. v.p. operations and sales, 1978-83, exec. v.p., 1983—. Mem. Fifth Ave. Assn. Republican. Episcopalian. Clubs: Rockaway Hunting, Lawrence Beach, U.S. Lawn Tennis, Colony, English-Speaking Union, Women's Nat. Republican. Home: 116 E 66th St New York NY 10021 Office: 715 Fifth Ave New York NY 10022

WALKER, SALLY LOU, electric company executive; b. Lubbock, Tex., June 24, 1956; d. Bruce and Dorothy Nell (Turner) Bagwell; m. Robert Pierce Walker, Oct. 1, 1982. B.A., Tex. Tech. U., 1978; B.A., Wayland Bapt. Coll., 1981. Univ. asst. First Bapt. Ch., Lubbock, Tex., 1974-76; asst. youth dir. Highland Bapt. Ch., Lubbock, 1976, youth dir., 1977-79; asst. minister edn. First Bapt. Ch., Plainview, Tex., 1979-81; bus. mgr. Dr. Randy Billings, Lubbock, 1981-83; bus. mgr. Acme Electric, Irving, Tex., 1983—; mgmt. cons. W. D. Turner Constrn., Lubbock, 1977-84. Author: The Magic of a Friend, 1980. Mem. Republican Nat. Com., 1977—. Mem. Nat. Assn. Female Execs., Nat.-Adv. Com. for Am. Security Council. Baptist. Avocations: photography; snow skiing; tennis; racquetball; designing hook rugs; writing poetry. Home: 5508 Ivy Hill Arlington TX 76016 Office: Acme Electric Co 3601 Conflans St Irving TX 75061

WALKER, SYLVIA CHRISTINE, corrosion engineer; b. Orange, Calif., July 4, 1954; d. Clarence Loring and Dorothy Mary (Greenwood) Hall; B.S. in Animal Sci., Calif. State Poly. U., 1974, M.S., 1979, M.B.A., 1983; postgrad. San Diego State U., 1979-81, San Jose State U., 1981-82; m. Ronald Raymond Walker, Sept. 9, 1978. Chem. technician Occidental Research Corp., La Verne, Calif., 1974-76; lectr. dept. chemistry. Calif. State Poly. U., Pomona, 1978; chemist Lockheed Aircraft Service Co., Carlsbad, Calif., 1979-81; research engr. Lockheed Missiles and Space Co., Sunnyvale, Calif., 1981-82; corrosion engr. Ameron, 1983—. Mem. Am. Chem. Soc., Nat. Assn. Corrosion Engrs., Gamma Sigma Delta, Phi Kappa Phi. Home: 2850 Amador Ave Ontario CA 91761

WALKER, TEMMY NATALIE, real estate company executive; b. Chgo., Mar. 18, 1935; d. George and Arlene (Cook) Rubenstein; m. Robert Harold Walker, June 2, 1957; children—Scott Graham, April Michele, Jillian Barri. B.A., U. Ill., 1957. Lic. real estate broker, Calif. Pres., Temma Creative Art, Chgo., 1957-72; real estate salesperson Harleigh Sandler, Los Angeles, 1973-74, real estate mgr. Fred Sands Realtors, Los Angeles, 1974-76, v.p., 1976-80, sr. v.p., 1980—; guest writer Los Angeles Times, 1979—, San Fernando Valley Daily News, 1979—. Mem. Nat. Assn. Realtors (fed. dist. coordinator 1983—), Calif. Assn. Realtors (dir. 1980—), San Fernando Valley Bd. Realtors (dir. 1980—, exec. com. 1982—, v.p. 1985, pres. 1986). Home: 5026 Veloz Ave Tarzana CA 91356 Office: Fred Sands Realtors 15477 Ventura Blvd Sherman Oaks CA 91403

WALKLIN, KAREN JOY, communications executive; b. Lincoln, Nebr.; d. Kenneth Russell and Joy Belle (Hill) McCaw; m. Larry John Walklin, Aug. 2, 1980; 1 child, Gregory John. B.A., U. Nebr., 1976. Prodn. asst. Sta. KRNU Radio, Lincoln, 1975-76; continuity asst. Stas. KOLN-TV/KGIN-TV, Lincoln, 1977, promotion asst., 1977-80, advt. media mgr., 1980, promotion mgr., 1981-82, dir. promotion and pub. relations, 1982-86, dir. creative services, 1986—. Bd. dirs. Lincoln/Lancaster County Heart Assn., 1982-85; dir., com. chmn. Fellowship Chs., 1983—. Mem. Broadcast Promotion and Mktg. Execs. (Ad awards 1981, 82, 83), Lincoln Advt. Fedn. (Ad awards 1981, 82), Am. Women in Radio and TV (pres. Cornhusker chpt. 1980-81, sec. treas. 1981—), Nebr. Broadcasters Assn., Soc. Profl. Journalists, Sigma Delta Chi (bd. dirs. 1986—), Mortar Bd., Alpha Epsilon Rho, Kappa Tau Alpha. Club. University. Office: Stas KOLN-TV/KGIN-TV 40th and W Sts Lincoln NE 68503

WALKO, ANN, college administrator; b. Newark; d. Alfred and Mary Lucy (Ciavarro) Murray; m. Michael Walko, Aug. 21, 1965; 1 son, Michael Edward. B.A. in Elem. Edn., Kean Coll., 1960; postgrad. U. Del., 1963; M.A. in Adminstrn., 1964; Ed.D., Rutgers U., 1983. Elem. tchr. N.J. Schs., 1960-63; asst. student teaching Kean Coll., Union, N.J., 1966-68, asst. dean students, 1968-81, certification officer, 1981-83, dean, 1983-84, asst. to v.p. for acad. affairs, 1985—. Adv. bd. Women in Support Essex County, Newark, 1982—; active Union County Women's Polit. Caucus, 1983, N.J. Assn. Elected Women Ofcls., 1982—, Union County Republican Women's Group, 1980—; mem. Child Rev. Placement Bd., Union County, Headstart Adv. Com., Union; mem.-at-large Boy Scouts Am. Recipient citation Union County Coordinating Agy. Higher Edn., 1983; resolution in honor of child care activities Union County Bd. Chosen Freeholders, 1983, proclamation in honor of sociol. study N.J. Assembly. Mem. Nat. Assn. Female Execs. (area coordinator), Nat. Assn. Women Deans, Adminstrs. and Counselors (newsletter editor 1981-83), Kean Coll. Profl. Women's Assn. (pres. 1977—), Nat. Soc. Educators and Scholars (adv. bd. 1980—), Phi Delta Kappa (pres. 1980-82, del. 1982-84), Kappa Delta Pi. Republican. Presbyterian. Club: Gran Centurions (scholarship dir. 1979-81). Office: Kean Coll Sch Edn B 102 Suite D Morris Ave Union NJ 07083

WALL, HELEN KATHARINE, personnel executive; b. Phila., Oct. 15, 1941; d. Milton and Carlyn (Ochs) Epstein; m. C. Robert Reichley, Jr., Aug. 29, 1964 (div. Jan. 1975); m. 2d James L. Wall, May 26, 1979; children—Susanne E., Melissa L. B.S., Temple U., 1963, postgrad., 1976-83. Tchr., Cooke Jr. High Sch., Phila., 1963-65; personnel adminstr. Oxford First Corp., Phila., 1977-78; benefits adminstr. Honeywell, Inc., Ft. Washington, Pa., 1978-79; personnel mgr. Smiths Industries, Inc., Malvern, Pa., 1979-83; employee relations mgr. Thomas & Betts Corp., Montgomeryville, Pa., 1983—. Tutor, classroom aide York Ave. Elem. Sch., Lansdale, Pa., 1971-73; dir. pub. relations LWV, Lansdale, 1972-76; leader jr. troop Girl Scouts U.S.A., North Wales, Pa., 1975-78; recruiter Am. Cancer Soc., North Wales/Lansdale, 1975-76. Phila. Bd. Edn. music scholar, 1959. Mem. Am. Soc. Personnel Adminstrs., North Penn Indsl. Relations Assn., Mfrs. Assn. Delaware Valley, AAUW. Office: Thomas & Betts Corp 121 Commerce Dr Montgomeryville PA 18936

WALL, JUDITH MARSHBURN, communications director; b. Bronx, N.Y., June 26, 1945; d. William Francis and Rita Theresa (Clifford) Marshburn; B.A. in Communications, U. Ga., 1969; M.B.A., City U. Seattle, 1982; m. Peter John Wall, May 2, 1970; 1 dau., Heather Dawn. Public info. dir. Bee County Coll., Beeville, Tex., 1970-72; women's editor Whidbey News Times, Oak Harbor, Wash., 1974-75; bd. dirs. Intruder Apparel, Inc., also owner Wrangler Wranch, Federal Way, Wash., 1975-78; asst. editor Federal Way News, 1976-78; communications coordinator Ednl. Service Dist. 121, Seattle, 1978—; communications cons. Bethel Sch. Dist., 1981—; dir. pub. info. Federal Way Sch. Dist., 1973—. Info. dir. Island County chpt. March of Dimes, 1974-75. Mem. Nat. Sch. Public Relations Assn., Wash. Press Women (various awards for photography and writing), Federal Way C. of C., Wash. Sch. Public Relations Assn. Republican. Roman Catholic. Club: Federal Way Soroptimists (nat. del. 1980, v.p. 1982, pres. 1983-84). Home: 30002 2d Pl SW Federal Way WA 98023 Office: 31455 28th Ave S Federal Way WA 98003

WALL, JULIA M(ARY), brokerage firm executive; b. N.Y.C., Ar. 8, 1948; d. John Edward and Mary (Hecht) Wall; m. Stevan John Zboyan, Aug. 1984. Student S.I. Community Coll., 1966-68, N.Y. Inst. Fin., 1968-69. Registered rep., option prin.; lic. ins. rep., N.J.; lic. real estate sales. Asst. to regional mgr. Aetna Life Ins. Co., N.Y.C., 1965-66, asst. to operation mgr. Hansen & Tidemann, N.Y.C., 1966-68; jr. trade Loeb, Rhoades & Co., N.Y.C., 1968-72; 2d v.p. Prudential-Bache Securities, N.Y.C., 1972—. Mem. Nat. Assn. Securities Dealers. Roman Catholic. Office: 100 Gold St New York NY 10292

WALL, MURIEL FRANCES, intercultural researcher; b. N.Y.C., Apr. 24, 1929; d. Charles and Fae (Zelesnick) Goldberg; m. George Jack Wall, Aug. 27, 1950; children—Barron Steven, Yvette Love, Suzanne Blondie. B.A., Hunter Coll., 1951; M.L.S., Rutgers U., 1969; Ed.D., NYU, 1979. Tchr. pub. schs., N.Y.C., 1951-65, multimedia tchr., 1960-65, media specialist, 1965-69; media cons. Hunter Coll. Tchrs. Library, N.Y.C., 1969-71; intercultural media dir. Rutgers U., New Brunswick, N.J., 1971-75; intercultural cons., dir. Info. Cons.

Assocs. ICA Pub., Hackensack, N.J., 1975—; media cons. Union City Bd. Edn. (N.J.), 1969-70; media cons. Project Best, N.Y.C., 1969-71; media researcher, cons. Dissemination Ctr., Bronx, N.Y., 1972-73. Editor newsletters; author monographs. Pres. Parent-Tchr. Orgn., Teaneck, N.J., 1965. Mem. ALA, Tchrs. of English to Speakers of Other Langs., Latin Americanist Ctr. for Latin Am. Studies, Global Perspectives Info. Exchange. Democrat. Jewish. Club: Singles Travel (pres. Hackensack 1983-84). Office: ICA Pubs Info Cons Assocs 303 W Pleasantview Ave Hackensack NJ 07601

WALL, NANCY LEE, real estate-land developer, medical consultant; b. Chesnee, S.C., June 28, 1944; d. Albert Lee and Sara Eleanor (Bush) Wall; student Furman U., 1962-63; B.S. in Med. Tech. and Chemistry, Lander Coll., 1966. Med. technologist Self Meml. Hosp., Greenwood, S.C., 1966-67; missionary med. technologist So. Bapt. Conv., Ghana, West Africa, 1967-69; chemistry technologist Alexandria (Va.) Hosp., 1969-70; spl. chem. tech., chemistry supr. Bapt. Hosp. System, Houston, 1970-71, med. tech. teaching coordinator, 1971-72; tech. sales rep. Abbott Labs., Houston, 1972-73, tech. liaison, 1974-76, internat. mktg. mgr. diagnostics div., South Pasadena, Calif., 1976-78; regulatory mgr. Alpha Therapeutic Corp., Pasadena, Calif., 1978-80, dir. quality mfg. and productivity dept., Los Angeles, 1980-83; pres. LeLynn Internat., 1982—; mem. staff 1984 Los Angeles Olympic Organizing Com., protocol mgr. judo. Bd. dirs. Via Verde Homeowners Assn., 1980, Erwin Lake Homeowners Assn., 1982; active Fight Against Multiple Sclerosis, 1978—. Recipient Abbott Labs. Presdl. award, 1975; Alpha Therapeutic Pres.'s award, 1981. Mem. Am. Assn. Clin. Chemists, Am. Assn. Clin. Pathologists, Am. Blood Resources Assn., Indsl. Soc. Pharm. Engrs., Nat. Assn. Female Execs., NOW. Home: 1640 Calle Miradero San Dimas CA 91773 Office: 1938 S Myrtle Ave Monrovia CA 91016

WALL, WENONIA ANN, educational counselor; b. Rockingham, N.C., Mar. 12, 1946; d. Limas and Mattie Lee (Sneed) W. B.A. in French, N.C. Central U., 1966, M.A. in Counseling, 1973. Registered practicing counselor, N.C. Tchr., Richmond County Schs., N.C., 1966-71, counselor, 1971—; neighborhood youth corps counselor Community Action Program, Southern Pines, N.C., summer 1974. Contbr. articles to profl. jours. Dep. dir. Dist. Eight Democratic Women, N.C., 1982-86; bd. dirs. Community Concert Assn., Rockingham, N.C., 1979-84, One-on-One Vol. Program, Rockingham, 1985. Mem. N.C. Assn. Educators (local pres. 1980-81, mem. legis. commn. 1985-88), NEA (elections com. 1981), N.C. Assn. Counseling and Devel., Alpha Pi Chi (pres. Alpha Lambda chpt. 1981-84). Avocations: reading; gardening; sewing. Home: Route 1 Box 569 Rockingham NC 28379

WALLACE, ANN C., health care administrator; b. Waterbury, Conn., Dec. 20, 1947; d. Frank and Muriel (Ackerman) Wallace. B.S. in Human Services, N.H. Coll., 1984. Lic. practical nurse New Medico Assoc., Waterbury, Conn., 1971-80; social worker New Medico Assocs., 1980-83, adminstr., 1983-85; adminstr. Athena Health Care Assocs., Waterbury, 1985—. Photographer. Mem. Am. Coll. Health Care Adminstrs., Nat. Assn. Female Execs. Home: 4 Oakland Ave Waterbury CT 06710

WALLACE, BARBARA LIVINGSTONE, chamber of commerce executive; b. Edmore, Mich., Apr. 7, 1941; d. Nuel Nichols and Ruth Lucille (Purdon) Donley; m. James Louis Wallace; 1 child, Wendy Ruth Borden. B.A., Mich. State U., 1964; postgrad. Central Mich. U., 1975-85. Social worker, asst. to bd. Oesterlin Home for Children, Springfield, Ohio, 1967-70; office mgr. Farmers Ins. Group, Boulder, Colo., 1971-74; adminstrv. asst. to dean Ferris State Coll., Big Rapids, Mich., 1974-77; exec. dir. crime prevention grant 720 Lilac, Big Rapids, 1980; exec. dir. Mich. Coalition To Prevent Shoplifting, 1981; exec. dir. Mecosta County Area C. of C., Big Rapids Mich., 1982—. Author; editor newsletter Ferris State Pharmacy Alumni, 1974-77, Mich. Coalition to Prevent Shoplifting, 1980, Mecosta County Area C. of C., 1982—. Author mag. Michigan Backroads, 1979. Sec. Western Mich. Crime Prevention Assn., Grand Rapids, 1980-85; nominations chmn. Internat. Soc. Crime, Louisville, 1982; state adv. bd. Distributive Edn. Clubs of Am., 1980—; tech. asst. Nat. Coalition to Prevent Shoplifting, 1981; lectr. crime prevention, 1980—; awards chmn. Internat. Soc. Crime Prevention Practitioners, Louisville, 1984; mem., co-chmn. fundraising Mecosta County Gen. Hosp. Aux., Big Rapids, 1978—; mem. crime prevention com. Mich. Commn. on Criminal Justice, Lansing, 1979-83; trustee cemetary bd. City of Big Rapids, 1979-84; sec. Big Rapids Indsl. Devel. Corp., 1982—; mem. Republican Women's Task Force, Lansing, 1982—, Mecosta County Council for the Arts, Big Rapids, 1982—; bd. dirs. Mecosta County Council for Humanities, Big Rapids, 1983-84; sec. West Central Mich. Community Growth Alliance, 1983—; mem. Mich. Sesquecentennial Commn., 1985—. Recipient Vol. of Yr. award Internat. Soc. Crime Prevention Practitioners, 1982, Outstanding Service award Mich. chpt. Distributive Edn. Clubs Am., 1983, Services to Hospitalized Vets., award, Med. Dist. 4, 1985; resolution Mich. Senate, 1984. Mem. Gen. Fedn. Women's Clubs (pres. Mich. 1984-86, bd. dirs. 1984—), Mich C. of C., Mich. C. of C. Execs. (bd. dirs. 1984—, scholar 1984, sec. 1986), U.S. C. of C., Town and Gown Council, Omicron Delta Kappa. Club: Big Rapids Women's (pres. 1978-80). Avocations: genealogy; ice skating; reading; swimming. Home: PO Box 520 Big Rapids MI 49307 Office: Mecosta County Area C of C 246 N State Big Rapids MI 49307

WALLACE, BARBARA RAPER, corporate professional; b. Greenwood, Miss., Aug. 31, 1953; d. Robert Erskin and Barbara (Kingsland) Raper; m. Arthur W. Ewell, Jan. 15, 1973; children—Arthur W. III, Gordon R.; m. Robert F. Wallace, Mar. 26, 1982. Student Memphis State U., 1971-73. Lic. ins. agt., Tenn. Adminstrv. asst. C & M Contractors, Memphis, 1979-83; sales asst. Morgan-Keegan & Co., Memphis, 1983-84; exec. sec. Walk Jones & Francis Mah, Inc., Memphis, 1984; adminstrv. asst. Correro Constrn. Enterprises, Memphis, 1984-85; prin., sales rep. Universal Liquidators, Memphis, 1985-86. Mem. Nat. Assn. Female Execs. Republican. Episcopalian. Home: 5367 Cottonwood Dr Memphis TN 38115 Office: Correro Constrn Enterprises 3639 New Getwell Rd Memphis TN 38119

WALLACE, BOBBIE FRANK, med. technologist; b. Golden, Tex., Feb. 20, 1932; d. Frank Messick and Charlotte Evelyn (Cathey) Wallace; B.A., Tex. Women's U., 1953. Chief med. technologist Callison Meml. Hosp., San Francisco, 1958-67; adminstrv. technologist Solano Labs., Berkeley, Calif., 1967-72; chief med. technologist M.D. Anderson Hosp., Houston, 1972-79; mgr. quality control ops. Technicon Corp., Middletown, Va., 1979-82; mgr. quality control Coulter Immunology, Hialeah, 1982—; clin. instr. U. Tex. Sch. Allied Health Scis., Houston, 1977-79. Vol. energy conservation workshop trainer Va. State U., Va. Tech. Extension Service, 1981. Lic. clin. lab. technologist, Calif. Mem. Am. Soc. for Med. Tech., Nat. Assn. for Female Execs. Home: 611 SW 71st Way Pembroke Pines FL 33023 Office: 440 W 20th St Hialeah FL 33010

WALLACE, BONNIE ANN, biophysics educator; b. Greenwich, Conn., Aug. 10, 1951; d. Arthur Victor and Maryjane Ann W. B.S. in Chemistry, Rensselaer Poly. Inst., 1973; M.Philosophy, Yale U., 1975, Ph.D. in Molecular Biophysics and Biochemistry, 1977. Postdoctoral research fellow Harvard Med. Sch., Boston, 1977-79; asst. prof. dept. biochemistry and molecular biophysics Columbia U., N.Y.C., 1979—; vis. scientist MRC Lab. Molecular Biology, Cambridge, Eng., 1978. Contbr. numerous articles to profl. jours. Jane Coffin Childs fellow, 1977-79; recipient Irma T. Hirschl award, 1980-84; Camille and Henry Dreyfus Tchr.-Scholar award, 1985. Mem. N.Y. Acad. Scis. (chmn. biophysics sect. 1983—), Biophys. Soc. (nat. council, Dayhoff award 1985), Am. Chem. Soc., Am. Crystallographic Assn., Sigma Xi, Phi Lamda Upsilon. Office: Dept Biochemistry and Molecular Biophysics Columbia U 630 W 168th St New York NY 10032

WALLACE, DEBORAH SUE, educator; b. Columbus, Ohio, Apr. 16, 1947; d. Richard S. and Mary E. (Clarke) W.; B.S. in Edn., Ohio U., 1969; M.A., Ohio State U., 1974, Ph.D., 1976. Tchr., Lancaster (Ohio) Public Schs., 1969-73, tchr. summer sch. program, 1971, 72; tutor neurologically handicapped, Lancaster, 1970-73; grad. research asst. Ohio State U., Columbus, 1973-74, grad. research asso. sch. projects, 1974, student tchr. supr., 1975-76, team leader parent tng. program, 1976; instr. Kent (Ohio) State U., summer, 1976; asso. prof. dept. spl. edn. Ga. State U., Atlanta, 1976—; cons. to various colls., schs. and rehab. instns., 1976—; panelist Sta. WOSU, 1975, WSB, 1983. reviewer The Directive Teacher, 1979—. Rep., Gov.'s Conf. Edn., State of Ga., 1980, 81, 82; v.p. Fulton County (Ga.) Young Democrats, 1977-78, pres., 1978-79; bd. dirs. Tommy Nobis Center for the Mentally Retarded, 1980—, v.p., pres. elect. Recipient Alumni Teaching award Ga. State U., 1982; Martha Holden Jennings scholar, 1972. Mem. Council for Exceptional Children, Council for Children with Behavior Disorders, NAACP, Pi Lambda Theta, Kappa Delta Epsilon (regional dir.). Methodist. Author teaching manuals; contbr. articles on edn. to profl. publs. Office: Georgia State U University Plaza Atlanta GA 30303

WALLACE, DORIS J., interviewing service company executive; b. Prague, Bohemia, Czechoslovakia, Oct. 30, 1923; came to U.S., 1948; d. Theodor W. and Jaroslava (Zandova) Jarsch; m. Aimel J. Wallace, Aug. 30, 1947; children—Raymond Gene, Julie Anne Wells. Student U. Vienna (Austria), 1942-44. Exec. sec., interpreter U.S. Mil. Govt. Prosecutor, Staubing, Bavaria, 1945-47; free lance interviewer Market Research, Indpls., 1958-67; proprietor/mgr. Wallace Interviewing Service, Indpls., Ft. Wayne, Ind., 1967—. Mem. Am. Mktg. Assn., Mktg. Research Assn. Republican. Methodist. Office: Wallace Interviewing Service 410 W Edgewood Ave Indianapolis IN 46217

WALLACE, ELIZABETH FORBES, travel industry executive; b. Malden, Mass., Oct. 19, 1952; d. William and Barbara B. (Duggan) Wallace; m. N. Duke Brobby, May 28, 1980 (div.); 1 dau., Alexis. B.A. in Photojournalism, Soviet Studies, Syracuse U., 1973. Asst. to pres. Visa Services, Washington, 1973-75, pres., owner Visa Advisors, 1975—; v.p. Wexita; fundraising mgr. Soviet Project, Werner Erhard & Assocs. Editor: Visaguide, 1983—. Mem. Women Execs. Internat. Travel Assn. Home: 3625 38th St NW Washington DC 20016

WALLACE, JANE HOUSE, geologist; b. Ft. Worth, Aug. 12, 1926; d. Fred Leroy and Helen Gould (Kixmiller) Wallace; A.B., Smith Coll., 1947, M.A., 1949; postgrad. Bryn Mawr Coll., 1949-52. Geologist, U.S. Geol. Survey, 1952—, chief Pub. Inquiries Offices, Washington, 1964-72, spl. asst. to dir., 1974—, Washington liaison Office of Dir., 1978—. Recipient Meritorious Service award Dept. Interior, 1971, Distinguished Service award, 1976. Mem. geol. socs. Am., Washington (treas. 1963-67), Sigma Xi (asso.). Home: 3003 Van Ness St NW Washington DC 20008 Office: Interior Bldg 19th and C Sts NW Washington DC Mail Address: US Geol Survey 103 Nat Center Reston VA 22092

WALLACE, JANE YOUNG (MRS. DONALD H. WALLACE), publishing company executive, editor; b. Geneseo, Ill., Feb. 17, 1933; d. Worling R. and Margaret C. (McBroom) Young; m. Donald H. Wallace, Aug. 24, 1959; children—Robert, Julia. B.S. in Journalism, Northwestern U., 1955, M.S., 1956. Editor house organ Libby McNeill & Libby, Chgo., 1956-58; prodn. editor Instns. Mag., Chgo., 1958-61, food editor, 1961-65, mng. editor, 1965-68, editor-in-chief, from 1968; editor Restaurants and Instns., from 1970; editorial dir. Hotels and Restaurants Internat. Mag., 1971—, Foodservice Equipment Specialist Mag., 1975—, Chain Report Newsletter, Fast Food and Restaurant Advt. and Mktg. Newsletter, 1980-83; v.p. Cahners Pub. Co., 1982—; cons. Nat. Restaurant Assn., dir., 1977—; cons. Nat. Inst. for Foodservice Industry.; vis. lectr. Fla. Internat. U.; bd. dirs. Ctr. for Research in Hospitality Industry. Editor: The Professional Chef, 1962, The Professional Chef's Book of Buffets, 1965; Contbr.: restaurant chpt. World Book Ency, 1975, Food Service Trends, American Quantity Cooking, 1976. Mem. com. investigation vocat. needs for food service tng. U.S. Dept. Edn., 1969; mem. Instnl. Food Editors' Conf., 1959—, pres., 1967; mem. hospitality industry edn. adv. bd. Ill. Dept. Edn., 1976, mem. adv. bd. Ill. sch. foodservice, 1978; mem. corp. adv. bd. Am. Dietetic Assn. Nutrition Found., 1981; trustee Presbyn. Ch., Barrington, Ill., 1983—. Recipient Jesse H. Neal award for best bus. press editorial, 1969, 70, 73, 76, 77. Fellow Soc. for Advancement Foodservice Research (dir. 1975—, sec. 1980); mem. Internat. Foodservice Mfrs. Assn., Nat. Assn. Foodservice Equipment Mfrs., Am. Bus. Press Assn. (chmn. editorial com. 1978), Am. Inst. Interior Designers (asso.), Women in Communications (v.p. Chgo. 1957-58), Les Dames d'Escoffier (charter mem.), Brotherhood of Knights of Vine (Gentlelady award 1980, 81), Gamma Phi Beta, Kappa Tau Alpha. Office: Cahners Pub Co 1350 E Touhy Ave Des Plaines IL 60018

WALLACE, JOAN EDAIRE SCOTT, social scientist, government official; b. Chgo., Nov. 8, 1930; d. William Edouard and Esther (Fulks) Scott; A.B. with honors, Bradley U., 1952; M.S.W. (Episcopal Youth Service fellow), Columbia U., 1954; postgrad. U. Chgo. Sch. Social Service Adminstrn., 1963-64; Ph.D. in Psychology (fellow), Northwestern U., 1973; D.Hum., U. Md., 1979; H.H.D. (hon.), U. Md.-Princess Anne, 1979; L.H.D. (hon.), Bowie State Coll., 1981; m. John H. Wallace, June 12, 1954 (div. Mar. 1977); children—Mark Scott, Eric Matthew, Victor Paul; m. 2d, Maurice A. Dawkins, Oct. 14, 1979. Social worker St. Mary's Home for Children, Chgo., 1954-58, casework dir., 1965-67; social worker United Charities Family Service Bur., Chgo., 1959-61; social work analyst Midway research project U. Chgo. Sch. Social Service Adminstrn., 1962-65; assoc. prof. social work Jane Addams Grad. Sch. Social Work, U. Ill., Chgo. Circle, 1967-73; assoc. prof. psychology Barat Coll., U. Ill., 1970-72; assoc. dean, prof. Howard U. Sch. Social Work, Washington, 1973-76; asst. sec. Dept. Agr., Washington, 1977-81; dir. Office of Internat. Cooperation and Devel., Washington, 1981—; dep. exec. dir. Nat. Urban League, 1975-76; v.p. bd. execs. Morgan State U., 1976-77; mem. Pres.'s Com. on Handicapped, N.Y.C. Mayor's Com. on Aging; cons. in field. Trustee, St. Mary's Services for Children; bd. dirs. Travelers Aid Soc. Recipient Robert S. Abbott award, 1948; Disting. Alumni award Bradley U.; Links Paragon award, Pres. Carter's Meritorious award, 1980, others. Office: Internat Cooperation and Devel 14th and Independence Ave SW Washington DC 20250

WALLACE, KATHLEEN MARIE, personnel executive; b. Chgo., May 2, 1955; d. Raymond William and Barbara Elaine (Justeson) Richardson; m. Michael Lee Wallace, Mar. 18, 1978. B.S. in Psychology, MacMurray Coll., 1977; M.A. candidate U. Tulsa. Mag card operator Arthur Andersen & Co., Chgo., 1977-78; sales asst., new account supr. Dean Witter Reynolds, Inc., Tulsa, 1978-79; personnel recruiter Bus. Resources and Exec. Search, Tulsa, 1979; dir. personnel State Fed. Savings and Loan, Tulsa, 1979-85; human resources rep. Agrico Chem. Co., Tulsa, 1985—. Leader spl. assignment Girl Scouts U.S.A., Tulsa, 1962-84. Recipient award of appreciation Girl Scouts U.S.A., Jacksonville, Ill., 1975. Mem. Inst. Fin. Edn. (pres. 1981-84), Tulsa Personnel Assn., Am. Soc. Personnel Adminstrn. Democrat. Roman Catholic. Lodge: Kiwanitas (bd. dirs. Tulsa 1982). Home: 2898-C E 51st Ave Tulsa OK 74105 Office: Agrico Chem Co PO Box 3166 Tulsa OK 74101

WALLACE, MARTHA REDFIELD, management consultant; b. Omaha, Dec. 27, 1927; d. Ralph J. and Lois (Thompson) Redfield; B.A. (Durant scholar), Wellesley Coll., 1949; M.A., Fletcher Sch. Law and Diplomacy, Tufts U., 1950; Litt. D. (hon.), Converse Coll., 1975; LL.D. (hon.), Occidental Coll., 1975, Pace U., 1975, Manhattan Coll., 1977. Instr. econs., asst. to dean Fletcher Sch. Econs., 1950-51; economist Dept. State, 1951-53; with RCA Internat., 1954-55; mem. editorial staff Fortune mag., 1955-57; with IBM, 1960-61; asst. dir. corp. devel. Time Inc., 1963-67; exec. dir., bd. dirs. Henry Luce Found., Inc., N.Y.C., 1967-83; pres. Redfield Assocs., 1983—; dir. Am. Can Co., Am. Express Co., Bristol-Myers Co., Chem. N.Y. Corp., N.Y. Telephone Co., 1972-84; dir. N.Y. Stock Exchange, 1977-83, mem. surveillance com., 1985—; trustee Bowery Savs. Bank 1972-81; mem. Conf. Bd., 1974—, bd. dirs., 1985—; mem. Nat. Com. U.S.-China Relations, 1975—, bd. dirs., 1986—; mem. Temp. Commn. N.Y.C. Fins., 1975-77, Brit.-Am. Com., 1976—, Trilateral Commn., 1978-86. Trustee Cultural Resources City of N.Y., 1977-81, chmn., 1978-81; trustee Williams Coll., 1974-86, N.Y.C. Citizens Budget Commn., 1976—; bd. dirs. Greater N.Y. Fund/United Way, 1975—, Am. Council/W. Ger., 1980—, N.Y.C. Partnership, 1980-86, Legal Aid Soc., 1983—, Internat. House, 1983—, Citizens Crime Commn., 1983—, Regional Plan Assocs., 1986—; mem. Phi Beta Kappa Assocs., 1985—; mem. sr. bus. adv. council Resources Inst.; chmn. membership Whitney Mus.; chmn. N.Y. Rhodes Scholar Selection com., 1983—. Mem. Am. Judicature Soc. (v.p., exec. com., dir. 1978, chmn. 1981-83, immediate past chmn., 1983-85), Council Fgn. Relations (dir. 1972-82), Council Founds. (dir. 1971-77), Found. Center (dir. 1971-77), Japan Soc. (dir. 1975-81, 83—), N.Y. Racing Assn. (dir. 1976—), Am. Acad. Polit. Scis., Regional Plan Assn. (bd. dirs. 1985—), Econ. Club, Phi Beta Kappa. Clubs: River, N.Y. Wellesley, Board Room. Home: 435 E 52d St New York NY 10022

WALLACE, MARY ELISABETH, political science educator; b. Oak Park, Ill., July 27, 1910; d. Malcolm William and Lillie May (Pitkin) W. B.A., U. Toronto, Ont., Can., 1931, Diploma in Social Sci., 1935; B.A., Oxford U., 1934; Ph.D., Columbia U., 1949. Social worker, 1935-45; mem. staff Sch. Social Work, U. Toronto, 1945-46; from lectr. to prof. polit. sci. U. Toronto, 1946-76, prof. emeritus polit. sci., 1976—. Editor: Readings in British Government, 1948; author: Goldwin Smith: Victorian Liberal, 1957; The British Caribbean: From the Decline of Colonialism to the End of Federation, 1977. Contbr. articles to learned jours. Fellow Royal Soc. Can.; mem. Toronto Symphony Orch. Assn., Can. Nature Fedn., Can. Assn. Internat. Affairs, Can. Wildlife Fedn. Mem. Liberal Party. Mem. United Ch. Can. Avocations: ornithology, music. Home: 421 Heath St E Toronto M4G 134 Canada

WALLACE, MICHELE FAITH, educator, writer, lecturer; b. N.Y.C., Jan. 4, 1952; d. Robert Earl Wallace and Faith Ringgold; B.A., CCNY, 1974. Book rev. researcher Newsweek Mag., N.Y.C., 1974-75; instr. journalism N.Y.U., 1976-78; author Black Macho and the Myth of the Superwoman, 1979; editor-at-large Essence Mag., 1983; vis. lectr. lit. U. Calif., San Diego, 1984; vis. asst. prof. English, U. Okla., Norman, 1984-85, asst. prof., 1985—. Contbr. articles, essays, short stories and poetry to newspapers and popular mags. including Ms., Esquire, The Village Voice, various anthologies; editor Women in Art, 1971. Pres., Art Without Walls, 1974; founding mem. Nat. Black Feminist Orgn., 1974; pres. WSABAL, 1970-76.

WALLACE, SALLY HANCOCK, library media specialist; b. Portland, Maine, Sept. 18, 1943; d. Owen Linwood and Lorayne Edna (Martin) H.; m. James Robert Wallace, May 15, 1965; children—Jennifer, James Stuart. B.A., Smith Coll., 1964; M.S., Towson State U., 1984. Research analyst Dept. Def., Washington, 1964-67; library media specialist Harford County Pub. Schs., Md., 1983—. Troop leader Central Md. council Girl Scouts U.S., 1982—. Democrat. Presbyterian. Club: Smith Coll. of Balt. (pres. 1984—). Avocations: reading; tennis; gardening; travel. Home: 808 Chestnut Glen Garth Towson MD 21204

WALLACE, SUZANNE L., communications executive; b. Bklyn., July 13, 1941; d. Sanford William and Helen Ross; m. Gene R. Wallace, Dec. 31, 1971; 1 child, Jonathan William. Student Queens Coll., N.Y., 1959-61. Lic. broadcast engr. 3d class. Media cons. BBD&O, N.Y.C., 1959-61; sales asst. Adam Young, N.Y.C., 1961-63, RKO Gen., N.Y.C., 1963-65; ops. dir. Sta. WOR-TV, N.Y.C., 1965-66; sales asst. Storer TV, N.Y.C., 1966-68; promotion dir. Della Reese Show, Los Angeles, 1968-70; prodn. asst. Mort Libov Prodns., Los Angeles, 1970-71; traffic dir. Sta. KHJ, Los Angeles, 1971-78, account exec., 1978-79; account exec. Sta. KIIS-FM, Los Angeles, 1979-80, nat. sales mgr., 1980-81, gen. sales mgr., 1981-82; nat. sales mgr. Sta. KFAC-AM/FM, Los Angeles, 1982—. Chair publicity Los Angeles Commn. on Status of Women, 1984; mem. steering com. PBS Your Children Our Children, 1983-84. Recipient cert. of recognition Mayor of Los Angeles, 1984. Mem. Am. Women in Radio and TV (v.p. Western area 1985—, chpt. pres. 1983-85). Office: Sta KFAC 6735 Yucca Los Angeles CA 90028

WALLACE, VONNA SYVETT, corporate contracting agent; b. Columbus, Ohio, June 11, 1947; d. Paris Allen and Dorothy Wallace; B.B.A., Ohio State U., 1969; M.S., Ga. Coll., 1977. Urban intern HUD, Chgo., 1969; asst. dept. mgr. ladies blouses and accessories Lazarus-Federated Dept. Stores, Columbus, 1970-73; buyer, cons. agreements and research and devel. agreements in semicondr. tech. Ford Motor Co., Dearborn, Mich., 1977-80; mgr. subcontract adminstrn. Space div. Gen. Electric Co., King of Prussia, Pa., 1980-85, corp. contracting agt., Bridgeport, Conn., 1985—. Served to capt. USAF, 1973-77. Mem. Nat. Contract Mgmt. Assn., Nat. Assn. Female Execs. Home: 335 Capt Thomas #75 West Haven CT 06516 Office: Gen Elec Co 1285 Boston Ave Bridgeport CT 06602

WALLACE, WANDA A., accounting educator, consultant, researcher; b. Kindley AFB, Bermuda, Aug. 19, 1953; d. Wayne R. and Alice L. (Anderson) Wilson; m. James J. Wallace, Nov. 3, 1972. B.B.A. magna cum laude, Tex. Christian U., Ft. Worth, 1972; M. Profl. Accountancy, 1974; Ph.D., U. Fla., 1978. Audit staff mem. Arthur Andersen & Co., Ft. Worth and Hartford, Conn., 1972, Ernst & Ernst Co. (now Ernst & Whinney), Jackson, Miss., 1973; research asst. U. Fla., Gainesville, 1976-77; instr. U. Ariz., Tucson, 1978; prof. U. Rochester (N.Y.), 1978-82; Corrigan prof. So. Meth. U., Dallas, 1982-85; Deborah D. Shelton systems prof. accounting Tex. A & M U., 1985—; cons. regression Price Waterhouse, N.Y.C., 1979—; cons. continuing edn. Peat, Marwick, Mitchell & Co., N.Y.C., 1980-81; cons. statis. techniques in litigation support Peterson & Co., Chgo., 1983—; cons. Arthur Andersen & Co., 1983—. Contbr. monographs, articles to profl. publs.; mem. editorial bd. Auditing: A Jour. of Practice and Theory, 1982—, others. Mem. Fulbright scholars screening com., 1985—. Recipient First Lit. award Am. Woman's Soc. C.P.A.s, 1981, 84, Wildman Gold medal, 1981, Cert. Disting. Performance, Inst. Mgmt. Acctg., 1980; grantee Peat, Marwick, Mitchell & Co., 1979-80, 82. Mem. Am. Acctg. Assn. (nat. council 1982-84, auditing sect. sec.-treas. 1983-84), Inst. Internal Auditors (bd. regents 1982-84, gold medal award 1981). Lutheran. Office: Dept Acctg Coll Bus Adminstrn Texas A & M Univ College Station TX 77843

WALLACH, ROCHELLE LAMM, financial services executive, publisher, author; b. Fargo, N.D., Apr. 16, 1948; d. Barney Eyles and Marion LaVerne (Peterson) Lamm; m. Alan Victor Wallach, Apr. 26, 1978; 1 child, David-Andrew. B.A., Loretto Heights Coll., 1970; M.B.A., U. Denver, 1980. Cert. fin. planner. Inst. salesman Kraft Foods, Inc., Ft. Worth, 1973-75; dir. adminstrn. Coll. Fin. Planning, Denver, 1975-77; regional v.p. Oppenheimer Mgmt., N.Y.C., 1977-80; exec. v.p., nat. sales mgr. Integrated Resources, Inc., N.Y.C., 1980-86; pres. Lamm Wallach Communications Group, Inc., Denver, 1985—. Author, pub.: On the Road Again, How to Succeed in the Competitive World of Wholesaling, 1985; author: On the Road Again, A Success Guide for Business Women Who Travel, 1985; author, producer video: Nanny Comes to Your House, How to Take Care of Your Newborn, 1986. Named Disting. Alumna, U. Denver, 1985. Mem. Inst. Cert. Fin. Planners, Internat. Assn. Fin. Planning (speakers bur.). Avocations: travel; writing; fishing; private pilot. Office: Lamm Wallach Communications Group 3892 S Grape St Denver CO 80237

WALLACH, SUSAN SILVERMAN, advertising executive, entrepreneur; b. N.Y.C., June 25, 1956; d. Marvin Edward and Sondra (Sherr) Silverman; m. Jordan L. Wallach, Jan. 7, 1978. B.S. in Advt., U. Fla., 1976. Copywriter, Fla. Sun Mktg., Sarasota, 1976-77; editor Sarasota Mag., 1977; sr. account exec. Sawyer & Assocs. Advt., Sarasota, 1977-80; mktg. dir. Investment Seminars, Inc., Bradenton, Fla., 1981; pres., account exec. Ward & Wallach Advt., Sarasota, 1981-85; v.p., account exec. Collateral Inc., Sarasota, 1985—; dir. v.p. SBV Advt. Fedn., Sarasota, 1979—. Copywriter advertisement Civilized Carpet Sale, 1983 (first pl. Addy award 1984). Precinct rep. Sarasota County Republican Exec. Com., 1980-83; mem. Sarasota County Civic League, 1984—. Jewish. Avocations: music, film. Office: Collateral Inc 330 S Pineapple Suite 110 Sarasota FL 33577

WALLACK, RINA EVELYN, labor lawyer; b. Pitts., July 16, 1949; d. Erwin Norman and Gloria A. (Schacher). in Nursing, Delta Coll., 1973; B.S. cum laude in Psychology, Eastern Mich. U., 1980; J.D. cum laude, Wayne State U., 1983. Registered nurse Mich.; bar: Calif. 1983. Psychiat. head nurse Ypsilanti State Hosp., Mich., 1973-77, instr., nursing educator, 1977-80; teaching asst. contracts Wayne State U., Detroit, 1981-83; legal asst. Wayne County Prosecutor's Office, 1982-83; atty. NLRB, Los Angeles, 1983-86, Paramount Pictures Corp., Los Angeles, 1986—. Contbr. articles to profl. jours. Instr., ARC, Mich., 1978-80. Recipient Am. Jurisprudence Book award, 1983; Order of Coif, 1983. Mem. ABA, Am. Trial Lawyers Assn., Mich., Calif. bar assns. Avocations: shooting movies; dancing; reading; photography. Office: Paramount Pictures Corp 5555 Melrose Ave Los Angeles CA 90038

WALLBAUM, JOAN MARGARET, computer company executive; b. Decatur, Ill., Dec. 18, 1938; d. Ralph Melvin and Margaret Bernice (Goveia) Funk; student parochial schs.; divorced. Tech. cons. State of Ill., Springfield, 1970-73; info. systems exec., data base adminstr. Ill. Dept. Public Aid, 1973-77; mgr. data base info. systems Philip Morris, Inc., Richmond, Va., 1977-81; dir. info. mgmt. Prime Computer Co., Natick, Mass., 1981—; mem. faculty Electronic Computer Programming Inst., 1972. Mem. Data Processing Mgmt. Assn. (v.p. 1982), Am. Mgmt. Assn., Inst. Cert. Computer Profls., Council Cert. Data Processing, Assn. Women in Computing (dir. 1983), Nat. Assn. Female Execs., Am. Contract Bridge League. Club: Framingham (Mass.) Bridge. Home: 16 Standish Rd Norfolk MA 02056 Office: Prime Computer Co Prime Park Natick MA 01760

WALLENT, JOAN FRANCES, executive and medical search consultant; b. Taunton, Mass., Nov. 3, 1945; d. John and Frances (Tumonis) Wallent; B.A., U. Chgo., 1966; postgrad. Harvard U., 1967-68 Psychol. Inst. N.Y.C., 1970. Research asst. Arthur D. Little, Inc., Cambridge, Mass., 1967-71; assoc. dir. admissions Emerson Coll., Boston, 1971-76; dir. admissions Bennett Coll., Millbrook, N.Y., 1976-77, Lake Erie Coll., Painesville, Ohio, 1977-79, Ottawa (Kans.) U., 1979-81; dir. human resources and physician recruitment Emergency Medicorp, Assoc. Group Physicians, Overland Park, Kans., 1981-83; pres. Search Unltd., Overland Park, 1983-85; human resources corp./physician recruiter Westworld Community Healthcare, Inc., Overland Park, 1985—. Mem. Nat. Assn. Coll. Admissions Counselors, New Eng. Assn. Coll. Admissions Counselors, N.Y. Assn. Coll. Admissions Counselors, Gt. Plains Assn. Coll. Admissions Counselors (pres.), Am. Assn. Coll. Registrars and Admissions Officers, Am. Personnel and Guidance Assn., Nat. Assn. Women Deans, Adminstrs. and Counselors, Am. Soc. Psychical Research, Am. Parapsychol. Assn., Am. Astrological Assn. Roman Catholic. Address: 10308 Metcalf Suite 225 Overland Park KS 66212

WALLER, JULIA REVA, financial aid counselor; b. Chgo., Aug. 24, 1950; d. Katie Lee (Waller) Richmond; 1 child, Kevin. B.A. in Psychology, Calif. State U.-Sacramento, 1982; M.A. in Edn., Calif. Poly State U.-San Luis Obispo, 1986. Youth supr. State of Ill., Chgo., 1972-74, caseworker, 1974-79; re-entry counselor Calif. State U., Sacramento, 1980-82, fin. aid advisor, 1981-83; fin. aid counselor Calif. Poly. State U., San Luis Obispo, 1983—. Treas. Detroit Area Neighborhood Council, Sacramento, 1981-82; mem. Operation PUSH, Chgo., 1971-76, Calif. Homemakers Assn., Sacramento, 1980-82, NAACP, San Luis Obispo. Marrion Muddox scholar, 1983-84; Herbert E. Collins scholar, 1984-85; Programs for Adult Students Admission and Re-entry scholar, 1981-82. Mem. Nat. Assn. Female Execs., Calif. Assn. Counseling and Devel., Western Assn. Student Fin. Aid Adminstrs., Calif. Assn. Student Fin. Aid Adminstrs. Pentecostal. Avocations: Directing plays; drama; book collecting. Home: 1260 Southwood Apt D San Luis Obispo CA 93401 Office: Calif Poly State University San Luis Obispo CA 93407

WALLER, NEOLA SHULTZ, educator; b. Okarche, Okla., Feb. 14, 1929; d. Lewis Ray and Alma Marie (Liebscher) Shultz; m. William Waller, Jr., May 28, 1949; children—Mary Ann, Jeffrey Scott. B.A., Okla. State U., 1949; M. in Teaching of Sci., Coll. William and Mary, 1972. Secondary math. tchr. Va. Beach City Pub. Schs., Va., 1963—. Mem. Virginia Beach Arts and Humanities Commn., 1978-79; chmn. bd. Baylake United Methodist Ch., Virginia Beach, 1982-83. Named Secondary Math. Tchr. of Yr. for Va., Va. Council Tchrs. of Math., 1985. Mem. AAUW (br. pres. 1979-81), Delta Kappa Gamma. Republican. Avocations: traveling; sewing; reading. Home: 1630 Arrowhead Point Rd Virginia Beach VA 23455 Office: Frank W Cox High Sch 2425 Shorehaven Dr Virginia Beach VA 23454

WALLER, WILHELMINE KIRBY, civic worker, orgn. ofcl.; b. N.Y.C., Jan. 19, 1914; d. Gustavus Town and Wilhelmine (Claflin) Kirby; ed. Chapin Sch., N.Y.C.; m. Thomas Mercer Waller, Apr. 7, 1942. Conservation chmn. Garden Club Am., 1959-61, pres., 1965-68, dir., 1968-71, chmn. nat. affairs com., 1968-74; mem. adv. com. N.Y. State Conservation Commn., 1959-70, dist. dir. Soil and Water Conservation, Westchester County, 1967-74, recipient Francis K. Hutchinson medal, 1971; mem. Nat. Adv. Com. Hwy. Beautification, 1965-68; mem. Lyndhurst council Nat. Trust Hist. Preservation, 1965-74; mem. Conservation Adv. Council, Bedford, N.Y., 1968-70; mem. Westchester County Planning Bd., 1970—; dir. Westchester Council Social Agys., 1970-72; mem. Rachel Carson council Nat. Audubon Soc., 1964—; v.p. Bedford Farmers Club, 1954-74; mem. Planning Bd. Bedford, 1953-57; mem. adv. com. to sec. of state UN Conf. on Human Environment, 1971-72; mem. N.Y. State Parks Adv. Com., 1971-72; adviser Gov. Rockefeller's Study Commn. Future of Adirondacks, 1968-70; mem. Citizens Adv. Com. on Environ. Quality, 1973-77; bd. govs. Nature Conservancy, 1970-77, vice chmn. Lower Hudson chpt., 1982—; trustee Mianus River Gorge; bd. dirs. Scenic Hudson, 1983—. Recipient award for More Beautiful America, Holiday mag., 1972; Conservation award Am. Motors, 1975. Mem. Nat. Soc. Colonial Dames, Huguenot Soc. Am., Daus. Cincinnati. Episcopalian. Club: Colony (N.Y.C.). Address: Tanrackin Farm Bedford Hills NY 10507

WALLIN, ANN LEWIS, educator; b. Haverstraw, N.Y., Dec. 9, 1937; d. Ernest Dalzell and Margaret Frances (Konecni) Lewis; B.S., U. Vt., 1958; M.S. in Counseling, U. Bridgeport, 1962, M.S. in Reading, 1976; 1 son, Jeffrey Orrick. Tchr., Fairfield (Conn.) Public Schs., 1959-61; free lance tchr. service workshops, Fairfield, 1974-77; pvt. practice diagnostic assessment and prescriptive teaching services, Fairfield, Westport, Conn., lectr. in field, coordinator Mid-Fairfield County Com. on Learning, 1974-77; sec. Council Exptl. Research in Reading, 1975-76; ednl. therapist Learning Help, Inc. and Ednl. Consulting Center, Westport, Conn., 1979-85; ednl. therapist, diagnostician, cons. Learning Help Inc.; cons. Skillbuilders, Inc., Essays and Applications. Cert. tchr., Conn. Mem. AAUW, Orton Soc., Conn. Assn. Children with Learning Disabilities, Am. Assn. Exec. and Profl. Women. Clubs: Ausable, Adirondack Mountain Res. Home and Office: 1 Merwins Ln Fairfield CT 06430

WALLIN, JUDITH KERSTIN, pediatrician, educator; b. Paris, Apr. 23, 1938; d. Theodore Bror and Ella Charlotte (Butler) Wallin; came to U.S., 1938; B.S. in Chemistry, Elizabethtown (Pa.) Coll., 1960; M.D., Temple U., 1964. Intern, Bellevue Hosp., N.Y.C., 1964-65, resident in pediatrics, 1965-67, attending pediatrician, 1967—; instr. pediatrics N.Y. U., 1967-71, asst. prof. clin. pediatrics, 1971-74, asso. prof., 1974—. Recipient Educate for Service through Profl. Achievement award, O.F. Stambaugh Alumni award Elizabethtown Coll., 1978. Diplomate Am. Bd. Pediatrics. Home: 300 E 33d St New York NY 10016 Office: Dept of Pediatrics Bellevue Hosp 27th St and 1st Ave New York NY 10016

WALLING, GEORGIA, psychotherapist b. Cedarhurst, N.Y.; d. William English and Anna (Strunsky) W.; student U. Paris, 1931-32, Vassar Coll., 1932-34; B.A., Rollins Coll., 1935; M.A., Columbia U., 1937, M.S. in Social Work, 1947. Caseworker, Family Service Soc., Atlanta, 1948-49, Bklyn. Bur. Social Service, 1951-53, Inwood House, N.Y.C., 1954-58; sr. psychiat. casework therapist Childrens Village, Dobb's Ferry, N.Y., 1959-60; asso. staff mem. Postgrad Center for Mental Health, N.Y.C., 1960-65; pvt. practice psychotherapy and psychoanalysis, N.Y.C. Mem. Nat. Assn. Social Workers, N.Y. State Soc. Clin. Social Work Psychotherapists, Postgrad. Psychoanalytic Soc., Nat. Accreditation Assn. for Psychoanalysis.

WALLING, SUSAN EILEEN FEMRITE, interior designer; b. Glenwood, Minn., Oct. 4, 1944; d. Sigvold Elmer and Sally Evangeline (Amundson) Femrite; B.S., U. Minn., 1966, cert. interior design, 1980; m. Greg Thomas Walling, Aug. 13, 1966; children—Christopher, Kari. Tchr., Roseville (Minn.) Public Schs., 1966-68, St. Louis Park (Minn.) Public Schs., 1968-73; interior designer Sue Walling Interiors, Edina, Minn., 1978-81; pres., interior designer SW Design, Inc., Mpls., 1981—. Pub. in Designer Mag., 1983, 84, 85. Active, Children's Health Center Aux., Friends of Mpls. Art Inst.; bd. life and growth Mt. Olivet Lutheran. Ch. Mem. Am. Soc. Interior Designers (assoc.). Club: Edina Country. Office: 925 Southgate Office Plaza 5001 W 80th St Minneapolis MN 55437

WALLIS, ELIZABETH SUSAN, air traffic control specialist; b. Tulsa, Dec. 20, 1953; d. Ralph David and Margaret Ella (Nolen) W. Student Drury Coll., 1972-73; B.S., U. Ark., 1976. Resident asst. U. Ark., Fayetteville, 1974-76; placement interviewer Okla. Employment Service, Tulsa, 1977-78; air traffic control specialist FAA Houston, 1978-84, regional staff specialist, Los Angeles, 1984-85, plans and programs specialist, Olathe, Kans., 1985, supervisory air traffic control specialist, 1986—. Mem. Profl. Women Controllers (central regional area dir. 1985-86), Air Traffic Control Assn., Nat. Assn. Female Execs., CAP. Avocations: Jazzercize; racquetball; travel. Office: FAA Kansas City Air Route Traffic Control Ctr 1801 E Loula St Olathe KS 61061

WALRAVEN, ELIZABETH ANN, social agency administrator; b. Schenectady, June 25, 1932; d. Clarence H. and Sara (Hollister) Linder; m. A. Emile Walraven, June 15, 1957; children—Peter, Mariann. B.A. in Econs., Wilson Coll., 1954. Ticket agt. KLM Royal Dutch Airlines, N.Y.C., 1955; engring. asst. AT&T Long Lines, White Plains, N.Y., 1956-57; membership dir. Schenectady Mus., 1973-74; adminstr. Home Furnishings Program, Schenectady, 1980-86; chmn. adv. council. Schenectady County Dept. Social Services, 1982—; bd. dirs. Family Found. Schenectady, Inc., pres., 1983-86, exec. v.p., 1986—; bd. dirs., officer Family and Child Service, Schenectady, 1963—, pres., 1972-74, 81-84, 1st v.p., 1984—; asst. to dir., 1986—; pres. Internat. Study Group, Brussels, 1977. Newsletter editor Internat. Sch. Brussels, 1976-77. Bd. dirs., officer Planned Parenthood, Schenectady, 1965-72; vol. ARC, Schenectady, 1979-84; bd. dirs. Hillside Elem. Sch. PTA. Mem. AAUW (bd. dirs. Schenectady chpt. 1965). Republican. Mem. Reformed Ch. in Am. Clubs: Queens Fort (pres. 1985-86), Jr. League (mem. exec. com., named Vol. of Yr. 1969), Garden (Schenectady). Avocations: rug hooking; embroidery. Home: 1248 Lenox Rd Schenectady NY 12308 Office: Family and Child Service Schenectady Inc 246 Union St Schenectady NY 12305

WALSCH, NELLIE LEE, steel warehousing exec.; b. Garrison, Ky., Mar. 18, 1920; d. Thomas Edgar and Essie Beatrice (Akers) Martin; student public and pvt. schs., also various coll. courses; m. Herman W. Walsch, Nov. 19, 1949; 1 son, Daniel Lee. With United Iron & Metal Co., Inc., Balt., from 1946, office mgr., bookkeeper div. Curtis Steel products Co.; corp. sec., bookkeeper Marlen Trading Co., Inc., Balt., Chesapeake Internat. Corp., Balt.; bookkeeper Curtis Export Corp., Balt., LSL Assos., Balt. Democrat. Methodist. Office: 4101 Curtis Ave Baltimore MD 21226

WALSH, ANNMARIE HAUCK, research organization executive; b. N.Y.C., May 5, 1938; d. James Smith and Annmarie (Kennedy) Hauck; B.A., Barnard Coll., 1961; M.A., Columbia U., 1969, Ph.D., 1971; m. John F. Walsh, Jr., Aug. 20, 1960; children—Peter Hauck, John David. Dir. Govs. N.Y., N.J. and Conn. Task Force Regional Planning, 1979-81; assoc. prof. polit. sci., dir. Center Urban and Policy Studies, CUNY Grad. Sch., 1972-79; mem. sr. staff Inst. Public Adminstrn., N.Y.C., 1961-72, pres., 1982—. Rep. N.Y. Fin. Control Bd., 1979-85; resource leader Presl. Mgmt. Intern Program, 1978-80. Mem. Nat. Acad. Public Adminstrn., Phi Beta Kappa. Roman Catholic. Club: Princeton (N.Y.C.). Author: Urban Government for the Paris Region, 1968; The Urban Challenge to Government: An International Comparison of Thirteen Cities, 1969; The Public's Business: The Politics and Practices of Government Corporations, 1978; also articles, monographs. Office: IPA 55 W 44th St New York NY 10023

WALSH, BEATRICE METCALFE PASSAGE, civic worker; b. Schenectady, Mar. 6, 1917; d. William Riley and Jessamine (Littlefield) Passage; student Western Res. U., 1941-42, Cleve. Community Coll., 1980—; m. Thomas Joseph Walsh, July 12, 1941; 1 dau., Joan Beatrice (Mrs. Peter Michael Waltz). Vol. worker ARC, 1941-46, 47-53; leader council Cleve. Beachwood (Ohio) Girl Scouts, 1952-57; vol. worker Community Chest, 1947-50; mem. women's com. Cleve. Orch., 1962—; ladies program chmn. Am. Chem. Soc., 1960, Am. Inst. Chem. Engrs., 1961, ladies program conv. com., 1969; mem. Orange Community Arts Council, 1969—, Pepper Pike Civic League, 1966—; ladies program co-chmn. Nat. Heat Transfer Conf., 1964; mem. women's com. Chagrin Valley Little Theater; mem., corr. sec. exec. bd. Case Western Res. U. Mem. Nat. Huguenot Soc., Nat. Soc. Founders and Patriots, Nat. Soc. New Eng. Women (sec. Cleve. Colony 1980—), Shaker Heights LWV, Case Faculty Wives (pres. 1958-59), Western Res. Rep. Women's Club, DAR, (Shaker chpt., corr. sec. 1962-64, registrar 1964-69, publicity chmn. 1968-70, chaplain 1969-71, librarian 1972-73, vice regent 1973-74, regent 1974-76, dir. 1985—, del. state conv. 1963, 64, 66, 69, 73, 74, 75, chmn. reception, del. nat. conv. 1964, 73, 74, 75), Friends of Orange Community Library, Daus. Am. Colonists (regent Charter Oak chpt. 1977-79, parliamentarian 1981-86), Nat. Soc. Daus. of Founders and Patriots Am., Order Crown of Charlemagne, Soc. Magna Charta Dames, Nat. Soc. New Eng. Women, Colonial Dames 17th Century, (corr. sec. 1985—), Nat. Soc. Women Descs. of Ancient and Honorable Arty. Co., Nat. Soc. Daus. 1812, Early Settlers of the Western Res., Western Res. Hist. Soc., Garden Center Greater Cleve. Presbyterian. Clubs: Blackbrook Country, Landerhaven Golf, Moreland Hills Golf, Landerwood Swim, Suburban Garden, Green Valley Garden (club rep. 1972-73, corr. sec. 1976-77); Case-Western Res. U. (exec. bd. 1981—); Univ. Women's. Home: 32555 Creekside Dr Pepper Pike Cleveland OH 44124

WALSH, CHERYL LEE, public relations manager; b. Lawrence, Mass., Mar. 11, 1954; d. Leo Emmanuel and Doris Marion (Thibodeau) Walsh. Cert. English, Wroxton Coll., Oxford, Eng., 1974; B.A. in Journalism/English, U. Mass., 1975; M.B.A., Suffolk U., 1982. Public relations staff Eastern States Expn., Springfield, 1976; dir. pub. relations Newbury Jr. Coll., Boston, 1976-79; assoc. dir. community relations, coordinator spl. events U. Mass., Amherst, 1979-84; dir. communications Wang Inst. Grad. Studies, Tyngsboro, Mass., 1984-85; mktg. communications mgr. IHRDC, 1985-86, Lisp Machine, Inc., Andover, Mass., 1986—. Contbg. editor: Your Career in Public Relations, 1983. Mem. Western Mass. Commn. on Tourism, Boston, 1983-84; bd. dirs. Amherst C. of C., 1979-81. Mem. Pub. Relations Soc. Am., Women in Communications, Publicity Club Boston, Inc. (v.p. membership 1983-84, co-chmn. bell ringer judging event 1986), Council for Advancement/Support Edn. Roman Catholic. Office: Lisp Machine Inc #4 6 Technology Dr Andover MA 01810

WALSH, DIANE, pianist; b. Washington, Aug. 16, 1950; d. William Donald and Estelle Louise (Stokes) W.; Mus.B., Juilliard Sch. Music, 1971; M.M., Mannes Coll. Music, 1982; m. Henry Forbes, 1969 (div. 1979); m. Richard Pollak, 1982. N.Y.C. debut Young Concert Artists Series, 1974; other appearances include: Kennedy Center for Performing Arts, Washington, 1976, Met. Museum, N.Y.C., 1976, Wigmore Hall, London, 1980; appeared with maj. orchs. worldwide, including St. Louis Symphony, Indpls. Symphony, San Francisco Symphony, Buffalo Philharmonic, Bavarian Radio Symphony of Munich, Berlin Radio Symphony, Radio Symphony Frankfurt, Radio Symphony Stuttgart; has toured Europe, N. Am., S. Am., Central Am.; founder Mannes Trio, 1982; recs. for Nonesuch Records, 1980, 82, Book-of-Month Records, 1985; mem. piano and chamber music faculty Mannes Coll. Music. Recipient 3d prize Busoni Internat. Piano Competition, Italy, 1974; 2d prize Mozart Internat. Piano Competition, Salzburg, Austria, 1975; 1st prize Munich Internat. Piano Competition, 1975; Naumburg Chamber Music award, 1986; Nat. Endowment Arts. grantee, 1981.

WALSH, DIANE BUSCH, lawyer; b. Butte, Mont., Feb. 21, 1954; d. Frank J. Busch and Margaret V. (McGreal) Shaffer; m. Kenneth Dale Walsh, Sept. 24, 1976. B.A. with honors, U. Mont., 1976, J.D., 1979. Bar: Mont. 1979, U.S. Dist. Ct. 1979, U.S. Tax Ct. 1982. Assoc. atty. McGarvey, Lence & Heberling, Kalispell, Mont., 1980—. Bd. dirs., vice-chmn. Flathead chpt. Mont. Wilderness Assn., Kalispell, Mont., 1981-83. Recipient Outstanding Service award Women's Law Caucus, Missoula, Mont., 1976; Piton Found. scholar, Denver, 1976-79. Mem. ABA, Mont. Bar Assn., N.W. Mont. Bar Assn., Phi Delta Phi, Psi Chi, Delta Gamma. Home: 213 Edgewood Dr Kalispell MT 59901 Office: McGarvey Lence & Heberling 745 S Main Kalispell MT 59901

WALSH, DOROTHY ANN, travel agency executive; b. Sheboygan, Wis., Jan. 8, 1945; d. Frank John and Sophia Mary (Schmitt) W. B.A., U. Wis.-Eau Claire, 1970. Mgr. Travel Services, Houston, 1975-77; travel cons. VIP Travel, Pasadena, Tex., 1977-78; mgr. Mex. Wholesalers, Houston, 1978; sec. Greater Houston Conv. and Visitors Council, Houston, 1978-80; sales sec. Grand Hotel, Houston, 1980; pres. Pan-A-Mexico, Inc., Houston, 1980-85; regional mgr. south/central sales Gaona Travel Corp., 1985—. Mem. Audubon Place Assn., Houston Exec. Women in Travel. Roman Catholic. Home: 3506 Aubudon Pl Houston TX 77006

WALSH, GERRY O'MALLEY, lawyer; b. Houston, Dec. 22, 1936; d. Frederick Harold and Blanche (O'Malley) Walsh. B.S., U. Houston, 1959; J.D., South Tex. Coll. Law, 1966. Bar: Tex. 1966, U.S. Dist. Ct. (so. and we. dists.) Tex. 1967. Elem. sch. tchr., Houston, 1959-65; instr. bus. law U. Houston, 1966-67; sole practice, Houston, 1966—; frequent lecturer before legal, jud. and civic orgns. Active various civic affairs, including Boy Scouts Am. Named Woman of Yr., Bus. and Profl. Women's Assn., Houston, 1973. Mem. ABA, Am. Judicature Soc., Criminal Def. Lawyers Assn., Tex. Criminal Lawyers Assn., Harris County Criminal Lawyers Assn., Tex. Trial Lawyers Assn., State Bar Tex., Houston Bar Assn., U. Houston Alumni Assn., S. Tex. Coll. Law Alumni Assn., Houston Zool. Soc., Houston Mus. Fine Arts, Iota Tau Tau, Zeta Tau Alpha. Office: 5400 Memorial Dr Suite 210 Houston TX 77007

WALSH, JANE ELLEN, health care official; b. Uniontown, Pa., Jan. 16, 1941; d. Albert Benton and Dorothy Rose (Ruble) McCann; B.A., Hood Coll., 1963; postgrad. Northwestern U., 1964-65; M.A., Antioch Coll., 1978; m. John Daniel Walsh, June 8, 1973; stepchildren—Christopher, Mark, Jonathan, Jennifer. Research asst. Cert. Nat. Interviewers, Chgo., 1963-64; project dir. Assn. Am. Med. Colls., Evanston, Ill., 1965-68; systems analyst Research Found. Mental Hygiene, Inc., Orangeburg, N.Y., 1968-72; systems analyst Nat. Center Health Services Research, Rockville, Md., 1972-73; research cordinator U. Calif., Berkeley, 1973-75; coordinator Pvt. Initiative in PSRO, San Francisco, 1975-76; cons., 1977-78; asso. dir. tech. services Western Consortium for Health Professions, Inc., San Francisco, 1978—; cons. health info. systems, health care evaluation, data sources. Recipient Martha Schaeffer Shaw award, 1960. Mem. Am. Public Health Assn., Assn. Health Services Research, Common Cause, Mus. Soc. San Francisco, Smithsonian Instn. Democrat. Presbyterian. Club: Highlands Country. Author: Introduction to Standard Mumps, 1978; developer automated system for storage and retrieval of clin. psychiat. data, 1969; designed mgmt. info. system for indigent care program; 1986; research on multi-splty. group practices delivering primary care, procedures for conducting concurrent quality assurance. Home: 50 Schooner Hill Oakland CA 94618 Office: 703 Market St Suite 535 San Francisco CA 94103

WALSH, JENNETTE, human resources risk manager, seminar speaker; b. Norfolk, Va., May 4, 1948; d. Walter Brown and Leona Irene (Place) McKee; m. Walter Lee Shawn, II, May 5, 1967 (div. 1985); children—Walter Heath, II, Travis Allan; m. Kermit Duane Walsh, Apr. 5, 1986. Cert. U. San Francisco, 1976; A.A., Tidewater Community Coll., 1982. Cert. personnel mgr. Personnel dir. Brooks Bros. Miller & Rhoades, Virginia Beach, VA., 1977-78; asst. dir. personnel Humana Inc., Virginia Beach, 1978-82; dir. personnel Va. Ctr. for Psychiatry, Hosp. Corp. Am., Norfolk, 1982-84; dir. benefits, risk mgr. Beverly Enterprises, Virginia Beach, 1984—; cons. Distributive Edn. Club Am., Virginia Beach, 1984-85. Contbr. oil paintings to exhbns. (hon. mention award 1979). Mem. Va. Assn. Hosp. Personnel Adminstrs., Nat. Assn. Female Execs. (network dir. Virginia Beach 1985). Avocations: oil painting; cross stitch; running; bicycling. Office: Beverly Enterprises 101 N Lynnhaven Rd Virginia Beach VA 23454

WALSH, LORRAINE MARIE, lawyer; b. San Francisco, Nov. 20, 1956; d. Walter Melvin and Bernadette (Kelly) Walsh. B.A., U. Calif.-Davis, 1978; J.D., U. Pacific McGeorge Sch. of Law, 1982. Bar: Calif., 1982. Atty., Contra Costa County, Martinez, 1984—. Mem. honors governing bd. Community Legal Services, McGeorge Sch. of Law, Sacramento, 1982. Mem. Calif. Bar Assn., ABA, San Francisco Queen's Bench, Phi Delta Phi, Prytanean Soc. Democrat. Roman Catholic. Home: 285 Del Amigo Rd Danville CA 94526 Office: County Counsel Contra Costa Adminstrn Bldg PO Box 69 Martinez CA 94553

WALSH, MARGARET M., answering service executive; b. Appleton, Wis., Nov. 26, 1920; d. Eugene J. and Anna M. (Finnegan) W.; student U. Wis. Extension, 1939, Spencerian Coll., 1940-41. Pres., owner Tel/Sec Inc., Appleton, 1949—; dir. Assoc. Appleton Bank. Founder, chmn. C.L.A.S.P., Inc. Mem. ATAE Inc. (pres. 1972-73), Sales and Mktg. Assn. NE Wis. (pres. 1979-80). Republican. Roman Catholic. Club: Riverview Country (pres. 1982-83). Home: 1125 S Oneida St Appleton WI 54915 Office: Tel/Sec Inc 516 W 6th St Appleton WI 54911

WALSH, MARILYN, lawyer, broadcasting co. exec.; B.A., Grinnell Coll., 1950; J.D., N.Y. U., 1957, LL.M., 1958, M.B.A., 1963. With U.S. Trust Co., 1951-53, Irving Trust Co., 1953-57; tax atty. Davies, Hardy, Ives and Lawther, 1958-64; with CBS, Inc., N.Y.C., 1964—, sr. tax atty., 1965-66, tax counsel, 1966-67, asst. treas., dir. tax sect., 1967-72, corporate v.p., dir. taxes, 1972—. Office: CBS Inc 51 W 52d St New York NY 10019

WALSH, MARY D. FLEMING, civic worker; b. Whitewright, Tex., Oct. 29, 1913; d. William Fleming and Anna Maud (Lewis) Fleming; B.A., So. Meth. U., 1934; LL.D., Tex. Christian U., 1979; m. F. Howard Walsh, Mar. 13, 1937; children—Richard, Howard, D'Ann Walsh Bonnell, Maudi Walsh Roe, William Lloyd. Pres. Fleming Found.; v.p. Walsh Found.; partner Walsh Co.; mem. Lloyd Shaw Found., Colorado Springs, Colo. Guarantor, Ft. Worth Arts Council, Ft. Worth Opera, Schola Cantorum Ft. Worth Ballet, Tex. Boys Choir Ft. Worth Theater; hon. mem. Opera Bd., hon. v.p.; co-founder Am. Field Service in Ft. Worth; mem. Tex. Commn. for Arts and Humanities, 1968-72, mem. adv. council, 1972-84; hon. bd. mem. Van Cliburn Internat. Piano Competition, Colorado Springs Day Nursery, Colorado Springs Symphony, Ft. Worth Arts Council, William Edrington Scott Theater; hon. chmn. Opera Guild Internat. Conf., 1976; 1st hon. chmn. Opera Ball, 1975; guarantor through the Walsh Found. the presentation of The Littlest Wiseman annually to City of Ft. Worth; hon. chmn. Tex. Christian U. Fine Arts Guild Spring Ballet, 1985. Recipient numerous awards, including Altrusa Civic award as 1st Lady of Ft. Worth, 1968, Streams & Valleys award, 1976-77, 78-79, 80, Opera award Girl Scouts, 1977, 78, 79; (with husband) Disting. Service award So. Bapt. Radio and TV Commn., 1972, NCCJ Brotherhood Citation, 1978, Royal Purple award Tex. Christian U., 1979; (with husband) appreciation award Southwestern Baptist Theol. Sem., 1981; (with husband) Sr. Citizen award, 1985; Med. Bldg. at Southwestern Bapt. Theol. Sem. and Library at Tarrant County Jr. Coll. N.W. named in honor (with husband); named (with husband) Patron of Arts in Ft. Worth, 1970, Edna Gladney Internat. Grandparents of 1972, spl. recognition award, Ft. Worth Ballet Assn., B.H. Carroll Founders award Southwestern Baptist Theol. Sem. Friends of Tex. Boys Choir, 1981. Mem. Ft. Worth Boys Club, Girls Service League (hon. life), Ft. Worth Children's Hosp., Jewel Charity Ball, Ft. Worth Pan Hellenic (pres. 1940), Opera Guild, Fine Arts Found. Guild Tex. Christian U., AAUW, Child Study Center, Tarrant County Aux. of Edna Gladney Home, YWCA (life), Ft. Worth Art Assn., Ft. Worth Ballet Assn. (hon. bd. dirs.), Tex. Boys Choir Aux., Round Table, Colorado Springs Fine Art Center, Am. Automobile Assn., Nat. Assn. Cowbelles, Rae Reimers Bible Study Class (pres. 1968), Tex. League Composers (hon. life), Chi Omega (pres. 1935-36), others. Baptist. Club: The Woman's (Club Fidelite). Home: 2425 Stadium Dr Fort Worth TX 76109 also 1801 Culebra Ave Colorado Springs CO 80907

WALSH, PEARL JERI LANE, editor, writer; b. Los Angeles, Nov. 9, 1914; d. John H. and Bertha (Frisch) Lane; cert. in pub. relations U. Calif. at Los Angeles, 1973; student Stanford U., 1964, U. So. Calif., 1939, Calif. State U.-Northridge, 1973; m. John Edward Walsh, Sept. 1951; 1 son, John Edward; 1 son by previous marriage, David Lane Nittinger. Tech. editor The Rand Corp., Santa Monica, Calif., 1947-50, Naval Weapons Center, China Lake, Calif., 1950-54; cons. editor Hawaiian Sugar Planters Exptl. Sta., Honolulu, 1964-65; tech. editor Mobil Research Corp., Dallas, 1967-68; tech. writer RCA Electromagnetic and Aviation Systems Corp., Van Nuys, Calif., 1968-71; free-lance editor McGraw-Hill Pub. Co., N.Y.C., 1950—; tech. writer C.E., U.S. Army, Los Angeles, 1974—; sr. writer U. Calif. Neuropsychiat. Inst. Program, Los Angeles, 1972-74; freelance supervisory editor Goodyear Pub. Co. subs. Prentice Hall Co., Palisades, Calif., 1971-80; pres. OR-Stat, Inc., Tarzana, Calif., 1960-67. Cert. travel cons.; recipient Outstanding award Naval Ordnance Test Sta., 1952; Spl. Act award Army Corps. Engrs., 1975. Mem. Soc. for Tech. Communication (sr.; publicity chmn. 26th internat. conf., mgr. nat. publicity com. 1984-85, pub. relations Los Angeles chpt. 1969—), So. Calif. Bookbuilders Assn. Publicity Club Los Angeles, Women in Communications, Am. Med. Writers Assn., Med. Mktg. Assn., Metric Assn. Author: Composition Standards, 1951; On Preparing Technical Papers, 1971. Inventor ratchet for Coxhead Varitype machine. Home: 8633 Balboa Blvd Northridge CA 91325 Office: 300 N Los Angeles St Los Angeles CA

WALSH, SUSAN FRANCES, psychiatric social worker; b. Fostoria, Ohio, Apr. 5, 1943; d. Edward Doty and Frances Elizabeth (Storey) W.; B.S., Ind. U., 1965; A.M., U. Chgo., 1968, Ph.D., 1984. Instr. social work Northwestern U. Med. Sch., also staff social worker Northwestern Meml. Hosp., Chgo., 1968-75; pvt. practice psychotherapy, Chgo., 1974—; assoc. dept. psychiatry Northwestern U. 1975—; coordinator outpatient services Inst. Psychiatry, Northwestern Meml. Hosp., 1975-85; field instr. U. Chgo., U. Ill., Chgo. Circle; lectr. U. Chgo., 1984—; pres. Susan Walsh, Ltd. Mem. Nat. Assn. Social Workers. Research on alternative to psychiat. hospitalization. Home: 3180 N Lake Shore Dr Chicago IL 60657 Office: 333 E Ontario St Chicago IL 60611

WALSH, WINIFRED CAMPBELL, former nursing administrator; b. Pawtucket, R.I., Nov. 10, 1919; d. Frank Owen and Charlotte Rose (Clark) Campbell; R.N., Roger Williams Sch. Nursing, 1940; postgrad. Yale U., 1941; m. Joseph A. Walsh, Oct. 30, 1943; children—Joseph A., Patrick F., Thomas J., E. Michael, Richard C., William A., Lawrence P. Staff nurse Homeopathic Hosp. R.I., 1940-41; head nurse Nat. Tumor Clinic, USPHS, Balt., 1941-44; supr./coordinator dept. phys. medicine and rehab. Mercy Hosp., Scranton, Pa., 1968-83; office mgr. State Auto Sales Inc., Dupont, Pa., 1983—. Vice pres., Goodwill Industries of Scranton, Inc., 1951-52; bd. dirs. Lackawanna County Welfare Council, Scranton Philharmonic Orch., Pa. Ballet Festival; active Friends of Scranton Public Library, Scranton chpt. ARC. Mem. Nat. Assn. Orthopedic Nurses (del./dir.), Orthopedic Nurses Assn., Assn. Rehab. Nurses, Nat. Assn. Female Execs., AMA Aux., Pa. Med. Soc. Aux. (treas., v.p.), Lackawanna Med. Soc. Aux. (pres.), Am. Mus. Natural History, Am. Assn. Ret. Persons, Am. Security Council Found., Irish Am. Cultural Inst., U.S. Congressional Adv. Bd. (charter), Early Am. Soc., Everhart Mus. Natural History, Sci. and Art, Smithsonian Assn., Broadway Theater League. Roman Catholic. Clubs: Scranton, Parliamentary Law, Country (Scranton); Skytop

(Pa.). Home: 337 1st St Blakely PA 18447 Office: State Auto Sales Dupont PA 18641

WALSH-JONES, PAMELA LEIGH, geologist; b. Frankfurt, W.Ger., July 1, 1957; d. William Walker and Gertraude Liebhilde (Hille) Walsh. B.S., Va. Poly. Inst., 1979; m. Malcolm Stuart Jones, June 2, 1984. With Esso Exploration, Houston, 1979-80; well logging engr. Core Labs., Houston, 1980-81, instr., Dallas, 1981-82, geologist, geochemist, Dallas, 1982—. Lutheran. Office: Core Labs Inc 1656 W Mockingbird St Suite 500 Dallas TX 75235

WALSTON, LOLA INGE, dietitian; b. Chgo., Jan. 26, 1943; d. Willy and Ingeborg (Smith) Neumann; m. Steven Ward Walston, Aug. 5, 1967; children—Bradley, Scott. B.S., No. Ill. U., 1965; M.S., U. Iowa, 1967. Registered dietitian. Asst. dietary dir. Alaska Hosp. Med. Ctr., Anchorage, 1975-78; cons. dietitian Mercer County Hosp., Coldwater, Ohio, 1979; profl. service cons. Health Care and Retirement Corp. Am., Lima, Ohio, 1981-84; dietary dir. Estes Health Care Ctr., Montgomery, Ala., 1979-80, Mercy Meml. Hosp., Urbana, Ohio, 1984—. Mem. com. Tecumseh council Boy Scouts Am., 1984. Mem. Am. Dietetic Assn., Ohio Dietetic Assn., Ohio Cons. Dietitians Health Care Facilities (chmn. 1982-84), Dayton Dietetic Assn., AAUW. Club: Hilltoppers (Fairborn, Ohio) (pres. 1982-83). Avocations: camping; sewing; knitting; crocheting; cooking. Office: Mercy Meml Hosp 904 Scioto St Urbana OH 43078

WALSTON, LYNN MAURYNE, banker; b. Indpls., Mar. 20, 1956; d. Frank, Jr. and Lula Lenora (Adams) Jameson; m. Gregory D. Walston, July 2, 1977 (div. Mar. 1985); children—Tamara J., Stacey V. Assoc. degree Ind. U., 1978; student bus. mgmt. Ind. U./Purdue U.-Indpls., part-time since 1982—. With Mchts. Nat. Bank, Indpls., since 1976—, bus. devel. officer, since 1982—, br. mgr., since 1982—, asst. v.p., since 1985—. Troop leader local Girl Scouts U.S., 1983—; vol. Planned Parenthood, Indpls., 1985—; treas. Riverside Park United Methodist Ch., 1984—. Recipient Vol. Service award Indpls. Humane Soc., 1983, Girl Scouts Just Friends Program, Indpls., 1985. Mem. Nat. Assn. Bank Women (scholar 1983, 85), Indpls. Urban Bankers, Nat. Assn. Female Execs. Democrat. Avocations: aerobics; bowling; reading. Home: 3211 N Sharon Ave Indianapolis IN 46222 Office: Merchants Nat Bank 6841 N Michigan Rd Indianapolis IN 46268

WALTER, MARY ELLEN, hardware supply executive; b. New Brighton, Pa., May 6, 1942; d. Robert C. and Louise S. (Matterness) Snyder; grad. Butler Community Coll.; married; 1 child. Sec., Fretz-Moon Tube Co., East Butler, Pa., 1960-63; sec. in advt. and fin. Am. Hardware Supply Co., Butler, Pa., 1963-75, customer service mgr., 1976—. Mem. Am. Soc. Profl. and Exec. Women, Nat. Assn. for Female Execs., Nat. Wildlife Fedn., Nat. Audubon Soc., Telecommunications Mgmt. Assn., Butler County Humane Soc., Western Pa. Conservancy, Internat. Customer Service Assn. Democrat. Roman Catholic. Home: 356G Whitestown Rd Butler PA 16001 Office: PO Box 1510 Butler PA 16003-1510

WALTER, MARY REGINA, electronics company executive, professional organization administrator; b. Balt., Jan. 13, 1947; d. Lawrence Leo and Mary Regina (Folk) Ireton; m. Philip M. Walter, Sept. 18, 1965; children—Michelle, Laura, Jennifer, Meghan. Student Stanford U., 1978, Notre Dame U., Balt., 1979-81. Vice pres., owner ASR Enterprises, Ltd., Balt., 1972—; ops. mgr. TOA Electronics, Balt., 1981—. Contbr. articles to profl. jours. Coordinator Ride-a-bike For The Retarded, Balt., 1978-80; tchr. Confrat. Christian Doctrine, Balt., 1973-78; officer Ladies of Notre Dame, Balt., 1973-76. Mem. Nat. Assn. Music Merchants, Electronics Reps. Assn., Nat. Sound Contractors Assn. Democrat. Roman Catholic. Club: Fallston. Avocations: writing poetry and short stories; family activities. Office: ASR Enterprises Ltd 8969 Yellow Brick Rd Baltimore MD 21237

WALTER, MAY ELIZABETH, retail company executive; b. N.Y.C.; d. Peter J. and Elizabeth (Shaub) W.; student NYU, Columbia U., 1920-30. Co-founder, treas., exec. v.p., vice chmn. Mut. Buying Syndicate, Inc., 1931-65; pres. Retail Marketers Advt., Inc., N.Y.C., 1966-67, cons., adviser, 1968-71. Sec., trustee, mem. exec. com. Am. Crafts Council, N.Y.C., 1962-77, hon. trustee, 1977—; adv. council Snite Mus. Art, U. Notre Dame. Recipient Salute to Women award Republican Women in Bus. and Professions, 1962. Home: 923 Fifth Ave New York NY 10021

WALTER, NOLA JANICE, rental company office manager; b. Eau Claire, Wis., Mar. 29, 1934; d. Robert Emmet and Adeline Victoria (Johnson) Rossman; student Dist. 1 Tech. Inst., Eau Claire, 1977-78; 1 dau., Rhea Carol. Exec. sec. W.H. Hobbs Supply Co., Eau Claire, 1952-54; jr. accountant C.A. Irwin Co., Eau Claire, 1954-61; legal sec. various attys. in Eau Claire, Mpls., 1963-73; office mgr. Bearson-Steinmetz Rentals, Eau Claire, 1974—; freelance artist, 1980-81. Recipient Gregg Shorthand certificate of merit, 1952, certs. of award in oil painting, 1977, 78; Gold, Silver and Bronze awards in competitive dancing, 1979, 80, 81. Mem. Nat. Wildlife Fedn., Am. Antiques and Crafts Soc., Nat. Trust for Historic Preservation, Mpls. Soc. Fine Arts, Smithsonian Assos., Am. Film Inst. Democrat. Congregationalist. Home: 825 Barland St Eau Claire WI 54701 Office: 315 E Madison St Eau Claire WI 54701

WALTERS, ANNA LEE, writer, administrator; b. Pawnee, Okla., Sept. 9, 1946; d. Luther and Juanita Mae (Taylor) McGlaslin; student U. N.Mex., 1977—; m. Harry Walters, June 1965; children—Anthony, Daniel. Dir. Navajo Community Coll. Press, Tsaile (Navajo Nation), Ariz., 1982—; contbg. author: The Man to Send Rainclouds, 1974, Warriors of the Rainbow, 1975, Shantih, 1976, The Third Woman, 1979, The Remembered Earth, 1979, American Indians Today, Thought, Literature, Art, 1981; co-author textbook: The Sacred Ways of Knowledge, Sources of Life, 1977; author: The Otoe-Missiouria Tribe, Centennial Memoirs, 1881-1981, 1981; Earth Power Coming, 1983; The Sun in not Merciful, 1985; contbr. articles to jours.; guest editor Frauen Offensive, 1978; also poet, feature writer. Office: Navajo Community Coll Press Tsaile AZ 86556

WALTERS, BARBARA, TV journalist; b. Sept. 25, 1931; d. Lou and Dena (Selett) Walters; grad. Sarah Lawrence Coll., 1953; L.H.D. (hon.), Ohio State U., 1971, Marymount Coll., 1975, Wheaton Coll., 1983; m. Lee Guber, Dec. 8, 1963 (div. 1976); 1 adopted dau. Jacqueline Dena. Formerly writer producer Sta. WNBC-TV then with Sta. WPIX and CBS-TV; joined Today Show, NBC, 1961, regular panel mem., 1963-74, co-host, 1974-76; newscaster ABC Evening News (now ABC World News Tonight), from 1976; now co-host 20/20, ABC; moderator Not for Women Only, nationally syndicated TV program; TV spls. include: Battle for the White House, 1976, Fidel Castro Speaks, 1977, A Farewell Visit with President and Mrs. Ford, 1977, Barbara Walters Specials. Hon. chmn. Nat. Assn. of Help for Retarded Children, 1970. Named to 100 Women of Accomplishment, Harper's Bazaar, 1967, 71, 200 Leaders of the Future, Time, 1974; America's 75 Most Important Women, Ladies' Home Jour., 1970, Woman of Yr. in Communications, 1974, Broadcaster of Yr. Internat. Radio & TV Soc., 1975, Woman of Yr. Theta Sigma Phi; recipient award of yr. Nat. Assn. TV Program Execs., 1975; Mass Media award Am. Jewish Com. Inst. Human Relations, 1975; Emmy, Nat. Acad. TV Arts and Scis., 1975, Matrix award N.Y. Women in Communications, 1977; Hubert H. Humphrey Freedom prize Anti-Defamation League-B'nai B'rith, 1978, others. Author: How To Talk With Practically Anybody About Practically Anything, 1970; contbr. articles to Good Housekeeping, Family Weekly, Ladies Home Jour., Reader's Digest. Barbara Walters coll. scholarship in broadcast journalism established by Ill. Broadcasters Assn., 1975. Address: care ABC 1330 Ave of Americas New York NY 10019*

WALTERS, CHRISTY CAMPBELL, state official; b. Santa Monica, Calif., Aug. 25, 1947; d. Neil F. Campbell. B.A., Smith Coll., 1969; diploma de langue francaise, Sorbonne U., Paris, 1968. Loan officer First Internat. Bank, Los Angeles, 1972-76, v.p., Hong Kong, v.p., br. mgr., Manila, Philippines, 1976-81, dir. corp. planning, Los Angeles, 1981-82; dir. Calif. Dept. Econ. and Bus. Devel., Sacramento, 1983—. Office: Calif Dept of Commerce 1121 L St Sacramento CA 95814

WALTERS, DIANNE, architect; b. Whitehall, Pa., Dec. 5, 1944; d. Merlin Paul and Margaret Roberta (Jacoby) W.; B.Arch., Va. Poly. Inst. and State U., 1967, M.B.A., 1979. Draftsman, Saunders & Pearson, Alexandria, Va., 1967-68, Bailey & Pye, Fairfax, Va., 1968-69, Cohen, Haft & Assos., Silver Spring, Md., 1969-70; instl. planner, constrn. engr. Va. Poly. Inst. and State U., Blacksburg, 1970-71; project architect H.D. Nottingham & Assos., McLean, Va., 1971-74; architect GSA, Washington, 1974-80, chief design programs br., 1980-82, dir. facilities mgmt. and support, 1982-85, dep. asst. com. design and constn., 1985—; mem. Nat. Evaluation Bd. on Architect-Engr. Selection. Recipient 2d Biennial Design award Gen. Services Adminstrn., 1975, Outstanding Performance award, 1978, 79, 83; registered architect, Va. Mem. Am. Inst. Plant Engrs., Nat. Acad. Sci., Alpha Rho Chi, Tau Sigma Delta. Author: (with others) Energy Conservation Guidelines for Existing Office Buildings, 1974. Editor: Day on Wheels, 1975. Home: 7915 Treeside Ct Springfield VA 22152 Office: General Services Administration 18th and F Sts NW Washington DC 20405

WALTERS, KAY LYNN, software devel. co. exec.; b. Big Spring, Tex., Nov. 27, 1942; d. Lesley Albert and La Verne (Holden) Clawson; B.A. in English, U. Tex., Arlington, 1974; M.B.A., So. Meth. U., 1978; children—David Ryan, Stephen Paul. Programmer, Bank of A. Levy, Oxnard, Calif., 1966-68; project leader 1st Data Processing, Big Spring, 1968-70, Results, Inc., Dallas, 1970-72; dir. application systems ENSERCH Corp., Dallas, 1973-80; mgr. devel. Performance Assos., Inc., Plano, Tex., 1980-81; v.p. Directions, Inc., Dallas, 1981—. Mem. So. Meth. U. M.B.A. Assn. Baptist. Office: 15301 Dallas Pkwy Suite 400 LB 23 Dallas TX 75248

WALTERS, LINDA ANN, nursing educator; b. Los Angeles, Sept. 3, 1940; d. Thomas and Lolita (Llora) Walters. B.S., Adelphi Coll., 1963; M.A., Columbia U., 1969; Ph.D. candidate NYU. R.N., N.Y. Pediatric sr. nurse NYU Med. Ctr., 1963-65; pediatric nurse clinician, clin. researcher Sloan-Kettering Inst., N.Y.C., 1965-67; pediatric instr. Montefiore Hosp. Affiliation, Bronx, N.Y., 1967-69; clin. nurse specialist in maternal and child health North Shore Hosp., Manhasset, N.Y., 1969-71; asst. prof. maternal and child health Bronx Community Coll., 1971-77; asst. prof. maternal and child health Pace U., Pleasantville, N.Y., 1977—; cons. research found. CUNY, 1978-79; writer Profl. Examination Service, N.Y.C., 1983—. Contbr. articles to profl. jours. Dist. bd. Health Systems Agy., N.Y.C., 1976-82; steering com. dist. bd. Comprehensive Health Planning, N.Y.C., 1973-76. Mem. AAUP, Nurses Assn. of Am. Coll. Obstetricians and Gynecologists, Nat. League Nursing, Am. Nurses Assn. (cert. in maternal and child health), Sigma Theta Tau, Delta Delta Delta. Democrat. Roman Catholic. Lodge: K.C. Office: Pace U Grad Div Nursing Bedford Rd Pleasantville NY 10570

WALTERS, MARY COON, state justice; b. Baraga, Mich., Jan. 29, 1922; d. Marvin Leonard and Nancy Claire (Conway) C.; m. Asa Lane Walters, July 9, 1952 (dec. June 1974); 1 child, Mark Richard. J.D., U. N.Mex., 1962. Bar: N.Mex. 1962, U.S. Ct. Appeals (10th cir.) 1962, U.S. Ct. Appeals (4th cir.) 1974, U.S. Supreme Ct. 1975. Practice law, Albuquerque, 1962-71, 73-79; judge N.Mex. Second Jud. dist. Ct., Albuquerque, 1971-72; judge N.Mex. Ct. Appeals, Santa Fe, 1979-81, chief judge, 1981-84; justice N.Mex. Supreme Ct., Santa Fe, 1984—. Served with WASPS, 1943-44; to 1st lt. USAF, 1951-55. Roman Catholic. Office: NMex Supreme Ct PO Box 848 Santa Fe NM 87501

WALTHER-KRAL, LUCY ENILDA, freelance consultant; b. Evanston, Ill., June 8, 1952; d. Cole Logsdon and Generosa Julia (Gordils) Walther; m. Roy A. Hamel, June 19, 1971 (div. 1981); m. 2d. Jerome F. Kral, May 15, 1982; 1 child, Natalie Amber. A.A. in Bus. Adminstrn., William R. Harper Coll., 1976, A.A.S. in Data Processing, 1981; B.S. in Bus. Adminstrn., Elmhurst Coll., 1984; postgrad. Northwestern U., 1985—. Sec., treas. Country Boys Ranch, Inc., Wheeling, Ill., 1966-72; adminstrv. asst. VRC North Lake County, North Chgo., 1972-74; adminstrv. asst. Baxter-Travenol Labs., Deerfield, Ill., 1974-75, bus. systems analyst, 1981-82, sr. info. ctr. cons., 1982—; exec. adminstr. Complete Equity Markets, Inc., Wheeling, Ill., 1976-80; freelance cons., instr., 1983—; project mgr. end-use computing services mgmt. info. systems automotive and indsl. electronics group Motorola, Inc., Schaumberg, Ill., 1984—; project leader parenteral systems Baxter Travenol Labs., Deerfield, Ill., 1985—; chmn. Travenol Personal Computer Club, Deerfield, Ill., 1982—; bldg. coordinator Travenol Crusade Mercy, Deerfield, Ill., 1983. Author: Information Center Guide to End-User Computing, 1983—; Travenol End-User Computing Newsletter. Recipient Outstanding Service award Baxter-Travenol Labs., 1982. Mem. Women in Mgmt., Am. Mgmt. Assn., Nat. Assn. Female Execs., Am. Mktg. Assn., Phi Theta Kappa. Republican. Methodist. Home: 1016 Heatherlea Dr E Palatine IL 60067

WALTHERS, MAUREEN ELIZABETH, editor; b. N.Y.C., Nov. 3; d. Thomas Michael Burns and Kathryn Elizabeth Bruce; children—John Thomas Walthers, Patricia Mack. Student pub. schs. With Ridgewood Times Newspaper (N.Y.), 1977—, editor, v.p., 1981—. Author: Our Community, Its History and People, 1976; author series: The Agony of Busheick, 1977. Vice pres. Greater Ridgewood Hist. Soc., 1975—, Greater Ridgewood Restoration Corp., 1975—; chmn. Pub. Safety Community Bd. 5, Queens, N.Y., 1977—.

WALTON, CARMELITA NOREEN, nurse; b. Chgo., Nov. 15, 1926; d. Elmo Augusta and Evelyn Mae (Terry) Desobrey; student St. Marys Coll., U. Notre Dame, 1943-45; grad. Cook County Sch. Nursing, 1949; student DePaul U., 1978-79; children from previous marriage—Michael Jerome. Head nurse, supr., nurse clinician Cook County Hosp., Chgo., 1951-71; supr. U. Chgo. Hosps./Clinics, 1963-68; dir. nursing Woodlawn Child Health Center, Chgo., 1968-69; dir. nursing prison health care Cermak Health Services, Cook County Jail, Chgo., 1973—. Recipient Superior Pub. Service award City of Chgo., 1984. Mem. Am. Nurses Assn. (cert. in nursing adminstrn., mem. Council Nursing Adminstrn.), Ill. Nurses Assn., Nat. League Nursing, Am. Pub. Health Assn., Am. Correctional Health Services Assn. Democrat. Roman Catholic. Home: 5050 LakeShore Dr S Apt 1608 Chicago IL 60615 Office: 2800 California Ave S Chicago IL 60608

WALTON, DANNA MOORE, lawyer; b. Texas City, Tex., Mar. 27, 1950; d. Dan Milton and Bennie Jo (Ellis) Moore; m. George Alan Walton, June 6, 1981; children—Jonathan Alan, Marleta Jo. B.A., Baylor U., 1971, J.D., 1974. Bar: Tex. 1974. Tchr., Alvin Ind. Sch. Dist. (Tex.), 1972; atty. Shell Oil Co., Houston, 1975-77, asst. cop. sec., 1977-81, atty., 1981—. Tchr., dir. So. Main Bapt. Ch., Houston, 1975—; pres. bd. dirs. Beckford Homeowners Assn., Houston, 1977-79. Mem. ABA, State Bar Tex., Houston Bar Assn., Houston Young Lawyers Assn., Phi Delta Phi (pres. 1977-78; Outstanding Mem. 1975). Home: 13003 Birch Grove Houston TX 77099 Office: Shell Oil Co 800 Louisiana St Houston TX 77002

WALTON, KARYL LAMONT, clin. social worker; b. Salt Lake City, Dec. 16, 1929; d. Robert Maxwell and Lucille Jane (Petersen) Lamont; B.A., U. Utah, 1951, cert. in social work, 1952, M.S.W., 1957; m. Kent L. Walton, Apr. 17, 1958; children—Kirk Lamont, Kristopher Leon, Katie Lynne. Caseworker adoption and foster care Ch. Jesus Christ of Latter-day Saints Relief Soc., 1951-56; probation officer Utah Juvenile Ct., 2d Dist., 1956-62; psychiat. social worker Family Service Soc., 1962-69, Head Start, 1965; psychiat. social worker Youth Services, 1969-70, with Dr. Thomas Hardy, Salt Lake City, 1970-80; clin. social worker pvt. practice 3rd Ave. Community Ctr., Salt Lake City, 1980—; pre-trial cons.; guest lectr. health class Hyland High Sch. Active PTA, 1967—; mem. Utah Heritage Found., 1976-78; pres. young women South 2d ward Ch. Jesus Christ of Latter-day Saints, 1959-61; bd. dirs. 3rd Ave. Community Ctr., 1984—. Mem. Nat. Assn. Social Workers (state com. licensure, recert. com. 1980-84), Phi Mu (pres. 1950-51), Lambda Delta Sigma. Home: 3068 Cascade Way Salt Lake City UT 84109 Office: 585 3d Ave Salt Lake City UT 84103

WALTON, SISTER MARA, school principal; b. Buffalo, Dec. 12, 1941; d. Joseph Dwight and Margaret Mary (Halloran) Walton. B.S. in Biology, Daemen Coll., 1965; M.A.T., Wash. State Coll., 1972; M.A. in Adminstrn., Ohio State U., 1980. Lic. tchr., N.Y.; lic. adminstr., N.Y. Tchr. sci. St. Aloysius Acad., New Lexington, Ohio, 1965-69, De Sales High Sch., Columbus, Ohio, 1979-80; tchr. sci. Buffalo Acad. of Sacred Heart, Buffalo, 1969-79, prin., 1980—; mem. N.Y. State adv. bd. Middle States Assn. of High Schs. and Colls. Named Outstanding Biology Tchr. of N.Y. State, Am. Biology Tchrs. Assn., 1973; Outstanding Young Educator, Amherst Jaycees, 1974. Mem. Nat. Sci. Tchrs. Assn., Nat. Biology Tchrs. Assn., Nat. Cath. Educators Assn. Roman Catholic. Avocations: tennis; gardening; needlepoint. Office: Buffalo Acad of Sacred Heart 3860 Main St Buffalo NY 14226

WALTON, PEGGY ANN, communications consultant, radio show host-producer, Realtor; b. Raymore, Mo., Dec. 8, 1932; d. Harry Francis and Esther (Wolf) Moneymaker. B.S. in Home Econs. cum laude, U. Nebr.-Omaha, 1954. Lic. salesman real estate, Va. Asst. dir. Dairy Council, Omaha, 1954-57; home economist Nebr. Wheat Commn., Lincoln, 1957-64; mgr. consumer info. Chem. Mfrs. Assn., Washington, 1964-81; Realtor, Shannon & Luchs, Falls Church, 1981—; exhibits coordinator-cons. Nestle Coordinating Ctr. for Nutrition, Washington, 1981—; host-producer Consumer Aware show Sta. WGTS-FM, Takoma Park, Md., 1983—; participant Internat. Trade Fair, Lausanne, Switzerland, 1959, South Am. nutritionists, 1960, Internat. Trade Fair, Cairo, 1961; product-acceptance explorer Nebr. Dept. Agr., Central and S.Am., 1962. Recipient First Place award in audio-video Am. Soc. Assn. Execs., 1979; named Friend of Extension, Dept. Agr., 1980. Mem. Am. Women in Radio and TV (nat. membership chmn. 1964-65), Am. Women in Radio and TV (Nebr. chpt. pres. 1962-64), Home Economists in Bus. (nat. sec. 1965-67, chmn. conv. program 1970), Nat. Home Fashions League (nat. sec. 1971-72, exec. v.p. 1972-73, local dir. 1967-69, Outstanding Mem. 1972), Nat. Fedn. Press Women (charter; Newsletter award 1976), Nat. Fedn. Press Women, Capital Press Women (bd. rep. 1973-74, radio award 1984), Soc. Consumer Affairs Profls.

WALTUCH, BARBARA ROSANNE, lawyer; b. New Haven, Aug. 6, 1938; d. Ben and Tillie (Schaffel) W. B.A. cum laude, So. Conn. State Coll., 1971; M.A., Columbia U., 1972; J.D., Yeshiva U., 1980. Bar: N.Y. 1981. Performer, Off-Broadway theatre, films, TV, summer stock, children's theatre and touring cos., N.Y.C., 1960-70; tchr. Kibbutz Gan Shmuel, Isreal, 1966-67, Harlem Early Childhood Ctr., N.Y.C., 1971-72, Brownsville Early Childhood Ctr., Bklyn., 1972-76; cons., lectr. CUNY, Queens, 1976-77; pvt. acting coach, also dir. classical vocal concert Alice Tully Hall, Lincoln Ctr., Bicentennial Concert, Grand Ballroom Waldorf Astoria and workshop prodns., N.Y.C., 1975-77; student def. atty. Legal Aid Soc., Bronx, N.Y., 1979-80; prin. law clk. to justice Supreme Ct. State N.Y., N.Y.C., 1981—. Contbg. author: Charges to the Jury and Requests to Charge in A Criminal Case; contbr. articles to profl. jours. Recipient acting awards European Film Festivals, 1964-65. Univ. scholar Yeshiva U., 1977-80. Mem. ABA, N.Y. State Trial Lawyers Assn., Asonia Reform Club N.Y. County. Democrat. Club: Women's City (N.Y.C.). Office: Supreme Ct State of NY 60 Centre St New York NY 100007

WALZ, BETTY MARION, personnel service executive, dental management consultant; b. Big Timber, Mont., July 23, 1934; d. Milton Sureno and Donna Marion (Chapel) Willard; m. John William Walz, Aug. 30, 1963 (div. 1977); children—Mrs. Jemell Guiles, Mrs. Shawn Hooks. Registered dental asst., Calif. Dental asst. various offices, Seattle and San Diego, 1953-75; dental office mgr. various offices, San Diego, 1975-80; dental mgmt. cons., San Diego, 1980-81; founder, pres. Profl. Fill-Ins/PFI Personnel Services, San Diego, 1980—. Mem. adv. bd. San Diego Community Coll. Dist., 1982—; leader San Diego-Imperial council Girl Scouts U.S., 1959-69; youth chmn. Jr. Women's Club, Chula Vista, Calif., 1968; vol. Flying Samaritans, 1975, 76, 82, 83. Recipient State Service award Jr. Women's Club, 1968, Girl Scouts Service award Jr. Women's Club, 1968. Mem. San Diego County Dental Assts. Soc., So. Calif. Dental Assts. Assn. (del. 1985), Am. Dental Assts. Assn., Women Bus. Owners Assn., Nat. Assn. Women Bus. Owners, Beta Sigma Phi. Republican. Mem. Religious Sci. Ch. Avocations: oil paintng; fishing; walking; travel. Home: 4201 Bonita Rd #238 Bonita CA 92002 Office: PFI Personnel Services 3737 Camino del Rio S #301 San Diego CA 92108

WANG, JOSEPHINE L. FEN, physician; b. Taipei, Republic of China, Jan 2, 1948; came to U.S., 1974; d. Pao-San and Ann-Nam (Chen) Chao; m. Chang-Yang Wang, Dec. 20, 1973; children—Edward, Eileen. M.D., Nat. Taiwan U., Taipei, 1974. Diplomate Am. Bd. Pediatrics, Am. Bd. Allergy and Immunology. Intern Nat. Taiwan U. Hosp., 1973-74; resident U. Ill. Hosp., Chgo., 1974-76; fellow Northwestern U. Med. Ctr., Chgo., 1976-78, instr. pediatrics, Chgo., 1978—; cons. Methodist Hosp. Ind., 1979—, Holy Cross Hosp., Chgo., 1978—, St. Anthony Hosp., 1985—. Mem. Am. Acad. Allergy. Office: 9012 Connecticut Dr Merrillville IN 46410 also 6815 W 95th St Oak Lawn IL 60453

WANGSGARD, LYNNDA M., librarian, dairy farmer; b. Ogden, Utah, Mar. 17, 1948; d. Samuel Lynnwood and Mildred (Masters) W. B.S., Weber State Coll., 1970; M.Library and Info. sci., Brigham Young U., 1976, M.P.A., 1983. Cert. secondary tchr., Utah. Intermural mgr. Weber State Coll., Ogden, 1969-70; fine arts librarian Weber County Library, Ogden, 1970-79, asst. library dir., 1979-85, dir., 1985—; mng. ptnr. Wangsgard Dairies, Huntsville, Utah, 1979—; del. Utah Gov.'s Conf. on Libraries, Salt Lake City, 1979; project dir. Utah Endowment for Humanities, Salt Lake City, 1979-80; mem. Utah Adv. Com. on Libraries and Info. Sci., Salt Lake City, 1980—; cons. Weber State Coll., 1983. Joint author Utah Plan for Library and Information Services, 1982. Chmn. Weber County Affirmative Action Com., 1972-76; mem. Utah Farm Bur., Salt Lake City, 1979—; bd. dirs. Weber LWV Ogden, 1983—. Recipient Beginning Profl. award Mountain Plains Library Assn., 1979, Utah Endowment for Humanities project grantee, 1978-80. Mem. ALA (council 1984-88), Mountain Plains Library Assn., Utah Library Assn. (dir. 1982-83, research award for jour. article 1983), Freedom to Read Found., Ogden C. of C. (women's council 1983—), AAUW, YWCA, Phi Kappa Phi, Phi Beta Mu. Home: 2737 Harrison Blvd Ogden UT 84403 Office: Weber County Library 2464 Jefferson Ave Ogden UT 84401

WANN, LOIS SUEL, newspaper editor, columnist, author: b. New Prague, Minn., Mar. 12, 1922; d. Arthur Joseph and Eleanor Irene (Remes) Suel; m. Eugene Charles Wann, Apr. 21, 1945; children—Eugene Charles, Arthur Suel. B.A. in English, Coll. of St. Catherine, 1943. Editor, columnist New Prague Times, 1943—, chmn. bd., 1981—; dir. Cath. Bull., St. Paul/Mpls., 1983—; chmn. bd. Suel Printing Co., 1981—. Bd. dirs. Queen Peace Hosp., New Prague, 1974-81. Mem. Press Women Minn., Nat. Assn. Press Women, St. Catherine's Alumnae Assn., Am. Legion Aux. Home: 24871 W Cedar Lake Dr New Prague MN 56071 Office: New Prague Times/Suel Printing Co 200 E Main St New Prague MN 56071

WANNEMACHER, PATRICIA COLLEEN, electrical contractor; b. Bloomington, Ill., Mar. 17, 1931; d. William and Louise (Ehrmantraut) O'Neil; m. Louis J. Wannemacher, Feb. 5, 1951; children—Steven, John, Jo Ann Reidy, Karen Arseneault. Grad. high sch., Bloomington. Ptnr., Wannemacher Electric, Bloomington, 1961-67, v.p. Wannemacher Electric, Inc., Bloomington, 1967-82, pres., 1982—. Mem. McLean County Bd., Ill., 1972-80, chmn. fin. com., 1978-80; mem. assoc. bd. Ill. Wesleyan U., Bloomington, 1984—; co-chmn. Children's Christmas Party for Unemployed, Bloomington, 1982—; mem. United Pvt. Industry Council, Pekin, Ill., Econ. Devel. Council Bloomington-Normal; mem. community bd. St. Joseph's Med. Ctr., Bloomington. Mem. McLean County C. of C. (pres. 1982-83), McLean County Elec. Contractors Assn., Ill. Assn. Women Contractors (1st v.p.). Republican. Roman Catholic. Avocations: reading, cooking, travel. Office: Wannemacher Electric Inc 210 Stillwell St PO Box 3726 Bloomington IL 61702

WARCHOL, JUDITH MARIE, secretarial service company executive; b. Chgo., Apr. 20; d. Michael Henry and Rose Therese (Vito) Schmidt Fitpold; m. Daniel August Warchol, Aug. 17, 1963; children—Kathleen Louise, Raymond Michael, Sherry Lynn. Exec. sec. N.W. Malt & Grain, Chgo., 1958-63; pres. Judy's Mailing & Secretarial Service, Northbrook, 1968—, Americano Motor Inn, Beaumont, Tex., 1976—; v.p. Golden Triangle Limo Service, Beaumont, 1982—; mng. ptnr. Warchol Investments, Beaumont, Tex., 1982—. Vice pres. Band Booster Club, Stanley Field Jr. High Sch., Northbrook, 1975-77; leader Blue Bird Group, Camp Fire Girls, Northbrook, 1971-76; bd. dirs. Stanley Field Jr. High Parent Tchr. Club, Northbrook, 1970-78; foster parent, Sierra Leone, 1978-85. Mem. Women in Mgmt., Nat. Assn. Secretarial Services, Mail Advertisers Assn., Northbrook C. of C. (bd. dirs. 1984-86). Republican. Roman Catholic. Avocations: boating; golf; tennis; fitness programs. Home: 3493 Techny Rd Northbrook IL 60062 Office: Judy's Mailing & Secretarial Service 3390 Commercial St Northbrook IL 60062

WARD, ADRIANNE GAY, nursing coordinator; b. Lubbock, Tex., Jan. 6, 1950; d. Wilson Bruhl and Gay Kathryn (Banks) Ward. B.S., Tex. Woman's U., 1972, M.S., 1979. Staff nurse The Meth. Hosp., Houston, 1972-74, head nurse, 1975-77, supr., 1979-82, nursing coordinator, staff devel. liaison Med. and Psychiat. Service, 1982—, lectr. med. seminar, 1975-78, Tex. Woman's U., 1978. Mem. Gulf Coast chpt. Kidney Found., 1972. Recipient Good Samaritan scholarship United Council Meth. Chs., 1968-72; The Meth. Hosp. Ednl. grantee, 1972. Mem. Philippine Nurses Assn. Met. Houston (mem. awards selection com. 1983), Am. Assn. Nephrology Nurses and Technicians, Sigma Theta Tau. Methodist. Office: Med Nursing Office The Methodist Hosp 6565 Fannin St Houston TX 77030

WARD, ANN TAYLOR, nurse; b. Cape Town, S. Africa, June 6, 1947; came to U.S., 1969; d. Ernest Edmund Peabody and Arline Dorothy (Kehl) Booth; m. Charles J. Taylor, Mar. 31, 1972 (div.); children—Jean-Ann, James; m. 2d, Albert E. Ward, Sept. 6, 1980. R.N., Sharley Cribb Coll. Nursing, S. Africa, 1968. Staff nurse Latter-Day Saints Hosp., Salt Lake City, 1969-73, oncology clin. coordinator, 1973-77, dir. quality assurance, 1977-80; quality assurance mgr. IHC Hosps. Inc., Salt Lake City, 1981-82; dir. Risk mgmt. and quality assurance Alta View Hosp., Sandy, Utah, 1982—; instr. Am. Cancer Soc., Salt Lake City, 1976-77. Mem. Utah Assn. Quality Assurance Profls. (treas. 1981-82, pres.-elect 1983-84), Nat. Assn. Quality Assurance Profls. Mem. Ch. of Jesus Christ of Latter-Day Saints. Office: Alta View Hosp 96605 1300 E Sandy UT 84070

WARD, CAROL ESTHER, ceramic supply company executive; b. Phoenix, Oct. 14, 1930; d. Stephen Raymond and Marjorie Edith (Taylor) Brooks; student public schs.; m. Cye Richard; children—Eileen Shepherd, Elaine Asmus, Stephen Hieb, Leslie Welson, Dawn. With Marjon Ceramic, Inc., Phoenix, 1957—, pres., owner, now chmn., chief exec. officer; condr. seminars, cons. in field; del. White Conf. Small Bus., 1980; moderator weekly bus. roundtable, 1978-79. Mem. Mayor Phoenix Com. Future Budget and Fin., 1980, Gov. Ariz. Blue Ribbon Com. Edn., 1979. Mem. Ariz. C. of C. (Small Bus. Person of Yr. award 1982), Ariz. Small Bus. Council (pres. 1979), Ariz. Ceramic Assn. (pres. 1964), Ariz. Bus. Alliance (pres. 1982), Ceramic Distbrs. Am. (pres. 1969), Nat. Ceramic Tchrs. Assn., Nat. Speakers Assn., Ariz. C. of C. (bd. dirs.), Sales and Mktg. Execs. Assn. Republican. Author: Original Designs by Carol, 1968, Ceramic Business Survival Kit, 1976; contbr. articles to profl. jours. Office: 3434 W Earll Dr Phoenix AZ 85017

WARD, CELIA AARON, clinical psychologist; b. Bklyn., Aug. 8, 1938; d. Philip and Frieda Aaron; B.B.A., City U. N.Y., 1960, M.S. in Edn., 1963; Ph.D., Yeshiva U., 1975; children—Lawrence David, Michael Jeffrey. Research asst. Yeshiva U., 1964; intern clin. psychology St. Elizabeths' Hosp., Washington, 1965-67, staff psychologist, 1967-69; mem. faculty Met. Mental Health Skills Center, The Washington Sch. Psychiatry, 1972-75; pvt. practice clin. psychology, Washington, 1967—; founder, dir. Loss Counseling Ctr. of Washington; asst. prof. George Washington U., 1982. USPHS fellow, 1964-65. Recipient Cert. of Leadership and Accomplishment D.C., State Fedn. Bus. and Profl. Women's Club. Mem. Nat. Assn. Women Bus. Owners, Washington Profl. Women's Coop., Am. Psychol. Assn., D.C. Psychol. Assn., Am. Group Psychotherapy Assn., Psychologists Interested in Study of Psychoanalysis. Home and Office: 3030 Q St NW Washington DC 20007

WARD, CHRISTINA YOUNG, public information specialist; b. Riverside, Calif., Jan. 12, 1949; d. Robert Warren Young and Charlotte Elinore (Allen) Zimmerman; m. Spencer Richard Ward, Mar. 5, 1982. A.A., Cottey Coll., 1969; B.S., U. Tulsa, 1971; postgrad. in Journalism, U. Nebr.-Lincoln, 1979-80. Cert. tchr., Oreg., Nebr. Tchr., Bellevue (Nebr.) Pub. Schs., 1972-79; researcher, assoc. producer Smeloff Teleprodns., Lincoln, 1980; franchising rep. Viacom Cablevision, Portland, Oreg., 1981-82; pub. info. officer Bur. Labor and Industries, Portland, 1983—. Bd. dirs. Ctr. Urban Edn., Portland, 1983—; active local, state, nat. polit. campaigns, 1975-78. PEO Sisterhood scholar, 1967-69. Mem. Women in Communications (dir., v.p. communications Portland 1983-84; Outstanding Service award 1983), Nat. Fedn. Local Dable Programmers, Delta Delta Delta. Office: Commissioner's Office Bur Labor and Industries 1400 SW 5th Ave Portland OR 97201*

WARD, DIANE KOROSY, lawyer; b. Cleve., Oct. 17, 1939; d. Theodore Louis and Edith (Bogar) Korosy; m. S. Mortimer Ward IV, July 2, 1960 (div. 1978); children—Christopher LaBruce, Samantha Martha; m. R. Michael Walters, June 30, 1979. A.B., Heidelberg Coll., 1961; J.D., U. San Diego, 1975. Bar: Calif. 1977, U.S. Dist. Ct. (so. dist.) Calif. 1977. Ptnr. Ward & Howell, San Diego, 1978-79, Walters, Howell & Ward, A.P.C., San Diego, 1979-81; mng. ptnr. Walters & Ward, A.P.C., San Diego, 1981—; dir., v.p. Oak Broadcasting Systems, Inc., 1982-83; dir. Elisabeth Kubler-Ross Ctr., Inc., 1983—. Pres. bd. dirs. Green Valley Civic Assn., 1979-80; bd. dirs. San Diego Mental Health Assn., Palomak-Pomerado Hosp. Found. Mem. ABA, Rancho Bernardo Bar Assn. (chmn. 1982-83), Lawyers Club San Diego, Profl. and Exec. Women of the Ranch (founder, pres. 1982—), Phi Delta Phi. Republican. Episcopalian. Club: Soroptimist Internat. (pres. chpt. 1979-80). Home: 16503 Avenida Florencia Poway CA 92064 Office: Walters & Ward 16776 Bernardo Center Dr Suite 214 San Diego CA 92128

WARD, DORIS ELIZABETH, biologist, educator, counselor; b. Charlotte N.C., Jan. 11, 1935; d. James Hopkins and Florie Kathryn Cofield; B.S., Howard U., 1966, postgrad. 1967-70; M.Ed. in Guidance and Counseling, Bowie State U., 1985; postgrad. U. Md., Summer 1985, George Washington U., 1985; m. Eddie Eugene Ward, Sept. 18, 1954; children—Eddie Eugene, Tanya Devonne, Tracia Lynnore, Tamara Elizabeth. Cert. sci. tchr. and guidance counselor, Md. Med. technician U.S. Dept. Agr., Washington, 1958-64, biol. lab. technician, Bethesda, Md., 1964-65; histologic tech. lab. instr. Howard U., Washington, 1966-67; biologist (histopathology technician) NIH, Bethesda, 1969-71; tchr. Our Lady Queen of Peace Sch., Washington, 1972-74; program analyst/mgmt. analysis IIIIS, Washington, 1974-82; career planning counselor Prince Georges Community Coll., Largo, Md., 1985—. Hospice vol.; mem. United Communities Against Poverty, Inc., 1982; developer, facilitator bereavement support ministry St. Joseph's Ch., Landover, Md., 1984; cons./vol., career counselor for transition and spl. needs populations Cerebral Palsy Assn. Prince Georges County, 1986. Recipient Tchr. Appreciation award Our Lady Queen of Peace Sch., 1974. Mem. Nat. Soc. Histotech., Am. Soc. Clin. Pathologists, Am. Assn. for Counseling and Devel., Nat. Career Devel. Assn., Chi Sigma Iota. Democrat. Roman Catholic. Home: 13003 Keverton Dr Upper Marlboro MD 20772

WARD, ERICA ANNE, lawyer, legal educator; b. Okiyama, Japan, Oct. 20, 1950; d. Robert Edward and Constance Regina (Barnett) W.; m. Ralph Joseph Gerson, May 20, 1979. B.A., Stanford U., 1972; J.D., U. Mich., 1975. Bar: Calif. 1975, D.C. 1975. Assoc. Wilmer, Cutler & Pickering, Washington, 1975-77; staff counsel U.S. Senate Ethics Com., Washington, 1977-78; exec. asst. gen. counsel U.S. Dept. Energy, Washington, 1978-79, counsellor to dep. sec., 1980; assoc. dir. energy and natural resources Domestic Policy Staff, White House, Washington, 1980-81; of counsel Skadden, Arps, Slate, Meagher & Flom, Washington, 1981—; adj. prof. law U. Mich., Ann Arbor, 1984. Editor 2 vols. Mich. Law Rev., 1975, contbr. article. Energy policy advisor Mondale for Pres., 1983-84. Recipient Outstanding Service medal U.S. Dept. Energy, 1981. Democrat. Jewish. Office: Skadden Arps Slate Meagher & Flom 919 18th St NW Washington DC 20006

WARD, ETTIE, legal educator; b. N.Y.C., Oct. 10, 1951; d. Jacob Benjamin and Hilda (Meltzer) W.; m. Alexander Rosenzweig, Nov. 13, 1977; 1 son, Robert Harry Rosenzweig. B.A., Barnard Coll., 1971; J.D., Columbia U., 1974. Bar: N.Y. 1975, U.S. Dist. Ct. (ea. and so. dists.) N.Y. 1975, U.S. Ct. Appeals (2d cir.) 1975, U.S. Supreme Ct. 1979. Assoc., Kaye, Scholer, Fierman, Hays & Handler, N.Y.C., 1974-82; asst. prof. Law Sch., St. John's U., N.Y.C., 1983—. Reporter 2d Cir. Com. Pretrial Phase of Civil Cases, 1984-86. Mem. ABA, Assn. Bar City N.Y., Fed. Bar Council. Office: St John's Univ Sch Law Grand Central and Utopia Pkwys Jamaica NY 11439

WARD, JANE ABERCROMBIE, property administration executive, consultant land systems; b. Phila., Oct. 5, 1930; d. Joseph Albert and Evelyn Holt (Harker) Abercrombie; m. Robert Dee Ward, Feb. 5, 1952 (div. 1972); 1 child, Lynda Susan. B.A., Ind. U., 1951. Sr. lease analyst Reynolds Mining Corp., Houston, 1954-62; landman Barnhart Co., Houston, 1973-77; adminstr. Pan Eastern Exploration Co., Houston, 1977-79; adminstrv. landman Kirby Exploration Co., Houston, 1980—. Author: User's Manual-Lease/Contract Information for Input, on-line computer system, 1984. Fund raiser Houston Grand Opera, 1973-74, Houston Zool. Soc., 1986, Mus. Fine Arts, Houston, 1985; tutor Literacy Advance. Mem. Am. Assn. Petroleum Landmen, Houston Assn. Petroleum Landmen, West Houston Assn. Petroleum Landmen, Nat., Houston assns. division order analysts. Democrat. Episcopalian. Avocations: classical music; bridge; word puzzles and games; baseball; numismatics. Home: 1360 Winrock #2402 Houston TX 77057

WARD, JANE PAMELA, psychiatric social worker; b. Sioux City, Iowa, Feb. 10, 1948; d. Robert James and Alice Noreen (Gullickson) Ward. B.A., Wartburg Coll., 1970; M.S.W., U. Iowa, 1975. Psychiat. therapist Community Mental Health Center of Scott County, Davenport, Iowa, 1975-76, coordinator of consultation and edn., 1976-77; dir. social work program Viterbo Coll., LaCrosse, Wis., 1977-79; asst. exec. dir., dir. social services Bremwood Luth. Children's Home, Waverly, Iowa, 1979-82; exec. dir. Three Crosses Ranch, Strawberry Point, Iowa, 1982-83; psychiat. pvt. practice and cons., 1983—; adj. prof. U. No. Iowa, Cedar Falls, 1983; asst. prof. U. Wis.-Oshkosh, 1984—; Mem. Gov.'s Commn. Planning Com. for Conf. on Children, Iowa, 1976; cons. South Central Community Justice Planning Commn., La Crosse, 1977, Viterbo Coll., 1979. Mem. Nat. Assn. Social Workers (dir. 1978-79), Bi-County Mental Health Assn. (dir. 1976), Acad. Cert. Social Workers, Nat. Registry Clin. Social Workers. Lutheran. Office: 329 Clow Faculty Dept Social Work U Wisconsin Oshkosh WI 54901

WARD, JEANNE PATRICIA, family counselor, consultant; b. Bklyn., Mar. 23, 1945; d. James Joseph and Grace Frances (Brennan) Lawton; m. Robert L. Bucher, June 11, 1966 (div. Aug. 1977); children—Barbara Anne, Laura Jeanne; m. Charles F. Ward Jr., Aug. 19, 1983. B.A. in Edn., St. Catherine's Coll., St. Paul, 1966; M.A. in Counseling and Psychology, Coll. St. Thomas, St. Paul, 1972. Tchr., Mpls. Pub. Schs., 1966-70; tchr. spl. edn. Duval County Schs, Jacksonville, Fla., 1977-79; instr. Fla. Jr. Coll., Jacksonville, 1977—; sch. counselor Duval County Schs., Jacksonville, 1979-83; pvt. practice family counseling, Jacksonville, 1983—; cons. direct mktg. tng. design and devel. Am. Transtech, Jacksonville, 1985—; founder, dir. Divorce Ministry Diocese of St. Augustine, Jacksonville, 1979-83; Fla. del. White House Conf. on Families, 1980; regular panelist WJXT, Channel 4, Jacksonville, 1982—. Author curriculum. Bd. dirs., chmn. personnel com. Child Guidance Clinic, Jacksonville, 1977—; bd. dirs. Girls Club of Jacksonville, 1981-83; chairperson Mayors Commn. on Status of Women, Jacksonville, 1985—. Mem. AAUW, Nat. Assn. Female Execs., ASTD, Nat. Council of Family Relations, Phi Delta Kappa. Democrat. Roman Catholic. Club: N.E. Fla. Soc. Parents of Visually Impaired Children (program chmn. 1985—). Home: 1651 Flager Ave Jacksonville FL 32207 Office: Am Transtech 8000 Baymeadows Way Jacksonville FL 32216

WARD, JUDITH LINDA BURTON, clinical psychologist; b. Des Moines, Apr. 20, 1953; d. Jack Duane and Carolyn Strimple Gillespie Burton; adopted dau. David Marvin Ward. B.A. in Psychology, Alma Coll., 1975; M.A. in Clin. Psychology, Marshall U., 1978. Psychology intern children's unit Community Mental Health Ctr., Huntington, W.Va., 1977; sr. therapist, adult out-patient unit Jefferson County Comprehensive Mental Health Ctr., Steubenville, Ohio, 1978-81, acting unit chief, 1981-82; prin. psychologist Martha's Vineyard Mental Health Ctr., Edgartown, Mass., 1982—; cons., condr. workshops in field. Mem. Am. Psychol. Assn. (asso.). Democrat. Office: 86 Main St PO Box 342 Edgartown MA 02539

WARD, MARGARET MOTTER, violist, violinist; b. Grand Rapids, Mich., Sept. 21, 1928; d. Gerrit and Dorris Alberta (Gilbert) VanRingelesteyn; student Mich. State U., 1946-49; Mus.B., Eastman Sch. Music, U. Rochester, 1952; m. Robert Paul Ward, June 17, 1978; children—Eva Lynne Motter, Phoebe Motter Baldini, Antonia Lee Motter, Charles Frederick Motter. Violinist, violist Grand Rapids (Mich.) Symphony, 1942-51; violist faculty quartet Mich. State U., 1947-49, Rochester (N.Y.) Philharm., 1951-53; instr. violin and viola U. N.C., Chapel Hill, 1953-56; violist Miami (Fla.) Symphony, 1962-64, LaQuartette, Miami, 1963-64; prof. violin and viola Conservatoire Nationale du Liban, Beirut and violist chamber orch. and quartet of Lebanese Conservatory, Beirut, 1964-66; pvt. tchr. violin and viola, Washington, 1967-78; instr. viola Montgomery Coll., 1970-74; violist Kennedy Center Opera House Orch., Washington, 1971—, Wolf Trap Filene Center Orch., Vienna, Va., 1971-83, Balt. Symphony, 1973-74, Am. Camerata for New Music, Wheaton, Md., 1974-85; founder, violist New Stringart Quartet, 1982-84; mem. Amateur Chamber Music Players, Inc. Mem. Alumni Assn. U. Rochester, Chamber Music Am. Home: 1101 Playford Ln Silver Spring MD 20901 Office: Opera House JF Kennedy Center Washington DC 20566

WARD, MARILYN ESTHER, marketing executive, consultant; b. Paris, Tex., Nov. 10, 1952; d. Houston Everett and Mable Esther (Rhoten) W.; m. John Joseph Sullins, Oct. 29, 1983. B.A. in Journalism, Ohio State U., 1976. Asst. editor Ohio Contractor Mag., Columbus, Ohio, 1976-77; dir. pub. relations United McGill Corp., Columbus, 1977-78; news editor Columbus Messenger, 1978-79; advt. mgr. Texocom, Inc., Garland, Tex., 1980-82; prodn. communications specialist San/Bar Corp., Garland, Tex., 1982-83; mgr. sales devel. VMX, Inc., Richardson, Tex., 1983-84, mgr. documentation systems, 1984—; cons. tech. mktg. Allard, Inc., Garland, 1982—. Author various tech. publs.; editor numerous indsl. and telecommunications articles numerous indsl., telecommunications sales brochures, pamphlets, 1976—. Mem. Soc. for Tech. Communication (sec. 1982-83), Internat. Orgn. for Women in Telecommunications, Am. Mgmt. Assn., Dallas Fine Arts Assn. Democrat. Office: VMX Inc 1241 Columbia Dr Richardson TX 75081

WARD, NANCY ELIZABETH, production executive, print consultant; b. Lima, Ohio, July 28, 1942; d. Marion Delbert Staup and Virginia Louise (Conner) Staup Meyers; m. Terry David Crider, Sept. 20, 1960 (div. 1972); children—Cristina, Heather, Jay; m. Kenneth Earl Ward, Dec. 20, 1980. Student in mktg., Edison State U., 1974-78; student in print mgmt., Cin. Tech. Coll., 1980-81. Prodn. dir. Lark Communications, Asheville, N.C., 1981-84, TMI Pub., Charlotte, N.C., 1984-85; prodn. mgr. print and advt. Uptons, Atlanta, 1985—; advisor graphics Western Carolina U., Culowhee, N.C., 1983. Prodn. dir. book: Fiberarts Design Book 2, 1982, Quiltmakers Art, 1983. Republican. Methodist. Avocations: antique collector; furniture refinishing; piano; ballet. Home: 1018 Autumn Crest Ct Stone Mountain GA 30083

WARD, NANCY P., answering service executive; b. Orange, N.J., June 14, 1938; d. Robert and Adele (Byrne) Prescott; m. Robert A. Ward, Jr., Oct. 3, 1964; children—Victoria, Jennifer, Robert, B.A., Wellesley Coll., 1960. Editorial asst. McGraw Hill Pub. Co., N.Y.C., 1960-61, Harper & Row Pub., N.Y.C., 1961-63; asst. office mgr. Hornblower Weeks/Hemphill-Noyes, N.Y.C., 1963-65; asst. sales mgr. Chemway Corp., Wayne, N.J., 1965-68; owner All Hours Answering Service (N.J.), 1968—; sec., v.p., dir. CGW Enterprises Advt. Agy., Butler, N.J., 1970—; v.p., dir. Litho Four Printing, Butler, 1970—, B.E.K., Inc., Butler and Wayne, N.J., 1970—; v.p., dir. N.J. Exchanges, Inc., Ridgewood, 1983—. Co-pres. Kinnelon Elem. Home and Sch. Assn. (N.J.), 1977-78, v.p., 1976-77; mem. Kinnelon Drug Adv. Council, 1979-82; troop leader Girl Scouts U.S.A., Kinnelon, 1982-84. Mem. Pompton Lakes C. of C., Oakland C. of C., West Milford C. of C., N.J. Mfrs. Assn. Republican. Episcopalian. Clubs: Wellesley of N.J.; Women of Smoke Rise (Kinnelon). Home: 393 Ski Trail Kinnelon NJ 07405 Office: All Hours Answering Service 817 Ringwood Ave Pompton Lakes NJ 07442

WARD, NATALIE JOY, educational consultant; b. Los Angeles, July 6, 1922; d. Leon and Bess Stromberg; B.A. magna cum laude, Pomona Coll., Claremont, Calif., 1943; M.A. with honors, Calif. State U., Los Angeles, 1956; Ed.D. with honors, UCLA, 1960; m. Oran W. Ward, June 3, 1943; children—Richard, Brian, Robert Wesley. Tchr., Pasteur Jr. High Sch., Los Angeles, 1945-56; mem. staff Los Angeles Unified Sch. Dist., 1956—, prin. Sepulveda Jr. High Sch., 1974-82, dir. instrn. region E, 1982-83; ednl. cons., 1983—; instr. Calif. State U.-Northridge, UCLA Extension; founder, counselor Choices Unltd. Mem. Futures Com. San Fernando Valley, 1981-82. Mem. Nat. Assn. Social Studies, Nat. Assn. Adminstrs. in Edn., Phi Beta Kappa, Delta Kappa Gamma, Pi Lambda Theta. Author: American History, Crisis and Conflict, 1971. Home: 1620 Pandora Ave Los Angeles CA 90024 Office: 6621 Balboa Blvd Van Nuys CA 91406

WARD, RACHEL, actress; b. Eng., 1957; m. Bryan Brown; 1 dau. Former model; movie debut in Three Blind Mice; other movies include: Night School, 1981, Sharky's Machine, 1981, Dead Men Don't Wear Plaid, 1982, The Final Terror, 1983, Against All Odds, 1984; TV miniseries: The Thorn Birds, 1983. Office: care Triad Artists Inc 16th Floor 10100 Santa Monica Blvd Los Angeles CA 90067

WARD, SALLY A(NN), state official; b. Springfield, Ill., July 9, 1951; d. Verdun and Marion L (Hult) Randolph. B.S. in Adminstrn. of Justice, So. Ill. U., 1972, M.S. in Adminstrn. of Justice, 1973. Mem. law enforcement faculty Western Ill. U., Macomb, 1973-76; budget and program analyst Ill. Bur. of Budget, Springfield, 1976-77; asst. to dir. Ill. Dept. Law Enforcement, Springfield, 1977-80; asst. to gov. State of Ill., Chgo., 1980-83; dir. Ill. Dept. of Employment Security, Chgo., 1983—; dirs. Ill. Job Tng. Coordination Council, Chgo., 1983—, Chgo. Pvt. Industry Council, 1983—; mem. cabinet Econ. Devel. Subcabinet, Springfield, 1983—; Mem. Interstate Conf. Employment Security Adminstrs. (chmn. pub. relations 1983, bd. dirs. 1985-86, mem. com. 1985-86), Internat. Assn. Personnel in Employment Security. Republican. Methodist. Office: Ill Dept Employment Security 910 S Michigan Chicago IL 60605

WARD, VENUS LORINE SAUNDERS, nursing firm executive, consultant; b. Silsbee, Tex., Oct. 29, 1923; d. James William and Esther (Frankland) Saunders; m. Frank Ward, Nov. 2, 1946; children—Frankie Lynn, VyAnn, David, Amber. Sec. cert. Cheniers Bus. Coll., 1943; lic. vocat. nurse diploma Lamar U., 1970. Medication nurse Doctors Hosp., Groves, Tex., 1970-71; intensive care nurse St. Mary's Hosp., Port Arthur, Tex., 1971-73, St. Elizabeth's Hosp., Beaumont, Tex., 1973-74; home health nurse Port Arthur Home Health, 1974-75; pvt. duty nurse Lic. Vocat. Nurse Registry Div. 31, Port Arthur, 1975-83; owner, operator Tex. Pvt. Duty Nursing, Port Neches, Tex., 1983—; cons. profl. nursing procedure. Mem. Port Neches C. of C., Retail Merchants, Greater Credit Bur. Beaumont. Democrat. Baptist. Lodge: Lions. Avocations: music; reading; swimming. Office: Tex Pvt Duty Nursing PO Box 462 Port Neches TX 77651

WARD, VIRGINIA LEE, consumer foods company executive; b. Grand Forks, N.D., Aug. 16, 1944; d. Vernol Lee Smith and Betty Louise (Scott) Perrin; m. William Edward Ward, Jr., July 23, 1977; children—Brian Scott Green, William E. Ward III, Andrew T. Ward, Wendy Helen Ward. B.S., U. N.D., 1966. Cert. tchr. Tchr. Ind. Sch. Dist. 279, Osseo, Minn., 1966-68; various mktg. mgmt. and human resource positions, IBM, 1973-81; dir. human resource planning The Pillsbury Co., Mpls., 1981-82, v.p. human resources, 1982—; trustee Voyageur Outward Bound, Mpls., 1981—; mem. human resource com. Nat. Food Processors, Washington, 1984—. Mem. benefit com. Children's Cancer Research, Mpls., 1985; fund raiser United Arts Council, St. Paul, 1985; mem. exec. com. Pillsbury PAC, 1984—; mem. Minn. Women's Polit. Campaign Fund, 1983-85. Recipient Leadership award Pillsbury Exec. Office, 1985, IBM Achievement award, 1981. Mem. Am. Soc. for Personnel Adminstrn., Am. Mgmt. Assn., Human Resource Planning Soc. (bd. dirs. 1982—, mem. exec. com., 1982—). Republican. Episcopalian. Clubs: Somerset (St. Paul); Mpls. Athletic. Avocations: backpacking, running, golfing, flyfishing, wildlife conservation. Home: 8580 Alverno Ave West Inver Grove Heights MN 55075 Office: The Pillsbury Co 2654 Pillsbury Ctr Minneapolis MN 55402

WARDEN, CAROLYN LEE, information scientist; b. Takoma Park, Md., Dec. 1, 1945; d. George Allie and Edith F. Lee; m. Joseph T. Warden, June 1, 1968; 1 son, Jeremy E.L. B.S., Furman U., 1967; M.A.T., Emory U., 1968; M.L.S., U. Western Ont., 1971. Cert. med. librarian. Library asst. U. Minn. Chemistry Library, Mpls., 1968-70; lectr. U. Western Ont. Sch. Library and Info. Sci., London, Can., 1971-72; asst. librarian, U. Calif. Biology Library, Berkeley, 1974, N.Y. State Med. Library, Albany, 1975-76; current awareness librarian Gen. Electric Corp. Research and Devel., Schenectady, 1976-77, search librarian, 1977—; mem. Chem. Abstracts Service User Council, Columbus, Ohio, 1983-86, RECON User Group U.S. Dept. Energy, 1978-81, BRS Tech. Subcom., 1977-80, N.Y.-N.J. Regional Med. Library Com. on Reference Services, 1980-82. Contbr. articles to profl. publs. U.S. Office Edn. fellow, 1967. Mem. ALA, Spl. Libraries Assn., Am. Soc. Info. Sci., Am. Chem. Soc. (div. chem. info.), Capital Dist. Library Council, Com. on Computer-Based Reference Services (chmn. 1978-79, sec. 1977-78). Office: Whitney Information Services General Electric Corp Research and Development PO Box 8 Schenectady NY 12301

WARDEN, CAROLYN MARIE, financial institution executive; b. Detriot, Oct. 29, 1956; s. William Haxton and Shirley Marie (Pressel) Warden. Student U. Heidelberg (W.Ger.), 1976; B.A., Albion Coll., 1978; postgrad. Xavier U., 1979, 83. Acct. Profl. Mgmt. Cons., Cin., 1978-79; examiner Nat. Credit Union Adminstrn., Grand Rapids, Mich., 1979-80, consumer examiner, Cin., 1980-82, fin. examiner, 1982; chief operating officer Emery Employees Fed. Credit Union, Cin., 1982-84; treas. Jefferson Bldg. and Savs. Bank, 1984-85; cons. Fedecomp, Inc., 1985—. Contbr. articles to newspapers and mags. Chmn., Kappa Alpha Theta Alumnae Philanthropies, Cin., 1980-82, editor, 1982-84. Webster scholar, 1977; Albion Coll. honor grantee, 1974-77. Mem. Cin. Profl. Mgrs. Assn. (chmn. 1982-86), Nat. Assn. Accts., AAUW. Republican. Methodist. Club: Bankers of Cin. Home: 2807 Linwood Ave Cincinnati OH 45208 Office: 3030 Clarendon Blvd Suite 300 Arlington VA 22201

WARDEN, WALDIA ANN, college president; b. New Orleans, Jan. 15, 1933; d. Walter Emmer and Lydia Eugenie (LeBlanc) W.; B.S., St. Mary's Dominican Coll., 1961; M.S. in Dietetics, St. Louis U., 1964. Joined Dominican Sisters, Congregation of St. Mary, Roman Cath. Ch., 1953; tchr. elem. schs., 1954-62; instr. foods and nutrition Dominican Coll., New Orleans, 1964-66, chmn. home econs. dept., 1966-69, asst. dean students, 1969-75, chmn. dept. home econs., 1975-78, chmn. Coll. Planning Council, 1972-76; dir. Rosaryville Center, Ponchatoula, La., 1979-81; pres. St. Mary's Dominican Coll., New Orleans, 1983—. Trustee, St. Mary's Dominican Coll., 1973-79, 83-86. Mem. La. Dietetic Assn. (editor jour. 1966-68), La. Leadership Conf. Women Religious, Am. Dietetic Assn., Am. Home Econs. Assn. Address: 580 Broadway New Orleans LA 70118

WARDINO, RAE DIANE, court administrative officer; b. Phila., Sept. 20, 1937; d. Angelo R. and Rose (DelBeato) Busillo; 1 dau., Angela Rose. A.D., St. Joseph's U., 1977, B.S., 1977. Adminstrv. asst. to med. dir. Phila. Common Pleas Ct., Phila., 1970-76, adminstr. mental health referrals, 1976—; lectr. St. Joseph's U., Phila., 1983-85; guest lectr. Pa. Assn. Probation, Parole, and Correction, The Fairmount Inst., Phila. Child Guidance Clinic, St. Joseph's U., Northeast Parents Support Group. Mem. Pa. Assn. Probation, Parole and Correction, 1984; chmn. grant com., bd. dirs. Intercommunity Action, Inc., 1972. Recipient Chapel of Four Chaplains Legion of Honor award, 1981; Service award, Northeast Parents Support Group, 1983; Meritorious Service award St. Joseph's U., 1983, Criminal Justice Alumni award, 1986. Mem. Criminal Justice Alumni (pres.), Cross Keys Fraternity (pres.). Office: Common Pleas Ct of Philadelphia Mental Health Referrals 1801 Vine St Philadelphia PA 19128

WARDLAW, KAREN NATACHA, lawyer; b. Nicholson, Ga., Oct. 8, 1939; d. Thomas Edward Watson and Helen Prescilla (Dillard) W.; m. Edward Wade Gebara, Oct. 30, 1965 (div. Apr. 1974); children—Wade Joseph, Karen Renee. B.B.A., U. Ga., 1960; J.D., Atlanta Law Sch., 1978. Bar: Ga. 1978. Claim approver John Hancock Ins. Co., Atlanta, 1960; mgmt. analyst USMC, Albany, Ga., 1960-65; tchr. Escambia County, Pensacola, Fla., 1969-70; real estate salesman Griswold Realty, Riverdale, Ga., 1973-78; sole practice law, Riverdale, 1978—. Mem. Ga. Women's Polit. Caucus. Mem. ABA, Clayton County Bar Assn., Ga. Bar Assn., DAR, UDC. Democrat. Baptist. Lodge: Order Eastern Star. Home: 7288 Monarch Dr Riverdale GA 30296 Office: 6585 Church St Riverdale GA 30274

WARD-MCLEMORE, ETHEL, research geophysicist, mathematician; b. Sylvarena, Miss., Jan. 22, 1908; d. William Robert and Frances Virginia (Douglas) Ward; B.A., Miss. Woman's Coll., 1928; M.A., U. N.C., 1929; postgrad. U. Chgo., 1931, Colo. Sch. Mines, 1941-42, So. Meth. U., 1962-64; m. Robert Henry McLemore, June 30, 1935; 1 dau., Mary Frances. Head math. dept. Miss. Jr. Coll., 1929-30; instr. chemistry, math. Miss. State Coll. for Women, 1930-32; research mathematician Humble Oil & Refining Co., Houston, 1933-36; ind. geophys. research, Tex. and Colo., 1936-42, Ft. Worth, 1946—; geophysicist United Geophys. Co., Pasadena, Cal., 1942-46; tchr. chemistry, physics, Hockaday Sch., Dallas, 1958-59, tchr. math., 1959-60; tchr. chemistry Ursuline Acad., Dallas, 1964-67, Hockaday Sch., 1968-69; geophys. cons., Dallas, 1957-77; bd. dirs. Geol. Info. Library of Dallas. Mem. Am. Math. Soc., Math. Assn. Am., Am. Geophys. Union, Seismol. Soc. Am., Soc. Exploration Geophysicists, AAAS, Soc. Indsl. and Applied Math., Am. Chem. Soc., Inst. Math. Statistics, Tex Acad. Sci. (dir.), Sigma Xi. Contbr. various articles to profl. jours.; author: China, 1983; also annotated bibliographies of sedimentary basis, 1981, 83. Home: 11625 Wander Ln Dallas TX 75230

WARDRIP, CAROL ANN, university secretary; b. Reno, Nov. 23, 1938; d. Thomas Henry and Alice Viola (Brooks) Dwyer; m. William G. Davis (dec.); 1 son, William; m. 2d, Robert Wardrip (div.); children—Jacqulyn Lee, Robert Lewis Jr. Cert. Reno Bus. Coll., 1956, UCLA Law Library Cataloging, 1966. Supervising sec. Farmers Ins. Group Br. Claims Office, Eureka, Calif., 1957-60; legal sec. various firms, Eureka, 1960-64; jury commr., law librarian, Humboldt County, Calif., 1964-66; sec., adminstrv. aide Humboldt State U. Marine Lab., Trinidad, Calif., 1966—. Recipient commendation Humboldt County Commn. on Status of Women, 1983; citation Internat. Women's Ctr., Santa Cruz, Calif., 1984. Mem. Calif. State Employees Assn. (chpt. sec. 1977-78, chpt. treas. 1983-85, newsletter editor 1978-82), Calif. Jury Commr.'s Assn. (bd. dirs.

1966), Am. Assn. Law Libraries. Democrat. Participated in legal action to ensure privacy rights for jurors, State of Calif., 1965-66. Home: PO Box 402 Trinidad CA 95570 Office: Marine Lab Humboldt State U PO Box 690 Trinidad CA 95570

WARE, CAROLYN BOGARDUS, university official and dean; b. Balt., Oct. 15, 1930; d. Eugene Wells and Carolyn Vassar (Taylor) Bogardus; m. Warren Reid Ware, Feb. 21, 1955 (div. 1960); 1 child, William Reid; m. James Rogers Garrison, Dec. 16, 1984. B.A., Western Res. U., 1952; M.Ed., U. Buffalo, 1963; Ph.D., Duke U., 1971. Cert phys. therapist. Asst. prof. phys. therapy U. N.C., Chapel Hill, 1963-66; asst. prof. anatomy SUNY-Downstate Med. Ctr., Bklyn., 1970-75; asst. dean health related professions SUNY-Buffalo, 1975-78; asst. v.p. acad. affairs SUNY-Binghamton, 1978-83; v.p. acad. affairs, dean faculty Cazenovia Coll., N.Y., 1983—; cons. N.Y. State Gerontology Ctr., Oxford, N.Y., 1983—. Recipient Sci. for Citizens grant NSF, 1981-83; teaching fellow Nat. Found., 1962-63, grad. study fellow Am. Phys. Therapy Assn./Vocat. Rehab. Assn., 1966-70; neurosci. grantee USPHS, 1976-78. Mem. AAUW, Soc. for Neurosci. Home: West Lake Rd Skaneateles NY 13152 Office: Cazenovia Coll Cazenovia NY 13035

WARE, CONSTANCE EVERETT, college administrator; b. Mineola, N.Y., Mar. 8, 1931; d. Charles Knox and Adele Constance (Shields) Everett; m. Richard Henry Ware, Sept. 26, 1953; children—Stephen Everett, Robert Francis, II, Philip Charles. B.A., Manhattanville Coll., 1952. Assoc. dir. devel. Trinity Coll., Hartford, Conn., 1974-77, dir. devel., 1977-83, v.p. devel., 1983—; lectr. Hartford Grad. Ctr., 1980—, Council Advancement and Support Edn., Washington, 1984; cons. Manhattanville Coll., Purchase, N.Y., 1985; cons. in field. Corporator Inst. of Living, Hartford, 1979—; bd. dirs. Greater Hartford ARC, 1980-84; trustee Convent Sch. of Sacred Heart, N.Y.C., 1978-82; v.p. Hartford Architecture Conservancy, 1975-83. Recipient Women in Leadership award YMCA, 1978, Vol. Recognition award United Way, 1980, Fellowship Leadership Conf. award Carnegie Found., 1978. Mem. Assn. Am. Colls. (nat. devel. com. 1978), Council Advancement and Support Edn. (participant conf. sr. devel. officers 1981), Nat. Soc. for Fund Raising Execs. (v.p. Hartford chpt. 1979-80). Republican. Roman Catholic. Clubs: University (Hartford); Princeton (N.Y.C.). Avocations: travel; tennis; gardening. Office: Trinity Coll 300 Summit St Hartford CT 06106

WARFIELD, JANET SMITH, title examiner, lawyer; b. Phila., Sept. 6, 1936; d. Norman Perry and Dorothy Imogene (Warfield) Smith; m. Alexander Stilwell Traub, III, Mar. 22, 1958 (div. May 1979); children—William Fairley, Stephen Alexander, Russell Perry. B.A., Swarthmore Coll., 1958; J.D. with honors, Rutgers U.-Camden, 1980. Bar: N.J. 1980. Research asst. Towers Perrin Forster & Crosby, Phila., 1959-61; research asst. Cumberland Advisors, Vineland, N.J., 1973-78; law clk., assoc. Cooper Perskie, April Niedleman Wagenheim & Weiss, Atlantic City, 1979-83; title examiner N.J. Realty Title Ins. Co., Toms River, 1984—. Am. Field Service exchange student, 1953. Mem. ABA, N.J. Bar Assn., Atlantic County Bar Assn., Ocean County Bar Assn., Pi Sigma Alpha. Office: New Jersey Realty Title Insurance Co 252 Washington St Toms River NJ 08753

WARFIELD, STEPHANIE ANN, artist; b. Sayre, Okla., July 31, 1953; d. Richard Lamont and Elizabeth Ann (Stout) W.; m. Gary Louis Mingle, June 3, 1978 (div.); m. Perry Walker House, Apr. 12, 1986. B.A. in Spanish, U. Tex., 1976. Cert. advt. design Art Inst. Houston. Freelance artist, Houston, 1980; prodn. artist Alphabet Publs., Houston, 1980; prodn. artist Encom Graphics, Houston, 1980-81; sr. prodn. artist Graphic Designer's Group, Houston, 1981-82; freelance artist r.e.d.h.o.t.s., Houston, 1982—; tchr. Houston Community Coll., 1982—; prodn. artist Houston City Mag., 1984—; ptnr., co-owner 2-d, design collaborative, Houston, 1985. Mem. NOW, 1982; mem., sponsor Christian Children's Fund, 1982—. Recipient award of Merit Design Schs. Internat. Design Conf., Aspen, Colo., 1980; Silver award Houston Advt. Fedn., 1980; Outstanding Achievement award Art Inst. Houston, 1980. Mem. Art Dirs. Club of Houston.

WARFORD, AUDREY MAE, account executive; b. Morristown, N.J., Dec. 9, 1945; d. Harold Crispin and Lucille Martha Chiancone. B.A., Montclair State Coll., 1967, M.A., 1971. Tchr. home econs. Union County Regional High Sch. Bd. Edn., 1967-69, Jonathan Dayton Regional High Sch., Springfield, N.J., 1970, 72; jr. mktg. research analyst Colgate Palmolive, N.Y.C., 1972; sales rep. Consumer Paper Product Westvaco, Los Angeles, 1973-77, with Paperboard Packaging Sales div., N.Y.C., 1977-84; account exec. Champion Internat. Corp., N.Y.C., 1984—; dir. Tiana Bay Apt. Owners, Hampton Bays, L.I., 1983-85. Mem. N.Y. State Senate Task, Manhattan, 1981—. Mem. Women in Sales. Republican. Home: 401 E 77th St New York NY 10021 Office: 805 3d Ave New York NY 10022

WARGOTZ, HELEN, psychoanalyst; b. N.Y.C., July 17, 1921; d. Louis and Eva (Weinglass) W.; m. Joseph De Marco, July 4, 1942. B.A., Hunter Coll., 1942; M.S.W., Columbia U., 1946. Case worker foster home dept. Jewish Child Care Assn., N.Y.C., 1946-47, psychiat. social worker VA Mental Hygiene Clinic, N.Y.C., 1947-48; 1st case worker mental retardation clinic Flower Hosp. Mental Hygiene Clinic, N.Y.C., 1950-51; psychiat. social worker Youth Bd. Pub. Sch. 140, L.I., 1951-52; family counselor Jewish Family Service, 1952-55; psychoanalytic psychotherapist L.I. Cons. Ctr., 1955-57; individual and group counselor N.Y. Guild for Jewish Blind, 1957-58; individual and group psychoanalytic psychotherapist, lectr., chmn. speakers' bur. Jamaica Ctr. for Psychotherapy (now Advanced Ctr. for Psychotherapy), 1958-68; psychoanalytic group therapist Mental Health Inst. N.Y.C., 1959-60; chief psychiat. social worker, supr., faculty Children's Clinic, N.Y. Sch. Psychiatry, 1962-63; individual and group counselor Shield David Sch. and Clinic, N.Y.C., 1966-69; chief psychiat. social worker 5th Ave. Ctr. for Counseling and Psychotherapy, N.Y.C., 1968-72; tng. psychoanalyst, faculty, supr., Tng. Inst. for Mental Health Practitioners, 1972-75; cons. N.Y. State Bur. of Disability Determinations, N.Y.C., 1974—; cons. Headstart, 1966; dir. profl. services Allied Teen-Age Guidance and Adult Counseling Service, N.Y.C., 1964—; team mem. evaluating children needing spl. edn. com. Handicapped, 1975—; supr. group therapy T. Reik Clinic, 1956-64; condr. parent edn. course Ft. Lee Adult High Sch., 1966-67; cons. Legal Aid Soc.; cons. on retirement Am. Mgmt. Assn. and various unions; radio and TV panelists. lectr. religious and sch. groups. Columnist: Teen Facts and Parent Strategy, L.I. Graphic Roosevelt Press; contbr. chpts. to book, textbook, articles to publs. Internat. profl. adv. com. Parents Without Partners, 1967—; pres., group discussion leader Club at 92d St., N.Y.C., 1967-68. Workshop fellow N.J. Montclair State Coll., 1966; Inst. for Curriculum in Adminstrn. of Community Mental Health Services fellow, 1971-73. Mem. Council of Psychoanalytic Psychotherapists (charter). Club: City of N.Y. (social welfare, health and hosp. coms. 1958—). Home: 510 E 86th St New York NY 10028

WARING, STAR LEE, lawyer; b. Misawa, Japan, Apr. 27, 1951; d. Robert Charles and Gwendolyn (Snapp) Waring; m. James Lloyd Kincaid, Sept. 27, 1981; 1 child, Andrew James. B.A., U. Colo., 1973; postgrad. U. Wis. Law Sch., 1976-77; J.D., U. Colo. 1979. Bar: Colo., 1979. Assoc. atty. Hall & Evans, Denver, 1979-81, Nossaman, Krueger & Knox, Denver, 1981-83; assoc. atty. Wagenlander & Assocs., Denver, 1983-85; of counsel Hayes & Phillips, Denver, 1985—; instr. water law Arapahoe Community Coll., Littleton, Colo., 1982; cons. atty. Sierra Club Legal Def. Fund, Denver, 1983-86. Recipient Am. Jurisprudence Book award-Contracts, Bancroft-Whitney, 1977, Am. Jurisprudence Book Award-Wills and Trusts, 1978. Mem. Colo. Bar Assn. (publs. com. 1983-84), Denver Bar Assn. Democrat. Presbyterian. Office: 1350 17th St Suite 450 Denver CO 80202

WARING, VIRGINIA, publisher, musician; b. Dinuba, Calif., Oct. 18, 1915; d. M. Rene and Elma (Merritt) Clotfelter; m. Livingston Hawley Gearhart, Feb. 28, 1940 (div. 1953); 1 child, Paul Alexander; m. Frederic Malcolm Waring, Dec. 2, 1954; 1 child, Malcolm Merritt. B.A. and B.Mus., Mills Coll., 1937; piano student of Robert Casadesus, Paris, 1937-39. Mem. 2-piano team Morley & Gearhart, 1940-53; owner Interior Design Assocs., East Stroudsburg, Pa., 1962-68; creative costume designer Fred Waring's Pennsylvanians, 1969-83, asst. condr. and master of ceremonies, 1980-83; chmn. bd. Fred Waring Enterprises, Delaware Water Gap; pres., owner Shawnee Press, Inc., Delaware Water Gap, Pa., 1983—; artistic dir. Fred Waring Summer Workshop, Pa. State U., 1985. Founding bd. dirs. Child Help U.S.A., 1965—; pres. bd. trustees Joanna Hodges Piano Competition, Palm Desert, Calif., 1983, 84, 85; bd. dirs. Palm Valley Sch., Palm Springs, Calif., 1967, 68, 69; founding bd. dirs. Pocono Arts Ctr., Stroudsburg, Pa., 1965-75. Mills Coll. scholar, 1934, 35, 36, 37; Fleischman Trustee Fund scholar, 1937-39. Mem. Am. Soc. Interior Designers, Music Pubs., Ch. Music Pubs. Assn., ASCAP. Republican. Avocations: needlework; tennis; golf. Home: The Gatehouse Shawnee-on-Delaware PA 18356 Office: Shawnee Press 1 Waring Dr Delaware Water Gap PA 18327

WARLICK, LANA STARNES, lawyer; b. Charlotte, N.C., Sept. 18, 1951; d. Marshall Cleveland and Dorothy Nell (Wright) Starnes; m. Robert Logan Warlick, Sr., Oct 14, 1979. A.B., U. N.C.-Chapel Hill, 1973, J.D., 1976. Bar: N.C. 1976. Ptnr., Ellis, Hooper, Warlick, Waters & Morgan, Jacksonville, N.C., 1976—. Mem. ABA, N.C. Bar Assn. (exec. council family law sect. 1981-84), N.C. Acad. Trial Lawyers (patron Raleigh 1983—). Democrat. Methodist. Clubs: Jacksonville (pres. 1981-82), Jr. Women's N.C. Home: 206 Aldersgate Rd Jacksonville NC 28540 Office: Ellis Hooper Warlick Waters & Morgan 313 New Bridge St Jacksonville NC 28541

WARMBRODT, EVELYN LORRAINE, nurse, educator; b. Dunkirk, N.Y., Nov. 28, 1925; d. Charles Henry and Maude Mary (Schrader) Schafer; m. William Walter Warmbrodt, June 18, 1949; children—Kenneth, Frederick, Sarah, Kurt. B.S. in Nursing Edn., U. Buffalo, 1951. R.N., N.Y. Head nurse Milliard Fillmore Hosp., Buffalo, 1947-48, Brooks Meml. Hosp., Dunkirk, N.Y., 1965-70; clin. instr. Boces Practical Nursing Sch., Dunkirk, 1970-71, Jamestown Sch. Practical Nursing (N.Y.), 1971—. Pres., 1st United Presbyn. Ch. Women's Assn., Dunkirk, 1965-66; clk. of session 1st United Presbyn. Ch., 1977-83. Mem. Am. Nurses Assn., NEA, Nat. Assn. United Presbyn. Women (life). Democrat. Club: Shorewood Country of Dunkirk (women's golf capt. 1981-83). Home: 5004 Morewood Rd Dunkirk NY 14048 Office: Jamestown Sch Practical Nursing Jamestown NY 14701

WARNATH, MAXINE AMMER, management consultant, educator; b. N.Y.C., Dec. 3, 1928; d. Philip and Jeanette Ammer; m. Charles Frederick Warnath, Aug. 20, 1952; children—Stephen Charles, Cindy Ruth. B.A., Bklyn. Coll., 1949; M.A., Columbia U., 1951, Ed.D., 1982. Lic. psychologist, Oreg. Various profl. positions Hunter Coll., U. Minn., U. Nebr., U. Oreg., 1951-62; asst. prof. psychology Oreg. Coll. Edn., Monmouth, 1962-77; assoc. prof. psychology, chmn. dept. psychology and spl. edn. Western Oreg. St. Coll., Monmouth, 1978-83, dir. organizational psychology program 1983—; cons., dir. Orgn. Research and Devel., Salem, Oreg., 1982—. Mem. Oreg. Psychol. Assn. (pres. 1980-81, pres.-elect 1979-80, legis. liaison 1977-78), Am. Psychol. Assn. (com. pre-coll. psychology 1970-74), Western Psychol. Assn. Office: Orgn Research and Devel 708 Rural Ave S Salem OR 97302

WARNER, CAROLYN, state education official; b. Aug. 5, 1930. Supt. public instrn. State of Ariz., 1974—. Mem. Ariz. Bd. Edn., Ariz. Bd. Regents, Council on Econ. Edn., Govtl. Commn. on Environment, Gov.'s Adv. Com. on Mgmt. Mem. Council of Chief State Sch. Officers, Western Correctional Assn. Clubs: Phoenix Execs., Democratic Women's. Office: 1535 W Jefferson Phoenix AZ 85007*

WARNER, CHARLENE WALLACE, publisher, editor, producer, director; b. Richmond, Va., Nov. 24, 1945; d. Charles and Carolease (Ballow) Wallace; m. Dennis Anthony Garrick Warner, June 8, 1968; children—Tarik, Thandi, Dia. B.A., Howard U., 1967; postgrad. studies U. W.I., Jamaica, 1968-69. Market research Carribean Research, Jamaica, 1969-70; market research coordinator Colgate, Palmolive, Jamaica, 1970-72; market research mgr. Nestles, Jamaica, 1972-77; owner, operator Cafe d Attic, Jamaica West, 1977-78; pub., editor Popcorn Mag., Richmond, Va., 1979-85; producer, dir. Popcorn Publs., Richmond, 1985—. Author: (songs) Depression, Hello Rainbow. Producer, dir. TV spl. Children of the Bahamas, 1985, TV programs Collector's Corner, Children's Corner. Recipient Outstanding Child Advocate, Delver Women's Club, 1982, Outstanding Service in Bus. award 31st Street Ch., 1982, Outstanding Child Advocate, State of Va., 1982-83, Outstanding in Youth Employment award Urban League, 1983. Mem. Am. Mktg. Assn., Carribean Market Research Assn., Richmond Media Soc., Am. Pubs. Assn., Am. Editor's Assn., Alpha Kappa Alpha. Anglican. Home: 9301 Carlway Ct Richmond VA 23228 Office: Popcorn Publ Corp 208 S Robinson St Richmond VA 23220

WARNER, CYNTHIA J., educator; b. East Chicago, Ind., Feb. 3, 1955; d. James and Eula (Freeman) W. A.A., Evansville U., 1974; B.S., Calumet Coll., 1978, Teaching Cert., 1980; postgrad. Ind. U. Tchr., Hammond High Sch., Ind. State sec. NAACP, East Chicago, 1968-69.. Mem. Alpha Kappa Alpha (pres. 1983—). Methodist. Home: 2808 E 141st St East Chicago IN 46312 Office: Hammond High Sch 5926 Calumet Ave Hammond IN 46320

WARNER, NAOMI RUTH, licensing consultant; b. N.Y.C., Nov. 6, 1939; d. Robert Louis and Lillian (Weinberg) Bernstein; m. Neil Warner, July 9, 1961; children—Juliet, James. A.B., Boston U., 1961; cert. interior design, N.Y. Sch. Interior Design, 1962; master fine arts cert. Ecole des Beaux Arts, Paris. Interior designer Naomi Shilkret Interiors, N.Y.C., 1966-72; prin. Naomi Warner Assocs., N.Y.C., 1972-74; publicity dir. Nandy Knits, N.Y.C., 1974-77, licensing dir. Harry N. Abrams, Inc., N.Y.C., 1977—; tchr. Parsons Sch. Design, N.Y.C., 1983, 84; lectr. Am. Women's Econ. Devel. Corp., N.Y.C., 1983. Mem. Licensing Industry Assn. (bd. dirs. 1981-84), Fashion Group. Home: 327 Central Park W New York NY 10025 Office: Harry N Abrams Inc 100 Fifth Ave New York NY 10011

WARNKEN, VIRGINIA MURIEL THOMPSON, social worker; b. Anadarko, Okla., Aug. 13, 1927; d. Sam Monroe and Ruth L. (McAllister) Thompson; A.B., Okla. U., 1946; M.S.W., Washington U., 1949; m. Douglas Richard Warnken, Sept. 16, 1957; 1 son, William Monroe. Med. social cons. Crippled Children's Services, Little Rock, 1950-54; supr. VA Hosp., Little Rock, 1954-55; asst. prof. U. Tenn. Sch. Social Work, Nashville, 1955-57; dir. social services N.Y. State Rehab. Hosp., Rockland County, 1957-58; asst. prof. U. Chgo. Sch. Social Service Adminstrn., 1958-59; free lance editor, 1960—; instr. evening div. Coll. of Notre Dame, Belmont, Calif., 1967-68; asso. Mills Hosp., San Mateo, Calif., 1978—; med. aux. Community Hosp., Pacific Grove, Calif., 1980—. Com. mem. C. of C. Miss Belmont Pageant, 1971-86, co-chmn., 1975-78. U.S. Children's Bur. scholar, 1947-49. Mem. Assn. Crippled Children and Adults (dir. 1952-55), Assn. Mentally Retarded (dir. 1953-55), Am. Assn. Med. Social Workers (practice chmn. 1954-55), Nat. Assn. Social Workers (dir. 1962-66), Acad. Cert. Social Workers, Am. Assn. Med. Social Workers, Nat. Rehab. Assn., Am. Psychol. Assn., Am. Orthopsychiat. Assn., Council Social Work Edn. Democrat. Presbyterian. Clubs: Carmel Valley Golf and Country, Peninsula Golf and Country, Monterey Golf and Country (Palm Desert, Calif.). Author: Annotated Bibliography of Medical Information and Terminology, 1956. Address: 1399 Bel Aire Rd San Mateo CA 94402

WARNS, MARIAN KINCAID, labor relations arbitrator, psychology educator; b. Louisville, Oct. 3, 1923; d. Horace L. and Laura (Law) Kincaid; B.A., U. Louisville, 1944, M.Ed., 1972, Ph.D., 1976; m. Carl Arthur Warns, Jr., Sept. 14, 1946. Asst. tng. dir. Richard Store Co., Miami, Fla., 1947-48; personnel and tng. dir. Kaufman Straus Co., Louisville, 1948-52; tchr., asst. coordinator Ahrens Trade High Sch., 1952-56; personnel, tng. dir. H.P. Selman Co., 1956-57; research asso. in arbitration Carl A. Warns Jr., 1957-64; indsl. psychology cons. Raymond Kemper & Assos., 1970-72; instr. psychology U. Louisville, 1972-76, adj. prof. indsl. psychology, 1983—; pvt. practice labor relations arbitrator, 1971—. Mem. Nat. Acad. Arbitrators (gov.), Am. Psychol. Assn., Am. Soc. Tng. Dirs., N.Y. Acad. Scis., Mortar Bd., Phi Kappa Phi, Psi Chi. Episcopalian. Contbr. articles in field to profl. jours. Home and Office: 312 Brunswick Rd Louisville KY 40207

WARREN, BONNIE, editor, writer; b. South Africa, Oct. 22, 1934; d. John Willis and Della Ruth (West) Warren; 1 son, Nathan Earl. Editorial rep. Better Homes and Gardens, New Orleans, 1968—, Woman's Day, 1976—; contbg. writer New Orleans Mag., 1967-77, columnist Around the Belt, 1967-77, editor, 1977-78; instr. creative writing for publ. Women's Center, Loyola U., New Orleans, 1976-78. Bd. dirs. Cultural Attractions Fund; mem. women's com. New Orleans Philharmonic Symphony Soc.; bd. dirs. France La. Festival; adv. com. Ponchartrain Mental Health Center, 1982—. Mem. New Orleans Art Assn. (pres.), New Orleans Mus. Art, Nat. Fedn. Press Women, Press Club New Orleans, Women in Communications, Nat. Writers Club. Recipient 1st place trophy New Orleans Press Club, best feature story, 1972, best sports column, 1971. Home and Office: 3652 River Oaks Dr New Orleans LA 70114

WARREN, DEBRA LYNN, social worker; b. Great Lakes, Ill., Sept. 22, 1960; d. Robert Ellis and Julia Marie (Brugioni) Warren; m. James Edward Schelinski, July 30, 1983. B.A. in Psychology, Lake Forest Coll., 1981, B.A. in Sociology and Anthropology, 1981; M.A., U. Chgo., 1983, postgrad. 1983—. Cert. social workers, Ill. Therapist/intake coordinator Bradley Counseling Ctr., Lake Villa, Ill., 1983-85; dir. North Suburban Counseling & Therapeutic Services, Lake Bluff, Ill., 1985—; cons. mem. Cons. Resource Assn., Lake Forest, 1985—. Co-author: (with Virginia Smiley) screenplay, Robots, 1986. Vol. coordinator Dem. Com. to Re-elect the Pres., Highland Park, 1980; religious edn. instr. St. James Ch., Highwood, Ill., 1979—; vice chmn. Youth Service Network, Gurnee, Ill., 1985-86, chmn., 1986—; bd. dirs. Lake County Domestic Violence Task Force, Waukegan, 1984—; bd. dirs. centennial com. City of Highwood. Mem. Acad. Cert. Social Workers, Nat. Assn. Social Workers, Ill. Soc. Clin. Social Work, Nat. Assn. Female Execs., Nat. Registry of Health Care Providers in Clin. Social Work. Democrat. Roman Catholic. Office: North Suburban Counseling & Therapeutic Services 11 N Skokie Hwy Lake Bluff IL 60044

WARREN, JANE ANNE, savings and loan executive; b. Glendale, Calif., Apr. 14, 1949; d. Edward John and Kathryn Marie (Hart) Hrinsin. Ed., Southington, Ohio pub. schs. Credit and collections mgr. Zales Jewelers, Paramus, N.J., 1976-79; credit coordinator Wyo. Nat. Bank, Casper, 1979-80; credit mgr. Provident Fed. Savs., Casper, 1980—. Founding dir. Surrey Ridge Townhouse Assn., Casper, 1983. Mem. Credit Women Internat. (pres. 1985-86, Credit Woman of Yr. 1985), Internat. Credit Assn. (bd. dirs. 1986). Republican. Avocations: scuba diving; rock climbing; skiing. Office: Provident Fed Box 1850 Casper WY 82602

WARREN, JEAN ELIZABETH, hospital executive; b. Phila., May 17, 1930; d. William Lawrence and Julia Evelyn (Bell) Hall; m. George Howard Warren Mar. 4, 1949 (div. Apr. 1962); children—Bruce Eric, Andrienne Lynn. Managerial Studies cert., Hofstra-Cornell Univs., 1979. Telephone operator N.Y. Telephone Co., Bklyn., 1952-61; telephone operator N.Y.C. Health and Hosp. Corp., Jamaica, N.Y., 1961-67, clinic supr., 1967-69, adminstrv. asst., 1969-74, acting asst. dir. grants, N.Y.C., 1974-76, Women, Infants and Children's program dir., Jamaica, 1976—; mem. health adv. bd. South Jamaica Ctr. for Children and Parents, 1978—. Recipient Significant Service award South Jamaica Ctr. for Children, 1978, 80, 84, Merit cert. N.Y. State Assembly, 1982; Recognition award Queens Hosp. Ctr., 1982. Mem. Nat. Assn. Female Execs., N.Y. State Women Infant Children's Assn. Democrat. Lutheran. Avocations: travel; cooking; sewing; swimming. Office: Queens Hosp Ctr WIC Program 114-02 Guy R Brewer Blvd Jamaica NY 11434

WARREN, JUDITH B., legal secretary, paralegal service executive, educator; b. Tuscaloosa, Ala., Dec. 29, 1943; d. Ezra Cantrell and Mary Virginia (Roberts) Beason; m. Lamar Wesley Warren, 1962; children—Richard Lamar, Randall Lee. Diploma, Alverson Draughon Coll., 1962; student Arapahoe Community Coll., 1972-73. Cert. profl. legal sec. Legal sec., Gulfport, Miss., 1968-71, Denver, 1971-72; legal asst., sec. to judge Dist. Ct. (2d jud. dist.) Colo., 1972-78; owner, mgr. Southwest Secretarial Service, Denver, 1978—; instr. Met. State Coll., Denver, 1979-83, paralegal adv. bd., 1978-83; instr. Arapahoe Community Coll., Littleton, Colo., 1974-79, paralegal adv. bd., 1973—; mem. paralegal adv. bd. Denver Paralegal Inst., 1978-82; instr. Program for Advanced Profl. Devel., Denver, 1973-79, Career Legal Secretarial Inst., Tulsa, 1984. Judge, Future Bus. Leaders of Am., Denver, 1984. Mem. Nat. Assn. Legal Secs., Denver Legal Secs. Assn. (Legal Sec. of Yr. 1981, pres. 1980-81), Colo. Legal Secs. (corr. sec. 1979-80, Legal Sec. of Yr. 1984), Nat. Assn. Legal Assts. (charter), Legal Assts. Colo. (charter, sec. 1977-78). Methodist. Home: 5333 S Jellsion St Littleton CO 80123 Office: Southwest Secretarial Service 5353 W Dartmouth Suite 303 Denver CO 80227

WARREN, JUNE ROCHELLE, state official; b. Detroit, Mar. 23, 1935; d. Frank J. and Lula B. Warren; B.S. in Occupational Therapy, Wayne State U., Detroit, 1959. Rehab. counselor, So. Calif., 1966-71; rehab. supr. Calif. Dept. Rehab., 1971-75, asst. dist. adminstr., 1975-76, dist. adminstr., Riverside, 1976-79, Los Angeles, 1979-81, asst. to dep. dir. adminstrv. services, Sacramento, 1981-82, chief rehab. engring. sect., 1983-85; chief of centralized services, field operation div., 1985—; mem. Los Angeles County Commn. Disabilities, 1979-81. Mem. Nat. Rehab. Assn., Nat. Rehab. Counselor Assn., Alpha Kappa Alpha. Methodist. Home: 8963 Amoruso Ave Fair Oaks CA 95628 Office: 830 K St Mall Sacramento CA 95814

WARREN, KENDRA S., computer systems programmer and analyst; b. Champaign, Ill., Aug. 28, 1954; d. Kenneth E. and Pat E. (Miduri) W.; m. James Robert Russell, Apr. 27, 1984. Cert. NSF Summer Linguistics Inst., No. Ariz. U., 1971; B.A. in Anthropology, Wright State U., 1975; postgrad. in info. mgmt. Wright State U., 1984—; also certs. from various U.S. Air Force and computer vendor tng. classes. Investigator, Smith & Schnacke, Attys. at Law, Dayton, Ohio, 1973-76; claims investigator State Farm Fire & Casualty, Dayton, 1976-79; computer programmer U.S. Air Force, Wright-Patterson AFB, Ohio, 1981-85, computer systems analyst, 1985—. Author application software, packages for use in vol. activities. Coordinator disaster vols. ARC, Dayton, 1979-84, chmn. disaster services, 1984—; precinct capt., mem. central com. Montgomery County Republican Party, Ohio, 1977-79, ward leader, mem. exec. com., 1979-81, also active election campaign coms., 1974-82; bd. dirs. Wright-Patterson AFB chpt. ARC, 1983—. Recipient citation for service Ohio Ho. of Reps., 1982. Sustained Superior Performance award USAF, 1983, 85, Disting. Service award Greater Dayton Jaycees, 1984; scholar NSF Summer Linguistics Inst., Flagstaff, 1971. Mem. Nat. Assn. Female Execs., Assn. Women in Computing.

WARREN, KIM LOREEN, marketing executive; b. Cedar Rapids, Iowa, Jan. 15, 1956; d. James Douglas and Saundra Jean (Foggy) Plotz. B.S. in Microbiology, U. Ariz., 1978; M.B.A., Northeastern U., Boston, 1986. Terr. mgr. Dart-Kraft, Inc., Glenview, Ill., 1979-81, No. New Eng. account mgr., 1982-83, Boston account mgr., 1983-84; mktg. mgr. Pauls Distbrs., Inc., Canton, Mass., 1985—. Editor, The Scoop newsletter, 1986. Mem. Fine Arts Mus., Com. to Elect Senator John Kerry, Boston, 1984, Com. to Elect City Councilman Dennis Quilty, Boston, 1982; mem. Bay Village Neighborhood Assn., Boston, 1983-86. Mem. Frozen Food Assn. New Eng. (exec. com.). Democrat. Christian. Club: New Eng. Backgammon. Avocations: piano; skiing; windsurfing. Home: 12 Melrose St Boston MA 02116 Office: Paul's Distbrs Inc 5 Whitman Rd Canton MA 02021

WARREN, LINDA CAROL, lawyer; b. Mt. Clemons, Mich., July 11, 1956; d. Robert Custer and Jeanette (Wattinger) Warren; m. J. William Edwards, Aug. 18, 1978. B.A., Memphis State U., 1978, J.D., 1981. Bar: Tenn. 1981. Legis. intern Tenn. Gen. Assembly, Nashville, 1978; staff atty. Memphis Area Legal Services, 1981-83; ptnr. Robilio, Less and Warren, Memphis, 1983—; instr. Shelby State Community Coll., Memphis, 1983—. Bd. dirs. Girls Club of Memphis, 1983-84; mem. Coalition for Econ. Justice for Women, Memphis, 1983-84. Mem. Memphis Bar Assn., Shelby County Assn., Grey Panther S. Democrat. Presbyterian. Home: 1551 Hope St Memphis TN 38111

WARREN, RITA SIMPSON, manufacturing company executive; b. Borger, Tex., Jan. 17, 1949; d. William D. and Bobbie J. (Hindman) S.; m. Harry E. Warren, Jr., June 10, 1978. B.A. in Sociology, U. Tex., 1977; M.B.A., North Tex. State U., 1982. Vice pres communications Tetra Pak Inc., Dallas, 1977-85; v.p. mktg. Devex Inc., Dallas, 1986—. Recipient various awards Dairy and Food Industries Supply Assn., 1979, 84, Soc. Visual Communication, 1979, Dallas Ad League TOPS, 1984. Mem. Pub. Relations Soc. Am., Internat. Assn. Bus. Communicators, Jaguar Owners Assn. S.W. (co-pres. 1979-83). Republican. Club: Tex. T Register (MG). Avocations: classic European automobiles, vintage racing, gardening. Office: Devex Inc Suite 1040 12720 Hillcrest Rd Dallas TX 75230-2010

WARRINGTON, BONNIE, legal assistant; b. Portland, Oreg., Nov. 30, 1930; d. Virgil F. and Lillian A. (Falconer) Baldwin; student U. Calif., 1949-52, U. Calif., Santa Barbara, 1976-79; children—Tracy Paul, Harry Wallace, Virgil Dennis. Coordinator family services USAF, Tex., Fla., Calif. and Wash., 1955-63; owner Secretarial Dispatch, Simi Valley, Calif., 1963-69; mgr. Simi Valley Western Union Office, 1964-67; substitute tchr. aide Simi Valley Unified Sch. Dist., 1967-69; with Youth Services City of Simi Valley, 1970-84; legal asst., 1984—. Bd. dirs. Ventura County Coalition Against Household Violence; mem. Simi Valley Women's Info. Network; chmn. Ventura County Commn. Human Concerns; mem. status of women adv. com. Ventura County Community Coll. Dist.; v.p. Ventura County Women's Commn. Friends. Recipient Woman of Yr. award Simi Valley C. of C., 1969; Woman of Yr. award Simi Valley Kiwanis Club, 1972; Silver Beaver award Boy Scouts Am., 1977; Nat. Adult Service award Camp Fire Girls, 1984. Mem. Channel Cities

Legal Assts. Assn., U. Calif.-Santa Barbara Alumni Assn. Address: PO Box 372 Simi Valley CA 93062

WARSHAUER, SANDRA CLAIRE, controller; b. Houston, Oct. 23, 1945; d. Raymond W. and Carolyn (Cotton) Thompson; m. Larry D. Lindemann, Nov. 22, 1975 (div. Aug. 1983); children—Aniesha Carol, Katy Marie; m. Philip Richard Warshauer, Nov. 3, 1984. Student Stephen F. Austin State U., U. Houston, Los Angeles City Coll. Office services dir. Maness Broome & Assocs., C.P.A.s, Temple, Tex., 1976-78; advt. mgr. Heck & Co., Temple, 1978-79; acct. Greenstein Logan & Co., Temple, 1979-81; pvt. practice acct., Temple, 1981-83; controller Minimax Research Corp., Berkeley, Calif., 1984—; acctg. cons. V & W Tool & Die, Inc. Mem. Profl. Secs. Internat., Nat. Assn. Female Execs., Am. Mgmt. Assn., Am. Electronics Assn. Republican. Baptist. Avocations: art; gourmet cooking; fishing; camping; travel. Home: 5335 San Simeon Pl Castro Valley CA 94552 Office: Minimax Research Corp 2150 Kittredge St Berkeley CA 94704

WARSHAVSKY, SUZANNE MAY, lawyer; b. N.Y.C., July 22, 1944; d. Charles F. and Charlotte (Ceaser) Goldman; m. Mordechai Warshavsky, June 7, 1964; children—Oren, Adam, Claire. B.A., Vassar Coll., 1965; J.D. cum laude, NYU, 1968. Bar: N.Y. 1968, U.S. Ct. Appeals (2d cir.) 1972, U.S. Supreme Ct. 1973. Assoc. atty. Dewey Ballantine Bushby Palmer & Wood, N.Y.C., 1968-73; assoc. Milgrim Thomajan Jacobs & Lee, P.C., N.Y.C., 1973-76; founder, prin. Warshavsky, Hoffman & Cohen, P.C., N.Y.C., 1976—; arbitrator Small Claims Ct., N.Y.C., 1975—. Mem. ABA, N.Y. State Bar Assn., City Bar N.Y., N.Y. Women's Bar Assn., Mag. Pubs. Assn. (legal affairs com. 1985—), Am. Arbitration Assn. (panel of arbitrators 1976-77). Home: 158 Gates Ave Montclair NJ 07042 Office: 500 Fifth Ave New York NY 10110

WARWICK, DIONNE, singer; b. East Orange, N.J., Dec. 12, 1941; m. Bill Elliott (div. 1975); 2 sons. Ed., Hartt Coll. Music, Hartford, Conn. As a teen-ager formed Gospelaires; then sang background for rec. studio, 1966; debut, Philharmonic Hall, N.Y. Lincoln Center, 1966; appearances include, London Palladium, Olympia, Paris, Lincoln Center Performing Arts, N.Y.C.; records include I'll Never Love This Way Again; albums include Valley of the Dolls and Others, 1968, Promises, Promises, 1975, Dionne, 1979, Then Came You, Friends, 1986; screen debut The Slaves, 1969, No Night, So Long, also, Hot! Live and Otherwise co-host; TV show Solid Gold; host: A Gift of Music, 1981; star: Dionne Warwick Spl. Recipient Grammy awards, 1969, 70, 80. Address: care Triad Artists Inc 10100 Santa Monica Blvd Los Angeles CA 90067

WARWICK, MARY ELLEN, chemical company executive; b. New Brunswick, N.J., Nov. 7, 1960; d. Frederick John and Barbara Ann (Cleary) Harris; m. John J. Warwick III, Mar. 17, 1984. B.A. in Econs. and Fin., Fairfield U., 1982. Conv. service mgr. Hyatt Hotels, New Brunswick, 1983-84; purchasing coordinator Cleary Chem. Corp., Somerset, N.J. 1984—. Mem. U.S. Soc. Notaries, Nat. Assn. Female Execs., Nat. Assn. for Women Bus. Owners, U.S. C. of C. Democrat. Roman Catholic. Avocations: photography; golf; needlepoint; cooking; travel. Home: 201 Kingsberry Dr Somerset NJ 08873 Office: W A Cleary Chem Corp 1049 Somerset St Somerset NJ 08873

WASHABAUGH, CATHERINE ANGELA BECKER, petroleum engineer; b. Detroit; Mar. 22, 1960; d. Julius Adrian and Julia (O'Sullivan) Becker; m. Thomas Robert Washabaugh, May 28, 1983. B.S. in Geol. Engring., Mich. Tech. U., 1982. Petroleum engr. Mich. Pub. Service Commn., Dept. Commerce, Lansing, 1982—. Mem. Mich. Basin Geol. Soc., Soc. Petroleum Engrs., Nat. Assn. Female Execs. Roman Catholic. Avocations: piano; triathlete; skiing; hiking; ballet; travel. Home: 8089 Miller Rd Swartz Creek MI 48473

WASHBURN, CLAUDIA ANN, biotech agriculture seed company research administrator, survey researcher; b. Hammond, Ind., June 27, 1948; d. Ivan Michael and Geraldine Pearl (Lewandowski) Krapac; m. Mark Fisher Washburn, Dec. 21, 1968. B.S., U. Ill., 1971, M.S., 1974. Lic. real estate sales. Various positions U. Ill. Survey Research Lab., Champaign, 1968-76; project mgr. Decision Making Info., Santa Ana, Calif., 1976-77; pres., owner The Research Place, Inc., Champaign, 1977-79; dist. office mgr. Dept. of Commerce U.S. Bur. of Census for 1980, Urbana, Ill., 1979-80; research assoc. U. Ill. Campus-wide Research Services Office, Champaign, 1980-81, exec. asst., Soviet Interview Project, 1981-84; mgr. research adminstrn. United AgriSeeds, Inc., Champaign, 1984—. Mem. Central City Commn., Champaign. Mem. ACLU, NOW, Twin Cities Bus. and Profl. Women (mem. various coms.), Am. Assn. Pub. Opinion Research, Am. Mktg. Assn. (sec., central Ill. chpt. chmn. publicity, chmn. spl. projects, bd. dirs. 1984—), Champaign-Urbana Personnel Adminstrs., Soc. Research Adminstrs. Democrat. Club: Champaign County Executive (mem. research com. 1984-85). Avocations: camping, canoeing, gardening, friends. Home: 1910 Stratford Dr Champaign IL 61821 Office: United AgriSeeds Inc PO Box 4011 Champaign IL 61820

WASHBURN, SUSAN LYNN, college administrator; b. Rahway, N.J., Apr. 13, 1951; d. Frank Edgar and Marie Josephine (Greene) W.; m. Christopher W. Talbot, Feb. 26, 1977 (div. 1983). A.B. in English and Latin, Franklin and Marshall Coll., 1973; M.S. in Indsl. Mgmt. and Mktg., Clarkson U., 1980. Asst. dir. devel. Franklin and Marshall Coll., Lancaster, Pa., 1973-74; coordinator corp. and found. support St. Lawrence U., Canton, N.Y., 1974-77; v.p. devel. Centenary Coll., Hackettstown, N.J., 1977-79; dir. devel. Evergreen State Coll., Olympia, 1979-85, dir. coll. relations and devel., 1983-85, v.p. devel. and adminstrv. services, 1985—; pub. speaker on fundraising and mktg. in higher edn., career devel., women's topics, time mgmt., and grantsmanship. Assoc. editor F&M Today, 1973-74 (Council for Advancement and Support Edn. First Place award tabloid category 1974); sr. editor The Centenarian, 1977-79; pub. Evergreen ReView, 1979-85. Mem. exec. bd. Franklin and Marshall Alumni Council, 1977-81; mem. Thurston County Econ. Devel. Council; bd. dirs. Olympia Downtown Devel. Assn., SAFEPLACE: Rape Relief/Women's Shelter Services. Mem. Council for Advancement and Support Edn. (mem. faculty Summer Insts. in Ednl. Fund Raising, 1980-81, chair dist. VIII conf., 1981, treas. dist. bd. dirs., 1980-84, chair-elect 1984-86, chair 1986-87), Olympia/Thurston County C. of C., Lacey C. of C., Northwest Devel. Officers Assn. Avocations: bicycling; hiking and backpacking; reading; gardening. Home: 4117 Park Dr SW Olympia WA 98502 Office: Evergreen State Coll Olympia WA 98505

WASHBURN-OSBORN, DAISY MARIE, missionary foundation executive; b. Merced, Calif., Sept. 23, 1925; d. Christopher Columbus and Clara Irene (Otis) Washburn; m. T.L. Osborn, Apr. 5, 1942; children—Marie LaVon (dec.), T.L. (dec.), LaDonna Carol Osborn-Nickerson, Mary Elizabeth (dec.). Student pub. schs., Los Banos; L.H.D., Bethel Christian Coll., 1983; D.D., (hon.), Zoe Coll., 1983. Co-founder, exec. adminstr., dir. overseas projects, pres. Osborn Found. (internat. missionary ch. orgn.), Tulsa, 1948—; speaker confs., convs., seminars. Internat. advisor and lifetime patron Christian Women's Fellowship Internat.; bd. regents Bethel Christian Coll. Office: PO Box 7572 Tulsa OK 74170*

WASHINGTON, BARBARA BUCKLEY, public relations specialist; b. Greenwood, Miss., Jan. 26, 1951; d. Luther B. and Cozetta (White) Buckley; m. Arthur M. Washington, June 5, 1971; children—Lynn Michelle, Celia Roxanne, Arthur Michael, Jr. B.A. in English, Spelman Coll., 1972. Traveling teller C.&S. Nat. Bank, Atlanta, 1970-71; reporter AP, Atlanta, 1972-77; sr. pub. info. specialist Ga. Power Co., Atlanta, 1977-81, editorial supr., 1981-85, sr. media programs specialist, 1985—. Mem. exec. bd., v.p. Arts Festival Atlanta, Inc.; asst. sec., bd. dirs. Atlanta Area Services for the Blind, United Way Met. Atlanta. Mem. Women in Communications. Democrat. Methodist. Club: Spelman Coll. Alumnae (pres. Atlanta 1980-82). Home: 1501 S Gordon St SW Atlanta GA 30310 Office: Georgia Power Co 333 Piedmont St PO Box 4545 Atlanta GA 30310

WASHINGTON, CAROL JUNE, labor department administrator, graphic artist; b. Freeport, N.Y., July 4, 1935; d. Bradford Martin and Marie Rose (Pizza) Critchley; m. Sam M. Ackerman, Mar. 12, 1954 (div. Sept. 1967); children—Joseph, Valerie, David; m. Samuel Robert Washington, Dec. 23, 1971 (dec. May 1978). B.S., Adelphi U., 1977, M.S.W., 1978. Prodn. mgr. Citizen Newspaper, Chgo., 1962-70; tng. coordinator SCLC/Com. for One Soc., Chgo., 1968-70; graphic artist Enlightment Press, N.Y.C., 1972-73; dir. program devel. Colony South Bklyn., 1973-79; dir. grants mgmt. N.Y. State Dept. Labor, Albany, 1980—; cons. numerous polit. campaigns, 1963—; Founder, dir. Chgo. Women's Liberation Ctr., 1968-70. Mem. NAACP, ACLU, Amnesty Internat., Nat. Women Polit. Caucus. Democrat. Jewish. Avocations: literature; writing; painting; graphics, theater. Home: 50 Morris St Albany NY 12208 Office: New York State Dept Labor Bldg 12 State Campus Albany NY 12240

WASHINGTON, CLOTEE WOODRUFF, job developer; b. Cleveland, Miss., May 3, 1947; d. Booker T. and Florida M. (Green) Woodruff; m. Robert Leflore, May 21, 1966 (div. Mar. 1976); 1 child, Vietta; m. David W. Washington, Apr. 6, 1979; 1 child, Rynetta. A.A., Coahoma Jr. Coll., 1971; student U. Miss., 1971-72, Miss. Valley State U., 1972-74, Delta State U., Cleveland, Miss., 1974-77. Ctr. adminstr. Bolivar County Project Headstart, Cleveland, Miss., 1966-78; exec. job developer Miss. Delta Council, Rosedale, 1979—; mem., cons. Bolivar County Welfare Council, 1983—; coordinator community services Miss. Delta Council, Rosedale, 1985—. Mem. Pace Election Commn., Miss., 1984-86; sec. Pace Voters League, 1985-86; research person Martin Luther King Elem. Sch. PTA, 1985-86; pub. relationist Delta Pace Planning for Tomorrow Club, 1985-86. Mem. Nat. Assn. Female Execs., Nat. Businesswomen Assn. Democrat. Baptist. Avocation: community service. Home: PO Box 188 507 Magnolia St Pace MS 38764 Office: Miss Delta Council 703 Bradford St Rosedale MS 38769

WASHINGTON, CONNIE MAY HENDERSON, public administrator; b. Chgo., June 3, 1934; d. Harold Edgar and Lillian Carrie (Haynes) Henderson; m. George Washington, Apr. 7, 1956; children—Sharon Maria, Matthew Anthony. B.A., Chgo. State U., 1981, M.S., 1984. X-ray technician U. Ill. Med. Ctr., Chgo., 1954-58; real estate property mgmt., Chgo., 1958-64; casework supr. Cook County Hosp., Chgo., 1964-67; with Chgo. Housing Authority, 1967—, program developer, 1981—. Mem. AAUW, Nat. Assn. Female Execs., Am. Forum for Internat. Study, Chgo. Archtl. Found., Nat. Assn. Housing and Redevel. Ofcls., Am. Correctional Assn., Phi Alpha Theta. Home: 7951 S Harvard Ave Chicago IL 60620 Office: Chgo Housing Authority 22 W Madison St Chicago IL 60602

WASHINGTON, JANICE CATCHINGS, accountant; b. Jackson, Miss., May 3, 1953; d. Roosevelt Benjamin and Willie Celeste (Dixon) Catchings; m. Allen Harold Washington, Aug. 5, 1978. B.S. in Acctg., Jackson State U., 1975; M.B.A., Ariz. State U., 1977. C.P.A., Ariz. Fin. mgmt. trainee Honeywell Info. Systems, Phoenix, 1975-77, fin. supr., 1977-79; fin. analyst Intel Corp., Phoenix, 1979-80, mktg. adminstrv. supr., 1981-83, mktg. adminstrv. mgr., 1983-85; owner J.C. Washington, C.P.A., Phoenix, 1985—; trustee First Instl., Phoenix, 1984—, cons., 1985. Recipient for #1 Customer Service, Intel Corp., 1984. Mem. Ariz. Soc. C.P.A.s, Black Women's Network (treas. 1983-84), Am. Inst. C.P.A.s, Jackson State U. Alumni Assn. (treas. 1977-79), Delta Sigma Theta (pres. 1978-79). Baptist. Avocations: bicycling, reading, dancing. Office: JC Washington CPA 3310 E Dahlia Dr Phoenix AZ 85032

WASHINGTON, JOYCE GUYNETH, roofing company executive; b. Turkey, Tex., Dec. 17, 1938; d. Ciecl Alven Edwards and Dovie A. (Couch) Basch; m. Raymond Elder Washington, Dec. 19, 1953; children—Joyce Kathleen, Charles Ray, Deloris Jane, Harold Blain, Linda Floreen, Alford Eugene. Owner, bookkeeper Washington Roofing Co., Lafayette, Oreg., 1970—. Democrat. Mem. Ch. of Christ. Clubs: Mem. Am. Assoc. Builders and Contractors, Home Builders Assn. Avocations: Stained glass, organ music, theatre. Home: Route 2 Box 153 Ash St Dayton OR 97114 Office: Washington Roofing Co 624 3rd St PO Box 518 Lafayette OR 97127

WASHINGTON, LINDA M., computer executive, marketing specialist; b. Savannah, Ga., Mar. 7, 1955; d. Joe Lee and Richardean (Williams) W. B.S., Savannah State Coll., 1975; M.S., Howard U., 1979; postgrad. George Washington U., 1982. Cert. computer scientist. Instr. Singer Link Div., Silver Spring, Md., 1977-79, programmer IBM, Manassas, Va., 1979-80; mktg. specialist Computer Scis. Corp., Rosslyn, Va., 1980-83; sr. systems cons. Wang Labs., Inc., Bethesda, Md., 1983-84, select mktg. rep., 1984—. Minister of music Hunter Meml. A.M.E. Ch., Suitland, Md., 1985—. Mem. Nat. Acad. Computer Scientists, Delta Sigma Theta (v.p. Savannah 1983—). Avocations: tennis; racquetball; backgammon; piano; music. Home: 2406D S Walter Reed Dr Arlington VA 22206

WASHINGTON, LINDA MARIE, production editor; b. Chgo., Apr. 26, 1960; d. Preston and Susie Lee (Edwards) W. B.A., Northwestern U., 1981; postgrad. in journalism Roosevelt U. Editorial asst. Commerce Clearing House, Inc., Chgo., 1981-83, prodn. editor ABA, Chgo., 1983—. Mem. AAUW, Nat. Assn. Female Execs. Democrat. Baptist. Home: 11712 S Laflin Chicago IL 60643 Office: Am Bar Assn 750 N Lake Shore Dr Chicago IL 60611

WASHINGTON, PATRICIA LEATREAL, educator, consultant; b. Md., Apr. 30, 1947; d. William Howard and Dorothy Lee Long; m. Robert Levi Reed, July 4, 1967 (dec. 1969); m. Lindsay Washington, Oct. 2, 1976; 1 child, Ryan Lewis. M.A. in Adminstrn. and Supervision, Morgan State U., 1977. Tchr. Balt. City Pub. Schs., 1967-69, 72-81, tchr. gifted children, 1981—; tchr. pvt. sch., Balt., 1969-72, cons. gifted and talented, 1982-85. Author curriculum unit: William Shakespeare, 1984, Drug Abuse Education, 1985. Dir-at-large Provinces Civic Assn., 1978-80. Recipient Tchr. of Yr. award NEA, 1971; Funds for Ednl. Excellence grantee, 1986. Mem. NEA, State Md. Internat. Reading Assn., Olympics of the Mind Assn., Nat. Assn. Gifted Children. Democrat. Baptist. Club: Bridge (v.p. 1980-84). Lodge: Eastern Star. Avocations: tennis; swimming; chess; ice skating; coin collecting.

WASHINGTON, VIVIAN EDWARDS, social worker, former govt. ofcl.; b. Claremont, N.H., Oct. 26, 1914; d. Valdemar and Irene (Quashie) Edwards; A.B., Howard U., 1938, M.A., 1946, M.S.W., 1956; m. George Luther Washington, Dec. 22, 1950; 1 son, Valdemar Luther. Tchr., guidance counselor, sch. social worker, asst. prin., prin. Edgar Allan Poe Sch. Program for Pregnant Girls, Balt., 1939-73; cons. Office Adolescent Pregnancy Programs, HEW, Washington, 1978-80, program devel. specialist, 1980-81; exec. dir. Balt. Council on Adolescent Pregnancy, Parenting and Pregnancy Prevention Inc., 1982—; cons. to adolescent parents. Bd. dirs. Nat. Alliance Concerned with Sch.-Age Parents, 1970-76, pres., 1970-72; bd. dirs. YWCA, Balt., 1966-69, United Way Central Md., 1971-80; bd. visitors U. Balt., 1978-80; adv. commn. on social services City of Balt., 1978-85; chmn. Md. Gov.'s Commn. on Children and Youth, 1972-77. Recipient Alumni award Howard U. Sch. Social Work, 1966; Clementine Peters award United Way, 1980; Sojourner Truth award Nat. Bus. and Profl. Women, 1979; Vashti Turley Murphy award Balt. chpt. Delta Sigma Theta, 1981; Balt.'s Best Blue and Silver award, 1983, Pvt. Sector Vol. Service award Pres. Reagan, 1984; Paul Harris fellow Balt. Rotary, 1985; United Way Community Service award, 1985. Mem. Nat. Assn. Social Work, LWV, Nat. Council Negro Women (life), Balt. Urban League, Balt. Mus. Art, Delta Sigma Theta (nat. treas. 1958-63, Las Amigas service award Balt. chpt. 1973). Democrat. Episcopalian. Club: Pierians. Contbr. articles to profl. jours. Home: 3507 Ellamont Rd Baltimore MD 21215

WASHINGTON-MORRIS, JOYCE ANN, insurance company executive; b. Fulton, Ky., Oct. 16, 1950; d. Thomas Dock and Lula Mae (Minor) Morris; m. Leroy Gill, June 15, 1968 (div. 1972); m. Eddie Earl Washington, Feb. 14, 1982; children—Latyana, Kai. Claim service rep. Allstate Ins. Co., St. Louis, 1971-73, property adjuster, 1973-75, operation and claim service supt., San Ramon, Calif., 1975-79, claim trainer, 1979-80, unit mgr., San Jose, Calif., 1980-84, dist. claim mgr., Daly City, Calif., 1984—. Exec. dir. Concerned Black Citizens, Fulton, Ky., 1970; founding mem., officer Black Adoption Agy., Oakland, 1980; mem. Bay Area USO, San Francisco, 1985. Mem. San Francisco Claim Mgr. Forum. Democrat. Avocations: sports; camping; outdoor activities; reading. Home: 8315 Ney Ave Oakland CA 94605 Office: Allstate Ins Co 375 Serramonte Plaza Daly City CA 94015

WASINGER, VIRGINIA LEE, quality engineer; b. Paris, Tex., Sept. 21, 1932; d. Theo Lee and Elizabeth Virginia (Cartter) White; B.B.A., Tarleton State U., 1978; children—Janet Wasinger Dickson, James, Richard, Lee Anne, Cynthia. Counselor, Nat. Bus. Con., Dallas, 1969; indsl. relations mgr. Voltaic Internat. Corp., 1969-71; property mgr. Sky-Harbour Lake Property, Granbury, Tex., 1974-75; owner Granbury Picture Framing, 1973-76; quality engr., documentation specialist Brown & Root Constrn., Glen Rose, Tex., 1979-83; quality assurance engr. UE&C, N.H., 1983—; pres. V-W Inc. of Del. Mem. Am. Assn. for Quality Control. Home: PO Box 129 Church and Warnock Bluffdale TX 76433 also PO Box 7057 Hampton NH 03842

WASKO, SUSAN NANCY, tax lawyer; b. Phila., Apr. 3, 1952; d. Stanley Joseph and Claire D. (Woodson) W. Student U. Salzburg (Austria), 1970-72; B.S. in Fgn. Service, Georgetown U., 1975; J.D., Gonzaga U., 1979; LL.M. in Taxation, U. Miami (Fla.), 1980. Bar: Pa. Law clk. Wash. State Atty. Gen.'s Office, Spokane, 1978-79; assoc. Alexander & Milne, Phila., 1980-83; tax law specialist, Office Assoc. Chief Counsel (Tech.) IRS, Washington, 1983-86; atty. Dist. Counsel IRS, Las Vegas, 1986—. Contbr. notes to Gonzaga Law Rev., 1978, editor spl. issue, 1979. Law Rev. Scholar, Gonzaga U., 1978-79. Mem. ABA, Fed. Bar Assn., Pa. Bar Assn., Phila. Bar Assn., Women's Bar Assn. D.C. Office: Dist Council IRS 550 E Charleston Blvd South Bldg Las Vegas NV 89104

WASOWICZ-PRINGLE, LIDIA CHERIE, editor, reporter; b. Krakow, Poland, Apr. 3, 1951; came to U.S., 1960, naturalized, 1967; d. Kazimierz and Janina (Wronska) Wasowicz; m. Douglas Hall Pringle, Nov. 13, 1982; 1 child, Alexandra Judith. B.A. with honors, U. Utah, 1973. Reporter, Deseret News, 1970-72; intern Salt Lake City Tribune, 1972, copy editor, 1972-73; UPI reporter, Salt Lake City, 1973-75; news reporter, broadcast editor Pacific div. UPI, San Francisco, 1975-78, news reporter, editor, 1978-81, Calif. desk editor, div. desk editor, 1982-83, Pacific Div. Sci. editor, 1983—. Rotary Club scholar, 1969; Russel S. Marriott scholar, 1969-73; Westminster Coll. Honors at Entrance scholar, 1969-70; Minute Women scholar, 1970-71; Maude May Babcock scholar, 1971-72; Sherwood Music Sch. scholar, 1969-73; Outstanding Calif. Journalist award, 1979; award for outstanding coverage Mt. St. Helens Volcano, 1980; UPI award for outstanding coverage of drug abuse in Marin County, 1980; 1st place competition in news reporting Peninsula Press Club, 1981, 1st place in investigative reporting, 1983, Cert. of Merit for splty. Story, 1984; 1st place feature writing competition Calif. State Fair, 1981; award for outstanding investigative reporting on Calif. prisons, 1981; Stanford U. and NEH profl. journalism fellow, 1981-82; 1st place Lincoln Steffens Journalism award for investigative reporting, 1984. Mem. Women in Communications, Mortar Board, Internat. Platform Assn., Smithsonian Assocs., Planetary Soc., Astron. Soc. Pacific, Phi Beta Kappa, Kappa Tau Alpha, Sigma Delta Chi (sec.-treas. 1972-73). Democrat. Roman Catholic. Author (with others): Violence in the 60's, 1972. Home: 949 Via Casitas Greenbrae CA 94904 Office: 1390 Market St San Francisco CA 94102

WASS, HANNELORE LINA, educational psychologist; b. Heidelberg, Ger., Sept. 12, 1926; came to U.S., 1957, naturalized, 1963; d. Herman and Mina (Lasch) Kraft; B.A., Tchrs. Coll., Heidelberg, 1951; M.A., U. Mich., 1960, Ph.D., 1968; m. Irvin R. Wass, Nov. 24, 1959 (dec.); 1 son, Brian C.; m. 2d, Harry H. Sisler, Apr. 13, 1978. Tchr., W.Ger. Univ. Lab. Schs., 1958-60; faculty U. Mich., Ann Arbor, 1958-60, U. Chgo. Lab. Sch., 1960-61, U. Mich., 1963-64, Eastern Mich. U., 1965-69, prof. ednl. psychology U. Fla., Gainesville, 1969—; cons., lectr. in field. Mem. Am. Psychol. Assn., Gerontol. Soc., Internat. Work Group Dying, Death and Bereavement, Forum Death Edn. and Counseling, Nat. Council on Aging, Fla. Council on Aging. Methodist. Author: The Professional Education of Teachers, 1974; Dying-Facing the Facts, 1979; Death Education: An Annotated Resource Guide, 1980; Helping Children Cope With Death, 1982, 2d edit., 1984; Death Education: An Annotated Resource Guide, vol. 2, 1984; Childhood and Death, 1984; founder, editor Death Studies, bi-monthly jour., 1977—; cons. editor Ednl. Gerontology, 1977—, Hemisphere Pub. Corp. subs. Harper & Row; contbr. articles to profl. jours. Home: 6014 NW 54 Way Gainesville FL 32606 Office: 1418 Norman Hall Univ Fla Gainesville FL 32611

WASSERMAN, CECILLE GOLDBERG, performing arts adminstrator; b. Boston, Nov. 19, 1934; d. William and Frances (Green) Goldberg; m. Herbert Wasserman, May 20, 1956; children—Julia A. (dec.), Emily A., Stefanie J., Wendy. B.S., Simmons Coll., 1955; postgrad. Juilliard Sch., 1983. Librarian, N.Y. Pub. Library, N.Y.C., 1955-60; lectr., coordinator Hunter Coll., N.Y.C., 1973-76; publicist Sarah Lawrence Coll., Bronxville, N.Y., 1977, Am. Symphony Orch., N.Y.C., 1979-81; exec. producer Music from Japan, N.Y.C., 1981—; pres. The Wasserman Office, N.Y.C., 1983—. Nat. bd. mem. Stress in Families Project, Harvard-NIMH, 1978-79; cons. Bd. Edn., N.Y.C., 1982. Illustrator: Letters from Helga, 1970. Bd. dirs. Performance Theatre Ctr., N.Y.C., 1979—; trustee Harrison (N.Y.) Pub. Library, 1970-72, The Emelin Theatre, Mamaroneck, N.Y., 1977-80; del. 1984 Democratic Nat. Conv. Mem. Women in Communication, Assn. Classical Music. Jewish. Office: The Wasserman Office 128 E 56th St New York NY 10022

WASSERMAN, ELEANOR ALMA, travel company executive; b. Southington, Conn., June 15, 1921; d. Gustave and Martha Helene (Mathof) Peltner; m. John Wasserman, Sept. 24, 1938; children—Nancy, John. Grad. exec. mgmt. travel program, Wellesley Coll., 1984. Travel organizer The Stanley Works, New Britain, Conn.; with World Wide Travel Service, Inc., New Britain, 1968—, pres., 1970—. Home: 472 Stanley St New Britain CT 06051 Office: World Wide Travel Service 117 W Main St New Britain CT 06051

WASSERMAN, ELVIRA, psychiatrist, psychotherapist; b. N.Y.C.; d. Charles W. and Zena (Berlin) W.; A.B., Hunter Coll., 1933; M.D., Women's Med. Coll. Pa., 1938; cert. N.Y. Sch. Psychiatry, 1962, Postgrad. Center for Mental Health, 1965; children—James G. Wallach, Lewis R. Wallach. Intern, Wilkes Barre (Pa.) Gen. Hosp., 1938-39; resident Creedmoor State Hosp., N.Y.C., 1959-62, supervising psychiatrist, 1962-65; practice medicine specializing in psychiatry, psychoanalysis and hypnoanalysis, N.Y.C., 1959-76, specializing in family, marital and child therapy, West Palm Beach, Fla., 1976—; asst. prof. guidance and counseling L.I.U., 1972-76; med. dir. Long Beach Mental Health Clinic, 1965-70, West Nassau Mental Health Clinic, 1970-76. Mem. Am. Psychiat. Assn., Internat. Soc. Clin. and Exptl. Hyponosis, Soc. Med. Analysts, N.Y. Council Child Psychiatry, Nat. League Am. Pen Women.

WASSERMAN, MARLIE P(ARKER), publisher; b. Chgo., Feb. 14, 1947; d. Theodore E. and Faye (Beller) Parker; m. Mark Wasserman, Nov. 24, 1968; children—Aaron David, Danielle Elizabeth. B.A., Duke U., 1969; M.A., Old Dominion U., 1970. Editor, U. Chgo. Press, 1970-78; sr. editor Rutgers U. Press, New Brunswick, N.J., 1978-83, asst. dir. and editor-in-chief, 1983—. Office: Rutgers U Press 30 College Ave New Brunswick NJ 08903

WASSERMAN, RACHEL ARONIN, marketing consultant; b. Chgo., July 25, 1937; d. Ben and Frieda (Horwich) Aronin; m. Norton Wasserman, June 12, 1957; children—Michael, Judith, Jonathan. Student Brandeis U., 1955-57; B.S., New Haven State Tchrs. Coll., 1959; M.Ed., Nat. Coll. Edn., 1973. Tchr. pub. and pvt. schs., Conn. and Ill., 1959-61, 70-74; engaged in grant mgmt. Northwestern U., Evanston, Ill., 1974-75; v.p. TRC Prodns., Inc., Skokie, Ill., 1975-79; video clinic mgr. AMA, Chgo., 1979-83, sr. mktg. services specialist, 1983-84. Bd. dirs. North Suburban Synagogue Beth El, Highland Park, Ill., 1966-72, pres. Beth El Sisterhood, 1968-70; bd. dirs. central br. Nat. Women's League, 1968-70; Midwest regional coordinator U.S. Holocaust Meml. Mus. Campaign, 1986. Mem. Am. Mktg. Assn., Health Scis. Communications Assn., Am. Assn. Med. Soc. Execs., Women's Am. ORT. Democrat. Club: East Bank (Chgo.). Lodge: Hadassah (life mem. Pioneer Women). Home: 1520 Forest Ave Highland Park IL 60035

WASSERMAN, RUTH, nurse; b. N.Y.C., Aug. 28, 1930; d. Harry and Dora W.; R.N., Bellevue Hosp., N.Y.C., 1948; B.S., Hunter Coll., N.Y.C., 1955; M.A., N.Y., U., 1958. Staff nurse Morrisania Hosp., N.Y.C., 1948-49, dir. nursing, 1969-76; charge nurse, supr.-tchr. Hosp. Joint Diseases, N.Y.C., 1951-55; supr., asst. dir. nursing Met. Hosp., N.Y.C., 1956-69; assoc. exec. dir. nursing service and edn. Met. Hosp. Center, 1977—; sec. Morrisania Hosp. Community Bd., 1972-76. Served with Army Nurse Corps, 1949-50. WHO Fellow, 1970. Mem. Am. Nurses Assn. (council nursing facilitators), N.Y. State Nurses Assn., Pub. Health Assn., Am. Hosp. Assn., Am. Soc. Nursing Services Adminstrs., Deans and Dirs. Greater N.Y., Bellevue Hosp., Hunter Coll., N.Y. U. alumni assns. Office: 1901 1st Ave New York NY 10029

WASSERMAN-GWIRTZMAN, SARINA, speech and language pathologist, consultant; b. Bronx, N.Y., May 13, 1944; d. Paul Joseph and Jean (Weinstein) Wasserman; m. Burton Gwirtzman, Aug. 27, 1985. B.A., Hunter Coll., 1966; M.A., CUNY, 1970, postgrad., 1979; postgrad. Yeshiva U., 1974, Hoffstra U., 1975, Mary Mount U., 1976. Lic. speech pathologist, N.Y. Speech/lang. therapist Bur. Speech Improvement, N.Y.C., 1966-69, co-dir. media unit, 1972-78; spl. project speech coordinator Grade Sch. Dist. 7, Bronx, 1969-70; chief speech-hearing-lang. pathologist Dept. Def. NATO Schs., Keflavik, Iceland, 1970-71; N.Y. State speech/lang. trainer Spl. Edn. Tng. and Resource Ctr., N.Y.C., 1978-82; program coordinator Citywide Speech Unit, N.Y.C., 1982—; pvt. practice speech-lang. pathology, N.Y.C., 1970—; instr. overseas div. U. Md., Keflavik, 1970-71, Manhattan Community Coll., N.Y.C., 1972; cons. N.Y. League for Hard of Hearing, N.Y.C., 1972-82, N.Y. State Edn.

Dept., Albany, 1978—, South Westchester-BOCES, Ardseley, N.Y., 1980—, Westchester County Med. Ctr., 1984—. Co-author filmstrips with workbook/manual. Contbr. to tng. manual. Fund raiser Concerned Individuals, Vet. Council, N.Y.C., 1978-83; election monitor Village Ind. Democrats, N.Y.C., 1976, 80; observer, writer Whale Rescue/Ocean Rescue, Trinity, Nfld., 1981. Mem. Am. Speech, Lang. and Hearing Assn., N.Y. State Speech, Hearing and Lang. Assn. (del. N.Y. State Schs. 1986—), N.Y.C. Speech, Hearing and Lang. Assn., Internat. Wine Club, U.S. Power Squadron.

WASSERSTEIN, WENDY, playwright; b. Bklyn., Oct. 18, 1950. B.A., Mt. Holyoke Coll.; M.A., CCNY, postgrad. Yale Drama Sch. Adapted John Cheever's "The Sorrows of Gin" for PBS TV series "Great Performances"; author of plays including: Any Woman Can't, Montpelier, Pazazz, When Dinah Shore Ruled the Earth, Uncommon Women and Others, Isn't It Romantic. Address: care Arlene Donovan International Creative Management 40 W 57th St New York NY 10019*

WASSERSTROM, EVELYN YAFFE (MRS. DEXTER JEROME WASSERSTROM), civic worker; b. Boston, Sept. 11, 1927; d. Joseph Harry and Tena (Drew) Yaffe; m. Dexter Jerome Wasserstrom, Dec. 25, 1948; children—Tena Lynn (dec.), Bruce Alan. Student Kansas City Art Inst., 1946-47, Kansas City Jr. Coll., 1946-47. Project dir. Housing Survey for Retarded, Kansas City Assn. for Retarded, 1969; pres. YWCA, Kansas City, Mo., 1964-65; co-chmn. Met. Action, 1969-80; mem. Kansas City Commn. Human Relations, 1979—; bd. dirs. Kansas City region NCCJ, 1963—, exec. dir., 1980—, Jewish chmn., 1973-76; bd. dirs. Jewish Community Relations Bur., 1969—, United Community Services, Inc., 1981-84; bd. dirs. Jewish Ednl. Council, 1970—, chmn., 1973-77; mem. adv. group Met. Jr. Coll., 1967-69; co-chmn. High Sch. Jewish Studies of Greater Kansas City, 1971-73; mem. Panel of Am. Women, 1966—; v.p. woman's div. Jewish Fedn. and Council of Greater Kansas City, pres. 1984-86, bd. govs., 1974—; bd. dirs. Vol. Action Center, 1974-84, Jewish Community Center, 1977—, pres., 1986—; chmn. Kansas City Mayor's Commn. Human Relations, 1982—; mem. Social Studies Adv. Com. Shawnee Mission Sch. Dist. Recipient Citation and Brotherhood award Kansas City sect. NCCJ, 1971, Disting. Missourian award Kansas City, 1980, Disting. Alumnus award BBG, 1977, Matrix award Kansas City chpt. Women in Communication, 1979, Woman of Achievement award Mid-Continent Council Girl Scouts, 1983, Commn. Status of Women award, 1984, Crisis Mgmt. award Am. Soc. Pub. Adminstrn. (Kansas City Chpt.) mem. Central Exchange. Mem. B'nai B'rith Women (internat. pres. 1978-80, counselor 1980-82). Home: 449 W Dartmouth Rd Kansas City MO 64113

WASWO, MARION MARGARET, association executive, library trustee; b. Bronx, N.Y., Oct. 23, 1917; d. William Joseph and Janette (Matthew) Fanshawe; m. Carl Waswo, Apr. 26, 1941; children—Janette, Nina, Karin, Carl, Rita. Student schs. Mineola, N.Y. Librarian North Bellmore Library (N.Y.), 1946-49, trustee, 1949-74, bd. pres., 1954-74; trustee Nassau Library System, Uniondale, N.Y., 1974-84, bd. pres., 1982-84; trustee N.Y. State Assn. Library Bd., Uniondale, 1980—, pres., 1986. Treas. United Cerebral Palsy Aux., Wantagh, N.Y., 1969-73; v.p. Wantagh Preservation Soc. 1984—. Recipient service awards North Bellmore Library, 1982, North Bellmore Community, 1974, Nassau Library System, 1984; citation, Nassau County Supr., 1974, Town of Hempstead, 1984, 85; Merit award United Cerebral Palsy of Nassau County, 1985. Mem. ALA, N.Y. Library Assn. Republican. Roman Catholic. Home: 2484 Beltagh Ave Bellmore NY 11710 Office: Nassau Library System 900 Jerusalem Ave Uniondale NY 11553

WATANABE, JUDITH NATSUE, controller; b. Honokaa, Hawaii, July 3, 1951; d. Alexander and Shinayo W. B.S., U. LaVerne-Calif., 1973. Asst. auditor First Nat. Bank Orange County, Calif., 1973-78; auditor Wells Fargo Bank, San Francisco, 1978, Community Bank, Huntington Park, Calif., 1978-79; asst. controller Heritage Bank, Anaheim, Calif., 1979-84; controller Beneficial Adminstrn. Co., Inc., Newport Beach, Calif., 1984—. Avocations: hiking; bowling; photography. Home: 21701 Flamenco Mission Viejo CA 92692 Office: Beneficial Adminstrn Co Inc 4201 Brich St Newport Beach CA 92660

WATANABE, RUTH, librarian, educator, writer; b. Los Angeles, May 12, 1916; d. Kohei and Iwa (Watanabe) W.; B.Mus., U. So. Calif., 1937, A.B., 1939, A.M., 1941, M.Mus., 1942; student Eastman Sch. Music, 1942-46, Columbia U., 1947; Ph.D., U. Rochester, 1952. Instr. piano, music theory, Los Angeles, 1934-41; counsellor, personnel work Eastman Sch. Music, U. Rochester, 1943-46, instr. music history, 1946-61, asso. prof. musicology, 1961-78, prof. music bibliography, 1978-84, instr. English, 1946-47, dir. music library workshop, 1956-84, also lectr. music U. Sch.; staff mem. in charge circulation Sibley Music Library, Rochester, N.Y., 1943-47, acting librarian, 1947-48, librarian, 1948-84, archivist, historian, 1984—; lectr. on music appreciation and music history, 1956—; lectr. Sch. Library Sci., Kent State U., summer 1968; cons. music libraries, 1968—; program annotator Rochester Philharmonic Orch., 1959—; in charge adult edn. Rochester Civic Music Assn.; adj. prof. Sch. Library Sci., SUNY, Geneseo, 1975-83; mem. overseers vis. com. Baxter Sch. Library Sci., Case Western Res. U., 1979-84. Pa.-Del. fellow AAUW, 1949-50; recipient citation for outstanding service to music librarianship, 1986. Mem. AAUW (v.p. Rochester br. 1964-65, mem. state bd. N.Y. State div. 1965-66, pres. Rochester br. 1969-71, fellowship com. 1968-74), Internat., Am. musicol. socs., Music Library Assn. (v.p. 1968-69, program chmn. 1970, pres. 1979-81), Internat. Assn. Music Libraries (2d v.p. commn. on conservatory libraries 1971-79), Assn. Coll. and Reference Librarians, U. Rochester Alumni Fedn. (bd. govs. 1958-61), Rochester Oratorio Soc. (dir. 1961-63, 70-74), Delta Kappa Gamma (v.p. chpt. 1973-76), Phi Beta Kappa (dir. Iota of N.Y. 1962-65, pres. 1977-78), Phi Kappa Phi, Mu Phi Epsilon (gen. chmn. nat. conv. 1956, nat. librarian, 1958-61), Pi Kappa Lambda (sec.-treas. chpt. 1975—), Delta Phi Alpha, Epsilon Phi. Club: Soroptimist (sec. 1956-57, pres. 1963-64). Author: Five Books of Italian Madrigals, 1956; Introduction to Research in Music, 1967; Antonio Il Verso: Madrigali a 5 voci, 1590, 1978; contbg. author: Music Library Handbook, 1966; Symphony Orchestras of America, 1986; Internat. Music Periodicals, 1987; Essays in Honor of Pauline Alderman, 1977; editor: Music Received. Home: 111 East Ave Rochester NY 14604 Office: 26 Gibbs St Rochester NY 14604

WATERMAN, DEBORAH ANN, lawyer; b. Columbus, Ohio, Dec. 4, 1956; d. William Vance and Frances Aileen (Raines) Waterman. B.A., Coll. William and Mary, 1978, J.D. with honors, 1981. Bar: Ohio 1981, W.Va. 1982. Researcher econ. issues Ohio Ednl. Broadcasting Network Columbus, 1980; assoc. Goodwin & Goodwin, Charleston, W.Va., 1981-83, Jenkins, Fenstermaker, Krieger, Kayes & Farrell, Huntington, W.Va., 1983-85; ptnr. Rhoads & Waterman, 1985—. Scholar Marshall-Wythe Sch. Law, Williamsburg, Va., 1979. Mem. ABA, W.Va. Bar Assn. (domestic law com. of legis. adv. group 1982), Pike County Bar Assn. (pres. 1986), Ohio State Bar Assn., Environ. Law Assn. (treas. Ohio State U. 1978-80), Internat. Law Soc. Pi Delta Phi (pres. coll. chpt. 1977-78), Kappa Delta (chmn. 1977-78). Office: 118 E 2d St Waverly OH 45690

WATERMAN, ROBERTA THERESA, retail executive; b. Beaver Falls, Pa., Apr. 28, 1937; d. Elvidio and Armandina (Piroli) Pellegrini; m. John Joseph Waterman, Sept. 30, 1961; children—Keith, Darcy, Craig, Kirk. Student Pasadena City Coll., 1955-57; A.A., Orange Coast Coll., 1971. Adminstrv. asst. Security Pacific, Los Angeles, 1959-61; mdse. mgr. J.C. Penney, Huntington Beach, Calif., 1970-75, sr. mdse. mgr., San Diego, 1975-78, personnel mgr., 1979-86, gen. mdse. mgr., Carlsbad, Calif., 1986—. Pres. PTO, Huntington Beach, Calif., 1964-67; sec. adv. com. Sch. Dist., Fountain Valley, Calif., 1966-68; pres. Huntington Valley Little League, Fountain Valley, 1967-69; sec. Pop Warner Youth Football, Huntington Beach, 1974-75. Recipient award of Merit Urban League, 1982, Twin Honoree award YWCA, 1984. Mem. Nat. Assn. Female Execs., Employment Mgmt. Assn., Internat. Assn. Personnel Women, Personnel Mgrs. Assn. (membership com. 1984-86), Am. Mgmt. Assn. Avocations: travel; tennis. Home: 709 Santa Rosita Solana Beach CA 92075

WATERS, ALICE HARROFF, financial consultant; b. Cleve., Jan. 15, 1944; d. Robert Eldridge and Alice (Kessener) Harroff; m. Sunny Collar Waters, Aug. 10, 1983. B.A. in Art History, Skidmore Coll., 1966. Dir. finance Collins Devel., N.Y.C., 1968-72; exec. v.p. Portfolio Mgmt., Houston, 1973-83; pvt. practice fin. cons., Dallas, 1983—; arbitrator, aquisitioner Funston Interest, Houston, 1984—; acting chief fin. officer Kittinger Co., Buffalo, 1984. Roman Catholic. Home and Office: 240 Canyon Valley Dr Richardson TX 75080

WATERS, BARBARA JEAN, gymnastics school adminstrator; b. Wheeling, W.Va., Dec. 6, 1950; d. John O. and Charlotte (Helling) W.; m. Donald Lamka, Aug. 4, 1973 (div. Sept. 1983); m. Gerald Joseph Todaro, July 20, 1985. B.S. in Edn., Ohio State U., 1972, M.Edn., 1974. Tchr. phys. edn. and health Hastings Jr. High Sch., Columbus, Ohio, 1972-74; pres., owner Universal Gymnasts, Inc., Columbus, 1974—; state rated judge U.S. Gymnastic Fedn., 1979-84. Mem. U.S. Gymnastic Fedn., U.S. Gymnastic Safety Assn., Delta Gamma. Republican. Club: PEO. Home: 8527 Pitlockry Ct Dublin OH 43017 Office: 4555 Knightsbridge Blvd Columbus OH 43214

WATERS, ELEANOR LOIS YOUMANS, librarian; b. Waycross, Ga., Aug. 25, 1928; d. Jacob Edward and Hazel Lois (Hendrix) Youmans; student Perry Bus. Sch., 1944-45, U. Wis., 1966, Loyola U., 1968; m. Thomas Edward Waters, Mar. 28, 1948; children—Belinda Waters Wheeler, Thomas Bruce, Sharon Waters Faircloth, Steven Edward. Sec. to supt. shipbuilding Brunswick Marine Constrn. Corp., Brunswick, Ga., 1945; library technician Nat. Marine Fisheries Service, Brunswick Lab., 1959-73, Ga. Dept. Nat. Resources Coastal Research Div., 1974—. Recipient Superior Performance award U.S. Dept. Interior, 1965, 68. Mem. Ga. Library Assn., Soc. for Bibliography Natural History. Presbyterian. Home: 2606 Starling St Brunswick GA 31520 Office: Ga Dept Natural Resources Coastal Resources Div 1200 Glynn Ave Brunswick GA 31520

WATERS, MAXINE, state legislator; b. St. Louis, Aug. 15, 1938; d. Remus and Velma (Moore) Carr; m. Sidney Williams, July 23, 1977; children by previous marriage—Edward, Karen. Grad. in sociology Calif. State U., Los Angeles. Former tchr. Head Start; mem. Calif. Assembly from dist. 48, 1976—, Democratic caucus chair, 1984. Mem. Dem. Nat. Com.; del. Dem. Nat. Conv., 1980; mem. Nat. Adv. Com. for Women, 1978—. Office: Calif State Assembly State Capitol Sacramento CA 95814*

WATERS, RUTH CRAMER, librarian, mayor; b. Mifflin, Pa., Dec. 15, 1916; d. William McCahan and Clara Esther (Hench) Cramer; A.B., Juniata Coll., Huntingdon, Pa., 1939; M.S., Pa. State U., 1957; m. James Kirk Waters, June 11, 1943 (div. 1950); children—James Kirk, Curtis William. Tchr. schs. in Pa., 1940-42, 44-53; chemist Carnegie Ill. Steel Co., Duquesne, Pa., 1942-43; librarian, 1953—; librarian Juniata High Sch., Mifflintow, Pa., 1970-80; ret., 1980; participant Kent U. seminar in socialist edn., Szeged, Hungary, and Moscow, USSR, 1970; mem. Juniata County Library Bd., 1972-78, pres., 1973-78; mem. Mifflin Borough Council, 1974-78, mayor, 1978—. Mem. Pa. Resolutions and Policy Com., 1976—; del. Pa. Borough Assn., 1976-78; past pres. Mifflin-Juniata Heart Assn.; chmn. public relations com. Juniata County Bicentennial Com., 1972-76; chmn. Juniata County cancer campaign Mifflin-Juniata Cancer Soc., 1982; mem. Mifflin-Juniata-Huntingdon County Mental Health/Mental Retardation, 1981—, Mifflin-Juniata-Huntingdon County Family Planning Bd. (now Women's Health Services), 1980—. Mem. Pa. Edn. Assn., NEA, Juniata County Edn. Assn. (past editor newsletter), ALA, Pa. Library Assn., Juniata County Hist. Soc. (pres. 1979—), Lewistown Bus. and Profl. Women's Club, Delta Kappa Gamma (past chpt. pres.). Democrat. Lutheran. Clubs: Mifflintown Women's Civic (past pres.); East Juniata Women's (past pres.). Author local newspaper column Purely Personal, 1971—; also radio programs. Home: 2 Main St Mifflin PA 17058 Office: Juniata High Sch Mifflintown PA 17059

WATKIN, VIRGINIA RUTH, banker; b. Pomona, Calif., Sept. 25, 1955; d. Charles Robertson Williams and Effie Ruth (Jones) Kettmann; m. Thomas Peter Watkin, Sept. 10, 1977. A.A., Mt. San Antonio Coll., 19—; postgrad. Calif. State U.-Fullerton, U. Guadalajara, Riverside City Coll. Mgmt. trainee Local Loan Co., La Puente, Calif., 1977, Morris Plan of Calif., Corona, 1977-78; cons. loan processor Glendale Fed. Riverside, Calif., 1978-81, cons. loan officer, Riverside and Downey, Calif., 1981-84, sr. cons. loan officer, Glendale, Calif., 1984—. Rep. Calif. Community and Jr. Coll. Assn., Walnut, 1975. Mem. Nat. Assn. Female Execs. Republican. Roman Catholic. Club: Soroptimists (v.p. 1982, pres. 1983) (Riverside). Avocations: reading; water skiing; fishing; camping; gourmet cooking. Office: Glendale Fed Savs and Loan 401 N Brand Blvd Glendale CA 91209

WATKINS, DORETTA, real estate executive; b. Pompton Plains, N.J., Apr. 12, 1944; d. Robert Lewis and Mary (Davis) Helmholtz; m. George Everett Watkins, Jan. 23, 1971; 1 child, Chad Everett. Student Newberry Coll., 1962-63. With Metro Cos., Atlanta, 1965—, v.p. metro mgmt., 1976-80, pres., 1980-84, v.p. corp. affairs, 1984—. Fellow Atlanta Bd. Realtors; mem. Inst. Real Estate Mgmt. (treas. Greater Atlanta chpt. 1978, v.p. 1979, pres. 1980, Mgr. of Yr. award 1980). Republican. Unitarian. Avocations: golf; sailing; snow skiing. Office: The Metro Cos 728 W Peachtree St Atlanta GA 30365

WATKINS, KATHLEEN PULLAN, educator; b. Somers Point, N.J., Oct. 17, 1949; d. James Henry and Joyce Marvel (Hampton) Pullan; B.A., Antioch U., 1974; Ed.M., Temple U., 1976, Ed.D., 1983; m. Ronald Cleophus Watkins, Apr. 15, 1968; children—Matthew David, Alyson Beth. Tchr.-dir. YWCA Parents Coop. Nursery, Phila., 1974-75; dir. Bernice Miller Day Care Center, Camden, N.J., 1975-76; coordinator Opportunities Industrialization Center CHILD Project, Phila., 1976; dir. day care tng. Community Coll. of Phila., 1977-81; instr. undergrad. div. Chestnut Hill Coll., Phila., 1979-80, prof. grad. edn., 1980—; instr. dir. Head Start child devel. assoc. tng. program, 1983-84; asst. prof. dept. child care Temple U., 1984—; partner ednl. cons. firm Durant & Watkins Assocs.; mem. Coll. of Phila., 1981—; trustee Union for Experimenting Colls. and Univs., 1975-76. Bd. dirs. Early Childhood Resource and Info. Ctr., N.Y. Pub. Library. Mem. Assn. for Supervision and Curriculum Devel., Infant Mental Health Assn. Roman Catholic. Research in field. Home: 263 W Tulpehocken St Philadelphia PA 19144 Office: Child Care Dept Sch Social Adminstrn Temple Univ Philadelphia PA 19122

WATKINS, SARA VAN HORN, oboist, conductor; b. Chgo., Oct. 12, 1945; d. John Edward and Virginia Pentland (Marthens) W.; B.Mus., Oberlin Conservatory Music, 1967; m. John Shirley-Quirk, Dec. 29, 1981; children—Benjamin Watkins Shirley-Quirk, Emily Sara Watkins Shirley-Quirk. Prin. oboist Honolulu Symphony Orch., 1969-73, Nat. Symphony Orch., Washington, 1973-81; solo oboist, condr., Europe, U.S., 1981—. Mem. Chgo. Fedn. Musicians.

WATMAN, CAROLYN PRESCOTT, personnel executive; b. Altus, Okla., July 5, 1944; d. John Carl and Helen Lorraine (Eikner) Prescott; B.B.A., U. Okla., 1966; postgrad. North Tex. State U.; M.A., U. N.Mex., 1985; m. Gerald S. Watman, July 31, 1975; 1 dau., Carrie Michele. Personel mgr. Neiman-Marcus, Dallas, 1966-72; dir. records and research Hockaday Sch., Dallas, 1972; dir. personnel and payroll Herman Marcus, Inc., Dallas, 1972-75; pvt. personnel cons., 1973-75; v.p. dir. Santa Fe Merc. Co., Inc., 1975-81; instr. mktg. mgmt. No. N.Mex. Community Coll., Espanola, 1981-83; instr. mktg. Los Alamos High Sch., 1983-85; instr. bus. adminstrn. Santa Fe Community Coll., 1984-85; personnel rep. Dillard Dept. Stores, Inc., 1985—. Mem. Profl. Distributive Edn. Clubs Am., Mktg. and Distributive Edn. Assn., Am. Vocat. Assn., N.Mex. Vocat. Assn. Unitarian Universalist.

WATROUS, ELEANOR BURNS, wholesale company executive; b. New Orleans, Nov. 9, 1914; d. John Thomas and Ellen Lacey (Burns); student Mercy Hosp. Sch. Nursing, 1930-32, Soule Bus. Coll., 1932-33; m. Herbert Leland Watrous, Dec. 5, 1960. Clk., Aleck Mattes, New Orleans, 1932-34; asst. purchasing agt. Hart Enterprises, New Orleans, 1934-39; price and quotation clk. Elec. Supply Co., New Orleans, 1939-49; sec., treas. Long Elec. Supply Co., New Orleans, 1949—, chmn. bd.; pres. Eleanor B. Long Realty Co., New Orleans, 1960—, chmn. bd. Named Citizen of Yr., Patrolmen Assn. New Orleans, 1970; recipient Humanitarian award Nat. Assn. Elec. Distbrs. Mem. Nat. Assn. Elec. Distbrs., So. Ind. Elec. Distbrs., La. Angus Assn., Nat. Angus Assn. Republican. Roman Catholic. Clubs: Covington Square C, Bogalusa Jeans and Queens, Eastern Star. Home: 23 Country Club Park Covington LA 70433 Office: PO Box 30320 New Orleans LA 70190

WATSKY, DONNA LOUISE, microbiologist; b. Lackawanna, N.Y., Aug. 4, 1944; d. Fred and Ida Caroline (Columbus) Kubiak; B.S., SUNY, Buffalo, 1966; M.S., Med. Coll. Va., Va. Commonwealth U., 1971; m. Michael Jay Watsky, Nov. 29, 1972; children—Joel Frederick, Tema Marie. Blood bank technician St. Joseph Mercy Hosp., Ann Arbor, Mich., 1966-67, asst. supr. chemistry, 1967-69; nightshift technologist St. Marys Hosp., Richmond, Va., 1969-71; supr. microbiology Anne Arundel Gen. Hosp., Annapolis, Md., 1971—, tchr. microbiology to nursing students, 1971-72; clin. instr. med. lab. tech. Prince Georges Community Coll., 1975-79; clin. rotation instr. med. tech. program U. Md., 1982—. Mem. Am. Soc. for Med. Tech., Md. Soc. Med. for Tech. (dir. 1981-82), Am. Soc. Microbiology, Omicron Sigma. Home: 290-C Hilltop Ln Annapolis MD 21403 Office: Anne Arundel Gen Hosp Franklin and Cathedral Sts Annapolis MD 21401

WATSON, ABBIE L., retired public health nurse; b. Greenville, Mich., July 27, 1905; d. Alfred T. and Effie (Henry) Watson; R.N., Harper Hosp. Sch. Nursing, Detroit, 1929; B.S. in Public Health Nursing, Wayne U., 1947; M.S. in Nursing Edn., Western Res. U., 1948. Clinic nurse outpatient dept. Harper Hosp., 1930-33; staff nurse, supr. Vis. Nurse Assn., Detroit, 1933-35, 38-42; supr. Tulare County Health Dept., Visalia, Calif., 1935-38; adminstrv. chief nurse, capt. Army Nurse Corps, AUS, 1942-46; exec. dir. Instructive Vis. Nurse Assn., Richmond, Va., 1948-57; dir. bur. pub. health nursing Instructive Vis. Nurse Assn. and City of Richmond, 1952-57; dir. bur. public health nursing pub. health div. Health and Hosp. Corp. of Marion County, Indpls., 1957-61; chief bur. pub. health nursing Public Health Dept. D.C., 1961-65; dir. pub. health nursing Met. Health Dept., Nashville, 1965-72. Mem. nursing services com. D.C. chpt. ARC, 1960-61; spl. services dept. D.C. Tb Assn., 1961—; club rep. Festival U.S.A. Winter Haven Bicentennial Com. Fellow Am. Public Health Assn. (past vice chmn., past research chmn. public health nursing sect. So. br.), Am. Sch. Health Assn., Royal Soc. Health (London); mem. Am. Nurses Assn., Nat. League Nursing (past chmn. program planning com. public health nursing biennial conv.), D.C. Public Health Assn. (1st v.p., chmn. constn. and by-laws com.), Polk County Fedn. Women's Clubs (pres. 1981-82). Club: Woman's of Winter Haven (rec. sec., pres. 1978-81). Contbr. articles to profl. publs. Address: 530 Ave K NE Winter Haven FL 33881

WATSON, ANDREA LOUISE, economist; b. Plymouth, Mass., Apr. 22, 1947; d. John Charles and Julia Louise (Avery) W.; B.A., U. Mass., 1969; M.A., Johns Hopkins U., 1972. Officer internat. staff Citibank, N.A., 1972-74; research assoc. Internat. Research & Tech., 1974-78; sr. analyst Bechtel, San Francisco, 1978-80, economist-fin., 1980-84, rep.-fin., 1984—. Mem. Nat. Assn. Bus. Economists, World Affairs Council No. Calif., Soc. Internat. Devel., Planning Forum. Democrat. Unitarian. Club: Commonwealth of Calif. Home: 1380 Sacramento St San Francisco CA 94109 Office: PO Box 3965 San Francisco CA 94119

WATSON, BARBARA CHRISTIE, furniture manufacturing executive; b. Seattle, Nov. 24, 1939; d. Lynn Gilbert and Maxine Bessie (Slaight) Murray; m. Grahame Edward Watson, Sept. 9, 1960; children—Sherian, Ruth, Heidi, Keith. Student pub. schs., Seattle. Draftsman, Boeing Co., Seattle, 1958-60; sec., treas. Watson & Assocs. Inc., Bainbridge Island, Wash., 1960—. Sec. Bainbridge Island Planning Adv. Council, 1972-74; mem. Econ. Devel. Council of Kitsap County, 1983. Mem. Bainbridge Island C. of C. (v.p. 1973, pres. 1974). Republican. Office: 12715 Miller Rd NE Bainbridge Island WA 98110

WATSON, BETTY SIMMONS, chemical company executive; b. Christiansburg, Va., May 30, 1939; d. James E. and V. Claudine (Cole) Simmons; B.S., Concord Coll., Athens, W.Va., 1960; postgrad Delta Coll., 1968-72, Saginaw Valley State Coll., 1977; children—James Robert, Cambrian Lou. With Dow Chem. Co., Midland, Mich., 1960—, biochemist, 1960-73, product rep. functional products and systems, 1974-76, sr. product rep., 1976-79, sales rep. agrl. products dept., Atlanta, 1979—. Mem. So. Agrl. Chem. Assn., Agrl. Chems. Assn. Ga., Ga. Plant Food Edn. Soc., Ga. Weed Control Soc., Ga. Entomol. Soc. Home: 312F Murphy Mill Rd Americus GA 31709 Office: Suite 2005 20 Perimeter Center E Atlanta GA 30346

WATSON, BRENDA JOYCE, communications company executive; b. Bluefield, W.Va., July 19, 1946; d. Harold and Juanita Hendricks; m. Solomon Brown Watson, IV, Apr. 28, 1984. B.A. in Bus. Sci., Bluefield State Coll., 1968; diploma mgmt., NYU, 1986. Personnel clk. New York Times, 1968-71, supr., clk., 1971-80, personnel asst., 1980-82, confidential staff asst., 1982-84, employment mgr., 1984—. Mem. bus. adv. council United Cerebral Palsy of N.Y.C., 1985—. Recipient cert. U. Mich., 1985, U. Chgo., 1984. Mem. Nat. Assn. Female Execs., Am. Mgmt. Assn., Newspaper Personnel Relations Assn., Am. Newspaper Pubs. Assn. Methodist. Avocations: art; fishing; hunting; travel. Home: 305 W 98th St New York NY 10025 Office: New York Times 229 W 43d St New York NY 10036

WATSON, CAROL DIANE, educator; b. Akron, Ohio, Oct. 30, 1946; d. Donald Devere and Edwina Marie Watson; B.A., U. Akron, 1968; M.A., Stanford U., 1975; Ph.D., Columbia U., 1980; 1 son, Thomas Tarikh Korula. Staff psychologist NYU Dental Sch., 1979-80; asst. prof. Grad. Sch. Mgmt., Rutgers U., Newark, 1980—; vis. asst. prof. Amos Tuck Sch. Bus. Adminstrn., Dartmouth Coll., Hanover, N.H., 1981-82. Mem. Am. Psychol. Assn., Acad. of Mgmt. Contbr. articles to profl. jours. Office: Rutgers Univ Grad Sch Mgmt Newark NJ 07102

WATSON, CATHERINE ELAINE, journalist; b. Mpls., Feb. 9, 1944; d. Richard Edward and LaVonne (Slater) W.; B.A. in Journalism, U. Minn., 1967, also postgrad.; M.A. in Teaching, Coll. of St. Thomas, 1971. Reporter, Mpls. Tribune, 1966-72, editor Picture mag., 1972-78, Travel-Adventure sect., 1978—; part-time instr. U. Minn. Sch. Journalism, 1974-78. Mem. Am. Newspaper Guild, Soc. Am. Travel Writers, Phi Beta Kappa, Kappa Tau Alpha, Alpha Omicron Pi. Contbr. articles to nat. mags. Office: 425 Portland Ave Minneapolis MN 55418

WATSON, DIANE EDITH, state legislator; b. Los Angeles, Nov. 12, 1933; d. William Allen Louis and Dorothy Elizabeth (O'Neal) Watson. B.A., UCLA, 1956; M.S., Calif. State U., Los Angeles. Tchr., sch. psychologist Los Angeles Unified Sch. Dist., 1960-69, 73-74; assoc. prof. dept. guidance Calif. State U., Los Angeles, 1969-71; health occupations specialist Bur. Indsl. Edn., Calif. Dept. Edn., 1971-73; mem. Los Angeles City Bd. Edn., 1975-78; mem. Calif. Senate from dist. 28, 1978—, chairperson health and welfare com., Legis. Black Caucus, joint commn. pub. rights and commn. on tchr. equality. Author: Health Occupations Instructional Units-Secondary Schools, 1975; Planning Guide for Health Occupations, 1975; co-author; Introduction to Health Care, 1976. Del. Democratic Nat. Conv., 1980. Recipient Mary Church Terrell award, 1976, Brotherhood Crusade award, 1981; named Alumnus of Yr., UCLA, 1980, 82, Senator of Yr., Calif. Trial Lawyers, 1982. Mem. Calif. Assn. Sch. Psychologists, Los Angeles Urban League, Calif. Tchrs. Assn., Calif. Commn. on Status Women. Roman Catholic. Office: Calif State Senate State Capitol Sacramento CA 95814*

WATSON, DIANE RITTENHOUSE, telecommunications company executive; b. Englewood, N.J., Mar. 2, 1949; d. George Virgil Rittenhouse and Lois Carol (McHale) Wagner; m. David Stewart Watson; children—David Stewart III, Michael Rittenhouse. Student La. State U., 1967-68, 68-74. With sales and mgmt. depts. Motorola C & E Inc., El Segundo, Calif., 1976-79; sales engr. CSC Inc., Anaheim, Calif., 1979-81; br. mgr. Executone, Anaheim, 1982-83; cons. Bryson-Watson Cons. Co., Anaheim, 1983-84; dist. mgr. GTE Sprint Communications, Gardena, Calif., 1984—. Sponsor, Sta. KCET-TV, Los Angeles, 1985-86, M.A.D.D., 1985-86, Los Angeles Mission, 1985-86; membership dir. Los Angeles Racquet Club, 1974-76. Mem. Internat. Orgn. Women in Telecommunications (1st v.p. 1984, founder Alpha chpt., pres. 1982, 83, nat. dir. fin. 1984-85), Women in Sales, Women in Mgmt. Republican. Mem. Ch. of Religious Sci. Club: Toastmasters (sec. 1980-81). Home: 2261 Ardemore Dr Fullerton CA 92633 Office: GTE Sprint Communications Corp 1025 W 190th St Gardena CA 90248

WATSON, GEORGIA BROWN, author; b. Atlanta; d. George C. and Willie (Willingham) Watson; B.S., Ga. So. Coll., 1946; M.A., George Peabody Coll., Vanderbilt U., 1947, Ph.D., 1949. Tchr., Ga. pub. schs., 1931-42; prof. psychology Ga. So. Coll., Statesboro, from, 1949, now emeritus prof., emeritus chmn. psychology dept.; postdoctoral research fellow Yale U., 1961-62. Served to maj. WAC, 1942-46. Mem. Internat. Platform Assn. Methodist. Author: How to Enjoy Retirement: Climb a Tree and Holler, 1979; Life in the Retirement Bed of Roses, 1982; Retirement Tracks: After Showing the Wisdom of Age, Leave in a Hurry, 1984; World War II in a Khaki Skirt, 1985; also articles. Home: 4 Preston Dr Statesboro GA 30458

WATSON, HELEN RICHTER, educator, ceramic artist; b. Laredo, Tex., May 10, 1926; d. Horace Edward and Helen Mary (Richter) Watson. B.A., Scripps Coll., 1947; M.F.A., Claremont Grad. Sch. and U. Ctr., 1949; postgrad. Alfred U., 1966; Swedish Govt. fellow Konstfackskolan, Stockholm, 1952-53. Mem. faculty Chaffey Coll., Ontario, Calif., 1950-52; chmn. ceramics Mt. San Antonio Coll., Walnut, Calif., 1955-57; prof., chmn. ceramics dept. Otis Art Inst., Los Angeles, 1958-81; mem. faculty Otis-Parsons Sch. Design, 1983—;

studio ceramic artist, Claremont, Calif. and Laredo, Tex., 1949—; design cons. Interpace, Glendale, Calif., 1963-64; artist-in-residence Clarement Men's Coll., 1977. Claremont Grad. Sch. fellow, 1948-49; Swedish Govt. grantee, 1952-53; recipient First Ann. Scripps Coll. Disting. Alumna award, Claremont, 1978. Mem. Artists Equity, Nat. Ceramic Soc., Am. Craftsmen's Council, Los Angeles County Mus. Art, Mus. Contemporary Art Los Angeles. Republican. Episcopalian. Address: 220 Brooks Ave Claremont CA 91711 also 1906 Houston St Laredo TX 78040

WATSON, JEAN KATHRYN, telephone company executive; b. Southbend, Ind., Nov. 29, 1928; d. Thomas and Rachel Evelyn (Murphy) Noonan; student Tyler Jr. Coll.; m. Jim Pat Watson, Jan. 4, 1974; children—Robert Anderson, Thomas Lee, Joseph Alan, Patricia Gipson. With United Telephone Co., Palestine, Tex., 1954—, traffic tng. supr., 1972-76, dist. comml. mgr., 1976-79, service center adminstr., 1979-80, tng. dir., 1980—. Bd. dirs. United Way, Athens, Tex., 1980—, Am. Heart Assn., State of Tex., 1980; area dir. Parents Without Partners, 1973. Mem. Am. Soc. Tng. and Devel., Am. Bus. Women's Assn. (treas., program chmn.), Bus. and Profl. Women's Orgn., Nat. Assn. Female Execs., Internat. Platform Assn. Republican. Baptist. Home: Box 6955 Tyler TX 75711 Office: PO Box 860 Palestine TX 75801

WATSON, JUANITA, nursing educator; b. Ephrata, Pa., July 5, 1946; d. Harry Augustus and Dorothy Mae (Leisey) Watson. Diploma in Nursing, Reading Hosp., 1967; B.S. in Nursing, U. Pa., 1970, M.S. in Nursing, 1973; postgrad. NYU, 1980—. Staff nurse Hosp. U. Pa., Phila., 1967-72; clin. nurse Student Health Hosp., U. Pa., Phila., 1972-73; instr. nursing Thomas Jefferson U., Phila., 1973-76, asst. prof. nursing, 1976-82; dir. continuing edn. St. Agnes Med. Ctr., Phila., 1982—. Nurses Ednl. Funds scholar, N.Y.C., 1968, Alumni Assn. scholar Reading Hosp. Sch. Nursing, 1968. Mem. Nat. League Nursing, Sigma Theta Tau (chpt. treas. 1972-74), Pi Lambda Theta. Democrat. Lutheran. Office: St Agnes Med Ctr 1900 S Broad St Philadelphia PA 19145

WATSON, KITTIE WELLS, speech communication educator; b. Newburgh, N.Y., July 31, 1953; d. Cody Usry and Bettie Richards (Todd) Watson. A.A., Gainesville Jr. Coll., 1973; B.S., U. Ga., 1975; M.A., Auburn U., 1977; Ph.D., La. State U., 1981. Cert. tchr., Ga. Grad. teaching asst. Auburn U. (Ala.), 1975-77, instr., 1977-79; instr. Tulane U., New Orleans, 1979-81, asst. prof. speech communication, 1981-85, assoc. prof., 1985—, also acting head dept. speech communication, 1981-82, chmn. dept., 1982-84, assoc. dir. Inst. for Study Intrapersonal Processes; staff writer and reviewer Prentice-Hall, Wm. C. Brown, Addison Wesley pub. cos.; co-owner, exec. v.p. SPECTRA Jewelry Creations; co-owner operator Rainbow River Studios. Mem. editorial bd. several jours. Author: Instructional Objectives and Evaluation, 1980; Effective Listening, 1983; Groups in Process, 3d edit., 1987; contbr. numerous articles to scholarly jours.; creator audio tapes: Watson-Barker Listening Test; Willing Yourself to Listen. Mem. Am. Council for Career Women. Recipient Mortar Bd. Teaching Excellence award Tulane U., 1982. Mem. Internat. Study of Intrapersonal Processes (assoc. dir.), Speech Communication Assn., Internat. Communication Assn., So. Speech Communication Assn., Eastern Speech Assn., Am. Soc. Tng. and Devel., Internat. Listening Assn. (mem.-at-large, chmn. research com.), Delta Delta Delta. Home: 701 Jefferson Ave Metairie LA 70001 Office: Dept Communication Newcomb Hall Tulane U New Orleans LA 70118

WATSON, MARY STONE, speech and drama educator; b. Marcellus, N.Y., May 24, 1909; d. James Horace and Ethel (Cowles) Stone; B.Oral English, Syracuse U., 1931; M.A., U. Md., 1965; m. Harry P. Watson, June 27, 1936; children—Ruth Watson Lancaster, Robert S., Rollin J., Harry P., Douglas J., Donald M., Sara L. High sch. tchr. English, speech, drama, N.Y., Pa., Md., 1931-37, 62-64; prof. speech Essex Community Coll., Baltimore County, Md., 1965-79, now emeritus, part-time instr., former head speech and drama dept.; lectr., condr. workshops in communications and therapeutic communication, 1965—; producer, anchor person Cable TV show The Best Is Yet To Be, 1981-82. Vol., YMCA Day Care, YMCA Summer Camp. Home: 108 W 39th St Apt 8 Baltimore MD 21210

WATSON, PAMELA GAHERIN, rehabilitation nurse; b. N.Y.C., Oct. 5, 1941; d. John Joseph and Rita (O'Brien) Gaherin; diploma Mass. Gen. Hosp. Sch. Nursing, 1964; B.S. in Nursing, Boston U., 1971, M.S., 1972, Sc.D. in Rehab. Counseling, 1982; m. Barron C. Watson, May 4, 1970; 1 child, Willis Fanning. Head nurse Yale-New Haven Hosp., 1964-66, Tufts-New Eng. Med. Center, Boston, 1966-67, instr. Boston U. Sch. Nursing, 1973-77, asst. prof., 1977-83, assoc. prof., 1983—, chmn. dept. rehab. nursing, 1978—. Bd. dirs. PTA, Peirce Sch., Newton, Mass., 1981-82; bd. dirs., cons. Extended Day Program, Newton, 1982-84. Mem. Am. Nurses Assn., Assn. Rehab. Nurses, Boston U. Sch. Nursing Alumni Assn. (dir. 1982-84), Internat. Assn. Enterostomal Therapy. Club: Cambridge Boat. Editor N.E. region Internat. Assn. Enterostomal Therapy Newsletter, 1981-83; assoc. editor: Jour. Enterostomal Therapy, 1984—; book rev. editor Rehab. Nursing, 1979-83; mem. editorial bd. Cancer Nursing, 1979—, Rehab. Nursing, 1979—; contbr. articles in field to profl. publs. Office: Boston U Sch Nursing 635 Commonwealth Ave Boston MA 02215

WATSON, PATRICIA LEONARD, party production and convention service company executive; b. Sanford, Fla., June 29, 1945; d. William Thomas and Letitia Summerlyn (Hopkins) Leonard; m. Lawrence Ray Watson, Sept. 4, 1965 (div. Oct. 1977); children—William Kirk, Scott Bradley; m. Charles Richard Covert, Jr., July 15, 1978. B.A., North Tex. State U., 1966. Tchr. Dallas Ind. Sch. Dist., 1966-68; real estate broker Larry Watson Realtors, Mesquite, Tex., 1970-72; founder, pres., chief exec. officer Magic by PTS, Inc., Dallas 1972—; chief exec. officer Conf. Mgmt. Assocs., Inc., Dallas, 1979—; mem. community service bd. Hotel Sales Mgrs. Assn., 1983. Chmn. tours com. Republican Nat. Conv., Dallas, 1984; mem. women's bd. Northwood Inst. Recipient Disting. Sales award Sales and Mktg. Execs. Internat., 1983, Disting. Service award Meeting Planners Internat., 1979, Hero award Meeting Planners Internat., 1980. Mem. Conv. Service and Sightseeing Network (v.p. 1984—), Profl. Conv. Mgrs. Assn., Am. Soc. Assn. Execs., Assn. Women Entrepreneurs of Dallas, Nat. Assn. Catering Execs., Alpha Phi. Avocations: cooking; reading. Home: 924 Villa Siete Mesquite TX 75181 Office: Magic by PTS Inc 3505 Turtle Creek Blvd Suite 113 Dallas TX 75219

WATSON, SHARON GITIN, psychologist, social services executive; b. N.Y.C., Oct. 21, 1943; d. Louis Leonard and Miriam (Myers) G.; B.A. cum laude, Cornell U., 1965; M.A., U. Ill., 1968, Ph.D., 1971; m. Eric Watson, Oct. 31, 1969; 1 child, Carrie Dunbar. Psychologist, City N.Y. Prison Mental Health, Riker's Island, 1973-74, Youth Services Center, County of Los Angeles Dept. Pub. Social Services, Los Angeles, 1975-77, dir. clin. services, 1978, dir. youth services center, 1978-80; exec. dir. Crittenton Ctr. for Young Women and Infants, 1980—; mem. adv. bd. High Risk Youth Project, Children's Hosp. of Los Angeles; mem. steering com. Los Angeles Children's Roundtable, Adolescent Pregnancy Child Watch Project, Child Welfare League Am. Western Region. Contbr. articles to profl. jours. USPHS fellow, 1965-68. Mem. Am. Psychol. Assn. Calif. Assn. Services for Children (pres., past chmn. budget and fin., mgmt. info. services, membership coms. sec., treas.), Assn. Children's Services Agys. of So. Calif. (sec., 1981-83, pres., 1984-85), Am. Mgmt. Assn. Cornell Alumni Assn. So. Calif., Pasadena Figure Skating Club (pres.). Home: 4056 Camino Real Los Angeles CA 90065 Office: 234 East Ave 33 Los Angeles CA 90031

WATSON, SHARON MYERS, journalist, communications company executive; b. Shreveport, La., Feb. 19, 1947; d. James S. and Myra (Posey) Myers; B.S. in Math., McNeese State U., Lake Charles, La., 1969, postgrad. in English, 1970-71; m. Larry Conrad Watson 1 son, Byron Lee. Edn. writer, Lake Charles (La.) American Press, 1969-70; copy editor, Dallas Morning News, 1971-72, club editor, 1972-76; pub. info. writer Blue Cross and Blue Shield of Tex., 1976-79; owner Watson Communications, 1979—. Bd. dirs. Hope Cottage, 1982—; mem. com. Dallas Vol. Ctr., 1980-84. Recipient AP award for team reporting, 1974, Austin Headliners award, 1973, AP award for spot news reporting, 1971, La. Press Women's awards, 1971. Mem. Women in Communications (Matrix award, 1976, pres. 1982-83, nat. v.p. fin. 1984—). Baptist. Home: 9314 Raeford Dallas TX 75243

WATSON, SKIRMANTE SEMETA, editor, freelance writer; b. Lithuania, Apr. 24, 1934; came to U.S., 1949, naturalized, 1955; d. Aleksas and Anele (Kruglinskaite) Semeta; corr. student Famous Writers Sch.; m. William Callear Robert Watson, Sept. 9, 1971. Dir. Gallery Gemini, Inc., Palm Beach, Fla., 1972-76; freelance art cons., Houston and N.Y.C., 1976-79; account exec. Spencer-Wood, Inc., public relations, N.Y.C., 1980-83; owner Wid & Skira Watson Assocs., pub. relations, N.Y.C., 1983—; N.Y.C. editor Palm Beach Mirror, weekly, 1980—; author articles on art, 1979—. Club: Ponciana (Palm Beach). Office: 40 Park Ave York NY 10016

WATSON, SUSAN RAE, retail executive; b. Burlington, Vt., May 2, 1942; d. Curtis Rae and Juanita Doris (Demick) MacLean; m. John Conrad Watson, June 12, 1965; children—Jill Rae, Scott Conrad. B.S. in Econs., Nasson Coll., Springvale, Maine, 1964. Exec. sec. Kemper Ins., Boston, 1964-65, Itek Corp., Burlington, Mass., 1965-68; founder, tchr. pvt. kindergarten, Derby Line, Vt., 1969-72; customs insp. Dept. Treasury, Derby Line, 1974-78; v.p., co-owner Habitation, Inc., Kitchenware, Newport, Vt., 1978—; v.p., sec. Newport Fuels, 1974—. Mem. Vt. Adv. Council for Handicapped, Montpelier, 1973-78; mem. Vt. Coalition of Handicapped, Burlington, 1978—; clk. Derby Sch. Bd. (Vt.), 1979-80, v.p., 1980-81, chmn., 1981-82; mem. Vt. Gov.'s Conf. on Edn., 1983. Mem. Memphremagog Bus. and Profl. Women, Vt. Retail Assn., Greater Newport Area C. of C. (exec. v.p., chmn. retail div. 1982-83), Mus. Fine Arts, Internat. Assn. Parents of Deaf, Alexander Graham Bell Assn. of Deaf. Republican. Episcopalian. Home: 173 Nelson Hills Dr Derby VT 05829 Office: Habitation Inc 48 Main St Newport VT 05855

WATSON, SYLVIA FRANCES, commercial painting company executive; b. Parkersburg, W.Va., Feb. 3, 1950; d. Thomas Elias and Alice (Michael) Coram; m. Leonard Grant Watson, Sept. 11, 1971; children—Janica, Sonya, Brian. A.A., W.Va. U., 1969; B.A., Marietta Coll., 1971; postgrad. Our Lady of the Lake, San Antonio, 1972-73; cert. constrn. drawings and quantity survey Columbus Tech. Inst., 1980. Teaching cert., Ohio, Tex. Asst. mgr. Truly Yours Gift Shop, Parkersburg, W.Va., 1969-70; intern socialworker W.Va. Dept. Welfare, Parkersburg, summer 1970; tchr. art San Antonio Sch. Dist., 1971-74; co-founder, v.p. New Day Painting, Inc., Columbus, Ohio, 1974—, co-founder, coordinator painting apprenticeship tng., 1983—. Recipient merit award San Antonio Sch. Dist., 1972, 73, 74; SBA bus. devel. grantee, 1983; recipient Best of Show award, painting and sculpture W.Va. U., Parkersburg, 1983. Mem. Women's Aux. Assoc. Builders and Contractors (bd. dirs. 1980-82), Assoc. Builders and Contractors (bus. devel. com. Central Ohio chpt.), Builders Exchange of Central Ohio, Nat. Assn. Female Execs., Nat. Assn. Minority Contractors. Roman Catholic. Avocations: art, reading; gardening. Office: New Day Painting Inc 3310 Morse Rd Suite 115 Columbus OH 43229

WATSON, TWILLA ORTMANN, educator; b. Plant City, Fla., Feb. 21, 1946; d. Wesley Westfield and Minnie Lee (Sapp) Ortmann; 1 child, Tony L. B.A., U. S. Fla., 1967, postgrad., 1980-81. Tchr. English, Horace Mann Jr. High Sch., Brandon, Fla., 1968-82, media specialist, video cameraman, 1982—; tchr. English, Operation Upgrade, Hillsborough County, Tampa, Fla., summers 1981—, cons. new jr. high sch. media ctrs., 1985—. Mem. Nat. Assn. Female Execs., Hillsborough County Assn. Sch. Library Media Specialists. Republican. Baptist. Avocations: piano; boating; collecting antiques. Home: 203 Cranberry Ln Brandon FL 33511 Office: Horace Mann Jr High Sch 409 E Jersey Ave Brandon FL 33511

WATSON-MELCHER, SHARON LUQUER, property management corporation executive; b. High Point, N.C., Sept. 17, 1945; d. Herbert and Tula (White) Luquer; m. Jerry Wesley Watson, Dec. 29, 1967 (div. Nov. 1976); m. Albert H. Melcher, Oct. 27, 1984. Student Mosely Flint Coll., Greensboro, N.C., 1983. Cert. property mgr. Asst. to mall mgr. Panama City Mall, Fla., 1976-77; resident mgr. John Crosland Mgmt., Charlotte, 1977-78, property mgr., 1978-80; property mgr. McGuire Properties, Charlotte, 1980-83; asst. dir. property mgmt. Steven D. Bell, Greensboro, N.C., 1983-85; pres. Gen. Property Mgmt. Corp., Durham, N.C., 1985—. Recipient pres. award Steven D. Bell & Co., 1984. Fellow Inst. Real Estate Mgmt.; mem. Greater Greensboro Bd. Realtors, Nat. Assn. Female Execs., Triangle Apt. Assocs. Methodist. Avocations: snow skiing; water skiing; dancing; reading. Home: 17 Cedar Creek Condos Jamestown NC 27282 Office: Gen Property Mgmt Corp 3514 University Dr Durham NC 27707

WATTS, BERTHA L., nurse; b. Lake City, Fla., Feb. 17, 1941; d. Ivory and Irene (Gainey) Ward; m. Johnny L. Watts, Sept. 20, 1958; children—Johnny, Tommy, Keith, Brenda, Sonya. A.Nursing, St. Petersburg Jr. Coll., 1977, student, 1983; student Tomlinson Vocat.-Tech. Sch. 1981. Nurse aid U. Fla., Gainesville, 1959-61, Bayfront Med. Ctr., St. Petersburg, 1967-68; nurse aid/ward clk. Palms of Pasadena Hosp., St. Petersburg, 1968-74, staff nurse, 1977-83, nurse mgr., 1983—. Vol. ARC, St. Petersburg. Named Woman of Yr., Am. Bus. Women's Assn., 1984. Mem. Concerned Women for Am., Am. Bus. Women's Assn. (v.p. 1984-85), Soc. for GI Asst. (pres.-elect 1986), Nat. Assn. Female Execs. Republican. Assemblies of God. Avocations: jewelry design; sewing; reading; photography. Home: 2326 23rd St S Saint Petersburg FL 33712 Office: Palms of Pasadena Hosp 1501 Pasadena Ave S Saint Petersburg FL 33707

WATTS, DORIS EARLENE, librarian; b. Palatka, Fla., Jan. 7, 1923; d. Charles Franklin and Elouise A.C. (Hagler) Foster; m. Fernand Cortez Watts, Aug. 30, 1950 (dec. 1955); children—Varick Steven, Franklin Cortez. A.B., Howard U., 1950; postgrad. Catholic U. Am., 1960-61, 65. With ICC, 1959—, editorial clk. 1959-60, library asst., 1960-61, cataloger, 1961-65, asst. librarian, 1965-70, librarian, 1970—. Recipient Spl. Achievement award ICC, 1983, 84. Mem. ALA, Delta Sigma Theta. Democrat. Methodist. Home: 2502 Perry St NE Washington DC 20018 Office: ICC 12th St and Constitution Ave NW Washington DC 20423

WATTS, EMILY STIPES, educator; b. Urbana, Ill., Mar. 16, 1936; d. Royal Arthur and Virginia Louise (Schenck) Stipes; student Smith Coll., 1954-56; A.B., U. Ill., 1958, M.A. (Woodrow Wilson Nat. fellow), 1959, Ph.D., 1963; m. Robert Allan Watts, Aug. 30, 1958; children—Benjamin, Edward, Thomas. Instr. English, U. Ill., Urbana, 1963-67, asst. prof. English, 1967-73, asso. prof., 1973-77, prof., 1977—, dir. grad. studies dept. English, 1977-79; bd. dirs. U. Ill. Athletic Assn., chmn., 1981-83; mem. faculty adv. com. Ill. Bd. Higher Edn., 1984—, vice chmn., 1986—. Guggenheim fellow, 1973-74. Mem. Authors Guild, Ill. Writers Assn., Phi Beta Kappa, Phi Kappa Phi, Republican. Presbyterian. Author: Ernest Hemingway and The Arts, 1971; The Poetry of American Women From 1632 to 1945, 1977; The Businessman in American Literature, 1982; contbr. articles on Jonathan Edwards and Anne Bradstreet to lit. jours. Home: 1009 W University Ave Champaign IL 61821 Office: 208 English Bldg U Ill 608 S Wright St Urbana IL 61801

WATTS, HELENA ROSELLE, military analyst; b. East Lynne, Mo., May 29, 1921; d. Elmer Wayne and Nellie Irene (Barrington) Long; m. Henry Millard Watts, June 14, 1940; children—Helena Roselle Watts Scott, Patricia Marie Watts Foble. B.A., Johns Hopkins U., 1952, postgrad., 1952-53. Assoc. engr., Westinghouse Corp., Balt., 1965-67; sr. analyst Merck, Sharp & Dohme, Westpoint, Pa., 1967-69; sr. engr. Bendix Radio div. Bendix Corp., Balt., 1970-72; sr. scientist Sci. Applications Internat. Corp., McLean, Va., 1975-84; mem. tech. staff The Mitre Corp., McLean, 1985—; adj. prof. Def. Intelligence Coll., Washington, 1984-85. Contbr. articles to tech. jours. Mem. IEEE, AAAS, Nat. Mil. Intelligence Assn., U.S. Naval Inst., Assn. Old Crows, Mensa. Republican. Roman Catholic. Avocations: photography; gardening; reading. Home: 4302 Roberts Ave Annandale VA 22003 Office: The Mitre Corp W 532 1820 Dolley Madison Blvd McLean VA 22102

WATTS, JOYCE LANNOM, university administrator; b. Los Angeles, June 1, 1942; d. Kenneth Loren and Elsie (Weston) Lannom; m. John Ransford Watts, Dec. 20, 1975. B.A. cum laude, Calif. State U.-Long Beach, 1976. Exec. asst. to pres. Calif. State U.-Long Beach, 1964-75, exec. dir. alumni affairs, 1976-79; mem. staff vice chmn. U.S. Commn. Civil Rights, 1975-76; regional adminstr. Career Research, Chgo., 1979-81; 2d v.p. No. Trust Co., Chgo., 1981-84; asst. dean, dir. career devel. and placement Kellogg Grad. Sch. Mgmt., Northwestern U., Evanston, Ill., 1984—. Mem. internat. bd. Chgo. Met. YMCAs; mem. bd. Community Adv. Council for Programs on Women, Northwestern U. Mem. Employment Mgmt. Assn., Coll. Placement Council, Midwest Coll. Placement Assn., AAUW (bd. dirs.), Women in Mgmt., Dorothy L. Sayers Soc. Home: 5510 N Sheridan Rd Chicago IL 60640 Office: Leverone Hall Northwestern U Evanston IL 60201

WATTS, LOU ELLEN, educator; b. Conway, S.C., Sept. 23, 1940; d. Bernie Louis and Dollie Ellen (Lemons) Overhultz; m. Ervin William Watts, Feb. 3, 1963; children—William Ashley. B. Music Edn., La. State U., 1962; postgrad. U. Ga., 1965, U. Ariz., 1972. Cert. elem. tchr., music tchr., Ind., Ga., La., Ariz. Music tchr. Westchester Twp. Sch., Chesterton, Ind., 1963-64; music cons. Clayton County Sch., Jonesboro, Ga., 1964-66; elem. and chorus tchr. Tucson Unified Sch. Dist., 1979—, intermediate head div. tchr., music cons., 1983-84, chorus dir., 1979-84; teacher, cons. archaeology, 1983—; exhibitor Nat. Sci. Tchrs. Conv., San Francisco, 1986. Pres., fine arts chmn., cons. Sahuaro Jr. Women's Club, Tucson, 1970-74; state consumer chmn., music award chmn. Ariz. Fedn. of Women's Club, 1970-72; mem. Tucson Panhellenic Council, 1971-72. Tucson Enrichment Fund grantee, 1983-84, 1984—. Recipient Clubwoman of the Year Ariz. Fedn. Jr. Women's Club, 1972; award for excellence in sci. teaching Ariz. Sci. Tchrs. Assn., 1985. Mem. Nat. Audubon Soc., Nat. Sci. Tchr. Assn., Music Educators Nat. Conf., Nat. Edn. Assn., Ariz. Edn. Assn., Tucson Edn. Assn., DAR, So. Ariz. Arabian Horse Assn., Delta Kappa Gamma (1st v.p.), Sigma Alpha Iota. Club: Young Astronauts (charter). Home and Office: 8740 E Summer Trail Tucson AZ 85749

WATTS, MARILYN, market research executive; b. N.Y.C., Oct. 16, 1931; d. Abraham and Bess (Golden) Silver; m. Daniel H. Watts, Sept. 4, 1954 (div. May 1967); 1 child, Fern Silver; m. Seymour Lieberman, Oct. 30, 1976. B.A., Columbia U., 1952; postgrad. NYU, 1954-59. Assoc. research dir. McCann-Erickson, N.Y.C., 1956-66; v.p., assoc. research dir. Grey Advt., N.Y.C., 1966-69; sr. v.p., research dir. Ketchum Advt., N.Y.C., 1969-74; v.p. mktg. services RCA, N.Y.C., 1974-82; sr. v.p. Lieberman Research, Inc., N.Y.C., 1982—. Mem. editorial bd. Jour. Advt. Research, Indsl. Mktg. Mgmt. Contbr. articles to profl. jours. Recipient Elizabeth Cutter Morrow award YWCA Acad. Women Achievers, N.Y.C. Mem. Market Research Council (pres. 1983-84), Assn. Nat. Advertisers (dir. 1980-82), Advt. Research Found. (chair pub. affairs council 1976-83), Conf. Bd., Am. Mktg. Assn., Nat. Cable TV Assn., Am. Assn. Pub. Opinion Research. Avocations: theatre; travel; tennis. Home: 211 Central Park W New York NY 10024 Office: Lieberman Research Inc 1140 Ave of Americas New York NY 10036

WATTS, MARSHA KAPNICKY, sales representative; b. Morgantown, W.Va., Oct. 7, 1956; d. Paul Nicholas and Iris Kathleen (Kelly) Kapnicky; m. Royce J. Watts, II, July 29, 1978 (div. Sept. 1981); m. 2d, A. James Wyatt, Jr., Jan. 7, 1984. B.S. in Journalism, W.Va. U., 1978. Sales rep., R.L. Polk Co., Richmond and Atlanta, 1978-79; sales rep. Designers Color, Inc., Atlanta, 1979-84; sr. sales rep. Techtron Imaging Network, Chgo. and Atlanta, 1984—. Mem. Atlanta Print Prodn. Assn., Nat. Assn. Female Execs., Atlanta Advt. Club, W.Va. U. Alumni Assn. Home: 909 Glasgow Dr Lilburn GA 30247 Office: Techtron Imaging Network Suite 4 1925 Century Blvd Atlanta GA 30345

WATTS, MARY ANN, educator; b. Harrisburg, Pa., Sept. 13, 1927; d. Major Allan and Ellana Susan (Robinson) Brown; B.S., Cheyney U., 1949; student Temple U., 1965-67, Pa. State U., 1969-72; m. Spencer R. Watts, June 23, 1951; children—Shelley Lynn, Allison Dee, Howard Allan. Tchr., Harrisburg Sch. Dist., 1949-51, 59-69, Balt. Sch. Dist., 1951-57, tchr. Reading (Pa.) Sch. Dist., 1969—, mem. sch. dist. dress and discipline code com., 1977-79; corr. Hamburg Item. Mem., Bernville Borough Council, 1976—, treas. Berks County Boroughs Assn., 1977—. Mem. Reading Edn. Assn., Pa. Edn. Assn., NEA, AAUW, Berks County Boroughs Assn., Pa. Elected Women's Assn., NAACP, LWV, Delta Sigma Theta. Democrat. Mem. United Ch. Christ. Clubs: Bernville Woman's (pres. 1978-80, 86-88, Woman of Yr. 1985), GNO of Harrisburg. Office: Reading Sch Dist 8th and Washington Sts Reading PA 19602

WATTS, VIVIAN EDNA, state legislator; b. Detroit, June 7, 1940; d. Edward William and Dorothy Beatrice (Price) Walker; m. David Allan Watts, Jan. 30, 1960; children—Cynthia, Jeffery. B.A., U. Mich., 1962. Pres., Fairfax Area LWV, 1975-77; dir. research Fairfax C. of C., 1977-79; legis. aide U.S. Congress, 1980, Va. Gen. Assembly, 1980-81; legislator Va. Ho. of Dels., 1982—, chmn. joint com. on in-state tuition, 1983. Editor, chmn. report Sch. Closing Task Force, 1978. Bd. dirs. Pre-Paid Legal Services, 1983—. Gov.'s Regulatory Reform Adv. Bd., 1982—, No. Va. Community Coll. Child Care Bd., 1980—; exec. bd. Nat. Capital United Way, 1976—; chmn. Tax and Revenue of Fairfax Fiscal Commn., 1978; founding mem. Fairfax Com. 100, 1975; chmn. 1978 Sch. Bond Referendum, 1978. Named Fairfax County Citizen of Year, Washington Star, 1978. Mem. No. Va. Consortium for Continuing Higher Edn. (dir.), Friends of Victim Assistance Network (dir.), No. Va. Coalition for Children (dir.), Bus. and Profl. Women. Democrat. Unitarian.

WAUGH, CAROL-LYNN RÖSSEL, writer, artist; b. Staten Island, N.Y., Jan. 5, 1947; d. Carl Frederick Leopold and Muriel Alice (Kiefer) Rössel; m. Charles Gordon Waugh, Nov. 11, 1967; children—Jenny-Lynn, Eric-Jon Rössel. B.A. in Humanities, SUNY-Binghamton, 1968; M.A. in Art History, Kent State U., 1979. Sewing instr. Singer Co., Augusta, Maine, 1971-72; instr. art history U. Maine, Augusta, 1977; art instr. Adult Edn., Winthrop, Maine, 1978; pvt. practice writer, artist, Winthrop, 1973—. Author: Petite Portraits, 1982; My Friend Bear, 1982; Octagon Houses of Maine, 1982; Teddy Bear Artists, 1984; (with Susanna Oroyan) Contemporary Artist Dolls, 1986; editor (with Isaac Asimov and Martin H. Greenberg) anthologies: The Twelve Crimes of Christmas, 1981, 2d edit. 1982, Japanese, Italian, Swedish edits.; Big Apple Mysteries, 1982, Japanese edit.; Show Business Is Murder, 1983, German edit.; Thirteen Horrors of Hallowe'en, 1983; Murder on the Menu, 1984; (with B. Pronzine and M.H. Greenberg) Manhattan Mysteries, 1986; co-author short story (in anthology); contbr. chpts. to books on dolls; reviewer children's books, art books, books about bears for various mags. and Sunday Sun-Jour., Lewiston-Auburn, Maine; authority on teddy bears; contbr. articles on dolls, teddy bears, antiques to mags.; lectr. in fields; sculptor original artist dolls, 1973—; exhibited watercolor paintings and photography. Justice of Peace, Kennebec County, Maine, 1972-78; mem. Kennebec County Democratic Com., Augusta, 1972-80. Buttonwood scholar, N.Y. Stock Exchange, 1964-68, 70-71; winner awards for original artist dolls. Mem. Soc. Children's Book Writers, Original Doll Artist Council Am. Home: 5 Morrill St Winthrop ME 04364

WAX, ROSALIE HANKEY, anthropologist, educator; b. Des Plaines, Ill., Nov. 4, 1911; d. Richard B. and Anna (Orb) Hankey; B.A. in Anthropology, U. Calif., Berkeley, 1942; Ph.D., U. Chgo., 1950; m. Murray L. Wax, Mar. 5, 1949. Chmn., Social Scis. II Coll., U. Chgo., 1956, examiner, 1947-55; acad. teaching asst. anthropology, 1946-47, instr. social scis., 1947-49, asst. prof., 1950-57; dir. Workshop on Am. Indian Affairs U. Colo., 1959-69; research assoc. Ogala Sioux Ednl. Research Project Emory U., 1962-64; assoc. prof. U. Kans., 1964-69, prof., 1970-73, assoc. dir. Indian Edn. Research Project, 1966-69; prof. dept. anthropology and sociology Washington U., St. Louis, 1973—; vis. lectr. U. Miami, 1959-62. Rockefeller Found. Humanities fellow, 1981-82; grantee in field. Fellow Am. Anthrop. Assn., AAAS (councilor 1973-74), Soc. Study Social Problems; mem. Am. Ethnol. Soc., Central States Anthrop. Soc., Soc. Applied Anthropology. Author: Magic, Fate and History: The Changing Ethos of the Vikings, 1969; Doing Fieldwork: Warnings and Advice, 1971. Office: Dept Anthropology Washington U Saint Louis MO 63130

WAXMAN, MARGERY HOPE, lawyer; b. N.Y.C., Oct. 21, 1942; d. Lee and Florence (Jackel) W.; m. Willard H. Mitchell, Apr. 4, 1982. A.B., Smith Coll., 1964; J.D. with honors, George Washington U., 1967. Bar: D.C. 1968, U.S. Supreme Ct. 1971. Law clk. U.S. Ct. Appeals for D.C. Circuit, 1967-68; assoc. firm Covington & Burling, 1968-72; asst. gen. counsel Office Consumer Affairs, 1972-73; assoc. dep. gen. counsel Cost of Living Council, 1973-74; exec. asst. to chmn. FTC, Washington, 1975, asst. dir., dep. dir., acting dir. Bur. Consumer Protection, FTC, 1976-77, exec. dir. FTC, 1977-79; gen. counsel Office Personnel Mgmt., Washington, 1979-81; dep. gen. counsel Dept. Treasury, 1981-86; ptnr. firm Sidley & Austin, Washington, 1986—. Mem. D.C. Bar, Adminstrv. Conf. U.S. (chmn. com. on pub. access and info.), ABA (chmn. spl. com. on lawyers in govt. 1982-83). Office: Sidley & Austin 1722 Eye St NW Washington DC 20006

WAYLOR, CHERYL WATSON, insurance company executive, consultant; b. Montreal, Que., Can., Sept. 8, 1943; came to U.S., 1954; d. Alan Douglas and Jean Mary (Hughes) Watson; m. Joseph Robert Earl Waylor, Apr. 5, 1969 (div. Feb. 1979). B.B.A., Ga. State U., 1980, postgrad. Supr. comml. underwriting Liberty Mut., Atlanta, 1969-74, supr. group health claims, 1974-76; instr. ins. DeKalb Community Coll., Clarkston, Ga., 1978-79; ops. analyst Kemper Group, Atlanta, 1979-81, div. officer services mgr., Overland Park, Kans., 1981-82, div. field systems mgr., 1982-85; cons. Waylor & Assocs., Overland Park, 1986—. Contbr. articles to profl. jours. Lectr. in field. Polit. speaker coordinator Kemper Group, Overland Park, 1982, 85, Ins. Women Greater Kansas City, 1986. Mem. Ins. Women of Greater Kansas City-Nat. Assn. Ins. Women (bd. dirs. 1985-86, Rookie of Yr. 1985), Nat. Assn. Female Execs. Republican. Club: Toastmasters (adminstrv. v.p., div. Obest evaluator 1985).

Avocations: sky diving; fencing; running; reading; travel. Home: 5300 W 103 Terr Overland Park KS 66207

WAYMIRE, ROBERTA ARLENE, construction company executive; b. Wimbledon, N.D., June 20, 1936; d. Gaylord and Huldah Evelyn (Ekstrand) Thorne; student Brigham Young U., 1953-54; m. Kenneth L. Waymire, Feb. 26, 1955; children—Thorne L., Kent L. Reporter, Democrat Herald, Albany, Oreg., 1955-56; with Waverly Constrn. Co., Inc., Tigard, Oreg., 1964—, v.p., 1982—. Mem. Portland Metro Homebuilders Assn. Republican. Home and office: 10185 SW Riverwood Ln Tigard OR 97223

WAYNE, AGNES LORENE, real estate firm executive; b. Henshaw, Ky., Jan. 14, 1922; d. James Anderson and Maudie Rudell (Hinton) Ledbetter; m. George William Wayne, Oct. 20, 1943 (dec. July 1977); children—Billy Tom, George Darrell, James Keith. Student pub. schs. Typist, Briggs Ind. Corp., Evansville, 1943-46; mgr. Tupperware home parties, Evansville, 1958-68; owner, broker Wayne Real Estate, Henderson, Ky., 1968—. Author: (poetry) Rememberances of Special Occasions, 1984; Cooking for the Fun of It, 1985. Bd. dirs. YMCA, 1973-74, v.p., 1975-76, pres., 1977-78; bd. dirs. United Way, 1979, gen. campaign chmn., 1982; active Democratic Women's Club, Henderson, 1980-85. Mem. Henderson C. of C. (bd. dirs., pres. community devel. 1980-85, Disting. Citizen of Yr. 1983), Bus. and Profl. Women's Club Henderson (chmn. legis. com. 1983-85, chmn. membership com. 1980, pres. 1974-75, Bus. Woman of Yr. 1974). Mem. Christian Ch. (Disciples of Christ). Avocations: swimming; cake decorating; gardening. Home: 2906 Green River Rd Henderson KY 42420

WAYNE, JANE ELLEN, manufacturing company executive; b. Phila., Apr. 6, 1936; d. Jesse Allen and Eleanor Mae (Brundle) Stump; student Grove City Coll., 1955, N.Y. U., 1956, Am. Acad. Dramatic Arts, 1957; m. Ronald R. Wayne, May 26, 1958 (div. 1967); 1 dau., Elizabeth Jo. Mem. promotion staff NBC, N.Y.C., 1957-65; mgr. V.I.P. div. N.Y. World's Fair, 1966; v.p. Abbot & Abbot Corp., wood mfrs., N.Y.C., 1974—; creator Beauty and Poise pvt. classes for bus. women, 1963-66. Mem. Sigma Delta Phi. Republican. Author: The Life of Robert Taylor, 1977; Kings of Tragedy, 1977; Tiffany, 1979; Lividia, 1979; The Love Gap, 1979; Kings of Tragedy II, 1982; Kings and Queens of Tragedy, 1983; The Barbara Stanwyck Story, 1985; contbr. to Nat. Enquirer, Harvey Mag. Home: 17-85 215th St Bayside Terrace NY 11360

WAYNE, KYRA PETROVSKAYA, author; b. Crimea, USSR, Dec. 31, 1918; came to U.S., 1948, naturalized, 1951; d. Prince Vasily Sergeyevich and Baroness Zinaida Fedorovna (Fon-Haffenberg) Obolensky; m. George J. Wayne, Apr. 21, 1961; 1 child, Ronald George. B.A., Leningrad Inst. Theatre Arts, 1939, M.A., 1940. Actress, concert singer, USSR, 1939-46; actress, U.S., 1948-51; enrichment lectr. Royal Viking Line cruises, Alaska-Can., 1985, Greek Islands-Black Sea, Russia/Europe, 1978-79, 81-82, 83-84, New Eng.-Can., 1985. Author: Kyra, 1959, Kyra's Secrets of Russian Cooking, 1960, The Quest for the Golden Fleece, 1962; Shurik, 1971, The Awakening, 1972, The Witches of Barguzin, 1975, Max, The Dog That Refused to Die, 1979 (Best Fiction award Dog Writers Assn. Am. 1980), Rekindle the Dreams, 1979. Founder, pres. Clean Air Program, Los Angeles County, 1971-72; mem. women's council KCET-Ednl. TV. Served to lt. Russian Army, 1941-43. Decorated Red Star, numerous other decorations USSR; recipient award Crusade for Freedom, 1955-56; award Los Angeles County, 1972. Mem. Soc. Children's Book Writers, Authors Guild, P.E.N., UCLA Med. Faculty Wives (pres. 1970-71, dir. 1971-75) UCLA Affiliates (life), Los Angeles Lung Assn. (life). Home: 234 S Rimpau Blvd Los Angeles CA 90004

WAYNE, OLGA MARCELLA, former Army official; b. Oct. 10, 1909; d. Walker William and Gertude (Hayes) Falconer; m. Richard Coker, Jan. 2 1930 (div. Jan. 1949); m. Marvin Daniel Wayne, July 6, 1956 (dec. Nov. 1980); children—Clive (dec.), Barbara Coker Sherrod. Student Ill. State U., Normal, 1929-31. Staffing technician U.S. Army Adminstrn. Ctr., East St. Louis, 1948-74. Dir. choir Mt. Zion Ch., East St. Louis, 1933-84; mem. exec. bd. Am. Cancer Soc., 1983—, chmn. transp. and rehab., 1983-86; dir., tchr. Mt. Zion Golden Tones, 1984—; mem. Sigma Gamma Rho, 1985—, Area Citizens Com. for Safety, 1982—; charter mem. Alta Sita Area Concerned Citizens, 1983—. Recipient Parent of Yr. award Project Speak, East St. Louis, 1982, Com. Service award Sigma Gamma Rho, 1985. Clubs: Libra, Bus. and Profl. Women's. Avocations: traveling; reading; music. Home: 3338 Bond Ave East Saint Louis IL 62207

WAYNS, ARLENE MORRIS, elderly service corporation executive; b. Phila., Jan. 22, 1947; d. Leroy and Helen (Morris) Lewis; m. Eugene Preston Wayns, Oct. 16, 1965 (dec. Sept. 1977); children—Kevin, Verland, Eugene. B.A., Temple U., 1978. Asst. mgr. Ctr. of Social Policy and Community Devel., Temple U., Phila., 1978-81; mgr. Stephen Smith Towers Apts. for the Elderly, Phila., 1981-85, exec. dir., 1985—; realtor assoc. Wilson & Wilson Assocs., Phila., 1983—; mgmt. cons. Stephen Smith Home for the Aged, Phila., 1985—; lectr. in field. Election judge City of Phila., 1975-76. Mem. Phila. Assn. Housing Mfrs. for the Elderly (pres. 1983—), Pa. Assn. Non-profit Homes for the Aging, (com. 1984—), Am. Assn. Housing for the Aging, Inst. Real Estate Mgmt. Avocations: aerobics; tennis; theater. Home: 1714 E Tulpehocken St Philadelphia PA 19138 Office: Stephen Smith Towers Apts for Elderly Inc 1030 Belmont Ave Philadelphia PA 19104

WEADOCK, LOUISE WEEKS, health manpower supply co. exec.; b. Greenwich, Conn., May 5, 1952; d. John Cullen and Sewall Boardman (Weeks) Weadock; B.S. in Nursing, Cath. U. Am., 1974; M.P.H., Johns Hopkins U., 1979. Clin. coordinator and head nurse Forbush Children's Center, Sheppard Pratt Hosp., Balt., 1976-78; dir. nursing Kimberly Nurses div., 1979-81; regional mgr. Nat. Med. Cons., N.Y.C., 1981, v.p. sales and ops., Overland Park, Kans., 1981—. Named top nat. saleswoman, 1980, 81. Mem. Am. Nurses Assn., Assn. for Exec. Females, Jr. League N.Y. Democrat. Roman Catholic. Clubs: L'Hirondelle Country, First Avenue Squash. Office: Nat Med Cons 8500 W 110th St Suite 600 Overland Park KS 66201

WEATHERFORD, CHERYL LORRAINE, building contractor, real estate broker; b. Waco, Tex., Nov. 25, 1947; d. Mary (Raper) Williams; divorced; children—Kelly Denise, Paxton David. Grad. high sch., Dallas. Lic. real estate broker. Building contractor, Dallas. Mem. Nat. Assn. Home Builders Tex., Home and Apartment Builders of Met. Dallas. Republican. Office: Cheryl Weatherford Inc PO Box 795192 Dallas TX 75379

WEATHERFORD, LYNDA SUE, offshore drilling company executive; b. Beaumont, Tex., Aug. 12, 1947; d. Ira Dewayne and Doris Annabel (Hingle) Weatherford. B.S. in Edn., U. Tex., 1969; M.Ed. in Counseling, Sam Houston State U., 1971. Secondary history tchr. Cypress-Fairbanks Ind. Sch. Dist., Houston, 1969-70, secondary Spanish tchr., 1971-73; dir. overseas family services Storm Drilling Co., Houston, 1973-74; mgr. compensation and relocation Zapata Offshore Co., Houston, 1975—. Mem. Houston Personnel Assn., Houston Compensation Assn. (membership chmn. 1983-84). Republican. Methodist. Office: Zapata Offshore Co PO Box 4240 Houston TX 72210

WEATHERUP, WENDY GAINES, insurance agent, writer; b. Glendale, Calif., Oct. 20, 1952; d. William Hughes and Janet Ruth (Neptune) Gaines; m. Roy Garfield Weatherup, Sept. 10, 1977; children—Jennifer, Christine. B.A., U. So. Calif., 1974; Lic. ins. agt. Ins. agt. Gaines Agy., Northridge, Calif., 1974—. Mem. fundraising com. Chatsworth Hills Acad., Calif., 1986. Mem. Nat. Assn. Female Execs., U. So. Calif. Alumni Assn., Alpha Gamma Delta. Republican. Methodist. Avocations: photography; travel; writing novels; computers. Home: 10016 Balboa Blvd Northridge CA 91325 Office: Gaines Agy 8448 Reseda Blvd Northridge CA 91324

WEAVER, BARBARA FRANCES, librarian; b. Boston, Aug. 29, 1927; d. Leo Francis and Nina Margaret (Durham) Weisse; B.A., Radcliffe Coll., 1949; M.L.S., U. R.I., 1968; M.Ed., Boston U., 1978; m. George Briggs Weaver, June 6, 1951 (dec. 1970); 1 dau., Valerie Susan. Tech. writer EG&G, Inc., Boston, 1951-59; head librarian Thompson (Conn.) Public Library, 1961-69; dir. Conn. State Library Service Center, Willimantic, 1969-72, regional adminstr. Central Mass. Regional Library System, Worcester, 1972-78; state librarian N.J. State Library, Trenton, 1978—; library cons., 1975—; pres. Val-A, Inc., Thompson, Conn., 1980—. Mem. ALA, N.J. Library Assn., Aircraft Owners and Pilots Assn. Office: New Jersey State Library 185 W State St Trenton NJ 08625

WEAVER, CAROL JEAN, lawyer; b. Bethlehem, Pa., Oct. 27, 1956; d. Thomas Allan and Gloria Mae (Frantz) Weaver. B.A., Temple U., 1978; J.D., U. Pitts., 1983. Bar: Pa. 1983. Sole practice, Easton, Pa., 1983—; dir. real estate investments cos., Easton, 1982—. Mem. Pa. Bar Assn., Pa. Trial Lawyers Assn., Assn. Trial Lawyers Am., ABA. Democrat. Office: 349 Ferry St Easton PA 18042

WEAVER, CYNTHIA, lawyer; b. Radford, Va., Apr. 10, 1958; d. Walter Scott and Ruth E. (Conner) W. A.B. with honors, Coll. William and Mary, 1980; J.D., Mercer U., 1983. Bar: Ga. 1983, Va. 83, U.S. Tax Ct. 1983. Assoc., Heard Leverett & Adams, P.C., Elberton, Calif., 1983—. Mem. Ga. Women's Lawyers Assn., Nat. Assn. Female Execs., Va. Bar Assn., Ga. Bar Assn., Ga. Trial Lawyers Assn., Assn. Trial Lawyers Am., ABA, Phi Delta Phi. Democrat. Methodist. Club: Elberton Country. Avocations: numismatics; tennis; golf; skiing; softball. Home: 750 Fleming Rd C-1 Elberton GA 30635 Office: Heard Leverett & Adams 25 Thomas St Elberton GA 30635

WEAVER, CYNTHIA MARIE, lawyer; b. Phila., Oct. 30, 1948; d. Lucien Russell and Antoinette Marie (Galizia) Favata; m. Wayne Andrew Weaver, June 26, 1971; children—Tiffany Marie, Meredith Anne. B.A., Adelphi U., 1970; secondary edn. cert. Bloomsburg State Coll., 1972; J.D., SUNY-Buffalo, 1977. Bar: Pa. 1977, U.S. Dist. Ct. (ea. dist.) Pa. 1983; secondary edn. teaching cert., Pa. Tchr., Bristol Jr./Sr. High Sch. (Pa.), 1970-72; law clk. Div. of Claims, State of N.Y., Buffalo, 1976; asst. pub. defender Bucks County, Doylestown, Pa., 1977-79, dep. pub. defender, 1979-81; sole practice, Newtown, Pa., 1982—; solicitor Children and Youth Agy., Bucks County, 1984—; speaker, panelist on various law related issues, Bucks County and Phila., 1977-81. Pres. bd. dirs. Preventative Rehab. Youth and Devel., Bristol, Pa., 1978-81; bd. dirs. Reaching-at-Problems Group Home, Chalfont, Pa., 1981—, Three Arches, Inc., Falls Twp., Pa., 1985; Youth Services Assn., Bucks County, 1984—. Recipient Trial Lawyer's award Erie County Bar Assn., 1977. Mem. ABA, Assn. Trial Lawyers Am., Bucks County Bar Assn. (dir. 1983—). Democrat. Roman Catholic. Club: Soroptimists (pres.) (Indian Rock). Office: 110 S State St Newtown PA 18940

WEAVER, ELIZABETH, financial service marketing executive; b. N.Y.C., Apr. 29, 1958; d. Leonard Joseph and Marie (Kelly) W.; m. Charles Theodore Sporing, Nov. 14, 1982. B.A., Marist Coll., 1980; postgrad. Adelphi U., 1982. Asst. mktg. Shearson Loeb Rhoades, N.Y.C., 1980-81; asst. v.p. mktg. E. F. Hutton, Garden City, N.Y., 1981—. Mem. Newcomer's Assn., Rockville Ctr., N.Y., 1982. Mem. Nat. Assn. Female Execs. Republican. Roman Catholic. Avocations: cross-country skiing; all-terrain vehicle riding.

WEAVER, ELIZABETH ANN, retailing executive; b. Dallas, July 13, 1948; d. Joseph Reuben and Elizabeth Louise (Costello) Weaver. B.A., U. Tex., 1970; M.B.A., So. Methodist U., 1982. Mgr. personnel areas Sanger Harris, Dallas, 1970-74, mgr. selling services, 1974-76, mgr. credit div. areas, 1976-83, asst. accounts payable mgr., 1983-84, group mgr. control div., 1984—. Mem. So. Meth. U. M.B.A. Alumni Assn., Catholic Alumni Club Dallas (pres. 1983-84), Sigma Sigma Sigma. Roman Catholic. Home: 4236 Colgate Ave Dallas TX 75225 Office: Sanger Harris 303 N Akard St Dallas TX 75201

WEAVER, GLENDA ROSE, nurse; b. Liberty, Tex., Jan. 2, 1944; d. Glenn Wood and Esther Augusta (Becker) W.; student Lamar U., 1961-62; diploma Hotel Dieu Sch. Nursing, 1963; B.S., St. Joseph's Coll., North Windham, Maine, 1986. Cert. nurse adminstr. Supr., Kersting Meml. Hosp., Liberty, Tex., 1963-65; sch. nurse Liberty Ind. Sch. Dist., 1965-71; dir. nursing service Chambers Meml. Hosp., Anahuac, Tex., 1971-76; asst. dir. nursing service North Shore Med. Plaza, Houston, 1976-78; dir. nursing service Kelsey-Seybold Clinic, Houston, 1978-82; nurse specialist-adminstrn. Baylor U. Coll. Medicine, Houston, 1982—. Mem. Tex. Hosp. Assn.-Nursing Service Adminstrs., ARC (past county first aid chmn. and disaster nurse chmn.). Methodist. Home: 2501 Westridge #145 Houston TX 77054 Office: 1200 Moursund Suite 185A Houston TX 77030

WEAVER, KITTY DUNLAP, author; b. Frankfort, Ky., Sept. 24, 1910; d. Arch Robertson and Rebecca (Johnson) Dunlap; student Sorbonne, Paris, summer 1930; A.B., William and Mary Coll., 1932; M.A., George Washington U., 1933; B.S., U. Md., 1947; postgrad. Georgetown U., U. Pa., George Washington U., 1964-67, Moscow U., 1983. m. Henry Byrne Weaver, June 29, 1933. Jr. high sch. tchr., 1931-32; poultry farmer, 1947-55; author, 1970—. Clubs: Sulgrave (Washington); River (N.Y.C.). Author: Lenin's Grandchildren, 1971; Russia's Future, 1981. Home: Glengyle Aldie VA 22001

WEAVER, LUCY MARLENE, county official; b. Defiance, Ohio, Oct. 25, 1933; d. Harold Henry and Erma Arvilla (Wheaton) Rulman; m. Gerald Floyd Weaver, Jan. 24, 1956; 1 child, Ann Michelle. Diploma in nursing St. Vincent's Hosp., Toledo, Ohio, 1954; B.S., Defiance Coll., 1976; M.S. and Edn. in Pub. Health, U. Toledo, 1978. R.N. Staff nurse Defiance Hosp., 1954-55; pub. health nurse Defiance County health Dept., 1955-60, supervising nurse, 1960-65, dir. nurses, 1965-73, asst. health commr., 1973-76, acting health commr., 1976-78, health commr. Gen. Health Dist., 1978—. Campaign chmn. Defiance County Tb and Health Assn., 1966; bd. dirs. Ret. Sr. Vol. Program, Defiance, 1985, Defiance Area Easter Seal Soc., 1985; sec. Defiance County Bd. Health, 1976—. Recipient Disting. Service award Defiance chpt. ARC, 1965. Mem. Ohio Pub. Health Assn. (Cert. of Honor 1980), N.W. Ohio Pub. Health Assn., Ohio Health Commrs. Assn. (dir.-at-large), Ohio Geneal. Soc. (treas. 1983—), St. Vincent's Med. Ctr. Alumni Assn., Defiance Coll. Alumni Assn. Republican. Roman Catholic. Avocations: genealogy; gardening; antiques. Home: 100 Northfield Ave Defiance OH 43512 Office: County Health Officer Defiance County Seat PO Box 860 Defiance OH 43512

WEAVER, MOLLIE LITTLE, lawyer; b. Alma, Ga., Mar. 11; d. Alfred Ross and Annis Mae (Bowles) Little; m. Jack Delano Nelson, Sept. 12, 1953 (div. May 1970); 1 dau., Cynthia Ann; m. 2d, Hobart Ayres Weaver, June 10, 1970. B.A. in History, U. Richmond, 1978; J.D., Wake Forest U., 1981. Bar: N.C. 1982, Fla. 1983; Cert. profl. sec.; cert. adminstrv. mgr. Supr., Western Electric Co., Richmond, Va., 1952-75; cons., owner Cert. Mgmt. Assocs., Richmond, 1975-76; sole practice, Ft. Lauderdale, Fla., 1982-86, Emerald Isle, N.C., 1986—. Author: Secretary's Reference Manual, 1973. Mem. adv. council to Bus. and Office Edn., Greensboro, N.C., 1970-73, adv. com. to bus. edn. Va. Commonwealth U., Richmond, 1977. Recipient Key to City of Winston-Salem, N.C., 1963; Epps award for scholarship, 1978. Mem. ABA, N.C. Bar Assn., Broward County Women Lawyers Assn., Fla. Bar Assn., Profl. Secs. Assn. (past pres.), Word Processing Assn. (v.p., founder Richmond 1973-75), Adminstrv. Mgmt. Soc. (com. chmn. Richmond, 1973-75), Phi Beta Kappa, Eta Sigma Phi, Phi Alpha Theta. Republican. Baptist. Home: 807 Ocean Dr Emerald Isle NC 28557

WEAVER, PAMELA SUE, insurance company supervisor; b. Sylvania, Ohio, June 9, 1962; d. Frank D. and L. Kay (Truesdell) W.; m. Edward L. Groskopf, Dec. 19, 1981 (div. 1984). Student pub. schs., Phoenix. Sr. rater, coder St. Paul Ins., Phoenix, 1980-83; asst. underwriter CIGNA Ins. Co., Phoenix, 1983; supr. comml. lines Eagle Star Ins. Co., Scottsdale, Ariz., 1984—. Home: PO Box 31307 Phoenix AZ 85046

WEAVER, RITA MARGARET, association executive; b. N.Y.C., Oct. 28, 1925; d. Newcomb and Lucy Elizabeth (Roche) Gaylord; B.A., N.Y. U., 1945; postgrad Lady Margaret Hall, Oxford (Eng.) U., 1945-46; m. Robert A. Weaver (dec.); children—Richard L.N., Michael Cameron. Concert pianist, 1940; reporter Nuremberg trials, 1946-48; syndicated columnist Fashions from New York, Escort Publs., London, 1949-51; actress, Off Broadway productions and summer stock, 1952-56; pres. Empire State chpt. Nat. Soc. Arts and Letters, N.Y.C., 1978-80, chmn. ballet career awards conv., 1980, v.p. and chmn. lit. career awards dinner and music career awards dinner, 1980-82, ways and means chmn. nat. bd., 1982-84, credentials chmn., 1986-84, credentials chmn., 1986-88, v.p., career awards chmn.; chmn. liaison internat. consulates, 1982-84, v.p. chmn. by laws, 1984-86, nat. dance com., 1984-86; producer Off-Broadway Musical, 1980; bd. dirs. Eleanor Gay Lee Gallery Found., N.Y.C., 1977, membership chmn., 1978-80, chmn. benefit com., 1981-82.

WEAVING, SUSAN CATHERINE, theatrical agency executive; b. Derby, Conn., Sept. 2, 1952; d. James Phillip and Genevieve (Strubbe) W.; m. Richard Kwinmartini, Aug. 1, 1980. B.F.A., U. Conn., 1974. Property mistress, stage mgr. Southbury Playhouse, Conn., 1970-73; pres. Kolmar/Luth Entertainment, Inc., N.Y.C., 1980-85; pres. Nat. Artists Mgmt. Co., booking agy., N.Y.C., 1985—; guest lectr. U. Wis., Madison, 1984; speaker in field. Avocation: gardening. Home: 600 W 52d St New York NY 10019 Office: Nat Artists Mgmt Co 165 W 46th St Suite 1202 New York NY 10036

WEBB, BETTY JO, school administrator; b. Plain Dealing, La., Apr. 6, 1945; d. Joe and Georgia V. (Little) W; 1 child, Arthur Ray. B.A. in Sociology, U. Minn., 1967, M.A. in Edn. Adminstrn., 1973, postgrad. 1979—. Social worker Pillsbury Services, Mpls., 1967-68, Hennepin County, Minn., 1968-69; social worker Mpls. Pub. Schs., 1969-72, asst. prin., 1972-81, prin., 1981—; compliance specialist Mpls. Schs., 1976-78. Bd. dirs. Domestic Abuse Project, Mpls., 1985; active Bus. Econ. Edn. Found., St. Paul, Choir dir. Wayman Ch., Mpls. Mem. Nat. Assn. Secondary Sch. Prins., Minn. Assn. Secondary Sch. Prins., Nat. Alliance Black Sch. Educators, Mpls. Prins. Forum, Phi Delta Kappa. Baptist. Avocations: golf; fishing; tennis; piano; singing. Home: 3668 Brookdale Dr Minneapolis MN 55443 Office: Mpls Pub Schs Franklin Jr High 1501 Aldrich Ave Minneapolis MN 55411

WEBB, ELIZABETH SHEFFIELD, legal assistant; b. Canton, Ohio, Dec. 2, 1957; d. Thomas Dudley and Verity Elizabeth (Voight) Webb O'Brien; A.B., Mt. Holyoke Coll., 1979. Legal asst. Willkie Farr & Gallagher, N.Y.C., 1979-82, legal asst. supr., 1983—. Legal asst. Community Law offices, N.Y.C., 1980-82; clerical asst. 17th Precinct Police Detective, N.Y.C., 1981-82; chmn. homeless shelter St. Bartholomew's Ch., N.Y.C., 1983—. Mem. N.Y. Jr. League. Home: 509 E 83d St Apt 3R New York NY 10028 Office: Willkie Farr & Gallagher 153 E 53d St New York NY 10022

WEBB, JOYCE ANN, lawyer; b. Lima, Ohio, July 22, 1955; d. Alfred E. and Miyuki (Sadaishi) W.; m. Danny E. Guisinger, Jr., Aug. 2, 1975 (div. 1984); m. 2d, James Dale Rainwater, Apr. 21, 1984. B.B.A., Fla. Atlantic U., 1980; M.B.A. in Fin., U. Houston, 1983, J.D., 1983. Bar: Tex. 1983. Assoc. Wyckoff, Russell, Dunn & Frazier, Houston, Summer 1982; assoc. Jack D. Nolan, Houston, 1983; ptnr. Clements, Fraser & Webb, Houston, 1984—. Recipient Paul Broughton Service award U. Houston Student Bar Assn., 1983. Mem. ABA, Tex. Bar Assn., Assn. Bus. Women of Am. Office: Clements Fraser & Webb 16850 Royal Crest Dr Houston TX 77058

WEBB, JUDITH ANN, educator; b. Lumberton, N.C., Dec. 13, 1942; d. Parker Dunford and Betty Lou (Humphrey) Jones; m. Charles Richard Webb, June 24, 1967; children—Tracey Renee, Stacey Dawn. B.A., Howard U., 1963, M.A., 1967; D.A., Cath. U., 1983. Grad. fellow Howard U., Washington, 1963-64; tchr. English, D.C. pub. schs., 1964—, now tchr. Coolidge Sr. High Sch.; City-wide dir. maxi-arts prodns. D.C. Congress Parents and Tchrs., 1976—. Author: Negro in Print—Bibliographic Survey, 1971; editor The Capitol Spotlight, 1981—; contbr. articles to curriculum guides. Mem. Adv. Neighborhood Commn., Washington; committeewoman Am. fgn. students internat. scholarships Washington br. Ams. Abroad, 1971-72. Named Outstanding Young Educator, D.C. Jaycees, 1968, Outstanding Tchr. of Yr., Research Club, Washington, 1975; recipient spl. commendation UN Assn. U.S.A., 1975. Mem. Nat. Council Tchr. of English, Internat. Thespian Soc. (state dir. 1978—, Earl W. Blank Excellence award 1981), Am. Theatre Assn., Assn. for Supervision and Curriculum Devel., Alpha Kappa Alpha. Democrat. Baptist. Home: 7408 8th St NW Washington DC 20012 Office: DC Public Schools Coolidge Senior High Sch 5th and Tuckerman Sts NW Washington DC 20011

WEBB, KATHARINE, counselor; b. Bklyn., Sept. 13, 1931; d. Joseph Norris and Thelma (Black) Norris Sharpton; m. John James Webb, May 25, 1956 (div. Aug. 1971); children—John, Tyra, Lori. B.S. in Home Econs., Hunter Coll., 1954, M.S. in Home Econs., 1957; M.S. in Guidance and Counseling, Western Mich. U., 1969; Ph.D. in Guidance and Psychol. Services, Ind. State U., 1972. Tchr. home econs. N.Y.C. Bd. Edn., Bklyn., 1954-65, counselor, 1965-68; counselor Ind. State U., Terre Haute, 1970-72; assoc. prof. counselor edn. SUNY-Brockport, 1972-79; mem. N.Y. State Commn. of Correction, Albany, 1979-85; dir. guidance and counseling N.Y. State Dept. Correctional Services, 1985—; mediator, arbitrator Community Dispute Ctr., Rochester, N.Y., 1973-79; mediator, fact-finder N.Y. State Pub. Employees Relations Bd., Albany, 1975-79. Pres. bd. dirs. Brockport Childcare Ctr. (N.Y.), 1973-74, Nat. Migrant Found., Inc., Albany, 1983-84; bd. dirs. YWCA of Rochester (N.Y.), 1975-77. Recipient cert. recognition YWCA of Rochester, 1975, cert. disting. service Urban League Rochester, 1976, award for disting. spl. programs SUNY Office Spl. Programs, Albany, 1978, award for support and contbns. Rochester Ednl. Opportunity Ctr., 1978, award for service Mental Health Assn. Rochester, 1979. Mem. Am. Correctional Assn., N.Y. State Personnel and Guidance Assn. (v.p. for profl. services 1979-80), Am. Assn. Counseling and Devel., Pub. Offender Counselor Assn., Assn. for Non-White Concerns, 100 Black Women, Delta Kappa Gamma Soc., Delta Sigma Theta. Democrat. Roman Catholic.

WEBB, LORRAYNE BETH, librarian; b. Fargo, Okla., Aug. 25, 1925; d. William Albert and Zella Elizabeth (Bernard) Webb. B.A., Tex. State Coll. for Women, 1947, B.L.S., 1948. Librarian San Marcos High Sch., Tex., 1948-49, Houston Ind. Sch. Dist., 1949-52; asst. librarian U. Tex. Dental Branch (now U. Tex. Health Sci. Ctr. at Houston), 1952-71, librarian, 1971—; mem. librarians' com. U. Tex. System, Austin, 1972. Bd. dirs. Unitex Credit Union, Houston, 1973—, chmn. credit com., 1973—; trustee Lake Venice Property Owners Assn., Sugar Land, Tex., 1978-83. Mem. Med. Library Assn. (chmn. So. regional group 1969), Tex. Library Assn., Tex. Public Employees Assn., Nat. Audubon Soc., Houston Audubon Soc., Armand Bayou Nature Ctr. Soc. Republican. Avocations: birding, conservation. Home: 107 Savoy Sugar Land TX 77478 Office: Univ Tex Health Sci Ctr at Houston Dental Branch 6516 John Freeman Ave Houston TX 77030

WEBB, MARILYN MARTHA, educational administrator; b. Derby, Conn., Jan. 15, 1938; d. Melvin Newton and Martha (Parker) Woodford; m. Charles Edward Headford, Apr. 21, 1978; children—Glenn Richard Webb, Randall Dana Webb. B.S. in Elem. Edn. with honors, Central Conn. State U., 1959, M.S. in Elem. Edn., 1971; diploma advanced profl. studies-edn. specialist So. Conn. State U., 1981; postgrad. in gifted edn. Coll. New Rochelle, 1979, 83, St. Leo Coll., Fla., 1984; postgrad. Fla. Atlantic U., 1986. Classroom tchr. Bd. Edn., Trumbull, Conn., 1959-61, Ansonia, Conn., 1967-80; substitute tchr., Trumbull and Ansonia, 1961-67; pres. Basics & Creativity, Inc., Margate, Fla., 1980—; dir. edn., owner Forest Acad. and Alphabet Acad., Margate, 1980—; coordinator Imagery Inst., Coll. New Rochelle, N.Y., 1984; guest lectr. St. Leo Coll., 1985, Nova U., 1984. cons. to tchrs. and developers gifted and creative programs in Conn., Fla., N.Y., Ohio, La., Va. Colombia, S.Am. and Alta., Can. Author, illustrator Fun and Facts, 1976; editorial cartoonist Suburban News, Shelton, Conn., 1964-66; feature writer, illustrator Bridgeport Post, Conn., 1966-72. Fine arts dir. Unitarian Ch., Stratford, Conn., 1978; ghost writer local and state politicians, Shelton, Conn., 1960's; charter mem. Sterling Theatre Found., 1960's; publicity work Huntington Hist. Soc., Shelton, 1971-76; founder Parents for Gifted Edn., Ansonia, 1977; designed, directed 1st girls' camping program YMCA Camp Tepee, Trumbull, 1960; mem. fin. devel. team Broward Mental Health Assn. Scholar, Central Conn. State Coll., 1958-59; author grant for gifted program State of Conn., 1978. Mem. Assn. for Supervision and Curriculum Devel., Nat. Assn. for Edn. Young Children (field test validator 1984-85, nat. acad. validator 1985-86), Broward Kindergarten and Nursery Assn., S. Fla. Assn. Pvt. Schs., Nat. Assn. for Gifted Children, Nat./State Leadership Tng. Inst. for Gifted and Talented, Council Exceptional Children, Fla. Assn. Gifted, U.S. Assn. Montessori Internationale, Broward Assn. for Children Under Six. Avocations: art, interior decoration, swimming, music, stitchery. Home: 1820 NW 33d St Oakland Park Fort Lauderdale FL 33309 Office: Alphabet and Forest Acads Basics and Creativity Inc 6050 SW 7th St Margate FL 33068

WEBB, SHARON LYNN, writer; b. Tampa, Fla., Feb. 29, 1936; d. William Wesley Talbott and Eunice Geraldine Tillman; m. W. Bryan Webb, Feb. 6, 1956; children—Wendy, Jerri, Tracey. Student Fla. So. Coll., 1953-56, U. Miami, 1962; ADN, Miami-Dade Sch. Nursing, 1972. Freelance writer, 1960-66; registered nurse South Miami Hosp., 1972-73, Union Gen. Hosp., Towns County Hosp., Blairsville, Ga., 1973-81. Author: RN, 1981; Earthchild, 1982; Earth Song, 1983; Ram Song, 1984; over 40 short stories. Mem. Author's Guild/League, Sci. Fiction Writers Am. (south/central dir., bd. dirs.).

WEBB, SHIRLEY ANN, accountant; b. Durant, Okla., July 21, 1951; d. Ned and Irene Marie (Pamplin) Dyer; m. Richard Dewayne Webb, Sept. 4, 1970; children—Melinda Diane, Amy Nicole. Student U. Okla. Accountant, Moak, Hunsaker Rouse, Thomas & Co., Oklahoma City, 1979-80, Red Land

Exploration Co., Oklahoma City, 1981-82; fin. officer, treas. United Bankers Mortgage Corp., Oklahoma City, 1983-86; controller Pool Mortgage Co., Oklahoma City, 1986—. Mem. Oklahoma City Assn. Profl. Mortgage Women, Oklahoma City Women Accts. Democrat. Baptist. Avocations: water skiing; golf; reading; sewing. Home: 1200 Live Oak Edmond OK 73034 Office: 5400 NW Grand Blvd Oklahoma City OK 73116

WEBB, THEORA GRAVES, public relations consulting executive; b. Norfolk, Va., July 21, 1941; d. Lemuel and Theora (Weaver) Graves. B.A., Wilson Coll., 1962. Chmn. modern langs. dept. William Henry High Sch., Dover, Del., 1962-64; abstractor-indexer, Rockville, Md., 1966-67; owner RML Translations, Acton, Mass., 1969-70; asst. dir. communications and pub. relations, acting dir. publs. br., spl. asst. to dep. supt., cons.-expert, instr. adult edn. pub. schs. D.C., 1971-78; regional coordinator, cons. Nat. Energy Edn. Day, Cedar Rapids, Iowa, 1979; projects mgr. U.S. Com. for Energy Awareness, Washington, 1980-83; dir. office pub. affairs Internat. Trade Adminstrn., U.S. Dept. Commerce, Washington, 1983—; mng. ptnr. HSW Communications. Chmn. Region II Women in Energy, 1982-83; mem. energy and econ. devel. com. nat. NAACP, 1980-83, energy task force Nat. Conf. Black Mayors, 1982-83; adv. council vol. services Dist. 7 Dept. Correctional Services, 1979-80; adv. bd. Linn County Jail Chaplaincy, 1979-80, Cedar Rapids YWCA, 1978-80. Mem. Am. Assn. Blacks in Energy, Md. State Right to Read Task Force, Nat. Sch. Pub. Relations Assn., Nat. Assn. Women's Bus. Owners. Council of 100, D.C. Right to Read Task Force, Black Career Women. Club: National Press. Home: 9029 Ottawa Pl Silver Spring MD 20910

WEBB, VIRGINIA ANN, computer systems programmer and analyst; b. Hot Springs, Ark., Oct. 31, 1944; d. Elvin Raymond and Ozie Marie (Cleaver) Baker; m. Jessie Leon Bates, Dec. 21, 1963 (div. 1964); m. Joseph Howard Webb, Mar. 27, 1965; children—Joseph A., Sandra M., Susan M., Kristy A. Student So. State Coll., 1962-63; A. in Gen. Edn., Garland County Coll., 1985. Computer systems operator Dilliard's Inc., Little Rock, 1976-78; computer systems operator Weyerhaeuser So. Div. Office, Hot Springs, 1978-83, programmer, analyst, 1983—. Baptist. Avocations: yoga; camping; reading; karate; traveling. Address: 311 Pine Meadow Loop Hot Springs AR 71901 Office: Weyerhaeuser So Div 811 Whittington St Hot Springs AR 71913

WEBB, VIRGINIA RUTH, technical writer/editor; b. Maryville, Tenn., Sept. 28, 1955; d. Eugene Leslie and Ruth Lillian (Freeman) Webb; B.A. in English magna cum laude, U. Tenn., 1977, M.A. in English, 1979. Asst. dir. engring. central services Washington U., St. Louis, 1979-81; tech. writer/editor action data services Control Data Corp., St. Louis, 1981—; instr. St. Louis Coll. Pharmacy, part-time 1986—. Mem. South Atlantic Modern Lang. Assn., S.E. Conf. Linguistics, Nat. Assn. Female Execs., Phi Beta Kappa, Phi Kappa Phi, Alpha Lambda Delta. Home: 7709 Shirley Dr Apt 2W Saint Louis MO 63105 Office: 7822 Bonhomme St Clayton MO 63105

WEBBER, HELEN, artist-designer; b. N.Y.C., June 18, 1928; d. David and Frieda (Berlin) Ross; children—Joel Benjamin, Daniel Saul, Rachel Frieda. B.A., Queens Coll., 1951; postgrad. Columbia U. Sch. Social Work, 1953; M.A., R.I. Sch. Design, 1963. Freelance artist-designer; tchr. design dept. Calif. Coll. Arts and Crafts, 1972-73; guest lectr. U. Calif.-Davis, 1978, Mills Coll., 1979, Coll. of Marin, 1980, U. Calif.-Santa Cruz, 1982-84; keynote speaker Am. Soc. Interior Designers, Tulsa, 1977, San Diego, Kansas City, 1982, Nat. Home Furnishings League, San Francisco, 1980, Chgo., 1982; lectr., exhibitor 6th Internat. Congress Women Architects, Paris, 1983. Prin. commissioned works in fabric collage tapestry, ceramic murals, for Philippine Comml. and Indsl. Bank, Manila, Security Pacific Bank, Panama City, Panama, Fluor Corp. Hdqrs., Irvine, Calif., tss Festivale and tss Tropicale; also sculptured ceramic murals and fountain; painted aluminum sculptures for Hoilday, Jubilee cruiseships, Carnival Cruise Lines, Miami, Fla., Bay Area Rapid Transit, Lafayette, Oakland, Calif., Lesley Coll., Cambridge, Mass., VA, Nat. Cemetery, Riverside, Calif., East Tex. Med. Ctr., Tyler, St. Patrick's Hosp., Lake Charles, La., Gatwick Penta Hotel, London, Radisson Hotel, Lexington, Ky., Jewish Home for Aged, Houston, TSUBMI restaurant, Tokyo; designer-artist textile, wallpaper, sheets, towels, children's games for Collins & Aikman, Burlington; designer ceramic sculpted tile, tufted carpet, mosaics. Author, illustrator Good-Night, Night, The Sea Is My Blanket, 1963, My Kite is the Magic Me, Summer Sun. Mem. Design Internat. (pres., co-founder San Francisco 1984-85), Women-in-Design Internat. (founder, pres. 1977-83, Outstanding Contbn. to Design award 1980). Office: Helen Webber Designs Designs 410 Townsend St San Francisco CA 94107

WEBBER, MARGARET BROWN, civic worker; b. McIntosh, Fla., Dec. 24, 1913; d. William Randolph and Roberta (Farra) Brown; m. William Beverly Webber, Oct. 24, 1938; children—William Beverly, Robert Franklin, Betsey Farra, Bruce Randolph. Student Converse Coll., 1930-32; B.A., Coll. William and Mary, 1934. Co-founder Multnomah Play Sch., Portland, Oreg., 1948; mem. Washington County Juvenile Adv. Com., Tri-County Community Council, Portland; bd. dirs. YWCA, Portland, 1964-79, mem. world service council, 1977—; bd. dirs. Tigard Community Youth Services, Codero House; mem. long-range planning com. Tigard Sch. Dist.; mem. budget and eval. coms. United Way, Columbia-Willamette, Portland, 1971-83; mem. Jud. Fitness Commn.; bd. dirs. Portland Youth Philharmonic; bd. assocs. Linfield Coll., McKinnville, Oreg. Recipient Lay Educator of Yr. award Tigard (Oreg.) Sch. Dist., 1969; Excellence in Action award Delta Kappa Gamma, Beaverton, Oreg., 1980. Democrat. Methodist.

WEBBER, PAMELA CLARK, construction scheduling company executive; b. Ft. Hood, Tex., Apr. 20, 1947; d. John Lanham and Alice Paula (Collier) Clark; student Radford Coll., 1965-68; m. David L. Webber, Sept. 24, 1976; 1 dau., Stacey Michele. Civil engring. technician with various cons. engrs., 1969-75; critical path method tech. adviser Winn & Assos., Richardson, Tex., 1974-75; v.p., sec.-treas. DLW Infosystems, Inc., Richardson, 1975—; pres. On Schedule, Inc. (WBE), 1983—. Mem. Beta Sigma Phi (sec. 1973). Republican. Episcopalian. Office: 1223 N Glenville Dr Richardson TX 75081

WEBB-PEABODY, SANDRA LORRAINE, insurance agency executive; b. Peabody, Mass., Oct. 13, 1951; d. Stanley Lincoln and Dorothy Pauline (Burnworth) Webb; m. William Nelson Peabody, Dec. 31, 1982; 1 son, Christopher Burns Peabody. B.A., Bates Coll., 1973. C.P.C.U.; cert. ins. counselor. Asst. to pres. Webb, Childs, McDonald Ins. Agy., Inc., Peabody, 1973-76, v.p., 1976—, treas., 1981—; dir. IIR/ACORD Corp., White Plains, N.Y., 1983-84, Acord Corp., Oradell, N.J., 1980-83. Pres. Peabody-Lynnfield YMCA, 1979; dir. Peabody chpt. ARC, 1981-82. Mem. Soc. C.P.C.U.s, Soc. Cert. Ins. Counselors, Peabody C. of C. (dir. 1979-80). Office: Webb Childs McDonald Insurance Agency Inc 24 Main St Peabody MA 01960

WEBER, BARBARA, financial executive; b. Bryn Mawr, Pa., Feb. 12, 1939; d. John Patrick and Margaret Veronica (Clune) Burke; m. Francis Owen Weber, Oct. 28, 1978; children—Richard, Jennifer, Charles, John, Deborah. B.A., Rosemont Coll., 1960. Broker, Jefferson Standard, Bethesda, Md., 1975-77; sr. v.p. Wallace Fin. Group, Bethesda, 1977-83; dir. agencies Home Life Ins. Co., Bethesda, 1983-84; pres. Md. Fin. Group, Balt., 1984—. Mem. Nat. Republican Congl. Com., 1986. Mem. Gen. Agts. and Mgrs. Assn. (treas.), Nat. Assn. Life Underwriters, Nat. Assn. Securities Dealers, Balt. Estate Planning Council, Balt. Assn. Fin. Planners, Internat. Assn. Fin. Planners. Roman Catholic. Club: Hunt Valley Country. Avocations: swimming; horseback riding. Home: 15 Glen Lyon Ct Phoenix MD 21131 Office: Md Financial Group 401 Washington Ave Suite 700 Towson MD 21204

WEBER, CAROL A., publisher; b. Washington, May 3, 1940; d. Harry Lee and Rosa Lee (McCannon) Almond; m. Romann H. John Weber, Aug. 6, 1966; 1 son, Romann Matthew. B.A. in English, Madison Coll. (now James Madison U.), 1962. Gen. assigment reporter Roanoke Times (Va.), 1962-64; gen. assignment reporter Miami Herald (Fla.), from 1964, successively edn. writer, investigative reporter, asst. city editor, Broward editor, to 1982, asst. mng. editor features, 1982-84, assoc. pub., 1985—. Mem. Com. of 100, Project Horizon Steering Com.; bd. dirs. Mus. Art, Broward Performing Arts Authority Found., Inc. Recipient various state, nat. awards for writing; named Woman of Yr., Women in Communication, Broward County, Fla., 1981. Office: The Miami Herald 1520 E Sunrise Blvd Fort Lauderdale FL 33304

WEBER, CECILIA ELIZABETH, set designer; b. Milw., Apr. 1, 1943; d. Kenneth E. and Eva S. (Scharmach) W. B.F.A., U. Wis.-Milw., 1966. Choreographer, Ballet Makers, 1971-73; set designer Sta. WMVS-WMVT-TV, 1973-85; tchr. Milw. Area Tech. Coll., 1973-85; v.p. Resort Unique, boarding kennel, Caledonia, Wis., 1986—; art dir. Scenic Design Studios, West Allis, Wis., 1981—; TV cons. Northwestern Mut. Life Ins. Co., 1982—. Editor, writer newsletter Shepherd Tales, 1983—. Mem. U.S. Inst. Theatre Tech., Internat. TV Assn., Am. Boarding Kennel Assn. (award 1985), German Shepherd Dog Club Am., German Shepherd Dog Club Wis., Therapy Dogs Internat. Avocations: breeding; showing and training champion German Shepherds. Office: Scenic Design Studios 2505 S 95th St West Allis WI 53227

WEBER, CHRISTINE LOIS, cosmetologist; b. Denver, Sept. 15, 1951; d. Thomas Allen and Ruth Lois (Smallcombe) W. A.A.S., Arapahoe Community Coll., 1971; student U. Colo., 1972-75; B.A., Loretto Heights Coll., 1976; grad. Columbine Beauty Sch., Lakewood, Colo., 1974. Founder, editor Who Knows newspaper, Littleton, Colo., 1970-72; dist. mgr. Montgomery Ward/Wendy, Ward, Denver, 1971-73; founder, pres. Sunshine Enterprises, Boulder and Denver, 1974—; mgr. Antoine Du Chez, Inc., Denver, 1980-81; founder, owner, mgr. Razzle Dazzle Hair, Denver, 1981—. Cons., lectr. Revlon Realistic, U.S., 1976-80, Helene Curtis, 1977—, Helen of Troy, 1983-85; image cons. Aurora Parks and Recreation, Colo., 1985—. Author: Let's Face It!, 1979. u. colo. scholar, 1972. Mem. Nat. Hairdressers and Cosmetologists Assn., Colo. Hairdressers and Cosmetologists Assn., Assn. Female Execs., Better Bus. Bur., Denver C. of C., Phi Theta Kappa. Roman Catholic. Clubs: Masters Swim; Phidippedes Track. Avocations: swimming; team triathlons; biking; photography; writing poetry; gardening. Office: Sunshine Enterprises 9042 E Amherst Dr Denver CO 80231

WEBER, DARLENE, restaurant executive; b. Milw., Jan. 5, 1930; d. Bert B. and Blanche (Corne) Harvey; student public schs., also specialized courses; m. Kurt Weber, Aug. 16, 1964; children—Kim, Jay, Kurt. Engaged in restaurant bus., 1948—; owner-mgr. White Tablecloth Restaurant, Cedarburg, Wis., 1966-69; pres., mgr. The Nantucket, Mequon, Wis., 1969-79; owner, mgr., corp. v.p. Nantucket Shores Restaurant, Milw., 1973—. Regional dir. Milw. Crusade, 1979; mem. council Christ Luth. Ch., Mequon, 1979. Mem. Wis. Restaurant Assn. (dir., v.p. Milw. chpt. 1982, now state bd. dirs.), Tempo. Club: Mequon Racquet.

WEBER, JANET M., nursing school administrator; b. Lansdale, Pa., Mar. 12, 1936; d. Russell H. and Naomi (Moyer) W. B.S. in Nursing, Grace Coll., 1960; diploma in nursing Washington County Hosp. Sch. Nursing, 1959; M.Ed., Duquesne U., 1969. Staff nurse, supr. Murphy Med. Ctr., Warsaw, Ind., 1959-60; coll. nurse Grace Coll., Winona Lake, Ind., 1959-60; med. surg. nursing instr. Washington County Hosp. Sch. Nursing, Hagerstown, Md., 1961-64; pvt. duty nurse Washington County Hosp., Hagerstown, 1964; chmn. founds. of nursing Presbyn. Univ. Hosp. Sch. Nursing, Pitts., 1963-72; curriculum coordinator Albert Einstein Med. Ctr. Sch. Nursing, Phila., 1972-73, assoc. dir., 1973-74, acting dir., 1974, dir., 1974—. Cons., Md. Bd. Higher Edn., 1981-82. Author: Assisting Students with Educational Deficiencies, 1975; The Faculty's Role in Policy Development, 1981. Mem. Pa. League Nursing (pres. 1982-86, bd. dirs. Area I, 1974-76), Washington County Hosp. Nurses Alumni Assn. (pres. 1962-64), Nat. League Nursing (bd. rev. 1980-84, chmn. elect council on diploma programs 1985—), Am. Hosp. Assn. Assembly Hosp. Schs., Hosp. Assn. Pa. (sec. council hosps. with schs. nursing 1979), Grace Coll. Alumni Assn., Duquesne U. Alumni Assn. Republican. Office: Albert Einstein Med Ctr Sch Nursing York and Tabor Rds Philadelphia PA 19141

WEBER, KATHY ANN, nurse; b. Bronx, N.Y., Feb. 5, 1955; d. Peter Charles and Frances Marie (Roberto) Wroblewski; m. Robert Michael Weber, May 4, 1979; 1 child, Sean Michael. B.S. in Nursing, Mount Saint Mary Coll., 1977. R.N., N.Y. Clin. instr. Suffolk Community Coll., Brentwood, N.Y., 1983-84; asst. head nurse North Shore U. Hosp., Manhasett, N.Y., 1984—, nurse recruiter, 1985—. Avocations: winter skiing; bicycling.

WEBER, LINDA JEAN, hospital association executive; b. Teaneck, N.J., May 4, 1958; d. Steven and Jean Ann (Govia) Wojciechowski; m. John Stephen Weber II, Oct. 9, 1983. B.A., Rider Coll., 1980. Program dir. Am. Cancer Soc., Lawrenceville, N.J., 1980-82; dir. car passenger safety programs N.J. Hosp. Assn., Princeton, 1983—. Vol., Am. Cancer Soc., Lawrenceville, 1983—; speaker communications dept. Rider Coll., Lawrenceville, 1980—; mem. Columbiettes, Hamilton, N.J., Mercer County Traffic Safety Com., Cranford, N.J., 1985—. Recipient Outstanding Pub. Info. award N.J. div. Am. Cancer Soc., 1982. Mem. Nat. Assn. Female Execs., N.J. Safety Belt Com., Hwy. Users Fedn., Nat. Child Passenger Safety Assn. (regional rep. 1983—, awards nominating com. 1986), Rider Coll. Alumni Assn. (telethon chmn. 1981). Roman Catholic. Home: 818 Quinton Ave Trenton NJ 08629 Office: NJ Hosp Assn 760 Alexander Rd Princeton NJ 08540

WEBER, MARGARET LAURA JANE, accountant; b. Fairview, Mo., Jan. 4, 1933; d. Mert James and Margaret Orr (Mortensen) Joel; m. James E. Jennings, Mar. 1953 (div.); children—James Edward Jennings, Janie Lea Franks, David Alan Jennings; m. Albert H. Weber, June 1956; children—Luhwanna Stonecipher, Margaret Anne Shadwick. A.A., Crowder Coll., Mo., 1972; postgrad. Mo. So. Coll., 1985. Teller, First State Bank, Joplin, Mo., 1951-53; clk. Mo. Lic. Dept., Joplin, 1954-57, U. Mo. Ext. Dept., Neosho, 1967-68; cashier Crowder Coll., Neosho, Mo., 1968-83, acct., 1983—. Mem., Newton County Welfare Com., 1984—. Mem. Am. Bus. Women's Assn. (Woman of Yr. 1982), Nat. Assn. Female Execs., Mo. Assn. Community Jr. Colls. (bd. dirs. 1978-82). Republican. Baptist. Home: Rt 6 Box 197 Neosho MO 64850 Office: Crowder Coll 601 Laclede Ave Neosho MO 64850

WEBER, MARY ELLEN HEALY, economist; b. San Francisco, May 28, 1943; d. Ignatius Bernard and Grace Marie (Hogan) Healy; B.A., Dominican Coll., 1965; postgrad. Nat. U. Mex., 1967, (vis. scholar) Stanford U., 1969-70, Cath. U. Chile, 1970-71, U. Chile, 1971-72; Ph.D., U. Utah, 1974; m. Stephen Francis Weber, Dec. 21, 1971. U. Utah teaching fellow, 1965-68; asst. prof. Smith Coll., 1972-75; country economist World Bank, IBRD, 1975-76; sr. economist Internat. Research & Tech. Corp., McLean, Va., 1976-78; dir. regulatory analysis, chief economist OSHA, U.S. Dept. Labor, Washington, 1979-84; pres. Weber Enterprises, 1984—. Social Sci. Research Council fgn. area fellow 1969-71. Mem. Am. Econ. Assn., Nat. Economists Club, Nat. Assn. Bus. Economists, Soc. Govt. Economists, Washington Women's Network. Roman Catholic.

WEBER, MARY HELEN, lawyer; b. Chgo., Sept. 24, 1950; d. Frank Joseph and Mary Helen (Suchy) Kryda; m. Roger Alan Weber, Aug. 11, 1973. B.A., Wellesley Coll., 1972; M.A., Harvard U., 1973; J.D., U. Cin., 1976. Bar: Ohio 1976, U.S. Dist. Ct. (so. dist.) Ohio 1976, U.S. Ct. Appeals (6th cir.) 1976, U.S. Tax Ct. 1977. Law clk. to judge U.S. Dist. Ct. (so. dist.) Ohio, Cin., 1976-77; atty. Cin. Dist. Counsel's Office, IRS, Cin., 1977-82, sr. atty., 1982-85, dep. regional counsel for tax litigation Central Region, 1985—. Contbr. articles to legal jours. Recipient Spl. Achievement Performance Bonus award Chief Counsel's Office, IRS, Washington, 1983, High Quality Increase award, 1982; Atty. of Quarter award Central Region Chief Counsel's Office, IRS, 1981; nominee Younger Fed. Lawyer award Fed. Bar Assn., 1983, 84; nominee James E. Markham Jr. award IRS, 1982. Mem. Order of Coif, ABA, U. Cin. Law Alumni Assn. (v.p., trustee 1983-85), Phi Beta Kappa. Clubs: Wellesley Coll. (pres. 1982-83), Radcliffe Coll. (treas. 1979-84), Harvard (bd. dirs. 1986—). Office: Regional Counsel's Office IRS Room 7510 Fed Office Bldg 550 Main St Cincinnati OH 45202

WEBER, MOLLY SMITH, editor; b. Durham, N.C., Sept. 4, 1957; d. H. Ralph and Sally Ann (Simmons) Smith; m. Walter Charles Weber, July 13, 1985. B.A. in Psychology, Yale U., 1979; M.A. in Edn., Stanford U., 1980. Dir. aquatics SUNY-Purchase, 1980-81; sales rep. Prentice-Hall, Inc., Englewood Cliffs, N.J., 1981-83; sales rep. West Ednl. Pub., St. Paul, 1983-85, editor, 1985—. Mem. Nat. Assn. Female Execs. Avocations: swimming; running; photography. Home: 309 E 70th Terr Kansas City MO 64113 Office: West Pub Co PO Box 411628 Kansas City MO 64141

WEBER, PATRICIA LOUISE BRADEN, marketing educator; b. Ft. Wayne, Ind., Oct. 31, 1945; d. Walter Frederick and Margaret June (Houk) Nagel, Jr.; m. Joseph Lou Braden, Aug. 23, 1969 (div. Feb. 1975); m. 2d, Walter Jacob Weber, Jr., July 20, 1981. B.S. in Bus. Adminstrn. with distinction, Ind. U., 1967, M.B.A., 1969, D.Bus.Adminstrn., 1973. Staff research assoc. div. research Sch. Bus. Adminstrn., Ind. U., Bloomington, 1967-70; adj. asst. prof. mktg. Coll. Bus., Eastern Mich. U., Ypsilanti, 1970, assoc. dean Coll. Bus., 1981—; mem. research faculty Grad. Sch. Bus. Adminstrn., U. Mich., Ann Arbor, 1970-81, asst. dir. div. research, 1980-81, adj. assoc. prof. mktg., 1974-81; subprogram coordinator Coastal Zone research Mich. Sea Grant Program, Ann Arbor, 1977—; mem. steering com. Minority Tech. Council Mich., Ann Arbor, 1982-83; mem. resource adv. com. Mich. changing economy program Mich. Dept. Commerce, Lansing, 1975-76; mem. subcoms. on competitive position, econ. growth and diversification, and statis. data Mich. Econ. Action Council, Lansing, 1975-76; dir. many sponsored research projects, cons. to govt., industry, bus. firms and profl. groups, 1970—. Author: Technological Entrepreneurship, 1977; (with Ramesh Gurnani) Data Processing in the Tax Function, 1980; also numerous tech. reports and articles in profl. jours. Program advisor Mich. Council for Arts, Detroit, 1978; bd. dirs. Child and Family Services of Washtenaw, Ann Arbor, 1983—, chmn. devel. com., 1984—. Mem. AAAS, Am. Inst. for Decision Scis. (chmn. Mktg. Track, Midwest AIDS), Am. Mktg. Assn. (chpt. v.p., dir. 1976-80, chmn. program com. 1977-78, editor chpt. membership directory 1977, Marketeer 1975-77; chpt. cert. of recognition 1976-79), Am. Statis. Assn., Internat. Council for Small Bus. (research adv. com. 1974-75), Mich. Tech. Council (research adv. bd. 1982-84), Soc. Automotive Engrs. (assoc. mem.; co-chmn. socio-tech. com. 1982—, sessions chmn. internat. congress 1982), Greater Detroit C. of C. (econ. devel. strategic planning com. 1982—), Eastern Mich. U. Women's Assn. (pres.-elect 1983—), Mich. Hist. Soc., Ann Arbor Art Assn. (dir., treas. 1980—), DAR, Alpha Gamma Delta, Beta Gamma Sigma, Omicron Delta, Alpha Lambda Delta. Home: PO Box 7775 Ann Arbor MI 48107 Office: 508 Pray-Harrold Bldg Coll of Bus Eastern Mich U Ypsilanti MI 48197

WEBER, YVONNE ROEBUCK, research administrator; educator; b. McKeesport, Pa., Oct. 22; d. Raymond Henry and Clara Maria (Roberts) Roebuck; B.A., U. Pitts., 1947, M.Litt., 1952, Ph.D., 1973; postgrad. Kent State U., 1950; Ecole Normale, Paris, 1953, Goethe Institut, 1960; m. William Frederick Weber, June 16, 1961; children—Laurel, Wendy. Tchr. French, German, English, history Carrollton (Ohio) High Sch., 1947-51, Canton, Ohio, 1951-52, Munhall (Pa.) High Sch., 1952-58, Wilkinsburg (Pa.) High Sch., 1958-61, Upper St. Clair (Pa.) High Sch., 1963-65; asst. prof. French and German, California (Pa.) State Coll., 1965-66, Point Park (Pa.) Coll., 1968-72; asst. prof., supr. edn. Washington and Jefferson Coll., 1976-79; head research project Delta Kappa Gamma Soc., Internat., Pitts., 1979-82. Recipient Good Citizenship award DAR, 1943; U. Pitts. scholar, 1943-47, Panhellenic Assn. scholar, 1946-47, disting. alumni award Sch. Edn., U. Pitts., 1985 Fulbright grantee to Germany, 1960; program scholar Nat. Endowment for the Humanities, Am. Library Assn., 1986; named Disting. Alumna, U. Pitts., 1971-82. Mem. Modern Lang. Assn., Doctoral Assn. Educators, Pa. State Modern Lang. Assn., Pa. Assn. Tchr. Educators, U.Pitts. Alumni Council, Delta Kappa Gamma Soc. Internat. (Scholarship 1972-73, Eunah Temple Holden Golden Anniversary award 1979), Mensa Internat., Pi Lambda Theta, Phi Delta Gamma, Zeta Tau Alpha. Club: McKeesport Coll. Author: A Beacon to the Future: Charting a Course for Advancement; contbr. articles to profl. jours. Home: 43 Dutch Ln Pittsburgh PA 15236

WEBSTER, CATHERINE ALICE, nurse, insurance examiner; b. San Rafael, Calif., Apr. 5, 1958; d. Robert E. and Helen L. (Niemeyer) W. A.S. in Nursing, Coll. of Marin, 1979; B.S. in Nursing, Sonoma State U., 1982. Registered nurse, Calif.; cert. pub. health nurse, Calif. Nurses aide Profl. Nurses Bur., San Rafael, 1978-79; staff nurse Novato Community Hosp., Calif., 1979-84; allergy nurse, office mgr., Novato, 1984—; ind. contractor, ins. examiner Hooper-Holmes, Inc., Hayward, Calif., 1983—, Am. Paraprofl. System, Walnut Creek, Calif., 1985—, Phys. Measurements Info., San Ramon, Calif.; R.N. evaluator Am. Claims Evaluations, Inc., Los Angeles. Avocations: miniatures; stamps; crafts; reading. Home and Office: PO Box 446 Novato CA 94948

WEBSTER, DIANE BARSTOW, newspaper editor; b. Fresno, Calif., Sept. 1, 1932; d. Richard Nason and Anna Laura (Dewhirst) Barstow; m. Gordon Morris Webster, Aug. 5, 1950; children—Gordon M., Norman G., Laura Webster Herzog. Reporter, The Fresno Bee, 1957-72, asst. women's editor, 1972-75, asst. to city editor, 1975-77, asst. met. editor, 1977-81, feature editor, 1981—. Republican. Methodist. Office: The Fresno Bee 1626 E St Fresno CA 93786

WEBSTER, JANICE MAY RAND, school administrator; b. Ashland, Maine, Jan. 19, 1931; d. Glen Clayton Rand and Irene (Collier) Rand Sawyer; m. Carleton Tucker, Aug. 26, 1950 (div. June 1969); children—Bruce Rand, Karen Marie, Colleen Patricia, Mary Lee Cary Tucker Mullen; m. Kent Day Webster, Aug. 21, 1969. B.S. in Edn., Gorham State Coll., 1969; M.S. in Guidance-Counselling, U. Maine, 1971; Ed.D., Vanderbilt U., 1985. Cert. tchr., guidance counselor, prin., supt., Maine. Tchr. English, Sanford Sch. System, Maine, 1969-77; tchr. English Ashland High Sch., Maine, 1977-80; guidance counselor Ashland High Sch. Dist. #32, 1980-82, prin., 1982—. Bd. dirs. Aroostook Mental Health Ctr., Caribou, Maine, 1980—. Mem. Nat. Assn. Secondary Prins., Maine Secondary Sch. Prins. Assn. Republican. Home: PO Box 405 Ashland ME 04732 Office: Ashland Sch Dist Box N Ashland ME 04732

WEBSTER, LAWANNA, cosmetician; b. Bluefield, W.Va., Sept. 17, 1938; d. Willie and Willie (Wade) Fitts; m. Anthony A. Webster, Oct. 8, 1960; children—Karen B., Anthony, Kimberly. Grad. Madame C.J. Walker Beauty Coll., 1960; B.A., Nat. Inst. Cosmetology, 1979; student Glancha Natural Cosmetic Sch., 1978. Owner, mgr. Webster Beauty Salon, Bluefield, W.Va., 1969—, LaSher's Boutique, Bluefield, 1984—; pres. Tri-City Cosmetician, Bluefield, 1966—. Active Girl Scouts U.S.A. Mem. Jackson Flowerttes Beauticians (sec. 1969-75), Va. Beauticians Assn., Nat. Beauty Culture League, Alpha Kappa Alpha. Democrat. Baptist. Club: Just Us (v.p.). Avocations: sewing; cooking; bowling; traveling; tennis. Address: 141 Clifford St Bluefield WV 24701

WEBSTER, LINDA KRISTOF, lawyer, army officer; b. Corpus Christi, Tex., Aug. 29, 1956; d. Paul Judson and Shirley Helen (Fitzgerald) Adams; m. Noel Ray Webster, Nov. 19, 1977; 1 child, David Ray. B.A. in History and Geography with highest honors, cert. secondary social studies, U. Okla., 1978; J.D., U. Tex., 1981. Bar: Tex. 1981. Entered as capt. U.S. Army, 1982; asst. Staff Judge Adv., Ft. Hood, Tex., 1982—, prosecutor, 1982-83, legal asst., 1983—. Contbr. articles to legal jours. Mem. ABA, Tex. Bar Assn., Assn. Am. Trial Lawyers, Am. Bus. Women's Assn. Democrat. Office: Office of Staff Judge Advocate Fort Hood TX 76544

WEBSTER, NANCY JOAN, personnel specialist; b. Geneva, Ohio, Jan. 21, 1949; d. Arthur Clair and Alice Mary (Falk) Eisbrenner; m. Bruce Alan Webster, June 15, 1968; children—Teresa Lynn, Melanie Marie. B.A. in Bus. Mgmt., Hiram Coll., 1985. Placement specialist Goodwill Industries, Ashtabula, Ohio, 1973-77, Ohio Job Service, Ashtabula, 1977-80; personnel specialist RMI Co., Ashtabula, 1980—; EEO affirmative action, 1984—; dir. C&W Custom Designs, Inc. Pub. relations chmn. Saybrook Elem. Sch. PTO, Ashtabula, 1976-78, carnival chmn., 1975-78, pres. 1976-78; sec. Mallory Sharon Metals Recreational Assn., Ashtabula, 1982-84; bd. dirs. United Way, Ashtabula County, 1976-79; vice chmn. allocations com., 1978-79, com. mem. priorities, nomination, Ohio Citizens Council, services innovations, 1977-80. Recipient Cert. of Appreciation, Goodwill Industries, 1975, Ashtabula County Vocat. Edn. Sch., 1985. Mem. Ashtabula County Personnel Assn. Republican. Roman Catholic. Avocations: consumer advocacy; volunteer work; home remodeling and repair. Office: RMI Co Metals Reduction Plant E 21 and State Rd PO Box 490 Ashtabula OH 44004

WEBSTER, SHARON B., polit. economist; b. Wildwood, Fla., Aug. 23, 1937; d. James McWilliams and Marion (Haulbrook) Boen; B.A., U. Fla., 1959; Ph.D., U. Va., 1965. Asst. prof. No. Mich. U., Marquette, 1962-64, U. Md., Marquette, 1964-66, Hollins (Va.) Coll., 1966-71; prof. Fed. Exec. Inst., Charlottesville, Va., 1971-72; program mgr. IRS, Washington, 1972-74; economist Econs., Statistics and Coop. Service, Washington, 1974-79; mem. Presdl. Commn. for Exec. Exchange, 1979-80; dir. internat. econs. Occidental Petroleum Corp., Los Angeles, 1980—. Mem. adv. bd. Pres.'s Carribbean Basin Initiative, 1982. Mem. Internat. Policy Inst. (v.p. 1977—), Internat. Assn. Energy Economists, Am. Assn. Agrl. Economists, Am. Polit. Sci. Assn., Nat. Assn. Bus. Economists, Internat. Studies Assn., Soc. Internat. Devel., Nat. Council Career Women. Contbr. articles to profl. jours. also: Occidental Petroleum Corp 10889 Wilshire Blvd Los Angeles CA 91504

WEBSTER-SCHOLTEN, C. PENNY, geologist, technical writer, geologist; b. Los Angeles, Oct. 10, 1940; d. Coleby Heliman and Sarah Yvonne (Craig) Webster; m. Donald Benjamin Scholten, Aug. 29, 1959; children—Jill Adair, Monica Lynn. A.A. in Geology with honors, Yavapai Coll., 1975; B.S. in Geology, No. Ariz. U., 1981, M.A. in Community Coll. Edn., 1982. Instr.

geology Yavapai Coll., Prescott, Ariz., 1976-77; geologist Cities Service Co., Tulsa, Okla., 1982-83; staff editor Am. Assn. Petroleum Geologists, Tulsa, 1983-84; tech. editor, writer Lawrence Livermore Nat. Lab., Livermore, Calif., 1985—. Mem. Am. Assn. Petroleum Geologists, Geol. Soc. Am., Assn. Earth Sci. Editors, No. Calif. Geol. Soc., Nat. Assn. Geology Tchrs., Sigma Gamma Epsilon (sec. 1980-81). Republican. Lutheran. Avocations: backpacking; mineral collecting; art and antique collecting. Office: Lawrence Livermore Nat Lab PO Box 5507 L-453 Livermore CA 94550

WECHMAN, CAROL ANN, insurance company executive; b. Floydsburg, Ky., Oct. 5, 1938; d. Fred Maurice and Frances Elizabeth (Robinson) Lindsey; m. Raymond Wechman, June 7, 1958; children—Raymond, Deborah Ann, Brian Maurice. Student pub. schs., LaGrange, Ky. Sec., Ky. Central Ins. Co., Anchorage, 1956; stenographer Fed. Bur. Investigation, Washington, 1956-57, Chrysler Corp., Missile Research Div., Huntsville, Ala., 1957-59; with Metlife Security Ins. Affiliate/Met. Life, Chatham, N.J., 1974-80, 82—, asst. v.p., 1984—. Mem. Nat. Assn. Female Execs. Methodist. Office: 97 Main St Chatham NJ 07928

WEDDELL, ROSE MARIE, nurse, administrator; b. Lincoln, Nebr., Mar. 16, 1940; d. Meredith Kruse and Virginia (Cook) W. Diploma Mercy Coll. Nursing, 1961; B.S. in Nursing, U. San Francisco, 1966; M.H.A., Baylor U., 1974. Nurse methods analyst Walter Reed Army Med. Ctr., Washington, 1976-79; dir. nursing Fox Army Hosp., Redstone Arsenal, Ala., 1982-84; asst. dir. nursing Wurzburg MEDDAC, Fed. Republic Germany, 1979-82, Moncrief Army Hosp., Ft. Jackson, S.C., 1984—; adminstrn. resident Letterman Army Med. Ctr. San Francisco, 1973-74; adv. bd. dirs. U. Ala., Huntsville, 1983-84. Mem. Nat. League for Nurses, Am. Nurses' Assn. (cert.), Am. Theater Organ Soc., Sigma Theta Tau, Beta Phi. Republican. Roman Catholic. Avocations: quilting; painting; cross stitch. Office: Moncreif Army Community Hosp Fort Jackson SC 29207

WEDGWORTH, RUTH SPRINGER, fertilizer company executive; b. Eaton Rapids, Mich., May 10, 1903; d. Clarence P. and Minnie L. (Washburn) Springer; student Mich. State U., 1921-23; LL.D. (hon.), U. Fla., 1965; H.H.D. (hon.), Fla. So. Coll., 1976; m. Herman H. Wedgworth, June 23, 1923; children—Helen Jean, George H., Barbara Ann. Pres., Wedgworth Farms, Inc., Belle Glade, Fla., 1938-80, Wedgworth's Inc., Belle Glade, 1954—, pres. Wedgworth Produce, Inc., Belle Glade, 1955-65; sec. Seminole Life Ins. Co., West Palm Beach, Fla., 1955-65; dir. Fla. Nat. Bank, Belle Glade, 1979—. Mem. Palm Beach County (Fla.) Bd. Edn., 1947-53; bd. dirs. Western Palm Beach County Hosp. Dist., 1940-47; chmn. Highlands Glades Drainage Dist., 1942-68; mem. Gov.'s Com. on Migrant Work, 1942-46; trustee Fla. So. Coll., 1970—; mem. migrant work com. Nat. Council Chs., 1948-56; leadership mem. Boy Scouts Am., 1979. Recipient Award of Merit, Gamma Sigma Delta, 1978; Council of Farmers Cooperatives award, 1979; named Woman of Yr. (Progressive Farmer, 1947), Belle Glade, Fla., 1975; award for excellence in industry and bus. Palm Beach County Com. on Status of Women, 1978; Disting. Service award, Fla. Farm Bur., 1979, Fla. Fruit and Vegetable Assn., 1958; Outstanding Service award for employment and community leadership Everglades Progressive Citizens, 1970; Achievement award, Lions, 1961. Mem. Fla. Fruit and Vegetable Assn., Fla. Hort. Soc., Fla. Soils Sci. Soc., Beta Sigma Phi. Methodist. Clubs: Belle Glade Women's, PEO, Lions (internat. hon.). Office: 651 NW 9th St Belle Glade FL 33430

WEDRAL, ELAINE REGINA, food chemist; b. Detroit, Feb. 29, 1944; d. Albert and Anna Amelia (Stalc) Maesso; B.S. with honors in Biochemistry, Purdue U., 1966; M.S. in Microbiology, Cornell U., 1968, Ph.D. in Food Chemistry, 1970; m. William Wedral, May 23, 1970. Quality control foreman, supr. Holloway House (Green Giant Food), Lafayette, Ind., 1964-65; chemist Campbell Soup Co., Chgo., 1966; mgr. microbiology Western Farmers Assn., Seattle, 1970-71; project coordinator nutrition and prodn. safety Libby McNeill & Libby Inc., Chgo., 1972-74, asso. dir. product devel., 1974-76, dir. research and devel., 1976, v.p. research and devel., 1979-80; v.p., dir. Westreco (Western Hemisphere Research Co. div. Nestle Inc.), New Milford, Conn., 1981—. Mem. Nat. Food Processors (sci. affairs council), Am. Meat Inst. (sci. research com. 1976-81), Grocery Mfrs. Am. (tech. rep. 1974-77). Contbr. articles to various publs. Office: Westreco Inc Boardman Rd New Milford CT 06776

WEE, ELIZABETH LIU, research biochemist; b. Manila, Nov. 7, 1941; d. Liu Gaw and Juana Leesuy; came to U.S., 1964; m. William G. Wee, June 24, 1967; children—Lawrence, Anthony. B.S. in Chem. Engring., Mapua Inst. Tech., Manila, 1963; M.S. in Chemistry, Northeastern U., 1967; Ph.D., U. Minn., 1971. Research assoc. U. Minn., Mpls., 1971, Children's Hosp. Med. Ctr., Cin., 1972—. Author: Current Topics in Developmental Biology, vol. 19, 1984; also articles. Mem. Teratology Soc. Office: Automation Research of Cin PO Box 19512 Cincinnati OH 45219

WEEKES, SHIRLEY M., artist; b. Buffalo, May 9, 1917; d. Ray Roscoe and Loretta Marie (Ent) Thompson; grad. Detroit Art Acad., 1939; m. Thomas Weekes, Mar. 27, 1942; children—Judith, Thomas. One woman shows: Frye Mus., Seattle, 1967, 72, Haines Gallery, Seattle, 1973, 75, Challis Gallery, Laguna Beach, Calif., 1970, 72, 74; group shows include: Frye Mus., 1965-69, 71-75, Seattle Art Mus., 1972; represented in permanent collections Frye Mus., Laguna Beach Mus. Art. Mem. N.W. Watercolor Soc., San Diego Watercolor Soc. Home: 40451 Calle Fiesta Rancho California CA 92390

WEEKS, BRIGITTE, newspaper book review editor; b. Whitchurch, Hants, Eng., Aug. 28, 1943; came to U.S., 1965; d. Jack and Margery May (Millett) W.; student Univ. Coll. of North Wales, Bangor, 1962-65; m. Edward A. Herscher, Sept. 6, 1969; children—Hilary, Charlotte, Daniel. Asst. editor Boston Mag., 1966-70; editor Kodansha Internat., Tokyo, 1969-72; editor Resources for the Future, 1973-74; asst. editor The Washington Post Book World, 1974-78, editor, 1978—; pres. Nat. Book Critics Circle. Office: The Washington Post Washington DC 20071

WEEKS, JANET HEALY, judge; b. Quincy, Mass., Oct. 19, 1932; d. John Francis and Sheila Josephine (Jackson) Healy; A.B. in Chemistry, Emmanuel Coll., Boston, 1954; J.D., Boston Coll., 1958; LL.D. (hon.), U. Guam, 1984; m. George Weeks, Aug. 29, 1959; children—Susan, George. Admitted to Mass. bar, 1958, Guam bar, 1972; trial atty. Dept. Justice, Washington, 1958-60; trial atty. firm Trapp & Gayle, Agana, Guam, 1971-73; partner firm Trapp, Gayle, Teker, Weeks & Freidman, Agana, 1973-75; judge Superior Ct. Guam, Agana, 1975—; chmn. task force cts., prosecution and defense Terr. Crime Commn., 1973-76; mem. Terr. Crime Commn. Bd., 1975-76, Guam Law Revision Commn., 1981—; rep. Nat. Conf. State Trial Judges, 1982. Mem. Catholic Sch. Bd. Guam, 1973. Mem. Nat. Assn. Women Judges (charter), Am. Judges Assn., Am. Bar Assn., Fed. Bar Assn. (chpt. sec. 1974), Guam Bar Assn. Club: Internat. (Guam). Office: Superior Ct Guam 110 W O'Brien Dr Agana Guam GU 96910

WEEKS, PATSY ANN LANDRY, librarian, teacher; b. Luling, Tex., Mar. 3, 1930; d. Lee and Mattie Wood (Callihan) Landry; m. Arnett S. Weeks, Dec. 2, 1950; children—Patsy Kate, Nancy Ann, Janie Marie. B.S., Southwest Tex. State U., San Marcos, 1951; M.L.S., Tex. Woman's U., Denton, 1979. Tchr. art, reading, math. Grandview Ind. Sch. Dist., Tex., 1950-52; tchr. phys. edn. Beaumont Ind. Sch. Dist., Tex., 1953; tchr. art, coll. algebra Cisco Jr. Coll., Tex., 1957-58; tchr. remedial reading Taylor County Schs., Tuscola, Tex., 1965-66; tchr. remedial reading Anson Ind. Sch. Dist. Tex., 1971-73; librarian Bangs Ind. Sch. Dist., Tex., 1973-79, learning resources coordinator, 1979—; adv. com. Edn. Service Ctr., 1978-83; coordinator Reading is Fundmental Program, 1978-83. Bd. dirs. Anson Pub. Library, Tex., 1971-72. Exhibitor oil paintings, pastels at Tex. fairs (1st prize 1952, 60). Mem. ALA, Assn. Library Service to children (Caldecott award com. 1986), Am. Assn. Sch. Librarians, Intellectual Freedom Round Table, Assn. Supervision and Curriculum Devel., Tex. Library Assn. (mem. intellectual freedom and profl. responsibility com. 1979-81, Tex. Bluebonnet award com. 1982-85), Tex. Assn. Sch. Librarians (media prodns. award com. 1985-86), Tex. Assn. Improvement Reading, Teenage Library Assn. Tex. (chmn. audio-visual award com. 1984), Tex. Assn. Sch. Library Adminstrs., Tex. State Tchr. Assn. (life), Kappa Pi, Alpha Chi, Beta Phi Mu, Delta Kappa Gamma. Baptist. Clubs: Bangs Progressive Women's (treas. 1974-76). Home: 110 Poco St Bangs TX 76823 Office: Bangs Ind Sch Dist PO Box 969 Bangs TX 76823

WEEKS, ROBBIE C., educator, administrator; b. Mulga, Ala., Oct. 13, 1936; d. Jesse Lewis and Ruby Pearl (Miles) Jackson; m. Cleophus James Weeks, June 10, 1956; children—Cleophus, Reginald Darnell. B.S., Daniel Payne Coll., Ala., 1966; M.Ed., Ala. State U., 1976; Advanced Study in Edn., U. Ala.-Birmingham, 1977. Cert. educator, administr., Ala. Instr. J.A. Davis Elem. Sch., Bessemer, Ala., 1968—, coordinator programs Bessemer City Sch. System, 1971—, supr. communications J.A. Davis Elem. Sch., 1979-83, coordinator workshops, 1984-85, coordinator creative writing, oratorical contests, sponsor Red Cross Club, 1985—. Contbr. articles to profl. jours., scripts for video presentations in edn.; editor: (sch. paper) Communications, 1979. Coordinator programs Allen Temple AME Ch., Bessemer, 1970—, steward, 1985—; mem. Unserv Council, Birmingham, Ala., 1984—; block capt. March of Dimes Mothers, Bessemer, 1986; pres. Bessemer Edn. Assn., 1985—. Mem. NEA, Nat. Assn. Female Execs., Ala. Edn. Assn. Democrat. Methodist. Club: Auxiliary (Bessemer). Lodge: Order Eastern Star. Avocations: writing; singing; speaking; sports; traveling. Home: 1314 21st Ave N Bessemer AL 35020

WEEMS, CATHLEEN, city official; b. Jasper, Ala., May 28, 1920; d. Rufus Hillard and Mary Elizabeth (Handley) Cornelius; m. Jesse James Weems, Feb. 7, 1942 (dec. 1978); children—Coletta Renea Weems Kirkpatrick. Student Walker Coll., 1960-61. Teller, Bank Cordova Citizens, Ala., 1938-42; with Indian Head Mills, Cordova, 1943-56, sec. to pres., 1957-59, sec. to So. Dist. pres. Natco Corp., Cordova, 1960-70; asst. to mgr. Health Care Center, HEW, Cordova, 1971-77; exec. dir., mgr. Cordova Housing and Cordova Manor, 1977—; exec. dir. Cordova Housing Authority, 1977—; sec., mgr. Cordova Manor Apts., 1977—; mgr. Cordova Park, 1977-82, Cordova Warrior River Apts., 1977-82. Sec., Citizens Group, Cordova, 1983—; active ARC; mem. Ala. Dept. Econ. and Community Affairs, Montgomery, Vol. & Info. Center of Community Resources, Birmingham. Fellow Nat. Assn. Housing Redevel. Officials, Nat. Assn. Female Execs.; mem. Ala. Housing & Urban Devel. Registration, Nat. Assn. Housing & Redevel. Democrat. Baptist. Clubs: Ladies Aux VFW, Order Eastern Star, Lioness. Avocations: music; travel; aerobics; ceramics. Home: 101 Stewart St Cordova AL 35550 Office: Cordova Housing Authority Route 2 Cook Blvd Cordova AL 35550

WEEMS, KATHARINE LANE, sculptor; b. Boston, Feb. 22, 1899; d. Gardiner Martin and Emma Louise (Gildersleeve) Lane; prep. edn. May Sch., Boston; art edn. Sch. of Museum of Fine Arts, Boston; pupil of Charles Grafly, Anna Hyatt Huntington, George Demetrios and Brenda Putman; m. F. Carrington Weems, Nov. 15, 1947. Prin. works include Dog Narcisse Noir, Museum Fine Arts, Boston, and Reading (Pa.) Mus., Kanagroo, Pa. Acad. Fine Arts, 12 foot bronze group Dolphins of the Sea Water Plaza, New Eng. Aquarium, Boston; rep. permanent collection: Greek Horse, Balt. Mus. Art; Bear, Spee Club, Harvard; Whippet, Glenbow Found. Mus.; Whippet and Fox, Colby Coll. Art Mus., Waterville, Maine; brick carvings and entrance doors, and 2 bronze rhinoceroses, Inst. of Biology, Harvard; sculpture on Lotta Fountain, Boston; small bronzes in pvt. collections; permanent exhbn. Weems Gallery Animal Sculpture, Mus. Sci., Boston; sculptor Goodwin medal Mass. Inst. Tech.; sculptor for U.S. Legion of Merit medal and medal for Merit, also Fincke Meml. medal Groton Sch. Mem. Mass. Art Commission, 1941-47. Decorated chevalier L'Ordre Nat. Merit (France); recipient bronze medal Sesqui-Centennial Exposition, Phila., 1926; Widener Meml. gold medal Pa. Acad. Fine Arts, 1927; honorable mention Paris (France) Salon, 1928; Joan of Arc gold medal Nat. Assn. Women Painters and Sculptors, 1928; hon. mention Grand Central Galleries, N.Y.C., 1929; bronze medal Boston Tercentenary Fine Arts Exhbn., 1930; Anna Hyatt Huntington prize Nat. Assn. Women Painters and Sculptors, 1931; Speyer prize NAD, 1931, 63, 72, Barnet prize, 1932; hon. mention Archtl. League of N.Y., 1942; Anonymous prize Nat. Assn. Women Artists, 1946; Saltus gold medal for merit Nat. Acad. Design, 1960; Lindsey Morris Meml. prize Nat. Sculpture Soc., 1960, Kalos Kagathos Found. sculpture prize, 1981; gold medal Nat. Arts Club, N.Y.C., 1961. N.A. Fellow Nat. Sculpture Soc. (council 1949); mem. Guild Boston Artists, Nat. Assn. Women Artists, Nat. Inst. Arts and Letters, Grand Central Art Galleries, Archtl. League, Am. Artists Profl. League, N. Shore Arts Assn., Huguenot Soc., Lords of Colonial Manors. Mass. Soc. Colonial Dames Am. Allied Artists Am. Clubs: Chilton (Boston); Cosmopolitan, Pen and Brush (N.Y.C.); Catherine Lorillard Wolfe. Home: PO Box 126 Manchester MA 01944

WEEMS, SUSAN GAYLE, radio sales executive; b. Billings, Mont., Nov. 17, 1943; d. Robert Prehn and Hariett (Hannel) Wilson; m. Charles R. Hurt, June 13, 1964 (div. 1975); children—Tamara Susan, Sharon Louise; m. Charles F. Weems, June 23, 1979; 1 child, Max. B.S., U. Mont., 1964. Pres. Interstate Talent Co., Knoxville, Tenn., 1968-75; prodn. mgr. Alex Cooley & Assocs., Atlanta, 1975-77; pres., chief exec. officer Joint Venture, Inc., Atlanta, 1977—; media asst. BDA/BBDO, Inc., Atlanta, 1980-83; regional mgr. Weiss & Powell, Inc., Atlanta, 1984—. Editor World of Arm Sports mag., 1985—, also various books, 1980—. Producer World's Wristwrestling Events, 1978—. Mem. Atlanta Broadcast Advertisers, Atlanta Radio Rep. Assn. (sec. 1984-85), Nat. Assn. Female Execs., Nat. Entrepreneur Assn. Republican. Roman Catholic. Avocations: music; photography. Home: 1716 Terrell Mill Rd S-4 Marietta GA 30067 Office: Weiss & Powell Inc 3355 Lenox Rd 750 Atlanta GA 30326

WEERGANG, ALIDA, cosmetology educator and administrator, consultant; b. Schiedam, Netherlands, Aug. 22, 1941; came to U.S., 1960, naturalized, 1970; d. Wouter and Alida H. (Dielamans) W. Lic. cosmetologist. Owner, ptnr. Continental Salon, Hudson and Nashua, N.H., 1963-83; ednl. dir. Continental Academie, Hudson, 1973—, pres., Manchester, N.H., 1982—; v.p. Continental Crimping, Inc., Hudson, 1983—. Editor: American Hair in Motion, 1985. Recipient Rose Dor du Paris award Festival Du Mondial, 1970. Mem. N.H. Hairdressers and Cosmetologists Assn. (1st v.p. 1983-84), Hair Am. Div. of Nat. Hairdressers and Cosmetologists Assn., (styles dir. 1977-79, hair Am. designer 1983-84, internat. judge 1984—), N.H. Fedn. Republican Women. Baptist. Clubs: Zonta, Lionesses (v.p. 1984-85). Avocations: gardening; traveling. Office: Continental Crimping Inc 102 Derry St Hudson NH 03051

WEESE, CYNTHIA ROGERS, architect educator; b. Des Moines, June 23, 1940; d. Gilbert Taylor and Catharine (Wingard) Rogers; m. Benjamin H. Weese, July 5, 1963; children—Daniel Peter, Catharine Mohr. B.S., Washington U., St. Louis, 1962, B.Arch., 1965. Registered architect., Ill. Pvt. practice architecture, Chgo., 1965-72, 1974-77; draftsperson, designer Harry Weese & Assocs., Chgo., 1972-74; prin. Weese Hickey Weese Ltd., Chgo., 1977—; design critic Ball State U., Muncie, Ind., Miami U., Oxford, Ohio, 1979, U. Wis.-Milw., 1980, U. Ill.-Chgo., 1981, Iowa State U., Ames, 1982. Mem. AIA (dir. Chgo. chpt. 1980-83, v.p. 1983-85, disting. bldg. awards 1977, 81, 82, 83, interior architecture award 1981, disting. service award 1978), Chgo. Women in Architecture Chgo. Networks, Alpha Rho Chi. Democrat. Club: Arts (Chgo.). Office: Weese Hickey Weese 230 E Ohio St Chicago IL 60611

WEGING, MARGARET HASIER, lawyer; b. Chgo., Oct. 15, 1953; d. John J. and Gloria (Neuman) Hasier; m. James E. Weging, Aug. 3, 1974. B.A., DePaul U., Chgo., 1974; J.D., Ill. Inst. Tech.-Chgo. Kent Coll. Law, 1979. Bar: Ill. 1979, U.S. Dist. Ct. (no. dist.) Ill. 1979, U.S. Ct. Appeals (7th cir.) 1979. Sr. atty. firm Osterkamp, Jackson & Hollywood, Chgo., 1977-82; sole practice, Oak Park, Ill., 1982—. Editor: Kenmore Rev., 1983. Mem. Chgo. Bar Assn., ABA, West Suburban Bar Assn., Royal History Soc. Am., Oak Park-River Forest C. of C., Delta Theta Phi. Democrat. Roman Catholic. Office: 401 South Blvd Oak Park IL 60302

WEGNER, MARY SUE, nuclear engineer; b. Centralia, Ill., Feb. 27, 1941; d. Clarence Frank and Mabel Arwood (Collie) Wehlage; A.A. in Physics, McLennan Community Coll., 1972; B.S. in Nuclear Engring., Tex A&M U., 1974; postgrad. Ga. Inst. Tech., 1980-81; m. Lloyd Arthur Wegner, May 7, 1961 (div.); children—Diana Teresa, Kathleen Marie, Karl David. Draftsman USAF, Keesler AFB, Miss., 1959-60; clk. Mid-State Electric Co., Alexandria, La., 1963-66; draftsman Dresser Indsl. Valve and Instrument div., Alexandria, 1966-67; aircraft insp. Gen. Dynamics, Waco, Tex., 1968-70; draftsman Lone Star Gas, Waco, 1971-72; nuclear field engr. Gen. Electric Co., Atlanta, 1974-81; nuclear engr. Nuclear Regulatory Commn., Bethesda, Md., 1981—. Served with USAF, 1959-60. Cert. governance Am. Nuclear Soc. Mem. Am. Nuclear Soc. (chmn. 1977). Home: 12205 Bond St Wheaton MD 20902 Office: Nuclear Regulatory Commn Office Inspection and Enforcement Washington DC 20555

WEGRZECKI, MARIA ANIELA, accountant; b. Warsaw, Poland, May 27, 1917; came to U.S., 1960, naturalized, 1964; d. Henryk Victor and Romana (Brzozowska) Olszewski; m. Lester L. Wegrzecki, July 2, 1960. M. Econs., Warsaw U., 1953; B.S.B.A., Lawrence Inst. Tech., Southfield, Mich., 1980. Fin. planner Polish Ministry Forestry and Lumber Industry, Warsaw, 1947-59; asst. to v.p. fin. Fellows Med. div. Chromalloy Am. Corp., Oak Park, Mich., 1963-78; asst. controller Alsar Aluminum Corp., Southfield, 1978-80; gen. acct. Engring. Soc. Detroit, 1980-82; compensation acct. Chevrolet-Can. Group, Gen. Motors Co., Warren, Mich., 1984—; cons. income taxes. Active Friends of Polish Art, Detroit, 1969—, pres., 1980-84; chmn. cultural exchange com. Am. Council Polish Cultural Orgns., Miami, Fla., 1984-85. Mem. Women Accts. Assn. (Detroit chpt.). Roman Catholic. Avocations: travel and touring. Home: 28551 San Marino Dr Southfield MI 48034

WEH, REBECCA ROBERTON, charter services administrator, computer consultant; b. Colorado Springs, Colo., Sept. 23, 1946; d. Eddie Joseph, Jr. and Roberta Louise (Aucoin) Roberton; m. Allen Edward Weh, July 5, 1968; children—Deborah, Ashley, Brian. B.S., U. N.M., 1969, postgrad. spl. edn., 1970-72, acctg., 1980-82. Tchr., Calvert Acad., Albuquerque, 1971-72, Albuquerque Pub. Sch., 1972-73; staff acct. McCarthy, Weems, C.P.A.s, Albuquerque, 1979-83; v.p., adminstrn. Charter Services, Albuquerque, 1983—; computer programmer various small bus., N.M., 1982—; instr. Computer Software Seminars, 1983—. Designer, developer Computer Programs for Bus., 1984—. Vol., N.M. Kidney Found., Albuquerque, 1972; mem. City of Albuquerque Beautification Com., 1982-84; vol. U.S. Senator P.V. Domenici Republican campaign, Albuquerque, 1983-84. Mem. Jr. League of Albuquerque (treas. 1984-85, nominating com. 1985-86, Service award), Kappa Alpha Theta (fin. adv. 1977-78, treas. 1977-82, Outstanding Alumni of Yr. 1980). Roman Catholic. Home: 1421 Kirby St NE Albuquerque NM 87112 Office: Charter Services Inc PO Box 25604 Albuquerque NM 87125

WEHMAN, MARTHA CLAIRE, advertising executive; b. Memphis, May 23, 1936; d. John Henry and Dorothy (Todd) W. B.J., U. Mo., 1957; student Memphis State Coll., 1953-55. Copywriter Sta. KBHS-AM-FM, Hot Springs, Ark., 1958-67, Sta. WDIA-AM and FM, Memphis, 1967-72; advt. v.p. Dorrity Advt., Memphis, 1972-81, Jan Gardner & Assocs., Memphis, 1981—; cons. Career Days, Memphis State U. Sch. Journalism, 1983-84. Mem. Memphis Advt. Fedn. (Pyramid award 1971, Gold cert. 1982), Am. Advt. Fedn. (newsletter editor 7th Dist. 1982-84). Presbyterian. Home: 1413 Somerset St Memphis TN 38104 Office: Jan Gardner & Associates Inc 3340 Poplar St Suite 229 Memphis TN 38111

WEHRLE, MARTHA GAINES, former state legislator; b. Charleston, W.Va., Nov. 30, 1925; d. Ludwell Ebersole and Betty (Chilton) Gaines; A.B., Vassar Coll., 1948; M.A., Harvard U., 1954; m. Russell Schilling Wehrle, Oct. 16, 1954; children—Michael H., Ebersole Gaines, Katherine S., Philip N., Martha Chilton. Tchr., W.Va. schs., 1949-50, Belmont (Mass.) Day Sch., 1951-53; mem. W.Va. Ho. of Dels., 1974-84, vice chmn. edn. com., 1976, chmn. constl. revision com., 1977-84, mem. fin. com.; dir. Kanawha Bank & Trust Co., 1984—. Bd. dirs. W.Va. Vocat. Edn. Found., United Way, Arthur B. Hodges Ctr., Inc.; mem. adv. council W.Va. Woman's Commn. Mem. LWV. Democrat. Episcopalian. Clubs: Kanawha Garden, Charleston Jr. League.

WEHUNT, JUDY ANN, city official; b. Acworth, Ga., Jan. 3, 1952; d. Lemon Juddy and Margaret Jean (Dills) Goddard; m. William Richard Wehunt, Jan. 15, 1978. Grad. high sch., Canton, Ga. Utility clk. City of Canton, 1970-76, asst. city clk. 1976-81, city clk., 1981—. Mem. Ga. Mcpl. Clks, and Fin. Officers (9th dist. bd. dirs. 1984—, chmn. membership com. 1984, cert.), Internat. Inst. Mcpl. Clks. (cert.), Canton Profl. Bus. Woman's Club (Profl. Bus. Woman of Day 1983), Cherokee County C. of C. Democrat. Baptist. Avocations: hiking; swimming; fishing; white water rafting; football. Home: PO Box 863 Canton GA 30114 Office: City of Canton PO Box 468 Canton GA 30114

WEI, KATHERINE, business executive; b. Peking, China, Oct. 4, 1930; came to U.S., 1949, naturalized, 1969; d. Kato and Alice (Chao) Yang Young; m. C.J. Shen (div.); children—Ada, Lawrence, Ava; m. Chung C Wei; children—Larry, Audrea. Diploma in Nursing, Shanghai Nursing Sch., 1949. Adminstr., Med. Office, J.F. Kennedy Airport, 1952-71; dir. pub. relations Falcon Shipping Group, Houston, 1971-80, sr. v.p., 1980—; pres. Monna Lisa Precision Corp., N.Y.C., 1968—, Wonderway, Houston, 1980—; lectr. in field. Author: (autobiography) Second Daughter, 1984. Pres., Am. Contract League Charity Found., Memphis, 1984—. Mem. Am. Contract Bridge League. Avocation: bridge. Address: 340 E 64th St New York NY 10021

WEIBLEN, JANET KATHERINE, mfg. co. exec.; b. Englewood, N.J., Feb. 16, 1941; d. Alfred Herman and Augusta Alma (Schellack) Weiblen; student Rapid Advancement program N.Y. U., 1957-58, Wittenberg U., 1958-59, Barnard Coll., 1959-61; B.A. summa cum laude, Fairleigh Dickinson U., 1976; m. Nov. 4, 1962 (div. 1974); children—Scott William Rusterholz, Lisa Michele Rusterholz. Asst. to dir. Fairleigh Dickinson U. Mental Health Center, Teaneck, N.J., 1973-76; asst. to v.p. Hanover Sq. Realty Investors, N.Y.C., 1976-78; traffic mgr. Kingsley & Keith Chem. Corp., Englewood Cliffs, N.J., 1978-79; corp. traffic mgr. Maidenform, Inc., Bayonne, N.J., 1979—; adj. prof. New Sch. Social Research. N.J. chmn. Nat. Humanities series Nat. Endowment for the Arts, 1971-72; pres. PTA, Waldwick, N.J., 1972-73; bd. dirs. YWCA, Bayonne, 1981. Mem. Nat. Council Phys. Distbn. Mgmt. (v.p.), Newark Traffic Club, Raritan Traffic Club, Hudson County Traffic Club, Nat. Assn. Female Execs., Delta Nu Alpha (local dir.). Lutheran. Contbr. article to profl. jour. Office: Maidenform Inc 154 Ave E Bayonne NJ 07002

WEIDA, DONNA LEE, computer company executive; b. Logansport, Ind., Oct. 29, 1939; d. Donald L. and Leila J. (Sweet) Kleckner; A.A., Orange Coast Coll. and Saddleback Coll., Mission Viejo, Calif., 1980; student Calif. State U.-Fullerton, 1983—; children—Mark, Traci, Teri, Sec., K.L.K. Mfg. Co., Logansport, 1957-60, 63-65; sec. Sch. Edn., Mich. State U., 1962-63; sec. Sch. Fine Arts, U. Calif., Irvine, 1966-69; co-organizer Plaza Vet. Clinic, Upland, Calif., 1969-70; mgr. Bob Bondurant Sch. High Performance Driving, Ontario (Calif.) Motor Speedway, 1970-73; mgr./pub. relations exec. Chuck Jones Racing, Costa Mesa, Calif., 1973; exec. sec. Dana Steel, Newport Beach, Calif., 1974; estimator/office mgr. Hardy & Harper, Tustin, Calif., 1975-76; controller/mgr. Gillen/Kloss Advt., Newport Beach, 1977-78; purchasing adminstr. Butler Housing, Irvine, 1979; controller/mgr. XMark Corp., Costa Mesa, 1980-81; adminstrv. mgr. Concept Devel., 1981; corp. sec., adminstrv. mgr. Personal Systems Tech., Inc., Laguna Hills, Calif., 1982-84, founder/owner Numbers & Words, Irvine, 1982-84; v.p. fin. Granada Group, Irvine, 1984—. Mem. Nat. Assn. Female Execs., Am. Soc. Profl. and Exec. Women, Beta Sigma Phi. Republican. Episcopalian. Home: 14241 Utrillo Dr Irvine CA 92714 Office: Granada Group 18002 Skypark Circle Irvine CA 92714

WEIDEL, LYNNE CATHERINE, consulting firm executive; b. Ridley Park, Pa., Sept. 13, 1946; d. Daniel Gossard and Antoinette Marie (Maccinile) W. B.A., U. Del., 1968; M.H.A., U. Minn., 1976. Dir. instl. planning Met. Hosps., Inc., Portland, Oreg., 1979-81, v.p., 1982-83; chief exec. officer Clackamas Health Care Consortium, Portland, 1982-83; prin. Weidel & Assocs., Portland, 1983—; sports network coordinator Inst. for Managerial and Profl. Women, Portland, 1980-81; mem. Multnomah sub-area council Northwest Oreg. Health Systems Agy., Portland, 1982-83; preceptor U. Minn., Mpls., 1982—. Bd. dirs. Portland YWCA, 1983-84; vol. mgmt. cons. Dougy Ctr., Portland, 1984—. Mem. Am. Coll. Hosp. Adminstrs., Am. Soc. Hosp. Planners, Oreg. Health Care Planning and Mktg. Assn. (steering com. 1984—). Republican. Club: Bergfunde Ski (Portland). Avocations: white water rafting; hiking. Office: Weidel & Assocs Suite 1-C 3930 Lake Grove Lake Oswego OR 97034

WEIDEMANN, CELIA JEAN, social scientist, international development consultant; b. Denver, Dec. 6, 1942; d. John Clement and Hazel (Van Tuyl) Kirlin; m. Wesley Clark Weidemann, July 1, 1972; 1 child, Stephanie Jean. B.S., Iowa State U., 1964; M.S., U. Wis.-Madison, 1970, Ph.D., 1973; postgrad. U. So. Calif., Washington, 1983. Advisor, UN Food & Agr. Orgn., Ibadan, Nigeria, 1973-77; ind. researcher, Asia and Near East, 1977-78; program coordinator, asst. prof., research assoc. U. Wis., Madison, 1979-81; chief institutional and human resources U.S. Agy. for Internat. Devel., Washington, 1982-85, team leader, cons., Sumatra, Indonesia, 1984; dir. fed. econs. program Midwest Research Inst., Washington, 1985—; cons. Internat. Ctr. for Research on Women, Kinshasa Zaire, 1986. Author: Planning Home Economics Curriculum for Social and Economic Development; contbr. chpts. to books and articles to profl. jours. Am. Home Econs. Assn. fellow, 1969-73. Mem. Soc. Internat. Devel., Am. Sociol. Assn., U.S. Dirs. of Internat. Agrl. Programs, Assn. for Women in Devel. (founder, bd. dirs.), Am. Home Econs. Assn. (Wis. internat. chmn. 1980-81), Internat. Fedn. Home Econs., Pi Lambda Theta, Omicron Nu. Roman Catholic. Avocations: mountain trekking; piano/pipe organ; canoeing; photography. Home: 2607 N 24th St Arlington VA 22207 Office: Midwest Research Inst 1750 K St NW Suite 250 Washington DC 20006

WEIDENFELD, SHEILA RABB, TV producer, author; b. Cambridge, Mass., Sept. 7, 1943; d. Maxwell M. and Ruth (Cryden) Rabb; B.A., Brandeis U., 1965; m. Edward L. Weidenfeld, Aug. 11, 1968; children—Nicholas Rabb, Daniel Rabb. Assoc. producer Metromedia, Inc., WNEW-TV, N.Y.C., 1965-68; talent coordinator That Show with Joan Rivers, NBC, N.Y.C., 1968-71; coordinator NBC network game programs, N.Y.C., 1968-71; producer Metromedia, Inc., WTTG-TV, Washington, 1971-73; creator/producer Take It From Here, NBC (WRC-TV), Washington, 1973-74; press sec. to first lady Betty Ford and spl. asst. to Pres. Gerald R. Ford 1974-77; mem. Pres.'s Adv. Commn. on Historic Preservation, 1977-81; TV producer, moderator On the Record, NBC-TV, WRC-TV, Washington, 1978-79; pres. D.C. Prodns., Ltd., 1978; mem. Sec. State's Adv. Commn. on Fgn. Service Inst., 1972-74. Corporator, Dana Hall Sch., Wellesley, Mass; bd. dirs. Wolf Trap Found., Women's Campaign Fund, 1978-79; bd. dirs. D.C. Contemporary Dance Theatre, 1986—, D.C. Republican Central Com., 1984—. Recipient awards for outstanding achievement in the media AAUW, 1973, 74; named hon. consul of Republic of San Marino to Washington. Mem. Washington Press Club, Am. Newspaper Women's Club, Am. Women in Radio and TV, Nat. Acad. TV Arts and Scis. (Emmy award 1972), Sigma Delta Chi. Author: First Lady's Lady, 1979. Home and office: 2903 Q St NW Washington DC 20007

WEIDENFELLER, GERALDINE CARNEY, speech therapist; b. Kearny, N.J., Oct. 12, 1933; d. Joseph Gerald and Catherine Grace (Doyle) Carney; B.S., Newark State U., 1954; postgrad. Northwestern U., summer 1956, U. Wis., summer 1960; M.A., N.Y. U., 1962; m. James Weidenfeller, Apr. 4, 1964; children—Anne, David. Speech pathologist Kearny (N.J.) Public Schs., 1954-61, North Brunswick (N.J.) Public Schs., 1961-65, Bridgewater (N.J.) Public Schs., 1969-72; speech therapist Somerset County Ednl. Commn., 1983—; real estate agt., N.J., 1982—; pvt. practice speech therapy, Somerville, N.J., 1980—. Vice pres. Rosary Soc., Hillsborough, N.J., 1986—. Mem. Am. Speech and Hearing Assn. Roman Catholic. Club: Toastmasters (winner dist. humorous speech contest 1984, sec. 1985, advanced Toastmaster 1986). Home: 3 Banor Dr Somerville NJ 08876

WEIDMAN, HAZEL HITSON, social anthropologist, educator; b. Taft, Calif., Aug. 3, 1923; d. Frederick Dhu and Estell May (Griesemer) Hitson; m. William Harold Weidman, Sept. 9, 1959; children—William Brook, Charles Dhu. B.Sc., Northwestern U., 1951; A.M., Radcliffe Coll., 1957, Ph.D., 1959. Asst. prof. Coll. William and Mary, Williamsburg, Va., 1964-65; asst. prof. U. Ala. Sch. Medicine, Birmingham, 1965-68; assoc. research prof. U. Hawaii, Honolulu, 1967-68; assoc. prof. U. Miami Sch. Medicine, Fla., 1968-72, prof. dept. psychiatry, 1972—, dir. Office Transcultural Edn. and Research, 1980—. Founding editor Med. Anthropology Newsletter, 1968-71; guest editor Social Sci. and Medicine, 1979. Contbr. articles to profl. jours., chpts. to books. Sec. Miccosukee Higher Edn. Exec. Com. of Miccosukee Corp., Miami, 1978-82; mem. adv. bd. Environ. Demonstration Ctr., Miami, 1981—; mem. mental health research edn. rev. com. NIMH, 1980-84. Predoctoral fellow Harvard U. Sch. Medicine, NIMH, Boston, 1957-59; research grantee The Commonwealth Fund, N.Y.C., 1971-76, research/tng. grantee Community Hosp. Edn. Council, Tallahassee, 1979-81. Fellow Am. Anthropol. Assn. (chmn. orgn. com. med. anthropology 1967-70), Soc. Applied Anthropology; mem. Soc. Psychol. Anthropology (bd. dirs. 1979-81), Soc. Med. Anthropology, World Fedn. Mental Health, Phi Beta Kappa. Office: Transcultural Edn and Research Dept Psychiatry U Miami Sch Medicine PO Box 016960 Miami FL 33101

WEIGHTMAN, JUDY MAE, lawyer; b. New Eagle, Pa., May 22, 1941; d. Morris and Ruth (Gutstadt) Epstein; children—Wayne, Randall, Darrell. B.S. in English, California U. of Pa., 1970; M.A. in Am. Studies, U. Hawaii, 1975; grantee in internat. relations Chaminade U., 1976; J.D., Richardson Sch. Law, 1981. Bar: Hawaii 1981. Tchr. Fairfax County Sch. (Va.), 1968-72, Hawaii Pub. Schs., Honolulu, 1973-75; lectr. Kapiolani Community Coll., Honolulu, 1975-76; instr. Olympic Community Coll., Pearl Harbor, Hawaii, 1975-77; lectr. Hawaii Pacific Coll., Honolulu, 1977-78; law clerk to atty. gen. Hawaii and Case, Kay and Lynch and Davis & Levin, 1979-81, to chief judge Intermediate Ct. Appeals, Honolulu, 1981-82; dep. pub. defender Office of Pub. Defender, Honolulu, 1982-84; staff atty. Dept. Commerce & Consumer Affairs, State of Hawaii 1984-86; pres., dir. Am. Beltwrap Corp., 1986—. Mem. Neighborhood Bd. No. 23 City and County Honolulu, 1976-77; vol. Legal Aid Soc., Honolulu, 1977-78; bd. dirs. women's div. Jewish Fedn., Protection and Advocacy Agy.; parent rep. Wheeler Internat. Adv. Council, Honolulu, 1975-77; membership dir. ACLU, 1977-78. Community scholar, Honolulu, 1980. Mem. ABA, Hawaii Women Lawyers, Hawaii Bar Assn., Am. Judicature Soc., Richardson Sch. Law Alumni Assn. (alumni rep. 1981-82), Phi Delta Phi (v.p. 1980-81). Democrat. Jewish. Clubs: Hadassah, Women's Guild.

WEIGLE, MARTA (MARY MARTHA), folklorist, educator; b. Janesville, Wis.; d. Richard D. Weigle. Student St. John's Coll., Annapolis, Md., 1961-62; A.B. cum laude in Social Relations, Harvard U. (Radcliffe Coll.), 1965; M.A., U. Pa., 1968, Ph.D., 1971. Asst. prof. anthropology and English U. N.Mex., Albuquerque, 1972-77, assoc. prof., 1977-83, prof. anthropology, English and Am. studies, 1983—, chmn. dept. Am. studies, 1984—; cons., lectr. in field; rev. panelist NEH. Author: Follow My Fancy: The Book of Jacks and Jack Games, 1970; The Penitentes of the Southwest, 1970; Spiders and Spinsters: Women and Mythology, 1982; editor: Echoes of the Flute, 1972; The Lightning Tree Southwestern Calendar for 1974, 1973; Hispanic Villages of Northern New Mexico, 1975; The Lightning Tree Bicentennial Southwestern Reader for 1976: An Anthology of Folklore with Weekly Calendar, Folklore Women's Communication, nos. 14, 15, 16, 17, 18, 19; (with Charles L. Briggs) Hispano Folklife of New Mexico: The Lorin W. Brown Fed. Writers' Project Manuscripts, 1978; New Mexicans in Cameo and Camera, 1985; author: (with David Johnson) Lightning & Labyrinth: An Introduction to Mythology, 1979, At the Beginning: American Creation Myths, 1980; (with Kyle Fiore) Santa Fe and Taos: The Writer's Era, 1982; contbr. numerous articles to revs. and papers to profl. jours.; cons.-editor Chamisal and Penasco: The Farm Security Adminstr. Photography of Russell Lee, 1985; Colonial Frontiers: Art and Life in Spanish New Mexico, 1982-83; assoc. editor Ancient City Press, 1972-74, ptnr. and editor, 1981—; mgr., co-owner Abacus Books, Inc., 1973-74; assoc. editor The Lightning Tree, Inc., 1974-76. Recipient award of honor Cultural Properties Rev. Com., State of N.Mex., 1976; Zia award N.Mex. Press Women, 1977; grantee: Nat. Endowment for Humanities, 1979-81; Exxon Edn. Found., 1979. Bd. dirs. Santa Fe Hist. Soc., 1977-81, Spanish Colonial Arts Soc., 1979—. Mem. N.Mex. Folklore Soc. (2d v.p. 1977-78, 1st v.p. 1978-79, pres. 1979-80, Roll of Honor 1978), Am. Folklore Soc. (editor Folklore Women's Communication 1977-79, editor publs., series, vols. 1-8, exec. bd. 1983-86). Office: Dept Am Studies U N Mex Albuquerque NM 87131

WEIHE, STARR CULVER, biology educator; b. Salisbury, Md.; d. Frederick A. and Violet (Timmons) Culver; m. Rudolph George Weihe, Oct. 20, 1967. B.A., Hood Coll., 1959; M.A., Duke U., 1961; Ed.D., Nova U., 1978. Biology asst. Fla. Presbyn. Coll., 1961-62; prof. biology St. Petersburg Jr. Coll., Fla., 1963—. Author profl. articles. Mem. St. Petersburg Symphony Guild, St. Petersburg Mus. Fine Arts. Hood Coll. scholar, 1958. Mem. AAAS, Am. Inst. Biol. Scis., Fla. Acad. Scis., Beta Beta Beta. Democrat. Methodist. Clubs: St. Petersburg Yacht, Lakewood Country. Avocation: piano. Home: 5108 Brittany Dr S Saint Petersburg FL 33715 Office: St Petersburg Jr Coll Saint Petersburg FL 33710

WEIL, MEHRI DANIELPOUR, sculptor; b. Teheran, Iran; d. Ibrahim and Akhtar (Farokh-Tavana) Moatamed; came to U.S., 1944, naturalized, 1950; student Art Students League, 1953-55, Phoenix Sch. of Design, 1954-56; m. Sayid Danielpour, Nov. 9, 1954 (dec.); children—Richard, Debbie; m. 2d, Mark R. Weil, July 1984. Freelance sculptor, Palm Beach, Fla., 1965—; tchr. sculpture Lighthouse Gallery and Sch. of Art, Tequesta, Fla., 1970—; owner, dir. Gallery Worth Ave., Palm Beach, 1975-80; major commns. include: portrait sculpture of His Highness, Crown Prince Reza, 1969, Her Imperial Majesty, Empress Farah of Iran (gold medal), 1969, Portrait bust of His Imperial Majesty, the Shah of Iran, 1970, Year of the Child sculpture West Palm Beach Public Library, 1979, sculpture Dusk, Govt. Ctr., West Palm Beach. Mem. Norton Mus. and Sch. Art, Worth Ave. Assn., Palm Beach C. of C. Home: 233 La Puerta Way Palm Beach FL 33480 also 8 O'Shaughnessy Ln Closter NJ 07624

WEIL, NANCY HECHT, psychologist, educator; b. Chgo., Apr. 15, 1936; d. Theodore R. and Jenice (Abrams) Hecht; student Cornell U., 1954-57; M.Ed., Nat. Coll. Edn., Ill., 1974; Ph.D., Northwestern U., 1976; postgrad. Chgo. Inst. Psychoanalysis, 1972-74; children—Lynda J., Edward S. Asso., Med. Sch., Northwestern U., 1977-80, asst. prof., 1976-77; asst. prof. continuing end. program Chgo. Inst. Psychoanalysis, 1976-77; lectr. Sch. Medicine, U. Chgo., 1978—; attending staff dept. psychiatry Michael Reese Hosp., 1978—; mental health cons.; vice-chair Ill. Mental Health Planning Bd., 1973-75; chmn. adv. council Ill. Dept. Mental Health 5-Yr. Plan, 1975-80. Bd. dirs. Chgo. Inst. Psychoanalysis, 1974—, Chgo. Focus. Fellow Am. Orthospsychiat. Assn.; mem. Am. Psychol. Assn., Ill. Psychol. Assn., Chgo. Assn. Psychoanalytic Psychology, AAUP. Contbr. articles to profl. jours.; lectr. applied psychoanalysis. Home: 1000 Lake Shore Plaza Apt 43A Chicago IL 60611 Office: 646 N Michigan Ave Chicago IL 60611

WEIL, SUZANNE S. FERN, broadcasting executive; b. Mpls., June 22, 1933; d. Maurice and Esther (Sperling) Swiller; m. Fred Weil, Jr., Sept. 14, 1952 (dec. 1983); 1 dau., Peggy. Student, U. Minn.-Mpls. Coordinator performing arts Walker Art Ctr., Mpls., 1969-76; dir. dance program Nat. Endowment for Arts, Washington, 1968-78; sr. v.p., mng. dir. Pub. Broadcasting Service, Washington, 1980-81, sr. v.p. programming, 1981—; mem. media adv. com. AIA, Washington, 1983—; dir. Nat. Arts Adv. Bd., Action for Children's TV, Boston, 1978—; cons. editor Jour. Arts ad Mgmt. and Law, Washington, 1982—. Bd. dirs. Cunningham Dance Found., N.Y.C., 1982—, Film in the Cities, St. Paul, 1976—, Guthrie. Theater, Mpls., 1982—, Twyla Tharp Dance Found., N.Y.C., 1978—; trustee Dance USA, Washington, 1982-83. Mem. Nat. Acad. TV Arts and Scis. Club: Mpls. Home: 2101 Connecticut Ave NW Washington DC 20008 Office: 475 L'Enfant Plaza SW Washington DC 20024

WEIMAR, DEBORAH MICHELE, hotel executive, educator; b. Newark, June 5, 1950; d. Patrick Raymond and Lillian (Senatore) Pico; m. Christopher Weimar, Oct. 10, 1972 (div. 1977); m. 2d, Merwyn Carroll, Feb. 10, 1978; 1 son, David Matthew. Exchange student U. London-Beford Coll., summer 1968; B.A. in Psychology, Kean Coll., 1972; M.S., Fairleigh-Dickerson Coll., 1974; student Lee Strasberg Theatre Inst., N.Y.C., 1976-78; Ph.D., Rutgers U., 1978; student Profl. Sch. Bus. and Real Estate, Union, N.J., 1980. Owner, gen. mgr. Georgian Inn-Hotel, Montclair, N.J., part-time 1974-83, full-time 1984—; corp. career counsellor Corp. Relocation Hotel, Montclair, 1984—; asst. prof. psychology Caldwell Coll. for Women, 1979; assoc. prof. Upsala Coll., East Orange, N.J., 1980-82. Contbr. articles in fields of career counseling and real estate bus. to mags. Adv. Students for Dem. Soc., Newark, 1968-71; mem. Deborah Hosps. Founds.; active NAACP, 1973-76; trustee N.J. Found. for Blind, 1976-78. Mem. Nat. Assn. Realtors (bd. dirs. 1981-83), Montclair Bd. Realtors, Nat. Assn. Female Execs., Nat. Assn. Hotel and Motel Execs., Montclair C. of C., N.J. Hotel and Motel Assn. (advt. com. 1983-84), Nat. Thespian Soc. Home: 2934 Colchester Rd North Cocoa FL 32926 Office: Georgian Inn-Hotel 37 N Mountain Ave Montclair NJ 07042

WEIMER, RITA JOYCE, reading educator; b. Boricourt, Kans., Aug. 25, 1933; d. Lovell Frank and Leona B. (McCoach) Click; m. Gerald Wayne Sullivan, Aug. 9, 1953 (div. June 1977); children—Lovell Wayne, Laura Beth; m. Robert J. Weimer, Dec. 2, 1977; children—Robyn, Scott, Sandra, Jody. B.S.Ed., Kans. State Tchrs. Coll., 1956; M.S.Ed., U. Kans., 1964, Ed.D., 1974. Instr. Army Edn. Ctr., Fed. Republic Germany, 1956-58; elem. tchr., pub. schs., Kans., 1959-60; tchr. bus. and English, pub. high sch., Topeka, 1960-66; instr. Kans. State U., Manhattan, 1966-74, asst. prof. reading, 1974—. Mem. Internat. Reading Assn., Internat. Reading Assn. (Kans. chpt.), Nat. Council Tchrs. English, Phi Delta Kappa. Episcopalian. Avocation: swimming. Home: 1741 Berglund Dr Clay Center KS 67432 Office: Kans State U Coll Edn 211 Bluemont Hall Manhattan KS 66506

WEINBERG, BARBARA BICKERSTAFFE, mayor; b. Boston; d. Herbert Powers and Florence (Jameson) Bickerstaffe; B.S., Boston U., 1958; postgrad. U. Conn., 1969-70; grad. Conn. Realtors Inst., 1973; m. Stanley Weinberg, Nov. 21, 1959; children—Leslie Jeanne, Susan Elizabeth. Founder, pres. B/W Realty Inc., Manchester, 1972—; mem. Manchester City Council, 1979-81; state coordinator Friendship Force; dep. mayor City of Manchester (Conn.), 1981-83, mayor, 1983—. Asst. state coordinator Carter Presdl. Primary, 1976, chmn. Com. for 31.3% Conn. presdl. campaign, 1976; bd. dirs. Friendship Force, Atlanta, also state dir., 1977; mem. Winograd Commn., Democratic Nat. Com., 1977-78, Mid-Term Conf., 1978; alt. del. Conn. State Dem. Conv., 1980; del. Dem. Nat. Conv., 1980; bd. dirs. Town Council, Manchester, 1979—, chmn. Housing Com., 1981—; bd. dirs. Manchester United Way. Charles Kettering fellow, 1981. Mem. Nat. Assn. Realtors, Women's Council Realtors (past pres. chpt.; service award), Conn. Assn. Realtors, Greater Hartford Bd. Realtors, Greater Hartford Multiple Listing Corp., Manchester Bd. Realtors (dir.; Realtor of Yr. 1981), Manchester Multiple Listing Corp. (dir.). Democrat. Methodist. Home: 157 Pitkin St Manchester CT 06040 Office: 164 E Center St Manchester CT 06040

WEINBERG, LILA SHAFFER, writer, editor; b. Chgo.; d. Sam and Blance (Hyman) Shaffer; m. Arthur Weinberg, Jan. 25, 1953; children—Hedy Merrill, Anita Michelle, Wendy Clare. Mng. editor Ziff-Davis Publishing Co., 1944-53; assoc. chief manuscript editor U. Chgo. Press, 1966-80, sr. manuscript editor (books), 1980—; mem. faculty Sch. New Learning DePaul U., 1976- ; instr. continuing edn. U. Chgo., 1984—. Author: (with Arthur Weinberg) The Muckrakers, 1961 (selected for spl. White House Library); Instead of Violence, 1963; Verdicts Out of Court, 1963; Passport to Utopia, 1968; Some Dissenting Voices, 1970; Clarence Darrow: A Sentimental Rebel, 1980 (Friends of Literature award 1980, Soc. Midland Authors best biography award 1980); contbr. articles to various publs. Recipient Social Justice award Clarence Darrow Community Ctr., 1981. Mem. Soc. Midland Authors (dir. 1977-82, v.p. 1982-83, pres. 1983-85), The Authors League. Office: Univ Chgo Press 5801 S Ellis Ave Chicago IL 60637

WEINBERG, PATRICIA ANN, educator; b. Dallas, Dec. 21, 1941; d. Warren Vernon and Charlene (McCarley) Stafford; student Tex. Women's U., 1960-61; B.S., U. Houston, 1972, M.Ed., 1976; postgrad. Houston Bapt. U., 1981—; children—Robin Christine, Sherry Lynn. Sec., Tex. A.&M. Engring. Expt. Sta., Bryan, Tex., 1961-62; nurse aide obstetrics ward St. Joseph's Hosp., Bryan, 1962-63; dr.'s asst./sec. Eugene J. Goldman, M.D., Houston, 1964-69; tchr. Spring Branch Ind. Sch. Dist., Houston, 1973-76, ednl. diagnostician, 1976-81, asst. dir. appraisal services, 1981—, tchr. adult continuing edn., 1980—; tutor grade sch. children. Mem. Hou-Met Diagnosticians (cert.), Council for Exceptional Children, Tex. Assn. Ednl. Diagnosticians, Tex. Tchrs. Assn., NEA, Assn. for Children with Learning Disabilities, Spring Branch Edn. Assn., Assn. Retarded Children, Phi Kappa Phi, Kappa Delta Pi. Clubs: Country Playhouse, Order of the Rainbow for Girls. Home: 7727 Fairdale Houston TX 77063 Office: 955 Campbell St Houston TX 77024

WEINBERG, SANDRA SUE, computer programmer; b. Miami Beach, Fla., Mar. 19, 1950; d. Irwin and Joyce Charlotte (Fleischer) W. A.A. in Math., Nassau Community Coll., 1970; B.A. in Psychology, Potsdam State U., 1972. Computer programmer Olivetti Corp., N.Y.C., 1972-74, Balt., 1974-76; systems programmer Eastern Airlines, Miami, 1976-82, sr. systems programmer, 1982-83, sr. programming specialist, 1983-84, programming systems specialist, 1984—. Named Employee of Month, Eastern Airlines Doral Computer Ctr. Site Com., 1985. Democrat. Jewish. Avocations: bowling; softball; fishing. Office: Eastern Airlines 9300 NW 36th St Miami FL 33178

WEINBERG, STEPHANIE GRANT, psychologist; b. N.Y.C., May 9, 1942; d. William D. and Gertrud Phyllis (Greenberg) Grant; student (Ill. State scholar) Northwestern U., 1959-61; A.B. with distinction in Psychology, Boston U., 1963, A.M. in Psychology (USPHS fellow), 1964, Ph.D. in Psychology, 1970. Teaching fellow Boston U., 1965-68, lectr., 1969-70; lectr. Boston State Coll., 1969; supr. behavior therapy Temple U. Med. Sch., Phila., 1971; asst. prof. psychology Trenton (N.J.) State Coll., 1970-72; research asso. Inst. Behavioral Research, Silver Spring, Md., 1972-73; research scientist, asst. prof. edn. Am. U., Washington, 1973-74; asst. prof. psychology U. Nev., Las Vegas, 1974-76; pvt. practice psychology and hypnosis, Las Vegas, 1974-81; postdoctoral intern in clin., family, and sch. psychology Johnson Assos., Auburn, Maine, 1981-82; asst. prof. psychology U. Maine at Presque Isle, 1982-83; asst. prof. SUNY-Oswego, 1983-84; pvt. practice psychology and hypnosis, Lewiston, Maine, 1984—. Lic. psychologist, D.C., Maine, Mass.; psychologist cert., Nev. Mem. Am. Soc. Clin. Hypnosis, Am. Psychol. Assn., Nat. Register Health Service Providers in Psychology, Internat. Soc. Hypnosis, Maine Psychol. Assn., Sigma Xi, Psi Chi. Address: care Remillard RFD 1 Box 780 Lewiston ME 04240

WEINBERG, SYDNEY STAHL, historian; b. N.Y.C., Oct. 2, 1938; d. David Leslie and Berenice (Jarvis) Stahl; B.A., Barnard Coll., 1960; M.A., Columbia U., 1964; Ph.D., 1969; m. Michael Weinberg, Sept. 1, 1957; children—Deborah Sara, Elisa Rachel. Instr. history N.J. Inst. Tech., 1967-69, asst. prof., 1969-72; asso. prof. history Ramapo Coll. N.J., Mahwah, 1972-74, prof., 1974—. Nat. Endowment for Humanities fellow, 1977-78. Mem. Inst. for Research in History, Middle Atlantic Radical Historians Orgn., Am. Hist. Assn., Orgn. Am. Historians, Am. Studies Assn. Contbr. articles to profl. jours. Home: 80 LaSalle St New York NY 10027 Office: Ramapo Coll NJ Mahwah NJ 07430

WEINBERG-ROBINOVITZ, ROBIN FRAN, insurance company executive, beauty consultant; b. Hartford, Conn., Apr. 30, 1955; d. Morton Irving and Hannah (Ettlinger) Weinberg; m. Bruce Ben Robinovitz, Oct. 2, 1983; 1 child, Joshua Michael. B.S. in Consumer Econs., U. Md., 1978. Group contract analyst Aetna Ins. Co., Hartford, Conn., 1978-82; sr. compliance analyst Paul Revere Ins. Co., Worcester, Mass., 1982-83; assoc. dir. mktg.-group ins. Mass. Mut. Ins. Co., Springfield, 1983—; cons. Mary Kay Cosmetics, Longmeadow, Mass., 1985—. U. Md. grantee, 1977. Mem. Nat. Assn. Bus. and Profl. Women, Nat. Assn. Female Execs. (bd. dirs.), Phi Kappa Phi, Omicron Nu. Jewish. Avocation: boating. Office: Mass Mut Ins Co 1295 State St Springfield MA 01111

WEINER, ANNETTE B., anthropologist; b. Phila., Feb. 14, 1933; d. Archibald W. and Phyllis (Stein) Cohen; children—Linda Matisse, Jonathan Weiner. B.A., U. Pa., 1968; Ph.D., Bryn Mawr Coll., 1974. Asst. prof. dept. anthropology U. Tex., Austin, 1974-80, assoc. prof., 1980-81; prof., chmn. dept. NYU, 1981—, David B. Kriser prof., 1985—; mem. Inst. Advanced Study, Princeton, N.J., 1980-81. Author: Women of Value, Men of Renown, New Perspectives in Trobriand Exchange, 1976. Grantee NIMH, Wenner-Gren Found. for Anthrop. Research, U. Tex.; Guggenheim fellow; NEH fellow; Am. Council Learned Socs. fellow. Fellow Am. Anthrop. Soc., Royal Anthrop. Soc. Gt. Brit.; mem. Am. Ethnol. Soc. Office: Dept Anthropology NYU 25 Waverly Pl New York NY 10003

WEINER, CLAIRE ZUNDELL, theatrical director; b. Worcester, Mass., June 19, 1933; d. Edward A. and Mary (Abramson) Shapiro; student Clark U., SUNY, Miami-Dade Coll.; m. Michael H. Weiner, Aug. 5, 1972; children by previous marriage—Aaryn Anne, Elliot Michael. Instr. fundamentals of theatre Dade County (Fla.) Community Sch. System, 1965-68; tchr. theatre arts Roberson Centre of the Arts, Binghamton, N.Y., 1969-70; artist-in-theatre Colgate U., Hamilton, N.Y., 1968-70; free lance feature writer Norwich (N.Y.) Eve. Sun, 1969-72; dir. Norwich Sr. High Theatre, 1968-72; dir. cultural activities for youth Norwich Youth Commn., 1969-72; resident dir., actress Gold Crown Dinner Theatre & Touring Co., Downey, Calif., 1972-76; dir. Theatre for Youth, City of Santa Clara (Calif.), 1979-80, The Center Players, Long Beach, Calif., 1977-78; mem. Miami Actors Co., Miami, Fla., 1965-68; mem. Gainesville (Fla.) Little Theatre, 1956-58, Jacksonville (Fla.) Little Theatre, 1958-62, Gallery Theatre, Coral Gables, Fla., 1961-62, Miami Beach Players, 1962-64, Arlington Players, Jacksonville, 1958-61; dir. Norwich Adult Weekly Summer Repertory Theatre, 1969-72, Norwich Weekly Children's Theatre in Mime, 1969-72; originator multi-sch. project Tino WorkShop Theatre, Fremont High Sch. Dist., 1980—; guest dir. West Valley Civic Light Opera, 1982; advisor N.Y. State Council on Arts, 1968-70; tchr. theatre arts Norwich Bd. Edn., summer 1970. Youth leader B'nai B'rith; reader for the blind San Jose Pub. Library. Mem. Am. Ednl. Theatre Assn., Internat. Platform Assn. Home: 1520 Branham Ln Apt 65 San Jose CA 95118

WEINER, MARCI, newspaper columnist; b. Phila., Nov. 1, 1942; d. Jacob and Martha (Blotstein) Cohen; B.S. (scholar), Temple U., 1964; postgrad. UCLA, 1966-68; m. Frederick P. Weiner, Jan. 13, 1975. Maj. stockholder Global Products Corp., Beverly Hills, Calif., 1977—; society columnist Good Life Newspapers, Cover to Cover Mag., Century City News; circulation mgr. Phila. Inquirer, 1970-72; banquet mgr. El Morocco, N.Y.C., 1972-74; semi-profl. singer. Mem. Variety Club, Opera Assos. Mem. Rolls Royce Owners Club, Los Angeles County Art Mus. Clubs: Pres.'s, Thalians, Hollywood Press. Office: PO Box 3687 Beverly Hills CA 90212

WEINER, MARCI KAREN, administrator; b. Elkton, Md., July 22, 1953; d. Robert William and June Doreen (Howcroft) Toth; m. Murray Weiner, Oct. 22, 1978; children—Stuart, Stanton, Adam. B.A., Western Md. Coll., 1974. Proprosal writer RTKL Assocs. Inc., Balt., 1974-76, Meyers & D'Aleo, Balt., 1976; word processing supr. pension dept. Merc. Safe Deposit and Trust Bank, Balt., 1976-78; asst. dir. Inhalation Therapy Services (ITS, Inc.), U. Md. Hosp., Balt., 1978—. Mem. Nat. Assn. Female Execs. Avocations: piano; reading; bicycling; swimming; arts/crafts. Office: ITS Inc care U Md Hosp Room NGE 11 22 S Greene St Baltimore MD 21201

WEINER, MINA RIEUR, civic worker; b. N.Y.C., Oct. 20, 1936; d. Charles Isaac and Gertrude (Levinson) Rieur; m. Stephen A. Weiner, Sept. 1, 1958; children—Karen Lessall, James Rieur. B.A., Cornell U., 1957. Mem. Cornell U. Council, Ithaca, N.Y., 1985—; exec. bd. dirs. LWV, Port Washington, N.Y., 1970-73; trustee Sands Point Civic Assn., N.Y., 1975-79; creator, coordinator Vols. in Port Schs., Port Washington, 1976-78; mem. Sands Point Planning Bd., 1977-81; bd. dirs. Port Washington Pub. Schs., 1979-85, v.p., 1979-81, pres., 1981-85; mem. State Legis. Network, N.Y. State Sch. Bds. Assn., 1980-85; founder Port Washington Youth Council; adv. bd. dirs. Mediation Alternative Project, Edn. Assistance Ctr., Port Washington, 1981—. Editor: Survey on Port Washington Pub. Schs., 1972-73. Contbr. articles to profl. jours. Avocations: reading; tennis. Home: 190 Harbor Rd Sands Point NY 11050

WEINGART, KAREN JOY, software services company executive; b. Nashville, Nov. 21, 1946; d. Louis and Sylvia (Packman) Sampson; m. Arnold G. Weingart, Aug. 11, 1968; children—Eli (dec.), Zoe Elizabeth. B.A. in Math., Adelphi U., 1968. Tchr. math. and sci. Mascoma Valley Regional High Sch., Enfield, N.H., 1967-68, Hanover High Sch. (N.H.), 1968-69; computer programmer Equitable Life, N.Y.C., 1970-72; computer systems analyst Irving Trust Co., N.Y.C., 1972-74; sr. cons. Automated Concepts Inc., N.Y.C., 1974-75, mgr. edn. products, N.Y.C., 1975-76, tech. dir. N.J. region, N.Y.C., 1976-77, v.p. Chgo. region, 1978-84, exec. v.p., 1981-84; pres. Synectics Inc. Chgo., 1984—. Author sales tng. program; co-author tech. course products; tech. research course developer. Home: Chicago IL Office: Synectics Inc 730 N Franklin Suite 303 Chicago IL 60610

WEINGROFF, DEBORAH MARY, municipal official; b. Hackensack, N.J., Dec. 23, 1952; d. Michael and Mary (Pokusa) Cajohn; m. Stephen Roy Weingroff, June 5, 1977. B.A., Stockton State Coll., 1976; A.S. Ocean County Coll., 1973. Mem. com. Twp. of Dover Mcpl. Ct., Toms River, N.J., 1973-78; asst. welfare dir. Twp. of Dover, Toms River, 1978—. Bd. dirs. Family Planning Ocean County, Toms River, 1977; chmn. Salvation Army, Toms River, 1983-84. Mem. Ocean Welfare League, Alumni Assn. Ocean County Coll. Mcpl. Welfare Assn. N.J. Jewish. Lodge: Sisterhood. Home: 81 Shady Nook Dr Toms River NJ 08753 Office: Twp of Dover Office Pub Assistance 33 Washington St Toms River NJ 08753

WEINKAUF, MARY LOUISE STANLEY, educator; b. Eau Claire, Wis., Sept. 22, 1938; d. Joseph Michael and Marie Barbara (Holzinger) Stanley; B.A., Wis. State U., 1961; M.A., U. Tenn., 1962, Ph.D., 1966; m. Alan D. Weinkauf, Oct. 12, 1962; children—Stephen, Xanti. Grad. asst., instr. U. Tenn., 1961-66; asst. prof. English, Adrian Coll., 1966-69; prof., head dept. English, Dakota Wesleyan U., Mitchell, S.D., 1969—. Mem. Mitchell Arts Council. Mem. Nat. Council Tchrs. English, S.D. Council Tchrs. English, Sci. Fiction Research Assn., Popular Culture Assn., Milton Soc., AAUW (div. pres. 1978-80), S.D. State Poetry Soc. (pres. 1982-83), Delta Kappa Gamma (pres. local chpt., mem. state bd. 1972—, state v.p. 1979-83, state pres. 1983-85), Sigma Tau Delta, Pi Kappa Delta, Phi Kappa Phi. Republican. Lutheran. Office: 507 Smith Hall Dakota Wesleyan U Mitchell SD 57301

WEINSHIENK, ZITA LEESON, judge; b. St. Paul, Apr. 3, 1933; d. Louis and Ada (Dubov) Leeson; m. Hubert Troy Weinshienk, July 8, 1956 (dec. 1983); children—Edith Blair, Kay Anne, Darcy Jill. Student, U. Colo., 1952-53; B.A. magna cum laude, U. Ariz., 1955; J.D. cum laude, Harvard U., 1958; Fulbright grantee U. Copenhagen, Denmark, 1959. Bar: Colo. 1959. Probation counselor, legal adviser, referee Denver Juvenile Ct., 1959-64; judge Denver County Ct., 1964-71; Denver dist. judge, 1972-79, U.S. dist. judge for dist. Colo., 1979—; Mem. Denver Anti-Crime Council; vis. com. Harvard Law Sch. Precinct com.-woman Denver Democratic Com., 1963-64. Named One of 100 Women in Touch with Our Time Harper's Bazaar Mag., 1971. Mem. ABA,

Colo., Denver bar assns., Nat. Conf. Fed. Trial Judges, Colo. Women's Bar Assn., Women's Forum of Colo., Harvard Law Sch. Assn., Denver League Women Voters, Soroptimist Club Denver, Bus. and Profl. Women's Club Denver (Woman of Yr. 1969), Order of Coif (hon. Colo. chpt.), Phi Beta Kappa, Phi Kappa Phi. Office: US Courthouse 1929 Stout St Denver CO 80294

WEINSTEIN, ANNE SPENCER, lawyer; b. Washington, Aug. 31, 1952; d. Sidney Durant and Frances (Vaeth) Spencer; m. Martin M. Weinstein, Dec. 28, 1974; children—Jeffrey, Andrea. B.A., Trinity Coll., 1974; J.D., George Washington U., 1979. Bar: Ill. 1981, U.S. Dist. Ct. (no. dist.) Ill. 1981. Research analyst Nat. Inst. for Advanced Studies, Washington, 1976-78; law clk. Debevoise & Liberman, Washington, 1978-79; sr. research atty. Callaghan & Co., Wilmette, Ill., 1981—. Mem. ABA, Chgo. Bar Assn. Home: 684 W Irving Park Rd Chicago IL 60613 Office: Callaghan & Co 3201 Old Glenview Rd Wilmette IL 60091

WEINSTEIN, CAROLE, training and educational specialist, consultant, educator; b. N.Y.C., Dec. 9, 1940; d. Arthur S. and Frances E. (Schwartz) W.; 1 son, Daniel Jason Baldwin. B.S., Bklyn. Coll., 1965; M.S., CCNY, 1976; student Columbia U., 1978-79. Cert. tchr. N.Y., 1965, N.J., 1976, Calif., 1977. Tchr. N.Y.C. pub. schs., 1965-69; specialist Human Resources Agy., N.Y.C., 1969-70; adult edn. trainer, cons. Higher Edn. Devel. Fund, N.Y.C., 1970-76, 78-80, CUNY Research Found., N.Y.C., 1980-82; tng. specialist Blue Cross & Blue Shield Co. of Greater N.Y., N.Y.C., 1982-85; ednl. specialist Deloitte Haskins & Sells, Exec. Office, N.Y.C., 1985—; cons.; adj. prof. Hunter Coll., N.Y.C., 1975-76, U. San Francisco, 1978, LaGuardia Community Coll., N.Y.C., 1980-81, N.Y.C. Tech. Coll., 1980-82, Pace U., N.Y.C., 1983-84, Baruch Coll., 1984, Grad. Sch. Mgmt. and Urban Professions and Adult div. New Sch. for Social Research, 1984, 85, 86. NYU Grad. Sch. Pub. Adminstrn., 1984, 85, 86. Author: Applied Writing, 1982; contbr. articles to profl. jours.; designer profl. tng. programs. Mem. Nat. Assn. Female Execs., Am. Soc. Tng. and Devel., Am. Assn. Adult and Continuing Edn. and Tech., Am. Assn. Bus. Communications, Assn. Ednl. and Communications Tech. Democrat. Jewish. Office: Deloitte Haskins & Sells 1114 6th Ave New York NY 10036

WEINSTEIN, CYNTHIA ALTMAN, pharmaceutical company physician executive; b. Bryn Mawr, Pa., May 19, 1954; d. Robert H. and Carole Joy (Betchen) Altman; m. Mark S. Weinstein, July 21, 1985; research student Hahnemann Med. Coll., 1971-72; B.S. with distinction, Pa. State U.-Jefferson Med. Coll., 1975, M.D., 1977. Intern, internal medicine Crozer-Chester Med. Center, Upland, Pa., 1977-78; resident in psychiatry U. Pa., Phila., 1978-79; asso. dir. clin. investigation, research and devel. SmithKline Beckman Corp., Phila., 1979-82, dir. Worldwide Project Mgmt. and Strategic Planning 1982-84; dir. worldwide Clin. Research Mgmt., 1984—; instr. dept. psychiatry and human behavior Jefferson Med. Coll., Phila., 1980—, assoc. prof., 1985—, asst. prof. pharmacology, 1984—, vol. faculty, 1974—. Bd. Affiliates for doctoral tng. program in teratology. Recipient Smith Kline & French Research and Devel. award, 1982; diplomate Nat. Bd. Med. Examiners. Mem. editorial bd. Jour. Clinical Pharmacology, Med. Communications. Fellow Am. Coll. Clinical Pharmacology. Mem. Am. Soc. for Clin. Pharm. and Therapeutics, Histamine Research Soc. of N. Am., Fed. of State Med. Bds., Am. Acad. Med. Dirs., AMA, Am. Med. Women's Assn. (Branch #25 chairperson, publicity com.), Pa. Med. Soc. (del.), Phila. County Med. Soc. (bd. dirs., chmn. continuing med. edn.), Am. Heart Assn. (council on clin. cardiology and laennec CV sound Soc.), Am. Psychiat. Assn., Am. Assn. of Psychiat. Adminstrs., Am. Coll. Neuropsychopharm., Am. Mgmt. Assn., Am. Med. Writers Assn., Soc. for Clin. Trials, Drug Info. Assn., Project Mgmt. Inst. Internat., J. Marion Sims Ob-Gyn Soc., Hobart Amory Hare Honor Med. Soc., Fedn. of Jewish Agys. (YLC cabinet, chmn. "Agenda for Leadership," LDC cabinet, Young Physicians, com. on health services, commn. on aging, chmn. LDC membership), Alumni Assn. of Jefferson Med. Coll. (exec. council). Contbr. articles in fields of medicine and mgmt. to profl. jours. and textbooks. Office: Smith Kline Beckman Corp 1500 Spring Garden St Philadelphia PA 19101

WEINSTEIN, JOYCE, artist; b. N.Y.C., June 7, 1931; d. Sidney and Rose (Bier) W.; student CCNY, 1948-50, Art Students League, 1948-52; m. Stanley Boxer, Nov. 28, 1952. Exhibited in one-women shows: Perdalma Gallery, N.Y.C., 1953-56, L.I. U., Bklyn., 1969, U. Calif.-Santa Cruz, 1969, T. Bortolazzo Gallery, Santa Barbara, Calif., 1972, Dorsky Gallery, N.Y.C., 1972, 74, Galerie Ariadne, N.Y.C., 1975, Gloria Cortella Gallery, N.Y.C., 1777, Meredith Long Contemporary Gallery, N.Y.C. 1978, 79, Martin Gerard Gallery, Edmonton, Alta., Can., 1981, 82, 84, Galerie Wentzel, Cologne, W.Ger., 1982, Haber Theodore Gallery, N.Y.C., 1983, 85, Cologne, W.Ger., 1982, Gallery One, Toronto, Ont., Can., 1983; group shows: Marlborough Gallery, N.Y.C., 1968, Bula Mus. Art, Calcutta, India, 1970, Rose Fried Gallery, N.Y.C., 1970, Hudson River Mus., 1971, Dorsky Gallery, 1972, Suffolk Mus., Stony Brook, N.Y., 1972, New York Cultural Center, 1973, Stamford (Conn.) Mus., 1973, Landmark Gallery, N.Y.C., 1974, Women's Interart Center, N.Y.C., 1974, 75, 78, New Sch. Social Research, N.Y.C., 1975, Bklyn. Mus., 1975, Galerie Areadne, N.Y.C., 1975, Fairleigh Dickinson U., Hackensack, N.J., 1976, Gloria Cortella, Inc., 1976, Edmonton Art Gallery Mus., 1977, 77, 83, Northeastern U., Boston, 1977, Lehigh (Pa.) U., 1977, Long Contemporary Gallery, 1977, 78, 79, 80, Mus. Modern Art, N.Y.C., 1981, Galerie Wentzel, Cologne, W.Ger., 1981-85, Martin Gerard Gallery, Edmonton, 1981, Gallery One, Toronto, 1981, Martin Girard Gallery, 1981-84, Haber Theodore Gallery, 1982-85, Queens Mus., N.Y.C., 1984, Jerald Melberg Gallery, Charlotte, N.C., 1984. also numerous univs. and colls.; represented in permanent collections: Pa. Acad. Fine Arts, N.J. State Mus., Ciba-Geigy Corp., New Sch. Social Research, Bula Mus. Art, U. Calif., Mus. Modern Art, N.Y.C., others; represented by Haber/Theodore Gallery, N.Y.C., Paul Kuhn Gallery, Calgary, Alta., Eva Conon Gallery, Highland Park, Ill., Hokin Gallery, Palm Beach and Miami, Fla., Galerie Ninety-Nine, Miami, Gallery One, Toronto, and Galerie Wentzel, Cologne, W. Ger.; exec. coordinator Women in Arts Found., Inc., 1975-79, 81-82, coordinating bd., 1983-84. Recipient Lambert Fund award Pa. Acad. Fine Arts, 1955; Susan B. Anthony award NOW, 1983. Home and Studio: 37 E 18th St New York NY 10003

WEINSTEIN, NANCY ANNE, box mfg. co. exec.; b. Richmond, Va., Oct. 21, 1925; d. Morris Hyman and Bertha (Batkins) W.; cert. commerce, U. Richmond, 1971. With C&O Ry., 1942-57; with Va. folding box div. WESTVACO, Richmond, 1957—, supr. acctg. dept., 1971—. Pres. Highland Springs Civic Assn., 1953-55, Highland Springs Jr. Women's Club, 1951-53; treas. Belmont Meth. Ch., Richmond, 1965-79; mem. budget and allocations com. United Way Greater Richmond, 1981—; trustee Ednl. Found. of Am. Women's Soc. C.P.A.s-Am. Soc. Women Accts., 1982-84. Mem. Am. Soc. Women Accts. (pres. Richmond chpt. 1978-80, chmn. nat. subcom. 1981). Republican. Club: Richmond Coin (past treas.). Home: 3556 Marquette Rd Richmond VA 23234 Office: 320 Hull St Richmond VA 23224

WEINSTEIN, PEGGY ANN, financial consultant; b. N.Y.C., Feb. 5, 1936; d. Jules Girden and Freda (Monastersky) Coe; m. Haim Weinstein, Apr. 10, 1960; children—David, Dani, Jonathan. Student Juilliard Sch., N.Y.C., 1952-55; B.S., Columbia U., 1957; M.A., Hunter Coll., 1965. Cert. tchr., N.Y., N.J. Tchr. music, choral dir. West Sch., Long Beach, N.Y., 1959-61; tchr. music, N.Y.C. Bd. Edn., 1962-67, Long Island Schs., N.Y., 1967-69; tchr. music, choral dir. Brandeis Sch., Lawrence, N.Y., 1970-81; account exec. East-West Oil & Gas Corp., N.Y.C., 1981-84; sales mgr. East-West Petroleum Corp., N.Y.C., 1984-85; sales mgr., fin. cons. P.G. Securities Corp., Lake Success, N.Y., 1985—; cons. P.G. Devel. Corp., N.Y.C. Committeeperson Nassau Democratic County Com., Merrick, N.Y., 1971—; del. Democratic Nat. Conv., 1976, 80; pres. Democratic Jewish Caucus, Nassau County, N.Y., 1977-78; v.p. Jewish Polit. Caucus, State N.Y., 1980—. Recipient Service award Hadassah, 1984. Lodge: Sisterhood Chav Shalom. Avocations: tennis; art; theatre; swimming; travel. Home: 72 Nancy Blvd Merrick NY 11566 Office: PG Securities Corp 1983 Marcus Ave Lake Success NY 11042

WEINSTEIN, SHARON SCHLEIN, public relations executive; b. Newark, Apr. 15, 1942; d. Louis Charles and Ruth Margaret (Franzblau) Schlein; B.A., U. Pa., 1964; M.A., New Sch. for Social Research, 1985; m. Elliott Weinstein, May 7, 1978. Sr. editor Merrill Lynch, N.Y.C., 1972-74; public relations officer Chase Manhattan Bank, N.Y.C., 1974-79; v.p. public relations and advt. Blyth Eastman Dillon, N.Y.C., 1979-80; mgr. corp. communications Sanford C. Bernstein & Co., N.Y.C., 1980-83; v.p. pub. relations Nat. Westminster Bank USA, N.Y.C., 1983—. Mem. Women Execs. in Public Relations, Women in Communications, Women's Econ. Roundtable. Home: 161 W 15th St New York NY 10011 Office: 175 Water St New York NY 10038

WEINTRAUB, GAIL COLEMAN, industrial cleaning company executive; b. Lancaster, Calif., July 11, 1954; d. Dickson Woodson and Marie A. (Roussy) Coleman; m. Alvin Allen Weintraub, Nov. 12, 1977; 1 dau., Lauren. B.S. in Bus. Adminstrn., U. Ark., 1977. Tax preparer H&R Block, Little Rock, 1977-78; supr. Lee Distbg., Little Rock, 1978-82; loan adminstr. Fairfield Communities, Inc., Little Rock, 1982—; pres., owner MidSouth Indsl. Cleaning, Little Rock, 1980—. Vol. March of Dimes, 1978—, Muscular Dystrophy, 1980—, ERA, 1981-82. Democrat. Jewish. Address: 617 Legato Dr Little Rock AR 72205

WEIR, BRENDA, advertising executive; b. Kermit, Tex., July 17, 1957; d. Joe B. and Dulcia F. (Williams) Murray; m. Samuel D. Weir, Aug. 26, 1978. B.A. summa cum laude, Tex. Tech. U., 1978. Publicity coordinator Tex. Tech. U. Continuing Edn., Lubbock, 1978-79; copywriter Weekley & Assocs., Ft. Worth, 1979-80; copy dir., account exec. Goodman & Assocs., Ft. Worth, 1980—. Mem. Arts Council Ft. Worth, Friends of Kimbell Art Mus., Ft. Worth, 1984. Recipient 1st, 2d, 3d place Addys, Ft. Worth Ad Club, 1979-84, Best of Show, 1979; Best of Entries, Advt. Artists Ft. Worth; 1st Place Dist. Addys, Am. Advt. Fedn., 1983. Mem. Am. Women in Radio/TV, Women in Communications, Tex. Tech. Mass Communications Alumni (pres. 1983-84), Alpha Delta Pi. Republican. Methodist. Office: Goodman & Assocs 601 Penn St Fort Worth TX 76102

WEIR, GLORIA JANE (MRS. N. LYLE EVANS), physician; b. Baton Rouge, Jan. 18, 1921; d. Claude Arnold and Peggy (Downing) W.; student Sullins Coll., 1936-37; B.S., La. State U., 1940, M.D., 1943; m. N. Lyle Evans, July 26, 1952; children—Peggy Jane, David Lyle. Intern, Charity Hosp. La., New Orleans, 1944, resident in pediatrics, 1949-51; pvt. practice medicine specializing in pediatrics, Baton Rouge, 1952-80; staff mem. Baton Rouge Gen. Med. Ctr., vice chief staff, 1965, vice chief pediatrics, 1969, chief pediatrics, 1970-71, now pediatric cons. Child Day Care Ctr.; mem. staff Our Lady of Lake Regional Med. Ctr., Baton Rouge, chief pediatrics, 1959-60, mem. instl. rev. bd.; mem. staff Women's Hosp., chief pediatrics, 1969-70; vis. staff Earl K. Long Meml. Hosp.; clin. asst. prof. pediatrics La. State U. Med. Sch.; pediatric cons. Baton Rouge Gen. Hosp. Child Day Care Center; chief med. cons. Disability Determination Services, Baton Rouge Area, State of La. Diplomate Am. Bd. Pediatrics. Fellow Am. Acad. Pediatrics (alt. state chmn. La. chpt. 1975-78); mem. AMA, La. 6th Dist., East Baton Rouge Parish med. socs., Am. Med. Women's Assn., Baton Rouge Women in Medicine, Baton Rouge Assn. for Retarded Citizens (bd. dirs.), La. Heart Assn., La., Baton Rouge (v.p. 1968-69, pres. 1969-70) pediatric socs., Cancer Soc. Baton Rouge (dir. 1963-67, 76-79), Sullins Alumnae Assn., La. State U. Med. Sch. Alumni Assns., Baton Rouge Civic Symphony Aux. (patron), Delta Zeta (mem. house corp.), La. State U. Alumni Fedn. Episcopalian. Club: Harlequins. Home: 5885 Eastwood Dr Baton Rouge LA 70806 Office: 2730 Wooddale Blvd PO Box 66498 Baton Rouge LA 70896

WEIR, KATHLEEN MICHELE, petroleum engineer consultant; b. Phila., Sept. 29, 1955; d. James Joseph and Catherine Theresa (McNeila) Weir; m. Dan Charles Vance, June 11, 1983. B.S. in Petroleum and Natural Gas Engring., Pa. State U., 1978. Engring. asst. Texaco Inc., New Orleans, summer 1976, Marathon Oil Co., Denver, summer 1977; petroleum engr. Amoco Prodn. Co., Houston, 1978-81; sr. petroleum engr. cons. Golden Engring., Inc., Houston, 1981—. Mem. Young Republicans, 1980. Mem. Soc. Petroleum Engrs., Soc. Profl. Well Log Analysts. Republican. Club: Tennis (Houston). Home: 807 Nashua St Houston TX 77008

WEISBERG, RENEE, cosmetics corporation executive; b. Glen Cove, N.Y., Mar. 16, 1947; d. Allan Jacob and Gertrude Clare (Gorman) Resler; m. Lawrence Paul Weisberg, Jan. 20, 1968; children—Todd Carey, Jodi Lynne. Grad. Taylor Bus. Inst., N.Y.C., 1965, Nat. Coll. Edn.-Chgo. Pres. Innova Labs., Inc., Phoenix, 1985—, Nat. Inst. Nail Tech., Phoenix, 1984—, The Nail Cons., Ltd., Phoenix, 1983—, The Nail Garden, Inc., Phoenix, 1980—; cons. Ariz. State Bd. Cosmetology, Phoenix, 1981; advisor Nat. Assn. Nail Artists, 1983. Patentee on miracryl, 1984. Author: Nailcare Training; Salon Owners Manual. Contbr. articles to profl. jours. Recipient Maimonides award ORT, Calif., 1979. Clubs: ORT, Hadassah.

WEISBERGER, BARBARA, choreographer, artistic director, educator; b. Bklyn., Feb. 28, 1926; d. Herman and Sally (Goldstein) Linshes; B.S., Pa. State U., 1945; L.H.D., Swarthmore Coll., 1970; D.F.A., Temple U., 1973; D.F.A., Kings Coll., 1978, Villanova U., 1978; m. Sol Spiller, 1945 (div. 1948); m. Ernest Weisberger, Nov. 15, 1949; children—Wendy, Steven. Performed with Met. Opera Ballet, N.Y.C., 1937, 38, Mary Binney Montgomery Co., Phila., 1940-42; tchr., dir. Wilkes-Barre (Pa.) Ballet Theatre, 1953; artistic dir., founder Wilkes-Barre Ballet Guild, 1957; ballet mistress, choreographer Ballet Co. of Phila. Lyric Opera, 1961-62; artistic dir., founder Pa. Ballet Co., 1962-82; founder, dir. Carlisle Project, 1984—. Choreographic works include: Judgment of Paris (Debussy, Griffes); Gingko Tree (Mendtner, Schubert); The Sorceress (Chopin); Quintet in Gay Minor (Gould); The Endless Curve (Debussy); Symphonic Variations (Franck); Italian Concerto, Bach; also operas for Phila. Lyric Opera Co., choreography for contemporary musical theatre. Ford Found. grantee, 1963, 65, 68, 71, 84. Named Distinguished Dau. of Pa., 1972; Distinguished Alumna, Pa. State U., 1972; recipient 46th ann. Gimbel Phila. award, 1978. Mem. Psi Chi. Home: 571 Charles Ave Kingston PA 18704 Office: 9 S Pitt Carlisle PA 17013

WEISBERG-SAMUELS, JANET SUSAN, psychologist; b. N.Y.C., Mar. 21, 1940; d. Morris and Vivian (Wank) Weisberg; m. Richard Samuels, Jan. 16, 1983; children—Debra, David. B.B.A., CCNY, 1960; M.S., CUNY, 1966; Ph.D., Yeshiva U., 1984. Cert. psychologist, sch. psychologist N.Y. State. Psychologist, Bklyn. Jewish Hosp., 1969-75; cons. N.Y. State Dept. Mental Hygiene, N.Y.C., 1978, N.Y.C. Bd. Edn., 1977—, Parent-Child Consultation Center, 1980—; psychologist Beth Israel Hosp., N.Y.C., 1975—, acting chief psychologist dept. child psychiatry, 1982-83, dir. Enuresis Clinic, 1981—; mem. faculty Mt. Sinai Med. Sch., N.Y.C., 1979—; pvt. practice in psychology, N.Y.C. Pres. Singles div. Park Ave. Synagogue, N.Y.C., 1980-83. Mem. Am. Psychol. Assn. Jewish. Office: 160 E 89th St New York NY 10128

WEISBURGER, ELIZABETH KREISER, chemist, editor; b. Greelane, Pa., Apr. 9, 1924; d. Raymond Samuel and Amy Elizabeth (Snavely) Kreiser; m. John H. Weisburger, Apr. 7, 1947 (div. May 1974); children—William Raymond, Diane Susan, Andrew John. B.S., Lebanon Valley Coll., Annville, Pa., 1944; Ph.D., U. Cin., 1947, D.Sc. (hon.), 1981. Research assoc. U. Cin., 1947-49; col. USPHS, 1951—; postdoctoral fellow Nat. Cancer Inst., Bethesda, Md., 1949-51, chemist, 1941-73, chief carcinogen metabolism and toxicology br., 1972-75, chief Lab. Carcinogen Metabolism, 1975-81, asst. dir. chem. carcinogenesis, 1981—; lectr. Found. for Advanced Edn. in Scis., Bethesda, 1980—; adj. prof. Am. U., Washington, 1982—. Asst. editor-in-chief Jour. Nat. Cancer Inst., 1971—; contbr. articles to profl. jours. Trustee Lebanon Valley Coll., 1970—, pres. bd. trustees, 1985—. Recipient Meritorious Service medal USPHS, 1973, Disting. Service medal, 1985; Hillebrand prize Chem. Soc. Washington, 1981. Fellow AAAS (nominating com. 1978-81); mem. Am. Chem. Soc. (Garvan medal 1981), Am. Assn. Cancer Research, Soc. Toxicology, Am. Soc. Biol. Chemists, Royal Soc. Chemistry, Grad. Women in Sci. (hon.), Iota Sigma Pi (hon.). Lutheran. Office: Nat Cancer Inst 9000 Rockville Pike Bethesda MD 20892

WEISE, ELIZABETH ANN, nurse; b. Balt., May 25, 1960; d. Richard Leroy and Letitia Lee (Dryden) W. B.S. in Nursing, U. Md., 1982. Lic. Md. Staff nurse Johns Hopkins Hosp., Balt., 1982—. Democrat. Episcopalian. Avocations: dancing; singing; sailing. Home: 617 St Johns Rd Baltimore MD 21210 Office: Johns Hopkins Hosp Marburg 3 601 N Wolfe St Baltimore MD 21205

WEISENBERG, DIANE RUTH, financial consultant, accountant; b. Bklyn., May 16, 1947; d. Irving and Rose (Greenberg) W. B.B.A., CUNY, 1969. Staff acct. Peat, Marwick, Mitchell & Co., N.Y.C., 1969-70; asst. controller Hawley Coal Mining Corp., N.Y.C., 1970-78; mgr. fixed assets NBC, Inc., N.Y.C., 1979-80; divisional controller Sentry Refining Co., Inc., N.Y.C., 1980-84. Home: 232 E 78th St New York NY 10021

WEISLER, RITA BERNSTEIN, beer distributing company executive; b. Charleston, S.C., Dec. 22, 1926; d. David and Bella (Rephan) Bernstein; m. Irving Aaron Weisler, Oct. 23, 1949 (dec. May 1966); children—Richard Harry, Ann, Paul Douglas. B.A., U. N.C.-Greensboro, 1947. Social worker N.Y. Hosp., N.Y.C., 1947-49; v.p. Rowan Distbg. Co., Salisbury, N.C., 1960-66, pres., 1966—. Vice pres. PTA of Frank B. John Sch., Salisbury, 1963-64; fundraiser Rowan County Heart Assn., Salisbury, 1967-72, Am. Cancer Soc., Salisbury, 1973-74, United Way of Rowan County, Salisbury, 1980-85, United Arts Council of Rowan County, 1984; active sisterhood Temple Israel, Salisbury. Recipient Full Line Drive award Miller Brewing Co., 1979, 80, Miller Master award Miller Brewing Co., 1982, 84. Mem. N.C. Beer Wholesalers Assn. (bd. dirs. 1973-77), Nat. Beer Wholesalers Assn., Rowan County Beer Wholesalers Assn. (chmn. 1982-84), AAUW (bd. dirs. Salisbury chpt. 1964-65). Avocations: white water rafting; interior decorating. Home: 234 W Colonial Dr Salisbury NC 28144 Office: Rowan Distbg Co PO Box 727 Salisbury NC 28144

WEISMAN, BARBARA, lawyer; b. Jersey City, N.J., Jan. 19, 1954; d. Albert and Estelle (Platt) W. B.A. magna cum laude, Douglass Coll., New Brunswick, N.J., 1975; J.D., Seton Hall Law Ctr., Newark, 1979. Bar: N.J. 1979, U.S. Supreme Ct. 1986. Law clk. Lamb Hartung Gallipoli & Coughlin, Jersey City, 1977-79; asst. prosecutor Hudson County Prosecutor's Office, Jersey City, 1980-82; atty. N.J. Solicitor's Office Port Authority of N.Y. & N.J., N.Y.C., 1982—. Mem. ABA, N.J. State Bar Assn., Hudson County Bar Assn. Home: 75 W 55th St Bayonne NJ 07002 Office: New Jersey Solicitor's Office Port Authority of NY and NJ 1 World Trade Ctr New York NY 10048

WEISMAN, JOANNE B. (SMITH), advertising and public relations executive; b. N.Y.C., Apr. 10, 1944; d. Daniel and Matilda S. (Rosenfeld) Smith; m. Lawrence C. Weisman, Sept. 10, 1967; children—Hilary Ann, Andrea Lynn. B.A., Boston U., 1965; M.A., Columbia U., 1967. Pres., The Editors, Chelmsford, Mass., 1977-84, chief exec. officer, Lowell, Mass., 1984—. Author: (juvenile) The Careful Kids, 1976; What's All This Fuss about Drugs?, 1985; My Stay at the Hospital, 1985; Accidents Do Happen, 1985. Bd. dirs. Merrimack Repertory Theatre, Lowell, 1980—, Lowell Girls' Club, 1983—. Recipient Kodak Kinsa award, 1980, 82. Mem. Chief Exec. Officers Club of Ctr. for Entrepreneurial Mgmt. Avocations: photography; writing; travel. Office: The Editors Inc 134 Middle St Lowell MA 01852

WEISS, ANDREA LEE MENDES, apparel retail executive; b. Roanoke Rapids, N.C., May 8, 1955; d. Toby Enos and Lucy Mae (Wren) Mendes; m. John Nicholas Baronian, II, Oct. 1, 1978 (dec. 1979); m. Richard M. Weiss, Apr. 12, 1981. B.F.A., Va. Commonwealth U., 1976; M.A. in Adminstrn. Sci., Johns Hopkins U., 1986. Gen. mgr. Petrie Stores, Inc., Seacaucus, N.J., 1979-81; dist. mgr. Commonwealth Trading, Inc., Stoughton, Mass., 1981-85; v.p. The Sporting Life, Inc., Alexandria, Va., 1985—. Mem. Internat. Council Shopping Ctrs., Nat. Retail Merchants Assn., Internat. Franchise Assn., Nat. Assn. Female Execs. Democrat. Club: Thoroughbred. Avocations: thoroughbred horse racing and breeding; art collecting. Office: Sporting Life Inc 5302 Eisenhower Ave Alexandria VA 22304

WEISS, CAREN CLARK, apparel company executive; b. Lebanon, Tenn., Jan. 4, 1956; d. Raymond John and Minnie Lou (Martin) Clark; m. Steven Fredrick Weiss, Mar. 12, 1983; 1 child, Alyssa Clark. B.A. in Econs., B.A. in Bus. Mgmt., N.C. State U., 1978. Mgmt. trainee So. Discount Co., Raleigh, N.C., 1978-79; methods analyst Blue Bell Inc., Greensboro, N.C., 1979-80; fabric buyer Wrangler Menswear Co., Greensboro, 1980-81, prodn. planner, 1981-83, mdse. assoc., 1983-84; mdse mgr. M & F Girbaud, N.Y.C., 1985-86; mgr. mktg. services M & F Girbaud, 1986—; dir. Blacker, Weiss Assocs., Balt., Blacker Weiss Industries, Salisbury, N.C. Mem. Nat. Assn. Female Execs. Republican. Methodist. Home: 4501 Kenbridge Dr Greensboro NC 27407 Office: M & F Girbaud 626 S Elm St Greensboro NC 27406

WEISS, DEBRA S., construction company executive; b. Three Rivers, Mich., Dec. 4, 1953; d. Harold E. and Winifred (Dunn) W. Student Albion Coll., 1972-73, Lake Superior State Coll., 1974-76; cert. Industrialized Housing Inst., Wausau, Wis., 1975. Lic. builder and mech. contractor, Mich. Sales mgr. Weiss Constrn., Inc., Alanson, Mich., 1976-80; owner, chmn. bd. dirs. Weiss Constrn., St. Ignace, Mich., 1980-84; corp. sec., supr. spl. projects Weiss Corp., St. Ignace, 1984—. Bd. dirs., treas. Eastern Upper Peninsula Pvt. Industry Council, Sault Ste. Marie, Mich., 1984-87, Downtown Devel. Authority, Mackinaw City, Mich., 1985-87; mem. St. Ignace Zoning Bd., 1984-86; mem. St. Ignace City Council, 1985—. Mem. NOW, St Ignace Bus. and Profl. Women (pres. 1980-81; Woman of Yr. 1980, Anna Howard Shaw award 1981, 82), Mich. Fedn. Bus. and Profl. Women. (mem. strategic long range planning com. 1985—; Outstanding Young Career Woman 1982), Silver Mountain Ski Assn (bd. dirs. 1982-85), St Ignace C. of C., St. Ignace Tourist Assn., Upper Peninsula Tourist and Recreation Assn., Silver Mountain Cross Country Club. Avocations: skiing, reading, rock repelling. Office: Weiss Constrn 99 Bertrand St Saint Ignace MI 49781

WEISS, DIANE, gift and wardrobe selection service executive; b. Middletown, N.Y., Aug. 12; d. Henry Wolfe and Shirley Angel (Angelowitz) Weiss. B.S., U. Fla., 1975. Assoc. buyer Burdine's Miami, Fla., 1977-78, buyer, mgr., 1978-81; with retail ops. Monet Jewelers, Southeast/Southwest, N.Y.C., 1981-83; pres., owner Present Co., Dallas, 1983—; designer copyright The Big D.G.O.P.ers, 1984. Fund raiser, 500 Inc, Dallas, 1983—; vote recruiter Concert Hall, Dallas, summer, 1982; active Betty Svboda Council Election, Dallas, winter, 1983; fund raiser Jewish Fedn., Dallas, 1982—. Home and Office: PO Box 670231 Dallas TX 75230

WEISS, DONNA JEAN, registered nurse; b. Utica, N.Y., Jan. 8, 1954; d. Paul Enoch and Jane Irene (Tomaino) Meyers; m. Jeffrey Glenn Weiss, Oct. 29, 1978; 1 child, Brian Paul. Diploma Nursing CVPH Champlain Valley Med. Ctr. Sch. Nursing, Plattsburg, N.Y., 1975; B.S., Russell Sage Coll., Troy, N.Y., 1985. Lic. R.N. Charge R.N. Glenridge Hosp., Scotia, N.Y., 1975-77; ICU nurse St. Lukes Meml. Hosp., Utica, N.Y., 1977-78; retail mgmt. Glenpeter Jewelers, Schenectady, N.Y., 1978-80; nurse cons. Dept. of Social Services N.Y. State, Albany, 1986—; mem. subs. staff YWCA Battered Women Shelter, Schenectady, 1985—; vol. recruiter Am. Heart Assn., Albany, 1985-86. Recipient Martha Karp Palmer award Russell Sage Coll., Troy, N.Y., 1985. Mem. N.Y. State Nurses Assn., Sigma Theta Tau. Avocations: cooking; fishing.

WEISS, DYANNE FAYE, public relations executive, media consultant; b. Los Angeles, July 25, 1958; d. Sidney Milton and Shirley Rose (Shapiro) W. Student UCLA, summers, 1975, 76; B.A. in Polit. Sci. cum laude, Calif. State U.-Northridge, 1982, now postgrad. Asst. account exec. Jackie Lapin & Assocs., Northridge, Calif., 1981-82; polit. media cons., Los Angeles, 1982-86; sr. account exec. Blaine Group, Los Angeles, 1983-85; sales communications specialist Farmers Ins. Group, 1985—. Third v.p. San Fernando Valley Young Republicans, 1984—; mem. Calif. Young Republicans, San Diego, 1983-84, Matador Alumni Assn., 1983-86. Mem. Internat. Assn. Bus. Communicators, Women in Communications, Calif. Bus. Women's Network, Pi Sigma Alpha. Jewish. Office: Farmers Ins Group 4680 Wilshire Blvd Los Angeles CA 90010

WEISS, FRANCINE KAREN, lawyer; b. Far Rockaway, N.Y., Aug. 23, 1949; d. Aaron and Rhoda Rose (Resnick) Weiss; m. Jacob Joseph Katzow, Feb. 3, 1979; children—Adrienne, Michelle. B.A., U. Calif.-Berkeley, 1971; LL.B., Loyola U., Los Angeles, 1974. Bar: Calif. 1975, D.C. 1977. Atty. Dept. Labor, Washington, 1974-77, EEOC, Washington, 1977-79; assoc. firm Seifman, Semo & Slevin, Washington, 1979-82; sole practice, Washington, 1982—; lectr. on age, sex discrimination, sex harassment. Author: (pamphlet) Age Discrimination against the older Women, 1984. Bd. dirs. Fed. Employed Women Legal and Edn. Fund. Mem. Women Labor Lawyers, Bar Assn. D.C., Women's Equity Action League, Older Women's League, Women's Legal Def. Fund, D.C. Womens Bar Assn. Home: 4020 51st St NW Washington DC 20016 Office: 1300 19th St NW Washington DC 20036

WEISS, JANET HARDCASTLE, auto dealerships business manager; b. San Jose, Calif., Sept. 8, 1935; d. C. Irvin and E. Berniece (Cottrell) Hardcastle; m. F. Douglas Weiss, Dec. 27, 1958 (div. 1968); children—Dana Christine, Kurt Douglas. B.A., San Jose State U., 1957. Tchr., Whisman Dist., Mountain View, Calif., 1957-58, Oakland Dist., Calif., 1960-61; cashier, sec. Himsl Volkswagen, San Jose, Calif., 1969-71; office mgr. Almaden Toyota, San Jose, 1971-74; bus. mgr., controller San Jose Datsun & Affiliate Cos., 1974—. Republican. Methodist. Avocations: reading, bridge. Home: 16470 Matilija Dr Los Gatos CA 95030 Office: San Jose Datsun & Affiliate Cos 4100 Stevens Creek Blvd San Jose CA 95129

WEISS, JANET MARGARET, psychologist; b. N.Y.C., Sept. 4, 1953; d. Edwin Franz and Marie (Dandreaux) W.; B.A., Sarah Lawrence Coll., 1975; M.A., Hofstra U., 1977; Ph.D., 1980; m. Richard J. Sullivan, Dec. 5, 1981.

Psychologist, West Nassau Community Mental Health Center, Elmont, N.Y., 1970-71; psychologist St. Christophers Home for Abused/Developmentally Delayed Children, Sea Cliff, N.Y., 1977-79; psychology intern Human Resources Sch., Albertson, N.Y., 1979-80; psychologist United Cerebral Palsy Children's Center, Jamaica, N.Y., 1980-81; sr. chief psychologist St. Christopher's Home Intermediate Care Facilities for Mentally Retarded, Ozone Park, N.Y., 1981—. N.Y. State fellow, 1971-75, 75-80. Mem. Am. Psychol. Assn., Nassau County Psychol. Assn., N.Y. State Psychol. Assn., Roman Catholic. Office: 186 Argyle Rd Stewart Manor NY 11530

WEISS, JUDITH ELLEN, real estate company executive; b. Cleve., Jan. 23, 1934; d. Hyman Jack and Nettie (Rich) Gelfand; m. Allen Joel Weiss, Feb. 22, 1953; children—Richard B., Cathy Lynn Weiss McCoy, Robert Scott. Student Phoenix Coll., 1953; grad. Realtors Inst., 1981. Lic. real estate broker. Sec., treas. gen. mgr. Red Canyon Realty, Inc., Sedona, Ariz., 1977—; gen. mgr. Young Ltd., Phoenix, 1967-77; dir. Sedona Villa, Bd. dirs. Ariz. Realtors Credit Union, Phoenix, 1979-82, Sedona/Oak Creek C. of C., 1980-83, Parkland Found., Sedona, 1985—; active mem. Womens Council Realtors, Sedona, 1985—. Named Realtor Assoc. of Yr. Sedona Verde Valley Bd. Realtors, 1979. Mem. Sedona-Oak Creek C. of C. (pres. 1984-85). Republican. Jewish. Office: Red Canyon Realty Inc PO Drawer CC Sedona AZ 86336

WEISS, JUDITH WYNNE, real estate executive; b. N.Y.C., Jan. 10, 1955; d. Benjamin and Belle (Eichler) Aronson. B.S. in Audiology and Communicative Disorders, Northwestern U., 1977; grad. Realtors Inst., 1979. Realtor Century 21 Frontier Realty, Rochester, Minn., 1978-80, ERA Buy-Rite Realty, Rochester, 1980—; sec. Rochester Sales Assocs., 1979-80; relocation coordinator Century 21 Frontier, Rochester, 1978-80. Del. Dist. Democratic Com., Rochester, 1978-80, county del., 1978-80. Mem. Rochester Bd. Realtors (membership, profl. standards and bylaws coms. 1980-82, bd. dirs., hon. chmn. bd.), Alpha Lambda Delta, Delta Delta Delta. Home: 11 Viking Village NW Rochester MN 55901 Office: ERA Buy-Rite Realty 315 Elton Hills Dr NW Rochester MN 55901

WEISS, MARILYN MAGALIFF, artist; b. Bklyn., Sept. 4, 1932; d. Max and Anna (Haber) Ackerman; B.S. magna cum laude, N.Y. U., 1953; m. Howard Jerry Weiss, Nov. 24, 1972; children—Jodi Kim Magaliff and Barry Todd Magaliff (twins). Exhibited one-woman shows: Alper-Goldberg Gallery, Cedarhurst, N.Y., 1977, Fred Leighton Madison Ltd., 1975, Port Washington (N.Y.) Library, 1974, Adelphi U., 1974, Hewlett Woodmere Library, 1972, Bodley Gallery, N.Y.C., 1983, exhibited in group shows Firehouse Gallery Nassau Community Coll., Garden City, 1971, Pallazzio Vechio, Florence, Italy, 1972, Palazzio Nat., Naples, Italy, 1972, Brockton (Mass.) Library, 1972, Roanoke (Va.) Fine Arts Center, 1972, Milliken U., 1972, U. Okla., 1973, Southeastern Ark. Art. and Sci. Center, 1973, Tuskegee Inst., 1974, Albrecht Gallery, 1974, Bergen Community Mus., 1974, 84, 85, Jesse Besser Mus., 1976, Central Wyo. Mus. Art, 1977, U. Wis., 1978, City Gallery, N.Y.C., 1981, Community Mus., 1974, Equitable Gallery, N.Y.C., 1979, Fed. Bldg., N.Y.C., 1979, 81-86, U.S. Painting Exhbn., 83-85, 85-87, Traveling Painting Exhbn. U.S.A., 1972-74, Traveling Watermedia Exhbn. U.S.A., 1976-78, Oil and Watermedia Exhbn., 1978-80, Cayuga Mus. History and Art, Auburn, N.D., 1983, Stephanie Roper Gallery, 1985, Sarah Lawrence Coll., 1985, Lighthouse Gallery, Fla., 1986, McPherson Coll., 1986, numerous others. Recipient maj. prize Suburban Art League Ann. Show, 1968, 71; Elizabeth Mosse Genius Found. prize for water media, 1983. Mem. Nat. Assn. Women Artists, Beta Gamma Sigma. Address: 1100 Park Ave New York NY 10128

WEISS, MYRNA GRACE, investment banker; b. N.Y.C., June 22, 1939; d. Herman and Blanche (Stiftel) Ziegler; m. Arthur H. Weiss; children—Debra Anne, Louise Esther. B.A., Barnard Coll., 1958; M.A., Hunter Coll., 1968; M.P.A., NYU, 1978. Dir. admissions Columbia Prep. Sch., N.Y.C., 1969-72; dir. PREP counselling NYU, N.Y.C., 1973-74; dept. head Heurtt Sch., N.Y.C., 1974-79; mgr. Met. Ins. Co., N.Y.C., 1979-84; mktg. exec. Rothschild, Inc., N.Y.C., 1984-85; pres. First Mktg. Capital Group Ltd., N.Y.C., 1985—; dir. First Woman's Bank; advisor Gov.'s Hwy. Safety Com., N.Y.C., 1985—. Bd. dirs. 92d St. YMCA, N.Y.C., 1972 , Nat. Choral Council, N.Y.C., 1982—, assoc. Am. Craft Mus., N.Y.C., 1980—. Mem. Fin. Women's Assn. N.Y. (pres. 1984-85), Women's Forum. Club: Economics (N.Y.C.). Office: First Mktg Capital Group Ltd 1056 Fifth Ave New York NY 10128

WEISS, NANCY JOAN, educator; b. Newark, Feb. 14, 1944; d. William and Ruth Sylvia (Puder) W. B.A. summa cum laude, Smith Coll., 1965; M.A., Harvard U., 1966, Ph.D., 1970. Asst. prof. history Princeton U., N.J., 1969-75, assoc. prof., 1975-82, prof., 1982—, master Dean Mathey Coll., 1982-86; mem. com. status black Ams. Nat. Acad. Scis./NRC, Washington, 1985—. Author: Charles Frances Murphy, 1858-1924: Respectability and Responsibility in Tammany Politics, 1968; Blacks in America: Bibliographical Essays, 1971; The National Urban League, 1910-1940, 1974; Farewell to the Party of Lincoln; Black Politics in the Age of FDR (Berkshire Conf. of Women Historians prize 1984), 1983. Trustee Smith Coll., Northampton, Mass., 1984—. Woodrow Wilson fellow, 1965; Charles Warren Ctr. for Studies in Am. History fellow, 1976-77; Radcliffe Inst. fellow, 1976-77. Mem. Am. Hist. Assn., Orgn. Am. Historians (chmn. status women hist. profession 1972-75), So. Hist. Assn., Phi Beta Kappa. Democrat. Jewish. Office: Princeton U Dept History Princeton NJ 08544

WEISS, NEOMA SHOTTS, insurance company representative; b. Rush Springs, Okla., May 9, 1933; d. Ulysses Winfred and Mildred (Simons) Shotts; m. Charles R. Weiss, June 10, 1951; children—Ronald Weiss, Troy D. Weiss. B.S., Central State U., Okla., 19—, M.S., 19—. Rep. ins. co. Neoma Weiss Ins. and Fin. Planning, Edmond, Okla., 1979—. Mem. Nat. Assn. Life Underwriters, Million Dollar Roundtale. Mem. Ch. of Christ. Home: 808 E Dr Edmond OK 73034 Office: Neoma Weiss Ins 1701 E 2d St Edmond OK 73034

WEISS, PAULINE EDITH, psychiatrist; b. N.Y.C., Nov. 23, 1931; d. Ellis H. and Freda (Teitlebaum) Liberman; B.A., Bklyn. Coll., 1952, M.S., 1958; M.D., Autonomous U., Guadalajara, Mex., 1973; m. Aaron Weiss, Nov. 26, 1964. Tchr. spl. edn. N.Y.C. Pub. Schs.; attending in psychiatry Roosevelt Hosp.; practice medicine specializing in psychiatry, N.Y.C.; psychoanalyst Karen Horney Inst.; staff psychiatrist St. Luke's-Roosevelt Hosp. Ctr.; asst. clin. psychiatrist Columbia U. Coll. Phys. and Surg. Recipient cert. of excellence N.Y.C Bd. Edn. Mem. Am. Psychiat. Assn., Am. Med. Women's Assn., Am. Acad. Psychoanalysis. Democrat. Jewish. Office: 240 Central Park S New York NY 10019

WEISS, SUZANNE TERRY, lawyer; b. N.Y.C., Apr. 16, 1946; d. Jerome and Mina Miriam (Stern) W.; m. Joel Jeffrey Margulies, Nov. 17, 1968 (div. 1972). B.F.A., NYU, 1968; J.D., N.Y. Law Sch., 1982. Bar: N.Y. 1983, U.S. Dist. Ct. (ea. and so. dists.) N.Y. 1983. Prodn. asst. sta. WOR-TV, N.Y.C., 1968-69; Asst. prodn. adminstr. Jules Power Prodn., 1969-71; prodn. asst., asst. traffic mgr. WMD Advt., 1971-72; freelance market researcher Research & Forecasts, 1973-76; timetable prodn. mgr., print prodn. asst. TDI/Winston Network, 1977-78; sole practice law, N.Y.C., 1983—. Contbr. editor book and radio series Prophecy for the Year 2000, 1967-72; topics editor, staff mem. Human Rights Jour., ABA, 1980-82. Recipient Human Rights award N.Y. Law Sch., 1982. Mem. ABA, N.Y. State Bar Assn., N.Y. County Bar Assn., Met. Women's Bar Assn., Assn. Bar City of N.Y. Democrat. Jewish. Home: 2 Horatio St Suite 906 New York NY 10014

WEISS, VERONICA CASS, photographic arts educator, art materials researcher; b. Standish, Mich., Jan. 5, 1927; d. Vincent Joseph and Mary Isabel (Verellen) White; m. James Frederick Cass, Feb. 19, 1949 (div. 1982); children—Marilynn deChant, Timothy J., Lewis F.; m. 2d, Heinz Rudolf Weiss, May 13, 1983; stepchildren—John S.V., Lois L. Cert., Eastman Kodak, Rochester, 1970, 71. Photographic Craftsman. Office mgr. Dirla Studio, Bay City, Mich., 1962-70; freelance retoucher Cass Retouching Service, Bay City, Mich., 1970-75; pres., Veronica Cass Acad. (and predecessor firm), Hudson, Fla., 1975—; cons., dir. photo mktg. Shiva, Inc., Torrance, Calif., 1983—; instr. West Coast Sch. Profl. Photography, Santa Barbara, 1977-82, Hawkeye Inst. Tech., Waterloo, Iowa, 1983—, Winona (Ind.) Sch. Profl. Photography, 1972-74. Author: Retouching From Start to Finish, 1979; Negative Retouching, 1984; patentee retouching dyes; pub. mag. VCI Retoucher's Guild, 1977. Mem. Profl. Photographers Am., Photo Mktg. Assn., Fla. Profl. Photographers, Am. Soc. Photography, Assn. Profl. Color Labs. Ecumenical. Office: Veronica Cass Inc 3779 New Jersey Ave PO Box 5519 Hudson FL 33567

WEISSBEIN, ELEANOR HIRSCH, real estate salesperson; b. N.Y.C., Nov. 17, 1929; d. Joseph and Clara (Kellmer) Hirsch; m. William Weissbein, June 18, 1950; children—Robert, Carol, Amy. B.A., NYU, 1950. Lic. real estate salesperson, N.J. Advt. and pub. relations positions Jewish Standard, newspaper, Teaneck, N.J., 1974-78; dir. community relations United Jewish Community Bergen County, River Edge, N.J., 1978-84; real estate sales rep. Atlantic Real Estate & Investment Corp., Paramus, N.J., 1984—. Editor newsletter JCRC Action Update, 1980-84. Mem. steering com. Ams. Concerned for Israel and Middle East, Bergen County, 1981-85; mem. Resource Ctr. for Holocaust and Genocide Studies, Bergen County, 1980-85; pres. Jewish Community Ctr. Paramus, 1976-78, named Woman of Yr., 1970. Recipient 30th Anniversary medal State of Israel Bonds, 1982. Club: Hadassah (v.p. 1969-71) (Paramus). Avocations: art collecting, travel.

WEISSBOURD, BERNICE TARG, family support agency executive; b. Chgo., Jan. 25, 1923; d. Max and Fannie (Wexler) Targ; m. Bernard BenZion Weissbourd, Oct. 31, 1946; children—Burt, Ruth, Robert, Richard. B.M., Am. Conservatory of Music, 1943; M.A., Columbia U., 1945. Tchr., Roosevelt U., Chgo., 1945-52; dir. Music for Children, Chgo., 1954-59; supr. King Family Ctr., Chgo., 1967-71; edn. dir. Child Care Center, Evanston, Ill., 1972-76; pres. Family Focus, Evanston, 1976—; pres. Family Resource Coalition, Chgo., 1981—; nat. task force mem. Child Devel. Assocs., Washington, 1984—; bd. dirs. Child Care Action Campaign, N.Y.C., 1984—; mem. adv. bd. Nat. Mental Health and Law Project; speaker/presenter Nat. Assn. for Edn. Young Children, others. Author: Creating Drop-in Centers: A Family Focus Model, 1979. Editor: Infants: Their Social Environments, 1981. Columnist Parents Mag., Two Year Olds, 1977—. Bd. dirs. People for the Am. Way, Washington, 1983—, Expressways Children's Mus., Chgo., 1982—, Erikson Inst., Loyola U., Chgo., 1965—, Northwestern U. Inst. for Psychiatry, Chgo., 1980—; mem. women's bd. U. Chgo., 1981—. Named Nat. Hon. Commr., Internat. Year of the Child, 1979; YWCA Outstanding award, 1981; Outstanding Woman award, Nat. Forum for Women, 1985; Chgo. UNICEF World of Children award, 1983. Fellow Am. Orthopsychiat. Assn., mem. Nat. Center for Clin. Infant Programs (dir.), Am. Pub. Welfare Assn. Jewish. Office: Family Resource Coalition 230 N Michigan Room 1625 Chicago IL 60601

WEISSMAN, ARLENE NANCY, market researcher, consultant; b. N.Y.C., Sept. 12, 1949; d. Stanley Robert and Bernice Frances (Grossman) W. B.A., Beaver Coll., 1971; M.A., U. Pa., 1973, Ph.D., 1979. Project dir. Depression Research Unit, U. Pa., Phila., 1973-77; project assoc. Am. Bd. Internal Medicine, Phila., 1977-79; sr. project dir. Chilton Research Services, Radnor, Pa., 1979-84; cons. Towers, Perrin, Forster & Crosby, Phila., 1984—; evaluator Research for Better Schs., Phila., 1972-73; cons. State Md. Dept. Personnel, Balt., 1975; lectr. U. Pa., Beaver Coll., Phila., 1974-81. Contbr. articles to profl. jours. Mem. Am. Mktg. Assn., Del. Valley Soc. Health Care Planning and Mktg. (pub relations com. 1984-85), Health Care Consortium, Beaver Alumni Assn. (rec. sec. 1984—, class agt. 1979—), Pi Lambda Theta (chpt. award 1974). Democrat. Jewish. Avocations: photography; tennis. Home: 736 Rodman St Philadelphia PA 19147

WEISSMAN, MICHELLE, general contractor; b. Denver, Sept. 3, 1947; d. Sidney Joseph and Shirley (Stoole) Walkovitz; m. Michael Steven Weissman, June 28, 1970. B.A. in Psychology, U. Colo., 1969; M.A. in Guidance and Counseling, U. Colo.-Denver, 1973. Lic. gen. contractor, Colo. Property mgr. ECD Co., Denver, 1970-73, Larwin Multihousing, Denver, 1973-75, Hera Investment, Denver, 1975-81; mng. ptnr., gen. contractor Constrn. Design, Denver, 1981—. Gen. contractor Safehouse Shelter for Battered Women, Denver, 1981. Mem. Rocky Mountain Associated Builders and Contractors (exec. bd. 1981—), Internat. Council Bldg. Ofcls., Nat. Fedn. Ind. Bus. Jewish. Office: Constrn Design 5250 Leetsdale Dr Suite 105 Denver CO 80222

WEISSMAN, RONEE FREEMAN, owner tour agency, speech pathologist; b. N.Y.C., Apr. 16, 1951; d. Jonas Herbert and Marion (Rosen) Freeman; B.A. magna cum laude, Queens Coll., 1973, M.A. in Speech Pathology, 1978; m. Eugene Weissman, Jan. 28, 1973; children—Ilana Nicole, Adam Scott. Tchr. high sch. speech, theatre and English, N.Y.C., 1973-75; speech pathologist Byram Hills Sch. Dist., Westchester, N.Y., part-time, 1979-80, E. Ramapo Sch. Dist., Rockland, N.Y., 1981-82; speech pathologist Vis. Therapy Assocs., 1983-84; owner, v.p., dir. Weissman Teen Tours, Inc., Ardsley, N.Y., 1974—. Youth dir., Sunday sch. tchr. Temple Israel, New Rochelle. Speech and hearing handicapped cert., speech arts cert., N.Y.; lic. speech pathologist, N.Y. Mem. Am. Speech, Lang. and Hearing Assn. (cert. clin. competency), N.Y. State Speech, Lang. and Hearing Assn., Internat. Platform Assn., Women's Bus. Orgn. of N.Y., Westchester Assn. Women Bus. Owners, Sales and Mktg. Execs. of Westchester, Phi Beta Kappa, Kappa Delta Pi. Home and Office: 517 Almena Ave Ardsley NY 10502

WEISSMAN, ROZANNE, public affairs director, writer; b. Cleve., Sept. 14, 1942; d. Jack and Gertrude (Hibshman) W. B.S. in Journalism, Ohio U., 1964. Reporter, Fairchild Publs. Inc., Cleve., 1964-66; pub. realtions/promotion specialist, feature writer Cleve. Plain Dealer, 1966-67; reporter Drug Research Reports, Washington, 1967, Consumer News Inc., Washington, 1968; press work Rep. Wayne Owens, Washington, 1974; investigative reporter Jack Anderson, Washington, 1974-75; lectr. Open U., Washington, 1978-80; spokesperson, media relations/community relations coordinator, head nat. communications network NEA, Washington, 1968-80; dir. pub. affairs Communications Workers Am., Washington, 1981—. Contbr. writings to coll. textbooks, edn. jours., publs. mags.; co-producer radio/TV series: Rewiring Your World, 1981-84; co-producer play: Lineman and Sweet Lightnin', 1983. Recipient Feature Writing awards Ednl. Press Assn., awards for articles, pub. relations, advt.; prize for environ./urban renewal proposal Cleve., Cleve. Press. Mem. Nat. Press Club, Fed. City Club, Pub. Relations Soc. Am., AFTRA, Washington Ind. Writers, Internat. Platform Assn. Internat. Policy Inst., Am. Women in Radio-TV, Network, Advt. Club Met. Washington, Touchdown Club. Democrat. Office: Communications Workers Am 1925 K St NW Washington DC 20006

WEISSMANN, HEIDI SEITELBLUM, radiologist, educator; b. N.Y.C., Feb. 4, 1951; d. Louis and June (Joseph) Seitel Bloom; m. Murray H. Weissmann, June 16, 1973; 1 dau., Lauren Erica. B.S. in Chemistry magna cum laude, Bklyn. Coll., CUNY, 1970; M.D., Mt. Sinai Sch. Medicine, N.Y.C., 1974. Diplomate Nat. Bd. Med. Examiners. Intern Montefiore Med. Ctr., Bronx, N.Y., 1974-75, resident in diagnostic radiology, 1975-78, resident in nuclear medicine, 1977-78; fellow in computerized transaxial tomography and ultrasonography N.Y. Hosp.-Cornell U. Med. Ctr., N.Y.C., 1978-79; instr. in radiology and nuclear medicine Albert Einstein Coll. Medicine and Montefiore Med. Ctr., Bronx, 1979-80, asst. prof. radiology and nuclear medicine, 1980-84, assoc. prof., 1984—; adj. attending Montefiore Med. Ctr., 1979—; chmn. Nuclear Medicine Grand Rounds: Greater N.Y., 1980—; physician coordinator Nuclear Medicine Technologist In-Service Tng. Program, 1982—; cons. NIH, 1984-86, NIH Diagnostic Radiology, 1985—. Assoc. editor Nuclear Medicine Ann., 5 vols., 1979-84, editor, 2 vols., 1985—; contbr. chpts. to books, articles to jours.; reviewer Jour. of Radiology, 1981-86, assoc. editor, 1986—; reviewer. Jour. of Nuclear Medicine, 1981—; contbr. audiovisual programs and films. Recipient Saul Horowitz, Jr., Meml. award (Disting. Alumnus award), Mt. Sinai Sch. Medicine, 1980, Pres.' award, Am. Roentgen Ray Soc., 1979, Berta Rubinstein, M.D., Resident award, 1978, others. Mem. Radiol. Soc. N.Am. (mem. subcom. for nuclear medicine of program com., 1981, 82, 83, chmn. 1984-86), Soc. Nuclear Medicine (trustee 1983—, sec.-treas. Correlative Imaging Council 1979-82, exec. bd. 1982-84, pres. 1984-86, mem. acad. council 1980—, task force on interrelationship between nuclear medicine and nuclear magnetic resonance 1983—, gov. Greater N.Y. chpt. 1983—, 2d ann. Tetalman award of Edn. and Research Found. 1982, mem., vice chmn. coms. and subcoms.), Soc. Gastrointestinal Radiologists, Am. Inst. Ultrasound in Medicine, N.Y. Acad. Scis., Assoc. Alumni Mt. Sinai Med. Ctr., Nuclear Radiology Club (chmn. 1983—). Phi Beta Kappa. Office: Montefiore Med Ctr 111 E 210th St Bronx NY 10467

WEITZEL, JACQUELINE NECHO, bus. research analyst; b. Phila., Oct. 16, 1927; d. Louis and Marie (Miglio) Necho; B.S. in Chemistry and Microbiology, U. Pa., 1949; M.S. in Info. Mgmt., Drexel U., 1968; m. Raymond A. Weitzel, June 3, 1952 (dec.); children—Pamela, Eric, Grant, James. Research chemist Dept. Agr., 1950-52; engring. librarian Widener U., 1964-66; info. analyst E.I. duPont de Nemours, Inc., 1966-71; sr. bus. research analyst Phila. Quartz Corp. (name now PQ Corp), Valley Forge, Pa., 1971—. Mem. Am. Chem. Soc., Nat. Assn. Bus. Economists, Chem. Mktg. Research Assn., Spl. Libraries Assn. (pres. Phila. chpt.). Office: PQ Corp Box 840 Valley Forge PA 19482

WELBIG, LYNN MARIE, college president; b. Dell Rapids, S.D., Nov. 7, 1936; d. John Jacob and Margaret L. (Hemmer) W. A.S., Presentation Coll., Aberdeen, S.D., 1958; B.S., No. State Coll., Aberdeen, 1968, M.S., 1974; Ph.D., Union Grad. Sch., Cin., 1977. Prin., St. Mary's Sch., Dell Rapids, 1969-71; dir. edn. Presentation Sisters, Aberdeen, 1971-74; prin. Holy Family Sch., Mitchell, S.D., 1974-76; pres. Presentation Coll., Aberdeen, 1977—; dir. Norwest, S.D. Bd. dirs. North Plains Hospice, Aberdeen, 1981—, McKennan Hosp., Sioux Falls, S.D., 1979—; mem. adv. council Resource Ctr. for Women, Aberdeen, 1984—; pres. S.D. Adv. Council Vocat. Edn., 1984-85. Mem. S.D. Assn. Pvt. Colls., Nat. Assn. Cath. Colls. and Univs., Aberdeen C. of C. (govt. com.). Avocations: wood and ceramic sculpture; outdoor sports. Office: Presentation Coll 1500 N Main Aberdeen SD 57401

WELCH, BETTY LEONORA, accountant; b. Missoula, Mont., July 18, 1961; d. George Oliver and Betty June (Dolton) W. B.B.A., U. Mont., 1983. C.P.A., Mont. Staff acct. Ellis & Assocs., Boise, Idaho, 1984; acct. Glacier Electric Coop., Cut Bank, Mont., 1984—; income tax cons. Mem. Nat. Assn. Female Execs., Am. Inst. C.P.A.s, Beta Gamma Sigma. Democrat. Roman Catholic. Avocations: skiing; sewing; reading; hunting. Office: Glacier Electric Coop Inc 410 E Main St Cut Bank MT 59427

WELCH, BRENDA SMEDLEY, hospital administrator, consultant; b. Nashville, Ark., May 24, 1949; d. Ellis and Easter (Roe) Smedley Hupertz; m. James Vernon Welch, May 23, 1981; children—Alisa, Shalice, Michael. A.A., Cuyahoga Community Coll., 1972, Assoc. Applied Scis., 1974; B.A., Cleve. State U., 1977; M.S.S.A., Case Western Res. U., 1984. Cert. alcoholism counselor. Alcoholism counselor Westside Community House, Cleve., 1980-81, Dept. Health, Cleve., 1981-83; program planner Neighborhood Ctrs. Assn., Cleve., 1983-84; substance abuse specialist United Labor Agy., Cleve., 1984; inpatient coordinator Ridgecliff Willow Ridge Hosp., Willoughby, Ohio, 1984—; dir. Heights Centre, Cleveland Heights, Ohio, 1984—. Author: In Father's House, 1980. Bd. dirs. Nat. Black Alcoholism Council, Cleve., 1980—. Mem. Nat. Assn. Female Execs. Democrat. Baptist. Avocations: Christian writings; poetry. Office: Ridgecliff Hosp/Willow Ridge 35900 Euclid Ave Willoughby OH 44094

WELCH, CAROL MAE, lawyer; b. Rockford, Ill., Oct. 23, 1947; d. Leonard John and LaVerna Helen (Ang) Nyberg; m. Donald Peter Welch, Nov. 23, 1968 (dec. Sept. 1976). B.A. in Spanish, Wheaton Coll., 1968; J.D., U. Denver, 1976. Bar: Colo. 1977, U.S. Dist. Ct. Colo. 1977, U.S. Ct. Appeals (10th cir.) 1977, U.S. Supreme Ct. 1981. Tchr., State Hosp., Dixon, Ill., 1969, Polo Community Schs., Ill., 1969-70; registrar Sch. Nursing Hosp. of U. Pa., Phila., 1970; assoc. Hall & Evans, Denver, 1977-81, ptnr., 1981—; mem. Colo. Supreme Ct. Jury Inst., Denver, 1982—; vice chmn. com. on conduct U.S. Dist. Ct., Denver, 1982-83, chmn., 1983-84; lectr. in field; speaker Women and Bus. Conf., Denver, 1982. Colo. state chair Def. Research Inst., 1985—. Named to Order St. Ives, U. Denver Coll. Law, 1977. Mem. Colo. Def. Lawyers Assn. (treas. 1982-83, v.p. 1983-84, pres. 1984-85), Denver Bar Assn., Colo. Bar Assn., ABA. Republican. Office: Hall & Evans 717 17th St Suite 2900 Denver CO 80202

WELCH, FERN STEWART, magazine editor; b. Redford, Mo., Aug. 13, 1934; d. Elza L. and Ruby I. (Bounds) DeMente; m. John M. Stewart III, May 24, 1954; children—Joni Stewart Olsen, Susan Stewart Caldwell, John D.; m. 2d, Kenneth A. Welch, Apr. 25, 1981. A.A., Phoenix Coll., 1953; student Ariz. State U., 1954, Phoenix Coll., 1965, Bellevue Community Coll., 1967, Lake Washington Community Coll., 1968. Writer/reporter, columnist Sammamish Valley News, Redmond Wash., 1967-71; staff writer, asst. to pub. relations dir. First Nat. Bank Oreg., Portland, 1971-72; asst. pub. relations dir. The Ariz. Bank, Phoenix, 1972-73, pub. relations dir., 1973-77; founder, prin. Fern Stewart and Assocs., Ltd., Phoenix, 1977—; editorial dir. Metro Phoenix Mag.; lectr. pub. relations. Bd. dirs. Central Ariz. chpt. ARC, 1976—, Combined Met. Arts and Scis.; mem. Arizonans for Cultural Devel., Scottsdale (Ariz.) Art Ctr. Assn., Valley Shakespeare Co. Recipient awards of merit and excellence Internat. Assn. Bus. Communicators, 1975-77. Mem. Pub. Relations Soc. Am., Women in Communications. Republican. Clubs: Phoenix Country, Plaza (Phoenix). Contbr. numerous articles to local and regional mags. Office: Fern Stewart and Assocs Ltd 4707 N 12th St Suite C Phoenix AZ 85014

WELCH, JEANNE MARIE, archeologist; b. Ramsey, N.J., Sept. 11, 1923; d. Lynus Randolph and Dorothy Delight (Leighton) Spadon; m. Francis Martin Welch, Dec. 1, 1942; children—James Francis, Michael Leighton. B.A. in English Lit., U. Wash., 1966, M.A. in Anthropology, 1968. Archeol. cons., Curtis, Wash., 1973-75; state archeologist State of Wash., Olympia, 1975-76, state conservator, 1977, dir. Office of Archeology/Hist. Preservation, 1977-81; pres. Western Heritage, Inc., Olympia, 1981—; sec.-treas. N.W. Heritage Found., Olympia, 1981—; lectr. in field; mem. project adv. com. Pacific Sci. Ctr. Trustee Makah Mus. Mem. Soc. Am. Archeology, Am. Soc. Conservation Archeology, Soc. Profl. Archeologists (qualifications rev. bd. 1982-83), Wash. Archeol. Research Ctr. (exec. com. 1985), Assn. Wash. Archeology, Nat. Conf. State Hist. Preservation Officers (past mem. rev. and compliance com.). Democrat. Roman Catholic. Avocations: physical fitness; flying; languages. Office: PO Box 6266 Olympia WA 98502

WELCH, KATHY JANE, oil company official; b. San Antonio, Aug. 5, 1952; d. John Dee and Pauline Ann (Overstreet) W.; m. John Thomas Unger, Jan. 8, 1977. B.A.S. in Computer Sci., So. Meth. U., 1974; M.B.A. in Fin., U. Houston, 1978. Programmer, analyst Tex. Instruments, Houston, 1974-76, project leader, 1976-78, br. mgr., 1978-81; mgr. systems and programming Global Marine, Houston, 1981-84, mgr. office automation, 1984-85, mgr. user systems, 1985—. Mem. Data Processing Mgmt. Assn., Am. Mgmt. Assn., Ops. Research Soc. Am., Assn. Women in Computing (pres. Houston chpt. 1986-87), Mensa, Beta Gamma Sigma. Office: Global Marine Inc PO Box 4577 Houston TX 77042

WELCH, MABEL ELIZABETH, college administrator; b. Excelsior Springs, Mo., Feb. 28, 1927; d. Bert William and Elsie (Malleis) Holmberg; m. Byron Welch, May 18, 1947; 1 son, Byron Eugene II. Student U. Houston, 1962-64, Houston Bapt. U., 1968-70, Office mgr. Guardian Mgmt., Houston, 1968-70; sec. Slaughter Industries, 1970-73; corp. sec. Welch Assocs., Inc., 1965—; dir. pub. affairs South Tex. Coll. Law, 1976—. Registrar, S.W. Inst. Fund Raising, Austin, Tex., 1974—; mem. ofcl. bd. Bethany Christian Ch., Houston, 1980—. Mem. Nat. Soc. Fund Raising Execs., Women in Communication, Tex. Pub. Relations Soc. Republican. Office: South Tex Coll Law 1303 San Jacinto Houston TX 77002

WELCH, MARY ANN, educational administrator; b. Rutland, Vt., Feb. 1, 1947; d. John Joseph and Yolanda Frances (Bove) Welch; A.B. in History, Smith Coll., 1969; M.A. in Student Personnel Adminstrn., Columbia U., 1977. Personnel counselor Manpower, Inc., N.Y.C., 1969-71; tchr. social studies Edmunds Jr. High Sch., Burlington, Vt., 1971-72; asst. dean students Smith Coll., Northampton, Mass., 1972-76; asso. dean students Douglass Coll./Rutgers State U., New Brunswick, N.J., 1977-78; dir. Weekend Coll., Trinity Coll., Burlington, from 1979; mem. Burlington Continuing Edn. Consortium. Bd. dirs. Greater Burlington Women's Network, 1981-82; mem. Save The Flynn Theater Project, 1981-82; vol. Vt. ETV Auction, 1981-82. Mem. Nat. Assn. Women Deans, Adminstrs. and Counselors.

WELCH, MARY EDDISON, town official; b. N.Y.C., Nov. 17, 1917; d. William Barton and Mary Corbin Eddison; m. E. Sohier Welch, Dec. 27, 1940; children—Edward S., William B., Mary C., Anne E. B.A., Bennington Coll., 1940; Adminstr., Mystic Valley Mental Health Ctr., Lexington, Mass., 1970-77; mem. Bd. Selectmen Town of Harvard, Mass., 1980-86. Bd. dirs. Girl Scouts U.S.A., N.Y.C., 1955-66; trustee Bennington Coll., Vt., 1964-71; bd. dirs. Minute Man Home Care Corp., Lexington, 1977-80. Democrat. Unitarian. Club: Chilton (Boston). Avocation: Sailing.

WELCH, MARY-SCOTT, writer; b. Chgo.; d. William Scott and Myrtle (Ferrin) Stewart; A.B. in English, U. Ill.; m. Barrett F. Welch (dec.); children—Farley, Laura Stewart, Margaret, Mary Barrett. Books include: Your First Hundred Meals, What Every Young Man Should Know, The Family Wilderness Handbook, Networking: The Great New Way for Women to Get Ahead; mem. staff Esquire-Coronet mag., Pageant mag., Look mag.; contbg. editor Glamour mag.; columnist Seventeen mag., McCall's mag., Vogue mag.; contbr. to mags. including Ladies Home Jour., Redbook, Ms., Modern Maturity, Working Woman, Woman's Day. Bd. advisors Working Women Edn. Fund, Inst. Women and Work of Cornell U. Served with USNR. Mem.

Authors Guild, Authors League, Am. Soc. Journalists and Authors, Women in Communications, Women's Inst. Freedom of Press, NOW (adv. bd.; past coordinator rape prevention com. N.Y.C.), Phi Beta Kappa, Kappa Kappa Gamma; also environ. and civil liberties orgns. Home and Office: 30 Waterside Plaza New York NY 10010 also 3520 S Ocean Blvd H-206 Palm Beach FL 33480

WELCH, NANCY RODGER, marriage, family and child therapist; b. Phila., June 9, 1931; d. Alexander Laing and Ann MacDonald (Patterson) Rodger; m. Oct. 31, 1954 (dec.); children—Rodger Laing, Scott David. B.A. with honors, Calif. Western U., 1973; M.A., U.S. Internat. U., 1976. Lic. family therapist, Calif. Intern juvenile div. Probation Dept., San Diego, 1975-76; family caseworker, intern Family Service Assn., San Diego, 1976-79; dep. dir. Navy Family Service, San Diego, 1981—; family therapist pilot program Family Service Ctr., U.S. Navy, 1979-80, dep. dir., 1980—. Com. mem. U.S. Naval Acad. Panel, 1975—; chmn. Outreach Com. Armed Services YMCA, San Diego, 1981-82; com. mem. bd. dirs. South Bay Family Network, South Bay Drug Abuse Bd., San Diego, 1983, Parents Resource Ctr. Mem. Am. Assn. Marriage and Family Therapists, Am. Orthopsychiat. Assn., Am. Psychol. Assn., Psi Chi. Episcopalian. Office: Navy Family Service Ctr Code 230 NAS Miramar San Diego CA 92145

WELDON, ANN BLAIN, journalist; b. Roanoke, Va., June 12, 1911; d. Samuel Stuart and Jean Maurice (Vaughan) Blain; student Nat. Bus. Coll., 1931, U. Va. Extension, 1932-36; m. Jack Weldon, Sept. 11, 1937; children—Ann Stuart, John Blain. Mem. secretarial, writing staffs Roanoke (Va.) Times and World News newspapers, 1933-41, also Sta. WDBJ-AM; corr. Times Publ. Co., St. Petersburg, Fla., 1965-70; religion writer St. Petersburg Evening Ind., 1970—; freelance writer on religious events, other subjects, 1969—. Tchr. Sunday Sch. Presbyn. Ch., 1928-64; bd. dirs. Aid to Refugees, 1983—. Mem. DAR, Religion Newswriters Assn., Fla. Press Women, (sec. 1981-83, 1st and 2d Place awards 1982, 1st Place award 1983), PEO, Sigma Delta Chi. Democrat. Clubs: garden, womens. Home: 5025 39th St S Saint Petersburg FL 33711 Office: 430 1st Ave S Saint Petersburg FL 33731

WELDON, BERNICE OLIVE MORTON, educator; b. Basin, Wyo., Feb. 25, 1915; d. Ray Royal and Olive Ethel (Robertson) Morton; B.A. in Social Studies and Classical Langs. (tuition scholar), Lewis and Clark Coll., Portland, Oreg., 1936; M.R.E. (William Gray scholar), Boston U., 1937; elem. tchr. cert., Oreg. Coll. Edn., 1955; m. Fay B. Weldon, May 16, 1939; children—Joseph, David, Philip, James, John, Michael. Instr. religion and Greek, Lewis and Clark Coll., 1937-38; dir. religious edn. Sheldon Jackson Sch., Sitka, Alaska, 1938-39; tchr. Liberty Elem. Sch., Sweet Home, Oreg., 1953-58; elem. sch. tchr., Austin, Minn., 1958—, specialist learning disabilities, 1968—. Precinct and county chmn. Minn. Ind. Republicans, 1976—, mem. state central com., 1980—, fin. chmn., 1980. Mem. NEA, Assn. Children Learning Disabilities, Orton Soc., Council Exceptional Children, World Future Soc., AAUW, Minn. Edn. Assn., Austin Edn. Assn., Bus. and Profl. Women, LWV, Audubon Soc. Presbyterian (elder). Home: 1806 5th Ave NW Austin MN 55912

WELDON, VIRGINIA VERRAL, medical school administrator, pediatric endocrinologist; b. Toronto, Ont., Can., Sept. 8, 1935; d. John Edward and Carolyn Edith (Swift) Verral; children—Ann Stuart, Susan Shaeffer. A.B., Smith Coll., 1957; M.D., SUNY-Buffalo, 1962; L.H.D. (hon.), Rush U. Intern, resident in pediatrics Johns Hopkins U. and Hosp. (fellow), 1962-67; instr. pediatrics Johns Hopkins U., Balt., 1967-68; from instr. to assoc. prof. Washington U., St. Louis, 1968-79, prof. pediatrics, 1979—, asst. vice chancellor med. affairs, 1975-81, assoc. vice chancellor med. affairs, 1981-83, dep. vice chancellor med. affairs, 1983—; co-dir. div. metabolism and endocrinology St. Louis Children's Hosp., 1973-77; cons. adv. com. endocrinology and metabolism FDA, 1973-76; mem. Mo. Health Manpower Planning Task Force, 1976—; mem. gen. clin. research ctr. adv. com. NIH, 1976-80, nat. adv. research resources council, 1980-84; dir. Centerre Trust Co. St. Louis, Southwestern Bell Corp., Gen. Am. Life Ins. Co. Commr. St. Louis Zool. Park; bd. dirs. St. Louis Regional Commerce and Growth Assn., St. Louis Regional Health Care Corp. Mem. AAAS, Endocrine Soc., Soc. Pediatric Research, Am. Pediatric Soc., Inst. Medicine, Sigma Xi. Office: Washington U Sch Medicine PO Box 8106 660 S Euclid Ave Saint Louis MO 63110

WELHAN, BEVERLY JEAN LUTZ, nursing educator, adminstrator; b. Phila., Dec. 7, 1950; d. Winfield E. and Mary Helen (James) Lutz; m. Joseph Welhan, Jan. 7, 1984; m. Robert John LeBar, Aug. 28, 1971 (div. July 1978); 1 child, James Benjamin. Diploma, Montgomery Hosp. Sch. Nursing, 1971; B.S.N., Gwynedd Mercy Coll., 1974; M.Ed., Lehigh U., 1977; M.S.N., Villanova U., 1983. Staff nurse recovery room Montgomery Hosp., Norristown, Pa., 1971-72; charge nurse North Penn Convalescent Residence, Lansdale, Pa., 1972-74; instr. med.-surg. nursing Episcopal Hosp., Phila., 1974-78; staff nurse Montgomery Hosp., Norristown, Pa., 1978-79; asst. dir. nursing edn. Episcopal Hosp., Phila., 1979—; part-time instr. Pa State U., 1983—; cons. Leonard M. Amodei, Phila., 1980-83, James Ciamaichelo, Phila., 1983—. Author: Testing Program for Scherer's Introductory Medical-Surgical Nursing, 1986. Mem. Nat. League Nursing, Am. Nurses Assn., Pa. Nurses Assn. Southeastern Pa. League for Nursing (mem. nominating com. 1982-83, bd. dirs. 1983—), Montgomery Hosp. Alumni Assn., Sigma Theta Tau, Phi Kappa Phi. Republican. Home: 506 E Godfrey Ave Philadelphia PA 19120 Office: Episcopal Hosp Sch Nursing Front St and Lehigh Ave Philadelphia PA 19125

WELLES, KELLY, advertising agency executive; b. Bellingham, Wash., June 10, 1948; d. Solon Richard and Elva Maria (Dibble) Boynton; student Sorbonne, Paris, 1966-67; B.A., U. Wash., Seattle, 1968; M.A. in Polit. Sci., New Sch. for Social Research, N.Y.C., 1974. Advt. copywriter Norton Simon Communication, N.Y.C., 1974-75; v.p., creative dir. Gordon & Shortt Advt., N.Y.C., 1976-79; exec. dir. advt. Paramount Pictures, N.Y.C., 1979-80; sr. copywriter, assoc. creative dir. William Esty Co., 1981-82; v.p., asso. creative dir. Bozell & Jacobs Advt., N.Y.C., 1982-84; chmn., pres. Welles's Connaught, Inc., 1984—; mass media cons. to Ford Found., 1976. Councillor, French C. of C., 1983-84; dir. media task force Co-ordination Com. for UN, 1983—; dir. media adv. council Univ. for Peace, 1986—; advisor Avon Found., 1983. Intern, UN, Geneva, SHAPE and NATO, Paris, The Common Market, Internat. Ct. at the Hague, 1966; recipient Casebook Print award, 1975; The One Show award, 1976; Effie award, 1979. Mem. Advt. Women of N.Y. (dir., 1979-80), N.Y. Women in Communications (bd. dirs. 1982-83), Ad Net (bd. dirs. 1984—), Ad Net Pub. Service Cum., (chmn.), TV Acad. Arts and Scis. (Emmy award judge 1980), Fgn. Policy Assn., Nat. Women's Polit. Caucus. Author: Analysis of Folk Art in Third World Communications, 1976; Analysis of African Training and Research Center for Women, 1976. Home: 425 E 63rd St New York NY 10021

WELLES, MELINDA FASSETT, educational psychologist, educator, consultant, artist; b. Palo Alto, Calif., Jan. 4, 1943; d. George Edward and Barbara Helena (Todd) W.; m. Robert Joseph Sbordone, June 30, 1972 (div. Aug. 1977). Student fine arts San Francisco Inst. Art, 1959-60, U. Oreg., 1960-62; B.A. in Fine Arts, UCLA, 1964, M.A. in Spl. Edn., 1971, Ph.D. in Ednl. Psychology, 1976; student fine arts and illustration Art Ctr. Coll. Design, 1977-80. Cert. ednl. psychologist, Calif. Asst. prof. Calif. State U., Northridge, 1979-82, Pepperdine U., Los Angeles, 1979-82; assoc. prof. counseling and spl. edn. U. So. Calif., Los Angeles, 1980—; mem. acad. faculty Pasadena City Coll., 1973-74, Art Ctr. Coll. Design, 1978—, UCLA Extension, 1980-84, Coll. Devel. Studies, Los Angeles, 1980—, El Camino Community Coll., Redondo Beach, Calif., 1982-86; cons. spl. edn.; pub. adminstrn. analyst UCLA Spl. Edn. Research Program, 1973-76; exec. dir. Atwater Park Ctr. Disabled Children, Los Angeles, 1976-78; coordinator Pacific Oaks Coll. in service programs for Los Angeles Unified Schs., Pasadena, 1978-81. Author, Calif. Dept. Edn. tech. reports, 1972-76. Editor: Teaching Special Students in the Mainstream, 1981. Group shows include: San Francisco Art Inst., 1960, U. Hawaii, 1978, Barnsdall Gallery, Los Angeles, 1979, 80; represented in various pvt. collections. HEW fellow, 1971-72; grantee Calif. Dept. Edn., 1975-76, Calif. Dept. Health, 1978. Mem. Calif. Assn. Neurologically Handicapped Children, Am. Council Learning Disabilities, Clearing House for Info. on Learning Disabilities, Calif. Scholarship Fedn. (life), Alpha Chi Omega. Democrat. Office: U So Calif WPH 601 Univ Park Los Angeles CA 90089

WELLES, NYDIA LELIA CANOVAS, psychologist; b. Buenos Aires, Argentina, Mar. 30, 1935; came to U.S., 1968, naturalized, 1977; d. Artemio Tomàs and Pura (Martìnez) Canovas; B.A. in Elem. Edn., Nat. Coll. Edn., Evanston, Ill., 1976; M.A. in Counseling Psychology, Northwestern U., 1977, now postgrad.; m. Lorant Welles, Oct. 21, 1967; 1 son, Lorant Esteban. Tchr. in Argentina, 1954-64; pvt. practice psychology, Argentina, 1964-67; social worker Cath. Charities, Chgo., 1971-75; translator SRA, Chgo., 1975; test adminstr. Ednl. Testing Service, 1975-76; Latin Am. Services supr. Edgewater Uptown Community Mental Health Council, Chgo., 1978—; research asst. Center Family Studies, 1978-79. Mem. Ill. Assn. for Hispanic Mental Health (co-founder), Phi Delta Kappa. Roman Catholic. Author papers in field. Home: 5255 W Winona St Chicago IL 60630

WELLS, BETTIE LOUISE, b. Ft. Hood, Killeen, Tex., Aug. 10, 1957; d. Louis Clarence and Bettie Mae (Harris) Wells. B.S. magna cum laude, Morgan State U., 1979; J.D., U. Houston, 1982. Bar: Tex. 1982. Computer scientist Procter & Gamble Co., Cin., 1976-77; acct. Morgan State U., Balt., 1977-79, St. Regis Paper Co., Houston, 1978-79; law clk. Shell Oil Co., Houston, 1979-82; assoc. Ross & Taylor, Houston, 1982-83; asst. atty. gen., Austin, Tex., 1983—. Mem. ABA, Nat. Bar Assn., Houston Bar Assn., Alpha Kappa Mu. Democrat. Baptist. Home: 3300 Parker Rd Austin TX 78741

WELLS, CLARA ELIZABETH, electronics company executive; b. Kokomo, Miss., July 16, 1923; d. Benjamin Alexander and Harriett Morgan (McLean) Lee; m. Robert Leonard Wells, Aug. 31, 1942 (dec. Sept 1964); children—Harriete Ann, John Robert, Richard Leonard. Student Massey Bus. Coll., 1956-57. Bookkeeper, Printing Industry Atlanta, 1957-59; v.p. Television Electronics Co., Atlanta, 1959-64, pres., 1964—. Exec. dir. Atlanta Dogwood Festival, 1985—; trustee The Prosperos, also v.p. Mem. Womens C. of C. (treas. 1979-81, 83-85), Bus. and Profl. Women Atlanta (pres. 1971-72), Bus. and Profl. Women Ga. (program chmn. 1972-73), Womens Commerce Club, Women Bus. Owners, Nat. Assn. Female Execs., Nat. Assn. Bus. and Ednl. Radio, Nat. Fedn. Ind. Bus., U.S. C. of C., Southeastern Motorola Service Sta. Assn. (co founder, sec. 1969—). Democrat. Methodist. Avocations: Swimming; reading. Home: 707 Sherwood Rd NE Atlanta GA 30324 Office: Television Electronics Co 1254 Techwood Dr NW Atlanta GA 30318

WELLS, FAY GILLIS, writer, lecturer, broadcaster; b. Mpls., Oct. 15, 1908; d. Julius Howells and Minnie Irene (Shafer) Gillis; student Mich. State Coll., 1925-28; m. Linton Wells, Apr. 1, 1935 (dec. 1976); 1 son, Linton Wells, II. Free-lance corr. in USSR for N.Y. Herald Tribune and AP, 1930-34, aviation mags., 1930-36; fgn. corr. N.Y. Herald Tribune, 1935-36, spl. Hollywood corr., 1937-38, syndicated boating columnist, 1960-62; contbr. book revs. Saturday Review, 1939-42; dep. chief of mission for U.S. Comml. Co., Portuguese W. Africa, 1942-46; White House corr. Storer Broadcasting Co., 1964-77; aircraft pilot, 1929; designer yacht interiors Alta Grant Samuels, 1958-62; now co-chmn. Internat. Forest of Friendship; hon. co-chmn. Nat. Air Heritage Council; mem. com. to select 1st journalist in space, 1985—. Recipient Sherman Fairchild Internat. Air Safety Writing award, 1965, Amelia Earhart medal, 1967, Golden Age of Flight award Nat. Air and Space Mus.-Dept. Transp., 1984, award Internat. Conf. Women Engrs. and Scientists, 1984. Mem. 1967. Mem. Aviation/Space Writers Assn., Am. Women in Radio and TV (pres. Washington chpt. 1968-69, CBS Charlotte Friel award 1972), Radio-TV Corrs. Assn., White House Corrs. Assn., Aircraft Owners and Pilots Assn., The Ninety-Nines (charter mem.; Most Valuable Pilot, Washington chpt. 1975), OX5 Aviation Pioneers (Outstanding Woman of Year award 1972), Internat. Soc. Woman Geographers, Broadcast Pioneers, Zonta Internat., Nat. Bus. and Profl. Womens Clubs, Nat. League Am. Pen Women, Nat. Aero. Assn. (named elder statesman 1984). Clubs: Georgetown, Overseas Press (founding mem. 1939), Am. Newspaper Women's, Nat. Press. Home: 4211 Duvawn St Alexandria VA 22310

WELLS, GLORIA TUCKER, food service administrator; b. Detroit, d. Fad Fred and Jonnie Belle (Jackson) Tucker; children—Darrell, Stephanie Townsel. B.S., Mich. State U., 1958. Staff dietitian N.Y. Hosp., 1959-60, El Camino Hosp., Mountain View, Calif., 1963-64; food service adminstr. Good Samaritan Hosp., San Jose, Calif., 1967—. Mem. Am. Dietetic Assn., Nutrition Today Assn. Office: 2425 Samaritan Dr San Jose CA 95124

WELLS, LUDMILLA GRICENKO, communications executive; b. Newark, June 28, 1954; d. Feodor and Lubow (Boyko) Gricenko; m. Peter Franklin Wells, June 2, 1974 (div. Aug. 1983). B.A., Eastern N.Mex. U., 1975; B.B.A., 1976; M.B.A., Fairleigh Dickinson U., 1981. Boutique mgr. Labels for Less, Irvington, N.J., 1970-73; free-lance comml. artist, Clovis, N.Mex., 1974-76; layout artist Gaylords Nat. Corp., Secaucus, N.J., 1976-79; copywriter Jamesway Corp., Secaucus, 1979-80; mgr. advt. and promotion Blue Cross and Blue Shield of N.J., Newark, 1980—; adj. prof. advt. Fairleigh Dickinson U., Madison, N.J., 1981-84; cons. L.G. Wells Advt. Co., West Orange, N.J. Bd. dirs. Occupational Ctr. of Essex County, Orange, N.J., 1982—; chmn. com. Maplewood Civic Assn., 1982-84. Mem. Advt. Club N.J., Am. Mktg. Assn. Russian Orthodox.

WELLS, MARY PHILLIPS, businesswoman; b. Wilson, N.C., Sept. 10, 1936; d. James Thurman and Lossie (Price) P.; m. Talmage Lee Wells, Oct. 15, 1955; children—James Talmage, Royce Lee, Tammy Wells, David Allen. Student N.C. State U. Dept. mgr. Montgomery Wards, Rocky Mount, N.C., 1962-65; office mgr. Infab, Inc., Spring Hope, N.C., 1965-70; bookkeeper/sec. One Hour Koretizing, Rocky Mount, 1970-74; owner OHK of Tarrytown, Rocky Mount, 1970, One Hour Koretizing, Rocky Mount, 1980—. Mem. com. Sml. Bus. Advoacry, Raleigh, 1983-85; mem. Internat. Fabricare, Silver Springs, Md., 1970—; pres. YWCA, Rocky Mount, 1984-85; bd. dirs. Uptown Assn., Rockymount, 1985, Rocky Mchts. Assn., 1985—, Rocky Mount Area C. of C., 1986—. Recipient Apprecation awards, United Cerebral Palsy, ARC; Pres. award, C. of C. Mem. N.C. Bus. and Profl. Women, Nashville Bus. and Profl. Women (pres., Woman of Yr. 1984), Nat. Assn. Female Execs., Rocky Mount Women Network (exec. com., Woman of Yr.). Baptist. Club: Altrusa. Home: Route 3 Box 351 Rocky Mount NC 27801 Office: One Hour Koretizing 202 Falls Rd Rocky Mount NC 27801

WELLS, PATRICIA BENNETT, business administration educator; b. Park River, N.D., Mar. 25, 1935; d. Benjamin Beekman Bennett and Alice Catherine (Peerboom) Bennett Breckinridge; A.A., Allan Hancock Coll., Santa Maria, Calif., 1964; B.S. magna cum laude, Coll. Great Falls, 1966; M.S., U. N.D., 1967, Ph.D., 1971; children—Bruce Bennett, Barbara Lea. Fiscal acct. USIA, Washington, 1954-56; public acct., Bremerton, Wash., 1956; statistician U.S. Navy, Bremerton, 1957-59; med. services accounts officer U.S. Air Force, Vandenberg AFB, Calif., 1962-64; instr. bus. adminstrn. Western New Eng. Coll., 1967-69; vis. prof. econs. Chapman Coll., 1971; vis. prof. systems Griffith AFB, 1973-74; assoc. prof. bus. Va. State U., 1973-74; assoc. prof. bus. adminstrn. Oreg. State U., Corvallis, 1974-82, prof., 1982—, univ. curriculum coordinator, 1984—, dir. adminstrv. mgmt. program, 1974-81, pres. Faculty Senate, 1981; cons. process tech. devel. Digital Equipment Corp., 1982. Pres., chmn. bd. dirs. Adminstrv. Office Services, Inc., Corvallis, 1976-83, Dynamic Achievement, Inc., 1983—. Cert. adminstrv. mgr. Mem. Am. Bus. Communication Assn. (mem. internat. bd. 1980-83, v.p. Northwest 1981, 2d v.p. 1982-83, 1st v.p. 1983-84, pres. 1984-85), Am. Bus. Women's Assn. (named Top Businesswoman in Nation 1980), Assn. Info. Systems Profls., Adminstrv. Mgmt. Soc., AAUP (chpt. sec. 1973, chpt. bd. dirs. 1982, pres. Oreg. conf. 1983-85), Am. Vocat. Assn. (nominating com. 1976), Associated Oreg. Faculties, Nat. Bus. Edn. Assn., Nat. Assn. Tchr. Edn. for Bus. Office Edn. (pres. 1976-77, chmn. public relations com. 1978-81), Corvallis Area C. of C. (v.p. chamber devel. 1985-86, Pres.'s award 1986), Sigma Kappa. Roman Catholic. Contbr. numerous articles to profl. jours. Office: 208 Bexell Coll Bus Oreg State U Corvallis OR 97331

WELLS, VALDA EVELYN, management consultant; b. N.Y.C., June 23, 1935; d. William Frederick and Valda Elva (Baldwin) W.; B.A. in Econs., N.Y. Sch. Social Research, N.Y.C., 1967. With Gen. Electric Co., N.Y.C., 1964-80, cons. internat. trade policy devel., 1973-75, mgr. internat. research programs, 1975-80; pres. Wellspring, N.Y.C., 1980—; co-dir. CW Assocs., 1983—; tchr. profl. communication. Mem. Women Bus. Owners N.Y., Ind. Citizens Research Found, Nat. Assn. Female Execs., Am. Soc. Profl. and Exec. Women, Internat. Platform Assn. Democrat. Presbyterian. Home: 36-19 Bowne St Flushing NY 11354 Office: PO Box 310 Flushing NY 11352

WELS, MARGUERITE SAMET (MRS. RICHARD H. WELS), interior decorator; b. N.Y.C.; d. Max and Bertha (Levine) Samet; student N.Y. U., 1937, N.Y. Sch. Interior Design, 1938-41; m. Richard H. Wels, Dec. 12, 1954; children—Susan Rebecca, Amy Elizabeth. Interior decorator—Marguerite Samet, N.Y.C., 1946-60; interior decorator, head Marguerite Samet Assos., 1960—; co-ordinator U.S. Army Spl. Services, 1942-46; cons. United Bowling Centers, Inc., Interboro Gen. Hosp. Active in William Alanson White Inst. Psychiatry, Psychoanalysis and Psychology, Am. Jewish Com., Islands Research Found. Mem. Am. Inst. Interior Designers (exec. bd., v.p. N.Y. Met. chpt.), Democratic Women's Workshop. Jewish. Clubs: Women's City, Woman Pays. Home: 911 Park Ave New York NY 10021

WELSH, CARYL FLETCHER, nurse; b. Glen Falls, N.Y., May 3, 1955; d. Gardner Bruce and Joan (Carlson) Fletcher; m. David Francis Welsh, Oct. 29, 1983. B.S., Wagner Coll., 1977. Lic. R.N., Calif. Nurse, Nassau Hosp., Mineola, N.Y., 1977-78, Albany Med. Ctr., N.Y., 1978-79; nursing coordinator Cedars-Sinai Med. Ctr., Los Angeles, 1979-83; dir. nursing Beaver Med. Clinic, Redlands, Calif., 1984; nurse Loma Linda Community Hosp., Calif., 1985—. Contbr. articles to profl. jours. Mem. Am. Assn. Critical Care Nurses, AAUW. Republican. Avocations: skiing; water sports; sewing; cooking; reading. Home: 125 N Lincoln St Redlands CA 92374

WELSH, DEBORAH CAMPBELL, lawyer; b. Leesburg, Va., Apr. 8, 1955; d. Tunis Henry and Doris (Williams) Campbell; m. Dennis Craig Welsh, Aug. 28, 1976; 1 child, Lyndsay Wray. B.A., U. Richmond, 1976, J.D., 1980. Bar: Va. 1980. Tchr., Chesterfield County pub. schs., Chesterfield, Va., 1976-77; assoc. Charles A. Ottinger, Leesburg, Va., 1980-84; sole practice law, Leesburg, 1984; ptnr. Kennedy, McAdams & Welsh, 1984—; dep. town atty., Leesburg, Va., 1985—. Bd. dirs. Loudoun County Youth Shelter, Leesburg, 1982—. Mem. Law Rev., mem. McNeill Law Soc., T.C. Williams Sch. Law, U. Richmond, 1978-80. Mem. ABA, Va. State Bar, Loudoun County Bar Assn. (sec. 1982-83), Va. Trial Lawyers Assn., Phi Beta Kappa, Pi Sigma Alpha, Kappa Delta Pi. Baptist. Clubs: Jr. Woman's (Leesburg); Women's Missionary Union. Home: 2 Phillips Dr NW Leesburg VA 22075 Office: 104 Church St SE Leesburg VA 22075

WELSH, DONITA ART, television station executive; b. Kansas City, Mo., Feb. 16, 1950; d. Donald Michael and J. Juanita Fern (Goodwin) Art; m. Michael Alan Shechtman, Nov. 16, 1972 (div. Feb. 1976); m. Stanley Marvin Welsh, Mar. 29, 1978. B.A., Pa. State U., 1972. Programming asst. Sta. WHYY-TV, Phila., 1973-76; dir. pub. programming Sta. WCVE-TV, Richmond, VA., 1976-78; program dir. Sta. WCTI-TV, Newbern, N.C., 1978-82; ops., program dir. Sta. WFLX-TV, West Palm Beach, Fla., 1982-84, station mgr., 1985—. Sec., Jupiter Farms Land and Homeowners Assn., Fla., 1982—. Grantee Corp. Pub. Broadcasting, 1976-78. Mem. Nat. Assn. TV Program Execs., Assn. Ind. TV Stations, Am. Film Inst., Am. Women in Radio and TV (v.p. elect chpt. 1985). Democrat. Methodist. Avocations: skiing; sailing; sewing; travel; photography. Home: PO Box 993 Jupiter FL 33468 Office: WFLX-TV Malrite of Fla 4130 Blue Heron Blvd West Palm Beach FL 33404

WELSH, DOROTHY DELL, educator, author; b. Pryor, Okla., Feb. 13, 1935; d. Roland Fields and Martha Gladys (Sheppard) Butler; m. James Robert Welsh, June 26, 1965; children—Pamela Jeanne (dec.), James Michael, Julie Marie. B.A., U. Okla., 1957, M.A., 1964; postgrad. Amarillo Coll., 1962, U. Tex.-Austin, 1983-84, Tex.-San Antonio, 1984. Newspaper reporter Pryor Jeffersonian (Okla.), 1955; tchr. English and journalism Classen High Sch., Oklahoma City, 1957-61, Henderson Jr. High Sch. (Nev.), 1961-62; dir. publs. Amarillo High Sch. (Tex.), 1962-64; tchr. English, Palmdale High Sch. (Calif.), 1964-65; tchr. English and journalism Desert High Sch., Edwards, Calif., 1965-66; lectr. English, San Antonio Coll., 1979—; reporter Swimming World mag., Los Angeles, 1980—. Editor The Cresent News, 1974-80, 83-86, The Swimmer's Ear, 1983-84, Off the Blocks, 1985-86; contbr. articles to profl. jours. Bd. dirs., publicity chmn. South Tex. Swimming Assn., Austin, 1982-84; info. com. Tex. Swimming Assn., San Antonio, 1983-84. Recipient Service award San Antonio Aquatic Club, 1983; Proficiency citation Superior work journalism Univ. Interscholastic League, Austin, 1964. Mem. Women in Communications, Inc., Journalism Educators Assn., Tex. Jr. Coll. Tchrs. Assn., AAUW (mem.-at-large), U. Okla. Assn., Coll. Conf. Tchrs. English, Mayes County Hist. Soc., Gamma Phi Beta (service award 1977, pres. 1972-73, v.p. 1973-74). Methodist. Home: 15102 Encinito Ave San Antonio TX 78232 Office: San Antonio Coll English Dept 1300 San Pedro San Antonio TX 78284

WELSH, JUDITH SCHENCK, educator; b. Patchogue, L.I., N.Y., Feb. 5, 1939; d. Frank W. and Muriel (Whitman) Schenck; B.Ed., U. Miami (Fla.), 1961, M.A. in English, 1968; m. Robert C. Welsh, Sept. 16, 1961; children—Derek Francis, Christopher Lord. Co-organizer Cataract Surg. Congress med. meetings, 1963-76; grad. asst. instr. Dale Carnegie Courses Internat., 1967; adminstr. Office Admissions, Bauder Fashion Coll., Miami, 1976-77, instr. communications, 1977—, also pub. coll. monthly paper; freelance writer regional and nat. publs.; guest speaker Optifair Internat., N.Y.C., 1980; guest speaker, mem. seminar faculty Optifair West, Anaheim, Calif., 1980, Optifair Midwest, St. Louis, 1980, Face to Face, Kansas City, Mo., 1981. Mem. Nat. Assn. Female Execs., Fla. Freelance Writers Assn., Nat. Writers Club (award), Delta Gamma. Congregationalist. Clubs: Coral Reef Yacht, Riviera Country, Royal Palm Tennis. Co-editor: The New Report on Cataract Surgery, 1969, Second Report on Cataract Surgery, 1974; editor: Surgidev's Cataract Surgery N.O.W., 1982—; contbr. Miami Today, 1985—. Home: 1600 Onaway Dr Miami FL 33133 Office: 1600 Onaway Dr Miami FL 33133

WELSH, SUE ANGELA, development and fund-raising specialist; b. N.Y.C., Nov. 10, 1938; d. Edward Thomas and Susan Bridget (Swanton) W.; B.A., Immaculate Heart Coll., 1960, Calif. secondary teaching credential, 1961; children—John Francis, Kieron Michael. Secondary sch. tchr. Los Angeles City Schs., 1960-77; field rep. Inter-Study, Los Angeles, 1977-78; dir. devel./community relations Poseidon Center for Troubled Adolescents with Learning Disabilities, Los Angeles, 1979—; dir. devel. Bilingual Found. Arts, 1983—, exec. dir., 1985—; adminstrv. coordinator Danzantes Unidos, 1978-82. Co-chmn. Irish Info. Com.; mem. Calif. Democratic Circle. Recipient Pub. Service to Youth in Watts award, 1964, Los Angeles County Human Relations award, 1965, Mexican Folklorico Arts Adv. award, 1979, Vol. Action Center award, 1982. Mem. Assn. for Children Who Learn Differently, Santa Monica-Westside Community Services Council (pres.). Home: 354 S Harvard Blvd Los Angeles CA 90020

WELSTEAD, JEAN MAUDIE, artist, educator; b. Fremont, Nebr., Nov. 22, 1922; d. Edward C. and Irene Elizabeth (Hooper) Olson; student Joslyn Art Mus., Omaha, 1962-64, Midland Luth. Coll., Fremont, 1970-74, St. Mary's Coll., Omaha, 1964-68; m. Marvin Glenn Welstead, Feb. 21, 1942; children—Robert L., Jon A. Legal sec. law firm, Fremont, 1940-42; staff hdqrs. office Northrup Aircraft Co., Hawthorne, Calif., 1943; civil service wartime rationing officer 3d Air Force, U.S. Air Force, Stuttgart, Ark., 1943-46; adminstrv. clk. merit system Dodge County Assistance Office, Fremont, 1946-48; art supr. Fremont Parks and Recreation, 1967-71; pvt. instr. art Fremont, 1967-71; publicity dir. Fremont Area Art Assn. Gallery, 1963-85; exhibited Sioux City Art Center, 1976-78, 2d Ann. Masters Touch Competitions, 1976, 4th Ann. Printmaking and Drawing Competition, Tulsa, 1977, Elden Gallery, Wesleyan U., 1976-77, Am. Bicentennial Exhbn., 1976, Sheldon Art Gallery, Lincoln, Nebr., 1985, Wesleyan U., Lincoln, 1986; exhibited in group show at Joslyn Biennial Juried Exhbn., 1986; represented in permanent collection Nebr. Artists, Appalachian State U., Boone, N.C., Wesleyan U., Lincoln, Nebr., Wayne State Coll. (Nebr.), Kearney State Coll. Chmn. Art from the Heart Viet Nam Amputees, Oakland Naval Hosp. (Calif.), 1968; active Boy Scouts Am., Republican party; pres. Linden Sch. PTA, 1955. Mem. Assn. Nebr. Art Clubs (award of excellence 1974-75, 76-79, Best of Show 1983, dir. 1974-75), Fremont Art Assn. (charter; organizer, pres. 1965-71, Community Art Service award 1985), Asso. Artists Omaha, Nat. League Am. Pen Women. Methodist. Club: Order of Eastern Star. Home: 1943 Parkview Dr Fremont NE 68025

WELTE, PATRICIA KATHRYN, counselor; b. Denver, Nov. 21, 1953; d. Joseph Francis and Rita Marie (Guthrie) Welte. B.S., Coll. St. Mary, Omaha, 1976; M.A., U. No. Colo., 1981. Tchr. 1st grad St. Joan of Arc Sch., Omaha, 1976; elem. tchr. St. Peter's Sch., Omaha, 1976-77, Greeley Catholic Sch., Colo., 1977-78, St. Josephs, Sch., Fort Collins, 1978-79; elem. counselor Highland Elem. Sch., Pierce, Colo., 1982—. Mem. Colo. Assn. Counseling and Devel., Colo. Sch. Counselors Assn. Democrat. Roman Catholic. Avocations: Cycling; reading; crafts.

WELTING, RUTH LYNN, singer; b. Memphis, Nov. 5, 1948; d. William Edwin and Mary Frances (Pugh) Welting; student Memphis State U., 1966-68, Juilliard Sch. Music, 1968-69; div. Mem. N.Y.C. Opera, 1971-73; appeared with Dallas Opera, Houston Symphony, San Francisco Symphony, Paris Opera, Salzburg Festival, Chgo. Lyric Opera, Met. Opera, Covent Garden, London, Netherlands Opera, San Francisco Opera, Teatro Colón, Buenos Aires, Teatro

Communale, Florence, Italy, others; soloist with Chgo. Symphony, Phila. Orch., San Francisco Symphony. Rockefeller grantee. Mem. Am. Guild Musical Artists. Office: The Lark Inc PO Box 240895 Memphis TN 38124

WELTY, EUDORA, author; b. Jackson, Miss.; d. Christian Webb and Chestina (Andrews) Welty; student Miss. State Coll. for Women; B.A., U. Wis., 1929; postgrad. Columbia Sch. Advt., 1930-31. Author: A Curtain of Green, 1941; The Robber Bridegroom, 1942; The Wide Net, 1943; Delta Wedding, 1946; The Golden Apples, 1949; The Ponder Heart, 1954; The Bride of the Innisfallen, 1955; The Shoe Bird, 1964; Losing Battles, 1970; One Time, One Place, 1971; The Optimist's Daughter, 1972 (Pulitzer prize 1973); The Eye of the Story, 1978; Collected Stories, 1980; One Writer's Beginnings, 1984; contbr. So. Rev., Atlantic Monthly, Harpers Bazaar, New Yorker. Recipient creative arts medal for fiction Brandeis U., 1966; Presdl. Medal of Freedom, 1979; Nat. Medal for Lit., 1980; Nat. Medal of Arts, 1986. Mem. Nat. Inst. Arts and Letters (Gold medal 1972), Am. Acad. Arts and Letters. Office: care Harvard U Press 79 Garden St Cambridge MA 02138

WEN, SHEREE HSIAO-RU, electronics company manager; b. Keelung, Taiwan, May 27, 1951; naturalized, 1982; d. Joong-Yu and Yu-Huang (Wang) Wen; Ph.D. in Materials Sci., U. Calif.-Berkeley, 1979. Mgr. materials characterization and analysis Thomas J. Watson Research Center, IBM, Yorktown Heights, N.Y., program mgr. for tech., corp. mfg. Recipient Robert Lansing Hardy gold medal, 1979; John E. Dorn Achievement award Am. Soc. Metals, 1978. Mem. AIME. Contbr. articles to profl. jours. Office: IBM Corporate Hdqrs 2000 Purchase St Purchase NY 10577

WENDEL, FAYE F., coin equipment manufacturing executive; b. Newark, Sept. 16, 1928; d. John Thomas and Sara Rose (Agliozzo) Fiorenza; m. Daniel C. Wendel, Nov. 26, 1949; children—Catherine C., Daniel C. III, Wayne J. Sec., P. Ballantine & Sons, Newark, 1946-49; head hostess, asst. to mgr. Bambergers-Carriage House Restaurant, 1971-74; sec. Peter Wendel & Sons, Inc., Irvington, N.J., 1961-78; sec. Wendel Industries, Inc., Union, N.J., 1978-80, pres., 1980—; pres. D.C. Wendel Corp., 1982—. Tchrs. aide St. Ann Sch.; asst. treas. Ladies Aux. St. Rose of Lima Ch., 1963. Mem. Short Hills Assn., Twig Group of Overlook Hosp., Rotary Assn., Am. Soc. Profl. and Exec. Women. Clubs: Republican, Short Hills Racquet. Home: 33 Quaker Rd Short Hills NJ 07078 Office: 1012 Greeley Ave N Union NJ 07083

WENDER, PHYLLIS BELLOWS, literary agent; b. N.Y.C., Jan. 6, 1934; d. Lee and Lillian (Frank) Bellows; B.A., Wells Coll., 1956; m. Ira Tensard Wender, June 24, 1966; children—Justin Bellows, Sarah Tensard. Dir. publicity Grove Press, 1958-60; dir. publicity Dell Pub. Co., 1960-63; theatrical agt. Artists Agy. Corp., N.Y.C., 1963-66, dir. N.Y. office, 1966-68; agt., pres. Wender & Assocs., 1968-81; lit. agt., partner Rosenstone/Wender, N.Y.C., 1981—. Trustee, Wells Coll., 1981—; bd. dirs. Fortune Soc., 1977-80; adv. council Just Women, Inc., 1982—. Mem. Women's Media Group. Club: Cosmopolitan (N.Y.C.). Home: 555 Park Ave New York NY 10021 Office: 3 E 48th St New York NY 10017

WENDT, ELIZABETH WARCZAK, insurance company officer; b. Chgo., Aug. 27, 1931; d. John George and Elizabeth Marion (Jankowski) Warczak; m. John Edward Wendt, Oct. 31, 1953 (div.); children—John Alan, Brian Arthur, James Michael. Student Loyola U.-Chgo., 1951-52; B.S.B.A., St. Mary-of-the-Woods Coll., 1980; postgrad. Chgo. Kent Coll. Law, 1981-82. Asst. to actuary Globe Life Ins. Co., Chgo., 1970-74, asst. compliance officer Globe Life/Ryan Ins. Group, Chgo., 1974—; mem. co. rep. FLMI Soc. Chgo., 1983—; mem. Life A&H Legis. Com. Consumer Credit Ins. Assn., Chgo., 1983—; co. rep., mem. Handout Com. Life & Health Compliance Assn., 1979—. Mem. United Farm Workers Support Com., Chgo.; Democratic judge of election. Fellow Life Mgmt. Inst.; mem. Inst. Distaff Execs. Assn., Nat. Assn. Ins. Women (dir. 1981-82) (Chgo.). Roman Catholic. Home: 5506 S Madison 11 Hinsdale IL 60521

WENGER, MICHELE JAY, educational administrator; b. Cin., Mar. 29, 1947; d. John Paul and Mildred Elizabeth (Zaus) W.; B.S., U. Cin., 1969, M.Ed., 1970; postgrad Xavier U., 1972-82, Coll. Mt. St. Joseph, 1980-81. With Cin. Public Schs., 1970—, dir. Right to Read, 1972—, project dir. minimum competencies in writing, 1978-81, sex desegregation, 1981-82. U. Cin. scholar, 1969-70, Betty Jane Hull scholar, 1968. Mem. Internat. Reading Assn., Nat. Coalition Sex Equity for Edn., Assn. Supervision and Carriculum Devel., Phi Delta Kappa (pres. U. Cin. chpt. 1982-86), Kappa Delta Pi (chpt. historian 1983-85). Home: 2435 Mustang Dr Unit 12 Cincinnati OH 45211 Office: 230 E 9th St Cincinnati OH 45202

WENGER, VICKI, interior designer; b. Indpls., Aug. 30, 1928. Ed. U. Nebr., Internat. Inst. Interior Design, Parsons in Paris. Pres., Vicki Wenger Interiors, Bethesda, Md., 1963-71, Washington, 1982—, pres. Beautiful Spaces Inc., Washington, 1982—; chief designer Creative Design, Capitol Heights, Md., 1969-84; lectr. Nat. Assn. Home Builders, 1983—; mem. programs com. D.C. Assn. Home Builders, 1983—. Author-host: (patented TV interior design show) Beautiful Spaces 1984. Designer Gourmet Gala, March of Dimes, Washington, 1984-86; designer decorator showcase Nat. Symphony Orch., Washington, 1983-85, Am. Cancer Soc., Washington, 1983. Mem. Am. Soc. Interior Designers (profl. mem.; mem. nat. bd. 1973-75, nat. examining com. 1977-78, pres. Md. chpt. 1976, mem. president's barrier free com. 1980), Nat. Trust Hist. Preservation, Smithsonian Instn. (sponsor), Friends of Corcoran Gallery (sponsor), Friends of Kennedy Ctr., Friends of Vieilles Maisons Françaises. Democrat. Presbyterian. Club: Pisces (Washington). Office: Vicki Wenger Interiors Beautiful Spaces Inc 3227 N St NW Washington DC 20007

WENIGER, KATHY L., commercial and residential interiors contractor; b. Morrillton, Ark., Oct. 19, 1949; m. Earl D. Weniger, May 15, 1981; 1 child, Chase Douglas. Student U. Ark.-Little Rock. Owner, pres. Kathy L. Brown & Assocs., Inc., Little Rock, The Workroom, Inc., Little Rock. Active Pvt. Industry Council, Little Rock. Mem. Nat. Assn. Female Execs., Associated Gen. Contractors. Baptist. Avocations: volunteer fund raiser; entertainer; painting. Home: One Treetops Ln #302 Little Rock AR 72202 Office: Kathy L Brown & Assocs Inc 3700 Cantrell Rd #100 Little Rock AR 72202

WENK, JENNY, advertising executive; b. Pitts., Dec. 29, 1942; d. Samuel Augustine and Jean Lois (Barnes) W.; B.A., U. Calif., Berkeley, 1964; M.B.A., Golden Gate U., 1980; m. Paul R. Allman, Dec. 31, 1981. Advt. promotion and research asst. Richmond (Calif.) Independent, 1965-67; sales promotion writer Dow Jones & Co., Inc., N.Y.C., 1968-70; mem. advt. sales staff Nat. Observer, San Francisco, 1970-74, advt. mgr. Pacific coast, 1974-77; advt. sales rep. Wall Street Jour., San Francisco, 1977—. Mem. San Francisco Women in Advt. (hon. mem., past pres.), San Francisco Advt. Club (dir. 1979-80), Seattle Women in Advt. (hon.). Presbyterian. Office: 220 Battery St San Francisco CA 94111

WENKE, MARY LOUISE, radio station executive; b. Pender, Nebr., Sept. 14, 1947; d. Clark Adolph and Jean Ann (Hogan) W. Student U. Nebr., 1965-68. Personnel cons. Welley Bus. Personnel, Denver, 1972-75; mktg. dir. Hilton Harvest House, Boulder, 1975-76; mktg. dir. Southglenn Mall, Littleton, Colo., 1976-78; creative services dir. Sta. KBPI/KNUS, Denver, 1979—; sec. Rocky Mountain Promotion Dirs. Assn., 1977-78. Trustee, sec. Mile High Transplant Bank, Denver, 1984—, Listen Found., Englewood, Colo., 1982—; trustee, pres. Com. for Denver Arts, 1979-83; mem. Jr. Symphony Guild, Denver Ctr. Alliance, Historic Denver. Republican. Episcopalian. Avocations: skiing; bridge; running. Home: 7341 S Columbine Way Littleton CO 80122 Office: KBPI/KNUS 4460 Morrison Rd Denver CO 80219

WENTE, VERGIE DEE, court ofcl.; b. Allison, Kans., Apr. 24, 1936; d. Virgil D. and Hazel (Storer) Wennihan; student Colby Community Coll., 1969-70; m. Lloyd Wente, July 23, 1953 (div. May 1966); children—Allen Charles, Rhonda Marie, Daniel Lloyd, Lynne LaRea. Bookmobile librarian N.W. Kans. Library System, Hoxie, 1968-70; clk. Dist. Ct. of Sheridan County, Hoxie, 1970-76; chief clk. 15th Jud. Dist. Kans., Hoxie, 1976—; mem. clks. adv. council Kans. Supreme Ct., 1979—. Honored by chief justice Supreme ct. for outstanding contbns. to Kans. Dist. Ct. Clks. and Adminstrs. Assn., 1981. Mem. Kans. Assn. Dist. Ct. Clks. and Adminstrs. (sec.-treas. 1978, v.p. 1979, pres. 1980, legis. chmn. 1981, chmn. 1982—, Mem. public edn. and info. 1981—, exec. com. 1982-84, President's award 1983), Nat. Assn. Ct. Adminstrs. (dir. 1982-84). Mem. Ch. of Christ. Home: 1417 Sheridan Ave Hoxie KS 67740 Office: Box 753 Hoxie KS 67740

WENTZ, CHARLOTTE MARIE, retired librarian; b. Dayton, Ohio, July 25, 1920; d. Walter Grover and Bessie Sunbeam (Stoner) Wentz; B.S. in Edn., U. Dayton, 1942; M.S. in Library Sci., Western Res. U., 1956; postgrad. U. Denver, Western Mich. U., 1966. Sec., Frigidaire div. Gen. Motors Corp., Dayton, 1942-50; tchr. Madison Elem. Sch., Trotwood, Ohio, 1950-52, Garfield Elem. Sch. Mason City, Iowa, 1952-55; librarian Madison High Sch., Trotwood, 1956-58, Madison High Sch., Madison, Ohio, 1958-59, Trotwood-Madison High Sch., Trotwood, 1959-67; library dir. Southwestern Mich. Coll., Dowagiac, Mich., 1967-85; bd. dirs. Dowagiac Public Library, 1975-85, chmn., 1977, 78. Mem. ALA, Southwestern Mich. Library Coop., Bus. and Profl. Women's Club (treas. 1969). Republican. Mem. Christian Ch. (Disciples of Christ). Home: 699A Outer Belle Rd Trotwood OH 45426

WENTZKY, PAULINE MOORE, retired nurse; b. Starr, S.C., June 29, 1920; d. Charley Franklin and Jessie Tiner (Speed) Moore; m. Roy Franklin Wentzky, Dec. 25, 1950 (dec.). R.N., Anderson County Meml. Hosp., 1942; student Anderson Coll., Duke U., 1949-50. Student nurse Anderson County Meml. Hosp. (S.C.), 1939-42, operating room staff nurse, 1942-47, head nurse, 1949, instr. nursing fundamentals, 1949-53, operating room supr., 1953-67, asst. head nurse, 1967-80; surg. asst. to Dr. J.W. Martin, Sr., Anderson, 1947-49. Mem. Am. Nurses Assn., S.C. Nurses Assn. Presbyterian. Home: Route 1 Crestview Rd Box 238 Anderson SC 29621

WERBIN, MARCIA NACHT, religious association executive; b. N.Y.C., Jan. 15, 1937; d. Jack and Ann (Musicant) Nacht; m. Aaron Werbin, Oct. 19, 1957; children—Sharon Alyse, Seth Richard. B.S., NYU, 1957; M.A., SUNY-StonyBrook, 1975, M.A.Ed., 1975. Exec. dir. Baron Hirsch Congregation, Memphis, 1979-81; coordinator Career Directions for Displaced Homemakers, Memphis, 1978-80; tchr. Middle Island Dist., N.Y., 1970-78, Ivy League Nursery Sch., Hauppauge, N.Y., 1969-70; exec. regional dir. Jewish Nat. Fund, Memphis, 1981—. Pres., You, Inc., Memphis, 1979—, Fem-Guide, Inc., Centereach, N.Y., 1976-78. Author: In the Interest of the Hour, 1975. Campaign planner Suffolk County Democratic Com., N.Y., 1973-75; researcher N.Y.C. Dem. Com., 1960, 68. Mem. AAUW, Am. Mgmt. Assn., Am. Assn. Fund Raising Execs.

WERNER, DEBBY HAY, advertising executive; b. Dallas, Dec. 8, 1952; d. Jess Thomas and Betty Jo (Peacock) Hay; 1 child, Jessica Kathryn. B.F.A., So. Meth. U., 1975. Vice pres. Dallas Market Ctr., 1975-83; pres. The Hay Agy. Inc., Dallas, 1983—. Bd. dirs. Dallas Democratic Forum, 1983, The Family Place, 1985, TACA, Inc., 1983—. Mem. Dallas Ad League, Fashion Group, Dallas Mus. Art, Dallas Communications Council. Democrat. Methodist. Home: 7226 Desco Dr Dallas TX 75225 Office: The Hay Agy Inc 2121 San Jacinto Tower Suite 800 Dallas TX 75201

WERNER, DIANE BARCELLONA, bank executive; b. Newark, Dec. 28, 1956; d. Frank and Grace (Bilancia) Barcellona. B.A., Rutgers U., 1978; student Emerson Coll., 1976-77. Publicity asst. N.J. Nightly News, Trenton, 1978-79; pub. info. writer N.J. Pub. TV, Trenton, 1979-80; account exec. Keyes Martin, Springfield, N.J., 1980-83; regional mktg. officer, asst. v.p. United Jersey Bank, N.A., Princeton, 1983—. Mem. Jr. League Montclair/Newark. Mem. Bank Mktg. Assn. Republican. Roman Catholic. Office: United Jersey Bank 301 Carnegie Ctr Princeton NJ 08542

WERNER, GLORIA S., librarian; b. Seattle, Dec. 12, 1940; d. Irving L. and Eva H. Stolzoff; B.A., Oberlin Coll., 1961; M.L., U. Wash., 1962; postgrad. UCLA, 1962-63; m. Newton Davis Werner, June 30, 1963; 1 son, Adam Davis. Reference librarian UCLA Biomed Library, 1963-64, asst. head pub. services dept., 1964-66, head pub. services dept., head reference div., 1966-72, asst. biomed. librarian public services, 1972-77, asso. biomed. librarian, 1977-78, biomed. librarian, assoc. univ. librarian, dir. Pacific S.W. regional Med. Library Service, 1979-83; asst. dean library services UCLA Sch. Medicine, 1980-83; assoc. univ. librarian for tech. services, 1983—; adj. lectr. UCLA Grad. Sch. Library and Info. Sci., 1977-83. Mem. ALA, Med. Library Assn., Assn. Acad. Health Sci. Library Dirs. (dir. 1981-83). Editor, Bull. Med. Library Assn., 1979-82, asso. editor, 1974-79; mem. editorial bd. Ann. Stats. Med. Sch. Libraries U.S. and Can., 1980-83. Office: Library Adminstrv Office U Research Library UCLA Los Angeles CA 90024

WERNER, KRISTINE ELLEN, programmer, analyst; b. Mineola, N.Y., July 24, 1959; d. Robert Paul and Evelyn Rose (Wentsch) Werner. A.A., Indian Valley Coll., Calif., 1980; B.A., Sonoma State U., Calif., 1982; M.B.A., Golden Gate U., San Francisco, 1985. Programmer, Calif. Pacific Ins., San Rafael, 1982-83; cons. self employed, Tiburon, 1983-85; office automation coordinator Hills Bros. Coffee, San Francisco, 1984-85; programmer analyst Hewlett-Packard, Roseville, Calif., 1985—. Author: (workshop) How to Start a Youth Group, 1984. Golden Gate U. merit scholar, 1984. Mem. Nat. Assn. Female Execs., Am. Mktg. Assn. (publicity dir. chpt. 1981-82). Democrat. Lutheran. Club: San Francisco Yacht. Avocations: sailing; aerobics; skiing; backpacking; youth counseling; crafts. Home: 3855 N Lake Shore Blvd Loomis CA 95650 Office: Hewlett Packard 8020 Foothills Blvd Roseville CA 95678

WERNER, PHYLLIS TENGDIN, editor, writer; b. Chgo., Dec. 20, 1923; d. Elmer Theodore and Agnes Minne Tengdin; m. Dean Franklin Werner, Oct. 14, 1945; children—Nancy Werner Bybel, Sallie Werner Wilson, Lynn Werner Driggers, Barbara Werner Douglas. A.A., Kansas City Jr. Coll., 1943; B.A., U. Okla., 1945; postgrad. U. Mo. Asst. prodn. dir. Carter Advt., Kansas City, Mo., 1945; reporter Daily Oklahoman, Oklahoma City, 1946-48; librarian Denver Post, 1948-49; reporter Dispatch Newspapers, North Kansas City, Mo., 1968-69; editor Central States Lutheran, Kansas City, Mo., 1979—; freelance writer, 1948—; del. to Luth. Ch. in Am. Biennial Convs., 1976, 78, 84. Vice pres. bd. govs. Kansas City Philharm., social chmn., 1980-82; past vice chmn Cockefair Chair (humanities) U. Mo., Kansas City; past pres. Philharm. Guild N.; past mem. Kansas City Mayor's Commn. for Human Relations, mem. commn. Sister Cities; mem. Lyric Opera Guild, Friends of Art, North Kansas City Hosp. Aux., Clay-Platte County (Mo.) Med. Aux. (past v.p.); bd. dirs. Mo. Citizens for Arts; legis. liaison Kansas City Symphony Guild, Kansas Interfaith Alliance, Luths. for Justice and Peace. Mem. World Assn. for Christian Communicators, Women in Communications, Inc., AAUW (v.p.), Hist. Kansas City Found., NCCJ (dir.), Ecumedia (vice chmn.), Gamma Phi Beta. Club: Central Exchange. Home and Office: 4609 N Main St Kansas City MO 64116

WERNER, VIVIAN, personnel manager; b. N.Y.C., June 5, 1942; d. Marcel A. and Renee (Cohn) Cordovi; children—Deborah Jill, David Scott; m. Robert Jay Golden, July 30, 1977. Grad. Katherine Gibbs Sch., 1963; B.S., Rutgers U., 1974. Pres., Research Systems Corp., N.Y.C., 1970-75; personnel counselor Snelling & Snelling, N.J., 1976-77; v.p., personnel mgr. Smith's Fifth Ave., N.Y.C., 1977—; guest lectr. Rutgers U., 1977-83; lectr. Katherine Gibbs Sch., 1978, Am. Mgmt. Assn., 1975, 76, 77. Contbr. articles to profl. jours.; assoc. editor Mktg. Rev., 1977-83. Office: Smiths Fifth Ave 17 E 45th St New York NY 10017

WERNICK, EDITH ELAINE, pianist, educator; b. Columbus, Ohio, July 30, 1944; d. Maurice and Evelyn (Stone) Wernick; pupil Loy Kohler, Jerry Lowder, George Haddad, Dave Wheeler, Lee Knoll. Pvt. tchr. piano, guitar, organ, accordian, Columbus, 1963—; instr. Van's Music Studio, Columbus, 1965-77; now tchr. Coyle's Music, Columbus. Rec. sec. Franklin County Young Democrats, 1976-77; fin. sec. women singles unit B'nai B'rith, 1977—; exec. com. Sabra Hadassah Edn. Com., 1977. Certificate in piano musicianship-pedagogy Nat. Piano Found. Mem. Music Tchrs. Nat. Assn., Nat. Piano Guild, Ohio, Columbus music tchrs. assns., Internat. Library Music Service for Profl. Music Tchrs., Nat. Honor Roll of Guild Tchrs. Jewish religion. Home: 496 S Hamilton Rd Apt 36 Columbus OH 43213 Office: PO Box 15753 Columbus OH 43215

WERNIKOFF, NANCY KASDON, speech/lang. pathologist; b. Cleve., Apr. 6, 1938; d. Eli David and Doree (Sands) Kasdon; B.A., N.Y. U., 1962; M.S. in Edn., Queens Coll., 1969; m. Sergio Wernikoff, Oct. 26, 1958; children—Laura Sue, Daniel Mark. Speech pathologist Speech Rehab. Inst., N.Y.C., 1962-63, acting speech supr. speech therapy dept., 1963-65; speech-lang. cons. pre-sch. program Pascack Valley (N.J.) Council Spl. Edn., 1976-77; cons. speech-lang. pathologist Ramsey (N.J.) Public Schs., 1978—; pvt. practice, 1967—; cons. in field. Mem. exec. bd. Archer Nursery Sch., Allendale, N.J., 1973-74; active local Boy Scouts Am., Girl Scouts U.S.A., 1972-78; mem. exec. bd. sisterhood Temple Beth Or, Washington Twp., N.J., 1976-81, mem. exec. bd. Temple Beth Or, 1981—. Recipient Griffith Hughes Meml. prize Washington Sq. Coll. of Arts and Scis., N.Y. U., 1962. Mem. Am. Speech, Lang. and Hearing Assn., N.J. Speech and Hearing Assn., Bergen County Speech and Hearing Assn. (co-founder), Speech and Hearing Study Group (co-founder). Home: 42 Somerset Dr Woodcliff Lake NJ 07675

WERTHEIM, AUDREY DARWIN, marketing, public relations executive; b. N.Y.C., Mar. 14, 1933; d. Hippolyte Maurice and Esther (Darwin) Wertheim. Student Erie Coll., Painesville, Ohio, 1950-53. Sec. publicity dept. Columbia Pictures, N.Y.C., 1958-60; exec. sec., editorial asst. Cholly Knickbocker column N.Y. Jour. Am., 1961-63; publicity dir. Sheraton Corp. Am., N.Y.C., 1963-66; spl. events promotion dir. ABC-TV, N.Y.C., 1965-67; propr. Wertheim & Assocs., N.Y.C., 1967—. Recipient numerous letters of commendation. Mem. Bahama Out Islands Assn. Republican. Episcopalian. Office: Ground Floor 227 E 57th St New York NY 10022

WERTHEIM, MARY CAROLE, advertising agency executive; b. Albuquerque, Dec. 25, 1939; d. Joseph and Stella (Mensio) May; m. Jerry Wertheim, Aug. 20, 1960; children—Jerry Todd, John Vincent. Student U. N.Mex., 1958-60, George Washington U., 1960-61. Treas. Werthco Ranch, N.Mex., 1972—; billing systems coordinator JGS&W, P.A., Santa Fe, 1973-74; founder, pres. Creative Images, LTD., Santa Fe, 1978—. Past mem. N.Mex. Com. Children and Youth, N.Mex. State Library Com. Recipient numerous awards for advt. prodn., 1978—. Mem. Santa Fe C. of C. (bd. dirs. 1983—, treas. 1984—), No. N.Mex. Advt. Fedn. (bd. dirs. 1981-82), Gen. Fedn. Women's Clubs (nat. bd. dirs. 1970-80), N.Mex. Fedn. Women's Clubs (state pres. 1976-78). Avocations: skiing; swimming; reading. Office: Creative Images Ltd 355 E Palace Ave Sante Fe NM 87501

WERTZ, ALTA HAPP, artist, educator; b. Kennewick, Wash., Feb. 19, 1921; d. Henry Lewis and Annie Elizabeth (Yates) Leckliter; student Bakersfield Jr. Coll., 1939-40; m. Richard Clarence Smith (div. 1961); children—Robin (Mrs. Bernard Charles Danylchuk), Alan Montgomery, Shelley (Mrs. Thomas William Stoye); m. 2d. William Morris Happ, Jan. 19, 1967 (dec. 1980); m. 3d Harvey William Wertz, Feb. 26, 1984. Instr. oil painting, adult edn. Palomar Coll., San Marcos, Calif., 1958-62; pvt. tchr., lectr. in field, 1962—; one-woman shows The Atheneaum, La Jolla, Calif., 1959, Jeane's Gallery, La Jolla, 1961, Palomar Coll., 1959-61, The Little Galleries, Escondido, Calif., 1964, La Pina Ltd., La Jolla, 1965, 66, 67, Gray's Gallery, Escondido, 1973, Carlsbad Oceanside Art League Gallery, 1973; exhibited in group shows San Diego Mus. Art, San Diego Art Inst., Riverside Mus. Art, San Bernardino Mus. Art, So. Calif. Expn., Del Mar, also various galleries represented in permanent collections; lectr. on psychology and symbology of color in music and art. Active Palomar Hosp. aux., 1957-59; pres. Showcase of Arts, Escondido, 1961-62; rep. to San Diego Council of Visual Arts, 1966-67, mem. Escondido Cultural Arts Com., 1972-73; chmn. Mission Valley (Calif.) Expn. Art, 1967; bd. dirs. Philos. Religious Free Library, 1970-74, Pala Mission Indian Sch., 1965-72. Huntington Hartford Found. fellow, Pacific Palisades, Calif., 1964. Recipient numerous other awards. Mem. San Diego Art Inst., San Diego Art Guild of Fine Arts Soc., San Diego Watercolor Soc., Nat. League of Am. Pen Women (pres. 1974-76), Watercolor West. Home: 11302 Moorpark St North Hollywood CA 91602

WERTZ, CHARLOTTE THERESE, paralegal; b. Springfield, Ill., July 11, 1959. B.S. in Music Edn., Duquesne U., 1980. Cert. paralegal. Paralegal Dickie, McCamey & Chilcote, Pitts., 1981—; advisor to bd. dirs. Pitts. Paralegal Assn., 1986—; rep. Triangle Corner Ltd., Pitts., 1985—. Author So You Want to be a Paralegal pamphlet, 1983. Editor Nat. Paralegal Reporter, 1984-85. Contbr. articles to newsletter. Mem. Pitts. Paralegal Assn. (pres. 1985-86, treas. 1983-85), Y-Net/YWCA (v.p. 1986—), Nat. Assn. Female Execs.

WERTZ, JANE KARR, broadcaster; b. Chgo., Aug. 16, 1934; d. Kenneth L. and Catharine C. (Carpenter) Karr; m. Edwin P. Neubauer, Aug. 10, 1956 (div. 1979); children—Kenneth Paul, Kathryn J., Keith E. (dec.); m. Charles W. Wertz, June 21, 1980. B.A., Beloit Coll., 1956. Tchr., Winnebago County Schs., Rockford, Ill., 1956-57; broadcaster Sta. WREX-TV, Rockford, 1964-80; pub. relations dir. Swedish Am. Hosp., Rockford, 1976-80; on air talent Beloit Cable TV, Wis., 1970-80, broadcaster, program dir. Sta. KSTS-TV, San Jose, Calif., 1981—; instr. San Jose State U., 1984—. Bd. dirs. Peninsula Ctr. for Blind, Palo Alto, Calif., 1981—. Mem. AFTRA, P.E.O. Sisterhood, Delta Gamma. Republican. Methodist. Home: 1010 Robin Way Sunnyvale CA 94087 Office: Sta KSTS-TV 2349 Bering Dr San Jose CA 95131

WESCHE-MONACO, PATRICIA, ballet teacher; b. N.Y.C., Oct. 13, 1952; d. Edward William and Gerta Henny (Flock) Wesche; m. Anthony Frank Monaco, Sept. 24, 1977; children—Michael Anthony, Nydia Nicole. Student (scholar) Am. Ballet Theatre Sch., N.Y.C., 1965-69. Dancer, Am. Ballet Theatre, N.Y.C., 1969-78; ballet tchr., Houston, 1978—; owner Am. Acad. of Dance, Spring, Tex., 1981—; dancer in film "Turning Point"; live work from Lincoln Ctr. Am. Ballet Theatre, N.Y.C., 1978—; TV appearances include Live from Lincoln Center, Dance in Am.; founder, dir. dance group North Houston Dance Theatre for local community and schs., Spring, 1982. Mem. Am. Guild Musical Artists, Screen Actors Guild, AFTRA. Office: Am Acad of Dance 18512 Kuykendahl Spring TX 77379

WESCHLER, ANITA, sculptor, painter; b. N.Y.C.; d. J. Charles and Hulda Eva (Mayer) W.; m. Herbert E. Solomon, Dec. 1944. Student Le Grand Verger, Lausanne; diploma Parsons Sch. Design, studied Nat. Acad., Art Students League, Columbia U., Pa. Acad. Fine Arts, Barnes Found. One-women shows include 14 in N.Y.C., 25 nationwide; group shows include Met. Mus. Art, N.Y.C., Mus. of Modern Art, Whitney Mus., Carnegie Inst., Phila. Mus. Art, San Francisco Mus. Art, Nat. Acad. and Inst. Arts and Letters, Riverside Mus., Bkyn. Mus., Newark Mus., Bucks County Council on Arts, Storm King Arts Ctr.; represented in permanent collections including Amherst Coll., Art Students League, Brandeis U., Inst. Achievement of Human Potential, Nebr. U., Norfolk U., Smithsonian Instn., Syracuse U., Wichita State U., Whitney Mus., Yale U., Met. Mus. Art, U. Iowa; represented in numerous pvt. collections. Fellow Mac Dowell Colony, Yaddo. Mem. Archtl. League, Artists Craftsman of N.Y., Fedn. Modern Painters and Sculptors (past exec. com.), Sculptors Guild (past exec. bd.), Internat. Assn. Art (U.S. com.), Internat. Inst. Arts and Letters, Fine Arts Fedn. N.Y. (del.). Art Students League. Address: 136 Waverly Pl New York NY 10014

WESENBERG, GLORIA ELEANE, health services administrator; b. Penzance, Cornwall, Eng., Apr. 10, 1927; came to U.S. 1929; d. Samuel Young and Mona Maude (Folkes) Dale; children—Gloria J. Hathaway, Vyvian M. Wesenberg, Carl P., Celia E., Barron V. Grad. Fisher Jr. Coll., 1947; B.S., J.F. Kennedy U., 1983, M.B.A., 1985. Health services adminstr. Kaiser Aluminum and Chem. Corp., Oakland, Calif., 1970—. Vol. Citizens for Dick Spees, Oakland, 1980; mem. San Francisco Opera Guild, Oakland Mus., Mus. Modern Art, Mus. Soc. Mem. Adminstrv. Mgmt. Soc. (treas.), Profl. Secs. Assn. (cert., v.p. 1971). Avocations: interior design; cross-country skiing; bicycling; gardening; sewing.

WESOLOWSKI, DEBORAH JEAN, nursing service hospital administrator; b. KraKow, Wis., Aug. 26, 1953; d. Elmer Robert and Dolores Marie (Strelecki) Majewski; m. Clarence Louis Wesolowski, Oct. 19, 1974. Diploma in nursing Holy Family Sch. of Nursing, Manitowoc, Wis., 1974; postgrad. in advanced studies in nursing and patient care adminstrn. U. Minn., 1980-82. Registered nurse. Staff nurse Community Meml. Hosp., Oconto Falls, Wis., 1974-76, head nurse med. surg. unit, 1976-79, asst. dir. nursing, 1979-81, dir. nursing, 1981—. Assisted with eye bank program Local Lions Club; lectr. St. Casimir Catholic Ch., KraKow; parish council chair of social concerns com. St. Casimir Cath. Ch., 1985. Mem. Am. Nurses Assn. (cert. in nursing adminstrn.), Wis. Orgn. Nurses Execs. (membership com.), Bay Area Dirs. Nursing. Avocations: needlework, crewel, counted cross-stitch, fishing, cross country skiing, swimming. Home: Route 1 Box 24 A Pulaski WI 54162 Office: Community Meml Hosp 855 S Main Oconto Falls WI 54154

WESS, GRACE IRENE BROWN (MRS. OTTO FRANCIS WESS), estimator, nurse, stables owner; b. Youngstown, Ohio, May 13, 1925; d. Floyd Raymond and Ruth (Walter) Brown; student Bliss Bus. Coll., 1942-43; LL.B., LaSalle U., 1952; grad. nurse's tng. Youngstown Hosp. Assn., 1974; m. Otto Francis Wess, June 11, 1949 (dec. Mar. 1969); children—Raymond Francis, Shannon Grace Wess Morello, Colleen Melody Wess Bloomingdale, Honey Lucile Wess Biondillo, Alyson Rae Wess Gilpin Carol Lynn Wess Sivley. Nurse's aid St. Elizabeth Hosp., Youngstown, 1938-42; traffic clk. B.F. Goodrich Co., Akron, Ohio, 1942-43; rate clk., traffic dept. Gen. Fireproofing

Co., Youngstown, 1947-49; pres., co-owner Jewels by Lady Grace, Detroit, 1949-63, Grayce's Treasure Chests, Youngstown, 1949-63, Grayce's Medicine Chests, Youngstown, 1949-63; indsl. and comml. bldg. estimator Ben Rudick & Son, Inc., Youngstown, 1963-71; freelance estimator, North Lima, Ohio, 1971—; newspaper columnist, various newspapers, 1963-68; nurse, 1974—; now staff nurse Drs. Hosp., Lake Worth, Fla.; owner Grace Wess Stables, Inc., Canfield, Ohio, 1949—. Democratic candidate for Mahoning County commr., 1973; bd. dirs. Missing Children Found., Tampa, Fla.; mem. legis. com. Palm Beach County, Mothers Against Drunk Driving. Served with WAVES, 1943-47. Mem. Am. Bus. Women's Assn. (pres. 1969-70, Woman of Yr. award 1970), Youngstown Bus. and Profl. Women's Club, U.S. Trotting Assn., Canfield Harness Horsemen's Assn., Ohio Harness Horsemen's Assn., Am. Legion, VFW, Def. Supply Assn., McGuffey Meml. Assn., Women in Constrn., Constrn. Specifications Inst., Internat. Platform Assn., Home and Sch. Assn., St. Charles Altar and Rosary Soc., Mahoning County Agrl. Soc., Am. German Club of Palm Beaches (Fla.), Youngstown Playhouse. Democrat. Roman Catholic. Lodges: Order Eastern Star (Grand Nurse of Fla. 1986-87), Grange. Home and office: 1008 Penn Grove Lake Worth FL 33461

WESSELMANN, JANINE CAROL, artist; b. Utica, N.Y., June 13, 1947; d. Robert A. and Anita G. (Ziegler) W. B.S. in Design, Cornell U., 1969; B.S. in Art Edn., Ladycliff Coll., 1980. Vol., Peace Corps, 1969; mem. faculty, head art dept. All Saints, St. Thomas, V.I., 1970-73; mem. faculty Ladycliff Coll., Highland Falls, N.Y., 1979-80; art dir. Tepfer Pub. Co., Danbury, Conn., 1980-85; designed murals for Pan Am. Hotel, Miami Beach, Fla.; instr. graphic arts, Switzerland, and Caribbean; art cons. Cunard Lines. Exhibited one-woman shows U.S., Europe, Caribbean. Chairwoman Art Circle. Recipient awards for painting Am. Bicentennial, Venice Art League, Nat. Design award for best mag. covers, 1985, Disting. Leadership award, 1985. Mem. Internat. Art Guild, Internat. Soc. Artists, Internat. Graphic Arts Edn. Found., Am. Woman's Club of Geneva. Studio: PO Box 627 West Redding CT 06896

WEST, ANNA LOUCHHEIM, public relations consultant; b. Phila., Dec. 5, 1953; d. Frank Pfeiffer and Betty (Meinel) Louchheim; B.A., Mt. Holyoke Coll., 1975; M.S., Boston U., 1980; m. Edward Foulke West, July 6, 1974; children—David Louchheim, Jonathan William. Public participation coordinator Delaware Valley Regional Planning Commn., 1975-77; public info. rep. New Eng. Power Co., 1977-79; sr. communications cons. Energy Research Group, Inc., 1979-83, v.p., 1983-84; prin. Kearns & West, Inc., 1984—. Mem. Pub. Relations Soc. Am. (pres. New Eng. chpt.). Home: 210 Litchfield Dr Carlisle MA 01741 Office: Lexington Sq Suite 5 1666 Massachusetts Ave Lexington MA 02173

WEST, BRENDA CAROL, university administrator; b. Hopkinsville, Ky., Aug. 17, 1944; d. Bedford Forrest and Eleanor (Stallons) Jones; m. William Taylor West, July 8, 1962; children—R. Michele, Deborah C. B.A. in Edn., U. Miss., 1976, M.Ed., 1977. Tchr. reading Intermediate Sch., Holly Springs, Miss., 1977-78; supr. learning ctr. Adult Day Sch., Wahiawa, Hawaii, 1978-80; records supr. alumni affairs U. Miss., University, 1981-83, asst. dir., 1983—. Com. chmn. Com. on Status of Women, University, 1982—. Univ. fellow U. Miss., 1976-77. Mem. AAUW (br. pres. 1981-83, state v.p. 1983-85), Council Advancement and Support Edn., U. Miss. Alumni Assn., Phi Kappa Phi (v.p. 1984-86), Kappa Delta Pi. Episcopalian. Avocations: reading; travel. Home: 2205 Haley St Oxford MS 38655 Office: Alumni Office U Miss University MS 38677

WEST, CAROLYN JO, land development company executive, financial consultant; b. Paducah, Ky., July 4, 1935; d. Joe Ed and Leona (Burks) Holly; m. William B. West, Sept. 28, 1957 (dec.); 1 dau., Holly Lynn Pierce. B.S., Pepperdine U., 1957; postgrad., Calif. State U.-Fullerton, 1965-67. Bookkeeper Quality Produce Co., Santa Ana, Calif., 1957-69; asst. mgr., controller Savi Devel. Corp., Orange, Calif., 1969-75; treas., controller So. Pacific Constrn. Co., Garden Grove, Calif., 1975-77; asst. controller, chief acct. Dunn Properties Corp., Santa Ana, 1977-79; v.p., treas., controller Saddleback Assocs. Inc., Santa Ana, 1979—; cons. Nantell Investments, Fountain Valley, Calif., 1977—; cons., chief fin. officer Gilmer Properties, Orange, 1980—; cons. investors, land developers., 1977—. Founder Helping Hands, Hillview Acres Children's Home, pres. 1963-67; leader trainer Girl Scouts U.S.A., Orange County, Calif., 1967-70; fund raiser, Orange County Democratic Com., 1968; speaker So. Calif. Women's Ch. Confs.; tchr. Bible classes, Ch. of Christ, Santa Ana and Garden Grove. Recipient outstanding service awards Girl Scouts U.S.A., 1969, Hillview Acres Children's Home, 1971. Mem. Delta Chi Omega (pres. 1954-55). Home: 8763 Rogue River Fountain Valley CA 92708 Office: Saddleback Assocs Inc PO Box 17899 Irvine CA 92713

WEST, DEBBIE JEAN, real estate sales broker; b. Conway, Ark., Nov. 8, 1953; d. L. and Juanita (Griffith) Kirkland; m. Ted. D. West, Apr. 15, 1972; children—Dana Renee, Jeffrey Dewayne. Student U. Ark., 1975, Paul Harris Sch. Real Estate, 1979. Sales assoc. Smithers Realty, Russellville, Ark., 1975-76, Rainey Realtors, Atkins, Ark., 1976-77, Ott-Longing Real Estate, Conway, 1977-79; sales mgr. Mack Realty, Greenbrier, Ark., 1979-80; real estate salesperson, assoc. broker C-21-Dunaway and Hart, Inc., Conway, 1980-81; co-owner, v.p. Stout Real Estate of Conway, Inc., 1981—. Named to Million Dollar Sales Club, 1979, 80, named life mem., 1983; named to Century 21 Million Dollar Sales Club, 1980. Mem. Conway C. of C., Am. Realtors Assn., Conway Bd. Realtors, Nat. Realtors, Nat. Realtors Assn. Baptist. Home: Route 6 Box 201A Conway AR 72032 Office: Stout Real Estate Co of Conway Inc Route 6 Box 201A Conway AR 72032

WEST, DOTTIE (DOROTHY MARIE MARSH), singer; b. McMinnville, Tenn., Oct. 11; d. William and Pelina (Jones) Marsh; m. William West, 1952 (div. 1972); children—Morris, Kerry, Shelly, Dale; m. Byron A. Metcalf, Aug. 27, 1973 (div. 1981). B.A. in Music, Tenn. Tech. Coll., 1956. Singing debut WEWS-TV, Cleve., 1956-60; singer 5-piece band Cross-Country, 1966—; performances include: Grand Ole Opry, 1962—, Memphis Symphony Orch., 1973, Kansas City Symphony, 1961-74, also Atlanta Symphony, Denver Symphony, New Orleans Symphony, TV appearances include: Eddy Arnold Special, Country Hit Parade, Music Country U.S.A., Hee-Haw, Glen Campbell Show, Jimmy Dean, Mike Douglas, Good Ole Nashville, Tonight Show, Kenny Rogers Spl., Hollywood Squares, Dukes of Hazzard, Barbara Mandrell, Ray Charles Spl., Good Morning Am., Solid Gold, Merv Griffin Show, Ernest Tubb Spl., Hee Haw, The Fall Guy, Circus of Stars, Bob Hope Spl. Country Comes Home, Love Boat; co-host award show Showtime Spl.; host weekly radio show This Week in Country Music; rec. artist Staeday Records, 1959-61, Atlantic Records, 1962, RCA, 1962—, United Artists Records, Permian Records. Recipient Grammy award female artist for Here Comes My Baby, 1965; named Number One Female Writer in U.S., Billboard Mag., 1974, Number One Female Performer in Eng., 1973, 74; Country Music Artist of Year, British Country Music Assn.; Coca Cola Country Girl, 1972—; Duet Artist of Yr. (with Kenny Rogers). Address: care Michael Brokaw Mgmt 3389 Camino de la Cumbre Sherman Oaks CA 91423

WEST, EUDORA MAY, bowling lanes proprietor, trucking company executive, accountant; b. Springfield, Colo., Nov. 8, 1939; d. T. L. Tucker and Leda May (Myers) Tucker; m. Sherrill D. West, June 24, 1962; children—Vicki, Mike. B.A. in Bus. Adminstrn., Colo. Coll., 1961. Acct., Sta. KZIX, Ft. Collins, Colo., 1963-64, Western Transp., Inc., Lamar, Colo., 1975—, corp. sec., 1976-83, v.p., 1984—; partner, corp. sec., acct. Royal Lanes, Inc., Springfield, Colo., 1978—. Mem. Southeastern Colo. Hosp. Aux., Springfield, Colo., 1982—; mem. Baca County Republican Party, Springfield, 1982—. Baptist. Home: 439 Pine St Springfield CO 81073 Office: Royal Lanes Inc 1165 Main St Springfield CO 81073 also Western Transp Inc 702 N Main St Lamar CO 81052

WEST, JOSEBELL LUCILLE, educator; b. Hialeah, Fla., Dec. 2, 1925; d. Willie and Willie Alfred (Thompson) Akers; student Oakwood Coll. Acad., 1946; early childhood certificate Broward Community Coll., 1963; m. Eddie West, Mar. 28, 1946; children—Frank A., Bernard E., Marva L., Dwayne E. Tchr., Mt. Olivet Seventh-Day Adventist Ch. Sch., Dania, Fla., 1951-52, West's Kindergarten, Dania, 1952-69; social educator Broward County (Fla.) Sch. Bd., Ft. Lauderdale, 1969—. Committeewoman, Dania Democratic Com., 1958-69; pres. Collins Elem. Sch. PTA, Dania, 1960-69, Bethune Elem. Sch. PTA, Hollywood, Fla., 1969-70; bd. dirs. Pathfinder, 1974-81. Mem. NEA, Am. Legion Aux., Concerned Citizens of Dania, Inc., 1974—. Seventh-Day Adventist (dep. dir.). Clubs: Cheerful Workers, Westside Civic of Dania (sec. 1959-65, pres. 1974—), Pathfinder (dir.), Dania Dem. Home: 621 NW 3d Terr Dania FL 33004 Office: 701 NW 31st Ave Fort Lauderdale FL 33311

WEST, JOYCE LOUISE, insurance company administrator; b. Gassaway, W.Va., Mar. 4, 1956; d. Esker Jerrell and Mary Madeline (Keener) Morris; m. Keith West, May 25, 1974. Cert., Ins. Inst. Am., 1980, Assoc. Los Control Mgmt., 1983. Typist, Erie Ins. Group (Pa.), 1975-80, loss control rep. 1980—, auditor, 1983—, class instr., 1983—. Mem. Nat. Assn. Ins. Women, Ins. Women Erie (v.p. 1983-84). Republican. Methodist. Office: Erie Ins Group PO Box 1699 100 Erie Ins Pl Erie PA 16530

WEST, KAREN, college administrator; b. Homestead, Pa., June 4, 1945; d. Elmer Howard and Margaret E. (Adelsperger) West; m. Donald L. Nelson (div. 1979); children—Bradford D., Keith L. A.A. in Humanities with honors, Jamestown Community Coll., 1980; B.S., SUNY-Empire State Coll., 1984. Exec. dir. ops. and pub. relations KND Leasing, Inc., Falconer, N.Y., 1975-80; affirmative action officer Jamestown Community Coll., N.Y., 1981-82, dir. community relations, 1980-84; exec. asst. to pres. coll. affairs SUNY-Fredonia, 1984—. Vice pres. bd. Jamestown Vis. Nurse Assn., 1982-84; bd. dirs. Jamestown Concert Assn., 1983-84; chmn. search and screen com. Chautauqua, Area council Girl Scouts U.S.A., 1984. Mem. SUNY Council Univ. Affairs and Devel. Avocations: reading; boating; snow skiing. Home: 81 Lakin Ave Jamestown NY 14701 Office: State Univ NY Coll Fredonia 143 Fenton Hall Fredonia NY 14063

WEST, KATHRYN MARIE, pianist; b. Lansing, Mich., Apr. 15, 1935; d. Harry Allen and Mabel Agnes (Dyer) Strait; student Central Mich. U., 1952-55, Eastern Mich. U., 1979-81; m. David Roche West, June 11, 1955; children—Julie, Martha, Nancy, Jean, Mark. Profl. accompanist Ann Arbor Civic Theatre, U. Mich. Gilbert and Sullivan Soc., U. Mich. Summer Theater, 1965-72, Comic Opera Guild, 1983; duo pianist with Naomi Donaldson, 1970-76, with Margaret Bond, 1972—; sec. Office of Pres. U. Mich., Ann Arbor, 1976-77, exec. sec., 1978-83; sec. U. Mich. Law Sch., Ann Arbor, 1984—; concerts in Kansas City, Mo., Ohio, Mich. Mem. Friends of Four Hand Music, Amateur Chamber Music Players, Sigma Alpha Iota. Home: 1105 Granger Ann Arbor MI 48104

WEST, LORETTA MARIE, underwriter; b. N.Y.C., Feb. 2, 1950; d. James L. and Alice (Richardson) West. A.B., Washington Coll., Chestertown, Md., 1972. Cert. profl. ins. woman. Disbursements cashier Middlesex Ins. Co., Concord, Mass., 1972-76, tech. asst., 1976-78, comml. lines underwriter, 1978-83; sr. comml. lines underwriter Sentry Ins. Co., Concord, 1983-86, large acct. underwriter, 1986—. Corr. sec. Framingham Republican Town Com. Mem. Nat. Assn. Ins. Women, Mass. Assn. Ins. Women (various coms. Middlesex and South Middlesex chpts., co-dir. South Middlesex chpt. 1986—; Woman of Yr. award Middlesex chpt. 1980). Roman Catholic. Home: 6 Prescott St Framingham MA 01701 Office: Sentry Insurance Route 2 Concord MA 01742

WEST, MARCIA ANN, broadcasting exec.; b. Seattle, Nov. 27, 1944; d. Byron Hale and Norma Ruth Harvey; B.A., W. Tex. State U., 1966, M.A., 1969; postgrad. U. Colo., 1971-76. Instr. Spanish, W. Tex. State U., 1966-68, U. Evansville (Ind.), 1969-71, U. Colo., Denver, 1971-76; host, co-producer Esta Semana, Sta. KRMA-TV, Denver, 1971-75; asso. editor La Luz mag., 1972—; producer, broadcaster KOA News, Denver, 1972-76; mgr. public affairs KOA Stas., Denver, 1976-78, program and public affairs dir., 1978—; publicity dir. Barney Ford Meml. Assn., 1976—; cons. in field. Bd. dirs. Cystic Fibrosis Found., Denver Opportunities Industrialization Center; mem. selection com. Minoru Yasui Vol. Awards for Denver; adv. bd. Denver Internat. Film Festival; mem. selection com. 10th Nat. Abe Lincoln awards; cons. Gov.'s Conf. Library Services. Recipient Abe Lincoln Merit award, 1977; Tummy award Denver Area Journalists Assn., 1972; Silver Bell award Nat. Advt. Council, 1981; Broadcast Preceptor's award San Francisco State U., 1983; named Outstanding Educator U. Colo., Denver, 1976; Outstanding Tchr. Fgn. Lang., W.Tex. State U., 1966; Best Public Affairs Producer, Denver Catholic Register, 1977; chosen media contributions winner Colo. Salute to Women, 1981. Mem. Am. Women in Radio and TV, Nat. Assn. Broadcasters, Colo. Broadcasters Assn., Nat. Alliance Businessmen, Nat. Assn. Program Execs. (selection com. awards 1978), Nat. Broadcasters Assn. for Community Affairs (regional v.p., nat. conf. chairperson 1980-81, pres. 1981-82, exec. com. 1983—), Leadership Denver, Denver C. of C. Author articles. Home: 61256 Cherry Creek Denver CO 80206 Office: 1044 Lincoln St Denver CO 80203

WEST, MARGUERITE ANN, county official; b. Dallas County, Iowa, Mar. 3, 1938; d. Joseph Leo and Marie Wilma (Knoll) Torsky; m. Jack Graham West, Sept. 8, 1956 (div. 1984); children—Michael Lester, Melanie Dawn, David Ray. Grad. high sch., Granger, Iowa. Stenographer, Bankers Life Co., Des Moines, 1955-57; office clk. Dallas County Clk. of Ct., Iowa, 1966-78; county recorder Dallas County, 1979—; sec. Dallas County Zoning Commn., 1977-78. Precinct committee-woman Dallas County Democrats, 1966-79. Mem. Dist. Recorders Assn. (sec. treas. 1981, vice chmn. 1982, chmn. 1983), Women's Polit. Caucus Dallas County. Lutheran. Avocations: dancing; sewing; reading; water skiing; camping. Home: 801 Warren St De Soto IL 50069 Office: Dallas County Recorder 801 Court St Adel IA 50003-1484

WEST, MARIANNE V., social worker; b. South Bend, Ind., Mar. 29, 1951; d. Leo William and Janet Irene (Grove) West; B.A., Ind. U., 1973; M.S.W., U. Ill., Chgo., 1975. Staff social worker St. Francis Hosp., Evanston, Ill., 1975-77; clin. social worker Health Care Assocs. for Women, Grants Pass, Oreg., 1977-78; pvt. practice clin. social work, Grants Pass, 1978-79; clin. social worker, dir. residence Mary Bartelme Home for Girls, Chgo., 1979-84, unit dir., 1981-84; program adminstr. Kaleidoscope, Inc., 1984—; instr. Rogue Community Coll., Grants Pass, 1978; cons. Josephine County Juvenile Dept., Grants Pass, 1978; fieldwork instr. Loyola U. Sch. Social Work, Chgo., 1979; cons. Chgo. YWCA, Chgo. Women Against Rape, 1976-77, 79—, Child Sexual Abuse Treatment and Tng. Ctr., Bolingbrook, Ill., 1984—; coordinator Parents Anonymous, Grants Pass, 1979; mem. governing bd. Cook County Child Sexual Abuse Task Force, Chgo., 1980-85. Cert. social worker, Ill.; registered clin. social worker, Oreg., 1978. Mem. AAUW, Acad. Cert. Social Workers, Alpha Xi Delta. Club: Order Eastern Star. Office: Kaleidoscope Inc 329 S Wood St Chicago IL 60612

WEST, MAUREEN BERNADETTE, computer consulting and software development company executive, data processing executive; b. Hoboken, N.J., May 21, 1948; d. Edward and Cecelia (O'Leary) Harney West; m. Stephan Chandler, June 14, 1969. B.S., SUNY 1972; student Manhattan Sch. Music, 1966-67, Suffolk Coll., 1967, Columbia U., 1969-70. Vice pres. ICS Group Inc., Torrance, Calif., 1981-83; exec. v.p. Data Dimensions, Los Angeles, 1983-84; pres., chmn. WCC, Inc., Los Angeles, 1980—. Editor software: Personnel Systems, 1983, Basic Tutorial, 1984, Date Stamp, 1984, Business Analyst, 1985. Avocations: chamber concerts; new music; art; opera; amateur radio. Office: WCC Inc 19531 Ventura Blvd Tarzana CA 91356

WEST, MOLLIE LOUISE, journalist; b. Detroit, Oct. 24, 1953; d. Frank Samuel and Mary Elizabeth (McKissick) W. B.A., U. Mich., 1976. Prodn. asst. NBC-WDIV-TV, Detroit, 1977-79; account exec. Daniel J. Edelman Pub. Relations, Chgo., 1980; intern reporter Detroit Free Press, 1979; gen. assignment reporter Ypsilanti Press (Mich.), 1979-80; free-lance writer Chgo. Tribune, also pub. relations div. Smith, Jones & Assocs., Chgo., also Inter-Service Mag., Washington, 1982—. Author: Stubborn Heart, 1984. Mem. Women in Communications (co-chmn. minority high sch. career conf. 1981, 82, rep. Ill. women's agenda 1983-84), Nat. Assn. Media Women. Home: 3427 N Elaine Pl Chicago IL 60657

WEST, SHARON MARIE, electrical engineer; b. Racine, Wis., May 5, 1959; d. Richard Irving and Virginia Margaret (Hansen) W. B.S. in Engring., U. Ill., 1981, M.S. in Engring., 1983. Registered profl. engr., Ill. Teaching asst. U. Ill., Champaign, 1981-83; engring. technician C.E., U.S. Army, Champaign, 1980-83; engr. Ill. Bell Telephone, Chgo., 1983-85, mgr., 1986—. Adminstrv. adviser Jr. Achievement, Downers Grove, Ill., 1985—; sci. fair judge Mus. Sci. and Industry, Chgo., 1985. Mem. Future Telephone Pioneers Am., Nat. Soc. Profl. Engrs., Western Soc. Engrs., Ill. Soc. Gen. Engrs., Ill. Soc. Profl. Engrs., Gamma Epsilon. Republican. Lutheran. Avocations: tennis; golf; jogging; composing music; playing piano. Office: Ill Bell Telephone Co 225 W Randolph St HQ26B Chicago IL 60606

WEST, SHIRLEY JEAN, real estate broker; b. Olney, Tex., July 10, 1937; d. Richard Hiram and Lois Lorene (Collins) Porter; m. George Edgar West, Mar. 22, 1956; children—Richie Lynn, Lori Leanne, Ami Sabrina. Student Odessa Coll., 1955, 56, 78. With Prudential Ins. Co., Odessa, 1955, Amoco Prodn. Co., Odessa, 1955-57, Abilene, Tex., 1957-61; dir. child devel. Crescent Park Bapt. Ch., Odessa, 1973-78; broker Goodwin Real Estate, Odessa, 1978-83, Eidson Wasson Lish Realtors, Odessa, 1983—. Mem. Odessa Bd. Realtors, Tex. Assn. Realtors, Nat. Assn. Realtors, Women's Council Realtors, Million Dollar Club. Republican. Baptist. Club: Odessa Racquetball and Health. Home: 2408 Quail Park Pl Odessa TX 79761 Office: Eidson Wasson Lish 3900 E 42d St Odessa TX 79762

WEST, TERRI LOUISE, communication specialist; b. Akron, Ohio, Sept. 5, 1948; d. Frank and Eileen Mae (Sprowls) West. B.S., Kent State U., 1971, M.A., 1972; Ph.D., U. Colo., 1983; Specialist in Aging, Inst. Gerontology, U. Mich., 1985. Instr., clin. supr. communication disorders U. Colo., Boulder, 1974-83; stroke rehab. program mgr. Meml. Med. Ctr., Long Beach, Calif.; pvt. practitioner communication disorders, aging, Los Angeles, 1984—; cons. Naomi Heller & Assocs., Santa Monica, Calif., 1984—, Boulder County Hospice, Colo., 1982-83. Mem. Am. Speech-Lang.-Hearing Assn. (cert. clin. competence speech-lang.), Am. Soc. Aging, Western Gerontol. Soc., Gerontol. Soc. Am. Avocations: reading, running. Home: 4380 Scandia Way Los Angeles CA 90065

WESTALL, PEGGY BURKE, real estate broker; b. Caliente, Nev., Feb. 3, 1929; d. John S. and Isabell (Morris) Burke; m. Alfred H. Westall; children—Lyn, Ann, Terry, Christine. Student U. Nev.-Reno. Co-chmn. adv. com. on sex discrimination in Nev. law, 1975-76; mem. transp. com. Nev. Assembly, Carson City, 1977-81, mem. govt. affairs com., 1977-79, mem. edn. com., 1979, chmn. legal functions, 1979-81, mem. taxation com., 1981, mem. ways and means com., 1981, mem. interim finance com., 1981-82, chmn. consumer advocate com., 1981-82, vice chmn. pub. records com., 1981-82, ret., 1982; candidate for Congress Dist. 2, No. Nev., 1982; real estate broker Westall Inc., Sparks, Nev. Mem. central com. Washoe Democratic Party, 1976-83. Mormons. Office: Westall Inc 1551 Pyramid Way Sparks NV 89431

WEST-ALLEN, M. DENISE, communications specialist; b. Riverside, Calif., Aug. 7, 1957; d. Harvey Dennis and Ruth Minnie (Turner) West; m. DeWayne David Allen, Nov. 24, 1979; 1 child, Neel Omar Allen. B.S. in Journalism, Northwestern U., 1979. Reporter/editor Macon News (Ga.), 1978; bur. reporter Newsweek, Atlanta, 1978; life/style editor LaPorte Herald Argus (Ind.), 1979-80; asst. editor Fairchild Publs., Chgo., 1980-81; editor Kemper Group, Long Grove, Ill., 1981-83; sr. corp. relations rep. Allstate Ins. Co., Northbrook, Ill., 1983—; editor/cons. Pres.'s Pvt. Sector Survey on Cost Control, Washington, 1982-83. Mem. Internat. Assn. Bus. Communicators (dir. Chgo. 1983-84, com. chairperson 1982-83, newsletter editor 1984-85), Delta Sigma Theta (rec. sec. Evanston-North Shore Alumnae chpt. 1983-85, regional rep. 1977-79). Democrat. Roman Catholic. Office: Allstate Ins Co Allstate Plaza N F3 Northbrook IL 60062

WESTBROOK, ANDREA, educational administrator; b. Gainesville, Ga., Mar. 27, 1949; d. Arthur Guy and Hazel Dean (Bradley) Parks; m. Harold Reece Westbrook, Jr., June 12, 1971; children—Reece, Mary Margaret. A.S., Gainesville Jr. Coll., 1969; M. Mktg. Distbn., U. Ga., 1974. Owner, pres. Fashion Consultants, Gainesville, 1975-781; mem. faculty Brenau Coll., Gainesville, 1981-82; coordinator career and profl. devel. and small bus. del. Gainesville Jr. Coll., 1982-85; dir. placement Lanier Area Tech. Sch., Gainesville, 1985—; research coordinator Elrod Mktg., Atlanta, 1976—; cons. Lanier Tech. Found., Gainesville, 1985—. Chmn. Council on Aging, Gainesville, 1985-86, Vol. Gainesville Recognition Celebration, 1985-86. Named Young Career Woman of Ga., Ga. Bus. Profl., 1974; elected to Distributive Edn. Hall of Fame, State Distributive Edn. dept., 1974; recipient cert. of appreciation Vietnam Vets. Leadership, Atlanta, 1984; Kellogg grantee Va. Poly. Inst. and State U., 1985. Mem. Nat. Assn. Female Execs., Ga. Coll. Placement Assn., Nat. Speakers Assn., Gainesville-Hall County C. of C., Am. Assn. Women in Community, LWV. Democrat. Baptist. Avocations: aerobics; dancing; story collecting. Home: 975 Longstreet Circle Gainesville GA 30501 Office: Lanier Area Tech Sch Mundy Mill Rd Oakwood GA 30566

WESTBROOK, GAYLE ROBINSON, lawyer; b. Wheeling, W.Va., May 19, 1947; d. William Francis and Elizabeth Marie (Naylor) Robinson; m. Robert Charles Westbrook, June 12, 1971; children—Shane Robert, Liam Patrick, Brittany Lynne. B.A. in Internat. Relations, U. Denver, 1969; J.D., U. Va., 1980. Bar: Ohio 1980, U.S. Dist. Ct. (so. dist.) Ohio, 1981. Assoc. Vorys, Sater, Seymour & Pease, Columbus, Ohio, 1980-83; gen. counsel Advanced Drainage Systems, Inc., Columbus, 1983—. Notes editor, mng. bd. Va. Jour. Internat. Law, Charlottesville, 1979-80, editorial bd., 1978-79; author article in law jour. Mem. ABA, Ohio State Bar Assn., Columbus Bar Assn., LWV (bd. dirs., chmn. internat. relations com. 1976-77), Am. Corp. Counsel Assn. (treas. 1984—), Thomas More Soc. Roman Catholic. Home: 3312 Cranston Dr Dublin OH 43017 Office: Advanced Drainage Systems Inc PO Box 21307 Columbus OH 43221

WESTBROOK, MABLE MARSHALL, frame shop/gallery owner; b. Loudon, Tenn., Mar. 16, 1924; s. Thomas Oliver and Beulah Gay (Watkins) Marshall; m. John Albert Westbrook, Feb. 28, 1948 (dec. Sept. 1982); 1 child, Edwin Marshall. B.S. in Chemistry, Maryville Coll., 1944. Chemist, U.S. Bur. Mines, Norris, Tenn., 1945-46, Carbide Carbon, Oak Ridge, Tenn., 1946-52; substitute tchr. Lenoir City System, Tenn., 1957-75; framer, owner Marbrook Frames, Lenoir City, 1975—. Den mother Boy Scouts Am., 1964-66; bd. dirs. Overlook Mental Health Assn., 1983—, Alternate Care Enterprises, 1985—. Mem. Profl. Framers, Gen. Fedn. Women's Clubs (pres. Tenn. fedn. 1982-84, chmn. arts nat. 1984-86). Methodist. Avocations: gardening; sewing; music; public speaking; travel. Home: Route 6 Box 549 Lenoir City TN 37771

WESTBROOKS, CYNTHIA TERRY, accountant; b. Cumming, Ga., Dec. 21, 1954; d. Seth Charles and Betty Jane (Padgett) Terry; m. Michael Wayne Westbrooks, Aug. 19, 1972; children—Amanda, Amy, Matthew. Student pub. schs. Alpharetta, Ga. Acct., Benson Chevrolet, Roswell, Ga., 1971-73; Jones Vinson Realty, Alpharetta, 1974-76, Monetary Systems, Atlanta, 1976-81, Travelanes, Inc., Dunwoody, Ga., 1981-84; owner, mgr. C. Westbrooks Bus. Services, Alpharetta, 1984—. mem. Assn. Women Entrepreneurs (treas. 1985—), N. Fulton C. of C., Womens Bus. Owners. Republican. Mem. choir Baptist Ch. Club: Womens. Avocations: skiing; track. Home: 11255 State Bridge Rd Alpharetta GA 30201

WESTBURY, JUNE ALWYN, Canadian government official; b. Hamilton, N.Z.; came to Can., 1948, naturalized, 1971; d. Philip William and Doris Myrtle (Halcrow) Cantwell; student Brain's Coll., Auckland; voice student of Mina Caldow; m. Peter W.A. Westbury, Oct. 22, 1949; children—Sheila Westbury Raffey, Pamela June, Jennifer Doris. Elected alderman, Ward I, Winnipeg (Man., Can.) City Council, 1969, vice chmn. Centennial Celebrations Com., 1970, mem. various Council coms., including Parks and Recreation, Health and Welfare, Housing and Urban Renewal, Utilities and Personnel, chmn. Health and Welfare Com., 1971, councillor, Roslyn Ward, City of Winnipeg, 1971-77, mem. various times Environ. and Works and Ops. Coms., Winnipeg Police Commn., Winnipeg Heritage Corp., chmn. subcom. on Group Homes, elected Corydon Ward, 1977, chmn. Adv. Com. on Hist. Bldgs., 1979; elected Liberal mem. Legis. Assembly, Man., Ft. Rouge Constituency, 1979-81. Founder, chmn. Laurier Club of Man., 1982—; bd. dirs. Winnipeg Mcpl. Hosps., 1970-79, 85—, chmn., 1971-75, vice chmn., 1977-78. Elected sec. (first woman) Liberal Party of Man., 1968-69, v.p. Liberal Party of Can., 1970-73; Liberal candidate Osborne Constituency, 1973; bd. dirs. Man. Health Orgns., Inc., 1970-76; bd. dirs. Can. Council Christians and Jews, Central Region, 1972—, chmn. program com., 1979-85, mem. Central Exec. Com., 1976-85, Nat. Exec., 1979-85; bd. dirs. Age and Opportunity Centres, 1972-76; adv. bd. YWCA, 1972-82; exec. Riverview Community Centre, 1973-74; commr. Nat. Capital Commn., Ottawa, 1976-82, mem. adv. com. on design, 1976-83; ofcl. Man. Track and Field Assn., 1978; mem. Task Force on Maternal and Child Health, 1979-82; dir. Epiphany pageant St. Alban's Anglican Ch., 1954-72; pres. Riverview-Ashland Home and Sch. Assn., 1967-69; edn. chmn. Royal Winnipeg Ballet Women's Com., 1967-69. Named Woman of Yr. in Politics and Govtl. Affairs, YWCA, 1979; recipient Melitta achievement award, 1982. Mem. Man. Hist. Soc., Heritage Can. Found. (bd. govs. 1982—).

WESTERHOLD, RUTH ELIZABETH, psychologist, educator; b. Youngstown, Ohio, Aug. 4, 1926; d. Samuel Gordon and Grace Elizabeth (Green) Meadows; B.S., Youngstown U., 1946; postgrad. Ohio U., 1947, U. Ill., 1947-49; Ph.D., So. Ill. U., 1978; m. Walter Charles Westerhold, June 1, 1949; children—Marsha L., Carl E. Chief clin. psychologist Alton (Ill.) State Hosp., 1952-55; psychologist St. Louis (Mo.) County Spl. Sch. Dist., 1963-68; chief psychologist Kaskaskia Spl. Edn. Dist., Centralia, Ill., 1968-78; dir. learning communications E. Miss. Jr. Coll., Scooba, 1978-83, consulting psychologist div. vocat. rehab. State of Ill., Alton, 1954-55. USPHS fellow, U. Ill., 1947-49. Cert. school psychologist, Mo., Ill. Mem. Am. Psychol. Assn., AAAS, Psi Chi Counselor, lectr., writer child-rearing, family, learning. Home: PO Box 135 Artesia MS 39736

WESTERMANN, MARY LOUISE, medical librarian, educator; b. N.Y.C., Mar. 11, 1953; d. A. Louis and Anne U. (Skelly) Morse; m. Karl S. Westermann, Jan. 18, 1975 (div.). B.S. in Biology, L.I.U., 1975, M.S. in L.S., 1976, M.P.A. in Health Care Adminstrn., 1986. Con. med. librarian Nassau-Suffolk Health Systems Agy., Melville, N.Y., 1976-77; dir. John N. Shell Library Nassau Acad. Medicine, Garden City, N.Y., 1977—; adj. prof. L.I.U., Greenvale, N.Y., 1983—, instr., 1976—; instr. Nassau County Library Assn., 1978—, Am. Assn. Physicians Assts., 1977—. Commentator monthly column: Cath. Library World. Recipient E. Hugh Behymer award L.I.U., 1976. Mem. Med. Library Assn. (sec. med. socs. sect. 1981-82, instr. continuing edn. 1982, chmn. med. soc. sect. 1986—; cert. health scis. librarianship), Spl. Libraries Assn. (sec. L.I. chpt. 1978-80, bd. dirs. 1982—), ALA, Cath. Library Assn. (instr. workshop), Suffolk-Nassau on-Line Retrievers (chmn. 1981), Med. and Sci. Libraries of L.I. (pres. 1980-81), Nassau County Library Assn. (chmn. health services com. 1978-81), Beta Beta Beta, Beta Phi Mu, Pi Alpha Alpha. Office: Nassau Acad Medicine 1200 Steward Ave Garden City NY 11530

WESTFALL, EVELYN JEAN, communications company executive; b. N.Y.C., Nov. 9, 1933; d. Walter Louis and Regina Catherine (Mordo) Heithaus; children—Laura Jean, Stephen Charles, Diane Gail. B.A. in Psychology, Coll. of New Rochelle (N.Y.), 1973, postgrad., 1973-74. Cert. tchr., N.Y. Exec. sec. Kwasha Lipton, Englewood Cliffs, N.J., 1954-69; asst. v.p., asst. to pres. Metromedia, Inc., N.Y.C., 1976—. Republican. Roman Catholic. Home: 1058 Boston Post Rd Rye NY 10580 Office: Metromedia Inc 205 E 67th St New York NY 10021

WESTFALL, MARSHA LYNNE, air force officer; b. Newark, Ohio, May 29, 1951; d. Kenneth M. and Vera Adeline (Myers) Westfall. B.A. in Social and Behavioral Scis., U. Tex., 1972, M.A. in Fgn. Langs., 1977. Commd. 2d lt. USAF, 1978, advanced through grades to capt., 1982; exec. officer 609th Tactical Control Squadron, Bad Munder Radar Sta., W.Ger., 1978-80; squadron sect. comdr. 314th Civil Engring. Squadron, Little Rock, 1980-82, exec. officer 62d Tactical Airlift Squadron, Little Rock, 1982; asst. prof. aerospace studies, comdt. cadets Detachment 055 Air Force ROTC, UCLA, 1982-85; comdr. 26th hdqrs. squadron Zweibrucken Air Force Base, Fed. Republic Germany, 1985—. Mem. citizens' adv. council Am. Inst. Cancer Research; chmn. chancellor's adv. com. on status of women UCLA; neighborhood chmn. Girl Scouts Am. ABA scholar Freedoms Found., Valley Forge, Pa., 1976, ABA scholar Sch. Comparative Politics and Ideologies, U. Colo., Boulder, 1977. Mem. Internat. Toastmistresses, Orgn. Counsellor and Advisers, Air Force Assn., Nat. Assn. Exec. Women, Speakers Bur., Alpha Omicron Pi (adv. sigma phi chpt.) Democrat. Office: 26th Hdqrs Squadron Bldg 35 Zweibrucken Air Base APO NY 09860-5000

WESTMORELAND, KATHLEEN, lawyer; b. Houston, Nov. 30, 1955; d. Hollis Glynn and Lillian Doris (Ambriz) Price; m. Kent Ewing Westmoreland, June 14, 1981. B.B.A. with honors, U. Tex., 1978; J.D. cum laude, U. Houston, 1981. Bar: Tex. 1981. Assoc., Ross, Griggs & Harrison, Houston, 1981—; mem. Arts Symposium Houston, Houston Ballet Guild; contbg. mem. Zool. Soc. Houston, Mus. Fine Arts Houston. Mem. Tex. Bar Assn., Houston Bar Assn., Houston Young Lawyers Assn., ABA, U. Houston Law Alumni Assn., U. Tex. Ex-Students Assn. (life), Phi Delta Phi. Office: Ross Griggs & Harrison Four Allen Center 1400 Smith St Suite 2800 Houston TX 77002

WESTNEY, OUIDA ELAINE, human development educator, researcher; b. Jamaica, W.I., June 20, 1929; came to U.S., 1955; d. James Ezekiel and Gertrude (Irving) Spleen; m. Lennox Samuel Westney, Dec. 19, 1954; children—Lennox Samuel, Irving Vaughan, Ouida Lenaine. R.N., Andrews Meml. Sch. Nursing, Jamaica, 1950; B.S. in Nursing, Columbia Union Coll., 1959; M.S. in Nursing, U. Md.-Balt., 1965; Ph.D., U. Md., College Park, 1972. R.N., Md. Staff nurse Andrews Meml. Hosp., Jamaica, 1951-55; head nurse psychiat. nursing Worcester State Hosp. (Mass.), 1955-57; instr. nursing Freedmen's Hosp. Sch. Nursing, Washington, 1960-63; asst. prof. nursing Sch. Nursing U. Md., Balt., 1966-67; assoc. prof. nursing Coll. Nursing, Howard U., Washington, 1971-74, assoc. prof. human devel., Sch. Human Ecology, 1974—, nursing edn. cons. Coll. Nursing, 1969-70. Contbr. chpt. to book, articles to publs. in field. Dir. family life Dept. Allegheny East Conf. Seventh-day Adventists, 1979-81; mem. Fairland Estates Citizens Assn., Silver Spring, Md., 1980—; trustee Loma Linda U., 1976-81, Columbia Union Coll., 1981—. Nurse research fellow USPHS, 1970-71; named Outstanding Faculty mem. Sch. Human Ecology, Howard U., 1979, 80, recipient award for outstanding and dedicated service, Grad. Student Assn. of Sch. Human Ecology, 1982. Mem. Am. Pub. Health Assn., AAUP, Nat. Council on Family Relations, Groves Conf. on Marriage and Family, Soc. for Research in Child Devel., Sigma Theta Tau. Office: Dept Human Devel Sch Human Ecology Howard U 2400 6th St NW Washington DC 20059

WESTON, DAWN THOMPSON, artist, researcher; b. Joliet, Ill., Apr. 15, 1919; d. Cyril C. and Vivian Grace Thompson; student (scholar) Penn Hall Jr. Coll., Chambersburg, Pa., 1937-38; B.S., Northwestern U., 1942, postgrad. in reading and speech pathology, 1960-61, M.A. in Edni. Adminstrn., 1970; postgrad. U. Ill., 1964; student Art Inst. Chgo., 1954, Pestalozzi-Froebel, Chgo., 1955, Phila. Inst. for Achievement Human Potential, 1963; m. Arthur Walter Weston, Sept. 10, 1940; children—Roger Lance, Randall Kent, Cynthia Brooke. Cert. tchr., Ill. Therapist, USN Hosp., Gt. Lakes, Ill., 1940-45; tchr. Holy Child and Waukegan (Ill.) High Schs., 1946-54; elem. and jr. high art dir. Lake Bluff (Ill.) Schs., 1954-58; pioneer ednl. dir. Grove Sch. for Brain-Injured, Lake Forest, Ill., 1958-66; one-woman shows: Evanston Woman's Club, Northwestern U., The Hein Co., Waukegan; numerous group shows, 1939-76. Represented in permanent collections: ARC, Victory Meml. Hosp., Waukegan, Sierra Assos., Chgo., numerous pvt. collections U.S., Can., Japan, Africa; works include: Poisonous Plants of Midwest set of etchings for Country Gentleman mag., 1956, Clouds mural, 1981; ind. researcher on shifting visual imagery due to trauma, 1982—; life mem. corp. Grove Sch., co-chmn. bd., 1983, chmn., 1984. Mem. Presdl. Gold Chain, Trinity Coll., 1979. Named Citizen of Yr., Grove Sch., 1978, room at sch. named in her honor, 1982; cert. tchr., Ill. Mem. Art Inst. Chgo., Deerpath Art League, Pi Lambda Theta. Methodist (del. Ann. Conf. 1982, 83). Research on uneven growth, 1969-70. Home and Office: 349 E Hilldale Pl Lake Forest IL 60045

WESTON, FRANCES, state legislator; b. Phila., Sept. 1, 1954; d. Alfred and Patricia Peteraf; B.A., Temple U., 1977; m. Edward Weston, May 20, 1977; 1 dau., Bridget Rose. Acctg. supr. J C Penney Regional Credit Office, Voorhees, N.J., 1976-80; mem. Pa. Ho. of Reps., 1980—. Committeewoman 41st Ward, Phila., 1973—. Mem. Phila. Council Republican Women, Polish Am. Citizens League. Roman Catholic. Club: Am. Legion Aux. Office: 7115 Torresdale St Philadelphia PA 19135

WESTON, JUDITH HELEN, fine arts firm executive; b. Phila., May 18, 1949; d. Kurt Louis and Hildegard (Salomon) Karo; m. Jeffrey Martyn Weston, May 19, 1968; 1 child, Shaun Alexander. Student Boston U., 1967-70; B.A. magna cum laude, U. Mass.-Boston, 1975. Lab. technician Herbert V. Shuster, Inc., North Quincy, Mass., 1975-77, sr. lab. technician, 1977-78; dir. ocular allergy lab. Eye Research Inst., Boston, 1979-85; cons., 1985; pres. Weston Fine Arts, Braintree, Mass., 1985—. Contbr. chpts. to books, monographs and jour. articles to profl. lit. Democrat. Jewish. Avocation: photography. Office: Weston Fine Arts 244 Middle St Braintree MA 02184

WESTON, PHYLLIS, art director; b. Cleve., Mar. 17, 1921; d. Armin and Wilma H. (Wasserman) Hornstein; m. Leo F. Weston, Oct. 18, 1953; children—H. Todd Cobey, John Cobey. Ed., Simmons Coll., Yale U. Director, A.B. Closson Jr. Co. Art Gallery, Cin., 1964—; art cons. Proctor & Gamble Co., Cin., 1983—; cons. and lectr. in art; mem. numerous art and civic orgns. Home: 4 Taft Rd Ln Cincinnati OH 45206 Office: 401 Race St Cincinnati OH 45202

WESTOVER, DIANA KAY, interior designer; b. Clovis, N.Mex., Aug. 24, 1953; d. Martin B. and Mary Catherine (Eberwein) Goodwin; m. Dan Oliver Westover, June 14, 1975; children—Jacqueline Diona, Danielle Leigh. Student Eastern N.Mex. U., 1971-73; Interior Design diploma LaSalle U., 1973; B.F.A. in Interior Design, N.Y. Sch. Interior Design, 1977. Mem. sales staff The Popular, El Paso, Tex., 1979-81; sales and design positions Hollon's, Lubbock, Tex., 1981-82, Spears, Lubbock, 1982-84; tchr. interior design N.Mex. Jr. Coll., Hobbs, 1985—; interior designer, buyer Callaway's Hobbs, 1985-86; interior designer Designers II, Hobbs, 1986—; set designer Miss N.Mex. Pagaent, Hobbs, 1984-85. Active Christian Women, Hobbs, Altar Soc., Hobbs, St. Joseph's Circle, Hobbs, Republican Women, Hobbs. Named Young Republican of Yr., Clovis, N.Mex., 1974. Roman Catholic. Avocations: tennis, reading, bicycling. Home: 1323 W Taos Hobbs NM 88240 Office: Designers II 1819 N Turner St Suite H Hobbs NM 88240

WESTPHAL, RUTH LILLY, educational audiovisual company executive, author, publisher; b. Glendale, Calif., July 27, 1931; d. Glen R. and Margaret E. (John) Lilly; m. H. Frederick Westphal, June 25, 1953. B.A. in Edn., UCLA, 1953; M.A. in Instructional System Tech., Chapman Coll., 1966. Cert. tchr. Calif. Tchr. pub. schs., Los Angeles, Glendale, Whittier, Calif., 1953-65; instuctional systems analyst Litton Industries, Anaheim, Calif., 1965-67; dir. devel. Trainex Corp., Garden Grove, Calif., 1967-69; owner, pres. Concept Media, Inc., Irvine, Calif., 1969—, Westphal Pub., Irvine, 1980—. Co-founder Friends of City Library, LaHabra, Calif., 1960-65; mem. Los Angeles County Mus. Art, 1975—, Laguna Beach Mus. Art, 1979—, Nautical Heritage Soc. Dana Point, Calif. 1982—. Author, editor numerous ednl. filmstrip programs. Author: Plein Air Painters of California: The Southland, 1982 (Western Books award 1982). Recipient numerous awards Info. Film Producers Am., Internat. Film and TV Festival N.Y., Chgo. Film Festival, Am. Jour. Nursing Media Festival, Author Recognition award U. Calif., 1983. Mem. Nat. Audiovisual Assn., Assn. Media Producers. Avocations: Art history. Office: Concept Media Inc 2493 DuBridge Ave Irvine CA 92714

WESTRATE, NANCY JOAN, service consultant; b. Paterson, N.J., Dec. 22, 1954; d. Vincent and Mae (Lill) Van Savage; m. Adrian John Westrate, June 20, 1981 (dec. Apr. 1982); 1 child, Kelly Ann. B.S. in Nursing, Villanova U., 19—. R.N., N.J. Nurse, Bergen Pines Hosp., Paramus, N.J., 1976-79, Hackensack Med. Ctr., N.J., 1979-81, Olsten Health Care, Hackensack, 1983-85; service cons. Meadowlands Health Care Ctr., Secaucus, N.J., 1985-86; rehab. specialist Gen. Rehab. Services, Inc., Teaneck, N.J., 1986—.

WETCHER, GOLDIE RAPPAPORT, psychotherapist, clinic administrator; b. Camden, N.J., July 12, 1939; d. Morris G. and Jean (Gordon) Cohen; m. Martin Paul Rappaport, June 7, 1959 (div. 1975); children—Karen Leah, Steven Aaron; m. Kenneth Wetcher, Apr. 11, 1976. B.A., Newcomb Coll., Tulane U., 1961, postgrad. Sch. Social Work, 1963; M.S.W., U. Houston, 1969-70. Psychotherapist Mental Health Mental Retardation, La Marque, Tex., 1970-72; psychotherapist Family Counseling Assoc. and Wetcher Clinic, Houston, 1972—. Organizer Crisis Mgmt. Service, Houston, 1984; active Bay Area Med., Houston, Orgn. Rehab. Tng., Houston; trustee Congregation Shaar Hashalom, Houston, 1984-85. Fellow Nat. Assn. Social Workers, Acad. Cert. Social Workers; mem. Houston Group Psychotherapy Assn. (tng. faculty), Am. Assn. Marriage and Family Therapists, Am. Group Psychotherapy Assn., Phi Beta Kappa, Phi Kappa Phi. Republican. Avocations: water sports; nutrition. Home: 2010 Port Royal Houston TX 77058 Office: Wetcher Clinic 16902 El Camino Real Suite 2C Houston TX 77058

WETHERBY, IVOR LOIS, librarian; b. Louisville, May 22, 1924; d. Luther Silas and Clara Marders (Hite) W.; A.B., Ky. Wesleyan Coll., 1944; M.S. in L.S. (AAUW fellow 1964-65), Fla. State U. 1965; S.Edn., Fla. Atlantic U., 1984; m. Herbert Charles Howard, July 4, 1947; children—Ivor Jane, Elizabeth Wetherby, John Allen, Luther Hite, Ann Dell. Various clerical and secretarial positions, 1944-50; tchr. Our Lady of Mercy Acad., Louisville, 1963-64; librarian Palm Beach Jr. Coll., Lake Worth, Fla., 1966-78; head librarian Sebring (Fla.) Public Library, 1978; health scis. reference librarian Miami-Dade Community Coll., Med. Center Campus, Miami, Fla., 1978—. Mem. Southeastern, Fla. library assns., Spl. Libraries Assn., DAR. Episcopalian. Home: 240 Galen Dr Apt 310 Key Biscayne FL 33149 Office: PO Box 014873 Miami FL 33101

WETSTONE, JANET MEYERSON, designer, journalist; b. Spartanburg, S.C.; d. Louis Alexander and Ella (Levinson) Meyerson; m. Richard J. Wetstone, Sept. 21, 1947 (div. Dec. 1973); children—John B., Gregory S., Linda Wetstone Sherman. Student U. Mo., 1946-47, Ga. State U., 1970-80. Interior designer Jan's Interiors, Atlanta, 1965-68; pres. Wetstone Crafts Co., Atlanta, 1968—; instr. women in bus. Emory U., 1972; cons. Plaid Enterprises Inc. Author: Rags to Riches with Mod-Podge, 1969; Specially Yours Decorating With Sheets, 1977; Needle-Podge Book, 1976; Creative Frame Maker, 1972; patentee craft paint, frame maker. Pres. edn. guild Ringling Mus., Sarasota, Fla., 1963-64, chairperson 1st creative art carnival, 1963-64; decorating chairperson Jimmy Carter Election Night, Atlanta, 1976; dir. communications Carter Mondale 1980 Campaign, Atlanta, 1980; chmn. visual arts Sarasota Centennial, 1985-86. Mem. United Inventors and Scientists Am., Women in Film (v.p. 1982-83), Fla. Assn. Realtors, Phi Sigma Sigma. Club: 1980 (Atlanta). Avocations: riding; painting; golf. Home: 3969 Glen Oaks Manor Dr Sarasota FL 33582

WETTERHAHN, KAREN ELIZABETH, chemistry educator; b. Plattsburgh, N.Y., Oct. 16, 1948; d. Gustave George and Mary Elizabeth (Thibault) W.; m. Leon H. Webb, June 19, 1982; children—Leon Ashley, Charlotte Elizabeth. B.S., St. Lawrence U., 1970; Ph.D., Columbia U., 1975. Chemist, Mearl Corp., Ossining, N.Y., 1970-71; research fellow Columbia U., N.Y.C., 1971-75, postdoctoral fellow, 1975-76; asst. prof. chemistry Dartmouth Coll., Hanover, N.H., 1976-82, assoc. prof., 1982-86, prof., 1986—. Contbr. articles to profl. jours., 1974—. A.P. Sloan fellow, 1981. Mem. Am. Chem. Soc., Am. Assn. Cancer Research, AAAS, N.Y. Acad. Scis. Office: Dartmouth Coll Dept Chemistry Hanover NH 03755

WEWER, DEE J., artist, educator, creative arts therapist; b. Mobile, Ala., Apr. 27, 1948; d. Gene B. and Juanita (Schmeckenbecher) Wewer; m. Doni Mitchell, Apr. 13, 1985. B.S., U. So. Miss., 1969; M.A., Am. U., 1974; postgrad. Georgetown U., 1981-82; Ph.D., Union Grad. Sch., 1986. With Dixie Press, Biloxi, Miss., 1968-70; tchr. St. Martin Public Sch., Biloxi, 1970; editor newspaper of Nat. War Coll., Ft. McNair, Washington, 1971-73; press and scheduling asso. and coordinator Nat. Fedn. State Chairmen, Office of Chmn., Republican Nat. Com., Washington, 1972-73; cons. Nat. Women's Edn. Fund, Nat. Women's Polit. Caucus, 1973-74; gen. mgr., treas. Printing Services Unltd., Washington, 1975; instr. Inst. Politics, Harvard U., Boston, 1976; media dir./prodn. mgr./creative group head Bailey, Deardourff & Assos., Washington, 1975-76; dir. mktg./account supr. Weitzman & Assos., Washington, 1976-78; dir. mktg. Britches of Georgetown, Washington, 1978-79; instr. Coll. Bus. and Mgmt., U. Md., College Park, 1980-83; v.p. public affairs AMF Head Sports Wear, Columbia, Md., 1979-81; exec. v.p. Sport-Obermeyer, Aspen, Colo., 1982-85; creativity coach, painter, writer, cons., 1985—; instr. Colo. Mountain Coll., 1985—; paintings represented by Aspen Artists Gallery, R Collection, Los Angeles, Sheehan & Assocs., Balt.; owner The Mitchell Wewer Design Group; dir. Monte/Edel Advt. Represented in permanent collection Aspen Art Mus. Charter mem. Aspen Initiative; active community affairs; vol. therapist Aspen Mental Health Clinic. Recipient Creative Design Distinction, Andy, Printing Industries Am., 1981; Distinctive Merit award Advt. Club of N.Y., 1980, Art Dirs. Club of Met. Washington, 1980; Clio awards, 1979; named Outstanding Working Woman, Glamour mag., 1978, Outstanding Tchr., Colo. Mountain Coll.; Nat. Newspaper Nat. Creativity award, 1974. Mem. Ski Industries of Am., Women in Advt. and Mktg., Am. Women in Radio and TV, Am. Mgmt. Assn., Advt. Club, Art Dirs. Club, NOW. Home: 790 W Hallem Aspen CO 81611 Office: 210-E Ventnor Ave Aspen CO 81611

WEXLER, ANNE, consulting company executive; b. N.Y.C., Feb. 10, 1930; d. Leon R. and Edith R. (Rau) Levy; B.A., Skidmore Coll., 1951, LL.D. (hon.), 1978; D.Sc. in Bus. (hon.), Bryant Coll., 1978; m. Joseph Duffey, Sept. 17, 1974; children by previous marriage—David Wexler, Daniel Wexler. asso. pub. Rolling Stone mag., 1974-76; personnel adv., 1976-77; dep. undersec. Dept. Commerce, 1977-78; asst. to Pres. U.S., 1978-81; chmn. Wexler, Reynolds, Harrison & Schule, Inc., Washington, 1981—; dir. New Eng. Electric System; adj. lectr. Kennedy Sch. Govt., Harvard U. Mem. nat. steering com. Carter/Mondale, 1976; mem. edn. and tng. council Democratic Nat. Com., 1976; bd. dirs. Pennsylvania Ave. Devel. Corp., Center Nat. Policy, Nat. Center Initiative Rev., Washington Campus; trustee Hampshire Coll.; vis. com. John F. Kennedy Sch. Govt., Harvard U.; bd. visitors U. Md. Sch. Pub. Policy. Named Outstanding Alumna, Skidmore Coll., 1972. Mem. Council Fgn. Relations. Jewish. Office: 1317 F St NW Suite 600 Washington DC 20004

WEXLER, JO SHEILA, advertising and marketing executive; b. Jan. 4, 1946; d. Isadore and Rella (Blaustein) W.; m. John Willis Fuller, Sept. 11, 1965; 1 son, Blair. B.A., Fla. State U., 1965; M.A. (grad. asst.), U. Fla., 1972; postgrad. U. Ga., 1972-73. Fashion artist Furchgott's, Jacksonville, Fla., 1967; advt. and pub. relations mgr. Jacksonville Area C. of C., 1972-74; mktg. dir. Jax Inc., Navy Fed. Credit Union, 1974-76; account supr. Abramson/Himelfarb Inc., Washington, 1976-81; v.p. mktg. Morgan Burchette Assocs., Inc., Alexandria, Va., 1981-85; pres. Wexler Mktg. Group, Alexandria, 1985—. Cellist, Jacksonville Symphony, 1967-76; cellist Arlington (Va.) Symphony, 1977—, chmn. bus. devel. com., 1983—, bd. dirs., 1984—. Recipient Pres.'s medal Fla. Pub. Relations Assn., 1975. Mem. Advt. Club. Met. Washington, Women in Advt. and Mktg. (dir. 1982-85, 86—, sec. 1983-85), Phi Kappa Phi. Democrat. Jewish. Office: Wexler Mktg Group Inc 712 N Armistead St Alexandria VA 22312

WEXLER, JUDIE GAFFIN, sociology educator, researcher; b. N.Y.C., Apr. 15, 1945; d. Isaac and Sara (Widensky) Pearlman; m. Howard M. Wexler, Mar. 11, 1973; children—Robyn, Matthew. B.A. in Sociology, Russell Sage U., Troy, N.Y., 1965; M.A. in Demography, U. Pa., 1966; Ph.D. in Sociology, U. Calif.-Berkeley, 1975. Researcher N.Y. Mental Health Dept., Albany, 1966-67; demographer City Planning Dept., San Francisco, 1967-68; assoc. prof. Holy Names Coll., Oakland, Calif., 1974—; cons. in field. Contbr. articles to profl. jours. Fellow Ford Found., NDEA. Mem. Am. Sociol. Assn., Am. Psychol. Assn. Home: 23 Cresta Vista Dr San Francisco CA 94127 Office: Holy Names Coll 3500 Mountain Blvd Oakland CA 94619

WEY, MISSY EGAN, entrepreneur, public relations executive, consultant; b. N.Y.C., Mar. 6, 1941; d. Edward Joseph and Ann Gertrude (Coakley) Egan; m. Thomas Alexander Wey, Nov. 26, 1976; children—Lynn, Richard, Edward, John. Student Manhattanville Coll., 1958-59, Coll. New Rochelle, 1978-81. Dir. fashion and spl. events I. Magnin, Los Angeles, 1970-72; dir. alumni affairs Manhaattanville Coll., Purchase, N.Y., 1972-76; dir. devel. Iona Coll., New Rochelle, N.Y., 1976-77; cons. Staley Robeson, Inc., White Plains, N.Y., 1978-79; dir. pub. relations and devel. Westchester Lighthouse, White Plains, 1979-81; pres. Missy Egan Wey Assocs., Larchmont, N.Y., 1981—; mem. adv. bd. Peoples Westchester Savings Bank, Hawthorne, N.Y., 1978—; spl. events cons., Mercy Coll., Dobbs Ferry, N.Y., 1981—; devel. cons. Burke Rehab. Ctr., White Plains, 1982—; devel./pub. relations cons. Clear View Sch., Scarborough, N.Y., 1983—. Recipient People on the Move award Spotlight mag., 1983. Mem. Council Advancement and Support Edn. (com. head.). Republican. Roman Catholic. Home: 18 Edgewood Ave Larchmont NY 10538

WEYAND, RUTH, lawyer; b. Grinnell, Iowa, Jan. 14, 1912; d. Lorenzo Dow and May (Grafton) W.; Ph.B., U. Chgo., 1930; J.D. cum laude, 1932; m. Leslie Sterling Perry, Sept. 29, 1947; children—Perry Weyand, Sterling Weyand. Bar: Ill. 1933, D.C. 1980, U.S. Supreme Ct. 1936; assoc. firm Gardner & Carton, Chgo., 1933, White and Hawxhurst. Chgo., 1933-35, Moses, Kennedy, Stein & Bachrach, Chgo., 1935-38; asst. gen. counsel NLRB, Washington, 1938-50; mem. firm Clifford D. O'Brien, Chgo., 1950-56, Leibik & Weyand, Chgo. and Washington, 1956-65; asst. gen. counsel Internat. Union Elec. Radio and Machine Workers, Washington, 1965-77; supervisory trial atty. Phila. Regional Litigation Center, EEOC, 1977-79, equal pay act counsel Office Gen. Counsel, EEOC, Washington, 1979—. Recipient Elizabeth Boyer award Women's Equity Action League, 1985, Georgina Smith award AAUP, 1985. Mem. ABA, Chgo. Bar Assn., Am. Assn. Trial Lawyers, NAACP (mem. nat. legal com. 1945-64). Democrat. Home: 1345 Douglass Ave Highland Beach Annapolis MD 21403 Office: Room 230 2401 E St NW Washington DC 20507

WEYHER, MARY JANE, civic worker; b. Salt Lake City, Dec. 26, 1947; d. John Walter and Helen (Brown) Jarman; m. William Carl Weyher, Nov. 27, 1970; children—Sam, Zach, Anna, Willy. Student Foothill Coll., 1966-67; B.A., U. Utah, 1971. Tchr. Neighborhood House, Salt Lake City, 1970-71, Head Start, 1972-74. Vice chmn. Dist. 3136 Republican party, 1984—, bd. dirs. Girls Village, 1984—, Sarah Daft Home, 1984—; mem. edn. com. Planned Parenthood, 1985—. Episcopalian. Avocations: skiing; swimming; reading; tennis. Home: 1442 Circle Way Salt Lake City UT 84103

WEYKER, KAY FRANCES STEVENS, construction company exec.; b. Hamburg, Iowa, Jan. 31, 1947; d. Roy Harland and Wanita (Killion) Sparks; children—Douglas Kent, Michelle De'Ann. With Warner Cable Co., Atchison County, Mo., 1965-78, system mgr., 1974-78; office mgr., gen. mgr. tng. Am. Heritage Cablevision, Council Bluffs, Iowa, 1979; gen. mgr. United Cable TV Sarpy County, Bellevue, Nebr., 1979-82; gen. mgr. United Cable TV of Scottsdale (Ariz.), 1982; mgr. Pacific S.W. Sales, Phoenix, 1982-83, Diprima Constrn., Satellite Beach, Fla., 1984—. Bd. dirs., sec. Bellevue Crimestoppers, 1981-82. Mem. Nebr. Cable Communications Assn. (dir. 1980-81, v.p. 1981-82), Mid Am. Cable TV Assn. (dir. 1981-82), Women in Cable, Nat. Assn. Female Execs. Clubs: Lioness, Eagles, Parents Without Partners. Office: 1199 S Patrick Dr Satellite Beach FL 32937

WHALEN, FLORENCE GOETZ, city official; b. Milw., Jan. 22, 1933; d. Fred William and Elsie Ann (Menne) Goetz; m. Richard Anthony Whalen, June 19, 1954; children—Patrick, Michael, Timothy, Terence. Student U. Wis.-Eau Claire, 1951-54. Mayor, City of Oconomowoc, Wis., 1976—; mem. Wis. Retirement Research Commn., 1984—, Wis. Unemployment Ins. Council, 1984—; bd. govs. Wis. Med. Malpractice Law Com., 1975-82, Wis. Expenditure Commn., 1985—. Named Outstanding Woman in Govt., Wis. Jaycee Women, 1984; Woman of Yr., Oconomowoc NOW, 1980; only woman in Wis. history to be elected to 5 consecutive terms as mayor. Mem. League Wis. Municipalities (chmn. ins trust 1983—, mem. exec. com. 1982-83, fin. and taxation com. 1979—), LWV (Wis. pres. 1973-75). Roman Catholic. Home: 406 W 3d St Oconomowoc WI 53066 Office: City of Oconomowoc Box 27 City Hall Oconomowoc WI 53066

WHALEN, LINDA LONG, lawyer; b. Connellsville, Pa., Mar. 24, 1954; d. Glenn Eugene and Joann Ruth (McNelis) Long; m. James Thomas Whalen, July 24, 1976 (div. 1981). B.A. in Polit. Sci. summa cum laude, Susquehanna U., 1976; J.D., U. Pitts., 1981. Bar: Pa. 1981, U.S. Dist. Ct. (we. dist.) Pa. 1981. Research asst. U. Pitts. Sch. Law, 1979-80; ptnr. Boyle & Whalen, Greensburg, Pa., 1981-83; sole practice, Greensburg, 1983—; mem. drafting com. for bankruptcy rules Western Dist. Pa., Pitts., 1983-84. Mem. sr. citizens housing com. 1st Luth. Ch., Greensburg, 1982-83, chmn. youth com., 1983-84; participant Law 4 You Phone-a-Thon Allegheny County/Channel 4 TV, Pitts., 1984; prof. continuing edn. div. County Community Coll.; bd. dirs. Ligonier Valley Learning Ctr., 1983-84, Am. Lung Assn. of Southwestern Pa., 1984—, Big Bros./Big Sisters of Westmoreland County, 1984—; pres. bd. dirs. Am. Performing Arts Theatre, 1985—. Mem. ABA, Pa. Bar Assn. (family law sect.), Westmoreland County Bar Assn. (family law div.). Democrat. Lutheran. Home: 117 W Otterman St Greensburg PA 15601 Office: 304 Coulter Bldg Greensburg PA 15601

WHALEN, LUCILLE, educator, librarian; b. Los Angeles, July 26, 1925; d. Edward Cleveland and Mary Lucille (Perrault) W.; B.A. in English, Immaculate Heart Coll., Los Angeles, 1949; M.S.L.S., Catholic U. Am., 1955; D.L.S., Columbia U., 1965. Tchr. elementary and secondary schs., Los Angeles, Long Beach, Calif., 1945-52; high sch. librarian Conaty Meml. High Sch., Los Angeles, 1950-52; reference/serials librarian, instr. library sci. Immaculate Heart Coll., 1955-58, dean Sch. Library Sci., 1958-60, 65-70; asso. dean Sch. Library and Info. Sci., SUNY-Albany, 1971-78, prof., 1978-83, assoc. dean, 1984—; dir. U.S. Office Edn. Insts. Mem. ALA (chmn. com. on accreditation 1976-78), Spl. Libraries Assn. (chmn. com. research 1974-80, chmn. social and human services sect. 1983-84), N.Y. Library Assn. (pres. sect. library educators 1976), Soc. Am. Archivist, Assn. Records Mgrs. and Adminstrs., ACLU, Common Cause, Amnesty Internat. Democrat. Roman Catholic. Office: Sch Library and Info Sci SUNY 135 Western Ave Albany NY 12222

WHALEN, MARION ELIZABETH, educational administrator; b. Jamaica, N.Y., Jan. 29, 1937; d. Elmer John and Bertha Irene (Beers) W.; B.S., SUNY-Plattsburgh, 1958, M.S., 1967; profl. diploma St. John's U., Jamaica, 1976. Elem. sch. tchr. Freeport (N.Y.) Schs., 1958-66, elem. sch. counselor, 1967-75; asst. dean women SUNY, Plattsburgh, 1966-67; asst. prin. Freeport High Sch., 1975—. Mem. Nat. Assn. Female Execs., Council Adminstrs. and Suprs., Freeport Adminstrs. Assn. (pres. 1982-85), SUNY-Plattsburgh Alumni Assn., St. John's U. Alumni Assn. Delta Kappa Gamma (chpt. pres. 1976-78;

Elsa Brookfield scholar 1975), Phi Delta Kappa. Contbr. articles to profl. jours. Home: 1 Toms Point Ln Bldg 5 Apt 9J Port Washington NY 11050 Office: Freeport High Sch Brookside Ave Freeport NY 11520

WHALEY, BARBARA BAYNARD, medical technology educator; b. Mobile, Ala., Apr. 2, 1945; d. H. Hugh Baynard and Frances Ethel (Deane) Whaley; B.S. in Biology, Spring Hill Coll., 1966; cert. med. tech. Providence Hosp. Sch. Med. Tech., 1967; M.S. in Clin. Pathology, U. Ala., Birmingham, 1970; postgrad. U. S. Ala., 1982-84, U. So. Miss., 1982-85. Hematology supr. Mobile Infirmary Lab., 1970, edn1. coordinator sch. med. tech., 1970-78, ednl. dir., 1978—, quality assurance dir., 1985—; site surveyor Nat. Accrediting Agy. for Clin. Lab. Scis.; vice chmn. hematology exam. sub-com. Nat. Cert. Agy. for Clin. Lab. Personnel; clin. instr. Auburn U., Judson Coll., Livingston U., Millsaps Coll., Miss. Coll., Mobile Coll., Morehead State U., Spring Hill Coll., U. W. Fla. Trustee Wilmer Hall Episcopal Children's Home, Mobile, 1977-80; dir. S.W. Ala. Health Systems Agy., 1977—, mem. exec. com., 1981—; lab. dir. Seale Harris Diabetic Camp, 1972. Cert. clin. lab. scientist Nat. Certification Agy. for Clin. Lab. Personnel. Mem. Am. Soc. Clin. Pathologists (cert. med. technologist), Am. Soc. for Allied Health Professions, Am. Soc. for Med. Tech. (del. annual meeting 1972-78, pres.'s council 1974-76, region III council, 1974-76, competency delineations com. 1975-77), Ala. State Soc. for Med. Tech. (numerous coms. including edn., scholarship, awards, bylaws, Sara Crowson Trust Fund, coordinator hematology sci. assembly 1971-74, pres. 1975, treas. 1978-80, registration chmn. 1979, dir. 1974-80), Mobile Bus. and Profl. Women's Club (v.p. 1980), Alpha Mu Tau. Asso. editor Am. Jour. Med. Tech., 1976-83. Home: 706 Westmoreland Dr W Mobile AL 36609 Office: PO Box 2144 Mobile AL 36652

WHALEY, CHARLOTTE TOTEBUSCH, publisher, editor, writer; b. Pitts., June 21, 1925; d. Charles R. and Elizabeth G. (Dunn) Totebusch; m. Gould Whaley, Jr., Aug. 24, 1951; children—John Gould, Robert Dunn. B.A., So. Meth. U., 1970, M.A., 1976. Editorial asst., Southwest Rev., S.M.U. Press, So. Meth. U., Dallas, 1971-72, asst. editor, 1972-74, assoc. editor, 1974-75, asst. to dir. S.M.U. Press, mng. editor Southwest Rev., 1975-81, editor Southwest Rev., 1981-83, asst. dir., editor SMU Press, 1981-82, editor, 1982-83; editor/pub. Still Point Press, 1984—. Mem. Assn. Am. Univ. Presses, AAUW (dir. pub. relations, Dallas div.), Nat. Assn. Women Bus. Owners, Assn. Women Entrepreneurs Dallas, Women in Scholarly Pub., Phi Beta Kappa asst. sec. So. Meth. U. chpt. 1979-82, pres. North Tex. chpt. 1982-84). Club: Staff. Home and Office: 4222 Willow Grove Rd Dallas TX 75220

WHALEY, JOAN FRANCES, editor; b. Evanston, Ill., Aug. 8, 1935; d. James Templeton and Elizabeth Markley (Dodson) Pettingell; student (scholar) Art Inst. Chgo. Sch. Art, 1949-53; B.A., Fla. Internat. U., 1976; M.A., Fla. Atlantic U., 1981. Promotion writer Edward Petry & Co., Inc., N.Y.C., 1954-56, Sta. WTVD-TV, Durham, N.C., 1956-57; reporter, feature writer Chicago Heights (Ill.) Star, 1958-59; editor, asso. editorial dir. Industry Pubs., Miami, Fla., 1973-82; dir. sales promotion and mktg. Fox Tennis Racquets Co., Inc., Manhattan Beach, Calif., 1982-83; editor Creative Age Publs., Van Nuys, Calif., 1983-86; exec. editor Nev. Bus. Outlook, Nev. State Recorder, 1986—; vis. instr. U. Miami, 1981. Janet Rice fellow, 1977. Mem. Women in Communications, Nat. Assn. Exec. Women, Sigma Delta Chi (pub. awareness chmn.), Phi Theta Kappa. Editor, contbg. author: The Idea Book, Planning, Building, Financing Tennis Clubs, Racket and Shoe Factory, 1972—, PGA Product Knowledge Book, 1979. Office: 628 E John St Suite 2 Carson City NV 89701

WHALEY, PEGGY ELAINE, editor, publisher; b. Cleveland, Tenn., Nov. 30, 1939; d. Edward Darrell and Pauline (Earley) Ellis; m. Leo Jackson Whaley, Mar. 29, 1957; children—Sherri, Angela, Traci. Student Cleveland Community Coll., 1963-65, Dalton Jr. Coll., 1970-72, also spl. classes. Office mgr. So. Gen. Products, Ringgold, Ga., 1967-73, also corp. officer; office mgr. Joe Goodson, C.P.A., Dalton, Ga., 1974-78; comptroller Profl. C & C, Dalton, 1980-83; owner, operator Whaley & Assocs., Dalton, 1983-85; editor, assoc. pub. S.E. Floor Covering, Dalton, 1985—. Editor, pub. Peggy Whaley News Report, 1982-85; contbg. editor Carpet and Rug Industry, 1974-85, America's Textiles, 1984-85. Publicity dir. LWV, Dalton, 1978-80; mem. bd. Dalton Regional Library, 1981-86, chmn. bd., 1985-86; Republican sec. and v.p., Dalton, 1970-80. Mem. N.Y. Bus. Press Editors, Inc., Nat. Assn. Accts. (v.p. communications 1984-85), Nat. Assn. Floor Covering Women (nat. bd. dirs.), Nat. Assn. Female Execs., Dalton C. of C. (mem. coms.), World Trade Council (local bd. dirs. 1984—). Lodges: Order Ea. Star (past matron), Toastmasters (local v.p. 1984—). Avocations: writing; swimming; tennis. Home: PO Box 205 Dalton GA 30722 Office: SE Floor Covering Mag PO Box 1206 300 Emory Sq Dalton GA 30720

WHALEY, REGENIA LEONA, public service company service representative; b. Charleston, S.C., Nov. 15, 1950; d. Daniel and Lovey Ann (Gilliard) Whaley. B.A., Hunter Coll., 1979. Overseas operator Am. Telephone and Telegraph Co., N.Y.C., 1969-71, 78-81, jr. service asst., 1971-73, sr. force clk., 1973-74, service asst., 1974-78, records clk., 1981-82, service rep., 1982—, trainer overseas operators traffic dept., 1974. Union steward Communications Workers Am. Local 1150, N.Y.C., 1982. Mem. Nat. Assn. Female Execs., Alliance of Black Telecommunications Employees. Baptist. Home: 511 Sunnyview Oval Keasbey NJ 08832

WHALLEY, ALICE SHEEHAN, immunodiagnostics researcher, biologist; b. Grand Rapids, Mich., Feb. 23, 1954; d. Donald James and Mildred Louise (Norton) Sheehan; m. Robert Aplin Mauss, Nov. 21, 1973 (div. 1981); m. Paul Leland Whalley, July 25, 1981; 1 child, James. B.A., Washington U.-St. Louis, 1976. Chemist Sigma Chem. Co., St. Louis, 1975-76; research assoc. U. Calif.-San Diego, 1977, research assoc. Salk Inst., San Diego, 1977-80; staff research assoc. U. Calif., San Diego, 1980-83; sr. research asst. II Johnson & Johnson, San Diego, 1983—. Contbr. articles to profl. jours.; patentee. Mem. Nat. Assn. Female Execs. Avocations: photography; computer programming; mystery novels. Home: 7994 Mission Vista Dr San Diego CA 92120

WHARTENBY, CATHERINE ENGLISH (MRS. CHARLES ALFRED WHARTENBY), business executive; b. Wellsboro, Pa., June 30, 1920; d. Robert Dean and Elizabeth Perpetua (Dwyer) English; B.S., Mansfield State Coll., 1941; J.D., Golden Gate U., 1968; m. Charles Alfred Whartenby, Feb. 9, 1946. Bar: Calif. 1969. Office employee Refractory Mica Products, Inc., Newark, 1941; clk. legal dept. 9th Service Command, Presidio of San Francisco, 1942-44; office sec., office mgr. Research Inst. Am., San Francisco, 1945-54; office sec. Conn. Gen. Life Ins. Co., San Francisco, 1954-62, asst. mgr., 1962-72, regional design cons. estate and bus. planning, No. Calif., 1973-74; regional design mgr. Western Regional Design Center, 1975-78, dir., 1981; dir. Southwestern Regional Design Center, Huntington Beach, Calif., 1978-80; dir. Qualified Plans, Design Services, 1982—; lectr. pension courses Am. Coll. Life Underwriters, 1969-71, instr. advanced estate planning course, 1973-74; faculty Practicing Law Inst., 1983. Mem. ABA, State Bar Calif. (vice chmn. ins. subcom. estate planning com. 1978-81), Am. Soc. C.L.U.s. Home: RD5 Box 303 Wellsboro PA 16901 Office: PO Box 834 19 Central Ave Wellsboro PA 16901

WHATLEY, ALICIA, environmental affairs executive, environmental and regulatory affairs consultant; b. Troy, Ala., May 15, 1951; d. Comer and Lillie (Grimes) Whatley. B.S., Tuskegee Inst. (Ala.), 1972; M.S., Chgo. State U., 1975; postgrad. U. Ill.-Chgo., 1977-78; Ph.D., Union U., Cin., 1981. Mgr. environ. concerns Sherwin Williams Co., Chgo., 1972-82; safety and regulatory affairs mgr. SCA Chem. Services, Chgo., 1982-84; pres. Whatley, Grimes & Assocs., Inc., Chgo., 1983—; cons. regulatory affairs David W. Young & Assocs., Olympia Fields, Ill., 1982—; cons. hazardous materials Gen. Dynamics Corp., Detroit, 1984—, Mid-Am. Environment Services, Inc., 1985—. Recipient Citation for Service, Jr. Achievement, 1975, 76; Cert. of Leadership, Met. YMCA Chgo., 1977, 78; Recognition of Achievement, Met. YMCA Chgo., 1978. Mem. Am. Coll. Toxicology, Am. Chem. Soc., AAAS, Nat. Assn. Women in Sci., Am. Soc. Safety Engrs., Am. Indsl. Hygiene Assn., N.Y. Acad. Sci., Iota Sigma Pi, Delta Sigma Theta. Office: 1130 S Plymouth Ct Chicago IL 60605

WHATLEY, JACQUELINE BELTRAM, lawyer; b. West Orange, N.J., Sept. 26, 1944; d. Quirino and Eliane (Gruet) Beltram; m. John W. Whatley, June 25, 1966. B.A., U. Tampa, 1966; J.D., Stetson U., 1969. Bar: Fla. 1969, Alaska 1971. Assoc. Gibbons, Tucker, McEwen Smith & Cofer, Tampa, Fla., 1969-71; sole practice, Anchorage, 1971-73; ptnr. Gibbons, Tucker, Miller, Whatley & Stein, P.A., Tampa, 1973-81, mng. ptnr., 1981—. Bd. dirs. Travelers Aid Soc.; bd. dirs. Tenn. Walking Horse Breeders and Exhibitors Assn., v.p., 1984—; trustee Keystone United Meth. Ch., 1986. Mem. ABA, Fla. Bar Assn., Alaska Bar Assn. Republican. Methodist. Club: Athena (Tampa). Home: PO Box 17595 Tampa FL 33682 Office: 606 Madison St Tampa FL 33602

WHEATLEY, MARGARET BISSON (PEGI WHITE), small business owner, personnel consultant; b. Washington, Dec. 27, 1941; d. Robert Omer Bisson and Margaret (Dysart) Redfield; m. Richard Withington Wheatley, Jr., June 5, 1971. B.S. in Psychology, Philosophy, Ripon Coll., 1963. Dep. probation officer Orange County, Calif., 1964-71; personnel cons., office mgr. James Holder Placement, San Francisco, 1972-77; owner Margaret Bisson Wheatley Designs, Mill Valley, Calif., 1976—; pres., co-owner, personnel cons. McCall Personnel Services, Inc., San Francisco, 1978—; dir., co-owner MTS/McCall Temporary Service, Inc., San Francisco, 1982—; ptnr. P&L Resources, San Francisco, 1983—. Mem. Calif. Assn. Personnel Cons. Republican. Commercial (bd. dirs. 1986-88). Avocations: tennis; international travel. Office: McCall Personnel Services Inc 369 Pine St Suite 700 San Francisco CA 94104

WHEELER, CAROL ESTELLE, educational administrator; b. Mobile, Ala., Sept. 9, 1936; d. Frederick G. and A. Estelle (Ryan) W.; A.B., Maryville Coll., St. Louis, 1958; M.A. in Philosophy, Georgetown U., 1971; M.A. in Edn., U. Chgo., 1976. Joined Sisters of Mercy, Roman Catholic Ch., 1959. Tchr., Mercy High Sch., Balt., 1961-68, Bishop Toolen High Sch., Mobile, 1968-69; asst. prin. Mercy High Sch., Balt., 1971-72, advisor to beginning tchrs., 1976-77, pres./prin., 1977—; supr. student tchrs. U. Chgo., 1974-75, adminstrv. asst. MST porgram, 1975-76; mem. profl. standards and tchr. edn. adv. bd. Md. Dept. Edn., 1984-86. Trustee Loyola Coll., Balt., 1982—, Mercy Hosp., Balt., 1985—, Cathedral Found. Bd., Archdiocese Balt., 1983—; del. provincial chpt. Sisters of Mercy, Balt., gen. chpt. Sisters of Mercy of the Union. Mem. Mercy Secondary Edn. Assn. (pres. 1983-87), Assocs. Research in Pvt. Edn., Assn. Supervision and Curriculum Devel., Nat. Assn. Secondary Sch. Prins., Nat. Cath. Edn. Assn. Office: Mercy High Sch 1300 E Northern Pkwy Baltimore MD 21239

WHEELER, DONNA MARIE, communications company executive; b. Boston, May 5, 1959; d. Richard Marston and Jane Marjorie (Flosdick) W. B.S. in Food and Natural Resources, U. Mass.-Amherst. Mgmt. trainee Hyatt Hotels, Long Beach, Calif., 1981; sales rep. Dunfey Hotel Corp., Boston, 1982-84; T&L Plus Communications, Framingham, Mass., 1983-84; sales rep. U.S. West Interline, Westwood, Mass., 1984-85, nat. account mgr., 1986—. Mem. Women in Telecommunications, Nat. Assn. Female Execs. Avocations: skiing; tennis; windsurfing. Home: 33 Lancaster Terr #104 Brookline MA 02146 Office: Interline 381 University Ave Westwood MA 02146

WHEELER, LENEA MAY, nursing educator; b. Brainerd, Minn., Sept. 19, 1934; d. Clinton Sardis and Blanche May (Potter) W. B.S. in Nursing, Coll. of St. Scholastica, 1956; M.S., St. Cloud State U., 1977. Staff nurse St. Mary's Hosp., Duluth, Minn., 1956-57; pub. health nurse Milw. Health Dept., 1957-59; project nurse U. Minn., Mpls., 1962-66, St. Paul Ramsey Hosp., 1966-68; R.N. instr. St. Cloud Hosp., Minn., 1959-62, St. Cloud Sch. Nursing, 1970—. Mem. exec. com. March Dimes, St. Cloud. Served as capt. U.S. Army, 1968-70, col. USAR, 1970—. Mem. Nat. League for Nursing, Am. Heart Assn. (bd. dirs.), Am. Amateur Karate Fedn., Phi Kappa Phi. Roman Catholic. Avocations: karate; swimming; study of Hispanic culture. Home: 2912 14th St N Saint Cloud MN 56301 Office; St Cloud Hosp Sch Nursing 1406 6th Ave N Saint Cloud MN 56301

WHEELER, PATTY NASH, newspaper publisher; b. Charlotte, N.C., Jan. 25, 1944; d. Benjamin Marion Nash and Ceil (Sypher) Murphy; m. Rowland McLamb Shelley, Aug. 17, 1968 (div. Feb. 1979); 1 son, Stephen Benjamin; m. 2d Thaddeus Alvin Wheeler, Jr., May 23, 1981. B.A. in Journalism, U. N.C., 1965. Lic. real estate broker, N.C. Reporter, News and Observer, Raleigh, N.C., 1965-67; writer, editor N.C. State U., Raleigh, 1968-70, 72-77; writer, alumni office Northwestern U., Evanston, Ill., 1970-71; dir. info. service N.C. Symphony, Raleigh, 1977-79; writer Carolina Country Mag., Raleigh, 1979-82; pub. Skyland Post, West Jefferson, N.C., 1982—; pres. Blue Ridge Communications, Inc., West Jefferson, 1982—. Bd. dirs. Northwest N.C. Devel. Assn., Winston-Salem, 1983-86, Ashe County Council on Aging, West Jefferson, 1983—; pres. Ashe County chpt. N.C. Symphony, West Jefferson, Raleigh, 1983, Nat. Com. for New River, 1985—; sec. Ashe County Performing Arts Bldg. Com., 1983—. Mem. N.C. Press Assn., Ashe County C. of C. (bd. dirs. 1983—). Democrat. Episcopalian. Home: PO Box 67 West Jefferson NC 28694 Office: Skyland Post PO Box 67 West Jefferson NC 28694

WHEELER, WENDY ROBIN, computer company executive; b. Washington, Aug. 25, 1953; d. Malcolm Frederick and Aurora Dorothy (Anas) Wheeler; m. Ian Stanley Reid, Aug. 16, 1986. B.A. in Modern Lang. and Lit., Trinity Coll., 1975. Mktg. rep. IBM, Waltham, Mass., 1975-80; product mgr. Prime Computer, Natick, Mass., 1980-82, asst. to pres., 1982-83, dir. product mktg., 1983-86, v.p. systems mktg., 1986—. Named 1984 Woman of Achievement in Bus. and Industry, Boston, YWCA, 1984. Mem. Profl. Council Cambridge, Women in Info. Processing. Office: Prime Computer Inc Prime Park Natick MA 01760

WHEELESS, CAROLYN RUDD, marketing executive, finance management consultant; b. Kingsport, Tenn., Aug. 7, 1954; d. Sedrick Selvin and Bonnie Ellen (Grove) Rudd; m. Richard Morelle Wheeless, Mar. 28, 1975. B.A. magna cum laude, High Point Coll., 1976. Dist. mgr. Chess King, Aurora, Ill., 1978-81, The Gap, Chevy Chase, Md., 1981-83; sr. dist. mgr. U.S. Shoe Corp., Wheaton, Md., 1983-86; v.p. fin. and mktg. RAMCO, Arlington, Va., 1984—; mgmt. cons. Hair Express, Glenburnie, Md., 1982-86, Pizazz, Arlington, Va., 1986, Richs Crown, Allentown, Md., 1985-86. Author: Old Man, 1976. Organizer Nat. Diabetes Assn., 1980-86, Catonsville High Sr. Class, Catonsville, 1984-86. Mem. Nat. Orgn. Female Execs. Republican. Baptist. Clubs: Ptnrs. for Peace, Alliance for Progress (Glenburnie, Md.). Avocations: travel; languages. Home: 1711 Massachusetts Ave Apt 406 Washington DC 20036 Office: Ramco 1225 Jefferson Davis Hwy Arlington VA 22202

WHELAN, ELAINE GILLIGAN, nurse, educator; b. Waltham, Mass., July 14, 1945; d. Thomas Joseph and Rose C. (Walker) Gilligan; m. James Michael Whelan, May 15, 1971; 1 son, Brian James. B.A., Jersey City State U., 1973, M.A., 1974; B.S. in Nursing Pace U., 1977; M.S. in Nursing, Seton Hall U., 1980. Instr. nursing Holy Name Hosp., Teaneck, N.J., 1967-74; staff nurse Holy Name Hosp., Teaneck, 1966, St. Elizabeth's Hosp., Brighton, Mass., 1967; assoc. prof. nursing Bergen Community Coll., Paramus, N.J., 1974—; clin. cons. Nurses Reference Library, 1981-83. Mem. Am. Nurses Assn. (mem. com. 1975-77), Holy Name Hosp. Alumni Assn., Jersey City State Alumni Assn., Pace U. Alumni Assn., Kappa Delta Pi, Sigma Theta Tau. Roman Catholic. Office: Bergen Community Coll 400 Paramus Rd Paramus NJ 07652

WHELAN, NANCY REYNOLDS, publishing company executive; b. Chgo., Feb. 11, 1947; d. Warren Jay and Mary Ellen (Seaman) Reynolds; m. Martin James Whelan, Feb. 12, 1972; children—Kimberly R., Michael B. B.A., Depauw U., 1969; cert. of mgmt. U. Balt., 1981. Mgmt. trainee Bankers Trust Co., N.Y.C., 1969-72; asst. cashier 1st State Bank of Miami, Fla., 1972-73; ops. officer Bank of Wheaton, Ill., 1974-76, cons., 1976-77; writer BAI, Rolling Meadow, Ill., 1977-78; pub. Microbanker, Inc., York, Pa., 1982—, editor and pub. Microbanker Research Letter, 1983—. Bd. dirs. Atkins House, York, 1979-82; fund-raiser Martin Meml. Library, York, 1984. Mem. Newsletter Assn., Ind. Bankers of Pa., Western Ind. Bankers. Club: Downtown (York). Avocations: pottery; roller skating. Office: Microbanker Inc 9-11 N Newberry St York PA 17401

WHELCHEL, SANDRA JANE, writer; b. Denver, May 31, 1944; d. Ralph Earl and Janette Isabelle (March) Everitt; m. Andrew Jackson Whelchel, June 27, 1965; children—Andrew Jackson, Anita Earlyn. B.A. in Elem. Edn., U. No. Colo., 1966; postgrad. Pepperdine Coll., 1971, UCLA, 1971. Elem. tchr. Douglas County Schs., Castle Rock, Colo., 1966-68, El Monte (Calif.) schs., 1968-72; br. librarian Douglas County Libraries, Parker, Colo., 1973-78; zone writer Denver Post, 1979-81; reporter The Express newspapers, Castle Rock, 1979-81; history columnist Parker Trail newspapers, 1985—; contbr. short stories and articles to various publs. including: Empire mag., Calif. Horse Rev., Jack and Jill, Child Life, Children's Digest; author non-fiction book: Your Air Force Academy, 1982; A Day in Blue, coloring book, 1984; A Day at the Cave, 1985; Pro Rodeo Hall of Champions and Museum of the American Cowboy, coloring book, 1985; Pikes Peak Country, coloring book, 1986; lectr. on writing. Mem. Internat. Order of Foresters, Nat. Writers Club (treas. Denver Metro chpt. 1985-86).

WHETSTONE, MARY ANNA, personnel executive; b. Tulsa, Sept. 8, 1930; d. Elgy Lee and Evelyn Amy (Teel) Barr; m. James E. Whetstone, Mar. 23, 1957; children—Byron W., Anita W. Whetstone Applegate. B.A., Phillips U., 1953. Personnel mgr. Foley's, Austin, Tex., 1968—. Contbr. articles to jours. Chmn. adv. council Redirected Homemakers, Austin, 1980-81; adv. bd. Ret. Sr. Vol. Program, Austin, 1981, Distributive Edn., Houston, 1974-77; precinct chmn. Republican Party, Austin, 1981. Mem. Am. Soc. Personnel Administrs., Austin Personnel Assn. (sec. 1983-84), Nat. Employer Services and Recreation Assn. (exec. bd. Capitol Area Recreation Council 1980-83). Mem. Christian Ch. Home: 506 S Fairfax Skiatook OK 74070 Office: Foley's 4300 Highland Mall Austin TX 78752

WHETSTONE, MARY ELLEN, educational administrator, educator; b. Stubenville, Ohio, Dec. 3, 1951; d. Wayne C. and Irene (Morgan) Keifer; m. Gerald Lee Whetstone, June 20, 1974; children—Renee, Suzette. B.S., Eastern Nazarene Coll., 1973. Sec. adult edn. Quincy Pub. Schs., Mass., 1972-74; tchr. Canton Pub. Schs., Ohio, 1980-82; prin., tchr. Trinity Christian Acad., Fitchburg, Mass., 1984—. Mem. Nazarene Youth Internat. (sec. 1979-81), Women Ministries (dir. 1984—), Children Ch. (dir. 1982-84). Home: 800 South St Fitchburg MA 01420

WHEWELL, DEBRA ANN, construction company executive; b. Jacksonville, Ill., May 1, 1962; d. John Albert and Patricia Ann (Howard) W. Student Western Ill. U., 1980-81. Bookkeeper, dispatcher Al's Ready Mix, Inc., Jacksonville, Ill., 1980-83, mgr., 1982-84; corporate officer Albert Whewell Builders, Inc., Jacksonville, 1984—. Mem. Nat. Assn. Female Execs. Roman Catholic. Club: Blackhawk (Jacksonville). Lodges: Am. Vets., Am. Legion. Avocations: reading; painting; writing. Home: 198 E Greenwood Ave Jacksonville IL 62650 Office: Albert Whewell Builders Inc Lincoln Square Shopping Ctr Jacksonville IL 62650

WHIGHAM, TERRI LEE, marketing executive; b. Riverside, Calif., May 8, 1953; d. Gordon Terrance and Virginia Lee (Warren) W.; student Merced Jr. Coll., 1979. Asst. to pres. BAC-Pritchard, Inc., Merced, Calif.; asst. to pres. Valley Sheet Metal, South San Francisco, Calif.; asst. to supt. Herman Christensen & Sons, San Carlos, Calif.; corp. treas. TransGlobal Mktg. Corp., San Francisco; now v.p. D&B Buying Group; pres. Internat. Trading Enterprises, Internat. Almond Brokerage. Mem. Nat. Assn. Female Execs., Nat. Sporting Goods Assn., Far West Ski Assn. Democrat. Methodist.

WHILEY, JOAN MARGARET, public relations writer, journalist; b. Vancouver, B.C., Can. Jan. 4, 1930; d. Alfred Ernest and Mary Margaret Mathews Scoby; B.A., U. B.C., 1951; m. John D. Whiley, Dec. 21, 1955 (div. Jan. 1965); children—Philip Vincent, Louise Margaret, Anthony John. Writer, Chiswell & Assos. Public Relations, London, 1954-57; freelance writer, 1958-65; writer Nordstrom's, Inc., Seattle, 1965-68; creative supr. Cole & Weber, Inc., Seattle, 1968-71; dir. public affairs Seattle City Light, 1973-78; mgr. mem. relations Wash. Public Power Supply System, Seattle, 1978-82; freelance writer, journalist, 1982—. Mem. bd. Univ. Dist. Community Council, 1979—. Mem. Pub. Relations Soc. Am. (accredited), Seattle Economists Club, Friends of the Earth, Mountaineers. Club: Wash. Athletic. Home: 5823 17th St NE Seattle WA 98105 Office: 1932 1st Ave Seattle WA 98101

WHILLOCK, RITA KIRK, communications educator; b. Springdale, Ark., Nov. 28, 1953; d. John William and Thelma Marie (Beard) Kirk; m. David Everett Whillock, June 30, 1978. B.S.E., U. Ark., 1975, M. Communication, 1977; postgrad. U. Mo., summer 1982. Cert. secondary tchr., Ark. Grad. asst. U. Ark., Fayetteville, 1976-77; tchr., dept. chmn. Rogers High Sch. (Ark.), 1977-79; communications prof. Kearney State Coll. (Nebr.), 1979-80; asst. to dean, prof. communications Stephen F. Austin State U., Nacogdoches, Tex., 1980—; tab room dir. U. Houston, 1982-84; coordinator Student Employment Service, Kearney, 1979-80; speechwriter, 1980-84, keynote speaker, 1978-84. Editor: Ideas, 1983-84. Counselor Women's Shelter of East Tex., Nacogdoches, 1982-84; dir. Media Arts Panel Spring Arts Festival, Nacogdoches, 1982-84; mem. Nacogdoches County Dem. Orgn., 1983-84; vol. Empty Stocking Fund., Nacogdoches, 1982-83. Mem. Women in Communication (sponsor 1983-84), Speech Communication Assn., Tex. Speech Communication Assn., So. Speech Communication Assn., Pi Kappa Delta (sponsor, coach 1980-84). Baptist.

WHINERY, DOROTHY COOKE (MRS. JAMES C. WHINERY), association executive; b. Louisville; d. Thomas and Abigail (Latimer) Cooke; B.S. in Music, Drake U., 1935; m. James Curtis Whinery, Oct. 9, 1938 (dec. Oct. 1955); 1 dau., Janet (Mrs. Jock Evan Thompson). Tchr. music pub. schs. Somers, Iowa, 1935-38; asst. buyer Younkers, Inc., Des Moines, 1941-45; nat. exec. sec. Sigma Alpha Iota, Des Moines, 1957—, nat. exec. bd., 1957—, mem. fin. planning group, 1981—. Bd. dirs. Des Moines Civic Music Assn., 1950-53, exec. sec., 1953-65. Recipient Sword Honor, 1950, Rose Honor, 1962, Ring Excellence, 1968, all Sigma Alpha Iota. Mem. Nat. Trust Hist. Preservation, Smithsonian Assos., Met. Mus. Art, Am. Bus. Women's Assn. Included in book Iowa Women at Work, 1979. Home: 1447 57th St Des Moines IA 50311 Office: 4119 Rollins Ave Des Moines IA 50312

WHIPPLE, BARBARA, graphic artist, writer; b. San Francisco, June 16, 1921; d. George Hoyt and Katharine Ball (Waring) W.; B.A., Swarthmore Coll., 1943; B.S., Rochester Inst. Tech., 1956; M.F.A., Temple U., 1961; m. John Schilling, Feb. 13, 1943 (div. 1956); children—Christine, Katharine; m. 2d, Grant Heilman, Aug. 14, 1961; 1 son, Hans. Tchr., Elizabethtown Coll., 1973-76, Franklin and Marshall Coll., 1974-76; grad. asst. Tyler Sch. Art, 1961; graphic artist; condr. workshops Adams State Coll., 1982, Colo. Graphic Arts Center, 1980, 82, Sangre de Cristo Art Ctr., Pueblo, Colo., 1985. One person shows include: Lebanon Valley Coll., 1973, Colo. Mountain Coll., 1979, Foothills Art Center, 1980, 84, Adams State Coll., 1982, West Nebr. Art Ctr., 1984; numerous invitational and group shows; co-author: Water Media Techniques, 1984; Water Media: Processes and Possibilities, 1986; bibliography: La Revue Moderne, 1969, Am. Artist, 1980, Colorado Outdoors, 1980; contbr. Am. Artist, 1971-80, contbg. editor, 1979-85. Bd. dirs. Swarthmore Coll., 1970-76; pres. Chaffee County LWV, 1980-81. Recipient 1st prize for prints Lancaster Open Juried Show, 1964, Best of Show award Liberal Religious Art, Denver, 1967, 1st prize for drawing Phila. Watercolor Club, 1979, others. Mem. Phila. Watercolor Club, Artists Equity, Foothills Art Center, Colo. Artists Assn., Nat. Mus. of Women in Arts (founding), Chaffee County Council on Arts. Home: PO Box 609 Buena Vista CO 81211 Office: 429 E Main St Buena Vista CO 81211

WHIPPLE, BEVERLY JEAN, medical clinic administrator; b. Portland, Oreg., Dec. 15, 1952; d. Kenneth C. and Myrtle Irene (Wales) W. Student Yakima Valley Coll., 1970-72; B.A. in Music with distinction, Central Wash. State Coll., 1975. Music tchr. West Valley Sch. Dist., Yakima, Wash., 1976-78; ind. truck driver, 1978-79; disc jockey Towne Plaza Disco, Yakima, 1979-80; co-founder, dir. Feminist Women's Health Ctr., Yakima, 1980-83, Everett, Wash., 1983-84, mem. quality assurance com., 1980—, exec. dir., pres., bd. dirs., 1984—. Conf. speaker Nat. Abortion Fedn., Atlanta, 1984, Nat. Lawyers Guild, Seattle, 1985, Nat. Women's Studies Assn., Seattle, 1985; inservice speaker Planned Parenthood Affiliates Wash., Olympia, 1985; witness sub-com. on civil and constl. rights U.S. Ho. of Reps., 1985; speaker numerous other civic orgns. Avocation: playing keyboard instruments and flute in rock and roll band. Office: Feminist Women's Health Ctr 2002 Englewood St Yakima WA 98902

WHIPPLE, CAROL OWEN, rancher, business cons.; b. Amarillo, Tex., Apr. 11, 1940; d. Wiley Ducoe and Marian (Hall) Owen; student U. Ariz., 1957-59,

Utah State U., 1960; m. Gordon S. Whipple, Mar. 26, 1980; children—Laura, Katherine, Randall. Owner, operator Creekwood Ranch, farming, horse and cattle breeders, Amarillo, 1960—; dir. Okla. Stud, Inc., Purcell, 1976-78, sec., 1978-80; sec. Rowel, Inc., comml. bldg. and property mgmt., Amarillo, 1975-79, pres., 1979—; owner, operator A New Idea, furniture leasing, 1979-80; pres. Sun Tans Unlimited, Inc., 1979-80; partner Whipple Assos., mgmt. cons., direct sales distbrs., 1981—; tng. cons. Neo-Life Tng. Center, Amarillo. Pres. Amarillo Girl Scout Council, 1974-78. Mem. Am. Soc. Profl. and Exec. Women, Nat. Assn. Female Execs., Am. Quarter Horse Assn., Appaloosa Horse Club, Internat. Entrepreneurs Assn., Nat. Fedn. Ind. Bus., Kappa Alpha Theta. Presbyterian. Home: Route 2 Box 370 Canyon TX 79015 Office: 4551 S Western St Suite 1 Amarillo TX 79109

WHIPPLE, ELEANOR BLANCHE, educational administrator, social worker; b. Bellingham, Wash., June 7, 1916; d. Charles William and Susan Blanche (Campbell) W.; B.A. in Sociology, U. Wash., 1938, M.S.W., 1949; Ph.D., Laurence U., 1982; m. Robert Auld Fowler, Oct. 1, 1938 (div. 1947); children—Lawrence William, Jeanice Marie Fowler Roosevelt. Founder, dir. Camp Cloud's End, Deception Pass, Wash., 1939-42; therapist Family Counseling Service, Seattle, 1949-58; field instr. U. Wash., Seattle, 1954-57; pvt. practice counselling, Burbank, Calif., 1958-60; social service dir. Hollygrove Children's Residential Treatment Center, Hollywood, Calif., 1960-66, exec. dir., 1966-81; adj. faculty Biola U., La Mirada, Calif., 1972-80; dean Grad. Sch. Calif. Christian Inst., Orange, 1981-85, pres., 1985—. Bd. dirs. Christian Fellowship for the Blind, Inc. Fellow Soc. Clin. Social Work, Royal Soc. Health; mem. Nat. Assn. Social Workers, Acad. Cert. Social Workers, N.Am. Assn. Christians in Social Work (immediate past pres. bd. dirs.). Contbr. articles in field to profl. publs. Home: 1105 Mound Ave Apt 9 South Pasadena CA 91030 Office: 1744 W Katella Ave Orange CA 92667

WHIPPLE, JACQUELINE CONANT, writer, media specialist; b. Columbus, Ohio, Mar. 31, 1921; d. William Horace and Gertrude Virginia (Bryant) Conant; A.B. magna cum laude, Mt. Holyoke Coll., 1943; postgrad. Art. Inst. Boston, 1974-79; m. David Collins Whipple, Sept. 6, 1944; children—Nancy, Roger, Leah, Benjamin. Reporter, Scarsdale (N.Y.) Inquirer, summers, 1939-43; scriptwriter radio dept. J. Walter Thompson Co., N.Y., 1943-45; reporter Washington Daily News, 1945-47; broadcast journalist, chief editorial writer Sta. WCRB-AM-FM, Waltham, Mass. and Boston, 1960-67; with Sch. div. Houghton Mifflin Co., Boston, 1967-86, retired; free land all media; jury now audio visual coordinator; jury chmn. excellence in pub. writing/support of edn. Council for Advancement and Support of Edn., Washington, 1981. Chmn. know your town Waltham LWV 1951, v.p., 1953; pres. Cohasset (Mass.) PTA, 1963. Recipient Tom Phillips award, UPI Broadcasters of Mass., 1963; cert. of merit Art Inst. Boston, 1976. Mem. Women in Communications. Democrat. Unitarian. Club: Cohasset Yacht. Contbr. articles to popular mags. Home: 119 N Main St Cohasset MA 02025

WHISENNAND, CYNTHIA SIMMONS, librarian; b. Dallas, Oct. 29, 1956; d. Mickey Thorne and Diane Katherine (Gale) Neel Simmons; m. Dietrich P. Whisennand, June 28, 1980. B.A., So. Meth. U., 1979; M.L.S., N. Tex. State U., 1985. Cert. tchr. Tex. Tchr., Dallas Ind. Sch. Dist., 1979-83; librarian Irving Ind. Sch. Dist., Tex., 1985—. Mem. dist. com. Mustang Dist. Council, Boy Scouts Am., Dallas, 1980—. Recipient Dist. award of Merit Boy Scouts Am., 1983. Mem. ALA, Assn. Supervision and Curriculum Devel., Nat. Assn. Female Execs., Tex. Library Assn. Republican. Mem. Disciple of Christ Ch. Avocations: judo; photography; music; shooting; computers. Home: 4702 Junius St Dallas TX 75246 Office: Lively Elem Sch 1800 Plymouth Dr Irving TX 76461

WHISKER, JUDITH WITHRODER, educational administrator; b. Hutchinson, Kans., July 26, 1943; d. L.A. and Mary C. (Colvin) Withroder; divorced; children—Jennifer, Jay. B.A., U. Kans., 1965. Exec. dir. March of Dimes, Hutchinson, 1974-75; dir. mktg. Central State Bank, Hutchinson, 1978-80; dir. resource development/personnel Hutchinson Community Coll., 1980—. Charter mem. Leadership Hutchinson class, 1984. Mem. Coll. and Univ. Personnel Assn., Nat. Council for Resource Devel. (state coordinator 1985—, asst. regional coordinator 1985—), Hutchinson C. of C. (chmn. Ambassadors 1985—). Episcopalian. Home: 1012 E 21st St Hutchinson KS 67502 Office: Hutchinson Community College 1300 N Plum St Hutchinson KS 67501

WHISMAN, JANET THOMPSON, artist, educator; b. Houston, Apr. 27, 1933; d. Lorance Porter Thompson and Aileen (Rayburn) Crafton; m. Meredith Everett Whisman, Dec. 30, 1961; 1 son, Meredith Benjamin. B.A., Rice U., 1955. Ptnr., Discount Art, Houston, 1970-72, pres., 1973-79; pres. Art. Land, Inc., Houston, 1980-81, Whisman Art Gallery, Houston, 1981—; artist. Elder, Northwest Christian Ch. (Disciples of Christ), Houston, 1981, 82, sec., 1980, 81, 82, historian, 1977, 78, 79. Republican. Home: 6807 Apple Valley Ln Houston TX 77069

WHISNANT, LELA RUTH, communications company executive; b. Asheville, N.C., Feb. 4, 1950; s. d. Clyde McCiver and Ruth (DePriest) W. B.A., Eckerd Coll., St. Petersburg, Fla., 1971; M.B.A., Wake Forest U., Winston-Salem, N.C., 1977. Cert. profl. estimator. Grad. asst. in stats. Wake Forest U., 1976-77; mfg. engr. Tex. Instruments Inc., Dallas, 1977-80, planning mgr. imager br., 1980-85; tech. planner DSC Communications, Plano, Tex., 1985—. Vice pres. N.C. Teenage Democrats, 1966-67. Mem. Nat. Assn. Female Execs., AAAS, Women in Electronics (bd. dirs. N. Tex. chpt. 1985—), Nat. Mgmt. Assn., Nat. Estimating Soc. Presbyterian. Home: 405 Nottingham Dr Richardson TX 75080 Office: DSC Communications 1000 Coit Rd Plano TX 75075

WHITAKER, CORINNE COOPER, financial executive; b. Stamford, Conn., Aug. 31, 1934; d. Samuel and Natalie Gordon; B.A. (Durant scholar), Wellesley Coll., 1956; postgrad. N.Y. Inst. Fin., 1972-73, U. Houston, 1974; children—Nanette Cooper McGuinness, Robin Cooper. Sr. account exec. Eppler, Guerin & Turner, Inc., Houston, 1972-76; fixed income liaison Loeb, Rhodes & Co., Los Angeles, 1976-77; cons. Edward T. Watkins & Co., Houston, 1977; account exec., asso. v.p. Bateman Eichler Hill Richards, Los Angeles, 1977-79; chmn. bd., chief adminstrv. officer Don C. Whitaker, Inc., Los Angeles, 1980-84; pres. Hillcreast Cons., Inc., 1984—; mem. Pacific Stock Exchange; organized seminars, courses in field; seminar coordinator Investment Dynamics series, Houston, 1975. Bd. dirs. women's div., nat. publicity chmn. Aerospace Med. Assn., 1964; lectr. African art, docent leader Rice U. Media Center Art to Schs. Program, 1974-75; mem. bus. and industry com. women's council Los Angeles Area C. of C., 1978. Recipient John Masefield award Wellesley Coll., 1956, Katherine Lee Bates award, 1956; Vol. Service award N.Y. Med. Coll., Flower and Fifth Ave. Hosps., 1958; Rookie of Yr. award Eppler Guerin & Turner, 1973, award of excellence, 1976, named to Millionaires Club 1973-75; commendation Houston Jr. C. of C., 1975; named to Century Club, Bateman Eichler Hill Richards Inc., 1978. Mem. Norton Simon Mus., Friends of Photography, Fellows of Contemporary Art, Ancient Arts Council, Soc. for Contemporary Photography, Nat. Mus. of Women in Arts (charter), Am. Crafts Council, Los Angeles Floor Brokers Assn. (founder), Phi Beta Kappa. Clubs: Wellesley Coll. Alumnae (chmn. spl. gifts div. Washington area 1964).

WHITAKER, DOROTHY EUSTACE, travel agent; b. Phila., Nov. 8, 1926; d. Robert Clifton Whitaker and Dorothy Veronica (Eustace) Whitaker-Hearn. Student UCLA, evenings 1949-58. Bus. office rep. Bell of Pa., Phila., 1945-48; pub. office rep. Gen. Telephone Co., Los Angeles, 1948-51; contract adminstr. York Corp., Phila., 1952-55, regional office mgr., Los Angeles, 1955-64; purchasing agt. Nat. Research Co., Gardena, Calif., 1965-68; travel agt. Talmage Tours, Phila., 1969-75; travel agt., mgr. Whitaker Travel, Ltd., Phila., 1975—; computer trainer ASTA Mktg. Services, Inc., 1981—; mem. adv. council Harcum Jr. Coll., Bryn Mawr, Pa., 1983—. Author: ADAM Computer tng. manual, 1982. Bd. dirs. Overbrook Farms Club, Phila., 1979—. Mem. Am. Soc. Travel Agts. (acctg. tchr. 1978—, nat. bd. dirs. 1984—, chmn. consumer affairs 1984—), Phila. Women's Travel Club (pres. 1974-76), Inst. Cert. Travel Agts. (cert. travel cons.). Republican. Roman Catholic. Avocations: history; bridge; travel. Home: 2125 N 63d St Philadelphia PA 19151 Office: Whitaker Travel Ltd 2125 N 63d St Overbrook PA 19151

WHITAKER, EILEEN MONAGHAN, artist; b. Holyoke, Mass., Nov. 22, 1911; d. Thomas F. and Mary (Doona) Monaghan; ed. Mass. Coll. Art, Boston; m. Frederic Whitaker. Ann. exhibits in nat. and regional watercolor shows; represented in permanent collections N.A.D., U.S. Internat. U., NAD, Charles and Emma Frye Mus., Seattle, Hispanic Soc., N.Y.C., Atlanta Art Mus., U. Mass., Norfolk (Va.) Mus., Springfield (Mass.) Mus. Art, Reading (Pa.) Art Mus., Okla. Mus. Art, St. Lawrence U., Wichita State U., pvt. collections. Recipient numerous major awards, including several awards Allied Artists Am., Providence Water Color Club, several awards Am. Watercolor Soc., Wong award Calif. Watercolor Soc., De Young Mus. award, Springville (Utah) Mus. Art award, Ranger Fund purchase prize, Orbrig prize NAD, silver medal Am. Watercolor Soc., Watercolor West; featured in Watson-Guptill books on watercolor, in various mags. including Am. Artist, Southwest Art, Artists of the Rockies and Golden West, others. Fellow Huntington Hartford Found., 1964. Academician NAD; mem. Am. Watercolor Soc., Providence Watercolor Club, Soc. Western Artists, Watercolor West (hon.), San Diego Watercolor Soc. (hon.). Home: 1579 Alta La Jolla Dr La Jolla CA 92037

WHITAKER, MARY RUTH, educator; b. Kansas City, Kans., Dec. 5, 1940; d. Floyd Edgar and Ruth Mary Fassnacht; B.S. in Edn., U. Kans., 1962, postgrad. in spl. edn., 1972-76; M.A., U. Mo., 1971; m. John C. Whitaker, Feb. 26, 1972; 1 dau., Lori. Tchr., Conn. and Kans., 1962-66; mem. staff Crittenton Center, Kansas City, Mo., 1972—, ednl. evaluation and resource coordinator, dir. edn., 1980, elem. program developer and tchr., 1980—; speaker, cons. in field. Chmn. ways and means com. Kansas City Young Matrons, 1973. Mem. Conf. Exceptional Children, AAUW, Alpha Chi Omega, Alpha Delta Kappa. Republican. Presbyterian. Club: Sertoma (pres. Johnson County 1981-83). Home: 3906 W 103d St Overland Park KS 66207 Office: 10918 Elm St Kansas City MO 64134

WHITAKER, SUSANNE KANIS, veterinary medical librarian; b. Clinton, Mass., Sept. 10, 1947; d. Harry and Elizabeth P. (Cantwell) Kanis; m. Daniel Brown Whitaker, Jan. 1, 1977. A.B. in Biology, Clark U., 1969; M.S. in Library Sci., Case Western Res. U., 1970. Cert. med. librarian. Regional reference librarian Yale Med. Library, New Haven, Conn., 1970-72; med. librarian Hartford Hosp., Conn., 1972-77; asst. librarian Cornell U. Coll. Vet. Medicine, Ithaca, N.Y., 1977-78, vet. med. librarian, 1978—. Mem. Med. Library Assn. (chmn. vet. med. libraries sect. 1984-85, sec., treas. 1983-84, directory editor 1984—), SUNY Council of Head Librarians (sec. 1981-83), Upstate N.Y. and Ontario Chpt. Med. Library Assn. Home: 502 The Parkway Ithaca NY 14850 Office: Flower Vet Library Cornell U NY State Coll Vet Medicine Ithaca NY 14853

WHITBECK, ELAINE ESTHER, lawyer; b. Fayetteville, N.C., Sept. 13, 1954; d. Robert Earl and Joanne Lee (Barber) Whitbeck; m. Lonnie Eugene Lindsey, Jan. 15, 1982. B.A. summa cum laude U. Va., 1976, J.D., 1979. Bar: Tex. 1979. Med. asst. Drs. Kress, Gardner, Turner & Maillis, Springfield, Va., 1971-74; protocol asst. to Sec. of Def., Dept. Def., Washington, 1975-76; research writer JAG Sch. and Research, Inc., Charlottesville, Va., 1977-78; trial litigator Vial, Hamilton et al, Dallas, 1979-82; corp. counsel Mary Kay Cosmetics, Inc., Dallas, 1982-86; asst. gen. counsel, asst. sec. Alcon Labs., Inc., Fort Worth, 1986—. Author handbook Securities Regulation, 1982; contbr. articles to profl. jours. Counselor Rape Crisis Ctr., Charlottesville and Dallas, 1974—, Child Care, Dallas, 1984 ; participant Leadership Tex.; atty./counselor Legal Assistance (Pro Bono), Charlottesville, 1978—. Echols scholar U. Va., 1974; recipient Tex. Leadership award Tex. Found., 1984. Mem. Assn. Trial Lawyers Am., Dallas Bar Assn., Tex. Lawyers Assn., ABA, Dallas Assn. Trial Lawyers, Dallas Assn. Young Lawyers, Nat. Assn. Female Execs., Dallas Area Women's Polit. Caucus, Am. Corp. Counsel Assn., Dallas Women of '85, Phi Beta Kappa, Phi Delta Phi. Republican. Roman Catholic. Clubs: U. Va. Alumni (Dallas); County Arts (Plano and Dallas); Las Colinas Sports. Home: 615 Waterview Dr Arlington TX 76016 Office: Alcon Labs Inc 6201 S Freeway Fort Worth TX 76116

WHITCOMB, RAE JEAN, hospital and laboratory supplies company executive; b. Sturgis, Mich., Mar. 21, 1940; d. Ralph Wilford and Velma Jeanette (Guernsey) Whitcomb; student Purdue U., 1958-60; M.T., Pontiac Gen. Hosp., 1961; student Robert Morris Coll., 1974-78, Marywood Coll., 1978. Teaching supr. Parkview Meml. Hosp., Ft. Wayne, Ind., 1961-68; sales rep. Gen. Diagnostics, Morris Plains, N.J., 1968-70; chief med. technologist Citizens Gen. Hosp., New Kensington, Pa., 1970-74, Sewickley (Pa.) Valley Hosp., 1974-79; sales rep Fisher Sci. Co., Pitts., 1979-81, eastern regional sales mgr., 1981-83, biomed. mktg. mgr., 1983—. Mem. Am. Soc. Clin. Pathologists, Am. Soc. Med. Tech., Pa. Soc. Med. Tech. Office: 711 Forbes Ave Pittsburgh PA 15219

WHITE, ANNE UNDERWOOD, geographer, consultant, researcher; b. Washington, Sept. 22, 1919; d. Norman and Anne Francis (Bayard) Underwood; m. Gilbert Fowler White, Apr. 28, 1944; children—William D., Mary B., Frances A. B.A., Vassar Coll., 1941. Jr. sociology sci. analyst U.S. Dept. Agr., Washington, 1942; econ. analyst, field examiner Nat. Labor Relations Bd., Washington, 1943-44; research asst. Gilbert F. White, Chgo., East Africa, 1966-72; editor Natural Hazards Research and Info. Ctr., Boulder, Colo., 1976-78; mem. profl. staff Inst. Behavioral Sci. U. Colo., Boulder, 1979—; cons. World Bank, Washington, 1980, U.S. AID, Nairobi, Kenya, 1982. Author: (with Gilbert F. White and David J. Bradley) Drawers of Water: Domestic Water Use in East Africa, 1972. Contbr. chpts. to books, articles to profl. jours. Mem., Boulder County Parks and Open Space Adv. Com., 1976-82, chmn., 1977; mem. Sunshine Fire Protection Dist. Bd., Boulder County, 1981-85; chairperson Boulder County Task Force on Services for Elderly, 1984; active mem. Women's Forum of Colo., Denver, 1976—, Women's Democratic Club, Boulder, Plan Boulder County. Mem. Assn. Am. Geographers, Soc. Women Geographers, Colo. Water Congress, Acad. Ind. Scholars. Home: 624 Pearl St 302 Boulder CO 80302 Office: Inst Behavioral Sci Box 482 U Colo Boulder CO 80309

WHITE, BERNICE ELIZABETH SMITH, govt. ofcl.; b. Balt., Feb. 27, 1924; d. Oscar and Georgia E. (Bell) Smith; B.S. in Edn., Coppin State Coll., 1945; postgrad. Johns Hopkins U., U. Md., George Washington U., Morgan State U.; m. George Alfred White, July 8, 1945; children—Myra Lorraine, Marlene Lenora White Baskerville. Tchr., Balt. City pub. schs., 1952-64; dir. community edn. div. Balt. City Community Relations Commn., 1964-67; ins. compliance specialist Social Security Adminstrn., Balt., 1967-69, dir. fed. women's program, 1969-72, community relations officer, 1972-78, chief hdqrs. coordination and liaison staff, office of govtl. affairs, 1978—. Bd. dirs. Health and Welfare Council Central Md., 1972-79, Med. Eye Bank of Md., 1973-79, Lexington Market Assn., 1980—, Balt. chpt. Young Audiences Inc., 1981—; past pres. United Presbyn. Women, Trinity Presbyn. Ch.; chmn. pres.'s com. Morgan State U. Choir. Recipient Public Service award Philomathians, 1973; Profl. award of Yr., Nat. Assn. Negro Bus. and Profl. Women, 1973; Disting. Woman award Delta Sigma Theta, 1974; Pres.'s award for disting. service Pres. Balt. City Council, 1981, others. Mem. Federally Employed Women (founder, 1st pres. Greater Balt. chpt.), Nat. Council Negro Women, NAACP, Balt. Urban League, Woman Power Inc. (Cert. of Merit 1973, 74), Les Grandes Dames (founder, pres. 1976—), Herbert M. Frisby Hist. Soc. (pres. 1974-78), Zeta Phi Beta (chmn. polit. action com. Atlantic region 1979-80, Woman of Yr. 1971, Meritorious Service award 1981). Democrat. Office: Social Security Adminstrn Room 4-H-5 West Highrise 6401 Security Blvd Baltimore MD 21235

WHITE, BEVERLY JEAN, state legislator; b. Salt Lake City, Sept. 28, 1928; d. Gustave R. and Helene (Sterzer) Larson; m. M. Floyd White, Apr. 8, 1947; children—Susan White Morris, Douglas Floyd, Robyn White Bauder, David Scott, Wendy Jo White McCleery. Mem. Utah Ho. of Reps., 1971—. Sec. Utah Dem. Party; Sunday Sch. tchr. Ch. of Jesus Christ of Latter Day Saints. Recipient Legislator of Year award Utah Social Workers, 1982, Woman of Year award Beta Sigma Phi, 1982. Mem. Nat. Order Women Legislators (past treas.), Utah Orgn. Women Legislators (treas.), Tooele Dem. Women's Orgn., Bus. and Profl. Women's Club. Club: Tooele Womans (past pres.).

WHITE, CAROL CUTTER, counselor, university administrator; b. Milw., Sept. 7, 1943; d. C. Theodore and Sara B. (Bullwinkel) Cutter; B.S., U. Wis.-Milw., 1966; M.A., U. Denver, 1969; postgrad. MacMurray Coll., 1971, Sangamon State U., 1972, Western Ky. U., 1979-82; m. Barton C. White, July 24, 1971. Personnel asst. First Wis. Nat. Bank, Milw., 1966-67, market researcher, summer 1968; head resident U. Denver, 1967-69; student activities coordinator U. Wis.-Milw., 1969-71; exec. dir. Morgan County Big Bros./Big Sisters Assn., Jacksonville, Ill., 1972-76; social services coordinator/dir. Vista project, Morgan County Housing Authority, 1976-79; asst. dir. Office Coop. Edn., Western Ky. U., Bowling Green, 1979—. Chair, Human Relations Commn., Jacksonville, 1978-79; chair Bowling Green Human Rights Commn., 1981—; pres. First Presbyn. Daycare Bd., 1977-78; deacon, 1977-79; vice chmn. Jacksonville-MacMurray Music Assn., 1977-78; publicity chmn. Jacksonville Conf. Chs., 1976-77. Recipient Outstanding Service award Big Bros./Big Sisters Assn., 1976; Presdl. award Jacksonville Jaycees, 1976; Service award Presbyn. Daycare Center, 1979. Mem. Coop. Edn. Assn. Ky. (dir., editor 1981—, Outstanding Mem. award 1983, v.p., pres. 1986-87), Midwest Coop. Edn. Assn. (state rep. 1986-87), Social and Community Services Congress Ill., Women's Alliance Western Ky. U., Alpha Sigma Alpha, Kappa Delta Pi. Presbyterian. Club: Little Sigma Soc. of Sigma Chi. Contbr. articles to profl. jours. Home: 2700 Thompson Dr Bowling Green KY 42101 Office: Office Coop Edn Western Ky Univ Bowling Green KY 42101

WHITE, CAROL JEAN MARSICANE, occupational therapist; b. Amsterdam, N.Y., Mar. 17, 1950; d. Albert Ralph and Virginia (Morrell) Marsicane; m. Ronald White, Aug. 18, 1973 (div. June 1979); children—Andrea Lynn, Leslie Ann. B.S., Utica Coll., Syracuse U., 1972. Therapy aide Marcy Psychiat. Clinic, N.Y., 1970-72, occupational therapist, 1972-74; occupational therapist Utica Psychiat. Clinic, N.Y., 1974; sr. occupational therapist Rome Devel. Ctr., N.Y., 1974-81; discipline coordinator Oswald D. Heck Devel. Ctr., Schenectady, 1981—; cons. Mohawk Valley Hosp., Ilion, N.Y., 1975-76, Folts Nursing Home, Herkimer, N.Y., 1977-81, Betsy Ross Health Care Facility, Rome, 1980-81, Mt. Loretto Nursing Home, Amsterdam, 1983-85, Bassett Hosp. Psychiat. Ctr., Cooperstown, N.Y., 1985—, St. Mary's Hosp. Psychiat. Ctr., Amsterdam, 1985—. Exec. bd. Amsterdam Day Care Ctr., 1983—; religion edn. instr. Our Lady Mt. Carmel Roman Catholic Ch., Amsterdam, 1984-86; pres. Barkley Elem. Sch. PTA, Amsterdam, 1985-86; adv. bd. Cert. Occupational Therapy Asst. program Maria Coll., Albany, 1985-86. Mem. Am. Occupational Therapy Assn., N.Y. State Occupational Therapy Assn., Capitol Dist. Occupational Therapy Assn. (scholarship chmn., exec. bd., developmental disabilities and geriatric liaison 1984—, pres.-elect 1986—), Sons of Italy, St. Sophia Soc. Avocations: traveling; crafts. Home: 18 Essex St Amsterdam NY 12010 Office: Oswald D Heck Devel Ctr Balltown and Consaul Rds Schenectady NY 12304

WHITE, CHERYL JEAN, disc jockey, radio executive; b. St. Louis, Jan. 1, 1956; d. Billy Lorene and Helene Elizabeth (Borman) White; student Ind. State U., Evansville, 1973-74. Producer daily program Woman's World, Sta. WROZ, Evansville, 1974-80, writer, producer weekly show Seeds and Stems, 1977-80, public service dir., 1977-80, disc jockey, 1973—; ops. mgr. Sta. WROZ-FM, 1985—. Vol., Easter Seal Telathon, 1978-81, Career Day Conf., Evansville Human Relations Commn., 1976-77; mem. PBS Spl. Talent Corps, 1981—; troop leader Girl Scouts U.S.A., 1979-80. Recipient cert. of merit Evansville Deaf Social Services Agy., 1980. Home: 1201 SE 1st St Evansville IN 47713 Office: PO Box 139 Evansville IN 47701

WHITE, CHRISTINA ANN, former state arts administrator; consultant; b. Providence, May 19, 1952; d. Edwin Frederick White and Julia Hope (Boutin) White Sjostrom; m. James Scott McNeil, May 3, 1980. B.S. in Art Edn., R.I. Coll., 1974; postgrad. in bus. adminstrn. U. R.I., 1982—. Cert. tchr., R.I. Owner, operator Jazzbo's, South Kingstown, R.I., 1974-77; grants officer, community coordinator R.I. Council on Arts, Providence, 1977-80, exec. dir., 1982-84; exec. dir. Providence Inner City Arts, 1980-82; bd. dirs. New Eng. Found. for Arts, Cambridge, Mass., 1982-84; cons. mktg. Alton Jones campus U. R.I., West Kingston, 1984. Bd. dirs. R.I. Feminist Theater, Providence, 1981-82, Autumnfest Steering com., Woonsocket, R.I., 1983-84, R.I. Arts Advs., Providence, 1984; adv. com. New Year's Portland, 1985. Recipient Design award R.I. Coll., 1974. Home: 24 Richardson St Portland ME 04103

WHITE, CLEATE MORRIS, muralist, designer, interior decorator; b. Yadkin, N.C., May 9, 1915; d. Robert H. and Elizabeth Jane (Shore) Plowman; m. Luther Coe, Dec. 23, 1933 (div. 1959); children—Gary Von, Janice Deone Sprinkle, Robert Lee; m. William White, Feb. 2, 1977. Student Fed. Art Sch., 1925-27. Creator of hand painted photographs, 1923—; executed murals from Fla. to Calif., 1959—, 3D 14K Gold murals for Ilalina Am. Club, 1982, ABC, N.Y.C., 1984; painted and designed sets for theatres, Palm Springs, Calif., 1962-70; interior decorator for Clarence Miller, Winston Salem, N.C., 1971-76; designed furniture, 14 K gold mural paintings, framed work in home open to public. Mem. Mil. Ladies Aux. Baptist. Avocations: writing songs; singing; dancing. Home: 4205 21st Way E New Port Richey FL 33552

WHITE, DIANNE CATHERINE, analyst, small business computer consultant; b. Bklyn., July 27, 1932; d. Tollis Alfred and Catherine (Guiliano) W. A.A.S. in Data Processing, Monroe Community Coll., 1980; B.S. in Bus. Mgmt., St. John Fisher, 1985. Programmer Greece Central Sch., 1979-81; computer cons., 1981-84; sr. analyst U. Rochester, 1984—. Mem. Rochester Friendship Council, Rochester, 1983—, Assocs. Teenage Diplomats, Rochester, 1983—. Mem. Assn. Computer Machinery (chmn. 1984—), Alpha Sigma Lambda. Avocations: reading; camping. Home: 14-10 Black Watch Trail Rochester NY 14450 Office: Univ Rochester 601 Elmwood Ave Rochester NY 14642

WHITE, DORA ELIZABETH, realtor, broker, owner; b. Chgo., Sept. 6, 1942; d. Wiley Henry and Lillie (Hatcher) Samuels; m. Norman White, Aug. 20, 1960 (div. 1981); children—Pamela Y., Brian L. Cert. in real esate Central YMCA Coll., 1964; Assoc. degree in Real Estate, Triton Coll., 1977; Course I Cert., Realtors Inst. Ill., 1981. Clk. typist Harris Trust & Savs. Bank, Chgo., 1960-67; broker, salesman Penny's Real Estate, Maywood, Ill., 1967-71; closing loan officer Kaufman & Broad Homes, Hinsdale, Ill., 1972-73; ind. real estate broker Chgo. and suburban Ill., 1973-78; owner, broker Century 21/All Am. Realty, Oak Park, Ill., 1979—. Bd. dirs. Am. Tennis Found. Mem. Nat. Assn. Market Developers (chpt. pres. 1983—), Nat. Assn. Realtors, Ill. Assn. Realtors, Oak Park Bd. Realtors, Century 21/Investment Soc. Mem. Church of Christ. Clubs: Century 21, Chgo. Prairie Tennis. Office: Century 21/All Am Realty 56 Chicago Ave Oak Park IL 60302

WHITE, DORIS ANNE, artist; b. Eau Claire, Wis., July 27, 1924; d. Ira and Mary (Dietz) White. B.F.A., Art Inst. Chgo.; student U. Berne (Switzerland). Group shows include: Met. Mus., N.Y.C., Pa. Acad. Fine Arts, Phila., Cleve. Inst. Art, Knickerbocker Artists, N.Y.C., Audubon Artists, N.Y.C., Nat. Acad. Design, N.Y.C., Washington Watercolor Assn., Walker Art Ctr., Mpls., Bergstrom Art Ctr., Neenah, Wis., Am. Watercolor Soc., N.Y.C., Art Inst. Chgo., Calif. Watercolor Soc., Allied Artists Am., N.Y.C., Butler Inst. Am. Art, Youngstown, Ohio, Smithsonian Inst., Washington, Art Alliance, Phila., Institute de Arte de Mexico, others; pvt. and corporate collections. Recipient Ranger Fund Purchase award Nat. Acad. Design, N.Y.C.; Medal of Honor, First award Knickerbocker Artists, N.Y.C.; Assoc. Mems. award Allied Artists Am. N.Y.C.; Purchase awards Walker Art Ctr. Biennial, Mpls., Butler Inst. Am. Art, Youngstown, Ohio; M. L. Jarrott Art Scholarship, Nat. League Am. Pen Women, Washington; First Purchase award Union League Club Chgo.; Grumbacher award Am. Watercolor Soc., Grand award, Paul Remmy award; Obrig award Nat. Acad. Design; Gimbel award Milw. Art Ctr. Mem. Nat. Acad. Design, Am. Watercolor Soc. (Gold medal of honor 1964). Methodist. Home: 2750 Church Rd Jackson WI 53037

WHITE, DOROTHY T., nursing educator; b. N.Y.C., Dec. 11, 1923; d. Joseph V. and Pearle E. (Salter) Raymond; diploma in nursing L.I. Coll. Hosp. Sch. Nursing, Bklyn.; B.S., M.A., Ed.D., Columbia U.; diploma, Inst. Ednl. Mgmt., Harvard U., 1982; m. G.M. White, Jan. 5, 1952. Prof. nursing Med. Coll. Ga., Augusta, 1971-77, dean Sch. Nursing, 1971-76; prof. Nova U., Ft. Lauderdale, Fla., 1977-78, dir. the Louise Mellen Inst. Nursing, 1977-78; prof. Calif. State U., Sacramento, 1978-79, chmn. div. nursing, 1978-79; prof. Hunter Coll.-City U. N.Y., Hunter-Bellevue Sch. Nursing, N.Y.C., 1979—, dean, 1979-82; cons. Office of Chancellor, City U. N.Y.; dir. Augusta Radiation Center, 1973-76; govtl. appointee Master Planning Com. for Nursing in Ga., 1971-75. Bd. dirs. Nurses House, Nurse Ednl. Fund; trustee Mt. St. Mary Coll., 1960-61, asso. trustee, 1961-65. Recipient citation Office of Sec. State of Ga., 1977; Cert. of Appreciation, U.S. Army Health Services Command, 1977. Mem. Group for Advancement in Nursing (founder), Am. Acad. Polit. and Social Scis., AAUW, Am. Assn. Women in Higher Edn., Am. Assn. Female Execs., Am. Assn. Higher Edn., AAUP, Am. Assn. Univ. Adminstrs., Nat. Assn. Women Deans, Adminstrs. and Counselors, N.Y. Acad. Scis. Author papers in field. Office: 440 E 26th St New York NY 10010

WHITE, ELIZABETH NORRIS, librarian; b. Buffalo, Tex., Sept. 11, 1931; d. Courtney R. and Gladys (Carder) Norris; m. Darwin Gayle White, Mar. 12, 1953; children—Debra, Lisa, Mark. B.A., La. Tech. U., 1952; L.M.S., Peabody/Vanderbilt U., 1968; Ed. Spec., Ga. State U., 1982. Tchr.'s cert., Ga. English tchr. Tioga High Sch., La., 1962-65; librarian Cohn High Sch.,

Nashville, Tenn., 1965-68, Berry Coll., Mt. Berry, Ga., 1968-69, Model High Sch., Rome, Ga., 1969—. Bd. dirs. Rome Little Theater, 1979. Mem. Ga. Assn. Educators, Floyd County Assn. Educators, NEA, Am. Library Assn., Beta Phi Mu, Kappa Delta Pi. Democrat. Baptist. Club: Berry Woman's (pres. 1970). Home: PO Box 426 Berry Coll Mount Berry GA 30149 Office: Model High Sch 3252 Calhoun Hwy Rome GA 30149

WHITE, ELLEN ELIZABETH, college administrator; b. Moultrie, Ga., Dec. 31, 1943; d. Burl and Hattie (Miller) Everett; m. Robert L. White, July 31, 1966; children—Crystal, Alison, Carmen. B.A., Paine Coll., Augusta, Ga., 1965; M.S., Xavier U., Cin., 1971; Ph.D., Fla. State U., 1985. Math. statistician, EPA, Cin., 1967-72; asst. institutional researcher Albany State Coll., Ga., 1973-78, dir. institutional advancement, 1981—. Bd. dirs. Girls Club/Boys Club, Albany, 1985—. Vols. in Albany, 1981—; mem. adv. bd. Sr. Citizens program, Albany, 1985—. Mem. Am. Ednl. Research Assn., Nat. Council on Measurement in Edn., Soc. Coll. and Univ. Planning. Methodist. Avocation: camping. Office: Albany State Coll 504 College Dr Albany GA 31707

WHITE, ETHYLE HERMAN (MRS. S. ROY WHITE), artist; b. San Antonio, Apr. 10, 1904; d. Ferdinand and Minnie (Simmang) Herman; ed. pvt. schs., instrs.; m. S. Roy White, Mar. 3, 1924 (dec.); children—De Lois Eileen (Mrs. William Marion Mohrle), Patsyruth (Mrs. Henry Wheeler). Exhibited numerous one-man, group shows, Tex.; represented pub. collections in U.S., pvt. collections in Switzerland, Germany, Sweden. Del. Internat. Com. Centro Studi E. Scambi Internationali. Mem. Anahuac Fine Arts Group, San Antonio, Beaumont, Galveston, Houston art leagues, Daus. Republic Tex., UDC, Pastel Soc. Tex., Watercolor Soc., Nat. League Am. Pen Women. Episcopalian. Mem. Order Eastern Star. Clubs: Fine Arts (Anahuac); Artist and Craftsmen (Dallas). Author, illustrator: Arabella. Author: Poet's Hour. Home: PO Box 176 Anahuac TX 77514

WHITE, FRANCINE BUSCEMI, lawyer; b. Chgo., Feb. 27, 1956; d. Salvatore and Johanna (Lietzow) Buscemi; m. William White. B.A. in Polit. Sci., Loyola U., Chgo., 1978; J.D., John Marshall Law Sch., 1982. Bar: Ill. 82. Law clk. to fed. magistrate U.S. Dist. Ct. (we. dist.) Ill., Rockford, 1982-83; sole practice, Rockford, 1982-82; asst. juvenile pub. defender Winnebago County, Rockford, 1983-84; assoc. Lawrence J. Ferolie & Assocs. Ltd., 1984—. Mem. allocations com. United Way, 1985. Mem. Am. Trial Lawyers Assn., Ill. Trial Lawyers Assn., Winnebago County Bar Assn. (young lawyers div. sec. 1984-85).

WHITE, GAIL (BROCKETT), poet, editor; b. Pensacola, Fla., Apr. 1, 1945; d. Robert and Jeanne Rosamund (Nelson) Brockett; m. Arthur Wilson White, Mar. 29, 1967. B.A. cum laude, Stetson U., 1967. Author chapbooks: Pandora's Box, 1976, Irreverent Parables, 1978, Fishing for Leviathan, 1982 (winner Wings Press competition 1982); Poetry editor Caraytid Mag., 1968-71, Piedmont Lit. Rev., 1983—. Recipient several prizes for poetry. Avocations: reading; travel; cats. Home and Office: 724 Bartholomew St New Orleans LA 70117

WHITE, GERMAINE, broadcasting executive; b. Dallas, Jan. 8, 1959; d. Julius Cornelius and Gloria (Smith) White. B.F.A., So. Meth. U., 1980. Cert. tchr., Tex. Resident advisor So. Meth. U., Dallas, 1979-80; student tchr. Dallas Ind. Sch. Dist., Dallas, 1980; sub. tchr. Richardson Ind. Sch. Dist., (Tex.), 1981; contract adminstrs. AFTRA/Screen Actors Guild, Dallas, 1981-84; account exec. WBAP Radio, Dallas, 1984—; mem. adv. bd. Two Byrds Pub. Co. Vice pres. edn. task force Dallas Urban League, 1983-84. Mem. Assn. Black Communicators (sec. 1983-84, exec. bd.), Music Ednl. Nat. Conf., Assn. Broadcast Execs. Tex., Sociology Club So. Meth. U., Mu Phi Epsilon, Delta Sigma Theta. Office: WBAP Radio 2730 Stemmons Freeway Suite 1108 Dallas TX 75207

WHITE, GLORIA WATERS, university administrator; b. St. Louis County, Mo., May 16, 1934; d. James Thomas and Thelma Celestine (Brown) W.; B.A., Harris-Stowe Tchrs. Coll., 1956; M.A., Washington U., St. Louis, 1963, M. Juridical Studies, 1980; m. W. Glenn White, Jan. 1, 1955; 1 dau., Terry Anita. Tchr., St. Louis Bd. Edn., 1956-63, psychol. counselor, 1963-67; dir. office spl. projects Washington U., 1967-76, asst. to asso. vice chancellor personnel and affirmative action, 1975—. Bd. dirs. Am. Assn. Affirmative Action, 1974-77; instl. chair Arts and Edn. Fund, 1975-84; mem. Eastern Dist. Mo. Desegregation and Adv. Com., 1981-82. Accredited exec. in personnel; cert. life counselor, life tchr; recipient citations Urban League, Pres.'s Council Youth Opportunities. Mem. Coll. and Univ. Personnel Assn. (v.p.; Creativity award 1981, Disting. Service award 1983), Am. Soc. Personnel Adminstrn., St. Louis Symphony Soc., Delta Sigma Theta. Roman Catholic. Home: 545 Del Price Ct Saint Louis MO 63124 Office: Box 1184 Saint Louis MO 63130

WHITE, INGRID ELISABETH, marketing consultant; b. Denison, Tex., Jan. 5, 1953; d. Dugan Dale and Eleonore Sophia (Leva) Whiting; m. Ronald White, May 12, 1973 (div. 1982). Assoc. B.B.A., Grayson Jr. Coll., 1973; B.B.A., U. Tex.-Arlington, 1974. Distbn. coordinator Anderson Clayton Foods, Dallas, 1974-76; prodn. supr. Container Corp. Am., Ft. Worth, 1976-78; owner, mgr. Exec. Careers Recruiting, Arlington, Tex., 1979-82; mktg. automation cons. Blue Cross, Blue Shield, Dallas, 1983—; ptnr. Commonwealth Enterprises Real Estate, 1983—. Mem. Sales and Mktg. Execs. Dallas, Tex. Personnel Assn. Republican. Lutheran.

WHITE, IRMA REED, writer, librarian; b. Nebraska City, Nebr., Mar. 4, 1897; d. Eustace Glen and Martha (Soper) Reed; B.A., U. Colo., 1919; M.A., Radcliffe Coll., 1926; m. Wilford L. White, June 12, 1922. Instr. English, U. Colo., 1922-24; instr. report writing Grad. Sch. Bus. Adminstrn. Harvard U., 1925-28; asst. head field sect. Office Price Adminstrn., editor, Washington, 1943-47; public info. specialist Bur. Census, 1958-69; writer Office Sec. Commerce, 1969-71, editor series Do You Know Your Economic ABCs, 1962-70; dir. press room Cost of Living Council, Washington, 1971-74; librarian firm Mayer, Brown & Platt, Washington, 1975—. Recipient Outstanding Achievement award Office Price Adminstrn., 1945; Silver medal Dept. Commerce, 1964, Creative Communication award, 1965; Excellence in Communications award Fed. Editors Assn., 1965, 66, 70; Oustanding Service award Cost of Living Council, 1972, 73; Public Service award SBA, 1978, Internat. Council Small Bus., 1978. Mem. Nat. Press Club, Nat. League Am. Pen Women (Nat. Achievement award 1966), Am. Newspaper Womens Club, PEO, Chi Omega. Contbr. articles to Ency. Brit., London Times, Christian Sci. Monitor, others. Office: Mayer Brown & Platt 2000 Pennsylvania Ave NW Washington DC 20006

WHITE, JEAN TILLINGHAST, state senator; b. Cambridge, Mass., Dec. 24, 1934; d. James Churchill Houlton and Clara Jean (Carter) Tillinghast; m. Robert D. Price, May 18, 1957 (div.); m. Peregrine White, June 6, 1970. B.A., Wellesley Coll., 1956. Supr., programmer Lumber Mut. Ins. Co., Cambridge, 1964-70; selectman, chmn. Town of Rindge (N.H.), 1975-80; clk. regulated revenues N.H. Ho. of Reps., Concord, 1978-80, vice chmn. regulated revenues, 1980-82; mem. N.H. Senate, 1982—, chmn. fin. com., v.p., treas. Perry White, Inc., Rindge, N.H., 1970—; dir. Peterborough Savings Bank (N.H.). Chmn., Rindge Friends of Library, 1972. Republican. Unitarian. Office: NH Senate Room 120 Concord NH 03301*

WHITE, JERUSHA LYNN, lawyer; b. Kansas City, Mo., Nov. 30, 1950; d. Riley Vaughn and Edith Blynn (Ringen) White; m. Larry D. Hancock, Jan. 5, 1969 (div. 1973); m. 2d Stephen Perry Wasson, Nov. 30, 1978 (div. 1985). A.S., Mo. State Fair Community Coll., 1974; B.S., Central Mo. State U., 1978; J.D., U. Mo.-Kansas City, 1981. Bar: Mo. 1981. With Montgomery Ward & Co., Sedalia, Mo., 1968-69, Parkhurst Mfg. Co., Sedalia, 1969-71, United Farm Agy., Sedalia, 1972-73, Montgomery Ward & Co., 1973-74, Howard Truck & Equipment Co., Sedalia, 1974-75, McGraw-Edison Co., Sedalia, 1975-76, Rival Mfg. Co., Sedalia, 1977-78; buyer Hotel Equipment Co., Century City, Calif., 1978; law clk. Legal Aid of Western Mo., Kansas City, 1979-80, Horowitz & Shurin, P.C., Kansas City, 1980-81; assoc. firm Steve Borel/Steve Streen, Kansas City, 1982-83; sole practice law, Sedalia, Mo., 1983-85; ptnr. Cope, Schuber & White, 1985—; dir. Home Equity Consultants, Inc., Sedalia, Queen City Mortgage Co., Sedalia. Mem. ABA, Mo. Bar Assn., Kansas City Bar Assn., Pettis County Bar Assn. Democrat. Presbyterian. Clubs: American Business Women's Assn., Bus. and Profl. Women's Orgn. Home: 907 S Prospect St Sedalia MO 65301 Office: 316 S Ohio Ave Sedalia MO 65301

WHITE, JOYCE L., medical technologist; b. Darlington, Wis., Sept. 2, 1938; d. William E. and Martha E. (Smith) Calverley; B.S., U. Wis., La Crosse, 1967; M.A., Central Mich. U., Mt. Pleasant, 1979; m. Raymond C. White, Jan. 30, 1960; children—Lorelei, Pamela, Lyall. Staff med. technologist Methodist Hosp., Peoria, Ill., 1960, St. Francis Med. Center, La Crosse, 1960-61; staff technologist, then head technologist LaCrosse Clinic, 1964-79; dir. lab. services Skemp-Grandview La Crosse Clinic, 1979—. Chmn. Pops Nite, Gt. River Festival Arts, 1974-82; coordinator Medieval World Banquet, 1979-81; chmn. German dinner Oktoberfest USA, 1977-81. Recipient various service and appreciation awards. Mem. Am. Soc. Med. Tech. (del. 1981-85), Am. Assn. Clin. Chemists, AAUW, Wis. Assn. Med. Tech. (dir. 1978-82, chmn. govt. liason com. 1980-82, pres. 1984-85; mem. of yr. 1986). Jehovah's Witness. Club: Jackson Hole (Wyo.) Racquet. Home: 1017 S 7th St La Crosse WI 54601 Office: 212 S 11th St LaCrosse WI 54601

WHITE, JUANITA GREER, university regent, legislator, educator; b. Atlanta, Nov. 19, 1905; d. Harry Goldsmith and Cleio E. (Greer) Greer; A.B., Agnes Scott Coll., 1926; Ph.D., Johns Hopkins U., 1929; m. Thomas Sherman White, June 6, 1935; 1 dau., Sally M. Prof. biology and chemistry, chmn. dept. sci. Mary Baldwin Coll., 1930-35; instr. anatomy and physiology Bennett Jr. Coll., 1935-38; research chemist Bell Labs., Murray Hill, N.J., 1943, De Luxe Labs., 20th Century-Fox Film Corp., N.Y.C., 43-46; instr. chemistry Hunter Coll. Sch. Gen. Studies, N.Y.C., 1943-44, 49-51; asso. prof. sci. Willimantic (Conn.) State Tchrs. Coll., 1951-52. Mem. Nev. Assembly, 1970-72; mem. exec. bd. ARC, Dutchess County, N.Y., 1940-44, Millbrook (N.Y.) Vis. Nurse Com., 1938-44, 46-50; mem. Nev. Gov.'s Com. on Aging, 1959-66; del. White House Conf. on Aging, 1961; mem. Nev. Gov.'s Com. on Med. Edn., 1963-64; edn. chmn. Nev. Gov.'s Commn. on Status of Women, 1963-66; dir. Nev. Tb and Respiratory Health Assn., 1963-73, pres., 1972-73; Nev. commr. Western Interstate Commn. Higher Edn., 1965-74, mem. exec. com., 1965-74; adv. com. Nat. Def. for Lang. Centers U.S. Office Edn., 1966-67; adv. com. S.W. Regional Lab. Edn. Research, 1967-74, Nev. Higher Edn. Commn., 1963-69, Nev. Edn. Commn., 1965, Clark County Health Planning Council, 1972-76; mem. governing body Clark County Health Services Agy., 1976-79, chmn. plan devel. com., 1977-79; mem. Nev. adv. com. Rural Devel. Program, 1973-74; regent U. Nev., 1963-71, adv. com. Coll. Med. Scis., 1975-83, hon. mem., 1983—; trustee Nevada So. Univ. Land Found., 1966-79. Recipient Disting. Nevadan award U. Nev., 1972; Outstanding Alumna award Agnes Scott Coll., 1980; Juanita White Hall U. Nev. at Las Vegas named in her honor, 1976. Mem. AAUW (dir. Nev. state div. 1957-67, state pres. 1963-65, nat. com. on social and econ. issues 1961-63, mem. internat. fellowships award com. 1964-73, chmn. internat. awards com. 1967-73, mem. edn. found. 1967-71), Phi Beta Kappa, Sigma Xi, Beta Sigma Phi (hon.). Republican. Episcopalian. Home: 639 Ave I Boulder City NV 89005

WHITE, JUDITH LOUISE, child services administrator, consultant; b. Lodi, Ohio, Feb. 27, 1939; d. Henry and Charlotte Virginia (Spahr) Schmelzer; m. Downer Dale White, Sept. 4, 1959; children—Mark, Kelly, Kristy, David. Child Devel. Assoc., Nat. Child Devel. Assoc. Consortium, Washington, 1979; A.A., Northland Pioneer Coll., Holbrook, Ariz., 1980; postgrad. No. Ariz. U., 1984—, Ariz. State U., 1985—. Tchr. head start, White Mountain Apache Head Start, Whiteriver, Ariz., 1976-80, child services coordinator, 1980—; cons. Nat. Indian Head Starts, 1980—; trainer Indian Child & Family Conf., Phoenix and Albuquerque, 1982-86; trainer Fetal Alcohol Syndrome-Indian Health Services, Whiteriver, 1984—; cons. Whiteriver Pub. Schs., 1984—; assoc. tchr. Northland Pioneer Jr. Coll., Holbrook, Ariz., 1985—. Mem. Coalition for Chronically Ill Children, Phoenix, 1985—. Mem. Council Exceptional Children, Nat. Assn. for Edn. Young Children, White Mt. Assn. for Edn. Young Children. Avocations: music; reading; free time; grandchildren. Home: Box 707 Whiteriver AZ 85941 Office: White Mountain Apache Head Start Box 738 Whiteriver AZ 85941

WHITE, JUDY A., journalist; b. Vallejo, Calif., Sept. 2, 1955; d. Andrew Beaton and Marion Lillieven (Hall) W. Student Heald Bus. Coll., 1973, Calif. Poly. State U.-San Luis Obispo, 1976-79. Free lance journalist Marysville, Calif., 1979-83; exec. sec. Fremont Med. Ctr., Yuba City, Calif., 1983-84; asst. editor Pacific Coast Jour., Sacramento, 1984; publicity dir. various events and fairs Calif. and Nev., 1979—; free lance journalist, Sacramento, 1984—. Contbr. articles to mags. Project leader 4-H, Marysville, 1985-86; mem. election bd. Yuba County, Marysville, 1985-86. Medal class champion Am. Horse Shows Assn., 1972-73, Internat. Stock Seat, 1972-73; year-end stock horse res. champion No. Calif. Horse Show Assn., 1973; champion stock horse Calif. State Horseman's Assn., Santa Rosa show, 1972. Mem. Sacramento Profl. Women's Network, Sacramento Zool. Soc. (author newsletter 1986—), Sigma Delta Chi and No. Calif. Chpt. Democrat. Roman Catholic. Clubs: Pacific Coast Cutting Horse Assn., Nat. Cutting Horse Assn. Avocations: showing horses; scuba diving; reading. Home: 7911 Orchard Woods Circle Sacramento CA 95828 Office: PO Box 1724 Marysville CA 95901

WHITE, JULIA CARSON, civic worker; b. Chgo., Dec. 9, 1922; d. William Waller and Julia McGowan (Brackett) Carson; m. Walter William White, June 11, 1943; children—Susan G., Florence C., White Little, Lavinia B. B.A. in Sociology, Barnard Coll., 1943. Internal control Julius Garfinckel, Washington, 1954-56; U.S. history tchr. Taipei Am. Sch., Taiwan, 1958-62; sec. cultural interests AAUW, Washington, 1964-69. Com. training, pub. relations Taipei Internat. Women's, Taiwan, 1969-71; edn., transp. Goals for Albuquerque, 1984—; pres. League of Women Voters, Albuquerque, 1979-81; reapportionment League of Women Voters of N.M., 1976—; democratic precinct and ward officer, Bernalillo County, N.M., 1976-79, 81-84; alto sect. N.M. Symphony Orch. Chorus. Mem. N.M. Assn. Univ. Women, AAUW, Am. Guild Organists. Episcopalian. Avocations: gardening, swimming, hiking, raising boxers. Home: 1535 Stanford Dr NE Albuquerque NM 87106

WHITE, KAREN LYNN, financial consultant, stockbroker; b. New Castle, Pa., July 22, 1952; d. Jay Clarence and Donna Rae (Gilvair) White; m. James Steven Cocolin, Oct. 2, 1982; 1 child, Anthony Jay DiMatteo White. B.S. in Econs., Bus., Allegheny Coll., 1981; student Edinboro State Coll., 1976-77; A.S.B., New Castle Bus. Coll., 1976. With Morgan's KFC Restaurant, New Castle, Pa., 1970-73, Arco Fill-N-Glow, Meadville, Pa., 1975-77; self employed pub. acct., artist, Meadville, 1976-82; sec., bookkeeper Sanray, Inc., Meadville, 1974-77; acct. Crawford County Office for Aging, Meadville, 1977-81; fin. cons. Merrill Lynch, Melbourne, Fla., 1982—; investment advisor 20/20 Investments, Melbourne, Fla., 1982-85, Triple P Investors, Palm Bay, Fla., 1982-85, Fortune Hunters, Melbourne, 1984-85, Investors Unltd., 1985. Active 1982 campaign to re-elect Rep. Marilyn-Evans-Jones, Melbourne, 1982. Nat. Bus. and Profl. Women's Found. scholar, 1981. Mem. C. of C. of S. Brevard (membership com. 1984-85), League Women Votrs, AAUW, Nat. Assn. Female Execs., Network of S. Brevard Profl. Women (past treas.). Republican. Baptist. Club: Soroptimist (past newsletter editor, past treas.). Avocations: plastic canvas needlework; painting; crochet. Home: 5040 Walker Ave Melbourne FL 32904 Office: Merrill Lynch 2200 S Front St Melbourne FL 32901

WHITE, KATHLEEN MAE, social worker; b. Lamar, Colo., Feb. 12, 1941; d. Cornelius William and Lillian Mae (Oswald) Hogan; A.A., U. Md., 1969; M.S.W., Our Lady of Lake U., 1976; B.S. cum laude, Tex. A. and I. U., 1972; m. Larry F. White, Mar. 30, 1959; children—Thomas William, Richard Edward, Judy Lynn, Ramona Marie. With Vol. Services, ARC, Wright Patterson AFB, Ohio, 1964-65, Randolph AFB, Tex., 1965-66, Sembach AFB, Ger., 1966-69; tchr. St. Augustines Cath. Sch., Laredo, Tex., 1970-71; social worker Tex. Dept. Public Welfare, San Antonio, 1972-74; tchr. Edgewood Ind. Sch. Dist., San Antonio, 1976-78; coordinator teenage mother's sch. Harlandale Ind. Sch. Dist., San Antonio, 1978-83; pvt. practice mental health social work, 1976—. VA stipend, 1975-76. Mem. Acad. Cert. Social Workers, Am. Assn. Social Workers, Am. Bus. Women's Assn., Our Lady of Lake U. Alumni Assn. Republican. Roman Catholic. Home: 261 Westway University City TX 78148 Office: 102 Genevieve St San Antonio TX 78285

WHITE, KATHY HURST, personnel executive; b. Spur, Tex., Sept. 20, 1944; d. Marion Clinton and Bernice Marie (Justice) Hurst; m. Danney Ray White, Feb. 18, 1968; (div. 1978); children—Andrea Dawn, Amy Michelle. B.A., U. Tex.-Austin, 1967. Civilian personnel, U.S. Army, 1967—, chief classification task force Army Communications Command, Sierra Vista, Ariz., 1978-81, chief position mgmt. and classification Army Health Services Command, San Antonio, 1981-83, chief Balt. field office Civilian Personnel Ctr., 1983—; speaker at symposia and confs. on women's career devel., equal employment programs; mem. blue-ribbon com. Fed. Women's Program, Ft. Meade, Md., 1984. Active Girl Scouts U.S.A., Ariz. and Tex., 1964-67, 79-81; performer ch. choirs, vocal ensembles, 1976—; asst. dir. youth choir Ch. of Castle Hills, San Antonio, 1981-83; vol. Rock Ch. Ministries, Balt., 1983—. Internat. exchange fellow Girl Scouts U.S.A., Greece, 1965; recipient awards Dept. of Army. Mem. Nat. Assn. Female Execs., Classification and Compensation Soc., Internat. Personnel Mgmt. Assn., Womens Clubs Am. (bd. adv. editors, named Outstanding Young Woman of Am. 1967). Club: Singles Alive in the Lord Together (Alexandria, Va.). Avocations: doll collecting. Home: 2842 Aspen Hill Rd Baltimore MD 21234 Office: Dept Field Office Desper Dept Army Suite 1114 31 Hopkins Plaza Baltimore MD 21201

WHITE, LELIA CAYNE, librarian; b. Berkeley, Calif., Feb. 22, 1921; d. James Lloyd and Eulalia Fulton (Douglass) Cayne; B.A., U. Calif., Berkeley, 1943, M.L.S., 1969; children by previous marriage—Douglass Fulton, Cameron Jane. Bibliographer, lectr., asso. U. Calif. at Berkeley Sch. Library and Info. Studies, 1969-72; reference librarian Berkeley-Oakland (Calif.) Service Systems, 1970-76, supervising librarian, 1973-76; dir. Oakland Public Library, 1976—. Bd. dirs. East Bay Negro Hist. Soc., Calif. Spanish Lang. Data Base, Project Asia, Nat. Ednl. Film Festival, Oakland Youth Works; mem. community adv. council Ombudsman, Inc.; mem. community services policy com. League Calif. Cities; mem. adv. com. U. Calif. Berkeley Sch. Library and Info. Studies; mem. adv. com. Mayor's Fgn. Investment program; mem. adv. bd. Internat. Trade Inst. of Vista Coll. Mem. ALA, Calif. Library Assn., Pub. Library Assn., Calif. Inst. Libraries, LWV, Oakland Dalian (China) Friendship City Soc. (pres.). Contbr. to Public Library User Education, 1983. Office: 125 14th St Oakland CA 94612

WHITE, MARCIA ELLEN, lawyer; b. Lockport, N.Y., Sept. 21, 1951; d. Richard Mark and Frances Elizabeth (Woods) W.; m. John Francis Kennedy, Jan. 1, 1982. B.S., Skidmore Coll. 1973; J.D., U. N.Mex., 1976. Bar: Alaska, 1977, N.Mex. 1979, U.S. Supreme Ct., 1982. Atty., Alaska Jud. Council, Anchorage, 1976-78; staff counsel Alaska Supreme Ct., Juneau, 1978-79; dep. atty. gen. State of N.Mex., Santa Fe, 1979-83, asst. atty. gen., 1983—, spl. prosecutor, 1983-86; mem. rules com. Supreme Ct. Appellate, Santa Fe, 1980—. Bd. dirs. El Dorado Community Improvement Assn., Santa Fe, 1983-85. NSF grantee, 1972; Dona Ana Bar Assn. scholar, 1974. Mem. N.Mex. Bar Assn., Alaska Bar Assn., ABA. Democrat. Home: 2 Conchas Loop El Dorado Santa Fe NM 87505 Office: NMex Atty Gen PO Drawer 1508 Santa Fe NM 87504

WHITE, MARGARET DELOIS DENNARD, educator; b. Chattanooga, Feb. 12, 1943; d. Fredc Lee Dennard and Cora E. (Boyd) Sublett; m. Joseph Clyde White, Jr., Sept. 9, 1961; children—Kimberly Elizabeth White Jackson, Joseph Clyde III. B.S., Tenn. State U., 1965; M.Ed., U. Tenn.-Chattanooga, 1973, postgrad., 1985—. Tchr.'s aide Chattanooga Pub. Schs., 1961-62, tchr., 1966—; cardiographic engr.'s aide TVA, Chattanooga, 1965-66. Hostess, United Negro Coll. Fund, 1983. Benwood Found. scholar, 1961. Mem. NEA, Tenn. Edn. Assn., Chattanooga Edn. Assn., NAACP, Chattanooga Urban League, Kappa Delta Phi. Democrat. Baptist. Club: Les Belle Dames Social (Chattanooga). Avocations: antiques; painting; sewing; interior decorating. Home: 4409 James Dr Chattanooga TN 37416 Office: DuPont Elem Sch Hixson Pike Chattanooga TN 37415

WHITE, MARGARET M., insurance agent; b. Ringwood, Hants., Eng., Apr. 3, 1939; came to U.S., 1963; d. John and Mary (Olding) W. Student London Sch. Econs., 1960. C.L.U. English tchr., student, Institut Catholique, Paris, 1962-63; sales mgr. ELHCO Industries, Danville, Calif., 1964-70; agt. Met. Life Ins. Co., Pleasant Hill, Calif., 1971-72, Prudential Ins. Co., San Rafael, Calif., 1972—. Active Big Sisters Am., Contra Costa County, 1982-84. Mem. Nat. Assn. Life Underwriters, Calif. Assn. Life Underwriters (trustee 1985—), Mt. Diablo Assn. Life Underwriters (pres. 1983-84), C.L.U. Soc. (membership chmn. 1982-84). Anglican. Avocations: travel; reading; languages; gourmet cuisine. Home: PO Box 5044 Petaluma CA 94952 Office: Prudential Ins Co 899 Northgate Suite 301 San Rafael CA 94903

WHITE, MARGARET RUTH, biochemist, biophysicist, government official; b. Handley, Tex., May 2, 1921; d. Theron Festus and Katie Irene (Pyeatt) W. A.A., North Tex. State U., 1940; Registered Lab. Technologist, Baylor U., Dallas, 1941; A.B. in Biochemistry, U. Calif.-Berkeley, 1948, postgrad. in biophysics, 1948-53. Lab. technologist St. Pauls Hosp., Dallas, 1941-43; lab. technologist, Lawrence Berkeley Lab., Berkeley, 1946-48, biochemist, biophysicist, 1948—; area mgr. Co2 research program Dept. Energy, 1981—. Contbr. articles to profl. publs. Served to 1st lt. WAC, 1943-46. Recipient numerous grants for cancer research and carcinogens, 1953—. Republican. Mem. Ch. of Christ. Avocations: gardening, hiking, fishing. Home: 36 Senior Ave Berkeley CA 94708 Office: U Calif Lawrence Berkeley Lab MS 29-100 1 Cyclotron Rd Berkeley CA 94720

WHITE, MARGIE PETERSON, retail manager; b. Nags Head, N.C., Nov. 5, 1946; d. John Caro and Alda (Moore) Peterson. B.S. in Edn., East Carolina U., Greenville, 1969. Successively sales clk., asst. mgr., mgr. The Galleon Esplanade, 20-store shopping ctr., 1963—; sec.-treas. The Cabana East, Inc. Bd. dirs. Outer Banks Health Ctr., 1972-78, N.C. Gov.'s Adv. Council for Distributive Edn., 1976-78, Outer Banks Hotline, 1980-84, Dare County Tourist Bur.; mem. N.C. Travel Council; pres. Outer Banks C. of C., 1980. Mem. Nat. Retail Mchts. Assn. (Fred Lazarus award), N.C. Coop. Edn. Assn. (bd. dirs., Employer of Yr. award 1978). Democrat. Club: Outer Banks Women's (v.p. 1972-74). Avocations; travel; music; reading. Home: Box 345 Kill Devil Hills NC 27948

WHITE, MARGITA EKLUND, communications consultant; b. Linköping, Sweden, June 27, 1937; d. Eyvind O. and Ella Maria (Eriksson) Eklund; came to U.S., 1948; B.A. magna cum laude in Govt., U. Redlands, 1959, LL.D. (hon.), 1977; M.A. in Polit. Sci. (Woodrow Wilson fellow), Rutgers U., 1960; m. Stuart Crawford White, June 24, 1961; children—Suzanne Margareta, Stuart Crawford Jr. Asst. to press sec. Richard M. Nixon Presdl. Campaign, Washington, 1960; adminstrv. asst. Whitaker & Baxter Advt. Agy., Honolulu, 1961-62; minority news sec. Hawaii Ho. of Reps., 1963; research asst. to Senator Barry Goldwater and Republican Nat. Com., 1963-64; research asst., writer Free Society Assn., 1965-66; research asst. to syndicated columnist Raymond Moley, 1967; asst. to Herbert G. Klein, White House dir. communications, 1969-73; asst. dir. USIA, 1973-75; asst. press sec. to Pres. Gerald R. Ford, 1975; asst. press sec. to Pres., dir. White House Office of Communications, Washington, 1975-76; commr. FCC, 1976-79; coordinator TV Operators Caucus, Inc.; dir. ITT, Taft Broadcasting Co. Bd. dirs. Rayonier Forest Resources, Golden Jubilee Commn. Telecommunications; U.S. del Internat. Telecommunications Union Plenipotentiary Conf., Nairobi, 1982; mem. Washington Women's Forum. mem. George Foster Peabody Adv. Bd., 1979-86; mem. adv. com. USIA pub. relations. Recipient Disting. Service award U. Redlands Alumni Assn., 1974; Superior Honor award USIA, 1975. Mem. Exec. Women in Govt. (founding mem., sec. 1975). Home: 7238 Evans Mill Rd McLean VA 22101 Office: 1730 M St NW Suite 407 Washington DC 20036

WHITE, MARILYN JANE, government official; b. Morristown, N.J., Dec. 27, 1944; d. Oliver D. and L. Josephine (Winter) Schmidt; B.A., Kans. State U., 1966; M.S., Ind. U., 1972; grad. Armed Forces Staff Coll., 1979, Nat. Def. U., 1981. Field services dir. U.S. Army Recreation Centers, Hdqrs. Dept. Army, Washington, 1972-76; mgmt. analyst Office of Adj. Gen., 1976-77, program analyst, 1977-79, orgnl. effectiveness specialist, Sec. of Army fellow, 1979-80; productivity improvement officer Office of Sec., Dept. Commerce, 1980-81; chief orgnl. effectiveness br. Office of Comptroller, Def. Communications Agy., Washington, 1981—; pres., chmn. bd. Performance Skills, Inc., Arlington, Va., 1981—; cons. career counseling. Mem. Organizational Devel. Network, Federally Employed Women, Inc. (Pentagon I chpt.), Fed. Orgnl. Devel. Network. Author: The Upward Mobility Kit, 1979; Moving Up: A Practical Guide for Women and Men Who Want to Move Up in the Federal Govt., 1981, 2d edit., 1984; Women to Women, 1986. Home: 1204 S Cleveland St Arlington VA 22204

WHITE, MARY ESTERLYN, chemist; b. Selma, Ala.; d. Frank Herman and Sadalure Elizabeth (Moore) W.; B.A., Dillard U., 1960; M.S., Fairleigh Dickinson U., 1971. Analyt. chemist Bristol Myers, Hillside, N.J., 1960-67; research scientist Lever Bros., Edgewater, N.J., 1968-75; asst. mgr. tapes and backings devel. Johnson & Johnson, New Brunswick, N.J., 1975—. Recipient Samuel B. Ullman award, 1956; mem. Dillard U. Dean's List, 1956-60; Philip B. Hofmann Research Scientist award, 1979. Mem. Am. Chem. Soc., N.Y.

Acad. Scis., Soc. Cosmetic Chemists, Sigma Xi, Alpha Kappa Alpha. Democrat. Baptist. Office: 501 George St New Brunswick NJ 08903

WHITE, NANCY, fashion consultant; b. Bklyn., July 25, 1916; d. Thomas J. and Virginia (Gillette) W.; student pvt. schs.; m. Ralph Delahaye Paine, Jr., July 25, 1947 (div. Dec. 1977); m. Clarence J. Dauphinot; children—Gillette Dauphinot Piper, Katharine Delahaye Paine. Fashion editor Pictorial Rev. mag., 1936-40; asst. fashion editor Good Housekeeping mag., 1940-47, fashion editor, 1947-57; asst. editor Harper's Bazaar, N.Y.C., 1957-58, editor-in-chief, 1958-71; fashion dir. Bergdorf Goodman, N.Y.C., 1972-74; dir. Gen. Mills; fashion cons., N.Y.C., 1974—; cons. fashion design Channel 13 Public TV; cons. spl. events Nat. Found. March of Dimes. Former mem. Nat. Council of Arts; mem. women's bd. Lighthouse for the Blind. Decorated knight Order Merit (Italy), Silver medal Merit (Spain); recipient N.Y. Designers award. Mem. Fashion Group (past pres.). Address: 3 E 77 St Apt 5C New York NY 10021

WHITE, NANCY ELIZABETH, psychotherapist, artist; b. San Angelo, Tex., Feb. 8, 1935; d. John William and Vivian Olive (Harrison) Whitten; m. Kirkwood Coulter Myers, Nov. 25, 1954 (dec.); children—Kirkwood Coulter, Nancy Elizabeth; m. 2d, Robert Arthur White, Apr. 25, 1959 (dec. Oct. 1977); children—Mark Hadley, John Bradford. B.F.A., U. Houston, 1976, M.A., 1978; Ph.D. in Clin. Psychology, Union Experimenting Colls. and Univs., Cleve., 1985. Profl. artist, Houston, 1970-77; art therapist Galveston County Hosp., Texas City, Tex., 1976-77; psychotherapist, Houston, 1978—; nat. seminar leader, Houston, 1983—; one-woman shows: Erdon Gallery, Houston, 1971, 72, Houston Bar Ctr., 1971; group shows include: Alfred Lee Gallery, Houston, 1975, Sol Del Rio Gallery, San Antonio, 1976. Recipient Merit award S.W. Watercolor Soc., 1976; 1st prize Jewish Community Ctr., 1976; citation Tex. Fine Arts, 1977; Merit award Watercolor Art Soc. Houston, 1977. Mem. Am. Assn. Marriage and Family Therapy, (clin.), Am. Assn. Sex Educators, Counselors and Therapists, Internat. Acad. Profl. Counseling and Psychotherapy, Am. Art Therapy Assn., Watercolor Art Soc. Houston. Republican. Mem. Unity Ch. Clubs: Profit Seekers Investment (treas. 1965-70), Memorial Forest Garden (pres. 1961-62) (Houston). Home: 9023 Briar Forest Dr Houston TX 77024 Office: 4600 Post Oak Pl Suite 157 Houston TX 77027

WHITE, NANCY RHODES, hotel and restaurant holding company executive, microelectronics company executive; b. Detroit, Jan. 17, 1941; d. Ike Smith and Verda Eudora (Hicks) Rhodes; m. Charles Buel Wetmore, Jr., Apr. 4, 1964 (div. 1976); children—Charles Buel III; m. Edward A. White, Oct. 6, 1979. B.B.A., U. Ariz., 1963; postgrad. SUNY-N.Y.C., 1963-64. Dir. pub. relations St. Joseph's Hosp., Phoenix, 1964-68; communications dir. Ariz. Hosp. Assn., Phoenix, 1970-72; staff asst. U.S. Senator Paul Fannin, Phoenix, 1975-76; communication dir. State Bar Ariz., Phoenix, 1976-83; pres. A.H.I., Inc., Fort Wayne, Ind., 1980—, White Technology, Phoenix, 1980—. Bd. dirs. Phoenix Behavioral Health Found., 1985—; trustee Desert Bot. Gardens, Phoenix, 1984—; bd. dirs. Community Network for Youth, Phoenix, 1983—; mem. Ariz. Republican. Caucus, Phoenix, 1982—. Mem. Young Press. Orgn., Am. Hotel Assn., Chaine Des Rotisseurs, Nat. Soc. Arts and Letters. Episcopalian. Clubs: Charter 100 (bd. dirs. 1981), Soroptimists, Jr. League (Phoenix). Home: 5780 Echo Canyon Circle Phoenix AZ 85018 Office: White Tech Inc 4246 E Wood St Phoenix AZ 85040

WHITE, PAMELA JANICE, lawyer; b. Elizabeth, N.J., July 13, 1952; d. Emmet Talmadge and June (Howlett) W. B.A., Mary Washington Coll., 1974; J.D., Washington and Lee U., 1977. Bar: Md. 1977, D.C. 1978, N.Y. 1983, U.S. Ct. Appeals (4th cir.) 1979, U.S. Ct. Appeals (D.C. cir.) 1981, U.S. Claims Ct., U.S. Supreme Ct. 1981, U.S. Ct. Appeals (2d cir.) 1983. Mgmt. intern adminstrv. br. IRS, Washington, 1974, 75; intern World Bank, Washington, 1973; law clk. Ober, Grimes & Shriver, Balt., 1976; assoc. Ober, Kaler, Grimes & Shriver, Balt., 1977-84, ptnr., 1985—, also Washington, N.Y.C., N.J., and Boston offices; mem. law council Washington and Lee U., 1983-87. Editor Notes and Comments Washington and Lee Law Rev., 1976-77; editor-in-chief Washington and Lee Law News, 1976-77. Mem. ABA (litigation and employment and labor law sects.), Md. State Bar Assn., D.C. Bar Assn., N.Y. State Bar Assn., Women's Bar Assn. Md. (bd. dirs. 1984-86, officer 1986—, outstanding contbn. award 1986), City Bar Assn. (young lawyers com., pub. edn. com. 1982-86), Fed. Bar Assn., Md. Assn. Def. Trial Counsel, Club: Merchants (Balt.). Home: 336 Rosebank Ave Baltimore 21212 Office: Ober Kaler Grimes & Shriver 10 Light St Baltimore MD 21202

WHITE, PATRICIA EARLY, lawyer; b. Amarillo, Tex., May 17, 1954; d. Allen and Frances Virginia (Ratliff) Early; m. George Howard White III, Aug. 22, 1981. B.A., magna cum laude, Vanderbilt U., 1976; J.D., Havard U., 1980, M.P.P., 1980. Bar: N.Y. 1981. Assoc. Webster & Sheffield, N.Y.C., 1980-82; dep. counsel N.Y.C. Comptroller's Office, 1982-84. Trustee, Vanderbilt U., 1976-80. Bd. dirs. City Kids Day Care Corner, Inc., N.Y.C., 1983-84; v.p. Women's Inst. Continuing Edn. at Am. Coll. in Paris, 1985, pres., 1986, bd. dirs., 1985-86. Ada Belle Stapleton scholar, 1974. Mem. Career Links Ltd., Hudson Group, N.Y., Phi Beta Kappa; Kappa Kappa Gamma. Democrat. Christian Scientist. Club: Harvard.

WHITE, RUTH BENNETT, nutritionist, educator, writer; b. Howe, Okla., Aug. 18, 1906; d. Ambrose L. and Sarah A. (Blevins) Bennett; m. Carl Milton White, Aug. 5, 1928; children—Sherril White Spencer, Caroline White Buchanan. B.A. with honors, Okla. Baptist U., 1928; M.S. (fellow), U. Iowa, 1930; postgrad. Cornell U., 1930-34, Columbia, 1955-56. Prin. Jr. High Sch., Heavener, Okla., 1926-27; surveyor of diets, research fellow N.Y. State 4-H Club camps, summer 1931-34; instr. nutrition Coll. Home Econs., Cornell U., Ithaca, N.Y., 1931-34; tchr. pub. schs., N.Y.C., 1956-58 Fort Lee (N.J.) High Sch., 1959-60; pub. lectr. foods and nutrition, 1931—; nutrition specialist for community programs N.Y. State Extension, 1931-34, Ankara, Turkey, 1960-61, Lagos, Nigeria, 1962-64; mem. Nat. Commn. on Revision of Home Econs. Curriculum, Fed. Republic of Nigeria, 1962-64. Author: If Food Could Talk, 1932; You and Your Food (text), 4th edit., 1976; Food and Your Future (text), 1972, 3d edit., 1985. Contbr. articles on nutrition to profl. jours. and newspapers. Mem. Leonia (N.J.) Bd. Edn., 1950-54. Recipient Alumni Achievement award Okla. Baptist U., 1975; named Woman of the Year, San Diego dist. Calif. Home Econs. Assn., 1973, 74; Woman of Achievement award Pres.'s Council Womens Service, Bus. and Profl. Clubs San Diego, 1973, 74. Mem. Am. Home Econs. Assn. (award for writing contbns. to home econs. profession 1984), Calif., Channel Islands home econs. assns., Internat. Fedn. Home Econs. (mem. council 1970-76), AAUW (del. nat. conv. 1984), Soc. Nutrition Edn., Nat. League Am. Pen Women, Pi Lambda Theta, Pi Kappa Delta. Democrat. Address: 2550 Treasure Dr Santa Barbara CA 93105

WHITE, RUTH MIRIAM WEIHS, trade and fin. co. exec.; b. Vienna, Austria; came to U.S., 1947, naturalized, 1952; d. Hugo and Ilka (Herzog) Weihs; B.A. in Bus. Adminstrn., St. John's U., Shanghai, China, 1947; postgrad. N.Y.U., CCNY; m. Paul White, Sept. 18, 1949. Exec. sec. to chmn. bd. Pan Am. Trade Devel. Corp., N.Y.C., 1947-49, mgr., 1949-53, asst. v.p., 1953-58, v.p., 1958-74, sr. v.p., 1974—; pres. Indsl. Crystal Corp. Office: 2 Park Ave New York NY 10016

WHITE, SANDRA ALINE, psychotherapist; b. N.Y.C., Jan. 14, 1937; d. Louis Schiffman and Molly Ruth (Singer) Schiffman David. B.A., Calif. State U.-Los Angeles, 1972, M.A., 1974; Ph.D., Calif. Grad. Inst., Los Angeles, 1983. Lic. marriage and family therapist, Calif.; cert. tchr. and counselor, Calif. Psychotherapist in pvt. practice, Los Angeles, 1975—; exec. dir. Ctr. for Applied Counseling, Los Angeles, 1983—; coordinator Human Services Network, Los Angeles, 1985—. Mem. Calif. Assn. Marriage and Family Therapists, Am. Assn. Counseling and Devel., Internat. Transactional Analysis Assn. Democrat. Jewish. Avocations: racquetball, yoga, reading, cooking, theatre. Office: Ctr for Applied Counseling 8170 Beverly Blvd Suite 200 Los Angeles CA 90048

WHITE, SANDRA JEANNE, elementary school educator; b. Peoria, Ill., May 23; d. Allen Noel Pate and Margaret Lucy (Stout) P.; m. Dale Eugene White Aug. 31, 1957; children—Cynthia Jeanne, Julie Ann Nelson. B.S. in Edn., Western Ill. U., 1967; M.S. in Edn., Ill. State U., 1974. Elem. tchr. Peoria Pub. Schs., 1967—; adj. instr. Ill. Central Coll. Bd. dirs., v.p., chmn. promotions Corn Stock Theatre; chmn. play selection com. Community Children's Theatre; active 1st United Meth. Ch., adminstrv. bd., council ministries, edn. chmn., mem. choir, tchr. Selected for 1981 Social Studies Colloquium Northwestern (Ill.) U., Follett Pub. Co.; Gov.'s Master Tchr. program nominee, 1984. Mem. AAUW, Peoria Edn. Assn., Ill. Edn. Assn., NEA (life), Assn. Supervision, Curriculum Devel., Ill. Assn. Supervision and Curriculum Devel. (editorial bd.), Ill. Assn. Tchr. Educators, Ill. Guidance and Personnel Assn., Ill. Prins. Assn., Delta Kappa Gamma, Phi Delta Kappa (newsletter editor Beta Psi chpt.). Club: Pilot Internat. (Peoria). Office: 1619 W Fredonia Peoria IL 61606

WHITE, SANDRA LAVENIA, municipal official; b. Birmingham, Ala., May 13, 1954; d. Luster and Viola Sanders; m. Lamont White, July 4, 1980; 1 child, Damion Lamont. B.A., S.W. Bus. Coll., Los Angeles, 19. Chief supr. dep. III, Mcpl. Ct. Beverly Hills, Calif., 1980—; pres. Sanmont Dame, Beverly Hills, 1984—. Recipient proclamation for saving a person's life, City of Beverly Hills, 1982. Office: Sanmont Dame 119 San Vicente Blvd Beverly Hills CA 90210

WHITE, SANDRA RICHARDS, sales engineer, chemist; b. Houston, Oct. 18, 1948; d. Earl Douglas and Joleta (Phillips) Lively; m. Gerald Robert White, Sept. 30, 1983; children by previous marriage—Laurie Joanna, Jamie Racquel. Student San Jacinto Coll., 1966-68; B.S. in Chemistry, Sam Houston State U., 1970; postgrad. Houston Bapt. U. Chemist, Sorbotec, Inc., Houston, 1971-72, Champion Papers, Inc., Pasadena, Tex., 1974-75, Core Labs, Inc., Houston, 1981-82; account rep. Foxboro Co., Houston, 1982—; lunar chemist at Lunar Receiving Lab., Johnson Space Ctr., Brown & Root-Northrup, Houston, 1970-71. Charter mem. Nat./State Leadership Tng. Inst. on Gifted and Talented, Ventura, Calif. 1979—; mem. Houston Mus. Natural Sci., Houston Contemporary Arts Mus. Sam Houston State U. research fellow, 1969-70. Mem. Soc. Women Engrs., Nat. Assn. Female Execs., Am. Chem. Soc., Instrument Soc. Am., Nat. Assn. Corrosion Engrs. Republican. Lutheran. Club: Christian Women's. Address: 5155 Cripple Creek Houston TX 77017 Office: Foxboro Co 6440 SW Freewy Houston TX 77074

WHITE, SARAH REBECCA, real estate broker; b. Columbia, Tenn., June 3, 1930; d. Douglas R. and Jimmy Pauline (Pigg) Parks; m. Charles Henry Fraser, June 10, 1949 (div. 1960); children—Linda Gail Fraser Johnson, Charles Henry; m. George Lawson White, Nov. 23, 1961; 1 child, Lloyd Anthony. Grad. high sch., Columbia, Tenn. Bookkeeper Sterchi Bros. Furniture, Columbia, 1952-54; salesperson Early Tire & Fishing, Columbia 1954-56; sec.-payroll M.C. West Mining Co., Columbia, 1956-64; salesperson Early & Akin Real Estate Agy., Columbia, 1966-72; owner, broker Early & White Realty, Columbia, 1972-74, White Realty, Columbia, 1974-81, White/Woodard, Columbia, 1981—. Sec. Fellowship of Christian Athletes, Columbia. Mem. Maury County Bd. Realtors (Realtor of Yr. 1983). Democrat. Methodist. Home: Route 4 Skyview Dr PO Box 784 Columbia TN 38401 Office: White/Woodard Realty 1300 Trotwood Ave Columbia TN 38401

WHITE, SHARON ELIZABETH, lawyer; b. Galveston, Tex., July 5, 1955; d. Edward and Clara (Haden) W. B.A., Baylor U., 1977; J.D., So. Meth. U., 1981. Bar: Tex. 1981. Assoc. Underwood, Wilson, Berry, Stein & Johnson, Amarillo, Tex., 1981—. Asst. editor-in-chief Southwestern Law Jour., 1980-81. Sec. bd. dirs. Amarillo council Girl Scouts Am., 1982-84, 3d v.p., 1984, 1st v.p., 1985—; bd. dirs. Amarillo Little Theatre, 1984—, treas., 1985—; grants chmn. Don Harrington Discovery Ctr., 1984—. Mem. Amarillo Bar Assn., ABA, Amarillo Area Estate Planning Council, Amarillo Symphony Guild, Amarillo Art Alliance, Panhandle Plains Hist. Soc., Phi Delta Phi, Delta Delta Delta. Republican. Presbyterian. Office: Underwood Wilson Berry Stein & Johnson PO Box 9158 Amarillo TX 79105

WHITE, STEPHANIE ALICE, federal legislative counsel, lawyer; b. Schenectady, Feb. 22, 1949; d. John Joseph and Elvira Louise (Geelan) Srodoski; m. Earl Timothy White (dec. Dec. 1983); 1 child, Katherine L. B.S., Empire State Coll., SUNY, 1977; J.D. magna cum laude, U. Bridgeport, 1981. Bar: Conn. 1982. Mem. Riccio & White, Bridgeport, Conn., 1982-84; atty. advisor to asst. sec., Office of Civil Rights, Dept. Edn., Washington, 1984-86; minority counsel Com. on D.C., U.S. Ho. of Reps., Washington, 1986—. Co-chmn. Embassy Sch., Parents' Orgn., Arlington, Va., 1985—. Named Grad. of Yr. Phi Delta Phi award, 1981. Mem. Conn. Bar Assn., Bridgeport Bar Assn., ABA. Republican. Roman Catholic. Home: 2907 Meadow Ln Falls Church VA 22042 Office: US Ho of Reps DC Com 1307 Longworth Bldg Washington DC 20515

WHITE, SUSIE, interior designer, company executive; b. Fairborn, Ohio, Dec. 3, 1948; d. Charles W. and Peggy (Adams) Friend; m. Spencer Lee White, Sept. 17, 1968 (div. 1977). A.A., Sinclair Coll., 1977; diploma N.Y. Sch. Design, 1977, cert. tng. Fashion Acad., 1983. Layout artist Kenco Printing, Dayton, Ohio, 1972-73; fashion and display coordinator Lerner's, Cin., 1974-76; interior designer Elder Beerman, Dayton, 1976-77; sr. designer Creative Design, Dallas, 1977-79; head interior design dept. Alpert Corp., Aurora, Colo., 1979-82; pres., interior designer Designer's Image, Aurora, 1982—. Contbr. articles to profl. jours. Coordinating designer Channel Six Auction House, Aurora, 1982. Mem. Homebuilding Assn. of Denver (Golden Nugget award southwest area 1984; McSam award Dallas 1979), Sales and Mktg. Council, Nat. Assn. Female Execs. Club: Colo. Backgammon (sec. 1984) (Aurora). Avocations: dollhouses; sewing; painting; cooking. Office: Designer's Image Prodns Inc 3250 Oakland St Unit D Aurora CO 80010

WHITE, WINIFRED DEMAREST (MRS. HERBERT A. WHITE), retired association executive, editor; b. N.Y.C.; d. Peter Edward and Margaret (McLaughlin) Demarest; A.B., Coll. New Rochelle, 1914; postgrad. in journalism Columbia U. Extension, 1916-18; m. Joseph S. Gifford, Aug. 29, 1925 (dec. Feb. 1948); m. 2d, Herbert A. White, Nov. 14, 1964 (dec. Oct. 1972). Tchr. English, speech Bryant High Sch., N.Y.C., 1914-17; asst. to bursar Rockefeller Inst. Med. Research, 1917-26; asst. editor, asst. to exec. sec. AIME, N.Y.C., 1947-59, editor, 1960—; exec. sec. Soc. Women Engrs., N.Y.C., 1961-73, assoc. life mem., 1973—; cons. copy editor IEEE, 1981—; freelance editor miscellaneous papers, 1959—; editorial proofreader, 1978—. Recipient Ursula Laurus citation Coll. New Rochelle, 1977, Angela Merici gold medal, 1984; cert. of recognition and White Glove award Soc. Women Engrs. Editor: Ironmaking Proc., Open Hearth Proc., Honors Book, 1950-63, Proc. Conf. on Women, 1971; copy editor Trans. of ASHRAE, 1976-81. Home: 12 E 97th St New York NY 10029

WHITEAKER, LINDA JOYCE, minister, educational administrator; b. Cookeville, Tenn., May 5, 1942; d. Beecher and Thelma Lee (Roberson) W. Student U. Hawaii, 1965, Hancock Jr. Coll., 1970—; Th.B., Clarksville Sch. Theology, 1980, M.Th., 1983; grad. Calif. Assn. Realtors, 1968. Lic. to ministry Ch. of God, 1960. Pastor, Ch. of God, Lahaina, Hawaii, 1962-64; dir. youth and Christian edn. Ch. of God, Hawaii, 1964-65; pastor Santa Maria Ch. of God, Calif., 1965—; owner/broker Lin*Etta Realty, Santa Maria, 1972—; builder. Founder, pastor, adminstr. Accelerated Christian Sch., 1976—; founder, pres. Lady Ministers Fellowship Internat., 1981—; mem. Santa Maria/Orcutt Gen. Plan Adv. Com., 1979-84, Santa Maria Planning Commn., 1984—; mem. congl. task force com. U.S. Ho. of Reps., 1983. Mem. Santa Maria Bd. Realtors (pres. 1978-79, legis. chmn. 1980), Calif. Assn. Realtors (bd. dirs. 1977-81), Nat. Assn. Realtors (bd. dirs. 1978-81), Santa Maria C. of C. (speakers club). Republican. Avocations: walking; collecting Bibles; travel; photography. Home: PO Box 1342 Santa Maria CA 93454 Office: PO Box 1342 Santa Maria CA 93454

WHITEBOOK, DENA KOENIGSBERG, psychotherapist; b. N.Y.C.; d. Louis and Yetta (Shapiro) Koenigsberg; B.A., Hunter Coll., N.Y.C., 1940; M.A., Pepperdine U., Los Angeles, 1976; m. Harold Plant, Oct. 30, 1943; children—Janet G., Richard P.; m. 2d, Edward F. Whitebook, Dec. 14, 1963. Sch. tchr., N.Y.C., 1945-47; crisis therapist Los Angeles Suicide Prevention Center, 1964-76; instr. UCLA Extension, 1975-77; pvt. practice psychotherapy, Beverly Hills, Calif., 1977—; dir. counseling Am. Inst. Family Relations, Los Angeles, 1978-82; tchr. human sexuality, clin. supr. LaVerne (Calif.) U. Extension, 1980-82; radio and TV panelist, 1967—; cons. in field. Mem. Am. Assn. Marriage and Family Therapists, Am. Assn. Sex Therapists, Educators and Counselors, Assn. Humanistic Psychology, Am. Assn. Suicidology, Internat. Assn. Suicide Prevention, Calif. Assn. Marriage and Family Therapists. Home: 320 N Maple Dr Beverly Hills CA 90210 Office: 9401 Wilshire Blvd Beverly Hills CA 90212

WHITEFIELD, CAROLYN LEE, lawyer; b. Texarkana, Ark., Mar. 1, 1946; d. William Parker, Sr. and Julia Arabella (Rayburn) Whitefield; B.S., So. State Coll., 1970; J.D., U. Ark., 1973; m. Jerry Allen McDowell, Sept. 21, 1974. Bar: Ark. 1973, Tex. 1974; sole practice, Texarkana, Ark., 1973—. Mem. ABA, Ark. Bar Assn., Tex. Bar Assn. Republican. Baptist. Home: Route 7 Box 536 Texarkana AR 75502 Office: Box 8007 State Line Plaza Room 611 Texarkana AR 75502

WHITE-HARRIS, JUDITH ANN, health occupations vocational educator; nurse; b. Springfield, Ohio, Mar. 6, 1939; d. Willis and Tennessee Bell (Poole) Martin; m. Allen G. Harris, Mar. 21, 1986; 1 child by previous marriage—Denise Marian White. R.N., Springfield City Hosp., 1960; postgrad. U. South Fla., 1978-85. R.N., Fla.; cert. tchr., Fla. Nurse, Dr. Robert Tapogna, Springfield, Ohio, 1960-62, Springfield City Hosp., 1962-65, Dr. Robert Beam, Springfield, 1965-75; ednl. coordinator, instr. med. assisting Sarasota Vocat. Ctr., Fla., 1977-82, instr. med. assisting program, chmn. dept., 1982-84, instr. health service occupations, placement coordinator health occupations, 1985—. Contbr. articles to profl. jours. Vol. Children's Breath Clinic, Sarasota, 1977-79, Kidney Found., Sarasota, 1982; vol. ARC, Sarasota, 1976-86, dir. Spl. Care unit, 1984-86. Named Outstanding Vocat. Tchr. Sarasota County Sch. Bd., 1985. Mem. Am. Vocat. Assn. (Outstanding Vocat. Tchr. Region II 1985), Health Occupations Educators (vice chmn. policy com. 1985-86), Nat. Assn. Health Occupations Tchrs. (v.p. Region II, 1984-86), Fla. Vocat. Assn. (bd. dirs. 1983-85, Pres. award 1984, Outstanding Vocat. Educator Region 23 award 1982), Health Occupations Educators Assn. Fla. (pres. 1983-84, chmn. legis. com. 1985-86), Sarasota County Vocat. and Adult Assn. (pres. 1978-80, editor newsletter, 1978-83), Am. Assn. Med. Assts., Nat. Assn. Female Execs. Democrat. Methodist. Avocations: swimming; pool-a-cize; knitting; sewing; biking. Home: 3846 Malec Circle Sarasota FL 33583 Office: Sarasota Vocat Ctr 4748 Beneva Rd Sarasota FL 33583

WHITEHEAD, ARDELLE COLEMAN, advertising and public relations executive; b. Carrollton, Ohio, May 13, 1917; d. James David and Gilsie Dale (Hendricks) Coleman; m. W. Wilson Whitehead, Mar. 9, 1974. B.S., Wittenberg U., 1938. Various advt. agy. and corp. exec. positions, N.Y.C., Los Angeles, until 1966; consumer affairs specialist Jennings/Thompson, Phoenix, 1966-73; pub. communications mgr. Valley Nat. Bank, Phoenix, 1974-76; pres. Whiteheads Inc., Phoenix, 1976—. Author, pub. various advt. booklets. Named Adperson of Yr., Phoenix, 1978. Mem. Women in Communications (chpt. dir. 1977—, named Woman of Achievement Phoenix chpt. and Far West region 1981), Pub. Relations Soc. Am. (chpt. dir. 1980-84, Percy award for excellence 1985). Clubs: Phoenix Advt. (dir. 1966-76, pres. 1974-75). Home: 337 E Pierson St Phoenix AZ 85012

WHITEHEAD, HELEN MAY, small business entrepreneur, marketing consultant; b. Harrisburg, Pa., Sept. 1, 1951; d. Warren Benjamin Engle and Priscilla Jean (Zinkan) Kohlhaas; m. Darell Roger Whitehead, Jan. 27, 1973; 1 child, Gregory James. A.A. in Liberal Arts, U. Md.-European div. Germany, 1978; certificado de Suficiencia, U. Zaragoza, Spain, 1978; B.S. in Mktg., Northeastern U., 1982; B.S. in Bus. Adminstrn. with high honors, Auburn U., 1983. Mgr., sales rep. M&S Indian Jewelry, Griesheim, Fed. Republic Germany, 1978-79; message distbn. shift supr. U.S. Air Force, Scott AFB, Belleville, Ill., 1971-75, communications detachment controller U.S. Air Force Europe, Ramstein, Fed. Republic Germany, 1975-78; tng. dept. coordinator Aviation Simulation Tech., Inc., Bedford, Mass., 1982-84; regional sales mgr. Huang's Trading Co., Skokie, Ill, 1984—; substitute tchr. Hanscom Primary Sch., Bedford, 1986—; pres., small bus. entrepreneur Uniques, Bedford, 1983—; speaker in field. Scholarship chairperson Hanscom Officers' Wives Club, Bedford, 1982-84. Served with U.S. Air Force, 1971-78, ETO. Mem. Nat. Assn. Female Execs., Alpha Sigma Lambda. Home: 11 Patterson Rd Bedford MA 01730

WHITEHORSE, KAREN SUE, insurance underwriter; b. Joplin, Mo., Aug. 14, 1949; d. Wilbur Richard and Wanda Mae (Hodkin) Collins; 1 child, Kelly Sue Hunter. Grad. Carthage High Sch., Mo., 1967. Cashier, sec. to controller Mo. So. State Coll., Joplin, 1973-76; teller Farm & Home Savs., Joplin, 1976-78; sewing instr. Singer, Joplin, 1978-80; mgr. Mid-Am. Banking, Springfield, Mo., 1980-83; field underwriter, registered rep. N.Y. Life Ins., N.Y.C., 1983—. Mem. adv. bd. Jane Chinn Home Health Care, Webb City, Mo., 1985—. Recipient awards N.Y. Life Ins. Mem. Million Dollar Round Table (provisional applicant), Nat. Assn. Life Underwriters (Nat. Sales Achievement award, Nat. Quality award, Nat. Health Quality award), Nat. Assn. Female Execs., Joplin C. of C., Southwest Mo. Assn. Life Underwriters (chmn. pub. relations 1981), Webb City C. of C. Republican. Methodist. Avocations: sewing; oil painting; knitting; crocheting. Home: 828 N Prospect St Webb City MO 64870 Office: N Y Life PO Box 227 Middlewest Bldg 1 S Main St Suite 100 Webb City MO 64870

WHITELEY, MARILYNN MAXWELL, education educator; b. Columbus, Ohio, Apr. 17, 1929; d. Marion Wilbur and Thelma (McGrady) Maxwell; children—Kay, Janet, Kenneth. B.S., East Carolina U., 1949; M.Ed., U. Tenn.-Chattanooga, 1975; Ed.D., U. Tenn., 1981. Tchr., Edgecombe County schs., N.C., 1949-51, Hamilton County schs., Tenn., 1966-69, Chattanooga pub. schs., 1969—; adj. prof. edn. U. Tenn., Chattanooga, 1980—. Delta Kappa Gamma scholar, 1974. Mem. Assn. Supervision and Curriculum Devel., Internat. Reading Assn., Nat. Council Tchrs. English, AAUW, United Teaching Profession, Phi Delta Kappa, Delta Kappa Gamma. Methodist. Home: 6433 Brookmeade Circle Hixson TN 37343

WHITESIDES, ELIZABETH IGLER (MRS. LAWSON EWING WHITESIDES), lawyer, club woman; b. Glendale, Ohio, Oct. 12, 1910; d. Herman Einhaus and Matilda (Voegtle) Igler; LL.B., U. Cin., 1932, J.D., 1967; m. Lawson Ewing Whitesides, June 29, 1935; children—Elizabeth Lawson (Mrs. David Garth Holdsworth), Lawson Ewing. Admitted to Ohio bar, 1932, U.S. Supreme Ct., 1968; pvt. practice law, Cincinnati, 1932—. Mem. Cin. Woman's Club; Town Club, Cin., mem. Glendale Lyceum; pres. Monday Class, Glendale, 1948-49, Glendale Village Gardeners, 1966-67. Mem. Cin. Council on World Affairs. Mem. Cin., Ky. hist. socs., Cin. Bar Assn., Order of Coif, Phi Delta Delta, Kappa Alpha Theta (pres. Cin. alumnae 1954-55). Episcopalian. Address: 840 Woodbine Ave Glendale Cincinnati OH 45246

WHITE-WARE, GRACE ELIZABETH, educator; b. St. Louis, Oct. 5, 1921; d. James Eathel, Sr. and Madree (Penn) White; B.A. in Edn., H.B. Stowe Tchrs. Coll., 1943; divorced; 1 son, James Otis Ware II (Oloye Kunle Adeyemon). Mgr. advt. Superior Press, St. Louis, 1935-39; tri-owner, v.p. Carolina Oil Co., St. Louis, 1938-42; with pub. relations Triangle Press, St. Louis, 1939-47, sales promotion, 1939-47; account supr. overtime payroll Bell Tel. Labs., Inc., N.Y.C., 1943-46; tchr. Dunbar Elem. Sch., St. Louis, 1946-47, Garfield Elem. Sch., Chgo., 1948-49, Betsy Ross Elem. Sch., Chgo., 1950-51, Lincoln Sch., Richmond, Mo., 1951, Dunbar Sch., Kinlock, Mo., 1952, Gladstone Elem. Sch., Cleve., 1954-61, Quincy Elem. Sch., Cleve., 1961-78, W.H. Brett Elem. Sch., Euclid Park, Ohio, 1979-82; head tchr. Head Start program, 1965; adult edn. tchr. Cleve. Bd. Edn., 1965-82; program coordinator Tutoring and Nutrition Project, Delta Sigma Theta, 1983—; tchr. TV Tonight Sch., lessons for adults, Cleve., 1972; tri-owner, v.p., social editor Style mag., St. Louis, 1947-49; owner/mgr. Wentworth Record Distbrs., Chgo., 1947-51; supr. accounts receivable div. Spiegel, Inc., Chgo., 1947-52; radio panelist Calling All Americans, Cleve., 1957-58; sec. bd. dirs. Hough Pub. Co., also Hough Area Devel. Corp., Cleve., 1968-69. Mem. child devel. parent bd. Greater Cleve. Neighborhood Centers Assn.; mem. fund raising com. Food First Program, co-chmn. woman's aux. Black Econ. Union, Cleve.; vice chmn. Cleve. com. Youth for Understanding Teenage Program; mem. Cleve. Council Human Relations; mem. Cleve. chpt. CORE; charter mem., fin. sec. Tots and Teens, Inc.; treas. Jr. Women's Civic League; mem. Cleve. bd. Afro-Am. Cultural and Hist. Soc.; women's aux. bd. Talbert Clinic and Day Care Center, Cleve.; adv. bd. Langston Hughes Library; mem. Forest City Hosp. Aux. Bd., also Women's Aux. Com. Forest City Hosp.; scholarship com. Women's Allied Arts Assn. Greater Cleve., 1972-74; mem. spl. com. Lake Erie council Girl Scouts U.S.A., 1982-84; co-coordinator Cuyahoga County Child Watch Project, 1982-83. Named Most Outstanding Vol. of Year, N.Y. Fedn. Settlements, 1944, Leading Tchr. of Community, Cleve. Call and Post, weekly newspaper, 1958; recipient Martha Holden Jennings scholar award Martha Holden Jennings Found., Cleve., 1966-67, Spl. Outstanding Tchrs. award, 1973; Outstanding Service award Black Econ. Union, 1970; Cert. of Appreciation, City of Cleve., 1973; Ednl. Service to Community award Urban League, 1986 Mem. Ohio, Cleve. edn. assns., Nat. Assn. Public Sch. Adult Edn., Nat. Assn. Minority Polit. women (treas. 1985—), NAACP, Phillis Wheatley Assn., Moreland Community Assn., Nat. Council Negro Women, Top Ladies of Distinction (pres. Cleve. 1980-82), Phi Delta Kappa (1st v.p. Cleve. 1971-73, Outstanding Achievement award 1975), Delta Sigma Theta (pres. Cleve. 1969-73), Delta Kappa Gamma, Eta Phi Beta (regional treas. 1979-83, nat. treas. 1984—). Democrat. Clubs: Novelette Bridge (pres. Cleve. 1973-77), Arewa Du-Du Bridge (treas. 1980—). Home: 14701 Milverton Rd Cleveland OH 44120

WHITING, ANN HARRIET, computer service executive; b. Chgo., July 31, 1936; d. Thomas Brent and Florence Harriet (Beals) Legg Thorstensen; m. Louis D. Straubel, June 23, 1956 (div. 1974); children—Michael, Rick; m. 2d, Robert Alan Whiting, Apr. 19, 1980. B.S., Mich. State U., 1962. Probation officer St. Joseph City Probate Ct., Centerville, Mich., 1960-62; police detective Kalamazoo Police Dept. (Mich.), 1962-77; security and safety supr. Indian River Meml. Hosp., Vero Beach, Fla., 1979-81; legal sec. state legislator R. Dale Patchett, Vero Beach, 1981-82; pres. Computer Creations By Ann, Inc., Vero Beach, 1982—. Mem. Republican Women Aware, Vero Beach; polit. campaign mgr. R. Dale Patchett, Vero Beach, 1982. Mem. Internat. Assn. Women Police (life). Christian Scientist. Home: 7605 McKenzie Terr Apt 1 Vero Beach FL 32962 Office: Computer Creations By Ann Inc PO Box 2290 Vero Beach FL 32960

WHITING, SUSAN FRANCES HIGGINS, hosp. public relations adminstr.; b. St. Cloud, Minn., July 6, 1945; d. Daniel Malachy and Mary Frances (Helget) Higgins; B.A. in Speech and Theatre Arts/Journalism, Manakato (Minn.) State U., 1967; m. Ward Harrison Whiting, May 25, 1968; children—Edward James, Ian Daniel. Copywriter, Better Homes and Gardens, Des Moines, 1967-68; asst. editor IBM, Rochester, Minn., 1968-70; publs. editor, dir. pubic relations Hubbard Milling Co., Mankato, 1970-73; instr. speech, dir. pubic relations Ohio No. U., Ada, 1973-79; dir. public relations and devel. St. Luke's Hosp., Maumee, Ohio, 1979—. Mem. Women in Communications, Public Relations Soc. Am., Am. Soc. Hosp. Public Relations, Ohio Soc. Hosp. Public Relations, Am. Mktg. Assn. Roman Catholic. Office: 5901 Monclova Rd Maumee OH 43537

WHITING-MARINCE, DIANE IRENE, art director, designer; b. Chgo., Aug. 10, 1957; d. David Elmer and Irene Grace (Pape) Whiting; m. Charles Douglas Marince, Nov. 26, 1983. B.S., A.S., So. Ill. U., 1980. Graphic designer Student Ctr. Graphics, Carbondale, Ill., 1979-80, Bob Bond and Others, Dallas, 1980-82; art dir. Studiographix, Irving, Tex., 1982-84, Source Communications Group, Dallas, 1984, Electronic Data Systems, Dallas, 1984—. Recipient cert. of excellence N.Y. Art Dirs. Club, 1983, Dallas Advt. League, 1982, Art Dirs. Club Tulsa, 1982. Mem. Dallas Soc. Visual Communications, Internat. Assn. Bus. Communicators, Women in Communications. Home: PO Box 801053 Dallas TX 75380

WHITLEY, ELIZABETH DURRELL, member staff U.S. Congress; b. Comanche County, Okla., May 2, 1953; d. Jesse W. and Ann (Marshall) W.; B.A. in Polit. Sci. and Am. History, Sweet Briar (Va.) Coll., 1975. Staff asst. scheduling office Office of the Vice Pres., Washington, 1973-74; legis. liaison Cook Industries, 1975-77; dir. scheduling John Warner for Senate campaign, Va., 1978; asst. dir., congressional liaison AIA, 1979; legis. dir. Office of U.S. Congressman Barry M. Goldwater, Jr., Washington, 1980-82; staff asst. to Senator Paul S. Trible, Jr., Washington, 1983-85; exec. v.p. Nat. Council Agrl. Employers, Washington, 1985—; researcher polit. campaigns; fund raiser. Bd. dirs. Am. Council Young Polit. Leaders, 1981-82; chmn. Sweet Briar Washington Job Resources Council, 1975-77. Mem. Women in Govt. Relations, Sweet Briar Alumnae Assn., Washington Jr. League. Republican. Presbyterian. Club: Capitol Hill. Office: 499 S Capitol St Washington DC 20003

WHITLEY, PEGGY CALDWELL, business executive; b. Cleveland, Tex., Aug. 21, 1945; d. Homer S. and Dorothy Jane (Bailes) Gilbert; m. Bob L. Caldwell, Apr. 12, 1967; children—Brian Lee, Brandon Lee; m. Donald Lynn Whitley, Jan. 21, 1984. Vice pres., dir. Agri-Sul, Inc., Mineola, Tex., 1969-78; v.p., dir. Agri-Sul Canada, Ltd., Calgary, Alta., 1974-78; owner Hickory Hut, Mineola, Tex., 1973-75; regulatory analyst Tex. Eastern Transmission Corp., Houston, 1978-84; owner Resource Mgmt. Dynamics, Humble, Tex., 1981-85; mgr. agrl. systems Gulf Markets Internat., Manama, Bahrain, 1984-85, mgr. fin. and adminstrn., water service div., 1986—. Mem. Am. Entrepreneurs Assn., Exec. Female, Am. Mgmt. Assn. Republican. Baptist. Home: PO Box 520 Coldsprings TX 77331 Office: PO Box 2709 Manama Bahrain

WHITLOCK, EVELYN PATRICIA, physician; b. Winston-Salem, N.C., Aug. 25, 1952; d. Coleman Morrison and Mary Louise (Merritt) Whitlock. A.B. with high distinction, Ind. U., Bloomington, 1974; M.D., Ind. U.-Indpls., 1979. Resident in Pathology St. Vincent's Hosp., Portland, Oreg., 1980-81; tchr. Nature's Cooking Sch., Portland, 1981-82; clinician Planned Parenthood, Portland, 1981-82; clinician in pvt. practice, nutrition and preventive medicine, Beaverton, Oreg., 1982-83; med. dir. Colgan Inst. Nutritional Sci., Carlsbad, Calif., 1983; dir. Health Access Systems, Inc., San Diego, 1984—; clinic cons. Lakeside Chiropractic Health Ctr., Lake Oswego, Oreg., 1982—; cons. PortaStat Services, Portland, 1984—. Contbr. Toys for Tots, 1983, Childhelp, 1983. Mem. Am. Holistic Med. Assn., N.W. Acad. Preventive Medicine, Orthomolecular Med. Soc., Mortar Bd., Phi Beta Kappa, Alpha Omega Alpha. Home: 1228 SW Cardinell Portland OR 97201

WHITLOCK, MARY ELLEN JENKINS (MRS. DOUGLAS WHITLOCK), social worker, travel cons.; b. Brownville, Nebr., Sept. 3, 1906; d. John Crisler and Mabel (Sapp) Jenkins; student Sullins Coll., 1923-24, Ferris Inst., 1924; A.B., Ind. U., 1927; m. Douglas Whitlock, June 18, 1929; children—Douglas Whitlock II, Marilyn Whitlock Long, Sandra (Mrs. Theodore G. Driscoll, Jr.). Case worker Children's Aid Soc., Detroit, 1927-28, head adoption dept., 1928-29; case supr. Asso. Charities Washington, 1929-32; co-owner, sec.-treas. Global Travel, Inc.; travel cons., 1973—. Mem. Women's Inaugural Com., Washington, 1953, 57. Chmn. women's com. Devereux Found., Devon, Pa., 1959-61. Mem. League Rep. Women, Nat. Fedn. Rep. Women, Family Service Assn. of Am., Goodwill Industries Assn., Mental Health Assn., Vis. Nurse Assn.; trustee Family and Child Services, Washington, 1951-65, 1st v.p., 1962-65; v.p. Episcopal Ch. Women of Washington, 1963-69, pres., 1969-72. Recipient award Alpha Omicron Pi, 1963; award Episcopal Diocese Washington, 1972. Mem. Ind. Soc. of Washington (mem. exec. bd. 1932—, award 1962), Ind. U. Alumni Assn., Alpha Omicron Pi. Republican. Episcopalian (vestrywoman 1968-71, 74-79). Clubs: Little Garden (pres. 1938-40), Wednesday (pres. 1940-42) (Sandy Spring, Md.); Internat. Neighbors (1st pres. 1956-58)) (Washington); Women of St. Thomas (pres. 1960-62). Home: The Westchester Apt 504-B 4000 Cathedral Ave NW Washington DC 20016

WHITLOCK, RUTH HENDRICKS SUMMERS, music educator; b. McAllen, Tex., May 10, 1934; d. Harold Glen and Lucile (McKee) Hendricks; B.A. (Theodore Presser scholar), Newcomb Coll., New Orleans, 1955; M.A., Occidental Coll., Los Angeles, 1970; Ph.D. (Mu Phi Epsilon grantee), N. Tex. State U., 1981; m. Robert Edward Whitlock, Jr., June 2, 1972; 1 son, Hal; stepchildren—Karen, Robert Edward, III. Music tchr., choral dir., supr. Tex. public schs., 1955-73; teaching fellow music edn. and choral music. N. Tex. State U., 1973-75; assoc. prof. music edn. Tex. Christian U., Ft. Worth, 1975—, dir. music edn. studies, 1985—; tchr. clinics and workshops; founder, steering com. Tex. Music Edn. Symposia, 1977, 85. Mem. Music Educators Nat. Conf., Am. Choral Dirs. Assn., Tex. Music Educators Conf., Tex. Music Educators Assn., Tex. Choral Dirs. Assn., Pi Kappa Lambda, Mu Phi Epsilon (Outstanding Faculty award 1979). Republican. Episcopalian. Author: Choral Insights-General Edition, 1982; Choral Insights-Renaissance Edition, 1982; Choral Insights-Baroque Edition, 1985; co-author: Guide to Writing Curriculum and Planning Instruction, 1985. Home: 2712 6th Ave Fort Worth TX 76110 Office: Dept Music Tex Christian U Fort Worth TX 76129

WHITLOW, MARION VIRGINIA, nursing educator; b. Johnstown, Pa., May 17, 1929; d. William Sercy and Mary Thelma (Hill) Holton; diploma in nursing St. Francis Hosp., Pitts. 1950; B.S. in Nursing, U. Pitts. 1966; M.S., U. Ind.-Purdue U., Indpls., 1977; m. Emery Whitlow, June 28, 1969; children—Cecily Patterson, Gary Patterson, Carol Patterson Upshur. Staff nurse St. Francis Hosp., 1950-52; staff nurse Mercy Hosp., Johnstown, 1956-58, 60-65, instr. pediatrics, 1966-69; assoc. prof. nursing Purdue U., Westville, Ind., 1980—. Mem. AAUW, Am. Nurses Assn. (council intercultural nursing), Harriet Tubman Nurse Assn. Michigan City (organizer), NAACP (sec. Michigan City 1971-73), Am. Nurses Found., Ind. Coalition Blacks in Higher Edn. (charter, sec.), Sigma Theta Tau. Democrat. Mem. African Methodist Episcopal Ch. Office: Purdue University North Central Westville IN 46390

WHITMAN, CLEMENTINE MCGOWIN, university administrator; oil company executive; b. Jackson, Ala., Apr. 15, 1943; d. Douglas DeVaughn and Juanita (Spann) McGowin; m. R. Wayne Whitman, Apr. 12, 1968 (div. July 1978). B.S., U. Ala., 1965. Teaching fellow U. Ala.-Tuscaloosa, 1965-68, fiscal asst., 1968-70; adminstrv. asst. U. Ala. Sch. Medicine, Birmingham, 1970-79; exec. asst. to internal medicine chmn. U. Tex. Med. Sch. Houston, 1979—, mem. employee relations com., 1979—, sec. com., 1979-82, chmn. com., 1983-84, 85-86; mem. pres.'s employee relations adv. council U. Tex. Health Sci. Ctr., 1983-87. Mem. U. Ala. Alumni Assn., U.S. Figure Skating Assn., Boat Owner's Assn. of U.S. Presbyterian. Club: Birmingham Figure Skating. Home: 2038 Hilton Head Dr Missouri City TX 77459 Office: Dept Internal Medicine U Tex Med Sch 6431 Fannin Houston TX 77030

WHITMAN, GAIL FELICIA, obstetrician/gynecologist; b. Gary, Ind., Sept. 15, 1949; d. David Myers and Annie Margaret (Mott) W.; B.A., U. Chgo., 171, M.D., 1976. Diplomate Am. Bd. Ob-Gyn. Resident in ob-gyn U. Chgo. Hosps. and Clinics/Chgo. Lying-In Hosp., 1976-80; staff obstetrician-gynecologist Hyde Park-Kenwood Community Health Center, Chgo., 1980-83; clin. instr. dept. ob-gyn Pritzker Sch. Medicine, U. Chgo., 1980-83; dir. young mothers' obstet. program Chgo. Lying-In-Hosp., 1980-83; pvt. practice ob-gyn, Chgo., 1980-83. Mem. exec. com. bd. mgrs. Chgo. Boys' Clubs; vice-chmn. First Congressional Dist. Health Task Force. Diplomate Nat. Bd. Med. Examiners. La Verne Noyes scholar, 1972-76; Nat. Med. fellow, 1972-73; recipient Searle Chemistry award, 1968. Fellow Am. Coll. Ob-Gyn; mem. Chgo. Med. Soc., Ill. Med. Soc., AMA, Cook County Physicians Assn., Prairie State Med. Soc., Nat. Med. Assn., Internat. Soc. Psychosomatic Ob-Gyn, U. Chgo. Alumni Assn., Chgo. Urban League, St. Jude League, Alpha Kappa Alpha, Alpha Gamma Pi. Mem. United Ch. of Christ. Office: 2050 Pfingston Rd Glenview IL 60025

WHITMAN, MARINA VON NEUMANN, economist; b. N.Y.C., Mar. 6, 1935; d. John and Mariette (Kovesi) von Neumann; B.A. summa cum laude, Radcliffe Coll., 1956; M.A., Columbia U., 1959, Ph.D., 1962; L.H.D., Russell Sage Coll., 1972, U. Mass., 1975, N.Y. Poly Inst., 1975, Baruch Coll., 1980; LL.D., Cedar Crest Coll., 1973, Hobart and William Smith Coll., 1973, Coe Coll., 1975, Marietta Coll., 1976, Rollins Coll., 1976, Wilson Coll., 1977, Allegheny Coll., 1977, Amherst Coll., 1978, Ripon Coll., 1980, Mt. Holyoke Coll., 1980; Litt.D., WilliamsColl., 1980; m. Robert Freeman Whitman, June 23, 1956; children—Malcolm Russell, Laura Mariette. Mem. faculty U. Pitts., 1962-79, prof. econs., 1971-73, distinguished pub. service prof. econs., 1973-79; v.p., chief economist Gen. Motors Corp., N.Y.C., from 1979, now group v.p. pub. affairs; sr. staff economist Council Econ. Advisers, 1970-71; mem. U.S. Price Commn., 1971-72; mem. Council Econ. Advisers, Exec. Office of Pres., 1972-73; dir. Mfrs. Hanover Trust Co., Procter & Gamble Co.; mem. President's Commn. for Nat. Agenda for Eighties; mem. Trilateral Commn.; mem. adv. com. on reform internat. monetary system Dept. Treasury, from 1977; mem. Consultative Group on Internat. Econs. and Monetary Affairs (Group of 30), from 1979; econ. adv. com. U.S. Dept. Commerce, from 1979. Bd. overseers Harvard Coll., 1972-78; trustee Princeton U., from 1979. Recipient Columbia medal for excellence, 1973; George Washington award Am. Hungarian Found., 1975; fellow Earhart Found., 1959-60, AAUW, 1960-61, NSF, 1968-70, also Social Sci. Research Council. Mem. Am. Econ. Assn. (exec. com. 1977-80), Commn. on Critical Choices for Ams., Atlantic Council (dir.), Council Fgn. Relations (dir. 1977—), Am. Fin. Assn. (dir. from 1979), Phi Beta Kappa. Author: Government Risk-Sharing in Foreign Investment, 1965; International and Interregional Payments Adjustment, 1967; Economic Goals and Policy Instruments, 1970; Reflections of Interdependence: Issues for Economic Theory and U.S. Policy; also articles; bd. editors Am. Econ. Rev., 1974-77; mem. editorial bd. Fgn. Policy. Office: Gen Motors Corp 767 Fifth Ave New York NY 10022

WHITMIRE, KATHRYN JEAN, mayor of Houston; b. Houston, Aug. 15, 1946; B.B.A. with honors, U. Houston, 1968, M.S. in Accountancy, 1970; m. James Whitmire (dec.). Audit mgr. Coopers & Lybrand, C.P.A.s, Houston, 1971-76; controller City of Houston, 1977-81, mayor, 1982—; mem. faculty bus. mgmt. U. Houston, 1976-77, mem. adv. com. Coll. Bus. Adminstrn., 1978-80; chmn. standing com. on arts U.S. Conf. Mayors, 1984—. Mem. adminstrv. bd. St. Paul's United Methodist Ch., Houston, 1972-75; bd. dirs., treas. Juvenile Diabetes Found., Houston, 1977; adv. bd. Houston YWCA, 1979-81, Houston Area Women's Center, 1978-79. Recipient Disting. Alumna award U. Houston, 1982. C.P.A., Tex. Mem. Am. Soc. Women Accountants (dir. 1972-73), Tex. Soc. C.P.A.s (dir. Houston chpt. 1973-75). Office: PO Box 1562 901 Bagby St Houston TX 77251

WHITMORE, EVONNE HOLLAND, broadcasting executive; b. Rock Mount, Va., July 23, 1951; d. John Alfred and Ruth (Cooper) Holland; m. Arthur Whitmore, III, May 26, 1974; children—Lathan Mc Kinely, Lauren Rae. B.A. in Polit. Sci., Norfolk State U.; M.A. in Journalism, Ohio State U., 1976. Instr., Norfolk State U., Va., 1976-79; radio news reporter WTAR Radio, Norfolk, 1979-81; television news reporter WVEC-TV, Norfolk, 1981-84; radio sta. mgr. WHOV-FM Hampton U., Va., 1984—, asst. prof., 1984—. Recipient cert. Achievement VFW, 1983, Women in Communication, 1985. Mem. Assn. Journalism Educators, Sigma Delta Chi, Alpha Kappa Alpha. Democrat. Baptist. Avocations: reading; gardening. Home: 958 Anna St Norfolk VA 23502 Office: WHOV-FM Hampton U Hampton VA 23668

WHITMORE, RUTH ANN, marketing/advertising agency executive; b. Saginaw, Mich., May 26, 1949; d. Calvin James and Violet Emma (Bessinger) W. B.A. in Advt. and Design, U. Mich., 1973. Researcher, Lou Gordon program Sta. WKBD-TV, Southfield, Mich., 1975-76, sta. advt. and promotion mgr., 1976-78; dir. advt. and promotion Sta. WRIF-FM, Southfield, 1978-81; creative services dir. Sta. WXYZ-TV, Southfield, 1981-84; pres. Whitmore Communications, Inc., Southfield, 1984—. Mem. media bd. Juvenile Diabetes Assn., Detroit, 1983-84. Mem. Am. Mktg. Assn. (v.p. Detroit 1982-84), Nat. Broadcast Promotion and Mktg. Execs. (mem. bd. 1982-84, Gold medallions 1981, 83, 84), Am. Women in Radio and TV (named Outstanding Woman in Media Support 1983), Adcrafters, Nat. Acad. TV Arts and Scis., Nat. Assn. Female Execs., Econ. Club, U. Mich. Alumnae Club. Avocations: photography; film; writing; literature. Home: 6430 Village Park Dr West Bloomfield MI 48034 Office: Whitmore Communications Inc 29260 Franklin Rd Suite 129 Southfield MI 48034

WHITNER, LILLIAN (LILLIE) MADDOX, interior designer, consultant; b. Birmingham, Ala.; d. Milton udoxious and Harriette (Newell Coleman) Maddox; m. James Harrison Whitner II, Feb. 27, 1923 (div. 1942); children—Harriette, James Harrison III, Lillian II. Sweet Briar Coll., Owner, operator Mary Lewis Dress Shop, Charlotte, N.C., 1939-42; researcher Fortune mag., Charlotte, 1942-45, Nat. Research Ctr., Denver, 1942-45; artist's rep., Charlotte, 1946-48; prin. Lillian Whitner's Interiors, Charlotte, 1948—. Exhibited at Mint Mus. Art, Charlotte, 1955; decorator Queen's Sorority House, Charlotte, 1958; Davidson Coll. frat. (N.C.), 1958; asst. decorator Gov's home, Charlotte, 1958. Pres. Alumnae Orgn. Sweet Briar Coll., Charlotte, 1932; asst. Handicraft Div. Regional Art, Mint Mus. Art, 1938-39; radio worker Community Chest, Charlotte, 1939-40. Mem. Am. Soc. Interior Designers (cert.), Mint Mus. Art. Presbyterian. Clubs: Charlotte Country, Jr. League Charlotte (soc. editor 1929-30, corr. sec. 1931-32, chmn. ways and means com. 1933-34, editor-in-chief 1935-36, chmn. local advt. 1940-41), Jr. League U.S.

WHITNEY, CONSTANCE CLEIN, psychologist; b. Seattle, Nov. 12, 1931; B.A., Stanford U., 1953; M.A., Washington U., St. Louis, 1977, Ph.D., 1984; children—Mark R., Caroline C. Writer, San Francisco Chronicle, 1953-55; dir. Am. Assn. UN, St. Louis, 1956-60; lectr. St. Louis Art Mus., 1960-71; producer KETC-TV, 1973-75; instr. U. Mo.-St. Louis, 1976-78; clin. asst. dept. psychiatry med. Sch., Washington U., 1977-80; research asst., teaching asst. Sch. Bus. Adminstrn., 1983-84, lectr. organizational behavior, fellow in mgmt., research assoc., 1984-86; bd. dirs. Adult Edn. Council of Greater St. Louis, 1977-82, Bd. dirs. women's com. St. Louis Symphony, 1959-63, Dance Concert Soc., 1965-70, Child Guidance Clinic, 1981-84, Stanford U. Alumni Assn., 1980—; exec. producer Forward-Looking Strategies for Women, 1986—; leadership cons. Girl Scouts Am., Greater Los Angeles, 1986—. Mem. Am. Personnel and Guidance Assn., Am. Psychol. Assn., Mo. Psychol. Assn., Assn. for Advancement Behavioral Therapy, AAUP, Am. Ednl. Research Assn., Internat. Soc. for Polit. Psychology, Am. Soc. Tng., Devel., Orgn. Behavioral Teaching Soc., Acad. Mgmt. St. Louis Art Mus. (life), Stanford Alumni Assn. (life). Clubs: Bus. and Profl. Women, St. Louis. Author: Effective Learning Skills, 1977; What is Treatment?, 1977; (with Brim and Wetzel) Social Network Characteristics of Hospitalized Depressed Patients, 1982; writer, dir. film Women and Money: Myths and Realities, 1976. Home: 10601 Wilshire Blvd Los Angeles CA 90024

WHITNEY, JANE, foreign service officer; b. Champaign, Ill., July 15, 1941; d. Robert F. and Mussette (Cary) W. B.A., Beloit Coll., 1963; C.D., U. Aix-Marseille, France, 1962. Joined Fgn. Service, U.S. Dept. State, 1965; vice consul, Saigon, Vietnam, 1966-68; career counselor Dept. State, 1968-70; spl. asst. Office of Dir. Gen., U.S. Dept. State, 1970-72; consul, Stuttgart, Fed. Republic Germany, 1972-74, Ankara, Turkey, 1974-76; spl. asst. Office of Asst. Sec. for Consular Affairs, U.S. Dept. State, 1976-77; mem. Bd. Examiners Fgn. Service, 1977-78, 79-81; consul, Munich, Fed. Republic Germany, 1978-79; consul, Buenos Aires, Argentina, 1981-82; ethics officer Office of Legal Adviser, U.S. Dept. State, 1982-85; advisor Office of Asst. Sec. for Diplomatic Security, U.S. Dept. State, 1985-86; dep. prin. officer, consul, Stuttgart, 1986—. Recipient awards Dept. State, 1968, 70, 81, 85. Democrat. Roman Catholic. Office: Am Consulate Gen APO New York NY 09154

WHITNEY, MYRNA-LYNNE, logistics engineer; b. Montreal, Que., Can., May 27, 1942; came to U.S., 1949, naturalized, 1962; d. Edmund W. and Florence S. (Richardson) Prasloski; B.A. magna cum laude, Calif. State U.-Northridge, 1971; M.S., Central Mo. State U., 1975; m. Richard A. Whitney, Jan. 2, 1977. Sec., Rockwell Internat., Canoga Park, Calif., 1962-69, methods and procedures analyst, 1976-77, environ. health and safety engr., 1977-79, system safety engr., 1979-81, developer missile support plan, 1981-84, tech. asst. space shuttle program, 1984; logistics specialist Dept. Air Force, 1984—. Served with USAF, 1971-74; maj. Res., 1975—. Decorated USAF Meritorious Service medal, Air Force Commendation medal. Mem. Am. Soc. Safety Engrs., System Safety Soc., Phi Kappa Phi. Office: Air Force Plant Rep Rocketdyne 6633 Canoga Ave Canoga Park CA 91304

WHITNEY, Q. LOUISE, cosmetology college executive; b. Artesia, N.Mex., Jan. 26, 1944; d. William Neil Jackson and Mary Lois (Pryor) Miller; children—Tammy, Lorrie, Billy, Orville, Jr., Christopher. Cert. cosmetology instr., N.Mex. Cosmetologist, Curl Cottage, Roswell, N.Mex., 1970-71, Dottie's Roswell, 1971-72, Maude's, Roswell, 1972-74, Lea's, Roswell, 1975-76; mgr. Louise's, Roswell, 1976-79; pres. Roswell Coll. Cosmetology, 1976—. Mem. Nat. Hairdressers and Cosmetologists Assn. (pres., v.p.), Tchr.'s Edn. Council, Nat. Assn. Cosmetology Schs., S.W. Assn. Fin. Aid Officers, Roswell C. of C. Democrat. Baptist. Office: Roswell Coll Cosmetology 112 N Virginia Roswell NM 88201

WHITNEY, RUTH REINKE, magazine editor; b. Oshkosh, Wis., July 23, 1928; d. Leonard G. and Helen (Diestler) Reinke; B.A., Northwestern U., 1949; m. Daniel A. Whitney, Nov. 19, 1949; 1 son, Philip. Copywriter edn. dept. circulation div. Time, Inc., 1949-53; editor-in-chief Better Living mag., 1953-56; asso. editor Seventeen magazine, 1956-62, exec. editor, 1962-67; editor-in-chief Glamour mag., N.Y.C., 1967—. Mem. Fashion Group, Am. Soc. Mag. Editors (pres. 1975-77), Women in Communication, Matrix award 1980), Alpha Chi Omega. Office: Glamour Mag Condé Nast Publs Inc 350 Madison Ave New York NY 10017

WHITSON, BETTY ANN, educational administrator; b. Canadian, Tex., May 15, 1937; d. Jack H. and Ruth Mary (King) W.; m. Paul R. Caillet, Sept. 18, 1960 (div. 1969). B.A., West Tex. U., 1958; B.S., U. Houston, 1963, M.Ed., 1977, Ed.D., 1979. Cert. tchr., Tex., Md. Tchr., Dalhart High Sch., Tex., 1958-59, Poolesville Jr. High Sch., Md., 1959-60, Southland Elem. Sch., Houston, 1963-76; teaching fellow U. Houston, 1976-79; asst. prin., tchr. Wainwright Elem. Sch., Houston, 1979—; vis. instr. U. St. Thomas, Houston, 1981. Contbr. research articles to profl. publs. Recipient Tchr. of Yr. award Wainwright Elem. Sch. 1982, Best Tchr. Made Mgmt. Program, Dept. Technology, Technology Fair, 1983, Excellence in Teaching award Tex. A&M U., 1985. Mem. Nat. Sci. Tchr. Assn., Computer Educator Assn., NEA, Tex. Edn. Assn., Tex. Classroom Tchrs. Democrat. Presbyterian. Avocations: birding; hiking; reading. Home: 1120 M D Anderson #6G Houston TX 77030 Office: Wainwright Elem Sch 5335 Milwee Houston TX 77092

WHITSON, LINDA JO, university administrator; b. Brownfield, Tex., Feb. 27, 1944; d. Ray Earl and Pauline Castleberry; B.A. in English, Tex. Tech. U., 1966; M.S. in Ednl. Psychology, Tex. A&M U., 1975, Ph.D. in Ednl. Adminstr., 1979; m. Robert E. Whitson, Aug. 30, 1963; children—Cristie Lynn, Susan Kimberly. Mem. adminstrv. staff Tex. A&M U. System, 1975-82, asst. to vice chancellor programs, 1978-82; cons. Spring Branch (Tex.) Sch. Dist., 1977; asst. to pres., asst. prof. edn. U. Tex., San Antonio, 1982-86, acting v.p. adminstrn., 1986—. Mem. Am. Assn. Higher Edn., Assn. Study Higher Edn., Am. Ednl. Research Assn., Assn. Women Deans, Adminstrs. and Counselors, Alpha Lambda Delta, Phi Kappa Phi, Kappa Delta Pi. Methodist. Office: Office of Vice Pres for Adminstr U Tex San Antonio TX 78285

WHITTEMORE, DOROTHY JANE, librarian; b. San Jose, Calif., Nov. 9, 1920; d. Glen James and Jane Dorothy (Katz) Gordon; A.B., San Jose State Coll., 1941, cert. of librarianship, 1942, postgrad., 1952-53; m. Robert Clifton Whittemore, June 15, 1959; children by previous marriage—Stanley Allen Lawton, Shirley Anne (Mrs. Anthony Kopcych). Sch. library supr. Piedmont (Calif.) Sch. Dist., 1942-43; asst. post librarian Presidio of San Francisco, 1943-49; jr. librarian San Jose (Calif.) State Coll., 1951-53; reference librarian Tulane U. Library, New Orleans, 1953-76, acting dir., 1976-78, asst. dir. public service, 1978-80, dir. Norman Mayer Bus. Library, 1980—. Dir., New Orleans chpt. LWV, 1964-66, dir. La. chpt., 1967-69, 73—; mem. citizens adv. com. City Planning Commn. of New Orleans, 1965-67; sec. New Orleans chpt. La. Consumers League, 1972-74; active Public Affairs Research Council; mem. adv. council La. State Bd. Nursing, 1977—. Council on Library Resources research grantee, 1972. Mem. Spl. Libraries Assn. (pres. La. chpt. 1975-77, sec.-treas. social welfare sect. 1977-79), La. Library Assn. (chmn. coll. and reference sect. 1968-69, exec. bd. 1973-74), New Orleans Library Club (past pres.), Am. Soc. Info. Sci., Nat. Microfilm Assn. Author: (with others) Citizen's Guide to Louisiana Government, 1969. Home: 7521 Dominican St New Orleans LA 70118 Office: Tulane U Library New Orleans LA 70118

WHITTEN, CYNTHIA LOU, typesetting company executive; b. Chgo., Mar. 30, 1953; d. George, Jr. and Betty Jean (Crabill) W.; m. Daniel Solis, Aug. 7, 1971 (div. Oct. 1978); m. Robert Jay Shutan, Apr. 1, 1985. Grad. high sch., Deerfield, Ill. Prodn. mgr. Addison Leader, Ill., 1972-73; editor Destination Publs. Ltd., Chgo., 1973-74; pres., owner PicaType Inc., Chgo., 1974—. Mem. Ill. Typographers Assn. (bd. dirs. 1980-86), Typographers Internat. Assn. (mem. exec. com. 1983-85). Avocations: reading, jogging. Office: PicaType Inc 7429 Western Ave Chicago IL 60645

WHITTIER, SARAJANE, social studies educator; b. North Manchester, Ind., Dec. 17, 1912; d. Charles and Ethel Clo (Free) Leckrone; m. C. Taylor Whittier, June 18, 1934; children—Chip, Tim, Cece, Penny. B.A., U. Chgo., 1934, M.A., 1946. Research sec. Oriental Inst., Chgo., 1935-39; tchr. pub. schs., Flossmoor, Ill., 1939-41, Sta. WSUN-TV, St. Petersburg, Fla., 1955-56, Sta. GWETA-TV, Washington, 1961-62; substitute tchr. pub. schs., Fla. and Md., 1962—. Co-author: Pasture Trails, 1941. Asst. monthly newsletter Supt.'s Digest, 1983-85. Pres., PTA, St. Petersburg, 1960's; Kans. chmn. Friends of J.F.K. Ctr., Topeka, 1969-75, Tex. chmn., San Antonio, 1975-82; guardian Camp Fire Girls, Chgo., 1936-41, Gaithersburg, Md., 1958-64; Sunday sch. tchr. Christian Ch., Chgo., 1926-34, St. Petersburg, 1950-57, pianist, San Antonio, 1975-82. U. Chgo. scholar, 1933-34. Mem. AAUW (past pres.). Republican. Avocations: acting; music; directing little theatres; photography; world traveling. Home: 756 Fairlawn Dr Gretna LA 70056

WHITTINGTON, MARY JAYNE GARRARD, journalist; b. Monteagle, Tenn., Aug. 13, 1915; d. William Mountjoy and Mabelle Moseley (Smith) Garrard; grad. Nat. Cathedral Sch., 1934; student King-Smith Studio Sch., 1934-35; m. William Madison Whittington, Jr., Dec. 27, 1945; children—Jamie Garrard Whittington Gasner, William Madison, Anna Aven. Contbg. editor Delta Rev., Memphis, 1964-69, Mississippi mag., 1977-82; freelance writer, columnist, Greenwood, Miss., 1956—. Mem. exec. bd. Greenwood Found. Arts, 1962-83; bd. govs. Greenwood Little Theatre, 1956-66, 75-82; trustee Ballet Miss.; bd. dirs. Mimi Garrard Dance Co., N.Y.C., Ctr. Study So. Culture, Internat. Ballet Competition III, Jackson, Miss., Mississippians for Ednl. TV, Friends of Art in Miss., Friends of Art Mus., Naples, Fla. Served to capt. WAC, 1942-45. Mem. Nat. League Am. Pen Women, So. Debutante Assembly, DAR, First Families Va., Delta Cotton Wives, Nat. Soc. Colonial Dames, Order Crown Am. Jr. Aux. (life), Kappa Pi (hon.). Clubs: Greenwood Garden, Greenwood Country. Address: 1000 Grand Blvd Greenwood MS 38930

WHITTLESEY, FAITH RYAN, ambassador, lawyer; b. Jersey City, Feb. 21, 1939; B.A., Wells Coll., 1960; J.D., U. Pa., 1963; postgrad. Acad. Internat. Law, The Hague, Netherlands; children—Amy, William, Henry. Substitute tchr. Phila. pub. schs., 1962-64; spl. asst. atty. gen., Pa. Dept. Justice, Phila., 1964-65; law clk. to judge U.S. Dist. Ct., Eastern Pa. Dist., 1965-66; spl. asst. atty. gen. Pa. Dept. Pub. Welfare, 1967-70; mem. Pa. Ho. of Reps., 1972-76; mem. Delaware County Council, Media, Pa., 1976-81; mem. firm Wolf, Block, Schorr and Solis-Cohen, Phila., 1980-81; ambassador to Switzerland, Bern, 1981-83; asst. for pub. liaison to Pres. U.S., Washington, 1983-85; ambassador to Switzerland, 1985. Address: Econ/Commercial Sta Switzerland US Dept State Washington DC 20520

WHITTLESEY, SUZANNE WOOD, psychiat. social worker; b. Oklahoma City, Sept. 16, 1942; d. William and Beryl Wood; B.S. in Nursing, San Francisco State Coll., 1965; M.S.W., U. Okla., 1975; m. W. A. Whittlesey, Apr. 13, 1963; children—Mark, Timothy. Nursing supr. Doctor's Gen. Hosp., Oklahoma City, 1970-73; psychiat. social worker, clin. instr. U. Okla., Oklahoma City, 1975-78, clin. asst. prof. psychiatry, 1980—. Mem. Nat. Assn. Social Workers, Okla. Health and Welfare Assn., Okla. Mental Health Assn., Assn. Clin. Social Workers. Home: 2313 Old Farm Rd Edmond OK 73034

WHITWORTH, JUNE ELIZABETH, advertising company executive; b. Vicksburg, Miss., Aug. 5, 1943; d. James Wesley and Doris Eleanor (Whitmire) Brannon; m. Charles Walton Whitworth, Mar. 14, 1963 (div. 1971); children—Clyde Wesley, Krista Lynn. Grad. Massey Bus. Coll., 1963; student LaGrange Coll., 1961-62, U. Ga., 1963-65. Corp. sales mgr., dir. catering Omni Hotel, Atlanta, 1975-78; Southeast regional mgr. Champion Internat. Retail, Atlanta, 1978-80; Southwest regional mgr. Pak 2000, Dallas, 1980-81; freelance cons., Dallas, 1981-82; mktg. dir. Lone Star Micro, Dallas, 1981-82; pres., owner June Whitworth & Assocs., Dallas, 1982—. Author, editor: Insights into Microcomputer Publications, 1983; Insights II, 1984. Named La. Hon. State Senator, 1976, Tex. Noble Women, 1984. Mem. Am. Assn. Advt. Agys., Dallas Advt. League, Dallas Advt. Profls., Sales and Mktg. Execs. Home: 5608 Bentwood Trail Dallas TX 75252 Office: June Whitworth & Assocs 3000 E Plano Pkwy Planos TX 75074

WHITWORTH, KATHRYNNE ANN, professional golfer; b. Monahans, Tex., Sept. 27, 1939; d. Morris Clark and Dama Ann (Robinson) Whitworth; student Odessa Jr. Coll., 1957. Mem. Ladies Profl. Golf Tour, 1959—; winner more than 88 ofcl. tournaments, 1965-71; winner Vare Scoring Trophy, 1965-67, 69, 71, 72; mem. adv. staff Walter Hagen Golf Co. Named Woman Athlete of Year, A.P., 1965, 66; Player of Year Ladies Profl. Golf Assn., 1966-69, 71-73; elected to Ladies Profl. Golf Assn. Hall of Fame, 1975, World Golf Hall of Fame, Tex. Sports Hall of Fame, Tex. Golf Hall of Fame, 1982, Women's Sports Found. Hall of Fame, 1984. first LPGA mem. to win over one million dollars. Mem. Ladies Profl. Golf Assn. (pres. 1967, 68, 70). Address: Ladies Profl Golf Assn 1250 Shoreline Dr Sugar Land TX 77478

WHORRALL, KAREN SUE, chemical engineer; b. Middletown, Ohio, Dec. 12, 1943; s. Neal Vincent and Margaret Olive (Long) Farnlacher; B.S.Chem. Engring., U. Cin., 1966; postgrad. Wright State U., 1967-70, Dayton Art Inst., 1966-70, Ind. U., 1970-71; m. William J. Whorrall, June 10, 1971; 1 son, David William. Process engr. Kimberly Clark Corp., West Carrollton, Ohio, 1966-70; chem. engr. mfg. tech. div., applied scis. dept. Naval Weapons Support Center, Crane, Ind., 1973-75,; pyrotechnic prodn. engr./environ. coordinator Crane Army Ammunition Activity, 1975-81; chem. engr. Naval Ammunition Prodn. Engring. Center, Crane, 1981-84, supervisory engr., 1984—; sci. instr. Northwood Inst., West Baden, Ind., 1972-73. Charter mem. Hoosier Hills chpt. Federally Employed Women, 1974—, pres., 1976. Lic. profl. engr., Ind. Mem. Am. Inst. Chem. Engrs. Patentee ecol. reclamation of pyrotechnic wastes (2). Home: Route 3 Shoals IN 47581 Office: Naval Ammunition Prodn Engring Center Crane IN 47522

WHORTON, BOBBIE ROSE, motel manager; b. Shreveport, La., Dec. 19, 1948; d. Walter Lawrence and Bobbie Louise (Campbell) Scarborough; m. C.G. Whorton, June 2, 1966; 1 child, Amanda Rose. Diploma, Shreveport Vocat. Tech. Sch., 1968, Ednl. Inst. Am. Hotel-Motel, Mich., 1983. Sales asst. Merrill Lynch, Shreveport, 1967-71; motel mgr. Best Western Airline Motor Inn, 1978—; realtor assoc. James Brown Real Estate, Bossier City, La., 1980—; dir. Bossier Bank & Trust, 1985—, Bossier Med. Ctr. Hosp., 1985—. Pres., Bossier City Quota Club, 1984—; dir. Women's Missionary Union, Airline Baptist Ch., 1985—; chmn. bldg. com. Airline Baptist Ch., 1986. Mem. Nat. Assn. Female Execs., Am. Hotel Motel Assn., C. of C. (v.p. mem. Bossier chpt. 1984—), Shreveport Bossier Hotel Motel Assn. (bd. dirs.), Shreveport Bossier Bd. Realtors Assn. Democrat. Am. Baptist. Lodge: Order Eastern Star. Home: 106 Fairmont Bossier City LA 71111 Office: Best Western Airline Motor Inn 1984 Airline Dr Bossier City LA 71112

WHORTON, COURTNEY, travel executive; b. Brunswick, Ga., July 27, 1947; d. James L. and Doris (Newman) Music; m. J. Leroy Whorton, July 31, 1971; 1 child, Julius Timothy. A.B. in Edn., Brunswick Jr. Coll., 1968; student Ga. So. Coll., 1969-71. Travel agt. Mary Miller Travel, Brunswick, Ga., 1969-72; travel mgr. Adventure Travel, St. Simons Island, Ga., 1972-74; corp. mgr. Gibson World Travel, Virginia Beach, Va., 1975-78, pres., owner, 1978—; pres., owner Gibson World Travel/Branch, 1984—. Treas. Virginia Beach Republican Club, 1985-86; bd. dirs. Red White & Blue Republican Club, 1986; mem. Pembroke Civic League, 1985-86; mem. PTA, 1984—. Mem. Nat. Assn. Profl. Saleswomen, Sales and Mktg. Execs., Contract Mgmt. Assn., Am. Bus. Women's Assn., Soc. of Travel Agts. in Govt., Assn. Retail Travel Agts. (pres. 1982-84). Advent Christian. Avocations: piano; collecting antiques. Home: 4616 Jeanne St Virginia Beach VA 23462 Office: Gibson World Travel 363 Independence Blvd Virginia Beach VA 23462

WIARDA, IEDA SIQUEIRA, political scientist, educator; b. Belo Horizonte, Brazil, Nov. 3, 1939; came to U.S., 1957, naturalized, 1968; d. Elvindo Dutra and Maria (Barros) S.; B.A., Nebr. Wesleyan U., 1960; M.A., U. Fla., 1962, Ph.D., 1968; m. Howard J. Wiarda, Feb. 4, 1964; children—Kristy Lynn, Howard Elvindo, Jonathan Siqueira. Research assoc. U. Mass., Amherst, 1972; faculty assoc. Smith Coll., 1978; now professorial lectr., course chmn. U. Mass., Amherst and Fgn. Service Inst., Dept. State; lectr. Bus. Council for Internat. Understanding, Am. U.; guest lectr. Nebr. Wesleyan U., U. Fla., New Coll., Fla., Mt. Holyoke Coll., Smith Coll.; cons. population policies. Grantee Ford Found., Rockefeller Found., NIH. Mem. Am. Polit. Sci. Assn., Latin Am. Studies Assn., Population Assn. Am., Am. Public Health Assn., New Eng. Council Latin Am. Studies, World Population Soc., World Future Soc., Conselho Nacional de Mulheres, Nat. Council Hispanic Women, Assn. for Women in Devel., Internat. Women's Health Coalition (dir.), Amherst Growth Com., Kestrel Fund, AAUW (v.p. Conn. Valley br.). Republican. Contbr. articles, chpts. to profl. publs. Home: 65 Chapel Rd Amherst MA 01002 Office: Polit Sci Dept U Mass Amherst MA 01003

WIBLE, JUDITH LAINE, psychiatrist; b. Portland, Ind., Oct. 7, 1940; d. John F. and June V. (Young) W.; student U. Houston, 1959-61; M.D., U. Tex., 1965; children—Pamela, Frederick. Intern, Jewish Hosp. and Med. Center, Bklyn., 1965-66; resident in psychiatry Phila. Psychiat. Center, Ancora Psychiat. Hosp., Hammonton, N.J., 1971-72, Phila. State Hosp., 1972-74; research psychiatrist Phila. Gen. Hosp., 1973-75; clin. dir., staff psychiatrist Phila. State Hosp., 1974-76; clin. asst. psychiatrist Pa. Hosp., Phila., 1976-77; inpatient unit dir. Dallas County Mental Health Center, Dallas, 1977-78; practice medicine specializing in psychiatry, Dallas, 1978—. Diplomate Am. Bd. Psychiatry and Neurology, Inc. Mem. Am. Med. Women's Assn., Am. Psychiat. Assn., Pres.'s Assocs. of Woman's Med. Coll. Pa., NOW, Nat. Women Polit. Caucus, Dallas C. of C., Alpha Epsilon Delta. Office: 13601 Preston Rd Dallas TX 75240

WICHELECKI, SANDRA MARIE, aerospace company executive; b. Chgo., Feb. 7, 1960; d. Edward Adam and Alivna H. (Nowicki) W. B.S. in Structural Engrng., U. Ill.-Chgo., 1983; postgrad. San Diego State U., 1985—. Assoc. engr. Convair div. Gen. Dynamics Corp., San Diego, 1983, engr., 1983—. Mem. ASCE, AIAA, Nat. Assn. Female Execs. Republican. Roman Catholic. Avocations: softball; racketball; golf; sailing. Home: 5141 Dawne St San Diego CA 92117 Office: Convair div Gen Dynamics Corp PO Box 85357 San Diego CA 92138

WICHER, CAMILLE PHYLLIS, nursing administrator; b. Buffalo, Dec. 11, 1955; m. Donald J. Wicher; 1 child, Christopher James. M.S. in Nursing, SUNY-Buffalo, 1983; postgrad. Sch. of Law, 1985—. Registered nurse, N.Y. Charge nurse intensive care unit Roswell Park Meml. Inst., Buffalo, 1977-79; dir. inservice edn. Buffalo Columbus Hosp., 1979-82, dir. nursing, 1982—; clin. instr. SUNY-Buffalo, 1981-82. Mem. Soc. Nursing Service Adminstrs. Democrat. Roman Catholic. Office: Buffalo Columbus Hosp 300 Niagara St Buffalo NY 14201

WICK, ERIKA ELISABETH, psychologist; b. Basel, Switzerland, July 31, 1937; d. Josef and Martha (Gabriel) W.; came to U.S., 1964, naturalized, 1970; Ph.D., U. Basel, 1964. Prof. psychology St. John's U., Jamaica, N.Y., 1976—. Mem. Am. Psychol. Assn., N.Y. Acad. Sci.; fellow Acad. Psychosomatic Medicine. Office: St John's U Jamaica NY 11439

WICKER, VERONICA DICARLO, judge; b. Monessen, Pa., Nov. 26, 1930; d. Vincent James and Rose Margaret DiCarlo; B.F.A., Syracuse U., 1952; J.D., Loyola U., New Orleans, 1966; m. Thomas Carey Wicker Jr; children—Cathy, Carey. U.S. magistrate Eastern dist. La., 1977-79; judge U.S. Dist. Ct. (ea. dist.) La., New Orleans, 1979—; participant Warren Conf., 1985, 86. Mem. vis. com. Loyola U. Sch. Law, New Orleans. Mem. ABA, La. Bar Assn., Fed. Bar Assn., New Orleans Bar Assn., Maritime Law Assn., Jefferson Parish Bar Aux., Fed. Judges Assn., Assn. Women Judges, Assn. Women Attys., Am. Justinian Soc. Jurists, Alpha Xi Alpha, Phi Mu. Office: US Courthouse Room C-508 500 Camp St New Orleans LA 70130

WICKS, MILDRED LEE, nursing educator; b. Vicksburg, Miss., Jan. 28, 1937; d. Moses Samuel and Mary Jesse (Lee) Simpkins; m. Richard Daniel Wicks, Apr. 12, 1956; children—Richard Anthony, Dayle, Michael, Kimberly, John. A.D. in Nursing, Community Coll. Allegheny County, 1970; B.S., Duquesne U., 1974; M.S. in Nursing Edn., U. Pitts., 1978. Staff nurse Montefiore Hosp., Pitts., 1970-71; clinic coordinator Manchester Health Ctr., Pitts., 1971-72; instr. Community Coll. Allegheny County, Pitts., 1972-81, assoc. prof., 1981—. Alt. del., White House conf. on Aging, 1981; bd. dirs. Hilltop YMCA, Pitts., 1979—, S.W. Community Mental Health/Mental Retardation, Pitts., 1981—. Mem. Nat. League Nursing, Sigma Theta Tau. Home: 239 Zara St Pittsburgh PA 15210 Office: Community Coll Allegheny County 808 Ridge Ave Pittsburgh PA 15212

WICKWIRE, PATRICIA JOANNE NELLOR, psychologist, educator; b. Sioux City, Iowa; d. William McKinley and Clara Rose (Pautsch) Nellor; B.A. cum laude, U. No. Iowa, 1951; M.A., U. Iowa, 1959; Ph.D., U. Tex., Austin, 1971; postgrad. U. So. Calif., UCLA, Calif. State U., Long Beach, 1951-66; m. Robert James Wickwire, Sept. 7, 1957; 1 son, William James. Tchr., Ricketts Ind. Schs., Iowa, 1946-48; tchr., counselor Waverly-Shell Rock Ind. Schs., Iowa, 1951-55; reading cons., head dormitory counselor U. Iowa, Iowa City, 1955-57; tchr., sch. psychologist, adminstr. S. Bay Union High Sch. Dist., Redondo Beach, Calif., 1962—, dir. student services and spl. edn.; cons. mgmt. and edn.; mem. Calif. Interagency Mental Health Council, exec. bd., 1968-72; chmn. Friends of Dominguez Hills (Calif.), 1981—; mem. exec. bd. Beach Cities Symphony Assn., 1970-82. Lic. ednl. psychologist, marriage, family and child counselor, Calif. Mem. AAUW (exec. bd., chpt. pres. 1962-72), Los Angeles County Dirs. Pupil Services (chmn. 1974-79), Los Angeles County Personnel and Guidance Assn. (pres. 1977-78), Calif. Personnel and Guidance Assn. (exec. bd. 1977-78), Assn. Calif. Sch. Adminstrs. (dir. 1977-81), Los Angeles County SW Bd. Dist. Adminstrs. for Spl. Edn. (chmn. 1976-81), Calif. Assn. Sch. Psychologist (dir. 1981—), Am. Psychol. Assn., Am. Assn. Sch. Adminstrs., Calif. Assn. for Measurement and Evaluation in Guidance (dir. 1981, pres. 1984-85), Am. Assn. Counseling and Devel., Assn. Measurement and Eval. in Guidance (Western regional editor 1983—), Calif. Assn. Counseling and Devel. (exec. bd. 1984—), Pi Lambda Theta, Alpha Phi Gamma, Psi Chi, Kappa Delta Pi, Sigma Alpha Iota. Contbr. articles in field to profl. jours. Home and Office: 2900 Amby Pl Hermosa Beach CA 90254

WIDDER, BETTE WIENBERG, nurse administrator; b. Lafayette County, Mo., June 20, 1929; d. Elmer Arthur and Lorene Mathilda (Bodenstab) Wienberg; B.S. cum laude, Linfield Coll., 1976; m. John Arthur Widder, July 7, 1953; children—John A., Anne Whiteley, Susan Jane, Scott Kevin. Acting supr. U. Mo. Hosps., 1951-52; mem. staff Arlington (Va.) Community Hosp., 1960-61, W. Jefferson Gen. Hosp., Marrero, La., 1965, dispensary 8th Naval Dist., 1965; mem. rehab. staff A. Holly Patterson Home, Uniondale, N.Y., 1969-70; mem. staff St. Vincent Hosp. and Med. Center, Portland, Oreg., 1972-78, asst. dir. nursing services, 1978—. Editor, pub. St. Vincent Nursing Newsletter. Contbr. articles to profl. jours. Mem. commn. on nursing edn. Oreg. Bd. Nursing; chmn. St. Vincent Nursing Safety Com., St. Vincent Safety Council. R.N., Oreg., N.Y., R.I., Va., La., Mo. Mem. SEE Internat., Am. Hosp. Assn., Oreg. Hosp. Assn., Am. Orgn. Nurse Execs., Oreg. Orgn. Nurse Execs. Home: 15095 NW Oakmont Loop Beaverton OR 97006 Office: 9205 SW Barnes Rd Portland OR 97225

WIDENER, PERI ANN, public relations manager; b. Wichita, Kans., May 1, 1956; d. Wayne Robert and LuAnne (Harris) W. B.S., Wichita State U., 1978; postgrad. Ala. A&M U., 1981. Advt. intern Associated Advt., Wichita, 1978; pub. relations asst. Fourth Nat. Bank, Wichita, 1978-79; mktg. support rep. Boeing Co., Wichita, 1979-83, pub. relations rep., Huntsville, Ala., 1983-85, pub. relations mgr., 1985—. Preston Huston scholar, Wichita State U., 1978; recipient Best Electronic Ad award Def. Electronics mag., 1982, Best Total Pub. Relations Program award Huntsville Press Club, 1985. Mem. Women in Communications, Pub. Relations Council Ala. (bd. dirs. 1985—), Internat. Assn. Bus. Communicators, Pub. Relations Soc. Am., Sigma Delta Chi. Club: Hunstville Press. Methodist. Office: The Boeing Co 220 Wynn Dr Huntsville AL 35807

WIDENER-BURROWS, DAWNE DELANE, marketing research executive; b. Hampton, Va., July 7, 1955; d. John Gordon and Sylvia Ann (Middleton) Widener; m. Lawrence B. Burrows, Jan. 1, 1980. B.S. in Journalism cum laude, U. Fla., 1976. Research analyst Rife Market Research, Miami, Fla., 1976-78; research mgr. Earle Palmer Brown & Assocs., Washington, 1978-79; v.p., research dir. Needham Harper & Steers, Washington, 1979-85; v.p. research Rosenthal, Greene & Campbell, Washington, 1985-86; prin. Migliara, Kaplan & Widener Assocs., Balt., 1986—; cons. Fairfax County C. of C., 1980-81. Mem. Mktg. Research Assn. (historian 1982-83, chpt. pres. 1985), Am. Mktg. Assn., Am. Assn. Advt. Agys., Bank Mktg. Assn. Democrat. Episcopalian. Home: 4607 Roxbury Dr Bethesda MD 20814 Office: Migliara Kaplan & Widener Assocs 305 W Chesapeake Ave Towson MD 21204

WIDENHOUSE, BONNIE TILLEY, real estate company executive; b. High Point, N.C., July 1, 1938; d. David Tilley and Leah Lucille (Davis) Bowen; m. Alton Glenn Widenhouse, Jr., May 24, 1958; 1 child, Brian Glenn. Student, Appalachian U., 1956-58, Queen's Coll., 1973-75. Buyer Belk Stores, Charlotte, N.C., 1958-64; pub. relations dir. Townsend Realty, Charlotte, 1971-74; v.p. Merrill Lynch Realty, Charlotte, 1974-83; pres., chief exec. officer Touchberry & Assocs., Charlotte, 1983—. Speaker, Real Estate One, Detroit, 1983—; bd. dirs. ARC, Charlotte, 1984—; Mission Air, Charlotte, 1985—; chmn. area div. Arts and Sci. Council Dr., Charlotte, 1985; chmn. econ. devel. Charlotte/Mecklenburg Citizens Forum, 1986; mem. steering com. White House Conf. Small Bus., 1986; mem. Travel and Tourism Council N.C., 1980-85. Mem. Women Bus. Owners, Nat. Homebuilders Assn., Speakers Assn., Charlotte C. of C. (bd. dirs. 1984—), Nat. Assn. Women Execs. (chmn. com. 1977-80). Republican. Presbyterian. Club: Jr. Womens (Charlotte) (pres. 1965-70). Office: Touchberry & Assocs Realtors 200 Queens Rd Charlotte NC 28204

WIDGOFF, MILDRED, physicist, educator; b. Buffalo, Aug. 24, 1924; d. Leo and Rebecca (Shulimson) W.; B.S., U. Buffalo, 1944; Ph.D., Cornell U., 1951; divorced; children—Eve Shapiro, Jonathan B. Shapiro. Research asso. Brookhaven Nat. Lab., Upton, N.Y., 1952-55; research fellow cyclotron lab. Harvard U., 1955-59; mem. faculty Brown U., 1959—, prof. physics, 1974—. Fellow Am. Phys. Soc.; mem. Phi Beta Kappa, Sigma Xi, Phi Kappa Phi. Office: Physics Dept Brown U Providence RI 02912

WIDICKER, GLENNA NELL, interior design firm executive; b. Jamestown, N.D.; d. Herman and Janiece W.; B.S., Andrews U., 1972. Owner, G.N. Designs, Vail, Colo., 1972-76; salesperson Contract Internat., Denver, 1976-79; Colo. real estate salesperson, 1972—; pres., owner Contract Design Ltd., Denver, 1979—; money broker, 1985-86; prin., broker movie prodn. co., 1986. Office: Contract Design Ltd 1948 S Quebec St Denver CO 80231

WIDING, CAROL SCHARFE, lawyer; b. South Orange, N.J., Dec. 18, 1941; d. Howard Carman and Marjorie (McConaghy) Scharfe; m. C. Jon Widing, July 2, 1966; 1 son, Daniel McClure. B.A., Wellesley Coll., 1964; M.Ed., Harvard U., 1965; J.D., Delaware Law Sch., Widener U., 1980. Bar: Del. 1981, Pa. 1981, Conn. 1984. Tchr. 4th-5th grades Frankin Sch., Lexington, Mass., 1964-65; pvt. tutor, Ibadan, Nigeria, 1965; tchr. 4th grade The Shipley Sch., Bryn Mawr, Pa., 1966-68, Pa. Adult Basic Edn. Acad., 1970-72; clk. Ridgely and Ridgely, P.A., Dover, Del., 1980; dep. atty. gen. representing state Child Protective Services in cases of child abuse and child neglect Office of Atty., Gen., Del. Dept. Justice, Wilmington, 1981-83; staff atty. UAW Legal Services Newark, Del., 1983; assoc. Hebb & Gitlin, P.C., Hartford, Conn., 1985—. Program chmn. Jr. League Phila., 1972; v.p. program AAUW, Middletown, Del., 1974; chmn. pub. relations and fundraising Lower New Castle County Med. Ctr., Middletown, 1980. Mem. ABA, Conn. Bar Assn., Hartford Assn. Women Attys., Pa. Bar Assn., Del. Bar Assn., Assn. Trial Lawyers Am. Democrat. Episcopalian. Office: Hebb & Gitlin PC One State St Hartford CT 06103

WIDMAYER, PATRICIA, consulting firm executive, education and public policy consultant; b. Buffalo, Jan. 21, 1943; d. C. Lane and Elizabeth M. (Gillgus) Ramsdell; m. Lawrence C. Widmayer, June 15, 1963; children—Carole Lane, Christopher Almon. B.A., Mich. State U., 1966, M.A., 1969, Ph.D., 1971. Instr. Oakland U., Rochester, Mich., 1971-72; research assoc. Office of the Speaker, Lansing, Mich., 1973-75; dist. staff dir. Congressman Bob Carr, Washington, 1975-77; dir. legis. Mich. dept. Edn., Lansing, 1977-82; dir. policy Office of Gov., Lansing, 1982-83; exec. dir. Gov.'s Commn. on Higher Edn., Lansing, 1983-85; pres. Widmayer and Assocs., Chgo., 1985—; trainer Nat. Women's Edn. Fund, Washington, 1982—; spl. project dir. colo. Commn. on Higher Edn., Denver, 1985-86; cons. Borg-Warner Found., Chgo., 1985—. Author numerous govt. papers, reports, 1977-85. Editor report: Putting our minds together, 1984. Vol. cons. to local, state and nat. campaigns and issue coalitions; coordinator Nat. Women's Polit. Caucus of Mich., 1975-80, Mich. Women's Assembly, 1976-84; bd. dirs. Econ. Devel. Corp., East Lansing, Mich., 1979-85. Inst. for Ednl. Leadership fellow George Washington U., Washington, 1978-79. Mem. Am. Assn. Higher Edn., Chgo. Women in Govt. Relations, Delta Delta Delta (officer 1968-85) Lodge: Zonta (officer 1978-81). Home: 420 Church St Evanston IL 60201 Office: Widmayer and Assocs 151 N Michigan Ave Suite 2416 Chicago IL 60601

WIDMER, LAURA BETH, mass communication educator; b. Moberly, Mo., May 6, 1956; d. John Richard and Gertrude (Roling) Widmer. B.S., Northwest Mo. State U., 1979; M.S., Iowa State U., 1983. Media asst. Earle Palmer Brown Advt. Agy., Washington, 1980; photo lab. instr. Iowa State U., Ames, 1981, instr. yearbook workshop, 1981—; publs. coordinator Clinton Sch. Dist. (Mo.), 1982-83; publs. dir., instr. Northwest Mo. State U., Maryville, 1983—, dir. summer publs. workshop, 1978—; instr. yearbook workshop Drake U., Des Moines, 1983, U. Mo., 1984—. Mem. Nat. Press Photographers Assn., Soc. Profl. Journalists, Mo. Press Women's Fedn., Collegiate Media Advisers. Roman Catholic. Home: 427 Lisa Ln Maryville MO 64468 Office: Northwest Mo State U 22 McCracken Hall Maryville MO 64468

WIDULSKI, LAURA JEAN, accountant; b. New Rochelle, N.Y., Sept. 5, 1961; d. William Paul and Rosemarie Claire (Biscoglio) W. A.S. in Acctg., Westchester Community Coll., 1980; B.B.A. in Acctg., Iona Coll., 1982; postgrad. Pace U., 1985—. C.P.A., N.Y. Staff acct. Litton Fin. Services, Stamford, Conn., 1982-83; asst. to controller, acct. Simon & Schuster Pub. Co., N.Y.C., 1983-85; auditor, staff acct. Lombardi & Palazzolo, C.P.A.s, Yonkers, N.Y., 1985—; mgr. VSL Tours, Inc. Mem. Nat. Assn. Female Execs., Fin. Club Pace U. Republican. Roman Catholic. Avocations: skiing; tennis; running; racquetball; singing. Home: 23 Myrtledale RD Scarsdale NY 10583 Office: Lombardi & Palazzolo CPAs 2128 Central Park Ave Yonkers NY 10583

WIDUP, CECELIA MABEL, mining company executive; b. South Bend, Ind., Dec. 26, 1944; d. Richard Elmer and Betty Frances (Wilson) W. B.S., Manchester Coll., 1966; M.B.A., Fordham U., 1975. Sec., Inco Ltd., N.Y.C., 1967-70, adminstrv. asst., 1970-72, supr. shareholder relations, 1972-74, mgr. shareholder relations, 1974-76, asst. sec, 1976—, mgr. shareholder services, 1976-81. Mem. Am. Soc. Corp. Secs., Corp. Transfer Agts. Assn. (bd. dirs.), Stock Transfer Assn., Canadian Corp. Shareholder Services Assn. (bd. dirs.), Assn. M.B.A. Execs., Nat. Assn. Female Execs. Republican. Episcopalian. Home: Apt 3-E 53 Irving Pl New York NY 10003 Office: Inco Ltd 1 New York Plaza New York NY 10004

WIEDEMAN, CONSTANCE R., real estate executive, lawyer; b. Roanoke, Va., Oct. 18, 1925; d. Riley Fisher and Mary Katharine (Bell) Spradlin; m. Alfred Burrell, Sept. 10, 1966; children—Craig, Jon. LL.B., Western State U., 1975. Pres. Connie Wiedeman, Inc., Kalilua, Hawaii, 1966-69; v.p. Real Property Investment Engring., Inc., Honolulu, 1969-75; v.p. Wiedemans, Realtors, Honolulu, 1980—; tchr., instr. Honolulu Bd. Realtors, 1966-84, cons., 1966-84. Author: For Sale By Owner Guide, 1979. Named Woman of Yr., Pali Bus. and Profl. Women, 1969. Mem. Honolulu Bd. Realtors, Nat. Assn. Realtors, ABA, Investment Group Realtors (1st v.p. 1984, Exchanger of Yr. 1966). Republican. Office: The Wiedemans PO Box 697 Honolulu HI 96809

WIEDEN, MARION ANNA, microbiologist; b. Cleve., Oct. 16, 1937; d. Joseph Frank and Anna Barbara (Bohac) Rusnak; B.S., U. Ariz., 1959; m. Walter Carl Wieden, Aug. 8, 1959; children—Mark David, Jill Ann, Matthew Joe. Microbiologist, St. Mary's Hosp., Tucson, 1961-63, chief microbiologist, 1963-68; chief microbiology sect. VA Hosp., Tucson, 1968—; adj. faculty health related professions U. Ariz., 1986—; chmn. Tucson Inter-hosp. Infections Control Com., 1974-77; mem. clin. lab. adv. bd. Ariz. State Dept. Health Services, 1983—. Registered microbiologist and clin. lab. specialist Nat. Registry, Am. Acad. Microbiology. Mem. Am. Soc. Med. Tech. (liaison officer for VA in Ariz.), Ariz. State Soc. Med. Tech. (Cert. of Merit 1975, 78, 79, 80, 83, 85, Cert. of Achievement 1980; Outstanding Contbns. to Microbiology award 1981, 85, Mem. of Yr. award 1981, state dir. 1976-79, 80-81, program chmn. 1981 conv., gen. chmn. 1983, 85, pres. Tucson chpt. 1980-81), Am. Soc. Microbiology (cert. specialist), Ariz. Soc. Microbiology (program chmn. Tucson br. 1979-81), Am. Pub. Health Assn., Assn. Practitioners in Infection Control, Am. Soc. Clin. Pathologists (various coms.), Smithsonian Instn., U. Ariz. Alumni Assn., Coccidioidomycosis, Study Group, Beta Beta Beta, Alpha Delta Pi. Roman Catholic. Contbr. articles to profl. jours. Address: 7180 N Cathedral Rock Pl Tucson AZ 85718

WIEDER, TAMARA, mattress company executive; b. Tucson, Apr. 29, 1952; d. Frank and Beatrice (Kornman) Berdofe; m. Irwin Wieder, Mar. 1, 1979; children—David Baruch, Molly Malka. B.A. in Performing Arts and Psychology, Goddard Coll., 1975. Dance dir. Goddard Coll., Montpelier, Vt., 1975-76; dance and English tchr. Jordan & Beit Shean, Israel, 1978-79; pres. Arise Futon Mattress Co., Inc., N.Y.C., 1980—. Mem. Am. Women's Econ. Devel. Corp. Jewish. Office: Arise Futon Mattress Co Inc 37 Wooster St New York NY 10013

WIEDL, SHEILA COLLEEN, biologist; b. Buffalo, Feb. 19, 1950; d. Frank George and Corinne Ruth (Nuskay) Wiedl; B.S., Daemen Coll., 1972; M.S., U. Notre Dame, 1974; Ph.D., SUNY-Buffalo, 1986. Instr., Holy Cross Jr. Coll., South Bend, Ind., 1973-74; research technician SUNY, Buffalo, 1975-78; entomol. asst. N.Y. State Health Dept., 1979-80; entomol. intern Ohio Dept. Health, 1981; prof. natural scis. Trocaire Coll., Buffalo, 1974-85; postdoctoral scientist Am. Cyanamid, Lederle Labs., Pearl River, N.Y., 1985—. Mem. N.Y. State Assn. Two-Year Colls., Assn. Gnotobiotics, N.Y. State Archeol. Assn. Roman Catholic. Club: Notre Dame Alumni. Contbr. articles to profl. jours. Home: 38 Park Terr Spring Valley NY 10977 Office: Lederle Labs Middletown Rd Pearl River NY 10965

WIEDLEA, JANE LEACH SMITH, civic worker; b. Battle Creek, Mich., Oct. 14, 1910; d. William Reynolds and Edith Pearl (Leach) Smith; A.B., Battle Creek Coll., 1933; postgrad. U. Mich., 1933; m. Clare Edgar Wiedlea, June 30, 1934; children—William Clare, Jane Reynolds, John Towle. Sch. librarian Willard Library, Battle Creek, 1927-29; desk librarian Battle Creek Coll., 1931-33, instr. history, 1933-35. Mem. Sturgis (Mich.) Public Library Bd., 1950-86, pres., 1955-60, 75-86; mem. Sturgis Hosp. Bd., 1969—, v.p., 1974-85, pres., 1985—; ; pres. Sturgis Hosp. Aux., 1969-70, life mem., 1970—; sec. S.W. Dist. Hosp. Aux. Bd., 1970-74; active St. John's Guild, St. John's Altar Guild; chmn. planning com. centennial yr. Episcopal Diocese of Western Mich., 1874-1974; bd. dirs. James Monroe Meml. Found., 1956-59. Named Citizen of Yr., 1970. Mem. DAR (Amos-Sturgis chpt. regent 1953-55, 73-75, nat. vice chmn. Am. History month 1955-58, state regent Mich. 1961-64, hon. state regent for life), U.S. Daus. of 1812, Daus. Colonial Wars, Daus. Am. Colonists. Republican. Episcopalian. Club: Polit. Study. Home: 400 Cottage Ave Sturgis MI 49091

WIEDMAN, MARY ELIZABETH, occupational therapist; b. Bonne Terre, Mo., Sept. 12, 1932; d. Edward Carl and Elva (Vinetta) Johnson; student N.W. Okla. State U., 1972-75, postgrad. 1979—; B.S. in Occupational Therapy, U. Okla. Health Sci. Center, 1978; postgrad. East Central U., 1985; m. Bill B. Wiedman, May 23, 1977; children—Michael Pinkley, Deborah Pinkley Lewis, Mark Pinkley, Susan Pinkley Schneider; stepchildren—Michael Wiedman, Jan Wiedman Schrock, Jill Wiedman Howard. Asst. for tng. Occupational Therapy in Ednl. Mgmt., Oklahoma City and Tulsa, 1981—; pvt. practice pediatric and rehab. therapy, Kiowa, Kans., 1979—; pvt. practice rehab. therapy Okla. Dept. Human Services, 1985—; occupational therapy cons. Achenbach Rehab. Center, Hardtner, Kans., 1979—, Cedar Crest Nursing Home, Kiowa and Medicine Lodge, Kans., 1985—; occupational therapist Northwestern Okla. Regional Edn. Service Ctr., Alva, 1978—; guest lectr. N.W. Okla. State U., 1978-79. Mem. World Fedn. Occupational Therapists, Am. Occupational Therapy Assn., Okla. Occupational Therapy Assn., Kans. Occupational Therapy Assn., Am. Occupational Therapy Found., Council Exceptional Children (charter mem. chpt.), Ctr. Study Sensory Integration Dysfunction, AAUW. Republican. Baptist. Home: 1011 Coats Kiowa KS 67070 Office: 1540 Davis St Alva OK 73717

WIEGAND, INGRID, videomaker, television producer; b. Vienna, Austria, Apr. 9, 1934; came to U.S. 1939, naturalized, 1955; d. Henry Peter and Katherine (Gerhardt) West; m. Robert Wiegand, Dec. 4, 1964; children—Indira, Pratap. B.A., NYU, 1954, postgrad., 1954-55. Indsl. sci. writer ITT, U. Pitts., and others, 1955-64; ind. filmmaker, 1964-70; videomaker, artist Pub. TV, Berlin Film Festival and others, 1971—; TV producer Pub. TV, Cable TV, 1981—; ednl. cons. Videomaker: Snapshots for an Indian Day, 1978; author: Professional Television Production, 1985; Critic, columnist TV and Media arts numerous newspapers, mags. Co-founder Soho Artists Assn., N.Y.C., 1969. Recipient Rockefeller Found. fellow, 1977; Vis. Video Artist award Synapse Found., 1978. Mem. Assn. Ind. Film and Videomakers, Found. Film and Video Arts. Avocations: flying; yoga. Home: 40 Harrison St 23F New York NY 10013

WIEL, CAROL LEE, sales and marketing executive; b. Washington, Mar. 11, 1943; d. John Myron and Alice Shelton (Trollinger) Ehrmantraut; m. Thomas Theodore, Sept. 5, 1964; children—Jeffrey Scott, Gregory Todd. B.A., U. Md., 1964. Tchr. St. Mary's County, Lexington Park, Md., 1965-72; owner, gen. mgr. Standard Sales Co., Nashville, 1977-82; mgr. Aladdin Industries, Nashville, 1982—. Bd. dirs. Nat. Assn. for Sight Conservation and Aid to Blind, Nashville, 1982. Mem. Am. Telemktg. Assn., Nat. Assn. Female Execs., Nat. Housewares Mfrs. Assn., Nashville Warehouse Investors, Nat. Wildlife Fedn. (assoc.), Delta Gamma Alumnae Assn. Republican. Avocations: tennis; windsurfing; aerobics. Home: 6043 Wellesley Way Brentwood TN 37027 Office: Aladdin Industries Inc 703 Murfreesboro Rd Nashville TN 37027

WIEMER-SUMNER, ANNE-MARIE, psychotherapist, educational administrator; b. Ger., Mar. 3, 1938; came to U.S., 1949, naturalized, 1956; d. Franz and Margaret (Neubacher) Wiemer; B.A., Hunter Coll., 1963; M.A., N.Y. U., 1965; cert. Psychoanalytic Individual and Group Therapy, Washington Square Inst. Psychotherapy, 1975, 76; m. Eric Eden Sumner, May 24, 1974; children—Erika, Trevor. Adminstrv. asst., counselor, asst. chmn. admissions N.Y. U., N.Y.C., 1956-69; asst. dean student Hunter Coll., N.Y.C., 1969-71; asso. dean students Cooper Union Advancement Art and Sci., N.Y.C., 1971—; supr. Washington Sq. Inst. for Psychotherapy, N.Y.C., 1977-81; pvt. practice psychotherapy, N.Y.C. Trustee Grace Ch. Sch., 1985—; bd. dirs. Washington Sq. Assn., The Caring Community. Mem. Council Psychoanalytic Psychotherapists, Am. Psychol. Assn., Am. Group Psychotherapy Assn., Am. Orthopsychiat. Assn., Internat. Assn. Group Psychotherapy, Nat. Accreditation Assn. and Am. Exam. Bd. Psychoanalysis, N.Y. State Assn. Practicing Psychotherapists, Nat. Assn. Women Deans and Counselors, Coll. Placement Council, Eastern Coll. Personnel Officers. Club: City. Home: 7-13 Washington Sq N New York NY 10003 Office: Cooper Union Cooper Sq New York NY 10003

WIENER, ANNABELLE, UN ofcl.; b. N.Y.C., Aug. 2, 1922; d. Philip and Bertha (Wrubel) Kalbfeld; ed. Hunter Coll.; married, Jan. 1, 1941; children—Marilyn Grunewald, Marjorie Petit, Mark. Chmn. UN Dept. Pub. Info., Nongovtl. Orgns. Exec. Com., spl. adviser to sec. gen. Internat. Women's Year Conf.; mem. exec. bd. Nongovtl. Orgns. Com. on Disarmament UN; bd. dirs. World Fedn. UN Assns., also founder, dir. art and philatelic program. Mem. Am. Fedn. Arts, Mus. Modern Art, Musee Nat. Message Biblique Marc Chagall, Am. Philatelic Soc., UN Philatelic Soc., UN Assn. U.S. Address: UN Hdqrs New York NY 10017

WIENER, MARJORIE SONIA, psychologist, telecommunications company executive; b. N.Y.C., Jan. 17, 1943; d. Philip Paul and Gertrude (Schler) W. B.S., Juilliard Sch., 1964, M.S., 1965; M.Phil., CUNY, 1981, Ph.D., 1981. Prin. flutist Met. Opera, N.Y.C., 1965-67; systems analyst AT&T, N.Y.C., 1967-70; grant research asst. NIMH, N.Y.C., 1973-77; instr. psychology Hunter Coll., N.Y.C., 1976-80; mgr. AT&T, Piscataway, N.J., 1982—; cons. Psychology Today mag., Washington, 1981—, Chesebrough-Pond's Inc., Conn., 1981, Medgar Evans Coll., N.Y.C., 1980; musician Israeli Dance Music, 1980. Contbr. articles to profl. jours. Mem. Am. Psychol Assn., N.Y. Acad. Scis., AAAS, Interplanetary Soc. Office: AT&T Communications 140 Centennial Ave Piscataway NJ 08854

WIERCIOCH, MARIANNE, lawyer; b. Chgo., June 29, 1958; d. Richard Stanley and Virginia Valentine (Lisiecki) Wiercioch, B.A. in Polit. Sci. and Journalism, Fla. Atlantic U., 1978; J.D., Pepperdine U., 1982; postgrad. in taxation U. Miami (Fla.). Bar: Fla. 1983. Sole practice, Boca Raton, Fla., 1985—; cons. So. Terr. Builders and Interiors, Boca Raton. Mem. Gold Coast Republican Club, Boca Raton. Mem. ABA, Fla. Assn. Women Lawyers, Fla. Bar Assn. Young Lawyers, Profl. Women's Assn., Women's Forum, Boca Raton C. of C., Baco Raton Bd. Realtors, Boca Raton Hist. Soc., Boca Raton Community Hosp. Aux., Singing Pines Mus., Delta Theta Phi, Pi Sigma Alpha, others. Republican. Office: PO Box 4215 Boca Raton FL 33429

WIESEMAN, MARY FOLLIARD, government official, lawyer; b. Washington, Sept. 14, 1942; d. Robert Joseph and Catherine Cecelia (Molly) Folliard; m. J. Theodore Wieseman, June 27, 1970; children—Theodore M., Moira G., Joseph H. A.B., Catholic U. Am., 1964, LL.B., 1967. Bar: D.C. 1968, Md. 1975. Atty., Dept. Justice, Washington, 1967-68; asst. U.S. atty. U.S. Atty.'s Office, Washington, 1968-71; legal counsel St. Elizabeth's Hosp., Washington, 1971-72; cons. Law Enforcement Assistance Adminstrn., Washington, 1974; atty. HEW, Washington, 1975-76; ptnr. Wieseman & Wieseman, Rockville, Md., 1975-83; acting gen. counsel Legal Services Corp., Washington, 1982-83; insp. gen. SBA, Washington, 1983—. Editorial bd. Cath. U. Law Rev., 1967. Mem. D.C. Bar, Bar State Md., Assn. Govt. Accts., Assn. Fed. Investigators. Republican. Roman Catholic. Office: SBA 1441 L St Washington DC 20416

WIESENBERG, JACQUELINE LEONARDI, lecturer; b. West Haven, Conn., May 4, 1928; d. Curzio and Filmenia Olga (Turriziana) Leonardi; m. Russel John Wiesenberg, Nov. 23; children—James Wynne, Deborann Donna. B.A., State U. N.Y. at Buffalo, 1970, postgrad., 1970-73, 80—. Interviewer, examiner Dept. Labor, New Haven, 1948-52; sec. W.I. Clark Co., Hamden, Conn., 1952-55; acct. VA Hosp., West Haven, 1956-60; acct.-commissary U.S. Air Force Missle Site, Niagara Falls, N.Y., 1961-62; tchr. Buffalo City Schs., 1970-73, 79; acct. Erie County Social Services, Buffalo, 1971-73; lectr., 1973—. Contbr. articles to CAP, U.S. Air Force mag., 1955-60. Capt., Nat. Found. March of Dimes, 1969—, com. mem. telethon, 1983-86; den mother Boy Scouts Am., 1961-68; chmn. Meals on Wheels, Town of Amherst, 1975-76; leader, travel chmn. Girl Scouts Am., 1968-77. Mem. Internat. Platform Assn., Am. Astrol. Assn., Western N.Y. Conf. Aging, Epsilon Delta Chi, Alpha Iota. Home: 14 Norman Pl Amherst NY 14226

WIESER, JOAN ELIZABETH, university official, employee development programs consultant; b. Fall River, Mass., Mar. 14, 1948; d. James Edward and Theresa (O'Gara) Lenaghan; m. Paul B. Wieser, Sept. 7, 1968. Student Triton Coll., River Grove, Ill., 1969-71, Brown U., 1973; M.B.A., U. Miami-Coral Gables, 1982. Cost acct. Sylvaniz Electric, Fall River, Mass., 1967-68; support staff mem. Alberto-Culver, Melrose Park, Ill., 1968-70; exec. sec. Profl. Marketers, Inc., Broadview, Ill., 1970-75; asst. mgr. East Providence Credit Union, R.I., 1975-84; asst. personnel dir. U. Miami, Coral Gables, 1984—, personnel dir. Med. Campus, Miami, 1984—; mem. credit com. U. Miami Credit Union, 1979—; cons. devel. employment skills John S. Koubek Ctr., Miami, 1981—; condr. workshops and seminars in field. Named Outstanding Young Women in Am., Sales & Mktg. Execs. of Ft. Lauderdale, Inc., 1983, Woman of Year Am. Bus. Women's Assn., 1984. Mem. U. Miami Women's Commn., Am. Bus. Women's Assn., Am. Mgmt. Assn., Am. Soc. Personnel Adminstrn., Am. Soc. Tng. and Devel. Club: Toastmasters Internat. (Coral Gables). Office: Univ of Miami Med Campus 1800 NW 10th Ave Miami FL 33101

WIESNER, JOAN R., state legislator. Mem. R.I. Senate from 27th dist., 1985—. Republican. Office: State Capitol Providence RI 02903*

WIEST, ELIZABETH HERMAN, nursing educator; b. Lancaster, Pa., July 3, 1936; d. Paul Lester and Elizabeth MacDonald (Woodburn) Herman; diploma Lancaster Gen. Hosp. Sch. Nursing, 1957; B.S.N., U. Md., 1966, M.S., 1968; Ed.D., U. Wyo., 1980; m. Donald K. Wiest, Mar. 8, 1980. Staff nurse Lancaster Gen. Hosp., 1957-63, Univ. Hosp., Balt., 1965-66; asst. prof. U. Md., Balt., 1967-74; asst. prof. U. Wyo., Laramie, 1974-80, assoc. prof., 1980-83, dir. off-campus nursing programs, 1983—. Bd. dirs., chmn. bd. Wyo. affiliate Am. Heart Assn., rep. N.W. Regional Heart Com., 1981—; exec. bd. Western Council Higher Edn. in Nursing, 1982-85. USPHS trainee, 1966-67; Kemper scholar, summer 1969. Mem. LWV, Am. Nurses Assn. (council on continuing edn.), Wyo. Nurses Assn. (pres. Dist. 12), Nat. League Nursing, Adult Edn. Assn. U.S., Wyo. Commn. Nursing and Nursing Edn., Lancaster Gen. Hosp. Nurses Alumni Assn., Summer Sch. Alumni Assn. Rutgers Summer Sch. Alcohol Studies, U. Wyo. Alumni Assn., Sigma Theta Tau. Republican. Lutheran. Home: 1930 Sheridan Laramie WY 82070 Office: U Wyo Sch Nursing Box 3065 Univ Sta Laramie WY 82071

WIGG, RISTIINA MARIA, librarian; b. Cheboygan, Mich., Nov. 16, 1946; d. Paul Alvar and Phyllis Elvira (Carlson) W.; m. Leon Edward Kotowski, Aug. 1981; 1 child, K. Zachary. B.A., Oakland U., 1968; A.M.L.S., Univ. Mich., 1971. Cert. librarian, Mich. Branch librarian Pontiac Library, Mich., 1968-70; cons. children's services Mid-Hudson Library System, Poughkeepsie, N.Y., 1971—. Author: (with others) We Want Sunshine in Our Houses, 1973. Treas. LWV, Poughkeepsie, 1973-75, Mid-Hudson Coalition for Free Choice, Poughkeepsie, 1976-84. Mem. ALA (John Newbery award com. 1986—), N.Y. Library Assn. (youth services sect., pres. 1981-83). Office: Mid-Hudson Library System 103 Market St Poughkeepsie NY 12601

WIGGERS, ANDREA VERN, banker; b. MacDill AFB, Fla., Apr. 16, 1948; d. Clifford Andrew and Amy Clifford (Taylor) Wiggers. Student, Radford Coll., 1966, Marjorie Webster Jr. Coll., 1967, Wright State U., 1969-70, U. Md. in Munich (W.Ger.), 1970-71. Supr., Woodward & Lothrop, Washington, 1971-74; adminstrv. asst. Nat. Capital Med. Found., Washington, 1974-76; exec. sec. Am. Security Bank, Washington, 1976-79, mgr., 1979-80, asst. treas., 1980-81, asst. v.p., 1981—. Mem. Nat. Speakers Assn., Nat. Assn. Bank Women, Am. Soc. Tng. and Devel. Episcopalian. Office: PO Box 922 Vienna VA 22180

WIGGINS, CAROLYN LEE, educator; b. N.Y.C., Dec. 8, 1947; d. Roedolphus and Hattie (Simmons) W. B.A., Antioch Coll., 1974, M.Ed., 1976; L.H.D. (hon.), Eastern Am. U., 1980. Cert. tchr., N.Y., Calif. Tchr., Morning Side Day Care Ctr., Inc., N.Y.C., 1969-76; early childhood specialist Laguardia Community Coll., Long Island City, N.Y., 1976-80; dir. Cathedral Pkwy. Pre-Sch., N.Y.C., 1980-82; ednl. cons. Concerned Parents Family Day Care, Bronx, N.Y., 1982-83; asst. exec. dir. Morning Side Head Start, N.Y.C., 1983-86; dir. edn. Concerned Parents Family Day Care, Inc., 1986—; cons. Harlem Interfaith Counseling Service, 1986—; adj. prof. Coll. of New Rochelle Sch. New Resources, 1983—; asst. chancellor Ednl. Theol. Consortium, N.Y.C., 1983—; pres. Ednl. Assocs., N.Y.C., 1985—. Author workbooks. Mem. Melrose Housing Devel. Block Assn., Bronx, N.Y., 1979—; mem. adv. com. Early Childhood Resource Info. Ctr., N.Y.C., 1984—; chmn. edn. com. Morisanic Urban Renewal Community Orgn., Bronx, 1980—; vice chmn. Concerned Parents Family Day Care, Inc., Bronx, 1984—. Mem. Nat. Assn. Edn. Young Children, Early Childhood Edn. Council N.Y., Assn. Black Women in Higher Edn., Assn. Black Educators of N.Y., United Negro Coll. Fund, Horace Mann Soc. Democrat. Avocations: reading; traveling. Office: Concerned Parents Family Day Care Inc Bronx NY 10459

WIGGINS, JUDITH HUGHES, pre-school educator; b. Columbus, Ohio, Dec. 11, 1942; d. Ernest Albert and Frances D. (Fairchild) Cady; m. Perry Daniel Wiggins, Nov. 2, 1984; children from previous marriage—Laura, Katherine, Jennifer. B.S. in Edn., Ohio State U., 1965. Cert. tchr., La. Tchr. pub. schs., Baton Rouge, 1967; owner, dir. Nursery Rhyme Day Care Ctr., Baton Rouge, 1978—; pres. Assn. Classroom Tchrs., Baton Rouge, 1978. Republican. Mem. Family Worship Ctr. Home: 3833 Valentine Rd Baton Rouge LA 70815 Office: Nursery Rhyme Day Care Ctr 3590 Jones Creek Baton Rouge LA 70816

WIGGINS-JONES, KATHLYN YVETTE, systems analyst; b. Memphis, Dec. 16, 1950; d. Mack C. and Texana R. (Ricks) Wiggins; B.S. in Fashion Merchandising, Memphis State U., 1972, M.Ed. in Distributive Edn., 1974; Ph.D. in Instructional Communications, SUNY-Buffalo, 1984; m. Young B. Jones, Feb. 11, 1978; children—Anaxet Yvette, Juliette Marie. Communications cons. N.Y. Telephone Co., Buffalo, 1974-76, mktg. adminstr. 1976-81, communications systems rep., 1981—. Active Urban League, NAACP; bd. dirs. Buffalo br. ARC, 1982—. Recipient cert. of appreciation United Negro Coll. Fund, 1979, cert. of salesmanship N.Y. Telephone Co., 1974. Mem. Nat. Assn. Female Execs, Am. Mktg. Assn., Curriculum Devel. and Instructional Media Club, Alpha Kappa Alpha. Democrat. Baptist. Author: Telecommunications Information for the Blind and Visually Impaired, 1981; developer video presentation Bell Mktg. Dept., 1981. Home: 22 University Ave Buffalo NY 14214 Office: 600 Main Pl Tower Main St Buffalo NY 14202

WIGHTMAN, NANCY MATTHEWS, swim school adminstrator; b. Las Vegas, Nev., Jan. 18, 1941; d. Arthur Elmer Matthews and Wilma Rose (Gustin) Matthews Firth; m. Edward F. Wightman, Nov. 16, 1968. B.A., U. Calif.-Riverside, 1963; M.A., Claremont Grad. Sch., 1969; postgrad. Union Coll., 1973. Teaching asst. Scripps Coll., Claremont, Calif., 1963-65; activities advisor, instr. Chico State Coll., Calif., 1965-67; residence dir. SUNY-Albany, 1967-69, quad coordinator, 1969-71; personnel dir. Environ. One Corp., Schenectady, 1972-73; dir. health, phys. edn. and recreation Troy-Cohoes YWCA, N.Y., 1973-78; pres. Swim Sch., Inc., Troy, 1978—; v.p. devel. U.S. Synchronized Swimming, Indpls., 1982—; head coach Troy Sculpins, Inc. Synchronized Swim Team, Troy, 1974—. Co-author: Better Synchronized Swimming for Girls, 1981. Bd. dirs. ARC, Troy, 1974—; mem. planning com. Robison Pool, Troy, 1984. Mem. U.S. Synchronized Swim. Democrat. Presbyterian. Avocations: sailing; swimming; crocheting; needlepoint. Office: The Swim Sch Inc 172 1st St Troy NY 12180

WIIG, ELISABETH HEMMERSAM, educator; b. Esbjerg, Denmark, May 22, 1935; came to U.S., 1957, naturalized, 1967; d. Svend Frederick and Ingeborg (Hemmersam) Nielsen; B.A., Statsseminariet Emdrupborg, 1956; M.A., Western Res. U., 1960; Ph.D., Case Western Res. U., 1967; postgrad. U. Mich., 1967-68; m. Karl Martin Wiig, June 10, 1958; children—Charlotte Elisabeth, Erik Daniel. Clin. audiologist Cleve. Hearing and Speech Center, 1959-60; instr. dept. phonetics Bergen (Norway) U., 1960-64; asst. prof. U. Mich., 1968-70; asst. prof. Boston, 1970-73, asso. prof., 1973-77, prof. dept. speech pathology and audiology, 1977—. Recipient Metcalf Cup and Prize for excellence in teaching Boston U., 1967; named hon. Ky. col. Fellow Am. Speech and Hearing Assn. (cert. of clin. competence in speech pathology and audiology); mem. Council on Exceptional Children, Mass. Speech-Lang.-Hearing Assn. (honors). Democrat. Lutheran. Author: Language Disabilities in Children and Adolescents, 1976; Language Assessment and Intervention for the Learning Disabled, 1980, 2d edit., 1984; CELF Screening Tests: Elementary and Secondary Levels, 1980; Clinical Evaluation of Language Functions, 1980; Let's Talk: Developing Prosocial Communication Skills, 1982; Let's Talk Inventory for Adolescents, 1983; Let's Talk for Children, 1983; Test of Language Competence, 1985. Office: Boston U 48 Cummington St Boston MA 02215

WIKE, BARBARA ANNE, township official; b. Altoona, Pa., Nov. 26, 1934; d. Gerald E. and Elizabeth (Zimmerman) Way; student Middlesex County Coll., 1977—, Rutgers U., 1981; m. Samuel E. Wike, Jr., Apr. 28, 1956; children—Samuel E. III, Robin Lynn. Office mgr. Boyer Bros., Altoona, 1952-56; exec. sec. to tax mgr. Mack Trucks, Plainfield, N.J., 1956-59; clk. Piscataway (N.J.) Planning Bd., 1967-69; exec. asst. to mayor, personnel officer for mcpl. govt., Piscataway, 1969—; exec. dir. Piscataway Community TV Ctr. Piscataway liaison N.J. Motion Picture and TV Devel. Commn.; trustee Piscataway Library, Rutgers Community Health Plan; past chmn. Piscataway Heart Fund Drive; mem. Piscataway Bicentennial Commn.; chmn. Middlesex County Ridesharing Task Force; mem. policy com. Head Start; mem. community relations Council Muhlenberg Hosp.; adv. com. Piscataway Adult Sch.; active Boy Scouts Am., Girl Scouts U.S. Recipient Disting. Woman in Bus. and Industry award Raritan Valley Regional C. of C., 1978; Disting Service award Piscataway Jaycees. Mem. Internat. City Mgmt. Assn., Piscataway C. of C. (pres. 1975-77, dir. 1974-78). Methodist. Lodge: Order of Eastern Star. Author: Piscataway Township Employee Handbook, 1976, Middlesex County Coll. Alumni Assn. Home: 62 Nelson Ave S Piscataway NJ 08854 Office: 455 Hoes Ln Piscataway NJ 08854

WIKE, D. ELAINE, business executive; b. Ridgecrest, Calif., Sept. 26, 1954; d. Robert G. and Jimmie Mae (Sallee) Field; student U. Houston, 1975-77; m. Mike Wike, Oct. 14, 1978; children—Mike II, Angelina Elaine. Legal sec. Morgan, Lewis & Bockius, Washington, 1977-78; legal asst. Alfred C. Schlosser & Co., Houston, 1972-77, 78-81, Jerry Sadler, atty., Houston, 1982-83; founder, owner DEW Profl. & Bus. Services, Houston, 1979—; office mgr. Law Offices Mike Wike, Houston, 1983—. Treas., Wilhelm Schole Parents Orgn., 1981-82; vol. campaign worker, (Ron Paul for Congress and Reagan for Pres.), 1975, 76; mem. Republican Presdl. Task Force. Mem. Young Ams. for Freedom, Nat. Notary Assn., Nat. Assn. Female Execs., Am. Soc., Notaries. Republican. Mem. Christian Ch. Office: 6001 Gulf Freeway Houston TX 77023

WILBORN, AURELIA, banker, accountant; b. Mobile, Ala., Oct. 18, 1948; d. Joseph and Cecilia (Matthews) Dabney; m. Anthony Outten, June 25, 1965; 1 son, Alexander; m. 2d, Donald Wilborn, Sept. 27, 1981. Grad. LaSalle Extension U., Chgo., 1982. Accounts receivable clk. CNA, Chgo., 1966-68, Maremont, Chgo., 1968-72, Interstate United, Chgo., 1972-75; investment processor Seaway Nat. Bank, Chgo., 1976-86; propr. Wilborn's Bookkeeping & Acctg. Services, Libra Mailing Co. Pollwatcher mayoral election, Chgo., 1983. Mem. Nat. Assn. Female Execs. Baptist, U.S. C. of C.

WILBURN, KATHRINE OWENS, lawyer; b. Opp, Ala., Nov. 18, 1955; d. H. Benton and Eddie Mae (McDuffie) Owens; m. Michael D. Wilburn, Sept. 6, 1981. A.A., George C. Wallace Jr. Coll., 1975; B.A. magna cum laude, Auburn U., 1977; J.D. cum laude, Cumberland Law Sch., 1980. Bar: Ala. 1980. Atty., So. Natural Gas Co., Birmingham, Ala., 1980—. Contbr. articles to profl. jours. Mem. ABA, Ala. Bar Assn., Ala. Assn. Corp. Counsel. Republican. Baptist (outreach leader 1983-84). Office: So Natural Gas Co PO Box 2563 Birmingham AL 35202

WILBURN, MARY NELSON, lawyer, writer; b. Balt., Feb. 18, 1932; d. David Alfred and Phoebe Blanche (Novotny) Nelson; A.B. cum laude, Howard U., 1952; M.A., U. Wis., 1955, J.D., 1975; m. Adolph Yarbrough Wilburn, Mar. 5, 1957; children—Adolph II, Jason David. Bar: Wis. 1975, U.S. Supreme Ct 1981. Lectr. U. Wis. Law Sch., 1975-77, 83, 84, 85; atty. adv. Bur. Prisons, Dept. Justice, 1977-82; chmn. Wis. State Parole Bd., Madison, 1986—; mem. steering com. Network Women Offenders, Women's Bur., Dept. Labor, 1981-82. Mem. Madison Met. Sch. Dist. Bd. Edn., 1975-77; bd. dirs. REP, Inc., Washington, 1978-82; assoc. mem. Schutz Am. Sch. Bd., Alexandria, Egypt, 1983-85. Mem. Fed. Bar. Assn. (nat. council 1981-82), Women's Bar Assn., Nat. Bar Assn., ABA, Dane County Bar Assn., Legal Assn. of Women, The Links, Inc., Am. Correctional Assn., Am. Assn. Access Profls., Nat. Assn. Blacks in Criminal Justice, Howard U. Alumni Assn., Alpha Kappa Alpha. Clubs: Nat. Lawyers (Washington); University (Madison). Contbr. to Cairo Today, 1983-84. Office: Wis Parole Bd 1 W Wilson St PO Box 7850 Madison WI 53707

WILCOX, BARBARA NELL, real estate broker; b. Luverne, Ala., June 15, 1933; d. Herman M. and Leona (Crowe) Bradshaw; m. Eddie F. Tucker, July 4, 1952 (div. 1974); children—Debra Joyce Tucker Strawser, Cathy Ann Tucker Hanson; m. 2d, Roy M. Wilcox, Aug. 20, 1976. Student Columbia Bible Coll., 1952. sec. Hanna Transfer Co., Tampa, Fla., 1965-69; salesman Ann Del Valle Realty Co., Tampa, 1969-76; broker Barbara Realty Inc., Tampa, 1976—; bd. dirs. Multiple Listing Services, Tampa, 1976—; past chmn. Landmark Bank Tampa, 1974-76, also stockholder's adv. bd.; adv. bd. Regency Bank of Fla., 1983—. Past trustee Lake Carroll Bapt. Ch., Tampa, 1977-78; Krewe of Venus, Sword of Hope Guild Am. Cancer Soc., 1983; adv. council Tampa Coll., 1984—. Recipient Whirlwind award for outstanding achievement U. Tampa, 1982; named Outstanding Women of Yr., Lake Carroll Bapt. Ch., Tampa, 1972. Mem. Sales and Mktg. Execs. Tampa (Top Salesman award, 1969-72), Tampa Bd. Realtors, Nat. Assn. Realtors (bd. dirs. 1976—), Tampa Women's Council, Tampa Com. of 100, Greater Tampa C. of C. Republican. Club: Green Jacket (Tampa). Office: Barbara Realty Inc 1046 W Busch Blvd Suite 300 Tampa FL 33612

WILCOX, CHERYL ANN, financial executive; b. Warren, Ohio, Dec. 24, 1948; d. Austin William and Anne Marie (Palo) Davis; m. Robert H.L. Wilcox, June 10, 1972 (dec. 1980). A.A.B., Youngstown U., 1972. Acct., Can. Dental Assn., Ottawa, Ont., 1977-78, Acctg. and Bus. Cons., Ft. Lauderdale, Fla., 1979-80; comptroller Cosby's Inc., Delray Beach, Fla., 1980-81; mortgage officer Spanish River Resort, Delray Beach, 1981-83; comptroller Marine Reins., Miami Beach, Fla., 1983-85, Marine R. Corp., Miami, 1985—; dir. Marine Reins. Corp., Marine R Corp.; sec.-treas. M.R. Cows Inc., 1984—; corp. sec. Northgate Plaza, Inc., Miami, 1985—. Bd. dirs. Big Bros./Big Sis. Broward, Ft. Lauderdale, 1985-86. Recipient Arion award Nat. Honor Soc., 1966; A-Rate award Ohio Solo Vocal Competition, State of Ohio, 1966. Mem. Nat. Assn. Female Execs., Women's Exec. Assn. Avocation: scuba diving. Office: Marine R Corp 11077 Biscayne Blvd Miami FL 33161

WILD, HEIDI KARIN, oil company executive; b. Detroit, July 28, 1948; d. Lauren Daggett and Eleanor Stephanie (Churchman) Wild; m. Francis Michael Robinson, Oct. 2, 1982. B.S., Western Mich. U., 1971; M.B.A., U. Hawaii, 1985. Tchr. secondary edn. St. Clair Sch. System, St. Clair Shores, Mich., 1971-74; personnel asst. Union Camp Corp., Kalamazoo, 1974-76; receptionist, typist Pacific Resources Inc., Honolulu, 1976-77, sec., 1977-78, adminstrv. asst., 1978, mktg. and supply analyst, 1978-80, coordinator light product supply and exchange, 1980-81, mfr. product supply, 1981-83, dir. product supply, 1983-85, gen. mgr. light products, 1985, gen. mgr. supply and distbn. 1985-86, mgr. crude and product supply ops., 1986—; dir. PRI Fed. Credit Union. Mem. Hawaii Soc. Corp. Planners, Navy League, Western Mich. U. Alumni Assn., Nat. Assn. Female Execs., Beta Gamma Sigma. Democrat. Clubs: Petroleum (Los Angeles); Honolulu, PRI Golf, Sierra. Avocations: golf, dominoes; craftwork; piano; travel. Office: Pacific Resources Inc 733 Bishop St 30th Fl Honolulu HI 96813

WILDE, PATRICIA, ballerina, ballet theatre executive; b. Ottawa, Can., July 16, 1928; naturalized, 1957; d. John Herbert and Eileen Lucy (Simpson) White; m. George Bardyguine, Dec. 14, 1953; children—Anya, Youri. Student, Profl. Children's Sch., N.Y.C. Mem. faculty Dance Educators Am.; tchr., performance coach Am. Ballet Theatre Co.; formerly ballet mistress; supr. opening Sch. Ballet of Grand Theatre de Geneve, Switzerland, 1969; tchr., rehearsed Ballet of Royal Opera, Stockholm, Sweden, 1970; tchr. Met. Opera Ballet, Dance Theatre Harlem, Am. Ballet Theatre Co. and Sch.; artistic dir. Pitts. Ballet Theatre, 1982—. Soloist, Ballet Russe de Monte Carlo, Marquis de Cuevas Ballet Co., Roland Petit Ballet de Paris, British Met. Ballet; ballerina, N.Y.C. Ballet, 1950-65; soloist, N.Y. Philharmonic Orch., 1962-65, six European tours, also tour of, Orient, numerous TV appearances, toured Russia with, N.Y.C. Ballet, 1962, commd. by N.Y. Philharmonic to choreograph ballets Festival, 1964; At The Ball, 1965, Viennese Evening, 1966, Petite Suite, 1967; dir., Am. Ballet Theater Sch., 1979—. Adminstr. scholarship fund Sch. Am. Ballet Group; mem. Nat. Bd. Regional Ballet; trustee Dance U.S.A. awards Dance Educators Am., 1957. Recipient Fashionplate award for Entertainment, Pitts., 1986. Mem. Am. Guild Mus. Artists, AFTRA. Office: Pitts Ballet Theatre 2900 Liberty Ave Pittsburgh PA 15201

WILDER, BARBARA ANN, nursing administrator; b. Ninevah, Ky., Nov. 22, 1936; d. Roosevelt and Evadena (Drury) Wash; m. Edward Rufus Lee, Dec. 5, 1957 (div. June 1968); children—Charles Edward Lee, Tamelia Diane Lee McKee; m. J. Lloyd Wilder, Oct. 8, 1969 (div. Apr. 1975). R.N., Fla. Hosp., Orlando, 1957; B.S.N. Fla. Internat. U., 1976. R.N., Fla., S.D., Okla., Ala., Tex., La., Colo., Va., Ill., Ga. Head psychiat. nurse Fla. Hosp., Orlando, 1957-66; psychiat. nurse therapist pvt. physician, Orlando and Wilford Hall USAF Med. Ctr., Lackland AFB, Tex., 1966-73; community health nurse Orange County Health Dept., Orlando, 1973-74; psychiat. head nurse Dodge Meml. Hosp., Miami Fla., 1976-77; rehab. specialist Ins. Co. N.Am., Hialeah,

Fla., 1976-77; nurse cons., 1977-78; psychiat. clin. nurse Gallup Indian Med. Ctr., N.Mex., 1978-80; psychiat. nurse clin. coordinator Indian Health Service, USPHS, Pine Ridge, S.D., 1980-81; dir. nursing USPHS Indian Hosp., Winnebago, Nebr., 1981-83; nurse cons. program specialist Health Care Fin. Adminstrn., HHS, Atlanta, 1983—. Vol. liaison officer Brevard Hosp., Melbourne, Fla., 1971-72; vol. ARC nurse Patrick AFB Hosp., Fla., 1971-72; safety and med. officer CAP, Miami, 1977-78; active PTA; mem. West River Mental Health Bd., S.D., 1980-81. Served to capt. USAF, 1969-70. Recipient award Aberdeen Indian Health Service, 1982. Mem. Am. Legion (sgt.-at-arms 1970-71), Fla. Psychiat. Women's Aux. (pres. 1971-72), Fla. Rehab. Nurses Assn. (chair bylaws com. 1976-77), Orange County Mental Health Assn. (dir.), Ga. Assn. Nurses in Long Term Care (assoc.), Mil. Surgeons U.S. (assoc.), Air Force Assn., Disabled Vets. Comdrs. Club. Lodge: Eagles. Home: PO Box 21223 Nashville TN 37221 Office: Columbia Corp 3401 West End Bldg Suite 360 Nashville TN 37203

WILDER, ELEANOR MARIE (NORA ROBERTS), writer; b. Washington, Oct. 10, 1950; d. Bernard Edward Robertson and Eleanor Margaret Harris; m. Ronald Eugene Aufdem-Brinke, Aug. 17, 1968 (div. 1985); children—Daniel, Jason; m. Bruce Allen Wilder, July 6, 1985. Grad. high sch., Silver Spring, Md. Legal sec. Wheeler & Korpec, Silver Spring, 1966-68; sec. R&R Lighting, Silver Spring, 1972-75; writer, 1979—. Author: The Heart's Victory, 1982; This Magic Moment, 1983; Untamed, 1983; A Matter of Choice, 1984. Mem. Washington Romance Writers, Romance Writers Am. (charter mem., Golden Medallion 1982-85). Democrat. Roman Catholic. Avocations: dancing, reading, films, sailing.

WILDER, JOANNE ROSS, lawyer; b. Rochester, N.Y., Dec. 8, 1942; d. Howard Evans and Ellen Joanne (Langer) Ross; m. Bruce Lord Wilder, Mar. 28, 1970; 1 son, Charles Ross. B.A., U. Md., 1964, J.D., 1969. Bar: Md. 1969, La. 1972, Pa. 1972. Staff atty. Legal Aid Bur., Balt., 1970-71; VISTA atty. New Orleans Legal Assistance Corp., 1971-72; staff atty. Neighborhood Legal Services Assn., Pitts., 1972-74, mng. atty., 1974-76; assoc. firm Raphael, Sheinberg & Barmen, P.A., Pitts., 1976-77; sole practice law, Pitts., 1977-78; prin. firm Wilder & Miller, P.C., Pitts., 1978—; clin. instr. U. Pitts. Sch. Law, 1978-80; lectr. continuing legal edn. program Pa. Bar Inst. and Bar Assn. Co-author: Pennsylvania Family Law Practice and Procedure Handbook. Contbr. articles to legal jours. Bd. dirs. Neighborhood Legal Services Assn., 1977—, pres., 1982-86. Recipient community Service award AAUW, 1982, Salute to Outstanding Woman in Law award Triangle Corner Ltd., 1984. Fellow Am. Acad. Matrimonial Lawyers; mem. ABA, Md. Bar Assn., La. Bar Assn., Pa. Bar Assn. (council family law sect. 1980—), Allegheny County Bar Assn. (chmn. family law sect. 1979-81), Women's Bar Assn. Md., Alpha Omicron Pi. Club: University (Pitts). Office: Wilder & Miller PC 816 Frick Bldg Pittsburgh PA 15219

WILDER, JOYCE ANN, lawyer; b. Mar. 10, 1950; d. Russell Roland and Theresa Marie (Beauregard) Wilder; m. Joseph M. Anderson, May 5, 1984. B.A. magna cum laude, Yale U., 1971; J.D., Cornell U., 1974; LL.M. in Taxation, Boston U., 1977. Bar: N.H. 1974. Assoc. Bell & Kennedy, Bell & Falk, Keene, N.H., 1974-76; mem. firm Smith, Connor & Wilder, P.C. and predecessors, Nashua, N.H., 1976, partner, 1978—. Mem. ABA, Nashua Bar Assn., N.H. Bar Assn., Am. Trial Lawyers Assn., N.H. Trial Lawyers Assn. Office: 47 Factory St Nashua NH 03061

WILDER, MARION BURT (MRS. RICHARD BETHELL WILDER), civic worker; b. N.Y.C.; d. George Frederick and Grace (Knight) Burt; student pvt. schs.; m. John Williams Morgan; 1 son, George Frederick; m. Richard Bethell Wilder, Oct. 27, 1972. Vice pres. Internat. Garden Club, Pelham, N.Y., 1961—; hon. pres. women's com. Judson Health Center, 1949—, bd. govs., 1946-60, hon. life mem. bd. govs.; bd. dirs. Samaritan Home for Aged, 1950-58; bd. govs. N.Y. Women's Bible Soc., 1947-57. Mem. Nat. Inst. Social Scis., Nat. Soc. Colonial Dames, Nat. Trust for Historic Preservation, Am. Fedn. Arts, Huguenot Soc. Am., Soc. Daus. Holland Dames (bd. govs.). Soc. of Four Arts. Clubs: Colony (N.Y.C.); Bath and Tennis, Everglades (Palm Beach, Fla.). Episcopalian. Home: 200 E 66th St New York NY 10021 also 389 S Lake Dr Palm Beach FL 33480 And Twin Brooks Kent CT 06757

WILDERMUTH, NANCY JANET, advertising executive; b. Bklyn., Aug. 2, 1956; d. George Frederick and Janet Neumann Wildermuth; student Centenary Coll., 1974-75; B.B.A. cum laude, Adelphi U., 1980. Mktg. adminstr., permissions editor Holt, Rinehart and Winston, CBS, Inc., N.Y.C., 1976-78, 78-79; account exec. N.Y. Yellow Pages, Inc., N.Y.C., 1980-81; account exec. Ad Forum, Inc., N.Y.C., 1981; advt. mgr. P.T.N. Pub. Corp., Woodbury, N.Y., 1982-84; advt. rep. Petersen Pub. Corp., 1984—. Mem. Am. Mktg. Assn., Mktg. and Advt. Club (pres.), Advt. Club N.Y., L.I. Advt. Club, Adelphi U. Alumni (dir.). Home: 30 Waterside Plaza Apt 37C New York NY 10010

WILDEY, SHARON ANN, lawyer; b. North Vernon, Ind., June 21, 1943; d. Murrell Edward and Virginia Lorane (Beach) W.; m. Edward Victer Mikesell, Feb. 23, 1975 (div. Apr. 1980); children—Tim, Heather, Brooke, Meredith. B.S., Ind. U., 1972, J.D., 1975. Bar: Ind. Assoc., Lubu, Sohaguchi & Wildey, South Bend, 1976-78, Wildey & Forsman, South Bend, 1978-81; founder, pres. Women's Legal Clinic, Inc., South Bend, 1980—. Editor Justicia, 1976. Recipient Roses award Ind. U. Women's Studies, 1979. Mem. Ind. Bar Assn., ABA, Assn. Trial Lawyers Am., Ind. Bar Found., Ind. Women's Polit. Caucus. Democrat. Mem. Soc. Friends. Office: Phelan Pope & John Ltd 180 N Wacker Dr Chicago IL 60606

WILENSKY, ROCHELLE LEAH, advertising executive; b. Jersey City; d. Murray and Ruth (Cohen) Weiss; m. Mark L. Wilensky; children—Alexa, Ryan. B.A. in psychology, Fairleigh Dickinson U., 1966; M.A., New Sch. Social Research, 1968. Advt. researcher Kenyon & Eckhardt Advt., N.Y.C., 1972-73; corporate researcher Bristol Myers Co., N.Y.C., 1973-76; mktg. researcher Am. Express Co., N.Y.C., 1976-82, Shearson Lehman Bros., N.Y.C., 1982-84; advt. researcher J. Walter Thompson, N.Y.C., 1984—. Contbr. articles to profl. jours. Mem. Am. Mktg. Assn. (sec. 1983-84), Fin. Women's Assn., Oratorio Soc. N.Y. (singing mem.). Jewish. Avocation: singing. Office: J Walter Thompson 466 Lexington Ave New York NY 10017

WILES, LAURENTIA RAMOS, businesswoman; b. Ewa, Honolulu, Feb. 28, 1924; d. Eugenio Lesperilles and Pelajia (Addion) R.; m. Henry Wiles, May 18, 1956. Cert., Honolulu Bus. Coll., 1942; diploma Dolores Premier Cosmetology Sch., San Francisco, 1944. Clk. typist, U.S. Army Civil Service, San Francisco, 1944-59; owner, mgr. Hobbitt Beauty Salon, San Francisco, 1956—. Community organizer Filipino Adult and Youth Cath. Orgn., San Francisco, 1959—; sr. commr. Commn. Status of Women of City and County San Francisco, 1975—; pres. Filipino Adult and Youth Cath. Orgn., 1970—, Filipino Community San Francisco, 1964-76, 84—; pres. Filipino Am. Coordinating Conf., 1976-82; bd. dirs. YWCA, San Francisco, 1970-81. Recipient Spl. Recognition resolution Calif. Senate, 1974, 76, 79; Key to City of Sacramento, 1970; Cert. of Honor, City and County of San Francisco, 1974, 79; Outstanding Woman Leadership plaque Philippine Consulate Gen., 1970. Democrat. Roman Catholic. Avocation: dancing. Home: 214 Rutland St San Francisco CA 94134 Office: Hobbitt Beauty Salon 323 Geary St Suite 820 San Francisco CA 94102

WILES, PAMELA ANN, communications company executive; b. Richmond, Va., Aug. 8, 1958; d. Alfred Lee and Mary Ann (Clark) W. A.A., Ferrum Jr. Coll., 1979; B.S., James Madison U., 1981. Part-owner, summer mgr. Saluda Market and Hardware, Va., 1976-82; automobile salesman Pence Briggs Nissan, Richmond, Va., 1982; account exec. AT&T Info. Systems, Richmond, 1983-84; assoc. mgr. AT&T Communications, Piscataway, N.J., 1984—. Mem. Nat. Assn. Female Execs., Smithsonian Assocs., Va. C. of C., Young Ams. for Freedom, Zeta Tau Alpha (life). Avocations: communications consulting, travel. Home: 6 Crossway Clinton NJ 08809 Office: AT&T Communications Tower I 100 Naricon Pl East Brunswick NJ 08816

WILEY, CAROL RICHARDSON, former library administrator; b. Flushing, L.I., N.Y., Jan. 5, 1946; d. Harry Alvin and Claire Amelia (Sepe) Richardson; A.A., Thomas A. Edison State Coll., 1979, B.S.B.A., 1982; m. Bennett John Wiley, Nov. 28, 1965; children—Jennifer, Julianne, Megan Jean. Sec. to dir. clin. investigation CIBA Pharm. Co., Summit, N.J., 1965-67; sec.-treas. Tuxford Corp., Westfield, N.J., 1971-79; dir. Watchung (N.J.) Public Library, 1980-82. Chmn. adult edn. program Wilson Meml. Ch., Watchung, N.J., 1977-81; sec. Watchung Borough Community Chest, 1977-82; mem. Christian Edn. com. Wilson Meml. Ch., 1977-81, mem. exec. bd., 1979, 80; adminstr. Otterbein United Meth. Ch., Lancaster, Pa., 1985—. Mem. ALA, Nat. Assn. Female Execs., N.J. Library Assn., Mensa. Republican. Home: 513 W Orange St Lititz PA 17543

WILEY, HANNAH CHRISTINE, dance educator, choreographer; b. Spokane, Wash., Aug. 21, 1950; d. Owen and Martha M. (Spille) W. B.A., U. Wash., 1973; M.A., NYU, 1981. Instr. in dance Cornish Inst. Allied Arts, Seattle, 1973-75; dancer, tchr. Ballet Folk Co., Moscow, Idaho, 1975-76; choreographer Empty Space Theatre, Seattle, 1975-77; asst. prof. dance Mt. Holyoke Coll., South Hadley, Mass., 1977-82, assoc. prof., 1982—; vis. prof. dance U. Wash., Seattle, summers 1980-86; artist in resident U. Idaho, Moscow, 1975-76; chairperson Five Coll. Dance Dept., Western Mass., 1982—; coordinator New Eng. Coll. dance Festival, Amherst, Mass., 1983-84. Choreographer numerous original ballets, 1977—; choreographer restaged ballet: Pas De Quatre (New Eng. Gala Concert 1984), 1980, 82, 84; manuscript reviewer Schirmer Books, N.Y.C., 1983. Mem. Council on Arts and Humanities, South Hadley, 1981-83. Recipient Research Materials award Capezio Ballet Markers and Ballet Internat., 1982; faculty grantee Mt. Holyoke Coll., 1978, 82, 85, faculty fellow, 1980. Mem. Am. Coll. Dance Festival Assn. (dir. 1983-84), Congress on Research in Dance, Nat. Dance Assn., AAHPER and Dance. Democrat. Unitarian. Office: Mount Holyoke Coll Dept Dance Kendall Hall South Hadley MA 01075

WILEY, HELEN BERNADETTE, interior designer; b. Herrin, Ill., May 15, 1944; d. Sidney and Margueritte Bernadette (Mathews) Jenkins; m. James Boyd Wiley, June 25, 1966; 1 child, Karen Bernadette. B.S., Bradley U., 1966. Interior designer C.S. Wo & Co., Honolulu, 1968-75; comml. rep. Sherwin-Williams Co., Honolulu, 1975-76; interior designer Very Spl. Environments, Honolulu, 1976-79; residential designer Midwest Furniture Corp., Denver, 1979-80; interior designer, owner Welcome Homes Interiors, Springfield, Ohio, 1980-86; pres. design firm The Focal Point, Inc., Springfield and Cin., 1986—. Active, Springfield Arts Council, S. Fountain Ave. Preservation Assn. Mem. Nat. Assn. Female Execs., Abilities Unlimited (sec.-treas. 1986—), Springfield/Clark County C. of C. (legis. affairs com.). Republican. Episcopalian. Avocations: art and sculpture collecting; equestrian riding. Home: 345 Upper Valley Pike Springfield OH 45504 Office: The Focal Point Inc 345 Upper Valley Pike Springfield OH 45504

WILEY, KAREN MARIE, personnel administrator; b. Kansas City, Mo., Apr. 26, 1955; d. James Amos and Lois Lucille (Fowler) W. B.S., Maryville Coll., Tenn., 1977; cert. U. Pitts., 1984; postgrad. St. Francis Coll., 1984—. Cert. tchr., Tenn. Paymaster Pitts. Brewing Co., 1980-84; personnel mgr. Jones & Brown, Inc., Pitts., 1985—. Mem. Am. Soc. Personnel Adminstrs. Avocations: shuttle weaving; reading. Home: 313 Garland St Pittsburgh PA 15218 Office: Jones & Brown Inc 2515 Preble Ave Pittsburgh PA 15233

WILEY, MICHELE MARY, university administrator; b. Boston, Feb. 21, 1944; d. Harold and Naomi Audrey (Schoville) Weiss; m. Harry James Wiley, Dec. 13, 1968; 1 son, Zachary Edward. B.S., U. Wis., 1966. Pub. safety specialist Nat. Safety Council, Chgo., 1966-68; writer Nixon-Agnew campaign, N.Y.C., 1968, info. rep. Portland State U. (Oreg.), 1968-75; assoc. dir. univ. relations Oreg. Health Scis. U., Portland, 1975-85; regional dir. capital campaign U. Calif., Berkeley, 1986—. Mem. Women in Communications (nat. dir. 1979-83, Clarion award 1977), Council for Advancement and Support Edn. (nat. trustee 1983—, News Writing award 1977, Mindpower award 1982), Am. Med. Colls. Group on Pub. Affairs Assn., Oreg. Assn. Broadcasters (ednl. assoc. 1978-85), Oreg. Newspaper Pubs. Assn. (ednl. assoc. 1978-85). Republican. Home: 18 St Benedict Ct San Ramon CA 94583 Office: Devel Office U Calif 2440 Bancroft Way Berkeley CA 94720

WILEY, SHIRLEY ANN, educator, musician; b. High Point, N.C.; d. Gus and Nannie L. W. B.S., Winston-Salem State Coll., 1960; M.S., N.C. Central U., 1966; postgrad. Harvard U., summer 1967, U. Bridgeport, 1975. Tchr. elem. sch. High Point City Schs., N.C., 1960-70, Bridgeport City Schs., Conn., 1970—, tchr. fgn. student, Bridgeport Bd. Edn., summer 1982, City of Bridgeport, summer 1983; music specialist Action for Bridgeport Community Devel., Bridgeport, summer 1974-78, Title XX program, Bridgeport, summer 1979-80; dir. youth choir Stratford Baptist Ch., 1974-79. Pres. YWCA (bus. and profl. club), High Point, 1967-68. Mem. NEA, Conn. Edn. Assn., Bridgeport Edn. Assn., N.C. Tchrs. Assn. (v.p. 1964-65), Alpha Kappa Alpha. Democrat. Baptist. Avocations: piano, organ. Home: 830 Wood Ave Bridgeport CT 06604

WILHELM, STEPHANIE ANNE, mobile catering company executive; b. Inglewood, Calif., Sept. 6, 1950; d. Robert Franklin and Eva Earl (Alexander) Wilhelm. A.A. in Phys. Therapy, Fullerton Coll., 1978; student San Antonio Coll., 1973, 80-84, U. Md., 1974-75, City Coll. Chgo., 1974. U. Tex., 1982-83. Commd. airman USAF, 1968, advanced through grades to staff sgt., 1975; document control clk., Offutt AFB, Nebr., 1969-70; personnel adminstr., Japan, 1970-72; telecommunications mgr., Kelly AFB, Tex., 1972-74; acctg. and fin. adminstr., Crete, 1974-75; instr. arts and crafts Anaheim Parks, Recreation and Arts Dept. (Calif.), 1976, instr. sports, spl. olympics coach 1976; exec. sec. Holovision Internat. Corp., Anaheim, 1976; exec. sec. Link Realtors, Fullerton, Calif., 1976; admissions clk. Fullerton Coll., 1976-77; dir. membership San Antonio Bd. Realtors, 1979-80; mfg. dir. Comp-Data Service, Inc., San Antonio, 1980-84; owner Charter Point Enterprises, San Antonio, 1983. Decorated Air Force Commendation medal. Mem. North San Antonio C. of C., Nat. Assn. Female Execs., Am. Entrepreneurs Assn. Democrat. Roman Catholic. Office: PO Box 380555 San Antonio TX 78280

WILHELM, WILLA METTA, educational media specialist; b. Jasper, Oreg., Sept. 10, 1912; d. Charles Elzie and Margaret Sephronia (Jacoby) Logsdon; B.S., U. Oreg., 1933, M.S., 1941; m. George August Wilhelm, June 21, 1941; 1 son, Daren Lyle (dec.). Tchr., Sprague River, Oreg., 1934-35, Canyonville (Oreg.) High Sch., 1935-37, Junction City (Oreg.) High Sch., 1937-41; mem. staff bus. office Convair Corp., San Diego, 1942-45; tchr. Riddle (Oreg.) Sch. System, 1945-47, supt., 1946-47; tchr. Lowell (Oreg.) High Sch., 1947-61, media specialist, 1961—, dir. high sch. paper (internat. 1st pl. award), 1947-60. Mem. Delta Zeta, Pi Lambda Theta. Republican. Clubs: Order Eastern Star, Rebekah. Home: 85501 Jasper Park Rd Pleasant Hill OR 97455

WILKERSON, MARILYN MACKENZIE, manufacturing company executive; b. Pitts., Apr. 13, 1952; d. Harry William and Ellen (Zitzman) Mackenzie; m. Wayne W. Lenigan, July 20, 1973 (div. Oct. 1978); m. William E. Wilerson, Oct. 1, 1982; one child, Derek. Student Allegheny County Community Coll., 1970-71; B.A., U. Pitts., 1973; career devel. courses Jackson Community Coll., 1974-75, Houston Baptist Coll., 1979-80, U. Houston, 1981—. With Haines, Lundberg & Waehler, Houston, 1978-80, Gen. Homes Corp., Houston, 1980, Emde Plumbing Co., 1980-81; customer service mgr. Palais Royal Co., Houston, 1981-83; v.p. sales/mktg. Equalizer Mfg. Co., Houston, 1983—; v.p. sales, sec./treas. First Nat. Holding Co., Houston, 1983—; sales mgr. Miramar Mktg. Co., Houston, 1983-84, Christmas Around the World, Houston, 1985-86. Contbr. poetry to various mags., 1970-76. Mem. Nat. Assn. Female Execs. Presbyterian.

WILKERSON, MARJORIE JOANN MADAR, insurance company executive, author, teacher, consultant; b. Spokane, Wash., Dec. 2, 1930; d. Joseph Robert and Margaret Muriel (McKee) Madar; m. Billy E. Wilkerson, Jan. 9, 1953; 1 child, Wesley James McEarl. Student U. Puget Sound, 1948; B.A., UCLA, 1949; postgrad. So. Meth. U., 1958. Mgmt. to agt. Travelers Ins. Cos., Houston and Dallas, 1952-63; sr. account agt. Allstate Ins. Cos., Tacoma, 1966—; cons in field; lectr. various colls. and univs. Author: Sex and Society, 1976. Editor publ. Chiropractic Edn., also newsletter. Pres., co-founder Pierce County Women's Polit. Caucus, Tacoma; newsletter editor bd. Caucus State of Wash., Seattle; lobbiest Caucus and prior for ERA, Olympia, Wash.; citizen lobbiest Worker Right to Know, Olympia, 1984-85; spokesperson Community effort to protect zoning, Gig Harbor, Wash., 1980-84; bd. dirs., sec. Beaumont Art Mus., Tex., 1954-57; pres. Walnut Hill League, N. Dallas, 1957-65; established first Girl Scout Program in Beaumont Girl Scouts U.S., 1955. Grantee activist to study Washington Commn. for Humanities, 1974-75. Recipient numerous sales awards Allstate Ins. Co.; named Divisional Agt. of Yr., 1984. Mem. Parent's Assn. Wash. State U., Alumni Assn. U. Puget Sound. Home: 5418 Wollochet Dr NW Gig Harbor WA 98335 Office: 15 Oregon Suite 304 Tacoma WA 98409

WILKES, A. RUTH HICKS, nurse; b. Upson County, Ga.; d. Lowell L. and Oddie M. Hicks; m. Michael D. Wilkes, Sept. 6, 1983. R.N., Cook County Hosp., Chgo., 1974; B.S., Coll. St. Francis, Joliet, Ill., 1978; M.S., DePaul U., Chgo., 1981. Staff nurse hosps. in Ill. and Calif., to 1980; nurse recruiter Jackson Park Hosp., Chgo., 1980-83, pres. elect nursing service adminstrn. group, 1982-83; condr. career counseling seminars. Mem. Nat. Black Nurses Assn. (chmn. scholarship com. chpt.), Am. Soc. Public Adminstrn., Nat. Assn. Female Execs., Chgo. Area Nurse Recruiters Assn., Alumni Assn. Coll. St. Francis, DePaul U. Alumni Assn. Home: 2217 Montevideo Dr Pittsburg CA 94565

WILKES, BEVERLY LAKE, lawyer; b. Boston, Apr. 25, 1949; d. Thomas E. and Ann W. Lake; B.A. in Math., Wheaton Coll., Norton, Mass., 1970; J.D., Fordham U., 1976; m. Lawrence R. Wilkes, Oct. 9, 1976. Photog. model Wilhelmina Models, Inc., N.Y.C., 1970-72; stockbroker E.F. Hutton & Co., Inc., N.Y.C., 1972-74; estate planner U.S. Trust Co., N.Y.C., 1974-76; admitted to N.Y. bar, 1977; corp. atty. Davis Polk & Wardwell, N.Y.C., 1976-82; fin. atty. Union Carbide Corp., Danbury, Conn., 1983—. Mem. ABA, Nat. Assn. Women Lawyers. Home: 115 Hemlock Hill Rd New Canaan CT 06840 Office: Union Carbide Corp 39 Old Ridgebury Rd Danbury CT 06817-0001

WILKES, HELEN TOWNSEND, artist; b. El Paso, Tex., 1904; d. Wilber and La Belle Frances (Read) Townsend; B.A., U. Calif., Berkeley, 1926; pupil of Sam. H. Harris, Katherine Shackelford, Robert Frame, Gay Maccoy, Lenard Kester; m. Peter F. Wilkes, 1927 (dec. 1969); children—Peter T. (dec.), Patricia Wilkes Wright; m. 2d, Kenneth Thomas Norwood, Aug. 14, 1978. One-woman shows: St. Mark's Gallery, Altadena, Calif., 1960, 62, 64, Main YWCA Gallery, Glendale, Calif., 1963, Tuesday Afternoon Club Gallery, Glendale, 1964, Glendale Fine Arts Gallery, 1968, Glendale Main Library Gallery, 1966; group exhbns. include: Greek Theatre, Los Angeles, 1961, Santa Paula (Calif.) C. of C., 1961, 63, Gallery Cezanne, Laguna Beach, Calif., 1972-74, Glendale Fine Arts Gallery, 1967-71; chmn., exhibit dir. Glendale All-City Art Show, 1960; gallery dir. St. Mark's Episcopal Ch., Altadena, 1957-63; coordinator Vincent Price shows, Glendale and Los Angeles, 1964; co-founder, v.p. Glendale Fine Arts Gallery, 1967; bd. dirs. Glendale Art Assn., 1955-56; mem. Gallery Cezanne, 1972-76; art juror, speaker, tchr. in field. Bd. govs. Glendale Symphony Orch. Assn., women's com. Glendale Symphony Orch., Glendale Philharm. Affiliates. Mem. PEO, Group Four Painters (co-founder 1976), Los Angeles Art Assn., Nat. Mus. Women in Arts (charter), Descanso Garden Guild, Contempos, Zeta Tau Alpha. Episcopalian. Address: 1831 Crestmont Ct Glendale CA 91208

WILKINS, ARLENE, social worker; b. Balt., Oct. 20, 1936; d. Joseph Martin and Alice Gertrude (Mickey) Martin Patterson; m. E.J. Wilkins, Jan. 15, 1963; children—Del, Deirdre, Justin, Patrick. B.A., Wilkes Coll., 1959; M.A., U. Pa., 1962. Social worker Children's Service Inc., Phila., 1960-62, Western Psychiat. Inst. and Clinic, Pitts., 1966-67, Bethesda United Presbyterian Ch., Pitts., 1967-70; clin. social worker Allegheny Gen. Hosp., Northview Heights Health Ctr., Pitts., 1967—. Program chmn. St. Andrew United Presbyn. Ch., Sewickley, Pa., 1981-83. Mem. Nat. Assn. Social Workers, Clin. Social Workers. Republican. Home: 416 College Park Dr Corapolis PA 15108 Office: Northview Heights Health Ctr 525 Mount Pleasant Rd Pittsburgh PA 15214

WILKINS, HELEN ELIZABETH, ballet company artistic director; b. Ottawa, Ont., Can., Mar. 3, 1943; came to U.S., 1964, naturalized 1967; d. Allan Archibald and Mary Emily (Marshall) Bailey; m. John Stephen Wilkins, Aug. 25, 1969; children—Darrell Allan, Daniel Stephen, Julia Kathleen. Student Nat. Ballet of Can., Toronto, 1960, Banff Sch. Fine Arts, Alta., 1956-62, U. Sask., 1962-64, Am. Ballet Theatre Sch., N.Y.C., Robert Joffrey Ballet, N.Y.C., Luigi Jazz Ctr., N.Y.C., 1964-67, Rosella Hightower Sch. of Ballet, Cannes, France, 1967, First Regional Am. Coll. Dance Festival, 1973, Internat. Ballet Competition, Jackson, Miss., 1979, Ballet mistress Fort Wayne Ballet, Inc., Ind., 1967-69; ballet tchr. Lois Smith Sch. dance, Toronto, 1970-71; co-founder, dir. Children's Arts Ctr., State College, Pa., 1971-73; ballet tchr. U. Sask. Ballet Sch., Saskatoon, 1974-76; asst. dir. Del. Regional Ballet Co., N.E. Regional Ballet Festival, 1978; ballet instr. Kent State U., 1978-80; dir. Canton Ballet Sch., Ohio, 1978-80; artistic dir. Olympic Ballet, Edmonds, Wash., 1981—; guest tchr. Mount Union Coll., Canton Ballet, Sally Wortman Sch. Ballet, Judy Bourn Sch. Dance, 1980-81, instr. Pacific Regional Ballet Festival, 1984. Editor: Basic Ballet Dictionary, 1980. Performer: Royal Alexander Theatre, Toronto, Music Carnival Inc., Cleve., Ballet Concepts Dance Co., N.Y.C., 1965-66, Pa. State U., 1972, First Regional Am. Coll. Dance Festival, Central Pa. Festival of Arts, 1973, Toronto Jewish Folk Choir, 1974. Choreographer: Carousel, Saskatoon, Summer Players, Sun Dance, Christmas Prayer and Celebration, U. Sask., 1975, Nutcracker, Solstice, Dulcet Pipes, Del. Regional Ballet Co., 1976-78, A Little Night Music, Players Guild of Canton, 1979, The Preacher Said We Could Dance, Canton Ballet Co., 1980, Rameau Suite, Haydn Study, Simcha, Alchemist's Dream, Endless Flight, Vienna Moon, Olympic Ballet, 1981—. Bd. dirs. Friends of Cultural Arts South Snohomish County (Wash.), Mem. Actors Equity. Avocation: family. Home: 1125 Sea Vista Pl Edmonds WA 98020 Office: Olympic Ballet 700 Main St Edmonds WA 98020

WILKINS, MADGE HANCOCK, research company executive; b. Ruby, S.C., Feb. 1, 1935; d. Carl E. and Annie (Campbell) Hancock; m. John A. Wilkins, Jr., Nov. 5, 1955 (div.); children—Anne Marie, D. Lynn, John III, Lisa. Student Wingate Coll., 1951-52, U. Tenn.-Chattanooga, 1970-71, Dell Sch. Med. Tech., 1952-53. Med. technician Gaston Meml. Hosp., Gastonia, N.C., 1953-54; Dr. D. Glenn, Gastonia, 1955-60; biol. technician Communicable Disease Ctr., Atlanta, 1961-62; researcher Mktg. Research, Atlanta, 1964-67, Chattanooga, 1968-71; owner Wilkins Research Services, Chattanooga, 1971—. Mem. Am. Mktg. Assn., Mktg. Research Assn., Chattanooga C. of C. Baptist. Home: 1921 Morris Hill Rd Chattanooga TN 37421 Office: Wilkins Research Services 1923 Morris Hill Rd Chattanooga TN 37421

WILKINSON, CANDACE FORKEL, accountant; b. Bartlesville, Okla., Mar. 13, 1950; d. Curt Emil and Chloe (Tidwell) F.; m. Thomas B. Wilkinson, IV, July 9, 1971; 1 child, Lauren Noel. B.A. in Math., Rice U., 1972; M. Profl. Acctg., U. Tex.-Austin, 1975. C.P.A., Tex. Acct., tax staff Arthur Young & Co., Houston, 1974-77; asst. treas. Gulf Interstate Co., Houston, 1977; asst. controller Ginther-Davis Interests, Houston, 1978; owner Candace F. Wilkinson, C.P.A., Houston, 1979—; treas. Women of Ch., First Presbyn. Ch., Houston, 1985—. Mem. Am. Inst. C.P.A.s, Phi Kappa Phi, Beta Alpha Psi. Republican. Presbyterian. Home: 8411 Roos Houston TX 77036 Office: 6009 Richmond #212 Houston TX 77057

WILKINSON, DORIS YVONNE, medical sociologist, health educator; b. Lexington, Ky.; d. Howard Thomas and Regina Lavonne Wilkinson; Ph.D., Case Western Res. U., 1968. Assoc. prof. sociology Macalester Coll. 1970-75, prof. 1975-77; exec. assoc. Am. Sociol. Assn. 1977-80; prof. sociology Howard U. 1980-84; prof. U. Ky., 1985—; bd. sci. counselors Nat. Cancer Inst., 1980-84; cons. Bd. overseers Case Western Res. U., 1982—. Author: Workbook for Introductory Sociology, 1968; editor: Black Revolt; Strategies of Protest, 1969, Black Male/White Female, 1975; co-editor The Black Male in America, 1977; contbr. articles to profl. jours. Social Sci. Research Council grantee, 1975, Nat. Inst. Edn. grantee, 1978-79. Mem. Am. Sociol. Assn., D.C. Sociol. Assn. (pres. 1982-83), Eastern Sociol. Soc. (v.p 1983-84), Soc. Study Social Problems (bd. 1982-84, v.p 1984-85), Am. Pub. Health Assn., Assn. Orthopsychiatry, Phi Beta Kappa. Office: U Ky Dept Sociology Lexington KY 40506

WILKINSON, HEI SOOK PARK, psychologist; b. Seoul, Korea, Oct. 11, 1947; came to U.S., 1970, naturalized, 1977; d. Woo Young and Seung Ui (Song) Park; B.A. summa cum laude, Ewha Womans U., 1969; M.A., George Peabody Coll. Tchrs., Vanderbilt U., 1973; postgrad. Merill-Palmer Inst., 1977; Ph.D., Saybrook Inst., 1981; m. Todd Scripps Wilkinson, Mar. 21, 1973; children—Todd Scripps, Gina Park. Korean lang. instr. Peace Corps, Fairleigh Dickinson U., 1970, cons. Peace Corps, Washington, 1971; tour guide UN, N.Y.C., 1971-72; liaison specialist Met. Davidson County Sch. System, Nashville, 1973-75; ednl. therapist Children's Ctr. Wayne County, Detroit, 1975-76; psychotherapist Lee M. Shulman Assocs., Royal Oak, Mich., 1978-84; psychologist Birmingham Clin., Mich., 1985—; psychol. cons. Mich. Dept. Social Services, 1978-82; cons. Bethany Internat. Adoptions, 1982—, Ams. for Internat. Aid and Adoption, 1982—; adj. faculty Union Grad. Sch., Cin., 1982—; faculty Inst. Advanced Pastoral Studies, Ecumenical Theol. Ctr., Detroit, 1984—. Mem. Korean Del. to UN World Youth Assembly, 1970. Mem. Am. Psychol. Assn., Assn. Humanistic Psychology, Korean Am. Women's Assn. Mich. (dir. 1983—). Home: 708 Parkman Dr Bloomfield Hills MI 48013 Office: 802 S Worth Birmingham MI 48011

WILKS, JACQUELIN HOLSOMBACK, educator; b. Oakdale, La., Jan. 18, 1950; d. Jack and Ida Mae (Bass) Holsomback; B.S., La. Coll., 1972; M.A.T., Okla. City U., 1982; postgrad. So. Bapt. Theol. Sem., Louisville, 1974, S.E. Mo. State U., 1977; counseling cert. Central State U., Edmond, Okla., 1983; m. Thomas M. Wilks, Jan. 28, 1972; children—Thomas David, Bryan Emerson. Sec. to adminstr. Allen Parish Hosp., Kinder, La., 1968-69; tchr. horseback riding, swimming Triple D Guest Ranche, Warren, Tex., 1969; singer, speaker Found. Singers, including TV and radio appearances, record albums, 1970-71; tchr. English, reading Pine Bluff (Ark.) High Sch., 1972-74; tchr. kindergarten Doyle Elem. Sch., East Prairie (Mo.) R-2 Sch. Dist., 1974-75; tchr. 1st grad Bertrand (Mo.) Elem. Sch., 1975-76; tchr. 6th grade sci. A.D. Simpson Sch., Charleston, Mo., 1976-78; dir. admissions and fin. aid Mo. Bapt. Coll., St. Louis, 1978-80; fin. adminstr. Control Data Inst., Control Data Corp., St. Louis, 1980-81; dir. tutorial services, instr. tutorial methods Okla. Bapt. U., 1981-83 instr. horsemanship St. Gregory's Jr. Coll., 1981; counselor Gordon Cooper Area Vocat. Tech. Sch., 1982-83, Shawnee Jr. High Sch. (Okla.), 1983-85; dir. Resource Ctr., instr. English, St. Gregory's Coll., Shawnee, Okla., 1985—; tutor for children under jurisdiction Juvenile Ct., Jefferson County, Ark., 1972-73, leader group counseling/therapy sessions, 1972. Choreographer, First Bapt. Ch. Youth Choir, Pine Bluff; v.p. St. Gregory's Coll. Therapeutic Horsemanship Program, 1981-82; Republican election judge. Recipient Kathryn Carpenter award La. Bapt. Conv., 1971; Real Scope award Realty World, St. Louis, 1980; lic. Realtor, Mo. Mem. Nat. Hist. Soc., Univ. Alliance Okla. Bapt. U., Nat. Assn. Fin. Aid Adminstrs., Nat. Assn. Admissions Counselors, Athenian Lit. Soc., Nat. Geog. Soc., Gamma Beta Phi, Kappa Delta, Phi Kappa Phi. Republican. Baptist. Clubs: Kathryn Boone Music, Civinette Booster. Home: Route 3 Box 143 Shawnee OK 74801 Office: St Gregory's Coll 1900 W MacArthur Shawnee OK 74801

WILKS, WANDA JEAN, secretary, educator; b. Syracuse, Kans., Dec. 28, 1945; d. Ervin Reed and Berthena Marie (Kinslow) Laney; m. Lloyd Ovitt Wells, Dec. 5, 1965 (div. Feb. 1981); children—Jeffrey Dale, Gari Sue, Chad Ovitt; m. Jimmie Wayne Wilks, Mar. 22, 1981. Student Southwestern U. Coll., Winfield, Kans., 1963-65; Wichita State U., 1984. Owner, operator W Wells Answering Service, Cheyenne Wells, Colo., 1969-77; part owner Wells Trucking Co.; legal sec. Max L. Dice, Johnson, Kans., 1966-68; clk. dist. ct. Cheyenne County, Cheyenne Wells, Colo., 1968-69; asst. adminstr. Contract Dept., Colo. Ind., A.C., Denver, 1977-78; sec. bookkeeper Beef City, McClave, Colo., 1978-80; tchr. Christian Ctr., Wichita, Kans., 1981-84; legal sec. Farm Credit Banks, Legal Div., Litigation Dept., Wichita, 1984—. Author (autobiography) Wanda's Wanderings. Drama dir. Christian Ctr., Wichita, 1981-84. Recipient Fast Start award Cosmetics Internat., 1975; ednl. grantee Southwestern Coll., 1963. Republican. Charismatic. Lodge: Rebekah's. Avocations: seamstress, dramatics, reading, crochet, ceramics.

WILL, JESSIE GERMAN, handwriting expert, document examiner; b. Muskogee, Okla., Oct. 8, 1912; d. William Paxton Zacheus and Mabel Gussie (Ward) German; student Ward Belmont Coll., 1929-30, Drake U., 1930-32; B.S., Okla. U., 1933; cert. Internat. Graphoanalysis Soc., 1968, master cert., 1973; m. Edward Ray Will, Sept. 29, 1934; children—Henry German, Margaret Ann Will Cornell. Handwriting expert, document examiner, Tulsa, 1970—; lectr. Oklahoma City U., 1972-78, Tri-County Tech. Sch., Bartlesville, Okla., 1977-81. Pres. local PTA, 1948-49, 55-58; bd. dirs. Tulsa WYWCA, 1963, Tulsa Philharmonic, 1964; mem. nat. panel advisers Nat. Forensic Center. Mem. PEO, (chpt. pres. 1962-63), Internat. Graphoanalysis Soc., Ind. Assn. Questioned Document Examiners (corr. sec. 1976-77), Tulsa Boys Home Women's Assn. (v.p. 1978-79), Internat. Assn. Forensic Scis., Kappa Alpha Theta (pres. alumni assn. 1961, coll. dist. pres. 1961-63), Mu Phi Epsilon. Republican. Mem. Disciples of Christ Ch. Expert witness in fed. and dist. cts. Kans. and Ark. Home and Office: 1727 E 31st St Tulsa OK 74105

WILL, MADELEINE C., government official; b. Hartford, Conn., Aug. 9, 1945; married; 3 children. B.A., Smith Coll., 1967; M.A., U. Toronto, 1969. Asst. sec. for spl. edn. and rehab. services Dept. Edn., Washington, 1983—; panelist White House Conf. on Aging, 1977; chmn. govt. affairs com. Montgomery County Assn. for Retarded Citizens, 1979; mem. govt. affairs com. Nat. Assn. Retarded Citizens; cons. Rock Creek Found. Office: Dept Edn Room 3006 330 C St SW Washington DC 20202

WILLACY, HAZEL MARTIN, lawyer; b. Utica, Miss., Apr. 20, 1946; d. Julious and Willie Thelma (Barnes) Martin; student Tougaloo Coll., 1963-64; B.A. in Econs., Smith Coll., 1967; J.D., Case Western Res. U., 1976; m. Aubrey Barrington Willacy, Mar. 18, 1967; children—Austin Keith, Louis Samuel. Admitted to Ohio bar, 1976; labor economist Bur. Labor Stats., U.S. Dept. Labor, 1967-70; assoc. firm Baker, Hostetler, Cleve., 1976-80; labor relations atty. Sherwin Williams Co., Cleve., 1980-82, asst. dir. labor relations, 1983—. Bd. dirs. YWCA, 1972, mem. fin. devel. com., 1976-80; bd. dirs., mem. recreation planning com. Shaker Heights Youth Ctr.; vis. com. bd. overseers student affairs Case Western Res. U. Mem. Am. Bar Assn. (labor law com.), Ohio Bar Assn. (labor law com.), Cleve. Bar Assn., Nat. Assn. Female Execs., Order of Coif. Clubs: Women's City, Law Wives (treas., 1979-80). Contbr. articles to legal publs. Office: 101 Prospect Ave Cleveland OH 44115

WILLADSEN, KAY A., marketing representative; b. Saginaw, Mich., May 11, 1947; d. W. Franklin and Elaine (Simkins) Brooks; m. Michael C. Willadsen, Dec. 5, 1964; children—Michael C., Erik J. A.A., McComb Coll., 1973; student Eastern Mich. U., 1977-78, U. Ill., 1979; B.B.A., Bowling Green State U., 1982; postgrad. Ind. U., 1983-85. Mktg. rep. Credit Bur. of Hancock County, Inc., Findlay, Ohio, 1983—. Choreographer dance Flowers and Confusion, 1974. Precinct del. Livingston County Republicans, Hamburg, Mich., 1976, state conv. del., 1976; treas. Hillcrest Gasline Project, Findlay, Ohio, 1984. Mem. Nat. Assn. Female Execs., Bowling Green Alumni Assn., Credit Grantors Assn. (dir. 1983-86). Methodist. Club: Women's Lions (dir. 1974-75). Avocations: dance; reading; investments. Home: 3210 Byrnwyck Dr Findlay OH 45840 Office: Credit Bur of Hancock Co Inc 118 E Sandusky S Findlay OH 45840

WILLARD-GALLO, KAREN ELIZABETH, molecular biologist; b. Oak Ridge, July 8, 1953; d. Harvey Bradford and Isabella Victoria (Rallis) Willard; student in microbiology U. Reading, Eng., 1973-74; A.B. in Biology, Randolph-Macon Woman's Coll., 1975; M.S. in Immunology, Va. Poly. Inst., 1978, Ph.D. in Molecular Biology, 1981; m. James Paul Gallo, July 31, 1982. Grad. teaching asst. Va. Poly. Inst., 1976-78; fellow Research Inst. in Cell Biology, Argonne Nat. Lab., Ill., 1977, lab. resident student assoc., 1978-81, postdoctoral fellow, 1981-82; research assoc. Ludwig Inst. for Cancer Research, Brussels, 1982-85; research scientist Internat. Inst. Cellular and Molecular Pathology, Brussels, Belgium, 1986—; cons. in field. Recipient award for teaching excellence Va. Poly. Inst., 1977, 78. Mem. Am. Soc. Cell Biology, Electrophoresis Soc. Contbr. chpts., articles to profl. publs.; patentee method for early detection infectious mononucleosis. Home: Ave Chevalier Jehan 117 1300 Wavre Belgium Office: Dept Biochemistry UCL 7539 Internat Inst Cellular and Molecular Pathology Ave Hippocrate 75 1200 Brussels Belgium

WILLAT, FELICE, corporate executive; b. Bklyn., June 28, 1944; d. Gene and Joyce (Terano) Bell Levinson; m. Al Barabas, Jan. 6, 1961 (div. 1978); 1 child, Bonnie; m. Boyd Willat, Dec. 31, 1978; children—Harper, Amber. Ed., Los Angeles City Coll. Free-lance prodn. coordinator for network TV, Los Angeles, 1974-80; pres., owner Harper House, Los Angeles, 1980—. Designer: Jour. calendar, Keeping Track, 1978; Personal organizer The Day Runner, 1981. Award for best selling calendar Retail Mktg. Report, 1985. Mem. Nat. Assn. Female Execs., Nat. Assn. Women Bus. Owners. Democrat. Club: Profl. Women's Breakfast Group (Westwood, Calif.). Avocations: Cooking; travel; early education. Home: 1414 N Harper Ave Los Angeles CA 90046 Office: Harper House 3562 Eastham Dr Culver City CA 90230

WILLBANKS, SUE SUTTON, investment executive, writer, artist; b. Luling, Tex., Sept. 24, 1935; d. William Herbert and Melba Ophelia (Ward) Sutton; m. Charles Walter Willbanks, Nov. 21, 1953 (dec. Feb. 1979); children—Jill Ann, Brenda Kay. B.S., Tex. Tech. U., 1955; M.A., U. Tex. Permian Basin, 1980. Cert. secondary, vocat. and elem. tchr., Tex. Tchr., Big Spring Ind. Sch. Dist., Tex., 1964-68, 1972-79, dept. chmn., 1980-82; owner, pres. Sutwill Co., Aiea, Hawaii, 1981—; pvt. practice psychotherapy, Tex., Hawaii, 1979—. Author short stories and poems. Contbr. articles to profl. jours. Organizer Silver Heels Vol. Fire Dept., Howard County, Tex., 1970-71; bd. dirs. Permian Basin Planned Parenthood Assn., Odessa, Tex., 1980-82; organist Immaculate Heart of Mary Ch., Big Spring, Tex., 1975-78; mem. United Cancer Council, 1984—. Mem. Nat. Assn. Female Execs., Psi Inst. Hawaii, The Am. Soc. Psychical Research, Planetary Citizens. Methodist. Avocations: interior decorating; acting. Home: 98-1457 B Kaahumanu St Aiea HI 96701

WILLBRAND, MARY LOUISE, speech pathologist, educator; b. Tulsa, Aug. 16, 1936; d. Raymond Richard and Wilma (Collins) Scott; m. Richard D. Rieke, June 24, 1979; 1 dau., Amy Dawn. A.A. in Drama, Christian Coll., 1956; student Mary Washington Coll., 1955, Tulsa U., 1957; B.S., U. Mo., 1958, M.A., 1969, Ph.D., 1972; postgrad. Stanford U., 1969. Speech clinician pub. schs., Moberly, Mo., 1958-61, Columbia, Mo., 1961-65, Cerebral Palsy Center, Fayette, Mo., 1967; tchr. speech and drama summer enrichment program, Columbia Mo., 1963-65; lang. clinician Inst. Childhood Aphasia, Palo Alto, Calif., 1969; instr. speech pathology U. Mo., Columbia, 1969-71; dir. speech-lang. pathology and audiology U. Utah, Salt Lake City, 1976-81, prof. speech pathology, 1973—; cons. to sch. dists. Mo., Wyo., Utah, Tex. Author: (with M.J. Mecham) Language Disorders in Children, 1979, Treatment of Language Disorders, 1985; (with R.D. Rieke) Teaching Oral Communication in Elementary Schools, 1983. Contbr. numerous articles to profl. jours. Vice pres., bd. dirs. Montessori Sch., Columbia, 1969-71; mem. exec. council Nat. Charity League, Salt Lake City, 1974-77; mem. home-sch. bd. Rowland Hall-St. Marks Sch., Salt Lake City, 1975-77; v.p., bd. dirs. Boy's Club Early Childhood Edn. Center, Salt Lake City, 1980—. Coll. Humanities grantee U. Utah, 1975, research com. grantee, 1981-83. Mem. Utah Speech and Hearing Assn. (pres.), Am. Speech-Lang-Hearing Assn. (visitor edn. tng. bd. site). Home: 1485 Sigsbee Ave Salt Lake City UT 84103 Office: 1201 Behavioral Sci Bldg Univ of Utah Salt Lake City UT 84112

WILLEFORD, CATHERINE PROCTOR, civic worker; b. Greenwood, S.C., Sept. 9, 1935; d. Benjamen Moye and Catherine Proctor; B.S., Winthrop Coll., 1957; M.S., La. State U., 1959; m. Brice J. Willeford, Jr., July 22, 1961; children—Brice J. III, Catherine Elizabeth. Instr., La. State U., 1957-58, Duke U., 1958-61; tchr. Cannon Jr. High Sch., Kannapolis, N.C., 1961-62; bd. dirs. Cabarrus County United Way, 1974-79, ARC, 1976-79, N.C. United Way, 1977-79; chmn. Womens Democratic County Com., 1973; chmn. Gov.'s Involvement Council, 1978-79; vice chmn. Democratic Precinct Com., Kannapolis, N.C., 1970-77; mem. planning bd. So. Piedmont Health Assn., 1978-79; chmn. Tchr. Parent Council, 1978-79; leader Girl Scouts U.S.A., 1970-78, Cub Scouts, 1969; soc. exec. bd. Cabarrus County ARC; sec. bd. Library Arts Council, 1977-79; bd. dirs. Old Courthouse Theatre, 1977—, Cabarrus-Concord Friends of Library; chmn. Episcopal Churchwomen, 1982, chmn. cookbook com., 1982—; Art Acquisition (Holt Collection), 1981—, Kannapolis Book Club II, 1982; bd. dirs. Cabarrus County chpt. Am. Cancer Soc., 1981—; co-chmn. Cabarrus Arts Council Ball, 1983; mem. YMCA Library Bd., Kanapolis, 1983-84. Co-editor; The Charmouse Cookbook, 1985. La. State U. fellow, 1957-58; recipient Gov.'s Spl. Vol. award, 1979. Mem. N.C. Hist. Assn., Internat. Platform Assn., DAR. Clubs: Friends of Library, Garden, Parnassus Book (chmn.), Cabarrus Country. Home: 1646 Eastwood St Kannapolis NC 28081

WILLEMS, CONSTANCE CHARLES, lawyer; b. Zuilen, Utrecht, Netherlands, Oct. 31, 1942; came to U.S., 1967, naturalized, 1977; d. Anton Henri and Maria (Van der Meys) Charles; m. Cornelis Franciscus Willems, May 25, 1965; 1 son, Maurice. B.A. in Sociology magna cum laude, U. New Orleans, 1974; J.D. with honors, Tulane U., 1977. Bar: La. 1977, U.S. Dist. Ct. (ea. dist.) La. 1977, U.S. Ct. Appeals (5th cir.) 1977, U.S. Supreme Ct. 1983. Assoc. McGlinchey, Stafford, Mintz, Cellini, and Lang, New Orleans, 1977-81, ptnr., 1982—. Mem. Task Force on Municipalization. Mem. ABA (mem. com. 1983), La. Assn. Women Attys., La. Bar Assn., New Orleans Bar Assn. Club: Holland (pres. 1980). Office: McGlinchey Stafford Mintz Cellini and Lang 630 Camp St New Orleans LA 70130

WILLETT, CATHY LENTZ, communications company executive; b. Russellville, Ala., Apr. 24, 1951; d. Wiley C. and DeEtta (Russell) L.; m. Donald James Godwin, Nov. 7, 1970 (div. Oct. 1977); children—Tara Colleen, Tamra Celeste; m. Kenneth Robert Willett, Oct. 16, 1982. Applications programmer Univ. Health Services Found., Birmingham, Ala., 1976-78; applications programmer Dyatron, Birmingham, 1978; systems programmer Central Bank of South, Birmingham, 1979-81; communication systems rep. So. Central Bell, Birmingham, 1981-82; tech. cons. AT&T Info. Systems, Birmingham, 1983-84; asst. mgr. product evaluation lab. Bell South Advanced Systems Inc., Birmingham, 1985—. Mem. Nat. Assn. Female Execs. Mem. Ch. of Christ. Avocations: Snow skiing; water skiing; painting; reading; calligraphy. Office: BellSouth Advanced Systems Inc 2001 Park Pl Suite 1200 Birmingham AL 35203

WILLETT, DONNA STRACHN, government official; b. Memphis, June 19, 1943; d. Edward Hadley and Sallie (Coffee) Strachn; m. Claude Sykes Haney, Jr., Mar. 8, 1963 (div. Mar. 1968); 1 child, Vicki Baker; m. Michael Jon Willett, May 10, 1975. Editorial asst. U.S. Army Corps of Engrs., Nashville, 1971-73, pub. info. specialist, 1973-76, asst. pub. affairs officer, 1976-80, pub. relations, 1980-85, pub. affairs officer South Pacific div., 1985—. Mem. Soc. Am. Military Engrs. Office: US Army Corps of Engrs 630 Sansome St San Francisco CA 94111

WILLEY, MYRTLE DENNEY, steel company executive; b. Jacksonville, Ill., July 7, 1918; d. Benjamin Harrison and Lora Edna (Burke) Denney; student Brown's Bus. Coll., 1935-36; m. George A. Corbett, Sept. 25, 1945 (div. 1964); 1 son, Michael Denney Corbett; m. Leland B. Willey, Sept. 14, 1972. Fashions buyer Emporium, Jacksonville, 1936-40; photographer Olin Mills Studio, Chattanooga, 1941-45; floor mgr. W.T. Grant Co., Jacksonville, 1945-50; with Peoples Water & Gas Co., Miami Beach, Fla., 1950-56; with T.W. Dick Co., Gardiner, Maine, 1956—, exec. v.p., 1968-76, pres., treas., gen. mgr., 1976—, owner, 1984—. corporator Gardiner Savs. Inst., 1974—. Chmn. fin. com., treas., exec. bd. Gardiner Gen. Hosp., 1975-80; treas. Gardiner Gen. Hosp. Women's Bd. Aux., 1973-80; budget com., dir. United Way, Augusta, Maine, 1975-81; pres. Kennebec Valley United Way, 1979-80; bd. dirs. Kennebec Valley Med. Ctr., 1980—, pres. Aux., 1980-82, 83—; mem. nat. women's bd. Northwood Inst., Midland, Mich., 1985—; patron Forum A, U. Maine, Augusta, 1974—, Portland (Maine) Symphony Orch., 1976—. Recipient Disting. Woman's medal Northwood Inst., 1985. Mem. Augusta Music Jazz Soc. (v.p. 1976—), Maine Good Roads Assn., Asso. Gen. Contractors, Small Bus. Assns. New Eng., Women Constrn. Owners and Execs. (v.p. 1984), Maine Soc. Entrepreneurs, Nat. Assn. Women in Constrn. (pres. chpt., mem. liaison com. 1982—), Maine State C. of C. (dir. 1979-82), Kennebec Valley C. of C. (dir. 1981—), Maine Better Transp. Assn. (v.p. 1983—). Republican. Episcopalian. Club: Zonta (pres. 1981-83, Dist. I treas. 1982—). Home: 2 Ash St Hallowell ME 04347 Office: 1 Summer St PO Box 60 Gardiner ME 04345

WILLEY, SHIRLEY FAYE (MRS. RICHARD WARREN WILLEY), antique dealer; b. Dawson, N.D., Aug. 5, 1933; d. Fern Clifford and Bessie Christine (Nord) Werner; student Pierce Coll., 1952, U. Calif. at Los Angeles, 1961; m. Richard Warren Willey, Feb. 25, 1967. Dir. mktg. and pub. relations Family of Artists, Rockton, Ill.; asst. corp. tng. dir. Bergner-Weise, Rockford, 1979—; program dir. Valley View, Rockford, 1981—; communications cons. Fairmont Hotel, San Francisco and Dallas, 1968-70, Beverly Hilton Hotel, Beverly Hills, Calif., 1964-67; chief communications Better 'n Nothing TV show, Grass Valley, Calif., 1968-69. Mgr. antique show for theatre restoration benefit, 1969; chmn. Nevada County chpt. Heart Assn., 1971—; entertainment chmn. Winnebago (Ill.) Sr. Citizens Days, 1982. Bd. dirs. Nevada County Liberal Arts Commn., cons., 1969-71. Recipient Meritorious service award Am. Heart Assn., 1971. Mem. Ch. of Religious Sci. (dir. 1967). Address: 150 W Russell Apt 9 Rockton IL 61072

WILLHOIT-RUDT, MARILYN JEAN, medical resources company executive; b. Paterson, N.J., Aug. 9, 1947; d. Robert and Eleanor Jean (Lewis) Houston; B.A. in Speech Correction, Trenton State Coll., 1968; M.A. in Audiology, U. Conn., 1970; m. Robert Norval Willhoit, Mar. 29, 1969 (div. 1978); m. 2d, Louis Lazare Rudt, Jan. 1, 1982. Grad. fellow U. Conn., Storrs, 1968-69; audiologist Grove Hill Clinic, New Britain, Conn., 1968-77, Hartford Hearing League, West Hartford, Conn., 1969-71, Gaylord Hosp., Wallingford, Conn., 1971-73, chmn. dept. speech and hearing, 1973-77; ednl. cons. Am. Electromedics Corp., Acton, Mass., 1978-79, nat. sales mgr., 1980-83; v.p. Micro Audiometrics Corp., Daytona Beach, Fla., 1983-86; pres. Med. Resources, Jacksonville, 1986—; part-time prof. So. Conn. State Coll., 1976-77; cons. Blue Cross of Conn., 1973-77, Pfeizer Industries, North Haven, Conn., Conn. State Dept. Health, Pehlps-Stokes Fund, Washington; profl. adv. Employees Ins. of Wasau, Conn.; public speaker in field; adv. bd. Profl. Standards Rev. Orgn., Conn. Mem. Am. Speech and Hearing Assn. (cert.), Conn. Speech and Hearing Assn. (award for spl. contbn. 1977), Nat. Assn. Bus. Planners, Nat. Assn. Small Bus. Mgrs., Am. Mgmt. Assn., Nat. Assn. Female Execs., Nat. Hearing Conservation Assn., Computer Users in Speech and Hearing. Author: Guidelines for the Provision of Speech, Hearing and Language Services State of Conn., 1977. Home: 116 Coral Way Port Orange FL 32019 Office: Medical Resources Inc 4791 Dusk Ct Jacksonville FL 32207

WILLIAM, SISTER MARIAN, college president. Pres., Immaculata Coll., Pa. Office: Immaculata Coll Immaculata PA 19345*

WILLIAMS, ADELLA JUDITH, educator, state representative; b. Barton, N.D., July 21, 1918; d. Bird J. and Clara (Adina Fluerog) Saude; m. Clifford James Williams, Aug. 31, 1941; children—Clark, Jerome, Konnie, Janet, Jane, Brian. B.A., Jamestown Coll., 1940. First class profl. teaching cert. Tchr., Lidgerwood, N.D., 1956-73; mem. N.D. Ho. of Reps., 1983-84, 85-86. Mem. Ret. Tchrs. Assn. (pres. 1978-83). Democrat. Methodist. Home: Route 1 Box 113 Lidgerwood ND 58053

WILLIAMS, ANGELA ANDERSON, health care administrator; b. Columbus, Ga., Aug. 12, 1956; d. Homer C. and Bernice Willene (Davis) Anderson; m. Charles Arthur Williams, June 3, 1978; children—Kimberly Faith, Angela Renee. A.A. in Nursing, Columbus Coll., Ga., 1977, B.S. in Health Sci., 1978; M.S. in Health Sci. Adminstrn., Jersey City State Coll., 1986; postgrad. SUNY-Albany, 1986—. Registered nurse Ga., Wash., N.J. Nursing supr. Stewart Webster Hosp., Richland, Ga., 1978; therapist St. Peters' Hosp., Olympia, Wash., 1979-80; anesthesia asst. St. Peter's Hosp., Olympia, 1980-82; head nurse Nutri-System Weight Loss Clinic, Columbus, Ga., 1983; staff nurse Vet.'s Med. Ctr., East Orange, N.J., 1984-85; asst. adminstr. North Jersey Community Union Health Ctr., Newark, 1985—. Tchr. Sunday Sch., Army Chapel, Bayonne, 1985-86. Mem. Am. Pub. Health Assn., Nat. Assn. Female Execs., Officer's Wives Club, ARC, N.J. Pub. Health Assn. Clubs: Internat Order Rainbow (Columbus), Order Eastern Star. Avocations: sewing; painting; restoring antiques. Home: 124 Goldsborough Village Bayonne NJ 07002 Office: North Jersey Community Union 105 Charlton St Newark NJ 07002

WILLIAMS, ANN E., marketing executive; b. Natchez, Miss., Apr. 9, 1952; d. Willie and Beatrice (Malone) McNair Stinson; m. Frank Williams, Jr., July 7, 1974; children—Timeka, Cherylyn. B.S., Tougaloo Coll., 1974. With Gen. Foods, White Plains, N.Y., 1973-83, group project supr., 1983; v.p. research projects Mktg. Viewpoints, Inc., White Plains, 1983—. Mem. Am. Mktg. Assn. Democrat. Baptist. Home: 70 Juniper Hill Rd White Plains NY 10607

WILLIAMS, ANNA FAY, economist, writer; b. Newark, July 23, 1935; d. Haney Fay and Mary Lillian Rodgers; B.S. in Journalism cum laude, U. Minn., 1957; M.A. in Broadcast Film Arts, So. Meth. U., 1968, M.A. econs., 1975; children—Paul C. Friedlander, Mark T. Friedlander. Editor, Richardson (Tex.) News, 1960; asst. editor Sun News, Sun Oil, Dallas, 1960-69; field research dir. Corp. for Public Broadcasting, Dallas-Ft. Worth, 1972-75; pres. Multi-Media, Inc., Dallas, 1968-70; instr. econs. So. Meth. U., Dallas, 1973-74, Richland Coll., Dallas, 1975-78, Northlake Coll., Irving, Tex., 1978-80; exec. and founding editor Solar Engring. Mag., Dallas, 1975-81; staff economist Keplinger Cos., energy cons., Houston, 1982-85; v.p. Tex. Commerce Bancshares, 1985—; presenter profl. paper 18th Intersoc. Energy Conversion Engring. Conf., 1983, 19th, 1984. Mem. Internat. Solar Energy Soc. (gen. chmn. ann. meeting Am. sect.), ASHRAE, Assn. Energy Engrs. (hon., chmn. regional tech. programs 1981—), Tex. Solar Energy Soc. (founder, dir. 1978-80), Center for Renewable Resources (officer, dir. 1978-80). Author: The Shared Time Strategy, 1966, Dallas Food Finds, 1974, Handbook of Photovoltaic Applications, 1985; also papers in field. Office: 707 Travis 10th Floor Houston TX 77002

WILLIAMS, ANNE M., lawyer, librarian; b. Mpls., Dec. 20, 1940; d. Kenneth Paul and Bette Jane (Linne) Martin; div.; children—Kathryn Malaika, Tara Lynn. B.A. cum laude, Mt. Holyoke Coll., 1962; diploma edn. Makerere U. Coll., Kampala, Uganda, 1963; M.L.S., SUNY-Buffalo, 1972, J.D. magna cum laude, 1975. Bar: N.Y. 1976. Tchr., Tchrs. for East Africa Program, Columbia U. and Kenya Govt., Wusi, 1963-65; library asst. N Kumbi Internat. Coll., Kabwe, Zambia, 1965-70; teaching asst. SUNY-Buffalo, 1973-75; law assoc. Phillips, Lytle et al, Buffalo, 1975-79; regional legal advisor U.S. AID, Swaziland, 1979-82, Morocco, 1983-86, Abidjan, Ivory Coast, 1986—. Pres., Parent/Tchr./Student Assn., Buffalo, 1977-78. Recipient Meritorious Honor award U.S. AID, 1981. Mem. ABA, Am. Soc. Internat. Law, Phi Beta Kappa. Episcopalian. Home and Office: REDSO/WA Abidjan ID Dept State Washington DC 20520

WILLIAMS, ANNIE JOHN, educator; b. Reidsville, N.C., Aug. 26, 1913; d. John Wesley and Martha Anne (Walker) W.; A.B., Greensboro Coll., 1933; M.A., U. N.C., Chapel Hill, 1939; postgrad. Appalachian State U., summer 1944, Duke U., summer 1936, (Shell Merit fellow) Cornell U., summer 1961. Tchr. math. Blackstone (Va.) Coll., 1934-35; tchr. pub. schs., Hoke High Sch., Raeford, N.C., 1935-37, Massey Hill High Sch., Fayetteville, N.C., 1937-42, Alexander Graham Jr. High Sch., Fayetteville, 1942-43, Carr Jr. High Sch., Durham, N.C., 1943-53; supr. math. N.C. Dept. Public Instrn., Raleigh, 1959-62; tchr. math. Durham High Sch., 1953-59, 62-78, ret., 1978; vol. in math. N.C. Sch. Sci. and Math., Durham, 1980—; adj. asst. prof. math. and sci. edn. N.C. State U., Raleigh, 1966-73. Recipient cert. of recognition, dept. math. N.C. State U., 1979; named Vol. of Yr., Key Vol. Program co-sponsored by Vol. Services Bur. and Durham Morning Herald, 1986. Mem. Nat. Council Tchrs. Math. (life), (dir. 1957-60), Math. Assn. Am. (life), N.C. Council Tchrs. Math. (W. W. Rankin Meml. award 1975), Internat. Platform Assn., Delta Kappa Gamma, Mu Alpha Theta (hon.). Methodist. Clubs: Pierian Lit. (sec. 1979-80, pres. 1980-81), Durham Woman's (co-chmn. internat. affairs dept. 1985—), DAR (chmn. chpt. Am. History Month 1980-82, corr. sec. chpt. 1982-84, chaplain chpt. 1984-86). Author: (with Brown and Montgomery) Algebra, First Course, 1963, Algebra, Second Course, 1963. Home and Office: 2021 Sprunt Ave Durham NC 27705

WILLIAMS, ANNIE RUTH, rehab. corp. exec.; b. Gadsden, Ala., Dec. 24, 1934; d. Erwin and Rosie L. (Sturns) Stevens; B.S. in Nursing Edn., Fresno State U., 1971, M.S. in Mental Health, 1972; M.S. in Counseling, Calif. State U., Los Angeles, 1976. Psychiat. nurse VA Hosp., Denver, 1965-69; supervising counselor Valley Med. Center, Fresno, Calif., 1969-70; asst. prof. Fresno State U., 1971-72; instr. for in-service edn. VA Hosp., Long Beach, Calif., 1972-75; asst. prof. Calif. State U., Los Angeles, 1975-78, also dir. tutorial program for minority students; rehab. counselor Profl. Counselors Inc., Santa Monica, Calif., 1978; pres., owner Rehab. Mgmt. Specialist, Inc., Long Beach, 1978—; cons. Los Angeles Regional Family Planning Council, Inc.; ednl. com. for ednl. seminar Calif. Assn. Rehab. Program, 1980-81. Registered nurse; cert. credentials rehab. counselor, pupil personnel counselor, community coll. instr., coll. counselor, student personnel worker. Mem. Am. Personnel and Guidance Assn., Calif. Personnel and Guidance Assn., Assn. Black Faculty and Staff of So. Calif., Nat. Rehab. Assn., Calif. Assn. Rehab. Profls., Council of Nurses Assn., NAACP, Alpha Nu (pres.), Theta Alpha Omega (rec. sec., com. chmn.). Democrat. Home: 13068 Sutton Cerritos CA 90701 Office: 3605 Long Beach Blvd Suite 201 Long Beach CA 90807

WILLIAMS, AUDREY JOAN, university administrator; b. Montreal, Que., Can., Mar. 6, 1929; d. William E. and Florence G. (Cunningham) W.; B.A., Marianopolis Coll., Montreal, 1950; B.Sc., McGill U., 1953, M.Sc., 1955. Tech. and analytical services Merck, Sharp & Dohme, Montreal, 1955-58, adminstrv. asst.-sci. services, 1958-61, market analyst, 1961-62, research group leader, 1962-69, sr. devel. scientist, 1969-71; univ. research officer Concordia U., Montreal, 1971-83, dir. research services, 1983—. NRC Can. Indsl. Research grantee, 1964-70. Mem. Chem. Inst. Can., Can. Assn. Univ. Research Adminstrs., Nat. Council Univ. Research Adminstrs., Can. Research Mgmt. Assn., Soc. Univ. Patent Adminstrs. Roman Catholic. Contbr. articles to sci. jours. Office: 1455 de Maisonneuve Blvd W Montreal PQ H3G 1M8 Canada

WILLIAMS, BARBARA ANN, printer; b. Roanoke, Va., Jan. 8, 1947; d. Floyd Allen and Louella (Brown) Hobson; m. Lawrence Arthur Williams, Dec. 13, 1967; children—Sophia Lynn, Sidney Lawrence, Sherry Lou. Lic. practical nursing cert. Burrell Meml. Sch. Practical Nursing, 1967. Pvt. duty nurse Burrell Meml. Hosp., Roanoke, 1966-70; mem. wrinkler-printing dept. Double Envelope Corp., Roanoke, 1970—; v.p. DECO Fed. Credit Union, Roanoke, 1980-81, pres., 1981-82, chief exec. officer, 1982—. Editor company annual report. Mem. youth adv. bd. Hill St. Bapt. Ch., Roanoke, 1979, pastor's aide, mem. Home & Fgn. Missionary Soc., 1983-84, v.p. flower club, 1984-85. Democrat. Avocations: interior decorating; floral arranging; aerobics; bicycling. Office: DECO Fed Credit Union PO Box 7000 Roanoke VA 24019

WILLIAMS, BARBARA ANNE, college president; b. Camden, N.J., Oct. 14, 1938; d. Frank and Laura Dorothy (Szweda) Williams. B.A. cum laude, Georgian Court Coll., 1963; M.L.S., Rutgers, The State U., 1965; M.A., Manhattan Coll., 1973; Ph.D. candidate, NYU, 1976—. Cert. English tchr., N.J. Joined Sisters of Mercy, 1957. Sec., Camden Catholic High Sch., N.J., 1956-57; registrar Georgian Court Coll., Lakewood, N.J., 1960-66, dir. library services, 1966-74, dean acad. affairs, 1974-80, pres., 1980—; dir. Assn. Independent Colls. and Univs. in N.J., Ind. Coll. Fund of N.J., N.J. Natural Gas Co., Diocesan Sch. Bd., Diocese of Trenton, N.J. Mem. adv. bd. Ocean County Center for Arts, Lakewood, N.J., 1983—; mem. Ocean County Pvt. Industry Council, 1983—. Named Outstanding Woman N.J. Assn. Women Business Owners, 1983. Mem. Assn. of Mercy Colls. (pres. 1981-83), Mercy Higher Edn. Colloquium (mem. exec. com. 1980—), Monmouth/Ocean Devel. Council (bd. dirs. 1981-84, humanitarian 1985), Ocean County Bus. Assn. (trustee 1982-84), Nat. Assn. Ind. Colls. and Univs. (secretariat 1981-83). Home and Office: Georgian Court Coll Lakewood NJ 08701

WILLIAMS, BARBARA ELAINE, publishing company official; b. Bartlesville, Okla., Aug. 12, 1952; d. B. Joe and Roy Marie (Smith) W.; m. Charles M. Ellertson, Apr. 20, 1985. B.A. cum laude, Duke U., 1974. Asst. to bus. mgr. Duke U. Press, Durham, N.C., 1974-75, prodn. asst., 1975-78, assoc. prodn. mgr., 1979-82, jours. mgr., 1982-85; prodn., design mgr. Menasha Ridge Press, 1985—; panelist Career Counseling Conf., Durham, 1983, 84. Photographer, Latent Image 3, 1976, Latent Image 4, 1978, Latent Image 5, 1980, N.C. Mus. Art Ann. Show, 1978, 79. Mem. Arts Sch. Gallery Com., Assn. Am. Univ. Presses (jours. com. 1983-85). Democrat. Office: Menasha Ridge Press Route 3 Box 450 Hillsborough NC 27278

WILLIAMS, BARBARA JEAN, typographer, graphic designer; b. Omaha, Nebr., Nov. 25, 1948; d. Arthur M. and Mary E. (Jensen) Pedersen; m. Loren Marion Williams, Dec. 29, 1968; children—Loren Benjamin, Jeffrey Clarke. B.S. in Botany, Iowa State U., 1969; postgrad. U. Nebr., 1969. Substitute tchr. Council Bluffs (Iowa) Pub. Schs., 1969-70; chief telex operator Singerwerke, Blankenloch, W.Ger., 1971-72; sec. Iowa State U., Ames, 1972; tchr. Gaffney (S.C.) Day Sch., 1972-74; composition dir. Kidd's Printing Co., Gaffney, 1979; owner, mgr. Typographics, Gaffney, 1979—; cons., type supplier several cos., 1979—. Choir dir. Saint Paul's Lutheran Ch., Gaffney, 1981; choir mem. Liedolsheim (W.Ger.) Gesangverein, 1971-72, Erlenbrunn (W.Ger.) Gesangverein, 1977-78. Recipient numerous Addy awards for typography and graphic arts, 1981-83. Mem. Nat. Assn. Female Execs., Nat. Assn. Self-Employed. Republican. Lutheran. Club: Spartanburg (S.C.) Kennel (sec. 1973-74). Home and Office: Route 2 Box 323 Gaffney SC 29340

WILLIAMS, BARBARA JUNE, lawyer, consultant; b. Lansing, Mich., Jan. 6, 1948; d. Ben Allan and Virginia Jane (Searing) W.; m. John Paul Halvorsen, Oct. 21, 1971. A.A., Stephens Coll., 1968; B.A., U. Ill.-Champaign, 1970; J.D., Rutgers U., 1974. Bar: N.J. 1974, N.Y. 1981. Assoc., Bookbinder, Coulagori & Bookbinder, Burlington, N.J., 1974-76, Law Offices of Cyrus Bloom, Newark, 1976-78, Warren, Goldberg, Berman & Lubitz, Princeton, N.J., 1978-84; with Rutgers U. Sch. Law, Newark, 1984-85; now assoc. Strauss & Hall, Princeton. Assoc. editor Rutgers Camden Law Jour., 1973-74. Contbr. articles to profl. jours. Mem. N.J. Citizens for Better Schs. Mem. Nat. Sch. Bds. Assn. (dir. nat. council sch. attys. 1981-86), ABA, N.J. Bar Assn. (dir. govt. law sect. 1981—), Mercer County Bar Assn., Princeton Bar Assn., N.J. Trial Lawyers Assn., NOW, Lawrence Arts Assn., Lawrence Twp. Republican Club. Home: 90 Denow Rd Lawrenceville NJ 08648 Office: Strauss & Hall 32 Nassau St Princeton NJ 08542

WILLIAMS, BARBARA LYNN, Realtor; b. Montrose, Colo., Nov. 25, 1944; d. Joe H. and Elsie Arlene Baldwin; grad. Am. Acad. Real Estate, 1973, Wyo. Real Estate Inst., 1977, Realtors Inst., 1979; children—Christine, Anisa Jo. Saleswoman, Western Realty Co., Durango, Colo., 1970-72; mng. broker Wedgwood Ltd., Realtors, Durango, 1973-74, pres., 1974-75; sales mgr. Coulter Agency, Gillette, Wyo., 1976-77, gen. sales mgr., 1977-78; broker, owner Real Estate Exchange, 1978—; dir. First Wyo. Bank of Gillette. Vice chmn. LaPlata County Republican Central Com., 1973-75, Campbell County Rep. Central Com., 1976-86; alt. del. Rep. Nat. Conv., 1980; mem. Region 9 Housing Com., 1974-75; mem. steering com. Sch. Dist. 9R, 1973-74; mem. Equal Opportunity Commn., 1980, dir. legis. com., legis. mortgage and fin. com., 1982; mem. Campbell County Econ. Devel. Corp., v.p., 1984-85. Lic. real estate broker, Colo., Wyo.; cert. residential specialist. Mem. LaPlata County Bd. Realtors (pres. 1974, dir. 1975—), Colo. Real Estate Bds. Assn. (dir. 1974-75), Nat. Assn. Realtors, Wyo. Bd. Realtors (dir. 1982), Campbell County Bd. Realtors (Realtor of Yr. 1981), Wyo. Assn. Realtors (pres. 1982, dir. 1980-84, chmn. profl. standards com. 1980), Nat. Inst. Real Estate Brokers, Durango C. of C., Gillette C. of C. (housing com. 1977-81). Clubs: Rep. Women's; Emblem (past sec., trustee); Newcomers (past dir.); Empire Investment (pres. 1977), Ambassador. Address: 5038 N 81st St Scottsdale AZ 85253

WILLIAMS, BERNICE MIE, computer programmer; b. Houston, June 7, 1956; d. Ella Mae Williams. B.S., MIT, 1978. Lic. ins. agt., real estate broker, Tex. Engr.-facilities Shell Oil Co., Houston, 1977-80; project engr. Air Products Co., Houston, 1980; design engr. Dow Chem. Corp., Houston, 1981; agt. J.C. Shorten, Realtor, Houston, 1983-84; computer programmer U. Tex.-Houston, 1985—; dir. Affluent Fin. Services, Gibraltor Home Improvement. Bd. dirs. Sr. Citizens Ctr., Houston, 1984; mem. ednl. council MIT, Cambridge, 1979-83. NSF fellow, 1983. (Houston). Home: 7330 Ashburn St Houston TX 77061 Office: 6723 Bertner Ave Houston TX 77030

WILLIAMS, BETTY, corporate professional; b. Los Angeles, Nov. 27, 1920; d. John D. Rasmussen and Muriel Grace (Kay) Winters; children—Derek Allen, Diane Lee Gilmore. Student Los Angeles City Coll., 1938-40, Occidental Coll., 1940, Los Angeles Jr. Coll. Bus., 1954-55, Loretta Young Way Sch. Modeling, 1959-61; Fellow of Religious Sci., Ernest Holmes Coll. Sch. Ministry, 1985. Lic. practitioner of religious sci. Exec. sec., asst. mgr. research dept. Los Angeles C. of C., 1957-63; exec. sec. McCann Erickson-Advt., Los Angeles, 1963-66, U. So. Calif., 1966-71, League of Calif. Cities, Los Angeles, 1972-77, Getty Oil Co. Texaco Inc., Los Angeles, 1980—; exec. sec., writer Soc. West Mag./Patte Barham Edn., Los Angeles, 1977-79; recording sec. So. Calif. Assn. C. of C. Mgrs., 1957-63, San Gabriel Valley Assn. C. of C., 1957-63; asst. mgr. Los Angeles C. of C. Alaska Good Will Tour, 1960. Author poetry, letters to high officials. Charter mem. Republican Presdl. Task Force, Washington, 1982; worker Rep. party, Los Angeles, 1978; mem. church choir Founder's Religious Sci. Ch., 1972-84, sec., practitioner, 1974-84. Mem. Am. Stats. Assn., Am. Mktg. Assn., Internat. Soc. Gen. Semantics, Classroom Tchrs. Gen. Semantics, League of Religious Sci. Practitioners. Avocations: singing; piano; dancing; swimming. Home: 820 Gramercy Pl Apt 11 Los Angeles CA 90005 Office: Texaco Inc 10 Universal City Plaza Universal City CA 91608

WILLIAMS, BETTY JEANE, home administrator; b. Los Angeles, Aug. 11, 1948; d. Charles and Jessie Mae (Howard) W.; A.A., Los Angeles Harbor Jr. Coll., 1970; B.A., Calif. State U., Dominguez Hills, 1973. Counselor, Compton (Calif.) Urban Corps, 1973-74, chief counselor, 1974-75, asst. dir., 1975-76, dir., 1976-78; manpower program dir. City of Compton, 1978-80; adminstr. Williams Home, Compton, 1980—; manpower cons. Chmn. Project Hope, Compton Community Coll., 1979—; mem. Vets. Employment Bd., 1983—; bd. dirs. Paul Robeson Players, 1979—, Mid-County Action Coalition, Employment Tng. Adv. Com.; active Century Club YMCA. Mem. Nat. Assn. Female Execs. Democrat. Baptist. Home: 318 W 121st St Los Angeles CA 90061 Office: 600 N Alameda Compton CA 90220

WILLIAMS, BETTY SUE, journalist; b. Waverly, Tenn., Aug. 20, 1941; d. Thomas Bruce and Ruby Lee W.; student George Peabody Tchrs. Coll., 1969-70, Fla. Keys Community Coll., 1979; Charles A. Tosch, III, m. Apr. 8, 1979; 1 dau., Lauren Elizabeth. Clearance service rep. Social Security Adminstrn., Nashville, 1961-67; real estate salesperson, pub. relations rep. Kenneth Boyd and Assos., also Computerized Apt. Locators Inc., Nashville, 1970-72; Sun Life editor Key West (Fla.) Citizen daily newspaper, 1973-80, 81—, feature writer, 1980-81; realtor assoc. Island Properties of Key West Inc., 1986—. Mem. com. United Way Fund, 1979; bd. dirs. Big Bros./Big Sisters Monroe County, 1982-84; sec. Hospice of the Fla. Keys Inc., 1984-86; pres. Key Haven Civic Assocs., Inc., 1986—. Recipient public service cert. award Key West Lions Club, 1979. Mem. Key West Art and Hist. Soc., Old Island Restoration Found. Democrat. Clubs: Key West Woman's, Key West Zonta. Home: 21 Beachwood Dr Key Haven Key West FL 33040 Office: Key West Citizen 515 Greene St Key West FL 33040

WILLIAMS, BEVERLY TOWNS, lawyer; b. Memphis, July 16, 1951; d. Edgar and Osa Lee (Weatherly) Towns; m. Andre Martin Williams, May 26, 1973. B.A., Smith Coll., 1973; M.S., U. Ill., 1975; J.D., U. Pa., 1978. Bar: Pa. 1979. Legal cons. Prudential Ins. Co., South Plainfield, N.J., 1978-79, asst. counsel, Fort Washington, Pa., 1981—; assoc. corp. counsel Houghton Mifflin Co., Boston, 1979-81. Sec., N.J. chpt. NAACP Legal Def. and Ednl. Fund, 1978; trustee Community Legal Services Phila. Mem. Nat. Bar Assn. (pres. women lawyers div. Phila. 1982—), Am. Corp. Counsel Assn., ABA, Pa. Bar Assn., Assn. Black Women Lawyers N.J. (sec. 1981-82). Democrat. Baptist. Club: Smith College of Phila. (bd. dirs.). Home: 112 Dogwood Ln Horsham PA 19044 Office: Prudential Ins Co Am PO Box 388 Fort Washington PA 19034

WILLIAMS, BLONDENIA JUANGINEE, air force officer, nurse; b. Charlotte, N.C., Mar. 12, 1951; d. John Wesley and Myrl (Raye) White; m. Edgar Willis Williams, Sept. 10, 1977; 1 child, Crystal Charlotte. B.S., N.C. A & T State U., 1973; M.S., St. Mary's U., San Antonio, 1981. R.N., Tex. Flight nurse N.C. Air Nat. Guard, Charlotte, 1975-76; mental health nurse L. Richardson Hosp., Greensboro, N.C., 1974-76, Santa Rosa Med. Ctr., San Antonio, 1976-77, State of Tex., 1977-82; commd. U.S. Air Force, 1982; advanced through grades to capt., 1982; mental health nurse Nurse Corp, Wichita Falls, Tex., 1982-83, San Antonio, 1983—. Recipient Sr. Nurse award badge Dept. Nursing, Sheppard AFB, Tex., 1983. Mem. Am. Nurses Assn., Soc. Air Force Mental Health Nurses, Nat. Bus. and Profl. Women's Assn., Nat. Assn. Female Execs. Democrat. Pentecostal. Club: Figure World, Inc. Lodge: Heroine of Jericho. Home: 2806 Lakebriar San Antonio TX 78222 Office: Wilford Hall Med Ctr Lackland AFB San Antonio TX 78236

WILLIAMS, CAROLE ANN, cytotechnologist; b. Duquesne, Pa., Apr. 14, 1934; d. Theodore Wylie and Dorothy Belle (Mehrmann) Williams; B.S., Chatham Coll., 1956; postgrad. Case-Western Res. U., 1956-57. Cytotechnologist, Clin. Path. Lab. of Paul Gross, Pitts., 1957-59; chief cytotechnologist, teaching supr. Presbyn. U. Hosp., Pitts., 1959-63; staff Pathology Lab. of Drs. Armanini & Wegner, Stockton, Calif., 1964; chief cytotechnologist, teaching supr. Hosp. of Good Samaritan, Los Angeles, 1964—; conductor workshops in field. Mem. Am. Soc. Clin. Pathologists (cytotech. exam. com. bd. registry 1978), Calif. Assn. Cytotechnologists (pres. 1967-68, 72-73), Internat. Acad. Cytology, Am. Soc. Cytology (Technologist of Yr. award 1981). Republican. Presbyterian. Home: 1200 Tellem Dr Pacific Palisades CA 90272 Office: 616 S Witmer St Los Angeles CA 90017

WILLIAMS, CASSANDRA DAHNE, distributing company executive; b. Middletown, Ohio, Sept. 5, 1945; d. Porter Winston and Zella Evelyn (Brewer) Adams; m. George Gilbert Williams, Dec. 23, 1967; 1 child, G. Zachary. B.S. Anderson Coll., 1967. Elem. tchr. West Central Corp., Anderson, Ind., 1967-73; sr. coordinator Shaklee Corp., San Francisco, 1972—. Recipient Altus award Shaklee Corp., 1983. Republican. Avocations: reading; crewel embroidery; hiking.

WILLIAMS, CECILE DUBOSE, telephone answering system company executive; b. Prichard, Ala., Aug. 28, 1941; d. Acey Cecil and Rozelle (Cunningham) DuBose; m. John William Armbruster, Jr., Feb. 1, 1962 (div. 1966); 1 child, Charles Alan; m. Richard L. Williams, May 15, 1968 (div. 1972); 1 child, Tracey Lee. Bus. cert. Soule Bus. Coll., 1960. Owner, mgr. Pascagoula Secretarial Exchange, Miss., 1961-77, Gulfport Answering Service, Miss., 1970-77; agt. Western Union Gulfport, 1971-83; mgr. Answerphone of Jackson, Inc., Miss., 1973-74; gen. mgr. Answer, Inc., New Orleans, 1975-76; owner, pres. Telephone Secretary, Inc., Houston, 1976—; pres., gen. mgr. Tel-Paging, Inc., Houston-Dallas-Fort Worth, 1979—; v.p. Cellular Systems, Inc., Houston, 1979—; cons. in field. Editor: Telephone Answering Service Operations, 1985. Vol. ARC, Pascagoula and Gulfport, 1966, Pascagoula Hosp. Aux., 1960-66; vol., donor CAP, Saraland, Ala., 1955-60, Methodist Ch., Houston, 1981—. Recipient Service award, 1976, Appreciation award, 1974. Mem. Assn. Telephone Exchanges, Telocator Network. Clubs: Consul's, Westwood (Austin, Tex.). Lodge: Altrusa. Avocations: cooking; dancing; bridge. Office: Telephone SecrInc 2000 West Loop South #1630 Houston TX 77027

WILLIAMS, CECILIA LEE PURSEL, optometrist; b. Lewisburg, Pa., Nov. 15, 1948; d. Lee LaVerne and Geraldine May (Steininger) Pursel; student Lycoming Coll., 1966-68; B.S. (Women's Aux. of Pa. Optometrists scholar 1968-70, Pa. State grantee 1968-70), Pa. Coll. Optometry, 1970, O.D. (Women's Aux. of Pa. Optometrists scholar 1970-72, Pa. State grantee 1970-72), 1972; m. Richard Lee Williams, May 17, 1975; 1 son, Kent Lee. Research optometrist in soft lens materials Gumpelmayer Optik, Vienna, Austria, 1973; optometrist Sterling Optical Co. Contact Lens Center, Washington, 1974-79; pvt. practice optometry, Springfield, Va., 1980—. Recipient Clin. Efficiency award Pa. Coll. Optometry, 1972; lic. and/or cert. optometrist, D.C., Pa., N.Y., N.J., Va. Mem. Optometric Center of Nation's Capital (dir. 1977-80), Am. Optometric Assn., Va. Optometric Assn., No. Va. Optometric Soc., Nat. Honor Soc. for Optometry, Omega Delta. Home: 3600 Wilton Hall Ct Alexandria VA 22310 Office: 6795A Springfield Mall Springfield VA 22150

WILLIAMS, CHARLOTTE EVELYN FORRESTER, civic worker; b. Kansas City, Mo., Aug. 7, 1905; d. John Dougal and Georgia (Lowerre) Forrester; student Kans. U., 1924-25; m. Walker Alonzo Williams, Sept. 25, 1926; children—Walker Forrester, John Haviland. Trustee, Detroit Grand Opera Assn., 1960—, dir., 1955-60; chmn. Grinnell Opera Scholarship, 1958-66; founder, dir., chmn. adv. bd. Cranbrook Music Guild, Inc., 1952-59, life mem., 1952—; bd. dirs. St. Peter's Home for Boys, Detroit, 1951-53, Detroit Opera Theater, 1959-61, Severo Ballet, 1959-61; Detroit dist. chmn. Met. Opera Regional Auditions, 1958-66; patron-mem. Met. Opera Nat. Council; mem. Central Opera Service, Met. Opera Guild; mem. Opera Guild Ft. Lauderdale (Fla.); trustee Detroit Grand Opera Assn.; mem. Fla. Atlantic U. Found.; past pres. Friends of Caldwell Playhouse, Boca Raton. Mem. Debbie-Rand Meml. Service League (life), Fla. Atlantic Music Guild (past pres.), DAR, English-Speaking Union, Vol. League Fla. Atlantic U., PEO, Order Eastern Star. Home: 1355 Fan Palm Rd Boca Raton FL 33432

WILLIAMS, CHERYL, health care administrator; b. Phila., Nov. 19, 1953; d. Dewey Howard Williams and Margaret Beatrice (Barnes) Johnson. B.A., Howard U., 1975. Plan rep. Newark Compre-Health, 1977-78; asst. systems analyst Health and Hosps. Corp., N.Y.C., 1978-79, systems analyst, 1979-80, sr. systems analyst, 1980-81; patient account mgr. North Central Bronx Hosp., N.Y., 1981-85; dir. patient accounts Woodhull Hosp., N.Y., 1985—. Democrat. Roman Catholic. Club: N.Y.C.-HHC P.C. (fin. com.). Home: PO Box 1488 New York NY 10027

WILLIAMS, COLEEN MARIE, educator of mentally handicapped; b. Ardmore, Okla., Feb. 9, 1956; d. Coley and Gladys M. (Russell) Devlin; m. Joey E. Williams, Feb. 23, 1977. A.S., Murray State Coll., 1976; B.S. in Edn., East Central Okla. State U., Ada, 1979. Fin. counselor local fed. savs. and loan co., Oklahoma City, 1980-81; model Barbara Cole Agy., Bristow, Okla., also Dallas, 1980-82; learning disabilities tchr. Southeast High Sch., Oklahoma City, 1981-82, tchr.-coordinator, workstudy, educable mentally handicapped, 1983—. Singer The Three Dimensions of Joy, Oklahoma City, 1983-85; voter registrar Oklahoma County. Mem. Central Okla. Assn. Tchr. Coordinators (v.p. 1985-86), Am. Fedn. Tchrs., Nat. Assn. Female Execs. Avocations: collecting miniatures; reading; listening to music; modeling. Office: Southeast High Sch 5401 S Shields St Oklahoma City OK 73129

WILLIAMS, CONSUELO CRUMP, administrator handicapped education; b. Chgo., Aug. 14, 1932; d. James Crump and Louise Washington Mitchell; m. Donald Crawford Williams, June 21, 1953; children—Tracey Dion, Donald Courtney. B.Ed., Chgo. Tchrs. Coll., 1953, postgrad., 1955-71; student U. Ill.-Chgo., 1968; M.S.Ed., No. Ill. U., 1979. With Bd. Edn. Chgo., 1953—, coop. work tng. tchr. coordinator Low Incidence Handicapped Ctr., 1976—; v.p., historian, The Guild, Chgo., 1971-81; chmn. leadership com. Chgo. chpt. Phi Delta Kappa, 1983—; CETA supr. Mayor's Summer Youth Employment Program, summer 1981, 82, 83. Adv. bd. Introspect Youth Inc.; Supt. nursery dept. Ebenezer Cradle Roll; mem. Bd. Christian Edn., Ebenezer Ch.; mem. vol. service aux. Urban Gateways. No. Ill. U. fellow, 1978. Mem. Theatre Exposure Council, Beverly Art Ctr., DuSable Mus., Phi Delta Kappa, Alpha Kappa Alpha, Delta Mu Sigma. Baptist. Home: 544 E 86th Pl Chicago IL 60619

WILLIAMS, DORIS CARSON, banker; b. Pitts., Sept. 19, 1949; d. Elmer D. and Doris (Tolbert) Carson; m. James Nathan Williams, Oct. 29. 1977. B.S. in Bus. and Data Processing, U. Hartford, 1972; grad. Nat. Sch. Fin. and Mgmt. Ctr. for Fin. Studies, 1983. Sr. mktg. rep. Control Data Corp., Pitts., 1974-79; instr. computer sci. Community Coll. Allegheny County, Pitts., 1980-81; asst. v.p. Dollar Bank, Pitts., 1979—; policy chmn. Pa. Minority Bus. Devel. Authority, Harrisburg, 1980—; mem. Pitts. Budget Commn., 1983-85; bd. dirs. Northside Devel. Corp., Pitts., 1985—. Chmn. Allegheny County Black Republicans, Pa., 1976—; dep. chmn. Pa. Rep. State Com., Harrisburg, 1982—; del. Rep. Nat. Conv., Dallas, 1984; speaker Pa. Rep. Speakers Bur. Named to Outstanding Young Women Am., U.S. Jaycees, 1984, 85; recipient Bus. Women of Yr. award Poise Found., 1985. Mem. Nat. Assn. Female Execs., NAACP, Northeasterners, Urban Bankers. Avocations: public speaking; reading; sewing. Home: 1431 Pennsylvania Ave Pittsburgh PA 15233

WILLIAMS, DORIS TERRY, health manpower development company executive; b. Middleburg, N.C., Oct. 26, 1951; d. Robert and Lucy (Hargrove) Terry; m. Thomas Williams, Aug. 29, 1981 (div. 1986); children—Adriel Lemuel, Lriel LaShawn. B.A., Duke U., 1972; M.Ed., N.C. State U., 1976, Ph.D. in Edn., 1983. Pub. relations N.C. Blue Cross/Blue Shield, 1972; tech. writer pub. relations Floyd B. McKissick Enterprises, Soul City, N.C., 1972-73; instr., counselor Vance-Granville Community Coll., Henderson, N.C., 1973-75, dir. adult basic edn., 1975-82, counselor, 1982-84; instr. Shaw U., Raleigh, N.C., 1978-83; assoc. dir. N.C. Health Manpower Devel. Co., Chapel Hill, N.C., 1984—. Contbr., editor Oracles of Truth, 1983—. Sec. bd. dirs. Sound and Print United WVSP radio sta., 1973—; mem. N.C. Black Women's Polit. Congress, Warren County, 1985; mem. N.C. Black Leadership Caucus; sec. Vance County Task Force on Domestic Violence, Vance County Task Force on Delinquency Prevention. Mem. Nat. Minority Health Affairs Assn., Nat. Assn. Female Execs., Am. Assn. Adult and Continuing Edn. Democrat. Mem. Apostolic Ch. Avocations: writing; travel; reading; acting. Home: PO Box 465 Manson NC 27553 Office: NC Health Manpower Devel Program 401 NCNB Plaza 136 E Rosemary St Chapel Hill NC 27514

WILLIAMS, DOROTHY ELLEN, educator; b. San Benito, Tex., July 27, 1940; d. Harry James, Jr. and Josephine Louise (Witherwax) W.; B.S., Tex. Woman's U., 1962; M.Ed., Our Lady of Lake Coll., San Antonio; 1968; mid-mgmt. cert. U. Tex., San Antonio, 1982; Ed.D., Tex. A&M U., 1985. Tchr., coach Harlandale Sch. Dist., San Antonio, 1962-68; instr. Sam Houston State U., Huntsville, Tex., 1968-69; tchr. Harlandale Sch. Dist., 1969-75; asst. athletic dir. San Antonio Sch. Dist., 1975-82; vice prin. M.L. King Middle Sch., San Antonio, 1982-85; prin. Harry Rogers Middle Sch., San Antonio, 1985—. Phi Delta Kappa. Mem. Nat. Assn. Secondary Sch. Prins., Tex. Assn. Secondary Sch. Prins., Nat. Fedn. Bus. and Profl. Women, Phi Kappa Phi, Methodist. Author articles in field. Home: PO Box 21292 San Antonio TX 78221 Office: 314 Galway San Antonio TX 78223

WILLIAMS, EDNA ALETA THEADORA JOHNSTON, journalist; b. Halifax, N.S., Can., Sept. 19, 1923; d. Clarence Harvey and Edna May (Lewis) Johnston; student Maritime Bus. Coll., 1943; m. Albert Murray Williams, Apr. 16, 1949 (dec.); children—Murleta, Norma, Martin, Charla, Kerrick, Renwick, Julia. Typist, Dept. Treasury (Navy), Halifax, 1944-49; with Bedford (N.S.) Mag., Halifax br., 1954-55, Presbyn. Office, New Glasgow, N.S., part-time, 1965-67, Thompson and Sutherland, New Glasgow, part-time, 1967-69; family editor, columnist and reporter New Glasgow Evening News, 1969—. Baptist rep. Pictou County Council of Churches, 1978-82, sec., 1980-82; pres. ch. aux. 2d United Bapt. Ch., 1979-83, organist, 1970—, chorus dir. Men's Choir, 1980—; organist St. James Anglican Ch., 1983-85; provincial pres. Women's Inst. of African United Bapt. Assn., 1983; mem. council Halifax YWCA; founding mem. Pictou County YM-YWCA, 1966—, bd. dirs., 1967-77, corr. sec., v.p., 1975-77, 1974-75; past pres., past provincial dir. Home and Sch.; past officer local interracial com.; bd. dirs. Black United Front. Mem. Can. Press Assn. Home: 230 Reservoir St New Glasgow NS B2H 4K4 Canada Office: Evening News 352 East River Rd New Glasgow NS B2H 5E2 Canada

WILLIAMS, ELEANOR JOYCE, government air traffic control specialist; b. College Station, Tex., Dec. 21, 1936; d. Robert Ira and Viola (Ford) Toliver; m. Tullie Williams, Dec. 20, 1955 (div. July 1978); children—Rodrick, Viola Williams Smith, Darryl, Eric, Dana, Sheila Williams Watkins, Kenneth. Student Prairie View A&M Coll., 1955-56, Anchorage Community Coll., 1964-65, U. Alaska-Anchorage, 1976. With FAA, 1965—, air traffic controller supr., San Juan, P.R., 1979-80, Anchorage, 1983-85, airspace specialist, Atlanta, 1980-83, Washington, 1985—. Sec. Fairview Neighborhood Council, Anchorage, 1967-69; mem. Anchorage Bicentennial Commn., 1975-76; bd. dirs. Mt. Patmos Youth Dept., Decatur, Ga., 1981-82. Recipient Mary K. Goddard award Anchorage Fed. Exec. Assn. and Fed. Women's Program, 1985, Sec.'s award Dept. transp., 1985. Mem. Bus. and Profl. Women U.S.A., Inc., Bus. and Profl. Women U.S.A., Inc. (North to the Future club) (charter pres. 1975-76), Blacks In Govt., Profl. Women Controllers Orgn., Nat. Assn. Female Execs., NAACP. Democrat. Baptist. Avocations: singing; sewing. Home: 6240 Edsall Rd Number 102 Alexandria VA 22312 Office: FAA 800 Independence AVE SW Washington DC 20591

WILLIAMS, ELIZABETH ANNEGA, communications executive; b. Bainbridge, Ga., May 22, 1955; d. Jack and Bertha (Wynn) Williams. B.S., Lane Coll., 1977; postgrad. Ind. U.-Indpls., 1980-82. Mgr. trainee McDonalds Restaurants, Indpls., 1978; account analyst Western Electric, Indpls., 1978-81, warehouse supr., 1981-82, bus. methods exec., 1982-83; customer service mgr. AT&T Consumer Products, Indpls., 1983-84; mktg. and sales exec. AT&T Technologies, Inc., Indpls., 1984-86; phone ctr. store mgr. AT&T Consumer Sales & Service, Jackson, Tenn., 1986—. Vol., Spl. Olympics, Indpls., 1983-85, Ind. Sch. for Blind, 1984. Mem. Am. Mgmt. Assn., Direct Mktg. Assn., Nat. Assn. Female Execs., Alpha Kappa Mu. Democrat. Christian Methodist Episcopal Ch. Clubs: NAACP, Zeta Phi Beta. Avocations: aerobics; jogging; photography; traveling. Home: 5 Fairfax Cove Jackson TN 38305 Office: AT&T Consumer Sales & Service 2021 N Highland Ave Jackson TN 38305

WILLIAMS, ELMA, retail executive; b. Carroll County, Va.; d. Preston and Macy (Goad) W.; A.B. with spl. honors, George Washington U., 1953; M.A. in Public Adminstrn., Am. U., 1961. Asst. program dir., asst. dir. ops. WTOP, CBS-Radio and TV, 1947-51; mem. pub. relations staff George Washington U., 1951-52; registrar Washington Sch. for Secs., 1953; exec. sec. Joint Econ. Com. of U.S. Congress, 1956-59; legis. info. specialist NEA, Washington, 1960-84; asst. mgr. Gem Tree Jewelry Store, Bethesda, Md., 1984—. Bd. dirs. Edn. Assocs. Fed. Credit Union, 1973-83, pres., 1975-77; bd. dirs. Met. Area Credit Union Mgmt. Assn., 1977-82, sec., 1977-82; bd. dirs. Kenwood Beach (Md.) Citizens Assn., 1981-84. Recipient Alumni Service award George Washington U., 1970. Mem. AAUW (br. publicity chmn. 1956-59), Am. News Women's Club, NEA (life), Columbian Women George Washington U. (pres. 1965-67), George Washington U. Alumni Assn. (dir. 1965-67, 69-70), Edn. Writers Assn., Ednl. Press Assn., Women's Joint Congressional Com. (chmn. 1974-76), Phi Delta Gamma (chpt. pres. 1973-74, nat. conv. chmn. 1980, nat. treas. 1980-84, nat. pres. 1984—, trustee 1980—), Pi Sigma Alpha. Mem. Nat. Woman's Party, Woman's Nat. Dem. Club, Twentieth Century Club. Office: Gem Tree 7720 Wisconsin Ave Bethesda MD 20814

WILLIAMS, EMILY JEAN, dietitian, educator; b. Indpls., July 18, 1928; d. Charles Emil and Vera Pearl (White) Rinsch; m. Donald Eugene Williams, Feb. 21, 1953; children—Donald Eugene, Ronald Owen. B.S. in Dietetics, Ind. U., 1950, M.S., 1979, Dr.Med. Scis., 1983. Registered dietitian. Dietetic intern U. Mich., 1951; therapeutic dietitian Ind. U., 1952-53; asst. prof. Ind. U.-South Bend, 1980, 81, grad. teaching asst., 1978-80; clin. assoc. Ind. U. Med. Ctr., Indpls., 1984—; therapeutic dietitian Desert Hosp., Palm Springs, Calif., 1965-66, 70-71, reviewer Diabetes Care Jour., 1985—; panel moderator Am. Dietetic Assn., New Orleans, 1985; lectr. in field. Author, editor: Diabetes Care and Education Practice Group Newsletter, 1985. Contbr. articles to profl. jours. Named Outstanding Mem., Alpha Xi Delta. Mem. Am. Dietetic Assn., Calif. Dietetic Assn., Am. Diabetes Assn., Palm Springs Hist. Soc., AAUW, Pi Lambda Theta. Republican. Clubs: Coachella Valley Panhellenic (pres.), Palm Springs Woman's (v.p.), P.E.O. Avocations: needlepoint. Home: 38-681 Bogert Trail Palm Springs CA 92264

WILLIAMS, ERIS ALAIDA ANDERSON, nursing educator; b. Union, N.D., Dec. 8, 1924; d. Andrew O. and Esther Sophia (Johnson) Anderson; m.

Ralph Oscar Williams; children—Kandela Groves, Kristie Lampton, Jack Fader. A.D.N. with honors, Everett Community Coll., 1970; B.S.N., U. Wash., 1973, M.S.N. in Adminstrn. and Edn., 1974. R.N., Wash. Nurse ob-gyn, nursery Island Hosp., Anacortes, Wash., 1966-68; head nurse medications Skagit Valley Hosp., Mt. Vernon, Wash., 1970-71; spl. duty nursing U. Wash. Hosp., 1972-74; asst. dir., dir. edn. Standring Hosp., Seattle, 1974-76; instr. nursing Highline Community Coll., Seattle, 1976-77; dir., coordinator nursing program Grays Harbor Coll., Aberdeen, Wash., 1977—; apptd. to State Bd. Practical Nurse Examiners, Dept. Licensing, Olympia, Wash., 1978-82; mem. transferability com. Wash. State Community Coll. Nursing Dirs., 1980-85, Wash. State Council on Nursing Edn., 1985—. Mem. Nat. League Nursing, Wash. State Nurses Assn., Am. Nurses Assn., Wash. Edn. Assn., NEA, Wash. State Vocat. Edn. Assn., Wash. State Health Occupations Assn. Lutheran. Home: 234 HoHum Ln Aberdeen WA 98520 Office: Grays Harbor Coll College Heights Aberdeen WA 98520

WILLIAMS, EUPHEMIA GOODLOW, nursing educator, consultant; b. Bagwell, Tex., Oct. 17, 1938; d. Otis John and Blanche M. (Pouge) Goodlow; m. James Altrice Williams, July 23, 1960; children—Caren, Christopher, Curt, Catherine. B.S., U. Okla., 1961; M.S., U. Colo., 1973, Ph.D., 1981. Staff nurse, head nurse VA Hosp., Oklahoma City, 1961-66; pub. health nurse Oklahoma City-County Health Dept., 1966-70; instr. U. Colo. Sch. Nursing, Denver, 1974-77, asst. prof., 1977-81; assoc. prof., chmn. dept. nursing Cameron U., Lawton, Okla., 1981-82; assoc. prof. nursing Met. State Coll., Denver, 1982-84, chmn. dept. nursing and health care mgmt., 1984—; workshop cons. S.D. State Health Dept., Pierre, 1975-76. Mem. profl. adv. com. Vis. Nurses' Assn., Boulder, 1978-81; mem. citizens adv. com. Boulder High Sch. (Colo.), 1978-79. Predoctoral nurse fellow HEW, 1978. Mem. Am. Nurses Assn., Am. Pub. Health Assn., Nat. League Nursing, Sigma Theta Tau. Democrat. Lutheran. Home: 961 15th St Boulder CO 80302 Office: Met State Coll Box 33 1006 11th St Denver CO 80204

WILLIAMS, EVELYN METOYER, educator; b. Evergreen, La., May 27, 1937; d. Steven and Alnetter T. Metoyer; B.S., Tex. So. U., 1959; M.Ed., So. U., 1965; Reading Specialist degree, U. So. Calif., 1979; m. Lindbergh Williams, Feb. 2, 1975. Master tchr. E. Baton Rouge Parish Sch. Dist., 1966-71; supr. aids and tchrs. Southeastern La. U. Lab. Sch., Hammond, 1971-73; asso. prof. So. Univ., New Orleans, 1973-74; Children's Center tchr., Los Angeles Unified Sch. Dist., 1977—, cons., tchr. in field. Com. mem. Calif. Tchrs. State Council; life mem. NAACP. Mem. NEA (women's caucus), Calif. Tchrs. Assn. (women's caucus), Black Women's Forum, Assn. for Supervision and Curriculum Devel., United Tchrs. Los Angeles; Internat. Reading Assn., Calif. Reading Assn., United Tchrs. Los Angeles, Phi Beta Kappa. Roman Catholic. Lodges: Order Eastern Star, Dau. of Isis.

WILLIAMS, FLORA L. ROUCH, consumer science educator, consultant; b. Tallahassee, Fla., Jan. 21, 1937; d. Noble J. and Dorothy (Rohrer) Rouch; m. Leiw K. Williams, June 26, 1960; children—Chadwick, Lora Lu, Matthew. B.S., Manchester Coll., 1959; M.S., Purdue U., 1964, Ph.D., 1969. Research asst. Purdue U., West Lafayette, Ind., 1965-67, asst prof., 1969-76, assoc. prof., 1976—; vis. prof. U. Calif-Davis, 1975-76; tchr., supr. West Lafayette Sch., 1963-67; tchr. Mishawaka Sch. (Ind.), 1959-63; cons. attys., Ind., 1971—, Family Service Agy., Lafayette, 1963-67, Farmers Home Adminstrn., So. Ill., 1979-82, United Way Counseling, Lafayette, 1980—. Co-author: The Family Economy, 1974; author: Guidelines to Financial Counseling, 1982; contbr. articles to profl. jours. Counselor Fin. Adv. Service, Purdue U. and Lafayette community, 1973—. Mem. Am. Council Consumer Interest, Am. Home Econs. Assn., Internat. Assn. Fin. Planners, Am. Econs. Assn., Kappa Delta Pi, Alpha Delta Kappa, Alpha Kappa Delta, Omicron Nu (pres. 1969). Democrat. Office: Consumer Sci and Retailing Matthews Hall Purdue U West Lafayette IN 47907

WILLIAMS, GENA KAY, automotive dealership executive; b. Fairfax, Va., Apr. 12, 1963; d. Leon Ellis and Vena Pearl (Hicks) W. B.S., U. Ariz., 1981; postgrad. Hofstra U., 1983. Controller TGI Friday's, Tuscon, Ariz., Westbury, N.Y., 1980-83; auto dealer, bus. mgr. Williams, Inc., Hampton, Va., 1983—. ROTC scholar U. Ariz., Tucson, 1979. Mem. Peninsula Assn. Credit Execs., Nat. Assn. Female Execs., Peninsula Women's Network, Mensa. Republican. Presbyterian. Avocation: photography. Office: Williams Inc 3233 W Mercury Blvd Hampton VA 23666

WILLIAMS, GLORIA J., hospital administrator; b. Lubbock, Tex., Jan. 25, 1950; d. Claude Milford and Florence Ann (Walker) Williams; m. Raymond Helams, Aug. 27, 1967 (div. Nov. 1973). B.B.A., Northeast La. U., 1976; M.B.A., U. Dallas, 1981. Acct., B.R. Wilson & Co., Winnsboro, La., 1971-72; officer mgr. McMahan Aviation, Inc., Monroe, La., 1973-77; staff auditor Lawhon, Thomas & Holmes, C.P.A.s, Dallas, 1978-79; corp. auditor ITV Corp., Dallas, 1979-82; dir. Parkland Hosp., Dallas, 1982—. Republican. Baptist. Home: 9254 Forest Ln #902 Dallas TX 75243

WILLIAMS, GWENDOLYN RENEE, nurse; b. Chattanooga, Apr. 10, 1953; d. Luther and Mary Elizabeth (Long) Burch; m. Samuel Williams, Jr., Oct. 31, 1976 (div. Mar. 1979); children—Anthony Hudson, Donald E., Samuel D. III. Student Community Coll. Allegheny County, 1972-75, Duquesne U., 1975; diploma South Side Hosp. Sch. Nursing, Pitts., 1979. Nurse, South Side Hosp., Pitts., 1979-80; pub. health nurse Allegheny County Health Dept., Pitts., 1980-83; renal dialysis nurse West Penn Hosp., Pitts., 1983—; facilitator Freedom from Smoking Program, Coop. Health Risk Reduction Program, Allegheny Health Dept., 1982-83. Author: Poems from a Black Heart, 1981. Club: Racquetball and Nautilus Fitness (Pitts.). Home: PO Box 5491 Pittsburgh PA 15206

WILLIAMS, HAZEL ALBERTA, handicrafts company executive; b. Kingsbury, Calif., Jan. 22, 1914; d. Albert John and Nellie Ethel (Haskell) Kaiser; m. Ray M. Pearson, June 16, 1935 (div. 1951); children—Sharon Wiborg, Gayle Merten; m. Jack K. Williams, Aug. 22, 1954. Student Los Angeles City Coll., 1935-37, UCLA, 1942-45, U. So. Calif. Gen. elementary tchr., Calif., 1932-49; pres. Hazel Pearson Handicrafts, Arcadia, Calif., 1950-85, chief exec. officer, 1980—; mem. Com. of 200, 1983—. Author over 150 handicraft instrn. books, 1970-83. Contbr. articles to trade mags. Program chair Sr. Citizens-Arcadia Presbyterian Ch., 1983—. Mem. Hobby Industry Assn. Am. (bd. dirs. 1970-74, meritorious award 1974, good egg award 1978), Soc. Craft Designers. Republican. Avocations: travel; craft lectures and displays; grandchildren. Home: 300 W Norman Ave Arcadia CA 91006

WILLIAMS, HAZEL MAY, real estate executive; b. San Diego, Oct. 21, 1926; d. William and Alice May (Yarno) Roth; B.A., San Diego State U., 1946; student West Valley Jr. Coll., 1970-73; grad. Realtors Inst.; m. Shelley S. Williams, Jr., Aug. 24, 1947; 1 dau., Christabel May. Vice pres. Shelley Williams Assos., Inc., Saratoga, Calif., 1968—. Active Los Gatos chpt. ARC, Community Hosp. Aux., West Valley Republican Women. Named Woman of Yr., Santa Clara chpt. Women's Council Realtors; cert. residential specialist, Realtor and broker; cert. real estate brokerage mgr. Mem. Nat. Assn. Realtors (dir. 1986—), Calif. Assn. Realtors (dir. 1974-79, 84, regional v.p. 1981, dir.-at-large 1983, chmn. policy com. 1985—), Los Gatos-Saratoga Bd. Realtors (pres. 1978, certs. of merit, Realtor of Yr. 1980), San Jose Real Estate Bd., Women's Council Realtors, Calif. Assn. Real Estate Tchrs., DAR (Los Gatos chpt.). Clubs: Saratoga Foothill, San Jose Women's. Office: 12960 Saratoga Sunnyvale Rd Saratoga CA 95070

WILLIAMS, HELEN BRUNSDALE, writer, publisher; b. Mpls., Nov. 12, 1926; d. Norman and Carrie (LaJord) Brunsdale; m. Percy Don Williams, Aug. 4, 1954; children—Anne Lucy, Margaret Frances, Elizabeth Helen. B.A., Vassar Coll., 1947. Advt. asst. Maico Hearing Aid Co., Mpls., 1947-48; reporter Great Bend (Kans.) Tribune, 1948-50; pub. relations staff Ramsey County Tb and Health Assn., St. Paul, 1950-51; reporter UP, Bismarck, N.D., 1952; asst. editor Cohen Publs., Mpls., 1953-54; freelance writer/poet, Houston, 1954—; co-founder Brown Rabbit Press, Houston, 1974—. Co-editor, pub.: (anthology) Christmas in Texas, 1979; The Leaf Raker, 1983; contbr. poems to North Country, Poetry View, (anthology) Poets Teaching, 1979. Clubs: Vassar (v.p. 1974-76), Tuesday Musical of Houston (com. chmn. 1981-83) (Houston). Home: 31 Briar Hollow Ln Houston TX 77027

WILLIAMS, HENRIETTA VER MEER, clinical psychologist; b. Pella, Iowa, Apr. 2, 1924; d. Otto Henry and Dena Catherine (Stadt) Ver Meer; B.A. in Philosophy, U. Iowa, 1944; M.A. in Psychology, U. Ill., 1946, Ph.D. in Exptl. Psychology, 1949; postgrad. in clin. psychology U. Md., 1966-67; m. Richard Hays Williams, Feb. 19, 1971; children—Marylie Catherine Williams Karlovac, Robert Harold, Frank Rendler. Counselor, U. Wis., Madison, 1945-51, lectr. dept. psychology, 1951-52; research psychologist NIMH, Bethesda, Md., 1965-67, postdoctoral intern in clin. psychology, 1967-68; staff psychologist, psychologist-in-charge of div. St. Elizabeth's Hosp., Washington, 1969-72, clin. adminstr., 1972-74; dir. psychol. services Pitt County Mental Health Center, Greenville, N.C., 1974-78; pvt. practice clin. psychology, asso. Nelson Clinic, Greenville, 1978—; cons. Alcoholic Rehab. Center, 1977-79, Regional Rehab. Center, Pitt Meml. Hosp., 1977-81, Devel. Evaluation Clinic, Med. Sch., 1980-84; clin. asst. prof. psychology Eastern Carolina U. Sch. Medicine, 1977—. Mem. vestry St. Luke's Episcopal Ch., Rockville, Md., 1968-71; mem. incorporating body, chmn. personnel com. St. Luke's Half-Way Houses, Rockville. Mem. Am. Psychol. Assn., Nat. Register Health Service Providers in Psychology, Phi Beta Kappa, Univ. Condominium Assn. (pres. 1980-82). Democrat. Clubs: PEO. Contbr. articles in field to profl. jours. Home: 111 Cardinal Dr Greenville NC 27834 Office: Nelson Clinic Suite 9 Med Pavilion Greenville NC 27834

WILLIAMS, IMA JO, home economist, civic worker; b. Bowie, Tex., Feb. 23, 1942; d. Herman Wayne and Clarice (Bilbrey) Tompkins; m. Robert Melvin Williams, Jan. 27, 1963; children—Stacy, Angie, Mark. B.A. in Home Econs., North Tex. State U., 1963. Home economist Lone Star Gas Co., Dallas, 1963-64, Mich. Consol. Gas Co., Ann Arbor, 1964-65; home econs. tchr. Milan High Sch., Mich., 1965-69; nutrition coordinator Shay Elem. Sch., Harbor Springs, Mich., 1979—; pres. Crooked Tree Arts Council, Petoskey, Mich., 1982-83, v.p. vols., 1983-84, fin. v.p., 1984-85; bd. dirs. Concerned Citizens for Arts, Detroit, 1983-86. Author (fairy tale): Petal, 1978. Performer local theatrical prodns., 1982—. Mem. AAUW (chmn. Mich. Ednl. Found. Program com. 1981-83, mem. nat. devel. com. 1983-85, Mich. cultural com. chmn. 1985-87). Republican. Methodist. Clubs: Garden (pres. 1979-81) (Harbor Springs); Antiques (Petoskey). Home: 6546 Lower Shore Dr Harbor Springs MI 49740

WILLIAMS, JANICE DENISE, physician; b. N.Y.C., Apr. 19, 1951; d. Ausborn John and Estelle (Mims) Williams. B.S., Fordham U., 1973. M.D., SUNY-Buffalo, 1977. Diplomate Am. Bd. Medicine and Surgery. Tchr. aide Bd. Edn. N.Y.C., Queens, 1973; extern surgery Harlem Hosp. Ctr., N.Y.C., 1974; resident ob-gyn Nassau County Med. Ctr., East Meadow, N.Y., 1977-81; attending phys. ob-gyn USPHS, Mt. Vernon, N.Y., 1981-84; attending phys. ob-gyn Mt. Vernon Neighborhood Health Ctr., 1981—; attending gynecologist Nat. Health Service Corp. USPHS, 1981-83; attending obstetrician-gynecologist Mt. Vernon Hosp., 1981—; clin. instr. Mt. Vernon Hosp., 1981-83. Leader Girl Scouts Am. N.Y.C., 1970-73; mem. NAACP, Jamaica, N.Y., 1982-83. Fellow N.Y. State med. Soc. (Westchester chpt.); mem. Student Nat. Med. Assn. (scholar 1974), AMA, Am. Women's Med. Assn., Am. Coll. Ob-Gyn, Susan Smith McKinney Steward Med. Soc., Nat. Residents Assn. Democrat. Methodist. Office: Mt Vernon Neighborhood Health Center 107 W 4th St Mt Vernon NY 10550

WILLIAMS, JEAN TAYLOR, artist; b. Town Creek, Ala., Mar. 27, 1912; d. Woodie Richard and Ella Ross (Harrison) Taylor; B.S., U. Montevallo, 1933; student Chgo. Art Inst., 1936; student of Robert Brackman, Noank, Conn., 1958-60; m. James Hayes Williams, June 18, 1935; children—James Richard, Hayes Taylor, Jean Williams Johnson. Art tchr. high sch., Ala., 1933-35; tchr. pvt. classes own studio, Birmingham, Ala., 1976—; art chmn. Mountain Brook Jr. High Sch., Birmingham, 1966; one-woman shows: Samford U., Nat. Soc. Arts and Letters; exhibited invitational Jerome Hines Exhbn., 1977; represented in numerous pvt. collections. Recipient grand award in oil painting State of Ala., 1961. Recipient Crusade citation for service Am. Cancer Soc., 1979. Mem. Am. Artists Profl. League (life), Nat. League Am. Pen Women (1st v.p. Birmingham br. 1982—), Nat. Soc. Arts and Letters (pres. Birmingham chpt. 1982—; organizer Ala. state art competition 1981, Ala. state piano competition 1982), Ala. Art League, Birmingham Art Assn. Presbyterian. Clubs: Vestavia Country, Turtle Point Yacht and Country, The Club. Address: 2801 Mountain Brook Pkwy Birmingham AL 35223

WILLIAMS, JERRY RUTH, telephone company manager; b. Bogalusa, La., Sept. 5, 1936; d. Charlie and Procula Marian (Norris) W.; Hutcherson; B.A. magna cum laude, So. U., 1957; M.Ed., U. Mo., St. Louis, 1969; m. Robert P. Williams, Jan. 25, 1959; 1 dau., Michelle Yvette. Tchr. English, New Orleans pub. schs., 1957-59; case worker Mo. Dept. Welfare St. Louis, 1960-61; tchr. St. Louis pub. schs., 1961-66; counselor Normandy Sch. Dist., St. Louis, 1969-78, dir. alt. learning program, 1975-76; staff trainer Title IX Workshop, 1977; staff supr. service costs Southwestern Bell Telephone Co., St. Louis, 1978-80, customer service supr. bus. installation control, 1980-82; asst. staff mgr. materials mgmt.-methods, 1982-84, customer services staff supr.-tng., 1984—; mem. Southwestern Bell Speakers Bur. Mem. Dist. Council on Ministries; bd. dirs. Wesley Found., Epworth Children's Home. Mem. United Meth. Women (unit pres. mem. exec. bd.), Phi Delta Kappa, Alpha Kappa Alpha, Kappa Delta Pi, Alpha Kappa Mu. Methodist. Club: Toastmasters (adminstrv. v.p. 1983-84). Home: 1967 Willow Lake Dr Chesterfield MO 63017 Office: 915 Olive 7th Floor Saint Louis MO 63101

WILLIAMS, JESSIE RUTH, purchasing executive; b. Warrensburg, Mo., Dec. 22, 1928; d. Rolla and Daisy Vine (Thomas) Close; B.S. in Bus. Edn., Central Mo. State Coll., 1967; m. Vernon Lyle Williams, May 8, 1950; 1 son, Lyle Eugene. With Montgomery Ward & Co., Kansas City, Mo., 1946-48, clk., Warrensburg, 1968-69; telephone operator United Telephone Co., Warrensburg, Mo., 1952-56, acctg. clk., 1958-62; purchasing dir. Johnson County Meml. Hosp., Warrensburg, Mo., 1969-84, material mgmt. dir., 1985; material mgmt. dir. Western Mo. Med. Ctr., Warrensburg, 1986—. Mem. Kansas City Area Hosp. Purchasing Dirs. (sec.-treas. 1976, pres. 1981, chmn. assoc. purchasing services 1984), Am. Hosp. Assn., Nat. Assn. Hosp. Purchasing Mgmt., Ozark Purchasing Group (sec. 1977). Baptist. Clubs: Club 46 Extention, Bus. and Profl. Women's (2d v.p. 1978—). Home: PO Box 170 Warrensburg MO 64093 Office: Burkarth Rd Warrensburg MO 64093

WILLIAMS, JOANNE WATERMAN, journalist, editor; b. Cin., Mar. 8, 1929; d. Ferdinand and Elsa Dorothy (Graef) Waterman; m. Galen Herschel Williams, Jr., Apr. 6, 1958; 1 child, Galen Stuart. B.A. in English, Miami U., Oxford, Ohio, 1951. Reporter, Tallahassee Democrat, Fla., 1958-60; asst. editor Sci. Research Assocs., Chgo., 1959-61; pub. relations dir. for fund raising cons., San Francisco, 1962-64; free-lance writer Pacific Sun, Mill Valley Record, Pacific Travel News, Mill Valley Sch. Dist., 1964-74; sr. editor Pacific Sun, Mill Valley, Calif., 1973-79; San Francisco corr. Working Woman mag., 1973-79; free lance writer, 1973-79; founding editor It's Your San Francisco, 1980—; editor Marin County directories, 1980—. Co-author: Women's Winning Doubles, 1985. Bd. pres. Community Health Ctr. of Marin, Fairfax, Calif., 1980-84; program and pub. info. chmn. Mill Valley Community Ctr., 1985, acting dir., 1985. Recipient Outstanding and Dedicated Service-Yr. of the Child award Marin Psychol. Assn., 1979, Resolution of Commendation Marin County Bd. Suprs., 1980, first-place journalism awards San Francisco Press Club, 1976, 78. Democrat. Club: Mill Valley Tennis. Avocations: tennis, swimming, running. Home: 75 Quarry Rd Mill Valley CA 94941 Office: It's Your San Francisco Ferry Bldg Suite 336 World Trade Ctr San Francisco CA 94111

WILLIAMS, JULIA BROOK, lawyer; b. Phila.; d. Franklin and Luvenia (Ruffin) W. B.A., Temple U., 1963; M.S.S.T., Am. U., 1971; J.D., NYU, 1974. Bar: N.Y. 1975, D.C. 1980. Atty., SEC, N.Y.C., 1974-78, Merck & Co., Inc., Rahway, N.J., 1978-80; corp. counsel U.S. Home Corp., Houston, 1980-84. Mem. ABA (mem. securities regulation com., small bus. com., real estate com.) Home: 1334 Ft Stevens Dr Apt 202 Washington DC 20011

WILLIAMS, JULIE BELLE, psychiatric social worker, psychologist; b. Algona, Iowa, July 29, 1950; d. George Howard and Leta Maribelle (Durschmidt) W.; B.A., U. Iowa, 1972, M.S.W., 1973. Social worker Psychopathic Hosp., Iowa City, 1971-72; OEO counselor YOUR, Webster City, Iowa, 1972; social worker Child Devel. Clinic, Iowa City, 1973; therapist Mid-Eastern Iowa Community Mental Health Center, Iowa City, 1973; psychiat. social worker Mental Health Center N. Iowa, Mason City, 1974-79, chief social worker, 1979-80; asst. dir. White Bear Lake (Minn.) Community Counseling Center, 1980-85, dir., 1985—; lectr., cons. in field. NIMH grantee, 1972-73. Mem. Nat. Assn. Social Workers, NOW, Acad. Cert. Social Workers, Am. Orthopsychiat. Assn., Am. Assn. Sex Educators, Counselors and Therapists, Phi Beta Kappa. Democrat. Home: 761 Cannon Ave Shoreview MN 55126 Office: 4739 Division Ave White Bear MN 55110

WILLIAMS, KAREN HARVEY, radio station executive; b. Longview, Tex., Aug. 22, 1948; d. Elton E. and Suann (Brown) Harvey; m. David Ray Williams, May 1, 1977; 1 child, Gina Michelle. Student pub. schs., Longview. Cashier, Longview Bank & Trust, 1965-74; office mgr., sec. to pres. and v.p. Sta. KYKX, Longview, 1974—, also cons. KYKX Big Bass Classic, 1985. Recipient Joe Travis award Dale Carnegie, Longview, 1972. Republican. Home: 1315 Princeton Longview TX 75601 Office: Sta KYKX PO Box 2727 1618 Judson Rd Longview TX 75606

WILLIAMS, KATHERINE LOUISE, computer geoscientist; b. Beaumont, Tex., Nov. 26, 1957; d. Dexter Earl and Marilyn Ann (Hughes) W. B.A. in Math., So. Meth. U., 1979. Actuary, A.S., Hansen, Inc., Dallas, 1979-80; sci. programmer, supr. Geophys. Services Inc., Dallas, 1980-83; computer geoscientist Standard Oil Production Co., Dallas, 1983—. So. Meth. U. scholar, 1975-79. Mem. Dallas Geophys. Soc., IEEE Computer Soc., ACM, Profl. Assn. Diving Instrs. (open water diver). Office: Standard Oil Production Co One Lincoln Ctr Suite 1200-LB25 5400 LBJ Freeway Dallas TX 75240

WILLIAMS, KATHRYN ULLRICH, public relations executive; b. Bklyn., Jan. 3, 1948; d. Charles Freeman and Eleanor Teresa (Bennett) Ullrich; m. Robert Ammon Williams, Jr., May 26, 1973 (div. July 1980). Student Tobe Coburn Sch., N.Y.C., 1966-68. Asst. mktg. rep. Allied Stores Mktg. Corp., N.Y.C., 1968-70; asst. pub. relations dir. Cone Mills Mktg. Corp., N.Y.C., 1970-71; office mgr. Pelican Films, N.Y.C., 1971-72; account exec., account supr. Rea Lubar Inc., N.Y.C., 1972-73, 75-77, v.p., 1980—; account exec. P.C.I., Miami, Fla. 1979-80; Mem. Fashion Group, Womens Fashion Fabrics Assn., Tobe Coburn Alumni Assn. (sec. 1982—). Democrat. Roman Catholic. Avocations: weaving; scuba diving. Home: 432 E 88th St Penthouse D New York NY 10128 Office: Rea Lubar Inc 15 W 38th St New York NY 10018

WILLIAMS, LESLIE JANE, chiropractic clinic executive; b. Kansas City, Mo., July 13, 1953; d. John William and Mildred May (Twist) Sebring; m. Larry Wayne Campbell (div.); children—Jeffery Lee, Cynthia Renee; m. John David Williams, Aug. 2, 1974; children—Annie May, John Floyd, Jeremy Daniel, Megan Lynn. Owner, dir. Williams Graphic Prodns., Kansas City, Kans., 1978—; chiropractic asst. Cleveland Chiropractic Coll., Kansas City, Mo., 1979, Clinic Masters, Independence, Mo., 1979; clin. acupuncturist Internat. Acad. Clin. Acupuncture, Overland Park, Kans., 1982; bus. mgr., dir. program devel. Chiropractic Accident Injury & Pain Clinic, Kansas City, 1978—. Mem. Internat. Acad. Clin. Acupuncture. Avocations: needle point; reading; travel; volley ball; racquet ball. Home: 7529 Greeley Kansas City KS 66109 Office: Chiropractic Accident Injury & Pain Clinic 5002 State Ave Kansas City KS 66109

WILLIAMS, LILLIE MAE, physician; b. Greenville, Ala., Mar. 24, 1947; d. J. D. and Lugene (Smith) Lewis; m. John A. Williams, Dec. 22, 1973; children—John, Joy, Jeanie. B.S. magna cum laude, Ala. A&M U., 1969; M.S. in Biology, U. Mich., 1970, M.S. in Zoology, 1972; M.D. U. Calif.-Irvine, 1980. Teaching fellow U. Mich., Ann Arbor, 1969-73; NIH trainee, 1969-72; teaching asst. UCLA, 1973-76; intern Martin Luther King, Jr.-Drew Med. Ctr., Los Angeles, 1980-81, resident in pediatrics 1981-83; practice medicine specializing in pediatrics, Los Angeles, 1983—; staff free clinic U. Calif.-Irvine Day Care Ctr., 1980; cons. Pleasant Hill Baptist Ch.; mem. Joint Council Interns and Residents Los Angeles County. Mem. AMA, Am. Acad. Pediatrics, Los Angeles Pediatric Soc., Jack and Jill Am., Delta Sigma Theta. Home: 8031 Ainsworth Ln La Palma CA 90623 Office: 12021 Wilmington Ave Los Angeles CA 90059

WILLIAMS, LINDA, retail consultant; b. Chgo., Dec. 10, 1948; d. Gilbert and Sallie (Daniels) Chaney; m. Brian Williams, Aug. 28, 1971; 1 child, Nikiya Noni. B.S., Loyola U., Chgo., 1972, Ed.M., 1980. Tchr. Chgo. Bd. Edn., 1971-82; investment mgr. Drexel Nat. Bank, Chgo., 1982-84; bus. cons. Southland Corp., San Diego, 1984—. Office: Southland Corp 7339 El Cajon Blvd Suite J San Diego CA 92041

WILLIAMS, LINDA S., microbiologist; b. Oxford, Miss., Aug. 29, 1946; d. Dewey Frank Sanders and Margarette Louise (Coleman) Tucker; m. John Hopkins Williams III, Feb. 26, 1969; children—Stephanie, John Hopkins IV. B.S., Miss. State U., 1969. Med. technologist North Miss. Med. Ctr., Tupelo, 1969-70, Petersburg Gen. Hosp., Va., 1974-75; tech. mgr. Gateway Community Hosp., St. Petersburg, Fla., 1976-81; owner, tech. dir. Med. Lab. Services, Clearwater, Fla., 1981-83; tech. dir. Central Med. Lab., Clearwater, 1983—; owner State Farm Ins. Agy.; infection control cons. numerous nursing homes. Sec., pastor, mem. parish com. Heritage United Methodist Ch., 1975—. Recipient plaque Am. Heart Assn., 1983. Mem. Am. Soc. Clin. Pathologists (assoc.), Am. Bus. Women's Assn., Fla. Health Care Assn., Nat. Assn. Female Execs., LWV, Republican. Clubs: Jr. League, Countryside Country (Clearwater). Home: 2733 Northridge Dr E Clearwater FL 33519

WILLIAMS, LINDA SUSAN, lawyer; b. Newark, Jan. 19, 1955; d. Claudius Richard and Mildred Ann (Daniels) Williams, Jr. B.A. in English Lit., Mt. Holyoke Coll., 1977; J.D., Seton Hall U., 1981. Bar: N.J. 1981. Law clk. Monmouth County, Freehold, N.J., 1981-82; supervising atty. Essex-Newark Legal Services, Newark, 1982—. Daniel A. Degnan scholar Setan Hall Sch. Law, 1979-81, Centennial scholar, 1978-81. Mem. Garden State Bar Assn. (sec. 1982-83, v.p. 1983-84), Assn. Black Women Lawyers N.J. (sec. 1982-83). Baptist. Home: 932 S 19th St Newark NJ 07108 Office: Essex Newark Legal Services 18 Rector St Newark NJ 07102

WILLIAMS, LORETTA FAYE, materials manager; b. Winnsboro, La., June 18, 1952; d. Earl and Jacqueline (Brown) W. B.S., Rutgers U., 1974, M.B.A., 1978. Asst. buyer Abraham & Straus, Bklyn., 1974-75; sr. buyer Sunshine Biscuits, Inc., N.Y.C.C., 1975-78; purchasing mgr. Life Savers, Inc., N.Y.C., 1978-82; contract mfg. mgr. Johnson & Johnson Baby Products, Skillman, N.J., 1982-84, purchasing and new product devel. mgr., 1984-86; materials mgr. Johnson & Johnson, Skillman, 1986—. Career cons. Douglass Alumnae Assn., 1981—; pres. bd. trustees Oak Hollow Homeowners Assn., 1984-86; mem. jud. bd. Douglass Coll. of Rutgers U., 1970-74; judge Point of Purchase Advt. Inst. ann. merchandising awards, 1979, 81. Paige and Frances Bradley l'Hommedieu scholar, 1972-74. Mem. Nat. Black M.B.A. Assn. (sec. 1980-82; Service award 1982), Nat. Assn. Female Execs., Assn. M.B.A. Execs., Soc. Plastic Engrs. (assoc.), Nat. Assn. Negro Bus. and Profl. Women. Baptist. Avocations: music; dance; cooking. Home: 4501 N Oaks Blvd North Brunswick NJ 08902 Office: Johnson & Johnson Grandview Rd Skillman NJ 08558

WILLIAMS, LOUISE ANITIA, advertising/graphic design co. exec.; b. Portland, Oreg., Mar. 31, 1942; d. Homer Bruce and Ora Ellen (Diehl) W.; student public schs., Beaverton, Oreg.; 1 dau., Tiffany Joy Wlecial. Med. asst., physicians' practice, 1963-64; adminstrv. asst. St. Vincent's Hosp., 1964-70; salesman, sales mgr., nat. sales mgr. Indsl. Systems, 1970; regional sales mgr. Peel O'Matique, 1971; bus. devel. rep. Imperial Bank, 1971-72; pvt. practice fin. cons., Los Angeles, 1972-73; sales rep. Printing Services, Granada Hills, Calif., 1976; partner Art, Love, Time & Money, Marina City, Calif., 1978-79; pres., sole stock holder Corporate Creative Services, Sherman Oaks, Calif., 1979—. Mem. Rep. Presdl. Task Force. Served with Hosp. Corps, USN, 1960-63. Mem. Nat. Assn. Female Execs., Los Angeles Ad Club, Women in Bus., Nat. Assn. Women Bus. Owners, Western Los Angeles C. of C., Sales and Mktg. Execs., Med. Mktg. Assn., Sherman Oaks C. of C., Clubs: Buckley Parents Assn., Mid Town Exec. (Los Angeles). Home: 177 S Water Wheelway Orange CA 92669 Office: PO Box 5973-396 15245 La Maida St Suite 303 Sherman Oaks CA 91403

WILLIAMS, M. A. HALL, newspaper publisher, editor; b. Jacksonville, Fla., Sept. 1, 1913; d. Andrew A. and Lillie (Hall) Williams. Student, Edward Waters Coll., 1930-32; B.S., Fla. A&M U., 1934; postgrad. Northwestern U., 1937-38. Tchr., Lake High Sch., Leesburg, Fla., 1934-37; tchr. Indsl./Roosevelt High Sch., West Palm Beach, Fla., 1937-56; founding pub., exec. editor Fla. Photo News, West Palm Beach, 1955—; mem. Black Media, Inc., N.Y.C., 1978. Mem. Urban League Palm Beach County, 1973—, Palm Beach County Community Action Council, 1970—, City Library Adv. Bd., Human Services Coalition, 1984—. Recipient Outstanding Community Service Plaque of Commendation, Links, Inc., 1980, Community Change Orgn., 1980. Delta Sigma Theta, 1980, Zeta Phi Beta, 1980; resolution commendation Palm Beach County Bd. Commrs., 1980; plaque commendation Fla. Conf. NAACP, 1982, Sickle Cell Found., 1983; cert of appreciation, Regional Social Security Office, 1983, Palm Beach County Bd. Commrs., 1983, others. Mem. Women in Communications, SCLC, NAACP, Community Round Table; S.E. Black Pubs.

Assn. (dir. 1979—). Democrat. Methodist. Clubs: Fla. Assn. Women's Clubs, Scalers. Address: Fla Photo News PO Box 1583-46 West Palm Beach FL 33402

WILLIAMS, MARCILLE GRAY, advertising and public relations agency executive; b. Tacoma, Apr. 15, 1947; d. Harold Franklin and Lucille Bessie (Price) Gray; student pub. schs., Tacoma. Pres., Spectra Advt. Inc., Newport Beach, Calif., 1973-76; exec. v.p. Reiser/Williams/deYong, Costa Mesa, Calif., 1977-79; mgr. mktg. communications Xerox Co., Dallas, 1979-83; sr. v.p. western ops. Strayton Corp., Santa Clara, Calif., 1983—. Author: The New Executive Woman, 1977. Office: 3333 Bowers Ave Suite 299 Santa Clara CA 95051

WILLIAMS, MARIAN ARETHA, teacher educator, consultant; b. Washington, May 11, 1941; d. Milton and Dorothy Mae (Thomas) W. B.A., Howard U., 1971, M.Ed., 1977, cert. in advanced edn., 1980, advanced degree in reading, 1986. Cert. secondary tchr., D.C. Lectr., Ctr. for Acad. Reinforcement, Howard U., Washington, 1977—; escort interpreter U.S. State Dept., Washington, 1980—; bd. advisors Adult Edn. Ctr., Washington, 1980-81; reading and study skills cons., Washington, 1979—. Named Outstanding Contbr. to Cross-Cultural Edn., Sr. Sodality of Holy Redeemer Ch., 1979. Mem. Internat. Reading Assn., Nat. Council Negro Women (life, Mary McLeod Bethune award 1986), Nat. Assn. Devel. Educators, Phi Delta Kappa. Democrat. Roman Catholic. Avocations: horseback riding; ice skating; camping; reading. Home: 3013 Vista St NE Washington DC 20018

WILLIAMS, MARILYN CRANE, real estate executive, Court official; b. Caldwell, N.J., Aug. 28, 1928; d. Raymond C. and Sadie A. (De Baun) Crane; m. Neal E. Williams, June 10, 1949; children—Laurie, Neal, Nancy, Mary. B.A., Conn. Coll., 1950; M.A., Eastern Conn. State U., 1971. Prof., Fields Meml. Sch., Fitchville, Conn., 1966—; ptnr. New Realty, East Lyme, Conn., 1975—; chief clk. Salem Probate Ct., Conn., 1982—. Pres. Creative Arts Fellowship, Salem, Conn., 1976. Treas. Bozrah Fedn. Tchrs., Conn., 1977—. Mem. Conn. Coll. Alumni Assn., Conn. Assn. Probate Clks. Democrat. Presbyterian. Club: Delta (Fitchville, Conn.). Avocations: music; swimming; camping; travel. Home: Skyline Dr Salem CT 06415 Office: Fields Meml Sch Fitchville CT 06334

WILLIAMS, MARILYN MURPHY, lawyer; b. Elizabeth, N.J., May 13, 1942; d. Thomas Patrick and Florence Ann (Weickhardt) Murphy; m. John James Williams, July 25, 1964; children—Patrick, Kathryn. B.S., U. Kans., 1964; M.L.S., Emporia State Coll., 1974; J.D., U. Mo. at Kansas City, 1979. Tchr., Shawnee Mission (Kans.) Sch. Dist., 1964-66, Virginia Beach, Va., 1967-68, Newport, R.I., 1969-70; librarian Center Sch. Dist., Kansas City, Mo., 1973-75; admitted to Kans. bar, 1979; partner Williams & Oberhelman, Mission, Kans., 1979-84; Kans. counsel Buck, Bohm, & Stein, P.C., 1983-84. Bd. dirs. Kans. Legal Services of Olathe, 1981-84. NDEA fellow, 1965. Mem. Am. Bar Assn., Kans. Bar Assn., Kans. Trial Lawyers Assn., Kansas City Bar Assn., Johnson County Bar Assn. (bench-bar com. domestic relations 1981—), Mid-Am. Family Mediation Assn. (pres. 1985-86). Republican. Home: 340 E Palm Ln #140 Phoenix AZ 85004 Office: 7199 W 98 Terrace Suite 130 Overland Park KS 66212

WILLIAMS, MARION MAXINE, college administrator, librarian; b. Scotts, Miss., Aug. 16, 1944; d. Abe and Nermer (Johnson) Holmes; m. J. C. Williams, Dec. 29, 1967; children—Anita, Kimberly, Janice, Jared, Erika, Nermer. B.S. in Social Studies, Alcorn A&M Coll., Lorman, Miss., 1967; postgrad. Miss. Coll., summer 1971; M.S. in History, Prairie View A&M Coll., 1974. Cert. tchr., Miss. Credit analyst Spiegel's Inc., Chgo., summers 1962, 64, 65, 66; tchr. Duncan Elem. Sch., Miss., 1967-68; secondary tchr. Vicksburg Pub. Schs., Miss., 1968-72; coordinator audio-visual lab. Prairie View A&M Coll., Tex., 1973-84, coordinator learning resources ctr., 1984—. Pres. Waller Schs. PTA, Tex., 1978-79, Prairie View chpt. Jack/Jill of Am., 1984-86; leader San Jacinto council Girl Scouts U.S.A., 1984—; sec. Top Ladies of Distinction, Prairie View, 1985-86; sec. Tchr. Corp. Community Adv. Bd., Prairie View, 1979. Recipient Human Relations award Tex. State Tchrs. Assn., Waller, 1979; COE Found. fellow Miss. Coll., Clinton, summer, 1971. Mem. Phi Delta Kappa, Phi Alpha Theta, Alpha Kappa Alpha (undergrad. adv. 1979-81). Roman Catholic. Home: PO Box 2092 Smith St Prairie View TX 77446

WILLIAMS, MARLA J., lawyer; b. Gary, Ind., June 29, 1952; d. Orlin K. and Ann B. (Snyder) W. A.B., Ind. U., 1974; J.D., Harvard U., 1980. Bar: Colo. Social worker Dept. Pub. Welfare, Gary, Ind., 1974-77; law clk., Judge James Richards, Hammond, Ind., summer 1970, Ruben & Proctor, Chgo., summer 1979; assoc. Holme Roberts & Owen, Denver, 1980—; mem. bd. student advisors Harvard Law Sch., Cambridge, Mass., 1978-80. Co-author articles in field. Hoosier scholar, 1970. Mem. ABA, Colo. Bar Assn., Denver Bar Assn., Untimely Motions, Colo. Women's Bar Assn. (bd. dirs. 1985—), Phi Beta Kappa. Club: Denver Athletic. Office: Holme Roberts & Owen 1700 Broadway Denver CO 80290

WILLIAMS, MARTHA LYNN, controller, numismatic executive; b. Dallas, Jan. 21, 1952; d. Joseph Raymond and Lola Betty (Jones) Burress; m. W. Crutchfield Williams II, Aug. 7, 1976. Student Houston Community Coll., 1984. Acctg. staff Met. Rare Coin Galleries, N.Y., 1973-74, Robert L. Hughes, Inc., Atlanta, 1974-75; daconis operator NASA, Houston, 1978-79; controller, fgn. exchange trader Tex. Fgn. Exchange, Houston, 1979-81; bullion trader, acct. Colonial Coins, Houston, 1982-84; controller Houston Numismatic Exchange, 1985—. Organizer Teen Club, Clear Lake Shores, Tex., 1984; pres. Clear Lake Shores Civic Club, 1984-86; charter sec. Seaside Lioness Club, 1978. Mem. Nat. Assn. Female Execs., Am. Numismatic Assn., Tex. Numismatic Assn. Republican. Methodist. Club: Kemah Bay Garden (treas. 1980). Lodge: Eastern Star (worthy matron 1982-83, sec. 1985—). Home: 915 Ivy Clear Lake Shores TX 77565 Office: Houston Numismatic Exchange 3486 Times Blvd Houston TX 77005

WILLIAMS, MARTHA OLIVER, accountant; b. Aberdeen, Miss., May 15, 1925; d. Christopher Lorenzo and Lydia Ercelle (Brown) Oliver; student So. Ark. U., 1974; m. Carl S. Williams, Dec. 15, 1946; children—Larry Carl, Mark Oliver. Office mgr.-acct. Ark. Chems., Inc., El Dorado, 1971—; broadcaster local TV and radio, 1955-65; tchr. So. Ark. U., El Dorado, 1978—; also lectr. Vice pres., membership chmn. Community Concert Assn., 1972-74; active PTA. Mem. Nat. League Am. Pen Women, Poets Roundtable Ark. Mem. Ch. of Christ. Author: Lines From Living, 1973; Windows, 1976; Time, Place and Emotion, 1983. Home: 1015 Harrison St El Dorado AR 71730 Office: Route 6 Box 98 El Dorado AR 71730

WILLIAMS, MARY EDWINA, communications company executive; b. Worcester, Mass., Jan. 18, 1950; d. Edward Joseph and Mary Theresa (Sullivan) W.; B.A., Clark U., Worcester, 1972; M.B.A., Anna Maria Coll., Paxton, Mass., 1979; grad. Tanglewood listening and analysis seminar Berkshire Music Center, Lenox, Mass., 1975, mgmt. seminar Am. Symphony Orch., 1975; m. Frederick Leroy Monahan, Jr., June 9, 1979; children—Caitlin Williams, Maura Williams Monahan. Mental hygiene therapist Hutchings Psychiat. Center, Syracuse, N.Y., 1972-75; bus. mgr., registrar Worcester Community Sch. Performing Arts, 1975-78; long-term substitute tchr. bus. dept. Sheehan High Sch., Wallingford, Conn., 1979-80; mktg. service cons. bus. dept. So. New Eng. Telephone Co., 1980-83, supr. support engring. dept., 1983—. Mem. Clark U. Alumni Council, also co-chmn. career counseling com.; trustee, mem. exec. com., chmn. public relations com. Edward St. Day Care Center, Worcester, 1976-78; bd. dirs. Wallingford Symphony Orch., 1980—. Club: Wallingford Jr. Women's (co-chmn. arts com. 1980-81, chmn. pub. affairs com. 1984-85). Address: 209 High St Wallingford CT 06492

WILLIAMS, MARY ELMORE, English and history educator; b. San Angelo, Tex., Sept. 19, 1931; d. Mortimer Taylor and Florrine (Gee) Elmore; m. Mark B. Williams, Sept. 6, 1951; children—John Mark, Mary Jean. A.A., San Angelo Coll., 1950; B.S., Tex. Christian U., 1951; M.S., Corpus Christi State U., 1983; postgrad. U. Chgo., 1954, Princeton U., 1961, Mansfield Coll., Oxford U., 1966. Tchr. 1st grade First Methodist Ch., Dallas, 1951-52; tchr. 8th grade Pleasant Grove Jr. High, Dallas, 1952-54; tchr. history Hamlin Jr. High Sch., Corpus Christi, 1958; tchr. 6th grade St. Christopher's Episcopal Sch., Lubbock, Tex., 1968; tchr. English and history Hamlin Jr. High, Corpus Christi, 1974—, coordinator Adopt-a-School Program, 1983—; cons. KEDT-TV Tex. History series The Lone Star, Corpus Christi, 1984-85; cons. textbook com. Corpus Christi Ind. Sch. Dist., 1983, 86; mem. curriculum writing team Corpus Christi Ind. Sch. Dist., 1985-86. Campaign coordinator Ruth Gill for Mayor, Corpus Christi, 1979; del. Gov.'s Commn. for Women, Corpus Christi Council for Women, San Antonio, 1985. Named Outstanding Tchr. Am. History-Tex., DAR, Corpus Christi, 1986. Mem. Assn. Curriculum and Devel., Corpus Christi Council Social Studies (v.p. 1981-83), Tex. Council Social Studies (conv. chmn. 1988), Corpus Christi C. of C. (events chmn. 1983), Phi Delta Kappa, AAUW (v.p. 1983-85, pres. 1986-88). Avocations: tennis; reading. Home: 601 Barracuda Pl Corpus Christi TX 78411 Office: Hamlin Jr High Sch 3900 Hamlin Dr Corpus Christi TX 78411

WILLIAMS, MARY IRENE, educator; b. Hugo, Okla., June 30, 1944; d. Primer and Hylar B. (Tarkington) Jackson; B.Bus. Edn., Langston U., 1967; M.S. in Bus. Edn., Emporia State U., 1973; postgrad. U. Nev., 1975-77; m. Lee A. William, Feb. 10, 1973; 1 dau., Monica Ariane. Bus. instr. Spokane (Wash.) Community Coll., 1967-69; Topeka West High Sch., 1970-71, tchr. bus. Highland Park High Sch., Topeka, Kans., 1972-73; instr. Clark County Community Coll., North Las Vegas, Nev., 1973-78, dir. bus. div., 1978—; cons. Scott Foresman Pub. Co., 1977-80; condr. seminars for Las Vegas C. of C., 1980. Recipient Educator of Yr. award, Bus. and Service award for edn. Clark County Community Coll., 1985. Mem. NEA, Am. Bus. Communication Assn., Nat. Bus. Edn. Assn., Am. Assn. Women in Community and Jr. Colls., Internat. Assn. Bus. Communicators, AAUW, Am. Assn. Female Execs. Office: 3200 E Cheyenne Ave North Las Vegas NV 89030

WILLIAMS, MARY JO, lawyer; b. Mpls., July 11, 1952; d. Maurice Robert and Louise Lorraine (Morrow) W. B.A., U. Minn., 1975; J.D., William Mitchell Coll. Law, 1979; LL.M., Boston U., 1980. Bar: Minn. 1980, U.S. Tax Ct. 1981. Tax research specialist Lurie, Eiger, Besikof, C.P.A.s, Golden Valley, Minn., 1980-82; tax counsel First Bank System, Mpls., 1983—; adj. prof. law William Mitchell Coll. Law, St. Paul, 1980-81. Treas. Art Ctr. Minn., Minnetonka, 1985—. Mem. Minn. Bar Assn., ABA. Roman Catholic. Office: First Bank System Inc 1300 First Bank Pl E Minneapolis MN 55402

WILLIAMS, MARY LOU NEWMAN, mus. and archives coordinator; b. Harleton, Tex., Dec. 21, 1918; d. Ray Maxie and Corine (Baker) Newman; A.A., Coll. of Marshall, 1935; B.A., Mary Hardin-Baylor U., 1937; postgrad. U. Tex., Austin, 1937-38; M.A., E. Tex. State U., 1961; m. Louis Booth Williams, Oct. 15, 1938; children—Joanne Williams Click, Louis B., Jr. English instr. Paris (Tex.) Jr. Coll., 1953-68, chmn. communications div., 1965-68, coordinator for devel. A.M. and Welma Aikin Regional Archives, 1977-83; English instr. E. Tex. State U., Commerce, 1970-74; coordinator for devel. R.F. Voyer Regional Mus., Honey Grove, Tex., 1977-84. Pres., McCuistion Regional Med. Center Aux., 1975-77; dist. bd. Nat. Multiple Sclerosis Soc.; mem. YWCA, Lamar County Hist. Commn. Winedale Mus. seminar scholar, 1977. Mem. AAUW, Am. Assn. State and Local History, Soc. Am. Archivists, Am. Assn. Museums, Tex. Assn. Museums, Tex. State Hist. Assn., N.E. Tex. Geneal. Soc., LWV, Paris Hist. Landmark Preservation Com., Phi Theta Kappa (hon.). Methodist. Clubs: Cosmos (pres. 1977), Paris Garden (pres. 1944), Garden Study (pres. 1955), Mary Emma Bible (pres. 1975, 80). Home: 3170 Laurel Ln Paris TX 75460

WILLIAMS, MELVA JEAN, oil and gas co. exec.; b. Burke, S.D., June 11, 1935; d. Wayne and Mildred Eva (Graham) Mulholland; grad. Roberta's Finishing Sch., Miami, Fla., 1950, Charron-Williams Comml. Coll., 1954; m. J.B. Williams, Apr. 29, 1977; children—Mark, Doris, Robin, Jeannie. With Southeastern Resources Corp., Ft. Worth and Rising Star, Tex., 1968—, pres., 1979-83, vice chmn. bd., 1983—, also dir.; with Delta Gas Co., Inc., Tchula, Miss., 1973-81, sec., treas., 1974-81, also dir.; with SERPCO, Inc., Fort Worth, 1977—, v.p., 1980-84, pres., 1984—, also dir.; sec., treas. J J & L Drilling Co., Inc., Ft. Worth and Cisco, Tex., 1979-82, also dir.; with Rising Star Processing Corporation, Fort Worth, sec. treas. 1981—, also dir.; with Brownwood Pipeline Corporation, Fort Worth, sec. treas. 1981—, also dir.; gen. partner B & W Real Estate Investments, Nashville, 1980—, F & W Real Estate Investments, Fort Worth, 1981—, Westward Properties, Ft. Worth; dir. Aero Modifications Internat., Inc., Ft. Worth and Waco, Tex. Republican. Home: 6150 Indigo Ct Fort Worth TX 76112 Office: 2201 Scott Ave Fort Worth TX 76103

WILLIAMS, MELVA L., actress, educator; b. Chgo., June 1, 1925; d. Oscar and Louvonia (Witcher) W. B.Ed., Chgo. State U., 1960, M.S. in Edn., 1967; Ed.D., Nova U., 1979. Musician with instrumental and vocal groups, 1945-60; actress radio, TV, stage and films, 1945—; tchr. Chgo. Pub. Schs., 1960-69, asst. prin., 1969—; mem. Goodman Theatre Repertory Co., Chgo., 1971-72, Milw. Repertory Co., 1974—, choral dir. various locations, 1960—; speech specialist; TV appearances include: Bird of the Iron Feather, Mike Royko at Best, A Matter of Principle; stage appearances include: A Raisin in the Sun, Native Son, Royal Family, Assassination (all Chgo.). Author: Soul Talk, 1970; (play) Play Doubletime for Me, 1974. Recipient nomination for Chgo. Emmy award, 1969; named Woman of Distinction in Edn. and Drama, Chgo. Citizens Scholarship Com., 1970; Service awards Model Cities Program, West Side Cluster High Schs., chs. and community orgns., Chgo. Mem. Chgo. State U. Alumni Assn., Nova U. Alumni Assn., Actors Equity, Screen Actors Guild, Am. Fedn. Musicians, AFTRA, Explorers Investment Group (bd. dirs.). Phi Delta Kappa.

WILLIAMS, MEREDITH JANE, philosophy educator; b. Anniston, Ala., July 29, 1947; d. Wilbur Eric and Martha Jane (Felgar) Swenson; m. Michael James Williams, Apr. 21, 1974; 1 son, Paul Hereward. Student Coll. William and Mary, 1965-67; B.A., NYU, 1969, Ph.D., 1974; M.A., U. Chgo., 1970. Asst. prof. philosophy Wesleyan U., Middletown, Conn., 1974-79, assoc. prof., 1979-85, chairperson dept. philosophy, 1983-84; assoc. prof. Northwestern U., Evanston, Ill., 1985—; vis. assoc. prof. U. Mich., Ann Arbor, spring 1983. Contbr. articles to profl. jours., 1976—. Mem. Am. Philos. Assn., Soc. for Philosophy and Psychology. Office: Northwestern U Dept Philosophy Evanston IL 60201

WILLIAMS, MILDRED JANE, librarian; b. Charlotte, N.C. Nov. 9, 1944; d. Leonard Augustus and Frances Edith (Long) W. B.A., Pfeiffer Coll., Misenheimer, N.C., 1966; M.S.L.S., U. N.C., 1968. Reference librarian Pub. Library Charlotte and Mecklenburg County (N.C.), 1967-70, assoc. dir., 1974-77; head dept. documents and serials Library of Davidson Coll. (N.C.), 1970-73; acting asst. dir. U. N.C.-Charlotte Library, 1977-78; pub. library cons. N.C. State Library, Raleigh, 1979-80, asst. state librarian, 1980-86, acting state librarian, 1986—. Mem. N.C. Library Assn. (2d v.p. 1983-85), Southeastern Library Assn., ALA. Democrat. Baptist. Office: State Library 109 E Jones St Raleigh NC 27611

WILLIAMS, MINNIE CALDWELL, retired educator; b. Chapel Hill, N.C., Feb. 25, 1917; d. Bruce and Minnie (Stroud) Caldwell; m. Peter Currington Williams Sr., Aug. 21, 1938; children—Peter Jr., Bruce, James, Jacqueline, Charles. B.S. in English, N.C. Central U., 1938, M.A. in Elem. Edn., 1942; postgrad. U. Ill., 1962, U. South Fla., 1965, Fla. State U., 1967. Cert. elem. tchr., N.C.; cert. spl. edn., Fla. Tchr. Weldon pub. schs., N.C., 1940-60, Pinellas County Sch., St. Petersburg, Fla., 1961-80, reading specialist, 1961-80, spl. edn. tchr., 1961-80. Exec. Democratic committeeman, Pinellas County, Fla., 1983-85, local campaign and poll worker; co-chairperson United Way Com. Recipient Ret. Tchrs. award Dixie Hollins High Sch., 1984; Ret. Tchrs. award NAACP, 1980; Panhellenic Service award Greek Orgn., 1980. Mem. Nat. Assn. Ret. Tchrs., Am. Bus. Women Assn., Profl. Bus. Women, Garden Club of St. Petersburg, Delta Sigma Theta (NAACP rep.), Kappa Delta Pi. Baptist. Avocations: Travel; reading; gardening; arts; bowling. Home: 1726 28th Ave S Saint Petersburg FL 33712

WILLIAMS, NELLIE JAMES BATT, educator; b. Nashville; d. Ivan C. and Lottie B. (Phillips) James; A.B., Stowe Coll., 1942; M.S., U. Ill., 1945; postgrad. Ill. Inst. Tech., 1959, 64, Oberlin Coll., 1965, St. Louis U., 1962, 63, 67, 68, Rockhurst Coll., 1972, Webster Coll., 1984, 85; m. Napoleon Williams, July 21, 1973; 1 son by previous marriage, Charles W. Batt, Jr. Tchr. Sumner High Sch., St. Louis, 1949-54, Handly High Sch., 1954-63; tchr., head mathematics dept. Northwest High Sch., St. Louis, 1963-76; instr., dept. head, Acad. Math. and Sci., St. Louis, 1976—; instr., head dept. Harris Teacher Coll., Forest Park Community Coll. Active NAACP, YWCA. NSF grantee, 1959, 62-65, 67, 72. Mem. Math. Club Greater St. Louis, Math. Assn. Am., Assn. Women in Math., Delta Sigma Theta (edn. com.). Methodist. Home: 7584 Amherst St Saint Louis MO 63130

WILLIAMS, PATRICIA ANN, insurance company manager; b. Dalton, Ga., July 17, 1950; d. John E. and Cecile (Caylor) W.; m. Perry L. Kiker, May 30, 1970 (div. June 1975). Grad. Dalton High Sch., 1968. Exec. sec. Dom, Inc., Dalton, 1969-77, Dorsett Carpet, Dalton, 1977-79; sales agt. Allstate Ins. Co., Chattanooga, 1979-83, asst. market sales mgr., Jackson, Miss., 1983-84, market sales mgr., Memphis, 1984—. Mem. Life Underwriters Tng. Council. Republican. Baptist. Avocations: travel; reading; crafts. Home: 2992 New London Dr Memphis TN 38115 Office: Allstate Ins Co Inc 6073 Mount Moriah #18 Memphis TN 38115

WILLIAMS, PATRICIA HILL, university administrator; b. Richmond, Va., May 3, 1939; d. Marshall Jerome and Virginia (O'Brien) H.; m. Arthur Esterbrook Williams, Sept. 6, 1958 (div. Aug. 1981); 1 child, Tory Therese. B.A., SUNY-Old Westbury, 1976; M.A., N.Y. Inst. Tech., 1981. Assoc. editor Babylon Beacon, N.Y., 1972-79; columnist, editor N.Y. Amsterdam News, N.Y.C., 1971-83; tchr. English, North Babylon Sch. Dist., N.Y., 1976-77; pub. info. officer Am. Cancer Soc., Melville, N.Y., 1977-80; dir. pub. relations and alumni affairs SUNY-Farmingdale, 1980—; cons. pub. relations N.Y. State Council Black Republicans, 1974—; dir. pub. relations L.I. Flower Show, 1983—; mem. exec. bd. SUNY Confedn. Alumni Assns., 1983—; bd. dirs. SUNY Coll. and Univ. Advancement and Devel. Council, 1984—. Contbr. poetry to anthologies. Producer videotapes. Mem. allocations com. United Way L.I., 1976—; mem. exec. bd. N.Y. State Council Black Reps., 1980—; pres. Babylon Council Black Reps., 1983—; trustee Babylon Council on Arts, 1976—. Recipient Woman of Yr. award Bethel African Methodist Episcopal Ch., 1980, Civic award NAACP, Amityville, N.Y., 1980, Pub. Relations award 100 Black Men, L.I., 1983, award of Excellence, L.I. Flower Show, 1983; W.K. Kellogg Internat. fellow, 1984-86. Mem. Ptnrs. of Ams. (v.p. L.I. com.), 100 Black Women (parliamentarian, charter mem. L.I. chpt. 1983—), Jack and Jill Am. (assoc., past pres. local chpt.), Alpha Kappa Alpha (chairperson women involved in global concerns com., chairperson connections com.). Episcopalian. Avocations: writing; tennis; travel. Home: 133 Millard Ave West Babylon NY 11704 Office: SUNY Adminstrn Bldg Farmingdale NY 11735

WILLIAMS, PATSY, real estate agency executive, broker; b. Corpus Christi, Tex., Apr. 11, 1940; d. Ralph Woodson and Velma Lee (Carter) West; m. Calvin O. Williams, Jan. 16, 1959; children—Roger Dale, Renee Diane Williams Meals. Cert. broker, Tex. Sec. Deer Park Ind. Sch. Dist., Tex., 1968-75; real estate salesman ERA, Palestine, Tex., 1977-79, broker, co-owner ERA Real Estate Ctr., Palestine, 1979—; owner, operator Pat Walkers Figure Salon, Crockett, Tex., 1981-83, Palestine, 1982-86. Mem. Palestine C. of C., Bus. and Profl. Women's Club. Republican. Baptist. Avocations: camping; reading; gardening. Home: Old Boston Rd Palestine TX 75801 Office: ERA Combined Assocs 114 E Palestine Ave Palestine TX 75801

WILLIAMS, PATTI MCBRIDE, diet center executive; b. Shreveport, La., July 31, 1950; d. William Andrew and Lucy Opal (Fussell) McBride; m. Richard Warren Williams, Aug. 25, 1973 (div.); 1 dau., Jennifer Nicole. B.S., La. State U., 1972; M.S., Northwestern State U. La., 1980. Bookkeeper, co-therapist W.A. McBride, M.D., Shreveport, La., 1972-77; dir. profl. and community relations Brentwood Hosp./Humana, Inc., Shreveport, 1979-85; owner, dir. Diet Ctr. of Shreveport, 1985—; part owner Diet Ctr. Shreveport. Mem. communications com. United Way, 1983, mem. budget com., 1985; publicity chmn. Shreveport Opera, 1981, 82, 83; bd. dirs. Mothers Against Drugs, 1982—; bd. dirs. Little Theater Guild, publicity chmn., 1985-86; past pres. St. Mary's Women Guild, St. Paul's Episcopal Ch.; bd. dirs. Explore 1981—, exec. dir., 1985-86. Recipient 1st place Newsletter award Nat. Hosp. Assn., 1980. Mem. Am. Women in Radio and TV (v.p. local chpt.), Pub. Relations Soc. Am. (pres. local chpt. 1984-86), Nat. Assn. Mental Health Info. Officers (communications awards 1980, 81), Jr. League Shreveport. Democrat. Office: Diet Ctr of Shreveport 2001 E 70th St Suite 506 Shreveport LA 71105

WILLIAMS, PEGGY FOWLER, management consultant; b. nr. Seymour, Tex., May 8, 1933; d. Leon Dockrey Fowler and Annie Bell (Williams) Dodd; B.S., North Tex. U., 1954; M.B.A., Rollins Coll., 1963; cert. of advanced study Am. Grad. Sch. Internat. Mgmt., Phoenix, 1980; m. George S. Moranz, June 5, 1953 (div. Aug., 1979); children—Leigh Ann, Walter Lochran. With Tex. Instruments, Dallas, 1957-58; with Temco Aircraft, Dallas, 1951-53, 55-57; owner Williams Cons. (formerly Moranz Cons.), Dallas, 1963—. Mem. UDC, Dallas Hist. Soc., AAUW, Nat. Assn. Female Execs., Am. Mgmt. Assn. Episcopalian. Club: Listener's. Address: PO Box 7173 Dallas TX 75209

WILLIAMS, PEGGY LENORE, circus clown; b. Madison, Wis., Nov. 3, 1948; d. Richard Eli and Harriet Jane (Edwards) Williams; student U. Wis., 1967-70; grad. Ringling Bros. Barnum & Bailey Clown Coll., 1970. Clown, Ringling Bros. Barnum and Bailey Circus, Washington, 1970-79, asst. performance dir., 1981—, staff instr. Clown Coll., 1974—; cons. in field; developer, tchr. courses on circus in the classroom Fordham U. Grad. Sch. Edn., summer 1985, 86. 1985. Author circus braille program, 1976—. Mem. Circus Fans of Am., Nat. Assn. Female Execs. Republican. Mem. Ch. of Jesus Christ of Latter-day Saints. First female to hold positions. Office: Ringling Bros Barnum and Bailey Circus 3201 New Mexico Ave NW Washington DC 20016

WILLIAMS, ROSE, public relations consultant; b. Chgo., Sept. 24, 1949; d. Bealie and Louise (Billingslea) W.; B.S. in Edn., U. Ill., 1971. Coordinator, mgr. mdsg. Playboy Enterprises, 1970-74; exec. asst. Bank Mktg. Assn., Chgo., 1974-79; dir. mktg. Chgo. Daily Defender, 1979-80; pres. RAW Enterprises, public relations, Chgo., 1980—; mem. speakers bur. Chgo. Bd. Edn., 1981-83; mem. host com., public relations co-chmn., Women's Bur., Dept. Labor, 1979-83; exec. council, chmn. publicity Provident Hosp. Aux., Chgo., 1981—; exec. council, co-chmn, public relations Chgo. PBS Sta. WTTW, 1981-84. Recipient Public Service award Nat. Council Negro Women, 1978, Dept. Labor, 1981. Mem. Nat. Assn. Female Execs. (network dir.), Nat. Assn. Media Women (past 1st v.p. Chgo. chpt.), Chgo. Assn. Commerce and Industry, Cosmopolitan C. of C. (v.p. pub. relations 1984-86, bd. dirs. 1983—, corp. sec. 1986), Publicity Club Chgo., Chgo. Fashion Exchange, Black Pub. Relations Soc. (treas. 1984—), Pub. Relations Soc. Am., Delta Sigma Theta. Address: 505 N Lake Shore Dr Chicago IL 60611

WILLIAMS, RUTH H., television broadcasting executive; b. Bklyn., Mar. 15, 1938; d. Oscar and Lillian (Steinberg) Forster; student schs., Los Angeles; children—Steven, Richard, Michael. Asst. studio mgr. Columbia Records, Los Angeles, 1966-71; West Coast adminstr. Custom div. RCA Records, Los Angeles, 1972-75; studio mgr. Motown Records, Los Angeles, 1975-80; central scheduling supr. Golden West TV/KTLA, 1980-85; ops. mgr. West Hollywood Paper, 1985—. Past mem. Los Angeles chpt. Coalition for Econ. Survival; commr. Rent Stabilization Bd. City of West Hollywood; founder, chair Citizens for Srs. Mem. Nat. Acad. Rec. Arts and Scis. Clubs: West Hollywood Dem., Stonewall Dem. Home: 7548 Lexington Ave West Hollywood CA 90046

WILLIAMS, SHARON, interior designer; b. Waukegan, Ill., Aug. 23, 1948; d. John Issac and Ruth (Robertson) Williams; B.S. in Bus. Edn. and Interior Design, Western Ill. U., 1970; postgrad. U. Minn., 1975, 79. Interior designer masterplan sales and interior design studio Dayton's Dept. Store, St. Paul, 1973-77; owner, pres., dir. interior design Sherry Williams-Ricks, Studio of Interior Design, Mpls., 1977—; mem. faculty dept. applied arts U. Wis.-Stout; mfrs. rep. contract and furnishings for instns. Recipient design and sales achievement award Dayton's Dept. Store, 1974. Mem. Am. Soc. Interior Designers, Mpls. Soc. Fine Arts, Mpls. Inst. Arts, Nat. Assn. Women Bus. Owners, Nat. Assn. Female Execs., Minn. Soc. AIA (interiors com.), Historic Preservation Soc., Greater Mpls. C. of C., North Suburban C. of C., Walker Art Ctr., Alpha Omicron Phi. Methodist. Home: 235 Mackubin Saint Paul MN 55102 Office: Sta 19 2001 University Ave SE Minneapolis MN 55414

WILLIAMS, SHERRY LYNNE, information services company executive; b. Midland, Tex., June 26, 1952; d. Marion Leo and Wanda Geraldine (Cox) Barnes; m. Stancle Edward Williams, June 26, 1969; 1 son, Paul Edward. B.B.A., U. Houston, 1976. Assoc. analyst Conoco, Houston, 1976-78; programmer/analyst Occidental Systems, Inc., Houston, 1978, Data Research, Inc., Houston, 1978-79; applications cons. Tymshare, Inc., Houston, 1980-82, bus. cons., 1982-83, area systems cons. ADP Thrift Services, Houston, 1984-85; nat. sales specialist McDonnell Douglas Communications Systems Co., Houston, 1985; mktg. mgr. Synercom, Sugar Land, Tex., 1985—. 1983. Vol. March of Dimes, Houston, 1983, Am. Cancer Soc., Houston, 1984. Named Applications Cons. of Yr., Tymshare, 1982. Mem. Nat. Assn. Female Execs., Assn. Info. Mgrs. Fin. Instns., Beta Gamma Sigma. Mem. Ch. of Christ. Home: 9415 Spellman Rd Houston TX 77031 Office: Synercom 10405 Corp Dr Sugar Land TX 77478Houston TX 77036

WILLIAMS, SHIRLEY MAE, non-profit organization administrator, clergy-woman; b. Portsmouth, Va., May 17, 1939; d. Sherman James Sheard and Helen Estelle (Weal) Sheard Davidson; m. Boris Eugene Williams, Nov. 2, 1968; children—Raymond, Diana, Paula. A.S. Camden County Coll., 1973; B.A., Rutgers U., 1976; postgrad. Antioch U., Phila., 1986—. Notary public, N.J.; ordained to ministry Holy Spirit Ch., 1980. Social work technician, nurse's aide Our Lady of Lourdes, Camden, N.J., 1962-71, community relations coordinator, social work asst., 1971-75; ctr. dir. Vols. of Am., Camden, 1975-78; tchr. N.J. Dept. Correction, Trenton, 1978-79; asst. exec. dir. Group Homes, Inc., Camden, 1979-81, exec. dir., 1981—; founder, pastor Holy Spirit Cathedral, Mt. Laurel, 1980—, lectr. Camden County Coll., 1977, Rutgers U., 1977; panelist television programs, 1985. Recipient citation, Solidarity Day award N.J. State Senate, 1985. Mem. Camden County Commn. on Women, LWV, Camden County Democratic Club. Lodge: Queen Esther (assoc. matron 1983-85). Home: 20 Hunters Dr Mount Laurel NJ 08054 Office: Group Homes Camden County Inc 35 S 29th St Camden NJ 08105

WILLIAMS, STEPHANIE KETHLEY, television news anchorwoman, lawyer; b. Austin, Tex., July 5, 1955; d. Jerre Stockton and Mary Pearl (Hall) W. B.A., U. Tex., 1977, J.D., 1980. Bar: Tex. 1980. Reporter, Sta. KLRN-TV, Austin, 1973-74; law clk. firm Clark, Thomas, Austin, 1978, Daughterty, Kuperman, Austin, 1979; news anchorwoman Sta. KTBC-TV, Austin, 1978-79; news anchorwoman, reporter Sta. KTBC-TV, Austin, 1980-82, Sta. KPRC-TV, Houston, 1982-85, KTBC-TV, Austin, 1985—; documentary reporter program on pub. sch. discipline State Bar Tex. Mem. Jr. League Houston. Mem. Women in Communications (Matrix award 1983), Travis County Bar Assn., Tex. Young Lawyers Assn. (co-chmn. pub. service programming com.), Delta Theta Phi, Sigma Delta Chi. Democrat. Methodist. Office: KTBC-TV PO Box 2223 Austin TX 78768

WILLIAMS, SYLVIA HILL, museum administrator; b. Lincoln University, Pa., Feb. 10, 1936; m. Charlton E. Williams. A.B., Oberlin Coll., 1957; cert. de Francais Parle Ecole Pract. de l'Alliance Francaise, Paris, 1962-63; M.A. in Primitive Art, NYU, 1975. Program cons. Nat. Assembly for Social Policy and Devel., N.Y.C., 1963-68; account exec. Harry L. Oram, Inc., N.Y.C., 1968-71; Mellon research fellow The Bklyn. Mus., 1971-73, assoc. curator, 1976-78, curator, 1978-83; dir. Smithsonian Inst. Nat. Mus. African Art, Washington, 1983—; lectr. African art New Sch. for Social Research, N.Y.C., 1979-80; adj. asst. prof. NYU, 1980. Author: Black South Africa, Contemporary Graphics, 1976. Contbr. author: African Art as Philosophy, 1974. Curator, organizer 5 major exhbns. and installations, 1973-81. Contbr. articles to profl. jours. Travel grantee Nat. Mus. Act, 1974. Mem. African Am. Mus. Assn., Assn. in Primitive and Pre-Columbian Art. Home: 141 12th St NE #9 Washington DC 20002 Office: Nat Mus of African Art Smithsonian Inst Washington DC 20560

WILLIAMS, VALENA MINOR, radio station official; b. New Orleans, Apr. 6, 1923; d. Norman Selby and Grace Claudia (Jones) Minor; m. John B. Williams, June 6, 1948 (dec. Oct. 1976); children—Valena Marie, Allison Grace, Jennifer Minor, Kimberley Susan. B.S., Bennett Coll., Greensboro, N.C., 1943; M.Jour., U. Calif.-Berkeley, 1981. Broadcaster Stas. WABQ, WHK, WTAM, Cleve., 1955-64; producer, coordinator univ. relations President's Office, U. Calif.-Berkeley, 1967-83; sta. mgr. Sta. KQED-FM, San Francisco, 1983—; pub. mem. Pub. Broadcasting Service, 1977-83; profl. mem. bd. dirs. Nat. Pub. Radio, 1985-87. Producer radio series U.C. Drum (African series), 1970-71, U.C. News Service, 1975-77. Recipient Golden Mike award McCall/Am. Women in Radio and TV, 1961. Home: 2207 Braemar Rd Oakland CA 94602

WILLIAMS, VEDA MARILEE, retired educational administrator; b. Tulsa, Aug. 10, 1929; d. Daniel Webster and Phyllis May (Shoup) Johnson; m. Robert LeRoy Williams, Dec. 17, 1952; children—Robert LeRoy II, John Phillip. B.A. in Journalism, U. Tulsa, 1951; M.Ed., N. Tex. State U., 1971. Cert. tchr., Okla., Ariz., Tex., secondary supr., Tex. Reporter, Tulsa Daily World, 1951-52, Enid News & Eagle (Okla.), 1953-54, Ariz. Record, Globe, 1956-57; advt. copywriter Keefe Advt. Agy., Tulsa, 1955; tchr. Sand Springs Pub. Schs. (Okla.), 1957-64, Saguaro High Sch., Scottsdale, Ariz., 1966-67; pub. info. dir. Richardson Pub. Schs. (Tex.), 1967-85. Mem. Nat. Sch. Pub. Relations Assn. (assoc.), Richardson Edn. Assn., Assn. Tex. Profl. Educators, Richardson C. of C. (edn. com. 1977-85), Mortar Board, Alpha Kappa Delta (corr. sec.). Republican. Episcopalian. Club: Altrusa (Richardson). Office: Richardson Independent School Dist 400 S Greenville Ave Richardson TX 75081

WILLIAMS, VERONICA MYRES, psychiatric social worker; b. Shreveport, La., May 11, 1947; d. McEura and Margie Virginia (Reagan) Myres; B.A., La. Tech. U., Ruston, 1969; M.S.W., U. Mich., Ann Arbor, 1977; m. John L. Williams, Jr., Nov. 30, 1969; children—Nicole Leann, Jennifer Lyn, Erica Maria. Probation counselor Citizens Probation Authority, Flint, Mich., 1970-72; unit dir., therapist Services to Overcome Drug Abuse Among Teenagers, Flint, 1972-74; psychiat. therapist Psycho-Therapeutic Treatment Clin., P.C., Flint, 1974-77: psychiat. social worker Hurley Med. Center, Flint, 1977-79; field instr. U. Mich., Flint, 1978-79; psychiat. social worker Inst. Mental Health, Flint, 1979-81, Psychotherapeutic Treatment Clinic, 1981-83; clin. social worker Flint Bd. Edn., 1979-83, Caddo Parish Sch. Bd., Shreveport, 1983-85, Flint Bd. Edn., 1986—; psychiat. therapist Mott Children's Health Ctr., 1986—. Cert. social worker, Mich. Mem. Nat. Assn. Social Workers, Acad. Cert. Social Workers, Mich. Edn. Assn., NEA. Democrat. Baptist. Club: Internat. 700. Office: Flint Bd Edn Flint MI 48502

WILLIAMS, VICTORIA ANNE VILCHEZ, lawyer; b. Tampa, Fla., Aug. 10, 1955; d. Angel and Mary Ida (Guarisco) Vilchez; m. Charles August Williams, Mar. 18, 1979; 1 child, Matthew Stephen. B.A., Fla. State U., 1977; J.D., Mercer U., 1980. Bar: Fla. 1980. Trial atty. Office Pub. Defender, Miami, Fla., 1980-83; sole practice law, Miami, 1983-84, Lake Worth, Fla., 1984-85; ptnr. Williams & Williams, Lake Worth, 1985—; rep. Nat. Conf. on Women and Law, Atlanta, 1978. Vol. Cath. Home for Children, Miami, 1983-84; mem. Council of Cath. Women, Miami, 1983-84. Recipient cert. of achievement 8th Nat. Conf. Juvenile Justice, 1981; Mercer U. grantee, 1977. Mem. ABA, Fla. Bar, Fla. Assn. Women Lawyers (sec., newsletter editor Palm Beach County chpt. 1985-86), Lake Worth Bar Assn., Palm Beach County Bar Assn., Fla. State U. Alumni Assn., Delta Theta Phi. Democrat. Roman Catholic. Club: Zonta (bd. dirs. 1985-86). Office: 521 Lake Ave Suite 1 Lake Worth FL 33460

WILLIAMS, YVONNE LAVERNE, educational executive, lawyer; b. Washington, Jan. 7, 1938; d. Smallwood Edmund and Verna Lucille (Rapley) W. B.A., Barnard Coll., 1959; M.A., Boston U., 1961; J.D., Georgetown U., 1977. Bar: D.C. 1980. Fgn. service officer USIA, Washington and abroad, 1961-65; dir. women's Africa commn. African-Am. Inst., N.Y.C., 1966-68; assoc. prof. African studies Benedict Coll., Columbia, S.C., 1968-70; press sec. Hon. Walter Fauntroy, U.S. Congress, Washington, 1970-72; dir. African-Am. Scholars Council, Washington, 1972-73; assoc. firm Leva, Hawes, Symington, Martin, Washington, 1977-79; asst. v.p. Brimmer & Co., Washington, 1980-82; assoc. dir. fed. relations, legal counsel Tuskegee Inst., Washington, 1982-83, v.p. fed. and internat. relations, legal counsel, 1983—. Vol., mem. Operation Crossroads Africa, N.Y.C. and Washington, 1960—; mem. Mayor's Internat. Task Force, Washington, 1982-83. African Research and Studies Program fellow, Boston U., 1960; Barnard Coll. scholar, 1955-57. Mem. ABA, Nat. Bar Assn., Nat. Assn. Coll. and Univ. Attys., Nat. Assn. State Univ. and Land Grant Colls., Assn. Univ. Dirs. Internat. Agrl. Programs, Democrat. Club: Barnard-in-Washington. Office: Washington Office Tuskegee U 11 DuPont Circle NW Suite 490 Washington DC 20036

WILLIAMS-MADDOX, JANICE HELEN, nurse; b. Boston, Nov. 27, 1936; d. Arthur Hamilton Wade and Edith Josephine (Weekes) Williams; B.S. in Nursing, Boston U., 1957; M.A., Atlanta U. Sch. Edn., 1971; M.Community Health, Emory U., 1976; m. Larry Maddox, May 21, 1977 (dec.). Staff nurse Beth Israel Hosp., Boston, 1957-58, N.Y. Hosp.-Cornell U. Med. Center, N.Y.C., 1958-59; ward supr. Jewish Meml. Hosp., Boston, 1959-61; staff and pvt. duty nurse Mass. Gen. Hosp., Boston, 1961-63; public health nurse Boston Health Dept., 1963-64; intravenous nurse Hughes Spalding Hosp., Atlanta, 1964-66; public health nurse Fulton County (Ga.) Health Dept., 1966-69; sr. tchr. Atlanta Southside Comprehensive Health Center, 1970-73, acting dir. edn., 1973-74, asso. dir. clin. nursing, 1974-76; asso. dir. mental health planning project So. Region Edn. Bd., Atlanta, 1976-78; nursing cons. Dept. Health and Human Services, Atlanta, 1978-81; head nurse VA Med. Center, Atlanta, 1982-85; br. mgr. Am. Home Health Care of Ga., Inc., Jonesboro, 1985—; evening coordinator, instr. for innovative practical nursing program for health para-profl. Atlanta Area Tech Sch., 1971-81; mem. admissions com. M.Community Health program Emory U. Sch. Medicine, 1979—. Mem. coms., including Women's Day com. Central United Meth. Ch., Atlanta. Recipient spl. recognition Am. Cancer Soc., 1975. Mem. Am. Assn. Health Planners, Nat. Assn. Female Execs. Office: Am Home Health Care Ga Inc 102 W Mimosa Dr Jonesboro GA 30236

WILLIAMSON, CONNIE MCDANIEL, home economist; b. Kent, Iowa, Dec. 15, 1943; d. John Nelson and Marjorie Gwendolen (Chandler) Davenport; B.S., Iowa State U., 1965, M.S., 1970; postgrad. U. Tenn., Knoxville, Colo. State U.; m. Gary L. McDaniel, July 31, 1966; 1 dau., Kerstin Ann; m. B.D. Butler, Sept. 15, 1985. Tchr. home econs., Iowa, Kans. and Tenn., 1965-78; extension agt. Colo. State U., Ft. Collins, 1978—. Mem. NEA, Nat. Assn. Extension Home Economists, Nat. Home Econs. Assn., Nat. Assn. Female Execs., Bus. and Profl. Women. Republican. Methodist. Clubs: Atlantic Golf and Country, Ft. Morgan Country, Order Eastern Star. Author curriculum guides, textbook and instrn. manuals, articles. Home: 194 27th Rd Grand Junction CO 81503 Office: 1001 N 2d St Friendship Hall Montrose CO 81401

WILLIAMSON, DONNA CONSTANCE, health care products company executive; b. Schenectady, June 6, 1952; d. Albert Carl and Aurelia Alexandra Erickson; m. Scott Howard Williamson, July 24, 1976; 1 child, Erik. B.S., Brown U., 1974; M.S., MIT, 1976. Dir. domestic planning Travenol Labs., Deerfield, Ill., 1980-82, dir. strategic planning, 1982-83; v.p. Baxter Travenol Labs., Inc., Deerfield, 1983-85, 85—; pres., chief exec. officer Omnis Surg., Northbrook, Ill., 1985. Editorial bd. Strategic Planning Mgmt., 1982—. Active Econ. Club, Chgo., 1982; chief crusader Crusade of Mercy, Chgo., 1983; regional gov. MIT Sloan Club, Chgo., 1984; bd. dirs. ARC, Chgo., 1984—. Recipient Leadership award YWCA, Chgo., 1980. Mem. Midwest Planning Assn. (adv. bd., speaker 1985), N.Am. Soc. Corp. Planning/The Planning Forum. Avocations: cross-country skiing; sailing; bicycling; tennis. Office: Baxter Travenol Labs 1 Baxter Pkwy Deerfield IL 60015

WILLIAMSON, DOROTHY JEAN, home economist, educator; b. Elmhurst, Ill., Jan. 11, 1939; d. Cecil M. and Mamie W. W. B.S., Western Mich. U., 1961; M.A., Mich. State U., 1968. Tchr. home econs. Grand Rapids Pub. Schs., Mich., 1961—; mem. adv. council Future Homemakers, East Lansing, Mich., 1972-74, 84-85, Simplicity Pattern Co., Niles, Mich., 1980-82; mem. adv. com. Instructional Devel. Edn. Assn., 1984-85. Author school curriculum. Recipient Cert. of Appreciation, U.S. 2d ROTC Region, 1982. Mem. Grand Rapids Edn. Assn., Mich. Edn. Assn., Grand Rapids Home Econs. Assn. (pres. 1981-83), Am. Home Econs. Assn., Mich. Educators Christian Fellowship (trustee 1985—). Avocations: hiking; traveling; reading; sewing.

WILLIAMSON, EVANGELINE FLOANN, vocational rehabilitation corporate executive; b. Ft. Wayne, Ind., Nov. 29, 1934; d. David Samuel and Anna Florence (Baker) McNelly; m. Clark Murray Williamson, Dec. 20, 1957 (div. 1964); 1 child, Dawn Valerie (dec.). B.A. with distinction, Transylvania U., 1956. Asst. dir. publs. ABA, Chgo., 1958-66; pres., owner Herringshaw-Smith, Inc., Chgo., 1966-77; internal cons. Monarch Printing Corp., Chgo., 1978-80, Callaghan & Co., Wilmette, Ill., 1980-82; v.p., co-owner Career Evaluation Systems, Inc., Niles, Ill., 1983—. Author: From Typist to Typesetter, 1978. Editor: Transylvania: Tutor to the West, 1975; editor, designer: Silversmiths, Jewelers, Clock and Watchmakers of Kentucky, 1785-1900, 1980. Bd. dirs., treas. West Central Assn., Chgo., 1976-77; bd. dirs. Martha Washington Hosp., Chgo., 1975-76, Mary Thompson Hosp., Chgo., 1977. Mem. Am. Voc. Assn., Nat. Rehab. Assn., Niles C. of C., Nat. Assn. Watch and Clock Collectors. Republican. Mem. Christian Ch. Avocations: antique clock and furniture collecting; writing. Office: Career Evaluation Systems Inc 7788 Milwaukee Ave Niles IL 60648

WILLIAMSON, JAYNE MICHELE, computer corporation executive; b. Chgo., Apr. 25, 1959; d. Prince Jackson and Jessye Mae (Nelson) Henderson; m. David W. Williamson, Dec. 14, 1984. Student pub. schs. Sec., IRS Dist. Counsel, Chgo., 1977-78; sec., office mgr. Real Estate Research, Chgo., Washington, 1978-83; adminstr. Price Waterhouse Co., Washington, 1983-84, IBM Corp., Bethesda, Md., 1985—; info. processing cons. For Your Info., Inc., Gaithersburg, Md., 1982—. Mem. Nat. Assn. Female Execs. Democrat. Roman Catholic. Avocations: creative writing; aerobics; reading. Home: 911 Clopper Rd Gaithersburg MD 20878 Office: IBM Corp 10401 Fernwood Rd Bethesda MD 20817

WILLIAMSON, KATHLEEN MARIE, accounting firm executive; b. Tarentum, Pa., Mar. 25, 1949; d. Stanley and Marguerite Bell (Gray) Nazaruk; m. Vern G. Williamson, Aug. 28, 1970; 1 child, Haze L. Student U. Pitts., 1967-70. Sec., various firms, Pitts., 1970-79; exec. asst. Sheppard, Anderson & Co., McKeesport, Pa., 1979-85; ptnr. Acctg. By Computer, McKeesport, 1985—. Bd. dirs., treas. Womansplace, McKeesport, 1979-81. Mem. Nat. Assn. Female Execs. Office: Acctg By Computer 505 Exec Bldg McKeesport PA 15132

WILLIAMSON, MIRIAM BEDINGER, medical librarian; b. Asheville, N.C., Nov. 18, 1919; d. Robert Dabney and Mary Julia (Smith) Bedinger; m. Robert Lewis Williamson, June 9, 1944 (div. June 1969); children—Robert Lewis Jr., John Bedinger, Ellen Richmond, Thomas Reid. B.A., Agnes Scott Coll., 1941; M. Christian Edn., Presbyn. Sch. Christian Edn., 1943; postgrad. U. Tenn., 1969. Ch. social worker, kindergarten tchr. N.E. Community Ctr., Italian Presbyn. Mission, Kansas City, Mo., 1943-44; med. librarian Blount Meml. Hosp., Maryville, Tenn., 1972—; tchr. vocat. edn. programs, adult reading program Alcoa, Blount County, Maryville sch. systems. Mem. Blount County unit Bread for the World; vol. worker Contact Teleministries of Blount County. Grantee Library Medicine, HEW, 1973, HHS, 1981, Blount County unit Am. Cancer Soc., 1982; recipient Outstanding Service award Vocat. Edn. Dept., 1983, 85; Blount Meml. Hosp. Aux. grantee, 1986. Mem. Med. Library Assn., Tenn. Hosp. Assn., Tenn. Health Sci. Library Assn., Knoxville Area Health Sci. Library Consortium. Democrat. Presbyterian. Home: 103 Hopi Dr Maryville TN 37801 Office: 907 Smoky Mountain Hwy Maryville TN 37801

WILLIAMSON, SHERRI REDIES, county official; b. Charlotte, N.C., Oct. 3, 1953; d. Robert F. and Sara F. (Riley) R.; m. Joe Linwood Williamson, Aug. 21, 1976. B.S. in Geography, East Carolina U., 1976. Trainee, Mecklenburg County, Charlotte, 1978-80; zoning insp. Charlotte-Mecklenburg County, Charlotte, 1980—. Vice-pres. local Homeowners Assn., 1981-84. Mem. N.C. Assn. Zoning Ofcls. (charter). Democrat. Roman Catholic. Club: Women's. Avocations: gourmet cooking; aerobics; gardening; camping; crafts. Office: PO Box 31097 Charlotte NC 28231

WILLINGHAM, GLORIA JEAN, nurse educator, administrator; b. Little Rock, Mar. 5, 1945; d. Ellis and Mary Lee Nelson; student So. Ill. U., 1963-66; R.N., St. Vincent Infirmary Sch. Nursing, Little Rock, 1970; B.S.N., SUNY, Albany, 1981; M. Nursing Sci., U. Ark., 1984; children—Gina Michele, Michael Damon, Christopher. Clin. nurse Brooke Army Med. Center, Ft. Sam Houston, Tex., 1970, 72-75; night charge nurse Albany (N.Y.) VA Hosp., 1971-72; staff nurse VA Med. Center, Little Rock, 1970, 75-78, clin. instr., 1978-83; assoc. chief trainee VA Hosp., Little Rock, 1983-84; assoc. chief nursing service for edn., VA Hosp., Shreveport, La., 1984—. chief instr. Med. Corpsmen Sch., Ark. Army N.G., now commd. maj. Dir. Christian edn. Miles Chapel, Little Rock, 1975-77; bd. dirs. Franklin Sch. PTA, chmn. City Beautiful, 1979-80; bd. dirs. Terry Sch. PTA, Little Rock, parliamentarian, adv. com., 1978-80, dist. rep., 1979-80; co-chmn. Christmas Bur., United Way Pulaski County, 1981; mem. research and planning com., 1981-82; v.p. alumni trustee bd.-regents external degrees SUNY, Albany, 1982-83, pres., 1983-85; mem. task force on regents external degrees and proficiency testing New York State Edn. Dept., 1983-84. Supt. Sunday sch. Lane Chapel C.M.E. Ch., Shreveport. Recipient Public Service award Miles Chapel Meth. Ch., 1976; suggestion awards VA, Little Rock, 1977; outstanding future nurse leadership award U Ark. Med. Sci. campus, 1984; R.N., Ark. Mem. Assn. Female Execs., Am. Soc. Profl. and Exec. Women, Am. Assn. Critical Care Nurses, Nat. Guard Officers Assn., Ark. Young Adminstr.'s Forum, Internat. Platform Assn. Methodist. Home: 9000 Rosedown Pl Shreveport LA 71118 Office: 510 E Stoner Ave Shreveport LA 71130

WILLINGHAM, JEANNE MAGGART, dancing instructor, ballet company executive; b. Fresno, Calif., May 8, 1923; d. Harold F. and Gladys (Ellis) Maggart. Student Tex. Woman's U., 1942; student profl. dancing schs. Dance tchr. Beaux Arts Dance Studio, Pampa, Tex., 1948—; artistic dir. Pampa Civic Ballet, 1972—. Mem. Tex. Arts and Humanities, Tex. Arts Alliance, Pampa C. of C. (fine arts com.), Pampa Fine Arts Assn. Home: 816 N Nelson St Pampa TX 79065 Office: Beaux Arts Dance Studio 315 N Nelson St Pampa TX 79065

WILLINGHAM, MARY MAXINE, fashion retailer; b. Childress, Tex., Sept. 12, 1928; d. Charles Bryan and Mary (Bohannon) McCollum; m. Welborn Kiefer Willingham, Aug. 14, 1950; children—Sharon, Douglas, Sheila. B.A., Tex. Tech U., 1949. Interviewer Univ. Placement Service, Tex. Tech U., Lubbock, 1964-69; owner, mgr., buyer Maxine's Accent, Lubbock, 1969—; speaker in field. Leader Campfire Girls, Lubbock, 1964-65; sec. Community Theatre, Lubbock, 1962-64. Named Outstanding Mcht., Fashion Retailor mag., 1971, Outstanding Retailer; recipient Golden Sun award Dallas Market, May 1985. Mem. Lubbock Symphony Guild, Ranch and Heritage Ctr. Club: Faculty Women's. Office: 10 Briercroft Ctr Lubbock TX 79412

WILLIS, DIANNA MARIE, physician; b. Ada, Okla., June 30, 1948; d. Wade Alexander and Ennie (Lewis) Watts; m. Donald Ray Willis, Dec. 14, 1968; 1 child, Erane Ennie. Cert. med. technologist, St. John's Hosp., 1970; B.S. in Med. Tech., East Central U., 1970, cert. specialist in hematology, 1975; D.O., Okla. Coll. Osteo. Medicine and Surgery, 1983. Intern Okla. Osteo. Hosp., Tulsa, 1983-84; staff physician Hillcrest Hosp., Tulsa, 1984—, Okla. Osteo. Hosp., Tulsa, 1984—, Okemah Community Hosp., 1985; med. Sapulda Indian Health Ctr., Okla., 1985—; lectr. in field. Lectr. Baptist Tng. Union, Tulsa, 1984. State of Okla. Bd. Regents grantee, 1980. Mem. Am. Osteo. Assn., Okla. Osteo. Assn., Tulsa Dist. Osteo. Soc., Am. Acad. Gen. Practitioners, Delta Omega. Democrat. Baptist. Club: 700 (Charleston, S.C.). Avocations: cross-stitching; quilting; camping; tennis. Office: 1125 E Cleveland Sapulpa OK 74066

WILLIS, ELLEN DEBORA, psychiatric nurse; b. Carbondale, Pa., Feb. 21, 1941; d. Niles John and Ruth Elizabeth (Farrell) Kiefer; R.N., Kings County Hosp. Sch. Nursing, 1960; postgrad. St. Joseph's Coll.; M.S., U. Scranton; m. Bernard J. Willis; 1 son, Edward John Enslin III. Staff nurse Kings County Hosp. Center, Bklyn., 1960-61; research asst. dept. cardiology Downstate Med. Center, U. Bklyn., 1961-63; pvt. duty nurse, N.Y.C., 1963; operating room nurse Scranton (Pa.) Gen. Hosp., 1963-64; asst. operating room supr. Carbondale (Pa.) Gen. Hosp., 1964-65, staff nurse, 1969-70; head nurse St. Joseph's Hosp., Carbondale, 1965-66, Horton Hosp., Middletown, N.Y., 1966-67, Middletown State Hosp., 1967-68; nursing supr. Farview State Hosp., Waymart, Pa., 1970-74, patient care coordinator, 1974-84, dir. nursing edn., 1984—. Commr., Econ. and Gen. Welfare Commn.; trustee Pa. Nurses Assn. Health and Welfare Fund. Cert. psychiat. mental health nurse. Mem. Am. Nurses Assn., Pa. Nurses Assn. (chmn. occupational unit state employees), Pa. Assn. Patient-Care Coordinators, Nat. Assn. Forensic Psychiat. Nurses, Am. Correctional Assn., Sigma Theta Tau. Home: 26 Old Gravity Rd Carbondale PA 18407 Office: Farview State Hospital PO Box 128 Waymart PA 18472

WILLIS, GAYLA SUE, administrative services company executive; b. Paris, Tex., Jan. 23, 1950; d. Marvin Dean and Eva Mae (Flick) Hughan; m. Ronald Eugene D'Olive, Nov. 8, 1975 (div. Oct. 1980); 1 child, Dusty Hugh; m. Gerald Wayne Willis, Apr. 1, 1983; 1 child, Rowdy Wayne. Student Southwestern Bus. U., 1968-69, Sam Houston State U., 1972-73. Cert. peace officer, Tex. Exec. sec. Harris County Sheriff's Dept., Houston, 1973-80; dep. sheriff Montgomery County Sheriff's Dept., Conroe, Tex., 1981-83; supr. office services and corp. purchasing, security dir., exec. sec. to pres. Lawrence Adminstrv. Services, Inc., Conroe, Tex., 1983—. Mem. Montgomery County Econ. Devel. Fair and Agr. Com. Mem. Am. Soc. for Indsl. Security, Sheriff's Assn. of Tex., Nat. Assn. Female Execs., Ladies Aux. to VFW. Republican. Baptist. Avocations: horses; ceramics; needlepoint; bowling; softball. Home: 403 Nursery Ln Willis TX 77378 Office: Lawrence Adminstrv Services Inc PO Box 2866 Conroe TX 77305

WILLIS, JANE MARLOW, journalist; b. Brandenburg, Ky., Mar. 8, 1942; d. James Mercer and Thelma (Marlow) W.; B.A., So. Meth. U., 1964; postgrad. (Mark Ethridge fellow), U. N.C., 1966, fire prevention and control Eastern Ky. U., 1976-78; mem. staff Meade County Messenger, Brandenburg, 1964—, editor, 1966—, pub., 1978-83. Former den mother local Cub Scouts; mem. drive com. Patton Museum Fund, 1965; mem. local com. Ky. Bicentennial, 1973; patron Pioneer Playhouse, Danville, Ky., 1972; mem. Brandenburg Vol. Fire Dept., 1975—, chmn. firemen's ball, 1977, chmn. Brandenburg Fire Sch., 1977, cert. fire fighter; group coordinator Brandenburg Unity Festival, 1975-76; participant 1977 inaugural parade, 1977 part-time instr. fire sci. Ky. Dept. Vocat. Edn. Mem. Ky., Western Ky. (pres. 1971) press assns., Nat. Newspaper Assn., Internat. oc. Fire Service Instrs. (charter mem. Ky. chpt., Dixie Firemen's Assn. (sch. com.), DAR, Women of Moose, Mensa, Sigma Delta Chi. Democrat. Methodist. Clubs: Falls City Corvette, Hillcrest Country. Editor: Since April Third, 1975; Meade County Messenger Happy Holidays Cookbook, 1975; Summertime and The Cookin' Is Easy, 1977. Co-author slide presentation, Does A Water Curtain Really Work?. Home: 321 Main St Brandenburg KY 40108 Office: Box 612 Brandenburg KY 40108

WILLIS, KATHLEEN B(ERYL), television research executive; b. Coventry, Eng., May 23, 1938; came to U.S., 1963; d. Percivil Edward and Ivy Plover (Parnel) W. Student in chemistry and physics U. Coventry, 1958-60. Market researcher W. R. Grace & Co., N.Y.C., 1963-65; media analyst J. Walter Thompson, N.Y.C., 1965-74; v.p. media analysis Grey Advt. Inc., N.Y.C., 1975-85; v.p., dir. mktg. AGB TV Research, Inc., 1985—; mem. radio/TV Research Council, N.Y.C., 1979—; Author reports: Media Decisions, 1970; Working Women, 1972; Singles, 1981; Cable Television, 1983; People Meter vs Diaries, 1985, others. Office: AGB TV Research Inc 555 Madison Ave New York NY 10021

WILLIS, LINDA ANTIONETTE, lawyer; b. May 12, 1954; d. James Robert and Lenolia Ione (Gladden) Willis; m. Luther Eugene Cobbs, June 16, 1972 (div. 1978); children—Luther Eugene, James Robert Willis-Cobbs; m. 2d Richard Allan Chambers, May 16, 1981. Student Wellesley Coll., 1971-72; B.A., DePaul U., Chgo., 1978, J.D., 1981. Bar: Ohio. Legal intern, Chgo., 1980-81; staff atty. Legal Aid Soc., Cleve., 1981-82; asst. pub. defender Cuyahoga County Pub. Defender's Office, Cleve., 1982—. Mem. legal redress com. NAACP, 1984; mem. exec. com. Cub Scouts, Warrensville Heights, Ohio, 1982; bd. dirs. Black Women Polit. Action Com., Cleve. Mem. Nat. Assn. Criminal Def. Lawyers, ABA, Norman S. Minor Bar Assn., Black Women Lawyers Assn., Pi Gamma Mu. Democrat. Baptist. Home: 3537 Raymont Blvd University Heights OH 44118 Office: Cuyahoga County Pub Defender's Office 1276 W 3d St Cleveland OH

WILLIS, LINDA MARIE, educational administrator; b. St. Louis, Oct. 26, 1950; d. Herman and Fannie Mae (Bell) Willis; m. Leslie LeRoy Willis, Apr. 12, 1973; 1 child, Lenci Yorel. B.S. in Edn., U. Mo., 1972. Cert. tchr., Mo. Circulation mgr. Scientist Inst., St. Louis, 1974-77; supr. academics St. Louis Job Corps, 1980-83, mgr. academics, 1983-84; faculty coordinator Watterson Coll., 1984—. Mem. Neighborhood Watch Assn., Berkeley, Mo.; contbr. City of Atlanta Children's Fund, 1981. Recipient commendation St. Louis Job Corps, 1983; cert. of recognition Mayor Maynard Jackson, Atlanta, 1981; named Staff Mem. of Month, St. Louis Job Corps, 1982. Mem. Nat. Assn. Female Execs. Democrat. Baptist. Home: 6701 Blackwalnut Ct Saint Louis MO 63134 Office: Watterson Skill Ctr 1408 N Kingshighway Blvd Saint Louis MO 63113

WILLIS, LOTTIE OPHELIA, educator; b. Caswell County, N.C., July 6, 1949; d. Elmer and Minnie (Mitchell) Jeffers; m. Marvin Gene Willis, June 30, 1973. B.S. in Bus. Edn., Livingstone Coll., Salisbury, N.C., 1971; M.S. in Intermediate Edn., N.C. A & T State U., 1976, M.S. in Edn. Adminstrn., 1985. Tchr., Caswell County Schs., N.C., 1971—. Mem. Big Bros. Big Sister, Yanceyville, 1983—. Mem. NEA, N.C. Assn. Educators, N.C. Council Tchrs. Math., Caswell County Assn. Educators (sec. 1982-83, v.p. 1983-84, pres. 1985-86), N.C. A&T U. Alumni, Alpha Kappa Alpha. Baptist. Club: Silhouette. Lodge: Order Eastern Star. Avocations: ceramics; reading; collecting antiques; tennis; bowling; travel; cooking. Home: PO Box 255 Yanceyville NC 27379

WILLIS, LOUISE MCKINNEY, petroleum company executive; b. Cooper, Tex., Nov. 12, 1924; d. Charles Martin and Birdie Floy (Griffin) McKinney; m. Glenn Harry Willis, May 7, 1948; children—Stephen Eric, Susan Renee, Mary Lynn, Glenda Ann. Student U. Okla., 1946-47. Instrument repair technician Tinker Field AFB, Okla., 1943-46; transit check clk. Fed. Res. Bank, Oklahoma City, 1948-50; sec. Southwestern Power Co., Tulsa, 1950-51, U.S. Govt. Agy., New Orleans, 1951-53; dist. mgr. World Book Encyclopedia, Dallas, 1972-78; v.p. Dor-Texan Petroleum, Dallas, 1980—. Mem. Dallas Opera Guild, 1984-85; pres. Dallas PTA, 1965-66, hon. life mem., 1975—; pres. St. Andrews Study Club, Dallas, 1968-69; chmn. Cotillion Park Bd., Dallas,

1964-66. Mem. Dallas C. of C. Baptist. Clubs: Petroleum, Dallas Athletic. Lodge: Order of Rainbow Girls (chmn. bd. dirs. 1973-76). Office: Dor-Texan Petroleum Inc 11081 Mandalay Dr Dallas TX 75228

WILLIS, SUSAN EADIE, nurse, educator; b. Balt., Nov. 17, 1949; d. Donald and Ruth Jacqueline (Hill) Eadie; m. David Larry Willis, July 25, 1970; children—Christopher Michael, Diana Lynn, Patrick Ryan, Cara Michele. A.A., St. Petersburg Jr. Coll., 1969, A.S. in Nursing, 1972; B.A. in Psychology, St. Leo Coll., Fla., 1979; B.S. in Nursing, U. South Fla., Tampa, 1981, now postgrad. R.N., cert. vocat. tchr., Fla. Staff nurse Morton Plant Hosp., Clearwater, Fla., 1972-73, 80-82, intravenous therapist, 1973-76; office nurse Dr. William Davis, Clearwater, 1976-80; instr. Pinellas Vocat. Tech. Inst., Clearwater, 1982—; also ARC nurse. Asst. author nursing modules for practical nurse program. Mem. Pinellas County PTA. Mem. Pinellas County Tchrs. Assn., Pinellas Assn. Vocat. Educators, Am. Nurses Assn., Fla. Nurses Assn., Assn. Operating Room Nurses. Republican. Home: 9 Ibis Circle Safety Harbor FL 33572

WILLISCROFT, BEVERLY RUTH, lawyer; b. Conrad, Mont., Feb. 24, 1945; d. Paul A. and Gladys L. (Buck) Williscroft; m. Kent J. Barcus, Oct. 1984. B.A. in Music, So. Calif. Coll., 1967; J.D., John F. Kennedy U., 1977. Elem. tchr., Sunnyvale, Calif., 1968-72; legal sec., legal asst. various law firms, Bay Area, 1972-77; admitted to Calif. bar, 1977; asso. firm Neil D. Reid, Inc., San Francisco, 1977-79; individual practice law, Concord, Calif., 1979—; exam. grader Calif. Bar, 1979—; real estate broker, 1980—; tchr. real estate King Coll., Concord, 1979-80; lectr. in field; judge pro-tem Mcpl. Ct., 1981—. Bd dirs. Contra Costa Musical Theatre, Inc., 1978-82, v.p. adminstrn., 1980-81, v.p. prodn., 1981-82; mem. community devel. adv. com. City of Concord, 1981-83, vice chmn., 1982-83, mem. status of women com., 1980-81, mem. redevel. adv. com., 1984—; co-chmn. Longshore Morning Forum, Concord, 1980-84; mem. exec. bd. Mt. Diablo council Boy Scouts Am., 1981-85. Named Woman of Achievement, Todos Santos Bus. and Profl. Women, Clayton, Calif., 1980, 81; award of merit, Bus. and Profl. Women, Bay Valley Dist., 1981. Mem. Concord C. of C. (dir., chmn. govt. affairs com. 1981-83, v.p. 1985-87), Calif. Women Lawyers, Calif. State Bar, Contra Costa County Bar Assn., Contra Costa Barristers. Clubs: Todos Santos Bus. and Profl. Women (co-founder, pres. 1983-84, pub. relations chmn. 1982-83), Soroptimists (fin. sec. 1980-81). Office: 2150-A East St Concord CA 94520

WILLMAN, VICTORIA LYNN (VICKI), bus company executive, tympanist; b. Helena, Mont., Apr. 21, 1959; d. Glenn Robert and Pearl Elaine (Martin) W. B.S. in Music, Mary Coll., Bismarck, N.D., 1981. Tchr. music Hatton Pub. Schs., N.D., 1981-82; pres., mgr. Bus. Services, Inc., Bismarck, 1982—; prin. tympanist Bismarck-Mandan Symphony Orch., Bismarck, 1982—; free-lance percussionist. Vol. coordinator, announcer and producer Saturday Classics program Prairie Pub. Radio, Bismarck, 1985—; mem. adv. com. Community Music Ctr., Bismarck, 1984—. Mem. Nat. Assn. Bus. Commn. Agts. (regional rep. 1984-85), Percussive Arts Soc. Inc., Gt. Plains Jazz Soc., Am. Fedn. Musicians (Local 229). Lutheran. Avocations: travel; jogging; jazz and classical music. Office: Bus Services Inc PO Box 638 1237 W Divide Ave Bismarck ND 58502

WILLNER, GERALDINE LISWOOD, association administrator; b. Bklyn., Sept. 16, 1923; d. Jacques and Rebecca (Goldman) Liswood; m. Sydney G. Willner, Sept. 8, 1943 (div. 1974); children—Elizabeth, David, Robert, Donald. B.S., NYU, 1951; postgrad. Antioch Coll., 1940-43. Cert. life, disability casulty ins. agt. Dep., Ind. Order of Foresters, Long Beach, Calif., 1976—; ct. dep. Ct. Palas Verdes, 1980-84, asst. mgr., Long Beach, 1982-83. Author video tape: The Gerry Willner Story, 1980, 81. Named Master Forester, annually, 1982—, Star Dep., Calif., Hawaii, 1980, Grand Forester, 1983, 84, 85, other honors. Democrat. Jewish. Home: 1030 Burlinghall Dr Long Beach CA 90807 Office: Ind Order of Foresters 4425 Atlantic #A25 Long Beach CA 90807

WILLOUGHBY, AVALEE, physical education and recreation educator; b. McComb, Miss.; d. John Cletus and Vertner (Tynes) Willoughby; B.S., La. State U., 1942; M.A., U. Fla., 1956; Ed.D., U. Ala., 1972. Tchr. phys. edn. Southwest Miss. Jr. Coll., Summit, 1944-51; phys. dir. YMCA, Birmingham, Ala., 1952-55; instr. phys. edn. U. Md., College Park, 1956-58; prof., chmn. div. health, phys. edn. and recreation Samford U., Birmingham, 1958—; also rehab. work with handicapped. Extensive work Aquatics, Ala. Spl. Olympics, ARC; mem. Gov.'s Commn. on Phys. Fitness. Named to Sports Hall Fame, S.W. Miss. Jr. Coll., 1972. Fellow AAHPER; mem. NEA, Ala. Assn. Health, Phys. Edn. and Recreation (pres. 1972-74, Honor award 1970, coordinator Ala. Sports Festival), Phi Kappa Phi, Delta Kappa Gamma; Kappa Delta Pi. Methodist. Club: Soroptomists. Home: 1841 Burning Tree Circle Birmingham AL 35226

WILLS, SUSAN ELISABETH, lawyer; b. Chgo., Mar. 29, 1948; d. Joseph A. and Selma E. (Seidel) Reddy; m. Frank E. Wills, Aug. 15, 1972; children—Susan Elisabeth, Joseph Corbin, D'Arcy Bowen. Premiere degree, U. Rouen (France), 1969; B.A., U. Miami, 1972, J.D. cum laude, 1978; LL.M. in Internat. and Comparative Law, Georgetown U., 1983. Bar: Fla. 1978. Asst. gen. counsel, asst. corp. sec. Air Fla., Inc., Miami, 1979-81; assoc. Galland, Kharasch, Morse & Garfinkle Washington, 1983-85. Contbr. articles to profl. jours. Vis. com. univ. libraries U. Miami Bd. Trustees, 1982; program asst. McLean Youth Track, 1983-84; team mother McLean Youth Soccer, 1983. Recipient Thomas Bradbury Chetwood S.J. prize Georgetown U. Law Ctr., 1983, 3 Am. Jurisprudence Book awards Lawyers Coop. Pub. Co., 1975, 76. Mem. ABA, Fla. Bar Assn., Phi Kappa Phi, Pi Delta Phi. Republican. Home: 1447 Oakview Dr McLean VA 22101

WILLSIE, BERTHA SPOONER, educator; b. Ashville, N.Y., May 15, 1921; d. Frank W. and Jeannette C. (Bergstresser) Spooner; B.A., Coll. Wooster, 1942; A.M., Cornell U., 1947; postgrad. Western Res. U., 1943, U. Buffalo, 1944-45, U. Havana, 1948, St. Bonaventure U., 1964-67; m. Robert L. Willsie, June 30, 1951; 1 dau., Anita Ruth. High sch. English and lang. tchr. Bemus Point High Sch., 1942-47; instr. French and Spanish, Alfred U. Extension, 1948-52; tchr. French, Spanish, Latin Falconer High Sch., 1952-56; tchr. Panama Central Sch., 1958-64; head fgn. lang. dept. Jamestown (N.Y.) Public Schs., 1964-76; instr. Spanish Chautauqua (N.Y.) Instn., 1976—. Mem. Bd. Edn., Chautauqua Central Sch., 1970-77; mem. Marvin Community House. Recipient Scholarships, Coll. Wooster, 1938-42, Cornell U., 1946-47. Mem. N.Y. State Fgn. Lang. Educators Council, Internat. Order King's Daus. and Sons, Chautauqua County Hist. Soc., Fenton Hist. Soc., DAR (chmn. com. on schs.), Phi Beta Kappa, Phi Sigma Iota, Delta Kappa Gamma. Methodist. Club: Eastern Star (matron). Home: Box 155 Stow NY 14785

WILLSON, MARION ELAINE, nursing instructor; b. Whitaker, Pa., May 20, 1939; d. Marion M. and Anna M. (Rehburg) Stuart; m. Donald M. Willson, May 19, 1961; children—Clinton, Ross. B.S.N., Slippery Rock U., 1978; M. Edn., Westminster Coll., 1983. Staff nurse Children's Hosp., Pitts., 1960-63, 66-67, Columbia Hosp., Pitts., 1969; office nurse Drs. Shaffer & Mansell, M.D.s, New Wilmington, Pa., 1972-74, Dr. Carlos Flores, New Wilmington, 1979-80; project coordinator Westinghouse Health Systems, Balt., 1979; nursing instr. Saint Francis Hosp., New Castle, Pa., 1980—; faculty MSHA-HEN State Bd. Rev., Youngstown, Ohio, 1982-86. Active Am. Heart Assn., Am. Cancer Soc., New Wilmington Presbyn. Ch. Recipient Vol. of Yr. award Midwest Pa. Heart Assn., 1979. Mem. Nat. League Nursing. Republican. Home: 445 W Neshannock Ave New Wilmington PA 16142

WILMER, MARY CHARLES, artist; b. Atlanta, Aug. 25, 1930; d. William Knox and Harriott Creighton (Thomas) Fitzpatrick; student Wellesley Coll., 1948-50; A.B., Agnes-Scott Coll., 1970; B.F.A., Coll. of Art, 1974; m. John Grant Wilmer, Dec. 28, 1950; children—John Grant, Knox Randolph, Charles Inman, Mary Catherine; m. 2d, Olin Grigsby Shivers, May 18, 1982. One-woman shows: Image South Gallery, 1974, Aronson Gallery, 1977, 79, Heath Gallery, 1982, Coach House Gallery, 1983; exhibited in group show: Colony Sq., 1975; portrait painter, 1974—. Bd. dirs. Hillside Cottages, 1963-65, Atlanta Child Services, 1965-68, Atlanta Coll. Art, 1965—, Atlanta Puppetry Arts, 1982—; co-chmn. Ga. Commn. Nat. Mus. of Women in the Arts, 1985—. Episcopalian. Club: Piedmont Driving. Address: 1 Vernon Rd Atlanta GA 30305

WILMORE, MARIE MCCLURG, government official; b. Tremont, Ohio, Jan. 27, 1940; d. Charles McClurg and Elsie Louisa (Ridder) McClurg Pearis; m. Jon Frederick Mattfeld, Nov. 30, 1957 (div. 1965); 1 son, Jon Frederick; m. Dhalmas Otto Wilmore, May 29, 1969 (dec. 1982); 1 dau., Laura Kathleen. Student No. Va. Community Coll., 1971-75. Clk. stenographer U.S. Air Force, Wright Patterson AFB, Ohio, 1957-62, sec.-stenographer, 1967-69, sec.-stenographer, Washington, configuration mgmt. specialist, 1970-72; with Dept. Navy, Washington, mgmt. analyst, 1974-82, dep. OEO officer, 1976-77, reports control analyst Naval Air Systems Command, 1977-82, staff asst. to dep. asst. Sec. Navy for res. affairs, 1981-82, petty officer USNR, 1979—; pres. Dhalmar Arabian Farm, Spotsylvania, Va., 1976—. Recipient Zero Defects awards, 1960, 63, 67; Sustained Superior Performance award Dept. Air Force, 1966, Dept. Navy, 1985; Air Force Unit Excellence award, 1969. Mem. Federally Employed Women, Va. Arabian Horse Assn., Eastern Amateur Arabian Horse Assn. Baptist. Office: Dept Navy Sea System Command (SEA62Y33G) Washington DC 20362

WILMOUTH, VICTORIA PRYTULAK, educator; b. Denver, Nov. 10, 1954; d. Donald and Shirley Ann (English) Prytulak; m. Robert Ellis Wilmouth, Jr., May 12, 1979; 1 child, Daniel Ellis. B.S., Old Dominion U., 1977, M.Ed. in Ednl. Adminstrn. and Supervision, 1986. Tchr. 7th grade Virginia Beach City Schs., Va., 1977-78, tchr. 5th grade, 1978-83, tchr. 6th grade, 1983—, grade chmn. White Oaks Elem. Sch., 1978-81, Woodstock Elem. Sch., 1985—. Participant Nat. Republican Com., 1982—. Mem. NEA, Virginia Edn. Assn., Virginia Beach Edn. Assn., Alpha Xi Delta (historian 1984-85). Episcopalian. Avocations: fishing; cooking; gardening. Home: 512 Bamboo Ln Virginia Beach VA 23452 Office: Woodstock Elem Sch 6016 Providence Rd Virginia Beach VA 23464

WILMS, NANCY ANDERSON, dermatologist; b. Battle Creek, Mich., July 19, 1950; d. Harold E. and Mary V. Anderson; m. Dale John Wilms, Sept. 5, 1976. B.A. cum laude, Andrews U., 1972; M.D., Loma Linda U., 1976. Diplomate: Am. Bd. Dermatology, 1982. Intern, Loma Linda U. (Calif.), 1976-77, resident in internal medicine, 1977-78; family practice staff Kaiser Permanente, San Bernardino, Calif., 1978; resident in dermatology Henry Ford Hosp., Detroit, 1978-81, staff, 1981-82; asst. prof. dermatology, pediatrics, pathology Loma Linda U., 1982—; cons. Jerry L. Pettis VA Hosp., Loma Linda, San Bernardino County Hosp., 1982—. Mem. AMA, Calif., Med. Assn., San Bernardino Med. Soc. Republican. Contbr. articles to profl. jours. Office: Faculty Medical Offices 11370 Anderson St Suite 2100 Loma Linda CA 92354

WILPON, BONNIE VIVIAN, research company executive; b. Coral Gables, Fla. July 31, 1952; d. Alvin H. and Evelyn H. (Klein) W. B.S. in Mgmt., Fla. State U., 1972; M.S., U. So. Fla. 1977; cert. completion U. Rennes 1968. Asst. youth cons. Natl. Assn. for Retarded Citizens, Arlington, Tex., 1970-71; asst. Develop. Disabilities Bur., Tallahassee, Fla., 1972-73; cons. Abt Assoc., Cambridge, Mass., 1973-75; program coordinator Project Community Sch., Waltham, Mass., 1973-75; program dir. Gulf Coast Epilepsy Found., Tampa, Fla., 1975-77; br. mgr. Walker Research Co., Tampa, 1977—; pres. East Lake Mchts. Assn., Tampa, 1980-83. Active Radio Reading Service for Blind, 1982—; bd. dirs. Angels Unaware Group Home, 1976—, Sta. WEDU-TV, Tampa 1978—. Recipient Pres.'s citation Walker Research Co., 1983; scholarship Am. Inst. for Fgn. Study, Rennes, France 1968. Mem. Bus. Profl. Women (Outstanding Career Woman 1981), Am. Mktg. Assn., Mensa, Phi Kappa Phi. Democrat. Club: Sunshine Postcard (Fla.). Home: 8310 Coors Pl Tampa FL 33615 Office: Walker Research Inc 5701 E Hillsborough Ave Tampa FL 33610

WILROY, HIABURNIA GAINES, title insurance company executive; b. DeSoto County, Miss., Apr. 22, 1929; d. Hubert Cornelius Gaines and Mattie Mae (Chamberlin) Gaines Troy; m. Leslie Lee Crawford, June 1, 1947 (div. June 1969); children—Leslie Lee, Jr., Richard Marvin; m. William Edwards Wilroy, Oct. 15, 1970 (div. Dec. 1985). B.B.A., U. Miss., 1979. Cert. profl. sec. Exec. sec. to county agt., Hernando, Miss., 1948-49; legal sec. W.E. Wilroy, Hernando, 1950-51, 53-57; chief clk. DeSoto County Agrl. Stblzn. and Conservation Service, Hernando, 1957-58; legal sec. Wilroy, Wilroy & Hagan, Hernando, 1958-69; corp. officer, asst. sec. Mid-South Title Ins. Corp., Memphis, 1969—. Mem. Profl. Secs. Internat. (treas. Memphis chpt. 1981-82, bd. dirs. 1984-85), Women's Soc. Christian Service (circle chmn. Hernando). Methodist. Club: Garden Study (sec.) (Hernando). Avocations: bridge, reading, needlepoint, knitting. Home: 96 Robinson St E PO Box 63 Hernando MS 38632 Office: Mid-South Title Ins Corp 1200 One Commerce Sq Memphis TN 38103

WILROY, JO ANN, librarian; b. Guntown, Miss., Dec. 7, 1935; d. Sam Doyle and Bertie Estele (Price) Patton; m. William Edwards Wilroy, Jr., Nov. 23, 1961; children—William Edwards, Lou Ann, Marcy, Blair. B.A.E., U. Miss., 1957, M.L.S., 1977; M.L.S., George Peabody Coll., 1978. Librarian, Haines City High Sch., Fla., 1957-58, Memphis Pub. Library, 1958-61; librarian, tchr. Whitehaven High Sch., Memphis, 1961-63; librarian 1st Regional Library, Hernando, Miss., 1967-79, asst. dir., 1979—. Pub. library editor Miss. Libraries, 1981—. Commr., Region II Mental Health Ctr., Oxford, Miss., 1978—; bd. dirs. DeSoto County Hist. Soc., Hernando. Mem. ALA, Southeastern Library Assn., Miss. Library Assn. (chair awards com. 1980, mem. legis. com. 1978, chair hospitality and conv. com. 1977, region sec. 1973, chair hospitality com. 1983, sec. pub. library sect. 1983), Beta Phi Mu. Methodist. Club: Hernando Women's. Avocations: travel, cooking; bridge. Home: PO Box 187 Hernando MS 38632

WILSON, ALICE BLAND, real estate consultant; b. Rainelle, W.Va., Apr. 1, 1938; d. Brady Floyd and Mildred Martha (George) Bland; m. Louis William Groves, Jr., Apr. 20, 1957 (div. 1981); children—Martha Rachel, Leonora Jayne; m. Glen Parten Wilson, Dec. 11, 1982. A.B., W.Va. U., 1959, postgrad. in microbiology, 1975-78. Contract adminstr. Washington Plate Glass Co., Washington, 1979-80; mem. acctg. staff Forbes Co., Washington, 1981; customer relations rep. Stern's Co., Wasington, 1982; real estate assoc. Merrill Lynch Realty Co., Washington, 1985—. Contbr. articles to Jour. Parasitology, Vol. coordinator John Glenn for Pres. campaign, Washington, 1983-84; mem. hospitality com. Women's Nat. Democratic Club, Washington, 1985—; mem. internat. adv. council ARC, Washington, 1985—. Mem. Washington Assn. Realtors (mem. residential sales com. 1985—). Avocations: flying; aerobics; nature study. Home: 433 New Jersey Ave SE Washington DC 20003 Office: Merrill Lynch Realty Co 2305 Calvert St NW Washington DC 20008

WILSON, ALMA D., state supreme court justice; b. Pauls Valley, Okla., May 25, 1917; d. William R. and Anna L. (Schuppert) Bell; m. William A. Wilson, May 30, 1948; 1 dau., Lee Anne. A.B., U. Okla., 1939, LL.B., 1941, J.D., 1970. Bar: Okla., 1941. Sole practice, Muskegee, 1941-43, Oklahoma City, 1943-47, Pauls Valley, 1948-69; judge Pauls Valley cpl. Ct., 1967-68; apptd. spl. judge, 1969-75, dist. judge, 1975-79, Dist. Ct. 21, Norman, Okla., 1975-83; assoc. justice Okla. Supreme Ct., Oklahoma City, 1983—. Mem. bd. visitors U. Okla., mem. alumni bd. dirs.; mem. Am. Legion Aux., Assistance League; trustee Okla. Meml. Union. Recipient Guy Brown award, 1974; Woman of Yr. award Norman Bus. and Profl. Women, 1975; elected to U. Okla. Hall of Fame, 1975. Mem. Garvin County Bar Assn. (past pres.), Okla. Bar Assn. (co-chmn. law and citizenship edn. com.), AAUW, Altrusa. Address: Supreme Ct of Okla 1 State Capitol Oklahoma City OK 73105*

WILSON, ANN, singer, recording artist; b. 1950; d. John and Lou Wilson; ed. Sammamish High Sch., Bellevue, Wash., Cornish Allied Inst. for Fine Arts, Seattle. Lead singer with rock group Heart, 1975—; albums include: Dreamboat Annie, 1975, Magazine, 1975, Little Queen, 1977, Dog and Butterfly, 1978, Bebe le Strange, 1980, Heart Live/Gr, Private Audition, 1982, Passionworks, 1983, Heart, 1985; single recs. include: Magic Man, 1976, Barracuda, 1977, Crazy on You, 1976, Straight On, 1978, Even It Up, 1980, Sweet Darlin, 1980, Tell It Like It Is, 1981, Unchained Melody, 1981; This Man is Mine, 1982, City's Burning, 1982, Bright Light Girl, 1982, How Can I Refuse, 1983, Sleep Alone, 1983, Almost Paradise, 1984, The Heat, 1984, What About Love, 1985, Never, 1985, These Dreams, 1986. Office: care Alan L Muller 219 1st Ave N Suite 333 Seattle WA 98109

WILSON, BERTHA, Canadian justice; b. Kirkcaldy, Scotland, Sept. 18, 1923; d. Archibald Wernham and Christina Noble; m. John Wilson, Dec. 14, 1945. Student, Aberdeen U., (Scotland), Tng. Coll. Tchrs. L.L.B., Faculty Law Dalhousie U., Halifax, N.S., L.L.D. (hon.), 1980; L.L.D. (hon.), Queen's U., 1983, U. Calgary, 1983, U. Toronto, 1984; D.H.L. (hon.), Mt. St. Vincent U., 1984; D.C.L. (hon.), U. Western Ont., 1984. Bar: N.S. 1958, Ont. 1959. Created Q.C., 1973; with firm Osler, Hoskin & Harcourt, Toronto, 1958-75, ptnr., 1968; apptd. Ont. Ct. Appeal, 1976-82; appted. Supreme Ct. Can., Ottawa, Ont., 1982—. Trustee, Clarke Inst. Psychiatry, 1972-75, Toronto Sch. Theology, 1975-81; chmn. Rhodes Scholarship Selection Com. for Ont., 1980-84. Mem. United Ch. of Can. Office: Supreme Ct Can Wellington St Ottawa ON K1A 0J1 Canada*

WILSON, BETTY ANDERSON, travel agency executive; b. Columbia, S.C., Oct. 31, 1940; d. Andrew Patrick and Alfree (George) Anderson; m. Hugh W. Wilson, III, June 6, 1964 (div. 1985); 1 child, Stephanie Paige. B.S., Winthrop Coll., 1962. Cert. profl. sec., 1969. Sec. dept. product devel. Cryovac div. W.R. Grace, Duncan, S.C., 1962-64; sec. to cashier Bankers Trust, Greenwood, S.C., 1965-66; sec. to pres. Palmer Coll., Charleston, S.C., 1966-71; travel agt. Wilson Travel Service, Summerville, S.C., 1976-78, mgr., 1978-85, pres., owner, 1985—. Mem. Am. Soc. Travel Agts. Avocations: travel; bridge; reading. Home: 308 S Main St Summerville SC 29483 Office: Wilson Travel Service Inc 120 S Main St Summerville SC 29483

WILSON, BEVERLEY CAROLE, fashion magazine executive; b. Richmond, Va., Nov. 11, 1953; d. Clarence Beverly and Marion (Martin) W. B.S. in Clothing and Textiles, Va. Poly. Inst. and State U., 1975; Assoc. in Occupational Studies, Tobe-Coburn Sch. Fashion, N.Y.C., 1976. Asst. to pres. Merchandising Motivation, Inc., N.Y.C., 1976-77; merchandising asst. Mademoiselle Mag., N.Y.C., 1977-78, merchandising editor, 1978-82, sr. merchandising editor, 1982-85, merchandising dir., 1985—. Mem. Fashion Group, Tobe-Coburn Alumni Assn. (exec. bd. 1980—; T award 1980), Va. Poly. Inst. Alumni Assn-Clothing and Textiles Grads. (Outstanding Alumni award 1985), Phi Upsilon Omicron. Avocations: collecting antique textiles, travel. Office: Mademoiselle Mag 350 Madison Ave New York NY 10017

WILSON, CANDACE, lawyer; b. Jacksonville, Fla., May 15, 1953; d. Carroll Joseph and Barbara Jane (Saxton) W.; m. Jack Dennis Suarez, May 1, 1976 (div. Aug. 1981). B.S. cum laude, Fla. State U., 1975; J.D. cum laude, Stetson U., 1979. Bar: Fla. 1979. Law clk. U.S. Bankruptcy Ct., Middle Dist. of Fla., Tampa, 1979-80; asst. counsel, office of gen. counsel City of Jacksonville (Fla.), 1980-82; assoc. Searcy, Facciolo & Hallows. P.A., Jacksonville, 1982—. Charles Dana scholar, 1976-79. Mem. ABA, Assn. Trial Lawyers Am., Fla. Bar Assn., Jacksonville Bar Assn., Acad. Fla. Trial Lawyers. Home: 10007 Sawgrass Dr E Ponte Vedra Beach FL 32082 Office: Searcy Facciolo & Hallows PA 1010 Blackstone Bldg Jacksonville FL 32202

WILSON, CAROL SCROGGINS, library literacy program administrator; b. Fayetteville, Ark., May 1, 1950; d. Jack Sam and Lelah Francine (Stewart) Scroggins; m. Jimmy Lee Jones, Dec. 25, 1969 (div. Feb. 1975); m. Joseph Walter Wilson, Mar. 19, 1980; 1 stepchild—Joseph Jeffrey. B.S. in Social Work, U. Ark., 1979, M.Ed., 1980; postgrad. U. San Francisco, 1984—. Research asst. Antaeus Research Inst., Fayetteville, 1980-81; mem. faculty Clovis Adult and Vocat. Edn., Calif., 1983—; mem. faculty women's studies Calif. State U.-Fresno, 1983-85; coordinator Library Literacy Program, Fresno, 1985—; advisor bd. dirs. McCarthy Inst. Learning and Edn., Madera, Calif., 1983—; founding mem. Literacy Coalition of Fresno, 1985—. Works of poetry include: Rain Goddess, 1984 (Golden Poet award 1985), Wishing Star, 1985. Mem. Central Calif. Forum Refugees, Fresno, 1986, Women's Caucus, Fresno, 1985; advisor Disabled Students Assn., Fresno, 1984; alt. Central Calif. Democratic Com., Fresno, 1983. Recipient certs. of recognition Coalition on Parenting Edn., 1979, Northwest Ark. Hospice, 1981. Mem. Nat. Assn. Female Execs., Am. Soc. Tng. and Devel., Nat. Assn. for Ethnic Studies, Council for Advancement Experiential Learning. Democrat. Lodge: Order Rosae Crucis (chpt. dep. master 1985-86, master 1986—). Avocations: writing; poetry; sewing. Home: 6541 N Teilman Fresno CA 93711 Office: Library Literacy Program 2420 Mariposa Fresno CA 93721

WILSON, CAROLYN SUE, respiratory therapy educator; b. Hot Springs, Ark., Aug. 28, 1946; d. Clarence E. and Alma Evelyn (Holt) Wilson. Student Lindenwood Coll. for Women, 1964; B.S. in Zoology, U. Ark.-Little Rock, 1970. Registered respiratory therapist Nat. Bd. for Respiratory Care. Respiratory therapist Methodist Hosp., Houston, 1971-75; supr. respiratory therapy Park Plaza Hosp., Houston, 1975-76; inservice coordinator respiratory therapy M.D. Anderson Hosp., Houston, 1976-78, asst. dir., 1978-81; asst. dir. pulmonary care Herman Hosp., Houston, 1981-83; clin. coordinator respiratory therapy Houston Community Coll., 1983—, cardiac life support instr. Am. Heart Assn., Houston, 1976—, advanced cardiac life support provider, 1982—. Vol. Harris County March of Dimes, Houston, 1981, team leader, 1982. Mem. Tex. Soc. Allied Health Profls., Tex. Assn. Jr. Coll. Tchrs., Am. Assn. Respiratory Therapy, Tex. Soc. Respiratory Therapy (pres. 1980-81, pres. Houston dist. 1977, state rep. 1978-79, dir. 1978-82, Dedicated Service award 1979, Pamela Poole Service award 1980). Democrat. Home: 5315 Willowbend Blvd Houston TX 77096 Office: Houston Community Coll 3100 Shenandoah Houston TX 77021

WILSON, CHARLOTTE JOYCE, financial services executive, marketing and communications consultant; b. Phila., Aug. 4, 1946; d. William and Charlotte Louise (Gettier) Todd; m. Richard Reynolds Wilson, July 12, 1969. B., Conn. Coll., New London, 1968; M.Ed., Lehigh U., Bethlehem, Pa., 1973; postgrad. U. Pa., Phila., 1977-79. Cert. tchr., Pa. Coordinator gifted curriculum Lower Moreland Sch. Dist., Huntingdon Valley, Pa., 1972-78; gifted resource dir. North Pa. Sch. Dist., Lansdale, 1978-81; dir. tng. and devel. Federated Investors Inc., Pitts., 1981-82, dir. product info. and market devel., 1982, asst. v.p. product devel., 1983—; mktg. cons. Kans. City Bank & Trust Co., Kansas City, Mo., 1983-84; author and producer film, 1986; communications cons. Republic Nat. Bank, N.Y.C., 1983-84, Union Nat. Bank, Albany, N.Y., 1983-84. Author: A Guide to Marketing Bank Services, 1983; contbr. in field. Bd. dirs. Abraxas Found., Pitts., 1983. Recipient Quality Circle Facilitator award Quality Circle Inst., 1982. Mem. Am. Mktg. Assn. (pres. 1986-84), Bus. Profl. Advt. Assn. (bd. dirs.), ASTD (chmn. community devel. 1982-84), AAUW. Republican. Episcopalian. Clubs: Econs., Advt. (Pitts.). Home: Upper Saint Clair PA 15241 Office: Federated Investors Inc 421 7th Ave Pittsburgh PA 15219

WILSON, DEBORAH ANN, international consulting company executive; b. Lincoln, Nebr.; d. Walter Woodrow Wilson and Betty Mae (Kister) Wood. B.A., Western Wash. State Coll., 1971, M.S., 1973, postgrad., U. Minn., 1973-77. Instr., U. Minn., Mpls., 1973-77; sr. research assoc. Minn. State, St. Paul, 1978; mgr. mktg. applications Comshare Inc., Mpls., 1978-83; mgr. market analysis West Pub., St. Paul, 1983-84; mgr. on line services CACI, Arlington, Va., 1984—; cons., Mpls., 1975-81. Mem. Am. Mktg. Assn. Avocations: weaving; raising parrots. Office: CACI Market Analysis Div 1815 N Fort Myer Dr Arlington VA 22209

WILSON, DIANE MONTGOMERY, human resource development consultant; b. Houston, Apr. 25, 1942; d. Ralph Wesley and Anna Ruth (Montgomery) Peterson; A.A. with honors, Johnson County Community Coll., 1973; B.S. in Journalism with highest distinction, U. Kans., 1976; m. James Timothy Wilson, July 25, 1964 (div. June 1981); children—Rebecca Lynn, Anthony Greg, Wendelle Marie. Asso. writer Golf Course Supts. Assn., Lawrence, Kans., 1976-77, asso. editor, 1977-78; copywriter Hallmark Cards, Inc., Kansas City, Mo., 1978-79; v.p. advt. and pub. relations The Wood Works, Inc., Overland Park, Kans., 1979-81; tng. cons. Marion Labs., 1985—; mgr. program devel. Western Auto, Kansas City, Mo., 1981-83, retail tng. mgr., 1983—; pres. Images, Overland Park, 1979-81, Phoenix Unltd., Overland Park, 1981-84. Bd. dirs. Mid-Continent council Girl Scouts U.S.A., 1976-80, 83—; chmn. Vol. Services Com., 1976-77; dir./producer Cable TV Programming for Leaders, 1974-77. Mem. Phi Beta Kappa. Am. Soc. for Tng. and Devel., toastmasters, Dimensions Unltd. (newsletter editor, nominating com. 1983-84), Kappa Tau Alpha, Phi Kappa Phi. Democrat. Mem. Unity Ch. Home: 13325 W 109th Terr Overland Park KS 66210 Office: 9300 Ward Pkwy Kansas City MO 64132

WILSON, DORIS LYNN, school district purchasing director; b. Long Beach, Calif., May 11, 1949; d. Rowe Francis and Annie Mae (Tunstill) Christopher; m. Louis Alan Wilson, Dec. 10, 1975 (div. Nov. 1985). Student Foothill Coll., 1966-67, DeAnza Coll., 1969-71. Cashier Navy Exchange, China Lake, Calif., 1965-66, Navy Exchange, Moffett Field, Calif., 1966-67; exec. sec. Varian Assocs., Palo Alto, Calif., 1967-75; salesperson Jorgensen Steel, Langhorne, Pa., 1976; exec. sec. Pennsbury Sch. Dist., Fallsington, Pa., 1976-82, dir. purchasing, 1982—. Mem. Pe. Assn. Sch. Bus. Ofcls. (Pa. registered sch. bus. specialist 1986, mem. conf. com.), Assn. Sch. Bus. Ofcls., Nat. Assn. Female Execs. Republican. Presbyterian. Avocations: needlecrafts; golf; spectator sports. Home: PO Box 92 Morrisville PA 19067 Office: Pennsbury Sch Dist Yardley Ave Box 338 Fallsington PA 19054

WILSON, ELIZABETH DOLAN NOLAN, investment company executive; b. Joplin, Mo., Mar. 9, 1909; d. John Lewis and Elizabeth (Hale) Dolan; m. Ralph Lauder Nolan, Oct. 17, 1929 (dec. Aug. 1971); children—Thomas Connor, John Keith; m. Alan Shepherd Wilson, Jr., Jan. 18, 1978. Student Drury Coll., 1927, 28, Kans. State Tchrs. Coll., 1927, 28. Famouse Artists Sch. Illustration and Design, 1960-63, Famous Artists Writers Sch., 1968, Inst. Children's Lit., 1975. Pres. Connor Investment Co., Joplin, 1971-79, also dir. Illustrator: Tales About Joplin, Short and Tall, 1962, 2d edit., 1968. Contbr. poetry, hist. articles and sports columns to profl. jours. Emeritus mem. women's aux. to bd. dirs. Drury Coll. Women's Aux., Springfield, Mo., 1961—, Joplin Hist. Soc. Dorothea B. Hoover Mus., Joplin; committeewoman Republican party, Joplin, 1964; bd. dirs. Spiva Art Ctr., 1956-60, 70-73. Republican. Presbyterian. Club: Twin Hills Golf and Country (Joplin). Avocations: golf; bridge. Home: 1240 Crest Dr Joplin MO 64801 Office: Connor Investment Co Joplin MO 64801

WILSON, EVELYN GAIL, retail chain official; b. Anniston, Ala., Aug. 9, 1945; d. John Haywood and Letty Bell (Johnson) Wildman; m. Jimmy Ray Rust, June 28, 1960 (dec. Mar. 1970); 1 son, Jimmy Ray; m. William O. Wilson, Jr., June 26, 1971; stepchildren—Andrew, Angela. Student Gadsden (Ala.) Bus. Coll., 1965, U. Ala.-Birmingham, 1975-76. Cert. profl. sec. Billing clk. Central Photocopy, Anniston, 1963; sec. Ch. of St. Michael and All Angels, Anniston, 1963-66; dist. sec. Ala. Vocat. Rehab. Service, Anniston, 1966-76; personnel adminstr. Super Valu Stores, Inc., Anniston, 1976—; instr. secretarial procedures Anniston Jr. Achievement, 1975; instr. written communication Am. Inst. Banking, 1981-82. Officer, mem. Wellborn Band Boosters, 1978-83, Wellborn Athletic Assn., 1970-83; dir. Boys Club Anniston, Inc., 1972, Anniston Football for Youth, 1975; bd. dirs. United Way of Calhoun County, mem. allocations com., 1985-86. Nat. Secs. Assn. scholar, 1963. Mem. Am. Soc. Personnel Adminstrs. (v.p. 1981-82), Internat. Mgmt. Assn. (sec. 1982-83, 1st v.p. 1985-86, sr. v.p. 1986-87), Nat. Secs. Assn. (pres. 1975-76, Sec. of Yr. 1976, 68), Anniston Area C. of C. Episcopalian. Home: 4212 Brian Dr Anniston AL 36201 Office: Super Valu Stores Inc Roberts Dr Industrial Park Anniston AL 36202

WILSON, FLORENCE DUNN (MRS. FLORENCE DUNN WILSON), civic worker; b. Erie, Pa.; d. Ira Jesse and Addie (Phillips) Dunn; student Harvard U., 1920, U. Wis., 1920-21, 22, 23, U. Mich., 1923; U. Pa., 1924, 25, 30; m. James Reid Wilson, Dec. 28, 1929 (dec. Oct. 1946); children—James Reid, Lowell Dunn. Mem. Phila. Hero Scholarship Com., 1960—, Washington Sq. West Civic Assn., 1963—, Emergency Aid Phila., 1958—; v.p. women's council United Cerebral Palsy Assn., 1965; mem. pub. relations Women's Flag Day Com., 1962—; bd. dirs. Phila. Assn. for Retarded Children, 1962—, v.p., 1962-63; bd. dirs. Phila. Centre City Residents Assn.; life bd. dirs. M.S. Walker Meml. Sch.; aux. chmn. legislature Parc Work Tng. Center Sch. Com.; bd. dirs. Pa. Council Republican Women; dir. polit. relations Rep. Women Pa., 1954-62, chmn. vols., 1964—, v.p., 1970-72, v.p., polit. chmn., 1974-77; Rep. committeewoman Phila., 1962—; past pres., bd. dirs. Phila. Assn. Ret. Citizens. Recipient Pub. Service awards Four Chaplains League, 1967, Phila. Assn. Retarded Children, 1963. Mem. D.A.R. (bd. mgrs. Phila. and state 1967-69, v.p. Americanism 1968—, rec. sec. Phila. 1972-73, del. state conv. 1972, dir. Pa., v.p. Americanism), Acad. Fine Arts, Colonial Hist. Soc., Penn's Town Hist. Soc., Pa. Soc. Daus. Founders and Patriots Am., Soc. Mayflower Descs., Commonwealth Pa., Colonial Daus. 17th Century, (corr. sec., dir., pub. relations Pa. chpt.), Nat. League Am. Pen Women (v.p. Phila. br. 1968—, historian 1971—, chmn. bicentennial com.), Phila. Soc. Preservation Landmarks. Clubs: Union League, Peale. Home: 329 S Smedley St Philadelphia PA 19103

WILSON, FRANCES HELEN, occupational therapist; b. Pitts., Oct. 17, 1929; d. J. Vernon and Margaret Hassler (Prugh) W.; B.A., Conn. Coll., 1951; advanced standing cert. Columbia Sch. Occupational Therapy, 1953. Therapist, Washington County Soc. Crippled Children and Adults, Washington, Pa., 1953-54; staff therapist Oakland VA Hosp., U. Pitts., 1955-66; supr. occupational therapy Aspinwall VA Hosp., Pitts., 1966-74, Oakland VA Hosp., Pitts., 1974-80; supr. occupational therapy clinic Aspinwal VA Hosp., Pitts., 1981-85. Active Jr. League Pitts., Inc. Mem. Am., Western Pa. (treas. 1967-69) occupational therapy assns. Republican. Presbyn. Clubs: Connecticut College (treas. 1971—), Twentieth Century (Pitts.). Home: 14 Devon Ln Ben Avon Heights Pittsburgh PA 15202

WILSON, JACKIE LYNN, educator; b. Houston, Sept. 22, 1933; d. John and Elton Jean (Spivey) Harris; B.A., Adelphi U., 1971; M.S., L.I. U., 1974; D.P.A., U. Colo., 1984; children—Robert, Patrick, Gregory. Detective, policewoman Nassau County (N.Y.) Police Dept., 1968-76; asst. prof. criminal justice L.I. U., 1973-76; asso. prof., chmn. dept. criminal justice Met. State Coll., Denver, 1976-85, prof. criminal justice and criminology, 1985—. Served with USAF, 1952-57. Mem. Internat. Assn. Black Women for Criminal Justice (pres.), Am. Criminal Justice Assn., Am. Assn. Criminology, Colo. Prison Assn. (exec. bd.), Colo. Assn. Probation Ofcls. (exec. bd.), Colo. Law Enforcement Officers Assn. (exec. bd.), Delta Sigma Theta, Delta Theta Kappa. Home: 255 Holly St Denver CO 80220 Office: 1000 11th St Denver CO 80204

WILSON, JACQUELINE ETHERIDGE, religious organization executive; b. Washington, Dec. 16, 1937; d. Robert B. and Bessie Lee (Dixon) Etheridge; m. John H. Wilson, Jr., Mar. 2, 1957; children—Margaret Cecelia, John H., Susan Elizabeth, Jacqueline Marie. A.B. in Elem. Edn., Cath. U. Am., 1966; M.Ed. in Adminstrn. and Supervision, Howard U., 1980. Typist law office, 1954-56; clk.-typist U.S. Army Corr. Unit, Pentagon, Washington, 1955; elem. sch. tchr. D.C. Pub. Schs., 1966-79; exec. dir. Office of Black Catholics, Archdiocese of Washington, 1979—; math. resource tchr. Benning Sch., 1966-69; mem. textbook evaluation com. D.C. Pub. Schs., 1971-73, cons. career devel. ctr., 1977-78; lectr. Washington Theol. Union, 1983, Office of Social Devel., 1982, Trinity Coll., 1983-84, Josephite Sem., Washington, 1981; cons. Black Cath. History Research Project, 1983—. Catechist, St. Gabriel Ch., 1963-81, charter mem., pres. parish council, 1971-77; master catechist, cons. Office of Religious Edn., 1981—; charter mem., pres., bd. dirs. Secretariat for Black Catholics, 1974-78; team mem. IMPAC Teen Retreats, 1976-79; mem. com. Africa and diaspora St. Augustine Ch., Washington, 1981—; mem. planning com. March on Washington, 1983; supporter Mt. Carmel Shelter for Homeless Women, 1982—; mem. children's programming adv. com. Sta. WDCA, 1984—; mem. Ctr. for Life Bd. Trustees, Providence Hosp. Editor Black Cath. News, 1979—. Recipient grants and awards D.C. Community Humanities Council, Archdiocese of Washington, Am. Bd. Cath. Missions. Mem. Assn. Supervision and Curriculum Devel., Nat. Black Child Devel. Inst., Nat. Urban League, NAACP, Nat. Assn. Black Cath. Adminstrs. (area coordinator 1977-79, 83—). Democrat. Home: 4342 G St SE Washington DC 20019

WILSON, JACQUELYN KAY, builders association administrator; b. Elizabethton, Tenn., Feb. 14, 1953; d. Stewart Jack and Mary Evelyn (Hyder) Carrouth; m. William Terry Garner, Sept. 3, 1972 (div. 1984); m. Robert Earl Wilson, Nov. 18, 1984. B.S in Fashion Design and Merchandising, Fla. State U., 1975. Profl. employment counselor Snelling & Snelling, Tallahassee, 1975-78; co-owner, bus. mgr. Capital City Plumbing Co., Inc., Tallahassee, 1978-80; interior designer Collier Interiors, Tallahassee, 1980-83; estimator, purchasing agt. Century Constrn. Corp., Tallahassee, 1983-85; exec. officer Tallahassee Builders Assn., 1985—; bd. dirs. Big Bend council Home Owners Warranty, 1983—, Tallahassee Housing Found., 1984—. Mem. Fla. State U. Booster Assn., 1975—, team leader fund drive, 1985; state judge Vocat./Indsl. Clubs Am., 1983; employer, supporter Leon County Master Plumbers Assn. apprenticeship program, Fla., 1978-80; mem. Citizens Adv. bd. Leon County Commn., 1985; mem. Leon County Republican Exec. Com. Mem. Nat. Assn. Women in Constrn. (nat. bd. dirs. 1984-85, WIC of Yr. 1979), Nat. Assn. Female Execs., Am. Soc. Assn. Execs., Fla. Soc. Assn. Execs., Tallahassee Soc. Assn. Execs., Fla. State U. Alumni Assn. Adventist. Club: Capital City Country. Avocations: sailing; bowling; sewing; arts and crafts. Office: Tallahassee Builders Assn 2522 Capital Circle NE #3 Tallahassee FL 32303

WILSON, JANE ELIZABETH GRIFFITH, business executive; b. Edgefield, S.C., Sept. 19, 1939; d. William Arthur and Elizabeth (Pritchard) Byrd; B.A., Winthrop Coll., 1961; M.A.T., U. N.C., 1965; postgrad. Duke U., 1962, Tex. A.&M. U., 1970-80; m. George Wayne Griffith, 1966 (dec. 1972); m. James Wesley Wilson, Sept. 1982. Tchr., Columbia (S.C.) Public Sch. System, 1961-63; biologist Nat. Marine Fisheries Lab., Oxford, Md., 1963-64; tchr. Texas City (Tex.) Ind. Sch. Dist., 1965-67, Galveston (Tex.) Coll., 1967-71; research asst. U. Tex. Med. Br., Galveston, 1972-73; spl. projects analyst Amoco Chem. Co., Alvin, Tex., 1974-82; pres. Griffith Enterprises, Hitchcock, Tex., 1981—; dir. edn. BTA Mus., 1982; pres. Savory Farm; George W. Griffith Scholarship Program dir., 1972-81; bd. dirs. Hitchcock Library, 1973-74; mem. City of Galveston Anti-litter Com., 1971-72. Mem. AAUW (state bd. 1972-74). Home: PO Box 305 Donalds SC 29638

WILSON, JANE FARISS, girls organization executive; b. Adamsville, Tenn., Mar. 6, 1928; d. Hugh David and Myrtle (Griffin) Fariss; A.A., Sullins Coll., 1947; B.A., U. Tenn., Chattanooga, 1949; postgrad. Scarrit Coll., 1973, Vanderbilt U. Grad. Sch. Mgmt., 1975, U. Chgo, 1977, N.Y.U., 1978, Harvard U. Bus. Sch., 1980, IBM Community Exec. Program; div.; children—David Lamar, Deborah Jane. Field dir., supr. Moccasin Bend council Girl Scouts U.S.A., Chattanooga, 1965-72, field exec. Cumberland Valley council, Nashville, 1972-76, exec. dir. Dogwood Trails council, Springfield, Mo., 1976-80, counselor Project Overview, Chattanooga, 1981, interim exec. dir. Flint River council, Albany, Ga., 1981-84, Green Hills council, Freeport, Ill., 1981, Maumee Valley council, Toledo, 1981-83, Pioneer Valley council, Springfield, Mass., 1984, Elkhart, Ind., 1985, Rochester, Minn., 1985; cons.; ch. sch. and religious edn. trainer. Mem. Springfield Community Planning Council, 1977-80. Mem. Adminstrv. Mgmt. Soc., Assn. Girl Scout Exec. Staff, Am. Guild Organists, Fellowship United Meths. in Music Worship and Other Arts, Bus. and Profl. Women, C of C., AAUW, Sigma Alpha Iota. Clubs: Zonta, Quota. Home and Office: PO Box 94 Osage Beach MO 65065

WILSON, JANET SUE, travel company executive; b. Clarksburg, W.Va., Oct. 28, 1934; d. Glenn Everett and Edna Marie Shaver; m. Alwin D. Wilson, Sept. 21, 1957 (div. Aug. 1959); 1 child, Virginia Marie. Student Davis & Elkins Coll., 1952-54, U. S. Fla., 1981. Travel mgr. Central W.Va. Auto Club, Clarksburg, 1954-57, Peninsula Motor Club, Sarasota, Fla., 1958-63; travel dir. Boyce Travel Agy., Sarasota, 1963-72; pres. Janet Wilson Travel Inc., Sarasota, 1972—; sec. First Step of Sarasota, 1978-79, pres., 1981-85. Chmn. Com. for an Elected Sheriff, Sarasota, 1985; bd. dirs. Crimewatch, Sarasota, 1985—. Recipient Crest award Am. Soc. Travel Agts., 1983, various awards from airlines and transp. cos. Mem. Phi Mu. Democrat. Presbyterian. Club: Altrusa (Sarasota) (treas. 1980-81). Avocations: needlepoint; profl. sports; books. Home: 6449 Kahana Way Sarasota FL 33583 Office: Janet Wilson Travel Inc 2136 Gulf Gate Dr Sarasota FL 33581

WILSON, JANIS KAY, promotion director; b. Anamosa, Iowa, Dec. 28, 1939; d. Clyde S. and Irma L. Wilson. B.F.A., Drake U., 1962. Copywriter, Chase Manhattan Bank, N.Y.C., 1962-66; presentation mgr. Newspaper Advt. Bur., N.Y.C., 1966-71; mktg./promotion mgr. Metromedia, N.Y.C., 1971-74; sr. promotion writer N.Y. Times, 1974-78; dir. mktg. services Crain Communications, N.Y.C., 1978-83; promotion dir. SRDS/MacMillan, Standard Rate & Data Service div. MacMillan, Wilmette, Ill., 1984—. Mem. Women's Design Group, Mag. Pubs. Assn., Internat. Newspaper Advt. and Mktg. Execs., Internat. Newspaper Pubs. Assn., Assn. Bus. Publs. Republican. Roman Catholic. Home: 801 Sylviawood Ave Park Ridge IL 60068 Office: Standard Rate & Data Service 3004 Glenview Rd Wilmette IL 60091

WILSON, JEAN MARIE HALEY, civic worker; b. Dallas, Oct. 16, 1921; d. William Eldred and Helen Marie (Littlepage) Haley; B.A., So. Meth. U., 1943; m. Edward Lewis Wilson, Jr., Mar. 19, 1943; children—Edward Lewis III, William Haley, Sarah. Bd. dirs. Dallas Symphony Orch. League, 1963—, sec., 1964-68, 1st v.p., 1968-72, vice-chmn. spl. projects, 1977—, rec. sec., 1984-85, 7th v.p., 1985-86; trustee Dallas Symphony Orch., 1976—; precinct chmn. Democratic Party, 1952-62; mem. Dallas County Dem. Exec. Com., 1952-62; bd. dirs. TACA (Com. for Fund Raising of the Arts), 1975—; mem. Southwestern hospitality bd. Met. Opera; charter mem., bd. dirs., North Tex. Herb Club, 1974-78. Mem. Women in Communications, Am. Symphony Orch. Leagues, Herb Soc. Am. (life), Am. Hort. Soc., Pewter Collectors Club Am., Internat. Platform Assn., Le Cercle Francaise of Dallas (hon. chmn. 1985—), Kappa Alpha Theta. Methodist. Home: 3501 Lexington Ave Dallas TX 75205 Office: 2909 Maple Ave Dallas TX 75201

WILSON, KAREN MIRTH MCKEE, naval officer; b. Hamdem, Conn., Apr. 13, 1945; d. Benjamin Franklin Moore and Dorothy Martha (Schumacher) Moore Mach-Brandt; A.S. in Acctg. and Bus. Mgmt., Southwestern Coll., Chula Vista, Calif., 1973; div.; 1 dau., Billie Jo. Enlisted in U.S. Navy, 1963, commd. chief warrant officer, 1979; personnel officer personnel support activity Naval Submarine Base, Groton, Conn., 1979-82; personnel officer USS Fulton, 1982-84; asst. dept. dir. MCA liaison/system mgmt. Enlisted Personnel Mgmt. Center, New Orleans, 1984—. Mem. Nat. Assn. Female Execs., Fleet Res. Assn. Republican. Presbyterian. Home: 208 Berry Wood Ct Slidell LA 70461 Office: Enlisted Personnel Mgmt Center Code 40A 4400 Dauphine St New Orleans LA 70159

WILSON, KATHERINE SCHMITKONS, biologist; b. Lorain, Ohio, Jan. 22, 1913; d. H. William and Katherine (Bauman) Schmitkons; A.B., Oberlin Coll., 1933; M.S., Northwestern U., 1935; Ph.D., Yale U., 1944; m. George E. Woodin, Nov. 23, 1961. Instr. biology Muskingum Coll., New Concord, Ohio, 1935-40; bot. researcher Yale U., 1941-44, Sessel fellow in biology, 1948-49, instr. biology, 1953-56; biologist div. research grants NIH, Bethesda, Md., 1956-58, scientist adminstr. genetics, 1958-77; ret., 1977; cons., lectr. genetics, 1978—. Recipient High Quality Service award HEW, NIH, 1966. Fellow AAAS, N.Y. Acad. Sci.; mem. Am. Soc. Human Genetics (spl. citation 1973), Genetics Soc. Am. (Service citation 1979), Environ. Mutagen Soc., Am. Inst. Biol. Scis., Am. Genetic Assn., Sigma Xi. Congregationalist. Club: PEO. Author: Botany—Principles and Problems, 5th ed., 1955; contbr. articles to profl. jours. Home: 77 235 Indiana Ave Palm Desert CA 92260

WILSON, LINDA SMITH, university administrator, chemist; b. Washington, Nov. 10, 1936; d. Fred M. and Virginia D. (Thompson) Smith; m. Malcolm C. Whatley, June 29, 1957 (div. 1969); 1 dau., Helen Katharine; m. Paul Allaby Wilson, Jan. 22, 1970; 1 stepdau., Beth Ann. B.A. with honors, Tulane U., 1957; Ph.D., U. Wis., 1962. Postdoctoral research assoc., research asst. prof. U. Md.-College Park, 1962-67; vis. asst. prof. U. Mo.-St. Louis, 1967-68; asst. to vice chancellor for research Washington U., St. Louis, 1968-69, asst. vice chancellor for research, 1969-74, assoc. vice chancellor for research, 1974-75; assoc. vice chancellor for research, assoc. dean Grad. Coll., U. Ill.-Urbana, 1975-85; v.p. for research U. Mich., Ann Arbor, 1985—; bd. dirs. Assn. for Biomed. Research, Washington, 1983—; mem. adv. bd. Nat. Coalition for Sci. and Tech., Washington, 1983—; mem. Nat. Commn. on Research, Washington, 1978-80; mem. com. on govt.-univ. relationships Nat. Acad. Sci., Washington, 1981-83; mem. council Gov.-Univ.-Research Roundtable, Washington, 1984-86; mem. nat. adv. council on research resources NIH, Bethesda, Md., 1978-82; mem. dirs. adv. council NSF, Washington, 1980—; bd. visitors Air U., Maxwell AFB, Montgomery, Ala., 1980-83; mem. council Inst. Medicine, Nat. Acad. Scis., 1986—; bd. dirs. Mich. Materials Processing Inst., 1985—. Contbr. articles to profl. jours. Bd. govs. Univ. YMCA, Champaign-Urbana, Ill., 1980-83. Named One of 100 Emerging Acad. Leaders, Am. Council on Edn., 1978. Fellow AAAS (dir. 1984-88); mem. Inst. Medicine-Nat. Acad. Scis., Nat Council Univ. Research Adminstrs., Soc. Research Adminstrn., Am. Chem. Soc. (bd. council com. on chemistry and pub. affairs 1978-80), Phi Beta Kappa, Sigma Xi, Phi Delta Kappa, Alpha Lambda Delta. Home: 2524 Blueberry Ln Ann Arbor MI 48103 Office: U Mich 4080 Fleming Adminstrn Bldg Ann Arbor MI 48109

WILSON, LISA ANN, accountant; b. Kansas City, Mo., June 10, 1957; d. Eugene Edmond and Ruth Pearl (Rhodes) Pasewark; m. Chris Lee Wilson, June 17, 1978; 1 child, Chase Tyler. B.B.A. in Acctg., Abilene Christian U., 1980. Acct., Houston Natural Gas, 1981-83; oil and gas revenue acct. Earlsboro Energies, Oklahoma City, Okla., 1983-84; owner, acct. Bittersweet Memories, 1984—. Republican. Mem. Christian Ch. Club: Sigma Theta Chi. Avocations: sewing; racquetball; swimming; horse-back riding. Home: 4009 NW 32nd St Oklahoma City OK 73112

WILSON, LIVIA GENE, manufacturing company marketing representative; b. Gaffney, S.C., Oct. 30, 1959; d. Lewis Eugene and Barbara Carolyn (Smawley) W. B.S. in Psychology, U. S.C., 1979; postgrad. Greenville Tech. Coll., 1982-85. Mng. dir. La Petite Acad., Spartanburg, S.C., 1979-80; with credit and collections dept. Spartan Express, Inc., Greer, S.C., 1980-81; personnel asst. Southeastern Kusan, Inman, S.C., 1981-83, customer rep., sales rep., Greenville, S.C., 1983-84, customer service mgr., 1984-85; mktg. rep. Steel Heddle Mfg. Co., Greenville, 1985—. Mem. Am. Mktg. Assn., Nat. Assn. Female Execs., Spartanburg County Council-Drafters/Engring. Republican. Methodist. Avocations: drawing; piano; reading; water skiing. Office: Steel Heddle Mfg Co Rutherford Rd Greenville SC 29602

WILSON, MARCELLE NADEAU, dinner theatre owner, theatrical producer, actress; b. St. Leonard, N.B., Can., Oct. 24, 1936; came to U.S., 1955, naturalized, 1965; d. Emile and Louise (Bouchard) Nadeau; student Fredericton (N.B.) Bus. Coll., 1954, Vallejo Jr. Coll., 1967, also modeling schs.; m. Charles H. Wilson, Nov. 25, 1970. Various secretarial and bookkeeping positions, 1955-68; owner, operator Timbers Cabaret Theatre, Goleta, Calif., 1970-73; owner, major stockholder Le P'tit Cabaret, Inc., dinner theatre, Santa Barbara, Calif., 1974—, also corp. sec.; producer over 100 plays since 1970; dir. One Flew Over the Cuckoo's Nest; Stalag 17, Funny Girl, others; acting roles include: Maggie in Cat on a Hot Tin Roof, Murielle Tate in Plaza Suite, Jenny Diver in The Threepenny Opera; Mr. Here First, Hoboland; playwright Only You, Lautrec, La Môme Piaf/Ses Chansons, ses Tristesses, The Games Actors Cry..., Hoboland, Me Here First. Recipient arts commendation plaque Santa Barbara News-Press, 1972, 73, Ventura County Actors award, 1973. Mem. Dramatists Guild. Roman Catholic. Playwright. Home: 416 E Valerio St Santa Barbara CA 93101 Office: 1826 Cliff Dr Santa Barbara CA 93109

WILSON, MARGARET CECELIA, word processing specialist, transcriptionist; b. Washington, Sept. 29, 1957; d. John Hans and Jacqueline Etheridge Wilson. B.A., Catholic U., 1984. Word processing operator Fulbright & Jaworski, Washington, 1978-81; word processing supr. Arthur Anderson & Co., Washington, 1981-82; word processing instr. People's Involvement Corp., Washington, 1981-82; word processing operator Arent, Fox et al., Washington, 1982-83; transcriptionist, Washington, 1978—; freelancer People Mag., Archdiocese of Washington, George Wash. U., BIL Assocs., Brookings Inst.; cons. Omni Info. Systems, Washington, 1982-83; adminstrv. asst. Am. Coll. Obstetricians and Gynecologists, 1984—; ct. reporter, 1984—; transcript coordinator Brookings Inst., 1978-80; lectr. in Afro-Am. history, Washington, 1981—; tutor, 1981—. Coordinator, Ward I Com. to Elect Douglas Moore, Washington, 1978; Ward IV Democrats, Washington, 1980; mem. Friends of Petworth Library, Washington, 1982—. Recipient John Earrell prize in history, 1984. Mem. Am. Hist. Assn., Orgn. Am. Historians, Pi Gamma Mu, Phi Alpha Theta. Roman Catholic. Contbr. articles to profl. jours. Office: The Workplace 1302 18th St NW Washington DC 20036

WILSON, MARGARET SULLIVAN, college official; b. Norwich, Conn., Mar. 21, 1924; d. John Joseph and Margaret Ellen (Connelly) Sullivan; m. William Robert Wilson, July 20, 1950 (dec.); children—Margaret Ellen, William Robert. B.S., Eastern Conn. State Coll., 1944; M.A. U. Conn., 1949. Reading cons. Greenwich (Conn.) Pub. Schs., 1948-50; asst. prof. early childhood, chmn. dept. early childhood Eastern Conn. State Coll., Willimantic, 1967-77, exec. asst. to pres., 1977-78, v.p. adminstrv. affairs, 1978-80, exec. dean, 1980—; del. White House Conf. on Children, 1970, 80; cons. Windham-Willimantic Child Care, 1971—; corporator Chelsea Groton Savs. Bank, Norwich, Conn. Mem. Conn. Mental Health Bd., 1979-83 mem. Norwich Hosp. Adv. Bd.; mem. Eastern Regional Mental Health Bd., 1976-83, chmn., 1979-81; chairperson rev. com. Conn. Health Coordinating Council; mem. Norwich Bd. Edn., 1954-69, 80-83; mem. vestry Ch. of Resurrection, Episcopal ch., Norwich; mem. Conn. Democratic Central Com., 1966-82, Dem. Town Com., 1966-82; chmn. Blue Ribbon Commn. To Establish Goals for U. Conn. Health Ctr., 1975-76; mem. Statewide Coordinating Com., Statewide Perinatal Services Com.; mem. adv. bd. Southeastern Conn. Day Care Programs; bd. dirs. Waterford Country Sch. Recipient Disting. Alumni award Eastern Conn. State U., 1972, Mental Health Bell award Conn. Mental Health Assn., 1972, Valient Women award Council Ch. Women, 1976, Woman of Yr. award Bus. and Profl. Women, 1978, Jefferson award Inst. Pub. Service, 1982. Mem. Norwich Area C. of C. (dir. 1979-81, Citizen of Yr. award 1970), Greater Willimantic C. of C. (bd. dirs.). Democrat. Home: 27 Canterbury Turnpike Norwich CT 06360 Office: 83 Windham St Willimantic CT 06226

WILSON, MARGERY LAUREN, editor, writer; b. Oxnard, Calif., Jan. 12, 1951; d. Loren George and Mary Brosius (Samuelson) Wilson; m. David Robert Gommel, Oct. 25, 1970 (div. 1979); 1 dau., Johanna Christiana. Student Santa Barbara City Coll., 1968-70, U. Mass., 1983—. Columnist, Santa Barbara News-Press (Calif.), 1964-65; writer, abstractor Leisure Abstracts and Horseman's Abstracts, Goleta, Calif., 1970-72; editor Winthrop Pubs., Cambridge, Mass., 1979-81; freelance writer, 1964—; co-founder, mng. editor Orthodox People Mag., Boston, 1980-84; exec. v.p. Internat. Orthodox Christian Writer's Guild, Cumberland, R.I., 1980-84; lit. cons. Inkfellows, Providence, Cumberland, 1981—. Author: Burgesses of Buck's County, 1983, others; editor Sex Roles and Human Behavior (K.F. Schaffer), 1981. Bd. dirs. youth com. Cambridge YWCA, 1983-84, mem. adv. council afterschool activities, 1983-84. Mem. New Eng. Historic Genealogy Soc., Bucks County Hist. Soc., Girl Scouts U.S.A. Democrat. Eastern Orthodox. Office: Orthodox People Mag 165 Park Dr Boston MA 02115

WILSON, MARJORIE PRICE, physician, academic administrator; b. Pitts., Sept. 25, 1924; student Bryn Mawr Coll., 1942-45; M.D., U. Pitts., 1949; m. Lynn Minford Wilson, Sept. 15, 1951; children—Lynn Deyo, Liza Price. Intern, U. Pitts. Med. Center Hosps., 1949-50; resident Children's Hosp. U. Pitts., 1950-51. Jackson Meml. Hosp., U. Miami Sch. Medicine, 1954-56; chief residency and internship div. edn. service Office of Research and Edn., VA, Washington, 1956, chief profl. tng. div., 1956-60, asst. dir. edn. service, 1960; chief tng. br. Nat. Inst. Arthritis and Metabolic Disease, NIH, 1960-63, asst. to assoc. dir. for tng. Office of Dir., NIH, 1963-64; assoc. dir. extramural programs Nat. Library Medicine, 1964-67; asso. dir. program devel. OPPD, NIH, 1967-69, asst. dir. program planning and evaluation, Bethesda, Md., 1969-70; dir. dept. instl. devel. Assn. Am. Med. Colls., Washington, 1970-81; sr. assoc. dean U. Md. Sch. Medicine, Balt., 1981-86, acting dean, 1984, vice dean, 1986—; mem. Inst. Medicine, Nat. Acad. Scis., 1974—; bd. visitors U. Pitts. Sch. Medicine, 1974—; mem. governing bd. Robert Wood Johnson Health Policy Fellowships, 1975—; mem. Nat. Bd. Med. Examiners, 1982—; mem. Md. Gov.'s Council on Toxic Substances, 1982—; trustee Analytic Services, Inc., Falls Church, Va., 1976—. Recipient Superior Service award NEW, 1970; P.S. Hench award U. Pitts., 1983. Fellow AAAS; mem. AMA, Assn. Am. Med. Colls., Am. Fedn. Clin. Research, Am. Med. Women's Assn., IEEE. Episcopalian. Contbr. articles to profl. jours. Office: U Md Sch Medicine Baltimore MD 21201

WILSON, MARTHA ROWENA, city official, real estate developer; b. Harrisburg, Pa., June 6, 1946; d. Joseph Cooper and Catherine (Stephan) McCune; m. E. Granger Wilson, Sept. 6, 1969 (div. Oct. 1981). B.S., Ithaca Coll., 1968; M.Ed., Springfield Coll., 1970. Tchr. earth sci. Easton High Sch., Md., 1970-72; dir. student services Hampshire Country Sch., Rindge, N.H., 1972-73; dir. Geneva Athletic Club, N.Y., 1973-78; dir. dept. recreation City of Geneva, 1978—; instr. Keuka Coll., Keuka Park, N.Y., 1983-84, Community Coll. Finger Lakes, Geneva, N.Y., 1985—; instr. trainer ARC, Rochester, N.Y., 1985—. Bd. dirs. Geneva YMCA, 1985—, Finger Lakes Sports-A-Rama, Geneva, 1985—. Fellow Genesee Recreation and Park Soc.; mem. Nat. Recreation and Park Assn. Republican. Episcopalian. Clubs: Kanadasaga Kennel, Zonta (pres. 1979-82), Seneca Yacht (Geneva). Avocations: sailing; raise and show English springer spaniels. Home: 394 W Lake Rd Clarks Point Geneva NY 14456 Office: Geneva Recreation Dept 666 S Exchange St Geneva NY 14456

WILSON, MARY EVE, children's librarian; b. Nashville, May 23, 1943; d. Alwin Curtis and Mary Usula (Glover) Hutcherson; B.S., Miss. State Coll. for Women, 1965; M.L.S., Vanderbilt U., 1968. Librarian, George Washington Carver High Sch., Newport News, Va., 1968-69; children's, young adult librarian Finkelstein Meml. Library, Spring Valley, N.Y., 1970-77; young adult services specialist Tampa-Hills County Pub. Library System, Tampa, Fla., 1977-82; asst. children's coordinator Sno-Isle Regional Library System, Marysville, Wash., 1985—; adj. prof. Grad. Sch. Library Sci., Fla. State U., 1981; aide to Fla. state senator Betty Castor, 1982-84; vis. prof. Peabody Coll., Vanderbilt U. Mem. Hills County Women's Polit. Caucus, 1980; del. Fla. Conf. on Children and Youth, 1981; bd. dirs. Northside Community Mental Health Complex, Tampa, 1981-84; mem. Fla. Alliance for Responsible Adolescent Parenting, 1978-82. Recipient vol. service award Hills County Children's Services, 1981. Mem. ALA (pres. young adult services div. 1981-82). Democrat. Episcopalian. Contbr. articles to profl. jours. Office: Sno-Isle Regional Library System PO Box 148 Marysville WA 98270

WILSON, MARY LUCY, nursing educator; b. Horton, Ala., Sept. 24, 1923; d. Martin Luther and Bertha Cleo (Medlock) Evans; m. Henry Boyle Wilson, June 4, 1959; children—Helen Boyce Wilson, Henry Boyce, Mary Madeline. B.S. in Nursing, U. Ala., 1954, M.S. in Nursing, 1958. Instr. nursing Pensacola Jr. Coll., Fla., 1965-67; dir. inservice edn. Baptist Hosp., Pensacola, 1969-72, clin. nurse specialist, 1972-75; dept. head nursing Jefferson Davis Jr. Coll., Birewton, Ala., 1974-76; clin. nurse specialist Baptist Hosp., Pensacola, 1976-83, patient edn. coordinator, 1983—; program coordinator. Active Disabled Am. Vets. Aux., Pensacola, 1962—; leader Girl Scouts U.S.A., Pensacola, 1967-73, Boy Scouts Am., 1968-70. Mem. Sigma Theta Tau. Democrat. Baptist. Avocations: gardening; swimming; aerobics; reading; needlework. Home: 920 Cranbrook Ave Pensacola FL 32505 Office: Bapt Hosp 1000 W Morono St Pensacola FL 32501

WILSON, MARY MARGARET, public relations executive; b. Dallas, Dec. 7, 1948; d. James B. and Marguerite (Getz) W. B.A., So. Meth. U., 1972, M.A., 1974. Psychol. assoc. Dallas Police Dept., 1973-76; pvt. practice psychology, Dallas, 1977; research assoc. Tex. A.&M. U., College Station 1978; asst. dir. communications United Way Tex.-Gulf Coast, Houston, 1980-86; dir. pub. relations Am. Productivity Ctr., Houston, 1986—; pres. Wilson & Assocs., Houston, 1977—; dir. E.C. Systems Co., Inc., 1981—; research asst. U. Tex. Med. Sch., Dallas, 1973-76. Vol., ARC, Dallas, 1965-70; mem. Houston Area Women's Ctr., 1982-83. Mem. Am. Psychol. Assn., Pub. Relations Soc. Am., Tex. Psychol. Assn., Nat. Assn. Female Execs., Houston Mus. Fine Arts.

WILSON, MAUREEN ANN, bookstore executive; b. Flushing, N.Y., Oct. 26, 1950; d. Michael Joseph and Cecilia Emily (Greifeld) W. Student pub. schs. Floral Park, N.Y. Dept. mgr. Alexander's Dept. Store, Valley Stream, N.Y., 1968-73, asst. personnel mgr., Manhattan, 1973-75; store mgr. B. Dalton Bookseller, Bayshore, N.Y., 1975-80, store mgr. Manhattan, 1981-85, gen. mgr. Flagship Store, N.Y.C., 1985—. Mem. Nat. Assn. Female Execs., Am. Booksellers Assn. Roman Catholic. Avocations: jogging; beach combing. Office: B Dalton Bookseller 666 Fifth Ave New York NY 10103

WILSON, MOLLIE CROSS HALEY, investment counselor; b. Charlotte, N.C., May 5, 1942; d. Shaffer and Mollie Flournoy (Cross) Haley; B.S. with honors in Bus. Adminstrn., U. Ark., Fayetteville, 1963, M.B.A., 1972, Ph.D. in Fin., 1979; m. Jack E. Grober. Grad. asst. U. Ark., Fayetteville, 1971-73, instr., 1974-79; assoc. Robert E. Kennedy, Inc., Fayetteville, 1971—; v.p. investment div. Mchts. Nat. Bank, Ft. Smith, Ark., 1979-83; pres. October Money Mgmt., 1983—; fin. cons. for public cos., Ark. Bd. dirs. Ark. Community Found., 1979-83, Ft. Smith Heritage Found., 1979-83. Chartered fin. planner, 1982. Bd. dirs. Ft. Smith Salvation Army, 1982—, vice chmn., 1986-87. Mem. Inst. Chartered Fin. Planners, Internat. Assn. Registered Fin. Planners, Ark. Soc. Fin. Mgrs. (bd. dirs., 1972—), Dallas Soc. Investment Analysts, Fin. Analysts Fedn., Western Ark. Estate Planning Council, Beta Gamma Sigma. Contbr. articles to publs. Home: # 9 Carthage Circle Fort Smith AR 72901 Office: PO Box 2605 Fort Smith AR 72902

WILSON, PATRICIA JANE, educator, librarian, educational and library consultant; b. Jennings, La., May 3, 1946; d. Ralph Harold and Wilda Ruth (Smith) Potter; m. Wendell Merlin Wilson, Aug. 24, 1968. B.S., La. State U., 1967; M.S. U. Houston-Clear Lake, 1979; Ed.D., U. Houston, 1985. Cert. tchr., learning resources specialist (librarian), Tex. Tchr., England AFB (La.) Elem. Sch., 1967-68, Edward White Elem. Sch., Clear Creek Ind. Schs., Seabrook, Tex., 1972-77; librarian C.D. Landolt Elem. Sch., Friendswood, Tex., 1979-81; instr./lectr. children's lit. U. Houston 1983—; with U. Houston/Clear Lake, 1984—. Trustee, Freeman Meml. Library, Houston, 1982—, v.p., 1985-86, pres., 1986-87; mem. Armand Bayou Nature Ctr., Houston, 1980—; bd. dirs. Sta. KUHT-TV, 1984—. Editor A Rev. Sampler, 1985-86; contbr. articles to profl. jours. Mem. ALA, Am. Assn. Sch. Librarians, Internat. Reading Assn., Nat. Council Tchrs. English, Tex. Joint Council Tchrs. English, Kappa Delta Pi, Alpha Delta Kappa, Phi Delta Kappa. Methodist. Club: Lakewood Yacht (Seabrook). Home: 1118 Appleford Dr Seabrook TX 77586

WILSON, PATRICIA POPLAR, electrical manufacturing company executive; b. Chgo., Sept. 20, 1931; d. George and Leona (O'Brien) Poplar; B.S., U. Wash., 1966, M.A., 1967, Ph.D., 1980; m. Chester Goodwin Wilson, Jan. 30, 1960; children—Susan Spadafora, Chester Wilson. Instr., U. Wash., Seattle, 1967-74; women's editor Nor'westing Mag., Seattle, 1969—; pres. Wilson & Assos. N.W. Inc., Seattle, 1974—; v.p. N.W. Mfg. & Supply, Inc., 1977—; pres. Trydor Sales Alberta Ltd., Can. Mem. Electric League. Episcopalian. Club: Seattle Yacht. Author: Household Equipment, Guide to Surplus Equipment. Contbr. articles to profl. jours. Office: 4045 7th Ave S Seattle WA 98108

WILSON, PAULA JEAN, lease administrator, marketing executive; b. Washington, Apr. 16, 1957; d. Marion Stanley and Frances Dolores (Higgs) Wills; m. Blaine Lee Wilson, Sept. 17, 1983. B.S., U. Md., 1979. Typist, Equifax Services, Oxon Hill, Md., 1975-77; receptionist, sec. The Ziegler Cos., Washington, 1977-79; lease adminstr., McLean, Va., 1979—. Roman Catholic. Avocations: bowling; going to beach. Office: The Ziegler Cos 8200 Greensboro Dr McLean VA 22102

WILSON, PHYLLIS STARR, magazine editor; b. New Orleans, Feb. 11, 1928; d. Daniel David and Anita (Garripy) Starr; B.A. in English, Tulane U., 1949; m. Hugh Hamilton Wilson, Dec. 24, 1958. Receptionist, asst. house organ Coca-Cola Co., New Orleans, 1949; sec., editor Weird Tales mag., N.Y.C., 1950; sec. Conde Nast Publs., N.Y.C., 1951-55, researcher, writer Vogue mag., 1955-62, writer Glamour mag., 1962-67, sr. editor copy and features, 1967-71, mng. editor, 1971-77; editor-in-chief Self mag., N.Y.C., 1977—; freelance writer, editor, 1955—. Recipient J.C. Penney-U. Mo. Journalism award for med. article, 1969; named one of outstanding women who have contbd. most to mag. pub. March of Dimes, 1982. Mem. Am. Soc. Mag. Editors. Democrat. Editor, researcher: The Artist in His Studio (Alexander Liberman), 1960; Moments Preserved (Irving Penn), 1960; editor: Glamour's Health and Beauty Book, 1972. Office: 350 Madison Ave New York NY 10017

WILSON, ROSE WILLOVENE CONFER, resource specialist, psychologist; b. Brackenridge, Pa., June 14, 1924; d. Irven J. and Marguerite Rose (Kelley) Confer; m. Clarence Wilson Jr., Feb. 27, 1945 (dec. 1955); children—Michael Carson Thomas, Clarence Patrick, James Robert, Marguerite Rose, Stephen Timothy. B.A., McNeese State U., 1963, M.Ed., 1971, Edn. Specialist, 1974, Ed.D., 1979. Tchr. LaGrange Middle Sch., Lake Charles, La., 1963-73, career edn. counselor, 1973-75; grad. asst., instr. counseling McNeese State U., Lake Charles, 1975-76, vis. lectr., 1977-78; guidance counselor Alfred M. Barbe High Sch., Lake Charles, 1976-77; with Calcasieu Parish Schs., Lake Charles, 1963—, coordinator occupational readiness, 1978-79, resource specialist, sch. psychologist, 1979—. Pres. Southwest La. Health Counseling Services, 1971-74, bd. dirs., 1974-79, mem. profl. adv. bd., 1979-85; mem. profl. adv. bd. La. Epilepsy Assn., 1979-81; chmn. Mayor's Com. Employment of Handicapped S.W. La., 1979-80; lay minister Eucharist, St. Margaret Roman Catholic Ch., Lake Charles, 1977—, mem. parish council, 1976-80, 81-83, sec., 1978-80. Recipient Freedom Found.'s Valley Forge Tchrs. medal, 1970; keys to City of Lake Charles from Mayor James Sudduth, 1973; Woman of Yr. award Quota Club Lake Charles, 1975; Outstanding Pub. Servant award Calcasieu Council 1207, K.C., 1980; cert. of award Lake Charles Assn. Retarded Citizens, 1980; S.W. La. Patriot of Yr. award, K.C., 1980; DAR Honor medal, 1981; Career Guild Regional Woman of Achievement award, 1981. Mem. La. Edn. Research Assn., Am. Assn. Counseling and Devel., La. Personnel and Guidance Assn., Am. Personnel and Guidance Assn., La. Sch. Counselors Assn., Am. Rehab. Counseling Assn., Assn. Counselor Edn. and Supervision, Am. Vocat. Guidance Assn., La. Vocat. Guidance Assn., Calcasieu Counselors Assn., La. Tchrs. Assn., Calcasieu Tchrs. Assn., Nat. Assn. Sch. Psychologists, Cath. Daus. Am. (vice regent 1972-73, Alpha Delta Kappa (pres. 1982-83), Phi Delta Kappa (pres. 1982-83), Quota (pres. 1982-83). Home: 1529 Tennessee St Lake Charles LA 70605 Office: 1120 W 18th St Lake Charles LA 70601

WILSON, RUBY LEILA, nurse, educator; b. Punxsutawney, Pa., May 29, 1931; d. Clark H. and Alda E. (Armstrong) W.; B.S. in Nursing Edn., U. Pitts., 1954; M.S.N., Case Western Res. U., 1959; Ed.D., Duke U., 1969. Staff nurse, asst. head nurse Allegheny Gen. Hosp., Pitts., 1951-52, night clin. instr., adminstrv. supr., 1951-55; staff nurse, asst. head nurse Fort Miley VA Hosp., San Francisco, 1957-58; instr. nursing Duke U. Sch. Nursing, Durham, N.C., 1955-57, asst. prof. med. surg. nursing, 1959-66, assoc. in medicine, 1963-66, prof. nursing, 1971—, dean Sch. Nursing, 1971-84, asst. to chancellor for health affairs, 1984—; asst. prof. dept. community and family medicine Duke U. Sch. Medicine, 1971—; cons., vis. prof. Rockefeller Found., Bangkok, 1969-71. Fellow Am. Acad. Nursing; mem. Am. Assn. Colls. Nursing, Am. Assn. Higher Edn., Am. Nurses Assn., Nat. League Nursing, N.C. Med. Care Commn., Inst. of Medicine, Assn. for Acad. Health Ctrs. (planning com.). Club: Torch. Contbr. articles to profl. jours. Office: Sch Nursing Duke Univ Durham NC 27710

WILSON, SHAREN, lawyer; b. Amarillo, Tex., Sept. 24, 1956; d. John Frank and Patsy Rae (Routh) W. A.S., Amarillo Coll., 1976; B.A., Tex. Tech. U., 1978, J.D., 1980. Bar: Tex. 1981. Asst. dist. atty. Tarrant County, Ft. Worth, 1981—; liaison Richland Hills Police Dept. (Tex.), 1982-85; instr. civil cts. tours Ft. Worth Ind. Sch. Dist., 1982-83; demonstration Tarrant County Legal Assts. Assn., 1983; speaker profl. socs. Mem. Tarrant County DWI Task Force, Tarrant County Area Agy. on Aging. Mem. ABA, State Bar Tex. (dist. 7A grievance com.), Tarrant County Bar Assn., Tarrant County Young Lawyers Assn., Tex. Dist. and County Attys. Assn., Delta Theta Phi, Delta Zeta. Democrat. Methodist. Home: 4417 El Campo Fort Worth TX 76107 Office: Tarrant County Dist Attys Office 200 W Belknap Fort Worth TX 76196

WILSON, SHIRLEY ANN, payroll administrator; b. Stratton, Colo., Apr. 17, 1935; d. Albert and Laura Evelyn (Noxon) Ward; m. William Herbert Wilson July 3, 1954 (dec. 1975); children—Robert, Janet, Bradley. Ed., Ft. Morgan Colo. schs. Cashier, then fin. asst. State of Colo. Dept. Higher Edn., 1969-77; acctg. mgr. U. So. Colo., Pueblo, 1977-80; acctg. supr., Penrose Hosp., Colorado Springs, 1981-85; acctg. supr. St. Luke's Health System, Phoenix, 1986—. Named Boss of Yr., Garden of the God's chpt. Am. Bus. Women Assn., 1983. Mem. Am. Payroll Assn., Am. Bus. Women's Assn. (pres. 1983-84). Republican. Avocations: reading; knitting. Home: 5350 E Taylor #161 Phoenix AZ 85008

WILSON, SONIA PATRICIA, nurse; b. Bluefields, Jamaica, Apr. 23, 1956; came to U.S., 1981; d. Joseph Egbert and Claris Elizabeth (Nesbet) W. R.N., Cornwall Sch. Nursing, Montego Bay, Jamaica, 1979. Nurse, Isaac Barrant Hosp., St. Thomas, Jamaica, 1979-80, Waterford Sec. Sch., St. Catherine, Jamaica, 1980-81, Jackson Meml. Hosp., Miami, 1981-83; pvt. duty nurse So. Nursing and Profl. Services, Miami, 1983—. Mem. Am. Nurses Assn. Methodist. Avocations: tennis. Home: 1500 NW 12th Ave #1405 Miami FL 33136

WILSON, SUSAN LEE, association executive; b. Fed. Republic Germany, Mar. 7, 1956 (parents Am. citizens); d. John Dale and Nancy Caroline (Cocking) Esher; m. Scott Edward Wilson, Nov. 1, 1980. B.S., Baker U., 1976. Asst. loan officer First Nat. Bank, Leavenworth, Kans., 1978-80; acct. Arlington Telecommunications, Va., 1981-83; fin. mgr. Am. Acad. Actuaries, Washington, 1983—. Mem. Am. Soc. Assn. Execs., Delta Delta Delta. Avocations: swimming, racquetball, tennis, sailing. Home: 7928 Caledonia St Alexandria VA 22309 Office: Am Acad Actuaries 1720 I St NW Washington DC 20009

WILSON, SUSAN NEUBERGER, educator, researcher; b. N.Y.C., Jan. 17, 1930; d. Harry H. and Katherine A. (Kridel) Neuberger; m. Donald M. Wilson, Apr. 6, 1957; children—Dwight, Katherine, Penelope. B.A., Vassar, 1951; M.S. in Edn., Bank Street Coll., 1976. Reporter LIFE Mag., N.Y.C., 1951-57; writer N.J. Office Econ. Opportunity, Trenton, 1964-67; pub. info. specialist Bank Street Coll., N.Y.C., 1976-78; program assoc. Nat. Assn. State Bds. Edn., Alexandria, Va., 1982—; v.p. N.J. State Bd. Edn. Trenton, 1977-82; exec. coordinator N.J. Network for Family Life Edn., 1985—. Mem. Lawrence Planning Bd., N.J., 1983—, Mercer County Commn. Status of Women, N.J., 1983—. Recipient Advocacy award N.J. Chpt. Nat. Commn. Prevention of Child Abuse, 1981, Advocacy award N.J. Family Planning Forum, 1982. Democrat. Episcopalian. Home: 4574 Province Line Rd Princeton NJ 08540

WILSON, TOMA COLLEEN, healthcare organization administrator; b. Salt Lake City, June 13, 1930; d. Thomas Richard and Luella Sophia (Metz) Robinson; divorced; children—Bruce, Lloyd (dec.), Deborah, Amy. B.A., U. Colo., 1969, M.P.A., 1981. Asst. adminstr. U. Colo. Sch. Medicine, Denver, 1964-74; adminstrv. dir. Estes Park Inst., Englewood, Colo., 1974-84, exec. dir., chief operating officer, sec.-treas., trustee, 1984—. Co-author: The Medical Staff and The Modern Hospital, 1985. Contbr. procs. Emerging Issues in Healthcare, 1986. Mortarboard Orgn. scholar, 1963. Mem. Assn. Western Hosps., AAAS. Republican. Avocations: golf; hiking; cross-country skiing; classical music; theater. Office: Estes Park Inst PO Box 400 Englewood CO 80151

WILSON, WILMA RUTH, utility company executive; b. East Chicago, Ind., June 20, 1950; d. William Vernon and Barbara Ann (Carson) Coward; m. Clyde Matthew Wilson, July 30, 1966; children—Dawn, Tracy. B.S. in Bus. Adminstr., Ind. U., 1980; postgrad. Purdue U., 1984-84. Engring. record clk. No. Ind. Pub. Service Co., Hammond, 1970-72, application credit clk., Gary, 1972-76, asst. to chief clk., 1976-78, personnel rep., 1978-84, system cons., Hammond, 1984—, mem. speakers bur., 1983-84; dir. No. Ind. Fed. Credit Union, Merrillville; edn. cons. Gary Vocat. Office Edn. Program, 1985—. Multimedia instr. ARC, Hammond, 1982—; loaned exec. Lake Area United Way, 1984—. Mem. Ind. U. Alumni Assn. Democrat. Baptist. Clubs: Xinos Beams, La Belle Femmes (Gary)(sec. 1983-84). Avocations: traveling; reading. Home: 3828 W 15th Ave Gary IN 46404 Office: No Ind Pub Service Co 5265 Hohman Ave Hammond IN 46320

WILSON-DUCLOS, CHRISTINE LOUISE, health administrator, consultant; b. Meyersdale, Pa., Apr. 27, 1953; d. Edmund George and Annemarie Jenny (Bohm) Wilson; m. David C. Duclos. B.A., U. Pitts., 1975, M.P.H., 1977. Edn./outreach supr. Planned Parenthood of Cambria Somerset, Johnstown, Pa., 1977-79; community organizer Family Planning Council Western Pa., Pitts., 1979; youth counselor VisonQuest Inc., Colorado Springs, Colo., 1980; cons., staff asst. Colo. Med. Polit. Action Com., Colo. Profl. Liability Trust, Colo. Med. Soc., Denver, 1980-81; cons.-coordinator Colo. Jail Health Care Project, Colo. Med. Soc., Denver, 1981—; site survey cons. Am. Health Care Cons. Inc., 1981—. Editor Jail Health Care Newsletter. Recipient hon. mention Gold Key awards Colo. chpt. Bus./Profl. Advt. Assn., 1981. Mem. Am. Correction Assn., Am. Correctional Health Services Assn., Am. Jail Assn., Am. Pub. Health Assn., Rocky Mountain Correctional Health Assn. (v.p., dir. 1983—), Nat. Assn. Female Execs. Home: 547 Detroit St Denver CO 80206 Office: Colo Jail Health Care Project 6825 E Tennessee Bldg 2 Suite 500 Denver CO 80224

WILSON-VLOTMAN, ANN LOUISE, special education educator; b. Broken Hill, N.S.W., Australia, Sept. 7, 1949; d. James Charles Oliver and Peggy Elise (Gibbins) Wilson; m. Willem Frederik Vlotman, Aug. 18, 1983; 1 child, Willem Frederik. B.Ed., Adelaide Coll. Advanced Edn., Australia, 1978; M.S., Western Oreg. State Coll., 1980; Ed.D., Utah State U., 1984. Cert. tchr. Utah; cert. parent-infant educator. Tchr., Australian Dept. Edn., Adelaide, 1971-76; lectr., supr. Adelaide Coll. Advanced Edn., 1978-79; instr. curriculum devel. Ski High Inst., Utah State U., Logan, 1983, project coordinator, 1983-85, cons., 1985; cons. spl. edn., Logan, 1985—. Co-author: (book) Educational Audiology Directory, 1985; Educational Audiology for the Hard of Hearing Child, 1986; (tng. manuals) Insite Home Visit Curriculum, 4 vols., 1985. Contbr. articles to profl. jours. Fulbright scholar, 1979-84. Mem. Alexander Graham Bell Assn. for the Deaf, Conv. Am. Instructors of the Deaf, Assn. Supervision Curriculum and Devel., AAUW, Nat. Assn. Female Execs., Phi Kappa Phi. Club: Toastmasters (sec.-treas. 1984-85, named Competent Toastmaster 1985). Avocations: reading; camping; gardening; travelling. Address: care Louis Berger Internat PO Box 798 Chittagong Bangladesh

WILTSE, GLADYS MAY, social worker; b. Denmark Twp., Mich., July 2, 1908; d. Norman John and Alice May (Levis) Garner; B.A., Eastern Mich. U., 1948; postgrad. U. Mich., 1955-69; m. Dorr Norman Wiltse, Nov. 11, 1932; children—Dorr Norman, Saire Christina Wiltse Keckler. Tchr. public high sch., Mayville, Mich., 1927-30, Vassar (Mich.) High Sch., 1930-33; social worker Tuscola County (Mich.) Bur. Social Aid, 1937-40, supr., 1940-44; area rep. Mich. Dept. Social Welfare Thumb Area, Caro, 1944-48; tchr. Caro High Sch., 1955-73; mem. Tuscola County Social Services Bd., 1952-85, chmn., 1954-68, vice chmn., 1968-79, 83-85; founder, sponsor Caro High Sch. History Club, 1958-73. Co-founder Watrousville-Caro Area Hist. Soc. and Museum, 1972. Recipient award of commendation Mich. Civil War Centnnial Graves Registration Com., 1965; Merit award Rotary Club, 1975; cert. appreciation Saginaw Inter-Tribal Assn., Inc., 1977; Outstanding Soc. Service award Watrousville-Caro Area Hist. Soc., 1982, numerous other awards. Mem. Mich. Counties Social Services Assn. (Meritorious award 1959, cert. commendation 1981), Caro Tchrs. Assn. (pres. 1956-57), Ret. Tchrs.' Assn., Indianfields Questers (pres. 1974-76), Tuscola County Med. Care Facility Forget Me Not Club, Cass River Gem and Mineral Soc., Saginaw Geneal. Soc. Clubs: Caro Garden (pres. 1977-78), DAR, Nat. Soc. Colonial Dames XVII Century, Nat. Soc. Daus. of Barons Runnemede, Huguenot Soc. Mich., Order of Crown of Charlemagne in U.S.A., Nat. Soc. Old Plymouth Colony Descs., Nat. Soc. Daus. Colonial Wars, Order Three Crusades, 1096-1192, Nat. Soc. Sons and Daus. of Pilgrims. Dames of the Court of Honor, Ancient and Honorable Artillery Co., Nat. Soc. of Magna Charta Dames, Colonial Daus., of the XVII Century. Home: 708 W Sherman St PO Box 143 Caro MI 48723

WILTSEE, SARAH, real estate broker, lecturer; b. Danville, Ky., Sept. 13, 1941; d. Joseph Perkins and Edith (Abbott) Gover; m. Charles Spinning Wiltsee, Sept. 6, 1969; children—Lisa, Beth, Eric, Kevin. Grad. Tex. Realtors Inst., 1976. Cert. residential specialist, real estate brokerage mgr. Sales mgr. Herman Waters, Realtors, Austin, Tex., 1976-77; pres., owner Sarah Wiltsee, Realtors, Austin, 1977-83; dir. brokerage Doyle Wilson & Assocs., Austin, 1983-84; v.p. brokerage Arbor Homes, Austin, 1984-85; gen. mgr. Bill Milburn, Realtors, Austin, 1985—. Mem. Austin Bus. Leaders Council, Forming the Future Study Group, Gov.'s Task Force on Energy. Mem. Austin Bd. Realtors (pres. 1984), Nat. Assn. Realtors (bd. dirs.), Tex. Realtors Found., Nat. Realtors Found., Tex. Assn. Realtors (v.p. region VIII 1986, various coms.), Austin Multiple Listing Service, Women's Council Realtors. Republican. Baptist. Club: Capital. Home: 5928 Highland Hills Dr Austin TX 78731 Office: Bill Milburn Realtors 13706 Research Blvd 310 Austin TX 78750

WILTSHIRE, BONNIE LOU, insurance company manager; b. Washington, July 19, 1956; d. Paul J. and Betty Jane (Newhouse) Bennett; m. Gregory Deane Wiltshire, July 6, 1979. B.S. cum laude, Towson State U., 19. Adminstrv. asst. Riggs, Counselman, Michaels & Downe, Inc., Balt., 1978-80; underwriter asst. Wye Ins. Corp., Towson, Md., 1980-81; mgmt. trainee to ops. mgr. mid-Atlantic region Tifco, Inc., Balt., 1981-86, corp. accounts receivable mgr., 1986—. Mem. Lutherville Community Assn., 1984—. Senatorial State scholar, 1974-75; Md. Gov.'s Scholastic Achievement award, 1974. Democrat. Baptist. Avocations: piano; needlecrafts; cooking; refinishing; gardening.

WILZACK, ADELE, state health official. Student Loyola Coll., R.N. diploma Mercy Hosp. Sch. Nursing, Balt., 1957; B.S. in Nursing, Mt. St. Agnes coll., 1959; M.S. in Nursing, U. Md., 1960; postgrad. in pub. adminstrn. U. So. Calif., 1976. Staff nurse Mercy Hosp., Balt., 1957-60, supr. non-profl. personnel, 1961-63, asst. dir. nursing services, 1963-65; project nurse operation REASON, Community Action Agy., Health and Welfare Council, Balt., 1965-67; asst. dir. bur. spl. home services Balt. City Health Dept., 1967-72, dir. bur. spl. home services, 1972-74, dir. health services for aging, 1974-76, asst. commr. health services for aging and med. care, 1976-79; asst. sec. for med. care programs Md. Dept. Health and Mental Hygiene, Balt., 1979-83, sec. dept., 1983—; assoc. faculty mem. U. Md. Sch. Nursing; vis. faculty mem. U. Mich. Inst. Gerontology, Ann Arbor; past mem. Md. Gov.'s Task Force on Med. Malprctice Ins., Md. Gov.'s Task Force on Health Care Cost Containment; past com. mem. and chmn. Central Md. Health Systems Agy.; past com. mem., past subcom. chmn. Md. Med. Assistance Adv. Com.; past chmn. Balt. City Sub-Area Adv. Council; past mem. regional adv. task force Johns Hopkins Hosp., task force on aging U. Md. Recipient award for outstanding contbns. to intergroup relations and dedicated humanitarian service to citizens of Balt. City, Balt. Community Relations Commn., 1978, Alumna of Yr. award Loyola Coll., 1978, Woman Mgr. of Yr., Conf. for Women in State Service, 1981; Merit scholar U. Md. Sch. Nursing. Mem. Md. Pub. Health Assn. (past mem. exec. com.), Am. Pub. Health Assn. (past mem. governing council state affiliate), Balt. City Med. Soc. (past mem. long-term care com.), Sigma Phi Sigma, Sigma Theta Tau. Office: Md Dept Health and Mental Hygiene 201 W Preston St Baltimore MD 21201

WIMBERLY, ZACQUELINE ELIZABETH, cattle farm executive; b. Cypress, Fla., Sept. 8, 1930; d. Ara Boyd and Viola Lula-Arthur (Hamilton) Sellers; m. William Ester, Sept. 10, 1948 (div. Oct. 1973); children—William Arthur, Tamaria Elizabeth; m. George Terrance Wimberly, Feb. 27, 1974. Student Chipola Jr. Coll., Marianna, Fla. Office mgr., Chavers-Fowhand Furniture, Marianna, 1949-56; teller, bookkeeping dept. Citizens State Bank, Marianna, 1955-65; with The Rhyne Co. Inc., Marianna, 1948-49; with Lehigh Portland Cement Co., Marianna, 1965-74; area mgr. Princess House Products, Marianna, 1977—; co-owner G & Z Charolais Farm, Marianna, 1974—. Clk., Eastside Bapt. Ch., Marianna, 1959—, tchr. Bible study, 1959—. Mem. Nat. Assn. Female Execs., Nat. Charolais Assn., Fla. Cowbelles, Jackson County Cattlemen's Assn. Avocations: travel; cattle farming; flower gardening; swimming. Home and Office: Route 1 Box 427 Marianna FL 32446

WINANDY, CAROL MARIE, designer; b. Chgo., Sept. 8, 1938; d. Thomas Pierre and Marie Ann (Diedling) W. B.A. in Fine Arts, Art Inst. Chgo., 1961; postgrad. U. Chgo., 1961. Dress designer Adrian Tabin, Chgo., 1961-62; lingerie designer Kellwood Co., Chgo., 1962-63, Phill-Maid Co., Chgo., 1963-65, Vassarette div. of Munsingwear, Mpls., 1965-67, O'Bryan Bros., Inc., Chgo., 1967-76; founder, pres. Tatsy Co., Chgo., 1976—. Patentee in field. Mem. Fashion Group, Internat. Old Lacers, Thimble Collectors Internat., Young Women of the Arts. Office: Tatsy Co Po Box 1401 Des Plaines IL 60017

WINANT, ETHEL WALD, broadcasting executive; b. Worcester, Mass., Aug. 5; d. William and Janice (Woolson) Wald; B.A., U. Calif., Berkeley; M.T.A., Whittier Coll.; children—William, Scott, Bruce. Dir. casting Talen Assos., N.Y.C., 1953-56; asso. producer Playhouse '90, CBS, Hollywood, Calif., 1956-60; asso. producer All Fall Down, MGM, Calif., 1960-61; producer Gt. Adventure, DBS, Hollywood, 1961-62; v.p. talent, dir. program devel. CBS, Hollywood, 1962-75; exec. producer Best of Families, PBS, N.Y.C., 1975-77, CBS movie A Time to Triumph, 1985; v.p. talent NBC, Burbank, Calif., 1978—, v.p. mini-series and novels for TV, 1979; sr. v.p. Metromedia Producers Co., 1981—; mem. adv. bd. Center for Advanced Film Studies, Am. Film Inst., 1981—, Procter & Gamble Gt. Am. Women. Bd. govs. Nat. Acad. TV Arts and Scis.; bd. dirs. Circle Repertory Theatre; mem. Pres.'s Commn. for Women; mem. Calif. Arts Council; cons. in field; mem. speakers bur. Braille Inst. Recipient Emmy award Nat. Acad. TV Arts and Scis., 1960; Disting. Alumni award Calif. Community Colls., 1981; named TV Woman of Yr., Conf. Personal Mgrs., 1974. Mem. Acad. TV Arts and Scis. (exec. com. 1981—), John Tracy Clinic, Women in Film (Crystal award 1979), Hollywood Radio and TV Soc. (dir. 1981—, sec. 1981—). Office: 5746 Sunset Blvd Los Angeles CA

WINCH, DEBRA LYNN CHAMPION, industrial engineer; b. Ishpeming, Mich., Aug. 25, 1956; d. Ruben Richard and Donna Mae (Benson) C.; B.S.B.A., Mich. Tech. U., 1979; m. Raymond F. Winch, Jr. Indsl. engr. Am. Can Co., Menasha, Wis., 1979-80, porcelain div. Franklin Mint Corp., Franklin Center, Pa., 1981-85, supr. credit union, 1982—. Adviser, Jr. Achievement, 1983. Mem. Houghton (Mich.) Bus. and Profl. Woman's Club (mem. legislative com. 1978-79), Phi Gamma Nu (v.p. 1977-79, Phila. chpt. alumni 1981—). Home: 138 Ridge Blvd Brookhaven PA 19015 Office: Franklin Mint Corp Porcelain Div Aston PA

WINCHELL, MARGARET WEBSTER ST. CLAIR, realtor; b. Clinton, Tenn., Jan. 26, 1923; d. Robert Love and Mayme Jane (Warwick) Webster; student Denison U., 1940, Miami U., Oxford (Ohio), 1947, 48; m. Charles M. Winchell, June 7, 1941; children—David Alan (dec.), Margaret Winchell Boyle; m. 2d, Robert George Sterrett, July 15, 1977 (dec. 1985). Saleswoman Fred K.A. Schmidt & Shirmer real estate, Cin., 1960-66, Cline Realtors, Cin., 1966-70; owner, broker Winchell's Showplace Realtors, Cin., 1972—; ins. agt. United Liberty Life Ins. Co., 1966—, dist. mgr., 1967-70, 77-82, regional mgr., 1982—; stockbroker Waddell & Reed, Columbus, Ohio, 1972—. Security Counselors; ins. broker, 1984, gen. agent; dir. Fin. Cons., 1984, 85, 86, 87. Treas., v.p. Parents without Partners, 1969, sec., 1968; pres. PTA; dir. Children's Bible Fellowship Ohio, 1953-76; dir. Child Evangelism Cin.; nat. speaker Child Evangelism Fellowship and Nat. Sunday Sch. Convs., 1955-57; pres. Christian Solos, 1974; chaplain Bethesda N. Hosp. Mem. Nat. Assn. Real Estate Bds. West Shell Realtors (v.p.), Womens Council Real Estate Bd. (treas.). Clubs: Alfonta, Travel go go, Guys and Gals Singles (founder, 1st pres.), Hamilton Singles (pres.). Home and Office: 8221 Margaret Ln Cincinnati OH 45242

WINCHESTER, ALMA ELIZABETH TATSCH (MRS. CLARENCE FLOYD WINCHESTER), civic worker, radio writer and broadcaster; b. Fredericksburg, Tex.; d. Otto August and Meta (Hohenberger) Tatsch; spl. student Am. Conservatory Music (Chgo.), 1937-38; m. Clarence Floyd Winchester, Sept. 25, 1943. Singer Chgo. Civic Opera Jr. Chorus, 1937-38; writer radio script Evans Fur Co., Chgo., 1941-42; writer Sta. KTSA, San Antonio, 1942-43; women's dir., writer, broadcaster Sta. KNOE, Monroe, La., 1944-45; writer, music lead ins Boyce Smith Show, Sta. WGN, Chgo., 1944; women's dir., writer, broadcaster Sta. WGGG, Gainesville, Fla., 1948-49; public relations Stokeley-Van Camp, Inc., Washington, 1954-55. Mem.

Salvation Army Aux., Washington; mem. women's bd. Providence Hosp., Washington, Pan-Am. liaison com. Women's Orgns., Washington, to 1981; mem. Women's Internat. Religious Fellowship in cooperation with UNESCO, UNICEF, schs., embassies; past pres. City of Hope Med. Research chpt. 56, Washington. Mem. Los Picaros (hon.). Mem. Christian Ch. Home: 2124 Sudbury Pl NW Washington DC 20012

WINCHESTER, VALINDA BLACKMON, state administrator; b. Richmond, Va., July 29, 1938; d. Thomas Franklin and Lucy Hazel (Lucas) Blackmon; m. Dan G. Mores, Dec. 28, 1985; m. Robert J. Winchester, Jr., June 14, 1958 (div. 1978); children—Jeffrey, Ellen, Kevin. M.A., Ariz. State U., 1981, M.P.A., 1982. Program coordinator Ariz. State U., 1982-85; intern Town of Guadalupe, Ariz., 1985; policy coordinator Ariz. Health Care Cost Containment System, Phoenix, 1985—; cons. Islamic Inst., Tempe, 1984. Bd. dirs. Phoenix Boys Choir, 1978. Mem. Am. Guild Organists. Democrat. Episcopalian. Avocation: vocalist. Home: 1411 S Marilyn Ann Dr Tempe AZ 85281 Office: Ariz Health Care Cost Containment System 801 E Jefferson St Phoenix AZ 85013

WINFIELD, BARBARA LABARGE, plastics consultant; b. Potsdam, N.Y., June 27, 1935; d. Clarence Lewis and Barbara (Pelsue) LaB.; m. Armand G. Winfield, July 23, 1966. B.S. in Art Edn., SUNY-Buffalo, 1958, postgrad., summer, 1959; postgrad. Columbia U., summer, 1960. Tchr. art Susquehanna Central Sch. Dist., Binghamton, N.Y., 1958-61, Conard High Sch., West Hartford, Conn., 1961-62, South Congl. Ch., Hartford, Conn., 1962-66; art dir. Fine Art Found. of Conn., Hartford, 1962-66; owner LaBarge Studios, Rocky Hill, Conn. and N.Y.C., 1962-68; pres. LaBarge Industries Ltd., West Babylon, N.Y., 1968-70, Finders Delightful Ltd., West Babylon, 1975-77; sec.-treas. Armand G. Winfield Inc., West Babylon and Santa Fe, N.Mex., 1966—; maker mus. replications for various Am. museums; designer, mfr. fashion jewelry, sculpture, housewares, indsl. products, toys, games, stage sets and costumes; plastics cons. Author, patentee in field. Mem. exec. com. to elect Dora Battle as Mayor of Santa Fe, 1981-82; aux. bd. Santa Fe Crime Stoppers Carnivals, 1983, 84. Recipient cert. of excellence in graphic design, Mead Library of Ideas, 1968. Mem. Soc. Plastics Engrs., (affiliate), Soc. Advancement Material and Process Engrng. (dir., co-chmn. membership Rio Grande chpt. 1985-86), Santa Fe C. of C. Club: Santa Fe Press (bd. dirs. 1983). Home: PO Box 1296 Santa Fe NM 87504 Office: 3 Siler Ln Santa Fe NM 87501

WINFREY, SUSAN VAUGHN, government official; b. Richmond, Va., June 12, 1946; d. Eddie Raymond and Hazel Isabelle (Axselle) Vaughn; B.Mus. Edn., Tex. Tech U., 1968; M.A. in Ednl. Adminstrn., U. Tex., El Paso, 1982. Music tchr., Ralls, Tex., 1968-69; elem. tchr., Grants, N.Mex., 1969-70; social studies tchr., Hatch, N.Mex., 1970-72; pastor's sec., El Paso, Tex. and Tampa, Fla., 1972-74; sec. Tarrant Bapt. Assn., Ft. Worth, 1974-75; substitute tchr. Ft. Worth Schs., 1975-76; social studies tchr., Pine Hill, N.Mex., 1976-79; cons. U. N.Mex., Albuquerque, 1980; tchr., El Paso, 1980-81; prin. Immanuel Bapt. Christian Sch., El Paso, 1981-83; with computer project liaison dept. Resource Mgmt. Office, U.S. Army Air Def. Arty. Sch., Ft. Bliss, Tex., 1984—; bd. mem. Tchr. Center, rural N.Mex., also travel rep. Mem. NEA, Tex. Classroom Tchrs. Assn., Assn. Individually Guided Edn. (facilitator), Assn. Supervision and Curriculum Devel., Nat. Assn. Female Execs. Baptist. Office: Bldg 2 Room 116 Fort Bliss TX 79916

WING, KYLENE SCARBOROUGH (MRS. ROBERT L. WING), columnist; b. Charlotte, N.C.; d. Kyle and Tomi (Riggs) Scarborough; grad. Stevens Schs. for Models, 1946-47, Ben Bard Acad. Theatre, Hollywood, Calif., 1952, Nat. Acad. Broadcasting Washington, 1957, UCLA Extension, 1965, Free U. Berlin Otto-Suhrz Inst. Extension, 1966. m. Robert L. Wing, Jan. 16, 1943; children—Susan, Jayme. Columnist, Kylene's Kalifornia Kapers, Inverness, Fla., 1965-66, Kylene's Kontinental Kapers, Berlin, Germany, 1966-68; publicity chmn. Am. Women's Club Founder patron Huntington Hartford Theatre; mem. Concerned Friend Nat. League Families POW-MIA, U.S. Congl. Adv. Bd. Recipient letter of Appreciation USAF, 1973. Mem. Planetary Soc., Hollywood C. of C., Freedom Found. at Valley Forge, Los Angeles World Affairs Council. Presbyn. Clubs: German American Women's, American Women's, American Yacht (all Berlin); Los Angeles Riding and Polo; Air Force Officers Wives; Bel-Air Republican Women's. Address: 3405 Blair Dr Hollywood CA 90026

WINGARD, KIMBERLY A., information manager; b. Seattle, May 23, 1956; d. Mervin Elliott Wingard and Patricia Ann (Pallett) Jorgensen. B.A., Calif. State U.-Northridge, 1980; M.S.L.S., U. So. Calif., Los Angeles, 1980-81. Library asst. Calif. State U.-Northridge, 1978-80; instr. Highline Community Coll., Seattle, 1981; info. analyst RMI ARCO, Anchorage, 1982, librarian Elmendorf AFB, Anchorage, 1982; cons., owner Applied Info. Mgmt., Anchorage, 1982-84; records analyst SOHIO Alaska Petroleum Co., Anchorage, 1983—. Mem. Assn. Records Mgrs. and Adminstrs. (v.p. Anchorage 1982-84, pres. 1984), ALA, Alaska Library Assn., Am. Soc. Info. Sci., Beta Phi Mu (scholarship award 1981, info. transfer subcom., com. on natural resources info. mgmt.). Clubs: Nordic Ski (Anchorage); Toastmasters. Home: PO Box 100121 Anchorage AK 99510 Office: SOHIO Pouch 6 612 Anchorage AK 99502

WINGATE, BETTY JEANINE, electrical construction company executive; b. Massillon, Ohio, June 1, 1930; d. Cletus and Beatrice Merle (Orr) Cutcher; m. James Preston Wingate, Apr. 20, 1956; children—Sheila, Steven, James, Mitchella, Cindy. Freelance model, Jacksonville, Fla., 1959-79; owner, operator dress shop, bridal gown rental shop, Jacksonville, 1976-84; pres. Jacksonville Heights Elect Constrn. Co., Inc., Jacksonville, 1970—; owner, operator Sr. Citizens Mobile Home Terr., Jacksonville, 1972—; instr. phys. fitness class, 1980. Republican. Mormon. Office: Jacksonville Heights Elec Constrn Co Inc 8917 Noroad Rd Jacksonville FL 32210

WINGATE, ELIZA CUNNINGHAM WEEKS, librarian, consultant; b. Washington, Sept. 25, 1943; d. Donald Weeks and Eliza Cunningham (Goddard) Weeks Bacas; m. Paul Shawn Wingate, Sept. 23, 1966; children—Rose Alice, Sierra Laurel. B.A. in Art, U. Calif.-Berkeley, 1965; M.L.S., Drexel U., 1983. Librarian circulation dept. film and resource library Ludington Pub. Library, Bryn Mawr, Pa., 1976-83; head librarian Belmont Hills Pub. Library (Pa.), 1983—; cons. New Gulph Childrens Ctr., Radnor, Pa., 1980—, Home Systems, Bryn Mawr, 1977—, Evergreen Fund, Rosemont, Pa., 1978—. Producer slide/tape: Penguins Don't Have Libraries, 1982. Active Lower Merion Resource Ctr., Bala-Cynwyd, Pa., 1974-76; v.p. Zero Population Growth, Phila., 1977-78; bd. dirs. New Gulph Children's Ctr., 1980—. Mem. AIA, Pa. Library Assn., Beta Phi Mu. Democrat. Home: 718 Old Lancaster Rd Bryn Mawr PA 19010 Office: Belmont Hills Pub Library 120 Mary Watersford Rd Belmont Hills PA 19004

WINGER, DEBRA, actress; b. Cleve., 1955; d. Robert and Ruth W. Student Calif. State U.-Northridge. Made 1st profl. appearance in Wonder Woman TV series, 1976-77; appeared in TV film Spl. Olympics, 1977; appeared in films Thank God It's Friday, 1978, French Postcards, 1979, Urban Cowboy, 1980, Cannery Row, 1982, An Officer and a Gentleman, 1982, Terms of Endearment, 1983, Mike's Murder, 1984. Served with Israeli Army, 1972. *

WINGERT, EMILY ANN, private detective; b. N.Y.C., Nov. 24, 1934; d. Edgar S. Peierls and Betsy (Vogel) Peierls Evans; B.S., Columbia U., 1961; widow; children—Laura, Edward, William. Cert. in security tng., retail security, security surveys, security mgmt., guard force mgmt., assets protection, phys. security. Pvt. cons. to art collectors and dealers, 1962-74; sec.-treas. Mark Ten Assocs., Inc., Montclair, N.J., 1974-75, pres., 1975—; pres. Centurion Tng. Inst., Inc., 1981—, W.C. Pubs., Inc., 1982-86, Trumpets Restaurant and Jazz Cafe, 1985—; gen. ptnr. WWZ Assocs. Ltd. Partnership, 1985—. Bd. dirs. Whole Theatre Co., Montclair, 1973, 82—; mem. bd. N. Essex Drug Abuse Council, 1970-73; residential fund chmn. Montclair chpt. ARC, 1972; mem. chmn.'s com. U.S. Senatorial Bus. Adv. Bd., 1981-82; co-founder Republican Presdl. Task Force, 1982—. Mem. Am. Soc. Indsl. Security (cert. protection profl., vice chmn. No. N.J. chpt. 1981, chmn. contract security com. 1980-81, chmn. security seminar com. 1982), Nat. Council Investigative and Security Services, N.J. Pvt. Detectives Assn., Am. Law Enforcement Officers Assn., Acad. Security Educators and Trainers, Nat. Assn. Female Execs., Am. Mgmt. Assn., Nat. Assn. Chiefs Police, Nat. Restaurant Assn., N.J. Restaurant Assn., Internat. Assn. Chiefs Police. Unitarian. Author basic security officer tng. manual, seminar materials, also audiovisual programs for security personnel. Office: 500 Bloomfield Ave Montclair NJ 07042

WINGERT, HANNELORE CHRISTIANE, chemical company executive; b. Karlsbad, Czechoslavakia, Feb. 9, 1942; came to U.S., 1962, naturalized, 1967; d. Andreas and Gisela Maria (Ciharz) Zwickel; m. Rudolf Wingert, Nov. 9, 1963; children—Angela, Helene, Christopher, Rudolf. I.B.A., Stadt. Berufsschule, Fed. Republic Germany, 1961; postgrad. in mgmt. Bergen Community Coll., 1983. Clk. various cos., N.J., 1963, bilingual sec., 1963-78; exec. sec., adminstrv. asst. Lurgi Corp., Hasbrouck Heights, N.J., 1978-81; sr. exec. sec. Degussa Corp., Teterboro, N.J., 1981-83, asst. product mgr. silica, 1983-85, asst. product mgr. H202, 1985—. Author community newsletter, 1972-73. Chmn. master planning com. High Crest Lake, West Milford, N.J., 1974-75; advisor Jr. Woman's Club Kinnelon-Butler, Butler, N.J., 1973-74. Mem. Am. Mgmt. Assn., TAPPI, Assn. Computing Machinery, Nat. Assn. Female Execs. Republican. Roman Catholic. Club: High Crest Lake Woman's (pres. 1972-73) (West Milford, N.J.). Home: 204 High Crest Dr West Milford NJ 07480 Office: Degussa Corp Route 46 J Hollister Rd Teterboro NJ 07608

WINGFIELD, CANDACE SUZANNE, architect; b. Alexandria, Va., Feb. 28, 1954; d. Joseph Daniel and Betty Jo (Elmore) W.; B.Arch., U. Cin., 1977. Archtl. apprentice J. Joseph Wagner, Assos., Troy, Ohio, 1973-77, architect, 1977—, in charge design, drafting dept., 1977—. Mem. adv. com. Upper Valley Joint Vocat. Sch., 1981—. Mem. Am. Bus. Women's Assn. (v.p. 1980-81, pres. 1981-82; named Woman of Year 1982), AIA, and the Architects Soc. of Ohio. Club: Women of Moose. Office: J Joseph Wagner Assos 25 S Norwich Rd Troy OH 45373

WINGO-DAVIS, MARIAN LEE, feminist therapist; b. Asheville, N.C., Sept. 16, 1944; d. Hugh Albert and Lee Ardis (English) Wingo; B.S. in Edn., Fla. State U., Tallahassee, 1966; M.S. in Human Devel. Counseling with honors George Peabody Coll., 1978; m. H.C. Davis, Aug. 28, 1966; children—Remi, Wade. Feminist therapist, human devel. counselor, San Antonio, 1980-82; dir. women's tng. programs Internat. Trainers, Educators and Cons., Inc., San Antonio, 1980-82, now cons; staff counselor Gulf Coast Family Counseling Agy., Pascagoula, Miss., 1983—; exec. bd. San Antonio Women's Credit Union, 1981—, San Antonio Women's Law Center, 1981—, Battered Women's Shelter of Bexar County, 1981—. Program chmn. Bexar County Women's Polit. Caucus, 1980-81; exec. bd. Gulf Coast Women's Center; bd. dirs. Pascagoula Women's Restitution Center. Recipient Today's Woman award San Antonio Light, Women's Network Profl. Devel. Leadership award, Lic. counselor. Mem. Nat. Feminist Therapist Assn., Assn. Women in Psychology, Town and Country Bus. and Profl. Women (Outstanding Citizen award), Women in Bus., NOW, Tex. Women's Polit. Caucus, Am. Assn. Counseling and Devel., Older Women's League, Am. Soc. Tng. and Devel. (asst. chairperson nat. women's network 1983-85, dir. women's network 1986—, regional coordinator 1981-83), Nat. Assn. Profl. Cons. Methodist. Home: 111 Mark Daniel Circle Ocean Springs MS 39564 Office: 408 Convent Pascagoula MS 39567

WINGROVE, BARBARA KESHIN, consulting company executive, computer systems consultant; b. N.Y.C., May 4, 1942; d. Jesse Gerald and Frieda Anna (Berkof) K.; m. James Russell Wingrove, Aug. 18, 1968; children—Robin Susanne, David James. B.A., U. Rochester, 1964. Programmer IBM, Zurich, Switzerland, 1963, systems analyst, Gaithersburg, Md., 1964-73, advt. mktg. rep., Rosslyn, Va., 1973-76; instr. Montgomery Coll., Rockville, Md., 1978-80; founder, pres. Win Data Cons. Ltd., Gaithersburg, 1980—; cons., trainer U. Va., Falls Church, 1982-84, Boeing Computer Service, Seattle, 1980—. Com. mem. Potomac Highlands Citizens Assn., Md., 1975—; team mgr. Montgomery Soccer Assn., Rockville, Md., 1983—; group aide Cub Scouts Am., Rockville, 1985, Girl Scouts Am., Rockville, 1983. Mem. Washington Ind. Computer Cons. (referral chmn. 1983), Ind. Computer Cons. Am., Met. Area Assn. Group Systems. Republican. Jewish. Clubs: Potomac Valley Skiers (Washington) (dir. 1981-83); Temple Beth Ami Sisterhood (Rockville, Md.). Avocations: skiing; gardening; children. Office: Win Data Cons Ltd 9001 Shady Grove Ct Gaithersburg MD 20877

WINICK, JANET MICHELE, gourmet food company executive; b. Bronxville, N.Y., Oct. 19, 1960; d. Eugene H. and Ina E. (Hodes) W. B.B.A., Emory U., 1982; postgrad. NYU, 1985—. Owner, pres. Isle Imports, Inc., N.Y.C., 1981—; distbn. mgr. Flying Foods, Internat., Inc., Long Island City, N.Y., 1983-86. Mem. Nat. Assn. Specialty Food Trade, Nat. Assn. Female Execs., Roundcircle for Women in Food Service, Nat. Mktg. Assn., Westchester Assn. Women Bus. Owners. Avocations: swimming, theatre. Home: 108 Thompson St New York NY 10012 Office: Isle Imports Inc 210 Fifth Ave New York NY 10010

WINICK, PAULINE, communications executive; b. N.Y.C., Sept. 19, 1946; d. Morris and Frances (Fox) Leiderman; m. Bruce Jeffrey Winick, June 19, 1966 (div. 1977); children—Margot Scott, Graham Douglas. B.A., Bklyn. Coll., 1966; M.A., NYU, 1971; A.S., Miami-Dade Community Coll., 1977. Tchr. N.Y.C. Pub. Schs., 1966-66, 69-74, Bloomington (Ind.) Pub. Schs., 1968-69; producer Sta. WPLG-TV, Miami, Fla., 1975-79; dir. Office of Communications, Metro-Dade County, Miami, Fla., 1979-86; exec. asst. city mgr. City of Miami, 1986—. Bd. dirs. Fla. Close-Up, Miami, 1979—; mem. exec. com. Leadership Miami Conf., 1980—; bd. dirs. LWV, Miami, 1980; mem. planning com. United Way, Miami, 1980—; bd. dirs. Anti-Defamation League, 1983. Mem. Nat. Acad. TV Arts and Scis. (bd. govs. Miami chpt.). Home: 11420 SW 72nd Ave Miami FL 33156 Office: Miami City Hall 3500 Pan American Dr Miami FL 33133

WINKEL, NINA, sculptor; b. Germany, May 21, 1905; d. Ernst and Augustine (Bauer) Koch; came to U.S., 1942, naturalized, 1945; student Staedel Mus. Art Sch., 1929-31; D.F.A. (hon.), SUNY, 1985; m. George J. Winkel, Dec. 15, 1934. Trustee, Sculpture Center, Inc., N.Y.C., 1946-69, pres., 1970-73, pres. emeritus, trustee, 1974—; one-man shows: Notre Dame U., 1954, Sculpture Center, N.Y.C., 1944, 47, 58, 72, Adirondack Mus., Elizabethtown, N.Y., 1976, Center Music Drama Art, Lake Placid, N.Y., 1977, Nat. Savs. Bank, Plattsburgh, N.Y., 1979, Carpenter and Painter Gallery, Elizabethtown, 1982, Allentown (Pa.) Art Mus., 1982, SUNY-Plattsburgh, 1983, 84, SUNY-Albany, 1984, Sculpture Ctr. Inc., N.Y.C., 1984; group shows: Met. Mus., Whitney Mus., Pa. Acad., San Francisco Mus., Va. Mus.; hon. adj. prof. SUNY-Plattsburgh, 1983. Juror for sculpture competition Winter Olympics 1980 in Lake Placid, 1978—; trustee Keene Valley Library Assn., 1967—, chmn. bi-centennial com., 1973-77; trustee Adirondack Mus., Elizabethtown, N.Y., 1978—. Recipient Samuel F.B. Morse Gold medal NAD, 1964, Artists Fund prize, 1979, Gold medal, 1982; Founders prize, Mrs. Louis Bennett prize Nat. Sculpture Soc.; Pen's Brush award Pen's Brush club, 1982. Fellow Nat. Sculpture Soc. (sec. 1965-68, Bronze medal 1967, 71, Purchase prize 1981); mem. Nat. Acad. Design (E. Watrous Gold medal 1945, 78, 83), Sculptors Guild, Center Music, Drama and Arts-Lake Placid. Home: Dunham Rd Keene Valley NY 12943

WINKELMAN, NANCY LEE, college official b. Balt., Nov. 16, 1929; d. Morris C. and Elizabeth J. (Hall) Winkelman. B.A., Western Md. Coll., 1951, M.Ed., 1969. Reporter The Post, Frederick, Md., 1951-53, Union Sun-Jour., Lockport, Md., 1953-55; reporter, producer Sta. WMAR-TV, Balt., 1955-57; dir. pub. relations Western Md. Coll., Westminster, 1957-73, Goucher Coll., Balt., 1973-75; dir. publs. Dickinson Coll., Carlisle, Pa., 1975—; editor numerous scholarly pubs. Mem. Council Advancement and Support Edn. (newsletter editor, dir., program dir.), LWV. Democrat. Methodist. Home: 141 Faith Circle Carlisle PA 17013 Office: Publications Office Dickinson College Carlisle PA 17013

WINKLER, NANCY ANN, bank executive; b. N.Y.C., Feb. 11, 1952; d. Andrew Melvin and Madeline Virginia (Mellon) Nordback; m. Herman Michael Winkler, Oct. 15, 1972; 1 child, Herman Andrew. B.B.A. in Acctg. and EDP, Pace Coll., 1972, M.B.A. in Acctg., 1976. With auditing dept. Bankers Trust Co., N.Y.C., 1972-82, v.p., 1979-82; v.p., unit head ALCO audit First Nat. Bank Chgo., 1982-83, sect. head ALCO and service products audit, 1984—, ALCO and staff depts. audit, 1985—; adj. instr. acctg. Pace U., 1977-82; instr. various audit rev. courses, 1980-81; speaker industry confs. Chartered bank auditor; C.P.A. Mem. Bank Adminstrn. Inst. (chartered bank auditor study group task force 1978-81, exam. com. 1982—), Inst. Internal. Auditors (N.Y.C. chpt.). Office: First Nat Bank of Chgo One First Nat Plaza Suite 0327 Chicago IL 60670

WINNER, ANNE MOORE WINDLE, sch. psychologist; b. West Chester, Pa., Sept. 4, 1921; d. Ernest Garfield and Sylvia Louise (Moore) Windle; B.A. in Philosophy, Swarthmore (Pa.) Coll., 1942; postgrad. scholar, Pa. Sch. Social Work, 1945-46; M.A. in Psychology (scholar), Bucknell U., Lewisburg, Pa., 1961; cert. of advanced study in communication disorders Johns Hopkins U., 1974; doctoral candidate Pa. State U., 1981—; m. Drexel Winner, Apr. 15, 1944 (dec. 1967); children—Catherine Winner Salam, David R., Hanna Winner Dunleavy, Rebecca Winner Diehl. Sch. psychologist II, Balt. City Schs., 1963—; cons. psychologist problems of children, pets; Md. rep. Internat. Sch. Psychology Com., 1981-84. Mem. Md. Psychol. Assn. (officer 1975, 76), Balt. City Assn. Sch. Psychologists (pres. 1980-82), Pa. Assn. Sch. Psychologists, Md. Assn. Sch. Psychologists, Am. Psychol. Assn. (asso.), Golden Retreiver Club Am. Quaker. Author articles in field. Address: 102 E Chestnut Hill Ln Reisterstown MD 21136

WINNER, NATHALIE, print advertising consultant; b. Flushing, N.Y.; d. Isidore and Anna (Marks) Baratz; B.B.A., CCNY. Advt. mgr. of wine and liquor Commentary Mag., N.Y.C., 1968-82; v.p. Aronson and Jonfry Co., pubs. reps., 1983—; wine and liquor print advt. cons.; nat. advt. mgr. Dining Out mag., 1984—. Mem. Met. Package Store Assn. of N.Y. (dir. public relations, lobbyist, chmn. legis. com.), N.Y. Fedn. Package Stores (sec.), Women of the Alcoholic Beverage Industry (public relations chmn., recipient Outstanding Achievement award), Internat. Platform Assn. Columnist various jours. incl. N.Y. Beverage Market, Ill. Beverage Jour., Conn. Beverage Jour., R.I. Beverage Jour., Spirits, Wine and Beer Mktg. Home: 888 Grand Concourse Bronx NY 10451 Office: PO Box 107 Bronx NY 10451

WINNICK, HELENE ANN, lawyer; b. Sacramento, Sept. 21, 1956; d. Byron Monroe and Estelle (Feinberg) W. A.A., Am. River Coll., Sacramento, 1975; B.A., UCLA, 1977; J.D., Southwestern U., Los Angeles, 1980. Bar: Calif. 1981, U.S. Tax Ct. 1982. Staff mem. U.S. Ho. of Reps., Los Angeles, 1976, Los Angeles Dept. Consumer Affairs, 1977; law clk. Rosenstock & Rosenstock, Los Angeles, 1979, Goller, Gillin & Menes, Los Angeles, 1979-80; v.p. Winns Sales Inc., Citrus Heights, Calif., 1977—; exec. dir. Quantum Ednl. Devel., Sacramento, 1981-82; assoc. Wohl Cinnamon & Hagedorn, Sacramento, 1980-82; sole practice, Sacramento, 1982—; prof. Pacific Coll. Legal Careers, Sacramento, 1983; lectr. in field U. Calif.-Davis, 1983. Mem. task force cable TV Council of Jewish Fedn., N.Y.C., 1982—; mem. Sacramento Regional Arts Council; bd. dirs. Religious Coalition for Cable TV, Sacramento, 1983—, Los Rios Community Coll. Found., Sacramento, 1984, Sacramento Community Cable Found. Mem. ABA, Calif. State Bar, Sacramento County Bar Assn., Women Lawyers Sacramento, Calif. Young Lawyers Assn. Democrat. Office: 555 University Ave Suite 290 Sacramento CA 95825

WINNING, CYNTHIA ANN, banker; b. Marietta, Ohio, Apr. 13, 1951; d. Theodore Charles and Ruth E. (Valentine) Bauer; student Marietta Coll., 1969-71; m. Theodore P. Winning, Sept. 18, 1975. Art dir. Jour. Am. Newspaper, Myrtle Beach, S.C., 1973-75; local origination dir. Channel II TV, Surfside Beach, S.C., 1975; media dir. Catalina Advt. Agy., Tucson, 1977-78; dir. Winning Advt., Tucson, 1979; dir. advt. Levitz Furniture, Tucson, 1978-79; mktg. product mgr. Citicorp, Denver, 1979-81; dir. mktg. Capital Cities Cable, Denver, 1981-83; dir. mktg. Daniel & Assocs., 1983-86; v.p. Citicorp, Denver, 1986—. Bd. dirs. Denver Internat. Film Festival. Recipient AdMaster Nat. Advt. award, 1973. Mem. Direct Mktg. Assn., Women in Cable, CTAM, Sports Car Club Am. (events dir.). Home: 1331 S Victor St Aurora CO 80012 Office: 5889 S Syracuse Circle Englewood CO 80111

WINSETT-YOUNG, VICTORIA LOUISE, advertising company public relations executive; b. Dallas, Feb. 6, 1950; d. Milo Asa and Louise Love (Metcalfe) Winsett; m. Robert Miles Young, May 27, 1983; 1 son, Christopher John Asa. A.A. in Merchandising, Wade's Coll., Dallas, 1970; student So. Methodist U., 1974-78. Copywriter Sugarman Internat., Dallas, 1969-71; promotion dir. Quandrangle, Dallas, 1971-74; account exec. Tracy-Locke, Dallas, 1974-78, account supr., 1978-80, mgr. pub. relations Tracy-Locke/BBDO, 1980-82; dir. pub. relations Cunningham & Walsh, Dallas, 1982-86; owner The Young Co., Dallas, 1986—; cons. pub. relations Krause & Assocs., Dallas, 1982—. Editor, Shop Talk, 1983; author ann. report Nat. Assn. Retarded Citizens, Dallas, 1981; vol. in pub. relations Consumer's Day Fair, Dallas C. of C., 1982; chmn. pub. relations Boys Club Am., Dallas, 1983; assoc. chmn. pub. relations Terrace Homeowners, Dallas, 1983. Mem. Pub. Relations Soc. Am. (assoc.), Tex. Pub. Relations Assn., Women in Communications, Inc. (profl.), Nat. Assn. Female Execs. Episcopalian. Address: 10806 Colbert Way Dallas TX 75218

WINSHIP, GLORIA GAIL, corporate official, farm owner; b. Augusta, Ga., July 29, 1952; d. William Tiran Winship and Gloria Zelda (Langford) Brantley; m. Thomas Toolen Brettel, Jr., June 26, 1971 (div. July 1979). Student in mgmt. and mktg. U. South Ala., Mobile, 1970-73; courses in fashion and modelling, N.Y.C., 1976-78. Cert. tchr., Ala. Owner, dir. Fashionique, Mobile, 1972-80, G.G.'s Boutique, Mobile, 1972-80; sales rep. L.M. Berry, Birmingham, Ala., 1980-81; govt. sales rep. Arnold Corp., Atlanta, 1981-84; with Norrell Printing, Inc., Atlanta, 1984—; also owner Sweet Sunshine Farms, 1983—. Mem. Pierrettes, Mobile, 1971-83. Mem. World Modeling Assn. (So. regional dir. 1980-81, judge internat. competition 1981-82, Dir. of Yr. 1979, 80, Sch. of Yr., 1980, Internat. Sch. of Yr. 1980, Celebrity of Tomorrow 1980), Phi Chi Theta (pres.). Republican. Roman Catholic. Home: 1530 Rucker Rd Alpharetta GA 30201 Office: Norrell Printing Inc 3092 Piedmont Rd NE Atlanta GA 30305

WINSLOW, HELEN CAUDLE, artist; b. New Salem, N.C., Mar. 24, 1916; d. Rufus Spurgeon and Nellie Sophia (Richardson) Caudle; B.A., Fla. So. Coll., 1936; student Art Students League, 1936-41, Otis Art Inst., Los Angeles, 1954-57; m. Randolph Winslow, Nov. 30, 1940; 1 dau., Joyce. Artist; juried exhbns. include; Frye Art Mus., Seattle, 1960, 62, 65, De Young Mus., San Francisco, 1968, 69, San Bernardino Mus., 1978; one woman shows include: Roberts Gallery, Los Angeles, 1966, Brentwood Gallery, Los Angeles, 1967-68, Vallis & Jensen, San Francisco, 1967, Gallery Fair, Mendocino, Calif., 1968-80, Austin Gallery, Scottsdale, Ariz., 1974-77; pvt. art tchr., 1956—; tchr. summer painting workshop, Rye, Colo., 1972-80. Recipient purchase award Los Angeles Ann. Art Festival, 1956, 2d prize Calif. State Fair, 1965, Wells Fargo award De Young Mus., 1969, 1st prize Beverly Hills Art League, 1974, spl. award San Bernardino Mus., 1978. Fellow Royal Soc. Arts; mem. Art Students League (life), Soc. Western Artists, Los Angeles Art Assn. Featured in article in S.W. Art Mag., 1977. Home: 9934 Westwanda Dr Beverly Hills CA 90210

WINSLOW, JOCELYNE VALIQUET, foreign language educator; b. Montreal, Que., Can., Jan. 1, 1917; came to U.S., 1951; d. Charles Napoleon and Jane Stewart (Vinson) Valiquet; m. Francis W. Bell, Nov. 9, 1951 (div. Dec. 1965); 1 child, Rene Francois Valiquet Bell; m. 2d Frank Jarnagin Winslow, Nov. 12, 1981. Grad. Ecole Normale Jacques Cartier, Montreal, 1935; student social, econ. and polit. sci. U. Montreal, 1940-42; Spanish Lang. cert., 1947; B.A., U. Houston-Dominican Coll., Houston, 1971; audio-visual teaching cert. Maryville Coll., St. Louis, 1969; cert. Ecole du Louvre, Paris, 1972, student Maxim's Cooking Sch., 1984. High sch. tchr. Inst. Fgn. Langs., Academie Notre Dame de Lourdes, Montreal, 1935-51, head fgn. lang. div., 1935-51; French instr. Alliance Francaise, Houston, 1965-66; head dept. French Inst., Duchesne Acad., Houston, 1966-71; tchr. high sch. fgn. langs. Kinkaid Sch., Houston, 1966-73; owner, instr. pvt. fgn. lang. sch., Houston, 1973—. Mem. Alliance Francaise, Am. Assn. Tchrs. French (many honor certs. 1971—), Mus. Fine Arts, Heritage Soc. Houston, Tex. Fgn. Lang. Assn., Friends of Bayou Bend, English Speaking Union, Pi Delta Phi (chpt. pres. 1971), Alpha Mu Gamma. Republican. Episcopalian. Club: Knife and Fork Soc. Home: 2660 Marilee Ln The Heritage Suite A43 Houston TX 77057

WINSTON, JUDITH ANN, lawyer; b. Atlantic City, Nov. 23, 1943; d. Edward Carl and Margaret Ann (Goodman) Marianno; B.A. (Nat. Competitive scholar), Howard U., Washington, 1966; J.D., Georgetown U., 1977; m. Michael Russell Winston, Aug. 10, 1963; children—Lisa Marie, Cynthia Eileen. Dir. EEO Project, Council Great City Schs., Washington, 1971-74; legal asst. Lawyers Com. for Civil Rights Under Law, Washington, 1975-77; admitted to D.C. bar, 1977, U.S. Supreme Ct. bar; spl. asst. to dir. Office for Civil Rights, HEW, Washington, 1977-79; exec. asst., legal counsel to chair U.S. EEO Commn., Washington, 1979-80; asst. gen. counsel U.S. Dept. Edn., 1980-86; dep. dir. Lawyers Com. for Civil Rights Under Law, 1986—; ednl. cons., 1974-77; guest lectr. Washington Coll. Law of Am. U. Trustee Family and Child Services of Washington; active NAACP Legal Def. and Ednl. Fund, 1968-79, Women's Legal Def. Fund, 1979. Mem. D.C. Bar Assn., Washington Council Lawyers, Washington Bar Assn., Nat. Bar Assn., Fed. Bar Assn., Phi Beta Kappa, Delta Theta Phi. Democrat. Episcopalian. Author: Desegregating Schools in the Great Cities: Philadelphia, 1970; Chronicle of a Decade

1961-1970, 1970; Desegregating Urban Schools: Educational Equality/Quality, 1970. Home: 1371 Kalmia Rd NW Washington DC 20012 Office: US Dept Edn 400 Maryland Ave SW Washington DC 20202

WINSTON, LISA JEANNE, advertising and public relations executive; b. Buffalo, June 16, 1956; d. Meyer John and Joan Adele (deForest) Winston. Student U. Miami-Fla., 1974; A.A.S. in Graphic Arts and Photography, Rochester Inst. Tech., 1977. Advt. coordinator Signore div. AVM, Ellicottville, 1980-82; mgr. sales promotion and advt. Alcas Cutlery Corp., Olean, N.Y., 1982—; guest lectr. mktg. St. Bonaventure U., Olean, 1985—. Editor Vector Blade, 1986—. Vice chmn. Alpac Polit. Action Com., Olean, 1984-86; mem. COFC Promotion & Mktg. Com., Olean, 1985-86, mem. subcoms., 1986. Mem. Nat. Assn. Female Execs., Direct Selling Assn., DSA Pub. Relations Com., Direct Mktg. Assn., Olean Indsl. Mgmt. Council. Republican. Office: Alcas Cutlery Corp 1116 E State St Olean NY 14760-0810

WINTER, ELIZABETH ANN, lawyer; b. Louisville, Jan. 19, 1949; d. James David and Mildred Gatliff (Conn) W.; m. Roger Owen Hooban, Jan. 24, 1971 (div. 1977). Student Calif. Luth. Coll., 1967-70; B.A., Ariz. State U., 1971; J.D., U. Tenn., 1975. Bar: Tenn. 1976. Pvt. practice law, Knoxville, 1976-78; atty. Title Ins. Co., Chattanooga, 1979-81, Lawyers Title & Escrow Inc., Chattanooga, 1981-85, Title Guaranty and Trust Co. Chattanooga, 1985—; lectr. Contbr. articles to profl. jours. Co-chmn. C. of C. Arts Festival, Chattanooga, 1984; mem. Ballet Guild, 1984, Landmark Chattanooga, 1984—, Chattanooga Venture, 1984; treas. Chattanooga Performing Arts Ctr., 1985; bd. dirs. Multiple Sclerosis. Mem. ABA, Tenn. Bar Assn., Chattanooga Land Title Assn. (pres. 1985), Chattanooga Bar Assn. (law com. 1984), Tenn. Paralegal Assn., Women's Council Realtors, Nat. Assn. Bond Lawyers, Jaycees. Republican. Lutheran. Club: Tenn. Valley Canoe. Home: PO Box 15132 Chattanooga TN 37415 Office: Title Guaranty and Trust Co Chattanooga 617 Walnut St Chattanooga TN 37402

WINTER, MARY DAVIDSON, lawyer, educator; b. Milw., Sept. 17, 1939; d. Arthur Harley and Janet Sherk (Harris) Davidson; m. Lawrence Edward Winter, July 7, 1960 (div. 1971); children—Anne, Catherine, William, Peter; m. 2d Charles Frederick Sweetland, June 11, 1977. A.B. cum laude, Stanford U., 1960; teaching cert. Portland State Coll., 1961; postgrad. Deutsche Sommerschule, Portland, 1961; J.D., U. Minn., 1975. Bar: Minn. 1975. U.S. Dist. Ct. Minn. 1975, U.S. Supreme Ct. 1982. Secondary tchr. Portland Pub. Schs. (Oreg.), 1961-63; student dir. U. Minn. Law Sch. Legal Aid Clinics, Mpls., 1974-75; sole practice, Mpls., 1975-80; clin. instr. William Mitchell Coll. Law, St. Paul, 1976-80; clin. supr. Hamline U. Law Sch., St. Paul, 1979—; family ct. referee Hennepin County, Mpls., 1980—; advisor Chrysalis, Mpls., 1982—. Contbr. articles to legal publs. Precinct chmn. Democratic Farm Labor Party, Edina, Minn., 1983-84, 86-87. Mem. ABA, Minn. State Bar Assn., Hennepin County Bar Assn. (chmn. community relations com. 1983-85), Assn. Trial Lawyers Am., Minn. Trial Lawyers Assn., Minn. Women Lawyers, Am. Acad. Matrimonial Lawyers (bd. govs. 1985-86). Lutheran. Club: Stanford of Minn. (pres. Mpls. 1977-78). Home: 5301 Evanswood Ln Edina MN 55436 Office: Hennepin County Govt Ctr Minneapolis MN 55487

WINTER, PATRICIA JOHANNA, lawyer; b. Atlanta, Nov. 6, 1949; d. Arthur Bruce and Eva Ann (Pirkle) Winter; m. Dennis Lee Holsapple, Nov. 15, 1980. Student Agnes Scott Coll., 1967-69; B.A., U. Nebr., 1971, J.D., 1975. Bar: Nebr. 1975. Assoc., Kutak Rock & Huie, Omaha, 1975-79, ptnr., 1979-81; atty. Northwestern Bell Telephone Co., Omaha, 1982—. Pres., Lawyers and Accts. for the Arts, Omaha, 1981-82; mem. Nebr. Assn. Community Theatres, Omaha, 1976-78; mem. Mayor's Lawyer Referral Service, Omaha Commn. on Status of Women, 1975-77. Mem. ABA, Nebr. State Bar Assn., Omaha Bar Assn., Order of the Coif, Phi Beta Kappa, Pi Sigma Alpha. Democrat. Episcopalian. Office: Northwestern Bell Telephone Co Legal Dept 1314 Douglas on the Mall Omaha NE 68102

WINTERLING, MARY ANN, educational adminstrator; b. Balt., Mar. 15, 1943; d. Leo George and Loretta Catherine (Novak) Winterling; B.A., Coll. Notre Dame, 1965; M.Ed., Johns Hopkins U., 1971, cert. advanced study in edn., 1980. Tchr., Balt. City Pub. Sch. No. 47, Hampstead Hill, 1965-74; asst. prin. Balt. City Pub. Sch. No. 150, Bentalou Elem. Sch., 1974-80, prin., 1980—; asst. prin. or. tchrs., 1970-79. Sec. S.E. Civic Orgn., 1972-73; mem. Adminstrs. Adv. Council, 1976-79. Mem. Assn. for Supervision and Curriculum Devel., Johns Hopkins U. Alumni Assn., Pub. Sch. Adminstrs. and Suprs. Assn., Pi Lambda Theta. Democrat. Roman Catholic. Club: Johns Hopkins. Office: 220 N Bentalou St Baltimore MD 21223

WINTERS, ALICE GRAHAM BUTLER (MRS. CARL S. WINTERS), civic worker; b. Linton, Ind., July 5, 1907; d. William Austin and Mary (Inman) Butler; A.B., Franklin Coll., 1932; spl. student U. Rochester, 1929-30, Colgate-Rochester Div. Sch., 1929-30; m. Carl S. Winters, May 23, 1925; children—Barbara (Mrs. Robert Kane), Janet (Mrs. Ralph Kuzmic), Linda (Mrs. Allen F. Jones). Minister junior ch., Jackson, Mich., 1931-39, 1st Bapt. Ch. Oak Park, Ill., 1939-59; lectr. Adult Edn. Council Chgo.; also freelance writer. Organizer, pres. Jackson (Mich.) Peace Council, 1933-35; pres. Jackson County LWV, 1935, Chgo. Drama League, 1948-50, Chgo. Mission Union, 1956-60; treas. Art Assocs. Oak Park, 1961-64; pres. Infant Welfare Soc., 1960-62; mem. Com. of 100, Nat. Council of Chs., 1963—; bd. dirs. Woman's Bd. Salvation Army, Chgo., 1960—, pres. bd., 1969—; bd. dirs. Women's Bd. Mental Health Assn., Chgo.; bd. dirs. Maywood (Ill.) Home and Hosp., 1940-62, v.p. bd., 1958-62; mem. woman's bd. Christian U. of Tokyo, 1963—. Recipient Outstanding Woman award Chgo. Assn. Commerce and Industry, 1976; citation for outstanding contbns. to humanity Franklin Coll., 1978; Disting. Service award Salvation Army Internat., 1980; Cert. of Recognition for outstanding service Comprehensive Community Services of Chgo., 1980; citation for achievement and influence Chautauqua Instn., 1982, Alice and Carl Winters Park named in their honor, 1985. Mem. Delta Zeta, Beta Sigma Phi, Kappa Delta. Clubs: Conference Club Presidents (bd. dirs. 1962—, chmn. pub. relations, sec.); 19th Century Woman's; Garden; Chautauqua (N.Y.) Women's; Oak Park Country; Zonta. Home: 404 N East Ave Oak Park IL 60602 also Packard Manor Chautauqua NY 14722

WINTERS, BARBARA JO, musician; b. Salt Lake City; d. Louis McClain and Gwendolyn (Bradley) Winters; A.B. cum laude, UCLA, 1960, postgrad., 1961; postgrad. Yale U., 1960. Mem. oboe sect. Pasadena (Calif.) Symphony, 1958-60; mem. oboe sect. Los Angeles Philharm., 1961—, now prin. oboist. Recs. movie, TV sound tracks. Home: 3529 Coldwater Canyon Studio City CA 91604 Office: 135 N Grand Ave Los Angeles CA 90012

WINTERS, BETH ANN, retired association executive; b. Monroe, Mich., June 12, 1918; d. John Joseph and Edith (Golden) Harrington; student U. Toledo; m. Edward R. 25, 1979; children—James W. Payne, III, Michael H. Winters, Penelope Ann Winters, Terrence J. Winters. Various clerical, bookkeeping and secretarial positions, 1934-58; clk. Monroe County (Mich.), 1959-63; owner Winters Office Aides, Monroe, Mich., 1963-65; acting exec. dir. Monroe County chpt. ARC, 1964, exec. dir., 1964-85, chmn. 1959-62; co-organizer Coordinating Council Agencies, Monroe, 1964. Bd. dirs. Friends Monroe County Zoo Assn., 1958-60, Monroe County Big Bros., 1968, Monroe County OEO, 1969, Mich. Welfare League, 1968, S.E. Mich. Tourist Assn., 1961; chmn. Monroe County Traffic and Safety Com., 1979; mem. Greater Monroe Council Alcoholism; treas. Alcohol and Substance Abuse Center, 1979-80. Recipient award ARC, 1960, 62, Camp Fire Girls, 1960; chpt. house named in her honor. Mem. Monroe County His. Soc. (sec. 1964-66), ARC Retirees, Art and Crafts League Monroe (vice chmn. 1958), Monroe County Bus. and Profl. Women, St. Patrick's Soc. Am. Irish (founder 1958, 1st pres. 1958-59), VFW Aux. Democrat. Roman Catholic. Club: Navy Mother's (charter, past dir.). Home: 443 N Macomb St Monroe MI 48161 Office: 202 S Macomb St Monroe MI 48161

WINTERS, DEBORAH ANN, radiologist; b. Garden City, Kans., Aug. 23, 1951; d. Wesley Chester and Ruby Irene (Vaughn) W.; m. Clyde Elam Marlin, Dec. 21, 1975; 1 child, Angela Michelle. B.A. cum laude, So. Missionary Coll., 1973; postgrad. Vol. State Community Coll., 1973-74, Middle Tenn. State U., 1974; M.D., Loma Linda U., 1978. Diplomate Am. Bd. Radiology, Nat. Bd. Med. Examiners. Records librarian Sta. WSMC, Collegedale, Tenn., 1969-71, 1972-73; computer operator Eaton, Yale & Towne, Gallatin, Tenn., 1973-74; resident in radiology Loma Linda U. (Calif.) Med. Center, 1979-82; practice medicine specializing in radiology Middle Tenn. Radiology Assocs., McMinnville. Mem. Am. Coll. Radiology, Radiol. Soc. N.Am., AMA, Warren County Med. Soc., Calif. Med. Assn., Tenn. Radiology Soc., Middle Tenn. Radiology Soc., Tenn. Med. Soc., So. Valley Radiol. Soc., Am. Assn. Women Radiologists, Loma Linda U. Women's Med. Aux. Alumni Assn., Nat. Soc. of Tole and Decorative Painters, San Diego Zool. Soc. Adventist. Office: River Park Hosp Sparta Hwy McMinnville TN 37110

WINTERS, MARY ANN, college administrator; b. Ancon, Panama, Apr. 28, 1948; came to U.S., 1951; d. Leonard McCrea and Selyn (Martin) W. B.A., Mt. St. Vincent, 1971; postgrad. New Sch. Social Research, 1983—. Tchr., Incarnation Sch., N.Y.C., 1970-74; co-dir. Washington Heights Ctr. for Action, N.Y.C., 1974-79; dir. Kingsbridge Heights Community Ctr., Bronx, 1975-79; devel. dir. Elizabeth Seton Coll., Yonkers, N.Y., 1982-85, Sch. of Holy Child, Rye, N.Y., 1985—. Mem. Council for Advancement and Support of Edn., Westchester Assn. Devel. Officers (v.p. 1985—), Westchester County Assn. Avocations: sailing; music. Office: Sch of Holy Child Westchester Ave Rye NY 10805

WINTERS, WENDY GLASGOW, social work educator sociologist; b. Norwalk, Conn., June 26, 1930; d. William and Gladys E. (Carter) Russell; B.S. with honors, Central Conn. State Coll., 1952; M.S., Columbia U. Sch. social work, 1954; Ph.D., Yale U., 1975; m. Irving J. Winters, Jr., June 14, 1975; children—Allison Lenore Glasgow, Roger DeCourey Glasgow, Jr. Chief social worker Baldwin-King schs. program Child Study Center, Yale U., 1968-75, instr., then asst. prof. social work, 1968-71, research asso., 1975-78, fellow Pierson Coll., 1969—; asso. prof., asst. dean acad. affairs Sch. Social Work, U. Conn., 1975-78; asso. prof. sociology and anthropology, adj. asso. prof. social work, dean coll. Smith Coll., 1979-84, assoc. prof. sociology and anthropology, prof. social work, 1984; mem. regional adv. council Conn. Dept. Children and Youth Services, 1975-78, chmn. evaluation subcom., 1977-78; adv. com. Conn. Commn. Higher Edn., 1976-77; bd. dirs. Leila Day Nurseries, Inc., New Haven, 1975-78; mem. juvenile justice adv. com. Conn. Justice Commn., 1977; bd. corporators Heritage/Northampton Instn. Savs., 1979—. Bd. dirs. Greater New Haven Urban League, 1969-71. Recipient various appreciation awards; NIMH research award, 1974; fellow Black Analysis, Inc., 1972-75, Yale U. Inst. Social and Policy Studies, 1974-75. Mem. Am. Orthopsychiat. Assn., Am. Sociol. Assn., Nat. Assn. Social Workers, New Eng. Minority Women Adminstrs., Alpha Kappa Alpha. Congregationalist. Author articles, coauthor book, reports in field. Home: 36 Paradise Rd Northampton MA 01060 Office: Neilson Library A-09 Smith Coll Northampton MA 01063

WINTERS-MALOLEPSY, TERRI, costume designer; b. Omaha, May 8, 1946; d. Henry C. and Mercedes (Royle) Winters; B.A. in Theatre, Edgewood Coll., Madison, Wis., 1968; M.A., U. Wis., Madison, 1972; M.F.A. in Theatre Design, Mich. State U., 1977; m. John F. Malolepsy, June 17, 1967; children—Jennifer Anne, Paul Michael. Instr. costume design Edgewood Coll., 1968-69, U. Mich., Flint, 1972-78; asst. prof. creative drama, costume design Memphis State U., 1979—, costume designer, makeup designer, 1968—; freelance costume designer, creative drama leader; costume designer Memphis Mud Island River Museum, 1981. Bd. dirs. Flint Hist. Theatre Assn., 1974-77, Coop. Threads Inc., 1969-72. Mem. Am. Theatre Assn., Univ. and Coll. Theatre Assn., U.S. Inst. Theatre Tech., AAUP (past univ. rep.). Office: Dept Theatre and Communication Arts Memphis State U Memphis TN 38152

WINTHROP, BARBARA SEVERY, chef, food consultant; b. Oceanside, Calif., Oct. 30, 1945; d. George Fairburn and Dorothy Mary (Severy) Winthrop. B.A., Hunter Coll., 1969. Dept. chmn. phys. edn. Parker Collegiate Inst., Bklyn., 1969-75; coach, tchr. Chapin Sch., N.Y.C., 1975-81; mgr. Servomation Corp., Stamford, Conn., 1981-82; chef Alpen Pantry, N.Y.C., 1982-83; head chef Bagels & Caviar, Bklyn., 1983-85, Heights Casino, Bklyn., 1985—; mem. Middle States Evaluation, N.Y.C., 1974. Vol. Democratic Party, 1985. Mem. NOW, Audubon Soc., Ms. Found. for Women, Wilderness Soc., Athletic Assn. Ind. Schs. Home: 50 Remsen St Brooklyn NY 11201 Office: Heights Casino 75 Montague St Brooklyn NY 11201

WINTZ, MILDRED MARY, environmental educator; b. Upper Darby, Pa., Feb. 25, 1932; d. George Lee and Mildred Ellen (Deering) Jenkins; B.Applied Arts, U. Pa., 1955; M.A. in Environ. Edn., Beaver Coll., 1979; postgrad. in curriculum theory Temple U., 1979—; m. Donald Wintz, July 31, 1954; children—Lisa Marie, Donald Lee, Donna Lee. Designer, John Reid Interiors, 1955-58; prin. Wintz Assocs., Huntingdon Valley, Pa., 1959—; dir. edn. Pennypack Watershed Assn., Huntingdon Valley, 1978—. Instr., CPR and first aid, ARC; trainer Girl Scouts U.S.A., Phila.; mem. environ. adv. commn. Upper Moreland Twp.; mem. Union League Phila. Recipient environ. award Pennypack Watershed Assn.; William Penn award Trefoil Soc., ARC. Cert. in elem. and secondary environ. edn., Pa. Mem. Am. Soc. Interior Designers, Assn. Interpretive Naturalists, Pa. Assn. Environ. Educators, Phila. Art Alliance, Land Mgmt. Task Force. Republican. Lutheran. Club: Huntingdon Valley Country. Author: Gray Fox Environmental Field Education Programs, 1976; Discovery Trek Environmental Field Education Programs, 1978—. Office: 2955 Edge Hill Rd Huntingdon Valley PA 19006

WIRSIG, JANE DEALY, writer; b. Boston, Aug. 22, 1919; d. James Bond and Anna B. (McQuillen) Dealy; B.A., Vassar Coll., 1941; M.S. (Vassar Coll. fellow 1941-42), Columbia U., 1942; m. Woodrow Wirsig, Dec. 11, 1942; children—Alan Robert, Guy Rodney, Paul Harold. Network radio newswriter CBS, 1942-43; free lance writer articles, short stories various mags., 1942—; editor Vassar Alumnae mag., 1952-53; editor, rewriter Companion in Paris, Woman's Home Companion, 1953-56; editor Wirsig, Gordon & O'Connor, Inc., Princeton, N.J., 1956-58; editorial cons. Ednl. Testing Service, Princeton, 1957-60, dir. publs., 1960-70, exec. dir. info. services and publs., 1971-74, sec. corp., 1974-81. Mem. exec. bd. George Washington council Boy Scouts Am., 1976-80. Mem. Am. Assn. Higher Edn., Greater Princeton C. of C. (dir. 1974—, v.p. 1976-80, chmn. 1980), Phi Beta Kappa. Club: Vassar (Central N.J. v.p. 1955-57). Home: 25 Gordon Way Princeton NJ 08540

WISCH, MARILYN JOAN, pension design firm executive; b. Bklyn., Oct. 13, 1942; d. Irving Elmer and Sylvia (Manzar) Chezar; m. Steven Charles Wisch, Sept. 19, 1965 (div. Nov. 1981); 1 child, Beth Allyson; m. Jerome Leonard Klein, Nov. 20, 1983. B.S., NYU, 1964; M.Ed., Adelphi U., 1976, paralegal employee benefits program, 1982. Art dir. Doyle Dane & Bernbach, N.Y.C., 1964-69; tchr. Baldwin Sch. Dist., N.Y., 1977; real estate saleswoman Village Homes, Rockville Centre, N.Y., 1978-82; cons., v.p., ptnr., owner Accu-Plan Adminstrs., Inc., Rockville Centre, 1983—; paralegal instr. Adelphi U., Garden City, N.Y., 1983—. Poll insp., Baldwin, 1977-78; v.p. Plaza PTA, Baldwin, 1978-79; v.p. Sisterhood, pres. Couples Club, Central Synagogue, Rockville Centre, 1978-81; vol. South Nassau Communities Hosp., Oceanside, N.Y., 1979-81. Mem. Nat. Assn. Female Execs. (network dir. 1985), Am. Soc. Pension Actuaries (coordinator for testing Rockville Centre 1986), Nat. Inst. Pension Adminstrs., Rockville Centre C. of C. Democrat. Jewish. Avocations: gardening; reading; needlecrafts; public speaking. Home: 1276 Surrey Ln Rockville Centre NY 11570 Office: Accu-Plan Adminstrs Inc 5 N Village Ave Rockville Centre NY 11570

WISE, EARNESTINE SPRINGER, traffic manager; b. Denton, Tex., Jan. 10, 1941; d. Earnest and Sarah Katherine (O'Neil) Springer; m. Carl L. Carpenter, Dec. 23, 1960 (div. 1971); children—Carl L., Shannon René; m. James Marrion Wise, June 15, 1973. Student So. Meth. U., 1972-74, Brookhaven Jr. Coll., 1980-82, U. Tex.-Dallas, 1982-86. Traffic mgr. Zoecon Corp., Dallas, 1971—. Mem. Am. Soc. Traffic and Logistics (cert. mem.; chpt. bd. dirs. 1982-84), Cert. Claims Profl. Accreditation Council (hon.), Delta Nu Alpha Transp. Club. Democrat. Baptist. Home: 13677 Rawhide Pkwy Dallas TX 75234 Office: Zoecon Corp 12200 Denton Dr Dallas TX 75234

WISE, ESTA ANN, health science consultant; b. Fairmont, W.Va., Apr. 30, 1938; d. William Harold and Iva G. (Hunt) Wageley; m. James R. Wise, Aug. 25, 1962; 1 child, James William. A.B. in Edn., Fairmont State Coll., 1961. Cons., owner Esta's, Massillon, Ohio, 1980—. Author: Search for Self, 1984. Mem. Christian Ch. Avocations: aerobics; reading; writing. Home: 7311 Knight St NW Massillon OH 44646

WISE, JANIE DENISE, communications consulting company executive; b. Frankfort, Ky., Dec. 15, 1945; d. Joseph William and Kathryn (Smither) W.; B.A. in Edn. and Psychology, U. Ky., 1971; postgrad. U. Louisville, 1971-72. Tchr., Taylorsville (Ky.) High Sch., 1970-72; mental health specialist mental health-retardation bd. Gardiner Lane Center, Louisville, 1972-73; alcohol counselor W.T. Edwards Hosp., Tampa, Fla., 1973-74; community edn. coordinator, counselor First Step, Inc., Sarasota, Fla., 1974-75; communications cons., coordinator Tri-County Alcoholism Services, Inc., Winter Haven, Fla., 1975-78; communications specialist, select account, area sales rep. Visual Products div. 3/M, St. Paul, 1978-80; owner, pres. Effective Communications Group, Tampa, Fla., 1980—. Bd. dirs. YMCA, Lakeland. Mem. Fla. Public Relations Assn., Fla. Fedn. Safety Orgns., Nat. Assn. Female Execs., Nat. Task Force on Women and Alcohol (bd. dirs.) Nat. Assn. Bus. and Indsl. Saleswomen (rep. Fla. office on women and alcohol Washington), Tampa C. of C., Small Bus. Council, U. Ky. Alumni Assn., AAUW, Aircraft Owners and Pilots Assn. Club: Porsche Club of Am. Home: 7893 Niagara Ave Tampa FL 33617 Office: PO Box 16623 Temple Terrace FL 33687

WISE, NANCY JOAN, lawyer; b. Oak Park, Ill., Aug. 5, 1950; d. Robert S. and Grace Ann (Ackerman) Wise. B.S., Wittenberg U., 1973; J.D., U. Dayton (Ohio), 1977. Bar: Ill. 1977. Atty., Ceco Corp., Oak Brook, Ill., 1977-84, asst. sec., 1981-84; asst. sec., atty. Ceco Industries, Inc., Oak Brook, 1984—. Casenote editor U. Dayton Law Rev., 1977. Mem. Chgo. Bar Assn., ABA.

WISE, WILMA MARK, credit bureau and employment agency executive; b. Frankfort, Ill., Mar. 13, 1926; d. Paul and Louise (Staedke) Mark; m. Perry Kenneth Wise, Sept. 5, 1948; children—Douglas Kent, Dennis Mark. Student, Met. Bus. Coll., 1943-44; grad. exec. devel. program Ind. U. Grad. Sch. Bus., 1975. Owner, ptnr. Naperville Credit Bur. (Ill.), 1958-70; gen. mgr., v.p. First Suburban Services, Naperville, 1970-75; pres., gen. mgr. Wise Suburban Services, Inc., divs. Snelling and Snelling, Wise Credit Bur., Wise Telephone Answering Service, Naperville, Ill., 1975—. Mem., pres. Naperville Dist. No. 203 Career Edn. Adv. Council, 1971—; mem. exec. com. North Central Coll. Community Fund Drive, 1980—, chmn., 1984-85; mem. exec. com. DuPage County Pvt. Industry Council, 1983—; 1st pres. Ill. Bus. Week, 1984. Recipient Woman of Achievement award Women in Mgmt., Oak Brook chpt., 1982; Internat. Key Leadership award Assoc. Credit Burs., 1979; named Boss of Year, Am. Bus. Women's Assn., 1979. Mem. Ill. Assn. Personnel Cons. (dir. 1976-81) Ill. Collector's Assn. (dir. 1982—, v.p. 1983-84, pres. 1985-86), Am. Collector's Assn., Internat. Fellowship Cert. Collectors, Associated Credit Burs. Inc. (award of excellence 1984), Associated Credit Burs. Ill. (dir. 1975—, pres. 1979-80), Women in Mgmt., Naperville C. of C. (dirs.), Downers Grove C. of C. (dirs. 1972-75), Naperville Organ Soc. Lutheran (mem. council 1978-84). Club: Cosmopolitan Dance (Naperville). Home: 7S410 Arbor Dr Naperville IL 60540 Office: 638-40 E Ogden Ave Twin Center Naperville IL 60540

WISEMAN, SHIRLEY JOAN MCVAY, government official; b. Gassville, Ark., June 17, 1937; d. L. R. and M. Maye (Powell) Byrd; grad. high sch.; m. L. McVay (div.); children—Larry, Sherri; m. 2d, Lynwood Wiseman, 1977. Owner, corp. sec. Wiseman Homes, Inc., Lexington, Ky., after 1965; gen. dep. asst. sec. housing Fed. Housing Commr. Mem. Lexington Real Estate Bd.; mem. exec. com. Com. to Insure Good Govt.; mem. adv. com. Water Quality Control Com. Mem. Republican Exec. Com., Fayette, Ky., 1966-72; mem. Fayette County Rep. Adv. Com., 1967-72; alt. del. Rep. Nat. Conv., 1972. Bd. dirs., treas. Lexington Housing for Handicapped. Mem. Lexington Home Builders Assn. (dir., pres.), Nat. Assn. Home Builders (nat. dir., vice chmn. standing com. for membership, membership chmn. 1978, mem. exec. com. 1978—, v.p. 1980—, v.p., sec. 1986—), Ky. Homebuilders Assn. (state membership chmn.), Lexington C. of C. (dir. 1977). Lodge: Order Eastern Star. Home: 337 11th St SE Washington DC 20003 Office: 451 7th St SW Room 9100 Washington DC 20410

WISHNER, KATHLEEN LAMBERT, physician; b. Modesto, Calif., June 11, 1943; d. Henry Oscar Lambert and Alyce (Littlefield) Lambert Daniells; m. Phillip Andrew Harris, Aug. 4, 1961 (div. 1973); children—Jeffrey John, Michael Lambert; m. William Jay Wishner, May 20, 1973. B.A., Calif. State U.-San Francisco, 1963; Ph.D., U. Calif.-San Francisco, 1968; M.D., U. So. Calif., 1976. Diplomate Nat. Bd. Med. Examiners, Am. Bd. Pediatrics. Intern, Children's Hosp. Los Angeles, 1976-77; resident Los Angeles County/U. So. Calif. Med. Ctr., 1977-78; fellow pediatric endocrinology City of Hope/Harbor-UCLA, 1978-79; asst. prof. U. Minn.-St. Paul, 1968-70, U. So. Calif., Los Angeles, 1970-73; teaching assoc. Georgetown U., Washington, 1973-74; staff physician City of Hope Med Ctr., Duarte, Calif., 1979-81; assoc. clin. prof. U. So. Calif., Los Angeles, 1984—; practice medicine specializing in pediatric endocrinology and clin. nutrition, Pasadena, Calif., 1981—cons. Panel on space sta. ops. medicine NASA, Am. Inst. Biol. Scis., 1983-85. Contbr. articles to profl. jours. NIH grantee, 1969-73, 69-72, 79-81. Mem. Am. Diabetes Assn. (dir. So. Calif. affiliate 1982—, pres.-elect 1986; Diabetes in Youth award 1985), Am. Dietetic Assn. (registered dietitian), Am. Inst. Nutrition, Calif. Med. Assn. (com. on accreditation and certification of continuing med. edn. 1985—), Los Angeles County Med. Assn. Democrat. Office: Pasadena Diabetes and Endocrinology Med Group 10 Congress St Suite 320 Pasadena CA 91105

WISNER, LINDA ANN, advertising agency executive, publishing company executive, interior designer; b. Sidney, N.Y., Apr. 28, 1951; d. Herbert and Ruth (Usher) W. B.A. in Theatre and Art, Macalester Coll., 1973, postgrad. in journalism, 1974; postgrad. in graphic design Mpls. Coll. Art and Design, 1973-74; postgrad. in advtg. and mktg. U. Minn., 1974. Designer, publs. asst. Macalester Coll., St. Paul, 1973-76; designer Stretch & Sew Inc., Eugene, Oreg., 1976-78; free-lance designer, Eugene, 1978-79; owner, creative dir. Wisner Assocs., Eugene, 1979—, Interludes, Eugene, 1981—; ptnr. Instant Interiors, Eugene, 1979—; chmn. Bus. Images Exhibit, Eugene, 1983. Designer, editor booklet series: Instant Interiors, 1979-83 (Woodie award 1980-83); designer, illustrator: Palmer/Pletsch Sewing Books, 1981-85. Ambassador, City of Eugene, 1985—; bd. dirs. Maude Kerns Art Ctr., Eugene, 1984-85, Oreg. Repertory Theatre, 1986—. Nat. Merit scholar Macalester Coll., 1969. Mem. Designers' Forum (pres. 1983-84, Designer of Yr. 1983), Sales and Mktg. Execs., Graphic Artists Guild, Exec. Bus. Women (pres. 1983-84), Mid Oreg. Ad Club (numerous certs. and trophy 1980-85), Eugene C. of C. Avocations: design; illustration; soft sculpture; event planning; catering. Office: Wisner Assocs 1991 Garden Ave Eugene OR 97403

WISNIEWSKI, DAWN MARIE, engineering firm accounting executive; b. Milw., Aug. 16, 1962; d. Richard and Barbara Joan (Hasselmaier) W. Student Sierra Coll, Rocklin, Calif., 1984—. Asst. bookkeeper G & G Enterprises, Ltd., Milw., 1979-80; acctg. asst. Kestly & Co., West Allis, Wis., 1980-81; asst. bookkeeper Republic-Dau, Milw., 1981-82; acctg. supr., data processing coordinator Culp Wesner Culp, Cameron Park, Calif., 1982—. Mem. Nat. Assn. Female Execs., Data Processing Mgmt. Assn. Avocations: reading; crocheting; sewing; theatre. Home: 4567 Benton Way Shingle Springs CA 95682 Office: Culp Wesner Culp 3461 Robin Ln Cameron Park CA 95682

WISNIEWSKI, LINDA, manufacturing company executive; dietitian; b. Medford, Wis., Jan. 15, 1952; d. Clarence and Elizabeth (Scheuer) W.; m. David P. Brinkman, Apr. 25, 1981; children—Sarah, Matthew. B.S., in Edn., No. Ill. U., 1973, M.S. in Nutrition, 1976. Registered dietitian, Ill. Extension adviser U. Ill., Champaign, 1973-74; home economist Jewel Foods, Melrose Park, Ill., 1976-78; technologist Quaker Oats, Barrington, Ill., 1978-82; owner A.C.E., Elburn, Ill., 1981—; owner LaDace, DeKalb, Ill., 1985—; instr. Waubonsee Community Coll., Sugar Grove, Ill., 1984—. Author mag. column, 1983. Mem. Am. Pet Products Mfg. Assn., Pet Industry Distbrs. Assn. Avocations: gourmet cooking; needle crafts; spinning. Home: 2446 Route 2 Maple Park IL 60151 Office: Am Cat Emporium PO Box 745 Elburn IL 60119

WISSER, ELLEN (B.), lawyer, educator; b. N.Y.C., May 7, 1930; d. Samuel and Essie (Chentko) Borenstein; m. Allen Wisser, Apr. 1, 1951; children—Ronni Ilise, Jamie Robert, Kerry Marc. Student Am. Acad. Dramatic Arts, N.Y.C., 1948-49; B.A. cum laude, Bklyn. Coll., 1953, M.A., 1955; J.D., U. Bridgeport (Conn.), 1982. Bar: Conn. 1983, U.S. Dist. Ct. Conn. 1984, U.S. Supreme Ct. Tchr. N.Y.C. Bd. Edn., 1953-62, Bridgeport Bd. Edn., 1963-84; sole practice, Westport, Conn., 1983—; legal cons., dir. Bridgeport Youth Law Edn. Program, 1983-85; dir. Conn. Consortium for Law-Related Edn., Inc., 1982—; speaker in field; dir. Westport Speech and Hearing Ctr., 1964-66. Mem. Mayor's Conf. on Status of Edn. 1984. Recipient Am. Jurisprudence awards, 1978-79. Mem. ABA, Conn. Bar Assn., (juvenile justice com. women's law com. 1984), Assn. Trial Lawyers Am., Conn. Trial Lawyers Assn., NEA (state del.-rep. assembly 1972-77, evaluator 1973), Conn. Edn. Assn. (dir. 1974-77, legis. comm. 1972-78, Bridgeport Edn. Assn. (v.p. 1973-74, 83-84, labor negotiator 1983, chmn. joint com. tchr. evaluation 1979-84), Phi Alpha Delta (treas. 1978-79, del. nat. conv. 1979). Home: 7 Black Birch Rd Westport CT 06880

WITCHEL, BARBARA MURIEL, college administrator, gerontology and psychology educator; d. Herman and Ann (Lotto) Goldfein; m. Sam Witchel;

children—Alexandra, Gregory, Phoebe, Emmett. B.A., NYU, 1953, M.A., 1955; Ed.D., Rutgers U., 1965. Cert. tchr. kindergarten-8th grade, N.Y. Tchr. pub. schs., Fairlawn and Caldwell, N.J., 1955-62; instr. Rutgers U., New Brunswick, N.J., 1962-64; assoc. prof. Kean Coll., Union, N.J., 1965-67; assoc. prof. gerontology Iona Coll., New Rochelle, N.Y., 1970—; dir. Iona Coll., Rockland Campus, Orangeburg, N.Y., 1983—; reviewer Adminstrn. Aging, Washington, 1979-85, N.Y. State Dept. Edn., Albany, 1983; mem. spl. adv. com. White House Conf. on Aging, 1980-81. Producer, host TV series The New Age: A Focus on the Older American, 1980; dir. spl. edn. program The University of the New Age, 1981-82. Mem. Passaic Bd. Edn., 1966-68, pres., 1967-69. Recipient Service award Passaic Bd. Edn., 1969; fellow Rutgers U., 1962-84; Iona Coll. fellow, Bryn Mawr, Pa., 1985. Mem. Am. Assn. Higher Edn., Gerontol. Soc., AAUP, Phi Delta Kappa, Kappa Delta Pi. Avocations: sculpting; reading science fiction; gardening. Home: 27 Myrtledale Rd Scarsdale NY 10583 Office: Iona Coll-Rockland Campus One Dutch Hill Rd Orangeburg NY 10962

WITCHER, JOHNNYE MURRAY, English educator, educational administrator; b. Montgomery, Ala., Nov. 4, 1933; d. James and Mattie (Robinson) Murray; m. Frederick Witcher, Jan. 28, 1955; children—Frederick Jr., Dierdre Valencia Anderson. B.S., Ala. State U., 1955; M.A., Atlanta U., 1963; Ed.D., Auburn U., 1983. Tchr., West Bainbridge Elem., Ga., 1955-56, Montgomery County Schs., Ramer, Ala., 1956-60, 61-67, DOD Schs., Rep. Phillipines, 1967-68, Sherman Ind. Schs., Tex., 1970-72, HopeWell City Schs., Va., 1972-75; tchr., dir., adminstr. Ala. State U., Montgomery, 1977—. Vice pres. membership Coalition 100 Black Women, Montgomery, 1984. Merrill Found. fellow, 1967. Mem. Nat. Council Tchrs. English, Conf. Coll. Communication and Composition, So. Assn. Ednl. Opportunity Personnel. Avocations: reading; piano. Home: 219 Conrad St Montgomery AL 36110 Office: Ala State U 915 S Jackson St Montgomery AL 36195

WITHERS, JEAN, service business advisor, trainer; b. Henderson, Tex., Apr. 24, 1944; d. Ruben and Thelma (Hardy) W. B. Radio-TV-Film, U. Tex.-Austin, 1970; M.B.A., Seattle U., 1981. Citizens info. officer Dept. Community Devel. City of Seattle, 1975-78; owner Communications Cons., Seattle, 1978-82; mgr. Fletcher & Assocs., Seattle, 1982-84; owner Jean Withers Assocs., Seattle, 1984—. Co-author: Marketing Planning Workbook for Service Businesses, 1987; Contbr. articles to profl. jours. Campaign mgr. Helen Sommers for State Legislature, Seattle, 1976; advisor Paul Schell for Mayor Campaign, Seattle, 1977, Lois North for King County Council, Seattle, 1978, Virginia Galle for Seattle City Council, 1985, Jane Noland for Seattle City Council, 1985; co-founder Seattle Women Bus. Owners, 1979; fundraiser Skyee Ski Sch. for Blind. Recipient Outstanding Employee of the Yr. award City of Seattle, 1976. Mem. Sales & Mktg. Execs. (chmn. publicity com. 1980-81, chmn. long range planning com., 1982-83, dir. 1981-82, regional officer 1984-85), Greater Seattle C. of C. (exec. and steering coms. small bus. council), NOW (co-pres. Seattle-King County chpt. 1974). Office: Jean Withers Assocs 2722 Eastlake Ave E Suite 320 Seattle WA 98102

WITHERSPOON, FREDDA LILLY, educator; b. Houston; d. Fred D. and Vanita E. (Meredith) Lilly; A.B., Bishop Coll.; M.S.W., Washington U., 1949, M.A. in Guidance and Counseling, 1954; Ph.D., St. Louis U., 1965; m. Robert L. Witherspoon; children—Robert L., Vanita. Social worker, supr. St. Louis City Welfare Office, Homer G. Phillips Hosp., 1943-50; tchr. English, guidance counselor St. Louis Public Schs., 1950-65; prof. student personnel services Forest Park Community Coll., St. Louis, 1965—; cons. Ednl. Testing Service, Princeton, N.J., Head Start program, 1965-68; counseling cons. St. Louis Job Corps Center for Women, 1966-68. Organizer teenage service guild Annie Malone Children's Home, 1964; v.p. St. Louis chpt. NAACP, 1969—, pres. Mo. Conf., 1973—; mem. Challenge of 70's Crime Commn., 1970-75; mem. adv. council Central Inst. for Deaf, 1970-78; mem. Mayor's Council Youth, 1970-75; dir. teens fund drive March of Dimes, 1960-72, Lily Day drive for Crippled Children, 1966-72; chpt. chmn., mem. speakers bur. United Way, 1969—. Bd. dirs. children's services City of St. Louis, Mo. Heart Assn., NAACP, Social Health Assn., Community Assn. Schs. for Arts, St. Louis Heart Assn., Girl Scouts; pres. St. Louis Met. YWCA, 1978-79, bd. dirs.; bd. dirs., vice-chmn. St. Louis Urban League, 1977—. Named woman of Year, Greyhound Bus Corp., 1967, St. Louis Argus, 1968, Nat. Outstanding Woman, Iota Phi Lambda, 1970; named Outstanding Woman of Achievement, Globe Dem., 1970, Outstanding Educator of Am., 1971, Nat. Top Lady Distinction, 1974; recipient Negro History award, 1971; George Washington Carver award, 1976; Health and Welfare Council award, 1975. Mem. NAACP (life, Nat. Outstanding Youth Adv. 1977), Am. Personnel and Guidance Assn., AAUP (pres. 1975—), AAUW, Nat. Assn. Women Deans and Counselors, Am. Sch. Counselors Assn., Am. Vocat. Guidance Assn., Assn. Measurement and Evaluation in Guidance, Nat. Assn. Jr. Colls., Nat. Faculty Assn. Jr. Colls., League Women Voters, Nat. Council Negro Women (life), Mo. Assn. Social Welfare, Jack and Jill, Mound City (pres. 1946-49), Nat. (pres. 1950, 82) bar auxs., Kappa Delta Pi, Iota Phi Lambda (nat. pres. 1977-81), Top Ladies of Distinction (organizer, pres. 1973-77), Continental Socs. (organizer 1981), Sigma Gamma Rho. Research on high sch. drop outs with police records, uses of group guidance techniques in jr. colls. Home: 20 Lewis Pl Saint Louis MO 63113

WITHROW, MARY ELLEN, state treasurer; b. Oct. 2, 1930; d. Clyde Welsh and Mildred Veletta (Stump) Hinamon; m. Norman David Withrow, Sept. 4, 1948; children—Linda Kay Withrow Rizzo, Leslie Ann Withrow Legge, Norma J., Rebecca S. Student U. Akron. Mem. Elgin Bd. Edn., Marion, 1969-73; dep. registrar County of Marion (Ohio), 1972-75, dep. auditor, 1976-77, county treas., 1977-83; treas. State of Ohio, Columbus, 1983—; chmn. Ohio Bd. Deposits, Columbus; mem. Ohio Pub. Facilities Commn., Pres., Marion County Democratic Club, 1976; mem. exec. com. Ohio Dem. Party, Columbus, 1983; mem. Dem. Nat. Com., 1984; mem. Columbus Area Women's Polit. Caucus, 1983; chairperson Ohio Women's Vote Task Force, 1984. Recipient award for investments Nat. Assn. County Officers, 1978. Mem. Dem. State Treas. Assn., Commrs. of Sinking Fund, Nat. Assn. State Treas. (exec. council), Mcpl. Treas. Assn. (hon.), Bus. and Profl. Women, Ohio Assn. County Treas. Club: Met. Women's (hon.) (Columbus). Office: Office State Treas 30 E Broad St Columbus OH 43215

WITHROW, PAMELA KAY, prison warden; b. Lafayette, Ind., Nov. 19, 1948; d. Charles Lewis and Edna Mae (Macy) W.; divorced; 1 child, John Cole Cordell. A.A., Lansing Community Coll., 1973; B.A., Mich. State U., 1975. Prison counselor Corrections Camp Program, Grass Lake, Mich., 1976-77; program analyst Program Bur. Mich. Dept. Corrections, Lansing, Mich., 1977-78; prison camp supr. Camp Brighton, Pinokney, Mich., 1978-81; adminstrv. asst. State Prison So. Mich., Jackson, 1981, asst. dep. warden, 1981-82; prison warden Mich. Dunes Correctional Facility, Holland, 1983—. Contbr. articles to profl publs. Sec., Nat. Orgn. for Women, Saugatuck, Mich., 1984, membership chair, 1985. Named Outstanding Young Woman Holland Jaycees, 1983; Commencement speaker Mich. State U., E. Lansing, 1983. Mem. Am. Correctional Assn., Mich. Corrections Assn. (corr. sec. 1984—, membership chair 1984—, conf. chair 1983, trustee 1982). Avocations: backpacking, camping, cross country skiing. Office: Mich Dunes Correctional Facility A6605 W 138th Ave Holland MI 49423

WITKIN, EVELYN MAISEL, geneticist; b. N.Y.C., Mar. 9, 1921; d. Joseph and Mary (Levin) Maisel; A.B., N.Y.U. 1941; M.A., Columbia U., 1943, Ph.D., 1947; D.Sc. (hon.), N.Y. Med. Coll., 1978; m. Herman A. Witkin, July 9, 1943 (dec. July 1979); children—Joseph, Andrew. Mem. staff genetics dept. Carnegie Inst., Washington, 1945-55; mem. faculty SUNY Downstate Med. Center, Bklyn., 1955-71, prof. medicine, 1968-71; prof. biol. scis. Rutgers U., Douglass Campus, 1971-79, Barbara McClintock prof. genetics, 1979—. Postdoctoral fellow Am. Cancer Soc., 1947-49; fellow Carnegie Instn., 1957; Selman A. Waksman lectr., 1960; grantee NIH, 1956—; recipient Prix Charles Leopold Mayer, French Acad. Scis., 1977; Lindback award, 1979. Fellow AAAS; mem. Nat. Acad. Scis., Am. Acad. Arts and Scis., Am. Genetics Soc., Am. Soc. Microbiology, Radiation Research Soc. Author articles, mem. profl. jour. editorial bds. Home: 88 Balcort Dr Princeton NJ 08540 Office: Waksman Inst Microbiology Rutgers U Piscataway NJ 08854

WITKIN-LANOIL, GEORGIA HOPE, psychologist, educator, author. Student Wellesley Coll., 1961-63; B.A. in Sociology, Barnard Coll., 1965; postgrad. in elem. edn. Hunter Coll., 1967-69; M.A. in Psychology, New Sch. for Social Research, 1970, Ph.D. in Psychology, 1977. Lic. clin. psychologist, N.Y. State. Asst. producer Grey Advt., N.Y.C., 1966-68; teaching asst. New Sch. for Social Research, 1968-69; adj. lectr. Lehman Coll., CUNY, 1971-72; assoc. prof. dept. social and behavioral sci. SUNY-Valhalla, 1972—, mem. vis. faculty criminal justice dept., 1972—; supr. residency program human sexuality program Mt. Sinai Sch. Medicine, N.Y.C., 1982—; former mem. vis. faculty U. Conn., NYU Coll. Dentistry, also others; assoc. prof. psychology Westchester Community Coll., Valhalla; presenter at profl. confs., also papers; pvt. practice clin. psychology, Scarsdale, N.Y. and N.Y.C.; appeared on various TV shows including Donahue, Today Show, Hour Mag. Author: The Female Stress Syndrome, 1984 (also Dutch, Japan, German, English, Spanish and Australian edits.); Coping with Stress; Human Sexuality; The Male Stress Syndrome, 1986. columnist Your Emotional Best, Health Mag., also mem. editorial adv. bd.; mem. editorial adv. bd. Jour. Preventive Psychiatry. Contbr. articles to profl. publs., mags. and newspapers. Mem. steering com. Westchester Community Coll. Found., 1973-75. Mem. AAAS, Soc. for Sex Therapy and Research, Westchester County Psychol. Assn., N.Y. Acad. Scis., Am. Assn. Sex Educators, Counselors and Therapists (cert. sex educator; mem. regional bd., exec. com.), Am. Assn. for Profl. Law Enforcement, Mensa, Criminal Justice Educators Assn. N.Y. State, Am. Soc. Criminology, World Future Soc., N.Y. State United Tchrs., Eastern Psychol. Assn., Am. Med. Writers Assn. Address: 1109 Post Rd Scarsdale NY 10583

WITORT, JANET LEE, lawyer; b. Cedar Rapids, Iowa, Mar. 10, 1950; d. Charles Francis and Phyllis Harriet (Wilber) Svoboda; m. Stephen Francis Witort, Oct. 27, 1979. Student U. Colo., 1968-69, U. Iowa, 1971; B.A., U. No. Colo., 1972; J.D., Loyola U., 1979. Bar: Ill. 1979. Paralegal, Fed. Nat. Mortgage Assn., Chgo., 1973-75, Sidley & Austin, Chgo., 1975-76; assoc. Frankel, McKay & Orlikoff, Chgo., 1979-81; atty. Mut. Trust Life Ins. Co., Oak Brook, Ill., 1981—; Midwest regional dir. Nat. Fedn. Paralegal Assns., Chgo., 1975-76; co. rep. Life and Health Compliance Assn., Chgo., 1981—. Author: (with others) The Legal Assistant-a Self Statement, 1974. Vol., Republican campaign, Chgo., 1974-76. Mem. ABA, Ill. Bar Assn., Women's Bar Assn., Chgo. Bar Assn., Chgo. Paralegal Assn. (sec. 1973-74), Ill. Paralegal Assn. (v.p. 1975-76), Phi Alpha Delta, Student Bar Assn. (class rep. 1976-77). Republican. Methodist. Office: Mut Trust Life Ins Co 1200 Jorie Blvd Oak Brook IL 60521

WITSHORK, LINDA KAY, educator, investor; b. Vincennes, Ind., June 27, 1947; d. John Henry and Lucille Anges (Sanders) W. Assoc. Sci., Vincennes U., 1966; B.S., Ind. State U., 1968, M.S., 1971, Specialist degree, 1975. Cert. tchr., Ind. Elem. tchr. Vincennes Sch., Ind., 1969-71; reading specialist South Knox Schs., Monroe City, Ind., 1971—; tchr. gifted children, summers 1983, 84, 85. Adviser Vincennes U., 1984—; tchr. St. Vincet Orphanage, Vincennes, summers 1969, 70; guest speaker in field. Mem. Mensa (gifted children coordinator 1985-86), Internat. Reading Council, Ind. State Tchrs. Assn. Lutheran. Avocation: travel. Home: 1020 State Rd 67 Vincennes IN 47591 Office: S Knox Schs PO 38 Monroe City IN 47557

WITSIL, ELIZABETH SMITH ALISON (MRS. WALTER EARLE WITSIL), former social worker; b. Wilmington, Del., Sept. 13, 1909; d. Alexander and Katharine Anna (Smith) Alison; A.B., Wilson Coll., 1931; postgrad. Columbia U., 1934-36; m. Walter Earle Witsil, Aug. 27, 1938 (dec. Feb. 1964); 1 child, Adah Elizabeth Witsil Unger; step-children—Walter Earle, Sarah Virginia Witsil Lloyd. Accounting clk. Remington Rand, Inc., Bridgeport, Conn., 1932-33; social case-worker Bridgeport Br.-New Eng. Home for Little Wanderers, 1933-36; social case worker Conn. Children's Aid Soc., Danbury, 1936-38; dir. membership, pub. relations and publicity YWCA, Bridgeport, 1964-75; dir. cultural tours and vols. Bridgeport Mus. Arts, Sci. and Industry, 1975-83. Mem. Bd. Fin. Fairfield (Conn.), 1955-79; mem. Fairfield Rep. Town Meeting, 1947-55; pres. bd. mgrs. Woodfield Maternity Home and Adoption Service, Bridgeport, 1954-57, mem. corp.; bd. dirs. Vis. Nurse Assn. Bridgeport, United Fund Council Eastern Fairfield County, Bridgeport Council Ch. Women, Child Guidance Center of Bridgeport, Conn. Conf. Social Work, Mountain Grove Cemetery Assn., Bridgeport; v.p. Fairfield Community Services; trustee Greater Bridgeport Symphony Soc., 1978—; mem. Sr. Citizens Tax Relief Com., Fairfield, 1980-85, Sr. Citizens Life Center Study and Bldg. Com., 1981-84; bd. assos. U. Bridgeport; mem. Republican Women's Assn. Fairfield. Mem. AAUW, LWV, DAR, Bridgeport Hosp. Aux. (pres. 1961-63), Delta Kappa Gamma (hon.). Presbyterian (trustee, elder). Clubs: Contemporary (sec. 1957-64, pres. 1976), Wilson Coll. Home: 235 Millard St Apt C3 Fairfield CT 06430

WITT, HELEN MERCER, government official, lawyer; b. Atlantic City, July 13, 1933; m. Edward A. Witt; 5 children. B.A., Dickinson Coll., 1955; J.D., U. Pitts., 1969. Mem. law firms Cleland, Hurtt & Witt, and Witt & Witt, 1970-74; asst. to chmn. U.S. Steel Corp./United Steelworkers Am. bd. arbitration, 1975-82; mem. Nat. Mediation Bd., 1983—. Office: Nat Mediation Bd 1425 K St NW Washington DC 20572

WITT, SANDRA JOHNSON, psychologist; b. Sanford, Fla., July 17, 1946; d. Elmer Hunter and Betty Malvina (Beeler) Johnson; B.A. with high honors in German, U. Fla., 1968, M.A. in German, 1969, Ph.D. in Psychology, 1978; M.A. in Psychology, Emory U., 1973; m. William Witt, Oct. 16, 1971; children—Amanda, Katherine. Internat. hostess and in-flight instr. Trans World Airlines, 1969-71; grad. teaching asst. Emory U., 1971-73; staff psychologist, dir. adult edn. Key Tng. Center, Lecanto, Fla., 1973-74; fellow Center for Gerontol. Studies and Programs, U. Fla., Gainesville, 1976, research asst. psychology dept., 1977, adj. asst. prof., 1978-79, asst. dir. testing and evaluation, coordinator basic skills program, 1981-83; test adminstr. State of Fla. Univ. System, 1983—; psychologist, dir. behavior mgmt. therapy Intermediate Care Facility, Sunland Tng. Center, Gainesville, 1979-81; dist. psychologist, devel. services program office Dept. Health and Rehabilitative Services, Gainesville, 1981; faculty U. Fla., 1984—; cons. psychologist for various orgns., univs., community mental health centers. Active in local elections; sch. adv. council rep. Alachua County Sch. System. Mem. Am. Psychol. Assn., Southeastern Psychol. Assn., Am. Assn. Mental Deficiency, Gerontol. Soc., Nat. Assn. Retarded Citizens, Phi Beta Kappa. Lutheran. Contbr. articles to profl. jours. Home: 2811 NW 37th Terr Gainesville FL 32605 Office: U Fla 134 Norman Hall Gainesville FL 32611

WITTE, MARY LEE, executive director legal services agency, lawyer; b. Madison, Wis., July 11, 1948; d. Harold Leo and Selma May (Dierckes) W.; m. Richard Scott Miko, June 7, 1970; 1 son, Stephen Joseph. B.A. cum laude, U. Wis., 1970; J.D. cum laude, DePaul U., 1974; M.A. cum laude, Webster Coll., 1977. Bar: Ill. 1974, U.S. Dist. Ct. (no. dist.) Ill. 1974, U.S. Ct. Mil. Appeals 1975. Dep. dir. Chgo. Vol. Legal Services Found. 1979-83, exec. dir. and atty., 1983—. Bd. dirs. Chgo. Law Enforcement Study Group, 1982—, Legal Clinic for Disabled, 1984, Ill. Citizens for Handgun Control, 1984. Served as capt. JAGC, U.S. Army, 1975-78. Mem. ABA, Ill. State Bar Assn., Chgo. Bar Assn., Womens Bar Assn. Ill., Mortar Board. Club: Executives (Chgo.). Office: Chgo Vol Legal Services Found 203 N Wabash Suite 2300 Chicago IL 60601

WITTELES, ELEONORA MEIRA, physicist; b. Jerusalem, July 14, 1938; d. Salomon and Rivka (Komornik) W.; B.S., Fordham U., 1962, M.S., 1963; M.S., N.Y.U., 1965; Ph.D. (research fellow), Yeshiva U., 1969. Postdoctoral fellow Bar-Ilan U., Israel, 1969-70, asst. prof., 1970-72; ind. cons., 1972-80; sr. research scientist Atlantic Richfield Co., Los Angeles, 1980-84; sr. staff engr. Hughes Aircraft Co., Los Angeles, 1984—. Mem. Am. Phys. Soc., AAAS, IEEE, IEEE Engring. in Medicine and Biology Soc., IEEE Magnetics Soc., Com. on Status of Women in Physics, N.Y. Acad. Scis. Research on solid state physics, superconductivity, applied material scis.; inventor med. instrumentation and cryogenic instrumentation. Home: 4714 Browndeer Ln Palos Verdes CA 90274 Office: 2000 El Segundo Blvd El Segundo CA 90245

WITTIG, SUSAN WEBBER, college administrator, English educator, author; b. Maywood, Ill., Jan. 2, 1940; d. John H. and Ai Lucille (Franklin) Webber; divorced; children—Robert, Robin, Michael. B.A., U. Ill., 1967; M.A., U. Calif.-Berkeley, 1969, Ph.D., 1972. Asst. to assoc. prof. English, U. Tex.-Austin, 1972-79, assoc. dean grad. sch., 1977-79; dean Newcomb Coll., New Orleans, 1979-81; prof. English, exec. asst. pres. Southwest Tex. State U., San Marcos, 1981-82, v.p. acad. affairs, 1982—. Author: Steps to Structure, 1975, Participating Reader, 1977, Narrative Structure in Medieval Non-cyclic Verse Romances, 1977. Danforth Found. grad. fellow, 1967-72; NEH grantee, 1985—. Mem. Inst. for Bus. and Profl. Communication (pres. 1976-79), Soc. for Values in Higher Edn., Council on Coll. Level Services Coll. Bd. Avocations: writing; reading. Office: Southwest Tex State Univ San Marcos TX 78667

WITTLER, SHIRLEY JOYCE, state official; b. Ravenna, Nebr., Oct. 10, 1927; d. Earl William and Minnie Ethel (Frink) Wade; student U. Nebr., 1944-47; m. LeRoy F. Wittler, Dec. 31, 1946; children—Julie Diane, Barbara Liane. Real estate saleswoman Harrington Assocs., Lincoln, Nebr., 1965-69; real estate broker Tom Searl Realty, Inc., Cheyenne, Wyo., 1970-76; dep. state treas. State of Wyo., 1976-78, state treas., 1978-83, state cons., 1983, commr. State Tax Commn., 1985—. Pres., LWV, Lincoln, 1965-69, state bd. dirs., 1970-72; fin. chmn. Republican Central Com. Laramie County, 1974-76; chmn. Laramie County Pres. Ford Com., 1976; Rep. precinct committeewoman, 1972-77; mem. Laramie County Library Bd., 1976, Community Devel. Adv. Bd., 1974-77. Mem. Cheyenne Bd. Realtors (pres. 1976, Cheyenne Realtor of Yr. 1974), Women's Civic League (treas. 1974, legis. chmn. 1975-76). Lutheran. Office: 1426 Herschler Bldg Cheyenne WY 82002

WITTLOCK, MARY LENORE, nurse; b. Chgo., July 29, 1932; d. Leonard Stanley and Mary Josephine (Palko) Boles; m. Charles Robert Wittlock, Oct. 2, 1954; children—Sandra, Scott, Geriann, Gary, Steven. Diploma, Norwegian Am. Hosp., Chgo., 1953. Registered nurse, Ill. Staff nurse obstetrics Norwegian Am. Hosp., Chgo., 1953-64; staff nurse obstetrics N.W. Hosp., Chgo., 1964-65, supr. med.-surg., 1965-77, critical care coordinator, 1977-83, asst. dir. critical care, 1983-85, dir. critical care services, 1985—. Scout leader Boy Scouts Am., Chgo., 1964-77, Girl Scouts U.S.A., Chgo., 1965-77. Mem. Am. Assn. Critical Care Nurses, Emergency Nurses Assn., Nat. Critical Care Inst. Democrat. Roman Catholic. Avocations: photography; camping; traveling. Office: NW Hosp 5645 W Addison St Chicago IL 60641

WITTSTOCK, LAURA WATERMAN, ednl. adminstr., journalist/writer, edn. cons.; b. Cattaraugus, Indian Reservation, N.Y., Sept. 11, 1937; d. Isaac and Clarinda (Jackson) Waterman; student San Francisco State Coll., 1961, Fla. Jr. Coll., 1964; m. Lloyd Wittstock, Aug. 30, 1970; children—Joe, Tedi, Arthur, James, Rosy. Copywriter, The Hecht Co., Washington, 1968-71; editor Legis. Review, Indian Legal Info. Devel. Service, Washington, 1971-73; project MEDIA designer/dir. Nat. Indian Edn. Assn., Mpls., 1973-77; ind. cons., edn. specialist, Mpls., 1976—; adminstr. Heart of the Earth Sch., Mpls., 1982—; mgr. Center V Satellite Office, Native Am. Research Inst., Inc., Mpls., 1981; lectr. in field. Bd. dirs. United Way, Mpls., Christian Sharing Fund, Mpls. Community-Bus. Employment Alliance, Met. U. Minority Services Program, St. Paul. Recipient award Best Merchandising Impression, May Cohens, Jacksonville, Fla., 1969. Mem. Am. Indian Bus. Devel. Corp. (dir. 1979-83), Nat. Commn. on Alcoholism and Alcohol Related Problems, Am. Indian Opportunities Industrialization Center (dir.). Editor, Indian Edn., 1973-74; contbr. articles to profl. jours. Office: Heart of the Earth School 1209 SE 4th St Minneapolis MN 55414

WITZKOSKE, GERTRUDE ANN (TRUDY), postmaster; b. Bremond, Tex., Dec. 13, 1937; d. Pete and Annie Elizabeth (Rekieta) Dutka; m. Clarence William Witzkoske, June 21, 1958; children—Mark, Paul. Student U. Houston, 1960, Massey Bus. Coll., 1967; A.S., North Houston Community Coll., 1975. With U.S. Postal Service, Porter, Tex., 1975-77, Houston, 1966-80, postal system examiner, 1979-80, postmaster, 1980—. Assoc. editor Lone Star Postmaster, 1982-86. Eucharistic minister Roman Catholic Ch., 1983-86; leader Boy Scouts Am., 1967-79; organizer Belmar Civic Club, 1965; vol. Am. Cancer Soc., Am. Heart Assn., Crisis Hot Line. Recipient Spl. Achievement award U.S. Postal Service, 1974, Bicentennial award, 1976. Mem. Nat. League Postmasters of U.S., Nat. Assn. Postmasters U.S. Exec. sec. Houston/Galveston Pastoral Council, 1972-73. Mem. Cath. Daughters Am. Democrat. Avocations: travel; costume design; flower arranging; gourmet cooking; stamp collecting. Home: 202 E Carby St Houston TX 77037 Office: US Postal Service 212 Loop 494 Porter TX 77365

WITZMAN, AUDREY LORAINE, educator; b. Galva, Ill., July 22, 1937; d. Clarence Gilbert and Gladys Bernice (Westlin) Peterson; B.A., Eureka Coll., 1958; M.Ed., Nat. Coll. Edn., 1962; Ph.D., Northwestern U., 1976; m. Thomas A. Witzman, Aug. 10, 1958; children—Johanna Marie, Jocelyn Anne. Public sch. tchr., Ill., 1958-67; asst. prof. early childhood edn. Northeastern Ill. U., Chgo., 1968-71; developer, owner/dir. Country Woods Nursery Sch. and Day Camp, Valparaiso, Ind., 1971—; prof. early childhood edn. Governors State U., University Park, Ill., 1979—. Chmn., Porter County (Ind.) Child Protection Team, 1980, 86; bd. dirs. Family House, Valparaiso, 1981—. Mem. Nat. Assn. for Edn. Young Children, Midwest Assn. Edn. Young Children (co-coordinator conf. Indpls. 1982, Ind. rep. to bd. 1981-83), Ind. Assn. for Edn. Young Children. Republican. Methodist. Home: 450 East 725 North Valparaiso IN 46383 Office: Div Edn Governors State University Park IL 60644

WODELE, PATRICIA J., county official; b. Durand, Wis., Oct. 1, 1943; d. Lyman John and Lila M. (Moline) Manor; m. Raymond Lester Davis, June 17, 1961 (dec. 1973); children—Sheri, Sheila, Shana; m. Dennis John Wodele, Dec. 28, 1974; 1 child, Shane. Student U. Wis., 1976. Bookkeeper, receptionist Pyrofax Gas Co., Durand, Wis., 1961-63; bookkeeper R.L. Davis Logging, Nelson, Wis., 1961-62; bookkeeper Nelson Sales, Wis., 1965-73, owner, operator, 1973-74; with payroll dept. L.A. Hogan Logging, 1973-74; treas. County of Buffalo, Alma, Wis., 1975—. Chmn. bd. dirs. Dist. 1 Voc., Tech. and Adult Edn.; treas. Nelson Little League, 1985—. Mem. Am. Vocat. Assn., Am. Community Coll. Assn., Wis. County Treas. Assn. (pres. 1978-79). Republican. Mem. Evang. Free Ch. Avocations: reading; travel. Home: Rural Route 1 Box 33-C Nelson WI 54756 Office: County of Buffalo 407 2nd St Alma WI 54610

WODLINGER, PATRICIA WHEELER, radio station executive; b. Kansas City, Mo., Jan. 7, 1952; d. John Osborne and Mary Jane (Smith) Wheeler; m. Kevin Mark Wodlinger, Oct. 29, 1977; children—John Louis, Anne Hartz. B.A., Georgetown U., 1974. With sales dept. Antares Broadcasting, Santa Barbara, Calif., 1976-77; with sales and prodn. dept. DeLuxe House, Santa Barbara, 1977-79; owner, sta. mgr. Monett Communications, Inc. Sta. KRMA-Sta. KKBL-FM, Monett, Mo., 1979—. Dir. radio commls., promotions. Pres. Artes Composit, Monett, 1982—. Mem. Monett C. of C., Monett Jaycee Women, Mo. Broadcasters, Nat. Radio Broadcasters Assn. Lutheran. Avocations: tennis; water and snow skiing; needlework. Home and Office: 1569 N Central St Monett MO 65708

WOEPPEL, PATRICE, rehabilitation counseling organization executive; b. Elmira, N.Y., Mar. 13, 1939; d. Oswald Joseph and Alice (O'Reilly) W.; m. Richard W. Berkeley, June 19, 1971 (div. July 1985); 1 child, S. Jamal. B.S., CCNY, 1966; M.S., Fordham U., 1980; postgrad. in edn., Nova U., 1985—. Cert. rehab. counselor Commn. on Rehab. Counselor Cert., Chgo., Fla., Pub. relations coordinator, office adminstr. Am. Mus. Natural History, N.Y.C., 1966; caseworker Westchester County Dept. Social Services, White Plains, N.Y., 1966-69; research asst. NYU Med. Ctr., N.Y.C., 1969-70; project dir. Van Etten drug treatment program Albert Einstein Coll. Medicine, Bronx, N.Y., 1970-76; program adminstr. Westchester County Dept. Community Mental Health, 1976-84; exec. dir., chief operating officer Early Childhood Devel. Assocs., Fort Lauderdale, Fla., 1984—; workshop presenter; mem. regional task force on children and youth N.Y. State Office Mental Health, 1977-84; mem. instrnl. rev. bd. N.Y. State Div. Substance Abuse Services, 1980-83; mem. steering com. Westchester County Task Force on Child Abuse/Neglect, 1980-84; bd. dirs. SCAN Am. of N.Y., Inc., 1982-84; v.p. Westchester Coalition on Teenage Pregnancy, Prevention and Parenting, 1982-84; mem. residential treatment facility adv. com. Hudson River region N.Y. State Office Mental Health, 1983-84; chmn. legis. com. Presch. Interagy. Council, 1985-86; co-chmn. ins. com. Fla. Child Care Provider's Forum, 1985-86; mem. Children's Prevention Task Force for State Health and Rehabilative Services, Dist. X, 1985—. Recipient achievement award Nat. Assn. Counties, 1980, 81; Ruth Benedict award for grad. study in anthropology, 1966; Edwin Michaelian scholar Pace U., 1984. Mem. Assn. Mental Health Adminstrs. (cert.), Fort Lauderdale C. of C. Democrat. Home: 2568 NW 99th Ave Coral Springs FL 33065 Office: 4137 N State Rd 7 Fort Lauderdale FL 33319

WOERNER, LOUISE, management consultant; b. Jackson, Tenn., June 2, 1942; d. Victor I. and Leland (Horner) W. B.S. cum laude, Trinity U., San Antonio, 1964; M.B.A., U. Chgo., 1965. Pres. Wheels, Inc., Key West, Fla., 1975—, L. Woerner, Inc. dba HCR, Rochester, N.Y., and Washington, 1978—, L. Woerner Co., Inc., Washington, 1978—; exec. v.p. J.A. Reyes Assocs., Inc., Washington, 1971-79; dir. communications Memphis Area C. of C., 1969-71; mgr. new bus., dir. pub. relations Allied Stores, Inc., Dallas, 1967-68; sr. assoc. D.R. Fagin & Assocs., Inc., Dallas, 1965-67; mem. small bus. and agrl. adv. council Fed. Res. Bank, N.Y.C., 1985—; mem. adv. council SBA, 1984—. Contbr. articles to profl. jours. Health Care Financing

Adminstrn. grantee; Gannett Found. grantee; named Outstanding Young Career Woman of Tex., 1968, Small Bus. Person of Yr., SBA, 1983, Bus. Adv. of Yr., 1983; recipient achievement award Wall St. Jour. Mem. Pvt. Industry Council, Bus. and Profl. Women's Club Dallas (Dist. 15 Woman of Yr. 1980, cert. of appreciation 1974), Rochester C. of C. Club: Zonta (dir. 1983-85) (Washington).

WOFFORD, ARLENE, nurse; b. Detroit, Dec. 28, 1949; d. William Joseph and Janina (Huczek) Wojkiewicz; m. James Coogan Wofford, Jan. 24, 1969 (div. May 1978); children—James William, Steven Jarett, Jeffrey Adam. R.N., Mercy Sch. of Nursing, Detroit, 1969; B.S. in Nursing, Mercy Coll., Detroit, 1982; postgrad. Madonna Coll., Livonia, Mich., 1984—. Registered nurse, Mich. Staff nurse St. Joseph Mercy Hosp., Detroit, 1969-77; nurse practitioner Hodaoi, M.D. and Assocs., Detroit, 1979-81; head nurse St. Joseph Mercy Hosp., also Samaritan Health Ctr., Detroit, 1977-85; nursing adminstrv. asst. Samaritan Health Ctr., Detroit, 1985—; nurse Profl. Care, Southfield, Mich., 1985—; head nurse Sinai Hosp., Detroit, 1985—; nurse cons. Borning Corp., Spokane, Wash., 1984—. Mem. Nat. League Nursing (Mich. chpt.), Nurse Assn. of Am. Coll. Obstetricians and Gynecologists, Mich. Assn. Concerned with Sch. Age Parents, Perinatal Assn. Mich. Democrat. Roman Catholic. Avocations: ceramics; needlework. Home: 8867 Sarasota St Redford MI 48239 Office: Sinai Hosp 6767 W Outer Dr Detroit MI 48235

WOHLSTETTER, ROBERTA, senior analyst defense research; b. Duluth, Minn., Aug. 22, 1912; d. Edmund Morris and Elsie Morgan; m. Albert Wohlstetter, June 7, 1939; 1 child, Joan. B.A., Vassar Coll., 1933; M.A., Columbia U., 1936. Cons. research Rand Corp., Santa Monica, Calif., 1949—; cons. Science Applications, Century City, Calif., 1974-79; sr. analyst def. research Research and Devel. Assocs., Marina del Rey, Calif., 1979—. Author: Pearl Harbor: Warning and Decision, 1962. Fellow AAUW, 1940-41. Recipient Bancroft award Columbia U., 1963. Named Los Angeles Times Woman of Year, 1963. Mem. Council Fgn. Relations, Internat. Council Internat. Inst. Strategic Studies (London), Internat. Council, Georgetown U. Csis. Office: Pan Heuristics Div Research and Devel Assos PO Box 9695 Marina del Rey CA 90295

WOJAHN, R. LORRAINE, state legislator; b. Wash. Mem. Wash. State Ho. of Reps., 1969-76; mem. Wash. State Senate from dist. 27, 1977—, mem. commerce and labor, rules, fin. instrns., ways and means coms. Democrat. Office: Wash State Senate State Capitol Olympia WA 98504*

WOJCIK, KATHLEEN LOUISE, state legislator; b. Chgo., July 15, 1936; d. George Frederick and Anna Marie (Nowak) Zorger; m. Norbert R. Wojcik, Aug. 25, 1956; children—Norbert R., Noreen. Student William R. Harper Coll., 1973. Exec. sec. to pres. E.L. Reibold Sales Promotion Agy., Chgo., 1956-60; real estate broker Quinlan & Tyson, Schaumburg, Ill., 1970-75; broker Kathleen L. Wojcik Realty, Schaumburg, 1976—; town clk., office mgr. Schaumburg Twp., Hoffman Estates, Ill., 1968-83; mem. Ill. Ho. of Reps., 1983—, spokesperson human services, 1985—. Chmn. Small Businessmen for Reagan/Bush, Schaumberg Twp., 1984; co-coordinator Schaumburg Twp. Women for Reagan, 1984; exec. sec. Rep. Orgn. Schaumburg, 1961-64, treas., 1963-65, precinct capt., 1968 ; v.p. St. Huberts Council Catholic Women. Fellow Nat. Conf. State Legislators, Am. Legis. Exchange Council, N.W. Suburban Assn. Commerce and Industry, Am. Businesswomens Assn., Ill. Realtors Assn. (legis. chmn.); mem. Twp. Clks. Ill. (pres. 1979—), Twp. Clks. Assn. Cook County (bd. dirs. 1973-82), DAR. Lodge: Moose. Avocation: golf. Office: 514 W Wise Rd Schaumburg IL 60193

WOJTAK, RUTH MARIE, retail company executive; b. Kenosha, Wis., Sept. 25, 1956; d. Richard Stanley and Anne Theresa (Steplyk) W. Assoc. Applied Sci., Gateway Tech. Inst., 1976; B.A., U. Wis.-Parkside, 1980. Transp. aide Kenosha Achievement Ctr. (Wis.), 1977; lifeguard U. Wis.-Parkside, Kenosha, 1980, library clk., 1978-80; asst. mgr. K Mart Corp., Troy, Mich., 1980—. Mem. Am. Mgmt. Assn., Nat. Assn. Female Execs., U. Wis.-Parkside Alumni Assn., Distributive Edn. Clubs Am. (parliamentarian 1976). Roman Catholic. Home: 1820 Duggleby St Davenport IA 52803 Office: K Mart 3530 3616 W Kimberly Rd #3441 Davenport IA 52806

WOLANIN, SOPHIE MAE, civic worker, tutor, scholar, lecturer; b. Alton, Ill., June 11, 1913; d. Stephen and Mary (Fijalka) Wolanin; student Pa. State Coll., 1943-44; cert. secretarial sci. U. S.C., 1946, B.S. in Bus. Adminstrn. cum laude, 1948; Ph.D. (hon.), Colo. State Christian Coll., 1972. Clk., stenographer, sec. Mercer County (Pa.) Tax Collector's Office, Sharon, 1932-34; receptionist, social sec., nurse-technician to Dr., N.Y.C., 1934-37; coil winder, assembler Westinghouse Electric Corp., Sharon, 1937-39; duplicator operator, typist, stenographer, 1939-44, confidential sec., Pitts., 1949-54; exec. sec., charter mem. Westinghouse Credit Corp., 1954-72, sr. sec., 1972-80; reporter WCC News, 1967-68, asst. editor, 1968-71, assoc. editor, 1971-74; student office sec. to dean U. S.C. Sch. Commerce, 1944-46, instr. math., bus. adminstrn., secretarial sci., 1946-48. Publicity and pub. relations chmn., corr. sec. South Oakland Rehab. Council, 1967-69; mem. nat. adv. bd. Am. Security Council; founder Center Internat. Security Studies Am. Security Council Edn. Found; charter mem. Republican Presdl. Task Force. Recipient various 1st prize awards Allegheny County Fair; gold plaque Westinghouse Credit Corp., 1968; citation Congl. Record, 1969; TWA, 1969; Gold medal for Community Service, London, 1973; Medal of Merit, Pres. Regan, 1982; Biographee of Yr. award Hist. Preservations of Am., 1986; numerous other plaques and certificates. Fellow Internat. Inst. Community Service (founder, life patron), U. S.C. Ednl. Found., Anglo-Am. Acad. (hon.), World Lit. Acad. (life); mem. Allegheny County Scholarship Assn. (life), Nat. Assn. Exec. Secs., Polish-Am. Numis. Assn., Polonus Philatelic Soc., Polish Inst. Arts and Scis. of Am., Inc. (assoc.), Allegheny County LWV, AAUW (life), Internat. Fedn. Univ. Women, Am. Mus. Natural History, (assoc.), N.E. Historic Geneal. Soc. (life), Anglo-Am. Hist. Soc. (founding charter mem.), Internat. Platform Assn., Nat. Hist. Soc. of Gettysburg (founding), Nat. Trust Historic Preservation, U. S.C. Alumni Assn. Ednl. Found. (gen. chmn. Tri-State area 1959, Pa. state fund chmn. 1967-68, pres.'s council 1972—), Smithsonian Assocs. (charter), UN Assn. U.S., Am. Bible Soc., Hypatian Lit. Soc., Acad. Polit. Sci. (life), Société Commemorative de Femmes Celebres, Bus. and Profl. Women's Club Pitts. (dir. 1963-80, editor Bull. 1963-65, treas. 1965-66, historian 1969-70, pub. relations 1971-80, Woman of Yr. Award 1972), Liturgical Conf. N. Am. (life), Am. Counselors Soc. (life), Westinghouse Vet. Employees Assn., Am. Acad. Social and Polit. Sci., Mercer County Hist. Soc. (life), Nat., Pa. (key club) fedns. bus. and profl. women's clubs, St. Paul's Cathedral Altar Soc., Assn. Nat. Archives, Early Am. Soc., Nat. Soc. Lit. and the Arts, Friends of Churchill Meml. Library in U.S., Met. Opera Guild (assoc.). Republican. Roman Catholic. Clubs: Jonathan Maxcy of U. S.C. (charter), University Catholic of Pitts., College of Sharon (hon.). Contbr. articles to newspapers. Home: 1608 Lafayette Rd Pittsburgh PA 15221

WOLANYK, SHEILA JANE, accountant, financial consultant; b. Niagara Falls, N.Y., Aug. 22, 1955; d. Peter Paul and Eva Jane (Fick) W. A.S.S., Bryant and Stratton Coll., 1979; B.S., Empire State U., 1981; postgrad. in bus. adminstrn. N.H. Coll., 1985—. Corp. acct. Econ. Devel., Buff, N.Y., 1981-83; corp. controller Buxton Corp., Brentwood, N.H., 1983-84; income tax preparer H&R Block, Exeter, N.H., 1984, 85; pvt. practice acctg., 1986—; real estate approval and fin. advisor Brown Realty, 1981; fin. cons. Green Tree Fin. Services, 1983. Mem. Nat. Assn. Pub. Accts., Nat. Health Fitness Assn. Democrat. Presbyterian. Home: PO Box 647 Route 156 Raymond NH 03077

WOLF, BARBARA ANNE, biological research administrator, biologist; b. N.Y.C., July 24, 1947; d. Boris and Molly (Gruberg) W.; B.A. magna cum laude (N.Y. State Regents scholar, Stanley Koncal award 1968), Queens Coll., City U. N.Y., 1968; Ph.D. in Biology, M.I.T., 1973; m. Robert Stanley Spiel, Aug. 25, 1973; children—Melissa Heather, Seth Brandon. Research asst. chem. synthesis Sloan-Kettering Inst. for Cancer Research, Rye, N.Y., 1967; teaching asst. cell biology M.I.T., Cambridge, 1969-70, supr. grad seminars, 1972-73; research asst. virology Rockefeller U., N.Y.C., 1973-75, fellow Nat. Cancer Inst., 1975-77, research assoc., oncological studies, summer, 1977; mgr. biol. services Revlon Research Center, Bronx, N.Y., 1977-80, dir. biol. services, 1981—; asso. prof. Coll. Pharmacy St. John's U., Queens, N.Y., 1981—. Mem. Am. Soc. Microbiologists, Soc. Toxicology, Am. Coll. Toxicology, N.Y. Soc. Electron Microscopists, Soc. of Cosmetic Chemists, Genetic Toxicology Assn., Environ. Mutagen Soc., AAAS, N.Y. Acad. Scis., Sigma Xi, Phi Beta Kappa, Beta Delta Chi. Contbr. articles on cell biology and oncology to sci. jours. Office: 2121 Route 27 Edison NJ 08818

WOLF, CAROLE BRUCE, educator; b. Houston, Mar. 20, 1944; d. Victor Van Buren and Susie Ellen (Fuller) Bruce; B.A., Stephen F. Austin State U., 1965, M.A. in English, 1968; Ph.D. in English (Truman Camp fellow), Tex. Tech U., 1982; m. John Charles Wolf, Oct. 21, 1967; children—Allan Bruce, Anne Elizabeth. Tchr. English, Marshall (Tex.) High Sch., 1965-66; teaching asst. in English, Stephen F. Austin State U., 1966-68; tchr. English, Castleberry Ind. Sch. Dist., Ft. Worth, 1968-72; instr. English, South Plains Coll., 1974, 79; instr. English, Tex. Tech U., Lubbock, 1975-79, lectr., 1980—; asst. archivist Southwest collection Tex. Tech. U., 1983-84; archivist Episcopal Diocese of Northwest Tex., 1984—; instr. Tarrant County Jr. Coll., 1969. Vol., Am. Cancer Soc.; leader South Plains council Cub Scouts Am.; pres. S.C. Episcopal Churchwomen, Lubbock, 1982-83, vestryman, 1986—. Mem. South Central Modern Lang. Assn. Episcopalian. Contbr. articles to profl. publs. Home: 3312 40th St Lubbock TX 79413

WOLF, DIANE WELFELD, accountant, real estate developer; b. New London, Conn., Dec. 10, 1943; d. Alvan and Faye P. Welfeld; B.S. U. Md., 1975; M. Taxation, U. Balt., 1982, postgrad. Law sch.; m. Morris Wolf, Dec. 18, 1977 (separated); children by previous marriage—Andrew, Amy Bereson. Acct., George Cox, C.P.A., 1979; pvt. practice acctg.; real estate developer, Owings Mills, Md.; v.p. MM Devel., MWW Devel.; v.p. Standard Bearer, Inc., Wolfland, Inc., Yacht for Charter, Cannes, France. C.P.A. Mem. Am. Inst. C.P.A.s, Md. Assn. C.P.S.s. Jewish. Home and Office: 11114 Verdant Ct Owings Mills MD 21117

WOLF, GERTRUDE OLSHAKER, librarian, journalist, poet; b. Bklyn., Sept. 27, 1923; d. Morris and Sarah Olshaker; B.A., Bklyn. Coll., 1944; children—Carol Jane, Laura Wolf Shur, Nancy Wolf Baumann, David Charles. Dir. prodn. Intersci. Pubs., N.Y.C., 1944; reporter, asst. to editor Somerset Messenger-Gazette, Somerville, N.J., 1944-46; assoc. editor Cosmetic & Drug Preview, 1946; editor-in-chief Citations, Comml. Investment Trust, N.Y.C., 1946-47; reporter, feature writer, asst. theater editor, drama critic Columbus (Ohio) Citizen, 1947-51; advt. copywriter Eaton Paper Corp., Pittsfield, Mass., 1951-52; suburban newspaper corr. Evening and Sunday Bull., Phila., 1966-69; reporter West Chester Daily Local News, 1966-67, Ardmore Main Line Times, 1968; reception desk clk. LaGuardia Med. Group, Jamaica, N.Y., 1971-80; clk. Queensborough Public Library, 1981—. Recipient writing awards. Mem. Phila. Press Assn. Author poetry: Golden Tinsel and the Stars, 1980; Seashells at Mantoloking, 1981; The First Snow of Winter, 1983; Lonely Landscape, 1984; Castle of Dreams, 1984; Movie Street Scene, 1985. Home: 40-04 157th St Flushing NY 11354

WOLF, ISABEL DRANE, food scientist, government official; b. Boston, Nov. 21, 1933; d. Louis Andrew and Anna (Whalen) Drane; B.S., Simmons Coll., 1955; M.S., U. Minn., 1971; m. Richard V. Lechowich, Jan. 21, 1983; children—Isabel, August L., Erika M. Wolf. Instr. dept. food sci. and nutrition U. Minn. 1972-79, asst. prof., 1979-81, assoc. prof., 1981—, extension food and nutrition specialist, 1972—; dir. Office of Consumer Advisor U.S. Dept. Agr., 1982-83, adminstr. Human Nutrition Info. Service, 1983-85, pvt. cons., 1985—. Mem. Inst. Food Technologists, Soc. Nutrition Edn., Nat. Nutrition Consortium, Minn. State Nutrition Council, Am. Home Econs. Assn. Author: (with N.W. Jerome, J.G. McCleery) Help Yourself - Choices in Food and Nutrition, 1981; contbr. articles to profl. jours. Office: 50 Harvard Ct White Plains NY 10605

WOLF, JOAN LEVIN, ballet teacher; b. Richmond, Va., July 28, 1933; d. Simon Jacob and Jean (Sturman) Levin; m. Harold Lawrence Wolf, May 6, 1956; children—Eric Andrew, Elizabeth Ann. Student Coll. William and Mary, 1951-54. Soloist, Richmond Civic Ballet Co., Va., 1949-57, pres., 1955-56; comml. artist Cargill & Wilson Advt. Agy., Richmond, 1954-56; owner Joan Wolf Sch. Ballet, River Edge, N.J., 1957-79, Hillsdale, N.J., 1963—; owner, dir. Joan Wolf Ballet Ensemble, 1964-82; artistic dir., choreographer Joan Wolf Ballet Co., Hillsdale and River Edge, 1972—. Trustee, Hackensack YMHA, 1969-70; bd. dirs. Pascack Valley Mental Health Ctr., 1975-77; chmn. Bikeway Commn. Woodcliff Lake, 1975—; mem. Bergen County Cultural Arts Commn., 1977-80. Recipient cert. of merit as profl. tchr. Nat. Acad. of Ballet, 1960; citation for outstanding cultural contbn. State of N.J., 1981; commendation Bergen County Freeholders, 1981. Mem. Hillsdale C. of C. (pres. 1968-71), Greater Pascack Valley C. of C. (trustee, chmn. Bikeway Commn. 1974—), Subject of book There's Always a Right Job for Every Woman (Roberta Roesch). Home: 12 Anderson Ct Woodcliff Lake NJ 07675 Office: 455 Hillsdale Ave Hillsdale NJ 07642

WOLF, MARTA SUSAN, librarian; b. Newark, Mar. 25, 1946; d. John Andrew and Gertrude Agnes (Kane) Turk; B.S., Bowling Green U., 1968; M.L.S., U. Tex., 1977; Library asst. serials dept. Bowling Green (Ohio) U. Library, 1968; sch. librarian Brooks Jr. Secondary Sch., Powell River, B.C., Can., 1968-69; asst. librarian U. Mich. Libraries, Ann Arbor, 1970-72; br. librarian Social Work Library, Gen. Libraries, U. Tex., Austin, 1972-75, cons. Center Social Work Research, Sch. Social Work, 1974-75, dir. info. services, 1975-79; asst. dir. Collection devel. Tex. State Library, Austin, 1980—; mem. Nat. Accreditation Com. for Info. and Referral Agys., 1977—; mem. Statewide Devel. Bd. for Establishment Tex. Info. and Referal Orgn., 1976. Mem. Spl. Libraries Assn., Am. Soc. Info. Sci., Alliance Info. and Referral Systems (mem. exec. com. Tex., mem. nat. standards com.), ALA, Tex. Library Assn., Austin On-Line Users Group, State Agy. Libraries of Tex. (pres. 1981-83), Assn. Specialized and Coop. Library Agys. (chmn. publs. com. 1982-84). Mem. editorial bd. Info. and Referral, Jour. Alliance Info. and Referral Systems, 1978—; editor Library Devels., jour. Tex. State Library, 1980—. Home: 1240 Barton Hills #114 Austin TX 78704 Office: Tex State Library PO Box 12927 Austin TX 78711

WOLF, MARY, training specialist; b. Camden, N.J., July 7, 1938; d. Harry S. and Reba (Braun) Elkins; B.S. in Edn., Temple U., 1960; M.A. in Human Devel., Fairleigh Dickinson U., 1979; children—Alan Eric, Lisa Caryl, Marla Beth. Tchr., Camden High Sch., 1960-61, W. Phila. High Sch., 1961-64; instr. World-Wide Ednl. Services, Newark, 1979; pres. Dynamic Lifestyles, Inc., Belmar, N.J., 1979—; tng. specialist Ocean County Coll., Toms River, N.J., 1979-81; tng. specialist Ocean County Employment and Tng. Adminstrn., Toms River, N.J., 1981-82; mgr. RCA, Eatontown, N.J., 1982-85; sr. orgnl. and tng. specialist RCA Astro Electronics, Princeton, N.J., 1985—; cons. in field. Mem. Am. Personnel and Guidance Assn., Am. Soc. Tng. and Devel., Nat. Soc. Performance and Instrn., Nat. Assn. Female Execs., Assn. Humanistic Psychology. Office: RCA Astro Electronics Princeton NJ

WOLF, MARY ZIETLOW, manufacturing company executive; b. New London, Wis., Feb. 26, 1950; d. Gordon Leo and Melane Mary (Simonis) Z.; student U. Wis., Stevens Point, 1968-70, part time, 1977-80; m. Rodney A. Wolf, 1980; children—Dirk, Wayne. Adminstrv. asst. K.F. Kellogg, Northfield, Ill., 1970-74; prodn. mgr. M.R. Ceramics, Inc., Iola, Wis., 1974-77; plant mgr. Weber Tackle Co., Stevens Point, Wis., 1977-81; v.p. Rodmar Co., Amherst Junction, Wis., 1981-85, Rodmar Mfg. Inc., Nelsonville, Wis., 1985—; owner/pres. Marzie Originals, Amherst Junction, 1977—. instr. adult evening tech. sch. Leader local area 4-H Club, 1973-78, key leader county level, 1976-78. Mem. Tomorrow River Fine Arts Council, sec., 1985-86. Mem. Nat. Assn. Female Execs., Nat. Assn. Tax Practitioners, Midwest Miniature Trade Assn. Roman Catholic. Home: 8946 Loberg Rd Amherst Junction WI 54407 Office: PO Box 68 Nelsonville WI 54458

WOLF, MONICA THERESIA, procedures analyst; b. W.Ger., Apr. 26, 1943; came to U.S., 1953, naturalized, 1959; d. Otto and Hildegard Maria (Heim) Bellemann; B.B.A., U. Albuquerque, 1986; m. Henry Wolf (div.); children—Clinton, Danielle. Developer Word Processing Center, Public Service of N.Mex., Albuquerque, 1971-74, word processing supr., 1974-78, budget coordinator, 1978-80, lead procedures analyst, 1980—. Adv. bd., student trainer APS Career Enrichment Center. Mem. Internat. Word Processing Assn., Nat. Assn. Female Execs., Nat. Rifle Assn., N.Mex. Shooting Sports Assn. Democrat. Club: Sandia Gun (adv. bd., coach). Instr. firearm safety and pistol marksmanship. Home: 305 Alamosa NW Albuquerque NM 87107 Office: 414 Silver Ave SW Albuquerque NM 87103

WOLF, ROSALIE JOYCE, paper company executive; b. Southampton, N.Y., May 8, 1941; d. Saul and Anne W.; A.B. (Durant scholar), Wellesley Coll., 1961; M.A. in Math., Northwestern U., 1962; m. Milton Stern, May 15, 1979; 1 dau., Dina G. Pruzansky. With Mobil Oil Corp., N.Y.C., 1962-77, asst. treas. internat., to 1977; v.p. venture capital group Donaldson, Lufkin & Jenrette, Inc., N.Y.C., 1977-79; asst. corp. controller Internat. Paper Co., N.Y.C., 1979-81, treas., 1981—. Recipient Tribute to Women in Internat. Industry award nat. bd. YWCA, 1981. Mem. Fin. Women's Assn. N.Y. (dir. 1981-82), Nat. Assn. Corp. Treasurers (dir. 1984—), Fin. Execs. Inst. (com. on corp. fin.), Treasurer's Group N.Y. (chmn. 1985-86, Phi Beta Kappa. Home: 115 E 87th St New York NY 10128 Office: Internat Paper Co 77 W 45th St New York NY 10036

WOLF, STEPHANIE RAY, foundation executive; b. N.Y.C., Feb. 29, 1948; d. Joseph and Ann (Dreeben) Neufeld; m. Arthur I. Wolf. B.A., Queens Coll., City U. N.Y., 1972; postgrad. New Sch., Golden Gate U. Grants analyst Wenner-Gren Found. Anthrop. Research, N.Y.C., 1969-72; grants adminstr., publs. mgr. Mus. Am. Indian/Heye Found., N.Y.C., 1972-74; coordinator CETA program Human Services Adminstrn., N.Y.C., 1974-76; exec. dir. S.H. Cowell Found., San Francisco, 1976—; chmn., founder Bay Area Women in Philanthropy, 1979-80; charter mem. Women and Founds./Corp. Philanthropy, 1977—; steering com. No. Calif. Grantmakers, 1980; cons. mgmt./fundraising for non-profit orgns. Mem. adv. bd. Whale Ctr., Tri-Valley Haven for Women, Acad. of Welders; trustee J.F. Kennedy U. Ctr. for Mus. Studies. Office: SH Cowell Found 260 California St Suite 501 San Francisco CA 94111

WOLFE, ANN, sculptor; b. Poland, Nov. 14, 1905; d. Jacob and Sarah (Szulmirski) Wolfe; B.A., Hunter Coll., 1926; studied sculpture Paris, 1932-33; m. Mark Graubard, Mar. 5, 1927; children—Jane Strovas, Maya Jones. One-man shows: Worcester (Mass.) Art Mus., 1939, Grace Horne Gallery, Boston, 1941, Whyte Gallery, Washington, 1946, Hamline U., St. Paul, 1951, Minn. State Fair, 1951, World Gallery, St. Paul, 1954, Walker Art Center, Mpls., 1955, Mpls. Inst. Arts, 1964, Adele Bednarz Galleries, Los Angeles, 1966, Stewart-Verde Galleries, San Francisco, 1966, West Lake Gallery, Mpls., 1970, Jewish Community Center, Mpls., 1970; group shows include Kraushaar Gallery, N.Y.C., Sculpture Center, N.Y.C., Fairweather Hardin Gallery, Chgo., Sears-Vincent Price Gallery, Chgo., 3d Sculpture Internat., Phila. Mus. Art, Pa. Acad. Fine Arts; represented in permanent collections CCNY, Hamline U., Colgate U., Nat. Mus. Korea, Seoul, Mus. Western Art, Moscow, Jerusalem Mus., Israel, Hartt Coll., U. Hartford (Conn.), Children's Hosp., St. Paul, Mt. Zion Temple, St. Paul, U. Minn., U. Calif., Berkeley, Mpls. Pub. Library, also numerous pvt. collections; tchr. sculpture; reviewer art publs. Worcester Telegram-Gazette, 1940-60. Recipient awards Allied Artists Am., 1936, Soc. Washington Artists, 1944, 45, Minn. State Fair, 1949, Mpls. Inst. Arts, 1951, Soc. Minn. Sculptors, 1955, Spring Salon, Mpls., 1957. Mem. Soc. Minn. Sculptors (past pres.). Home: 2928 Dean Pkwy Minneapolis MN 55416

WOLFE, ANTOINETTE, sales executive; b. San Bernadino, Calif., Feb. 7, 1954; d. Dennis and Smila Rose (Janich) Prokopis; m. John Edward Wolfe, Sept. 16, 1972 (div. 1983); children—Jason, Dennis. Student pub. schs., Gary, Ind. With classified advt. sales staff Mpls. Star & Tribune, 1972—, classified field auto sales rep., 1981—. Recipient Pub.'s award trophy, Mpls. Star & Tribune, 1983, Pub.'s Club and award, 1984-85. Mem. Nat. Assn. Female Execs. Democrat. Greek Orthodox. Avocations: horseback riding; writing poetry. Home: 42 17th Ave N Hopkins MN 55343 Office: Mpls Star & Tribune 425 Portland Ave S Minneapolis MN 55488

WOLFE, BARBARA AHMAJAN, stock brokerage executive, administrator; b. Providence, Aug. 1, 1943; d. Michael Ashod and Liberty (Hagopian) A.; m. Thomas Francis Wolfe, Apr. 7, 1984. B.A., Mills Coll., 1965. Mktg. analyst Calif. Blue Shield, San Francisco, 1967-70; research analyst Pacific Maritime Assn., San Francisco, 1970-73; corp. adminstr. Lawrence Systems, Inc., San Francisco, 1973-75; analyst Stanford Research Inst., Calif., 1975; exec. v.p., adminstr. Charles Schwab & Co., San Francisco, 1976—, dir.; corp. sec. Charles Schwab & Co., 1976—. Bd. govs. Mills Coll., Oakland, Calif., 1977-80. Home: 1221 Jones St HC3 San Francisco CA 94109 Office: Charles Schwab & Co Inc 101 Montgomery St San Francisco CA 94104

WOLFE, BARBRA ANN, bank marketing director; b. N.Y.C., Oct. 25, 1956; d. Edward Patrick and Dorothy Ann (Hennessy) W.; m. Brian Francis Cheverko, Oct. 11, 1986. B.A. in Polit. Sci. magna cum laude, SUNY-Stony Brook, 1978; M.B.A. in Mktg. Mgmt., Baruch Coll., CCNY, 1985. Consumer relations mgr. Citibank, N.Y.C., 1978-79, priority services account rep., 1980-81; mktg. coordinator 1st Nationwide Savs., N.Y.C., 1982-84, sr. mktg. coordinator, 1984-85, area mktg. dir., 1985—. Mem. Nat. Assn. Female Execs., Assn. M.B.A. Execs., Pi Sigma Alpha. Republican. Office: 1st Nationwide Savs 1790 Broadway New York NY 10019

WOLFE, CAROLINE MARGARET, nurse; b. Toledo, Dec. 9, 1943; d. Russet John and Angela Frances (Kelly) DuMont; m. Warren Dwight Wolfe, Dec. 29, 1973; children—Mark Russet, Jeremy Dean, Jason Kelly. Diploma in nursing St. Vincent Hosp., Toledo, 1964; B.S. in Nursing, Mary Manse Coll., Toledo, 1966. Registered nurse, Ohio. Staff nurse, asst. head nurse ICU, Maumee Valley Hosp., Toledo, 1964-69; asst. head nurse hemodialysis Med. Coll. of Ohio, Toledo, 1969-71, head nurse hemodialysis, 1971-73, head nurse renal unit, 1973-75, staff nurse renal unit, 1978-81, transplant nurse coordinator, 1981—. Mem. Am. Nephrology Nurses Assn., N.Am. Transplant Coordinators Orgn., Kidney Found. Northwestern Ohio (pres. 1970-72, sec. 1973-74). Democrat. Avocations: skiing, reading, bowling. Home: 4562 Westbourne Dr Toledo OH 43623 Office: Med Coll of Ohio CS 10008 Toledo OH 43699

WOLFE, CORINNE HOWELL, retired social worker; b. El Paso, Tex., Dec. 15, 1912; d. David Emerson and Clara (Schultz) Howell; B.A., U. Tex., El Paso, 1933; M.S.W., Tulane U., 1944; LL.D. (hon.), N.Mex. State U., 1983; m. Howard Clark Wolfe, Jr., Feb. 29, 1936. Social worker Tex. Dept. Public Welfare, 1933-45, Family Service Assn., Ft. Worth, 1945-46, VA, Dallas, 1946-48; dir. staff devel. and tng. Social and Rehab. Service, HEW, Washington, 1948-72; prof. social work N.Mex. Highlands U., Las Vegas, 1972-82, ret., 1982; cons. social services, social work edn. Mem. adv. panel N.Mex. Community Corrections. Recipient Disting. Service award HEW, 1973; Outstanding Alumni award Tulane U., 1975; named N.Mex. Vol. of Yr., 1983. Mem. Nat. Assn. Social Workers (Nat. Social Worker Yr. 1986), Council Social Work Edn. (Disting. Service award 1972), N.Mex. Alliance Mentally Ill, Northern N.Mex. Civil Liberties Union (chair), N.Mex. Human Services Coalition (co-chair), Council Social Work Edn., Am. Public Welfare Assn., Nat. and Internat. Conf. on Social Welfare, Santa Fe Living Treasure. Democrat. Methodist. Contbr. articles to profl. jours. Home: 2509 Avenida de Isidro Santa Fe NM 87505

WOLFE, DEBORAH ANN, lawyer; b. Detroit, May 4, 1955; d. Adam and Mary A. (Smyth) Wolfe. Student Ariz. State U.-Tempe, 1973-76; B.A. in Polit. Sci., Bus. Tex. Christian U., Ft. Worth, 1977; postgrad. So. Meth. U., 1977-78; J.D., U. San Diego, 1980. Bar: Calif. 1981, Ariz. 1982. Sole practice, San Diego, 1981-83; ptnr. Kremer & Wolfe, San Diego, 1983—; judge F. Lee Bailey Moot Ct. Competition, San Diego, 1984. Floutist, San Diego City Guard Band, 1981—, Grossmont Sinfonia, La Mesa, 1982-83; Classical/Chamber Music Quartet, San Diego, 1983. Author: (with Kremer and Craig) Handling Your Own Divorce, 1984. Mem. ABA, Assn. Trial Lawyers Am., Calif. Trial Lawyers Assn., San Diego Trial Lawyers Assn. Republican. Club: Lawyers (San Diego). Office: Kremer & Wolfe 8316 Clairemont Mesa Blvd San Diego CA 92111

WOLFE, DEBORAH CANNON PARTRIDGE, government education consultant; b. Cranford, N.J.; d. David Wadsworth and Gertrude (Moody) Cannon; 1 son, Roy. B.S., N.J. State Coll., 1937; M.A., Tchrs. Coll. Columbia U., 1938, Ed.D., 1945; postgrad. Vassar Coll., 1944-45, U. Pa., 1950-51, Union Theol. Sem., 1952-54, Jewish Sem. Am., 1953; hon. doctorate Seton Hall U., Coll. New Rochelle, Morris Brown U., Jersey City State Coll.; LL.D., Kean Coll., 1981, Stockton Coll., 1984. Former prin., tchr. pub. schs., Cranford, also Tuskegee, Ala.; faculty Tuskegee Inst., Grambling Coll., NYU, Fordham U., U. Mich., Tex. Coll., Columbia U.; supervision and adminstrn. curriculum devel., social studies U. Ill., summers; prof. edn., affirmative action officer Queens Coll.; prof. edn. and children's lit. Wayne State U., summer; edn. chief U.S. Ho. of Reps. Com. on Edn. and Labor, 1962—; lectr. Princeton U., 1957-58; Fulbright prof. Am. lit., NYU; U.S. rep. to 1st World Conf. on Women in Politics; editorial cons. Macmillan Pub. Co.; cons. Ency. Brit.; adv. bd. Ednl. Testing Service; assoc. minister 1st Bapt. Ch., Cranford, N.J.; mem. State Bd. Edn., 1964—; mem. N.J. Bd. Higher Edn., 1967—, now vice chmn.; mem. nat. adv. panel on vocat. edn. HEW; mem. citizen's adv. com. to Bd. Edn., Cranford; mem. Citizen's Adv. Com. on Youth Fitness; mem. Pres.'s Adv. Com. on Youth Fitness; mem. White House Conf. Children and Youth, 1950, 60, White House Conf. Edn., 1955, White House Conf. Aging, 1960,

White Conf. Civil Rights, 1966, White House Conf. on children, 1970; mem. Adv. Council for Innovations in Edn.; chmn. exec. com. Non-Govtl. Representations to UN; v.p. nat. Alliance for Safer Cities; cons. VISTA Corp, OEO. Contbr. articles to ednl. publs. Bd. dirs. Cranford Welfare Assn., Community Ctr., 1st Bapt. Ch., Cranford Community Ctr. Migratory Laborers, Hurlock, Md.; trustee Sci. Service, Seton Hall U.; mem. Pub. Broadcasting Authority. Recipient Nat. Achievement award Nat. Assn. Negro Bus. and Profl. Women's Clubs, 1958; Women of Yr. award Delta Beta Zeta, Morgan State Coll., 1959; Woman of Courage award Radcliffe Coll., 1984; Community Service award Jersey City, 1985; Chancellor's Service award Seton Hall U., 1985; Outstanding Educator award Stockton State Coll., 1985; Outstanding Prof. award Dept. Edn., Queens Coll. of CUNY, 1985. Mem. Council Nat. Orgns. Children and Youth, Am. Council Human Rights (v.p.), NCCJ, Nat. Panhellenic Council (bd. dirs.), Nat. Assn. Black Educators (pres.), NEA (life), LWV, N.Y. Tchrs. Assn., Am. Tchrs. Assn., Fellowship So. Churchmen, AAUW (nat. edn. chmn.), AAUP, Internat. Reading Assn., Comparative Edn. Soc., Am. Acad. Polit. and Social Sci., Internat. Assn. Childhood Edn., Nat. Soc. Study Edn., Am. Council Edn. (commn. fed. relations), Assn. Supervision and Curriculum, Devel. (rev. council), AAAS (chmn. tchr. edn. com.) Nat. Alliance Black Educators (pres.), Alliance of Black Clergywomen (pres., founder), NAACP, Internat. Platform Assn., Ch. Women United (UN rep., mem. exec. com.), UN Assn.-U.S.A. (exec. com.), Delta Kappa Gamma (chmn. world fellowship com.), Kappa Delta Pi (chmn. ritual com., sec. Ednl. Found.; trustee Edn. Devel. Ctr.), Pi Lambda Theta, Zeta Phi Beta (internat. pres. 1954, chmn. edn. found. 1974—, Achievement award Atlantic region 1959). Home: 62 S Union Ave Cranford NJ 07016 Office: Queens Coll CCNY New York NY 11367

WOLFE, GOLDIE BRANDELSTEIN, realtor; b. Linz, Austria, Dec. 20, 1945; d. Albert and Regina (Sandman) Brandelstein; student U. Ill., Urbana, 1963-64; B.S. in Bus. Adminstrn. cum laude, Roosevelt U., 1967; postgrad. Grad. Sch. Bus. U. Chgo., 1968-69; 1 dau., Alicia Danielle Schuyler. Account research mgr. J. Walter Thompson, advt., Chgo., 1967-71, asso. account exec., 1971-72; account exec. Needham, Harper & Steers Advt. Inc., Chgo., 1972; real estate broker, office leasing dept. Arthur Rubloff & Co., Chgo., 1972—, asst. v.p., 1975-77, v.p. office leasing, 1977-80, sr. v.p., 1980—, also dir. Chmn. services group Chgo. Public TV, 1974-75; bd. dirs. realty div. Jewish United Fund, 1976-77, chmn. realty div., 1986; bd. dirs. Michael Reese Hosp. Med. Research Inst. Council, 1979—; bd. governors Met. Housing Planning Commn. Recipient Salesman of Yr. award Chgo. Real Estate Bd., 1981, 82, 83. Recipient Rubloff's Top Producer award, 1981-82, 83, mem. Chgo. Council Fgn. Relations, Young Execs. Club Chgo. (program chmn. 1980-81), Chgo. Real Estate Bd., Nat., Ill. assns. Realtors, Am. Mktg. Assn., Urban Land Inst., Roosevelt U. Alumni Assn. (bd. govs.), Chgo. Network. Clubs: Economic, Standard (Chgo.). Home: 1332 Sutton Pl Chicago IL 60610 Office: care Arthur Rubloff & Co 111 W Washington St Chicago IL 60602

WOLFE, HARRIET MUNRETT, lawyer; b. Mt. Vernon, N.Y., Aug. 18, 1953; d. Lester John Francis Jr. and Olga Harriet (Miller) Munrett; m. Charles Briant Wolfe, Sept. 10, 1983. B.A., U. Conn., 1975; postgrad., Oxford U. (Eng.), 1976; J.D., Pepperdine U., 1978. Bar: Conn. 1979. Assoc. legal counsel, asst. sec. Citytrust, Bridgeport, Conn., 1979—; mem. govt. relations com. Electronic Funds Transfer Assn., Washington, 1983—. Mem. Conn. Bar Assn. (mem. legis. com. banking law sect.), ABA, Am. Trial Lawyers Assn., Conn. Bankers Assn. (trust legis. com.), Guilford Flotilla Coast Guard Aux., U.S. Yacht Racing Union, Phi Alpha Delta Internat. (Frank E. Gray award 1978, Shepherd chpt. Outstanding Student award 1977-78). Home: 26 Farm View Dr Madison CT 06443 Office: Legal Dept Citytrust 961 Main St Bridgeport CT 06601

WOLFE, JANICE E., government executive; b. Racine, Ohio, Aug. 25, 1939; d. Donald Clark and Erline (Sargent) W. A.B. in Govt., Ohio U., 1961; J.D., Ohio State U., 1964. Bar: Ohio 1964. Atty. examiner Ohio Dept. Liquor Control, Columbus, 1964; asst. atty. gen., Columbus, Ohio, 1965-72; dist. counsel SBA, 1972-80, dep. dist. dir., Chgo., 1980-83, dist. dir., Washington, 1983—. Recipient SBA awards. Office: SBA 1111 18th St NW Washington DC 20036

WOLFE, JEAN ELIZABETH, medical artist; b. Newark, Oct. 3, 1925; d. Arthur Howard and Ethel (Harper) W. B.S., Russell Sage Coll., 1947; student Pratt Inst., 1949-50; diploma U. Rochester Sch. Medicine and Dentistry, 1955; M.F.A. (W. B. Saunders fellow 1955-56), U. Pa., 1973, M.A. (hon.), 1973, postgrad., 1980. Instr. Pembroke Coll. Brown U., 1947-49; mem. faculty Kimberley Sch., Upper Montclair, N.J., 1950-52; freelance med. illustration Studio N.Y. Med. Coll., 1956-60; instr. Pratt Inst., 1958-59; asso. in med. illustration in ophthalmology U. Pa. Sch. Medicine, 1960-72, research asst. prof. med. art, 1972-85; freelance med. and sci. illustrator, 1985—; guest lectr. Johns Hopkins Med. Sch., 1973, NIH, Beaver Coll., 1984; guest artist U.S. Air Force Acad., 1971. Exhbns. include: Pratt Inst. Galleries, Bklyn., 1958, N.Y. Med. Coll., 1958, Assn. Med. Illustrators, 1961-70, AMA, N.Y.C., 1965, Phila., 1965, ACS, Atlantic City, 1965, Research Study Club Los Angeles, 1966, Phila. Art Alliance, 1967, U. Pa. Opthalmol. Soc., 1967-68, Cayuga Mus. History and Art, 1968, Pensacola Art Center, 1969, FAA Aero. Center, Okla., 1970, Scheie Eye Inst., 1972-75, Assn. Med. Illustrators Traveling Salon, 1977-79, Moore Coll. Art, 1985; illustrations in med. books, jours., mags., pharm. house publs.; represented in permanent collection Phila. Coll. Physicians, Mutter Mus., Francis A. Countway Med. Library, Harvard U. Recipient Merit cert. AMA; Appreciation cert. ACS; 1st prize Pensacola Art Center and Am. Heart Assn., 1969. Mem. Phila. Art Alliance, Assn. Med. Illustrators (bd. govs. 1970—, chmn. bd. govs. 1974-75, vice chmn. bd. 1973-74, chmn. nominating com. 1972-73, Ralph Sweet, Tom Jones awards), Assn. for Computing Machinery Spl. Interest Group in Graphics, Soc. Illustrators N.Y., AAUP. Studio: William Henry Apts Beech 222 Malvern PA 19355

WOLFE, JOAN LUEDDERS, non-profit organizations consultant, writer; b. Detroit, May 2, 1929; d. William R. and Mary Lucinda (Deane) Luedders; B.A., in Econs., U. Mich., 1951; D.Public Service (hon.), Western Mich. U., 1973; m. Willard Wolfe, June 26, 1953; children—John Roberts, Peter Harper (dec.). Founder, chmn. West Mich. Environ. Action Council, exec. dir., 1971-73; mem. Mich. Natural Resources Commn., 1973-82; bd. dirs. Dyer Ives Found., 1984—, Mich. Wetlands Found., 1984—. Author: Making Things Happen: The Guide for Members of Volunteer Organizations, 1981. Pres., Belmont Sch.-Community Club, Newcomers Club Grand Rapids, Grand Rapids Audubon Club, Mich. Pesticide Council. Recipient Environ. Quality award Mich. Soc. Internal Medicine, 1970; Conservation award Am. Motors Corp., 1973; others. Mem. AAAS, Mich. Assn. Vol. Adminstrs., Nat. Audubon Soc. (nat. bd. dirs. 1982—).

WOLFE, LAURA CARNES, builders hardware manufacturing company executive; b. Jefferson, S.C., Aug 13, 1936; d. John Howard and Lottie Lula (Killough) Carnes; m. John Beasley Benton (dec. 1970); m. Elton Edwin Wolfe Jr., Apr. 2, 1972 (div. 1976); children—Deborah Elizabeth, Benton Parker. Student, U. S.C., 1955-56. Clk., Sears Roebuck, Florence, S.C., 1954-55; receptionist Am. Textile Mfrs. Inst., Charlotte, N.C., 1961-67, Pilot Life, Charlotte, 1958-60; sec. Chas. T. Main Inc, Charlotte, 1961-67; treas., mgr. Chipper Service, Lancaster, S.C., 1967-68; credit mgr. Buensod Div. Aeronca Inc., Pineville, N.C., 1968-72; export internat. credit analyst Scovill Inc., Monroe, N.C., 1972—. Pres. Lancaster County Heart Assn., 1981. Mem. Internat. Assn. Execs. in Fin., Credit and Internat. Bus., Nat. Assn. Credit Mgmt., Am. Legion Aux. Democrat. Baptist. Club: Evening Garden, (pres. 1981-83) (Lancaster). Avocations: reading; gardening; travel; swimming. Home: 419 Churchill Dr Lancaster SC 29720

WOLFE, LYNNELLE YVONNE, fast food chain executive; b. Bemidji, Minn., Feb. 23, 1961; d. Max Merideth and Yvonne Carol (Benson) W. Student Oxford U., 1982; B.S., Bemidji State U., 1983. Opening team mem. Internat. Dairy Queen Inc., Mpls., 1983-84, ops. specialist, 1984—. Mem. Nat. Assn. Female Execs. Lutheran. Avocations: softball; travel; reading; dance; spectator sports. Office: Am Dairy Queen Corp 5701 Green Valley Dr Bloomington MN 55437

WOLFE, MARGARET RIPLEY, historian, educator, consultant; b. Kingsport, Tenn., Feb. 3, 1947; d. Clarence Estill and Gertrude Blessing Ripley; B.S. magna cum laude, East Tenn. State U., 1967, M.A., 1969; Ph.D. (Haggin fellow), U. Ky., 1974; m. David Early Wolfe, Dec. 17, 1966; 1 dau., Stephanie Ripley. Instr. history East Tenn. State U., 1969-73, asst. prof., 1973-77, assoc. prof., 1977-80, prof., 1980—. Mem. Tenn. Com. for Humanities, 1983-85. Recipient Disting. Faculty award East Tenn. State U., 1977; East Tenn. State U. Found. research award, 1979, Alumni cert. merit, 1984. Mem. Orgn. Am. Historians, So. Assn. Women Historians (pres. 1983-84, exec. com. 1984-86), So. Hist. Assn., Tenn. Hist. Soc. Author: Lucius Polk Brown and Progressive Food and Drug Control; Tennessee and New York City, 1908-1920; 1978; An Industrial History of Hawkins County, Tennessee, 1983; contbr. articles to profl. jours. Office: E Tenn State U Kingsport Center Kingsport TN 37660

WOLFE, RINNA EVELYN, educator; b. Bklyn., May 2, 1925. B.B.A., CCNY, 1957; M.A. in Creative Arts, San Francisco State U., 1966. With Charles Stores, N.Y.C., 1944-54, Raylass Dept. Stores, N.Y.C., 1955-59; classroom and resource tchr. Mt. Diablo Schs. (Calif.), 1960-65, Danville Schs. (Calif.), 1965-67, Berkeley Schs. (Calif.), 1967-80; extension tchr. U. Calif., 1968-78. Author: From Children With Love, 1970; The Singing Pope, 1980 (presented to Pope John Paul, Apr. 1982). Organizer R.E.A.P. (program for older adults), Berkeley Jewish Community Ctr.; Point Found. fellow, 1976. Mem. Am. PEN Women, Nat. Book Assn.

WOLFE, SANDRA ROSE, administrative coordinator; b. Fort Wayne, Ind., May 15, 1937; d. Douglas Daniel and Eleanor Emily (Ross) Seely; m. Paul S. Grossman, Apr. 2, 1976 (dec. 1981). Student Internat. Bus. Coll., 1955-56. Co-mgr. family owned hotel, Fort Wayne, 1957-67; sec., bookkeeper for presiding justice cir. ct., Fort Wayne, 1967-69; asst. to mgr. Marriott Hotel, Fort Wayne, 1970-73; sec. to Allen County Council, Fort Wayne, 1973-75; adminstrv. coordinator Bd. Commrs., Fort Wayne, 1975—, mem. Cabinet, 1985—; mem. adv. com. Allen County CETA, 1976-83. Dep. registrar voter registration, Fort Wayne, 1983-84; bd. dirs. Allen County Ct. Appointed Spl. Advocate, 1986—. Republican. Clubs: Allen County Rep., Allen County Women's Rep. Avocations: travel; golf; gardening. Office: Allen County Bd Commrs Room 200 City-County Bldg 1 Main St Fort Wayne IN 46802

WOLFE, TRACEY DIANNE, distbg. co. exec.; b. Dallas, June 13, 1951; d. George F. Wolfe and Helen Ruth Cline Lemons; B.S. in Edn. and Social Sci., East Tex. State U., Commerce, 1973, M.S. in Elem. Edn., 1976; 1 son, Bronson Alan. Asst. to dir. student devel. East Tex. State U., 1973-74; corp. sec., v.p. Wolfe Distbg. Co., beer distbrs., Terrell, Tex., 1974—. Mem. Kappa Delta (alumnae v.p. 1978-79, alumnae treas. 1979-81, province pres. 1980-82). Republican. Methodist. Home: 3316 Lakeside Dr Rockwall TX 75087 Office: 100 Metro Dr Terrell TX 75160

WOLFF, DEBORAH H(OROWITZ), lawyer; b. Phila., Apr. 6, 1940; d. Samuel and Anne (Manstein) Horowitz; m. Morris H. Wolff, May 15, 1966; children—Michelle Lynn, Lesley Anne. B.S., U. Pa., 1962, M.S., 1966; postgrad., Sophia U., Tokyo, 1968; J.D., Villanova U., 1979. Tchr. Overbrook High Sch., Phila., 1962-68; homebound tchr. Lower Merior Twp., Montgomery County, 1968-71; asst. dean U. Pa., Phila., 1975-76; law clk. firm Stassen, Kostos and Mason, Phila., 1977-78; assoc. firm Spencer, Sherr, Moses and Zuckerman, Norristown, Pa., 1980-81; ptnr. Deborah H. Wolff, Esquire, 1981—; lectr. law and estate planning, Phila., 1980—; Recipient 3d ann. Community Service award Phila. Mayor's Com. for Women, 1984; named Pa. Heroine of Month, Ladies Home Jour., July 1984. Founder Take a Brother Program; bd. dirs. Germantown Jewish Ctr.; high sch. sponsor World Affairs Club, Phila., 1962-68; mem. exec. com. Crime Prevention Assn., Phila., 1965—; bd. dirs. U. Pa. Alumnae Bd., Phila., 1965—. Mem. ABA, Pa. Bar Assn., Phila. Bar Assn., Montgomery County Bar Assn., Phila. Women's Network, Bus. Women's Network. Club: Cosmopolitan (membership com. Phila.). Home: 422 W Mermaid Ln Philadelphia PA 19118

WOLFF, JANET LOEB, advertising executive; b. San Francisco; d. Albert I. and Aurene (Goddard) Loeb; student U. Paris; grad. Finch Coll.; m. James A. Wolff, June 24, 1946; children—James Alexander, John, Barbara Ann, Timothy Grant. Copywriter, J. Walter Thompson Co., N.Y.C., Crompton Co., N.Y.C.; now exec. v.p. William Esty Co. Inc., N.Y.C.; mem. Fashion Group, N.Y.C. Mem. Bus. Council, N.Y.C. Named Advt. Woman of Yr., Advt. Women of N.Y., 1968. Author. What Makes Women Buy, 1958; Let's Imagine series, 1960. Office: 100 E 42d St New York NY 10017

WOLFF, JOAN MITTELMARK, retail store official; b. N.Y.C., Dec. 8, 1929; d. Seymour and Sadye (Fingeroth) Mittelmark; children—Steven, Melissa, Stacey. B.A., Syracuse U., 1952. Tournament dir. Kodel Mixed Doubles Tennis, Macy's White Plains, N.Y., 1977-78, spl. events and pub. relations mgr., White Plains, 1978-82, Stamford, Conn., 1982—. Pres. Central Sch. PTA, Larchmont, N.Y., 1970-72; mem. White Plains Tricentennial Ball Com., 1983; dir. Stamford chpt. ARC, 1984, Stamford Commn. on Aging, 1983—. Mem. Women in Communications, Pub. Relations Soc. Fairfield. Club: Midday (Stamford). Home: 11 Village Green Port Chester NY 10573 Office: Macys 151 Broad St Stamford CT 06901

WOLFF, JOANNE SLAY, human resource management consultant; b. Detroit, Apr. 2, 1953; d. Lorenzo and Mahala (Rowell) Slay; m. Mervin Gary Wolff, July 22, 1978; 1 dau., Garen S. B.S. in Psychology, Tenn. State U., 1976; M.A. in Library and Info. Sci., U. Toledo, 1979; postgrad. Entrepreneur Inst., U. Detroit, 1986. Drug abuse counselor Comprehensive Neighborhood Health Services Methadone Clinic, Detroit, 1974-75; on-site data collector W.O.M-.A.N., Detroit, 1976-77; info. and referral specialist Toledo Mental Health Ctr., 1977; acting dir. Learning Resource Ctr., John Wesley Coll., Owosso, Mich., 1978-79; program specialist sch. and community affairs Mich. Dept. Edn., Lansing, 1980-81; co-owner, founder Wolff-Harris Research and Cons., Detroit, 1980-81; pres., founder J.S. Wolff Co., Detroit, 1981—; founder and developer In-House Workshops, at home, 1984. Recipient Outstanding Service award NCCJ, 1984. Democrat. Baptist. Avocations: tennis; chess. Home and Office: 8051 Third Ave Detroit MI 48202

WOLFF, SIDNEY CARNE, astronomer, observatory administrator; b. Sioux City, Iowa, June 6, 1941; d. George Albert and Ethel (Smith) Carne; m. Richard J. Wolff, Aug. 29, 1962. B.A., Carleton Coll., 1962, D.S. (hon.), 1985; Ph.D., U. Calif.-Berkeley, 1966. Postgrad. research fellow Lick Observatory, Santa Cruz, Calif., 1969; asst. astronomer U. Hawaii, Honolulu, 1967-71, assoc. astronomer, 1971-76; astronomer, assoc. dir. Inst. for Astronomy, Honolulu, 1976-83, acting dir., 1983-84; dir. Kitt Peak Nat. Observatory, Tucson, Ariz., 1984—. Author: The A-Type Stars—Problems and Perspectives, 1983. Contbr. numerous articles to sci. jours. Mem. Astron. Soc. of the Pacific (pres. 1984—, bd. dirs. 1979-85), Am. Astron. Soc. (council mem. 1983—), Internat. Astron. Union (com. 29 mem.). Office: Kitt Peak Nat Observatory PO Box 26732 Tucson AZ 85726

WOLFF, SUSAN (JOEY), communications and new products marketing executive; b. N.Y.C., Apr. 11, 1944; d. Seymour Barnett and Julia (Weiner) Joseph; m. Ivan Lawrence Wolff, June 18, 1967; 1 son, Adam Gregory. B.S. with honors, Cornell U., 1966; M.S. with honors, NYU, 1968. Mgr. mktg. research Mattel, Inc., Hawthorne, Calif., 1968-74; mgr. new product research Gillette Co., Boston, 1975-76; mktg. mgr. new products AT&T Consumer Products, Basking Ridge, N.J., 1977-81, dir. mktg. Advanced Mobile Phone Service, Inc. subs. AT&T, Basking Ridge, 1981-83; pres. Wolff Assocs. Inc., Mountain Lakes, N.J., 1983—; mng. dir. Solomon-Wolff Assocs. Inc., Mountain Lakes, N.J., 1984—. NDEA fellow NYU, 1966-68. Mem. Cornell U. Alumni Assn. (pres. 1981—). Republican. Office: Wolff Assocs Inc 165 Laurel Hill Rd Mountain Lakes NJ 07046

WOLFGRAM, DEBORAH DIANE, investment researcher; b. Iowa City, June 9, 1959; d. William Curtis and Janet (Johnson) McLeod; m. Douglas Edward Wolfgram, Dec. 29, 1982. B.S., Calif. State U.-Long Beach, 1981; postgrad. U. Calif.-Irvine, 1982—. Systems analyst Analytic Investment Mgmt., Irvine, 1981—; dir. Microtex Industries, Inc., Costa Mesa, Calif. Mem. Phi Eta Sigma, Alpha Lambda Delta. Republican. Presbyterian. Home: 2810 Serang Pl Costa Mesa CA 92626 Office: Analytic Investment Mgmt 2222 Martin #230 Irvine CA 92715

WOLFMAN, BRUNETTA REID, community college president; b. Clarksdale, Miss., Sept. 4, 1931; d. Willie Orlando and Belle Victoria (Allen) Griffin Reid; m. Burton Wolfman, Oct. 4, 1952; children—Andrea, Jefferey. B.A., U. Calif.-Berkeley, 1957, M.A., 1968, Ph.D., 1971; D.H.L. (hon.), Boston, U., 1983; D.P. (hon.), Northeastern U., 1983; D.L. (hon.), Regis Coll., 1984, Stonehill Coll., 1985; D.H.L. (hon.), Suffolk U., 1985. Asst. dean faculty Dartmouth Coll., Hanover, N.H., 1972-74; asst. v.p. acad. affairs U. Mass., Boston, 1974-76; acad. dean Wheelock Coll., Boston, 1976-78; cons. Arthur D. Little, Cambridge, Mass., 1978; dir. policy planning Dept. Edn., Boston, 1978-82; pres. Roxbury Community Coll., Boston, 1983—; dir. U.S. Trust Bank, Boston, 1982, Harvard Community Health Plan. Author: Roles, 1983. Bd. overseers Wellesley (Mass.) Coll., 1981; bd. dirs. Boston-Fenway Program, 1977, Freedom House, Boston, 1983; co-chmn. NCCJ, Boston, 1983, Boston Pvt. Industry Council, 1983; bd. overseers Boston Symphony Orch., Mus. Fine Arts, Boston. Recipient Freedom award NAACP No. Calif., 1971; Amelia Earhart award Women's Edn. and Indsl. Union, Boston, 1983; Humanitarian award Alpha Kappa Alpha, Boston, 1984. Mem. Adult Edn. Assn. U.S.A., Am. Sociol. Assn., Am. Ednl. Research Assn., Am. Council on Edn. (bd. dirs.), AAUW, Black Women for Policy Action, 1976, Greater Boston, C. of C. (edn. com. 1982), Pi Lambda Theta, Alpha Kappa Alpha. Democrat. Home: 276 Marlborough St Boston MA 02116 Office: Roxbury Community Coll 625 Huntington Ave Boston MA 02115

WOLFSON, FRANCES LOUISE, insurance company executive; b. Miami, Fla., June 9, 1932; d. Mitchell and Frances Louise (Cohen) Wolfson; B.A., Bennington (Vt.) Coll., 1953; children—Jeri Louise, Jacquelyn Frances. Sec., treas., dir. Gen. Ins. Corp., Miami Beach, Fla.; pres. Frances W. Cary Antiques, Marine R. Corp., M.R. Cows, Inc. Past mem. nat. adv. bd. Big Bros.-Big Sisters Am.; bd. dirs. Up With People; past pres. women's guild U. Miami; founder/mem. Mt. Sinai Hosp., Miami Beach. Mem. Daus. Confederacy. Clubs: Jockey, Ocean Reef, Palm Bay, Princeton, Country Club of Asheville. Home: 11111 Biscayne Blvd Miami FL 33181 Office: 11077 Biscayne Blvd Suite 200 Miami FL 33161

WOLICKI, NANCY FRIEDA, staff mem. U.S. Senate, lawyer; b. Chgo., Sept. 8, 1953; d. Samuel and Ingrid (Rappel) W.; B.A. in Journalism and Sociology, U. Ariz., 1974, J.D., 1977. Admitted to Ariz. bar, 1977; law clk. firm Verity, Smith & Kearns, Tucson, 1976-77, Ariz. Ct. Appeals, 1977-78; legis. asst. fgn. policy and armed services health, staff atty. Billy Carter investigation to U.S. Sen. Dennis DeConcini, 1979-81; staff dir. Senate Subcom. on Alcoholism and Drug Abuse, Washington, 1981-84; mem. staff Senator Gordon J. Humphrey, Washington, 1984—. Recipient William Spaid Meml. award U. Ariz. Coll. Law, 1977, Senate commendation for Billy Carter investigation, 1980. Mem. Am. Bar Assn., Ariz. Bar Assn., Phi Kappa Phi. Jewish. Office: 531 Hart Senate Office Bldg Washington DC 20510

WOLK, JOAN MARCIA, technical writer, document analyst, editor; b. Pitts., Dec. 2, 1947; d. Samuel David and Rhoda (Levy) Kopelman; m. Stephen Selis Wolk, Oct. 25, 1970 (div. Sept. 1979); 1 child, Jason. B.A. in English, Ohio U., 1969; postgrad. Linguistic Inst. Ohio State U., 1970; M.A. in Linguistics, U. Mass., 1970. Tchr. English, chmn. dept. Prince George County Bd. Edn., Upper Marlboro, Md., 1970-73; editor, 1977-81; sr. tech. writer Boeing Computer Services, Vienna, Va., 1981-85, document analyst, 1985—. Democrat. Jewish. Avocations: parapsychology/metaphysics; concerts; theater; opera; walking. Office: Boeing Computer Services 7980 Boeing Ct Vienna VA 22180

WOLOTKIEWICZ, MARIAN MARGARET, writer, editor, lawyer; b. Camden, N.J., Apr. 22, 1954; d. Edward J. and Rita J. Wolotkiewicz; m. Paul J. Sagan, Mar. 31, 1984. B.A., Mt. Holyoke Coll., 1976; cert. legal asst. tng. program U. Mass., 1975; J.D., Suffolk U., 1979. Manuscript editor law div. Little, Brown & Co., Boston, 1979-84. Mem. Mass. Bar Assn., Mass. Women's Bar Assn. Editor newsletter Women's Bar Assn., 1979-83; mng. editor newsletter, tax sect. Mass. Bar Assn., 1978-83; founder, pres. Barrister Pub., Inc., 1981—. Office: 21 Dunster Dr Stow MA 01775

WOLPE, CLAIRE FOX, civic worker, psychotherapist; b. N.Y.C., June 24, 1909; d. David and Pauline (Hirsch) Fox; A.B., Mills Coll., 1930; M.A., U. So. Calif., 1936, M.S.W., 1965; Ph.D., Marquette U., 1970; postgrad. Smith Coll., summer 1931, Columbia U., summer 1963, U. Mexico City, summer 1964; m. Arthur S. Wolpe, Dec. 25, 1932 (dec. Mar. 1962); children—Ruth (Mrs. Roy Rose), Sheri (Mrs. Jerome Langer). Student advisor Jewish student orgn. UCLA, 1931-33; with Travelers Aid, Los Angeles, 1934; med. social work Los Angeles County Gen. Hosp., 1934-38; with USPHS, 1938; social worker Los Angeles County Health Dept., 1938-39; psychiat. social worker Gateways Psychiat. Hosp. and Mental Health Center, Los Angeles, 1962-63, 65-66; exec. dir. Bay Cities Mental Health Center, Los Angeles, 1966-68; supr. Airport Marina Counseling Service; pvt. practice. Mem. Mayors Com. on Civil Def. 1950-52, Wilshire Coordinating Council, 1954-58; leader Girl Scouts U.S.A., 1954-58; mem. regional bd. NCCJ, 1951-55. Bd. dirs. So. Calif. Mental Health Assn., 1955-58, Los Angeles chpt. A.R.C., 1951-53, Community Relations Conf. So. Calif., 1950-60, Los Angeles Jewish Fedn. Council, 1952-58, B'nai B'rith Anti-Defamation League, 1973—, Hillel Assn., 1973—. Fellow Soc. Clin. Social Workers, Am. Assn. Orthopsychiatry; mem. Nat. Assn. Social Workers, Psychotherapy Assn. So. Calif. (dir. 1967—, pres.-elect 1984), Calif. Marriage, Family and Child Counseling Assn., Am. Group Psychotherapy Assn., Los Angeles Transactional Analysis Soc. (sec.-treas. 1966-68), Psi Chi. Jewish religion. Mem. B'nai B'rith Women. Home and office: 234 Orange Dr Los Angeles CA 90036

WOLYNIEC, CONSTANCE, business owner, consultant; b. N.Y.C., Jan. 17, 1954; d. Adolph B. and Marion (Jankowsky) W. B.S. cum laude in Bus. Adminstrn., Ithaca Coll., 1974; M.B.A., Babson Coll., 1978. Systems mktg. rep. Control Data Corp., Boston, 1974-78, sales trainer, Greenwich, Conn., 1978-80; dir. Strategic Projects, internat. market entry and devel. co., St. John, V.I., 1980—; owner The Clothing Studio Mongoose Jct., St. John, 1984—. Mem. Mensa. Lutheran. Home: Casa Tova Saint John VI 00830 Office: Strategic Projects Box 713 Saint John VI 00830

WOMBLE, LAUREL KINARD, school psychologist; b. Greenville, Tex., Dec. 13, 1954; d. Hugh Street and Lois Annette (Farrer) Kinard; m. James Michael Womble, June 14, 1975. B.A., Ga. State U., 1976, M.Ed., 1980, Ed.S., 1983. Acct. analyst Robinson-Humphrey Co., Inc., Atlanta, 1976-79; assoc. psychologist Forsyth County Schs., Cumming, Ga., 1980—; diagnostician, cons. Dept. Offender Rehab., Atlanta, 1983; diagnostician Hodges Learning Lab., Atlanta, 1984. Mem. Ga. Assn. Sch. Psychologists (state rep. 1984-85), Nat. Assn. Sch. Psychologists, Ga. Psychol. Assn. Republican. Baptist. Clubs: West Paces Racquett (Atlanta); Pinetree Country (Kennesaw, Ga.). Avocations: flying; racquetball; running; skydiving; traveling; photography. Home: 155 E Lake Point Kennesaw GA 30144 Office: Forsyth County Bd Edn 101 School St Cumming GA 30130

WOMBLE, MELODIE LYNN, utility executive; b. Rockville Centre, N.Y., Mar. 19, 1945; d. Harold and Sylvia (Ross) Lisses; B.A. in English and Journalism, Fla. State U., 1967; M.Ed., U. Miami, 1970; postgrad. Nova U., 1978; m. Gary W. Womble, June 10, 1967 (dec. 1978). Tchr. Dade County Public Schs., Miami, Fla., 1967-69; asst. communications research Dallas Ind. Sch. Dist., 1970-73; editor Sports Digest, Miami, 1974; evaluation specialist Evaluator Dade County Public Schs., Miami, 1975-77; sr. coordinator Fla. Power and Light Corporate Communications Dept., 1977—; instr. U. Miami, 1979; officer dir. Abba El Prodns., 1984—. Charter mem. Fla. AWARE Com., chmn., 1978, 86, program chmn. state meetings, 1979, 80, 83, 85; mem. steering com. Downtown Prayer Breakfast. NDEA fellow, 1970. Mem. Internat. Assn. Bus. Communication (co-chmn. regional meeting 1979), Women in Communication (moderator seminar 1980, 81, 84), LWV (bd. dirs. legislative liaison 1980-83), Greater Miami C. of C., Fla. C. of C. (adviser, energy task force com. 1983-84), Leadership Miami Alumni Assn. Author profl. papers. Office: PO Box 029100 Miami FL 33152

WOMMACK, KAREN ANN, realtor; b. Morgantown, Ky., Sept. 19, 1949; d. Glendell Elmore and Myrtie Joette (Harper) Hawes; m. Jerry Don Wommack, July 22, 1967; children—Jay Harrison, Kandice Joette. Cert. Draughon's, 1968; cert. Grad. Realtors Inst., 1978. Cert. residential specialist, Ky. Realtor, Gallery of Homes, Gilbertsville, Ky., 1976-80; realtor, owner Century 21 So. Heritage, Gilbertsville, 1980—. Pres. Marshall County Women Democrats, Benton, Ky., 1982, sec., 1983. Mem. Ky.-Barkley Lake Bd. Realtors (chmn. multi-list 1983-84, bd. dirs. 1983—, sec.-treas. 1981-82, realtors polit. action com. 1985), Benton C. of C. (bd. dirs. 1983-85). Baptist. Home: Route 7 Benton KY 42025 Office: Century 21 So Heritage Route 1 Gilbertsville KY 42044

WONCH, DIANE ELIZABETH, nurse, educator; b. Buffalo, May 24, 1947; d. Charles William and Ruth Catherine (Besser) W.; student Medaille Coll., 1965-69; A.S., Trocaire Coll., 1971; B.S. in Nursing, D'Youville Coll., Buffalo, 1976; M.S. in Nursing, SUNY-Buffalo, 1978, postgrad., 1980—. Elem. sch. tchr., East Aurora, N.Y., 1968-69; nursing asst., practical nurse Orchard Park (N.Y.) Nursing Home, 1969-71; with Roswell Park Meml. Cancer Inst.,

Buffalo, 1971—, staff nurse, 1971-74, head nurse, 1974-75, clin. nurse specialist, 1975-78, dir. staff devel., 1978-83, dir. nursing edn., 1983—; asst. prof. SUNY, Buffalo, 1981-82; cons. law firm for nursing related cases; vol. lectr. Am. Cancer Soc.; vol. instr. ARC; cons. Buffalo and Erie County, Girl Scouts U.S.A. Recipient Anne Walker Sengbusch Leadership award, 1977; Disting. Alumna award Trocaire Coll., 1985; USPHS 1975-76. Mem. Am. Nurses Assn., N.Y. State Nurses Assn. (dir. dist. 1), D'Youville Alumni Assn., Am. Heart Assn., Oncology Nursing Soc., Buffalo Zool. Soc., Nat. Audubon Soc., Buffalo Soc. Natural Scis., SUNY Buffalo Alumni Assn., Sigma Theta Tau. Office: 666 Elm St Buffalo NY 14263

WONG, BETTY JEAN, state education administrator; b. Leland, Miss., Mar. 15, 1949; d. Suey Henry and Pon Chu (Lam) Wong; B.S., Miss. State U., 1971; M.Ed., Delta State U., 1973. Asst. gen. mgr. Sta. WJPR, Greenville, Miss., 1972-73; career devel. specialist Greenville Municipal Sch. Dist., 1973-74; instrnl. materials specialist research/curriculum unit Miss. State U., Jackson, 1974-76, research specialist, 1976-77, research/curricula specialist, 1977-79; coordinator tchr. edn. vocat. div. Miss. Dept. Edn., Jackson, 1979-80, asst. state dir. supportive services sect. vocat. div., 1980-85, div. dir., 1985—; cons. on career edn. Mem. Am., Miss. (exec. bd., chmn. profl. devel. task force, chmn. conv. 1980) personnel and guidance assns., Am. Vocat. Assn. (named one of 16 Outstanding Women in Vocat. Adminstrn. 1983, mem. policy bd. guidance sect.), Miss. Vocat. Assn., AAUW (handbook chairperson 1975-77). Baptist. Contbr. articles to profl. publs.; also handbook. Home: 1137 Woodfield Dr Jackson MS 39211 Office: PO Box 771 Vocat Div Jackson MS 39205

WONG, ELAINE DANG, financial executive; b. Canton, China, June 3, 1936 (parents Am. citizens); d. Robert G. and Fung Heong (Woo) Dang; A.A. (Rotary scholar), Coalinga Coll., 1956; B.S. (AAUW scholar, Grad. Resident scholar), U. Calif., Berkeley, 1958, teaching credential, 1959; m. Philip Wong, Nov. 8, 1959; children—Elizabeth, Russell, Roger, Edith, Valerie. Tchr. acctg. San Mateo (Calif.) High Sch., 1959-60; acct., 1960-75; substitute tchr. Richmond County Schs., Augusta, Ga., 1975-77; comptroller Central Savannah River Area, United Way, Augusta, 1977-82; asst. controller Hammermill Hardwoods div. Hammermill Paper Co., Augusta, 1982-84; controller SFN Communications of Augusta, Inc. (WJBF-TV), 1984-85, K.F. Wong Co., Augusta, 1985—; cons. small bus.; pvt. tutor acctg. Panel judge Jr. Achievement Treas. award, 1980, 81; treas. Chinese Lang. Sch., 1973-75, Merry Neighborhood Sch., 1974-75; bd. dirs. YWCA, Augusta, 1977-78. Recipient Achievement award Bank of Am., 1954. Mem. Nat. Assn. Accts. (dir. 1978—, treas. 1982-84, v.p. 1984-85), Chinese Assn. Republican. Presbyterian.

WONG, LINDA YUNWAI, nurse; b. Kowloon, Hong Kong, Oct. 28, 1958; came to U.S., 1968, naturalized, 1974; d. Roland Po Sum and Jean Mankit (Hong) W. B.S. in Nursing, U. Calif.-San Francisco, 1980. R.N., Calif. Nurse, Cedars-Sinai Med. Ctr., West Hollywood, Calif., 1981-82, On Lok Sr. Health Services, San Francisco, 1983-84, 85—. Vol. student adviser Nurses Christian Fellowship, Pasadena, Calif., 1981-82; vol. missionary Youth with a Mission, Sunland, Calif., 1983. Avocation: running. Home: 14 Idora Ave San Francisco CA 94127

WONG, MARGARET WAI, lawyer; b. Hong Kong, July 27, 1950; d. Mien Lin and Kuan Kuo (Kwan) Hwang; m. Kam M. Chan, Jan. 3, 1983. A.A., Ottumwa Heights Coll. (Iowa), 1971; B.Sc. in Chemistry-Biology, Western Ill. U., 1973; J.D., SUNY-Buffalo, 1976. Bar: Ohio 1977, N.Y. 1977, D.C. 1980, U.S. Dist. Ct. 1980, U.S. Ct. Appeals (6th cir.) 1983. Instr. bus. law SUNY-Fredonia, 1977; mgmt. trainee Central Nat. Bank, Cleve., 1977-78; chief legal and fin. officer Buffalo City Govt., 1979-80; assoc. Berger & Kirchenbaum, Cleve., 1980-81; prin. Margaret W. Wong & Assocs., Cleve., 1981—; co-founder, co-owner Pearl of the Orient Restaurant, Cleve., 1978—, Richmond Apothecary, Cleve., 1983—. Contbr. articles to legal jours. Trustee, Women Space, Cleve., 1982—, Fedn. Community Planning, Cleve., 1983-84, Women City Club, Cleve., 1983—, Orgn. Chinese Ams., Cleve., 1983—, Cleve. Council Human Relations, 1983—; sec., trustee Chinese Assn. Greater Cleve., 1980—. Named one of Top Ten Outstanding Young Women, Glamour mag., 1983; YWCA Career Woman of Yr., 1984. Mem. Fed. Bar Assn. (sec., trustee chpt. 1983—), ABA, N.Y. State Bar Assn., D.C. Bar Assn., Cuyahoga County Bar Assn., Cleve. Bar Assn., Ohio Bar Assn., Cleve. Trial Lawyers Assn., Am. Assn. Immigration Lawyers. Club: Zonta (trustee 1983-84) (Cleve.). Home: 2491 Euclid Heights Blvd Cleveland Heights OH 44106 Office: 330 Standard Bldg Cleveland OH 44113

WONG, MARY ANN, information systems specialist; b. Hartford, Conn.; d. Toy S. and Bo Yuk (Kwan) W.; B.S. magna cum laude, Bklyn. Coll., 1975; postgrad. Pace U. Programmer, Texaco, Inc., N.Y.C., 1975-77; programmers-analyst Inco Inc., N.Y.C., 1977-80, systems analyst, 1980-81, info. systems mgr. Inco U.S. Inc., N.Y.C., 1981—. Mem. Nat. Assn. Female Execs. Inc., Asian Mgmt. and Bus. Assn., Asian Fin. Soc. Office: One New York Plaza New York NY 10004

WONG, PAULINE LEIN, veterinary anesthesiologist; b. Coronado, Calif. May 2, 1949; d. Edward G. and Ellen G. Wong. B.S., Sch. Vet. Medicine, U. Calif.-Davis, 1973, D.V.M., 1975. Intern, Coll. Vet. Medicine, U. Ga., Athens, 1976-77; resident in surgery, dept. small animal clin. scis. Coll. Vet. Medicine, U. Minn., St. Paul, 1977-80; resident in anesthesia, critical patient care, Vet. Med. Teaching Hosp., U. Calif., Davis, 1980-83, vis. lectr. dept. surgery, 1983—, clinic. anesthesiologist, 1983—; lectr. seminars. Contbr. articles in field to jours. San Diego County Jr. Horseman's Assn. Scholar, 1967; grantee San Diego County Heart Assn., 1968; Hart scholar, 1972-73. Mem. AVMA, Calif. Coll. Vet. Anesthesiologists (diplomate 1985), Calif. Vet. Med. Assn., Internat. Anesthesia Research Soc., Vet. Cricital Care Soc., Phi Zeta. Home: 720 Adams St #4 Davis CA 95616 Office: Sch Vet Medicine U Calif Davis CA 95616

WOO, OLGA FOON, pharmacologist, educator; b. San Francisco, Apr. 8, 1949; d. Robert Duck and Foon (Wong) Woo. A.B. in Art History, U. Calif.-Berkeley, 1970; Pharm.D., U. Calif.-San Francisco, 1974. Registered pharmacologist, Calif. Asst. prof. Med. Coll. Va., Richmond, 1975-78; asst. prof. and pediatric drugs specialist U. Wash. Children's Hosp. and Med. Ctr., Seattle, 1979-81; pediatric and poison info. cons. and specialist San Francisco Bay Area Regional Poison Control Ctr., 1981—; clin. prof. U. Calif.-San Francisco, 1981—; mem. quality assurance rev. com. Med. Coll. Va., 1975-78; reviewer. Author/editor: Guidebook to OTC Drugs, 1974; editor: The Pharmacy Script (newsletter), 1978-80. Active docent Asian Art Soc., San Francisco, 1981—, Mus. Soc. San Francisco, 1981—, Graphics Art Council San Francisco, 1982—. Mem. Am. Assn. Colls. Pharmacy, Am. Pharm. Assn., Calif. Pharm. Assn., N.Y. Acad. Sci., AAAS. Contbr. articles to profl. jours. Office: San Francisco Poison Control Ctr 1001 Potrero Ave 1E86 San Francisco CA 94110

WOO, SUSAN LI, real estate broker, developer; b. Wuchang, China, Feb. 5, 1932; d. Tieh-Tseng Li and Yung-Hsien Chou; m. William R. Woo, May 15, 1954; children—David, Patrick, Sharon. Student Ginling Coll., Nanking, China, 1947-49; B.A., Coll. of Notre Dame, Belmont, Calif., 1971. Sec., Aid Refugee Chinese Intellectuals, Hong Kong, 1956-58, Calif. Hydronics Corp., San Francisco, 1959-61, data processor, 1961-63; pres. Susan Woo Realty, Inc., San Mateo, Calif., 1974—. Mem. Internat. Real Estate Fedn., Nat. Assn. Realtors. Clubs: Circlon (San Mateo), Commonwealth of Calif. Lodge: Zonta of Midpeninsula. Office: 520 El Camino Real San Mateo CA 94402

WOOCHER, LOIS M., lawyer; b. N.Y.C., Aug. 19, 1946; d. Milton and Sylvia Woocher; m. Perry R. Karfunkel, Jan. 16, 1972; 1 dau., Robin Woocher Karfunkel. B.A., U. Mass., 1968; J.D., Columbia U., 1971. Bar: N.Y. 1972, Mass. 1972. Atty. N.H. Legal Assistance, Inc., Nashua, N.H., 1972; atty. FTC, Boston, 1973-78; assoc. Brown, Prifti, Leighton & Cohen, Boston, 1979; atty. J.C. Penney Co. Inc., N.Y.C., 1980—; faculty lectr. debt collection law and practice ABA-Am. Law Inst., 1983; atty., adviser VOICE, Nashua, N.H., 1972. Contbr. articles to profl. publs. Pres. Charles River Park Tenants Assn., Boston, 1973-76. Mem. ABA (corp. banking and bus. com.), Assn. Bar City N.Y. (sect. consumers affairs com. 1982), Columbia Law Sch. Assn. N.J., Boston City Bar Assn. (antitrust law sect. 1979), N.Y. State Bar Assn. (corp. counsel, banking, corp. and bus. law sects.). Club: Saddle River Valley Newcomers (N.J.). Office: JC Penney Co 1301 Ave of Americas New York NY

WOOD, ANNE BOLLES, recording studio executive; b. Cambridge, Mass.; d. Russell Abner and Anna (Broberg) W. A.B., Harvard U.; M.S., Simmons Coll. Former divisional mdse. mgr. Sanger Harris, Dallas, Gimbels, N.Y.C.; former v.p., div. mdse. mgr. Franklin Simon, N.Y.C.; pres. Mastermind Rec. Studios, N.Y.C., 1982—. Mem. Fashion Group, Audio Engring. Soc., Soc. Profl. Rec. Studios. Club: Harvard (N.Y.C.). Home: 944 Park Ave New York NY 10028 Office: Mastermind Studios 1650 Broadway New York NY 10019

WOOD, BARBARA LOUISE, psychologist; b. Staunton, Va., Nov. 28, 1949; d. William Earle and Caroline Estelle (Marks) W.; B.A. in Psychology, Carnegie-Mellon U., 1971; M.A. in Counseling (EDPA fellow), U. Minn., 1974; Ph.D. in Counseling, U. Md., 1979; student Assn. for Psychoanalytic Study, 1980—; m. Philip Bond Ray, Aug. 2, 1981. Counselor Kenyon Coll., Gambier, Ohio, 1976-77; psychol. counselor Am. U., Washington, 1977; cons. Temple Hills (Md.) Counseling Center, 1977-79; profl. assoc. Univ. Counseling Center, U. Md., College Park, 1977-79, teaching asst., 1977, 79, instr., 1978-84, adj. asst. prof., 1985—; dir. Greenbelt-College Park (Md.) Counseling Center, 1979—; pvt. practice psychology, Chevy Chase, Md., 1982—. Mem. Am. Personnel and Guidance Assn., Am. Coll. Personnel Assn., Am. Psychol. Assn., Washington Psychologists for Psychoanalysis, Phi Kappa Phi. Democrat. Roman Catholic. Contbr. articles to profl. publs. Home: 16704 Baederwood Ln Rockville MD 20855 Office: 35 Wisconsin Circle Suite 310 Chevy Chase MD 20815

WOOD, CONSTANCE RICE, psychiatric social worker; b. Marlboro, Mass., Feb. 1, 1922; d. John Edward and Helen Bullard (Ellis) Rice; A.B., Syracuse U., 1943; M.S.W., Boston U., 1973; m. Robert K. Wood, Mar. 18, 1944; children—Robert K. Jr., Jeffrey Bullard, Durinda Rice. Clinician, psychiat. social worker Monadnock Family and Mental Health Service, Keene, N.H., 1972—; pvt. practice psychiat. social work, Keene, 1975—; owner Tavern Antiques, Keen, 1981—. Mem. adv. bd. Monadnock Area Women's Crisis Service, 1980-82; founding mem. Keene Center for Human Concerns, 1969, Women's Crisis Center, Keene, 1977-79; N.H. del. Nat. Democratic Conv., 1968, mem. exec. bd. N.H., Dem. Party, 1969-72, chmn. Cheshire County Dem. Party, 1972; pres. bd. trustees Keene Unitarian-Universalist Ch., 1969; recorder N.H. Women's Polit. Caucus, 1974. Mem. Nat. Assn. Social Workers, NOW, Nat. Women's Polit. Caucus, ACLU, LWV, Women's Internat. League for Peace and Freedom. Home: 63 Arch St Keene NH 03431 Office: 331 Main St Keene NH 03431

WOOD, DIANNE JEANETTE, business educator; b. Valley City, N.D., Apr. 21, 1948; d. Norman Fredrick and Avis Minnie (Eggert) Potter; m. William E. Wood; children from previous marriage—Lisa Marie Lee, Jodie Ann Lee, Larry Norman Lee. B.S.Ed., Valley City State Coll., 1980; M.B.A., Moorhead State U., 1983. Co-owner, mgr. Sheyenne Lodge, Valley City, N.D., 1981—; instr. Valley City State Coll., 1983-85, coordinator small bus. ctr., 1984—, asst. prof., 1986—, asst. to pres., 1985-86. Counselor, SCORE N.D., 1984—; coordinator N.D. Women's Bus. Ownership, 1985—. Mem. Commn. on Status of Women, Valley City, 1984—; mem. Epworth Methodist Edn. Com., 1983-84, United Ministries in Higher Edn., 1985-86. Mem. Am. Mgmt. Assn., NEA, N.D. Higher Edn. Assn., C. of C. Valley City (chmn. hospitality com. 1983-84), AAUW, Bus. and Profl. Women (pres. 1984-85). Avocations: conservation; equestrian; athletics. Home: RR 2 Valley City ND 58072 Office: Valley City State Coll College St Valley City ND 58072

WOOD, EDNA LUELLA (SELBE), retired nurse, educator; b. Phillipsburg, Kans., Apr. 24, 1925; d. John Carlyle and Cora Jane (Reese) Selbe; R.N. diploma St. Francis Hosp. Sch. Nursing, Topeka, 1946; B.S. in Nursing Edn. (Coll. fellow), St. Mary Coll., Leavenworth, Kans., 1948; M.S. in Health Edn., So. Ill. U., Carbondale, 1972; m. Elmer Leroy Wood, June 6, 1948; children—Carolyn Ann, Wanda Lee, John Leslie. Sch. nurse St. Mary Coll., 1946-48; supr. Meml. Hosp. Cheyenne, Wyo., 1947, 48, staff nurse obstetrics, 1951-55; staff nurse Invenson Meml. Hosp., Laramie, Wyo., 1949-51; with VA Nursing Service, 1955-85, asst. chief nursing service VA Med. Center, Cheyenne 1962-66, chief nursing service, Grand Junction, Colo., 1967-70, Marion, Ill., 1970-76, asso. chief nursing service for edn. Colmery-O'Neil VA Med. Center, Topeka, 1976-85; mem. numerous health-related coms.; mem. Task Force Continuing Edn. for Nurses in Kans., 1980; mem. Kans. Planning Com. for Nurses, 1982; mem. adj. faculty U. Kans. Sch. Nursing, Ft. Hays State U. Sch. Nursing. Mem. Gov.'s Com. for Nurses in Wyo., 1960-66, pres. Wyo. League for Nursing, 1962-66; mem. consumer planning com. U. So. Ill. Sch. Medicine, 1970-72. Recipient Dir.'s commendation for superior performance VA Med. Center, Cheyenne, 1964; hon. recognition plaque So. Ill. Nurses, 1976, Washburn U. Honor Soc. for Nursing, 1980, Eta Kappa chpt. Sigma Theta Tau, 1983; hon. plaque Task Force Continuing Edn. for Nurses, 1982. Mem. Am. Nurses Assn., Kans. State Nurses Assn., Nat. League Nursing, Am. Hosp. Assn. for Health Manpower, Nursing Orgn. VA. Mem. Christian Ch. (Disciples of Christ). Clubs: Toastmistress (Cheyenne); Wider Horizons Toastmistress (Grand Junction). Contbr. articles to profl. jours. Home: 730 NW 35th Topeka KS 66617

WOOD, EMMA LOU, real estate managment company executive; b. Jasonville, Ind., Sept. 29, 1935; d. Leo William and Elizabeth (White) Warrick; student Ind. U., 1957-72; m. C.J. Wood, Jan. 31, 1966 (dec.); children—Elizabeth Marie, Charles John; m. Thomas B. McNulty, Sept. 4, 1985. Bookkeeper, Place & Co., South Bend, Ind., 1959-65; pres. C.J. Wood, Inc., South Bend, 1976—. Mem. South Bend C. of C. Clubs: Orchard Hills Country (Niles, Mich.); Knollwood Country (Granger, Ind.). Office: C J Wood Inc 1119 S Franklin St South Bend IN 46624

WOOD, ETHEL LENORA, nurse; b. St. Louis, Sept. 28, 1935; d. Oscar and Bettie Sue (Johnson) White; m. Eugene William Wood, Jr., Feb. 1, 1959; children—Eugene W. III, Karen, Stephen Oscar. Student, Minot State Tchrs. Coll., N.D., 1953-54; Diploma, Jewish Hosp. Sch. Nursing, St. Louis, 1958; postgrad. UCLA Sch. Pub. Health, 1972, B.S. in Nursing program, Marquette U., Milw., 1975-77. Registered profl. nurse, N.Y., Tex., Ga., Wis., Mo. Staff nurse Vet.'s Hosp., St. Louis, 1958-59; staff nurse Ft. Gordon Army Hosp., Ga., 1959-61; head nurse St. John's Hosp., St. Louis, 1961-63, Barnes Hosp., St. Louis, 1962-63; sch. nurse St. Louis Bd. Edn., 1964-67; occupational nurse McDonnell Douglas Corp., St. Louis, 1963-64, IBM, Kingston, N.Y., 1967-68; pub. health nurse, sch. nurse Milw. Dept. Health, 1968-70; nurse cons. State of Wis., Madison, 1970-73; staff nurse Vet.'s Hosp., Milw., 1973-75; pvt. duty nurse, Houston, 1977-79; pub. health nurse City of Houston Dept. Health, 1979-81; instr. nursing Houston Community Coll., 1982-84; sch. nurse Aldines Ind. Sch. Dist., Houston, 1984—; Author: Dual Roles: Professional and Parenting. Fund raiser Am. Cancer Assn., Houston, 1977-85; active United Fund, Houston. Jewish Hosp. Nursing scholar, 1955. Mem. Am. Nurses Assn., Am. Occupational Health Nurses Assn., Iota Phi Lambda (pres. 1974-75). Avocations: Travelling; cooking; reading. Home: 1710 Willow Mill Dr Missouri City TX 77489 Office: PO Box 807 Missouri City TX 77459

WOOD, FAY S., electronics co. exec.; b. Phila.; d. Paul and Dorothy Wiener; B.A. in English, 1967; grad. exec. mgmt. course RCA Corp., 1977; children—Deborah, Esther. Real estate sales rep., 1968-70; cons. Hearing Centers, Inc., 1970-72; dist. sales mgr. Beltone Hearing Aid Centers, Inc., 1972-76; v.p. PhD Hearing Centers, Inc.; with RCA Service Co., 1976-79, sales mgr., 1977-79, regional sales mgr., N.Y. dist., 1979—; v.p. sales and mktg. Full Line Repair Centers, Inc., 1979-81, pres., 1981—; v.p. sales and mktg. Quantech Electronics Corp. Mem. N.Y.C. Commn. on Status of Women. Recipient audiology cert. Dahlberg Electronics, Master Cons. award Beltone Electronics; 1st degree Black Belt in Tae Kwon Do Karate; named Regional Mgr. of Yr., RCA Service Co. Mem. AAUW, LWV, Nat. Assn. Female Execs., Nat. Fedn. Bus. and Profl. Women, NOW, Nat. Fedn. Bus. and Profl. Women. Club: B'nai B'rith. Office: 73 E Merrick Rd Freeport NY 11520

WOOD, JACALYN KAY, educational consultant; b. Columbus, Ohio, May 25, 1949; d. Carleston John and Grace Anna (Schumacher) W. B.A., Georgetown Coll., 1971; M.S., Ohio State U., 1976; Ph.D., Miami U., 1981. Elem. tchr. Bethel-Tate Schs., Ohio, 1971-73, Columbus (Ohio) Christian Sch., 1973-74, Franklin (Ohio) Schs., 1974-79; teaching fellow Miami U., Oxford, Ohio, 1979-81; cons. intermediate grades Erie County Schs., Sandusky, Ohio, 1981— presenter tchr. inservice tng. Mem. council Sta. WVIZ-TV, 1981—; mem. exec. com. Perkins Community Schs., 1981—; mem. community adv. bd. Sandusky Vols. Am., Sandusky Soc. Bank. Mem. Am. Businesswomen's Assn. (local pres. 1985), Assn. Supervision and Curriculum Devel., Internat. Reading Assn., Ohio Sch. Suprs. Assn. (regional pres. 1986, state pres. 1986-87), Phi Delta Kappa (local sec. 1985). Lutheran. Home: 4512 7 Venice Heights Blvd Sandusky OH 44870 Office: 2902 Columbus Ave Sandusky OH 44870

WOOD, JOYCE ANN MLAKER, hosp. histologist; b. Warren, Ohio, Mar. 11, 1946; d. John and Anna (Poncer) Mlaker; student Ohio U., 1964-66; cert. Northside Hosp., 1967; m. Robert Vaughn Wood, May 6, 1978. Lab. asst. Northside Hosp., Youngstown, Ohio, 1966-67, histologist, 1967-71; supr. histology Bethesda Meml. Hosp., Boynton Beach, Fla., 1971—. Mem. Am. Soc. Clin. Pathologist (affiliate), Fla. State Histology Soc., Nat. Soc. Histotech. Home: 3919 Edgar Ave Boynton Beach FL 33436 Office: Bethesda Meml Hosp 2815 S Seacrest Blvd Boynton Beach FL 33435

WOOD, KATHLEEN ANN STUDT, teacher educator; b. Lansing, Mich., Aug. 20, 1943; d. Robert E. and Georgia (Preston) Studt; B.A., Trevecca Nazarene Coll., 1966; M.A., Wayne State U., 1972, postgrad., 1976—; M.Ed., U. Detroit, 1974; children—Elizabeth David. Tchr., Southfield (Mich.) Christian Sch., 1972-75; child therapist Met. Guidance Center, Farmington, Mich., 1975-76; instr. John Wesley Coll., Farmington, also dir. lab. sch. for early learners; asst. prof. early childhood edn. Mt. Vernon (Ohio) Nazarene Coll., 1976—; guest prof. summer workshops Eastern Nazarene Coll., 1979-80; presenter workshops seminars, 1969—; adviser Head Start and Social Services Day Care and Infant Programs, 1979—. Mem. Am. Assn. Colls. for Tchrs. Edn., Ohio Assn. Colls for Tchr. Edn., Nat. Assn. Edn. Young Children, Council Exceptional Children, Assn. Children with Learning Disabilities, Am. Personnel and Guidance Assn., Nazarene Assn. Tchr. Edn. Office: Mt Vernon Nazarene Coll Mt Vernon OH 43050

WOOD, KATHLEEN DORAN, producer, performer; b. Morristown, N.J., June 27, 1946; d. Arthur Francis and Blanche Evaline (Knapp) Ringwood; 1 son, Peter Shawn. B.S. in Elem. Edn., West Chester State Coll. (Pa.), 1975; M.A. in Speech Communications and Pub. Relations Mgmt., U. Houston, 1982. Cert. tchr. Caseworker, Montgomery County Bd. Assistance, Norristown, Pa., 1972-80, adminstrv. asst. Montgomery County Drug/Alcoholism, 1979-80; tchr. spl. edn. Jeanne Pfeifer Sch., Houston, 1980-81; prodn. coordinator Sta. KUHT-TV, Houston, 1981, D.W. Frederickson, Inc., Houston, 1981-82; producer Storer Cable TV, Houston, 1982-85; coordinator Vols. in Pub. Schs., Houston, 1983-84; producer, cons. Columbia Cable TV, Rosenberg, Tex., 1983; traffic mgr. Cook Sound Prodns. Inc., 1986—; cons. pub. relations Retinitis Pigmentosa & Lion's Eye Bank, Houston, 1981-84; lectr. U. St. Thomas, Houston, 1984. Editor, writer (newsletter) Access, 1982-84; reporter asst. editor: (newsletter) Hotline, 1982-84; host, producer Access, Dear Subscriber, Community News, 1983-84. Press asst. Jack Heard for Mayor Campaign, Houston, 1981; mem. Atkinson Sch. PTA, Houston, 1981-86; spokesperson KUHT-TV auction, 1981-84; actress Pasadena Little Theatre, 1984-86; mem. U.S.A. Sports Assn., Houston, 1983; founding mem., steering com. Houston Theatre Alliance, 1985-86. Named hon. sheriff's dep. Harris County Sheriff's Office, Houston, 1981. Mem. Women in Cable (exec. bd. 1982-84, chmn. publicity 1982-84), Women in Theatre Network Houston (founding mem., pres. 1985-86), Houston Bus. Com. for Ednl. Excellence (co-chmn. publicity 1985-86). Republican. Roman Catholic. Clubs: Towering Texans, Clear Lake Area Ski (publicity asst. 1982-84) (Houston). Home: 9810 Tiltree Street Houston TX 77075

WOOD, KATHLEEN OLIVER, writer and editor; b. Mt. Kisco, N.Y., Sept. 17, 1921; d. Eli Leslie and Melba Antoinette (Gislason) Oliver; student Swarthmore Coll., 1938-39, Antioch Coll., 1940-41, U. N.Mex., 1949, Cleve. Coll., 1960-61; m. John Thornton Wood, June, 1941 (div. 1947); children—Mark Thornton, Jonna Grim, Karen Wood Weston; m. 2d, Clifford Emanuel Huff, June, 1948 (div. 1955). Tech. sec. Gray Iron Founders Soc., Cleve., 1955-57; tchr. Whiting Bus. Coll., Cleve., 1957-62; editorial asst. Chem. Rubber Co., Cleve., 1966; editor, writer Jefferson Ency., World Pub. Co., Cleve., 1967-68; disc jockey, announcer Sta. WCLV-FM, Cleve., 1968-69; communications coordinator, writer, editor Highlights newsletter University Circle, Inc., Cleve., 1971-81; talk-show hostess, announcer Sta. WERE-AM, Cleve., 1972-73; free-lance writer, editor, cons., 1981—; tchr. Project LEARN; tutor VIP program. Hostess weekly radio show, CRRS, Cleve. Soc. for Blind; taper books for Library of Congress Service for Visually Handicapped; treas. Cleve. Beautiful Com., 1980, sec., 1982; v.p. Cleve. Cultural Garden Fedn.; trustee E. Cleve. Community Theatre. Mem. Pub. Relations Soc. Am., Internat. Assn. Bus. Communicators, Women's Advt. Club Cleve. (past pres., editor Weathervane 1982-83), Women in Communication, World Assn. Women Journalists and Writers (congress coordinator), MENSA, Early Settlers. Quaker. Clubs: Zonta Internat. (past pres. Cleve., dir. Area 3 Dist. V, 1984-86), Women's City. Author: Greenwood, 1967; editor, pub. Frog in the Milk Pan (Marie Wallace), 1963; editor Graffiti Mag., 1967, Office Gal Mag., 1962-63, Smorgasbrain Mag., 1968. Home: 3118 E Overlook Rd Cleveland Heights OH 44118 Office: PO Box 5612 Cleveland OH 44101

WOOD, LARRY (MARY LAIRD WOOD), journalist, educator, environmental consultant; b. Sandpoint, Idaho; d. Edward Hayes and Alice (McNeel) Small; children—Mary, Marcia, Barry. B.A. magna cum laude, U. Wash., Seattle, 1938, M.A. with highest honors, 1940; postgrad. Stanford U., 1941-42, 78-79, U. Calif.-Santa Cruz, 1975, U. Minn, 1970-71; postgrad. U. Calif.-Berkeley, 1943-44, cert. of photography, 1971; postgrad. in journalism U. Wis.-Madison. 1971-72, U. Ga., 1972-73. By-line columnist Oakland (Calif.) Tribune, San Francisco Chronicle, 1946—; feature writer Western region Christian Sci. Monitor and CSM Syndicate, 1973—, Times-Mirror Syndicate, 1975—, also Donnelly Bus. Publs., Oak Brook, Ill.; contbg. editor Travelday mag., regional corr., contbg. editor Spokane Mag., 1976—; Calif. corr. Seattle Times Sunday mag.; stringer Off Duty, mag. for mil.; contbg. author Fawcett Boating Books; feature writer Meridian Bus. Publs.; free lance writer for various nat. mags. including Parents', Sports Illus., Popular Mechanics, Mechanix Illus., Oceans, Sea Frontiers, TV Guide, Woman's Day, Am. Home, nat. travel, bus., fashion, home/garden, archtl. and environ. mags., 1946—; writings syndicated Internat. Communications Agy., and USIA, 1981—; author, reviewer series Focus on Sci., Charles Merrill Pub. Co., 1982—; feature, archtl. writer Calif. Today, 1979—; feature and travel writer San Jose (Calif.) Mercury News, 1979—, Odyssey Travel mag., AAA, Motorland, Westways, 1982—, Chevron, USA, Accent, People, Parade, Travel & Leisure, Industrial Progress, Your Home, Fodor Travel Guides to San Francisco and Calif., 1981—. Contbg. editor Fashion Showcase, Dallas, Country Roads; contbg. editor, feature writer Linguapress; dir. pub. relations No. Calif. Assn. Phi Beta Kappa, 1969—; judge Am. Book Awards, 1980—, Nat. Assn. Real Estate Editors, 1979—, others; prof. journalism San Diego State U., 1974—; asst. prof. journalism Calif. State U., Hayward, fall 1977; vis. prof. journalism San Jose State U., spring 1976; asst. prof. sci./environ. journalism U. Calif. extension, 1978—; pub. relations dir./cons. in field of sci., environ. affairs and recreation numerous firms, instns. and assns.; syndicated news stories and features on AM radio, 350 stas. in U.S. and Can.; participant, speaker nat. profl. confs. Public relations dir. YWCA, YM-YW USO, Seattle, 1942-46, YWCA, Oakland, Calif., 1946-56, Children's Home Soc. Calif., 1946-56, Children's Med. Ctr. No. Calif., 1946-70, Eastbay Regional Park Dist., 1946-58, Calif. Spring Garden Show, 1946-58, Girl Scouts U.S.A., Oakland, 1948-56; speaker for ednl. insts., profl. groups, 1946—; sec. Jr. Center of Arts, Oakland, 1952—; vol. public relations Am. Cancer Soc., YMCA, Oakland, 1946-52; pub. relations writer ARC, 1946-56, cons. Oakland Park Dept., Bay Area Hosp. Assn., 1946-75, Soc. Profl. Journalists Nat. Bd. Hist. Sites, 1985—, KRON-TV, 1985—; pub. relations account exec. March of Dimes, 1946-58; bd. dirs. Camp Fire Girls, Oakland, Joaquin Miller PTA, Oakland; del. 1st Conf. on Sci. in Nat. Parks, San Francisco, 1979, Nat. Park Service-Nat. Trust Hist. Preservation joint conf., 1982, 1st Internat., C., Hydrofoil Conf., N.S., Can., 1982. Recipient citations U.S. Forest Service, 1975, Nat. Park Service, 1976; award for feature on Adapt-A-Horse program U.S. Forest Service, 1977-78; citation for Sea Grant, article in Oceans Mag., 1980; Citation Am. Youth Hostels, 1982, numerous other awards. Mem. Pub. Relations Soc. Am. (cons. acad. 1984—), Nat. Sch. Pub. newspapers com. 1969—), Nat. Acad. TV Arts Relations Assn., Environ. Cons. N.Am., Internat. Environ. Cons., Internat. Oceanographic Soc., Am. Assn. Edn. in Journalism (nat. mag. and newspapers com. 1969—), Nat. Acad. TV Arts and Scis., AAAS, Am. Soc. Med. Writers, Nat. Trust Hist. Preservation, Am. Women in Radio and TV, Nat. Council Advancement Sci. Writing, U. Wash. Ocean Scis. Alumni Assn. (charter, named to Hall of Fame 1984), Investigative Reporters and Editors, Soc. Am. Travel Writers, Nat. Press Photographers Assn., Eastbay Women's Press Club, Nat. Assn. Sci. Writers, Calif. Writers Assn., San Francisco Press Club, Mortar Bd., Women in Communication (Woman of Year, Eastbay 1952, regional pres. 1970-71, regional v.p., nat. bd. 1975-79, speaker nat. conv. 1980), Calif. Assn. Environ. Profls., Found. Am. Communications (del.), Phi Beta Kappa (pub. relations dir. No. Calif. 1969—), Phi Beta Kappa Alumni, Chi Omega, Pi Lambda Theta, Sigma Delta Chi. Author: Pacific Coast Waterfronts, 1974; Railroads of the West, 1975; Restoration in the West, 1976; America's Endangered Animals, 1976; Great Zoos of the World, 1976; Showcase Cities of the West, 1977; America at the 1980 Olympics; America's Estuaries; Sylvia Earle—Woman Aquanaut; co-author Bell & Howell sci. texts, 1984; others Home: 6161 Castle Dr Oakland CA 94611

WOOD, LINDA GAYE, real estate development company executive; b. South Haven, Mich., May 12, 1959; d. Gene A. and Beatrice (McKamey) W.; m. Terry M. Shaw, July 20, 1980 (div. 1982). Corr. student broker registration U. San Francisco, 1985. Sr. loan processor Shearson Am Express Mktg., San Diego, 1977-80; office mgr. Lomas & Nettleton Mfg. Co., San Diego, 1980-81; escrow coordinator Barratt Developers, San Diego, 1981-83, Tara Escrow Inc., 1983-84; sales mgr. real estate devel. Watt Industries Inc., Rancho Sante Fe, Calif, 1984-85; sales and mktg. mgr. Buie Corp., Laguna Niguel, Calif., 1985—. Mem. Orange County Sales and Mktg. Council (bd. dirs. 1985—), Assn. Profl. Mktg. Women (rec. sec. 1984-85), Nat. Assn. Female Execs. Republican. Avocations: Swimming; walking; hiking; travel; cycling.

WOOD, LUCILLE, physical education educator; b. Louisville, Miss., Jan. 9, 1931; d. George S. and Collie Edna (Myres) W.; A.A., East Central Jr. Coll., 1951; B.S., U. So. Miss., 1953, M.A., 1955; postgrad. Instr. phys. edn., basketball, tennis coach Copiah-Lincoln Jr. Coll., Wesson, Miss., 1953-56; mem. phys. edn. dept. East Central Jr. Coll., Decatur, Miss., 1956—, chmn. dept., 1961-78, coach women's basketball, tennis, 1968—; mem. Stayfree Nat. Jr. Coll. Selection Com., 1980, 81. Named E. Central Jr. Coll. Alumnus of Year, 1964, Miss. Jr. Coll. Women's Basketball All-Star Coach, 1978, 81, Miss. Assn. Coaches Coach of Year, 1979, Nat. Jr. Coll. Coach of Yr. Top 20, 1979. Mem. Jr. Coll. Miss. Women's Basketball Coaches (pres.), NEA, Miss. Assn. Educators, Miss. Jr. Coll. Faculty Assn., Miss. Folklore Soc., Nat. Jr. Coll. Coaches Assn., U. So. Miss. Alumni Assn., Miss. Farm Bur., East Central Jr. Coll. Alumni Assn. (pres., v.p.), Delta Kappa Gamma. Coach champion teams, 1968, 70, 73, 76, 79, regional tournament teams, 1973, 77, 78, 79, 80. Home: Rt 2 Box 303 Louisville MS 39339 Office: East Central Jr Coll Decatur MS 39327

WOOD, MARGARET E., financial company executive; b. Freeland, Pa., Mar. 21, 1921; d. Thomas J. and Stella R. (Daubert) Williams; Bus. degree, McCann Sch. Bus., 1939; m. Raymond W. Wood, May 20, 1944; children—Thomas H., Richard W. Asst. v.p. Dominick & Dominick, Inc., Boston, 1970-73; v.p., div. mgr. F.L. Putnam & Co., Inc. of Boston, Salem, N.H., 1973-81, Buttonwood Securities Corp. of Mass., Boston, Salem, N.H. div., 1981—; dir. BankEast Guaranty Savs. Bank. Trustee Haverhill YWCA. Office: Buttonwood Securities Corp 1 Manor Pkwy Salem NH 03079

WOOD, MONICA LONGMORE, packaged goods executive; b. Fountainbleau, France, Apr. 3, 1955; came to U.S., 1957; d. Floyd Thenford and Marion (Longmore) Wood; m. Edward Louis Hibshman, Aug. 12, 1983. A.A., Dade Community Coll., 1974; B.S. magna cum laude, U. Fla., 1976; M.B.A. magna cum laude, U. Miami, 1979. Elem. tchr. Dade County Sch. System, Miami, Fla., 1976-78; analyst mktg. research Burger King Corp., Miami, 1979-80, sr. analyst mktg. research, 1980-82, asst. mgr. consumer research, 1982-83, mgr. nat. advt. and sales promotions, 1983-85; mgr. market research Campbell's Soup Co., 1985—. Mem. exec. com. Republican party, 1984—. Mem. Am. Mktg. Assn. (pres. elect 1984-85), Greater Miami C. of C., Phi Kappa Phi, Beta Gamma Sigma. Office: Campbell's Soup Co 1 Campbell Park Camden NJ 18305

WOOD, NANCY E(LIZABETH), psychologist, educator; b. Martins Ferry, Ohio; d. Donald Sterret and Orne (Erwin) W.; B.S., Ohio U., 1943, M.S., 1947; Ph.D., Northwestern U., 1952. Coordinator clin. services, also Lang Found., Cleve. Hearing and Speech Center, 1952, assoc. dir. lang. disorders, 1959-60; asso. prof. Western Res. U., 1952-60; specialist speech and hearing disorders U.S. Office Edn., Washington, 1960-62; chief research Neurol. and Sensory Disease Chronic Diseases USPHS, Washington, 1963-64; dir. research John Tracy Clinic, Los Angeles 1964-65; prof. lang. pathology and otolaryngology U. So. Calif., 1966-72, chmn. grad. program communicative disorders, 1972-75, prof. journalism, 1975—. Fellow Internat. Council Women Psychologists, Am. Psychol. Assn., Soc. Research in Child Devel., Am. Speech and Hearing Assn. (mem. exec. com.); mem. Council Exceptional Children and Youth, Delta Kappa Gamma. Author: Language Disorders in Children; Delayed Speech and Language Development; Verbal Learning; Signs and Symbols; contbr. articles to profl. jours. Office: 305 Grace Ford Salvatori Hall U So Calif Los Angeles CA 90089

WOOD, REBECCA LOUISE, financial executive; b. Farmington, N.Mex., Feb. 22, 1956; d. Darby Lindsey West and Donna Beth (Johnson) Padilla; m. Charles Ray Wood, Feb. 5, 1972; children—Angela, Wilson. Student San Juan Coll., Framington, N.Mex., 1982-86. Sec. B&G Electric Co., Inc., Farmington, 1978-80; bookkeeper West Main Auto, Farmington, 1980-81; fin. mgr. P&A Inc., Farmington, 1981—. Active PTA, Girl Scouts U.S.A., Farmington. Avocations: painting, sports, sewing, music, reading. Home: 2601 Cliffside Dr Farmington NM 87401 Office: P&A Inc 768 US Hwy 64 Farmington NM 87401

WOOD, ROBERTA SUSAN, foreign service officer; b. Clarksdale, Miss., Oct. 4, 1948; d. Robert Larkin and Dorothy Eloise (Shelton) Wood; B.A. with distinction, Southwestern U., Memphis, 1970; postgrad. Nat. U. Cuyo, Mendoza, Argentina, 1970-71; M.P.A., Harvard U., 1980. Joined U.S. Fgn. Service, 1972; service in Manila, Naples and Turin, Italy and Port-au-Prince, Haiti; mgmt. analyst Dept. State, Washington, 1980-84; U.S. consul gen., Jakarta, Indonesia, 1984—. Fulbright scholar, 1970-71. Mem. Am. Fgn. Service Assn., Consular Officers Assn., Friends of Nat. Zoo, DAR, Friends of Kennedy Center, Planned Parenthood Washington, Phi Beta Kappa. Office: American Embassy Jakarta Box 1 APO San Francisco CA 96356

WOOD, SANDRA ELAINE, systems analyst, programmer; b. Lynchburg, Va., June 27, 1944; d. William Lewis and Mattie Lou Wood; diploma exec. sec. course Phillips Bus. Coll., Lynchburg, 1970; B.A. in Bus. Adminstrn./Mgmt. cum laude, Lynchburg Coll., 1982, postgrad. 1982. Various clerical and secretarial positions, 1962-66; with Owens-Ill., Inc., 1966—, data processing supr./programmer, Big Island, Va., 1974-76, data processing systems-analyst/programmer, 1977—. Sec. Bedford County Transp. Safety Commn., 1974—. Named Outstanding Alumna, Phillips Bus. Coll., 1972. Mem. Profl. Secs. Internat. (Sec. of Yr. award Lynchburg chpt. 1971, chpt. pres. 1974, coordinator S.E. Dist. Conf. 1981-82), Data Processing Mgmt. Assn. (chpt. pres. 1980), CPS Assos., Am. Biog. Inst. Research Assn., Gold Key Honor Soc. Democrat. Methodist. Address: Owens-Ill Inc Big Island VA 24526

WOOD, SARAH YOUNGBLOOD, librarian; b. Dallas, Jan. 19, 1920; d. George Quincy and Lela Pearl (Brownlee) Youngblood; m. John Ralph Wood, June 29, 1948 (dec. May 1975). B.A., Tex. Woman's U., 1968, M.L.S., 1972. Library clk. Greenhill Sch., Dallas, 1962-68, asst. librarian, 1968-70; head librarian Hockaday Sch., Dallas, 1970—. Mem. evaluation com. Ind. Schs. Assn. of Southwest, 1971, 82. Mem. Dallas County Librarians Assn. (sec. 1981-82), Tex. Library Assn. (publs. com. 1973-74), ALA (program com. nat. conv. 1983-84), Cum Laude, Soc., Beta Phi Mu. Republican. Methodist. Home: 7015 Fisher Rd Dallas TX 75214 Office: Hockaday Sch Inc 11600 Welch Rd Dallas TX 75229

WOOD, SUSAN BARNETT, technical writer and editor, publisher and business consultant; b. Astoria, N.Y., Oct. 2, 1950; d. Sydney and Ruth (Savitsky) Barnett; m. Aubrey Nelson Wood, II, Oct. 16, 1970 (div. 1977); m. R. Lee Easter, Dec. 31, 1980. Student Queens Coll.-CUNY, 1967-69, New Sch. Social Research, 1968-69, Sir George Williams Coll., Montreal, 1972-74. Researcher, Buttenheim Pub., N.Y.C., 1968-69, Factory Mut., Montreal, Que., Can., 1969-71; asst. mgr. Gray Security Services, Miami, Fla., 1974-76; adminstrv. asst. Unltd. Yacht Service, Miami, 1976-78; adminstrv. mgr. Grove House Inc., Coconut Grove, Fla., 1978-80; pres. SPEC-EDIT, Inc., Coral Gables, 1980—, dir. Spl. Systems Design Group, Inc., Miami, 1981—; editor SPEC-TOPICS Quar., 1981— (publs. awards 1982, 83); editor, co-author jour. articles; contbg. author constrn. manual (hon. mention award 1983). Bd. dirs. Grove House, Inc., Coconut Grove, 1982—. Mem. Constrn. Specifications Inst. (editor 1982-84, publs. award 1983, chpt. orgn. cert., Miami 1983, region orgn. cert. S.E. Region 1983, pres.' cert. Miami 1983, dir. Miami chpt. 1983—), Fla. Freelance Writers Assn., Nat. Bldg. Mus. Democrat. Office: 29 Barton St Somerville MA 02144

WOOD, SUSANNE MARY, retail company executive; b. Detroit, Aug. 9, 1944; d. Samuel and Joyce Sara (Kendell) Mackey; m. Henry James Wood, June 17, 1960 (div. Oct. 1977); children—Anne Marie, Henry Thomas, Karen Susanne, Samuel Stephens. Lic. practical nurse diploma Shapero Sinai Hosp., Detroit, 1968; student Oakland Community Coll., 1975-78; cert. operating room technician Pontiac Gen. Hosp. (Mich.), 1974. Nurse, Pontiac Gen. Hosp., 1973-79; dir. Met. Flint Nurse Service (Mich.), 1979-80; owner, operator Holly Wood Products (Mich.), 1980—. Mem. Nat. Wood and Pallet Assn., Soc. Packaging Engrs., Nat. Orgn. Women Bus. Owners, Aircraft Owner's Pilots Assn., 99's Internat. Republican. Baptist. Club: Deer Lake Raquet (Clarkston, Mich.). Home: 16110 Tucker Rd Holly MI 48442

WOOD, VIRGINIA MARGARET, nurse; b. N.Y.C., Jan. 1, 1936; d. Ivan Smyrna and Louise Catherine (Straub) W.; adopted children—Margaret Theresa, Christine Louise. Diploma Capital City Sch. Nursing, 1957; B.S. in Nursing, U. Nev., 1970; M.Ed. in Allied Health, U. Fla., 1979; Ph.D. in Nursing Adminstrn., Columbia Pacific U., 1983. Staff nurse D.C. Gen. Hosp., Washington, 1957-58, USPHS Indian Health Service, Whiteriver and Phoenix, Ariz., 1958-61, U.S. Air Force, Nellis AFB, Las Vegas, Nev., 1961-63; staff nurse, supr. VA Hosp., Phoenix, 1970-72; nurse instr. VA Hosp., Columbia, Mo. and Gainesville, Fla., 1972-79; nurse educator USPHS Indian Health Service, Whiteriver, 1979-80, dir. nurses, San Carlos, Ariz., 1980—. Served to capt. USAF, 1963-68; maj. U.S. Army, 1975-79. Recipient Supr. of Yr. award USPHS Indian Health Service, 1983. Mem. Am. Nurses Assn., Nat. League Nursing, Ariz. Soc. Ariz. Nursing Service Adminstrs. (nominating com. 1983-84), Phi Kappa Phi, Pi Lambda Theta. Republican. Roman Catholic. Avocations: reading; sewing; walking. Home: Box N San Carlos AZ 85550 Office: USPHS Indian Health Service Hosp Box 208 San Carlos AZ 85550

WOOD, VIVIAN POATES, mezzo-soprano, educator, author; b. Washington, Aug. 19, 1923; d. Harold P. and Mildred G. (Patterson) W.; student Walter Anderson, Antioch Coll., 1953-55; student of Denise Restout, Saint-Leu-La-Fôret, France and Lakeville, Conn., 1960-62, 64-70, Paul A. Pisk, 1968-71, Paul Ulanowsky, N.Y.C., 1958-68, Elemer Nagy, 1965-68, Vyautas Marijosius, 1967-68; B.Mus., Hartt Coll. Music, 1968; postgrad. (fellow) Yale U., 1968; Mus.M. (fellow), Washington U., St. Louis, 1971, Ph.D. (fellow), 1973. Debut in recital series Internat. Jeunesse Musicals Arts Festival, 1953, solo fellowship Boston Symphony Orch., Berkshire Music Center, Tanglewood, 1964, St. Louis Symphony Orch., 1969, Washington Orch., 1949, Bach Cantata Series Berkshire Chamber Orch., 1964, Yale Symphony Orch., 1968; appearances in U.S. and European recitals, oratorios, operas, radio and TV, 1953-68; appeared as soloist in Internat. Harpsichord Festival, Westminister Choir Coll., Princeton, N.J., 1973; appeared as soloist in meml. concert, Landowska Center, Lakeville, 1969; prof. voice U. So. Miss., Hattiesburg, 1971—, asst. dean Coll. Fine Arts, 1974-76, acting dean, 1976-77; guest prof. Hochschule für Musik, Munich, Germany, 1978-79; prof. Italian Internat. Studies Program, Rome, summers 1985—; Miss. coordinator Alliance for Arts Edn., Kennedy Center Performing Arts, 1974—. Mem. Miss. Gov.'s Adv. Panel for Gifted and Talented Children, 1974—; mem. 1st Miss. Gov.'s Conf. on the Arts, 1974—; bd. dirs. Miss. Opera, 1974—. Recipient Young Am. Artists Concert award N.Y.C., 1955; Wanda Landowska fellow, 1968-72. Mem. Nat. Assn. Tchrs. of Singing, Am. Musicological Soc., Golden Key, Mu Phi Epsilon, Delta Kappa Gamma, Tau Beta Kappa (hon.), Pi Kappa Lambda. Democrat. Episcopalian. Author: Poulenc's Songs: An Analysis of Style, 1978. Home: 3017 Navajo Circle Hattiesburg MS 39401 Office: South Station Box 8264 Coll Fine Arts U So Miss Hattiesburg MS 39401

WOOD, WENDY DEBORAH, filmmaker; b. N.Y.C., Oct. 4, 1940; d. John Meyer and Marion Emily (Peters) W.; B.A. cum laude, Vassar Coll., 1962; M.A., Stanford U., 1964; m. William Dismore Chapple, Dec. 7, 1963; 1 son, Samuel Eliot. Teaching asst. Stanford U., 1962-64; photographer, film editor Bristol (Eng.) U., 1964-66, asst. dir. Internat. Conf. Film Schs., 1966; research asst. biology dept. U. Conn., Storrs, 1970-72; sr. program devel. specialist, writer, producer, dir. video and film audio visual services Aetna Life & Casualty Co., Hartford, Conn., 1972—; pres. Chapple Films, Inc., 1972—; films include: Yankee Craftsman, 1972; Alcoholism, Industry's Costly Hangover, 1974; Draggerman's Haul, 1975; Flight Without Wings, 1977; Auto Insurance Affordability (2 awards), 1981; Where Rivers Run to the Sea (award), 1981; Our Town is Burning Down (6 awards), 1982; Wellness at the Worksite, 1984 (4 awards); Welcome to the Aetna Institute, 1985 (3 awards); Aenhance, 1985 (3 awards). Recipient CINE Golden Eagle award Council on Internat. Non-theatrical Events, 1972, 76, 83, 1st Place award Indsl. Photography, 1974, cert. Outstanding Creativity U.S. TV Commls. Festival, 1974, EFLA award Am. Film Festival, 1974, 76, Dir.'s Choice award Sinking Creek Film Festival, 1975, award Columbus Film Festival, 1975, award Excellence Life Ins. Advtrs. Assn., 1975, Silver Screen award U.S. Indsl. Film Festival, 1976, 81, 1st place award Conn. Film Festival, 1977, 1st prize Nat. Outdoor Travel Film Festival, 1978, 1st pl. Houston Film Festival, 1982, CINE Golden Eagle, 1982, award Am. Film Festival, 1982, N.Y. Film Festival, 1982, 83, 86, others. Mem. Info. Film Producers Am. (nat. dir.; pres. chpt. 1981-82; Cindy award 1971, 72, 81, 82, 85), Assn. Ind. Video and Film Producers, Internat. Quorum Motion Picture Producers, Women in Communications, Audio Visual Communicators (pres. Conn. chpt. 1985). Republican. Quaker. Home: Star Route Chaplin CT 06235 Office: Aetna Life & Casualty Co Creative Services-Corp Communications 151 Farmington Ave Hartford CT 06115

WOODARD, BARBARA THOMAS, government official; b. Havana, Ill., May 31, 1944; d. Robert Lee and Alta Mae (Johnson) Thomas; student U. Nev., Las Vegas, 1974—; Assoc. Gen. Studies (hon.), Clark County Community Coll., 1984. Assoc. Arts Social Sci. (hon.), 1985. With AEC, Las Vegas, Nev., 1968—, (name changed to Energy Research and Devel. Adminstrn., 1975, Dept. of Energy, 1977—), adminstrv. asst., mgr.'s office, 1977—. Vol. Univ. Med. Ctr. So. Nev., Las Vegas. Mem. Fed. Women's Program Adv. Council, 1974-75. Recipient High Quality Achievement award U.S. Dept. Energy, 1979, also Superior Job Performance award, 1981, 82, 83, 85, cert. Appreciation for exemplary performance, 1970, 84. Mem. Clark County Community Coll. Honor Soc., Nat. Mus. Women in Arts (charter). Roman Catholic. Office: PO Box 14100 Las Vegas NV 89114

WOODARD, CAROL JANE, educator; b. Buffalo, Jan. 19, 1929; d. Harold August and Violet Maybelle (Landsittel) Young; B.A., Hartwick Coll., 1950; M.A., Syracuse U., 1952; Ph.D., State U. N.Y. at Buffalo, 1972, postgrad. Bank St. Coll., 1976, Harvard U., 1977; m. Ralph Arthur Woodard, Aug. 19, 1950; children—Camaron Jane, Carsen Jane, Cooper Ralph. Tchr., Orchard Park, N.Y., 1950-51, Danville, Ind., 1951-52, Akron, N.Y., 1952-54, Amherst (N.Y.) Coop. Nursery Sch., 1967-69; dir. Garden Nursery Sch., Williamsville, N.Y., 1955-65; asst. prof. early childhood edn. State U. Coll. at Buffalo, 1969-72, lab. demonstration tchr. and student teaching supr., 1969-76, assoc. prof., 1972-79, prof., 1979—; cons. Lutheran Ch. Am., Villa Maria Coll., Erie Community Coll., Headstart Tng. Programs, pub. sch. systems, numerous workshops. Mem. alumni bd. dirs. Hartwick Coll., Oneonta, 1976, 1977, trustee, 1978—; cons. bus., civic orgns. in child care. Recipient faculty grant State U. N.Y., 1974-75, Shield grant, 1977; certified tchr., N.Y. Mem. Nat. Assn. Edn. Young Children, Early Childhood Edn. Council Western N.Y., Assn. Childhood Edn. Internat., Pi Lambda Theta, Pi Delta Kappa. Author 7 books for young children, 2 textbooks; co-author nat. curriculum for ch. sch. for 3 yr-olds; author booklet for parents: You Can Help Your Baby Learn; contbr. numerous articles to profl. jours. Home: 1776 Sweet Rd East Aurora NY 14052 Office: State U Coll 1300 Elmwood Ave Bacon Hall #301 Buffalo NY 14222

WOODARD, DOROTHY MARIE, insurance broker; b. Houston, Feb. 7, 1932; d. Gerald Edgar and Bessie Katherine (Crain) Floeck; student N.Mex. State U., 1950; m. June 19, 1950 (dec.); m.2d, Norman W. Libby, July 19, 1982. Ptnr., Western Oil Co., Tucumcari, N.Mex., 1950—; owner, mgr. Woodard & Co., Las Cruces, N.Mex., 1959-67; agt., dist. mgr. United Nations Ins. Co., Denver, 1968-74; agt. Western Nat. Life Ins. Co., Amarillo, Tex., 1976—. Exec. dir. Tucumcari Indsl. Commn., 1979—; dir. Bravo Dome Study Com., 1979—; regional bd. dirs. N.Mex., Eastern Plains Council Govts., 1979—, Resource Conservation and Devel., El llana Estacado, 1980—; panel mem. N.Mex. R.R. Planning Conf., 1981. Mem. N.Mex. Indsl. Devel. Execs. Assn., Tucumcari C. of C. Club: Mesa Country. Home: PO Box 823 Tucumcari NM 88401 Office: PO Box 1003 Tucumcari NM 88401

WOODARD, MARTHA VIRGINIA, buyer; b. Bethesda, Md., Aug. 19, 1959; d. Frederick A. and Joanne V. (Latta) Alworth. B.S., Tex. Christian U., 1981. Asst. buyer Sanger Harris Dept. Store, Dallas, 1982-83, 84—, mdse. analyst, 1983-84. Pres., Episcopal Young Churchmen, San Diego, 1976-77; mem. Dist. Atty.'s Youth Adv. Co., San Diego, 1976-77. Recipient Achievement award Bank of Am., 1977; Alpha Delta Pi Scholar, 1980-81. Mem. Am. Mktg. Assn., Am. Home Econs. Assn., Am. Legion Aux., Alpha Delta Pi. Republican. Episcopalian. Home: 8307 Meadow Rd Apt 2098 Dallas TX 75231 Office: Sanger Harris 1400 Federal St Dallas TX 75205

WOODARD, MARY ACE, public administrator, nurse; b. Scranton, Pa., Nov. 13, 1935; d. Eugene Patrick and Katharine Anne (Hayes) Kelly; m. John Henry Ace, Jan. 7, 1957 (dec. Sept. 1980); children—Michael, Kathryn; m. William D. Woodard III, Sept. 28, 1985. R.N., Mercy Hosp. Sch. Nursing, 1956; B.S. in Health Care Adminstrn., East Tex. State U., 1980; M.A. in Pub. Adminstrn., U. Tex.-Arlington, 1982. R.N., Pa., Md. Staff nurse Dept. of Army, Stuttgart, W.Ger., 1957-58; supr./head nurse Riddle Meml. Hosp., Lima, Pa., 1962-68; indsl. nurse Burroughs Corp., Paoli, Pa., 1968-70; mgmt. analyst Soc. Security Adminstrn., Balt., 1971-74, staff assoc., 1974-76; tchr. surveyor tng. Tulane U., New Orleans, 1974, U. Md., 1974; mem. steering com. Fed. Exec. Bd. for Tex. State Fair, Dallas, 1979-83; mem. pub. info. officers Fed. Exec. Bd., Dallas, 1979-83; tchr. behavior modification workshop Essex Community Coll., Md., 1974. Author: Supplemental Security Income Systems, 1975; A Guide for Hospital Auxilians (Ark. Traveler award 1981), 1979. outreach dir. Oak Grove Baptist Ch., Churchville, Md., 1975; mem. Young Life Adult Council, Dallas, 1978; mem. coll. and youth coms. Cliff Temple, Dallas, 1979. Recipient High Performance award Medicare Bureau, 1972, Nat. Beneficiary Services award Health Care Financing Adminstrn., 1982, Sustained Superior Performance award Health Care Financing Adminstrn., 1977, 84; recipient scholarship Scranton C. of C., 1953. Mem. Am. Soc. Pub. Adminstrn., Assn. Pub. Policy Analysis and Eval., Am. Pub. Welfare Assn., Pi Sigma Alpha. Clubs: Brookhaven Country, Positive Strokes Racquet (Dallas). Home: 3018 Adolph St Dallas TX 75204 Office: Health Care Financing Adminstrn 1200 Main Tower Bldg Dallas TX 75202

WOODARD, NINA ELIZABETH, banker; b. Los Angeles, Apr. 3, 1947; d. Alexander Rhodes and Harriette Jane (Power) Mathews; m. John David Woodard, Mar. 17, 1966; children—Regina M., James D. Student pub. schs., Los Angeles. Dental asst. Los Angeles, 1965-66; with Security Pacific Nat. Bank, Marina Del Rey, Calif., 1968-69; with First Interstate Bank, Casper, Wyo., 1971—, adminstr. asst. personnel, 1975-78, asst. v.p., asst. mgr. personnel, 1978-82, v.p., dir. mktg. and personnel, 1982-84, v.p., mgr. human resources, 1984—; instr. mktg. Am. Inst. Banking, 1983, Casper Coll., 1982. Mem. Civil Service Commn., City of Casper, 1983—; bd. dirs. YMCA, 1984—, Downtown Devel. Assn.; chmn. Wyo. Steering Com. on Bus. Edn.; pres. Downtown Casper Assn. Named Bus. Woman of Yr., Bus. and Profl. Women, 1982, Young Career Woman, 1975. Mem. Nat. Assn. Bank Women, Bus. and Profl. Women (dist. dir.), Am. Soc. Personnel Adminstrn. (regional v.p., chmn. Wyo. steering com. for bus. edn. 1985-86, accredited sr. profl. in human resources). Republican. Roman Catholic. Lodge: Order Eastern Star.

WOODARD, SUSAN DUKES, college director; b. Orangeburg, S.C., Feb. 10, 1946; d. William Walter, Jr. and Margaret (Crevensten) Dukes; m. William Leicester Woodard, Dec. 12, 1964; children—William L. Jr., Christopher Crevensten. Student St. Mary's Jr. Coll., Raleigh, N.C., 1964-65; B.A., Converse Coll., 1970. Owner, operator Candy Cupboard, Spartanburg, S.C., 1968-70; elem. tchr., Woodruff, S.C., 1970-71; test analyst Orangeburg City Schs., S.C., 1972-73; secondary tchr. Wade Hampton Acad., Orangeburg, 1973-76; asst. dir. alumnae affairs Converse Coll., Spartanburg, 1978-79, dir. alumnae affairs, 1979—. Bd. dirs., v.p. Mental Health Assn., Spartanburg, 1976—; sec. Women of Ch., Redeemer Episcopal Ch., Orangeburg, 1974-75, Jr. League of Orangeburg, 1972-77. Mem. Council for Advancement and Support Edn., Alumnae Dirs. and Pres. Together, S.C. Network Women Adminstrs., Pi Gamma Mu, Gamma Sigma. Club: Converse Campus (pres. 1983-84). Avocations: church youth work; active sports; needlework; reading. Home: 33 Summercreek Dr Spartanburg SC 29302 Office: Converse Coll 580 E Main St Spartanburg SC 29301

WOODARD, WANDA CAROLYN, housing authority clerk, special services supervisor; b. Magnolia, Ark., Jan. 19, 1956; d. Carroll Martin and Dorothy Nell (Baskin) W. Student Ayers Bus. Sch., 1974. Cert. pub. housing mgr. Sec., Tex. Eastern, Shreveport, La., 1975; bookkeeper Kelso Equipment Co., Magnolia, 1975-76; supr. Magnolia Housing Authority, Ark., 1976—. Recipient Aging Services award Area Agy. on Aging, 1985. Baptist. Home: PO Box 186 Magnolia AR 71753 Office: Housing Authority of City of Magnolia Ark PO Box 488 Magnolia AR 71753

WOODARD, WILMA C., state legislator; b. Harnett County, N.C., Nov. 18, 1934; d. Claude Cummings and Lutheria (Searcy) Cummings; m. Warden Lewis Woodard, Jr., 1952; children—Mary Ellen Ward, Albert, Richard. A.B., N.C. State U., 1969. Formerly mem. N.C. Ho. of Reps.; mem. N.C. Senate from dist. 14, 1983—. Former vice chmn. planning bd. Town of Garner, N.C.; Garner rep. to Raleigh-Wake Land Use Code Commn.; mem. adv. bd. Wake County CETA; bd. dirs. N.C. State U. Recipient B.F. Brown award N.C. State U., 1969. Mem. N.C. State Mus. Natural History, Women's Forum N.C. Methodist. Democrat. Office: NC State Senate State Capitol Raleigh NC 27611*

WOODBRIDGE, ANNIE SMITH, retired teacher and librarian; b. Wingo, Ky., July 7, 1915; d. Ernest Herbert and Flora Susan (Parrish) Smith; B.A., Murray State Coll., 1935; M.A., Peabody Coll., 1936; postgrad. U. Wis., Tex. State Coll. for Women, U. Ky., Sorbonne, Universidad Interamericana; m. Hensley C. Woodbridge, Aug. 28, 1953; 1 dau., Ruby Susan Woodbridge Jung. Tchr. Cadiz High Sch., 1936-37, David Lipscomb Coll., 1937-43, Bethel Coll., 1943-46, Murray State Coll., 1946-54, 59-65; instr. So. Ill. U., Carbondale, 1966-74, researcher Morris Library, 1974-85. Mem. NOW, Midwest Latin Am. Studies Assn., Ellen Glasgow Soc., Soc. Study of Midwestern Lit. Democrat. Mem. Ch. of Christ. Editor: (with others) Collected Short Stories of Mary Johnston; contbr. articles jours and newsletters. Home: 1804 W Freeman St Carbondale IL 62901 Office: Morris Library Southern Illinois University Carbondale IL 62901

WOODBURY, MARGARET CLAYTOR, physician, university administrator; b. Roanoke, Va., Oct. 30, 1937; d. John Bunyan and Roberta Morris (Woodfin) Claytor; m. Lawrence DeWitt Young, 1959 (div.); children—Laura Ruth, Lawrence DeWitt Jr.; m. 2d, David Henry Woodbury, Jr., Nov. 30, 1968; 1 child, David Henry III. A.B. cum laude, Mt. Holyoke Coll., 1958; postgrad. Albany Med. Coll., 1958-60; M.D., Meharry Med. Coll., 1962. Diplomate Am. Bd. Internal Medicine, Nat. Bd. Med. Examiners. Asst. chief medicine-endocrinology USPHS, S.I., N.Y., 1967-68; chief out-patient clinic USPHS Hosp., Detroit, 1968-69; med. officer-in-charge USPHS Out-patient Clinic, Detroit, 1969-71; instr. internal medicine-endocrinology U. Mich., Ann Arbor, 1969-80, asst. prof. internal medicine-endocrinology and metabolism, 1980—, asst. dean student and minority affairs, 1983—; project dir. Health Careers Opportunity Program/Assistance to Increase Matriculation and Earn Degrees, 1984—; cons. Bryant Neighborhood Clinic, Ann Arbor, 1978; vis. lectr. Morehouse Med. Coll., Atlanta, 1980-82; minority recruitment officer Admissions U. Mich. Med. Sch., Ann Arbor, 1975-83; mem. Adv. Com. on Affirmative Actions Program, 1982-85, chair, 1984-85. Contbr. chpts. to books, articles to profl. jours. Vol. Democratic Party, Ann Arbor, 1972—, co-chair precinct, 1973; parent rep. Engring. Indsl. Support Program, Ann Arbor, 1978-82; vol. Nat. Council Negro Women, Ann Arbor, 1974-76; mentor Ann Arbor Alliance for Achievement in Acads. and the Arts, sec., 1982-83; trustee Mt. Holyoke Coll., 1985—. Recipient Biochemistry award Albany Med. Coll. (N.Y.), 1958-60; pediatrics prize Meharry Med. Coll., Nashville, 1960-62; Alumni medal of honor Mt. Holyoke Coll., 1983. Mem. Nat. Med. Assn., Am. Med. Women's Assn., Nat. Minority Health Assn. (charter), Alpha Omega Alpha. Presbyterian. Club: Mt. Holyoke (press rep. 1973-76, pres. 1976-80). Office: U Mich PO Box 025 Furstenberg Med Center Ann Arbor MI 48109

WOODCOCK, RUTH MILLER, religious organization executive; b. Harrisburg, Pa., Sept. 1, 1927; d. Evan Jones and Ruth (Wills) Miller; 1 dau., Deborah. B.A., Wells Coll., 1949; M.A., Fletcher Sch. Law and Diplomacy, 1950. Assoc. exec. dir. Community Action Agy., Harisburg, Pa., 1964-69, YWCA of City N.Y., 1969-75, Ch. Women United in U.S.A., N.Y.C., 1975-80, McBurney YWCA, N.Y.C., 1980-81; exec. dir. YWCA Retirement Fund, Inc., N.Y.C., 1981-86; assoc. gen. sec. for adminstrn. and fin. Nat. Council Chs. of Christ, 1986—. Vol. Tri-County Welfare Council, Harrisburg, 1960s, Susquehanna council Girl Scouts U.S.A., 1960s, YMCA and YWCA Day Care Corp., N.Y.C., 1970s; nat. bd. dirs. Am. Friends Service Com., Phila., 1980s, Women in Community Service, Washington, 1980s. Rotary Found. fellow, Geneva, 1950-51. Quaker. Office: Nat Council Chs of Christ 475 Riverside Dr New York NY 10015

WOODHOUSE, GAY VANDERPOEL, lawyer; b. Torrington, Wyo., Jan. 8, 1950; d. Wayne Gaylord and Sally (Rouse) Vanderpoel; m. Randy Leon Woodhouse, Nov. 26, 1983. B.A. with honors, U. Wyo., 1972, J.D., U. Wyo., 1977. Bar: Wyo., 1978. Dir. legal services U. Wyo. Law Sch., Laramie, 1976-77; intern Donald E. Jones Law Office, Torrington, 1977-78, atty., 1978; asst. atty. gen., Cheyenne, Wyo., 1978-84, sr. asst. atty. gen., 1984—; chmn. Telephone Consumer Panel, Cheyenne, 1982-84. Mem. Substance Abuse Task Force, Cheyenne, 1984; sec. Pathfinder Bd. Dirs., Cheyenne, 1985. Mem. Wyo. State Bar Assn., ABA. Republican. Avocations: swimming; water-skiing; stained glass. Home: 13432 Stewart Rd Cheyenne WY 82009 Office: Office Atty Gen 123 State Capitol Cheyenne WY 82002

WOODHULL, NANCY JANE, newspaper editor; b. Perth Amboy, N.J., Mar. 1, 1945; d. Harold and Mertie May Cromwell; student Trenton (N.J.) State Coll., 1963-64; m. William D. Watson; 1 dau., Tennie Watson. Reporter, editor News, Tribune, Woodbridge, N.J., 1964-72; reporter Detroit Free Press, 1973-75; mng. editor Times-Union, Rochester, N.Y., 1979-80, Democrat and Chronicle, Rochester, 1980-82; mng. editor enterprise U.S.A. Today, Washington, 1982—. Recipient numerous awards N.J. Newspaperwoman's Assn. Mem. Am. Soc. Newspaper Editors, AP Mng. Editors Assn. Office: USA Today 1000 Wilson Blvd Arlington VA 22209

WOODLIEF, EILEEN YOUNTS, banker; b. San Rafael, Calif., Mar. 2, 1954; d. Jack L. and Lynda C. (Adams) W.; m. David Eugene Foster, Dec. 1, 1974 (div. June 1978); m. Michael Phillip Younts, Aug. 31, 1979. B.A. cum laude, San Francisco State U., 1976. Salesperson Now Jewelery, San Francisco, 1973-79; customer service rep. Wells Fargo Bank, Oakland, Calif., 1980-82, electronic data processor, 1982-83, gen. ledger systems, San Leandro, 1983, asst. ops. officer, Oakland, 1983-85, bus. banking officer, 1985—. Mem. Nat. Assn. Female Execs., Music Masters Am. Republican. Clubs: Wells Fargo (chpt. sec. 1983-84) (San Leandro); Dimond Main Wells (pres. 1985-86) (Oakland). Avocations: song writing; poetry; guitar; tennis; volleyball. Office: Wells Fargo Bank PO Box 2707 Oakland CA 94602

WOOD-MACY, CANDY-LOUISE, accountant; b. Townsville, Queensland, Australia, Feb. 16, 1960; came to U.S. 1964; d. Peter and Roma Elaine (Pomeroy) Wood; m. John G. Macy, II, June 24, 1984. B.A., Franklin & Marshall Coll., 1982. Advanced acct. Ernst & Whinney, White Plains, N.Y., 1982-84; tax/fin. acct. James P. Kelly & Co., Rye, N.Y., 1984-85; gen. acct. Am. ACMI, Stamford, Conn., 1985; sr. acct. Fisher Camuto, Stamford, 1985—; gen. acctg. supr. Don Travel, White Plains, N.Y.; tax/acctg. services Frank LaRusso C.P.A., Mammaroneck, N.Y., 1985-86, Zinsner Real Estate, Rye, N.Y., 1984-86. Alumni admissions officer Franklin & Marshall Coll., 1982-86. Mem. Fairfield Network of Exec. Women, Nat. Assn. Female Execs. Presbyterian. Home: 68 Mulberry St Stamford CT 06907 Office: Don Travel White Plains NY

WOODRING, BARBARA CROSS, nursing educator; b. Balt., Jan. 26, 1944; d. Robert N. and Evelyn (Smith) Cross; m. Richard C. Woodring, Aug. 26, 1967. Diploma in nursing Union Meml. Hosp. Sch. Nursing, 1963; B.S.N. cum laude, Grace Coll., 1966; M.S., St. Francis Coll., Ft. Wayne, Ind., 1970; M.Ed., Johns Hopkins U., 1975; M.A., Ed.D., Ball State U., 1983. R.N. Staff nurse Union Meml. Hosp., Balt., 1963-65, mem. faculty, coordinator Sch. Nursing, 1966-67, 70-73; faculty coordinator Parkview Meth. Sch. Nursing, Ft. Wayne, 1967-70; asst. prof. Allegheny Community Coll., Pitts., 1975-77; prof., chmn. dept. nursing Grace Coll., Winona Lake, Ind., 1977-84; ednl. coordinator Children's Meml. Med. Ctr., Chgo., 1984—; adj. prof. ctr. for Nursing, Northwestern U., Chgo., 1985—. Roberta Lee Ball scholar, 1963; AAUW scholar, 1960. Mem. Nat. League Nursing, Am. Nurses Assn., Phi Beta Kappa, Sigma Tau Theta, Pi Lambda Theta. Mem. Grace Brethren Ch. Home: 6108 W Giddins Chicago IL 60630 Office: 2300 Childrens Plaza Chicago IL 60614

WOODRING, CAROLE LYN, psychologist, consultant; b. State College, Pa., Nov. 7, 1945; d. Charles Elmer and Helen Pauline W.; m. Eric Marvin Berg, May 30, 1970; children—Nicole Leslie Woodring, Adam Trevor Woodring, Jessica Lynne Woodring. B.A., Pa. State U., 1967; M.A., Columbia U., 1969. Foster caseworker Dauphin County Child Care Agy., Harrisburg, Pa., 1967-68; personnel asst. dir. Conf. Bd., Inc., N.Y.C., 1969-70; mgr. tng. design and validation Chem. Bank N.Y. Trust Inc., N.Y.C., 1970-73; tng. cons. 1st Union Corp., Charlotte, N.C., 1978-79; adj. prof. Sacred Heart Coll., Belmont, N.C., 1978-80; dir., officer Fortune Cons., 1977-81; pvt. cons., Matthews, N.C., 1979—; officer pres. J.N. Adams & Assos., 1982—. Trustee, Charlotte Montessori Sch., 1980-83, pres., 1981-83; mem. parent council bd. Charlotte Latin Sch., 1984-85. Mem. Assn. for Psychol. Type, AAUW (past dir.), Am. Psychol. Assn. (assoc.), Sigma Sigma Sigma (past chpt. pres.). Presbyterian. Home: 239 Science Park Rd State College PA 16801 Office: 315 S Allen St Suite 222 State College PA 16801

WOODRUFF, CAROLYN JOHNSON, lawyer; b. Tuscaloosa, Ala., June 14, 1955; d. Thomas Theo and Dorothy Carolyn (Lewis) Johnson; m. William Walter Woodruff, III, May 30, 1981. B.A. summa cum laude, Tenn. Temple U., 1977; M.A., Bob Jones U., 1979; J.D. with high honors, Duke U., 1983. Bar: N.C. 1983; C.P.A., N.C. Prof., Bob Jones U., Greenville, S.C., 1977-80; assoc. Tuggle Duggins Meschan & Elrod, P.A., Greensboro, N.C., 1983—. Research and mng. editor Duke Law Jour., 1982-83. Mem. ABA, N.C. Bar Assn., Greensboro Bar Assn., N.C. Assn. C.P.A.s. Republican. Baptist. Office: Tuggle Duggins Meschan & Elrod PA 228 W Market St Greensboro NC 27402

WOODRUFF, GEORGIA DELORES (WILBUR), nursing edn. adminstr.; b. Port Arthur, Tex., Mar. 31, 1926; d. Clarence Nelson and Gertrude Alice (Sewell) Wilbur; diploma St. Mary's Hosp. Sch. Nursing, 1948; A.A., Lamar Coll., 1947; m. James Calvin Woodruff, Sept. 27, 1957. Staff nurse various hosps. in Tex. and Ariz., 1948-61; nurse, Park Place Hosp., Port Arthur, Tex., 1961-65; dir. of nurses Newton County (Tex.) Hosp., 1966-67; dir. Home Health Assistance, Inc., Kirbyville, Tex., 1967-71; dir. Home Health-Home Care, Newton, Tex., 1972-76; inservice edn. dir. Mary Dickerson Hosp., Jasper, Tex., 1976—. Mem. Am., Tex. nurses assns., Nat. League Nurses. Democrat. Mem. Pentecostal Ch. Home: 511 Mays St Jasper TX 75951 Office: Mary Dickerson Hospital 1001 Dickerson Dr Jasper TX 75951

WOODRUFF, JUNE YVONNE, insurance agency executive; b. Bellflower, Calif., Jan. 26, 1930; d. Archie Leo and Virginia (Walton) Herrick; m. Ervin Dee Woodruff, Sept. 9, 1951; 1 son, Ervin Dee. A.A., Santa Ana Coll., 1950; B.A., Loma Linda U., 1951. Tchr., Rogue River Acad., Medford, Oreg., 1958-65; asst. librarian So. Oreg. Coll., 1966; sec. Sch. Dist. 549C, Medford, 1967-69; ins. agt. AAA of Oreg., Coos Bay, 1970-75; pres., ins. agt. Woodruff & Assocs., Inc., North Bend, Oreg., 1978—. Mem. Ind. Ins. Agts. Southwest Oreg., Ind. Agts. Oreg., Nat. Ind. Agts., Am. Bus. Women's Assn. (past treas., past chmn. edn. com.), Phi Beta Psi (past treas.). Republican. Lutheran. Club: Soroptomists (chmn. UN affairs 1981—, chmn. edn. com. 1983—). Home: 647 Shore Pines Heights Coos Bays OR 97420 Office: Woodruff & Assocs Inc 1860 Virginia Ave Suite 10 North Bend OR 97459

WOODRUFF, MARIAN DAVIS, former state legislator, art gallery ofcl.; b. Boston, Dec. 15, 1922; d. Harvey Nathaniel and Alice Marion (Rohde) Davis; m. Bliss Woodruff, Sept. 27, 1952; children—Nathaniel Rohde, William Watts, Davis Miller, Charlotte Bliss. B.A., Smith Coll., 1945. Guide, Met. Mus. Art, N.Y.C., 1945-46; lectr. Mus. Art, R.I. Sch. Design, Providence, 1946-51; dir. edn. Currier Gallery Art, Manchester, N.H., 1962-66, 70—; program dir. Nashua Arts and Sci. Center, N.H., 1968-69; mem. N.H. Ho. of Reps. from 18th Dist., 1973-76; instr. White Pines Coll., Chester, N.H., 1979-81, 86; field reviewer Inst. Mus. Services, 1985—. Mem. visual arts com. N.H. Commn. Arts; mem. White Mountain Environment Com., Nat. Alliance Arts Edn., Arts Advocacy Com., Nashua Conservation Commn., 1978-80; bd. dirs. Daniel Clark Found., pres., 1977-81; bd. dirs. United Health Systems Agy., 1978-81, Studio Potter, Inc., 1985—; mem. council Nashua League Craftsmen; mem. council League N.H. Craftsmen, 1979—, 84, bd. dirs., 1984—; founding mem. Nashua LWV; bd. dirs. Nashua Headstart. Mem. Am. Assn. Mus., Order Women Legislators, N.H. Micological Soc. (pres. 1978-80). Democrat. Unitarian-Universalist. Clubs: Appalachian Mountain, Randolph Mountain. Home: 587 Maple St Manchester NH 03104 Office: 192 Orange St Manchester NH 03104

WOODRUFF, MARTHA JOYCE, temporary nursing service executive; b. Unadilla, Ga., Jan. 3, 1941; d. Metz Loy and Helen (McCorvey) Woodruff. B.A., Shorter Coll., 1963; M.A., U. Tenn.-Knoxville, 1972. Tchr., Albany High Sch. (Ga.), 1963-69; instr. U. Tenn.-Knoxville, 1970-72; asst. prof. Valdosta State Coll. (Ga.), 1972-76; coordinator Staff Builders, Atlanta, 1976-78; pres., owner Med. Personnel Pool, Knoxville, 1978—, Personnel Pool of Knoxville, Inc., 1985—; mem., adviser Owners Adv. Council, Personnel Pool of Am., Ft. Lauderdale, Fla., 1980-82. Mem. Nat. League for Nursing, Franchise Owners Assn., Knoxville C. of C. (com. for cost containment 1982—), Blount County C. of C. (retirement com. 1983, mem. indsl. relations com. 1983). Republican. Methodist.

WOODRUM, PATRICIA ANN, librarian; b. Hutchinson, Kans., Oct. 11, 1941; d. Donald Jewell and Ruby Pauline (Shuman) Hoffman; m. Clayton Eugene Woodrum, Mar. 31, 1962; 1 child, Clayton Eugene II. B.A., Kans. State Coll., 1963; M.L.S., U. Okla., 1966. Head of reference Tulsa City-County Library, 1966-67, chief of extension, 1967-70, chief pub. services, 1970-73, asst. dir., 1973-76, dir., 1976—. Bd. dirs. Univ. Ctr. at Tulsa, 1982—, vice chmn., 1982-83; bd. dirs. Tulsa Area Council on Aging, 1973—, Okla. Health Systems Agy. Council, 1975—, Downtown Tulsa Unlimited, Tulsa Council for Internat. Visitors. Mem. ALA (mem. council 1978-81, com. accreditation 1985—), Pub. Library Assn. (nat. conf. chmn. 1986), Okla. Library Assn. (pres. 1978-79, Disting. Service award 1982), Tulsa Met. C. of C., Leadership Tulsa Alumni. Republican. Episcopalian. Avocations: skiing; backpacking; swimming. Office: Tulsa City-County Library 400 Civic Center Tulsa OK 74103

WOODS, ALISON SCOTT, systems engineering administrator; b. Chgo., July 28, 1952; d. Eugene Henri and Erma Lee (Willis) Scott; m. Charles Raymond Woods, May 7, 1982; children—Jamel, Jihan, Asia. B.A., Carleton Coll., Northfield, Minn., 1974. Systems engr. IBM, Mpls., 1974-79, Houston, 1979-81; regional rep., Houston, 1981-83, systems engring. mgr., Fort Worth, 1983—. Recipient IBM awards, 1977, 78, 81, 83, 85. Mem. Ch. of Christ. Home: 3925 Willow Way Rd Fort Worth TX 76133 Office: IBM 201 Main St 10th Floor Fort Worth TX 76102

WOODS, BARBARA LEE, lithographic company executive; b. Phoenix, Nov. 13, 1942; d. Samuel Thomas and Eunice Kathryn (Looney) Staggs; m. Frank B. Woods, Apr. 19, 1963; 1 child, Stephen Craig. Cert., Durham Bus. Coll., 1964; grad. Plaza Three Modelling Sch., 1983. Sec., First Nat. Life Ins. Co., Phoenix, 1963-65; escrow sec. Stewart Title Co., Phoenix, 1966-69; escrow sec. Minn. Title Co., Phoenix, 1970-72, escrow officer, br. mgr., 1972-75; sec. Franklin Press, Phoenix, 1976-78; co-owner, dir. corp. communications Woods Lithographics, Phoenix, 1978—. Bd. dirs. Phoenix Ad Club; bd. dirs., mem. celebrity auction com. Cystic Fibrosis Found., Phoenix; mem. steering com. Women for Warner, Phoenix, 1986. Mem. Phoenix Soc. Communicating Arts, Phoenix Ad Club, Nat. Assn. Women Bus. Owners, Nat. Assn. Female Execs. Republican. Baptist. Clubs: Arizona, Moon Valley Country (Phoenix). Avocations: walking; piano; calligraphy; hiking. Office: Woods Lithographics Inc 3433 W Earll Dr Phoenix AZ 85017

WOODS, BRENDA GENE, nursing adminstrator; b. Durham, N.C., Nov. 17, 1958; d. Gene Berkley and Frances Mae (Robinson) W. Student Va. Commonwealth U., 1976-78; B.S., Hampton Inst., 1982; postgrad Sch. Nursing, 1985—. R.N., N.C., Va. nurse asst. VA, Hampton, 1978-79; profl. nurses asst. Duke U. Hosp., Durham, N.C., 1980-81; ICU nurse Whittaker Meml. Hosp., Newport News, Va., 1982; adminstrv. supr. Hillcrest Convalescent, Durham, 1983; nursing supr. Hillhaven LaSalle, Durham, 1984; nurse Duke U. Hosp., Durham, 1982—. Hampton U. scholar, 1985-86. Mem. Nat. League Nursing (com. chmn.), Am. Nurses Assn. (del. conv. 1984), Nat. Black Nurses Assn., Am. Heart Assn., Chi Eta Phi. Democrat. Baptist. Office: Hampton U Sch Nursing Hampton VA 23607

WOODS, DIANE HOLLIS, university official; b. Altadena, Calif., Apr. 17, 1956; d. Richard Owen and Barbara (Hoffman) Hollis; m. Michael Gage Woods, Aug. 16, 1980. B.A., Ottawa U., 1978; postgrad. U. So. Calif., 1984—. Exec. asst. Fuller Theol. Sem., Pasadena, Calif., 1979-80; corp. legal sec. Barger and Wolen, Los Angeles, 1980-81; employment counselor Lynn Carol Employment Agy., Pasadena, 1981-82; asst. to dean Annenberg Sch. Communications, U. So. Calif., Los Angeles, 1982-85, asst. dir. continuing legal edn. programs, 1985—. Sec.-treas. sanctuary choir Pasadena Covenant Ch., 1984—. Mem. Am. Mgmt. Assn., Nat. Assn. Female Execs., Women in Mgmt. Democrat. Avocations: writing; photography; needlework; travel. Office: U So Calif Advanced Profl Program Law 105-D University Park Los Angeles CA 91101

WOODS, ELAINE MARIE, health clinic administrator; b. Abilene, Tex., Jan. 13, 1948; d. Clifford Utah and Christine Clair (Walter) Woods. B.S., Loyola U., 1970, M.S., 1974, Ph.D., 1979. Wardmaster Gen. Lenord Wood Army Hosp., St. Roberts, Mo., 1979-80; non-commd. officer in charge Finten Army Air Field Dispensary, Finten, Germany, 1980-82; wardmaster HSC 8th Med. Bn., Bad Kreuznach, Germany, 1982-83; non-commd. officer in charge outpatient clinic USA Health Clinic, Dugway, Utah, 1983—. Served with U.S. Army, 1976-83. Decorated Army Commendation medal (3). Democrat. Roman Catholic. Home: Route 7 Box 356 Abilene TX 79605 Office: USA Health Clinic Dugway UT 84022

WOODS, EVELYN LOCKETT, telephone company executive; b. Lafayette, La., Nov. 3, 1949; d. Bethel Louis and Evelyn Rose (Jones) Lockett; m. Gregory C. Frazier, Nov. 30, 1974 (div.); m. Richard Charles Woods, Oct. 12, 1985; children—Keli Frazier, Kendra Frazier. B.A. in Math., Engring., U. Houston, 1972. Cert. tchr., Tex. Tchr., Houston Ind. Sch. Dist., 1972-74; computer programmer Ill. Bell Telephone Co., Chgo., 1976-80, EDP auditor, 1980-82, mgr., 1982-84, dist. mgr., 1984—. Named Up & Coming Black Bus. & Profl. Women, Dollar & Sense Mag., 1985. Mem. Bell Mgmt. Women, Delta Sigma Theta. Democrat. Roman Catholic. Office: Ill Bell Telephone Co 225 W Randolph HQ 14B Chicago IL 60606

WOODS, GERALDINE PITTMAN, consultant NIH; b. West Palm Beach, Fla.; d. Oscar and Susie (King) Pittman; student Talladega Coll., 1938-40; B.S. in Zoology, Howard U., 1942; M.A., Radcliffe Coll. and Harvard Biol. Lab., 1943, Ph.D. in Neuro-embryology, 1945; D.Sc. (hon.), Benedict Coll., 1977; m. Robert I. Woods, Jan. 30, 1945; children—Jan, Jerri, Robert I. Instr., Howard U., Washington, 1945-46. Pres. Los Angeles chpt. Jack and Jill, 1954-56; pres. Aux. to Med., Dental and Pharm. Assn. So. Calif., 1951-54, state pres., 1955; mem. Lulaby Guild Children's Home Soc.; past mem. local met. bd., chmn. pub. affairs com. YWCA; mem. nat. adv. council Gen. Med. Scis. Inst. NIH, 1964-68, cons., 1969—, mem. gen. research support adv. com., div. research resources, 1971-74, 77-78; mem. fgn. service officers selection bds. Dept. State, 1967; nat. 1st v.p. Delta Sigma Theta, 1958-63, nat. pres., 1963-67, pres. Los Angeles Alumnae chpt., 1952-56, pres. Research and Edn. Found., 1983; mem. LWV, NAACP (life); mem. nat. bd. Nat. Council Negro Women (life); mem. regional com. Girl Scouts U.S.A., 1969-75, nat. bd., 1975—; v.p. Community Relations Conf. So. Calif.; exec. com. Leadership Conf. Civil Rights; chmn. def. adv. com. Women in Services, 1968; mem. air pollution manpower devel. adv. com. EPA, 1973-75; chmn. bd. trustees Howard U., 1975—, recipient Postgrad. Achievement award, 1978, Achievement award, 1980; trustee Calif. Mus. Found., Calif. Mus. Sci. and Industry, Atlanta U.; active Minority Access to Research Careers program; mem. Calif. Postsecondary Edn. Commn.; bd. dirs. Nat. Commn. Certification Physicians Assts. Named Woman of Year, Zeta Phi Beta, 1954; Meritorious Achievement award Nat. Panhellenic Council, 1966; spl. awards presented by Iota Phi Lambda, Howard U. Alumni Assn., Nat. Assn. Colored Women, Pres. Johnson's Council on Youth Opportunity; tribute 2nd Western States Minority Biomed. Support Program U. Calif., San Diego, 1977; Minerva award Los Angeles Alumnae chpt. Delta Sigma Theta, 1978, Mary Church Terrell award, 1979; Scroll of Merit, Nat. Med. Assn., 1979; Atlanta U. chemistry scholarship named in her honor; named one of 20 Famous Black Scientists, Nabisco. Mem. Nat. Acad. Scis., N.Y. Acad. Scis., Inst. Medicine (dir. Robert Wood Johnson Health Policy Fellowships 1973—), AAAS, AAUP, Fedn. Am. Scientists, Nat. Sci. Inst., Phi Beta Kappa. Congregationalist. Home: 12065 Rose Marie Ln Los Angeles CA 90049

WOODS, HARRIETT, lieutenant governor; b. Cleve., June 2, 1927; student U. Chgo. Coll.; B.A., U. Mich., 1949; m. James B. Woods, Jan. 2, 1953; 3 children. Newspaper reporter, St. Louis; producer TV sta., St. Louis; mem. Mo. Senate, 1976-84; lt. gov. of Mo., 1984—; mem. Mo. State Hwy. Commn., Mo. State Transp. Commn. Active University City (Mo.) Council, Nat. League of Cities, Mo. Mcpl. League, St. Louis County Mcpl. League, LWV, civic orgns. St. Louis and University City. Democrat; Democratic nominee for U.S. Senate, 1982. Office: Missouri State Capitol Jefferson City MO 65101

WOODS, LAURIE, lawyer; b. N.Y.C., Nov. 18, 1947; d. William M. and Sylvia Leona (Bottstein) W.; m. John W. Corwin, June 1, 1968; children—Robert Woods-Corwin, James Woods-Corwin. B.A., New Sch.-N.Y.C., 1969; J.D., Boston U., 1973. Bar: N.Y., 1974. Staff atty. MFY Legal Services, N.Y.C., 1973-79; exec. dir. Nat. Ctr. on Women and Family Law, N.Y.C., 1979—; bd. dirs. N.Y. Women Against Rape, 1982—, Feminist Legal Strategies Project, Washington, 1983—. Contbr. articles in field to publs. Bd. dirs. Gingerbread Day Care Ctr., N.Y.C., 1982-83. Mem. ABA, N.Y. State Bar Assn., Assn. Bar City N.Y., N.Y. Women's Bar Assn. Office: Nat Ctr on Women and Family Law 799 Broadway Room 402 New York NY 10003

WOODS, MARY CAROLINE MCGONAGILL, geologist, editor; b. Amarillo, Tex. Jan 29, 1921; d. Frank E. and Willie M. (Stroud) McGonagill. B.A. in Geology, U. Tex., 1942; postgrad. geology, environ. studies U. Calif.-Davis, 1971, 75, 76. Registered geologist Calif. Geol. technician Pure Oil Co., Ft. Worth, 1943-47; sec. Geol. dept. U. So. Calif., Los Angeles, 1947-49; ground water geologist U.S. Bur. Reclamation, Sacramento, 1964-73; geologist Calif. Div. Mines and Geology, Sacramento, 1974—, editor-in-chief Calif. Geology mag., 1976—; com. mem. Gov.'s Emergency Task Force Earth-Quake Preparedness, Calif., 1981-83. Contbr. numerous articles to Calif. Geology mag. Mem. Assn. Engring. Geologists, Assn. Earth Sci. Editors, Nat. Assn. Geology Tchrs., AAUW. Office: Calif Div Mines Geology 1416 9th St Room 1341 Sacramento CA 95814

WOODS, PATRICIA ANN, microbiologist; b. Akron, Ohio, Aug. 25, 1953; d. Theodore Nathaniel and Marion Henrietta (Albert) W.; A.A., Glendale Community Coll., 1974; B.S. in Microbiology, U. Ariz., 1975. Microbiologist, U.S. Dept. Health and Human Services, Centers for Disease Control, Hepatitis Labs., Phoenix, 1976-83, mgr. fed. women's program hepatitis lab., 1980, viral gastroenteritis lab., Atlanta, 1983—. Leader Girl Scouts U.S.A., 1979-81; sec. Fed. Women's Program Interagy. Council, 1981-82. Mem. Am. Soc. Microbiology, Am. Soc. Med. Tech., Ariz. Med. Lab. Assn. (Lawrence Jessop Meml. award for microbiology 1974; pres. 1980). Republican. Clubs: United Fedn. of Doll Clubs. Home: 106 Regency Woods Dr Atlanta GA 30319 Office: 1600 Clifton Rd Atlanta GA 30333

WOODS, RUTH DIAL, educational administrator; b. Pembroke, N.C., May 22, 1937; s. A.G. and Ruby (Carter) D.; m. James Ray Roberts, Sept. 6, 1955 (div. 1971); children—Constance Susan, Stephanie Rose; m. Noah Woods, Feb. 16, 1973; children—Noah Ollin, Aaron Reuben. A.B. in Spanish, English, Meredith Coll., 1962; M.A. Ed. in Ednl. Adminstrn. and Supervision, Pembroke State U., 1981. Cert. tchr., ednl. media specialist, prin., supr. Sec. U.S. Commn., Bethesda, Md., 1955, Ford Motor Co., Dearborn, 1956-58; comml. biller Blair Transit Mich. Express, Detroit, 1955-56; fed. programs adminstr. N.C. Fund, Durham, 1965-67; program dir. New Careers Project Tri-County Community Action, Inc., Rockingham, N.C., 1968, communications coordinator, 1968; area dir. Southeastern Community Action Programs, Inc., 1968-70; dir. Lumberton Ctr. N.C. Manpower, Inc., Chapel Hill, 1970-72; program planning and devel. officer Lumbee Regional Devel. Assn., Inc., Pembroke, 1972; ednl. media specialist Fairgrove Sch. Robeson County Bd. Edn., Lumberton, N.C., 1972-77, program cons., 1977, dir. Indian edn., 1977-82, asst. supt. div. compensatory edn., 1982—; Gubernatorial appointment to adv. council Robeson County Unit, N.C. Dept. Corrections; mem. state evaluation com. on tchr. edn. N.C. State Dept. Pub. Instrn., cons. in field. Mem. spl. com. on minority presence Girl Scouts U.S.A.; mem. N.C. state coordinating com. Internat. Women's Yr., del. nat. conf., N.C. state co-chmn., mem. continuing com. of conf.-nat. commn. women; chmn. Spotlight on Women Conf., N.C. Fed. Bus. and Profl. Women's Clubs, so. area v.p.; pres. Pembroke Bus. and Profl. Women's Club; chmn. 1978 Fall Forum, N.C. Council Women's Orgns.; corr. sec. N.C. United for Equal Rights Amendment, 1978; chmn. planning com. N.C. State Commn. Indian Affairs, 1970, mem. commn., 1979-82; chmn. planning com. State Plan for Indian Library and Info. Services, Nat. Indian Edn. Assn.; mem. planning com. for Native Am. Women's Seminar, United Methodist Ch.; mem. adv. council OHOYO Resource Ctr., Wichita, Tex.; bd. govs. N.C. Univ., 1985—. Recipient Woman of Yr. award Pembroke Bus. and Profl. Women's Club, 1978, Gov.'s award for Community Leadership, N.C. Human Relations Commn., 1978, Henry Berry Lowry award Lumbee Regional Devel. Assn., 1980. Mem. N.C. Assn. Educators (Robeson County Unit), NEA, Nat. Indian Edn. Assn., N.C. Library Assn., Southeastern Library Assn., N.C. Consortium on Indian Edn., N.C. Women's Forum, N.C. Women's Polit. Caucus, Native Am. Women's Caucus, Women's Equity Action League, Pembroke Bus. and Profl. Women's Club. Democrat. Avocations: reading; quilting; gardening. Home: Rt 2 Box 142 Pembroke NC 28372 Office: Robeson County Bd Edn PO Box 1328 Lumberton NC 28359

WOODS, SANDRA KAY, brewing company real estate executive; b. Loveland, Colo., Oct. 11, 1944; d. Ivan H. and Florence L. (Betz) Harris; m. Gary A. Woods, June 11, 1967; children—Stephanie Michelle, Michael Harris. B.A., U. Colo., 1966, M.A., 1967. Personnel mgmt. specialist CSC, Denver, 1967; asst. to regional dir. HEW, Denver, 1968-69; urban renewal rep. HUD, Denver, 1970-73, dir. program analysis, 1974-75, asst. regional dir. community planning and devel., 1976-77, regional dir. fair housing, 1978-79; mgr. eastern facility project Adolph Coors Co., Golden Colo., 1980, dir. real estate, 1981, v.p. corp. real estate, 1982—; pres. Industries for Jefferson County (Colo.), 1985. Mem. Exec. Exchange, The White House, 1980; bd. dirs. Golden Local Devel. Corp. (Colo.), 1981-82; fundraising dir. Coll. Arts and Scis., U. Colo., Boulder, 1982-83; mem. exec. bd. NCCJ, Denver, 1982-84; v.p. Women in Bus., Inc., Denver, 1982-83; mem. steering com. 1984 Yr. for All Denver Women, 1983-84. Named Outstanding Young Women Am., U.S. Jaycees, 1974, 78. Mem. Indsl. Devel. Resources Council (bd. dirs. 1986), Am. Mgmt. Assn., Denver C. of C. (co-chairperson steering com. for water 1982-84, Disting. Young Exec. award 1974, mem. Leadership Denver, 1976-77), Denver Women's Forum, Phi Beta Kappa, Pi Alpha Alpha. Republican. Presbyterian. Club: PEO (Loveland, Colo.). Office: Adolph Coors Co Corp Real Estate 807 Golden CO 80401

WOODS, SUSANNE, educator; b. Honolulu, May 12, 1943; d. Samuel Ernest and Gertrude (Cullom) W.; B.A. in Polit. Sci., UCLA, 1964, M.A. in English, 1965; Ph.D. in English and Comparative Lit. (Woodrow Wilson fellow 1968-70), Columbia U., 1970; M.A. (hon.), Brown U., 1978. Asst. editor Rand Corp., Calif., 1963-65; instr. Ventura (Calif.) Coll., 1965-66; lectr. CUNY, 1967-69; asst. prof. U. Hawaii, 1969-72; asst. prof. Brown U., Providence, 1972-77, asso. prof. English, 1977-83, prof., 1983—, dir. grad. studies, 1986—; vis. asso. prof. U. Calif., 1981-82. Active various polit. campaigns, 1960-64, 68-76, 84; mem. staff Senator Daniel K. Inouye, 1963. Bronson fellow, 1976; Huntington Library fellow, 1979-80, 81; Clark Library fellow, 1981; Huntington-NEH fellow, 1984-85. Mem. MLA (chmn. div. Seventeenth Century English lit., 1982, del. assembly 1983-86), N.E. MLA (chmn. English Renaissance sect. 1978, Milton sect. 1983), Renaissance Soc. Am., Milton Soc., Spenser Soc., Alpha Gamma Delta. Democrat. Episcopalian. Club: Athenaeum (Pasadena, Calif.). Author: English Versification, 1983; Natural Emphasis, 1984; contbr. numerous articles to profl. jours.; reviewer for various profl. jours. including Renaissance Quar., Jour. of English and Germanic Philology, Women's Rev. of Books; reader for PMLA jour., SEL jour., also various presses. Office: Box 1852 Brown U Providence RI 02912

WOODS, WENDY, reporter, editor; b. Newark, Nov. 16, 1952; d. Julian Jonathan and Eileen Margaret (Woods) A.; m. Nicholas Cobalt Gorski, May 29, 1983. Student Wilkes Coll., Wilkes-Barre, Pa., 1970-72; B.A. in Film, Syracuse U., 1976. News reporter Sta. WILK, Wilkes-Barre, 1971-72; reporter, anchor Sta. WIXT-TV, Syracuse, N.Y., 1975-81; corr. Cable News Network, San Francisco, 1981-82; news reporter Sta. KGO-TV (ABC), San Francisco, 1982—; lectr. in field. Editor newsletter Newsbytes, 1983—(Best Online Publ. award Computer Press Assn. 1985). Recipient best environ. reporting award Central N.Y. Environ. Assn., 1979; best reporting under deadline pressure award Syracuse Press Club, 1980, best investigative reporting award, 1981. Mem. AFTRA, Acad. TV Arts and Scis., Nat. Assn. Broadcast Employees and Technicians, San Francisco Pub. TV. Democrat. Roman Catholic. Club: Sierra.

WOODSIDE, LISA NICOLE, college dean; b. Portland, Oreg., Sept. 7, 1944; d. Lee and Emma (Wenstrom) W.; student Reed Coll., 1962-65; M.A., U. Chgo., 1968; Ph.D. (Am. Assn. Papyrology grantee, S. Maude Kaemmerling fellow), Bryn Mawr Coll., 1972; cert. Harvard U. Inst. for Ednl. Mgmt., 1979; m. John S. Bilinski, Jr., June 8, 1973. Mem. dean's staff Bryn Mawr Coll., 1970-72; asst. prof. Widener U., Chester, Pa., 1972-77, asso. prof. humanities, 1978-83, asst. dean student services, 1972-76, asso. dean, 1976-79, dean,

1979—; acad. dean Holy Family Coll., Phila., 1983—; accreditor Commn. on Higher Edn., Middle States Assn., 1979-83. City commr. for community relations Chester, 1980-83; mem. Adult Edn. Council Phila.; trustee YWCA. Mem. Am. Assn. Higher Edn., Council Ind. Colls., Eastern Assn. Coll. Deans, Pa. Assn. Colls. and Tchr. Educators, AAUW (univ. rep. 1975-83), Phi Eta Sigma, Alpha Sigma Lambda. Episcopalian. Club: Am. Fox Terrier. Home: 217 Avondale Rd Wallingford PA 19086 Office: Holy Family Coll Torresdale Philadelphia PA 19114

WOODSON, MARY P., technical writer; b. Watermill, N.Y., Dec. 25, 1937; d. Clifford Rudolph and Lessie (Parker) Finney; m. Charles L. Woodson, Feb. 26, 1956; children—Patricia, Dennis, Mary Eileen. B.A. in Psychology, SUNY-Stony Brook, 1971. Document analyst Aspen Pubs., Rockville, Md, 1978-79; assoc. lexicographer Aspen Pubs., 1979-81, tech. writer, 1981—; documentation cons., founder, chief exec. officer Mary Woodson Documentation, Germantown, Md., 1983—. Author numerous tech. manuals. Tutor, Montgomery City Schs., Rockville, 1981. Recipient Cert. of Appreciation, Suffolk County Dept. Welfare, 1973. Mem. Washington Ind. Computer Cons., U.S. Entrepreneur Assn., Tandy Users Group, Bus. and Profl. Women. Episcopalian. Avocations: playing guitar; theater; dancing; reading. Address: 11469 Appledowre Way Germantown MD 20874

WOODSON, RUBY GARRARD, educational administrator, chemistry educator; b. Dothan, Ala., June 22, 1931; d. David and Ella Mae (McClendon) Garrard; m. William Dallas Woodson, Dec. 22, 1956 (div. May 1970); 1 child, William. B.S. in Chemistry, Fla. A&M U., 1951; M.A. in Edn., Am. U., 1959. Tchr. chemistry Moton High Sch., Brooksville, Fla., 1951-52; tchr. math. and sci. Pub. Sch. of D.C., 1953-66; tchr., chmn. dept. sci. Western High Sch., Washington, 1966-69; assoc. prof. chemistry. U. Md., College Park, 1970-71; tchr., chmn. sci. dept. Wilson High Sch., Washington, 1969-73; founder, dir. Cromwell Acad., Washington, 1973—; cons. Office of Edn., Washington, 1974-76. Author: Some Recent Advances in the Teaching of High School Chemistry, 1979. Attendee First Black Polit. Conv., Gary, Ind., 1971; participant Congl. Black Caucus Conv., Washington, 1981-84. Amos Lewis scholar, 1948; NSF grantee, 1957, 63, 67, 71; Mem. Nat. Assn. Secondary Sch. Prins., NEA, Black Child Devel. Assn., Parents Assn. Inc. (pres. 1977-85). Roman Catholic. Avocations: travel; theater; swimming. Home: 3202 McKinley St NW Washington DC 20015 Office: Cromwell Acad 3100 Military Rd NW Washington DC 20015

WOODSON, WILBERTA, consultant; b. Tecumseh, Nebr., Sept. 7, 1939; d. Charles Wilber and Edith Mildred Woodson; student Coll. of Emporia, 1957-61; B.A., Wichita State U., 1963; M.A., U. Hawaii, 1966; postgrad. U. Conn., 1968, U. Ill., 1969-70; M.S., U. San Francisco, 1981; children—Rebecca Louise. Research asst., computer programmer U. Hawaii, Honolulu, 1964-66; computer programmer Newport News (Va.) Shipbldg., 1967; computer programmer econ. research U. Ill., Urbana, 1969-70; cons. Ventura County Mental Health, Ventura, Calif., 1973-78; tech. writer Mohawk Data Scis., Los Gatos, Calif., 1978-79; documentation specialist Tandem Computers, Cupertino, Calif., 1979-84; documentation specialist Oracle Corp., Menlo Park, Calif., 1984-85; cons., 1985—. Mem. Nat. Assn. Female Execs., Soc. Tech. Communication, Profl. and Tech. Cons. Assn. Democrat. Unitarian. Home: 1056 Queensbrook Dr San Jose CA 95129

WOODSWORTH, ANNE, university administrator; b. Fredericia, Denmark, Feb. 10, 1941; d. Thorvald Ernst and Roma Yrea (Jensen) Lindner; m. Sverre Egil Lunder; m. Peter Ross Woodsworth (div.); 1 dau., Yrsa Anne. B.F.A., U. Man., 1962; B.L.S., U. Toronto, 1964; M.L.S., 1969. Med. librarian Toronto Western Hosp., 1969-70; head reference dept. U. Toronto, 1970-74; research and planning officer Ont. Ednl. Communications Authority, Toronto, 1974-75; personnel dir. Toronto Pub. Library, 1975-78; dir. libraries York U., Toronto, 1978-83; assoc. provost U. Pitts., 1983—; pres. Info. Cons., Toronto, 1974-83. Author: Project Progress: A Study, 1981; The Alternative Press in Canada, 1972; also jour. articles and revs. Bd. dirs. Population Research Found., 1980-83. Isbister scholar, 1961; grantee Ont. Arts Council, 1974, Can. Council, 1974. Mem. Assn. Research Libraries (bd. dirs. 1981-84), Can. Assn. Research Libraries (pres. 1981-83). Office: Cathedral of Learning U Pitts Pittsburgh PA 15260

WOODWARD, DEBORAH BOROS, writer, consultant; b. Cleve., May 13, 1950; d. Albert George and Rhoda Beatrice (West) Boros; m. Arthur Quincy Woodward III, May 6, 1973. B.A., U. Mich., 1973. Freelance writer, Richmond, Va., 1975-78; editor Richmond Mag., Va., 1978-79; owner, operator Deborah Woodward Ltd., Richmond, 1979-84; ptnr. Rudisill, Inc., Alexandria, Va., 1985—. Scriptwriter, assoc. producer documentary film The Common Wealth of Women, 1985 (finalist Am. Film Festival). Mem. Washington Ind. Writers. Avocations: dance; renovating Victorian homes. Office: Rudisill Inc 2039 W Grace St Richmond VA 23220

WOODWARD, FAE BLANCHE, journalist; b. Santa Ana, Calif., Nov. 15, 1925; d. Louis George and Rhoda Miranda (Morris) Willits; m. Billy J. Woodward, Nov. 24, 1947; children—Billy, Bobby, Tonni, Clarissa, Kevin, Woodra. Cub reporter, society editor Progress Bull., Pomona, Calif., 1944-48; society editor Telegram Tribune, San Luis Obispo, Calif., 1948-49; Corcoran corr. Fresno Bee (Calif.), 1953-54; corr. Ukiah (Calif.) Daily Jour., 1956-58, 61-64, teletypesetter, 1960, 71, lifestyles editor, 1971—. Tenderfoot leader, mem. tng. com. Sonoma-Mendocino council Boy Scouts Am., 1967—; mem. young women's program Ch. of Jesus Christ of Latter-day Saints, Ukiah, 1981—; mem. sch. adv. com. compensatory edn. Ukiah Unified Sch. Dist., 1974-77, also adv. com. photograpy, 1979—. Recipient Golden Rule award Calif. Assn. for Retarded, 1980; Disting. Achievement Pub. Info. award North Coast Coordinating Council Devel. Disabilities, 1980, Silver Beaver award Boy Scouts Am., 1983. Mem. Calif. Press Women's Assn. Republican. Home: 6785 W Hwy 20 Star Route 2 Ukiah CA 95482 Office: Ukiah Daily Jour 590 S School St Ukiah CA 95482

WOODWARD, GRETA CHARMAINE, construction company executive, rental and investment property manager; b. Congress, Ohio, Oct. 28, 1930; d. Richard Thomas and Grace Lucetta (Palmer) Duffey; m. John Jay Woodward, Oct. 29, 1949; children—Kirk Jay, Brad Ewing, Clay William. Bookkeeper, Kaufman's Texaco, Wooster, Ohio, 1948-49; office mgr. Holland Furnace Co., Wooster, 1948-49; acctg. clk. Columbus and So. Ohio Electric, Columbus, 1949-50; interviewer, clk. State Ohio Bur. Employment Services, Columbus, 1950-51; clk. Def. Constrn. Supply Ctr. (U.S. Govt.) (formerly Columbus Gen. Depot), 1951-52; treas. Woodward Co., Inc., Reynoldsburg, Ohio, 1963—. Newspaper columnist Briarcliff News, 1960-63. Active Reynoldsburg PTA, 1960-67. Methodist. Avocations: bike-riding; crocheting; writing poetry; stock-market; financial magazines. Office: Woodward Excavating Co Inc 7320 Tussing Rd Reynoldsburg OH 43068

WOODWARD, ISABEL AVILA, writer; b. Key West, Fla., Mar. 14, 1906; d. Alfredo and Isabel (Lopez) Avila; student Fla. State Coll. for Women, 1925, A.B. in Edn., 1938; cert. in teaching Spanish, U. Miami, 1961; summer study U. Fla., Eckerd Coll.; postgrad. St. Lawrence U., U. Miami; m. Clyde B. Woodward, June 6, 1944 (dec.); children—Joy Avis Ball, Greer Isabel Woodward Sucke. Tchr., Key West, 1927-42, remedial reading cons., 1941-42; reading tchr., asst. reading lab. and clinic St. Lawrence U., summer 1941; Spanish translator U.S. Office of Censorship, Miami, 1943; tchr. Central Beach Elem. Sch., Miami Beach, Fla., 1943-44, Silver Bluff Elem. Sch., 1943-50, Henry West Lab. Sch., Coral Gables, Fla., 1955-57, Dade Demonstration Sch., Miami, 1957-61; author 125 sch. radio lessons for teaching Spanish, Dade County Elem. Schs., 1961; tchr. Spanish Workshop for Fla.; speaker poetry and short story writing, 1977; guest lectr. on writing the short story Fla. Inst. Tech., Jensen Beach, 1981; freelance writer; contbr. to Listen Mag., Sunshine Mag., Lookout Mag., Christian Sci. Monitor, Miami Herald, Three/Four, Child Life, Wee Wisdom, Fla. Wildlife, Young World; sponsor Port St. Lucie Jr. Woman's Club, 1983. Recipient Honoris Causa award Alpha Delta Kappa, 1972-74, award Contra Costa Times, Calif., 1985; named one of 5 Outstanding Fla. Tchrs., 1972-74. Mem. Nat. League Am. Pen Women (1st v.p. Greater Miami br. 1974-76, historian 1978—, librarian 1978—, awards for writing 1973, 74, 77, 1st and 3d place state writing awards for adult and juvenile fiction 1983, state 1st prize short story 1985), AAUW, Alpha Delta Kappa, Psi Psi Psi. Address: 1950 Palm City Rd Apt 6-301 Stuart FL 33497

WOODWARD, MELINDA ELLICE, state mental health administrator; b. Atlanta, May 8, 1943; d. Richard Lewis and Helen (Beal) W.; m. James Merwyn Burke, Dec. 11, 1972 (div. 1976). A.B., Radcliffe Coll. Harvard U., 1965; M.P.A., Princeton U., 1969. Planner Vera Inst. Justice, N.Y.C., 1969-71; planner/cons. Oreg. Corrections Div., Salem, 1971-72; planner/cons. Oreg. Mental Health Div., Salem, 1972-78, dep. asst. adminstr., 1978-80, asst. adminstr., 1980-85; dir. support services Fairview Tng. Ctr., Salem, 1985—. A.P. Gordon traveling fellow, Mexico, 1964; Fulbright scholar, Argentina, 1965-66. Democrat. Office: Fairview Tng Ctr 2250 Strong Rd SE Salem OR 97310

WOODWELL, MARGOT BELL, broadcasting company executive; b. Pitts., Mar. 5, 1936; d. Davitt Stranahan and Marian (Whieldon) Bell; m. William Herron Woodwell, June 24, 1960; children—Davitt Bell, William Herron, James Ross. A.B., Vassar Coll., 1957. Dir. community support Sta. WQED, Pitts., 1978-84, v.p., sta. mgr., 1984—. Pres. bd. trustees St. Edmunds Acad., Pitts., 1972-75; pres. bd. trustees Episcopal Diocese Pitts., 1975-78, mem. standing com., 1982—; chmn. Episcopal Diocese Renewal Fund, Pitts., 1980—; trustee Vassar Coll., Poughkeepsie, N.Y., 1982—. Mem. Nat. Soc. Fund Raising Execs. Republican. Office: Sta-WQED 4802 5th Ave Pittsburgh PA 15217

WOODWORTH, GENE BOSWELL, educator; b. Collinwood, Tenn., Oct. 11, 1926; d. Carl and Vida (Langford) Boswell; B.S., Middle Tenn. State U., 1968, M.A., 1975; children—Jill, Camille, Patricia, John. Tchr., Tullahoma (Tenn.) Sch. System, 1968—. Named Tchr. of Yr., Tullahoma, Tenn., 1984-85. Mem. Assn. for Supervision and Curriculum Devel., NEA, Tenn. Edn. Assn., Tullahoma Edn. Assn., Middle Tenn. Edn. Assn., AAAS, Bus. and Profl. Women Manchester (Woman of Yr. 1985-86). Democrat. Methodist. Home: 704 Madison St Manchester TN 37355 Office: Tullahoma West Middle Sch Tullahoma TN 37388

WOODY, CAROL CLAYMAN, mfg. co. ofcl; b. Bristol, Va., May 20, 1949; d. George Neal and Ida Mae (Nelms) Clayman; B.S. in Math., Coll. William and Mary, Williamsburg, Va., 1971; M.B.A. with distinction (IBM Corp. fellow 1978, Stephen Bufton Meml. Ednl. Found. grantee 1978-79), Wake Forest U., 1979; m. Robert William Woody, Aug. 19, 1972. Programmer trainee GSA, 1971-72; systems engr. Citizens Fidelity Bank & Trust Co., Louisville, 1972-75; programmer/analyst-tng. coordinator Blue Bell, Inc., Greensboro, N.C., 1975-79; mgr. adminstrv. info. systems and tech. services J.E. Baker Co., York, Pa., 1979-81, mgr. adminstrv. info. systems and tech. services, 1981-82; fin. design supr. Lycoming div. AVCO, Stratford, Conn., 1982—; mem. Data Processing Standards Bd., 1977, CICS/VS Adv. Council, 1975, Health Resources Planning and Devel., 1980—. Bd. dirs. Ruth Gasnell Ednl. Found., 1981—. Mem. Am. Bus. Woman's Assn. (chpt. v.p. 1978-79; Merit award 1978), Nat. Assn. Female Execs., Delta Omicron (alumni pres. 1973-75, regional chmn. 1979—). Republican. Presbyterian. Author various manuals. Office: 550 S Main St Stratford CT 06497

WOODY, KATHLEEN JOANNA, lawyer; b. Honolulu, May 3, 1949; d. Edward Franklin and Norma Lee (Harris) W. A.B. magna cum laude, U. Miami, 1973, J.D., 1976; LL.M., Columbia U., 1981; postgrad. Oxford U., 1982. Vice pres., tax cons. Franklin Tax Service, Inc., Silver Spring, Md., 1967-76; real estate agt., sales mgr. Pershing Real Estate Co., Silver Spring, 1972-76; admitted to Fla. bar, 1976, D.C. bar, 1977, U.S. Tax Ct. bar, 1977, U.S. Supreme Ct. bar, 1980; atty. Office Comptroller of Currency, Washington, 1976-78, N.Y.C., 1979-80; mem. faculty New Sch. for Social Research, N.Y.C., 1980; teaching fellow, dir. tng. internat. tax program Harvard Law Sch., 1981-82; mem. faculty Inst. Comparative Law, U. San Diego, 1982; ptnr. firm Woody & Woody, Washington, 1982; adj. prof. law Georgetown U. Sch. Law. Mem. Internat. Bar Assn., ABA, D.C. Bar Assn., Fed. Bar Assn., Am. Arbitration Assn. (arbitrator), Assn. Bar City N.Y. Baptist. Club: St. Bartholomew's Community (N.Y.C.). Contbr. articles to profl. jours.

WOODY, MARSHA, dance educator; b. Oklahoma City, Dec. 25, 1935; d. Doyle L. and Paulene (Lambert) W.; m. Marion Frank Zummo, Dec. 30, 1956; 1 child, Monique Woody. Student Lamar U., 1954-55, Joffrey Sch., N.Y.C., 1956-58, Sch. Am. Ballet, N.Y.C., 1977, David Howard Sch., N.Y.C., 1975, Harkness Sch., N.Y.C., 1968. Cert. Dance Masters Am., Tex. Assn. Tchrs. Dance. Tchr. dance sch., Beaumont, Tex., 1952-55; owner, dance dir. Marsha Woody Acad., Beaumont, 1956—; founder, artistic dir. Beaumont Civic Ballet, 1971—; lectr. in field; performing mem. Southwest Regional Ballet, 1981, mem. Honor Co., 1982; field judge Am. Ballet Competition, 1983. Produced (profl. dancers) Robert La Fosse, Am. Ballet Theatre, N.Y.C., Edmund La Fosse, Royal Winnipeg Ballet of Can., Kristine Richmond, Houston Ballet. Bd. dirs. Beaumont Arts Related Curriculum, Beaumont Med. Surg. Hosp., 1985—; panel advisor Tex. Commn. Arts in Austin, 1984-85. Mem. Beaumont Symphony Guild, Beaumont Community Theatre, Beaumont Opera Buffs, Beaumont Ballet Soc. Republican. Roman Catholic. Clubs: Beaumont Country, Tower (Beaumont). Avocations: travel; collecting antiques; knitting; swimming; skiing. Office: Marsha Woody Acad 3717 Calder St Beaumont TX 77706

WOODY, MARY FLORENCE, nursing educator, university administrator; b. Chambers County, Ala., Mar. 31, 1926; d. Hugh Ernest and May Lillie (Gilliland) W.; diploma Charity Hosp. Sch. Nursing, 1947; B.S., Columbia U., 1953, M.A., 1955. Staff nurse Wheeler Hosp., Lafayette, Ala., 1947-48; polio nurse Willard Parker Hosp., N.Y.C., 1949; staff nurse, supr. VA Hosp., Montgomery, Ala., 1950-53; faculty mem., field supr., nursing dept. Tchrs. Coll., Columbia U., N.Y.C., 1955-56; asst. dir. nursing Emory U. Hosp., clin. asst. prof. Emory U. Sch. Nursing, Atlanta, 1956-68; asst. dir., then dir. nursing Grady Meml. Hosp., Atlanta, 1968-79; dean, prof. Sch. Nursing, Auburn (Ala.) U., 1979—; chmn. Ga. Statewide Master Planning Com. for Nursing and Nursing Edn., 1971-75; faculty preceptor patient care adminstrn. Sch. Public Health, U. Minn., 1977-79. Recipient Spl. Recognition, 5th Dist. and Ga. Nurses Assn., 1978. Fellow Am. Acad. Nursing (charter); mem. Am. Nurses Assn., Nat. League Nursing, Am. Heart Assn., Sigma Theta Tau. Democrat. Chmn. bd. dirs. Am. Jour. Nursing Co., 1978-83. Office: Sch Nursing Auburn U Auburn AL 36849

WOOLCOCK, OZEIL FRYER, journalist, educator, editor; b. Atlanta, Nov. 25; d. John Perry and Carrie (Moreland) F. B.A., Clark Coll., Atlanta, 1932; postgrad. Atlanta U. Journalist, Atlanta Daily World, 1945—; educator pub. schs., Atlanta, 1951-74; reporter Nat. Ret. Tchrs., Ga. Ret. Tchrs., Atlanta Ret. Tchrs., 1974—. Contbr. articles to world Travel By-Weekly, 1979—, also editor. Recipient achievement service awards Clark Coll., 1982, 83, Journalist award Delta Sigma Theta, 1981, 82, Community Service plaque High Mus. of Art, 1983, Conf. of Black Mayors, 1983. Mem. Soc. Profl. Journalists, Nat. Assn. Media Women (corr. sec. 1980-82). Episcopalian.

WOOLDRIDGE, MARY JANE, fashion writer, photo stylist; b. Raleigh, N.C., Apr. 3, 1958; d. Oscar Bailey Wooldridge, Jr. and Martha Jane (Clarke) Wooldridge Jordan. A.B. in History, Duke U., 1980; summer study New Coll., Oxford, England, 1979. Gen. reporter, intern News & Observer, Raleigh, 1979-80; fashion writer N.Y. Times Mag., N.Y.C., 1980-81; freelance writer N.Y.C., 1981-82; asst. Eloit Janeway, Economist, N.Y.C., 1982-83; fashion writer, photo stylist Miami Herald, Fla., 1983—. Author (with others) Best Publications, 1982, also articles. Mem. N.C. Youth Adv. Bd., Raleigh, 1975-76; chmn. N.C. State Youth Councils, 1975-76. Angier B. Duke scholar Duke U., 1978-80. Democrat. Mem. Interdenominational Ch. Avocations: photography, horseback riding; sewing; design; travel. Office: Miami Herald 1 Herald Plaza Miami FL 33101

WOOLDRIDGE, RHONDA WELFARE, writer and editor; b. Raleigh, N.C., May 4, 1957; d. Fred Griffith and Nancy (Cook) Welfare; m. Peter William Wooldridge, Dec. 19, 1981; 1 child, Zachary. B.S., Northwestern U., 1979. Staff editor Am. Nuclear Soc., LaGrange Park, Ill., 1979-81; staff writer Tuscaloosa News (Ala.), 1982-85; tech. editor Research Triangle Inst., Research Triangle Park, N.C., 1986—. Recipient 1st Place Newswriting award Ala. AP, 1982, 2d Place, 1983. Mem. Women in Communications, West Ala. Registry Interpreters for the Deaf, Kappa Delta. Baptist. Home: 1719-C E Cornwallis Rd Durham NC 27713 Office: Research Triangle Inst PO Box 12194 Research Triangle Park NC 27709

WOOLF, ESTHER BARASCH, real estate executive; b. Russia, Dec. 24, 1913; came to U.S., 1921; d. Hyman and Celia (Mandelbaum) Barasch; grad. high sch.; 1 dau., Louise Gersen Sharir. Office asst., then office mgr. F & P Mgmt. Co. 1932-37; asst. to pres. L.V. Hoffman & Co., Inc., 1937-42; with Marx Realty & Improvement, N.Y.C., 1942-43; with Williams & Co., Inc. and Williams Real estate Co., Inc., N.Y.C., 1943—, successively adminstrv. v.p., fin. v.p., sr. v.p. fin. and adminstrn., also dir.; dir. L.F. Rush, Inc., Teaneck, N.J. Mem. Local Bd. 5, 1982—; mem. Assn. for a Better N.Y.; mem. U.S. Congl. Adv. Bd. Mem. Real Estate Bd. N.Y., Bldg. Owners and Mgrs. Assn. N.Y. (budget com.). Jewish. Home: 240 Central Park S New York NY 10019 Office: 530 Fifth Ave New York NY 10036

WOOLFE, ELIZABETH ARMSTRONG, community coll. adminstr.; b. Orlando, Fla., Jan. 18, 1929; d. William and Alice Lucy (Metcalf) Armstrong; B.S., Fla. State U., 1950, M.S., 1967; Ed.D. (Charles S. Mott fellow 1974), Fla. Atlantic U., 1979; m. Robert Cecil Woolfe, July 30, 1950; children—Robert Craig, Richard Stephen (dec.), Randall Clark, Russell Cameron. Home service rep. Fla. Power & Light Co., 1960-62; extension home econs. agt. Palm Beach County (Fla.), also U. Fla., 1964-66; from program specialist to tchr. Palm Beach County Sch. Bd., 1966-70, county staff resource tchr. dept. adult and community edn., 1972-74; asst. prof. Indian River Community Coll., 1970-72; part-time instr., then coordinator continuing edn. Palm Beach Jr. Coll., 1976-81, dir. continuing edn. II, North Campus, 1981—. Deacon, Immanuel Presbyn. Ch., Palm Beach Gardens, Fla., 1959-82. Named Woman of Year Bus. and Profl. Women, 1985. Mem. Am. Assn. Community and Jr. Colls., Fla. Assn. Community Colls. (chmn. region 1986-88), Am. Assn. Women Community and Jr. Colls., Assn. Continuing Higher Edn., Am. Soc. Tng. and Devel., AAUW, (mem. div. bd. 1986-88), Fla. Assn. Community Colls., Fla. Assn. Community Edn., Fla. Fedn. Women's Clubs (jr. dist. dir. 1962-64), Palm Beach County Panhellenic (pres. 1959-60), Greater W. Palm Beach C. of C., No. Palm Beach Gardens C. of C., RSVP (bd. dirs. 1985-88). Alpha Lambda Delta, Kappa Delta Pi, Omicron Nu, Phi Delta Kappa, Alpha Chi Omega. Democrat. Club: Palm Beach Gardens Soroptomist (chmn. youth citizenship com. 1980-82, dir. 1982—, v.p. 1985-86, pres. 1986-87). Home: 59 Ironwood Way N Palm Beach Gardens FL 33418 Office: 3160 PGA Blvd Palm Beach Gardens FL 33410

WOOLFOLK, ELIZABETH CARROW, speech pathologist researcher, consultant; b. Houston, Sept. 18, 1927; d. Arthur Maurice and Mary Constance (Ruiz) Carrow; m. Robert Moore Woolfolk, Jr., Nov. 9, 1974; 1 dau., Amelie Robinson. B.A., Our Lady of the Lake U., 1949; M.A., U. Tex., 1950; Ph.D., Northwestern U., 1955. Founder, dir. Harry Jersig Ctr., San Antonio, 1955-68; prof., chmn. speech Our Lady of the Lake U., San Antonio, 1960-68, v.p., 1967-69; assoc. prof. otolaryngology Baylor Coll. Medicine, Houston, 1969-73; prof., head speech pathology U. Tex., Austin, 1973-74; research cons., Houston, 1974—; mem. adv. council Sch. Communication, U. Tex., Austin, 1975-78. Author: (with Joan Lynch) Integrative Approach to Language Disorders in Children, 1982; contbr. articles to various publs.; editor Jour. Speech and Hearing Disorders, 1968-74. Trustee Our Lady of the Lake U., San Antonio, 1977-79; bd. dirs. Sch. for Deaf Children, Houston, 1981—. Recipient Matrix award Theta Sigma Pi, 1969; Jack L. Bangs Meml. award Tex. Speech and Hearing Assn., 1976. Fellow Am. Speech and Hearing Assn. (mem. publs. bd. 1968), Tex. Speech and Hearing Assn. (pres. 1962). Republican. Roman Catholic.

WOOLLACOTT, MARJORIE HINES, neuroscientist; b. Long Beach, Calif., Aug. 25, 1946; d. Laurence Robert and Helen Virginia (Carson) Hines; student U. Redlands, 1963-65; A.B. magna cum laude with honors extraordinary in organic chemistry, U. So. Calif., 1969, Ph.D. (NIH fellow), 1973. NIH summer trainee in neurophysiology U. So. Calif., 1968; NIH postdoctoral fellow U. Oreg., 1973-76, Alfred P. Sloan postdoctoral research asso. in neurophysiology, 1975-76, asso. prof. phys. edn. and neurosci., 1980—; asst. prof. Va. Poly. Inst. and State U., 1976-77; sr. research asso. Neurol. Scis. Inst., Portland, Oreg., 1977-80; Arthur Vining Davis fellow in marine invertebrate neurophysiology Santa Catalina Marine Lab., 1971. Mem. exec. com. Siddha Meditation Center, Eugene. M.I.T. Neurosci. Research Program fellow, 1977; NIH grantee, 1978-80, 85—; Med. Research Found. Oreg. grantee, 1979-80, 81-82; Fyssen Found. France grantee, 1982-83; Calif. State Personnel Bd. grantee, 1982. Mem. Soc. Neurosci., AAAS, Am. Coll. Sports Medicine, Phi Beta Kappa. Contbr. chpts., articles to profl. publs. Home: 1628 Lawrence St Eugene OR 97401 Office: Esslinger Hall U Oreg Eugene OR 97403

WOOLLEY, CATHERINE (JANE THAYER), author; b. Chgo., Aug. 11, 1904; d. Edward Mott and Anna L. (Thayer) W.; A.B., UCLA, 1927. Advt. copywriter Am. Radiator Co., N.Y.C., 1927-31; freelance writer, 1931-33; copywriter, editor house organ Am. Radiator & Standard San. Corp., N.Y.C., 1933-40; desk editor Archtl. Record, 1940-42; prodn. editor SAE Jour., N.Y.C., 1942-43; pub. relations writer NAM, N.Y.C., 1943-47; instr. juvenile writing Cape Cod Writers Conf., 1965, 66; instr. workshop in juvenile writing Truro Center for the Arts, summers 1977, 78. Trustee, Truro Pub. Libraries, 1974-84; mem. Passaic Bd. Edn., 1953-56, Passaic Redevel. Agy., 1952-53. Mem. Authors League Am., Friends of Truro Libraries, Truro Hist. Soc., Vols. for AIM, Kenilworth Soc. Democrat. Author juvenile books (under name Catherine Woolley): I Like Trains, 1944, rev., 1965; Two Hundred Pennies, 1947; Ginnie and Geneva, 1948; David's Railroad, 1949; Schoolroom Zoo, 1950; Railroad Cowboy, 1951; Ginnie Joins In, 1951; David's Hundred Dollars, 1952; Lunch for Lennie, 1952 (pub. as L'Incontentabile Gigi in Italy); The Little Car that Wanted a Garage, 1952; The Animal Train and Other Stories, 1953; Holiday on Wheels, 1953; Ginnie and the New Girl, 1954; Ellie's Problem Dog, 1955; A Room for Cathy, 1956; Ginnie and the Mystery House, 1957; Miss Cathy Leonard, 1958; David's Campaign Buttons, 1959; Ginnie and the Mystery Doll, 1960; Cathy Leonard Calling, 1961; Look Alive, Libby!, 1962; Ginnie and Her Juniors, 1963; Cathy's Little Sister, 1964; Libby Looks for a Spy, 1965; The Shiny Red Rubber Boots, 1965; Ginnie and the Cooking Contest, 1966; Ginnie and the Wedding Bells, 1967; Chris in Trouble, 1968; Ginnie and the Mystery Cat, 1969; Libby's Uninvited Guest, 1970; Cathy and the Beautiful People, 1971; Cathy Uncovers a Secret, 1972; Ginnie and the Mystery Light, 1973; Libby Shadows a Lady, 1974; Ginnie and Geneva Cookbook, 1975; (under name Jane Thayer) The Horse with the Easter Bonnet, 1953; The Popcorn Dragon, 1953; Where's Andy?, 1954; Mrs. Perrywinkle's Pets, 1955; Sandy and the Seventeen Balloons, 1955; The Chicken in the Tunnel, 1956; The Outside Cat, 1957, 83 (English edit. 1958); Charley and the New Car, 1957; Funny Stories To Read Aloud, 1958; Andy Wouldn't Talk, 1958; The Puppy Who Wanted a Boy, 1958, revised edit., 1986; The Second-Story Giraffe, 1959; Little Monkey, 1959; Andy and His Fine Friends, 1960; The Pussy Who Went To the Moon, 1960 (English edit. 1961); A Little Dog Called Kitty, 1961 (English edit. 1962, 75); The Blueberry Pie Elf, 1961 (English edit. 1962); Andy's Square Blue Animal, 1962; Gus Was a Friendly Ghost, 1962 (English edit. 1971, Japanese edit. 1982); A Drink for Little Red Diker, 1963; Andy and the Runaway Horse, 1963; A House for Mrs. Hopper; the Cat that Wanted to Go Home, 1963; Quiet on Account of Dinosaur, 1964 (English edit. 1965, 74); Emerald Enjoyed the Moonlight, 1964 (English edit. 1965); The Bunny in the Honeysuckle Patch, 1965 (English edit. 1966); Part-Time Dog, 1965 (English edit. 1966); The Light Hearted Wolf, 1966; What's a Ghost Going to Do?, 1966 (English edit. 1972, Japanese edit. 1982); The Cat that Joined the Club, 1967 (Brit. edit. 1968); Rockets Don't Go to Chicago, Andy, 1967; A Contrary Little Quail, 1968; Little Mr. Greenthumb, 1968 (Brit. edit. 1969); Andy and Mr. Cunningham, 1969; Curious, Furious Chipmunk, 1969; I'm Not a Cat, Said Emerald, 1970 (Brit. edit. 1971); Gus Was a Christmas Ghost, 1970 (Brit. edit. 1973, Japanese edit., 1982), Mr. Turtle's Magic Glasses, 1971; Timothy and Madam Mouse, 1971 (Brit. edit. 1972); Gus and the Baby Ghost, 1972 (Brit. edit. 1973, Japanese edit. 1982); The Little House, 1972; Andy and the Wild Worm, 1973; Gus Was a Mexican Ghost, 1974 (Brit. edit. 1975, Japanese edit. 1982); I Don't Believe in Elves, 1975; The Mouse on the Fourteenth Floor, 1977; Gus Was a Gorgeous Ghost, 1978; Where is Squirrel?, 1979; Try Your Hand, 1980; Applebaums Have a Robot, 1980; Clever Raccoon, 1981; Gus Was a Real Dumb Ghost, 1982; contbr. stories to juvenile anthologies, sch. readers, juvenile mags. Home: Higgins Hollow Rd Truro MA 02666

WOOLLEY, HELEN MACK, librarian; b. El Paso, Tex., Oct. 18, 1929; d. Collin MacDonnel and Ada Dean (Pilcher) Lovelady; m. Jean Albert Woolley, June 1, 1949; children—John Allen, Lynda Jean Woolley Fisk, Penny Anne Woolley Poston, Rebecca Dean Woolley Mead. B.S. in Elem. Edn. with honors, Tex. Tech U., 1970; postgrad. Eastern N.Mex. U., 1971-74, U. Albuquerque, 1976-77, U. N.Mex., 1978-79, West Tex. State U., 1984. Cert. elem. tchr., Tex., N.Mex. Migrant tchr., tchr. 3d grade pub. sch., Tucumcari, N.Mex., 1970-74; kindergarten tchr. Curiosity Shop, Albuquerque, 1975-77; tchr. math. and sci. jr. high sch., tchr. 5th grade, Moriarity, N.Mex., 1977-79; children's librarian Killgore Pub. Library, Dumas, Tex., 1980-85; head librarian Moore County Libraries, 1985—. Bible sch. tchr. Ch. of Christ, Tex., Wyo., La., N.Mex., 1950—; troop leader Girl Scouts U.S.A., 1963-74, day camp dir., Spur, Tex., 1966; adult leader 4-H, Morton, Tex., 1966-69; asst. coordinator Pilot Internat., Dumas, 1985. Recipient spl. service award Amarillo council Girl

Scouts U.S.A., 1985. Mem. Tex. Library Assn., AAUW (pres. Dumas 1982-84), Phi Theta Kappa, Phi Kappa Phi. Republican. Avocations: calligraphy; gardening; sewing; camping; antique automobiles. Home: 1106 Phillips Dumas TX 79029 Office: Killgore Meml Library 124 S Bliss Dumas TX 79029

WOOLLEY, MARY TRUDEL, public relations executive; b. Neptune, N.J.; d. LeRoy and Elizabeth Etta (Reading) Trudel; B.A. magna cum laude, CCNY, 1968; m. Jon Howard Woolley, Aug. 8, 1965; children—Won Gil, Joshua. Vice pres., partner Firestone Assos., public relations, N.Y.C., 1968-77; exec. v.p. Rowland Co., Inc., N.Y.C., 1977—. Mem. Fashion Group, Phi Beta Kappa. Democrat. Mem. Christian Ch. (Disciples of Christ). Office: 415 Madison Ave New York NY 10017

WOOLSEY, JOANNE CAROL, writer; b. Phila., June 1, 1957; d. William Frederick and Rosemary Ann (Reilly) Woolsey. B.A., Lehigh U., 1979. Editorial asst. Phila. Nat. Bank, 1979-80, staff writer/communications specialist, 1980—. Sec. to bd. Young Leaders of Phila., 1983-84. Mem. Women in Communications (chmn. publs. adv. com. to nat. exec. bd. 1983-84, nat. conf. communications chmn. 1983). Republican. Episcopalian. Home: 7100 Oxford Ave Apt 60 Philadelphia PA 19111 Office: Philadelphia Nat Bank 1 N 5th St Philadelphia PA 19101

WOOLSEY, MARY BETH, financial planner; b. Pasadena, Calif., Mar. 20, 1948; d. Charles Cramer and Mary Elizabeth (Sawyer) W.; A.B. in Psychology, UCLA, 1971; M.B.A. in Fin., U. San Francisco, 1980; m. Gary Franklin Calame, Mar. 13, 1982. Sr. buyer Geyser Peak Winery, Geyserville, Calif., 1974-75; buyer Calif. & Hawaiian Sugar Co., San Francisco, 1976-78, fin. analyst, 1978-80; regional fin. analyst Foremost McKesson, San Francisco, 1981-82; strategic planning mgr. San Francisco Newspaper Agy., 1982-84; budget and strategic planning cons., San Francisco, 1984-85; personal fin. planner IDS/Am. Express, San Francisco, 1985—; mem. faculty Golden Gate U., 1980-81; condr. small bus. mktg. workshop Alameda C. of C., 1981; cons. to small bus. Mem. allocation panel United Way, San Francisco. Mem. Planning Forum (v.p. seminars), Planning Execs. Inst. Democrat. Christian Scientist. Office: 345 Oakes Blvd San Leandro CA 94577

WOOLSTON, EVELYN DORIS, arts administrator, public relations specialist; b. Boston, Nov. 8, 1925; d. Paul Hermann and Louise Martha (Gesch) Franz; m. John Woolston, Apr. 7, 1945; (div. 1967); 1 son, Peter Christopher; m. 2d Robert Franklin May, Feb. 1, 1984. B.A., Emerson Coll., 1947. Asst. merchandising mgr. Sta. WCSC-TV-AM, Charleston, S.C., 1954-57; mgr. promotions and merchandising, Knight Broadcasting, Inc., Portsmouth, N.H., 1957-61; asst. advt. dir. Hahn Shoes, Landover, Md., 1961-70; advt. dir. W & J Sloane, Inc., Washington, 1970-76, exec. dir. Capitol Ballet, Inc., Washington, 1977-80; freelance arts adminstr., Washington, 1980—. Exec. dir. Off the Circle Theatre Co., Washington, 1982-84; chmn., coordinator fund-raising project League of Washington Theatres, 1984-85; bd. dirs. D.C. Contemporary Dance Theatre, 1985—. League Washington Theatres, Helen Hayes Awards, co-chmn. Washington Theatre Fortnight, 1986—; fund raiser various arts orgns., Washington, 1961—; Mem. Emerson Coll. Alumni Assn. (mem. exec. bd. 1984—). Republican. Club: ARTS Club of Washington (chmn. drama 1982-83). Avocations: theatre; travel; reading; Japanese literature; swimming. Home and Office: 2734 34th Pl NW Washington DC 20007

WOOTEN, MARTHA MARIE, systems engineering executive, consultant; b. Gadsden, Ala., Apr. 4, 1951; d. Garland Wesley and Rada Lenderman Mauldin; 1 child, Andre Collin Gray. B.S. in Math. and Psychology with spl. honors in Psychology, Jacksonville State U., 1977; M.S. in Indsl. Engring., U. Ala.-Tuscaloosa, 1979. Human factors engr. Tex. Instruments, Inc., Dallas, 1979-81, project mgr., 1983-85, also tech. spokesperson, 1985; mgr. quality assurance Mary Kay Cosmetics, Inc., Dallas, 1981-83; asst. v.p. systems engring. Tng. Gallery, Inc., Dallas, 1985—, also cons., 1980-81, 85; developer, presenter workshop/seminars, 1979-85. Scholar, Jacksonville State U., Ala., 1975. Mem. Human Factors Soc. (past pres. North Tex. chpt.), Am. Assn. Artificial Intelligence, IEEE, Dallas Women's Found. Mem. Unity Ch. Avocations: scuba diving; water skiing; tennis; painting; dancing. Home: 12690 Hillcrest Apt 1100 Dallas TX 75230 Office: Tng Gallery Inc 12800 Hillcrest Dallas TX 75230

WORBOIS, LOIS EVELYN, newspaper editor; b. Mt. Pleasant, Pa., June 30, 1930; d. Edwin Thomas and Louvina Elizabeth (May) Butler; m. Robert John Worbois, Feb. 3, 1951; children—James, Cheryl, John (dec.), Susanne, Allen. Freelance writer Light & Life Press, Winona Lake, Ind., 1969-71; soc. editor News Dispatch, Jeannette, Pa., 1972-75; reporter Standard Observer, Irwin, Pa., 1976-79, woman's editor, 1979—. Author: The Thorn, 1977. Mem. Sr. Community Service Projects adv. bd. Westmoreland County Community Coll., 1976—; mem. Health and Welfare Council, Westmoreland County, 1980—. Mem. DAR, Soc. Profl. Journalists. Republican. Methodist. Club: Gideons Internat. Aux. (v.p. 1972, sec. 1979) (Westmoreland County). Home: 2849 Schade Hill Rd North Huntingdon PA 15642 Office: Standard Observer Westmoreland Jours Inc PO Box 280 Irwin PA 15642

WORD, LINDA LEE, lawyer, trust administrator; b. Alice, Tex., Nov. 2, 1948; d. William Adams and Alberta Jean (Boucher) W. B.A., U. Tex.-Austin, 1970; J.D., South Tex. Coll. Law, 1982. Bar: Tex. 1982. Flight attendant Pan Am World Airways, Los Angeles, 1971-79; assoc. Drummond & Assocs., Houston, 1982-83; trust adminstr. Frost Nat. Bank, San Antonio, 1983—. Vol. Prison Fellowship Family Ministry, San Antonio; area vol. Children's Heart Inst. So. Tex., Corpus Christi; bd. dirs. Lighthouse for Blind, San Antonio, Holy Cross Ctr., San Antonio, 1984—. Mem. State Bar Tex., ABA, Bexar County Women's Bar Assn., San Antonio Bar Assn., San Antonio Young Lawyer's Assn. Republican. Home: 2619 Waterford San Antonio TX 78217 Office: Frost Nat Bank PO Box 1600 San Antonio TX 78296

WORDEN, KAREN MARTHA, radio station executive; b. McCloud, Calif., Mar. 7, 1939; d. Albert Eric and Vivienne Maxine (Serpa) Copitzky; m. Tom Worden, Aug. 20, 1960; 1 child, Eric Clint. Student Shasta Coll., 1958; grad. Tng. Sch., 1978. Owner, operator dancing sch., 1955-57; bookkeeper Woodard Acctg. Co., 1958-60; salesperson, office mgr. Sta. KQEN, Roseburg, Oreg., 1962-70; sales mgr. Sta. KRSB, Roseburg, 1970—; owner, operator antique shop, estate service, 1969—; mem. Oreg. Sch. Fin. Forum; gen. mgr. KRSB/KYES W.R.R. Inc., Broadcast House, Inc., 1980—; pres. Broadcast House, Inc., 1982—; dir. Umpqua Community Coll. Found., Douglas County, Oreg., 1983—; abstract nature photographer. Represented by Lawrence Gallery, Salishan, Gleneden Beach, Oreg., Maude Kern Art Gallery, Eugene, Oreg.; exhibited in group shows at Umpqua Valley Arts Gallery, Woman's Art Festival of Douglas County, 1981, 82, 83, Susan Berry Art Festival, 1984, Umpqua Valley Art Festival, 1980-84. Oreg. del. Republican Nat. Conv., Kansas City, Kans., 1976; chmn. phone bank operation Douglas County Rep. Party, 1976; vice chmn. Oreg. Rep. Party, 1977-79; vol. chmn. Douglas County Rep. Central Com., 1972-79; active Rep. campaigns; vol. Douglas County Hist. Soc. Recipient award in human relations Dale Carnegie Inst., 1978, award State of Oreg. Poetry Competition, 1976, photography award, County of Douglas, 1983-84. Mem. Nat. Assn. FM Broadcasters, Nat. Assn. Broadcasters, Oreg. Assn. Broadcasters, Radio Advt. Bur., So. Oreg. Resource Alliance (bd. dirs.), Roseburg C. of C. Roman Catholic. Club: Zonta. Home: 2144 SE Kline St Roseburg OR 97470 Office: KRSB/KYES Radio 829 SE Cass Ave Roseburg OR 97470

WORDEN, KATHARINE COLE, sculptor; b. N.Y.C., May 4, 1925; d. Philip Gillette and Katharine (Pyle) Cole; student Potters Sch., Tucson, 1940-42, Sarah Lawrence Coll., 1942-44; m. Frederic G. Worden, Jan. 8, 1944; children—Rick, Dwight, Philip, Barbara, Katharine. Sculptures exhibited Royce Galleries, Galerie Françoise Besnard (Paris), Cooling Gallery, London, Galerie Schumacher, Munich, Selected Artists Gallery, N.Y.C., Art Inst. Boston, Reid Gallery, Nashville, Weiner Gallery, N.Y.C., 1976, 77, Desraches Gallery, Montreal, Que., Can., 1977, 78, Boston Athanaeum, 1979, Gilcrease Mus., Tulsa, Galerie des Capucies, Paris, Grand Palaisi, Paris, Dakar and Bathurst, Africa; House of Humor and Satire, Gabrova, Bulgaria, 1983, Bay

---

Club Mall, Newport, R.I., 1984; represented in numerous pvt. collections. Occupational therapist psychopathic ward Los Angeles County Gen. Hosp., 1953-57; headstart vol., Watts, Calif., 1965-67; tchr. sculpture Watts Towers Art Center, 1967-69; participant White House Women Doers Luncheon meeting, 1968; dir. Cambridgeport Problem Center, Cambridge, Mass., 1969-71; dir. Stride Rite Corp. Trustee, Communication Research Inst., Miami, Fla., 1960-69, chmn. bd., 1966-69; bd. dirs. Boston Center for the Arts, Child and Family Services of Newport County; bd. overseers Boston Mus. Fine Arts, 1978-83; trustee Newport Art Mus., 1985—. Mem. Common Cause (Mass. adv. bd. 1971-72, dir. 1974-75), Mass. Civil Liberties Union (exec. bd. 1973-74, 76-78, dir. 1976-77, trustee found. 1977-78). Home: 24 Fort Wetherill Rd Jamestown RI 02835

WORFEL, CYNTHIA JEAN, cruise line sales executive; b. Detroit, May 3, 1944; d. William Vernon and Jean Rose (Felts) Hicks; m. Thomas Robert Worfel, Dec. 27, 1965 (div. May 1974); 1 son, William Benjamin. B.A., Mich. State U., 1966, postgrad., 1967-69. Tchr. elem. edn. Grand Rapids (Mich.) Bd. Edn., 1965-70; cons. elem. intern program Mich. State U., East Lansing, 1970-74; cons. sales Travel Industry, Grand Rapids, 1974-77; regional sales rep. Carnival Cruise Lines, Chgo., 1977-79, regional sales mgr., 1979-81, dir. sales, 1981—; revisions cons. environ. edn. State of Mich., 1970. Named Outstanding Educator, Grand Rapids Edn. Assn., 1970. Mem. Chgo. Travel Women's Club. Democrat. Office: Carnival Cruise Lines 3915 Biscayne Blvd Miami FL 33137

WORKMAN, LAURAL ANN, retail association executive; b. Monrovia, Calif., Feb. 13, 1960; d. Robert and Laura Louise (Benton) W. B.Mus., U. Oreg., 1983. Acctg. clk. Renfield Importers, N.Y.C., 1981-82; adminstrv. asst. Internat. Council Shopping Ctrs., N.Y.C., 1983-84, meetings mgr., 1984-85, western meetings dir., San Francisco, 1986—. Co-author: Guide to ICSC Idea Exchanges, 1985. Mem. NOW, Nat. Assn. Female Execs., Phi Beta (pres. 1981-82). Democrat. Avocations: classical musician; tennis; traveling; swimming. Home: 500 Stanyan St Apt 602 San Francisco CA 94117 Office: Internat Council Shopping Ctrs 500 Stanyan St Apt 602 San Francisco CA 94117

WORRELL, AUDREY MARTINY, psychiatrist, state official; b. Phila., Aug. 12, 1935; d. Francis Aloysius and Dorothy (Rawley) Martiny; m. Richard Vernon Worrell, June 14, 1958; children: Philip Vernon, Amy Elizabeth. M.D., Meharry Med. Coll., 1960. Diplomate Am. Bd. Psychiatry and Neurology. Dir. capitol region Mental Health Ctr., Hartford, Conn., 1974-77; acting regional dir. Region IV, State Dept. Mental Health, 1976-77; asst. chief psychiatry VA Med. Ctr., Newington, Conn., 1977-78, acting chief psychiatry, 1978-79, chief psychiatry, 1978-80; dir. Capitol Regional Mental Health Facilities, Hartford, Conn., 1980-81; clin. prof. psychiatry U. Conn., 1981—; commr. State Dept. Mental Health, Hartford, 1981—. Contbr. articles to profl. jours. Bd. dirs. Transitional Services, Buffalo, 1973-74, ARC, Buffalo, 1973-74, Child and Family Services, Hartford, 1972-73; co-chmn. United Way/Combined Health Appeal, State of Conn., 1983, 84; active Child Welfare Inst. Adv. Bd., Hartford, 1983—, Conn. Prison Bd., Hartford, 1984-85. Recipient Leadership award Conn. Council Mental Health Ctrs., 1983; Outstanding Contbn. award to Health Services YWCA, Hartford, 1983; chmn. Gov.'s Task Force on Mental Health Policy, 1982—; mem. Gov.'s Task Force on Homeless, 1983—. Mem. New Eng. Mental Health Commrs. Assn., Am. Med. Women's Assn., Conn. Assn. Mental Health and Aging, Conn. Coalition for Homeless Inc., Conn. Rehab. Assn., Am. Assn. Psychiat. Adminstrs., Am. Hosp. Assn., AMA, Am. Orthopsychiat. Assn., Am. Pub. Health Assn., Assn. Mental Health Adminstrs., Hosp. and Community Psychiatry Service, Corporators of Inst. of Living of Hartford, Am. Psychiat. Assn., Conn. Psychiat. Soc., NASMHPD (sec., bd. dirs. 1982—), Am. Coll. Psychiatrists, Am. Coll. Mental Health Adminstrs. Democrat. Office: Dept of Mental Health 90 Washington St Hartford CT 06106*

WORRELL, GAIL GARRETT, medical illustrator and graphic designer; b. Queens, N.Y., Apr. 11, 1946; d. Wayne Oliver and Gloria Elizabeth (Titscher) Garrett; B.S. in Design, U. Cin., 1969. Graphic designer Alpha Designs, Inc., Cin., 1969-73; med. illustrator and supr. Good Samaritan Hosp., Cin., 1973—; free-lance cons. designer. Recipient various awards Tulsa Art Dirs. Show, 1977, 1st prize Am. Occupational Med. Assn. exhibit, 1976, 2d prize Ohio Med. Assn. exhibit, 1977, bronze plaque Ohio Med. Assn., 1978, Hull award AMA, 1980. Club: Soroptimist Internat. Illustrator: Vascular Surgery, Vol. 2 (John J. Cranley, M.D.); contbr. illustrations to med. texts. Home: 3850 Clifton Ave Cincinnati OH 45220 Office: Good Samaritan Hosp 3217 Clifton Ave Cincinnati OH 45220

WORSHAM, PATRICIA DUNHAM, financial analyst; b. Ann Arbor, Mich., Aug. 7, 1951; d. Perry Orlando and Norma Ann (Niendorf) Dunham; m. Michael L. Worsham, Mar. 26, 1984; 1 child, Andrew. Student Central Mich. U., 1969-72; B.B.A. U. Tenn., 1980; M.B.A., Vanderbilt U., 1982. C.P.A., Tenn. Head teller Huron Valley Bank, Ann Arbor, Mich., 1974-77; market researcher Alladin Industries, Nashville, 1981; fin. analyst Ingram Industries, Nashville, 1982—. Long range planner United Way Nashville and Davidson County, 1984-85; mem. Ladies Hermitage Soc., Nashville, 1985. Republican. Presbyterian. Avocations: arts and crafts; piano. Office: Ingram Industries Inc 4304 Harding Rd Nashville TN 37205

WORSHAM-KELLEY, JANET JEAN, crime prevention and detection equipment company executive; b. Coral Gables, Fla., Nov. 23, 1955; d. Robert Joe and Christine Edith (Skipper) Worsham; m. Mitchell Patrick Kelley, Sept. 27, 1981. Student pub. schs., Miami, Fla. Prodn. staff Criminalistics, Inc., Miami, Fla., 1971-73, asst. mgr. office, 1973-78, v.p. adminstrv., 1978-84, pres., 1984—. Co-patentee fingerprint powder. Named Miss Directory, Opa Locka C. of C., 1974. Mem. Nat. Assn. Female Execs. Republican. Baptist. Office: Criminalistics Inc 7560 NW 82 St Miami FL 33166

WORTHING, MARCIA LYNN, cosmetics company executive; b. Columbus, Ohio, Jan. 8, 1943; d. Ford Buxton and Dorothy Jean (Leonard) W.; m. Ronald Martin Foster, Jr., Dec. 15, 1973; children—Christopher Worthing, Geoffrey Worthing. B.A., Calif. State U., 1965. Tchr., San Francisco, 1966-67; editorial asst. Am. Mgmt. Assn., N.Y.C., 1967-69; publs. editor Merrill Lynch Pierce Fenner & Smith, N.Y.C., 1969-72; publs. editor Avon Products, Inc., N.Y.C., 1972-73, supr. personnel, 1973-74, mgr. employment, 1974-76, mgr. tng., 1976-78, dir. personnel, 1978-81, gen. mgr. hqrs., 1981-82, v.p. personnel, 1982-84, v.p. human resources, 1984—. Office: Avon Products Inc 9 W 57th St New York NY 10019*

WORTHINGTON, MARY EMMONS, clinical psychologist; b. San Jose, Calif., Apr. 17, 1922; d. Grover Carlton and Helen Keith (Boulware) Emmons; B.A., Vanderbilt U., 1942; M.L.A., U. So. Calif., 1972; M.A., Pepperdine U., 1975; Ph.D., Fla. Inst. Tech., 1981; m. John Worthington, July 4, 1942; children—Jon, Gina. Librarian, Internat. Grad. U., Lugano, Switzerland, 1976-77; dir. and clin. psychologist High Plains Comprehensive Community Mental Health Center, Osborne, Kans., 1978—; lectr. Pepperdine U., UCLA, Ft. Hays U., Internat. Grad. U. Founder and pres. Friends of Long Beach Library; neighborhood chmn. Girl Scouts U.S.A., 1978-82; mem. Area Agy. on Aging, Osborne, 1981-82; chair bd. trustees UTESA Med. Sch., Dominican Republic; mem. Gov.'s Com. on Drunk Driving. Lic. marriage, family and child therapist, Calif. Mem. Am. Psychol. Assn., Osborne C. of C., Hospice, Osborne County Hosp. Aux., Gamma Phi Beta, Sigma Beta Pi, Psi Chi. Democrat. Methodist. Clubs: PEO (chpt. CR), Fidelia (pres. 1981-82). Home: 318 S 2d St Osborne KS 67473 Office: High Plains Comprehensive Community Mental Health Center 121 W Main St Osborne KS 67473

WORTMAN, JUDITH ANN, professional society administrator, lobbyist; b. Detroit, Aug. 26, 1940; d. Marion Edgar and Laura (Pauline) Stallsmith; m. David Morris Wortman, Feb. 13, 1971. B.S. in Nursing, Wayne State U., 1962; M.A. in Med. Jurisprudence, George Washington U., 1979. R.N., Mich. Dir. long-term care project JWK Internat., Annandale, Va., 1977-78; editor Patient and Health Edn., Robert Brady Co., Bowie Md., 1978-79; dir. fed. relations Calif. State U., Washington, 1979-83; mgr. pub. responsibilities Am. Inst. Biol.

Scis., Washington, 1984-85; dir. Associated Natural Sci. Instns., Washington, 1986—; cons. Ency. Brit. Corp., Chgo., 1979, Inst. Contemporary Studies, San Francisco, 1983-85. Editorial bd. Grants Mag., San Diego, 1979-83. Vol. health-related orgns., Montgomery County, Md., 1984—. Mem. Women in Govt. Relations. Club: Woodmont Country (Rockville, Md.). Home: 8621 Lancaster Dr Bethesda MD 20814 Office: The Associated Natural Sci Instns 499 S Capitol St Suite 110 Washington DC 20003

WOS, SUSAN MARIE, microbiologist, researcher; b. Buffalo, Dec. 2, 1955; d. Anthony Lucas and Florence Angeline (Woloszyn) W. B.A., SUNY-Buffalo, 1977, M.A., 1980, Ph.D., 1983. Med. lab. technician Erie County Med. Ctr., Buffalo, 1974-79; research technician N.Y. State Dept. Health, Albany, 1979-83; postdoctoral fellow Wadsworth Ctr. Labs./Research, Albany, 1983-84; research microbiologist E.I. duPont de Nemours & Co., Wilmington, Del., 1984—; presentor nat. sci. meetings, 1980—. Author column Infectious Disease Inst. News, 1982; also articles, chpts. Vol. E.J. Meyer Meml. Hosp., Buffalo, 1973-74, Friends of Saratoga Performing Arts Ctr., N.Y., 1981-82. N.Y. State Regents scholar SUNY-Buffalo, 1973-77. Mem. Am. Soc. Microbiology, N.Y. Acad. Sci., Buffalo Collegium of Immunology, Am. Soc. Virology. Avocations: travel; microcomputers; photography. Office: E I duPont de Nemours & Co Dept Biomed Products Glasgow Research Lab Wilmington DE 19898

WOULFE, MARGARET FRANCES, lawyer; b. Chgo., Feb. 14, 1957; d. James Joseph and Yvonne Elizabeth (Kenney) Woulfe. B.S. cum laude, Ill. State U., 1979; J.D., U. Ill., 1982. Bar: Ill. 1982, U.S. Dist. Ct. (no. dist.) Ill. 1982, U.S. Ct. Appeals (7th circuit), 1983. Mem. law firm Chadwell & Kayser, Ltd., Chgo., 1982—; instr. DePaul U. Coll. Law and IIT Chgo.-Kent Law Sch., Chgo., 1983; legal talk show guest WIND Radio, 1983. Mem. ABA, Ill. Bar Assn., Chgo. Bar Assn., Women's Bar Assn., Chgo. Council Fgn. Relations, Nat. Assn. Female Execs. Roman Catholic. Clubs: Sierra, River. Home: 957 W Montana St Chicago IL 60614 Office: Chadwell & Kayser Ltd 8500 Sears Tower Chicago IL 60606

WOULFF, NINA, clinical psychologist; b. Bronx, N.Y., Oct. 5, 1949; d. Sholem and Sylvia (Siegal) W.; B.A. cum laude in Psychology and English, CCNY, 1970; Ph.D. in Psychology, U. Maine, 1975. Staff psychologist, br. dir. Atlantic Child Guidance Centre, Dartmouth, N.S., Can., 1975—; lectr. and dept. psychiatry. Dalhousie U., Halifax, N.S., Can., 1980—; leader assertiveness tng. groups, Mt. St. Vincent U., Halifax, 1977—; assoc. fellow, supr. Inst. Rational-Emotive Therapy, N.Y.C., 1980—; child psychologist for CBC radio call-in program. Mem. Am. Psychol. Assn., Can. Psychol. Assn., Phi Beta Kappa. Author papers in field. Office: 277 Pleasant St Suite 204 Dartmouth NS B2Y 4B7 Canada

WRAGG, JOANNA DICARLO, newspaper editor; b. Batavia, N.Y., Nov. 3, 1941; d. Anthony Joseph and Josephine (Ruffino) DiCarlo; m. Otis O. Wragg, III, Dec. 21, 1963; children—Otis O. IV, LaMae. B.A., Fla. State U., 1963. Tchr., Nova Schs., Ft. Lauderdale, Fla., 1963, Pinellas Schs., Safety Harbor, Fla., 1965-68; social worker State of Fla., Lakeland, 1968-70; journalist Lakeland Ledger, 1969-72; editorial writer, then chief editorial writer Miami News, 1972-78; editorial dir. Sta. WPLG-TV, Miami, 1978; editorial writer Miami Herald, 1978-80, assoc. editor, 1980—; pub. speaker. Contbr. articles newspapers. Recipient Pulitzer prize, 1983, Robert F. Kennedy award Robert F. Kennedy Journalism Found., 1971, Disting. Service award Sigma Delta Chi, 1971. Mem. Nat. Conf. Editorial Writers, Women in Communications. Unitarian. Clubs: Zonta, Miami Forum. Office: Miami Herald 1 Herald Plaza Miami FL 33101*

WRAY, SUSAN STEWART, public relations executive; b. Ft. Worth, Aug. 5, 1946; d. Malcolm and Jean (James) Stewart. Student U. Tulsa, 1964-65; B.A., U. N.D., 1968; M.A., Colo. State U., 1970. Bus. adminstr. pvt. dental practice, Denver, 1973-79; state coordinator Nat. Unity Campaign/John Anderson, Denver, 1980; pub. relations advisor Met. Denver Child Dental Care Assn., 1980-82; pub. info. dir. Met. Denver Dental Soc., 1980-82; pub. relations coordinator Dental Health Colo./Am., Denver and Phoenix, 1982-83; pres. Profl. Images Pub. Relations, Los Altos, Calif., 1980—, pres. Stewart Seminars for Health Care Profls., 1981—; v.p. mktg. and pub. relations JSB & Assocs., 1984—; editor, publ. dir. Complementary Medicine Mag., 1985—; pub. relations adv. Nat. Found. Nutritional Research, Denver, 1982-84; cons. Linus Pauling Inst. Sci. and Medicine, Palo Alto, Calif., 1983-85, Personal Best Corp., Vancouver, B.C., 1982-83. Vol., Com. to Elect Gary Hart with Denver, 1976, 78, Gary Hart for Senate, Denver, 1976. Served to lt. USAF, 1970-72. Recipient Spl. Achievement award Internat. Acad. Preventive Medicine, 1980, 82. Mem. Pub. Relations Soc. Am. (Counselors Acad.), Internat. Acad. Bus. Communicators, Nat. Speakers Assn., Meeting Planners Internat. Republican. Episcopalian. Office: PO Box 4351 Mountain View CA 94040

WREGE, JULIA BOUCHELLE, tennis coach; b. Charleston, W.Va., Apr. 11, 1944; d. Dallas Payne and Mary Louise (Hagan) Bouchelle; m. Douglas Ewart Wrege, July 13, 1968; children—Dallas Ewart, Shannon Bouchelle. B.S. in Physics, Ga. Inst. Tech., 1965, M.S. in Physics, 1967. Systems analyst Gen. Electric Apollo Systems, Daytona Beach, Fla., 1967-68; med. scientist Space Instruments Research, Atlanta, 1968-70; head tennis profl. Riverside Tennis Club, Atlanta, 1971-72, Am. Adventures, Roswell, Ga., 1972-75, Hampton Farms Tennis Club, Marietta, Ga., 1975-79; head women's tennis coach Georgia Inst. Tech., Atlanta, 1979—; stadium chmn., umpire, referee U.S. Tennis Assn., Atlanta, 1977—. Author: Tournament Manual, 1977. Pres. Dickerson Middle Sch. Parent-Tchr.-Student Assn., Marietta, Ga., 1982—. Named Umpire of Yr., Ga. Tennis Assn., 1978, So. Tennis Assn., 1978; Ga. Tennis Coach of Yr., Assn. Intercollegiate Athletics for Women-Ga. Tennis Coaches Assn., 1981, 82, 83. Mem. U.S. Profl. Tennis Assn. (pres. 1980), U.S. Tennis Assn., Intercollegiate Tennis Coaches Assn., Ga. Tennis Assn. (pres. 1976-81), Atlanta Lawn Tennis Assn., Atlanta Profl. Tennis Assn., Alpha Xi Delta, Sigma Pi Sigma. Republican. Episcopalian. Home: 1366 Little Willeo Rd NE Marietta GA 30067 Office: Georgia Tech Athletic Assn 150 3d St Atlanta GA 30332

WREN, CHARLOTTE, real estate broker, consultant; b. Bklyn., July 22, 1947; d. George and Mary Courdy; m. Charles Wren, Oct. 1970 (div. 1979); children—Christopher, Casey. Student Jones Real Estate Coll., 1981, U. Colo., 1982, 85. Lic. real estate broker, investment specialist. Realtor assoc. Bauer's Brokerage, Grand Junction, Colo., 1981-82, Century 21 Hallmark, Grand Junction, 1982-83; broker assoc. Century 21 Old Homestead Realty, Grand Junction, 1983-86; property mgr., project coordinator, leasing Kroh Bros. Devel. Co., Englwood, Colo., 1983-85; asset mgr. asst. Valley Fed. Savs. & Loan, Grand Junction, 1985; broker-owner Real Estate Services Co., Grand Junction, 1986—; exchanger Colo. West Exchanger, Grand Junction, 1982-83. Commr. City of Grand Junction Housing Authority, 1981-82; bd. dirs. Mesa County Women's Network. Recipient Top Residential Sales Assn. award Century 21 Western Slope Broker's Council, 1983. Mem. Nat. Assn. Realtors, Inst. Creative Mktg., USSA Ski Assn./Powderhorn Racing Club (bd. dirs. 1982, 85). Avocations: travel; skiing; water sports. Office: Real Estate Services Co 602 Rico Way Grand Junction CO 81506

WREN, PAMELA ANNE PORTER, physical therapist; b. Florence, Colo., July 17, 1951; d. Ivan Raymond and Reba Betty (Kintner) Porter; m. Donald Gregory Wren, Nov. 24, 1973; children—Amber Lea, Ashlie Kaye, Alexandria Anne. Student, Hendrix Coll., 1969-71; B.S., U. Central Ark., 1973. Lic. physical therapist. Physical therapist, clin. coordinator Meml. Hosp., North Little Rock, Ark., 1973-74; staff phys. therapist Central Baptist Hosp., Little Rock, 1974-75; co-owner, operator Conway Phys. Therapy Clinic, P.A., Ark., 1975—; clin. instr. U. Central Ark. Sch. Phys. Therapy, Conway and Little Rock, 1973—; cert. childbirth educator Prepared Childbirth of Conway, 1976-81. Mem. personnel nominating com. 1st Methodist Ch., Conway, 1977-79, mem. pastor staff relations com., 1981-82, sec. bd. trustees, 1985—; v.p. Conway Jaycettes, 1975-77; mem. Yokefellows Bible Study, Conway, 1982-84. Mem. Am. Phys. Therapy Assn. (sec. Ark. chpt. 1977-79), Am. Soc. Psychoprophylaxis in Obstetrics, Internat. Childbirth Educators Assn., LWV (2d v.p. Conway chpt. 1979-82, 1st v.p. 1986—). Club: PEO Sisterhood (Conway). Avocations: tennis; swimming; golf; needlework. Home: 4 Oakdale

Circle Conway AR 72032 Office: Conway Phys Therapy Clinic PA 1404 Caldwell Conway AR 72032

WRIDE, ANH THU, electrical engineer; b. Saigon, Vietnam, Sept. 28, 1955; came to U.S., 1975; d. Lieu V. and Thinh T. (Duong) Doan; m. Bernard R. Wride, Apr. 29, 1978; 1 child, Eric S. B.A. magna cum laude, Brigham Young U., 1977; B.S. in Elec. Engring. magna cum laude, Weber State U., 1984. Electronic technician Communication Certification Lab., Salt Lake City, 1980-81, tech. project leader, 1981-83, engring. mgr., 1984—. Mem. IEEE, Pi Delta Phi. Office: Communication Certification Lab 1940 Alexander St Salt Lake City UT 84120

WRIGHT, ALMA MCINTYRE, magazine editor; b. Knoxville, Tenn., July 31, 1909; d. William Mobry and Theresa (Biagiotti) McIntyre; B.S. in Edn., U. Tenn., 1932; m. Robert Oliver Wright, Feb. 17, 1931; 1 son, Robert Oliver. Writer stories, articles on African violets, house plants, 1947—; editor African Violet Mag., 1947-63, The Master List of African Violets, 1962, GSN (Gesneriad-Saintpaulia News), 1963-86, publs. of Saintpaulia Internat., 1963 (rec. sec. 1963), Am. Gesneria Soc., Inc., 1963; exec. dir. African Violet Soc. Am., Inc., 1960-63; pres. Indoor Gardener Pub. Co., Inc., 1963—. Mem. Am. Hort. Soc., Inc. (hon. v.p. 1954), Am. Gesneria Soc. (rec. sec.), African Violet Soc. Am., Inc. (hon. life mem., rec. sec. 1946-48, nat. pres. 1948-49, membership sec. 1953-63). Home: The Meadows 7914 Gleason Rd Condominium 1075 Knoxville TN 37919 Office: 1800-1802 Grand Ave Knoxville TN 37901

WRIGHT, ANNA BEEBE, nurse; b. Burlington, Iowa, Sept. 8, 1925; d. Charles Howard and Ruth Ernestine (Bovell) Beebe; m. Donald Carlyle Wright, July 28, 1946; children—Jacalyn Gale, Bradley Carlyle. Student Burlington Jr. Coll. (Iowa), 1943-44; R.N., U. Iowa, 1947. Staff nurse University Hosp., Iowa City, 1947-49; staff nurse Stormont-Vail Hosp., Topeka, Kans., 1949-51, clin. instr., staff nurse, 1951-53, 53-58; staff nurse University Hosp., Iowa City, 1958-60; head nurse, staff nurse Meml. Hosp., Topeka, Kans., 1964-71, charge nurse, 1971-85; clinic vol. Am. Heart Assn., 1979, 82. Mem. Am. Assn. Critical Care Nurses. Republican. Methodist. Home: 3719 Munson St Topeka KS 66604

WRIGHT, BESSIE MARGARET, nursery exec.; b. Centralia, Kans., May 23, 1905; d. Onbey Roscoe and Sarah Elizabeth (Shrontz) Roberts; student public schs., Rupert, Idaho; m. Loyd K. Wright, Feb. 6, 1924; 1 son, John Robert. Partner, treas. Kimberly Nurseries, Inc., Twin Falls, Idaho, 1924—. Sunday sch. tchr., 1946-56. Mem. Nat. Fedn. Ind. Bus., Twin Falls C. of C., Am. Nurserymen, Idaho Nursery Assn., Archaeol. Inst. Am., Twin Falls Hist. Soc. (dir.), Nat. Assn. Watch and Clock Collectors, Franklin Mint Collectors Soc., Smithsonian Soc. Republican. Methodist. Club: Daus. of Nile. Author: Me and My Other Self (autobiography). Home: PO Box L Kimberly ID 83341 Office: Kimberly Nurseries Inc Route 3 Addison Ave E Twin Falls ID 83301

WRIGHT, CAROLE YVONNE, chiropractor, consultant; b. Long Beach, Calif., July 12, 1932; d. Paul Burt and Mary Leoan (Staley) Fickes; 1 dau., Morgan Michelle. D. Chiropractic, Palmer Coll., Davenport, Iowa, 1975. Instr. Palmer Coll., 1975-76; dir., owner Wright Chiropractic Clinic, Rocklin, Calif., 1978—, Woodland, Calif., 1980-81; dir., co-owner Ft. Sutter Chiropractic Clinic, Sacramento, 1985—; cons. in field; lectr., speaker on radio programs, at seminars. Contbr. articles to profl. jours. Chmn. Harold Michaels for Congress campaign, Alameda, Calif., 1972; dist. dir. 14th Congl. Dist., 1983—. Mem. Internat. Chiropractic Assn. Calif. (bd. dirs. 1978-81, pres. 1983-85), Palmer Coll. Alumni Assn. (Calif. state pres. 1981-83), Rocklin C. of C. (bd. dirs. 1979-81), Chiropractic Info. Bur. Downtown Sacramento (pres. 1986—), Rocklin-Loomis Bus. and Profl. Women. Republican. Avocations: reading; travel. Home: 4270 Cavitt Stallman Rd Roseville CA 95678 Office: Wright Chiropractic Clinic 3175 Sunset Blvd Suite 105 Rocklin CA 95677

WRIGHT, CYNTHIA SUSANNE (CINDY), oil company executive, rental partnership executive; b. Bartlesville, Okla., May 31, 1955; d. Tommey Ansier, Jr. and Mary Effie (Dean) Yokley; m. Gary Dean Wright, Aug. 21, 1976; 1 child, Brandon Jackson. B.S., Okla. State U., 1977. Unit asst. to dean of library Okla. State U., Stillwater, 1977-78; mgr. Yorktowne Apts., Stillwater, 1977-79; exec. sec. to pres. Univ. Bank, Stillwater, 1978-79; law firm office mgr. Wheatley & Freid Profl. Corp., Stillwater, 1979-81; controller Carberry Distributors, Inc., Stillwater, 1981—. Bartlesville Women's Club scholar, Okla., 1974-77. Mem. Okla. State U. Alumni Assn., Beta Upsilon Sigma. Republican. Mem. Ch. of Christ. Club: Sooner Wives (bd. officer programs 1979-80). Avocations: cooking; investing in stock market; softball. Home: 1603 Berkshire Stillwater OK 74074 Office: Carberry Distributors Inc 515 S Kelly PO Box 1777 Stillwater OK 74076

WRIGHT, DEBBIE KAY, lawyer, state official; b. Roanoke Rapids, N.C., Apr. 17, 1955; d. Henry Floyde and Gladys Doreatha (Porch) Wright. B.S. Biology, Western Carolina U. Cullowhee, N.C., 1973-77; M.A., Wake Forest U., Winston-Salem, N.C., 1977-78; J.D., U. N.C., 1983. Bar: N.C. 1983. Jr. exec. Thalimers Dept. Store, Winston-Salem, 1978-80; legal intern North Central Legal Assn. Program, Durham, N.C., 1981-82; pro diem dist. atty. Wake County Dist. Atty.'s Office (N.C.), Raleigh, 1983-84; assoc. atty. gen. N.C. Dept. Justice, 1984—; tutor U. N.C. Sch. Law, Chapel Hill, 1981;13 ; participant Domestic Law Clinic, Chapel Hill, 1980-83. Staff aide Edmisten for Gov. campaign, Durham, 1984. Named Chief Justice Honor Ct. U. N.C. Sch. Law, 1982; scholar N.C. Bd. Govs., 1977, Dobson scholar in biology, Western Carolina U. 1977. Mem. ABA, N.C. Bar Assn., N.C. Assn. Black Lawyers, Mortar Bd. Baptist. Home: 1131 A Lupine Ct Raleigh NC 27606

WRIGHT, DEIEDRE ANNE, real estate broker; b. Houston, Aug. 14, 1953; d. Chester A. and Fay Joyce (Gaines) W. B.A., Tex. So. U., 1975, M.S., 1985; postgrad. in social gerontology Tex. A&M U., 1985—. Geophys. data technician Exxon Co., U.S.A., Houston, 1974-78; computer programmer/analyst City of Houston, 1978-81; real estate broker Wright Real Estate, Houston, 1981—. Active Gulf Coast Community Services, Houston, 1978—. Mem. Nat. Assn. Realtors, Tex. Assn. Realtors, Houston Bd. Realtors, Research Assn. Minority Profs., Am. Sociol. Assn., Southwest Sociol. Assn., Alpha Kappa Delta (chpt. pres. 1984-85, chpt. sec. 1985—), Delta Sigma Theta, Sigma Delta Chi. Avocations: tennis; swimming; cycling. Office: Wright Real Estate Co PO Box 1532 Houston TX 77251

WRIGHT, DIANA LOUISE, communications company manager; b. Bklyn., Oct. 25, 1946; d. Eugene and Lula (Owens) W. B.A. in Psychology, Plattsburgh State U., 1968. Asst. youth service coordinator Clinton County Youth Commn., Plattsburgh, N.Y., 1968; tng. and devel. mgr. AT&T, N.Y.C., 1969-72, asst. editor, 1973-77, mgr. pub. relations, 1978-80, account exec., 1981-83; nat. account mgr., 1984—. Recipient Significant Sales award AT&T, 1979, 80, 82, 84. Mem. Nat. Assn. Female Execs., Soc. Consumer Affairs Profls. Avocations: interior decorating; antiques; landscape design. Home: 24 Grant Ave Cresskill NJ 07620 Office: AT&T 32 Ave of the Americas New York NY

WRIGHT, ELEANORE REIDELL, physician; b. Mattoon, Ill., June 17, 1915; d. Joseph Emanual and Mabel Edna (Eckerly) Reidell; B.S., U. Ill., 1938, B.M., 1940, M.D., 1941, cert. hosp. adminstr., 1959; m. Curtis Wright, Mar. 21, 1941; m. 2d, Arthur O. Hecker, Feb. 11, 1955 (dec.); children—Carolyn Pearson, Eleanore H., Sarah Lawrence, Deborah O'Connell, Curtis. Intern, Augustana Hosp., Chgo., 1940-41; resident Ypsilanti (Mich.) State Hosp., 1950-52, Trenton (N.J.) State Hosp., 1952-54; mem. staff Friends Hosp., Phila., 1954-55; asst. supt. Embreeville (Pa.) Hosp., 1955-70, supt., 1970-71; dir. Eastern Pa. Mental Health programs, 1962-65; lectr. U. Ill., 1941-43, Women's Med. Coll., Phila., 1954-68. Chmn. Cecil Republicans, Inc., 1973; pres. Cecil County Soc. Prevention Cruelty to Animals, 1973-75, 76-78, 79-81; bd. dirs. Foster Care, Cecil County; sec. found. Cecil Community Coll. Grantee in field. Cert. hosp. adminstr. Md. Mem. AMA, Am. Psychiat. Assn., Pa. Psychiat. Assn., Chester County Med. Soc., Am. Coll. Neurol. Psychiatry. Presbyterian. Contbr. articles to profl. jours. Home: 1657 Elk Forest Elkton MD 21921

WRIGHT, ESTELLA VIOLA HARRISON (MRS. WILLIAM M. WRIGHT), sculptor; b. Riceville, Ga.; d. Elijah and Elicia (Butler) Harrison; student Art Student's League, 1937, 48-50, (scholar) Newark Mus., 1961, summer 1962, Nat. Acad. Sch. Fine Arts, 1962, NAD, fall 1962; m. William M. Wright, Apr. 24, 1928 (dec.). One-man shows at various banks, also Scott's Auditorium; exhibited in group shows: Artists of Am. at Master Inst., 1941, Audubon Artists Ann., 1942, NAD, 1962, Art Exhbn. Springfield (Mass.), 1962, Countee Cullen Public Library, 1963, Lynn Kottler Gallery, N.Y.C., 1973 others; commd. work includes bas relief in plaster, 1976, trophy for Boy Scouts Am., Bklyn., 1977; life-size works various persons, including George Washington Carver, Thomas Bethune, also portrait busts including Eubie Blake, Booker T. Washington, Mary McLoed Bethune; represented in permanent collections: Schromberg Collection, N.Y.C. Public Library, Public Sch. 92, N.Y.C. Mus., also pvt. collections. Bd. dirs. Gray lady Harlem Hosp., N.Y.C., 1951—. Recipient certificate of public service State of N.Y., 1958, citation for meritorious service Bklyn. Women's Council, 1963. Mem. Art Students League (life), John Brown Meml. Assn., Rosicrucian Anthrosophic League Sch. Philosophy. Home: 226 W 138th St New York NY 10030 Office: Art Student League 215 W 57th St New York NY 10019

WRIGHT, FRANCES JANE, educational psychologist; b. Los Angeles, Dec. 22, 1943; d. step-father John David and Evelyn Jane (Dale) Brinegar. B.A., Long Beach State U., 1965, secondary tchr. cert., 1966; M.A., Brigham Young U., 1968, Ed.D., 1980; postdoctoral U. Nev., 1970, U. Utah, 1972-73, Utah State U., 1985—. Cert. tchr., adminstr. Utah. Asst. dir. Teenpost Project, San Pedro, Calif., 1966; caseworker Los Angeles County, 1966-67; self-care inservice dir. Utah State Tng. Sch., American Fork, Utah, 1968, vocat. project designer, 1968; tchr. mentally handicapped Santa Ana Unified Schs., Calif., 1968-69; state specialist intellectually handicapped State Office Edn., Salt Lake City, 1969-70; vocat. counselor Manpower, Salt Lake City, 1970-71; tchr. severely handicapped Davis County Schs., Farmington, Utah, 1971-73, diagnostician, 1973-74, resource elem. tchr., 1974-78; instr. Brigham Young U., Salt Lake City, 1976—; resource tchr. jr. high Davis County Schs., Farmington, 1978—; ednl. cons., Murray, Utah, 1973—; cons. and lectr. in field. Author curriculums in spl. edn.; contbr. articles to profl. jours. Named Profl. of Yr., Utah Assn. for Children with Learning Disabilities, 1985. Mem. Assn. Children/Adults with Learning Disabilities (del. 1979-85, nat. nominating com. 1985-86), NEA, Nat. Assn. Female Execs., Utah Assn. Children/Adults with Learning Disabilities (exec. bd. 1978-84, profl. adv. bd. 1985—), Council Exceptional Children (div. learning disabilities, behavioral disorders), Utah Ednl. Assn., Davis County Edn. Assn. Democrat. Mormon. Lodge: Job's Daughters. Avocations: geneology research; horseback riding; sketching; crafts; reading. Home: 5212 Gravenstein Park Murray UT 84123 Office: Kaysville Jr High Sch Kaysville UT 84037

WRIGHT, GERALDINE HATHAWAY (JERE), public relations consultant; b. Salem, Oreg., Aug. 25, 1926; Gail A. and Mary R. (Peterson) H.; B.A., U. Md., 1947; postgrad. YWCA Profl. Sch., 1950; children—Gaile Rosamond, Winfield Grant, Carter Lee. Asso. dir. Internat. Festival of Mime, 1981; cons. United Cable TV, 1981, Fairfax Symphony Orch., 1979-81, STRAIGHT, Inc., 1981-83, Clews Comminication, 1985-86, Children's Hospice Internat.; devel. cons. Wolf Trap Found. for Performing Arts, Wolf Trap Farm Park, 1975-79; pub. relations cons. to Mrs. Jouett Shouse, founder, chmn. Wolf Trap Farm Park for the Performing Arts, 1969-72; acting dir. Fairfax County Council of the Arts, 1973-74; public relations cons. So. Rural Action, 1971-73; YWCA Teen-Age dir., Washington, 1949-54; guest lectr. arts mgmt. Am. U., Washington, 1981—. Vice pres. Fairfax County Council of the Arts, 1969-70, adv. bd., 1972-76; bd. dirs. YWCA of Fairfax County, 1960-66, program chmn. and children's theatre chmn., 1962-65; chmn. Leopold Stokowski's No. Va. Concert, 1963; co-chmn. Community Communications Conf., Washington, 1973; chmn. No. Va. Communications Conf., 1975; bd. dirs. No. Va. Community Found., 1979—, others; co-chmn. Internat. Children's Festival at Wolf Trap, 1983, Women of Yr., Nat. Capital Area YWCAs. Recipient Nat. Public Relations Service award Public Relations Soc. Am., 1974, Pres.'s Citation and Thoth award, 1973; Cert. of Appreciation for service Fairfax Council Council of Arts, 1974. Mem. Fairfax County C. of C., Nat. Collegiate Players, No. Va. Press Club, Capital Speakers Club, Delta Delta Delta, Alpha Psi Omega. Episcopalian. Clubs: Fairfax Symphony Assn., Wolf Trap Assn. Author: (with Harold M. Shaw) Smokey Bear and Ranger Hal, LP, 1970; producer; Tribute to Freedom with Senator Everett M. Dirksen, 1972; lyracist, author, various children's stories. Address: 11060 Thrush Ridge Rd Reston VA 22090

WRIGHT, HELEN KENNEDY, editor, librarian; b. Indpls., Sept. 23, 1927; d. William Henry and Ida Louise (Crosby) Kennedy; m. Carl F. Prince, Sept. 18, 1950 (div. 1967); 1 child, Carl Freeman Prince; m. Samuel Arthur Wright, Sept. 5, 1970. B.A., Butler U., 1945, M.S., 1950; M.S.L.S., Columbia U., 1952. Pub. librarian N.Y. Pub. Library, N.Y.C., 1952-53; young adults librarian Bklyn. Pub. Library, 1953-54; cataloger U. Utah, Salt Lake City, 1954-57; librarian Chgo. Pub. Library, 1957-58; mem. staff pub. dept. ALA, Chgo., 1958—; cons. Macmillan Ednl. Corp., N.Y.C., 1985. Contbr. to books. Mem. Phi Kappa Phi, Kappa Delta Pi, Phi Chi Nu. Avocations: psychology of reading; mosaics. Home: 1138 W Illinois St Chicago IL 60643 Office: ALA 50 E Huron St Chicago IL 60611

WRIGHT, JACQUELINE STUCKER, law librarian; b. Euclid, Ohio, Nov. 5, 1933; d. John H. and Betsy (Delaney) Stucker; children—Robert R., John F., David S. B.A., U. Ark., 1955, M.L.I.S., 1985; J.D., U. Okla., 1973. Bar: Okla. 1974, Ark. 1978. Asst. gen. counsel Okla. Assn. Mcpl. Attys., Norman, 1974-76; law clk. Okla. Ct. Appeals, Oklahoma City, 1975-76, Ark. Supreme Ct., Little Rock, 1976-77; instr. U. Ark. Sch. Law, Little Rock, 1977-78; law clk. U.S. Dist. Ct., Little Rock, 1979; librarian Ark. Supreme Ct., Little Rock, 1979—; vice-chair employees ins. adv. com. State of Ark., 1979—. Author: Handbook for Appellate Advocacy, 1980. Mem. Ark. Assn. Women Lawyers (treas. 1978-79, rec. sec. 1980-81, pres. 1981-82), Democrat. Episcopalian. Club: Altrusa (v.p. 1982-84) (Little Rock). Office: Supreme Ct Library Justice Bldg Little Rock AR 72201

WRIGHT, JAIME, grocery distribution company executive; b. Oklahoma City, July 9, 1949; d. J. Ben and Barbara J. (Birmingham) W. B.A., East Carolina U., 1975, M.A., 1977. Instr. sociology Craven Community Coll., New Bern, N.C., 1976-78; assoc. dir. Northeastern N.C. Profl. Standards Rev. Orgn., New Bern, 1978-80; adj. prof. sociology East Carolina U., Greenville, N.C., 1975-82; mgmt. succession adminstr. Food Lion, Salisbury, N.C., 1982-86; corp. tng. mgr. McLane Co., Temple, Tex., 1986—. Active Council on Status of Women, Carteret County, N.C., 1980-82; vol. VA Hosp., Salisbury, N.C., 1985. Named Young Career Woman of Yr., Bus. and Profl. Women, Havelock, N.C., 1978; East Carolina U. scholar, 1976, grantee, 1977. Mem. Am. Soc. Tng. and Devel. Republican. Office: McLane Co PO Drawer 80 Temple TX 76501

WRIGHT, JANET H., management company executive; b. Lansing, Mich., May 5, 1936; d. Alfred E. and Olive (Woodry) H.; m. Paul E. Peterson, Dec. 20, 1959 (div. Dec. 1971); Andrew, Russell, Timothy; m. Thompson T. Wright, May 11, 1973; stepchildren—Robert, William, Debra, Holly, Diane, Donna, Thompson. Ed. Mich. State U., 1954-59. Cert. expn. mgr. Engaged in radio, TV and ice show prodn. and pub. relations, 1958-73; asst. dir. convs. Profl. Photographers Am., Des Plaines, Ill., 1975-78; pres. The Wright Orgn., Inc., Des Plaines, 1978—. Officer, Des Plaines Sister Cities Internat., 1983—; rec. sec. Des Plaines Sesquicentennial, 1984-85; judge U.S. Figure Skating Assn., 1978—; mem. DuPage Figure Skating Club, 1984—. Mem. Nat. Assn. Expn. Mgrs. (bd. dirs. 1985—, chpt. pres. 1983, chpt. bd. dirs. 1979-84), Meeting Planners Internat., Trade Show Bur., LWV (chpt. officer), P.E.O. (organizing chpt. pres. 1962). Avocation: figure skating. Office: Wright Orgn 716 Lee St Des Plaines IL 60016

WRIGHT, JANET SCRITSMIER, investment consultant; b. Pomona, Calif., May 21, 1960; d. Jerome Lorenzo and Mildred Joan (Lloyd) Scritsmier; m. James Calvin Wright, Mar. 26, 1983; children—Justin Michael, Corey Gray. Student Calif. State Poly. U., 1978-79. Vice pres. sales E.L.A. Co., Industry, Calif., 1979-84; investment cons. Cameron Properties Inc., Covina, Calif., 1980—. Asst. instr. Dale Carnegie Sales Course, 1981-82, Human Relations, 1983. Republican. Mormon. Avocation: snow skiing. Home: 2454 N Cameron Ave Covina CA 91724

WRIGHT, JEAN VERLICH, writer, public relations executive; b. McKeesport, Pa., July 5, 1950; d. Matthew Louis and Irene (Tomko) Verlich; student Bucknell U., 1968-69; B.A., U. Pitts., 1971; m. S(tanley) Wayne Wright, Sept. 29, 1979. Press sec. Com. to Re-elect President, S.W. Pa., 1972; adminstrv. asst. Pa. Rep. James B. Kelly III, 1972-73; reporter Beaver (Pa.) County Times, 1973-74; proofreader Ketchum, MacLeod & Grove, Pitts., 1975-76; community relations specialist, PPG Industries, Pitts., 1976-77, editor PPG News, 1977-79, sr. staff writer, 1979-84, communications coordinator, 1984-85; pub. relations assoc. Glass Group, 1986—. Mem. Internat. Assn. Bus. Communicator (dir. Pitts. chpt. 1981, v.p. public relations Pitts. chpt. 1982, v.p. Pitts. chpt. 1985, pres. Pitts. chpt. 1986), Aviation/Space Writers Assn., Phi Beta Kappa, Delta Zeta. Office: One PPG Pl 32 E Pittsburgh PA 15272

WRIGHT, JEANNE JASON, editor, publishing executive; b. Washington, June 24, 1934; d. Robert Stewart and Elizabeth (Gaddis) Jason; m. Benjamin Hickman Wright, Oct. 30, 1965. B.A., Radcliffe Coll., 1956; M.A., U. Chgo., 1958. Cert. social worker, N.Y. Psychiat. social worker various mental health facilities, 1958-70; gen. mgr. Black Media, Inc., N.Y.C., 1970-74, pres., 1974-75; pres. Black Resources, Inc., N.Y.C., 1975—; exec. editor New Nat. Black Monitor, N.Y.C., 1975—. Mem. planning com. 1st Black Power Conf., Newark, 1966, 2d conf., Phila., 1967; bd. dirs. YWCA, N.Y.C., 1968-69; mem. planning com. First Internat. Black Cultural and Bus. Expn. Greater N.Y. Operation Breadbasket, 1971. Recipient Pres.'s award Nat. Assn. Black Women Attys., 1977; 2d ann. Freedom's Jour. award U. D.C. Dept. Communicative and Performing Arts, 1979. Mem. Nat. Assn. Media Women (Media Woman of Year 1984), Nat. Assn. Social Workers, Inc., AAAS, Acad. Cert. Social Workers, Inc., Alpha Kappa Alpha, U. Chgo. Alumni Assn. Democrat. Clubs: Radcliffe of N.Y., Harvard of N.Y., Newswomen's of N.Y. Office: 410 Central Park W Ph C New York NY 10025

WRIGHT, JEANNE STALLINGS, advertising manager; b. Birmingham, Ala., June 12, 1930; d. Millard and Irma (Hitchcock) Stallings; m. John Leo Wright, Jr., Apr. 15, 1950; children—Debra Carmack, John Wright, Teresa Roberson, Maureen Spears, Mark. Student U. Ala., 1947-49, Gulf State Art Sch., 1949-50. File clerk Birmingham News, 1949-50, promotion and research, 1953-57; tchr. Our Lady of Sorrows Sch., Birmingham, 1962-63; advt. sales Birmingham News, 1967, telephone sales mgr., 1971, asst. classified advt. mgr., 1976, classified advt. mgr., 1983—. Mem. Salvation Army Women's Aux. Mem. Assn. Profl. Saleswomen (charter, sec.), Sales and Mktg. Execs. Club, So. Classified Advt. Mgrs. Assn., (dir.), Am. Newspaper Classified Mgrs. Assn. Democrat. Roman Catholic. Home: 4300 10th Ave S Birmingham AL 35222 Office: Birmingham News Co 2400 4th Ave N Birmingham AL 35222

WRIGHT, JEANNIE BIRD, financial planner; b. Greensboro, N.C., Sept. 10, 1950; d. Ignacio and Lucy (Jennette) Bird; m. John V. Wright, Mar. 9, 1974 (div. 1978). B.A., Emory U., 1972. Cert. fin. planner; C.L.U.; chartered fin. cons. Fin. planner FSC Adv. Corp., Atlanta, 1972-74; dir. personal fin. planning Robinson Humphrey Co., Inc., Atlanta, 1974—; instr. Emory U., 1984. Bd. dirs., pres. Clairmont North Homeowners Assn., Atlanta, 1982-83. Mem. Internat. Assn. Fin. Planning (v.p. 1981-82), Atlanta Assn. Women in Securities (pres. 1982), Atlanta Women's Network. Avocations: traveling; birdwatching; sailing.

WRIGHT, JOSEPHINE ROSA BEATRICE, musicologist; b. Detroit, Sept. 5, 1942; d. Joseph Le Vander and Eva Lee Garrison W.; Mus.B., U. Mo., Columbia, 1963, M.A., 1967; Mus.M., Pius XII Acad., Florence, Italy, 1964; Ph.D., N.Y.U., 1975. Instr. music York Coll., CUNY, 1972-75, asst. prof., 1975; asst. prof. Afro-Am. studies in musicology Harvard U., Cambridge, Mass., 1976-81; asso. dir. integration of Afro-Am. folk arts with music project, Nat. Endowment Humanities, 1979-82; assoc. prof. music Coll. of Wooster, 1981—; panelist, cons. on music Mass. Council of Arts and Humanities, 1978-80; cons. Nat. Endowment Humanities, 1982-83, Ohio Humanities Council, 1986. Mem. AAUW, Am. Musicol. Soc., Internat. Musicol. Assn., Coll. Music Soc., Assn. for Study of Afro-Am. Life and History, Sonneck Soc., U. Mo. Faculty of Arts and Sci. Alumni Assn. (trustee 1982-85), Pi Kappa Lambda. Democrat. Episcopalian (vestry). Author: Ignatius Sancho (1729-1780), An Early African Composer in England: The Collected Edition of His Music in Facsimile, 1981; editor of new music: The Black Perspective in Music, 1979—; co-editor: The Bicentennial Issue of The Black Perspective in Music, 1976. Contbr. articles to profl. jours. Office: Dept Music Coll of Wooster Wooster OH 44691

WRIGHT, JUDITH MITCHELL, management consultant; b. Balt.; d. John Armitage and Mary (Bowen) Mitchell; R.N., Church Home and Hosp. Sch. Nursing, 1970; m. Harold Russell Wright, Jr., Aug. 15, 1970; children—Alexander Bowen, Morgan du Val Watkins Team leader Good Samaritan Hosp., Balt., 1970-73; patient care coordinator Keswick Home for Incurables, Balt., 1974-76; owner, pres. The Wright Group. Co chmn. Druid Hill tennis project Jr. League Balt., 1977, 78, bd. dirs., 1980-84, asst. treas., 1982-83, treas., 1983-84, also mem. exec. bd.; chmn. security Balt. Internat. Indoor Tennis Championships, 1978; co-chmn. ops. 1st Nat. Grand Prix Tennis Classic, 1979, chmn. ops., 1980, asst. chmn., 1981; com. chmn. Troop 500, Boy Scouts Am., 1985-86; v.p. Brooke Army Med. Ctr. Women's Aux., 1985-86. Republican. Episcopalian. Club: Woman's of Roland Park (pres. jr. dept. 1982-83, bd. govs. 1982-84). Home and Office: 425 Graham Rd Fort Sam Houston TX 78234

WRIGHT, JUDITH RAE, accountant; b. Paoli, Ind., Feb. 16, 1929; d. Samuel Earl and Bernice Louise (Lomax) Hudelson; m. James Edward Walters, July 11, 1947 (div. June 1971); children—Jamie Jo, Jennifer Rae; m. 2d, George Ralph Wright, Feb. 20, 1972 (dec. Apr. 1977). Student Northwood Inst., West Baden, Ind., 1968-69, Ind.-U.-Purdue U., Indpls., 1973-74. Acct., Ind. Hwy. Commn., Indpls., 1969-75, Ind. Dept. Correction, Indpls., 1975-76, Ind. Dept. Pub. Welfare, Indpls., 1976-78, Ind. Office Social Services, Indpls., 1978-79; acct. supr. Ind. Dept. Pub. Welfare, Indpls., 1979-84. Mem. Assn. Govt. Accts., Am. Legion Aux., Kappa Kappa Kappa. Republican. Mem. Christian Ch. Office: Indiana Dept of Public Welfare 100 N Senate Ave Room 708 Indianapolis IN 46204

WRIGHT, KATIE HARPER, educational administrator, journalist; b. Crawfordsville, Ark., Oct. 5, 1923; d. James Hale and Connie Mary (Locke) Harper; B.A., U. Ill., 1944; M.Ed., 1959; Ed.D., St. Louis U., 1979; m. Marvin Wright, Mar. 21, 1952; 1 dau., Virginia K. Jordan. Elem. and spl. edn. tchr. East St. Louis (Ill.) Pub. Schs., 1944-65, dir. Dist. 189 Instructional Materials Program, 1965-71, dir. spl. edn. Dists. 188, 189, 1971-77, asst. supt. programs, 1977-79; adj. faculty Harris/Stowe State Coll., 1980; cons. to numerous workshops, seminars in field; mem. study tour People's Republic of China, 1984. Mem. Ill. Commn. on Children, 1973-85, East St. Louis Bd. Election Commrs.; pres. bd. dirs. St. Clair County Mental Health Center, 1970-72; bd. dirs. River Bluff council Girl Scouts, 1979—, nat. bd. dirs., 1981-84; bd. dirs. United Way, 1979—, Urban League, 1979—; pres. bd. trustees East St. Louis Public Library, 1972-77; charter mem. Coalition of 100 Black Women; mem. coordinating council ethnic affairs Synod of Mid-Am., Presbyn. Ch. U.S.A; charter mem. Metro East Links Group; charter mem. Gateway chpt. The Links, Inc. Recipient Lamp of Learning award East St. Louis Jr. Wednesday Club, 1965; Outstanding Working Woman award Downtown St. Louis, Inc., 1967; Ill. State citation for ednl. document Love is Not Enough, 1974; Delta Sigma Theta citation for document Good Works, 1979; award Nat. Council Negro Women, 1983; Girl Scout Thanks badge, 1982; Community Service award Met. East Bar Assn., 1983; named Woman of Achievement, St. Louis Globe Democrat, 1974, Outstanding Adminstr. So. region Ill. Office Edn., 1975. Mem. Am. Libraries Trustees Assn. (regional v.p. 1978-79, nat. sec. 1979-80), Ill. Commn. on Children, Mensa, Council for Exceptional Children, Top Ladies of Distinction, Delta Sigma Theta (chpt. pres. 1960-62), Kappa Delta Pi (pres. So. Ill. U. chpt. 1973-74), Phi Delta Kappa (Service Key award 1984, chpt. pres. 1984-85), Iota Phi Lambda, Pi Lambda Theta (chpt. pres. 1985—). Republican. Presbyterian. Club: East St. Louis Women's (pres. 1973-75). Contbr. articles to profl. jours.; feature writer St. Louis Argus Newspaper, 1979—. Home: 733 N 40th St East Saint Louis IL 62205

WRIGHT, KAY MORROW, computer information systems educator; b. Baytown, Tex., Sept. 28, 1942; d. Morris Robinson and Martha (Whiteman) Morrow; m. Terry Frank Wright, June 4, 1966; children—Stephanie Lynn, Stacie Cole. B.A. in Math., U. Tex., 1964. Programmer, Bankers Life, Des Moines, 1966-68; programmer analyst Enjay Fibers and Laminates Co., Odenton, Md., 1968-69; dir. data processing Mercy Hosp. Med. Ctr., 1975-78, planning coordinator, 1978-79, computer planning coordinator, 1979-81, systems cons., 1981-82; mktg. assoc. XL-DP, Inc., Des Moines, 1982-84; instr. Coll. Bus. Adminstrn., Drake U., Des Moines, 1984—. Bd. dirs. Iowa Soc. To Prevent Blindness, 1977-83, Mercy Hosp. Credit Union, 1978-80; benefit chmn. Flip for Sight, 1977-81. Mem. Data Processing Mgmt. Assn., Iowa Health Computer Assn. (founding pres. 1978-79), Electronic Computing Health Oriented, Province Alumnae Iowa, Wis. (dir. 1979-84), League Attys. Wives, Delta Zeta (nat. networking chmn. 1984—). Democrat. Methodist. Office: 351 Aliber Hall Drake U Des Moines IA 50311

WRIGHT, LEOLA MARIE, educator; b. Alexandria, La., Nov. 14; d. James Hunter and Elnora (Boxter) Lofton; m. Francis Hawthorne Wright (dec. June 1974); children—Ted Hawthorne, Francine Elaine, Hugh Gilbert. B.A., Huston Tillotson Coll., 1935; M.A. in Edn., Howard U., 1952; postgrad. Catholic U. Am., Tex. A&I U., Del Mar Coll. All level permanent life teaching cert., Tex. Tchr. music Kingsville Ind. Sch. Dist., Tex., 31 yrs.; pianist ch. sch. King Star Baptist Ch., Kingsville. Organizer, pres. Afro-Am. Hist. and Cultural Com. of Kingsville, 1974—; mem. council Camp Fire, Inc., Kingsville. Recipient Leadership award Afro-Am. Hist. and Cultural Com. Kingsville, 1984; Service award Kingsville Ind. Sch. Dist., 1985, Outstanding Tchr. award, 1984-85; award for ch., community and sch. services King Star Bapt. Ch., 1985. Mem. Tex. Music Educators Assn., Tex. State Tchrs. Assn., NEA, AAUW, Assn. Study Afro-Am. Life and History (life), Community Concerts Kingsville, Howard U. Prestige Clubs, Alpha Kappa Alpha. Baptist. Avocation: community work, especially with young people. Home: PO Box 300 Kingsville TX 78363

WRIGHT, LILYAN BOYD, educator; b. Upland, Pa., May 11, 1920; d. Albert Verlenden and Mabel (Warburton) Boyd; B.S., Temple U., 1942, M.Ed., 1946; Ed.D., Rutgers U., 1972; m. Richard P. Wright, Oct. 23, 1942; 1 dau., Nicki Warburton (Mrs. Arthur Scott Vanek). Tchr. health and phys. edn. Woodbury (N.J.) High Sch., 1942-43, Glen-Nor High Sch., Glenolden, Pa., 1944-46, Chester (Pa.) High Sch., 1946-54; chmn. women's dept. health and phys, edn. Union (N,J.) High Sch., 1954-61; with Trenton State Coll., 1961—, head women's program health and phys. edn., 1967-77, chmn. dept. health, phys. edn. and recreation, 1977—; mem. N.J. State Com. Div. Girls and Women's Sports, 1958-80; chmn. New Atlantic Field Hockey Sectional Umpiring, 1981-85; chmn. New Atlantic Field Hockey Assn., 1985—. Active Chester United Fund; water safety, first aid instr. ARC Scholarship in her honor N.J. Athletic Assn. Girls, 1971; named to Hall of Fame, Temple U., 1976. Mem. AAHPER (chmn. Eastern dist. assn. div. girls and women's sports, sec. to council for services Eastern dist. 1979-80, chmn. 1980-81, N.J. rep. to council for convs. 1984-85), N.J. AHPER (pres. 1974-75, past pres. 1975-76, v.p. phys. edn. div., Disting. Service and Leadership award 1969, Honor Fellow award 1977), N.J. Women's Lacrosse Assn. (umpiring chmn. 1972-76), Nat. Assn. Phys. Edn. in Higher Edn., Eastern Assn. Phys. Edn. Coll. Women, AAUP, North Jersey, Central Jersey bds. women's ofcls., Am., Pa. (v.p. 1953-54), Chester (pres. 1949-54) fedns. tchrs., U.S. (exec. com.), North Jersey (past pres.) field hockey assns., Kappa Delta Epsilon, Delta Psi Kappa (past pres. Phila. alumni chpt.), Kappa Delta Pi. Episcopalian. Home: 260 Green Valley Rd Langhorne PA 19047 Office: Trenton State College Trenton NJ 08625

WRIGHT, MARGARET ADA BENNETT, business executive; b. Camden, N.J., Dec. 20, 1918; d. John Henry and Margaret Catherine (Bloxsom) Bennett. B.S., Glassboro State Coll., 1940; M.A., St. Mary's U., 1970; Ph.D., U. Tex., 1976. Cert. elem., secondary tchr., N.J., Tex.; lic. profl. counselor, Tex.; nat. cert. counselor. Tchr. elem. and secondary schs., N.J., 1940-42, 46-48, Tex., 1966-70; adminstr. Student Aid Library and Counseling Ctr., Minnie Stevens Piper Found., San Antonio, 1970-73; counselor Incarnate Word Coll., San Antonio, 1974-75; exec. dir. Tex. Personnel and Guidance Assn., Austin, 1976-79; pres. New Outlook Inc., 1979—; asst. prof. dept. counseling and human services Grad. Sch., St. Mary's U., 1981-85; producer/dir. ann. conf. Women of 80's, 1980-82. Editor, mng. editor counselor's newsletters and profl. jours. Contbr. articles to profl. jours. Author: Programs Emphasizing Positive Personal Development, 1981. Editor newsletter Women in Bus. Active grad. com. instl. self-study St. Mary's U., 1970-72; bd. dirs. St. Mary's Alumni Assn., 1974-77, Las Palmas YWCA, San Antonio, 1982-84, San Antonio Women's Law Ctr., 1974-78, pres. 1978. Served with USNR (WAVES), 1942-46. Mem. Am. Assn. Counseling and Devel., Nat. Vocat. Guidance Assn. Republican. Home: PO Box 29221 San Antonio TX 78229

WRIGHT, MARY RUTH (MRS. WILLIAM KEMP WRIGHT), psychologist; b. St. Louis, Apr. 2, 1922; d. Leon Carl and Gwendolyn (Travis) Brown; R.N., Washington U., St. Louis, 1944; B.S., U. Houston, 1966, M.A., 1967; Ph.D., Union Grad. Sch., 1978; m. William Kemp Wright, Feb. 10, 1945; children—Gwendolyn, Veronica, Victoria, Jennifer. Instr. surgery Washington U. Sch. Nursing, 1944-45, U.S. Cadet Nurse Corps, USPHS, 1944; instr. pediatrics Children's Meml. Hosp., Chgo., 1945-46; teaching fellow U. Houston, 1965-66; instr. S. Tex. Jr. Coll., Houston, 1967-70; mental health cons. St. Joseph Mental Hosp., Houston, 1966-67; staff psychol. services Almeda Clinic, Houston, 1966-70; pvt. practice marriage and family counselor, Houston, 1970—; med.-psychol. researcher and writer, 1970—; psychologist Vasectomy Clinic, Houston Dept. Health, 1971—; clin. asst. prof. psychology, dept. otorhinolaryngology and communicative scis. Baylor Coll. Medicine, Houston, 1979. Recipient spl. award Security Agy., 1945. Mem. Am. Psychol. Assn., Am. Assn. Marriage and Family Counselors, Am. Assn. Sex Educators and Counselors, Internat. Council Psychologists, Nat. Council Family Relations, Nat. Assn. Social Workers, Mental Health Assn. Houston and Harris County (dir.). Contbr. articles to profl. jours. Home: 3671 Del Monte St Houston TX 77019 Office: 633 Hermann Profl Bldg Houston TX 77030

WRIGHT, PATRICIA GEORGIA, accountant; b. Manchester, Jamaica, Feb. 25, 1949; d. James Alexander Wright and Blanche Leonie (Wilson) W. B.Sc., Long Island U., 1980, M.B.A., 1986. Asst. resident mgr. Hedonism II/Couples, Jamaica, 1976-78; exec. asst. mgr. Lotus Tours N.Y., 1978-80; sr. acct. Am. Fedn. Arts, N.Y.C., 1980-83; fin. controller Internat. Ctr. Photography, N.Y.C., 1983—; cons. in field. Contbr. research in field. Mem. Am. Mgmt. Assn., Am. Assn. Museums, CPA Candidates Assn., ARC Assn., Jr. C. of C. Home: 330 E 19th St Brooklyn NY 11226 Office: 1130 Fifth Ave New York NY 10128

WRIGHT, PAULA CHRISTINE, educator; b. Cleve., Jan. 2, 1955; d. Paul R. and Gertrude R. (Christman) W. A.B. in French, John Carroll U., 1978, postgrad in edn., 1980—. French and Spanish tchr. Glen Oak Sch. for Girls, Gates Mills, Ohio, 1978-79, Upward Bound Project, Case Western Res. U., Cleve., 1980—, Kirk Middle Sch., East Cleveland, Ohio, 1980-81, Shaw High Sch., East Cleveland, 1981-84, Shaker Heights High Sch., Ohio, 1984-85; Midwest del. Fgn. Lang. Tchrs. Inst., NEH, Purdue U., summer 1985. Recipient excellence in teaching award Case Western Res. U., 1983; named Tchr. of Yr., Univ. Project Upward Bound, 1984. Vice-pres., treas. St. Dominic Choir, 1984-85. Democrat. Roman Catholic. Club: Fortuna Investment II (treas 1976-83) (Cleve.). Avocations: reading; needlework. Office: 15911 Aldersyde Rd Shaker Heights OH 44120

WRIGHT, ROSE MARIE, controller; b. Boston, July 14, 1947; d. James Melbourne and Viola Margaret Stevenson; B.S.B.A. magna cum laude, Wright State U., 1973; postgrad. Ohio State U., 1979-80; m. Thew Wright, III, July 14, 1971. Sr. acct. Peat, Marwick, Mitchell & Co., Cin., 1973-76; supervising sr. auditor Borden, Inc., Columbus, Ohio, 1976-79; mgr. internal auditing Ohio Med. Indemnity Mut., Columbus, 1979; controller, chief fin. officer Agfoods, Inc., Columbus, 1980—. Trustee, Epilepsy Assn. Franklin County, 1981-82, treas., 1982-83. C.P.A., Ohio. Mem. Am. Inst. C.P.A.s, Ohio Soc. C.P.A.s, Acctg. Research Assn., Nat. Soc. Accts. for Coops., Nat. Council Phys. Distbn. Mgmt., Nat. Council Farmer Coops (legal, tax and acctg. com.). Club: Continental Athletic. Office: Agfoods Inc 3775 Zane Trace Dr Columbus OH 43228

WRIGHT, SARAH BIRD, educator, writer; b. Wilmington, N.C., Nov. 25, 1933; d. Richard Oscar and Elise (Martin) Grant; m. R.L. Wright, Sept. 7, 1963; 1 child, Alexander Grant. A.B., Bryn Mawr Coll., 1955; M.A., Duke U., 1958. Tchr. English composition and lit. Boston U., 1959-60; research asst. linguistics Harvard U. Computation Lab., 1960-62; copy editor Beacon Press and Allyn & Bacon, Boston, 1963-70; instr. English, U. Richmond, Va., 1981—. Contbr. to newspapers and mags. including Christian Sci. Monitor, N.Y. Times, Accent on Living, Newsday, Toronto Globe & Mail, Chgo. Tribune other jours. Dist. councilor Bryn Mawr Coll. Alumnae Assn., 1975-78; vol. Va. Mus., 1980-81. Mem. Authors Guild N.Y., MLA. Episcopalian. Club: Richmond Woman's. Home: 3505 Old Gun Rd Midlothian VA 23113 Office: English Dept Room 405 Ryland Hall U Richmond Richmond VA 23227

WRIGHT, SHARON SUE POTTER, banker; b. Dallas, Mar. 4, 1940; d. Millard M. and Gladys P. (Potter); student N. Tex. State U., 1958-59, U. Tex., Arlington, 1960-62, Am. Inst. Banking, 1963; m. Robert E. Wright, Apr. 28, 1965; children—Deborah Sue, David Michael. Exec. sec. First Nat. Bank, Duncanville, Tex., 1962-63, Trinity Nat. Bank, Dallas, 1963-65; ops. officer Exchange Bank and Trust, Dallas, 1965-76; v.p. Nat. Bank of Commerce of Dallas, 1976-80; sr. v.p., cashier Tex. Am. Bank, Dallas, 1980—. Bd. dirs. Cedar Hill (Tex.) Youth Assn., 1966-78. Mem. Nat. Assn. Bank Women, Am. Inst. Banking, Bankers Adminstrn. Inst., Am. Bankers Assn., Cedar Hill C. of C. Mem. Churches of Christ. Office: Tex Am Bank 6300 Harry Hines Blvd Dallas TX 75235

WRIGHT, SUSAN WEBBER, law educator; b. Texarkana, Ark., Aug. 22, 1948; d. Thomas Edward and Betty Jane (Gary) Webber; m. Robert Ross Wright, III, May 21, 1983. B.A., Randolph-Macon Woman's Coll., 1970; M.P.A., U. Ark., 1972, J.D. with high honors, 1975. Bar: Ark. 1975. Law clk. U.S. Ct. Appeals 8th Circuit, 1975-76; asst. prof. law U. Ark.-Little Rock, 1976-78, assoc. prof., 1978-83, prof., 1983—, asst. dean, 1976-78; vis. assoc. prof. Ohio State U., Columbus, 1981, La. State U., Baton Rouge, 1982-83; mem. adv. com. U.S. Ct. Appeals 8th Circuit, St. Louis, 1983—. Author: (with R. Wright) Land Use in a Nutshell, 1978, 2d edit., 1985; editor-in-chief Ark. Law Rev., 1975; contbr. articles to profl. jours. Mem. ABA, Ark. Bar Assn., Pulaski County Bar Assn., Ark. Assn. Women Lawyers (v.p. 1977-78). Episcopalian. Office: Sch Law Univ Ark 400 W Markham St Little Rock AR 72201

WRIGHT-SCHULZ, MARILYN KAY, advertising agency executive, marketing consultant, public relations specialist; b. Bath, N.Y., Dec. 1, 1944; d. Elmer Edward Wright and Louise Emma (Buckley) Hastings; m. Elton Schulz, Sept. 30, 1967 (div. 1982); children—Steven Edward, Christina Louise; m. George Scott, June 22, 1985. A.A., Alfred Tech. U., 1964; B.A., Syracuse U., 1966. Coordinator internal pub. relations Eastman Kodak Co., Rochester, N.Y., 1966-70; freelance writer, Rochester, 1975-83, tech. writer, 1977—; program producer, host Radio and Cable TV, Rochester, 1980-83; dir. pub. relations WGMC Radio, Greece, N.Y., 1980-83; pres., owner Pilgrim Assocs. Rochester, 1982—; cons. County Sch. Bd. Assn., Rochester, 1979-81; editor Rochester Sesquicentennial Book, 1984. Chmn. 10th Anniversary Com., Greece, N.Y., 1977; pres. PTA, Greece, 1978-79; bd. dirs. YMCA, Downtown Promotion Council, Ctr. for Ednl. Devel.; v.p. Community Ednl. Adv. Council, Greece, 1979-81; bd. dirs. Nat. Tech. Inst. for Deaf. Recipient Cert. of Merit, County Sch. Bd., Rochester, 1981. Mem. Women in Communications, Inc., Rochester C. of C., Rochester Women's Council. Republican. Episcopalian. Home: 49 Cloverland Dr Rochester NY 14610 Office: Pilgrim Assocs 3300 Monroe Ave Rochester NY 14618

WRIGHTSON, MARJORY BEATRICE, real estate broker; b. Portland, Oreg., Apr. 15, 1926; d. Edwin and Marjory (Green) Smith; m. William Vaughn Wrightson, Sept. 17, 1949; children—William C., Marjory Ann, Robert E., David A., Susan L. Real estate sales tng. Lane Community Coll. Office worker Charles F. Berg Co., Portland, 1944-46, Robert Bros., Portland, 1946-47, Portland Clinic, 1947-49; part-time office worker and sales rep. Oreg. Pacific & Eastern R.R., Cottage Grove, Bauder & Young Co., Cottage Grove, 1969-73; acct. M.L. Sizemore, C.P.A., Cottage Grove, 1967-73; pres., broker Bohemia Realty, Inc., Cottage Grove, 1981—. Democratic precinct chmn., 1984-85; bd. dirs. South Lane Maintenance, 1985. Mem. Cottage Grove Bd. Realtors (sec. 1977, v.p. 1981, pres. 1982, treas. 1985—, certs. of appreciation). Episcopalian. Lodge: Order Eastern Star (worthy matron 1984-85). Avocations: painting; golf; gardening; crafts. Home: 201 Talemena Dr Cottage Grove OR 97424 Office: Bohemia Realty Inc 636 Jefferson St Cottage Grove OR 97424

WRIGLEY, ELIZABETH SPRINGER (MRS. OLIVER K. WRIGLEY), found. exec.; b. Pitts., Oct. 4, 1915; d. Charles Woodward and Sarah Maria (Roberts) Springer; B.A., U. Pitts., 1935; B.S., Carnegie Inst. Tech., 1936; m. Oliver Kenneth Wrigley, June 16, 1936 (dec. July 26, 1978). Procedure analyst U.S. Steel Corp., Pitts., 1941-43; Research asst. The Francis Bacon Found., Inc., Los Angeles, 1944, exec., 1945-50, trustee, 1950—, dir. research, 1951-53, pres., 1954—. Mem. Renaissance Soc. Am., Modern Humanities Research Assn., Am. Cryptogram Assn., Alpha Delta Pi. Presbyn. Mem. Order Eastern Star, Damascus Shrine. Editor: The Skeleton Text of the Shakespeare Folio L.A. (W. C. Arensberg), 1952; (with David W. Davies) A Concordance to the Essays of Francis Bacon, 1973. Compiler: Short Title Catalogue Numbers in the Library of the Francis Bacon Foundation, 1958, supplement, 1967, Lee Bernard Collection in American Political Theory, 1972; compiler, pub. Wing Numbers in the Francis Bacon Library, 1959. Home: 4805 N Pal Mal Ave Temple City CA 91780 Office: 655 N Dartmouth Ave Claremont CA 91711

WRINGER, PAULA HARMON, educator; b. Princeton, Ind., Aug. 23, 1945; d. Roderick Allen and Emily Lou (Williams) Harmon; B.Nursing, U. Evansville, 1967, M.S., 1975; m. Ralph Dean Wringer, Dec. 9, 1967; children—Brian Allen, Edra Lynn. Unit supr. Norman Beatty Psychiat. Hosp., Westville, Ind., 1967-70; instr. nursing Purdue-North Central Campus, Westville, 1970-73; instr. nursing U. Evansville (Ind.), 1973-75, Olney (Ill.) Community Coll., 1975-76; asst. prof. nursing Purdue U., West Lafayette, Ind., 1976—, acting head baccalaureate program, 1982-83, dir. div. family centered nursing, 1983—; cons. Lafayette Home Hosp., 1978. Sec. Am. Heart Assn., Tippecanoe unit, 1979-82, v.p., 1982—; mem. adv. bd. Tippecanoe County Elderly Ombudsman, 1979—. Mem. Nat. League Nursing, Am. Nurses Assn., Central Ind. Health Systems Agy., Sigma Theta Tau, Alpha Tau Delta. Baptist. Club: Order Eastern Star. Office: Purdue U Sch Nursing West Lafayette IN 47907

WROBEL, BONNIE JANE, film company executive; b. Akron, Ohio, Jan. 25, 1941; d. George Mayfield Reed and Grace Jane (Gercevic) Morrison; m. Joseph Stanley Wrobel, Jan. 28, 1959 (div. July 1971); children—Vicki Jayne, Eric Joseph, Teri Jo Huston. A.A. in Bus. Law, Los Angeles Valley Coll., 1974; B.A. in Bus. Adminstrn., U. Akron, 1964. Sec. Los Angeles Valley Coll. Business-women's Assn., 1973-74; ops. mgr. TV bus. affairs dept. Columbia Pictures Industries, Burbank, Calif., 1984—. Recipient award of Merit Columbia Pictures Industries, 1977. Mem. Women in Film, Women of Motion Picture Industry, Nat. Assn. Female Execs., Kappa Kappa Gamma (sec. 1962-64). Democrat. Roman Catholic. Avocation: interior design. Home: 20838 Satinwood Dr Saugus CA 91350 Office: Columbia Pictures Industries 306 Columbia Plaza North Burbank CA 91505

WROBLESKI, JEANNE PAULINE, lawyer; b. Phila., Feb. 14, 1942; d. Edward Joseph and Pauline (Popelak) Wrobleski; m. Robert J. Klein, Dec. 3, 1979. B.A., Immaculata Coll., 1964; M.A., U. Pa., 1966; J.D., Temple U., 1975. Bar: Pa. 1975. Pvt. practice law, Phila., 1975—. Mem. Commn. on Women and the Legal Profession, 1986. Rhea Liebman scholar, 1974. Mem. AAUW, ABA, Phila. Bar Assn. (chmn. women's rights com. 1986, com. on jud. selection and reform 1986, investigative com. of commn. jud. selection and retention 1986), Pa. Bar Assn., Alpha Psi Omega, Lambda Iota Tau. Democrat. Clubs: Lawyers, Peale. Office: Kohn Savett Marion & Graf PC 2400 One Reading Ctr 1101 Market St Philadelphia PA 19107

WROBLOWA, HALINA STEFANIA, electrochemist; b. Gdansk, Poland, July 5, 1925; came to U.S., 1960, naturalized, 1970; M.Sc., U. Lodz (Poland), 1949; Ph.D., Warsaw Inst. Tech., 1958; 1 child, Krystyna Wrobel-Knight. Chmn. dept. prep. studies U. Lodz, 1950-53; adj. Inst. for Phys. Chemistry, Acad. Scis., Warsaw, Poland, 1958-60; dep. dir. electrochemistry lab. Energy Inst., U. Pa., Phila., 1960-67, dir. electrochemistry lab., 1968-75; prin. research scientist Ford Motor Co., Dearborn, Mich., 1978—; cons. to industry and mcpl. authorities, 1970-78. Served with Polish Underground Army, 1943-45. Decorated Silver Cross of Merit with Swords. Mem. Electrochem. Soc., Internat. Electrochem. Soc., Mensa, Sigma Xi. Contbr. chpts. to books, articles to profl. jours., patent lit. Home: 5924 Dunmore Dr West Bloomfield MI 48033 Office: Ford Motor Co SRL S-2079 PO Box 2053 Dearborn MI 48121

WRUBEL, BARBARA, lawyer, educator, former editor; b. N.Y.C., Aug. 16, 1942; d. Harold and Rose (Friedberg) Kolsky; m. Peter Stefan Wrubel, July 30, 1966; 1 dau., Dana. B.A. cum laude, Queens Coll., N.Y.C., 1964; postgrad. U. Calif.-Berkeley, 1964-65; J.D., Fordham U., 1981. Bar: N.Y. 1982, U.S. Dist. Ct. (so. dist.) N.Y. 1982, U.S. Dist. Ct. (ea. dist.) N.Y. 1983. Atty., Skadden, Arps, Slate, Meagher & Flom, N.Y.C., 1981; adj. assoc. prof. law NYU, N.Y.C., 1982—, Fordham U. Sch. Law, N.Y.C., 1981—; lectr. Am. Law Inst., Practising Law Inst., ABA, 1982—; editor edn. books, N.Y.C., 1965-78; freelance photographer. Author: (with Leon J. Saul) Psychodynamics of Hostility, 1976; columnist (with Sheila L. Birnbaum) on products liability Nat. Law Jour., 1981—; contbr. articles to law publs.; editor Law Rev. Fordham U., 1980-81. Mem. Assn. Bar City N.Y., ABA, N.Y. Bar Assn., Fed. Bar Council, Women's Bar Assn. State N.Y. Home: 351 E 84th St New York NY 10028 Office: Skadden Arps Slate Meagher & Flom 919 3d Ave New York NY 10022

WRUCHA, MARGARET ANN, social worker; b. Weatherford, Okla., July 28, 1943; d. Roy Willis and Lucille (Nikkel) North; m. Jerry A. Wrucha, Nov. 12, 1977; children—Andrew James Ryan III, Jenifer Lynn White. B.A. in Social Studies, Southwestern Okla. State U., 1965, B.A. in Sociology, 1968. Social worker Dept. Inst. Social and Rehab. Services, Oklahoma City, 1971-73, supr., 1973-78; tng. supr. Dept. Human Services, Oklahoma City, 1978-80, social service supr., 1980-84, county dist. programs supr., 1984-85, programs field rep., 1985—. Recipient recognition of assistance Vietnamese Am. Assn., Oklahoma City, 1985. Mem. Am. Pub. Welfare Assn., Okla. Health and Welfare Assn. (treas. central region 1985-86), Res. Officers Assn. Ladies, Sigma Kappa Alumnae. Republican. Avocations: sailing; reading; cooking. Home: Box C-4200 Suite 281 Scottsdale AZ 85261 Office: Dept Human Services PO Box 25352 Oklahoma City OK 73125

WU, ESTHER UN-WAH, aerospace executive; b. Pasadena, Calif., Feb. 24, 1960; d. Wilson and Louise (Cheng) Wu. B.S. in Pub. Adminstrn., U. So. Calif., 1982; M.S. in Pub. Health, UCLA, 1984. Supr. corp. disability plans Security Pacific Corp., Los Angeles, 1983-84; research assoc. Robert Wood Johnson Found., U. Lowell, Mass., 1984; sr. employee benefits rep. McDonnell Douglas Corp., Long Beach, Calif., 1984—. Contbr. chpt. to book in field. Com. mem. data collection Employers Health Care Coalition Los Angeles, 1984—; mem. Orange County Health Care Coalition, 1984—. Mem. Am. Soc. Pub. Adminstrn., Am. Pub. Health Assn., U. So. Calif. Pub. Adminstrn. Support Group. Democrat. Lutheran. Avocation: tennis. Home: 1270 Grand Vista Pl Monterey Park CA 91754 Office: McDonnell Douglas Corp 3855 Lakewood Blvd 126-20 Long Beach CA 90846

WU, FELICIA YING-HSIUEH, biochemist, educator; b. Taipei, Taiwan, Feb. 27, 1939; came to U.S., 1961, naturalized, 1976; d. I-Sung and Ti (Yen) Chen; m. Cheng-Wen Wu, Nov. 10, 1963; children—David, Faith, Albert. B.S., Nat. Taiwan U., 1961; M.S., U. Minn., 1963; Ph.D., Case Western Res. U., 1969. Med. technician dept. biochemistry U.S. Naval Med. Research Unit No. 2, Taipei, Taiwan, 1963-65; research assoc. in biochemistry and molecular biology Cornell U., Ithaca, N.Y., 1969-71; research assoc. dept. pharmacology Yale U., New Haven, 1971-72; assoc. dept. biophysics Albert Einstein Coll. Medicine, Bronx, N.Y., 1972-73, instr., 1973-78, asst. prof. dept. biochemistry, 1978-79; vis. prof. dept. molecular biology Institut Pasteur, Paris, and Unite de physicochimie macromoleculaire Institut Gustave-Roussy, Villejuif, France, 1979-80; assoc. prof. pharm. sci. SUNY-Stony Brook, 1980—, W.J. and F.M. Catacosinos prof., 1980. Contbr. articles to profl. jours. Mem. Am. Soc. Biol. Chemists, Biophys. Soc., Am. Chem. Soc., Soc. Chinese Bioscientists in Am., Assn. Women in Sci., Internat. Assn. for Women in Bioscis. Office: SUNY Dept Pharmacological Scis HSC 7T-182 Stony Brook NY 11794

WU, LINDA YEE CHAU, sculptor; b. Canton, China, July 4, 1919. Student, Calif. Sch. Fine Arts, 1939-42, NAD, 1942-44, Columbia U. Sch. Painting and Sculpture, 1944-50. Exhibited in group shows: Allied Arts Am. Ann. Exhibits, 1947—, Audubon Artists Ann. Exhibits, NAD Ann. Exhibits, Nat. Sculpture Soc. Ann Exhibits, Internat. Sculpture Third, Phila. Art Mus., 1949; dean students N.Y. Chinese Sch., 1960-74, prin., 1974—; represented collections Bas-relief Chinese Community, N.Y., 1952, portrait Sam Y. Ong, Republican Club, Chinatown, N.Y., 1975. Recipient Anna Hyatt Huntington Gold medal Catharine Lorillard Wolfe Art Club, 1968. Mem. NAD (Dessier Greerprize for sculpture 1965), Nat. Sculpture Soc., Allied Artists Am. (Gold medal of honor for sculpture 1973), Knickerbocker Artists (chmn. jury sculpture awards 1974). Office: care Nat Sculpture Soc 15 E 26th St New York NY 10010

WU, MARGARET ANNE, computer scientist, educator; b. Chgo., Apr. 11, 1935; d. Aloys Joseph and Beatrice Rose (Kubal) Schlosser; B.S. in Math., Ill. Inst. Tech., 1956; M.S. in Math., Northwestern U., 1958; Ph.D. in Computer Sci., U. Iowa, 1980; m. Shih-Yen Wu, June 24, 1967; children—Jennifer, Gregory. Research computer scientist IIT Research Inst., Chgo., 1958-67; research assoc. U. Iowa, 1967-71, vis. asst. prof. mgmt. sci., 1979—. Mem. Assn. Computing Machinery, IEEE Computer Soc. Author: Computers and Programming: An Introduction, 1973; Introduction to Computer Data Processing, 1975, 2d edit., 1979; Introduction to Computer Data Processing with Basic, 1980. Office: Phillips Hall University of Iowa Iowa City IA 52242

WU, TERESITA GO, physician; b. Tarlac, Philippines, Oct. 31, 1946; came to U.S., 1974, naturalized, 1983; d. Li and Virginia (Co) Go; m. Raymond K. Wu, Nov. 21, 1978; children—Tonna, Andrew. B.A., Southwestern U., Philippines, 1967; M.D., U. of East, Quezon City, Philippines, 1972. Resident physician Met. Hosp., Manila, 1972-74; pediatric resident Lincoln Med. Ctr., Bronx, 1974-76; psychiat. resident Kingsboro Psychiat. Ctr., Bklyn., 1976-79; staff physician Brookhaven Hosp., Patchogue, N.Y., 1980; part-time gen. practice medicine, Dix Hills, N.Y., 1979—. Contbr. articles to med. and religious jours. Recipient award for Acad. Superiority, Most Honorable Sorority of the Squirette of Hippocrates, 1969. Mem. AMA, Internat. Assn. Med. Specialists. Home: 486 Wolf Hill Rd Dix Hills NY 11746

WUESTE, PATRICIA, lawyer; b. San Antonio, Dec. 11, 1953; d. Gus Michael and W. Cecelia (Goodwin) Wuester. B.A., Incarnate Word Coll., 1975; J.D., St. Mary's U., 1978. Bar: Tex. 1978, U.S. Dist. Ct. (we. dist.) Tex. 1982. Mem. Law Office R. Ritter, San Antonio, Tex., 1978—. Active Tex. Women's Polit. Caucus, Bexar County Womens Polit. Caucus; mem. Ursuline Acad. Sch. Bd. Named Outstanding Advocate, St. Mary's Sch. Law, 1978. Mem. ABA, Tex. Bar Assn., San Antonio Bar Assn., Bexar County Women's Bar Assn. (pres. elect), St. Mary's Law Alumni Assn., San Antonio Young Lawyers, Nat. Order Barristers, Delta Theta Phi. Democrat. Roman Catholic. Club: Altrusa. Home: 403 Shropshire San Antonio TX 78217 Office: Law Office Robert Ritter 1026 W Hildebrand San Antonio TX 78201

WUJCIK, VALERIE HAMILTON, insurance company executive; b. Camden, N.J., June 2, 1957; d. Joseph Edwin and Patricia (Bard) H. Student Camden County Coll., Rutgers U., 1980—. Receptionist, State Farm Ins., Pennsauken, N.J., 1975-76, sec., 1976-77, claims adjuster, 1977-82, auto ins. claims investigator, mgr., 1982—. Vol., Birthright, Collingswood, N.J., 1980—. Mem. South Jersey Claim Assn. Republican. Roman Catholic. Home: 106B Mulberry Cove Mount Laurel NJ 08054 Office: Wheelways Ins Program 259 E Lancaster Ave Wynnewood PA 19096

WUKELIC, MARTI ANNE, club training executive; b. Steubenville, Ohio, Jan. 6, 1954; d. Daniel A. and Anne (Vein) W.; m. Robert John Wiggins, Apr. 6, 1985, A.A., Bauder Coll., Miami, Fla., 1974; postgrad. U. Colo.-Denver, 1977-79; B.A., U. So. Calif., 1986. Asst. advt. mgr., buying asst. Madison's Inc., Columbus, Ohio, 1974-77; children's theatre coordinator Theatre Under Glass, Denver, 1978-80; restaurant mgr. Silverado Resort, Napa, Calif., 1980-84; asst. dir. human resources Amfac Hotel, Los Angeles, 1984-85; tng. dir. Marina City Club, Marina del Rey, Calif., 1985—. Active Abalone Alliance, San Luis Obisbo, Calif., 1981, People for Am. Way, Washington, Foster Parent Plan; telephone coordinator Common Cause; campaign worker Hart for Pres., Calif., 1984. Recipient Area Chmn. of Yr. award March of Dimes, Napa/Solano County, 1984. Mem. Am. Soc. Tng. and Devel., Nat. Assn. Female Execs. Avocations: watercolor painting; photography; computer-ized video; reading; model trains. Office: Marina City Club 4333 Admiralty Way Marina del Rey CA 90292

WULBRECHT ZADVINSKIS, DOREEN MARIE, entrepreneur, training consultant; b. Detroit, May 25, 1955; d. Donald John and Gladys Estell (Keichinger) W. B.A.E., Eastern Mich. U., 1977. Lic. real estate cons., Mich. With McBee Systems, Grand Rapids, Mich., 1978; with New Dimension in Edn., Houston, 1979-80, regional mgr., 1980; salesman Pitney Bowes, Grand Rapids, 1980-81; owner Wulbrecht Carpet Wholesalers, Grand Rapids, 1981-85; owner Fantasies Gift Store, 1986—; condr. seminars in field; lectr. in field; cons. in field. Contbr. articles to profl. jours. Vol. Arts Council Festival, Grand Rapids, 1984, supr., 1985. Recipient Top Salesperson award Pitney Bowes, 1980, 81; Top Producer, McBee Systems, 1978; Top Mgr., New Dimensions in Edn., 1979, Sales award, 1979. Mem. Nat. Speakers Assn. Republican. Roman Catholic. Avocations: reading; photography; biking. Home: 15023 154th St Grand Haven MI 49417 Office: Fantasies 301 N Harbor Grand Haven MI 49417

WULF, SHARON ANN, marketing executive; b. New Bedford, Mass., Aug. 23, 1954; d. Daniel Thomas and Norma Dorothy (McCabe) Vieira; B.S. cum laude in Acctg., Providence Coll., 1976; M.B.A., Northeastern U., 1977; Ph.D., Columbia Pacific U., 1984; m. Stanley A. Wulf, Oct. 1, 1983. M.B.A. intern Laventhal & Horwath, C.P.A., Providence, 1977; jr. fin. analyst Polaroid Corp., Waltham, Mass., 1977-78, fin. analyst, Freetown, Mass., 1978-79, Cambridge, Mass., 1979-81; sr. fin. analyst Digital Equipment Corp., Stow Mass., 1981-83, fin. devel. program mgr., Maynard, Mass., 1983-84; strategic fin. mgr. Digital Equipment Corp., Maynard, Mass., 1984-86, strategic mktg. mgr., Hudson, Mass., 1986—; v.p. fin., treas. Edizioni, Ltd., Boston, 1981-82; pres. Wulf Assocs. lectr. fin. acctg. Southeastern Mass. U., 1979-81; adj. prof. managerial fin., mgmt. and cost acctg. Northeastern U., 1979—; lectr. communications Shirley C. Martin Modeling Studio, New Bedford, 1979-81. Chmn. public support and fund raising com. New Bedford chpt. ARC. Mem. Nat. Assn. Female Execs. (dir.), Providence Coll. Alumni Assn. (treas. 1981-82), Phi Sigma Tau. Home: 902 Salem End Rd Framingham MA 01701 Office: Digital Equipment Corp 77 Reed Rd Hudson MA 01749

WULFF, LOIS YVONNE, medical librarian; b. Seattle, Nov. 23, 1940; d. Arthur Ray and Audrey June (Carpenter) Roark; B.S., Washington State U., 1962; M.L.S., U. Wash., 1963; postgrad. Syracuse U., 1969-70; m. Barry Kahn, Dec. 18, 1971 (dec. 1982). Intern, then head documents div. Ohio State U., 1963-67; spl. project investigator U. Wash., 1968-69; staff asst., head search unit Johns Hopkins Med. Instns., 1971-72; project coordinator, asst. to dir., coordinator health sci. libraries U. Minn., 1973-77; head librarian Alfred Taubman Med. Library, U. Mich., 1978—, coordinator Med. and Sci./Tech. Libraries, 1981—. Gaylord fellow, 1969-70. Mem. Med. Library Assn., ALA, Assn. Acad. Health Sci. Library Dirs., Assn. Coll. and Research Libraries. Office: 1135 E Catherine St Ann Arbor MI 48109

WUNSCH, EILEEN KATHRYN, rehabilitation administrator; b. Scranton, Pa., Feb. 9, 1949; d. Linus C. and Kathryn (Keser) Wunsch. B.A. in Communication Arts and Secondary Edn., Marywood Coll., 1970; M.S. in Vocat. Rehab. Counseling, U. Scranton, 1973. Cert. rehab. counselor. Tchr. communications arts Abington Heights Jr. High Sch., Clarks Summit, Pa., 1970-71; tchr. various subjects and spl. edn. Scranton Sch. Dist. (Pa.), 1971-73; rehab. counselor Kurtz Tng. Ctr., Bethlehem, Pa., 1973-79; dir. rehab. Crawford Rehab. Services, Allentown, Pa., 1979—; lectr., mem. curriculum adv. com. U. Scranton, 1980—, Pa. State U.; lectr. State College, 1982—. Mem. Ins. Assn. Lehigh Valley, Allentown, 1982—; mem. com. Channel 39 Auction, Bethlehem, 1981-84; pres. Lehigh Valley Claims Assn., 1982-83; bd. dirs. Pa. Playhouse, Bethlehem, 1983-85. Mem. Nat. Assn. Rehab. Profls. in Pvt. Sector (pres. Pa. chpt. 1983-86), Pa. Rehab. Counseling Assn. (pres. 1982-83), Pa. Rehab. Assn. (pres. 1979-80), Nat. Rehab. Counseling Assn. Roman Catholic. Office: Crawford Rehab Services 1501 N Cedar Crest Blvd Allentown PA 18104

WURSTER, THELMA PAULINE, nurse; b. Celina, Ohio, June 9, 1932; d. Francis Q. and Mary Lee (Kindel) Wade; R.N., Miami Valley Hosp., Dayton, Ohio, 1953; B.S. in Nursing, Marquette U., Milw., 1961; M.Ed. in Profl. Devel., U. Wis., Whitewater, 1982; postgrad. Coll. of St. Joseph, Joliet, Ill.; m. Charles Wayne Wurster, Aug. 18, 1952. Staff and head nurse hosps. in Ohio and Wis., 1953-80; dir. operating rm. Milw. Children's Hosp., 1966-78, asst. dir. nursing, 1979-80; supr. operating room Eye Inst., Milw. County Med. Complex, Wauwatosa, Wis., 1980—. R.N., Ohio, Wis. Mem. Assn. Operating Room Nurses, AAUW, Phi Delta Kappa. Republican. Club: Kettle Moraine Curling (Hartland, Wis.). Contbr. articles to profl. jours. Home: 1932 Moraine End Delafield WI 53018 Office: 8700 W Wisconsin Ave Wauwatosa WI 53226

WURSTNER, JUDY REBECCA PAYNE, hospital administrator; b. Nashville, Dec. 30, 1947; d. Jacob Allen and Mattie Glyndon (Lane) Payne; m. Carl Everett Woodall, July 12, 1966 (div. 1980); 1 child, Ryan Curtis; m. Roland David Wurstner, May 29, 1982. Assoc. in Nursing, Fayetteville Tech. Inst., 1975; B.S. in Nursing, U. Tex. Health Sci. Ctr., 1978; M.S. in Mgmt., Troy State U., 1981. Staff nurse Cape Fear Valley Hosp., Fayetteville, N.C., 1975, nursing record analyst, 1975-76; clinician II, Bexar County Hosp., San Antonio, 1976-79; dir. operating room, recovery room, central supply Humana Hosp.-Fort Walton Beach, Fort Walton Beach, Fla., 1979-80; assoc. exec. dir. nursing Humana Hosp., Ft. Walton Beach, 1980-86, Humana Hosp. Med. City Dallas, 1986—; real estate salesperson, Fort Walton Beach, 1985. Sr. leader Girl Scouts Am.; bd. dirs. Ft. Walton Beach chpt. Am. Heart Assn., 1985—. Scholar Vanderbilt U., 1965. Named Dist. IX Student Nurse of Year, N.C. Student Nurses Assn., 1975. Mem. Am. Bus. Women's Assn. (pres. 1983-84), Fla. Nurses Assn., Am. Nurses Assn., Assn. Operating Room Nurses, Fla. Soc. Hosp. Nursing Service Adminstrs., Am. Orgn. Nursing Execs., Am. Hosp. Assn., Fla. Hosp. Assn. (nursing adv. com. 1985), Sigma Theta Tau. Republican. Methodist. Clubs: Zonta (mem. bd.) (Ft. Walton Beach). Avocations: flying; water activities; writing poetry. Office: Humana Hosp Med City Dallas 7777 Forrest Ln Dallas TX 75230 Office: Humana Hosp Fort Walton Beach 1000 Mar Walt Dr Fort Walton Beach FL 32548

WURZBERGER, SUZANNE ALICE WELLS, shop owner; b. Bridgeport, Conn., June 7, 1938; d. Daniel Marcus and Sarah Evelyn (French) Wells; m. Albert George Wurzberger, May 2, 1959; children—Carolsue, Albert John. A.S., Vt. Coll., 1958; diploma Internat. Corr. Sch., 1979. Owner, operator Norton House, Wilmington, Vt., 1966—. Author Living History Assn. Jour., 1982. Pres. Parent Tchrs. Club, Wilmington, Vt., 1974-75; troop leader brownies Girl Scouts U.S.A., Wilmington, 1967. Mem. Women Bus. Owners of Vt., Nat. Assn. Female Execs., Am./Internat. Quilt Assn. Republican. Congregationalist. Clubs: Ch. Guild (pres.), Green Mt. Quilters Guild. Avocations: sewing; snowshoeing. Home: Stowe Hill Rd RFD 1 Box 105 Wilmington VT 05363 Office: Norton House 1836 Country Store Village Wilmington VT 05363

WURZEL, RUTH SCHWARTZ, paralegal; b. N.Y.C., June 8, 1944; d. Philip and Mildred (Chernoff) Schwartz; m. Mark Raymond Wurzel, Nov. 13, 1965; children—Stephanie Rae, Alicia Dawn, Seth Michael. B.S., NYU, 1966; paralegal cert., Watterson Coll., 1986. Cert. paralegal, Calif. Tchr. N.Y.C. Bd. Edn., 1966-67; owner Ruth Wurzel Invitations, Granada Hills, Calif., 1981—; paralegal Leon Laufer, Los Angeles, 1985—. Vice pres. North Valley Jewish Community Ctr., Granada Hills, 1983-85 (Outstanding Bd. Mem. 1984, Spl. Recognition award 1981), Jewish Community Ctrs.-Camp JCA, Los Angeles, 1985—; trustee, bd. dirs. Jewish Community Ctrs. of Greater Los Angeles, 1984-85. Mem. Los Angeles Paralegal Assn. (bd. dirs., chmn. Westside sect.), Nat. Assn. Female Execs. Republican. Avocations: community theatre; camping; river rafting; miniature collecting. Home: 16301 Keeler Dr Granada Hills CA 91344

WUSNACK, PRIMA THOMAS, librarian; b. Picayune, Miss., Mar. 14, 1949; d. Charles A. and Jessie Don (Welsh) Thomas; B.A. with honors in Edn., U. Miss., 1974; M.S. in Library Sci., U. So. Miss., 1981; 1 son, Charles Joseph. Librarian, Coast Episcopal High Sch., Pass Christian, Miss., 1974-75, Christ Episcopal Day Sch., Bay St. Louis, Miss., 1974-75; dir. Hancock County Library System, Bay St. Louis, 1975—; mem. adv. com. S. Mi-s. Conf. on Libraries and Info. Sci.; group leader Miss. Gov.'s Conf. on Libraries and Info. Sci. Mem. ALA, Miss. Library Assn., Kappa Delta Pi. Clubs: Altrusa (treas. 1978-79) (Bay St. Louis/Waveland). Office: Hancock County Library System 312 Hwy 90 Bay Saint Louis MS 39520

WUTHRICH, HELEN MARIE, wholesale candy and tobacco executive; b. Houghton, Mich., Aug. 30, 1927; d. Albert J. and Elsie L. (Brunner) Gitzen; m. John P. Wuthrich, June 27, 1953; children—Joan, Robert, Patricia. Student Suomi Coll., Mich., 1945-47. Sec., Gitzen Co., Houghton, 1946-76, v.p., 1976-83, pres., 1983—. Vice-pres., Houghton Housing Commn., 1982-83; mem. Downtown Devel. Authority, 1985. Mem. Houghton-Hancock Bus. and Profl. Women's Club. Office: Gitzen Co 44 N Dodge St Houghton MI 49931

WYAND, REBECCA GUYTON, principal; b. Frederick, Md., Dec. 1, 1936; d. Garland Sylvester and Mary Manzella (Coblentz) Guyton; s. Ralph William Wyand, Aug. 1956; children—Ralph W., David M. B.A., Shepherd Coll., 1961; M.A., Shippensburg U., 1968. Tchr., U.S. Army Dept. Sch., Verona, Italy, 1957-58; tchr. Washington County Bd. Edn., Hagerstown, Md., 1958-59, Fred County Bd. Edn., Middletown, Md., 1961-62, 64; supr. Heritage Acad., Hagerstown, Md., 1969-73; prin. Broadfording Christian Acad., Hagerstown, 1973—; speaker in field. Author: Victory Drill Manual, 1972. Unit leader Concerned Women for Am., Washington County, Md., 1984—; vol. Republican Com., Md., 1984. Mem. Am. Assn. Christian Schs. Avocations: biographical reading; biking; walking; studying. Home: 827 Oak Hill Ave Hagerstown MD 21740 Office: Broadfording Christian Acad Route 4 Box 261C Hagerstown MD 21740

WYATT, ADDIE L., labor leader; b. Bookhaven, Miss., Mar. 8, 1924; d. Ambrose and Maggie (Nolan) Cameron; student pub. and pvt. schs., Chgo.; LL.D. (hon.), Anderson (Ind.) Coll., 1976; m. Claude S. Wyatt, Jr., 1940; children—Renaldo, Claude S., Emmett Cameron, Willie Cameron, Bluet Cameron (dec.), Audrey Dandridge, Maude Davis. Employee in meat packing and food industry, Chgo., 1941-54; internat. rep. United Packinghouse Workers Union (merged with Amalgamated Meat Cutters 1968), Chgo., 1954-74, pres. local 56, 1953-55; dir. women's affairs dept. Amalgamated Meat Cutters and Butcher Workmen N.Am. (merged with Retail Clks. Internat. Union, name now United Food & Comml. Workers Internat. Union), AFL-CIO-CLC, Chgo., from 1974, internat. v.p., 1976-84, former dir. civil rights and women's affairs dept.; exec. v.p. Coalition Labor Union Women; advisor, labor instr. Roosevelt U., Chgo.; labor com. advisor Chgo. Urban League; served as a labor advisor to Dr. Martin Luther King, Jr., Dr. Ralph Abernathy, Rev. Jesse L. Jackson. Mem. Ill. Commn. on Status of Women, Ill. Pub. Health Survey Commn.; youth leader for Altgeld Gardens, Chgo. Housing Authority, 1945-55; apptd. to Internat. Women's Year Commn., 1977; mem.-at-large Democratic Nat. Com.; mem. bd. advisors Alliance to Save Energy, Citizens for Day Care, People United to Serve Humanity; mem., advisor women's orgn. Nat. Assn. Ch. of God; minister of music Vernon Park Ch. of God, Chgo. Recipient Image award League Black Women, 1973; Disting. Labor Leader award Woodlawn Orgn., Chgo.; Service award Women's Bd. NAACP; named one of 12 Women of Yr., Time Mag., 1975; Black Book award, 1977; Ebony Mag. citation, 1977; one of 9 Women of Year, Ladies' Home Jour., 1977; recipient numerous other awards and citations. Mem. Coalition of Black Trade Unionists, Nat. Commn. on Working Women, Ams. for Dem. Action (del.-at-large), NAACP (v.p.), Nat. Council Negro Women, Interdenoml. Ministers Wives.

WYATT, BARBARA POWERS, association executive, author; b. Salem, N.J., Dec. 4, 1931; d. Byron Lippincott and Marguerite (Richmond) Powers; m. Frederic Alliger Wyatt, June 30, 1956; children—Scott Richmond, Todd Alliger, Frederic Talmadge. Student Douglas Coll., 1949-50; cert. in teaching, Clarke Conservatory of Music, 1953; A.A., Los Angeles Community Coll., 1975. Tchr. Salem High Sch. (N.J.), 1953-55; airline stewardess TransWorld Airlines, Kansas City, Mo., 1955-56; v.p. Wyatt Mgmt. Cons., North Hollywood, Calif., 1962-73; tchr. Viewpoint Sch., Calabasas, Calif., 1973-81; program dir. Voices for Freedom, Toluca Lake, Calif., 1980-81; program dir. Action Agy., Washington, 1981—; pres. Mussatti-Wyatt, Toluca Lake, 1978—. Author: What Comes Next?, 1969; editor: We Came Home—POWs of Vietnam, 1973; author, creator California Historical Coloring Book, 1978. Pres. POW Pubs., Toluca Lake, 1973-81; bd. dirs. Young Vols. in Action, Missing and Exploited Children's Program. Republican. Baptist. Office: Action Agy 806 Connecticut Ave Washington DC 20525*

WYATT, DEBORAH DENISE, publisher; b. Highland Park, Mich., Aug. 28, 1956; d. Joseph Herbert and Maxine Winnefred (Armstrong) W. B.A. in English and Sociology, Albion Coll., 1978. Products editor Scranton-Gillette Communications, Chgo., 1978, mng. editor, 1979; writer, researcher Interlochen Ctr. for Arts, Mich., 1980; founder, pres., pub., editor Prism Publs., Inc., Traverse City, Mich., 1981—; regional corr. The Mich. Woman, 1984-85; exec. editor Sleeping Bear Dunes Nat. Lakeshore, 1984. Mem. Human Rights Commn., Traverse City, 1984. Mem. Traverse City, C. of C., Phi Beta Kappa. Avocations: fiction writing; reading; cross-country skiing; bicycling; swimming. Home: 508 Webster St Traverse City MI 49684 Office: Prism Publs Inc 121 S Union St Traverse City MI 49684

WYATT, KATHRYN ELIZABETH BENTON, psychologist, educator; b. Danville, Va., May 11, 1928; d. Joseph Nelson and Margaret (Davis) Benton; B.A., Randolph Macon Woman's Coll., Lynchburg, Va., 1949; M.Ed., U. Va., 1952; M.A., U. N.C., Greensboro, 1974, Ph.D., 1977; m. Landon Russell Wyatt, Aug. 30, 1952; children—Margaret Wyatt Scott, Landon Russell, III, Elizabeth Benton. Instr., then asst. prof. psychology Stratford Coll., Danville, 1949-74, chmn. dept., 1963-74; prof. psychology Danville Community Coll., 1977—. Mem. Danville Sch. Bd.; deacon, tchr. 1st Bapt. Ch., Danville; pres. so. dist. Va. Sch. Bds. Assn. Mem. Am. Psychol. Assn., Soc. Research Child Devel., Southeastern Psychol. Assn., Va. Psychol. Assn., Va. Acad. Sci. Clubs: Friends Danville Pub. Library, Jr. Wednesday (pres.), Gabriella, Wayside Garden, Shakespeare. Author articles in field. Home: 301 Magnolia St Danville VA 25441 Office: Danville Community Coll Danville VA 24541

WYATT, KATRINA HOLLAND, computer software company executive; b. Shawnee, Okla., May 3, 1945; d. Blair Eugene and Kathryn (Keller) Holland; m. Larry Lee Wyatt, Feb. 14, 1976. B.B.A., Robert Morris Coll., 1976. Programmer Alcoa, Pitts., 1977-78, systems analyst, 1978-80, staff auditor, 1980-82; account mgr. Cullinet Software, Pitts., 1982-83, customer support mgr., 1983-84, regional support mgr., Phila., 1984—; fin. dir. Old Allegheny Festival Choir, Pitts., 1980-82; mem. fin. com. Allegheny Towne Corp., Pitts., 1982-83. NDEA scholar U. Wis., 1964. Mem. Data Processing Mgmt. Assn., Nat. Assn. Female Execs. Avocations: choral singing; piano; stained glass window making; interior decorating. Office: Cullinet Software Inc Scott Plaza II, 4th Floor Philadelphia PA 19113

WYATT, MARTHA, judge; b. Phila., July 21, 1939; d. Leon and Freda (Moed) Goldstein; m. E. Malcolm Wyatt, June 24, 1961; children—Rachel, Ruth, Mark. B.A., St. John's Coll., Annapolis, Md., 1961; postgrad. Peabody Conservatory Music, Balt., 1962, Grad. Inst. St. John's Coll., Santa Fe, N.Mex., 1971; J.D., U. Md.-Balt., 1976. Bar: Md. 1977, U.S. Dist. Ct. Md. 1978, D.C. 1979. Intern, Atty. Gen.'s Office, Annapolis, 1976-77; mem. Legum, Cochran, Chartrand & Wyatt, P.A., Annapolis, 1977-82, Blumenthal, Delavan, Offutt & Moodispaw, P.A., Annapolis, 1982-84; judge Md. Dist. Ct., Annapolis, 1984—. Contbr. articles to profl. jours. Pres. Women's Law Ctr., Annapolis, 1978-82; chmn. Md. Commn. for Women, Balt., 1981-84; mem. subcom. on comparable worth Gov.'s Commn. on Compensation, 1983-84. Mem. Women's Bar Assn. Md. (dir.). Office: 580 Taylor Ave Annapolis MD 21403

WYATT, ROSE MARIE, financial planner, psychiatric and medical social worker; b. San Angelo, Tex., Feb. 16; d. James Odis and Annie LaVernia (Lott) W.; B.A. (Ford Found. scholar, 1953-57), Fisk U., 1957; M.S., U. So. Calif., 1963; M.A., M.S.W. (univ. scholar 1970-72, United Charities scholar 1970-72), U. Chgo., 1972; postgrad. in indsl. psychology Ill. Inst. Tech., 1976—. Elem. tchr. Chgo. Bd. Edn., 1959-63, clin. social worker, 1979—; adult program dir. Chgo. YWCA, 1963-64; youth counselor Chgo. Commn. on Youth Welfare, 1964-66; supervising social worker for Head Start, Chgo. Com. on Urban Opportunity, 1966; social worker Chgo. Commn. on Youth Welfare, 1966-68, Jewish Vocat. Service, 1968; social worker Sch. Community Relations, Detroit Public Schs., 1968-70; social worker United Charities, 1972-74; clin. social worker Rosman-Wyatt and Assos., Chgo., 1980—, pres., 1981—; instr. dept. corrections Chgo. State U., 1972—. Adv. bd. United Charities, Calumet Area, program com. chmn., 1974-80; vol. Assn. of Community Agts. 1968-70, Southside Sr. Citizens Coalition, Chgo., 1963-66, Roseland Health Planning Com., 1974-76, Teen Pregnancy Caucus, 1978-82; mem. social work adv. council Chgo. Bd. Edn., 1976. Recipient Outstanding Employee award for med.-social work services Maternal and Child Health Services div. HEW; 1971. Mem. Nat. Assn. Social Workers, Acad. Cert. Social Workers, Ill. Cert. Social Workers, Chgo. Psychol. Club, Ill Acad. Criminology, NEA, Ill. Assn. Sch. Social Workers, Am. Assn. Mental Deficiency, Qualified Mental Retardation Profls., Fisk U. Alumni Assn., Alpha Kappa Alpha. Roman Catholic. Clubs: Am. Bridge Assn., Civenos Bridge.

WYCHE, MARY GREEN (MRS. EDMOND WYCHE, JR.), educator; b. Norfolk, Va., Oct. 29, 1938; d. George Herbert and Lillian Louise (Vaughn) Green; student Norfolk State Coll., 1955-57; B.S., Howard U., 1959; postgrad. N.Y. U., 1960; M.Ed., So. U., 1962; postgrad. Ind. U., 1963, U. Ill., 1964, Temple U., 1968, U. Del., 1973; Ph.D., U. Md., 1983; m. Edmond Wyche, Jr., June 3, 1978. Health and phys. edn. tchr. Newport News (Va.) City Schs., 1959-61, East Baton Rouge Parish, 1962-63; instr. health and phys. edn. Dillard U., New Orleans, 1963-65, Va. State Coll., Petersburg, 1965-67; asst. prof. health and phys. edn. Del. State Coll., Dover, 1967-70, assoc. prof., chmn. health and phys. edn., 1970—, mem. Grad. Sch. council, 1981-82, 85-86. Mem. State Health Adv. Com. Recipient award Dover YMCA, 1968, Plaque Phys. Edn. Major's Club, 1970-73, grant, DuPont Co., 1973. Mem. Am. Assn. (mem. nat. com. 1969-71), Del. (mem. scholarship com. 1970, pres. profl. award) assns. health, phys. edn. and recreation, Nat., Eastern assns. health, phys. edn. and recreation, Nat. Parks and Recreation Assn., Delta Sigma Theta. Democrat. Roman Catholic. Clubs: Delicadoes (Norfolk); Racquet, Indoor Tennis, Colonial (Dover). Home: 600 Carriage Ln Dover DE 19901

WYCKOFF, BEVERLY A., banker, lawyer; b. Williams AFB, Ariz., May 13, 1956; d. Daniel McCoy and Betty Jean (Stumpf) Wyckoff. B.A., Yale U., 1978; J.D., U. Miami (Fla.), 1981. Bar: Ill. 1981. Trust adminstr. Am. Nat. Bank & Trust Co., Chgo., 1981-82, trust officer, 1982-84, 2d v.p., 1984—. Mem. Women's Bar Assn. Ill. (mem. com. rights of women 1983-86), Chgo. Bar Assn., Ill. Bar Assn., Friends Lincoln Park Boat Club (treas., dir. 1983—). Republican. Home: 429 W Wellington Ave Chicago IL 60657 Office: American Nat Bank and Trust Co 33 N LaSalle St Chicago IL 60690

WYCKOFF, DIANE PLANCON, educational administrator, librettest, producer, choreographer; b. Bridgeport, Conn., Aug. 1, 1936; d. William Kenneth and Sara Ruth (Carew) Plancon; m. John William Greene Wyckoff, June 28, 1968 (div. June 1975); children—John, Jeanne, Christopher, Anne, Sara Peter. Grad. Am. Theatre Wing, 1956; student Jose Limon, Valerie Bettis, Alvin Ailey, Sergievsky, Volodine, Aron Frankel and Eva Brown, N.Y.C. and Conn., 1954-56. Actress, dancer various prodns. summer stock, legitimate theatre, TV, radio, 1952-60; dance dir. Easton Grange Hall (Conn.), 1961-62; cons., producer arts tours for schs., chs., convalescent homes, So. Conn., 1962—; founder, artistic dir. Wyckoff Sch. Ballet, Fairfield, Conn., 1969-75; dir. dance, prodns. Judeo-Christian Women Eastern Fairfield County (Conn.), 1975-76; founder, dir. New Horizons, Greater Ballet Co. Inner-City Dance Program, Bridgeport, Conn., 1976-77; co-founder, bd. dirs. Fairfield Commn. on Arts, Inc., 1978-80, chmn. programs com., 1978; founder, bd. dirs. dance Alliance Fairfield, Inc., 1978-80, sec., 1978; exec. dir. Fine Art Acad. in Fairfield, 1979—; adminstrv. dir. Conn. Grand Opera, 1981; bd. advs. Fine Art Acad. in Fairfield, 1982—; choreographer for various assns., univs., So. Conn., 1957—; co-founder, bd. dirs. Arts in So. Conn., Inc., Fairfield, 1984; artist in residence Greater Bridgeport Ballet Co., 1976-77. Choreographer, dir. 35 student dance-theatre prodns., 1961-84; librettest, choreographer, dir., costumer original ballets: The Dragon, 1975; Sunmae Dancer, 1979; producer 7 dance, music, theatre, art, sculpture galas: Gala: 1 to 7, 1977-84. Honoree 10 groups Human Rights Day Observance, Bridgeport, 1975; Conn. Com. on Arts grantee, 1980—. Mem. Actors Equity Assn., Fine Art Acad. Guild, Westport-Weston Arts Council, Fairfield C. of C. (Festival of Arts com.), Easton Grange (life), Profl. Dance Tchrs. Assn., Nat. Soc. Lit. and Arts. Republican. Office: Fine Art Acad in Fairfield Mill Hill Sch Mill Hill Terr Southport CT 06490

WYCKOFF, JUANITA CHARLENE, retired textiles educator; b. Luray, Kans., Sept. 24, 1915; d. William S. and Bertha (McKanna) W.; B.S., Kans. State U., 1940; M.S., Colo. State U., 1959. Tchr., Gove (Kans.) Rural High Sch., 1940, Luray (Kans.) Community High Sch., 1941-42, Decatur Community High Sch., Oberlin, Kans., 1944-46, Oswego (Kans.) High Sch., 1946-48, Cherryvale (Kans.) High Sch., 1948-57; asst. prof. textiles and clothing Mankato (Minn.) State U., 1959-82, ret., 1982; mem. adv. bd. Secondary Home Econs. Dist. No. 77, Mankato. Mem. Centenary Meth. Choir. Mem. NEA, Minn. Edn. Assn., Mankato State U. Interfaculty Assn., Am. Home Econs. Assn., Minn. Home Econs. Assn., Assn. Coll. Prof. Textiles and Clothing, United Meth. Women, Delta Kappa Gamma, Phi Upsilon Omicron, Methodist. Home: 225 Heather Ln Apt 6 Mankato MN 56001

WYLIE, HAZEL RUSSELL, continuing education programs administrator; b. Denison, Tex., Oct. 24, 1919; d. George Dewey and Bertha (Higdon) Hagans; m. John Coakey Russell, Oct. 11, 1941 (dec. Dec. 1951); 1 dau., K. Jayne Russell Larkin; m. 2d O.D. Wylie, July 30, 1966. B.S., North Tex. State U., 1940, M.Ed., 1953; postgrad. So. Meth. U., 1968, U. Del., 1957, others. Tchr., Nacogdoches (Tex.) Ind. Sch. Dist., 1940-42, Liberty Common Sch. Dist., Bowie County, Tex., 1946-52; tchr., adminstr. Dallas Ind. Sch. Dist., 1952-80, short course instr., 1980—; real estate broker, Dallas, 1980—. Mem. Classroom Tchrs. Dallas (pres. 1957-58), Tex. Classroom Tchrs. (dir. 1957-59), Tex. State Tchrs. Assn., NEA, Ret. Tchrs. Assn. Democrat. Presbyterian. Club: Zonta Internat. (pres. Dallas II chpt. 1982-83).

WYLIE, HELEN JEANNE, writer, editor; b. Los Angeles, Sept. 18, 1935; d. Frank and Mary Sue (Valle) Mormino; m. Arthur Payne (div.); children—Gary Lee Payne, Jacqueline Marie Payne Wedel, William Thomas Payne; m. James Marshal Wylie, July 18, 1976; 1 child, Lance Terrill. Student pub. schs., Los Angeles. Mktg. dir., v.p. FWF Enterprises div. of State Mut. Savings and Loan, Los Angeles, 1973-76; editor, pub. Statesman's Mag., Los Angeles, 1976-84, also contbr. articles; pres. Straight Shot Communications, Inc., Houston, 1984-85; free-lance writer and editor, Houston, 1985—; cons. Statesman's Club Internat., Los Angeles, 1976-84, Janus Assocs., Houston, 1985-86. Regent, Nat. Republican Woman's Club, Washington, 1985-86; active Statue of Liberty/Ellis Island Found., Internat. Fund Animal Welfare, Meml. West Rep. Woman's Club, Houston, 1985—. Mem. Nat. Film Inst., Nat. Assn. Exec. Women. Roman Catholic. Club: University (Houston). Avocations: tennis; kerry blue terriers. Home: 1 Lazee Trail Houston TX 77024 Office: J M Wylie & Assocs 800 Gessner Suite 285 Houston TX 77024

WYLIE, KATHLEEN SUSAN, utility executive; b. Valpraiso, Fla., Sept. 22, 1957; d. Ivan D. and Dot O. (Cobb) White; m. Samuel John Wylie III, June 2, 1979. B.A. cum laude, Angelo State U., 1978, also M.S. Adminstrv. clk. GTE-SW, San Angelo, Tex., 1978-79, adminstrv. clk. trainer, 1979-80, product asst., 1980-81, product analyst, 1981-82, market research analyst, 1982—. Campaign worker Com. to Re-elect Gov. Clements, San Angelo, 1982. Mem. Am. Mktg. Assn. (telephone chmn., newsletter chmn.), Alpha Mu Gamma, Alpha Lambda Delta. Republican. Presbyterian. Home: 2535 Baylor St San Angelo TX 76904 Office: GTE-SW 2701 S Johnson St San Angelo TX 76904

WYMAN, LOTTE ANN NOVAK, civic worker; b. Vienna, Austria, Aug. 15, 1925; d. Josef and Hertha (Wallnstorfer) Novak; B.A., Barnard Coll., 1947; 1 dau., Leslie Andrea. Grey Lady, ARC, 1947-55; treas. Women's Assn. First Presbyn. Ch., Greenwich, Conn., 1963-65, chmn. mission interpretation program, 1975-77; bd. dirs. Friends of Sunny Hill Sch. for Phys. and Emotionally Handicapped Children, Greenwich, 1960—; bd. dirs. YWCA, Greenwich, 1963-78, 81—, chmn. world fellowship, 1965, mem. bldg. com., 1965-70, pres., 1967-70; bd. dirs. Drug Liberation Program of Greater Stamford, 1970-74, Community Chest, Greenwich, 1967-70, Community Forum, Greenwich, 1970—; bd. dirs. Turtle Bay Music Sch., N.Y.C., 1970-80; bd. dirs. Greenwich Arts Council, 1974-79, pres., 1976-79; bd. dirs. Neuberger Mus., SUNY, 1979—, M.I.T. Council for the Arts, 1980—, World Service Council YWCA, 1983—; bd. dirs. Met. Opera Assn., 1980—, adv. dir., 1982—; mem. Purchase Coll. Found., 1983—; cons. Nat. Exec. Service Corps, 1984—; elder 1st Presbyn. Ch. Greenwich, 1986—; mem. Bd. Parks and Recreation, Greenwich, 1986—. Mem. N.Y. Zool. Soc., Ch. Women United (v.p. 1971-72). Republican. Presbyterian. Clubs: Greenwich Country; Stratton Mountain (Vt.) Country. Home: Baldwin Farms North Greenwich CT 06830

WYNDEWICKE, KIONNE ANNETTE, educator; b. Preston, Miss.; d. Clifton Thomas and Missouria (Jackson) Johnson; student Columbia Coll., Chgo., 1972; B.S., Ill. State Normal U., 1961; postgrad. Williams Coll., Williamstown, Mass., 1972; M.Ed., Nat. Coll. Edn., 1982; m. Eugene C. Moorer, Sept. 23, 1961 (div.). Social worker Cook County Dept. Pub. Aid, 1961; tchr. reading Chgo. Bd. Edn., 1961—; asst. to news dir. WCIU-TV, 1972-74; asst. women's editor Chgo. Defender, 1970-72; social sec. Dr. William R. Clarke, 1972—; part-time photog. model, fashion commentator, pub. relations cons., pub. speaker. Co-chmn. installation Profl. Women's Aux.,

Provident Hosp., 1961, corr. sec., 1969, publicity chmn., 1969-72, 74-77. Selected one of 13 persons in U.S. to attend Innovative Tchr. Tng. Seminar, funded by Henry Luce Found. at Williams Coll., 1972; one of 25 Black women of Chgo. to receive Kizzy award, 1977; recipient Outstanding Community Service award Beatrice Caffrey Youth Service, Inc., 1978. Mem. Ill. Speech and Theatre Assn., WTTW Channel 11 Ednl. TV, Mus. Contemporary Art, Speech Communication Assn. Am., YWCA. Lutheran. Contbr. articles to local newspapers. Office: 707 E 37th St Chicago IL 60653

WYNKOOP, SUSANNE HELENE, rehabilitation counselor; b. Teaneck, N.J., May 3, 1930; d. Rossman Hoffman and Hildegard M. (Korn) W.; grad. in inter-cultural affairs U. San Carlos and Guatemalan-Am. Inst., Guatemala City, 1950; M.A. in Vocat. Rehab., Counseling and Guidance, Goddard Coll., Plainfield, Vt., 1972. With Easter Seal Soc. of N.J., Hackensack, 1958—, asst. to exec. dir., 1958-66, Bergen County field rep., 1971-76, dir. office skills evaluation and tng. program, 1966-84, dir. community relations and ednl. services Assoc. Craftsmen/Easter Seal Soc., 1976-84, dir. profl. services, 1981-84, dir. office skills, 1966-84, dir. equipment loan, info. and referral services, 1984—. Bd. govs. Hackensack Med. Center, 1980—; mem. Bergen County Human Services Planning Council, 1982—, vice chmn., 1985—; evening membership dept. rep. N.J. Fedn. Women's Clubs, 1972-74, vice chmn. 9th Dist., 1970-72; bd. dirs. Bergen County Office on Handicapped, 1978-80; corr. sec. Bergen Community Mus., 1972-74; sec. to bd. dirs. Mental Health Consultation Center of Bergen County, 1958-68. Cert. rehab. counselor. Mem. Am. Personnel and Guidance Assn., Nat. Rehab. Assn., Easter Seal Exec. Assn. Clubs: Hackensack Women's, Jr. Woman's of Hackensack (pres. 1957-58). Creator one-handed typing system. Home: 76 Louis St Hackensack NJ 07601 Office: 171 Atlantic St Hackensack NJ 07601

WYNN, DEBRA KAY, bank software company executive; b. Winters, Tex., Nov. 1, 1950; d. Lumis Meryle and Christene Vena (Goolsby) Campbell; m. George Latham, Nov. 25, 1969 (div. Jan. 1972); children—Leidra, Tashi; m. Alan Bailey Wynn, Mar. 29, 1975; 1 child, Dustin. A.A., Mesa Community Coll., 1978. Cert. data processor. Customer rep. Escom, Phoenix, 1978; programmer trainee Ariz. Bank, Tempe, 1978-79, programmer, 1979-80, sr. programmer, 1980-82; systems analyst Republic Bank, Dallas, 1982; v.p. Directions, Dallas, 1982—, bank cons., 1982—. Systems analyst systems devel. CPCS NON-MICR, 1984. Campaign leader United Way at G.E., Albuquerque, 1975; bd. dirs. Good Neighbor Fund at G.E., Albuquerque, 1975. Recipient award Ariz. Bank, 1980. Mem. Exec. Females, Bank Adminstrn. Inst. Club: 4-H (Murphy, Tex.) (food leader 1983-84). Lodge: Women of Moose (chairwoman 1976-77). Avocations: racquetball; swimming; water skiing; horseback riding. Office: Directions 15301 N Dallas Pkwy Suite 400 Dallas TX 75248

WYNN, GRACE ROSE, insurance consultant; b. Milw., Feb. 7, 1937; d. Joseph Frank and Evelyn Valerie (Stefanski) Wysocki; Student U. Wis.-Milw., 1961-63. C.L.U. Office mgr. A.R. Korbel, Milw., 1961-65; sales asst. Korbel Corp., Milw., 1961-68; ins. agt. Central Life Assurance Co., Milw., 1968—; owner, assoc. G.R. Wynn C.L.U. & Assocs., Milw., 1970-80, 83—; ptnr. Wynn & Mottl C.L.U., Milw., 1980-83; class moderator Life Underwriting Training Council, Washington, 1984. Named to Pres.'s Cabinet Central Life Assurance Co., Des Moines, 1972—. Mem. Agts. Adv. Council Central Life Ins. Co., chmn., 1979-85. Mem. Estate Counselors Forum, Million Dollar Round Table (life and qualifying), Milw. Assn. Life Underwriters (dir. 1979-83), Women's Leaders Round Table (life and qualifying), C.L.U. Milw. chpt., Nat. Assn. Life Underwriters (Nat. Quality Sales Achievement award 1971—). Republican. Roman Catholic. Club: Florentine Opera (Milw.). Avocations: Opera; music; tennis; skiing; bicycling. Home: 929 N Astor Milwaukee WI 53202 Office: G R Wynn CLU & Assoc 400 N Broadway Milwaukee WI 53202

WYNNE, MARIE VICTORIA, insurance company executive; b. Niskayauna, N.Y., Feb. 7, 1952; d. Edward Robert and Winifred Louise (Ayres) Hoffman; m. Robert James Wynne, Jr., Aug. 19, 1978; children—Conor Karol, Brittany Landers. Student Fashion Inst. Tech., SUNY-N.Y.C., 1969-70. Sales assoc. Macy's Dept. Store, Colonie, N.Y., 1972-75; ticket rep. New Eng. Whalers, Boston, 1975; asst. underwriter Royal Globe, Boston, 1975-76, underwriter, 1977-79; sr. underwriter Comml. Union, Boston, 1979—. Active Big Sister Assn., 1975-79, Clamshell Alliance, 1979-83. Mem. Boiler and Machinery Assn. Boston (pres. 1983-84, Presdl. award 1985), Union Concerned Scientists. Democrat. Roman Catholic. Club: Mariners. Home: 209 River Rd Winthrop MA 02152 Office: Commercial Union Ins Co 600 Atlantic Ave Boston MA 02110

WYNNE, MARTHA VIRGINIA, corporation finance executive; b. Dallas, Nov. 18, 1951; d. Robert Edwards and Rubye Floyd (Davis) W. B.J., U. Tex., 1972; M.B.A., U. Houston, 1981. Speechwriter, Lt. Gov. Wm. P. Hobby, Jr., Austin, Tex., 1973; with prodn. dept. Tracy-Locke, BBDO, Dallas, 1973-77; equity analyst Fayez Sarofim & Co., Houston, 1977-81; v.p. corp. fin. Rotan Mosle Inc., Houston, 1981-85; corp. fin. mgr. Gen. Electric Credit Corp., Dallas, 1985—. Mem. editorial bd. John Wiley & Sons, 1985—. Pres., founder ENCORPS, Houston, 1979-80; treas. Houston Bus. Forum; bd. dirs. Houston Symphony League, 1979. Mem. Houston Soc. Fin. Analysts (bd. dirs.), Houston Grand Opera Guild. Avocations: investments; reading; travel. Office: 15301 Dallas Pkwy Suite 1100 Dallas TX 75248

WYNNS, JOYCE RAINES (JOY), medical centers administrator, educator; b. Greenville, S.C., Nov. 24, 1944; d. William Roy and Joyce (Ellison) Raines; m. Robert Sanders Wynns, Aug. 21, 1965 (div. 1975); children—Ellison, Robert Sanders, Frank Brannon. B.A. in Home Econs., Brenau Coll., 1967; A.D. in Bus. and Computers, Greenville Tech. Coll., 1977; postgrad. in Pub. and Pvt. Mgmt., Birmingham So. Coll., 1985—. Guidance counselor Project T-Square, Allendale, S.C., 1967-69; supr. expanded food and nutrition program Extension Service Clemson U., Allendale, 1974-75; instr. nutrition Greenville Tech. Coll., S.C., 1975; programmer Harbert Internat., Birmingham, Ala., 1977-81; programmer-analyst Baptist Med. Ctrs., Birmingham, 1981-83, sr. analyst-programmer, 1983-86; adj. faculty Jefferson State Jr. Coll., Birmingham, 1985. Treas. Exodus Ch. Sch. Class, 1985-86; mem. Pizitz Middle Sch. PTO, 1984-86, Vestavia Hills High Sch. PTO, 1983-86, Lakeshore Rehab. Placement Com., 1982-85. Mem. Data Processing Mgrs. Assn. (membership attendance dir. Birmingham 1985-86), Healthcare Fin. Mgmt. Assn., Nat. Assn. Female Execs., Gamma Phi Beta. Clubs: Epicureans (pres. Allendale 1971-72), Moonlight Garden (pres. Fairfax, S.C. 1970-71). Avocations: studying; walking; tennis; swimming; reading. Home: 1748 Carovel Circle Birmingham AL 35216 Office: Bapt Med Ctrs 3201 4th Ave S Birmingham AL 35222

WYNSTRA, NANCY ANN, lawyer, health services executive; b. Seattle, June 25, 1941; d. Walter S. and Gaile E. (Cogley) W. B.A. cum laude, Whitman Coll., 1963; LL.B. cum laude, Columbia U., 1966. Bar: Wash. 1966, D.C. 1969, Ill. 1979. With appellate sect., civil div. U.S. Dept. Justice, Washington, 1966-67; TV corr.-legal news Sta. WRC, NBC and Sta. WTOP, CBS, Washington, 1967-68; spl. asst. Corp. Counsel, D.C., Washington, 1968-70; dir. planning and research D.C. Superior Ct., Washington, 1970-78; spl. advisor White House Spl. Action Office for Drug Abuse Prevention, Washington, 1973-74; fellow Drug Abuse Council, 1974-75; gen. counsel Michael Reese Hosp. and Med. Ctr., Chgo., 1978-83; sr. v.p., gen. counsel Allegheny Health Services, Inc., Pitts., 1983—; cons. various drug abuse programs. Contbr. articles to profl. jours. Mem. ABA, Nat. Health Lawyers Assn. (bd. dirs.), Am. Soc. Hosp. Attys., Others. Presbyterian. Home: 120 Richland Ln Pittsburgh PA 15208 Office: Allegheny Health Services Inc 320 E North Ave Pittsburgh PA 15208

WYSE, JOY BARTULA, talent agency executive; b. Fort Worth, Sept. 4, 1934; d. Adam Paul Bartula and Eula Scott (Tankersley) Bartula Mayer; m. Donald J. Wyse, Oct. 22, 1955; children—Paula Scott, Donna Hill, Bennett Casey, Adam. Grad. high sch., Los Angeles. Sports coordinator Los Angeles Examiner, 1952-53; sec. Lockheed Co., Burbank, Calif., 1953-55; freelance writer, Studio City, Calif., 1955-69; owner, operator Joy Wyse Agy., Dallas, 1969—. Democrat. Roman Catholic. Office: Joy Wyse Agy 2600 Stemmons St Suite 127 Dallas TX 75207

XETHALIS, EILEEN SCANLON, accountant; b. New Castle, Pa., May 8, 1943; d. Thomas Edward and Martha Irene (Posivach) Scanlon; B.A., N.Y.U., 1982; m. Demetrios L. Xethalis, July 11, 1966; children—Sofia Demetria, Lambros Demetrios. Sec.-treas. Flowers by Demetrios, Inc., Hightstown, N.J., 1967—; mem. controllers council Bus. Planning Bd. Key leader Capital Funds campaign Princeton Day Sch., 1976-77; v.p. Arts and Exhibits Parents Assn., 1977-79, class parent, 1981. Mem. Am. Mgmt. Assn., Nat. Assn. Accts. Nat. Fedn. Ind. Bus., Mfg. Jewelers Assn. Am. Republican. Greek Orthodox. Club: Skyview Country. Home: 182 Stockton St Hightstown NJ 08520 Office: 182 Stockton St Hightstown NJ 08520

XIFARAS, STELLA ROBERTA, development firm executive; b. Dorchester, Mass., Mar. 1, 1958; d. Robert Louis and Barbara Ann (Fay) Xifaras. Student Am. Internat. Coll., 1976-78, Deree Pierce Coll., Athens, Greece, 1978-79; cert. Kinyon Cambell, 1982; Paralegal program Newbury Jr. Coll., 1982; B.S., Northeastern U., 1985. Salesperson Diros Realty, Inc., New Bedford, Mass., 1979-80; with Top of the Hub Restaurant, Boston, 1980; developer apprentice Amvex, Inc. (Amvest, Inc.), New Bedford and Westport, Mass., 1982—, pres., 1984—. Mem. New Bedford Jaycees, U.S. Chess Fedn., Fall River Rod and Gun Club. Republican. Office: Amvex Inc 827 Am Legion Hwy Westport MA 02790

YACHER, NANCY TERRELL STEERE, educator; b. McMinnville, Oreg., Mar. 22, 1935; d. Horace Clifford and Mary Margaret (Newsom) Terrell; student Linfield Coll., 1953-55; B.A. summa cum laude in English, Lewis and Clark Coll., 1957; M.A. in Am. Studies (Danforth fellow, scholar), U. Pa., 1960; postgrad. (Danforth Grad. Woman fellow), U. Kans., 1972-78; m. Sherman L. Yacher, Oct. 5, 1979; children by previous marriage—John Tierney Steere, Robert Terrell Steere. Program asst. Am. Friends Service Com., Phila., 1957-58, 60-61; asst. instr. English dept. U. Kans., Lawrence, 1975-78, lectr., 1985—; asst. prof. English, Washburn U., Topeka, 1980—. Mem. regional selection com. Danforth Assocs. Program, 1972-74; bd. dirs. Gainesville (Fla.) Women for Equal Civil Rights, 1962-67; chmn. Lawrence Community Nursery, 1968-69; v.p. Schwegler Sch. PTA, Lawrence, 1970-71; bd. dirs. Lawrence Environ. Improvement Assn., 1970-72. Danforth Assoc., 1963-75. Mem. Nat. Council Tchrs. of English, Soc. for Values in Higher Edn., Assocs. Religion and Intellectual Life, Inst. for Theol. Encounter with Sci. and Tech., Sigma Tau Delta. Home: 1749 W 20th St Lawrence KS 66046 Office: 157 Morgan Hall Washburn U Topeka KS 66621

YACOBIAN, SONIA SIMONE, metals company executive; b. Cairo, Egypt, Feb. 13, 1943; came to U.S., 1966, naturalized, 1971; d. Simon and Lucy (Guendimian) Samsonian; divorced; children—Tatiana, Richard. B.S., Lycee of Cairo, 1962; B.B.A., U. Cairo, Egypt, 1965; student Pace U., 1978-80. Asst. mgr. new accounts Lincoln Savs. & Loan, Los Angeles, 1973-77; sr. acct. U.S. Industries, N.Y.C., 1977-81; dep. mgr. French C. of C., N.Y.C., 1981-82; mgr. mktg. Samancor Metals, New Rochelle, N.Y., 1982-84; pres. NIDDAM Inc., New Hyde Park, N.Y., 1984—. Mem. Assn. Profl. Women in Metal. Republican. Orthodox Christian. Home: 37 Wintergreen Dr Dix Hills Long Island NY 11746 Office: NIDDAM Inc PO Box 877 Melville NY 11747

YACOVONE, ELLEN ELAINE, savings and loan executive; b. Ithaca, N.Y., Aug. 4, 1951; d. Wilfred Elliott and Charlotte Frances (Fox) Drew; m. Richard Daniel Yacovone, June 2, 1979; stepchildren—Christopher Daniel, Kimberly Marie. Student Broome Community Coll., 1973-80; cert. Inst. Fin. Edn., Chgo., 1974. Sec. to exec. v.p. Ithaca Savs., N.Y., summer 1968; mortgage clk. Citizens Savs. Bank, 1968-69; with Lincoln Bank, Van Nuys, Calif., 1970-71; asst. bookkeeper Henry's Jewelers, Binghamton, N.Y., 1971-74; teller, br. supt., br. mgr. Fist Fed. Savs., Binghamton, N.Y., 1974-82, v.p., central regional sales mgr., 1982—. Mem. Gov.'s Commn. on Domestic Violence, Albany, N.Y., 1983—; bd. dirs. S.O.S. Shelter, Inc., Endicott, N.Y., 1979—, pres., 1982-83, treas., 1985-86; vol. United Way of Broome County, Binghamton, 1976—, WSKG Pub. TV, Conklin, N.Y., 1974—. Named Young Careerist, Triple Cities Bus. and Profl. Women, 1977; Woman of Achievement, Broome County Status of Women Council, 1981. Mem. Triple Cities Bus. and Profl. Women (pres. 1979-81), Sales and Mktg. Execs., Broome County C. of C., Broome County Bankers Assn. (bd. dirs. 1979—, pres. 1983-84), Inst. Fin. Edn. (bd. dirs. 1976—, pres. 1984-85). Republican. Methodist. Avocations: exercise; camping; wood working; gardening; needlecrafts. Home: 1169 Taft Ave Endicott NY 13760 Office: 32 Washington Ave Endicott NY 13760

YAEGER, BILLIE PATRICIA, advertising sales executive; b. Boston, Mar. 17, 1949; d. Harold Stern and Marie Frances (Levenson) Y. Student Logos Bible Coll. Office mgr., Northeast rep. Ticketron, Inc., Boston, 1968-73; owner, mgr. Performance King, Natick, Mass., 1973-74, House of Portraits, Lakeland, Fla., 1974-75, employment counselor Snelling & Snelling, Lakeland, 1975-77; advt. sales account exec. The Ledger/N.Y. Times, Lakeland, Fla., 1977—. Recipient Chmn. of Bd. award N.Y. Times, 1984, 85. Mem. Nat. Assn. Female Execs. Republican. Avocations: photography; writing; waterskiing.

YAGODA, (STELLA) AQUILLA, government administrator; b. Cherokee, Ala., July 31, 1941; d. William Payne and Stella Elizabeth (Waldrep) Wadkins; m. Rudolph Jon Yagoda, Nov. 23, 1963; 1 child, Paul Anthony. Diploma Larimore Bus. Coll., Florence, Ala., 1960. Personnel clk. IRS, N.Y.C., 1966-73; personnel asst. Bur. Alcohol, Tobacco and Firearms, Dept. Treasury, N.Y.C., 1973-75, personnel mgmt. specialist, 1975-79, personnel officer, 1979-85, equal employment mgr., 1985—; sec. Fed. Women's Program, 1984-85; EEO mgr. EEO sub-com. Fed. Exec. Bd., N.Y.C., 1985—. Counselor Youth Orgn., Taylor, Pa., 1982-86; active Ch. Women United, Scranton, Pa., 1985-86; pres. United Methodist Women, Taylor, 1985-86. Recipient Superior Work Performance award Bur. Alcohol, Tobacco and Firearms, 1984. Mem. Hispanic Orgn., Nat. Assn. Female Execs., Nat. Labor Relations Soc., Image, Fed. Employed Women. Avocations: reading; crafts; photography. Home: 37-16 84th St Jackson Heights NY 11372 Office: Bur Alcohol Tobacco and Firearms 6 World Trade Ctr Room 620 New York NY 10048

YALICH, BARBARA LU, college administrator; b. Jetmore, Kans., Dec. 10, 1930; d. Kenneth Albert and Alice Charlotte (Rasmussen) Neeley; m. Milo Yalich, Nov. 24, 1950; children—Nicholas Milo, Janelli Ann Yalich Betts. Ind. piano tchr., Colorado Springs, Colo., 1959-69; exec. dir. Mental Health Assn., Colorado Springs, 1970-72, Health Assn., Colorado Springs, 1972-73; dir. ann. fund Colo. Coll., Colorado Springs, 1973-75, dir. alumni relations, 1975-85, dir. devel., 1985—; dir. United Bank Colorado Springs; mem. adv. com. Inasmuch Found., Oklahoma City, 1982—. Pres. Jr. League Colorado Springs Inc., 1964-66; regional bd. dirs. Assn. Jr. Leagues Inc., N.Y.C., 1966-68, internat. pres., 1968-70; bd. dirs. Citizens Goals, Colorado Springs, 1975-85; mem. Colorado Springs Centennial Commn., 1976. Recipient Silver Bell award Assistance League, 1975. Mem. Council for Advancement and Support Edn. (dist. chmn. 1985-86). Republican. Episcopalian. Clubs: Broadmoor Golf (Colorado Springs); Denver. Home: 2134 Clarkson Dr Colorado Springs CO 80909 Office: Colo Coll Office Alumni Relations Colorado Springs CO 80903

YALOW, ROSALYN SUSSMAN, medical physicist; b. N.Y.C., July 19, 1921; d. Simon and Clara (Zipper) Sussman; A.B., Hunter Coll., 1941; M.S., U. Ill., 1942, Ph.D., 1945, D.Sc. (hon.), 1974; hon. degrees: D.Sc., Phila. Coll. Pharmacy and Sci., 1976, N.Y. Med. Coll., 1976, Med. Coll. Wis., Milw., 1977, Yeshiva U., 1977, Southampton Coll., 1978, Bucknell U., 1978, Princeton U., 1978, Jersey City State Coll., 1979, Med. Coll. Pa., 1979, Manhattan Coll., 1979; D.Hum.Lett., Hunter Coll., 1978, Sacred Heart U., Conn., 1978, St. Michael's Coll., Vt., 1979, Johns Hopkins U., 1979, U. Vt., U. Hartford, Rutgers U., 1980, Rensselaer Poly. Inst., St. Lawrence U., Colgate U., U. So. Calif., 1981, Clarkson Coll., 1982, U. Md. at Balt., 1982, Tel Aviv U., 1985, Claremont U., 1986, Mills Coll., 1986; D.Honoris Causa, U. Claude Bernard, Lyon, France, 1979, U. Ghent, 1984; D.Med., Med. U. S.C., 1981; LL.D., Beaver Coll., 1982, U. Miami, 1983, Washington U., St. Louis, 1983, Adelphi U., 1983, U. Alta. (Can.), 1983, Columbia U., 1984, SUNY, 1984; m. A. Aaron Yalow, June 6, 1943; children—Benjamin, Elanna. Asst. in physics U. Ill., Urbana, 1941-43, instr., 1944-45; lectr., temp. asst. prof. physics Hunter Coll., N.Y.C., 1946-50; physicist, asst. chief radioisotope service VA Hosp., Bronx, N.Y., 1950-70, chief nuclear medicine service, 1970-80, dir. Solomon A. Berson Research Lab., 1973; sr. med. investigator VA, 1972; research prof. dept. medicine Mt. Sinai Sch. Medicine, CUNY, 1968-74, Disting. Service prof., 1974-79, Solomon A. Berson disting. prof.-at-large, 1986—; disting. prof.-at-large, Albert Einstein Coll. Medicine, Yeshiva U., N.Y.C., 1979-85, prof. emeritus, 1985—; chmn. dept. clin. scis. Montefiore Hosp. and Med. Center, Bronx, 1980-85; cons. radioisotope unit VA Hosp., Bronx, 1947-50, Lenox Hill Hosp., N.Y.C., 1952-62; mem. subcom. 13, Nat. Com. Radiation Protection, 1957—; sec. U.S. Nat. Com. Med. Physics, 1963-67; med. adv. bd. Nat. Pituitary Agy., 1968-71; endocrinology study sect. NIH, 1969-72; IAEA expert Instituto Energia Atomica, Sao Paulo, Brazil, 1970; cons. subcom. human applications of radioactive materials N.Y.C. Dept. Health, 1972—; bd. sci. counselors NIAMD, NIH, 1972-75; mem. task force immunology and disease NIAID, NIH, 1972-73; mem. com. for evaluation of NPA, NRC, 1973-74; WHO cons. Radiation Medicine Center, Bombay, India, 1978. Bd. dirs. N.Y. Diabetes Assn., 1974. Recipient Nobel prize, 1977; Dickson prize U. Pitts., 1971; Gairdner Found. Internat. award, 1971; Koch award Endocrine Soc., 1972; Commemorative medallion Am. Diabetes Assn., 1972, Rosalyn S. Yalow Research and Devel. award, 1978; Anachem award Detroit Assn. Analytical Chemists, 1973; Dr. Albion O. Bernstein award Med. Soc. N.Y. State, 1974; Sci. Achievement award AMA, 1975; VA Exceptional Service award, 1975, 78; A. Cressy Morrison award N.Y. Acad. Scis., 1975; Disting. Achievement award Modern Medicine, 1976; Albert Lasker Basic Med. Research award, 1976; La Madonnina Internat. prize, Milan, 1976; Torch of Learning award Am. Friends of Hebrew U., 1978; Gratum Genus Humanum Gold medal World Fedn. Nuclear Medicine and Biology, 1978; Virchow Gold medal Virchow-Pirquet Med. Soc., 1978; G. von Hevesy medal, 1978; citation of esteem St. John's U., 1979; Achievement in Life award Ency. Britannica, 1980; ann. gold medal award Phi Lambda Kappa, 1980; Theobald Smith award, 1982; Pres.'s Cabinet award U. Detroit, 1982; John and Samuel Bard award in medicine and sci. Bard Coll., 1982; Disting. Research award Dallas Assn. Retarded Citizens, 1982; numerous others. Fellow Clin. Soc. of N.Y. Diabetes Assn. (hon.), N.Y. Acad. Sci. (chmn. biophysics div. 1964-65), Am. Coll. Radiology (asso.); mem. Radiation Research Soc., Am. Assn. Physicists in Medicine, Biophys. Soc., Am. Diabetes Assn., Am. Physiol. Soc., Endocrine Soc. (council; pres.-elect 1977, pres. 1978), Soc. Nuclear Medicine, Nat. Acad. Scis., Am. Acad. Arts and Scis., Harvey Soc. (hon.), French Acad. Medicine (fgn. asso.), Sigma Xi (hon.), Phi Beta Kappa (hon.), Sigma Pi Sigma, Pi Mu Epsilon, Sigma Delta Epsilon. Editorial bd. Endocrinology, 1967-72; co-editor Hormone and Metabolic Research, 1973—; editorial adv. council Acta Diabetologica Latina, 1975-77; editorial bd. Mt. Sinai Jour. Medicine, 1976-79, Diabetes, 1976-79; editorial adv. bd. Ency. Universalis, 1978; contbr. numerous articles to profl. jours. Home: 3242 Tibbett Ave Bronx NY 10463 Office: 130 W Kingsbridge Rd Bronx NH NY 10468

YAMADA, AYAKO LOUISE, librarian; b. Topaz, Utah, Sept. 11, 1943; d. Masao and Yoneko (Masuda) Y. B.S., Western Res. U., 1965; M.S. in Library Sci., Case Western Res. U., 1968. Librarian Cuyahoga County Pub. Library, Cleve., 1965-73, San Jose City Library (Calif.), 1974, Alameda County Pub. Library, Castro Valley, Calif., 1974-80, San Leandro Community Library (Calif.), 1981, San Mateo County Library, Belmont, Calif., 1982—; host Cable TV show, Pacifica, Calif., 1983—. Contbr. articles to newspapers. Recipient Five Yrs. Disting. Service award Alameda County, 1980. Mem. Assn. Children's Librarians, Calif. Library Assn., ALA, Ohio Library Assn., Beta Phi Mu. Home: 707 Continental Circle Apt 1626 Mountain View CA 94040 Office: San Mateo County Library 25 Tower Rd Belmont CA 94002

YAMANI, ELAINE REIKO, computer-peripherial company executive; b. Ogden, Utah, Apr. 2, 1945; d. Joe and Chieko (Kato) Yamani; m. Victor G. Sugihara, Aug. 10, 1970 (div. June 1973); 1 dau., Jo Ann Renae. B.S. in English and Psychology, Weber State U., 1965, A.A., 1967; postgrad. U. Utah, 1975-79. Personnel generalist Weber State U., Odgen, Utah, 1973-78; personnel specialist Cutter Lab., Ogden, 1978-81; human resource mgr. Iomega, Ogden, 1981-83, compensation and benefits mgr., 1983-85; dir. human resources Cericor Inc., 1983-85, Hewlett-Packard, 1985—. Mem. No. Utah Personnel Assn. (pres. 1980-81), now 2d v.p.). Club: Soroptimist (sec. 1981). Office: Hewlett Packard Lake Side Plaza One 5215 Wiley Post Way Salt Lake City UT 84116

YANCEY, ANNE RICHARDSON, civic worker; b. Brookline, Mass., Feb. 12, 1913; d. Otis Weld and Lucile (Johnston) Richardson; B.A., Vassar Coll., 1936; m. Charles Stephen Yancey, Apr. 9, 1942; children—Sherod Anne, Charles Stephen. Researcher, asst. sec. Mass. Investors Trust, Boston, 1937-40; researcher Harvard Sch. Pub. Health, 1942-45; partner, co-adminstr. Fairlawn Nursing Home, 1963-73; pres. Dalmin Devel. Corp., Dallas, 1973—. Mem. Boston Jr. League, 1932-45; mem. Dallas Jr. League, 1945—, 1st v.p., 1952-54; pres. Dallas Vis. Nurse Assn., 1952-54; 1st v.p. Children's Bur., Dallas, 1945-47; bd. dirs. Dallas Planned Parenthood, 1956-58, Dallas Soc. Crippled Children, 1954-60; exec. bd. Community Council Greater Dallas, 1955-65, 1st v.p., 1959-61, chmn. family and children's div., 1957-59; Gov.'s Com. White House Conf. Children and Youth, 1960; mem. Linz Award Com., Dallas, 1961; bd. dirs. Dallas Civic Opera Guild, 1965-72, Council World Affairs, 1964-65, Island Nursing Home, Deer Isle, Maine, 1975—, Nat. Conservancy, 1977—; class fund chmn. Vassar Coll., Poughkeepsie, N.Y., 1977—, active Dallas Mus. Fine Arts, Dallas Symphony Orch. League, Friends of Library. Licensed nursing home adminstr., Tex. Mem. Am. Coll. Nursing Home Adminstrs., Nat. Assn. Jr. Leagues Am., Nat. Soc. Colonial Dames Am., Pan Am. Round Table (dir. 1964-65), Am. Hort. Soc. Episcopalian. Clubs: Dallas Women's, Dallas Garden, Garden Club Fedn. Maine (dir.), Evergreen Garden (pres. 1964-65), Boston Vassar, Harpswell Garden, Dallas Vassar. Home: Route 1 Box 827 South Harpswell ME 04079

YANDELL, VIRGINIA L., animal health products executive; b. Hawthorne, Calif., Aug. 9, 1927; d. John R. and Winnie B. (McNabb) Ford; m. Lunsford P. Yandell, July 16, 1945; children—Laura L. Powell, Carol Jead Edgar. Ed. Bishop High Sch., Calif. Sales clk. Wall's Livestock, Visalia, Calif., 1964-67, div. mgr., 1967-69; exec. sec. Walco, Porterville, Calif., 1969-70, exec. sec., v.p., 1970-83, v.p., personnel mgr., 1983—. Avocations: horseback riding; fishing; trap shooting. Home: 31295 Meadowlark Ln Porterville CA 93257 Office: Walco Internat Inc 846 N Main St Porterville CA 93257

YANEZ, JEQUETTA SUE, computer software company official, consultant, business proprietor; b. Elkins, Ark., Oct. 1, 1944; d. Charles Vaugh and Ellen Louisa (Davenport) Ledbetter; m. Anthony V. Yanez, Mar. 7, 1985; 1 child, Carol Lynn. A.A., Golden West Coll., 1982; student Calif. State U.-Long Beach., 1983—. Data control mgr. CTC Computer Co., Los Angeles, 1969-71; ops. mgr. Computer Dimensions, Los Angeles, 1971-72; Western region client services dir. Users Inc., Los Angeles, 1972—. Author: Technical and User Manuals, Reports Manual, 1977; Users Guide, 1977; conversion Guide, 1982; Terminal Operations, 1982. Mem. Nat. Assn. Female Execs., Am. Soc. Tng. and Devel., Golden Key Nat. Honor Soc. Republican. Office: Users Inc 970 W 190th St Torrance CA 90520

YANEZ, LINDA REYNA, lawyer; b. Rio Hondo, Tex., Nov. 30, 1948; d. David A. Reyna and Angela (Zavala) Sauzameda; m. Eusebio P. Compian, June 8, 1971 (div. Aug. 1973); 1 dau., Regina Marisa; m. Emilio S. Yanez, Aug. 28, 1975; 1 dau., Amparo Monique. B.A. in Inter-Am. Studies, Pan Am. Coll., 1970; J.D., Tex. So. U., 1976. Bar: Ill. 1977, Tex. 1980. Intern, Cabinet Com. on Opportunity for Spanish Speaking, Washington, 1970-71; tchr. bilingual edn. Weslaco Pub. Schs. (Tex.), 1971-72; tchr. migrant edn. Nebr. Dept. Edn., Bayard, 1972-73; staff atty. Legal Assistance Found. of Chgo., 1976-79; dir. immigration project Tex. Rural Legal Aid, Inc., Brownsville, 1979-81; sole practice, Brownsville, 1981—; leader immigration seminar faculty U. Tex. Law Sch., Austin, 1982-84; counsel Border Assn. for Refugees from C.Am., Edinburg, Tex., 1983—. Mem. com. Gov.'s Task Force on Workers Compensation for Farm Workers, Austin, 1983; mem. Mexican Am. Democrats, Brownsville, 1982—; panelist Women and the Law Nat. Conf., Washington, 1982-83. Mem. Mexican Am. Lawyers Assn. (dir. 1978-79), Tex. Bar Assn.-Concern of the Spanish Speaking (dir. 1982-83), ABA, Cameron County Bar Assn., Assn. Trial Lawyers Am., Am. Immigration Lawyers Assn. Democrat. Roman Catholic.

YANGER, NADINE DIANE, educational administrator; b. Elizabeth, N.J., Aug. 25, 1942; d. Benjamin Thomas and Margaret Mary (Talias) Y. B.A., Kean Coll. of N.J., 1964, postgrad., 1982; M.A., Seton Hall U., 1973. Tchr., Elizabeth, N.J., 1964—, tchr. elem. remedial reading, 1964-71, pre-kindergarten cons., 1971-76, coordinator-supr. Title I, 1976-81, basic skills coordinator elem. schs., 1981—; pres. Central Adminstrv. Council; treas. Elizabeth Adminstrv. and Supervisory Council; exec. bd. Union County Head Start. Grantee, U. P.R., 1967; recipient ESEA Title I award, 1980. Mem. Prins. and Suprs. Assn., Nat. Assn. Elem. Sch. Adminstrs., Elizabeth Adminstrv. and Supervisory Council, Kean Coll. Alumni Assn., Seton Hall U. Alumni Assn. Roman Catholic. Clubs: Coll. of N.J., Metuchen Singles, What's Your Racket. Office: Christopher Columbus Sch 15 239 S 5th St Elizabeth NJ 07202

YANISH, ELIZABETH YAFFE, sculptor; b. St. Louis; d. Sam and Fannie May (Weil) Yaffe; student Washington U., 1941, Denver U., 1960; pvt. studies; m. Nathan Yanish, July 5, 1944; children—Ronald, Marilyn Ginsburg, Mindy. One-woman shows: Woodstock Gallery, London, 1973, Internat. House, Denver, 1963, Colo. Women's Coll., Denver, 1975, Contemporaries Gallery,

Santa Fe, 1963, So. Colo. State Coll. Pueblo, 1967, others; exhibited in group shows: Salt Lake City Mus., 1964, 71, Denver Art Mus., 1961-75, Oklahoma City Mus., 1969, Joslyn Mus., Omaha, 1964-68, Lucca (Italy) Invitational, 1971, others; represented in permanent collections: Colo. State Bank, Bmh Synagogue, Denver, Denver Womens Coll., Har Ha Shem Congregation, Boulder, Colo., Faith Bible Chapel, Denver, others. Chmn. visual arts Colo. Centennial-Bicentennial, 1974-75; pres. Denver Council Arts and Humanities, 1973-75; mem. Mayor's Com. on Child Abuse, 1974-75; co-chmn. visual arts spree Denver Pub. Schs., 1975; trustee Denver Center for the Performing Arts, 1973-75; chmn. Concerned Citizens for Arts, 1976; pres. Beth Israel Hosp. Aux., 1985-87; bd. dirs. Srs., Inc. Recipient McCormick award Ball State U., Muncie, Ind., 1964, Purchase award Colo. Women's Coll., Denver, 1963, Tyler (Tex.) Mus., 1963, 1st prize in sculpture 1st Nat. Space Art Show, 1971; Humanities scholar Auraria Libraries, U. Colo., Denver. Mem. Artists Equity Assn., Rocky Mountain Liturgical Arts, Allied Sculptors Colo., Allied Arts Inc. Hist. Denver, Symphony Guild, Parks People, Beth Israel Aux. Jewish. Home: 131 Fairfax St Denver CO 80220

YANNELL, ROSEMARY KUULEI, property manager; b. San Diego, Apr. 16, 1955; d. Edward James and Antarina Larn (Young) Moore; m. John Ivan Yannell, Sept. 1, 1979; children—Ian Everest, Sean Maru. Student pub. schs., San Diego. Sec. Wailea Devel. Co., Kihei, Hawaii, 1977-78, Amfac Property Corp., Lahaina, Hawaii, 1979-80, projects coordinator, 1980-81, shopping ctr. mgr., 1981-83, resort adminstrn. mgr., 1983, property mgr., 1983—; mem. Amfac Archtl. Review Com., 1983—. Composer var. songs (hon. mention, lyrics, Am. Song Festival, 1979). Recruiter/participant March of Dimes (3d place moneymaker 1982); recruiter Charity Walk Hawaii Hotel Assn., 1983. Mem. Internat. Council Shopping Ctrs., Kaanapali Beach Operators Assn., Am. Mktg. Assn., Nat. Orgn. Women Execs. Democrat. Office: Amfac Property Corp 2530 Kekaa Dr Lahaina HI 96761

YANNELLO, CHERYL ANNETTE, candy company executive, lawyer; b. Buffalo, Jan. 29, 1947; d. Guy Raymond and Grace Alberta (Barone) Yannello. B.A., Lynchburg Coll., 1968; M.A., SUNY-Stonybrook, 1973; cert. of study N.Y. State Sch. Indsl. and Labor Relations, 1977; J.D., Ohio No. U., 1980. Bar: Ill. 1981. Tchr., West Islip Pub. Sch. (N.Y.), 1968-78; assoc. Klein, Thrope & Jenkins, Ltd., Chgo., 1980-82; indsl. relations mgr. E.J. Brach & Sons, Chgo., 1982-83, asst. v.p. indsl. relations, 1984—; counselor Cornell-N.Y. State Sch. Indsl. and Labor Relations, Farmingdale, 1976-77. Officer, pres. West Islip Tchrs. Assn., 1968-78. Mem. ABA, Ill. Bar Assn., Delta Kappa Gamma (Ruth Mack Haven scholar 1979). Office: E J Brach & Sons 4656 W Kinzie St Chicago IL 60644

YANNELLO, JUDITH ANN, federal judge; b. Buffalo, Mar. 27, 1943; d. Guy Raymond and Grace Alberta (Barone) Y.; B.A., Barnard Coll., 1964; J.D., Cornell U., 1967. Admitted to N.Y. bar, 1967, D.C. bar, 1970, U.S. Supreme Ct. bar, 1971, also various fed. cts.; law clk. U.S. Ct. Claims, Washington, 1967-68, trial judge, 1977-82, judge, 1982—; trial atty. civil div. Dept. Justice, Washington, 1968-73; assoc. firm Hudson, Creyke, Koehler & Tacke, Washington, 1973-76; adminstrv. judge Armed Services Bd. Contract Appeals, Washington, 1976-77; adj. prof. law Potomac Sch. Law, 1980; speaker, lectr. in field. Recipient Meritorious Service award Dept. Justice, 1972. Mem. Am. Bar Assn., Fed. Bar Assn. (chmn. Ct. Claims com. 1974-76, Disting. Service award 1975), D.C. Bar Assn. (Cert. of Appreciation 1976), N.Y. State Bar Assn., D.C. Bar, Exec. Women in Govt. Club: Zonta. Contbr. articles to profl. jours.; co-editor, contbg. author: Manual for Practice in U.S. Court of Claims, 1976.

YANNELLO, KAREN, lawyer; b. Buffalo, May 8, 1952; d. Guy R. and Grace A. (Barone) Y. B.A., Coll. William and Mary, 1974; J.D., U. Va., 1977. Bar: Va. 1977, D.C. 1979. Sr. editor Michie-Bobbs Merrill Law Pub. Co., Charlottesville, Va., 1977-80; lawyer Office of Gen. Counsel, U.S. Dept. Def., Washington, 1980—; pres. sr. profl. women's group Office of Sec. Def., 1983-86. Mem. ABA, Va. State Bar Assn., D.C. Bar Assn., Phi Beta Kappa.

YANOFSKY, BRENDA LEE, psychologist; b. Boston, May 10, 1950; d. Abraham and Martha (Yakus) Y.; B.A. cum laude, U. Mass., 1971; M.Ed. cum laude, Tufts U., 1973; cert. advanced grad. studies Boston U., 1974, Ed.D., 1985. Counselor, Newton North High Sch., Newtonville, Mass., 1972-76; psychologist State of Mass., 1974-76, Oak Park (Mich.) Schs., 1976—; instr. Eastern Mich. U., 1977-81, Mercy Coll., 1982—; psychologist Jensen Counseling, Farmington Hills, Mich., 1980—; psychologist Lakewood Clinic, Birmingham, Mich., 1984—; bd. dirs. Multi-Service Center, Newton, Mass., 1974-76. Mem. Am. Psychol. Assn., Am. Personnel and Guidance Assn., Mental Health Profs. Assn., Mich. Alcohol and Addiction Assn.

YANTIS, KATHLEEN MARY, naval officer; b. Gouverneur, N.Y., Dec. 15, 1951; d. Clifford Alexander and Isabelle Marjorie (Howard) Hance; B.S. in Psychology, St. Lawrence U., 1974; m. Micheal Dee Yantis, Dec. 28, 1976; Commd. ensign U.S. Navy, 1974, advanced through grades to lt. comdr., 1983; communications watch officer, Naval Communications Area Master Sta. Eastern Pacific, 1974-76; message center officer, comdr. Oceanographic Systems Atlantic, 1977-78; asst. officer in charge Nav. Aids Support Unit, 1979-80; asst. officer in charge Naval Telecommunications Center, Hampton Roads, Norfolk, Va., 1980-82; assigned to Naval Postgrad. Sch., Monterey, Calif., 1982-84. Mem. Armed Forces Communications and Electronics Assn., Nat. Assn. Female Execs. Office: SMC 1935 Naval Postgrad Sch Monterey CA 93940

YARBOROUGH, EMILY CLARK, broadcasting executive; b. Maryville, Tenn., Jan. 21, 1952; d. Frank Proffitt and Mary Amner (Wilson) Clark; m. William Dewey Yarborough, Oct. 3, 1981; 1 child, Mary Page. B.S. in Advt., U. Tenn., 1974. Advt. asst. Proffit's Dept. Store, Inc., Maryville, 1974-75; continuity dir. Sta. WTVK-TV, Knoxville, Tenn., 1975-76, promotion mgr., 1976—, mem. affiliate promotion adv. com. NBC, region II, 1980-83; judge Greater Charleston Advt. Club Addy awards, S.C., 1979. Bd. dirs. Girls' Club of Am., Blount County chpt., 1985—; mem. pub. edn. and pub. relations com. East Tenn. chpt. Am. Heart Assn., Knoville, 1979—. Recipient Addy award Greater Knoxville Advt. Club, 1976, 80, 83, award of Merit Broadcaster's Promotion Assn., 1978. Mem. Broadcast Promotion and Mktg. Execs. Assn., Knoxville C. of C. (community affairs council 1985—). Republican. Presbyterian. Clubs: Gen. Federated Women's Clubs, Tenn. Federated Women's Clubs, Jr. Chilhowee (internat. affairs chmn. 1982-84, rec. sec. 1984-85) (Maryville). Avocations: travel; jogging; jazzercise; photography. Home: 106 Piedmont Circle Maryville TN 37801 Office: WTVK PO Box 1388 Knoxville TN 37901

YARBROUGH, ANDRYETTA WELLS, state official; b. New Orleans, Mar. 14, 1937; d. David Nelson Wells and Edna Helen (Edwards) Dumas; m. Herman Walter Yarbrough, Dec. 18, 1965; children—Marlon Nelson, Ayra T., Elka M. B.A., Dillard U., New Orleans, 1958; M.P.H., Tulane U., 1974. Cert. tchr., La. Tchr., Orleans Pub. Schs., New Orleans, 1958-69; tng. mgr. Family Health Found., New Orleans, 1969-74; research assoc. Tulane U., New Orleans, 1972-82; health planner Med. Care Ctr., New Orleans, 1974-77; exec. dir. Genetic Disease Ctr., New Orleans, 1977-84; confidential asst. Dept. Health and Human Resources, Baton Rouge, La., 1984—; cons. Boone, Young & Assocs., N.Y.C., 1979-84. Author: Research Manual, 1977; co-author; Human Sexuality and Patient education, 1974; Patient Recruitment and Maintenance, 1974. Ministry dir. Bd. Christian Edn., New Orleans, 1980—. Recipient Outstanding Services award New Orleans Pub. Schs., 1976-81; Cert. of Appreciation, City of New Orleans, 1980-83; named hon. capt. New Orleans Police Force, 1982. Mem. Am. Soc. Tng. and Devel., Movement to Obtain Reform in Edn. (pres.), Female Execs. in Govt., Am. Pub. Health Assn., Health Edn. Council New Orleans, Delta Sigma Theta. Baptist. Avocations: sewing; drawing; reading; walking; ceramics. Home: 4401 Dreux Ave New Orleans LA 70126 Office: Dept Health and Human Resources PO Box 3776 Baton Rouge LA 70821

YARBROUGH, JOYCE LENORE, management consultant; b. Bowling Green, Ky., Oct. 7, 1948; d. William S. Yarbrough and Hortense Lenore (Bullock) Jackson; B.A., Fisk U., 1970; M.B.A., Golden Gate U., 1977. Spl. projects coordinator Econ. Opportunity Council, San Francisco, 1971-77; sales/statistician Macy's of Calif., San Francisco, 1971—; mgmt. cons. C.J. & Assos. Enterprises Inc., San Francisco, 1977-78; pres. Le Nore Co., Inc., 1978—; adminstrv. ops. supr. Bur. Census, U.S. Dept. Commerce, 1980; market researcher Western Pacific Industries, 1981—; dist. sales rep. Calif. State Lottery, 1985—. Co-founder Scott-Wada Youth Fund; bd. dirs. Urban League San Francisco, 1973-79, Mental Assn. San Francisco, 1972-79; panelist United Way of Bay Area, 1971-76; treas. Westside Community Mental Health Center, 1976-79; sec. Cath. Youth Orgn., 1977—; sec. Black Agenda Council San Francisco, 1984—. Mem. Mortar Bd. Home: 100 Font Blvd Apt 1K San Francisco CA 94132 Office: PO Box 15117 San Francisco CA 94115

YARBROUGH, MARTHA CORNELIA, music educator; b. Waycross, Ga., Feb. 8, 1940; d. Henry Elliott and Jessie (Sirmans) Y.; B.M.E., Stetson U., 1962; M.M.E., Fla. State U., 1968, Ph.D., 1973. Choral dir. Ware County High Sch., Waycross, Ga., 1962-64, Glynn Acad., Brunswick, Ga., 1964-70; asst. choral dir. Fla. State U., 1970-72; cons. in music Muscogee County Sch. Dist., Columbus, Ga., 1972-73; cons. in tchr. edn. Psycho-Edno. Cons., Inc., Tallahassee, 1972-73; asst. prof. music edn., dir. univs. choruses and oratorio soc. Syracuse U., 1973-76, assoc. prof. music edn., 1976-83, prof., 1983-86, acting asst. dean Coll. Visual and Performing Arts, 1980-82, acting dir. Sch. Music, 1980-82, chmn. music edn., 1982-86; prof. music La. State U., Baton Rouge, 1986—, coordinator music, edn., 1986—. Mem. Music Educators Nat. Conf., N.Y. State Sch. Music Assn., Am. Ednl. Research Assn., AAUP, Pi Kappa Lambda, Phi Beta, Kappa Delta Pi. Co-author: Competency-Based Music Education, 1980; mem. editorial com. Jour. Research in Music Edn.; contbr. articles to profl. jours., chpts. in books. Office: Sch Music La State U Baton Rouge LA 70803

YASSNEY, SHIRLEE T., food store chain executive; b. Russellville, Ky., Nov. 27, 1936; d. Lawrence Edward and Ida Dell (Rager) Utley; m. John Herbert Gfeller, Nov. 13, 1954 (div. June 1962); 1 child, Patricia; m. Joe Quinnion Yassney, Oct. 1, 1966; 1 child, Amy. Cert. Supervisory Devel. Inst., 1983. Group leader Rockwell Internat., Russellville, 1964-72; owner, mgr. Ky's Copper Kettle, Russellville, 1972-74; mgr. Cato's, Russellville, 1974-75; coordinator, Russellville C. of C., 1976-77, also bd. dirs.; supr. Minit Mart Foods, Inc., Bowling Green, Ky., 1979—. Named Ky. col. and named to hon. com. of agr. State of Ky., 1976; named mounted rifleman State of Ky., 1978; recipient Appreciation award City of Russellville, 1981. Mem. Exec. Female. Democrat. Lodge: Order Ea. Star. Avocations: reading; gardening. Home: 715 Crittenden Circle Russellville KY 42276 Office: Minit Mart Foods Inc PO Box 1177 Bowling Green KY 42101

YATES, DIANE GREINER, librarian; b. Lancaster, Pa., Nov. 16, 1939; d. Arthur Kreider and Catherine Mae (Hersh) Greiner; m. Robert James Yates, Aug. 13, 1960; children—Robert, Andrew, Karen. B.A., Grove City Coll., 1961; M.L.S., U. Pitts., 1972. Cert. pub. librarian, Pa. Hotel rep. Glenn Fawcett, Inc., San Francisco, 1961-63; bookmobile librarian Carnegie Library, Pitts., 1963; reference librarian North Hills Library, Glenshaw, Pa., 1969-81, library dir., 1981—. Contbr. articles to mags., book revs. to local newspapers and Voice of Youth Advocates. Bd. dirs. Zoar Home. Mem. Pa. Library Assn. (chmn. various coms. and task forces), ALA, AAUW, Musical Box Soc. Republican. Office: North Hills Library 1822 Mount Royal Blvd Glenshaw PA 15116

YATES, GAYLE GRAHAM, educator, writer; b. Wayne County, Miss., May 6, 1940; d. Robert C. and Gleta (Jones) Graham; B.A., Millsaps Coll., 1961; M.A.T., Vanderbilt U., 1962; Ph.D., U. Minn., 1973; m. Herschel Wilson Yates, Jr., July 21, 1961; children—Natasha, Stiles. Mem. Faculty English dept. Boston U., 1964-67; vis. scholar Cambridge U., 1973-74, 78; chmn. women's studies U. Minn., Mpls., 1976-81, assoc. prof. women's studies and Am. studies, 1981—, founding mem. Big Ten panel on women's studies. Mem. Minn. Gov.'s Adv. Com. on Families, 1980-82. Named Alumna of Yr., Millsaps Coll., 1976. Mem. Am. Studies Assn. (chmn. women's com. 1981-83), Women Historians of Midwest, Nat. Women's Studies Assn. Democrat. Methodist. Author: What Women Want: The Ideas of the Movement, 1975; editor: Harriet Martineau on Women, 1984. Home: 4105 Vincent Ave S Minneapolis MN 55410 Office: Am Studies 104 Scott Hall U Minn 72 Pleasant Ave SE Minneapolis MN 55455

YATES, MARSIEA WARREN, city official; b. Long Beach, Calif., Sept. 14, 1947; d. J. Claude and Ethelyne (Yarbrough) Warren; m. Tom Boyd Yates, Dec. 11, 1971 (div. Jan. 1984); stepchildren—Karen, Steven, Kristine, Hope Melanie. B.A. U. Ala.-Birmingham, 1974, M.A., 1977; Records clk. Orange County Sheriff's Dept., Santa Ana, Calif., 1968-71; adminstrv. officer, police officer U. Ala. Police Dept., Birmingham, 1971-74; adminstrv. coordinator faculty devel. Project on Teaching and Learning in Univ. Coll., U. Ala., Birmingham, 1974-76; asst. dir. aux. service U. Ala., Birmingham, 1976-78; info. mgr. Fort Collins Police Dept., Colo., 1979-82; mgr. integrated network services City of Ft. Collins, 1982—; cons. office automation, telecommunications; instr. Colo. State U., 1982—, U. No. Colo., 1982—; cons. human aspects of tech. Author: Criminal Record Security for Colorado Criminal Justice Agencies, 1981, rev. edit., 1983. Contbr. articles to profl. jours. Mem. bus and industry team United Way Campaign, Ft. Collins, 1984; creator Reader's Theatre, Ft. Collins Nursing Homes, 1985—. Mem. Assn. Info. Mgrs., Office Automation Soc. Internat., Urban and Regional Info. Systems Assn., Interex. Republican. Episcopalian. Avocations: stained glass designer and artisan; scuba diver; traveler. Home: 3500 Rolling Green Apt I-35 Fort Collins CO 80525 Office: City of Fort Collins 300 La Porte Ave Fort Collins CO 80521

YATES, ROWENA RAQUEL, nurse; b. Whittier, Calif., Feb. 18, 1959; d. Maclovio and Diane Elise (Doran) Lopez; m. Timothy Shawn Yates, Mar. 13, 1981. B.S. in Nursing cum laude, Tex. Women's U., 1981. Critical care nurse intern Parkland Hosp., Dallas, 1981-82, staff nurse neurosurg. intensive care unit, 1982, asst. nurse coordinator, 1982—. Contbg. author: Critical Care Nursing: Body-Mind-Spirit, 2d edit. Mem. Am. Assn. Critical Care Nurses, Sigma Theta Tau. Home: 3475 High Vista Dr Dallas TX 75234 Office: Parkland Meml Hosp 5201 Harry Hines Blvd Dallas TX 75235

YATES, VIRGINIA WOODCOCK, asphalt maintenance company executive; b. Burgaw, N.C., Feb. 21, 1955; d. Hubert Leon and LaVerne (DeBose) Woodcock; m. Donald Page Millis, July 29, 1974 (div. May 1977) 1 child, Donald Glendon; m. Raymond Wesley Yates, Jr., Dec. 2, 1978; 1 child, Wesley Leon. Mgr., Stewart & Everrett, Wilmington, N.C., 1973-76; clk. Herne Lincoln, Wilmington, 1976-77; account exec. Jefferson, Pilot Broadcasting, Wilmington, 1977-79; owner, operator Coastal Line & Striping Systems, Inc., Wilmington, 1979-84, pres., chmn., 1984—. Mem. N.C. Seal Coating Assn. (sec., treas. 1984-85), Nat. Assn. Women in Constrn. (dir. 1985—), Assn. Gen. Contractors, Neyra Adv. Bd., Sealmore Seminar Circuit (instr. 1983—). Democrat. Baptist. Lodge: Woodmen of the World. Office: Class Inc PO Box 4141 Wilmington NC 28406

YBARRA, DEBBI HUFFMAN, construction company executive; b. Riverside, Calif., Mar. 25, 1951; d. Clarence Houston and Gloria Marie (Aston) Huffman; m. Anthony Fuentes Ybarra, Jan. 31, 1981; children—Kelly Lee, Lindsey Marie. Student Calif. State U., San Bernardino, 1969-70. Bookkeeper, Roy O. Huffman Roof Co., Riverside, 1971-72, sec.-treas., 1972-75, v.p., 1975-77, pres., chief exec. officer, 1977—. Bd. dirs. Riverside City Coll. Found., 1985, Riverside Rape Crisis Ctr., 1982-83, Childhelp U.S.A., 1982-84; chmn. bd. dirs. Riverside City Coll. Civic Light Opera, 1984-85; mem. citizens com. Calif. Baptist Coll., 1982—. Named Outstanding Young Woman of Am., 1983. Mem. Roofing Contractors Assn. of San Bernardino and Riverside Counties (pres. 1982, 83, 86), Roofing Contractors Assn. of Calif. (bd. dirs. 1982-83). Republican. Roman Catholic. Club: Jr. League of Riverside (bd. dirs. 1984-85). Home: 5519 Inspiration Dr Riverside CA 92506 Office: Roy O Huffman Roof Co 5971 Jurupa Ave Riverside CA 92504

YEAGER, PATRICIA MARGARET, univ. adminstr.; b. Detroit, July 24, 1941; d. William Hugh and Kathleen Grace (McKee) Sullivan; B.A. with high distinction, U. Mich., Dearborn, 1973; m. Frederick Carl Yeager, Aug. 17, 1963; children—Gwendolyn Grace, Elizabeth Brooke, Emily Anne. Mem. adminstrv. staff U. Mich., Dearborn, 1973—, adminstrv. asst. II, 1977-79, dir. Engring. Projects Office, 1979—, acting dir. profl. devel. program, 1980—, interim dir. sponsored research, 1981—; trustee Met. Detroit Sci. and Engring. Coalition, 1980—; grant reviewer Nat. Action Council Minorities in Engring., 1982. Recipient Outstanding Engring. Edn. Achievement award Mich. Soc. Profl. Engrs., 1980. Mem. Nat. Assn. Female Execs., Am. Soc. Engring. Edn., Soc. Women Engrs. (asso.), Nat. Assn. Minority Engring. Project Adminstrs., Alumni Assn. U. Mich., Alumni Assn. U. Calif., LWV (chpt. 1st v.p. 1970-72), Gamma Phi Beta. Club: Detroit Yacht. Office: U Michigan 4901 Evergreen St Dearborn MI 48128

YEARGIN-ALLSOPP, MARSHALYN, medical epidemiologist, pediatrician; b. Greenville, S.C., May 17, 1948; d. Grady Andrew and Willie Mae (Blocker) Yeargin; m. Ralph Norman Allsopp, Apr. 5, 1975; children—Timothy Chandler, Whitney Marisha. Student Bennett Coll., 1964-66; B.A., Sweet Briar Coll., 1968; M.D., Emory U., 1972. Diplomate Am. Bd. Pediatrics. Intern Montefiore Hosp., Bronx, N.Y., 1972-73, resident, 1973-75; instr. pediatrics Albert Einstein Coll. Medicine, Bronx, 1975-77, asst. prof. pediatrics, 1977-78, 80-81; pediatrician Montefiore-Morrisania Comprehensive Health Care Ctr., Bronx, 1975-78, Louise Wise Adoption Agy., N.Y.C., 1975-80, Children's Evaluation and Rehab. Ctr., Rose F. Kennedy Ctr., Bronx, 1980-81; officer USPHS, 1981—, comdr., 1983—; epidemiologic intelligence service officer birth defects br. Ctrs. for Disease Control, Atlanta, 1981-83, preventive medicine resident, 1982-84, med. epidemiologist, 1984—; pediatric cons. Clayton County Early Intervention Program, Jonesboro, Ga., 1983—; med. dir. Easter Seal Presch. Program, Atlanta, 1981-83; physician Com. on Handicapped, N.Y.C., 1979-81, United Cerebral Palsy Program, Bronx, 1980-81. Bd. overseers Sweet Briar Coll., 1981—; bd. dirs. Neighborhood Arts Ctr., Atlanta, 1984—; mem. prevention edn. com. Retarded Citizens, Atlanta, 1984—; mem. fundraising campaign Greater Atlanta YWCA, 1985. Fellow Am. Acad. Pediatrics, Am. Acad. Cerebral Palsy and Devel. Medicine; mem. AMA, Atlanta Med. Assn., Jack and Jill of Am., Phi Beta Kappa, Delta Sigma Theta. Home: 2931 Pine Valley Circle East Point GA 30344 Office: Ctrs for Disease Control Chamblee-5 1600 Clifton Rd Atlanta GA 30333

YEARY, TERRI LYN, insurance company executive; b. LaFayette, Ind., Jan. 2, 1953; d. Robert Eugene and Betty Lou (Truman) Strader; m. Jack Yeary, Sept. 18, 1982; 1 dau., Tiffani Leigh. Grad. high sch. Claims sec. Am. States Ins. Co., Cleve., 1972-75; with group dept. Reliance Ins. Co., Cleve., adminstrv. asst. PIE Mut. Ins. Co., Cleve., 1975-79, underwriting mgr., 1979—; treas. Rogers Ins. Consultants, Cleve., 1976-79. Office: PIE Mut Ins Co 1365 Ontario Ave Suite 602 Cleveland OH 44114

YEATER, CAROL RAE, psychiatric nurse; b. Glendale, W.Va., Sept. 13, 1952; d. Robert Ormsby and Rosalee Lena (Kelly) Y. A.S. in Sci. and Nursing, W.Va. No. Community Coll., 1975; student W. Liberty State Coll., 1976-78; B.A., U. South Fla., Tampa, 1985; postgrad. U. South Fla. R.N. Staff nurse Ohio Valley Med. Ctr., Wheeling, W.Va., 1975-80, Morton Plant Hosp., Clearwater, Fla., 1980—. Mem. NOW (convenor 1973-75), Phi Kappa Phi, Pi Gamma Mu. Democrat. Avocations: swimming; attending plays; concerts; women's cultural events. Home: 11315 112th Ave N Largo FL 33544

YEAZELL, RUTH BERNARD, educator; b. N.Y.C., Apr. 4, 1947; d. Walter and Annabelle (Reich) Bernard; B.A. with high honors, Swarthmore Coll., 1967; M.Phil. (Woodrow Wilson fellow), Yale U., 1970, Ph.D., 1971; m. Stephen C. Yeazell, Aug. 14, 1969 (div. 1980). Asst. prof. English, Boston U., 1971-74; asst. prof. English, UCLA, 1975-77, asso. prof., 1977-80, prof., 1980—. Guggenheim fellow, 1979-80. Mem. MLA, AAUP (supervising com. English Inst. 1983-86). Author: Language and Knowledge in the Late Novels of Henry James, 1976; Death and Letters of Alice James, 1981; asso. editor Nineteenth-Century Fiction, 1977-80; editor: Sex, Politics, and Science in the 19th Century Novel, 1986. Home: 329 Veteran Ave Los Angeles CA 90024 Office: Dept English UCLA Los Angeles CA 90024

YEH, JUDITH ELAINE, mechanical engineer, educator; b. Toronto, Can., Nov. 11, 1953, came to U.S., 1956, naturalized, 1963; d. Paul Pao and Beverley Pamela (Eng) Y. B.S.M.E., Calif. State U.-Fullerton, 1981. Summer computer analyst TRW, Redondo Beach, Calif., 1973; summer cons. Ford Aerospace, Newport Beach, Calif., 1976; student engr. Rockwell Internat., Downey, Calif., 1978-79; assoc. engr. Lockheed Aircraft, Burbank, Calif., 1981-82; mech. engr. Mattel Toys, Hawthorne, Calif., 1982-83; contract mech. engr. Rockwell Internat., Anaheim, Calif., 1983-84; Contract mech. engr. Hughes Aircraft, 1984; desing engr. advanced tech. div. HTL Industries, Duarte, Calif., 1984—. Contr. to Calif. Engr. Mag., 1972. Sec. Californians for Nonsmokers Rights, 1976—; sec. Chinese Assn. Orange County, 1983. Recipient cert. of appreciation Orange Coast Coll., 1976; Nat. Merit Scholar, 1971. Mem. Soc. Women Engrs. (pres. UCLA chpt. 1973-74), ASME (assoc.), Chinese Engrs. and Scientists Assn. So. Calif., Engring. Soc. U. Calif. (sec. 1971-78), Alpha Gamma Delta. Republican. Baptist.

YEKEL, PENNY LYNN, newspaper editor, printing manager; b. Alliance, Nebr., July 14, 1951; d. Clarence Fred and Betty Jean (Broich) Y. B.A., Chadron State Coll., 1973; M.A., U. Nebr.-Lincoln, 1977; postgrad. Nebr. Western Coll. Residence dir. Nebr. Wesleyan U., Lincoln, 1973-74; with Youth Program, NW Nebr. Community Action, Chadron, 1974-75; with patient intake Panhandle Mental Health, Scottsbluff, Nebr., 1975-76; reporter, sales rep. Bus. Farmer Inc., Scottsbluff, 1976-78, editor, 1978—, gen. mgr., 1980—; pub. Nebr. Wheat Power Broker, Ogallala, 1983—. Author profl. jours. Bd. dirs. Am. Cancer Soc., Scottsbluff, 1982, United Way, 1983-84; mem. W. Nebr. Arts Ctr., 1980—, Scotts Bluff County Fair Bd., 1983—, Outriders, 1983—. Recipient award Gt. Navy of Nebr., Gov. Nebr., 1982; Meritorious Service to 4-H, Nebr. Extension Council, 1983; Appreciation award Nebr. Stock Growers Assn., 1982. Mem. Western Dist. Press Assn. (pres. 1982-83), Nat. Fedn. Press Women, Nebr. Assn. Press Women, Nebr. Press Assn., Scottsbluff C. of C., AAUW, Bus. and Profl. Women, Sigma Delta Chi. Lutheran. Club: Soroptimists (officer 1982-83). Home: 3905 Ave D Scottsbluff NE 69361 Office: Bus Farmer Inc 1617 Ave A Scottsbluff NE 69361

YELENICK, MARY THERESE, lawyer; b. Denver, May 17, 1954; d. John Andrew and Maesel Joyce (Reed) Y. B.A. magna cum laude, Colo. Coll., 1976; J.D. cum laude, Georgetown U., 1979. Bar: D.C. 1979, U.S. Dist. Ct. D.C. 1980, U.S. Ct. Appeals (D.C. cir.) 1981, N.Y. 1982, U.S. Dist. Ct. (so. and ea. dists.) N.Y. 1982. Law clk. to presiding justices Superior Ct. D.C., 1979-81; assoc. Chadbourne & Parke, N.Y.C., 1981—. Editor Jour. of Law and Policy Internat. Bus., 1978-79. Mem. Phi Beta Kappa. Democrat. Roman Catholic. Home: 310 E 46th St New York NY 10017 Office: Chadbourne & Parke 30 Rockefeller Plaza New York NY 10112

YELLEN, LINDA, film director writer, producer; b. Forest Hills, N.Y., July 13, 1949; d. Seymour and Bernice (Mittelman) Y. B.A. magna cum laude, Barnard Coll., 1969; M.F.A. in Film, Columbia U., 1971, Ph.D. in Lang., Lit. and Communications, 1975. Mem. film faculty Columbia U., N.Y.C., 1971-73, Barnard Coll., 1971-73, Yale U., 1970-71, CUNY, 1974; prin. Chrysalis-Yellen Prodns., Inc., N.Y.C., 1982—. Producer, dir. films: Prospera, 1969; Come Out, Come Out, 1971; Looking Up, 1978; producer, dir., co-writer film: Prisoner Without a Name, Cell Without A Number, NCB-TV, 1983 (Peabody award; Writers Guild nominee for best screenplay); exec. producer, producer CBS network spls.: Hard Hat and Legs, 1980; Mayflower: The Pilgrims Adventure, 1979; Playing For Time, 1980 (Emmy award for best dramatic spl., Peabody award, Christopher award); exec. producer, producer, co-writer CBS network spl.: The Royal Romance of Charles and Diana, 1982; exec. producer, producer CBS-TV movie: Second Serve: The Renee Richards Story, 1986; contbr. articles to N.Y. Times, Village Voice, Interview, Hollywood Reporter. Mem. Dirs. Guild Am. (exec. council), Writers Guild Am., Acad. TV Arts and Scis. Office: William Morris Agy 151 El Camino Dr Beverly Hills CA 90069

YELLIN, JUDITH, electrologist; b. Balt., Feb. 21, 1930; d. Jack and Sarah (Grebow) Levin; m. Sidney Yellin, Jan. 1, 1950; children—David, Paul, Tamar. Student U. Md., 1948-50, Catonsville Community Coll., 1969-71. Mgr. credit dept. Lincoln Co., Balt., 1956-59; office mgr. Seaview Constrn. Co., 1960-62; owner, operator Yellin Telephone Soliciting Agy., 1963-65; mgr. Liberty Antique Shop, 1967-69; owner, mgr. Judith Yellin Electrology, 1973—; chief examiner Md. State Bd. Electrology, 1978-81. Mem. Am. Electrolysis Assn., Md. Assn. Profl. Electrologists. Avocations: travel; reading; collecting-Haitian and art deco-nouveau art. Home: 6232 Blackstone Ave Baltimore MD 21209 Office: Judith Yellin Electrology 1401 Reisterstown Rd Baltimore MD 21208

YEO, URSULA MURIEL, industrial engineer; b. Bad Kreuznach, Fed. Republic Germany, May 24, 1957; came to U.S., 1958; d. Kenneth Daniel and Hanna Beate (Leven) Moore; m. Steven Brent Yeo, May 3, 1979. A.A., Harrisburg Area Community Coll., 1977; B.S. in Indsl. Engring., Pa. State U., 1979. Looper (trainee) Bethlehem Steel Corp., Balt., 1979-82; chief indsl. engring. staff U.S. Coast Guard Yard, Balt., 1983—. Mem. Inst. Indsl. Engrs. (rec. sec. 1978-79, treas. 1981-82, v.p. membership 1982-83, bd. dirs. 1983-84, v.p. membership 1986—). Republican. Lutheran. Avocations: needlework; sewing; quilting; photography; travel. Home: 373 Phirne Rd Glen Burnie MD 21061

YERACARIS, BERNICE LEVENFELD, psychologist; b. Detroit, Sept. 16, 1920; d. Mitchell Abe and Florence Berman Levenfeld; m. Constantine A. Yeracaris, Sept. 12, 1949; children—Flora, Yoryos, Panos, Anthony. Student Roosevelt U., 1940-42; B.A., U. Chgo., 1944, postgrad. 1947-49. Pvt. practice psychol. therapy, Buffalo, 1951—; instr. Cornell Extension Sch. Labor and Mgmt., 1949-50, U. Buffalo, 1949-50. Diplomate Am. Bd. Psychotherapy. Mem. Am. Psychol. Assn., N.Y. State Psychol. Assn., Psychol. Assn. Western N.Y., Council Advancement Profl. Psychology, Nat. Register Health Service Providers in Psychology, Mental Health Assn. Erie County, Sex, Info. and Edn. Council. Address: 485 Norwood Ave Buffalo NY 14222

YESENOSKY, CATHY SUSAN, systems consultant; b. N.Y.C., Oct. 25, 1952; d. Herman G. and Ruth R. (Rothenstein) Gelfand; m. Stephen Michael Yesenosky, Aug. 21, 1983. B.A. cum laude, Queens Coll., 1973; Cert. in Bus. Mgmt., NYU, 1976, M.B.A., 1985. Sr. programmer Fed. Res. Bank, N.Y.C., 1973-76; sr. systems analyst Depository Trust Co., N.Y.C., 1976-77; sr. tech. writer Bankers Trust Co., N.Y.C., 1977-78; sr. cons. Interactive Data Corp., N.Y.C., 1978-80; bus. systems planner, corp. systems liaison Smith, Barney, Harris, Upham, N.Y.C., 1980-83; systems cons. Merrill, Lynch & Co., N.Y.C., 1983-85; mgr. profl. support systems Bear Stearns & Co., N.Y.C., 1985-86, planning mgr. Equitable Life Assurance Soc., N.Y.C., 1986—. Community bd. Am. Mus. Natural History, Mcpl. Art Soc. Mem. Nat. Assn. Female Execs., Women in Data Processing, Women in Computing, Mensa, Concert/Theatre Club, Am. Mus. Natural History, Met. Mus. Art, Whitney Mus., Cooper-Hewitt Mus., Mus. of Modern Art, South St. Seaport Mus. Democrat. Jewish. Club: Hadassah. Home: 30 W 61st St New York NY 10023 Office: 663 3d Ave New York NY 10017

YIH, MAE DUNN, state legislator; b. Shanghai, China, May 24, 1928; d. Chung Woo and Fung Wen (Feng) Dunn; m. Stephen W.H. Yih, 1953; children—Donald, Daniel. B.A., Barnard Coll., 1951; postgrad. Columbia U., 1951-52. Asst. to bursar Barnard Coll., N.Y.C., 1952-53; mem. Oreg. Ho. of Reps. from 36th dist., 1977-83, Oreg. Senate from 19th dist., 1983—. State Democratic precinct woman; mem. Clover Ridge Elem. Sch. Bd., Albany, Oreg., from 1969, Albany Union High Sch. Bd., from 1975; mem. adv. com. Environ. Health Dept., Linn County, Oreg., from 1977. Mem. AAUW, LWV, Linn County Citizens for Retarded, Linn County Mental Health Assn., Oreg. Sch. Bd. Assn. Episcopalian. Office: Oreg Senate State Capitol Salem OR 97310*

YIM, MARY ANCILLA, library dir., educator; b. Honolulu, Feb. 17, 1927; d. Ernest K. and Wai Shan (Ching) Y.; student St. Francis Normal Sch., Maria Regina Coll., 1948-52; B.S. in Edn., U. Dayton, 1957; M.S. in L.S., Cath. U. Am., 1962; postgrad. U. Hawaii, Honolulu, 1961-69; cert. advanced studies in instructional adminstrn. SUNY, Oswego, 1975. Joined Third Order of St. Francis, 1948; sec., receptionist, real estate, ins. and law office, Honolulu, 1944-48; tchr. St. Paul's Ch., Whitesboro, N.Y., 1950-52; tchr.-librarian St. Joseph's High Sch., Hilo, Hawaii, 1952-65, prin., 1965-71; asst. prin. Oswego (N.Y.) Cath. High Sch., 1971-75; dir. library Maria Regina Coll., Syracuse, N.Y., 1975—, instr., 1976-79, asst. prof., 1979-82, asso. prof., 1982—. NDEA grantee in English, U. Hawaii, 1964. Mem. ALA, Cath. (chpt. pres. 1980-82; facilitator continuing edn. program 1982—), N.Y. library assns., Assn. Coll. and Research Libraries. Office: 1024 Court St Syracuse NY 13208

YINGLING, ADRIENNE ELIZABETH, communications company executive; b. Hershey, Pa., June 10, 1959; d. Richard Terry Yingling and Dolores Jean (Ott) Brown. Student N.C. State U., Raleigh, 1983—. Lic. real estate assoc., N.C. Asst. mgr. Fast Face, Raleigh, 1979-80; statis. analyst S.P.A.R., Elmsford, N.Y., 1980-81; relocation dir., sales assoc. Realty World, Cary, N.C., 1981-83; product mgr. Southeastern Electronics, Raleigh, 1983-84; results acct. No. Telecom, Research Triangle Park, N.C., 1984—. Stage technician Raleigh Little Theater, 1983—. Mem. Nat. Assn. Female Execs., Nat. Assn. Accts., N.C. State U. Acctg. Soc., Phi Kappa Phi, Gamma Beta Phi. Republican. Unitarian. Avocations: photography; watercolor painting; reading; aerobics; dance. Home: 1341 Chester Rd Apt C Raleigh NC 27608 Office: No Telecom 4600 Emperor Blvd Norrisville NC 27560

YOCHAM, WANDA JUNE BURLESON, theol. sem. adminstr.; b. Rankin, Tex., Oct. 29, 1934; d. Wesley Hardin and Vivian May Lee (Hickerson) Burleson; student San Angelo Coll., 1953-54, Austin Community Coll., 1974-75, U. Ky. Coll. Bus. Mgmt. Inst., 1977-78, 79; div.; children—James, Kathy. Claims clk. Legal div. Tex. Bd. Hosps. and Schs., Austin Tex., 1959-61; office mgr. George T. Barr Comml. Food Equipment, Orlando, Fla., 1962-64; bus. officer Episcopal Theol. Sem., Austin, Tex., 1964—. Treas., bd. dirs. Ctr. for Hispanic Ministries. Mem. So. Assn. Coll. and Univ. Bus. Officers. Republican. Episcopalian. Address: Episcopal Theol Sem Southwest Box 2247 Austin TX 78767

YOCHEM, LINDA ANN, management training company executive; b. Charleston, S.C., Nov. 2, 1948; d. Harry Dillard and Ella Ruth (Summer) Y.; m. John Randal Harbin, Jan. 23, 1966 (div. June 1982); children—Kenneth Randal, Keith Foster. B.B.A. cum laude, Lander Coll., 1979; postgrad Augusta Coll., 1983, M.S. in Mktg. Mgmt., U. S.C., 1986. Cert. Purchasing Mgr. Sec., Piedmont Tech. Coll., Greenwood, S.C., 1967-70, G.E. Moore Contracting Co., Greenwood, S.C., 1971-73; sec., asst. Drs. Brockington & Baker, Greenwood, S.C., 1973-75; office mgr. So. Calculating Machines, Greenwood, 1975-79, v.p. sales, 1979-81; purchasing supr. Prof. Med. Products, Greenwood, 1982-85; seminar leader Yochem Assocs., Greenwood, 1985—. Mem. Nat. Assn. Purchasing Mgmt., Nat. Assn. Female Execs., Am. Mktg. Assn., PMAC-V, AAUW. Club: Four Seasons Garden (pres. 1976-77). Office: 204 Windtree Rd Greenwood SC 29646

YOCK, NORMA IRIS, counselor, educator; b. Pekin, Ill., Apr. 18, 1920; d. John Battista and Pauline (Gianessi) Lami; m. John Matthew Yock, June 1, 1946 (dec. July 1957); 1 child, Julie Ann. B. in Music Edn., Ill. Wesleyan U., 1941; M.A., Bradley U., Peoria, Ill., 1961; specialist cert. Ill. State U., 1961, 63; U. Louisville, 1965, U. Ill., 1975. Cert. sch. counselor. Supr. music, art High Sch., Venice, Ill., 1941-45; dir. vocal music Edison Jr. High Sch., Pekin, 1952-58; supr. music Pekin Pub. Schs., 1958-62; counselor Pekin Community High Sch., 1962-84; sales rep. Sutton Travel Services, 1984—. Pres., Pekin Jr. Women's Club, 1948-50; Pekin Civic Chorus, 1959—; bd. dirs. YWCA, Am. Cancer Soc., 1983—, Channel 47, Peoria, Ill., 1983—. Cited for Outstanding Contbn. to Sch. and Community, Pekin Community High Sch. Bd. of Edn., 1984; chmn. United Way, 1985. Recipient Outstanding Achievement award YWCA, 1982. Mem. Altrusa Internat., NEA, Ill. Edn. Assn., Tri-County Guidance, Federated Bus. and Profl. Women's Club (pres. 1970-75), Delta Kappa Gamma (pres. 1961-64), Sigma Alpha Iota (pres. 1940-44). Republican. Roman Catholic. Avocations: music; reading; travel. Home: 1314 State St Pekin IL 61554 Office: 34 S Capitol St Pekin IL 61554

YODER, CAROLYN PATRICIA, editor; b. Greenwich, Conn., July 2, 1953; d. Rufus Wayne and Kathryn Louise (Mulhollen) Y. B.A., Washington U., St. Louis, 1975; M.A., U. Iowa-Iowa City, 1979. Editorial asst. D.C. Heath & Co., Lexington, 1979-81; publs. asst. Internat. Human Resources Devel. Corp., Boston, 1981-82, prodn. editor, 1982-83; asst. editor Cobblestone, Cobblestone Pub., Inc., Peterborough, N.H., 1983, editor, 1983-84, editor-in-chief, 1984—, editor-in-chief Faces, 1984—, Classical Calliope, 1984—. Contbr. illustrations to Sojourner, Women, Lake Hope, Off Our Backs. Mem. Bookbuilders of Boston (prodn. coordinator winning book and cover New England Book Show 1983), Assn. Earth Sci. Editors, Greater Boston Rights and Permissions Group, Soc. Scholarly Pub., Ednl. Press Assn. Am. Democrat. Office: Cobblestone Publishing Inc 20 Grove St Peterborough NH 03458

YODER, DORIS ELAINE, food company executive; b. Los Angeles, Sept. 23, 1931; d. John Charles and Bertha (Koenig) Allen; m. Willard Harding, Feb. 12, 1966; 1 son, Paul Thomas; stepchildren—Mark Douglas, Nancy Anne. Student East Los Angeles Coll., 1960-62, Woodbury Coll., 1965-66; B.S., U. Beverly Hills, 1981, M.S. in Acctg., 1983. Office adminstr. Northington, Inc., West Los Angeles, Calif., 1950-55, Bonded Products Co., Los Angeles, 1955-60; owner, operator C & D Plastics, Monterey Park, Calif., 1960-64; bookkeeper Kold Kist Foods, Los Angeles, 1964-76, office mgr., controller, 1976-85, v.p. adminstrn. and fin., 1985—. Violinist, All Cities Orch., 1947-50; 1st violinist Huntington Park Symphony Orch., 1950-53; 2d violinist San Gabriel Symphony Orch., 1953-56. Mem. Am. Mgmt. Assn. Lutheran. Home: 353 De La Fuente Monterey Park CA 91754 Office: 5356 Jillson St Los Angeles CA 90022

YODER, PATRICIA ELLEN, nurse; b. Norristown, Pa., Mar. 24, 1953; d. Edward Luther and Janet Ellen (Brooks) Wood; m. Roger Grove Yoder, May 12, 1973; children—Susan Jennifer, Bethany Laura, Joshua Christopher, Kathleen Marie, David Dominic. Student Muhlenberg Coll., 1971-73, Coll. Misericordia, 1985; A.A., Luzerne County Community Coll., 1983. R.N., Pa. Charge nurse St. Joseph's Hosp., Hazleton, Pa., 1983-85, Birchwood Nursing Ctr., 1985—. Tchr. Trinity Ch. and Newport Ch., Nanticoke, 1984—; choir dir. Newport Ecumenical Choir, Nanticoke, 1984—; bd. dirs. nursing services Wyo. Valley Red Cross, Wilkes-Barre, Pa., 1984—. Roman Catholic. Avocations: needlework; cooking; writing; reading. Home: 29 E Kirmar Ave Nanticoke PA 18634

YOHE, MARY SCARAMASTRA, human resources executive; b. Scranton, Pa., July 9, 1949; d. Vincent Matthew and Irene Anne (Heckman) Scaramastra; m. Bradley Eugene Yohe, Dec. 21, 1969; 1 son, Gregory Daniel. Student Lock Haven State U., 1967-69; B.S., Mt. St. Mary's Coll., 1981. Bookkeeper, Robert Hall, Inc., State College, Pa., 1971-73; asst. indsl. relations mgr. Worthington div. McGraw-Edison Co., Taneytown, Md., 1973-74, human resource mgr., 1974—. Commr. Econ. Devel. Com., Carroll County, Md., 1981—; adviser Carroll County Vocat. Edn. Council, 1981—; pres. procurement com. Carroll County Sheltered Workshop, 1980-82. Recipient Community Service award United Way of Central Md., Balt., 1978, 79, 80, 81, 82, 83, Am. Heart Assn., 1981, 82. Mem. Carroll County Personnel Assn. (pres. 1980-83), Am. Soc. Personnel Adminstrs., Am. Bus. Women's Assn., Carroll County C. of C., Hanover Area C. of C. Republican. Roman Catholic.

YOPCONKA, NATALIE ANN CATHERINE, computer specialist, educator; b. Taylor, Pa., July 21, 1942; d. Michael Joseph and Natalie Ann Lucille (Panek) Yopconka; B.S., U. Md., 1965; M.B.A., George Washington U., 1976; postgrad. numerous courses. Mgmt. analyst, adminstrv. trainee U.S. Dept. Commerce, Maritime Adminstrn., Washington, 1965-67; computer programmer, computer specialist Dept. Labor, Washington, 1967-78; instr. computer sci. Assn. for Computing Machinery, Washington, 1978; instr. computer sci. Montgomery Coll., Takoma Park and Rockville, Md., 1979; sr. programmer analyst Dynamic Data Processing, Inc., Silver Spring, Md., 1979; instr. Nat. Bus. Sch., Inc., Alexandria, Va., 1980; cons. McLeod Corp., Washington, 1980; lectr. computer sci., coop. coordinator U. Md., College Park, 1980-81; sr. adminstrv. applications analyst programmer, Data Transformation Corp., Washington, 1981; sr. systems analyst Singer Link Simulation Systems div., Silver Spring, 1981-82; self-employed distbr. and accessory designer, 1982-83; market researcher Washington Fin. Service, 1982-83; lectr. computer info. and systems sci. U. D.C., Rockville, Md., 1983; prof computer programming and mgmt. info. systems Benjamin Franklin U., Washington, 1983; researcher Info. U.S.A., Potomac, Md., 1983-85; self-employed admissions rep. Brook-Wein Bus. Inst., Washington, 1985; self-employed distbr., Hyattsville, Md., 1979—. Mem. Takoma Park Disability Com.; Mayor's Com. on Energy, Housing and Planning, 1980-81; mem. choir Our Lady of Sorrows Ch. Mem. EDP Auditors Assn., Assn. for Computing Machinery (edn. com., instr. 1978-79, 1980-81), Data Processing Mgmt. Assn., Fed. Automatic Data Processing Users Group, Am. Automobile Assn., IEEE Computer Soc., Internat. Biog. Assn., Am. Biog. Inst. Research Assn., Phi Delta Gamma (scholarship com., social com., hospitality com. 1977-78, 1980-81, 82—). Clubs: Cath. Alumni, Fed. Poets. Home and office: 7401 New Hampshire Ave Apt 1115 Hyattsville MD 20783

YORBURG, BETTY (MRS. LEON YORBURG), educator; b. Chgo., Aug. 27, 1926; d. Max and Hannah (Bernstein) Gitelman; Ph.B., U. Chgo., 1945, M.A., 1948; Ph.D., New Sch. Social Research, 1968; m. Leon Yorburg, June 23, 1946; children—Harriet, Robert. Instr., Coll. New Rochelle, 1966-67; lectr. City Coll. and Grad. Center, City U. N.Y., 1967-69, asst. prof., 1969-73, asso. prof. sociology dept., 1973-77, prof., 1978—; research asst. Prof. Clifford Shaw, Chgo. Area Project, 1946-47. Mem. Am., Eastern sociol. assns., Am. Council Family Relations. Author: Utopia and Reality, 1969; The Changing Family, 1973; Sexual Identity: Sex Roles and Social Change, 1974; The New Women, 1976; Introduction to Sociology, 1982; Families and Societies, 1983. Home: 20 Earley St City Island NY 10464 Office: Sociology Dept City Coll NY 138th and Convent Ave New York NY 10031

YORDANOFF, DORIS MARIE, nurse, educator; b. Houston, Jan. 15, 1930; d. Frank Joseph and Susie Lucille (Guinn) Blakeslee; m. Theo Yordanoff, Jr., Apr. 27, 1979; children by previous marriage—Debbie Martin, Mike Collins, Mitzie Collins. B.S. in Nursing, Dominican Coll., 1954; M.Edn., U. Houston, 1961. Registered nurse, Tex. Social and health dir. Sacred Heart Dominican Coll., Houston, 1951-52, clin. instr. pediatrics, 1952-57; staff nurse City Health Dept., Houston, 1958-59; head nurse pediatrics isolation unit St. Joseph Hosp., Houston, 1959-61, charge nurse 3-11, 1962-63, staff nurse relief med. units, 1963-73, dir. nursing edn., 1973—; instr. health occupations Houston Ind. Sch. Dist., 1961-62; sophomore coordinator nursing faculty Dominican Coll. and U. St. Thomas, Houston, 1963-73; cons. Sisters of Charity, 1976, 78. Contbr. articles to profl. jours. Sec., Houston Assn. Children with Learning Disabilities, 1965-68; chmn. St. Augustine CCD program, Houston, 1966-67; tchr. St. John Vianney CCD program, 1975-76; mem. Meml. Club Townhouse Assn., Houston, 1979-81. St. Joseph Hosp. edn. scholar, 1951. Mem. Am. Nurses Assn., Tex. Hosp. Assn., Houston Assn. for Nursing Service Adminstrn., Assoc. Nursing Alumni (pres. 1980-84). Democrat. Roman Catholic. Club: Nursing Honor Soc. Home: 14423 Misty Meadow Houston TX 77079 Office: Saint Joseph Hosp 1919 LaBranch St Houston TX 77002

YORK, CAROLYN KAYE, writer; b. Greenfield, Ohio, May 21, 1929; d. James Mortimer and Michal Oviatt (Porter) Y.; m. Earl J. Hicks, Oct. 28, 1950 (dec. 1974); children—Sharon Lee Hicks Szymanski, Warren York (dec.), Diana Marie. B.A., Miami U., Oxford, Ohio, 1950. Copywriter, broadcaster sta. WMOH-AM, Hamilton, Ohio, 1950-56; exec. sec. newsletter First Presbyn. Ch., Middletown, Ohio, 1957-58; traffic dir., broadcaster sta. WPFB and WPFB-FM, Middletown, 1958-62; account exec., broadcasters news sta. WFOL-FM and WENW, Fairfield, Ohio, 1962-68; asst. editor Miami Alumnus, Miami U. 1968-82, editorial asst., alumni affairs univ. relations, 1982—; editor newsletter Ohio Community Theatre Assn., 1972-74. Actress, soprano Miami U. Summer Theatre, 1969—, bd. dirs., 1967-85; co-founder Big Bros. and Sisters of Hamilton and Vicinity, Inc., 1968, chmn. bd., 1976-78; co-founder Oxford Area Community Theatre, 1979, Hamilton chpt. Parents Without Partners, 1966; elder Presbyn. Ch.; county officer Republican Party, 1976-82. Mem. Women in Communications (profl. advisor Miami U., Nat. Advisor of Yr. 1977, co-founder Miami U. chpt. 1977), Alpha Epsilon Rho, Delta Zeta Alumnae (pres. Oxford 1970, 81). Home: 808 Clover Circle Oxford OH 45056 Office: Miami Univ Oxford OH 45056

YORK, DONNA JEAN, newspaper publisher; b. Salmon, Idaho, Mar. 14, 1935; d. Clell Mace and Mary Lou (Matthews) Riddle; children—Debbie Lynn, James Wesley, Carla Jo. B.S., Tex. Eastern U., 1976. Editor, Kerens (Tex.) Tribune, 1976-77, pub. owner, 1977—. Named Woman of Year, Am. Bus. Women's Assn., 1984; Profl. and Bus. Women's Assn. scholar, 1976; Tex. Coll. scholar, 1975; recipient Silver Key award Mont. State U., 1952, 53. Mem. Kerens C. of C. (dir. 1980-82), Am. Bus. Women's Assn. (pres. 1982), Sigma Delta Chi. Club: Kerens Pioneer Literary (corr. sec. 1983-84). Home: 605 Gray Ln Kerens TX 75144 Office: Kerens Tribune 116 S Colket St Kerens TX 75144

YORK, JANET BREWSTER, nurse, family and sex therapist; b. N.Y.C., Mar. 5, 1941; d. Edward Cox and Janet (Stone) Brewster; A.A. with honors, Briarcliff Coll., 1961; R.N. with highest honors, U. Iowa, 1965; B.A. summa cum laude, Marymount Manhattan Coll., 1975; M.A. with honors, N.Y.U., 1978; m. Albert Thompson York, Mar. 31, 1962 (dec.); children—Clifton Gaston, Torrance Brewster; 1 child, Justin Brigham. Nurse, Manhattan Eye, Ear and Throat Hosp., N.Y.C., 1966-74; nurse, counselor Washington Free Clinic, 1969-71; family therapist Ackerman Family Inst., N.Y.C., 1976-80; sex therapist N.Y. Med. Coll., Flower Fifth Ave. Hosp., N.Y.C., 1976-78; individual practice family, marriage and sex therapy, N.Y.C., 1978—; supr. sex therapy NYU Med. Ctr., 1982—. Fellow in sex edn., counseling and therapy, marital and family therapy Internat. Council Sex Edn. and Parenthood, Am. U., 1981. Mem. Am. Soc. Sex Therapy and Research, Am. Assn. Marriage and Family Therapists (asso.), Am. Assn. Sex Edn., Counseling and Therapy, Soc. for Sci. Study Sex, Sex Info. and Edn. Council U.S. Clubs: Lawrence Beach, Rockaway Hunting. Contbr. articles to profl. jours. Home: 155 E 72d St New York NY 10021

YORK, MARGARET RUTH ASHTON (MRS. GORDON C. YORK), occupational therapist; b. Reynoldsburg, Ohio, June 9, 1911; d. George Edward and Mary Ruth (Abbott) Ashton; A.A., Los Angeles City Coll., 1933; postgrad. UCLA, 1940; B.S., U. So. Calif., 1958, certificate occupational therapy, 1959; m. Edward T. Randall, Nov. 2, 1938 (dec. Mar. 1968); m. Gordon C. York, Mar. 26, 1973; 1 stepdau., Paulette Marie. Audio-visual specialist U. Calif. Extension, Los Angeles, 1940-56; registered occupational therapist Bur. Crippled Children Services, Schs. for Physically Handicapped, Calif. Dept. Public Health, El Monte, Burbank and Ontario, 1959-63; supervising occupational therapist Crippled Children Services, Orange County Health Dept., Santa Ana, Calif., 1963-74, ret., 1974. Hon. clin. faculty Sargent Coll. Allied Health Professions, Boston U., Sch. Allied Health Professions, Loma Linda U. Mem. South Orange County Regional Citizens Mental Health Adv. Bd., 1975. Mem. Audio-Visual Assn. So. Calif. (v.p. 1955-56), So. Calif. (sec. 1960-61), Orange County (sec. 1969-70) occupational therapy assns. Episcopalian. Club: Pilot (v.p. 1955) (Westwood Village, Calif.). Home: 320-F Avenida Carmel Laguna Hills CA 92653

YORK, MARY ALICE, banker; b. Windber, Pa., Nov. 13, 1949; d. John Joseph and Lillian Elaine (Mihalick) Hutsky; m. George York, June 20, 1976. B.S., Youngstown State U., 1972; M.Ed., Cleve. State U., 1976. Tng./adminstrn. specialist CitiBank, N.A., N.Y.C., 1978-80; sr. officer Citizens Union Nat. Bank and Trust Co., Lexington, Ky., 1981-82, v.p., dir. human resources, 1982-86; compensation and benefits adminstr. Gallatin Bank (Penn Bancorp), Uniontown, Pa., 1986—. Contbr. articles to profl. jours. Lay rep. Ky. Council of Chs., Lexington, 1984—. Grantee Cleve. State U., 1975-76. Mem. Am. Soc. Personnel Adminstrs., Am. Compensation Assn. Democrat. Eastern Orthodox. Office: Gallatin Nat Bank 2 W Main St Uniontown PA 15401

YORK, RUTH B., educator; b. Boston, June 20, 1924; d. V. Everett and Beatrice C. (McGuire) Y. A.A., Graceland Coll., 1943; B.A., U. Iowa, 1945, M.A., 1947; Ph.D., Columbia U., 1963. Instr. Graceland Coll., Lamoni, Iowa, 1947-56; asst. prof. Ill. Coll., Jacksonville, 1956-59; lectr., then asst. prof. Columbia U., N.Y.C., 1959-65; asst. prof. U. Calif.-Davis, 1965-71, lectr., 1971-82, sr. lectr., chmn., 1981—, com. French XX Bibliography, 1961—. Contbr. articles and revs. to profl. jours. Fulbright fellow, 1954; Columbia U. Pres.'s fellow, 1959, 60; Samuel Fels Found. fellow, 1962. Mem. MLA, Am. Assn. Tchrs. French, Philological Assn. Pacific Coast, Assn. Internat. des Amis de Valery Larbaud, Phi Beta Kappa, Pi Delta Phi, Phi Sigma Iota, Lambda Delta Pi. Home: 818 Barcelona Davis CA 95616 Office: Dept French and Italian U Calif Davis CA 95616

YORK, SUSAN REBECCA, accountant; b. Pensacola, Fla., Nov. 28, 1956; d. Avin Huey and Peggy Laura (Jernigan) York. B.S. in Phys. Edn., U. Fla., 1977; M.S. in Accountancy, U. Houston, 1983. C.P.A. Sci. tchr., swimming and softball coach Hampton City Schs. (Va.), 1977-79; phys. edn. tchr., volleyball and basketball coach North Forest Ind. Sch. Dist., Houston, 1979-81; sr. tax acct. Arthur Andersen & Co., Houston, 1983-85, Gibraltar Savs. Assn., Houston, 1986—. Mem. Am. Inst. C.P.A.s, Tex. Soc. C.P.A.s, Houston Soc. C.P.A.s, Beta Alpha Psi, Sigma Kappa. Baptist. Home: 6200 Renwick St Apt 429 Houston TX 77081 Office: Gibraltar Savs Assn 13401 North Freeway Houston TX 77252

YORKE, MARIANNE R., lawyer, real estate executive; b. Ridley Park, Pa., Nov. 4, 1948; d. Joseph George and Catherine Veronica (Friel) Yorke. B.A., West Chester U., 1970; J.D., Temple U., 1980; postgrad. U. Pa., 1983—. Bar: Pa. 1981. Real estate mgr. CIGNA Service Co., Phila., 1981-85, asst. dir., 1985—; real estate atty. Garfinkel & Volpicelli, Phila., 1980-81; ptnr. Yorke/Eisenman, Real Estate, Phila., 1976—; lectr. Women in the Arts, 1982—. Contbr. articles to profl. jours. Solicitor, Pa. Ballet, Phila., 1983—, United Way, Phila., 1983—; mem. adv. panel for econ. devel. Lutheran Settlement House, 1986—. Woodrow Wilson fellow nominee, 1970. Mem. ABA (forum on constrn. 1982—), Pa. Bar Assn. (condominium and zoning coms. 1982—), Phila. Bar Assn., Phila. Women Real Estate Attys., Nat. Assn. Corp. Real Estate Execs. (comml. council), Women's Law Caucus, NOW, German Soc., Phi Alpha Delta. Republican. Roman Catholic. Office: Cigna Real Estate Dept 1600 Arch St Philadelphia PA 19103

YOSHA, LINDA OLIVIERI, banker; b. Chgo., Feb. 25, 1953; d. Joseph John and Adelaide Teresa (Leonard) Olivieri; B.A., Elmhurst Coll., 1976; m. Larry Yosha, Aug. 22, 1981. With East Side Bank & Trust Co., Chgo., 1968—, full-time 1977—, v.p. mktg. and personnel, 1982—. Mem. Nat. Assn. Bank Women, Bank Mktg. Assn., Ill. Bankers Assn., Chgo. Bank Women Assn. Office: Eastside Bank & Trust 10635 Ewing St Chicago IL 60617

YOSKOWITZ, CAROL MAGIL, insurance company executive; b. Washington, Oct. 11, 1949; d. Herbert and Adele Elaine (Liebman) Magil; m. Irving Benjamin Yoskowitz, Feb. 11, 1973; 1 son, Stephen Michael. Student Bryn Mawr Coll., 1971, Emory U., 1972. Mgmt. trainee Dept. Def., Washington, 1972-73, trainer, 1973-74; chief tng. Naval Security Group, Washington, 1974-75; chief civilian tng. U.S. Mil. Acad., West Point, N.Y., 1975-77; dir. employee relations Chief Naval Ops., Washington, 1977-79; asst. dir. employee assitance program CIGNA, Hartford, Conn., 1979—. Named Dept. Def. Youth Rep. to White House, 1973. Mem. Am. Soc. for Tng. and Devel. (sec. 1983, exec. bd. dirs. Central Conn. chpt. 1983), Am. Soc. Personnel Adminstrn., Bryn Mawr Coll. Alumni Assn. (chmn. info. Hartford 1982—, jr. v.p. Washington 1973-75). Office: CIGNA Hartford CT 06152

YOSS, LINDA S., lawyer; b. N.Y.C., July 10, 1947; d. Hyman J. and Edna (Mitzner) Yoss. B.B.A., Pace U., 1977; J.D., St. John's U., Jamaica, N.Y., 1982. Bar: N.Y. 1983. Sole practice, Maspeth, N.Y., 1982—. Mem. ABA, N.Y. State Bar Assn., Queens County Bar Assn., Bklyn. Bar Assn. Office: 36-35 167th Street Flushing NY 11358

YOST, FELICITY OLDAKOWSKA, painter, graphic designer; b. Washington, Mar. 24, 1950; d. Charles Woodruff and Irena (Oldakowska) Y. A.A., Pine Manor Coll., 1970; student Ecole Du Louvre, Paris, 1970-72, Ecole des Beaux Arts, Paris, 1970-72, Atelier Bagneux, Paris, 1970-72, Sch. Visual Arts, N.Y.C., 1976-80. Researcher, Look Mag., N.Y.C., 1969; photographer Am. Library in Paris, 1970-72; portrait painting tchr. Sch. Visual Arts, N.Y.C., 1981-82; graphic designer UN, N.Y.C., 1973—; mem. UN Study Group II, Carnegie Endowment, N.Y.C., 1974-76. Exhibited in group shows at United Nations, 1974-79, Scaf Gallery, 1974, S.I. Mus., 1975, Nat. Arts Club, 1976, Berkshire Art Assn., 1977, Harkness House for the Ballet Arts, 1977. Mem. Artists' Space. Democrat. Club: UN Art Club (N.Y.C.) (pres. 1976-79, v.p. 1975-76). Avocations: bodybuilding; reading. Home: 310 E 23rd St New York NY 10010

YOST, HELEN MARGUERITE, religious organization social worker; b. San Diego, Oct. 16, 1918; d. Don Merlin Lee and Susie Marguerite (Sims) Y. A.A., Pasadena Jr. Coll., 1939; B.S., UCLA, 1948, postgrad., 1950-52. Girls worker Pasadena Settlement, 1948-52; program dir. YWCA, 1952-56; field dir., div. dir. CYO, Archdiocese of Los Angeles, 1956-84; dir., coordinator dept. aging Catholic Charities, Los Angeles, 1980—. Del., Calif. Council Statehouse Conf. Children and Youth, 1980, Statehouse Conf. on Aging, 1981; mem. spl. task force on elder abuse Los Angeles County Area Agy. Aging, 1985—; chmn. evaluation com. Calif. Sr. Legis., 1984—. Served with U.S. Navy, 1943-45. Recipient Genemerenti medal Pope John Paul II, 1985, Friend of Youth award CYO, Los Angeles, 1982. Mem. Am. Camping Assn. (Disting. Service award 1980), Am. Area Agy. Aging (adv. council, historian 1983-85, rec. sec. 1985—), Calif. Conf. Cath. Charities, Nat. Conf. Cath. Charities, Nat. Assn. Female Execs., So. Calif. Interfaith Coalition Aging (pres. 1983-84, v.p. 1984-86). Delta Zeta. Club: Soroptimist (rec. sec. 1977). Avocations: dancing; reading. Home: 1425 E Orange Grove Blvd Apt 10 Pasadena CA 91104 Office: Dept Aging Cath Charities 1400 W 9th St Los Angeles CA 90015

YOST, MARY WALTON, import export company executive; b. Ann Arbor, Mich., Dec. 21, 1941; d. Fielding Harris and Mary Louise (Gray) Y.; m. Edward Douglas Parsons, Dec. 29, 1962 (div. 1976); children—Catherine Ann, Donald Keith. B.A., DePauw U., 1963; postgrad. U. Calif.-San Diego, 1982—. Tchr., Los Angeles Schs., U.S. Mil. overseas and domestic, 1963-75; acctg. supr. Computer Automation, Inc., Irvine, Calif., 1976-79; adminstrv. sec. The Mitre Corp., San Diego, 1980-81; ch. adminstr. Christ Ch. Unity, San Diego, 1982-83; pres. Markets for Design, Internat., San Diego, 1983—. Contbr. articles in field to trade publs. Sec., Libertarian party, region 20, San Diego, 1981-82; del. Libertarian Conv., Long Beach, Calif., 1982. Mem. Am. Mgmt. Assn., World Trade Assn., Nat. Assn. Female Execs., Greater San Diego C. of C., Mid-City C. of C., Nat. Assn. Women Bus. Owners. Libertarian. Mem. Unity Ch. Club: GROW (profit. chmn. 1983—) (San Diego). Office: Markets for Design Internat 1958 Sunset Cliffs Blvd #196 San Diego CA 92107

YOST, NANCY LYNN, architect; b. Santa Monica, Calif., Mar. 25, 1954; d. Stewart William and Marilyn Austin (Judson) Y.; student Ohio State U., 1972-73, U. Oreg., 1973-76; B.Arch., Boston Archtl. Center, 1981. Designer, William B. Morris, Cleve., 1972, Claude Miquelle Assocs., Melrose, Mass., 1976-77; job capt. Kubitz & Pepi, Wellesley, Mass., 1977-78; project mgr. Gelardin/Bruner/Cott, Cambridge, Mass., 1978-80; sr. assoc. architect Boston Archtl. Team, Inc., 1980-84; prin. Hresko Yost Assocs., Inc., Boston, 1984—. Mem. AIA, Boston Soc. Architects, Nat. Trust Hist. Preservation. Office: 110 Broad St Boston MA 02110

YOULE, JESSICA JEANNE, lawyer; b. Elmhurst, Ill., July 29, 1946; d. John Clinton and Jeanne (Eadie) Thomson Y.; m. Mark Smith, Sept. 1, 1968 (div. Oct. 1973); m. Robert Elliott, Mar. 1, 1974 (div. July 1977); 1 child, Alexandra Tapeats; m. Samuel McClung, June 22, 1979 (div. July 1983); m. Sherman Cawley II, 1 child, Graham Dexter. B.A. cum laude, Carleton Coll., 1968; M.Ed., Springfield Coll., 1972; cert. advanced grad. study, 1973; J.D. cum laude, Ariz. State U., 1983. Bar: Ariz., 1983, U.S. Dist. Ct. (Ariz.), 1983. Service rep. Bell Telephone Co., Elgin, Ill. and Mpls., 1964-69; admissions counselor Judson Coll., Elgin, Ill., 1969-70; asst. dir., counselor, tchr. Exptl. Individual Instrn. Program, Wilbraham, Mass., 1971-73; co-mgr., co-owner, v.p., sec.-treas. Ariz. Raft Adventures, Inc., Flagstaff, Ariz., 1974-85; atty., law clk. Bruce Meyerson, Ariz. Ct. Appeals, Phoenix, 1983-84; assoc., Lewis and Roca, Phoenix, 1984—; dir. Ariz. Raft Advt., Inc., Flagstaff, 1974-85. Author, editor Ariz. State Law Jour., 1981-83. Counselor, vol. Planned Parenthood, Flagstaff, Ariz., 1978; charter mem. Planned Parenthood Council Central and No. Ariz.; vol. counselor, pub. relations, Augusta, Ga., 1978; student mem. Ariz. State U. Law Sch. Curriculum Com., Tempe, 1981-83. Pedrick scholar Ariz. State U. Coll. Law, Tempe, 1981, 82, 83. Mem. ABA, Am. Soc. Profl. and Exec. Women, Ariz. Bar Assn., Western River Guides Assn. (guide, outfitter), Friends of the River, Order of Coif. Democrat. Mem. Ch. of Christ. Home: 3846 N 60th Pl Scottsdale AZ 85251 Office: Lewis and Roca 100 W Washington St Phoenix AZ 85003

YOUNATHAN, MARGARET TIMS, nutritionist, educator; b. Clinton, Miss., Apr. 25, 1926; d. Peter Asbury and Eula Lee (Tatum) Tims; B.A., U. So. Miss., 1946, B.S., 1950; M.S., U. Tenn., 1951; Ph.D., Fla. State U., 1958; m. Ezzat S. Younathan, Aug. 11, 1958; children—Janet Nadya, Carol Miriam. Instr., food and nutrition Oreg. State U., 1951-55; postdoctoral research asso. Fla. State U., 1958-59; sr. nutritional cons. Ark. Dept. Health, Little Rock, 1962-68; instr. pediatrics U. Ark. Sch. Medicine, Little Rock, 1962-65, asst. prof. pediatrics, 1965-68; asso. prof. food and nutrition Sch. Home Econs., La. State U., 1971-79, prof., 1979—. Am. Inst. Nutrition grantee, 1965; La. State U. Council on Research summer faculty grantee, 1980. Mem. Inst. Food Technologists, Am. Inst. Nutrition, Am. Dietetic Assn., Am. Home Econs. Assn., La. Home Econs. Assn. (pres. dist. D. 1981-82), Sigma Xi, Phi Kappa Phi, Gamma Sigma Delta, Omicron Nu, Phi Upsilon Omicron. Mem. Christian Ch. (Disciples of Christ). Contbr. articles on food and nutrition research to profl. jours. Home: 1048 Castle Kirk Dr Baton Rouge LA 70808 Office: Sch Home Econs La State U Baton Rouge LA 70803

YOUNCE, ALICE BARRON, nurse educator; b. Troy, Pike County, Ala.; d. Jan. 18, 1953; d. Archie and Margaret Louise (Berry) Barron; m. Dale Richard Younce, Oct. 10, 1980; children—William Robert, Margaret Mae. B.S. in Nursing, Troy State U., 1975; M.S. in Nursing, U. Ala.-Birmingham, 1981. Staff nurse U. South Ala. Med. Ctr., Mobile, 1975; pub. health nurse Mobile Bd. Health, 1975-77; instr. Providence Hosp., Mobile, 1977-81, Mobile Coll., 1983—. cons in field. Nat. Nursing Student scholar, 1971-75; Am. Legion scholar, 1971-75; Ala. Bd. Nursing scholar, 1979. Mem. Nurses Assn. of Am., Coll. Obstetricians and Gynecologists, Ala. State Nurses Assn. Republican. Baptist. Home: 6103 Appaloosa Dr Mobile AL 36609 Office: Mobile Coll Box 13220 Mobile AL 36613

YOUNG, ANN ELIZABETH O'QUINN, historian, educator; b. Waycross, Ga.; d. James Foster and Pearl Elizabeth (Sasser) O'Quinn; student Shorter Coll.; B.A., M.A., U. Ga., Ph.D., 1965; m. Robert William Young, Aug. 18, 1968; children—Abigail Ann, Leslie Lynn. Asst. prof. history Kearney (Nebr.) State Coll., 1965-69, assoc. prof., 1969-72, prof., 1972—; participant Inst. on Islam, Middle East and World Politics, U. Mich., summer 1984. Mem. Am. Hist. Assn., NEA, PEO, World History Assn., Phi Alpha Theta, Delta Kappa Gamma (chpt. pres. 1978-79), Phi Mu. Republican. Presbyterian. Contbg. author Dictionary of Georgia Biography. Office: Dept History Kearney State Coll Kearney NE 68849

YOUNG, BARBARA NAIMAN, psychiatrist; b. S.I., N.Y., June 23, 1939; d. John Zygmund and Rose Marie (Burchie) Naiman; A.B., Immaculata Coll., 1961; M.D., Med. Coll. Pa., 1966; postgrad. Phila. Psychoanalytic Inst.; children—Andrew, Christopher, Timothy. Intern, Women's Med. Coll. Pa., 1966-67; resident in adult psychiatry Med. Coll. Pa., Phila., 1969-71, chief resident, 1970-71, clin. asst. prof., dir. Child and Adolescent Psychiat. Clinic, 1976-79, fellow in child psychiatry Psychiat. Inst., 1971-73; candidate in adult and child psychoanalysis Phila. Psychoanalytic Inst., 1971—; clin. asst. prof. Rutgers Med. Coll.; pvt. practice psychiatry, Pa. and Moorestown, N.J., 1974—; psychiat. cons. Center Early Childhood Services, Phila., 1979-81; sch. cons. Germantown Friends Sch., Phila., 1974-76; adolescent group and individual psychotherapist Cath. Home for Girls, Phila., 1973-77; sch. cons. Eastern Pa. Psychiat. Inst., 1971-73. Mem. Am. Psychiat. Assn., Am. Psychoanalytic Assn., New Jersey Psychiat. Assn., Phila. Psychiat. Soc., Phila. Psychoanalytic Inst. Candidates' Orgn. (pres. 1976-77). Roman Catholic. Office: 214 W Main St Moorestown NJ 08057

YOUNG, BETTY STANSBURY, magazine advertising director, foodwriter; b. Columbus, Ohio, Nov. 11, 1940; d. Earl and Helen Marie (Chalfant) Stansbury; B.S., Ohio State U., 1962; m. Robert Anthony Young, Oct. 7, 1967; children—Elizabeth Marie, Jeanne Louise. Acting dir., home economist Home Service dept. Mich. Consol. Gas Co., Detroit, 1962-69; commodity exhibits coordinator Mich. State Fair, 1970; cons. Waste King-Universal, Amana Refrigeration, Crowley's, Franciscan, 1971-79; educator Macomb County Community Coll., Wayne County Community Coll., Henry Ford Community Coll., Marygrove Coll., Hudson's, Grosse Pointe Continuing Edn., 1972-82; promotion cons., exec. dir. Mich. Wine Inst., 1975-77; pres. Culinary Consultants, Inc., Detroit, 1980-84; sr. advt. dir. assoc. pub. Intratech Communications, 1981-85; advt. dir., food writer Heritage: A Journal of Grosse Pointe Life, 1985—. Grosse Pointe Meml. Ch. (Mich.). Mem. Am. Home Econs. Assn., Mich. Home Econs. Assn., Detroit Home Economists in Bus. (chmn. 1979-80), Detroit Home Economists in Action (founder, pres. 1974-76), Detroit Adcraft Club. Editor: The American Wine Soc. Jour., 1978-81; No Second Fiddle Cookbook, 1970. Producer Microwave Show, 1979. Address: 1168 Yorkshire St Grosse Pointe MI 48230

YOUNG, BILLIE GAYLE, transportation analyst; b. Dallas, July 24, 1952; d. Garland C. and Jorena (Moore) Myles; m. Aaron Young, Sr., July 7, 1970; children—Aaron, Adam Richard. B.B.A., Tex. So. U., 1980. Acctg. clk. Aramco Service Co., Houston, 1979-80, invoice auditor, 1980-81, transp. analyst, 1981—. Treas., Riverside Cowboys-Little League Football, Houston, 1982-83. Republican. Baptist. Mem. Am. Soc. Women Accts. (telephone chmn. Houston 1983-84). Home: 11422 Herald Sq Dr Houston TX 77099

YOUNG, COLLEEN MARA, sales manager; b. Jacksonville, N.C., Feb. 18, 1962; d. Martin Victor and Joyce Josephine (McManus) Y. B.A. in Econs., U. Calif.-Davis, 1983, B.A. in Internat. Relations, 1983. Staff writer Pub. Affairs, U. Calif., Davis, 1981-82; career counselor Advt. Services, U. Calif., Davis, 1982-83; computer system mgr. Pacific Bell, San Francisco, 1983-84, sales mgr. 1984-85; writer, Boise, Idaho, 1985—; dir. data processing Mercy Hosp., Nampa, Idaho. Author: A Little Mischief, 1985. Vol., Sta. KAID Pub. TV, 1985-86. Mem. Nat. Assn. Female Execs., Omicron Delta Epsilon, Pi Sigma Alpha. Republican. Roman Catholic. Club: U. Calif. Women's Honor Soc. Avocations: book collecting; the arts; equestrian.

YOUNG, DIANNE, police officer; b. Memphis, Sept. 1, 1956; d. John Henry Tunstall and Rebecca T. (Taylor) Tunstall Young. Student U. Miss., 1975-78, U. Houston, 1983—. Peace officer, Tex. With J.C. Penney Co., Detroit, 1977-78, Houston, 1979-80; patrol officer Houston Police Dept., 1980-81; juvenile investigator, 1982—. Mem. Afro-Am. Police Officers Houston (Officer of Month 1982), Houston Police Patrolmen Union, Stanza Peterson Dancers. Democrat. Baptist. Home: 1201 Wilcrest St Apt 14 Houston TX 77042 Office: 61 Riesner St Houston TX 77042

YOUNG, DOLORES SALLY, advertising photography company executive; b. Camden, N.J., Mar. 4, 1932; d. Herman Carl and Rayetta (Glading) Brandt; B.A. in Journalism and Advt. with honors, Douglass Coll., Rutgers U., 1954; m. Robert Arthur Young, July 17, 1959. Chief copywriter Koos Bros. Furniture Showplace, Rahway, N.J., 1954-62; co-owner, sec.-treas. Bob Young Photography, Inc., Rahway, N.J., 1962—; N.J. account exec. Graphics 3, Inc., Jupiter, Fla., 1974-78; trustee Jal-Con, Inc., conv. chmn., 1981. Trustee, First Unitarian Soc., Plainfield, N.J., v.p., 1983-84. Recipient Advt. award Asbury Park (N.J.) Press, 1954, Best Lamp Ad award Nat. Lamp Council, 1959, Socrates award for furniture advt., 1956; N.J. State scholar, 1951-54; Desi award, 1978. Mem. AAUW, NOW, Art Dirs. Club N.J. (co-chmn. communications art seminar 1978), N.J. Schola Cantorum (bd. govs.), ACLU. Home: 116 Cleveland Ave Colonia NJ 07067 Office: 1445 Main St Rahway NJ 07065

YOUNG, GAIL ADALINE, association executive; b. N.Y.C., June 8, 1948; d. Robert William and Virginia Adaline (Guy) Y. B.S. in Speech, Emerson Coll., 1971. Asst. to alumni dir. Adelphi Coll., Garden City, N.Y., 1973; asst. to sr. v.p. Hill & Knowlton Inc., N.Y.C., 1973-81; account exec. Glick Lorwin, Inc., N.Y.C., 1981-82; assoc. dir. for pub. affairs and program devel. USO Met. N.Y., N.Y.C., 1982—; pub. relations cons. New Yorkers for Dearie, N.Y.C., 1981; mem. alumni adv. bd. dirs. Floating Hosp., N.Y.C., 1979-81. Mem. Emerson Coll. Alumni Assn. (v.p. N.Y. chpt. 1983—), Pub. Relations Soc. Am. (co-chmn. publicity com. N.Y.C. 1979-80). Club: N.Y. Press (by-line ball com. 1980-83, co-chmn. Christmas fundraising program 1982-83). Home: 321 E 45th St #14C New York NY 10017 Office: USO Met NY 140 West St New York NY 10007

YOUNG, GERTRUDE GOLDEN, corporate secretary; b. Stockdale, Tex., Aug. 10, 1926; d. John and Agnes (Christa) Golden; student Rhodes Bus. Sch., 1945; m. Beryl Young, Apr. 26, 1945; 1 child, Sally Ann Young Hoopes. With S.W. Bell Telephone, Houston, 1943-44; receptionist Linde Air Products, Houston, 1945-46; with Selby-Leigh Accts., Houston, 1947; with Courtney & Co., Inc., Houston, 1947—, sec.-treas., 1964—; sec. Courtney Enterprises, Inc., 1982—; dir. Gulf Coast Rentals, Inc., 1962—. Mem. So. Baptist Woman's Missionary Union (past tchr. girls' aux.). Home: 1018 Kern St Houston TX 77009 Office: 5322 Ashbrook St Houston TX 77081

YOUNG, HOLLY PEACOCK, lawyer; b. Indpls., Sept. 21, 1949; d. John Edward and Sylvia (Griffith) Peacock; m. Gregory Glenn Young, Sept. 2, 1972; children—Reagan Wheelock, Trevor Griffith. Student Dartmouth Coll., 1969-70; B.A., Conn. Coll., 1971; M.A., U. Tex., 1973; J.D., So. Meth. U., 1982. Bar: Tex. 1983; state water program mgr. EPA, Dallas, 1973-75, 75-77; asst. mgr. Menlo Sport, Menlo Park, Calif., 1977-79; dir. Hindostan Whetstone Co., Bedford, Ind.; with Jour. Air Law and Commerce, 1980-82. Bd. dirs. Montessori Sch. of Park Cities, 1983—; bd. advisors Cottonwood Gulch Found., 1982—. Recipient Bronze medal EPA, 1974. Mem. ABA, Tex. Bar Assn., Dallas Bar Assn. Episcopalian. Home: 4711 Cherokee Trail Dallas TX 75209

YOUNG, JENNIFER JESS, personnel administrator; b. St. Louis, Jan. 16, 1947; d. Harry Melvin and Dorothy G. (Bailey) Y.; m. Ronald Moore, Mar. 21, 1975 (div. 1979). B.A. with distinction, Purdue U., 1968, student Madrid U., 1967-68; postgrad. So. Meth. U., 1975-78. Unit recreation dir. ARC, Vietnam, 1968-69; employee relations asst. Mobil Oil Corp., Dallas, 1970-74; compensation adminstr. InterFirst Bank, Dallas, 1974-76, internat. compensation adminstr., 1976-78, sect. head compensation, 1978-80, v.p., dept. head compensation and benefits, 1980-85, dept. mgr. employment/employee relations, 1985—. Mem. steering com. Dallas Com. For Fgn. Visitors; vol. arbitrator Dallas Better Bus. Bur.; mem. draft bd. U.S. SSS; program chmn. Dallas Bus. Group on Health; bd. mgmt., mem. pub. relations and mktg. com. Dallas YMCA. Mem. Am. Compensation Assn., 4th Inf. Div. (v.p. Tex. chpt.). Club: Dallas Ski (bd. dirs.). Home: PO Box 50515 Dallas TX 75250 Office: InterFirst Corp PO Box 8300 Dallas TX 75283-1062

YOUNG, JOAN CRAWFORD, advertising agency executive; b. Hobbs, N.Mex., July 30, 1931; d. William B. and Ora Maydelle (Boone) Crawford; student Tex. Tech. U., 1949; B.A. in Journalism, Hardin Simmons U., 1952. Reporter, Lubbock (Tex.) Avalanche-Jour., 1952-54; promotion dir. Sta. KCBD-TV, Lubbock, 1954-61; space buyer, account exec. Ward Hicks Advt., Albuquerque, 1961-71; v.p. Mellekas & Assos Advt., Albuquerque, 1971-78; pres. J. Young Advt., Albuquerque, 1978—. Bd. dirs. N.Mex. Symphony Orch., 1970-73, United Way of Greater Albuquerque, 1985—. Recipient Am. Advt. Fedn. Silver medal award, 1977. Mem. N.Mex. Advt. Fedn. (dir. 1976-78), Am. Women in Radio and TV (dir. Zia chpt. 1978), Greater Albuquerque C. of C. (dir. 1983-85). Republican. Author: (with Louise Allen and Audre Lipscomb) Radio and Television Continuity Writing, 1962. Home: 3425 Avenida Charada NW Albuquerque NM 87107 Office: 303 Roma NW Albuquerque NM 87102

YOUNG, JOANNE WHEELER, lawyer; b. Columbus, Ga., Dec. 18, 1949; d. Mason James and Helen (Bullardo) Young; m. Bruce Edward Foreman, Apr. 29, 1978; 1 dau., Maureen Lynn. B.A. cum laude, Wesleyan U., 1971; J.D., Georgetown U., 1974. Bar: N.Y. 1975, D.C. 1975. Field dir. Wis. Gubernatorial Campaign, Madison, 1970; asst. to dean admissions Wesleyan U., Middletown, Conn., 1971; intern EPA, Washington, 1972; summer assoc. Beekman & Bogue, N.Y.C., 1973; judicial clk. Hon. F.B. Ugast, Washington, 1974-75; trial atty. CAB, Washington, 1976-77; sole practice, Washington, 1977-81; ptnr. Barrett Smith Schapiro Simon & Armstrong, Washington, 1981—; chmn. Regional Airline Assn., Washington, 1983—, vice chmn., 1982-83. Contbr. articles to profl. jours. Trustee, Wesleyan U., 1983—; pres. Washington Alumni Club, Wesleyan U., 1980—; chmn. Wesleyan U. Alumni Council Clubs Com., 1981-83. Mem. Women's Bar Assn., N.Y. State Bar Assn., D.C. Bar Assn., Fed. Bar Assn., ABA, Phi Beta Kappa. Episcopalian. Clubs: City Tavern, Pisces. Home: 2905 28th St NW Washington DC 20008 Office: Barrett Smith Schapiro Simon & Armstrong 1201 Pennsylvania Ave NW Washington DC 20004

YOUNG, JUDITH GAIL, sales company executive, import executive; b. Chgo., Nov. 6, 1942; d. Ben and Ruth (Golberg) Young; m. Dennis A. Bell, Nov. 6, 1977. B.A., Roosevelt U., 1964. Tchr. Chgo. Bd. Edn., 1965-73; sales rep. T.E. Simmons & Assocs., Chgo., 1973-77; owner, pres. Joy Internat. Corp., Chgo., 1977—; pres. Lyric Internat. Corp., Chgo., 1983—; v.p. Herald Internat. Travel Service, Hong Kong, 1982—, Chefmate Housewares, 1985—; design cons. Taipan Herald Ltd., Hong Kong, 1983—. Mem. vocat. bus. com. Rich Daley for Mayor, Chgo., 1983; mem. women's com. Ann Stephan for Ward Committeeman, Chgo., 1983; fundraiser Mental Health Assn. Chgo., 1982-83, Chgo. Council Fgn. Relations, 1977—. Recipient Outstanding Performance award Randix Industries Ltd., 1980. Mem. Nat. Assn. Female Execs. Democrat. Jewish. Clubs: Internat., Variety (Chgo.). Office: Joy Internat Corp 8 W Division St Suite 201 Chicago IL 60610

YOUNG, JUDITH TAYLOR, nursing administrator; b. Pineville, W.Va., June 15, 1949; d. Edmond Eli and Imogene (Bradford) Taylor; m. Donald Wayne Young, Nov. 13, 1976; 1 dau., Marleina Ann. Student Towson State U., 1967-68; R.N., Union Meml. Hosp., Balt., 1971. Staff nurse Union Meml. Hosp., Balt., 1971-72, 73-75; out-patient supr. North Charles Gen. Hosp., Balt., 1972-73; emergency room charge nurse North Arundel Hosp., Glen Burnie, Md., 1975-77; charge nurse Md. Manor Nursing Home, Glen Burnie, 1978-82, dir. nursing, 1982—; speaker/leader Md. Manor Family Counsel, Glen Burnie, 1983—; speaker Community Awareness Seminar, Glen Burnie, 1983—. Author: Geriatric Nursing Assistant Teaching Program, 1983. Democrat. Baptist. Office: Md Manor Nursing Home 7575 E Howard Rd Glen Burnie MD 21061

YOUNG, KAREN SUE, newspaper editor; b. Centerville, Iowa, Sept. 9, 1937; d. Victor Lee and Margaret E. (Darrah) Cleeton; m. Bernard L. Young, Aug. 30, 1954; children—Vicky Sue, Darrah, James Ray Young. Grad. high sch. Typist, Seymour Herald, Iowa, 1969-77, editor, ptnr., 1977—. Sec., Seymour Community Club, since 1980—, local Baptist women's ch. orgn., since 1950—, also sec. Sunday sch. Mem. Iowa Newspaper Assn. (award 1980). Club: GEG (Seymour). Home: Rt 1 Box 193 Seymour IA 52590

YOUNG, LINDA KAY, mathematics educator; b. Ft. Worth, Tex., June 12, 1953; d. Helen Marie (Washington) Johnson; m. Victor Earl Young, May 25, 1974; children—Victor Earl, Jr., Twynette Latrice. B.S., Bishop Coll., Dallas, 1975; M.S., Tex. Women's U., 1984. Operator, The Treas., Dallas, 1969-70; office asst. IRS, Ft. Worth, 1970-72; math. tchr., Ft. Worth Inds. Sch. Dist., 1975—. Methodist. Home: 7221 Greenspan St Dallas TX 75232

YOUNG, LUCY CLEAVER, physician; b. Wheeling, W.Va., Aug. 8, 1943. B.S. in Chemistry, Wheaton Coll. (Ill.), 1965; M.D., Ohio State U., 1969. Diplomate Am. Bd. Family Practice. Rotating intern Riverside Meth. Hosp., Columbus, Ohio, 1969-70; resident Trumbull Meml. Hosp., Warren, Ohio, 1970-71; practice medicine specializing in family practice, West Chicago, Ill., 1971-73, Paw Paw and Mendota, Ill., 1973-78; co-founder and med. dir. Wholistic Health Ctr. of Mendota, 1976-78; asst. med. dir. Met. Life Ins. Co., Gt. Lakes Head Office, Aurora, Ill., 1979-80; med. dir. Commonwealth Life Ins. Co., Louisville, 1980-85; assoc. prof. U. Ill. Abraham Lincoln Sch. Medicine, 1976-79; faculty monitor MacNeal Meml. Hosp. Family Practice Ctr. (Ill.), 1979-80; faculty preceptor U. Louisville Family Practice Dept., 1981-85; mem. staffs Central DuPage Hosp., Winfield, Ill., 1971-73, Mendota Community Hosp., 1973-80. Fellow Am. Acad. Family Practice; mem. Jefferson County Med. Assn., Am. Med. Women's Assn., Christian Med. Soc. Office: PO Box 1300 Chalmette LA 70044

YOUNG, MACHERÉ ANONA, hosp. ofcl.; b. Stoneville, N.C., Oct. 23, 1951; d. James Mark and Susie Elenor (Carter) Spencer; Western Mich. U., 1970-72, student Grand Rapids (Mich.) Jr. Coll., 1973-74; m. Westley Al Young, Mar. 29, 1971; 1 son, Allen Ruffin. Interviewer, Nat. Opinion Research Center, 1973-74; pres. Madison/Hall Neighborhood Assn., 1974-76; agt. Pearson-Cook Real Estate, 1975-76; mem. citizens participation task force Grand Rapids City Commn., 1977; adminstrv. asst. Grand Rapids Public Schs., 1976-81; environ. services supr. St. Mary's Hosp., Grand Rapids, 1981—. Democrat. Baptist. Home: 500 Umatilla St SE Grand Rapids MI 49507 Office: 200 Jefferson Ave Grand Rapids MI 49503

YOUNG, MARGARET ALETHA MCMULLEN (MRS. HERBERT WILSON YOUNG), social worker; b. Vossburg, Miss., June 13, 1916; d. Grady Garland and Virgie Aletha (Moore) McMullen; B.A. cum laude, Columbia Bible Coll., 1949; grad. Massey Bus. Coll., 1958; M.S.W., Fla. State U., 1965; postgrad. Jacksonville U., 1961-62, Tulane U., 1967; m. Herbert Wilson Young, Aug. 19, 1959. Dir. Christian edn. Eau Claire Presbyn. Ch., Columbia, S.C., 1946-51; tchr. Massey Bus. Coll., Jacksonville, Fla., 1954-57, office mgr., 1957-59; social worker, unit supr. Fla. div. Family Services, St. Petersburg, 1960-66, dist. casework supr., 1966-71; social worker, project supr., program supr. Project Playpen, Inc., 1971-81, pres. bd., 1982-83, cons., 1986—; mem. council Child Devel. Ctr., 1983—; mem. transitional housing com., Religious Community Services, 1984—. Mem. Acad. Cert. Social Workers, Nat. Assn. Social Workers (pres. Tampa Bay chpt. 1973-74), Fla. Assn. for Health and Social Services (pres. chpt. 1971), Nature conservancy. Democrat. Presbyn. Rotary Ann (pres. 1970-71). Home: 330 Roebling Rd N Belleair Clearwater FL 33516 Office: 4140 49th St N Saint Petersburg FL 33709

YOUNG, MARJORIE WILLIS, writer, journalist, lecturer; b. Mansfield, Ohio; d. John Edgar and Mary Adelle (Reiter) Willis; student agr. Cornell U., 1924; student Art Students League, 1925-27, Cooper Union, 1925-27, Columbia U., 1927, 43, Sorbonne, U. Paris, 1928-30, Japanese Lang. Sch., Tokyo, 1934-35, N.Y. U., 1944; m. James Russell Young, Oct. 2, 1934; 1 son, Willis Patterson. Columnist in Far East, Internat. News Service, 1938-41; feature writer King Features Syndicate, 1939, Saturday Pictorial Rev., 1941-45; asst. tech. dir. motion picture Behind the Rising Sun, 1943; research dept. Believe It or Not, 1946-48; feature editor and columnist The Sunday Star, Wilmington, Del., 1946-48; promotion dir. David McKay Pub. Co., 1945-48; lectr. Nat. Concert and Artists Corp., 1942-43; feature writer Anderson (S.C.) Independent, 1949-73; feature writer Anderson Daily Mail, 1949-73, asso. editor The New South, ann. spl. edit. of Daily Mail, 1966-73; editor The Safety Jour., Anderson, 1953—; program moderator Decorating for a Holiday, Sta. WAIM-TV, 1953-55, safety program moderator WAIM-TV, 1953—, program moderator How to Cut and Sew, 1954-55, travel feature program WAIM-WCAC-FM, 1973-82; travel editor Quote mag., 1977-80; editor Vets. of Safety news page, What's What monthly; dir. Capitol City Communications, Inc. Spl. scroll dir. Chinese War Orphans Relief, 1941-45; publicity dir. Crusade for Children, State of Del., 1948; publicity chmn. S.C. Indsl. Nurses Assn., 1953; dir. S.C. 4-H Club TV Safety Program, 1953; coordinator Ann. S.C. State Landmark Conf., 1979. Bd. dirs. Anderson Heritage, Inc. Recipient various awards for safety activities including Disting. Service award S.C. Occupational Safety Council, 1973. Mem. U. S.C. Caroliniana Soc., Writers Assn. Am., Am. Women in Radio and TV, Nat. Recreation Assn., S.C. Recreation Soc. (v.p. and program dir. 1954-56), Anderson County Hist. Soc. (pres. 1978-80), Am. Soc. Safety Engrs., Vets. Safety Internat., (pres. 1979), DAR, Colonial Dames of the XVII Century. Episcopalian. Clubs: Am. News Women's, Nat. Press (Washington); Overseas Press of Am.; Cornell Women's (N.Y.C.). Author: Decorating for Joyful Occasions, 1952; It's Time for Christmas Decorations, 1957; Fodor's Tour Guide of South Carolina, 1966-68, Tour Guide of Georgia, 1966-67; Japanese American Cook Book, 1972; The Cateechee Trail, 1975; South Carolina's Women Patriots of the American Revolution, 1975; Mystery of the Ivory Eagle, 1980. Editor: Textile Leaders, 1963. Home: 2003 Laurel Dr Anderson SC 29621 Office: Safety Jour PO Box 4189 Anderson SC 29622

YOUNG, MARLENE A(NNETTE), association executive, lawyer; b. Portland, Oreg., Mar. 3, 1946; d. Hardy Shelby and Eunice Jean (Gregory) Y.; m. Abdullah S. Ritai, June 3, 1973 (div. 1981); m. John H. Stein, Jan. 1, 1986. B.S., Portland State U., 1967; Ph.D., Georgetown U., 1973; J.D., Williamette U., 1975. Bar: Oreg. 1975. Research dir. div. pub. safety Multnomah County, Portland, Oreg., 1975-77; sole practice law, Wilsonville, Oreg., 1975-81; exec. dir. Applied Systems Research and Devel., Inc., Wilsonville, 1976-81; exec. dir. Nat. Orgn. for Victim Assistance, Washington, 1981—; instr. Portland State U., 1979, U. Utah, Salt Lake City, 1976-78; cons. Univ. Research Corp., Washington, 1979-83; instr. Essex Community Coll., Balt., 1972-83; dir. Silver Leaf Farms, Inc., Wilsonville, 1970-73, accounts mgr. Silver Leaf Inn, 1973-75. Editor: Justice and Older Americans, 1977; contbr. articles to pubs. Bd. visitors Willamette Coll. Law, 1981-83; mem. planning commn. City of Wilsonville, 1979-81, Ways and Means Com., 1977-79; bd. dirs. Chemeketa Community Coll., 1979, Oreg. State Council on Alcoholism; mem. Clackamas County Community Devel. Adv. Com.; chmn. adv. com. on aging City of Portland. Recipient Pub. Policy award Victims Com. World Fedn. Mental Health, 1983, Founders award Nat. Orgn. for Victim Assistance, 1982, Pres.'s award, 1981. Mem. World Soc. Victimology (adv. bd.; von Hentig award 1985), World Fedn. for Mental Health (sci. com. on victims), Nat. Coalition Against Sexual Assault, ABA (land use com. local govt. sect., victims com. criminal justice sect.), Oreg. State Bar Assn., Am. Soc. Criminology, Am. Sociol. Assn., Am. Polit. Sci. Assn., Gerontol. Soc., Western Gerontol. Soc. Office: Nat Orgn for Victim Assistance 717 D St NW Washington DC 20004

YOUNG, MARY ELIZABETH, historian, educator; b. Utica, N.Y., Dec. 16, 1929; d. Clarence Whitford and Mary (Tippit) Young; B.A., Oberlin Coll., 1950; Ph.D. (Robert Shalkenbach Found. grantee, Ezra Cornell fellow), Cornell U., 1955. Instr., Ithaca (N.Y.) Coll., part-time, 1954-55; instr. Ohio State U., Columbus, 1955-58, asst. prof., 1958-63, assoc. prof., 1963-69, prof., 1969-73; prof. history U. Rochester (N.Y.), 1973—. Recipient Louis Pelzer prize, 1955; Social Sci. Research Council grantee, 1968-69. Mem. Am. Hist. Assn., Orgn. Am. Historians, Am. Antiquarian Soc., Soc. of Historians of Early Republic (exec. bd.), Am. Studies Assn. Author: Redskins, Ruffle-shirts and Rednecks, 1961; co-editor and contbr: The Frontier in Am. Devel.: Essays in Honor of Paul W. Gates, 1969. Office: Dept History U Rochester Rochester NY 14627

YOUNG, MARY LOU, writer; b. Plainfield, N.J., May 3, 1940; d. John F. and Helen M. (Cole) O'Brien; student Nathaniel Hawthorne Coll., Antrim, N.H., 1977-78; div.; children—Michelle Lynn Young Reifsnyder, Conrad John Young. Office mgr. Far Packaging Co., South Plainfield, N.J., 1958-60; co-owner, treas. Young Advt. Agy., Inc., Concord, N.H., 1967-74; assoc. editor Horse of Course mag., Temple, N.H., 1976-78; editor, dir. promotion and publs. Am. Morgan Horse Assn., Inc., Westmoreland, N.Y., 1978-80; dir. Kirkland Art Center, Clinton, N.Y., 1981-82; freelance writer, 1982—; lectr. advt. and mktg. within horse industry. Mem. Parks and Recreation Commn., Gilmanton, N.H., 1970-72; pres. Gilmanton PTA, 1973; mem. adv. bd. Mohawk Valley Community Coll., Utica, N.Y., 1980. Recipient award Grand Nat. Morgan Horse Show Com., 1979. Mem. Am. Horse Publs., Am. Soc. Bus. Press Editors, Nat. Audiovisual Assn., Nat. Bus. Circulation Assn. Ghost writer; contbr. articles to profl. jours., newspapers, mags. Office: On The Park Clinton NY 13323

YOUNG, MARY SUE, housing administrator, social worker; b. Clovis, N.Mex., Aug. 18, 1939; d. Leland L. and Louise (Miller) McMillon; m. Abraham Young, Nov. 26, 1969 (div. 1977); children—Luana Elizabeth, Malia Diane. Student Ill. Wesleyan U., 1957-58; B.S., Okla. State U., 1961; M.S.W., St. Louis U., 1967. Vol., Peace Corps, Colombia, 1963-65; sch. social worker State of Ill., East St. Louis, 1967-69; social worker III, State of Hawaii, Honolulu, 1969-72; social work sr. State of Ga., Macon, 1977-79; adminstr. St Paul Apts., Inc., Macon, 1979—, St. Paul Village, Inc., 1982—. Foster parent, 1972-77; assault team vol. Crisis Line, Macon, 1983—. HEW grantee, 1965-67. Mem. Ga. Gerontol. Soc. (edn. com. 1984), Ga. Assn. Homes and Services for Aging (sec. 1982—), Am. Assn. Homes for Aging (del. 1985-86), Episcopal Soc. Ministry for Aging, Nat. Assn. Social Workers. Democrat. Episcopalian. Avocations: swimming; travel. Home: 634 Woodridge Dr Macon GA 31204 Office: 1330 Forsyth St Macon GA 31201

YOUNG, PATSY KIKUE, state legislator; b. Maui, Hawaii, Oct. 29, 1929. Ed. U. Hawaii. Mem. adv. council Leeward Sch., 1966-70; rep. State Constl. Conv., 1968; bd. regents U. Hawaii, 1971; mem. staff Hawaii Senate, 1966-71; mem. Hawaii Ho. of Reps., from 1972; now mem. Hawaii Senate from 23d dist., also sgt.-at-arms. Democrat. Office: Hawaii Senate State Capitol Honolulu HI 96813*

YOUNG, PAULA ERNESS, educational administrator; b. Memphis, Sept. 20, 1957; d. Ernest Leroy and Carrie Louise (Watson) Y. B.A., Memphis State U., 1978; M.P.A., Altanta U., 1981. Social counselor Memphis Dept. Human Services, 1978-79; congl. intern U.S. Rep. Harold Ford of Tenn., Memphis, summer 1980; asst. dir. grants, contracts clearinghouse and conf. exhibits mgr. Nat. Assn. for Equal Opportunity in Higher Edn., Washington, 1981-83; dir. research and proposal writing Clark Coll., Atlanta, 1984—; cons. C.A.R.E., Atlanta, 1986. Mem. polit. action com. Cascade United Meth. Ch., Atlanta, 1985; troop leader, vol. Girl Scouts U.S.A., 1985-86. Woodrow Wilson fellow, 1981-83, 85-87. Mem. Nat. Assn. Negro Bus. and Profl. Women's Clubs, Nat. Council Negro Women (youth com. 1982-83), Toastmasters Internat., Alpha Kappa Alpha. Democrat. Avocations: ceramic artwork. Office: Clark Coll 240 James Brawley Dr SW Atlanta GA 30314

YOUNG, PHYLLIS ETHERIDGE, government official; b. Washington, Jan. 22, 1940; d. Robert Bruce and Bessie (Dixon) Etheridge; children—Rose Kathryn Young, Beverly Adelaide Young. Student, Dunbarton Coll., 1957-59; B.S. in Math., Howard U., 1961, M.S., 1966; postgrad. Am. U., 1973-74. Math. asst. Ops. Evaluation Group, Arlington, Va., 1961-65; math. statistician Bur. Pub. Rds., Fed. Hwy. Adminstrn., McLean, Va., 1965-75, safety info. br. chief, Washington, 1975-82, chief performance evaluation br., 1982—; cons. Adv. Council Careers, 1977-78, Commn. chmn. Adv. Neighborhood Commn. 4C, Washington, 1978-85; at-large mem. D.C. Bd. Edn., 1985—, pres. Parents United for Full Sch. Funding, Washington, 1980-81, Area 2A Council, D.C. PTA, 1983-85; ward 4 rep. Citizens Planning Coalition, Inc., 1982—; mem. Mayor's com. com. on Edn. and Buget Resources, Blacks in Govt., Conf. Minority Transit Ofcls., NOW, Nat. Assn. Female Execs., Nat. Council of Negro Women, Alpha Kappa Alpha. Home: 4503 Iowa Ave NW Washington DC 20011 Office: Fed Hwy Adminstrn HHS-22 400 7th St SW Washington DC 20590 also 415 12th St NW Washington DC 20004

YOUNG, SARAH COLGLAZIER, community services exec.; b. Salem, Ind., July 20, 1937; d. Donald Lee and Phyllis Irma (Hansen) Colglazier; B.S.N., Duke U., 1959; M.A. in Edn. and Human Develop. Holy Names Coll., Oakland, Calif., 1983. Staff nurse Duke U. Med. Center, Durham, N.C., 1959-60, Riverside Meth. Hosp., Columbus, Ohio, 1961-62; pvt. duty nurse, Columbus, 1962-66, Oakland, 1966-68; asst. dir. nurses Booth Meml. Home, Oakland, 1968-71; program coordinator Creative Health Resources, Walnut Creek, Calif., 1977; adminstrv. asst. Pleasant Hill (Calif.) C. of C., 1978-79; community liaison to Contra Costa County Bd. Suprs., Concord, Calif., 1979-81, asst. to county supervisor, 1981-82; planner, cons. community programs. Pleasant Hill sponsor Red Cross Youth Vols., 1966-68; chmn. Pleasant Hill City Devel. Com., 1971-76; founding mem., pres. Pleasant Hill Hist. Soc., 1973-82; bd. dirs. Pleasant Hill Bicentennial Commn., 1975-76; chmn. Pleasant Hill Citizens' Forum, 1973, vice chmn., 1976; founding mem. Contra Costa Nurses Community Action Group, Contra Costa Health Forum, 1981-82; founding mem., bd. dirs. Pleasant Hill Arts Council, 1974-76, 78-79, 81-82, service award 1976; community coordinator Adult Health Multiphasic Screening Program, 1974-76; developer awards program Pleasant Hill Beautification Com., 1975-76; consumer rep. Contra Costa Central Dist. council Alameda-Contra Costa Health Systems Agy., 1978-81, mem. governing body, 1979-86 recognition of service award, 1979; vice-chairperson community adv. council Mt. Diablo Hosp. Med. Center, 1979-82, Community Adv. Council rep. to Mt. Diablo Hosp. Planning Com., 1979-82; sec. bd. dirs. Mt. Diablo Edn. Fund., Mt. Diablo Unified Sch. Dist., 1982-83; bd. dirs. Contra Costa Alliance for the Arts, 1982-83; treas. Pleasant Hill Hist. and Cultural Ctr., 1984-86; exec. dir. Love Is The Answer of Contra Costa, 1985-86; Named Pleasant Hill Citizen of Yr., 1973, lifetime citizen, 1976; 15th ann. appreciation award City of Pleasant Hill, 1976; recipient commendation Calif. State Legislature, 1976. Mem. Calif. Nurses Assn. (dir. 1974-76, service award 1976), AAUW (dir. Pleasant Hill br. 1966-76, 81-83), Am. Soc. of Aging , Calif. Specialists on Aging, Pleasant Hill C. of C. (hon. life mem.). Methodist. Club: Commonwealth. Home and office: 1884 Cannon Dr Walnut Creek CA 94596

YOUNG, SHARON LEE, lawyer, savings and loan executive; b. Sheridan, Wyo., May 9, 1943; d. Andrew and Lottie Fern (Shipley) Suchta; m. Howard W. Young. Sept. 25, 1964; children—Ronda Lee, Jarrett Lynn. B.S. with honors in Journalism, U. Wyo., 1965, B.A. with honors in Polit. Sci., 1976, J.D., 1979. Bar: Wyo. 1979, Colo. 1980, U.S. Dist Ct. Colo. 1980, U.S. Dist. Ct. Wyo. 1979. Mng. editor Rawlins Daily Times (Wyo.), 1965-67; reporter, photographer Riverton Ranger (Wyo.), 1967-68; dir. mktg. Arctic First Fed., Fairbanks, Alaska, 1972-76; v.p., corp. counsel Valley Fed. Savs. & Loan Assn., Grand Junction, Colo., 1979—; instr. comml. law. Inst. Fin. Edn., Grand Junction, 1984. Contbg. author: Those Good Years at Wyoming University, 1965. Mem. ABA, Wyo. State Bar, Colo. Bar Assn., Mesa County Bar Assn. Home: 2673 Catalina Dr Grand Junction CO 81506 Office: Valley Federal Savings & Loan Assn 225 N 5th St Grand Junction CO 81501

YOUNG, SHERRY DUKE, talent agent; b. Center, Tex., Aug. 30, 1927; d. Horace Campbell and Alice (Rudd) Duke; m. Thomas R. Young, Jr., June 15, 1957 (dec. 1981); 1 son, Michael H. B.A., Stephen F. Austin U., 1944; postgrad. San Francisco State Coll., 1966. Jr. astrologist Civil Service, Houston, 1944-45; womens auditor Sta. KELD, Little Rock, 1945-48; fashion coordinator Richs, Atlanta, 1954-56; buyer I. Magnins, San Francisco, 1968-71, pres., owner Sherry Young, Inc., Houston, 1979—; mem. Regional Home Fashion Group Internat., Houston, 1951-56; fashion show cons., producer 1971—. Contbr. articles to various publs. Mem. Mayor's Com., Los Angeles, 1961-64. Mem. Fashion Group Internat., Motion Picture Council Houston, Nat. Assn. Female Execs. Republican. Roman Catholic.

YOUNG, SHIRLEY JEAN, small business owner; b. Galveston, Tex., Mar. 18, 1944; d. Rufus H. and Ena I. (Carter) Y. Histologic technician St. Mary's Hosp., Galveston, 1963; clk.-typist Am. Oil Co., Texas City, 1967-68, Am. Nat. Ins. Co., Galveston, 1969-75; med. sec. U. Tex. Med. Br., Galveston, 1975-83; owner WORDS ETC Word Processing Service, Galveston, 1983—; cons. Art From The Heart, Livingston, Tex., 1984—. Mem. Nat. Fedn. for Decency, 1984—. Mem. Nat. Assn. Female Execs., Computer Entrepreneur Assn. Am., Am. Soc. Clin. Pathologists (assoc.). Baptist. Clubs: 700, 1000 (Virginia Beach, Va.). Home: 2311 71st St Galveston TX 77551 Office: WORDS ETC Word Processing Service 6608 Stewart Rd Suite 308 Galveston TX 77551

YOUNG, SONIA WINER, editor; b. Chattanooga, Tenn., Aug. 20, 1934; d. Meyer D. and Rose (Demby) Winer; m. Melvin A. Young, Feb. 24, 1957; 1 child, Melanie Anne. B.A., Sophie Newcomb Coll., 1956; M.Ednl. Psychology, U. Tenn.-Chattanooga, 1966. Cert. speech and hearing specialist Am. Speech and Hearing Assn. Speech therapist Chattanooga-Hamilton County Speech and Hearing Ctr., 1961-66, ednl. psychology, 1966-78; staff psychologist Chattanooga Testing and Counseling Services, 1978-80; ins. rep. Mut. Benefit Life Ins. Co., Chattanooga, 1980-84; columnist Chattanooga Times, 1982-84; community affairs reporter Sta. WRCB-TV, Chattanooga, 1983-84; pub. relations and promotions dir. Purple Ladies, Inc., Chattanooga, 1984—; cons. psychology Ga. Dept. Human Resources, also Cheerhaven Sch., Dalton, 1970-78; adj. prof. psychology U. Tenn.-Chattanooga, 1971-80. Pres. Chattanooga Opera Guild, 1973-74, Chattanooga Opera Assn., 1979-80; bd. dirs., sec. Chattanooga-Hamilton County Bicentennial Library, 1977-79; pres. Little Theatre of Chattanooga, 1984—, bd. dirs., 1974—; v.p. Girls Club, Chattanooga, 1979-80; bd. dirs. Chattanooga Symphony Guild, Mizpah Congregation, Chattanooga Area Literacy Council; mem. alumni council U. Tenn.-Chattanooga; mem. selection com. Leadership Chattanooga, 1984-86; sec. Allied Arts Greater Chattanooga, 1978-80, residential campaign chmn., 1985; bd. dirs. Chattanooga Ctr. for the Dance. Recipient Disting. Citizens award City of Chattanooga, 1975; Steakley award Little Theatre, Chattanooga, 1982. Mem. Phi Beta Kappa (pres. Chattanooga chpt. 1978-79). Jewish. Home: 1025 River Hills Circle Chattanooga TN 37415 Office: The Little Theatre 400 River St Chattanooga TN 37405

YOUNG, SUSAN JEAN, music specialist; b. Chgo., Nov. 9, 1940; d. Walter Lawrence and Grace Helen (Blue) Pennie; B.Mus.Ed. (scholar), Northwestern U., 1962; M.Mus.Ed. (grad. scholar), Am. Conservatory of Music, Chgo., 1974; m. Peter R. Young, Jr., June 23, 1962; children—Laura Jane, Beth Ann. Music specialist Skokie (Ill.) Sch. Dist., 1962-63, Northbrook (Ill.) Sch. Dist., 1974—; pvt. piano tchr., 1963-74; pres. Stevenson High Choral Guild, 1979-81; mem. music com. Long Grove Ch.; music dir., choir dir. Wheeling Community Ch., 1981—; music dir. Northbrook Children's Theatre, 1981—, Glenview Community Theatre, Northbrook Community Theatre; dir. Northbrook Youth Chorale. Mem. Music Educators Nat. Conf., Ill. Music Educators Assn., Ill. Music Tchrs. Assn., Music Tchrs. Nat. Assn., Am. Choral Dirs. Assn., Soc. Am. Musicians, Delta Kappa Gamma, Mu Phi Epsilon. Home: 957 Alden Ln Buffalo Grove IL 60089 Office: 1475 Maple Ave Northbrook IL 60062

YOUNG, TOMMIE MORTON, media services educator; b. Nashville. B.A. cum laude, Tenn. State U., 1951; M.L.S., George Peabody Coll. for Tchrs., 1955; Ph.D., Duke U., 1977; postgrad. U. Okla., 1967, U. Nebr., 1968. Coordinator, Young Adult Program, Lucy Thurman br. YWCA, 1951-52; instr. edn. Tenn. State U., Nashville, 1956-59; instr., coordinator media program Prairie View Coll. (Tex.), 1959-61; asst. prof. edn., assoc. prof. English, dir. IMC Ctr., U. Ark.-Pine Bluff, 1965-69; asst. prof. English and edn., dir. learning lab., N.C. Central U., Durhan, 1969-74; prof., dir./chairperson library media services and dept. ednl. media, dir. Afro-Am. Family Project, N.C. Agrl. and Tech. State U., Greensboro, 1975—; pres. World Assocs., Inc., Greensboro: dir. workshops, grants. Contbr. research papers, articles to profl. jours. Nat. chmn. Com. to Re-Elect the Pres.; past sec. Fedn. Colored Women's Clubs; bd. dirs. southwestern div. ARC, dir. Volun-Teens; chairperson learning resources com. Task Force Durham Day Care Assn.; bd. dirs., chairperson schs. div. Durham County Unit Am. Cancer Soc.; past mem. adv. bd. dirs. YMCA, Atlanta; 1st v.p. Durham br. NAACP; mem. U.S. Civil Rights Commn.; past bd. dirs. YWCA, Nashville, Atlanta; bd. dirs. NIH, N.C. Council of the Arts; mem. Guilford County Involvement Council; chmn. N.C. adv. com. U.S. Civil Rights Com., N.C. Civil Rights Network; N.C. chmn. Civil Rights Commn. Recipient awards ARC, 1968, 73, NAACP, 1973, HEW, 1978, U.S. Commn. on Civil Rights, 1982. Mem. Assn. Childhood Ednl. Internat., Comparative and Internat. Edn. Assn., Archives Assoc., ALA (past pres.), N.C. Assn. Coll. and Research Librarians, Internat. Platform Assn., Nat. Hist. Soc., NEA, AAUW (honor award 1983, pres. Greensboro br., chairperson internat. relations com.), Zeta Phi Beta (chairperson polit. action com. eastern region, nat. grammateus, Polit. and Civic Service award 1974, Outstanding Social-Polit. Service award 1982, Woman of Yr. 1977). Home: 4303 King Arthur Pl Greensboro NC 27405

YOUNG, VANEICA YVONNE, chemist; b. Topeka, Feb. 18, 1947; d. Jesse Lee and Blanche Beatrice (Hardy) Y.; B.A., U. Kans., 1969; M.S., U. Mo., Kansas City, 1972, Ph.D., 1976; Postdoctoral research asso., vis. asst. prof. Purdue U., West Lafayette, Ind., 1976-78; asst. prof. chemistry Tex. A&M U., College Station, 1978-84; asst. prof. chemistry U. Fla., Gainesville, 1984—; cons. NASA, Johnson Space Center, 1980—. NSF summer research fellow, 1970; grantee Petroleum Research Fund, 1979-81, Robert A. Welch Found., 1979-84, NSF, 1985—. Mem. Am. Chem. Soc., AAAS, N.Y. Acad. Scis., Soc. Applied Spectroscopy, Am. Phys. Soc., Am. Vacuum Soc., Microbeam Analysis Soc., Phi Lambda Upsilon. Contbr. articles to profl. jours.

YOUNG, VERONICA LESLEY, film maker, publishing and video company executive, media consultant; b. Tarset, Eng., Aug. 5, 1945; d. Stephen I. and Josephine (Demming) Y.; came to U.S., 1972. B.A., U. Melbourne (Australia), 1967, diploma in social studies, 1966. Researcher, BBC-TV, London, 1970-72, field producer, N.Y.C., 1973-75; producer, dir., writer Sta. WGBH-TV, Boston, 1977-80; producer Time Life Video, Time Inc., N.Y.C., 1980, dir. informational programming, 1980-82, assoc. dir. new bus. devel., 1983-84. Producer, dir., writer films: Nova: The Pinks and the Blues (Am. Psychol. Found. Nat. Media award 1981); A World of Difference: B.F. Skinner and the Good Life; Blindness: Five Points of View; dir. film Emily Dickinson, 1985. Mem. Writers Guild Am., Am. Soc. Tng. and Devel., Women in Film Orgn. Home and Office: 250 Mercer St #B1002 New York NY 10012

YOUNGBERG, RUTH MAE, nurse; b. Clearwater, Nebr., Sept. 30, 1921; d. Byron DeForest and Mary Jane (Kletke) Brown; R.N., Lincoln Gen. Hosp. Sch. Nursing, 1943; m. Ira Burnell Youngberg, Sept. 13, 1969; children—Carol Hall Gleason, Mary Hall Hughes, Janet Hall Hays. Office nurse, Lincoln, Nebr., 1947-58; staff nurse Porters Hosp., Denver, 1958-59; head nurse, obstetrical supr. Lincoln Gen. Hosp., 1959-74; maternal child health nurse cons. Nebr. State Health Dept., Lincoln, 1974-77; head nurse labor and delivery Lincoln Gen. Hosp., 1977-85. Mem. Nurses Assn. Am. Coll. Obstetricians and Gynecologists (past vice-chmn. Nebr., past membership chmn. Nebr.), Am. Nurse Assn., Nebr. Perinatal Orgn. (dir., past pres.), Great Plains Orgn. Perinatal Health Care (past sec.), Lincoln Gen. Hosp. Alumni Assn. Republican. Methodist. Home: 400 S 46th St Lincoln NE 68510

YOUNGBLOOD, ARLENE LOIS, public relations specialist; b. Lancashire, Eng., Feb. 10, 1957; d. Alvin Lee and Christine A. (Gallimore) Youngblood. B.J., U. Tex.-Austin, 1979. Various positions Sta. KLRN-TV, Austin, 1975-78, asst. TV traffic mgr., 1979; reporter Daily Texan, Austin, 1978, Villager Newspaper, Austin, 1978-79; reporter, mng. editor Loquacity Mag., Austin, 1978-79; opening day coordinator United Way Schenectady County, Schenectady, N.Y., 1980; tng. specialist advt. and pub. relations Gen. Electric Co., Schenectady, 1979-81; asst. coordinator services Richmond State Sch. (Tex.), 1982-84; mgmt. instr. Courses Tex. Gov.'s Office Mgmt. Devel. Ctr., 1985—. Vice pres. adv. bd. Tex. Youth Commn., Richmond, 1983-84; sec. Martin Luther King Voter's League, Richmond, 1983-84; youth sponsor Mt. Carmel Baptist Ch., Richmond, 1982-84; pres. United Methodist Youth Fellowship, 1974-76. Georgia Lucas scholar U. Tex., 1975; Delta Sigma Theta scholar. Mem. Women in Communications (chpt. v.p. 1977-78), NAACP. Democrat. Home: 8216 Research Blvd #232 Austin TX 78758

YOUNGBLOOD, KATIE BETH HUNTER, physician; b. Borger, Tex., Mar. 13, 1934; d. Russell McRae and Theo (Dees) Hunter; B.A., Rice U., 1958; M.D., U. Tex., 1969; m. James Luther Youngblood, July 25, 1954; children—Linda Kay Youngblood Jones, Thomas Hunter, Carey Elizabeth Youngblood Harnden, Susan Bernice. Intern, Meml. Bapt. Hosp., Houston, 1969-70; gen. practice medicine Magliolo Clinic, Houston, 1970-73, Clear Lake Family Practice Clinic, Houston, 1973-83, Youngblood-Incalcatera Clinic, Houston, 1983—; chief staff Humana Hosp., Clear Lake, 1986; staff physician Clear Lake Hosp.; dir. First City Bank of Clear Lake. Trustee, Clear Creek Ind. Sch. Dist. Sch. Bd., 1979—. Recipient Johanna Blumel Meml. award U. Tex. Med. Br., 1968; diplomate Am. Bd. Family Practice. Fellow Am. Acad. Family Physicians (com. on minority health affairs and Indian health subcom. 1984-86); mem. AMA (Physician's Recognition award 1976), Tex., Galveston County med. assns., Am. Med. Women's Assn., Tex. Acad. Family Practice Physicians, (dir.), Sigma Xi. Presbyterian. Office: 1066 Hercules Houston TX 77058

YOUNGBLOOD, SARA W., real estate broker, government and political relations representative; b. Anahuac, Tex., Sept. 7, 1933; d. Grover C. and Martha (Watson) Willcox; m. Robert E. Youngblood, Sept. 12, 1952 (div. 1966); children—Kim, Karen, Kevin, Kathy, Kay. Student Baylor U., 1951-52; B.A., Lamar U., 1968; postgrad. Univ. Estudios Superiores, Monterrey, Mex., 1968, U. of the Americas, Mexico City, 1969. Cert. tchr., Tex.; lic. real estate broker, Tex. Tchr. French High Sch., Beaumont, Tex., 1968-70, Clear Creek High Sch., NASA, Houston, 1970-73; dir. Region 4 Tex. State Tchrs. Assn., San Antonio, 1973-80; pvt. practice real estate sales Sara W. Youngblood & Assocs., Inc., San Antonio, 1980—; mem. campaign orgn. Lt. Gov. Bill Hobby, San Antonio, 1976—; cons. Farm Adv. Com. Tex. Land Commr., Austin, 1986, Bill Hobby, 1976—. Fund raiser United Way, San Antonio, 1985, Democratic Party, 1980-86. Mem. Nat. Assn. Realtors, Tex. Assn. Realtors, San Antonio Bd. Realtors (govt. relations com. 1980-86), Farm and Land Inst., Tex. State Tchrs. Assn. (life). Avocation: hand crafts. Home: Rte 1 Box 1342 Boerne TX 78006 Office: Sara W Youngblood & Assocs Inc 7800 IH10West Suite 500 San Antonio TX 78230

YOUNGER, JANICE LYNN, association executive; b. Austin, Tex., Feb. 4, 1950; d. Dewey George and Mary Annette (Padgett) Younger, Jr. B.A. in Biology, U. Calif.-Santa Barbara, 1972; med. Technologist, U. Tex.-Houston, 1973. Advt. and pub. relations mgr. Boehringer Mannheim Diagnostics, Houston, 1977-82; v.p. ops. Fitness, Internat., Kingwood, Tex., 1982-83; conv. sales mgr. Greater Houston Conv. and Visitors Council, 1983—. Mem. Am. Soc. Clin. Pathology, Chi Omega. Republican. Presbyterian. Home: 10047 Westpark St Apt 6 Houston TX 77042

YOUNGER, JUDITH TESS, lawyer, educator, labor arbitrator; b. N.Y.C., Dec. 20, 1933; d. Sidney and Kate (Greenbaum) Weintraub; m. Irving Younger, Jan. 21, 1955; children—Rebecca, Abigail. B.S., Cornell U., 1954; J.D., NYU, 1958; LL.D. (hon.), Hofstra U., 1974. Bar: N.Y. 1958, D.C. 1983, Minn. 1985, U.S. Dist. Ct. (ea. dist.) N.Y. 1960, U.S. Dist. Ct. (so. dist.) N.Y. 1960, U.S. Ct. Appeals (2d cir.) 1960, U.S. Supreme Ct. 1962. Law clk. U.S. Dist. Ct. (so. dist.) N.Y., 1958-60; assoc. Chadbourne, Park, Whiteside & Wolff, N.Y.C., 1960-62; mem. Younger & Younger and successors, N.Y.C., 1960-67; adj. asst. prof. law NYU, 1967-69; asst. atty. gen. State of N.Y., N.Y.C., 1969-70; assoc. prof. law Hofstra U., 1970-72, prof. law, assoc. dean, 1972-74; prof. law, dean Syracuse U., 1974-75; prof. law Cornell U., 1975-85, dep. dean, 1975-78; adviser Am. Law Inst., Phila., 1977-84; prof. U. Minn. Sch. Law, 1985—; chmn. tenured tchr. hearings State of N.Y., 1979—; mem. screening com. Fulbright applications Council Internat. Exchange Scholars, Washington, 1981-84; mem. Gov. Rockefellers panel to screen candidates for Ct. Claim judges, 1973-74. Author: (with Irving Younger) How to Take and Pass a Law School Examination, 1981; contbr. articles to profl. jours. Trustee Cornell U., 1974-78; bd. dirs. Tompkins County Arts Council, Ithaca, N.Y., 1979-81, v.p., 1980-81. Mem. ABA, N.Y. State Bar Assn., N.Y.C. D.C., Minn. bar assns., AAUP (v.p. Cornell chpt. 1978-79). Office: U Minn Law Sch 229 19th Ave S Minneapolis MN 55455

YOUNG KRZUS, LESLIE ANN, writer, editor; b. Casper, Wyo., Oct. 4, 1960; d. Earl Allan and Floy Ella (Muender) Young; m. Michael Krzus, Dec. 31, 1982. A.A. in Psychology with honors, Mesa Coll., Grand Junction, Colo., 1980; B.A. in Advt. and Pub. Relations, (with honors, U. Tulsa, 1981. Summer intern Quarter Horse Jour., Amarillo, Tex., 1981; publs. editor Autumn Revolution, Tulsa, 1982; bus. and oil writer Tulsa World, 1982; editor Calgary (Alta.) Alumni Mag., U. Calgary, 1983—; freelance writer Horse Sense, Toronto, Colo. Cowboy, Palisade, Colo., Eastern/Western Quarter Horse Jour., Middleboro, Mass., Wild Rose Quarter Horse Jour., Calgary. Conf. scholar Council Advancement and Support of Edn., 1984; Scripps-Howard scholar, 1981. Mem. Internat. Assn. Bus. Communicators, Women in Communications, Sigma Delta Chi. Roman Catholic. Office: Calgary Alumni Affairs 2500 University Dr NW Calgary AB T2N 1N4 Canada

YOUNG LIVELY, SANDRA LEE, home health service executive; b. Rockport, Ind., Dec. 31, 1943; d. William Cody and Flora Juanita (Carver) Thorpe; m. Kenneth Leon Doom, May 4, 1962 (div. 1975); children—Patricia, Anita, Elizabeth. A.S., Vincennes U., 1979. Nursing aide, nurse Forest Del Nursing Home, Princeton, Ind., 1975-80; charge nurse Welborn Bapt. Hosp., Evansville, Ind., 1979-80, 82-83; staff nurse Longview Regional Hosp., Tex., 1980-82; dir. home health R.H. Laird Hosp., Kilgore, Tex., 1985—; staff nurse, asst. dir. Leizure Lodge Home Health, Overton, Tex., 1983-84. Mem. Nat. Assn. Female Execs., Vincennes U. Alumni Assn., Smithsonian Instn. Avocations: writing; reading; cake decorating; house plants. Home: PO Box 641 1011 Cheyenne Gladewater TX 75647 Office: R H Laird Meml Hosp 1612 S Henderson Kilgore TX 75662

YOUNGS, LINDA MILLER, lawyer; b. Worcester, Mass., May 13, 1942; d. James Wesley Miller and Hope (Norman) Connell; m. J. William T. Youngs, Jr., June 24, 1967; children—J. William Theodore III, Hope Eleanor. A.B., Wellesley Coll., 1963; M.Sc., U. Pa., 1966; J.D., Gonzaga U., 1975. Bar: Wash. 1975. City atty. City of Bellevue, Wash., 1981-84; of counsel Davis Wright & Jones, Bellevue, 1984—. Mem. ABA, Seattle-King County Bar Assn., Wash. Women Lawyers (dir. 1982). Democrat. Home: 10014 SE 16th St Bellevue WA 98004 Office: 110 110th Ave NE Bellevue WA 98004

YOUNGS-BILICKI, BETTIE B., educator, author, consultant; b. Belmond, Iowa, Mar. 24, 1948; d. Everett H. and Arlene B. Burres; Ed.D., Drake U., 1978; Ph.D., Walden U., 1976; m. Peter A. Bilicki; 1 dau., Jennifer Leigh. Program specialist Des Moines Public Schs., 1970-77; internat. ednl. cons. Batten, Batten, Hudson & Swab, 1977-78; adminstr. Iowa Dept. Social Services, 1978-80; adminstr. San Diego State U., 1980—, prof. ednl. adminstrn., 1980—, founder, dir. Internat. Mgmt. and Leadership Inst., 1978-85; bd. dirs HED Inst., 1977-80; mem. Nat. Council Adminstrv. Women Edn., 1981—. Recipient Edn. Press award for excellence in ednl. journalism, 1980; named Tchr. of Yr., Iowa Dept. Public Instrn., 1976; Margaret Mann fellow, 1978. Mem. Nat. Assn. Life-Long Learning, NEA, Delta Kappa Gamma, Phi Delta Kappa. Author: The Nurturing Response: How to Help Youngsters Cope with Stress, 1984. Contbr. articles to profl. jours. Home: 6876-33 Caminito Montanoso San Diego CA 92119 Office: Dept Ednl Adminstrn San Diego State Univ San Diego CA 92182

YOUNGWIRTH, JONI CLARICE, consultant; b. Sioux Falls, S.D., Feb. 12, 1950; d. John Wesley and Clarice Lillian (Stoen) Yttreness; B.S., S.D. State U., 1972; M.S., Boston U., 1977, M.B.A., 1984; m. Stephen A. Youngwirth, Apr. 5, 1975; 1 child, Nicole Elise. Dir. dietary services New Eng. Deaconness Assn., Concord, Mass., 1975-76; project coordinator New Eng. Deaconness Hosp., Boston, 1978-81, mem. computer applications devel. team, 1981-82; mgr. mktg. services Organizational Dynamics Inc., Burlington, Mass., 1982—; cons. in field. Corp. treas. Paint Rock Pool Corp., 1983-84. Served with USAF, 1972-75. Mem. Women in Mgmt., Am. Women in Computing, Am. Dietetic Assn., Mass. Dietetic Assn., Am. Soc. Tng. and Devel., LWV (dir. chpt. 1980-82, state program specialist 1985—), Am. Mgmt. Assn. New Eng. Apple Tree Club, Chi Omega. Unitarian. Home: 21 Partridge Rd Lexington MA 02173 Office: 5 Burlington Woods Burlington MA 01803

YOUNKER, DONNA LEE, educator; b. Evanston, Ill., Feb. 7, 1932; d. Fred Lee and Florence (Jett) Y.; B.A., Baylor U., 1952; M.A., So. Meth. U., 1958; Ph.D., U. Tex., 1964. Vis. prof. Purdue U., Lafayette, Ind., 1964; faculty Central State U., Edmond, Okla., 1966—, asso. prof. philosophy of edn., 1966-78, prof., 1978—, mem. faculty senate, 1971-72; tchr. Ind. Sch. Dist., Dallas, 1958-60; lectr. U. Tex., 1962-64, Fellow Philosophy of Edn. Soc.; mem. Southwestern Philosophy of Edn. Soc. (pres. 1971-72), History of Edn. Soc., Am. Ednl. Studies Assn., Am. Ednl. Research Assn., DAR (regent Samuel King chpt. 1980-82), Phi Delta Kappa. Methodist. Home: 1404 Mockingbird Ln Edmond OK 73034

YOUNKER, MARY LOU, accountant, counselor, advocate; b. Meeker, Colo., Nov. 6, 1940; d. James Wilson and Mary Anna (Ross) Y.; m. Robert Lee Grim, Jan. 7, 1961 (div. 1966); children—Robin Denise, Rita Anna; m. Wayne McGuire, Dec. 9, 1971 (div. 1976); 1 child, Shann L. Acct. Diamond Constrn. Co., Sacramento, Calif., 1964-73, Adonis Pools Contractor, Sacramento, 1973-75; counselor, advocate, acct. Rape Relief Hotline, Portland, 1976-80; sr. acct. Turner Ranches Water and Sanitation Co., Mesa, Ariz., 1980-84; controller SDI Community Developer, Inc., Stockton, Calif., 1984—. Developed pegboard system for constrn. co., 1974. Bd. dirs. Bradley Angle House, Friends of Family, Who Farm, Rape Relief Hot Line, Bus. Women Am. Club: Cowbells. Avocations: camping; hunting; fishing; sewing; leather work. Home: 820 San Miguel Ave Stockton CA 95210 Office: SDI Community Developer Inc 1545 St Marks Plaza Suite 1 Stockton CA 95207

YOUNT, ELOISE ADKINS, nurse; b. Salisbury, Md., June 12, 1943; d. Marion Carlton and Dorothy Mae (Moore) Adkins; Lic. Practical Nurse, Appalachian Sch. Practical Nurses, 1966; R.N. with academic honors, Ky. State U., 1972; m. Eugene Edward Yount, May 19, 1962; children—Eugene Edward, Rhonda Marie. Nurses aide Peninsula Gen. Hosp., Salisbury, Md., 1962; nurses aide, student practical nurse, lic. practical nurse Kings Daus. Meml. Hosp., Frankfort, Ky., 1965-72, relief asst. dir., critical care unit staff nurse, 1972—, head nurse, 1980—, asst. dir. nursing, 1982—; instr. cardiopulmonary resuscitation, inservice tng.; part time nurse Woodford County Hosp., Bendix Westinghouse Air Brake Co.; relief nurse Schenley Distillery. Guard,

Aux. Fraternal Order of Police, 1974—. Certified coronary care, trauma and transp. of critically ill. Mem. Am. Assn. Critical Care. Home: Route 9 Jamesway Frankfort KY 40601 Office: Kings' Daughters Dr Frankfort KY 40601

YOUNT, FLORENCE JANE, lawyer; b. Enid, Okla., Dec. 13, 1926; d. William Edward and Florence Evelyn (McCully) Y.; B.A., State U. Iowa, 1948; J.D., S. Tex. Coll. Law, 1958; cert. Parker Sch. Fgn. and Comparative Law, Columbia U., 1976. Bar: Tex. 1958. Atty. Ginther, Warren & Co., Houston, 1959-70; supr. internat. contracts Eastern Hemisphere Petroleum div. Conoco, Inc., N.Y.C., Stamford, Conn., 1970-75; sr. atty. Cities Service Co., Houston, 1975-83; contracts supr. Marathon Internat. Oil Co., Houston, 1984—; adviser to Internat. Law Socs. of three Houston law schs.; bd. dirs. S. Tex. Law Jour., Inc., v.p., 1969, 77, 84, 85, pres., 1970, 78, 79. Bd. dirs. Park Ave. Christian Ch., N.Y.C., 1971-73, First Christian Ch., Houston, 1977; active Vols. of Shelter, N.Y.C., 1973-75; precinct chmn., asso. legal counsel, chmn. rules com. Harris County (Tex.) Republican Party, 1958-68. Recipient Distinguished Alumnus award S. Tex. Coll. Law, 1976; Houston Matrix award, 1978; named One of 100 Top Corporate Women, Bus. Week, 1976, One of Five Outstanding Career Women, Bus. and Profl. Women's Club Houston, 1976. Mem. Am., Tex. (contbg. editor Internat. Law Newsletter), Houston bar assns., South Tex. Coll. Law Alumni Assn. (dir. 1977-80), Zool. Soc. Houston. Mem. Christian Ch. Contbr. articles to law jours.

YOUNT, KATHY SUE, radio executive; b. Greenville, Ky., July 11, 1957; d. Leon Dean and Daris (Cook) Harden; m. James Darrell Yount, July 30, 1976; children—Deana Kay, Jamie Lee. Student U. Ky., 1976, U. Louisville, 1977. Announcer Sta. WCND, Shelbyville, Ky., 1977-78, news dir., 1978-81, asst. mgr., 1981—. Mem. Ky. Broadcasters Assn., Louisville Area Radio Stas., Shelbyville C. of C. (bd. dirs. 1984-86), Downtown Shelbyville Bus. Assn. (pres.), Science Hill Bus. and Profl. Women (pres.). Democrat. Mem. Ch. of Christ. Avocations: reading; cooking. Home: Route 3 Box 109 Shelbyville KY 40065 Office: Sta WCND 416 Main St Shelbyville KY 40065

YOUNTS, PATTY LOU, interior designer executive, researcher; b. Lexington, N.C., Feb. 20, 1950; d. Wayne Lohr and Rosetta Mae (Myers) Y. B.S., U. N.C.-Greensboro, 1972; postgrad. in Mktg., Wake Forest U., Winston-Salem, N.C., 1976. Apprentice draftsman and interior designer Paul T. Briggs, AIA, Lexington, 1971, in-house designer, specifer, 1972-74; part-time interior designer Watkins Office Interiors, Winston-Salem, 1972-74; ptnr. IN-Ex Designs, Inc., 1974-75, corp. officer, head, 1975-81, pres., owner, 1981—. dir. Industry Gen. Tire, GF Bus. Systems, Armstrong Industries, Mid-State Tile; guest speaker univs. Adv. bd. Lexington Meml Hosp., 1984—, Western Carolina U., 1983—. Recipient N.C. AIA awards for Sch. Planning, 1977, 79. Sperry and Hutchinson scholar, 1968-72, honorary scholar, U. N.C.-Greensboro, 1971-72. Mem. Inst. Bus. Designers (mem., chmn. various coms., pres. Carolinas chpt. 1977-80, 82-84), Am. Soc. Interior Designers, Color Mktg. Group (chairholder 1985). Lexington C. of C. (com. chmn. 1980, bd. dirs. 1981-84). Democrat. Mem. United Ch. of Christ. Avocations: water skiing, golf. Office: Design Cons 302 W Center St Lexington NC 27292

YOUTZ, CAROL ANN, banker attorney; b. Canton, Ohio, June 17, 1953; d. Charles Burton and Florence Nancy (Parks) Youtz; student Baldwin-Wallace Coll., 1971-72; B.S. magna cum laude in Acctg., U. Akron, 1979, J.D. U. Akron Sch. Law., 1985. New accounts counselor The Harter Bank & Trust Co., Canton, Ohio, 1973-75; litigation, corp. and pension paralegal Krugliak, Wilkins, Griffiths & Dougherty Co., Canton, 1975-80; tax and ins. analyst Diebold, Inc., Canton, 1980-81; trust adminstr. Bank One of Akron, N.A., 1981-82, asst. trust officer, 1983-84; employee benefits officer Fidelity Bank, 1984—; mem. Akron Pension Council, 1979-82. Mem. Tuscarawas Philharmonic Orch., 1978-80, Main Line Symphony Orch., 1985—. Mem. Am. Bar Assn., Akron Pension Council, Beta Alpha Psi, Beta Gamma Sigma, Alpha Sigma Lambda. Mem. United Ch. of Christ. Club: Order of Eastern Star. Home: 288 Iven Ave Apt 3C St Davids PA 19087 Office: Fidelity Bank Broad & Walnut Sts Philadelphia PA 19109

YU, ANNE RAMONA WING-MUI, psychologist; b. Hong Kong, Apr. 9, 1948; came to U.S., 1968, naturalized, 1974; d. Hing-wan and Sin-wah (Yau) Y.; B.A. with honors in Psychology, Ohio U., 1971; M.A. in Clin. Psychology, So. Ill. U., 1975. Psychol. examiner Delta Counseling & Guidance Center, Monticello, Ark., 1975-76; psychologist Mid-Nebr. Community Mental Health Ctr. (name now Mid-Plains Ctr. for Profl. Services), Grand Island, 1977—; supr. satellite clinic Loup Valley Mental Health Center, Loup City, Nebr., 1977-79; project dir. Protection from Domestic Abuse, 1978-79; pres. Grand Island Task Force on Domestic Violence and Sexual Assault, Inc., 1980-82; mem. Fellows of Menninger Found., 1983-84; bd. dirs. Com. Against Child Sexual Assault, 1983—. Bd. dirs. YWCA, 1983—; mem. Central Nebr. Agr.-in-Transition Adv. Bd., 1986. Mem. Am. Assn. Marriage and Family Therapy (v.p. Nebr. div. 1981-83, pres.-elect 1983-85, pres. 1985-87), AAUW (dir. 1983—, pres. Grand Island 1983-85, v.p. Nebr. 1985-87), Am. Psychol. Assn., Asian Am. Psychol. Assn. Home: 1524 Coventry Ln Apt 97 Grand Island NE 68801 Office: 914 Baumann Dr Grand Island NE 68801

YU, LINDA, newswoman, television anchorwoman; b. Xian, China, Dec. 1, 1946; B.A. in Journalism, U. So. Calif., 1968; m. Richard K. Baer, June 1982. With Sta. KTLA-TV, Los Angeles, Sta. KABC-TV, Los Angeles; news anchor, reporter Sta. KATU-TV, Portland, Oreg.; gen. assignment reporter Sta. KGO-TV, San Francisco; with Sta. WMAQ-TV, Chgo., 1979-84, gen. assignment reporter, weekend anchor, 1979-80, co-anchor Monday-Friday edit. NEWSCENTER5, 4:30 PM, 1980-81, co-anchor NEWSCENTER5, 10:00 PM, 1981-84; co-anchor Eyewitness News, WLS-TV, Chgo., 1984—; spl.: Linda Yu in China, 1980; anchor WLS-TV, Chgo., 1984—. Recipient Chgo. Emmy award, 1981, 82. Office: WLS-TV 190 N State St Chicago IL 60601

YUENGLING, ELIZABETH ROSE, hospital administrator; b. N.Y.C., Apr. 7, 1960; d. John Anthony and May Elizabeth (Fox) Y. Student, Nassau Community Coll., 1978-79, U. Houston, 1982—. Notary pub. Security asst. Hermann Hosp., Houston, 1980-81, supr. security, 1981-85, asst. dir. security, 1985—. Recipient employee awards, 1982-84. Fellow Nat. Notary Assn., Nat. Locksmith Assn., Internat. Assn. for Hosp. Security, Am. Soc. for Indsl. Security, 100 Club of Houston. Republican. Roman Catholic. Avocations: softball; volleyball; fencing. Home: PO Box 66394 Houston TX 77006

YUHAS, SUSAN MARIE, nurse; b. Patauxant, Md., July 8, 1945; d. William F. and Ruth F. (Schlenker) Pfeifer; m. John James Yuhas, June 8, 1968; children: John Sandor, Kenneth Karolyi. R.N., Lankenau Sch. Nursing, Phila., 1966; student U. Pitts., 1970. Lic. nurse, Pa. 1966, Ga. 1982. Night charge nurse ICU, Presbyn. Hosp., Pitts., 1966-68; staff nurse hemodialysis VA Hosp., Pitts., 1968-69, hemodialysis home tng. nurse, 1969-73, coordinator, 1973-77; advisor Am. Assn. Nephrology Nurses and Techs., Marietta, Ga., 1982, chmn. Found., 1984-86; owner Custom Covers. Mem. Bd. Nephrology Examiners in Nursing and Tech. (fin. advisor 1974-76). Mem. Am. Assn. Nephrology Nurses and Technicians (regional v.p. 1973-75, nat. treas. 1975-77, chpt. chair 1977-78, pres.-elect 1978-79, pres. 1979-80). Contbr. articles to profl. jours. Lutheran.

YUKL, TRUDY ANN, medical social worker, counseling psychologist; b. Portsmouth, N.H., Feb. 5, 1947; d. Francis Joseph and Dorothy Helen (Pluff) Y. B.A. in psychology, U. Ky., 1969; M.S. in Counseling, Suffolk U., 1984; postgrad. in counseling psychology, Harvard U., 1984-85, Boston U., 1985—. Med. social worker Mass. Gen. Hosp., Boston, 1969—, co-founder, dir. Indian Clinic, 1973—; cons. Boston Indian Council, 1973—; lectr. in field. Contbr. articles to profl. jours. Health adv. bd. Tecumseh House, Boston, 1980—; active Homeless Coalition, Boston, 1984-85. Recipient Outstanding Profl. Human Services award, 1974-75; nominated Disting. Alumni, U. Ky., 1985. Mem. Nat. Assn. Social Workers, Mass. Psychol. Assn. Avocations: travel; photography; music; native American culture; dancing; swimming. Office: Mass Gen Hosp Social Service Dept Fruit St Boston MA 02114

ZABRISKIE, VIRGINIA M., art dealer; b. N.Y.C. Student, Washington Sq. Coll.; B.A., NYU; M.A., NYU Inst. Fine Arts. Dir., Zabriskie Gallery, 1954—. Mem. Art Dealers Assn. (dir.). Address: 724 Fifth Ave New York NY 10019

ZACCONE, SUZANNE MARIA, graphics company executive; b. Chgo., Oct. 23, 1957; d. Dominic Robert and Lorretta F. (Urban) Z. Student pub. schs., Downers Grove. Sales sec. Brookeridge Realty, Downers Grove, 1975-76; sales cons. Kafka Estates Inc., Downers Grove, 1975-76; adminstrv. asst. Chem. Dist., Inc., Oakbrook, Ill., 1976-77; sales rep., mgr. Anographics Corp., Burr Ridge, Ill., 1977-85; pres. Graphic Solutions, Inc., Downers Grove, 1985—. Recipient Outstanding Sales Performance award Anographics Corp., 1981; named Rep. of Yr., 1982, 83, 84, 85. Mem. Women in Mgmt., Nat. Assn. Female Execs., Sales and Mktg. Execs. of Chgo., Women Entrepreneurs of DuPage. Avocations: reading; sailing; cooking; needlepoint. Office: Graphic Solutions Inc 5117 Main St Downers Grove IL 60515

ZACHARY, ANDREA ANNE, geneticist; b. Cleve., Sept. 25, 1946; d. Anthony A. and Audrey J. (Klaus) Z. B.S., Ohio State U., 1967, M.S., 1969; Ph.D., Case Western Res. U., 1982. Research asst. Ohio State U., Columbus, 1969-70; technologist Cleve. Clinic Found., 1970-74, supr. lab., 1974-81, project scientist, 1981-82, staff, 82-84, assoc. lab. dir., 1984-85, lab. co-dir., 1985—; ad-hoc cons. NIH, 1986—. Co-editor: AACHT Laboratory Manual, 1981. Author audio-visual program on immunogenetics, 1983. Contbr. articles to profl. jours. and chpts. to scholarly tests. Grantee Kidney Found. of Ohio, 1984, Cleve. Clinic Found., 1985. Mem. Am. Soc. for Histocompatibility and Immunogenetics (councillor 1977-78, 83—, edn. program faculty 1971-83, 85), Genetics Soc. Am., Am. Soc. Human Genetics, Transplant Soc. of Northeast Ohio, Genetics Soc. Am., Audubon Soc., Nat. Wildlife Fedn. Avocations: nature photography, cross-country skiing, music, leather carving. Office: Cleve Clinic Found 9500 Euclid Ave Cleveland OH 44106

ZACHERT, VIRGINIA, psychologist, emeritus educator; b. Jacksonville, Ala., Mar. 1, 1920; d. Rev. R. E. and Cora H. (Massee) Z.; student Norman Jr. Coll., 1937; A.B., Ga. State Woman's Coll. (now Valdosta State Coll.), 1940; M.A., Emory U., 1947; Ph.D., Purdue U., 1949. Statistician, Davison-Paxon Co., Atlanta, 1941-44; research psychologist Mil. Contracts, Auburn Research Found., Ala. Poly. Inst.; indsl. and research psychologist Sturm & O'Brien, cons. engrs., 1958-59; research project dir. Western Design, Biloxi, Miss., 1960-61; self-employed cons. psychologist, Norman Park, Ga., 1961-71, Good Hope, Ga., 1971-77, Augusta, Ga., 1977—; research asso. med. edn. Med. Coll. Ga., Augusta, 1964-66, asso. prof., 1966-70, prof., 1970-84, prof. emeritus, 1984—, mem. Acad. Council, 1976-79, exec. com., 1979-84, chmn.-elect, 1982, chmn., 1983; mem. Ga. Psychology Bd., 1974-79, pres., 1978; adj. prof. McCormick Theol. Sem., 1977-80. Ga. del. White House Conf. on Aging, 1981; exec. com. Sr. Citizens Council, 1981, adv. council, 1982; chmn. Augusta Mayor's Sr. Citizens Adv. Bd., 1982—. Served as aerologist USN, 1944-46, aviation psychologist USAF 1949-54, mem. air tng. command adv. bd. 1967-72. Named Alumna of Yr., Valdosta State Coll., 1980; diplomate Am. Bd. Profl. Psychology. Fellow Am. Psychol. Assn. (com. on profl. practice 1982-84, continuing edn. sponsor approvals com. 1982—), AAAS; mem. Nat. Soc. Programmed Instruction (nat. sec. 1968, adv. bd. 1969-71), AAUP (pres. med. chpt. 1978-81), Gerontol. Soc. Am., Nat. Council on Aging, New Bordeaux Cottage Assn. (pres. 1981—), Sigma Xi (pres. Med. Coll. Ga. chpt. 1980-81). Baptist. Club: RSVP Augusta (v.p. 1982). Author programmed instruction texts. Home: 1126 Highland Ave Augusta GA 30904 Office: Dept Obstetrics and Gynecology Med Coll GA Augusta GA 30912

ZACHRISSON, RUTH CONERLY, illustrator, artist; b. Marshall, Tex., Oct. 27, 1908; d. Thomas Preston and Elizabeth (Davis) C.; m. Theodore N. Smith, 1929 (dec. 1944); 1 dau., Sharon Elizabeth Wolf; m. 2d Arvid Zachrisson, Apr. 1946 (dec.). Student Sullins Coll., Art Students League, N.Y.C. Formerly art dir. Titche Goettingers. Group shows include: Witte Mus., San Antonio, 1953. represented in permanent collections: Marshall Hist. Mus. (Tex.), Alamo, San Antonio; illustrator War Bonds; guest tchr. Columbia U., N.Y.C., Chgo. Art Inst., Witte Mus., San Antonio. Author: Drawing the Fashion Figure, 1937. Recipient 2d Best Portrait award Witte Mus.; Best Layout award Fiesta of San Jacinto Assn., 1953. Mem. Art Students League (best portrait and best painting awards). Methodist. Home: 8403 Burkhart St Houston TX 77055

ZAFFARANO, DIANA MARIE, financial executive; b. Abington, Pa., Sept. 21, 1955; d. Albert Vincent and Mary Virginia (Piccarilli) Z. A.A. Sci., Montgomery County Community Coll., 1975; B.B.A., Temple U., 1977. Adminstrv. sec. Montgomery Pub. Co., Ft. Washington, Pa., 1968-76; acctg. clk. Narco Avionics, Ft. Washington, 1970-76; in-charge acct. Coopers & Lybrand, Phila., 1976-80; sr. fin. auditor Rorer Group Inc., Ft. Washington, 1980—. Mem. Nat. Acctg. Assn. (bd. dirs. 1977—). Home: 1214 Hartranft Ave Fort Washington PA 19034 Office: Rorer Group Inc 500 Virginia Dr Fort Washington PA 19034

ZAGORSKI, HILDEGARD MARIE, stock market analyst; b. Hamburg, Germany, Oct. 14, 1931; came to U.S., 1932; d. Otto and Lisbeth Auguste (Henkis) Riege; m. Walter Theodore Zagorski, Aug. 14, 1956 (div. Oct. 1964); 1 son, Theodore. Student in acctg., security analysis N.Y. Inst. Fin., summer 1969. Registered rep. Supr., Howard Johnson, N.Y.C., 1960-69; stock market analyst Prudential Bache Securities, Inc., N.Y.C., 1969—. Republican. Lutheran. Office: Prudential Bache Securities 1 Seaport Plaza New York NY 10292

ZAGORSKI, SHIRLEY ANN, travel agent; b. Burlington, Iowa, Sept. 25, 1936; d. Howard O. and Cleo (Menefee) Griffith; m. Stanley W. Zagorski; children—Gregory, Stephen, Christopher, Stacey. Student U. Iowa, 1958. Mgr., Singer Travel, Bridgeport, Conn., 1976-80; owner, mgr. Executive World Travel, Trumbull, Conn., 1980—; pres., Travel Temporaries, Trumbull, 1982—; v.p. Travel Careers, New Canaan, 1982—. Cert. travel agt. Mem. Assn. Retail Travel Agts., Inst. Cert. Travel Agts., Cruise Lines Internat. Assn., Internat. Air Transport Assn., Airlines Reporting Assn. Republican. Roman Catholic. Avocations: painting; reading. Home: 8 Arbutus Ln Trumbull CT 06611 Office: Executive World Travel Ltd 6515 Main St Trumbull CT 06611

ZAGORZYCKI, MARIA TERESA, physician; b. Trenton, N.J., Dec. 18, 1953; d. John M. and Janina Zofia (Jaworski) Z.; B.A. in Biochemistry with distinction in all subjects, Cornell U., 1975; M.D., George Washington U., 1979. Diplomate Am. Bd. Ob-Gyn. Intern, UCLA Hosp., 1979-80, resident in ob-gyn., 1980-82, chief resident in ob-gyn., 1982-83, asst. clin. prof. ob-gyn, 1983—. Fellow Am. Coll. Ob-Gyn, Inter-Am. Coll. Physicians and Surgeons; mem. Am. Fertility Soc., Am. Med. Women's Assn., Am. Assn. Gynecologic Laproscopists, Los Angeles County Obstetrical and Gynecol. Soc., Phi Delta Epsilon. Club: Cornell of So. Calif. Office: 14624 Sherman Way Suite 408 Van Nuys CA 91405

ZAHM, BERNICE SCHULTZ, ednl. adminstr.; b. Cleve., May 25, 1919; d. Sam and Lillian (Levin) Schultz; B.A., Ohio State U., 1941; M.A. in Ednl. Guidance, Calif. State U., Los Angeles; Ph.D. in Human Behavior, U.S. Internat. U., San Diego, 1972; m. Nathan R. Zahm, 1939 (dec. 1979); children—Stephen, Barbara Tchr. pub. schs., Los Angeles, 1952-53; pvt. remedial educator, 1953—; founder Zahm Sch. and Ednl. Guidance Center, Los Angeles, 1956—; speaker, lectr. profl. assns., 1965—; cons. to pvt. and pub. schs., 1965—. Recipient award for contbn. to remedial edn. County of Los Angeles, 1964. Mem. Am. Psychol. Assn., Calif. Psychol. Assn. (chmn. ednl. div.). Calif. Assn. Sch. Psychologists, Calif. Assn. Marriage and Family Counselors, Am. Personnel and Guidance Assn. Psychologists for Social Responsibility (co-chmn., steering com. 1984). Contbr. articles to profl. jours. Originator multilectic approach to edn. Address: 4422 Sherman Oaks Circle Sherman Oaks CA 91403

ZAHN, ALICE MANNING, bank consultant executive; b. Siloam Springs, Ark., Dec. 12, 1931; d. William Granville and Stella Eunice (Phelps) Gibbs; m. Stauss Franklin Manning, July 30, 1950 (div. 1978); children—Janna Sue, James Wesley, Michael Jay; m. James Robert Zahn, June 23, 1984. Mem. ops. officer Citizens Nat. Bank, Okmulgee, Okla., 1962-76; prin. Profit Tech., Houston, 1976—. Democrat. Baptist. Home: 3406 Shoreside Dr Crosby TX 77532 Office: Profit Tech Corp 25211 Grogan's Mill Rd The Woodlands TX 77380

ZAIDUONDO-GONZALEZ, BELEN, gerontologist, ednl. adminstr.; b. San Juan, P.R., Sept. 29, 1937; d. Roberto Zalduondo and Agustina González; A.D. in Secretarial Sci., Universidad de P.R., 1971; B.B.A., Internat. Inst. of Am., 1974; M.S., Centro Caribeno de Estudios Postgraduados, P.R., 1977, Ph.D., 1982; children—Carmen B. Candelario, Luis Roberto Candelario. Sec., Dept. of Agr., Commonwealth of P.R., 1957-60, adminstrv. sec. Land Authority, 1960-66, adminstrv. sec., Dept. Agr., 1966-68, exec. dir. and asst. to vice pres. Senate of Commonwealth P.R., 1972-77; prof. devel. of individual, chair World U., Hato Rey, P.R., 1977-80; dir. grad. studies Caribbean Center for Advance Studies, Miami, Fla., 1980—, prof., 1980-82; appeared in various TV and radio programs, P.R., 1980-82. Mem. Am. Psychol. Assn., Nat. Assn. of P.R. Women, P.R. Psychol. Assn., Nat. Assn. for Hispanic Aging, Assn. for Gerontology in Higher Edn., Latin Bus. and Profl. Women, Sociedad Interamerican de Psicologia. Mem. Evangelical Ch. Contbr. articles on gerontology to profl. jours. Office: 960 SE 26 Reparto Metropolitano Rio Piedras PR

ZAIS, EDITH MOREIN, university official; b. Providence, Apr. 8, 1931; d. Samuel Joshua and Sona Morein; A.B., Brown U., 1952; M.A. in Teaching, R.I. Coll., 1964; 6th year diploma edn. U. Conn., 1968; m. Robert S. Zais, Sept. 14, 1952; children—Louis Scott, Roberta Susan. Tchr. English, E. Providence (R.I.) Sr. High Sch., 1964-66; staff writer Willimantic (Conn.) Chronicle, 1966-67; tchr. reading Crestwood Schs., Mantua, Ohio, 1969-70; coordinator learning devel. program Kent (Ohio) State U., 1970—, instr. Exptl. Coll., 1973—; mem. admissions com. Northeastern Ohio Univs. Coll. Medicine, 1979-81; project co-dir. spl. services disadvantaged students Dept. Edn., 1978—. Mem. Nat. Assn. Women Deans, Adminstrs. and Counselors, Internat. Reading Assn., Assn. Children and Adults with Learning Disabilities, LWV (chmn. edn. com. Kent chpt. 1976-78), Omicron Delta Kappa. Home: 431 Wilson Ave Kent OH 44240 Office: Kent State U Kent OH 44242

ZAISER, SALLY SOLEMMA VANN, financial executive; b. Birmingham, Ala., Jan. 18, 1917; d. Carl Waldo and Einnan (Herndon) Vann; student Birmingham-So. Coll., 1933-36, Akron Coll. Bus., 1937; m. Foster E. Zaiser, Nov. 11, 1939. Acct., A. Simionato, San Francisco, 1958-65; head acctg. dept. Richard T. Clarke Co., San Francisco, 1966; acct. John Howell-Books, San Francisco, 1967-72, sec., treas., 1972-83, fin. dir., 1982-85; sec. Great Eastern Mines, Inc., Albuquerque, 1969-80, dir., 1980—. Contbr. articles to profl. and trade jours. Braille transcriber for ARC, Kansas City, Mo. 1941-45; vol. worker ARC Hosp. Program, Sao Paulo, Brazil, 1952; bd. dirs. Gleeson Library Assocs., 1984—. Mem. Book Club Calif., Gleeson Library Assocs. (dir. 1984—), Calif. Hist. Soc., U. Tex. Library Assocs., Yale Library Assocs., Theta Upsilon. Republican. Episcopalian. Contbr. articles to hist. jours. Home: 355 Serrano Dr San Francisco CA 94132 Office: 440 Post St San Francisco CA 94102

ZAITZ, JOAN SALWEN, lawyer; b. N.Y.C., June 29, 1951; d. Sidney and Ruth (Starr) Salwen; m. Alan S. Zaitz, Oct. 18, 1980; 1 child, Jacob Salwen. A.B. cum laude, Syracuse U., 1973; J.D., U. Pa., 1976. Bar: N.Y. 1977. Assoc. Louis E. Cherico, White Plains, N.Y., 1977-80, Joel Martin Aurnou, White Plains, 1980-82; sole practice, Hartsdale, N.Y., 1983-84, Scarsdale, N.Y., 1984—. Mem. N.Y. State Bar Assn., White Plains Bar Assn. (bd. dirs. 1982—), Westchester County Bar Assn. (bd. dirs. lawyer referral service 1983-84), Pi Sigma Alpha. Home and Office: 2 Crawford Ln Scarsdale NY 10583

ZAJICEK, BARBARA JEANNE, health care company executive; b. Peoria, Ill., Jan. 12, 1932; d. Gale Edward and Thelma Beatrice (Drury) Allen; student public schs.; m. Albert F. Zajicek, July 5, 1973; children—Gregg Hahn, Lisa Jeffries, Dana Hahn. Office supr., then exec. asst. to pres. Larry Smith & Co., Northfield, Ill., 1970-74, 76-77; asst. to pres., leasing agt. Devel. Control Corp., Northfield, 1974-76; bus. mgr. EMSCO, Ltd., Des Plaines, Ill., 1978—; dir., v.p./asst. sec.-treas. Midwest Med. Mgmt., Mem. Emergency Medicine Mgmt. Assn. (pres.-elect), Nat. Assn. Free-Standing Emergency Centers. Republican. Lutheran. Home: 619 Hillside Rd Glenview IL 60025 Office: 999 E Touhy Ave Suite 145 Des Plaines IL 60018

ZALESKI, JEAN, artist; b. Malta; d. John M. and Carolina (Micallef) Busuttil; studied Art Students League, N.Y.C., 1956-59, New Sch. Social Research, 1967-69, Moore Coll. Art, 1970-71, Parsons Sch. Design, 1974-75, Pratt Inst., 1975-76; children—Jeffrey, Philip, Susan. Art dir. Studio 733, Great Neck, N.Y., 1963-67; dir. Naples Art Studio (Italy), 1972-73; corp. sec. Women in Arts, 1974-75, exec. coordinator, 1976-78; adj. lectr. Hofstra U., 1977—, Bklyn. Coll., 1974-75, Cooper Union, 1986; represented by Elaine Starkman Gallery, N.Y.C.; one-woman shows include: Galleria Stuciv, Florence, Italy, 1976, Adelphi U., 1975, Women in Arts Gallery, N.Y.C., 1975, Il Gabbiano Gallery, Naples, 1973, Wallnuts Gallery, Phila., 1971, Neikrug Gallery, N.Y.C., 1970, Alonzo Gallery, 1979, Va. Center for Creative Arts, Sweet Briar, 1981, Hodgell Galleries, Sarasota, Fla., 1982, Elaine Starkman Gallery, N.Y.C., 1986; group exhbns. include Art: U.S.A., N.Y.C., 1969, Internat. Art Exhbn., Cannes, France, 1969, Frick Mus., Pitts., 1970, NAD, N.Y.C., 1970-71, Phila. Mus. Art, 1971, Am. Women Artists, Palazzo Vecchio, Florence, Italy, 1972, Internat. Women's Arts Festival, Milan Italy (Gold medal), 1973, Bklyn. Mus., 1975, Sweet Briar Coll., 1977, CUNY, 1978, Mus. Hudson Highlands, 1982, Pace U. Gallery, 1982, Bayly Mus., Charlottesville, Va., 1986; represented in permanent collections Easter Seal Human Resource Center, N.Y., Hofstra U., N.Y. Pub. Library, Bklyn. Poly. Inst., Met. Mus. Art, Va. Center Creative Arts, Sweet Briar. Recipient Susan B. Anthony award NOW, N.Y.C., 1986. Mem. Artists Equity, Internat. Assn. Art, Nat. Women's Caucus for Art.

ZALEWSKI, CLAIRE JEAN, educator; b. Cambridge, Mass., July 17, 1945; d. Stephen Charles and Magdalena Veronica (Senukevicz) Budwitis; m. John B. Graham, Jr., Aug. 8, 1980. B.A., Boston Coll., 1967; Ed.M., Boston U., 1971, Ed.D., 1978. Tchr. Karlsruhe Am. Elem. Sch., Fed. Republic Germany, 1968-69; tchr. Lexington Pub. Schs., Mass., 1969-72, elem. math specialist, 1972—instr. Middlesex Community Coll., Bedford, Mass., 1973; instr. Lesley Coll., Cambridge, 1982—, Brandeis U., 1983—, Boston U., 1984; workshop leader for local, state and nat. confs., Boston to Hawaii, 1972—; cons. D.C. Health and Co., Houghton Mifflin Co., Allyn and Bacon, 1978—, Children's TV Workshop, N.Y.C., Walt Disney Ednl. Media, Burbank, Calif., others; Mem. Boston U. Sch. Edn. Alumni Exec. Bd., 1976—, pres., 1982-84; chmn. math., sci. profl. adv. group on cert. to Mass. Commn. Edn., 1975-77. Recipient Vol. Tchr. Leadership award Lexington Public Schs., 1973-76, Presdl. awards Mass. Math. State Dir., 1984, 85, 86. Mem. Boston Area Math. Specialists (pres., treas. 1978—), Assn. Tchrs. Math. Eastern Mass. (dir. 1979-81, pres. 1983-85), Nat. Council Tchrs. Math. (chmn. com.), Nat. Council Suprs. Math., Assn. Supervision and Curriculum Devel., Lexington Edn. Assn. Mass. Tchrs. Assn., NEA. Club: Women Radio Operators New Eng. Home: 53 Williams Rd Lexington MA 02173 Office: Curriculum Resource Center Bowman Sch 9 Philip Rd Lexington MA 02173

ZALI, LILA, ballet company executive. Founder, dir. Ballet Pacifica, Laguna Beach, Calif. Office: Ballet Pacifica 1863 S Coast Hwy Laguna Beach CA 92651*

ZAMBOUKOS, CYNTHIA SOTERIA, travel consultant, paralegal; b. San Francisco, June 17, 1957; d. James Neal and Nafsika Vasiliki (Katsoulos) Zamboukos. B.A. in French and Italian, San Francisco State U., 1980. Asst. sec.-treas. Pacific Am. Group, Inc., San Francisco, 1977-84; freelance travel cons. and paralegal, San Francisco, 1984—. Mem. Nat. Assn. Female Execs., Nat. Notary Assn., Alliance Francaise, Hellenic Am. Profl. Soc., San Francisco Assn. Legal Assts. Democrat. Greek Orthodox.

ZAMER, BELINDA ROSE, human resource development specialist, psychology educator; b. Washington, Oct. 26, 1953; d. Fred Elias and Yvonne Rose (Habib) Z. A.A., Prince George's Coll., Largo, Md., 1973; B.A., Catholic U., 1974; M.A., George Washington U., 1976, Ed.D., 1983. Asst. dir., sr. therapist Navy Dept., Washington, 1976-78; employee relations staff EPA, Washington, 1978-82, psychologist, 1982-84; asst. prof. George Washington U., 1983—; instr. U. Md., College Park, 1984; assoc. prof. U-Va., 1984—; lectr. Marymount Coll., 1986; guest speaker faculty in-service tng. program U.S. Air Force Acad., 1985; cons. WHO, NIMH Study Ctr., Washington; cons IBM, 1985. Bd. dirs. Prince George's Mental Health Assn., Cheverly, Md., 1974; exec. adv. bd. County Council Mental Health, Upper Marlboro, Md., 1975; bd. dirs. NIMH, Adelphi, Md., 1975. Catholic U. Bd. Trustees fellow, 1975, Health and Human Services of Washington grantee, 1976. Mem. AAUW (Outstanding Young Career Woman 1982-83), Nat. Council Exec. Women, Literacy Council Prince George County, Prince George's County Bus. and Profl. Women (exec. bd. 1983), So. Prince George's Bus. and Profl. Women, Nat. Assn. Female Execs., Phi Beta Kappa (v.p. 1975-76), Psi Chi (v.p. 1976).

ZANES, RUTH LEE, marketing consultant; b. N.Y.C., Feb. 16, 1935; d. Morris Harris and Bertha Clara (Steifel) Bernstein; m. Marc Weissman, Aug. 21, 1956 (div. 1966); children—Glenn, Lee; m. George William Zanes, June 17, 1970. B.A., Bklyn. Coll., 1956; postgrad. New Sch. for Social Research, 1956-57. Project dir. James M. Vicary Co., N.Y.C., 1957-60; dir. research Gilbert Mktg. Group, N.Y.C., 1960-64; account research supr. Foote Cone & Belding, N.Y.C., 1964-66; research account exec. Grey Advt., N.Y.C., 1966-68; mgr. corp. and advt. research Clairol, Inc., N.Y.C., 1968-70; mgr. market research Chesebrough-Pond's, Greenwich, Conn., 1970-73; mgr. consumer research Avon Products, N.Y.C., 1973-74; pres. Zanes & Assocs., Inc., Ft. Lee, N.J., 1974—; adj. prof. Jersey City State Coll., 1985. Contbr. articles to profl. jours. Founder, mem. adv. bd. Los Niños project Pan Am. Devel. Found., 1983-85. Mem. Am. Mktg. Assn., Mktg. Research Assn. (bd. dirs. 1980-81), Qualitative Research Cons., Advt. Women N.Y. Home: 7000 Boulevard E Guttenberg NJ 07093 Office: Zanes & Assocs Inc 1350 15th St Fort Lee NJ 07024

ZANESKI, PATRICIA MARIE, media coordinator; b. New Britain, Conn., May 11, 1956; d. Victor Joseph and Anne Elizabeth (Rulevich) Z. B.S., Central Conn. State Coll., 1982. Clk., Heublein, Inc., Hartford, Conn., 1976-77, sr. clk. spirits group, 1977-78, mktg. analyst grocery products group, Farmington, Conn., 1978-81, media coordinator corp. group, 1981-84, adminstr. spot TV and print, 1985-86; adminstr. nat. TV, Nabisco Brands Inc., 1986—. Roman Catholic. Office: Nabisco Brands Inc Nabisco Brands Plaza Parsippany NJ 07054

ZANETOS, JOANNE MARIE, nurse; b. Columbus, Ohio, Aug. 30, 1956; d. Robert Norman and Joan Cecilia (Mauck) Troyer; m. Timothy James Zanetos, May 13, 1978; 1 child, Thomas William. A.A. in Nursing, Columbus Tech. Inst., 1976, cert. in Am. sign lang. of blind and deaf; cert. John Robert Powers Modeling and Finishing Sch., 1982. R.N. Nurse Doctors Hosp., Columbus, 1976-78, Convacare, Inc., Columbus, 1978-80, Health Care Personnel, Columbus, 1980—. Painter forget-me-knot porcelain plate, 1979 (Gammie award, blue ribbon Columbus Ceramics Festival), porcelain cardinals, 1981 (Gammie award, blue ribbon), Bd. dirs. Women's Assn. of Columbus Symphony Orch., 1984—, mem. Young Assocs. of Women's Assn., 1981—, treas., 1985, mem. numerous coms., chmn. property acquisitions for auction Columbus Symphony Orch. League, 1985—, mem. social com., 1984-85; active mem. Condr.'s Club, 1983—; charter mem. Zephyrus League Central Ohio Lung Assn., 1983—, chmn. various coms.; pub. relations chmn. Columbus Greats We Love Exec. Com., 1984-85. Recipient meritorious commendation Doctors Hosp. West, 1978. Roman Catholic. Avocations: china painting; playing piano; water skiing; ceramics; dancing. Home: 4620 Elan Ct Columbus OH 43220

ZANINI, DEBRA JUST, textile personnel analyst and consultant; b. Chgo., Feb. 28, 1960; d. Jim P. and Susan Mary (Piotrowski) Just; m. Andrew Joseph Zanini, Dec. 14, 1985. Student schs. Clearwater, Fla. Cons. Just Mgmt. Services, Clearwater, to present. Active Republican Nat. Com. Mem. Nat. Assn. Female Execs. Office: Just Mgmt Services Inc PO Box 207 Clearwater FL 33517

ZANNETOS, CLOTILDE CHAVES, college administrator; b. Cambridge, Mass., June 20, 1936; d. Americo and Irene (Beers) Chaves; m. Zenon S. Zannetos, June 23, 1956; children—Cynthia Zannetos Peltier, Ianthe T., Christopher Z., Stephen S. B.S., Simmons Coll., 1958. Asst. to pres. Regis Coll., Weston, Mass., 1980, dir. 1980-84, v.p. resources and planning, 1984—. Contbr. articles to profl. jours. Fundraiser Sen. Edward M. Kennedy, Boston, 1980. Mem. Women in Devel. (mem. exec. bd. 1983—), Nat. Soc. Fundraisers, Mass. Soc. Fundraisers, Council for the Advancement and Support of Edn., Soc. Coll. and Univ. Planners. Greek Orthodox Christian. Clubs: Hellenic Women's (Boston). Avocations: gourmet cooking; needlecraft. Home: 164 Country Dr Weston MA 02193

ZANOPOULO, JOANNA SOTIRI, market research company executive, real estate developer; b. Alexandria, Egypt, Mar. 26, 1950; came to U.S., 1969, naturalized, 1985; d. Stavro Michaelidis and Mary (Iliadis); m. Sotiri B. Zanopoulo, June 9, 1973; children—Byron, Stephanie. B.A., Douglass Coll., Rutgers U., 1973; M.B.A., Fairleigh Dickinson U., 1978. Mktg. trainee Am. Cyanamid, Stamford, Conn., 1973-74, tech. sales rep. Cy/Ro div., Wallingford, Conn., 1974-78; v.p. Signet Research, Scarsdale, N.Y., 1978-80, pres., chmn. bd., Cliffside Park, N.J., 1980—; v.p. Sibco, Inc., Cliffside Park, 1984—, also dir. Named Nat. Salesperson of Yr., Cyro Industries, 1977. Mem. Am. Mktg. Assn., Mktg. Research Dir. Assn., Mktg. Research Assn., Philoptochos Archidiocesan Soc. Greek Orthodox. Avocations: tennis; opera. Office: Signet Research Inc 613 Anderson Ave Cliffside Park NJ 07010

ZANOTTI, DAWN MARIE, retail chain executive; b. Quincy, Mass., Dec. 3, 1961; d. Donald John and Lorelei Elena (Perry) Z. B.A. in Econs., U. N.H., 1984. Polit. research asst. Nat. Assn. Mfrs., Washington, 1983; dept. mgr. Bradlees, Somerville, Mass., 1984—. Mem. Nat. Assn. Female Execs., Omicron Delta Epsilon, Phi Chi Theta. Democrat. Roman Catholic. Avocations: tennis; racquetball; writing. Home: 128 Cain Ave Braintree MA 02184 Office: Bradlees 180 Somerville Ave Somerville MA 02143

ZAPATA, CELIA CORREAS, Hispanic literature educator; b. Mendoza, Argentina; married; children—Carol, Martin. B.A. summa cum laude, Escuela Normal, Tomas Gody Cruz, Mendoza, 1951; B.A. summa cum laude, U. Cuyo, Mendoza, 1965; Ph.D. summa cum laude in Hispanic Literatures, U. Calif.-Irvine, 1971. Instr. Spanish, Santa Ana Jr. Coll., Calif., 1964-65; assoc. Spanish, U. Calif.-Irvine, 1965-68; educator in Hispanic literature San Jose State U., Calif., 1969—, prof., 1978—; participant seminars in field; assoc. editor San Studies, 1978-83; dir. Com. Inter-Am. Women Writers, 1976. Author: Cantos, 1968; Cruz del Sur, 1976; Ensayos Hispanoamericanos, 1978; Tiempo Ajeno, 1980; Detrás de la Reja, 1980; El Trascender Cristiano en la Poética de Leopoldo Panero, 1983; numerous poems, short stories. Contbr. articles, revs. to profl. publs. Founding mem. Council Latin Am. Studies, Calif. State U. System, 1978; juror Hispanic Narrative and Poetry Contest, Instituto Literario y Cultural Hispanico, Chapman Coll., Orange, Calif., 1980; panelist, reviewer NEH, 1981—; mem. com. Mex. Am. Heritage of Santa Clara County, 1982; spl. guest Third Conf. Inter-Am. Women Writers, Universidad Autonoma de Mex., 1981; invited guest Library of Congress, Washington, 1978. Mem. Assn. Tchrs. of Spanish and Portuguese, Pacific Coast Council on Latin Am. Studies, Phological Assn. of Pacific Coast, Ctr. Inter-Am. Women Writers (founder), Latin Am. Studies Assn., Council of Latin Am. Studies. Office: San Jose State U Fgn Lang Dept Washington Sq San Jose CA 95192

ZARNEGAR, ZOHREH TAHEREH, medical educator, researcher, psychologist; b. Ghazvin, Iran, Aug. 27, 1951; d. Gholam-Ali and Esmat (Sadband) Z. B.A. in Psychology, Tehran U. (Iran), 1972; M.A. in Psychology, Mich. State U., 1976; Ph.D. in Ednl. Psychology, U. So. Calif., 1982. Research asst. UNESCO, Tehran, 1969-73; asst. dir. tribal mobile libraries Inst. Intellectual Devel. of Children and Young Adults, Tehran, 1973-74; asst. prof. Tchrs. U., Tehran, 1972-74; pvt. practice research cons., Los Angeles, 1976—; clin. asst. prof. U. So. Calif. Sch. Medicine, Los Angeles, 1981-85, student counselor, 1981-85; asst. v.p. Security Pacific Corp., 1984-85, fin. coordinator, research assoc., 1985—. asst. psychologist Razi Mental Hosp., Tehran, 1970-72; speaker in field. Author: (with Ahmad Fattahi Pour) Theories of Adult Education, 1973. Scholar U. Tehrean, 1968-72, 75-80. Fellow Am. Ednl. Research Assn.; mem. Am. Psychol. Assn., Am. Studies Assn., Union of Concerned Scientists, N.Y. Acad. Scis., Bus. Vols. for Arts. Office: H16-70 333 S Hope Los Angeles CA 90071

ZARRELLA, NANCY FAY CHATMAS, department store executive; b. Marlin, Tex., Aug. 25, 1950; d. James George and Fay Pauline (Nunley) Chatmas; m. John Michael Zarrella, Sept. 5, 1981. B.S., U. Tex., 1972. Asst. Buyer exec. tng. program Joske's Dept. Stores, Dallas, 1972, buyer misses sportswear, 1973; buyer sportswear Dillard's, Ft. Worth, 1974-78; buyer jr. sportswear Margo's, Dallas, 1978-82, div. mdse. mgr. intimate apparel and shoes, 3 Beall Bros., Dallas, 1982—; pres., ptnr. Rentex Property Mgmt., Inc., 1985—; ptnr., owner Zarrella & Assocs., Dallas, 1981—; bd. dirs. DFW Rand Group, Inc., Dallas, 1983-84, membership chmn., 1983-84, social chmn., 1983-85. Bd. dirs. Dallas aux. Edna Gladney Ctr., 1986—, asst. pub. relations chair, 1986—. Office: Zarrella & Assocs PO Box 225071 Dallas TX 75265

ZARRO, JANICE ANNE, lawyer; b. Newark, June 30, 1947; d. Samuel James and Elma Dora (Monaco) Zarro; m. Bobby Charles Wood, Nov. 7, 1977. B.A., Rutgers U., 1969; J.D., Chgo.-Kent Coll. Law, 1973. Bar: Pa. 1974. Counsel Jud. Com. House of Reps., Washington, 1973-77; counsel, mem. profl. staff Senate Labor Human Resources Com., Washington, 1977-80; dir. fed. affairs Avon Products, Inc., N.Y.C., 1980-81, Washington, 1982—; mem. legis. affairs com. Health Industry Mfrs. Assn., Washington, 1983—; chmn. subcom. on compliance Direct Selling Assn., Washington, 1983—, mem. govt. relations com., 1980—; mem. adv. bd. Congl. Hispanic Caucus, Washington, 1983. Bd. dirs. YMCA Met. Washington, 1978-80, fundraiser, 1977-83, mem. personnel com., 1980—, chmn. personnel com. 1978-80; bd. dirs. Children's Found., 1985—. Mem. ABA, Pa. Bar Assn., Woman Bus. Com. Overseas Edn. Fund, Women in Govt. Relations. Roman Catholic. Office: Avon Products Inc 1660 L St NW Suite 915 Washington DC 20036

ZATZKIS, ANDREA BETH, metaphysician, counselor-consultant, researcher, photographer; b. Shreveport, La., July 10, 1944; d. Isadore and Min (Frumer) Horowitz; div. 1971; 1 child, Scott. Student U. Miami, Coral Gables, Fla., 1962-63, IBM Sch., 1963, La. State U., 1966-67, Esalen Inst., Big Sur, Calif., 1979-85; Ph.B., Internat. Inst. Metapsychology, 1979. Ordained to ministry (non-denominational), 1979. IBM operator paleontology dept. Chevron Oil Co., New Orleans, 1963; ad exec. A.R. Agy. and Mag., New Orleans, 1966; investment advisor Landy Investment Co., Dallas, Shreveport, New Orleans, 1966-78; employment mgr., exec. pub. relations O.T.I. Services, New Orleans, 1969-71; entertainment exec. Rivertown Prodns., New Orleans, San Diego, Dallas, 1969-76; employment exec., pres., owner Helix Employment Agy., San Diego; metaphys. cons., researcher, lectr. Internat. Assn. Metapsychology, San Diego, 1979—; counselor-cons. holistic healing, nutrition, astrology, cartology, clairvoyance, psychometry, others; cons. forensic investigations, med. doctors and lawyers; parapsychol. researcher and cons., U.S. and abroad. Vol. hosp. and hospice work, aged, victims and families of victims of violent crimes. Mem. Internat. Promoters Assn., Nat. Mgmt. Assn., Communicating Arts Group, Internat. Assn. Metapsychology, Nat. Assn. Female Execs., Smithsonian Assocs., Sigma Delta Tau. Avocations: photography; writing; trapshooting; bicycling; fishing. Office: PO Box 2109 Del Mar CA 92014 also Astrology Counseling Ctr 1545 S Wells Ave #202 Reno NV 89502

ZAWISLAK, BARBARA JOAN, communication systems executive; b. Mpls., Oct. 24, 1939; d. Theodore Raymond and Josephine Dorothy (Traczyk) Z.; Various positions Northwestern Bank, Mpls., 1957-65; clerical coordinator Graco, Inc., Mpls., 1965-70; v.p. Leasing Services, Inc., Mpls., 1970-81; dir. personnel, comptroller M & W Inc., Mpls., 1971-81; pres., owner Arklo Distbrs. Inc., Mpls., 1977—; treas. Micro Communication Systems, Inc., Mpls., 1982—; pvt. cons. personnel and fin. Writer romance, mystery novels. Bd. dirs., v.p., librarian, treas. Al-Anon, St. Mary's Rehab. Center; sec., adv. bd. St. Mary's Rehab. Center. Club: Breakfast Club Mpls. Home: Minneapolis MN 55432 Office: Minneapolis MN 55432

ZAYACHEK, MARY KATHERINE, hospital administrator, nurse; b. Jersey City, Aug. 18, 1943; d. Chester Charles and Olga Pauline (Miko) Fabian; m. Jon Martin Zayachek, Sept. 24, 1966; children—Lea, Keith, Joel. B.S., Russell Sage Coll., 1965; M.Mgmt., Southwestern U., 1985. R.N., N.J. Charge nurse St. Barnabas Med. Ctr., Livingston, N.J., 1965-66; nurse critical care Spohn Hosp., Corpus Christi, Tex., 1966-67, Overlook Hosp., Summit, N.J., 1968-74; clin. instr. Passaic County Community Coll., Paterson, N.J., 1975-76, Clara Maass Sch. Nursing, Belleville, N.J., 1975; asst. adminstr. Mountainside Hosp., Montclair, N.J., 1976-80, utilization supr. quality assurance, 1980-85, asst. adminstr., 1985-86, asst. v.p., 1986—; guest lectr. William Paterson Coll., Wayne, N.J., 1978. Guest cons. nursing mag. Bd. dirs. Health Adv. Bd., Montclair, 1981-83; sec. PTA Council, Montclair; v.p. PTA, Grove St. Sch., Montclair. Mem. Nat. Assn. Quality Assurance Profls. (cert.), N.J. Assn. Quality Assurance Profls. (north region rep., chmn. nominating com., treas. 1983-85, nominating com. 1985—). Roman Catholic. Avocations: sailing; jogging; aerobic dance. Office: Mountainside Hosp Bay and Highland Ave Montclair NJ 07042

ZAYDON, JEMILLE ANN, educator; b. Peckville, Pa., Feb. 21, 1940; d. Joseph and Catherine Ann (Hazzouri) Z.; student Barry Coll. for Women, 1957-59; B.S., Marywood Coll., 1963; M.S. in Edn., Wilkes Coll., 1978; doctoral candidate Temple U. Tchr. St. Hugh Elementary Sch., Coconut Grove, Fla., 1963-64; Allapattah Elementary Sch., Miami, 1964-65, Columbus Elementary Sch., Westfield, N.J., 1965-66; communications instr. Keystone Job Corps, Drums, Pa., 1966-73; vol. instr. Keystone Rehab. Center, Scranton, Pa., 1970-71; curriculum cons. for mentally retarded, Vienna, Austria, 1974; prof. English and reading Lackawanna Jr. Coll., Scranton, 1974—, head dept. English, speech and reading, 1976—, chmn. dept. arts, humanities and social studies, 1977—; prof. English, U. Scranton, 1981—; communications instr. Lackawanna County Vocat. Tech. Sch., 1974—. Supr. recreation program, Hazleton, Pa., summer 1968; founder, adviser Keystone Kourier, 1967-69. Sec. Fedn. Youth, William W. Scranton, 1963; supr. students Heart Fund campaign, 1968-71; developer program mentally retarded Allied Services for Handicapped Scranton, 1973; Class rep. Marywood Coll. Fund Dr., 1978; active ARC, March of Dimes, Heart Fund, Leukemia and United Fund drives, also Sickle Cell Anemia Found. Bd. dirs. Michael F. Harrity Meml. Fund., 1969-73; mem. exec. bd. Northeastern Pa. Environ. Council, also co-chmn. public edn. and funding. Recipient Staff Mem. of Year award, Job Corps, 1969, Humanitarian award, 1980; Educators award Dade County, 1973, 75; named Tchr. of Yr., 1973; Service scholar, Barry Coll., 1958; Mem. Nat., Pa. State edn. assns., Beta Lambda Tau, Sigma Tau Delta, Theta Chi Beta (charter pres. 1961-63), Lambda Iota Tau (life). Democrat. Roman Catholic (instr. Confraternity Christian Doctrine 1956-71). Editor Lebanese Am. Jour., 1957-63. Home: 608 N Main Ave Scranton PA 18504

ZBOROWSKI, BEVERLY JEAN, civic worker; b. Gary, Ind., Apr. 23, 1948; d. Stephan Joseph and Mary Helen (Petrovich) Soohey; m. Joseph Richard Zborowski, Aug. 10, 1968; children—Annemarie Nicole, Natalie Joelle, Nicholas Joseph. B.S., Ind. U., 1970; M.S., Purdue U., 1975. Life lic. in elem. edn., Ind. Elem. tchr. Portage Twp. Schs., Ind., 1970-73; pres. Country Neighbors chpt. Porter County Extension Homemakers, Hebron, Ind., 1981-83; 1st pres. elected bd. Porter Twp. Sch. Bd., 1982-85; sec. Porter County Vocat. Edn. Com., Ind., 1984—. Mem. Sigma Beta (sec. Gamma Rho chpt. 1982-84). Republican. Roman Catholic. Avocations: gourmet cooking; photography; creative needlework; reading. Office: Porter Twp Sch Corp 208 S 725 W Hebron IN 46341

ZDUNCZYK, ELIZABETH ELEANOR, real estate company executive; b. Torrington, Conn., Sept. 16, 1910; d. John Walter and Rose (Kukulka) Klemba; m. Joseph Anthony Zdunczyk, Nov. 17, 1934; children—Elizabeth Ann, David Thomas. Student pub. schs. Waterbury and Southington, Conn. Mem. Conn. Ho. of Reps., 1950-54; tax collector Bd. Tax Rev., City of Southington, 1965-82; pres. E-Z Real Estate, Southington, 1960—; Democratic party nominee for Conn. Sec. of State, 1955; dir. Southington Savs. and Loan Assn. Chmn. bloodmobile, vol. canteen Southington ARC, 1950-83; bd. dirs., 1960—; pres. Bradley Meml. Hosp. Aux., 1957-58; chmn. jury commn. Southington, 1963-69; vice-chmn. Southington Dem. Town Com., 1964—; mem. Dem. State Central Com., 1972—. Recipient Gold medal Unico Club, 1955. Roman Catholic.

ZEANAH, PAULA LYNN DOYLE, nurse; b. Anderson, S.C., Dec. 20, 1952; d. Robert Hugh and Phyllis Ann (Cliver) Doyle; R.N., Piedmont Hosp., 1973; B.S. in Nursing, Med. Coll. Ga., 1975; M.Sc. in Nursing, U. Va., 1979; m. Charles H. Zeanah, Jr., Nov. 3, 1979; 1 dau., Emily Hunter. Staff nurse pediatric ICU Grady Hosp., Atlanta, 1973-75; pediatric nurse practitioner Dekalb-Grady Clinic, Atlanta, 1976-77; head nurse pediatric clinic Duke U. Med. Center, 1979-80; inservice coordinator Children's Hosp., Stanford, Calif., 1980-81, acting dir. nursing, 1981-82, inservice coordinator, 1982—. Mem. Am. Nurses Assn., Nat. League Nursing, Nat. Assn. Pediatric Nurse Assocs. and Practitioners, Assn. Care of Children's Health, AAAS. Democrat. Office: Children's Hosp 520 Willow Rd Palo Alto CA 94304

ZEBOOKER, NINA, manufacturing executive, artist; b. Phila., May 13, 1954; d. Eli Philip and Janet (Reibstein) Zebooker; m. William Frank Ephraim, May 9, 1982. B.F.A., R.I. Sch. Design, 1976. Ptnr., Best Friend Products, Phila., 1977—. Mem. Am. Pet Products Mfrs. Assn., Pet Industry Joint Adv. Council. Office: Best Friend Products 940 New Market St Philadelphia PA 19123

ZEDEK, MARGARET, travel agent; b. San Francisco, Apr. 28, 1935; d. Everett Floyd and Dorothy (Asbury) Teeters; m. Frank Anthony Zedek, Sept. 8, 1957; children—Theresa, Frank Jr., Stacy, David. A.A., San Francisco City Coll., 1954; student Coll. Marin, 1965. Supr. news bur. Pacific Telephone & Telegraph Co., San Francisco, 1953-62; asst. to pres. Hurricane Internat., San Francisco, 1964-67; sec. Firemans Fund, San Rafael, Calif., 1972-78; travel agt., owner, pres. Dimensions in Travel, Inc., Novato, Calif., 1978—, West Wind Travel, San Rafael, 1984—. Active St. Vincent's Sch., Marin Forum. Mem. Assn. Retail Travel Agts., Am. Soc. Travel Agts. Democrat. Roman Catholic. Office: West Wind Travel 910 Irwin St San Rafael CA 94901

ZEE, CAROL ANN, systems and energy company executive; b. Los Angeles, June 24, 1951; d. Zygmund John and Helen (Brasky) Z.; B.A. in Chemistry, Occidental Coll., 1973. Mem. tech. staff TRW Electronics and Def. Sector, TRW Inc., Redondo Beach, Calif., 1974-78, sect. head, project mgr., 1978-80, mem. mgmt. team satellite-to-satellite laser communication system, 1980-84; asst. chief engr. Systems Engring. and Devel. Div., 1985—. Active local politics and coastal land use planning issues. Mem. Am. Chem. Soc., Soc. Women Engrs., AIAA. Contbr. articles on environ. impact of hazardous waste disposal and synfuel technologies to profl. jours. Home: 432 1st St Manhattan Beach CA 90266 Office: TRW One Space Park 134/10831 Redondo Beach CA 90278

ZEEMAN, JOAN JAVITS, writer, inventor; b. N.Y.C., Aug. 17, 1928; d. Benjamin Abraham and Lily (Braxton) Javits; m. John Huibert Zeeman III, Mar. 20, 1954; children—Jonathan, Andrea Zeeman Deane, Eloise Zeeman Scharff, Phoebe, Merrily Margaret. B.A., Vassar Coll., 1949; M.Ed., U. Vt., 1976. Pub. relations exec. Benjamin Sonnenberg, N.Y.C., 1949-51; freelance writer, 1952—. Bd. dirs. Performing Arts Repertory Theatre, N.Y.C., 1953-83. Author: The Compleat Child, 1964. Lyricist musical plays: Young Abe Lincoln, 1961; Hotel Passionato, 1965; song lyricist: Santa Baby, 1953. Patentee Alphocube. Trustee Profl. Children's Sch. Mem. ASCAP, Dramatists Guild. Club: Vassar (sec. 1978-84, v.p. 1984—) (Westchester, N.Y.). Home and Office: 520 Hommocks Rd Larchmont NY 10538

ZEHNER, JEAN COLGAN, chemist; b. Donora, Pa., July 12, 1919; d. Howard Oliver and Garnett Farquhar (Colvin) Colgan; A.B., Wilson Coll., 1941; m. Lisle A. Zehner, Jr., Mar. 14, 1941; 1 son, Lisle A. III. Fellow, Mellon Inst. Indsl. Research, Pitts., 1941-58; dir. testing bur. May Dept. Stores, Pitts., 1958-75, v.p. consumer affairs, 1975—; mem. adv. council U.S. Consumer Product Safety Commn.; mem. tech. and consumer affairs coms. Nat. Retail Mchts. Assn. Trustee Wilson Coll., 1970—; bd. dirs. Easter Seal Soc., 1963-79. Named Woman of Yr., Pitts. Advt. Club, 1969. Mem. Pa. C. of C. (dir. 1978—), Am. Chem. Soc., Am. Assn. Textile Technology, Soc. Consumer Affairs Profls., Am. Assn. Textile Chemists and Colorists, Pitts. Advt. Club. Democrat. Presbyterian. Clubs: N.Y. Chemists, 20th Century, Pitts. Coll. Office: 400 5th Ave Pittsburgh PA 15219

ZEIGLER, JEANINE BAHRAM PATTON, guidance counselor; b. Chgo., Nov. 9, 1928; d. Lester H. and Florence (Toney) Bahram; B.A., Mich. State U., 1965, M.A., 1969; m. Daniel J. Patton, Jr. (dec.); children—Daniel J., Deborah J., Denise J.; m. 2d, Lamar Henry Zeigler, June 19, 1971. Successively elementary tchr., sch. social worker, elementary sch. prin. Battle Creek (Mich.) public schs., 1965-77; guidance counselor So. U., New Orleans, 1977—, asst. prof., Chmn. bd. dirs. Bethany Day Care Center, New Orleans, 1978—; hon. chmn. Battle Creek Cancer Crusade, 1976; bd. dirs. Y Center, Battle Creek, 1974-77. Recipient various service awards. Mem. Assn. Supervision and Curriculum Devel., Am. Personnel and Guidance Assn., Am. Coll. Personnel Assn., Am. Assn. Non-White Concerns, AAUW (pres. Battle Creek br. 1974-76 membership v.p. La. div. 1981—, pres. New Orleans br. 1984-86, nat. membership com., pres. La. div. 1986), La Assn. Coll. and Univ. Student Personnel Adminstrs., Urban League, Nat. Council Negro Women (bd. dirs.), Moneychangers Investment Club (pres. 1981—), Delta Sigma Theta. Methodist. Clubs: Nat. Smart Set, Internat. Y Men's (New Orleans). Office: 6400 Press Dr New Orleans LA 70126

ZEILINGER, ELNA RAE, educator; b. Tempe, Ariz., Mar. 24, 1937; d. Clayborn Eddie and Ruby Elna (Laird) Simpson; B.A. in Edn., Ariz. State U., 1958, M.A. in Edn., 1966, Ed.S., 1980; m. Philip Thomas Zeilinger, June 13, 1970; children—Shari, Chris. Bookkeeper, First Nat. Bank of Tempe, 1955-56; with registrar's office Ariz. State U., 1956-58; piano tchr., recreation dir. City of Tempe, tchr. Thew Sch., Tempe, 1958-61, elem. tchr. Mitchell Sch., 1962-74, intern prin., 1976, personnel intern, 1977; specialist in gifted edn. Tempe Elem. Schs., 1977—; grad. asst. ednl. adminstrn., Iota Workshop coordinator Ariz. State U., 1978; presenter Ariz. Gifted Conf., 1978-81, Nat. Assn. Gifted Children, Phila., 1983; condr. survey of gifted programs, 1980; reporter public relations Tempe Sch. Dist., 1978-80, Access com. for gifted programs, 1981-83, dist. adv. com. to gifted program 1982-84. Freedom Train com. Ariz. Bicentennial Commn., 1975-76. Named Outstanding Leader in Elem. and Secondary Schs., 1976 Ariz. Cattle Growers scholar, 1954-55; Elks scholar, 1954-55; recipient Judges award Tempe Art League, 1970, Best of Show, Scottsdale Art League, 1976. Mem. Council Exceptional Children, Ariz. Assn. Gifted and Talented, Ariz. Sch. Adminstrs., Tempe Hist. Assn. (liaison 1975), Scottsdale Artists League, Tempe Art League, Am. Bus. Women's Assn. (Woman of Yr., Tierra del Sol chpt. 1983), Tempe Edn. Assn. (sec. 1983-84), Phi Kappa Phi, Pi Lambda Theta, Kappa Delta Pi, Phi Delta Kappa, Kappa Delta. Democrat. Congregationalist. Club: Eastern Star. Author: Leadership Role of the Principal in Gifted Programs: A Handbook, 1980; Classified Personnel Handbook, 1977, also reports and monographs. Home: 610 E Colgate St Tempe AZ 85283 Office: 1975 E Cornell St Tempe AZ 85283

ZEITLAN, MARILYN LABB, lawyer; b. N.Y.C., Sept. 17, 1938; d. Charles and Florence Labb; m. Barrett M. Zeitlan, Apr. 14, 1957; children—Adam, Daniel. B.A., Queens Coll., 1958, M.S., 1970; J.D. (fellow 1976), Hofstra U., 1978. Bar: N.Y. 1979. Tchr., N.Y.C., 1958-61; Sole practice, N.Y., 1979—. Contbr. articles to profl. jours. Commr./chairperson East Hills Environ. Com. (N.Y.), 1971-74, 74-75; v.p. League Women Voters, Roslyn, N.Y., 1974-75; co-founder Roslyn Environ. Assn., 1970. Assoc. editor Hofstra Law Rev., 1976-78. Mem. ABA N.Y. State Bar Assn. Nassau County Bar Assn. (matrimonial com.), Nassau-Suffolk Women's Bar Assn., Phi Beta Kappa. Office: Marilyn L Zeitlan Esq 98 Cutter Mill Rd Great Neck NY 11021

ZEKMAN, TERRI MARGARET, graphic designer; b. Chgo., Sept. 13, 1950; d. Theodore Nathan and Lois (Bernstein) Z.; B.F.A., Washington U., St. Louis, 1971; postgrad. Art Inst. Chgo., 1974-75; m. Alan Daniels, Apr. 12, 1980. Graphic designer (on retainer) Recycled Paper Products, Chgo., 1970—; apprenticed graphic designer Helmuth, Obata & Kassabaum, St. Louis, 1970-71; graphic designer Container Corp., Chgo., 1971; graphic designer/art dir./photographer Cuerden Advt. Design, Denver, 1971-74; art dir. Darcy, McManus & Masius Advt., Chgo., 1975-76; freelance graphic designer Image Response Design Firm, Goldsmith, Yamasaki & Specht Design, Playboy Enterprises, Chgo., 1976-77; art dir. Garfield Linn Advt., Chgo., 1977-78; graphic designer Keiser Design Group, Van Noy & Co., Los Angeles, 1978-79; owner Graphic Design Studio, Los Angeles, 1979—. Recipient cert. of merit St. Louis Outdoor Poster Contest, 1970, Denver Art Dirs. Club, 1973.

ZELASKO, NANCY FABER, university administrator; b. N.Y.C., June 4, 1951; d. Robert David and Elaine Margaret (Affleck) Faber; B.S. in Linguistics, Georgetown U., Washington, 1973, M.S. in Sociolinguistics, 1975, Ph.D. candidate, Georgetown U.; m. Franciszek Jozef Zelasko, Nov. 28, 1975. Substitute tchr. D.C. Public Schs., 1973-74, research asst. div. bilingual edn., 1974-76, program specialist, 1976-78, acting adminstrv. officer, 1978-79, project dir. bilingual tng. grant, 1979-80; asst. dir. Georgetown U. Bilingual Edn. Service Center, 1980—; co-chair 12th Ann. Internat. Bilingual Bicultural Edn. Conf., 1983; cons. sch. dists. Recipient outstanding performance rating D.C. Public Schs., 1978-79. Mem. Nat. Assn. Female Execs., TESOL, D.C. Assn. Bilingual Edn. (pres. 1981-83), Nat. Assn. Bilingual Edn. (spl. recognition award 1979-80, sec. 1984-85, treas. 1985-86). Editor NABE News, 1981—. Office: Suite 100 2139 Wisconsin Ave NW Washington DC 20007

ZELAZNY, CLAUDIA DENE, small business owner; lecturer; b. Denver, Sept 28, 1945; d. Robert W. and Ila Dene (Bittick) Arrendiell; m. Charles Leslie Zelazny, June 25, 1967; 1 child, Kelsey Joy. B.S., U. Tex., 1967. Tchr., Dallas Pub. Schs., 1967-71; adminstrv. asst. Jewish Welfare Fedn., Dallas, 1978-79; publicist BSI, Inc., Dallas, 1979-80; pres. The Clarry Corp., Dallas, 1980—. Fitness columnist Park Cities News, Park Cities People. Bd. dirs. Younger Set, Dallas, 1971-77, service v.p., 1976; bd. dirs. Jewish Welfare Fedn., Dallas, 1973-77; mem. Young Women's Leadership Cabinet, N.Y.C., 1977; chair Israel Task Force Community Relations Council, Dallas, 1980. Mem. I.D.E.A.S. Jewish. Avocations: travel; reading; gardening; bird-watching; shell collecting. Home: 4217 Melissa Ln Dallas TX 75229 Office: Clarry Corp 4420 Lovers Ln Dallas TX 75225

ZELCER, LOLY, neckwear company executive; b. Havana, Cuba, Oct. 2, 1935; came to U.S., 1960, naturalized, 1965; d. Zizie and Hela (Kodner) Shaftal; m. Isaac Zelcer; children—Alan, Elena, Robin. Exec. Isaco Internat. Corp., Miami, Fla. Home: 1215 N Biscayne Point Rd Miami Beach FL 33141 Office: Isaco Internat Corp 228 NE 2d St Miami FL 33132

ZELENY, MARJORIE PFEIFFER (MRS. CHARLES ELLINGSON ZELENY), psychologist; b. Balt., Mar. 31, 1924; d. Lloyd Armitage and Mable (Willian) Pfeiffer; B.A., U. Md., 1947; M.S., U. Ill., 1949, postgrad., 1951-54; m. Charles Ellingson Zeleny, Dec. 11, 1950 (dec.); children—Ann Douglas, Charles Timberlake. Vocational counseling psychologist VA, Balt., 1947-48; asst. U. Ill. at Urbana, 1948-50, research asso. Bur. Research, 1952-53; chief psychologist dept. neurology and psychiatry Ohio State U. Coll. Medicine, Columbus, 1950-51; research psychologist, cons., Tucson, Washington, 1954—. Mem. Am., D.C. psychol. assns., A.A.A.S., Soc. for Psychol. Study Social Issues, D.A.R., Mortar Bd., Delta Delta Delta, Sigma Delta Epsilon, Psi Chi, Sigma Tau Epsilon. Roman Catholic. Home: 6825 Wemberly Way McLean VA 22101

ZELEPSKY, ANNETTE MARIE, data processing executive; b. Fort Wayne, Ind., Aug. 9, 1958; d. Paul Joseph and Catherine Anne (Amato) Findlay; m. Sept. 26, 1981 (div. Dec. 1985); 1 child, Jacqueline Anne. B.S. in Mgmt., U. Akron, 1980, Assoc. Applied Sci. in Data Processing, 1978. Student system programmer U. Akron Computer Ctr., Ohio, 1977-80; system programmer Diebold, Inc., North Canton, Ohio, 1980-81; mgr. operating systems Central Nat. Bank, Cleve., 1981-85; mgr. system software AAA Mich., Dearborn, 1985—; project officer Share/TSM project, Chgo., 1985—; tutor Akron/Summit Tutorial Program, 1977. Mem. Nat. Assn. Female Execs. Avocations: jazzercise; sports cars. Home: 12450 Will Mill Dr Brighton MI 48116 Office: AAA Mich 1 Auto Club Dr Dearborn MI 48126

ZELL, DOLORES PFAFFENDORF, educational administrator; b. Miami, Fla., July 13, 1944; d. George and Pearl (Watford) Pfaffendorf; B.S. in Edn., William Carey Coll., 1969; M.A. in Coll. Personnel Adminstrn., U. Miami, 1971, postgrad., 1977—; m. Don Richard Zell, Aug. 16, 1969. Placement dir. William Carey Coll., Hattiesburg, Miss., 1967-69; asst. dir. Pearson Hall, U. Miami (Fla.), 1969-70; customer service rep. Burdines, Miami, 1970-76; tchr. A.L. Lewis Elem. Sch., Miami Public Schs., 1970-75, area coordinator sch. vol. program, 1975-77, tchr. R.R. Moton Elem. Sch., 1979-80, Coral Reef Elem. Sch., 1979; asst. prin. Opa Locka Elem. Sch., Dade County (Fla.) Public Schs., 1980-81, Vineland and Bel Aire Elem. Sch., 1983-84; legis. aide state rep. Dexter Lehtinen, Fla., 1981—; adj. prof. Fla. Internat. U., Miami-Dade Community Coll. Coordinator Lehtinen legis. campaign, 1978, 80. Tchr. Sunday Sch., Bapt. Ch.; officer Young Democrats; mem. S. Dade Democratic Club. Mem. Dade County Sch. Adminstrs. Assn., Am. Bus. Women's Assn., Assn. Elem. Sch. Prins., Assn. Supervision and Curriculum Devel., Internat. Reading Assn., Nat. Sch. Vol. Program, Inc., S. Dade Reading Council, Phi Delta Kappa. Club: Briar Bay. Contbr. articles in field to profl. jours. Home: 13323 SW 103 Pl Miami FL 33176 Office: 18 House Office Bldg The Capitol Tallahassee FL 32301

ZELLEM, SUZANNE, nurse administrator; b. Hollis, N.Y., Apr. 25, 1955; d. Charles and Mary Irene (Bonin) Welch; m. Ronald Theodore Zellem, July 30, 1977. B.S. in Nursing, Molloy Coll., Rockville Centre, N.Y., 1977; postgrad. Villanova U. (Pa.), 1984—. Staff nurse II Emory U. Hosp., Atlanta, 1978-80; staff nurse Roxborough Meml. Hosp., Phila., 1980; nurse practitioner U. Pa., Phila., 1981; instr. nursing Presbyterian Sch. Nursing, Phila., 1981-84; program developer, div. edn. and research Hahnemann U. Hosp., Phila., 1984—. Mem. Am. Nurses Assn., Am. Assn. Neurosci. Nurses, Sigma Theta Tau. Office: Hahnemann U Hosp Dept Nursing Broad and Vine Sts Philadelphia PA 19102

ZELLERBACH, MERLA, writer; b. San Francisco, Aug. 27, 1930; d. Elliot M. and Lottie G. Burstein; m. Fred Goerner; 1 child, Gary. Free-lance writer, San Francisco, 1961—; featured columnist —My Fair City— in San Francisco Chronicle, 1962—; regular panelist Sta. ABC-TV game show —Oh My Word—, 1965-70; lectr., leader creative writing seminars. Author: The Wildes of Nob Hill, 1986; Love the Giver, 1987; Love in a Dark House, 1961; co-author: Detox, 1984; Type 1/Type 2 Allergy Relief Program, 1983. Contbr. articles to mags. Mem. adv. bd. dirs. Leukemia Soc. Am., 1975—. Office: San Francisco Chronicle San Francisco CA 94119

ZELLERS, BETTY-JANE, machinery company executive; b. Newark, Mar. 25; d. William Elmer and Marie Matilda (Steigman) Zellers. Student acctg. Rutgers U., 1955, Bloomfield Coll., 1976-82. With Abrasive Machine & Supply Co., Newark, 1947—, office mgr., 1966-68, credit mgr., 1968, corp. credit mgr., 1968—, corp. sec., v.p. fin., 1968—. Active Nat. Women's Party, 1982—; bd. dirs. Newark Day Care Center, 1971-77. Mem. N.J. Assn. Credit and Fin. Mgmt. (pres. 1974-76), N.J. Credit Women's Group (pres. 1972-74), Metals and Indsl. Supplies Group (chmn. 1971-73), Exec. Women N.J., Am. Soc. Women Accts., Greater Newark C. of C. Nat. Assn. Credit Mgmt. (legis. council 1980—), Ironbound Mfrs. Assn. (dir. 1980-83). Republican. Lutheran. Lodge: Order Eastern Star. Home: 2021 Balmoral Ave Union NJ 07083 Office: Abrasive Machine & Supply Co Inc 261 South St Newark NJ 07114

ZEMBA, DOROTHY IRENE, oil and mining company executive; b. Cuyahoga Falls, Ohio, Nov. 20, 1928; d. Raymond Clarence and Anna Frances (Knapp) Dorner; m. John Zemba, Mar. 10, 1951 (dec. Nov. 1978); children—John Raymond, Joel Dennis. Student pub. schs., Akron, Ohio. Sec. Akron Bd. Edn., 1946-47; with printing office Ohio Match Co., Wadsworth, 1947-48; payroll clk. Akron Parcel Co., 1948-50; payroll clk. Ace Rubber Co., Akron, 1950-53, acct., 1953-77; exec. v.p. Gasoil Energy, Inc., Canton, Ohio, 1977-82; corp. sec. Davage Oil & Gas Co., Phoenix, 1982—, also dir.; dir. Profile Mgmt., Inc., Canton; cons. Sq. Circle Devel. Corp., Phoenix, 1985. Mem. Nat. Assn. Female Execs., Am. Soc. Profl. and Exec. Women, Precious Moments Club, Goebel Collectors. Republican. Lutheran. Club: Riker-Bartlett (Fort Collins, Colo.). Avocations: collecting antiques, art and limited editions of pewter, glass and porcelain. Home: 6015 W Pierce St Phoenix AZ 85043

ZEMBICKI, CHRISTINE ROSE, librarian; b. Passaic, N.J., June 21, 1949; d. Edward S. and Czestawa (Skora) Z. B.A., William Paterson Coll. of N.J., 1971; M.L.S., Rosary Coll., River Forest, Ill., 1973. Circulation, interlibrary loan librarian N.J. Inst. Tech., Newark, 1973-81, head reference librarian, 1981—. Pres., Most Sacred Heart Parish Council, Wallington, N.J., 1984—. Mem. N.J. Library Assn., Roman Catholic. Office: N J Inst Tech 323 Dr Martin Luther King Jr Blvd Newark NJ 07102

ZEMEL, HELENE LEVEY, educator, career consultant; b. N.Y.C., Jan. 3, 1947; d. Theodore Abraham and Sylvia Leah (Bernbach) Levey; B.A. cum laude, Hofstra U., 1968; M.A. (teaching fellow), Queens Coll., 1972; m. Leonard S. Zemel, Nov. 27, 1974. Piano instr., concert artist, 1968-77; asst. adminstr. society, group and council activities IEEE, 1977-78, adminstr. conf. activities and publs., 1978-83; pres. Rite-Word Resume and Career Guidance Services, Forest Hills, N.Y., 1984—; instr. Adelphi Inst., Astoria, N.Y., 1985—. Mem. N.Y. League Bus. and Profl. Women (rec. sec. 1981-82, treas. 1982-83), Delta Mu Delta. Democrat. Jewish. Home and Office: 102-40 67th Rd Forest Hills NY 11375

ZEMKE, CAROL MARY, college administrator; b. Rochester, Minn., Mar. 12, 1936; d. Kenneth Norman and Anna Matilda (Evjen) Molde; m. Leonard Henry Zemke, Mar. 15, 1958; children—Thomas Leonard, Jay David. A.A., North Hennipen Coll., 1973; student Concordia Coll., 1985—. Lab. technician Mayo Clinic, Rochester, Minn., 1954-58; tchr. of arts and crafts to handicapped, Div. of Vocat. Adminstrn., Mankato, Minn., 1958-62; dir. Lutheran Ctr., U. Minn.-Mpls., 1983; dir. pub. relations Concordia Coll., St. Paul, 1983—. Author, shortstory book, 1985. Contbr. articles to profl. jours. Editor, sch. quarterly, 1983. Sec. Midway Civic and Commerce Assn., St. Paul, 1985; pres. Lutheran Women's Missionary League, Minn., 1978-82, v.p., 1974-84; chmn. promotion com. Midway Civic & Commerce Assn., 1984—; sec. Twin Cities Chpt. Religious Pub. Relations Council, Mpls., St. Paul, 1985—. Recipient Silver Angel award, Religion in Media, Hollywood, Calif., 1984, Appreciation for Promotion award Midway Civic & Commerce Assn., St. Paul, 1985. Republican. Clubs: Fed. Women's (Rapidan, Minn.) (pres. 1960-64), U. of Minn. Extension (Mpls.) (pres. 1968-70). Avocations: tennis; golfing; swimming; boating; sewing; reading. Home: 8325 33rd Ave N Minneapolis MN 55427 Office: Concordia Coll Hamline & Marshall Sts St Paul MN 55104

ZENOFF, ELYCE HOPE, legal educator; b. Milw., Feb. 2, 1930; d. Ben and Gertrude (Rothstein) Z.; m. Charles B. Ferster, May 17, 1964; children—William, Andrea, Sam, Warren. B.S., U. Wis., 1951; J.D., Northwestern U., 1954. Bar: Ill. 1954, D.C. 1968, U.S. Supreme Ct. 1961. Research atty. Am. Bar Found. Chgo., 1956-59; atty. AMA, Chgo., 1959-61; counsel U.S. Senate Subcom. on Constl. Rights, Washington, 1961-62; atty. U.S. Commn. on Civil Rights, Washington, 1962-64; faculty George Washington U., Washington, 1964—, prof. law, 1969—. Mem. ABA, D.C. Bar Assn. Democrat. Author: Mental Impairment and Legal Incompetency, 1968, Readings in Law and Psychiatry, 2d edit., 1975, Sanctions, Sentencing and Corrections, 1982. Contbr. numerous articles to profl. jours. Office: George Washington Law Sch 700 20th St NW Washington DC 20052

ZENOFF, KATHRYN E., lawyer; b. Chgo., July 30, 1946; d. A.J. and Dorothy J. (Raftenberg) Z.; m. Arthur Rettig, July 30, 1972; children—Rebecca Lauren, Max Louis. B.A. cum laude, Stanford U., 1968; J.D., Columbia U., 1971. Bar: N.Y. 1972, Ill. 1972. Assoc. Aranow, Bordsky, Bohlinger, Benetar & Einhorn, N.Y.C., 1971-75, Zenoff, Westler & Zenoff, Chgo., 1975-77; asst. states atty. Cook County, Ill., Chgo., 1977-78; chief juvenile (asst. states atty.) Winnebago County, Rockford, Ill., 1982—; part-time instr. in law Ill. Inst. Tech., Chgo. Kent Coll. Law, 1976-77; vol. atty. Child Adv. Assn. Chgo., 1976-77, Community Law Office, Harlem, N.Y.C., 1971-74. Bd. dirs. Local Planning Bd. Youth Services, Rockford, 1984; mem. LWV, Rockford, 1981-84. Participant Internat. Fellows Program, Columbia U., 1970. Mem. Chgo. Bar Assn. (chmn. juvenile law com. 1980-81, bench bar relations com., evaluation of jud. candidates com., consumer and credit com. 1975-81), Winnebago County Bar Assn., N.Y. County Lawyers Assn. (spl. com. women's rights 1974-75).

ZEPEDA, DORA FRANCISCA, educator, businesswomen; b. Melvin, Tex., Oct. 10, 1932; d. Eulalio and Feliz (Rodriguez) Z. B.S., Howard Payne U., 1959; M.A., Tex. A&I U., 1976. Cert. tchr., Tex. Elem. tchr., Midland, Tex., 1960—. Bd. dirs. Ballet Folklorico of Midland, 1984—. Mem. West Tex. Assn. Bilingual Edn., Mex.-Am. Profl. Assn., League Latin-Am., Midland Hispanic C. of C., Nat. Assn. Female Execs., Tex. State Tchrs. Assn., NEA. Republican. Baptist. Avocations: reading; music; guitar.

ZERBO, DONNA MARIE, lawyer, accountant; b. N.Y.C., July 28, 1952; d. Albert James and Frances Rose (Piccio) LaSalvia; m. Louis Nicholas Zerbo, May 17, 1975; children—Matthew Joseph, Nicholas Louis. B.A. in Acctg. and Econs. magna cum laude, Queens Coll., 1974; J.D. cum laude, Fordham U., 1979; LL.M. in Taxation, NYU, 1985. Bar: N.Y. 1980; C.P.A., N.J. Sr. asst. tax acct. Deloitte Haskins & Sells, N.Y.C., 1974-76; lectr. bus. law, taxation and acctg. Bloomfield Coll. (N.J.), 1977-78; law clk. U.S. Dist. Ct., Newark, 1978; assoc. Cleary Gottlieb Steen & Hamilton, N.Y.C., 1979-82; assoc. Morgan Lewis & Bockius, N.Y.C., 1982-84; founding ptnr., cons. Zerbo & Co., C.P.A., Fairfield, N.J., 1983—; assoc. Cadwalader, Wickersham & Taft, N.Y.C., 1984—; researcher N.Y. State Legis. Law Revision Com., N.Y.C., 1978. Bd. dirs. Cath. Guardian Soc., 1984. Recipient Francis X. Thaddeus award Fordham U., 1979. Mem. ABA, N.Y. State Bar Assn., AAUP. Republican. Roman Catholic. Office: Cadwalader Wickersham & Taft 1 Wall St New York NY 10004

ZERKLE, WYNN THI, savings executive; b. Saigon, South Vietnam, Sept. 25, 1963; came to U.S., 1965; d. Rodger Wells and Hue T. (Pham) Wells Johnson; m. Rick T. Zerkle, May 13, 1983. Grad. high sch. Asst. mgr. Pic-A-Dilly, Fairfield, Calif., 1980-82; teller Am. Savs., Huntington Beach, Calif., 1983-84, in-br. trainer new accounts, El Cajon, Calif., 1984-85, savs. supr., 1985—. Republican. Roman Catholic. Office: Am Savs 591 Camino de la Reina San Diego CA 92108

ZETTICK, ELAINE PETUCH, marketing executive; b. Phila., Feb. 6, 1934; d. Peter Samuel and Tatiana (Losew) Petuch; m. John S. Zettick, July 26, 1952; children—Audrie L., Dorothea L. Student pub. schs., Darby Borough, Pa. Co-owner, founder Jet Spltys. Co., Levittown, Pa., 1966-80; exec. dir. Bucks County Bicentennial Com. (Pa.), 1974-77; commr., County of Bucks, Doylestown, Pa., 1980-84, chmn., 1981, 83, vice chmn., 1980, 82; pres. Zettick Mktg. Corp., 1984—. Trustee Southeastern Pa. Transp. Authority, also chmn. conflict of interest com., mem. other coms.; del. Republican Nat. Conv., 1980, mem. com. on permanent orgn.; bd. suprs. Middletown Twp. (Pa.), 1977-83, vice chmn. bd. dirs., 1979; commr. Bucks County Govt. Study Commn., 1977-78; county commr. Neshaminy Water Resources Authority, 1978-80, Bucks County Hist. Tourist Commn., 1977-80; various polit. activities including co-chmn. Coyne for Congress, 1980; chmn. People for Heinz, Buck County, 1982; bd. dirs. Del. Valley Philharm. Orch., 1965—; adv. bd. dirs. St. Mary Hosp., mem. golf tournament com., 1981, 82; bd. dirs. United Way Bucks County; past sr. adviser, past mem. nominating com. Girl Scouts U.S.A.; spl. gifts chmn. Am. Heart Assn., 1982; co-chmn. ann. dinner Bucks County Council on Alcoholism, 1981; hon. chairperson of Mother's March, March of Dimes, 1981, 82; chmn. judges com. Miss Am. Preliminary, Miss Bucks County Scholarship Pageant, 1976, 77, 78, 79; mem. ann. ball com. Lower Bucks County Hosp., 1969-79; past gen. chmn. 1st through 5th Ann Art Exhibit and Antiques Auction and 1776 Fair, Washington Crossing Found.; mem. tavern com. ann. dinner, Hist. Fallsington. Mem. Pa. State Assn. County Commrs. (legis. com. 1980, 83, chmn. 1981, exec. com. 1981, 2d v.p. 1983), Nat. Assn. Counties (human services policy steering com. 1982, 83, intergovtl. affairs and local determination steering com. 1982, 83), Nat. Conf. Rep. Ofcls., Women Ofcls., Pa. Elected Women's Assn., Splty. Advt. Assn. Internat., Advt. Splty. Inst., Am. Legion Aux., Lower Bucks County Women's Bowling Assn. (bd. dirs., parliamentarian, chmn. 1st program ad book), Central Bucks C. of C., Lower Bucks C. of C. (bd. dirs. 1971-77, 83-84, past chmn. conv. and visitor com., legis., membership, spl. projects coms.), Pennridge C. of C., Upper Bucks C. of C. Lodge: Soroptimists (Lower Bucks County). Home: 116 Forsythia Dr E Levittown PA 19056 Office: Adminstrn Bldg Doylestown PA 18901

ZICH, SUE SCHAAB, nursing administrator; b. Buffalo, Oct. 18, 1946; d. Milan Harvey and Mary Margaret (Olmsted) Schaab; B.S. in Nursing, Villa Maria Coll., 1968; m. Timothy John Zich, Nov. 25, 1976; children—John Paul Trottman, Scott Francis Trottman. Staff nurse, charge nurse, team leader Children's Hosp., Buffalo, 1968-71; staff nurse plasmapheresis unit Roswell Park Meml. Inst., Buffalo, 1971-72, 73-75; staff devel. coordinator Episcopal Ch. Home, Buffalo, 1975-77; pediatric unit charge nurse Loudoun Meml. Hosp., Leesburg, Va., 1977; nursing instr. No. Va. Mental Health Inst., Falls Church, 1977-78; dir. nursing service Barcroft Inst., Falls Church, Va., 1978—. Troop com. mem., den leader, den leader coach, dist. mem. Prince William Dist. Boy Scouts Am., day camp dir. Cub Scout Camp Tomahawk, 1983—. Recipient Key Leader award Prince William dist. Boy Scouts Am., 1982, Den Leader Tng. award, 1982, 85, award of merit, 1985. Mem. Dir. Nurses Group No. Va. (sec.-treas. 1980-81, v.p. 1981—), Nat. Campers and Hikers Assn., Friends of Nat. Zoo, Smithsonian Assocs., Met. Washington Soccer Referees Assn., Va. High Sch. League Ofcl., Villa Maria Coll. Alumnae Assn. (life, past pres. Buffalo chpt.), St. Edmund's Ladies Guild (pres. 1972-73, advisor 1973-74). Roman Catholic. Home: 9709 Evans Ford Rd Manassas VA 22111-2633 Office: 2960 Sleepy Hollow Rd Falls Church VA 22044

ZIDEK, BERNICE LOUISE (MRS. STEPHEN P. ZIDEK), wire manufacturing company executive; b. Chgo., Oct. 10, 1906; d. Albert and Bessie (Kaberna) Vonder; diploma Englewood (Ill.) Secretarial Coll., 1923; m. Stephen Paul Zidek, July 22, 1925; children—Louise Ann Zidek Pavlin, Charles Edward. Asst. to asst. mgr. Emerson Drug Co., Chgo., 1923-24; office mgr. Van Dyke Industries, Chgo., 1936-38; ptnr. Midland Metal Products Co., Chgo., 1941—. Troop leader to leader trainer Lone Tree Area council Girl Scouts U.S.A., 1938-68. Recipient Thank You award Girl Scouts U.S.A., 1957. Mem. Nat., Fla. State assns. parliamentarians, Am. Guild Flower Arrangers, Nat. Council State Garden Clubs (life), Fla. Fedn. Garden Clubs (life), Nat. Council Flower Show Judges (cert. master judge), Freedoms Found. at Valley Forge, Insight for the Blind, Inc. Republican. Roman Catholic. Clubs: Bauhinia Garden Circle (pres. 1965-67), Federated Garden Circles of Ft. Lauderdale (pres. 1974-75), Coral Springs Garden (pres. 1985-86), Moraine Valley (Ill.) Parliamentary Unit, Women's Civic Coral Ridge Yacht (Ft. Lauderdale); Country of Coral Springs. Home: 2791 NW 112th Ave Coral Springs FL 33065

ZIELINSKI, JOAN, state official; b. New Bedford, Mass., Dec. 24, 1948; d. John and Adele Zielinski; m. Kenneth N. Gross, May 30, 1981. A.B. in Sociology, Emmanuel Coll., Boston, 1970; M.A. in Sociology UCLA, 1975; Ph.D. in Mktg., U. New South Wales, Kensington, Australia, 1980. Lectr. mktg. U. New South Wales, Kensington, 1975-80; asst. prof. mktg. Wharton Sch., U. Pa., Phila., 1980-85; exec. dir. N.J. State Lottery, Trenton, 1985—; cons. in field. Author: Consumer Behavior, 1984. Contbr. articles to profl. publs. Mem. Women's Polit. Caucus, N.J., Republican Task Force, N.J., Polish Am. Rep. Caucus, N.J. Mem. Am. Mktg. Assn. (bd. dirs. Phila. chpt. 1984—). Office: NJ State Lottery CN041 Trenton NJ 08625

ZIERCHER, JULIA ANN, managing editor; b. St. Louis, June 28, 1937; d. Herbert William and Elizabeth Ziercher. B.A., Washington U., St. Louis, 1959; M.S. in English Lit., U. Wis.-Madison, 1962. Jr. high sch. English tchr. Huntington, N.Y., 1960-63, Ladue, Mo., 1963-65; copy editor Surgery jour., C.V. Mosby Co., St. Louis, 1965-66; sr. editing supr. McGraw-Hill Book Co., St. Louis and N.Y.C., 1966-72; sales rep. Alex Taylor & Co. Inc., N.Y.C., 1972-74; copy editing supr. Harper & Row, N.Y.C., 1974-77; mng. editor children's books, E.P. Dutton, N.Y.C., 1977—. Office: EP Dutton Inc 2 Park Ave New York NY 10016

ZIETLOW, CHARLOTTE THIELE, county official, retail store executive; b. Milw., Oct. 21, 1934; d. Gilbert Amadeus and Margaret Agnes (Ernst) Thiele; m. Paul N. Zietlow, Aug. 28, 1957; children—Rebecca, Nathan. B.A., Valparaiso U. 1957; M.A., U. Mich., 1959, Ph.D., 1969. Mem. faculty U. Mich., Ann Arbor, 1958-62; vis. lectr. Ind. U., Bloomington, 1967-68; owner, operator Goods, Inc., Bloomington, 1973—; county commr. Monroe County, Ind., 1981—; pres., bd. dirs. Ind. Family Health Council, Indpls., 1979—; chmn., bd. dirs. Ind. Acad. in Pub. Service, Indpls., 1981—. Author monograph: A Critical Edition of the Gothic Version of the Book of Romans, 1969. Mem. Bloomington City Council, 1971-75; candidate for U.S. Congress, 7th dist. Ind., 1978. Named Newsmaker of Yr., Bloomington Herald-Telephone, 1984. Mem. Assn. Ind. Counties (Achievement award 1984), Ind. Assn. County Bd. Commrs. (bd. dirs., dist. pres. 1985—), AAUW (pres. club 1976-77). Democrat. Avocations: needlework; cooking; sewing; piano; reading. Home: 213 S Bryan Bloomington IN 42401 Office: Monroe County Monroe County Courthouse Bloomington IN 47401

ZIKMUND, BARBARA BROWN, minister, educator; b. Ann Arbor, Mich., Oct. 16, 1939; d. Henry Daniels and Helen (Langworthy) Brown; m. Joseph Zikmund II, Aug. 26, 1961; 1 child, Brian Joseph. B.A., Beloit Coll., 1961; B.Div., Duke U., 1964, Ph.D., 1969; Dr.Div. (hon.), Doane Coll., 1984, Chgo. Theol. Sem., 1985. Ordained to ministry United Ch. of Christ, 1964. Instr. Albright Coll., Reading, Pa., 1966-67, Temple U., Phila., 1967-68, Ursinus Coll., Collegeville, Pa., 1968-69; asst. prof. religion studies Albion Coll., Mich., 1970-75; asst. prof. ch. history, dir. studies Chgo. Theol. Sem., 1975-80; dean and assoc. prof. ch. history Pacific Sch. Religion, Berkeley, Calif., 1981-85, dean and prof. ch. history, 1985—; chmn. United Ch. of Christ Hist. Council, 1983-85, mem. council for ecumenism, 1983—; mem. Nat. Council Chs. Commn. on Faith and Order, 1979—, World Council of Chs. Programme Theol. Edn., 1984—. Author: Discovering the Church, 1983. Editor: Hidden Histories in the UCC, 1984; (with Manschreck) American Religious Experience, 1976. Contbr. articles to profl. jours. Mem. City Council, Albion, Mich., 1972-75. Woodrow Wilson fellow, 1964-66; NEH grantee, 1974-75; issues implementation grantee Assn. Theol. Schs., 1983-84. Mem. Assn. Theol. Schs. (v.p. 1984-86), Am. Soc. Ch. History (council), Internat. Assn. Women Ministers (v.p. 1977-79), AAUW (v.p. 1973-75). Democrat. Home: 1281 Peachwood Ct San Bruno CA 94066 Office: Pacific Sch Religion 1798 Scenic Ave Berkeley CA 94709

ZILBERBERG, BARBARA, school psychologist; b. Kenya, Sept. 15, 1943; came to U.S., 1950, naturalized, 1957; d. Isidore and Sophie (Werner) Zysman; B.A. cum laude, City U. N.Y., Bklyn. Coll., 1964; M.A., New Sch. for Social Research, 1966; cert. sch. psychologist, Montclair State Coll., 1981; m. Charles Zilberberg, Sept. 2, 1965; 1 dau., Julie Marlene. Intern psychologist Central Islip N.Y. State Hosp., 1965-66; sr. clin. psychologist Kings Park State Hosp., N.Y., 1966-68; psychologist Bonnie Brae Residential Treatment Center, Millington, N.J., 1977-78; sch. psychologist Sayreville (N.J.) Public Schs., 1981—. Bd. dirs. PTA, 1973-82; troop leader Girl Scouts U.S.A., community cons., 1975-79; mem. Friends of Thirteen; Cert. sch. psychologist, N.J. Mem. Am. Psychol. Assn., N.J. Assn. Sch. Psychologists, Nat. Assn. Sch. Psychologists, Mensa, Psi Chi. Home: 469 Stratford Rd Union NJ 07083 Office: Truman School 1 Taft Pl Parlin NJ 08859

ZILE, KAREN RAE, fiber optic systems marketing manager; b. Dayton, Ohio, Jan. 19, 1958; d. William and Sharon Rae (Ferrigan) Z. A.A. in Gen. Edn., Fla. Jr. Coll., Jacksonville, 1978; B.S. summa cum laude in Bus. Adminstrn., U. Fla.-Gainesville, 1981; M.B.A. with high honors, U. Central Fla., 1986. Programmer, Riverside Hosp., Jacksonville, Fla., 1974-77; salesperson Body Shop Sportwear, Jacksonville, 1977-78; asst. buyer Tee-To-Green Sportswear, Gainesville, 1980-81; dir. advt. Fla. Software, Orlando, Fla., 1981-83; nat. account mgr. Stromberg-Carlson, Lake Mary, Fla., 1982—; cons. U. Central Fla., Orlando, 1983. Mem. Am. Mktg. Assn., Am. Mgmt. Assn., U. Fla. Alumni Assn., Phi Kappa Phi, Beta Gamma Sigma. Democrat. Club: Gator (Orlando). Office: Stromberg-Carlson Corp 400 Rinehart Rd Lake Mary FL 32746

ZILIN, SADYE JOHANNA, lawyer; b. Amsterdam, N.Y.; d. Nikodimas A. and Mary M. (Russell) Z.; B.S. cum laude, SUNY, Albany, 1942; LL.B., J.D., Union U., Albany, 1946; m. David S. Mackay, Aug. 20, 1949; children—James Russell, David Bruce, Marianne R., Robert W. Bar: N.Y. 1947, U.S. Dist. Ct. (no. dist.) N.Y. 1947. Assoc. Fitzsimmons & Wilsey, 1947-49; sole practice, Albany, 1949—; mem. Original Albany County Charter Commn. Mem. Albany County Bar Assn., SUNY Albany Alumni Assn., Albany Law Sch. Alumni Assn., West Point Parents Club Capital Dist., Assn. West Point Grads. (Parents). Club: Bus. and Profl. Women's (Albany). Address: 144 Cardinal Ave Albany NY 12209

ZIMET, CONSTANCE, writer, producer, actress, advertising creative director; b. Indpls., Nov. 22, 1941; d. Max Eugene and Ruby Estelle (Sagalowsky) Z.; m. Victor Isaac Ziskin, (div. 1979); 1 son, Zachary Louis. Student Briarcliff Coll., Briarcliff Manor, N.Y., 1960-61, N.Y. Sch. Interior Design, 1963, N.Y. Sch. Social Research, 1965. Vice pres. devel. Magnum Prodns., N.Y.C., Mpls. and Tampa, Fla., 1981-82; v.p. King George Prodns., N.Y.C., 1981-82; pres. Musad Prodns., Miami, Fla., 1980-82, Zimcon Prodns., Miami, 1982—; ptnr., pres. CeeZee Prodns., Miami, 1983—; sec.-treas. Maruco Enterprises, Inc., Miami, 1984—; ptnr., v.p. Diversity, Inc., Miami, 1983—; tchr., lectr. workshops Studio Ctr., Miami, 1979-81; lectr. music U. Miami, 1982; writer, producer, talent record album Poetica Erotica, 1983; writer soap opera Winds of Love, 1982; books include: Shampoo, Soap, Shampoo and You, 1983; writer, talent TV and radio commls., 1961—; advt. jingle singer maj. advertisers, 1961-70; singer's contractor various rec. cos. including Columbia Records, 1964-69; rec. artist Colpix Records, Pickwick Records, Golden records, other maj. children's labels; voice-over talent on nat., regional and local comml. campaigns, 1961—. Mem. Screen Actors Guild, AFTRA (dir., tchr., lectr.), Assn. Can. TV and Radio Artists, Writers Guild Am. Jewish. Office: The Ad Tram 15251 NE 18th Ave North Miami Beach FL 33162

ZIMMELMAN, JOANE FALK, insurance investigations company executive, consultant; b. Bklyn., July 10, 1929; d. Harry Herman and Ida Irene (Rabinowitz) Falk; m. Charles Kenneth Zimmelman, Jan. 27, 1947; children—Teri Lynn Jewell, Steven Craig. B.A., UCLA, 1951, M.A., 1956. Vice pres. Emard & Skrifvars, Inc., Los Angeles, 1974-80; pres. J.F. Zimmelman & Assocs., Inc., Canoga Park, Calif., 1980—. Mem. adv. bd. Los Angeles City Council, 1982; art dir., membership dir. P.T.A., 1963-64; area organizer Muscular Dystrophy, City of Hope, 1961-63. Recipient First Place awards P.T.A. Calif., 1965, 66. Mem. Calif. Assn. Lic. Investigators. Club: Senatorial (Washington). Avocations: yachting; gardening; crocheting.

ZIMMER, BEVERLY CLARK, credit manager; b. Covington, Ohio, Dec. 21, 1935; d. L. Eugene and Lois Mae (Houser) Clark; m. Dale Monroe Zimmer, Oct. 29, 1955; children—Connie Jo, Lois Jean, Ross Monroe, Kirk Douglas. Student pub. schs., Covington. Sec., mgr. DeKalb Research Agy., Greenville, Ohio, 1968-74; mgr. Duriron Employees Fed. Credit Union, Dayton, Ohio, 1975-79; mgr. credit and collections Unibraze Corp., Covington, 1979—. Republican candidate for Darke County treas., 1984. Mem. Greenville Bus. and Profl. Women (treas. 1983, 1st v.p. 1984), Dayton Credit Women's Group, Nat. Assn. Credit Mgmt. Republican. Lutheran. Lodge: Women of Moose. Home: 6453 Dull Rd Arcanum OH 45304 Office: Box 194 7502 W US Route 41 Covington OH 45318

ZIMMER, CAROLE GETZOFF, broadcaster; b. N.Y.C., Dec. 29, 1943; d. Alexander and Frances Evelyn (Kramer) G.; B.A., Hunter Coll., 1965; Editorial asst. Pageant Mag., N.Y.C., 1965, asso. editor, 1966, photoeditor, 1967; mem. dance and drama workshop La Mama ETC., N.Y.C., 1967-70; host A Woman's Place and New Morning, Sta. WPLJ, ABC, N.Y.C., 1975-80; reporter/anchor, 1980-83; asso. producer 20/20, ABC-TV, N.Y.C., 1979-80; writer/field producer Eyewitness News, Sta. WABC-TV, 1983; reporter/

anchor News of New York, Sta. WNYC-TV, 1984-85; free-lance broadcaster, 1985—; tchr. women in media course New Sch. for Social Research, 1977-80. Recipient Grace Schulberg Essay prize Hunter Coll., 1965, Women in Media prize. Mem. AFTRA, Actors Equity, Screen Actors Guild, Am. Women in Radio and TV. Democrat. Jewish. Author: The Natural Cook's First Book, 1973; contbr. articles to mags., 1970-80, including Ms., Village Voice, Harper's, Cosmopolitan.

ZIMMER, JANET ROSE, lawyer; b. Lancaster, Pa., Apr. 14, 1949; d. Robert Clare and Rose Evelyn (Williams) Zimmer. A.B. magna cum laude, Duke U., 1971; J.D., Georgetown U., 1975. Bar: D.C. 1975. Tchr. English, Eastern Lancaster County Sch. Dist., Pa., 1971-72; atty./advisor U.S. SEC, Div. Corp. Fin., Washington, 1975-78, spl. counsel and br. chief Div. Market Regulation, 1978-80; assoc. Rogers & Wells, Washington, 1980-82; assoc. Seward & Kissel, Washington, 1982-85, ptnr., 1986—. D.C. chmn. Robert L. Burch for (Ohio) State Senate, 1984. Nat. Merit scholar, 1967-71. Mem. ABA (sect. corp., banking and bus. law, com. on fed. regulation of securities), D.C. Bar Assn., Women's Bar Assn. D.C., Kappa Delta Pi. Club: Sierra (No. Va. conservation com. mem. 1980). Office: Seward & Kissel 818 Connecticut Ave NW Washington DC 20006

ZIMMER, SUZANNE, day care center administrator; b. N.Y.C., Sept. 4, 1928; d. Nathan and Jennie (Cohen) Chasan; 1 child, Susan C. B.S., NYU, 1949, M.A., 1953; postgrad., Columbia U., 1950-51. Dir. Fuld Day Nursery, Newark, 1951-55, Head Start, East Orange, West Orange, South Orange, N.J., 1965; exec. dir. Community Day Nursery, East Orange, 1957—; mem. panel Children's Bur. Rev. Grants, Washington, 1966-67; chmn. Bd. Pub. Welfare, Trenton, 1983; day care cons. Council of Jewish Women, Newark, 1970, Hoboken Bd. Edn., N.J., 1971. Pres. Day Care Coordinating Council, Essex County, N.J., 1977; chmn. Timothy Still Program, Upsala Coll., East Orange, 1975, Essex County adv. bd. Youth and Family Service, Newark, 1982, chmn. planning com. Community Mental Health Ctr., South Orange, 1981. Mem. Nat. Assn. Social Workers, Children's Def. Fund, Assn. of Children of N.J., Acad. Cert. Social Workers, East Orange Day Care Coalition. Avocations: swimming; reading; knitting; walking; sewing. Home: 131 Sagamore Rd Millburn NJ 07041 Office: Community Day Nursery 115 S Munn Ave East Orange NJ 07018

ZIMMERMAN, BARBARA JO, pharmaceutical company representative; b. Johnson City, Tenn., Nov. 6, 1948; d. Richard Thomas and Mildred (Adams) Z. B.S., East Tenn. State U., 1970, M.S., 1976. Cert. Secondary tchr., Tenn. Tchr. English, Central High Sch., Blountville, Tenn., 1970-80; pharm. salesperson Marion Labs., Inc., Kansas City, Mo., 1980—, field trainer, 1984—. Leader, People to People Internat., 1973-80; active LWV of Sullivan County, 1975—, Democratic Women Sullivan County, 1984—. Recipient Marion Ring award Marion Labs., 1982, 84, Marion Jr. Sales Achievers award Marion Labs., 1982. Mem. Sullivan County Edn. Assn. (rep. 1978-80), Tri-Cities Pharm. Orgn. Home: 4580 Old Stage Rd Kingsport TN 37664 Office: Marion Labs Inc 10236 Bunker Ridge Rd Kansas City MO 64134

ZIMMERMAN, BEVERLY MAY MCKAY, nursing educator; b. Rochester, N.Y., Mar. 2, 1939; d. James Kenneth and Gertrude Florence (Ritchie) McKay; m. Abraham Abba Zimmerman, Oct. 5, 1968; children—Lisa Marie, Sarah Ritchie. Cert. Pediatric Nurse, Rutgers U., 1975; cert. in Family Therapy, N.J. Ctr. Family Studies, 1983; B.S., Cornell U., 1963; M.Ed., Columbia, 1968, Ed.D., 1980. Instr. N.Y. Hosp., White Plains, 1964-66, Cornell U., N.Y.C., 1968-69; asst. prof. Seton Hall U., South Orange, N.J., 1976-81; assoc. prof. nursing, Fairleigh Dickinson U., Rutherford, N.J., 1981—, asst. dean Maxwell Becton Coll. Liberal Arts, 1985—; pvt. practice family therapy, Millburn, N.J., 1983—. Bd. dirs., treas. New Providence LWV, New Providence, N.J., 1970-76; bd. dirs., pres. Jefferson Sch. PTA, Summit N.J., 1976-81. Computer grantee Fairleigh Dickinson U., 1983, 1984. Mem. Am. Nurses Assn., N.J. State Nurses Assn., Am. Orthopsychiat. Assn., N.J. Soc. Cert. Clin. Specialists Psychiat. Mental Health Nursing. Democrat. Presbyterian. Home: 1 Canterbury Ct Warren NJ 07060 Office: Fairleigh Dickinson U 188 Montross Ave Rutherford NJ 07070

ZIMMERMAN, BRENDA GAIL, association executive, word processing consultant; b. Peoria, Ill., Jan. 25, 1950; d. Charles Franklin and Mary Jeanette (Hardy) Hendrickson. Assoc. Applied Sci., Ill. Central Coll., 1974; cert. Adminstr.'s Guide to Word Processing, 1980, Personnel Law Seminar, 1985; postgrad. Inst. Orgn. Mgmt., 1986. Tchr. East Peoria Day Care Ctr., Ill., 1974-75; supr. office clks. St. Francis Med. Ctr., Peoria, Ill., 1976-78; adminstrv. asst. Greater Detroit C. of C., 1978, word processing supr., 1978-83, office mgr., 1983—; instr. Word Processing, Detroit, 1978—, Art of Dictation, Detroit, 1978—. Author Supervisors Guide to Word Processing, 1980, Word Processing Training Course, 1983. Mem. Nat. Assn. Female Execs., Internat. Soc. Wang Users, Assn. Info. Systems Profls., Wang Office Systems Users Soc., Phi Theta Kappa. Republican. Baptist. Avocations: baseball; reading; writing. Home: 1204 E Harwood St Madison Heights MI 48071 Office: Greater Detroit C of C 600 W Lafayette St Detroit MI 48226

ZIMMERMAN, DIANE LEENHEER, law educator, lawyer; b. Newton, N.J., Apr. 16, 1941; d. Adrian and Mildred Eleanor (Booth) Leenheer; m. Earl A. Zimmerman, Sept. 24, 1960 (div. Aug. 1982); m. 2d, Cavin P. Leeman, Feb. 18, 1984. B.A., Beaver Coll., Glenside, Pa., 1963; J.D., Columbia U., 1976. Bar: N.Y. 1977, U.S. Supreme Ct. 1983. Reporter, Newsweek mag., N.Y.C., 1963-71; spl. features writer N.Y. Daily News, N.Y.C., 1971-73; law clk. U.S. Dist. Ct. (ea. dist.) N.Y., Bklyn., 1976-77; asst. prof. law NYU, N.Y.C., 1977-80, assoc. prof., 1980-82, prof., 1982—; mem. faculty Practicing Law Inst., N.Y.C., 1979, 84; mem. subcom. on cts.' environment 2d Cir. Adv. Planning Com., N.Y.C., 1979-80; legal adviser Reporters Com. for Freedom of Press, Washington, 1984—. Articles and book rev. editor Columbia Law Rev., 1975-76. Recipient citation of merit Columbia U. Sch. Journalism, 1972; Kent scholar and Stone scholar, 1973-76. Mem. Am. Law Inst., Assn. Bar City N.Y. (chairperson com. civil rights 1981-83), Fed. Bar Council (asst. sec. 1982-84), Met. Women Law Tchrs. Assn. (pres. 1979-83), Soc. Am. Law Tchrs., ACLU, Women's Polit. Caucus. Office: NYU Sch Law 40 Washington Sq S New York NY 10012

ZIMMERMAN, ELIZABETH THAYER, educator; b. Colorado Springs, Colo., Jan. 8, 1907; d. Harry Stanley and Mary Elizabeth (Brown) Thayer; B.A., U. Colo., 1928; m. Austin M. Zimmerman, Dec. 26, 1934; children—Edward Austin, John Jeffrey. Lectr. horticulture, botany, ecology Morton Arboretum, Lisle, Ill., 1956—, instr., 1961—. Rec. sec. Conservation Council Chgo., 1961—; trustee Morton Arboretum, Lisle, Ill., Ill. chpt. Nature Conservancy, 1962—. Recipient Award for Horticulture, 1963, Conservation, 1965; Eloise Payne Luquer medal Garden Club Am., 1971. Mem. Chgo. Hort. Soc. (dir., trustee, mem. exec. com., pres. women's bd., award 1982), Delta Gamma. Home: Brae Burn Farm Barrington Hills PO Algonquin IL 60102

ZIMMERMAN, EVELYN NELLIE, county supervisor; b. Pittsville, Wis., Jan. 8, 1922; d. Herman John and Margaret Johanna (Cook) Christensen; m. George Glen Zimmerman, Mar. 26, 1938 (dec. Apr. 1976); children—Nancy Zimmerman Wyman, Dorene Zimmerman Russell, Kathleen Zimmerman Chansley, George Herman. Student Mid-State Tech., Wisconsin Rapids, 1977-78, 85-86, U. Wis.-Stevens Point, 1978-79. Pvt. practice sewing and designing, Wisconsin Rapids, 1962-81; mem. Wood County Bd. Suprs., Wisconsin Rapids, 1978-86; clk. Family Natural Foods, Wisconsin Rapids, 1981-85. Mem. child support and veterans services Bd. Social Services, Wisconsin Rapids, 1978-86, chairperson, 1982-86; mem. Wood County Health Com., 1978-86, sec., 1978-80, 84-86, vice-chmn., 1980-84; vice chmn. Wis. Social Services Bd., 1982-85; chmn. Area Comprehensive Health, Wood County, Wis., 1979-83, sec. Transp. Com., 1980-82; chmn. Community Options Program, 1983-86; clk. election bd. Wood County, 1949-62, 73-80; trustee Moravian Ch., Wisconsin Rapids, 1976-83. Mem. Wisconsin Rapids Bus. & Profl. Women's Club (treas. 1973-75, 2d vice chmn. 1975-77, 1st vice chmn. 1977-79, bd. dirs. 1979-82), North Central Dist. Social Services Assn. (pres. 1985-86), Wis. Child Support Enforcement Assn. Democrat. Avocations: creative writing; sewing; reading; swimming. Home: 2330 6th St S Wisconsin Rapids WI 54494

ZIMMERMAN, FRANCES ADDIE HOWELL, state government official; b. Kansas City, Mo., Oct. 10, 1930; d. Dewey J. and Louise Frances (Wydick) Howell; Asso. Degree, Park Coll., Parkville, Mo., 1944; student Rockhurst Coll., 1970, U. Mo., Kansas City, 1972, U. Mich., 1976, 77, U. Houston, 1977, U. Kans., 1979; m. Eugene R. Zimmerman, Aug. 10, 1945 (dec.); children—Donald, Nancy Zimmerman Giller, Robert J., Laura Zimmerman Scott. Dir. public relations program, county organizer Am. Cancer Soc., Kansas City, Mo., 1959-60; public relations, Mo. Employment Service, 1962-75; instr., art dir. Regional Tng. Center, U.S. Dept. Labor, Overland Pk., Kans., 1975-80, public relations and employer com. coordinator, Kansas, Mo., 1980—; cons. in field. Pres., Scarritt Sch. PTA, 1950; bd. dirs. Shawnee Mission (Kans.) High Sch., 1960; v.p. women's polit. caucus Jefferson City Commn. on Status of Women, 1983. Mem. Internat. Assn. Personnel (v.p. Mo. 1975, exec. bd. internat. award of merit Mo. 1975), Am. Soc. Trainers (charter mem. orgnl. devel. media div.), Mid-Am. Assn. of Assn. Execs., Nat. Assn. Female Execs., Nelson Gallery Art, Kansas City C. of C., Urban League Greater Kansas City, Personal Dynamics Assn., Park Coll. Alumni Assn. Art Dirs. Club Kansas City, Nelson Gallery Art Soc. Baptist. Clubs: Kansas City Art Dirs., Overland Park Lioness, Soroptimist Internat. Home: 10658 Century Ln Overland Park KS 66212 Office: 1411 Main St Kansas City MO 64105

ZIMMERMAN, GRACE HENRIETTA, county treasurer, educator; b. Monticello, Iowa, Nov. 29, 1928; d. Menno John and Anna Frances (Caspers) Mcenk; m. Paul Henry Zimmerman, June 7, 1948; children—Diana Carol, Andrew James, Bradley Emil. B.A., U. Iowa, 1968. Tchr. Midland Sch., Wyoming, Iowa, 1953-78; county treas. Jones County, Anamosa, Iowa, 1981—; dir. Burroughs Computer User Group, Des Moines, 1982—. Active Jones County Democrats, 1978—. Named Outstanding Educator, Nat. Edn. Governing Bd., 1976, Outstanding Farm Spokesperson, Chem. Co., 1978. Mem. Bus. Profl. Women, NEA, County Officers Assn. (v.p. 1983—, pres. 1985—), Anamosa C. of C., Jones County Hist. Soc., Izaak Walton League (sec. Wapsiketa chpt. 1981—). Lutheran. Club: Cow Belles (pres. 1979-82). Avocations: public speaking; gardening; bowling; dancing. Home: Rural Route 2 Monticello IA 52310 Office: Jones County Treas PO Box 79 Anamosa IA 52205

ZIMMERMAN, JANICE MARIE, savings and loan executive; b. Chgo., June 27, 1958; d. Edward Chester and Frances (Baranowski) Pawlowski; m. Michael Scott Daniel, May 25, 1980 (div. Oct. 1983); m. Daniel Victor Zimmerman, Sept. 7, 1985. B.S. in Fin., Eastern Ill. U., 1980; M.S. in Fin., St. Louis U., 1987. Asst. examiner Fed. Res. Bank, Chgo., 1980-82; fin. analyst Fed. Res. Bank St. Louis, 1982-84; v.p., treas. Illini Fed., Fairview Heights, Ill., 1984—. Mem. Fin. Mgrs. Soc., Nat. Orgn. Female Execs. Republican. Roman Catholic. Club: Creve Coeur Racquet (Mo.). Avocations: reading; golfing; writing. Office: Illini Fed 6550 N Illinois St Fairview Heights IL 62208

ZIMMERMAN, JEAN, lawyer; b. Berkeley, Calif., Dec. 3, 1947; d. Donald Scheel Zimmerman, Jr. and Phebe Jean (Reed) Doan; m. Gilson Berryman Gray III, Nov. 25, 1982; children—Charles Donald Buffum and Catherine Elisabeth Phebe (twins); stepchildren—Alison Travis, Laura Rebecca, Gilson Berryman. Student Mich. State U., 1965-66; B.S. in B.A., U. Md., 1970; J.D., Emory U., 1975. Bar: Ga. 1975, D.C. 1976, N.Y. 1980. Asst. mgr. investments FNMA, Washington, 1970-73; assoc. counsel Fuqua Industries, Inc., Atlanta, 1976-79; assoc. Sage Gray Todd & Sims, N.Y.C., 1979-84; asst. gen. counsel J. Henry Schroder Bank & Trust Co., N.Y.C., 1984—. Founder, officer ERA Ga., Altanta, 1977-79. Mem. N.Y. State Bar Assn., ABA, Ga. Assn. Women Lawyers (dir. 1977-79), LWV, DAR. Democrat. Office: J Henry Schroder Bank & Trust Co One State St New York NY 10004

ZIMMERMAN, JULIET GOODFRIEND, marketing company executive, consultant; b. Phila., Dec. 20, 1941; d. David Joseph and Theresa Miriam (Hirschberg) Goodfriend; m. Robert Harris Zimmerman, May 10, 1964; children—Erica June, J. Micah. B.A. cum laude with honors, Bryn Mawr Coll., 1963. With Smith Kline & French, Phila., 1963-65; asst. to pres. Acad. Natural Scis., Phila., 1965-67; pub. relations officer Inst. Cancer Research, Fox Chase, Pa., 1967-71; group mktg. mgr. Booz-Allen & Hamilton-Nat. Analysts, Phila., 1972-79; pres. Strategic Mktg. Corp., Bala Cynwyd, Pa., 1980—; cons. on health care; cons. to med. products industry. Campaign mgr. candidates for local commrs., Lower Merion, Pa.; bd. dirs. Albert Einstein Med. Ctr., Phila., 1984—, Beth David, Phila., 1980-83; vice chmn. Ctr. Autistic Children, Phila., 1982—. Mem. Pharm. and Med. Supplies Mktg. Research Groups (com. chmn. 1973—), Am. Mktg. Assn., Pharm. Advt. Council, AAAS, Am. Med. Writers Assn., Forum Exec. Women (charter), Phila. Women's Network, LWV (div. 1968-73). Clubs: Cosmopolitan (Phila.); Alumni of Phila. of Bryn Mawr Coll. (pres. 1971-73). Research on mktg. Office: Strategic Mktg Corp 50 Monument Rd Suite 303 Bala Cynwyd PA 19004

ZIMMERMAN, MARGOT LURIE, nonprofit organization administrator; b. Williamsport, Pa., Oct. 3, 1935; d. David Harris and Frances (Jacobson) L.; m. M. Paul Zimmerman, Aug. 18, 1957; children—Jeffrey, John, Julie. B.A., Cornell U., 1956; M.A., NYU, 1957. Program officer World Edn., N.Y.C., 1971-75; researcher, writer George Washington U. Med. Ctr., Washington, 1975-76; lectr. U. Ill. at Washington, 1976-77; seminar dir. Ctr. Devel. and Population Activities, Washington, 1976-78; program officer Program Intro. and Adaptation of Contraceptive Tech. and Program Appropriate Tech. in Health, Washington, 1980-83, dir., 1983—; cons. Internat. Devel. Study Ctr., Battle Meml. Inst., Washington, 1978-81; mem. exec. com. Mysore State Family Planning Assn., Bangalore, India, 1966-81; instr. Inst. Mass. Communications and Journalism, Teheran, Iran, 1969-71. Contbr. articles to health and family planning jours. Mem. Am. Pub. Health Assn., Population Assn. Am., Soc. Internat. Devel., Nat. Council Internat. Health, Pi Lambda Theta, Phi Alpha Theta. Jewish. Avocations: tennis; art; travel; reading. Home: 7902 Rocton Ave Chevy Chase MD 20815 Office: PIACT/PATH 1255 23d St NW Washington DC 20037

ZIMMERMAN, PATRICIA A(NNE), personnel director; b. N.Y.C., Apr. 22, 1935; d. Frank Alvin and Agnes (Healy); m. Michael P. Forde, May 29, 1956 (div.); children—Michael, Patricia Virginia; m. 2d Victor C. Zimmerman, July 2, 1970. Student Hunter Coll., 1953-56. Dir. benefits and compensation May Co., St. Louis, 1970-78; personnel mgr. Calgon Corp., St. Louis, 1978—; personnel dir. Petrie Stores, N.Y.C., 1976-78. Bd. dirs. YMCA, St. Louis; co-chmn. N.W. County YMCA, 1984; coordinator Inroads, St. Louis; judge Jr. Achievement, St. Louis, 1979. Recipient Leadership award YMCA, 1983; named Coordinator of Yr., Inroads, 1982. Mem. Indsl. Relations Assn., Personnel Assn. St. Louis. Republican. Office: Calgon Corp 7501 Page Ave Saint Louis MO 63166

ZIMMERMANN, CAROLINE A., advertising agency executive, author; b. Amityville, N.Y., Oct. 19, 1944; d. H. Paul and Frances (Short) Z. B.A., Ga. State U., 1966. Mgr. Christian Herald Pub. Co., N.Y.C., 1960-64; v.p. William Steiner Assocs., N.Y.C., 1964-69; pres. Zimmermann Direct, Inc., N.Y.C., 1969—; chmn. pub. relations Direct Mktg. Day in N.Y., 1982—. Author: How To Break Into The Media Professions, 1981; Fun with Your Camera, 1981. Office: Zimmermann Direct Inc 342 Madison Ave Suite 1916 New York NY 10173

ZIMMERMANN, KRISTINE, food company executive; b. Seebach, Austria, Sept. 5, 1946; d. Franc and Kristina (Breznik) Medved; m. William Zimmermann, June 23, 1968 (div.). B.S., Coll. St. Catherine, St. Paul, 1968; postgrad. bus. adminstrn. U. Minn. Tchr. math. Mpls. Public Schs., 1968-69; research data processing mgr. Pillsbury, Mpls., 1969-76; mktg. research mgr. Green Giat Co., Jonathan, Minn., 1976-77; mktg. research mgr. Internat. Multifoods, Mpls., 1977-79; dir. mktg. research Land O'Lakes, Arden Hills, Minn., 1979—; pres., owner A&W Restaurant, Mpls., 1981—. Mem. communications adv. bd. U. Minn., 1984—. Dwan Found. scholar, 1964-68. Mem. Am. Mktg. Assn., Advt. Research Found., Women in Foodservice, Pi Mu Epsilon. Club: Greenway Athletic (adv. bd. 1984—). Home: 210 W Grant St #316 Minneapolis MN 55403 Office: Land O'Lakes 4001 Lexington Ave N Arden Hills MN

ZIMMERMANN, PATRICIA JEANNE, lawyer; b. Chgo., Feb. 18, 1940; d. Stanley Marion and Jean (Hallas) Dudek; B.A. in Psychology, No. Ill. U., 1962; J.D., U. Wis., 1985; children—Kimberly Chi, Jacqueline Michele, Bradford William. Research asst. psychology Yale U., 1962-63; dir. govtl. affairs Madison (Wis.) C. of C., 1977-80; owner, operator Printing Plus, Madison, 1980-83; legis. cons. housing industry in Dane County, 1980-85; litigation atty. Blumenthal & Milliken, Riverside, Calif., 1985—. Vice pres. Eagle Heights Council, 1969; bd. dirs. Dane County LWV, 1972; alderman Madison City Council, 1973-77; program dir. Capitolaires All Girl Drum and Bugle Corps, 1976-78. Recipient cert. of appreciation for service City of Madison, 1977, cert. of recognition Madison Women's Issues Com., 1977. Mem. Nat. Assn. Female Execs. Republican. Roman Catholic. Editor Metropolitan, 1980-82. Home: 138 E Briardale Orange CA 92665 Office: 3890 10th St Riverside CA 92501

ZIMNY, SUSAN LYNN, marketing coordinator; b. Chgo., June 13, 1958; d. Florian John and Josephine LaVern (Prondzinski) Z. B.S., U. Ill., Urbana, 1981. Classified advt. counselor Chgo. Tribune Co., 1979; student intern Instrn. TV, Urbana, 1979-80; classified advt. sales rep. Downtown Lakeshore News, Chgo., 1980; mktg. coordinator The Blood Ctr. of No. Ill., Glenview, Ill., 1981—. Women in Communications scholar, 1980, Ill. Gen. Assembly Scholar, 1976-80. Mem. Women in Communications (chmn. hospitality 1983-85, membership 1985-86), Northwest Press Club (chmn. seminar 1982), Lit. Vols. of Chgo., Chgo. Hosp. Pub. Relations Soc., Assn. Blood Donor Recruiters. Home: 4812 N Linder St Apt 3A Chicago IL 60630 Office: The Blood Ctr of No Ill 1255 N Milwaukee Ave Glenview IL 60025

ZINDEL, BONNIE, writer; b. N.Y.C., May 3, 1943; d. Jack and Claire (Bromberg) Hildebrand; m. Paul Zindel, Oct. 25, 1973; children—David, Lizabeth. B.A. in Psychology, Hofstra U., 1964. Dir. pub. relations The Cleveland Play House, Cleve., 1969-72; producer show Intermission Feature, Boston Symphony, sta. WCLV-FM, Cleve., 1970-72. Author: A Star for the Latecomer, 1980; Hollywood Dream Machine, 1984; playwright I Am A Zoo-Jewish Repetory Theatre-The Troupe Theatre, 1976; Lemons in the Morning, A.M. Back Alley Theatre, 1983, The Latecomer, 1985. Mem. Playwrights Unit-Actors Studio, Women in Film. Office: care Curtis Brown 575 Madison Ave New York NY 10022

ZINGARO, KATHLEEN GAIL, human resources executive; b. Phila., Sept. 21, 1953; d. Joseph C. and Connie (Chiarizio) Z. Payroll/personnel adminstr. Star Sprinkler Co., Phila., 1974-77; personnel mgr. Star Porcelain Co., Trenton, N.J., 1977-81, Heinemann Electric Co., Lawrenceville, N.J., 1981—. Adv. bd. pub. relations com. Salvation Army, Trenton, N.J., 1982-84; loaned exec. Delaware Valley United Way, Trenton, 1983-84; adv. com. Assn. Advancement Mental Health, Princeton, N.J., 1983-84; indsl. relations com. N.J. Dept. Labor and Industry, Trenton, 1983-84, vocat. guidance adv. com. N.J. Dept. Edn., Trenton, 1983-84. Recipient Superior Merit award Am. Soc. Personnel Adminstrn., 1983, 84. Mem. Delaware Valley Personnel Assn. (v.p. membership 1980-81, pres. 1982-84), N.J. Bus. and Industry Assn. (indsl. relations com. 1983-84), Indsl. Relations Research Assn., Am. Soc. Personnel Adminstrn. (legis. liaison 1984-86). Office: Heinemann Electric Co PO Box 6800 Lawrenceville NJ 08648

ZINN, BARBARA LYNNE, department store administrator; b. Jersey City, June 4, 1951; d. Sidney and Ruth Jean (Riker) Genser; m. David H. Zinn, Jan. 15, 1972 (div. 1984). Student Douglass Coll., Rutgers U., 1969-72. Buyer better sportswear Abraham & Straus, Bklyn., 1973-76; buyer Miss Bergdorf Sportswear dept. Bergdorf Goodman, N.Y.C., 1976-77; buyer better dresses and suits Bambergers, Newark, 1977-79, buyer moderate shoes, 1979-82, mdse. councillor/buyer jr. and moderate shoes, 1982-84, mdse. councillor moderate shoes, 1984-85, mdse. adminstr. for moderate and jr. shoes, 1985—. Recipient Outstanding Corp. Group. Performance award Brown Shoe Co., 1980, 81, 82. Mem. Women's Accessory Council, Fashion Group.

ZIOBRO, MARTHA JANE, engineer; b. McKeesport, Pa., Oct. 29, 1954; d. Michael Francis and Stella (Hutsko) Ziobro; A.A., U. Fla., 1974, B.Bldg. Constrn., 1976. Constrn. mgmt. asst. TVA, Hartsville Nuclear Project, 1976-79, asst. laborer supt., 1979-82, asst. supt., asst. project engr., 1983; resident engr. Gresham Smith & Ptnrs., 1984—. Sec., Cath. Youth Orgn., 1971. Clearwater chpt. Women in Constrn., scholar, 1972; recipient H.H. Block award dept. bldg. constrn. U. Fla., 1976. Mem. Student Contractors and Builders Assn. (pres. 1976), Nat. Mgmt. Assn. Home: 328 Trina St Gallatin TN 37066 Office: 3310 West End Nashville TN 37202

ZIPF, DEBORAH WEST, magazine editor, parliamentarian; b. Boston, Dec. 24, 1936; d. Elmer Dalton and Dorothy Lois (Barton) West; m. Robert Zipf, Nov. 25, 1961; children—George West, Catherine Welcome. A.B., Middlebury Coll., 1958; M.A., Fla. State U., 1959. Editor, N.Y. State Congress of Parents and Tchrs., Inc., Albany, 1980-85, editorial advisor, v.p., 1985—. Various positions PTA, Scarsdale, N.Y., 1969—. Mem. LWV, Am. Inst. Parliamentarians, Village Club, Sierra Club, Phi Beta Kappa, Phi Kappa Phi. Democrat. Avocations: piano; skating. Home: 22 Gorham Rd Scarsdale NY 10583 Office: NY State PTA 119 Washington Ave Albany NY 12210

ZIPKIN, DAPHNA, telecommunications company executive, consultant; b. Afula, Jezreel Valley, Israel, July 18, 1943; came to U.S., 1955, naturalized, 1961; d. Axel Samuel and Shulamith (Narod) Golde; m. Charles Richard Zipkin, Aug. 15, 1965 (div. Dec. 1978); children—Ilan David, Daniella Ann, Ronen Israel, B.A., U. Calif.-Berkeley, 1965. Exec. sec. IBM Corp., Los Angeles, San Francisco, 1965-70; adminstrv. asst. The Gap Stores, Inc., San Bruno, Calif., 1979-80; sales rep. Day & Night Communications, San Francisco, 1981-83, United Technologies, San Jose, Calif., 1983-84; area sales mgr. Introlink, Sacramento, Calif., 1984-85; western region mgr. XEL Communications, Aurora, Colo., 1985—; pres., owner DZ Cons. Service, Millbrae, Calif., 1984—. Vol. ARC, San Francisco, Philippines, 1960—, Kibbutz Mishmar Ha'Emek, Israel, 1978-79; mem. Jewish Community Fedn., 1980—. Recipient Professionalism award IBM Corp., Los Angeles, 1966; named Sales Rep. of Yr., Day and Night Communications, San Francisco, 1982. Mem. Women in Telecommunications, Nat. Assn. Female Execs., Nat. Assn. Profl. Saleswomen. Democrat. Jewish. Avocations: Israeli folk dancing; writing poetry; art collecting; theatre. Home: 451 Helen Dr Millbrae CA 94030

ZIPKOWITZ, FAY, librarian; b. N.Y.C., Nov. 11, 1938. B.A. in English, L.I. U., 1958; M.S.L.S., Case Western Res. U., 1959; M.A. in English, U. Mass., 1970; D.A. (Acad. Library Adminstrn.), Simmons Coll., 1977. Asst. librarian Cleve. Pub. Library, 1959-63; archivist Abba Hillel Silver Meml. Arch. and Library, The Temple, Cleve., 1964-66; document reference librarian U. Mass., 1975-77, library systems analyst, 1973-75, head info. processing, 1970-73, sr. cataloger, 1968-70, asst. dir., 1966-68; coordinator library systems Worcester Area Coop. Library, 1977-80; dir. R.I. Dept. State Library Services, Providence, 1981—. Contbr. articles to profl. jours. Chmn. bd. N.E. Documents Conservation Ctr., 1984—. Mem. ALA, ACRL, ASCLA (bd. dirs. 1985-86), LAMA, ACRL (pres. 1980-81), Operation Friendship. Council on Library Resources fellow, 1973. Address: State Library 95 Davis St Providence RI 02908*

ZIPPEL, MARY-ELLA HOLST, religious educator; b. Detroit, Oct. 12, 1934; d. Spencer and Ruth Catherine (McCullough) Holst; B.A., U. Toledo, 1959; M.A., N.Y.U., 1970; m. Bert Zippel, Jan. 18, 1969 (dec. May 1985); children—Patricia Hall, Darcy Hall. Sr. counselor, employment specialist N.Y. Dept. Labor, 1962-75; religious edn. dir. Unitarian Ch. of All Souls, 1976—; mem. Unitarian Universalist Hist. Scholarship Com. Bd. mgrs. Soc. for Aging, 1974—; bd. dirs. Yorkville Common Pantry, 1982—. Contbg. editor Conversations. . . Journal of Women and Religion; contbr. poetry to lit. jours. Home: 150-74 Village Rd Jamaica NY 11432 Office: Unitarian Ch of All Souls 1157 Lexington Ave New York NY 10021

ZIPSNIS, KATE CONGDON, state health administrator; b. Pensacola, Fla., June 27, 1943; d. Frederick M. and Irwin Congdon; B.A., Calif. State Coll., Long Beach, 1964; M.P.H., U. Tex., Houston, 1973; m. Steven M. Zipsnis, Mar. 10, 1979; children—Fearn S. Smith, Sarah K. Smith. Coordinator home health program Upjohn Co., Houston, 1971-73; drug abuse counselor Nueces County Mental Health Mental Retardation Center, Corpus Christi, Tex., 1973-75; drug abuse planner Coastal Bend Council Govts., Corpus Christi, 1975-77; planner, program mgr. Ariz. Dept. Health Services, Phoenix, 1977-81, mgr. state cert. of need program, 1981-82, exec. staff to dir. Div. Family Health Services, 1982—; cons. Nat. Inst. Drug Abuse. USPHS fellow, 1965; USPHS trainee, 1973. Mem. Tex. Assn. Drug Abuse Services (dir.), Am. Public Health Assn., Phi Kappa Phi. Home: 8662 E Bonnie Rose Scottsdale AZ 85253 Office: 1740 W Adams Phoenix AZ 85007

ZIRGER, MILDRED LEE, preschool owner; b. Topeka, Oct. 20, 1934; d. Myron Alvin and Ruth Lucile (Harrington) Powell; m. William Joseph Zirger, July 28, 1957; 1 child, Elizabeth Ruth. B.A. in Home Econs., Washburn U., 1957. Owner, operator Country Day Presch., Topeka, 1954—. Mem. Nat. Assn. Young Children, Kans. Assn. Edn. Young Child, Topeka Ann. Edn. Young Child (treas. 1985-86), Zeta Tau Alpha. Republican. Methodist. Club: Zonta Internat. Lodge: Order Eastern Star (worthy matron 1972). Avocations:

animals; travel; arts and crafts; music. Home: 2510 SW 37th St Topeka KS 66611 also 13608 S Locust St Olathe KS 66062 Office: Country Day Presch 2500 SW 37th St Topeka KS 66611

ZIRKELBACH, NANCY ELEANOR, educator; b. Rochester, N.Y., Aug. 17, 1945; d. Harris Joseph and Dolores Rose (Kane) Fulton; m. Richard Gerald Zirkelbach, July 17, 1971; children—Tracey, Lora. B.A. in History, Nazareth Coll., Rochester, 1967; postgrad. Utah State U., Idaho State U., SUNY-Brockport. Third grade tchr. St. Anne's, Rochester, 1967-69, Joanna Perrin, Fairport, N.Y., 1969-71, L.M. Steen, Bogota, N.J., 1971-72, Ucon, Idaho, 1979-81; fourth grade tchr. Gwyn-nor, North Wales, Pa., 1973-74; second grade tchr. Cloverdale, Idaho Falls, Idaho, 1981—, math. textbook com., 1984, chmn. 5 yr. state evaluation, 1985. Sec. Idaho Falls Ski Tng. Facility, Idaho, 1984. Republican. Roman Catholic. Home: 3725 Wanda St Idaho Falls ID 83401

ZIROT, HAZEL MARGARET, insurance executive; b. Hanover, Pa., Aug. 14, 1942; d. Clarence Hayward and Hazel Mary (Rogers) Fluharty; m. John William Zirot, Oct. 17, 1966 (dec.); children—Lisa Lynn, Lori Leigh. Student Ohio U., 1960-62, Western Mont. State Coll., 1962; certs. Dale Carnegie, Fla. Ins. Sch.; diploma Life Underwriters Training Council. Registered rep., risk mgmt. specialist. Bookkeeper, Central Bookkeeping, Columbus, Ohio, 1965-67; sales rep. Met. Ins. Co., Beaver Falls, Pa., 1973-74, branch mgr. trainee, Orange Park, Fla., 1983—, also sales rep. Creator, designer Apple Dumpling Originals doll, 1982. Com. mem. Life Underwriters Polit. Action Com., Jacksonville, 1985. Recipient sales award Met., 1983, Pacesetter award Met., 1984, Orlando Region Exec. Exec. Club designation Met., 1984, Field Builder award Met., 1984. Mem. Nat. Assn. Female Execs., Nat. Life Underwriters Assn., Fla. Life Underwriters Assn., Jacksonville Life Underwriters Assn., Met. Presidents Advisory Bd., Advanced Underwriting Associate Group Met., Jacksonville C. of C., South Council C. of C. Roman Catholic. Avocations: making dolls, volunteer teaching. Office: Met Ins Cos 38C Blanding Blvd Orange Park FL 32073

ZISSER, CAROLYN SCHIFREEN, lawyer; b. Phila., Mar. 25, 1947; d. Clement Soloman and Rita (Fuld) Schifreen; m. Elliot Zisser, June 20, 1971; children—Jonathan Clement, Leah Rachel (dec.), Alison Rebecca. Student Skidmore Coll., 1965-67; B.A. with honors in Philosophy, NYU, 1969; J.D. with honors, George Washington U., 1972. Bar: Fla. 1972. Staff atty. Duval County Legal Aid,. Jacksonville, Fla., 1972-75; mng. atty. Carolyn S. Zisser, P.A., Jacksonville, 1975—; instr. Fla. Jr. Coll., 1976-78; lectr. in field. Bd. dirs. Beth Shalom Congregation, 1976-78. Mem. ABA, Fla. Bar Assn., Jacksonville Bar Assn., Jacksonville Beaches C. of C. (dir. 1982—). Democrat. Jewish. Clubs: Ponte Vedra, Sawgrass. Office: 302 3d St Suite 6 Neptune Beach FL 32233

ZOBEL, RYA WEICKERT, federal judge; b. Zwickau, Germany, Dec. 18, 1931; d. Paul J. K. and Elizabeth Weickert; A.B. cum laude, Radcliffe Coll., 1953; LL.B., Harvard U., 1956; m. Hiller B. Zobel, Nov. 23, 1973; children—Andrea Elizabeth Featherston, David Stephen Featherston, Scott Alexander Featherston; 4 stepchildren. Law clk. to Chief Judge George C. Sweeney, U.S. Dist. Ct., Dist. Mass., 1956-66; asso. firm Hill & Barlow, Boston, 1967-73; asso. firm Goodwin, Procter & Hoar, Boston, 1973-75, partner, 1976-79; judge U.S. Dist. Ct., Dist. Mass., 1979—. Fellow Am. Bar Found., Acad. Matrimonial Lawyers Am. (gov. Mass. chpt. 1978-79); mem. Am. Bar Assn., Mass. Bar Assn., Boston Bar Assn. (council 1973-76). Office: Room 1802 John W McCormack Post Office and Courthouse Boston MA 02109*

ZOBLE, ADRIENNE KAPLAN, advertising agency executive; b. Newark, July 11, 1940; d. Herman Israel and Ada (Goodglass) Kaplan; B.A., Rutgers U., Newark, 1963; m. Jacob Manus Zoble, Aug. 23, 1962; children—Allison Leigh, Jennifer Hope. Sec. media dept., broadcast estimator J. Walter Thompson Co., N.Y.C., 1961-64; asst. buyer, buyer Maxon, Inc., N.Y.C., 1964; media dir. Bruce Friedlich & Co., N.Y.C., 1965-66; media dir. Keyes, Martin & Co., Springfield, N.J., 1966-76; owner Adrienne Zoble Advt., Bridgewater, N.J., 1977—; mem. Active Corps Execs., U.S. SBA, 1977—. Mem. LINK (founder, past pres.), N.J. Assn. Women Bus. Owners (founder, past pres. Central N.J.), Raritan Valley C. of C. (trustee, chmn. small bus. council), Am. Bus. Assn. (trustee). Office: 380 Foothill Rd Bridgewater NJ 08807

ZOLA, DEBIE ROSE, learning disabilities educator, financial executive; b. Youngstown, Ohio, Mar. 20, 1952; d. Louis Maron and Rose Marie (Joseph) Ellis; m. Eugene Matthew Zola, Mar. 17, 1973; children—Justin, Michael. B.S. in Edn., Youngstown State U., 1974, Kent State U., 1976. Learning disabilities tchr. Youngstown Bd. Edn., 1975; learning disabilities specialist Campbell Bd. Edn., Ohio, 1975—; v.p. The Oven Works, Inc., Youngstown, 1977—, Justin Time Cleaners, Youngstown, 1977—; piano tchr., Youngstown, 1973-74; camp counselor Mahoning County Sch., Youngstown, summer 1970. Author: Learning Disabilities, 1975. Recipient cert. of commendation for NASA Tchr. in Space Project, State Ohio Supt. Pub. Instrn. and dir. NASA Lewis Research Ctr., 1985. Mem. Campbell Edn. Assn. (bldg. rep. 1976-77), Ohio Edn. Assn., NEA. Maronite Catholic. Avocations: piano; needlepoint; handcrafts. Home: 292 Upland Ave Youngstown OH 44504 Office: Penhale Primary Sch 281 Penhale Ave Campbell OH 44405

ZOLBER, KATHLEEN KEEN (MRS. MELVIN L. ZOLBER), educator; b. Walla Walla, Wash., Dec. 9, 1916; d. Wildie H. and Alice (Johnson) Keen; B.S. in Foods and Nutrition, Walla Walla Coll., 1941; M.A., Wash. State U., 1961; Ph.D., U. Wis., 1968; m. Melvin L. Zolber, Sept. 19, 1937. Dir. food service Walla Walla Coll., 1941-50, mgr. coll store, 1951-59, asst. prof. food and nutrition, 1959-62, asso. prof., 1962-64; asso. prof. nutrition Loma Linda (Calif.) U., 1964-72, prof. nutrition, 1972-84, prof. nutrition, program dir., 1984—, dir. dietetic edn., 1967-84, dir. dietetics Med. Center, 1972-84; bd. dirs. Nat. Nutrition Consortium, Washington, 1979-83. Mead Johnson grantee, 1965-67; recipient Alumna of Year award Walla Walla Coll., 1977; Dolores Nyhus award Calif. Dietetic Assn., 1978; named Outstanding Faculty Lectr., Loma Linda U., 1979. Mem. Am. Dietetic Assn. (chmn. Commn. on Accreditation 1976-79, dir. 1979-81, pres. 1982-83), Am. Public Health Assn., Am. Home Econs. Assn., Inst. Food Tech., Am. Mgmt. Assn., AAUP, Soc. Food Service Research, Soc. Personnel Adminstrn., Sigma Xi, Omicron Nu, Delta Omega. Address: PO Box 981 Loma Linda CA 92354

ZOLLA, BETTY ELLEN, dietitian, consultant; b. Chgo., July 11, 1925; d. William M. and Miriam (Siegel) Brodsky; m. Edward M. Zolla, Jr., July 4, 1945 (div. Feb. 1977); children—Edward M. III, Wendy Miriam, Debra Ann. B.S., Mundelein Coll., Chgo., 1945; postgrad. U. Iowa, 1971-72, UCLA, 1971-72, U. Calif.-Northridge, 1971-72. Registered dietitian. Dietitian trainee U. So. Calif. Med. Ctr., 1972-74; instr. diabetes teaching program Century City Hosp., Los Angeles, 1974-76; cons. dietitian Skilled Nursing Facilities, Los Angeles, 1974-79, Bd. & Care Facilities, Los Angeles, 1974—; nutrition cons. Physicians in Pvt. practice, 1974—, Vis. Nurse Assn. Los Angeles, 1975—, Dialysis Ctrs., Los Angeles, 1975—, Verdugo Hills Vis. Nurse Assn., 1977—; guest lectr. coll.; cons. in field. Mem. editorial staff Nutrition & the M.D., 1975-81. Contbr. articles to profl. publs. Dietitian vol. Pediatric Pavilion, Los Angeles County-U. So. Calif. Med. Ctr., 1974-75; mem. nursing and nutrition subcoms. San Fernando Valley unit Am. Cancer Soc., Calif., 1977-79, guest lectr., 1980-81. Mem. Am. Dietetic Assn. (instr. diabetes teaching program 1974-76), Calif. Dietetic Assn., Soc. Nurtrition Edn., Greater Los Angeles Nutrition Council, So. Calif. Kidney Found. (sci. adv. council), Nat. Kidney Found. (council renal nutrition), End Stage Renal Disease (network 4, coordinating council), Cons. Nutritionists So. Calif. Avocations: sailing; oil painting; photography; travel.

ZOLLA, SUSAN PENECALE, construction company executive; b. Philadelphia, June 24, 1946; d. Michael Anthony and Martha (Kelly) Penecale; m. Edward M. Zolla, July 3, 1971; children—Alissa, Miriam, Anne. B.A. in History and Psychology, Bucknell U., 1968; M.A. in Edn. Adminstrn., U. So. Calif., 1976. Lic. gen. contractor, Calif. Tchr. history Santa Ana Schs., Calif., 1969-72, sch. adminstr., 1972-75; real estate developer, Los Angeles, 1976—; project mgr., co-owner Horizon Constrn., Culver City, Calif., 1984—. Author: Get Help! The Complete Guide to Household Help, 1984. Pres. Crestwood Hills Pre-Sch., Los Angeles, 1980-81; speaker Senator Campbell's Conf. on Women, Orange County, Calif., 1984, 85; mem. governing bd. Camp Good Times, Los Angeles, 1984-85, 86. Mem. Women in Constrn., Bucknell U. Alumni Assn. (fundraising rep. 1984). Office: Horizon Constrn 8825 National Blvd Culver City CA 90232

ZOLLER, ANN LANGE, poet, writer; b. Clinton, Iowa, Jan. 28, 1940; d. Arthur A. and Margaret (Myklebust) Lange; m. Robert P. Zoller, June 10, 1962 (div. Sept. 1984); children—Kristen Ann, Kimberly Kay. B.A., U. Iowa, 1962. Cert. tchr., Iowa: High sch. English tchr., Cedar Rapids, Iowa, 1962-64; pub. poet, Tulsa, 1981—; poetry editor Nimrod jour., Tulsa, 1984—. Author: (poetry) New Pony on a Carousel, 1983 (Pegasus award 1984); Answers from the Bowing Moon, 1985; (chapbook of poems) Artists in Residence, 1982. Contbr. to anthologies and lit. mags. Bd. dirs. PTA, Tulsa, 1971—. Mem. Poetry Soc. Am., Am. Acad. Poets, Nat. Fedn. Poetry Socs., Okla. State Poetry Soc. Avocations: fishing; golf; boating. Home: 6717 S Evanston St Tulsa OK 74136

ZOLOTOW, CHARLOTTE, author, editor; b. Norfolk, Va., June 26, 1915; d. Louis J. and Ella F. (Bernstein) Shapiro; m. Maurice Zolotow, Apr. 14, 1938 (div. 1969); children—Stephen, Ellen. Ed. U. Wis. Editor children's book dept. Harper & Bros., 1938-44; sr. editor Harper & Row, 1962-76, v.p., assoc. pub. Jr. Books, 1976-81, editorial cons., 1981—; editorial dir. Charlotte Zolotow Books, N.Y.C.; author: (children's books) The Park Book, 1944, Do You Know What I'll Do?, 1958; Big Brother, 1960; The Quarreling Book, 1963, The Sky Was Blue, 1963, Someday, 1965, When I Have A Little Girl, 1965; Big Sister and Little Sister, 1966, If It Weren't For You, 1966; When I Have A Son, 1967; The Hating Book, 1969; A Father Like That, 1971; Janey, 1973, My Grandson Lew, 1974, The Summer Night, 1974; The Unfriendly Book, 1975; May I Visit?, 1976, Someone New, 1978; If You Listen, 1980, Say It, 1980, The Song, 1982, I Know a Lady, 1984, numerous others. Recipient Gold medal for editorial excellence Harper & Row, 1975; Christopher award, 1974; Kerlan award, 1986. Mem. PEN, Authors Guild, Coffee House. Jewish. Office: 10 E 53d St New York NY 10022

ZONKA, CONSTANCE ZIPPRODT, public relations executive; b Evanston, Ill., May 23, 1937; d. Herbert Edward and Agnes Irene (Turpin) Zipprodt; m. Leif B. Sorensen, June 29, 1959 (div. Mar. 1964); children—Heidi Liselotte; m. Robert F. Zonka, Aug. 5, 1970 (div. June 1982) 1 son, Milo Matthew. B.A., U. Fla., 1958; student Smith Coll., 1955-56; postgrad U. Chgo., 1958-59. Dir. publicity WIND Radio, Chgo., 1962-64; Midwest asst. pub. relations dir. Time Inc., Chgo., 1964-66; account exec. D.J. Edelman, Inc., Chgo., 1966-69; pres. Connie Zonka & Assocs., Chgo., 1970—; dir. Facets Multimedia, Chgo., 1983—; mem. adv. com. Passage Theatre, Chgo., 1982—; coordinator Chgo. Communications, 1974—. Mem. benefit com. Midwest Women's Ctr., Chgo., 1983-86. Mem. NOW, Nat. Assn. Female Execs., Nat. Assn Women Bus. Owners., Pub. Relations Soc. Am., Publicity Club Chgo. (Golden Trumpet award 1980, Merit award 1982). Democrat. Clubs: Arts, Chgo. Press. Home: 1655 N Vine St Chicago IL 60614 Office: Zonka & Assocs 1655 N Vine St Chicago IL 60614

ZOOK, MARTHA FRANCES HARRIS, nursing administrator; b. Topeka, Nov. 15, 1921; d. Dwight Thacher and Helen Muriel (Houston) Harris; R.N., Meriden (Conn.) Hosp. Sch. Nursing, 1947; student U. Kans., 1948-49, Kans. State U., 1960-61, Barton County Community Coll., 1970-73; B.A., Stephens Coll., 1977; postgrad. Ft. Hays State U., 1978-79; m. Paul Warren Zook, July 2, 1948; children—Mark Warren, Mary Elizabeth Zook Hughey. Staff nurse Stormont Hosp., Topeka, 1947-48; staff nurse Watkins Meml. Hosp., Lawrence, Kans., 1948-49; nursing supr. Larned State Hosp., 1949-53, sect. supr., 1956-57, dir. nursing, 1958-61, 83—; sect. nurse Sedgewick Sect., 1961-76, clin. instr. nursing edn., 1976-77, dir. nursing edn., 1977-83; clinic nurse for podiatrist; sect. supr. Dillon Bldg., Larned, 1957-58; Mem. Am. Nurses Assn., Dist. VII Kans. Nurses Assn., Nat. League Nursing, Kans. League Nursing, Kans. Orgn. Nurse Execs., AAUW. Republican. Roman Catholic. Home: 1109 Johnson St Larned KS 67550 Office: Route 3 Box 89 Larned State Hosp Larned KS 67550

ZOON, KATHRYN EGLOFF, biochemist; b. Yonkers, N.Y., Nov. 6, 1948; d. August R. and Violet T. (Pollock) Egloff; B.S. (N.Y. State Regents fellow), Rensselaer Poly. Inst., 1970; Ph.D. (fellow), Johns Hopkins U., 1975; m. Robert A. Zoon, Aug. 22, 1970; children—Christine K, Jennifer R. Interferon research fellow NIH, Bethesda, Md., 1975-77, staff fellow, 1977-79, sr. staff fellow, 1979-80; sr. staff fellow div. biochem. biophysics Bur. Biologics, FDA, Bethesda, 1980-83; research chemist div. virology Office of Biologics Research and Rev., FDA, 1983—, now also chief immunology lab. Mem. Internat. Soc. Interferon Research. Roman Catholic. Contbr. numerous articles on research in biol. chemistry to sci. jours.; editor Interferon Research, 1980—. Office: Div Virology Office of Biologics Research and Rev Bldg 29A Room 2A17 8800 Rockville Pike Bethesda MD 20205

ZOPF, EVELYN LANOEL MONTGOMERY, guidance counselor; b. Laurel, Miss., July 10, 1932; d. Arthur LaNoel and Ruby Lee (Lewis) Montgomery; Mus. B. in Edn., U. So. Miss., 1953, M.A., 1954; m. Paul Edward Zopf, Jr., Aug. 5, 1956; 1 son, Eric Paul. Guidance counselor U. So. Miss., 1953-54, U. Fla., 1954-56; tchr. New Orleans City Schs., 1956-57; pub. sch. music tchr., band dir., choral dir. Putnam County Schs., Fla., 1957-59; pvt. music tchr. voice, pino, clarinet and trumpet, 1953-61; substitute tchr. Guilford County Schs., 1959—; mem. arts series com. Guilford Coll., 1973-77; interim choir dir. New Garden Friends Meeting, 1961, chmn. music com., 1974-76; adviser to fgn. students, 1954-56, 59-62. Vol., ARC, Boy Scouts Am.; mem. U. Fla. Union Bd., 1955-56; precinct del. County Democratic Conv., 1977, 79, precinct worker, 1980, campaign worker, 1980; bd. dirs. Greensboro Friends of Music, 1970-71, Greensboro chpt. N.C. Symphony Bd., 1979—. Recipient Best Citizen award Miss. So. Coll., 1953. Mem. United Soc. of Friends Women (pres. 1979-81), Internat. Fellowship Quaker Women, Guilford Coll. Community Chorus, Phi Mu. Clubs: Women's Soc. (dir. 1978—), Guilford Coll. Arts Appreciation (v.p. 1980-81, pres. 1981-82), Guilford Gourmet. Home: 815 George White Rd Greensboro NC 27410

ZOUHARY, KATHLEEN MAHER, lawyer; b. Greenville, Ohio, June 28, 1951; d. Thomas Richard and Mary (Brown) Maher; b. Jack Zouhary, Oct. 21, 1978; children—Kathleen Marie, Alexis Jacqueline. B.A. in Polit. Sci. cum laude, Miami U., Oxford, Ohio, 1973; J.D. cum laude, U. Notre Dame, 1976. Bar: Ohio 1976. Assoc., Fuller & Henry, Toledo, 1976-81, ptnr., 1981-85; v.p., gen. counsel St. Luke's Hosp., Maumee, Ohio, 1985—. Gen. chmn. Tribute to Women and Industry, Toledo, 1984, honoree, 1982; bd. dirs. Women Involved in Toledo, 1981-83; trustee Toledo Legal Aid Soc., 1977—. Mem. Am. Soc. Hosp. Attys., ABA, Ohio Bar Assn., Toledo Bar Assn., Miami Presidents Club, St. Luke's Hosp. Pacesetter Club, Phi Beta Kappa. Office: St Luke's Hosp 5901 Monclava Rd Maumee OH 43537

ZOZAYA, JULIA SOTO, media consultant; b. Kingman, Ariz., Mar. 23, 1926; d. Francisco Cuesta and Maria (Blanca) Soto; m. Steve Mike Zozaya, Jan. 3, 1945; 1 child, Steve Mike. Student Lamson Bus. Coll., Phoenix, 1959-60, Phoenix Coll., 1960. Adminstr. employee relations Zozaya Constrn. Co., 1960-66; state info. specialist Ariz. Dept. Econ. Security, 1966-82; pres. Am. Internat. Devel. Corp., Inc., Phoenix, 1972-83; owner, gen. mgr. Sta.-KNNN-FM, Phoenix, 1982-84; media cons. Am. Internat. Diversified, Phoenix, 1984—; spl. Ariz. del. White House Conf. on Aging, 1971, Mich. Com. on Employment Handicapped, 1976-78; cons. White House Conf. on Small Bus., 1978-80. Bd. dirs. Nat. Caucus on Aging, 1971; bd. dirs. Dept. Labor Spl. Com. on Women, 1967-69, Ariz. Health Planning Com., 1976-79, Pres.'s Com. for Employment Handicapped, 1978-81, Project SER, 1979-81, Nat. Health Planning Council, 1977-82, Ariz. Dept. Edn. Div. Handicapped; 1st v.p. Ariz. Fedn. of Blind, 1964; state publicity chairperson League United Latin Am. Citizens, 1967-68, nat. v.p., 1969-71, past bd. dirs., past newsletter editor, nat. dir. aging and housing, women's affairs, 1972-74. Recipient citation of merit, Gov. Ariz., 1968, 78, 83, Traditional Dress and Jewelry award Apache Tribe, 1968; various awards League United Latin Am. Citizens, including Woman of Yr. award, 1969, 80; Ring award Hopi Tribe, 1970, Outstanding Citizen award Image, Inc., 1977, cert. appreciation Epsilon Sigma Alpha Internat., 1978, Diana award Epsilon Sigma Alpha Internat., 1979, Goodwill Ambassador's award Ariz. Lion's Club, 1979, cert. appreciation Ariz. Adv. Council on Vocat. Edn., 1980, 82. Mem. Am. Assn. Tng. and Devel., Am. Women in Radio and TV, Nat. Assn. Broadcasters, Statewide Reading Service for Blind and Handicapped-Sun Sounds, Ariz. Town Halls, Chicano Por la Causa, Mujer (outstanding citizen award 1976), Nat. Hispanic C. of C. (founder, 1st v.p. 1977), Ariz. Mexican C. of C. (incorporator, pres. 1972-80, Disting. Service award 1971, 50th Anniversary Service award 1979). Democrat. Roman Catholic. Avocations: music; dance; history and culture. Home: 4548 W Osborn Rd Phoenix AZ 85031

ZOZOM, ELIZABETH, graphic designer, sculptor; b. Bayonne, N.J., June 12, 1955; d. Andrew Zozom and Ada (Cooper) Smith. Assoc. in Specialized Tech., Art Inst. Phila., 1975; student Pa. Acad. Fine Arts, 1977-78. Asst. art dir. Phila. Mag., 1975-76; designer, proofreader Stephenson Bros. Printers, Phila., 1980-81; designer, proofreader Running Press Book Pubs., Phila., 1981-82, design dir., 1982-83, dir. prodn. and design, 1983—. Exhibited group shows including: Pratt Inst., N.Y.C., 1972, Provident Bank, Phila., 1974, Women's Art League Phila., 1976, Gallery 3 1/2 & 4, Phila., 1976, Etage, Phila., 1977, Art Inst. Phila., 1977, Old City Art Spring Festival, Phila., 1978, Race Gallery, Phila., 1979. Editor: Masterpieces, 1981; The Ultimate Sandwich Book, 1982; Bed and Breakfast Cookbook, Best of the Realist, Designer books including: Cat Notebook II, Computer Dictionary, Concerning the Jews, Cook's Notebook, Country Notebook (3d Pl. award Phila. Book Clinic 1983), Gardener's Notebook, Grandparent's Journal; Horse Notebook; I Ching Records; Intelligent Idiot's Guide to Home Video Equipment, Overnight Guide to Public Speaking; Tales of Peter Rabbit; Teacher Brother's Modern-Day Almanac, Teddy Bear Journal I (1st place award Phila. Book Clinic 1984), and II, Unicornis (1st place award Phila. Art Dirs. Club 1985), Velveteen The Unabridged Edgar Allan Poe, The Unpublished Lenny Bruce, Young Aspiring Professional's Fast-Track Handbook; designer Velveteen Rabbit Calendar, 1983 (1st place award Phila. Book Clinic 1982, Neographic Silver award 1983), Woman's Journal, Writers on Writing. Mem. Phila. Book Clinic, Art Dirs. Club Phila. Office: Running Press Book Pubs 125 S 22d St Philadelphia PA 19103

ZUCHELKOWSKI, HEIDI MARIE, hairstylist; b. Keonigshofen, Bavaria, Germany, Nov. 7, 1945; came to U.S., 1978; d. Guenten and Rosa (Woerlein) Venus; m. Thomas Edward Zuchelkowski, May 21, 1966; 1 child, Andrea. Grad. Staetische Beau-Schule, Rothenburg, W. Ger., 1959. Hairstylist Salon Piaiika, Rothenburg, 1959-63, Wiese, Bad-Homburg, 1963-67, Maria's Couffires, Aberdeen, Md., 1969-72, Salon Steiger, Hanau, Ger., 1972-77, Internat. Coffires, Aberdeen, 1978-79; owner, mgr. Hair Odyssey, Aberdeen, 1979—. Office: Hair Odyssey 14 Aberdeen Shopping Plaza Aberdeen MD 21001

ZUCKER, ISABEL SCHNAPPER (MRS. MYRON ZUCKER), horticultural journalist; b. Phila.; d. Henry and Johanna (Neugass) Schnapper; B.S., Cornell U., 1926, postgrad. 1927-28; m. Myron Zucker, Jan. 28, 1929; children—Judith Zucker Clark, Ralph, Jack. Owner flower shops, Great Neck and Little Neck, N.Y., 1926-29, landscape firm, 1929-40; garden editor The Detroit Times, 1941-60; editor Question Box, Flower Grower mag., 1961-62; dir. Nat. Garden Bur., Bloomfield Hills, Mich., 1962-72; columnist indoor plants Horticulture mag., 1977-79; sec., treas., dir. Myron Zucker Engring. Co., Myron Zucker, Inc., both Bloomfield Hills; tchr., counselor Camp Pontiac, Mich. Conservation-Corrections Program, 1954—. Recipient plaque All Am. Selections, 1971; honor plaque award Am. Seed Trade Assn. 1958; named Garden Writer of Year, Am. Assn. Nurserymen, 1964. Fellow Royal Hort. Soc. (Great Britain), Garden Writers Assn. Am. (editor Bull. 1949-69, pres. 1969-71, 1st recipient Hall of Fame award 1980), Am. Hort. Soc. (citation 1967; Hall of Fame 1981); mem. Mich. (medal 1966), Mass. hort. socs., Internat., Am. socs. hort. sci., Internat. Lilac Soc. (dir. 1972-76, award of merit 1975, honors and achievements award 1980). Author: Flowering Shrubs, 1966; Four Seasons of Fun for Youngsters, 1969. Home and Office: 708 W Long Lake Rd Bloomfield Hills MI 48013

ZUCKER, JEAN MAXSON, nurse; b. Dunmore, Pa., Aug. 9, 1925; d. Earl L. and Florence M. (Cromwell) Maxson; R.N., Kings County Hosp. Center, 1948; cert. gerontol. nurse; children—Lawrence F., Pamela J., Diane K. Pvt. duty nurse various locations, N.Y., N.J., 1959-64; indsl. nurse Bendix Corp., Eatontown, N.J., 1955; asst. head nurse Point Pleasant Hosp., N.J., 1964-66; head nurse intensive and CCU, VA Hosp., Ft. Howard, Md., 1974-78; clin. nurse USPHS Hosp., Balt., 1978-81; nursing supr. VA Hosp. Center, Ft. Howard, 1981—; tchr. in field. Mem. Am., Md. nurses assns., Am. Assn. Critical Care Nurses. Democrat. Methodist.

ZUCKER, PHOEBE SUE, nutritional counsellor, diet center executive; b. Milw., Jan. 19, 1932; d. Joseph Aaron and Hannah (Seltzer) Berman; m. Gordon Leslie Zucker, Nov. 22, 1951; children—Laurel, Denise, Charles I. B.S., U. Wis., 1954; postgrad. Pa. State U., 1955-56. Reference librarian Glens Falls Library, N.Y., 1972; gen. librarian Tempe Pub. Library, Ariz., 1972-75; pres. Mont. Diet Ctrs., Inc., Butte, 1975—; mem. profl. adv. bd. Diet Ctr., Inc., Rexburg, Idaho, 1978—. Mem. Butte Mayor's Com., 1984—; active local unit Am. Cancer Soc. Recipient award Diet Ctr., Inc., Missoula, Mont., 1984. Mem. AAUW, U. Wis. Alumni Assn., Univ. Women at Mont. Tech. Avocations: cross-country skiing; cycling; swimming; walking; reading. Home: 1140 W Platinum St Butte MT 59701

ZUCKERMAN, LINDA ELISE, instructional materials company executive; b. N.Y.C., Oct. 9, 1950; d. Arthur and Claire (Roth) Zuckerman. Student Manhattan Community Coll., 1967-68, H.H. Lehman Coll., 1968-72. Adminstrv. mgr. J.B. Kass & Co., N.Y.C., 1972-74; asst. personnel dir. Morningside House Aging in Am., N.Y.C., 1974-78; outplacement Cons. Re-Placements Unltd., N.Y.C., 1978-80; profl. edn. supr. Coopers & Lybrand, N.Y.C., 1980-81; cons. Tng. Systems Design, N.Y.C., 1982—. Contbr. articles to profl. jours. Bronx student coordinator Ottinger for N.Y. State Senator, 1970. Mem. Am. Soc. for Tng. and Devel., Am. Soc. Personnel Adminstrn., Nat. Assn. Female Execs. Democrat.

ZUCKERMAN, MADELINE MARY, public relations advertising executive; b. N.Y.C., Dec. 3, 1947; d. Sterling and Ann (Tunno) Botenus; m. Leonard Zuckerman, Mar. 8, 1970; children—Jennifer, Matthew. Grad., Collegiate Bus. Sch., N.Y.C., 1967; student N.Y. Sch. Interior Design, 1970, NYU, 1969. Asst. to corp. pub. relations dir. Burlington Industries, N.Y.C., 1966-68; v.p., ptnr. Letitia Baldridge Enterprises, Inc., N.Y.C., 1968-75; owner, pres. Madeline Zuckerman Pub. Relations Advt., Tustin, 1977—. Contbg. editor Orange County Illustrated Mag., 1977. Bd. dirs. Orange County Trauma Soc., Am. Heart Assn. Named Young Achiever, Glamour Mag., 1975. Mem. Women in Communications (v.p.), Exec. Women Internat. (bd. dirs.), Pub. Relations Soc. Am., Exec. Internat., Indsl. League Orange County, Newport Harbor Area C. of C., Irvine C. of C. Club: Orange County Press. Home: 9722 Willow Glen Circle Santa Ana CA 92705 Office: Madeline Zuckerman Pub Relations Advt 18231 Irvine Blvd Tustin CA 92680

ZUCKERMAN, MARILYN ROSE, telecommunications official; b. Newark, Jan. 8, 1939; d. Morris and Ruth (Lilien) Levy; children—Lisa Karen, Sarah Lynn. B.A., Douglass Coll., New Brunswick, N.J., 1960. Programmer, analyst RCA, Morrestown, N.J., 1960-61; system programmer IEC, Paramus, N.J., 1961-62; systems analyst Bell Labs., Whippany, N.J., 1962-63; sr. systems analyst Am. Hoechst Corp., Bridgewater, N.J., 1974-76, dir. MIS edn., 1976-79; staff mgr. AT&T, Basking Ridge, N.J., 1979-81, dist. mgr., Parsiappany, N.J., 1981—. Author: Business Systems Advisor, 1980; designer, author exec. seminars. Adv. bd. Fairleigh Dickinson U., 1974-79, Middlesex County Coll., Somerville, N.J., 1976-79; sec. N.J. Democratic Com., 1980-82; bd. dirs. ACLU, N.J., 1970-75. Mem. Am. Soc. Tng. and Devel., Exec. Women N.J., Women in Telecommunications. Democrat. Jewish. Office: AT&T 99 Jefferson Rd Parsippany NJ 07054

ZUCKERMAN, SHELLEY JOY, public relations company executive; b. Bklyn., Dec. 28, 1953; d. Max and Zelda (Steck) Zuckerman; m. Barry Spector, July 6, 1986. B.A. in Journalism, U. R.I., 1974; M.S. in TV and Radio, Syracuse U., 1975. Account exec. Hill & Knowlton, N.Y.C., 1978-80; asst. dir., press relations Am. Stock Exchange, N.Y.C., 1980-82; exec. v.p. Lobsenz-Stevens Pub. Relations, N.Y.C., 1982—. Mem. Internat. Assn. Bus. Communications (mem. com.), Women Execs. in Pub. Relations. Democrat. Jewish. Avocations: skiing; scuba diving; tennis. Home: 420 E 80th St New York NY 10021 Office: Lobsenz-Stevens Inc 460 Park Ave S New York 10016

ZUEFELDT, JOEANN DAUGHERTY, security specialist; b. Dallas, Nov. 9, 1933; d. Wilma Elson and Anna L. (Dickson) Daugherty; m. Dan Lewis Zuefeldt, Jan. 15, 1954; children—Joyce Ann Zuefeldt Fiaccone, Dan Lewis, Jr. B.S. in Elem. Edn., Tex. Wesleyan U., 1971; Assoc., U. Tex.-Arlington, 1952; Assoc. in Criminal Justice, Tarrant County Jr. Coll., 1974. With LTV Aerospace and Def. Co., Dallas, 1960—, sr. security specialist, 1979—. Trustee, v.p. and sec. bd. Birdville Ind. Sch. Dist., Ft. Worth, 1978—. Mem. Am. Soc. for Indsl. Security. Deomocrat. Baptist. Avocations: photography; hiking; mountain climbing; camping. Home: 4016 Doeline St Ft Worth TX 76117 Office: LTV Aerospace and Def Co 9314 W Jefferson Blvd Dallas TX 75265

ZUELOW, MARGO JEANNE, writer, researcher; b. Eau Claire, Wis., Mar. 8, 1938; d. Ivan Eugene and Alice May (Krause) Chamberlain; m. Edwin Hanke, June 30, 1984; children—Cynthia Jeanne, James Fredrick. Elementary sch. tchr., Minn., Oreg. and Alaska, 1962-74; instr. edn. Kuskokwim Community Coll., U. Alaska, Bethel, 1974-76; grad. teaching fellow U. Oreg., 1976-77; supr. adult edn. Alaska Dept. Edn., Juneau, 1977-78; dean instrn. Kenai Peninsula Community Coll., Soldotna, Alaska, from 1978; program researcher Rural Edn. div. U. Alaska; now writer, researcher history books. Mem. Kenai C. of C., Phi Delta Kappa Democrat. Club: Soroptomists. Home: 4939 Rhoads Ave Santa Barabara CA 93111

ZUGBY, LILLIAN COURY, librarian; b. Lowell, Mass., Sept. 10, 1911; d. Peter M. and Nellie (Batal) Coury; m. Emile Zugby, May 27, 1939 (dec.); children—Robert C., Donald E. B.S.E., U. Lowell, 1933; grad. Wood's Bus. Coll., 1927; M.L.S., Catholic U., 1964; postgrad. U. Md., 1966-68. Jr. profl. asst. USDA, Washington, 1935-44; tchr. pub. schs. Prince George County, Md., 1954-58; librarian, prof. Montgomery Coll., Takoma Park, Md., 1959-83, head pub. service, dir. reference dept. Montgomery Coll. Library, 1971-83; cons. Learning Resources, 1971-76. Mem. NEA, ALA, Md. Library Assn., AAUP, Nat. Faculty Assn. Democrat. Roman Catholic.

ZUGICH, VIRGINIA ALBINA, city clerk; b. Pisek, N.D., Feb. 18, 1931; d. James and Albina Anna (Dvorak) Votava; m. Henry Richard Zugich, June 17, 1950 (dec. 1973); children—Catherine Ann, Michael Henry, Christine Marie. Cert. Mcpl. clk. Village clk. Sturtevant, Wis., 1974-78; exec. sec. Am. Planning Agy., Racine, Wis., 1978; asst. dir. Northside Redevelopment Corp., Racine, 1979; clk., treas. City Lake Mills, Wis., 1979-83; city clk. City Muskegon, Mich., 1985—; chmn. Wis. Mcpl. Treas. Cert. Inst., 1982-83; dist. dir. Wis. Mcpl. Clks. Assn., 1982-83. Mem. Cable TV Adv. Com., Lake Mills, 1981-83, Madison Braille Inst., Wis., 1981-82; neighborhood chmn. Racine County council Girl Scouts U.S., Sturtevant, 1958-61; profl. vocalist on tour, 1983-84. Mem. Internat. Inst. Mcpl. Clks. (vice chmn. profl. status 1985—, membership dir., 1981-82, agenda and minutes com., 1980-81), Mich. Mcpl. Clks. Assn. Avocations: community theater; choir; hiking; reading; crafts. Office: City Muskegon 933 Terrace St Muskegon MI 49441

ZUGOR, OLGA, design company executive; b. Budapest, Hungary, Nov. 7; came to U.S., 1956, naturalized, 1962; d. Laszlo and Olga (Ricker) Nagy; student of art, Hungary and Ger.; children—Andre, Christina. Designer, Color & Line, Gloria Buce Assos., G&L Studio, Everfast Co.; stylist various cos.; pres. Decorative Concept Inc., N.Y.C., 1977—; exhibited batik painting, Washington, N.Y. Mus. Contemporary Crafts, Silvermine (Conn.) Guild Artist; exhibited prints traveling exhibit N.Y. State Council on Arts, also Tapei (Taiwan) Mus. Home: 110 East End Ave New York NY 10028

ZUKOWSKI, LUCILLE KATHRYN, mathematician, emerita educator; b. Millinocket, Maine, Nov. 2, 1916; d. Percy J. and Winnifred A. (Ball) Pinette; B.A. cum laude, Colby Coll., 1937, M.A., 1971; M.A., Syracuse U., 1943; postgrad. Harvard U., 1946, Bryn Mawr Coll., 1947-48, U. Mich., Ann Arbor, 1954-55; m. Walter H. Zukowski, Dec. 26, 1955; 1 dau., Mary Lucille. Teaching asst. Syracuse U., 1941-43; prof. dept. math. Colby Coll., Waterville, Maine, 1943-44, 45-82, prof. emerita, 1982—, chmn. dept., 1971-82; vis. prof. Robert Coll., Istanbul, Turkey, 1965-66, Iranzamin Coll., Tehran, Iran, 1972-73; prof. NSF Summer Insts., 1958-70; corporator Waterville Savs. Bank, 1980—, People's Heritage Bank, 1980—; chmn. adv. com. Mount Merici Acad., 1979—. NSF Summer Inst. fellow U. Colo., 1953. Mem. Math. Assn. Am., Soc. Indsl. and Applied Math., Phi Beta Kappa, Sigma Xi. Roman Catholic. Office: Colby Coll Waterville ME 04901

ZUMMO, MARY ANN (IVY), real estate firm executive; b. Chgo., Jan. 31, 1943; d. Anthony and Mary (Cravatta) Iovinelli; m. Peter Salvatore Spina, June 12, 1963 (div. 1972); children—James Spina, Peter Spina, Gina Spina; m. Michael Anthony Zummo, May 11, 1985. Real estate broker Real Estate Tng. Inst., Dallas, 1980, mgmt. specialist, 1984; real estate broker Harper Coll., 1977. Hair designer Northlake Beauty Salon, Dallas, 1973, Hairstyles by MaryAnn, Chgo., 1975-78; real estate saleswoman Plano Real Estate, Tex., 1978-80; real estate broker Century 21 Heritage, Plano, 1980-81, mgr., 1980—. Editor Women Council of Realtors Communicator, 1985-86, Counselor Crisis Ctr. Collin County, Plano, 1982-86, bd. dirs., 1984-86; campaign dir. League Republican Women, Collin County, 1982. Mem. Nat. Assn. Female Execs., Women's Council Realtors (treas. 1983-84, v.p. 1984-85, pres. 1985-86, Woman of Yr. 1985), Collin County Bd. Realtors (bd. dirs. 1984—, Realtor of Yr. 1984). Roman Catholic. Avocations: jogging; aerobics. Office: Century 21 Heritage 2801 W Parker Rd Plano TX 75023

ZUMWALT, NANCY EILEEN WILLIAMS, nurse, public health administrator; b. Ferndale, Mich., Aug. 14, 1927; d. Joseph A. and Marcella N. (Wahl) Williams; diploma Highland Park Gen. Hosp. Sch. Nursing, 1948; R.N., B.A., Eastern Ill. U., 1976, M.S. Ed. in Community Counseling, 1980; m. Bruce G. Zumwalt, Jan. 28, 1950; children—Marcy Kugler, B. Joseph, Frank, John. Various positions in nursing profession, 1948-77; dir. Iroquois Meml. Hosp. Home Health Agency, Watseka, Ill., 1968-71, dir. nursing Vermilion County Health Dept., Danville, Ill., 1971-74; adminstr. Iroquois County Health Dept., Watseka, 1974-77; instr. health occupations Iroquois Area Career Center, Watseka, 1980—; past pres. Ill. Council Home Health Services, Ill. Assn. Local Health Dept. Nursing Adminstrs. Mem. regional bd., sec. East Central Ill. Health Service Agy.; mem. exec. bd. Iroquois County Mental Health Center; v.p. Iroquois County Heart Assn. Mem. Iroquois Meml. Hosp. Aux., Health Occupations Students Am. Methodist. Club: Am. Legion Aux. Home: Rural Route 2 Sheldon IL 60966 Office: Iroquois Area Cancer Ctr Watseka IL 60970

ZUPAN, BONITA KATHIRINE, travel agency executive; b. Cleve., June 2; d. Joseph Frank and Francesca Marie (Poropat) Klaus; m. Terrance David Zupan, June 29, 1968; children—Terrance David Jr., Tisa Nicole Shalimar. Hair stylist Ingrid Hair Stylists, Parma, Ohio, 1968-70; pres. Pass Travel, Banning, Calif., 1978—. Vol. Cleve. Big Sisters, 1975; probation officer Calif. Dept. Pub. Social Services, 1978, worker for abused children, 1979; mem. Banning Pregnancy Hotline, 1984; mem. Precious Blood Sch. Bd., 1980—, pres., 1982-83. Club: Banning Jr. Women (ways and means com. 1977-80). Roman Catholic. Office: Pass Travel 1184 W Ramsey St Banning CA 92220

ZUPANCIC, CHRISTINE ANN, furniture company executive; b. Maple Heights, Ohio, July 5, 1957; d. Joseph John and Eva Marie (Sudick) Z. A.A., Art. Inst. Pitts., 1978; student, Florence, Italy, 1977. Layout artist, artist Gordon's Jewelers, Houston, 1978-79; art dir., artist Weiner's Clothing, Houston, 1979-81; art dir. Finger's Furniture, Houston, 1981—. Mem. Mus. Fine Arts, Houston Opera Guild. Roman Catholic. Club: Slovenian/American (Houston). Avocations: painting; plastic casting jewelry; photography. Office: Finger's Furniture Co PO Box 194 Houston TX 77001

ZURBUCHEN, SUSAN JANE, arts consultant; b. Madison, Wis., June 28, 1949; d. Herbert August and Ruth Helen (Pfaffenbach) Z. B.A. in Speech and Theatre, Lakeland Coll., Sheboygan, Wis., 1970; M.A. in Theatre Arts, U. Minn., 1972. Salesperson Keebler Co., Elmhurst, Ill., 1975; regional coordinator Office Criminal Justice Programs, Traverse City, Mich., 1976-77; bus. mgr. Old Town Playhouse, Traverse City, 1978-81; dir. adminstrn. Ind. Arts Commn., Indpls., 1982-85; arts cons. PAX/Indpls. 1985—; arts cons. Pan Am Arts Festival, Indpls., 1985—; actress, dir. Traverse City Civic Players, 1976-81; grantsmanship Cons. Grand Traverse County (Mich.), 1977-81; spl. events cons. LWV, Traverse City, 1980-81. Puppeteer syndicated TV show Time for Timothy—PuppetVision, 1982—. Bd. dirs. Criminal Justice Adv. Council, Traverse City, 1976-82, Rainbow House, Inc., Cadillac, Mich., 1977-79; pres. bd. dirs Women's Resource Ctr., Traverse City, 1977-80; bd. dirs. Julian Ctr., 1986—, Arts Unlimiting, 1986—. Mem. LWV (bd. dirs. 1981-82), Nat. Assn. Female Execs., Am. Theatre Assn. Mem. United Ch. of Christ. Office: PAX/Indpls 4475 Allisonville Rd Indianapolis IN 46287

ZURYLO, BEVERLY ANISOWICZ, bursar, sports columnist, writer; b. Northampton, Mass., Oct. 18, 1947; d. Chester Stanley and Christine Constance (Szarkowski) Anisowicz; m. Joseph Eugene Zurylo, Apr. 12, 1969 (div. 1980). A.A., Greenfield Community Coll., 1971; B.A. magna cum laude, U. Mass., 1973. Bursar, Smith Coll., Northampton, Mass., 1977—; columnist Pro Football Weekly, Chgo., 1979—; free-lance writer, 1981—; pres. Investments Unlimited, Northampton, 1976, 78-80; sports talk show host radio stas., Mass., 1982-84. Author: Beefcake and Lifeslices, 1986. Mem. Nat. Assn. Accts. (v.p. communications 1975-78), Phi Beta Kappa. Avocations: whale watching; interspecies communication; scuba diving; photography. Home: RFD 1 16 Laurel Mountain Rd Haydenville MA 01039 Office: Smith College College Hall 5 Northampton MA 01063

ZUSSY, NANCY LOUISE, state library official; b. Tampa, Fla., Mar. 4, 1947; d. John D. and Patsy (Stone) Roche; m. Roderick G Swartz, Dec. 12, 1985. A.A., St. Petersburg Jr. Coll., 1967; B.A. in Edn., U. Fla., 1969; M.A. in L.S., U. South Fla., 1977, M.S. in Mgmt., 1980. Cert. in librarianship, Wash. Ednl. evaluator State of Ga., Atlanta, 1969-70; media specialist DeKalb County Schs., Atlanta, 1970-71; researcher Ga. State Library, Atlanta, 1971; asst. to dir., reference librarian Clearwater Pub. Library (Fla.), 1978-80; dir. of libraries, 1978-80; dep. state librarian Wash. State Library, Olympia, 1981-86, state librarian, 1986—; mem. Consortium for Automated Library Services, Olympia, 1982—, chmn., 1983—. Bd. dirs. Thurston-Mason County Community Mental Health Ctr., Olympia, 1982-84, treas., 1983-84. Mem. ALA, Wash. Library Assn., Pacific Northwest Library Assn. Office: Wash State Library AJ-11 Olympia WA 98504

ZVARA, DIANE MARY, oil company executive; b. Lexington, Mass., Sept. 16, 1959; d. John and Rose Mary (Stillwell) Zvara. B.B.A., Baylor U., 1981. Exec. sec. Aerospace Systems, Inc., Burlington, Mass., 1976-81; oil and gas lease analyst Amoco Prodn. Co., Houston, 1981—. Baptist. Club: Desk and Derrick (Houston). Home: 14680-B Perthshire Rd Houston TX 77079 Office: Amoco Prodn Co Room 7134 PO Box 3092 Houston TX 77253

ZWEIGENTHAL, GAIL, magazine editor; b. N.Y.C., Feb. 27, 1944; d. Joseph and Bessie (Lang) Z. B.A., Tufts U., 1965. Editorial asst. Gourmet mag., N.Y.C., then assoc. editor, sr. editor, now mng. editor. Office: Gourmet Mag Conde Nast Publs Inc 560 Lexington Ave New York NY 10022

ZWENIG, FRANCES ANNE, legislative assistant, lawyer; b. N.Y.C., July 11, 1945; d. Eugene Amos and Sara Frances (Moore) Z. A.B., Coll. William and Mary, 1967; M.A., Fletcher Sch. Law and Diplomacy, Medford, Mass., 1971; J.D., Duke U., 1974. Bar: Ga. 1974, Calif. 1976. Vol., Peace Corps, Thailand, 1967-69; co-dir. Student Adv. Com. on Internat. Affairs, Washington, 1970-71; mng. atty. Atlanta Legal Aid Soc., 1974-76; atty. Calif. Rural Legal Assistance Program, San Francisco, 1976; atty., lobbyist Ralph Nader's Congress Watch, Washington, 1976-79, Bldg. Trades Dept. AFL-CIO, Washington, 1980-81; dir. pub. policy People for the Am. Way, Washington, 1981-84; exec. dir. Environ. Safety Council, Washington, 1984-85; adminstrv. asst. to Rep. W. Wyche Fowler, Jr., 1985—; cons. Food Research and Action Ctr., Washington, 1977-79. Pres. Stanton Manor Condo Assn., Washington, 1982-85. Mem. Phi Beta Kappa.

ZWICKER, DENISE ALLEN, advertising and business writer; b. Lubbock, Tex., Dec. 26, 1952; d. Edward Easton and Isla Fern (Smedley) Allen; m. George Haggas Zwicker, July 27, 1974. B.A. magna cum laude, Baylor U., 1974. Dir. merchandising Houston Post, 1974-76; creative dir. Cummings Advt. Agy., Inc., Houston, 1976-77; freelance advt., pub. relations writer, Bellaire, Tex., 1977—; author articles, scripts, speeches, brochures. Holder 7 college scholarships. Mem. Internat. Assn. Bus. Communicators (v.p., dir. Houston chpt. 1980, 84, numerous writing awards, local, regional and nat., named Communicator of Yr. Houston chpt. 1979), Women in Communications, (Headliner award Houston chpt. 1986), Women's Network Group (exec. dir. 1986). Episcopalian. Home and Office: 4525 Sunburst St Bellaire TX 77401

ZWICKL, JUDITH ELLEN, computer consultant; b. Denver, June 13, 1949; d. Arthur Hoober and Julia Lorraine (Koester) Neumann; m. Ronald Dean Zwickl, June 13, 1970. B.S., Colo. State U., 1971; M.B.A., U. N.H., 1976. Service rep. New Eng. Telephone Co., Dover, N.H., 1972-75; account rep. ADP Network Services, Balt., 1977-79, cons. Western div., San Francisco, 1979-80; mem. staff Los Alamos Nat. Lab., 1983-86, assoc. group leader, 1984-86; software specialist III, Digital Equipment Corp., 1986—. Mem. credit com. Los Alamos Credit Union, 1981-83, chmn., 1982-83, mem. supervisory com., 1983-85, chmn., 1984-85, bd. dirs., 1985—. Mem. Balt.Econ. Soc. (rec. sec. 1978-79). Home: 314 Potrillo Dr Los Alamos NM 87544

ZWILICH, ELLEN TAAFFE, composer; b. Miami, Apr. 30, 1939; d. Edward Porter and Ruth (Howard) Taaffe; m. Joseph Zwilich, June 22, 1969 (dec. June 1979). B.Mus., Fla. State U., 1960, M.Mus., 1962; D.Mus. Arts, Juilliard Sch., 1975; studied violin with Roger Sessions, Elliott Carter, Richard Burgin and Ivan Galamian. Violinist Am. Symphony, N.Y.C., 1965-73; composer-in-residence Festival of Contemporary Music, Ind. State U., 1985. Composer: Sonata in Three Movements, 1973-74; String Quartet, 1974; Clarino Quartet, 1977; Chamber Symphony, 1979; Passages (for Soprano and Chamber Ensemble), 1981; String Trio, 1982; Symphony 1: 3 Movements for Orch., 1982; Divertimento, 1983; Einsame Nacht, 1971; Emlékezet, 1978; Im Nebel, 1972; Passages for Soprano and Orch., 1982; Trompeten, 1974; Fantasy for Harpsicord, 1983; Intrada, 1983; Prologue and Variations, 1983. Double Quartet for Strings, 1984; Celebration for Orch., 1984. Recipient Elizabeth Sprague Coolidge Chamber Music prize, 1974; Gold medal G.B. Viotti, Vercelli, Italy, 1975; citation Ernst von Dohnanyi, Fla. State U., 1981; Pulitzer prize, 1983; Nat. Inst. Arts and Letters award, 1984; Martha Baird Rockefeller Fund rec. grantee, 1977, 79, 82; Guggenheim fellow, 1981. Mem. Am. Fedn. Musicians (hon. life), Am. Music Ctr. (bd. dirs., v.p. 1982-84), Internat. League Women Composers. Home: 600 W 246th St Riverdale NY 10471 Office: American Music Ctr 250 W 54th St Rm 300 New York NY 10019

ZWIREN, JAN MARIE, advertising executive; b. Columbus, Ohio, May 22, 1944; d. Justin Bernard and Annabell Lee (Slyh) Reichert. A.S., Fashion Inst. Tech., 1965; student Wharton Sch. Bus., Phila., 1970, 71, 72, 75. Copywriter, Rike's Dept. Store, Dayton, Ohio, 1966-67; copywriter John Wanamaker, Phila., 1967-69; promotion dir. Menley & James Labs., Phila., 1969-74; v.p. mktg. Helen Curtis Industries, Chgo., 1974-79; pres. Jan Zwiren Agy., Chgo., 1979-82; chmn. Zwiren & Wagner Agy., Chgo., 1983—. Contbr. articles to profl. jours. Named Ad Women of Yr., Chgo. Tribune, 1981; recipient awards Clio's, Addys, Chgo. Ad Club. Mem. Nat. Assn. Women Bus. Owners, Am. Assn. Advt. Agencies, Chgo. Advt. Club, Am. Advt. Fedn., NOW, LWV. Methodist. Clubs: Chgo. Yacht, Womens. Office: Zwiren & Wagner Advt 840 N Michigan Ave Chicago IL 60611

ZYKAN, MARY SUSAN, solid waste disposal company owner; b. St. Louis, Oct. 7, 1946; d. Edward Patrick and Edna Elenora (Showalter) Schneider; m. Robert Walter Zykan, Mar. 27, 1965; children—Robert, Ronald, Steven, Karen. Grad. high sch., Overland, Mo. Sec. Greater St. Louis Foster Parent Assn., 1969-72, v.p., 1973-76; treas. Met. San. Haulers Assn., 1975-78; owner R & Z Hauling Service, St. Ann, Mo., 1965—; waste industry advisor Bi-State Devel. Agy., St. Louis, 1977-78; com. mem. St. Louis County Solid Waste Adv. Com., 1977-78; waste industry advisor Mo. Dept. Natural Resources Task Force, 1982-83. Editor newsletter Greater St. Louis Foster Parent Assn., 1970-76. Vol. Emergency Foster Home, St. Louis County Welfare Agy., Mo., 1972-74; planner, guest speaker Forest Park Community Coll. Waste Conf., 1980. Recipient Service awards St. Louis County Juvenile Ct., 1973, 78. Mem. Nat. Solid Waste Mgmt. Assn. (pres. Mo. chpt. 1981-82, legis. sec. 1985, chmn. solid waste legis. com. 1984-85), Met. San. Haulers Assn. (pres. 1985, bd. dirs. 1974-85, service award 1979), Nat. Fedn. Ind. Bus., Mo. Waste Coalition (conf. exhibit com. 1982). Lutheran. Club: Am. Bdll. Avocations: bowling; swimming; bell collecting; writing. Home: 10319 Millwood St Saint Ann MO 63074 Office: R & Z Hauling Service 10319 Millwood St Saint Ann MO 63074